Employment, Hours, and Earnings

States and Areas, 2005

Employment, Hours, and Earnings

States and Areas, 2005

EDITOR
Diane Werneke

ASSOCIATE EDITOR
Mary Meghan Ryan

ISBN: 1-886222-25-8

Printed by Automated Graphic Systems, Inc., White Plains, MD, on acid-free paper that meets the American National Standards Institute Z39-48 standard.

2006 2005 4 3 2 1

BERNAN PRESS
4611-F Assembly Drive
Lanham, MD 20706
800-274-4447
email: info@bernan.com
www.bernanpress.com

CONTENTS

PREFACE

Bernan Press is pleased to present this special edition of its *U.S. Handbook of Labor Statistics*. The Bernan Press edition of *Employment, Hours, and Earnings: States and Areas, 2005* brings together the wealth of employment data compiled by the Bureau of Labor Statistics (BLS) and expands on the traditional BLS volume *Employment, Hours, and Earnings: State and Areas*, which was last published in 1994. This is the first printed volume of industry employment data under the new North American Industry Classification System (NAICS). Other features include:

- Over 200 tables presenting historical data on employment, hours, and earnings by state and on select local areas within each state;

- Detailed industry data organized monthly on a non-seasonally adjusted basis;

- An introduction page for each state highlighting salient data and noteworthy trends;

- A concise technical guide that explains the sources, definitions, changes, and other pertinent facts about the data, as well as references for further guidance; and

- An appendix detailing geographical components.

The employment, hours, and earnings data introduced in this handbook give a robust and timely picture of the 50 states and the District of Columbia, as well as the nation's largest metropolitan areas. These data can be used to analyze key factors affecting state and local economies, as well as to compare the impact of national cyclical trends with what occurs at the local level. They allow the user to answer such questions as, what compositional changes have occurred in a particular labor market from 1990 to 2003? How was employment in a specific area affected by the 1990–1991 and 2001 recessions? As the recessions did not affect all states and areas equally or at the same time, nor did they recover at the same time.

These data are valuable for use in both the public and private sectors. On a public-policy level, these data can be used to determine the health of the economy, and the need for federally assisted programs. State and local jurisdictions use the data to determine needs for services, including training and unemployment assistance, as well as for planning and budgetary purposes. For private industry, this information can be used to identify suitable states and localities when making decisions on plant locations, wholesale and retail trade outlets, and to locate a particular sector base.

Diane Werneke has edited this edition, in association with Mary Meghan Ryan.

Diane Werneke was formerly an economist and senior congressional liaison at the Federal Reserve Board and has also served on the House Budget Committee, the President's Commission on Employment and Unemployment Statistics, and in the International Labor Office in Geneva, Switzerland, specializing in macroeconomic and labor market policy and analysis. She holds a B.A. from the University of California at Berkeley and an M.A. from The George Washington University, both in economics.

Mary Meghan Ryan is a data analyst with Bernan Press. She received her bachelor's degree in economics from the University of Maryland and is a former economist with the American Economics Group. Additionally, Ms. Ryan has worked as a research assistant for FRANDATA. Ms. Ryan is also an associate editor of the eighth edition of *Business Statistics of the United States* and the first edition of *Vital Statistics of the United States*, both published by Bernan Press.

Bernan Press's editorial and production departments, under the direction of Tamera Wells-Lee, did the copy editing, layout, and graphics preparation. Katherine DeBrandt provided assistance on various editorial aspects of the publication. Kara Prezocki, the production team leader, capably managed the production aspects of this volume as well as prepared the graphics and cover design. Production assistant Rebecca Zayas helped Kara in coordinating this project. With support from Automated Graphics Systems and Publications Professionals, Kara and Rebecca assisted the editor tremendously with finalizing this publication.

As always, special thanks are due to the many federal agency personnel who assisted us in obtaining the data, provided excellent resource on their Web sites, and patiently answered our questions.

INTRODUCTION:
TRENDS IN EMPLOYMENT

Over the 1990–2003 period, the U.S. economy experienced two recessions, one in 1990–1991 and another in 2001. In both contractionary periods, total employment declined substantially and the unemployment rate rose. Following the earlier recession, nonfarm payroll employment expanded sharply, led by strong growth in the service-providing sector, and from 1992 to 2000 over 23 million jobs were added to the economy, with service sector jobs accounting for 89 percent of the growth. Each service-providing industry added jobs during this period, while jobs in the goods-producing sector edged up slightly as growth in construction employment was offset by languishing manufacturing and mining employment.

Following the 2001 recession, the recovery in employment was unusually slow. In fact, nonfarm employment continued to contract until the autumn of 2003, at which time expanding employment in the service-providing sector offset continuing declines in the goods sector, especially in manufacturing.

Regional patterns of employment change varied. In general, the Midwest had the largest contraction of jobs in both recessions, followed by the Northeast, which was affected more by the 1990–1991 recession than the one in 2001. In the South, employment growth slowed during the first contraction, but did not decline; unlike in 2001 when a net contraction in jobs occurred. The pattern was the opposite in the West, where employment declined in 1991 but continued to grow in 2001, albeit much more slowly.

Patterns of employment change also varied from state to state. While most states' total nonfarm payroll employment tended to mirror national and regional patterns, the two recessions had differing impacts, reflecting the industrial composition of employment. In general, states dependent on goods-producing industries fared worse than those with large service sector employment.

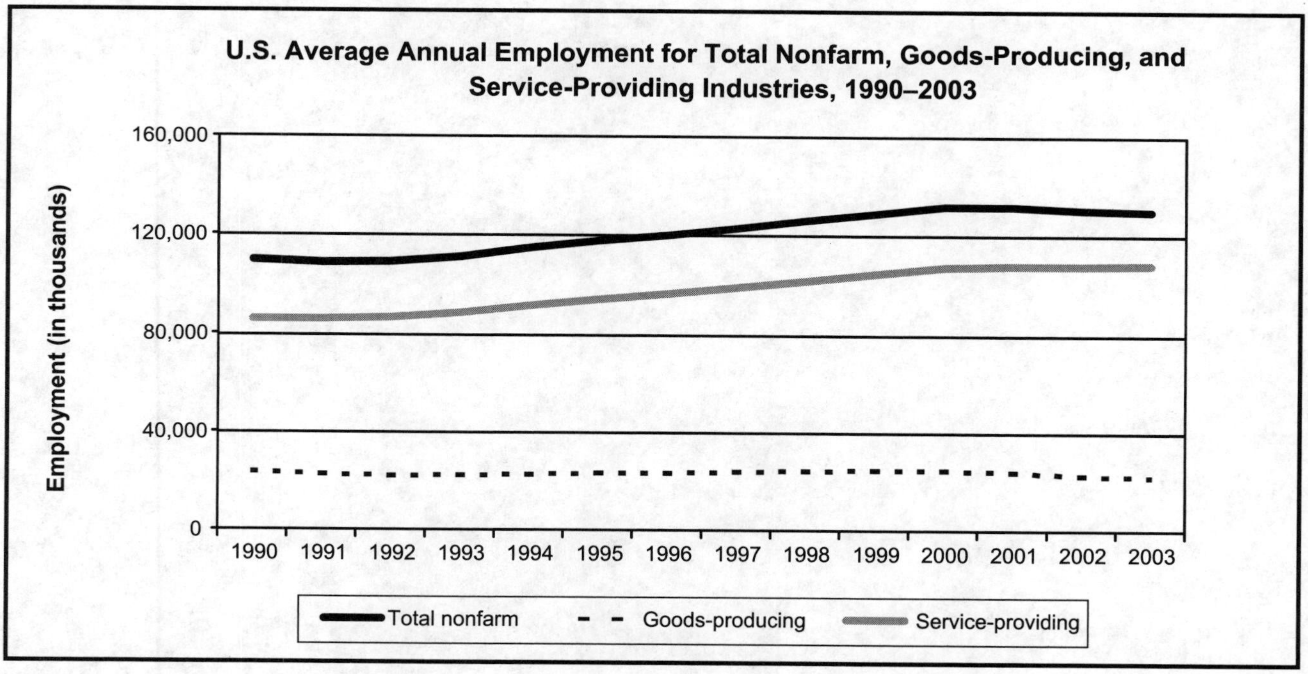

TECHNICAL NOTES

OVERVIEW

This publication presents monthly and annual average data on employment, hours, and earnings by major industry categories for each state and for the largest metropolitan areas. The industry data is based on the new North American Industry Classification System (NAICS), which is discussed in greater detail on page xiii, and for various reasons does not go back before 1990. As a result, the employment data are presented on a monthly and annual basis from 1990 to 2003. For similar reasons, the hours and earnings data are only available from 2001. Unemployment rates are presented for each state for 1990, 2001, and 2003. As noted in the introduction, recessions began in both 1990 and 2001.

The Bureau of Labor Statistics (BLS), which is the statistical agency within the U.S. Department of Labor, conducts the Current Employment Statistics (CES) survey to provide national, state, and local nonfarm employment data by industry, and hours and earnings data for nonfarm workers in the private sector. The unemployment data come from the Local Area Unemployment Statistics (LAUS) Program, which provides monthly employment and unemployment data for approximately 7,200 areas.

Both the employment, hours, and earnings series and the unemployment rate data are derived from federal-state cooperative data collection efforts in which state employment security agencies prepare data using concepts, definitions, and technical procedures prescribed by the BLS. Although the estimation of the two data sets are based on differing methodologies, more fully described below, their inclusion together in this publication is intended to provide a broad overview of state and local labor market conditions.

THE CURRENT EMPLOYMENT STATISTICS (CES) SURVEY–EMPLOYMENT, HOURS, AND EARNINGS DATA

The Current Employment Statistics (CES) survey is commonly referred to as the establishment or payroll survey. These estimates are derived from a sample of about 160,000 private nonfarm businesses, such as factories, offices, and stores, as well as federal, state, and local government entities, covering about 400,000 individual worksites and about one-third of all nonfarm payroll employees. These establishments are classified on the basis of their primary activity by major industry groupings in accordance with NAICS. For an establishment engaging in more than one activity, the entire employment of the establishment is included under the industry indicated by principal activity.

All establishments of 1,000 employees or more are asked to participate in the survey, along with a representative sample of smaller businesses. Sample respondents extract the requested data from their payroll records, which must be maintained for a variety of tax and accounting purposes, and submit this information to both the state and to the BLS (BLS Form 790). This information is collected on a supplement to the quarterly unemployment insurance tax reports filed by employers. Statewide samples range from nearly 40,000 sample units in California to about 1,500 in smaller states.

All the states' samples are combined to form a collective sample for developing national industry estimates. However, state estimation procedures are designed to produce accurate data for each individual state. The BLS independently develops the national series and does not force state estimates to sum to the national total. Because each state series is subject to larger sampling and nonsampling errors than the national series, summing them cumulates individual state level errors and can cause significant distortions at an aggregate level. As a result of these statistical limitations, the BLS does not compile a "sum of states" employment series and cautions users that doing so can result in a series that is subject to a relatively large and volatile error structure.

As detailed in the 1997 *BLS Handbook of Methods* (updated in 2003 at <www.bls.gov/opub/hom/>), the employment data are estimated at the publication "cell" level, which is a micro industrial class of industry and aggregated up to broader levels of industry detail such as "manufacturing, trade, government," etc. What the BLS publishes is a "guaranteed" aggregation of the cells that aggregate to the broad categories of "goods-producing," "service-providing," "total nonfarm," and "total private." The monthly data are published using a "link-relative" technique in which a ratio of current month employment to that of the previous month is computed from a sample of establishment reporting for both periods. The estimates of the data for the current month are obtained by multiplying the estimates of the previous month by these ratios. Information on this complex procedure is also summarized in *Employment and Earnings*, published monthly by the BLS, and available by monthly subscription, or for specific information by telephone at (202) 691-6559.

Data in this volume are available on a current basis in the BLS monthly release, *Regional and State Employment and Employment*, available on the BLS Web site at <www.bls.gov/sae> or by contacting the BLS at (202) 691-6559 or (202) 691-5902. These releases are also available by subscription by contacting the BLS Office of Publications at (202) 691-5200.

Concepts

Industries

Nonfarm employment includes all goods-producing and service-providing employment. Total private includes goods-producing plus private service-producing industries. The goods-producing sector includes natural resources and mining, construction, and manufacturing. Construction and mining were often combined to form one industry for a variety of reasons, including the size of the area and the availability of reliable data. The service-providing sector includes both private service-providing and government employment. Private service sector employment includes trade, transportation, and utilities, which is comprised of wholesale trade, retail trade, and transportation and utilities; information; financial activities; professional and business services; educational and health services; leisure and hospitality; and other services. Government employment includes those employed at the federal, state, or local level. Industry subcategories are available on the BLS Web site <www.bls.gov/sae>.

Employment

Employment is the total number of persons employed either full or part-time in nonfarm business establishments during a specific payroll period. Temporary employees are included. Members of the Armed Forces, agricultural workers, the self-employed, and unpaid family workers are excluded. The data refer to all persons who worked during, or received pay, for any part of the pay period that includes the 12th of the month, a standard for all federal agencies collecting employment data from business establishments.

Workers who are on paid sick leave (when pay is received directly from the employer); who are on paid holiday or vacation; or who worked during only part of the specified pay period, even though they are unemployed or on strike during the rest of the pay period, are all counted as employed by the establishment survey. Persons on the payroll of more than one establishment during the pay period are counted in each establishment that reports them, whether the duplication is due to turnover or dual jobholding.

Persons are considered employed if they receive pay for any part of the pay period, but they are excluded if they receive no pay at all for the pay period. Those excluded from the employed include persons on layoff, on leave without pay, or on strike for the entire pay period, and persons who were hired but have not yet started work during the pay period.

The CES government employment statistics refer to civilian government employees only. Employees of the Central Intelligence Agency, the National Security Agency, the National Imagery and Mapping Agency, and the Defense Intelligence Agency are excluded.

Hours and Earnings

The hours and earnings data series for states are based on reports of gross private payrolls and the corresponding paid hours for production workers, primarily in the manufacturing industries. Because not all sample respondents report production worker hours and earnings data, insufficient sample sizes preclude hours and earnings data from many sectors in many states. Therefore, the data available and thus published vary from state to state.

The CES collects data for production workers in manufacturing and in natural resources and mining industries. In manufacturing, the production worker classification covers employees, up to the level of working supervisors, who engage directly in the manufacture of the establishment's product. Among those excluded from this category are persons in executive and managerial positions and persons engaged in activities such as accounting, sales, advertising, routine office work, professional and technical functions, and "force-account construction." (Force-account construction is construction work performed by an establishment, engaged primarily in some business other than construction, for its own account and use of its employees.)

In construction, the term construction workers applies to persons up through the level of working supervisors, who are engaged directly in a construction project, either at the site or in shops or yards, at jobs ordinarily performed by members of the construction trades. Excluded from this category of construction workers are executive and managerial personnel, professional and technical employees, and other employees in routine office employment.

For private service-providing industries, earnings and hours data are collected only for nonsupervisory workers, which exclude executive, managerial, and supervisory positions.

Payrolls are reported *before deductions of any kind*, including Social Security, unemployment insurance, group health insurance, withholding taxes, retirement plans, or union dues. Included in the payroll report of earnings is pay for all hours worked, including overtime, shift premiums, and pay for vacations, holidays, and sick leave. Bonuses, commissions, and other non-cash payments are excluded unless they are earned and paid directly by the firm. Employee benefits paid by the employer, tips, and payment in kind are also excluded.

Total hours during a pay period that include the 12th of

the month for these workers covers all hours worked (including overtime hours), and hours paid for holidays, vacations, and sick leave. Total hours differs from the concept of scheduled hours worked because the average weekly hours are derived from paid total hours that reflect the effects of such factors as unpaid absenteeism, labor turnover, part-time work, and strikes, as well as fluctuations in work schedules.

Average hourly earnings are derived by dividing gross payrolls by total hours, reflecting the actual earnings of workers, including premium pay. They differ from wage rates, which are the amounts stipulated for a given unit of work or time. Average hourly earnings do not represent total labor costs per hour because they exclude retroactive payments and irregular bonuses, employee benefits, and the employer's share of payroll taxes. Earnings for those employees not included in the production worker or nonsupervisory categories are not reflected in the estimates.

Average weekly earnings are derived by multiplying average weekly hours by average hourly earnings.

It should be noted that in the context of the historical data long-term trends in the hours and earnings data also reflect structural changes such as the changing mix of full- and part-time employees and of highly paid and lower wage workers within a business as well as across an industry.

Metropolitan Areas

The general concept of a Metropolitan Statistical Area (MSA) is that of a core area containing a large population nucleus, together with adjacent communities having a high degree of economic and social integration. A Primary Metropolitan Statistical Area (PMSA) is an urban area within a very large metropolitan area. A statistical area may include localities from neighboring states. For example, Fort Smith MSA in Arkansas includes Sequoyah County, Oklahoma.

The standard definition of a MSA is determined by the Office of Management and Budget (OMB), which updates the definition, based on the decennial census as well as updated information provided by the Census Bureau between the censuses.

As of February 2005, the BLS provided employment data for 288 MSAs, which were not seasonally adjusted, according to procedures established by the OMB in its circular on the subject, June 30, 1996. These employment estimates were updated by the BLS in March 2005 (too late for the release of this publication) based on the 2000 census and the February 18, 2004 OMB issuance of new definitions and standards for MSAs. As a result, the BLS added 49 new MSAs.

The geographic boundary area components are shown in the Appendix.

Revisions to the Data

North American Industry Classification System (NAICS)

The most far-reaching revision of the CES data occurred with the change in the industrial classification system from the Standard Industrial Classification (SIC) to the North American Industry Classification System (NAICS). The industries for states and areas are classified in accordance with the 2002 NAICS, which replaced in January 2003 the 60-year-old SIC system. This change altered how establishments are classified into industries to more fully reflect the current composition of U.S. businesses. NAICS was adopted as the standard measure of industry classification by the statistical agencies of the United States, Canada, and Mexico in order to enhance comparability of economic data across the North American Free Trade Association (NAFTA) trade area. These revisions were so profound as to preclude the linkage of the present NAICS to the old SIC, and the BLS consequently has not updated the SIC data nor linked, for the most part, the historical SIC data with the current NAICS data. The employment data in this publication, using the NAICS classification, commence with 1990 and are fully consistent for all subsequent years. Data from the old SIC industrial classification have not been updated and are no longer available. Therefore, the user is advised to contact the BLS if seeking to use employment, hours, and earnings data prior to this time.

Benchmark revisions

Employment estimates are adjusted annually to a complete count of jobs, called benchmarks, which are derived primarily from tax reports that are submitted by employers who are covered under state unemployment laws (which cover most establishments). In this re-anchoring of sample-based employment estimates to full population counts, the original sample-based estimates are replaced with the benchmark data from the previous year. The benchmark information is used to adjust monthly estimates between the new benchmark and the preceding one, thereby preserving the continuity of the series, and also to establish the level of employment for the new benchmark month.

The data in this publication reflect the benchmark revisions made in February 2004, changing the data for 2003 and preceding years from previous estimates. The new benchmark revisions were released at the national level in February and at the state and local level in March 2005, changing the data from 2004.

Monthly revisions

Initial monthly estimates are calculated from an incomplete sample and are subject to revision in the subsequent month when more sample data are available. Revisions for preliminary statewide employment data are generally small, but users who wish to update the data available in this publication for monthly data are advised to consult the most recent BLS information available on their Web site as noted on page xi.

Seasonal adjustment

Over the course of a year, the size of a state's employment level undergoes sharp fluctuations because of changes in the weather, reduced or expanded production, harvests, major holidays, and so on. Because these seasonal events follow a more or less regular pattern each year, the data may be adjusted to eliminate these seasonal influences on data trends. These adjustments make it easier to observe the cyclical and other nonseasonal movements in the data series, but it is important to note that the seasonally adjusted series are only an approximation based on past experience and that the seasonally adjusted data have a broader margin of error than the unadjusted data because they are subject not only to sampling and other errors but to the seasonal adjustment process as well.

The data presented in this publication are not seasonally adjusted and therefore the month-to-month variations in the data contain seasonal variations that may distort these month-to-month comparisons. The BLS plans to provide seasonally adjusted state data for the major industry groups as time series data are accumulated over a duration long enough to produce accurate results under the BLS seasonal adjustment program. Therefore, for monthly comparison purpose, the user is recommended to observe month-to-month patterns using year-to-year comparisons for the monthly data.

The BLS also provides total nonfarm employment data on a seasonally adjusted basis at the state level. As noted above, these data will allow for a basis of consistent comparison over time. However, data for the disaggregated subsectors appear in their unadjusted form until the time series data are available for a period sufficient to enable reliable seasonal adjusted data. The BLS also publishes some data series on a seasonally adjusted basis at the state level by industry and will continue to add series over the near term. Subsequent versions of this volume will incorporate seasonally adjusted data when it becomes available on a comprehensive basis.

Data for MSAs are also not seasonally adjusted because the sample sizes do not allow for reliable estimates for seasonal adjustment factors.

THE LOCAL AREA UNEMPLOYMENT STATISTICS (LAUS) PROGRAM—PROVIDING UNEMPLOYMENT DATA

The Local Area Unemployment Statistics (LAUS) program provides monthly and annual estimates for unemployment rates, as well as labor force, employment, and unemployment totals for states and many local areas. These unemployment data are not available by industry.

The concepts and definitions underlying the LAUS program come from the Current Population Survey (CPS), the household survey that is the official measure of the U.S. labor force. The LAUS models combine current and historical data from the CPS, the CES, and the State Unemployment Insurance (UI) Systems. There are numerous conceptual and technical differences between the household and establishment surveys, and estimates of monthly employment change from these two surveys usually do not match in size or even direction. As a result, the unemployment rates presented in the header page are not directly comparable to the employment data. However, this publication is including these data for the annual averages of 1990, 2001, and 2003 to provide complementary information on labor market conditions in states. Monthly and annual data are available from the BLS Web site at <www.bls.gov/lau> and available by telephone at (202) 691-6392. A full description of the differences between the two surveys as well as guidance on the complex methods used to obtain the LAUS data on unemployment rates is provided by the BLS at <www.bls.gov/lau/laufaq.htm> as well as in the *BLS Handbook of Methods* at <www.bls.gov/opub/hom/>.

ALABAMA AT A GLANCE

(Population and total nonfarm employment numbers in thousands)

Population, Census 2000:	4,447.1
Total nonfarm employment, 2003:	1,874.8
Change in total nonfarm employment	
(Number)	
1990–2003:	239.0
1990–2001:	272.9
2001–2003:	-33.9
(Compound annual rate of change)	
1990–2003:	1.1%
1990–2001:	1.4%
2001–2003:	-0.9%
Unemployment rate	
1990:	6.3%
2001:	4.8%
2003:	5.8%

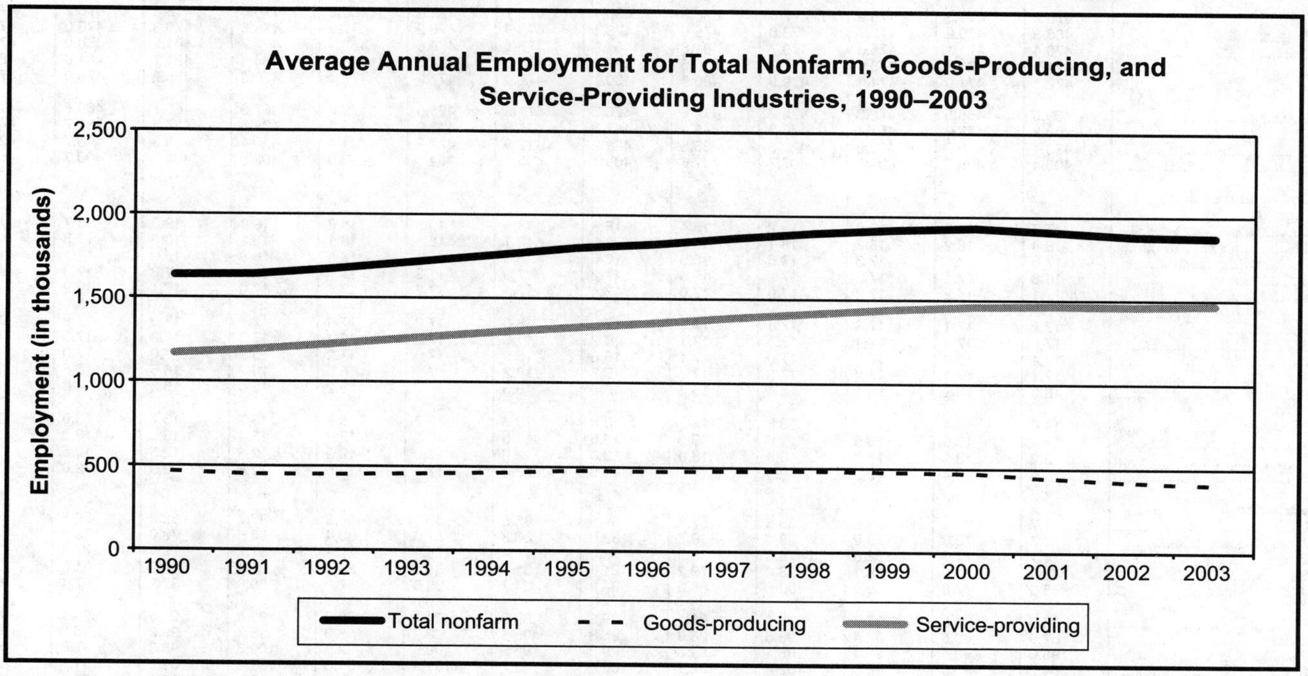

After showing slow growth during the 1990–1991 recession, total nonfarm payroll employment grew steadily during the strong recovery and expansion that followed. Despite an increase in service-providing employment, total nonfarm employment declined by over 55,000 from 2000 to 2003. These job losses were in the goods-producing industries, particularly manufacturing.

Employment by Industry: Alabama

(Numbers in thousands. Not seasonally adjusted.)

Industry	January	February	March	April	May	June	July	August	September	October	November	December	Annual Average
STATEWIDE													
Total nonfarm													
1990	1606.0	1608.0	1615.3	1635.3	1646.0	1647.8	1638.9	1632.8	1646.8	1648.7	1652.7	1651.0	1635.8
1991	1616.8	1616.9	1628.6	1636.4	1644.9	1644.0	1641.0	1638.5	1652.5	1660.0	1662.4	1662.4	1642.0
1992	1637.9	1643.8	1654.1	1665.3	1676.5	1674.4	1671.7	1677.7	1681.4	1700.0	1702.8	1706.7	1674.4
1993	1676.6	1688.9	1696.0	1714.8	1718.8	1720.8	1714.8	1713.0	1725.0	1740.0	1744.9	1747.5	1716.8
1994	1711.7	1720.1	1734.3	1747.9	1752.6	1762.7	1752.0	1756.8	1779.1	1781.0	1806.1	1797.5	1758.5
1995	1769.5	1776.7	1789.5	1800.3	1806.0	1813.8	1796.2	1799.2	1813.5	1818.1	1829.1	1832.0	1803.7
1996	1793.8	1800.4	1814.3	1822.7	1830.3	1827.7	1822.0	1827.6	1838.0	1848.1	1859.4	1859.3	1828.6
1997	1830.0	1836.0	1853.8	1863.2	1871.2	1868.7	1861.8	1861.9	1875.4	1885.5	1891.8	1895.4	1866.2
1998	1860.9	1869.7	1884.1	1903.5	1908.7	1913.6	1889.2	1894.4	1907.7	1910.3	1915.5	1919.8	1898.1
1999	1883.8	1895.4	1910.8	1919.3	1922.8	1924.9	1917.5	1916.1	1931.7	1930.8	1937.1	1943.6	1919.5
2000	1903.3	1910.4	1929.1	1931.3	1945.0	1941.0	1922.4	1928.7	1941.2	1936.3	1941.9	1943.7	1931.2
2001	1894.4	1903.9	1914.8	1919.6	1921.2	1918.6	1897.5	1905.2	1910.2	1903.5	1908.1	1907.9	1908.7
2002	1859.7	1868.4	1882.6	1888.3	1891.6	1886.1	1872.4	1879.8	1888.3	1889.9	1897.0	1894.8	1883.2
2003	1857.0	1863.9	1875.0	1878.8	1882.2	1875.7	1862.1	1869.3	1880.9	1882.3	1885.0	1886.1	1874.8
Total private													
1990	1282.6	1282.3	1287.8	1304.6	1311.5	1326.3	1313.8	1322.8	1320.7	1317.8	1319.3	1320.0	1309.1
1991	1285.2	1283.3	1293.9	1300.7	1306.8	1313.8	1314.4	1322.8	1322.0	1322.2	1322.9	1325.0	1309.4
1992	1302.7	1305.4	1314.4	1325.7	1333.2	1340.3	1337.8	1347.8	1349.2	1357.3	1358.8	1364.8	1336.5
1993	1337.0	1345.1	1351.2	1371.2	1372.9	1382.4	1379.7	1386.8	1388.5	1395.7	1398.5	1403.3	1376.0
1994	1367.1	1373.9	1387.3	1399.5	1403.6	1415.9	1413.5	1426.4	1436.7	1432.7	1442.4	1451.0	1412.5
1995	1425.1	1428.7	1441.4	1452.7	1457.5	1470.5	1461.2	1471.5	1475.6	1472.3	1482.5	1487.1	1460.5
1996	1451.1	1454.6	1467.3	1475.0	1481.5	1488.1	1486.5	1497.5	1499.6	1502.0	1511.3	1514.9	1485.8
1997	1484.4	1487.5	1503.7	1512.6	1519.1	1525.9	1522.1	1529.7	1533.0	1535.4	1540.0	1546.4	1520.0
1998	1512.3	1518.7	1531.8	1553.1	1557.1	1568.7	1554.9	1561.0	1562.0	1560.7	1563.4	1568.8	1551.0
1999	1533.9	1542.3	1555.8	1563.7	1568.6	1577.3	1575.2	1578.1	1581.2	1577.0	1582.2	1589.5	1568.7
2000	1551.7	1556.0	1570.8	1574.7	1580.3	1592.6	1583.9	1592.0	1590.8	1583.0	1588.0	1589.8	1579.5
2001	1542.9	1548.5	1559.6	1564.4	1566.0	1570.1	1557.7	1563.8	1557.7	1547.8	1551.5	1551.3	1556.8
2002	1507.2	1512.5	1526.0	1530.0	1534.1	1534.8	1531.1	1537.2	1532.0	1529.7	1535.4	1533.4	1528.6
2003	1498.7	1501.9	1512.1	1515.4	1518.9	1521.3	1517.7	1522.9	1519.9	1518.8	1521.2	1523.0	1515.9
Goods-producing													
1990	461.1	459.7	460.6	469.6	472.0	477.7	468.7	472.4	470.9	468.0	463.9	460.2	467.1
1991	444.7	443.4	445.2	449.0	451.5	456.2	452.1	456.9	455.7	455.9	453.3	449.9	451.2
1992	442.0	442.1	444.5	446.6	448.6	450.8	446.6	452.8	453.6	459.0	456.9	455.2	449.9
1993	445.7	449.2	451.2	457.1	457.6	462.3	457.0	458.5	457.8	459.0	457.4	455.3	455.7
1994	443.7	446.7	451.1	456.7	459.5	465.2	462.5	469.6	474.1	472.7	475.0	475.4	462.7
1995	470.9	471.3	476.2	477.5	476.8	480.1	475.7	479.8	480.9	478.0	478.3	476.2	476.8
1996	468.5	470.2	472.7	473.6	475.0	476.1	472.5	476.2	477.9	478.5	479.3	476.0	474.7
1997	470.4	471.1	476.5	479.7	481.8	481.9	477.1	479.6	481.4	482.7	481.2	480.0	478.6
1998	474.9	475.8	478.9	487.7	486.5	488.2	478.9	484.5	484.7	484.3	481.7	481.0	482.3
1999	472.1	471.9	474.1	479.5	480.9	480.7	477.4	477.9	478.4	476.3	475.9	476.0	476.8
2000	469.5	469.5	472.3	472.2	472.5	476.7	471.9	475.0	473.3	467.6	465.7	464.6	470.9
2001	448.8	448.8	451.4	450.3	449.4	447.6	441.8	443.9	443.0	436.6	434.4	431.7	444.0
2002	420.1	419.9	422.5	422.3	423.5	422.2	418.9	421.9	421.4	420.1	418.3	415.7	420.6
2003	408.4	408.2	409.7	407.7	407.6	406.1	402.1	404.1	403.8	402.5	401.3	400.7	405.1
Natural resources and mining													
1990	17.7	17.8	18.0	18.2	18.4	18.6	18.9	18.8	18.8	19.1	19.0	18.7	18.5
1991	18.4	18.2	18.2	18.1	17.9	18.0	18.1	18.1	18.1	18.2	18.0	17.8	18.1
1992	17.6	17.5	17.5	17.5	16.9	16.6	16.5	16.4	16.8	16.8	16.9	17.1	17.0
1993	16.8	17.1	17.2	17.2	17.0	17.2	17.3	17.3	17.5	17.4	17.6	17.3	17.2
1994	17.1	17.2	17.2	17.0	17.0	17.4	17.1	17.2	17.4	17.0	17.1	17.2	17.2
1995	17.2	17.1	17.3	17.4	17.5	17.8	18.0	17.9	17.9	17.7	17.9	17.9	17.6
1996	17.5	17.4	17.4	17.1	17.1	17.2	17.3	17.2	17.4	17.3	17.3	17.3	17.3
1997	17.1	16.9	17.0	17.0	17.1	16.8	16.9	17.0	17.2	16.9	17.0	17.0	17.0
1998	17.1	17.1	17.2	17.5	17.7	17.8	17.2	17.1	16.9	16.9	16.6	16.5	17.1
1999	16.2	16.2	16.1	15.4	15.4	15.5	15.3	15.2	15.2	15.0	15.0	14.8	15.4
2000	14.6	14.4	14.4	13.8	13.7	13.8	13.7	13.7	13.7	13.7	13.7	13.6	13.9
2001	13.4	13.5	13.5	13.6	13.5	13.5	13.5	13.5	13.5	13.4	13.3	13.3	13.5
2002	13.2	13.1	13.2	13.0	13.0	13.0	12.9	13.0	12.9	12.6	12.5	12.5	12.9
2003	12.5	12.4	12.5	12.5	12.5	12.5	12.4	12.5	12.6	12.6	12.6	12.6	12.5
Construction													
1990	81.7	83.0	84.6	85.8	87.3	89.5	86.8	87.5	84.9	83.7	82.2	80.8	84.8
1991	74.7	75.8	78.0	79.4	79.7	82.0	80.8	81.3	80.4	80.5	78.0	75.8	78.9
1992	71.1	71.7	72.8	74.8	75.9	75.8	76.4	78.1	77.9	81.7	79.4	77.4	76.1
1993	72.0	74.0	75.1	78.8	79.2	81.1	81.7	81.1	80.7	83.1	82.2	81.0	79.2
1994	75.9	77.8	79.9	82.8	83.0	84.9	84.7	86.5	87.8	86.8	87.9	87.1	83.8
1995	85.0	84.5	87.7	88.6	88.1	89.3	89.3	90.6	90.6	91.8	91.5	90.1	88.9
1996	87.9	89.6	92.4	93.6	95.6	95.8	95.8	98.2	98.8	98.7	99.2	96.8	95.2
1997	93.0	93.5	96.4	98.1	99.3	99.3	98.6	99.8	99.9	100.6	98.3	97.3	97.8
1998	94.7	95.6	98.0	102.4	102.1	102.9	100.7	101.9	101.6	102.4	101.9	101.7	100.5
1999	98.9	100.4	102.8	103.1	104.0	103.7	105.0	105.0	106.0	106.0	105.2	105.4	103.8
2000	101.1	101.7	103.6	104.6	105.0	106.8	107.3	108.3	109.4	107.2	106.6	105.9	105.6
2001	101.6	102.7	104.8	106.6	107.7	107.9	106.3	106.2	105.8	104.7	104.4	102.1	105.1
2002	96.8	98.3	100.5	99.7	100.9	100.0	100.3	101.4	102.1	102.7	101.1	99.2	100.3
2003	97.3	97.6	99.3	98.4	98.9	98.8	98.8	99.7	100.6	100.1	99.2	98.8	98.9

Employment by Industry: Alabama—*Continued*

(Numbers in thousands. Not seasonally adjusted.)

Industry	January	February	March	April	May	June	July	August	September	October	November	December	Annual Average
STATEWIDE—*Continued*													
Manufacturing													
1990	361.7	358.9	358.0	365.6	366.3	369.6	363.0	366.1	367.2	365.2	362.7	360.7	363.8
1991	351.6	349.4	349.0	351.5	353.9	356.2	353.2	357.5	357.2	357.2	357.3	356.3	354.2
1992	353.3	352.9	354.2	354.3	355.8	358.4	353.7	358.3	358.9	360.5	360.6	360.7	356.8
1993	356.9	358.1	358.9	361.1	361.4	364.0	358.0	360.1	359.6	358.5	357.6	357.0	359.3
1994	350.7	351.7	354.0	356.9	359.5	362.9	360.7	365.9	368.9	368.9	370.0	371.1	361.8
1995	368.7	369.7	371.2	371.5	371.2	373.0	368.4	371.3	372.4	368.5	368.9	368.2	370.3
1996	363.1	363.2	362.9	362.9	362.3	363.1	359.4	360.8	361.7	362.5	362.8	361.9	362.2
1997	360.3	360.7	363.1	364.6	365.4	365.8	361.6	362.8	364.3	365.2	365.9	365.7	363.8
1998	363.1	363.1	363.7	367.8	366.7	367.5	361.0	365.5	366.2	365.0	363.2	362.8	364.6
1999	357.0	355.3	355.2	361.0	361.5	361.5	357.1	357.7	357.2	355.3	355.7	355.8	357.5
2000	353.8	353.4	354.3	353.8	353.8	356.1	350.9	353.0	350.2	346.7	345.4	345.1	351.4
2001	333.8	332.6	333.1	330.1	328.2	326.2	322.0	324.2	323.7	318.5	316.7	316.3	325.5
2002	310.1	308.5	308.8	309.6	309.6	309.2	305.7	307.5	306.4	304.8	304.7	304.0	307.4
2003	298.6	298.2	297.9	296.8	296.2	294.8	290.9	291.9	290.6	289.8	289.5	289.3	293.7
Service-providing													
1990	1144.9	1148.3	1154.7	1165.7	1174.0	1170.1	1170.2	1160.4	1175.9	1180.7	1188.8	1190.8	1168.7
1991	1172.1	1173.5	1183.4	1187.4	1193.4	1187.8	1188.9	1181.6	1196.8	1204.1	1209.1	1212.5	1190.9
1992	1195.9	1201.7	1209.6	1218.7	1227.9	1223.6	1225.1	1224.9	1227.8	1241.0	1245.9	1251.5	1224.5
1993	1230.9	1239.7	1244.8	1257.7	1261.2	1258.5	1257.8	1254.5	1267.2	1281.0	1287.5	1292.2	1261.1
1994	1268.0	1273.4	1283.2	1291.2	1293.1	1297.5	1289.5	1287.2	1305.0	1308.3	1331.1	1322.1	1295.8
1995	1298.6	1305.4	1313.3	1322.8	1329.2	1333.7	1320.5	1319.4	1332.6	1340.1	1350.8	1355.8	1326.9
1996	1325.3	1330.2	1341.6	1349.1	1355.3	1351.6	1349.5	1351.4	1360.1	1369.6	1380.1	1383.3	1353.9
1997	1359.6	1364.9	1377.3	1383.5	1389.4	1386.8	1384.7	1382.3	1394.0	1402.8	1410.6	1415.4	1387.6
1998	1386.0	1393.9	1405.2	1415.8	1422.2	1425.4	1410.3	1409.9	1423.0	1426.0	1433.8	1438.8	1415.9
1999	1411.7	1423.5	1436.7	1439.8	1441.9	1444.2	1440.1	1438.2	1453.3	1454.5	1461.2	1467.6	1442.7
2000	1433.8	1440.9	1456.8	1459.1	1472.5	1464.3	1450.5	1453.7	1467.9	1468.7	1476.2	1479.1	1460.3
2001	1445.6	1455.1	1463.4	1469.3	1471.8	1471.0	1455.7	1461.3	1467.2	1466.9	1473.7	1476.2	1464.8
2002	1439.6	1448.5	1460.1	1466.0	1468.1	1463.9	1453.5	1457.9	1466.9	1469.8	1478.7	1479.1	1462.7
2003	1448.6	1455.7	1465.3	1471.1	1474.6	1469.6	1460.0	1465.2	1477.1	1479.8	1483.7	1485.4	1469.6
Trade, transportation, and utilities													
1990	314.2	311.2	312.0	312.8	314.6	318.6	317.4	319.4	318.9	318.1	323.3	327.3	317.3
1991	318.4	315.2	318.1	318.0	319.7	319.9	320.1	321.5	321.4	322.6	327.1	331.3	321.1
1992	318.0	316.6	318.3	321.1	324.0	326.1	326.1	327.2	327.1	329.1	333.8	340.3	325.6
1993	326.7	326.0	326.9	332.3	332.5	334.8	335.1	338.5	339.6	343.6	348.6	354.6	336.6
1994	340.9	339.3	340.8	343.0	344.6	347.8	346.6	349.5	352.7	353.4	359.6	365.8	348.7
1995	351.7	349.4	351.3	354.9	356.6	360.7	358.1	360.8	363.0	363.1	370.6	375.5	359.6
1996	361.4	358.8	361.1	361.0	362.2	365.3	364.6	367.6	367.9	369.7	375.7	381.4	366.4
1997	368.3	364.7	368.5	367.8	370.5	372.2	372.5	373.7	374.6	378.0	384.4	390.4	373.8
1998	371.7	370.4	373.9	378.6	380.1	383.6	379.0	378.7	381.1	381.5	386.1	391.1	379.7
1999	376.1	376.5	380.6	379.0	380.7	383.9	383.8	384.7	386.5	386.7	390.7	396.4	383.8
2000	381.2	379.5	381.6	380.5	384.0	386.0	383.0	384.1	384.8	386.0	392.6	396.2	385.0
2001	379.5	377.3	379.5	379.0	380.4	381.9	378.1	378.6	376.9	377.9	384.4	387.2	380.1
2002	370.7	368.9	371.6	369.7	370.6	370.1	370.6	369.6	368.2	369.8	376.6	380.5	371.4
2003	365.6	363.7	366.7	367.9	369.1	370.8	372.4	373.1	372.4	375.3	378.2	381.7	371.4
Wholesale trade													
1990	67.5	67.6	67.8	68.3	68.4	69.2	68.8	69.3	69.2	69.0	68.9	68.8	68.6
1991	67.1	67.0	67.6	67.6	67.6	67.6	67.7	67.9	68.0	68.0	67.6	67.5	67.6
1992	66.4	66.5	67.2	67.7	67.9	68.2	68.1	68.1	68.1	68.5	68.2	68.6	67.8
1993	67.6	67.7	67.9	68.6	68.7	69.0	70.0	72.0	72.4	72.6	72.7	73.1	70.2
1994	72.1	72.5	72.8	73.0	73.1	73.8	72.5	74.8	75.4	75.1	75.7	76.2	73.9
1995	75.1	75.5	76.0	76.6	76.9	77.7	76.0	77.4	78.0	77.7	78.0	78.5	77.0
1996	77.5	77.8	78.2	78.0	77.9	78.5	77.4	79.5	79.4	79.7	79.5	79.7	78.6
1997	78.9	79.2	79.6	80.2	80.7	80.9	79.0	81.0	81.1	81.3	81.4	81.8	80.4
1998	80.6	80.9	81.1	82.2	82.3	83.0	82.2	82.0	82.2	81.8	81.7	82.2	81.9
1999	81.3	81.5	82.1	82.0	82.0	82.5	82.8	82.8	83.3	83.0	83.0	83.7	82.5
2000	83.0	83.2	83.7	83.2	83.7	84.1	83.9	84.2	84.2	84.3	84.5	84.7	83.9
2001	83.7	84.0	83.8	83.6	83.5	83.4	82.9	82.8	82.4	82.0	81.4	81.3	82.9
2002	79.5	79.1	79.1	78.3	78.2	78.2	78.1	78.1	78.0	77.6	77.8	78.0	78.3
2003	76.4	76.3	76.6	76.3	76.7	76.9	76.9	76.8	77.1	77.2	77.3	77.0	76.7
Retail trade													
1990	189.0	185.9	186.3	186.8	188.0	190.2	190.0	191.6	191.4	190.7	196.4	200.3	190.6
1991	192.3	189.0	190.7	191.0	192.1	192.0	192.1	193.3	193.1	194.6	199.2	203.0	193.5
1992	191.5	190.1	191.0	193.7	196.0	196.9	196.0	197.1	196.9	198.5	203.7	208.9	196.7
1993	198.0	197.0	197.5	201.5	201.3	202.4	201.8	203.0	203.6	206.9	211.8	217.6	203.5
1994	206.3	204.3	205.2	206.4	207.6	209.4	209.9	210.3	212.7	213.1	218.5	224.3	210.7
1995	213.2	210.9	212.2	214.7	216.0	218.6	217.9	219.1	220.5	220.2	227.4	231.4	218.5
1996	219.7	216.4	218.6	218.8	220.0	222.3	222.5	222.8	222.9	224.3	230.5	236.2	222.9
1997	225.0	221.3	224.6	222.3	224.0	225.2	227.1	227.7	228.3	230.2	236.4	241.4	227.8
1998	224.9	222.8	225.4	229.8	230.8	233.0	228.9	229.1	230.8	230.8	235.8	240.1	230.2
1999	227.5	227.4	230.7	228.6	230.4	233.1	232.5	233.7	235.3	234.9	239.6	244.4	233.2
2000	231.1	229.0	230.6	230.4	232.6	233.8	231.2	231.9	232.9	234.0	240.3	243.8	233.5
2001	229.2	226.0	227.9	227.4	228.6	229.7	227.0	227.4	226.5	228.1	235.5	238.2	229.3
2002	226.4	225.0	227.3	225.5	225.8	225.2	225.3	224.1	223.0	225.3	231.9	235.7	226.7
2003	223.5	222.2	224.8	226.7	226.9	228.1	229.3	230.3	229.5	231.8	234.8	238.8	228.8

Employment by Industry: Alabama—*Continued*

(Numbers in thousands. Not seasonally adjusted.)

Industry	January	February	March	April	May	June	July	August	September	October	November	December	Annual Average
STATEWIDE—*Continued*													
Transportation and utilities													
1990	57.7	57.7	57.9	57.7	58.2	59.2	58.6	58.5	58.3	58.4	58.0	58.2	58.2
1991	59.0	59.2	59.8	59.4	60.0	60.3	60.3	60.3	60.3	60.0	60.3	60.8	60.0
1992	60.1	60.0	60.1	59.7	60.1	61.0	62.0	62.0	62.1	62.1	61.9	62.8	61.2
1993	61.1	61.3	61.5	62.2	62.5	63.4	63.3	63.5	63.6	64.1	64.1	63.9	62.9
1994	62.5	62.5	62.8	63.6	63.9	64.6	64.2	64.4	64.6	65.2	65.4	65.3	64.1
1995	63.4	63.0	63.1	63.6	63.7	64.4	64.2	64.3	64.5	65.2	65.2	65.6	64.2
1996	64.2	64.6	64.3	64.2	64.3	64.5	64.7	65.3	65.6	65.7	65.7	65.5	64.9
1997	64.4	64.2	64.3	65.3	65.8	66.1	66.4	65.0	65.2	66.5	66.6	67.2	65.6
1998	66.2	66.7	67.4	66.6	67.0	67.6	67.9	67.6	68.1	68.9	68.6	68.8	67.6
1999	67.3	67.6	67.8	68.4	68.3	68.3	68.5	68.2	67.9	68.8	68.1	68.3	68.1
2000	67.1	67.3	67.3	66.9	67.7	68.1	67.9	68.0	67.7	67.7	67.8	67.7	67.6
2001	66.6	67.3	67.8	68.0	68.3	68.8	68.2	68.4	68.0	67.8	67.5	67.7	67.9
2002	64.8	64.8	65.2	65.9	66.6	66.7	67.2	67.4	67.2	66.9	66.9	66.8	66.4
2003	65.7	65.2	65.3	64.9	65.5	65.8	66.2	66.0	65.8	66.3	66.1	65.9	65.7
Information													
1990	31.4	31.5	31.5	31.6	31.9	32.1	32.0	32.0	31.9	31.6	31.8	31.8	31.8
1991	31.0	31.0	31.0	30.9	30.8	30.7	30.6	30.5	30.4	30.4	30.3	30.2	30.7
1992	29.9	29.9	29.9	30.0	30.1	30.4	30.5	30.3	30.3	30.4	30.6	30.8	30.3
1993	30.1	30.0	30.1	30.1	30.0	30.3	30.3	30.4	30.4	30.5	30.5	30.8	30.3
1994	30.3	30.5	30.7	30.4	30.5	30.8	30.9	30.9	31.0	30.8	30.9	31.1	30.7
1995	30.8	30.8	31.0	31.1	31.1	31.5	31.4	31.4	31.2	31.2	31.3	31.5	31.2
1996	31.1	31.1	31.1	31.7	31.9	31.8	31.9	31.8	31.7	31.6	31.8	32.1	31.6
1997	31.6	31.7	31.8	31.7	31.7	32.1	32.5	32.6	32.6	32.6	32.6	32.8	32.2
1998	32.6	32.9	32.4	32.2	32.4	32.5	32.6	32.4	32.5	32.7	32.7	33.1	32.6
1999	33.2	33.4	33.7	33.5	34.0	34.2	34.5	34.5	34.2	34.3	34.4	34.6	34.0
2000	34.2	34.3	34.8	34.7	35.0	35.5	36.0	36.3	36.2	36.4	36.6	37.0	35.6
2001	36.8	36.7	36.8	36.3	36.4	36.3	35.8	35.6	35.1	34.9	35.0	35.0	35.9
2002	34.7	34.4	34.6	34.3	34.2	34.2	34.1	33.7	33.2	33.2	33.2	33.1	33.9
2003	32.5	32.6	32.6	31.6	31.7	31.8	31.8	31.5	31.1	31.4	31.6	31.5	31.8
Financial activities													
1990	79.7	79.7	79.6	80.2	80.4	80.9	80.9	80.9	80.6	79.9	79.5	79.7	80.2
1991	77.6	77.6	78.0	77.8	78.3	78.9	79.6	79.9	79.6	79.3	79.2	79.6	78.8
1992	79.1	79.2	79.4	79.4	79.9	80.5	80.6	80.4	80.1	80.2	80.3	80.9	80.0
1993	80.1	80.3	80.8	80.8	81.0	82.0	82.2	82.6	82.3	82.2	82.3	82.6	81.6
1994	81.1	81.3	81.8	82.8	83.1	83.8	83.8	83.8	83.5	82.9	83.0	83.6	82.9
1995	82.6	82.7	83.3	83.7	83.6	84.4	84.1	84.1	83.5	83.3	83.6	84.0	83.6
1996	82.8	83.2	83.5	83.9	84.5	85.6	86.0	86.5	86.4	86.5	87.0	87.9	85.3
1997	87.8	88.2	89.2	89.3	90.0	90.8	91.2	91.7	92.2	92.3	92.6	93.7	90.8
1998	92.5	92.8	93.4	93.8	94.4	94.8	95.1	95.2	94.7	94.7	94.8	95.7	94.3
1999	96.1	96.6	97.1	97.1	97.6	98.2	98.0	98.0	97.7	98.1	98.0	98.7	97.6
2000	97.3	97.3	98.0	98.5	98.7	99.3	100.0	100.0	99.4	99.4	99.4	99.8	98.9
2001	96.9	97.0	97.4	97.9	98.3	99.0	99.0	98.9	98.3	97.7	97.5	98.0	98.0
2002	96.8	96.4	96.7	97.3	97.6	97.8	97.9	97.8	97.0	97.0	96.8	97.2	97.2
2003	95.9	95.5	95.7	96.0	96.4	97.0	97.7	97.7	97.0	96.7	96.8	97.2	96.6
Professional and business services													
1990	110.9	111.9	113.5	115.7	115.7	118.3	117.2	118.5	118.8	120.3	120.1	120.4	116.8
1991	117.7	118.0	119.5	119.6	118.9	120.1	122.0	122.9	123.4	124.0	123.8	124.2	121.2
1992	125.0	126.4	127.9	130.5	129.6	131.1	132.3	134.0	134.4	133.6	132.1	132.5	130.8
1993	132.8	134.9	135.7	138.3	136.4	137.1	138.2	138.4	138.7	139.9	139.5	139.3	137.4
1994	136.4	138.0	139.7	139.6	137.9	139.8	140.4	142.3	143.8	143.7	144.1	145.1	140.9
1995	143.3	145.3	146.1	147.2	148.8	149.5	150.0	151.4	152.1	152.4	152.6	152.7	149.3
1996	147.3	148.8	151.8	153.2	154.8	155.4	156.8	159.3	159.4	159.9	160.7	160.7	155.7
1997	154.6	157.0	159.3	160.1	160.1	162.5	163.3	165.6	165.6	165.1	164.3	165.2	161.9
1998	161.6	164.1	167.3	169.9	170.4	173.9	174.0	175.5	174.9	175.4	174.4	174.6	171.3
1999	170.9	173.2	175.6	177.2	176.8	178.8	179.1	180.3	181.0	181.1	181.3	181.6	178.1
2000	176.5	178.6	181.6	183.5	182.2	184.8	184.2	186.8	187.8	187.1	186.5	185.8	183.8
2001	181.8	183.9	186.3	186.3	185.2	186.9	186.1	188.6	187.6	186.0	184.0	183.4	185.5
2002	177.5	179.2	183.2	184.5	184.2	185.8	186.1	189.2	188.4	188.7	187.7	186.3	185.1
2003	182.7	184.4	186.0	186.4	186.4	186.9	186.0	187.5	187.2	188.3	187.4	187.1	186.3
Educational and health services													
1990	125.2	126.4	126.9	127.4	127.2	126.8	126.5	127.6	129.8	131.6	132.9	133.4	128.5
1991	131.1	132.5	133.7	134.2	134.6	133.6	134.3	135.2	137.2	138.0	137.9	138.7	135.1
1992	138.9	139.6	140.4	141.1	141.4	140.5	140.6	141.7	143.8	145.0	145.0	145.4	142.0
1993	144.7	146.0	146.6	147.7	147.7	147.1	147.2	148.1	150.1	150.9	151.2	151.6	148.2
1994	149.2	150.6	151.7	152.4	151.9	150.6	151.5	152.1	154.8	155.0	155.8	156.4	152.7
1995	155.5	157.0	157.8	158.6	158.6	158.1	157.3	158.6	160.7	161.7	163.1	163.4	159.2
1996	160.5	161.7	162.5	162.9	162.5	161.6	161.4	162.5	164.7	165.6	167.0	167.7	163.4
1997	166.6	168.0	168.4	170.0	170.0	169.4	169.6	170.3	172.1	173.6	174.7	174.7	170.6
1998	171.7	172.4	172.3	173.5	172.7	171.6	170.0	170.4	171.8	171.8	173.1	172.8	172.0
1999	169.3	171.1	171.1	172.1	171.4	170.8	170.2	170.1	172.5	173.7	175.4	175.6	171.9
2000	172.1	173.4	174.1	175.1	175.0	175.0	175.3	175.9	177.4	177.3	178.6	178.1	175.6
2001	171.8	174.8	174.9	176.9	176.3	175.8	175.9	176.8	179.1	179.8	182.5	182.4	177.3
2002	177.1	180.9	181.2	183.2	182.5	182.2	181.0	182.7	185.0	185.9	188.3	187.1	183.1
2003	184.4	186.2	186.5	187.7	187.3	185.4	185.1	185.3	187.5	187.7	189.4	187.8	186.6

Employment by Industry: Alabama—*Continued*

(Numbers in thousands. Not seasonally adjusted.)

Industry	January	February	March	April	May	June	July	August	September	October	November	December	Annual Average
STATEWIDE—*Continued*													
Leisure and hospitality													
1990	100.2	101.8	103.3	106.5	108.5	110.2	109.7	110.3	108.0	106.6	106.2	105.8	106.4
1991	103.0	104.0	106.2	108.8	110.4	112.0	112.7	112.7	111.2	109.0	108.4	108.2	108.9
1992	107.4	109.1	111.3	113.8	116.0	117.4	117.3	117.5	115.9	115.5	116.2	115.5	114.4
1993	112.6	114.0	114.9	118.9	121.1	122.6	123.1	123.4	122.2	121.6	121.3	120.9	119.7
1994	117.6	118.9	122.1	125.1	126.7	128.6	129.0	129.2	128.1	125.6	125.5	124.9	125.1
1995	122.7	124.5	127.5	131.0	132.8	136.2	134.7	135.0	133.4	131.5	131.2	131.6	131.0
1996	128.3	128.9	132.0	135.5	136.9	138.5	139.7	139.8	137.8	136.4	135.8	135.2	135.4
1997	132.0	133.5	136.1	140.4	142.8	144.9	143.7	144.2	142.6	139.7	139.0	138.5	139.8
1998	136.2	138.9	142.0	145.5	148.2	151.1	151.9	150.7	148.5	146.2	146.3	145.7	145.9
1999	141.4	144.2	147.5	149.0	150.4	153.3	154.1	154.1	152.1	148.0	147.3	147.0	149.0
2000	141.8	143.5	147.3	149.1	151.7	153.6	151.8	152.4	150.5	147.8	147.3	146.7	148.6
2001	143.1	145.3	148.8	152.6	154.8	157.1	155.4	155.5	152.2	149.8	148.9	149.0	151.0
2002	144.3	146.2	149.2	151.9	154.6	155.9	156.3	156.2	153.5	150.3	150.1	149.6	151.5
2003	146.1	148.0	151.5	154.5	156.4	158.6	158.4	159.3	157.1	153.8	153.6	154.2	154.2
Other services													
1990	59.9	60.1	60.4	60.8	61.2	61.7	61.4	61.7	61.8	61.7	61.6	61.4	61.1
1991	61.7	61.6	62.2	62.4	62.6	62.4	63.0	63.2	63.1	63.0	62.9	62.9	62.6
1992	62.4	62.5	62.7	63.2	63.6	63.5	63.8	63.9	64.0	64.5	63.9	64.2	63.5
1993	64.3	64.7	65.0	66.0	66.6	66.2	66.6	66.9	67.4	68.0	67.7	68.2	66.5
1994	67.9	68.6	69.4	69.5	69.4	69.3	68.8	69.0	68.7	68.6	68.5	68.7	68.9
1995	67.6	67.7	68.2	68.7	69.2	70.0	69.9	70.4	70.8	71.1	71.8	72.2	69.8
1996	71.2	71.9	72.6	73.2	73.7	73.8	73.6	73.8	73.8	73.8	74.0	73.9	73.3
1997	73.1	73.3	73.9	73.6	72.2	72.1	72.2	72.0	71.9	71.4	71.2	71.1	72.3
1998	71.1	71.4	71.6	71.9	72.4	73.0	73.4	73.6	73.8	74.1	74.3	74.8	73.0
1999	74.8	75.4	76.1	76.3	76.8	77.4	78.1	78.5	78.8	78.8	79.2	79.6	77.5
2000	79.1	79.9	81.1	81.1	81.2	81.7	81.7	81.5	81.4	81.4	81.3	81.6	81.1
2001	84.2	84.7	84.5	85.1	85.2	85.5	85.6	85.9	85.5	85.1	84.8	84.6	85.1
2002	86.0	86.6	87.0	86.8	86.9	86.6	86.2	86.1	85.3	84.7	84.4	83.9	85.9
2003	83.1	83.3	83.4	83.6	84.0	84.7	84.2	84.4	83.8	83.1	82.9	82.8	83.6
Government													
1990	323.4	325.7	327.5	330.7	334.5	321.5	325.1	310.0	326.1	330.9	333.4	331.0	326.7
1991	331.6	333.6	334.7	335.7	338.1	330.2	326.6	315.7	330.5	337.8	339.5	337.4	332.6
1992	335.2	338.4	339.7	339.6	343.3	334.1	333.9	329.9	332.2	342.7	344.0	341.9	337.9
1993	339.6	343.8	344.8	343.6	345.9	338.4	335.1	326.2	336.5	344.3	346.4	344.2	340.7
1994	344.6	346.2	347.0	348.4	349.0	346.8	338.5	330.4	342.4	348.3	363.7	346.5	346.0
1995	344.4	348.0	348.1	347.6	348.5	343.3	335.0	327.7	337.9	345.8	346.6	344.9	343.2
1996	342.7	345.8	347.0	347.7	348.8	339.6	335.5	330.1	338.4	346.1	348.1	344.4	342.9
1997	345.6	348.5	350.1	350.6	352.1	342.8	339.7	332.2	342.4	350.1	351.8	349.0	346.2
1998	348.6	351.0	352.3	350.4	351.6	344.9	334.3	333.4	345.7	349.6	352.1	351.0	347.1
1999	349.9	353.1	355.0	355.6	354.2	347.6	342.3	338.0	350.5	353.8	354.9	354.1	350.8
2000	351.6	354.4	358.3	356.6	364.7	348.4	338.5	336.7	350.4	353.3	353.9	353.9	351.7
2001	351.5	355.4	355.2	355.2	355.2	348.5	339.8	341.4	352.5	355.7	356.6	356.6	352.0
2002	352.5	355.9	356.6	358.3	357.5	351.3	341.3	342.6	356.3	360.2	361.6	361.4	354.6
2003	358.3	362.0	362.9	363.4	363.3	354.4	344.4	346.4	361.0	363.5	363.8	363.1	358.8
Federal government													
1990	65.4	65.0	66.1	66.1	68.6	67.5	67.8	65.0	64.3	63.9	63.9	63.8	65.6
1991	62.8	62.9	62.9	63.6	63.4	64.0	64.4	64.4	64.6	64.5	64.6	64.2	63.9
1992	63.5	63.3	63.4	63.5	63.4	63.6	63.5	62.9	62.7	63.1	63.0	63.1	63.3
1993	61.6	61.7	61.7	60.7	60.5	60.7	60.9	60.7	60.0	59.7	59.7	59.7	60.6
1994	59.3	59.2	59.1	58.8	58.4	58.5	58.5	58.3	58.3	57.6	57.3	57.3	58.4
1995	56.6	56.4	56.3	56.1	56.3	56.2	56.2	56.2	56.0	55.8	55.6	55.7	56.1
1996	55.1	55.0	54.9	55.0	54.9	55.0	55.0	55.0	54.6	54.0	53.8	54.0	54.7
1997	54.6	54.4	54.6	54.4	54.4	54.4	54.3	54.5	54.3	54.2	54.7	54.4	54.4
1998	54.1	53.8	54.0	53.8	54.0	54.2	54.2	54.2	54.3	54.9	55.6	55.9	54.4
1999	53.7	53.6	54.0	53.7	52.9	52.9	52.9	53.0	52.9	52.8	52.8	53.1	53.2
2000	52.4	52.4	54.9	53.6	61.1	52.8	54.7	52.4	51.4	51.4	51.3	51.8	53.4
2001	51.3	51.2	51.3	51.3	51.4	51.7	51.8	51.7	51.7	51.3	51.5	51.6	51.5
2002	51.2	50.9	50.9	50.9	50.9	51.2	51.3	51.1	50.9	51.0	51.3	51.4	51.1
2003	50.7	50.6	50.3	49.9	49.9	50.4	50.6	50.5	50.4	50.5	50.4	50.7	50.4
State government													
1990	87.7	89.2	89.2	90.9	90.7	85.9	85.3	85.3	89.7	93.6	94.6	92.5	89.6
1991	93.5	94.5	94.6	94.0	94.7	89.6	88.4	88.1	91.4	96.5	96.7	94.4	93.0
1992	94.3	96.4	96.4	95.5	97.5	91.0	91.0	90.4	92.8	98.7	98.7	96.1	94.9
1993	96.0	98.2	98.3	98.5	98.3	93.7	92.7	92.2	93.0	99.5	100.2	97.9	96.5
1994	98.1	99.5	99.5	100.0	99.6	94.8	94.7	96.7	98.9	103.1	103.5	100.3	99.1
1995	100.1	102.3	101.9	102.0	101.2	95.5	94.8	95.2	95.8	100.4	100.5	98.7	99.0
1996	97.6	100.3	100.5	99.9	99.1	93.0	93.6	93.9	94.7	99.9	100.6	96.8	97.5
1997	97.7	99.7	99.9	100.4	99.8	93.9	93.7	94.1	95.4	99.9	100.0	97.0	97.6
1998	97.7	99.4	99.5	98.0	97.5	92.8	92.7	92.5	94.8	94.6	95.1	93.3	95.7
1999	96.0	97.7	98.2	98.1	96.4	91.9	91.8	92.4	96.4	98.4	98.7	97.3	96.1
2000	96.3	98.4	98.7	98.0	97.0	91.7	89.3	89.3	95.9	98.3	98.0	97.6	95.7
2001	96.1	98.8	98.7	97.9	96.4	91.5	91.1	92.9	97.4	99.7	99.5	99.0	96.6
2002	96.7	99.3	99.5	100.6	98.5	94.2	94.3	94.7	99.9	102.2	102.2	101.7	98.7
2003	100.0	102.7	103.4	104.0	102.6	95.4	96.5	97.5	103.2	104.4	104.2	103.2	101.4

Employment by Industry: Alabama—*Continued*

(Numbers in thousands. Not seasonally adjusted.)

Industry	January	February	March	April	May	June	July	August	September	October	November	December	Annual Average
STATEWIDE—*Continued*													
Local government													
1990	170.3	171.5	172.2	173.7	175.2	168.1	172.0	159.7	172.1	173.4	174.9	174.7	171.5
1991	175.3	176.2	177.2	178.1	180.0	176.6	173.8	163.2	174.5	176.8	178.2	178.8	175.7
1992	177.4	178.7	179.9	180.6	182.4	179.5	179.4	176.6	176.7	180.9	182.3	182.7	179.8
1993	182.0	183.9	184.8	184.4	187.1	184.0	181.5	173.3	183.5	185.1	186.5	186.6	183.6
1994	187.2	187.5	188.4	189.6	191.0	193.5	185.3	175.4	185.2	187.6	202.9	188.9	188.5
1995	187.7	189.3	189.9	189.5	191.0	191.6	184.0	176.3	186.1	189.6	190.5	190.5	188.0
1996	190.0	190.5	191.6	192.8	194.8	191.6	186.9	181.2	189.1	192.2	193.7	193.6	190.7
1997	193.3	194.4	195.6	195.8	197.9	194.5	191.7	183.6	192.7	196.0	197.1	197.6	194.2
1998	196.8	197.8	198.8	198.6	200.1	197.9	187.4	186.7	196.6	200.1	201.4	201.8	197.0
1999	200.2	201.8	202.8	203.8	204.9	202.8	197.6	192.6	201.2	202.6	203.4	203.7	201.5
2000	202.9	203.6	204.7	205.0	206.6	203.9	194.5	195.0	203.1	203.6	204.6	204.5	202.7
2001	204.1	205.4	205.2	206.0	207.4	205.3	196.9	196.8	203.4	204.7	205.6	206.0	203.9
2002	204.6	205.7	206.2	206.8	208.1	205.9	195.7	196.8	205.5	207.0	208.1	208.3	204.9
2003	207.6	208.7	209.2	209.5	210.8	208.6	197.3	198.4	207.4	208.6	209.2	209.2	207.0
BIRMINGHAM													
Total nonfarm													
1990	393.9	395.4	397.3	400.1	401.4	402.5	402.0	399.8	403.0	404.4	404.8	406.8	401.0
1991	399.2	399.7	402.3	401.1	401.8	401.3	402.1	401.2	404.2	404.5	406.8	407.8	402.7
1992	400.3	401.6	403.1	407.4	409.5	410.3	408.6	408.0	411.7	414.1	414.5	417.2	408.9
1993	409.1	410.1	411.2	415.5	417.0	418.7	419.3	417.4	421.8	424.5	427.0	429.4	418.4
1994	419.5	421.2	423.9	425.8	427.6	429.7	430.0	429.4	435.0	435.4	439.6	441.5	429.9
1995	435.0	435.6	439.1	439.8	440.5	443.9	442.5	441.7	445.1	446.9	450.5	452.1	442.7
1996	443.0	443.8	446.6	448.2	450.2	449.9	450.5	450.4	453.5	456.2	458.2	460.8	450.9
1997	453.6	455.4	459.1	461.2	462.3	464.0	462.1	461.7	464.5	469.4	472.6	474.5	463.4
1998	463.6	466.0	469.5	472.8	475.4	476.5	472.6	471.3	473.8	476.2	478.7	480.9	473.1
1999	470.7	473.6	476.5	479.4	480.9	482.4	482.1	481.0	485.5	486.1	488.5	491.5	481.5
2000	478.4	480.2	483.3	483.3	486.4	486.7	485.2	484.3	488.1	488.7	490.6	491.2	485.5
2001	482.9	483.8	486.7	486.6	487.7	489.0	483.1	482.4	482.6	483.8	485.2	486.5	485.0
2002	476.2	476.6	479.5	479.0	479.1	478.5	477.1	475.8	477.1	477.3	480.3	479.9	478.0
2003	468.8	470.5	473.0	473.2	474.2	473.8	472.2	474.3	475.5	478.9	479.3	480.4	474.5
Total private													
1990	331.9	333.1	334.8	336.9	338.0	342.0	340.1	341.0	339.4	339.9	340.0	341.8	338.2
1991	334.8	333.7	335.9	335.5	336.2	337.8	339.4	340.2	339.0	338.5	340.5	341.5	337.8
1992	334.9	335.5	336.8	340.6	342.2	344.3	343.3	344.3	344.5	346.1	346.5	349.5	342.4
1993	341.6	342.7	343.8	348.0	349.3	352.5	354.1	354.1	355.0	356.7	359.2	361.5	351.5
1994	351.8	353.5	355.9	357.8	359.3	362.6	363.8	364.5	367.1	366.1	369.3	371.8	362.0
1995	366.4	366.8	370.1	370.9	371.8	375.6	376.5	377.2	377.7	378.0	381.2	382.7	374.6
1996	374.1	374.8	377.3	378.8	380.6	381.9	384.0	385.5	385.7	386.4	387.9	390.6	382.3
1997	384.1	385.7	389.0	391.8	392.7	395.5	395.9	396.5	397.2	399.5	402.1	404.2	394.5
1998	394.0	396.4	399.8	403.6	405.7	407.6	406.8	406.8	406.7	407.3	409.5	411.2	404.6
1999	402.4	405.0	407.9	410.1	412.3	414.6	415.9	415.9	417.5	417.2	419.2	421.9	413.3
2000	409.5	411.1	413.9	413.8	415.6	418.9	418.4	418.8	419.3	418.8	420.9	421.4	416.7
2001	413.4	413.8	416.6	416.8	417.6	419.9	415.9	415.6	413.5	413.4	414.8	416.1	415.6
2002	406.4	406.6	409.2	408.8	408.5	408.8	409.7	408.8	407.1	406.1	408.6	408.2	408.1
2003	397.6	398.8	400.9	400.6	401.5	402.9	402.8	404.9	402.9	405.3	405.4	406.0	402.4
Goods-producing													
1990	79.6	80.9	80.5	82.0	82.5	83.5	82.6	82.7	82.2	81.3	80.2	80.0	81.5
1991	79.3	78.7	79.4	79.5	79.1	79.5	79.2	79.1	78.6	77.9	77.7	77.2	78.8
1992	75.1	75.1	74.9	75.7	75.6	76.1	74.7	75.1	75.2	76.2	76.0	75.9	75.5
1993	74.0	74.6	74.8	75.8	76.5	77.2	77.3	77.5	77.6	78.1	78.6	78.4	76.7
1994	76.7	77.1	77.8	78.2	78.9	79.6	79.9	79.8	81.0	80.3	81.0	81.1	79.3
1995	80.8	80.6	82.2	82.1	81.9	82.6	82.6	82.5	82.7	82.8	82.8	82.2	82.2
1996	81.8	81.7	82.5	82.7	83.1	83.5	83.9	84.0	83.8	83.0	83.0	82.7	83.0
1997	81.5	82.5	83.2	83.8	83.9	84.2	83.7	83.7	84.0	84.6	84.5	85.0	83.7
1998	83.6	83.9	84.9	84.9	85.3	85.6	84.6	84.3	84.3	84.7	84.6	84.3	84.6
1999	83.4	83.8	84.0	84.6	85.5	84.9	85.1	84.9	85.3	85.1	85.5	85.8	84.8
2000	84.2	84.4	85.2	86.2	86.6	87.5	87.2	87.2	87.3	86.7	86.7	86.2	86.3
2001	82.0	81.4	81.9	81.6	81.4	81.3	79.5	79.3	78.9	78.6	78.0	78.0	80.2
2002	75.4	74.7	75.3	75.9	75.6	75.5	75.3	75.2	74.8	75.2	74.9	74.1	75.2
2003	72.9	72.8	73.4	73.1	73.0	72.9	72.5	73.2	72.8	72.7	72.1	71.7	72.7
Construction and mining													
1990	25.7	25.8	26.1	26.1	26.4	26.9	26.6	26.7	26.2	25.9	25.6	25.7	26.1
1991	25.2	25.1	25.4	25.8	25.6	25.9	26.2	26.3	25.8	25.4	25.1	24.8	25.6
1992	23.4	23.3	23.3	23.9	23.8	24.0	23.9	24.0	24.1	24.6	24.2	24.2	23.9
1993	22.8	23.2	23.3	24.1	24.3	25.0	25.3	25.4	25.4	25.8	25.9	25.8	24.7
1994	24.7	25.1	25.6	25.8	26.0	26.5	26.9	27.1	27.2	26.7	27.0	26.8	26.3
1995	26.2	26.3	27.4	27.0	26.9	27.6	28.1	28.2	28.2	28.3	28.6	28.4	27.6
1996	28.1	28.2	28.9	29.1	29.5	29.9	30.5	31.4	31.2	30.3	30.2	30.0	29.8
1997	28.9	29.4	29.9	30.5	30.6	31.1	31.2	31.4	31.4	31.4	31.2	31.2	30.7
1998	30.3	30.5	31.2	31.0	31.3	32.0	31.5	31.3	31.3	31.3	31.1	31.0	31.2
1999	30.6	31.1	31.4	31.9	32.3	31.7	31.8	31.7	32.1	32.1	32.0	32.2	31.7
2000	31.4	31.6	32.2	32.6	32.8	33.6	33.8	33.8	34.0	33.3	33.4	33.2	33.0
2001	32.5	32.6	33.2	33.4	33.6	33.7	33.0	32.9	32.7	32.6	32.3	32.4	32.9
2002	30.7	31.0	31.4	32.3	32.2	32.0	32.4	32.3	32.2	32.8	32.6	32.0	32.0
2003	31.7	31.8	32.4	32.3	32.0	32.0	32.4	32.9	32.9	32.8	32.3	32.3	32.3

Employment by Industry: Alabama—*Continued*

(Numbers in thousands. Not seasonally adjusted.)

Industry	January	February	March	April	May	June	July	August	September	October	November	December	Annual Average
BIRMINGHAM—*Continued*													
Manufacturing													
1990	53.9	55.1	54.4	55.9	56.1	56.6	56.0	56.0	56.0	55.4	54.6	54.3	55.4
1991	54.1	53.6	54.0	53.7	53.5	53.6	53.0	52.8	52.8	52.5	52.6	52.4	53.2
1992	51.7	51.8	51.6	51.8	51.8	52.1	50.8	51.1	51.1	51.6	51.8	51.7	51.6
1993	51.2	51.4	51.5	51.7	52.2	52.2	52.0	52.1	52.2	52.3	52.7	52.6	52.0
1994	52.0	52.0	52.2	52.4	52.9	53.1	53.0	52.7	53.8	53.6	54.0	54.3	53.0
1995	54.6	54.3	54.8	55.1	55.0	55.0	54.5	54.3	54.5	54.5	54.2	53.8	54.6
1996	53.7	53.5	53.6	53.6	53.6	53.6	53.4	52.6	52.6	52.7	52.8	52.7	53.2
1997	52.6	53.1	53.3	53.3	53.3	53.1	52.5	52.3	52.6	53.2	53.3	53.8	53.0
1998	53.3	53.4	53.7	53.9	54.0	53.6	53.1	53.0	53.0	53.4	53.5	53.3	53.4
1999	52.8	52.7	52.6	52.7	53.2	53.2	53.3	53.2	53.2	53.0	53.5	53.6	53.1
2000	52.8	52.8	53.0	53.6	53.8	53.9	53.4	53.4	53.3	53.4	53.3	53.0	53.3
2001	49.5	48.8	48.7	48.2	47.8	47.6	46.5	46.4	46.2	46.0	45.7	45.6	47.3
2002	44.7	43.7	43.9	43.6	43.4	43.5	42.9	42.9	42.6	42.4	42.3	42.1	43.2
2003	41.2	41.0	41.0	40.8	41.0	40.9	40.1	40.3	39.9	39.9	39.8	39.4	40.4
Service-providing													
1990	314.3	314.5	316.8	318.1	318.9	319.0	319.4	317.1	320.8	323.1	324.6	326.8	319.5
1991	319.9	321.0	322.9	321.6	322.7	321.8	322.9	322.1	325.6	326.6	329.1	330.6	323.9
1992	325.2	326.5	328.2	331.7	333.9	334.2	333.9	332.9	336.5	337.9	338.5	341.3	333.4
1993	335.1	335.5	336.4	339.7	340.5	341.5	342.0	339.9	344.2	346.4	348.4	351.0	341.7
1994	342.8	344.1	346.1	347.6	348.7	350.1	350.1	349.6	354.0	355.1	358.6	360.4	350.6
1995	354.2	355.0	356.9	357.7	358.6	361.3	359.9	359.2	362.4	364.1	367.7	369.9	360.6
1996	361.2	362.1	364.1	365.5	367.1	366.4	366.6	366.4	369.7	373.2	375.2	378.1	368.0
1997	372.1	372.9	375.9	377.4	378.4	379.8	378.4	378.0	380.5	384.8	388.1	389.5	379.7
1998	380.0	382.1	384.6	387.9	390.1	390.9	388.0	387.0	389.5	391.5	394.1	396.6	388.5
1999	387.3	389.8	392.5	394.8	395.4	397.5	397.0	396.1	400.2	401.0	403.0	405.7	396.7
2000	394.2	395.8	398.1	397.1	399.8	399.2	398.0	397.1	400.8	402.0	403.9	405.0	399.3
2001	400.9	402.4	404.8	405.0	406.3	407.7	403.6	403.1	403.7	405.2	407.2	408.5	404.9
2002	400.8	401.9	404.2	403.1	403.5	403.0	401.8	400.6	402.3	402.1	405.4	405.8	402.9
2003	395.9	397.7	399.6	400.1	401.2	400.9	399.7	401.1	402.7	406.2	407.2	408.7	401.7
Trade, transportation, and utilities													
1990	91.2	89.9	90.2	89.3	89.5	90.3	89.9	90.1	90.0	90.6	91.9	93.4	90.5
1991	88.1	87.1	87.4	87.2	87.6	87.7	88.2	88.5	88.2	88.3	89.9	91.2	88.3
1992	87.9	87.4	87.6	88.2	88.9	89.3	89.2	89.5	89.4	90.1	91.0	93.4	89.3
1993	89.6	89.1	89.3	91.0	91.0	91.6	91.5	91.6	92.0	92.7	94.2	96.2	91.7
1994	92.2	91.6	91.9	92.0	92.3	93.3	94.2	94.2	95.0	95.0	96.9	98.9	94.0
1995	95.5	94.8	95.3	95.3	95.3	96.5	96.5	96.8	97.3	97.3	99.9	101.2	96.8
1996	97.3	96.3	96.8	97.0	97.2	97.8	97.5	97.5	97.9	98.6	100.1	102.0	98.0
1997	98.9	98.0	99.0	98.2	98.7	99.3	100.3	99.8	100.8	102.0	103.5	105.3	100.3
1998	100.3	100.0	100.9	103.2	104.0	104.6	102.3	102.5	102.9	102.9	104.7	106.5	102.9
1999	102.1	102.4	103.2	103.1	103.3	104.2	104.2	104.2	104.9	105.2	106.7	108.4	104.3
2000	103.8	103.1	103.3	102.2	103.0	103.1	102.7	102.6	103.7	104.2	106.1	107.1	103.7
2001	105.7	104.5	105.1	103.8	104.4	104.9	103.8	103.7	103.1	103.3	105.3	106.6	104.5
2002	103.0	102.2	102.7	101.2	101.4	101.3	101.7	101.6	100.8	101.6	103.9	105.3	102.2
2003	101.1	100.7	101.2	100.7	101.2	101.8	102.3	102.7	102.3	103.3	104.3	105.5	102.2
Wholesale trade													
1990	26.0	25.9	25.9	25.6	25.5	25.6	25.4	25.5	25.4	25.7	25.6	25.6	25.6
1991	23.5	23.5	23.6	23.5	23.5	23.4	23.7	23.8	23.7	23.4	23.3	23.3	23.5
1992	23.3	23.3	23.4	23.4	23.6	23.7	23.7	23.7	23.6	23.9	23.8	23.9	23.6
1993	23.7	23.7	23.8	24.2	24.2	24.3	24.3	24.3	24.4	24.7	24.8	24.9	24.3
1994	24.7	24.7	24.8	24.7	24.8	25.0	25.4	25.4	25.5	25.6	25.7	25.9	25.2
1995	25.5	25.7	26.0	25.8	25.9	26.1	26.1	26.1	26.2	26.1	26.3	26.4	26.0
1996	26.1	26.3	26.4	26.5	26.5	26.6	26.7	26.7	26.8	26.9	26.8	27.0	26.6
1997	26.8	27.1	27.2	27.3	27.4	27.5	27.5	27.6	27.5	27.5	27.5	27.6	27.4
1998	27.2	27.4	27.4	27.4	27.5	27.7	27.5	27.5	27.5	27.2	27.3	27.6	27.4
1999	27.5	27.5	27.7	27.8	27.8	28.0	28.0	28.0	28.3	28.1	28.1	28.4	27.9
2000	28.0	28.1	28.2	27.5	27.6	27.7	27.7	27.7	27.9	27.8	27.9	27.9	27.8
2001	30.3	30.4	30.5	30.2	30.2	30.2	29.9	29.7	29.7	29.4	29.3	29.2	29.9
2002	29.2	29.1	29.1	28.9	28.8	28.8	28.8	28.9	28.6	28.5	28.6	28.6	28.8
2003	28.3	28.3	28.3	28.2	28.3	28.4	28.4	28.3	28.5	28.5	28.7	28.6	28.4
Retail trade													
1990	47.3	46.2	46.5	46.1	46.3	46.8	46.7	46.9	47.0	47.2	48.6	50.1	47.1
1991	46.5	45.5	45.7	45.7	45.9	45.9	46.4	46.7	46.5	47.2	48.8	49.9	46.7
1992	47.1	46.6	46.8	47.6	47.9	48.1	48.0	48.4	48.2	48.8	49.9	51.7	48.3
1993	48.6	48.1	48.2	49.5	49.5	49.8	49.6	49.8	50.0	50.5	51.9	53.8	49.9
1994	50.4	49.8	49.9	50.1	50.2	50.8	51.4	51.5	52.1	52.1	53.7	55.6	51.5
1995	53.2	52.2	52.4	52.5	52.4	53.3	53.2	53.5	53.9	53.7	56.0	57.0	53.6
1996	53.7	52.5	52.9	52.9	53.1	53.8	53.3	53.3	53.3	54.0	55.6	57.2	53.8
1997	54.4	53.4	54.3	53.0	53.3	53.8	54.7	54.6	55.0	55.6	57.0	58.6	54.8
1998	54.2	53.7	54.3	56.5	56.9	57.5	55.7	55.7	56.0	56.1	57.8	59.2	56.1
1999	55.5	55.8	56.4	56.1	56.5	57.4	57.1	57.2	57.6	57.7	59.2	60.8	57.3
2000	57.1	56.4	56.6	56.6	57.0	57.2	56.6	56.7	57.5	58.1	59.8	60.9	57.5
2001	56.5	55.2	55.7	54.9	55.4	55.9	55.2	55.2	54.8	55.3	57.5	58.7	55.9
2002	56.0	55.4	55.8	54.8	54.9	54.9	55.3	55.0	54.6	55.6	57.7	59.0	55.8
2003	55.5	55.2	55.6	55.5	55.7	56.2	56.6	57.1	56.7	57.5	58.4	59.7	56.6

Employment by Industry: Alabama—*Continued*

(Numbers in thousands. Not seasonally adjusted.)

Industry	January	February	March	April	May	June	July	August	September	October	November	December	Annual Average
BIRMINGHAM—*Continued*													
Transportation and utilities													
1990	17.9	17.8	17.8	17.6	17.7	17.9	17.8	17.7	17.6	17.7	17.7	17.7	17.7
1991	18.1	18.1	18.1	18.0	18.2	18.4	18.1	18.0	18.0	17.7	17.8	18.0	18.0
1992	17.5	17.5	17.4	17.2	17.4	17.5	17.5	17.4	17.6	17.4	17.3	17.8	17.5
1993	17.3	17.3	17.3	17.3	17.3	17.5	17.6	17.5	17.6	17.5	17.5	17.5	17.4
1994	17.1	17.1	17.2	17.2	17.3	17.5	17.4	17.3	17.4	17.3	17.5	17.4	17.3
1995	16.8	16.9	16.9	17.0	17.0	17.1	17.2	17.2	17.2	17.5	17.6	17.8	17.2
1996	17.5	17.5	17.5	17.6	17.6	17.4	17.5	17.5	17.8	17.7	17.7	17.8	17.6
1997	17.7	17.5	17.5	17.9	18.0	18.0	18.1	17.6	18.3	18.9	19.0	19.1	18.1
1998	18.9	18.9	19.2	19.3	19.6	19.4	19.1	19.3	19.4	19.6	19.6	19.7	19.3
1999	19.1	19.1	19.1	19.2	19.0	18.8	19.1	19.0	19.0	19.4	19.4	19.2	19.1
2000	18.7	18.6	18.5	18.1	18.4	18.2	18.4	18.2	18.3	18.3	18.4	18.3	18.4
2001	18.9	18.9	18.9	18.7	18.8	18.8	18.7	18.8	18.6	18.6	18.5	18.7	18.7
2002	17.8	17.7	17.8	17.5	17.7	17.6	17.6	17.7	17.6	17.5	17.6	17.7	17.7
2003	17.3	17.2	17.3	17.0	17.2	17.2	17.3	17.3	17.1	17.3	17.2	17.2	17.2
Information													
1990	14.3	14.2	14.3	14.4	14.5	14.5	14.5	14.6	14.4	14.4	14.4	14.3	14.4
1991	14.0	13.9	14.0	14.0	14.0	14.1	13.9	13.9	13.8	13.8	13.7	13.7	13.9
1992	13.2	13.2	13.2	13.4	13.4	13.4	13.5	13.4	13.4	13.4	13.5	13.5	13.4
1993	13.6	13.5	13.5	13.5	13.4	13.5	13.7	13.6	13.6	13.8	13.8	13.9	13.6
1994	13.7	13.7	13.8	13.6	13.7	13.7	13.7	13.7	13.7	13.8	13.8	13.8	13.7
1995	13.9	13.8	13.9	13.9	13.9	13.9	14.0	13.9	13.8	13.8	13.8	13.8	13.9
1996	13.7	13.7	13.7	14.1	14.2	14.0	14.0	13.8	13.8	13.7	13.6	13.7	13.8
1997	13.5	13.7	13.7	13.5	13.5	13.6	13.8	13.8	13.9	14.0	14.0	13.9	13.7
1998	13.9	14.1	13.5	13.3	13.2	13.4	13.4	13.5	13.7	13.8	13.8	13.9	13.6
1999	13.9	14.0	14.1	14.3	14.4	14.6	14.5	14.5	14.6	14.5	14.5	14.5	14.4
2000	14.4	14.4	14.5	14.2	14.2	14.4	14.8	14.9	14.8	15.1	15.2	15.3	14.7
2001	15.4	15.5	15.7	15.6	15.7	15.7	15.6	15.6	15.4	15.5	15.5	15.4	15.6
2002	15.4	15.3	15.5	15.3	15.2	15.2	15.3	15.1	14.9	15.1	15.0	14.8	15.2
2003	14.4	14.3	14.3	13.5	13.4	13.5	13.5	13.5	13.3	13.6	13.7	13.7	13.7
Financial activities													
1990	31.1	31.2	31.4	31.4	31.4	31.7	31.6	31.4	31.3	30.8	30.5	30.8	31.2
1991	30.4	30.3	30.4	30.3	30.4	30.7	31.1	31.1	31.0	30.8	31.0	31.1	30.7
1992	30.7	30.7	30.9	30.9	31.0	31.2	31.1	31.0	30.9	30.9	31.0	31.3	31.0
1993	30.9	31.0	31.1	30.9	31.1	31.5	31.7	31.8	31.7	31.7	31.8	32.0	31.4
1994	31.1	31.1	31.2	31.8	31.9	32.1	32.3	32.3	32.4	32.1	32.0	32.3	31.9
1995	31.7	31.7	31.8	32.0	32.1	32.3	32.2	32.1	31.8	31.9	32.0	32.3	32.0
1996	31.9	32.2	32.1	32.4	32.6	32.9	33.1	33.3	33.3	33.5	33.7	34.1	32.9
1997	33.8	34.1	34.5	34.6	34.7	34.9	34.9	35.0	35.0	35.7	36.0	36.2	35.0
1998	36.0	36.0	36.4	36.4	36.6	36.8	37.3	37.3	37.1	36.9	36.9	37.3	36.8
1999	37.9	38.0	38.3	38.6	38.6	38.8	38.7	38.7	38.6	38.8	38.8	39.0	38.6
2000	38.4	38.5	38.6	38.8	38.8	39.0	39.5	39.5	39.3	39.0	39.0	39.1	39.0
2001	39.1	39.3	39.3	39.7	39.8	40.1	40.0	40.1	39.8	39.8	39.7	39.8	39.7
2002	39.6	39.4	39.3	39.5	39.6	39.7	39.7	39.7	39.5	39.6	39.7	39.9	39.6
2003	38.8	38.7	38.6	38.9	39.0	39.2	39.4	39.4	39.2	39.5	39.4	39.4	39.1
Professional and business services													
1990	37.9	38.2	39.3	39.1	39.2	40.2	40.1	40.4	40.0	40.8	40.6	40.9	39.7
1991	41.4	41.3	41.7	41.3	41.4	41.7	41.8	42.1	41.8	42.1	42.3	42.4	41.8
1992	42.1	42.3	42.6	43.7	43.7	44.4	44.8	45.0	45.4	44.6	43.5	43.9	43.8
1993	43.8	44.0	44.0	44.5	44.3	45.0	45.6	45.5	45.8	46.2	46.2	46.3	45.1
1994	45.5	46.1	46.3	46.8	46.8	47.8	47.5	48.3	48.4	49.2	49.4	49.2	47.6
1995	49.5	49.9	50.2	50.2	50.8	51.0	52.8	53.4	53.8	53.8	54.1	54.0	52.0
1996	52.1	53.2	53.6	53.1	53.3	53.3	54.8	56.4	56.1	56.6	56.4	56.6	54.6
1997	56.1	56.3	56.8	58.1	57.8	58.9	58.4	59.0	59.0	58.7	59.4	59.5	58.2
1998	57.5	58.6	59.5	59.0	59.0	59.2	61.0	61.3	61.2	60.9	61.4	61.0	60.0
1999	60.2	60.6	60.8	60.6	60.7	61.4	61.8	62.0	62.4	63.2	63.1	63.3	61.7
2000	60.5	61.0	61.5	61.8	61.6	62.5	62.2	62.7	62.9	62.4	62.4	62.1	62.0
2001	61.4	61.7	62.3	62.8	62.9	63.7	63.4	63.5	63.1	63.1	62.9	62.9	62.8
2002	61.7	61.9	62.7	62.5	62.1	62.3	61.4	61.6	61.1	60.5	60.3	60.0	61.5
2003	58.6	59.2	59.5	59.3	59.4	59.7	59.9	60.4	60.0	60.8	60.5	60.2	59.7
Educational and health services													
1990	37.5	37.9	38.0	38.3	38.2	38.3	38.2	38.2	38.8	39.4	39.8	39.8	38.5
1991	39.5	40.0	40.3	40.4	40.3	40.1	40.4	40.6	41.1	41.7	41.9	42.1	40.7
1992	42.2	42.4	42.6	42.9	43.0	42.8	42.7	43.1	43.6	44.1	44.2	44.3	43.2
1993	43.9	44.3	44.7	44.9	44.8	44.7	45.3	45.1	45.5	45.8	45.9	46.0	45.1
1994	45.2	45.8	46.0	45.9	45.8	45.7	45.8	45.7	46.4	46.1	46.4	46.6	46.0
1995	46.1	46.7	46.7	46.6	46.6	46.8	46.1	46.2	46.5	46.8	47.0	47.0	46.6
1996	46.2	46.5	46.8	46.8	46.8	46.5	46.5	46.8	47.6	48.0	47.9	48.3	47.1
1997	48.1	48.5	48.8	49.7	49.8	49.7	49.9	50.5	50.6	50.8	51.0	51.0	49.9
1998	49.8	50.2	50.1	50.6	50.7	50.3	50.7	50.4	50.5	50.4	50.2	50.3	50.4
1999	48.7	49.1	49.2	49.3	49.3	49.4	49.5	49.3	49.8	49.7	49.8	50.1	49.4
2000	49.6	50.2	50.3	50.4	50.4	50.3	51.1	51.2	51.4	51.6	51.8	51.6	50.8
2001	50.7	51.6	51.7	52.1	51.8	51.6	51.6	51.4	52.1	52.5	53.1	53.0	51.9
2002	52.0	53.2	53.4	53.6	53.3	53.1	54.5	54.0	55.1	54.7	55.0	54.6	53.9
2003	53.9	54.7	54.9	54.9	54.6	54.2	54.1	54.1	54.5	54.7	54.7	54.1	54.4

Employment by Industry: Alabama—*Continued*

(Numbers in thousands. Not seasonally adjusted.)

Industry	January	February	March	April	May	June	July	August	September	October	November	December	Annual Average
BIRMINGHAM—*Continued*													
Leisure and hospitality													
1990	23.0	23.4	23.6	24.9	25.1	25.6	25.3	25.6	25.0	24.8	24.7	24.8	24.7
1991	24.1	24.3	24.5	24.7	25.2	25.7	26.1	26.2	26.1	25.6	25.7	25.6	25.3
1992	25.6	26.2	26.7	27.4	28.1	28.3	28.4	28.3	28.0	28.2	28.7	28.6	27.7
1993	27.3	27.6	27.8	28.6	29.3	29.8	29.6	29.5	29.4	28.9	29.3	29.2	28.9
1994	27.9	28.3	29.0	29.4	29.8	30.3	30.3	30.4	30.1	29.8	30.0	30.0	29.6
1995	29.3	29.6	30.3	30.8	31.1	32.2	31.8	31.7	31.2	31.0	30.8	31.3	30.9
1996	30.3	30.2	30.7	31.4	31.8	32.2	32.5	32.1	31.8	31.4	31.5	31.5	31.5
1997	30.7	30.9	31.2	32.6	33.1	33.7	33.4	33.2	32.7	32.6	32.7	32.4	32.4
1998	32.3	32.9	33.8	35.2	35.8	36.3	35.8	36.0	35.5	36.1	36.2	36.0	35.2
1999	34.2	35.0	36.0	37.1	37.8	38.3	38.7	38.9	38.6	37.4	37.4	37.3	37.2
2000	35.4	36.1	36.8	36.6	37.5	38.1	36.9	36.9	36.4	36.2	36.2	36.3	36.6
2001	35.8	36.5	37.3	37.7	38.1	38.9	38.1	38.1	37.3	36.8	36.6	36.7	37.3
2002	35.5	35.9	36.3	37.0	37.4	37.7	37.6	37.5	37.1	35.8	36.1	36.0	36.7
2003	34.9	35.4	36.0	37.0	37.6	38.1	37.6	38.1	37.7	37.8	38.0	38.6	37.2
Other services													
1990	17.3	17.4	17.5	17.5	17.6	17.9	17.9	18.0	17.7	17.8	17.9	17.8	17.7
1991	18.0	18.1	18.2	18.1	18.2	18.3	18.7	18.7	18.4	18.3	18.3	18.2	18.3
1992	18.1	18.2	18.3	18.4	18.5	18.8	18.9	18.9	18.6	18.6	18.6	18.6	18.5
1993	18.5	18.6	18.6	18.8	18.9	19.2	19.4	19.5	19.4	19.5	19.4	19.5	19.1
1994	19.5	19.8	19.9	20.1	20.1	20.1	20.1	20.1	20.1	19.8	19.8	19.9	19.9
1995	19.6	19.7	19.7	20.0	20.1	20.3	20.5	20.6	20.6	20.6	20.8	20.9	20.3
1996	20.8	21.0	21.1	21.3	21.6	21.7	21.7	21.6	21.4	21.6	21.7	21.7	21.4
1997	21.5	21.7	21.8	21.3	21.2	21.2	21.5	21.5	21.2	21.1	21.0	20.9	21.3
1998	20.6	20.7	20.7	21.0	21.1	21.4	21.7	21.5	21.5	21.6	21.7	21.9	21.3
1999	22.0	22.1	22.3	22.5	22.7	23.0	23.4	23.4	23.3	23.3	23.4	23.5	22.9
2000	23.2	23.4	23.7	23.6	23.5	24.0	24.0	23.8	23.5	23.6	23.5	23.7	23.6
2001	23.3	23.3	23.3	23.5	23.5	23.7	23.9	23.9	23.8	23.8	23.7	23.7	23.6
2002	23.8	24.0	24.0	23.8	23.9	24.0	24.2	24.1	23.8	23.6	23.7	23.5	23.9
2003	23.0	23.0	23.0	23.2	23.3	23.5	23.5	23.5	23.1	22.9	22.7	22.8	23.1
Government													
1990	62.0	62.3	62.5	63.2	63.4	60.5	61.9	58.8	63.6	64.5	64.8	65.0	62.7
1991	64.4	66.0	66.4	65.6	65.6	63.5	62.7	61.0	65.2	66.0	66.3	66.3	64.9
1992	65.4	66.1	66.3	66.8	67.3	66.0	65.3	63.7	67.2	68.0	68.0	67.7	66.5
1993	67.5	67.4	67.4	67.5	67.7	66.2	65.2	63.3	66.8	67.8	67.8	67.9	66.9
1994	67.7	67.7	68.0	68.0	68.3	67.1	66.2	64.9	67.9	69.3	70.3	69.7	67.9
1995	68.6	68.8	69.0	68.9	68.7	68.3	66.0	64.5	67.4	68.9	69.3	69.4	68.2
1996	68.9	69.0	69.3	69.4	69.6	68.0	66.5	64.9	67.8	69.8	70.3	70.2	68.6
1997	69.5	69.7	70.1	69.4	69.6	68.5	66.2	65.2	67.3	69.9	70.5	70.3	68.9
1998	69.6	69.6	69.7	69.2	69.7	68.9	65.8	64.5	67.1	68.9	69.2	69.7	68.5
1999	68.3	68.6	68.6	69.3	68.6	67.8	66.2	65.1	68.0	68.9	69.3	69.6	68.2
2000	68.9	69.1	69.4	69.5	70.8	67.8	66.8	65.5	68.8	69.9	69.7	69.8	68.8
2001	69.5	70.0	70.1	69.8	70.1	69.1	67.2	66.8	69.1	70.4	70.4	70.4	69.4
2002	69.8	70.0	70.3	70.2	70.6	69.7	67.4	67.0	70.0	71.2	71.7	71.7	70.0
2003	71.2	71.7	72.1	72.6	72.7	70.9	69.4	69.4	72.6	73.6	73.9	74.4	72.0
Federal government													
1992	10.0	10.0	10.0	9.9	9.9	9.9	10.1	10.1	10.2	10.3	10.2	10.3	10.1
1993	9.9	9.8	9.8	9.9	9.8	9.8	9.8	9.8	9.8	9.7	9.6	9.7	9.8
1994	9.6	9.5	9.5	9.5	9.6	9.5	9.9	9.9	10.0	10.0	10.1	10.1	9.8
1995	10.0	10.0	10.0	9.9	9.9	10.0	10.0	10.0	10.1	10.2	10.3	10.4	10.1
1996	10.2	10.2	10.2	10.3	10.2	10.3	10.4	10.4	10.1	10.1	10.1	10.2	10.2
1997	10.0	9.9	10.0	10.0	10.1	10.0	10.0	10.0	10.0	10.1	10.2	10.2	10.0
1998	10.0	9.9	9.8	9.8	9.8	9.8	9.7	9.6	9.6	10.0	10.3	10.5	9.9
1999	9.8	9.7	9.6	10.0	9.4	9.3	9.3	9.4	9.5	9.7	9.8	10.1	9.6
2000	9.7	9.6	9.7	9.7	11.0	9.3	9.6	9.2	9.1	9.1	9.1	9.2	9.5
2001	9.1	9.1	9.1	9.0	8.9	9.0	9.0	9.0	9.0	8.9	8.9	9.0	9.0
2002	8.8	8.7	8.7	8.6	8.6	8.6	8.6	8.6	8.6	8.9	9.0	9.0	8.7
2003	8.8	8.7	8.7	8.6	8.6	8.6	8.7	8.7	8.7	8.8	8.9	9.0	8.7
State government													
2001	22.2	22.4	22.4	22.3	22.4	22.0	21.9	22.0	22.1	23.0	22.8	22.7	22.4
2002	22.6	22.7	22.9	22.9	22.9	22.8	22.7	22.4	22.9	23.1	23.3	23.3	22.9
2003	23.1	23.5	24.0	24.5	24.5	23.4	24.1	24.2	24.7	25.2	25.4	25.5	24.3
Local government													
2001	38.2	38.5	38.6	38.5	38.8	38.1	36.3	35.8	38.0	38.5	38.7	38.7	38.1
2002	38.4	38.6	38.7	38.7	39.1	38.3	36.1	36.0	38.5	39.2	39.4	39.4	38.4
2003	39.3	39.5	39.4	39.5	39.6	38.9	36.6	36.5	39.2	39.6	39.6	39.9	38.9

Employment by Industry: Alabama—*Continued*

(Numbers in thousands. Not seasonally adjusted.)

Industry	January	February	March	April	May	June	July	August	September	October	November	December	Annual Average
HUNTSVILLE													
Total nonfarm													
1990	154.7	155.3	155.2	158.3	158.6	158.8	159.2	157.8	159.0	158.0	159.4	159.1	157.8
1991	156.2	154.3	154.1	155.7	157.0	157.4	156.1	155.9	158.0	157.7	158.5	159.3	156.7
1992	156.9	155.4	156.7	158.6	161.0	162.1	159.7	162.5	162.8	162.7	163.3	163.9	160.5
1993	162.6	164.0	163.8	165.0	164.2	163.4	162.6	163.9	163.7	164.0	164.9	164.6	163.9
1994	161.3	161.6	162.9	162.9	162.9	162.8	159.2	163.2	164.2	163.8	165.4	165.0	162.9
1995	162.5	163.2	164.1	165.7	166.9	166.6	163.5	165.3	167.2	166.3	168.1	168.1	165.6
1996	165.1	165.1	167.8	168.7	168.4	169.0	165.8	169.0	170.0	169.3	170.7	171.4	168.4
1997	168.3	169.7	171.7	171.7	172.7	173.6	171.6	175.1	175.5	176.3	175.9	176.6	173.2
1998	172.7	173.4	174.9	177.9	178.3	178.7	175.2	178.0	178.7	180.2	180.4	180.4	177.4
1999	177.1	177.0	178.5	180.4	180.7	180.8	178.5	180.8	182.9	182.9	183.8	184.7	180.7
2000	181.2	182.6	184.1	184.9	185.6	185.0	182.0	184.4	185.8	186.8	187.9	188.4	184.9
2001	181.5	184.5	186.7	186.8	186.6	187.2	184.5	186.9	187.6	187.0	187.2	187.4	186.2
2002	181.4	181.6	183.2	184.6	184.9	185.4	183.5	185.8	186.2	186.4	187.6	187.5	184.8
2003	185.5	186.5	187.8	188.2	188.8	188.0	186.6	188.6	190.1	189.9	190.1	190.2	188.3
Total private													
1990	115.8	116.1	116.7	118.4	118.6	119.9	119.6	119.9	120.2	119.3	120.4	120.7	118.8
1991	118.0	116.0	115.9	117.2	118.3	118.6	118.4	119.3	119.4	119.1	119.7	120.7	118.4
1992	118.7	117.0	117.9	119.7	121.4	122.5	121.3	124.2	123.4	123.2	123.6	124.5	121.5
1993	123.1	123.8	123.5	125.8	124.7	124.9	124.0	125.5	124.5	124.5	125.0	125.2	124.5
1994	121.2	121.7	122.8	122.3	122.5	123.6	120.8	124.7	124.9	123.9	124.5	125.2	123.2
1995	122.9	123.0	123.9	125.6	126.8	127.2	124.9	127.2	128.1	127.5	128.9	129.0	126.3
1996	126.2	126.0	128.6	129.7	129.5	130.5	128.2	131.3	132.0	131.4	132.7	133.5	130.0
1997	130.0	131.0	132.6	132.8	133.6	135.3	134.0	137.3	136.9	137.5	137.0	137.8	134.7
1998	134.1	134.4	135.7	138.5	138.8	139.5	136.4	139.6	139.2	140.2	140.0	140.1	138.0
1999	136.9	136.7	137.8	139.8	140.1	141.0	139.6	141.8	142.6	142.5	143.6	144.8	140.6
2000	141.7	142.3	143.7	144.4	144.6	145.4	143.0	145.6	146.0	146.8	147.7	148.3	145.0
2001	142.5	144.8	146.8	147.0	146.4	147.2	145.5	147.6	147.3	146.6	146.7	146.7	146.3
2002	141.7	141.6	143.3	144.5	144.8	145.2	144.5	146.6	145.8	145.7	146.6	146.7	144.8
2003	144.7	145.0	146.3	146.9	147.6	147.5	147.1	148.5	148.6	148.5	148.6	148.8	147.3
Goods-producing													
1990	40.8	40.8	40.9	41.4	41.3	41.9	41.8	41.8	41.4	41.1	41.3	41.4	41.3
1991	40.4	38.8	38.4	39.6	39.8	39.7	39.1	39.3	39.3	39.0	38.8	38.7	39.2
1992	41.9	40.2	40.3	41.5	41.8	42.0	40.2	42.4	42.0	42.1	42.2	42.5	41.6
1993	41.8	42.3	42.2	43.1	42.8	42.8	41.5	43.0	42.2	41.8	41.8	41.6	42.2
1994	39.9	40.3	41.0	40.8	40.9	41.3	38.4	42.0	41.8	41.9	41.7	41.6	41.0
1995	41.1	41.2	41.5	42.2	42.5	42.5	40.8	42.5	42.9	42.8	43.0	42.9	42.2
1996	42.5	42.6	43.5	43.6	43.9	44.0	41.8	44.0	44.3	44.1	44.3	44.1	43.6
1997	43.2	43.6	43.9	44.3	44.6	45.6	43.6	45.6	45.5	46.1	45.9	45.7	44.8
1998	44.8	44.6	44.7	46.6	46.2	46.0	42.5	45.0	44.5	44.5	43.9	43.5	44.7
1999	43.5	42.8	42.9	43.3	43.3	43.2	41.6	43.1	43.4	43.5	43.6	43.8	43.2
2000	43.7	43.7	43.8	43.7	43.6	43.9	42.3	44.1	43.8	44.2	44.1	44.0	43.7
2001	41.9	43.3	43.7	43.6	43.3	43.6	42.1	43.3	42.7	41.9	41.6	41.4	42.7
2002	40.9	41.0	40.8	41.0	41.0	40.9	39.7	41.1	40.5	40.2	40.0	39.7	40.6
2003	39.0	38.9	38.5	38.5	38.5	38.4	37.3	38.2	37.9	37.8	37.6	37.7	38.1
Construction and mining													
1990	6.2	6.3	6.4	6.3	6.4	6.6	6.6	6.6	6.5	6.4	6.4	6.4	6.4
1991	5.8	5.9	5.8	5.6	5.8	5.9	6.1	6.1	6.0	6.0	5.9	5.8	5.9
1992	5.3	5.3	5.2	5.3	5.3	5.3	5.4	5.4	5.4	5.5	5.5	5.4	5.4
1993	5.1	5.5	5.4	5.8	5.9	6.0	6.0	6.0	5.9	5.9	5.9	5.8	5.8
1994	5.4	5.5	5.7	5.8	5.8	5.9	5.9	6.0	5.9	5.8	5.8	5.7	5.8
1995	5.5	5.4	5.5	5.6	5.7	5.7	5.7	5.7	5.7	5.6	5.6	5.6	5.6
1996	5.3	5.4	5.7	5.8	5.8	6.0	6.1	6.1	6.1	6.0	6.0	5.9	5.9
1997	5.5	5.7	5.8	6.1	6.1	6.2	6.3	6.4	6.4	6.4	6.2	6.1	6.1
1998	5.9	6.0	6.1	6.6	6.6	6.7	6.7	6.7	6.6	6.6	6.5	6.6	6.5
1999	6.5	6.6	6.7	6.8	6.8	7.0	7.0	7.0	7.1	7.0	7.0	7.1	6.9
2000	6.9	7.0	7.2	7.2	7.3	7.5	7.4	7.4	7.4	7.3	7.1	7.1	7.2
2001	7.0	7.1	7.3	7.5	7.6	7.7	7.7	7.5	7.5	7.2	7.2	7.1	7.4
2002	6.7	6.7	6.7	7.0	7.2	7.3	7.5	7.4	7.3	7.4	7.3	7.2	7.1
2003	6.9	6.8	6.9	7.0	7.2	7.2	7.3	7.3	7.3	7.4	7.4	7.5	7.1
Manufacturing													
1990	34.6	34.5	34.5	35.1	34.9	35.3	35.2	35.2	34.9	34.7	34.9	35.0	34.9
1991	34.6	32.9	32.6	34.0	34.0	33.8	33.0	33.2	33.3	33.0	32.9	32.9	33.4
1992	36.6	34.9	35.1	36.2	36.5	36.7	34.8	37.0	36.6	36.6	36.7	37.1	36.2
1993	36.7	36.8	36.8	37.3	36.9	36.8	35.5	37.0	36.3	35.9	35.9	35.8	36.5
1994	34.5	34.8	35.3	35.0	35.1	35.4	32.5	36.0	35.9	36.1	35.9	35.9	35.2
1995	35.6	35.8	36.0	36.6	36.8	36.8	35.1	36.8	37.2	37.2	37.4	37.3	36.6
1996	37.2	37.2	37.8	37.8	38.1	38.0	35.7	37.9	38.2	38.1	38.3	38.2	37.7
1997	37.7	37.9	38.1	38.2	38.5	39.4	37.3	39.2	39.1	39.7	39.7	39.6	38.7
1998	38.9	38.6	38.6	40.0	39.6	39.3	35.8	38.3	37.9	37.9	37.4	36.9	38.3
1999	37.0	36.2	36.2	36.5	36.5	36.2	34.6	36.1	36.3	36.5	36.6	36.7	36.3
2000	36.8	36.7	36.6	36.5	36.3	36.4	34.9	36.7	36.4	36.9	37.0	36.9	36.5
2001	34.9	36.2	36.4	36.1	35.7	35.9	34.4	35.8	35.2	34.7	34.4	34.3	35.3
2002	34.2	34.3	34.1	34.0	33.8	33.6	32.2	33.7	33.2	32.8	32.7	32.5	33.4
2003	32.1	32.1	31.6	31.5	31.3	31.2	30.0	30.9	30.6	30.4	30.2	30.2	31.0

Employment by Industry: Alabama—*Continued*

(Numbers in thousands. Not seasonally adjusted.)

Industry	January	February	March	April	May	June	July	August	September	October	November	December	Annual Average
HUNTSVILLE—*Continued*													
Service-providing													
1990	113.9	114.5	114.3	116.9	117.3	116.9	117.4	116.0	117.6	116.9	118.1	117.7	116.5
1991	115.8	115.5	115.7	116.1	117.2	117.7	117.0	116.6	118.7	118.7	119.7	120.6	117.4
1992	115.0	115.2	116.4	117.1	119.2	120.1	119.5	120.1	120.8	120.6	121.1	121.4	118.9
1993	120.8	121.7	121.6	121.9	121.4	120.6	121.1	120.9	121.5	122.2	123.1	123.0	121.7
1994	121.4	121.3	121.9	122.1	122.0	121.5	120.8	121.2	122.4	121.9	123.7	123.4	122.0
1995	121.4	122.0	122.6	123.5	124.4	124.1	122.7	122.8	124.3	123.5	125.1	125.2	123.5
1996	122.6	122.5	124.3	125.1	124.5	125.0	124.0	125.0	125.7	125.2	126.4	127.3	124.8
1997	125.1	126.1	127.8	127.4	128.1	128.0	128.0	129.5	130.0	130.2	130.0	130.9	128.4
1998	127.9	128.8	130.2	131.3	132.1	132.7	132.7	133.0	134.2	135.7	136.5	136.9	132.7
1999	133.6	134.2	135.6	137.1	137.4	137.6	136.9	137.7	139.5	139.4	140.2	140.9	137.5
2000	137.5	138.9	140.3	141.2	142.0	141.1	139.7	140.3	142.0	142.6	143.8	144.4	141.2
2001	139.6	141.2	143.0	143.2	143.3	143.6	142.4	143.6	144.9	145.1	145.6	146.0	143.5
2002	140.5	140.6	142.4	143.6	143.9	144.5	143.8	144.7	145.7	146.2	147.6	147.8	144.3
2003	146.5	147.6	149.3	149.7	150.3	149.6	149.3	150.4	152.2	152.1	152.5	152.5	150.1
Trade, transportation, and utilities													
1990	21.6	21.4	21.3	21.8	21.9	22.1	22.1	22.1	22.3	22.0	22.5	22.9	22.0
1991	21.8	21.4	21.5	21.3	21.5	21.5	21.4	21.6	21.7	21.7	22.3	22.8	21.7
1992	20.8	20.5	20.7	20.8	21.0	21.1	21.2	21.3	21.2	21.3	21.7	22.4	21.2
1993	21.0	21.0	20.9	21.3	21.4	21.5	21.4	21.5	21.5	21.9	22.3	23.0	21.6
1994	21.6	21.6	21.7	21.3	21.6	21.8	21.8	21.9	22.2	22.2	22.7	23.4	22.0
1995	22.3	22.0	22.0	22.3	22.4	22.7	22.6	22.8	23.2	23.0	24.1	24.5	22.8
1996	23.3	22.6	23.1	23.4	23.7	24.0	24.0	24.1	24.1	24.2	25.2	26.0	24.0
1997	24.5	24.2	24.6	24.2	24.5	24.9	24.9	25.1	25.3	25.7	26.4	27.2	25.1
1998	25.2	24.9	25.4	25.9	26.0	26.1	26.0	26.2	26.7	27.2	27.9	28.4	26.3
1999	26.8	26.8	27.2	27.3	27.4	27.6	27.5	27.7	27.9	28.0	28.6	29.0	27.7
2000	27.5	27.5	27.7	27.4	27.6	27.6	27.5	27.5	27.8	28.4	29.3	29.8	28.0
2001	28.4	28.0	28.5	28.5	28.8	29.2	29.1	29.5	29.5	29.6	30.2	30.2	29.1
2002	28.8	28.4	28.9	28.7	28.8	28.7	28.8	28.9	28.8	29.5	30.3	30.7	29.1
2003	29.3	28.9	29.3	29.6	29.9	30.0	30.0	30.0	30.3	30.4	30.6	30.8	29.9
Wholesale trade													
1990	4.2	4.2	4.2	4.3	4.3	4.4	4.4	4.4	4.4	4.4	4.4	4.4	4.3
1991	4.1	4.1	4.1	4.1	4.1	4.1	4.1	4.1	4.1	4.2	4.2	4.2	4.1
1992	3.8	3.9	4.0	4.0	4.0	4.0	4.0	4.0	4.0	4.1	4.1	4.1	4.0
1993	3.9	4.0	4.1	4.1	4.2	4.2	4.0	4.1	4.1	4.1	4.1	4.1	4.1
1994	4.1	4.2	4.3	4.2	4.3	4.3	4.3	4.3	4.4	4.4	4.4	4.5	4.3
1995	4.5	4.5	4.5	4.5	4.6	4.6	4.6	4.6	4.6	4.6	4.7	4.7	4.6
1996	4.7	4.6	4.7	4.7	4.7	4.8	4.7	4.8	4.8	4.8	4.9	4.9	4.8
1997	4.9	4.9	4.9	4.8	4.8	4.9	4.9	4.9	4.9	4.9	4.9	5.0	4.9
1998	4.9	4.9	4.9	4.9	4.9	4.8	4.9	4.8	4.9	4.8	4.8	4.8	4.9
1999	4.7	4.8	4.8	4.8	4.8	4.9	4.9	4.9	4.9	5.0	5.0	5.0	4.9
2000	5.0	5.0	5.1	5.0	5.1	5.0	5.1	5.1	5.2	5.1	5.2	5.2	5.1
2001	5.9	5.9	6.0	5.9	5.9	5.9	5.8	5.9	5.8	5.7	5.7	5.7	5.8
2002	5.7	5.7	5.8	5.7	5.7	5.6	5.6	5.6	5.4	5.4	5.3	5.3	5.6
2003	5.4	5.4	5.5	5.4	5.5	5.5	5.5	5.4	5.4	5.4	5.4	5.4	5.4
Retail trade													
1990	15.7	15.4	15.3	15.7	15.7	15.8	15.8	15.8	15.9	15.7	16.2	16.6	15.8
1991	15.9	15.5	15.6	15.4	15.6	15.6	15.5	15.7	15.7	15.7	16.2	16.7	15.8
1992	15.2	14.8	14.9	15.0	15.2	15.3	15.4	15.4	15.3	15.4	15.7	16.4	15.3
1993	15.3	15.2	15.0	15.4	15.3	15.4	15.5	15.5	15.5	15.9	16.4	17.1	15.6
1994	15.7	15.6	15.6	15.3	15.5	15.7	15.7	15.8	16.1	16.1	16.6	17.2	15.9
1995	16.2	15.9	15.9	16.2	16.2	16.4	16.3	16.5	16.9	16.7	17.7	18.1	16.6
1996	17.0	16.4	16.7	17.1	17.4	17.5	17.5	17.5	17.5	17.6	18.4	19.3	17.5
1997	17.8	17.5	17.9	17.5	17.7	18.0	17.9	18.1	18.1	18.5	19.1	19.8	18.2
1998	18.0	17.7	18.1	18.5	18.6	18.8	18.6	18.8	19.2	19.7	20.4	20.8	18.9
1999	19.3	19.2	19.5	19.5	19.7	19.7	19.7	19.9	20.1	20.1	20.7	21.1	19.9
2000	19.8	19.7	20.0	19.7	19.8	19.9	19.7	19.7	19.9	20.5	21.2	21.7	20.1
2001	19.6	19.3	19.6	19.8	20.1	20.4	20.5	20.8	20.9	21.1	21.8	21.8	20.5
2002	20.6	20.2	20.5	20.4	20.5	20.5	20.5	20.6	20.7	21.4	22.3	22.7	20.9
2003	21.2	20.9	21.2	21.6	21.8	21.9	21.9	22.0	22.3	22.4	22.5	22.7	21.8
Transportation and utilities													
1990	1.7	1.8	1.8	1.8	1.9	1.9	1.9	1.9	2.0	1.9	1.9	1.9	1.9
1991	1.8	1.8	1.8	1.8	1.8	1.8	1.8	1.8	1.9	1.8	1.9	1.9	1.8
1992	1.8	1.8	1.8	1.8	1.8	1.8	1.8	1.9	1.9	1.8	1.9	1.9	1.8
1993	1.8	1.8	1.8	1.8	1.9	1.9	1.9	1.9	1.9	1.9	1.8	1.8	1.9
1994	1.8	1.8	1.8	1.8	1.8	1.8	1.8	1.8	1.7	1.7	1.7	1.7	1.8
1995	1.6	1.6	1.6	1.6	1.6	1.7	1.7	1.7	1.7	1.7	1.7	1.7	1.7
1996	1.6	1.6	1.7	1.6	1.6	1.7	1.8	1.8	1.8	1.8	1.9	1.8	1.7
1997	1.8	1.8	1.8	1.9	2.0	2.0	2.1	2.1	2.3	2.3	2.4	2.4	2.1
1998	2.3	2.3	2.4	2.5	2.5	2.5	2.5	2.6	2.6	2.7	2.7	2.8	2.5
1999	2.8	2.8	2.9	3.0	2.9	3.0	2.9	2.9	2.9	2.9	2.9	2.9	2.9
2000	2.7	2.8	2.6	2.7	2.7	2.7	2.7	2.7	2.7	2.8	2.9	2.9	2.7
2001	2.9	2.8	2.9	2.8	2.8	2.9	2.8	2.8	2.8	2.8	2.7	2.7	2.8
2002	2.5	2.5	2.6	2.6	2.6	2.6	2.7	2.7	2.7	2.7	2.7	2.7	2.6
2003	2.7	2.6	2.6	2.6	2.6	2.6	2.6	2.6	2.6	2.6	2.7	2.7	2.6

Employment by Industry: Alabama—*Continued*

(Numbers in thousands. Not seasonally adjusted.)

Industry	January	February	March	April	May	June	July	August	September	October	November	December	Annual Average
HUNTSVILLE—*Continued*													
Information													
1990	2.6	2.6	2.6	2.6	2.6	2.7	2.6	2.6	2.7	2.7	2.7	2.7	2.6
1991	2.7	2.7	2.7	2.5	2.5	2.6	2.5	2.5	2.5	2.5	2.5	2.5	2.6
1992	2.4	2.4	2.4	2.4	2.4	2.4	2.4	2.4	2.4	2.4	2.4	2.4	2.4
1993	2.3	2.3	2.3	2.3	2.3	2.4	2.3	2.3	2.3	2.3	2.3	2.3	2.3
1994	2.3	2.3	2.3	2.2	2.2	2.3	2.3	2.3	2.3	2.3	2.3	2.3	2.3
1995	2.3	2.3	2.3	2.3	2.4	2.4	2.4	2.4	2.4	2.4	2.4	2.4	2.4
1996	2.4	2.4	2.4	2.3	2.3	2.3	2.4	2.4	2.3	2.4	2.4	2.4	2.4
1997	2.4	2.4	2.4	2.5	2.4	2.4	2.6	2.6	2.6	2.6	2.6	2.6	2.5
1998	2.5	2.5	2.6	2.5	2.5	2.6	2.6	2.6	2.6	2.6	2.7	2.7	2.6
1999	2.6	2.6	2.6	2.6	2.7	2.7	2.7	2.7	2.7	2.6	2.6	2.7	2.7
2000	2.8	2.8	2.8	2.9	2.9	3.0	2.9	2.9	2.8	2.7	2.7	2.7	2.8
2001	2.7	2.8	2.7	2.8	2.8	2.7	2.7	2.7	2.6	2.5	2.5	2.5	2.7
2002	2.5	2.4	2.4	2.4	2.5	2.5	2.4	2.4	2.4	2.4	2.4	2.4	2.4
2003	2.4	2.4	2.4	2.3	2.3	2.3	2.3	2.3	2.3	2.2	2.2	2.2	2.2
Financial activities													
1990	4.3	4.3	4.4	4.5	4.4	4.5	4.5	4.5	4.5	4.5	4.5	4.5	4.5
1991	4.6	4.6	4.5	4.5	4.6	4.6	4.6	4.6	4.6	4.6	4.6	4.6	4.6
1992	4.4	4.4	4.4	4.4	4.5	4.5	4.6	4.6	4.6	4.6	4.6	4.6	4.5
1993	4.6	4.6	4.6	4.7	4.7	4.7	4.7	4.8	4.7	4.8	4.8	4.8	4.7
1994	4.8	4.8	4.8	4.8	4.8	4.8	4.8	4.8	4.7	4.7	4.8	4.8	4.8
1995	4.7	4.7	4.8	4.8	4.9	4.9	4.8	4.8	4.8	4.7	4.7	4.7	4.8
1996	4.8	4.8	4.8	4.8	4.8	4.8	4.8	4.8	4.9	4.8	4.9	4.9	4.8
1997	5.0	5.0	5.0	5.2	5.2	5.3	5.3	5.3	5.4	5.4	5.5	5.5	5.3
1998	5.5	5.5	5.5	5.5	5.6	5.5	5.6	5.6	5.5	5.5	5.6	5.6	5.5
1999	5.7	5.7	5.7	5.8	5.8	5.8	5.8	5.8	5.8	5.8	5.8	5.9	5.8
2000	5.7	5.8	5.8	5.8	5.8	5.8	5.8	5.8	5.8	5.9	5.9	5.9	5.8
2001	5.7	5.8	5.8	5.8	5.8	5.8	5.9	5.9	5.9	5.8	5.8	5.9	5.8
2002	5.7	5.7	5.7	5.8	5.8	5.8	5.8	5.8	5.7	5.8	5.8	5.8	5.8
2003	5.8	5.8	5.8	5.8	5.9	5.9	5.9	5.9	5.9	5.8	5.8	5.8	5.8
Professional and business services													
1990	26.2	26.3	26.6	26.9	27.0	27.2	27.2	27.3	27.7	27.7	27.8	27.8	27.1
1991	27.3	27.2	27.2	27.3	27.5	27.7	28.2	28.6	28.8	29.0	29.2	29.6	28.1
1992	28.2	28.4	28.8	29.4	29.8	30.3	30.8	31.3	31.2	31.0	30.8	30.6	30.1
1993	31.6	31.7	31.5	31.7	30.6	30.2	30.6	30.4	30.2	30.5	30.5	30.1	30.8
1994	29.8	29.8	29.8	29.7	29.5	29.9	30.0	30.0	30.3	29.5	29.6	29.8	29.8
1995	29.4	29.5	29.5	29.8	29.9	29.8	29.7	29.8	29.6	29.7	29.6	29.3	29.6
1996	28.7	29.0	29.8	29.9	28.9	29.2	29.2	29.5	29.6	29.6	29.6	29.9	29.4
1997	28.9	29.5	29.9	29.7	30.0	29.4	29.8	30.5	30.1	30.1	29.1	29.2	29.7
1998	29.0	29.4	29.8	29.8	29.8	30.6	31.0	31.4	30.9	31.5	30.9	30.8	30.4
1999	29.9	29.9	30.2	31.4	31.2	31.4	31.9	32.1	32.2	32.0	32.3	32.4	31.4
2000	31.7	31.7	32.2	33.2	32.9	32.9	32.6	33.1	33.6	34.0	34.2	34.1	33.0
2001	32.7	32.8	33.6	33.2	32.5	32.8	32.6	33.1	33.0	33.4	32.9	32.7	32.9
2002	31.5	31.3	32.2	32.8	32.9	33.5	33.8	34.2	33.9	33.9	34.0	34.0	33.2
2003	34.4	35.0	35.9	35.6	35.7	35.7	36.1	36.4	36.6	36.7	36.8	36.7	35.9
Educational and health services													
1990	6.2	6.4	6.4	6.5	6.5	6.4	6.4	6.4	6.6	6.8	6.9	6.9	6.5
1991	6.8	6.8	6.9	6.9	6.9	6.9	6.9	7.1	7.2	7.1	7.2	7.3	7.0
1992	6.8	6.8	6.9	6.9	7.0	7.0	7.0	6.9	7.0	7.0	7.0	7.1	7.0
1993	7.0	7.1	7.2	7.2	7.2	7.3	7.3	7.3	7.3	7.4	7.4	7.5	7.3
1994	7.3	7.4	7.5	7.3	7.3	7.2	7.1	7.2	7.4	7.5	7.5	7.5	7.4
1995	7.5	7.6	7.7	7.7	7.8	7.8	7.6	7.8	7.9	8.0	8.0	8.0	7.8
1996	7.8	7.8	8.0	8.1	8.2	8.2	8.1	8.3	8.4	8.4	8.5	8.4	8.2
1997	8.4	8.5	8.6	8.6	8.7	8.8	8.9	9.0	9.1	9.2	9.2	9.2	8.9
1998	9.1	9.1	9.2	9.1	9.2	9.1	9.0	9.1	9.2	9.4	9.5	9.5	9.2
1999	9.2	9.4	9.5	9.5	9.5	9.6	9.5	9.6	9.7	9.8	9.8	9.9	9.6
2000	9.8	9.9	10.0	9.9	10.0	10.0	10.0	10.2	10.3	10.3	10.2	10.3	10.1
2001	10.3	11.0	11.1	11.2	11.2	10.8	10.8	10.9	11.4	11.5	11.8	11.9	11.2
2002	11.1	11.5	11.6	11.8	11.4	11.5	11.6	11.6	12.1	12.0	12.1	12.1	11.7
2003	12.2	12.3	12.3	12.6	12.6	12.2	12.4	12.4	12.5	12.4	12.5	12.5	12.4
Leisure and hospitality													
1990	9.8	10.0	10.2	10.3	10.5	10.5	10.5	10.7	10.5	10.1	10.2	10.1	10.3
1991	9.7	9.9	10.1	10.5	10.8	10.9	10.9	10.8	10.5	10.4	10.3	10.4	10.4
1992	9.6	9.7	9.8	9.7	10.2	10.5	10.3	10.5	10.2	10.0	10.1	10.1	10.1
1993	9.9	10.0	10.0	10.6	10.7	10.9	11.0	11.1	11.1	10.5	10.7	10.6	10.6
1994	10.4	10.3	10.5	10.9	10.9	11.0	11.1	11.1	11.0	10.6	10.7	10.6	10.8
1995	10.5	10.6	11.0	11.3	11.7	11.8	11.8	11.8	11.9	11.5	11.6	11.7	11.4
1996	11.3	11.3	11.4	12.0	12.1	12.4	12.3	12.5	12.7	12.3	12.2	12.2	12.1
1997	12.0	12.2	12.6	12.8	12.8	13.3	13.4	13.5	13.3	12.8	12.8	12.9	12.9
1998	12.6	12.9	13.0	13.5	13.8	13.9	13.9	13.9	14.0	13.5	13.5	13.6	13.5
1999	13.2	13.4	13.5	13.6	13.8	14.2	14.2	14.2	14.3	14.1	14.2	14.3	13.9
2000	13.7	14.0	14.4	14.6	14.8	15.2	14.9	15.1	14.8	14.2	14.2	14.4	14.5
2001	13.6	13.8	14.1	14.6	14.7	15.1	15.1	15.0	14.9	14.6	14.7	14.9	14.6
2002	13.9	14.0	14.4	14.7	15.1	15.1	15.2	15.3	15.1	14.7	14.8	14.8	14.8
2003	14.4	14.5	14.9	15.3	15.4	15.7	15.8	15.9	15.6	15.7	15.7	15.7	15.3

Employment by Industry: Alabama—*Continued*

(Numbers in thousands. Not seasonally adjusted.)

Industry	January	February	March	April	May	June	July	August	September	October	November	December	Annual Average
HUNTSVILLE—*Continued*													
Other services													
1990	4.3	4.3	4.3	4.4	4.4	4.6	4.5	4.5	4.5	4.4	4.5	4.4	4.4
1991	4.7	4.6	4.6	4.6	4.7	4.7	4.8	4.8	4.8	4.8	4.8	4.8	4.7
1992	4.6	4.6	4.6	4.6	4.7	4.7	4.8	4.8	4.8	4.8	4.8	4.8	4.7
1993	4.9	4.8	4.8	4.9	5.0	5.1	5.2	5.1	5.2	5.3	5.2	5.3	5.1
1994	5.1	5.2	5.2	5.3	5.3	5.3	5.3	5.4	5.2	5.2	5.2	5.2	5.2
1995	5.1	5.1	5.1	5.2	5.2	5.3	5.2	5.3	5.4	5.4	5.5	5.5	5.3
1996	5.4	5.5	5.6	5.6	5.6	5.6	5.6	5.7	5.7	5.6	5.6	5.6	5.6
1997	5.6	5.6	5.6	5.5	5.4	5.6	5.5	5.7	5.6	5.6	5.5	5.5	5.6
1998	5.4	5.5	5.5	5.6	5.7	5.7	5.8	5.8	5.8	6.0	6.0	6.0	5.7
1999	6.0	6.1	6.2	6.3	6.4	6.5	6.4	6.6	6.6	6.7	6.7	6.8	6.4
2000	6.8	6.9	7.0	6.9	7.0	7.0	7.0	6.9	7.1	7.1	7.1	7.1	7.0
2001	7.2	7.3	7.3	7.3	7.3	7.2	7.2	7.2	7.3	7.3	7.2	7.2	7.3
2002	7.3	7.3	7.3	7.3	7.3	7.2	7.2	7.3	7.3	7.2	7.2	7.2	7.3
2003	7.2	7.2	7.2	7.2	7.3	7.3	7.3	7.4	7.5	7.5	7.4	7.4	7.3
Government													
1990	38.9	39.2	38.5	39.9	40.0	38.9	39.6	37.9	38.8	38.7	39.0	38.4	39.0
1991	38.2	38.3	38.2	38.5	38.7	38.8	37.7	36.6	38.6	38.6	38.8	38.6	38.3
1992	38.2	38.4	38.8	38.9	39.6	39.6	38.4	38.3	39.4	39.5	39.7	39.4	39.0
1993	39.5	40.2	40.3	39.2	39.5	38.5	38.6	38.4	39.2	39.5	39.9	39.4	39.4
1994	40.1	39.9	40.1	40.6	40.4	39.2	38.4	38.5	39.3	39.9	40.9	39.8	39.8
1995	39.6	40.2	40.2	40.1	40.1	39.4	38.6	38.1	39.1	38.8	39.2	39.1	39.4
1996	38.9	39.1	39.2	39.0	38.9	38.5	37.6	37.7	38.0	37.9	38.0	37.9	38.4
1997	38.3	38.7	39.1	38.9	39.1	38.3	37.6	37.8	38.6	38.8	38.9	38.8	38.6
1998	38.6	39.0	39.2	39.4	39.5	39.2	38.8	38.4	39.5	40.0	40.4	40.3	39.4
1999	40.2	40.3	40.7	40.6	40.6	39.8	38.9	39.0	40.3	40.4	40.2	39.9	40.1
2000	39.5	40.3	40.4	40.5	41.0	39.6	39.0	38.8	39.8	40.0	40.2	40.1	39.9
2001	39.0	39.7	39.9	39.8	40.2	40.0	39.0	39.3	40.3	40.4	40.5	40.7	39.9
2002	39.7	40.0	39.9	40.1	40.1	40.2	39.0	39.2	40.4	40.7	41.0	40.8	40.1
2003	40.8	41.5	41.5	41.3	41.2	40.5	39.5	40.1	41.5	41.4	41.5	41.4	41.0
Federal government													
1992	19.4	19.4	19.4	19.6	19.6	19.8	19.8	19.8	19.6	19.5	19.5	19.5	19.6
1993	19.1	19.1	19.1	18.2	18.3	18.4	18.5	18.6	18.3	18.2	18.3	18.4	18.5
1994	18.2	18.2	18.2	17.9	17.6	17.6	17.4	17.4	17.3	17.2	17.2	17.2	17.6
1995	16.9	16.9	16.9	16.9	16.9	16.8	16.8	16.7	16.7	16.4	16.5	16.5	16.7
1996	16.3	16.3	16.3	16.1	16.1	16.1	16.1	16.1	16.0	15.7	15.7	15.7	16.0
1997	15.5	15.5	15.5	15.2	15.2	15.2	15.4	15.3	15.3	15.2	15.3	15.2	15.3
1998	15.0	15.2	15.2	15.4	15.6	15.7	15.8	15.8	15.9	15.8	15.8	15.9	15.6
1999	15.7	15.6	15.7	15.5	15.4	15.5	15.5	15.5	15.5	15.4	15.5	15.5	15.5
2000	15.3	15.4	15.4	15.4	15.8	15.3	15.5	15.3	15.2	15.4	15.3	15.5	15.4
2001	15.4	15.4	15.4	15.4	15.5	15.6	15.6	15.6	15.6	15.4	15.5	15.5	15.5
2002	15.4	15.3	15.3	15.3	15.4	15.5	15.5	15.4	15.4	15.3	15.4	15.4	15.4
2003	15.3	15.3	15.2	15.1	15.2	15.4	15.4	15.4	15.4	15.4	15.4	15.4	15.3
State government													
2001	4.6	5.0	5.1	4.6	4.7	4.5	4.3	4.5	5.1	5.2	5.2	5.2	4.8
2002	4.7	4.9	4.8	4.9	4.7	4.7	4.3	4.4	5.2	5.5	5.6	5.4	4.9
2003	5.5	5.8	5.8	5.7	5.4	4.6	4.6	5.0	5.8	5.8	5.8	5.8	5.4
Local government													
2001	19.0	19.3	19.4	19.8	20.0	19.9	19.1	19.2	19.6	19.8	19.8	20.0	19.6
2002	19.6	19.8	19.8	19.9	20.0	20.0	19.2	19.4	19.8	19.9	20.0	20.0	19.8
2003	20.0	20.4	20.5	20.5	20.6	20.5	19.5	19.7	20.3	20.2	20.3	20.2	20.2
MOBILE													
Total nonfarm													
1990	171.2	172.3	173.6	175.4	178.6	179.8	178.7	177.3	178.7	178.9	180.0	181.1	177.1
1991	177.7	178.5	180.4	183.3	184.5	185.6	185.6	184.3	185.8	187.5	187.9	187.4	184.0
1992	184.2	184.5	186.2	187.1	188.3	189.9	190.8	190.2	187.9	191.8	193.1	193.0	188.9
1993	189.4	190.3	192.1	195.2	195.7	197.6	198.1	196.9	197.3	199.9	201.7	202.4	196.4
1994	196.2	197.6	201.0	203.1	203.4	205.5	203.8	202.8	204.3	203.5	206.6	205.7	202.8
1995	202.6	203.6	205.8	207.6	209.2	211.5	208.6	207.7	207.8	210.1	211.9	212.0	208.2
1996	207.8	209.3	211.3	212.6	213.8	215.0	212.9	214.1	214.6	215.4	216.7	216.6	213.3
1997	214.1	214.4	217.7	219.7	221.4	222.3	221.5	220.4	220.6	222.3	222.2	224.1	220.1
1998	218.9	220.7	223.6	225.6	226.3	227.9	225.4	225.2	226.3	226.5	227.1	228.3	225.2
1999	223.6	224.8	228.0	228.4	229.5	231.3	230.5	229.2	229.8	229.9	230.0	230.1	228.8
2000	224.5	225.7	228.8	229.6	232.1	233.3	232.2	232.6	233.3	232.6	234.2	233.2	231.0
2001	225.7	226.5	228.7	230.4	230.8	232.1	230.4	231.0	229.8	227.0	228.2	228.8	229.1
2002	220.8	222.4	225.4	226.2	226.9	228.0	225.9	225.3	224.8	225.3	225.6	224.8	225.1
2003	221.0	221.6	223.7	225.0	225.9	226.7	225.7	224.4	224.8	225.2	224.7	224.4	224.4

Employment by Industry: Alabama—*Continued*

(Numbers in thousands. Not seasonally adjusted.)

Industry	January	February	March	April	May	June	July	August	September	October	November	December	Annual Average
MOBILE—*Continued*													
Total private													
1990	141.8	142.7	143.9	144.8	147.4	150.9	148.3	149.5	148.4	148.0	148.9	149.5	147.0
1991	146.2	146.9	148.8	151.7	152.7	154.3	155.0	155.6	154.6	155.8	155.9	155.5	152.8
1992	152.0	152.2	153.9	154.5	155.6	157.6	157.9	158.1	158.3	159.5	160.4	160.3	156.7
1993	156.8	157.7	159.4	162.2	162.7	164.6	166.1	165.8	165.6	167.4	168.4	169.0	163.8
1994	162.4	164.0	167.3	168.9	169.2	171.8	171.1	171.3	171.8	169.8	170.6	171.9	169.2
1995	168.3	169.0	171.5	173.0	174.5	177.3	176.3	175.9	175.6	175.8	177.6	178.1	174.4
1996	173.6	175.2	177.0	178.2	179.3	181.2	180.1	181.7	181.5	181.3	182.3	182.8	179.5
1997	179.7	179.9	183.2	184.8	186.4	187.9	187.5	187.4	187.0	187.1	186.9	189.0	185.6
1998	184.6	185.9	188.6	190.5	191.0	192.8	191.7	191.7	191.1	190.9	191.2	192.4	190.2
1999	188.2	189.1	192.1	192.6	193.8	196.0	195.6	194.9	194.2	193.7	193.6	193.8	193.1
2000	188.5	189.5	192.2	193.3	194.8	197.9	197.6	198.3	197.8	196.6	198.0	197.0	195.1
2001	190.2	190.9	193.0	194.9	195.8	197.3	196.4	196.9	194.8	191.9	192.9	193.4	194.0
2002	185.3	186.8	189.8	190.6	191.3	192.6	191.5	190.7	189.0	189.3	189.5	188.7	189.6
2003	184.9	185.2	187.4	188.5	189.4	190.5	190.7	189.6	188.7	188.8	188.5	188.2	188.3
Goods-producing													
1990	38.0	38.1	38.3	39.1	40.0	41.3	40.0	40.5	39.8	39.8	39.9	40.0	39.6
1991	38.5	39.1	39.5	39.9	40.5	41.1	41.2	41.8	41.3	42.3	41.6	41.1	40.7
1992	39.5	39.2	39.6	39.8	39.8	40.7	40.5	40.8	41.0	41.9	41.7	40.8	40.4
1993	39.8	40.1	40.6	41.0	40.8	41.5	41.9	41.6	41.4	41.1	41.2	41.3	41.0
1994	39.6	40.4	41.3	41.5	41.4	42.1	41.7	42.3	42.6	42.0	42.2	42.0	41.6
1995	41.5	41.2	41.8	41.7	41.8	42.0	41.6	41.4	41.4	41.6	42.1	42.2	41.7
1996	41.3	42.2	42.6	42.7	43.1	43.2	42.6	43.2	43.6	43.7	43.9	43.7	43.0
1997	42.9	42.7	43.4	43.7	44.1	43.9	44.0	44.4	44.3	44.7	44.3	44.7	43.9
1998	44.6	44.8	45.5	45.6	45.4	45.2	44.7	45.2	45.1	45.6	45.5	45.6	45.2
1999	44.9	44.6	45.1	45.1	44.9	44.9	44.6	44.2	43.9	44.1	44.0	43.7	44.5
2000	43.1	43.5	43.7	43.5	43.7	44.3	43.8	44.2	44.6	44.6	44.7	44.3	44.0
2001	42.0	41.9	42.1	41.9	41.8	41.8	41.5	42.0	41.9	41.0	40.9	40.7	41.6
2002	38.2	37.9	38.4	38.9	38.9	38.7	38.4	38.2	38.4	38.9	38.6	38.1	38.5
2003	37.1	36.7	36.8	36.4	36.5	36.2	36.1	35.8	35.8	35.9	36.0	35.8	36.2
Construction and mining													
1990	11.7	11.6	11.6	12.3	12.8	13.6	12.5	12.9	12.4	12.3	12.5	12.5	12.4
1991	11.7	12.1	12.6	13.3	13.7	14.2	14.2	14.3	14.1	15.2	14.4	13.9	13.6
1992	12.9	12.9	13.1	13.5	13.5	13.9	14.0	14.3	14.4	15.2	15.1	14.3	13.9
1993	13.5	13.7	14.2	14.5	14.4	14.9	14.9	14.5	14.2	14.3	14.6	14.6	14.4
1994	13.8	14.4	15.0	15.3	15.1	15.7	15.6	15.9	16.1	15.7	15.9	15.7	15.4
1995	15.7	15.4	15.8	15.6	15.6	15.7	15.4	15.5	15.4	15.5	16.0	15.8	15.6
1996	15.8	16.4	16.6	16.7	17.0	17.0	16.8	17.0	17.3	17.3	17.5	17.5	16.9
1997	16.8	16.4	16.7	17.1	17.4	17.6	17.7	18.1	17.9	18.1	17.8	17.9	17.5
1998	17.5	17.6	18.1	18.4	18.1	17.9	17.7	17.7	17.4	18.0	18.1	18.1	17.9
1999	17.7	17.9	18.3	18.7	18.6	18.5	18.3	18.1	18.2	18.2	18.2	18.0	18.2
2000	17.4	17.7	17.9	17.9	18.0	18.5	18.3	18.5	18.8	18.8	18.7	18.4	18.2
2001	17.2	17.3	17.4	17.7	17.4	17.1	17.0	17.1	17.1	16.7	16.8	16.6	17.1
2002	15.1	15.2	15.6	16.2	16.3	16.1	16.1	16.1	16.3	16.6	16.5	16.1	16.0
2003	15.6	15.6	15.8	15.7	15.7	15.6	15.8	15.7	15.8	15.8	15.7	15.5	15.6
Manufacturing													
1990	26.3	26.5	26.7	26.8	27.2	27.7	27.5	27.6	27.4	27.5	27.4	27.5	27.2
1991	26.8	27.0	26.9	26.6	26.8	26.9	27.0	27.5	27.2	27.1	27.2	27.2	27.0
1992	26.6	26.3	26.5	26.3	26.3	26.8	26.5	26.5	26.6	26.7	26.6	26.5	26.5
1993	26.3	26.4	26.4	26.5	26.4	26.6	27.0	27.1	27.2	26.8	26.6	26.7	26.7
1994	25.8	26.0	26.3	26.2	26.3	26.4	26.1	26.4	26.5	26.3	26.3	26.3	26.2
1995	25.8	25.8	26.0	26.1	26.2	26.3	26.2	25.9	26.0	26.1	26.1	26.4	26.1
1996	25.5	25.8	26.0	26.0	26.1	26.2	25.8	26.2	26.3	26.4	26.4	26.2	26.1
1997	26.1	26.3	26.7	26.6	26.7	26.3	26.3	26.3	26.4	26.6	26.5	26.8	26.5
1998	27.1	27.2	27.4	27.2	27.3	27.3	27.0	27.5	27.7	27.6	27.4	27.5	27.4
1999	27.2	26.7	26.8	26.4	26.3	26.4	26.3	26.1	25.7	25.9	25.8	25.7	26.3
2000	25.7	25.8	25.8	25.6	25.7	25.8	25.5	25.7	25.8	25.8	26.0	25.9	25.8
2001	24.8	24.6	24.7	24.2	24.4	24.7	24.5	24.9	24.8	24.3	24.1	24.1	24.5
2002	23.1	22.7	22.8	22.7	22.6	22.6	22.3	22.1	22.1	22.3	22.1	22.0	22.5
2003	21.5	21.1	21.0	20.7	20.8	20.6	20.3	20.1	20.0	20.1	20.3	20.3	20.5
Service-providing													
1990	133.2	134.2	135.3	136.3	138.6	138.5	138.7	136.8	138.9	139.1	140.1	141.1	137.6
1991	139.2	139.4	140.9	143.4	144.0	144.5	144.4	142.5	144.5	145.2	146.3	146.3	143.4
1992	144.7	145.3	146.6	147.3	148.5	149.2	150.3	149.4	146.9	149.9	151.4	152.2	148.5
1993	149.6	150.2	151.5	154.2	154.9	156.1	156.2	155.3	155.9	158.8	160.5	161.1	155.4
1994	156.6	157.2	159.7	161.6	162.0	163.4	162.1	160.5	161.7	161.5	164.4	163.7	161.2
1995	161.1	162.4	164.0	165.9	167.4	169.5	167.0	166.3	166.4	168.5	169.8	169.8	166.5
1996	166.5	167.1	168.7	169.9	170.7	171.8	170.3	170.9	171.0	171.7	172.8	172.9	170.4
1997	171.2	171.7	174.3	176.0	177.3	178.4	177.5	176.0	176.3	177.6	177.9	179.4	176.1
1998	174.3	175.9	178.1	180.0	180.9	182.7	180.7	180.0	181.2	180.9	181.6	182.7	179.9
1999	178.7	180.2	182.9	183.3	184.6	186.4	185.9	185.0	185.9	185.8	186.0	186.4	184.3
2000	181.4	182.2	185.1	186.1	188.4	189.0	188.4	188.4	188.7	188.0	189.5	188.9	187.0
2001	183.7	184.6	186.6	188.5	189.0	190.3	188.9	189.0	187.9	186.0	187.3	188.1	187.5
2002	182.6	184.5	187.0	187.3	188.0	189.3	187.5	187.1	186.4	186.4	187.0	186.7	186.7
2003	183.9	184.9	186.9	188.6	189.4	190.5	189.6	188.6	189.0	189.3	188.7	188.6	188.1

Employment by Industry: Alabama—*Continued*

(Numbers in thousands. Not seasonally adjusted.)

Industry	January	February	March	April	May	June	July	August	September	October	November	December	Annual Average
MOBILE—*Continued*													
Trade, transportation, and utilities													
1990	41.6	41.5	41.8	41.7	42.2	43.2	42.4	42.7	42.7	42.4	43.0	43.5	42.4
1991	41.6	41.5	41.5	41.7	41.9	42.2	42.4	42.6	42.4	42.4	43.5	43.9	42.3
1992	41.9	41.9	42.1	41.6	42.2	42.7	43.0	42.9	42.7	43.3	44.3	45.0	42.8
1993	43.3	43.1	43.3	43.9	44.0	44.2	44.5	44.5	44.6	46.1	47.2	47.6	44.7
1994	45.0	44.8	45.3	45.6	46.0	46.8	46.9	46.6	46.9	46.9	47.8	48.7	46.4
1995	47.0	46.9	47.3	47.4	47.8	48.5	48.8	48.8	49.0	49.0	49.8	50.3	48.4
1996	48.8	48.3	48.1	48.5	48.5	49.4	49.1	49.7	49.5	49.3	50.0	50.6	49.2
1997	49.1	48.7	49.4	49.8	50.3	50.9	51.6	51.3	51.4	51.5	52.4	53.3	50.8
1998	51.0	50.6	51.3	51.3	51.6	52.3	52.0	51.6	51.8	51.8	52.0	52.7	51.7
1999	50.5	50.7	51.4	51.1	51.5	52.0	52.6	52.5	52.4	52.6	52.9	53.6	52.0
2000	51.4	51.2	51.7	51.5	52.4	53.0	53.4	53.4	53.1	53.0	54.3	54.6	52.8
2001	51.6	51.1	51.4	51.1	51.3	51.5	51.1	50.7	50.0	50.1	51.2	51.8	51.1
2002	49.6	49.3	50.0	50.0	50.0	50.4	50.3	49.8	49.4	49.6	50.4	50.9	50.0
2003	48.7	48.4	48.9	49.4	49.5	50.1	50.6	50.4	50.2	50.9	51.2	51.4	49.9
Wholesale trade													
1990	8.3	8.3	8.3	8.4	8.5	8.7	8.6	8.6	8.6	8.6	8.6	8.5	8.5
1991	8.0	8.0	8.0	8.1	8.1	8.2	8.3	8.3	8.2	8.3	8.3	8.3	8.2
1992	8.1	8.1	8.1	8.1	8.2	8.3	8.3	8.3	8.3	8.3	8.3	8.4	8.2
1993	8.2	8.1	8.2	8.1	8.2	8.3	8.3	8.3	8.3	8.4	8.5	8.5	8.3
1994	8.2	8.3	8.3	8.4	8.5	8.6	8.6	8.7	8.7	8.7	8.8	8.9	8.6
1995	8.7	8.7	8.8	8.9	9.0	9.1	9.1	9.1	9.2	9.2	9.2	9.2	9.0
1996	9.1	9.0	9.1	9.1	9.1	9.4	9.1	9.2	9.1	9.1	9.1	9.1	9.1
1997	9.1	9.0	9.1	9.3	9.4	9.5	9.6	9.5	9.5	9.4	9.5	9.5	9.4
1998	9.2	9.1	9.2	9.5	9.6	9.8	9.5	9.4	9.4	9.4	9.3	9.4	9.4
1999	9.2	9.3	9.3	9.5	9.5	9.5	9.6	9.5	9.5	9.5	9.5	9.7	9.5
2000	9.7	9.7	9.8	9.7	9.8	9.9	9.8	9.8	9.8	9.8	9.9	9.9	9.8
2001	10.6	10.5	10.5	10.5	10.6	10.6	10.7	10.6	10.4	10.5	10.3	10.4	10.5
2002	10.2	10.1	10.1	10.2	10.2	10.3	10.3	10.3	10.2	10.2	10.2	10.2	10.2
2003	10.0	10.0	10.0	10.1	10.2	10.3	10.3	10.3	10.3	10.4	10.5	10.5	10.2
Retail trade													
1990	25.7	25.6	25.9	25.8	26.1	26.7	26.2	26.5	26.5	26.1	26.9	27.3	26.3
1991	25.6	25.2	25.3	25.4	25.6	25.8	25.8	25.9	25.7	26.0	26.9	27.2	25.9
1992	25.5	25.5	25.6	25.5	26.0	26.1	26.1	26.1	26.1	26.5	27.6	28.1	26.2
1993	26.7	26.5	26.6	27.1	27.1	27.0	27.3	27.3	27.4	28.5	29.4	29.9	27.6
1994	28.0	27.7	28.0	28.4	28.6	29.1	29.3	29.0	29.2	29.3	30.1	30.8	29.0
1995	29.2	29.1	29.3	29.4	29.6	30.1	30.4	30.5	30.4	30.2	31.1	31.6	30.1
1996	30.1	29.7	29.8	30.0	30.1	30.6	30.6	30.9	30.8	30.7	31.5	32.1	30.6
1997	30.6	30.1	30.8	30.9	31.2	31.7	32.3	32.2	32.1	32.1	33.0	33.5	31.7
1998	31.5	31.2	31.6	31.7	31.8	32.1	31.8	31.5	31.6	31.4	31.8	32.4	31.7
1999	30.8	30.9	31.5	31.1	31.5	32.0	32.2	32.3	32.2	32.2	32.7	33.2	31.9
2000	31.4	31.2	31.5	31.5	32.1	32.6	32.7	32.6	32.4	32.3	33.4	33.8	32.3
2001	31.1	30.7	30.9	30.6	30.7	31.0	30.5	30.2	29.8	29.9	31.2	31.7	30.7
2002	30.2	30.1	30.6	30.6	30.6	30.9	30.6	30.3	30.1	30.2	31.0	31.5	30.6
2003	29.6	29.4	29.9	30.4	30.4	30.8	31.0	30.9	30.7	31.1	31.4	31.7	30.6
Transportation and utilities													
1990	7.6	7.6	7.6	7.5	7.6	7.8	7.6	7.6	7.6	7.7	7.5	7.7	7.6
1991	8.0	8.3	8.2	8.2	8.2	8.2	8.3	8.4	8.5	8.1	8.3	8.4	8.3
1992	8.3	8.3	8.4	8.0	8.0	8.3	8.6	8.5	8.3	8.5	8.4	8.5	8.3
1993	8.4	8.5	8.5	8.7	8.7	8.9	8.9	8.9	8.9	9.2	9.3	9.2	8.8
1994	8.8	8.8	9.0	8.8	8.9	9.1	9.0	8.9	9.0	8.9	8.9	9.0	8.9
1995	9.1	9.1	9.2	9.1	9.2	9.3	9.3	9.2	9.4	9.6	9.5	9.5	9.3
1996	9.6	9.6	9.2	9.4	9.3	9.4	9.4	9.6	9.6	9.5	9.4	9.4	9.5
1997	9.4	9.6	9.5	9.6	9.7	9.7	9.7	9.6	9.8	10.0	9.9	10.3	9.7
1998	10.3	10.3	10.5	10.1	10.2	10.4	10.7	10.7	10.8	11.0	10.9	10.9	10.6
1999	10.5	10.5	10.6	10.5	10.5	10.5	10.8	10.7	10.7	10.9	10.7	10.7	10.6
2000	10.3	10.3	10.4	10.3	10.5	10.5	10.9	11.0	10.9	10.9	11.0	10.9	10.7
2001	9.9	9.9	10.0	10.0	10.0	9.9	9.9	9.9	9.8	9.7	9.7	9.7	9.9
2002	9.2	9.1	9.3	9.2	9.2	9.2	9.4	9.2	9.1	9.2	9.2	9.2	9.2
2003	9.1	9.0	9.0	8.9	8.9	9.0	9.3	9.2	9.2	9.4	9.3	9.2	9.1
Information													
1990	2.7	2.7	2.7	2.7	2.7	2.7	2.7	2.7	2.7	2.6	2.6	2.6	2.7
1991	2.7	2.7	2.7	2.8	2.8	2.8	2.7	2.6	2.6	2.8	2.8	2.8	2.7
1992	2.7	2.8	2.8	2.7	2.8	2.8	2.8	2.8	2.8	2.9	2.9	2.8	2.8
1993	2.7	2.7	2.7	2.8	2.8	2.8	2.9	2.9	3.0	2.9	3.0	3.0	2.9
1994	2.9	3.0	3.0	3.0	3.0	3.1	3.1	3.2	3.2	3.0	3.0	3.1	3.1
1995	3.1	3.1	3.1	3.2	3.1	3.2	3.3	3.2	3.1	3.1	3.1	3.2	3.2
1996	3.1	3.1	3.1	3.3	3.4	3.4	3.4	3.4	3.4	3.2	3.3	3.3	3.3
1997	3.3	3.3	3.3	3.4	3.4	3.5	3.5	3.6	3.6	3.5	3.5	3.6	3.5
1998	3.7	3.7	3.6	3.6	3.6	3.5	3.7	3.7	3.7	3.7	3.6	3.8	3.7
1999	3.8	3.8	3.8	3.8	4.0	3.9	4.0	3.9	4.0	4.0	4.1	4.1	3.9
2000	3.9	3.9	3.9	4.0	4.0	4.1	4.0	4.0	4.0	4.0	4.0	4.0	4.0
2001	4.1	4.0	4.0	3.8	3.7	3.7	3.6	3.5	3.5	3.4	3.4	3.5	3.7
2002	3.3	3.3	3.3	3.3	3.3	3.3	3.2	3.2	3.1	3.1	3.1	3.1	3.2
2003	3.1	3.1	3.1	3.0	3.0	3.0	3.0	3.0	2.9	2.9	2.9	2.9	3.0

Employment by Industry: Alabama—*Continued*

(Numbers in thousands. Not seasonally adjusted.)

Industry	January	February	March	April	May	June	July	August	September	October	November	December	Annual Average
MOBILE—*Continued*													
Financial activities													
1990	8.0	8.0	8.1	8.1	8.2	8.3	8.1	8.0	8.1	8.1	8.4	8.5	8.2
1991	8.6	8.6	8.7	8.8	8.8	8.9	9.0	8.9	8.8	8.9	8.9	9.0	8.8
1992	9.0	8.9	8.9	9.1	9.1	9.1	9.2	9.1	9.1	9.2	9.1	9.1	9.1
1993	9.1	9.2	9.2	9.6	9.7	9.8	9.9	9.9	9.8	9.9	9.9	10.0	9.7
1994	9.7	9.8	9.9	10.0	10.0	10.1	10.1	10.0	10.0	9.9	9.9	9.9	9.9
1995	9.8	9.9	10.0	10.0	9.9	10.1	10.2	10.1	10.1	10.1	10.2	10.1	10.0
1996	9.8	9.9	10.1	10.1	10.3	10.5	10.3	10.4	10.3	10.3	10.3	10.5	10.2
1997	10.5	10.6	10.8	10.9	11.2	11.1	10.8	10.9	11.0	11.0	10.9	11.1	10.9
1998	10.5	10.6	10.8	10.7	10.9	11.0	11.1	11.1	10.9	10.8	10.9	10.9	10.9
1999	10.8	10.9	11.0	11.1	11.1	11.3	11.4	11.4	11.4	11.2	11.3	11.3	11.2
2000	11.1	11.1	11.4	11.7	11.8	12.0	12.1	12.2	12.0	12.0	12.0	12.0	11.8
2001	11.9	12.1	12.2	12.5	12.6	12.8	12.8	12.7	12.4	12.2	12.2	12.3	12.4
2002	12.0	12.0	12.2	12.3	12.5	12.7	12.6	12.5	12.2	12.0	12.0	12.1	12.3
2003	12.0	12.0	12.1	12.3	12.4	12.7	12.8	12.7	12.4	12.2	12.1	12.0	12.3
Professional and business services													
1990	12.9	13.2	13.2	13.7	13.8	14.1	14.0	14.4	14.4	14.8	14.7	14.7	14.0
1991	14.6	14.8	15.1	15.7	15.5	15.7	15.9	15.7	15.6	16.1	16.0	15.7	15.5
1992	15.9	15.9	16.4	16.9	16.9	17.0	17.1	17.2	17.2	17.2	17.2	17.6	16.9
1993	16.9	17.2	17.6	17.9	17.9	18.4	18.5	18.4	18.3	18.5	18.5	18.6	18.1
1994	17.4	17.7	18.4	18.3	18.2	18.5	18.4	18.5	18.8	18.7	18.5	18.9	18.4
1995	17.7	18.1	18.5	19.1	19.7	20.2	19.7	19.7	19.8	19.6	19.7	19.6	19.3
1996	18.9	19.2	19.8	19.9	19.8	20.2	20.4	20.6	20.7	20.8	21.0	21.0	20.2
1997	20.8	21.2	21.4	21.5	21.4	21.8	21.2	21.2	21.0	21.3	21.0	21.2	21.3
1998	20.8	21.1	21.6	22.5	22.3	22.8	22.8	22.9	22.9	23.3	23.5	23.8	22.5
1999	23.1	23.3	23.9	23.7	24.0	24.3	24.0	24.0	24.1	24.5	24.1	24.0	23.9
2000	23.5	23.7	24.1	24.7	24.6	25.2	24.7	25.0	25.1	25.3	25.2	24.7	24.7
2001	24.2	24.7	25.3	25.8	25.8	26.0	26.1	26.8	26.9	25.7	25.6	25.4	25.7
2002	24.6	25.2	25.7	25.2	25.0	25.3	25.8	26.2	25.8	26.2	25.9	25.2	25.5
2003	25.4	25.6	26.0	26.2	26.2	26.4	26.2	26.2	25.9	26.0	25.6	25.6	25.9
Educational and health services													
1990	16.0	16.2	16.3	15.5	15.5	15.7	15.5	15.8	16.0	16.2	16.5	16.5	16.0
1991	16.3	16.4	16.6	17.1	17.1	17.2	17.2	17.4	17.6	17.8	17.8	17.9	17.2
1992	17.9	18.0	18.1	18.2	18.1	18.4	18.3	18.4	18.8	18.8	18.8	18.9	18.4
1993	19.0	19.1	19.2	19.5	19.4	19.5	19.4	19.5	19.8	20.3	20.3	20.4	19.6
1994	20.2	20.2	20.3	20.3	20.3	20.2	20.3	20.3	20.4	20.3	20.4	20.5	20.3
1995	20.5	20.7	20.8	20.8	20.9	20.9	20.8	21.0	21.2	21.6	21.6	21.8	21.1
1996	21.3	21.7	21.7	21.4	21.4	21.3	21.0	21.1	21.3	21.6	21.7	21.9	21.5
1997	21.8	21.9	22.3	22.4	22.4	22.5	22.6	22.5	22.7	22.9	22.9	23.1	22.5
1998	22.6	22.8	22.8	23.1	23.1	23.0	22.6	22.5	22.8	22.7	22.8	22.7	22.8
1999	22.6	22.6	22.8	22.8	23.0	23.0	22.7	22.9	23.2	23.1	23.2	23.2	22.9
2000	22.7	22.7	22.8	22.5	22.4	22.7	22.8	23.0	23.0	23.1	23.2	23.3	22.9
2001	22.9	23.3	23.3	23.7	23.7	24.0	24.1	24.3	24.4	24.4	24.8	25.0	24.0
2002	23.8	24.6	24.8	25.0	24.9	25.2	24.3	24.3	24.7	24.7	25.0	24.8	24.7
2003	24.5	24.8	24.9	25.4	25.3	25.1	25.3	24.8	25.8	25.8	25.7	25.6	25.2
Leisure and hospitality													
1990	13.5	13.9	14.4	14.7	15.6	16.2	16.2	16.0	15.2	14.6	14.3	14.2	14.9
1991	14.1	14.1	14.9	15.7	16.1	16.6	16.7	16.6	16.1	15.3	15.0	14.9	15.5
1992	14.9	15.3	15.8	16.0	16.5	16.9	17.0	16.9	16.3	15.7	16.1	15.8	16.1
1993	15.7	15.9	16.3	16.9	17.3	17.9	18.4	18.3	17.7	17.5	17.3	17.1	17.2
1994	16.8	17.1	18.0	19.0	19.2	19.9	19.8	19.6	19.0	18.0	17.8	17.6	18.5
1995	17.7	18.0	18.7	19.5	19.9	20.8	20.5	20.3	19.3	19.0	19.0	18.9	19.3
1996	18.6	18.9	19.6	20.2	20.5	21.0	21.3	21.3	20.4	20.1	19.8	19.6	20.1
1997	19.2	19.4	20.4	21.1	21.6	22.2	22.0	21.7	21.0	20.1	19.9	19.9	20.7
1998	19.6	20.4	21.0	21.6	22.0	22.9	22.6	22.4	21.5	20.6	20.6	20.5	21.3
1999	20.3	20.8	21.6	22.5	22.7	23.9	23.5	23.2	22.4	21.3	21.0	20.9	22.0
2000	20.0	20.4	21.4	22.2	22.6	23.3	23.5	23.2	22.7	21.5	21.4	21.0	21.9
2001	20.5	20.7	21.5	22.9	23.7	24.2	24.0	23.6	22.5	22.0	21.8	21.8	22.4
2002	21.1	21.6	22.4	22.8	23.5	24.1	24.2	23.6	22.6	21.9	21.7	21.9	22.6
2003	21.5	21.9	22.9	23.1	23.6	24.3	24.2	24.0	23.1	22.4	22.2	22.2	22.9
Other services													
1990	9.1	9.1	9.1	9.3	9.4	9.4	9.4	9.4	9.5	9.5	9.5	9.5	9.4
1991	9.8	9.7	9.8	10.0	10.0	9.8	9.9	10.0	10.2	10.2	10.3	10.2	10.0
1992	10.2	10.2	10.2	10.2	10.2	10.0	10.0	10.0	10.4	10.5	10.3	10.3	10.2
1993	10.3	10.4	10.5	10.6	10.8	10.5	10.6	10.7	11.0	11.1	11.0	11.0	10.7
1994	10.8	11.0	11.1	11.2	11.1	11.1	10.8	10.8	10.9	11.0	11.0	11.2	11.0
1995	11.0	11.1	11.3	11.3	11.4	11.6	11.4	11.4	11.7	11.8	12.1	12.0	11.5
1996	11.8	11.9	12.0	12.1	12.3	12.2	12.0	12.0	12.3	12.3	12.3	12.2	12.1
1997	12.1	12.1	12.2	12.0	12.0	12.0	11.8	11.8	12.0	12.1	12.0	12.1	12.0
1998	11.8	11.9	12.0	12.1	12.1	12.1	12.2	12.3	12.4	12.4	12.3	12.4	12.2
1999	12.2	12.4	12.5	12.5	12.6	12.7	12.8	12.8	12.8	12.9	13.0	13.0	12.7
2000	12.8	13.0	13.2	13.2	13.3	13.3	13.3	13.3	13.3	13.1	13.2	13.1	13.2
2001	13.0	13.1	13.2	13.2	13.2	13.3	13.2	13.3	13.2	13.1	13.0	12.9	13.1
2002	12.7	12.9	13.0	13.1	13.2	12.9	12.7	12.9	12.8	12.9	12.8	12.6	12.9
2003	12.6	12.7	12.7	12.7	12.9	12.7	12.5	12.7	12.6	12.7	12.8	12.7	12.6

Employment by Industry: Alabama—*Continued*

(Numbers in thousands. Not seasonally adjusted.)

Industry	January	February	March	April	May	June	July	August	September	October	November	December	Annual Average
MOBILE—*Continued*													
Government													
1990	29.4	29.6	29.7	30.6	31.2	28.9	30.4	27.8	30.3	30.9	31.1	31.6	30.1
1991	31.5	31.6	31.6	31.6	31.8	31.3	30.6	28.7	31.2	31.7	32.0	31.9	31.3
1992	32.2	32.3	32.3	32.6	32.7	32.3	32.9	32.1	29.6	32.3	32.7	32.7	32.2
1993	32.6	32.6	32.7	33.0	33.0	33.0	32.0	31.1	31.7	32.5	33.3	33.4	32.6
1994	33.8	33.6	33.7	34.2	34.2	33.7	32.7	31.5	32.5	33.7	36.0	33.8	33.6
1995	34.3	34.6	34.3	34.6	34.7	34.2	32.3	31.8	32.2	34.3	34.3	33.9	33.8
1996	34.2	34.1	34.3	34.4	34.5	33.8	32.8	32.4	33.1	34.1	34.4	33.8	33.8
1997	34.4	34.5	34.5	34.9	35.0	34.4	34.0	33.0	33.6	35.2	35.3	35.1	34.5
1998	34.3	34.8	35.0	35.1	35.3	35.1	33.7	33.5	35.2	35.6	35.9	35.9	35.0
1999	35.4	35.7	35.9	35.8	35.7	35.3	34.9	34.3	35.6	36.2	36.4	36.3	35.6
2000	36.0	36.2	36.6	36.3	37.3	35.4	34.6	34.3	35.5	36.0	36.2	36.2	35.9
2001	35.5	35.6	35.7	35.5	35.0	34.8	34.0	34.1	35.0	35.1	35.3	35.4	35.1
2002	35.5	35.6	35.6	35.6	35.6	35.4	34.4	34.6	35.8	36.0	36.1	36.1	35.5
2003	36.1	36.4	36.3	36.5	36.5	36.2	35.0	34.8	36.1	36.4	36.2	36.2	36.0
Federal government													
1990	3.2	3.2	3.3	3.3	3.7	3.5	3.5	3.2	3.2	3.2	3.2	3.2	3.3
1991	3.2	3.2	3.2	3.2	3.2	3.2	3.2	3.2	3.2	3.3	3.2	3.3	3.2
1992	3.2	3.2	3.2	3.3	3.2	3.2	3.3	3.3	3.3	3.3	3.2	3.2	3.2
1993	3.2	3.1	3.2	3.2	3.1	3.2	3.2	3.2	3.2	3.2	3.1	3.2	3.2
1994	3.1	3.1	3.1	3.1	3.1	3.1	3.1	3.1	3.1	3.1	3.1	3.1	3.1
1995	3.1	3.0	3.0	3.0	3.0	3.0	3.0	3.0	3.0	3.0	3.0	3.0	3.0
1996	3.0	3.0	3.0	3.0	3.0	3.0	3.0	3.0	3.0	3.0	3.0	3.0	3.0
1997	2.9	2.9	2.9	2.9	2.9	2.9	2.9	2.8	2.8	2.8	2.8	2.9	2.9
1998	2.8	2.8	2.8	2.7	2.7	2.7	2.7	2.7	2.7	2.9	2.9	2.9	2.8
1999	2.8	2.8	2.8	2.8	2.8	2.8	2.8	2.8	2.8	2.8	2.9	2.9	2.8
2000	2.8	2.9	3.1	3.0	4.0	2.9	3.2	2.9	2.8	2.8	2.8	2.8	3.0
2001	2.8	2.8	2.8	2.8	2.8	2.8	2.8	2.8	2.8	2.8	2.7	2.8	2.8
2002	2.7	2.7	2.7	2.7	2.7	2.7	2.8	2.9	2.9	2.9	2.9	2.9	2.8
2003	2.8	2.8	2.8	2.8	2.8	2.8	2.9	2.9	2.9	2.9	2.8	2.9	2.8
State government													
2001	10.5	10.5	10.6	10.4	10.2	10.1	10.2	10.2	10.3	10.3	10.5	10.4	10.4
2002	10.6	10.6	10.6	10.5	10.5	10.3	10.3	10.3	10.6	10.7	10.7	10.6	10.5
2003	10.6	10.7	10.6	10.7	10.6	10.4	10.2	10.2	10.6	10.6	10.5	10.4	10.5
Local government													
2001	22.2	22.3	22.3	22.3	22.0	21.9	21.0	21.1	21.9	22.0	22.1	22.2	21.9
2002	22.2	22.3	22.3	22.4	22.4	22.4	21.3	21.4	22.3	22.4	22.5	22.6	22.2
2003	22.7	22.9	22.9	23.0	23.1	23.0	21.9	21.7	22.6	22.9	22.9	22.9	22.7
MONTGOMERY													
Total nonfarm													
1990	132.0	132.6	133.4	134.8	135.7	135.7	136.8	135.9	135.9	136.1	137.1	137.0	135.3
1991	133.4	132.3	132.5	133.3	133.9	135.2	135.5	135.8	135.3	136.6	137.3	137.3	134.9
1992	135.9	137.2	137.9	138.2	138.8	138.4	139.7	140.1	139.4	141.4	141.6	142.7	139.3
1993	140.1	141.2	142.2	142.9	143.3	143.2	143.5	143.7	143.9	145.4	146.2	147.3	143.6
1994	143.6	144.2	145.7	147.0	146.8	146.6	145.9	146.5	147.4	147.7	149.6	149.4	146.7
1995	146.8	147.8	148.3	149.7	150.6	151.4	149.2	150.3	150.3	150.7	151.6	152.9	150.0
1996	149.8	151.5	152.6	153.6	154.3	154.0	154.3	154.6	154.4	154.4	155.4	156.1	153.8
1997	154.2	154.7	156.5	156.4	156.9	156.5	157.2	156.7	157.7	158.9	159.9	160.7	157.2
1998	157.6	158.0	159.3	160.4	160.8	161.5	161.2	161.2	161.7	161.7	163.0	163.6	160.8
1999	161.7	162.5	164.0	164.8	165.1	165.4	164.9	164.9	165.5	164.8	165.5	166.4	164.6
2000	163.0	164.0	165.5	165.5	166.9	166.9	164.5	164.4	165.1	165.2	165.9	166.3	165.3
2001	162.9	163.7	164.9	165.4	165.8	165.2	164.5	164.4	164.3	164.8	165.5	166.0	164.8
2002	161.5	162.3	162.8	163.5	163.2	162.8	163.3	163.5	163.2	163.5	164.6	165.2	163.3
2003	161.6	162.1	162.6	163.5	164.2	163.6	162.9	163.1	163.2	163.9	164.8	164.7	163.3
Total private													
1990	98.0	98.1	98.6	99.8	100.3	101.1	101.9	102.2	102.0	101.1	101.6	101.5	100.5
1991	97.5	97.0	96.8	97.5	98.0	99.1	99.6	100.7	100.5	100.3	100.7	100.8	99.0
1992	99.3	100.1	100.8	101.1	101.6	102.2	102.5	103.3	103.3	104.1	104.3	105.3	102.3
1993	103.2	103.9	104.7	105.7	105.9	106.5	106.8	107.4	107.8	108.4	109.1	110.2	106.6
1994	106.9	107.3	108.5	109.6	109.5	109.7	109.3	110.3	110.7	110.6	111.5	112.3	109.7
1995	111.2	111.3	112.0	113.2	113.9	114.6	113.2	114.6	114.6	114.4	115.2	116.4	113.7
1996	114.2	114.8	115.9	117.1	117.8	118.7	118.1	118.9	118.4	117.7	118.7	119.5	117.5
1997	117.8	117.9	119.3	119.2	119.5	120.2	121.0	120.6	121.5	122.1	122.8	123.6	120.5
1998	120.7	120.9	121.9	123.0	123.5	125.0	124.7	125.2	125.4	125.2	126.0	126.5	124.0
1999	125.0	125.5	126.6	127.1	127.5	128.3	128.4	128.5	128.9	127.5	128.0	129.1	127.5
2000	125.9	126.6	127.6	128.3	129.3	130.3	128.7	128.8	129.0	128.9	129.5	130.1	128.6
2001	126.0	126.3	127.5	127.8	128.1	128.7	127.8	128.0	127.5	127.1	127.7	128.1	127.6
2002	124.0	124.4	124.9	125.3	125.3	125.8	126.2	126.3	125.5	125.1	126.0	126.3	125.4
2003	123.1	123.3	123.9	125.0	125.6	126.4	125.5	125.8	125.2	125.3	125.7	125.8	125.0

Employment by Industry: Alabama—*Continued*

(Numbers in thousands. Not seasonally adjusted.)

Industry	January	February	March	April	May	June	July	August	September	October	November	December	Annual Average
MONTGOMERY—*Continued*													
Goods-producing													
1990	23.5	23.7	23.8	24.0	24.4	24.6	24.7	24.9	24.9	24.4	24.0	23.8	24.2
1991	22.4	21.8	21.3	22.1	22.1	22.8	22.6	23.4	23.3	23.1	23.0	22.5	22.5
1992	21.8	21.9	22.1	22.1	22.2	22.4	22.7	22.8	22.9	23.1	23.1	23.2	22.5
1993	22.6	22.8	23.0	23.1	23.1	23.3	23.5	23.5	23.6	23.6	23.6	23.6	23.3
1994	23.4	23.5	23.6	23.6	23.7	23.7	23.5	24.0	24.1	24.0	24.3	24.4	23.8
1995	24.4	24.6	24.7	24.8	25.0	25.2	24.1	25.3	24.9	24.9	25.0	25.1	24.8
1996	24.6	24.7	24.8	25.3	25.4	25.5	25.4	25.5	25.0	24.9	24.8	24.4	25.0
1997	24.3	24.5	24.7	24.5	24.6	24.9	25.2	24.8	24.7	24.7	24.7	24.5	24.7
1998	24.4	24.5	24.6	25.2	25.1	25.5	25.4	25.7	25.4	25.7	25.7	25.8	25.3
1999	25.6	25.5	25.5	25.8	26.0	26.1	26.0	25.6	25.7	25.2	25.3	25.4	25.6
2000	25.2	25.4	25.7	26.1	26.4	26.7	26.1	26.0	25.9	26.0	26.0	26.0	26.0
2001	25.5	25.6	25.6	25.4	25.4	25.5	25.0	25.0	25.0	24.7	24.6	24.4	25.1
1992	24.1	24.2	24.5	24.7	24.8	24.9	24.8	24.9	24.8	24.6	24.4	24.5	24.6
2003	24.0	24.0	24.1	24.3	24.7	24.7	24.7	24.9	24.8	24.7	24.9	24.7	24.5
Construction and mining													
1990	7.2	7.3	7.4	7.8	8.1	8.3	8.3	8.3	8.0	7.6	7.3	7.2	7.7
1991	6.5	6.6	6.7	7.0	6.8	7.2	7.0	7.0	7.0	6.9	6.9	6.8	6.9
1992	6.4	6.5	6.6	6.7	6.8	6.9	7.2	7.3	7.1	7.3	7.1	7.2	6.9
1993	6.7	6.8	6.9	7.0	7.1	7.2	7.4	7.4	7.4	7.5	7.4	7.4	7.2
1994	7.2	7.3	7.3	7.5	7.6	7.7	7.5	7.7	7.7	7.6	7.7	7.7	7.5
1995	7.7	7.6	7.7	7.8	7.9	8.1	8.2	8.3	8.2	8.1	8.2	8.3	8.0
1996	8.3	8.4	8.6	8.8	9.0	9.1	9.1	9.2	8.8	8.7	8.7	8.4	8.8
1997	8.3	8.4	8.5	8.5	8.5	8.8	9.0	8.9	8.8	8.7	8.5	8.3	8.6
1998	8.2	8.2	8.3	8.7	8.6	8.9	8.9	9.1	8.9	9.0	8.9	9.0	8.7
1999	8.6	8.5	8.6	8.6	8.7	8.7	8.8	8.9	8.9	8.9	8.9	8.9	8.8
2000	8.8	8.8	8.9	9.0	9.2	9.3	8.9	8.9	8.8	8.8	8.8	8.8	8.9
2001	8.6	8.6	8.7	8.8	8.9	9.1	9.2	9.2	9.2	9.0	9.0	8.9	8.9
2002	8.5	8.6	8.8	8.8	8.9	8.9	8.9	8.9	8.8	8.8	8.4	8.3	8.7
2003	8.1	8.1	8.2	8.3	8.7	8.7	8.7	8.9	8.8	8.8	9.0	8.9	8.5
Manufacturing													
1990	16.3	16.4	16.4	16.2	16.3	16.3	16.4	16.6	16.9	16.8	16.7	16.6	16.5
1991	15.9	15.2	14.6	15.1	15.3	15.6	15.6	16.4	16.3	16.2	16.1	15.7	15.7
1992	15.4	15.4	15.5	15.4	15.4	15.5	15.5	15.5	15.8	15.8	16.0	16.0	15.6
1993	15.9	16.0	16.1	16.1	16.0	16.1	16.1	16.1	16.2	16.1	16.2	16.2	16.1
1994	16.2	16.2	16.3	16.1	16.1	16.0	16.0	16.3	16.4	16.4	16.6	16.7	16.3
1995	16.7	17.0	17.0	17.0	17.1	17.1	15.9	17.0	16.7	16.8	16.8	16.8	16.8
1996	16.3	16.3	16.2	16.5	16.4	16.4	16.3	16.3	16.2	16.2	16.1	16.0	16.3
1997	16.0	16.1	16.2	16.0	16.1	16.1	16.2	15.9	15.9	16.0	16.2	16.2	16.1
1998	16.2	16.3	16.3	16.5	16.5	16.6	16.5	16.6	16.5	16.7	16.8	16.8	16.5
1999	17.0	17.0	16.9	17.2	17.3	17.4	17.2	16.7	16.8	16.3	16.4	16.5	16.9
2000	16.4	16.6	16.8	17.1	17.2	17.4	17.2	17.1	17.1	17.2	17.2	17.2	17.0
2001	16.9	17.0	16.9	16.6	16.5	16.4	15.8	15.8	15.8	15.7	15.6	15.5	16.2
2002	15.6	15.6	15.7	15.9	15.9	16.0	15.9	16.0	16.0	15.8	16.0	16.2	15.9
2003	15.9	15.9	15.9	16.0	16.0	16.0	16.0	16.0	16.0	15.9	15.9	15.8	15.9
Service-providing													
1990	108.5	108.9	109.6	110.8	111.3	111.1	112.1	111.0	111.0	111.7	113.1	113.2	111.0
1991	111.0	110.5	111.2	111.2	111.8	112.4	112.9	112.4	112.0	113.5	114.3	114.8	112.3
1992	114.1	115.3	115.8	116.1	116.6	116.0	117.0	117.3	116.5	118.3	118.5	119.5	116.8
1993	117.5	118.4	119.2	119.8	120.2	119.9	120.0	120.2	120.3	121.8	122.6	123.7	120.3
1994	120.2	120.7	122.1	123.4	123.1	122.9	122.4	122.5	123.3	123.7	125.3	125.0	122.9
1995	122.4	123.2	123.6	124.9	125.6	126.2	125.1	125.0	125.4	125.8	126.6	127.8	125.1
1996	125.2	126.8	127.8	128.3	128.9	128.5	128.9	129.1	129.4	129.5	130.6	131.7	128.7
1997	129.9	130.2	131.8	131.9	132.3	131.6	132.0	131.9	133.0	134.2	135.2	136.2	132.5
1998	133.2	133.5	134.7	135.2	135.7	136.0	135.8	135.5	136.3	136.0	137.3	137.8	135.6
1999	136.1	137.0	138.5	139.0	139.1	139.3	138.9	139.3	139.8	139.6	140.2	141.0	139.0
2000	137.8	138.6	139.8	139.4	140.5	140.2	138.4	138.4	139.2	139.2	139.9	140.3	139.3
2001	137.4	138.1	139.3	140.0	140.4	139.7	139.5	139.4	139.3	140.1	140.9	141.6	139.6
2002	137.4	138.1	138.3	138.8	138.4	137.9	138.5	138.6	138.4	138.9	140.2	140.7	138.7
2003	137.6	138.1	138.5	139.2	139.5	138.9	138.2	138.2	138.4	139.2	139.9	140.0	138.8
Trade, transportation, and utilities													
1990	27.1	26.7	26.7	26.7	26.8	27.1	27.3	27.3	27.2	27.0	27.8	27.9	27.1
1991	25.3	25.1	25.3	24.9	25.3	25.5	25.6	25.8	25.8	25.9	26.3	26.7	25.6
1992	25.7	25.8	25.9	26.3	26.7	26.9	26.9	26.8	26.6	27.1	27.3	28.0	26.7
1993	26.8	26.6	26.7	27.2	27.2	27.6	27.6	27.8	27.7	28.0	28.6	29.1	27.6
1994	28.0	27.9	27.9	28.5	28.5	28.7	28.7	28.8	29.0	29.2	29.5	30.0	28.7
1995	29.2	28.6	28.8	29.2	29.4	29.8	29.5	29.5	29.5	29.6	30.2	30.7	29.5
1996	29.6	29.0	29.3	29.5	29.8	30.4	30.3	30.5	30.6	30.5	31.1	31.6	30.2
1997	30.8	30.3	30.6	30.5	30.6	30.9	31.1	30.9	31.4	32.0	32.7	33.3	31.3
1998	31.3	31.0	31.3	31.4	31.8	32.2	31.7	31.6	31.9	31.9	32.4	32.8	31.8
1999	31.6	31.5	31.8	31.9	32.2	32.8	33.1	33.2	33.3	32.8	33.1	33.8	32.6
2000	32.2	32.0	32.1	32.0	32.4	32.6	32.1	32.1	32.1	32.1	32.8	33.2	32.3
2001	31.3	31.3	31.7	31.8	31.9	32.0	31.7	31.7	31.6	32.1	32.6	33.0	31.9
2002	30.8	30.4	30.6	30.5	30.4	30.3	30.7	30.6	30.4	30.4	31.1	31.5	30.6
2003	29.5	29.4	29.8	30.5	30.4	30.6	30.7	30.6	30.4	30.7	31.1	31.3	30.4

Employment by Industry: Alabama—*Continued*

(Numbers in thousands. Not seasonally adjusted.)

Industry	January	February	March	April	May	June	July	August	September	October	November	December	Annual Average
MONTGOMERY—*Continued*													
Wholesale trade													
1990	6.2	6.2	6.2	6.3	6.5	6.5	6.4	6.5	6.4	6.2	6.3	6.2	6.3
1991	5.9	5.9	5.9	5.8	5.8	5.9	6.0	6.0	6.0	6.0	6.0	6.0	5.9
1992	5.9	5.9	6.0	5.8	5.9	5.9	5.9	5.9	5.8	5.9	5.8	5.8	5.9
1993	5.7	5.7	5.7	5.8	5.8	5.9	5.9	5.9	5.8	5.8	5.9	5.9	5.8
1994	5.7	5.8	5.8	5.8	5.8	5.8	5.9	5.9	5.9	5.7	5.7	5.7	5.8
1995	6.0	5.9	6.0	6.1	6.2	6.3	6.2	6.2	6.2	6.2	6.1	6.2	6.1
1996	6.1	6.1	6.1	6.1	6.2	6.3	6.3	6.3	6.3	6.2	6.3	6.3	6.2
1997	6.2	6.2	6.2	6.2	6.2	6.2	6.2	6.2	6.2	6.2	6.2	6.2	6.2
1998	6.0	6.0	6.1	6.0	6.1	6.2	6.1	6.1	6.2	6.2	6.1	6.1	6.1
1999	6.1	6.1	6.2	6.3	6.3	6.3	6.5	6.4	6.5	6.3	6.3	6.4	6.3
2000	6.4	6.4	6.4	6.3	6.4	6.5	6.4	6.5	6.4	6.4	6.4	6.4	6.4
2001	6.7	6.8	6.8	6.9	6.9	6.9	6.9	7.0	6.9	7.0	7.0	7.1	6.9
2002	6.7	6.7	6.7	6.9	6.8	6.8	6.7	6.6	6.6	6.6	6.6	6.6	6.7
2003	6.3	6.3	6.3	6.6	6.6	6.6	6.7	6.7	6.7	6.7	6.7	6.7	6.5
Retail trade													
1990	17.1	16.7	16.7	16.5	16.4	16.5	16.8	16.7	16.6	16.6	17.2	17.4	16.8
1991	15.0	14.9	15.0	14.9	15.2	15.2	15.2	15.4	15.5	15.5	15.9	16.2	15.3
1992	15.4	15.4	15.4	16.0	16.2	16.3	16.0	16.0	15.9	16.3	16.6	17.2	16.1
1993	16.3	16.2	16.3	16.6	16.5	16.6	16.6	16.8	16.8	17.2	17.7	18.2	16.8
1994	17.4	17.2	17.2	17.4	17.5	17.5	17.3	17.4	17.6	17.7	18.0	18.6	17.6
1995	17.8	17.4	17.5	17.7	17.8	17.9	17.8	17.8	17.8	17.9	18.6	19.0	17.9
1996	18.1	17.6	17.9	17.9	18.1	18.4	18.3	18.5	18.6	18.7	19.2	19.7	18.4
1997	19.1	18.6	18.9	18.6	18.7	18.8	19.0	19.2	19.2	19.6	20.3	20.9	19.2
1998	19.2	18.9	19.1	19.2	19.4	19.5	18.9	18.9	19.1	19.0	19.7	20.1	19.3
1999	19.0	18.8	19.1	18.9	19.2	19.6	19.7	20.0	20.1	19.8	20.2	20.8	19.6
2000	19.4	19.2	19.3	19.2	19.4	19.4	19.1	19.1	19.2	19.2	20.0	20.4	19.4
2001	18.4	18.2	18.4	18.3	18.4	18.5	18.3	18.3	18.4	18.6	19.2	19.5	18.5
2002	18.0	17.7	17.9	17.6	17.6	17.5	17.8	17.8	17.8	17.9	18.7	19.2	18.0
2003	17.6	17.6	18.0	18.3	18.2	18.3	18.3	18.3	18.1	18.2	18.6	18.8	18.1
Transportation and utilities													
1990	3.8	3.8	3.8	3.9	3.9	4.1	4.1	4.1	4.2	4.2	4.3	4.3	4.0
1991	4.4	4.3	4.4	4.2	4.3	4.4	4.4	4.4	4.3	4.4	4.4	4.5	4.4
1992	4.4	4.5	4.5	4.5	4.6	4.7	5.0	4.9	4.9	4.9	4.9	5.0	4.7
1993	4.8	4.7	4.7	4.8	4.9	5.1	5.1	5.1	5.1	5.0	5.0	5.0	4.9
1994	4.9	4.9	4.9	5.3	5.2	5.4	5.5	5.5	5.5	5.8	5.8	5.7	5.4
1995	5.4	5.3	5.3	5.4	5.4	5.6	5.5	5.5	5.5	5.5	5.5	5.5	5.5
1996	5.4	5.3	5.3	5.5	5.5	5.7	5.7	5.7	5.7	5.6	5.6	5.6	5.6
1997	5.5	5.5	5.5	5.7	5.7	5.9	5.9	5.5	6.0	6.2	6.2	6.2	5.8
1998	6.1	6.1	6.1	6.2	6.3	6.5	6.7	6.6	6.6	6.7	6.6	6.6	6.4
1999	6.5	6.6	6.5	6.7	6.7	6.9	6.9	6.8	6.7	6.7	6.6	6.6	6.7
2000	6.4	6.4	6.4	6.5	6.6	6.7	6.6	6.5	6.5	6.5	6.4	6.4	6.5
2001	6.2	6.3	6.5	6.6	6.6	6.6	6.5	6.4	6.3	6.5	6.4	6.4	6.4
2002	6.1	6.0	6.0	6.0	6.0	6.0	6.2	6.2	6.0	5.9	5.8	5.7	6.0
2003	5.6	5.5	5.5	5.6	5.6	5.7	5.7	5.6	5.6	5.8	5.8	5.8	5.6
Information													
1990	2.3	2.3	2.3	2.3	2.3	2.3	2.3	2.3	2.3	2.3	2.3	2.3	2.3
1991	2.4	2.4	2.4	2.5	2.5	2.5	2.5	2.5	2.5	2.5	2.5	2.5	2.5
1992	2.4	2.4	2.4	2.4	2.4	2.5	2.4	2.5	2.5	2.5	2.5	2.5	2.5
1993	2.5	2.5	2.5	2.5	2.5	2.6	2.5	2.5	2.5	2.6	2.6	2.6	2.5
1994	2.6	2.6	2.7	2.6	2.6	2.7	2.6	2.7	2.6	2.7	2.7	2.7	2.7
1995	2.7	2.7	2.7	2.7	2.7	2.7	2.7	2.8	2.8	2.8	2.8	2.8	2.7
1996	2.8	2.8	2.8	2.8	2.8	2.8	2.8	2.8	2.8	2.8	2.8	3.0	2.8
1997	2.9	2.9	2.9	2.9	2.9	3.0	3.1	3.0	3.0	3.0	3.0	3.1	3.0
1998	3.1	3.1	3.1	3.0	3.1	3.1	3.1	3.0	3.0	3.0	3.0	3.1	3.1
1999	3.1	3.2	3.2	3.2	3.2	3.2	3.3	3.3	3.3	3.3	3.3	3.3	3.2
2000	3.3	3.3	3.4	3.3	3.4	3.5	3.5	3.5	3.5	3.5	3.5	3.6	3.4
2001	3.5	3.4	3.4	3.3	3.3	3.3	3.3	3.2	3.2	3.1	3.2	3.2	3.3
2002	3.2	3.2	3.2	3.1	3.1	3.1	3.0	2.9	2.9	2.8	2.8	2.9	3.0
2003	2.8	2.7	2.7	2.7	2.8	2.8	2.7	2.7	2.6	2.6	2.4	2.5	2.6
Financial activities													
1990	8.0	8.0	8.0	8.1	8.1	8.2	8.3	8.3	8.3	8.2	8.2	8.2	8.2
1991	8.1	8.0	8.0	7.9	7.9	8.0	8.1	8.1	8.0	7.9	7.9	7.9	8.0
1992	7.9	7.9	8.0	7.9	7.9	8.0	8.0	8.0	7.9	8.0	8.0	8.1	8.0
1993	8.0	8.0	8.0	8.0	8.1	8.2	8.2	8.3	8.3	8.3	8.3	8.4	8.2
1994	8.3	8.3	8.4	8.4	8.4	8.5	8.4	8.4	8.3	8.2	8.3	8.3	8.4
1995	8.2	8.2	8.2	8.3	8.3	8.4	8.4	8.3	8.3	8.3	8.4	8.4	8.3
1996	8.4	8.4	8.5	8.5	8.6	8.8	8.8	8.9	8.9	8.9	9.0	9.1	8.7
1997	9.1	9.1	9.2	9.2	9.3	9.4	9.2	9.2	9.3	9.6	9.6	9.7	9.3
1998	9.7	9.8	9.8	10.0	10.1	10.2	10.2	10.3	10.2	10.3	10.4	10.4	10.1
1999	10.5	10.6	10.7	10.8	10.8	10.9	11.0	11.0	10.9	11.0	11.0	11.1	10.9
2000	10.8	10.7	10.7	10.8	10.8	11.0	10.9	10.9	10.9	10.9	10.9	10.9	10.9
2001	10.8	10.7	10.7	10.6	10.7	10.8	10.8	10.8	10.8	10.7	10.7	10.7	10.7
2002	10.7	10.7	10.7	10.6	10.6	10.6	10.7	10.6	10.5	10.5	10.5	10.5	10.6
2003	10.4	10.4	10.4	10.3	10.4	10.5	10.4	10.5	10.5	10.4	10.4	10.5	10.4

Employment by Industry: Alabama—*Continued*

(Numbers in thousands. Not seasonally adjusted.)

Industry	January	February	March	April	May	June	July	August	September	October	November	December	Annual Average
MONTGOMERY—*Continued*													
Professional and business services													
1990	9.3	9.3	9.4	10.0	9.9	10.1	10.2	10.3	10.2	10.2	10.2	10.1	9.9
1991	10.5	10.5	10.6	10.4	10.3	10.5	10.5	10.5	10.6	10.6	10.6	10.5	10.5
1992	10.9	11.1	11.2	11.0	10.8	11.0	11.0	11.2	11.2	11.1	11.1	11.1	11.1
1993	11.2	11.5	11.8	11.8	11.6	11.6	11.8	11.8	11.9	12.2	12.2	12.4	11.8
1994	11.8	11.9	12.4	12.7	12.5	12.5	12.5	12.7	12.6	12.4	12.6	12.7	12.4
1995	12.7	12.8	12.9	13.3	13.3	13.3	13.2	13.2	13.3	13.4	13.3	13.4	13.2
1996	13.3	14.0	14.2	14.5	14.7	14.7	14.6	14.9	14.8	14.5	14.6	14.8	14.5
1997	14.6	14.9	15.2	15.3	15.3	15.3	15.9	16.1	16.3	16.2	16.1	16.3	15.6
1998	15.8	15.9	16.1	16.2	16.3	16.8	17.1	17.4	17.5	17.3	17.5	17.5	16.8
1999	17.2	17.3	17.5	17.2	17.0	17.1	16.4	16.7	16.7	16.5	16.7	16.7	16.9
2000	16.5	16.8	16.9	17.1	17.2	17.2	17.1	17.2	17.3	17.6	17.6	17.7	17.2
2001	17.0	17.0	17.4	17.6	17.6	17.8	17.7	17.9	17.7	17.4	17.2	17.3	17.5
2002	16.4	16.5	16.6	16.9	16.8	16.8	16.8	17.1	17.0	17.4	17.2	17.1	16.9
2003	17.3	17.5	17.4	17.5	17.6	17.7	16.9	17.0	16.9	16.9	17.0	17.0	17.2
Educational and health services													
1990	12.6	12.7	12.8	13.3	13.2	13.0	13.2	13.3	13.6	13.6	13.6	13.7	13.2
1991	13.6	13.8	13.8	13.9	14.0	13.8	14.0	14.2	14.4	14.5	14.5	14.7	14.1
1992	14.7	14.8	14.9	14.8	14.8	14.6	14.7	15.0	15.3	15.4	15.4	15.5	15.0
1993	15.5	15.6	15.7	15.8	15.9	15.6	15.5	15.9	16.2	15.8	15.9	16.0	15.8
1994	15.3	15.4	15.5	15.6	15.6	15.3	15.2	15.4	15.9	16.0	16.0	16.1	15.6
1995	16.1	16.3	16.3	16.4	16.4	16.2	16.3	16.5	16.9	16.7	16.8	16.9	16.5
1996	16.8	17.0	17.0	16.7	16.7	16.6	16.3	16.4	16.7	16.7	16.8	17.1	16.7
1997	17.0	17.0	17.2	17.1	17.0	16.8	16.7	16.8	17.0	17.0	17.0	17.0	17.0
1998	16.9	16.8	16.9	17.0	16.7	16.7	16.7	16.8	17.2	16.9	17.0	17.0	16.9
1999	17.2	17.3	17.4	17.3	17.4	17.0	17.1	17.2	17.6	17.6	17.7	17.7	17.4
2000	17.2	17.4	17.4	17.7	17.7	17.5	17.4	17.3	17.6	17.4	17.4	17.3	17.4
2001	17.0	17.2	17.2	17.4	17.5	17.3	17.3	17.5	17.6	17.7	18.0	18.0	17.5
2002	17.6	17.9	17.8	17.9	17.8	17.8	17.9	18.0	18.1	18.0	18.4	18.2	18.0
2003	17.9	18.1	18.0	17.9	17.8	17.7	17.6	17.7	17.9	18.0	17.9	17.9	17.8
Leisure and hospitality													
1990	8.7	8.8	9.0	8.9	9.0	9.1	9.2	9.1	8.8	8.9	8.9	8.9	8.9
1991	8.5	8.7	8.8	9.0	9.1	9.2	9.4	9.3	9.1	9.1	9.2	9.2	9.1
1992	9.2	9.4	9.5	9.7	9.9	9.9	9.9	10.0	10.0	9.9	10.0	9.9	9.8
1993	9.7	10.0	10.1	10.3	10.5	10.6	10.6	10.5	10.5	10.7	10.7	10.8	10.4
1994	10.2	10.4	10.6	10.7	10.7	10.8	10.8	10.7	10.7	10.7	10.7	10.8	10.7
1995	10.6	10.8	11.1	11.3	11.5	11.6	11.4	11.4	11.5	11.3	11.3	11.6	11.3
1996	11.2	11.4	11.7	12.3	12.3	12.2	12.2	12.2	12.1	11.9	12.1	12.1	12.0
1997	11.7	11.8	12.0	12.3	12.4	12.5	12.4	12.4	12.4	12.2	12.2	12.2	12.2
1998	12.0	12.3	12.5	12.6	12.8	12.9	12.9	12.8	12.7	12.6	12.5	12.4	12.6
1999	12.1	12.4	12.7	13.0	13.0	13.2	13.4	13.4	13.2	12.9	12.7	12.8	12.9
2000	12.5	12.7	13.0	12.9	13.1	13.2	13.0	13.3	13.2	13.0	12.9	12.9	13.0
2001	12.8	13.0	13.4	13.6	13.7	13.9	13.7	13.6	13.4	13.2	13.2	13.3	13.4
2002	13.0	13.2	13.2	13.4	13.5	13.8	13.8	13.8	13.5	13.2	13.4	13.4	13.4
2003	13.1	13.1	13.3	13.6	13.7	13.9	13.9	13.9	13.8	13.8	13.8	13.7	13.6
Other services													
1990	6.5	6.6	6.6	6.5	6.6	6.7	6.7	6.7	6.7	6.5	6.6	6.6	6.6
1991	6.7	6.7	6.6	6.8	6.8	6.8	6.9	6.9	6.8	6.7	6.7	6.8	6.8
1992	6.7	6.8	6.8	6.9	6.9	6.9	6.9	7.0	6.9	7.0	6.9	7.0	6.9
1993	6.9	6.9	6.9	7.0	7.0	7.0	7.1	7.1	7.1	7.2	7.2	7.3	7.1
1994	7.3	7.3	7.4	7.5	7.5	7.5	7.6	7.6	7.5	7.4	7.4	7.3	7.4
1995	7.3	7.3	7.3	7.2	7.3	7.4	7.6	7.6	7.4	7.4	7.4	7.5	7.4
1996	7.5	7.5	7.6	7.5	7.5	7.7	7.7	7.7	7.5	7.5	7.5	7.4	7.6
1997	7.4	7.4	7.5	7.4	7.4	7.4	7.4	7.4	7.4	7.4	7.5	7.5	7.4
1998	7.5	7.5	7.6	7.6	7.6	7.6	7.6	7.6	7.5	7.5	7.5	7.5	7.6
1999	7.7	7.7	7.8	7.9	7.9	8.0	8.1	8.1	8.2	8.2	8.2	8.3	8.0
2000	8.2	8.3	8.4	8.4	8.3	8.6	8.6	8.5	8.5	8.4	8.4	8.5	8.4
2001	8.1	8.1	8.1	8.1	8.0	8.1	8.3	8.3	8.2	8.2	8.2	8.2	8.2
2002	8.2	8.3	8.3	8.2	8.3	8.5	8.5	8.4	8.3	8.2	8.2	8.2	8.3
2003	8.1	8.1	8.2	8.2	8.2	8.5	8.6	8.5	8.3	8.2	8.2	8.2	8.2
Government													
1990	34.0	34.5	34.8	35.0	35.4	34.6	34.9	33.7	33.9	35.0	35.5	35.5	34.7
1991	35.9	35.3	35.7	35.8	35.9	36.1	35.9	35.1	34.8	36.3	36.6	36.5	35.8
1992	36.6	37.1	37.1	37.1	37.2	36.2	37.2	36.8	36.1	37.3	37.3	37.4	37.0
1993	36.9	37.3	37.5	37.2	37.4	36.7	36.7	36.3	36.1	37.0	37.1	37.1	36.9
1994	36.7	36.9	37.2	37.4	37.3	36.9	36.6	36.2	36.7	37.1	38.1	37.1	37.0
1995	35.6	36.5	36.3	36.5	36.7	36.8	36.0	35.7	35.7	36.3	36.4	36.5	36.3
1996	35.6	36.7	36.7	36.5	36.5	35.3	36.2	35.7	36.0	36.7	36.7	36.6	36.3
1997	36.4	36.8	37.2	37.2	37.4	36.3	36.2	36.1	36.2	36.8	37.1	37.1	36.7
1998	36.9	37.1	37.4	37.4	37.3	36.5	36.5	36.0	36.3	36.5	37.0	37.1	36.8
1999	36.7	37.0	37.4	37.7	37.6	37.1	36.5	36.4	36.6	37.3	37.5	37.3	37.1
2000	37.1	37.4	37.9	37.2	37.6	36.6	35.8	35.6	36.1	36.3	36.4	36.2	36.7
2001	36.9	37.4	37.4	37.6	37.7	36.5	36.7	36.4	36.8	37.7	37.8	37.9	37.2
2002	37.5	37.9	37.9	38.2	37.9	37.0	37.1	37.2	37.7	38.4	38.6	38.9	37.9
2003	38.5	38.8	38.7	38.5	38.6	37.2	37.4	37.3	38.0	38.6	39.1	38.9	38.3

Employment by Industry: Alabama—*Continued*

(Numbers in thousands. Not seasonally adjusted.)

Industry	January	February	March	April	May	June	July	August	September	October	November	December	Annual Average
MONTGOMERY—*Continued*													
Federal government													
1990	7.3	7.3	7.4	7.5	7.7	7.8	7.6	7.3	7.3	7.3	7.3	7.3	7.4
1991	7.2	7.1	7.2	7.2	7.2	7.3	7.4	7.4	7.4	7.5	7.5	7.5	7.3
1992	7.5	7.5	7.5	7.6	7.5	7.6	7.6	7.6	7.6	7.6	7.6	7.7	7.6
1993	7.5	7.5	7.4	7.5	7.5	7.6	7.6	7.6	7.3	7.2	7.3	7.3	7.4
1994	7.2	7.2	7.3	7.3	7.3	7.3	7.3	7.2	7.2	7.1	7.0	7.1	7.2
1995	7.0	6.9	6.8	6.8	6.9	6.9	6.9	6.9	6.9	6.9	6.8	6.9	6.9
1996	6.8	6.8	6.7	6.8	6.8	6.9	7.0	7.0	7.1	7.1	7.0	7.0	6.9
1997	7.0	7.0	7.1	7.0	7.1	7.2	7.1	7.2	7.2	7.1	7.1	7.2	7.1
1998	7.0	7.0	7.0	7.1	7.1	7.2	7.2	7.2	7.2	7.1	7.2	7.2	7.1
1999	7.1	7.1	7.1	7.1	7.1	7.2	7.3	7.3	7.2	7.2	7.2	7.2	7.2
2000	7.1	7.1	7.2	7.2	7.7	7.3	7.4	7.2	7.1	7.0	7.1	7.1	7.2
2001	7.1	7.0	7.0	7.0	7.1	7.1	7.2	7.2	7.1	7.1	7.1	7.1	7.1
2002	7.0	7.0	7.0	7.0	7.0	7.0	7.1	6.9	6.8	6.8	6.8	6.9	6.9
2003	6.8	6.7	6.6	6.4	6.4	6.5	6.7	6.5	6.4	6.4	6.4	6.5	6.5
State government													
2001	17.0	17.5	17.6	17.7	17.7	16.7	17.3	17.0	17.2	17.9	18.0	18.1	17.5
2002	17.9	18.2	18.3	18.5	18.2	17.5	18.2	18.2	18.1	18.7	18.8	18.9	18.3
2003	18.7	19.0	19.0	19.0	19.0	17.8	18.5	18.4	18.6	18.9	19.3	19.0	18.7
Local government													
2001	12.8	12.9	12.8	12.9	12.9	12.7	12.2	12.2	12.5	12.7	12.7	12.7	12.7
2002	12.6	12.7	12.6	12.7	12.7	12.5	11.8	12.1	12.8	12.9	13.0	13.1	12.6
2003	13.0	13.1	13.1	13.1	13.2	12.9	12.2	12.4	13.0	13.3	13.4	13.4	13.0
TUSCALOOSA													
Total nonfarm													
1990	65.8	63.8	66.4	67.2	67.4	65.6	65.4	66.6	68.6	68.2	68.4	68.1	66.8
1991	66.3	66.7	66.8	67.6	66.7	65.9	65.2	65.2	67.2	67.9	67.9	67.8	66.8
1992	66.0	66.7	66.9	66.8	66.5	64.5	64.7	65.6	66.7	67.5	67.5	68.0	66.5
1993	66.2	67.9	68.1	69.2	69.0	67.7	67.9	68.7	69.9	71.5	71.9	72.0	69.2
1994	69.5	70.4	71.0	71.5	71.4	70.2	69.7	70.6	72.4	72.7	73.6	73.5	71.4
1995	71.3	72.3	72.7	72.9	73.4	72.5	72.2	73.3	74.5	75.1	75.4	75.1	73.4
1996	73.3	74.1	74.5	75.3	75.4	73.8	74.0	75.2	76.5	77.0	77.7	77.5	75.4
1997	76.1	77.4	78.5	78.3	78.5	77.8	76.5	77.7	79.5	79.7	80.3	80.0	78.4
1998	78.4	79.5	80.1	80.5	80.9	80.0	79.1	80.6	82.2	82.7	82.4	83.1	80.8
1999	80.8	82.1	83.1	82.7	82.2	81.4	81.1	81.9	83.1	82.9	83.9	83.9	82.4
2000	82.6	83.2	83.7	84.0	84.2	82.6	81.4	81.8	83.4	83.5	84.0	84.2	83.2
2001	82.3	83.2	83.6	83.8	83.5	81.8	81.2	81.8	83.4	83.4	83.2	83.0	82.9
2002	81.4	82.3	83.4	83.4	83.4	81.6	80.9	81.7	83.4	83.8	84.1	84.0	82.8
2003	82.6	83.2	84.1	82.2	82.9	80.7	80.1	80.6	82.3	82.9	82.4	82.3	82.1
Total private													
1990	45.2	43.1	45.6	46.2	46.3	46.5	46.4	47.2	47.8	47.2	47.3	47.0	46.3
1991	45.4	45.3	45.6	46.2	45.3	45.9	45.6	45.5	45.8	46.2	46.1	46.1	45.8
1992	44.7	45.0	45.1	45.3	44.9	44.1	44.5	45.1	45.0	45.5	45.5	46.1	45.1
1993	44.7	45.8	46.1	46.9	47.0	47.2	47.4	47.7	47.9	48.9	49.2	49.3	47.3
1994	47.7	48.2	48.4	48.8	49.1	49.2	49.2	49.7	50.2	50.3	50.9	51.2	49.4
1995	49.8	50.3	50.7	51.5	52.2	52.4	52.5	53.0	53.0	53.5	53.7	53.4	52.2
1996	52.3	52.5	52.8	53.7	54.0	54.0	54.4	54.8	55.1	55.7	56.1	56.2	54.3
1997	54.6	55.4	56.3	56.2	56.9	57.3	56.6	56.9	57.4	57.5	57.9	58.0	56.8
1998	56.5	57.0	57.5	58.5	59.3	59.7	58.7	59.6	60.1	60.4	59.9	60.6	59.0
1999	58.8	59.5	60.2	60.2	60.3	60.8	60.8	60.9	60.7	60.5	61.4	61.3	60.5
2000	60.5	60.8	61.1	61.4	61.5	61.4	61.1	61.3	61.1	61.1	61.5	61.5	61.2
2001	60.3	60.4	60.8	60.9	60.9	60.9	60.3	60.8	60.7	60.5	60.4	60.0	60.6
2002	59.2	59.6	60.5	60.6	60.7	60.7	60.4	60.6	60.8	60.9	61.1	60.9	60.5
2003	60.1	60.2	60.9	59.2	59.9	59.5	59.4	59.5	59.6	60.0	59.5	59.5	59.7
Goods-producing													
1990	16.9	14.8	17.5	17.7	17.7	17.9	18.0	18.0	18.0	18.0	17.7	17.6	17.5
1991	16.9	16.7	17.0	17.1	16.7	16.9	17.0	16.9	17.0	17.0	16.8	16.7	16.9
1992	16.0	16.2	16.2	16.3	15.9	15.6	15.6	15.7	15.6	15.9	15.9	16.0	15.9
1993	15.7	16.1	16.4	16.5	16.6	16.8	17.0	17.1	17.1	17.2	17.0	16.8	16.7
1994	16.7	16.8	16.9	16.8	16.9	17.2	17.2	17.4	17.4	17.3	17.4	17.5	17.1
1995	17.2	17.3	17.5	17.9	18.2	18.1	18.3	18.4	18.3	18.6	18.3	18.1	18.0
1996	18.1	18.0	18.0	18.6	18.8	19.0	18.9	18.9	18.9	19.2	19.2	19.1	18.7
1997	19.0	19.2	19.6	19.6	19.9	20.2	19.8	19.8	19.9	19.6	19.6	19.7	19.7
1998	19.5	19.8	19.8	20.4	21.0	21.1	20.7	21.2	21.3	21.5	21.1	21.3	20.7
1999	20.9	21.2	21.3	21.5	21.7	21.9	21.9	21.8	21.7	21.3	21.4	21.3	21.5
2000	21.4	21.5	21.6	21.6	21.6	21.7	21.5	21.3	21.1	21.0	21.0	21.0	21.4
2001	20.8	20.8	21.0	20.8	20.7	20.7	20.3	20.4	20.1	20.2	20.1	20.0	20.5
2002	19.8	20.1	20.3	20.3	20.5	20.6	20.5	20.7	20.6	20.7	20.6	20.5	20.4
2003	20.6	20.7	20.9	19.5	20.2	19.8	19.8	19.7	19.6	19.8	19.9	20.0	20.0

Employment by Industry: Alabama—*Continued*

(Numbers in thousands. Not seasonally adjusted.)

Industry	January	February	March	April	May	June	July	August	September	October	November	December	Annual Average
TUSCALOOSA—*Continued*													
Construction and mining													
1990	7.6	7.9	8.0	8.2	8.2	8.4	8.5	8.4	8.5	8.5	8.4	8.3	8.2
1991	8.0	7.8	7.8	7.8	7.6	7.7	7.8	7.7	7.7	7.7	7.5	7.5	7.7
1992	7.0	6.9	6.9	7.0	6.5	6.3	6.3	6.3	6.3	6.5	6.5	6.6	6.6
1993	6.6	6.7	6.8	6.8	6.9	7.0	7.1	7.1	7.1	7.2	7.1	6.9	6.9
1994	6.9	7.1	7.2	7.0	7.0	7.2	7.1	7.2	7.2	7.2	7.2	7.2	7.1
1995	7.1	7.1	7.3	7.7	7.9	7.7	7.9	8.0	8.0	8.1	7.9	7.8	7.7
1996	7.7	7.6	7.6	8.1	8.2	8.3	8.2	8.2	8.1	8.5	8.4	8.3	8.1
1997	8.4	8.5	8.6	8.6	8.8	8.9	8.2	8.2	8.2	7.9	7.8	7.8	8.3
1998	7.8	7.9	7.9	8.6	9.1	9.0	8.8	8.9	9.0	9.1	8.7	8.7	8.6
1999	8.5	8.7	8.8	8.5	8.6	8.7	8.6	8.6	8.7	8.2	8.2	8.1	8.5
2000	8.2	8.3	8.4	8.3	8.3	8.3	8.0	7.9	7.9	8.0	7.9	7.9	8.1
2001	8.0	8.1	8.3	8.3	8.3	8.3	8.0	8.0	7.9	7.9	7.9	7.9	8.1
2002	8.1	8.3	8.6	8.7	8.9	9.0	8.9	9.2	9.1	9.3	9.2	9.2	8.9
2003	9.4	9.4	9.6	8.9	8.9	8.5	8.3	8.2	8.1	8.2	8.1	8.0	8.6
Manufacturing													
1990	9.3	6.9	9.5	9.5	9.5	9.5	9.5	9.6	9.5	9.5	9.3	9.3	9.2
1991	8.9	8.9	9.2	9.3	9.1	9.2	9.2	9.2	9.3	9.3	9.3	9.2	9.2
1992	9.0	9.3	9.3	9.3	9.4	9.3	9.3	9.4	9.3	9.4	9.4	9.4	9.3
1993	9.1	9.4	9.6	9.7	9.7	9.8	9.9	10.0	10.0	10.0	9.9	9.9	9.8
1994	9.8	9.7	9.7	9.8	9.9	10.0	10.1	10.2	10.2	10.1	10.2	10.3	10.0
1995	10.1	10.2	10.2	10.2	10.3	10.4	10.4	10.4	10.3	10.5	10.4	10.3	10.3
1996	10.4	10.4	10.4	10.5	10.6	10.7	10.7	10.7	10.8	10.7	10.8	10.8	10.6
1997	10.6	10.7	11.0	11.0	11.1	11.3	11.6	11.6	11.7	11.7	11.8	11.9	11.3
1998	11.7	11.9	11.9	11.8	11.9	12.1	11.9	12.3	12.3	12.4	12.4	12.6	12.1
1999	12.4	12.5	12.5	13.0	13.1	13.2	13.3	13.2	13.0	13.1	13.2	13.2	13.0
2000	13.2	13.2	13.2	13.3	13.3	13.4	13.5	13.4	13.2	13.0	13.1	13.1	13.2
2001	12.8	12.7	12.7	12.5	12.4	12.4	12.3	12.4	12.2	12.3	12.2	12.1	12.4
2002	11.7	11.8	11.7	11.6	11.6	11.6	11.6	11.5	11.5	11.4	11.4	11.3	11.6
2003	11.2	11.3	11.3	10.6	11.3	11.3	11.5	11.5	11.5	11.6	11.8	12.0	11.4
Service-providing													
1990	48.9	49.0	48.9	49.5	49.7	47.7	47.4	48.6	50.6	50.2	50.7	50.5	49.3
1991	49.4	50.0	49.8	50.5	50.0	49.0	48.2	48.3	50.2	50.9	51.1	51.1	49.9
1992	50.0	50.5	50.7	50.5	50.6	48.9	49.1	49.9	51.1	51.6	51.6	52.0	50.5
1993	50.5	51.8	51.7	52.7	52.4	50.9	50.9	51.6	52.8	54.3	54.9	55.2	52.5
1994	52.8	53.6	54.1	54.7	54.5	53.0	52.5	53.2	55.0	55.4	56.2	56.0	54.3
1995	54.1	55.0	55.2	55.0	55.2	54.4	53.9	54.9	56.2	56.5	57.1	57.0	55.4
1996	55.2	56.1	56.5	56.7	56.6	54.8	55.1	56.3	57.6	57.8	58.5	58.4	56.6
1997	57.1	58.2	58.9	58.7	58.6	57.6	56.7	57.9	59.6	60.1	60.7	60.3	58.7
1998	58.9	59.7	60.3	60.1	59.9	58.9	58.4	59.4	60.9	61.2	61.3	61.8	60.1
1999	59.9	60.9	61.8	61.2	60.5	59.5	59.2	60.1	61.4	61.6	62.5	62.6	60.9
2000	61.2	61.7	62.1	62.4	62.6	60.9	59.9	60.5	62.3	62.5	63.0	63.2	61.9
2001	61.5	62.4	62.6	63.0	62.8	61.1	60.9	61.4	63.3	63.2	63.1	63.0	62.4
2002	61.6	62.2	63.1	63.1	62.9	61.0	60.4	61.0	62.8	63.1	63.5	63.5	62.4
2003	62.0	62.5	63.2	62.7	62.7	60.9	60.3	60.9	62.7	63.1	62.5	62.3	62.1
Trade, transportation, and utilities													
1990	11.8	11.7	11.6	11.5	11.5	11.6	11.7	11.9	12.2	11.8	12.0	12.0	11.8
1991	11.1	11.1	11.0	11.2	11.1	11.2	11.0	11.1	11.0	11.4	11.6	11.8	11.2
1992	11.3	11.3	11.2	11.2	11.3	11.2	11.4	11.3	11.2	11.3	11.3	11.7	11.3
1993	11.1	11.3	11.2	11.2	11.2	11.5	11.6	11.7	11.6	12.3	12.4	12.6	11.6
1994	11.9	11.7	11.8	11.9	12.0	12.1	12.1	12.1	12.3	12.4	12.8	13.2	12.2
1995	12.4	12.3	12.4	12.4	12.7	12.8	12.9	13.0	13.0	13.0	13.6	13.7	12.9
1996	13.0	12.9	12.9	13.0	13.0	13.0	13.3	13.3	13.5	13.7	14.2	14.5	13.4
1997	13.4	13.3	13.5	13.5	13.6	13.6	13.7	13.8	14.0	14.0	14.3	14.5	13.8
1998	13.5	13.3	13.6	13.8	13.9	14.0	14.0	14.1	14.2	14.2	14.4	14.6	14.0
1999	13.9	13.9	14.0	14.1	14.1	14.2	14.0	14.1	14.1	14.3	14.7	14.8	14.2
2000	14.3	14.0	14.1	14.3	14.4	14.4	14.2	14.4	14.3	14.3	14.6	14.7	14.3
2001	14.0	13.9	14.0	14.0	14.1	14.1	14.0	14.0	14.0	14.1	14.3	14.3	14.1
2002	13.9	13.8	14.0	13.8	13.8	13.8	13.6	13.5	13.6	13.6	13.9	14.1	13.8
2003	13.7	13.3	13.5	13.5	13.5	13.5	13.7	13.7	13.7	13.7	14.0	14.0	13.6
Wholesale trade													
1990	1.8	1.8	1.8	1.7	1.7	1.7	1.7	1.7	1.8	1.7	1.7	1.7	1.7
1991	1.7	1.7	1.6	1.5	1.5	1.5	1.5	1.5	1.5	1.6	1.6	1.6	1.6
1992	1.5	1.6	1.5	1.5	1.6	1.5	1.5	1.5	1.5	1.5	1.5	1.6	1.5
1993	1.5	1.6	1.5	1.6	1.6	1.6	1.7	1.7	1.7	1.7	1.7	1.8	1.6
1994	1.6	1.6	1.6	1.6	1.6	1.7	1.7	1.7	1.7	1.7	1.7	1.7	1.7
1995	1.7	1.7	1.7	1.7	1.7	1.7	1.7	1.8	1.8	1.7	1.8	1.8	1.7
1996	1.7	1.8	1.8	1.9	1.9	1.9	1.9	1.9	1.9	2.0	2.0	2.0	1.9
1997	1.9	1.9	1.9	1.9	1.9	1.9	1.9	1.9	1.9	2.0	2.0	2.0	1.9
1998	2.0	1.9	1.9	1.9	1.9	1.9	1.9	1.9	1.9	1.9	1.9	1.9	1.9
1999	1.9	1.9	1.9	1.9	1.9	1.9	1.9	1.9	1.9	1.9	1.9	1.9	1.9
2000	1.9	1.8	1.8	1.9	1.9	1.9	1.9	1.9	1.9	1.9	1.8	1.8	1.9
2001	2.0	2.0	2.0	2.0	2.0	2.0	2.0	2.0	2.0	2.0	2.0	2.0	2.0
2002	2.0	2.0	2.0	2.0	2.0	2.0	2.0	2.0	2.0	2.0	2.0	2.0	2.0
2003	2.0	1.9	1.9	1.9	2.0	1.9	2.0	1.9	2.0	2.0	2.0	2.0	1.9

Employment by Industry: Alabama—*Continued*

(Numbers in thousands. Not seasonally adjusted.)

Industry	January	February	March	April	May	June	July	August	September	October	November	December	Annual Average
TUSCALOOSA—*Continued*													
Retail trade													
1990	8.3	8.2	8.1	8.1	8.1	8.2	8.3	8.5	8.6	8.4	8.6	8.6	8.3
1991	7.7	7.7	7.7	8.0	7.9	8.0	7.9	7.9	7.9	8.1	8.3	8.5	8.0
1992	8.1	8.0	8.0	8.0	8.0	8.1	8.2	8.1	8.1	8.1	8.2	8.4	8.1
1993	8.0	8.1	8.1	8.0	8.0	8.2	8.2	8.3	8.2	8.9	9.0	9.1	8.3
1994	8.6	8.4	8.5	8.6	8.8	8.8	8.8	8.8	9.0	9.1	9.5	9.9	8.9
1995	9.1	9.0	9.1	9.1	9.3	9.4	9.4	9.4	9.5	9.5	10.0	10.1	9.4
1996	9.6	9.4	9.4	9.4	9.3	9.3	9.5	9.5	9.6	9.7	10.2	10.5	9.6
1997	9.6	9.5	9.6	9.6	9.7	9.6	9.7	9.8	9.9	9.9	10.2	10.4	9.8
1998	9.3	9.2	9.4	9.5	9.6	9.7	9.6	9.7	9.8	9.7	9.9	10.1	9.6
1999	9.5	9.5	9.6	9.7	9.7	9.8	9.7	9.8	9.8	10.0	10.4	10.6	9.8
2000	10.1	9.9	10.0	10.1	10.2	10.2	9.9	10.0	10.0	10.1	10.4	10.5	10.1
2001	9.6	9.5	9.6	9.6	9.7	9.7	9.6	9.6	9.6	9.8	10.0	10.1	9.7
2002	9.8	9.7	9.9	9.7	9.7	9.7	9.5	9.4	9.5	9.5	9.8	10.0	9.7
2003	9.6	9.4	9.5	9.6	9.5	9.6	9.6	9.7	9.7	9.7	9.9	10.0	9.6
Transportation and utilities													
1990	1.7	1.7	1.7	1.7	1.7	1.7	1.7	1.7	1.8	1.7	1.7	1.7	1.7
1991	1.7	1.7	1.7	1.7	1.7	1.7	1.6	1.7	1.6	1.7	1.7	1.7	1.7
1992	1.7	1.7	1.7	1.7	1.7	1.6	1.7	1.7	1.6	1.7	1.6	1.7	1.7
1993	1.6	1.6	1.6	1.6	1.6	1.7	1.7	1.7	1.7	1.7	1.7	1.7	1.7
1994	1.7	1.7	1.7	1.7	1.6	1.6	1.6	1.6	1.6	1.6	1.6	1.6	1.6
1995	1.6	1.6	1.6	1.6	1.7	1.7	1.8	1.8	1.7	1.8	1.8	1.8	1.7
1996	1.7	1.7	1.7	1.7	1.8	1.8	1.9	1.9	2.0	2.0	2.0	2.0	1.9
1997	1.9	1.9	2.0	2.0	2.0	2.1	2.1	2.1	2.2	2.1	2.1	2.1	2.1
1998	2.2	2.2	2.3	2.4	2.4	2.4	2.5	2.5	2.5	2.6	2.6	2.6	2.4
1999	2.5	2.5	2.5	2.5	2.5	2.5	2.4	2.4	2.4	2.4	2.4	2.3	2.4
2000	2.3	2.3	2.3	2.3	2.3	2.3	2.4	2.5	2.4	2.3	2.4	2.4	2.4
2001	2.4	2.4	2.4	2.4	2.4	2.4	2.4	2.4	2.4	2.3	2.3	2.2	2.4
2002	2.1	2.1	2.1	2.1	2.1	2.1	2.1	2.1	2.1	2.1	2.1	2.1	2.1
2003	2.1	2.0	2.1	2.0	2.0	2.0	2.1	2.1	2.0	2.0	2.1	2.0	2.0
Information													
1990	0.8	0.8	0.8	0.8	0.9	0.9	0.8	0.9	0.9	0.8	0.9	0.8	0.8
1991	0.8	0.8	0.8	0.8	0.8	0.8	0.8	0.8	0.8	0.8	0.8	0.8	0.8
1992	0.8	0.8	0.8	0.8	0.8	0.8	0.8	0.8	0.8	0.9	1.0	1.0	0.8
1993	0.8	0.9	0.9	0.9	0.8	0.8	0.8	0.8	0.8	0.8	0.9	0.9	0.8
1994	0.8	0.9	0.9	0.9	0.9	0.9	0.9	0.9	0.9	0.9	0.9	0.9	0.9
1995	0.9	0.9	0.9	0.9	0.9	1.0	1.0	1.0	1.0	1.0	1.0	1.0	1.0
1996	0.9	0.9	0.9	0.9	1.0	1.0	0.9	0.9	0.9	0.9	0.9	0.9	0.9
1997	0.8	0.8	0.8	0.8	0.9	0.9	0.8	0.8	0.8	0.8	0.8	0.9	0.8
1998	0.9	1.0	1.0	1.1	1.1	1.1	1.1	1.1	1.1	0.9	0.9	0.9	1.0
1999	0.9	0.9	1.0	0.9	1.0	1.0	1.0	1.0	1.0	1.0	1.0	1.0	1.0
2000	1.0	1.1	1.1	1.1	1.1	1.1	1.1	1.1	1.1	1.1	1.1	1.2	1.1
2001	1.3	1.3	1.3	1.3	1.3	1.3	1.2	1.2	1.2	1.2	1.2	1.1	1.2
2002	1.1	1.1	1.1	1.1	1.1	1.1	1.1	1.0	1.0	1.0	1.0	1.0	1.1
2003	1.0	1.0	1.0	1.0	1.0	1.0	1.0	1.0	1.0	1.0	1.0	1.0	1.0
Financial activities													
1990	2.0	2.0	2.0	2.1	2.1	2.1	2.1	2.2	2.2	2.1	2.1	2.1	2.1
1991	2.1	2.1	2.1	2.2	2.1	2.2	2.1	2.1	2.1	2.1	2.1	2.1	2.1
1992	2.1	2.1	2.1	2.1	2.1	2.1	2.1	2.2	2.2	2.1	2.1	2.2	2.1
1993	2.2	2.2	2.2	2.2	2.2	2.2	2.2	2.2	2.2	2.2	2.2	2.3	2.2
1994	2.1	2.1	2.1	2.1	2.2	2.2	2.2	2.3	2.2	2.3	2.3	2.3	2.2
1995	2.3	2.3	2.3	2.3	2.3	2.4	2.4	2.4	2.4	2.4	2.4	2.4	2.4
1996	2.4	2.4	2.5	2.4	2.4	2.5	2.5	2.5	2.5	2.5	2.5	2.5	2.5
1997	2.5	2.5	2.6	2.5	2.5	2.6	2.5	2.5	2.5	2.6	2.6	2.6	2.5
1998	2.6	2.6	2.6	2.6	2.6	2.6	2.6	2.6	2.6	2.7	2.7	2.7	2.6
1999	2.6	2.7	2.7	2.7	2.8	2.8	2.8	2.8	2.7	2.7	2.8	2.8	2.7
2000	2.7	2.7	2.7	2.7	2.7	2.7	2.8	2.7	2.7	2.8	2.8	2.8	2.7
2001	2.7	2.7	2.7	2.8	2.8	2.8	3.0	3.0	2.9	2.9	2.9	2.9	2.8
2002	2.9	2.9	2.9	2.9	2.9	2.9	3.0	3.0	2.9	3.0	3.0	3.0	2.9
2003	3.0	3.1	3.0	3.0	3.1	3.1	3.1	3.1	3.1	3.1	3.0	3.0	3.0
Professional and business services													
1990	3.2	3.2	3.2	3.3	3.3	3.3	3.4	3.4	3.4	3.3	3.4	3.3	3.3
1991	3.5	3.6	3.5	3.6	3.5	3.5	3.6	3.6	3.6	3.5	3.5	3.5	3.5
1992	3.6	3.6	3.7	3.6	3.6	3.5	3.7	3.8	3.9	3.8	3.8	3.8	3.7
1993	3.8	3.9	3.9	4.2	4.2	4.2	4.1	4.2	4.2	4.2	4.2	4.2	4.1
1994	4.3	4.4	4.5	4.6	4.5	4.5	4.5	4.5	4.6	4.5	4.5	4.4	4.5
1995	4.4	4.5	4.6	4.7	4.7	4.8	4.7	4.7	4.7	4.7	4.6	4.6	4.6
1996	4.5	4.6	4.7	4.6	4.6	4.6	4.6	4.7	4.7	4.6	4.6	4.5	4.6
1997	4.3	4.6	4.6	4.7	4.8	4.7	4.7	4.8	4.8	4.9	5.1	4.8	4.7
1998	4.8	4.9	4.8	4.8	4.8	5.0	4.6	4.7	4.8	4.9	4.7	4.9	4.8
1999	4.6	4.7	4.8	4.9	4.7	4.7	4.9	4.9	4.8	4.8	5.0	4.9	4.8
2000	5.0	5.1	5.0	5.1	4.9	4.9	5.0	5.0	5.1	4.9	4.9	4.8	5.0
2001	4.8	4.9	4.9	4.9	4.8	4.9	4.9	5.1	5.2	5.0	4.9	4.8	4.9
2002	4.7	4.9	5.2	5.2	5.1	5.1	5.0	5.1	5.2	5.1	5.1	5.0	5.1
2003	5.4	5.4	5.5	5.4	5.3	5.3	5.3	5.4	5.4	5.4	5.4	5.1	5.3

Employment by Industry: Alabama—*Continued*

(Numbers in thousands. Not seasonally adjusted.)

Industry	January	February	March	April	May	June	July	August	September	October	November	December	Annual Average
TUSCALOOSA—*Continued*													
Educational and health services													
1990	2.9	2.9	2.9	3.0	3.0	3.0	2.9	2.9	3.0	3.2	3.2	3.3	3.0
1991	3.2	3.3	3.3	3.4	3.3	3.4	3.3	3.2	3.4	3.5	3.4	3.4	3.3
1992	3.4	3.4	3.4	3.5	3.6	3.5	3.5	3.5	3.6	3.7	3.7	3.7	3.5
1993	3.7	3.7	3.7	3.9	3.9	3.8	3.8	3.8	3.9	3.9	4.0	4.0	3.8
1994	3.9	4.0	4.0	4.2	4.2	4.1	4.1	4.1	4.2	4.3	4.3	4.3	4.1
1995	4.3	4.4	4.4	4.4	4.4	4.4	4.3	4.4	4.5	4.7	4.7	4.7	4.5
1996	4.6	4.7	4.7	4.8	4.8	4.7	4.9	4.9	4.9	4.9	4.9	4.9	4.8
1997	4.9	4.9	5.0	5.0	5.0	5.0	4.9	4.9	5.0	5.1	5.1	5.2	5.0
1998	5.1	5.1	5.2	5.2	5.2	5.1	5.0	5.0	5.1	5.2	5.2	5.2	5.1
1999	5.1	5.2	5.3	5.3	5.3	5.3	5.3	5.3	5.4	5.4	5.4	5.5	5.3
2000	5.3	5.4	5.4	5.3	5.4	5.4	5.4	5.5	5.5	5.5	5.6	5.6	5.4
2001	5.6	5.6	5.6	5.7	5.7	5.7	5.7	5.8	5.8	5.8	5.8	5.7	5.7
2002	5.7	5.4	5.5	5.7	5.7	5.7	5.6	5.6	5.7	5.8	5.8	5.8	5.7
2003	5.6	5.7	5.7	5.7	5.7	5.7	5.6	5.5	5.6	5.6	5.6	5.6	5.6
Leisure and hospitality													
1990	4.7	4.8	4.8	5.0	5.0	4.9	4.8	5.1	5.2	5.1	5.2	5.1	5.0
1991	5.0	5.0	5.1	5.1	5.0	5.0	5.0	5.1	5.2	5.1	5.1	5.0	5.1
1992	4.8	4.9	5.0	5.0	4.8	4.7	4.7	5.0	5.0	5.0	4.9	4.9	4.9
1993	4.8	5.0	5.1	5.3	5.3	5.1	5.1	5.2	5.3	5.5	5.6	5.6	5.2
1994	5.2	5.4	5.3	5.4	5.5	5.3	5.3	5.5	5.8	5.7	5.8	5.7	5.5
1995	5.5	5.7	5.7	6.0	6.0	5.9	5.9	6.1	6.1	6.1	6.1	5.9	5.9
1996	5.8	6.0	6.1	6.3	6.3	6.0	6.1	6.4	6.5	6.7	6.6	6.6	6.3
1997	6.5	6.9	6.9	6.9	7.0	7.0	6.9	7.1	7.2	7.2	7.2	7.1	7.0
1998	6.9	7.0	7.2	7.3	7.4	7.4	7.4	7.6	7.7	7.6	7.5	7.5	7.4
1999	7.3	7.4	7.6	7.3	7.2	7.3	7.3	7.4	7.4	7.4	7.4	7.3	7.4
2000	7.1	7.2	7.3	7.4	7.5	7.3	7.3	7.5	7.6	7.6	7.6	7.5	7.4
2001	7.3	7.4	7.5	7.6	7.7	7.6	7.4	7.5	7.7	7.5	7.5	7.5	7.5
2002	7.3	7.5	7.6	7.7	7.7	7.5	7.7	7.8	7.9	7.8	7.7	7.5	7.6
2003	7.2	7.4	7.7	7.5	7.5	7.4	7.3	7.5	7.6	7.7	7.0	7.2	7.4
Other services													
1990	2.9	2.9	2.8	2.8	2.8	2.8	2.7	2.8	2.9	2.9	2.8	2.8	2.8
1991	2.8	2.7	2.8	2.8	2.8	2.9	2.8	2.7	2.7	2.8	2.8	2.8	2.8
1992	2.7	2.7	2.7	2.8	2.8	2.7	2.7	2.8	2.7	2.8	2.8	2.8	2.8
1993	2.6	2.7	2.7	2.7	2.8	2.8	2.8	2.7	2.8	2.8	2.9	2.9	2.8
1994	2.8	2.9	2.9	2.9	2.9	2.9	2.9	2.9	2.8	2.9	2.9	2.9	2.9
1995	2.8	2.9	2.9	2.9	3.0	3.0	3.0	3.0	3.0	3.0	3.0	3.0	3.0
1996	3.0	3.0	3.0	3.1	3.1	3.2	3.2	3.2	3.2	3.2	3.2	3.2	3.1
1997	3.2	3.2	3.3	3.2	3.2	3.3	3.3	3.2	3.2	3.3	3.2	3.2	3.2
1998	3.2	3.3	3.3	3.3	3.3	3.4	3.3	3.3	3.3	3.4	3.4	3.5	3.3
1999	3.5	3.5	3.5	3.5	3.5	3.6	3.6	3.6	3.6	3.6	3.7	3.7	3.6
2000	3.7	3.8	3.9	3.9	3.9	3.9	3.8	3.8	3.7	3.9	3.9	3.9	3.8
2001	3.8	3.8	3.8	3.8	3.8	3.8	3.8	3.8	3.8	3.8	3.7	3.7	3.8
2002	3.8	3.9	3.9	3.9	3.9	4.0	3.9	3.9	3.9	3.9	4.0	4.0	3.9
2003	3.6	3.6	3.6	3.6	3.6	3.7	3.6	3.6	3.6	3.7	3.6	3.6	3.6
Government													
1990	20.6	20.7	20.8	21.0	21.1	19.1	19.0	19.4	20.8	21.0	21.1	21.1	20.5
1991	20.9	21.4	21.2	21.4	21.4	20.0	19.6	19.7	21.4	21.7	21.8	21.7	21.0
1992	21.3	21.7	21.8	21.5	21.6	20.4	20.2	20.5	21.7	22.0	22.0	21.9	21.4
1993	21.5	22.1	22.0	22.3	22.0	20.5	20.5	21.0	22.0	22.6	22.7	22.7	21.8
1994	21.8	22.2	22.6	22.7	22.3	21.0	20.5	20.9	22.2	22.4	22.7	22.3	22.0
1995	21.5	22.0	22.0	21.4	21.2	20.1	19.7	20.3	21.5	21.6	21.7	21.7	21.2
1996	21.0	21.6	21.7	21.6	21.4	19.8	19.6	20.4	21.4	21.3	21.6	21.3	21.1
1997	21.5	22.0	22.2	22.1	21.6	20.5	19.9	20.8	22.1	22.2	22.4	22.0	21.6
1998	21.9	22.5	22.6	22.0	21.6	20.3	20.4	21.0	22.1	22.3	22.5	22.5	21.8
1999	22.0	22.6	22.9	22.5	21.9	20.6	20.3	21.0	22.4	22.4	22.5	22.6	22.0
2000	22.1	22.4	22.6	22.6	22.7	21.2	20.3	20.5	22.3	22.4	22.5	22.7	22.0
2001	22.0	22.8	22.8	22.9	22.6	20.9	20.9	21.0	22.7	22.9	22.8	23.0	22.3
2002	22.2	22.7	22.9	22.8	22.7	20.9	20.5	21.1	22.6	22.9	23.0	23.1	22.3
2003	22.5	23.0	23.2	23.0	23.0	21.2	20.7	21.1	22.7	22.9	22.9	22.8	22.4
Federal government													
1990	1.9	1.9	1.9	2.0	2.1	2.0	2.0	1.9	1.8	1.9	1.9	1.9	1.9
1991	1.8	1.8	1.8	1.9	1.9	1.9	1.9	1.9	1.9	1.9	1.9	1.9	1.9
1992	1.9	1.9	1.9	1.9	1.9	1.9	1.9	1.9	1.9	1.9	1.9	1.9	1.9
1993	1.8	1.8	1.8	1.8	1.8	1.8	1.9	1.9	1.9	1.9	1.8	1.9	1.8
1994	1.8	1.8	1.7	1.8	1.7	1.7	1.7	1.7	1.7	1.7	1.7	1.7	1.7
1995	1.6	1.6	1.6	1.7	1.7	1.7	1.6	1.6	1.6	1.6	1.6	1.6	1.6
1996	1.6	1.6	1.6	1.6	1.6	1.6	1.6	1.6	1.6	1.6	1.6	1.6	1.6
1997	1.6	1.6	1.6	1.6	1.6	1.6	1.6	1.6	1.6	1.6	1.5	1.5	1.6
1998	1.5	1.5	1.5	1.5	1.5	1.5	1.5	1.5	1.5	1.5	1.5	1.5	1.5
1999	1.5	1.5	1.5	1.5	1.5	1.5	1.5	1.5	1.5	1.5	1.5	1.5	1.5
2000	1.5	1.5	1.6	1.6	1.9	1.6	1.6	1.5	1.5	1.4	1.5	1.5	1.6
2001	1.4	1.4	1.4	1.5	1.5	1.5	1.5	1.5	1.5	1.5	1.4	1.4	1.5
2002	1.4	1.4	1.4	1.4	1.4	1.4	1.4	1.4	1.4	1.4	1.4	1.4	1.4
2003	1.4	1.4	1.4	1.4	1.4	1.4	1.4	1.4	1.4	1.4	1.4	1.4	1.3

Employment by Industry: Alabama—*Continued*

(Numbers in thousands. Not seasonally adjusted.)

Industry	January	February	March	April	May	June	July	August	September	October	November	December	Annual Average
TUSCALOOSA—*Continued*													
State government													
2001	10.4	11.1	11.1	11.1	10.8	9.0	9.1	9.6	10.8	11.1	11.1	11.1	10.5
2002	10.5	11.0	11.0	11.0	10.9	9.1	9.2	9.7	10.9	11.3	11.4	11.3	10.6
2003	10.7	11.2	11.3	11.2	11.2	9.2	9.3	9.7	10.8	10.9	10.9	10.8	10.6
Local government													
2001	10.2	10.3	10.3	10.3	10.3	10.4	10.3	9.9	10.4	10.3	10.3	10.5	10.3
2002	10.3	10.3	10.5	10.4	10.4	10.4	9.9	10.0	10.3	10.2	10.2	10.4	10.3
2003	10.4	10.4	10.5	10.4	10.4	10.6	10.0	10.0	10.5	10.6	10.6	10.6	10.4

Average Weekly Hours by Industry: Alabama

(Not seasonally adjusted.)

Industry	January	February	March	April	May	June	July	August	September	October	November	December	Annual Average
STATEWIDE													
Natural resources and mining													
2001	45.3	43.9	43.0	43.2	43.9	45.1	45.8	46.1	45.5	45.4	45.8	45.3	44.8
2002	43.3	43.3	44.2	45.2	44.4	45.3	46.6	45.4	46.1	45.4	46.9	39.4	44.6
2003	43.0	42.9	43.3	42.7	43.5	45.1	44.3	45.1	46.3	45.1	45.6	42.8	44.1
Manufacturing													
2001	40.9	39.9	40.6	40.6	40.8	41.1	41.1	41.6	41.5	41.2	41.1	41.1	41.0
2002	40.7	40.6	40.9	41.8	42.1	41.5	41.5	41.8	42.0	41.1	41.2	41.7	41.4
2003	41.7	41.6	41.3	41.4	41.7	41.1	40.4	40.8	40.9	40.2	40.5	40.7	41.0
BIRMINGHAM													
Manufacturing													
2001	42.7	41.6	42.2	40.9	41.1	42.8	42.7	42.2	42.4	42.0	41.9	41.7	42.0
2002	42.3	42.9	43.3	42.8	42.4	43.4	42.8	43.2	43.9	42.9	41.9	41.5	42.8
2003	42.2	41.7	41.0	42.1	42.6	42.2	42.0	42.1	41.4	42.3	42.1	42.6	42.1
MOBILE													
Manufacturing													
2001	42.8	43.3	43.1	41.5	41.8	40.6	41.6	40.8	42.4	42.6	43.9	44.2	42.3
2002	43.0	42.6	43.5	43.2	41.4	41.9	41.2	42.5	43.4	42.1	42.1	46.0	42.7
2003	43.7	43.4	45.0	42.5	41.8	41.6	39.4	40.7	40.7	40.9	39.7	40.1	41.7

Average Hourly Earnings by Industry: Alabama

(Dollars, not seasonally adjusted.)

Industry	January	February	March	April	May	June	July	August	September	October	November	December	Annual Average
STATEWIDE													
Natural resources and mining													
2001	17.55	17.51	17.23	16.88	16.97	17.28	17.18	17.13	16.96	16.84	17.14	17.17	17.15
2002	17.15	17.16	17.31	17.20	17.23	17.41	16.80	16.87	16.74	16.45	15.81	16.06	16.85
2003	17.18	17.04	17.55	17.83	17.66	17.74	17.49	18.30	18.39	18.08	17.66	17.14	17.68
Manufacturing													
2001	12.56	12.45	12.57	12.67	12.80	12.82	12.81	12.89	12.90	12.84	12.85	13.00	12.76
2002	12.87	12.88	12.94	13.01	13.12	13.14	13.19	13.19	13.23	13.16	13.15	13.34	13.10
2003	13.28	13.19	13.44	13.45	13.44	13.46	13.39	13.59	13.86	14.02	13.82	13.83	13.56
BIRMINGHAM													
Manufacturing													
2001	13.74	13.41	13.50	13.38	13.32	13.67	13.73	13.70	13.65	13.58	13.49	13.43	13.55
2002	13.40	13.44	13.44	13.33	13.30	13.29	13.39	13.21	13.43	13.43	13.40	13.75	13.40
2003	13.92	14.36	14.48	14.37	14.24	14.40	14.61	14.60	14.92	14.77	14.94	15.21	14.56
MOBILE													
Manufacturing													
2001	13.73	13.64	13.53	13.89	13.97	14.04	14.05	13.93	14.02	14.26	14.34	14.35	13.98
2002	14.05	13.99	14.07	14.20	14.28	14.38	14.66	14.95	15.29	15.26	15.41	15.72	14.69
2003	15.36	15.27	14.46	14.88	15.02	14.36	14.11	13.77	14.29	14.85	14.92	15.56	14.75

Average Weekly Earnings by Industry: Alabama

(Dollars, not seasonally adjusted.)

Industry	January	February	March	April	May	June	July	August	September	October	November	December	Annual Average
STATEWIDE													
Natural resources and mining													
2001	795.02	768.69	740.89	729.22	744.98	779.33	786.84	789.69	771.68	764.54	785.01	777.80	768.32
2002	742.60	743.03	765.10	777.44	765.01	788.67	782.88	765.90	771.71	746.83	741.49	632.76	751.51
2003	738.74	731.02	759.92	761.34	768.21	800.07	774.81	825.33	851.46	815.41	805.30	733.59	779.69
Manufacturing													
2001	513.70	496.76	510.34	514.40	522.24	526.90	526.49	536.22	535.35	529.01	528.14	534.30	523.16
2002	523.81	522.93	529.25	543.82	552.35	545.31	547.39	551.34	555.66	540.88	541.78	556.28	542.34
2003	553.78	548.70	555.07	556.83	560.45	553.21	540.96	554.47	566.87	563.60	559.71	562.88	555.96
BIRMINGHAM													
Manufacturing													
2001	586.70	557.86	569.70	547.24	547.45	585.08	586.27	578.14	578.76	570.36	565.23	560.03	569.10
2002	566.82	576.58	581.95	570.52	563.92	576.79	573.09	570.67	589.58	576.15	561.46	570.63	573.52
2003	587.42	598.81	593.68	604.98	606.62	607.68	613.62	614.66	617.69	624.77	628.97	647.95	612.98
MOBILE													
Manufacturing													
2001	587.64	590.61	583.14	576.44	583.95	570.02	584.48	568.34	594.45	607.48	629.53	634.27	591.35
2002	604.15	595.97	612.05	613.44	591.19	602.52	603.99	635.38	663.59	642.45	648.76	723.12	627.26
2003	671.23	662.72	650.70	632.40	627.84	597.38	555.93	560.44	581.60	607.37	592.32	623.96	615.08

ALASKA AT A GLANCE

(Population and total nonfarm employment numbers in thousands)

Population, Census 2000:	626.9
Total nonfarm employment, 2003:	299.7
Change in total nonfarm employment	
(Number)	
1990–2003:	61.7
1990–2001:	51.3
2001–2003:	10.4
(Compound annual rate of change)	
1990–2003:	1.8%
1990–2001:	1.8%
2001–2003:	1.8%
Unemployment rate	
1990:	7.0%
2001:	6.2%
2003:	7.7%

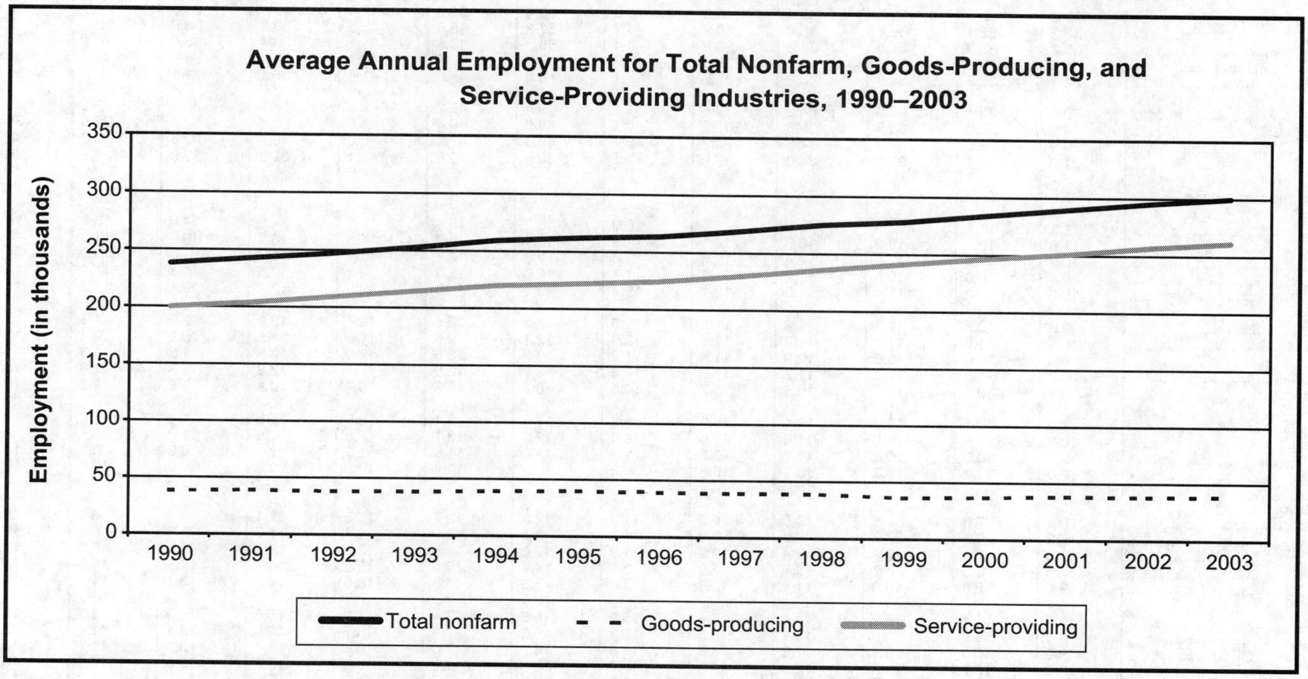

Unlike many other states, Alaska did not experience a drop-off in nonfarm payroll employment during the recessionary periods of 1990–1991 and 2001. However, for much of the 1990s, Alaska's growth lagged behind the U.S. average. From 1994 to 1996, the slowdown was attributable to low growth in the service-providing industries, while from 1998 to 1999, it was due to a sharp slowdown in the goods-producing sector.

Employment by Industry: Alaska

(Numbers in thousands. Not seasonally adjusted.)

Industry	January	February	March	April	May	June	July	August	September	October	November	December	Annual Average
STATEWIDE													
Total nonfarm													
1990	213.9	220.5	225.4	232.8	240.6	252.7	257.2	256.6	249.4	240.0	234.7	233.1	238.0
1991	223.4	228.5	231.1	236.6	245.6	253.6	261.6	261.3	253.7	242.8	237.6	236.9	242.7
1992	228.5	234.7	237.9	243.4	250.1	258.5	265.8	264.5	258.4	246.5	239.4	238.3	247.1
1993	232.0	238.0	241.7	246.0	253.3	264.0	271.1	270.7	264.9	256.7	249.6	246.0	252.8
1994	238.8	246.7	249.5	251.9	259.9	271.5	277.6	278.6	274.1	260.2	253.5	249.6	259.3
1995	241.9	249.1	250.6	254.0	264.4	276.5	281.9	282.7	275.4	263.1	254.2	250.1	261.9
1996	242.1	248.8	251.9	256.9	267.7	277.4	284.1	283.8	276.2	264.9	256.8	252.4	263.5
1997	247.0	253.2	256.0	261.4	272.7	283.0	289.3	288.1	281.9	271.1	262.2	258.9	268.7
1998	254.9	261.4	264.7	268.0	279.6	287.7	293.8	293.0	287.4	275.5	268.0	265.6	274.9
1999	258.1	263.2	267.0	270.7	281.5	290.4	296.4	296.6	292.3	278.4	271.2	268.1	277.8
2000	260.9	268.2	271.7	276.0	288.5	298.5	305.4	304.8	297.5	284.3	275.7	274.4	283.8
2001	264.8	274.2	276.8	281.9	293.4	303.8	311.7	312.4	305.1	290.4	280.2	277.3	289.3
2002	271.1	280.3	283.5	287.0	297.7	308.5	315.1	315.8	309.8	297.3	287.9	286.0	295.0
2003	279.0	285.3	288.3	290.2	303.7	313.7	319.4	319.7	313.4	301.0	291.9	290.2	299.7
Total private													
1990	145.8	149.5	153.7	160.3	168.9	181.9	187.9	187.3	177.4	167.6	163.1	161.1	167.0
1991	154.6	156.9	159.5	164.1	173.6	183.1	192.8	192.1	181.3	168.7	163.8	162.6	171.0
1992	156.2	161.1	163.9	168.5	175.9	186.0	196.0	193.7	184.6	171.4	164.8	164.3	173.8
1993	158.2	163.3	166.6	170.3	177.6	190.2	200.3	198.4	189.7	179.9	173.4	170.7	178.2
1994	164.8	171.9	174.5	176.4	184.8	198.6	207.4	207.0	199.6	185.5	179.3	175.8	185.4
1995	169.5	175.5	176.9	179.8	190.1	203.9	213.3	212.3	202.6	188.9	180.6	177.2	189.2
1996	170.3	175.5	177.8	182.2	193.9	204.4	214.4	213.5	203.3	190.0	182.7	178.4	190.5
1997	174.4	178.9	181.6	186.5	198.3	210.7	219.8	218.0	208.5	196.5	188.2	184.7	195.5
1998	182.1	187.1	190.2	193.0	203.4	215.1	223.3	222.8	213.7	200.6	193.6	190.9	201.3
1999	185.9	189.3	192.4	195.0	205.3	217.9	226.2	226.6	218.4	203.3	196.6	193.4	204.1
2000	188.2	193.7	195.8	200.0	210.9	225.0	234.0	233.4	223.1	208.7	200.3	198.9	209.3
2001	189.1	195.9	197.6	201.6	212.1	225.7	236.1	236.3	225.1	209.5	199.7	197.1	210.5
2002	193.4	199.8	202.2	204.9	215.6	228.2	239.3	238.4	227.8	215.1	205.7	202.9	214.4
2003	199.1	203.2	205.3	207.1	220.1	232.5	242.4	241.9	230.7	218.2	209.4	207.1	218.1
Goods-producing													
1990	27.4	29.4	31.9	35.9	39.1	45.2	51.3	49.6	42.8	37.2	34.5	32.7	38.0
1991	30.8	32.3	34.0	36.2	40.5	44.3	52.3	50.6	44.4	36.5	32.9	31.7	38.8
1992	29.5	33.6	35.0	37.2	38.7	43.7	51.1	48.5	42.5	36.1	31.6	30.3	38.1
1993	29.2	33.4	35.2	35.7	36.6	42.9	51.0	48.8	43.2	39.6	33.8	31.2	38.3
1994	30.6	36.0	36.6	35.0	37.1	43.9	51.2	49.9	45.0	40.0	35.0	31.0	39.2
1995	30.2	35.3	35.5	35.4	38.9	45.0	53.4	51.8	45.9	40.6	35.0	31.5	39.8
1996	30.3	35.1	36.1	36.8	40.2	44.1	51.2	49.6	43.8	38.3	33.6	29.8	39.0
1997	30.2	33.9	34.9	36.2	39.2	44.4	50.7	48.5	44.1	39.4	33.6	30.1	38.7
1998	31.8	35.8	36.5	36.2	38.0	42.5	48.7	47.7	44.1	39.1	34.8	31.5	38.8
1999	31.1	33.3	34.6	33.9	35.7	39.1	46.3	45.9	41.8	36.1	31.1	28.0	36.4
2000	28.5	32.1	32.5	34.2	36.5	41.4	49.0	48.2	43.4	37.7	32.5	30.2	37.1
2001	29.9	35.0	35.5	35.6	37.2	41.7	49.9	49.4	44.6	38.4	32.4	29.8	38.3
2002	30.9	35.0	35.3	34.5	36.2	40.9	48.9	47.9	43.6	39.2	33.8	31.0	38.1
2003	31.2	34.7	35.3	34.0	37.2	43.2	50.1	49.0	44.1	39.3	33.9	31.2	38.6
Natural resources and mining													
1990	11.1	11.5	12.5	13.6	14.4	16.0	16.2	16.4	15.5	14.9	14.0	13.2	14.1
1991	11.8	12.2	13.0	13.8	14.1	14.8	15.1	15.3	14.8	13.9	13.0	12.3	13.6
1992	10.9	11.4	12.0	12.4	12.6	12.8	12.8	12.7	12.4	11.7	11.3	10.8	11.9
1993	9.4	10.0	10.5	11.2	11.2	11.7	12.0	12.3	12.1	12.5	11.7	11.1	11.3
1994	10.8	11.2	11.4	11.8	12.1	12.4	12.4	12.5	12.6	12.7	12.1	11.2	11.9
1995	9.9	10.8	11.1	11.2	11.5	12.0	12.3	12.6	12.4	12.6	12.0	11.3	11.6
1996	10.4	11.0	11.7	11.6	11.6	12.0	12.1	12.0	11.9	11.5	10.9	10.4	11.4
1997	9.5	10.0	10.6	10.9	11.5	11.9	12.2	12.5	12.9	12.3	11.2	11.3	11.4
1998	10.7	11.0	11.2	11.7	11.8	12.2	12.6	12.9	12.8	12.8	12.3	12.0	12.0
1999	10.3	10.4	10.7	10.5	10.7	10.8	10.7	10.6	10.7	10.2	9.6	9.2	10.3
2000	8.9	10.1	10.3	10.4	10.9	11.2	11.7	12.1	12.8	11.8	11.4	11.5	11.0
2001	10.5	11.5	11.6	11.8	12.0	12.3	12.2	12.1	12.0	11.8	11.2	10.7	11.6
2002	10.5	10.7	10.8	11.1	10.9	11.1	11.6	11.5	11.2	11.1	10.8	10.5	11.0
2003	10.0	10.2	10.3	10.2	10.4	10.2	10.3	10.4	10.2	10.3	9.9	10.0	10.2
Construction													
1990	6.8	7.0	7.6	8.5	9.9	11.9	12.3	12.7	12.5	11.1	9.6	8.5	9.8
1991	7.3	7.3	7.7	8.2	9.8	11.5	12.3	13.0	13.1	11.9	9.6	8.6	10.0
1992	7.0	7.1	7.3	8.4	10.2	11.9	13.0	13.9	13.4	12.2	10.1	9.3	10.3
1993	7.9	8.3	8.7	9.7	11.9	13.7	14.7	15.5	15.2	14.3	12.5	10.9	11.9
1994	9.5	9.8	10.3	11.1	12.5	14.1	15.6	16.5	16.0	14.8	13.1	11.4	12.8
1995	9.7	10.1	10.2	11.3	13.6	15.9	16.6	17.4	16.9	15.8	13.0	11.2	13.4
1996	9.4	9.7	9.9	11.1	13.5	15.3	16.2	17.3	16.7	15.3	13.1	11.4	13.2
1997	9.9	9.9	9.9	11.3	13.8	15.6	16.5	17.3	16.6	16.0	13.1	11.7	13.4
1998	10.5	10.7	11.2	12.0	14.0	15.8	16.8	17.2	16.6	15.6	13.6	12.1	13.8
1999	11.0	10.5	11.2	12.5	14.1	15.9	17.2	17.9	17.3	16.1	14.0	12.4	14.1
2000	11.1	11.5	11.8	12.5	14.3	16.6	17.0	17.7	16.6	15.8	13.3	12.5	14.2
2001	10.9	11.5	12.1	13.3	14.9	17.2	18.2	19.0	18.1	16.8	14.1	13.1	14.9
2002	12.2	12.4	12.8	13.4	15.8	18.1	19.0	19.6	18.9	17.7	15.5	14.3	15.8
2003	12.5	12.7	13.1	14.6	17.3	19.2	20.2	20.7	20.2	18.5	16.4	15.3	16.7

Employment by Industry: Alaska—*Continued*

(Numbers in thousands. Not seasonally adjusted.)

Industry	January	February	March	April	May	June	July	August	September	October	November	December	Annual Average
STATEWIDE—*Continued*													
Manufacturing													
1990	9.5	10.9	11.8	13.8	14.8	17.3	22.8	20.5	14.8	11.2	10.9	11.0	14.1
1991	11.7	12.8	13.3	14.2	16.6	18.0	24.9	22.3	16.5	10.7	10.3	10.8	15.1
1992	11.6	15.1	15.7	16.4	15.9	19.0	25.3	21.9	16.7	12.2	10.2	10.2	15.8
1993	11.9	15.1	16.0	14.8	13.5	17.5	24.3	21.0	15.9	12.8	9.6	9.2	15.1
1994	10.3	15.0	14.9	12.1	12.5	17.4	23.2	20.9	16.4	12.5	9.8	8.4	14.4
1995	10.6	14.4	14.2	12.9	13.8	17.1	24.5	21.8	16.6	12.2	10.0	9.0	14.7
1996	10.5	14.4	14.5	14.1	15.1	16.8	22.9	20.3	15.2	11.5	9.6	8.0	14.4
1997	10.8	14.0	14.4	14.0	13.9	16.9	22.0	18.7	14.6	11.1	9.3	7.1	13.9
1998	10.6	14.1	14.1	12.5	12.2	14.5	19.3	17.6	14.7	10.7	8.9	7.4	13.0
1999	9.8	12.4	12.7	10.9	10.9	12.4	18.4	17.4	13.8	9.8	7.5	6.4	11.8
2000	8.5	10.5	10.4	11.3	11.3	13.6	20.3	18.4	14.0	10.1	7.8	6.2	11.8
2001	8.5	12.0	11.8	10.5	10.3	12.2	19.5	18.3	14.5	9.8	7.1	6.0	11.7
2002	8.2	11.9	11.7	10.0	9.5	11.7	18.3	16.8	13.5	10.4	7.5	6.2	11.3
2003	8.7	11.8	11.9	9.2	9.5	13.8	19.6	17.9	13.7	10.5	7.6	5.9	11.7
Service-providing													
1990	186.5	191.1	193.5	196.9	201.5	207.5	205.9	207.0	206.6	202.8	200.2	200.4	199.9
1991	192.6	196.2	197.1	200.4	205.1	209.3	209.3	210.7	209.3	206.3	204.7	205.2	203.8
1992	199.0	201.1	202.9	206.2	211.4	214.8	214.7	216.0	215.9	210.4	207.8	208.0	209.0
1993	202.8	204.6	206.5	210.3	216.7	221.1	220.1	221.9	221.7	217.1	215.8	214.8	214.4
1994	208.2	210.7	212.9	216.9	222.8	227.6	226.4	228.7	229.1	220.2	218.5	218.6	220.0
1995	211.7	213.8	215.1	218.6	225.5	231.5	228.5	230.9	229.5	222.5	219.2	218.6	222.1
1996	211.8	213.7	215.8	220.1	227.5	233.3	232.9	234.2	232.4	226.6	223.2	222.6	224.5
1997	216.8	219.3	221.1	225.2	233.5	238.6	238.6	239.6	237.8	231.7	228.6	228.8	229.9
1998	223.1	225.6	228.2	231.8	241.6	245.2	245.1	245.3	243.3	236.4	233.2	234.1	236.0
1999	227.0	229.9	232.4	236.8	245.8	251.3	250.1	250.7	250.5	242.3	240.1	240.1	241.4
2000	232.4	236.1	239.2	241.8	252.0	257.1	256.4	256.6	254.1	246.6	243.2	244.2	246.6
2001	234.9	239.2	241.3	246.3	256.2	262.1	261.8	263.0	260.5	252.0	247.8	247.5	251.1
2002	240.2	245.3	248.2	252.5	261.5	267.6	266.2	267.9	266.2	258.1	254.1	255.0	256.9
2003	247.8	250.6	253.0	256.2	266.5	270.5	269.3	270.7	269.3	261.7	258.0	259.0	261.1
Trade, transportation, and utilities													
1990	43.0	43.3	43.9	44.9	47.5	50.4	50.8	51.2	50.0	48.4	48.1	48.1	47.4
1991	45.1	44.8	45.3	46.1	48.6	50.6	51.5	51.8	50.4	49.4	49.4	49.2	48.5
1992	46.5	46.4	46.9	47.8	50.8	52.1	53.2	53.2	52.2	49.6	49.7	50.0	49.8
1993	47.4	47.1	47.4	48.3	51.2	53.1	54.3	54.4	53.6	51.7	51.7	51.7	50.9
1994	49.2	49.4	50.7	52.0	54.3	57.0	58.0	58.2	57.8	54.6	54.4	55.1	54.2
1995	52.1	52.0	52.5	53.3	55.9	58.6	59.1	59.5	58.3	55.2	54.2	54.3	55.4
1996	51.8	51.2	51.2	52.7	56.2	59.0	59.3	59.7	57.8	55.6	54.6	54.9	55.3
1997	52.5	52.1	52.6	54.1	57.6	60.4	61.4	61.4	59.6	57.2	56.8	56.9	56.8
1998	54.5	54.4	55.3	56.5	60.0	62.5	62.9	63.2	61.3	58.5	57.9	58.2	58.7
1999	55.5	55.8	56.2	57.4	60.6	63.9	64.3	64.6	63.3	59.7	59.5	59.1	59.9
2000	56.5	56.6	57.1	57.8	61.3	63.9	64.7	65.2	63.3	60.1	59.0	59.1	60.3
2001	55.6	55.3	55.7	57.8	61.2	64.0	65.6	65.5	63.4	60.5	58.8	58.7	60.2
2002	56.6	57.0	57.9	58.8	62.4	64.9	66.3	66.4	64.1	61.2	59.4	59.3	61.2
2003	57.2	56.9	57.3	58.6	62.3	64.3	65.8	65.9	63.7	61.2	59.8	59.6	61.1
Wholesale trade													
1990	5.1	5.3	5.4	5.4	5.7	5.9	6.1	6.0	5.7	5.6	5.5	5.5	5.6
1991	5.1	5.1	5.2	5.2	5.4	5.6	5.7	5.6	5.5	5.8	5.7	5.7	5.4
1992	5.4	5.4	5.5	5.6	5.8	6.0	6.2	6.1	5.9	5.6	5.6	5.6	5.7
1993	5.4	5.5	5.6	5.6	5.8	6.0	6.2	6.3	6.0	5.7	5.6	5.7	5.7
1994	5.5	5.6	5.6	5.6	5.8	6.0	6.4	6.4	6.2	5.8	5.8	5.9	5.8
1995	5.8	5.9	5.9	6.1	6.2	6.4	6.8	6.9	6.6	6.2	6.1	6.1	6.2
1996	6.0	6.0	6.0	6.1	6.3	6.6	6.9	6.8	6.5	6.3	6.1	6.2	6.3
1997	5.9	5.9	6.0	6.0	6.2	6.5	6.5	6.5	6.2	5.9	6.0	5.9	6.1
1998	5.9	6.0	6.1	6.0	6.3	6.4	6.8	6.8	6.5	6.1	6.1	6.0	6.2
1999	6.0	6.1	6.1	6.1	6.2	6.6	6.9	6.8	6.6	6.2	6.1	6.0	6.3
2000	6.0	6.1	6.2	6.1	6.2	6.4	6.8	6.8	6.5	6.1	6.0	6.0	6.2
2001	5.9	5.9	5.9	6.0	6.2	6.4	7.0	6.9	6.4	6.0	5.9	5.9	6.2
2002	5.7	5.7	5.8	6.1	6.2	6.5	7.0	6.9	6.4	6.0	5.9	5.9	6.2
2003	6.0	5.9	5.9	5.9	6.1	6.3	6.5	6.5	6.3	6.0	6.0	6.0	6.1
Retail trade													
1990	24.2	24.0	24.2	25.0	26.1	27.3	27.4	27.6	26.9	26.4	26.9	27.1	26.0
1991	25.4	25.0	25.3	25.6	26.7	27.4	28.0	28.1	27.1	27.0	27.6	27.5	26.7
1992	25.7	25.2	25.4	25.7	27.0	28.0	28.5	28.3	27.7	27.1	27.7	27.9	27.0
1993	25.9	25.4	25.5	26.0	27.3	28.7	29.3	29.3	28.9	28.8	29.6	29.7	27.8
1994	27.9	27.6	28.6	29.5	30.6	31.8	32.3	32.5	32.1	30.8	31.4	31.8	30.5
1995	29.8	29.3	29.6	30.0	31.7	33.2	33.2	33.2	32.5	31.5	31.7	31.9	31.4
1996	30.2	29.3	29.2	30.0	31.7	33.3	33.5	33.6	32.6	31.8	32.1	32.3	31.6
1997	30.5	29.7	29.8	30.6	32.4	34.0	34.4	34.1	32.8	32.4	32.6	33.0	32.1
1998	30.9	30.3	30.7	31.6	33.2	34.7	34.5	34.1	33.4	32.5	32.9	33.5	32.6
1999	31.5	31.3	31.6	32.2	33.4	35.4	35.5	35.4	35.0	34.0	34.3	34.5	33.6
2000	32.1	31.7	32.0	32.4	33.9	35.1	35.2	35.1	34.4	33.5	33.6	33.8	33.5
2001	31.5	31.0	31.1	32.0	33.4	34.9	35.1	35.1	34.3	33.5	33.4	33.4	33.2
2002	32.0	31.9	32.2	32.6	34.2	35.4	35.8	35.6	34.9	34.3	34.0	34.2	33.9
2003	32.3	32.1	32.2	32.8	34.3	35.6	36.2	35.8	35.1	34.6	34.3	34.3	34.1

Employment by Industry: Alaska—*Continued*

(Numbers in thousands. Not seasonally adjusted.)

Industry	January	February	March	April	May	June	July	August	September	October	November	December	Annual Average
STATEWIDE—*Continued*													
Transportation and utilities													
1990	13.7	14.0	14.3	14.5	15.7	17.2	17.3	17.6	17.4	16.4	15.7	15.5	15.7
1991	14.6	14.7	14.8	15.3	16.5	17.6	17.8	18.1	17.8	16.6	16.1	16.0	16.3
1992	15.4	15.8	16.0	16.5	18.0	18.1	18.5	18.8	18.6	16.9	16.4	16.5	17.1
1993	16.1	16.2	16.3	16.7	18.1	18.4	18.8	18.8	18.7	17.2	16.5	16.3	17.3
1994	15.8	16.2	16.5	16.9	17.9	19.2	19.3	19.3	19.5	18.0	17.2	17.4	17.7
1995	16.5	16.8	17.0	17.2	18.0	19.0	19.1	19.4	19.2	17.5	16.4	16.3	17.7
1996	15.6	15.9	16.0	16.6	18.2	19.1	18.9	19.3	18.7	17.5	16.4	16.4	17.3
1997	16.1	16.5	16.8	17.5	19.0	19.9	20.5	20.8	20.6	18.9	18.2	18.0	18.5
1998	17.7	18.1	18.5	18.9	20.5	21.4	21.6	22.3	21.4	19.9	18.9	18.7	19.8
1999	18.0	18.4	18.5	19.1	21.0	21.9	21.9	22.4	21.7	19.5	19.1	18.6	20.0
2000	18.4	18.8	18.9	19.3	21.2	22.4	22.7	23.3	22.4	20.5	19.4	19.3	20.5
2001	18.2	18.4	18.7	19.8	21.6	22.7	23.5	23.5	22.7	21.0	19.5	19.4	20.8
2002	18.9	19.4	19.9	20.1	22.0	23.0	23.5	23.9	22.8	20.9	19.5	19.2	21.1
2003	18.9	18.9	19.2	19.9	21.9	22.4	23.1	23.6	22.3	20.6	19.5	19.3	20.8
Information													
1990	5.2	5.2	5.3	5.3	5.5	5.6	5.5	5.5	5.6	5.6	5.6	5.6	5.4
1991	5.5	5.6	5.6	5.6	5.6	5.8	5.8	5.7	5.7	5.7	5.7	5.7	5.6
1992	5.6	5.5	5.6	5.6	5.7	5.4	5.5	5.5	5.5	5.5	5.4	5.5	5.5
1993	5.3	5.3	5.4	5.4	5.6	5.7	5.7	5.6	5.6	5.5	5.4	5.4	5.4
1994	5.4	5.4	5.4	5.5	5.5	5.6	5.7	5.7	5.6	5.5	5.4	5.5	5.5
1995	5.4	5.3	5.4	5.3	5.4	5.5	5.5	5.4	5.4	5.4	5.4	5.4	5.4
1996	5.3	5.3	5.5	5.5	5.6	5.6	5.7	5.7	5.6	5.6	5.4	5.4	5.5
1997	5.6	5.6	5.6	5.7	5.8	5.9	6.1	6.0	5.9	5.9	5.9	5.9	5.8
1998	6.2	5.9	6.0	6.0	6.0	6.1	6.1	6.1	6.3	6.2	6.3	6.4	6.1
1999	6.3	6.3	6.4	6.4	6.9	6.9	7.2	7.2	7.2	7.3	7.3	7.3	6.8
2000	7.5	7.5	7.5	7.5	7.5	7.7	7.7	7.6	7.5	7.4	7.4	7.5	7.5
2001	7.3	7.4	7.4	7.2	7.4	7.5	7.5	7.5	7.3	7.3	7.3	7.2	7.4
2002	6.9	6.8	6.9	7.1	7.1	7.2	7.4	7.2	7.2	7.1	7.0	7.1	7.1
2003	6.8	6.8	6.8	6.9	7.0	7.1	7.2	7.0	6.9	6.9	6.9	7.0	6.9
Financial activities													
1990	10.0	10.0	10.2	10.3	10.8	11.1	10.9	11.0	10.9	11.0	10.8	10.8	10.6
1991	10.5	10.4	10.5	10.8	11.1	11.4	11.7	11.8	11.6	11.4	11.5	11.5	11.1
1992	11.5	11.4	11.6	12.0	12.3	12.7	12.7	12.9	12.7	12.5	12.2	12.3	12.2
1993	12.1	12.1	12.2	12.4	12.6	13.2	13.5	13.6	13.3	13.1	12.9	13.0	12.8
1994	12.5	12.7	12.8	13.0	13.3	13.6	13.4	13.4	13.2	12.5	12.3	12.0	12.8
1995	11.4	11.4	11.2	11.4	11.8	12.0	12.0	12.2	12.1	11.7	11.4	11.4	11.6
1996	11.1	11.1	11.1	11.3	11.8	12.2	12.7	12.8	12.7	12.4	12.3	12.3	11.9
1997	12.2	12.3	12.4	12.6	13.2	13.7	13.9	14.0	13.7	13.1	12.9	12.9	13.0
1998	12.8	12.7	12.8	13.2	13.5	14.1	14.2	14.4	13.9	13.9	13.6	13.7	13.5
1999	13.5	13.4	13.6	13.5	13.7	14.3	14.4	14.6	14.2	14.0	13.7	13.8	13.8
2000	13.5	13.5	13.6	13.6	13.8	14.5	14.5	14.6	14.2	14.0	13.7	13.8	13.9
2001	13.4	13.4	13.4	13.6	14.0	14.5	14.3	14.5	14.0	13.7	13.5	13.5	13.8
2002	13.2	13.1	13.4	13.3	13.7	14.2	14.3	14.4	14.2	14.0	13.9	13.8	13.8
2003	13.7	13.7	13.9	14.0	14.4	14.8	14.9	15.1	14.7	14.5	14.4	14.5	14.4
Professional and business services													
1990	16.5	17.1	17.5	18.1	18.8	19.8	19.1	19.4	19.0	18.5	18.0	18.1	18.3
1991	18.5	19.0	19.1	18.9	19.4	19.9	20.3	20.6	19.6	18.9	18.3	18.2	19.2
1992	18.1	18.4	18.6	18.8	18.9	19.9	20.3	20.4	19.7	19.1	18.5	18.6	19.1
1993	18.5	18.9	19.1	19.7	20.3	21.2	21.0	21.2	20.9	19.7	19.5	19.4	19.9
1994	19.2	19.7	19.8	20.3	20.8	21.8	22.2	22.5	22.1	21.0	20.7	20.8	20.9
1995	20.4	20.7	20.9	21.3	22.1	23.4	23.6	23.7	23.6	22.8	22.1	21.6	22.1
1996	20.9	21.3	21.5	22.0	22.7	23.4	23.6	24.0	23.6	22.5	21.8	21.6	22.4
1997	20.7	21.1	21.5	21.9	22.8	23.6	23.8	23.9	23.3	22.3	21.8	21.7	22.3
1998	21.4	21.9	22.2	22.6	23.7	24.2	24.9	25.0	24.2	23.0	22.5	22.3	23.1
1999	22.1	22.4	22.7	23.1	24.2	25.6	24.8	25.4	24.8	23.6	23.4	23.2	23.7
2000	22.2	22.7	23.0	23.6	24.6	26.1	26.1	26.0	25.3	24.7	23.8	24.0	24.3
2001	21.2	21.8	22.0	22.2	23.1	24.2	24.5	24.7	23.6	22.4	21.7	21.7	22.8
2002	21.2	21.8	22.0	22.2	23.1	24.0	23.9	24.2	23.2	22.6	22.0	21.9	22.7
2003	22.0	21.9	22.2	22.4	23.9	24.7	24.4	24.7	23.6	23.1	22.3	22.4	23.1
Educational and health services													
1990	15.9	16.2	16.3	16.6	16.8	16.9	16.4	16.6	16.7	17.1	17.2	17.2	16.6
1991	16.9	17.1	17.2	17.5	17.4	17.4	17.0	17.2	17.3	17.6	17.7	17.7	17.3
1992	17.6	17.8	17.9	18.0	18.0	18.0	17.9	18.1	18.4	18.4	18.4	18.6	18.0
1993	18.2	18.7	18.8	18.8	18.9	18.8	18.8	18.7	18.8	19.0	19.3	19.3	18.8
1994	18.7	19.2	19.3	19.3	19.5	19.4	19.2	19.4	19.7	19.6	19.8	20.0	19.4
1995	19.8	20.3	20.3	20.4	20.6	20.6	20.5	20.4	20.5	20.5	20.7	20.8	20.4
1996	20.5	20.7	20.9	21.1	21.3	21.3	21.4	21.3	21.5	21.5	21.6	21.5	21.2
1997	21.8	22.1	22.3	22.6	22.9	22.8	22.6	22.8	22.8	22.8	22.9	22.9	22.6
1998	23.0	23.3	23.4	23.4	23.8	23.6	23.1	23.2	23.4	23.5	23.6	23.9	23.4
1999	23.7	24.0	24.2	24.2	24.6	24.6	24.6	24.7	24.8	25.0	25.0	25.3	24.5
2000	25.2	25.8	25.8	25.7	26.0	26.0	25.6	25.8	26.0	26.0	26.1	26.4	25.8
2001	26.5	27.0	27.2	27.4	27.7	28.0	28.1	28.3	28.4	28.6	28.9	29.0	27.9
2002	29.0	29.4	29.7	30.1	30.5	30.8	30.8	31.0	30.8	31.2	31.5	31.9	30.6
2003	31.5	32.3	32.5	32.7	33.0	32.9	33.0	33.2	33.0	33.3	33.7	33.9	32.9

Employment by Industry: Alaska—*Continued*

(Numbers in thousands. Not seasonally adjusted.)

Industry	January	February	March	April	May	June	July	August	September	October	November	December	Annual Average
STATEWIDE—*Continued*													
Leisure and hospitality													
1990	18.1	18.4	18.7	19.6	21.2	23.6	24.5	24.5	23.0	20.6	19.5	19.3	20.9
1991	18.5	18.7	18.8	19.8	21.6	24.0	24.8	25.0	23.1	20.1	19.3	19.7	21.1
1992	18.3	18.8	19.1	19.9	22.1	24.5	25.4	25.5	23.9	20.5	19.5	19.4	21.4
1993	18.2	18.4	19.0	20.3	22.6	25.0	25.9	26.0	24.4	21.4	20.9	20.8	21.9
1994	19.4	19.7	20.0	21.2	24.1	26.9	27.5	27.9	26.1	22.3	21.7	21.5	23.1
1995	20.4	20.6	21.1	22.4	25.1	28.4	28.9	29.0	26.6	22.4	21.4	21.8	24.0
1996	20.4	20.6	21.2	22.3	25.5	28.1	29.7	29.6	27.4	23.3	22.7	22.2	24.4
1997	21.1	21.4	21.8	22.9	26.0	29.2	30.4	30.5	28.3	24.9	23.5	23.4	25.2
1998	21.6	22.2	22.9	23.8	27.1	30.6	32.0	31.7	29.4	25.1	23.6	23.6	26.1
1999	22.6	22.9	23.3	24.7	27.9	31.7	32.6	32.5	30.4	25.7	24.7	24.7	26.9
2000	23.1	23.6	24.2	25.5	28.9	32.9	34.1	33.9	31.2	26.6	25.5	25.5	27.9
2001	23.8	24.5	24.7	26.0	29.3	33.5	34.1	34.2	31.7	26.7	25.3	25.4	28.3
2002	24.0	24.9	25.0	26.9	30.5	34.3	35.7	35.4	33.0	28.3	26.7	26.6	29.3
2003	25.6	25.7	26.0	27.1	30.8	34.0	35.5	35.5	33.3	28.6	27.1	27.3	29.7
Other services													
1990	9.7	9.9	9.9	9.6	9.2	9.3	9.4	9.5	9.4	9.2	9.4	9.3	9.4
1991	8.8	9.0	9.0	9.2	9.4	9.7	9.4	9.4	9.2	9.1	9.0	8.9	9.1
1992	9.1	9.2	9.2	9.2	9.4	9.7	9.9	9.6	9.7	9.7	9.5	9.6	9.4
1993	9.3	9.4	9.5	9.7	9.8	10.3	10.1	10.1	9.9	9.9	9.9	9.9	9.8
1994	9.8	9.8	9.9	10.1	10.2	10.4	10.2	10.0	10.1	10.0	10.0	9.9	10.0
1995	9.8	9.9	10.0	10.3	10.3	10.4	10.3	10.3	10.2	10.3	10.4	10.4	10.2
1996	10.0	10.2	10.3	10.5	10.6	10.7	10.8	10.8	10.9	10.8	10.7	10.7	10.5
1997	10.3	10.4	10.5	10.5	10.8	10.7	10.9	10.9	10.8	10.9	10.8	10.9	10.7
1998	10.8	10.9	11.1	11.3	11.3	11.5	11.4	11.5	11.1	11.3	11.3	11.3	11.2
1999	11.1	11.2	11.4	11.8	11.7	11.8	12.0	11.7	11.9	11.9	11.9	12.0	11.7
2000	11.7	11.9	12.1	12.1	12.3	12.5	12.3	12.1	12.2	12.2	12.3	12.4	12.1
2001	11.4	11.5	11.7	11.8	12.2	12.3	12.1	12.2	12.1	11.9	11.8	11.8	11.9
2002	11.6	11.8	12.0	12.0	12.1	11.9	12.0	11.9	11.7	11.5	11.4	11.3	11.8
2003	11.1	11.2	11.3	11.4	11.5	11.5	11.5	11.5	11.4	11.3	11.3	11.2	11.4
Government													
1990	68.1	71.0	71.7	72.5	71.7	70.8	69.3	69.3	72.0	72.4	71.6	72.0	71.0
1991	68.8	71.6	71.6	72.5	72.0	70.5	68.8	69.2	72.4	74.1	73.8	74.3	71.6
1992	72.3	73.6	74.0	74.9	74.2	72.5	69.8	70.8	73.8	75.1	74.6	74.0	73.3
1993	73.8	74.7	75.1	75.7	75.7	73.8	70.8	72.3	75.2	76.8	76.2	75.3	74.6
1994	74.0	74.8	75.0	75.5	75.1	72.9	70.2	71.6	74.5	74.7	74.2	73.8	73.8
1995	72.4	73.6	73.7	74.2	74.3	72.6	68.6	70.4	72.8	74.2	73.6	72.9	72.7
1996	71.8	73.3	74.1	74.7	73.8	73.0	69.7	70.3	72.9	74.9	74.1	74.0	73.0
1997	72.6	74.3	74.4	74.9	74.4	72.3	69.5	70.1	73.4	74.6	74.0	74.2	73.2
1998	72.8	74.3	74.5	75.0	76.2	72.6	70.5	70.2	73.7	74.9	74.4	74.7	73.6
1999	72.2	73.9	74.6	75.7	76.2	72.5	70.2	70.0	73.9	75.1	74.6	74.7	73.6
2000	72.7	74.5	75.9	76.0	77.6	73.5	71.4	71.4	74.4	75.6	75.4	75.5	74.4
2001	75.7	78.3	79.2	80.3	81.3	78.1	75.6	76.1	80.0	80.9	80.5	80.2	78.9
2002	77.7	80.5	81.3	82.1	82.1	80.3	75.8	77.4	82.0	82.2	82.2	83.1	80.6
2003	79.9	82.1	83.0	83.1	83.6	81.2	77.0	77.8	82.7	82.8	82.5	83.1	81.6
Federal government													
1990	18.1	18.2	18.5	18.7	19.0	19.5	19.7	19.0	18.8	18.4	18.2	18.6	18.7
1991	17.9	17.9	17.9	18.3	18.9	19.6	19.6	19.6	19.5	19.5	19.2	19.2	18.9
1992	18.8	18.8	18.8	19.2	19.6	20.3	20.2	20.2	20.0	19.8	19.5	19.4	19.5
1993	19.4	19.4	19.4	19.6	20.0	20.7	21.0	20.9	20.6	19.9	19.6	19.5	20.0
1994	18.7	18.6	18.6	18.8	19.0	19.4	19.5	19.1	18.9	18.3	17.8	18.1	18.7
1995	17.6	17.4	17.4	17.4	17.8	18.4	18.1	18.0	17.6	17.2	16.9	17.1	17.5
1996	16.8	16.7	16.7	17.1	17.6	18.0	18.0	17.9	17.6	17.2	17.0	17.1	17.3
1997	16.8	16.8	16.9	16.9	17.6	18.0	18.1	18.1	17.7	17.1	17.0	17.1	17.3
1998	16.8	16.8	16.8	16.9	17.6	17.9	17.9	17.9	17.6	16.7	16.6	16.6	17.1
1999	16.2	16.3	16.3	16.7	17.2	17.6	17.5	17.3	17.3	16.9	16.5	16.6	16.8
2000	16.2	16.4	17.1	16.8	18.1	18.0	18.0	17.9	17.1	16.7	16.5	16.7	17.1
2001	16.3	16.2	16.3	16.4	16.9	17.6	17.6	17.4	17.3	16.5	16.3	16.9	16.8
2002	15.9	15.9	16.0	16.1	16.6	17.4	17.6	17.3	17.3	16.7	16.7	17.6	16.8
2003	16.5	16.5	16.8	16.8	17.3	17.9	17.9	17.8	17.7	17.0	16.8	17.7	17.2
State government													
1990	19.7	21.6	21.8	21.9	20.8	21.5	21.7	21.4	22.1	21.8	21.8	21.5	21.4
1991	19.9	21.8	21.8	22.2	20.9	20.9	20.9	20.7	21.8	22.1	22.1	22.2	21.4
1992	21.9	22.3	22.6	22.6	21.5	21.3	20.4	20.6	22.0	21.9	21.7	21.1	21.6
1993	21.3	21.8	21.9	22.1	21.6	20.9	20.2	20.7	22.1	22.2	22.1	21.4	21.5
1994	21.6	22.1	22.1	22.3	21.6	20.5	20.7	21.1	22.2	22.2	21.9	21.1	21.6
1995	21.4	22.0	22.1	22.3	21.9	20.6	20.1	20.4	21.7	22.0	21.9	21.3	21.4
1996	21.2	22.0	22.1	22.3	20.6	21.6	20.9	20.3	21.4	22.1	22.0	21.8	21.5
1997	21.2	22.0	22.1	22.4	20.9	20.8	20.0	20.1	21.4	21.5	21.5	21.4	21.2
1998	20.7	21.6	21.7	22.1	22.3	20.8	21.2	20.4	21.8	22.0	21.9	22.0	21.5
1999	21.2	21.9	22.2	22.4	22.4	21.1	21.0	20.5	21.9	22.1	22.1	21.9	21.7
2000	21.1	22.1	22.4	22.6	22.7	21.3	21.4	21.2	22.4	22.8	22.7	22.5	22.1
2001	21.5	22.8	23.1	23.3	23.5	22.1	22.3	21.9	23.7	23.7	23.7	23.5	22.9
2002	22.5	23.9	24.1	24.4	23.5	23.4	22.9	23.3	24.6	24.4	24.3	24.0	23.8
2003	23.7	24.3	24.6	24.9	24.2	23.8	23.4	23.0	24.7	24.5	24.4	24.0	24.1

Employment by Industry: Alaska—*Continued*

(Numbers in thousands. Not seasonally adjusted.)

Industry	January	February	March	April	May	June	July	August	September	October	November	December	Annual Average
STATEWIDE—*Continued*													
Local government													
1990	30.3	31.2	31.4	31.9	31.9	29.8	27.9	28.9	31.1	32.2	31.6	31.9	30.8
1991	31.0	31.9	31.9	32.0	32.2	30.0	28.3	28.9	31.1	32.5	32.5	32.9	31.2
1992	31.6	32.5	32.6	33.1	33.1	30.9	29.2	30.0	31.8	33.4	33.4	33.5	32.0
1993	33.1	33.5	33.8	34.0	34.1	32.2	29.6	30.7	32.5	34.7	34.5	34.4	33.0
1994	33.7	34.1	34.3	34.4	34.5	33.0	30.0	31.4	33.4	34.2	34.5	34.6	33.5
1995	33.4	34.2	34.2	34.5	34.6	33.6	30.4	32.0	33.5	35.0	34.8	34.5	33.7
1996	33.8	34.6	35.3	35.3	35.6	33.4	30.8	32.1	33.9	35.6	35.1	35.1	34.2
1997	34.6	35.5	35.4	35.6	35.9	33.5	31.4	31.9	34.3	36.0	35.5	35.7	34.6
1998	35.3	35.9	36.0	36.0	36.3	33.9	31.4	31.9	34.3	36.2	35.9	36.1	34.9
1999	34.8	35.7	36.1	36.6	36.6	33.8	31.7	32.2	34.7	36.1	36.0	36.2	35.0
2000	35.4	36.0	36.4	36.6	36.8	34.2	32.0	32.3	34.9	36.1	36.2	36.3	35.2
2001	37.9	39.3	39.8	40.6	40.9	38.4	35.7	36.8	39.0	40.7	40.5	39.8	39.1
2002	39.3	40.7	41.2	41.6	42.0	39.5	35.3	36.8	40.1	41.1	41.2	41.5	40.0
2003	39.7	41.3	41.6	41.4	42.1	39.5	35.7	37.0	40.3	41.3	41.3	41.4	40.2
ANCHORAGE													
Total nonfarm													
1990	103.5	105.8	107.6	108.6	111.1	115.6	115.4	115.8	115.5	114.0	112.2	111.4	111.3
1991	106.4	108.1	108.9	109.4	112.3	115.8	116.7	117.4	115.7	114.2	112.5	113.2	112.5
1992	108.7	110.1	110.3	111.4	113.7	116.3	117.6	117.9	117.3	115.2	113.5	114.2	113.8
1993	110.7	112.0	112.5	114.4	117.7	120.4	120.8	121.4	121.5	120.2	119.4	119.1	117.5
1994	114.5	115.8	116.5	118.2	120.5	123.0	123.3	124.4	124.2	121.1	119.9	120.1	120.1
1995	115.9	116.7	117.2	118.1	120.6	124.3	123.5	124.5	123.5	121.5	119.5	119.7	120.4
1996	115.8	115.9	116.5	117.9	121.3	124.3	124.2	124.9	124.4	123.2	122.1	121.9	121.0
1997	117.5	118.3	118.9	121.2	124.5	127.6	127.6	127.9	127.1	125.9	125.2	125.5	123.9
1998	122.2	123.7	124.6	126.3	130.1	132.3	132.0	131.9	131.9	130.3	129.6	129.8	128.7
1999	125.2	125.4	126.9	128.2	131.7	134.8	134.5	135.2	134.4	132.5	131.9	132.1	131.0
2000	127.6	128.4	130.0	132.0	135.5	138.3	137.5	138.7	138.4	135.8	134.5	135.2	134.3
2001	131.4	132.9	133.5	136.5	140.0	143.5	142.0	142.6	141.8	139.7	137.4	137.8	138.3
2002	133.5	135.8	136.4	138.3	141.6	145.1	143.6	144.3	144.9	143.0	141.5	140.9	140.7
2003	137.6	138.2	139.1	139.9	143.2	145.9	144.4	145.3	145.7	144.8	143.4	143.4	142.6
Total private													
1990	77.7	79.0	80.6	81.6	84.4	89.0	88.5	89.2	88.4	86.4	85.1	84.4	84.5
1991	80.4	81.1	82.0	82.3	85.2	89.0	90.0	90.6	88.3	86.1	84.3	84.3	85.3
1992	80.8	81.7	81.9	82.8	85.5	88.2	89.6	89.9	88.6	86.2	84.4	85.3	85.4
1993	81.6	82.6	83.3	84.8	88.0	91.3	92.3	92.5	92.0	90.3	89.6	89.3	88.1
1994	85.5	86.6	87.3	88.9	91.2	94.4	95.3	96.3	95.5	92.3	91.3	91.4	91.3
1995	87.6	88.0	88.6	89.5	92.0	96.1	96.4	97.2	95.8	93.4	91.5	91.5	92.3
1996	88.0	88.1	88.6	89.9	93.7	96.5	97.3	97.9	97.0	95.0	94.0	93.7	93.3
1997	89.8	90.2	90.8	92.9	96.7	99.6	100.9	100.9	99.3	97.7	96.7	96.7	96.0
1998	93.8	94.9	95.9	97.3	100.7	103.9	104.3	104.5	103.3	101.4	100.6	100.6	100.1
1999	97.0	96.4	98.0	98.9	102.3	106.8	107.2	108.1	106.0	103.7	103.1	103.0	102.5
2000	99.2	99.7	100.9	102.4	105.7	109.9	109.8	110.9	109.6	106.8	105.5	106.1	105.5
2001	102.9	103.9	104.4	106.3	109.6	114.4	113.9	114.7	112.3	110.3	107.8	108.0	109.0
2002	104.6	106.2	106.7	108.2	111.7	115.2	116.3	116.7	114.8	112.6	111.1	110.4	111.2
2003	107.5	107.7	108.3	109.4	112.9	115.5	116.5	117.3	115.5	114.3	112.8	112.7	112.5
Goods-producing													
1990	8.7	9.1	9.6	10.1	10.8	12.4	12.8	12.9	12.9	12.0	11.0	10.2	11.0
1991	9.3	9.4	9.6	10.0	11.0	12.3	12.9	13.1	12.4	11.5	10.2	9.9	10.9
1992	8.8	8.9	9.0	9.5	10.5	11.6	12.2	12.2	11.8	11.0	9.7	9.7	10.4
1993	9.2	9.5	9.8	10.3	11.3	12.5	13.4	13.9	13.5	13.1	11.7	11.0	11.6
1994	10.6	10.8	11.0	11.2	11.9	12.9	13.8	14.2	13.8	12.6	11.6	11.0	12.1
1995	9.8	10.1	10.4	10.4	12.0	13.3	13.9	14.3	13.6	12.7	11.1	10.5	11.8
1996	9.5	9.7	9.7	10.1	11.6	12.7	13.2	13.8	13.5	12.7	11.4	10.4	11.5
1997	9.7	9.7	9.6	10.4	11.6	12.5	13.1	13.5	13.0	12.8	11.0	10.5	11.4
1998	10.5	10.7	10.8	11.0	12.1	13.2	13.7	13.9	13.6	13.1	12.0	11.3	12.1
1999	9.8	9.5	10.1	10.6	11.6	12.9	13.9	14.2	13.6	12.6	11.4	10.9	11.7
2000	9.9	10.0	10.2	10.6	11.5	12.9	13.3	13.7	13.0	12.3	11.1	11.0	11.6
2001	10.7	11.0	11.2	12.2	13.1	14.3	14.4	14.7	14.1	13.3	11.8	11.5	12.7
2002	11.1	11.2	11.3	11.7	12.9	14.0	14.4	14.5	14.2	13.3	12.2	11.7	12.7
2003	10.8	10.8	11.0	11.4	12.7	13.4	14.0	14.5	14.2	13.5	12.2	11.8	12.5
Natural resources and mining													
1990	3.7	3.9	4.0	4.0	3.9	3.8	3.9	3.9	4.0	4.1	4.0	3.9	3.9
1991	3.9	4.0	4.0	4.1	4.1	4.2	4.3	4.4	4.2	3.9	3.8	3.9	4.0
1992	3.6	3.6	3.7	3.6	3.5	3.6	3.6	3.3	3.3	3.2	3.1	3.1	3.4
1993	3.3	3.4	3.4	3.4	3.4	3.5	3.5	3.6	3.6	3.7	3.5	3.5	3.4
1994	3.5	3.5	3.5	3.4	3.3	3.3	3.2	3.2	3.2	3.0	2.9	2.8	3.2
1995	2.7	2.8	2.9	2.7	2.7	2.7	2.7	2.8	2.7	2.8	2.7	2.8	2.7
1996	2.6	2.7	2.7	2.6	2.6	2.6	2.5	2.5	2.5	2.5	2.4	2.4	2.5
1997	2.3	2.3	2.3	2.5	2.5	2.5	2.6	2.5	2.5	2.4	2.3	2.4	2.4
1998	2.9	3.0	3.1	3.0	3.0	3.1	3.2	3.3	3.2	3.1	3.0	3.0	3.0
1999	2.3	2.4	2.5	2.3	2.4	2.7	2.8	3.0	3.0	2.8	2.8	3.0	2.6
2000	2.3	2.4	2.4	2.3	2.3	2.6	2.7	2.9	2.9	2.7	2.8	2.9	2.6
2001	3.4	3.4	3.4	3.6	3.6	3.8	3.5	3.3	3.1	3.2	3.1	3.0	3.4
2002	2.8	2.8	2.8	2.9	2.9	2.9	2.9	2.8	2.7	2.6	2.5	2.4	2.8
2003	2.3	2.3	2.4	2.2	2.1	2.1	2.1	2.2	2.2	2.3	2.2	2.2	2.2

Employment by Industry: Alaska—*Continued*

(Numbers in thousands. Not seasonally adjusted.)

Industry	January	February	March	April	May	June	July	August	September	October	November	December	Annual Average
ANCHORAGE—*Continued*													
Construction													
1990	3.6	3.8	4.2	4.5	5.1	6.4	6.5	6.8	6.9	6.1	5.2	4.6	5.3
1991	3.9	4.0	4.1	4.3	5.1	6.0	6.2	6.4	6.3	5.9	4.8	4.4	5.1
1992	3.7	3.8	3.7	4.2	5.2	6.0	6.2	6.5	6.4	6.0	4.9	4.7	5.1
1993	4.4	4.6	4.8	5.2	6.2	7.1	7.7	8.1	8.0	7.5	6.5	5.8	6.3
1994	5.4	5.6	5.8	6.0	6.7	7.5	8.4	8.7	8.5	7.7	6.8	6.1	6.9
1995	5.1	5.3	5.4	5.7	7.0	8.1	8.7	9.1	8.7	7.9	6.5	5.8	6.9
1996	5.0	5.1	5.1	5.5	6.9	8.0	8.5	9.1	8.9	8.2	7.1	6.2	6.9
1997	5.6	5.6	5.4	6.0	7.2	8.0	8.4	8.9	8.5	8.5	6.9	6.3	7.1
1998	5.8	5.8	5.8	6.0	7.0	7.9	8.3	8.4	8.2	7.9	7.0	6.4	7.0
1999	5.9	5.5	5.9	6.5	7.3	8.2	8.9	9.2	8.7	8.0	6.9	6.2	7.2
2000	5.9	5.9	6.0	6.5	7.3	8.3	8.5	8.7	8.2	7.8	6.6	6.4	7.1
2001	5.7	6.0	6.2	6.9	7.7	8.6	9.0	9.4	9.1	8.3	7.0	6.8	7.6
2002	6.5	6.6	6.7	7.0	8.1	9.2	9.6	9.8	9.6	8.9	8.0	7.6	8.1
2003	6.8	6.9	6.9	7.4	8.7	9.4	10.0	10.4	10.1	9.4	8.3	7.9	8.5
Manufacturing													
1990	1.4	1.4	1.4	1.6	1.8	2.2	2.4	2.2	2.0	1.8	1.8	1.7	1.8
1991	1.5	1.4	1.5	1.6	1.8	2.1	2.4	2.3	1.9	1.7	1.6	1.6	1.7
1992	1.5	1.5	1.6	1.7	1.8	2.0	2.4	2.4	2.1	1.8	1.7	1.9	1.8
1993	1.5	1.5	1.6	1.7	1.7	1.9	2.2	2.2	1.9	1.9	1.7	1.7	1.7
1994	1.7	1.7	1.7	1.8	1.9	2.1	2.2	2.3	2.1	1.9	1.9	2.1	1.9
1995	2.0	2.0	2.1	2.0	2.3	2.5	2.5	2.4	2.2	2.0	1.9	1.9	2.1
1996	1.9	1.9	1.9	2.0	2.1	2.1	2.2	2.2	2.1	2.0	1.9	1.8	2.0
1997	1.8	1.8	1.9	1.9	1.9	2.0	2.1	2.1	2.0	1.9	1.8	1.8	1.9
1998	1.8	1.9	1.9	2.0	2.1	2.2	2.2	2.2	2.2	2.1	2.0	1.9	2.0
1999	1.6	1.6	1.7	1.8	1.9	2.0	2.2	2.0	1.9	1.8	1.7	1.7	1.8
2000	1.7	1.7	1.8	1.8	1.9	2.0	2.1	2.1	1.9	1.8	1.7	1.7	1.8
2001	1.6	1.6	1.6	1.7	1.8	1.9	1.9	2.0	1.9	1.8	1.7	1.7	1.8
2002	1.8	1.8	1.8	1.8	1.9	1.9	1.9	1.9	1.9	1.8	1.7	1.7	1.8
2003	1.7	1.6	1.7	1.8	1.9	1.9	1.9	1.9	1.9	1.8	1.7	1.7	1.8
Service-providing													
1990	94.8	96.7	98.0	98.5	100.3	103.2	102.6	102.9	102.6	102.0	101.2	101.2	100.3
1991	97.1	98.7	99.3	99.4	101.3	103.5	103.8	104.3	103.3	102.7	102.3	103.3	101.5
1992	99.9	101.2	101.3	101.9	103.2	104.7	105.4	105.7	105.5	104.2	103.8	104.5	103.4
1993	101.5	102.5	102.7	104.1	106.4	107.9	107.4	107.5	108.0	107.1	107.7	108.1	105.9
1994	103.9	105.0	105.5	107.0	108.6	110.1	109.5	110.2	110.4	108.5	108.3	109.1	108.0
1995	106.1	106.6	106.8	107.7	108.6	111.0	109.6	110.2	109.9	108.8	108.4	109.2	108.5
1996	106.3	106.2	106.8	107.8	109.7	111.6	111.0	111.1	110.9	110.5	110.7	111.5	109.5
1997	107.8	108.6	109.3	110.8	112.9	115.1	114.5	114.4	114.1	113.1	114.2	115.0	112.4
1998	111.7	113.0	113.8	115.3	118.0	119.1	118.3	118.0	118.3	117.2	117.6	118.5	116.5
1999	115.4	115.9	116.8	117.6	120.1	121.9	120.6	121.0	120.8	119.9	120.5	121.2	119.3
2000	117.7	118.4	119.8	121.4	124.0	125.4	124.2	125.0	125.4	123.5	123.4	124.2	122.7
2001	120.7	121.9	122.3	124.3	126.9	129.2	127.6	127.9	127.7	126.4	125.6	126.3	125.6
2002	122.4	124.6	125.1	126.6	128.7	131.1	129.2	129.8	130.7	129.7	129.3	129.2	128.0
2003	126.8	127.4	128.1	128.5	130.5	132.5	130.4	130.8	131.5	131.3	131.2	131.6	130.1
Trade, transportation, and utilities													
1990	23.8	23.9	24.4	24.8	25.9	27.1	27.0	27.1	26.6	26.0	26.1	26.1	25.7
1991	24.3	24.2	24.6	24.5	25.7	26.4	27.0	27.1	26.7	26.6	26.4	26.6	25.8
1992	25.2	25.1	25.3	25.3	26.3	26.7	27.0	27.2	27.0	26.8	26.9	27.1	26.3
1993	25.4	25.4	25.4	25.4	26.5	27.0	27.5	27.3	27.4	27.3	28.0	28.1	26.7
1994	26.6	26.7	27.1	27.6	28.4	29.2	29.7	29.8	29.8	29.1	29.2	29.5	28.5
1995	28.5	28.2	28.2	28.5	28.6	29.6	29.8	30.1	29.8	29.7	29.6	29.8	29.2
1996	28.4	27.9	27.8	28.1	29.1	29.9	29.7	30.0	29.7	29.6	30.0	30.3	29.2
1997	28.8	28.5	28.7	29.2	30.0	30.7	30.8	30.9	30.7	30.6	31.3	31.6	30.1
1998	29.9	29.8	30.3	30.8	31.3	31.8	31.5	31.9	31.7	31.7	32.1	32.4	31.2
1999	30.9	30.6	31.1	31.3	31.6	32.5	32.6	33.0	32.7	32.2	33.0	33.1	32.0
2000	31.2	31.1	31.4	31.9	32.7	32.9	32.8	33.5	33.5	32.9	33.0	33.0	32.4
2001	31.4	31.0	31.1	31.4	32.3	33.4	33.5	33.6	33.3	33.3	32.8	33.0	32.5
2002	31.5	31.7	32.0	32.3	33.0	33.5	34.1	34.4	34.1	33.7	33.4	33.3	33.1
2003	32.1	31.9	31.9	32.2	32.8	33.4	33.9	34.0	33.7	33.5	33.5	33.5	33.0
Wholesale trade													
1990	3.6	3.6	3.7	3.7	3.8	4.0	4.0	4.0	3.9	3.9	3.8	3.8	3.8
1991	3.4	3.4	3.5	3.5	3.6	3.6	3.6	3.6	3.6	3.9	3.8	3.8	3.6
1992	3.6	3.7	3.7	3.8	3.9	4.0	4.0	4.0	3.9	3.9	3.8	3.8	3.8
1993	3.7	3.8	3.8	3.8	3.9	4.0	3.9	3.9	3.9	3.9	3.8	3.9	3.8
1994	3.8	3.8	3.8	3.8	3.9	4.0	4.1	4.1	4.1	4.0	3.9	3.9	3.9
1995	3.9	4.0	4.0	4.3	4.3	4.4	4.4	4.4	4.4	4.3	4.3	4.3	4.2
1996	4.2	4.2	4.2	4.3	4.4	4.5	4.6	4.5	4.4	4.3	4.3	4.4	4.3
1997	4.1	4.0	4.1	4.1	4.2	4.4	4.1	4.0	4.0	3.9	4.1	4.1	4.0
1998	4.1	4.1	4.2	4.2	4.3	4.4	4.4	4.3	4.3	4.2	4.3	4.3	4.2
1999	4.4	4.4	4.5	4.5	4.5	4.7	4.7	4.7	4.6	4.5	4.5	4.5	4.5
2000	4.2	4.2	4.3	4.5	4.5	4.6	4.6	4.7	4.5	4.4	4.4	4.4	4.4
2001	4.6	4.6	4.6	4.7	4.8	4.8	4.9	4.9	4.8	4.7	4.6	4.6	4.7
2002	4.5	4.5	4.5	4.6	4.7	4.8	4.8	4.8	4.7	4.6	4.6	4.5	4.6
2003	4.5	4.5	4.5	4.5	4.6	4.7	4.8	4.7	4.7	4.6	4.5	4.5	4.6

Employment by Industry: Alaska—*Continued*

(Numbers in thousands. Not seasonally adjusted.)

Industry	January	February	March	April	May	June	July	August	September	October	November	December	Annual Average
ANCHORAGE—*Continued*													
Retail trade													
1990	12.7	12.6	12.7	13.1	13.5	13.9	13.8	13.9	13.7	13.5	14.0	14.1	13.4
1991	13.2	13.1	13.2	13.1	13.6	13.8	14.2	14.3	14.0	13.8	14.1	14.1	13.7
1992	13.1	12.8	12.9	12.9	13.4	13.7	13.9	13.9	13.9	13.9	14.3	14.3	13.5
1993	12.9	12.7	12.7	12.8	13.4	13.8	14.0	13.9	14.0	14.2	15.1	15.1	13.7
1994	14.1	14.1	14.4	14.6	15.0	15.4	15.7	15.9	15.9	15.5	15.9	16.1	15.2
1995	15.3	14.9	14.9	15.0	15.5	16.0	16.0	16.1	15.9	16.1	16.5	16.6	15.7
1996	15.5	15.0	14.9	15.1	15.7	16.3	16.3	16.4	16.2	16.3	16.7	16.9	15.9
1997	15.8	15.5	15.6	15.8	16.4	16.9	17.0	16.9	16.6	16.8	17.3	17.5	16.5
1998	15.9	15.7	16.0	16.2	16.5	17.0	16.8	16.8	16.7	16.8	17.2	17.6	16.6
1999	16.2	15.9	16.2	16.1	16.3	17.2	17.4	17.4	17.2	17.2	18.0	18.2	16.9
2000	16.7	16.4	16.6	17.0	17.4	17.6	17.4	17.5	17.7	17.4	17.7	17.7	17.2
2001	16.6	16.2	16.2	16.4	16.7	17.2	17.2	17.3	17.2	17.3	17.3	17.5	16.9
2002	16.5	16.5	16.5	16.7	17.1	17.4	17.5	17.6	17.6	17.9	17.9	18.0	17.3
2003	17.0	16.9	16.9	17.0	17.2	17.6	17.8	17.8	17.7	17.8	18.1	18.2	17.5
Transportation and utilities													
1990	7.5	7.7	8.0	8.0	8.6	9.2	9.2	9.2	9.0	8.6	8.3	8.2	8.4
1991	7.7	7.7	7.9	7.9	8.5	9.0	9.2	9.2	9.1	8.9	8.5	8.7	8.5
1992	8.5	8.6	8.7	8.6	9.0	9.0	9.1	9.3	9.2	9.0	8.8	9.0	8.9
1993	8.8	8.9	8.9	8.8	9.2	9.2	9.6	9.5	9.5	9.2	9.1	9.1	9.1
1994	8.7	8.8	8.9	9.2	9.5	9.8	9.9	9.8	9.8	9.6	9.4	9.5	9.4
1995	9.3	9.3	9.3	9.2	8.8	9.2	9.4	9.6	9.5	9.3	8.8	8.9	9.2
1996	8.7	8.7	8.7	8.7	9.0	9.1	8.8	9.1	9.1	9.0	9.0	9.0	8.9
1997	8.9	9.0	9.0	9.3	9.4	9.4	9.7	10.0	10.1	9.9	9.9	10.0	9.5
1998	9.9	10.0	10.1	10.4	10.5	10.4	10.3	10.8	10.7	10.7	10.6	10.5	10.4
1999	10.3	10.3	10.4	10.7	10.8	10.6	10.5	10.9	10.9	10.5	10.5	10.4	10.5
2000	10.3	10.5	10.5	10.4	10.8	10.7	10.8	11.3	11.3	11.1	10.9	10.9	10.7
2001	10.2	10.2	10.3	10.3	10.8	11.4	11.4	11.4	11.3	11.3	10.9	10.9	10.9
2002	10.5	10.7	11.0	11.0	11.2	11.3	11.8	12.0	11.8	11.2	10.9	10.8	11.2
2003	10.6	10.5	10.5	10.7	11.0	11.1	11.3	11.5	11.3	11.1	10.9	10.8	10.9
Information													
1990	2.8	2.8	2.9	3.0	3.1	3.2	3.1	3.1	3.2	3.2	3.2	3.2	3.0
1991	3.1	3.2	3.2	3.2	3.2	3.3	3.3	3.3	3.2	3.3	3.3	3.2	3.2
1992	3.2	3.2	3.2	3.2	3.3	2.9	3.0	2.9	2.9	2.9	2.9	3.0	3.0
1993	2.9	2.9	2.9	3.0	3.0	3.0	3.1	3.1	3.1	3.0	3.0	3.0	3.0
1994	3.0	3.0	3.0	3.1	3.1	3.1	3.1	3.1	3.1	3.0	3.0	3.0	3.0
1995	2.8	2.8	2.8	2.8	2.8	2.9	2.9	2.8	2.8	2.8	2.8	2.8	2.8
1996	2.8	2.8	2.9	3.0	3.0	3.0	3.1	3.0	3.0	3.0	2.9	3.0	2.9
1997	3.0	3.1	3.1	3.2	3.2	3.4	3.6	3.4	3.4	3.3	3.4	3.5	3.3
1998	3.5	3.5	3.5	3.5	3.5	3.6	3.5	3.6	3.7	3.7	3.8	3.9	3.6
1999	3.9	3.9	3.9	3.9	4.7	4.7	4.8	4.7	4.7	4.6	4.6	4.7	4.4
2000	4.9	4.9	4.9	4.8	4.9	5.0	4.9	4.9	4.9	4.7	4.7	4.9	4.8
2001	4.8	4.8	4.9	4.7	4.7	4.8	5.0	5.0	4.9	4.8	4.8	4.8	4.8
2002	4.5	4.5	4.5	4.6	4.7	4.7	4.9	4.7	4.7	4.7	4.7	4.7	4.7
2003	4.5	4.5	4.5	4.5	4.6	4.6	4.7	4.6	4.5	4.6	4.6	4.7	4.6
Financial activities													
1990	6.7	6.6	6.7	6.8	6.9	7.1	7.1	7.1	7.1	7.0	7.0	7.0	6.9
1991	6.9	6.9	6.9	6.9	7.0	7.1	7.2	7.1	7.1	6.9	6.9	6.9	6.9
1992	6.5	6.5	6.5	6.9	7.1	7.2	7.2	7.3	7.2	6.9	6.9	7.0	6.9
1993	6.9	6.9	7.0	7.1	7.3	7.5	7.4	7.5	7.4	7.3	7.3	7.3	7.2
1994	7.3	7.3	7.3	7.5	7.8	7.9	7.8	7.8	7.7	7.5	7.5	7.5	7.5
1995	7.4	7.4	7.4	7.5	7.6	7.8	7.7	7.8	7.8	7.5	7.4	7.4	7.5
1996	7.3	7.3	7.4	7.4	7.6	7.7	7.8	7.7	7.6	7.4	7.3	7.4	7.4
1997	7.1	7.1	7.1	7.2	7.5	7.7	7.9	7.8	7.6	7.4	7.5	7.4	7.4
1998	7.3	7.4	7.4	7.6	7.8	8.0	8.0	8.0	7.8	8.0	7.9	7.9	7.7
1999	7.8	7.7	7.8	7.7	7.8	8.2	8.2	8.2	8.0	7.8	7.7	7.7	7.8
2000	7.7	7.7	7.7	7.8	7.9	8.2	8.2	8.1	8.1	7.8	7.8	7.9	7.9
2001	8.3	8.4	8.4	8.5	8.6	8.9	8.7	8.7	8.6	8.3	8.3	8.4	8.5
2002	8.1	8.1	8.2	8.2	8.4	8.6	8.6	8.6	8.5	8.4	8.5	8.5	8.4
2003	8.4	8.5	8.7	8.8	8.8	9.0	9.0	9.0	8.9	8.9	8.8	8.8	8.8
Professional and business services													
1990	11.6	12.0	12.2	12.6	13.1	13.6	13.4	13.6	13.4	13.3	13.0	13.1	12.9
1991	13.2	13.5	13.6	13.4	13.8	14.1	14.1	14.4	13.8	13.3	13.1	13.0	13.6
1992	12.8	13.1	13.1	13.2	13.1	13.8	14.2	14.2	13.8	13.5	13.1	13.3	13.4
1993	13.1	13.4	13.5	13.8	14.2	14.6	14.6	14.6	14.6	14.0	13.9	13.9	14.0
1994	13.8	14.1	14.1	14.4	14.6	15.1	15.1	15.3	15.0	14.5	14.3	14.5	14.5
1995	13.8	14.0	14.1	14.4	14.6	15.5	15.2	15.4	15.4	15.1	14.9	14.8	14.7
1996	14.2	14.5	14.6	14.8	15.1	15.4	15.3	15.5	15.4	15.2	14.7	14.8	14.9
1997	14.3	14.6	15.0	15.2	15.7	16.1	16.1	16.0	15.7	15.3	15.0	15.0	15.3
1998	14.8	15.1	15.2	15.4	15.8	16.0	16.4	16.3	16.1	15.5	15.3	15.3	15.6
1999	15.3	15.3	15.4	15.6	16.3	17.1	16.4	16.8	16.4	16.1	16.0	15.8	16.0
2000	15.3	15.4	15.7	16.0	16.6	17.6	17.3	17.3	17.0	16.9	16.4	16.5	16.5
2001	15.1	15.5	15.4	15.7	16.3	17.2	17.1	17.3	16.5	16.2	15.6	15.7	16.1
2002	15.3	15.8	15.7	15.8	16.4	16.9	16.6	16.9	16.4	16.1	15.7	15.6	16.1
2003	15.4	15.4	15.5	15.4	16.4	16.7	16.6	16.6	16.1	16.1	15.8	15.7	16.0

Employment by Industry: Alaska—*Continued*

(Numbers in thousands. Not seasonally adjusted.)

Industry	January	February	March	April	May	June	July	August	September	October	November	December	Annual Average
ANCHORAGE—*Continued*													
Educational and health services													
1990	8.7	8.9	9.0	9.0	9.1	9.2	8.8	9.0	9.1	9.2	9.3	9.2	9.0
1991	8.7	8.9	9.0	9.0	9.1	9.1	8.9	9.0	9.0	9.1	9.2	9.2	9.0
1992	9.2	9.4	9.3	9.2	9.2	9.1	9.0	9.1	9.3	9.3	9.3	9.4	9.2
1993	9.3	9.6	9.5	9.7	9.8	9.8	9.6	9.5	9.6	9.7	9.8	9.8	9.6
1994	9.2	9.5	9.5	9.5	9.5	9.5	9.3	9.4	9.5	9.5	9.6	9.7	9.4
1995	9.5	9.7	9.7	9.8	9.8	9.8	9.7	9.7	9.7	9.8	9.9	9.9	9.7
1996	10.0	10.1	10.1	10.3	10.5	10.6	10.4	10.3	10.4	10.4	10.6	10.7	10.3
1997	10.7	10.9	10.9	11.1	11.4	11.4	11.4	11.4	11.4	11.3	11.5	11.5	11.2
1998	11.5	11.6	11.7	11.7	12.0	12.0	11.7	11.7	11.8	12.1	12.1	12.3	11.8
1999	12.2	12.2	12.3	12.4	12.6	12.7	12.6	12.5	12.6	12.7	12.8	13.0	12.5
2000	13.1	13.3	13.3	13.2	13.3	13.5	13.3	13.5	13.6	13.5	13.7	13.8	13.4
2001	14.2	14.4	14.5	14.6	14.8	14.9	14.9	15.0	15.0	15.2	15.3	15.4	14.9
2002	15.5	15.7	15.8	15.9	16.0	16.2	16.3	16.4	16.2	16.3	16.5	16.5	16.1
2003	16.5	16.9	17.1	17.2	17.3	17.4	17.2	17.4	17.4	17.6	17.8	18.0	17.3
Leisure and hospitality													
1990	10.6	10.8	10.9	10.9	10.9	11.6	11.7	11.7	11.5	11.2	11.0	11.1	11.1
1991	10.8	10.8	10.9	11.1	11.1	12.1	12.1	12.2	11.8	11.2	11.0	11.4	11.3
1992	10.6	11.0	11.0	11.0	11.4	12.1	12.3	12.4	12.0	11.2	11.1	11.2	11.4
1993	10.3	10.4	10.6	10.9	11.3	12.0	12.0	12.0	11.8	11.2	11.2	11.5	11.2
1994	10.5	10.6	10.7	11.0	11.2	11.8	11.7	12.0	11.9	11.5	11.5	11.6	11.3
1995	11.3	11.2	11.4	11.5	11.9	12.5	12.4	12.4	12.0	11.2	11.2	11.6	11.7
1996	11.1	11.1	11.4	11.3	11.9	12.2	12.7	12.6	12.4	11.8	12.2	12.2	11.9
1997	11.6	11.6	11.6	11.9	12.4	12.9	13.0	13.1	12.7	12.1	12.1	12.3	12.2
1998	11.5	11.9	12.1	12.3	13.2	14.2	14.5	14.2	13.8	12.5	12.5	12.6	12.9
1999	12.3	12.4	12.5	12.3	12.6	13.5	13.5	13.6	13.0	12.7	12.6	12.8	12.8
2000	12.2	12.3	12.6	13.1	13.6	14.4	14.7	14.8	14.4	13.5	13.5	13.7	13.5
2001	13.1	13.4	13.5	13.8	14.2	15.1	14.6	14.7	14.3	13.6	13.6	13.6	14.0
2002	13.1	13.7	13.5	14.0	14.6	15.5	15.6	15.5	15.1	14.5	14.5	14.5	14.5
2003	14.2	14.1	14.0	14.2	14.6	15.1	15.2	15.3	15.1	14.5	14.5	14.6	14.6
Other services													
1990	4.8	4.9	4.9	4.4	4.6	4.8	4.6	4.7	4.6	4.5	4.5	4.5	4.6
1991	4.1	4.2	4.2	4.2	4.3	4.6	4.5	4.4	4.3	4.2	4.2	4.1	4.2
1992	4.5	4.5	4.5	4.5	4.6	4.8	4.7	4.6	4.6	4.6	4.5	4.6	4.5
1993	4.5	4.5	4.6	4.6	4.6	4.9	4.7	4.6	4.6	4.7	4.7	4.7	4.6
1994	4.5	4.6	4.6	4.6	4.7	4.9	4.8	4.7	4.7	4.6	4.6	4.6	4.6
1995	4.5	4.6	4.6	4.6	4.7	4.7	4.8	4.7	4.7	4.6	4.6	4.7	4.6
1996	4.7	4.7	4.7	4.9	4.9	5.0	5.1	5.0	5.0	4.9	4.9	4.9	4.8
1997	4.6	4.7	4.8	4.7	4.9	4.9	5.0	4.8	4.8	4.9	4.9	4.9	4.8
1998	4.8	4.9	4.9	5.0	5.0	5.1	5.0	4.9	4.8	4.8	4.9	4.9	4.9
1999	4.8	4.8	4.9	5.1	5.1	5.2	5.2	5.1	5.0	5.0	5.0	5.0	5.0
2000	4.9	5.0	5.1	5.0	5.2	5.4	5.3	5.1	5.1	5.2	5.3	5.3	5.1
2001	5.3	5.4	5.4	5.4	5.6	5.8	5.7	5.7	5.6	5.6	5.6	5.6	5.6
2002	5.5	5.5	5.7	5.7	5.7	5.8	5.8	5.7	5.6	5.6	5.6	5.6	5.7
2003	5.6	5.6	5.6	5.7	5.7	5.9	5.9	5.9	5.6	5.6	5.6	5.6	5.7
Government													
1990	25.8	26.8	27.0	27.0	26.7	26.6	26.9	26.6	27.1	27.6	27.1	27.0	26.8
1991	26.0	27.0	26.9	27.1	27.1	26.8	26.7	26.8	27.4	28.1	28.2	28.9	27.2
1992	27.9	28.4	28.4	28.6	28.2	28.1	28.0	28.0	28.7	29.0	29.1	28.9	28.4
1993	29.1	29.4	29.2	29.6	29.7	29.1	28.5	28.9	29.5	29.9	29.8	29.8	29.3
1994	29.0	29.2	29.2	29.3	29.3	28.6	28.0	28.1	28.7	28.8	28.6	28.7	28.7
1995	28.3	28.7	28.6	28.6	28.6	28.2	27.1	27.3	27.7	28.1	28.0	28.2	28.1
1996	27.8	27.8	27.9	28.0	27.6	27.8	26.9	27.0	27.4	28.2	28.1	28.2	27.7
1997	27.7	28.1	28.1	28.3	27.8	28.0	26.7	27.0	27.8	28.2	28.5	28.8	27.9
1998	28.4	28.8	28.7	29.0	29.4	28.4	27.7	27.4	28.6	28.9	29.0	29.2	28.6
1999	28.2	29.0	28.9	29.3	29.4	28.0	27.3	27.1	28.4	28.8	28.8	29.1	28.5
2000	28.4	28.7	29.1	29.6	29.8	28.4	27.7	27.8	28.8	29.0	29.0	29.1	28.7
2001	28.5	29.0	29.1	30.2	30.4	29.1	28.1	27.9	29.5	29.4	29.6	29.8	29.2
2002	28.9	29.6	29.7	30.1	29.9	29.9	27.3	27.6	30.1	30.4	30.4	30.5	29.5
2003	30.1	30.5	30.8	30.5	30.3	30.4	27.9	28.0	30.2	30.5	30.6	30.7	30.0
Federal government													
1990	10.4	10.5	10.6	10.4	10.5	10.7	10.8	10.4	10.4	10.6	10.5	10.6	10.5
1991	10.3	10.3	10.3	10.3	10.6	10.8	10.8	10.7	10.8	11.1	11.0	11.1	10.6
1992	10.9	10.9	10.9	11.0	11.2	11.4	11.4	11.4	11.3	11.5	11.4	11.4	11.2
1993	11.6	11.6	11.5	11.7	11.7	11.9	12.1	12.1	12.1	11.9	11.9	11.9	11.8
1994	11.2	11.2	11.2	11.2	11.2	11.3	11.3	11.2	11.1	11.0	10.8	11.0	11.1
1995	10.7	10.7	10.7	10.5	10.6	10.7	10.5	10.4	10.3	10.2	10.1	10.4	10.4
1996	10.0	9.9	9.8	9.9	10.0	10.2	10.2	10.1	10.1	10.0	10.0	10.1	10.0
1997	9.8	9.8	9.8	9.8	9.9	10.1	10.1	10.1	10.0	9.9	10.0	10.2	9.9
1998	9.9	9.9	9.9	9.9	10.3	10.3	10.2	10.2	10.1	9.8	9.9	10.0	10.0
1999	9.7	9.8	9.7	9.7	9.8	10.0	10.0	9.9	9.9	9.9	9.8	10.1	9.8
2000	9.7	9.8	9.9	9.8	10.1	10.1	10.1	10.2	9.8	9.7	9.7	9.9	9.9
2001	9.7	9.6	9.6	9.6	9.7	9.9	9.9	9.8	9.8	9.5	9.5	9.7	9.7
2002	9.4	9.4	9.4	9.3	9.4	9.7	9.7	9.6	9.7	9.7	9.7	9.9	9.6
2003	9.7	9.7	9.8	9.6	9.7	9.9	9.9	9.9	9.8	9.8	9.8	10.0	9.8

Employment by Industry: Alaska—*Continued*

(Numbers in thousands. Not seasonally adjusted.)

Industry	January	February	March	April	May	June	July	August	September	October	November	December	Annual Average
ANCHORAGE—*Continued*													
State government													
1990	7.0	7.7	7.8	7.9	7.3	7.4	7.2	7.4	8.0	8.0	8.2	7.9	7.6
1991	7.3	8.1	8.1	8.2	7.7	7.5	7.4	7.6	8.0	8.3	8.3	8.4	7.9
1992	8.2	8.4	8.4	8.4	7.7	7.8	7.7	7.7	8.3	8.2	8.2	8.0	8.0
1993	8.1	8.2	8.2	8.3	8.2	7.6	7.5	7.8	8.3	8.4	8.4	8.2	8.1
1994	8.2	8.4	8.4	8.4	8.2	7.6	7.6	7.8	8.3	8.4	8.3	8.1	8.1
1995	8.1	8.4	8.4	8.4	8.2	7.6	7.4	7.7	8.2	8.3	8.3	8.1	8.0
1996	8.1	8.3	8.3	8.3	7.5	7.7	7.6	7.7	8.0	8.4	8.3	8.3	8.0
1997	8.1	8.3	8.3	8.4	7.9	7.9	7.4	7.6	8.2	8.2	8.3	8.3	8.0
1998	8.1	8.3	8.3	8.5	8.6	8.0	8.2	7.9	8.7	8.7	8.7	8.7	8.3
1999	8.4	8.7	8.7	8.7	8.8	8.3	8.2	8.1	8.7	8.8	8.8	8.7	8.5
2000	8.6	8.8	8.8	8.9	9.0	8.4	8.3	8.3	8.9	9.1	9.1	9.0	8.7
2001	8.7	9.1	9.1	9.2	9.3	8.8	8.8	8.6	9.5	9.5	9.6	9.5	9.1
2002	9.2	9.5	9.5	9.6	9.1	9.4	9.1	9.5	9.9	9.8	9.8	9.7	9.5
2003	9.6	9.7	9.8	9.8	9.3	9.3	9.2	9.2	9.7	9.7	9.7	9.7	9.6
Local government													
1990	8.4	8.6	8.6	8.7	8.9	8.5	8.9	8.8	8.7	9.0	8.4	8.5	8.6
1991	8.4	8.6	8.5	8.6	8.8	8.5	8.5	8.5	8.6	8.7	8.9	9.4	8.6
1992	8.8	9.1	9.1	9.2	9.3	8.9	8.9	8.9	9.1	9.3	9.5	9.5	9.1
1993	9.4	9.6	9.5	9.6	9.8	9.6	8.9	9.0	9.1	9.6	9.5	9.7	9.4
1994	9.6	9.6	9.6	9.7	9.9	9.7	9.1	9.1	9.3	9.4	9.5	9.6	9.5
1995	9.5	9.6	9.5	9.7	9.8	9.9	9.2	9.2	9.2	9.6	9.6	9.7	9.5
1996	9.7	9.6	9.8	9.8	10.1	9.9	9.1	9.2	9.3	9.8	9.8	9.8	9.6
1997	9.8	10.0	10.0	10.1	10.0	10.0	9.2	9.3	9.6	10.1	10.2	10.3	9.8
1998	10.4	10.6	10.5	10.6	10.5	10.1	9.3	9.3	9.8	10.4	10.4	10.5	10.2
1999	10.1	10.5	10.5	10.9	10.8	9.7	9.1	9.1	9.8	10.1	10.2	10.3	10.0
2000	10.1	10.1	10.4	10.9	10.7	9.9	9.3	9.3	10.1	10.2	10.2	10.2	10.1
2001	10.1	10.3	10.4	11.4	11.4	10.4	9.4	9.5	10.2	10.4	10.5	10.6	10.4
2002	10.3	10.7	10.8	11.2	11.4	10.8	8.5	8.5	10.5	10.9	10.9	10.9	10.5
2003	10.8	11.1	11.2	11.1	11.3	11.2	8.8	8.9	10.7	11.0	11.1	11.0	10.7

Average Weekly Hours by Industry: Alaska

(Not seasonally adjusted.)

Industry	January	February	March	April	May	June	July	August	September	October	November	December	Annual Average
STATEWIDE													
Natural resources and mining													
2001	47.5	44.6	46.4	48.0	46.9	48.6	47.4	48.8	45.9	48.4	47.3	45.6	47.1
2002	45.8	47.1	48.1	48.9	47.5	49.5	49.1	48.4	46.3	41.9	41.9	41.5	46.4
2003	41.0	41.4	41.7	43.9	42.5	41.7	41.6	42.2	44.8	43.6	45.5	40.4	42.5
Construction													
2001	37.5	36.9	38.5	38.1	45.8	43.3	44.7	48.5	44.8	43.9	37.2	38.6	42.2
2002	38.0	40.4	39.9	38.7	40.7	43.2	42.8	44.0	44.5	41.2	38.4	39.7	41.3
2003	38.9	39.4	38.9	40.0	44.4	43.3	44.5	45.6	44.8	43.5	37.6	38.3	42.1
Manufacturing													
2001	31.2	47.1	52.0	33.8	32.0	37.6	49.1	50.9	44.6	43.8	33.8	34.3	43.1
2002	32.8	45.4	46.3	36.9	34.8	29.2	40.0	44.3	33.5	31.3	29.8	30.2	37.4
2003	22.8	46.2	38.0	38.7	44.0	39.7	51.5	49.1	46.2	39.5	38.0	39.0	42.8
Trade, transportation, and utilities													
2001	32.8	34.6	35.3	34.7	33.9	35.7	36.1	36.6	35.6	34.3	33.3	34.0	34.8
2002	32.5	33.6	33.5	32.3	32.3	35.6	34.1	34.4	34.8	33.6	33.4	33.6	33.7
2003	32.7	34.2	33.8	34.3	34.5	36.2	35.4	35.6	35.1	34.0	34.9	33.7	34.6
Wholesale trade													
2001	34.9	34.5	37.0	40.2	37.9	39.2	40.0	37.9	39.0	36.8	37.3	39.2	37.9
2002	36.7	39.5	38.8	39.9	40.3	42.5	40.7	39.6	40.6	37.9	38.3	38.1	39.5
2003	37.4	38.9	37.2	38.8	38.5	39.6	38.8	39.2	38.3	37.9	38.8	36.9	38.4
Retail trade													
2001	33.2	36.0	36.6	34.6	34.5	36.5	35.8	37.7	36.4	34.9	34.2	34.3	35.4
2002	33.1	34.1	34.0	31.9	32.0	32.8	32.8	33.4	33.3	32.4	32.8	32.5	32.9
2003	32.2	33.4	32.5	33.2	34.0	35.0	34.5	35.0	34.0	33.5	33.7	32.4	33.6
Transportation and utilities													
2001	31.3	32.1	32.6	33.2	31.7	33.4	35.4	34.4	33.3	32.3	30.4	31.7	32.7
2002	29.9	30.8	31.1	30.7	30.7	38.7	34.3	34.5	35.7	34.7	33.0	34.6	33.4
2003	32.4	34.4	35.4	35.1	34.4	37.5	35.9	35.6	36.2	33.8	36.3	35.3	35.3
Financial activities													
2001	35.8	35.0	35.4	35.6	35.7	34.8	35.8	35.6	34.0	35.5	33.8	33.5	35.1
2002	34.0	33.0	33.2	34.2	32.8	34.3	31.8	34.0	36.8	32.9	34.6	37.9	34.1
2003	35.4	38.0	38.5	36.8	36.9	38.2	35.4	37.6	36.8	37.8	35.9	34.6	36.8

Average Hourly Earnings by Industry: Alaska

(Dollars, not seasonally adjusted.)

Industry	January	February	March	April	May	June	July	August	September	October	November	December	Annual Average
STATEWIDE													
Natural resources and mining													
2001	26.71	27.83	27.73	27.60	27.88	27.69	27.33	26.88	27.24	27.46	27.46	27.66	27.46
2002	27.75	28.12	27.63	27.73	27.60	27.66	27.96	27.79	27.62	26.84	29.72	29.22	27.94
2003	29.91	31.41	30.86	30.19	30.04	31.10	30.76	29.99	29.03	28.85	30.35	29.69	30.17
Construction													
2001	25.10	25.59	26.90	26.22	25.41	27.87	27.56	27.15	28.23	27.18	24.91	24.71	26.66
2002	24.96	24.96	25.71	25.82	26.64	26.13	26.50	26.81	28.38	27.08	26.84	28.11	26.64
2003	27.23	27.11	27.97	29.72	29.83	29.47	29.96	30.02	29.45	29.20	29.05	28.28	29.16
Manufacturing													
2001	15.30	11.36	10.39	12.31	13.46	12.21	10.36	11.14	11.09	11.55	15.13	16.13	11.70
2002	15.50	11.75	11.78	13.54	14.54	14.40	13.16	12.85	13.01	13.21	14.69	15.20	13.24
2003	14.10	12.21	11.73	12.05	12.25	12.73	11.90	11.64	11.41	12.11	13.51	13.82	12.16
Trade, transportation, and utilities													
2001	14.64	14.30	14.28	14.88	15.15	15.24	15.28	15.19	15.63	15.54	15.96	15.98	15.19
2002	15.59	15.67	16.17	16.27	16.18	16.09	16.01	16.08	16.34	16.09	15.78	15.64	16.00
2003	15.67	15.75	15.59	15.63	15.69	15.12	15.78	16.11	15.97	15.58	15.66	15.65	15.68
Wholesale trade													
2001	17.56	17.49	18.57	17.98	17.41	18.23	18.11	18.16	19.74	18.34	18.33	19.10	18.26
2002	17.52	17.14	18.02	18.40	18.12	17.91	17.07	17.93	18.39	17.71	17.88	17.42	17.79
2003	17.92	18.52	17.75	18.02	18.01	17.34	18.04	18.10	18.06	17.32	16.72	16.45	17.68
Retail trade													
2001	12.97	12.38	12.07	12.94	13.70	13.28	13.13	13.10	13.45	13.66	14.22	14.03	13.25
2002	13.94	14.07	14.36	14.58	14.93	14.96	14.60	14.47	14.46	14.44	14.08	14.03	14.41
2003	13.94	13.85	13.70	13.65	13.64	13.21	13.03	13.43	13.75	13.28	13.24	13.50	13.51
Transportation and utilities													
2001	16.86	17.16	17.30	17.32	17.07	17.90	17.95	18.04	18.32	18.29	18.87	18.93	17.85
2002	18.39	18.43	19.19	18.72	17.78	17.21	17.97	18.13	18.78	18.55	18.48	18.21	18.28
2003	18.29	18.44	18.28	18.37	18.54	17.65	19.69	19.97	19.03	19.42	19.93	19.46	18.94
Financial activities													
2001	18.28	18.45	18.43	18.86	19.02	19.37	19.26	18.47	21.76	19.89	22.47	20.86	19.57
2002	21.21	21.38	21.24	21.48	21.71	20.71	20.45	19.66	19.79	19.31	19.37	18.85	20.39
2003	18.28	18.35	18.31	18.53	18.20	18.22	18.64	20.52	19.84	19.61	21.37	20.85	19.22

Average Weekly Earnings by Industry: Alaska

(Dollars, not seasonally adjusted.)

Industry	January	February	March	April	May	June	July	August	September	October	November	December	Annual Average
STATEWIDE													
Natural resources and mining													
2001	1268.73	1241.22	1286.67	1324.80	1307.57	1345.73	1295.44	1311.74	1250.32	1329.06	1298.86	1261.30	1293.37
2002	1270.95	1324.45	1329.00	1356.00	1311.00	1369.17	1372.84	1345.04	1278.81	1124.60	1245.27	1212.63	1296.42
2003	1226.31	1300.37	1286.86	1325.34	1276.70	1296.87	1279.62	1265.58	1300.54	1257.86	1380.93	1199.48	1282.23
Construction													
2001	941.25	944.27	1035.65	998.98	1163.78	1206.77	1231.93	1316.78	1264.70	1193.20	926.65	953.81	1125.05
2002	948.48	1008.38	1025.83	999.23	1084.25	1128.82	1134.20	1179.64	1262.91	1115.70	1030.66	1115.97	1100.23
2003	1059.25	1068.13	1088.03	1188.80	1324.45	1276.05	1333.22	1368.91	1319.36	1270.20	1092.28	1083.12	1227.64
Manufacturing													
2001	477.36	535.06	540.28	416.08	430.72	459.10	508.68	567.03	494.61	505.89	511.39	553.26	504.27
2002	508.40	533.45	545.41	499.63	505.99	420.48	526.40	569.26	435.84	413.47	437.76	459.04	495.18
2003	321.48	564.10	445.74	466.34	539.00	505.38	612.85	571.52	527.14	478.35	513.38	538.98	520.45
Trade, transportation, and utilities													
2001	480.19	494.78	504.08	516.34	513.59	544.07	551.61	555.95	556.43	533.02	531.47	543.32	528.61
2002	506.68	526.51	541.70	525.52	522.61	572.80	545.94	553.15	568.63	540.62	527.05	525.50	539.20
2003	512.41	538.65	526.94	536.11	541.31	547.34	558.61	573.52	560.55	529.72	546.53	527.41	542.53
Wholesale trade													
2001	612.84	603.41	687.09	722.80	659.84	714.62	724.40	688.26	769.86	674.91	683.71	748.72	692.05
2002	642.98	677.03	699.18	734.16	730.24	761.18	694.75	710.03	746.63	671.21	684.80	663.70	702.71
2003	670.21	720.43	660.30	699.18	693.39	686.66	699.95	709.52	691.70	656.43	648.74	607.01	678.91
Retail trade													
2001	430.60	445.68	441.76	447.72	472.65	484.72	470.05	493.87	489.58	476.73	486.32	481.23	469.05
2002	461.41	479.79	488.24	465.10	477.76	490.69	478.88	483.30	481.52	467.86	461.82	455.98	474.09
2003	448.87	462.59	445.25	453.18	463.76	462.35	449.54	470.05	467.50	444.88	446.19	437.40	453.94
Transportation and utilities													
2001	527.72	550.84	563.98	575.02	541.12	597.86	635.43	620.58	610.06	590.77	573.65	600.08	583.70
2002	549.86	567.64	596.81	574.70	545.85	666.03	616.37	625.49	670.45	643.69	609.84	630.07	610.55
2003	592.60	634.34	647.11	644.79	637.78	661.88	706.87	710.93	688.89	656.40	723.46	686.94	668.58
Financial activities													
2001	654.42	645.75	652.42	671.42	679.01	674.08	689.51	657.53	739.84	706.10	759.49	698.81	686.91
2002	721.14	705.54	705.17	734.62	712.09	710.35	650.31	668.44	728.27	635.30	670.20	714.42	695.30
2003	647.11	697.30	704.94	681.90	671.58	696.00	659.86	771.55	730.11	741.26	767.18	721.41	707.30

ARIZONA AT A GLANCE

(Population and total nonfarm employment numbers in thousands)

Population, Census 2000:	5,130.6
Total nonfarm employment, 2003:	2,289.3
Change in total nonfarm employment	
(Number)	
1990–2003:	806.3
1990–2001:	782.0
2001–2003:	24.3
(Compound annual rate of change)	
1990–2003:	3.4%
1990–2001:	3.9%
2001–2003:	0.5%
Unemployment rate	
1990:	5.3%
2001:	4.7%
2003:	5.7%

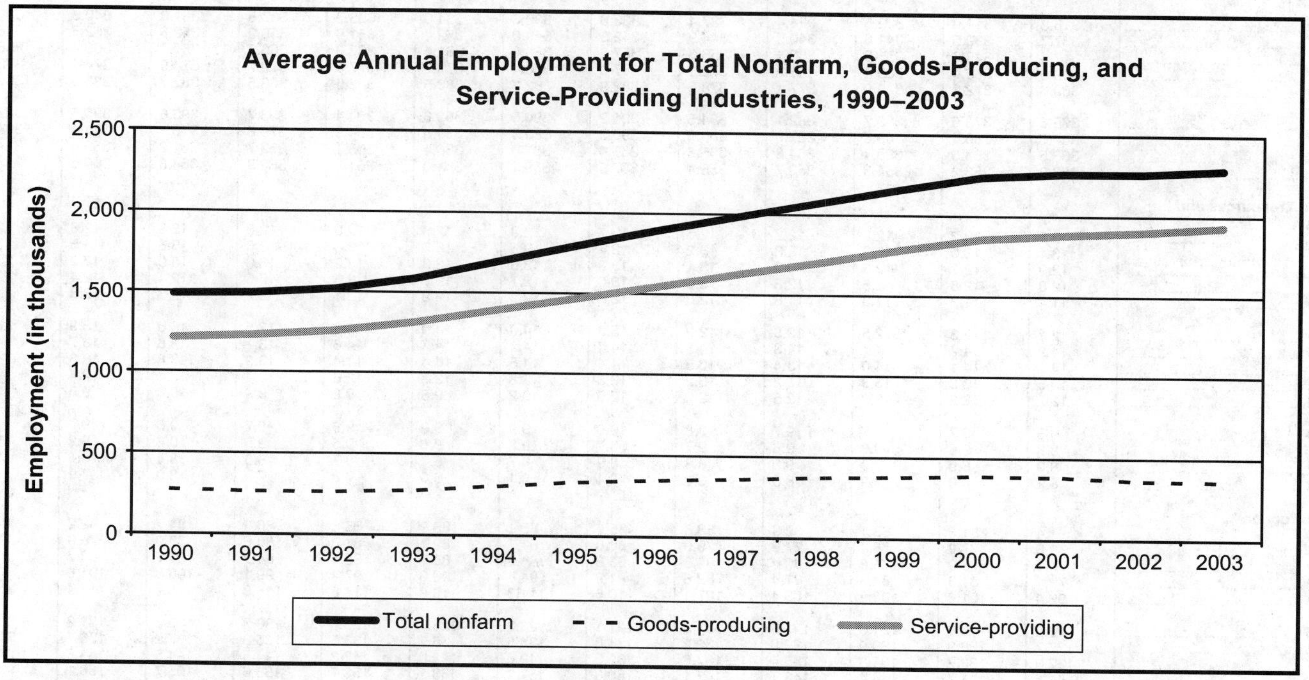

Total nonfarm payroll employment growth was sluggish in the early 1990s due to the 1990–1991 recession. However, it responded strongly to economic recovery through 2000, as Arizona's job growth outpaced the U.S. average. After 2000, employment growth slowed sharply, largely due to a decline in the number of manufacturing jobs. The service-providing sector also slowed considerably. However, by 2003 a recovery was apparent in a broad range of goods and services industries.

Employment by Industry: Arizona

(Numbers in thousands. Not seasonally adjusted.)

Industry	January	February	March	April	May	June	July	August	September	October	November	December	Annual Average
STATEWIDE													
Total nonfarm													
1990	1455.4	1476.6	1489.4	1494.8	1500.6	1470.6	1444.5	1454.6	1487.0	1499.2	1513.0	1511.4	1483.0
1991	1479.0	1493.7	1503.3	1497.5	1497.5	1473.7	1445.6	1458.1	1489.6	1508.3	1521.4	1527.2	1491.2
1992	1484.3	1501.8	1512.2	1522.0	1525.7	1500.7	1484.5	1494.3	1535.4	1538.3	1547.7	1558.3	1517.1
1993	1518.4	1547.7	1565.3	1583.3	1588.5	1567.1	1550.2	1560.1	1602.3	1627.4	1643.0	1659.8	1584.4
1994	1624.0	1652.3	1672.4	1684.8	1684.7	1672.1	1657.4	1680.6	1713.5	1732.6	1757.2	1772.7	1692.0
1995	1734.7	1769.5	1784.0	1785.4	1794.2	1779.7	1757.0	1773.7	1810.8	1834.0	1851.7	1869.2	1795.3
1996	1836.7	1871.4	1887.0	1874.8	1885.8	1870.2	1848.6	1877.3	1907.4	1924.9	1956.6	1966.5	1892.2
1997	1919.9	1955.1	1973.0	1975.1	1981.8	1960.9	1935.0	1955.8	1999.9	2029.1	2055.8	2073.5	1984.5
1998	2017.2	2045.7	2068.0	2070.1	2075.7	2054.2	2022.9	2051.7	2096.5	2111.6	2135.1	2147.8	2074.7
1999	2094.7	2128.7	2143.6	2162.2	2161.6	2148.3	2127.4	2142.7	2182.1	2204.2	2222.7	2238.5	2163.0
2000	2184.1	2220.3	2239.7	2240.3	2253.5	2224.9	2192.9	2218.5	2259.3	2274.6	2293.1	2311.5	2242.7
2001	2239.4	2275.4	2291.5	2287.0	2279.8	2251.8	2216.2	2243.8	2266.6	2269.7	2276.8	2281.5	2265.0
2002	2228.2	2251.8	2268.3	2279.9	2276.0	2250.9	2209.5	2245.4	2265.9	2282.2	2310.9	2311.9	2265.1
2003	2253.0	2279.4	2292.3	2290.6	2292.4	2262.9	2232.9	2265.6	2295.8	2319.5	2338.5	2348.9	2289.3
Total private													
1990	1206.1	1214.2	1224.1	1226.3	1228.3	1232.0	1215.8	1220.0	1224.3	1226.3	1236.7	1235.2	1224.1
1991	1216.0	1218.3	1223.4	1216.8	1217.3	1217.3	1206.2	1211.5	1214.1	1223.3	1234.7	1242.4	1220.1
1992	1211.3	1218.2	1226.9	1236.2	1240.9	1242.7	1239.3	1239.8	1248.0	1251.2	1259.1	1270.5	1240.3
1993	1240.3	1254.6	1269.6	1288.7	1294.1	1297.7	1292.7	1296.4	1311.9	1327.4	1340.7	1359.5	1297.8
1994	1336.7	1352.2	1370.3	1382.9	1385.7	1397.1	1391.8	1402.0	1413.3	1427.4	1447.5	1465.8	1397.7
1995	1431.1	1452.0	1467.2	1464.5	1473.3	1487.3	1474.6	1483.8	1495.3	1512.6	1529.9	1546.8	1484.8
1996	1522.8	1541.2	1555.1	1554.2	1565.9	1572.3	1564.9	1576.8	1585.4	1597.3	1620.9	1635.7	1574.3
1997	1604.9	1625.2	1640.4	1635.6	1642.2	1648.6	1642.4	1650.3	1664.6	1686.2	1708.3	1727.5	1656.3
1998	1679.2	1695.3	1714.7	1719.7	1726.2	1736.5	1729.3	1735.4	1744.6	1756.8	1770.8	1790.3	1733.2
1999	1748.5	1767.2	1781.2	1798.9	1803.1	1812.9	1805.3	1812.2	1819.8	1836.0	1852.3	1870.1	1808.9
2000	1825.5	1848.7	1863.0	1862.1	1870.4	1880.7	1860.5	1876.2	1886.5	1895.6	1913.0	1930.5	1876.0
2001	1873.9	1891.5	1906.4	1900.3	1896.2	1898.2	1875.5	1882.9	1879.2	1876.1	1880.1	1886.0	1887.2
2002	1845.9	1856.5	1871.6	1879.4	1881.3	1879.7	1859.0	1871.4	1869.2	1877.2	1898.5	1906.2	1874.7
2003	1864.2	1875.4	1888.5	1887.2	1890.6	1888.2	1881.5	1889.3	1897.3	1913.0	1931.3	1941.4	1895.7
Goods-producing													
1990	270.4	270.6	272.2	270.7	272.4	275.3	275.0	277.1	276.1	275.5	274.0	270.5	273.3
1991	266.4	263.0	263.1	261.1	261.9	263.4	264.9	266.6	264.5	264.9	264.6	263.4	263.9
1992	256.2	256.6	257.0	260.2	262.6	264.6	265.0	265.6	265.6	265.3	264.5	263.7	262.2
1993	258.5	260.5	264.8	267.8	271.0	273.7	276.6	279.0	280.6	283.6	285.1	288.3	274.1
1994	285.3	287.6	292.1	296.0	299.3	304.7	305.9	309.5	311.2	314.6	316.6	318.7	303.4
1995	315.3	319.0	322.5	324.4	327.4	333.6	330.6	334.0	335.7	337.5	337.8	340.8	329.8
1996	337.7	339.5	341.6	340.5	344.9	349.5	349.0	352.4	351.6	350.9	352.6	352.6	346.9
1997	347.4	349.9	351.9	350.1	353.3	357.8	360.0	361.4	363.3	366.7	367.4	369.4	358.2
1998	365.0	366.0	369.4	368.2	372.1	377.0	376.4	377.6	377.8	376.7	374.6	374.7	372.9
1999	369.6	372.2	373.9	377.1	378.5	382.9	382.7	383.5	382.5	383.5	382.7	383.6	379.3
2000	375.6	378.6	380.7	382.1	384.5	391.2	390.5	393.6	394.4	393.7	393.6	395.5	387.8
2001	384.7	386.4	389.8	387.9	388.6	390.5	389.3	389.6	384.9	379.8	375.1	371.4	384.8
2002	363.5	363.5	365.1	364.8	365.6	367.4	367.0	368.4	365.1	362.7	361.2	359.4	364.5
2003	353.9	353.2	354.5	353.7	355.4	357.6	359.1	361.0	361.2	362.7	364.8	366.5	358.6
Natural resources and mining													
1990	12.3	12.2	12.2	12.2	12.5	12.7	12.8	12.8	12.9	12.8	12.8	12.8	12.5
1991	13.1	13.0	12.8	12.8	13.2	13.4	13.5	13.5	13.4	13.6	13.6	13.5	13.2
1992	12.9	12.7	12.6	12.8	13.1	13.3	13.5	13.3	13.2	13.0	13.0	12.9	13.0
1993	12.8	12.6	12.5	12.8	13.0	13.0	12.7	12.7	12.5	12.5	12.4	12.4	12.6
1994	11.4	11.3	11.3	11.8	12.0	12.2	12.2	12.2	12.1	12.2	12.3	12.3	11.9
1995	12.1	12.3	12.5	12.8	12.9	13.2	14.0	14.0	13.9	13.5	13.6	13.9	13.2
1996	14.2	14.2	14.1	14.3	14.5	14.7	14.7	14.7	14.6	13.7	13.8	13.7	14.2
1997	14.0	14.1	14.0	13.4	13.5	14.4	14.5	14.4	14.4	13.9	13.8	13.8	14.0
1998	13.5	13.3	13.3	13.2	13.2	13.3	12.8	12.7	12.6	12.4	12.4	12.4	12.9
1999	12.2	12.2	12.2	12.5	12.6	12.6	10.2	9.8	9.8	9.9	10.0	9.6	11.1
2000	9.6	9.7	9.7	9.7	9.8	10.0	9.9	9.9	9.8	9.7	9.6	9.7	9.7
2001	9.6	9.6	9.6	9.6	9.7	9.7	9.6	9.6	9.5	9.5	9.4	9.2	9.6
2002	8.9	8.9	8.9	9.0	8.8	8.9	8.7	8.7	8.7	8.6	8.4	8.4	8.7
2003	8.2	8.0	7.9	8.0	8.0	8.1	8.1	8.0	7.9	7.9	8.0	7.9	8.0
Construction													
1990	81.4	81.6	83.1	82.9	83.8	85.6	85.1	86.9	86.8	86.0	84.7	82.2	84.1
1991	79.5	77.9	78.4	77.9	79.0	80.0	81.7	82.1	81.3	80.8	80.9	79.9	79.9
1992	76.5	76.9	78.6	80.4	82.6	83.8	84.9	85.7	85.4	84.9	84.7	83.7	82.3
1993	79.1	81.3	84.5	87.4	89.6	91.9	94.5	96.0	97.4	99.1	100.0	101.6	91.8
1994	99.4	101.2	103.9	105.4	107.4	110.6	111.3	113.2	114.5	115.8	116.7	117.4	109.7
1995	116.5	118.6	121.0	121.0	123.3	127.1	126.3	128.7	129.3	130.3	130.2	131.2	125.2
1996	127.7	128.9	129.9	129.2	132.2	134.8	134.8	136.9	136.5	136.9	137.2	136.7	133.4
1997	132.3	133.7	135.3	135.4	137.6	139.3	140.8	142.0	142.3	144.5	144.5	144.8	139.3
1998	141.3	141.7	144.4	143.7	147.1	150.3	151.7	153.1	153.7	155.6	155.7	156.1	149.5
1999	152.3	154.1	155.2	158.3	159.1	162.3	163.7	164.5	164.6	165.4	165.0	165.0	160.7
2000	159.6	161.2	162.9	164.3	166.7	170.3	169.9	171.9	172.5	172.9	172.1	173.4	168.1
2001	166.5	168.8	172.4	172.1	173.6	176.7	177.5	179.6	177.3	174.9	172.9	170.4	173.6
2002	167.0	167.4	169.7	170.1	172.0	174.0	174.1	176.6	174.8	174.3	173.9	172.4	172.2
2003	168.7	169.0	170.5	171.7	174.2	176.4	177.6	179.7	180.6	182.4	183.8	184.7	176.6

Employment by Industry: Arizona—*Continued*

(Numbers in thousands. Not seasonally adjusted.)

Industry	January	February	March	April	May	June	July	August	September	October	November	December	Annual Average
STATEWIDE—*Continued*													
Manufacturing													
1990	176.7	176.8	176.9	175.6	176.1	177.0	177.1	177.4	176.4	176.7	176.5	175.5	176.5
1991	173.8	172.1	171.9	170.4	169.7	170.0	169.7	171.0	169.8	170.5	170.1	170.0	170.7
1992	166.8	167.0	165.8	167.0	166.9	167.5	166.6	166.6	167.0	167.4	166.8	167.1	166.8
1993	166.6	166.6	167.8	167.6	168.4	168.8	169.4	170.3	170.7	172.0	172.7	174.3	169.6
1994	174.5	175.1	176.9	178.8	179.9	181.9	182.4	184.1	184.6	186.6	187.6	189.0	181.7
1995	186.7	188.1	189.0	190.6	191.2	193.3	190.3	191.3	192.5	193.7	194.0	195.7	191.3
1996	195.8	196.4	197.6	197.0	198.2	200.0	199.5	200.8	200.5	200.3	201.6	202.2	199.1
1997	201.1	202.1	202.6	201.3	202.2	204.1	204.7	205.0	206.6	208.3	209.1	210.8	204.8
1998	210.2	211.0	211.7	211.3	211.8	213.4	211.9	211.8	211.5	208.7	206.5	206.2	210.5
1999	205.1	205.9	206.5	206.3	206.8	208.0	208.8	209.2	208.1	208.2	207.7	209.0	207.4
2000	206.4	207.7	208.1	208.1	208.0	210.9	210.7	211.8	212.1	211.1	211.9	212.4	209.9
2001	208.6	208.0	207.8	206.2	205.3	204.1	202.2	200.4	198.1	195.4	192.8	191.8	201.7
2002	187.6	187.2	186.5	185.7	184.8	184.5	184.2	183.1	181.6	179.8	178.9	178.6	183.5
2003	177.0	176.2	176.1	174.0	173.2	173.1	173.4	173.3	172.7	172.4	173.0	173.9	174.0
Service-providing													
1990	1185.0	1206.0	1217.2	1224.1	1228.2	1195.3	1169.5	1177.5	1210.9	1223.7	1239.0	1240.9	1209.7
1991	1212.6	1230.7	1240.2	1236.4	1235.6	1210.3	1180.7	1191.5	1225.1	1243.4	1256.8	1263.8	1227.2
1992	1228.1	1245.2	1255.2	1261.8	1263.1	1236.1	1219.5	1228.7	1269.8	1273.0	1283.2	1294.6	1254.8
1993	1259.9	1287.2	1300.5	1315.5	1317.5	1293.4	1273.6	1281.1	1321.7	1343.8	1357.9	1371.5	1310.3
1994	1338.7	1364.7	1380.3	1388.8	1385.4	1367.4	1351.5	1371.1	1402.3	1418.0	1440.6	1454.0	1388.5
1995	1419.4	1450.5	1461.5	1461.0	1466.8	1446.1	1426.4	1439.7	1475.1	1496.5	1513.9	1528.4	1465.4
1996	1499.0	1531.9	1545.4	1534.3	1540.9	1520.7	1499.6	1524.9	1555.8	1574.0	1604.0	1613.9	1545.3
1997	1572.5	1605.2	1621.1	1625.0	1628.5	1603.1	1575.0	1594.4	1636.6	1662.4	1688.4	1704.1	1626.3
1998	1652.2	1679.7	1698.6	1701.9	1703.6	1677.2	1646.5	1674.1	1718.7	1734.9	1760.5	1773.1	1701.7
1999	1725.1	1756.5	1769.7	1785.1	1783.1	1765.4	1744.7	1759.2	1799.6	1820.7	1840.0	1854.9	1783.6
2000	1808.5	1841.7	1859.0	1858.2	1869.0	1833.7	1802.4	1824.9	1864.9	1880.9	1899.5	1916.0	1854.8
2001	1854.7	1889.0	1901.7	1899.1	1891.2	1861.3	1826.9	1854.2	1881.7	1889.9	1901.7	1910.1	1880.1
2002	1864.7	1888.3	1903.2	1915.1	1910.4	1883.5	1842.5	1877.0	1900.8	1919.5	1949.7	1952.5	1900.6
2003	1899.1	1926.2	1937.8	1936.9	1937.0	1905.3	1873.8	1904.6	1934.6	1956.8	1973.7	1982.4	1930.7
Trade, transportation, and utilities													
1990	315.5	314.4	316.1	314.1	315.6	315.7	310.3	311.4	314.0	314.6	322.5	325.0	315.7
1991	312.5	310.7	311.2	310.2	311.2	311.3	305.9	306.4	306.6	309.3	316.6	322.5	311.2
1992	312.1	310.0	310.6	309.8	310.8	309.5	308.5	308.3	309.9	310.8	317.1	322.4	311.6
1993	307.0	306.7	307.8	312.0	311.9	311.9	313.0	313.4	317.8	325.1	333.5	341.3	316.7
1994	330.9	330.6	333.5	334.6	336.5	338.7	340.6	342.3	345.3	348.6	358.8	367.1	342.2
1995	354.8	354.8	355.8	353.7	355.6	357.0	356.1	357.7	358.8	365.6	374.1	380.9	360.4
1996	370.2	369.2	369.7	370.6	373.0	372.8	371.4	373.8	374.7	381.3	393.9	401.4	376.8
1997	386.7	385.6	387.7	386.8	388.5	389.1	387.8	388.9	391.5	397.9	410.0	418.4	393.2
1998	401.0	400.7	402.4	402.5	402.9	404.6	402.2	404.6	408.3	413.4	422.2	431.5	408.0
1999	415.2	414.5	416.1	418.4	418.4	419.2	419.9	421.0	422.2	429.9	440.3	450.4	423.7
2000	432.5	433.1	432.2	429.5	430.5	433.6	430.6	433.7	436.4	442.2	455.7	464.0	437.8
2001	444.1	441.9	440.9	439.7	438.4	438.5	434.8	434.9	434.7	439.1	447.2	452.5	440.6
2002	437.2	434.0	436.7	437.4	439.1	439.9	435.3	436.8	438.1	442.1	452.9	460.9	440.9
2003	442.6	441.7	442.7	440.2	440.6	440.0	438.0	439.4	440.8	447.3	458.7	464.5	444.7
Wholesale trade													
1990	63.2	63.6	63.8	62.9	63.4	63.5	62.3	62.2	61.9	61.8	62.1	62.1	62.7
1991	60.1	59.9	60.1	59.0	59.1	59.3	58.7	58.4	58.3	59.2	59.9	60.5	59.3
1992	59.6	59.9	60.4	60.1	60.2	60.0	60.1	59.7	60.0	59.8	60.7	61.0	60.1
1993	60.1	60.6	61.3	61.1	61.0	61.1	60.8	60.5	60.8	61.6	62.9	63.7	61.2
1994	63.9	64.4	65.1	65.4	65.5	65.9	65.6	66.2	67.1	68.1	69.2	70.0	66.3
1995	70.7	71.9	72.7	72.3	72.9	73.3	72.8	72.9	73.6	74.5	75.0	76.3	73.2
1996	76.1	77.6	78.5	78.6	79.5	79.5	79.0	79.0	79.5	80.1	81.5	82.7	79.3
1997	81.9	83.2	84.0	83.7	84.0	84.6	83.8	83.9	84.5	85.3	86.9	87.9	84.4
1998	86.6	87.6	88.4	89.1	88.4	89.0	88.1	88.1	89.0	88.9	89.7	90.7	88.6
1999	89.9	90.9	91.4	91.4	91.0	91.1	91.0	91.1	91.3	92.5	93.1	95.6	91.6
2000	94.4	95.3	95.8	93.6	93.7	94.3	93.9	93.9	94.4	95.4	97.1	98.7	95.0
2001	97.6	98.3	98.5	97.3	96.3	95.8	94.8	94.6	94.0	94.0	94.3	95.2	95.9
2002	94.2	94.4	95.0	93.5	94.3	94.0	93.4	93.4	93.3	94.0	94.6	95.4	94.1
2003	94.3	94.6	94.4	92.9	93.1	92.6	91.8	91.8	91.8	92.5	93.2	94.0	93.1
Retail trade													
1990	196.4	194.6	195.5	195.2	195.9	195.9	192.2	193.2	195.5	196.0	203.5	206.0	196.6
1991	194.5	192.8	193.2	192.4	192.8	192.3	187.3	188.4	189.4	192.2	198.3	202.9	193.0
1992	193.5	191.0	190.6	189.6	190.2	189.0	188.6	188.9	190.8	191.6	197.3	202.5	191.9
1993	193.8	192.3	192.3	195.4	194.3	193.6	195.4	196.0	199.2	203.7	210.4	216.6	198.5
1994	208.0	206.7	208.0	209.0	209.9	211.4	214.0	214.7	216.8	219.3	228.3	235.4	215.1
1995	223.8	222.4	222.6	220.7	221.5	222.1	221.2	222.7	223.3	226.8	234.4	240.1	225.1
1996	230.6	227.7	227.2	228.5	229.6	228.9	227.8	229.4	229.8	233.8	244.7	250.6	232.3
1997	239.4	236.8	237.5	237.3	237.9	237.6	236.9	237.8	239.1	244.0	253.7	260.7	241.5
1998	246.5	245.0	245.6	244.1	244.9	245.2	244.1	245.7	247.9	253.0	260.6	268.3	249.2
1999	254.9	252.6	253.1	254.8	254.6	254.5	254.7	255.8	257.3	261.1	270.8	278.2	258.5
2000	264.3	264.2	263.5	263.2	263.9	265.7	262.8	265.2	267.1	271.4	282.3	288.4	268.5
2001	270.0	266.8	265.7	265.6	264.7	265.1	262.9	263.3	264.2	269.0	277.4	282.4	268.1
2002	268.9	265.6	267.0	268.6	269.2	269.4	265.8	266.8	268.4	270.6	280.7	287.8	270.7
2003	271.5	270.3	271.4	270.8	271.1	271.3	270.3	271.6	273.0	277.6	288.4	293.6	275.1

Employment by Industry: Arizona—*Continued*

(Numbers in thousands. Not seasonally adjusted.)

Industry	January	February	March	April	May	June	July	August	September	October	November	December	Annual Average
STATEWIDE—*Continued*													
Transportation and utilities													
1990	55.9	56.2	56.8	56.0	56.3	56.3	55.8	56.0	56.6	56.8	56.9	56.9	56.3
1991	57.9	58.0	57.9	58.8	59.3	59.7	59.9	59.6	58.9	57.9	58.4	59.1	58.7
1992	59.0	59.1	59.6	60.1	60.4	60.5	59.8	59.7	59.1	59.4	59.1	58.9	59.5
1993	53.1	53.8	54.2	55.5	56.6	57.2	56.8	56.9	57.8	59.8	60.2	61.0	56.9
1994	59.0	59.5	60.4	60.2	61.1	61.4	61.0	61.4	61.4	61.2	61.3	61.7	60.8
1995	60.3	60.5	60.5	60.7	61.2	61.6	62.1	62.1	61.9	64.3	64.7	64.5	62.0
1996	63.5	63.9	64.0	63.5	63.9	64.4	64.6	65.4	65.4	67.4	67.7	68.1	65.1
1997	65.4	65.6	66.2	65.8	66.6	66.9	67.1	67.2	67.9	68.6	69.4	69.8	67.2
1998	67.9	68.1	68.4	69.3	69.6	70.4	70.0	70.8	71.4	71.5	71.9	72.5	70.1
1999	70.4	71.0	71.6	72.2	72.8	73.6	74.2	74.1	73.6	76.3	76.4	76.6	73.5
2000	73.8	73.6	72.9	72.7	72.9	73.6	73.9	74.6	74.9	75.4	76.3	76.9	74.2
2001	76.5	76.8	76.7	76.8	77.4	77.6	77.1	77.0	76.5	76.1	75.5	74.9	76.6
2002	74.1	74.0	74.7	75.3	75.6	76.5	76.1	76.6	76.4	77.5	77.6	77.7	76.0
2003	76.8	76.8	76.9	76.5	76.4	76.1	75.9	76.0	76.0	77.2	77.1	76.9	76.6
Information													
1990	32.3	32.6	32.3	33.1	33.3	33.7	33.4	33.2	32.9	32.4	32.7	32.6	32.8
1991	31.8	31.8	32.0	31.0	30.9	31.2	31.5	31.2	31.0	30.7	30.7	31.0	31.2
1992	30.0	30.0	30.2	30.0	30.3	30.5	29.9	29.8	29.8	29.5	29.8	30.2	30.0
1993	29.9	30.2	30.5	30.1	30.1	30.7	31.1	31.2	30.9	30.7	30.9	31.3	30.6
1994	30.7	30.8	31.2	31.3	31.8	32.2	32.3	32.5	32.7	33.4	34.0	34.3	32.2
1995	34.2	35.2	35.3	34.9	35.6	36.2	35.3	35.6	35.8	35.9	36.7	36.7	35.6
1996	36.3	36.4	36.6	36.7	37.6	37.9	38.6	38.9	38.8	39.1	39.5	40.3	38.0
1997	40.4	41.0	41.0	40.7	40.8	41.0	41.1	41.3	41.3	41.6	42.3	42.8	41.2
1998	42.4	42.8	43.1	42.8	43.2	43.5	43.5	43.8	43.6	43.5	44.2	45.1	43.4
1999	44.7	45.9	45.6	46.2	47.2	47.2	47.4	48.0	47.8	47.7	49.0	48.8	47.1
2000	51.6	52.6	54.8	55.1	55.6	55.6	55.1	55.1	54.5	53.6	54.1	54.6	54.3
2001	53.7	54.9	54.4	54.4	53.8	54.2	53.7	53.8	53.2	53.0	54.0	53.2	53.9
2002	53.2	53.2	52.7	52.7	52.3	51.7	51.6	51.4	50.6	49.9	50.7	50.8	51.7
2003	49.6	49.9	50.1	50.0	49.8	49.9	49.5	48.9	48.6	48.6	48.8	48.8	49.4
Financial activities													
1990	97.5	98.0	98.7	99.3	99.3	99.3	99.2	99.5	98.6	98.1	98.0	97.5	98.5
1991	97.1	97.8	97.6	95.6	95.8	95.9	96.8	97.2	96.3	97.3	97.4	97.8	96.8
1992	92.3	92.7	93.3	93.4	94.2	94.3	96.2	95.8	96.2	96.9	97.6	98.7	95.1
1993	97.6	98.5	99.6	101.1	101.6	102.2	102.3	102.4	103.0	103.5	104.3	105.9	101.8
1994	106.4	107.3	108.1	108.4	108.9	109.7	108.5	108.6	108.5	108.2	108.5	109.3	108.3
1995	106.2	106.9	107.7	108.0	107.7	108.7	109.1	109.4	110.1	112.0	112.5	114.1	109.3
1996	114.5	115.5	116.3	116.3	116.9	118.3	119.9	121.1	121.1	122.3	123.5	125.3	119.2
1997	125.9	127.7	129.6	130.0	130.2	130.7	132.2	132.5	133.4	135.5	137.0	139.4	132.0
1998	135.2	135.9	137.6	140.3	140.8	141.3	143.6	144.1	144.2	145.3	146.4	148.1	141.9
1999	142.9	143.9	144.4	145.7	146.2	147.4	148.6	148.9	149.1	150.0	150.8	151.9	147.4
2000	147.2	149.9	149.9	149.2	150.1	151.6	150.5	151.4	152.0	152.7	153.0	154.4	150.9
2001	149.2	150.8	152.3	152.4	152.8	153.5	154.4	154.6	154.7	154.6	155.3	156.3	153.4
2002	153.2	154.7	154.2	155.2	154.6	154.5	154.2	154.4	154.5	155.7	157.7	158.6	155.1
2003	156.5	157.4	158.9	158.1	159.0	159.3	159.8	159.8	159.9	160.2	161.2	161.1	159.3
Professional and business services													
1990	138.4	139.8	142.6	143.3	142.2	144.2	144.3	144.7	144.0	142.4	142.3	142.9	142.5
1991	144.0	145.8	146.8	147.8	146.9	148.1	145.2	147.9	148.2	149.0	150.1	151.6	147.6
1992	151.1	153.6	157.0	160.0	160.6	162.4	161.9	162.5	164.3	164.5	164.6	167.8	160.8
1993	161.5	165.4	168.9	173.7	174.8	177.2	173.4	174.6	176.1	177.9	178.7	183.1	173.7
1994	178.2	182.6	185.9	190.9	189.3	193.5	192.7	195.4	196.6	198.6	202.1	206.5	192.6
1995	203.6	210.2	213.8	214.0	215.5	220.1	217.4	219.8	221.4	226.0	229.3	232.8	218.6
1996	229.3	236.4	239.8	238.8	242.8	247.7	245.8	248.1	249.8	251.6	254.3	256.8	245.1
1997	246.9	254.6	257.9	260.1	262.5	267.2	267.0	270.7	272.3	274.8	277.2	281.0	266.0
1998	266.5	271.6	276.9	278.8	279.4	284.7	285.8	287.1	288.0	289.6	292.5	296.4	283.1
1999	288.7	295.1	299.7	304.3	305.4	309.6	309.1	311.4	312.6	313.4	315.7	319.0	307.0
2000	309.5	316.1	321.9	324.6	328.2	329.2	325.4	329.8	330.6	331.6	332.5	335.2	326.2
2001	319.1	324.5	328.7	326.4	324.1	324.7	318.1	318.4	317.3	314.5	310.6	312.2	319.9
2002	303.6	307.7	313.1	316.9	315.9	316.7	313.7	317.2	315.5	314.8	317.2	317.2	314.1
2003	308.8	313.2	317.3	318.1	319.0	319.8	320.7	321.4	324.4	326.2	324.6	326.1	320.0
Educational and health services													
1990	132.1	133.8	134.8	135.5	135.6	135.9	133.3	133.3	135.4	137.1	138.3	138.4	135.2
1991	139.3	140.7	141.4	141.2	141.2	141.6	140.8	141.1	143.4	145.4	146.9	147.2	142.5
1992	144.7	145.9	146.7	148.5	148.8	148.7	149.2	149.0	151.2	152.1	152.6	154.2	149.3
1993	152.8	155.2	155.1	156.2	156.5	156.3	155.7	155.4	158.9	159.6	161.1	161.8	157.0
1994	158.5	160.8	161.8	161.7	161.8	162.4	160.3	161.4	164.1	165.7	167.4	168.5	162.8
1995	164.6	166.8	168.1	167.5	168.4	169.6	167.7	168.1	171.9	172.8	174.2	175.8	169.6
1996	173.3	176.2	178.6	177.8	178.8	178.3	178.2	180.3	183.8	185.0	187.4	188.4	180.5
1997	187.7	190.3	191.7	190.8	190.3	190.1	186.3	187.4	191.3	192.8	194.6	195.7	190.7
1998	193.3	196.4	198.1	197.6	197.3	197.2	196.2	197.2	200.3	202.7	204.2	205.3	198.8
1999	202.2	204.5	205.6	206.2	206.3	206.0	204.2	205.8	209.2	210.9	212.4	213.2	207.2
2000	208.7	211.4	212.1	211.1	211.3	210.6	208.1	211.2	213.7	214.8	215.8	217.7	212.2
2001	214.5	216.8	218.6	218.5	218.2	218.5	215.3	220.1	221.8	223.5	225.3	227.6	219.9
2002	227.3	229.4	230.7	230.0	231.6	231.0	226.9	232.0	233.9	237.5	239.9	240.7	232.6
2003	239.8	242.5	243.1	243.8	244.5	243.9	243.3	247.3	249.1	251.5	253.1	253.6	246.3

Employment by Industry: Arizona—*Continued*

(Numbers in thousands. Not seasonally adjusted.)

Industry	January	February	March	April	May	June	July	August	September	October	November	December	Annual Average
STATEWIDE—*Continued*													
Leisure and hospitality													
1990	156.7	161.2	163.3	163.6	163.0	160.7	154.0	154.3	156.9	158.0	160.6	159.8	159.3
1991	158.5	161.8	164.3	163.2	162.9	158.8	155.2	155.7	158.9	160.6	162.2	162.6	160.3
1992	159.7	164.0	166.2	168.4	167.3	165.7	161.2	161.7	163.8	165.6	166.2	166.7	164.7
1993	166.3	170.4	174.2	178.5	179.0	176.3	171.5	172.1	176.3	179.1	179.6	180.2	175.2
1994	179.7	185.2	189.9	190.5	188.6	185.6	180.7	181.7	184.2	187.5	189.0	189.8	186.0
1995	189.4	195.2	199.7	198.2	199.2	197.2	193.5	194.2	196.9	196.5	198.6	198.5	196.4
1996	198.5	204.3	208.3	209.2	207.3	203.0	197.4	198.1	201.8	202.8	205.4	206.6	203.5
1997	206.2	211.6	215.8	213.1	212.2	207.9	203.1	203.8	207.0	212.1	214.9	215.8	210.2
1998	211.1	216.3	220.7	222.2	222.3	218.8	212.5	212.5	213.8	216.5	217.3	218.9	216.9
1999	215.1	219.8	223.8	228.4	227.8	226.0	218.7	219.3	221.7	224.6	225.6	226.9	223.1
2000	224.1	229.3	233.2	233.2	232.4	230.1	222.6	224.1	227.6	229.4	230.3	230.6	228.9
2001	226.7	232.8	236.9	236.9	235.4	231.7	224.4	225.6	226.5	227.4	227.9	228.0	230.0
2002	223.0	228.4	232.5	235.7	235.2	230.8	224.3	225.1	225.3	228.3	232.6	232.2	229.5
2003	228.0	232.2	235.8	237.1	235.7	231.0	225.8	225.9	227.5	230.7	234.1	234.6	231.5
Other services													
1990	63.2	63.8	64.1	66.7	66.9	67.2	66.3	66.5	66.4	68.2	68.3	68.5	66.3
1991	66.4	66.7	67.0	66.7	66.5	67.0	65.9	65.4	65.2	66.1	66.2	66.3	66.2
1992	65.2	65.4	65.9	65.9	66.3	67.0	67.4	67.1	67.2	66.5	66.7	66.8	66.4
1993	66.7	67.7	68.7	69.3	69.2	69.4	69.1	68.3	68.3	67.9	67.5	67.6	68.3
1994	67.0	67.3	67.8	69.5	69.5	70.3	70.8	70.6	70.7	70.8	71.1	71.6	69.7
1995	63.0	63.9	64.3	63.8	63.9	64.9	64.9	65.0	64.7	66.3	66.7	67.2	64.8
1996	63.0	63.7	64.2	64.3	64.6	64.8	64.6	64.1	63.8	64.3	64.3	64.3	64.1
1997	63.7	64.5	64.8	64.0	64.4	64.8	64.9	64.3	64.5	64.8	64.9	65.0	64.5
1998	64.7	65.6	66.5	67.3	68.2	69.4	69.1	68.5	68.6	69.1	69.4	70.3	68.0
1999	70.1	71.3	72.1	72.6	73.3	74.6	74.7	74.3	74.7	76.0	75.8	76.3	73.8
2000	76.3	77.7	78.2	77.3	77.8	78.8	77.7	77.3	77.3	77.6	78.0	78.5	77.7
2001	81.9	83.4	84.8	84.1	84.9	86.6	85.5	85.9	86.1	84.2	84.7	84.8	84.7
2002	84.9	85.6	86.6	86.7	87.0	87.7	86.0	86.1	86.2	86.2	86.3	86.4	86.3
2003	85.0	85.3	86.1	86.2	86.6	86.7	85.3	85.6	85.8	85.8	86.0	86.2	85.9
Government													
1990	249.3	262.4	265.3	268.5	272.3	238.6	228.7	234.6	262.7	272.9	276.3	276.2	258.9
1991	263.0	275.4	279.9	280.7	280.2	256.4	239.4	246.6	275.5	285.0	286.7	284.8	271.1
1992	273.0	283.6	285.3	285.8	284.8	258.0	245.2	254.5	287.4	287.1	288.6	287.8	276.7
1993	278.1	293.1	295.7	294.6	294.4	269.4	257.5	263.7	290.4	300.0	302.3	300.3	286.6
1994	287.3	300.1	302.1	301.9	299.0	275.0	265.6	278.6	300.2	305.2	309.7	306.9	294.3
1995	303.6	317.5	316.8	320.9	320.9	292.4	282.4	289.9	315.5	321.4	321.8	322.4	310.4
1996	313.9	330.2	331.9	320.6	319.9	297.9	283.7	300.5	322.0	327.6	335.7	330.8	317.8
1997	315.0	329.9	332.6	339.5	339.6	312.3	292.6	305.5	335.3	342.9	347.5	346.0	328.2
1998	338.0	350.4	353.3	350.4	349.5	317.7	293.6	316.3	351.9	354.8	364.3	357.5	341.4
1999	346.2	361.5	362.4	363.3	358.5	335.4	322.1	330.5	362.3	368.2	370.4	368.4	354.1
2000	358.6	371.6	376.7	378.2	383.1	344.2	332.4	342.3	372.8	379.0	380.1	381.0	366.6
2001	365.5	383.9	385.1	386.7	383.6	353.6	340.7	360.9	387.4	393.6	396.7	395.5	377.8
2002	382.3	395.3	396.7	400.5	394.7	371.2	350.5	374.0	396.7	405.0	412.4	405.7	390.4
2003	388.8	404.0	403.8	403.4	401.8	374.7	351.4	376.3	398.5	406.5	407.2	407.5	393.7
Federal government													
1990	45.1	44.9	45.8	47.4	50.1	47.1	47.0	46.3	45.2	44.6	44.1	44.6	46.0
1991	44.1	44.1	44.2	45.1	45.7	45.2	44.7	45.9	46.0	45.7	45.5	45.7	45.1
1992	45.3	45.2	45.1	45.3	45.7	44.9	44.6	46.0	46.1	45.8	45.6	45.5	45.4
1993	45.2	44.9	48.8	45.2	45.5	44.2	44.1	45.1	45.5	45.3	44.8	45.2	45.3
1994	44.4	44.3	43.8	44.7	45.2	43.9	43.7	44.7	45.0	44.9	44.6	44.9	44.5
1995	43.5	43.4	42.9	43.9	44.7	43.5	43.0	44.0	44.1	43.7	43.5	44.0	43.6
1996	44.8	44.8	45.1	43.7	44.0	42.9	42.4	43.5	43.8	43.3	43.1	43.8	43.7
1997	43.2	43.1	43.2	43.7	44.1	43.1	43.1	44.1	44.4	44.1	44.2	44.0	43.6
1998	43.9	43.4	43.5	44.0	44.7	43.8	44.6	44.9	45.0	44.7	44.6	45.9	44.4
1999	47.0	47.1	46.4	47.6	47.3	47.0	46.4	47.4	47.5	47.2	46.9	47.3	47.0
2000	46.3	46.6	49.8	50.1	56.8	48.6	49.2	47.6	47.4	47.1	47.1	48.3	48.7
2001	47.1	47.0	47.4	47.5	48.4	49.0	48.4	48.9	49.0	48.6	48.5	49.6	48.3
2002	48.1	47.8	48.2	48.3	48.9	49.7	49.0	49.5	49.4	49.9	50.1	51.4	49.2
2003	49.8	49.9	50.1	50.1	50.7	51.4	50.9	51.3	51.4	51.0	50.8	51.8	50.8
State government													
1994	69.0	73.4	74.6	74.5	72.5	70.0	68.8	69.6	74.9	76.4	78.3	77.9	73.3
1995	72.7	76.2	77.2	77.4	77.1	70.6	68.8	67.6	75.6	77.0	77.2	76.8	74.5
1996	74.1	79.0	78.8	73.7	73.7	72.0	70.3	70.8	75.9	80.3	77.9	79.9	75.5
1997	76.1	79.5	80.1	81.7	81.4	76.0	66.4	69.4	76.2	80.6	82.4	81.6	77.6
1998	78.5	81.7	82.7	82.8	80.0	75.9	68.5	71.4	77.7	84.6	86.4	84.5	79.5
1999	81.6	85.8	86.2	86.2	82.3	80.3	73.1	76.4	83.7	89.0	88.9	86.7	83.3
2000	85.1	88.9	89.7	90.0	88.4	83.8	79.5	79.1	88.6	91.3	90.3	89.6	87.0
2001	87.3	90.2	90.0	90.5	88.8	85.2	79.4	80.6	89.8	92.7	93.0	90.8	88.2
2002	89.1	92.2	91.8	92.2	90.8	86.0	82.5	80.3	87.6	91.4	90.4	89.9	88.7
2003	86.0	89.3	89.2	89.2	88.3	83.4	77.9	78.9	86.9	90.7	89.7	89.5	86.6

Employment by Industry: Arizona—*Continued*

(Numbers in thousands. Not seasonally adjusted.)

Industry	January	February	March	April	May	June	July	August	September	October	November	December	Annual Average
STATEWIDE—*Continued*													
Local government													
1994	173.9	182.4	183.7	182.7	181.3	161.1	153.1	164.3	180.3	183.9	186.8	184.1	176.4
1995	187.4	197.9	196.7	199.6	199.1	178.3	170.6	178.3	195.8	200.7	201.1	201.6	192.2
1996	195.0	206.4	208.0	203.2	202.2	183.0	171.0	186.2	202.3	204.0	214.7	207.1	198.5
1997	195.7	207.4	209.4	214.2	214.1	193.2	183.1	192.1	214.7	218.3	220.9	220.5	206.9
1998	215.6	225.3	227.1	223.6	224.8	198.0	180.5	200.0	229.2	225.5	233.3	227.1	217.5
1999	217.6	228.6	229.8	229.5	228.9	208.1	202.6	206.7	231.1	232.0	234.6	234.4	223.6
2000	227.2	236.1	237.2	238.1	237.9	211.8	203.7	215.6	236.8	240.6	242.7	243.1	230.9
2001	231.1	246.7	247.7	248.7	246.4	219.4	212.9	231.4	248.6	252.3	255.2	255.1	241.3
2002	245.1	255.3	256.7	260.0	255.0	235.5	219.0	244.2	259.7	263.7	271.9	264.4	252.5
2003	253.0	264.8	264.5	264.1	262.8	239.9	222.6	246.1	260.2	264.8	266.7	266.2	256.3
PHOENIX													
Total nonfarm													
1990	991.7	1004.6	1012.4	1020.3	1023.9	1012.2	991.5	994.3	1016.3	1023.0	1034.3	1032.3	1013.0
1991	1008.7	1017.0	1021.6	1012.2	1010.9	999.0	982.3	984.7	1001.6	1015.0	1025.2	1030.5	1009.0
1992	1001.3	1011.2	1017.7	1022.1	1024.2	1015.4	1002.1	1005.7	1030.2	1033.6	1040.4	1048.1	1021.0
1993	1019.1	1038.1	1050.4	1063.9	1066.0	1069.1	1063.6	1061.2	1081.7	1099.4	1112.4	1124.7	1070.8
1994	1092.2	1112.5	1124.5	1131.8	1132.8	1135.2	1125.9	1134.7	1154.0	1169.8	1189.1	1201.0	1141.9
1995	1176.8	1201.0	1212.1	1213.1	1220.2	1212.9	1196.2	1206.1	1237.0	1259.8	1274.1	1288.4	1224.8
1996	1274.2	1294.1	1304.1	1295.2	1303.4	1296.0	1284.4	1298.6	1324.6	1338.3	1365.3	1371.7	1312.4
1997	1339.3	1363.8	1375.1	1374.5	1379.7	1366.1	1352.3	1360.8	1391.7	1411.4	1433.4	1448.0	1383.0
1998	1412.5	1432.6	1447.7	1449.7	1456.4	1443.8	1427.9	1443.3	1477.5	1485.7	1505.5	1514.9	1458.1
1999	1479.5	1502.9	1512.6	1522.5	1522.5	1513.9	1504.6	1513.0	1537.3	1549.8	1564.0	1576.9	1524.9
2000	1534.7	1558.7	1570.7	1573.5	1583.7	1564.7	1545.5	1565.2	1592.7	1603.1	1616.9	1631.9	1578.4
2001	1582.2	1606.8	1617.8	1611.9	1607.7	1589.3	1566.4	1583.9	1597.4	1600.4	1602.3	1606.0	1597.7
2002	1566.5	1581.4	1592.8	1605.7	1601.5	1589.6	1562.0	1585.3	1596.9	1608.3	1632.1	1631.3	1596.1
2003	1587.2	1606.3	1614.7	1615.6	1617.6	1599.4	1580.8	1602.5	1621.3	1639.3	1653.7	1662.2	1616.7
Total private													
1990	855.3	860.4	866.7	872.4	873.0	874.8	862.4	865.0	869.2	871.7	880.9	879.6	869.2
1991	861.4	863.1	867.4	857.5	856.4	854.6	846.1	848.3	851.3	858.0	866.9	873.1	858.6
1992	850.5	855.7	861.1	865.9	868.4	870.4	865.7	865.7	872.4	876.5	882.9	891.5	868.8
1993	866.8	878.0	889.4	902.8	905.1	909.2	907.6	910.2	922.4	934.6	945.7	959.7	910.9
1994	934.5	948.5	959.8	968.9	970.1	977.2	975.0	982.5	992.8	1004.7	1021.6	1035.3	980.9
1995	1015.9	1031.1	1041.8	1041.3	1048.3	1058.2	1048.5	1056.9	1066.8	1086.6	1100.3	1114.5	1059.1
1996	1104.6	1118.5	1127.1	1123.5	1131.7	1136.7	1134.3	1143.4	1151.7	1161.2	1181.5	1194.6	1142.4
1997	1172.0	1187.1	1197.5	1197.2	1201.9	1206.4	1198.5	1204.9	1216.3	1232.1	1251.6	1267.4	1211.0
1998	1233.8	1246.2	1260.3	1263.2	1267.7	1274.1	1272.4	1276.9	1284.7	1295.9	1308.0	1322.4	1275.4
1999	1295.8	1310.2	1319.3	1328.6	1330.2	1337.3	1332.1	1337.4	1342.6	1352.1	1365.3	1376.8	1335.6
2000	1342.4	1359.2	1370.4	1372.2	1378.0	1384.7	1371.4	1383.6	1392.1	1399.5	1412.7	1426.3	1382.7
2001	1387.3	1400.4	1410.8	1404.4	1401.2	1402.9	1383.8	1389.2	1387.4	1385.8	1386.8	1391.1	1394.3
2002	1359.3	1366.7	1377.6	1388.3	1389.0	1389.5	1373.2	1381.7	1379.7	1385.5	1402.9	1408.0	1383.5
2003	1375.4	1384.3	1392.7	1393.4	1396.2	1393.5	1389.5	1395.1	1401.0	1413.3	1427.0	1434.6	1399.7
Goods-producing													
1990	195.5	195.7	196.7	196.7	197.6	199.7	199.1	200.2	199.7	199.4	198.2	195.7	197.8
1991	193.2	190.4	190.5	187.9	188.0	188.1	189.4	190.5	189.6	190.3	190.5	189.8	189.8
1992	184.6	184.8	184.9	187.5	189.2	191.1	190.5	191.4	191.8	192.1	191.5	191.5	189.2
1993	187.0	188.5	191.6	194.2	196.0	198.1	201.6	202.9	204.2	206.3	207.2	209.6	198.9
1994	205.0	207.1	210.0	212.5	214.6	218.3	219.7	222.6	224.5	226.9	229.0	230.6	218.4
1995	228.5	231.2	233.5	235.6	238.3	242.9	241.2	244.4	246.0	247.8	247.9	251.0	240.6
1996	249.6	251.1	252.6	251.3	254.1	257.3	257.2	259.8	260.1	258.2	260.1	260.6	256.0
1997	257.8	259.6	260.9	260.3	263.0	266.6	267.6	269.6	271.0	273.5	275.2	276.9	266.8
1998	275.1	276.6	278.7	277.5	279.8	283.4	283.8	284.1	284.4	283.2	281.9	281.9	280.8
1999	277.9	279.5	280.6	283.0	283.2	285.8	284.9	285.9	284.6	284.4	283.9	284.4	283.1
2000	278.8	281.3	283.0	282.9	284.8	288.9	288.4	290.1	290.8	290.8	290.6	291.5	286.8
2001	285.3	286.7	288.3	287.1	287.3	288.3	287.2	287.3	283.5	278.6	274.4	271.4	283.8
2002	265.8	265.5	266.3	266.6	267.1	268.6	268.3	268.7	266.1	263.6	262.5	260.8	265.8
2003	257.3	256.9	257.1	257.3	258.9	260.4	261.4	263.6	263.6	265.2	267.1	268.3	261.4
Natural resources and mining													
1990	4.5	4.5	4.5	4.5	4.5	4.5	4.5	4.5	4.6	4.5	4.5	4.5	4.5
1991	5.1	5.1	5.1	4.8	5.0	5.0	5.1	5.1	5.0	5.1	5.1	5.1	5.0
1992	4.1	4.2	4.2	4.3	4.3	4.4	4.3	4.3	4.3	4.2	4.1	4.1	4.2
1993	4.2	4.2	4.2	4.3	4.3	4.2	4.2	4.2	4.2	4.2	4.1	4.2	4.2
1994	3.7	3.6	3.7	4.0	4.0	4.0	4.1	4.1	4.1	4.2	4.2	4.2	3.9
1995	4.7	4.7	5.0	5.0	5.1	5.1	5.8	5.8	5.8	5.5	5.6	5.9	5.3
1996	6.3	6.3	6.3	6.4	6.4	6.4	6.5	6.5	6.4	5.5	5.5	5.5	6.1
1997	6.1	6.1	6.1	5.4	5.4	6.1	6.2	6.1	6.1	5.6	5.6	5.6	5.8
1998	5.6	5.5	5.5	5.3	5.4	5.3	4.9	4.8	4.8	4.7	4.7	4.8	5.1
1999	4.7	4.7	4.7	4.9	4.9	4.9	2.7	2.4	2.2	2.3	2.3	2.1	3.5
2000	2.4	2.4	2.4	2.4	2.4	2.4	2.4	2.4	2.4	2.4	2.4	2.4	2.4
2001	2.5	2.4	2.5	2.4	2.4	2.4	2.3	2.4	2.3	2.3	2.3	2.3	2.4
2002	2.3	2.3	2.3	2.3	2.3	2.3	2.2	2.3	2.1	2.1	2.0	2.0	2.2
2003	2.0	2.0	1.9	2.0	2.0	2.0	2.0	2.0	2.0	2.0	2.0	2.0	2.0

Employment by Industry: Arizona—*Continued*

(Numbers in thousands. Not seasonally adjusted.)

Industry	January	February	March	April	May	June	July	August	September	October	November	December	Annual Average
PHOENIX—*Continued*													
Construction													
1990	55.2	55.3	56.3	56.2	56.6	58.0	57.8	58.9	59.1	58.6	57.7	56.0	57.1
1991	53.6	52.0	52.1	51.7	52.1	52.2	53.6	54.0	53.9	53.8	54.0	53.4	53.0
1992	50.9	50.9	52.0	53.8	55.4	56.5	57.2	58.2	58.1	58.2	57.8	57.4	55.5
1993	53.8	55.3	57.6	59.6	60.9	62.4	64.5	65.8	67.0	68.1	68.7	69.7	62.7
1994	68.1	69.5	71.1	72.1	73.3	75.2	75.7	77.5	78.8	80.4	81.2	81.8	75.3
1995	81.0	82.6	83.8	84.3	86.1	88.9	88.6	90.7	91.3	92.8	92.4	93.3	87.9
1996	92.0	93.0	93.5	92.0	93.9	95.9	95.7	97.4	97.4	97.7	98.2	97.9	95.3
1997	95.5	96.6	97.6	97.8	98.9	100.2	101.2	102.3	102.8	104.4	104.9	105.4	100.6
1998	103.6	104.3	105.9	105.9	107.7	110.4	111.9	112.8	113.4	114.7	115.1	115.1	110.0
1999	112.4	113.8	114.8	116.7	116.7	118.9	119.9	120.9	121.3	121.4	121.1	121.1	118.2
2000	117.0	118.4	119.8	121.1	122.9	124.8	124.5	125.5	126.1	126.8	126.0	126.7	123.3
2001	122.8	124.9	127.1	127.6	128.9	131.3	131.8	133.4	131.3	128.8	126.7	124.5	128.3
2002	122.2	122.2	123.7	124.6	126.1	127.9	128.2	129.5	128.5	127.4	127.1	126.0	126.1
2003	123.7	124.0	124.6	125.7	127.8	129.6	130.5	132.7	133.2	134.9	136.4	137.0	130.0
Manufacturing													
1990	135.8	135.9	135.9	136.0	136.5	137.2	136.8	136.8	136.0	136.3	136.0	135.2	136.2
1991	134.5	133.3	133.3	131.4	130.9	130.9	130.7	131.4	130.7	131.4	131.4	131.3	131.7
1992	129.6	129.7	128.7	129.4	129.5	130.2	129.0	128.9	129.4	129.7	129.6	130.0	129.4
1993	129.0	129.0	129.8	130.3	130.8	131.5	132.9	132.9	133.0	134.0	134.4	135.7	131.9
1994	133.2	134.0	135.2	136.4	137.3	139.1	139.9	141.0	141.6	142.3	143.6	144.6	139.0
1995	142.8	143.9	144.7	146.3	147.1	148.9	146.8	147.9	148.9	149.5	149.9	151.8	147.3
1996	151.3	151.8	152.8	152.9	153.8	155.0	155.0	155.9	156.3	155.0	156.4	157.2	154.4
1997	156.2	156.9	157.2	157.1	158.7	160.3	160.2	161.2	162.1	163.5	164.7	165.9	160.3
1998	165.9	166.8	167.3	166.3	166.7	167.7	167.0	166.5	166.2	163.8	162.1	162.0	165.6
1999	160.8	161.0	161.1	161.4	161.6	162.0	162.3	162.6	161.1	160.7	160.5	161.2	161.3
2000	159.4	160.5	160.8	159.4	159.5	161.7	161.5	162.2	162.3	161.6	162.2	162.4	161.1
2001	160.0	159.4	158.7	157.1	156.0	154.6	153.1	151.5	149.9	147.5	145.4	144.6	153.2
2002	141.3	141.0	140.3	139.7	138.7	138.4	137.9	136.9	135.5	134.1	133.4	132.8	137.5
2003	131.6	130.9	130.6	129.6	129.1	128.8	128.9	128.9	128.4	128.3	128.7	129.3	129.4
Service-providing													
1990	796.2	808.9	815.7	823.6	826.3	812.5	792.4	794.1	816.6	823.6	836.1	836.6	815.2
1991	815.5	826.6	831.1	824.3	822.9	810.9	792.9	794.2	812.0	824.7	834.7	840.7	819.2
1992	816.7	826.4	832.8	834.6	835.0	824.3	811.6	814.3	838.4	841.5	848.9	856.6	831.7
1993	832.1	849.6	858.8	869.7	870.0	871.0	862.0	858.3	877.5	893.1	905.2	915.1	871.8
1994	887.2	905.4	914.5	919.3	918.2	916.9	906.2	912.1	929.5	942.9	960.1	970.4	923.5
1995	948.3	969.8	978.6	977.5	981.9	970.0	955.0	961.7	991.0	1012.0	1026.2	1037.4	984.1
1996	1024.6	1043.0	1051.5	1043.9	1049.3	1038.7	1027.2	1038.8	1064.5	1080.1	1105.2	1111.1	1056.4
1997	1081.5	1104.2	1114.2	1114.2	1116.7	1099.5	1084.7	1091.2	1120.7	1137.9	1158.2	1171.1	1116.1
1998	1137.4	1156.0	1169.0	1172.2	1176.6	1160.4	1144.1	1159.2	1193.1	1202.5	1223.6	1233.0	1177.2
1999	1201.6	1223.4	1232.0	1239.5	1239.3	1228.1	1219.7	1227.1	1252.7	1265.4	1280.1	1292.5	1241.7
2000	1255.9	1277.4	1287.7	1290.6	1298.9	1275.8	1257.1	1275.1	1301.9	1312.3	1326.3	1340.4	1291.6
2001	1296.9	1320.1	1329.5	1324.8	1320.4	1301.0	1279.2	1296.6	1313.9	1321.8	1327.9	1334.6	1313.9
2002	1300.7	1315.9	1326.5	1339.1	1334.4	1321.0	1293.7	1316.6	1330.8	1344.7	1369.6	1370.5	1330.3
2003	1329.9	1349.4	1357.6	1358.3	1358.7	1339.0	1319.4	1338.9	1357.7	1374.1	1386.6	1393.9	1355.3
Trade, transportation, and utilities													
1990	223.8	222.8	224.1	223.6	224.6	224.8	221.1	221.8	224.0	224.6	230.8	232.6	224.8
1991	219.9	219.3	219.6	216.9	217.1	216.9	212.9	212.8	213.0	214.0	219.3	223.6	217.1
1992	216.6	215.1	214.9	213.7	213.9	213.1	212.3	211.9	213.0	214.0	218.3	221.9	214.8
1993	209.2	209.5	210.7	214.5	213.9	214.2	215.8	216.4	219.3	224.4	230.5	235.5	217.8
1994	226.6	227.1	229.0	231.7	233.2	234.4	235.5	236.9	239.5	242.5	250.3	256.1	236.9
1995	248.2	248.1	248.9	248.6	249.9	251.1	250.5	251.7	253.1	258.7	264.9	269.5	253.6
1996	263.6	262.8	263.0	264.2	266.1	266.2	266.5	268.4	269.2	274.7	284.0	289.7	269.8
1997	278.2	277.5	279.1	280.3	281.2	281.4	280.3	281.1	283.2	287.1	296.3	303.3	284.0
1998	292.2	291.3	292.3	291.7	292.4	293.4	292.0	294.7	297.4	301.9	307.8	314.2	296.7
1999	303.6	304.2	304.6	306.3	306.8	307.2	308.1	309.1	309.9	315.8	323.7	329.7	310.7
2000	316.9	317.0	316.3	315.6	316.2	318.7	316.3	318.7	321.1	324.7	334.2	340.7	321.3
2001	326.1	324.3	323.4	323.2	322.7	323.0	320.5	320.8	320.7	324.6	330.0	333.0	324.4
2002	321.6	318.8	320.9	322.7	324.0	325.3	322.2	323.2	324.6	326.9	335.0	340.3	325.5
2003	326.5	325.4	325.5	324.9	325.4	324.8	323.9	324.8	325.9	330.3	337.8	342.2	328.1
Wholesale trade													
1990	50.8	51.0	51.2	50.8	51.4	51.7	51.1	51.0	50.7	50.7	50.8	50.6	50.9
1991	47.3	47.1	47.3	46.2	46.3	46.5	46.6	46.3	46.4	46.9	47.4	47.6	46.8
1992	46.8	47.1	47.4	47.6	47.9	47.8	48.0	47.7	48.0	47.9	48.1	48.1	47.7
1993	46.6	47.0	47.7	48.6	48.6	48.9	49.3	49.0	49.2	49.6	50.1	50.4	48.7
1994	50.3	50.9	51.5	52.5	52.8	53.4	53.4	53.9	54.6	55.4	56.1	56.5	53.4
1995	57.0	57.9	58.6	59.0	59.7	60.2	59.9	60.3	60.9	61.6	61.8	62.0	59.9
1996	61.8	63.2	63.9	64.8	65.7	66.0	65.7	65.7	66.1	66.5	67.2	67.6	65.3
1997	67.1	68.1	68.8	68.8	69.4	70.0	69.7	69.9	70.4	70.6	71.3	71.9	69.6
1998	71.3	72.0	72.6	72.7	72.8	73.5	73.5	73.6	74.3	74.2	74.3	74.4	73.2
1999	73.9	74.8	75.1	75.3	75.6	75.9	76.0	76.1	76.2	76.8	77.2	77.6	75.8
2000	76.7	77.4	77.9	77.6	77.6	78.4	78.5	78.7	79.0	79.5	80.0	80.7	78.5
2001	80.3	80.9	80.9	80.4	80.4	79.9	79.4	79.3	78.6	78.4	78.2	78.1	79.6
2002	76.9	77.1	77.6	78.0	78.9	79.0	78.8	78.8	78.7	78.9	79.1	79.0	78.4
2003	77.9	78.0	77.8	77.4	77.9	77.6	77.3	77.3	77.2	77.3	77.5	77.5	77.6

Employment by Industry: Arizona—*Continued*

(Numbers in thousands. Not seasonally adjusted.)

Industry	January	February	March	April	May	June	July	August	September	October	November	December	Annual Average
PHOENIX—*Continued*													
Retail trade													
1990	130.0	128.4	128.9	129.6	129.7	129.7	127.2	127.7	129.3	129.8	135.7	137.6	130.3
1991	127.7	127.3	127.5	125.7	125.6	125.0	120.8	121.3	122.0	123.6	128.2	131.7	125.5
1992	125.3	123.4	122.8	121.6	121.4	120.5	119.7	119.6	121.1	121.9	126.2	130.0	122.7
1993	123.2	122.5	122.6	124.5	123.2	122.7	124.1	124.7	126.7	129.9	135.3	139.3	126.5
1994	132.5	131.8	132.5	134.6	135.1	135.5	136.9	137.5	139.3	141.6	148.5	153.6	138.2
1995	146.1	144.9	144.9	144.1	144.5	145.0	144.4	145.3	145.8	148.7	154.4	159.1	147.2
1996	154.3	151.6	151.2	151.7	152.4	151.8	152.0	153.2	153.3	156.9	165.1	170.2	155.3
1997	161.3	159.5	159.9	161.3	161.2	160.5	159.7	160.1	161.2	164.9	172.7	178.7	163.4
1998	169.2	167.5	167.7	166.1	166.4	166.4	165.5	167.3	169.0	173.2	178.8	184.8	170.1
1999	175.0	174.4	174.1	175.1	174.7	174.3	174.4	175.4	176.6	179.5	186.8	192.4	177.7
2000	182.8	182.5	182.2	181.8	182.3	183.6	181.1	182.7	184.3	187.0	195.2	200.5	185.5
2001	187.8	185.2	184.4	184.3	183.1	183.8	182.2	182.4	183.2	187.5	193.6	197.1	186.2
2002	187.2	184.3	185.3	186.4	186.5	186.8	184.1	184.8	186.3	187.7	195.5	201.0	188.0
2003	189.0	187.9	188.2	188.2	188.4	188.3	187.7	188.5	189.6	192.8	200.3	204.8	191.1
Transportation and utilities													
1990	43.0	43.4	44.0	43.2	43.5	43.4	42.8	43.1	44.0	44.1	44.3	44.4	43.6
1991	44.9	44.9	44.8	45.0	45.2	45.4	45.5	45.2	44.6	43.5	43.7	44.3	44.7
1992	44.5	44.6	44.7	44.5	44.6	44.8	44.6	44.6	43.9	44.2	44.0	43.8	44.4
1993	39.4	40.0	40.4	41.4	42.1	42.6	42.4	42.7	43.4	44.9	45.1	45.8	42.5
1994	43.8	44.4	45.0	44.6	45.3	45.5	45.2	45.5	45.6	45.5	45.7	46.0	45.1
1995	45.1	45.3	45.4	45.5	45.7	45.9	46.2	46.1	46.4	48.4	48.7	48.4	46.4
1996	47.5	48.0	47.9	47.7	48.0	48.4	48.8	49.5	49.8	51.3	51.7	51.9	49.2
1997	49.8	49.9	50.4	50.2	50.6	50.9	50.9	51.1	51.6	51.6	52.3	52.7	51.0
1998	51.7	51.8	52.0	52.9	53.2	53.5	53.0	53.8	54.1	54.5	54.7	55.0	53.3
1999	54.7	55.0	55.4	55.9	56.5	57.0	57.7	57.6	57.1	59.5	59.7	59.7	57.1
2000	57.4	57.1	56.2	56.2	56.3	56.7	56.7	57.3	57.8	58.2	59.0	59.5	57.3
2001	58.0	58.2	58.1	58.5	59.2	59.3	58.9	59.1	58.9	58.7	58.2	57.8	58.6
2002	57.5	57.4	58.0	58.3	58.6	59.5	59.3	59.6	59.6	60.3	60.4	60.3	59.1
2003	59.6	59.5	59.5	59.3	59.1	58.9	58.9	59.0	59.1	60.2	60.0	59.9	59.4
Information													
1990	23.3	23.5	23.3	23.9	24.0	24.3	24.3	24.1	23.9	23.6	23.9	23.7	23.8
1991	23.3	23.4	23.6	22.6	22.5	22.9	23.0	22.7	22.6	22.2	22.3	22.5	22.8
1992	21.8	21.7	21.9	21.6	21.8	22.1	21.5	21.4	21.6	21.3	21.5	21.8	21.6
1993	21.4	21.7	22.1	21.6	21.8	22.4	22.8	22.8	22.6	22.4	22.5	22.8	22.2
1994	21.7	21.8	22.3	22.3	22.6	23.1	23.3	23.4	23.6	23.7	23.9	24.3	23.0
1995	24.0	24.5	24.7	24.3	24.7	25.5	24.8	25.0	25.3	25.2	25.5	25.9	24.9
1996	25.4	25.5	25.8	25.9	26.4	27.0	27.6	27.8	27.6	27.8	28.0	28.8	26.9
1997	28.8	29.3	29.4	29.4	29.4	29.8	29.8	29.8	29.9	30.2	30.5	30.8	29.7
1998	30.7	31.0	31.3	31.0	31.2	31.4	31.7	32.1	32.1	32.1	32.4	32.9	31.6
1999	33.2	33.9	34.1	34.6	35.3	35.5	35.6	36.0	36.0	35.8	36.1	36.3	35.2
2000	39.3	40.0	42.4	42.8	43.1	43.2	42.8	42.6	42.2	41.3	41.7	42.3	41.9
2001	41.3	42.4	42.1	42.4	41.6	42.1	41.6	41.5	41.1	41.0	41.4	40.8	41.6
2002	40.7	40.5	40.1	40.4	39.9	39.4	39.4	39.1	38.3	37.7	38.3	38.5	39.4
2003	37.5	37.7	38.0	38.1	37.9	38.0	37.5	37.0	36.7	36.6	36.6	36.5	37.3
Financial activities													
1990	78.5	78.8	79.5	80.3	80.4	80.6	80.3	80.4	79.5	79.6	79.6	79.2	79.7
1991	78.8	79.5	79.8	77.5	77.6	77.6	78.5	78.4	77.9	78.6	78.6	78.9	78.4
1992	74.0	74.5	74.7	75.1	75.8	75.8	77.6	77.2	77.4	78.2	78.6	79.4	76.5
1993	79.2	79.9	80.8	82.5	82.7	83.3	83.5	83.6	84.0	84.5	85.3	86.6	82.9
1994	85.8	86.9	87.2	87.5	87.9	88.2	87.6	87.7	87.7	87.4	87.8	88.3	87.5
1995	85.9	86.4	86.8	87.0	86.6	87.6	88.1	88.4	88.9	90.9	91.5	92.7	88.4
1996	93.3	94.2	94.6	95.0	95.6	96.7	98.3	99.7	99.8	101.6	102.7	104.3	97.9
1997	105.5	106.9	108.4	108.9	109.2	109.4	110.7	110.6	111.3	112.5	114.1	115.9	110.2
1998	112.4	113.5	114.8	116.9	117.1	117.4	120.7	120.6	120.7	121.4	122.4	124.1	118.5
1999	120.9	121.7	122.3	123.1	123.2	124.4	125.1	125.4	125.4	126.0	126.8	127.8	124.3
2000	122.5	124.7	124.7	124.8	125.6	127.0	126.1	126.7	127.5	127.9	128.6	129.8	126.3
2001	125.9	127.4	128.6	128.2	128.9	129.4	130.1	130.7	131.4	130.9	131.3	132.4	129.6
2002	129.8	131.0	130.4	131.7	130.8	130.9	130.3	130.5	130.3	131.6	133.3	134.0	131.2
2003	132.2	132.8	134.0	133.5	134.1	134.3	134.7	134.8	134.7	135.1	136.1	136.3	134.4
Professional and business services													
1990	107.1	108.1	109.5	110.4	110.0	111.0	111.2	112.3	111.9	110.3	110.6	110.8	110.2
1991	110.6	111.8	113.1	114.0	113.5	114.4	111.5	113.6	113.9	114.6	115.2	116.3	113.5
1992	115.1	117.3	120.3	123.0	123.8	125.3	124.3	124.8	126.2	125.9	126.1	128.0	123.3
1993	122.4	125.4	128.5	131.7	133.0	135.2	132.2	132.8	134.7	135.4	136.7	140.2	132.3
1994	135.0	138.7	141.1	145.7	144.9	148.1	147.5	149.6	150.4	152.9	155.8	158.7	147.3
1995	156.4	161.0	164.1	164.4	166.4	169.8	167.8	170.1	171.8	177.1	180.3	182.8	169.3
1996	182.3	188.3	191.0	188.9	192.1	195.8	194.9	196.2	198.0	200.7	203.4	205.9	194.7
1997	197.3	203.6	206.4	209.2	211.3	215.1	213.5	216.7	218.0	220.6	223.0	225.6	213.3
1998	212.5	216.1	220.7	221.5	222.4	226.0	227.7	228.3	229.7	232.8	236.0	238.7	226.0
1999	233.3	238.2	241.5	246.1	247.1	250.1	249.9	251.9	253.2	252.9	255.0	256.7	247.9
2000	248.6	253.8	258.2	262.0	265.3	265.7	264.1	268.3	268.8	270.7	271.1	272.8	264.1
2001	260.1	264.2	267.8	265.4	263.7	263.8	257.3	257.7	257.4	253.9	250.1	251.4	259.4
2002	244.1	247.5	252.3	256.2	256.0	256.4	253.2	256.2	254.7	254.2	255.8	255.9	253.5
2003	248.3	252.8	256.2	256.8	257.8	257.5	259.0	259.4	261.4	263.2	261.8	262.9	258.1

Employment by Industry: Arizona—*Continued*

(Numbers in thousands. Not seasonally adjusted.)

Industry	January	February	March	April	May	June	July	August	September	October	November	December	Annual Average
PHOENIX—*Continued*													
Educational and health services													
1990	87.9	89.2	90.2	91.8	91.9	91.7	90.2	90.1	91.5	92.2	92.9	92.8	91.0
1991	93.4	94.1	94.7	94.2	94.4	94.4	93.8	94.1	95.2	96.8	97.6	98.1	95.0
1992	96.7	97.4	98.0	98.9	99.3	99.1	99.2	99.2	100.6	100.8	101.3	102.6	99.4
1993	100.8	102.6	102.4	103.4	103.5	103.5	103.3	102.9	105.5	106.1	106.8	107.4	104.0
1994	103.4	105.6	106.1	105.4	105.4	105.7	104.8	105.6	107.6	108.5	109.5	110.4	106.5
1995	108.1	110.3	111.2	111.6	112.1	112.6	110.4	111.0	113.4	115.2	115.8	116.9	112.3
1996	115.3	117.4	118.5	117.8	118.8	118.4	118.4	120.1	122.6	122.3	124.3	124.5	119.8
1997	123.6	125.5	126.1	125.3	125.2	125.0	121.7	122.6	125.2	126.0	127.1	127.8	125.0
1998	125.5	127.8	129.1	129.3	129.1	129.3	128.6	129.9	131.8	133.4	134.4	135.2	130.2
1999	133.2	134.9	135.5	133.5	133.5	134.3	133.4	134.3	136.4	137.2	138.5	139.0	135.3
2000	134.5	136.5	137.6	136.8	137.1	136.9	135.3	137.0	138.5	138.9	139.6	141.1	137.4
2001	139.9	141.5	142.8	142.7	142.5	143.4	140.7	144.1	144.9	146.1	147.1	148.9	143.7
2002	148.5	149.9	151.0	150.8	152.0	152.3	149.5	152.7	154.0	156.9	158.7	159.4	153.0
2003	158.4	160.1	160.8	161.0	161.4	161.8	161.7	164.0	165.2	166.5	167.3	167.5	163.0
Leisure and hospitality													
1990	103.1	105.8	106.6	107.2	105.8	103.8	98.0	97.9	100.3	103.1	105.9	105.5	103.5
1991	103.5	105.8	107.0	105.4	104.5	101.0	97.9	97.5	100.4	102.3	103.9	104.4	102.8
1992	102.9	105.9	107.1	107.6	105.9	104.7	101.2	100.9	102.7	105.3	106.5	107.1	104.8
1993	107.8	110.6	112.8	113.9	113.5	111.5	107.6	108.6	111.9	115.1	116.5	117.3	112.2
1994	117.3	121.2	123.7	122.2	120.0	117.3	114.0	114.1	116.7	119.6	121.8	123.1	119.2
1995	122.9	126.9	129.6	127.0	127.5	125.3	122.3	122.8	125.0	126.4	128.8	129.6	126.1
1996	130.3	133.9	135.9	134.8	132.8	129.4	125.4	125.8	129.1	130.4	133.4	135.2	131.3
1997	135.6	138.9	141.2	138.6	137.3	133.5	129.1	129.2	132.3	136.6	139.8	141.4	136.1
1998	139.8	143.5	146.3	147.5	147.1	144.0	138.8	138.5	140.0	142.1	143.9	146.0	143.1
1999	143.9	147.2	149.6	150.8	149.5	147.6	142.6	142.5	144.5	146.4	147.9	149.2	146.8
2000	147.8	150.9	152.7	152.8	151.0	148.9	143.7	145.6	148.6	150.3	151.8	152.7	149.7
2001	151.7	155.7	158.7	156.7	155.2	152.3	146.5	147.0	148.3	151.3	152.9	153.6	152.5
2002	148.9	153.1	155.5	158.0	157.1	153.8	148.9	149.6	149.8	152.7	157.3	157.0	153.5
2003	154.2	157.4	159.3	160.1	158.7	154.6	150.5	150.5	152.2	155.0	158.7	159.2	155.9
Other services													
1990	36.1	36.5	36.8	38.5	38.7	38.9	38.2	38.2	38.4	38.9	39.0	39.3	38.1
1991	38.7	38.8	39.1	39.0	38.8	39.3	39.1	38.7	38.7	39.2	39.5	39.5	39.0
1992	38.8	39.0	39.3	38.5	38.7	39.2	39.1	38.9	39.1	38.9	39.1	39.2	38.9
1993	39.0	39.8	40.5	41.0	40.7	41.0	40.8	40.2	40.2	40.4	40.2	40.3	40.3
1994	39.7	40.1	40.4	41.6	41.5	42.1	42.6	42.6	42.8	43.2	43.5	43.8	41.9
1995	41.9	42.7	43.0	42.8	42.8	43.4	43.4	43.5	43.3	45.3	45.6	46.1	43.6
1996	44.8	45.3	45.7	45.6	45.8	45.9	46.0	45.6	45.3	45.5	45.6	45.6	45.5
1997	45.2	45.8	46.0	45.2	45.3	45.6	45.8	45.3	45.4	45.6	45.6	45.7	45.5
1998	45.6	46.4	47.1	47.8	48.6	49.2	49.1	48.7	48.6	49.0	49.2	49.4	48.2
1999	49.8	50.6	51.1	51.2	51.6	52.4	52.5	52.3	52.6	53.6	53.4	53.7	52.0
2000	54.0	55.0	55.5	54.5	54.9	55.4	54.7	54.6	54.6	54.9	55.1	55.4	54.8
2001	57.0	58.2	59.1	58.7	59.3	60.6	59.9	60.1	60.1	59.4	59.6	59.6	59.3
2002	59.9	60.4	61.1	61.9	62.1	62.8	61.4	61.7	61.9	61.9	62.0	62.1	61.6
2003	61.0	61.2	61.8	61.7	62.0	62.1	60.8	61.0	61.3	61.4	61.6	61.7	61.5
Government													
1990	136.4	144.2	145.7	147.9	150.9	137.4	129.1	129.3	147.1	151.3	153.4	152.7	143.7
1991	147.3	153.9	154.2	154.7	154.5	144.4	136.2	136.4	150.3	157.0	158.3	157.4	150.3
1992	150.8	155.5	156.6	156.2	155.8	145.0	136.4	140.0	157.8	157.1	157.5	156.6	152.1
1993	152.3	160.1	161.0	161.1	160.9	159.9	156.0	151.0	159.3	164.8	166.7	165.0	159.8
1994	157.7	164.0	164.7	162.9	162.7	158.0	150.9	152.2	161.2	165.1	167.5	165.7	161.0
1995	160.9	169.9	170.3	171.8	171.9	154.7	147.7	149.2	170.2	173.2	173.8	173.9	165.6
1996	169.6	175.6	177.0	171.7	171.7	159.3	150.1	155.2	172.9	177.1	183.8	177.1	170.0
1997	167.3	176.7	177.6	177.3	177.8	159.7	153.8	155.9	175.4	179.3	181.8	180.6	171.9
1998	178.7	186.4	187.4	186.5	188.7	169.7	155.5	166.4	192.8	189.8	197.5	192.5	182.6
1999	183.7	192.7	193.3	193.9	192.3	176.6	172.5	175.6	194.7	197.7	198.7	200.1	189.3
2000	192.3	199.5	200.3	201.3	205.7	180.0	174.1	181.6	200.6	203.6	204.2	205.6	195.7
2001	194.9	206.4	207.0	207.5	206.5	186.4	182.6	194.7	210.0	214.6	215.5	214.9	203.4
2002	207.2	214.7	215.2	217.4	212.5	200.1	188.8	203.6	217.2	222.8	229.2	223.3	212.7
2003	211.8	222.0	222.0	222.2	221.4	205.9	191.3	207.4	220.3	226.0	226.7	227.6	217.1
Federal government													
1995	18.3	18.3	18.4	18.5	18.6	18.6	17.9	17.9	18.0	17.9	18.2	18.7	18.2
1996	18.4	18.4	18.7	18.7	18.8	18.8	18.7	18.9	18.9	18.9	19.0	19.7	18.8
1997	19.1	19.0	19.1	19.1	19.0	19.1	19.2	19.3	19.4	19.5	19.6	19.5	19.2
1998	19.9	19.5	19.5	19.3	19.4	19.3	19.4	19.6	19.7	19.8	19.8	20.9	19.6
1999	20.8	20.4	20.0	20.7	20.1	19.9	20.0	20.1	20.2	20.1	20.2	21.0	20.2
2000	20.3	20.3	20.9	21.4	25.7	20.8	21.7	20.2	20.0	20.0	20.2	21.1	21.0
2001	20.3	20.2	20.3	20.3	20.4	20.4	20.5	20.5	20.6	20.8	20.6	21.4	20.5
2002	20.6	20.5	20.5	20.3	20.4	20.7	20.6	20.6	20.7	21.6	21.9	22.8	20.9
2003	21.9	21.7	21.7	21.6	21.6	21.6	21.6	21.6	21.6	21.6	21.7	22.4	21.7

Employment by Industry: Arizona—*Continued*

(Numbers in thousands. Not seasonally adjusted.)

Industry	January	February	March	April	May	June	July	August	September	October	November	December	Annual Average
PHOENIX—*Continued*													
State government													
1994	37.1	38.6	39.5	38.7	39.0	36.5	35.6	35.5	38.8	39.7	41.0	39.8	38.3
1995	37.9	39.9	39.8	39.9	39.7	36.3	36.3	36.6	40.3	41.2	41.4	40.6	39.1
1996	39.4	41.8	41.6	38.0	38.1	38.2	37.3	37.4	40.5	42.9	41.6	41.5	39.8
1997	38.8	41.1	41.1	42.0	42.0	38.2	38.2	38.3	41.5	42.5	43.5	42.8	40.8
1998	40.0	42.3	42.5	42.6	42.5	40.3	39.2	39.3	42.1	43.0	43.5	43.5	41.7
1999	41.1	43.7	43.9	43.9	43.6	40.7	40.2	40.5	43.4	45.1	44.4	44.5	42.9
2000	42.0	44.4	44.6	44.6	44.4	41.4	40.6	40.8	44.9	46.4	45.5	45.1	43.7
2001	43.6	45.4	45.4	45.6	45.3	42.4	42.0	42.4	45.8	48.1	47.6	46.0	45.0
2002	44.7	47.4	47.2	47.0	46.5	43.5	44.2	43.1	46.0	48.3	47.2	47.1	46.0
2003	43.6	46.4	46.7	46.6	46.4	43.4	41.7	41.8	45.3	48.0	47.1	47.3	45.4
Local government													
1994	102.0	106.9	106.7	105.6	105.2	102.9	96.7	98.2	103.7	106.7	107.9	106.7	104.1
1995	104.7	111.7	112.1	113.4	113.6	99.8	93.5	94.7	111.9	114.1	114.2	114.6	108.1
1996	111.8	115.4	116.7	115.0	114.8	102.3	94.1	98.9	113.5	115.3	123.2	115.9	111.4
1997	109.4	116.6	117.5	116.2	116.8	102.4	96.5	98.3	114.5	117.4	118.6	118.3	111.8
1998	118.8	124.6	125.4	124.6	126.8	110.1	96.9	107.5	131.0	127.0	134.2	128.1	121.2
1999	121.8	128.6	129.4	129.3	128.6	116.0	112.3	115.0	131.1	132.5	134.1	134.6	126.1
2000	130.0	134.8	134.8	135.3	135.6	117.8	111.8	120.6	135.7	137.2	138.5	139.4	130.9
2001	131.0	140.8	141.3	141.6	140.8	123.6	120.1	131.8	143.6	145.7	147.3	147.5	137.9
2002	141.9	146.8	147.5	150.1	145.6	135.9	124.0	139.9	150.5	152.9	160.1	153.4	145.7
2003	146.3	153.9	153.6	154.0	153.4	140.9	128.0	144.0	153.4	156.4	157.9	157.9	150.0
TUCSON													
Total nonfarm													
1990	250.1	253.6	255.9	252.3	254.3	245.3	241.3	246.6	252.2	254.1	256.4	257.4	251.6
1991	252.5	255.5	260.6	258.9	260.0	251.3	247.6	252.9	261.6	264.0	267.1	267.6	258.3
1992	260.5	264.4	265.6	267.2	268.1	256.1	254.4	257.2	267.3	268.0	270.8	273.1	264.3
1993	267.5	272.9	274.8	274.6	275.5	268.9	262.0	264.8	276.2	281.5	284.3	287.1	274.1
1994	285.5	291.0	292.1	292.3	289.8	282.3	279.2	289.6	295.3	296.8	299.8	303.3	291.4
1995	298.2	303.1	305.3	306.3	305.8	299.0	293.0	297.9	300.4	304.8	307.5	310.3	302.6
1996	302.0	306.5	309.2	309.2	310.5	305.1	296.9	303.3	307.4	309.5	312.1	314.7	307.2
1997	307.1	312.0	314.7	315.5	317.2	310.2	305.8	310.2	315.7	322.6	325.9	327.6	315.3
1998	319.3	323.7	326.9	326.9	326.8	322.9	314.3	319.0	322.5	326.1	329.3	332.3	324.1
1999	324.5	330.4	333.0	337.9	337.3	335.4	325.5	331.8	337.6	345.2	348.7	350.0	336.4
2000	345.0	350.0	352.9	351.3	352.0	348.0	339.8	343.3	349.0	352.9	356.6	358.5	349.9
2001	344.2	349.9	352.6	352.7	351.1	344.6	336.8	342.3	347.3	346.9	350.3	350.7	347.5
2002	344.1	347.4	348.3	350.0	349.2	341.6	332.2	338.9	344.9	348.7	352.3	353.0	345.9
2003	343.6	346.7	348.8	348.1	348.0	340.3	332.8	338.3	345.8	350.2	353.7	355.2	346.0
Total private													
1990	195.8	197.0	198.5	194.5	195.7	195.8	192.7	194.2	195.2	195.5	196.7	197.3	195.7
1991	197.8	197.6	199.0	197.5	198.3	197.9	197.5	199.6	200.3	201.4	204.1	204.6	199.6
1992	200.2	201.0	201.9	203.3	203.9	202.5	202.4	202.5	203.7	204.9	206.5	208.5	203.4
1993	205.9	208.0	209.4	208.5	209.1	209.0	207.3	208.7	211.4	214.8	217.0	220.4	210.7
1994	218.2	221.5	223.3	224.9	224.6	225.3	225.1	225.6	227.0	229.2	231.2	234.7	225.8
1995	230.5	233.2	235.1	234.8	234.5	235.8	231.0	231.5	232.1	234.8	237.5	239.6	234.2
1996	233.7	235.6	237.8	237.6	238.5	237.0	235.7	236.8	237.7	238.5	242.1	242.4	237.7
1997	237.5	240.4	242.3	241.0	242.1	241.5	242.0	243.6	245.9	249.1	251.2	252.8	244.1
1998	247.6	250.1	252.4	252.1	252.3	253.3	252.3	252.3	252.7	252.3	254.4	258.0	252.4
1999	252.2	255.1	257.3	261.4	263.1	264.4	262.5	263.4	265.1	269.4	271.8	274.8	263.3
2000	270.2	273.0	274.7	272.8	272.3	273.3	270.2	272.5	273.5	274.7	277.5	279.5	273.6
2001	268.6	271.3	273.2	273.0	271.8	271.0	269.5	270.6	269.6	268.3	269.9	270.5	270.6
2002	266.4	267.5	268.4	268.8	268.8	267.2	264.4	266.4	267.0	268.3	270.9	271.8	268.0
2003	264.9	265.6	267.3	267.0	266.9	266.8	264.2	265.5	267.8	269.6	272.9	274.4	267.7
Goods-producing													
1990	42.7	42.4	42.6	41.7	42.4	42.6	42.7	43.0	42.6	43.2	42.9	42.7	42.6
1991	42.0	41.7	42.1	41.6	42.0	42.7	43.0	42.9	42.1	42.3	42.3	41.6	42.1
1992	40.5	40.6	40.4	40.4	40.5	40.3	41.0	40.7	40.2	39.7	39.5	39.6	40.2
1993	39.3	39.6	40.2	39.9	40.3	40.8	40.7	41.4	41.6	41.9	42.4	43.4	40.9
1994	43.9	44.4	45.0	45.7	46.3	47.1	47.6	47.7	47.9	48.0	47.8	48.3	46.6
1995	49.7	49.9	50.3	50.4	50.1	50.7	49.7	49.9	49.8	50.7	50.5	50.6	50.1
1996	48.9	48.9	48.8	49.2	49.7	50.0	50.2	50.6	50.2	50.5	50.4	50.2	49.8
1997	49.4	49.6	50.1	49.2	49.9	50.6	50.6	50.7	50.9	51.4	51.0	51.2	50.3
1998	49.9	50.1	50.7	50.4	51.1	51.5	51.8	51.8	51.4	51.1	51.1	51.2	51.0
1999	50.8	51.4	52.1	52.7	53.4	54.6	55.3	55.5	56.1	56.9	56.7	57.2	54.3
2000	56.1	56.2	56.8	56.7	56.6	57.7	57.9	58.5	58.5	58.2	58.5	59.1	57.5
2001	56.9	57.1	57.7	57.5	57.7	58.2	58.4	58.7	58.1	57.3	56.7	56.0	57.5
2002	55.1	54.5	54.6	54.4	54.7	55.0	54.9	55.1	54.7	54.2	54.0	53.9	54.6
2003	53.0	52.3	52.7	52.2	52.5	53.0	53.0	52.8	52.9	52.8	52.9	53.2	52.8

Employment by Industry: Arizona—*Continued*

(Numbers in thousands. Not seasonally adjusted.)

Industry	January	February	March	April	May	June	July	August	September	October	November	December	Annual Average
TUCSON—*Continued*													
Natural resources and mining													
1990	2.2	2.2	2.1	2.1	2.2	2.2	2.2	2.2	2.2	2.2	2.3	2.3	2.2
1991	2.3	2.3	2.3	2.3	2.4	2.4	2.4	2.4	2.4	2.5	2.5	2.5	2.3
1992	2.5	2.5	2.4	2.4	2.5	2.4	2.5	2.5	2.4	2.4	2.5	2.5	2.4
1993	2.5	2.4	2.4	2.3	2.3	2.3	2.1	2.1	2.0	2.0	2.0	2.0	2.2
1994	2.0	2.0	2.0	2.0	2.0	2.0	2.1	2.0	2.0	2.0	2.0	2.1	2.0
1995	2.1	2.1	2.1	2.2	2.2	2.3	2.3	2.2	2.2	2.3	2.2	2.2	2.2
1996	2.3	2.3	2.2	2.2	2.3	2.3	2.3	2.3	2.2	2.2	2.2	2.2	2.2
1997	2.2	2.2	2.2	2.1	2.2	2.3	2.3	2.2	2.2	2.2	2.2	2.2	2.2
1998	2.1	2.1	2.1	2.1	2.1	2.1	2.1	2.1	2.0	2.0	2.0	2.0	2.0
1999	2.0	2.0	2.0	2.0	2.0	2.0	1.8	1.8	1.9	1.9	1.9	1.8	1.9
2000	1.8	1.8	1.8	1.8	1.8	1.8	1.8	1.8	1.8	1.8	1.8	1.8	1.8
2001	1.8	1.8	1.8	1.8	1.8	1.8	1.8	1.8	1.7	1.7	1.7	1.7	1.8
2002	1.7	1.6	1.6	1.6	1.6	1.6	1.4	1.4	1.5	1.4	1.4	1.4	1.5
2003	1.3	1.1	1.2	1.1	1.2	1.2	1.2	1.2	1.1	1.1	1.1	1.1	1.2
Construction													
1990	14.6	14.4	14.6	14.6	15.1	15.4	15.1	15.3	15.1	15.3	15.0	14.7	14.9
1991	14.7	14.7	15.0	14.7	15.0	15.5	15.8	15.8	15.3	15.0	15.2	14.8	15.1
1992	14.3	14.4	14.6	14.4	14.6	14.7	15.2	15.0	14.6	14.4	14.5	14.5	14.6
1993	14.1	14.4	14.6	14.9	15.2	15.8	16.2	16.4	16.5	16.7	17.0	17.7	15.7
1994	17.5	17.9	18.3	18.4	18.7	19.1	19.2	19.1	19.1	19.1	19.0	19.2	18.7
1995	20.2	20.4	20.6	20.3	20.3	20.8	20.4	20.7	20.6	21.0	21.0	21.2	20.6
1996	19.8	19.8	19.9	20.2	20.5	20.7	20.7	20.8	20.5	20.6	20.4	20.4	20.3
1997	19.8	19.9	20.1	19.8	20.3	20.7	20.9	21.0	21.0	21.3	21.1	21.1	20.5
1998	20.2	20.2	20.6	19.8	20.5	20.7	20.8	20.7	20.8	20.7	20.7	21.0	20.5
1999	20.4	20.8	21.1	21.7	22.1	22.5	22.6	22.6	22.8	23.1	22.9	23.0	22.1
2000	22.3	22.3	22.6	22.5	22.5	23.0	23.1	23.5	23.4	23.1	23.0	23.3	22.8
2001	21.9	22.2	22.6	22.3	22.5	22.9	23.3	23.6	23.5	22.9	22.6	22.3	22.7
2002	21.9	21.8	22.0	21.8	22.2	22.6	22.9	23.3	23.0	23.0	23.0	23.0	22.5
2003	22.5	22.3	22.4	22.4	22.7	23.1	23.1	23.0	23.1	23.2	23.3	23.5	22.9
Manufacturing													
1990	25.9	25.8	25.9	25.0	25.1	25.0	25.4	25.5	25.3	25.7	25.6	25.7	25.4
1991	25.0	24.7	24.8	24.6	24.6	24.8	24.8	24.7	24.4	24.8	24.6	24.3	24.6
1992	23.7	23.7	23.4	23.6	23.4	23.2	23.3	23.2	23.2	22.9	22.5	22.6	23.2
1993	22.7	22.8	23.2	22.7	22.8	22.7	22.4	22.9	23.1	23.2	23.4	23.7	22.9
1994	24.4	24.5	24.7	25.3	25.6	26.0	26.3	26.6	26.8	26.9	26.8	27.0	25.9
1995	27.4	27.4	27.6	27.9	27.6	27.6	27.0	27.0	27.0	27.4	27.3	27.2	27.3
1996	26.8	26.8	26.7	26.8	26.9	27.0	27.2	27.5	27.5	27.7	27.8	27.6	27.1
1997	27.4	27.5	27.8	27.3	27.4	27.6	27.4	27.5	27.7	27.9	27.7	27.9	27.5
1998	27.6	27.8	28.0	28.5	28.5	28.7	28.9	29.0	28.6	28.4	28.4	28.2	28.3
1999	28.4	28.6	29.0	29.0	29.3	30.1	30.9	31.1	31.4	31.9	31.9	32.4	30.3
2000	32.0	32.1	32.4	32.4	32.3	32.9	33.0	33.2	33.3	33.3	33.7	34.0	32.8
2001	33.2	33.1	33.3	33.4	33.4	33.5	33.3	33.3	32.9	32.7	32.4	32.0	33.0
2002	31.5	31.1	31.0	31.0	30.9	30.8	30.6	30.4	30.2	29.8	29.6	29.5	30.5
2003	29.2	28.9	29.1	28.7	28.6	28.7	28.7	28.6	28.7	28.5	28.5	28.6	28.7
Service-providing													
1990	207.4	211.2	213.3	210.6	211.9	202.7	198.6	203.6	209.6	210.9	213.5	214.7	209.0
1991	210.5	213.8	218.5	217.3	218.0	208.6	204.6	210.0	219.5	221.7	224.8	226.0	216.1
1992	220.0	223.8	225.2	226.8	227.6	215.8	213.4	216.5	227.1	228.3	231.3	233.5	224.1
1993	228.2	233.3	234.6	234.7	235.2	228.1	221.3	223.4	234.6	239.6	241.9	243.7	233.2
1994	241.6	246.6	247.1	246.6	243.5	235.2	231.6	241.9	247.4	248.8	252.0	255.0	244.7
1995	248.5	253.2	255.0	255.9	255.7	248.3	243.3	248.0	250.6	254.1	257.0	259.7	252.4
1996	253.1	257.6	260.4	260.0	260.8	255.1	246.7	252.7	257.2	259.0	261.7	264.5	257.4
1997	257.7	262.4	264.6	266.3	267.3	259.6	255.2	259.5	264.8	271.2	274.9	276.4	264.9
1998	269.4	273.6	276.2	276.5	275.7	271.4	262.5	267.2	271.1	275.0	278.2	281.1	273.1
1999	273.7	279.0	280.9	285.2	283.9	280.8	270.2	276.3	281.5	288.3	292.0	292.8	282.0
2000	288.9	293.8	296.1	294.6	295.4	290.3	281.9	284.8	290.5	294.7	298.1	299.4	292.3
2001	287.3	292.8	294.9	295.2	293.4	286.4	278.4	283.6	289.2	289.6	293.6	294.7	289.9
2002	289.0	292.9	293.7	295.6	294.5	286.6	277.3	283.8	290.2	294.5	298.3	299.1	291.3
2003	290.6	294.4	296.1	295.9	295.5	287.3	279.8	285.5	292.9	297.4	300.8	302.0	293.2
Trade, transportation, and utilities													
1990	45.6	45.6	46.0	44.9	45.2	45.1	44.2	44.6	45.1	44.8	45.9	46.2	45.2
1991	45.6	44.9	45.4	45.7	45.9	45.8	45.7	46.2	46.5	47.1	48.7	49.3	46.4
1992	47.3	47.1	47.4	47.7	48.0	47.7	47.4	47.6	48.1	48.5	49.8	50.5	48.0
1993	48.9	48.4	48.3	48.0	48.0	48.2	48.3	48.4	49.3	50.5	51.8	53.1	49.2
1994	50.7	51.1	51.3	50.1	50.3	50.6	52.0	51.7	51.8	51.9	52.9	54.0	51.5
1995	51.7	51.6	51.5	51.2	51.4	51.3	50.3	51.0	50.5	51.8	53.2	54.0	51.6
1996	51.3	51.2	51.1	50.4	50.6	50.3	49.3	49.6	49.7	50.3	51.9	52.3	50.6
1997	50.5	50.5	50.6	49.5	49.8	49.8	49.6	49.9	50.5	51.7	53.0	53.4	50.7
1998	50.8	50.9	51.1	51.3	51.4	51.5	51.3	51.5	51.9	52.2	53.6	54.6	51.8
1999	53.8	52.5	52.9	52.8	52.9	53.3	52.9	53.1	53.1	54.0	55.3	56.2	53.5
2000	54.2	54.0	53.8	53.5	53.7	53.8	54.1	54.7	54.9	56.0	57.9	58.9	54.9
2001	55.7	55.2	55.1	55.0	55.0	54.9	54.6	54.6	54.9	54.9	56.5	57.6	55.3
2002	54.1	53.8	53.8	54.0	54.4	54.2	53.5	53.6	53.5	54.4	55.9	57.0	54.4
2003	54.0	54.0	54.4	54.0	53.9	53.8	53.2	53.4	53.5	54.4	56.8	57.1	54.4

Employment by Industry: Arizona—*Continued*

(Numbers in thousands. Not seasonally adjusted.)

Industry	January	February	March	April	May	June	July	August	September	October	November	December	Annual Average
TUCSON—*Continued*													
Wholesale trade													
1990	6.2	6.3	6.3	6.0	6.0	6.0	5.9	5.8	5.8	5.6	5.5	5.5	5.9
1991	6.1	6.1	6.1	6.0	6.0	6.0	6.1	6.1	6.1	6.0	6.1	6.2	6.0
1992	5.9	6.0	6.1	5.9	6.0	6.0	6.0	6.0	6.1	6.1	6.1	6.0	6.0
1993	6.1	6.1	6.1	6.1	6.2	6.2	6.0	6.1	6.1	6.3	6.3	6.4	6.1
1994	6.2	6.2	6.3	6.4	6.4	6.4	6.6	6.6	6.7	6.7	6.7	6.6	6.4
1995	6.6	6.6	6.7	6.8	6.8	6.8	6.6	6.6	6.6	6.8	6.8	6.9	6.7
1996	6.9	6.9	7.0	6.7	6.8	6.8	6.7	6.7	6.7	6.8	6.8	6.9	6.8
1997	6.6	6.7	6.7	7.0	7.0	7.0	6.9	7.0	7.0	7.2	7.3	7.3	6.9
1998	7.0	7.0	7.1	7.1	7.2	7.2	7.1	7.0	7.1	7.2	7.2	7.2	7.1
1999	7.1	7.2	7.2	7.2	7.3	7.3	7.3	7.3	7.3	7.5	7.5	7.6	7.3
2000	7.6	7.6	7.6	7.2	7.3	7.4	7.4	7.4	7.4	7.4	7.5	7.6	7.4
2001	7.3	7.3	7.4	7.4	7.4	7.5	7.4	7.4	7.4	7.3	7.4	7.4	7.4
2002	7.5	7.4	7.4	7.2	7.3	7.3	7.2	7.3	7.3	7.4	7.4	7.4	7.3
2003	7.2	7.3	7.3	7.3	7.3	7.2	7.2	7.1	7.2	7.2	7.2	7.2	7.2
Retail trade													
1990	33.7	33.8	34.1	33.3	33.5	33.4	32.6	33.1	33.6	33.5	34.7	35.0	33.6
1991	34.4	33.6	34.0	33.9	34.0	33.8	33.4	33.9	34.2	34.8	36.2	36.7	34.4
1992	34.9	34.6	34.6	34.5	34.7	34.5	34.7	34.9	35.2	35.5	36.8	37.6	35.2
1993	36.0	35.5	35.3	34.9	34.7	34.8	35.2	35.3	36.0	37.0	38.0	39.2	35.9
1994	37.2	37.4	37.5	36.1	36.2	36.5	37.6	37.4	37.4	37.4	38.5	39.6	37.4
1995	37.6	37.5	37.2	36.7	36.7	36.6	35.9	36.4	36.4	37.2	38.6	39.3	37.1
1996	36.5	36.3	36.1	35.8	36.0	35.7	34.9	35.1	35.3	35.5	37.0	37.3	35.9
1997	36.2	35.9	35.9	34.7	34.8	34.8	34.7	35.2	35.3	36.2	37.4	37.8	35.7
1998	36.1	36.2	36.2	36.2	36.3	36.1	35.7	36.1	36.1	36.5	37.8	38.7	36.5
1999	38.5	37.0	37.3	37.0	37.1	37.4	36.9	37.1	37.2	37.8	39.2	40.0	37.7
2000	38.0	37.9	37.7	37.8	37.9	37.9	37.7	38.3	38.6	39.6	41.3	42.1	38.7
2001	39.0	38.5	38.3	38.3	38.2	38.1	37.9	37.9	38.3	38.6	40.1	41.3	38.7
2002	39.1	38.8	38.8	39.1	39.4	39.2	38.6	38.6	38.7	39.2	40.7	41.8	39.3
2003	39.0	38.9	39.3	38.9	38.8	38.8	38.3	38.7	38.7	39.5	41.9	42.2	39.4
Transportation and utilities													
1990	5.7	5.5	5.6	5.6	5.7	5.7	5.7	5.7	5.7	5.7	5.7	5.7	5.6
1991	5.1	5.2	5.3	5.8	5.9	6.0	6.2	6.2	6.2	6.3	6.4	6.4	5.9
1992	6.5	6.5	6.7	7.3	7.3	7.2	6.7	6.7	6.8	6.9	6.9	6.9	6.8
1993	6.8	6.8	6.9	7.0	7.1	7.2	7.1	7.0	7.2	7.2	7.5	7.5	7.1
1994	7.3	7.5	7.5	7.6	7.7	7.7	7.8	7.7	7.7	7.8	7.7	7.8	7.6
1995	7.5	7.5	7.6	7.7	7.9	7.9	7.8	8.0	7.5	7.8	7.8	7.8	7.7
1996	7.9	8.0	8.0	7.9	7.8	7.8	7.7	7.8	7.7	8.0	8.1	8.1	7.9
1997	7.7	7.9	8.0	7.8	8.0	8.0	8.0	7.7	8.2	8.3	8.3	8.3	8.0
1998	7.7	7.7	7.8	8.0	7.9	8.2	8.5	8.4	8.7	8.5	8.6	8.7	8.2
1999	8.2	8.3	8.4	8.6	8.5	8.6	8.7	8.7	8.6	8.7	8.6	8.6	8.5
2000	8.6	8.5	8.5	8.5	8.5	8.5	9.0	9.0	8.9	9.0	9.1	9.2	8.7
2001	. . .	9.4	9.4	9.3	9.4	9.3	9.3	9.3	9.2	9.0	9.0	8.9	. . .
2002	7.5	7.6	7.6	7.7	7.7	7.7	7.7	7.7	7.5	7.8	7.8	7.8	7.7
2003	7.8	7.8	7.8	7.8	7.8	7.8	7.7	7.6	7.6	7.7	7.7	7.7	7.7
Information													
1990	5.1	5.1	5.1	5.2	5.4	5.4	5.1	5.1	4.9	4.8	4.8	4.8	5.0
1991	4.9	4.9	4.9	4.8	4.7	4.7	4.8	4.9	4.9	4.9	4.9	4.9	4.8
1992	4.6	4.6	4.6	4.8	4.8	4.8	4.8	4.8	4.8	4.8	4.8	4.9	4.7
1993	4.8	4.8	4.8	4.9	4.9	5.0	5.0	5.0	5.0	5.0	5.0	5.0	4.9
1994	5.5	5.5	5.4	5.5	5.5	5.5	5.3	5.4	5.4	5.7	5.9	5.8	5.5
1995	6.0	6.3	6.4	6.5	6.8	6.5	6.3	6.4	6.2	6.5	7.1	6.6	6.4
1996	6.8	6.8	6.7	6.7	7.0	6.6	6.7	6.8	6.9	6.9	7.3	7.3	6.8
1997	7.3	7.6	7.5	7.3	7.3	7.0	7.1	7.4	7.3	7.5	7.7	7.8	7.4
1998	7.7	7.8	7.7	7.7	7.8	7.7	7.6	7.4	7.3	7.3	7.6	8.0	7.6
1999	7.4	7.9	7.5	7.5	7.7	7.5	7.8	7.9	7.7	7.8	8.5	8.1	7.7
2000	7.9	8.1	8.0	8.0	8.1	8.0	7.9	8.1	7.8	7.8	7.8	7.8	7.9
2001	7.8	7.8	7.8	7.7	7.7	7.6	7.6	7.7	7.7	7.6	7.8	7.9	7.7
2002	7.9	8.0	8.0	7.9	8.0	7.8	7.8	7.9	7.8	7.8	7.9	7.8	7.9
2003	7.6	7.7	7.5	7.4	7.5	7.4	7.6	7.5	7.5	7.6	7.7	7.7	7.6
Financial activities													
1990	12.2	12.2	12.3	11.8	11.9	11.9	11.9	12.0	12.0	11.7	11.5	11.5	11.9
1991	11.4	11.3	11.0	10.8	10.9	11.1	11.3	11.5	11.4	11.4	11.5	11.6	11.2
1992	10.9	11.0	11.1	10.8	10.9	10.9	10.9	11.0	11.0	10.9	11.0	11.2	10.9
1993	10.7	10.8	10.9	10.9	10.9	11.1	11.0	11.0	11.1	11.3	11.3	11.5	11.0
1994	11.8	11.8	11.9	12.0	12.0	12.0	11.9	11.8	11.7	11.6	11.6	11.6	11.8
1995	11.3	11.4	11.6	11.5	11.4	11.6	11.3	11.4	11.5	11.9	11.9	12.1	11.5
1996	12.1	12.2	12.4	12.4	12.4	12.4	12.6	12.4	12.4	12.1	12.1	12.2	12.3
1997	12.0	12.1	12.4	12.4	12.5	12.5	12.6	12.7	12.8	13.5	13.6	13.8	12.7
1998	12.9	12.7	12.8	13.1	13.2	13.3	13.1	13.2	13.4	13.7	13.8	13.9	13.2
1999	13.2	13.4	13.5	13.4	13.6	13.7	14.3	14.2	14.2	14.5	14.6	14.8	13.9
2000	14.6	14.8	14.9	14.6	14.6	14.7	14.9	15.0	15.0	15.2	14.8	14.8	14.8
2001	14.2	14.4	14.5	14.8	14.7	14.7	14.8	14.5	14.1	14.2	14.3	14.3	14.5
2002	14.0	14.1	14.2	14.2	14.4	14.3	14.2	14.3	14.4	14.7	14.7	14.8	14.4
2003	14.8	14.9	15.1	15.0	15.1	15.2	14.9	15.0	15.1	15.3	15.3	15.3	15.1

Employment by Industry: Arizona—*Continued*

(Numbers in thousands. Not seasonally adjusted.)

Industry	January	February	March	April	May	June	July	August	September	October	November	December	Annual Average
TUCSON—*Continued*													
Professional and business services													
1990	21.1	21.1	21.2	21.3	21.2	21.4	21.5	21.8	21.6	21.5	21.3	21.4	21.3
1991	22.7	23.0	23.2	23.4	23.6	23.5	23.1	23.9	23.9	23.9	24.1	24.2	23.5
1992	24.5	24.7	25.0	25.2	25.3	25.3	25.6	25.6	25.8	26.4	26.6	27.2	25.6
1993	26.5	27.3	27.5	28.5	28.0	28.1	27.6	28.0	27.8	29.0	28.9	29.5	28.0
1994	28.9	30.0	30.4	30.9	30.1	30.5	30.4	30.8	31.1	31.6	32.2	33.4	30.8
1995	32.7	33.9	34.3	34.3	33.7	34.4	33.4	33.5	33.5	33.8	33.8	34.3	33.8
1996	32.5	33.0	33.2	34.1	34.5	34.5	35.2	35.5	35.6	34.5	34.9	34.5	34.3
1997	33.9	34.6	34.9	36.2	36.4	36.7	37.8	38.2	38.6	38.1	38.2	38.6	36.8
1998	38.6	39.6	40.3	40.9	40.6	41.9	42.0	42.3	42.1	40.3	40.0	41.2	40.8
1999	39.0	40.2	40.7	40.6	40.9	41.5	40.9	41.1	41.2	41.8	42.2	43.1	41.1
2000	42.3	43.4	44.6	44.2	44.1	44.5	42.8	43.4	43.3	42.8	43.0	43.3	43.4
2001	41.0	42.2	42.4	42.3	41.5	41.6	41.4	41.4	40.5	40.6	40.5	40.3	41.3
2002	40.4	41.0	41.3	41.5	40.9	41.1	41.2	41.9	42.0	42.0	42.4	42.2	41.5
2003	40.6	40.6	40.7	40.9	40.7	41.3	40.8	41.1	41.8	42.2	42.1	42.5	41.3
Educational and health services													
1990	29.6	30.1	30.3	29.6	29.7	30.0	29.1	29.1	29.8	30.5	30.9	31.1	29.9
1991	30.9	31.0	31.3	31.2	31.2	31.1	31.1	31.3	32.3	32.0	32.3	32.3	31.5
1992	31.5	31.7	31.8	32.5	32.7	32.4	32.6	32.4	32.8	33.4	33.3	33.5	32.5
1993	34.0	34.2	34.2	33.5	33.7	33.5	33.6	33.8	34.3	34.4	34.8	34.9	34.0
1994	34.8	35.1	35.3	35.9	35.9	36.0	35.3	35.5	36.0	36.3	36.7	37.0	35.8
1995	34.7	35.2	35.3	35.0	35.3	35.8	35.5	35.2	36.0	35.6	36.2	36.7	35.5
1996	36.3	36.4	37.8	37.1	37.4	37.2	37.0	37.2	37.8	38.3	38.8	39.2	37.5
1997	37.4	37.8	38.1	38.7	38.7	38.6	38.1	38.3	39.0	39.3	39.7	39.8	38.6
1998	40.3	40.7	40.9	40.6	40.5	40.3	40.0	39.9	40.3	40.1	40.4	40.6	40.3
1999	39.5	40.2	40.4	42.9	42.9	42.2	41.5	41.5	41.9	42.5	42.4	42.7	41.7
2000	42.4	42.5	42.3	41.8	41.6	41.4	41.0	41.6	42.1	42.2	42.4	42.4	41.9
2001	40.7	41.0	41.6	41.5	41.4	41.3	41.3	41.7	42.2	42.4	42.9	43.2	41.8
2002	42.9	43.4	43.4	43.4	43.7	43.4	42.7	43.5	43.9	44.0	44.3	44.3	43.6
2003	44.3	44.9	45.0	45.3	45.5	45.2	45.0	45.7	46.3	46.5	46.8	47.1	45.6
Leisure and hospitality													
1990	29.6	30.5	31.0	29.9	29.7	29.2	28.2	28.5	29.2	29.1	29.4	29.6	29.4
1991	29.9	30.4	30.6	29.5	29.5	28.4	28.0	28.4	28.9	29.3	29.9	30.3	29.4
1992	30.6	31.0	31.2	31.2	31.0	30.1	29.0	29.4	30.1	30.4	30.6	30.7	30.4
1993	30.8	31.9	32.3	32.3	32.4	31.4	30.6	30.3	31.5	32.0	32.2	32.4	31.6
1994	32.2	33.1	33.5	34.3	34.0	32.9	31.9	32.1	32.5	33.4	33.5	33.9	33.1
1995	34.3	34.7	35.4	35.8	35.7	35.3	34.2	33.9	34.5	34.2	34.5	35.0	34.7
1996	35.2	36.3	37.0	36.8	36.0	35.0	33.9	34.0	34.5	35.0	35.8	35.8	35.4
1997	36.2	37.3	37.8	37.0	36.7	35.4	35.2	35.6	35.9	36.6	37.0	37.2	36.4
1998	36.4	37.2	37.7	36.9	36.4	35.5	34.9	34.9	35.0	36.1	36.3	36.3	36.1
1999	36.6	37.4	37.9	39.0	39.0	38.4	36.8	37.2	38.1	38.9	39.1	39.7	38.1
2000	39.8	40.9	41.3	41.0	40.6	39.9	38.5	38.4	39.0	39.6	40.1	40.0	39.9
2001	38.5	39.7	40.0	40.0	39.4	38.1	36.9	37.4	37.6	37.0	36.9	36.9	38.2
2002	37.8	38.4	38.8	38.7	37.9	36.7	35.5	35.6	36.2	36.8	37.3	37.4	37.3
2003	36.4	36.9	37.5	37.6	37.1	36.2	35.1	35.4	36.1	36.3	36.8	37.0	36.5
Other services													
1990	9.9	10.0	10.0	10.1	10.2	10.2	10.0	10.1	10.0	9.9	10.0	10.0	10.0
1991	10.4	10.4	10.5	10.5	10.5	10.6	10.5	10.5	10.3	10.5	10.4	10.4	10.4
1992	10.3	10.3	10.4	10.7	10.7	11.0	11.1	11.0	10.9	10.8	10.9	10.9	10.7
1993	10.9	11.0	11.2	10.5	10.9	10.9	10.5	10.8	10.8	10.7	10.6	10.6	10.7
1994	10.4	10.5	10.5	10.5	10.5	10.7	10.7	10.6	10.6	10.7	10.6	10.7	10.5
1995	10.1	10.2	10.3	10.1	10.1	10.2	10.3	10.2	10.1	10.3	10.3	10.3	10.2
1996	10.6	10.8	10.8	10.9	10.9	11.0	10.8	10.7	10.6	10.9	10.9	10.9	10.8
1997	10.8	10.9	10.9	10.7	10.8	10.9	11.0	10.8	10.9	11.0	11.0	11.0	10.8
1998	11.0	11.1	11.2	11.2	11.3	11.6	11.6	11.3	11.3	11.5	11.6	12.2	11.4
1999	11.9	12.1	12.3	12.5	12.7	13.2	13.0	12.9	12.8	13.0	13.0	13.0	12.7
2000	12.9	13.1	13.0	13.0	13.0	13.3	13.1	12.8	12.9	12.9	13.0	13.2	13.0
2001	13.8	13.9	14.1	14.2	14.4	14.6	14.5	14.6	14.5	14.3	14.3	14.3	14.3
2002	14.2	14.3	14.3	14.7	14.8	14.7	14.6	14.5	14.5	14.4	14.4	14.4	14.5
2003	14.2	14.3	14.4	14.6	14.6	14.7	14.6	14.6	14.6	14.5	14.5	14.5	14.5
Government													
1990	54.3	56.6	57.4	57.8	58.6	49.5	48.6	52.4	57.0	58.6	59.7	60.1	55.8
1991	54.7	57.9	61.6	61.4	61.7	53.4	50.1	53.3	61.3	62.6	63.0	63.0	58.6
1992	60.3	63.4	63.7	63.9	64.2	53.6	52.0	54.7	63.6	63.1	64.3	64.6	60.9
1993	61.6	64.9	65.4	66.1	66.4	59.9	54.7	56.1	64.8	66.7	67.3	66.7	63.3
1994	67.3	69.5	68.8	67.4	65.2	57.0	54.1	64.0	68.3	67.6	68.6	68.6	65.5
1995	67.7	69.9	70.2	71.5	71.3	63.2	62.0	66.4	68.3	70.0	70.0	70.7	68.4
1996	68.3	70.9	71.4	71.6	72.0	68.1	61.2	66.5	69.7	71.0	70.0	72.3	69.4
1997	69.6	71.6	72.4	74.5	75.1	68.7	63.8	66.6	69.8	73.5	74.7	74.8	71.2
1998	71.7	73.6	74.5	74.8	74.5	69.6	62.0	66.7	69.8	73.8	74.9	74.3	71.6
1999	72.3	75.3	75.7	76.5	74.2	71.0	63.0	68.4	72.5	75.8	76.9	75.2	73.0
2000	74.8	77.0	78.2	78.5	79.7	74.7	69.6	70.8	75.5	78.2	79.1	79.0	76.2
2001	75.6	78.6	79.4	79.7	79.3	73.6	67.3	71.7	77.7	78.6	80.4	80.2	76.8
2002	77.7	79.9	79.9	81.2	80.4	74.4	67.8	72.5	77.9	80.4	81.4	81.2	77.9
2003	78.7	81.1	81.5	81.1	81.1	73.5	68.6	72.8	78.0	80.6	80.8	80.8	78.2

Employment by Industry: Arizona—*Continued*

(Numbers in thousands. Not seasonally adjusted.)

Industry	January	February	March	April	May	June	July	August	September	October	November	December	Annual Average
TUCSON—*Continued*													
Federal government													
1995	8.4	8.4	8.4	8.4	8.5	8.3	8.4	8.5	8.6	8.5	8.4	8.5	8.4
1996	8.0	8.0	8.0	8.1	8.1	8.0	8.0	8.2	8.3	8.3	8.3	8.5	8.1
1997	8.5	8.5	8.5	8.5	8.5	8.4	8.4	8.5	8.6	8.5	8.6	8.7	8.5
1998	8.6	8.5	8.6	8.7	8.8	8.7	8.7	8.7	8.8	8.7	8.8	9.0	8.7
1999	8.9	8.9	9.1	9.0	8.9	9.0	8.9	9.1	9.1	9.0	9.0	9.2	9.0
2000	9.1	9.2	9.5	9.4	10.6	9.4	9.5	9.2	9.1	8.9	9.0	9.2	9.3
2001	9.0	8.9	8.9	9.0	9.0	9.1	9.0	9.3	9.3	9.1	9.2	9.3	9.1
2002	9.3	9.2	9.1	9.0	9.0	9.2	9.0	9.1	9.1	9.3	9.3	9.4	9.2
2003	9.3	9.4	9.5	9.5	9.5	9.5	9.7	9.7	9.7	9.9	10.0	9.8	9.6
State government													
1994	24.4	25.7	25.0	25.6	24.0	24.7	24.0	24.4	25.6	25.9	26.5	26.5	25.1
1995	25.4	26.4	26.4	26.3	26.4	24.7	22.7	21.4	24.4	24.8	24.8	25.2	24.9
1996	25.1	25.4	25.8	26.0	26.1	24.4	22.0	22.5	23.1	25.1	23.8	26.0	24.6
1997	25.0	25.3	25.9	27.9	27.7	27.0	17.2	20.5	23.4	25.0	25.3	25.3	24.6
1998	25.2	25.6	26.0	25.4	25.5	23.5	17.2	21.0	22.7	26.2	26.5	26.2	24.2
1999	25.4	26.4	26.6	27.2	24.7	25.4	19.0	22.6	24.9	27.6	28.1	26.3	25.3
2000	27.2	28.0	28.1	28.2	28.2	26.5	22.8	23.0	26.9	28.0	28.2	28.4	26.9
2001	27.5	27.9	28.5	28.5	28.3	26.7	22.0	22.9	27.2	27.4	28.5	28.5	27.0
2002	27.8	28.1	28.0	28.6	28.5	26.6	22.2	23.1	26.7	28.1	28.3	28.4	27.0
2003	27.8	28.2	28.1	28.4	28.5	26.5	22.7	23.6	27.2	28.5	28.5	28.6	27.2
Local government													
1994	34.3	35.3	35.2	33.2	32.7	23.9	21.8	31.2	34.4	33.3	33.8	33.5	31.8
1995	33.9	35.1	35.4	36.8	36.3	30.1	30.8	36.4	35.3	36.7	36.8	37.0	35.0
1996	35.2	37.5	37.6	37.5	37.8	35.7	31.2	35.8	38.3	37.6	37.9	37.8	36.6
1997	36.1	37.8	38.0	38.1	38.9	33.4	38.2	37.7	37.9	40.1	40.7	40.8	38.1
1998	37.9	39.5	39.9	40.7	40.2	37.4	36.1	37.0	38.3	38.9	39.6	39.1	38.7
1999	38.0	40.0	40.0	40.3	40.6	36.6	35.1	36.7	38.5	39.2	39.8	39.7	38.7
2000	38.5	39.8	40.6	40.9	40.9	38.8	37.3	38.6	39.5	41.3	41.9	41.4	39.9
2001	39.1	41.8	42.0	42.2	42.0	37.8	36.3	39.5	41.2	42.1	42.7	42.4	40.8
2002	40.6	42.6	42.8	43.6	42.9	38.6	36.6	40.3	42.1	43.0	43.8	43.4	41.7
2003	41.6	43.5	43.9	43.2	43.1	37.5	36.2	39.5	41.1	42.2	42.3	42.4	41.4

Average Weekly Hours by Industry: Arizona

(Not seasonally adjusted.)

Industry	January	February	March	April	May	June	July	August	September	October	November	December	Annual Average
STATEWIDE													
Construction													
2001	35.6	36.7	37.4	36.9	37.8	38.2	37.9	37.6	37.5	37.2	36.5	36.2	37.1
2002	37.0	37.1	37.7	37.5	37.8	37.3	36.9	37.9	37.0	37.9	37.5	38.0	37.5
2003	37.4	36.3	37.3	37.9	37.7	38.3	37.5	38.0	37.3	37.8	36.9	37.6	37.5
Manufacturing													
2001	40.6	40.1	40.4	39.5	39.4	39.8	39.9	40.8	40.9	40.7	40.4	40.5	40.3
2002	40.1	39.9	40.3	40.4	40.0	40.2	40.3	39.9	39.8	39.7	39.8	39.9	40.0
2003	40.4	39.2	40.0	40.4	40.6	40.7	39.8	40.1	40.5	40.6	41.3	41.3	40.4
Trade, transportation, and utilities													
2001	33.1	32.9	33.1	33.5	32.6	32.8	33.4	33.1	33.0	33.0	32.7	33.5	33.1
2002	33.1	33.3	33.5	33.3	33.4	33.6	33.5	33.6	33.6	33.6	33.3	34.1	33.5
2003	33.9	33.9	33.9	33.9	34.1	34.6	34.6	34.8	34.2	34.7	34.5	34.8	34.3
Wholesale trade													
2001	38.2	38.6	38.5	39.2	38.1	38.7	39.9	38.7	39.1	39.9	39.3	39.7	39.0
2002	39.9	41.1	39.9	39.9	38.9	37.9	36.8	37.8	38.9	39.0	38.4	39.6	39.0
2003	40.2	39.3	39.6	38.9	39.3	39.3	39.6	39.6	38.9	38.3	39.2	40.4	39.4
Retail trade													
2001	30.5	30.5	30.5	30.6	30.3	30.6	30.9	30.9	30.4	30.1	30.4	31.3	30.6
2002	30.6	30.9	31.2	31.1	31.4	31.7	31.9	31.6	31.3	31.4	31.0	31.9	31.3
2003	30.9	31.4	31.0	31.4	31.3	32.1	32.0	32.1	31.6	32.3	31.6	32.0	31.6
PHOENIX													
Construction													
2001	36.1	37.2	37.8	37.4	38.3	38.6	38.5	38.5	38.5	38.1	37.5	37.4	37.9
2002	38.0	38.2	38.8	38.4	38.6	38.2	37.2	38.1	37.4	38.1	37.5	38.1	38.0
2003	37.6	36.7	37.7	38.2	38.1	38.4	37.6	38.1	37.7	38.0	37.5	38.5	37.8
Manufacturing													
2001	40.1	39.6	39.7	38.9	38.3	38.6	38.6	39.5	40.0	40.1	39.2	39.5	39.3
2002	38.7	38.6	39.1	39.4	39.4	39.9	39.3	39.4	39.2	39.1	39.3	39.7	39.2
2003	39.7	38.4	39.3	39.9	39.9	40.4	39.4	39.4	39.7	40.1	41.0	40.9	39.9
Wholesale trade													
2001	38.5	38.6	38.4	39.6	38.4	38.7	39.9	38.9	39.9	39.7	39.5	40.2	39.2
2002	40.2	41.3	41.2	40.7	41.2	41.1	39.9	39.6	40.8	39.9	38.7	39.9	40.4
2003	40.5	39.2	39.5	38.6	38.9	38.7	39.3	38.9	38.0	37.4	38.2	38.3	38.8
Retail trade													
2001	30.1	29.9	30.1	30.2	29.9	30.4	30.5	30.7	30.2	29.9	30.5	31.4	30.3
2002	30.8	31.3	31.5	31.4	32.0	32.2	32.4	31.8	31.3	31.4	31.0	32.3	31.6
2003	31.4	31.7	31.5	31.9	31.8	32.5	32.4	32.2	32.1	32.7	31.8	32.0	32.0
TUCSON													
Construction													
2001	33.3	34.3	35.3	34.4	35.4	36.5	35.4	34.5	34.0	34.7	33.7	32.7	34.5
2002	33.0	33.2	33.9	34.1	34.1	35.1	34.9	35.9	35.6	36.7	36.9	36.9	35.0
2003	36.2	35.1	36.1	36.3	37.0	37.5	37.8	37.8	37.5	37.7	36.6	37.7	37.0
Manufacturing													
2001	42.1	41.2	41.8	40.9	41.0	41.6	41.8	42.1	42.6	41.9	42.3	42.3	41.8
2002	42.2	41.8	41.5	41.6	40.9	41.6	42.7	41.4	41.7	41.8	41.9	41.4	41.7
2003	42.6	41.3	42.4	42.5	42.0	41.6	41.1	42.3	43.2	43.3	43.4	43.6	42.4
Trade, transportation, and utilities													
2001	32.2	33.1	33.1	33.0	32.6	32.2	32.6	32.6	32.3	32.5	31.7	32.3	32.5
2002	31.4	30.8	31.4	31.7	31.0	31.3	30.9	31.0	31.5	32.2	31.6	32.0	31.4
2003	31.5	32.0	31.3	31.6	31.6	32.2	32.4	32.4	32.3	32.5	32.3	33.0	32.1

Average Hourly Earnings by Industry: Arizona

(Dollars, not seasonally adjusted.)

Industry	January	February	March	April	May	June	July	August	September	October	November	December	Annual Average
STATEWIDE													
Construction													
2001	15.45	15.46	15.56	15.56	15.18	14.80	14.75	14.40	14.50	14.46	14.46	14.76	14.94
2002	14.42	14.28	14.22	14.31	14.25	14.21	14.32	14.37	14.53	14.59	14.78	14.82	14.43
2003	14.89	14.87	14.98	15.03	15.13	15.40	15.35	15.24	15.39	15.16	15.23	15.38	15.18
Manufacturing													
2001	13.48	13.50	13.70	13.71	13.72	13.73	13.89	13.76	14.01	13.94	14.09	14.11	13.80
2002	14.06	14.10	14.14	14.04	14.16	14.22	14.18	14.09	14.13	14.16	14.16	14.50	14.16
2003	14.41	14.26	14.28	14.23	14.33	14.33	14.44	14.48	14.34	14.45	14.61	14.33	14.38
Trade, transportation, and utilities													
2001	12.90	13.05	13.11	13.03	12.96	12.94	12.76	12.97	13.18	12.99	13.08	13.14	13.01
2002	12.97	13.07	13.12	13.11	13.13	13.17	13.10	13.07	13.38	13.26	13.29	13.09	13.15
2003	13.40	13.42	13.53	13.34	13.46	13.51	13.49	13.42	13.58	13.45	13.84	13.45	13.49
Wholesale trade													
2001	15.44	15.90	15.62	15.52	15.05	15.32	14.97	15.38	15.59	15.12	14.92	15.24	15.34
2002	15.06	14.85	14.93	15.38	15.65	16.12	16.58	16.19	16.49	16.22	16.37	16.51	15.85
2003	16.01	16.00	16.48	16.32	16.65	17.15	17.11	17.25	17.66	17.50	18.03	17.49	16.97
Retail trade													
2001	11.08	11.25	11.46	11.38	11.27	11.30	10.96	11.29	11.44	11.21	11.55	11.36	11.30
2002	11.17	11.35	11.35	11.27	11.25	11.27	11.11	11.17	11.41	11.34	11.33	11.12	11.26
2003	11.41	11.47	11.55	11.52	11.58	11.56	11.53	11.32	11.47	11.47	11.77	11.42	11.51
PHOENIX													
Construction													
2001	16.08	16.00	16.14	16.12	15.76	15.37	15.28	14.89	15.02	14.94	14.93	15.21	15.47
2002	15.01	14.78	14.80	14.94	14.88	14.81	14.94	14.91	15.08	15.14	15.38	15.38	15.00
2003	15.41	15.47	15.49	15.61	15.72	16.02	16.01	15.84	15.91	15.79	15.86	15.90	15.76
Manufacturing													
2001	13.32	13.32	13.56	13.59	13.56	13.43	13.69	13.52	13.78	13.72	13.87	13.88	13.60
2002	13.92	13.92	13.92	13.83	13.93	13.91	13.81	13.81	13.68	13.74	13.70	13.95	13.84
2003	13.96	13.94	13.98	13.83	13.93	13.92	13.93	13.76	13.64	13.82	13.90	13.67	13.85
Wholesale trade													
2001	15.91	16.39	16.23	16.47	15.98	16.35	15.86	16.34	16.71	16.21	16.09	16.55	16.26
2002	16.16	16.05	15.91	16.39	16.66	17.16	17.67	17.37	17.76	17.29	17.66	17.87	16.99
2003	17.33	17.81	17.98	17.71	18.04	18.58	18.15	18.26	18.56	18.32	18.87	18.30	18.15
Retail trade													
2001	11.78	11.93	12.14	12.12	11.95	11.97	11.61	11.96	12.12	11.87	12.23	12.04	11.98
2002	11.68	12.00	11.99	11.92	11.82	11.88	11.56	11.71	12.05	11.96	11.97	11.72	11.85
2003	11.95	12.04	12.16	12.13	12.15	12.08	12.04	11.82	11.97	11.97	12.33	11.96	12.05
TUCSON													
Construction													
2001	13.06	13.14	13.14	13.25	12.85	12.46	12.59	12.57	12.22	12.35	12.32	12.56	12.70
2002	12.59	12.50	12.34	12.41	12.32	12.31	12.38	12.55	12.51	12.53	12.55	12.41	12.45
2003	12.42	12.49	12.56	12.72	12.95	13.06	13.03	13.11	13.47	13.34	13.43	13.81	13.05
Manufacturing													
2001	14.79	14.79	14.91	14.63	14.87	14.93	14.82	14.93	15.34	14.90	15.06	15.35	14.94
2002	14.89	15.01	15.36	15.16	15.26	15.28	15.05	15.10	15.29	15.28	15.41	15.87	15.24
2003	15.56	15.09	15.04	15.13	15.10	14.97	14.92	15.37	15.44	15.31	15.24	15.00	15.18
Trade, transportation, and utilities													
2001	12.15	12.08	12.04	11.75	11.71	11.82	11.82	12.04	12.03	11.98	11.87	11.74	11.92
2002	11.87	11.91	12.14	12.10	12.05	11.96	12.32	12.22	12.28	12.11	12.03	11.86	12.07
2003	12.14	12.14	12.01	11.93	11.97	12.14	12.44	12.55	12.70	12.70	12.43	12.32	12.29

Average Weekly Earnings by Industry: Arizona

(Dollars, not seasonally adjusted.)

Industry	January	February	March	April	May	June	July	August	September	October	November	December	Annual Average
STATEWIDE													
Construction													
2001	550.02	567.38	581.94	574.16	573.80	565.36	559.03	541.44	543.75	537.91	527.79	534.31	554.27
2002	533.54	529.79	536.09	536.63	538.65	530.03	528.41	544.62	537.61	552.96	554.25	563.16	541.13
2003	556.89	539.78	558.75	569.64	570.40	589.82	575.63	579.12	574.05	573.05	561.99	578.29	569.25
Manufacturing													
2001	547.29	541.35	553.48	541.55	540.57	546.45	554.21	561.41	573.01	567.36	569.24	571.46	556.14
2002	563.81	562.59	569.84	567.22	566.40	571.64	571.45	562.19	562.37	562.15	563.57	578.55	566.40
2003	582.16	558.99	571.20	574.89	581.80	583.23	574.71	580.65	580.77	586.67	603.39	591.83	580.95
Trade, transportation, and utilities													
2001	426.99	429.35	433.94	436.51	422.50	424.43	426.18	429.31	434.94	428.67	427.72	440.19	430.63
2002	429.31	435.23	439.52	436.56	438.54	442.51	438.85	439.15	449.57	445.54	442.56	446.37	440.53
2003	454.26	454.94	458.67	452.23	458.99	467.45	466.75	467.02	464.44	466.72	477.48	468.06	462.71
Wholesale trade													
2001	589.81	613.74	601.37	608.38	573.41	592.88	597.30	595.21	609.57	603.29	586.36	605.03	598.26
2002	600.89	610.34	595.71	613.66	608.79	610.95	610.14	611.98	641.46	632.58	628.61	653.80	618.15
2003	643.60	628.80	652.61	634.85	654.35	674.00	677.56	683.10	686.97	670.25	706.78	706.60	668.62
Retail trade													
2001	337.94	343.13	349.53	348.23	341.48	345.78	338.66	348.86	347.78	337.42	351.12	355.57	345.78
2002	341.80	350.72	354.12	350.50	353.25	357.26	354.41	352.97	357.13	356.08	351.23	354.73	352.44
2003	352.57	360.16	358.05	361.73	362.45	371.08	368.96	363.37	362.45	370.48	371.93	365.44	363.72
PHOENIX													
Construction													
2001	580.49	595.20	610.09	602.89	603.61	593.28	588.28	573.27	578.27	569.21	559.88	568.85	586.31
2002	570.38	564.60	574.24	573.70	574.37	565.74	555.77	568.07	563.99	576.83	576.75	585.98	570.00
2003	579.42	567.75	583.97	596.30	598.93	615.17	601.98	603.50	599.81	600.02	594.75	612.15	595.73
Manufacturing													
2001	534.13	527.47	538.33	528.65	519.35	518.40	528.43	534.04	551.20	550.17	543.70	548.26	534.48
2002	538.70	537.31	544.27	544.90	548.84	555.01	542.73	544.11	536.26	537.23	538.41	553.82	542.53
2003	554.21	535.30	549.41	551.82	555.81	562.37	548.84	542.14	541.51	554.18	569.90	559.10	552.62
Wholesale trade													
2001	612.54	632.65	623.23	652.21	613.63	632.75	632.81	635.63	666.73	643.54	635.56	665.31	637.39
2002	649.63	662.87	655.49	667.07	686.39	705.28	705.03	687.85	724.61	689.87	683.44	713.01	686.40
2003	701.87	698.15	710.21	683.61	701.76	719.05	713.30	710.31	705.28	685.17	720.83	700.89	704.22
Retail trade													
2001	354.58	356.71	365.41	366.02	357.31	363.89	354.11	367.17	366.02	354.91	373.02	378.06	362.99
2002	359.74	375.60	377.69	374.29	378.24	382.54	374.54	372.38	377.17	375.54	371.07	378.56	374.46
2003	375.23	381.67	383.04	386.95	386.37	392.60	390.10	380.60	384.24	391.42	392.09	382.72	385.60
TUCSON													
Construction													
2001	434.90	450.70	463.84	455.80	454.89	454.79	445.69	433.67	415.48	428.55	415.18	410.71	438.15
2002	415.47	415.00	418.33	423.18	420.11	432.08	432.06	450.55	445.36	459.85	463.10	457.93	435.75
2003	449.60	438.40	453.42	461.74	479.15	489.75	492.53	495.56	505.13	502.92	491.54	520.64	482.85
Manufacturing													
2001	622.66	609.35	623.24	598.37	609.67	621.09	619.48	628.55	653.48	624.31	637.04	649.31	624.49
2002	628.36	627.42	637.44	630.66	624.13	635.65	642.64	625.14	637.59	638.70	645.68	657.02	635.51
2003	662.86	623.22	637.70	643.03	634.20	622.75	613.21	650.15	667.01	662.92	661.42	654.00	643.63
Trade, transportation, and utilities													
2001	391.23	399.85	398.52	387.75	381.75	380.60	385.33	392.50	388.57	389.35	376.28	379.20	387.40
2002	372.72	366.83	381.20	383.57	373.55	374.35	380.69	378.82	386.82	389.94	380.15	379.52	379.00
2003	382.41	388.48	375.91	376.99	378.25	390.91	403.06	406.62	410.21	412.75	401.49	406.56	394.51

ARKANSAS AT A GLANCE

(Population and total nonfarm employment numbers in thousands)

Population, Census 2000:	2,673.4
Total nonfarm employment, 2003:	1,143.7
Change in total nonfarm employment	
(Number)	
1990–2003:	220.3
1990–2001:	230.3
2001–2003:	-10.0
(Compound annual rate of change)	
1990–2003:	1.7%
1990–2001:	2.0%
2001–2003:	-0.4%
Unemployment rate	
1990:	6.8%
2001:	4.7%
2003:	5.9%

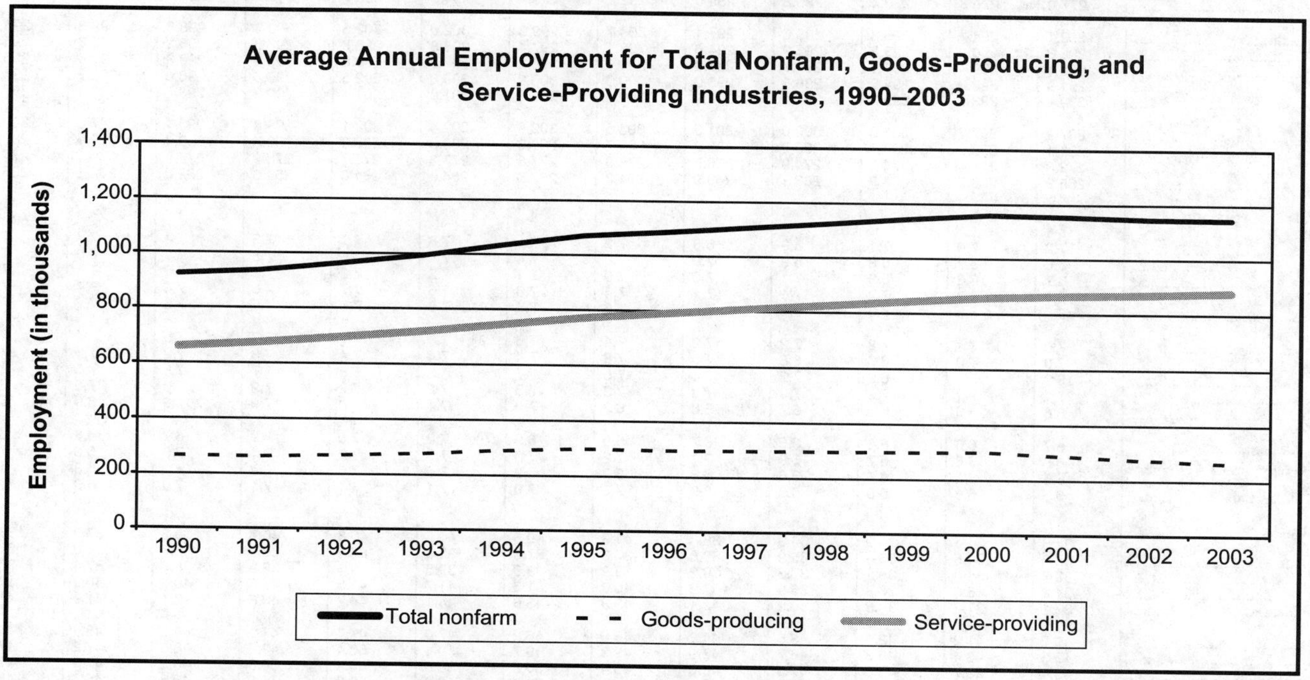

Total nonfarm payroll employment expanded steadily between 1990 and 2000. The number of jobs in the goods-producing sector rose significantly following the 1990–1991 recession, before flattening in the mid-1990s and dropping during the 2001 recession. This pattern was attributable to the decline in manufacturing jobs. Manufacturing's share of Arkansas' total employment fell from nearly 24 percent in 1990 to 18 percent in 2003. After 1999, job growth slowed in the service-producing sector due in part to declines in trade, transportation, and utilities. However, the service-producing sector continued to add jobs, especially in educational and health services, where employment increased by 53 percent from 1990 to 2003.

Employment by Industry: Arkansas

(Numbers in thousands. Not seasonally adjusted.)

Industry	January	February	March	April	May	June	July	August	September	October	November	December	Annual Average
STATEWIDE													
Total nonfarm													
1990	895.3	902.1	911.7	918.7	928.0	933.1	920.0	927.7	940.4	937.2	935.8	931.8	923.4
1991	905.4	916.2	925.8	931.8	937.7	942.5	929.8	939.8	951.4	955.0	950.9	950.1	936.3
1992	932.0	941.6	951.0	960.1	968.9	970.8	958.1	962.3	975.4	980.3	978.1	978.0	963.0
1993	957.6	969.7	978.3	989.2	995.3	997.5	989.9	996.1	1010.1	1014.2	1014.2	1015.2	993.9
1994	992.2	999.7	1012.4	1026.2	1037.4	1040.8	1031.6	1040.0	1058.7	1056.3	1056.6	1056.7	1034.0
1995	1038.8	1049.0	1059.4	1065.0	1069.6	1076.0	1059.9	1071.2	1086.9	1085.2	1084.7	1086.2	1069.3
1996	1059.9	1065.3	1076.4	1082.4	1091.0	1093.5	1079.8	1090.4	1099.3	1097.5	1099.3	1096.9	1085.9
1997	1069.2	1079.2	1090.6	1101.5	1108.2	1107.6	1097.4	1107.1	1118.7	1123.1	1121.4	1123.2	1103.9
1998	1094.1	1103.1	1112.2	1120.1	1126.8	1128.5	1116.1	1121.1	1134.0	1136.9	1136.5	1136.7	1122.1
1999	1112.1	1121.9	1132.0	1139.7	1142.7	1144.6	1134.5	1141.2	1153.1	1156.6	1159.6	1163.2	1141.7
2000	1135.6	1143.8	1158.4	1158.7	1166.5	1168.3	1148.2	1156.6	1168.4	1168.1	1167.4	1163.1	1158.5
2001	1139.8	1147.3	1157.0	1160.8	1162.8	1161.3	1143.9	1151.5	1159.6	1155.5	1154.2	1151.0	1153.7
2002	1125.3	1132.8	1144.1	1148.4	1155.3	1155.0	1138.2	1143.2	1157.2	1151.7	1151.8	1152.4	1146.3
2003	1128.7	1133.1	1140.4	1142.7	1149.0	1144.0	1129.3	1139.8	1154.6	1154.4	1154.5	1153.5	1143.7
Total private													
1990	738.8	741.8	749.1	757.3	763.8	775.7	773.7	779.5	778.0	773.7	771.2	768.0	764.2
1991	744.7	751.1	759.8	765.9	771.9	782.0	780.8	787.7	785.9	785.9	781.5	780.7	773.1
1992	766.2	771.4	779.9	789.3	798.3	806.2	805.1	807.1	807.1	808.7	806.1	805.7	795.9
1993	788.8	796.7	804.9	815.8	821.9	830.4	833.9	837.1	838.9	840.8	839.8	840.9	824.1
1994	821.8	825.2	837.3	850.5	861.5	869.2	872.7	878.0	882.7	878.3	877.5	878.1	861.0
1995	863.7	870.4	879.6	885.0	889.1	900.1	896.7	904.0	907.5	903.5	902.7	904.3	892.2
1996	881.5	883.7	894.2	899.7	908.1	917.3	910.5	917.5	917.2	913.1	913.9	911.6	905.6
1997	888.1	894.1	904.7	914.9	922.6	926.6	925.8	932.8	933.7	935.4	932.9	935.0	920.5
1998	910.3	915.7	924.4	932.1	938.7	946.2	945.7	947.1	946.7	945.7	944.6	946.8	937.0
1999	926.0	932.5	941.4	949.4	952.9	960.1	960.7	962.6	964.3	964.5	966.6	970.9	954.3
2000	947.1	952.0	964.0	965.3	969.2	977.9	971.9	975.2	977.1	973.6	972.2	968.7	967.8
2001	948.5	951.8	960.5	963.7	966.4	970.3	965.1	969.1	963.8	956.5	954.0	951.2	960.1
2002	930.4	933.8	944.1	949.6	956.8	962.1	957.7	959.7	961.0	952.6	951.3	952.1	950.9
2003	932.0	932.8	939.0	941.7	948.1	949.5	945.5	952.6	953.8	952.1	951.9	951.1	945.8
Goods-producing													
1990	257.9	258.4	259.0	261.4	264.4	270.2	268.9	269.7	270.4	268.5	266.3	264.1	264.9
1991	255.1	256.8	259.3	259.5	260.2	264.5	264.5	267.8	266.6	267.4	264.9	264.0	262.5
1992	260.6	261.5	264.6	266.6	269.6	272.9	272.1	271.8	270.8	271.7	270.7	270.7	268.6
1993	266.1	268.7	272.4	273.7	275.5	278.7	280.2	281.0	281.3	281.9	281.7	281.8	276.9
1994	277.0	276.8	280.4	285.3	289.0	292.2	293.7	294.9	296.7	295.8	294.4	294.3	289.2
1995	292.1	294.1	295.8	296.6	297.1	300.7	299.3	302.0	302.6	300.3	298.8	298.3	298.1
1996	291.3	290.9	293.3	293.9	294.6	298.1	297.4	298.8	298.6	297.8	296.2	294.3	295.4
1997	288.1	289.4	291.1	294.7	297.3	299.6	299.2	300.3	299.8	299.2	296.8	297.6	296.0
1998	291.8	293.2	294.8	296.3	298.0	300.9	300.3	299.8	299.5	297.6	296.0	296.7	297.0
1999	292.4	293.6	295.2	297.1	298.3	300.4	301.3	301.0	301.1	299.9	298.8	299.9	298.2
2000	297.2	297.7	301.0	300.0	301.3	303.5	302.5	302.4	302.1	299.8	298.1	297.0	300.2
2001	291.1	288.9	290.7	290.0	289.9	290.7	289.0	289.8	287.3	283.7	280.4	279.0	287.5
2002	273.3	273.4	274.6	274.9	276.7	278.9	277.8	277.3	276.7	273.1	270.9	270.1	274.8
2003	265.2	263.5	263.9	263.1	263.9	264.3	263.5	264.6	264.8	264.0	262.6	262.1	263.8
Natural resources and mining													
1990	7.2	7.0	7.1	6.9	6.9	7.2	7.5	7.6	7.7	7.5	7.4	7.4	7.2
1991	6.6	6.7	6.8	6.9	7.0	7.2	7.4	7.5	7.5	7.3	7.2	6.9	7.0
1992	6.7	6.6	6.8	7.1	7.0	7.0	7.1	7.2	7.2	7.3	7.2	7.1	7.0
1993	6.8	6.9	7.2	7.1	7.1	7.4	7.6	7.6	7.7	7.6	7.4	7.4	7.3
1994	6.9	6.8	7.0	7.3	7.4	7.6	7.6	7.6	7.6	7.5	7.3	7.2	7.3
1995	7.0	7.1	7.2	7.2	7.2	7.4	7.6	7.8	7.7	7.7	7.5	7.4	7.4
1996	7.0	7.0	6.9	6.8	7.0	7.3	7.4	7.4	7.4	7.3	7.2	7.1	7.1
1997	6.9	6.9	6.9	7.2	7.4	7.5	7.7	7.8	7.8	7.7	7.5	7.5	7.4
1998	7.1	7.1	7.2	7.3	7.3	7.3	7.3	7.2	7.2	7.2	7.0	7.0	7.1
1999	6.6	6.6	6.6	6.7	6.8	6.9	7.0	7.1	7.0	7.0	6.9	6.9	6.8
2000	6.7	6.6	6.6	6.5	6.7	6.9	6.9	7.0	7.0	6.9	6.7	6.8	6.7
2001	6.5	6.6	6.7	6.9	7.1	7.2	7.3	7.3	7.2	7.1	7.0	6.8	7.0
2002	6.5	6.5	6.6	6.6	6.8	6.9	6.9	7.0	7.0	6.9	6.9	6.8	6.8
2003	6.5	6.6	6.6	6.8	6.9	7.0	7.0	7.1	7.1	7.1	7.0	6.9	6.9
Construction													
1990	34.5	34.4	34.9	36.3	38.4	41.3	40.5	40.5	40.8	40.7	39.3	37.9	38.2
1991	32.8	34.5	35.8	35.9	35.6	37.3	37.8	38.0	37.4	38.6	36.3	36.0	36.3
1992	33.7	35.0	36.2	37.3	39.2	39.9	39.6	39.5	39.1	39.9	38.0	37.6	37.9
1993	34.2	35.0	36.3	36.9	37.9	40.0	41.5	41.7	41.5	41.5	40.5	40.2	38.9
1994	37.1	37.2	39.5	40.9	42.1	43.3	43.6	44.1	44.2	43.8	42.1	41.9	41.6
1995	40.2	41.2	42.5	43.5	44.2	46.0	46.2	47.0	47.7	47.1	45.6	45.6	44.7
1996	42.3	43.4	45.3	46.7	47.9	49.3	49.7	50.1	50.4	49.9	48.5	47.2	47.5
1997	43.4	43.7	45.0	47.3	48.6	49.4	50.3	50.8	50.4	50.3	48.2	47.9	47.9
1998	44.6	45.0	46.1	47.6	48.8	49.7	50.3	50.0	50.0	49.6	48.8	48.6	48.2
1999	46.5	47.6	49.2	50.2	51.0	51.7	52.6	52.4	52.4	52.0	51.3	51.6	50.7
2000	50.3	50.7	53.0	52.5	53.4	54.5	54.1	54.5	55.0	53.9	52.8	52.0	53.0
2001	49.6	49.9	52.2	52.9	54.4	55.3	56.1	56.6	55.7	54.4	53.9	53.3	53.7
2002	51.3	51.7	53.2	54.0	55.2	56.6	57.1	57.1	56.0	54.2	53.0	52.2	54.3
2003	49.3	48.7	49.5	50.1	51.3	51.7	52.0	52.5	52.3	51.1	50.3	49.7	50.7

Employment by Industry: Arkansas—*Continued*

(Numbers in thousands. Not seasonally adjusted.)

Industry	January	February	March	April	May	June	July	August	September	October	November	December	Annual Average
STATEWIDE—*Continued*													
Manufacturing													
1990	216.2	217.0	217.0	218.2	219.1	221.7	220.9	221.6	221.9	220.3	219.6	218.8	219.3
1991	215.7	215.6	216.7	216.7	217.6	220.0	219.3	222.3	221.7	221.5	221.4	221.1	219.1
1992	220.2	219.9	221.6	222.2	223.4	226.0	225.4	225.1	224.5	224.5	225.5	226.0	223.6
1993	225.1	226.8	228.9	229.7	230.5	231.3	231.1	231.7	232.1	232.8	233.8	234.2	230.6
1994	233.0	232.8	233.9	237.1	239.5	241.3	242.5	243.2	244.9	244.5	245.0	245.2	240.2
1995	244.9	245.8	246.1	245.9	245.7	247.3	245.5	247.2	247.2	245.5	245.7	245.3	246.0
1996	242.0	240.5	241.1	240.4	239.7	241.5	240.3	241.3	240.8	240.6	240.5	240.0	240.7
1997	237.8	238.8	239.2	240.2	241.3	242.7	241.2	241.7	241.6	241.2	241.1	242.2	240.7
1998	240.1	241.1	241.5	241.4	241.9	243.9	242.7	242.6	242.3	240.8	240.2	241.1	241.6
1999	239.3	239.4	239.4	240.2	240.5	241.8	241.7	241.5	241.7	240.9	240.6	241.4	240.7
2000	240.2	240.4	241.4	241.0	241.2	242.1	241.5	240.9	240.1	239.0	238.6	238.2	240.3
2001	235.0	232.4	231.8	230.2	228.4	228.2	225.6	225.9	224.4	222.2	219.5	218.9	226.9
2002	215.5	215.2	214.8	214.3	214.7	215.4	213.8	213.2	213.7	212.0	211.0	211.1	213.7
2003	209.4	208.2	207.8	206.2	205.7	205.6	204.5	205.0	205.4	205.8	205.3	205.5	206.2
Service-providing													
1990	637.4	643.7	652.7	657.3	663.6	662.9	651.1	658.0	670.0	668.7	669.5	667.7	658.5
1991	650.3	659.4	666.5	672.3	677.5	678.0	665.3	672.0	684.8	687.6	686.0	686.1	673.8
1992	671.4	680.1	686.4	693.5	699.3	697.9	686.0	690.5	704.6	708.6	707.4	707.3	694.4
1993	691.5	701.0	705.9	715.5	719.8	718.8	709.7	715.1	728.8	732.3	732.5	733.4	717.0
1994	715.2	722.9	732.0	740.9	748.4	748.6	737.9	745.1	762.0	760.5	762.2	762.4	744.8
1995	746.7	754.9	763.6	768.4	772.5	775.3	760.6	769.2	784.3	784.9	785.9	787.9	771.1
1996	768.6	774.4	783.1	788.5	796.4	795.4	782.4	791.6	800.7	799.7	803.1	802.6	790.5
1997	781.1	789.8	799.5	806.8	810.9	808.0	798.2	806.8	818.9	823.9	824.6	825.6	807.8
1998	802.3	809.9	817.4	823.8	828.8	827.6	815.8	821.3	834.5	839.3	840.5	840.0	825.1
1999	819.7	828.3	836.8	842.6	844.4	844.2	833.2	840.2	852.0	856.7	860.8	863.3	843.5
2000	838.4	846.1	857.4	858.7	865.2	864.8	845.7	854.2	866.3	868.3	869.3	866.1	858.3
2001	848.7	858.4	866.3	870.8	872.9	870.6	854.9	861.7	872.3	871.8	873.8	872.0	866.2
2002	852.0	859.4	869.5	873.5	878.6	876.1	860.4	865.9	880.5	878.6	880.9	882.3	871.5
2003	863.5	869.6	876.5	879.6	885.1	879.7	865.8	875.2	889.8	890.4	891.9	891.4	879.9
Trade, transportation, and utilities													
1990	191.1	190.5	191.3	192.1	193.6	195.8	195.4	196.9	196.1	196.2	197.6	198.4	194.5
1991	192.7	191.4	193.3	194.9	197.5	199.1	198.3	199.0	198.8	198.3	198.8	199.6	196.8
1992	193.7	193.2	194.5	197.0	199.4	201.2	201.2	202.0	202.9	203.8	204.6	206.3	199.9
1993	197.7	198.0	199.2	201.5	203.4	205.0	205.6	207.0	208.0	209.7	211.2	213.0	204.9
1994	204.6	204.0	206.7	208.8	214.0	215.8	217.1	218.2	220.2	219.6	222.0	225.2	214.6
1995	217.3	216.6	219.0	220.2	221.8	223.5	223.0	224.3	226.1	227.4	229.4	232.0	223.3
1996	223.4	221.6	224.0	224.8	227.9	229.3	227.5	229.0	229.0	229.8	233.4	234.7	227.8
1997	225.0	224.4	227.1	228.7	230.6	230.9	230.2	230.6	232.6	234.8	237.7	239.5	231.0
1998	229.1	227.8	230.6	232.2	234.2	235.6	235.4	236.6	236.9	238.0	240.8	243.4	235.0
1999	233.8	233.3	236.1	237.6	238.6	240.4	240.3	241.3	241.6	242.8	246.2	249.4	240.1
2000	237.8	237.8	239.9	240.5	241.3	243.1	241.3	242.2	242.6	243.5	245.8	247.6	241.9
2001	238.6	237.5	240.4	241.5	242.5	243.2	241.4	241.7	240.9	241.2	243.7	244.6	241.4
2002	236.9	236.9	239.8	240.4	242.0	242.5	241.6	241.4	241.8	240.4	243.0	244.4	240.9
2003	236.2	235.3	236.7	237.4	238.2	238.5	238.6	239.6	240.9	242.5	245.1	246.7	239.6
Wholesale trade													
1990	38.1	38.3	38.5	38.5	38.7	39.3	39.3	39.2	38.9	38.6	38.6	38.4	38.7
1991	38.1	38.2	38.6	38.9	39.3	39.9	39.6	39.4	39.1	39.1	38.9	38.7	38.9
1992	38.2	38.3	38.5	38.7	39.0	39.6	39.4	39.2	39.0	39.3	39.1	39.0	38.9
1993	38.5	38.8	39.1	39.5	39.8	40.2	40.1	39.9	39.7	40.0	39.8	39.8	39.6
1994	39.3	39.5	40.0	40.3	40.6	41.0	41.1	40.9	41.0	40.7	40.5	40.6	40.4
1995	40.4	41.0	41.5	42.0	42.2	42.8	42.6	42.6	42.4	42.2	42.0	42.2	41.9
1996	41.4	41.8	42.4	42.5	42.7	43.2	42.9	42.9	42.6	42.7	42.7	42.8	42.5
1997	42.0	42.1	42.7	43.2	43.7	44.0	43.9	43.9	43.6	44.0	43.9	43.8	43.4
1998	43.5	43.8	44.3	44.7	45.0	45.5	45.2	45.1	44.8	44.4	44.1	44.3	44.5
1999	43.7	44.1	44.7	44.9	45.2	45.7	45.6	45.3	45.1	45.0	44.8	45.1	44.9
2000	44.6	44.9	45.6	45.6	45.9	46.7	46.4	46.2	46.2	45.9	45.6	45.6	45.7
2001	45.1	45.3	45.8	45.8	45.9	46.3	46.1	45.9	45.5	45.3	45.0	44.9	45.6
2002	44.2	44.2	44.8	44.9	45.1	45.6	45.3	45.2	45.3	44.9	44.6	44.6	44.9
2003	43.9	44.1	44.4	44.4	44.7	45.2	44.8	44.7	44.9	44.7	44.4	44.5	44.6
Retail trade													
1990	102.6	101.8	101.9	102.6	103.5	104.3	103.9	105.0	104.5	104.2	106.0	107.3	103.9
1991	103.3	101.9	103.0	104.1	105.8	106.3	105.9	106.4	106.2	105.7	107.0	108.2	105.3
1992	104.1	103.6	104.7	106.5	108.1	108.8	108.7	109.4	109.7	110.6	112.2	114.0	108.3
1993	108.2	108.0	108.6	109.9	110.7	111.7	112.2	113.4	113.6	114.4	116.5	118.1	112.1
1994	112.6	111.6	113.3	115.0	117.3	117.6	118.4	119.4	120.4	119.5	122.5	124.1	117.6
1995	118.3	117.4	118.6	119.0	120.5	121.1	119.6	121.3	122.4	123.4	125.7	127.4	121.2
1996	121.0	119.8	121.6	122.1	124.6	125.4	124.3	125.1	125.0	125.7	129.1	130.5	124.5
1997	123.4	122.7	124.5	125.2	126.1	126.0	125.4	126.7	127.0	128.2	131.2	132.6	126.5
1998	125.0	123.3	125.1	126.0	127.2	127.9	127.4	128.2	128.4	129.6	132.8	134.5	127.9
1999	127.7	126.7	128.7	129.7	130.0	131.0	130.4	131.3	131.4	133.0	136.0	138.3	131.1
2000	130.2	130.2	131.2	131.6	132.3	132.9	131.7	132.6	132.5	133.1	135.9	137.4	132.6
2001	130.5	129.0	130.9	131.5	132.4	132.5	130.9	130.8	130.3	130.3	133.5	134.6	131.4
2002	128.6	127.5	129.1	129.7	130.8	130.7	130.1	129.5	129.4	128.8	131.8	133.5	130.0
2003	127.1	126.0	126.8	127.4	128.0	128.0	128.4	129.1	129.9	130.7	133.7	135.2	129.2

Employment by Industry: Arkansas—*Continued*

(Numbers in thousands. Not seasonally adjusted.)

Industry	January	February	March	April	May	June	July	August	September	October	November	December	Annual Average
STATEWIDE—*Continued*													
Transportation and utilities													
1990	50.4	50.4	50.9	51.0	51.4	52.2	52.2	52.7	52.7	53.4	53.0	52.7	51.9
1991	51.3	51.3	51.7	51.9	52.4	52.9	52.8	53.2	53.5	53.5	52.9	52.7	52.5
1992	51.4	51.3	51.3	51.8	52.3	52.8	53.1	53.4	54.2	53.9	53.3	53.3	52.6
1993	51.0	51.2	51.5	52.1	52.9	53.1	53.3	53.7	54.7	55.3	54.9	55.1	53.2
1994	52.7	52.9	53.4	53.5	56.1	57.2	57.6	57.9	58.8	59.4	59.0	60.5	56.5
1995	58.6	58.2	58.9	59.2	59.1	59.6	60.8	60.4	61.3	61.8	61.7	62.4	60.1
1996	61.0	60.0	60.0	60.2	60.6	60.7	60.3	61.0	61.4	61.4	61.6	61.4	60.8
1997	59.6	59.6	59.9	60.3	60.8	60.9	60.9	60.0	62.0	62.6	62.6	63.1	61.0
1998	60.6	60.7	61.2	61.5	62.0	62.2	62.8	63.3	63.7	64.0	63.9	64.6	62.5
1999	62.4	62.5	62.7	63.0	63.4	63.7	64.3	64.7	65.1	64.8	65.4	66.0	64.0
2000	63.0	62.7	63.1	63.3	63.1	63.5	63.2	63.4	63.9	64.5	64.3	64.6	63.5
2001	63.0	63.2	63.7	64.2	64.2	64.4	64.4	65.0	65.1	65.6	65.2	65.1	64.4
2002	64.1	65.2	65.9	65.8	66.1	66.2	66.2	66.7	67.1	66.7	66.6	66.3	66.1
2003	65.2	65.2	65.5	65.6	65.5	65.3	65.4	65.8	66.1	67.1	67.0	67.0	65.9
Information													
1990	17.2	17.4	17.4	17.4	17.4	17.8	18.0	18.0	17.9	18.0	18.0	18.0	17.7
1991	17.8	17.8	17.7	17.5	17.8	18.0	18.0	17.9	17.7	17.6	17.0	17.0	17.6
1992	16.5	16.3	16.3	16.6	16.7	17.0	17.2	16.8	16.8	16.8	16.6	16.3	16.6
1993	16.4	16.4	16.3	16.7	16.6	16.9	17.1	17.1	17.0	17.0	17.0	16.9	16.7
1994	16.6	16.6	16.7	16.8	16.9	17.5	17.5	17.6	17.7	17.5	17.6	17.4	17.2
1995	17.3	17.6	17.6	17.7	17.7	18.3	18.4	18.5	18.4	18.3	18.5	18.4	18.0
1996	18.1	18.1	18.4	18.3	18.4	18.9	18.8	18.7	18.5	18.4	18.6	18.7	18.4
1997	18.2	18.3	18.5	18.7	18.8	19.1	19.3	18.9	18.7	18.9	18.9	18.7	18.7
1998	18.5	18.7	18.7	18.9	18.9	19.1	19.1	19.1	18.7	19.2	19.2	19.4	18.9
1999	19.1	19.2	19.2	19.2	19.4	19.6	20.0	20.0	19.9	20.0	20.2	20.2	19.6
2000	19.9	19.9	20.1	19.8	20.1	20.4	20.6	21.0	21.1	21.2	21.4	21.5	20.5
2001	21.2	21.2	21.0	20.8	20.8	20.9	21.1	21.1	21.0	20.8	20.9	20.8	21.0
2002	20.8	20.5	20.2	20.2	20.2	20.5	20.4	20.3	20.2	20.2	20.4	20.3	20.4
2003	20.1	20.1	20.1	20.0	20.1	20.3	20.4	20.4	20.2	20.2	20.4	20.3	20.2
Financial activities													
1990	39.6	39.5	39.7	40.0	40.2	40.8	40.6	40.7	39.9	40.1	40.1	40.1	40.1
1991	39.4	39.5	39.8	39.9	40.4	40.8	40.9	40.8	40.6	40.3	40.3	40.5	40.2
1992	40.1	40.2	40.4	40.6	40.9	41.4	41.4	41.4	41.1	41.1	41.1	41.4	40.9
1993	40.8	40.8	41.2	41.5	41.9	42.3	42.4	42.5	42.3	42.7	42.8	43.1	42.0
1994	42.5	42.5	42.9	43.2	43.6	43.9	44.2	44.3	44.1	44.0	43.9	44.2	43.6
1995	43.9	43.9	44.2	44.3	44.5	45.1	45.1	45.2	44.8	45.0	44.9	45.2	44.6
1996	44.6	44.6	45.1	45.3	45.7	46.3	46.1	46.1	45.8	45.8	45.9	46.1	45.6
1997	45.8	45.9	46.3	46.5	46.9	46.9	47.1	47.2	46.8	47.0	46.9	47.1	46.7
1998	47.1	47.1	47.6	47.5	47.7	48.1	47.9	47.9	47.5	48.0	48.1	48.4	47.7
1999	47.7	47.9	48.3	48.6	48.9	49.4	49.4	49.4	49.0	49.3	49.3	49.9	48.9
2000	49.1	49.1	49.4	49.6	49.5	50.1	49.6	49.4	49.2	49.1	49.1	49.4	49.3
2001	48.7	48.9	49.0	49.1	49.4	49.8	49.8	49.7	49.6	49.2	49.4	49.9	49.4
2002	49.4	49.2	49.5	49.5	49.7	50.0	50.0	49.9	49.8	49.3	49.4	49.8	49.6
2003	49.4	49.4	49.6	49.8	50.1	50.6	50.9	50.9	50.6	50.4	50.5	50.7	50.2
Professional and business services													
1990	53.6	54.5	55.2	57.0	57.1	58.3	58.6	59.8	59.3	58.0	57.2	56.8	57.1
1991	53.5	54.8	55.7	57.4	57.7	58.9	59.0	60.3	60.3	60.6	60.1	59.9	58.1
1992	58.6	59.3	60.3	61.9	63.2	63.4	63.3	64.3	64.5	64.9	64.3	63.6	62.6
1993	64.0	65.2	65.4	68.2	69.0	70.0	70.8	70.9	71.2	70.4	69.3	70.2	68.7
1994	69.1	70.6	73.0	74.1	73.8	74.9	75.9	76.9	77.2	77.1	76.3	75.5	74.5
1995	73.5	75.6	76.5	77.2	77.2	79.0	78.6	80.3	80.4	79.9	79.1	78.4	77.9
1996	76.7	78.4	79.4	80.4	81.7	82.7	82.2	84.3	83.8	83.1	82.2	81.3	81.3
1997	79.3	81.2	83.1	84.1	84.7	85.6	87.7	91.1	90.5	91.5	90.1	89.9	86.5
1998	87.1	88.4	89.5	91.4	91.9	93.7	96.0	95.9	95.7	94.8	93.5	92.3	92.5
1999	91.3	92.8	94.2	95.5	95.5	96.9	97.6	99.4	100.0	101.2	101.2	100.8	97.2
2000	98.3	99.4	101.4	100.2	100.9	102.4	101.9	103.9	104.2	103.2	102.6	100.5	101.5
2001	100.9	102.4	102.6	102.1	102.4	103.0	102.3	104.0	102.7	100.7	99.6	98.3	101.8
2002	96.4	96.9	99.1	100.4	101.2	102.4	102.3	103.3	104.5	103.7	102.6	102.9	101.3
2003	101.0	101.5	102.0	103.1	104.3	104.4	102.5	105.3	105.1	104.1	103.4	102.3	103.3
Educational and health services													
1990	88.3	87.7	90.2	90.6	90.9	90.1	90.0	91.3	93.1	94.2	95.0	94.5	91.3
1991	93.6	95.2	95.8	95.9	95.9	95.6	95.3	96.4	98.3	100.9	101.6	101.7	97.1
1992	100.7	101.9	102.3	102.8	103.1	101.9	101.7	102.9	104.5	105.8	106.2	105.8	103.3
1993	104.2	105.2	105.5	106.3	106.5	106.0	106.0	106.6	108.6	110.6	111.2	110.2	107.2
1994	109.8	110.3	110.4	111.4	111.5	109.8	109.0	110.4	112.6	113.0	113.6	112.3	111.1
1995	112.7	113.7	114.4	114.4	114.0	113.4	112.8	114.2	117.3	117.6	118.4	118.8	115.1
1996	116.7	118.3	118.9	119.0	119.2	118.7	116.7	117.8	121.1	121.0	121.4	121.5	119.1
1997	119.9	121.4	122.0	122.4	121.9	120.4	119.0	120.3	123.1	123.9	124.4	124.5	121.9
1998	122.7	124.4	124.7	124.6	124.2	122.6	121.5	122.7	124.9	125.9	126.3	126.2	124.2
1999	124.5	125.7	126.0	126.1	125.5	124.1	123.5	123.8	126.5	127.4	127.8	127.9	125.7
2000	125.5	126.9	127.7	127.7	127.0	126.0	124.9	125.4	128.9	129.3	129.6	129.1	127.3
2001	127.8	130.0	130.4	131.0	130.5	129.6	129.3	130.8	132.9	134.0	134.4	134.5	131.3
2002	133.0	133.8	135.0	135.4	135.3	134.1	133.2	134.9	137.4	137.9	138.6	138.7	135.6
2003	137.3	138.6	139.6	139.5	139.7	137.7	136.7	138.9	141.4	142.0	142.4	142.4	139.7

Employment by Industry: Arkansas—*Continued*

(Numbers in thousands. Not seasonally adjusted.)

Industry	January	February	March	April	May	June	July	August	September	October	November	December	Annual Average
STATEWIDE—*Continued*													
Leisure and hospitality													
1990	58.8	61.3	63.6	66.0	67.1	68.8	68.3	69.2	67.5	64.9	63.1	62.1	65.0
1991	58.7	61.4	63.8	66.3	67.5	69.7	69.3	70.3	68.7	66.4	64.5	63.6	65.8
1992	61.7	64.5	66.6	68.8	70.2	72.4	72.0	72.1	70.9	68.9	67.2	66.2	68.4
1993	64.5	67.1	69.2	72.2	73.3	75.2	75.2	75.7	74.6	73.2	71.4	70.5	71.8
1994	67.5	69.6	71.9	75.2	76.8	78.6	78.6	79.4	78.0	75.6	74.0	73.4	74.8
1995	71.3	73.1	75.6	78.0	79.8	82.5	82.0	82.3	81.0	78.4	77.2	76.5	78.1
1996	74.3	75.2	78.0	81.0	83.3	85.4	83.9	85.1	83.1	80.2	79.2	77.8	80.5
1997	75.0	76.5	79.3	82.2	84.5	85.7	84.8	86.1	84.2	82.2	80.3	79.7	81.7
1998	76.2	77.9	79.9	82.3	84.5	86.0	85.3	85.1	83.7	82.5	81.0	80.4	82.0
1999	77.4	79.9	82.0	84.5	85.6	87.4	86.6	86.1	85.0	83.0	82.3	81.8	83.4
2000	78.9	80.6	83.5	86.5	87.8	90.4	89.4	89.4	87.8	86.5	84.8	82.9	85.7
2001	79.7	82.3	85.3	88.3	89.8	91.3	90.7	90.6	88.5	86.4	85.2	83.7	86.8
2002	80.5	82.8	85.2	88.0	90.6	92.0	91.0	91.3	89.6	87.5	85.9	85.3	87.5
2003	82.6	84.3	86.6	88.1	90.8	92.1	91.8	91.9	90.1	88.5	87.1	86.1	88.3
Other services													
1990	32.3	32.5	32.7	32.8	33.1	33.9	33.9	33.9	33.8	33.8	33.9	34.0	33.3
1991	33.9	34.2	34.4	34.5	34.9	35.4	35.5	35.2	34.9	34.4	34.3	34.4	34.6
1992	34.3	34.5	34.9	35.0	35.2	36.0	36.2	35.8	35.6	35.7	35.4	35.4	35.3
1993	35.1	35.3	35.7	35.7	35.7	36.3	36.6	36.3	35.9	35.3	35.2	35.2	35.6
1994	34.7	34.8	35.3	35.7	35.9	36.5	36.7	36.3	36.2	35.7	35.7	35.8	35.7
1995	35.6	35.8	36.5	36.6	37.0	37.6	37.5	37.2	36.9	36.6	36.4	36.7	36.7
1996	36.4	36.6	37.1	37.0	37.3	37.9	37.9	37.7	37.3	37.0	37.0	37.2	37.2
1997	36.8	37.0	37.3	37.6	37.9	38.4	38.5	38.3	38.0	37.9	37.8	38.0	37.7
1998	37.8	38.2	38.6	38.9	39.3	40.2	40.2	40.0	39.8	39.7	39.7	40.0	39.3
1999	39.8	40.1	40.4	40.8	41.1	41.9	42.0	41.6	41.2	40.9	40.8	41.0	40.9
2000	40.4	40.6	41.0	41.0	41.3	42.0	41.7	41.5	41.2	41.0	40.8	40.7	41.1
2001	40.5	40.6	41.1	40.9	41.1	41.8	41.5	41.4	40.9	40.5	40.4	40.4	40.9
2002	40.1	40.3	40.7	40.8	41.1	41.7	41.4	41.3	41.0	40.5	40.5	40.6	40.8
2003	40.2	40.1	40.5	40.7	41.0	41.6	41.1	41.0	40.7	40.4	40.4	40.5	40.7
Government													
1990	156.5	160.3	162.6	161.4	164.2	157.4	146.3	148.2	162.4	163.5	164.6	163.8	159.2
1991	160.7	165.1	166.0	165.9	165.8	160.5	149.0	152.1	165.5	169.1	169.4	169.4	163.2
1992	165.8	170.2	171.1	170.8	170.6	164.6	153.0	155.2	168.3	171.6	172.0	172.3	167.1
1993	168.8	173.0	173.4	173.4	173.4	167.1	156.0	159.0	171.2	173.4	174.4	174.3	169.7
1994	170.4	174.5	175.1	175.7	175.9	171.6	158.9	162.0	176.0	178.0	179.1	178.6	172.9
1995	175.1	178.6	179.8	180.0	180.5	175.9	163.2	167.2	179.4	181.7	182.0	181.9	177.1
1996	178.4	181.6	182.2	182.7	182.9	176.2	169.3	172.9	182.1	184.4	185.4	185.3	180.2
1997	181.1	185.1	185.9	186.6	185.6	181.0	171.6	174.3	185.0	187.7	188.5	188.2	183.3
1998	183.8	187.4	187.8	188.0	188.1	182.3	170.4	174.0	187.3	191.2	191.9	189.9	185.1
1999	186.1	189.4	190.6	190.3	189.8	184.5	173.8	178.6	188.8	192.1	193.0	192.3	187.4
2000	188.5	191.8	194.4	193.4	197.3	190.4	176.3	181.4	191.3	194.5	195.2	194.4	190.7
2001	191.3	195.5	196.5	197.1	196.4	191.0	178.8	182.4	195.8	199.0	200.2	199.8	193.7
2002	194.9	199.0	200.0	198.8	198.5	192.9	180.5	183.5	196.2	199.1	200.5	200.3	195.4
2003	196.7	200.3	201.4	201.0	200.9	194.5	183.8	187.2	200.8	202.3	202.6	202.4	197.8
Federal government													
1990	22.0	21.9	23.3	22.7	25.0	23.9	23.9	22.4	22.2	21.9	21.9	22.0	22.7
1991	21.8	21.8	21.8	22.1	22.5	23.1	22.9	22.8	22.5	22.6	22.6	22.6	22.4
1992	22.5	22.5	22.5	22.5	22.6	22.9	22.7	22.5	22.1	22.0	21.6	22.0	22.3
1993	21.6	21.6	21.5	21.6	21.6	21.7	21.6	21.3	21.3	21.2	21.2	21.2	21.4
1994	20.9	20.9	20.9	21.3	21.4	21.8	21.5	21.7	21.4	21.4	21.3	21.3	21.3
1995	20.8	20.7	20.9	21.2	21.3	21.6	21.6	21.6	21.5	21.5	21.3	21.3	21.2
1996	20.9	20.9	20.9	21.1	21.2	21.3	21.4	21.3	21.1	21.2	21.2	21.2	21.1
1997	20.8	20.8	20.9	21.0	20.8	21.0	21.1	21.0	20.9	21.0	21.2	21.2	20.9
1998	20.5	20.4	20.4	20.4	20.4	20.5	20.6	20.6	20.6	22.6	22.8	21.0	20.9
1999	20.5	20.4	20.8	20.6	20.5	20.8	20.7	20.7	20.6	21.0	21.2	21.2	20.7
2000	20.9	21.0	23.0	21.6	25.7	25.0	23.6	23.7	20.8	21.0	21.1	21.4	22.4
2001	21.0	20.8	20.9	20.9	21.0	21.2	21.4	21.1	21.0	21.3	21.2	21.3	21.1
2002	21.0	20.8	20.7	20.6	20.7	21.2	21.2	20.9	20.6	21.0	21.0	21.1	20.9
2003	20.8	20.7	20.8	20.9	21.0	21.2	21.6	21.3	21.3	21.2	21.0	21.2	21.1
State government													
1990	46.8	49.8	50.3	50.0	49.8	46.9	46.5	46.9	51.0	51.9	52.1	51.6	49.4
1991	48.9	52.2	52.5	52.5	51.6	48.8	48.7	49.9	53.4	54.4	54.4	54.1	51.7
1992	51.2	54.6	55.1	54.8	54.0	50.5	50.3	50.9	55.4	56.5	56.5	56.3	53.8
1993	53.5	56.5	56.8	56.5	55.7	51.7	52.3	53.4	57.2	56.8	57.2	56.9	55.3
1994	54.1	57.3	57.5	57.0	56.3	53.0	53.4	54.7	58.2	58.4	58.6	58.2	56.3
1995	56.3	59.1	59.5	59.4	58.9	55.7	54.6	56.8	59.9	60.6	60.8	60.5	58.5
1996	58.1	60.7	60.7	60.7	60.0	56.0	55.2	56.9	60.7	61.8	62.2	61.9	59.5
1997	59.2	61.8	62.0	62.3	60.8	57.7	56.8	58.0	61.7	63.2	63.3	63.0	60.8
1998	60.3	62.8	63.1	62.7	62.2	58.4	57.7	58.7	62.8	63.5	63.6	63.5	61.6
1999	61.3	63.7	63.9	63.3	62.6	58.6	58.2	59.2	63.6	64.6	64.8	64.0	62.3
2000	61.7	64.2	64.4	64.7	64.2	59.1	57.5	59.6	63.8	65.3	65.3	64.2	62.8
2001	62.2	65.1	65.7	66.2	65.0	61.1	59.0	61.2	65.4	67.0	67.4	66.8	64.3
2002	63.4	66.8	67.3	66.8	65.8	61.5	59.4	61.1	65.4	65.9	66.7	66.4	64.7
2003	64.0	67.1	67.7	67.0	66.2	61.5	60.0	61.8	67.0	67.5	67.6	67.2	65.4

Employment by Industry: Arkansas—*Continued*

(Numbers in thousands. Not seasonally adjusted.)

Industry	January	February	March	April	May	June	July	August	September	October	November	December	Annual Average
STATEWIDE—*Continued*													
Local government													
1990	87.7	88.6	89.0	88.7	89.4	86.6	75.9	78.9	89.2	89.7	90.6	90.2	87.0
1991	90.0	91.1	91.7	91.3	91.7	88.6	77.4	79.4	89.6	92.1	92.4	92.7	89.0
1992	92.1	93.1	93.5	93.5	94.0	91.2	80.0	81.8	90.8	93.1	93.9	94.0	90.9
1993	93.7	94.9	95.1	95.3	96.1	93.7	82.1	84.3	92.7	95.4	96.0	96.2	92.9
1994	95.4	96.3	96.7	97.4	98.2	96.8	84.0	85.6	96.4	98.2	99.2	99.1	95.2
1995	98.0	98.8	99.4	99.4	100.3	98.6	87.0	88.8	98.0	99.6	99.9	100.1	97.3
1996	99.4	100.0	100.6	100.9	101.7	98.9	92.7	94.7	100.3	101.4	102.0	102.2	99.5
1997	101.1	102.5	103.0	103.3	104.0	102.3	93.7	95.3	102.4	103.5	104.0	104.0	101.5
1998	103.0	104.2	104.3	104.9	105.5	103.4	92.1	94.7	103.9	105.1	105.5	105.4	102.6
1999	104.3	105.3	105.9	106.4	106.7	105.1	94.9	98.7	104.6	106.5	107.0	107.1	104.3
2000	105.9	106.6	107.0	107.1	107.4	106.3	95.2	98.1	106.7	108.2	108.8	108.8	105.5
2001	108.1	109.6	109.9	110.0	110.4	108.7	98.4	100.1	109.4	110.7	111.6	111.7	108.2
2002	110.5	111.4	112.0	111.4	112.0	110.2	99.9	101.5	110.2	112.2	112.8	112.8	109.7
2003	111.9	112.5	112.9	113.1	113.7	111.8	102.2	104.1	112.5	113.6	114.0	114.0	111.4
FAYETTEVILLE-SPRINGDALE													
Total nonfarm													
1990	96.8	98.1	98.8	99.5	100.3	100.7	100.1	101.1	102.3	103.0	102.9	102.8	100.5
1991	99.2	100.7	101.6	102.7	103.3	103.6	102.4	103.6	105.2	106.1	106.0	105.5	103.3
1992	103.6	104.8	105.4	107.0	108.0	108.5	107.6	108.6	110.3	111.6	112.2	112.4	108.3
1993	109.5	111.0	112.3	113.9	115.2	114.8	114.5	116.7	118.2	118.8	119.7	120.0	115.3
1994	116.7	118.5	119.9	122.1	123.2	124.0	124.0	125.6	127.3	127.4	128.5	128.4	123.8
1995	126.1	128.2	128.9	130.2	130.9	131.1	130.4	132.1	133.3	133.5	133.7	134.6	131.0
1996	130.4	131.7	132.7	134.0	135.1	135.2	133.5	135.9	137.4	136.8	138.3	138.7	134.9
1997	133.9	135.6	136.8	138.0	138.8	137.5	137.4	138.8	140.3	142.1	141.8	141.4	138.5
1998	137.1	137.6	139.4	140.4	141.5	141.9	141.7	142.2	143.7	145.0	145.8	146.0	141.8
1999	141.4	143.1	144.4	146.4	146.9	147.8	147.7	148.6	150.1	151.4	152.8	152.8	147.8
2000	148.3	150.2	152.5	152.4	153.9	155.0	152.7	153.7	155.4	156.2	157.0	156.1	153.6
2001	157.0	159.2	160.8	162.7	163.5	163.3	161.2	162.4	163.6	164.3	164.9	164.7	162.3
2002	161.6	164.7	166.9	167.9	169.2	169.5	167.3	169.2	171.2	170.3	170.6	170.6	168.3
2003	167.9	169.3	170.1	170.3	171.3	172.4	170.4	172.5	174.4	175.4	176.3	175.8	172.2
Total private													
1990	82.3	82.8	83.4	84.2	84.9	86.3	86.2	86.9	86.7	87.1	86.9	86.9	85.3
1991	84.3	84.7	85.5	86.8	87.8	88.7	88.5	89.4	89.8	90.3	90.4	90.1	88.0
1992	89.3	89.4	89.8	91.5	92.7	93.7	93.8	94.4	94.8	95.6	96.3	96.5	93.1
1993	94.4	95.0	96.3	97.8	99.2	99.8	100.1	101.9	102.3	102.7	103.4	103.8	99.7
1994	101.7	102.5	103.7	105.8	107.0	108.2	108.7	110.2	110.9	110.5	111.4	111.4	107.6
1995	110.0	110.9	111.6	112.9	113.5	114.1	114.1	115.4	115.1	115.1	115.0	116.0	113.6
1996	113.3	113.3	114.1	115.5	116.6	117.6	116.4	118.3	118.8	117.7	119.1	119.2	116.6
1997	116.0	116.4	117.7	118.5	119.6	119.2	119.6	120.6	121.1	122.5	122.1	121.5	119.5
1998	118.7	118.2	120.1	121.1	122.1	123.1	124.0	124.3	124.4	125.3	126.0	126.3	122.8
1999	122.9	123.6	125.0	126.8	127.4	129.1	129.8	130.2	130.5	131.5	132.7	132.7	128.5
2000	129.4	130.2	132.1	132.3	133.4	134.9	134.1	134.8	135.2	135.5	136.3	135.8	133.7
2001	137.3	138.4	139.9	141.8	142.6	143.5	142.8	143.1	142.6	142.8	143.3	143.1	141.8
2002	141.1	143.1	145.4	146.4	147.9	149.0	148.4	149.3	149.6	149.0	149.1	149.3	147.3
2003	146.6	147.0	147.6	148.7	149.8	150.7	150.3	151.6	151.6	152.4	153.1	152.7	150.2
Goods-producing													
1990	29.3	29.6	29.7	29.9	30.1	30.4	30.6	30.6	30.6	30.8	30.6	30.6	30.2
1991	29.3	29.6	29.6	30.2	30.2	30.5	30.1	30.6	30.6	30.8	30.9	30.8	30.2
1992	30.8	30.6	30.8	30.8	31.2	31.6	32.0	32.0	32.2	32.3	32.7	32.9	31.6
1993	32.3	32.6	32.9	33.5	34.2	34.4	34.8	35.1	35.2	35.0	35.2	35.5	34.2
1994	35.0	35.2	35.3	36.0	36.1	36.5	36.7	37.0	37.1	37.0	37.4	37.4	36.3
1995	37.6	37.8	37.9	38.2	38.3	38.5	38.5	38.6	38.0	38.0	38.0	38.2	38.1
1996	37.4	37.3	37.3	37.5	37.5	37.9	37.6	38.0	38.1	37.6	38.0	38.0	37.6
1997	37.1	37.1	37.3	37.3	37.5	37.5	37.5	37.5	37.7	37.9	37.4	37.2	37.4
1998	36.3	36.0	36.3	36.6	36.9	37.4	37.5	37.3	37.3	37.3	37.3	37.5	36.9
1999	36.8	37.2	37.2	37.6	37.9	38.3	38.7	38.6	38.8	38.7	38.7	38.9	38.1
2000	38.5	38.7	39.2	39.5	39.6	39.7	39.6	39.5	39.3	39.2	39.0	39.0	39.2
2001	39.3	39.4	39.5	39.4	39.6	39.8	39.8	39.6	39.6	39.3	39.3	39.0	39.5
2002	38.3	38.3	38.4	38.5	38.7	39.0	38.8	39.0	38.7	38.4	38.3	38.3	38.6
2003	37.8	37.7	37.7	37.7	37.7	37.8	38.1	38.3	38.3	38.3	38.4	38.1	38.0
Construction and mining													
1990	3.3	3.4	3.4	3.5	3.6	3.7	3.7	3.7	3.5	3.5	3.4	3.4	3.5
1991	3.1	3.3	3.4	3.8	3.9	4.0	3.9	3.9	3.8	3.9	3.8	3.9	3.7
1992	3.9	3.8	4.0	4.0	4.1	4.2	4.3	4.3	4.3	4.4	4.4	4.4	4.1
1993	4.2	4.3	4.4	4.5	4.7	4.9	5.1	5.2	5.2	5.1	5.0	5.1	4.8
1994	5.0	5.0	5.1	5.3	5.4	5.6	5.6	5.7	5.6	5.5	5.5	5.6	5.4
1995	5.6	5.7	5.9	5.8	6.0	6.1	6.1	6.2	6.1	6.2	6.1	6.2	6.0
1996	5.8	5.9	6.1	6.3	6.3	6.6	6.5	6.6	6.6	6.4	6.3	6.3	6.3
1997	5.9	5.9	6.0	6.1	6.2	6.2	6.3	6.3	6.2	6.2	5.9	5.9	6.0
1998	5.5	5.5	5.5	5.8	6.0	6.3	6.3	6.3	6.1	6.1	6.0	6.1	5.9
1999	5.9	6.0	6.1	6.2	6.3	6.6	6.8	6.8	6.8	6.7	6.8	6.8	6.5
2000	6.5	6.6	6.9	7.0	7.1	7.2	7.2	7.1	7.1	7.1	7.0	6.9	7.0
2001	7.2	7.3	7.4	7.6	7.8	8.1	8.2	8.2	8.1	8.0	8.0	7.9	7.8
2002	7.7	7.8	7.8	7.8	7.9	8.1	8.0	8.0	7.8	7.6	7.6	7.6	7.8
2003	7.3	7.2	7.4	7.7	7.8	7.9	8.0	8.2	8.2	8.1	8.1	8.1	7.8

Employment by Industry: Arkansas—*Continued*

(Numbers in thousands. Not seasonally adjusted.)

Industry	January	February	March	April	May	June	July	August	September	October	November	December	Annual Average
FAYETTEVILLE-SPRINGDALE—*Continued*													
Manufacturing													
1990	26.0	26.2	26.3	26.4	26.5	26.7	26.9	26.9	27.1	27.3	27.2	27.2	26.7
1991	26.2	26.3	26.2	26.4	26.3	26.5	26.2	26.7	26.8	26.9	27.1	26.9	26.5
1992	26.9	26.8	26.8	26.8	27.1	27.4	27.7	27.7	27.9	27.9	28.3	28.5	27.4
1993	28.1	28.3	28.5	29.0	29.5	29.5	29.7	29.9	30.0	29.9	30.2	30.4	29.4
1994	30.0	30.2	30.2	30.7	30.7	30.9	31.1	31.3	31.5	31.5	31.9	31.8	30.9
1995	32.0	32.1	32.0	32.4	32.3	32.4	32.4	32.4	31.9	31.8	31.9	32.0	32.1
1996	31.6	31.4	31.2	31.2	31.2	31.3	31.1	31.4	31.5	31.2	31.7	31.7	31.3
1997	31.2	31.2	31.3	31.2	31.3	31.3	31.2	31.2	31.5	31.7	31.5	31.3	31.3
1998	30.8	30.5	30.8	30.8	30.9	31.1	31.2	31.0	31.2	31.2	31.3	31.4	31.0
1999	30.9	31.2	31.1	31.4	31.6	31.7	31.9	31.8	32.0	32.0	31.9	32.1	31.6
2000	32.0	32.1	32.3	32.5	32.5	32.5	32.4	32.4	32.2	32.1	32.0	32.1	32.3
2001	32.1	32.1	32.1	31.8	31.8	31.7	31.6	31.4	31.5	31.3	31.3	31.1	31.7
2002	30.6	30.5	30.6	30.7	30.8	30.9	30.8	31.0	30.9	30.8	30.7	30.7	30.8
2003	30.5	30.5	30.3	30.0	29.9	29.9	30.1	30.1	30.1	30.2	30.3	30.0	30.2
Service-providing													
1990	67.5	68.5	69.1	69.6	70.2	70.3	69.5	70.5	71.7	72.2	72.3	72.2	70.3
1991	69.9	71.1	72.0	72.5	73.1	73.1	72.3	73.0	74.6	75.3	75.1	74.7	73.0
1992	72.8	74.2	74.6	76.2	76.8	76.9	75.6	76.6	78.1	79.3	79.5	79.5	76.6
1993	77.2	78.4	79.4	80.4	81.0	80.4	79.7	81.6	83.0	83.8	84.5	84.5	81.1
1994	81.7	83.3	84.6	86.1	87.1	87.5	87.3	88.6	90.2	90.4	91.1	91.0	87.4
1995	88.5	90.4	91.0	92.0	92.6	92.6	91.9	93.5	95.3	95.5	95.7	96.4	92.9
1996	93.0	94.4	95.4	96.5	97.6	97.3	95.9	97.9	99.3	99.2	100.3	100.7	97.2
1997	96.8	98.5	99.5	100.7	101.3	100.0	99.9	101.3	102.6	104.2	104.4	104.2	101.1
1998	100.8	101.6	103.1	103.8	104.6	104.5	104.2	104.9	106.4	107.7	108.5	108.5	104.8
1999	104.6	105.9	107.2	108.8	109.0	109.5	109.0	110.0	111.3	112.7	114.1	113.9	109.7
2000	109.8	111.5	113.3	112.9	114.3	115.3	113.1	114.2	116.1	117.0	118.0	117.1	114.4
2001	117.7	119.8	121.3	123.3	123.9	123.5	121.4	122.8	124.0	125.0	125.6	125.7	122.8
2002	123.3	126.4	128.5	129.4	130.5	130.5	128.5	130.2	132.5	131.9	132.3	132.3	129.7
2003	130.1	131.6	132.4	132.6	133.6	134.6	132.3	134.2	136.1	137.1	137.9	137.7	134.2
Trade, transportation, and utilities													
1990	22.5	22.4	22.4	22.7	22.7	23.1	23.1	23.4	23.2	23.1	23.4	23.5	22.9
1991	22.8	22.6	22.6	23.1	23.3	23.4	23.2	23.1	23.0	22.9	22.9	22.8	22.9
1992	22.5	22.4	22.3	22.9	23.3	23.7	23.5	23.5	23.5	23.8	23.9	24.2	23.2
1993	23.4	23.4	23.6	23.9	24.2	24.3	24.6	24.9	25.2	25.5	26.0	26.2	24.6
1994	25.2	25.1	25.4	25.9	26.4	26.8	27.1	27.3	27.3	27.1	27.5	27.8	26.5
1995	27.1	27.3	27.4	27.7	27.8	28.1	28.1	28.4	28.4	29.0	29.3	29.7	28.1
1996	28.8	28.5	28.7	28.8	29.2	29.5	29.6	29.8	29.8	29.8	30.6	30.8	29.4
1997	29.3	29.1	29.2	29.2	29.5	29.4	29.3	29.2	29.5	30.1	30.5	30.7	29.5
1998	29.4	28.9	29.4	29.6	29.9	30.2	30.5	30.6	30.8	31.1	31.7	31.9	30.3
1999	30.8	30.5	30.9	31.3	31.5	31.7	32.0	32.3	32.1	32.3	33.0	33.2	31.8
2000	31.8	31.7	32.3	32.5	32.9	33.2	32.8	33.2	33.3	33.6	34.4	34.7	33.0
2001	34.9	35.0	35.7	36.7	36.7	37.0	37.1	37.2	37.0	38.0	38.8	38.8	36.9
2002	38.8	40.0	41.0	41.1	41.6	41.8	41.7	41.7	42.0	41.5	41.9	42.1	41.3
2003	41.3	41.2	41.4	41.7	41.8	41.8	42.1	42.4	42.3	42.8	43.4	43.6	42.2
Wholesale trade													
1990	3.1	3.0	3.0	3.1	3.1	3.2	3.2	3.2	3.1	3.1	3.2	3.1	3.1
1991	3.1	3.1	3.1	3.2	3.3	3.3	3.3	3.3	3.2	3.3	3.3	3.2	3.2
1992	3.2	3.2	3.2	3.2	3.3	3.4	3.3	3.4	3.3	3.3	3.2	3.2	3.2
1993	3.3	3.2	3.3	3.3	3.4	3.4	3.5	3.5	3.5	3.5	3.5	3.6	3.4
1994	3.5	3.5	3.5	3.6	3.7	3.8	3.8	3.9	3.8	3.7	3.8	3.8	3.7
1995	3.8	3.9	3.9	3.9	4.0	4.1	4.1	4.1	4.0	4.0	4.0	4.0	3.9
1996	4.1	4.1	4.1	4.2	4.3	4.4	4.3	4.3	4.3	4.3	4.4	4.4	4.2
1997	4.4	4.3	4.3	4.4	4.5	4.6	4.7	4.6	4.5	4.6	4.6	4.7	4.5
1998	4.6	4.5	4.6	4.6	4.8	4.9	4.9	4.9	4.8	4.7	4.7	4.8	4.7
1999	4.8	4.7	4.8	4.8	5.0	5.1	5.4	5.4	5.3	5.3	5.4	5.4	5.1
2000	5.5	5.4	5.6	5.7	5.9	6.1	6.1	6.1	6.1	6.0	6.2	6.1	5.9
2001	6.1	6.1	6.1	6.2	6.3	6.6	6.6	6.6	6.4	6.7	6.6	6.7	6.4
2002	6.6	6.7	6.8	6.8	7.0	7.1	7.2	7.1	7.3	7.2	7.1	7.1	7.0
2003	7.2	7.3	7.3	7.3	7.3	7.7	7.7	7.8	7.8	7.8	7.8	7.9	7.6
Retail trade													
1990	10.2	10.1	10.1	10.3	10.4	10.6	10.6	10.7	10.8	10.7	10.9	11.0	10.5
1991	10.2	10.2	10.2	10.4	10.5	10.6	10.5	10.5	10.6	10.5	10.7	10.8	10.4
1992	10.6	10.6	10.8	11.2	11.5	11.7	11.5	11.5	11.6	11.7	11.9	12.1	11.3
1993	11.4	11.4	11.5	11.7	11.8	11.9	11.9	12.1	12.3	12.5	12.9	13.0	12.0
1994	12.4	12.3	12.5	12.8	13.1	13.2	13.4	13.4	13.5	13.4	13.8	13.9	13.1
1995	13.3	13.3	13.2	13.4	13.4	13.5	13.4	13.6	13.9	14.4	14.6	15.0	13.7
1996	14.2	13.9	14.2	14.1	14.4	14.6	14.9	15.0	15.1	15.3	15.8	16.0	14.7
1997	14.7	14.5	14.6	14.6	14.7	14.6	14.7	14.7	15.0	15.5	15.9	16.0	14.9
1998	14.8	14.4	14.7	14.9	14.9	15.0	15.1	15.1	15.3	15.7	16.2	16.3	15.2
1999	15.3	15.1	15.3	15.5	15.5	15.5	15.5	15.7	15.7	16.2	16.6	16.9	15.7
2000	15.9	15.8	16.0	16.2	16.3	16.3	16.0	16.4	16.4	16.4	16.9	17.3	16.3
2001	16.7	16.5	16.8	17.0	17.0	16.9	16.9	16.9	16.9	17.2	17.7	17.7	17.0
2002	16.9	16.7	17.0	17.2	17.3	17.3	17.2	17.2	17.3	17.4	17.9	18.2	17.3
2003	17.2	16.9	17.1	17.2	17.3	17.2	17.4	17.5	17.6	17.7	18.2	18.5	17.5

Employment by Industry: Arkansas—*Continued*

(Numbers in thousands. Not seasonally adjusted.)

Industry	January	February	March	April	May	June	July	August	September	October	November	December	Annual Average
FAYETTEVILLE-SPRINGDALE—*Continued*													
Transportation and utilities													
1990	9.2	9.3	9.3	9.3	9.2	9.3	9.3	9.5	9.3	9.3	9.3	9.4	9.3
1991	9.5	9.3	9.3	9.5	9.5	9.5	9.4	9.3	9.2	9.1	8.9	8.8	9.2
1992	8.7	8.6	8.3	8.5	8.5	8.6	8.7	8.6	8.6	8.8	8.8	8.9	8.6
1993	8.7	8.8	8.8	8.9	9.0	9.0	9.2	9.3	9.4	9.5	9.6	9.6	9.1
1994	9.3	9.3	9.4	9.5	9.6	9.8	9.9	10.0	10.0	10.0	9.9	10.1	9.7
1995	10.0	10.1	10.3	10.4	10.4	10.5	10.6	10.7	10.5	10.6	10.7	10.7	10.4
1996	10.5	10.5	10.4	10.5	10.5	10.5	10.4	10.5	10.4	10.2	10.4	10.4	10.4
1997	10.2	10.3	10.3	10.2	10.3	10.2	9.9	9.9	10.0	10.0	10.0	10.0	10.1
1998	10.0	10.0	10.1	10.1	10.2	10.3	10.5	10.6	10.7	10.7	10.8	10.8	10.4
1999	10.7	10.7	10.8	11.0	11.0	11.1	11.1	11.2	11.1	10.8	11.0	10.9	11.0
2000	10.4	10.5	10.7	10.6	10.7	10.8	10.7	10.7	10.8	11.2	11.3	11.3	10.8
2001	12.1	12.4	12.8	13.5	13.4	13.5	13.6	13.7	13.7	14.1	14.5	14.4	13.5
2002	15.3	16.6	17.2	17.1	17.3	17.4	17.3	17.4	17.4	16.9	16.9	16.8	17.0
2003	16.9	17.0	17.0	17.2	17.2	16.9	17.0	17.1	16.9	17.3	17.4	17.2	17.1
Information													
1990	1.7	1.7	1.6	1.7	1.7	1.7	1.7	1.7	1.7	1.8	1.7	1.8	1.7
1991	1.7	1.6	1.6	1.6	1.7	1.7	1.7	1.7	1.7	1.7	1.7	1.7	1.6
1992	1.7	1.7	1.7	1.7	1.7	1.8	1.8	1.8	1.8	1.8	1.8	1.8	1.7
1993	1.7	1.7	1.7	1.8	1.8	1.8	1.8	1.8	1.8	1.8	1.9	2.0	1.8
1994	2.0	1.9	1.9	1.9	1.9	1.9	1.8	1.9	1.9	1.8	1.9	1.9	1.8
1995	1.8	1.8	1.8	1.9	1.9	1.9	1.9	2.0	1.9	1.9	1.9	2.0	1.8
1996	1.9	1.9	1.9	2.0	2.0	2.0	2.0	2.0	2.0	1.9	1.9	1.9	1.9
1997	1.9	1.9	1.9	1.9	1.9	1.9	2.0	2.0	2.0	2.0	2.0	2.0	1.9
1998	1.9	1.9	2.0	1.9	1.9	2.0	2.1	2.1	2.1	2.1	2.1	2.1	2.0
1999	2.1	2.1	2.1	2.1	2.1	2.1	2.1	2.1	2.1	2.1	2.2	2.2	2.1
2000	2.2	2.2	2.2	2.1	2.1	2.1	2.2	2.3	2.2	2.3	2.3	2.3	2.2
2001	2.4	2.4	2.4	2.4	2.4	2.4	2.4	2.4	2.3	2.3	2.3	2.3	2.4
2002	2.3	2.3	2.3	2.3	2.3	2.3	2.3	2.2	2.2	2.2	2.2	2.2	2.3
2003	2.2	2.2	2.2	2.2	2.2	2.3	2.3	2.3	2.3	2.3	2.3	2.3	2.3
Financial activities													
1990	3.2	3.2	3.3	3.3	3.4	3.4	3.5	3.4	3.4	3.5	3.5	3.5	3.3
1991	3.3	3.3	3.4	3.4	3.5	3.5	3.5	3.6	3.5	3.5	3.5	3.5	3.4
1992	3.5	3.6	3.6	3.6	3.7	3.8	3.8	3.8	3.8	3.9	3.9	3.9	3.7
1993	3.8	3.9	3.9	4.0	4.1	4.1	4.1	4.2	4.2	4.2	4.2	4.2	4.0
1994	4.2	4.2	4.3	4.4	4.5	4.5	4.5	4.6	4.6	4.6	4.6	4.6	4.4
1995	4.6	4.6	4.7	4.7	4.8	4.9	4.8	4.9	4.8	4.8	4.8	4.9	4.7
1996	4.9	5.0	5.0	5.1	5.2	5.3	5.3	5.3	5.3	5.1	5.2	5.2	5.1
1997	5.2	5.1	5.2	5.1	5.2	5.2	5.2	5.2	5.2	5.3	5.3	5.3	5.2
1998	5.3	5.2	5.4	5.5	5.5	5.5	5.5	5.6	5.5	5.5	5.6	5.6	5.4
1999	5.5	5.5	5.5	5.6	5.6	5.7	5.7	5.7	5.6	5.7	5.8	5.9	5.7
2000	5.8	5.8	5.9	5.8	5.9	5.9	5.8	5.7	5.8	5.8	5.8	5.9	5.8
2001	6.0	6.0	6.0	6.0	6.1	6.1	6.2	6.2	6.2	6.2	6.2	6.3	6.1
2002	6.3	6.3	6.4	6.3	6.4	6.4	6.4	6.4	6.4	6.4	6.4	6.4	6.4
2003	6.3	6.4	6.4	6.4	6.4	6.5	6.7	6.7	6.7	6.7	6.7	6.7	6.6
Professional and business services													
1990	9.2	9.2	9.4	9.6	9.6	10.2	9.9	10.1	9.9	9.7	9.6	9.4	9.6
1991	9.8	9.8	10.1	10.0	10.4	10.6	10.9	11.0	11.1	11.3	11.3	11.1	10.6
1992	10.8	10.8	11.0	11.7	11.8	11.8	12.0	12.3	12.4	12.5	12.7	12.4	11.8
1993	12.3	12.5	13.1	13.0	13.1	13.3	13.3	13.9	13.7	13.8	13.8	13.5	13.2
1994	13.4	13.8	14.2	14.3	14.6	15.0	15.3	15.8	15.9	15.9	15.9	15.8	14.9
1995	15.3	15.5	15.6	15.8	15.7	16.0	16.0	16.4	16.4	16.1	15.8	15.7	15.8
1996	15.3	15.3	15.5	15.8	16.1	16.5	15.9	16.4	16.5	16.2	16.2	16.2	15.9
1997	16.4	16.8	17.2	17.8	17.7	17.8	18.7	19.4	19.1	19.3	19.3	19.1	18.2
1998	19.2	19.4	19.9	19.8	19.8	20.3	20.8	20.9	20.8	20.9	20.9	20.9	20.3
1999	20.5	20.5	21.1	21.6	21.6	22.4	22.7	22.9	23.0	23.5	23.8	23.6	22.3
2000	22.9	23.1	23.4	23.2	23.3	24.0	24.3	24.4	24.7	24.3	24.4	24.1	23.8
2001	25.2	25.4	25.5	26.3	26.4	26.7	26.4	26.3	25.9	25.1	24.9	24.9	25.8
2002	24.4	24.8	25.5	25.9	26.2	26.6	26.7	26.8	27.0	27.1	26.9	26.9	26.2
2003	26.4	26.7	26.7	27.2	27.4	27.8	27.2	27.4	27.4	27.5	27.3	27.2	27.2
Educational and health services													
1990	6.8	7.0	7.0	7.0	7.1	7.1	6.9	7.0	7.1	7.6	7.6	7.6	7.1
1991	7.5	7.7	7.9	7.9	8.0	8.2	8.2	8.4	8.7	9.2	9.2	9.2	8.3
1992	9.3	9.4	9.4	9.5	9.5	9.5	9.2	9.3	9.4	9.7	9.8	9.8	9.4
1993	9.7	9.7	9.7	9.8	9.8	9.8	9.5	9.6	9.8	10.3	10.4	10.5	9.8
1994	10.4	10.5	10.6	10.7	10.7	10.7	10.3	10.4	10.6	11.0	11.0	11.1	10.6
1995	11.1	11.1	11.2	11.2	11.2	10.8	10.9	11.0	11.4	11.4	11.5	11.6	11.2
1996	11.5	11.6	11.6	11.7	11.8	11.4	11.3	11.5	11.7	12.2	12.2	12.2	11.7
1997	12.1	12.2	12.2	12.2	12.3	12.0	11.7	11.7	12.0	12.5	12.4	12.4	12.1
1998	12.3	12.4	12.4	12.5	12.5	12.3	12.0	12.1	12.2	12.6	12.7	12.7	12.3
1999	12.5	12.6	12.7	12.7	12.7	12.6	12.3	12.3	12.5	13.0	13.1	12.9	12.7
2000	12.8	13.1	13.1	13.1	13.1	13.2	12.6	12.8	13.0	13.4	13.5	13.4	13.1
2001	13.6	13.8	13.9	13.9	14.0	14.0	13.6	13.8	13.9	14.4	14.4	14.6	14.0
2002	14.5	14.5	14.7	14.6	14.7	14.7	14.3	14.6	14.7	15.1	15.3	15.3	14.8
2003	15.1	15.2	15.3	15.3	15.6	15.6	15.2	15.4	15.6	16.0	16.2	16.2	15.6

Employment by Industry: Arkansas—*Continued*

(Numbers in thousands. Not seasonally adjusted.)

Industry	January	February	March	April	May	June	July	August	September	October	November	December	Annual Average
FAYETTEVILLE-SPRINGDALE—*Continued*													
Leisure and hospitality													
1990	6.6	6.7	6.9	7.0	7.2	7.3	7.3	7.5	7.6	7.4	7.3	7.2	7.1
1991	6.7	6.9	7.1	7.4	7.5	7.6	7.6	7.7	7.9	7.7	7.7	7.8	7.4
1992	7.4	7.6	7.7	8.0	8.2	8.2	8.2	8.4	8.4	8.3	8.2	8.1	8.0
1993	7.8	7.9	8.1	8.4	8.6	8.6	8.6	8.9	8.9	8.7	8.5	8.5	8.4
1994	8.1	8.4	8.6	9.2	9.3	9.3	9.4	9.6	9.8	9.5	9.5	9.2	9.1
1995	9.0	9.2	9.4	9.7	10.0	10.1	10.1	10.2	10.4	10.1	10.0	10.1	9.8
1996	9.7	9.9	10.3	10.7	10.9	11.0	10.8	11.3	11.4	11.0	11.0	10.9	10.7
1997	10.2	10.4	10.8	11.1	11.5	11.4	11.2	11.6	11.6	11.4	11.2	10.8	11.1
1998	10.3	10.4	10.6	11.1	11.4	11.2	11.4	11.5	11.5	11.6	11.5	11.4	11.1
1999	10.6	11.0	11.3	11.7	11.8	12.0	11.9	11.8	12.0	11.8	11.7	11.6	11.6
2000	11.1	11.2	11.6	11.7	12.0	12.3	12.3	12.4	12.4	12.4	12.4	12.0	12.0
2001	11.5	11.9	12.3	12.5	12.8	12.9	12.7	13.0	13.1	13.0	12.9	12.7	12.6
2002	12.0	12.3	12.5	13.0	13.3	13.5	13.5	13.8	13.9	13.6	13.4	13.4	13.2
2003	12.8	13.0	13.2	13.4	13.9	14.0	13.9	14.2	14.2	14.0	14.0	13.8	13.7
Other services													
1990	3.0	3.0	3.1	3.0	3.1	3.1	3.2	3.2	3.2	3.2	3.2	3.3	3.1
1991	3.2	3.2	3.2	3.2	3.2	3.2	3.3	3.3	3.3	3.2	3.2	3.2	3.2
1992	3.3	3.3	3.3	3.3	3.3	3.3	3.3	3.3	3.3	3.3	3.3	3.4	3.3
1993	3.4	3.3	3.3	3.4	3.4	3.5	3.4	3.5	3.5	3.4	3.4	3.4	3.4
1994	3.4	3.4	3.4	3.4	3.5	3.5	3.6	3.6	3.7	3.6	3.6	3.6	3.5
1995	3.5	3.6	3.6	3.7	3.8	3.8	3.8	3.9	3.8	3.8	3.7	3.8	3.7
1996	3.8	3.8	3.8	3.9	3.9	4.0	3.9	4.0	4.0	3.9	4.0	4.0	3.9
1997	3.8	3.8	3.9	3.9	4.0	4.0	4.0	4.0	4.0	4.0	4.0	4.0	3.9
1998	4.0	4.0	4.1	4.1	4.2	4.2	4.2	4.2	4.2	4.2	4.2	4.2	4.1
1999	4.1	4.2	4.2	4.2	4.2	4.3	4.4	4.5	4.4	4.4	4.4	4.4	4.3
2000	4.3	4.4	4.4	4.4	4.5	4.5	4.5	4.5	4.5	4.5	4.5	4.4	4.5
2001	4.4	4.5	4.6	4.6	4.6	4.6	4.6	4.6	4.6	4.5	4.5	4.5	4.6
2002	4.5	4.6	4.6	4.7	4.7	4.7	4.7	4.8	4.7	4.7	4.7	4.7	4.7
2003	4.7	4.6	4.7	4.8	4.8	4.9	4.8	4.9	4.8	4.8	4.8	4.8	4.8
Government													
1990	14.5	15.3	15.4	15.3	15.4	14.4	13.9	14.2	15.6	15.9	16.0	15.9	15.1
1991	14.9	16.0	16.1	15.9	15.5	14.9	13.9	14.2	15.4	15.8	15.6	15.4	15.3
1992	14.3	15.4	15.6	15.5	15.3	14.8	13.8	14.2	15.5	16.0	15.9	15.9	15.1
1993	15.1	16.0	16.0	16.1	16.0	15.0	14.4	14.8	15.9	16.1	16.3	16.2	15.6
1994	15.0	16.0	16.2	16.3	16.2	15.8	15.3	15.4	16.4	16.9	17.1	17.0	16.1
1995	16.1	17.3	17.3	17.3	17.4	17.0	16.3	16.7	18.2	18.4	18.7	18.6	17.4
1996	17.1	18.4	18.6	18.5	18.5	17.6	17.1	17.6	18.6	19.1	19.2	19.5	18.3
1997	17.9	19.2	19.1	19.5	19.2	18.3	17.8	18.2	19.2	19.6	19.7	19.9	18.9
1998	18.4	19.4	19.3	19.3	19.4	18.8	17.7	17.9	19.3	19.7	19.8	19.7	19.0
1999	18.5	19.5	19.4	19.6	19.5	18.7	17.9	18.4	19.6	19.9	20.1	20.1	19.3
2000	18.9	20.0	20.4	20.1	20.5	20.1	18.6	18.9	20.2	20.7	20.7	20.3	20.0
2001	19.7	20.8	20.9	20.9	20.9	19.8	18.4	19.3	21.0	21.5	21.6	21.6	20.5
2002	20.5	21.6	21.5	21.5	21.3	20.5	18.9	19.9	21.6	21.3	21.5	21.3	21.0
2003	21.3	22.3	22.5	21.6	21.5	21.7	20.1	20.9	22.8	23.0	23.2	23.1	22.0
Federal government													
1990	1.4	1.4	1.4	1.4	1.6	1.5	1.5	1.4	1.4	1.4	1.4	1.4	1.4
1991	1.4	1.4	1.4	1.4	1.4	1.4	1.4	1.4	1.4	1.4	1.4	1.4	1.4
1992	1.4	1.4	1.4	1.4	1.4	1.5	1.5	1.4	1.4	1.4	1.4	1.5	1.4
1993	1.5	1.4	1.4	1.4	1.5	1.4	1.5	1.5	1.4	1.4	1.5	1.5	1.4
1994	1.5	1.4	1.5	1.5	1.4	1.5	1.5	1.5	1.5	1.5	1.5	1.5	1.4
1995	1.5	1.5	1.5	1.5	1.5	1.6	1.6	1.6	1.6	1.5	1.6	1.5	1.5
1996	1.6	1.6	1.6	1.6	1.6	1.6	1.6	1.6	1.6	1.6	1.6	1.7	1.6
1997	1.6	1.6	1.6	1.6	1.6	1.6	1.6	1.6	1.6	1.6	1.6	1.7	1.6
1998	1.6	1.6	1.6	1.6	1.6	1.6	1.5	1.6	1.6	1.7	1.7	1.6	1.6
1999	1.6	1.6	1.6	1.6	1.6	1.6	1.6	1.6	1.6	1.6	1.6	1.6	1.6
2000	1.6	1.6	1.8	1.6	2.1	2.1	1.9	1.9	1.6	1.6	1.6	1.6	1.8
2001	1.6	1.6	1.6	1.6	1.6	1.6	1.6	1.7	1.6	1.7	1.7	1.7	1.6
2002	1.7	1.7	1.7	1.7	1.7	1.7	1.7	1.7	1.7	1.7	1.7	1.8	1.7
2003	1.7	1.7	1.8	1.8	1.8	1.8	1.8	1.8	1.8	1.8	1.9	1.9	1.8
State government													
1990	5.3	6.0	6.0	5.9	5.7	5.0	5.3	5.5	6.0	6.3	6.3	6.2	5.7
1991	5.3	6.1	6.2	6.1	5.7	5.4	5.7	6.0	6.6	6.6	6.5	6.4	6.0
1992	5.5	6.5	6.7	6.5	6.2	5.9	5.9	6.2	6.8	7.0	6.9	6.8	6.4
1993	5.9	6.8	6.8	6.8	6.5	5.8	6.2	6.4	6.9	6.7	6.8	6.8	6.5
1994	5.6	6.6	6.7	6.7	6.6	6.3	6.8	6.8	6.8	7.0	7.1	7.0	6.6
1995	6.1	7.1	7.1	7.1	7.1	6.7	7.1	7.3	7.8	7.9	8.0	8.0	7.2
1996	6.6	7.8	7.8	7.8	7.6	6.9	7.0	7.3	7.8	8.1	8.1	8.1	7.5
1997	6.7	8.0	7.8	8.2	7.7	6.9	7.3	7.5	7.9	8.1	8.1	8.1	7.6
1998	6.8	7.6	7.5	7.5	7.5	7.0	7.2	7.1	7.6	7.7	7.7	7.6	7.4
1999	6.6	7.5	7.4	7.5	7.3	6.7	7.0	7.1	7.5	7.6	7.8	7.7	7.3
2000	6.7	7.8	7.9	7.8	7.6	7.2	7.1	7.1	7.6	8.0	7.9	7.4	7.5
2001	7.0	8.0	8.0	8.0	7.9	6.8	6.5	7.2	7.9	8.1	8.2	8.1	7.6
2002	7.1	8.1	8.0	8.0	7.7	6.9	6.5	7.3	8.2	7.5	7.6	7.3	7.5
2003	7.5	8.4	8.5	7.6	7.3	7.4	7.0	7.6	8.6	8.7	8.6	8.4	8.0

Employment by Industry: Arkansas—*Continued*

(Numbers in thousands. Not seasonally adjusted.)

Industry	January	February	March	April	May	June	July	August	September	October	November	December	Annual Average
FAYETTEVILLE-SPRINGDALE—*Continued*													
Local government													
1990	7.8	7.9	8.0	8.0	8.1	7.9	7.1	7.3	8.2	8.2	8.3	8.3	7.9
1991	8.2	8.5	8.5	8.4	8.4	8.1	6.8	6.8	7.4	7.8	7.7	7.6	7.8
1992	7.4	7.5	7.5	7.6	7.7	7.4	6.4	6.6	7.3	7.6	7.6	7.6	7.3
1993	7.7	7.8	7.8	7.9	8.0	7.8	6.7	6.9	7.6	8.0	8.0	7.9	7.6
1994	7.9	8.0	8.0	8.1	8.2	8.0	7.0	7.1	8.1	8.4	8.5	8.5	7.9
1995	8.5	8.7	8.7	8.7	8.8	8.7	7.6	7.8	8.8	9.0	9.1	9.1	8.6
1996	8.9	9.0	9.2	9.1	9.3	9.1	8.5	8.7	9.2	9.4	9.5	9.7	9.1
1997	9.6	9.6	9.7	9.7	9.9	9.8	8.9	9.1	9.7	9.9	10.0	10.1	9.6
1998	10.0	10.2	10.2	10.2	10.3	10.2	9.0	9.2	10.1	10.3	10.4	10.5	10.0
1999	10.3	10.4	10.4	10.5	10.6	10.4	9.3	9.7	10.5	10.7	10.7	10.8	10.4
2000	10.6	10.6	10.7	10.7	10.8	10.8	9.6	9.9	11.0	11.1	11.2	11.3	10.7
2001	11.1	11.2	11.3	11.3	11.4	11.4	10.3	10.4	11.5	11.7	11.7	11.8	11.3
2002	11.7	11.8	11.8	11.8	11.9	11.9	10.7	10.9	11.7	12.1	12.2	12.2	11.7
2003	12.1	12.2	12.2	12.2	12.4	12.5	11.3	11.5	12.4	12.5	12.7	12.8	12.2
FORT SMITH													
Total nonfarm													
1990	76.8	77.6	79.0	80.5	81.5	82.7	82.8	82.2	82.2	80.2	79.7	79.2	80.3
1991	78.1	78.6	79.5	80.1	81.9	83.1	82.7	83.3	81.9	81.1	81.5	81.7	81.1
1992	80.2	80.4	81.9	82.8	84.0	84.8	83.6	84.3	83.8	83.9	84.4	84.0	83.1
1993	83.1	84.2	85.0	86.2	87.0	88.1	87.4	86.7	87.4	87.1	87.4	87.6	86.4
1994	86.3	86.3	87.4	90.0	90.5	92.0	92.0	91.9	93.0	92.5	92.9	92.4	90.6
1995	91.1	91.3	91.6	92.3	92.4	93.4	92.5	93.2	93.5	93.3	93.2	93.4	92.6
1996	92.0	91.6	92.3	93.4	94.2	94.6	93.9	95.6	94.7	95.0	94.8	94.1	93.8
1997	93.2	93.8	94.8	95.4	96.3	96.3	95.8	96.6	96.4	97.0	96.5	96.6	95.7
1998	94.8	95.7	96.2	96.9	97.8	97.7	97.9	98.1	98.0	98.9	98.5	97.9	97.3
1999	96.9	97.6	98.7	100.0	100.1	100.8	100.2	101.4	101.3	101.6	100.7	100.7	100.0
2000	99.5	99.9	101.5	102.0	102.7	102.8	101.0	103.0	103.3	102.1	102.5	102.3	101.8
2001	101.3	101.9	102.4	102.8	103.4	103.3	101.6	102.8	102.6	101.7	101.4	101.0	102.2
2002	99.0	99.5	100.2	100.2	101.3	101.8	99.6	100.8	101.5	100.4	100.3	100.0	100.4
2003	98.9	98.6	99.4	99.3	100.1	100.3	98.9	99.3	100.4	100.5	100.6	100.3	99.7
Total private													
1990	68.5	69.1	70.5	71.9	72.7	74.3	75.5	74.8	73.6	71.5	70.9	70.6	71.9
1991	69.4	69.8	70.6	71.1	72.8	74.3	75.0	75.4	73.1	72.0	72.4	72.8	72.3
1992	71.3	71.2	72.7	73.5	74.7	75.7	75.6	76.0	74.5	74.4	74.9	74.6	74.0
1993	73.7	74.6	75.4	76.7	77.5	78.9	79.2	78.4	78.1	77.8	78.0	78.3	77.2
1994	77.0	76.9	77.9	80.5	80.9	82.8	83.8	83.5	83.5	82.9	83.4	82.9	81.3
1995	81.6	81.7	82.0	82.9	82.8	84.6	84.1	84.4	84.1	83.8	83.5	83.7	83.2
1996	82.5	82.0	82.6	83.7	84.5	85.5	85.5	86.5	84.8	85.0	84.8	84.2	84.3
1997	83.5	83.9	84.8	85.5	86.3	87.0	86.9	87.3	86.3	86.9	86.5	86.6	85.9
1998	85.0	85.6	86.3	86.7	87.6	88.2	89.0	88.6	87.9	88.4	88.0	87.7	87.4
1999	86.7	87.2	88.3	89.6	89.9	91.2	91.1	91.7	90.9	91.1	90.2	90.2	89.8
2000	89.1	89.2	90.7	91.2	91.5	92.3	91.6	92.8	92.7	90.8	91.1	90.9	91.1
2001	90.2	90.5	91.0	91.4	92.0	92.3	91.6	92.5	91.5	90.2	90.0	89.7	91.1
2002	88.0	88.4	89.0	88.9	89.9	90.6	89.8	90.4	90.2	88.9	88.8	88.5	89.3
2003	87.4	87.0	87.8	87.7	88.3	88.8	88.4	88.6	88.9	88.8	88.9	88.8	88.3
Goods-producing													
1990	26.9	27.5	27.8	29.5	29.6	30.6	30.8	30.3	29.8	28.3	27.9	27.7	28.8
1991	27.2	27.0	27.4	27.9	29.0	29.2	29.2	29.3	28.3	27.6	27.6	27.9	28.1
1992	27.6	27.4	28.1	28.2	28.4	29.0	28.4	28.0	27.8	27.8	28.0	28.2	28.0
1993	27.9	28.3	28.8	29.6	29.9	30.0	30.0	29.8	29.7	29.6	29.6	29.6	29.4
1994	29.2	29.1	29.4	30.8	31.4	32.3	32.7	32.6	32.8	32.6	32.5	32.2	31.4
1995	32.3	32.0	32.0	32.2	32.0	32.5	32.2	32.2	32.1	32.1	31.8	31.8	32.1
1996	31.4	31.0	31.1	32.1	31.9	32.4	32.4	32.6	32.2	32.3	32.0	31.5	31.9
1997	31.8	31.9	32.0	32.3	32.5	32.6	32.5	32.6	32.4	31.7	31.6	31.8	32.1
1998	31.5	31.7	31.9	32.0	32.0	32.4	32.3	32.0	31.9	31.7	31.6	31.7	31.8
1999	31.7	31.8	32.0	33.0	33.1	33.5	33.4	33.5	33.4	33.4	33.0	33.1	32.9
2000	33.0	32.8	32.9	32.9	33.0	33.1	33.3	33.5	33.4	32.7	32.8	32.9	33.0
2001	32.7	32.7	32.6	33.2	33.1	33.2	33.0	33.0	32.8	32.4	32.1	32.2	32.8
2002	31.8	31.8	31.6	31.1	31.4	31.7	31.5	31.3	31.3	30.9	31.0	30.8	31.4
2003	30.7	30.5	30.5	30.1	30.4	30.7	30.9	31.1	31.3	31.5	31.6	31.5	30.9
Natural resources and mining													
1990	0.9	0.9	0.9	0.9	0.9	0.9	0.9	0.9	1.0	1.0	1.0	1.0	0.9
1991	0.9	0.9	0.9	0.9	0.9	0.9	0.8	0.8	0.8	0.8	0.8	0.8	0.8
1992	0.8	0.8	0.8	0.8	0.7	0.8	0.7	0.8	0.7	0.8	0.8	0.8	0.7
1993	0.8	0.8	0.8	0.8	0.8	0.8	0.8	0.8	0.8	0.8	0.8	0.8	0.8
1994	0.8	0.8	0.9	0.9	0.9	1.0	1.0	0.9	0.9	1.0	0.9	0.9	0.9
1995	0.9	0.8	0.8	0.8	0.8	0.8	0.8	0.8	0.9	0.9	0.8	0.8	0.8
1996	0.8	0.8	0.8	0.8	0.8	0.8	0.9	0.8	0.8	0.8	0.8	0.8	0.8
1997	0.8	0.8	0.8	0.9	0.9	0.8	0.8	0.9	0.9	0.9	0.9	0.9	0.8
1998	0.9	0.9	0.9	0.9	0.8	0.8	0.8	0.7	0.7	0.7	0.7	0.7	0.7
1999	0.7	0.7	0.7	0.7	0.6	0.7	0.7	0.7	0.7	0.7	0.7	0.7	0.6
2000	0.7	0.7	0.7	0.7	0.7	0.8	0.7	0.7	0.7	0.7	0.8	0.9	0.7
2001	0.9	0.9	1.0	1.0	1.0	1.0	1.1	1.1	1.1	1.0	1.0	1.0	1.0
2002	0.9	0.9	0.9	0.9	0.9	0.9	0.9	0.9	0.9	0.9	0.9	0.9	0.9
2003	0.8	0.9	0.9	0.9	1.0	1.0	1.0	1.0	1.1	1.0	1.0	1.0	1.0

Employment by Industry: Arkansas—*Continued*

(Numbers in thousands. Not seasonally adjusted.)

Industry	January	February	March	April	May	June	July	August	September	October	November	December	Annual Average
FORT SMITH—*Continued*													
Construction													
1990	2.6	2.6	2.6	2.6	2.6	2.8	2.9	2.8	2.8	2.8	2.8	2.8	2.7
1991	2.5	2.6	2.7	2.8	2.8	2.8	3.0	3.0	3.0	3.0	2.9	2.9	2.8
1992	2.7	2.6	2.7	2.6	2.6	2.8	2.8	2.8	2.8	2.8	2.7	2.8	2.7
1993	2.6	2.7	2.7	2.8	2.9	3.0	3.2	3.2	3.1	3.1	3.2	3.2	2.9
1994	3.0	3.1	3.1	3.3	3.4	3.6	3.6	3.6	3.6	3.4	3.4	3.4	3.3
1995	3.3	3.3	3.4	3.4	3.4	3.5	3.5	3.5	3.5	3.5	3.5	3.5	3.4
1996	3.3	3.3	3.4	3.8	4.0	4.1	4.1	4.1	4.0	4.1	4.0	4.0	3.8
1997	3.8	3.8	3.8	3.9	4.0	4.1	4.1	4.1	4.1	4.0	3.9	3.9	3.9
1998	3.8	3.9	3.9	4.0	4.0	4.2	4.2	4.1	4.1	3.9	3.9	3.9	3.9
1999	3.8	3.8	3.8	3.8	3.9	4.0	4.1	4.1	4.1	4.1	4.1	4.2	3.9
2000	4.2	4.1	4.2	4.1	4.1	4.1	4.2	4.3	4.4	4.2	4.2	4.1	4.1
2001	4.3	4.5	4.7	4.8	4.9	4.9	5.0	5.0	4.9	4.9	4.8	4.6	4.8
2002	4.4	4.4	4.5	4.5	4.6	4.7	4.7	4.7	4.6	4.5	4.5	4.4	4.5
2003	4.3	4.2	4.3	4.4	4.4	4.6	4.7	4.8	4.8	4.7	4.7	4.7	4.6
Manufacturing													
1990	23.4	24.0	24.3	26.0	26.1	26.9	27.0	26.6	26.0	24.5	24.1	23.9	25.2
1991	23.8	23.5	23.8	24.2	25.3	25.5	25.4	25.5	24.5	23.8	23.9	24.2	24.4
1992	24.1	24.0	24.6	24.8	25.1	25.4	24.9	24.4	24.3	24.2	24.5	24.6	24.5
1993	24.5	24.8	25.3	26.0	26.2	26.2	26.0	25.8	25.8	25.7	25.6	25.6	25.6
1994	25.4	25.2	25.4	26.6	27.1	27.7	28.1	28.1	28.3	28.2	28.2	27.9	27.1
1995	28.1	27.9	27.8	28.0	27.8	28.2	27.9	27.9	27.7	27.7	27.5	27.5	27.8
1996	27.3	26.9	26.9	27.5	27.1	27.5	27.4	27.7	27.4	27.4	27.2	26.7	27.2
1997	27.2	27.3	27.4	27.5	27.6	27.7	27.6	27.6	27.4	26.8	26.8	27.0	27.3
1998	26.8	26.9	27.1	27.1	27.2	27.4	27.3	27.2	27.1	27.1	27.0	27.1	27.1
1999	27.2	27.3	27.5	28.5	28.6	28.8	28.6	28.7	28.6	28.6	28.2	28.2	28.2
2000	28.1	28.0	28.0	28.1	28.2	28.2	28.4	28.5	28.3	27.8	27.8	27.9	28.1
2001	27.5	27.3	26.9	27.4	27.2	27.3	26.9	26.9	26.8	26.5	26.3	26.6	27.0
2002	26.5	26.5	26.2	25.7	25.9	26.1	25.9	25.7	25.8	25.5	25.6	25.5	25.9
2003	25.6	25.4	25.3	24.8	25.0	25.1	25.2	25.3	25.4	25.8	25.9	25.8	25.4
Service-providing													
1990	49.9	50.1	51.2	51.0	51.9	52.1	52.0	51.9	52.4	51.9	51.8	51.5	51.4
1991	50.9	51.6	52.1	52.2	52.9	53.9	53.5	54.0	53.6	53.5	53.9	53.8	52.9
1992	52.6	53.0	53.8	54.6	55.6	55.8	55.2	56.3	56.0	56.1	56.4	55.8	55.1
1993	55.2	55.9	56.2	56.6	57.1	58.1	57.4	56.9	57.7	57.5	57.8	58.0	57.0
1994	57.1	57.2	58.0	59.2	59.1	59.7	59.3	59.3	60.2	59.9	60.4	60.2	59.1
1995	58.8	59.3	59.6	60.1	60.4	60.9	60.3	61.0	61.4	61.2	61.4	61.6	60.5
1996	60.6	60.6	61.2	61.3	62.3	62.2	61.5	63.0	62.5	62.7	62.8	62.6	61.9
1997	61.4	61.9	62.8	63.1	63.8	63.7	63.3	64.0	64.0	65.3	64.9	64.8	63.5
1998	63.3	64.0	64.3	64.9	65.8	65.3	65.6	66.1	66.1	67.2	66.9	66.2	65.4
1999	65.2	65.8	66.7	67.0	67.0	67.3	66.8	67.9	67.9	68.2	67.7	67.6	67.0
2000	66.5	67.1	68.6	69.1	69.7	69.7	67.7	69.5	69.9	69.4	69.7	69.4	68.8
2001	68.6	69.2	69.8	69.6	70.3	70.1	68.6	69.8	69.8	69.3	69.3	68.8	69.4
2002	67.2	67.7	68.6	69.1	69.9	70.1	68.1	69.5	70.2	69.5	69.3	69.2	69.0
2003	68.2	68.1	68.9	69.2	69.7	69.6	68.0	68.2	69.1	69.0	69.0	68.8	68.8
Trade, transportation, and utilities													
1990	15.6	15.2	15.4	15.4	15.6	15.7	15.8	15.6	15.7	15.7	16.0	16.1	15.6
1991	15.6	15.4	15.4	15.2	15.4	15.7	15.5	15.6	15.7	15.7	16.0	16.1	15.6
1992	15.4	15.2	15.4	15.7	15.9	16.0	16.0	16.0	15.9	16.0	16.1	16.5	15.8
1993	15.8	15.8	15.9	16.4	16.4	16.4	16.5	16.7	16.7	17.0	17.2	17.4	16.5
1994	16.8	16.7	17.0	17.7	17.9	18.2	18.0	18.1	18.4	18.3	18.7	18.7	17.8
1995	18.0	17.9	17.9	17.8	17.9	18.0	17.9	18.0	18.2	18.2	18.5	18.7	18.0
1996	18.6	18.2	18.4	18.5	18.7	18.9	18.9	19.1	18.8	19.2	19.6	19.8	18.8
1997	19.1	19.3	19.6	19.5	19.5	19.7	19.5	19.4	19.3	19.7	20.0	20.1	19.5
1998	19.1	19.0	19.2	19.0	19.2	19.2	19.2	19.4	19.1	19.6	19.7	19.8	19.2
1999	19.0	18.9	19.2	18.8	18.9	19.3	19.2	19.5	19.4	19.4	19.6	19.7	19.2
2000	19.5	19.4	19.8	19.9	19.8	20.0	19.6	19.9	20.0	19.7	20.0	20.1	19.8
2001	19.6	19.6	19.8	19.5	19.7	19.6	19.6	19.5	19.6	19.4	19.8	19.8	19.6
2002	19.1	18.9	19.0	19.0	19.2	19.3	19.4	19.5	19.4	19.5	19.9	20.0	19.4
2003	19.2	19.3	19.7	19.7	19.7	19.7	19.8	19.7	19.8	19.8	20.0	20.4	19.7
Wholesale trade													
1990	2.7	2.7	2.7	2.7	2.8	2.8	2.8	2.7	2.7	2.7	2.7	2.7	2.7
1991	2.7	2.7	2.7	2.7	2.7	2.8	2.7	2.7	2.7	2.7	2.7	2.7	2.7
1992	2.6	2.6	2.6	2.7	2.7	2.7	2.7	2.7	2.7	2.7	2.7	2.7	2.6
1993	2.7	2.7	2.7	2.8	2.8	2.8	2.8	2.8	2.8	2.8	2.7	2.7	2.7
1994	2.7	2.7	2.8	2.9	2.8	2.9	2.9	2.9	2.9	2.9	2.9	2.9	2.8
1995	2.9	2.9	2.9	2.9	2.9	2.9	2.8	2.8	2.8	2.8	2.8	2.8	2.8
1996	2.9	2.9	3.0	2.9	2.9	3.0	3.0	3.0	2.9	2.9	2.9	2.9	2.9
1997	2.9	2.9	2.9	2.9	2.9	3.0	3.0	3.0	3.0	3.2	3.2	3.2	3.0
1998	3.1	3.1	3.1	3.1	3.1	3.1	3.1	3.1	3.0	3.1	3.0	3.0	3.0
1999	2.8	2.8	2.8	2.9	2.9	3.0	3.0	3.0	3.0	2.9	2.9	3.0	2.9
2000	2.9	2.9	3.0	3.0	3.0	3.1	3.0	3.0	3.0	3.0	3.0	3.0	2.9
2001	3.2	3.2	3.2	3.2	3.2	3.2	3.2	3.2	3.2	3.2	3.2	3.2	3.2
2002	3.1	3.1	3.1	3.1	3.1	3.1	3.1	3.2	3.1	3.2	3.2	3.2	3.1
2003	3.2	3.2	3.2	3.2	3.2	3.2	3.2	3.2	3.2	3.2	3.2	3.3	3.2

Employment by Industry: Arkansas—*Continued*

(Numbers in thousands. Not seasonally adjusted.)

Industry	January	February	March	April	May	June	July	August	September	October	November	December	Annual Average
FORT SMITH—*Continued*													
Retail trade													
1990	9.0	8.7	8.8	9.0	9.1	9.2	9.2	9.2	9.1	9.0	9.3	9.4	9.0
1991	9.0	8.7	8.7	8.8	8.9	9.0	8.9	8.9	9.0	9.0	9.2	9.3	8.9
1992	8.8	8.6	8.8	9.0	9.1	9.1	9.1	9.1	9.0	9.1	9.2	9.5	9.0
1993	9.0	9.0	9.1	9.4	9.4	9.4	9.4	9.5	9.5	9.7	10.0	10.1	9.4
1994	9.6	9.5	9.6	9.8	10.0	10.0	10.0	10.2	10.4	10.4	10.7	10.7	10.0
1995	10.2	10.0	10.0	10.1	10.2	10.3	10.2	10.3	10.4	10.5	10.7	10.9	10.3
1996	10.5	10.2	10.3	10.5	10.7	10.7	10.7	10.9	10.7	11.0	11.3	11.5	10.7
1997	10.9	11.0	11.3	11.4	11.4	11.4	11.3	11.2	11.1	11.1	11.4	11.5	11.2
1998	10.7	10.5	10.6	10.7	10.8	10.9	10.9	11.0	10.8	11.0	11.2	11.3	10.8
1999	10.8	10.6	10.9	11.0	11.0	11.3	11.1	11.3	11.2	11.2	11.4	11.5	11.1
2000	10.9	10.9	11.2	11.3	11.2	11.2	11.3	11.5	11.5	11.3	11.6	11.7	11.3
2001	10.9	10.9	11.1	11.1	11.2	11.1	11.1	11.0	11.1	10.9	11.3	11.4	11.1
2002	10.8	10.6	10.7	10.7	10.8	10.8	10.9	10.8	10.8	10.8	11.2	11.3	10.9
2003	10.7	10.7	11.0	11.0	11.0	11.0	11.0	11.0	11.0	11.0	11.2	11.4	11.0
Transportation and utilities													
1990	3.9	3.8	3.9	3.7	3.7	3.7	3.8	3.7	3.9	4.0	4.0	4.0	3.8
1991	3.9	4.0	4.0	3.7	3.8	3.9	3.9	4.0	4.0	4.0	4.1	4.1	3.9
1992	4.0	4.0	4.0	4.0	4.1	4.2	4.2	4.2	4.2	4.2	4.2	4.3	4.1
1993	4.1	4.1	4.1	4.2	4.2	4.2	4.3	4.4	4.4	4.5	4.5	4.6	4.3
1994	4.5	4.5	4.6	5.0	5.1	5.3	5.1	5.0	5.1	5.0	5.1	5.1	4.9
1995	4.9	5.0	5.0	4.8	4.8	4.8	4.9	4.9	5.0	4.9	5.0	5.0	4.9
1996	5.2	5.1	5.1	5.1	5.1	5.2	5.2	5.2	5.2	5.3	5.4	5.4	5.2
1997	5.3	5.4	5.4	5.2	5.2	5.3	5.2	5.2	5.2	5.4	5.4	5.4	5.3
1998	5.3	5.4	5.5	5.2	5.3	5.2	5.2	5.3	5.3	5.5	5.5	5.5	5.3
1999	5.4	5.5	5.5	4.9	5.0	5.0	5.1	5.2	5.2	5.3	5.3	5.2	5.2
2000	5.7	5.6	5.6	5.6	5.6	5.7	5.3	5.4	5.5	5.4	5.4	5.4	5.5
2001	5.5	5.5	5.5	5.2	5.3	5.3	5.3	5.3	5.3	5.3	5.3	5.2	5.3
2002	5.2	5.2	5.2	5.2	5.3	5.4	5.4	5.5	5.5	5.5	5.5	5.5	5.4
2003	5.3	5.4	5.5	5.5	5.5	5.5	5.6	5.5	5.6	5.6	5.6	5.7	5.5
Information													
1990	1.3	1.3	1.3	1.3	1.3	1.3	1.4	1.3	1.3	1.3	1.3	1.3	1.3
1991	1.3	1.3	1.3	1.4	1.3	1.3	1.4	1.4	1.4	1.4	1.4	1.4	1.3
1992	1.4	1.4	1.4	1.4	1.4	1.4	1.4	1.4	1.4	1.4	1.4	1.4	1.4
1993	1.3	1.3	1.3	1.3	1.3	1.4	1.4	1.4	1.4	1.4	1.4	1.4	1.3
1994	1.4	1.4	1.4	1.4	1.4	1.5	1.4	1.5	1.5	1.4	1.5	1.5	1.4
1995	1.4	1.4	1.4	1.4	1.4	1.5	1.5	1.5	1.5	1.5	1.5	1.5	1.4
1996	1.5	1.5	1.5	1.5	1.5	1.6	1.6	1.6	1.6	1.6	1.6	1.6	1.5
1997	1.6	1.6	1.6	1.6	1.6	1.6	1.5	1.5	1.5	1.5	1.5	1.5	1.5
1998	1.5	1.6	1.6	1.6	1.6	1.6	1.6	1.6	1.6	1.6	1.6	1.6	1.5
1999	1.7	1.7	1.7	1.8	1.8	1.8	1.9	1.9	1.8	1.8	1.8	1.8	1.7
2000	1.8	1.8	1.8	1.8	1.8	1.9	1.8	1.8	1.8	1.9	1.9	1.9	1.8
2001	2.0	2.0	1.9	1.9	1.9	1.8	1.8	1.8	1.8	1.8	1.8	1.8	1.9
2002	1.7	1.8	1.8	1.8	1.8	1.8	1.7	1.7	1.7	1.7	1.7	1.7	1.7
2003	1.7	1.7	1.7	1.6	1.7	1.7	1.6	1.6	1.6	1.6	1.6	1.6	1.6
Financial activities													
1990	2.9	2.8	2.9	2.7	2.7	2.7	2.8	2.7	2.7	2.8	2.8	2.8	2.7
1991	2.8	2.8	2.8	2.6	2.6	2.7	2.7	2.7	2.7	2.7	2.7	2.7	2.7
1992	2.8	2.8	2.8	2.8	2.8	2.8	2.8	2.8	2.8	2.8	2.8	2.8	2.8
1993	2.8	2.8	2.8	2.8	2.9	2.9	3.0	3.0	3.0	3.0	3.0	3.0	2.9
1994	3.0	3.0	3.0	3.0	3.1	3.1	3.2	3.1	3.2	3.2	3.2	3.2	3.1
1995	3.2	3.2	3.2	3.1	3.1	3.2	3.1	3.2	3.1	3.1	3.1	3.2	3.1
1996	3.1	3.1	3.1	3.2	3.2	3.3	3.3	3.3	3.3	3.3	3.3	3.3	3.2
1997	3.3	3.3	3.3	3.2	3.3	3.3	3.3	3.3	3.3	3.3	3.2	3.2	3.2
1998	3.3	3.3	3.3	3.2	3.3	3.3	3.3	3.3	3.3	3.3	3.3	3.3	3.2
1999	3.4	3.4	3.4	3.5	3.5	3.5	3.5	3.5	3.5	3.5	3.5	3.6	3.4
2000	3.5	3.5	3.5	3.3	3.3	3.4	3.5	3.5	3.5	3.4	3.5	3.5	3.4
2001	3.5	3.5	3.6	3.5	3.6	3.6	3.5	3.5	3.5	3.5	3.5	3.5	3.5
2002	3.5	3.5	3.5	3.5	3.5	3.6	3.6	3.6	3.6	3.5	3.6	3.6	3.6
2003	3.6	3.6	3.6	3.6	3.6	3.6	3.6	3.6	3.6	3.6	3.6	3.6	3.6
Professional and business services													
1990	5.4	5.6	5.9	6.5	6.7	6.8	6.8	7.1	7.0	6.4	5.9	5.9	6.3
1991	5.6	5.9	6.2	6.3	6.5	6.7	7.1	7.3	7.0	6.5	6.6	6.6	6.5
1992	6.3	6.3	6.7	7.0	7.3	7.3	7.5	7.7	7.7	7.8	7.7	7.2	7.2
1993	7.5	7.6	7.6	7.9	8.0	8.1	8.4	8.1	8.1	7.9	7.8	7.8	7.9
1994	7.7	7.7	7.9	7.9	7.0	7.4	7.5	7.4	7.4	7.3	7.1	7.0	7.4
1995	6.8	7.0	6.9	7.8	7.6	8.2	7.9	8.2	8.2	8.1	7.9	7.8	7.7
1996	7.3	7.2	7.4	8.1	8.6	8.5	8.5	9.1	8.5	8.3	8.1	7.9	8.1
1997	7.5	7.5	7.7	7.9	8.2	8.5	8.8	9.2	9.0	9.8	9.3	9.3	8.5
1998	9.0	9.3	9.3	9.8	10.1	10.0	10.7	10.6	10.6	11.0	10.7	10.2	10.1
1999	10.0	10.3	10.4	11.1	11.0	11.2	11.2	11.5	11.2	11.6	10.9	10.8	10.9
2000	10.5	10.7	11.5	11.5	11.6	11.8	11.2	11.8	11.7	11.4	11.1	10.9	11.3
2001	10.7	10.9	11.0	10.8	10.9	11.0	10.9	12.0	11.3	10.9	10.6	10.1	10.9
2002	10.0	10.3	10.6	10.6	10.9	10.8	10.4	10.9	11.0	10.4	9.9	9.6	10.5
2003	9.6	9.4	9.4	9.7	9.8	9.9	9.6	9.8	10.0	9.8	9.6	9.2	9.7

Employment by Industry: Arkansas—*Continued*

(Numbers in thousands. Not seasonally adjusted.)

Industry	January	February	March	April	May	June	July	August	September	October	November	December	Annual Average
FORT SMITH—*Continued*													
Educational and health services													
1990	8.6	8.7	8.9	8.0	8.0	8.2	9.0	8.9	8.2	8.8	8.8	8.9	8.5
1991	9.2	9.3	9.3	9.3	9.5	9.9	10.2	10.1	9.3	9.7	9.8	9.9	9.6
1992	9.8	9.8	9.9	9.9	10.1	10.2	10.6	11.2	10.1	10.1	10.3	10.0	10.1
1993	10.2	10.4	10.4	9.8	9.9	10.8	10.7	10.2	9.9	10.0	10.2	10.1	10.2
1994	10.4	10.4	10.4	10.4	10.6	10.6	11.1	11.1	10.7	10.7	10.8	10.8	10.6
1995	11.0	10.9	11.0	11.0	11.1	11.3	11.4	11.1	11.1	11.1	11.2	11.2	11.1
1996	11.3	11.4	11.3	10.3	10.3	10.3	10.5	10.4	10.3	10.4	10.4	10.4	10.6
1997	10.8	10.8	10.9	10.8	10.7	10.8	11.0	10.9	10.8	11.0	11.1	11.0	10.8
1998	11.2	11.3	11.3	11.2	11.3	11.4	11.5	11.4	11.4	11.3	11.4	11.4	11.3
1999	11.5	11.5	11.5	11.1	11.2	11.4	11.5	11.4	11.4	11.5	11.5	11.5	11.4
2000	11.4	11.5	11.5	11.6	11.6	11.6	11.7	11.8	11.9	11.8	11.9	11.8	11.6
2001	12.0	12.1	12.1	12.3	12.4	12.4	12.3	12.4	12.4	12.4	12.4	12.5	12.3
2002	12.4	12.5	12.6	12.7	12.7	12.8	12.8	13.0	13.0	13.0	13.0	13.1	12.8
2003	13.0	12.9	13.0	13.1	13.0	12.9	12.6	12.6	12.5	12.5	12.5	12.6	12.8
Leisure and hospitality													
1990	5.2	5.4	5.7	5.9	6.2	6.3	6.2	6.2	6.3	5.6	5.6	5.3	5.8
1991	5.1	5.4	5.5	5.7	5.8	6.0	6.0	6.3	6.0	5.7	5.6	5.5	5.7
1992	5.3	5.6	5.7	5.8	6.0	6.1	6.0	6.1	6.0	5.7	5.8	5.7	5.8
1993	5.4	5.6	5.8	6.2	6.4	6.5	6.3	6.4	6.5	6.1	6.1	6.2	6.1
1994	5.8	5.9	6.1	6.6	6.7	6.8	7.0	6.8	6.7	6.6	6.8	6.7	6.5
1995	6.3	6.5	6.7	6.9	7.0	7.1	7.2	7.4	7.2	6.9	6.7	6.7	6.8
1996	6.5	6.7	6.9	7.2	7.4	7.5	7.3	7.5	7.2	7.0	6.9	6.8	7.0
1997	6.5	6.6	6.8	7.4	7.6	7.5	7.3	7.4	7.1	7.0	6.9	6.8	7.0
1998	6.5	6.5	6.7	7.0	7.2	7.3	7.3	7.3	7.1	7.0	6.8	6.8	6.9
1999	6.5	6.7	7.1	7.4	7.5	7.5	7.3	7.4	7.3	7.0	6.9	6.8	7.1
2000	6.5	6.6	6.8	7.2	7.4	7.4	7.5	7.5	7.4	7.0	7.0	6.9	7.1
2001	6.7	6.7	7.0	7.2	7.4	7.6	7.4	7.3	7.2	6.9	6.9	6.9	7.1
2002	6.7	6.8	7.0	7.3	7.5	7.6	7.4	7.5	7.3	7.1	6.9	6.9	7.2
2003	6.8	6.8	7.1	7.1	7.3	7.4	7.4	7.4	7.3	7.2	7.2	7.1	7.2
Other services													
1990	2.6	2.6	2.6	2.6	2.6	2.7	2.7	2.7	2.6	2.6	2.6	2.6	2.6
1991	2.6	2.7	2.7	2.7	2.7	2.8	2.9	2.7	2.7	2.7	2.7	2.7	2.7
1992	2.7	2.7	2.7	2.7	2.8	2.9	2.9	2.8	2.8	2.8	2.8	2.8	2.7
1993	2.8	2.8	2.8	2.7	2.7	2.8	2.9	2.8	2.8	2.8	2.7	2.8	2.7
1994	2.7	2.7	2.7	2.7	2.8	2.9	2.9	2.9	2.8	2.8	2.8	2.8	2.7
1995	2.6	2.8	2.9	2.7	2.7	2.8	2.9	2.8	2.7	2.8	2.8	2.8	2.7
1996	2.8	2.9	2.9	2.8	2.9	3.0	3.0	2.9	2.9	2.9	2.9	2.9	2.9
1997	2.9	2.9	2.9	2.8	2.9	3.0	3.0	3.0	2.9	2.9	2.9	2.9	2.9
1998	2.9	2.9	3.0	2.9	2.9	3.0	3.1	3.0	2.9	2.9	2.9	2.9	2.9
1999	2.9	2.9	3.0	2.9	2.9	3.0	3.1	3.0	2.9	2.9	3.0	2.9	2.9
2000	2.9	2.9	2.9	3.0	3.0	3.1	3.0	3.0	3.0	2.9	2.9	2.9	2.9
2001	3.0	3.0	3.0	3.0	3.0	3.1	3.1	3.0	2.9	2.9	2.9	2.9	3.0
2002	2.8	2.8	2.9	2.9	2.9	3.0	3.0	2.9	2.9	2.8	2.8	2.8	2.9
2003	2.8	2.8	2.8	2.8	2.8	2.9	2.9	2.8	2.8	2.8	2.8	2.8	2.8
Government													
1990	8.3	8.5	8.5	8.6	8.8	8.4	7.3	7.4	8.6	8.7	8.8	8.6	8.3
1991	8.7	8.8	8.9	9.0	9.1	8.8	7.7	7.9	8.8	9.1	9.1	8.9	8.7
1992	8.9	9.2	9.2	9.3	9.3	9.1	8.0	8.3	9.3	9.5	9.5	9.4	9.0
1993	9.4	9.6	9.6	9.5	9.5	9.2	8.2	8.3	9.3	9.3	9.4	9.3	9.2
1994	9.3	9.4	9.5	9.5	9.6	9.2	8.2	8.4	9.5	9.6	9.5	9.5	9.2
1995	9.5	9.6	9.6	9.4	9.6	8.8	8.4	8.8	9.4	9.5	9.7	9.7	9.3
1996	9.5	9.6	9.7	9.7	9.7	9.1	8.4	9.1	9.9	10.0	10.0	9.9	9.5
1997	9.7	9.9	10.0	9.9	10.0	9.3	8.9	9.3	10.1	10.1	10.0	10.0	9.7
1998	9.8	10.1	9.9	10.2	10.2	9.5	8.9	9.5	10.1	10.5	10.5	10.2	9.9
1999	10.2	10.4	10.4	10.4	10.2	9.6	9.1	9.7	10.4	10.5	10.5	10.5	10.1
2000	10.4	10.7	10.8	10.8	11.2	10.5	9.4	10.2	10.6	11.3	11.4	11.4	10.7
2001	11.1	11.4	11.4	11.4	11.4	11.0	10.0	10.3	11.1	11.5	11.4	11.3	11.1
2002	11.0	11.1	11.2	11.3	11.4	11.2	9.8	10.4	11.3	11.5	11.5	11.5	11.1
2003	11.5	11.6	11.6	11.6	11.8	11.5	10.5	10.7	11.5	11.7	11.7	11.5	11.4
Federal government													
1990	1.7	1.7	1.6	1.8	1.9	1.8	1.8	1.7	1.6	1.6	1.6	1.6	1.7
1991	1.6	1.6	1.6	1.7	1.8	1.8	1.8	1.7	1.7	1.8	1.8	1.7	1.7
1992	1.8	1.8	1.8	1.8	1.9	1.9	1.9	1.9	1.9	1.9	1.9	1.9	1.8
1993	1.9	1.8	1.8	1.8	1.7	1.7	1.6	1.6	1.6	1.5	1.5	1.5	1.6
1994	1.5	1.5	1.5	1.5	1.6	1.7	1.7	1.6	1.5	1.4	1.4	1.4	1.5
1995	1.4	1.3	1.3	1.3	1.4	1.4	1.4	1.5	1.4	1.3	1.4	1.4	1.3
1996	1.3	1.4	1.4	1.4	1.4	1.4	1.4	1.5	1.4	1.4	1.4	1.4	1.4
1997	1.4	1.4	1.4	1.4	1.4	1.4	1.4	1.4	1.4	1.3	1.3	1.3	1.3
1998	1.3	1.3	1.2	1.3	1.3	1.3	1.3	1.3	1.3	1.5	1.5	1.3	1.3
1999	1.3	1.3	1.3	1.3	1.3	1.3	1.3	1.3	1.3	1.3	1.3	1.3	1.3
2000	1.3	1.4	1.5	1.4	1.8	1.7	1.6	1.6	1.3	1.3	1.3	1.3	1.4
2001	1.3	1.3	1.3	1.3	1.3	1.3	1.3	1.3	1.3	1.3	1.2	1.2	1.3
2002	1.1	1.1	1.1	1.1	1.1	1.2	1.1	1.3	1.2	1.3	1.3	1.3	1.2
2003	1.3	1.3	1.3	1.3	1.3	1.3	1.3	1.3	1.3	1.3	1.3	1.3	1.3

Employment by Industry: Arkansas—*Continued*

(Numbers in thousands. Not seasonally adjusted.)

Industry	January	February	March	April	May	June	July	August	September	October	November	December	Annual Average
FORT SMITH—*Continued*													
State government													
1990	1.0	1.1	1.2	1.2	1.2	1.1	1.1	1.1	1.3	1.3	1.3	1.2	1.1
1991	1.1	1.2	1.3	1.3	1.2	1.1	1.1	1.1	1.2	1.2	1.2	1.2	1.1
1992	1.1	1.2	1.2	1.3	1.2	1.1	1.1	1.1	1.3	1.3	1.3	1.3	1.2
1993	1.2	1.3	1.3	1.3	1.3	1.3	1.3	1.2	1.3	1.3	1.4	1.3	1.2
1994	1.3	1.3	1.4	1.4	1.3	1.2	1.2	1.2	1.4	1.4	1.4	1.4	1.3
1995	1.3	1.4	1.4	1.4	1.4	1.3	1.3	1.2	1.4	1.4	1.5	1.4	1.3
1996	1.3	1.4	1.4	1.4	1.4	1.3	1.2	1.2	1.5	1.5	1.5	1.4	1.3
1997	1.3	1.4	1.4	1.4	1.4	1.3	1.3	1.3	1.5	1.5	1.4	1.4	1.3
1998	1.3	1.5	1.4	1.5	1.5	1.3	1.3	1.4	1.5	1.5	1.5	1.5	1.4
1999	1.6	1.6	1.6	1.6	1.4	1.3	1.3	1.4	1.6	1.6	1.6	1.5	1.5
2000	1.5	1.6	1.6	1.6	1.6	1.3	1.3	1.3	1.6	1.6	1.6	1.6	1.5
2001	1.4	1.6	1.6	1.6	1.6	1.5	1.4	1.4	1.5	1.7	1.7	1.7	1.6
2002	1.6	1.7	1.8	1.9	1.9	1.8	1.7	1.7	1.8	2.0	2.0	1.9	1.8
2003	1.8	1.9	1.9	1.9	2.0	1.9	1.7	1.7	1.9	2.0	2.0	2.0	1.9
Local government													
1990	5.6	5.7	5.7	5.6	5.7	5.5	4.4	4.6	5.7	5.8	5.9	5.8	5.5
1991	6.0	6.0	6.0	6.0	6.1	5.9	4.8	5.1	5.9	6.1	6.1	6.0	5.8
1992	6.0	6.2	6.2	6.2	6.2	6.1	5.0	5.3	6.1	6.3	6.3	6.2	6.0
1993	6.3	6.5	6.5	6.4	6.5	6.2	5.3	5.5	6.4	6.5	6.5	6.5	6.2
1994	6.5	6.6	6.6	6.6	6.7	6.3	5.3	5.6	6.6	6.8	6.7	6.7	6.4
1995	6.8	6.9	6.9	6.7	6.8	6.1	5.7	6.1	6.6	6.8	6.8	6.9	6.5
1996	6.9	6.8	6.9	6.9	6.9	6.4	5.8	6.4	7.0	7.1	7.1	7.1	6.7
1997	7.0	7.1	7.2	7.1	7.2	6.6	6.2	6.6	7.2	7.3	7.3	7.3	7.0
1998	7.2	7.3	7.3	7.4	7.4	6.9	6.3	6.8	7.3	7.5	7.5	7.4	7.1
1999	7.3	7.5	7.5	7.5	7.5	7.0	6.5	7.0	7.5	7.6	7.6	7.7	7.3
2000	7.6	7.7	7.7	7.8	7.8	7.5	6.5	7.3	7.7	8.4	8.5	8.5	7.7
2001	8.4	8.5	8.5	8.5	8.5	8.2	7.3	7.6	8.3	8.5	8.5	8.4	8.3
2002	8.3	8.3	8.3	8.3	8.4	8.2	7.0	7.4	8.3	8.2	8.2	8.3	8.1
2003	8.4	8.4	8.4	8.4	8.5	8.3	7.5	7.7	8.3	8.4	8.4	8.2	8.2
LITTLE ROCK-NORTH LITTLE ROCK													
Total nonfarm													
1990	247.2	248.3	249.9	250.5	254.1	255.8	251.7	254.9	256.6	255.7	257.0	256.6	253.1
1991	250.7	253.0	254.7	254.2	256.3	258.1	254.5	257.3	260.3	261.3	260.5	260.8	256.8
1992	256.2	258.1	260.4	262.7	265.1	266.8	264.2	264.9	267.5	268.3	268.5	268.8	264.2
1993	264.4	266.6	267.7	269.4	270.7	272.8	270.7	271.4	274.0	275.6	276.6	276.9	271.4
1994	271.1	271.8	274.7	277.4	280.7	282.4	282.2	284.2	287.6	286.3	288.4	288.3	281.2
1995	282.8	285.5	288.2	288.7	290.0	293.5	288.9	292.2	294.5	293.9	296.2	296.6	290.9
1996	290.7	292.0	294.1	294.8	298.3	301.0	296.4	299.0	300.5	300.5	301.7	302.2	297.6
1997	294.4	296.8	300.0	301.3	303.5	304.3	302.3	304.8	306.5	308.0	307.7	309.7	303.2
1998	302.2	304.1	305.9	307.3	309.2	309.9	306.8	308.7	310.5	311.6	312.3	312.9	308.4
1999	307.1	309.1	311.8	311.6	313.0	314.9	312.9	314.3	316.0	316.5	319.0	320.6	313.9
2000	312.6	313.5	315.7	315.9	316.7	318.4	314.6	316.1	317.5	317.7	318.0	317.5	316.2
2001	317.2	318.9	320.9	320.8	321.2	321.8	318.4	319.7	320.0	319.6	319.7	319.0	319.8
2002	312.5	313.4	315.7	316.9	318.9	319.0	314.7	315.6	318.1	318.0	318.5	319.9	316.8
2003	312.9	313.8	316.3	317.2	318.5	318.5	313.5	317.3	320.5	320.1	318.9	318.0	317.1
Total private													
1990	198.9	199.1	200.4	201.3	204.1	206.2	205.5	208.1	206.8	205.7	206.7	206.1	204.0
1991	200.3	201.8	203.3	203.1	205.1	207.8	207.5	209.5	208.9	208.8	207.9	208.1	206.0
1992	204.2	205.1	207.1	209.4	212.1	214.6	214.3	214.7	214.7	214.6	214.8	214.7	211.6
1993	210.6	211.9	212.9	214.9	216.4	219.5	219.6	220.2	219.9	221.0	221.7	222.1	217.5
1994	216.8	216.9	219.4	222.2	225.6	227.9	229.2	230.5	231.6	230.1	231.9	231.9	226.1
1995	226.8	228.8	230.7	231.4	233.1	236.9	235.1	237.7	237.8	236.7	239.0	239.1	234.4
1996	233.6	234.6	236.4	237.1	240.5	243.8	240.9	242.7	242.5	242.1	243.1	243.4	240.0
1997	235.9	237.6	240.4	241.7	244.5	245.7	245.7	247.3	247.5	248.5	247.6	249.6	244.3
1998	242.7	243.9	245.6	247.0	249.3	251.2	250.7	251.5	250.9	251.4	251.9	252.6	249.0
1999	246.9	248.7	250.7	251.1	252.8	254.9	255.5	255.7	256.0	255.7	258.0	259.4	253.8
2000	252.2	252.9	255.0	254.9	255.5	257.7	257.1	257.7	256.8	256.7	256.6	256.1	255.8
2001	256.0	257.1	258.7	258.4	259.4	260.8	259.5	260.1	258.5	257.2	256.9	256.2	258.2
2002	250.3	250.5	252.5	253.8	255.8	257.0	255.2	255.6	255.7	255.0	255.0	256.2	254.4
2003	250.1	250.6	252.8	253.5	255.4	256.2	254.9	257.4	257.1	256.3	255.0	254.4	254.5
Goods-producing													
1990	41.1	40.8	40.9	40.9	42.0	42.9	42.7	43.3	43.2	42.9	42.7	42.1	42.1
1991	40.8	40.9	41.3	41.0	41.3	42.3	42.4	42.9	43.1	43.2	42.6	42.4	42.0
1992	41.5	41.4	42.6	42.8	43.6	44.0	44.4	44.3	43.8	43.8	43.7	43.5	43.2
1993	42.6	42.8	43.4	43.3	43.6	44.8	45.1	45.0	45.0	44.9	44.9	44.5	44.1
1994	43.7	43.8	44.3	45.1	46.2	47.1	47.4	47.7	48.4	48.1	47.9	47.9	46.4
1995	46.9	47.1	47.3	47.8	47.9	48.8	48.3	48.9	48.7	48.1	48.0	47.8	47.9
1996	47.0	47.0	47.4	47.5	48.1	48.9	48.8	48.8	48.6	48.6	48.1	47.9	48.0
1997	46.1	46.4	46.7	47.2	47.8	48.4	48.5	48.6	48.3	48.1	47.5	47.6	47.6
1998	46.5	46.8	47.2	47.3	47.8	48.5	48.7	48.7	48.5	48.7	48.4	48.8	47.9
1999	47.3	47.7	48.3	48.4	48.9	49.1	49.4	49.1	48.8	48.7	48.7	48.8	48.6
2000	47.7	47.6	48.3	47.8	47.8	48.4	48.3	48.2	47.7	47.2	47.0	46.7	47.7
2001	46.1	46.1	46.7	46.6	46.8	47.0	46.4	46.7	46.4	46.0	44.8	44.5	46.2
2002	43.8	43.6	43.7	44.6	44.8	44.9	44.1	44.1	43.6	43.4	42.7	42.5	43.8
2003	41.3	41.3	41.8	41.8	42.1	42.5	42.4	42.4	42.0	41.8	40.8	41.1	41.8

Employment by Industry: Arkansas—*Continued*

(Numbers in thousands. Not seasonally adjusted.)

Industry	January	February	March	April	May	June	July	August	September	October	November	December	Annual Average
LITTLE ROCK-NORTH LITTLE ROCK—*Continued*													
Construction and mining													
1990	10.4	10.3	10.5	10.9	11.5	12.5	12.4	12.6	12.4	12.0	12.0	11.6	11.5
1991	10.5	10.9	11.1	10.9	11.2	11.8	11.9	12.0	11.8	11.7	11.3	11.4	11.3
1992	10.9	11.1	11.5	11.8	12.5	12.6	13.0	12.9	12.7	12.6	12.2	12.0	12.1
1993	11.2	11.5	11.8	11.9	12.1	13.0	13.2	13.0	12.8	12.7	12.5	12.3	12.3
1994	11.6	11.6	12.1	12.6	13.3	13.7	13.8	14.0	14.0	13.7	13.4	13.4	13.1
1995	12.8	12.9	13.3	13.7	13.8	14.5	14.6	14.7	14.5	14.3	14.2	14.1	13.9
1996	13.5	13.8	14.3	14.6	14.9	15.4	15.5	15.7	15.5	15.4	15.1	15.0	14.8
1997	13.9	14.1	14.3	14.7	15.3	15.6	15.7	15.8	15.5	15.3	14.8	14.8	14.9
1998	14.1	14.2	14.6	14.8	15.2	15.8	15.9	15.7	15.6	15.8	15.6	15.8	15.2
1999	15.1	15.3	15.9	15.9	16.3	16.4	16.6	16.5	16.3	16.3	16.2	16.2	16.1
2000	15.6	15.6	15.9	15.8	15.9	16.3	16.3	16.2	16.0	15.9	15.9	15.7	15.9
2001	15.3	15.4	16.0	16.3	16.8	17.1	17.4	17.5	17.5	17.3	17.2	17.1	16.7
2002	16.5	16.5	16.7	17.8	18.0	18.4	17.7	17.5	17.3	17.3	16.9	16.8	17.3
2003	16.3	16.3	16.7	16.9	17.3	17.6	17.6	17.6	17.3	17.3	17.1	16.8	17.1
Manufacturing													
1990	30.7	30.5	30.4	30.0	30.5	30.4	30.3	30.7	30.8	30.9	30.7	30.5	30.5
1991	30.3	30.0	30.2	30.1	30.1	30.5	30.5	30.9	31.3	31.5	31.3	31.0	30.6
1992	30.6	30.3	31.1	31.0	31.1	31.4	31.4	31.4	31.1	31.2	31.5	31.5	31.1
1993	31.4	31.3	31.6	31.4	31.5	31.8	31.9	32.0	32.2	32.2	32.4	32.2	31.8
1994	32.1	32.2	32.2	32.5	32.9	33.4	33.6	33.7	34.4	34.4	34.5	34.5	33.3
1995	34.1	34.2	34.0	34.1	34.1	34.3	33.7	34.2	34.2	33.8	33.8	33.7	34.0
1996	33.5	33.2	33.1	32.9	33.2	33.5	33.3	33.1	33.1	33.2	33.0	32.9	33.1
1997	32.2	32.3	32.4	32.5	32.5	32.8	32.8	32.8	32.8	32.8	32.7	32.8	32.6
1998	32.4	32.6	32.6	32.5	32.6	32.7	32.8	33.0	32.9	32.9	32.8	33.0	32.7
1999	32.2	32.4	32.4	32.5	32.6	32.7	32.8	32.6	32.5	32.4	32.5	32.6	32.5
2000	32.1	32.0	32.4	32.0	31.9	32.1	32.0	32.0	31.7	31.3	31.1	31.0	31.8
2001	30.8	30.7	30.7	30.3	30.0	29.9	29.0	29.2	28.9	28.7	27.6	27.4	29.4
2002	27.3	27.1	27.0	26.8	26.8	26.5	26.4	26.6	26.3	26.1	25.8	25.7	26.5
2003	25.0	25.0	25.1	24.9	24.8	24.9	24.8	24.8	24.7	24.5	23.7	24.3	24.7
Service-providing													
1990	206.1	207.5	209.0	209.6	212.1	212.9	209.0	211.6	213.4	212.8	214.3	214.5	211.0
1991	209.9	212.1	213.4	213.2	215.0	215.8	212.1	214.4	217.2	218.1	217.9	218.4	214.7
1992	214.7	216.7	217.8	219.9	221.5	222.8	219.8	220.6	223.7	224.5	224.8	225.3	221.0
1993	221.8	223.8	224.3	226.1	227.1	228.0	225.6	226.4	229.0	230.7	231.7	232.4	227.2
1994	227.4	228.0	230.4	232.3	234.5	235.3	234.8	236.5	239.2	238.2	240.5	240.4	234.7
1995	235.9	238.4	240.9	240.9	242.1	244.7	240.6	243.3	245.8	245.8	248.2	248.8	242.9
1996	243.7	245.0	246.7	247.3	250.2	252.1	247.6	250.2	251.9	251.9	253.6	254.3	249.5
1997	248.3	250.4	253.3	254.1	255.7	255.9	253.8	256.2	258.2	259.9	260.2	262.1	255.6
1998	255.7	257.3	258.7	260.0	261.4	261.4	258.1	260.0	262.0	262.9	263.9	264.1	260.4
1999	259.8	261.4	263.5	263.2	264.1	265.8	263.5	265.2	267.2	267.8	270.3	271.8	265.3
2000	264.9	265.9	267.4	268.1	268.9	270.0	266.3	267.9	269.8	270.5	271.0	270.8	268.5
2001	271.1	272.8	274.2	274.2	274.4	274.8	272.0	273.0	273.6	273.6	274.9	274.5	273.6
2002	268.7	269.8	272.0	272.3	274.1	274.1	270.6	271.5	274.5	274.6	275.8	277.4	273.0
2003	271.6	272.5	274.5	275.4	276.4	276.0	271.1	274.9	278.5	278.3	278.1	276.9	275.4
Trade, transportation, and utilities													
1990	55.6	54.8	55.0	55.1	55.6	55.7	55.9	56.3	56.0	55.9	56.9	57.4	55.8
1991	56.2	56.0	56.2	56.3	56.8	57.0	57.3	57.8	57.3	57.2	57.7	58.5	57.0
1992	56.7	56.5	56.8	57.1	57.3	57.6	57.8	58.2	58.4	58.3	58.8	59.6	57.7
1993	57.1	57.1	57.2	57.5	57.9	58.4	58.4	58.6	58.7	59.0	59.8	60.6	58.3
1994	58.4	57.9	58.5	58.4	59.6	60.1	60.7	61.0	61.3	61.1	62.4	63.1	60.2
1995	61.2	61.2	61.6	61.8	62.0	62.7	62.7	63.5	64.0	64.5	65.6	66.0	63.0
1996	63.5	63.0	63.3	63.6	64.4	64.8	63.5	64.1	64.2	64.9	66.2	67.1	64.3
1997	64.2	63.9	64.4	64.6	65.0	65.0	64.8	64.6	65.3	66.3	67.1	68.3	65.2
1998	65.1	65.0	65.2	65.4	66.1	66.2	66.1	66.6	66.9	67.3	68.4	69.3	66.4
1999	66.5	66.3	66.6	66.6	67.1	67.7	68.0	68.4	68.6	69.1	70.7	72.1	68.1
2000	68.7	69.0	68.8	69.0	68.9	69.2	69.2	69.4	69.3	70.0	70.6	71.5	69.5
2001	69.9	69.3	69.7	69.6	69.7	70.0	69.3	69.3	69.1	69.0	70.0	70.3	69.6
2002	67.8	67.4	67.9	68.0	68.2	68.2	67.4	67.3	67.4	67.2	68.3	69.1	67.9
2003	66.8	66.3	66.6	66.4	66.5	66.5	66.4	66.8	67.5	67.6	67.9	68.7	67.0
Wholesale trade													
1990	13.1	13.2	13.2	13.2	13.2	13.3	13.5	13.5	13.4	13.3	13.4	13.4	13.3
1991	13.3	13.4	13.5	13.4	13.6	13.7	13.7	13.7	13.5	13.3	13.3	13.3	13.4
1992	13.1	13.2	13.3	13.2	13.2	13.3	13.3	13.3	13.3	13.3	13.3	13.3	13.2
1993	13.2	13.3	13.4	13.4	13.5	13.5	13.4	13.3	13.3	13.4	13.3	13.4	13.3
1994	13.1	13.1	13.2	13.2	13.2	13.4	13.6	13.5	13.5	13.3	13.3	13.3	13.3
1995	13.1	13.3	13.4	13.5	13.4	13.6	13.7	13.8	13.8	13.8	13.8	13.8	13.5
1996	13.6	13.6	13.7	13.6	13.6	13.7	13.7	13.8	13.7	13.8	13.8	14.0	13.7
1997	13.7	13.6	13.8	13.8	13.9	14.0	14.0	14.0	13.9	13.9	13.8	13.9	13.8
1998	13.9	14.0	14.0	14.1	14.2	14.3	14.4	14.4	14.3	14.1	14.0	14.1	14.1
1999	14.1	14.3	14.3	14.3	14.4	14.7	14.8	14.9	15.0	14.9	15.1	15.3	14.7
2000	15.4	15.5	15.7	15.8	15.9	16.1	16.2	16.3	16.4	16.4	16.2	16.3	16.0
2001	16.5	16.5	16.5	16.5	16.5	16.7	16.6	16.6	16.6	16.2	16.2	16.2	16.5
2002	16.1	16.1	16.2	16.2	16.2	16.2	16.1	16.1	16.0	15.9	15.8	15.9	16.1
2003	15.8	15.8	15.8	15.7	15.8	15.8	15.9	15.9	16.0	15.9	15.7	15.8	15.8

Employment by Industry: Arkansas—*Continued*

(Numbers in thousands. Not seasonally adjusted.)

Industry	January	February	March	April	May	June	July	August	September	October	November	December	Annual Average
LITTLE ROCK-NORTH LITTLE ROCK—*Continued*													
Retail trade													
1990	29.2	28.4	28.5	28.4	28.6	28.7	28.7	29.0	28.7	28.6	29.4	29.9	28.8
1991	29.2	28.8	28.8	28.8	29.1	29.2	29.4	29.7	29.5	29.4	29.9	30.6	29.3
1992	29.2	28.9	29.0	29.2	29.4	29.5	29.6	29.9	30.1	30.2	30.8	31.5	29.7
1993	29.2	29.0	29.0	29.3	29.4	29.7	29.7	30.0	30.0	30.3	31.2	31.8	29.8
1994	30.1	29.6	30.0	30.3	30.7	30.8	30.8	31.1	31.5	31.3	32.4	33.0	30.9
1995	31.5	31.0	31.0	30.9	31.3	31.6	31.4	31.8	32.1	32.4	33.5	34.0	31.8
1996	32.0	31.6	31.8	32.1	32.8	33.1	32.1	32.3	32.4	32.8	34.1	34.8	32.6
1997	32.8	32.5	32.8	32.9	33.1	32.9	32.6	33.1	33.0	33.5	34.5	35.5	33.2
1998	32.9	32.6	32.8	32.8	33.3	33.5	33.2	33.6	33.8	34.3	35.6	36.4	33.7
1999	34.4	34.0	34.3	34.3	34.6	35.0	34.7	35.0	35.0	35.4	36.7	37.8	35.1
2000	34.8	35.0	34.6	34.6	34.7	34.9	34.5	34.7	34.5	35.2	36.0	36.8	35.0
2001	35.3	34.9	35.3	35.2	35.4	35.5	34.8	34.7	34.6	34.8	36.0	36.5	35.3
2002	34.4	34.1	34.5	34.5	34.8	34.9	34.4	34.2	34.3	34.2	35.4	36.1	34.7
2003	34.0	33.5	33.7	33.8	33.9	34.0	33.9	34.2	34.7	35.0	35.5	36.2	34.4
Transportation and utilities													
1990	13.3	13.2	13.3	13.5	13.8	13.7	13.7	13.8	13.9	14.0	14.1	14.1	13.7
1991	13.7	13.8	13.9	14.1	14.1	14.1	14.2	14.4	14.3	14.5	14.5	14.6	14.1
1992	14.4	14.4	14.5	14.7	14.7	14.8	14.9	15.0	15.0	14.8	14.7	14.8	14.7
1993	14.7	14.8	14.8	14.8	15.0	15.2	15.3	15.3	15.4	15.3	15.3	15.4	15.1
1994	15.2	15.2	15.3	14.9	15.7	15.9	16.3	16.4	16.3	16.5	16.7	16.8	15.9
1995	16.6	16.9	17.2	17.4	17.3	17.5	17.6	17.9	18.1	18.3	18.3	18.2	17.6
1996	17.9	17.8	17.8	17.9	18.0	18.0	17.7	18.0	18.1	18.3	18.3	18.3	18.0
1997	17.7	17.8	17.8	17.9	18.0	18.1	18.2	17.5	18.4	18.9	18.8	18.9	18.1
1998	18.3	18.4	18.4	18.5	18.6	18.4	18.5	18.6	18.8	18.9	18.8	18.8	18.5
1999	18.0	18.0	18.0	18.0	18.1	18.0	18.5	18.5	18.6	18.8	18.9	19.0	18.4
2000	18.5	18.5	18.5	18.6	18.3	18.2	18.5	18.4	18.4	18.4	18.4	18.4	18.4
2001	18.1	17.9	17.9	17.9	17.8	17.8	17.9	18.0	17.9	18.0	17.8	17.6	17.9
2002	17.3	17.2	17.2	17.3	17.2	17.1	16.9	17.0	17.1	17.1	17.1	17.1	17.1
2003	17.0	17.0	17.1	16.9	16.8	16.7	16.6	16.7	16.8	16.7	16.7	16.7	16.8
Information													
1990	7.2	7.3	7.3	7.3	7.3	7.3	7.3	7.3	7.3	7.4	7.5	7.4	7.3
1991	7.4	7.4	7.3	7.2	7.2	7.2	7.2	7.2	7.1	7.1	6.6	6.5	7.1
1992	6.3	6.3	6.2	6.3	6.3	7.2	6.6	6.3	6.3	6.3	6.3	6.3	6.3
1993	6.3	6.3	6.3	6.3	6.3	6.4	6.4	6.4	6.4	6.3	6.4	6.4	6.3
1994	6.2	6.2	6.3	6.3	6.3	6.4	6.3	6.3	6.4	6.4	6.5	6.5	6.3
1995	6.7	6.7	6.7	6.8	6.8	7.0	6.9	6.9	6.9	7.0	7.1	7.1	6.8
1996	7.1	7.1	7.1	7.0	7.1	7.2	7.3	7.3	7.2	7.2	7.4	7.5	7.2
1997	7.4	7.5	7.6	7.6	7.7	7.8	7.8	7.8	7.8	7.8	7.9	7.9	7.7
1998	7.9	8.0	8.0	8.0	8.0	8.1	8.0	8.0	8.0	8.0	8.1	8.3	8.0
1999	8.2	8.3	8.3	8.3	8.3	8.5	8.6	8.5	8.5	8.6	8.7	8.7	8.5
2000	8.4	8.5	8.5	8.5	8.6	8.8	8.8	9.0	9.0	9.1	9.2	9.1	8.8
2001	9.4	9.4	9.2	9.0	9.1	9.1	9.3	9.3	9.3	9.2	9.2	9.1	9.2
2002	9.2	9.2	9.1	9.1	9.1	9.2	9.1	9.1	9.1	9.3	9.3	9.3	9.2
2003	9.3	9.2	9.3	9.3	9.4	9.4	9.4	9.4	9.3	9.4	9.4	9.4	9.4
Financial activities													
1990	16.2	16.1	16.2	16.2	16.3	16.5	16.4	16.4	16.2	16.2	16.2	16.3	16.2
1991	16.2	16.3	16.3	16.2	16.4	16.5	16.6	16.5	16.5	16.2	16.3	16.4	16.3
1992	16.3	16.3	16.4	16.6	16.7	16.8	16.9	16.8	16.8	16.8	16.8	16.9	16.6
1993	16.8	16.8	16.9	17.0	17.1	17.1	17.1	17.2	17.1	17.4	17.4	17.4	17.1
1994	17.2	17.2	17.3	17.3	17.4	17.4	17.4	17.4	17.4	17.3	17.3	17.4	17.3
1995	17.4	17.4	17.4	17.4	17.4	17.5	17.6	17.7	17.6	17.6	17.6	17.8	17.5
1996	17.7	17.8	17.9	17.8	17.9	18.1	17.9	18.0	18.0	18.2	18.2	18.2	17.9
1997	17.8	17.8	18.0	18.3	18.3	18.2	18.3	18.3	18.2	18.2	18.2	18.4	18.1
1998	18.7	18.8	18.9	18.6	18.6	18.7	18.5	18.5	18.3	18.5	18.6	18.6	18.6
1999	18.4	18.6	18.7	18.8	19.0	19.1	19.1	19.1	19.0	19.0	18.9	19.1	18.9
2000	18.7	18.7	18.7	18.5	18.5	18.6	18.7	18.7	18.5	18.3	18.2	18.4	18.5
2001	18.9	18.9	19.0	19.0	19.1	19.2	19.2	19.1	19.0	18.8	18.9	19.1	19.0
2002	18.9	18.9	19.0	18.9	18.9	19.0	19.1	19.1	19.1	19.0	19.0	19.2	19.0
2003	19.0	19.1	19.0	19.2	19.3	19.5	19.6	19.7	19.6	19.6	19.6	19.6	19.4
Professional and business services													
1990	23.9	24.1	24.3	24.9	25.2	25.5	25.6	26.2	25.7	25.0	25.1	25.0	25.0
1991	22.7	22.9	23.1	23.2	23.4	23.8	24.0	24.5	24.5	24.9	24.6	24.5	23.8
1992	24.0	24.1	24.2	24.9	25.6	25.7	25.5	26.0	25.9	25.9	25.8	25.8	25.2
1993	26.1	26.4	26.2	27.4	27.8	28.2	28.6	28.4	28.2	28.2	27.9	28.5	27.6
1994	27.8	28.3	29.0	30.3	30.7	31.3	32.1	32.5	32.3	32.3	32.4	31.9	30.9
1995	30.2	31.1	31.7	31.6	31.8	32.4	32.7	33.3	33.3	32.7	32.9	32.8	32.2
1996	32.2	32.9	33.1	33.0	33.4	33.9	34.1	34.6	34.6	34.6	34.3	33.9	33.7
1997	33.0	33.8	34.5	34.1	34.6	34.8	35.8	37.3	37.1	37.0	36.4	36.4	35.4
1998	34.5	34.7	35.1	36.1	36.4	37.2	38.0	38.1	37.7	36.9	36.4	35.6	36.3
1999	35.7	36.2	36.7	36.4	36.4	36.8	37.0	37.8	38.6	38.6	38.9	38.6	37.3
2000	38.0	38.2	38.9	38.3	38.7	39.0	39.3	40.0	40.0	40.0	39.9	38.9	39.1
2001	39.4	40.2	40.0	39.5	39.4	39.3	39.7	40.1	39.7	39.0	38.7	38.4	39.5
2002	37.2	37.1	37.7	37.7	38.2	38.8	38.9	39.3	39.6	39.8	39.2	39.7	38.6
2003	38.8	38.9	39.5	39.6	40.1	39.8	39.3	40.9	40.4	40.4	39.6	38.3	39.6

Employment by Industry: Arkansas—*Continued*

(Numbers in thousands. Not seasonally adjusted.)

Industry	January	February	March	April	May	June	July	August	September	October	November	December	Annual Average
LITTLE ROCK-NORTH LITTLE ROCK—*Continued*													
Educational and health services													
1990	27.6	28.5	28.5	28.4	28.8	28.8	28.3	28.7	29.0	29.3	29.6	29.5	28.7
1991	29.4	30.2	30.4	30.5	30.7	30.8	30.2	30.5	31.0	31.2	31.5	31.3	30.6
1992	31.4	31.9	32.0	32.0	32.3	32.0	31.8	31.9	32.6	33.0	33.1	32.9	32.2
1993	32.3	32.7	32.8	32.9	32.9	33.0	32.7	33.1	33.3	34.0	34.2	33.8	33.1
1994	33.4	33.5	33.4	33.4	33.5	33.0	32.6	32.9	33.4	33.5	33.8	33.7	33.3
1995	33.4	34.1	34.2	33.9	34.1	34.4	33.6	34.1	34.6	34.8	35.3	35.3	34.3
1996	34.5	35.1	35.3	35.2	35.5	35.7	34.7	35.1	35.7	35.2	35.6	35.6	35.2
1997	35.1	35.7	36.0	36.0	36.4	36.1	35.5	35.6	36.2	36.4	36.5	36.5	36.0
1998	36.3	36.7	36.7	36.8	36.8	36.7	36.1	36.4	36.9	37.2	37.5	37.5	36.8
1999	36.9	37.1	37.2	37.2	37.2	37.1	36.9	36.7	37.0	37.0	37.2	37.2	37.1
2000	36.5	36.7	36.8	36.9	36.9	36.8	36.6	36.3	36.8	36.8	36.8	36.7	36.7
2001	37.3	37.8	38.0	38.2	38.2	38.4	38.3	38.4	38.7	39.1	39.3	39.1	38.4
2002	38.6	38.9	39.2	39.2	39.4	39.2	39.2	39.4	40.2	40.0	40.1	40.1	39.5
2003	39.6	40.1	40.4	40.5	40.6	40.6	40.5	40.7	41.5	41.3	41.4	41.1	40.7
Leisure and hospitality													
1990	17.4	17.5	18.2	18.5	18.9	19.2	19.1	19.7	19.3	18.9	18.5	18.2	18.6
1991	17.4	17.8	18.4	18.5	19.0	19.6	19.3	19.6	19.2	18.8	18.4	18.3	18.6
1992	17.8	18.4	18.6	19.3	19.8	20.5	20.3	20.3	20.1	19.7	19.5	19.3	19.4
1993	19.1	19.4	19.7	20.0	20.4	20.9	20.6	20.9	20.8	20.8	20.8	20.5	20.3
1994	20.0	19.8	20.3	21.0	21.5	21.9	22.0	22.1	21.9	21.1	21.2	21.1	21.1
1995	20.7	20.8	21.2	21.4	22.2	23.1	22.3	22.4	21.9	21.4	21.9	21.7	21.7
1996	21.1	21.1	21.5	22.3	23.3	24.2	23.7	23.8	23.4	22.7	22.6	22.4	22.6
1997	21.6	21.7	22.3	22.9	23.5	24.0	23.6	23.8	23.4	23.4	22.8	23.1	23.0
1998	22.3	22.4	22.7	23.0	23.7	23.7	23.3	23.3	22.8	23.0	22.7	22.7	22.9
1999	22.0	22.5	22.9	23.3	23.7	24.1	24.1	23.9	23.4	22.9	23.2	23.1	23.3
2000	22.5	22.5	23.2	24.1	24.2	24.7	24.2	24.1	23.7	23.7	23.3	23.2	23.6
2001	23.2	23.6	24.0	24.6	25.1	25.4	25.1	25.0	24.3	24.2	24.0	23.8	24.4
2002	22.9	23.5	23.9	24.3	25.0	25.2	24.9	24.8	24.3	24.2	24.2	24.2	24.3
2003	23.4	23.7	24.1	24.6	25.2	25.6	25.2	25.4	24.8	24.4	24.4	24.4	24.6
Other services													
1990	9.9	10.0	10.0	10.0	10.0	10.3	10.2	10.2	10.1	10.1	10.2	10.2	10.1
1991	10.2	10.3	10.3	10.2	10.3	10.6	10.5	10.5	10.2	10.2	10.2	10.2	10.3
1992	10.2	10.2	10.3	10.4	10.5	10.8	11.0	10.9	10.8	10.8	10.8	10.4	10.5
1993	10.3	10.4	10.4	10.5	10.4	10.7	10.7	10.6	10.4	10.4	10.3	10.4	10.4
1994	10.1	10.2	10.3	10.4	10.4	10.7	10.7	10.6	10.5	10.3	10.4	10.3	10.4
1995	10.3	10.4	10.6	10.7	10.9	11.0	11.0	10.9	10.8	10.6	10.6	10.6	10.7
1996	10.5	10.6	10.8	10.7	10.8	11.0	10.9	11.0	10.8	10.7	10.7	10.8	10.7
1997	10.7	10.8	10.9	11.0	11.2	11.4	11.4	11.3	11.2	11.3	11.2	11.4	11.1
1998	11.4	11.5	11.8	11.8	11.9	12.1	12.0	11.9	11.8	11.8	11.8	11.8	11.8
1999	11.9	12.0	12.0	12.1	12.2	12.5	12.4	12.2	12.1	11.8	11.7	11.8	12.1
2000	11.7	11.7	11.8	11.8	11.9	12.2	12.0	12.0	11.8	11.6	11.6	11.6	11.8
2001	11.8	11.8	12.1	11.9	12.0	12.4	12.2	12.2	12.0	11.9	12.0	11.9	12.0
2002	11.9	11.9	12.0	12.0	12.2	12.5	12.5	12.5	12.4	12.1	12.2	12.1	12.2
2003	11.9	12.0	12.1	12.1	12.2	12.3	12.1	12.1	12.0	11.8	11.9	11.8	12.0
Government													
1990	48.3	49.2	49.5	49.2	50.0	49.6	46.2	46.8	49.8	50.0	50.3	50.5	49.1
1991	50.4	51.2	51.4	51.1	51.2	50.3	47.0	47.8	51.4	52.5	52.6	52.7	50.8
1992	52.0	53.0	53.3	53.3	53.0	52.2	49.9	50.2	52.8	53.7	53.7	54.1	52.6
1993	53.8	54.7	54.8	54.5	54.3	53.3	51.1	51.2	54.1	54.6	54.9	54.8	53.8
1994	54.3	54.9	55.3	55.2	55.1	54.5	53.0	53.7	56.0	56.2	56.5	56.4	55.0
1995	56.0	56.7	57.5	57.3	56.9	56.6	53.8	54.5	56.7	57.2	57.2	57.5	56.4
1996	57.1	57.4	57.7	57.7	57.8	57.2	55.5	56.3	58.0	58.4	58.6	58.8	57.5
1997	58.5	59.2	59.6	59.6	59.0	58.6	56.6	57.5	59.0	59.5	60.1	60.1	58.9
1998	59.5	60.2	60.3	60.3	59.9	58.7	56.1	57.2	59.6	60.2	60.4	60.3	59.3
1999	60.2	60.4	61.1	60.5	60.2	60.0	57.4	58.6	60.0	60.8	61.0	61.2	60.1
2000	60.4	60.6	60.7	61.0	61.2	60.7	57.5	58.4	60.7	61.0	61.4	61.4	60.4
2001	61.2	61.8	62.2	62.4	61.8	61.0	58.9	59.6	61.5	62.4	62.8	62.8	61.5
2002	62.2	62.9	63.2	63.1	63.1	62.0	59.5	60.0	62.4	63.0	63.5	63.7	62.4
2003	62.8	63.2	63.5	63.7	63.1	62.3	58.6	59.9	63.4	63.8	63.9	63.6	62.7
Federal government													
1990	9.6	9.6	9.6	9.8	10.2	9.9	9.8	9.6	9.6	9.6	9.6	9.7	9.7
1991	9.4	9.4	9.5	9.5	9.6	9.8	9.8	9.7	9.7	9.8	9.8	9.8	9.6
1992	9.8	9.8	9.8	9.7	9.8	9.8	9.5	9.5	9.5	9.5	9.4	9.7	9.6
1993	9.6	9.6	9.6	9.5	9.6	9.6	9.6	9.5	9.5	9.5	9.5	9.6	9.5
1994	9.5	9.5	9.5	9.5	9.5	9.6	9.8	9.8	9.7	9.7	9.7	9.8	9.6
1995	9.6	9.6	9.8	10.0	9.9	10.0	10.0	10.0	10.0	9.9	9.9	10.0	9.8
1996	9.7	9.7	9.7	9.8	9.9	9.9	9.9	9.9	9.8	9.7	9.8	9.8	9.8
1997	9.8	9.8	9.8	9.8	9.7	9.7	9.7	9.6	9.6	9.6	9.8	9.9	9.7
1998	9.6	9.5	9.4	9.4	9.3	9.4	9.5	9.5	9.5	9.8	10.0	10.0	9.5
1999	9.6	9.5	9.9	9.5	9.4	9.5	9.4	9.5	9.4	9.5	9.7	9.9	9.6
2000	9.6	9.5	9.6	9.5	10.1	10.3	9.9	10.0	9.4	9.4	9.6	10.0	9.7
2001	9.7	9.5	9.7	9.6	9.5	9.7	9.7	9.6	9.5	9.6	9.6	9.7	9.6
2002	9.7	9.5	9.5	9.4	9.4	9.4	9.4	9.2	9.1	9.3	9.3	9.4	9.4
2003	9.3	9.2	9.3	9.3	9.4	9.4	9.5	9.5	9.4	9.4	9.3	9.4	9.4

Employment by Industry: Arkansas—*Continued*

(Numbers in thousands. Not seasonally adjusted.)

Industry	January	February	March	April	May	June	July	August	September	October	November	December	Annual Average
LITTLE ROCK-NORTH LITTLE ROCK—*Continued*													
State government													
1990	20.5	21.1	21.3	21.2	21.2	20.7	20.8	20.9	21.8	21.8	22.0	22.0	21.2
1991	21.9	22.5	22.4	22.3	22.2	21.2	21.5	22.0	22.6	23.0	23.1	23.0	22.3
1992	22.5	23.2	23.3	23.3	22.9	22.1	22.4	22.3	23.4	23.8	23.8	23.9	23.0
1993	23.6	24.2	24.2	24.0	23.7	22.8	23.0	22.9	24.1	24.0	24.1	24.0	23.7
1994	23.9	24.2	24.5	24.2	24.0	23.3	23.9	24.3	24.9	24.7	24.8	24.7	24.2
1995	24.8	25.3	25.6	25.3	24.9	24.4	24.0	24.3	25.2	25.3	25.4	25.5	25.0
1996	25.3	25.5	25.6	25.6	25.5	24.7	24.6	25.0	25.9	26.2	26.3	26.4	25.5
1997	26.4	26.8	27.1	26.9	26.4	26.0	25.6	26.1	26.9	27.1	27.4	27.3	26.6
1998	27.1	27.6	27.8	27.6	27.2	26.2	25.7	26.3	27.1	27.3	27.4	27.3	27.0
1999	27.6	27.9	28.0	27.5	27.4	26.8	26.3	26.7	27.7	27.9	27.9	27.8	27.5
2000	27.5	27.7	27.7	27.8	27.4	26.6	26.1	26.4	27.5	27.7	27.8	27.5	27.3
2001	27.5	28.1	28.2	28.3	27.9	26.9	26.8	27.4	28.0	28.3	28.5	28.4	27.9
2002	28.0	28.8	29.0	29.0	28.9	27.9	27.3	27.9	28.6	28.8	29.2	29.4	28.6
2003	28.7	29.2	29.3	29.2	28.7	27.9	27.6	28.1	28.9	29.2	29.3	29.2	28.8
Local government													
1990	18.2	18.5	18.6	18.2	18.6	19.0	15.6	16.3	18.4	18.6	18.7	18.8	18.1
1991	19.1	19.3	19.5	19.3	19.4	19.3	15.7	16.1	19.1	19.7	19.7	19.9	18.8
1992	19.7	20.0	20.2	20.3	20.3	20.3	18.0	18.4	19.9	20.4	20.5	20.5	19.8
1993	20.6	20.9	21.0	21.0	21.0	20.9	18.5	18.8	20.5	21.1	21.3	21.2	20.5
1994	20.9	21.2	21.3	21.5	21.6	21.6	19.3	19.6	21.4	21.8	22.0	21.9	21.1
1995	21.6	21.8	22.1	22.0	22.1	22.2	19.8	20.2	21.5	22.0	21.9	22.0	21.6
1996	22.1	22.2	22.4	22.3	22.4	22.6	21.0	21.4	22.3	22.5	22.5	22.6	22.1
1997	22.3	22.6	22.7	22.9	22.9	22.9	21.3	21.8	22.5	22.8	22.9	22.9	22.5
1998	22.8	23.1	23.1	23.3	23.4	23.1	20.9	21.4	23.0	23.1	23.0	23.0	22.7
1999	23.0	23.0	23.2	23.5	23.4	23.7	21.7	22.4	22.9	23.4	23.4	23.5	23.1
2000	23.3	23.4	23.4	23.7	23.7	23.8	21.5	22.0	23.8	23.9	24.0	23.9	23.4
2001	24.0	24.2	24.3	24.5	24.4	24.4	22.4	22.6	24.0	24.5	24.7	24.7	24.1
2002	24.5	24.6	24.7	24.7	24.8	24.7	22.8	22.9	24.7	24.9	25.0	24.9	24.4
2003	24.8	24.8	24.9	25.2	25.0	25.0	21.5	22.3	25.1	25.2	25.3	25.0	24.5

Average Weekly Hours by Industry: Arkansas

(Not seasonally adjusted.)

Industry	January	February	March	April	May	June	July	August	September	October	November	December	Annual Average
STATEWIDE													
Manufacturing													
2001	40.7	39.7	39.7	39.2	40.0	40.1	39.9	40.2	40.3	39.8	39.0	39.9	39.9
2002	39.6	39.3	39.8	39.5	40.3	39.7	39.3	40.1	40.3	39.6	38.7	40.2	39.7
2003	39.7	39.0	39.1	39.5	39.3	39.8	39.1	40.2	40.5	39.7	39.3	40.4	39.6
FAYETTEVILLE-SPRINGDALE													
Manufacturing													
2001	43.7	41.6	41.2	42.3	41.8	41.8	41.8	40.4	40.8	39.9	40.7	39.9	41.3
2002	39.1	40.0	39.9	39.5	40.2	40.4	39.3	39.8	39.6	38.7	37.9	38.9	39.4
2003	39.0	38.1	39.1	38.3	39.1	38.9	40.6	41.1	41.1	39.4	39.3	39.2	39.4
FORT SMITH													
Manufacturing													
2001	40.6	38.9	38.8	38.6	40.4	40.3	39.8	39.4	39.4	39.7	38.2	40.3	39.5
2002	40.1	38.9	40.5	40.3	43.0	41.3	38.1	41.2	40.1	39.8	39.7	43.5	40.5
2003	41.0	37.2	38.9	40.9	40.5	42.1	40.7	41.1	44.1	40.7	39.8	41.8	40.7
LITTLE ROCK													
Manufacturing													
2001	40.2	39.1	39.8	39.1	39.0	39.4	40.5	41.2	41.3	39.8	36.2	39.1	39.6
2002	38.1	37.2	38.2	38.1	39.2	40.0	40.3	42.4	41.9	39.7	38.6	40.9	39.5
2003	40.7	41.5	40.9	41.6	41.3	41.7	39.5	42.1	41.6	40.4	41.7	42.5	41.3

Average Hourly Earnings by Industry: Arkansas

(Dollars, not seasonally adjusted.)

Industry	January	February	March	April	May	June	July	August	September	October	November	December	Annual Average
STATEWIDE													
Manufacturing													
2001	12.79	12.71	12.73	12.80	12.74	12.87	13.02	12.96	12.97	12.97	13.04	13.20	12.90
2002	13.12	13.09	13.13	13.26	13.25	13.39	13.52	13.38	13.34	13.34	13.42	13.41	13.30
2003	13.39	13.54	13.69	13.79	13.71	13.68	13.75	13.58	13.48	13.33	13.35	13.38	13.55
FAYETTEVILLE-SPRINGDALE													
Manufacturing													
2001	12.27	12.43	12.37	12.14	12.18	12.31	12.54	12.71	12.79	12.90	13.00	13.05	12.55
2002	13.04	13.03	13.08	13.13	13.11	13.30	13.25	13.29	13.20	13.33	13.47	13.52	13.23
2003	13.30	13.46	13.62	13.68	13.82	13.85	13.70	13.50	13.21	13.20	13.17	13.04	13.46
FORT SMITH													
Manufacturing													
2001	12.89	12.83	12.74	12.84	12.94	12.87	13.00	13.05	13.02	12.96	12.89	13.28	12.94
2002	12.98	13.42	13.41	13.60	13.57	13.81	13.81	13.47	13.41	13.54	13.66	13.99	13.56
2003	14.13	14.22	14.27	13.99	13.94	13.51	13.76	13.52	13.64	13.31	13.29	13.30	13.73
LITTLE ROCK													
Manufacturing													
2001	13.01	12.99	12.97	12.96	12.78	12.85	12.94	12.85	12.75	12.80	12.52	12.80	12.86
2002	12.64	12.74	12.82	12.92	13.10	13.09	13.13	13.50	13.51	13.63	13.81	13.76	13.22
2003	13.81	13.63	13.96	13.73	13.82	13.67	13.67	14.16	13.99	13.85	13.67	13.79	13.81

Average Weekly Earnings by Industry: Arkansas

(Dollars, not seasonally adjusted.)

Industry	January	February	March	April	May	June	July	August	September	October	November	December	Annual Average
STATEWIDE													
Manufacturing													
2001	520.55	504.59	505.38	501.76	509.60	516.09	519.50	520.99	522.69	516.21	508.56	526.68	514.71
2002	519.55	514.44	522.57	523.77	533.98	531.58	531.34	536.54	537.60	528.26	519.35	539.08	528.01
2003	531.58	528.06	535.28	544.71	538.80	544.46	537.63	545.92	545.94	529.20	524.66	540.55	536.58
FAYETTEVILLE-SPRINGDALE													
Manufacturing													
2001	536.20	517.09	509.64	513.52	509.12	514.56	524.17	513.48	521.83	514.71	529.10	520.70	518.32
2002	509.86	521.20	521.89	518.64	527.02	537.32	520.73	528.94	522.72	515.87	510.51	525.93	521.26
2003	518.70	512.83	532.54	523.94	540.36	538.77	556.22	554.85	542.93	520.08	517.58	511.17	530.32
FORT SMITH													
Manufacturing													
2001	523.33	499.09	494.31	495.62	522.78	518.66	517.40	514.17	512.99	514.51	492.40	535.18	511.13
2002	520.50	522.04	543.11	548.08	583.51	570.35	526.16	554.96	537.74	538.89	542.30	608.57	549.18
2003	579.33	528.98	555.10	572.19	564.57	568.77	560.03	555.67	601.52	541.72	528.94	555.94	558.81
LITTLE ROCK													
Manufacturing													
2001	523.00	507.91	516.21	506.74	498.42	506.29	524.07	529.42	526.58	509.44	453.22	500.48	509.26
2002	481.58	473.93	489.72	492.25	513.52	523.60	529.14	572.40	566.07	541.11	533.07	562.78	522.19
2003	562.07	565.65	570.96	571.17	570.77	570.04	539.97	596.14	581.98	559.54	570.04	586.08	570.35

CALIFORNIA AT A GLANCE

(Population and total nonfarm employment numbers in thousands)

Population, Census 2000:	33,871.6
Total nonfarm employment, 2003:	14,410.2
Change in total nonfarm employment	
(Number)	
1990–2003:	1,910.4
1990–2001:	2,102.1
2001–2003:	191.7
(Compound annual rate of change)	
1990–2003:	1.1%
1990–2001:	1.4%
2001–2003:	-0.7%
Unemployment rate	
1990:	5.8%
2001:	5.4%
2003:	6.8%

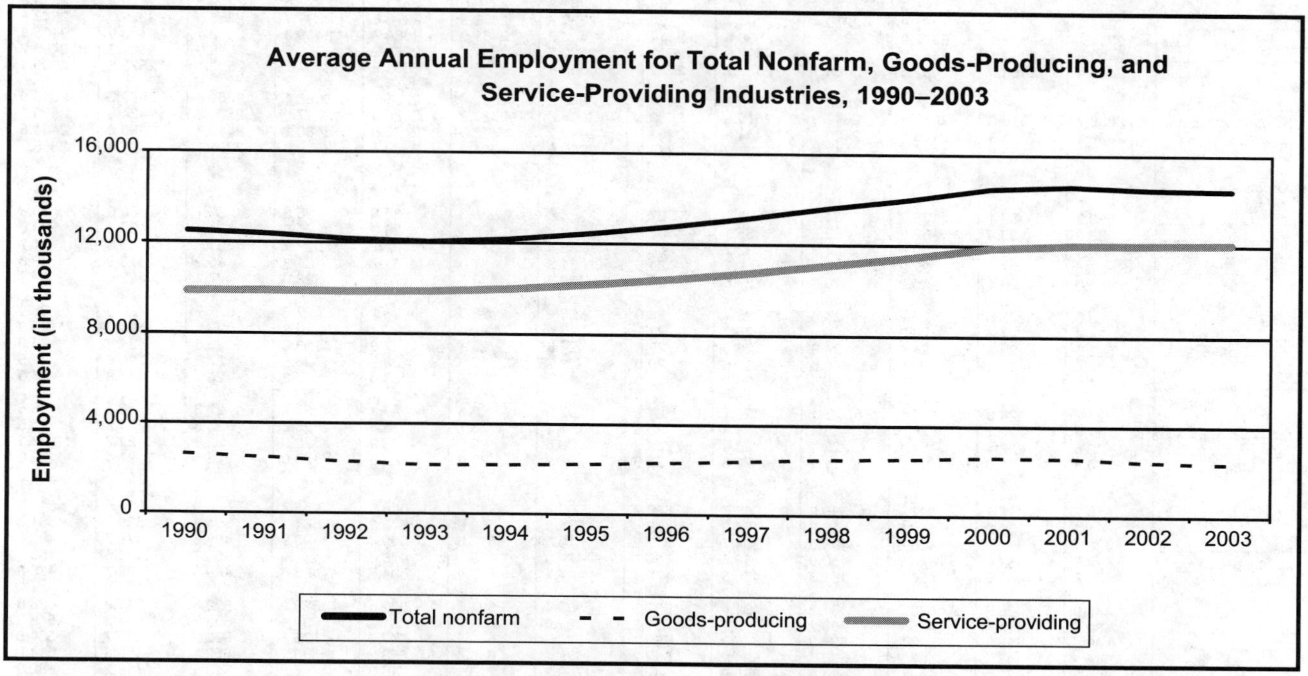

In 2003, California's total nonfarm employment exceeded 14.4 million, with nearly 84 percent in the services sector. Most of the job losses in recent years were in the goods-producing sector, particularly in manufacturing industries. Service sector job growth has been sluggish since 2000. A job contraction was particularly notable in the information industry and in professional and business services, which employed over 137,000 fewer people in 2003 than it did in 2000.

Employment by Industry: California

(Numbers in thousands. Not seasonally adjusted.)

Industry	January	February	March	April	May	June	July	August	September	October	November	December	Annual Average
STATEWIDE													
Total nonfarm													
1990	12290.1	12360.0	12437.2	12463.4	12526.7	12583.9	12493.8	12471.2	12546.7	12580.9	12610.2	12633.5	12499.8
1991	12311.5	12328.6	12360.2	12366.3	12387.3	12418.5	12308.2	12299.7	12369.3	12379.5	12389.7	12388.4	12358.9
1992	12058.5	12075.4	12174.1	12182.4	12204.8	12229.8	12134.9	12086.9	12144.6	12160.4	12195.3	12195.4	12153.5
1993	11933.9	11968.8	12007.1	11992.9	12036.0	12097.4	12014.3	12009.7	12090.1	12080.3	12121.5	12192.5	12045.4
1994	11882.6	11983.9	12089.2	12087.6	12146.8	12216.8	12113.0	12136.9	12258.3	12249.3	12332.9	12416.1	12159.5
1995	12082.5	12232.6	12314.1	12319.8	12415.1	12503.4	12348.8	12420.7	12566.7	12528.1	12635.3	12696.8	12422.0
1996	12411.6	12540.7	12635.5	12617.0	12738.2	12807.3	12675.4	12738.0	12853.2	12873.6	12993.5	13036.3	12743.4
1997	12710.7	12852.3	12988.8	13036.7	13138.6	13213.4	13094.1	13142.1	13264.9	13288.7	13354.7	13470.9	13129.7
1998	13203.4	13306.1	13423.6	13455.9	13575.8	13663.8	13569.6	13626.9	13753.2	13766.1	13862.7	13946.6	13596.1
1999	13574.9	13697.5	13819.9	13870.7	13964.1	14040.2	13978.7	14006.5	14122.3	14180.2	14268.8	14377.4	13991.8
2000	14030.7	14170.1	14323.4	14354.0	14493.4	14599.8	14450.0	14521.9	14645.0	14649.8	14760.9	14859.1	14488.2
2001	14513.5	14598.0	14713.1	14650.1	14697.5	14752.3	14494.8	14534.8	14551.8	14549.5	14569.2	14598.9	14601.9
2002	14237.6	14328.0	14459.1	14448.7	14531.1	14581.6	14352.9	14404.4	14465.9	14505.6	14575.1	14604.0	14457.8
2003	14238.8	14302.1	14381.3	14386.5	14443.1	14502.2	14299.3	14360.7	14425.6	14506.1	14534.6	14541.6	14410.2
Total private													
1990	10243.8	10292.3	10348.9	10361.5	10396.5	10459.0	10478.2	10505.3	10500.4	10485.8	10501.5	10526.9	10425.0
1991	10225.5	10223.9	10239.1	10241.6	10258.0	10291.5	10291.3	10319.2	10307.8	10274.3	10273.3	10274.3	10268.3
1992	9960.7	9956.0	10043.2	10051.5	10069.9	10099.7	10104.0	10098.7	10082.4	10059.9	10081.7	10087.6	10057.9
1993	9848.0	9864.6	9896.7	9882.3	9919.5	9985.4	10007.1	10032.7	10049.4	9992.6	10012.0	10087.3	9964.8
1994	9800.1	9875.9	9971.8	9966.8	10016.0	10088.6	10095.2	10144.4	10196.6	10136.2	10208.2	10294.8	10066.2
1995	9977.2	10104.8	10176.5	10179.0	10268.8	10360.7	10321.6	10422.1	10494.0	10406.3	10500.4	10568.8	10315.0
1996	10310.3	10413.0	10499.2	10478.8	10589.6	10664.7	10646.7	10732.3	10764.3	10734.7	10837.8	10889.2	10630.1
1997	10582.9	10698.9	10818.6	10864.3	10957.2	11040.8	11046.5	11114.1	11148.5	11128.4	11174.9	11292.6	10989.0
1998	11064.3	11144.8	11242.8	11271.4	11378.6	11469.3	11484.9	11564.6	11612.1	11567.3	11638.3	11722.4	11430.1
1999	11374.0	11462.2	11561.1	11598.9	11688.1	11774.4	11814.3	11870.5	11919.9	11913.1	11971.2	12081.5	11752.4
2000	11748.4	11859.0	11982.0	12004.4	12093.9	12239.6	12224.0	12312.7	12365.6	12313.6	12398.9	12499.4	12170.1
2001	12170.6	12231.5	12329.3	12242.4	12279.4	12332.9	12201.4	12249.8	12192.7	12128.7	12122.1	12158.0	12219.9
2002	11815.0	11878.2	11979.9	11958.2	12034.1	12089.5	11993.9	12062.3	12057.9	12038.7	12091.9	12129.3	12010.7
2003	11787.7	11835.9	11896.7	11909.2	11968.8	12030.8	11956.5	12045.9	12057.3	12085.8	12105.0	12124.9	11983.7
Goods-producing													
1990	2598.2	2609.5	2625.2	2636.6	2649.3	2669.7	2675.8	2688.1	2677.3	2645.6	2616.4	2594.9	2640.6
1991	2500.1	2492.0	2477.9	2481.6	2486.7	2499.1	2497.2	2517.0	2506.5	2475.7	2441.0	2404.8	2481.6
1992	2316.7	2305.0	2331.6	2325.9	2330.0	2340.2	2345.6	2345.4	2328.5	2305.4	2263.3	2229.3	2313.9
1993	2162.6	2172.2	2181.0	2174.8	2183.5	2200.1	2203.8	2217.8	2211.7	2179.3	2165.3	2154.5	2183.9
1994	2098.0	2114.7	2145.8	2156.5	2172.2	2197.5	2222.4	2242.1	2249.3	2217.3	2208.6	2210.4	2186.2
1995	2136.6	2175.8	2195.6	2198.2	2218.3	2249.7	2261.3	2299.6	2314.5	2277.6	2279.8	2270.4	2239.8
1996	2224.4	2245.3	2267.8	2270.4	2304.7	2330.7	2333.7	2366.9	2373.8	2351.1	2353.5	2339.3	2313.5
1997	2284.2	2322.1	2353.9	2357.6	2388.4	2414.5	2446.5	2481.9	2484.7	2449.8	2439.4	2443.0	2405.5
1998	2402.5	2412.1	2446.7	2460.5	2492.3	2523.4	2532.7	2557.4	2566.2	2540.0	2528.9	2521.2	2498.7
1999	2455.4	2466.9	2492.5	2498.1	2520.7	2549.2	2565.8	2588.2	2601.2	2584.7	2572.5	2573.5	2539.1
2000	2512.1	2527.2	2554.7	2565.6	2590.3	2638.5	2648.9	2674.6	2681.7	2658.1	2658.8	2669.3	2615.0
2001	2606.7	2615.0	2635.9	2612.3	2619.8	2632.5	2608.0	2620.9	2590.8	2547.5	2508.3	2484.6	2590.1
2002	2406.2	2415.9	2433.6	2426.4	2444.8	2462.6	2447.2	2472.5	2462.8	2436.1	2413.7	2396.0	2434.8
2003	2335.7	2332.8	2346.6	2342.5	2357.0	2375.2	2360.5	2384.3	2380.7	2366.8	2351.1	2335.4	2355.7
Natural resources and mining													
1990	33.2	33.1	33.3	34.8	36.3	37.8	38.6	38.3	38.8	38.2	37.1	35.6	36.3
1991	33.2	33.0	32.3	33.8	35.1	36.4	36.9	36.5	36.0	35.6	34.4	32.3	34.6
1992	30.1	30.0	29.9	31.3	32.7	33.6	33.4	33.1	32.7	32.1	31.5	30.3	31.7
1993	27.5	27.4	27.2	28.6	29.7	31.0	31.3	31.8	31.7	31.2	30.9	28.8	29.8
1994	26.0	25.4	25.2	26.6	27.6	28.6	28.3	28.6	28.7	28.0	27.1	25.6	27.1
1995	23.6	23.8	24.2	24.4	25.4	26.9	28.2	28.0	28.1	27.6	27.5	25.8	26.1
1996	24.4	24.2	24.3	24.7	26.1	27.2	27.4	27.4	27.1	26.9	26.2	24.3	25.9
1997	23.5	23.7	24.1	24.9	26.0	27.0	27.8	28.1	27.8	26.9	26.3	24.8	25.9
1998	24.4	23.7	25.8	26.6	27.6	29.0	29.7	29.8	29.9	28.5	27.8	26.6	27.5
1999	24.6	23.8	24.2	25.5	26.9	27.8	27.2	27.6	28.0	27.3	26.7	25.8	26.3
2000	24.2	24.0	24.0	25.1	26.7	27.5	27.9	28.3	28.1	27.7	27.3	26.7	26.5
2001	24.6	24.1	24.2	25.1	26.4	26.8	26.4	26.7	26.6	26.2	25.6	24.2	25.5
2002	22.5	22.4	22.1	22.1	23.0	23.6	23.6	23.9	23.9	23.8	23.6	22.7	23.1
2003	20.8	21.0	21.0	21.0	21.8	22.8	22.9	23.0	22.8	23.0	22.6	21.4	22.0
Construction													
1990	616.7	617.3	627.9	636.2	645.7	658.9	660.8	666.2	666.5	656.7	646.8	634.5	644.5
1991	561.0	556.2	548.6	550.3	562.3	572.4	574.5	580.9	576.2	564.7	554.8	539.8	561.8
1992	482.1	471.1	486.8	495.0	504.7	512.9	510.1	512.6	509.4	496.9	488.5	472.7	495.2
1993	424.5	434.8	446.2	450.0	458.5	466.5	472.3	478.5	478.4	471.2	465.7	460.6	458.9
1994	434.8	441.6	456.2	461.3	466.3	479.1	487.7	497.4	504.7	496.5	489.8	487.7	475.3
1995	444.9	466.2	472.7	481.5	491.4	507.0	509.4	524.6	529.8	523.8	522.6	511.8	498.8
1996	482.6	484.4	488.8	493.2	509.2	521.3	522.6	537.0	541.2	539.4	538.7	524.6	515.3
1997	499.5	515.8	528.1	533.9	547.9	559.1	572.3	587.5	592.0	578.3	570.2	569.7	554.5
1998	546.2	545.3	567.2	576.6	594.2	617.2	635.4	648.4	653.2	663.2	662.1	658.6	614.0
1999	630.3	630.0	645.0	654.3	670.9	687.6	703.3	713.1	716.8	717.6	713.5	712.2	682.9
2000	676.0	676.9	689.3	703.5	719.5	742.9	747.5	760.3	767.2	762.1	762.6	764.7	731.0
2001	737.4	741.6	758.8	765.2	781.5	796.6	798.6	813.1	803.0	795.9	783.7	772.1	778.9
2002	735.4	741.8	752.3	755.8	770.0	782.4	782.4	800.8	797.1	795.0	789.4	780.0	773.5
2003	754.3	751.6	764.1	769.1	785.5	800.6	801.4	815.7	813.7	812.6	804.3	792.8	788.8

Employment by Industry: California—*Continued*

(Numbers in thousands. Not seasonally adjusted.)

Industry	January	February	March	April	May	June	July	August	September	October	November	December	Annual Average
STATEWIDE—*Continued*													
Manufacturing													
1990	1948.3	1959.1	1964.0	1965.6	1967.3	1973.0	1976.4	1983.6	1972.0	1950.7	1932.5	1924.8	1959.8
1991	1905.9	1902.8	1897.0	1897.5	1889.3	1890.3	1885.8	1899.6	1894.3	1875.4	1851.8	1832.7	1885.2
1992	1804.5	1803.9	1814.9	1799.6	1792.6	1793.7	1802.1	1799.7	1786.4	1776.4	1743.3	1726.3	1787.0
1993	1710.6	1710.0	1707.6	1696.2	1695.3	1702.6	1700.2	1707.5	1701.6	1676.9	1668.7	1665.1	1695.2
1994	1637.2	1647.7	1664.4	1668.6	1678.3	1689.8	1706.4	1716.1	1715.9	1692.8	1691.7	1697.1	1683.8
1995	1668.1	1685.8	1698.7	1692.3	1701.5	1715.8	1723.7	1747.0	1756.6	1726.2	1729.7	1732.8	1714.9
1996	1717.4	1736.7	1754.7	1752.5	1769.4	1782.2	1783.7	1802.5	1805.5	1784.8	1788.6	1790.4	1772.4
1997	1761.2	1782.6	1801.7	1798.8	1814.5	1828.4	1846.4	1866.3	1864.9	1844.6	1842.9	1848.5	1825.1
1998	1831.9	1843.1	1853.7	1857.3	1870.5	1877.2	1867.6	1879.2	1883.1	1848.3	1839.0	1836.0	1857.2
1999	1800.5	1813.1	1823.3	1818.3	1822.9	1833.8	1835.3	1847.5	1856.4	1839.8	1832.3	1835.5	1829.9
2000	1811.9	1826.3	1841.4	1837.0	1844.1	1868.1	1873.5	1886.0	1886.4	1868.3	1868.9	1877.9	1857.5
2001	1844.7	1849.3	1852.9	1822.0	1811.9	1809.1	1783.0	1781.1	1761.2	1725.4	1699.0	1688.3	1785.6
2002	1648.3	1651.7	1659.2	1648.5	1651.8	1656.6	1641.2	1647.8	1641.8	1617.3	1600.7	1593.3	1638.2
2003	1560.6	1560.2	1561.5	1552.4	1549.7	1551.8	1536.2	1545.6	1544.2	1531.2	1524.2	1521.2	1544.9
Service-providing													
1990	9691.9	9750.5	9812.0	9826.8	9877.4	9914.2	9818.0	9783.1	9869.4	9935.3	9993.8	10038.6	9859.3
1991	9811.4	9836.6	9882.3	9884.7	9900.6	9919.4	9811.0	9782.7	9862.8	9903.8	9948.7	9983.6	9877.3
1992	9741.8	9770.4	9842.5	9856.5	9874.8	9889.6	9789.3	9741.5	9816.1	9855.0	9932.0	9966.1	9839.6
1993	9771.3	9796.6	9826.1	9818.1	9852.5	9897.3	9810.5	9791.9	9878.4	9901.0	9956.2	10038.0	9861.5
1994	9784.6	9869.2	9943.4	9931.1	9974.6	10019.3	9890.6	9894.8	10009.0	10032.0	10124.3	10205.7	9973.2
1995	9945.9	10056.8	10118.5	10121.6	10196.8	10253.7	10087.5	10121.1	10252.2	10250.5	10355.5	10426.4	10182.2
1996	10187.2	10295.4	10367.7	10346.6	10433.5	10476.6	10341.7	10371.1	10479.4	10522.5	10640.0	10697.0	10429.9
1997	10426.5	10530.2	10634.9	10679.1	10750.2	10798.9	10647.6	10660.2	10780.2	10838.9	10915.3	11027.9	10724.2
1998	10800.9	10894.0	10976.9	10995.4	11083.5	11140.4	11036.9	11069.5	11187.0	11226.1	11333.8	11425.4	11097.5
1999	11119.5	11230.6	11327.4	11372.6	11443.4	11491.0	11412.9	11418.3	11521.1	11595.5	11696.3	11803.9	11452.7
2000	11518.6	11642.9	11768.7	11788.4	11903.1	11961.3	11801.1	11847.3	11963.3	11991.7	12102.1	12189.8	11873.2
2001	11906.8	11983.0	12077.2	12037.8	12077.7	12119.8	11886.8	11913.9	11961.0	12002.0	12060.9	12114.3	12011.7
2002	11831.4	11912.1	12025.5	12022.3	12086.3	12119.0	11905.7	11931.9	12003.1	12069.5	12161.4	12208.0	12023.0
2003	11903.1	11969.3	12034.7	12044.0	12086.1	12127.0	11938.8	11976.4	12044.9	12139.3	12183.5	12206.2	12054.4
Trade, transportation, and utilities													
1990	2405.8	2383.4	2385.1	2385.9	2392.5	2407.7	2415.4	2416.1	2415.6	2437.7	2477.6	2512.1	2419.6
1991	2398.6	2364.1	2358.6	2348.2	2353.3	2367.7	2371.8	2371.2	2374.7	2381.4	2422.7	2456.6	2380.7
1992	2362.9	2323.2	2327.7	2330.3	2337.7	2346.6	2347.8	2343.0	2342.7	2351.9	2399.3	2435.3	2354.0
1993	2347.5	2318.5	2309.9	2307.9	2309.3	2322.9	2329.0	2327.0	2330.1	2342.8	2380.2	2426.3	2337.6
1994	2311.6	2298.1	2304.8	2303.3	2313.9	2331.8	2339.6	2351.4	2361.5	2376.1	2437.5	2485.5	2351.3
1995	2365.2	2357.3	2360.3	2352.9	2367.0	2387.4	2380.5	2399.6	2412.5	2413.2	2469.1	2513.6	2398.2
1996	2414.2	2408.2	2409.2	2397.6	2421.9	2444.2	2432.9	2444.9	2456.8	2463.8	2527.1	2576.5	2449.8
1997	2462.2	2460.3	2472.2	2474.0	2492.1	2509.9	2508.5	2500.4	2529.9	2541.1	2591.5	2649.5	2516.0
1998	2554.8	2534.1	2540.0	2527.3	2553.9	2573.4	2575.0	2589.9	2601.0	2603.1	2658.0	2707.4	2584.8
1999	2585.1	2584.8	2592.3	2589.1	2609.0	2626.2	2640.7	2655.2	2665.5	2682.6	2727.4	2783.4	2645.1
2000	2668.7	2662.0	2673.4	2668.5	2686.6	2713.8	2715.6	2726.8	2734.2	2742.6	2803.2	2861.4	2721.4
2001	2753.8	2732.1	2743.1	2727.2	2733.2	2752.1	2733.7	2736.4	2736.5	2733.2	2770.7	2807.5	2746.6
2002	2697.4	2679.9	2694.3	2691.0	2706.8	2726.3	2712.1	2719.4	2727.5	2730.2	2781.7	2829.9	2724.7
2003	2699.7	2681.5	2685.0	2680.4	2692.2	2711.7	2704.1	2720.8	2731.6	2755.4	2786.5	2815.3	2722.0
Wholesale trade													
1990	543.1	544.5	545.9	550.6	550.4	553.0	550.4	549.8	549.2	555.7	554.9	557.1	550.4
1991	553.7	554.0	553.3	553.8	555.1	555.2	554.2	552.8	551.9	554.9	553.6	551.8	553.7
1992	543.9	542.2	544.9	547.0	548.4	549.3	547.9	547.0	544.1	545.6	546.5	546.4	546.1
1993	540.0	541.2	543.0	538.6	540.7	542.6	542.0	542.0	539.9	539.5	540.3	542.0	541.0
1994	534.0	538.5	543.2	540.0	542.2	545.9	546.3	549.8	551.0	547.7	549.7	553.4	545.1
1995	543.8	550.0	553.8	553.8	557.5	561.6	557.7	560.7	563.0	556.6	559.6	562.4	556.7
1996	557.0	562.6	567.6	567.6	573.2	577.7	576.2	578.7	579.5	579.9	583.2	586.5	574.1
1997	577.9	584.3	590.1	592.1	596.6	598.9	598.8	602.4	601.0	600.8	600.9	603.2	595.6
1998	602.0	606.0	609.4	610.5	615.0	619.1	615.3	616.3	618.8	617.2	618.8	620.4	614.1
1999	613.8	619.1	623.1	624.1	626.6	631.3	631.5	632.6	632.8	633.1	633.8	636.1	628.2
2000	629.3	634.9	639.3	639.1	642.5	649.0	647.7	649.9	651.5	649.3	650.3	655.7	644.9
2001	655.8	661.6	664.8	661.0	660.6	665.1	659.0	658.2	656.2	655.3	652.1	652.3	658.5
2002	644.0	647.4	651.5	651.4	653.8	656.4	652.7	654.7	654.9	651.8	652.3	653.8	652.1
2003	644.3	646.4	649.4	651.5	653.6	656.3	651.6	654.0	654.0	652.7	651.3	651.9	651.4
Retail trade													
1990	1449.6	1424.7	1422.0	1416.3	1420.9	1429.2	1435.6	1436.6	1434.5	1449.6	1490.5	1518.4	1444.0
1991	1410.5	1378.8	1373.9	1362.7	1364.0	1373.9	1374.1	1376.2	1380.4	1384.4	1425.8	1461.5	1388.9
1992	1386.0	1349.1	1349.3	1348.0	1351.9	1358.2	1359.1	1354.9	1357.3	1366.2	1411.6	1447.0	1369.9
1993	1371.2	1342.6	1332.8	1335.6	1332.8	1340.1	1343.2	1341.5	1345.5	1353.8	1392.9	1436.9	1355.7
1994	1344.1	1326.3	1325.9	1324.7	1331.4	1340.6	1341.2	1348.1	1354.9	1368.3	1426.9	1473.3	1358.8
1995	1377.3	1359.9	1354.2	1347.2	1354.8	1365.9	1360.3	1374.4	1381.6	1387.7	1439.3	1480.6	1381.9
1996	1403.0	1387.8	1379.7	1369.0	1382.8	1396.1	1386.1	1394.2	1402.4	1407.0	1466.3	1511.7	1407.2
1997	1420.8	1409.1	1411.8	1408.0	1416.7	1427.4	1428.4	1438.0	1443.0	1449.7	1499.6	1553.4	1442.2
1998	1466.6	1440.5	1439.9	1428.6	1445.1	1455.5	1460.6	1471.5	1477.1	1482.3	1536.4	1582.4	1473.9
1999	1479.0	1471.4	1473.6	1465.3	1478.6	1488.7	1497.6	1509.0	1519.3	1526.9	1572.3	1625.3	1508.9
2000	1530.7	1518.6	1523.7	1516.6	1529.2	1545.6	1547.8	1555.9	1561.6	1572.7	1631.3	1678.8	1559.4
2001	1581.0	1557.2	1561.3	1549.2	1555.3	1568.6	1559.0	1562.5	1565.4	1564.7	1614.9	1654.3	1574.4
2002	1567.7	1545.1	1557.5	1551.4	1561.3	1575.3	1566.6	1570.3	1578.8	1585.2	1637.4	1683.7	1581.7
2003	1576.6	1558.1	1558.3	1553.9	1561.1	1574.6	1572.6	1585.3	1593.3	1616.7	1650.0	1678.8	1589.9

Employment by Industry: California—*Continued*

(Numbers in thousands. Not seasonally adjusted.)

Industry	January	February	March	April	May	June	July	August	September	October	November	December	Annual Average
STATEWIDE—*Continued*													
Transportation and utilities													
1990	413.1	414.2	417.2	419.0	421.2	425.5	429.4	429.7	431.9	432.4	432.2	436.6	425.2
1991	434.4	431.3	431.4	431.7	434.2	438.6	443.5	442.2	442.4	442.1	443.3	443.3	438.2
1992	433.0	431.9	433.5	435.3	437.4	439.1	440.8	441.1	441.3	440.1	441.2	441.9	438.1
1993	436.3	434.7	434.1	433.7	435.8	440.2	443.8	443.5	444.7	449.5	447.0	447.4	440.9
1994	433.5	433.3	435.7	438.6	440.3	445.3	452.1	453.5	455.6	460.1	460.9	458.8	447.3
1995	444.1	447.4	452.3	451.9	454.7	459.9	462.5	464.5	467.9	468.9	470.2	470.6	459.6
1996	454.2	457.8	461.9	461.0	465.9	470.4	470.6	472.0	474.9	476.9	477.6	478.3	468.5
1997	463.5	466.9	470.3	473.9	478.8	483.6	481.3	460.0	485.9	490.6	491.0	492.9	478.2
1998	486.2	487.6	490.7	488.2	493.8	498.8	499.1	502.1	505.1	503.6	502.8	504.6	496.9
1999	492.3	494.3	495.6	499.7	503.8	506.2	511.6	513.6	513.4	522.6	521.3	522.0	508.0
2000	508.7	508.5	510.4	512.8	514.9	519.2	520.1	521.0	521.1	520.6	521.6	526.9	517.2
2001	517.0	513.3	517.0	517.0	517.3	518.4	515.7	515.7	514.9	513.2	503.7	500.9	513.6
2002	485.7	487.4	485.3	488.2	491.7	494.6	492.8	494.4	493.8	493.2	492.0	492.4	491.0
2003	478.8	477.0	477.3	475.0	477.5	480.8	479.9	481.5	484.3	486.0	485.2	484.6	480.7
Information													
1990	385.4	390.6	385.2	386.3	386.8	388.3	391.5	391.6	391.7	395.5	397.7	396.8	390.6
1991	395.1	395.7	399.1	398.7	397.5	400.3	395.4	395.7	394.4	394.9	391.8	387.5	395.5
1992	385.1	387.1	392.0	388.5	387.8	386.0	383.5	383.4	380.2	389.2	394.0	393.3	387.5
1993	381.7	385.2	387.4	377.3	376.2	384.9	388.5	392.0	391.7	389.4	388.2	392.0	386.2
1994	381.0	389.0	393.7	393.5	395.4	399.7	397.4	401.1	400.5	398.7	400.8	399.2	395.8
1995	403.4	415.4	413.4	402.9	412.5	416.9	413.3	420.6	430.4	416.1	421.3	424.8	415.9
1996	409.4	419.2	427.8	422.9	425.5	431.6	432.3	442.9	441.8	443.1	452.8	444.1	432.8
1997	444.8	450.2	457.3	456.2	459.2	464.1	464.7	466.7	469.8	466.9	467.9	472.7	461.7
1998	467.4	476.2	478.8	468.5	473.1	477.6	480.8	487.9	491.4	491.5	497.0	503.2	482.8
1999	504.4	501.7	506.3	503.6	513.4	511.0	520.1	527.6	523.2	523.4	533.5	540.5	517.4
2000	536.7	549.4	559.3	561.7	571.6	579.0	579.0	589.1	586.8	591.3	601.6	599.6	575.4
2001	586.8	588.3	589.7	570.9	557.3	554.3	537.2	534.3	529.0	523.9	523.4	522.5	551.4
2002	510.1	511.3	519.8	502.6	502.3	501.6	484.6	490.5	481.4	487.8	495.8	479.4	497.3
2003	479.8	486.5	481.0	472.0	475.0	466.3	461.6	471.0	461.2	464.6	472.6	464.7	471.4
Financial activities													
1990	819.8	824.6	829.2	821.9	823.2	825.7	822.2	822.5	823.9	815.8	812.5	821.0	821.9
1991	818.2	817.8	821.2	812.8	812.1	810.6	810.4	813.4	804.5	796.6	795.0	795.0	809.0
1992	784.5	789.5	797.1	792.3	793.8	794.8	786.1	789.3	784.3	788.3	790.6	792.9	790.3
1993	785.3	785.1	784.9	784.3	786.2	791.0	787.6	789.0	788.8	784.6	785.7	791.6	787.0
1994	785.9	789.6	792.2	777.9	774.3	773.0	768.5	768.0	763.6	748.8	748.4	752.9	770.3
1995	739.0	742.4	744.2	741.1	743.0	746.5	741.3	743.4	743.5	738.3	740.7	743.8	742.3
1996	734.6	742.0	744.6	744.4	745.1	748.9	741.8	745.2	743.9	740.4	744.3	739.3	742.9
1997	729.8	728.4	735.3	733.5	738.5	743.2	747.8	751.1	748.7	754.8	757.1	763.8	744.3
1998	752.2	759.6	766.3	764.4	770.1	774.4	776.5	780.4	781.6	782.5	787.2	792.3	774.0
1999	783.2	789.7	793.6	791.4	795.1	799.1	793.4	794.7	793.4	790.7	793.4	800.2	793.2
2000	785.4	790.9	794.7	788.7	792.2	799.2	793.3	797.8	797.0	796.5	797.8	807.5	795.1
2001	817.7	825.7	833.3	830.9	834.0	840.3	833.9	837.6	836.2	840.3	843.1	849.8	835.2
2002	834.8	840.4	843.7	844.8	848.5	853.5	852.3	857.6	857.9	860.0	866.3	873.7	852.8
2003	866.1	871.3	876.2	880.1	886.2	890.8	891.5	896.4	894.5	895.6	895.7	896.8	886.8
Professional and business services													
1990	1480.5	1499.5	1513.8	1506.9	1509.9	1517.7	1520.8	1525.0	1527.0	1526.4	1528.1	1536.5	1516.0
1991	1498.9	1510.3	1518.8	1507.1	1500.9	1500.8	1513.0	1518.0	1519.9	1518.5	1516.7	1521.4	1512.0
1992	1472.9	1484.0	1503.4	1501.1	1497.1	1507.0	1514.6	1515.2	1518.2	1521.8	1527.6	1528.1	1507.6
1993	1505.2	1515.9	1527.2	1525.6	1530.9	1537.5	1552.5	1560.0	1568.7	1555.1	1552.3	1567.7	1541.6
1994	1525.8	1553.1	1575.8	1572.0	1572.7	1584.9	1586.8	1596.9	1610.5	1606.3	1616.8	1634.9	1586.4
1995	1590.6	1624.4	1643.6	1642.5	1655.0	1673.7	1667.4	1689.8	1702.0	1691.5	1707.1	1725.7	1667.8
1996	1691.3	1711.9	1733.2	1725.7	1740.6	1757.7	1772.5	1788.1	1798.6	1798.7	1816.2	1832.2	1763.9
1997	1786.1	1816.1	1844.9	1862.0	1869.5	1888.5	1902.3	1926.8	1927.5	1929.9	1936.2	1972.3	1888.5
1998	1943.8	1969.6	1992.5	2005.9	2016.7	2034.4	2053.0	2079.0	2088.1	2075.8	2085.9	2099.1	2037.0
1999	2022.9	2042.7	2066.5	2091.9	2098.0	2123.2	2137.8	2152.3	2160.5	2163.0	2172.2	2198.8	2119.2
2000	2133.0	2163.9	2195.4	2217.7	2226.3	2263.7	2261.9	2288.8	2296.9	2288.9	2298.6	2316.3	2246.0
2001	2203.3	2216.2	2233.5	2202.9	2206.3	2212.6	2178.5	2184.4	2168.8	2148.4	2138.1	2144.4	2186.4
2002	2090.4	2103.7	2126.3	2109.0	2111.9	2119.9	2106.0	2121.9	2118.4	2115.3	2122.7	2126.3	2114.3
2003	2060.1	2073.3	2090.9	2090.2	2094.4	2108.0	2097.4	2122.3	2131.4	2140.3	2142.4	2147.0	2108.1
Educational and health services													
1990	1085.1	1101.9	1108.1	1114.5	1112.4	1111.3	1100.6	1107.7	1118.4	1141.1	1149.6	1145.3	1116.3
1991	1139.7	1150.7	1154.8	1157.8	1155.2	1147.7	1140.0	1137.1	1150.5	1171.2	1172.8	1174.0	1154.3
1992	1163.5	1179.3	1186.6	1190.7	1188.2	1180.7	1175.9	1172.1	1183.3	1183.5	1192.0	1195.7	1182.6
1993	1182.2	1190.9	1195.5	1191.5	1190.2	1190.3	1189.8	1186.6	1197.7	1206.4	1211.4	1216.7	1195.8
1994	1193.6	1208.0	1218.6	1212.2	1215.2	1210.2	1193.2	1193.1	1216.1	1220.7	1228.8	1234.4	1212.0
1995	1206.3	1228.8	1236.7	1243.4	1249.5	1244.3	1221.9	1223.9	1245.3	1250.0	1257.7	1259.3	1238.9
1996	1238.7	1262.1	1270.9	1267.2	1274.2	1266.1	1249.3	1252.0	1268.3	1270.7	1275.4	1279.3	1264.5
1997	1260.1	1281.4	1291.0	1297.9	1303.1	1294.0	1273.6	1273.1	1285.8	1309.9	1312.6	1318.0	1291.7
1998	1296.9	1320.4	1323.8	1333.4	1341.2	1331.8	1313.3	1311.8	1329.8	1345.9	1353.6	1357.7	1330.0
1999	1333.0	1359.4	1367.3	1371.7	1374.8	1370.6	1353.3	1348.4	1373.8	1384.2	1390.3	1392.9	1368.3
2000	1375.5	1400.3	1410.2	1399.3	1401.8	1392.2	1372.1	1374.1	1411.5	1411.1	1417.9	1410.3	1398.0
2001	1405.5	1429.8	1443.6	1440.8	1449.9	1440.6	1413.5	1433.9	1453.2	1473.7	1486.3	1491.5	1446.8
2002	1465.5	1491.7	1503.0	1496.2	1504.4	1491.2	1474.3	1477.0	1500.2	1518.7	1531.0	1532.7	1498.8
2003	1502.6	1524.4	1534.8	1545.4	1547.6	1537.4	1509.0	1510.7	1535.4	1558.5	1563.1	1566.8	1536.3

Employment by Industry: California—*Continued*

(Numbers in thousands. Not seasonally adjusted.)

Industry	January	February	March	April	May	June	July	August	September	October	November	December	Annual Average
STATEWIDE—*Continued*													
Leisure and hospitality													
1990	1062.2	1072.2	1087.7	1095.4	1106.8	1121.6	1132.4	1135.6	1127.0	1105.2	1102.7	1104.8	1104.5
1991	1064.8	1080.4	1094.9	1119.5	1135.7	1146.2	1146.0	1149.6	1139.7	1119.1	1117.1	1120.0	1119.4
1992	1070.1	1081.5	1094.4	1114.2	1124.8	1132.4	1141.9	1142.9	1136.1	1114.7	1110.6	1111.1	1114.6
1993	1081.6	1089.9	1101.4	1114.7	1134.4	1147.0	1146.0	1151.6	1148.0	1127.2	1121.3	1131.6	1124.6
1994	1095.1	1109.6	1121.8	1134.7	1152.2	1167.3	1167.3	1171.1	1167.8	1144.0	1142.8	1151.6	1143.8
1995	1121.0	1137.5	1154.0	1168.5	1190.0	1205.3	1206.2	1214.4	1209.7	1186.3	1189.1	1196.2	1181.5
1996	1171.8	1191.0	1207.5	1211.6	1235.0	1239.7	1245.2	1251.3	1238.8	1226.6	1226.8	1236.9	1223.5
1997	1185.8	1202.8	1221.8	1238.3	1257.1	1274.5	1256.3	1265.1	1251.6	1227.5	1224.8	1226.9	1236.0
1998	1204.4	1224.9	1239.4	1254.2	1268.4	1285.7	1291.0	1295.7	1288.2	1263.4	1263.1	1276.1	1262.9
1999	1232.9	1253.1	1273.1	1285.6	1305.2	1318.3	1327.4	1327.9	1322.8	1305.3	1301.9	1311.7	1297.1
2000	1264.6	1286.9	1309.0	1317.5	1336.8	1358.8	1365.1	1372.0	1365.2	1337.8	1333.2	1344.3	1332.6
2001	1312.7	1332.8	1351.7	1359.6	1376.9	1393.3	1395.7	1400.3	1376.2	1360.6	1351.9	1357.3	1364.0
2002	1318.1	1335.3	1355.4	1382.3	1403.3	1419.2	1410.0	1417.2	1402.9	1384.1	1375.0	1385.6	1382.4
2003	1346.1	1362.9	1376.7	1391.1	1405.6	1426.3	1426.9	1434.4	1417.4	1399.6	1389.0	1395.5	1397.6
Other services													
1990	406.8	410.6	414.6	414.0	415.6	417.0	419.5	418.7	419.5	418.5	416.9	415.5	415.6
1991	410.1	412.9	413.8	415.9	416.6	419.1	417.5	417.2	417.6	416.9	416.2	415.0	415.7
1992	405.0	406.4	410.4	408.5	410.5	412.0	408.6	407.4	409.1	405.1	404.3	401.9	407.4
1993	401.9	406.9	409.4	406.2	408.8	411.7	409.9	408.7	412.7	407.8	407.6	406.9	408.2
1994	409.1	413.8	419.1	416.7	420.1	424.2	420.0	420.7	427.3	424.3	424.5	425.9	420.5
1995	415.1	423.2	428.7	429.5	433.5	436.9	429.7	430.8	436.1	433.3	435.6	435.0	430.6
1996	425.9	433.3	438.2	439.0	442.6	445.8	439.0	441.0	442.3	440.3	441.7	441.6	439.2
1997	429.9	437.6	442.2	444.8	449.3	452.1	446.8	449.0	450.5	448.5	445.4	446.4	445.2
1998	442.3	447.9	455.3	457.2	462.9	468.6	462.6	462.5	465.8	465.1	464.6	465.4	460.0
1999	457.1	463.9	469.5	467.5	471.9	476.8	475.8	476.2	479.5	479.2	480.0	480.5	473.2
2000	472.4	478.4	485.3	485.4	488.3	494.4	488.1	489.5	492.3	487.3	487.8	490.7	486.7
2001	484.1	491.6	498.5	497.8	502.0	507.2	500.9	502.0	502.0	501.1	500.3	500.4	498.9
2002	492.5	500.0	503.8	505.9	512.1	515.2	507.4	506.2	506.8	506.5	505.7	505.7	505.7
2003	497.6	503.2	505.5	507.5	510.8	515.1	505.5	506.0	505.1	505.0	504.6	503.4	505.8
Government													
1990	2046.3	2067.7	2088.3	2101.9	2130.2	2124.9	2015.6	1965.9	2046.3	2095.1	2108.7	2106.6	2074.8
1991	2086.0	2104.7	2121.1	2124.7	2129.3	2127.0	2016.9	1980.5	2061.5	2105.2	2116.4	2114.1	2090.6
1992	2097.8	2119.4	2130.9	2130.9	2134.9	2130.1	2030.9	1988.2	2062.2	2100.5	2113.6	2107.8	2095.6
1993	2085.9	2104.2	2110.4	2110.6	2116.5	2112.0	2007.2	1977.0	2040.7	2087.7	2109.5	2105.2	2080.6
1994	2082.5	2108.0	2117.4	2120.8	2130.8	2128.2	2017.8	1992.5	2061.7	2113.1	2124.7	2121.3	2093.2
1995	2105.3	2127.8	2137.6	2140.8	2146.3	2142.7	2027.2	1998.6	2072.7	2121.8	2134.9	2128.0	2107.0
1996	2101.3	2127.7	2136.3	2138.2	2148.6	2142.6	2028.7	2005.7	2088.9	2138.9	2155.7	2147.1	2113.3
1997	2127.8	2153.4	2170.2	2172.4	2181.4	2172.6	2047.6	2028.0	2116.4	2160.3	2179.8	2178.3	2140.7
1998	2139.1	2161.3	2180.8	2184.5	2197.2	2194.5	2084.7	2062.3	2141.1	2198.8	2224.4	2224.2	2166.1
1999	2200.9	2235.3	2258.8	2271.8	2276.0	2265.8	2164.4	2136.0	2202.4	2267.1	2297.6	2295.9	2239.3
2000	2282.3	2311.1	2341.4	2349.6	2399.5	2360.2	2226.0	2209.2	2279.4	2336.2	2362.0	2359.7	2318.1
2001	2342.9	2366.5	2383.8	2407.7	2418.1	2419.4	2293.4	2285.0	2359.1	2420.8	2447.1	2440.9	2382.0
2002	2422.6	2449.8	2479.2	2490.5	2497.0	2492.1	2359.0	2342.1	2408.0	2466.9	2483.2	2474.7	2447.1
2003	2451.1	2466.2	2484.6	2477.3	2474.3	2471.4	2342.8	2314.8	2368.3	2420.3	2429.6	2416.7	2426.5
Federal government													
1990	354.5	353.8	357.9	367.1	384.3	383.8	376.2	364.0	353.3	349.5	349.1	351.8	362.1
1991	345.2	345.2	346.3	346.7	347.4	348.8	350.2	349.9	348.3	347.7	346.2	348.2	347.5
1992	342.9	342.1	342.2	343.5	345.0	347.0	350.0	349.5	348.9	347.5	344.5	347.4	345.9
1993	339.7	338.1	337.3	336.7	336.4	338.1	336.6	335.6	332.9	331.8	334.2	336.6	336.2
1994	327.4	328.0	326.3	325.5	325.7	326.2	326.0	325.0	324.2	321.8	319.5	323.1	324.9
1995	314.8	314.5	314.2	313.1	312.9	313.8	313.7	312.4	311.0	308.8	305.3	308.6	311.9
1996	301.4	300.9	300.3	296.8	297.7	296.5	294.9	294.7	293.4	290.3	289.6	293.7	295.9
1997	286.3	285.3	284.8	288.0	287.2	287.8	286.0	285.0	283.6	279.1	278.7	283.3	284.6
1998	271.7	270.0	270.1	269.8	271.0	271.2	273.9	274.7	274.9	272.9	272.3	277.7	272.5
1999	268.8	270.0	270.2	276.0	268.3	268.2	271.7	271.2	271.3	266.7	266.4	271.9	270.1
2000	265.1	265.9	272.4	275.7	318.8	286.5	277.1	273.6	260.0	258.1	259.0	262.3	272.9
2001	253.6	252.4	252.9	253.2	253.6	255.6	257.0	256.4	256.2	254.3	253.6	253.2	254.3
2002	251.7	250.9	252.5	253.1	253.1	255.7	255.0	253.8	253.4	254.0	254.1	257.7	253.8
2003	256.9	258.5	260.7	260.2	261.3	262.1	259.6	258.8	257.1	257.3	255.5	256.8	258.7
State government													
1990	377.3	380.5	384.5	386.0	388.6	386.5	371.8	369.6	375.8	387.6	389.7	386.3	382.0
1991	383.6	389.0	395.5	396.0	396.5	395.7	378.0	374.0	376.8	386.3	386.7	382.9	386.8
1992	380.7	386.8	390.7	390.1	391.9	389.0	371.7	370.0	375.0	385.5	389.3	388.0	384.1
1993	385.6	388.2	390.4	389.5	391.3	390.2	378.0	375.3	378.1	389.7	391.7	389.0	386.4
1994	388.7	393.4	398.0	399.5	401.9	401.6	386.9	383.0	387.5	402.2	403.7	402.3	395.7
1995	401.9	405.5	407.1	408.5	409.6	409.4	392.8	388.4	394.6	407.7	409.3	407.1	403.5
1996	403.4	406.7	409.9	410.9	411.8	413.6	391.6	391.7	397.2	409.8	414.5	407.3	405.7
1997	405.5	410.0	415.4	414.4	415.7	413.2	393.6	391.2	398.1	411.5	418.4	410.8	408.2
1998	404.6	409.6	417.2	416.2	418.9	418.1	399.9	396.3	405.0	423.2	426.2	421.2	413.0
1999	418.0	424.2	431.3	431.3	435.1	434.3	414.9	414.4	419.4	437.6	441.0	438.1	428.3
2000	431.5	437.0	443.5	449.5	449.6	449.5	431.9	431.1	435.3	451.9	455.9	453.8	443.4
2001	449.6	455.0	463.4	463.4	465.2	466.9	448.7	448.7	456.6	470.5	473.9	471.9	461.1
2002	465.4	470.2	479.5	477.8	479.6	478.7	457.8	457.7	463.0	477.4	481.2	477.4	472.1
2003	471.1	474.8	481.0	479.4	479.1	479.6	458.6	456.0	460.6	473.7	475.1	469.8	471.6

Employment by Industry: California—*Continued*

(Numbers in thousands. Not seasonally adjusted.)

Industry	January	February	March	April	May	June	July	August	September	October	November	December	Annual Average
STATEWIDE—*Continued*													
Local government													
1990	1314.5	1333.4	1345.9	1348.8	1357.3	1354.6	1267.6	1232.3	1317.2	1358.0	1369.9	1368.5	1330.7
1991	1357.2	1370.5	1379.3	1382.0	1385.4	1382.5	1288.7	1256.6	1336.4	1371.2	1383.5	1383.0	1356.4
1992	1374.2	1390.5	1398.0	1397.3	1398.0	1394.1	1309.2	1268.7	1338.3	1367.5	1379.8	1372.4	1365.7
1993	1360.6	1377.9	1382.7	1384.4	1388.8	1383.7	1292.6	1266.1	1329.7	1366.2	1383.6	1379.6	1358.0
1994	1366.4	1386.6	1393.1	1395.8	1403.2	1400.4	1304.9	1284.5	1350.0	1389.1	1401.5	1395.9	1372.6
1995	1388.6	1407.8	1416.3	1419.2	1423.8	1419.5	1320.7	1297.8	1367.1	1405.3	1420.3	1412.3	1391.6
1996	1396.5	1420.1	1426.1	1430.5	1439.1	1432.5	1342.2	1319.3	1398.3	1438.8	1451.6	1446.1	1411.8
1997	1436.0	1458.1	1470.0	1470.0	1478.5	1471.6	1368.0	1351.8	1434.7	1469.7	1482.7	1484.2	1447.9
1998	1462.8	1481.7	1493.5	1498.5	1507.3	1505.2	1410.9	1391.3	1461.2	1502.7	1525.9	1525.3	1480.5
1999	1514.1	1541.1	1557.3	1564.5	1572.6	1563.3	1477.8	1450.4	1511.7	1562.8	1590.2	1585.9	1541.0
2000	1585.7	1608.2	1625.5	1624.4	1631.1	1624.2	1517.0	1504.5	1584.1	1626.2	1647.1	1643.6	1601.8
2001	1639.7	1659.1	1667.5	1691.1	1699.3	1696.9	1587.7	1579.9	1646.3	1696.0	1719.6	1715.8	1666.5
2002	1705.5	1728.7	1747.2	1759.6	1764.3	1757.7	1646.2	1630.6	1691.6	1735.5	1747.9	1739.6	1721.2
2003	1723.1	1732.9	1742.9	1737.7	1733.9	1729.7	1624.6	1600.0	1650.6	1689.3	1699.0	1690.1	1696.2
BAKERSFIELD													
Total nonfarm													
1990	164.7	165.6	166.8	169.5	170.9	171.8	171.0	169.3	172.7	174.3	175.0	176.9	170.7
1991	176.0	176.6	177.9	178.0	178.7	179.5	175.3	174.0	177.4	177.6	178.3	178.0	177.2
1992	172.8	172.6	174.4	174.8	174.9	175.7	171.8	169.8	173.1	173.0	173.4	173.5	173.3
1993	168.1	168.3	169.2	170.4	170.9	173.2	168.3	167.8	169.3	170.4	170.7	172.3	169.9
1994	167.1	167.6	168.9	170.4	171.8	174.7	169.0	168.6	171.9	172.1	173.4	174.2	170.8
1995	168.9	169.4	170.9	172.1	172.9	175.5	172.9	172.1	174.8	173.7	174.7	175.2	172.7
1996	170.4	171.6	173.3	174.8	176.1	177.3	172.9	172.8	175.5	177.4	178.2	178.2	174.8
1997	175.3	176.6	178.8	178.5	180.2	182.1	177.8	176.3	180.4	181.4	181.6	181.7	179.2
1998	180.2	180.6	181.4	183.3	184.9	187.5	183.6	182.8	184.8	186.6	187.3	188.1	184.2
1999	184.4	183.8	187.0	188.7	188.8	192.2	186.8	186.6	189.8	191.3	192.6	194.0	188.8
2000	189.8	190.8	192.7	193.0	195.1	196.0	191.3	191.0	195.0	196.9	198.4	199.2	194.1
2001	199.3	200.1	201.5	202.2	202.9	205.3	197.9	200.1	201.8	204.2	205.8	205.8	202.2
2002	202.2	202.8	205.3	205.8	206.7	208.2	201.8	202.4	203.2	206.2	208.0	208.5	205.1
2003	204.9	205.2	207.8	207.6	208.5	208.2	204.3	205.2	206.4	207.7	208.4	207.8	206.8
Total private													
1990	121.3	121.6	122.3	124.3	125.2	126.6	129.1	129.2	129.7	129.5	130.0	131.2	126.6
1991	131.2	131.0	131.5	131.6	132.0	133.0	132.5	131.9	131.6	131.4	131.5	131.4	131.7
1992	126.8	126.2	127.5	127.8	127.9	129.2	129.0	128.8	128.2	127.0	127.4	127.5	127.7
1993	123.0	122.8	123.2	124.1	124.8	125.1	125.2	125.4	124.7	123.7	123.6	124.9	124.2
1994	121.0	121.4	121.7	122.8	124.3	125.8	124.8	125.2	126.2	124.7	125.1	125.9	124.0
1995	122.0	121.8	122.8	123.8	124.7	125.8	127.9	128.0	128.9	126.1	126.4	127.1	125.4
1996	123.3	124.0	125.0	126.4	127.6	129.2	129.0	129.3	129.1	129.0	129.3	129.5	127.5
1997	127.0	128.1	129.8	129.5	130.7	132.7	132.2	132.6	132.8	132.4	131.8	132.4	131.0
1998	130.8	130.9	131.9	133.3	135.2	137.5	137.9	137.8	137.6	137.2	137.3	137.9	135.4
1999	134.3	133.7	136.2	137.6	137.9	139.4	140.0	140.3	140.7	140.2	140.5	141.8	138.5
2000	137.9	138.9	139.9	140.3	141.8	143.0	144.6	145.0	144.4	143.7	144.5	145.7	142.4
2001	146.1	146.2	147.3	147.6	148.3	149.7	149.5	149.8	149.3	149.4	150.2	150.1	148.6
2002	147.1	147.5	148.8	149.2	150.4	151.1	150.0	150.7	150.3	150.5	151.1	151.7	149.9
2003	148.4	149.1	151.0	151.6	152.9	152.9	153.3	154.2	154.4	153.8	153.7	153.2	152.4
Goods-producing													
1990	32.7	32.9	33.4	33.8	34.0	34.5	35.0	35.2	35.2	34.7	34.8	35.1	34.2
1991	34.2	34.3	34.4	34.6	34.6	35.0	34.6	34.4	34.0	33.7	33.4	33.2	34.2
1992	30.8	30.4	30.8	31.0	30.8	31.2	31.3	31.2	30.7	30.6	30.4	30.2	30.7
1993	28.4	28.3	28.8	28.8	29.0	29.1	29.3	29.9	29.5	29.4	29.2	29.4	29.0
1994	27.6	28.2	28.3	28.2	28.6	28.9	28.1	28.6	29.1	28.2	28.0	28.5	28.3
1995	27.4	27.6	28.0	28.4	28.4	28.3	29.3	29.3	29.6	28.8	29.0	29.1	28.6
1996	28.0	27.7	27.9	28.4	28.9	29.3	29.4	29.3	29.1	29.1	28.8	28.9	28.7
1997	28.0	28.5	29.0	28.8	29.3	29.6	29.8	30.4	30.3	29.9	29.8	29.5	29.4
1998	28.6	28.1	27.9	28.7	29.1	29.5	30.0	29.8	29.4	29.6	29.4	29.3	29.1
1999	28.0	27.7	28.5	28.4	28.5	28.7	29.1	29.4	29.2	28.8	28.6	28.8	28.6
2000	28.5	28.9	29.5	29.8	30.4	30.9	31.4	31.5	31.6	31.5	31.5	31.9	30.6
2001	31.6	31.8	32.2	32.6	32.8	33.1	33.2	33.5	33.3	32.9	32.6	32.3	32.6
2002	31.9	31.9	32.2	32.2	32.4	32.8	33.0	33.2	33.3	33.5	33.5	33.6	32.8
2003	33.5	33.7	33.8	34.0	34.2	34.1	34.3	34.7	34.8	34.5	34.2	34.0	34.2
Natural resources and mining													
1990	11.7	11.9	11.9	11.9	12.0	12.2	12.4	12.3	12.3	12.5	12.3	12.0	12.1
1991	12.5	12.4	12.4	12.4	12.3	12.3	11.8	11.5	11.3	11.5	11.4	11.4	11.9
1992	10.9	10.9	11.0	11.0	10.8	11.0	10.9	10.8	10.9	10.8	10.6	10.5	10.8
1993	10.2	10.1	10.0	10.0	10.0	10.1	10.2	10.3	10.3	10.3	10.4	10.6	10.2
1994	10.2	10.0	10.0	10.3	10.4	10.5	9.9	10.1	10.1	10.0	10.0	10.2	10.1
1995	10.1	9.9	10.0	9.9	9.9	10.0	10.4	10.1	10.1	9.9	10.0	9.9	10.0
1996	10.0	9.8	9.8	9.9	10.0	10.0	10.1	9.9	9.8	9.8	9.8	9.8	9.8
1997	9.7	9.8	9.9	9.9	9.8	9.9	10.0	10.2	10.1	9.7	9.8	9.6	9.8
1998	9.6	9.3	8.8	8.8	8.8	8.9	8.9	8.7	8.2	8.0	7.9	7.7	8.6
1999	7.4	7.1	7.4	7.4	7.3	7.3	7.2	7.4	7.5	7.1	7.2	7.4	7.3
2000	7.6	7.8	8.0	7.8	7.9	8.0	8.4	8.6	8.6	8.5	8.6	8.7	8.2
2001	8.5	8.5	8.6	8.6	8.6	8.7	8.7	8.8	8.7	8.7	8.6	8.5	8.6
2002	8.2	8.0	7.9	7.8	7.7	7.8	7.9	7.9	7.9	7.9	7.9	7.9	7.9
2003	7.8	7.9	7.9	7.9	8.0	7.9	7.9	7.9	7.8	7.8	7.8	7.9	7.9

Employment by Industry: California—*Continued*

(Numbers in thousands. Not seasonally adjusted.)

Industry	January	February	March	April	May	June	July	August	September	October	November	December	Annual Average
BAKERSFIELD—*Continued*													
Construction													
1990	11.1	11.0	11.5	11.8	11.9	12.1	12.7	13.1	13.3	12.3	12.6	13.1	12.2
1991	11.7	11.8	11.8	12.2	12.2	12.5	12.4	12.6	12.3	11.7	11.6	11.3	12.0
1992	9.8	9.6	9.8	9.9	9.8	9.8	10.0	10.1	9.6	9.6	9.7	9.7	9.7
1993	8.5	8.5	9.0	9.1	9.2	9.1	9.3	9.8	9.5	9.4	9.3	9.3	9.1
1994	8.3	9.0	9.1	8.6	8.7	8.9	8.8	9.1	9.5	8.8	8.6	8.8	8.8
1995	8.0	8.4	8.7	9.0	9.1	8.9	9.3	9.6	9.9	9.3	9.5	9.4	9.0
1996	8.7	8.5	8.7	8.8	9.1	9.4	9.2	9.2	9.2	9.2	9.0	8.9	8.9
1997	8.2	8.5	8.7	8.8	9.2	9.5	9.9	10.1	10.0	10.0	9.8	9.9	9.3
1998	9.3	9.0	9.2	9.4	9.7	10.0	10.3	10.4	10.4	10.8	10.6	10.9	10.0
1999	10.1	10.0	10.3	10.4	10.5	10.8	11.0	11.0	10.9	11.1	10.9	11.0	10.6
2000	10.6	10.7	10.8	11.1	11.5	11.8	12.0	12.0	12.1	12.1	12.1	12.3	11.5
2001	12.1	12.3	12.7	13.0	13.1	13.2	13.3	13.6	13.4	13.1	13.0	12.9	12.9
2002	12.9	13.1	13.4	13.3	13.4	13.5	13.4	13.5	13.3	13.3	13.5	13.4	13.3
2003	13.2	13.2	13.3	13.5	13.6	13.6	13.7	14.0	14.0	13.9	13.7	13.7	13.6
Manufacturing													
1990	9.9	10.0	10.0	10.1	10.1	10.2	9.9	9.8	9.6	9.9	9.9	10.0	9.9
1991	10.0	10.1	10.2	10.0	10.1	10.2	10.4	10.3	10.4	10.5	10.4	10.5	10.2
1992	10.1	9.9	10.0	10.1	10.2	10.4	10.4	10.3	10.2	10.2	10.1	10.0	10.1
1993	9.7	9.7	9.8	9.7	9.8	9.9	9.8	9.8	9.7	9.7	9.5	9.5	9.7
1994	9.1	9.2	9.2	9.3	9.5	9.5	9.4	9.4	9.5	9.4	9.4	9.5	9.3
1995	9.3	9.3	9.3	9.5	9.4	9.4	9.6	9.6	9.6	9.6	9.5	9.8	9.4
1996	9.3	9.4	9.4	9.7	9.8	9.9	10.1	10.2	10.1	10.1	10.0	10.2	9.8
1997	10.1	10.2	10.4	10.1	10.3	10.2	9.9	10.1	10.2	10.2	10.2	10.0	10.1
1998	9.7	9.8	9.9	10.5	10.6	10.6	10.8	10.7	10.8	10.8	10.9	10.7	10.4
1999	10.5	10.6	10.8	10.6	10.7	10.6	10.9	11.0	10.8	10.6	10.5	10.4	10.6
2000	10.3	10.4	10.7	10.9	11.0	11.1	11.0	10.9	10.9	10.9	10.8	10.9	10.8
2001	11.0	11.0	10.9	11.0	11.1	11.2	11.2	11.1	11.2	11.1	11.0	10.9	11.0
2002	10.8	10.8	10.9	11.1	11.3	11.5	11.7	11.8	12.1	12.3	12.1	12.3	11.6
2003	12.5	12.6	12.6	12.6	12.6	12.6	12.7	12.8	13.0	12.8	12.7	12.4	12.7
Service-providing													
1990	132.0	132.7	133.4	135.7	136.9	137.3	136.0	134.1	137.5	139.6	140.2	141.8	136.4
1991	141.8	142.3	143.5	143.4	144.1	144.5	140.7	139.6	143.4	143.9	144.9	144.8	143.0
1992	142.0	142.2	143.6	143.8	144.1	144.5	140.5	138.6	142.4	142.4	143.0	143.3	142.5
1993	139.7	140.0	140.4	141.6	141.9	144.1	139.0	137.9	139.8	141.0	141.5	142.9	140.8
1994	139.5	139.4	140.6	142.2	143.2	145.8	140.9	140.0	142.8	143.9	145.4	145.7	142.4
1995	141.5	141.8	142.9	143.7	144.5	147.2	143.6	142.8	145.2	144.9	145.7	146.1	144.1
1996	142.4	143.9	145.4	146.4	147.2	148.0	143.5	143.5	146.4	148.3	149.4	149.3	146.1
1997	147.3	148.1	149.8	149.7	150.9	152.5	148.0	145.9	150.1	151.5	151.8	152.2	149.8
1998	151.6	152.5	153.5	154.6	155.8	158.0	153.6	153.0	155.4	157.0	157.9	158.8	155.1
1999	156.4	156.1	158.5	160.3	160.3	163.5	157.7	157.2	160.6	162.5	164.0	165.2	160.1
2000	161.3	161.9	163.2	163.2	164.7	165.1	159.9	159.5	163.4	165.4	166.9	167.3	163.4
2001	167.7	168.3	169.3	169.6	170.1	172.2	164.7	166.6	168.5	171.3	173.2	173.5	169.5
2002	170.3	170.9	173.1	173.6	174.3	175.4	168.8	169.2	169.9	172.7	174.5	174.9	172.3
2003	171.4	171.5	174.0	173.6	174.3	174.1	170.0	170.5	171.6	173.2	174.2	173.8	172.7
Trade, transportation, and utilities													
1990	32.7	32.3	32.5	32.2	32.5	32.6	33.4	33.6	33.8	33.9	34.4	34.8	33.2
1991	35.8	35.4	35.2	34.6	34.9	35.1	35.1	34.9	35.1	35.7	36.6	36.5	35.4
1992	35.0	34.3	34.3	34.0	34.4	34.5	34.4	34.6	34.5	34.4	35.1	35.5	34.5
1993	34.2	34.1	33.7	34.4	34.3	34.3	34.5	34.4	34.4	34.4	34.9	35.9	34.4
1994	33.8	33.3	33.2	33.5	33.8	34.1	34.2	34.4	34.3	33.5	34.3	34.7	33.9
1995	33.6	33.0	33.1	32.9	33.4	34.0	34.9	35.1	35.3	34.6	35.2	35.5	34.2
1996	33.8	33.7	33.9	33.9	34.2	34.6	34.6	35.0	35.0	34.9	35.7	36.0	34.6
1997	35.5	35.2	35.4	34.9	35.2	35.8	35.3	35.3	35.8	35.5	35.5	36.0	35.4
1998	35.3	35.1	35.4	35.0	35.7	36.1	35.5	35.7	35.8	36.3	37.0	37.2	35.8
1999	35.4	34.9	35.5	35.7	36.0	36.4	36.8	37.0	37.4	37.2	37.7	38.3	36.5
2000	36.2	36.2	36.3	36.5	36.9	37.0	37.6	37.8	37.6	37.6	38.3	38.8	37.2
2001	38.3	37.8	38.0	38.1	38.2	38.6	38.4	38.2	38.1	38.6	39.2	39.3	38.4
2002	38.0	37.8	38.1	38.5	38.8	39.1	39.3	39.3	39.4	39.3	39.9	40.4	39.0
2003	38.6	38.7	39.2	39.2	39.5	39.8	40.0	39.9	40.0	40.2	40.6	40.7	39.7
Wholesale trade													
1990	6.3	6.1	6.2	6.1	6.2	6.2	6.4	6.4	6.5	6.7	6.7	6.8	6.3
1991	6.7	6.6	6.3	6.2	6.1	6.1	6.2	6.1	6.1	6.2	6.2	6.1	6.2
1992	6.3	6.1	6.1	5.8	5.9	5.7	5.7	5.7	5.9	5.7	5.8	5.8	5.8
1993	5.8	5.8	5.7	5.7	5.7	5.7	5.8	5.7	5.7	5.8	5.9	6.1	5.7
1994	5.9	5.9	5.9	5.9	5.9	5.8	5.8	5.8	5.6	5.5	5.5	5.5	5.7
1995	5.6	5.6	5.7	5.4	5.5	5.5	5.9	5.9	5.8	5.5	5.6	5.6	5.6
1996	5.6	5.5	5.6	5.6	5.7	5.8	5.8	5.7	5.6	5.5	5.5	5.5	5.6
1997	5.9	6.0	6.1	5.9	5.9	6.0	5.9	5.9	5.8	5.8	5.7	5.7	5.8
1998	5.8	5.9	5.8	5.6	5.6	5.7	5.6	5.6	5.5	5.3	5.3	5.4	5.5
1999	5.4	5.3	5.4	5.4	5.4	5.5	5.6	5.6	5.5	5.5	5.6	5.6	5.4
2000	5.5	5.5	5.5	5.6	5.7	5.7	5.8	5.8	5.7	5.8	5.8	5.8	5.6
2001	5.7	5.7	5.7	5.9	5.9	6.0	5.9	5.9	5.9	6.0	6.0	6.0	5.8
2002	6.0	6.0	6.0	6.0	6.0	6.1	6.3	6.3	6.3	6.2	6.0	6.1	6.1
2003	5.9	5.9	6.0	6.0	6.1	6.2	6.3	6.2	6.2	6.3	6.2	6.2	6.1

Employment by Industry: California—*Continued*

(Numbers in thousands. Not seasonally adjusted.)

Industry	January	February	March	April	May	June	July	August	September	October	November	December	Annual Average
BAKERSFIELD—*Continued*													
Retail trade													
1990	21.1	20.8	20.9	20.7	20.8	20.9	21.3	21.3	21.5	21.4	22.0	22.4	21.2
1991	23.1	22.9	22.9	22.5	22.8	22.8	22.7	22.6	22.7	23.1	24.1	24.1	23.0
1992	22.5	22.1	21.9	21.8	22.1	22.3	22.3	22.4	22.2	22.3	22.9	23.3	22.3
1993	22.1	21.9	21.5	21.9	21.6	21.5	21.8	21.9	21.9	21.8	22.3	23.1	21.9
1994	21.8	21.3	21.2	21.3	21.6	21.7	21.5	21.8	21.8	21.6	22.4	22.9	21.7
1995	21.9	21.3	21.2	21.1	21.2	21.4	22.0	22.1	22.1	22.0	22.8	23.2	21.8
1996	21.7	21.5	21.4	21.5	21.6	21.8	21.8	22.2	22.3	22.1	22.9	23.3	22.0
1997	22.4	22.0	22.1	21.9	22.1	22.3	22.1	22.3	22.5	22.4	22.7	23.2	22.3
1998	22.5	22.0	22.2	21.7	22.2	22.7	22.1	22.2	22.3	22.7	23.4	23.6	22.4
1999	22.6	22.3	22.6	22.1	22.4	22.5	22.7	23.0	23.2	23.0	23.6	24.2	22.8
2000	22.7	22.6	22.7	22.6	22.9	23.0	23.1	23.2	23.2	23.3	24.1	24.6	23.1
2001	24.3	23.9	24.0	24.0	24.0	24.3	24.0	23.8	23.8	24.2	24.8	25.1	24.1
2002	24.0	23.7	24.0	24.4	24.6	24.8	24.5	24.5	24.6	24.6	25.4	25.9	24.6
2003	24.4	24.4	24.5	24.4	24.6	24.7	24.6	24.6	24.7	25.1	25.5	25.7	24.8
Transportation and utilities													
1990	5.3	5.4	5.4	5.4	5.5	5.5	5.7	5.9	5.8	5.8	5.7	5.6	5.5
1991	6.0	5.9	6.0	5.9	6.0	6.2	6.2	6.2	6.3	6.4	6.3	6.3	6.1
1992	6.2	6.1	6.3	6.4	6.4	6.5	6.4	6.5	6.4	6.4	6.4	6.4	6.3
1993	6.3	6.4	6.5	6.8	7.0	7.1	6.9	6.8	6.8	6.8	6.7	6.7	6.7
1994	6.1	6.1	6.1	6.3	6.3	6.6	6.9	6.8	6.9	6.4	6.4	6.3	6.4
1995	6.1	6.1	6.2	6.4	6.7	7.1	7.0	7.1	7.4	7.1	6.8	6.7	6.7
1996	6.5	6.7	6.9	6.8	6.9	7.0	7.0	7.1	7.1	7.3	7.3	7.2	6.9
1997	7.2	7.2	7.2	7.1	7.2	7.5	7.3	7.1	7.5	7.3	7.1	7.1	7.2
1998	7.0	7.2	7.4	7.7	7.9	7.7	7.8	7.9	8.0	8.3	8.3	8.2	7.7
1999	7.4	7.3	7.5	8.2	8.2	8.4	8.5	8.4	8.7	8.7	8.5	8.5	8.1
2000	8.0	8.1	8.1	8.3	8.3	8.3	8.7	8.8	8.7	8.5	8.4	8.4	8.3
2001	8.3	8.2	8.3	8.2	8.3	8.3	8.5	8.5	8.4	8.4	8.4	8.2	8.3
2002	8.0	8.1	8.1	8.1	8.2	8.2	8.5	8.5	8.5	8.5	8.5	8.4	8.3
2003	8.3	8.4	8.7	8.8	8.8	8.9	9.1	9.1	9.1	8.8	8.9	8.8	8.8
Information													
1990	3.2	3.3	3.3	3.4	3.5	3.6	3.7	3.6	3.5	3.7	3.7	3.7	3.5
1991	3.7	3.6	3.6	3.7	3.7	3.7	3.7	3.6	3.6	3.4	3.4	3.4	3.5
1992	3.4	3.4	3.4	3.4	3.3	3.4	3.4	3.4	3.3	3.5	3.6	3.6	3.4
1993	3.4	3.4	3.3	3.3	3.3	3.3	3.3	3.3	3.3	3.1	3.1	3.1	3.2
1994	3.1	3.1	3.1	3.1	3.2	3.2	3.1	3.2	3.1	3.1	3.1	3.1	3.1
1995	3.0	3.0	3.0	2.9	2.9	3.0	2.8	2.8	2.8	2.8	2.7	2.6	2.8
1996	2.4	2.4	2.4	2.3	2.3	2.3	2.4	2.4	2.3	2.3	2.3	2.3	2.3
1997	2.3	2.3	2.4	2.4	2.4	2.5	2.7	2.6	2.6	2.6	2.6	2.6	2.5
1998	2.5	2.5	2.5	2.4	2.4	2.4	2.5	2.5	2.4	2.4	2.5	2.5	2.4
1999	2.5	2.5	2.4	2.4	2.3	2.4	2.5	2.4	2.4	2.4	2.4	2.5	2.4
2000	2.5	2.5	2.5	2.5	2.5	2.5	2.6	2.5	2.5	2.5	2.5	2.5	2.5
2001	2.5	2.5	2.5	2.6	2.6	2.7	2.6	2.5	2.5	2.5	2.5	2.5	2.5
2002	2.6	2.6	2.6	2.6	2.6	2.6	2.5	2.4	2.4	2.5	2.5	2.5	2.5
2003	2.6	2.6	2.6	2.6	2.6	2.6	2.7	2.7	2.6	2.6	2.6	2.6	2.6
Financial activities													
1990	6.8	6.9	6.8	6.7	6.7	6.8	6.9	6.9	6.9	6.8	6.8	6.8	6.8
1991	7.2	7.1	7.1	7.2	7.2	7.2	7.0	7.0	6.9	6.9	6.9	6.9	7.0
1992	6.7	6.7	6.8	6.7	6.6	6.7	6.8	6.8	6.7	6.4	6.5	6.5	6.6
1993	6.2	6.3	6.3	6.3	6.3	6.3	6.3	6.3	6.2	6.1	6.1	6.1	6.2
1994	6.2	6.2	6.2	6.3	6.3	6.3	6.2	6.2	6.2	6.1	6.1	6.2	6.2
1995	6.1	6.1	6.1	6.2	6.1	6.1	6.4	6.3	6.4	6.4	6.5	6.7	6.2
1996	6.7	6.8	6.8	6.8	6.9	6.8	6.8	6.8	6.8	6.8	6.8	6.8	6.8
1997	6.6	6.7	6.8	6.8	6.8	6.9	6.9	7.0	7.0	6.9	6.8	6.9	6.8
1998	7.1	7.2	7.3	7.5	7.6	7.8	7.7	7.8	7.8	7.7	7.6	7.7	7.5
1999	7.7	7.7	7.8	7.6	7.6	7.7	7.7	7.7	7.7	7.5	7.5	7.6	7.6
2000	7.6	7.7	7.7	7.5	7.6	7.5	7.6	7.5	7.5	7.5	7.5	7.6	7.5
2001	7.6	7.6	7.6	7.7	7.7	7.9	7.8	7.8	7.8	7.8	7.8	7.9	7.7
2002	7.7	7.8	7.9	8.0	8.0	8.0	8.0	8.0	8.0	8.0	8.1	8.2	8.0
2003	8.1	8.1	8.2	8.3	8.4	8.4	8.3	8.4	8.3	8.3	8.4	8.3	8.3
Professional and business services													
1990	15.6	15.9	15.7	16.9	17.1	17.3	17.7	17.8	17.9	17.9	17.5	18.0	17.1
1991	17.4	17.4	17.5	17.6	17.5	17.6	17.4	17.5	17.3	17.0	16.8	16.7	17.3
1992	17.2	17.5	17.7	17.5	17.4	17.7	17.3	17.2	17.4	16.6	16.5	16.5	17.2
1993	16.3	16.3	16.5	16.5	16.6	16.7	17.1	16.8	16.8	16.4	16.2	16.3	16.5
1994	16.5	16.5	16.4	16.8	16.7	17.1	17.5	16.9	17.5	17.7	17.5	17.3	17.0
1995	16.9	16.8	16.9	17.2	17.4	17.6	17.7	17.7	17.8	16.8	16.4	16.6	17.1
1996	16.6	16.9	17.1	17.7	17.6	18.2	18.2	17.8	17.8	17.9	18.0	18.0	17.6
1997	17.9	18.1	18.4	19.1	19.1	19.3	19.4	19.4	19.1	19.5	19.7	20.0	19.0
1998	19.3	19.5	19.8	20.1	20.2	20.9	21.7	22.0	22.2	21.9	21.3	21.8	20.8
1999	21.2	21.3	21.7	22.2	22.2	22.4	21.8	21.5	21.6	22.0	22.1	22.6	21.8
2000	22.1	22.1	22.1	21.9	21.9	22.2	22.2	22.5	22.2	22.0	22.4	22.5	22.1
2001	23.1	23.1	23.2	22.7	22.7	23.0	22.6	23.0	22.7	23.2	23.5	23.5	23.0
2002	23.2	23.3	23.4	22.8	22.6	22.6	21.9	22.3	21.9	21.6	21.4	21.3	22.4
2003	20.7	20.7	21.2	21.4	21.5	21.6	21.5	21.8	22.1	22.0	21.9	21.7	21.5

Employment by Industry: California—*Continued*

(Numbers in thousands. Not seasonally adjusted.)

Industry	January	February	March	April	May	June	July	August	September	October	November	December	Annual Average
BAKERSFIELD—*Continued*													
Educational and health services													
1990	12.6	12.7	12.7	12.8	12.8	13.1	13.5	13.3	13.4	13.8	13.8	13.9	13.2
1991	14.1	14.3	14.5	14.2	14.2	14.3	14.3	14.4	14.5	14.7	14.6	14.8	14.4
1992	14.6	14.8	15.0	15.0	15.1	15.4	15.8	15.8	15.9	16.0	16.0	16.1	15.4
1993	15.4	15.5	15.6	15.4	15.5	15.4	14.8	14.9	14.9	14.9	14.8	14.9	15.1
1994	14.6	14.8	14.9	14.9	15.1	15.2	15.2	15.3	15.5	15.7	15.7	15.8	15.2
1995	15.5	15.6	16.0	15.7	15.6	15.4	15.4	15.3	15.5	15.6	15.6	15.7	15.5
1996	15.5	15.6	15.7	15.9	16.0	16.0	15.9	15.9	16.0	16.0	15.9	15.9	15.8
1997	15.8	16.0	16.2	16.0	16.0	16.2	16.2	16.2	16.3	16.4	16.3	16.4	16.1
1998	16.8	17.1	17.3	17.2	17.2	17.4	17.2	17.1	17.1	17.0	17.0	17.1	17.1
1999	17.3	17.3	17.5	18.1	18.1	18.2	18.3	18.4	18.4	18.4	18.6	18.5	18.0
2000	18.6	18.9	19.0	19.1	19.2	19.4	19.5	19.4	19.5	19.2	19.2	19.3	19.1
2001	20.1	20.3	20.3	19.9	19.9	20.0	20.3	20.3	20.3	20.3	20.4	20.5	20.2
2002	20.1	20.3	20.4	20.7	20.9	21.0	20.6	20.8	20.8	20.9	21.0	21.1	20.7
2003	20.9	21.1	21.2	21.3	21.4	21.4	21.4	21.6	21.6	21.5	21.4	21.5	21.4
Leisure and hospitality													
1990	12.6	12.5	12.7	13.4	13.5	13.4	13.6	13.6	13.8	13.5	13.8	13.8	13.3
1991	13.6	13.7	14.0	14.5	14.6	14.6	15.0	14.7	14.8	14.6	14.5	14.6	14.4
1992	13.9	13.9	14.2	14.8	14.9	14.9	14.6	14.5	14.4	14.3	14.2	14.0	14.3
1993	14.0	13.8	13.9	14.4	14.7	14.8	14.6	14.6	14.4	14.3	14.3	14.2	14.3
1994	14.2	14.3	14.6	14.8	15.3	15.6	15.3	15.4	15.2	15.1	15.0	15.0	14.9
1995	14.4	14.5	14.5	15.0	15.4	15.7	15.8	15.8	15.8	15.5	15.3	15.2	15.2
1996	14.8	15.2	15.4	15.6	15.9	16.1	15.9	16.1	16.1	16.0	15.9	15.7	15.7
1997	15.1	15.4	15.6	15.5	15.8	16.3	15.8	15.7	15.6	15.2	14.9	14.8	15.4
1998	15.0	15.1	15.3	15.9	16.3	16.6	16.5	16.1	16.2	15.7	15.9	15.8	15.8
1999	15.6	15.7	16.1	16.3	16.3	16.7	16.8	17.0	17.1	17.2	16.8	16.7	16.5
2000	15.9	16.1	16.2	16.4	16.7	16.9	17.1	16.9	16.7	16.6	16.4	16.4	16.5
2001	16.4	16.5	16.9	17.2	17.5	17.6	17.7	17.6	17.5	17.2	17.3	17.3	17.2
2002	16.8	16.9	17.3	17.6	18.1	18.2	17.9	17.9	17.8	17.7	17.6	17.7	17.6
2003	17.3	17.4	17.9	17.9	18.3	18.1	18.2	18.1	17.9	17.6	17.5	17.5	17.8
Other services													
1990	5.1	5.1	5.2	5.1	5.1	5.3	5.3	5.2	5.2	5.2	5.2	5.1	5.1
1991	5.2	5.2	5.2	5.2	5.3	5.5	5.4	5.4	5.4	5.4	5.3	5.3	5.3
1992	5.2	5.2	5.3	5.4	5.4	5.4	5.4	5.3	5.3	5.2	5.1	5.1	5.2
1993	5.1	5.1	5.1	5.0	5.1	5.2	5.3	5.2	5.2	5.1	5.0	5.0	5.1
1994	5.0	5.0	5.0	5.2	5.3	5.4	5.2	5.2	5.3	5.3	5.4	5.3	5.2
1995	5.1	5.2	5.2	5.5	5.5	5.7	5.6	5.7	5.7	5.6	5.7	5.7	5.5
1996	5.5	5.7	5.8	5.8	5.8	5.9	5.8	6.0	6.0	6.0	5.9	5.9	5.8
1997	5.8	5.9	6.0	6.0	6.1	6.1	6.1	6.0	6.1	6.4	6.2	6.2	6.0
1998	6.2	6.3	6.4	6.5	6.7	6.8	6.8	6.8	6.7	6.6	6.6	6.5	6.5
1999	6.6	6.6	6.7	6.9	6.9	6.9	7.0	6.9	6.9	6.7	6.8	6.8	6.8
2000	6.5	6.5	6.6	6.6	6.6	6.6	6.6	6.9	6.8	6.8	6.7	6.7	6.6
2001	6.5	6.6	6.6	6.8	6.9	6.8	6.9	6.9	7.1	6.9	6.9	6.8	6.8
2002	6.8	6.9	6.9	6.8	7.0	6.8	6.8	6.8	6.7	7.0	7.1	6.9	6.9
2003	6.7	6.8	6.9	6.9	7.0	6.9	6.9	7.0	7.1	7.1	7.1	6.9	6.9
Government													
1990	43.4	44.0	44.5	45.2	45.7	45.2	41.9	40.1	43.0	44.8	45.0	45.7	44.0
1991	44.8	45.6	46.4	46.4	46.7	46.5	42.8	42.1	45.8	46.2	46.8	46.6	45.5
1992	46.0	46.4	46.9	47.0	47.0	46.5	42.8	41.0	44.9	46.0	46.0	46.0	45.5
1993	45.1	45.5	46.0	46.3	46.1	48.1	43.1	42.4	44.6	46.7	47.1	47.4	45.7
1994	46.1	46.2	47.2	47.6	47.5	48.9	44.2	43.4	45.7	47.4	48.3	48.3	46.7
1995	46.9	47.6	48.1	48.3	48.2	49.7	45.0	44.1	45.9	47.6	48.3	48.1	47.3
1996	47.1	47.6	48.3	48.4	48.5	48.1	43.9	43.5	46.4	48.4	48.9	48.7	47.3
1997	48.3	48.5	49.0	49.0	49.5	49.4	45.6	43.7	47.6	49.0	49.8	49.3	48.2
1998	49.4	49.7	49.5	50.0	49.7	50.0	45.7	45.0	47.2	49.4	50.0	50.2	48.8
1999	50.1	50.1	50.8	51.1	50.9	52.8	46.8	46.3	49.1	51.1	52.1	52.2	50.2
2000	51.9	51.9	52.8	52.7	53.3	53.0	46.7	46.0	50.6	53.2	53.9	53.5	51.6
2001	53.2	53.9	54.2	54.6	54.6	55.6	48.4	50.3	52.5	54.8	55.6	55.7	53.6
2002	55.1	55.3	56.5	56.6	56.3	57.1	51.8	51.7	52.9	55.7	56.9	56.8	55.2
2003	56.5	56.1	56.8	56.0	55.6	55.3	51.0	51.0	52.0	53.9	54.7	54.6	54.5
Federal government													
1990	12.2	12.2	12.3	12.7	13.2	13.1	13.0	12.4	12.3	12.2	12.2	12.3	12.5
1991	12.1	12.0	12.1	12.1	12.2	12.4	12.5	12.4	12.4	12.2	12.2	12.1	12.2
1992	12.0	12.0	11.9	12.0	12.0	12.2	12.1	12.0	11.9	11.8	11.8	11.7	11.9
1993	11.5	11.5	11.4	11.5	11.5	11.7	11.8	11.8	11.7	11.7	11.6	11.7	11.6
1994	11.4	11.5	11.3	11.5	11.5	11.5	11.6	11.6	11.6	11.5	11.5	11.5	11.5
1995	11.3	11.3	11.3	11.2	11.3	11.4	11.4	11.4	11.3	11.1	11.0	11.0	11.2
1996	10.6	10.6	10.6	10.6	10.7	10.7	10.8	10.8	10.7	10.5	10.4	10.4	10.6
1997	10.1	10.1	10.1	10.0	10.2	10.3	10.4	10.4	10.3	10.2	10.1	10.1	10.1
1998	9.9	9.7	9.7	9.6	9.6	9.7	9.9	9.9	9.8	9.7	9.7	9.6	9.7
1999	9.6	9.6	9.6	9.8	9.7	9.8	10.0	10.0	9.9	9.7	9.7	9.7	9.7
2000	9.5	9.5	9.8	9.9	10.5	9.8	9.8	9.6	9.5	9.4	9.4	9.4	9.6
2001	9.3	9.3	9.3	9.3	9.4	9.4	9.6	9.6	9.6	9.4	9.4	9.4	9.4
2002	9.3	9.3	9.4	9.4	9.5	9.6	9.8	9.9	9.8	9.8	9.8	9.8	9.6
2003	9.8	9.7	9.8	9.7	9.8	9.8	9.8	9.8	9.8	9.7	9.6	9.6	9.7

Employment by Industry: California—*Continued*

(Numbers in thousands. Not seasonally adjusted.)

Industry	January	February	March	April	May	June	July	August	September	October	November	December	Annual Average
BAKERSFIELD—*Continued*													
State government													
1990	4.0	4.0	4.0	4.0	4.0	4.0	3.9	3.8	3.9	4.0	4.1	4.0	3.9
1991	4.2	4.3	4.4	4.5	4.6	4.6	4.5	4.6	4.7	4.7	4.7	4.6	4.5
1992	4.8	4.8	4.8	4.8	4.8	4.8	4.6	4.6	4.6	4.8	4.8	4.8	4.7
1993	4.8	4.8	5.0	5.1	5.1	5.2	5.2	5.3	5.4	5.5	5.5	5.5	5.2
1994	5.5	5.6	5.6	5.7	5.7	5.7	5.7	5.6	5.7	5.8	6.0	5.9	5.7
1995	5.9	5.9	5.9	5.9	5.9	5.9	5.8	5.7	5.8	5.9	6.0	5.9	5.8
1996	6.0	6.1	6.2	6.2	6.3	6.2	6.1	6.1	6.2	6.3	6.3	6.1	6.1
1997	6.1	6.2	6.2	6.3	6.3	6.4	6.2	6.1	6.3	6.3	6.4	6.2	6.2
1998	6.3	6.5	6.5	6.6	6.6	6.5	6.4	6.3	6.4	6.6	6.6	6.6	6.4
1999	6.6	6.6	6.6	6.6	6.7	6.7	6.6	6.5	6.6	6.8	6.8	6.8	6.6
2000	6.8	6.9	6.9	6.8	6.8	6.9	6.7	6.7	6.8	7.0	7.0	6.9	6.8
2001	7.0	7.1	7.0	7.0	7.1	7.0	6.9	6.9	6.9	7.2	7.1	7.1	7.0
2002	7.1	7.2	7.2	7.2	7.2	7.2	7.0	6.9	6.9	7.2	7.3	7.3	7.1
2003	7.3	7.4	7.4	7.3	7.3	7.4	7.0	7.0	6.9	7.2	7.2	7.2	7.2
Local government													
1990	27.2	27.8	28.2	28.5	28.5	28.1	25.0	23.9	26.8	28.6	28.7	29.4	27.5
1991	28.5	29.3	29.9	29.8	29.9	29.5	25.8	25.1	28.7	29.3	29.9	29.9	28.8
1992	29.2	29.6	30.2	30.2	30.2	29.5	26.1	24.4	28.4	29.4	29.4	29.5	28.8
1993	28.8	29.2	29.6	29.7	29.5	31.2	26.1	25.3	27.5	29.5	30.0	30.2	28.8
1994	29.2	29.1	30.3	30.4	30.3	31.7	26.9	26.2	28.4	30.1	30.8	30.9	29.5
1995	29.7	30.4	30.9	31.2	31.0	32.4	27.8	27.0	28.8	30.6	31.3	31.2	30.1
1996	30.5	30.9	31.5	31.6	31.5	31.2	27.0	26.6	29.5	31.6	32.2	32.2	30.5
1997	32.1	32.2	32.7	32.7	33.0	32.7	29.0	27.2	31.0	32.5	33.3	33.0	31.7
1998	33.2	33.5	33.3	33.8	33.5	33.8	29.4	28.8	31.0	33.1	33.7	34.0	32.5
1999	33.9	33.9	34.6	34.7	34.5	36.3	30.2	29.8	32.6	34.6	35.6	35.7	33.8
2000	35.6	35.5	36.1	36.0	36.0	36.3	30.2	29.7	34.3	36.8	37.5	37.2	35.1
2001	36.9	37.5	37.9	38.3	38.1	39.2	31.9	33.8	36.0	38.2	39.1	39.2	37.1
2002	38.7	38.8	39.9	40.0	39.6	40.3	35.0	34.9	36.2	38.7	39.8	39.7	38.5
2003	39.4	39.0	39.6	39.0	38.5	38.1	34.2	34.2	35.3	37.0	37.9	37.8	37.5
FRESNO													
Total nonfarm													
1990	231.4	234.0	236.0	240.9	242.7	244.6	244.3	246.6	252.6	250.0	248.3	247.9	243.2
1991	243.6	245.0	246.3	248.8	249.6	248.7	245.8	248.1	251.7	250.0	247.5	246.3	247.6
1992	242.0	242.5	245.5	248.4	252.8	250.5	256.1	258.5	259.1	253.4	252.4	252.8	251.1
1993	245.4	248.0	249.7	254.6	255.7	254.5	257.4	259.8	262.4	259.3	257.4	258.4	255.2
1994	249.6	250.4	254.8	256.2	257.6	260.8	261.9	263.8	266.0	262.8	261.6	262.5	259.0
1995	254.6	257.9	260.3	262.9	265.9	268.8	270.0	272.7	275.8	272.2	271.4	270.5	266.9
1996	262.7	263.7	265.8	268.4	272.0	273.1	275.3	277.0	277.6	272.1	271.2	270.4	270.7
1997	263.6	267.4	269.2	271.9	275.4	275.7	279.2	280.8	280.7	277.3	275.1	275.1	274.2
1998	267.5	268.4	271.5	273.9	277.4	280.0	280.7	285.5	287.5	285.2	284.8	285.6	279.0
1999	274.9	276.6	280.3	284.1	287.4	292.4	294.4	295.6	295.6	295.0	294.4	294.7	288.7
2000	287.9	291.3	293.7	295.3	298.5	299.2	300.1	300.4	302.3	302.0	302.2	302.6	297.9
2001	295.2	297.5	300.2	301.7	304.0	305.8	306.1	308.4	306.6	306.3	307.2	306.9	303.8
2002	299.5	302.9	305.9	308.9	312.7	313.9	312.9	316.0	316.5	316.1	316.8	315.4	311.5
2003	306.7	308.8	311.7	314.1	317.5	320.7	316.8	317.1	316.6	316.8	316.4	315.2	314.9
Total private													
1990	177.2	179.5	180.4	183.7	185.6	188.5	192.3	194.4	196.7	192.7	191.0	190.9	187.7
1991	187.4	186.9	187.1	188.9	189.9	190.2	192.6	194.5	195.0	192.3	190.1	189.2	190.3
1992	185.7	184.9	187.1	189.3	192.8	194.0	201.5	203.8	201.1	194.7	193.9	194.2	193.5
1993	186.8	188.4	189.7	193.9	195.3	197.0	202.0	204.3	203.6	199.0	197.2	198.0	196.2
1994	189.9	189.6	193.3	194.5	195.7	199.7	204.3	206.5	205.9	201.3	200.0	200.9	198.4
1995	192.6	194.5	195.9	198.1	200.9	204.3	208.9	211.5	212.5	206.6	206.1	205.7	203.1
1996	198.1	198.2	199.7	202.2	205.3	207.5	212.5	214.9	212.8	207.2	206.8	206.0	205.9
1997	199.6	201.8	203.1	205.6	208.7	209.9	216.1	218.5	216.6	211.1	209.3	209.7	209.1
1998	202.6	202.7	204.9	206.8	210.0	213.1	217.0	222.1	222.0	217.5	217.1	217.4	212.7
1999	207.9	208.3	211.0	214.1	217.1	223.1	227.1	229.3	227.5	223.6	223.2	223.8	219.6
2000	216.9	218.6	220.1	221.5	223.5	226.9	229.5	231.2	230.9	227.9	227.9	228.6	225.2
2001	221.5	223.1	224.8	225.6	228.4	229.8	232.7	235.8	233.2	230.7	230.3	230.7	228.8
2002	223.5	225.5	227.5	229.8	232.9	234.7	237.2	240.9	240.5	237.3	237.8	237.2	233.7
2003	229.5	229.8	232.3	234.5	238.0	240.7	239.9	241.3	240.9	238.5	238.4	237.8	236.8
Goods-producing													
1990	40.0	41.0	41.9	43.6	44.5	45.3	46.2	47.6	48.6	47.7	45.2	44.2	44.6
1991	42.5	42.2	41.6	42.5	42.9	43.6	45.1	46.7	47.1	44.7	42.8	41.6	43.6
1992	39.0	38.5	39.5	39.6	40.4	40.9	43.1	44.6	44.2	41.5	40.4	39.7	40.9
1993	36.4	37.2	37.9	39.3	40.1	41.1	42.5	44.7	44.4	42.3	41.3	40.5	40.6
1994	38.2	37.8	39.2	39.1	39.6	41.1	42.3	43.8	43.7	41.4	39.7	39.3	40.4
1995	37.1	37.9	38.3	39.1	40.1	41.2	44.1	45.2	45.0	42.6	42.0	40.8	41.1
1996	38.5	38.3	38.7	39.4	41.0	41.3	44.6	46.0	45.2	42.2	41.3	40.3	41.4
1997	38.9	39.7	40.1	41.8	42.8	42.8	46.3	47.8	47.4	44.2	43.1	42.5	43.1
1998	40.3	40.1	41.3	42.2	43.6	44.9	47.4	48.5	48.9	48.2	47.2	47.0	44.9
1999	43.1	43.2	43.7	45.1	46.1	46.8	48.7	49.8	50.0	49.3	48.2	47.5	46.7
2000	44.9	45.0	44.9	45.3	45.9	47.3	50.6	51.1	50.4	48.5	48.1	47.5	47.4
2001	45.9	46.1	46.5	46.7	47.8	48.1	50.2	52.1	51.2	49.0	47.2	47.1	48.2
2002	45.5	45.8	46.4	46.8	48.4	49.0	50.4	53.0	53.2	50.2	49.5	48.6	48.9
2003	47.4	47.5	48.4	48.6	50.5	51.7	52.0	52.9	52.7	50.5	48.9	48.2	49.9

Employment by Industry: California—*Continued*

(Numbers in thousands. Not seasonally adjusted.)

Industry	January	February	March	April	May	June	July	August	September	October	November	December	Annual Average
FRESNO—*Continued*													
Natural resources and mining													
1990	0.8	0.8	0.8	0.9	0.9	1.0	1.0	0.9	1.0	1.0	1.0	0.9	0.9
1991	0.9	0.9	0.8	0.9	0.9	0.9	0.9	0.9	0.9	0.9	0.9	0.8	0.8
1992	0.7	0.7	0.7	0.8	0.8	0.8	0.8	0.8	0.8	0.8	0.8	0.7	0.7
1993	0.6	0.7	0.6	0.6	0.7	0.7	0.7	0.7	0.7	0.7	0.6	0.6	0.6
1994	0.6	0.6	0.6	0.6	0.6	0.6	0.6	0.6	0.6	0.7	0.6	0.6	0.6
1995	0.6	0.6	0.6	0.6	0.6	0.7	0.7	0.7	0.7	0.7	0.7	0.7	0.6
1996	0.6	0.6	0.6	0.6	0.6	0.6	0.6	0.6	0.6	0.6	0.6	0.5	0.5
1997	0.6	0.6	0.6	0.6	0.6	0.6	0.6	0.6	0.7	0.6	0.6	0.5	0.6
1998	0.5	0.5	0.5	0.4	0.4	0.4	0.4	0.4	0.4	0.4	0.4	0.4	0.4
1999	0.4	0.3	0.3	0.4	0.4	0.4	0.4	0.5	0.5	0.5	0.5	0.5	0.4
2000	0.4	0.4	0.4	0.4	0.5	0.5	0.5	0.5	0.5	0.5	0.5	0.4	0.4
2001	0.4	0.4	0.4	0.4	0.4	0.5	0.5	0.5	0.5	0.5	0.4	0.4	0.4
2002	0.4	0.4	0.3	0.4	0.4	0.4	0.3	0.4	0.4	0.3	0.4	0.3	0.4
2003	0.3	0.2	0.2	0.2	0.3	0.3	0.3	0.3	0.3	0.3	0.3	0.3	0.3
Construction													
1990	14.0	14.2	15.0	15.6	16.0	16.6	17.1	17.1	17.0	17.1	16.6	16.4	16.0
1991	15.0	15.2	15.0	15.4	15.7	16.0	15.9	15.9	15.5	14.9	14.7	14.4	15.3
1992	12.6	12.3	13.1	13.3	13.8	14.0	13.9	13.9	13.8	13.4	13.1	13.1	13.3
1993	11.3	11.7	12.4	13.0	13.3	13.6	13.5	13.7	13.6	13.6	13.4	13.2	13.0
1994	12.4	12.2	12.9	13.1	13.1	13.6	13.4	13.6	13.4	12.9	12.5	12.4	12.9
1995	10.9	11.5	11.8	12.7	13.0	13.7	13.7	13.8	13.8	13.7	13.6	13.2	12.9
1996	12.2	12.0	12.3	12.7	13.3	13.7	13.4	13.7	13.3	13.0	12.8	12.2	12.8
1997	11.6	12.1	12.5	12.9	13.0	13.3	14.0	14.3	14.1	13.4	13.2	13.1	13.1
1998	12.4	11.8	12.9	13.2	14.1	14.7	15.4	15.9	15.7	16.1	15.8	15.7	14.4
1999	14.6	14.6	15.2	15.8	16.0	16.4	16.8	16.7	16.8	16.8	16.7	16.7	16.0
2000	15.4	15.3	15.4	15.9	16.2	16.9	17.1	17.3	17.6	16.9	17.1	17.1	16.5
2001	16.1	16.3	16.6	17.0	17.6	18.2	18.0	18.4	18.1	18.2	17.8	17.8	17.5
2002	17.5	17.7	18.1	18.4	18.8	18.8	18.9	19.1	18.8	18.8	19.0	18.8	18.6
2003	18.5	18.6	19.2	19.4	20.0	20.8	20.8	21.0	20.7	20.5	20.5	20.4	20.0
Manufacturing													
1990	25.2	26.0	26.1	27.1	27.6	27.7	28.1	29.6	30.6	29.6	27.6	26.9	27.6
1991	26.6	26.1	25.8	26.2	26.3	26.7	28.3	29.9	30.7	28.9	27.2	26.4	27.4
1992	25.7	25.5	25.7	25.5	25.8	26.1	28.4	29.9	29.6	27.3	26.5	25.9	26.8
1993	24.5	24.8	24.9	25.7	26.1	26.8	28.3	30.3	30.1	28.0	27.3	26.7	26.9
1994	25.2	25.0	25.7	25.4	25.9	26.9	28.3	29.6	29.7	27.8	26.6	26.3	26.8
1995	25.6	25.8	25.9	25.8	26.5	26.8	29.7	30.7	30.5	28.2	27.7	26.9	27.5
1996	25.7	25.7	25.8	26.1	27.1	27.0	30.6	31.7	31.3	28.6	27.9	27.6	27.9
1997	26.7	27.0	27.0	28.3	29.2	28.9	31.7	32.9	32.6	30.2	29.3	28.9	29.3
1998	27.4	27.8	27.9	28.6	29.1	29.8	31.6	32.2	32.8	31.7	31.0	30.9	30.0
1999	28.1	28.3	28.2	28.9	29.7	30.0	31.5	32.6	32.7	32.0	31.0	30.3	30.2
2000	29.1	29.3	29.1	29.0	29.2	29.9	33.0	33.3	32.3	31.1	30.5	30.0	30.4
2001	29.4	29.4	29.5	29.3	29.8	29.4	31.7	33.2	32.6	30.3	29.0	28.9	30.2
2002	27.6	27.7	28.0	28.0	29.2	29.8	31.2	33.5	34.0	31.1	30.1	29.5	30.0
2003	28.6	28.7	29.0	29.0	30.2	30.6	30.9	31.6	31.7	29.7	28.1	27.5	29.6
Service-providing													
1990	191.4	193.0	194.1	197.3	198.2	199.3	198.1	199.0	204.0	202.3	203.1	203.7	198.6
1991	201.1	202.8	204.7	206.3	206.7	205.1	200.7	201.4	204.6	205.3	204.7	204.7	204.0
1992	203.0	204.0	206.0	208.8	212.4	209.6	213.0	213.9	214.9	211.9	212.0	213.1	210.2
1993	209.0	210.8	211.8	215.3	215.6	213.4	214.9	215.1	218.0	217.0	216.1	217.9	214.5
1994	211.4	212.6	215.6	217.1	218.0	219.7	219.6	220.0	222.3	221.4	221.9	223.2	218.5
1995	217.5	220.0	222.0	223.8	225.8	227.6	225.9	227.5	230.8	229.6	229.4	229.7	225.8
1996	224.2	225.4	227.1	229.0	231.0	231.8	230.7	231.0	232.4	229.9	229.9	230.1	229.3
1997	224.7	227.7	229.1	230.1	232.6	232.9	232.9	233.0	233.3	233.1	232.0	232.6	231.1
1998	227.2	228.3	230.2	231.7	233.8	235.1	233.3	237.0	238.6	237.0	237.6	238.6	234.0
1999	231.8	233.4	236.6	239.0	241.3	245.6	245.7	245.8	245.6	245.7	246.2	247.2	241.9
2000	243.0	246.3	248.8	250.0	252.6	251.9	249.5	249.3	251.9	253.5	254.1	255.1	250.5
2001	249.3	251.4	253.7	255.0	256.2	257.7	255.9	256.3	255.4	257.3	260.0	259.8	255.6
2002	254.0	257.1	259.5	262.1	264.3	264.9	262.5	263.0	263.3	265.9	267.3	266.8	262.6
2003	259.3	261.3	263.3	265.5	267.0	269.0	264.8	264.2	263.9	266.3	267.5	267.0	264.9
Trade, transportation, and utilities													
1990	50.5	50.6	50.2	51.5	52.0	52.5	53.0	52.8	52.9	52.6	54.0	54.7	52.2
1991	52.2	51.2	51.5	51.9	51.9	51.8	52.9	52.9	52.5	52.6	53.4	53.0	52.3
1992	51.8	50.9	51.4	52.7	53.9	54.4	55.1	54.6	54.9	54.9	55.5	55.6	53.8
1993	53.2	53.2	53.0	54.1	54.1	54.7	55.3	55.9	55.5	55.1	55.5	56.1	54.6
1994	53.1	52.6	53.4	53.9	54.4	55.6	56.5	56.9	57.0	56.4	57.3	57.4	55.3
1995	54.4	54.3	54.4	54.9	55.2	55.7	56.2	56.3	56.5	55.9	56.8	56.9	55.6
1996	54.9	54.1	54.0	54.5	55.2	55.5	56.4	56.7	56.2	55.4	56.3	56.4	55.4
1997	54.1	54.7	54.6	54.1	54.7	55.0	56.0	56.2	56.3	55.6	56.4	56.7	55.3
1998	53.9	52.8	53.3	54.0	54.4	55.2	55.0	56.5	56.9	56.3	57.4	57.9	55.3
1999	54.6	53.8	54.6	54.5	55.2	55.9	56.8	56.9	57.1	57.0	58.1	58.8	56.1
2000	55.7	55.6	56.0	55.9	56.6	57.3	57.6	58.1	58.3	58.1	59.3	59.8	57.3
2001	56.9	56.6	57.1	57.4	57.9	58.2	58.6	59.2	59.1	59.2	60.1	60.3	58.3
2002	57.4	57.2	57.3	58.0	58.1	59.1	59.8	60.3	60.4	60.8	62.1	62.4	59.4
2003	59.1	58.6	59.0	60.0	60.6	61.5	61.9	62.3	62.3	62.7	63.6	63.8	61.3

Employment by Industry: California—*Continued*

(Numbers in thousands. Not seasonally adjusted.)

Industry	January	February	March	April	May	June	July	August	September	October	November	December	Annual Average
FRESNO—*Continued*													
Wholesale trade													
1990	11.9	12.0	11.9	12.2	12.5	12.6	12.8	12.7	12.7	12.4	12.5	12.5	12.3
1991	12.2	11.9	12.1	11.9	12.2	12.0	12.3	12.4	12.3	12.1	11.9	11.8	12.0
1992	11.9	11.9	12.1	12.3	12.7	12.7	12.9	12.8	12.7	12.6	12.3	12.4	12.4
1993	12.4	12.5	12.6	12.5	12.8	12.7	13.2	13.1	13.0	12.8	12.5	12.7	12.7
1994	12.3	12.1	12.4	12.8	12.8	13.2	13.0	13.0	13.0	12.5	12.5	12.6	12.6
1995	12.4	12.5	12.6	12.6	12.6	13.0	13.0	12.8	12.6	12.3	12.2	12.1	12.5
1996	11.9	11.8	11.7	11.6	11.9	12.0	11.9	11.9	11.6	12.0	11.8	11.7	11.8
1997	11.7	11.9	12.1	11.8	12.0	12.2	12.6	12.5	12.1	11.8	11.7	11.5	11.9
1998	11.8	11.7	11.9	12.2	12.3	12.6	12.5	12.8	12.7	12.5	12.7	12.4	12.3
1999	12.2	12.1	12.4	12.2	12.3	12.7	13.0	12.9	12.6	12.8	12.8	12.6	12.5
2000	12.2	12.3	12.4	12.6	12.7	12.8	12.9	13.0	12.8	12.6	12.6	12.6	12.6
2001	12.2	12.3	12.4	12.6	12.6	12.7	13.0	13.2	12.9	12.7	12.5	12.4	12.6
2002	12.4	12.4	12.5	12.9	12.9	13.3	13.4	13.5	13.4	13.6	13.5	13.5	13.1
2003	12.9	12.8	13.0	13.3	13.5	13.7	14.0	14.1	14.1	14.0	13.9	13.8	13.6
Retail trade													
1990	29.8	29.6	29.6	30.3	30.6	30.8	31.0	30.7	30.9	31.3	32.5	33.2	30.8
1991	31.0	30.4	30.5	30.8	30.7	30.7	31.1	30.9	30.5	30.5	31.4	31.8	30.8
1992	31.2	30.3	30.5	31.2	31.7	32.2	32.3	31.8	31.9	31.9	32.7	33.4	31.7
1993	31.8	31.5	31.1	31.8	31.5	31.9	31.8	32.0	31.7	31.8	32.7	33.4	31.9
1994	31.3	30.9	31.0	31.0	31.4	31.9	32.7	33.0	33.1	33.2	34.3	34.7	32.3
1995	32.8	32.5	32.2	32.4	32.5	32.6	33.1	33.2	33.4	33.9	34.8	35.1	33.2
1996	33.4	32.7	32.6	32.9	33.1	33.3	33.9	33.9	33.7	33.6	35.0	35.2	33.6
1997	33.1	33.3	33.0	32.7	33.1	33.0	33.2	33.6	33.8	34.1	35.1	35.6	33.6
1998	33.5	32.6	32.6	32.9	33.1	33.1	33.2	33.8	34.1	34.1	35.2	36.0	33.6
1999	33.3	32.8	33.2	33.3	33.7	33.8	33.9	33.8	34.3	34.6	36.0	36.7	34.1
2000	34.2	34.2	34.4	34.0	34.4	34.9	34.8	35.0	35.3	35.5	36.8	37.4	35.0
2001	35.1	34.8	35.0	35.1	35.4	35.6	35.4	35.6	35.8	36.1	37.4	37.8	35.7
2002	35.4	35.2	35.2	35.2	35.4	35.8	35.9	36.1	36.2	36.5	37.9	38.4	36.1
2003	36.3	35.9	36.0	36.4	36.6	37.2	37.3	37.5	37.6	38.0	39.2	39.6	37.3
Transportation and utilities													
1990	8.8	9.0	8.7	9.0	8.9	9.1	9.2	9.4	9.3	8.9	9.0	9.0	9.0
1991	9.0	8.9	8.9	9.2	9.0	9.1	9.5	9.6	9.7	10.0	10.1	9.4	9.3
1992	8.7	8.7	8.8	9.2	9.5	9.5	9.9	10.0	10.3	10.4	10.5	9.8	9.6
1993	9.0	9.2	9.3	9.8	9.8	10.1	10.3	10.8	10.8	10.5	10.3	10.0	9.9
1994	9.5	9.6	10.0	10.1	10.2	10.5	10.8	10.9	10.9	10.7	10.5	10.1	10.3
1995	9.2	9.3	9.6	9.9	10.1	10.1	10.1	10.3	10.5	9.7	9.8	9.7	9.8
1996	9.6	9.6	9.7	10.0	10.2	10.2	10.6	10.9	10.9	9.8	9.5	9.5	10.0
1997	9.3	9.5	9.5	9.6	9.6	9.8	10.2	10.1	10.4	9.7	9.6	9.6	9.7
1998	8.6	8.5	8.8	8.9	9.0	9.5	9.3	9.9	10.1	9.7	9.5	9.5	9.2
1999	9.1	8.9	9.0	9.0	9.2	9.4	9.9	10.2	10.2	9.6	9.3	9.5	9.4
2000	9.3	9.1	9.2	9.3	9.5	9.6	9.9	10.1	10.2	10.0	9.9	9.8	9.6
2001	9.6	9.5	9.7	9.7	9.9	9.9	10.2	10.4	10.4	10.4	10.2	10.1	9.9
2002	9.6	9.6	9.6	9.9	9.8	10.0	10.5	10.7	10.8	10.7	10.7	10.5	10.2
2003	9.9	9.9	10.0	10.3	10.5	10.6	10.6	10.7	10.6	10.7	10.5	10.4	10.4
Information													
1990	5.0	5.0	5.0	4.9	5.0	5.0	5.0	5.0	5.0	5.1	5.1	5.2	5.0
1991	5.1	5.1	5.2	5.2	5.2	5.1	5.1	5.1	5.1	5.1	5.0	5.0	5.1
1992	5.2	5.2	5.2	5.2	5.3	5.3	5.3	5.2	5.3	5.2	5.3	5.4	5.2
1993	5.4	5.4	5.4	5.3	5.2	5.3	5.2	5.2	5.2	5.1	5.1	5.2	5.2
1994	5.2	5.1	5.2	5.2	5.2	5.2	5.3	5.3	5.2	5.2	5.3	5.3	5.2
1995	5.2	5.2	5.3	5.2	5.3	5.3	5.3	5.3	5.4	5.3	5.3	5.3	5.2
1996	5.5	5.5	5.6	5.1	5.1	5.1	5.4	5.3	5.2	5.4	5.4	5.4	5.3
1997	5.3	5.4	5.4	5.4	5.6	5.6	5.7	5.6	5.5	5.6	5.5	5.6	5.5
1998	5.7	5.6	5.5	5.3	5.5	5.6	5.7	5.6	5.6	5.7	5.6	5.6	5.5
1999	5.5	5.5	5.4	5.4	5.4	5.4	5.6	5.6	5.4	5.6	5.7	5.8	5.5
2000	5.4	5.5	5.5	5.5	5.5	5.6	5.7	5.7	5.7	5.7	5.7	5.7	5.6
2001	6.1	6.0	6.0	5.7	5.7	5.6	5.7	5.6	5.5	5.3	5.4	5.4	5.6
2002	5.5	5.4	5.5	5.4	5.3	5.3	5.2	5.2	5.1	5.2	5.2	5.1	5.3
2003	4.6	4.6	4.6	4.6	4.6	4.6	4.7	4.8	4.7	4.7	4.8	4.8	4.7
Financial activities													
1990	12.8	12.9	12.9	13.2	13.1	13.3	13.3	13.4	13.5	13.6	13.5	13.5	13.2
1991	13.8	13.7	13.8	13.4	13.4	13.3	13.2	13.2	13.1	13.1	13.0	13.1	13.3
1992	13.3	13.4	13.5	13.3	13.4	13.3	13.3	13.5	13.4	13.2	13.2	13.4	13.3
1993	13.4	13.4	13.6	13.7	13.7	13.8	13.7	13.6	13.6	13.6	13.6	13.8	13.6
1994	13.4	13.4	13.4	13.2	13.2	13.3	13.4	13.4	13.3	13.3	13.5	13.6	13.3
1995	13.4	13.4	13.5	13.5	13.7	13.9	13.4	13.4	13.5	13.5	13.5	13.6	13.5
1996	13.3	13.3	13.3	13.4	13.2	13.4	13.3	13.5	13.4	13.5	13.5	13.5	13.3
1997	13.1	13.2	13.3	13.2	13.3	13.4	13.6	13.6	13.4	13.5	13.5	13.6	13.3
1998	12.9	12.9	13.0	13.0	13.0	13.2	13.1	13.5	13.4	13.5	13.5	13.7	13.2
1999	13.4	13.4	13.5	13.7	13.8	13.8	13.9	13.8	13.9	13.9	13.9	13.9	13.7
2000	14.1	14.3	14.3	13.9	13.9	14.2	14.1	14.1	14.2	14.1	14.1	14.3	14.1
2001	14.5	14.7	14.8	14.8	14.9	15.0	15.1	15.0	14.9	14.6	14.6	14.7	14.8
2002	14.4	14.4	14.5	14.9	15.0	15.0	15.2	15.3	15.1	14.8	14.9	14.9	14.9
2003	14.5	14.5	14.5	14.9	15.0	15.1	15.1	15.2	15.0	14.9	14.9	14.9	14.9

Employment by Industry: California—*Continued*

(Numbers in thousands. Not seasonally adjusted.)

Industry	January	February	March	April	May	June	July	August	September	October	November	December	Annual Average
FRESNO—*Continued*													
Professional and business services													
1990	16.7	16.7	16.7	16.9	17.0	17.2	17.9	18.1	18.1	18.1	18.3	18.2	17.4
1991	18.3	18.4	18.4	18.9	19.1	19.1	19.3	19.5	19.1	19.1	18.8	18.7	18.8
1992	19.1	19.1	19.3	19.9	20.1	20.4	20.8	20.8	20.5	20.2	20.2	20.3	20.0
1993	20.2	20.0	20.1	21.0	21.3	21.2	21.5	21.3	21.2	21.1	20.6	20.9	20.8
1994	20.3	20.7	21.0	21.5	21.6	22.2	22.3	22.3	22.1	22.1	22.0	22.6	21.7
1995	21.9	22.2	22.2	22.6	22.8	23.4	23.1	23.3	23.7	23.8	23.5	23.8	23.0
1996	22.5	22.7	22.9	23.1	23.3	23.8	22.9	23.0	22.8	22.8	22.5	22.2	22.8
1997	22.0	22.4	22.6	23.6	23.8	24.1	24.5	24.6	24.3	24.4	24.1	24.6	23.7
1998	24.1	24.4	24.3	25.0	25.0	25.6	25.0	25.8	25.9	25.6	25.4	25.5	25.1
1999	25.0	25.2	25.4	26.0	26.0	26.3	26.1	26.5	26.3	26.2	26.3	26.6	25.9
2000	26.8	26.9	27.1	28.4	28.2	28.5	27.6	27.8	27.9	28.1	27.6	28.0	27.7
2001	25.6	25.7	25.6	25.6	25.7	26.3	25.6	25.8	25.5	26.0	26.0	26.2	25.8
2002	26.2	26.7	26.7	27.3	27.5	27.6	27.4	27.8	27.6	28.1	28.1	28.1	27.4
2003	27.9	27.8	28.1	28.1	28.2	28.2	27.6	27.5	27.6	27.6	28.0	27.9	27.9
Educational and health services													
1990	24.6	25.1	25.2	25.0	24.8	25.8	26.8	27.5	28.1	26.0	25.6	25.7	25.8
1991	26.9	27.1	27.1	27.5	27.3	27.1	26.9	26.9	27.2	27.5	27.3	27.5	27.1
1992	27.8	27.8	28.0	27.9	28.1	28.1	31.7	33.0	30.2	28.3	28.2	28.4	28.9
1993	28.2	28.6	28.6	29.0	28.8	28.8	31.6	31.3	31.3	30.2	29.7	30.1	29.6
1994	28.9	29.1	29.2	29.1	29.2	29.3	31.5	31.7	31.0	30.3	29.8	30.0	29.9
1995	29.4	30.0	30.1	30.0	30.3	30.7	32.3	33.2	33.6	32.2	31.4	31.5	31.2
1996	30.8	31.1	31.3	31.5	31.8	32.3	34.4	34.8	34.5	33.8	33.7	34.1	32.8
1997	33.4	32.3	32.6	32.4	32.7	32.7	34.1	34.5	33.9	32.6	32.2	32.4	32.9
1998	31.9	32.4	32.7	32.5	32.7	32.5	34.6	35.5	34.6	33.5	33.2	33.1	33.2
1999	32.5	32.9	33.3	33.9	34.0	37.6	37.6	38.6	36.7	34.9	34.3	34.3	35.0
2000	34.0	34.6	34.8	34.9	34.9	35.1	34.8	34.9	35.5	35.5	35.6	35.8	35.0
2001	35.4	35.9	36.2	36.8	36.8	36.7	36.9	37.2	37.6	37.6	38.0	38.0	36.9
2002	37.0	37.7	38.2	38.5	38.6	38.5	38.8	38.8	39.4	39.6	39.9	39.9	38.7
2003	39.3	39.6	40.0	40.3	40.0	39.9	39.8	39.9	40.4	40.5	40.6	40.7	40.1
Leisure and hospitality													
1990	18.2	18.3	18.6	19.0	19.4	19.9	20.1	20.0	20.2	19.4	19.2	19.2	19.2
1991	19.0	19.3	19.6	19.7	20.2	20.6	20.4	20.4	20.5	20.0	19.8	19.9	19.9
1992	19.7	20.0	20.2	20.5	21.3	21.5	21.9	21.8	21.9	21.1	20.7	21.2	20.9
1993	20.3	20.6	21.0	21.4	21.9	22.2	22.1	22.2	22.0	21.5	21.1	21.2	21.4
1994	20.8	20.9	21.7	22.2	22.3	22.9	22.7	22.8	23.0	22.1	21.9	22.2	22.1
1995	21.1	21.3	21.8	22.4	23.0	23.8	24.2	24.1	23.9	22.5	22.7	23.0	22.8
1996	22.1	22.5	23.1	24.4	24.8	25.0	24.9	24.8	24.6	23.7	23.6	23.7	23.9
1997	22.9	23.7	24.0	24.6	25.2	25.6	25.7	25.7	25.2	24.6	24.0	23.9	24.5
1998	23.7	24.1	24.2	24.0	24.8	25.3	25.8	26.0	25.8	23.8	24.0	23.8	24.6
1999	23.6	23.7	24.3	24.5	25.6	26.2	27.7	27.1	26.9	25.6	25.3	25.8	25.5
2000	25.4	25.7	26.2	26.4	27.2	27.8	28.2	28.2	27.4	26.7	26.3	26.2	26.8
2001	25.6	26.1	26.6	26.6	27.3	27.8	28.4	28.1	27.1	26.8	26.7	26.7	26.9
2002	25.9	26.1	26.5	26.2	27.1	27.6	27.7	27.4	26.8	26.2	25.8	25.7	26.6
2003	24.8	25.2	25.5	25.8	26.7	27.3	27.1	26.9	26.3	25.8	25.8	25.6	26.1
Other services													
1990	9.4	9.9	9.9	9.6	9.8	9.5	10.0	10.0	10.3	10.2	10.1	10.2	9.9
1991	9.6	9.9	9.9	9.8	9.9	9.6	9.7	9.8	10.4	10.2	10.0	10.4	9.9
1992	9.8	10.0	10.0	10.2	10.3	10.1	10.3	10.3	10.7	10.3	10.4	10.2	10.2
1993	9.7	10.0	10.1	10.1	10.2	9.9	10.1	10.1	10.4	10.1	10.3	10.2	10.1
1994	10.0	10.0	10.2	10.3	10.2	10.1	10.3	10.3	10.6	10.5	10.5	10.5	10.2
1995	10.1	10.2	10.3	10.4	10.5	10.3	10.3	10.7	10.9	10.8	10.9	10.8	10.5
1996	10.5	10.7	10.8	10.8	10.9	11.1	10.6	10.8	10.9	10.4	10.5	10.4	10.7
1997	9.9	10.4	10.5	10.5	10.6	10.7	10.2	10.5	10.6	10.6	10.5	10.4	10.4
1998	10.1	10.4	10.6	10.8	11.0	10.8	10.4	10.7	10.9	10.9	10.8	10.8	10.6
1999	10.2	10.6	10.8	11.0	11.0	11.1	10.7	11.0	11.2	11.1	11.4	11.1	10.9
2000	10.6	11.0	11.3	11.2	11.3	11.1	10.9	11.3	11.5	11.2	11.2	11.3	11.1
2001	11.1	11.6	11.6	12.0	12.3	12.1	12.2	12.8	12.3	12.2	12.3	12.3	12.0
2002	11.6	12.2	12.4	12.7	12.9	12.6	12.7	13.1	12.9	12.4	12.3	12.5	12.5
2003	11.9	12.0	12.2	12.2	12.4	12.4	11.7	11.8	11.9	11.8	11.8	11.9	12.0
Government													
1990	54.2	54.5	55.6	57.2	57.1	56.1	52.0	52.2	55.9	57.3	57.3	57.0	55.5
1991	56.2	58.1	59.2	59.9	59.7	58.5	53.2	53.6	56.7	57.7	57.4	57.1	57.2
1992	56.3	57.6	58.4	59.1	60.0	56.5	54.6	54.7	58.0	58.7	58.5	58.6	57.5
1993	58.6	59.6	60.0	60.7	60.4	57.5	55.4	55.5	58.8	60.3	60.2	60.4	58.9
1994	59.7	60.8	61.5	61.7	61.9	61.1	57.6	57.3	60.1	61.5	61.6	61.6	60.5
1995	62.0	63.4	64.4	64.8	65.0	64.5	61.1	61.2	63.3	65.6	65.3	64.8	63.7
1996	64.6	65.5	66.1	66.2	66.7	65.6	62.8	62.1	64.8	64.9	64.4	64.4	64.8
1997	64.0	65.6	66.1	66.3	66.7	65.8	63.1	62.3	64.1	66.2	65.8	65.4	65.1
1998	64.9	65.7	66.6	67.1	67.4	66.9	63.7	63.4	65.5	67.7	67.7	68.2	66.2
1999	67.0	68.3	69.3	70.0	70.3	69.3	67.3	66.3	68.1	71.4	71.2	70.9	69.1
2000	71.0	72.7	73.6	73.8	75.0	72.3	70.6	69.2	71.4	74.1	74.3	74.0	72.6
2001	74.1	74.8	75.8	76.1	75.6	76.0	73.4	72.6	73.4	75.6	76.9	76.2	75.0
2002	76.0	77.4	78.4	79.1	79.8	79.2	75.7	75.1	76.0	78.8	79.0	78.2	77.7
2003	77.2	79.0	79.4	79.6	79.5	80.0	76.9	75.8	75.7	78.3	78.0	77.4	78.1

Employment by Industry: California—*Continued*

(Numbers in thousands. Not seasonally adjusted.)

Industry	January	February	March	April	May	June	July	August	September	October	November	December	Annual Average
FRESNO—*Continued*													
Federal government													
1990	9.5	9.9	10.6	11.5	11.0	11.0	10.6	10.3	10.0	10.2	10.1	10.0	10.3
1991	10.0	10.8	11.5	11.8	11.5	11.1	10.7	10.9	10.7	10.6	10.3	10.3	10.8
1992	10.2	10.6	11.1	11.7	12.3	12.2	12.4	12.1	12.1	12.1	11.7	11.7	11.6
1993	12.0	12.1	12.2	12.3	12.2	12.2	12.1	12.0	11.9	12.0	11.7	12.0	12.0
1994	11.9	12.2	12.1	12.2	12.0	11.8	11.8	11.7	11.7	11.5	11.1	11.1	11.7
1995	11.5	11.9	12.2	12.3	12.2	12.0	12.0	11.9	12.0	12.1	11.8	11.7	11.9
1996	12.1	11.9	12.0	12.4	12.4	11.9	12.0	11.6	11.5	11.5	11.3	11.3	11.8
1997	11.4	11.7	11.8	12.0	11.7	11.5	11.4	11.1	11.2	11.1	11.0	11.0	11.4
1998	10.9	11.0	11.2	11.4	11.4	11.1	11.0	10.9	10.8	10.9	10.8	10.9	11.0
1999	10.6	11.2	11.3	11.8	11.4	11.2	11.0	10.9	10.8	11.5	11.1	11.0	11.1
2000	11.4	12.2	12.6	12.5	13.5	11.5	11.6	11.2	11.4	11.6	11.6	11.5	11.8
2001	12.1	12.3	12.4	12.5	12.3	12.2	12.1	11.9	11.9	12.0	11.8	11.7	12.1
2002	12.1	12.6	12.8	12.9	13.3	13.1	12.8	12.4	12.4	12.6	12.6	12.6	12.7
2003	12.5	13.5	13.9	14.1	14.1	14.1	14.1	14.1	12.6	12.6	12.4	12.4	13.4
State government													
1990	6.8	6.7	6.9	7.0	7.2	6.7	6.3	6.3	7.3	7.7	7.7	7.7	7.0
1991	7.1	7.5	7.7	7.8	7.9	7.9	7.2	7.0	7.6	7.7	7.5	7.4	7.5
1992	6.9	7.3	7.5	7.6	7.6	7.2	6.9	6.7	6.9	7.3	7.2	7.3	7.2
1993	7.3	7.2	7.4	7.4	7.5	7.2	6.9	6.8	7.4	7.6	7.5	7.5	7.3
1994	7.0	7.3	7.7	7.8	7.7	7.7	7.5	7.0	7.5	8.2	8.2	8.4	7.6
1995	8.0	8.2	8.5	8.8	8.8	8.8	8.4	8.3	9.0	9.2	9.2	9.2	8.7
1996	8.8	9.1	9.3	9.3	9.4	9.2	8.9	8.7	9.3	9.5	9.4	9.5	9.2
1997	9.0	9.3	9.5	9.5	9.6	9.2	9.0	8.9	9.1	9.6	9.6	9.6	9.3
1998	9.6	9.3	9.7	9.7	9.8	9.8	9.3	9.1	9.5	10.1	10.1	10.2	9.6
1999	10.1	9.8	10.2	10.3	10.5	10.6	9.9	9.7	10.1	10.7	10.6	10.7	10.2
2000	10.6	10.4	10.7	10.8	10.9	11.0	10.5	10.2	10.8	11.3	11.4	11.4	10.8
2001	11.3	11.0	11.4	11.6	11.8	11.7	11.0	10.9	11.2	11.8	11.9	11.8	11.4
2002	11.7	11.4	11.8	11.9	12.0	12.1	11.2	11.0	11.1	11.8	11.8	11.7	11.6
2003	11.6	11.6	11.7	11.7	11.7	11.7	11.0	10.8	11.0	11.4	11.4	11.3	11.4
Local government													
1990	37.9	37.9	38.1	38.7	38.9	38.4	35.1	35.6	38.6	39.4	39.5	39.3	38.1
1991	39.1	39.8	40.0	40.3	40.3	39.5	35.3	35.7	38.4	39.4	39.6	39.4	38.9
1992	39.2	39.7	39.8	39.8	40.1	37.1	35.3	35.9	39.0	39.3	39.6	39.6	38.7
1993	39.3	40.3	40.4	41.0	40.7	38.1	36.4	36.7	39.5	40.7	41.0	40.9	39.5
1994	40.8	41.3	41.7	41.7	42.2	41.6	38.3	38.6	40.9	41.8	42.3	42.1	41.1
1995	42.5	43.3	43.7	43.7	44.0	43.7	40.7	41.0	42.3	44.3	44.3	43.9	43.1
1996	43.7	44.5	44.8	44.5	44.9	44.5	41.9	41.8	44.0	43.9	43.7	43.6	43.8
1997	43.6	44.6	44.8	44.8	45.4	45.1	42.7	42.3	43.8	45.5	45.2	44.8	44.3
1998	44.4	45.4	45.7	46.0	46.2	46.0	43.4	43.4	45.2	46.7	46.8	47.1	45.5
1999	46.3	47.3	47.8	47.9	48.4	47.5	46.4	45.7	47.2	49.2	49.5	49.2	47.7
2000	49.0	50.1	50.3	50.5	50.6	49.8	48.5	47.8	49.2	51.2	51.3	51.1	49.9
2001	50.7	51.5	52.0	52.0	51.5	52.1	50.3	49.8	50.3	51.8	53.2	52.7	51.4
2002	52.2	53.4	53.8	54.3	54.5	54.0	51.7	51.7	52.5	54.4	54.6	53.9	53.4
2003	53.1	53.9	53.8	53.8	53.7	54.2	51.8	50.9	52.1	54.3	54.2	53.7	53.3
LOS ANGELES-LONG BEACH													
Total nonfarm													
1990	4128.9	4154.9	4178.2	4162.7	4162.7	4159.7	4116.9	4092.6	4101.9	4121.2	4121.5	4127.5	4135.7
1991	3996.0	3999.8	4012.7	3999.1	3991.4	3992.3	3956.5	3941.9	3962.3	3973.9	3982.9	3984.1	3982.7
1992	3808.3	3818.2	3840.8	3822.1	3816.9	3814.9	3783.7	3760.4	3780.4	3795.3	3802.2	3810.6	3804.5
1993	3720.5	3726.0	3725.0	3703.3	3698.2	3714.3	3687.1	3677.7	3706.1	3696.5	3704.6	3732.0	3707.6
1994	3635.6	3672.8	3704.6	3696.5	3701.2	3709.0	3679.4	3677.1	3715.1	3716.5	3746.2	3769.0	3701.9
1995	3677.9	3730.0	3747.1	3734.8	3752.6	3762.4	3710.7	3718.3	3768.8	3758.0	3788.0	3810.0	3746.6
1996	3703.9	3743.0	3775.9	3770.6	3792.1	3799.4	3762.8	3770.4	3810.8	3817.9	3853.0	3862.1	3788.5
1997	3779.7	3820.6	3854.5	3852.4	3865.0	3874.8	3839.0	3846.5	3880.4	3902.0	3919.3	3945.6	3865.0
1998	3864.8	3901.4	3930.7	3928.5	3953.7	3961.5	3916.2	3920.7	3955.9	3969.3	4000.5	4018.9	3943.5
1999	3914.1	3956.4	3980.8	3996.0	4008.2	4007.4	3983.1	3974.2	4006.0	4040.9	4068.8	4099.2	4002.9
2000	3992.9	4031.9	4063.3	4070.3	4088.5	4080.9	4037.6	4047.1	4083.5	4097.3	4125.0	4146.9	4072.1
2001	4064.6	4089.2	4123.4	4098.8	4093.3	4095.2	4025.7	4032.4	4050.7	4064.4	4064.5	4080.7	4073.5
2002	3983.6	4004.9	4042.9	4040.0	4048.3	4047.2	3982.2	3992.9	4021.3	4039.1	4058.6	4060.4	4026.8
2003	3964.8	3982.4	4004.0	4000.1	4003.8	3999.5	3949.4	3959.8	3975.2	4005.8	4018.9	4017.9	3990.1
Total private													
1990	3592.7	3615.7	3634.2	3616.9	3609.5	3607.4	3582.8	3577.4	3574.6	3578.7	3576.6	3584.9	3596.0
1991	3455.6	3458.9	3467.3	3453.6	3445.2	3444.4	3426.7	3427.4	3431.1	3430.5	3436.1	3437.5	3442.9
1992	3264.4	3272.3	3293.7	3276.4	3271.1	3268.0	3253.8	3246.1	3250.5	3255.2	3260.3	3269.4	3265.1
1993	3184.2	3188.8	3187.2	3165.4	3160.1	3174.0	3167.2	3170.6	3185.5	3165.4	3170.0	3196.2	3176.2
1994	3101.8	3136.3	3164.8	3156.9	3160.5	3166.9	3158.2	3167.6	3189.2	3180.1	3208.4	3227.7	3168.2
1995	3139.5	3187.5	3203.9	3191.1	3208.7	3217.8	3187.1	3206.7	3242.5	3221.7	3251.7	3272.1	3210.9
1996	3175.4	3208.3	3240.9	3233.1	3252.9	3259.0	3242.3	3260.8	3280.8	3279.3	3311.7	3321.5	3255.5
1997	3245.1	3280.2	3311.1	3309.1	3320.6	3329.9	3320.7	3336.5	3348.3	3363.3	3375.6	3403.6	3328.7
1998	3327.6	3364.8	3386.8	3383.2	3406.2	3413.4	3390.1	3405.2	3423.3	3421.7	3445.9	3462.3	3402.5
1999	3363.3	3399.8	3418.6	3422.3	3438.5	3440.9	3434.5	3438.4	3460.6	3470.9	3489.2	3518.4	3441.3
2000	3417.8	3451.1	3475.0	3480.5	3483.4	3495.3	3477.9	3494.6	3510.8	3514.5	3533.5	3555.8	3490.9
2001	3471.7	3492.5	3517.5	3492.0	3485.2	3486.2	3450.3	3458.6	3462.1	3459.7	3457.5	3470.4	3475.3
2002	3378.4	3398.3	3427.9	3425.3	3431.5	3432.2	3397.0	3413.6	3422.7	3429.2	3444.9	3447.8	3420.7
2003	3357.5	3373.7	3388.8	3389.3	3393.7	3389.1	3366.2	3388.0	3392.3	3409.6	3420.8	3422.6	3391.0

Employment by Industry: California—*Continued*

(Numbers in thousands. Not seasonally adjusted.)

Industry	January	February	March	April	May	June	July	August	September	October	November	December	Annual Average
LOS ANGELES-LONG BEACH—*Continued*													
Goods-producing													
1990	973.2	980.8	986.2	978.5	974.1	972.9	968.9	960.6	956.5	954.0	942.0	930.8	964.9
1991	903.8	903.2	901.3	898.7	895.3	895.7	881.7	881.1	879.8	880.0	876.0	864.4	888.4
1992	825.5	828.7	834.5	828.0	823.1	823.5	813.1	809.2	808.6	800.3	792.8	786.9	814.5
1993	772.3	771.3	768.5	764.8	761.3	760.5	752.9	753.9	754.2	748.8	743.6	741.1	757.8
1994	724.1	733.5	739.7	737.6	738.0	740.2	739.3	738.9	742.7	741.1	744.3	747.1	738.9
1995	724.7	739.3	746.9	746.3	747.7	749.8	740.7	742.7	748.9	742.8	745.3	745.0	743.3
1996	733.0	737.3	746.0	739.1	743.4	745.8	736.7	740.9	746.2	745.3	749.5	747.0	742.5
1997	732.6	744.3	751.4	747.7	750.5	751.3	755.0	759.7	761.6	759.0	757.5	758.4	752.4
1998	753.9	763.3	768.4	761.2	769.1	770.6	765.0	765.5	766.9	767.1	767.7	766.2	765.4
1999	744.1	750.3	758.3	755.3	756.5	759.7	754.5	752.9	757.7	756.5	754.1	754.8	754.6
2000	740.0	745.7	752.0	750.0	749.0	754.8	744.7	744.2	746.9	742.3	741.3	745.5	746.4
2001	730.8	730.8	735.2	730.8	728.5	728.7	716.4	716.3	712.2	703.7	696.7	692.2	718.5
2002	674.6	678.6	683.9	679.3	679.7	680.0	668.2	670.3	670.3	666.2	663.4	661.0	673.0
2003	646.1	646.1	648.6	644.4	643.2	642.5	633.1	631.9	630.6	627.7	628.0	624.6	637.2
Natural resources and mining													
1990	8.4	8.5	8.4	8.4	8.4	8.4	8.4	8.2	8.1	8.1	7.8	7.3	8.2
1991	7.0	7.0	6.8	6.9	7.0	7.0	6.8	6.7	6.6	6.7	6.6	6.6	6.8
1992	6.2	6.0	5.9	5.8	5.9	6.1	6.1	5.9	6.0	6.0	5.9	5.9	6.0
1993	5.7	5.7	5.6	5.6	5.7	5.6	5.5	5.6	5.3	4.9	5.0	4.8	5.4
1994	4.4	4.4	4.3	4.2	4.2	4.2	4.2	4.2	4.2	4.1	4.2	4.2	4.2
1995	4.1	4.3	4.2	4.1	4.1	4.1	4.1	4.0	4.1	4.1	4.2	4.2	4.1
1996	4.2	4.2	4.1	3.7	3.8	3.8	3.7	3.7	3.7	3.8	3.8	3.8	3.9
1997	3.5	3.5	3.6	3.4	3.5	3.5	3.5	3.5	3.4	3.4	3.4	3.6	3.5
1998	3.4	3.5	3.5	3.4	3.4	3.5	3.4	3.5	3.5	3.5	3.5	3.6	3.5
1999	3.5	3.4	3.5	3.4	3.4	3.5	3.4	3.4	3.4	3.3	3.3	3.5	3.4
2000	3.4	3.4	3.4	3.3	3.4	3.4	3.3	3.3	3.3	3.3	3.3	3.6	3.4
2001	3.9	3.8	3.8	3.8	3.8	3.8	3.8	3.8	3.8	3.8	3.8	3.8	3.8
2002	3.8	3.8	3.8	3.5	3.6	3.6	3.7	3.7	3.7	3.7	3.8	3.8	3.7
2003	3.8	3.9	3.9	3.8	3.8	3.8	3.8	3.8	3.7	3.6	3.6	3.6	3.8
Construction													
1990	148.4	149.1	151.0	145.8	145.2	146.6	146.2	144.8	145.3	141.8	139.0	137.9	145.1
1991	132.2	133.4	133.1	131.6	132.3	132.1	130.3	131.3	129.9	128.6	127.9	125.5	130.7
1992	114.2	112.8	115.9	114.1	113.7	113.6	111.8	112.0	111.5	111.3	109.1	108.2	112.4
1993	100.1	102.5	103.4	102.7	102.5	102.9	102.7	103.7	103.6	102.5	101.6	101.9	102.5
1994	98.2	103.5	107.0	106.9	106.4	107.7	110.0	112.0	113.6	113.4	114.1	114.7	109.0
1995	105.4	110.2	112.1	113.5	114.7	116.1	113.6	115.7	116.3	113.3	112.9	112.8	113.1
1996	105.7	106.6	107.4	106.8	108.4	109.1	107.6	109.0	110.7	109.7	110.3	109.1	108.4
1997	104.1	107.3	108.6	107.9	109.8	110.1	112.1	114.2	114.6	112.4	112.7	113.7	110.6
1998	110.1	111.8	113.3	113.6	116.6	118.7	120.7	122.6	123.1	125.3	126.2	126.6	119.1
1999	120.9	121.6	124.0	122.9	125.3	126.2	128.5	129.7	130.7	131.2	130.4	131.3	126.9
2000	126.4	126.8	128.5	128.6	130.1	132.3	130.9	133.2	134.7	135.4	135.9	137.3	131.7
2001	132.4	132.4	134.4	134.7	136.3	137.8	138.0	140.5	139.4	139.6	138.4	138.0	136.8
2002	132.8	132.9	134.6	132.9	133.7	134.5	133.2	136.2	136.5	136.3	135.1	134.8	134.5
2003	130.9	129.9	131.7	132.6	133.5	134.6	135.2	135.8	136.2	134.6	133.7	132.8	133.5
Manufacturing													
1990	816.4	823.2	826.8	824.3	820.5	817.9	814.3	807.6	803.1	804.1	795.2	785.6	811.6
1991	764.6	762.8	761.4	760.2	756.0	756.6	744.6	743.1	743.3	744.7	741.5	732.3	750.9
1992	705.1	709.9	712.7	708.1	703.5	703.8	695.2	691.3	691.1	683.0	677.8	672.8	696.2
1993	666.5	663.1	659.5	656.5	653.1	652.0	644.7	644.6	645.3	641.4	637.0	634.4	649.8
1994	621.5	625.6	628.4	626.5	627.4	628.3	625.1	622.7	624.9	623.6	626.0	628.2	625.7
1995	615.2	624.8	630.6	628.7	628.9	629.6	623.0	623.0	628.5	625.4	628.2	628.0	626.2
1996	623.1	626.5	634.5	628.6	631.2	632.9	625.4	628.2	631.8	631.8	635.4	634.1	630.3
1997	625.0	633.5	639.2	636.4	637.2	637.7	639.4	642.0	643.6	643.2	641.4	641.1	638.3
1998	640.4	648.0	651.6	644.2	649.1	648.4	640.9	639.4	640.3	638.3	638.0	636.0	642.9
1999	619.7	625.3	630.8	629.0	627.8	630.0	622.6	619.8	623.6	622.0	620.4	620.0	624.3
2000	610.2	615.5	620.1	618.1	615.5	619.1	610.5	607.7	608.9	603.6	602.1	604.6	611.3
2001	594.5	594.6	597.0	592.3	588.4	587.1	574.6	572.0	569.0	560.3	554.5	550.4	577.8
2002	538.0	541.9	545.5	542.9	542.4	541.9	531.3	530.4	530.1	526.2	524.5	522.4	534.8
2003	511.4	512.3	513.0	508.0	505.9	504.1	494.1	492.3	490.7	489.5	490.7	488.2	500.0
Service-providing													
1990	3155.7	3174.1	3192.0	3184.2	3188.6	3186.8	3148.0	3132.0	3145.4	3167.2	3179.5	3196.7	3170.9
1991	3092.2	3096.6	3111.4	3100.4	3096.1	3096.6	3074.8	3060.8	3082.5	3093.9	3106.9	3119.7	3094.3
1992	2982.8	2989.5	3006.3	2994.1	2993.8	2991.4	2970.6	2951.2	2971.8	2995.0	3009.4	3023.7	2990.0
1993	2948.2	2954.7	2956.5	2938.5	2936.9	2953.8	2934.2	2923.8	2951.9	2947.7	2961.0	2990.9	2949.8
1994	2911.5	2939.3	2964.9	2958.9	2963.2	2968.8	2940.1	2938.2	2972.4	2975.4	3001.9	3021.9	2963.0
1995	2953.2	2990.7	3000.2	2988.5	3004.9	3012.6	2970.0	2975.6	3019.9	3015.2	3042.7	3065.0	3003.2
1996	2970.9	3005.7	3029.9	3031.5	3048.7	3053.6	3026.1	3029.5	3064.6	3072.6	3103.5	3115.1	3046.0
1997	3047.1	3076.3	3103.1	3104.7	3114.5	3123.5	3084.0	3086.8	3118.8	3143.0	3161.8	3187.2	3112.6
1998	3110.9	3138.1	3162.3	3167.3	3184.6	3190.9	3151.2	3155.2	3189.0	3202.2	3232.8	3252.7	3178.1
1999	3170.0	3206.1	3222.5	3240.7	3251.7	3247.7	3228.6	3221.3	3248.3	3284.4	3314.7	3344.4	3248.4
2000	3252.9	3286.2	3311.3	3320.3	3339.5	3326.1	3292.9	3302.9	3336.6	3355.0	3383.7	3401.4	3325.7
2001	3333.8	3358.4	3388.2	3368.0	3364.8	3366.5	3309.3	3316.1	3338.5	3360.7	3367.8	3388.5	3355.0
2002	3309.0	3326.3	3359.0	3360.7	3368.6	3367.2	3314.0	3322.6	3351.0	3372.9	3395.2	3399.4	3353.8
2003	3318.7	3336.3	3355.4	3355.7	3360.6	3357.0	3316.3	3327.9	3344.6	3378.1	3390.9	3393.3	3352.9

Employment by Industry: California—*Continued*

(Numbers in thousands. Not seasonally adjusted.)

Industry	January	February	March	April	May	June	July	August	September	October	November	December	Annual Average
LOS ANGELES-LONG BEACH—*Continued*													
Trade, transportation, and utilities													
1990	804.6	799.8	799.3	788.0	786.0	787.7	791.1	787.6	789.0	785.5	800.4	817.7	794.7
1991	777.6	769.4	769.6	769.7	769.0	773.1	771.4	768.7	770.5	776.6	788.5	800.5	775.4
1992	745.6	741.9	742.0	735.0	734.8	736.3	732.9	730.9	731.5	737.2	745.2	756.0	739.1
1993	729.2	720.4	715.2	709.3	707.0	708.6	705.2	704.9	707.3	711.8	722.7	735.8	714.8
1994	700.0	696.6	698.2	700.8	702.4	704.2	705.4	708.2	712.4	715.8	731.7	744.9	710.1
1995	714.3	713.2	713.5	710.1	711.6	713.1	710.1	713.0	719.7	721.4	735.4	749.8	718.8
1996	719.5	719.4	719.6	715.1	718.7	723.2	714.9	718.0	724.1	728.6	744.6	759.7	725.5
1997	735.7	734.8	736.9	736.4	737.7	738.6	737.8	740.1	741.4	751.1	762.1	779.4	744.3
1998	754.0	750.1	749.9	743.7	753.3	756.3	751.3	755.6	757.8	760.3	774.8	787.8	757.9
1999	757.6	758.3	760.3	758.3	762.3	766.7	764.2	767.2	772.3	782.3	791.1	805.3	770.5
2000	776.4	775.6	777.4	774.0	775.2	779.7	779.1	782.6	785.6	790.9	803.3	817.3	784.8
2001	792.7	787.1	790.0	787.1	786.3	790.1	784.5	785.4	788.0	786.4	793.7	806.0	789.7
2002	776.3	772.4	774.3	776.5	778.7	782.6	778.2	780.9	784.4	783.0	794.9	809.6	782.7
2003	774.2	770.6	770.4	768.5	770.2	774.2	769.9	772.7	778.0	787.4	790.6	799.1	777.2
Wholesale trade													
1990	232.2	232.4	232.5	229.8	228.8	229.0	228.2	226.6	226.6	225.4	223.7	224.5	228.3
1991	221.5	221.8	221.1	224.3	223.7	223.7	221.8	221.4	220.3	222.9	222.9	221.8	222.3
1992	211.7	211.9	212.9	210.7	210.5	210.8	207.8	207.6	206.6	207.8	207.1	207.5	209.4
1993	204.5	204.6	203.5	200.8	201.0	200.7	199.2	199.0	198.7	200.2	201.1	201.6	201.2
1994	197.6	198.7	200.4	201.4	201.3	201.4	200.9	202.0	202.7	202.3	203.8	204.3	201.4
1995	202.3	203.9	205.3	203.5	204.1	203.8	202.7	203.1	204.4	203.2	203.9	205.8	203.8
1996	201.6	204.5	205.8	204.7	205.6	206.4	204.2	204.9	206.5	205.8	206.9	208.0	205.4
1997	207.8	209.9	212.0	212.1	212.7	212.8	214.4	215.6	215.0	215.3	215.3	216.7	213.3
1998	213.3	215.1	216.2	213.5	216.3	216.8	214.9	215.5	216.1	216.6	217.1	217.8	215.8
1999	215.4	215.9	217.6	216.8	217.0	218.5	217.0	217.2	218.2	218.8	219.0	220.3	217.6
2000	217.0	218.4	219.7	218.0	218.0	219.3	220.0	220.6	220.6	219.2	219.2	219.6	219.1
2001	217.6	219.3	219.5	220.0	219.6	221.7	220.1	219.3	219.5	219.3	218.3	218.8	219.4
2002	215.5	216.4	218.3	217.6	217.2	218.0	217.4	217.7	218.5	216.6	216.8	217.6	217.3
2003	213.9	214.5	215.0	214.4	214.8	216.0	213.2	213.5	214.1	214.2	214.2	214.6	214.4
Retail trade													
1990	413.9	407.4	405.6	398.7	397.6	398.7	402.3	400.9	400.3	397.0	414.0	428.9	405.4
1991	397.0	389.3	388.4	387.7	387.3	390.0	388.6	387.6	389.4	392.3	403.1	416.3	393.1
1992	382.3	376.0	374.9	370.1	370.1	371.5	371.7	370.4	371.0	374.7	383.4	393.8	375.8
1993	372.6	364.4	361.4	359.1	356.7	357.9	356.7	356.8	358.4	359.4	369.3	380.8	362.8
1994	354.3	348.9	348.4	351.1	351.4	353.1	353.2	354.6	357.3	359.6	373.4	385.8	357.6
1995	361.3	356.9	354.4	353.7	354.2	355.2	353.2	356.2	359.5	362.1	374.5	387.1	360.7
1996	366.0	361.3	358.7	356.0	358.1	360.1	356.0	358.0	361.4	364.5	379.1	392.5	364.3
1997	370.1	366.1	364.9	364.6	364.7	365.1	364.8	366.2	366.6	371.4	382.0	396.8	370.3
1998	375.0	368.9	366.4	364.4	369.3	371.0	368.7	371.7	372.9	375.1	388.3	400.8	374.4
1999	373.8	372.6	373.2	371.3	373.7	375.3	377.1	379.2	382.7	385.9	394.8	408.5	380.7
2000	387.2	384.2	384.8	382.4	383.2	386.3	386.7	388.8	391.2	394.2	406.6	419.6	391.3
2001	398.6	392.1	393.0	388.7	389.4	391.6	389.1	390.9	392.0	392.2	403.9	416.2	394.8
2002	395.5	389.3	391.9	391.9	393.6	396.5	393.6	394.8	397.7	398.6	410.7	423.8	398.2
2003	396.1	392.2	392.0	391.0	392.1	395.3	393.9	396.7	400.2	410.0	413.0	421.9	399.5
Transportation and utilities													
1990	158.5	160.0	161.2	159.5	159.6	160.0	160.6	160.1	162.1	163.1	162.7	164.3	161.0
1991	159.1	158.3	160.1	157.7	158.0	159.4	161.0	159.7	160.8	161.4	162.5	162.4	160.0
1992	151.6	154.0	154.2	154.2	154.2	154.0	153.4	152.9	153.9	154.7	154.7	154.7	153.9
1993	152.1	151.4	150.3	149.4	149.3	150.0	149.3	149.1	150.2	152.2	152.3	153.4	150.8
1994	148.1	149.0	149.4	148.3	149.7	149.7	151.3	151.6	152.4	153.9	154.5	154.8	151.1
1995	150.7	152.4	153.8	152.9	153.3	154.1	154.2	153.7	155.8	156.1	157.0	156.9	154.2
1996	151.9	153.6	155.1	154.4	155.0	156.7	154.7	155.1	156.2	158.3	158.6	159.2	155.7
1997	157.8	158.8	160.0	159.7	160.3	160.7	158.6	158.3	159.8	164.4	164.8	165.9	160.8
1998	165.7	166.1	167.3	165.8	167.7	168.5	167.7	168.4	168.8	168.6	169.4	169.2	167.8
1999	168.4	169.8	169.5	170.2	171.6	172.9	170.1	170.8	171.4	177.6	177.3	176.5	172.2
2000	172.2	173.0	172.9	173.6	174.0	174.1	172.4	173.2	173.8	177.5	177.5	178.1	174.4
2001	176.5	175.7	177.5	178.4	177.3	176.8	175.3	175.2	176.5	174.9	171.5	171.0	175.5
2002	165.3	166.7	164.1	167.0	167.9	168.1	167.2	168.4	168.2	167.8	167.4	168.2	167.2
2003	164.2	163.9	163.4	163.1	163.3	162.9	162.8	162.5	163.7	163.2	163.4	162.6	163.3
Information													
1990	177.9	183.4	181.9	196.2	195.4	195.5	177.4	180.8	180.7	187.9	188.7	188.0	186.2
1991	190.1	190.9	194.7	184.1	181.3	184.1	175.9	178.6	181.9	169.7	169.1	168.8	180.8
1992	163.2	166.2	170.2	170.4	170.4	166.8	161.5	162.7	161.6	174.2	177.3	176.4	168.4
1993	165.1	168.3	170.5	161.1	160.2	168.4	170.2	174.0	174.7	173.7	170.9	173.1	169.2
1994	164.0	171.3	175.2	177.3	177.7	178.5	177.2	181.3	182.3	180.9	182.7	177.7	177.2
1995	178.5	190.2	187.7	178.6	184.4	186.3	186.9	194.7	204.7	195.1	197.1	200.0	190.4
1996	183.7	192.8	200.3	197.5	197.4	199.9	201.4	210.5	210.8	204.9	211.9	202.6	201.1
1997	207.1	210.5	215.5	211.3	211.0	213.5	215.6	215.2	219.5	218.0	217.8	220.4	214.6
1998	210.7	217.7	219.2	212.8	205.9	207.1	208.0	214.6	217.9	217.8	220.8	223.0	214.6
1999	229.0	242.2	234.8	232.5	238.8	231.8	236.7	242.2	234.8	234.5	238.4	239.1	236.2
2000	232.9	238.0	239.8	238.3	240.4	239.6	240.7	246.8	244.6	247.0	254.4	249.0	242.6
2001	239.4	243.9	245.4	235.2	223.8	223.5	217.6	217.3	218.6	215.2	217.5	217.7	226.2
2002	209.8	212.6	220.5	208.3	207.7	207.9	198.1	205.5	199.1	206.4	213.8	197.9	207.3
2003	201.1	205.1	203.4	199.9	202.0	193.3	191.5	200.4	192.3	196.8	203.7	196.0	198.8

Employment by Industry: California—*Continued*

(Numbers in thousands. Not seasonally adjusted.)

Industry	January	February	March	April	May	June	July	August	September	October	November	December	Annual Average
LOS ANGELES-LONG BEACH—*Continued*													
Financial activities													
1990	283.2	283.9	285.5	281.4	280.8	281.4	277.2	283.7	279.2	276.2	273.6	277.6	280.3
1991	269.9	268.7	269.7	267.5	266.8	266.4	266.5	266.7	265.5	263.3	261.8	262.3	266.3
1992	249.0	250.5	252.7	250.0	250.6	251.3	250.5	250.4	247.7	249.8	249.9	252.1	250.4
1993	245.7	245.4	245.1	244.5	243.8	244.7	243.0	242.8	243.0	240.3	240.5	242.6	243.5
1994	240.1	240.6	241.4	238.2	236.8	236.1	233.3	234.1	234.0	229.9	230.5	232.2	235.6
1995	228.4	229.9	230.3	228.4	229.1	229.0	227.6	228.4	228.1	227.3	228.5	228.8	228.7
1996	221.7	223.3	224.2	223.8	224.4	224.5	221.2	222.8	222.2	221.4	222.3	223.5	222.9
1997	210.5	212.1	213.8	212.6	213.2	213.3	214.5	215.9	214.6	219.1	219.6	221.1	215.0
1998	211.2	213.8	215.6	217.3	219.2	220.1	217.9	218.9	218.8	220.8	223.1	224.0	218.4
1999	219.1	220.5	222.0	219.7	220.7	222.1	220.1	219.9	219.7	222.2	222.0	223.8	221.0
2000	218.3	219.5	219.5	219.4	219.5	220.1	217.4	218.0	218.0	217.7	217.5	219.9	218.7
2001	226.2	227.7	229.3	228.3	228.1	229.2	227.2	229.8	229.3	230.1	230.3	231.8	228.9
2002	228.1	229.7	230.7	231.4	232.0	233.2	232.7	233.3	233.7	234.1	235.1	237.1	232.6
2003	235.4	236.3	237.3	239.9	240.5	241.2	240.8	241.7	240.7	240.8	241.0	241.8	239.8
Professsional and business services													
1990	539.6	545.2	551.1	542.5	541.6	539.7	542.2	538.9	539.6	541.9	540.1	540.4	541.9
1991	514.5	518.7	519.1	514.4	513.1	507.6	513.0	515.1	516.6	512.2	511.1	513.9	514.1
1992	499.3	488.9	493.2	490.4	490.3	491.4	494.5	493.0	493.8	496.8	498.7	500.2	494.2
1993	492.3	497.2	498.7	499.0	498.5	498.6	500.1	501.2	505.5	495.3	496.3	502.5	498.8
1994	497.3	506.9	514.2	505.6	504.0	505.6	504.0	506.2	512.1	512.3	515.6	521.5	508.8
1995	504.8	515.0	519.7	517.1	518.7	522.9	514.4	519.8	524.5	520.2	525.1	525.6	519.0
1996	514.0	518.6	525.3	525.5	530.0	531.0	537.0	538.5	541.7	542.3	545.8	549.2	533.2
1997	531.0	539.5	546.7	552.4	555.3	559.9	558.9	563.9	566.1	572.1	574.8	578.5	558.3
1998	566.9	576.7	585.0	583.8	583.1	586.4	587.3	591.1	591.2	587.7	590.0	592.5	585.1
1999	560.6	560.0	566.9	581.8	581.4	587.3	590.0	591.6	596.8	594.6	600.3	608.3	585.0
2000	577.8	584.1	588.8	595.7	592.9	597.4	600.2	605.0	606.6	609.3	609.6	610.5	598.2
2001	586.4	591.7	597.2	587.4	592.4	589.2	584.1	589.4	587.5	585.0	581.9	583.6	587.9
2002	568.5	570.8	576.8	577.9	577.6	577.4	573.0	576.5	576.6	574.8	574.7	575.7	575.0
2003	560.0	560.7	567.0	565.2	563.8	564.7	565.1	573.3	572.4	575.3	575.7	578.1	568.4
Educational and health services													
1990	379.5	387.1	388.6	389.5	387.4	383.0	375.8	377.0	381.9	388.4	388.5	389.5	384.7
1991	370.4	376.8	376.5	376.3	373.4	367.4	365.8	365.0	366.1	379.9	379.8	380.2	373.1
1992	360.5	369.1	370.6	367.3	365.1	360.0	358.3	358.1	366.7	360.4	360.6	361.6	363.2
1993	360.1	362.7	362.9	358.0	356.4	354.3	358.4	357.0	363.4	362.9	364.6	367.1	360.7
1994	362.4	367.0	370.2	368.3	368.2	365.3	360.9	360.7	367.5	367.1	369.9	369.9	366.5
1995	364.8	369.3	371.0	372.9	373.4	370.1	365.2	364.1	372.1	374.0	377.1	378.0	371.0
1996	373.5	380.5	384.5	387.3	387.5	382.5	380.6	380.2	387.0	385.4	387.0	386.4	383.5
1997	384.4	392.1	394.0	390.4	388.9	385.7	378.6	380.1	384.5	386.1	385.6	384.6	386.3
1998	385.5	392.6	393.0	400.5	402.7	396.9	386.5	385.5	396.2	397.8	399.9	397.6	394.6
1999	396.3	405.3	407.4	404.1	401.7	395.4	390.9	389.5	403.3	408.2	409.3	410.1	401.8
2000	407.4	416.1	419.4	422.3	420.2	412.3	406.6	407.9	418.3	420.4	420.8	423.0	416.2
2001	418.2	428.8	433.1	432.3	431.6	425.2	422.0	424.6	434.3	443.5	445.5	447.0	432.1
2002	437.5	446.1	449.2	454.2	453.5	445.9	440.3	441.3	452.5	459.5	461.9	463.0	450.4
2003	448.6	457.7	461.3	464.2	462.6	455.9	449.8	451.2	461.9	469.3	470.6	470.5	460.3
Leisure and hospitality													
1990	298.6	298.7	303.6	304.2	307.4	310.8	313.3	312.3	311.5	307.4	306.2	305.6	306.6
1991	294.8	295.9	301.0	305.9	309.2	312.8	315.8	315.7	314.5	310.6	311.2	309.7	308.1
1992	290.9	295.6	297.6	301.9	303.1	304.0	309.6	309.2	308.0	304.7	304.4	304.3	302.8
1993	290.7	293.4	295.5	298.3	302.1	307.4	306.6	306.3	306.0	302.7	301.6	303.7	301.2
1994	290.5	295.4	299.5	302.7	306.6	309.3	311.0	311.1	310.3	305.3	305.2	305.8	304.4
1995	296.7	300.7	304.0	305.7	310.8	313.2	312.5	314.6	313.8	309.8	311.3	313.2	308.9
1996	301.9	306.5	309.7	314.0	320.0	320.3	320.8	320.0	318.6	322.0	320.9	323.5	316.5
1997	315.9	317.6	322.3	326.9	331.8	335.6	329.6	330.8	329.6	326.0	326.7	329.5	326.9
1998	315.0	319.0	322.7	329.5	336.2	338.7	338.8	339.2	337.4	334.0	333.7	335.1	331.6
1999	322.9	328.4	332.4	334.6	339.8	339.9	341.0	338.9	338.4	335.8	337.2	339.8	335.8
2000	328.9	334.8	339.2	340.9	345.6	349.4	349.3	350.5	350.0	346.8	346.4	350.0	344.3
2001	337.1	340.4	343.8	347.5	350.5	355.1	355.6	353.7	349.5	351.6	348.5	348.7	348.5
2002	341.9	344.6	347.7	352.7	355.8	358.0	360.2	360.1	359.4	358.3	355.1	356.9	354.2
2003	348.4	352.2	355.0	361.6	364.9	370.0	370.1	371.3	369.9	365.9	365.2	367.0	363.5
Other services													
1990	136.1	136.8	138.0	136.6	136.8	136.4	136.9	136.5	136.2	137.4	137.1	135.3	136.7
1991	134.5	135.3	135.4	137.0	137.1	137.3	136.6	136.5	136.2	138.2	138.6	137.7	136.7
1992	130.4	131.4	132.9	133.4	133.7	134.7	133.4	132.6	132.6	131.8	131.4	131.9	132.5
1993	128.8	130.1	130.8	130.4	130.8	131.5	130.8	130.5	131.4	129.9	129.8	130.3	130.4
1994	123.4	125.0	126.4	126.4	126.8	127.7	127.1	127.1	127.9	127.7	128.5	128.6	126.9
1995	127.3	129.9	130.8	132.0	133.0	133.4	129.7	129.4	130.7	131.1	131.9	131.7	130.9
1996	128.1	129.9	131.3	130.8	131.5	131.8	129.7	129.9	130.2	129.4	129.7	129.6	130.2
1997	127.9	129.3	130.5	131.4	132.2	132.0	130.7	130.8	131.0	131.9	131.5	131.7	130.9
1998	130.4	131.6	133.0	134.4	136.7	137.3	135.3	134.8	137.1	136.2	135.9	136.1	134.9
1999	133.7	134.8	136.5	136.0	137.3	138.0	137.1	136.2	137.6	136.8	136.8	137.2	136.5
2000	136.1	137.3	138.9	139.9	140.6	142.0	139.9	139.6	140.8	140.1	140.2	140.6	139.7
2001	140.9	142.1	143.5	143.4	144.0	145.2	142.9	142.1	142.7	144.2	143.4	143.4	143.1
2002	141.7	143.5	144.8	145.0	146.5	147.2	146.3	145.7	146.7	146.9	146.0	146.6	145.6
2003	143.7	145.0	145.8	145.6	146.5	147.3	145.9	145.5	146.5	146.4	146.0	145.5	145.8

Employment by Industry: California—*Continued*

(Numbers in thousands. Not seasonally adjusted.)

Industry	January	February	March	April	May	June	July	August	September	October	November	December	Annual Average
LOS ANGELES-LONG BEACH—*Continued*													
Government													
1990	536.2	539.2	544.0	545.8	553.2	552.3	534.1	515.2	527.3	542.5	544.9	542.6	539.8
1991	540.4	540.9	545.4	545.5	546.2	547.9	529.8	514.5	531.2	543.4	546.8	546.6	539.9
1992	543.9	545.9	547.1	545.7	545.8	546.9	529.9	514.3	529.9	540.1	541.9	541.2	539.4
1993	536.3	537.2	537.8	537.9	538.1	540.3	519.9	507.1	520.6	531.1	534.6	535.8	531.4
1994	533.8	536.5	539.8	539.6	540.7	542.1	521.2	509.5	525.9	536.4	537.8	541.3	533.7
1995	538.4	542.5	543.2	543.7	543.9	544.6	523.6	511.6	526.3	536.3	536.3	537.9	535.7
1996	528.5	534.7	535.0	537.5	539.2	540.4	520.5	509.6	530.0	538.6	541.3	540.6	533.0
1997	534.6	540.4	543.4	543.3	544.4	544.9	518.3	510.0	532.1	538.7	543.7	542.0	536.3
1998	537.2	536.6	543.9	545.3	547.5	548.1	526.1	515.5	532.6	547.6	554.6	556.6	541.0
1999	550.8	556.6	562.2	573.7	569.7	566.5	548.6	535.8	545.4	570.0	579.6	580.8	561.6
2000	575.1	580.8	588.3	589.8	605.1	585.6	559.7	552.5	572.7	582.8	591.5	591.1	581.3
2001	592.9	596.7	605.9	606.8	608.1	609.0	575.4	573.8	588.6	604.7	607.0	610.3	598.2
2002	605.2	606.6	615.0	614.7	616.8	615.0	585.2	579.3	598.6	609.9	613.7	612.6	606.1
2003	607.3	608.7	615.2	610.8	610.1	610.4	583.2	571.8	582.9	596.2	598.1	595.3	599.2
Federal government													
1990	69.5	69.2	69.9	71.9	77.8	78.6	75.9	73.0	69.3	68.8	68.8	69.6	71.9
1991	68.3	67.9	67.7	67.9	68.4	68.2	68.8	69.0	69.3	69.3	69.2	70.7	68.7
1992	69.2	68.7	68.7	68.6	68.7	68.7	69.6	69.7	69.4	69.4	68.7	69.8	69.1
1993	67.5	67.2	67.1	66.9	66.7	67.0	66.5	66.6	66.8	65.5	65.5	66.7	66.7
1994	65.2	65.5	65.3	65.3	65.2	65.2	64.2	64.2	64.2	64.4	64.1	65.7	64.9
1995	63.7	63.7	63.6	63.5	63.4	63.8	63.5	63.6	63.0	62.9	62.5	64.0	63.4
1996	62.4	62.4	62.2	61.9	61.7	61.1	60.6	60.5	60.5	59.8	59.7	61.4	61.2
1997	58.7	58.3	58.1	58.2	58.2	58.2	57.9	57.8	57.8	56.4	56.3	58.3	57.9
1998	55.1	54.8	54.7	54.9	55.3	55.3	56.5	56.8	57.4	57.0	56.9	59.0	56.1
1999	56.4	56.3	56.2	62.2	56.6	56.5	56.1	56.2	56.6	56.5	56.5	58.8	57.1
2000	56.3	56.5	57.5	59.0	73.3	57.0	58.4	56.0	55.2	54.9	54.9	56.2	57.9
2001	54.7	54.6	54.6	54.0	53.9	53.9	54.6	54.6	54.5	54.3	54.3	54.2	54.3
2002	53.9	53.7	53.9	53.5	53.5	53.6	53.7	53.6	53.3	54.8	55.7	56.5	54.1
2003	56.2	56.1	56.0	55.9	55.6	55.4	55.2	55.0	54.8	55.3	54.9	55.4	55.5
State government													
1990	69.6	70.6	70.8	71.0	71.7	71.3	68.2	67.1	67.3	69.5	70.9	70.4	69.9
1991	69.8	70.0	72.4	72.1	72.5	72.1	67.9	67.7	69.4	69.2	69.2	68.9	70.1
1992	67.7	69.3	69.5	69.5	69.8	69.9	65.9	65.9	66.1	68.1	68.8	68.9	68.3
1993	68.9	69.2	69.2	69.0	69.4	69.3	66.8	65.5	65.4	68.5	68.8	69.4	68.3
1994	69.3	68.3	69.5	69.8	70.3	70.1	67.9	65.9	66.6	69.8	70.7	71.6	69.2
1995	70.6	71.5	71.3	71.2	71.6	71.2	68.2	67.2	68.1	70.9	71.9	71.7	70.5
1996	70.6	70.8	71.3	71.2	71.2	72.0	66.9	67.4	68.3	70.8	72.3	71.2	70.3
1997	70.8	71.1	72.5	71.8	72.3	71.9	67.9	67.2	68.5	71.2	73.3	72.3	70.9
1998	71.4	71.9	73.7	73.5	73.7	73.8	69.9	69.1	69.8	74.4	75.0	74.6	72.6
1999	73.2	74.1	75.5	75.6	76.3	76.5	72.5	71.7	72.5	77.0	77.5	77.0	75.0
2000	75.6	76.4	77.8	78.3	77.5	78.2	76.0	75.0	74.6	77.6	79.2	78.9	77.1
2001	78.9	78.9	81.0	79.8	79.8	80.9	76.3	76.1	78.0	80.7	81.9	81.3	79.4
2002	80.0	80.3	82.4	81.5	81.7	82.3	77.4	78.1	78.9	81.6	82.8	82.3	80.8
2003	80.7	81.4	83.0	82.3	82.3	82.5	77.7	78.0	78.0	80.7	81.3	80.6	80.7
Local government													
1990	397.1	399.4	403.3	402.9	403.7	402.4	390.0	375.1	390.7	404.2	405.2	402.6	398.1
1991	402.3	403.0	405.3	405.5	405.3	407.6	393.1	377.8	392.5	404.9	408.4	407.0	401.1
1992	407.0	407.9	408.9	407.6	407.3	408.3	394.4	378.7	394.4	402.6	404.4	402.5	402.0
1993	399.9	400.8	401.5	402.0	402.0	404.0	386.6	375.0	388.4	397.1	400.3	399.7	396.4
1994	399.3	402.7	405.0	404.5	405.2	406.8	389.1	379.4	395.1	402.2	403.0	404.0	399.7
1995	404.1	407.3	408.3	409.0	408.9	409.6	391.9	380.8	395.2	402.5	401.9	402.2	401.8
1996	395.5	401.5	401.5	404.4	406.3	407.3	393.0	381.7	401.2	408.0	409.3	408.0	401.5
1997	405.1	411.0	412.8	413.3	413.9	414.8	392.5	385.0	405.8	411.1	414.1	411.4	407.6
1998	410.7	409.9	415.5	416.9	418.5	419.0	399.7	389.6	405.4	416.2	422.7	423.0	412.3
1999	421.2	426.2	430.5	435.9	436.8	433.5	420.0	407.9	416.3	436.5	445.6	445.0	429.6
2000	443.2	447.9	453.0	452.5	454.3	450.4	425.3	421.5	442.9	450.3	457.4	456.0	446.2
2001	459.3	463.2	470.3	473.0	474.4	474.2	444.5	443.1	456.1	469.7	470.8	474.8	464.4
2002	471.3	472.6	478.7	479.7	481.6	479.1	454.1	447.6	466.4	473.5	475.2	473.8	471.1
2003	470.4	471.2	476.2	472.6	472.2	472.5	450.3	438.8	450.1	460.2	461.9	459.3	463.0
OAKLAND													
Total nonfarm													
1990	858.6	861.2	864.8	869.4	874.8	882.1	879.3	878.4	888.3	893.2	899.0	901.5	879.2
1991	878.4	879.7	879.3	879.1	880.0	883.1	872.7	872.2	877.9	881.4	886.1	885.9	879.6
1992	861.6	864.4	869.9	870.2	872.7	872.8	863.9	862.1	871.6	875.0	878.3	879.6	870.1
1993	862.9	868.2	870.8	871.4	875.1	878.8	868.7	868.6	873.3	876.6	881.1	886.6	873.5
1994	862.7	868.0	874.8	875.0	877.4	878.5	869.3	872.6	881.1	882.8	890.6	896.1	877.4
1995	874.5	887.2	890.8	888.9	893.5	901.3	894.2	897.8	908.5	903.7	912.2	917.0	897.4
1996	895.6	902.4	904.3	904.9	912.7	921.2	912.8	915.0	923.2	926.8	937.0	941.1	916.4
1997	919.2	929.0	937.4	940.1	947.6	952.1	944.3	947.2	959.4	959.0	963.9	973.9	947.7
1998	949.4	954.9	963.5	967.5	974.1	979.9	972.5	977.3	987.2	988.3	996.4	1003.2	976.1
1999	978.7	985.8	994.3	1000.9	1009.4	1012.6	1006.6	1010.2	1016.9	1019.8	1024.9	1035.7	1007.9
2000	1012.7	1019.4	1027.6	1035.8	1044.1	1054.4	1043.6	1048.5	1054.3	1056.3	1065.0	1073.3	1044.5
2001	1052.0	1057.3	1065.7	1059.8	1060.0	1062.9	1050.7	1051.3	1050.4	1048.7	1047.6	1050.6	1054.7
2002	1025.3	1031.8	1039.0	1036.3	1040.5	1045.5	1033.4	1036.5	1042.5	1045.9	1049.5	1051.5	1039.8
2003	1024.5	1028.6	1032.4	1027.1	1028.9	1031.2	1014.3	1014.8	1019.4	1023.1	1025.7	1026.4	1024.7

Employment by Industry: California—*Continued*

(Numbers in thousands. Not seasonally adjusted.)

Industry	January	February	March	April	May	June	July	August	September	October	November	December	Annual Average
OAKLAND—*Continued*													
Total private													
1990	692.7	692.5	695.5	698.6	702.3	710.7	716.9	718.9	720.4	724.4	728.8	732.7	711.2
1991	709.7	709.1	707.8	707.1	707.7	712.0	710.7	711.9	711.5	712.0	715.5	716.5	710.9
1992	693.5	693.3	696.9	697.5	700.1	700.7	701.3	701.8	704.0	702.8	705.4	707.5	700.4
1993	693.8	695.6	697.8	698.1	702.0	707.0	705.9	706.6	707.2	706.1	710.4	716.7	703.9
1994	694.6	697.4	702.9	702.2	704.1	706.8	706.9	709.4	713.6	710.7	717.3	723.7	707.4
1995	704.1	714.1	717.8	716.3	720.6	729.5	731.4	736.5	741.5	733.0	740.5	747.1	727.7
1996	727.3	731.5	734.8	734.9	742.8	752.7	752.5	754.1	756.1	756.8	765.4	770.2	748.2
1997	751.8	758.6	766.4	769.7	777.2	783.3	785.1	786.2	792.4	790.0	793.5	804.2	779.8
1998	782.2	786.1	793.5	796.1	802.0	810.8	811.6	816.7	818.5	817.7	822.6	829.9	807.3
1999	808.2	811.8	819.9	824.1	832.1	836.8	840.4	844.8	846.0	845.8	849.0	860.4	834.9
2000	838.2	842.6	849.0	857.0	862.3	873.1	873.7	877.6	881.1	879.0	886.4	896.1	868.0
2001	876.5	878.8	885.3	877.5	878.6	883.3	879.1	878.7	873.6	866.2	865.3	868.4	875.9
2002	843.6	847.2	852.6	848.4	852.6	859.5	858.1	861.4	859.8	858.3	861.5	864.9	855.7
2003	839.3	841.5	844.4	840.2	842.4	846.4	840.4	843.3	841.8	841.6	844.1	846.3	842.6
Goods-producing													
1990	155.1	154.3	154.9	156.1	158.1	160.1	161.2	161.2	161.5	159.7	158.8	157.6	158.2
1991	150.8	148.9	148.4	147.8	147.8	149.9	151.9	151.9	152.3	151.0	149.3	148.0	149.8
1992	142.6	140.8	143.4	141.2	142.5	144.0	144.6	144.3	144.3	141.7	140.3	138.4	142.3
1993	134.8	135.2	136.6	137.0	138.1	139.6	140.0	140.2	140.3	138.2	137.9	136.5	137.8
1994	132.9	131.3	133.3	136.4	136.6	137.7	139.6	141.1	142.2	140.6	140.4	140.8	137.7
1995	137.7	142.0	142.1	141.0	142.2	144.6	146.9	148.8	149.6	148.5	149.0	149.5	145.1
1996	147.6	149.2	150.2	150.7	152.8	156.1	156.8	157.7	158.0	157.2	156.9	155.8	154.0
1997	155.2	158.1	159.5	159.5	160.9	162.8	163.9	164.6	166.9	165.5	164.5	166.5	162.3
1998	163.6	161.9	164.2	167.1	168.3	171.7	173.6	174.1	174.1	174.7	173.7	172.9	169.9
1999	167.2	166.1	168.6	172.3	174.3	175.8	176.6	177.7	178.4	179.0	178.1	179.4	174.4
2000	174.9	175.7	175.9	179.1	181.2	185.6	186.4	188.3	190.4	190.6	191.6	192.6	184.3
2001	188.7	189.0	190.4	187.9	187.5	187.9	185.3	185.2	182.5	178.9	176.3	174.4	184.5
2002	166.1	167.1	167.6	170.1	171.2	174.1	173.8	175.7	174.7	173.8	171.5	170.5	171.4
2003	164.6	164.6	165.6	164.5	164.8	165.2	164.7	166.5	166.1	166.1	166.3	165.0	165.3
Natural resources and mining													
1990	3.4	3.4	3.4	3.1	3.2	3.2	3.2	3.2	3.1	3.2	3.2	3.1	3.2
1991	3.0	3.1	3.0	3.1	3.1	3.1	3.2	3.1	3.1	3.2	3.2	3.1	3.1
1992	3.4	3.4	3.4	3.4	3.3	3.3	3.3	3.3	3.2	3.0	3.0	2.9	3.2
1993	3.1	3.1	3.1	3.1	3.1	3.1	3.1	3.1	3.1	3.1	3.1	3.0	3.0
1994	2.6	2.4	2.4	2.7	2.8	2.8	2.7	2.8	2.9	2.9	2.9	2.9	2.7
1995	2.5	2.6	2.6	2.4	2.4	2.4	2.4	2.4	2.5	2.3	2.3	2.4	2.4
1996	2.3	2.3	2.2	2.3	2.3	2.3	2.3	2.3	2.3	2.3	2.3	2.3	2.2
1997	2.5	2.5	2.5	2.4	2.4	2.4	2.4	2.4	2.4	2.4	2.4	2.5	2.4
1998	3.3	3.3	3.3	1.8	1.7	1.7	1.7	1.8	1.7	1.8	1.9	1.9	2.1
1999	1.9	1.9	1.9	2.6	2.8	2.9	2.0	2.3	2.4	2.4	2.5	2.5	2.3
2000	2.3	2.4	2.4	2.4	2.4	2.4	2.4	2.4	2.3	2.3	2.4	2.4	2.3
2001	1.8	1.8	1.8	1.7	1.7	1.6	1.6	1.5	1.5	1.5	1.4	1.4	1.6
2002	1.3	1.3	1.3	1.3	1.3	1.2	1.1	1.1	1.0	1.0	1.0	1.0	1.2
2003	0.8	0.8	0.8	0.8	0.8	0.8	0.8	0.8	0.8	0.8	0.8	0.8	0.8
Construction													
1990	48.3	47.6	48.3	49.6	50.7	52.0	50.9	51.3	51.4	50.5	49.8	48.6	49.9
1991	44.6	44.0	44.6	44.8	45.0	46.2	46.9	47.6	47.6	47.2	45.5	44.8	45.7
1992	40.5	39.1	40.5	40.0	41.0	41.8	42.4	42.4	42.6	41.4	40.9	39.4	41.0
1993	36.3	37.2	38.6	39.4	40.5	41.2	42.1	42.7	42.3	41.7	41.3	40.0	40.2
1994	37.5	37.3	38.4	39.9	39.5	40.1	41.2	42.0	42.6	41.7	41.1	40.2	40.1
1995	37.6	40.6	40.0	40.3	41.1	42.1	43.6	45.2	45.4	44.9	44.9	44.2	42.4
1996	42.9	42.5	42.4	42.8	44.1	46.3	48.2	48.9	49.4	48.9	48.4	46.5	45.9
1997	44.8	46.8	47.5	47.2	48.2	49.3	50.0	50.6	52.0	50.7	49.7	50.0	48.9
1998	46.3	45.7	47.9	50.2	51.5	53.6	56.4	57.5	57.7	57.9	57.5	56.5	53.2
1999	55.4	54.2	55.8	57.9	59.8	60.8	62.1	62.9	63.0	63.0	62.6	62.7	60.0
2000	59.7	59.4	60.1	62.9	64.2	66.2	67.8	69.0	70.0	69.3	68.7	68.3	65.4
2001	66.7	67.2	68.9	69.4	70.7	71.8	71.8	72.4	71.6	70.0	68.8	67.4	69.7
2002	61.9	63.0	63.5	65.1	66.0	68.1	68.1	69.8	69.3	69.1	68.0	67.3	66.6
2003	64.6	65.2	66.2	65.4	65.9	66.8	67.3	69.2	68.9	69.2	69.2	67.9	67.2
Manufacturing													
1990	103.4	103.3	103.2	103.4	104.2	104.9	107.1	106.7	107.0	106.0	105.8	105.9	105.0
1991	103.2	101.8	100.8	99.9	99.7	100.6	101.8	101.2	101.6	100.6	100.6	100.1	100.9
1992	98.7	98.3	99.5	97.8	98.2	98.9	98.9	98.6	98.5	97.3	96.4	96.1	98.1
1993	95.4	94.9	94.9	94.5	94.5	95.3	94.8	94.4	94.9	93.4	93.5	93.5	94.5
1994	92.8	91.6	92.5	93.8	94.3	94.8	95.7	96.3	96.7	96.0	96.4	97.7	94.8
1995	97.6	98.8	99.5	98.3	98.7	100.1	100.9	101.2	101.7	101.3	101.8	102.9	100.2
1996	102.4	104.4	105.6	105.6	106.4	107.5	106.3	106.5	106.3	106.0	106.2	107.0	105.8
1997	107.9	108.8	109.5	109.9	110.3	111.1	111.5	111.6	112.5	112.4	112.4	114.0	110.9
1998	114.0	112.9	113.0	115.1	115.1	116.4	115.5	114.8	114.7	115.0	114.3	114.5	114.6
1999	109.9	110.0	110.9	111.8	111.7	112.1	112.5	112.5	113.0	113.6	113.0	114.2	112.1
2000	112.9	113.9	113.4	113.8	114.6	117.0	116.2	116.9	118.1	119.0	120.5	121.9	116.5
2001	120.2	120.0	119.7	116.8	115.1	114.5	111.9	111.3	109.4	107.4	106.1	105.6	113.1
2002	102.9	102.8	102.8	103.7	103.9	104.8	104.6	104.8	104.4	103.7	102.5	102.2	103.6
2003	99.2	98.6	98.6	98.3	98.1	97.6	96.6	96.5	96.4	96.1	96.3	96.3	97.4

Employment by Industry: California—*Continued*

(Numbers in thousands. Not seasonally adjusted.)

Industry	January	February	March	April	May	June	July	August	September	October	November	December	Annual Average
OAKLAND—*Continued*													
Service-providing													
1990	703.5	706.9	709.9	713.3	716.7	722.0	718.1	717.2	726.8	733.5	740.2	743.9	721.0
1991	727.6	730.8	730.9	731.3	732.2	733.2	720.8	720.3	725.6	730.4	736.8	737.9	729.8
1992	719.0	723.6	726.5	729.0	730.2	728.8	719.3	717.8	727.3	733.3	738.0	741.2	727.8
1993	728.1	733.0	734.2	734.4	737.0	739.2	728.7	728.4	733.0	738.4	743.2	750.1	735.6
1994	729.8	736.7	741.5	738.6	740.8	740.8	729.7	731.5	738.9	742.2	750.2	755.3	739.6
1995	736.8	745.2	748.7	747.9	751.3	756.7	747.3	749.0	758.9	755.2	763.2	767.5	752.3
1996	748.0	753.2	754.1	754.2	759.9	765.1	756.0	757.3	765.2	769.6	780.1	785.3	762.3
1997	764.0	770.9	777.9	780.6	786.7	789.3	780.4	782.6	792.5	793.5	799.4	807.4	785.4
1998	785.8	793.0	799.3	800.4	805.8	808.2	798.9	803.2	813.1	813.6	822.7	830.3	806.1
1999	811.5	819.7	825.7	828.6	835.1	836.8	830.0	832.5	838.5	840.8	846.8	856.3	833.5
2000	837.8	843.7	851.7	856.7	862.9	868.8	857.2	860.2	863.9	865.7	873.4	880.7	860.2
2001	863.3	868.3	875.3	871.9	872.5	875.0	865.4	866.1	867.9	869.8	871.3	876.2	870.2
2002	859.2	864.7	871.4	866.2	869.3	871.4	859.6	860.8	867.8	872.1	878.0	881.0	868.5
2003	859.9	864.0	866.8	862.6	864.1	866.0	849.6	848.3	853.3	857.0	859.4	861.4	859.4
Trade, transportation, and utilities													
1990	176.4	173.5	173.1	173.5	173.9	175.8	178.3	178.2	178.5	181.8	185.8	189.3	178.1
1991	185.0	181.6	180.2	177.8	177.9	178.7	177.9	178.8	178.0	180.5	184.5	186.6	180.6
1992	177.2	175.4	174.8	175.3	175.6	175.7	177.0	176.8	177.5	177.8	180.9	183.5	177.2
1993	180.1	178.2	177.7	176.1	176.6	177.6	177.1	176.4	176.7	177.4	180.3	185.1	178.2
1994	177.1	177.0	177.2	175.8	176.0	176.5	178.0	178.7	179.5	182.8	187.2	190.9	179.7
1995	181.4	180.3	180.4	180.2	180.3	181.7	182.6	184.0	184.9	185.7	190.5	193.9	183.8
1996	183.8	183.2	183.0	183.4	185.1	187.3	186.4	186.1	186.3	188.3	193.7	197.2	186.9
1997	189.2	188.1	189.3	189.5	190.6	191.6	192.4	193.0	194.2	194.1	199.0	204.1	192.9
1998	195.0	194.0	194.7	191.3	192.5	194.1	194.5	196.0	196.2	196.0	199.3	203.8	195.6
1999	200.4	199.5	200.0	198.4	199.7	200.7	202.4	204.0	204.6	203.7	207.2	212.1	202.7
2000	202.8	201.2	202.2	204.5	206.2	207.9	208.1	208.1	208.4	208.8	214.1	219.4	207.6
2001	213.0	211.6	212.1	210.2	209.3	210.5	209.1	208.0	208.1	206.6	209.5	211.7	209.9
2002	204.5	203.1	203.7	201.6	202.7	204.0	203.5	203.0	203.8	205.0	208.8	211.8	204.6
2003	200.9	198.7	198.0	195.9	196.2	197.7	196.1	196.6	196.9	197.4	199.7	202.4	198.0
Wholesale trade													
1990	40.2	39.9	39.9	40.6	40.8	41.0	41.5	41.5	41.5	42.3	42.3	42.1	41.1
1991	41.2	41.5	41.5	41.0	41.1	41.1	40.6	40.5	40.2	40.8	40.6	40.7	40.9
1992	40.7	40.7	40.9	41.7	41.9	41.9	41.7	41.4	41.7	41.3	41.2	41.4	41.3
1993	41.1	41.2	41.4	40.8	40.9	41.3	41.1	41.1	41.1	40.7	40.9	41.1	41.0
1994	40.5	40.9	41.2	41.0	41.0	41.2	41.4	41.6	41.9	41.3	41.2	41.6	41.2
1995	41.0	41.4	41.7	42.3	42.4	42.6	42.5	42.6	42.9	42.3	42.6	42.9	42.2
1996	41.9	42.4	43.0	43.3	43.6	44.1	44.4	44.3	43.9	45.1	45.2	45.3	43.8
1997	45.1	45.4	45.7	46.3	46.5	46.6	46.5	46.4	46.8	47.2	47.3	47.6	46.4
1998	47.4	48.2	49.0	50.2	50.3	50.6	50.1	50.3	50.5	50.3	50.4	50.4	49.8
1999	51.4	51.8	52.0	51.2	51.3	51.6	51.4	51.7	51.4	51.3	51.3	51.5	51.4
2000	51.2	51.4	52.3	53.3	53.6	54.1	54.5	54.6	54.8	54.5	54.6	55.2	53.6
2001	56.0	56.6	56.8	56.1	55.8	55.8	55.3	55.1	55.1	54.4	54.2	54.1	55.4
2002	53.4	53.7	53.9	52.9	53.2	53.3	53.0	52.9	52.8	52.6	52.8	52.9	53.1
2003	51.6	51.6	51.7	51.6	51.3	51.3	50.8	50.7	50.7	50.6	50.8	50.9	51.1
Retail trade													
1990	104.0	101.4	101.1	100.3	100.6	101.7	103.3	103.2	103.2	105.1	109.2	112.6	103.8
1991	108.3	104.6	103.6	103.4	103.3	104.0	103.4	104.4	104.1	104.9	108.7	110.8	105.2
1992	103.4	101.5	100.7	100.5	100.3	100.5	101.2	101.1	101.6	102.4	105.3	108.0	102.2
1993	104.7	102.6	102.0	101.5	101.4	102.1	102.1	101.8	102.1	103.3	106.2	110.1	103.3
1994	102.3	101.0	100.7	100.0	99.9	100.2	100.7	100.8	101.0	103.5	107.6	110.6	102.3
1995	103.8	102.0	101.4	101.2	101.3	102.0	101.9	102.9	102.8	104.1	108.1	111.3	103.5
1996	104.1	102.7	101.9	102.3	103.1	104.3	103.0	103.0	103.5	103.5	108.4	111.6	104.2
1997	105.0	103.3	103.7	103.7	104.3	104.9	106.0	106.2	107.3	105.7	110.2	115.0	106.2
1998	107.0	105.1	105.0	102.4	102.9	103.8	104.6	105.7	105.5	105.4	108.7	112.6	105.7
1999	107.4	106.0	106.3	105.7	106.5	107.3	109.8	110.8	112.1	110.5	113.7	118.3	109.5
2000	110.5	109.0	109.2	109.9	111.3	112.0	111.6	111.3	111.3	112.6	117.4	121.1	112.2
2001	114.6	112.7	112.7	112.3	112.0	113.1	112.9	112.3	112.2	111.6	115.5	117.5	113.2
2002	111.2	109.4	109.9	109.6	110.3	111.0	111.2	110.9	111.9	112.9	116.8	119.4	112.0
2003	111.7	109.6	109.1	107.9	108.4	109.2	108.8	109.3	109.4	109.9	112.2	114.5	110.0
Transportation and utilities													
1990	32.2	32.2	32.1	32.6	32.5	33.1	33.5	33.5	33.8	34.4	34.3	34.6	33.2
1991	35.5	35.5	35.1	33.4	33.5	33.6	33.9	33.9	33.7	34.8	35.2	35.1	34.4
1992	33.1	33.2	33.2	33.1	33.4	33.3	34.1	34.3	34.2	34.1	34.4	34.1	33.7
1993	34.3	34.4	34.3	33.8	34.3	34.2	33.9	33.5	33.5	33.4	33.2	33.9	33.8
1994	34.3	35.1	35.3	34.8	35.1	35.1	35.9	36.3	36.6	38.0	38.4	38.7	36.1
1995	36.6	36.9	37.3	36.7	36.6	37.1	38.2	38.5	39.2	39.3	39.8	39.7	37.9
1996	37.8	38.1	38.1	37.8	38.4	38.9	39.0	38.8	38.9	39.7	40.1	40.3	38.8
1997	39.1	39.4	39.9	39.5	39.8	40.1	39.9	40.4	40.1	41.2	41.5	41.5	40.2
1998	40.6	40.7	40.7	38.7	39.3	39.7	39.8	40.0	40.2	40.3	40.2	40.8	40.0
1999	41.6	41.7	41.7	41.5	41.9	41.8	41.2	41.5	41.1	41.9	42.2	42.3	41.7
2000	41.1	40.8	40.7	41.3	41.3	41.8	42.0	42.2	42.3	41.7	42.1	43.1	41.7
2001	42.4	42.3	42.6	41.8	41.5	41.6	40.9	40.6	40.8	40.6	39.8	40.1	41.2
2002	39.9	40.0	39.9	39.1	39.2	39.7	39.3	39.2	39.1	39.5	39.2	39.5	39.5
2003	37.6	37.5	37.2	36.4	36.5	37.2	36.5	36.6	36.8	36.9	36.7	37.0	36.9

Employment by Industry: California—*Continued*

(Numbers in thousands. Not seasonally adjusted.)

Industry	January	February	March	April	May	June	July	August	September	October	November	December	Annual Average
OAKLAND—*Continued*													
Information													
1990	30.2	30.0	30.0	29.2	29.3	29.3	29.8	29.5	29.5	29.9	29.8	29.9	29.7
1991	29.8	29.9	30.0	32.1	32.3	32.6	32.1	31.9	32.0	32.1	32.1	31.4	31.5
1992	30.5	29.6	29.3	29.2	29.5	29.2	29.4	29.5	29.0	29.6	29.7	29.6	29.5
1993	29.3	29.1	29.0	29.1	29.2	29.4	29.2	28.6	28.4	28.5	28.6	28.8	28.9
1994	28.4	28.6	28.6	28.9	29.2	29.5	29.5	29.6	29.5	29.1	29.2	29.1	29.1
1995	29.1	29.1	29.3	29.1	29.6	29.5	28.8	28.8	29.0	28.8	29.1	29.3	29.1
1996	29.0	28.8	29.1	29.0	29.2	29.7	29.9	30.1	29.9	30.3	30.7	30.7	29.7
1997	30.6	30.9	31.3	31.9	32.4	32.6	32.8	32.8	33.1	34.1	33.9	34.3	32.5
1998	33.9	34.4	34.3	33.9	33.7	34.0	34.3	34.4	34.5	34.4	34.6	35.1	34.2
1999	33.4	33.8	34.0	34.3	34.5	34.7	35.4	35.3	35.4	35.8	36.3	37.3	35.0
2000	37.2	37.8	38.3	38.4	39.4	40.2	39.0	39.3	39.3	39.4	39.5	39.6	38.9
2001	39.7	39.3	39.2	38.3	38.1	37.3	38.2	37.8	37.3	36.0	35.9	35.7	37.7
2002	36.6	36.5	36.4	35.5	35.7	35.7	34.5	34.3	33.9	34.2	34.4	34.4	35.2
2003	33.8	34.3	33.2	32.7	32.4	32.4	31.9	31.7	31.1	31.2	31.3	31.1	32.3
Financial activities													
1990	56.9	56.7	57.1	56.8	57.3	57.1	58.3	58.2	58.0	57.9	57.3	57.7	57.4
1991	57.2	57.4	57.1	55.9	54.7	54.4	54.0	53.9	54.0	53.3	53.4	53.7	54.9
1992	53.6	54.3	54.8	54.1	54.5	54.7	53.5	54.3	54.3	54.3	54.4	54.5	54.2
1993	53.6	53.5	53.4	53.6	53.6	54.1	54.5	54.6	54.1	53.3	53.4	53.5	53.7
1994	53.8	53.8	53.8	53.1	52.7	52.5	52.1	51.9	51.5	50.8	50.5	50.5	52.2
1995	50.1	50.4	50.5	50.8	50.6	50.9	50.9	50.9	50.8	50.5	50.3	50.5	50.6
1996	48.9	49.5	49.9	50.2	50.2	50.7	50.3	50.1	49.9	49.7	49.8	49.9	49.9
1997	48.3	48.3	48.2	48.5	48.8	49.3	49.1	49.6	49.8	49.8	50.0	50.6	49.1
1998	47.9	48.4	48.1	48.1	48.4	48.9	48.5	48.8	49.0	49.1	49.5	50.3	48.7
1999	49.4	49.7	50.2	50.0	50.6	50.6	50.4	50.5	50.2	49.6	49.5	49.7	50.0
2000	50.3	50.8	50.7	50.4	50.4	50.7	50.3	50.4	50.3	50.5	50.6	51.6	50.5
2001	56.1	56.8	57.5	57.6	57.8	58.4	59.3	59.5	59.5	59.7	60.0	60.4	58.5
2002	59.0	59.4	59.6	60.8	61.5	62.2	62.7	63.6	63.8	64.9	65.8	66.6	62.5
2003	67.3	67.8	68.3	67.8	68.2	68.3	67.7	67.8	67.7	67.8	67.7	67.9	67.9
Professional and business services													
1990	102.8	103.7	105.3	105.2	105.9	107.4	108.8	109.2	109.7	111.5	111.8	113.4	107.8
1991	107.2	108.5	109.2	111.7	112.2	112.7	112.8	113.1	113.3	112.3	112.8	113.6	111.6
1992	109.6	110.0	110.6	112.2	111.8	111.5	112.5	113.0	114.5	114.0	114.3	114.5	112.3
1993	112.2	112.9	113.8	114.4	114.5	115.1	115.6	117.9	118.5	119.7	120.2	122.1	116.4
1994	115.5	117.1	118.5	118.0	118.1	119.2	119.1	119.7	121.2	119.7	120.8	122.2	119.0
1995	117.8	119.9	121.5	120.9	122.2	124.1	125.5	127.3	128.7	124.9	125.5	126.2	123.7
1996	124.6	124.2	124.7	122.8	123.8	126.0	129.5	131.7	133.1	133.6	134.9	137.4	128.8
1997	133.5	134.9	137.3	139.6	140.8	142.5	146.0	146.6	148.0	145.8	145.8	147.1	142.3
1998	143.6	146.3	148.4	150.1	149.6	151.4	152.3	154.6	154.9	154.6	156.1	157.4	151.6
1999	152.3	154.1	156.3	158.7	158.6	159.9	161.2	162.0	162.4	164.2	164.8	167.3	160.1
2000	163.0	164.6	167.3	169.7	168.3	170.2	171.4	172.7	173.8	173.2	173.8	174.2	170.1
2001	162.5	162.5	163.5	160.1	159.7	160.6	158.1	158.0	156.7	156.1	154.7	155.7	159.0
2002	151.0	151.5	153.0	150.5	149.9	150.3	148.5	149.4	148.6	147.4	147.1	147.9	149.6
2003	142.8	143.6	145.1	144.0	143.3	144.3	143.6	143.5	143.0	142.6	142.5	142.7	143.4
Educational and health services													
1990	84.5	86.3	86.1	87.8	86.9	88.8	87.7	89.3	89.8	90.2	92.6	92.1	88.5
1991	88.3	90.6	90.1	91.3	91.6	91.3	90.2	89.7	90.3	92.3	92.9	92.2	90.9
1992	91.6	93.2	93.1	93.7	93.4	93.1	92.5	91.5	92.6	94.0	95.0	95.7	93.2
1993	94.6	96.0	96.0	96.1	96.0	96.7	95.1	94.3	95.6	96.1	97.2	97.7	95.9
1994	95.2	96.6	97.2	96.1	96.1	95.3	93.5	92.8	94.8	94.6	96.2	96.4	95.4
1995	95.9	98.2	98.4	97.4	97.6	99.0	96.2	95.9	97.8	97.1	98.3	98.3	97.5
1996	96.3	97.9	98.2	98.3	98.8	98.8	95.9	94.8	96.0	96.7	98.0	97.8	97.2
1997	96.7	99.1	101.0	101.1	101.9	101.2	98.8	97.7	99.1	101.6	101.6	101.6	100.1
1998	103.1	105.0	105.6	105.9	107.5	106.6	103.9	103.7	105.0	107.0	108.1	108.6	105.8
1999	107.8	109.8	109.9	108.6	109.5	109.6	108.2	108.6	109.4	109.1	109.5	109.8	109.1
2000	108.5	109.8	110.8	110.8	111.2	111.1	109.2	109.6	111.2	111.2	111.9	113.1	110.7
2001	109.0	111.0	111.9	111.0	112.1	112.2	112.1	112.6	113.8	114.4	114.7	115.4	112.5
2002	113.8	115.7	116.9	113.2	113.5	112.8	113.9	114.0	115.2	115.1	116.0	115.9	114.7
2003	114.5	116.4	117.3	118.2	118.6	117.5	116.1	116.4	117.7	118.1	118.6	119.1	117.4
Leisure and hospitality													
1990	60.7	61.8	62.6	62.6	63.6	64.5	64.9	65.4	65.3	64.9	64.4	64.3	63.7
1991	62.9	64.3	64.7	62.9	63.6	64.6	64.0	64.9	64.1	63.3	63.5	63.9	63.8
1992	61.8	62.9	63.6	64.6	65.5	65.2	64.3	64.9	64.3	64.4	63.9	64.3	64.1
1993	62.5	63.4	63.9	64.2	66.3	66.5	66.4	66.6	65.9	65.4	65.3	65.5	65.1
1994	64.1	65.1	66.0	65.6	66.9	67.5	66.1	66.5	65.7	64.9	64.5	65.4	65.6
1995	64.1	65.6	66.7	68.1	69.0	70.2	70.6	71.0	71.1	68.5	68.8	70.1	68.6
1996	68.1	69.4	70.1	70.8	72.8	73.3	73.5	73.2	72.6	71.2	71.5	71.6	71.5
1997	69.0	69.3	69.6	69.6	71.4	72.6	71.6	71.3	70.7	69.0	68.8	69.8	70.2
1998	65.4	66.2	67.2	69.1	71.2	72.8	73.4	73.8	73.5	72.3	71.9	72.3	70.7
1999	67.8	68.5	70.2	71.2	73.9	74.3	74.6	75.0	73.9	73.1	72.5	73.4	72.3
2000	71.0	71.8	72.5	72.5	73.7	75.1	76.4	76.6	75.6	73.3	73.0	73.4	73.7
2001	74.2	74.7	76.2	77.4	78.5	80.0	80.4	80.8	79.1	77.8	77.4	77.9	77.8
2002	76.0	76.7	78.0	79.2	80.4	82.1	82.4	82.7	81.3	80.1	80.0	80.2	79.9
2003	78.2	78.5	79.3	79.3	80.8	82.4	82.4	82.7	81.6	80.9	80.6	80.7	80.6

Employment by Industry: California—*Continued*

(Numbers in thousands. Not seasonally adjusted.)

Industry	January	February	March	April	May	June	July	August	September	October	November	December	Annual Average
OAKLAND—*Continued*													
Other services													
1990	26.1	26.2	26.4	27.4	27.3	27.7	27.9	27.9	28.1	28.5	28.3	28.4	27.5
1991	28.5	27.9	28.1	27.6	27.6	27.8	27.8	27.7	27.5	27.2	27.0	27.1	27.6
1992	26.6	27.1	27.3	27.2	27.3	27.3	27.5	27.5	27.5	27.0	26.9	27.0	27.1
1993	26.7	27.3	27.4	27.6	27.7	28.0	28.0	28.0	27.7	27.5	27.5	27.5	27.5
1994	27.6	27.9	28.3	28.3	28.5	28.6	29.0	29.1	29.2	28.2	28.5	28.4	28.4
1995	28.0	28.6	28.9	28.8	29.1	29.5	29.9	29.8	29.6	29.0	29.0	29.3	29.1
1996	29.0	29.3	29.6	29.7	30.1	30.8	30.2	30.4	30.3	29.8	29.9	29.8	29.9
1997	29.3	29.9	30.2	30.0	30.4	30.7	30.5	30.6	30.6	30.1	29.9	30.2	30.2
1998	29.7	29.9	31.0	30.6	30.8	31.3	31.1	31.3	31.3	29.6	29.4	29.5	30.4
1999	29.9	30.3	30.7	30.6	31.0	31.2	31.6	31.7	31.7	31.3	31.1	31.4	31.0
2000	30.5	30.9	31.3	31.6	31.9	32.3	32.9	32.6	32.1	32.0	31.9	32.2	31.8
2001	33.3	33.9	34.5	35.0	35.6	36.4	36.6	36.8	36.6	36.7	36.8	37.2	35.7
2002	36.6	37.2	37.4	37.5	37.7	38.3	38.8	38.7	38.5	37.8	37.9	37.6	37.8
2003	37.2	37.6	37.6	37.8	38.1	38.6	37.9	38.1	37.7	37.5	37.4	37.4	37.7
Government													
1990	165.9	168.7	169.3	170.8	172.5	171.4	162.4	159.5	167.9	168.8	170.2	168.8	168.0
1991	168.7	170.6	171.5	172.0	172.3	171.1	162.0	160.3	166.4	169.4	170.6	169.4	168.6
1992	168.1	171.1	173.0	172.7	172.6	172.1	162.6	160.3	167.6	172.2	172.9	172.1	169.7
1993	169.1	172.6	173.0	173.3	173.1	171.8	162.8	162.0	166.1	170.5	170.7	169.9	169.5
1994	168.1	170.6	171.9	172.8	173.3	171.7	162.4	163.2	167.5	172.1	173.3	172.4	169.9
1995	170.4	173.1	173.0	172.6	172.9	171.8	162.8	161.3	167.0	170.7	171.7	169.9	169.7
1996	168.3	170.9	169.5	170.0	169.9	168.5	160.3	160.9	167.1	170.0	171.6	170.9	168.1
1997	167.4	170.4	171.0	170.4	170.4	168.8	159.2	161.0	167.0	169.0	170.4	169.7	167.8
1998	167.2	168.8	170.0	171.4	172.1	169.1	160.9	160.6	168.7	170.6	173.8	173.3	168.8
1999	170.5	174.0	174.4	176.8	177.3	175.8	166.2	165.4	170.9	174.0	175.9	175.3	173.0
2000	174.5	176.8	178.6	178.8	181.8	181.3	169.9	170.9	173.2	177.3	178.6	177.2	176.5
2001	175.5	178.5	180.4	182.3	181.4	179.6	171.6	172.6	176.8	182.5	182.3	182.2	178.8
2002	181.7	184.6	186.4	187.9	187.9	186.0	175.3	175.1	182.7	187.6	188.0	186.6	184.2
2003	185.2	187.1	188.0	186.9	186.5	184.8	173.9	171.5	177.6	181.5	181.6	180.1	182.1
Federal government													
1990	31.0	30.8	30.9	31.3	32.3	32.5	31.6	31.1	30.4	30.1	30.1	30.1	31.0
1991	30.3	30.3	30.3	30.4	30.3	30.3	30.4	30.4	30.3	30.0	30.2	30.3	30.2
1992	29.9	30.0	30.2	30.3	30.3	30.3	30.3	30.3	30.3	30.1	30.1	30.6	30.2
1993	29.6	29.4	29.4	29.5	29.2	29.2	29.0	29.0	28.6	28.4	28.1	28.9	29.0
1994	28.3	28.1	28.1	28.2	28.1	27.8	27.8	28.0	28.1	28.2	28.2	28.8	28.1
1995	28.1	27.9	27.6	26.9	26.8	26.6	26.4	26.5	26.6	25.9	25.8	26.5	26.8
1996	25.4	25.3	25.2	24.9	24.8	24.7	24.4	24.4	24.2	23.9	24.0	24.7	24.6
1997	23.4	23.4	23.2	22.8	22.1	22.1	21.8	21.7	21.4	20.8	21.0	21.6	22.1
1998	20.6	20.4	20.5	20.8	21.0	20.9	20.9	20.9	21.0	21.1	21.0	21.7	20.9
1999	20.7	20.4	20.1	20.4	20.2	20.2	20.3	20.4	20.4	19.9	20.3	21.2	20.3
2000	20.3	20.1	20.5	21.2	24.0	24.2	21.3	22.2	19.5	19.4	19.5	19.7	20.9
2001	19.5	19.5	19.5	20.0	19.9	19.8	18.7	18.8	18.8	18.7	18.7	18.8	19.2
2002	18.6	18.5	18.6	18.4	18.4	18.4	18.4	18.4	18.3	18.8	18.8	19.3	18.6
2003	18.9	18.9	19.0	18.9	18.9	18.9	17.9	17.8	17.6	17.7	17.6	17.9	18.3
State government													
1990	40.2	41.1	41.2	41.3	41.3	39.8	40.1	40.0	40.8	40.8	41.2	40.5	40.6
1991	40.5	41.0	41.2	41.3	41.0	39.5	39.6	40.1	39.9	40.4	40.5	40.0	40.4
1992	40.0	40.7	41.3	41.2	41.0	39.9	40.1	40.6	42.0	43.4	43.6	42.8	41.3
1993	41.8	43.2	43.6	43.7	43.3	42.5	42.6	42.9	42.8	42.6	42.8	41.9	42.8
1994	41.3	43.0	43.7	44.0	43.9	43.0	42.8	43.4	43.0	44.0	44.5	43.8	43.3
1995	43.6	44.7	44.3	44.5	44.3	43.6	43.1	43.0	42.9	44.0	44.2	43.3	43.7
1996	43.2	44.3	43.8	44.1	43.8	42.4	42.3	42.3	42.9	43.3	43.5	43.0	43.2
1997	42.4	43.2	44.0	43.6	43.3	42.3	42.1	42.1	42.9	43.3	43.6	43.4	43.0
1998	42.7	43.3	44.0	44.3	44.1	42.2	43.4	43.3	44.2	44.6	45.3	44.9	43.8
1999	43.6	45.4	46.1	46.2	46.4	45.6	44.9	45.1	45.4	45.9	46.3	45.7	45.5
2000	44.5	46.1	46.6	46.7	46.6	45.1	45.2	45.3	45.1	46.4	46.6	46.1	45.8
2001	45.2	46.7	47.1	47.7	47.6	46.4	46.9	47.1	47.4	48.5	48.1	48.3	47.2
2002	47.4	49.0	49.4	49.7	49.7	48.6	48.5	48.5	49.2	49.5	49.9	49.3	49.1
2003	48.7	49.2	49.6	49.6	49.3	48.3	48.1	47.3	48.7	49.2	48.9	48.2	48.8
Local government													
1990	94.7	96.8	97.2	98.2	98.9	99.1	90.7	88.4	96.7	97.9	98.9	98.2	96.3
1991	97.9	99.3	100.0	100.3	101.0	101.3	92.0	89.8	96.2	99.0	99.9	99.1	97.9
1992	98.2	100.4	101.5	101.2	101.3	101.9	92.2	89.4	95.3	98.7	99.2	98.7	98.1
1993	97.7	100.0	100.0	100.1	100.6	100.1	91.2	90.1	94.7	99.5	99.8	99.1	97.7
1994	98.5	99.5	100.1	100.6	101.3	100.9	91.8	91.8	96.4	99.9	100.6	99.8	98.4
1995	98.7	100.5	101.1	101.2	101.8	101.6	93.3	91.8	97.5	100.8	101.7	100.1	99.1
1996	99.7	101.3	100.5	101.0	101.3	101.4	93.6	94.2	100.0	102.8	104.1	103.2	100.2
1997	101.6	103.8	103.8	104.0	105.0	104.4	95.3	97.2	102.7	104.9	105.8	104.7	102.7
1998	103.9	105.1	105.5	106.3	107.0	106.0	96.6	96.4	103.5	104.9	107.5	106.7	104.1
1999	106.2	108.2	108.2	110.2	110.7	110.0	101.0	99.9	105.1	108.2	109.3	108.4	107.1
2000	109.7	110.6	111.5	110.9	111.2	112.0	103.4	103.4	108.6	111.5	112.5	111.4	109.7
2001	110.8	112.3	113.8	114.6	113.9	113.4	106.0	106.7	110.6	115.3	115.5	115.1	112.3
2002	115.7	117.1	118.4	119.8	119.8	119.0	108.4	108.2	115.2	119.3	119.3	118.0	116.5
2003	117.6	119.0	119.4	118.4	118.3	117.6	107.9	106.4	111.3	114.6	115.1	114.0	115.0

Employment by Industry: California—*Continued*

(Numbers in thousands. Not seasonally adjusted.)

Industry	January	February	March	April	May	June	July	August	September	October	November	December	Annual Average
SACRAMENTO													
Total nonfarm													
1990	539.1	541.7	546.4	549.7	555.2	560.0	557.5	557.9	564.3	564.3	566.7	568.6	555.9
1991	558.9	557.9	558.7	560.2	563.4	568.3	566.1	566.2	571.1	567.8	569.2	568.0	564.6
1992	543.8	543.1	547.4	551.8	554.5	558.4	557.2	555.3	558.4	556.5	558.6	559.9	553.7
1993	546.2	548.5	551.9	551.4	551.1	553.7	553.6	554.6	557.6	558.8	560.1	564.1	554.3
1994	553.7	557.3	562.9	565.2	566.7	573.0	571.2	572.3	575.2	574.1	578.2	582.0	569.3
1995	570.7	576.8	581.3	582.2	584.0	589.0	583.2	589.4	594.1	592.9	600.0	600.0	586.9
1996	591.9	594.3	599.4	599.3	602.9	608.1	603.1	609.6	611.5	610.1	616.6	616.3	605.2
1997	604.9	609.4	616.3	618.7	622.5	627.4	626.0	630.9	635.3	633.0	636.8	641.4	625.2
1998	628.1	632.1	641.0	643.7	647.5	654.1	653.4	656.8	659.6	662.9	668.9	676.5	652.0
1999	662.6	671.1	676.2	679.4	681.9	690.6	689.2	692.0	694.8	692.6	696.9	703.6	685.9
2000	688.1	692.6	699.3	701.7	707.7	715.8	708.0	715.1	717.1	716.3	724.3	730.6	709.7
2001	714.2	717.3	726.1	726.8	728.6	735.0	734.0	737.1	734.1	735.2	741.4	745.0	731.2
2002	728.8	730.4	739.9	738.5	744.6	748.1	744.6	746.2	748.2	747.3	752.1	753.0	743.5
2003	742.4	743.4	747.4	750.8	752.7	758.1	752.7	753.0	753.8	755.9	759.3	758.9	752.4
Total private													
1990	378.1	379.7	383.5	386.4	391.5	396.7	399.6	402.4	404.0	402.4	404.2	406.9	394.6
1991	396.6	395.9	395.2	395.5	399.5	403.9	407.0	409.0	409.0	406.1	407.4	406.7	402.6
1992	385.0	382.2	386.2	390.0	392.6	397.3	398.9	398.3	398.7	395.9	395.4	398.3	393.2
1993	384.4	385.7	389.0	390.9	392.2	395.5	399.2	400.1	399.4	398.9	399.7	404.5	394.9
1994	394.2	394.7	400.5	402.0	402.8	408.5	410.5	413.0	413.6	409.7	413.3	417.5	406.6
1995	405.9	410.6	414.2	414.3	416.6	421.8	423.1	428.1	429.1	426.3	432.0	432.4	421.2
1996	425.0	427.8	431.2	431.6	435.0	440.7	440.8	446.5	446.0	442.2	447.6	448.4	438.5
1997	436.8	440.0	444.6	447.7	450.9	457.5	461.3	465.9	466.2	463.5	466.5	472.0	456.0
1998	459.6	461.9	468.7	471.1	474.5	481.9	484.3	488.0	489.0	489.6	494.0	500.9	480.2
1999	488.1	492.0	496.0	499.9	501.5	508.9	514.4	515.7	515.4	513.7	517.8	523.9	507.2
2000	510.3	512.5	516.8	519.6	522.2	530.3	531.6	536.5	536.9	534.3	541.2	547.6	528.3
2001	532.6	534.2	539.8	539.2	541.2	547.0	548.3	549.6	543.8	544.3	548.7	552.2	543.4
2002	537.8	538.0	542.6	541.1	546.3	551.0	551.9	553.1	553.9	552.9	557.6	559.1	548.8
2003	550.8	550.1	553.9	557.4	559.0	565.0	563.0	564.8	564.1	565.0	568.0	568.6	560.8
Goods-producing													
1990	68.7	69.9	71.4	72.6	74.6	76.6	76.6	77.3	77.8	75.1	73.2	71.1	73.7
1991	66.8	66.2	65.0	66.5	68.4	70.0	70.5	71.0	71.2	70.9	69.5	67.2	68.6
1992	59.7	58.7	60.2	61.4	62.4	63.5	64.5	64.7	64.3	64.0	62.9	60.4	62.2
1993	56.2	56.7	57.4	57.9	59.3	60.5	62.1	63.5	62.5	62.5	61.6	60.5	60.0
1994	57.5	57.2	59.4	60.7	62.3	64.1	65.4	66.4	66.7	65.6	64.4	63.4	62.7
1995	59.8	61.9	62.5	62.7	64.0	65.9	69.5	71.4	71.6	70.4	70.6	69.3	66.6
1996	67.4	67.5	68.2	69.5	71.5	72.9	73.2	74.8	75.0	74.7	74.6	72.5	71.8
1997	69.3	70.6	72.2	73.0	74.7	77.2	78.8	81.1	80.9	80.1	79.1	78.4	76.2
1998	74.9	74.7	77.2	77.6	79.7	82.1	84.0	85.4	85.8	86.2	86.2	85.3	81.5
1999	83.7	83.5	85.0	86.4	87.9	89.7	91.4	92.4	92.5	92.5	92.0	91.5	89.0
2000	88.0	88.0	89.3	90.4	92.5	94.7	95.4	97.6	97.5	97.3	97.4	97.4	93.7
2001	94.3	94.9	96.9	98.3	100.6	103.0	103.3	103.7	102.4	101.7	99.9	98.3	99.7
2002	94.2	94.2	95.4	96.1	98.5	99.6	100.6	102.1	102.1	101.4	100.6	99.0	98.7
2003	95.4	96.4	98.1	99.4	101.0	102.8	102.4	103.8	103.6	103.0	102.1	100.5	100.7
Natural resources and mining													
1990	0.3	0.4	0.4	0.5	0.6	0.7	0.7	0.7	0.7	0.6	0.6	0.5	0.5
1991	0.7	0.7	0.7	0.7	0.8	0.8	0.8	0.8	0.8	0.8	0.8	0.7	0.7
1992	0.6	0.5	0.5	0.6	0.7	0.8	0.9	0.8	0.8	0.8	0.8	0.7	0.7
1993	0.5	0.5	0.5	0.6	0.7	0.7	0.8	0.8	0.8	0.8	0.7	0.7	0.6
1994	0.6	0.5	0.6	0.6	0.6	0.6	0.6	0.6	0.7	0.6	0.6	0.5	0.5
1995	0.3	0.4	0.4	0.4	0.4	0.5	0.6	0.6	0.6	0.6	0.5	0.4	0.4
1996	0.4	0.3	0.4	0.4	0.5	0.5	0.5	0.5	0.5	0.5	0.5	0.4	0.4
1997	0.3	0.3	0.4	0.4	0.4	0.5	0.5	0.5	0.5	0.5	0.5	0.4	0.4
1998	0.4	0.4	0.4	0.4	0.4	0.4	0.5	0.5	0.5	0.6	0.5	0.4	0.4
1999	0.4	0.4	0.4	0.5	0.6	0.6	0.6	0.6	0.6	0.6	0.6	0.6	0.5
2000	0.5	0.5	0.5	0.6	0.6	0.6	0.6	0.6	0.6	0.6	0.6	0.6	0.5
2001	0.5	0.5	0.5	0.6	0.6	0.6	0.6	0.6	0.6	0.6	0.5	0.5	0.5
2002	0.5	0.5	0.5	0.5	0.5	0.5	0.5	0.5	0.5	0.6	0.6	0.6	0.5
2003	0.4	0.4	0.4	0.4	0.5	0.5	0.5	0.5	0.5	0.5	0.5	0.5	0.5
Construction													
1990	34.6	35.4	36.8	38.1	40.0	41.5	40.9	41.6	42.1	39.4	37.9	36.4	38.7
1991	31.6	31.2	30.3	31.2	32.7	33.9	34.0	34.3	34.2	33.5	32.4	31.0	32.5
1992	25.7	24.8	26.0	27.6	28.9	29.7	29.8	29.6	29.4	28.7	27.9	25.8	27.8
1993	22.3	22.8	23.6	24.0	25.2	26.1	26.8	27.6	27.3	27.5	26.9	25.7	25.4
1994	23.8	23.6	25.1	26.1	27.4	28.7	29.1	29.6	29.7	29.5	28.3	27.4	27.3
1995	24.3	26.1	26.4	27.3	28.3	29.7	29.6	30.5	30.6	30.0	29.6	28.1	28.3
1996	26.9	26.9	27.1	28.4	29.9	31.1	31.2	32.5	32.6	32.8	32.5	30.4	30.1
1997	28.4	29.2	30.5	31.3	32.5	33.7	34.8	36.2	36.3	35.8	34.7	33.9	33.1
1998	31.3	31.0	33.2	33.4	35.2	37.5	39.3	40.5	41.0	41.8	41.8	41.2	37.2
1999	38.7	38.5	40.1	42.0	43.6	45.1	46.4	47.1	47.0	46.7	46.2	45.6	43.9
2000	43.1	42.6	43.8	46.2	48.0	50.2	50.1	51.3	51.5	51.1	51.1	50.8	48.3
2001	48.8	49.4	51.3	53.2	55.2	57.2	57.8	59.1	58.1	57.3	56.1	54.6	54.8
2002	51.8	52.3	53.3	54.1	56.3	57.5	58.2	59.8	59.9	59.7	59.2	57.6	56.6
2003	55.6	56.4	58.1	59.3	60.8	62.5	62.5	63.7	63.6	63.0	62.6	61.3	60.8

Employment by Industry: California—*Continued*

(Numbers in thousands. Not seasonally adjusted.)

Industry	January	February	March	April	May	June	July	August	September	October	November	December	Annual Average
SACRAMENTO—*Continued*													
Manufacturing													
1990	33.8	34.1	34.2	34.0	34.0	34.4	35.0	35.0	35.0	35.1	34.7	34.2	34.4
1991	34.5	34.3	34.0	34.6	34.9	35.3	35.7	35.9	36.2	36.6	36.3	35.5	35.3
1992	33.4	33.4	33.7	33.2	32.8	33.0	33.8	34.3	34.1	34.5	34.2	33.9	33.6
1993	33.4	33.4	33.3	33.3	33.4	33.7	34.5	35.1	34.4	34.2	34.0	34.1	33.9
1994	33.1	33.1	33.7	34.0	34.3	34.8	35.7	36.2	36.3	35.5	35.5	35.5	34.8
1995	35.2	35.4	35.7	35.0	35.3	35.7	39.3	40.3	40.4	39.8	40.5	40.8	37.7
1996	40.1	40.3	40.7	40.7	41.1	41.3	41.5	41.8	41.9	41.4	41.6	41.7	41.1
1997	40.6	41.1	41.3	41.3	41.8	43.0	43.5	44.4	44.1	43.8	43.9	44.1	42.7
1998	43.2	43.3	43.6	43.8	44.1	44.2	44.2	44.4	44.3	43.8	43.9	43.7	43.8
1999	44.6	44.6	44.5	43.9	43.7	44.0	44.4	44.7	44.9	45.2	45.2	45.3	44.5
2000	44.4	44.9	45.0	43.6	43.9	43.9	44.7	45.7	45.4	45.6	45.7	46.0	44.9
2001	45.0	45.0	45.1	44.5	44.8	45.2	44.9	44.0	43.7	43.8	43.3	43.2	44.3
2002	41.9	41.4	41.6	41.5	41.7	41.6	41.9	41.8	41.7	41.1	40.8	40.8	41.5
2003	39.4	39.6	39.6	39.7	39.7	39.8	39.4	39.6	39.5	39.5	39.0	38.7	39.5
Service-providing													
1990	470.4	471.8	475.0	477.1	480.6	483.4	480.9	480.6	486.5	489.2	493.5	497.5	482.2
1991	492.1	491.7	493.7	493.7	495.0	498.3	495.6	495.2	499.9	496.9	499.7	500.8	496.0
1992	484.1	484.4	487.2	490.4	492.1	494.9	492.7	490.6	494.1	492.5	495.7	499.5	491.5
1993	490.0	491.8	494.5	493.5	491.8	493.2	491.5	491.1	495.1	496.3	498.5	503.6	494.2
1994	496.2	500.1	503.5	504.5	504.4	508.9	505.8	505.9	508.5	508.5	513.8	518.6	506.5
1995	510.9	514.9	518.8	519.5	520.0	523.1	513.7	518.0	522.5	522.5	529.4	530.7	520.3
1996	524.5	526.8	531.2	529.8	531.4	535.2	529.9	534.8	536.5	535.4	542.0	543.8	533.4
1997	535.6	538.8	544.1	545.7	547.8	550.2	547.2	549.8	554.4	552.9	557.7	563.0	548.9
1998	553.2	557.4	563.8	566.1	567.8	572.0	569.4	571.4	573.8	576.7	582.7	591.2	570.4
1999	578.9	587.6	591.2	593.0	594.0	600.9	597.8	599.6	602.3	600.1	604.9	612.1	596.8
2000	600.1	604.6	610.0	611.3	615.2	621.1	612.6	617.5	619.6	619.0	626.9	633.2	615.9
2001	619.9	622.4	629.2	628.5	628.0	632.0	630.7	633.4	631.7	633.5	641.5	646.7	631.4
2002	634.6	636.2	644.5	642.4	646.1	648.5	644.0	644.1	646.1	645.9	651.5	654.0	644.8
2003	647.0	647.0	649.3	651.4	651.7	655.3	650.3	649.2	650.2	652.9	657.2	658.4	651.7
Trade, transportation, and utilities													
1990	95.9	94.9	95.4	97.7	98.3	99.6	100.4	101.0	101.8	102.7	104.9	106.8	99.9
1991	99.4	97.8	97.9	96.4	97.2	98.4	98.2	98.8	98.9	97.8	100.5	101.0	98.5
1992	94.8	92.1	92.5	94.8	95.7	96.5	97.0	96.6	96.5	96.2	98.0	100.1	95.9
1993	92.2	91.4	91.6	92.6	92.7	93.7	93.8	93.7	93.6	94.7	96.4	98.5	93.7
1994	93.2	92.1	92.7	93.7	94.0	95.4	95.0	95.6	95.9	96.4	99.5	101.9	95.4
1995	97.1	96.4	96.6	96.3	96.6	97.3	96.8	97.7	97.7	97.1	100.2	102.0	97.6
1996	96.9	97.1	97.4	97.4	98.0	99.0	99.1	99.5	99.2	99.1	102.6	104.3	99.1
1997	99.9	99.1	99.8	101.2	102.0	103.2	103.9	104.4	105.0	104.9	107.7	110.5	103.4
1998	104.4	103.3	104.6	104.3	105.3	106.7	106.5	107.7	107.5	108.7	111.7	114.4	107.0
1999	109.2	109.0	109.2	109.8	110.5	111.9	113.8	114.2	114.5	114.5	117.3	120.5	112.8
2000	114.9	113.8	114.1	114.7	114.8	115.7	116.4	117.9	118.2	118.2	122.9	125.8	117.2
2001	119.7	118.0	118.3	118.0	118.3	120.0	119.5	119.5	119.7	120.0	123.4	125.4	119.9
2002	118.2	117.1	118.1	118.4	118.9	120.2	120.5	120.7	121.0	121.7	125.0	127.0	120.6
2003	122.3	120.4	120.6	121.0	121.3	122.9	123.0	123.6	123.5	124.2	126.4	127.6	123.1
Wholesale trade													
1990	16.2	16.5	16.5	16.3	16.4	16.6	16.9	16.9	16.9	17.0	17.1	17.1	16.7
1991	18.5	18.5	18.6	17.1	17.3	17.5	17.5	17.5	17.5	17.6	17.7	17.5	17.7
1992	17.5	17.3	17.4	17.6	17.8	17.9	18.1	17.8	17.6	17.6	17.5	17.4	17.6
1993	16.7	16.9	17.0	16.6	16.8	16.9	16.4	16.6	16.5	16.5	16.4	16.6	16.6
1994	16.3	16.4	16.5	16.6	16.7	16.8	16.8	16.9	16.9	16.8	16.9	17.0	16.7
1995	16.6	16.7	16.9	17.1	17.3	17.4	17.1	17.2	17.1	17.2	17.5	17.5	17.1
1996	16.9	17.1	17.3	17.4	17.5	17.8	18.0	18.3	18.1	17.9	17.9	17.9	17.6
1997	17.9	17.7	17.8	18.7	18.7	18.8	18.9	19.1	19.1	18.8	18.7	18.8	18.5
1998	18.4	18.4	18.7	18.5	18.5	18.7	18.4	18.6	18.6	18.6	18.6	18.7	18.5
1999	18.9	19.1	19.2	19.3	19.5	19.7	20.1	20.2	20.2	19.9	19.9	20.0	19.6
2000	19.7	19.7	19.8	20.1	20.1	20.3	20.2	20.3	20.3	20.5	20.5	20.7	20.1
2001	20.8	21.1	21.2	21.4	21.3	21.5	21.6	21.7	21.6	21.6	21.6	21.5	21.4
2002	20.9	21.1	21.3	21.1	21.1	21.1	21.0	21.0	20.8	20.9	21.0	20.9	21.0
2003	21.2	21.2	21.2	21.3	21.2	21.3	21.0	21.1	21.0	20.8	20.8	20.7	21.1
Retail trade													
1990	67.4	66.0	66.3	68.8	69.3	70.3	70.5	71.1	71.8	72.7	74.8	76.7	70.4
1991	68.2	66.6	66.5	66.4	67.1	68.0	67.6	68.1	68.3	67.3	69.8	70.5	67.8
1992	64.9	62.5	62.7	64.8	65.4	66.0	66.2	66.3	66.4	66.0	68.0	70.2	65.7
1993	63.5	62.3	62.4	63.8	63.8	64.4	64.7	64.4	64.4	65.2	67.1	69.0	64.5
1994	64.6	63.5	63.7	64.7	65.0	66.2	65.6	66.0	66.4	67.0	70.0	72.1	66.2
1995	67.5	66.6	66.5	66.0	66.3	66.8	66.6	67.4	67.5	66.9	69.7	71.4	67.4
1996	67.3	67.0	67.0	66.7	67.4	68.1	68.1	68.0	68.1	68.3	71.7	73.2	68.4
1997	68.8	68.1	68.5	68.6	69.4	70.3	70.7	71.0	71.5	71.7	74.7	77.3	70.8
1998	72.1	71.0	71.7	71.4	72.2	73.3	73.4	74.3	74.2	75.1	78.0	80.6	73.9
1999	75.2	74.7	74.7	74.9	75.5	76.5	77.6	77.8	78.2	78.6	81.3	84.2	77.4
2000	79.1	77.9	78.1	78.4	78.7	79.4	80.2	81.4	81.7	81.9	86.2	88.5	80.9
2001	82.6	80.8	80.9	81.1	81.6	82.8	82.4	82.3	82.7	83.0	86.5	88.5	82.9
2002	83.0	81.7	82.5	82.6	82.9	84.1	84.5	84.7	85.4	86.2	89.3	91.5	84.9
2003	86.9	84.9	85.1	85.3	85.5	86.9	87.5	87.9	87.9	88.7	90.8	92.2	87.5

Employment by Industry: California—*Continued*

(Numbers in thousands. Not seasonally adjusted.)

Industry	January	February	March	April	May	June	July	August	September	October	November	December	Annual Average
SACRAMENTO—*Continued*													
Transportation and utilities													
1990	12.3	12.4	12.6	12.6	12.6	12.7	13.0	13.0	13.1	13.0	13.0	13.0	12.7
1991	12.7	12.7	12.8	12.9	12.8	12.9	13.1	13.2	13.1	12.9	13.0	13.0	12.9
1992	12.4	12.3	12.4	12.4	12.5	12.6	12.7	12.5	12.5	12.6	12.5	12.5	12.4
1993	12.0	12.2	12.2	12.2	12.1	12.4	12.7	12.7	12.7	13.0	12.9	12.9	12.5
1994	12.3	12.2	12.5	12.4	12.3	12.4	12.6	12.7	12.6	12.6	12.6	12.8	12.5
1995	13.0	13.1	13.2	13.2	13.0	13.1	13.1	13.1	13.1	13.0	13.0	13.1	13.0
1996	12.7	13.0	13.1	13.3	13.1	13.1	13.0	13.2	13.0	12.9	13.0	13.2	13.0
1997	13.2	13.3	13.5	13.9	13.9	14.1	14.3	14.3	14.4	14.4	14.3	14.4	14.0
1998	13.9	13.9	14.2	14.4	14.6	14.7	14.7	14.8	14.7	15.0	15.1	15.1	14.5
1999	15.1	15.2	15.3	15.6	15.5	15.7	16.1	16.2	16.1	16.0	16.1	16.3	15.7
2000	16.1	16.2	16.2	16.2	16.0	16.0	16.0	16.2	16.2	15.8	16.2	16.6	16.1
2001	16.3	16.1	16.2	15.5	15.4	15.7	15.5	15.5	15.4	15.4	15.3	15.4	15.6
2002	14.3	14.3	14.3	14.7	14.9	15.0	15.0	15.0	14.8	14.6	14.7	14.6	14.7
2003	14.2	14.3	14.3	14.4	14.6	14.7	14.5	14.6	14.6	14.7	14.8	14.7	14.5
Information													
1990	14.2	14.3	14.4	14.5	14.6	14.6	14.7	14.7	14.8	14.8	14.7	14.7	14.5
1991	14.7	14.8	14.9	14.9	14.8	14.8	14.9	14.8	14.9	14.6	14.8	14.7	14.8
1992	14.9	14.9	15.0	15.1	15.2	15.3	15.6	15.5	15.6	15.7	15.7	16.0	15.3
1993	16.0	16.1	16.1	16.1	16.4	16.4	16.5	16.5	16.5	16.2	16.2	16.4	16.2
1994	16.3	16.4	16.5	16.2	16.2	16.4	16.5	16.5	16.4	16.3	16.4	16.6	16.3
1995	16.5	16.6	16.7	16.9	16.9	16.9	16.6	16.6	16.7	16.3	16.5	16.6	16.6
1996	16.3	16.3	16.4	16.2	16.4	16.7	16.7	16.8	16.6	16.4	16.4	16.4	16.4
1997	16.2	16.1	16.2	16.1	16.2	16.1	16.1	16.2	16.1	16.2	16.4	16.5	16.2
1998	16.1	16.1	16.2	16.3	16.5	16.5	16.4	16.5	16.6	16.8	17.0	17.1	16.5
1999	17.2	17.3	17.4	17.4	17.6	17.6	17.7	17.5	17.5	17.6	17.7	17.7	17.5
2000	17.5	17.4	17.3	17.3	17.2	17.3	17.4	17.5	17.5	17.5	17.6	17.7	17.4
2001	19.6	19.7	20.1	20.8	20.9	20.9	21.7	22.0	21.9	22.6	22.6	22.6	21.2
2002	22.9	22.6	22.5	22.4	22.6	22.4	22.2	21.6	21.3	21.2	20.8	20.5	21.9
2003	20.7	20.8	20.6	20.3	20.6	20.7	20.6	20.4	20.1	20.1	20.2	20.2	20.4
Financial activities													
1990	36.8	37.2	37.5	37.2	37.9	38.4	38.5	38.4	38.7	38.6	38.7	38.8	38.0
1991	39.3	39.4	39.3	40.4	40.5	40.8	40.5	40.7	40.3	40.1	40.5	40.3	40.1
1992	39.0	39.2	39.8	39.0	39.3	39.4	39.2	39.6	39.4	38.9	38.8	39.0	39.2
1993	39.0	39.0	39.3	39.3	39.5	39.8	40.0	40.0	40.5	40.5	40.3	40.7	39.8
1994	40.3	40.4	40.7	39.5	39.2	39.4	39.0	39.0	38.6	37.6	37.7	37.6	39.0
1995	37.3	37.7	37.9	37.8	37.6	37.8	37.2	37.5	37.4	37.3	37.4	38.0	37.5
1996	37.9	38.7	39.1	39.9	40.0	40.3	40.1	40.5	40.2	39.8	40.1	40.6	39.7
1997	40.1	40.6	40.9	42.8	43.0	43.4	44.5	44.9	45.1	44.7	45.0	45.5	43.3
1998	45.9	46.4	47.1	48.2	48.7	49.4	50.0	50.3	50.6	50.9	50.3	50.7	49.0
1999	49.8	50.0	50.2	50.5	50.5	50.2	50.3	50.5	50.2	49.1	49.5	50.0	50.0
2000	49.0	49.4	49.6	49.2	49.3	49.4	48.7	49.0	48.8	47.5	47.9	48.6	48.8
2001	48.4	48.8	49.2	48.8	48.9	49.3	49.3	49.7	49.3	49.8	50.0	50.3	49.3
2002	49.8	50.1	50.4	50.9	50.8	51.1	51.8	52.3	53.0	53.9	54.5	55.0	52.0
2003	55.1	55.7	55.9	56.2	56.5	56.7	57.1	57.5	56.9	56.9	56.9	56.9	56.5
Professional and business services													
1990	47.8	48.0	48.6	48.5	49.1	49.3	50.1	50.9	50.8	51.2	52.0	53.2	49.9
1991	53.4	53.9	54.3	54.2	54.4	54.8	56.3	56.1	56.4	56.5	56.2	56.3	55.2
1992	53.2	53.5	54.0	54.0	53.6	54.1	54.6	54.2	54.7	54.2	54.1	54.5	54.0
1993	54.0	54.6	54.9	55.1	55.0	55.1	56.3	56.0	56.1	56.2	56.3	57.1	55.5
1994	56.3	57.3	58.3	59.3	59.4	60.3	62.3	62.7	62.9	62.9	64.1	64.1	60.8
1995	63.1	64.4	65.5	66.4	67.1	68.3	67.1	68.8	69.4	68.3	69.2	67.8	67.1
1996	68.7	69.9	70.5	67.8	68.9	69.4	70.4	72.4	72.1	71.9	72.7	72.6	70.6
1997	72.8	73.3	73.8	72.7	72.7	73.9	74.8	75.7	76.4	77.0	78.1	79.7	75.0
1998	78.6	79.8	79.7	81.1	82.0	83.1	83.5	84.2	84.9	84.9	85.7	86.7	82.8
1999	84.6	85.8	87.4	88.6	88.5	90.5	91.8	92.1	92.3	92.6	92.5	93.3	90.0
2000	91.7	93.1	94.9	96.0	96.2	98.2	97.4	98.1	97.8	96.6	97.1	97.6	96.2
2001	90.6	91.3	92.3	90.7	90.9	91.1	91.8	91.3	89.6	88.6	88.8	89.0	90.5
2002	85.9	86.9	89.1	87.7	87.6	89.0	89.1	89.0	89.5	87.0	87.4	87.4	88.0
2003	86.5	86.9	87.1	87.9	87.9	89.4	88.0	88.8	89.4	89.3	90.1	89.7	88.4
Educational and health services													
1990	47.8	48.1	48.3	48.5	48.8	49.1	49.7	49.8	50.3	51.0	51.5	52.0	49.5
1991	52.3	52.1	51.8	52.6	52.7	53.1	52.8	53.2	53.9	54.2	54.1	54.2	53.0
1992	52.7	53.0	53.4	54.2	54.3	55.1	54.6	54.5	55.5	55.4	55.4	55.8	54.4
1993	55.8	55.7	56.4	56.3	56.5	56.5	55.9	56.1	56.5	56.7	56.8	56.9	56.3
1994	56.2	56.5	56.9	57.2	57.5	57.3	55.8	56.0	56.4	56.5	56.8	57.4	56.7
1995	57.2	57.9	58.4	56.8	56.8	57.1	57.6	57.9	58.5	58.4	58.9	59.1	57.8
1996	58.7	59.4	59.4	60.2	59.5	60.5	59.5	59.7	60.5	59.8	60.3	60.2	59.8
1997	59.3	60.1	60.7	60.6	60.4	60.8	60.5	59.8	59.6	59.6	59.8	60.0	60.1
1998	58.7	59.8	60.6	60.2	59.9	60.2	59.9	59.5	60.1	61.0	61.6	61.4	60.2
1999	60.9	61.9	61.6	61.6	62.0	62.5	61.9	61.7	62.2	62.8	63.4	64.0	62.2
2000	63.4	63.6	63.6	63.8	63.8	64.1	65.3	65.3	66.1	67.7	67.9	68.5	65.2
2001	68.3	68.8	69.5	70.3	71.2	70.8	69.9	70.3	70.8	71.0	72.1	71.1	70.3
2002	72.5	71.4	71.7	70.9	72.8	71.7	71.3	70.9	71.9	73.0	74.2	73.2	72.1
2003	74.4	72.7	73.7	75.3	75.4	75.1	74.5	73.3	75.0	75.8	76.5	76.1	74.8

Employment by Industry: California—*Continued*

(Numbers in thousands. Not seasonally adjusted.)

Industry	January	February	March	April	May	June	July	August	September	October	November	December	Annual Average
SACRAMENTO—*Continued*													
Leisure and hospitality													
1990	47.6	47.7	48.0	47.4	47.9	48.6	49.0	49.8	49.3	48.6	49.0	50.1	48.5
1991	51.9	52.5	52.7	50.8	51.6	52.1	53.4	53.9	52.8	51.8	51.7	53.1	52.3
1992	51.8	52.1	52.3	52.1	52.6	53.8	53.4	53.2	52.6	51.8	51.0	53.0	52.4
1993	52.1	52.9	53.8	54.0	53.1	53.7	54.3	54.0	53.6	52.1	52.2	54.5	53.3
1994	55.0	55.5	56.2	56.0	54.7	55.8	56.3	56.6	56.6	54.9	55.3	57.3	55.8
1995	55.9	56.5	57.3	57.2	57.3	58.0	57.9	58.2	57.9	58.3	59.1	59.3	57.7
1996	59.2	58.8	59.6	59.7	59.5	60.5	60.8	61.5	61.4	59.8	59.9	60.7	60.1
1997	58.2	58.8	59.3	59.8	60.2	60.8	60.4	61.3	60.5	58.9	58.5	59.3	59.6
1998	58.7	59.1	59.8	59.9	58.5	59.7	60.1	60.7	59.8	57.6	57.9	61.5	59.4
1999	59.5	60.9	61.3	61.8	60.4	62.0	62.5	62.2	61.1	59.9	60.6	61.9	61.1
2000	61.8	62.6	63.1	63.4	63.2	65.4	65.9	66.1	65.4	64.5	65.5	67.0	64.4
2001	66.8	67.3	67.9	66.5	64.3	65.5	66.6	67.0	64.1	64.3	65.7	69.3	66.2
2002	68.5	69.3	69.4	68.8	68.3	70.4	70.0	70.5	69.1	68.3	68.8	70.6	69.3
2003	71.1	71.5	72.1	70.9	69.7	70.6	71.0	71.0	69.6	69.6	69.8	71.8	70.7
Other services													
1990	19.3	19.6	19.9	20.0	20.3	20.5	20.6	20.5	20.5	20.4	20.2	20.2	20.1
1991	18.8	19.2	19.3	19.7	19.9	19.9	20.4	20.5	20.6	20.2	20.1	19.9	19.8
1992	18.9	18.7	19.0	19.4	19.5	19.6	20.0	20.0	20.1	19.7	19.5	19.5	19.4
1993	19.1	19.3	19.5	19.6	19.7	19.8	20.3	20.3	20.1	20.0	19.9	19.9	19.7
1994	19.4	19.3	19.8	19.4	19.5	19.8	20.2	20.2	20.1	19.5	19.1	19.2	19.6
1995	19.0	19.2	19.3	20.2	20.3	20.5	20.4	20.0	19.9	20.2	20.1	20.3	19.9
1996	19.9	20.1	20.6	20.9	21.2	21.4	21.0	21.3	21.0	20.7	21.0	21.1	20.8
1997	21.0	21.4	21.7	21.5	21.7	22.1	22.3	22.5	22.6	22.1	21.9	22.1	21.9
1998	22.3	22.7	23.5	23.5	23.9	24.2	23.9	23.7	23.7	23.5	23.6	23.8	23.5
1999	23.2	23.6	23.9	23.8	24.1	24.5	25.0	25.1	25.1	24.7	24.8	25.0	24.4
2000	24.0	24.6	24.9	24.8	25.2	25.5	25.1	25.0	25.6	25.0	24.9	25.0	24.9
2001	24.9	25.4	25.6	25.8	26.1	26.4	26.2	26.1	26.0	26.3	26.2	26.2	25.9
2002	25.8	26.4	26.0	25.9	26.8	26.6	26.4	26.0	26.0	26.4	26.3	26.4	26.3
2003	25.3	25.7	25.8	26.4	26.6	26.8	26.4	26.4	26.0	26.1	26.0	25.8	26.1
Government													
1990	161.0	162.0	162.9	163.3	163.7	163.3	157.9	155.5	160.3	161.9	162.5	161.7	161.3
1991	162.3	162.0	163.5	164.7	163.9	164.4	159.1	157.2	162.1	161.7	161.8	161.3	162.0
1992	158.8	160.9	161.2	161.8	161.9	161.1	158.3	157.0	159.7	160.6	163.2	161.6	160.5
1993	161.8	162.8	162.9	160.5	158.9	158.2	154.4	154.5	158.2	159.9	160.4	159.6	159.3
1994	159.5	162.6	162.4	163.2	163.9	164.5	160.7	159.3	161.6	164.4	164.9	164.5	162.6
1995	164.8	166.2	167.1	167.9	167.4	167.2	160.1	161.3	165.0	166.6	168.0	167.6	165.7
1996	166.9	166.5	168.2	167.7	167.9	167.4	162.3	163.1	165.5	167.9	169.0	167.9	166.6
1997	168.1	169.4	171.7	171.0	171.6	169.9	164.7	165.0	169.1	169.5	170.3	169.4	169.1
1998	168.5	170.2	172.3	172.6	173.0	172.2	169.1	168.8	170.6	173.3	174.9	175.6	171.7
1999	174.5	179.1	180.2	179.5	180.4	181.7	174.8	176.3	179.4	178.9	179.1	179.7	178.6
2000	177.8	180.1	182.5	182.1	185.5	185.5	176.4	178.6	180.2	182.0	183.1	183.0	181.4
2001	181.6	183.1	186.3	187.6	187.4	188.0	185.7	187.5	190.3	190.9	192.7	192.8	187.8
2002	191.0	192.4	197.3	197.4	198.3	197.1	192.7	193.1	194.3	194.4	194.5	193.9	194.7
2003	191.6	193.3	193.5	193.4	193.7	193.1	189.7	188.2	189.7	190.9	191.3	190.3	191.6
Federal government													
1990	30.3	30.0	30.1	30.1	30.7	30.4	29.5	28.7	28.4	28.0	28.0	28.2	29.3
1991	28.1	27.7	27.7	27.6	27.1	26.9	27.0	26.8	26.6	26.8	26.5	26.9	27.1
1992	25.3	25.1	25.1	24.4	24.3	24.6	24.8	25.0	25.0	24.8	24.6	24.7	24.8
1993	24.8	24.7	24.2	22.5	22.5	21.0	20.8	20.9	20.9	20.6	20.2	20.5	21.9
1994	19.9	20.2	20.0	19.7	20.0	20.2	20.6	20.6	20.8	20.4	20.6	20.9	20.3
1995	20.9	20.9	20.8	20.5	20.3	20.4	20.2	20.1	20.1	19.9	19.6	19.8	20.2
1996	19.6	19.5	19.5	19.4	19.3	19.4	19.0	18.9	18.9	18.7	18.7	18.9	19.1
1997	18.9	18.9	18.8	18.6	18.6	18.7	18.5	18.4	18.2	18.0	18.0	18.1	18.4
1998	17.9	17.9	17.7	17.1	17.1	16.8	16.7	16.7	16.5	16.0	15.9	16.0	16.8
1999	15.8	15.7	15.6	15.2	15.2	15.0	14.8	14.6	14.3	13.4	13.4	13.4	14.7
2000	13.2	13.1	13.3	13.2	15.1	15.0	13.4	13.6	11.8	11.1	10.9	11.0	12.8
2001	10.9	10.7	10.6	10.3	10.1	10.3	10.4	10.3	10.3	10.1	10.1	10.2	10.3
2002	10.2	10.0	10.1	9.9	9.9	10.0	9.8	9.6	9.5	9.5	9.5	9.4	9.8
2003	9.2	9.2	9.2	9.1	9.2	9.3	9.3	9.3	9.3	9.4	9.4	9.4	9.3
State government													
1990	68.7	68.8	69.0	69.4	68.9	68.7	68.4	68.3	68.7	69.4	69.5	68.3	68.8
1991	69.5	69.3	70.0	70.9	70.2	70.2	69.0	68.6	69.4	69.0	68.5	67.7	69.3
1992	68.0	68.8	68.8	69.6	69.7	68.5	68.2	68.1	69.2	69.2	70.0	70.0	69.0
1993	70.2	70.2	70.6	70.4	68.8	70.1	70.7	70.7	70.6	71.3	71.3	70.7	70.4
1994	72.0	73.8	73.4	73.7	73.8	74.1	73.7	73.4	74.1	73.8	74.2	74.2	73.6
1995	74.4	75.0	75.4	76.6	76.4	75.9	75.4	75.2	76.0	75.9	76.1	76.0	75.6
1996	76.0	76.2	76.5	76.6	76.1	76.1	75.1	75.4	76.0	75.9	75.8	75.5	75.9
1997	75.8	76.6	76.8	76.3	76.0	76.2	75.1	74.8	75.7	75.6	75.8	75.6	75.8
1998	75.1	76.1	77.0	76.5	76.5	76.6	76.5	76.0	77.6	77.9	78.2	77.9	76.8
1999	78.0	79.2	80.0	80.0	80.0	80.0	80.1	80.6	81.3	81.1	81.3	81.0	80.2
2000	80.7	81.3	81.7	81.8	81.8	81.5	81.4	81.7	82.0	82.8	83.3	83.4	81.9
2001	83.1	84.0	85.3	85.9	86.1	86.3	86.5	86.8	87.3	87.5	88.1	88.0	86.2
2002	87.3	87.7	88.5	88.6	88.3	87.6	86.8	86.5	86.8	87.2	87.3	86.6	87.4
2003	86.0	86.5	86.5	86.0	85.4	84.9	83.7	83.1	83.2	83.4	83.2	82.3	84.5

Employment by Industry: California—*Continued*

(Numbers in thousands. Not seasonally adjusted.)

Industry	January	February	March	April	May	June	July	August	September	October	November	December	Annual Average
SACRAMENTO—*Continued*													
Local government													
1990	62.0	63.2	63.8	63.8	64.1	64.2	60.0	58.5	63.2	64.5	65.0	65.2	63.1
1991	64.7	65.0	65.8	66.2	66.6	67.3	63.1	61.8	66.1	65.9	66.8	66.7	65.5
1992	65.5	67.0	67.3	67.8	67.9	68.0	65.3	63.9	65.5	66.6	68.6	66.9	66.6
1993	66.8	67.9	68.1	67.6	67.6	67.1	62.9	62.9	66.7	68.0	68.9	68.4	66.9
1994	67.6	68.6	69.0	69.8	70.1	70.2	66.4	65.3	66.7	70.2	70.1	69.4	68.6
1995	69.5	70.3	70.9	70.8	70.7	70.9	64.5	66.0	68.9	70.8	72.3	71.8	69.7
1996	71.3	70.8	72.2	71.7	72.5	71.9	68.2	68.8	70.6	73.3	74.5	73.5	71.6
1997	73.4	73.9	76.1	76.1	77.0	75.0	71.1	71.8	75.2	75.9	76.5	75.7	74.8
1998	75.5	76.2	77.6	79.0	79.4	78.8	75.9	76.1	76.5	79.4	80.8	81.7	78.0
1999	80.7	84.2	84.6	84.3	85.2	86.7	79.9	81.1	83.8	84.4	84.4	85.3	83.7
2000	83.9	85.7	87.5	87.1	88.6	89.0	81.6	83.3	86.4	88.1	88.9	88.6	86.5
2001	87.6	88.4	90.4	91.4	91.2	91.4	88.8	90.4	92.7	93.3	94.5	94.6	91.2
2002	93.5	94.7	98.7	98.9	100.1	99.5	96.1	97.0	98.0	97.7	97.7	97.9	97.5
2003	96.4	97.6	97.8	98.3	99.1	98.9	96.7	95.8	97.2	98.1	98.7	98.6	97.8
SAN DIEGO													
Total nonfarm													
1990	949.2	956.5	962.6	962.8	969.4	970.4	962.5	965.1	972.8	973.4	977.2	977.7	966.6
1991	962.2	964.0	965.5	964.9	967.4	969.7	958.2	957.3	962.9	959.5	960.2	958.9	962.5
1992	940.0	943.5	948.8	951.3	952.4	956.1	944.6	939.0	946.4	947.4	952.4	950.3	947.6
1993	937.0	939.9	943.0	941.7	946.2	954.1	943.4	944.1	948.4	951.6	953.9	961.2	947.0
1994	937.4	944.5	951.1	950.8	954.1	961.3	949.7	953.3	962.4	959.4	965.7	973.6	955.2
1995	947.2	959.8	966.4	971.1	978.2	987.2	975.4	982.5	988.9	986.5	997.1	1002.1	978.5
1996	981.1	989.1	991.9	998.0	1007.3	1013.6	1003.7	1009.7	1011.5	1014.1	1025.0	1029.8	1006.2
1997	1015.8	1026.7	1036.7	1043.2	1053.4	1062.5	1055.3	1061.6	1066.4	1068.8	1075.6	1085.3	1054.2
1998	1066.7	1076.8	1083.0	1093.3	1104.2	1112.0	1105.0	1110.1	1115.7	1125.9	1132.2	1140.6	1105.4
1999	1116.5	1126.6	1137.8	1145.6	1153.4	1159.7	1151.1	1150.4	1160.4	1170.0	1177.7	1185.0	1152.8
2000	1164.0	1173.7	1184.2	1184.7	1197.1	1203.0	1185.6	1188.4	1198.8	1206.3	1215.1	1224.9	1193.8
2001	1196.9	1205.6	1214.0	1217.7	1225.6	1229.6	1211.1	1213.2	1216.6	1225.4	1231.0	1234.5	1218.4
2002	1206.9	1217.6	1224.4	1230.8	1237.5	1244.2	1220.8	1225.6	1225.6	1237.5	1245.5	1251.7	1230.7
2003	1221.4	1228.0	1234.4	1238.8	1243.7	1249.2	1237.2	1244.4	1243.7	1253.4	1252.9	1256.1	1241.9
Total private													
1990	775.1	779.9	783.6	783.0	786.6	789.7	795.4	797.8	796.4	792.9	795.0	795.8	789.2
1991	781.7	782.9	782.7	783.2	785.2	787.5	787.9	788.2	784.7	780.0	780.6	779.0	783.6
1992	759.8	761.9	765.5	767.7	769.5	772.0	775.1	771.4	771.2	767.1	770.9	769.0	768.4
1993	756.8	759.1	761.0	760.1	763.8	771.3	771.8	775.8	772.1	771.4	772.4	779.9	767.9
1994	756.9	762.8	767.8	767.1	769.8	775.2	779.0	782.3	782.7	774.8	779.4	787.5	773.7
1995	761.2	771.8	777.2	781.9	788.3	796.6	799.4	808.4	805.1	798.3	807.1	813.4	792.3
1996	792.3	797.8	799.7	804.1	812.9	818.6	823.2	831.5	824.5	822.6	830.4	835.9	816.1
1997	824.3	832.8	840.9	848.3	857.6	866.5	872.1	881.8	878.7	874.8	879.7	889.8	862.2
1998	874.3	882.0	886.3	896.9	906.1	913.8	919.9	926.1	924.7	927.8	932.4	940.8	910.9
1999	918.5	925.9	934.8	943.2	950.1	957.5	960.9	965.7	965.8	967.4	972.2	980.1	953.5
2000	956.9	965.5	973.6	975.5	983.6	993.5	990.4	996.0	997.4	997.4	1003.6	1013.0	987.2
2001	986.9	993.0	999.3	1000.8	1006.3	1011.6	1008.7	1011.9	1006.9	1006.9	1009.9	1013.8	1004.6
2002	987.0	994.8	1000.7	1007.7	1014.7	1021.0	1010.1	1015.2	1012.7	1016.1	1022.7	1029.2	1011.0
2003	1000.5	1005.2	1009.6	1014.4	1020.0	1025.5	1025.3	1033.3	1029.4	1033.1	1033.2	1036.0	1022.1
Goods-producing													
1990	185.5	185.4	186.6	184.8	185.5	185.5	186.2	185.4	184.5	182.4	180.6	178.5	184.2
1991	171.3	170.7	169.9	171.3	171.4	171.0	169.3	168.9	168.5	168.1	166.6	164.4	169.2
1992	160.6	160.4	161.1	160.2	159.8	159.4	159.0	158.0	153.5	152.9	151.8	149.4	157.1
1993	146.4	147.4	147.7	147.4	147.5	148.5	147.9	147.3	147.0	148.6	147.4	148.1	147.6
1994	144.7	144.7	145.2	146.9	146.3	147.4	148.3	149.3	150.8	149.3	149.0	149.9	147.6
1995	143.8	146.8	148.4	149.1	149.5	150.3	152.9	155.8	156.0	154.9	155.7	156.1	151.6
1996	151.6	151.9	151.9	154.7	156.8	157.9	157.8	159.7	159.8	160.3	161.4	161.9	157.1
1997	159.8	162.1	163.9	165.6	168.1	170.3	172.4	174.6	174.9	172.4	173.1	174.7	169.3
1998	176.4	177.9	180.0	181.2	184.0	186.4	186.9	187.8	187.5	189.0	188.3	188.5	184.4
1999	184.9	185.4	186.8	187.3	189.2	191.3	192.0	192.4	191.7	194.0	193.9	193.5	190.2
2000	188.2	189.1	189.5	190.5	191.9	194.5	193.2	194.2	194.1	194.4	195.0	196.5	192.5
2001	192.9	193.8	195.0	194.9	196.0	196.2	195.9	196.4	194.1	193.8	192.8	191.4	194.4
2002	188.0	188.3	189.3	189.3	190.9	191.8	189.3	189.9	188.9	188.0	187.7	186.9	189.0
2003	182.1	180.5	182.9	183.0	184.8	186.2	186.9	188.1	186.8	187.6	187.2	187.3	185.3
Natural resources and mining													
1990	0.6	0.6	0.6	0.6	0.7	0.7	0.6	0.6	0.6	0.6	0.6	0.6	0.6
1991	0.6	0.6	0.5	0.5	0.5	0.5	0.5	0.5	0.5	0.5	0.4	0.4	0.5
1992	0.4	0.4	0.4	0.4	0.4	0.4	0.4	0.4	0.4	0.4	0.4	0.4	0.4
1993	0.4	0.4	0.4	0.4	0.4	0.4	0.4	0.4	0.4	0.4	0.4	0.4	0.4
1994	0.4	0.3	0.3	0.3	0.3	0.3	0.3	0.3	0.3	0.3	0.3	0.3	0.3
1995	0.3	0.3	0.3	0.3	0.3	0.3	0.3	0.3	0.3	0.3	0.3	0.3	0.3
1996	0.3	0.3	0.3	0.3	0.3	0.3	0.3	0.3	0.3	0.3	0.3	0.3	0.3
1997	0.4	0.3	0.4	0.3	0.4	0.3	0.4	0.4	0.4	0.3	0.3	0.3	0.3
1998	0.3	0.3	0.3	0.3	0.3	0.3	0.3	0.3	0.3	0.3	0.3	0.3	0.3
1999	0.3	0.3	0.3	0.3	0.3	0.3	0.3	0.3	0.3	0.3	0.3	0.3	0.3
2000	0.3	0.3	0.3	0.3	0.3	0.3	0.3	0.3	0.3	0.3	0.3	0.3	0.3
2001	0.3	0.3	0.3	0.3	0.3	0.3	0.3	0.3	0.3	0.3	0.3	0.3	0.3
2002	0.3	0.3	0.3	0.3	0.3	0.3	0.3	0.3	0.3	0.3	0.3	0.3	0.2
2003	0.3	0.3	0.3	0.3	0.3	0.3	0.3	0.3	0.3	0.3	0.3	0.3	0.3

Employment by Industry: California—*Continued*

(Numbers in thousands. Not seasonally adjusted.)

Industry	January	February	March	April	May	June	July	August	September	October	November	December	Annual Average
SAN DIEGO—*Continued*													
Construction													
1990	61.7	61.5	62.1	61.1	61.5	61.2	60.6	60.7	60.1	57.8	57.1	56.4	60.1
1991	51.5	50.7	49.8	48.8	49.5	50.0	50.5	51.1	50.3	49.0	48.6	47.1	49.7
1992	44.0	42.9	44.2	44.7	45.8	46.1	45.5	45.6	45.6	44.3	43.8	42.7	44.6
1993	38.8	39.7	40.4	40.8	41.2	42.1	41.8	41.5	41.7	41.6	40.8	41.4	40.9
1994	39.4	39.6	40.2	40.8	40.6	41.5	42.2	42.9	43.9	43.2	43.0	43.7	41.7
1995	39.8	41.6	42.1	43.0	43.5	44.8	45.5	47.0	47.2	46.3	46.8	46.5	44.5
1996	44.2	44.1	44.1	44.5	46.1	46.6	46.6	48.0	48.3	48.3	48.3	48.4	46.4
1997	47.0	48.5	48.9	48.8	50.3	51.3	53.7	55.3	56.1	53.8	54.0	54.5	51.8
1998	52.5	53.4	54.8	57.2	59.1	61.0	62.1	63.3	63.6	65.2	65.0	65.3	60.2
1999	62.5	62.8	63.7	64.5	65.9	67.4	69.0	69.9	69.6	69.9	69.7	69.2	67.0
2000	66.3	67.0	67.1	67.2	68.2	70.0	70.7	71.8	72.1	71.5	71.8	72.9	69.7
2001	72.2	72.4	73.0	73.8	75.4	75.8	76.1	77.3	76.3	76.9	76.3	75.7	75.1
2002	73.5	73.2	73.9	75.2	76.8	77.7	77.0	78.2	77.6	77.9	77.8	78.0	76.4
2003	75.9	74.5	76.2	76.5	78.7	80.0	81.7	82.9	82.0	82.4	82.0	82.2	79.6
Manufacturing													
1990	123.2	123.3	123.9	123.1	123.3	123.6	125.0	124.1	123.8	124.0	122.9	121.5	123.4
1991	119.2	119.4	119.6	122.0	121.4	120.5	118.3	117.3	117.7	118.6	117.6	116.9	119.0
1992	116.2	117.1	116.5	115.1	113.6	112.9	113.1	112.0	107.5	108.2	107.6	106.3	112.1
1993	107.2	107.3	106.9	106.2	105.9	106.0	105.7	105.4	104.9	106.6	106.2	106.3	106.2
1994	104.9	104.8	104.7	105.8	105.4	105.6	105.8	106.1	106.6	105.8	105.7	105.9	105.5
1995	103.7	104.9	106.0	105.8	105.7	105.2	107.1	108.5	108.5	108.3	108.6	109.3	106.8
1996	107.1	107.5	107.5	109.9	110.4	111.0	110.9	111.4	111.2	111.7	112.8	113.2	110.3
1997	112.4	113.3	114.6	116.5	117.4	118.7	118.3	118.9	118.4	118.3	118.8	119.9	117.1
1998	123.6	124.2	124.9	123.7	124.6	125.1	124.5	124.2	123.6	123.5	123.0	122.9	123.9
1999	122.1	122.3	122.8	122.5	123.0	123.6	122.7	122.2	121.8	123.8	123.9	124.0	122.8
2000	121.6	121.8	122.1	123.0	123.4	124.2	122.2	122.1	121.7	122.6	122.9	123.3	122.5
2001	120.4	121.1	121.7	120.8	120.3	120.1	119.5	118.8	117.5	116.6	116.2	115.4	119.0
2002	114.2	114.8	115.1	113.8	113.8	113.8	112.0	111.4	111.0	109.8	109.6	108.6	112.3
2003	105.9	105.7	106.4	106.2	105.8	105.9	104.9	104.9	104.5	104.9	104.9	104.8	105.4
Service-providing													
1990	763.7	771.1	776.0	778.0	783.9	784.9	776.3	779.7	788.3	791.0	796.6	799.2	782.3
1991	790.9	793.3	795.6	793.6	796.0	798.7	788.9	788.4	794.4	791.4	793.6	794.5	793.2
1992	779.4	783.1	787.7	791.1	792.6	796.7	785.6	781.0	792.9	794.5	800.6	800.9	790.5
1993	790.6	792.5	795.3	794.3	798.7	805.6	795.5	796.8	801.4	803.0	806.5	813.1	799.4
1994	792.7	799.8	805.9	803.9	807.8	813.9	801.4	804.0	811.6	810.1	816.7	823.7	807.6
1995	803.4	813.0	818.0	822.0	828.7	836.9	822.5	826.7	832.9	831.6	841.4	846.0	826.9
1996	829.5	837.2	840.0	843.3	850.5	855.7	845.9	850.0	851.7	853.8	863.6	867.9	849.0
1997	856.0	864.6	872.8	877.6	885.3	892.2	882.9	887.0	891.5	896.4	902.5	910.6	884.9
1998	890.3	898.9	903.0	912.1	920.2	925.6	918.1	922.3	928.2	936.9	943.9	952.1	920.9
1999	931.6	941.2	951.0	958.3	964.2	968.4	959.1	958.0	968.7	976.0	983.8	991.5	962.6
2000	975.8	984.6	994.7	994.2	1005.2	1008.5	992.4	994.2	1004.7	1011.9	1020.1	1028.4	1001.2
2001	1004.0	1011.8	1019.0	1022.8	1029.6	1033.4	1015.2	1016.8	1022.5	1031.6	1038.2	1043.1	1024.0
2002	1018.9	1029.3	1035.1	1041.5	1046.6	1052.4	1031.5	1035.7	1036.7	1049.5	1057.8	1064.8	1041.7
2003	1039.3	1047.5	1051.5	1055.8	1058.9	1063.0	1050.3	1056.3	1056.9	1065.8	1065.7	1068.8	1056.7
Trade, transportation, and utilities													
1990	169.6	168.5	168.8	168.0	169.5	171.0	172.2	172.5	172.0	172.7	175.9	178.4	171.5
1991	175.0	173.2	172.5	169.9	170.6	172.4	173.1	172.0	171.3	169.2	172.2	174.5	172.1
1992	166.1	165.1	165.8	165.6	166.8	167.5	169.9	168.7	170.2	168.8	173.8	176.3	168.7
1993	170.3	168.4	167.8	168.1	168.3	170.2	171.3	171.1	171.3	172.0	174.8	179.2	171.0
1994	170.1	169.9	170.1	169.7	170.7	171.7	172.2	173.1	173.4	172.9	177.8	182.7	172.8
1995	172.2	171.2	171.2	171.6	172.9	175.3	174.4	176.8	177.2	177.0	182.7	186.4	175.7
1996	177.0	175.3	174.4	174.9	177.0	178.5	176.9	178.4	178.0	179.0	184.7	188.6	178.5
1997	182.2	182.1	183.1	182.8	184.9	186.8	187.7	188.0	190.1	190.4	195.0	199.5	187.7
1998	184.8	183.1	182.6	184.6	186.8	188.1	187.1	188.1	189.0	189.3	193.7	197.6	187.9
1999	189.0	188.6	188.9	190.8	192.2	192.7	194.4	194.9	194.3	196.8	201.4	206.3	194.1
2000	198.1	198.4	198.5	198.8	200.9	202.4	201.7	201.6	202.0	204.3	210.2	214.8	202.6
2001	208.1	206.6	206.5	206.5	207.6	209.0	208.5	208.4	207.7	209.8	213.1	216.3	209.0
2002	206.6	205.4	206.3	207.3	208.1	209.2	207.1	207.5	207.3	207.8	212.6	217.6	208.6
2003	205.7	204.7	205.0	205.5	206.5	207.2	207.9	209.5	209.9	212.5	213.3	215.2	208.6
Wholesale trade													
1990	31.3	31.8	32.0	32.1	32.4	32.6	32.7	32.7	32.5	32.5	32.3	31.9	32.2
1991	31.9	32.2	31.8	30.8	30.9	31.0	31.3	31.1	30.9	30.7	30.5	30.2	31.1
1992	30.2	30.4	30.7	30.5	30.8	30.7	31.1	30.9	31.3	30.9	31.0	30.8	30.7
1993	29.9	30.2	30.3	30.3	30.3	30.3	30.4	30.3	30.4	30.4	30.4	30.7	30.3
1994	30.6	31.1	31.4	30.8	31.1	31.1	31.6	31.7	31.9	31.5	31.8	32.2	31.4
1995	32.4	33.1	33.1	33.6	33.9	33.8	33.2	33.3	33.5	33.6	33.7	33.7	33.4
1996	32.3	31.7	31.8	31.5	31.6	31.7	31.7	31.8	31.8	32.2	32.6	32.5	31.9
1997	32.5	33.0	33.2	33.7	34.0	33.9	34.0	34.1	34.1	34.4	34.1	34.4	33.7
1998	33.4	33.7	33.8	34.6	35.0	35.2	34.8	34.8	34.9	34.9	35.2	35.5	34.6
1999	35.3	35.6	35.9	36.6	36.9	37.2	37.1	37.2	37.0	37.2	37.5	37.9	36.7
2000	38.4	38.8	38.6	39.0	39.4	39.8	39.1	39.0	39.0	39.1	39.3	39.7	39.1
2001	40.5	41.0	41.1	41.2	42.3	42.8	41.3	41.4	41.2	41.5	41.5	41.7	41.4
2002	40.4	40.8	40.9	41.4	41.6	41.8	41.4	41.6	41.4	41.5	41.6	41.6	41.3
2003	40.9	41.2	41.4	41.5	41.7	41.7	41.3	41.4	41.1	41.1	41.1	41.2	41.3

Employment by Industry: California—*Continued*

(Numbers in thousands. Not seasonally adjusted.)

Industry	January	February	March	April	May	June	July	August	September	October	November	December	Annual Average
SAN DIEGO—*Continued*													
Retail trade													
1990	114.4	113.0	112.9	112.3	113.3	114.2	115.0	115.3	115.1	115.9	119.3	121.9	115.2
1991	116.4	114.4	113.6	112.4	112.6	113.8	113.9	113.6	113.9	112.5	115.9	118.8	114.3
1992	110.8	109.4	109.4	109.4	109.9	110.0	111.2	110.4	112.1	111.9	116.7	119.2	111.7
1993	115.0	113.1	112.1	112.0	111.7	112.6	113.3	113.5	113.7	114.5	117.5	121.3	114.1
1994	113.6	112.5	111.8	112.2	112.5	112.6	112.4	113.4	113.6	114.3	119.1	123.3	114.2
1995	114.3	112.6	112.2	111.9	112.6	114.1	113.5	115.4	115.9	116.3	121.6	125.1	115.4
1996	118.6	117.3	116.1	116.3	117.5	118.2	117.0	118.1	117.9	118.9	124.1	127.8	118.9
1997	122.2	121.5	121.5	120.5	121.5	122.8	123.8	125.2	126.2	127.4	132.2	136.3	125.0
1998	124.1	122.3	121.8	121.5	122.6	123.4	122.7	123.5	124.4	125.8	130.0	133.9	124.6
1999	125.9	125.3	125.3	124.3	125.4	126.0	126.8	128.0	128.5	130.1	134.3	138.8	128.2
2000	131.2	131.0	130.9	129.9	131.1	131.9	131.7	132.3	133.1	135.6	141.1	145.2	133.7
2001	136.3	134.2	133.6	133.1	133.3	134.1	134.3	134.8	135.0	135.6	139.7	143.1	135.5
2002	136.1	134.2	134.9	135.1	135.8	137.0	136.2	137.1	138.1	138.7	143.6	148.8	138.0
2003	138.6	137.3	137.0	137.0	137.6	138.1	139.0	140.3	140.9	143.6	144.4	146.3	140.0
Transportation and utilities													
1990	23.9	23.7	23.9	23.6	23.8	24.2	24.5	24.5	24.4	24.3	24.3	24.6	24.1
1991	26.7	26.6	27.1	26.7	27.1	27.6	27.9	27.3	26.5	26.0	25.8	25.5	26.7
1992	25.1	25.3	25.7	25.7	26.1	26.8	27.6	27.4	26.8	26.0	26.1	26.3	26.2
1993	25.4	25.1	25.4	25.8	26.3	27.3	27.6	27.3	27.2	27.1	26.9	27.2	26.5
1994	25.9	26.3	26.9	26.7	27.1	28.0	28.2	28.0	27.9	27.1	26.9	27.2	27.1
1995	25.5	25.5	25.9	26.1	26.4	27.4	27.7	28.1	27.8	27.1	27.4	27.6	26.8
1996	26.1	26.3	26.5	27.1	27.9	28.6	28.2	28.5	28.3	27.9	28.0	28.3	27.6
1997	27.5	27.6	28.4	28.6	29.4	30.1	29.9	28.7	29.8	28.6	28.7	28.8	28.8
1998	27.3	27.1	27.0	28.5	29.2	29.5	29.6	29.8	29.7	28.6	28.5	28.2	28.5
1999	27.8	27.7	27.7	29.9	29.9	29.5	30.5	29.7	28.8	29.5	29.6	29.6	29.1
2000	28.5	28.6	29.0	29.9	30.4	30.7	30.9	30.3	29.9	29.6	29.8	29.9	29.7
2001	31.3	31.4	31.8	32.2	32.0	32.1	32.9	32.2	31.5	32.7	31.9	31.5	31.9
2002	30.1	30.4	30.5	30.8	30.7	30.4	29.5	28.8	27.8	27.6	27.4	27.2	29.3
2003	26.2	26.2	26.6	27.0	27.2	27.4	27.6	27.8	27.9	27.8	27.8	27.7	27.3
Information													
1990	21.4	21.5	21.5	21.2	21.4	21.7	22.0	22.1	21.9	22.0	21.9	22.1	21.7
1991	22.6	22.8	22.7	22.5	22.5	22.6	22.8	22.7	22.6	22.5	22.4	22.1	22.5
1992	22.4	22.4	22.4	22.2	22.3	22.5	22.1	21.8	22.0	22.1	22.3	22.3	22.2
1993	22.4	22.5	22.3	22.5	22.9	23.0	23.0	23.1	23.0	23.0	23.1	23.4	22.8
1994	23.2	23.3	23.5	23.8	23.9	24.2	24.4	24.5	24.5	24.6	24.8	25.0	24.1
1995	24.3	24.6	24.9	25.5	25.9	26.5	26.5	26.6	26.6	26.7	27.2	27.8	26.0
1996	26.9	26.9	27.3	27.2	27.6	28.0	28.2	28.2	28.2	28.8	29.0	29.3	27.9
1997	29.1	29.0	29.3	30.4	31.0	31.5	30.7	31.0	31.1	31.4	31.3	31.8	30.6
1998	31.8	33.6	32.4	33.5	33.9	34.5	34.9	35.2	35.3	35.4	35.6	35.8	34.3
1999	35.3	35.2	35.7	36.0	36.5	36.9	37.0	37.0	37.0	35.6	35.8	36.5	36.2
2000	37.1	37.8	38.8	39.4	40.3	41.0	39.6	39.6	39.7	38.8	39.0	39.0	39.1
2001	39.1	39.1	39.3	39.2	39.1	39.3	38.7	38.7	38.1	38.0	38.3	38.3	38.7
2002	38.0	38.0	38.2	38.1	38.0	37.8	37.0	36.7	36.3	38.3	38.3	38.0	37.7
2003	37.6	37.9	37.3	37.0	37.0	37.0	37.0	37.0	36.8	36.8	36.8	36.4	37.1
Financial activities													
1990	65.8	66.3	66.6	66.0	66.2	66.3	64.5	64.5	64.7	64.1	64.0	65.0	65.3
1991	63.3	63.9	64.9	64.0	64.3	65.1	64.1	64.1	63.8	62.9	62.7	62.5	63.8
1992	60.9	61.6	61.7	61.2	61.4	61.3	60.8	61.1	61.0	60.7	60.9	60.8	61.1
1993	60.8	61.2	61.2	60.9	61.3	61.8	61.8	62.1	61.9	61.5	61.4	61.7	61.4
1994	60.2	60.4	60.4	59.8	59.5	58.3	58.2	58.3	57.6	56.7	56.6	56.7	58.5
1995	55.9	56.2	56.7	56.8	57.1	57.1	58.1	58.4	58.2	57.3	57.6	57.7	57.2
1996	57.6	58.1	58.3	58.5	58.7	58.7	59.4	59.6	59.4	59.6	60.0	60.0	58.9
1997	59.4	60.1	60.7	60.9	61.4	61.9	62.9	63.4	63.4	64.5	64.3	65.1	62.3
1998	63.4	64.2	64.8	64.9	65.5	64.6	67.4	68.0	67.8	66.8	66.8	67.2	65.9
1999	68.5	69.0	69.6	70.1	70.5	70.9	70.9	71.2	70.9	70.9	71.0	71.8	70.4
2000	70.0	70.5	70.8	70.9	71.1	71.5	71.2	71.3	71.1	71.5	71.8	72.1	71.1
2001	70.1	70.9	71.3	71.4	71.7	72.3	72.5	73.0	72.5	72.5	72.9	73.4	72.0
2002	72.1	73.0	73.4	73.9	74.6	75.1	75.0	75.7	75.7	76.3	77.3	77.9	75.0
2003	77.5	78.2	78.6	79.6	80.6	81.0	81.3	81.8	81.5	81.7	81.8	81.9	80.5
Professional and business services													
1990	120.0	121.6	123.1	124.4	124.5	124.7	124.0	125.3	125.5	125.0	125.4	126.2	124.1
1991	122.2	122.9	122.4	122.9	121.6	121.0	122.3	123.0	123.2	122.4	122.0	121.7	122.3
1992	119.5	120.4	121.3	122.0	121.4	121.9	123.8	123.6	125.1	126.0	126.3	125.7	123.0
1993	126.1	126.9	127.8	126.5	126.6	127.0	125.6	126.9	127.2	126.9	127.2	127.8	126.8
1994	126.2	129.3	131.0	130.0	129.7	130.0	129.9	130.9	131.2	131.0	131.3	132.1	130.2
1995	129.1	132.8	133.6	134.2	134.8	135.6	135.7	137.2	136.9	136.6	137.8	138.5	135.2
1996	136.3	138.7	139.8	141.0	142.4	143.2	145.0	146.6	146.4	146.2	146.6	147.3	143.2
1997	146.4	149.2	150.6	153.2	153.9	154.0	156.2	158.8	158.7	159.6	160.3	161.5	155.2
1998	164.2	166.9	167.8	170.7	171.3	172.6	172.9	175.0	177.1	178.5	178.8	181.3	173.0
1999	175.6	178.4	180.5	183.0	182.8	184.9	187.3	189.1	189.8	188.7	189.0	190.6	184.9
2000	186.9	189.0	192.4	191.3	191.9	194.2	195.7	198.6	200.1	199.8	200.2	201.8	195.1
2001	195.8	198.2	199.2	197.9	198.0	198.5	196.1	197.5	197.8	198.6	200.3	200.5	198.2
2002	197.5	200.5	201.7	200.6	200.7	202.1	200.7	202.5	202.0	203.0	204.0	204.9	201.7
2003	199.5	201.8	201.8	201.5	200.3	201.3	200.2	202.2	202.1	202.8	202.6	203.0	201.6

Employment by Industry: California—*Continued*

(Numbers in thousands. Not seasonally adjusted.)

Industry	January	February	March	April	May	June	July	August	September	October	November	December	Annual Average
SAN DIEGO—*Continued*													
Educational and health services													
1990	80.3	81.9	82.1	83.2	83.4	82.7	83.4	83.6	85.0	87.0	88.2	88.0	84.0
1991	86.5	87.2	87.8	88.7	88.9	88.2	88.5	88.4	89.6	90.0	90.4	90.3	88.7
1992	90.4	92.2	92.3	93.9	93.9	95.1	93.8	91.3	93.1	92.6	93.4	92.9	92.9
1993	91.2	92.0	92.2	93.1	93.0	94.6	94.4	94.6	92.1	93.9	93.8	94.3	93.2
1994	93.1	94.3	94.9	94.8	95.1	97.9	97.2	95.5	95.4	95.3	95.7	96.1	95.4
1995	94.5	96.1	96.4	97.7	98.2	99.9	99.3	98.4	97.1	97.3	97.6	97.6	97.5
1996	97.0	98.4	98.6	98.3	98.3	99.0	100.2	100.4	98.7	99.2	99.7	100.1	98.9
1997	100.2	101.9	102.5	102.3	102.3	103.0	104.1	104.7	101.9	103.6	103.7	104.6	102.9
1998	103.9	104.9	105.4	107.1	107.0	107.7	108.2	107.8	105.5	108.3	109.3	109.6	107.0
1999	107.9	109.8	110.8	111.8	112.2	112.0	110.9	111.0	114.9	115.0	114.9	115.3	112.2
2000	113.7	115.6	116.0	115.0	115.6	115.1	114.3	114.2	115.1	116.3	116.3	116.8	115.3
2001	111.4	112.8	114.4	115.0	116.2	116.1	115.6	115.7	117.4	118.8	119.1	119.4	115.9
2002	117.8	120.2	120.3	120.6	121.0	120.1	117.4	117.2	118.5	120.6	121.1	121.2	119.7
2003	119.8	120.5	121.2	121.8	122.5	122.2	120.3	120.9	122.2	123.9	124.4	124.7	122.0
Leisure and hospitality													
1990	99.5	101.2	101.3	101.9	102.6	104.0	108.6	110.0	108.5	105.8	105.1	103.5	104.3
1991	106.9	108.1	108.5	109.6	111.5	112.2	112.8	114.1	111.1	110.3	109.9	109.5	110.3
1992	106.3	105.9	106.8	108.6	109.8	110.2	111.0	112.4	112.2	110.1	108.7	108.2	109.1
1993	106.1	106.7	107.8	107.3	109.8	111.2	112.6	115.8	115.1	111.2	110.4	111.0	110.4
1994	105.4	106.8	108.1	107.5	109.8	110.5	113.0	115.0	114.2	109.7	109.2	109.8	109.9
1995	106.9	108.9	110.4	111.7	114.4	115.8	116.3	118.9	117.2	113.1	112.8	113.5	113.3
1996	110.9	112.7	113.5	113.0	115.2	115.5	117.8	120.1	116.2	112.2	111.3	111.8	114.1
1997	111.4	111.9	113.9	115.8	118.4	119.9	118.9	121.6	119.2	114.7	114.1	114.6	116.2
1998	112.1	113.2	114.3	115.8	117.8	118.9	122.5	124.2	122.9	121.0	120.2	120.8	118.6
1999	118.0	119.9	122.5	124.0	126.1	127.3	126.6	128.3	126.1	124.9	124.7	124.5	124.4
2000	121.8	123.5	125.5	127.4	129.6	131.8	132.0	134.2	132.9	130.3	129.1	129.4	128.9
2001	126.7	128.3	129.6	131.6	132.7	134.0	135.5	136.4	133.1	130.5	128.6	129.4	131.3
2002	123.7	125.5	127.0	131.9	134.8	137.3	137.5	140.3	138.3	136.3	135.8	136.6	133.8
2003	132.9	135.9	136.8	138.8	140.6	142.1	143.9	146.0	142.6	140.2	139.5	139.6	139.9
Other services													
1990	33.0	33.5	33.6	33.5	33.5	33.8	34.5	34.4	34.3	33.9	33.9	34.1	33.8
1991	33.9	34.1	34.0	34.3	34.4	35.0	35.0	35.0	34.6	34.6	34.4	34.0	34.4
1992	33.6	33.9	34.1	34.0	34.1	34.1	34.7	34.5	34.1	33.9	33.7	33.4	34.0
1993	33.5	34.0	34.2	34.3	34.4	35.0	35.2	34.9	34.5	34.3	34.3	34.4	34.4
1994	34.0	34.1	34.6	34.6	34.8	35.2	35.8	35.7	35.6	35.3	35.0	35.2	34.9
1995	34.5	35.2	35.6	35.3	35.5	36.1	36.2	36.3	35.9	35.4	35.7	35.8	35.6
1996	35.0	35.8	35.9	36.5	36.9	37.8	37.9	38.5	37.8	37.3	37.7	36.9	37.0
1997	35.8	36.5	36.9	37.3	37.6	39.1	39.2	39.7	39.4	38.2	37.9	38.0	37.9
1998	37.7	38.2	39.0	39.1	39.8	41.0	40.0	40.0	39.6	39.5	39.7	40.0	39.4
1999	39.3	39.6	40.0	40.2	40.6	41.5	41.8	41.8	41.1	41.5	41.5	41.6	40.8
2000	41.1	41.6	42.1	42.2	42.3	43.0	42.7	42.3	42.4	42.0	42.0	42.6	42.1
2001	42.8	43.3	44.0	44.3	45.0	46.2	45.9	45.8	46.2	44.9	44.8	45.1	44.8
2002	43.3	43.9	44.5	46.0	46.6	47.6	46.1	45.4	45.7	45.8	45.9	46.1	45.6
2003	45.4	45.7	46.0	47.2	47.7	48.5	47.8	47.8	47.5	47.6	47.6	47.9	47.2
Government													
1990	174.1	176.6	179.0	179.8	182.8	180.7	167.1	167.3	176.4	180.5	182.2	181.9	177.3
1991	180.5	181.1	182.8	181.7	182.2	182.2	170.3	169.1	178.2	179.5	179.6	179.9	178.9
1992	180.2	181.6	183.3	183.6	182.9	184.1	169.5	167.6	175.2	180.3	181.5	181.3	179.2
1993	180.2	180.8	182.0	181.6	182.4	182.8	171.6	168.3	176.3	180.2	181.5	181.3	179.0
1994	180.5	181.7	183.3	183.7	184.3	186.1	170.7	171.0	179.7	184.6	186.3	186.1	181.5
1995	186.0	188.0	189.2	189.2	189.9	190.6	176.0	174.1	183.8	188.2	190.0	188.7	186.1
1996	188.8	191.3	192.2	193.9	194.4	195.0	180.5	178.2	187.0	191.5	194.6	193.9	190.1
1997	191.5	193.9	195.8	194.9	195.8	196.0	183.2	179.8	187.7	194.0	195.9	195.5	192.0
1998	192.4	194.8	196.7	196.4	198.1	198.2	185.1	184.0	191.0	198.1	199.8	199.8	194.5
1999	198.0	200.7	203.0	202.4	203.3	202.2	190.2	184.7	194.6	202.6	205.5	204.9	199.3
2000	207.1	208.2	210.6	209.2	213.5	209.5	195.2	192.4	201.4	208.9	211.5	211.9	206.6
2001	210.0	212.6	214.7	216.9	219.3	218.0	202.4	201.3	209.7	218.5	221.1	220.7	213.7
2002	219.9	222.8	223.7	223.1	222.8	223.2	210.7	210.4	212.9	221.4	222.8	222.5	219.7
2003	220.9	222.8	224.8	224.4	223.7	223.7	211.9	211.1	214.3	220.3	219.7	220.1	219.8
Federal government													
1990	47.2	47.3	48.5	49.3	51.2	50.1	50.4	49.5	49.2	49.3	49.2	49.3	49.2
1991	47.9	47.8	47.8	47.2	47.1	47.2	47.1	47.2	47.2	46.7	46.3	46.1	47.1
1992	45.4	45.3	45.2	45.3	45.2	45.6	45.4	45.4	45.4	45.4	45.5	45.4	45.3
1993	44.9	44.4	44.4	44.2	44.1	44.2	44.2	44.2	44.4	44.3	44.3	44.5	44.3
1994	44.2	44.4	44.5	44.8	45.1	45.6	45.6	45.6	45.9	46.1	46.1	46.5	45.3
1995	45.6	45.5	45.7	45.5	45.6	45.8	45.9	45.9	46.0	46.0	45.6	45.8	45.7
1996	45.3	45.4	45.4	46.3	46.3	46.1	46.2	46.1	46.0	45.6	45.6	45.6	45.8
1997	45.5	45.2	45.1	44.8	44.5	44.5	45.2	44.5	44.1	43.9	44.0	44.3	44.6
1998	43.6	43.4	43.4	43.2	43.3	43.2	43.4	43.4	43.2	42.8	43.1	43.5	43.2
1999	42.7	42.6	43.1	42.3	42.2	42.1	42.5	42.3	42.4	42.5	42.6	42.8	42.5
2000	42.4	42.3	42.6	42.4	46.1	42.1	42.3	41.2	41.0	40.8	40.7	40.7	42.0
2001	40.3	40.0	40.0	39.9	40.1	40.1	40.3	40.2	40.3	40.3	40.3	40.1	40.1
2002	40.2	39.9	40.0	39.8	39.9	40.0	40.0	39.9	39.8	40.4	40.7	40.9	40.1
2003	40.5	41.5	42.6	42.9	43.0	42.8	43.2	43.0	42.9	43.1	43.1	43.2	42.7

Employment by Industry: California—*Continued*

(Numbers in thousands. Not seasonally adjusted.)

Industry	January	February	March	April	May	June	July	August	September	October	November	December	Annual Average
SAN DIEGO—*Continued*													
State government													
1990	27.7	27.8	28.5	28.5	28.7	28.8	26.5	26.6	27.6	28.6	29.0	28.9	28.1
1991	28.8	29.1	30.2	29.9	29.8	30.1	28.4	27.6	28.3	29.3	29.1	29.2	29.1
1992	28.7	29.3	29.8	29.9	29.9	30.0	27.8	27.7	28.1	29.4	29.8	29.8	29.1
1993	29.7	29.6	30.3	30.1	30.2	30.6	28.9	28.1	28.9	30.4	30.6	30.2	29.8
1994	30.1	29.9	30.6	30.6	30.8	31.0	29.2	28.6	29.4	30.4	31.0	31.1	30.2
1995	30.8	31.3	31.5	31.6	31.6	31.8	30.3	29.1	30.2	31.2	31.8	31.6	31.0
1996	31.4	31.3	32.0	32.0	32.1	32.6	29.7	29.7	29.9	31.4	32.2	31.3	31.3
1997	31.4	31.4	32.2	31.9	32.5	32.1	29.6	29.3	29.6	31.5	32.4	31.8	31.3
1998	31.8	31.8	32.5	32.6	33.2	33.0	30.5	30.3	31.0	33.4	33.6	33.1	32.2
1999	33.1	33.5	33.9	33.9	34.5	34.4	31.7	31.5	32.3	34.7	35.2	34.8	33.6
2000	34.2	34.5	35.3	35.9	35.7	35.9	33.2	33.0	33.9	35.7	36.3	35.9	34.9
2001	35.2	35.9	37.0	37.0	37.4	37.5	33.0	33.0	34.9	37.3	38.1	37.4	36.1
2002	37.3	37.8	39.0	38.4	38.5	38.2	35.5	35.6	36.5	38.4	38.9	38.5	37.7
2003	37.8	38.4	39.1	38.9	39.1	38.9	36.3	36.3	36.9	38.7	38.8	38.6	38.2
Local government													
1990	99.2	101.5	102.0	102.0	102.9	101.8	90.2	91.2	99.6	102.6	104.0	103.7	100.0
1991	103.8	104.2	104.8	104.6	105.3	104.9	94.8	94.3	102.7	103.5	104.2	104.6	102.6
1992	106.1	107.0	108.3	108.4	107.8	108.5	96.3	94.5	101.7	105.5	106.2	106.1	104.7
1993	105.6	106.8	107.3	107.3	108.1	108.0	98.5	96.0	103.0	105.5	106.6	106.6	104.9
1994	106.2	107.4	108.2	108.3	108.4	109.5	95.9	96.8	104.4	108.1	109.2	108.5	105.9
1995	109.6	111.2	112.0	112.1	112.7	113.0	99.8	99.1	107.6	111.0	112.6	111.3	109.3
1996	112.1	114.6	114.8	115.6	116.0	116.3	104.6	102.4	111.1	114.5	116.8	117.0	112.9
1997	114.6	117.3	118.5	118.2	118.8	119.4	108.4	106.0	114.0	118.6	119.5	119.4	116.0
1998	117.0	119.6	120.8	120.6	121.6	122.0	111.2	110.3	116.8	121.9	123.1	123.2	119.0
1999	122.2	124.6	126.0	126.2	126.6	125.7	116.0	110.9	119.9	125.4	127.7	127.3	123.2
2000	130.5	131.4	132.7	130.9	131.7	131.5	119.7	118.2	126.5	132.4	134.5	135.3	129.6
2001	134.5	136.7	137.7	140.0	141.8	140.4	129.1	128.1	134.5	140.9	142.7	143.2	137.4
2002	142.4	145.1	144.7	144.9	144.4	145.0	135.2	134.9	136.6	142.6	143.2	143.1	141.8
2003	142.6	142.9	143.1	142.6	141.6	142.0	132.4	131.8	134.5	138.5	137.8	138.3	139.0
SAN FRANCISCO													
Total nonfarm													
1990	934.6	935.1	939.7	941.9	943.0	948.9	950.0	943.6	949.4	955.6	960.0	965.5	947.2
1991	935.8	934.6	936.5	938.1	938.9	938.9	938.2	937.4	939.5	943.1	945.2	948.3	939.5
1992	911.8	907.9	913.9	915.0	914.0	917.0	914.1	912.7	912.5	913.8	919.0	921.1	914.4
1993	900.9	901.8	903.6	903.9	907.5	910.2	906.4	903.9	910.3	912.6	915.0	923.2	908.2
1994	889.4	893.2	899.6	899.9	902.9	907.7	901.7	901.3	904.8	907.8	913.1	922.3	903.6
1995	894.2	901.5	907.0	905.5	912.8	918.1	916.3	920.2	925.6	923.2	932.3	941.1	916.4
1996	922.4	930.8	940.1	937.1	943.3	950.1	948.8	951.1	955.3	956.2	967.6	975.5	948.1
1997	953.1	962.7	970.6	977.4	983.4	989.8	984.5	983.9	991.3	993.7	1000.6	1010.9	983.4
1998	984.4	989.6	994.5	1002.4	1008.5	1016.3	1017.0	1017.3	1021.5	1023.9	1031.3	1040.2	1012.2
1999	1015.7	1023.9	1032.3	1030.7	1036.8	1043.0	1040.5	1040.0	1045.3	1048.6	1056.1	1067.4	1040.0
2000	1041.1	1055.1	1068.2	1070.2	1079.3	1088.6	1085.8	1090.5	1096.2	1094.8	1104.4	1111.1	1082.1
2001	1075.4	1080.6	1087.8	1071.2	1069.2	1068.0	1047.1	1041.3	1036.2	1026.0	1021.9	1021.8	1053.8
2002	988.0	988.6	994.0	990.5	993.9	993.0	981.0	981.3	980.0	981.5	987.3	986.2	987.1
2003	955.2	957.3	957.0	955.7	956.8	959.2	946.1	947.8	948.6	948.5	949.7	951.3	952.8
Total private													
1990	797.6	796.5	799.6	801.5	801.5	807.5	813.4	811.2	811.8	816.2	818.9	823.5	808.2
1991	797.4	795.4	795.9	797.3	798.2	800.1	802.7	803.4	802.5	803.8	805.2	807.6	800.7
1992	776.9	772.1	777.0	778.8	778.4	782.9	783.5	784.1	781.9	782.7	786.5	788.6	781.1
1993	770.8	770.6	771.9	771.9	775.4	779.3	780.2	780.5	783.4	783.5	785.6	793.9	778.9
1994	763.0	765.7	771.3	771.3	773.7	778.6	776.9	778.9	780.7	779.9	785.2	793.8	776.5
1995	768.6	774.6	780.2	778.5	785.9	791.1	793.7	799.2	803.5	799.3	807.5	815.3	791.4
1996	799.6	806.6	814.7	811.6	817.7	824.3	827.2	830.5	832.6	832.5	842.1	849.7	824.0
1997	829.1	838.5	845.4	852.2	857.7	864.3	862.7	863.3	869.1	868.9	874.7	887.8	859.4
1998	863.7	868.2	872.2	879.7	884.8	892.4	896.4	897.0	900.3	900.0	906.0	914.2	889.5
1999	892.6	898.5	905.5	903.3	909.2	917.5	917.9	918.2	921.9	922.3	927.9	939.0	914.4
2000	915.6	928.5	940.0	936.0	942.4	953.4	957.1	961.1	966.8	963.5	970.7	977.1	951.0
2001	946.5	951.4	957.2	940.2	938.1	937.2	919.8	914.9	905.8	894.2	889.0	889.0	923.6
2002	856.0	856.2	859.2	855.9	858.9	858.5	851.9	852.8	848.9	847.2	852.0	851.1	854.1
2003	822.5	823.9	823.1	822.2	823.1	825.5	818.6	820.5	820.5	819.3	820.4	822.1	821.8
Goods-producing													
1990	102.4	102.3	103.8	103.3	103.6	104.8	103.8	104.5	105.0	105.6	105.0	104.0	104.0
1991	97.5	98.6	98.7	96.8	97.2	97.8	97.8	98.3	98.2	98.7	98.5	96.9	97.9
1992	91.3	90.2	91.4	91.9	91.7	92.9	92.7	92.7	91.9	90.8	90.8	89.3	91.4
1993	86.4	86.9	87.7	88.1	88.3	88.7	88.3	88.8	89.2	89.3	89.3	88.7	88.3
1994	85.8	86.1	87.2	87.1	87.2	88.7	89.4	90.7	90.8	89.9	89.9	90.0	88.5
1995	86.9	88.3	89.3	88.6	89.4	90.9	90.8	92.1	93.2	92.8	93.0	92.7	90.6
1996	90.6	91.0	92.6	92.7	93.6	95.7	96.5	97.9	98.4	98.5	99.6	99.0	95.5
1997	96.7	98.0	99.1	98.4	99.3	100.2	101.5	102.5	103.4	102.4	102.5	103.6	100.6
1998	101.1	101.5	102.5	102.8	103.6	105.3	106.5	106.6	107.2	107.3	107.6	107.3	104.9
1999	104.4	104.6	105.9	103.9	104.8	106.3	107.0	107.4	108.3	107.3	107.7	107.5	106.2
2000	104.4	105.4	107.0	106.1	106.2	106.8	107.5	108.1	109.0	108.1	108.6	109.3	107.2
2001	105.0	105.3	106.9	105.6	104.8	105.2	104.3	104.2	102.9	101.4	99.8	99.2	103.7
2002	95.8	96.0	96.8	95.4	95.5	96.1	95.0	95.6	94.7	94.0	93.2	91.4	95.0
2003	89.6	89.2	88.3	88.5	88.4	89.2	89.4	89.7	90.0	90.1	90.0	89.5	89.3

Employment by Industry: California—*Continued*

(Numbers in thousands. Not seasonally adjusted.)

Industry	January	February	March	April	May	June	July	August	September	October	November	December	Annual Average
SAN FRANCISCO—*Continued*													
Natural resources and mining													
1990	6.3	6.3	6.4	6.4	6.3	6.3	5.4	6.2	6.3	6.4	6.3	6.3	6.2
1991	1.5	1.5	1.4	1.2	0.5	0.5	1.2	1.4	1.2	0.7	0.4	1.4	1.1
1992	0.5	0.5	0.5	0.5	0.5	0.5	0.6	0.6	0.6	0.6	0.6	0.6	0.6
1993	0.6	0.5	0.6	0.6	0.5	0.5	0.5	0.5	0.4	0.4	0.5	0.5	0.5
1994	0.5	0.5	0.5	0.5	0.4	0.4	0.4	0.4	0.5	0.4	0.4	0.5	0.5
1995	0.4	0.5	0.4	0.5	0.4	0.4	0.4	0.3	0.4	0.4	0.4	0.5	0.4
1996	0.4	0.4	0.4	0.5	0.4	0.5	0.5	0.4	0.5	0.4	0.4	0.5	0.4
1997	0.5	0.6	0.5	0.5	0.5	0.5	0.4	0.4	0.4	0.5	0.4	0.5	0.5
1998	0.5	0.5	0.4	0.5	0.4	0.4	0.5	0.4	0.3	0.4	0.3	0.3	0.4
1999	0.3	0.4	0.4	0.3	0.4	0.3	0.3	0.3	0.3	0.3	0.3	0.2	0.3
2000	0.1	0.2	0.2	0.2	0.2	0.2	0.2	0.1	0.2	0.2	0.1	0.2	0.2
2001	0.2	0.2	0.2	0.2	0.2	0.2	0.2	0.2	0.2	0.2	0.2	0.2	0.2
2002	0.2	0.2	0.2	0.2	0.2	0.2	0.2	0.2	0.2	0.2	0.2	0.2	0.2
2003	0.2	0.2	0.2	0.2	0.2	0.2	0.2	0.2	0.2	0.2	0.2	0.2	0.2
Construction													
1990	31.2	31.0	31.8	32.1	32.5	32.9	33.2	33.1	33.4	32.8	32.5	31.9	32.4
1991	30.5	31.0	30.9	30.2	31.3	31.4	31.3	31.7	31.8	32.2	32.1	30.3	31.2
1992	27.5	26.7	27.0	28.2	28.1	28.7	28.5	28.8	28.7	27.9	28.0	27.1	27.9
1993	24.9	25.2	25.6	25.8	25.9	26.1	26.6	27.1	27.5	27.3	27.1	26.9	26.3
1994	25.2	25.1	25.4	25.5	25.7	26.6	27.2	27.9	28.3	28.0	27.6	27.4	26.7
1995	25.5	26.3	26.9	26.9	27.5	28.6	29.2	30.1	30.8	29.9	29.6	29.2	28.4
1996	28.6	28.7	29.3	29.6	30.4	31.5	32.6	33.6	33.8	33.8	34.0	33.4	31.6
1997	32.9	33.6	34.4	34.5	35.0	35.8	37.0	38.0	38.4	37.6	37.0	37.2	36.0
1998	35.6	35.6	37.0	37.5	38.4	39.9	41.2	41.9	42.3	42.1	42.2	41.7	39.6
1999	39.9	39.7	40.6	41.0	41.8	43.0	43.8	44.6	45.3	44.5	44.9	45.3	42.9
2000	43.3	43.5	45.0	43.4	44.1	45.4	46.5	47.2	47.6	47.1	47.1	47.3	45.6
2001	46.0	46.3	47.8	47.1	47.2	48.0	48.5	49.1	48.9	48.1	47.1	46.8	47.6
2002	44.6	44.7	45.2	45.0	45.2	45.9	45.7	46.6	46.1	45.6	44.7	43.5	45.2
2003	43.3	42.9	42.4	42.9	43.1	43.7	44.1	44.3	44.6	44.4	44.0	43.8	43.6
Manufacturing													
1990	64.9	65.0	65.6	64.8	64.8	65.6	65.2	65.2	65.3	66.4	66.2	65.8	65.4
1991	65.5	66.1	66.4	65.4	65.4	65.9	65.3	65.2	65.2	65.8	66.0	65.2	65.6
1992	63.3	63.0	63.9	63.2	63.1	63.7	63.6	63.3	62.6	62.3	62.2	61.6	62.9
1993	60.9	61.2	61.5	61.7	61.9	62.1	61.2	61.2	61.3	61.6	61.7	61.3	61.4
1994	60.1	60.5	61.3	61.1	61.1	61.7	61.8	62.4	62.0	61.5	61.9	62.1	61.4
1995	61.0	61.5	62.0	61.2	61.5	61.9	61.2	61.7	62.0	62.5	63.0	63.0	61.8
1996	61.6	61.9	62.9	62.6	62.8	63.7	63.4	63.9	64.1	64.3	65.2	65.1	63.4
1997	63.3	63.8	64.2	63.4	63.8	63.9	64.1	64.1	64.6	64.3	65.1	65.9	64.2
1998	65.0	65.4	65.1	64.8	64.8	65.0	64.8	64.3	64.6	64.8	65.1	65.3	64.9
1999	64.2	64.5	64.9	62.6	62.6	63.0	62.9	62.5	62.7	62.5	62.5	62.0	63.0
2000	61.0	61.7	61.8	62.5	61.9	61.2	60.8	60.8	61.2	60.8	61.4	61.8	61.4
2001	59.0	59.0	59.1	58.5	57.6	57.2	55.8	55.1	54.0	53.3	52.7	52.4	56.1
2002	51.0	51.1	51.4	50.2	50.1	50.0	49.1	48.8	48.4	48.2	48.3	47.7	49.5
2003	46.1	46.1	45.7	45.4	45.1	45.3	45.1	45.2	45.2	45.5	45.8	45.5	45.5
Service-providing													
1990	832.2	832.8	835.9	838.6	839.4	844.1	846.2	839.1	844.4	850.0	855.0	861.5	843.2
1991	838.3	836.0	837.8	841.3	841.7	841.1	840.4	839.1	841.3	844.4	846.7	851.4	841.6
1992	820.5	817.7	822.5	823.1	822.3	824.1	821.4	820.0	820.6	823.0	828.2	831.8	822.9
1993	814.5	814.9	815.9	815.8	819.2	821.5	818.1	815.1	821.1	823.3	825.7	834.5	819.9
1994	803.6	807.1	812.4	812.8	815.7	819.0	812.3	810.6	814.0	817.9	823.2	832.3	815.0
1995	807.3	813.2	817.7	816.9	823.4	827.2	825.5	828.1	832.4	830.4	839.3	848.4	825.8
1996	831.8	839.8	847.5	844.4	849.7	854.4	852.3	853.2	856.9	857.7	868.0	876.5	852.6
1997	856.4	864.7	871.5	879.0	884.1	889.6	883.0	881.4	887.9	891.3	898.1	907.3	882.8
1998	883.3	888.1	892.0	899.6	904.9	911.0	910.5	910.7	914.3	916.6	923.7	932.9	907.3
1999	911.3	919.3	926.4	926.8	932.0	936.7	933.5	932.6	937.0	941.3	948.4	959.9	933.7
2000	936.7	949.7	961.2	964.1	973.1	981.8	978.3	982.4	987.2	986.7	995.8	1001.8	974.9
2001	970.4	975.3	980.9	965.6	964.4	962.8	942.8	937.1	933.3	924.6	922.1	922.6	950.1
2002	892.2	892.6	897.2	895.1	898.4	896.9	886.0	885.7	885.3	887.5	894.1	894.8	892.2
2003	865.6	868.1	868.7	867.2	868.4	870.0	856.7	858.1	858.6	858.4	859.7	861.8	863.4
Trade, transportation, and utilities													
1990	193.3	189.9	189.5	190.0	190.1	191.3	193.8	192.9	192.9	194.5	198.4	201.2	193.1
1991	190.4	188.3	187.0	187.3	187.3	187.5	187.8	188.3	187.7	188.7	190.4	193.2	188.6
1992	185.3	181.2	180.9	179.1	178.6	179.7	180.3	179.7	179.0	179.8	183.4	186.5	181.1
1993	178.7	176.5	175.2	174.9	174.8	176.1	176.9	176.1	176.5	177.5	180.3	184.7	177.3
1994	174.5	172.6	172.2	172.1	172.0	172.8	172.7	173.0	173.2	175.4	179.1	182.9	174.3
1995	174.2	173.8	173.6	170.8	172.5	173.4	173.1	173.9	174.1	174.6	178.7	182.1	174.5
1996	175.0	175.0	175.6	174.7	175.8	177.0	178.4	177.4	178.9	179.0	183.7	187.0	178.1
1997	180.3	180.6	181.8	183.0	183.5	185.8	184.4	183.3	185.3	186.4	190.2	195.6	185.0
1998	187.7	185.2	185.5	185.9	186.7	188.1	187.4	188.0	187.3	187.5	191.9	195.1	188.0
1999	186.6	185.4	185.6	184.9	186.3	187.6	187.2	187.2	187.4	187.8	190.5	195.4	187.6
2000	188.7	187.8	188.9	188.2	189.2	190.6	191.7	191.7	191.8	190.2	194.5	198.0	190.9
2001	190.5	188.6	189.1	187.8	188.1	188.7	187.0	186.3	185.4	182.1	182.8	183.8	186.6
2002	177.1	175.4	175.3	173.1	173.5	174.1	173.9	173.3	173.3	173.5	176.7	178.5	174.8
2003	172.7	170.6	169.9	168.4	168.9	169.2	167.8	167.7	167.1	166.6	168.9	171.0	169.1

Employment by Industry: California—*Continued*

(Numbers in thousands. Not seasonally adjusted.)

Industry	January	February	March	April	May	June	July	August	September	October	November	December	Annual Average
SAN FRANCISCO—*Continued*													
Wholesale trade													
1990	38.2	38.2	38.4	39.1	39.1	39.3	39.5	39.4	39.6	39.8	39.9	39.9	39.2
1991	38.7	38.8	38.8	39.3	39.5	39.2	39.0	38.8	38.7	38.9	38.5	38.5	38.8
1992	37.3	37.2	37.4	36.1	35.9	36.0	36.0	35.9	35.7	35.7	35.6	35.6	36.2
1993	35.0	35.0	35.1	35.3	35.3	35.5	35.6	35.5	35.4	35.0	35.1	35.2	35.2
1994	34.6	34.7	34.8	34.7	34.6	34.9	34.8	34.9	35.0	35.4	35.6	35.8	34.9
1995	34.8	35.3	35.6	34.2	34.3	34.5	34.4	34.4	34.7	34.7	35.0	35.2	34.7
1996	34.6	35.0	35.3	35.1	35.3	35.4	35.3	35.2	35.4	35.2	35.5	35.8	35.2
1997	35.0	35.2	35.5	35.5	35.7	36.0	35.6	35.8	35.4	35.9	36.0	36.3	35.6
1998	35.2	35.1	35.3	34.2	34.3	34.5	34.0	34.1	34.0	33.7	33.9	33.9	34.3
1999	33.3	33.7	33.7	32.9	33.0	33.2	32.8	32.7	32.9	32.5	32.6	32.8	33.0
2000	31.9	32.2	32.4	31.8	31.9	31.9	32.2	32.1	32.2	32.1	32.2	32.6	32.1
2001	31.5	31.8	31.7	31.4	31.3	31.2	30.9	30.7	30.7	30.6	30.7	30.6	31.1
2002	29.6	29.7	29.7	29.1	29.1	29.0	28.9	28.9	28.8	28.6	28.3	28.3	29.0
2003	27.9	27.9	27.8	27.7	27.9	27.9	27.5	27.7	27.6	27.7	27.8	27.9	27.8
Retail trade													
1990	97.1	93.4	92.8	92.1	92.4	93.2	95.1	94.8	94.5	95.4	99.2	102.0	95.1
1991	91.9	89.7	88.6	88.0	87.3	87.7	88.5	88.9	88.9	89.2	91.3	94.1	89.5
1992	88.3	85.0	84.0	83.6	83.3	84.0	84.2	83.9	83.5	84.5	88.4	91.5	85.3
1993	85.3	83.3	82.6	82.3	82.2	82.9	83.9	83.5	83.6	84.1	87.7	91.9	84.4
1994	83.2	82.0	81.6	81.4	81.5	81.9	82.0	82.4	82.4	83.7	87.4	91.1	83.3
1995	84.5	83.5	83.1	81.8	82.9	83.5	83.4	84.2	84.2	84.6	88.1	91.1	84.5
1996	85.9	85.2	84.8	83.7	84.6	85.8	86.8	86.2	87.1	87.4	91.2	94.3	86.9
1997	88.6	88.1	88.6	89.6	89.1	91.1	90.4	90.9	91.3	90.9	94.5	99.2	91.0
1998	93.2	91.0	90.7	92.1	93.0	93.9	93.9	94.7	94.0	94.8	98.8	103.0	94.4
1999	96.0	95.1	95.1	95.3	96.1	96.9	97.5	97.5	97.5	97.7	100.9	105.3	97.5
2000	99.6	98.2	98.4	98.5	99.1	100.5	101.2	101.4	101.3	101.3	105.0	108.0	101.0
2001	102.9	100.7	101.2	100.2	100.3	101.1	100.7	100.2	99.9	98.1	100.9	103.3	100.7
2002	98.0	96.3	96.6	95.8	96.0	96.6	96.3	95.9	96.1	96.4	100.0	102.0	97.2
2003	97.1	95.5	94.9	93.7	94.1	94.7	94.2	94.3	94.2	94.0	96.2	97.9	95.1
Transportation and utilities													
1990	58.0	58.3	58.3	58.8	58.6	58.8	59.2	58.7	58.8	59.3	59.3	59.3	58.7
1991	59.8	59.8	59.6	60.0	60.5	60.6	60.3	60.6	60.1	60.6	60.6	60.6	60.2
1992	59.7	59.0	59.5	59.4	59.4	59.7	60.1	59.9	59.8	59.6	59.4	59.4	59.5
1993	58.4	58.2	57.5	57.3	57.3	57.7	57.4	57.1	57.5	58.4	57.5	57.6	57.6
1994	56.7	55.9	55.8	56.0	55.9	56.0	55.9	55.7	55.8	56.3	56.1	56.0	56.0
1995	54.9	55.0	54.9	54.8	55.3	55.4	55.3	55.3	55.2	55.3	55.6	55.8	55.2
1996	54.5	54.8	55.5	55.9	55.9	55.8	56.3	56.0	56.4	56.4	57.0	56.9	55.9
1997	56.7	57.3	57.7	57.9	58.7	58.7	58.4	56.6	58.6	59.6	59.7	60.1	58.3
1998	59.3	59.1	59.5	59.6	59.4	59.7	59.5	59.2	59.3	59.0	59.2	58.2	59.2
1999	57.3	56.6	56.8	56.7	57.2	57.5	56.9	57.0	57.0	57.6	57.0	57.3	57.0
2000	57.2	57.4	58.1	57.9	58.2	58.2	58.3	58.2	58.3	56.8	57.3	57.4	57.7
2001	56.1	56.1	56.2	56.2	56.5	56.4	55.4	55.4	54.8	53.4	51.2	49.9	54.8
2002	49.5	49.4	49.0	48.2	48.4	48.5	48.7	48.5	48.4	48.5	48.4	48.2	48.6
2003	47.7	47.2	47.2	47.0	46.9	46.6	46.1	45.7	45.3	44.9	44.9	45.2	46.2
Information													
1990	28.0	27.9	27.9	27.9	28.1	28.4	29.0	28.5	28.4	28.6	28.6	28.8	28.3
1991	28.4	28.3	28.7	30.4	30.3	30.6	30.7	30.8	30.6	31.2	31.3	31.3	30.2
1992	28.6	28.6	28.9	29.2	29.2	29.5	28.5	28.9	28.6	29.6	29.8	30.1	29.1
1993	30.2	30.4	30.3	30.3	31.0	31.0	31.3	31.4	31.5	31.4	31.7	31.8	31.0
1994	31.8	32.1	32.3	30.9	31.1	31.5	31.2	30.8	31.1	31.1	31.0	31.6	31.3
1995	33.3	32.5	32.8	33.0	33.3	33.8	33.0	33.1	33.4	32.8	33.1	33.4	33.1
1996	32.5	33.0	33.1	33.2	33.6	33.8	33.3	33.6	33.7	33.4	34.0	34.4	33.4
1997	34.6	35.2	35.3	35.6	35.7	36.1	35.8	35.9	36.0	37.0	37.3	37.7	36.0
1998	38.5	38.8	39.2	39.9	40.4	41.0	41.0	41.3	41.6	41.8	42.2	42.7	40.7
1999	43.2	44.3	44.8	45.0	45.9	46.9	49.3	50.1	51.3	52.3	53.5	55.1	48.4
2000	55.4	57.3	59.3	60.7	62.8	64.8	65.4	66.4	66.8	66.3	66.9	66.9	63.2
2001	70.0	69.3	68.7	64.0	61.8	61.0	57.1	55.8	54.0	53.9	52.7	52.0	60.0
2002	51.6	50.9	50.9	50.3	51.0	51.1	51.2	51.3	51.1	49.4	49.7	49.5	50.7
2003	48.0	48.1	47.9	47.3	47.5	47.0	46.8	46.7	46.5	46.0	46.2	46.1	47.0
Financial activities													
1990	99.3	99.1	99.5	99.3	99.1	99.8	101.5	100.0	99.7	100.0	99.8	99.5	99.7
1991	97.4	98.0	97.5	97.9	98.0	97.6	98.2	97.1	96.2	95.1	95.0	94.8	96.9
1992	93.9	93.9	94.5	95.1	94.7	94.9	93.7	93.6	93.3	94.2	94.5	94.3	94.2
1993	96.3	96.6	96.5	96.3	96.5	96.7	96.3	95.9	95.6	95.7	96.0	96.3	96.2
1994	94.6	95.0	95.3	94.2	94.1	94.3	94.1	94.0	93.4	92.1	92.3	92.6	93.8
1995	91.4	91.9	91.8	92.1	92.4	92.6	92.9	93.1	93.6	93.4	93.7	94.4	92.7
1996	93.4	94.1	94.5	93.8	93.8	94.2	93.0	93.2	93.1	92.8	93.5	93.3	93.5
1997	92.7	92.5	92.9	92.7	93.2	94.1	94.8	94.9	94.8	94.7	94.7	96.3	94.0
1998	94.3	95.1	95.5	94.7	95.6	95.9	96.7	96.7	96.9	96.5	97.3	97.9	96.0
1999	97.1	97.4	97.4	96.4	97.0	97.6	96.7	96.7	96.5	96.6	97.1	97.8	97.0
2000	95.4	95.7	96.2	96.1	96.8	98.2	97.9	97.0	97.6	98.5	98.3	98.9	97.2
2001	102.6	103.1	104.4	103.9	103.2	103.5	101.6	100.9	100.4	100.1	99.9	99.7	101.9
2002	97.4	97.1	97.2	96.2	95.6	95.8	95.1	95.2	94.1	93.6	93.2	93.3	95.3
2003	91.0	91.3	91.4	90.9	90.9	91.0	90.4	90.3	90.2	90.5	90.3	90.3	90.7

Employment by Industry: California—*Continued*

(Numbers in thousands. Not seasonally adjusted.)

Industry	January	February	March	April	May	June	July	August	September	October	November	December	Annual Average
SAN FRANCISCO—*Continued*													
Professional and business services													
1990	164.1	166.1	165.7	165.8	166.2	169.0	169.1	169.2	169.4	169.4	168.7	171.0	167.8
1991	172.7	172.0	172.8	171.7	170.1	170.5	171.3	171.2	171.6	172.6	173.0	173.3	171.9
1992	168.3	168.0	169.8	170.8	169.3	171.5	175.6	175.7	175.1	174.4	175.0	174.6	172.3
1993	170.1	170.3	171.3	170.3	170.1	171.9	171.6	172.3	173.0	171.9	172.0	173.5	171.5
1994	163.7	165.7	167.3	169.1	169.1	170.1	169.3	170.9	171.6	169.9	170.9	173.4	169.2
1995	167.5	170.7	172.5	172.3	173.7	174.9	177.0	178.5	179.7	179.1	180.5	182.9	175.7
1996	185.0	188.1	190.3	189.3	190.8	192.7	194.2	196.4	195.8	196.3	198.6	200.4	193.1
1997	194.4	198.0	200.0	200.8	201.6	203.6	203.4	205.7	205.6	204.8	206.0	209.1	202.7
1998	202.9	205.1	205.7	209.4	209.7	212.6	214.4	215.2	215.0	214.9	216.2	218.6	211.6
1999	214.3	217.8	219.9	221.0	222.2	225.4	224.9	226.2	225.5	227.2	228.4	231.1	223.6
2000	227.7	232.4	236.2	237.2	238.3	242.9	243.8	247.4	248.3	248.5	249.4	250.9	241.9
2001	232.2	233.7	233.5	226.1	224.0	223.1	217.5	214.7	210.5	206.1	204.5	204.9	219.2
2002	192.5	192.3	192.3	191.0	189.8	189.5	187.4	186.6	184.6	183.7	186.1	185.3	188.4
2003	179.0	179.5	178.9	178.7	178.0	178.2	176.5	176.8	176.9	176.3	176.5	176.8	177.7
Educational and health services													
1990	83.8	84.3	85.2	86.1	85.6	84.1	85.0	84.5	84.9	86.3	86.1	86.5	85.2
1991	83.7	84.9	85.2	85.6	85.8	85.2	87.1	87.0	86.7	87.4	87.7	88.1	86.2
1992	84.8	86.0	87.1	87.3	87.1	85.7	86.3	86.0	85.5	85.6	85.8	85.9	86.0
1993	85.3	86.3	86.8	86.4	86.6	85.7	87.0	86.7	86.7	86.7	86.9	87.6	86.5
1994	85.1	86.3	86.9	87.6	87.7	87.1	87.0	86.5	86.6	87.5	87.9	88.7	87.0
1995	85.1	87.1	88.0	89.1	89.5	89.1	89.7	89.7	89.9	89.8	90.6	90.8	89.0
1996	88.5	90.2	91.3	91.2	90.9	90.9	91.1	90.3	90.2	90.4	90.8	92.2	90.6
1997	91.2	93.1	93.3	94.6	96.4	94.5	95.3	92.5	94.2	96.5	97.0	97.1	94.6
1998	96.3	98.7	98.5	98.8	99.4	97.7	97.8	95.8	97.8	99.5	98.8	98.7	98.1
1999	97.6	100.2	101.0	100.7	99.9	99.6	99.4	97.2	98.9	98.9	99.5	99.7	99.3
2000	96.8	100.0	100.0	94.4	94.1	92.9	93.6	92.5	93.5	94.3	95.7	95.8	95.3
2001	92.5	94.8	95.8	96.3	96.6	95.6	95.1	95.2	96.1	97.1	98.3	98.5	95.9
2002	96.1	97.8	98.3	97.8	98.1	95.9	95.5	95.3	96.1	98.4	99.4	99.1	97.3
2003	95.6	97.3	98.0	98.4	98.0	97.4	97.5	96.7	97.5	98.5	99.4	99.5	97.8
Leisure and hospitality													
1990	91.3	91.3	92.0	93.6	93.2	94.1	94.8	95.3	95.5	95.8	96.1	96.5	94.1
1991	91.9	90.9	91.2	91.9	93.8	95.1	93.8	94.9	95.6	94.3	93.6	93.7	93.3
1992	88.7	88.3	88.3	89.7	92.1	92.7	90.6	91.6	92.6	92.1	91.2	91.3	90.7
1993	87.9	88.2	88.3	90.2	92.2	93.1	92.4	93.0	94.4	94.6	93.0	94.8	91.8
1994	91.0	91.1	92.8	93.1	95.1	96.1	95.4	94.9	95.8	95.9	96.5	96.8	94.5
1995	93.9	94.1	95.8	96.3	98.2	99.2	99.5	100.9	101.8	99.6	100.4	101.6	98.4
1996	98.5	98.9	100.4	99.7	101.9	102.6	103.2	104.2	105.0	104.4	104.2	105.6	102.3
1997	101.3	102.6	104.0	107.5	107.8	109.5	108.1	108.7	109.9	107.4	107.3	108.2	106.8
1998	103.8	104.6	105.4	107.5	108.5	110.3	111.8	112.7	113.6	111.0	110.6	112.3	109.3
1999	107.5	108.1	110.1	111.1	113.0	114.6	113.4	113.7	114.1	112.1	111.2	112.0	111.7
2000	108.0	110.1	112.3	113.0	114.6	116.5	116.8	117.7	119.6	117.0	116.3	116.2	114.8
2001	113.2	115.5	117.1	116.1	118.9	119.2	117.1	117.9	116.7	113.7	111.5	111.5	115.7
2002	106.8	107.7	109.2	112.9	116.0	116.7	114.9	116.9	116.2	115.9	114.9	114.8	113.6
2003	108.8	109.4	110.1	111.7	113.0	115.1	112.8	115.2	114.8	113.8	111.5	111.1	112.3
Other services													
1990	35.4	35.6	36.0	35.5	35.6	36.0	36.4	36.3	36.0	36.0	36.2	36.0	35.9
1991	35.4	34.4	34.8	35.7	35.7	35.8	36.0	35.8	35.9	35.8	35.7	36.3	35.6
1992	36.0	35.9	36.1	35.7	35.7	36.0	35.8	35.9	35.9	36.2	36.0	36.6	35.9
1993	35.9	35.4	35.8	35.4	35.9	36.1	36.4	36.3	36.5	36.4	36.4	36.5	36.0
1994	36.5	36.8	37.3	37.2	37.4	38.0	37.8	38.1	38.2	38.1	37.6	37.8	37.5
1995	36.3	36.2	36.4	36.3	36.9	37.2	37.7	37.9	37.8	37.2	37.5	37.4	37.0
1996	36.1	36.3	36.9	37.0	37.3	37.4	37.5	37.5	37.5	37.7	37.7	37.8	37.2
1997	37.9	38.5	39.0	39.6	40.2	40.5	39.4	39.8	39.9	39.7	39.7	40.2	39.5
1998	39.1	39.2	39.9	40.7	40.9	41.5	40.8	40.7	40.9	41.5	41.4	41.6	40.6
1999	41.9	40.7	40.8	40.3	40.1	39.5	40.0	39.7	39.9	40.1	40.0	40.4	40.2
2000	39.2	39.8	40.1	40.3	40.4	40.7	40.4	40.3	40.2	40.6	41.0	41.1	40.3
2001	40.5	41.1	41.7	40.4	40.7	40.9	40.1	39.9	39.8	39.8	39.5	39.4	40.3
2002	38.7	39.0	39.2	39.2	39.4	39.3	38.9	38.6	38.8	38.7	38.8	39.2	39.0
2003	37.8	38.5	38.6	38.3	38.4	38.4	37.4	37.4	37.5	37.5	37.6	37.8	37.9
Government													
1990	137.0	138.6	140.1	140.4	141.5	141.4	136.6	132.4	137.6	139.4	141.1	142.0	139.0
1991	138.4	139.2	140.6	140.8	140.7	138.8	135.5	134.0	137.0	139.3	140.0	140.7	138.7
1992	134.9	135.8	136.9	136.2	135.6	134.1	130.6	128.6	130.6	131.1	132.5	132.5	133.2
1993	130.1	131.2	131.7	132.0	132.1	130.9	126.2	123.4	126.9	129.1	129.4	129.3	129.3
1994	126.4	127.5	128.3	128.6	129.2	129.1	124.8	122.4	124.1	127.9	127.9	128.5	127.0
1995	125.6	126.9	126.8	127.0	126.9	127.0	122.6	121.0	122.1	123.9	124.8	125.8	125.0
1996	122.8	124.2	125.4	125.5	125.6	125.8	121.6	120.6	122.7	123.7	125.5	125.8	124.1
1997	124.0	124.2	125.2	125.2	125.7	125.5	121.8	120.6	122.2	124.8	125.9	123.1	124.0
1998	120.7	121.4	122.3	122.7	123.7	123.9	120.6	120.3	121.2	123.9	125.3	126.0	122.6
1999	123.1	125.4	126.8	127.4	127.6	125.5	122.6	121.8	123.4	126.3	128.2	128.4	125.5
2000	125.5	126.6	128.2	134.2	136.9	135.2	128.7	129.4	129.4	131.3	133.7	134.0	131.0
2001	128.9	129.2	130.6	131.0	131.1	130.8	127.3	126.4	130.4	131.8	132.9	132.8	130.2
2002	132.0	132.4	134.8	134.6	135.0	134.5	129.1	128.5	131.1	134.3	135.3	135.1	133.1
2003	132.7	133.4	133.9	133.5	133.7	133.7	127.5	127.3	128.1	129.2	129.3	129.2	131.0

Employment by Industry: California—*Continued*

(Numbers in thousands. Not seasonally adjusted.)

Industry	January	February	March	April	May	June	July	August	September	October	November	December	Annual Average
SAN FRANCISCO—*Continued*													
Federal government													
1990	35.9	35.5	35.6	36.3	37.1	37.6	36.4	35.7	35.5	35.1	35.2	35.5	35.9
1991	35.6	35.4	35.5	35.5	35.5	35.7	35.9	35.9	35.8	35.6	35.7	36.3	35.7
1992	33.6	33.5	33.5	33.4	33.3	32.9	33.3	33.1	32.7	32.4	32.1	32.5	33.0
1993	31.8	31.5	31.4	31.4	31.3	31.2	30.8	30.5	30.5	30.1	29.9	30.3	30.8
1994	29.2	29.5	29.5	29.8	29.9	29.9	29.3	28.9	28.6	28.0	27.8	28.4	29.0
1995	27.3	27.2	27.1	27.0	26.6	26.5	26.3	26.2	26.0	25.7	25.6	26.5	26.5
1996	25.1	25.2	25.2	25.3	25.3	25.4	24.9	25.4	25.4	24.9	25.1	26.1	25.2
1997	24.7	24.7	24.7	24.6	24.6	24.6	24.6	24.6	24.6	24.2	24.4	25.7	24.6
1998	24.0	24.0	24.1	23.9	24.0	24.0	24.3	24.5	24.6	24.5	24.8	25.9	24.3
1999	24.5	24.8	24.5	24.5	24.4	24.3	24.1	24.0	24.0	23.9	24.0	24.9	24.3
2000	24.0	23.9	24.1	25.3	27.7	28.6	25.9	26.7	24.1	24.1	24.6	25.6	25.3
2001	22.4	22.2	22.4	21.7	21.8	21.9	22.7	22.6	22.7	22.3	22.3	22.4	22.2
2002	22.3	22.2	22.4	22.0	22.1	22.3	22.6	22.5	22.5	22.8	22.7	23.2	22.5
2003	22.8	22.8	22.8	22.6	22.8	22.8	22.2	22.2	22.2	22.1	22.0	22.4	22.5
State government													
1990	28.2	27.9	28.5	28.5	28.5	28.6	29.1	29.0	29.4	29.6	29.9	30.0	28.9
1991	30.1	29.8	30.7	30.6	30.7	30.9	30.1	30.0	30.0	30.5	30.4	30.2	30.3
1992	30.3	30.1	30.7	30.7	30.7	30.9	30.0	29.8	28.8	28.5	28.9	29.0	29.8
1993	28.7	28.7	28.8	28.8	28.6	28.4	28.2	27.7	27.9	28.2	28.3	27.9	28.3
1994	27.9	27.7	28.2	28.1	28.1	28.2	27.5	27.2	27.3	29.1	28.3	28.0	27.9
1995	28.1	27.6	28.1	28.3	27.9	28.2	27.3	26.8	27.0	27.4	27.5	27.5	27.6
1996	27.3	27.3	27.6	27.7	27.7	28.1	26.9	26.7	27.1	27.4	28.0	27.6	27.4
1997	27.6	27.5	27.9	28.1	28.1	28.1	27.1	26.9	26.8	27.7	27.7	23.6	27.2
1998	23.5	23.1	23.6	23.9	23.7	23.9	22.7	22.5	22.9	23.7	24.0	23.5	23.4
1999	23.5	23.1	23.8	24.1	24.0	24.0	23.0	22.9	23.1	23.9	24.3	24.0	23.6
2000	23.8	23.2	24.0	28.7	28.6	28.7	27.5	27.7	28.0	28.3	28.9	28.5	27.1
2001	28.4	28.0	28.8	29.5	28.8	29.3	28.3	28.5	28.9	29.4	30.0	29.6	28.9
2002	29.7	29.2	30.0	30.2	30.0	30.2	29.4	29.6	29.6	30.4	30.6	30.4	29.9
2003	30.3	30.0	30.8	30.9	30.7	30.9	30.4	29.8	29.5	30.4	30.4	30.3	30.4
Local government													
1990	72.9	75.2	76.0	75.6	75.9	75.2	71.1	67.7	72.7	74.7	76.0	76.5	74.1
1991	72.7	74.0	74.4	74.7	74.5	72.2	69.5	68.1	71.2	73.2	73.9	74.2	72.7
1992	71.0	72.2	72.7	72.1	71.6	70.3	67.3	65.7	69.1	70.2	71.5	71.0	70.3
1993	69.6	71.0	71.5	71.8	72.2	71.3	67.2	65.2	68.5	70.8	71.2	71.1	70.1
1994	69.3	70.3	70.6	70.7	71.2	71.0	68.0	66.3	68.2	70.8	71.8	72.1	70.0
1995	70.2	72.1	71.6	71.7	72.4	72.3	69.0	68.0	69.1	70.8	71.7	71.8	70.8
1996	70.4	71.7	72.6	72.5	72.6	72.3	69.8	68.5	70.2	71.4	72.4	72.1	71.3
1997	71.7	72.0	72.6	72.5	73.0	72.8	70.1	69.1	70.8	72.9	73.8	73.8	72.0
1998	73.2	74.3	74.6	74.9	76.0	76.0	73.6	73.3	73.7	75.7	76.5	76.6	74.8
1999	75.1	77.5	78.5	78.8	79.2	77.2	75.5	74.9	76.3	78.5	79.9	79.5	77.5
2000	77.7	79.5	80.1	80.2	80.6	77.9	75.3	75.0	77.3	78.9	80.2	79.9	78.5
2001	78.1	79.0	79.4	79.8	80.5	79.6	76.3	75.3	78.8	80.1	80.6	80.8	79.0
2002	80.0	81.0	82.4	82.4	82.9	82.0	77.1	76.4	79.0	81.1	82.0	81.5	80.7
2003	79.6	80.6	80.3	80.0	80.2	80.0	74.9	75.3	76.4	76.7	76.9	76.5	78.1
SAN JOSE													
Total nonfarm													
1990	803.3	807.5	810.5	811.8	815.5	817.9	819.0	821.2	815.3	818.7	817.4	816.7	814.5
1991	808.1	809.1	808.3	806.7	808.1	807.5	804.9	807.0	802.9	803.5	802.1	801.3	805.7
1992	782.4	780.2	787.7	790.2	792.8	796.5	795.2	796.1	793.9	794.2	796.6	799.4	792.1
1993	784.8	787.8	792.2	790.8	795.5	800.4	798.8	799.2	798.8	798.5	802.4	809.5	796.5
1994	784.1	789.4	793.5	794.8	799.5	803.1	799.0	802.5	803.5	804.6	808.1	817.3	799.9
1995	794.8	805.6	814.1	818.1	826.1	835.7	835.8	843.4	845.3	846.0	855.0	862.6	831.8
1996	849.7	860.6	867.2	869.9	878.9	884.0	884.8	886.9	884.2	889.3	897.7	904.5	879.8
1997	887.9	899.5	911.5	915.9	923.1	933.3	932.5	935.3	935.6	941.6	947.1	956.0	926.6
1998	941.7	947.2	954.2	953.8	959.5	964.1	961.1	958.6	955.7	956.2	959.8	964.0	956.3
1999	949.7	955.0	962.0	960.7	965.9	971.3	974.6	976.6	977.5	981.6	986.7	993.9	971.2
2000	985.9	994.8	1009.3	1009.4	1022.4	1037.4	1041.8	1043.4	1045.9	1047.4	1055.9	1066.0	1029.9
2001	1040.9	1044.0	1048.4	1030.2	1025.5	1021.9	999.7	988.2	972.2	962.4	954.7	953.3	1003.5
2002	919.4	919.9	925.1	915.2	913.7	912.0	900.3	893.9	886.3	885.6	882.6	879.6	902.8
2003	859.0	858.0	859.1	858.5	859.7	861.7	852.8	848.7	846.9	848.4	849.2	848.5	854.2
Total private													
1990	714.6	718.9	721.1	722.5	724.4	726.9	731.1	732.8	726.9	729.0	727.1	727.2	725.2
1991	718.8	719.5	717.8	716.5	718.0	719.0	717.6	719.2	715.0	714.0	712.5	712.2	716.6
1992	694.5	691.2	697.8	700.3	702.6	706.6	706.6	709.0	706.2	706.2	708.5	710.4	703.3
1993	698.3	699.8	703.4	702.1	706.3	711.4	711.8	712.6	713.1	711.4	713.6	720.5	708.6
1994	695.9	700.4	703.6	704.6	709.0	713.2	713.0	717.2	717.6	716.4	719.9	729.4	711.6
1995	708.0	718.3	726.2	729.9	737.0	746.7	747.7	758.4	759.9	757.6	765.6	773.9	744.1
1996	762.5	772.7	778.4	781.4	789.8	795.6	798.0	803.3	800.1	801.6	809.0	816.8	792.4
1997	800.5	810.8	821.9	826.0	832.7	844.0	844.5	850.5	849.5	852.1	857.2	867.1	838.0
1998	853.6	858.5	864.1	863.8	869.3	875.2	872.9	873.8	869.4	866.0	868.8	873.2	867.3
1999	859.1	863.8	869.8	868.2	872.9	880.2	883.7	889.0	888.9	889.1	893.2	900.3	879.8
2000	892.0	901.2	913.6	914.0	925.9	938.0	946.5	953.3	956.2	952.6	960.7	971.2	935.4
2001	947.6	950.2	953.7	935.2	929.2	926.5	906.8	897.7	879.7	866.2	857.3	856.1	908.8
2002	822.5	822.1	826.1	815.1	813.5	812.1	803.4	799.7	791.0	786.9	783.5	781.0	804.7
2003	761.3	761.4	761.8	761.3	762.8	765.5	760.2	759.0	756.1	754.5	754.7	754.8	759.5

Employment by Industry: California—*Continued*

(Numbers in thousands. Not seasonally adjusted.)

Industry	January	February	March	April	May	June	July	August	September	October	November	December	Annual Average
SAN JOSE—*Continued*													
Goods-producing													
1990	275.8	275.1	274.2	278.1	277.4	277.9	281.4	281.8	279.2	278.7	275.5	272.7	277.3
1991	272.9	272.9	271.1	269.2	267.8	267.5	267.1	268.4	265.9	261.6	257.8	255.5	266.4
1992	251.6	249.6	250.8	252.3	251.5	252.0	254.6	255.5	253.9	250.1	249.4	247.7	251.5
1993	245.8	245.8	245.9	244.6	245.3	247.3	246.8	247.6	248.3	244.5	244.2	244.7	245.9
1994	238.1	237.7	238.3	236.0	237.8	239.6	242.3	244.4	243.6	241.6	240.7	243.0	240.2
1995	238.1	240.5	242.3	242.8	245.2	250.0	255.1	261.4	262.6	260.4	261.4	262.3	251.8
1996	261.4	264.5	265.0	267.1	269.5	271.9	273.1	275.7	274.7	273.5	274.1	274.4	270.4
1997	272.4	275.1	278.0	277.5	280.9	284.7	287.1	290.3	288.2	289.4	289.5	291.6	283.7
1998	288.3	289.2	290.3	287.7	289.5	290.4	290.2	290.0	288.3	283.4	281.9	280.1	287.4
1999	276.5	276.2	277.6	274.9	275.5	277.8	281.6	283.6	283.9	282.9	282.6	283.2	279.6
2000	281.7	284.2	288.6	289.8	293.2	299.1	303.1	306.7	309.6	309.9	311.9	314.1	299.3
2001	306.6	306.7	305.6	300.7	297.1	295.1	287.9	283.9	277.4	271.9	265.9	263.8	288.5
2002	255.5	251.7	252.8	248.3	248.0	247.5	245.2	243.3	239.2	235.3	230.7	227.0	243.7
2003	222.0	219.7	219.0	218.7	217.4	217.3	216.4	214.9	214.1	212.5	210.6	209.3	216.0
Natural resources and mining													
1990	0.2	0.2	0.2	0.3	0.2	0.2	0.3	0.3	0.2	0.3	0.3	0.3	0.2
1991	0.3	0.3	0.3	0.2	0.2	0.2	0.2	0.2	0.2	0.2	0.2	0.2	0.2
1992	0.2	0.2	0.2	0.2	0.3	0.3	0.3	0.3	0.3	0.3	0.2	0.2	0.2
1993	0.2	0.2	0.2	0.2	0.2	0.2	0.2	0.2	0.2	0.2	0.2	0.2	0.2
1994	0.2	0.2	0.2	0.2	0.2	0.2	0.2	0.2	0.2	0.2	0.2	0.2	0.2
1995	0.1	0.1	0.1	0.1	0.1	0.1	0.1	0.1	0.1	0.1	0.1	0.1	0.1
1996	0.1	0.1	0.1	0.1	0.1	0.1	0.2	0.2	0.2	0.2	0.2	0.2	0.1
1997	0.1	0.1	0.2	0.2	0.2	0.2	0.2	0.2	0.2	0.2	0.2	0.2	0.1
1998	0.1	0.1	0.1	0.1	0.2	0.2	0.2	0.2	0.2	0.2	0.2	0.2	0.1
1999	0.2	0.2	0.2	0.2	0.2	0.2	0.2	0.2	0.2	0.2	0.2	0.2	0.2
2000	0.2	0.2	0.2	0.2	0.2	0.2	0.2	0.2	0.2	0.2	0.2	0.3	0.2
2001	0.2	0.2	0.2	0.2	0.2	0.2	0.2	0.2	0.2	0.2	0.2	0.2	0.2
2002	0.3	0.3	0.3	0.2	0.2	0.2	0.2	0.2	0.2	0.2	0.2	0.2	0.2
2003	0.2	0.2	0.2	0.2	0.2	0.2	0.2	0.2	0.2	0.2	0.2	0.2	0.2
Construction													
1990	27.5	27.0	27.3	28.6	28.6	29.1	29.7	29.8	29.5	29.5	29.0	28.3	28.6
1991	27.5	27.2	27.1	27.4	27.5	28.0	28.2	28.4	27.9	27.8	27.5	27.1	27.6
1992	26.1	24.8	26.0	26.6	27.2	28.0	28.2	28.9	29.2	28.9	28.1	27.1	27.4
1993	24.9	25.3	25.7	25.6	26.0	26.9	27.4	27.8	28.0	27.5	27.1	27.1	26.6
1994	25.1	24.7	25.6	25.1	25.6	26.6	26.9	27.3	27.7	27.6	27.1	26.9	26.3
1995	24.3	25.2	25.6	26.1	27.2	28.6	30.0	31.3	31.6	31.6	31.6	31.5	28.7
1996	30.2	30.3	30.3	30.9	32.0	33.0	32.9	34.1	34.0	34.1	34.1	33.8	32.4
1997	32.6	33.0	34.1	35.0	36.0	36.9	38.0	39.3	39.3	37.3	37.0	37.3	36.3
1998	37.6	37.1	38.3	39.4	40.5	41.6	42.0	42.9	43.3	44.0	43.7	43.2	41.1
1999	41.7	41.0	42.3	42.9	43.9	45.0	46.2	46.8	47.0	46.5	46.0	45.9	44.6
2000	43.6	43.7	44.9	45.3	46.2	47.6	48.5	49.3	50.3	49.9	50.1	49.8	47.4
2001	49.1	48.9	49.5	49.0	48.8	49.0	48.2	48.5	47.0	46.2	45.2	44.2	47.8
2002	41.8	41.4	42.2	41.6	42.4	43.1	43.3	44.3	43.3	42.3	41.6	40.0	42.3
2003	38.1	37.8	38.1	38.1	38.4	39.0	39.6	40.3	40.5	39.7	38.7	37.3	38.8
Manufacturing													
1990	248.1	247.9	246.7	249.2	248.6	248.6	251.4	251.7	249.5	248.9	246.2	244.1	248.4
1991	245.1	245.4	243.7	241.6	240.1	239.3	238.7	239.8	237.8	233.6	230.1	228.2	238.6
1992	225.3	224.6	224.6	225.5	224.0	223.7	226.1	226.3	224.4	220.9	221.1	220.4	223.9
1993	220.7	220.3	220.0	218.8	219.1	220.2	219.2	219.6	220.1	216.8	216.9	217.4	219.0
1994	212.8	212.8	212.5	210.7	212.0	212.8	215.2	216.9	215.7	213.8	213.4	215.9	213.7
1995	213.7	215.2	216.6	216.6	217.9	221.3	225.0	230.0	230.9	228.7	229.7	230.7	223.0
1996	231.1	234.1	234.6	236.1	237.4	238.8	240.0	241.4	240.5	239.2	239.8	240.4	237.7
1997	239.7	242.0	243.7	242.3	244.7	247.6	248.9	250.8	248.7	251.9	252.3	254.1	247.2
1998	250.6	252.0	251.9	248.2	248.8	248.6	248.0	246.9	244.8	239.2	238.0	236.7	246.1
1999	234.6	235.0	235.1	231.8	231.4	232.6	235.2	236.6	236.7	236.2	236.4	237.1	234.8
2000	237.9	240.3	243.5	244.3	246.8	251.3	254.4	257.2	259.1	259.8	261.6	264.0	251.6
2001	257.3	257.6	255.9	251.5	248.1	245.9	239.5	235.2	230.2	225.5	220.5	219.4	240.5
2002	213.4	210.0	210.3	206.5	205.4	204.2	201.7	198.8	195.7	192.8	188.9	186.8	201.2
2003	183.7	181.7	180.7	180.4	178.8	178.1	176.6	174.4	173.4	172.6	171.7	171.8	177.0
Service-providing													
1990	527.5	532.4	536.3	533.7	538.1	540.0	537.6	539.4	536.1	540.0	541.9	544.0	537.2
1991	535.2	536.2	537.2	537.5	540.3	540.0	537.8	538.6	537.0	541.9	544.3	545.8	539.3
1992	530.8	530.6	536.9	537.9	541.3	544.5	540.6	540.6	540.0	544.1	547.2	551.7	540.5
1993	539.0	542.0	546.3	546.2	550.2	553.1	552.0	551.6	550.5	554.0	558.2	564.8	550.6
1994	546.0	551.7	555.2	558.8	561.7	563.5	556.7	558.1	559.9	563.0	567.4	574.3	559.6
1995	556.7	565.1	571.8	575.3	580.9	585.7	580.7	582.0	582.7	585.6	593.6	600.3	580.0
1996	588.3	596.1	602.2	602.8	609.4	612.1	611.7	611.2	609.5	615.8	623.6	630.1	609.4
1997	615.5	624.4	633.5	638.4	642.2	648.6	645.4	645.0	647.4	652.2	657.6	664.4	642.8
1998	653.4	658.0	663.9	666.1	670.0	673.7	670.9	668.6	667.4	672.8	677.9	683.9	668.8
1999	673.2	678.8	684.4	685.8	690.4	693.5	693.0	693.0	693.6	698.7	704.1	710.7	691.6
2000	704.2	710.6	720.7	719.6	729.2	738.3	738.7	736.7	736.3	737.5	744.0	751.9	730.6
2001	734.3	737.3	742.8	729.5	728.4	726.8	711.8	704.3	694.8	690.5	688.8	689.5	714.9
2002	663.9	668.2	672.3	666.9	665.7	664.5	655.1	650.6	647.1	650.3	651.9	652.6	659.1
2003	637.0	638.3	640.1	639.8	642.3	644.4	636.4	633.8	632.8	635.9	638.6	639.2	638.2

Employment by Industry: California—*Continued*

(Numbers in thousands. Not seasonally adjusted.)

Industry	January	February	March	April	May	June	July	August	September	October	November	December	Annual Average
SAN JOSE—*Continued*													
Trade, transportation, and utilities													
1990	127.0	126.1	125.6	125.0	125.2	125.8	126.7	126.4	125.9	126.8	129.0	131.7	126.7
1991	126.8	124.1	123.7	124.8	125.3	126.3	125.4	125.9	125.9	125.8	128.7	130.7	126.1
1992	124.6	121.5	121.9	122.3	122.9	123.5	123.8	123.6	123.5	124.5	127.5	130.3	124.1
1993	125.4	124.1	123.4	123.1	123.8	124.3	124.0	123.8	124.1	123.9	126.8	129.8	124.7
1994	121.3	120.9	120.6	120.8	121.8	121.9	121.8	122.8	123.5	124.7	127.8	130.7	123.2
1995	124.5	124.4	124.4	125.5	125.8	126.8	126.0	127.1	127.5	127.8	131.0	134.8	127.1
1996	130.1	131.2	131.5	132.4	133.7	135.0	136.2	136.5	136.3	137.3	140.4	143.6	135.3
1997	137.0	137.2	138.3	138.8	139.3	141.2	141.3	140.5	141.3	142.0	145.5	149.5	140.9
1998	143.2	141.7	142.0	140.7	141.4	142.3	142.7	143.6	142.8	142.9	145.9	148.3	143.1
1999	144.3	144.3	144.0	143.2	143.7	144.2	146.0	146.6	146.8	147.5	150.1	153.3	146.1
2000	149.3	148.2	148.8	148.2	148.9	149.6	150.6	150.9	150.9	149.7	153.1	156.3	150.3
2001	150.4	148.3	149.1	146.2	145.7	146.0	144.6	143.0	141.9	140.3	142.6	144.6	145.2
2002	136.8	135.3	135.8	133.9	133.9	133.7	133.3	132.9	132.7	132.4	134.4	136.4	134.3
2003	129.6	127.8	127.5	127.7	127.8	128.6	127.7	128.2	128.1	128.0	130.5	131.7	128.6
Wholesale trade													
1990	37.9	37.9	38.1	37.9	37.6	37.5	37.6	37.0	36.6	36.9	36.5	35.9	37.2
1991	36.5	36.4	36.3	36.3	36.3	36.2	36.0	36.0	35.9	36.2	36.1	35.9	36.1
1992	35.8	35.9	36.0	35.8	36.0	35.9	35.9	35.9	35.6	36.2	36.0	36.0	35.9
1993	35.9	35.7	35.6	35.4	35.4	35.6	35.1	35.0	34.9	34.1	34.3	34.0	35.0
1994	33.3	33.7	33.7	34.2	34.4	34.5	34.5	35.0	35.1	35.1	35.2	35.3	34.5
1995	35.2	35.7	36.1	36.3	36.7	37.0	36.6	36.7	36.7	36.6	36.7	37.0	36.4
1996	36.8	37.7	38.1	38.5	38.8	39.1	40.0	40.3	40.1	40.2	40.6	41.0	39.2
1997	40.7	41.0	41.5	41.6	41.7	42.1	42.2	42.4	42.1	42.3	42.5	42.6	41.8
1998	42.2	42.3	42.6	42.6	42.6	42.7	42.7	42.6	42.5	42.3	42.3	41.9	42.4
1999	42.1	42.6	42.3	42.1	41.8	41.9	42.6	42.5	42.4	42.4	42.3	42.3	42.2
2000	42.4	42.6	42.6	42.5	42.6	42.4	42.4	42.3	42.0	41.9	41.6	41.4	42.2
2001	42.2	42.3	42.6	41.3	40.9	40.7	40.7	40.5	39.9	39.3	38.8	38.7	40.6
2002	38.1	37.6	37.7	36.7	36.5	36.0	35.4	35.0	34.4	34.1	33.5	33.1	35.7
2003	32.7	32.6	32.9	33.4	33.7	33.9	33.8	33.9	33.8	33.6	33.8	33.4	33.5
Retail trade													
1990	75.4	74.5	73.7	73.2	73.6	74.3	75.0	75.3	75.2	75.5	78.2	81.5	75.4
1991	75.9	73.3	73.0	73.9	74.2	75.2	74.6	75.0	75.4	74.9	77.9	79.9	75.2
1992	75.0	71.8	72.2	72.8	73.1	73.7	73.6	73.5	73.8	74.2	77.3	80.1	74.2
1993	75.7	74.4	73.7	73.7	74.2	74.4	74.1	73.8	74.2	74.9	77.6	80.9	75.1
1994	73.6	72.8	72.5	72.6	73.0	73.1	72.6	73.0	73.6	74.7	77.9	80.5	74.1
1995	75.3	74.5	74.1	74.8	74.5	75.1	74.4	75.1	75.4	75.7	78.7	82.0	75.8
1996	78.1	78.2	78.0	77.9	78.6	79.6	79.7	79.7	79.8	80.4	83.1	85.8	79.9
1997	80.1	79.9	80.4	80.6	80.8	82.0	82.2	82.5	82.5	82.5	85.8	89.5	82.4
1998	84.5	82.9	82.7	81.2	81.9	82.6	83.0	84.0	83.1	83.5	86.5	89.3	83.7
1999	85.3	84.7	84.6	84.2	84.8	85.0	86.1	86.7	86.8	87.5	90.1	93.3	86.5
2000	89.9	88.6	89.1	88.1	88.9	89.6	90.6	90.8	91.2	90.1	93.7	96.9	90.6
2001	91.1	88.9	89.3	88.0	87.9	88.4	87.4	86.2	86.0	85.7	88.8	91.0	88.2
2002	84.2	83.1	83.5	82.4	82.2	82.5	82.7	82.8	83.2	83.1	85.8	88.2	83.6
2003	82.6	81.0	80.5	79.9	79.9	80.3	79.8	80.1	80.2	80.3	82.7	84.3	81.0
Transportation and utilities													
1990	13.7	13.7	13.8	13.9	14.0	14.0	14.1	14.1	14.1	14.4	14.3	14.3	14.0
1991	14.4	14.4	14.4	14.6	14.8	14.9	14.8	14.9	14.6	14.7	14.7	14.9	14.6
1992	13.8	13.8	13.7	13.7	13.8	13.9	14.3	14.2	14.1	14.1	14.2	14.2	13.9
1993	13.8	14.0	14.1	14.0	14.2	14.3	14.8	15.0	15.0	14.9	14.9	14.9	14.4
1994	14.4	14.4	14.4	14.0	14.4	14.3	14.7	14.8	14.8	14.9	14.7	14.9	14.5
1995	14.0	14.2	14.2	14.4	14.6	14.7	15.0	15.3	15.4	15.5	15.6	15.8	14.8
1996	15.2	15.3	15.4	16.0	16.3	16.3	16.5	16.5	16.4	16.7	16.7	16.8	16.1
1997	16.2	16.3	16.4	16.6	16.8	17.1	16.9	15.6	16.7	17.2	17.2	17.4	16.7
1998	16.5	16.5	16.7	16.9	16.9	17.0	17.0	17.0	17.2	17.1	17.1	17.1	16.9
1999	16.9	17.0	17.1	16.9	17.1	17.3	17.3	17.4	17.6	17.6	17.7	17.7	17.3
2000	17.0	17.0	17.1	17.6	17.4	17.6	17.6	17.8	17.7	17.7	17.8	18.0	17.5
2001	17.1	17.1	17.2	16.9	16.9	16.9	16.5	16.3	16.0	15.3	15.0	14.9	16.3
2002	14.5	14.6	14.6	14.8	15.2	15.2	15.2	15.1	15.1	15.2	15.1	15.1	15.0
2003	14.3	14.2	14.1	14.4	14.2	14.4	14.1	14.2	14.1	14.1	14.0	14.0	14.2
Information													
1990	20.6	20.7	20.9	21.0	21.0	21.1	21.4	21.4	21.0	21.3	21.3	21.4	21.0
1991	21.1	21.3	21.2	21.4	21.4	21.4	21.3	21.1	21.0	21.7	21.8	21.8	21.3
1992	21.5	21.6	21.5	21.2	21.3	21.8	21.8	21.8	21.7	22.4	22.4	22.4	21.7
1993	22.7	22.6	22.9	22.8	22.9	23.0	23.4	23.4	23.4	23.5	23.6	24.0	23.1
1994	23.4	23.4	23.3	23.4	23.5	23.7	23.6	23.9	23.8	23.6	23.5	23.6	23.5
1995	23.9	24.0	24.3	24.5	24.6	25.0	24.3	24.4	24.7	24.5	25.1	25.4	24.5
1996	25.2	25.2	25.3	25.4	25.5	25.7	26.2	26.4	26.2	26.7	27.0	27.5	26.0
1997	27.3	27.5	27.8	28.0	28.4	28.6	28.3	28.5	28.2	28.1	28.3	28.7	28.1
1998	28.9	29.3	29.6	28.4	28.6	29.0	29.0	29.1	29.0	28.8	29.0	29.3	29.0
1999	29.7	30.1	30.8	30.8	31.3	32.1	32.9	33.6	34.0	34.0	34.8	35.5	32.4
2000	36.8	37.6	39.1	40.0	41.4	43.0	44.1	44.9	45.5	46.0	46.5	47.0	42.6
2001	46.4	46.1	46.0	43.7	43.3	42.7	41.3	40.6	39.5	38.2	37.5	37.2	41.8
2002	36.9	36.8	36.6	35.6	34.8	34.1	33.4	33.1	32.7	32.3	32.4	32.0	34.2
2003	31.6	31.9	31.5	31.1	31.2	31.2	30.8	30.7	30.4	30.2	30.7	30.3	31.0

Employment by Industry: California—*Continued*

(Numbers in thousands. Not seasonally adjusted.)

Industry	January	February	March	April	May	June	July	August	September	October	November	December	Annual Average
SAN JOSE—*Continued*													
Financial activities													
1990	32.5	32.9	32.8	32.7	33.2	33.4	33.2	33.1	32.9	32.7	32.3	32.7	32.8
1991	32.8	32.8	32.7	33.2	33.1	32.9	32.9	33.0	32.7	32.2	32.2	32.3	32.7
1992	31.5	31.6	32.0	31.8	32.0	32.1	32.2	32.6	32.2	32.8	33.0	33.1	32.2
1993	32.4	32.7	32.6	32.7	32.8	33.1	32.7	32.7	32.8	32.7	32.7	32.8	32.7
1994	31.8	32.0	31.9	31.6	31.4	31.4	30.8	30.8	30.6	30.6	30.5	30.7	31.1
1995	29.9	30.3	30.3	30.5	30.6	30.7	30.5	30.5	30.4	30.4	30.5	30.7	30.4
1996	30.6	30.9	31.2	31.4	31.4	31.7	31.6	31.7	31.6	31.5	31.7	32.0	31.4
1997	31.0	31.3	31.8	31.8	32.3	32.5	32.5	32.7	32.4	32.9	33.2	33.2	32.3
1998	33.2	33.7	33.8	33.7	33.9	34.2	33.7	33.8	33.8	33.7	34.1	34.5	33.8
1999	34.2	34.3	34.6	34.4	34.7	34.5	34.1	34.3	33.9	33.9	33.9	34.1	34.2
2000	33.3	33.7	33.9	33.8	33.8	34.2	34.3	34.1	34.0	34.0	34.2	34.4	33.9
2001	34.1	34.4	34.8	34.9	35.1	35.5	35.4	35.9	35.6	35.3	35.5	35.8	35.1
2002	35.0	35.2	35.2	34.7	35.1	35.0	35.0	35.2	34.8	34.8	34.7	34.7	35.0
2003	34.2	34.3	34.5	34.6	34.9	34.9	34.9	34.9	34.9	35.0	35.0	35.1	34.8
Professional and business services													
1990	112.7	114.8	116.2	113.5	114.1	115.2	115.7	116.8	116.3	115.7	115.7	115.5	115.1
1991	113.8	113.4	114.0	114.7	114.3	115.2	116.5	116.5	116.3	117.4	118.3	118.8	115.7
1992	115.9	116.5	118.5	118.3	119.1	121.0	119.8	120.8	121.6	121.6	122.3	122.7	119.8
1993	122.4	123.6	124.8	124.4	125.2	126.1	126.6	126.6	127.1	128.1	128.7	131.0	126.2
1994	127.8	130.0	130.6	132.3	132.5	133.1	133.7	135.0	136.5	135.3	137.6	140.8	133.7
1995	135.0	138.2	141.0	142.6	144.6	147.0	148.4	150.9	152.6	151.7	154.8	157.3	147.0
1996	155.1	156.6	158.9	157.9	160.2	161.4	164.5	166.3	166.1	166.9	168.7	170.6	162.7
1997	167.9	170.6	173.8	177.5	177.8	180.8	183.7	186.2	188.7	188.2	188.8	191.8	181.3
1998	189.7	191.4	192.7	195.1	195.7	197.5	198.5	199.3	198.7	199.2	200.5	202.6	196.7
1999	198.9	200.5	201.7	204.4	205.5	208.4	208.8	210.7	210.5	210.0	212.0	214.0	207.1
2000	212.0	216.1	219.5	218.1	222.9	228.2	229.4	232.6	232.6	230.1	232.4	235.5	225.7
2001	227.3	228.4	229.0	221.2	217.2	215.5	208.3	204.4	198.5	193.5	189.5	187.4	210.0
2002	178.7	179.0	178.9	175.8	173.8	173.8	172.1	171.0	169.3	169.0	168.4	168.2	173.2
2003	164.7	164.7	164.9	164.4	165.1	166.1	164.0	165.1	164.2	162.2	162.6	163.2	164.3
Educational and health services													
1990	70.1	72.3	72.5	72.3	72.8	72.0	70.0	70.3	69.3	72.2	72.6	72.7	71.5
1991	73.4	75.1	75.0	74.5	75.2	74.2	72.4	72.7	72.3	75.2	76.1	75.8	74.3
1992	73.7	74.2	75.1	75.8	75.9	75.2	72.9	72.9	72.3	74.5	75.5	76.1	74.5
1993	71.9	72.3	72.8	73.3	73.1	73.6	75.1	74.9	74.1	77.7	78.1	78.6	74.6
1994	76.1	77.4	77.8	78.0	78.1	78.1	76.1	75.6	75.0	77.5	78.5	78.6	77.2
1995	76.8	79.2	80.1	78.3	78.7	78.7	75.5	75.6	74.4	77.2	78.0	78.3	77.5
1996	76.9	79.4	78.7	79.5	79.9	79.5	76.2	76.4	75.7	78.7	80.2	80.5	78.4
1997	79.4	81.2	81.7	82.3	82.5	82.6	79.4	79.9	79.2	81.9	83.0	83.8	81.4
1998	82.5	84.5	85.2	85.0	85.6	85.4	82.0	81.7	82.3	84.8	85.0	86.3	84.1
1999	85.0	86.5	87.2	86.2	86.8	86.2	83.4	83.3	83.1	85.9	86.4	86.1	85.5
2000	86.4	86.9	86.9	85.8	86.5	83.7	83.3	82.3	82.6	85.4	86.0	86.7	85.2
2001	87.1	88.5	89.7	89.1	90.1	90.0	87.9	88.8	88.8	91.6	92.4	93.2	89.7
2002	88.8	91.5	92.5	92.5	92.5	92.0	88.9	89.1	88.8	91.3	92.4	92.4	91.1
2003	90.7	92.8	93.5	92.8	93.0	93.0	91.5	91.3	91.4	93.9	94.1	94.3	92.7
Leisure and hospitality													
1990	53.9	54.8	56.3	57.5	58.2	58.8	59.6	59.8	59.1	58.7	58.1	58.1	57.7
1991	55.6	57.1	57.4	55.8	57.8	58.1	58.4	58.0	57.1	56.6	54.3	53.9	56.6
1992	52.9	53.3	54.7	55.2	56.2	57.1	57.4	57.6	56.7	56.3	54.5	54.3	55.5
1993	54.3	54.9	56.9	57.5	59.1	59.6	59.3	59.6	59.3	57.2	55.5	55.6	57.4
1994	54.1	55.4	57.2	58.6	59.9	61.1	60.4	60.4	60.4	59.2	57.4	58.1	58.5
1995	56.4	57.8	59.8	61.2	62.7	63.8	63.0	63.6	62.6	60.7	59.7	60.2	60.9
1996	58.5	59.7	62.2	62.1	63.8	64.3	64.0	64.2	63.7	60.8	60.9	62.1	62.1
1997	60.4	62.3	64.6	65.1	66.2	67.7	66.6	66.7	65.9	64.1	63.3	62.8	64.6
1998	62.0	62.7	64.1	66.8	68.0	69.4	69.9	69.6	68.2	66.9	66.2	66.0	66.6
1999	64.5	65.7	67.4	68.4	69.4	70.5	70.6	70.7	70.8	69.0	67.4	68.3	68.5
2000	66.7	68.3	70.2	71.4	72.3	72.9	74.3	74.4	74.1	71.3	70.4	70.4	71.3
2001	69.6	71.6	73.3	73.4	74.5	75.2	75.0	74.6	71.8	69.2	67.7	67.8	71.9
2002	65.0	66.4	67.9	68.1	69.2	69.8	69.3	69.0	67.8	66.6	65.0	65.0	67.4
2003	64.1	65.4	66.2	67.3	68.6	69.5	70.0	69.3	68.3	68.0	66.5	66.4	67.5
Other services													
1990	22.0	22.2	22.6	22.4	22.5	22.7	23.1	23.2	23.2	22.9	22.6	22.4	22.6
1991	22.4	22.8	22.7	22.9	23.1	23.4	23.6	23.6	23.8	23.5	23.3	23.4	23.2
1992	22.8	22.9	23.3	23.4	23.7	23.9	24.1	24.2	24.3	24.0	23.9	23.8	23.6
1993	23.4	23.8	24.1	23.7	24.1	24.4	23.9	24.0	24.0	23.8	24.0	24.0	23.9
1994	23.3	23.6	23.9	23.9	24.0	24.3	24.3	24.3	24.2	23.9	23.9	23.9	23.9
1995	23.4	23.9	24.0	24.5	24.8	24.7	24.9	24.9	25.1	24.9	25.1	24.9	24.5
1996	24.7	25.2	25.6	25.6	25.8	26.1	26.2	26.1	25.8	26.2	26.0	26.1	25.7
1997	25.1	25.6	25.9	25.0	25.3	25.9	25.6	25.7	25.6	25.5	25.6	25.7	25.5
1998	25.8	26.0	26.4	26.4	26.6	27.0	26.9	26.7	26.3	26.3	26.2	26.1	26.3
1999	26.0	26.2	26.5	25.9	26.0	26.5	26.3	26.2	25.9	25.9	26.0	25.8	26.1
2000	25.8	26.2	26.6	26.9	26.9	27.3	27.4	27.4	26.9	26.2	26.2	26.8	26.7
2001	26.1	26.2	26.2	26.0	26.2	26.5	26.4	26.5	26.2	26.2	26.2	26.3	26.2
2002	25.8	26.2	26.4	26.2	26.2	26.2	26.2	26.1	25.7	25.2	25.5	25.3	25.9
2003	24.4	24.8	24.7	24.7	24.8	24.9	24.9	24.6	24.7	24.7	24.7	24.5	24.7

Employment by Industry: California—*Continued*

(Numbers in thousands. Not seasonally adjusted.)

Industry	January	February	March	April	May	June	July	August	September	October	November	December	Annual Average
SAN JOSE—*Continued*													
Government													
1990	88.7	88.6	89.4	89.3	91.1	91.0	87.9	88.4	88.4	89.7	90.3	89.5	89.3
1991	89.3	89.6	90.5	90.2	90.1	88.5	87.3	87.8	87.9	89.5	89.6	89.1	89.1
1992	87.9	89.0	89.9	89.9	90.2	89.9	88.6	87.1	87.7	88.0	88.1	89.0	88.7
1993	86.5	88.0	88.8	88.7	89.2	89.0	87.0	86.6	85.7	87.1	88.8	89.0	87.8
1994	88.2	89.0	89.9	90.2	90.5	89.9	86.0	85.3	85.9	88.2	88.2	87.9	88.2
1995	86.8	87.3	87.9	88.2	89.1	89.0	88.1	85.0	85.4	88.4	89.4	88.7	87.7
1996	87.2	87.9	88.8	88.5	89.1	88.4	86.8	83.6	84.1	87.7	88.7	87.7	87.3
1997	87.4	88.7	89.6	89.9	90.4	89.3	88.0	84.8	86.1	89.5	89.9	88.9	88.5
1998	88.1	88.7	90.1	90.0	90.2	88.9	88.2	84.8	86.3	90.2	91.0	90.8	88.9
1999	90.6	91.2	92.2	92.5	93.0	91.1	90.9	87.6	88.6	92.5	93.5	93.6	91.4
2000	93.9	93.6	95.7	95.4	96.5	99.4	95.3	90.1	89.7	94.8	95.2	94.8	94.5
2001	93.3	93.8	94.7	95.0	96.3	95.4	92.9	90.5	92.5	96.2	97.4	97.2	94.6
2002	96.9	97.8	99.0	100.1	100.2	99.9	96.9	94.2	95.3	98.7	99.1	98.6	98.1
2003	97.7	96.6	97.3	97.2	96.9	96.2	92.6	89.7	90.8	93.9	94.5	93.7	94.8
Federal government													
1990	13.3	13.3	13.3	13.3	13.9	14.2	14.0	13.5	13.0	13.1	13.0	12.8	13.3
1991	12.7	12.7	12.7	12.8	12.8	12.9	12.9	12.8	12.8	12.8	12.7	12.7	12.7
1992	12.6	12.6	12.7	12.6	12.6	12.6	12.7	12.7	12.8	12.5	12.4	12.6	12.6
1993	12.4	12.3	12.3	12.3	12.3	12.5	12.4	12.5	12.6	12.6	12.7	13.0	12.4
1994	13.2	13.3	13.4	13.4	13.4	13.5	13.2	13.1	13.1	13.0	13.0	12.9	13.2
1995	12.8	12.7	12.7	13.1	13.1	13.2	13.3	13.3	13.2	13.1	13.0	13.1	13.0
1996	13.0	13.0	12.9	12.6	12.5	12.2	12.0	12.0	12.0	12.1	12.2	12.3	12.4
1997	12.1	12.1	12.1	12.2	12.2	12.2	12.0	11.9	11.8	11.7	11.7	11.7	11.9
1998	11.4	11.3	11.2	11.1	11.2	11.1	11.3	11.4	11.4	11.4	11.3	11.5	11.3
1999	11.4	11.5	11.3	11.4	11.3	11.4	11.4	11.4	11.4	11.3	11.3	11.7	11.4
2000	11.5	11.5	11.7	11.3	12.7	14.0	11.9	12.5	10.7	10.6	10.6	10.8	11.6
2001	10.6	10.6	10.6	10.4	10.4	10.4	10.2	10.2	10.2	10.2	10.2	10.2	10.3
2002	10.1	10.1	10.1	10.6	10.5	10.5	10.4	10.3	10.2	10.4	10.3	10.4	10.3
2003	10.3	10.3	10.3	10.1	10.1	10.1	10.0	9.9	9.9	9.9	9.9	10.0	10.1
State government													
1990	8.7	8.5	8.7	8.8	8.9	9.0	7.9	7.8	8.0	8.6	8.8	8.8	8.5
1991	8.7	8.3	8.9	8.9	9.0	9.0	8.1	7.8	8.1	8.5	8.4	8.3	8.5
1992	8.2	7.8	8.2	8.4	8.2	8.2	7.5	7.3	7.6	8.0	8.0	8.1	7.9
1993	7.9	7.9	7.9	7.8	8.1	8.1	7.5	7.4	7.5	8.0	8.1	8.0	7.8
1994	7.9	7.6	8.1	8.2	8.4	8.4	7.5	7.4	7.5	8.1	8.1	8.1	7.9
1995	8.0	7.7	8.0	7.9	7.9	8.0	7.4	7.2	7.2	7.8	7.8	7.8	7.7
1996	7.5	7.2	7.6	7.7	7.6	7.7	7.0	6.9	7.1	7.6	7.7	7.5	7.4
1997	7.4	7.3	7.6	7.6	7.6	7.6	6.9	6.8	6.9	7.6	7.6	7.6	7.3
1998	7.3	7.1	7.5	7.7	7.7	7.6	7.0	6.7	7.0	7.6	7.7	7.7	7.3
1999	7.6	7.1	7.7	7.8	7.8	7.9	7.2	7.1	7.2	8.0	8.0	8.1	7.6
2000	7.8	7.3	7.9	7.9	8.0	8.0	7.2	7.1	7.1	7.8	8.0	8.0	7.6
2001	7.9	7.4	7.8	7.8	8.0	8.0	7.4	7.3	7.3	8.0	8.1	8.2	7.7
2002	8.1	7.7	8.3	8.3	8.5	8.4	7.6	7.6	7.8	8.4	8.4	8.5	8.1
2003	8.3	7.7	8.2	8.1	8.2	8.1	7.4	7.2	7.5	7.9	7.9	7.8	7.9
Local government													
1990	66.7	66.8	67.4	67.2	68.3	67.8	66.0	67.1	67.4	68.0	68.5	67.9	67.4
1991	67.9	68.6	68.9	68.5	68.3	66.6	66.3	67.2	67.0	68.2	68.5	68.1	67.8
1992	67.1	68.6	69.0	68.9	69.4	69.1	68.4	67.1	67.3	67.5	67.7	68.3	68.2
1993	66.2	67.8	68.6	68.6	68.8	68.4	67.1	66.7	65.6	66.5	68.0	68.0	67.5
1994	67.1	68.1	68.4	68.6	68.7	68.0	65.3	64.8	65.3	67.1	67.1	66.9	67.1
1995	66.0	66.9	67.2	67.2	68.1	67.8	67.4	64.5	65.0	67.5	68.6	67.8	67.0
1996	66.7	67.7	68.3	68.2	69.0	68.5	67.8	64.7	65.0	68.0	68.8	67.9	67.5
1997	67.9	69.3	69.9	70.1	70.6	69.5	69.1	66.1	67.4	70.2	70.6	69.6	69.1
1998	69.4	70.3	71.4	71.2	71.3	70.2	69.9	66.7	67.9	71.2	72.0	71.6	70.2
1999	71.6	72.6	73.2	73.3	73.9	71.8	72.3	69.1	70.0	73.2	74.2	73.8	72.4
2000	74.6	74.8	76.1	76.2	75.8	77.4	76.2	70.5	71.9	76.4	76.6	76.0	75.2
2001	74.8	75.8	76.3	76.8	77.9	77.0	75.3	73.0	75.0	78.0	79.1	78.8	76.5
2002	78.7	80.0	80.6	81.2	81.2	81.0	78.9	76.3	77.3	79.9	80.4	79.7	79.6
2003	79.1	78.6	78.8	79.0	78.6	78.0	75.2	72.6	73.4	76.1	76.7	75.9	76.8
STOCKTON													
Total nonfarm													
1990	146.1	147.1	148.4	150.7	152.5	153.2	156.6	159.1	157.9	154.8	153.0	153.0	152.7
1991	151.2	151.8	150.8	152.6	154.5	155.0	156.7	160.7	161.9	157.9	155.1	154.1	155.1
1992	150.2	149.1	150.7	152.0	153.3	153.9	159.5	162.6	161.5	156.4	155.2	153.1	154.7
1993	151.7	152.2	153.1	154.9	155.7	156.4	159.7	162.3	161.4	157.4	156.1	153.6	156.2
1994	151.5	151.6	153.8	155.3	156.0	156.5	160.8	163.9	164.1	159.8	157.9	156.7	157.3
1995	154.4	155.5	156.5	158.1	160.4	160.3	160.3	165.2	167.1	162.7	162.8	160.4	160.3
1996	157.2	157.3	158.4	160.1	162.2	163.2	165.3	168.4	170.6	167.3	166.6	165.3	163.4
1997	160.3	161.5	163.4	164.4	167.3	169.0	170.0	172.7	173.6	169.1	168.4	169.2	167.4
1998	165.3	165.9	167.8	167.8	169.2	170.4	170.2	177.0	179.2	176.0	174.2	174.8	171.4
1999	170.6	171.1	173.4	175.4	177.0	178.3	179.2	184.4	187.0	183.8	181.9	182.0	178.6
2000	178.2	178.8	180.4	182.5	184.0	187.1	188.5	191.5	191.5	189.7	188.5	189.3	185.8
2001	186.0	186.4	188.1	189.2	191.4	193.3	191.7	195.3	194.1	193.0	192.3	191.9	191.0
2002	187.4	188.7	190.5	190.5	193.6	194.7	194.2	197.0	199.0	199.2	199.2	199.5	194.5
2003	194.2	194.8	196.8	196.6	197.8	199.0	195.5	197.2	200.6	199.7	199.4	199.5	197.6

Employment by Industry: California—*Continued*

(Numbers in thousands. Not seasonally adjusted.)

Industry	January	February	March	April	May	June	July	August	September	October	November	December	Annual Average
STOCKTON—*Continued*													
Total private													
1990	113.9	113.9	114.8	116.7	117.4	118.3	122.7	125.6	124.3	120.9	119.1	118.9	118.8
1991	117.3	117.8	116.4	117.9	119.6	120.1	122.6	128.2	127.6	123.1	120.0	118.7	120.7
1992	115.2	114.4	115.7	116.7	118.1	119.0	124.7	127.6	126.8	121.5	120.4	119.8	119.9
1993	117.0	117.2	118.2	119.7	120.7	121.7	127.9	130.0	127.9	123.4	122.0	121.0	122.2
1994	117.7	117.5	120.0	120.9	121.6	122.7	129.0	131.7	130.2	125.6	123.6	123.6	123.6
1995	120.3	121.3	122.1	123.6	125.9	126.5	128.5	132.8	133.3	129.5	128.9	127.2	126.6
1996	123.7	123.5	124.7	126.2	128.2	130.1	133.4	136.3	136.8	132.9	131.8	131.4	129.9
1997	126.0	126.7	128.4	129.1	131.9	134.1	137.9	140.5	140.6	134.5	133.6	134.3	133.1
1998	130.8	131.0	132.8	132.7	134.1	135.7	137.4	143.6	144.2	140.4	138.6	139.1	136.7
1999	135.2	135.4	137.5	139.3	140.8	142.7	145.2	150.3	151.0	147.6	145.5	146.0	143.0
2000	141.8	142.3	143.6	145.5	146.3	150.1	152.1	154.7	154.7	152.3	151.0	151.8	148.8
2001	148.4	148.5	149.9	150.7	152.3	154.4	153.5	156.0	155.2	153.3	152.4	152.1	152.2
2002	147.5	148.5	149.9	150.0	152.5	154.2	156.7	158.5	159.2	158.7	158.3	158.4	154.4
2003	153.7	154.3	156.3	156.3	157.6	159.1	158.8	160.4	161.6	160.1	159.7	159.9	158.2
Goods-producing													
1990	32.0	32.0	32.5	32.5	32.6	33.7	36.5	39.1	37.7	34.3	32.6	31.6	33.9
1991	29.9	30.1	29.3	29.6	30.5	31.1	34.4	37.2	36.3	31.9	29.9	28.7	31.5
1992	27.7	27.3	27.8	28.5	29.4	30.1	34.0	35.8	35.0	29.5	28.4	27.6	30.0
1993	26.6	26.7	27.2	27.5	27.8	28.5	33.3	35.0	33.1	29.0	27.7	27.2	29.1
1994	25.7	25.6	26.7	27.8	28.0	28.7	32.8	34.3	32.7	29.9	28.0	27.8	29.0
1995	26.3	26.7	27.1	28.1	28.6	29.4	30.9	34.1	32.8	30.3	29.4	28.4	29.3
1996	26.9	26.8	27.0	28.3	29.2	30.1	32.8	34.9	34.3	32.2	30.5	29.3	30.1
1997	28.2	28.5	28.9	29.1	29.9	31.1	33.4	36.0	35.5	31.1	30.4	29.9	31.0
1998	28.6	28.3	29.3	29.7	30.5	31.5	33.2	37.5	36.9	32.9	32.0	31.8	31.8
1999	30.5	30.5	31.5	32.5	32.9	33.9	35.6	39.6	39.8	36.7	34.8	34.7	34.4
2000	33.3	33.0	33.5	34.1	34.7	36.9	39.2	41.2	40.2	38.0	37.1	36.4	36.4
2001	34.7	34.7	34.9	35.2	36.0	37.1	36.6	38.5	37.5	36.3	35.2	34.4	35.9
2002	32.9	33.0	33.1	32.9	33.8	35.0	35.6	36.5	36.3	35.4	35.3	34.3	34.5
2003	32.4	32.7	33.5	33.6	34.3	35.0	35.9	36.8	36.6	34.8	34.5	33.9	34.5
Natural resources and mining													
1990	0.1	0.1	0.1	0.1	0.1	0.1	0.1	0.1	0.1	0.1	0.1	0.1	0.1
1991	0.1	0.1	0.1	0.1	0.2	0.2	0.2	0.2	0.2	0.1	0.2	0.1	0.1
1992	0.1	0.1	0.1	0.1	0.2	0.2	0.1	0.1	0.1	0.2	0.1	0.1	0.1
1993	0.1	0.1	0.1	0.1	0.1	0.1	0.1	0.1	0.1	0.1	0.1	0.1	0.1
1994	0.1	0.1	0.1	0.1	0.1	0.1	0.1	0.1	0.1	0.1	0.1	0.1	0.1
1995	0.1	0.1	0.1	0.1	0.1	0.1	0.1	0.1	0.1	0.1	0.1	0.1	0.1
1996	0.1	0.1	0.1	0.1	0.1	0.1	0.1	0.1	0.1	0.1	0.1	0.1	0.1
1997	0.1	0.1	0.1	0.1	0.1	0.1	0.1	0.1	0.1	0.1	0.1	0.1	0.1
1998	0.1	0.1	0.1	0.1	0.1	0.1	0.1	0.1	0.1	0.1	0.1	0.1	0.1
1999	0.1	0.1	0.1	0.1	0.1	0.1	0.1	0.1	0.1	0.1	0.1	0.1	0.1
2000	0.1	0.1	0.1	0.1	0.1	0.2	0.2	0.2	0.2	0.2	0.2	0.2	0.1
2001	0.2	0.2	0.2	0.2	0.2	0.2	0.2	0.2	0.2	0.2	0.2	0.2	0.1
2002	0.2	0.2	0.2	0.2	0.2	0.2	0.2	0.2	0.2	0.2	0.2	0.2	0.2
2003	0.2	0.2	0.2	0.2	0.2	0.2	0.2	0.2	0.2	0.2	0.2	0.2	0.2
Construction													
1990	9.4	9.2	9.4	9.6	9.7	9.9	9.5	9.8	9.9	9.6	9.2	8.9	9.5
1991	7.4	7.2	6.9	7.5	7.8	8.1	7.8	8.3	8.1	7.6	7.3	7.1	7.5
1992	6.1	5.8	6.1	6.5	6.9	6.9	7.2	7.3	7.1	6.6	6.4	5.9	6.5
1993	5.2	5.3	5.7	5.8	6.1	6.3	6.6	6.6	6.5	6.4	6.3	6.0	6.0
1994	5.5	5.4	5.8	6.1	6.3	6.5	6.9	6.9	6.9	6.7	6.3	6.2	6.2
1995	5.4	5.7	5.8	6.5	6.6	6.9	7.0	7.2	7.3	6.7	6.7	6.1	6.4
1996	5.9	5.8	5.9	6.4	6.9	6.9	7.1	7.3	7.5	7.5	7.7	6.8	6.8
1997	6.7	7.1	7.4	7.3	7.8	8.3	8.4	8.3	8.4	8.1	7.9	7.7	7.7
1998	7.0	7.0	7.8	8.1	8.5	9.1	9.6	9.8	9.9	9.6	9.8	9.7	8.8
1999	9.1	9.0	9.6	10.3	10.6	11.1	11.0	11.2	11.2	11.0	10.8	10.9	10.4
2000	10.5	10.2	10.4	10.9	11.2	12.0	12.4	12.5	12.4	12.4	12.4	12.4	11.6
2001	11.9	12.2	12.7	13.1	13.5	13.9	14.0	14.2	13.7	13.6	13.2	12.7	13.2
2002	11.9	12.1	12.4	12.9	13.5	13.9	14.1	14.3	14.2	14.3	14.3	14.0	13.5
2003	13.1	13.2	13.8	14.1	14.4	14.9	14.9	15.1	15.0	15.1	15.2	14.7	14.5
Manufacturing													
1990	22.5	22.7	23.0	22.8	22.8	23.7	26.9	29.2	27.7	24.6	23.3	22.6	24.3
1991	22.4	22.8	22.3	22.0	22.5	22.8	26.4	28.7	28.0	24.2	22.4	21.5	23.8
1992	21.5	21.4	21.6	21.9	22.3	23.0	26.7	28.4	27.8	22.7	21.9	21.6	23.4
1993	21.3	21.3	21.4	21.6	21.6	22.1	26.6	28.3	26.5	22.5	21.3	21.1	22.9
1994	20.1	20.1	20.8	21.6	21.6	22.1	25.8	27.3	25.7	23.1	21.6	21.5	22.6
1995	20.8	20.9	21.2	21.5	21.9	22.4	23.8	26.8	25.4	23.5	22.6	22.2	22.7
1996	20.9	20.9	21.0	21.8	22.2	23.1	25.6	27.5	26.7	24.6	22.7	22.4	23.2
1997	21.4	21.3	21.4	21.7	22.0	22.7	24.9	27.6	27.0	22.9	22.4	22.1	23.1
1998	21.5	21.2	21.4	21.5	21.9	22.3	23.5	27.6	26.9	23.2	22.1	22.0	22.9
1999	21.3	21.4	21.8	22.1	22.2	22.7	24.5	28.3	28.5	25.6	23.9	23.7	23.8
2000	22.7	22.7	23.0	23.1	23.4	24.7	26.6	28.5	27.6	25.4	24.5	23.8	24.6
2001	22.6	22.3	22.0	21.9	22.3	23.0	22.4	24.1	23.6	22.5	21.8	21.5	22.5
2002	20.8	20.7	20.5	19.8	20.1	20.9	21.3	22.0	21.9	20.9	20.8	20.1	20.8
2003	19.1	19.3	19.5	19.3	19.7	19.9	20.8	21.5	21.4	19.5	19.1	19.0	19.8

Employment by Industry: California—*Continued*

(Numbers in thousands. Not seasonally adjusted.)

Industry	January	February	March	April	May	June	July	August	September	October	November	December	Annual Average
STOCKTON—*Continued*													
Service-providing													
1990	114.1	115.1	115.9	118.2	119.9	119.5	120.1	120.0	120.2	120.5	120.4	121.4	118.7
1991	121.3	121.7	121.5	123.0	124.0	123.9	122.3	123.5	125.6	126.0	125.2	125.4	123.6
1992	122.5	121.8	122.9	123.5	123.9	123.8	125.5	126.8	126.5	126.9	126.8	125.5	124.7
1993	125.1	125.5	125.9	127.4	127.9	127.9	126.4	127.3	128.3	128.4	128.4	126.4	127.0
1994	125.8	126.0	127.1	127.5	128.0	127.8	128.0	129.6	131.4	129.9	129.9	128.9	128.3
1995	128.1	128.8	129.4	130.0	131.8	130.9	129.4	131.1	134.3	132.4	133.4	132.0	130.9
1996	130.3	130.5	131.4	131.8	133.0	133.1	132.5	133.5	136.3	135.1	136.1	136.0	133.3
1997	132.1	133.0	134.5	135.3	137.4	137.9	136.6	136.7	138.1	138.0	138.0	139.3	136.4
1998	136.7	137.6	138.5	138.1	138.7	138.9	137.0	139.5	142.3	143.1	142.2	143.0	139.6
1999	140.1	140.6	141.9	142.9	144.1	144.4	143.6	144.8	147.2	147.1	147.1	147.3	144.2
2000	144.9	145.8	146.9	148.4	149.3	150.2	149.3	150.3	151.3	151.7	151.4	152.9	149.3
2001	151.3	151.7	153.2	154.0	155.4	156.2	155.1	156.8	156.6	156.7	157.1	157.5	155.1
2002	154.5	155.7	157.4	157.6	159.8	159.7	158.6	160.5	162.7	163.8	163.9	165.2	160.0
2003	161.8	162.1	163.3	163.0	163.5	164.0	159.6	160.4	164.0	164.9	164.9	165.6	163.1
Trade, transportation, and utilities													
1990	29.5	28.9	29.2	29.8	30.3	30.8	31.7	31.9	32.0	31.9	31.7	32.0	30.8
1991	31.8	31.5	31.2	31.4	31.7	32.3	32.5	33.5	33.4	33.5	33.0	33.0	32.4
1992	31.8	31.0	31.3	31.9	32.4	33.0	34.3	34.9	34.7	34.6	34.9	34.7	33.2
1993	33.5	33.2	33.3	33.9	34.0	34.4	36.0	36.2	36.3	36.1	36.1	36.2	34.9
1994	34.4	34.1	34.7	35.1	35.3	35.7	37.2	37.6	37.5	37.2	37.4	37.4	36.1
1995	35.5	35.5	35.4	35.4	35.8	35.8	36.7	37.5	38.2	37.8	37.9	37.7	36.6
1996	36.3	35.8	35.8	36.0	36.4	37.0	38.2	38.5	38.4	37.8	38.1	38.5	37.2
1997	36.1	36.0	36.3	37.0	37.8	38.3	39.7	39.8	39.6	38.9	38.9	39.2	38.1
1998	37.8	37.3	37.3	37.5	37.8	38.1	38.7	40.0	40.1	39.9	39.8	39.7	38.6
1999	38.6	38.1	38.4	39.2	39.8	40.4	41.0	41.7	41.6	41.8	41.8	42.0	40.3
2000	40.5	40.1	40.1	40.5	40.8	41.4	42.5	42.5	42.6	42.6	43.2	43.8	41.7
2001	42.9	42.2	42.6	42.7	43.2	43.8	44.2	44.6	44.4	44.1	44.3	44.3	43.6
2002	42.8	42.5	42.7	43.3	43.8	44.5	45.3	45.8	46.0	46.6	46.7	47.0	44.8
2003	45.7	45.5	45.8	46.0	46.2	46.5	46.9	47.7	47.9	48.0	47.8	48.1	46.8
Wholesale trade													
1990	6.1	6.1	6.1	6.6	6.7	6.7	7.2	7.2	7.4	7.4	6.9	6.7	6.7
1991	5.9	6.0	6.0	5.9	5.9	5.9	6.0	6.1	6.2	6.4	5.9	5.6	5.9
1992	5.6	5.6	5.7	6.0	6.1	6.1	6.4	6.4	6.5	6.6	6.4	6.0	6.1
1993	5.9	5.9	5.9	5.8	5.8	5.8	6.2	6.2	6.2	6.2	6.2	5.6	5.9
1994	5.5	5.5	5.6	5.6	5.6	5.8	6.3	6.5	6.4	6.4	6.3	5.8	5.9
1995	5.7	5.8	5.8	6.2	6.1	6.1	6.6	6.6	6.7	6.6	6.3	6.0	6.2
1996	5.8	5.7	5.8	5.8	5.9	6.0	6.4	6.5	6.4	6.3	6.1	5.9	6.0
1997	5.7	5.7	5.8	6.1	6.3	6.4	6.4	6.5	6.4	6.4	5.9	5.8	6.1
1998	5.9	5.9	5.9	6.2	6.2	6.4	6.6	6.7	6.6	6.6	6.3	6.1	6.2
1999	6.2	6.1	6.2	6.1	6.2	6.3	6.4	6.5	6.4	6.4	6.2	6.0	6.2
2000	6.2	6.2	6.3	6.3	6.3	6.5	6.7	6.7	6.7	6.6	6.5	6.3	6.4
2001	6.2	6.2	6.3	6.5	6.6	6.9	6.9	7.1	7.0	7.1	6.9	6.8	6.7
2002	6.5	6.6	6.6	6.8	6.9	7.2	7.5	7.6	7.7	7.8	7.6	7.5	7.2
2003	7.6	7.7	7.8	7.9	7.9	7.9	7.9	8.0	8.0	8.1	7.9	8.1	7.9
Retail trade													
1990	17.8	17.2	17.3	17.5	17.8	17.7	17.8	17.9	18.0	18.1	18.7	19.3	17.9
1991	19.8	19.3	19.1	19.1	19.4	19.6	19.4	19.9	19.8	20.0	20.3	20.7	19.7
1992	19.9	19.2	19.2	19.0	19.1	19.2	19.6	20.0	19.8	20.1	20.5	20.9	19.7
1993	20.0	19.5	19.5	20.0	20.0	20.1	20.5	20.6	20.6	20.6	21.0	21.8	20.3
1994	20.3	20.1	20.3	20.5	20.4	20.4	20.6	20.5	20.6	20.6	21.3	21.9	20.6
1995	20.5	20.3	20.2	19.8	20.2	20.2	20.2	20.4	20.8	21.0	21.7	22.0	20.6
1996	20.8	20.5	20.4	20.3	20.5	20.8	21.0	21.1	21.2	21.2	22.0	22.6	21.0
1997	20.6	20.4	20.6	20.7	21.1	21.3	21.7	21.7	21.7	21.9	22.7	23.3	21.4
1998	21.8	21.2	21.3	21.0	21.2	21.4	21.5	22.3	22.3	22.3	22.8	23.0	21.8
1999	21.5	21.3	21.4	22.3	22.6	22.7	22.5	22.7	22.6	23.0	23.7	24.2	22.5
2000	23.0	22.7	22.6	22.9	23.1	23.2	23.6	23.5	23.5	24.0	25.0	25.7	23.5
2001	24.4	23.9	24.1	24.1	24.4	24.6	24.6	24.5	24.7	24.5	25.3	25.6	24.5
2002	24.3	24.0	24.2	24.4	24.6	24.6	24.7	24.7	24.9	25.2	25.8	26.4	24.8
2003	25.1	24.9	25.1	24.9	24.8	25.0	24.9	25.0	25.1	25.3	25.8	26.2	25.2
Transportation and utilities													
1990	5.6	5.6	5.8	5.7	5.8	6.4	6.7	6.8	6.6	6.4	6.1	6.0	6.1
1991	6.1	6.2	6.1	6.4	6.4	6.8	7.1	7.5	7.4	7.1	6.8	6.7	6.7
1992	6.3	6.2	6.4	6.9	7.2	7.7	8.3	8.5	8.4	7.9	8.0	7.8	7.4
1993	7.6	7.8	7.9	8.1	8.2	8.5	9.3	9.4	9.5	9.3	8.9	8.8	8.6
1994	8.6	8.5	8.8	9.0	9.3	9.5	10.3	10.6	10.5	10.2	9.8	9.7	9.5
1995	9.3	9.4	9.4	9.4	9.5	9.5	9.9	10.5	10.7	10.2	9.9	9.7	9.7
1996	9.7	9.6	9.6	9.9	10.0	10.2	10.8	10.9	10.8	10.3	10.0	10.0	10.1
1997	9.8	9.9	9.9	10.2	10.4	10.6	11.6	11.6	11.5	10.6	10.3	10.1	10.5
1998	10.1	10.2	10.1	10.3	10.4	10.3	10.6	11.0	11.2	11.0	10.7	10.6	10.5
1999	10.9	10.7	10.8	10.8	11.0	11.4	12.1	12.5	12.6	12.4	11.9	11.8	11.5
2000	11.3	11.2	11.2	11.3	11.4	11.7	12.2	12.3	12.4	12.0	11.7	11.8	11.7
2001	12.3	12.1	12.2	12.1	12.2	12.3	12.7	13.0	12.7	12.5	12.1	11.9	12.3
2002	12.0	11.9	11.9	12.1	12.3	12.7	13.1	13.5	13.4	13.6	13.3	13.1	12.7
2003	13.0	12.9	12.9	13.2	13.5	13.6	14.1	14.7	14.8	14.6	14.1	13.8	13.8

Employment by Industry: California—*Continued*

(Numbers in thousands. Not seasonally adjusted.)

Industry	January	February	March	April	May	June	July	August	September	October	November	December	Annual Average
STOCKTON—*Continued*													
Information													
1990	2.5	2.5	2.5	2.7	2.7	2.7	2.7	2.7	2.7	2.7	2.7	2.8	2.6
1991	2.7	2.7	2.7	2.7	2.7	2.8	2.7	2.6	2.6	2.6	2.6	2.6	2.6
1992	2.3	2.3	2.3	2.3	2.2	2.3	2.3	2.3	2.3	2.3	2.4	2.4	2.3
1993	2.4	2.4	2.4	2.5	2.5	2.5	2.5	2.5	2.5	2.4	2.4	2.5	2.4
1994	2.4	2.4	2.4	2.4	2.4	2.5	2.5	2.5	2.5	2.6	2.6	2.6	2.4
1995	2.6	2.6	2.6	2.5	2.6	2.6	2.5	2.5	2.5	2.5	2.5	2.5	2.5
1996	2.5	2.5	2.5	2.5	2.6	2.6	2.5	2.5	2.5	2.4	2.5	2.5	2.5
1997	2.5	2.5	2.5	2.5	2.5	2.6	2.6	2.5	2.5	2.4	2.4	2.5	2.5
1998	2.5	2.5	2.5	2.4	2.4	2.5	2.5	2.5	2.6	2.6	2.5	2.7	2.5
1999	2.7	2.7	2.7	2.7	2.8	2.8	2.7	2.7	2.7	2.7	2.7	2.8	2.7
2000	2.9	3.0	2.9	2.9	3.0	3.0	3.0	3.1	3.0	3.1	3.1	3.1	3.0
2001	3.4	3.4	3.4	3.3	3.3	3.3	3.4	3.3	3.1	3.1	3.0	3.0	3.2
2002	3.2	3.2	3.2	3.1	3.1	3.1	3.1	3.0	3.0	3.0	3.0	3.1	3.1
2003	3.0	3.0	2.9	2.9	2.9	2.9	2.9	2.8	2.8	2.8	2.9	2.9	2.9
Financial activities													
1990	9.1	9.1	9.3	9.3	9.3	9.2	9.5	9.3	9.3	9.3	9.3	9.3	9.2
1991	9.0	9.0	8.9	9.0	9.0	9.0	8.9	9.3	9.2	9.1	9.1	9.1	9.0
1992	9.1	9.0	9.0	8.7	8.7	8.5	8.5	8.6	8.5	8.7	8.7	8.8	8.7
1993	8.7	8.6	8.6	8.7	8.7	8.9	9.0	9.0	8.9	8.8	8.9	9.0	8.8
1994	8.7	8.7	8.7	8.6	8.6	8.5	8.5	8.5	8.4	8.1	8.0	8.1	8.4
1995	8.2	8.2	8.1	8.0	8.2	8.3	8.1	8.1	8.2	8.1	8.1	8.1	8.1
1996	8.0	8.0	7.9	8.1	8.1	8.2	8.1	8.2	8.1	8.1	8.0	8.1	8.0
1997	8.1	8.1	8.2	8.3	8.3	8.5	8.5	8.4	8.4	8.3	8.3	8.3	8.3
1998	8.1	8.0	8.1	8.2	8.2	8.2	8.2	8.2	8.2	8.3	8.2	8.3	8.1
1999	8.3	8.2	8.3	8.4	8.3	8.5	8.4	8.4	8.4	8.4	8.4	8.5	8.3
2000	8.4	8.5	8.5	8.4	8.4	8.4	8.4	8.4	8.5	8.5	8.5	8.6	8.4
2001	8.6	8.7	8.7	8.9	8.8	8.9	8.9	8.9	8.8	8.9	9.0	9.2	8.8
2002	9.0	9.1	9.0	9.2	9.3	9.3	9.5	9.6	9.6	9.7	9.7	9.8	9.4
2003	9.9	9.9	10.0	10.1	10.1	10.2	9.9	9.9	9.8	9.8	9.8	10.0	10.0
Professional and business services													
1990	9.0	9.0	9.3	9.2	9.2	9.1	9.3	9.6	9.5	9.0	9.0	9.2	9.2
1991	9.8	9.9	9.8	10.3	10.2	10.1	10.1	10.4	10.6	10.5	10.2	10.2	10.1
1992	10.0	10.0	10.3	10.2	10.1	10.1	10.3	10.5	10.4	10.6	10.4	10.4	10.2
1993	10.7	10.6	10.8	10.7	11.1	11.2	11.2	11.4	11.3	11.0	10.7	10.8	10.9
1994	10.7	10.8	11.1	11.4	11.3	11.2	11.7	12.2	12.0	11.4	11.2	11.2	11.3
1995	11.0	11.1	11.3	11.4	11.6	11.6	12.0	12.2	12.4	12.4	12.6	12.5	11.8
1996	12.0	12.1	12.8	12.2	12.3	12.5	12.6	12.8	13.2	13.0	13.1	13.4	12.6
1997	13.3	13.4	13.7	13.6	13.9	14.0	14.0	14.2	14.3	14.1	14.0	14.5	13.9
1998	13.9	14.1	14.5	14.5	14.7	14.9	15.0	15.3	15.5	15.9	15.8	15.9	15.0
1999	15.4	15.7	15.9	15.6	15.8	16.0	16.5	16.7	16.7	16.4	16.4	16.5	16.1
2000	16.1	16.2	16.6	16.8	16.5	16.8	16.7	17.2	17.4	17.5	16.9	17.3	16.8
2001	16.6	16.5	16.7	16.9	16.7	17.0	16.9	17.1	17.5	17.1	16.7	17.1	16.8
2002	16.5	16.6	17.1	16.9	16.9	16.9	17.4	17.6	17.8	17.7	17.5	18.1	17.3
2003	17.7	17.8	18.3	17.5	17.5	17.6	17.6	17.5	18.0	17.9	17.8	18.1	17.8
Educational and health services													
1990	16.0	16.5	16.0	16.7	16.6	16.0	16.0	15.9	16.1	17.2	17.5	17.6	16.5
1991	17.4	17.9	17.8	17.9	17.9	17.0	16.5	17.1	17.5	18.0	18.0	17.9	17.5
1992	17.7	18.2	18.3	18.0	17.8	17.4	17.3	17.4	17.9	18.4	18.5	18.7	17.9
1993	18.0	18.7	18.8	18.9	18.7	18.2	17.8	17.8	18.1	18.9	19.0	18.1	18.4
1994	19.0	18.9	19.1	18.2	18.3	17.9	17.8	17.9	18.8	18.7	18.7	18.8	18.5
1995	19.1	19.4	19.6	20.0	20.3	19.8	19.2	19.3	19.9	19.5	19.7	19.3	19.5
1996	19.5	19.7	19.7	20.2	20.4	20.0	19.5	19.7	20.7	20.3	20.5	20.6	20.0
1997	19.6	20.0	20.2	19.9	20.3	19.9	20.1	20.0	20.9	21.0	21.0	21.2	20.3
1998	21.1	21.8	21.9	21.3	21.2	20.8	20.1	20.3	21.3	21.7	21.5	21.7	21.2
1999	21.0	21.4	21.6	21.6	21.5	21.0	20.9	21.1	21.6	22.0	22.0	22.0	21.4
2000	21.4	22.0	22.1	22.3	22.3	22.4	21.3	21.4	22.0	22.3	22.1	22.4	22.0
2001	21.7	22.4	22.5	22.5	22.5	22.3	21.9	21.6	22.2	22.6	22.9	22.9	22.3
2002	22.5	23.3	23.5	23.0	23.2	22.6	22.8	22.8	23.3	23.6	23.6	23.6	23.2
2003	23.5	23.7	23.8	23.9	24.0	23.6	22.8	22.8	23.6	24.0	24.1	24.1	23.7
Leisure and hospitality													
1990	11.1	11.3	11.3	11.7	12.0	12.0	12.1	12.2	12.1	11.7	11.6	11.6	11.7
1991	11.8	11.7	11.8	11.9	12.5	12.6	12.5	13.0	12.9	12.4	12.1	12.1	12.2
1992	11.5	11.5	11.6	12.0	12.4	12.3	12.7	12.8	12.7	12.1	11.9	12.0	12.1
1993	12.0	11.9	12.0	12.4	12.7	12.7	12.8	12.7	12.4	12.0	12.0	12.0	12.3
1994	11.7	11.9	12.2	12.2	12.6	13.0	13.2	13.3	13.0	12.5	12.7	12.6	12.5
1995	12.6	12.7	12.9	13.1	13.6	13.6	13.6	13.6	13.8	13.5	13.4	13.4	13.3
1996	13.2	13.2	13.5	13.4	13.7	14.0	14.0	14.0	13.9	13.6	13.6	13.5	13.6
1997	12.8	12.8	13.1	13.1	13.5	13.9	13.8	13.7	13.5	13.1	13.0	13.1	13.2
1998	13.4	13.5	13.7	13.6	13.7	14.0	14.0	14.1	13.9	13.5	13.2	13.4	13.6
1999	13.1	13.3	13.5	13.6	13.9	14.2	14.2	14.2	14.3	13.8	13.8	13.8	13.8
2000	13.5	13.8	14.1	14.6	14.7	15.1	14.9	14.8	14.8	14.3	14.3	14.3	14.4
2001	14.6	14.7	15.1	15.1	15.6	15.7	15.6	15.8	15.6	15.2	15.3	15.3	15.3
2002	14.6	14.8	15.2	15.4	16.1	16.3	16.5	16.6	16.6	16.2	16.1	16.1	15.9
2003	15.3	15.5	15.8	16.1	16.4	16.8	16.7	16.7	16.7	16.7	16.7	16.8	16.4

Employment by Industry: California—*Continued*

(Numbers in thousands. Not seasonally adjusted.)

Industry	January	February	March	April	May	June	July	August	September	October	November	December	Annual Average
STOCKTON—*Continued*													
Other services													
1990	4.7	4.6	4.7	4.8	4.7	4.8	4.9	4.9	4.9	4.8	4.7	4.8	4.7
1991	4.9	5.0	4.9	5.1	5.1	5.2	5.0	5.1	5.1	5.1	5.1	5.1	5.0
1992	5.1	5.1	5.1	5.1	5.1	5.3	5.3	5.3	5.3	5.3	5.2	5.2	5.2
1993	5.1	5.1	5.1	5.1	5.2	5.3	5.3	5.4	5.3	5.2	5.2	5.2	5.2
1994	5.1	5.1	5.1	5.2	5.1	5.2	5.3	5.4	5.3	5.2	5.0	5.1	5.1
1995	5.0	5.1	5.1	5.1	5.2	5.4	5.5	5.5	5.5	5.4	5.3	5.3	5.2
1996	5.3	5.4	5.5	5.5	5.5	5.7	5.7	5.7	5.7	5.5	5.5	5.5	5.5
1997	5.4	5.4	5.5	5.6	5.7	5.8	5.8	5.9	5.9	5.6	5.6	5.6	5.6
1998	5.4	5.5	5.5	5.5	5.6	5.7	5.7	5.7	5.7	5.6	5.6	5.6	5.5
1999	5.6	5.5	5.6	5.7	5.8	5.9	5.9	5.9	5.9	5.8	5.6	5.7	5.7
2000	5.7	5.7	5.8	5.9	5.9	6.1	6.1	6.1	6.2	6.0	5.8	5.9	5.9
2001	5.9	5.9	6.0	6.1	6.2	6.3	6.0	6.2	6.1	6.0	6.0	5.9	6.0
2002	6.0	6.0	6.1	6.2	6.3	6.5	6.5	6.6	6.6	6.5	6.4	6.4	6.3
2003	6.2	6.2	6.2	6.2	6.2	6.5	6.1	6.2	6.2	6.1	6.1	6.0	6.2
Government													
1990	32.2	33.2	33.6	34.0	35.1	34.9	33.9	33.5	33.6	33.9	33.9	34.1	33.8
1991	33.9	34.0	34.4	34.7	34.9	34.9	34.1	32.5	34.3	34.8	35.1	35.4	34.4
1992	35.0	34.7	35.0	35.3	35.2	34.9	34.8	35.0	34.7	34.9	34.8	33.3	34.8
1993	34.7	35.0	34.9	35.2	35.0	34.7	31.8	32.3	33.5	34.0	34.1	32.6	33.9
1994	33.8	34.1	33.8	34.4	34.4	33.8	31.8	32.2	33.9	34.2	34.3	33.1	33.6
1995	34.1	34.2	34.4	34.5	34.5	33.8	31.8	32.4	33.8	33.2	33.9	33.2	33.6
1996	33.5	33.8	33.7	33.9	34.0	33.1	31.9	32.1	33.8	34.4	34.8	33.9	33.5
1997	34.3	34.8	35.0	35.3	35.4	34.9	32.1	32.2	33.0	34.6	34.8	34.9	34.2
1998	34.5	34.9	35.0	35.1	35.1	34.7	32.8	33.4	35.0	35.6	35.6	35.7	34.7
1999	35.4	35.7	35.9	36.1	36.2	35.6	34.0	34.1	36.0	36.2	36.4	36.0	35.6
2000	36.4	36.5	36.8	37.0	37.7	37.0	36.4	36.8	36.8	37.4	37.5	37.5	36.9
2001	37.6	37.9	38.2	38.5	39.1	38.9	38.2	39.3	38.9	39.7	39.9	39.8	38.8
2002	39.9	40.2	40.6	40.5	41.1	40.5	37.5	38.5	39.8	40.5	40.9	41.1	40.1
2003	40.5	40.5	40.5	40.3	40.2	39.9	36.7	36.8	39.0	39.6	39.7	39.6	39.4
Federal government													
1990	5.7	5.7	5.7	5.9	6.2	6.1	6.0	5.6	5.5	5.5	5.4	5.5	5.7
1991	5.6	5.4	5.4	5.4	5.4	5.3	5.2	5.2	5.2	5.3	5.3	5.6	5.3
1992	5.3	5.3	5.3	5.3	5.3	5.2	5.2	5.3	5.4	5.5	5.5	5.5	5.3
1993	5.4	5.4	5.3	5.4	5.1	5.1	4.8	4.8	4.7	4.7	4.7	4.8	5.0
1994	4.5	4.5	4.5	4.6	4.6	4.6	4.6	4.6	4.6	4.7	4.7	4.8	4.6
1995	4.6	4.5	4.4	4.4	4.4	4.4	4.3	4.3	4.3	4.3	4.3	4.3	4.3
1996	4.1	4.1	4.1	4.3	4.2	4.2	4.3	4.3	4.3	4.4	4.4	4.5	4.2
1997	4.6	4.6	4.6	4.6	4.6	4.6	4.6	4.6	4.5	4.5	4.5	4.6	4.5
1998	4.4	4.3	4.3	4.3	4.3	4.3	4.3	4.3	4.3	4.3	4.2	4.3	4.3
1999	4.2	4.1	4.1	4.0	4.0	4.0	3.9	3.9	3.9	3.8	3.8	3.9	3.9
2000	3.7	3.7	3.7	3.8	4.2	3.8	3.8	3.7	3.6	3.6	3.6	3.6	3.7
2001	3.7	3.7	3.7	3.9	4.0	4.2	4.3	4.2	4.2	4.2	4.2	4.2	4.0
2002	4.2	4.2	4.2	4.1	4.1	4.1	4.1	4.1	4.1	4.1	4.1	4.2	4.1
2003	4.2	4.0	3.9	3.9	3.9	3.9	3.9	3.9	3.9	3.9	3.9	4.0	3.9
State government													
1990	4.5	4.5	4.5	4.6	4.6	4.7	4.7	4.7	4.6	4.6	4.6	4.6	4.6
1991	4.6	4.6	4.7	4.8	4.8	4.8	4.9	4.9	5.0	5.0	5.0	5.0	4.8
1992	5.0	5.0	5.0	5.0	5.0	5.0	5.0	5.0	5.0	5.0	5.0	5.0	5.0
1993	4.9	4.9	4.9	4.9	4.9	4.9	5.0	5.0	4.9	4.9	4.9	4.8	4.9
1994	4.8	4.9	4.8	4.9	4.9	4.9	4.9	4.9	4.9	4.9	4.9	4.9	4.8
1995	4.9	4.9	4.9	4.9	4.9	4.9	4.9	4.9	4.8	4.6	4.5	4.5	4.8
1996	4.4	4.2	4.2	4.2	4.2	4.2	4.2	4.2	4.2	4.2	4.2	4.2	4.2
1997	4.1	4.1	4.2	4.2	4.2	4.2	4.2	4.2	4.2	4.2	4.2	4.2	4.1
1998	4.1	4.1	4.2	4.2	4.2	4.2	4.2	4.2	4.2	4.2	4.2	4.2	4.1
1999	4.2	4.2	4.2	4.3	4.3	4.3	4.3	4.3	4.3	4.3	4.3	4.3	4.2
2000	4.3	4.3	4.3	4.3	4.4	4.4	4.4	4.4	4.4	4.4	4.4	4.4	4.3
2001	4.4	4.4	4.4	4.4	4.5	4.5	4.5	4.5	4.5	4.5	4.5	4.5	4.4
2002	4.5	4.5	4.5	4.4	4.4	4.4	4.5	4.5	4.5	4.5	4.5	4.5	4.5
2003	4.4	4.4	4.3	4.3	4.2	4.2	4.2	4.2	4.2	4.1	4.1	4.1	4.2
Local government													
1990	22.0	23.0	23.4	23.5	24.3	24.1	23.2	23.2	23.5	23.8	23.9	24.0	23.4
1991	23.7	24.0	24.3	24.5	24.7	24.8	24.0	22.4	24.1	24.5	24.8	24.8	24.2
1992	24.7	24.4	24.7	25.0	24.9	24.7	24.6	24.7	24.3	24.4	24.3	22.8	24.4
1993	24.4	24.7	24.7	24.9	25.0	24.7	22.0	22.5	23.9	24.4	24.5	23.0	24.0
1994	24.5	24.7	24.5	24.9	24.9	24.3	22.3	22.7	24.4	24.6	24.7	23.4	24.1
1995	24.6	24.8	25.1	25.2	25.2	24.5	22.6	23.2	24.7	24.3	25.1	24.4	24.4
1996	25.0	25.5	25.4	25.4	25.6	24.7	23.4	23.6	25.3	25.8	26.2	25.2	25.0
1997	25.6	26.1	26.2	26.5	26.6	26.1	23.3	23.4	24.3	25.9	26.1	26.1	25.5
1998	26.0	26.5	26.5	26.6	26.6	26.2	24.3	24.9	26.5	27.1	27.2	27.2	26.3
1999	27.0	27.4	27.6	27.8	27.9	27.3	25.8	25.9	27.8	28.1	28.3	27.8	27.3
2000	28.4	28.5	28.8	28.9	29.1	28.8	28.2	28.7	28.8	29.4	29.5	29.5	28.8
2001	29.5	29.8	30.1	30.2	30.6	30.2	29.4	30.6	30.2	31.0	31.2	31.1	30.3
2002	31.2	31.5	31.9	32.0	32.6	32.0	28.9	29.9	31.2	31.9	32.3	32.4	31.5
2003	31.9	32.1	32.3	32.1	32.1	31.8	28.6	28.7	30.9	31.6	31.7	31.5	31.3

Employment by Industry: California—*Continued*

(Numbers in thousands. Not seasonally adjusted.)

Industry	January	February	March	April	May	June	July	August	September	October	November	December	Annual Average
VALLEJO-FAIRFIELD-NAPA													
Total nonfarm													
1990	133.0	132.8	133.4	136.3	138.6	139.9	141.0	140.0	141.2	140.0	140.0	139.9	138.0
1991	135.9	136.8	137.2	138.4	139.2	139.8	140.5	140.1	140.7	140.6	139.7	138.9	138.9
1992	136.9	137.9	139.2	140.2	141.3	143.4	143.7	142.6	143.6	143.5	142.4	141.4	141.3
1993	138.2	138.6	139.8	139.5	140.9	142.1	142.0	141.4	142.2	142.0	141.2	141.0	140.7
1994	136.5	138.0	138.8	139.9	141.1	143.0	142.4	140.9	142.4	142.1	141.4	141.2	140.6
1995	136.5	139.0	139.3	139.4	141.2	143.4	142.6	143.6	144.8	143.6	143.7	142.8	141.6
1996	138.7	140.6	141.7	141.1	144.7	146.8	146.5	146.2	147.7	146.2	146.9	146.7	144.4
1997	142.5	144.7	146.9	146.6	149.3	151.9	151.2	151.7	154.2	153.5	153.8	154.8	150.0
1998	148.3	149.5	152.1	154.1	156.0	158.4	158.5	159.5	161.6	160.4	161.0	161.0	156.7
1999	157.1	158.8	160.8	162.7	165.0	167.4	166.7	167.1	168.2	169.5	169.9	169.5	165.2
2000	164.8	166.2	168.3	171.3	172.3	175.4	174.0	174.6	175.5	174.2	175.3	175.0	172.2
2001	171.3	173.0	175.6	176.9	179.4	180.8	179.8	180.9	182.6	180.0	178.9	177.4	178.0
2002	173.4	176.1	178.6	180.6	182.7	183.6	183.0	183.3	184.6	184.2	183.5	182.2	181.3
2003	178.3	179.8	181.2	182.7	184.1	185.6	184.0	184.0	184.6	184.7	183.3	183.0	182.9
Total private													
1990	94.4	94.3	94.9	98.0	100.0	100.6	102.8	103.9	104.1	103.0	102.7	102.9	100.1
1991	99.1	99.3	99.8	100.8	101.4	102.0	102.6	103.3	103.6	103.1	102.1	101.3	101.5
1992	99.6	100.3	101.4	102.5	103.5	105.3	106.6	106.1	106.8	106.3	105.2	104.4	104.0
1993	102.1	102.1	103.3	103.2	104.8	106.0	106.7	106.6	107.4	106.5	105.7	105.6	105.0
1994	101.7	103.0	103.8	105.0	106.3	107.9	108.6	108.4	109.1	107.9	107.0	107.1	106.3
1995	102.8	104.9	105.3	105.6	107.4	109.6	110.3	112.1	113.0	111.4	111.4	110.8	108.7
1996	107.3	108.7	109.5	110.1	113.4	115.4	116.3	117.2	117.7	115.7	115.9	115.5	113.5
1997	112.2	113.8	115.6	115.7	118.2	120.4	121.2	122.4	123.8	122.3	122.5	123.2	119.2
1998	117.1	118.0	120.4	122.1	124.0	126.1	127.6	129.3	129.9	128.3	128.2	128.3	124.9
1999	124.5	125.6	127.3	128.7	131.0	133.2	134.6	135.2	135.5	136.1	136.0	135.5	131.9
2000	131.5	132.2	134.2	136.7	137.6	140.0	140.8	141.9	142.5	140.3	140.7	140.4	138.2
2001	137.1	138.7	140.6	141.3	143.4	144.9	146.1	147.0	146.9	144.1	143.2	141.7	142.9
2002	137.8	140.0	141.7	143.2	145.3	146.9	146.8	147.9	148.6	147.8	147.3	146.5	145.0
2003	143.2	144.3	145.3	146.8	148.2	149.7	148.6	149.2	149.6	149.1	148.0	147.9	147.5
Goods-producing													
1990	21.9	21.9	22.2	22.8	23.6	24.3	25.0	25.3	25.7	24.7	23.7	23.0	23.6
1991	20.8	21.7	21.6	21.7	22.5	23.0	23.4	24.0	23.8	23.9	23.0	22.5	22.6
1992	20.5	20.8	21.4	22.2	22.5	23.5	24.3	24.2	24.5	23.0	22.3	21.6	22.5
1993	21.1	21.5	22.0	22.0	22.7	23.3	23.9	24.0	24.3	23.6	22.8	22.3	22.7
1994	21.4	21.9	22.1	23.0	23.5	24.0	25.4	25.4	25.5	24.8	23.7	23.3	23.6
1995	22.2	23.2	23.5	23.1	23.8	24.6	25.6	26.3	26.7	25.9	25.4	24.7	24.5
1996	23.7	24.2	24.5	25.2	26.5	27.4	28.1	28.5	29.2	28.1	27.4	27.4	26.6
1997	25.6	26.2	26.9	27.4	28.3	29.0	29.8	30.4	31.1	29.6	29.2	29.4	28.5
1998	27.2	27.6	28.7	29.2	29.9	30.6	31.7	31.8	32.3	31.8	30.6	30.4	30.1
1999	29.5	29.9	30.3	31.1	31.8	32.8	33.7	33.5	33.9	34.5	33.7	33.3	32.3
2000	32.2	32.2	32.5	33.4	33.6	34.8	35.3	35.5	36.3	36.0	35.7	34.9	34.3
2001	35.0	35.0	35.7	35.7	36.2	37.0	36.8	37.1	37.2	35.8	35.1	34.0	35.8
2002	33.7	34.6	34.9	35.1	35.9	36.2	36.8	37.3	37.7	36.7	35.5	34.7	35.8
2003	34.1	34.5	34.7	34.8	35.2	35.6	35.6	35.8	36.0	36.2	35.7	35.2	35.3
Natural resources and mining													
1990	0.3	0.3	0.3	0.3	0.3	0.4	0.4	0.4	0.4	0.4	0.4	0.4	0.3
1991	0.3	0.4	0.4	0.4	0.4	0.4	0.4	0.4	0.4	0.4	0.3	0.4	0.3
1992	0.3	0.3	0.3	0.4	0.4	0.4	0.4	0.4	0.4	0.4	0.4	0.3	0.3
1993	0.3	0.3	0.3	0.4	0.4	0.4	0.4	0.4	0.3	0.3	0.3	0.3	0.3
1994	0.3	0.3	0.3	0.3	0.3	0.3	0.3	0.3	0.3	0.3	0.3	0.3	0.3
1995	0.3	0.3	0.3	0.3	0.3	0.3	0.3	0.3	0.4	0.3	0.4	0.4	0.3
1996	0.4	0.4	0.4	0.4	0.4	0.4	0.4	0.4	0.4	0.4	0.4	0.4	0.4
1997	0.4	0.4	0.4	0.4	0.5	0.5	0.5	0.5	0.5	0.5	0.5	0.5	0.4
1998	0.4	0.5	0.4	0.4	0.4	0.4	0.4	0.4	0.4	0.4	0.4	0.4	0.4
1999	0.4	0.4	0.4	0.4	0.4	0.4	0.4	0.4	0.4	0.5	0.5	0.5	0.4
2000	0.4	0.4	0.4	0.4	0.4	0.4	0.4	0.5	0.5	0.5	0.5	0.5	0.4
2001	0.5	0.5	0.5	0.4	0.4	0.4	0.4	0.4	0.4	0.4	0.3	0.3	0.4
2002	0.3	0.3	0.3	0.3	0.3	0.3	0.3	0.3	0.3	0.3	0.3	0.3	0.3
2003	0.3	0.4	0.4	0.4	0.4	0.4	0.4	0.4	0.4	0.4	0.4	0.4	0.4
Construction													
1990	9.4	9.2	9.4	9.7	10.2	10.3	10.0	10.1	10.2	9.9	9.6	9.0	9.7
1991	8.5	9.4	9.2	9.0	9.7	9.9	9.7	10.2	10.2	9.9	10.0	9.6	9.6
1992	8.1	8.2	8.8	8.9	9.0	9.4	9.1	9.3	9.3	9.1	8.9	8.3	8.9
1993	7.4	7.6	8.0	7.8	8.2	8.4	8.5	8.6	8.7	8.7	8.7	8.3	8.2
1994	7.9	8.1	8.2	8.7	8.8	8.9	9.1	9.1	9.2	9.0	8.6	8.3	8.7
1995	7.1	7.7	7.9	7.4	7.9	8.4	8.8	9.0	9.0	8.8	8.9	8.2	8.2
1996	7.5	7.6	7.8	7.9	8.5	8.8	8.8	9.2	9.3	9.7	9.6	9.6	8.6
1997	8.9	9.2	9.5	9.5	9.8	10.1	10.5	10.8	10.8	10.7	10.6	10.7	10.0
1998	9.5	9.4	10.4	10.3	10.6	11.0	11.0	11.1	11.3	11.2	11.0	11.0	10.6
1999	10.5	10.6	10.8	11.4	11.5	12.1	12.5	12.5	12.5	12.9	12.8	12.6	11.8
2000	12.2	11.9	12.0	12.8	12.8	13.4	13.8	13.8	14.0	14.5	14.6	14.3	13.3
2001	14.0	13.8	14.3	14.4	14.8	15.1	15.1	15.2	15.1	14.4	14.4	13.8	14.5
2002	13.9	14.5	14.5	14.6	15.1	15.3	15.5	16.0	16.2	15.8	15.4	15.1	15.2
2003	14.5	14.7	14.9	15.1	15.4	15.7	15.9	16.1	15.9	16.2	16.0	15.7	15.5

Employment by Industry: California—*Continued*

(Numbers in thousands. Not seasonally adjusted.)

Industry	January	February	March	April	May	June	July	August	September	October	November	December	Annual Average
VALLEJO-FAIRFIELD-NAPA—*Continued*													
Manufacturing													
1990	12.2	12.4	12.5	12.8	13.1	13.6	14.6	14.8	15.1	14.4	13.7	13.6	13.5
1991	12.2	12.1	12.2	12.5	12.7	12.9	13.5	13.6	13.3	13.7	12.9	12.6	12.9
1992	12.4	12.4	12.4	13.0	13.2	13.8	14.8	14.6	14.7	13.5	13.0	13.0	13.4
1993	13.4	13.5	13.6	13.7	14.0	14.5	15.0	15.0	15.3	14.5	13.8	13.7	14.2
1994	13.2	13.4	13.6	14.0	14.4	14.8	16.0	16.0	16.0	15.5	14.8	14.7	14.7
1995	14.8	15.2	15.3	15.4	15.6	15.9	16.5	17.0	17.3	16.8	16.1	16.1	16.0
1996	15.8	16.2	16.3	16.9	17.6	18.2	18.9	18.9	19.5	18.0	17.4	17.4	17.5
1997	16.3	16.6	17.0	17.5	18.0	18.4	18.8	19.1	19.8	18.4	18.1	18.2	18.0
1998	17.3	17.7	17.9	18.5	18.9	19.2	20.3	20.3	20.6	20.2	19.2	19.0	19.0
1999	18.6	18.9	19.1	19.3	19.9	20.3	20.8	20.6	21.0	21.1	20.4	20.2	20.0
2000	19.6	19.9	20.1	20.2	20.4	21.0	21.1	21.2	21.8	21.0	20.6	20.1	20.5
2001	20.5	20.7	20.9	20.9	21.0	21.5	21.3	21.5	21.7	21.0	20.4	19.9	20.9
2002	19.5	19.8	20.1	20.2	20.5	20.6	21.0	21.0	21.2	20.6	19.8	19.3	20.3
2003	19.3	19.4	19.4	19.3	19.4	19.5	19.3	19.3	19.7	19.6	19.3	19.1	19.4
Service-providing													
1990	111.1	110.9	111.2	113.5	115.0	115.6	116.0	114.7	115.5	115.3	116.3	116.9	114.3
1991	115.1	115.1	115.6	116.7	116.7	116.8	117.1	116.1	116.9	116.7	116.7	116.4	116.3
1992	116.4	117.1	117.8	118.0	118.8	119.9	119.4	118.4	119.1	120.5	120.1	119.8	118.7
1993	117.1	117.1	117.8	117.5	118.2	118.8	118.1	117.4	117.9	118.4	118.4	118.7	117.9
1994	115.1	116.1	116.7	116.9	117.6	119.0	117.0	115.5	116.9	117.3	117.7	117.9	116.9
1995	114.3	115.8	115.8	116.3	117.4	118.8	117.0	117.3	118.1	117.7	118.3	118.1	117.0
1996	115.0	116.4	117.2	115.9	118.2	119.4	118.4	117.7	118.5	118.1	119.5	119.3	117.8
1997	116.9	118.5	120.0	119.2	121.0	122.9	121.4	121.3	123.1	123.9	124.6	125.4	121.5
1998	121.1	121.9	123.4	124.9	126.1	127.8	126.8	127.7	129.3	128.6	130.4	130.6	126.5
1999	127.6	128.9	130.5	131.6	133.2	134.6	133.0	133.6	134.3	135.0	136.2	136.2	132.8
2000	132.6	134.0	135.8	137.9	138.7	140.6	138.7	139.1	139.2	138.2	139.6	140.1	137.8
2001	136.3	138.0	139.9	141.2	143.2	143.8	143.0	143.8	145.4	144.2	143.8	143.4	142.1
2002	139.7	141.5	143.7	145.5	146.8	147.4	146.2	146.0	146.9	147.5	148.0	147.5	145.6
2003	144.2	145.3	146.5	147.9	148.9	150.0	148.4	148.2	148.6	148.5	147.6	147.8	147.7
Trade, transportation, and utilities													
1990	25.3	24.9	24.7	25.0	25.3	25.3	25.7	25.8	25.9	25.9	26.6	27.3	25.6
1991	26.1	25.4	25.5	25.3	25.1	25.0	25.5	25.6	25.8	25.9	26.4	26.4	25.6
1992	26.4	25.9	26.0	26.5	26.7	26.9	27.5	27.2	27.4	28.0	28.7	28.9	27.1
1993	27.8	27.2	27.0	27.1	27.3	27.7	27.8	27.7	27.9	27.9	28.2	28.9	27.7
1994	26.7	26.6	26.5	26.6	26.9	27.2	27.2	27.0	27.2	27.2	28.1	28.6	27.1
1995	26.3	26.2	26.3	26.1	26.7	27.1	27.4	27.6	28.1	28.0	28.7	29.5	27.3
1996	27.7	27.7	27.7	27.2	27.8	28.3	28.6	28.8	28.7	28.4	29.3	29.5	28.3
1997	28.9	28.7	29.0	28.7	29.2	29.8	29.7	29.8	30.2	30.2	31.1	31.7	29.7
1998	29.8	29.5	29.4	29.5	29.7	30.2	29.8	30.5	30.5	30.2	31.2	31.4	30.1
1999	30.3	30.0	30.1	30.2	30.7	31.0	31.0	31.3	31.2	31.5	32.3	32.4	31.0
2000	30.6	30.4	30.4	31.0	31.3	31.4	31.7	31.8	31.8	31.6	32.7	33.4	31.5
2001	31.8	31.7	31.7	31.9	32.2	32.5	33.2	33.2	33.2	33.3	34.0	34.3	32.7
2002	32.1	32.0	32.2	32.5	32.9	33.2	33.2	33.4	34.0	34.4	35.4	35.8	33.4
2003	34.2	33.7	33.5	34.0	34.2	34.7	35.0	35.2	35.6	35.4	36.0	36.9	34.9
Wholesale trade													
1990	2.6	2.6	2.6	2.6	2.6	2.7	2.7	2.7	2.7	2.6	2.6	2.7	2.6
1991	2.6	2.6	2.6	2.8	2.8	2.8	2.8	2.8	2.8	2.7	2.8	2.7	2.7
1992	2.6	2.7	2.7	2.9	3.0	3.0	3.0	3.0	2.9	3.0	3.0	2.9	2.8
1993	2.9	2.9	2.9	2.9	2.9	2.9	3.0	2.9	2.9	2.7	2.7	2.7	2.8
1994	2.7	2.7	2.7	2.7	2.8	2.8	2.8	2.8	2.8	2.8	2.9	2.9	2.7
1995	2.8	2.9	2.9	3.2	3.3	3.3	3.3	3.3	3.4	3.3	3.5	3.6	3.2
1996	3.3	3.4	3.4	3.4	3.5	3.6	3.6	3.6	3.7	3.8	3.8	3.7	3.5
1997	3.8	3.8	3.8	3.9	4.1	4.2	4.1	4.1	4.1	4.2	4.2	4.2	4.0
1998	3.9	3.9	3.9	4.2	4.2	4.4	4.2	4.3	4.3	4.3	4.2	4.2	4.1
1999	4.3	4.3	4.3	4.6	4.7	4.7	4.6	4.6	4.6	4.7	4.7	4.6	4.5
2000	4.5	4.5	4.6	5.0	5.0	4.9	4.9	5.0	4.9	4.9	4.9	4.8	4.8
2001	4.8	4.9	5.0	5.0	5.1	5.1	5.3	5.3	5.3	5.3	5.3	5.3	5.1
2002	4.9	5.2	5.1	5.1	5.1	5.2	5.2	5.3	5.6	5.6	5.6	5.4	5.3
2003	5.3	5.3	5.3	5.4	5.4	5.4	5.7	5.7	6.0	5.6	5.6	5.6	5.5
Retail trade													
1990	19.0	18.8	18.4	18.6	18.8	18.6	19.0	19.0	19.1	19.2	19.9	20.6	19.0
1991	19.5	18.9	19.0	18.6	18.4	18.2	18.7	18.9	18.9	19.4	19.9	20.1	19.0
1992	19.8	19.3	19.3	19.5	19.6	19.7	19.9	19.7	19.9	20.5	21.0	21.4	20.0
1993	20.6	20.0	20.0	19.9	19.9	20.1	20.1	20.0	20.3	20.4	20.9	21.5	20.3
1994	19.6	19.4	19.5	19.4	19.6	19.6	19.7	19.6	19.8	19.9	20.8	21.5	19.8
1995	19.6	19.4	19.3	18.9	19.4	19.4	19.7	19.7	20.2	20.3	20.7	21.3	19.8
1996	20.1	20.0	19.9	19.5	19.9	20.0	20.1	20.3	20.1	20.1	21.0	21.4	20.2
1997	20.7	20.4	20.6	20.3	20.5	20.8	20.7	20.9	21.0	21.1	21.9	22.6	20.9
1998	21.2	20.8	20.7	20.5	20.8	21.0	20.8	21.2	21.2	21.2	22.2	22.8	21.2
1999	21.6	21.3	21.5	21.1	21.5	21.6	21.7	21.7	21.7	22.0	22.8	23.4	21.8
2000	21.8	21.6	21.5	21.8	22.0	22.2	22.1	22.3	22.4	22.3	23.6	24.2	22.3
2001	22.8	22.6	22.5	22.6	22.8	23.0	23.5	23.5	23.5	23.6	24.4	24.9	23.3
2002	23.2	22.8	23.0	23.2	23.6	23.8	23.8	23.8	24.0	24.2	25.0	25.7	23.8
2003	23.9	23.5	23.3	23.6	23.7	24.2	24.3	24.4	24.5	24.7	25.4	26.2	24.3

Employment by Industry: California—*Continued*

(Numbers in thousands. Not seasonally adjusted.)

Industry	January	February	March	April	May	June	July	August	September	October	November	December	Annual Average
VALLEJO-FAIRFIELD-NAPA—*Continued*													
Transportation and utilities													
1990	3.7	3.5	3.7	3.8	3.9	4.0	4.0	4.1	4.1	4.1	4.1	4.0	3.9
1991	4.0	3.9	3.9	4.0	3.9	4.0	4.0	4.0	4.1	4.1	4.1	4.0	4.0
1992	4.1	4.1	4.2	4.2	4.3	4.4	4.6	4.5	4.5	4.3	4.5	4.4	4.3
1993	4.3	4.3	4.1	4.3	4.5	4.6	4.7	4.7	4.7	4.8	4.6	4.7	4.5
1994	4.4	4.5	4.3	4.5	4.5	4.8	4.7	4.6	4.6	4.5	4.4	4.2	4.5
1995	3.9	3.9	4.1	4.0	4.0	4.4	4.4	4.6	4.5	4.4	4.5	4.6	4.2
1996	4.3	4.3	4.4	4.3	4.4	4.7	4.9	4.9	4.9	4.5	4.5	4.4	4.5
1997	4.4	4.5	4.6	4.5	4.6	4.8	4.9	4.8	5.1	4.9	5.0	4.9	4.7
1998	4.7	4.8	4.8	4.8	4.7	4.8	4.8	5.0	5.0	4.7	4.8	4.4	4.7
1999	4.4	4.4	4.3	4.5	4.5	4.7	4.7	5.0	4.9	4.8	4.8	4.4	4.6
2000	4.3	4.3	4.3	4.2	4.3	4.3	4.7	4.5	4.5	4.4	4.2	4.4	4.3
2001	4.2	4.2	4.2	4.3	4.3	4.4	4.4	4.4	4.4	4.4	4.3	4.1	4.3
2002	4.0	4.0	4.1	4.2	4.2	4.2	4.2	4.3	4.4	4.6	4.8	4.7	4.3
2003	5.0	4.9	4.9	5.0	5.1	5.1	5.0	5.1	5.1	5.1	5.0	5.1	5.0
Information													
1990	2.1	2.1	2.1	2.1	2.1	2.1	2.1	2.1	2.0	2.0	2.0	2.0	2.0
1991	1.9	1.9	2.0	2.0	2.0	2.0	2.0	2.0	2.0	2.0	2.0	2.0	1.9
1992	2.0	2.0	2.0	2.0	2.0	2.0	2.0	2.0	2.0	2.0	2.0	2.1	2.0
1993	2.1	2.1	2.1	2.0	2.1	2.1	2.1	2.2	2.1	2.1	2.1	2.1	2.1
1994	2.1	2.1	2.1	2.2	2.2	2.3	2.3	2.3	2.2	2.2	2.2	2.2	2.2
1995	2.2	2.2	2.2	2.2	2.2	2.2	2.3	2.3	2.3	2.3	2.4	2.3	2.2
1996	2.3	2.3	2.4	2.3	2.3	2.3	2.4	2.4	2.4	2.4	2.4	2.4	2.3
1997	2.4	2.4	2.4	2.3	2.4	2.4	2.4	2.4	2.4	2.4	2.4	2.5	2.4
1998	2.4	2.4	2.4	2.5	2.6	2.6	2.6	2.6	2.5	2.5	2.5	2.5	2.5
1999	2.5	2.5	2.4	2.4	2.6	2.6	2.5	2.5	2.5	2.3	2.3	2.4	2.4
2000	2.5	2.5	2.5	2.5	2.5	2.6	2.5	2.5	2.5	2.5	2.6	2.5	2.5
2001	2.5	2.5	2.5	2.6	2.6	2.6	2.6	2.6	2.6	2.6	2.6	2.6	2.5
2002	2.5	2.5	2.5	2.5	2.6	2.6	2.5	2.5	2.6	2.7	2.8	2.9	2.6
2003	2.7	2.7	2.7	2.7	2.7	2.7	2.7	2.7	2.7	2.8	2.8	2.8	2.7
Financial activities													
1990	5.4	5.4	5.4	5.4	5.5	5.5	5.6	5.6	5.6	5.6	5.7	5.7	5.5
1991	5.7	5.7	5.6	5.7	5.7	5.7	5.7	5.6	5.7	5.5	5.5	5.6	5.6
1992	5.5	5.5	5.6	5.6	5.6	5.7	5.7	5.7	5.7	5.9	5.8	5.9	5.6
1993	5.7	5.7	5.7	5.7	5.8	5.8	5.7	5.7	5.8	5.7	5.8	5.7	5.7
1994	5.7	5.8	5.8	5.7	5.7	5.8	5.8	5.8	5.7	5.6	5.5	5.4	5.6
1995	5.5	5.6	5.5	5.6	5.7	5.8	5.7	5.7	5.7	5.6	5.7	5.7	5.6
1996	5.6	5.7	5.7	5.5	5.6	5.7	5.7	5.7	5.7	5.7	5.7	5.6	5.6
1997	5.6	5.7	5.7	5.6	5.7	5.8	5.7	5.7	5.7	5.7	5.7	5.7	5.6
1998	5.6	5.5	5.6	5.9	5.9	6.0	6.0	6.0	6.0	6.1	6.1	6.2	5.9
1999	6.0	6.0	6.0	6.1	6.1	6.3	6.2	6.3	6.3	6.2	6.2	6.3	6.1
2000	6.4	6.4	6.5	6.5	6.5	6.6	6.4	6.5	6.4	6.4	6.4	6.5	6.4
2001	6.3	6.4	6.4	6.5	6.6	6.7	6.8	6.8	6.8	6.8	6.8	6.9	6.6
2002	7.0	7.0	7.0	7.3	7.4	7.5	7.8	7.9	8.0	8.1	8.3	8.4	7.6
2003	8.3	8.3	8.4	8.6	8.6	8.7	8.5	8.5	8.5	8.5	8.6	8.6	8.5
Professional and business services													
1990	7.5	7.7	7.7	8.0	8.2	8.0	7.9	8.2	8.2	8.2	8.2	8.3	8.0
1991	8.6	8.5	8.7	8.9	8.8	8.7	8.7	8.9	8.8	8.7	8.5	8.6	8.7
1992	9.0	9.2	9.3	9.1	9.0	9.1	9.2	9.2	9.3	9.5	9.2	9.1	9.2
1993	9.0	8.9	9.2	8.9	8.8	9.0	9.0	9.0	9.0	9.1	9.0	9.1	9.0
1994	9.2	9.5	9.7	10.1	10.1	10.1	9.9	10.1	10.2	10.0	9.8	10.0	9.8
1995	10.2	10.4	10.4	11.1	11.0	11.1	10.5	11.1	11.0	10.9	10.7	10.6	10.7
1996	10.5	10.6	10.7	11.3	11.6	11.8	12.0	12.2	12.2	11.6	11.6	11.6	11.4
1997	11.3	11.5	11.9	11.8	12.2	12.4	12.6	12.8	12.5	12.3	12.3	12.3	12.1
1998	12.4	12.4	12.5	12.9	12.9	13.2	14.0	14.3	14.2	14.6	14.8	14.9	13.5
1999	14.6	14.7	14.9	15.0	15.1	15.2	16.1	16.5	16.3	16.6	16.6	16.7	15.6
2000	16.5	16.4	16.7	17.8	17.7	17.8	17.8	17.9	17.9	17.2	17.4	17.1	17.3
2001	16.6	16.7	16.7	16.7	16.7	16.8	17.4	17.8	17.9	17.1	16.9	17.0	17.0
2002	16.9	17.3	17.5	17.5	17.4	17.5	17.3	17.4	17.0	16.9	16.8	16.6	17.2
2003	16.3	16.4	16.4	16.5	16.3	16.4	16.3	16.4	16.6	16.0	15.7	16.0	16.3
Educational and health services													
1990	13.8	13.9	14.2	14.8	15.0	14.8	15.2	15.5	15.6	15.6	16.0	16.0	15.0
1991	15.8	15.9	16.0	16.0	16.1	16.0	15.3	15.2	15.9	15.6	15.8	15.8	15.8
1992	15.9	16.4	16.4	16.2	16.2	16.2	16.0	16.1	16.5	16.4	16.4	16.5	16.3
1993	16.5	16.8	16.9	16.7	16.7	16.6	16.3	16.4	16.6	16.6	16.6	16.8	16.6
1994	16.6	16.7	16.9	16.5	16.6	16.7	16.5	16.4	16.8	16.6	16.7	16.8	16.6
1995	16.3	16.5	16.7	16.4	16.5	16.8	16.4	16.6	16.9	16.9	17.0	17.0	16.6
1996	17.3	17.5	17.7	16.9	17.2	17.3	16.8	16.9	17.1	17.2	17.4	17.3	17.2
1997	17.5	17.7	17.8	17.6	18.0	18.2	17.7	17.8	18.5	18.6	18.7	19.1	18.1
1998	18.4	18.9	19.1	18.8	19.0	18.9	19.2	19.4	19.8	19.2	19.3	19.6	19.1
1999	19.3	19.4	19.5	19.6	19.6	19.6	19.8	20.0	20.2	20.1	20.4	20.5	19.8
2000	20.3	20.6	20.7	20.3	20.6	20.7	20.9	21.4	21.6	21.3	21.4	21.4	20.9
2001	21.4	21.8	21.9	22.3	22.7	22.4	22.0	22.1	22.4	22.4	22.4	22.4	22.1
2002	22.2	22.7	22.7	22.8	23.0	23.0	22.1	22.1	22.5	22.7	22.9	22.7	22.6
2003	23.2	23.6	23.6	23.8	24.0	23.7	22.8	22.9	23.2	23.8	23.8	23.6	23.5

Employment by Industry: California—*Continued*

(Numbers in thousands. Not seasonally adjusted.)

Industry	January	February	March	April	May	June	July	August	September	October	November	December	Annual Average
VALLEJO-FAIRFIELD-NAPA—*Continued*													
Leisure and hospitality													
1990	13.9	13.8	14.0	15.2	15.6	15.9	16.7	16.7	16.4	16.0	15.5	15.5	15.4
1991	15.0	15.0	15.2	15.8	16.0	16.5	17.0	16.9	16.6	16.0	15.3	15.0	15.9
1992	14.9	15.1	15.3	15.6	16.1	16.4	16.8	16.6	16.5	16.4	15.7	16.5	16.0
1993	14.9	15.0	15.5	15.9	16.6	16.7	16.9	16.7	16.6	16.4	16.0	15.7	16.1
1994	15.1	15.4	15.7	15.8	16.3	16.8	16.6	16.6	16.3	16.4	16.0	15.9	16.0
1995	15.5	16.0	16.0	16.5	16.9	17.4	17.8	17.9	17.5	16.9	16.6	16.3	16.7
1996	15.5	15.8	15.9	16.9	17.5	17.7	17.8	17.8	17.5	17.3	17.1	16.8	16.9
1997	16.1	16.6	17.0	17.3	17.3	17.7	18.4	18.6	18.4	18.3	17.9	17.4	17.5
1998	16.5	16.8	17.6	18.2	19.0	19.4	19.2	19.6	19.4	18.7	18.5	18.2	18.4
1999	17.3	18.0	18.9	19.2	20.0	20.4	20.2	20.0	20.1	19.6	19.2	18.7	19.3
2000	17.9	18.5	19.6	19.9	20.1	20.7	20.7	20.7	20.3	19.8	19.0	19.1	19.6
2001	18.4	19.4	20.3	20.3	21.2	21.7	22.2	22.3	21.6	20.8	20.2	19.3	20.6
2002	18.2	18.7	19.6	20.2	20.7	21.4	21.5	21.6	21.1	20.8	20.1	19.9	20.3
2003	19.1	19.6	20.4	20.8	21.5	22.1	22.1	22.1	21.5	20.9	19.9	19.4	20.8
Other services													
1990	4.5	4.6	4.6	4.7	4.7	4.7	4.6	4.7	4.7	5.0	5.0	5.1	4.7
1991	5.0	5.0	5.0	5.1	4.9	4.9	4.8	4.8	4.9	5.1	5.0	4.9	5.0
1992	5.0	5.1	5.1	5.1	5.1	5.2	5.1	5.0	5.1	5.3	5.3	5.2	5.1
1993	5.0	5.0	5.0	5.0	4.9	4.9	5.0	5.0	5.1	5.2	5.2	5.0	5.0
1994	4.9	5.0	5.0	5.1	5.0	5.0	4.9	4.8	5.2	5.1	5.0	4.9	4.9
1995	4.6	4.8	4.7	4.6	4.6	4.6	4.6	4.6	4.8	4.9	4.9	4.7	4.7
1996	4.7	4.9	4.9	4.8	4.9	4.9	4.9	4.9	4.9	5.0	5.0	4.9	4.8
1997	4.8	5.0	4.9	5.0	5.1	5.1	4.9	4.9	5.0	5.2	5.2	5.1	5.0
1998	4.8	4.9	5.1	5.1	5.0	5.2	5.1	5.1	5.2	5.2	5.2	5.1	5.0
1999	5.0	5.1	5.2	5.1	5.1	5.3	5.1	5.1	5.0	5.3	5.3	5.2	5.1
2000	5.1	5.2	5.3	5.3	5.3	5.4	5.5	5.6	5.7	5.5	5.5	5.5	5.4
2001	5.1	5.2	5.4	5.3	5.2	5.2	5.1	5.1	5.2	5.3	5.2	5.2	5.2
2002	5.2	5.2	5.3	5.3	5.4	5.5	5.6	5.7	5.7	5.5	5.5	5.5	5.5
2003	5.3	5.5	5.6	5.6	5.7	5.8	5.6	5.6	5.5	5.5	5.5	5.4	5.6
Government													
1990	38.6	38.5	38.5	38.3	38.6	39.3	38.2	36.1	37.1	37.0	37.3	37.0	37.8
1991	36.8	37.5	37.4	37.6	37.8	37.8	37.9	36.8	37.1	37.5	37.6	37.6	37.4
1992	37.3	37.6	37.8	37.7	37.8	38.1	37.1	36.5	36.8	37.2	37.2	37.0	37.3
1993	36.1	36.5	36.5	36.3	36.1	36.1	35.3	34.8	34.8	35.5	35.5	35.4	35.7
1994	34.8	35.0	35.0	34.9	34.8	35.1	33.8	32.5	33.3	34.2	34.4	34.1	34.3
1995	33.7	34.1	34.0	33.8	33.8	33.8	32.3	31.5	31.8	32.2	32.3	32.0	32.9
1996	31.4	31.9	32.2	31.0	31.3	31.4	30.2	29.0	30.0	30.5	31.0	31.2	30.9
1997	30.3	30.9	31.3	30.9	31.1	31.5	30.0	29.3	30.4	31.2	31.3	31.6	30.8
1998	31.2	31.5	31.7	32.0	32.0	32.3	30.9	30.2	31.7	32.1	32.8	32.7	31.7
1999	32.6	33.2	33.5	34.0	34.0	34.2	32.1	31.9	32.7	33.4	33.9	34.0	33.2
2000	33.3	34.0	34.1	34.6	34.7	35.4	33.2	32.7	33.0	33.9	34.6	34.6	34.0
2001	34.2	34.3	35.0	35.6	36.0	35.9	33.7	33.9	35.7	35.9	35.7	35.7	35.1
2002	35.6	36.1	36.9	37.4	37.4	36.7	36.2	35.4	36.0	36.4	36.2	35.7	36.3
2003	35.1	35.5	35.9	35.9	35.9	35.9	35.4	34.8	35.0	35.6	35.3	35.1	35.5
Federal government													
1990	14.6	14.5	14.3	14.2	14.4	14.4	13.8	13.3	13.1	12.6	12.4	12.2	13.6
1991	12.4	12.4	12.4	12.4	12.4	12.3	12.5	12.5	12.5	12.2	12.2	12.2	12.3
1992	12.1	11.9	12.1	12.1	12.1	12.0	12.0	12.1	12.1	12.1	12.0	11.8	12.0
1993	11.5	11.4	11.4	11.3	11.2	11.0	10.9	10.9	10.9	10.9	10.8	10.7	11.0
1994	10.6	10.1	9.9	9.8	9.7	9.6	9.3	9.0	8.9	8.8	8.7	8.7	9.4
1995	8.6	8.5	8.3	8.1	8.0	7.8	7.6	7.4	6.9	6.5	6.4	6.2	7.5
1996	6.0	5.9	5.9	4.9	4.9	4.9	4.9	5.0	4.9	4.9	4.9	4.9	5.1
1997	4.7	4.7	4.7	4.5	4.6	4.7	4.6	4.7	4.7	4.7	4.7	4.7	4.6
1998	4.5	4.4	4.4	4.5	4.5	4.6	4.7	4.7	4.7	4.8	4.8	4.7	4.6
1999	4.6	4.6	4.8	4.9	4.9	4.9	5.0	5.0	4.7	4.8	4.8	4.9	4.8
2000	4.8	4.8	4.8	4.9	5.3	5.5	5.0	5.2	4.7	4.8	4.7	4.7	4.9
2001	4.7	4.7	4.7	4.8	4.7	4.8	4.9	4.9	4.8	4.8	4.9	4.9	4.8
2002	4.9	4.9	4.9	4.8	4.8	4.9	4.8	4.9	4.9	4.9	4.9	4.9	4.9
2003	4.8	4.8	4.8	4.7	4.7	4.7	4.6	4.6	4.6	4.6	4.6	4.6	4.7
State government													
1990	6.5	6.5	6.5	6.5	6.5	6.6	6.6	6.6	6.6	6.5	6.5	6.5	6.5
1991	6.6	6.6	6.6	6.7	6.8	6.8	6.8	6.8	6.8	6.7	6.7	6.7	6.7
1992	6.8	6.8	6.8	6.7	6.7	6.7	6.7	6.6	6.6	6.6	6.6	6.6	6.6
1993	6.5	6.5	6.4	6.3	6.2	6.2	6.3	6.4	6.3	6.4	6.3	6.2	6.3
1994	6.2	6.3	6.3	6.3	6.3	6.3	6.3	6.3	6.3	6.2	6.3	6.3	6.2
1995	6.4	6.4	6.3	6.3	6.4	6.4	6.3	6.4	6.5	6.5	6.5	6.5	6.4
1996	6.5	6.5	6.7	6.5	6.6	6.5	6.5	6.6	6.6	6.7	6.8	6.7	6.6
1997	6.6	6.8	6.8	6.8	6.7	6.7	6.7	6.8	6.8	6.9	6.9	6.9	6.7
1998	7.0	7.0	7.0	7.0	7.0	7.0	6.9	6.8	6.9	7.0	7.0	7.0	6.9
1999	7.0	7.0	7.1	7.1	7.1	7.1	7.1	7.2	7.2	7.3	7.3	7.3	7.1
2000	7.4	7.4	7.4	7.4	7.3	7.2	7.2	7.2	7.3	7.4	7.4	7.4	7.3
2001	7.4	7.4	7.4	7.4	7.4	7.3	7.4	7.4	7.5	7.6	7.5	7.5	7.4
2002	7.5	7.5	7.6	7.6	7.6	7.5	7.6	7.6	7.6	7.6	7.6	7.6	7.6
2003	7.6	7.6	7.6	7.6	7.6	7.5	7.6	7.6	7.6	7.7	7.6	7.6	7.6

Employment by Industry: California—*Continued*

(Numbers in thousands. Not seasonally adjusted.)

Industry	January	February	March	April	May	June	July	August	September	October	November	December	Annual Average
VALLEJO-FAIRFIELD-NAPA—*Continued*													
Local government													
1990	17.5	17.5	17.7	17.6	17.7	18.3	17.8	16.2	17.4	17.9	18.4	18.3	17.6
1991	17.8	18.5	18.4	18.5	18.6	18.7	18.6	17.5	17.8	18.6	18.7	18.7	18.3
1992	18.4	18.9	18.9	18.9	19.0	19.4	18.4	17.8	18.1	18.5	18.6	18.6	18.6
1993	18.1	18.6	18.7	18.7	18.7	18.9	18.1	17.5	17.6	18.2	18.4	18.5	18.3
1994	18.0	18.6	18.8	18.8	18.8	19.2	18.2	17.2	18.1	19.2	19.4	19.1	18.6
1995	18.7	19.2	19.4	19.4	19.4	19.6	18.4	17.7	18.4	19.2	19.4	19.3	19.0
1996	18.9	19.5	19.6	19.6	19.8	20.0	18.8	17.4	18.5	18.9	19.3	19.6	19.1
1997	19.0	19.4	19.8	19.6	19.8	20.1	18.7	17.8	18.9	19.6	19.7	20.0	19.3
1998	19.7	20.1	20.3	20.5	20.5	20.7	19.3	18.7	20.1	20.3	21.0	21.0	20.1
1999	21.0	21.6	21.6	22.0	22.0	22.2	20.0	19.7	20.8	21.3	21.8	21.8	21.3
2000	21.1	21.8	21.9	22.3	22.1	22.7	21.0	20.3	21.0	21.7	22.5	22.5	21.7
2001	22.1	22.2	22.9	23.4	23.9	23.8	21.4	21.6	23.4	23.5	23.3	23.3	22.9
2002	23.2	23.7	24.4	25.0	25.0	24.3	23.8	22.9	23.5	23.9	23.7	23.2	23.9
2003	22.7	23.1	23.5	23.6	23.6	23.7	23.2	22.6	22.8	23.3	23.1	22.9	23.2
VENTURA													
Total nonfarm													
1990	224.7	225.9	227.7	228.1	230.2	231.7	231.1	230.6	230.4	231.7	234.3	236.9	230.2
1991	231.0	230.7	229.8	230.0	230.4	232.6	232.8	228.9	229.5	229.2	229.2	230.1	230.3
1992	223.7	223.5	226.2	226.7	228.1	228.9	227.0	224.5	226.4	227.3	228.2	228.3	226.5
1993	223.1	224.4	226.9	227.5	228.7	228.3	227.7	224.0	226.0	227.1	228.7	231.0	226.9
1994	226.0	228.1	230.8	231.7	233.0	235.4	233.7	233.5	235.7	235.4	237.4	238.6	233.2
1995	232.6	235.0	236.6	238.2	237.7	239.3	238.0	235.7	236.6	238.2	239.4	240.1	237.2
1996	233.9	236.4	236.6	237.4	240.1	239.0	236.9	236.0	236.8	238.4	241.0	242.1	237.8
1997	235.5	238.0	240.5	242.9	244.9	245.3	238.9	241.5	242.6	246.8	247.0	248.9	242.7
1998	244.8	245.4	247.6	250.1	252.1	253.3	254.4	252.7	255.4	255.4	257.5	259.4	252.3
1999	255.3	256.2	257.4	261.4	263.1	265.1	264.3	263.6	266.7	267.8	270.0	272.5	263.6
2000	267.4	267.9	270.3	273.3	275.2	277.2	275.5	274.3	277.4	278.4	279.9	283.1	274.9
2001	277.3	277.1	278.8	279.0	280.6	280.9	279.3	277.8	279.6	281.4	283.0	284.5	279.9
2002	277.7	279.6	280.4	280.2	281.7	283.8	281.1	278.3	282.4	282.9	286.9	286.9	281.8
2003	279.7	280.1	282.4	283.7	285.9	287.4	283.0	281.8	284.0	284.4	286.1	285.1	283.6
Total private													
1990	182.1	182.5	183.8	184.1	185.2	186.7	186.9	186.6	186.4	187.4	189.6	192.0	186.1
1991	186.9	186.1	184.9	184.8	185.4	187.0	186.8	185.5	185.0	184.5	184.2	184.3	185.4
1992	178.8	178.5	181.0	181.1	182.3	183.4	182.2	181.9	182.7	183.0	183.1	183.2	181.7
1993	179.2	180.3	182.7	183.3	184.5	184.5	184.5	184.2	185.0	184.3	185.0	187.2	183.7
1994	183.3	185.0	187.6	187.8	189.2	191.8	191.5	193.2	195.3	192.9	194.0	195.2	190.5
1995	189.7	192.0	193.4	193.5	194.0	195.2	195.3	195.3	195.4	195.1	195.6	196.5	194.2
1996	191.1	192.1	192.7	193.9	195.7	195.3	194.5	194.9	194.9	193.9	196.6	197.7	194.4
1997	192.1	193.9	196.2	198.3	200.3	201.3	199.7	200.8	201.1	202.3	202.5	204.3	199.4
1998	201.2	201.9	203.7	207.3	209.1	210.7	211.9	212.5	213.1	212.0	213.2	214.8	209.2
1999	211.1	212.0	213.2	217.0	219.2	221.1	220.9	222.0	222.8	224.0	225.4	227.6	219.6
2000	223.3	223.3	225.3	228.0	229.5	232.2	232.3	233.0	234.5	233.8	234.8	237.8	230.6
2001	231.5	231.5	233.4	234.3	235.7	236.7	234.4	235.1	235.4	235.8	236.4	237.7	234.8
2002	231.8	233.1	234.4	234.5	236.1	237.7	237.3	236.6	238.0	237.8	240.2	241.3	236.6
2003	234.2	234.6	236.3	237.9	239.3	241.4	240.1	240.3	240.4	240.7	242.0	241.4	239.1
Goods-producing													
1990	52.6	52.6	53.1	52.4	52.1	52.7	51.4	50.7	50.2	50.2	50.6	50.8	51.6
1991	47.6	47.2	46.3	47.1	47.5	48.1	48.0	47.2	46.7	46.0	45.9	45.3	46.9
1992	42.4	42.2	43.2	43.5	44.0	44.5	43.9	43.9	43.8	43.7	43.5	43.0	43.4
1993	40.5	41.3	41.7	41.3	42.1	42.0	41.8	42.5	42.6	42.6	42.1	41.7	41.8
1994	40.7	41.4	42.6	42.5	43.2	44.2	43.7	44.8	45.5	45.4	45.1	44.9	43.6
1995	43.3	44.7	44.9	44.1	44.5	44.7	44.5	44.8	45.0	45.2	45.2	45.0	44.6
1996	43.5	43.8	43.8	45.7	46.6	46.5	46.6	46.9	47.0	46.6	46.8	46.3	45.8
1997	46.2	46.8	47.6	48.6	49.4	49.8	49.9	50.6	50.6	50.4	50.0	49.8	49.1
1998	49.7	49.4	50.4	51.8	52.5	53.5	53.3	53.8	53.8	53.3	53.4	53.2	52.3
1999	52.7	52.9	53.3	54.3	54.8	55.5	55.5	55.7	56.5	56.2	56.3	56.1	54.9
2000	55.4	55.2	55.7	56.4	57.1	58.2	58.5	58.8	59.5	59.2	58.8	59.0	57.6
2001	57.3	57.3	57.8	57.7	57.9	58.2	57.5	57.8	57.7	57.3	56.4	55.7	57.3
2002	54.0	54.7	54.7	54.4	54.8	55.2	54.4	54.0	54.2	53.7	54.2	54.0	54.4
2003	52.9	52.7	53.2	53.8	54.3	55.0	55.4	55.1	54.9	54.7	54.8	54.2	54.3
Natural resources and mining													
1990	1.8	1.7	1.8	1.8	1.8	1.8	1.9	1.9	1.9	1.9	1.9	1.9	1.8
1991	2.3	2.3	2.3	2.3	2.3	2.3	2.3	2.2	2.2	2.2	2.2	2.1	2.2
1992	1.9	1.8	1.9	2.1	2.1	2.1	2.1	2.1	2.0	2.0	1.9	2.0	2.0
1993	2.0	1.9	1.9	2.0	2.0	2.0	2.0	2.1	2.0	1.9	1.9	1.9	1.9
1994	2.1	2.0	2.0	2.1	2.0	2.1	2.0	2.0	2.0	2.0	2.0	2.0	2.0
1995	1.8	1.8	1.8	1.9	1.9	1.8	1.9	1.8	1.9	1.8	1.8	1.8	1.8
1996	1.8	1.8	1.8	1.7	1.7	1.6	1.6	1.6	1.6	1.6	1.6	1.6	1.6
1997	1.6	1.6	1.6	1.6	1.6	1.6	1.6	1.6	1.6	1.5	1.5	1.5	1.5
1998	1.6	1.6	1.6	1.1	1.1	1.1	1.2	1.2	1.1	1.1	1.1	1.1	1.2
1999	1.1	1.1	1.1	1.0	1.0	1.0	0.9	0.9	0.9	0.8	0.9	0.9	0.9
2000	0.8	0.8	0.8	0.8	0.8	0.8	0.8	0.8	0.8	0.8	0.8	0.8	0.8
2001	0.8	0.8	0.8	0.8	0.8	0.8	0.8	0.8	0.8	0.8	0.8	0.8	0.7
2002	0.7	0.7	0.7	0.7	0.7	0.7	0.7	0.7	0.7	0.7	0.7	0.6	0.7
2003	0.6	0.6	0.6	0.6	0.6	0.6	0.6	0.6	0.6	0.6	0.6	0.6	0.6

Employment by Industry: California—*Continued*

(Numbers in thousands. Not seasonally adjusted.)

Industry	January	February	March	April	May	June	July	August	September	October	November	December	Annual Average
VENTURA—*Continued*													
Construction													
1990	17.6	17.3	17.5	16.6	16.1	16.4	16.0	15.6	15.2	15.1	15.0	15.1	16.1
1991	13.0	12.7	12.4	12.0	12.2	12.5	12.2	12.1	11.9	12.1	11.9	11.9	12.2
1992	9.9	9.6	10.2	10.0	10.4	10.8	10.4	10.7	10.6	10.3	10.1	9.9	10.2
1993	8.2	8.8	9.3	8.8	9.3	9.2	9.3	9.5	9.5	9.8	9.7	9.4	9.2
1994	8.6	9.3	10.0	9.4	9.9	10.1	10.5	11.1	11.4	11.3	11.1	11.2	10.3
1995	10.0	11.0	11.1	11.1	11.3	11.4	11.4	11.7	11.5	11.8	11.6	11.5	11.2
1996	10.5	10.4	10.1	10.4	10.7	10.9	10.9	11.2	11.2	11.0	11.0	10.5	10.7
1997	10.3	10.7	11.0	11.3	11.6	11.8	11.8	12.4	12.1	11.9	11.6	11.5	11.5
1998	11.2	11.0	11.6	12.3	12.5	13.2	13.8	14.4	14.3	14.5	14.5	14.5	13.1
1999	13.9	13.7	14.0	13.7	14.2	14.5	15.1	15.4	15.7	15.6	15.4	15.2	14.7
2000	14.3	14.1	14.3	14.8	15.3	16.0	16.1	16.3	16.7	16.2	15.9	16.0	15.5
2001	15.1	15.0	15.4	15.7	16.1	16.5	16.4	16.9	16.9	16.6	16.2	16.0	16.0
2002	15.3	15.8	15.5	15.3	15.4	15.6	15.8	15.8	15.9	16.0	16.0	15.9	15.7
2003	15.3	15.1	15.4	16.0	16.8	17.1	17.5	17.5	17.2	16.9	17.1	16.9	16.6
Manufacturing													
1990	33.2	33.6	33.8	34.0	34.2	34.5	33.5	33.2	33.1	33.2	33.7	33.8	33.6
1991	32.3	32.2	31.6	32.8	33.0	33.3	33.5	32.9	32.6	31.7	31.8	31.3	32.4
1992	30.6	30.8	31.1	31.4	31.5	31.6	31.4	31.1	31.2	31.4	31.5	31.1	31.2
1993	30.3	30.6	30.5	30.5	30.8	30.8	30.5	30.9	31.1	30.9	30.5	30.4	30.6
1994	30.0	30.1	30.6	31.0	31.3	32.0	31.2	31.7	32.1	32.1	32.0	31.7	31.3
1995	31.5	31.9	32.0	31.1	31.3	31.5	31.2	31.3	31.6	31.6	31.8	31.7	31.5
1996	31.2	31.6	31.9	33.6	34.2	34.0	34.1	34.1	34.2	34.0	34.2	34.2	33.4
1997	34.3	34.5	35.0	35.7	36.2	36.4	36.5	36.6	36.9	37.0	36.9	36.8	36.0
1998	36.9	36.8	37.2	38.4	38.9	39.2	38.3	38.2	38.4	37.7	37.8	37.6	37.9
1999	37.7	38.1	38.2	39.6	39.6	40.0	39.5	39.4	39.9	39.8	40.0	40.0	39.3
2000	40.3	40.3	40.6	40.8	41.0	41.4	41.6	41.7	42.0	42.2	42.1	42.2	41.3
2001	41.4	41.5	41.6	41.2	41.0	40.9	40.3	40.1	40.0	39.9	39.4	38.9	40.5
2002	38.0	38.2	38.5	38.4	38.7	38.9	37.9	37.5	37.6	37.0	37.5	37.5	38.0
2003	37.0	37.0	37.2	37.2	36.9	37.3	37.3	37.0	37.1	37.2	37.1	36.7	37.1
Service-providing													
1990	172.1	173.3	174.6	175.7	178.1	179.0	179.7	179.9	180.2	181.5	183.7	186.1	178.6
1991	183.4	183.5	183.5	182.9	182.9	184.5	184.8	181.7	182.8	183.2	183.3	184.8	183.4
1992	181.3	181.3	183.0	183.2	184.1	184.4	183.1	180.6	182.6	183.6	184.7	185.3	183.1
1993	182.6	183.1	185.2	186.2	186.6	186.3	185.9	181.5	183.4	184.5	186.6	189.3	185.1
1994	185.3	186.7	188.2	189.2	189.8	191.2	190.0	188.7	190.2	190.0	192.3	193.7	189.6
1995	189.3	190.3	191.7	194.1	193.2	194.6	193.5	190.9	191.6	193.0	194.2	195.1	192.6
1996	190.4	192.6	192.8	191.7	193.5	192.5	190.3	189.1	189.8	191.8	194.2	195.8	192.0
1997	189.3	191.2	192.9	194.3	195.5	195.5	189.0	190.9	192.0	196.4	197.0	199.1	193.5
1998	195.1	196.0	197.2	198.3	199.6	199.8	201.1	198.9	201.6	202.1	204.1	206.2	200.0
1999	202.6	203.3	204.1	207.1	208.3	209.6	208.8	207.9	210.2	211.6	213.7	216.4	208.6
2000	212.0	212.7	214.6	216.9	218.1	219.0	217.0	215.5	217.9	219.2	221.1	224.1	217.3
2001	220.0	219.8	221.0	221.3	222.7	222.7	221.8	220.0	221.9	224.1	226.6	228.8	222.5
2002	223.7	224.9	225.7	225.8	226.9	228.6	226.7	224.3	228.2	229.2	232.7	232.9	227.5
2003	226.8	227.4	229.2	229.9	231.6	232.4	227.6	226.7	229.1	229.7	231.3	230.9	229.4
Trade, transportation, and utilities													
1990	40.9	40.4	40.6	40.1	40.9	41.2	41.8	41.8	41.7	42.2	43.3	44.9	41.6
1991	43.9	42.9	42.4	40.9	41.3	42.2	41.8	41.2	41.2	40.7	41.5	42.8	41.9
1992	40.7	39.7	40.2	40.9	41.0	40.8	40.3	39.9	40.2	40.2	41.0	42.1	40.5
1993	40.9	40.0	40.1	39.9	39.7	39.9	39.9	39.9	39.8	40.1	41.1	42.6	40.3
1994	41.0	40.5	41.2	41.0	41.3	41.9	41.7	42.0	42.7	42.5	43.7	45.2	42.0
1995	43.3	43.1	42.9	43.2	43.3	43.5	43.0	43.2	43.3	43.6	44.5	45.6	43.5
1996	43.5	43.0	42.8	42.4	43.0	42.9	42.9	42.8	42.8	43.3	44.8	46.3	43.3
1997	44.2	44.3	44.6	45.2	45.3	45.3	44.4	44.3	44.5	44.8	45.5	47.2	44.9
1998	44.7	44.3	44.6	44.9	44.9	45.3	44.9	44.9	45.0	45.4	46.2	47.8	45.2
1999	45.2	44.8	45.2	46.5	47.0	47.1	46.7	46.9	46.8	47.6	49.0	50.4	46.9
2000	48.6	48.3	48.4	48.8	48.9	49.3	49.3	49.5	49.8	50.1	51.9	53.4	49.6
2001	50.9	50.3	50.5	50.5	50.2	50.2	49.9	50.4	50.2	50.8	52.0	53.1	50.7
2002	51.8	51.5	51.5	50.6	50.9	51.4	50.8	51.0	51.1	51.7	53.0	54.2	51.6
2003	51.5	51.3	51.3	51.1	51.3	51.5	51.2	51.6	51.7	52.7	53.2	54.1	51.9
Wholesale trade													
1990	7.3	7.5	7.5	7.6	7.9	8.0	8.1	8.2	8.0	8.2	8.1	8.5	7.9
1991	8.3	8.2	8.2	7.5	7.6	7.9	7.9	7.7	7.5	7.3	7.3	7.2	7.7
1992	7.2	7.1	7.3	8.5	8.4	8.4	8.4	8.3	8.3	8.0	8.1	8.2	8.0
1993	7.6	7.7	7.8	7.7	7.8	7.8	7.7	7.7	7.4	7.4	7.3	7.3	7.6
1994	7.6	7.6	7.9	8.0	8.0	8.1	8.0	8.1	8.0	7.8	7.7	7.8	7.8
1995	7.7	8.1	8.2	8.8	8.8	8.9	8.8	8.9	8.7	8.5	8.5	8.5	8.5
1996	8.2	8.4	8.5	8.3	8.4	8.4	8.5	8.4	8.3	8.1	8.3	8.5	8.3
1997	8.3	8.6	8.7	8.7	8.8	8.9	8.7	8.7	8.6	8.5	8.5	8.6	8.6
1998	8.4	8.6	8.8	9.1	9.1	9.3	9.1	8.9	8.9	9.1	9.0	9.0	8.9
1999	8.7	8.9	9.1	9.6	9.7	9.6	9.6	9.5	9.4	9.7	9.7	9.7	9.4
2000	9.6	9.8	9.9	10.2	10.3	10.4	10.5	10.5	10.6	10.6	10.8	10.8	10.3
2001	10.8	11.0	11.2	11.1	11.0	11.0	11.0	11.2	10.9	10.9	11.0	11.1	11.0
2002	11.6	11.9	11.8	11.6	11.7	11.7	11.5	11.6	11.5	11.6	11.8	11.8	11.7
2003	11.7	11.8	12.0	12.1	12.1	12.2	11.7	11.8	11.7	11.6	11.7	11.8	11.9

Employment by Industry: California—*Continued*

(Numbers in thousands. Not seasonally adjusted.)

Industry	January	February	March	April	May	June	July	August	September	October	November	December	Annual Average
VENTURA—*Continued*													
Retail trade													
1990	28.9	28.2	28.1	27.5	27.8	28.0	28.5	28.3	28.4	28.7	29.8	30.8	28.5
1991	30.1	29.2	28.8	27.8	28.0	28.4	28.2	28.1	28.3	28.1	28.8	29.7	28.6
1992	27.7	26.9	26.9	26.6	26.6	26.7	26.6	26.5	26.6	26.7	27.4	28.2	26.9
1993	27.5	26.6	26.5	26.5	26.3	26.4	26.8	26.8	26.9	27.1	28.0	29.2	27.0
1994	27.4	26.8	27.1	26.9	27.1	27.5	27.9	28.2	28.9	28.9	30.1	31.1	28.1
1995	29.6	29.0	28.7	28.6	28.6	28.7	28.6	28.8	29.0	29.6	30.4	31.3	29.2
1996	29.6	28.9	28.5	28.3	28.9	29.0	29.1	29.2	29.3	29.9	31.1	32.1	29.4
1997	30.5	30.3	30.4	30.6	30.8	30.8	30.5	30.5	30.7	30.9	31.7	33.0	30.8
1998	31.0	30.3	30.3	30.4	30.4	30.6	30.7	30.9	31.0	31.0	31.9	33.1	30.9
1999	31.1	30.5	30.6	31.4	31.8	32.0	31.9	32.2	32.2	32.6	33.9	35.0	32.1
2000	33.5	33.0	33.0	32.9	33.0	33.3	33.5	33.7	33.8	34.0	35.3	36.5	33.7
2001	33.9	33.1	33.1	33.0	33.0	33.2	33.3	33.5	33.7	34.1	35.3	36.3	33.7
2002	34.3	33.6	33.7	33.3	33.5	33.9	33.6	33.7	34.0	34.4	35.3	36.5	34.2
2003	34.1	33.8	33.7	33.5	33.7	33.8	33.9	34.2	34.3	35.5	35.9	36.6	34.4
Transportation and utilities													
1990	4.7	4.7	5.0	5.0	5.2	5.2	5.2	5.3	5.3	5.3	5.4	5.6	5.1
1991	5.5	5.5	5.4	5.6	5.7	5.9	5.7	5.4	5.4	5.3	5.4	5.9	5.5
1992	5.8	5.7	6.0	5.8	6.0	5.7	5.3	5.1	5.3	5.5	5.5	5.7	5.6
1993	5.8	5.7	5.8	5.7	5.6	5.7	5.4	5.4	5.5	5.6	5.8	6.1	5.6
1994	6.0	6.1	6.2	6.1	6.2	6.3	5.8	5.7	5.8	5.8	5.9	6.3	6.0
1995	6.0	6.0	6.0	5.8	5.9	5.9	5.6	5.5	5.6	5.5	5.6	5.8	5.7
1996	5.7	5.7	5.8	5.8	5.7	5.5	5.3	5.2	5.2	5.3	5.4	5.7	5.5
1997	5.4	5.4	5.5	5.9	5.7	5.6	5.2	5.1	5.2	5.4	5.3	5.6	5.4
1998	5.3	5.4	5.5	5.4	5.4	5.4	5.1	5.1	5.1	5.3	5.3	5.7	5.3
1999	5.4	5.4	5.5	5.5	5.5	5.5	5.2	5.2	5.2	5.3	5.4	5.7	5.4
2000	5.5	5.5	5.5	5.7	5.6	5.6	5.3	5.3	5.4	5.5	5.8	6.1	5.5
2001	6.2	6.2	6.2	6.4	6.2	6.0	5.6	5.7	5.6	5.8	5.7	5.7	5.9
2002	5.9	6.0	6.0	5.7	5.7	5.8	5.7	5.7	5.6	5.7	5.9	5.9	5.8
2003	5.7	5.7	5.6	5.5	5.5	5.5	5.6	5.6	5.7	5.6	5.6	5.7	5.6
Information													
1990	7.4	7.4	7.4	7.7	7.6	7.8	8.6	8.5	8.5	8.6	8.7	8.1	8.0
1991	7.8	7.8	7.6	7.1	7.1	7.2	6.8	6.7	6.7	6.6	6.5	6.4	7.0
1992	6.9	6.7	6.9	6.4	6.4	6.4	6.6	6.6	6.6	6.6	6.5	6.5	6.5
1993	7.0	6.9	7.0	6.7	6.6	6.4	6.7	6.6	6.7	6.3	6.4	6.4	6.6
1994	6.9	6.7	6.7	6.3	6.4	6.6	6.2	6.2	6.2	5.9	6.0	6.3	6.3
1995	6.1	6.0	6.4	6.0	6.1	6.5	6.2	6.2	6.4	6.1	6.1	6.3	6.2
1996	5.8	5.7	6.1	5.8	5.9	6.1	5.9	5.9	6.2	5.9	6.0	6.5	5.9
1997	6.0	6.1	6.5	6.2	6.4	6.8	6.6	6.7	6.7	6.5	6.6	6.6	6.4
1998	6.6	6.7	6.8	6.9	6.9	7.0	7.4	7.4	7.4	7.4	7.4	7.5	7.1
1999	7.7	7.9	7.9	8.2	8.1	8.5	8.4	8.4	8.4	8.1	8.2	8.3	8.1
2000	7.8	7.8	7.9	7.6	7.7	7.8	7.9	7.9	8.0	8.1	8.1	8.3	7.9
2001	8.3	8.3	8.5	8.3	8.5	8.6	8.5	8.4	8.3	8.2	8.2	8.2	8.3
2002	8.3	8.3	8.4	8.3	8.3	8.2	8.0	7.9	7.8	7.8	7.8	7.8	8.1
2003	7.5	7.4	7.4	7.1	7.1	7.0	7.0	7.0	6.9	6.8	6.8	6.8	7.1
Financial activities													
1990	11.5	12.2	12.3	12.7	12.8	12.5	12.2	12.1	12.1	12.6	12.0	12.1	12.2
1991	12.8	13.4	14.1	14.4	14.5	14.3	13.8	13.6	13.5	14.1	13.6	13.7	13.8
1992	13.7	14.1	14.1	13.6	13.4	13.2	12.5	12.6	12.6	13.0	12.5	12.5	13.1
1993	12.5	12.8	13.7	14.2	14.3	14.2	14.0	13.5	13.4	13.4	13.2	13.1	13.5
1994	13.5	13.9	14.2	14.2	13.9	14.0	13.5	13.0	13.2	13.2	13.0	13.1	13.5
1995	12.8	12.7	12.7	13.1	13.2	13.1	13.3	13.1	13.0	12.9	12.8	13.0	12.9
1996	13.0	13.1	12.8	12.5	12.5	12.5	12.5	12.5	12.6	12.3	12.3	12.4	12.5
1997	12.6	12.9	12.9	12.5	12.6	12.8	12.7	12.8	13.1	13.6	13.6	13.8	12.9
1998	13.7	14.0	14.0	14.5	14.6	14.8	14.8	14.8	14.9	15.2	15.3	15.2	14.6
1999	15.8	15.8	15.8	16.2	16.3	16.3	16.2	16.3	16.1	16.3	16.2	16.4	16.1
2000	16.2	16.1	16.3	16.4	16.6	16.7	16.9	17.0	17.0	17.1	17.0	17.2	16.7
2001	18.5	18.7	19.0	19.1	19.2	19.6	19.7	20.0	20.1	20.5	20.6	20.9	19.6
2002	20.9	21.1	21.4	21.8	22.0	22.2	22.5	22.7	22.8	22.9	23.2	23.3	22.2
2003	22.5	22.7	23.1	23.2	23.4	23.8	23.6	23.9	23.7	23.6	23.4	23.3	23.4
Professional and business services													
1990	25.8	25.7	25.5	26.2	26.3	26.1	26.6	27.1	27.2	27.1	27.4	28.0	26.5
1991	27.6	27.4	27.2	27.7	27.1	26.7	27.3	27.8	27.9	27.7	27.5	27.1	27.4
1992	27.2	27.3	27.6	27.0	27.2	27.4	28.0	28.1	28.1	28.2	27.9	27.8	27.6
1993	27.7	28.3	28.9	29.5	29.7	29.8	30.3	30.0	30.6	30.7	30.8	31.7	29.8
1994	30.3	30.8	31.7	32.0	32.2	32.5	32.9	33.4	34.1	33.9	34.4	34.2	32.7
1995	33.2	33.6	33.9	33.9	33.4	33.7	33.9	33.8	33.5	33.6	33.6	33.2	33.6
1996	33.0	33.3	33.6	33.6	33.5	33.6	33.0	33.3	33.1	32.6	32.8	32.8	33.1
1997	30.8	30.8	31.1	31.5	31.6	31.8	31.7	32.0	32.2	32.8	32.3	32.5	31.7
1998	33.5	34.0	34.0	34.8	35.0	34.9	36.1	36.3	36.2	35.8	35.4	35.6	35.1
1999	34.8	35.1	35.1	35.9	36.3	36.4	37.0	37.3	37.3	37.9	37.7	37.9	36.5
2000	38.2	38.1	38.6	40.2	40.1	40.6	40.2	40.0	40.2	39.5	39.3	39.8	39.5
2001	37.1	36.9	37.2	37.3	37.6	37.8	37.2	36.8	37.0	36.8	36.9	37.3	37.1
2002	35.9	36.1	36.3	36.7	36.8	36.9	36.8	36.4	36.7	36.6	36.9	37.0	36.6
2003	35.9	35.9	36.4	36.6	36.8	37.3	36.5	36.6	36.6	36.4	37.2	36.9	36.6

Employment by Industry: California—*Continued*

(Numbers in thousands. Not seasonally adjusted.)

Industry	January	February	March	April	May	June	July	August	September	October	November	December	Annual Average
VENTURA—*Continued*													
Educational and health services													
1990	17.1	17.1	17.4	17.9	18.0	18.2	18.3	18.2	18.4	19.0	19.3	19.5	18.2
1991	18.7	18.9	18.9	19.2	19.2	19.3	19.5	19.5	19.6	19.9	20.0	20.0	19.3
1992	20.0	20.2	20.4	20.5	20.7	20.8	20.9	20.6	21.1	21.7	21.9	21.9	20.8
1993	21.9	22.2	22.1	22.4	22.4	22.3	21.6	21.5	22.0	22.3	22.4	22.5	22.1
1994	22.5	22.8	21.9	22.2	22.3	22.4	22.5	22.5	22.2	22.1	21.9	22.0	22.2
1995	21.5	22.0	22.0	22.4	22.6	22.6	22.8	22.7	22.9	22.7	22.6	22.6	22.4
1996	22.1	22.6	22.7	23.4	23.4	22.7	22.3	22.0	22.2	22.7	22.7	22.4	22.6
1997	22.0	22.5	22.6	23.3	23.6	23.3	23.0	23.0	22.9	23.4	23.5	23.4	23.0
1998	22.4	22.7	22.8	23.1	23.2	23.1	23.6	23.4	24.0	23.7	24.1	23.9	23.3
1999	23.4	23.7	23.5	23.5	23.8	24.1	23.8	23.8	24.3	24.4	24.5	24.7	23.9
2000	23.8	24.1	24.3	24.0	24.1	24.2	24.0	24.2	24.5	24.3	24.4	24.5	24.2
2001	24.4	24.7	24.6	25.3	25.6	25.5	25.4	25.3	25.6	25.8	25.9	25.9	25.3
2002	25.4	25.5	25.7	25.9	26.0	25.9	26.3	26.3	27.0	27.3	27.2	27.1	26.3
2003	27.0	27.3	27.5	27.9	28.0	28.1	27.7	27.6	28.1	28.6	28.8	28.6	27.9
Leisure and hospitality													
1990	19.5	19.9	20.2	19.9	20.2	20.8	20.4	20.6	20.7	20.2	20.7	20.9	20.3
1991	20.3	20.2	20.2	20.4	20.6	21.0	21.3	21.2	21.1	21.2	21.0	20.8	20.7
1992	19.8	20.1	20.4	21.0	21.3	21.9	21.7	21.8	21.9	21.5	21.7	21.3	21.2
1993	20.6	20.7	21.0	21.0	21.4	21.5	21.8	21.8	21.5	20.7	20.9	21.0	21.1
1994	20.3	20.8	21.1	21.2	21.5	21.7	22.5	22.7	22.8	21.5	21.6	21.2	21.5
1995	21.2	21.5	22.2	22.3	22.5	22.6	22.9	22.8	22.7	22.4	22.3	22.3	22.3
1996	21.8	22.1	22.4	21.9	22.2	22.4	22.6	22.7	22.4	21.9	22.6	22.4	22.2
1997	21.6	21.7	22.0	22.1	22.4	22.5	22.2	22.1	21.9	21.8	21.9	21.9	22.0
1998	21.7	21.9	22.0	22.2	22.7	22.9	22.4	22.5	22.4	22.0	22.2	22.4	22.2
1999	22.4	22.6	23.1	22.9	23.3	23.6	23.7	23.9	23.8	24.1	24.0	24.3	23.4
2000	23.8	24.2	24.5	24.8	25.2	25.5	25.7	25.8	25.7	25.8	25.6	25.7	25.1
2001	25.6	25.8	26.1	26.6	27.0	27.1	26.8	27.0	26.8	26.6	26.5	26.7	26.5
2002	25.8	26.1	26.5	26.8	27.2	27.6	28.1	28.0	28.0	27.6	27.5	27.5	27.2
2003	26.7	27.0	27.1	27.5	27.7	27.9	28.0	27.9	27.9	27.5	27.4	27.3	27.5
Other services													
1990	7.3	7.2	7.3	7.2	7.3	7.4	7.6	7.6	7.6	7.5	7.6	7.7	7.4
1991	8.2	8.3	8.2	8.0	8.1	8.2	8.3	8.3	8.3	8.3	8.2	8.2	8.2
1992	8.1	8.2	8.2	8.2	8.3	8.4	8.3	8.4	8.4	8.1	8.1	8.1	8.2
1993	8.1	8.1	8.2	8.3	8.3	8.4	8.4	8.4	8.4	8.2	8.1	8.2	8.2
1994	8.1	8.1	8.2	8.4	8.4	8.5	8.5	8.6	8.6	8.4	8.3	8.3	8.3
1995	8.3	8.4	8.4	8.5	8.4	8.5	8.7	8.7	8.6	8.6	8.5	8.5	8.5
1996	8.4	8.5	8.5	8.6	8.6	8.6	8.7	8.8	8.6	8.6	8.6	8.6	8.5
1997	8.7	8.8	8.9	8.9	9.0	9.0	9.2	9.3	9.2	9.0	9.1	9.1	9.0
1998	8.9	8.9	9.1	9.1	9.3	9.2	9.4	9.4	9.4	9.2	9.2	9.2	9.1
1999	9.1	9.2	9.3	9.5	9.6	9.6	9.6	9.7	9.6	9.4	9.5	9.5	9.4
2000	9.5	9.5	9.6	9.8	9.8	9.9	9.8	9.8	9.8	9.7	9.7	9.9	9.7
2001	9.4	9.5	9.7	9.5	9.7	9.7	9.4	9.4	9.7	9.8	9.9	9.9	9.6
2002	9.7	9.8	9.9	10.0	10.1	10.3	10.4	10.3	10.4	10.2	10.4	10.4	10.2
2003	10.2	10.3	10.3	10.7	10.7	10.8	10.7	10.6	10.6	10.4	10.4	10.2	10.5
Government													
1990	42.6	43.4	43.9	44.0	45.0	45.0	44.2	44.0	44.0	44.3	44.7	44.9	44.1
1991	44.1	44.6	44.9	45.2	45.0	45.6	46.0	43.4	44.5	44.7	45.0	45.8	44.9
1992	44.9	45.0	45.2	45.6	45.8	45.5	44.8	42.6	43.7	44.3	45.1	45.1	44.8
1993	43.9	44.1	44.2	44.2	44.2	43.8	43.2	39.8	41.0	42.8	43.7	43.8	43.2
1994	42.7	43.1	43.2	43.9	43.8	43.6	42.2	40.3	40.4	42.5	43.4	43.4	42.7
1995	42.9	43.0	43.2	44.7	43.7	44.1	42.7	40.4	41.2	43.1	43.8	43.6	43.0
1996	42.8	44.3	43.9	43.5	44.4	43.7	42.4	41.1	41.9	44.5	44.4	44.4	43.4
1997	43.4	44.1	44.3	44.6	44.6	44.0	39.2	40.7	41.5	44.5	44.5	44.6	43.3
1998	43.6	43.5	43.9	42.8	43.0	42.6	42.5	40.2	42.3	43.4	44.3	44.6	43.0
1999	44.2	44.2	44.2	44.4	43.9	44.0	43.4	41.6	43.9	43.8	44.6	44.9	43.9
2000	44.1	44.6	45.0	45.3	45.7	45.0	43.2	41.3	42.9	44.6	45.1	45.3	44.3
2001	45.8	45.6	45.4	44.7	44.9	44.2	44.9	42.7	44.2	45.6	46.6	46.8	45.1
2002	45.9	46.5	46.0	45.7	45.6	46.1	43.8	41.7	44.4	45.1	46.7	45.6	45.3
2003	45.5	45.5	46.1	45.8	46.6	46.0	42.9	41.5	43.6	43.7	44.1	43.7	44.6
Federal government													
1990	11.8	11.8	11.8	12.0	12.6	12.2	12.4	12.6	12.2	12.0	12.0	12.0	12.1
1991	12.0	12.0	12.0	12.2	12.2	12.3	12.5	12.5	12.5	12.5	12.4	12.4	12.2
1992	12.3	12.2	12.2	12.4	12.3	12.4	12.2	12.1	12.2	12.1	11.9	12.0	12.1
1993	11.6	11.5	11.4	11.4	11.3	11.3	11.2	11.3	11.4	11.3	11.3	11.3	11.3
1994	10.9	10.9	10.9	10.9	10.9	11.0	10.9	10.9	10.8	10.6	10.6	10.6	10.8
1995	10.4	10.4	10.4	10.4	10.5	10.5	10.5	10.4	10.4	10.3	10.2	10.2	10.3
1996	9.9	9.9	9.8	9.9	9.9	10.0	9.9	9.9	9.8	9.8	9.8	9.7	9.8
1997	9.4	9.4	9.3	9.3	9.2	9.3	9.3	9.2	9.2	9.2	9.1	9.1	9.2
1998	8.9	8.8	8.8	8.8	8.8	8.8	8.8	8.7	8.7	8.7	8.7	8.7	8.7
1999	8.5	8.5	8.5	8.7	8.4	8.4	8.6	8.6	8.7	8.5	8.5	8.3	8.5
2000	8.1	8.0	8.1	8.3	9.1	8.2	8.2	8.1	8.0	8.0	8.0	8.0	8.1
2001	8.0	7.9	7.9	7.9	7.9	7.9	8.0	8.0	8.0	8.0	8.0	8.0	7.9
2002	8.0	7.8	7.9	7.8	7.8	7.9	7.8	7.8	7.8	7.9	7.9	7.9	7.9
2003	8.0	8.0	7.9	7.7	7.8	7.8	7.7	7.7	7.8	7.7	7.6	7.7	7.8

Employment by Industry: California—*Continued*

(Numbers in thousands. Not seasonally adjusted.)

Industry	January	February	March	April	May	June	July	August	September	October	November	December	Annual Average
VENTURA—*Continued*													
State government													
1990	3.5	3.5	3.5	3.6	3.6	3.6	3.7	3.7	3.7	3.7	3.7	3.7	3.6
1991	3.7	3.7	3.7	3.7	3.8	3.8	3.7	3.7	3.7	3.7	3.7	3.7	3.7
1992	3.7	3.7	3.7	3.8	3.8	3.8	3.8	3.8	3.8	3.8	3.8	3.7	3.7
1993	3.7	3.7	3.6	3.7	3.7	3.7	3.7	3.6	3.7	3.6	3.6	3.5	3.6
1994	3.5	3.5	3.5	3.4	3.4	3.4	3.4	3.4	3.4	3.5	3.5	3.5	3.4
1995	3.5	3.5	3.4	3.5	3.5	3.4	3.5	3.4	3.4	3.5	3.4	3.4	3.4
1996	3.4	3.4	3.4	3.4	3.4	3.4	3.4	3.4	3.4	3.3	3.3	3.2	3.3
1997	3.1	3.1	3.1	3.1	2.9	2.3	2.0	2.0	1.9	1.9	1.9	1.9	2.4
1998	1.9	1.9	1.9	1.9	1.9	1.9	1.9	1.8	1.9	1.8	1.8	1.8	1.8
1999	1.8	1.8	1.8	1.8	1.8	1.8	1.8	1.8	1.8	1.8	1.8	1.7	1.7
2000	1.7	1.7	1.7	1.7	1.7	1.7	1.7	1.7	1.7	1.7	1.7	1.7	1.7
2001	1.7	1.7	1.7	1.7	1.8	1.8	1.9	1.9	2.0	1.9	1.9	1.9	1.8
2002	1.9	1.9	1.9	2.0	2.0	2.0	2.0	2.0	2.1	2.1	2.1	2.1	2.0
2003	2.0	2.0	2.2	2.2	2.2	2.2	2.2	2.2	2.3	2.3	2.3	2.3	2.2
Local government													
1990	27.3	28.1	28.6	28.4	28.8	29.2	28.1	27.7	28.1	28.6	29.0	29.2	28.4
1991	28.4	28.9	29.2	29.3	29.0	29.5	29.8	27.2	28.3	28.5	28.9	29.7	28.8
1992	28.9	29.1	29.3	29.4	29.7	29.3	28.8	26.7	27.7	28.4	29.4	29.4	28.8
1993	28.6	28.9	29.2	29.1	29.2	28.8	28.3	24.9	25.9	27.9	28.8	29.0	28.2
1994	28.3	28.7	28.8	29.6	29.5	29.2	27.9	26.0	26.2	28.4	29.3	29.3	28.4
1995	29.0	29.1	29.4	30.8	29.7	30.2	28.7	26.6	27.4	29.3	30.2	30.0	29.2
1996	29.5	31.0	30.7	30.2	31.1	30.3	29.1	27.8	28.7	31.4	31.3	31.5	30.2
1997	30.9	31.6	31.9	32.2	32.5	32.4	27.9	29.5	30.4	33.4	33.5	33.6	31.6
1998	32.8	32.8	33.2	32.1	32.3	31.9	31.8	29.7	31.7	32.9	33.8	34.1	32.4
1999	33.9	33.9	33.9	33.9	33.7	33.8	33.0	31.2	33.4	33.5	34.3	34.9	33.6
2000	34.3	34.9	35.2	35.3	34.9	35.1	33.3	31.5	33.2	34.9	35.4	35.6	34.4
2001	36.1	36.0	35.8	35.1	35.2	34.5	35.0	32.8	34.2	35.7	36.7	36.9	35.3
2002	36.0	36.8	36.2	35.9	35.8	36.2	34.0	31.9	34.5	35.1	36.7	35.6	35.4
2003	35.5	35.5	36.0	35.9	36.6	36.0	33.0	31.6	33.5	33.7	34.2	33.7	34.6

Average Weekly Hours by Industry: California

(Not seasonally adjusted.)

Industry	January	February	March	April	May	June	July	August	September	October	November	December	Annual Average
STATEWIDE													
Manufacturing													
2001	39.4	39.8	39.8	39.2	39.5	39.4	39.2	39.7	39.9	39.6	39.4	40.0	39.6
2002	38.5	39.1	39.8	39.6	39.5	40.0	39.0	39.9	40.2	39.8	40.0	40.4	39.6
2003	39.1	39.5	39.6	39.4	39.7	40.0	39.2	39.7	39.8	39.8	40.5	40.1	39.7
BAKERSFIELD													
Manufacturing													
2001	40.1	38.2	39.2	40.9	40.7	40.0	41.1	39.8	40.0	39.3	39.6	41.3	40.0
2002	39.9	38.8	39.8	40.1	40.8	39.0	38.0	38.6	36.9	35.7	36.1	37.7	38.4
2003	36.4	36.4	37.2	35.7	37.3	35.8	36.0	35.9	35.1	35.9	37.2	36.9	36.3
FRESNO													
Manufacturing													
2001	40.3	40.5	40.6	40.0	40.7	40.5	40.2	41.4	41.1	39.6	40.1	41.5	40.5
2002	40.1	39.1	39.4	39.9	39.8	41.0	40.1	40.8	41.1	40.0	39.5	39.6	40.1
2003	39.0	38.5	39.7	38.7	38.9	38.8	39.4	40.6	40.6	39.0	40.8	40.1	39.5
LOS ANGELES-LONG BEACH													
Manufacturing													
2001	39.8	39.9	40.1	39.2	39.7	39.4	39.3	39.3	39.6	39.5	39.4	39.9	39.6
2002	38.7	39.7	40.2	40.0	39.8	40.3	39.7	40.3	40.6	40.3	40.5	40.6	40.0
2003	40.0	39.7	40.1	40.0	39.9	39.6	39.0	39.4	40.0	39.8	40.4	40.1	39.8
OAKLAND													
Manufacturing													
2001	39.8	40.9	40.8	40.9	41.9	41.5	43.6	41.3	41.0	41.6	41.6	41.5	41.3
2002	43.2	41.1	42.1	42.7	43.3	42.7	41.1	41.6	41.4	40.7	42.1	42.1	42.0
2003	41.7	40.7	41.1	40.6	40.2	40.4	40.3	40.5	41.7	41.4	41.8	41.7	41.0
SACRAMENTO													
Manufacturing													
2001	37.5	37.7	37.6	38.0	38.2	38.3	38.5	39.1	39.3	40.0	40.1	39.9	38.7
2002	38.4	39.4	38.3	38.4	39.0	39.8	38.7	39.0	40.7	39.6	39.4	40.4	39.2
2003	39.7	39.4	40.1	39.6	39.9	40.5	39.2	40.7	40.9	39.9	40.8	40.9	40.1
SAN DIEGO													
Manufacturing													
2001	40.6	40.9	41.3	40.0	40.5	40.4	39.7	39.1	39.5	39.1	39.1	39.7	40.0
2002	38.3	39.7	40.8	40.4	40.1	40.7	39.4	40.0	39.4	39.6	39.2	40.8	39.9
2003	39.3	40.3	39.5	39.7	40.6	40.7	39.5	39.6	39.4	39.8	39.8	39.6	39.8
SAN FRANCISCO													
Manufacturing													
2001	38.2	38.2	36.6	36.7	36.8	35.8	36.8	36.1	36.8	37.1	37.2	38.0	37.0
2002	35.8	35.6	35.1	35.3	35.3	36.2	35.4	36.2	36.1	37.4	36.8	37.7	36.1
2003	36.0	36.5	36.6	37.1	36.9	36.7	36.7	37.1	37.1	37.3	38.5	38.9	37.1
SAN JOSE													
Manufacturing													
2001	39.4	40.4	40.7	39.4	39.2	39.1	38.1	40.1	40.8	40.2	39.0	40.3	39.7
2002	38.8	39.0	40.3	39.4	39.9	40.4	38.7	39.7	40.1	39.7	39.4	40.0	39.6
2003	38.5	40.4	40.9	40.8	40.6	41.5	40.3	41.1	40.9	41.0	41.2	41.2	40.7
STOCKTON													
Manufacturing													
2001	37.6	38.2	38.3	38.6	39.4	38.5	37.9	39.6	40.6	39.7	38.4	37.9	38.7
2002	37.3	37.7	38.9	38.9	38.6	38.7	37.3	37.9	38.3	39.1	39.2	40.8	38.5
2003	39.6	39.8	40.4	40.5	39.8	40.6	40.0	41.4	39.1	40.5	39.9	39.8	40.1
VALLEJO-FAIRFIELD-NAPA													
Manufacturing													
2001	40.8	38.8	39.1	37.6	38.2	36.5	39.1	38.6	37.5	37.6	38.8	38.2	38.4
2002	38.5	39.4	40.9	40.7	41.5	40.5	39.8	41.2	44.9	40.4	40.0	39.9	40.7
2003	39.3	39.4	40.2	40.0	40.5	41.1	41.1	40.4	40.8	41.3	41.0	40.1	40.4
VENTURA													
Manufacturing													
2001	42.5	42.4	41.8	41.7	40.8	41.3	42.0	41.4	42.0	41.4	42.2	42.3	41.8
2002	41.8	41.5	42.2	41.3	41.7	42.0	42.9	41.9	44.1	43.5	43.2	42.9	42.4
2003	42.0	41.3	41.2	40.7	41.3	42.1	41.3	41.4	41.6	41.9	42.5	41.8	41.6

Average Hourly Earnings by Industry: California

(Dollars, not seasonally adjusted.)

Industry	January	February	March	April	May	June	July	August	September	October	November	December	Annual Average
STATEWIDE													
Manufacturing													
2001	14.50	14.47	14.48	14.56	14.59	14.72	14.85	14.76	14.80	14.78	14.84	14.99	14.69
2002	15.02	14.94	14.87	14.89	14.85	14.89	14.86	14.76	14.80	14.79	14.93	15.12	14.89
2003	15.02	14.97	14.97	14.92	14.95	15.03	15.10	15.05	15.07	15.05	15.15	15.26	15.05
BAKERSFIELD													
Manufacturing													
2001	17.53	17.40	17.28	17.35	17.12	16.95	16.82	16.75	16.66	16.86	17.07	16.99	17.06
2002	16.74	16.56	16.52	16.28	16.13	16.17	16.03	15.86	15.70	15.51	15.59	15.54	16.04
2003	15.46	15.39	15.56	15.52	15.30	15.34	15.32	15.35	15.48	15.45	15.43	15.46	15.42
FRESNO													
Manufacturing													
2001	13.07	12.93	12.93	13.03	13.01	13.16	13.08	12.94	12.85	12.85	12.96	13.01	12.98
2002	12.92	12.97	13.10	13.16	13.19	13.15	13.23	13.26	13.20	13.33	13.29	13.26	13.18
2003	13.16	13.21	13.25	13.29	13.23	13.26	13.21	13.04	12.96	13.18	13.27	13.31	13.19
LOS ANGELES-LONG BEACH													
Manufacturing													
2001	12.78	12.78	12.78	12.76	12.82	13.03	13.12	13.17	13.26	13.19	13.26	13.35	13.02
2002	13.22	13.17	13.14	13.05	13.04	13.02	13.11	13.11	13.17	13.16	13.19	13.33	13.14
2003	13.21	13.27	13.20	13.17	13.17	13.30	13.35	13.32	13.38	13.41	13.40	13.41	13.30
OAKLAND													
Manufacturing													
2001	17.74	17.48	17.66	17.66	17.85	17.85	17.71	17.67	17.86	17.72	17.89	18.00	17.75
2002	18.23	18.26	18.26	18.41	18.14	18.21	18.04	18.18	18.14	17.86	17.99	18.22	18.16
2003	18.26	18.13	18.27	18.25	18.29	18.48	18.40	18.40	18.47	18.32	18.33	18.33	18.33
SACRAMENTO													
Manufacturing													
2001	14.74	14.32	14.27	14.49	14.79	14.80	15.00	15.11	15.41	15.47	15.54	15.64	14.97
2002	15.74	15.88	15.94	15.81	15.82	15.72	15.88	15.79	15.69	15.63	15.71	15.76	15.78
2003	15.53	15.78	15.59	15.66	15.62	15.69	15.79	16.02	15.86	16.12	16.19	16.25	15.85
SAN DIEGO													
Manufacturing													
2001	15.27	15.02	15.05	14.97	15.10	14.90	15.05	14.89	14.99	15.10	15.28	15.44	15.09
2002	15.44	15.35	15.15	15.44	15.23	15.13	15.17	15.02	15.04	15.04	15.14	15.04	15.18
2003	14.86	15.02	14.98	15.06	14.85	14.80	14.77	14.87	15.03	14.87	14.93	14.91	14.91
SAN FRANCISCO													
Manufacturing													
2001	14.10	14.20	14.41	14.42	14.43	14.34	14.30	14.31	14.05	14.16	14.16	14.61	14.29
2002	14.86	14.57	14.54	14.46	14.71	14.68	14.90	14.95	14.95	14.88	14.98	14.86	14.78
2003	14.98	14.87	14.90	14.84	14.87	15.01	15.19	15.30	15.33	15.36	15.29	15.36	15.11
SAN JOSE													
Manufacturing													
2001	19.14	19.19	19.09	19.28	19.49	19.70	19.86	20.03	20.26	20.46	20.65	20.90	19.81
2002	20.69	20.72	20.77	20.80	20.85	20.89	20.90	20.93	20.99	21.01	21.09	21.14	20.89
2003	20.93	21.06	21.02	20.88	20.98	21.14	20.92	20.93	21.02	21.17	21.24	21.21	21.04
STOCKTON													
Manufacturing													
2001	13.33	13.06	13.11	13.22	13.28	13.27	13.35	13.34	13.15	13.23	13.28	13.35	13.25
2002	13.44	13.48	13.45	13.59	13.58	13.52	13.65	13.58	13.46	13.45	13.47	13.55	13.52
2003	13.47	13.43	13.51	13.67	13.90	14.01	14.15	14.11	14.00	13.83	14.04	14.10	13.86
VALLEJO-FAIRFIELD-NAPA													
Manufacturing													
2001	15.52	15.48	15.54	15.59	15.76	15.35	15.63	15.48	15.75	16.07	15.98	16.23	15.69
2002	16.33	16.05	15.71	15.99	16.10	16.64	16.24	16.37	16.41	16.25	16.54	16.88	16.29
2003	16.69	16.44	16.33	16.44	16.55	16.66	16.76	16.87	16.98	17.09	16.92	17.04	16.73
VENTURA													
Manufacturing													
2001	15.34	15.22	15.12	15.24	15.44	15.13	15.13	15.23	15.49	15.49	15.57	15.62	15.33
2002	15.51	15.44	15.56	15.68	15.59	15.75	15.61	15.90	15.78	15.83	15.95	15.98	15.72
2003	15.81	15.90	15.89	15.77	15.92	15.86	15.84	16.01	15.83	15.91	15.93	15.99	15.89

Average Weekly Earnings by Industry: California

(Dollars, not seasonally adjusted.)

Industry	January	February	March	April	May	June	July	August	September	October	November	December	Annual Average
STATEWIDE													
Manufacturing													
2001	571.30	575.91	576.30	570.75	576.31	579.97	582.12	585.97	590.52	585.29	584.70	599.60	581.72
2002	578.27	584.15	591.83	589.64	586.58	595.60	579.54	588.92	594.96	588.64	597.20	610.85	589.64
2003	587.28	591.32	592.81	587.85	593.52	601.20	591.92	597.49	599.79	598.99	613.58	611.93	597.49
BAKERSFIELD													
Manufacturing													
2001	702.95	664.68	677.38	709.62	696.78	678.00	691.30	666.65	666.40	662.60	675.97	701.69	682.40
2002	667.93	642.53	657.50	652.83	658.10	630.63	609.14	612.20	579.33	553.71	562.80	585.86	615.94
2003	562.74	560.20	578.83	554.06	570.69	549.17	551.52	551.07	543.35	554.66	574.00	570.47	559.75
FRESNO													
Manufacturing													
2001	526.72	523.67	524.96	521.20	529.51	532.98	525.82	535.72	528.14	508.86	519.70	539.92	525.69
2002	518.09	507.13	516.14	525.08	524.96	539.15	530.52	541.01	542.52	533.20	524.96	525.10	528.52
2003	513.24	508.59	526.03	514.32	514.65	514.49	520.47	529.42	526.18	514.02	541.42	533.73	521.01
LOS ANGELES-LONG BEACH													
Manufacturing													
2001	508.64	509.92	512.48	500.19	508.95	513.38	515.62	517.58	525.10	521.01	522.44	532.67	515.59
2002	511.61	522.85	528.23	522.00	518.99	524.71	520.47	528.33	534.70	530.35	534.20	541.20	525.60
2003	528.40	526.82	529.32	526.80	525.48	526.68	520.65	524.81	535.20	533.72	541.36	537.74	529.34
OAKLAND													
Manufacturing													
2001	706.05	714.93	720.53	722.29	747.92	740.78	772.16	729.77	732.26	737.15	744.22	747.00	733.08
2002	787.54	750.49	768.75	786.11	785.46	777.57	741.44	756.29	751.00	726.90	757.38	767.06	762.72
2003	761.44	737.89	750.90	740.95	735.26	746.59	741.52	745.20	770.20	758.45	766.19	764.36	751.53
SACRAMENTO													
Manufacturing													
2001	552.75	539.86	536.55	550.62	564.98	566.84	577.50	590.80	605.61	618.80	623.15	624.04	579.34
2002	604.42	625.67	610.50	607.10	616.98	625.66	614.56	615.81	638.58	618.95	618.97	636.70	618.58
2003	616.54	621.73	625.16	620.14	623.24	635.45	618.97	652.01	648.67	643.19	660.55	664.63	635.59
SAN DIEGO													
Manufacturing													
2001	619.96	614.32	621.57	598.80	611.55	601.96	597.49	582.20	592.11	590.41	597.45	612.97	603.60
2002	591.35	609.40	618.12	623.78	610.72	615.79	597.70	600.80	592.58	595.58	593.49	613.63	605.68
2003	584.00	605.31	591.71	597.88	602.91	602.36	583.42	588.85	592.18	591.83	594.21	590.44	593.42
SAN FRANCISCO													
Manufacturing													
2001	538.62	542.44	527.41	529.21	531.02	513.37	526.24	516.59	517.04	525.34	526.75	555.18	528.73
2002	531.99	518.69	510.35	510.44	519.26	531.42	527.46	541.19	539.70	556.51	551.26	560.22	533.56
2003	539.28	542.76	545.34	550.56	548.70	550.87	557.47	567.63	568.74	572.93	588.67	597.50	560.58
SAN JOSE													
Manufacturing													
2001	754.12	775.28	776.96	759.63	764.01	770.27	756.67	803.20	826.61	822.49	805.35	842.27	786.46
2002	802.77	808.08	837.03	819.52	831.92	843.96	808.83	830.92	841.70	834.10	830.95	845.60	827.24
2003	805.81	850.82	859.72	851.90	851.79	877.31	843.08	860.22	859.72	867.97	875.09	873.85	856.33
STOCKTON													
Manufacturing													
2001	501.21	498.89	502.11	510.29	523.23	510.90	505.97	528.26	533.89	525.23	509.95	505.97	512.78
2002	501.31	508.20	523.21	528.65	524.19	523.22	509.15	514.68	515.52	525.90	528.02	552.84	520.52
2003	533.41	534.51	545.80	553.64	553.22	568.81	566.00	584.15	547.40	560.12	560.20	561.18	555.79
VALLEJO-FAIRFIELD-NAPA													
Manufacturing													
2001	633.22	600.62	607.61	586.18	602.03	560.28	611.13	597.53	590.63	604.23	620.02	619.99	602.50
2002	628.71	632.37	642.54	650.79	668.15	673.92	646.35	674.44	736.81	656.50	661.60	673.51	663.00
2003	655.92	647.74	656.47	657.60	670.28	684.73	688.84	681.55	692.78	705.82	693.72	683.30	675.89
VENTURA													
Manufacturing													
2001	651.95	645.33	632.02	635.51	629.95	624.87	635.46	630.52	650.58	641.29	657.05	660.73	640.79
2002	648.32	640.76	656.63	647.58	650.10	661.50	669.67	666.21	695.90	688.61	689.04	685.54	666.53
2003	664.02	656.67	654.67	641.84	657.50	667.71	654.19	662.81	658.53	666.63	677.03	668.38	661.02

COLORADO AT A GLANCE

(Population and total nonfarm employment numbers in thousands)

Population, Census 2000:	4,301.3
Total nonfarm employment, 2003:	2,150.4
Change in total nonfarm employment	
(Number)	
1990–2003:	629.6
1990–2001:	704.6
2001–2003:	-75.0
(Compound annual rate of change)	
1990–2003:	2.7%
1990–2001:	3.5%
2001–2003:	-1.7%
Unemployment rate	
1990:	5.1%
2001:	3.9%
2003:	6.2%

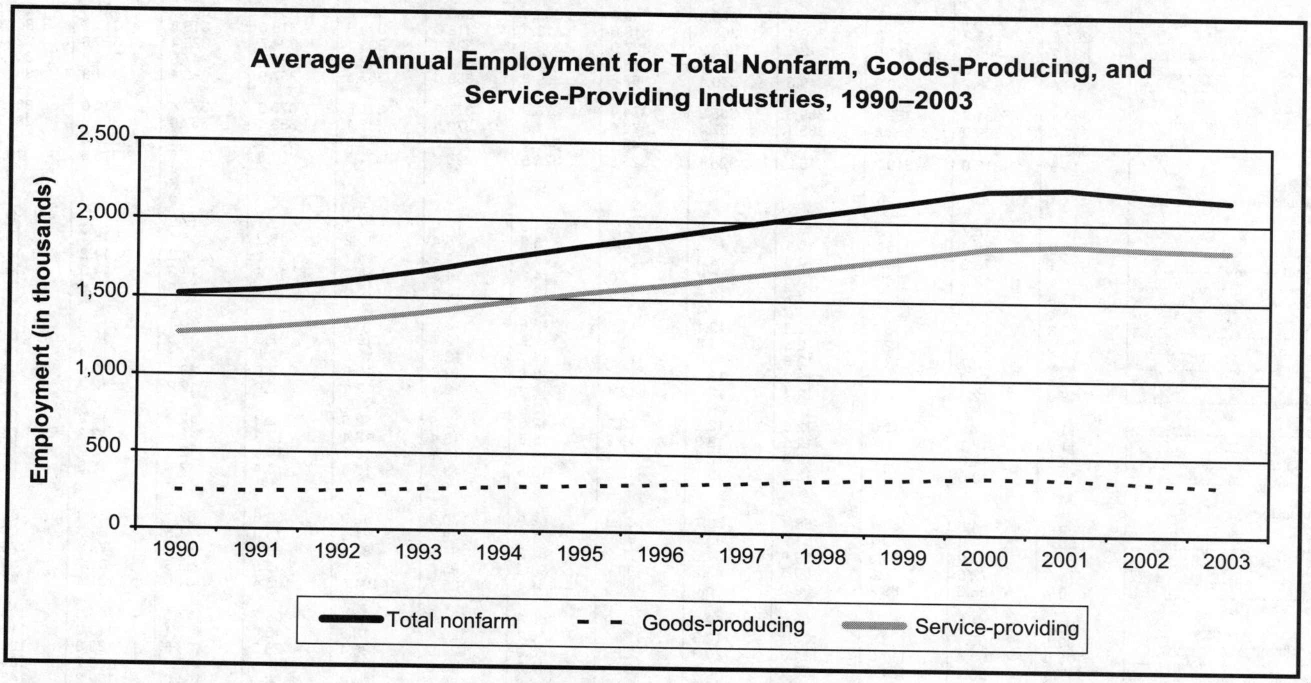

Nonfarm payroll employment grew steadily throughout the 1990s, but fell off during the 2001 recession with sharp declines in private sector employment. Manufacturing and, to a lesser extent, construction, were hard-hit by the 2001 recession, and service sector jobs also slowed significantly. However, construction employment grew rapidly in the 1990s and accounted for 7 percent of Colorado's employment in 2003, up from about 4 percent in 1990.

Employment by Industry: Colorado

(Numbers in thousands. Not seasonally adjusted.)

Industry	January	February	March	April	May	June	July	August	September	October	November	December	Annual Average
STATEWIDE													
Total nonfarm													
1990	1478.0	1490.9	1502.7	1506.5	1517.0	1537.2	1521.6	1531.5	1535.2	1532.0	1544.5	1553.5	1520.8
1991	1513.2	1520.1	1529.1	1530.4	1533.0	1555.5	1543.5	1548.2	1554.9	1558.8	1568.5	1584.7	1544.9
1992	1545.9	1557.9	1569.0	1578.5	1584.4	1605.9	1603.4	1607.5	1615.6	1623.3	1627.5	1644.7	1596.9
1993	1609.9	1627.1	1642.7	1655.7	1651.3	1678.2	1677.9	1685.0	1688.9	1697.2	1704.1	1730.3	1670.7
1994	1688.9	1704.9	1719.3	1735.1	1737.8	1766.6	1761.7	1771.9	1779.9	1782.7	1797.1	1824.4	1755.9
1995	1774.3	1793.2	1811.5	1811.3	1815.5	1848.2	1836.6	1848.6	1858.0	1855.2	1867.5	1893.0	1834.4
1996	1841.1	1856.0	1874.7	1879.8	1889.6	1913.9	1898.7	1916.9	1920.5	1919.2	1935.7	1958.3	1900.4
1997	1913.5	1932.0	1947.4	1944.8	1960.0	1990.1	1990.2	1997.3	2003.5	2008.7	2019.7	2046.5	1979.5
1998	1996.7	2012.1	2026.6	2031.6	2040.7	2068.4	2070.5	2073.4	2076.6	2079.8	2089.1	2115.3	2056.7
1999	2068.1	2090.1	2099.0	2122.6	2115.3	2147.2	2144.1	2144.4	2147.5	2151.2	2160.7	2188.3	2131.5
2000	2133.2	2155.0	2180.2	2186.8	2201.1	2232.8	2226.1	2237.8	2238.3	2236.2	2250.1	2273.3	2212.6
2001	2209.1	2221.3	2235.1	2229.1	2230.7	2260.5	2238.6	2238.7	2224.0	2204.9	2202.2	2210.6	2225.4
2002	2147.2	2158.0	2171.3	2180.2	2189.5	2212.6	2192.0	2198.0	2187.3	2177.1	2181.3	2196.0	2182.5
2003	2129.6	2133.6	2137.5	2138.0	2145.3	2166.7	2153.8	2161.5	2155.9	2156.9	2159.3	2167.1	2150.4
Total private													
1990	1210.2	1211.8	1221.5	1223.9	1231.0	1257.0	1261.9	1274.4	1259.7	1249.5	1258.0	1269.8	1244.0
1991	1238.0	1235.3	1242.7	1242.6	1243.1	1270.3	1276.0	1284.1	1272.1	1266.6	1275.5	1293.6	1261.6
1992	1264.1	1265.8	1274.5	1284.3	1287.4	1313.8	1329.1	1333.5	1324.1	1322.7	1326.2	1345.5	1305.9
1993	1321.0	1327.3	1341.1	1352.6	1347.4	1381.5	1397.6	1405.6	1394.7	1392.9	1399.4	1427.2	1374.0
1994	1397.1	1402.6	1415.8	1429.0	1432.0	1467.9	1480.8	1489.5	1481.0	1475.5	1489.4	1518.6	1456.6
1995	1480.2	1487.7	1503.5	1503.5	1506.0	1544.7	1550.6	1560.9	1552.5	1543.2	1554.7	1581.4	1530.7
1996	1541.3	1545.0	1560.9	1566.0	1573.2	1605.4	1607.9	1626.1	1611.2	1602.9	1617.6	1642.0	1591.6
1997	1605.5	1615.3	1628.7	1625.5	1638.2	1674.8	1690.9	1700.7	1687.2	1684.0	1693.9	1722.1	1663.9
1998	1681.6	1688.6	1701.4	1706.0	1711.9	1747.1	1763.1	1769.0	1754.1	1749.4	1756.7	1783.9	1734.4
1999	1748.0	1760.1	1767.4	1790.1	1780.3	1819.5	1831.9	1833.6	1817.9	1814.8	1823.9	1850.7	1803.2
2000	1809.4	1819.6	1839.5	1845.3	1852.0	1895.2	1904.9	1915.2	1900.5	1892.3	1904.8	1928.0	1875.6
2001	1877.0	1877.2	1890.1	1883.8	1882.1	1916.4	1910.4	1908.5	1876.5	1851.5	1846.4	1855.5	1881.3
2002	1803.1	1803.1	1813.1	1822.0	1827.2	1856.9	1853.3	1857.5	1830.8	1812.3	1815.4	1831.3	1827.2
2003	1779.1	1773.1	1775.0	1776.8	1779.1	1811.1	1815.9	1822.8	1799.9	1792.1	1794.7	1804.4	1793.7
Goods-producing													
1990	240.8	239.3	240.7	244.3	248.9	255.1	256.8	258.8	256.6	256.2	254.7	252.1	250.3
1991	241.6	239.8	240.6	240.0	244.4	248.9	251.6	253.9	252.2	252.3	250.4	247.6	246.9
1992	240.1	240.1	240.9	246.4	251.5	255.8	260.1	260.6	260.6	262.1	259.4	255.2	252.7
1993	249.1	249.4	253.1	257.6	263.1	270.1	276.1	278.1	279.0	279.7	277.1	275.3	267.3
1994	268.2	266.6	269.0	276.1	281.5	289.3	291.4	293.3	293.9	294.9	294.8	290.2	284.1
1995	283.4	284.1	286.7	289.7	293.5	299.9	302.6	303.7	303.9	304.0	303.5	302.7	296.5
1996	291.8	293.2	297.8	300.1	306.3	313.0	313.0	316.8	314.5	315.5	315.8	313.7	307.6
1997	304.2	306.3	311.0	312.5	320.9	327.0	333.2	334.0	333.1	334.5	329.4	329.6	323.0
1998	324.7	325.8	330.5	335.7	341.7	348.8	351.3	352.5	352.3	350.7	347.6	346.8	342.4
1999	336.6	338.7	340.9	349.3	350.4	357.6	359.3	359.0	357.1	357.9	356.1	354.8	351.5
2000	348.1	351.3	357.1	359.3	365.9	374.4	376.0	377.3	375.6	375.3	372.4	372.0	367.1
2001	359.2	359.0	362.8	363.1	367.4	372.9	371.8	370.5	365.1	359.1	352.9	346.5	362.5
2002	332.6	331.7	335.2	338.9	344.7	349.1	348.4	348.1	342.3	339.2	334.1	329.3	339.5
2003	316.6	313.8	313.2	315.3	320.1	325.6	325.5	325.6	321.5	321.3	317.7	313.6	319.2
Natural resources and mining													
1990	16.7	16.7	16.7	16.8	17.0	17.4	17.6	17.5	17.1	17.1	17.2	17.0	17.0
1991	16.0	15.4	15.2	15.1	15.2	15.3	15.3	15.4	15.2	15.2	15.1	15.1	15.2
1992	14.1	13.9	13.7	14.0	14.0	14.1	14.2	14.2	14.1	14.1	14.2	14.2	14.0
1993	14.1	13.8	13.7	13.5	13.7	13.9	14.2	14.3	14.3	14.2	14.3	14.3	14.0
1994	13.9	13.8	13.5	13.7	13.7	13.8	13.5	13.6	13.8	13.8	13.8	14.0	13.7
1995	13.5	13.4	13.2	13.2	13.1	13.5	13.8	13.5	13.3	13.2	13.1	13.0	13.3
1996	12.5	12.5	12.7	12.5	12.6	12.8	12.6	12.7	12.6	12.5	12.5	12.6	12.6
1997	12.6	12.7	12.8	12.8	13.0	13.4	13.7	13.6	13.5	13.5	13.3	13.4	13.2
1998	13.2	13.2	13.4	13.2	13.5	13.7	13.8	13.6	13.6	13.2	13.1	13.0	13.4
1999	12.6	12.5	12.7	12.4	12.3	12.4	12.2	12.1	12.1	12.2	12.2	12.2	12.3
2000	11.9	11.9	12.0	12.0	12.2	12.3	12.5	12.5	12.5	12.3	12.2	12.2	12.2
2001	11.9	12.1	12.4	12.5	12.8	13.2	13.5	13.4	13.4	13.3	13.4	13.3	12.9
2002	12.9	12.8	12.9	12.8	12.9	13.1	13.2	13.1	13.1	13.0	12.8	12.7	12.9
2003	12.5	12.6	12.7	12.8	13.1	13.3	13.5	13.6	13.5	13.4	13.4	13.0	13.1
Construction													
1990	55.7	54.6	55.7	58.4	62.7	66.8	68.0	70.0	68.9	68.6	67.1	64.3	63.4
1991	58.4	57.8	59.4	61.9	65.5	69.1	71.3	72.7	71.5	73.0	71.5	68.7	66.7
1992	63.3	63.9	65.0	69.9	74.6	78.2	81.3	81.9	82.1	83.0	80.7	76.6	75.0
1993	71.3	72.5	76.6	80.5	85.2	89.7	94.2	95.6	95.0	95.9	93.5	91.7	86.8
1994	86.7	85.6	88.2	92.3	96.0	101.5	104.1	105.1	104.5	105.4	104.0	101.4	97.9
1995	93.9	94.0	96.6	98.5	102.0	106.9	109.3	110.7	109.9	108.7	107.5	106.0	103.7
1996	99.1	100.4	103.8	107.1	112.3	117.4	118.1	120.4	118.6	118.0	117.1	113.9	112.2
1997	106.0	108.4	111.6	114.3	120.3	125.3	128.0	129.0	128.4	128.5	123.5	123.0	120.5
1998	117.9	120.5	124.2	128.1	133.4	138.8	142.8	143.7	143.5	142.9	140.5	138.7	134.6
1999	133.1	135.4	138.7	145.1	147.2	153.7	156.2	156.7	154.6	155.0	154.0	152.2	148.5
2000	146.5	149.6	154.8	157.7	163.9	170.4	171.5	172.8	171.2	170.6	167.7	165.9	163.6
2001	159.1	159.4	163.1	165.3	169.7	175.2	175.7	176.1	172.9	169.6	165.4	160.3	167.7
2002	150.5	151.3	154.5	158.8	164.3	168.4	168.5	168.8	164.5	162.2	158.5	154.3	160.4
2003	145.2	143.1	143.4	145.6	150.4	155.4	156.2	156.2	153.5	153.2	149.8	145.5	149.8

Employment by Industry: Colorado—*Continued*

(Numbers in thousands. Not seasonally adjusted.)

Industry	January	February	March	April	May	June	July	August	September	October	November	December	Annual Average
STATEWIDE—*Continued*													
Manufacturing													
1990	168.4	168.0	168.3	169.1	169.2	170.9	171.2	171.3	170.6	170.5	170.4	170.8	169.8
1991	167.2	166.6	166.0	163.0	163.7	164.5	165.0	165.8	165.5	164.1	163.8	163.8	164.9
1992	162.7	162.3	162.2	162.5	162.9	163.5	164.6	164.5	164.4	165.0	164.5	164.4	163.6
1993	163.7	163.1	162.8	163.6	164.2	166.5	167.7	168.2	169.7	169.6	169.3	169.3	166.5
1994	167.6	167.2	167.3	170.1	171.8	174.0	173.8	174.6	175.6	175.7	177.0	174.8	172.5
1995	176.0	176.7	176.9	178.0	178.4	179.5	179.5	179.5	180.7	182.1	182.9	183.7	179.5
1996	180.2	180.3	181.3	180.5	181.4	182.8	182.3	183.7	183.3	185.0	186.2	187.2	182.9
1997	185.6	185.2	186.6	185.4	187.6	188.3	191.5	191.4	191.2	192.5	192.6	193.2	189.3
1998	193.6	192.1	192.9	194.4	194.8	196.3	194.7	195.2	195.2	194.6	194.0	195.1	194.4
1999	190.9	190.8	189.5	191.8	190.9	191.5	190.9	190.2	190.4	190.7	189.9	190.4	190.7
2000	189.7	189.8	190.3	189.6	189.8	191.7	192.0	192.0	191.9	192.4	192.5	193.9	191.3
2001	188.2	187.5	187.3	185.3	184.9	184.5	182.6	181.0	178.8	176.2	174.1	172.9	181.9
2002	169.2	167.6	167.8	167.3	167.5	167.6	166.7	166.2	164.7	164.0	162.8	162.3	166.1
2003	158.9	158.1	157.1	156.9	156.6	156.9	155.8	155.8	154.5	154.7	154.5	155.1	156.2
Service-providing													
1990	1237.2	1251.6	1262.0	1262.2	1268.1	1282.1	1264.8	1272.7	1278.6	1275.8	1289.8	1301.4	1270.5
1991	1271.6	1280.3	1288.5	1290.4	1288.6	1306.6	1291.9	1294.3	1302.7	1306.5	1318.1	1337.1	1298.0
1992	1305.8	1317.8	1328.1	1332.1	1332.9	1350.1	1343.3	1346.9	1355.0	1361.2	1368.1	1389.5	1344.2
1993	1360.8	1377.7	1389.6	1398.1	1388.2	1408.1	1401.8	1406.9	1409.9	1417.5	1427.0	1455.0	1403.4
1994	1420.7	1438.3	1450.3	1459.0	1456.3	1477.3	1470.3	1478.6	1486.0	1487.8	1502.3	1534.2	1471.8
1995	1490.9	1509.1	1524.8	1521.6	1522.0	1548.3	1534.0	1544.9	1554.1	1551.2	1564.0	1590.3	1537.9
1996	1549.3	1562.8	1576.9	1579.7	1583.3	1600.9	1585.7	1600.1	1606.0	1603.7	1619.9	1644.6	1592.7
1997	1609.3	1625.7	1636.4	1632.3	1639.1	1663.1	1657.0	1663.3	1670.4	1674.2	1690.3	1716.9	1656.5
1998	1672.0	1686.3	1696.1	1695.9	1699.0	1719.6	1719.2	1720.9	1724.3	1729.1	1741.5	1768.5	1714.4
1999	1731.5	1751.4	1758.1	1773.3	1764.9	1789.6	1784.8	1785.4	1790.4	1793.3	1804.6	1833.5	1780.1
2000	1785.1	1803.7	1823.1	1827.5	1835.2	1858.4	1850.1	1860.5	1862.7	1860.9	1877.7	1901.3	1845.5
2001	1849.9	1862.3	1872.3	1866.0	1863.3	1887.6	1866.8	1868.2	1858.9	1845.8	1849.3	1864.1	1862.9
2002	1814.6	1826.3	1836.1	1841.3	1844.8	1863.5	1843.6	1849.9	1845.0	1837.9	1847.2	1866.7	1843.1
2003	1813.0	1819.8	1824.3	1822.7	1825.2	1841.1	1828.3	1835.9	1834.4	1835.6	1841.6	1853.5	1831.3
Trade, transportation, and utilities													
1990	299.9	296.5	297.5	298.6	304.1	304.5	304.0	306.9	306.5	306.6	312.6	317.6	304.6
1991	305.2	300.7	301.1	299.7	300.4	303.9	304.3	306.3	305.5	306.9	312.7	318.9	305.4
1992	307.6	303.6	304.7	306.6	308.0	311.0	313.5	314.2	314.3	315.5	320.5	328.3	312.3
1993	315.9	315.0	316.5	319.1	318.3	323.2	325.6	327.1	326.0	329.1	335.6	344.7	324.7
1994	331.0	330.1	331.0	334.4	336.8	341.8	345.8	348.2	348.3	348.5	356.7	368.2	343.4
1995	351.2	349.7	351.9	353.0	354.4	359.3	360.7	363.1	363.8	365.5	372.7	382.0	360.6
1996	368.5	365.9	366.8	365.9	367.5	370.0	369.6	374.5	373.8	371.9	381.2	389.6	372.1
1997	375.6	372.7	373.3	372.1	374.2	378.0	382.3	384.2	382.9	385.1	392.5	402.7	381.3
1998	386.2	383.7	384.1	383.9	385.6	389.7	394.0	394.1	392.8	397.0	404.5	413.1	392.4
1999	398.2	397.0	396.8	399.1	397.7	402.8	405.5	406.1	405.2	406.4	416.3	427.1	404.9
2000	410.1	409.1	409.3	411.2	412.1	416.8	416.5	420.6	419.7	423.7	435.1	443.0	418.9
2001	425.2	420.3	421.4	420.2	420.7	425.2	423.8	423.6	420.7	419.8	425.4	429.3	423.0
2002	409.0	405.3	406.4	408.1	410.3	415.0	413.7	413.6	410.6	409.8	418.3	424.6	412.1
2003	405.6	401.6	400.8	399.5	399.5	402.5	403.4	405.2	404.2	404.1	410.7	411.8	404.1
Wholesale trade													
1990	71.3	71.5	71.9	72.2	72.7	73.4	72.8	73.2	73.4	73.7	73.8	73.5	72.7
1991	71.8	71.8	72.0	71.2	71.5	72.2	72.3	72.4	72.6	72.8	72.8	73.2	72.2
1992	73.1	72.9	73.4	73.6	74.2	74.7	75.3	75.2	75.5	75.5	75.5	75.8	74.5
1993	75.0	75.5	76.0	76.4	76.8	77.5	77.7	77.5	77.6	78.0	78.2	78.9	77.1
1994	77.7	78.3	78.7	78.9	79.7	80.7	81.3	81.7	82.0	81.7	82.3	83.3	80.5
1995	81.9	82.6	83.3	83.2	83.6	84.4	84.4	84.4	84.5	84.7	84.7	85.3	83.9
1996	83.6	84.4	85.1	84.7	84.2	85.1	85.8	86.6	86.8	87.3	87.8	88.4	85.8
1997	87.6	88.3	88.8	88.2	88.8	89.6	90.5	90.9	90.6	91.0	90.8	91.2	89.7
1998	89.4	90.9	92.2	92.4	92.9	92.7	92.9	93.0	92.9	93.4	93.2	93.8	92.5
1999	93.5	94.2	94.0	93.9	93.6	94.3	94.8	94.8	94.6	94.8	95.2	96.1	94.5
2000	96.9	97.5	98.4	98.9	99.8	100.6	99.3	99.6	99.4	100.2	100.5	101.1	99.4
2001	100.0	100.8	101.0	100.5	100.4	100.7	100.1	100.0	99.2	98.5	98.1	98.0	99.8
2002	95.7	95.7	95.7	95.6	95.7	95.8	95.6	95.1	94.5	93.9	93.7	94.0	95.1
2003	92.8	92.3	92.4	92.3	92.3	92.7	92.6	92.4	92.4	92.1	91.1	91.2	92.2
Retail trade													
1990	170.3	166.6	166.6	167.4	172.4	171.4	171.7	173.7	172.9	172.5	178.2	182.6	172.1
1991	172.6	168.1	168.0	168.1	168.5	170.7	171.0	172.8	171.7	173.0	178.4	183.2	172.1
1992	173.5	169.6	169.4	171.0	172.0	174.0	175.6	176.0	175.7	176.7	181.3	187.3	175.1
1993	177.2	175.7	176.1	178.2	177.5	181.0	182.0	183.7	182.8	185.5	191.5	197.7	182.4
1994	187.6	185.4	186.0	188.7	190.1	193.4	196.5	198.3	198.3	199.9	206.8	215.0	195.5
1995	202.5	199.7	200.3	201.4	202.4	206.1	207.9	209.3	209.9	210.9	217.2	223.7	207.6
1996	214.4	210.6	210.6	211.2	214.3	216.0	215.2	218.8	218.6	217.6	225.5	231.7	217.0
1997	220.3	216.8	217.2	216.6	218.5	221.3	224.0	224.9	223.9	225.4	231.7	240.2	223.4
1998	227.6	224.4	224.2	223.6	225.3	229.1	232.4	231.9	230.5	232.9	240.3	247.3	230.8
1999	235.2	233.3	233.3	234.5	233.8	238.5	239.9	239.9	238.8	240.3	248.2	256.4	239.3
2000	240.5	238.6	238.1	238.6	239.1	242.6	242.7	246.1	245.6	248.5	257.9	264.6	245.2
2001	247.0	242.0	242.8	242.3	243.1	246.7	245.6	244.9	243.6	244.0	250.9	255.3	245.7
2002	240.2	236.4	237.6	239.1	240.8	244.9	243.5	243.5	241.3	241.3	249.1	254.5	242.7
2003	238.7	235.4	234.6	234.6	235.6	238.3	238.6	240.3	239.6	239.4	246.1	247.3	239.0

Employment by Industry: Colorado—*Continued*

(Numbers in thousands. Not seasonally adjusted.)

Industry	January	February	March	April	May	June	July	August	September	October	November	December	Annual Average
STATEWIDE—*Continued*													
Transportation and utilities													
1990	58.3	58.4	59.0	59.0	59.0	59.7	59.5	60.0	60.2	60.4	60.6	61.5	59.6
1991	60.8	60.8	61.1	60.4	60.4	61.0	61.0	61.1	61.2	61.1	61.5	62.5	61.0
1992	61.0	61.1	61.9	62.0	61.8	62.3	62.6	63.0	63.1	63.3	63.7	65.2	62.5
1993	63.7	63.8	64.4	64.5	64.0	64.7	65.9	65.9	65.6	65.6	65.9	68.1	65.2
1994	65.7	66.4	66.3	66.8	67.0	67.7	68.0	68.2	68.0	66.9	67.6	69.9	67.4
1995	66.8	67.4	68.3	68.4	68.4	68.8	68.4	69.4	69.4	69.9	70.8	73.0	69.1
1996	70.5	70.9	71.1	70.0	69.0	68.9	68.6	69.1	68.4	67.0	67.9	69.5	69.2
1997	67.7	67.6	67.3	67.3	66.9	67.1	67.8	68.4	68.4	68.7	70.0	71.3	68.2
1998	69.2	68.4	67.7	67.9	67.4	67.9	68.7	69.2	69.4	70.7	71.0	72.0	69.1
1999	69.5	69.5	69.5	70.7	70.3	70.0	70.8	71.4	71.8	71.3	72.9	74.6	71.0
2000	72.7	73.0	72.8	73.7	73.2	73.6	74.5	74.9	74.7	75.0	76.7	77.3	74.3
2001	78.2	77.5	77.6	77.4	77.2	77.8	78.1	78.7	77.9	77.3	76.4	76.0	77.5
2002	73.1	73.2	73.1	73.4	73.8	74.3	74.6	75.0	74.8	74.6	75.5	76.1	74.3
2003	74.1	73.9	73.8	72.6	71.6	71.5	72.2	72.5	72.2	72.6	73.5	73.3	72.8
Information													
1990	51.7	52.1	51.6	51.2	51.4	52.0	52.4	52.5	52.2	52.3	52.6	53.0	52.0
1991	48.7	48.7	49.2	49.4	49.9	50.4	50.6	50.9	50.7	49.7	49.9	50.2	49.8
1992	50.2	50.6	50.8	51.1	51.4	51.6	51.8	51.8	51.7	51.5	51.6	52.2	51.3
1993	50.6	50.6	50.6	53.0	53.1	54.0	54.2	54.0	54.0	54.8	55.1	55.7	53.3
1994	56.8	57.4	57.8	56.8	57.3	58.3	59.2	59.7	59.8	61.0	62.3	63.3	59.1
1995	64.5	65.6	66.1	64.2	63.7	64.1	64.4	63.9	63.8	63.5	64.2	65.5	64.5
1996	65.8	66.4	66.5	67.1	67.5	68.2	68.2	68.6	68.7	69.3	70.3	68.5	67.9
1997	69.4	69.7	69.8	71.7	72.4	73.6	72.1	72.7	72.1	77.9	81.2	82.2	73.7
1998	81.7	82.0	83.4	83.8	85.0	85.4	87.4	88.1	88.9	89.0	89.9	91.7	86.4
1999	89.9	90.7	91.3	94.8	95.5	96.2	98.5	99.4	100.0	101.5	102.9	103.6	97.0
2000	102.1	103.7	105.0	106.0	107.1	108.8	110.3	111.0	111.2	111.3	112.0	112.8	108.4
2001	113.2	112.8	112.0	110.3	109.3	109.3	106.6	105.5	103.8	102.2	101.7	100.5	107.3
2002	98.1	97.0	96.2	95.2	94.1	93.7	91.7	91.0	89.9	89.3	89.4	88.6	92.9
2003	86.5	86.1	85.7	85.0	84.9	85.0	84.8	84.4	83.9	84.4	84.3	84.2	84.9
Financial activities													
1990	104.6	105.3	106.5	104.6	103.5	104.5	104.4	104.8	103.6	102.9	103.4	104.5	104.3
1991	104.3	104.1	104.7	103.5	102.5	104.2	104.8	104.9	103.8	103.8	104.5	107.1	104.3
1992	105.8	106.2	106.9	107.8	106.9	108.7	109.0	109.3	108.6	108.4	109.2	111.0	108.1
1993	111.9	112.7	113.5	113.4	112.3	114.2	115.4	115.9	115.9	116.3	117.3	120.4	114.9
1994	120.2	120.2	121.1	120.7	119.9	121.5	121.7	122.0	121.0	120.7	120.3	122.7	121.0
1995	120.9	121.3	121.6	118.5	118.2	120.1	119.9	120.7	120.8	122.0	123.1	125.5	121.1
1996	123.8	125.1	126.2	127.2	126.9	128.7	128.0	129.1	128.5	128.6	129.7	132.9	127.9
1997	131.3	131.9	133.0	132.7	133.0	135.1	136.3	137.1	136.4	136.9	137.7	140.5	135.2
1998	139.1	140.0	140.6	140.8	140.6	142.5	144.9	145.2	144.2	143.8	144.9	147.1	142.8
1999	145.4	146.5	146.8	148.7	146.8	148.4	148.7	148.3	146.4	146.2	147.1	149.2	147.4
2000	146.3	147.1	147.7	146.5	145.8	147.3	147.1	147.3	146.3	146.2	147.0	149.6	147.0
2001	147.0	147.7	149.0	148.7	148.1	149.7	149.4	148.9	147.4	147.3	147.5	149.2	148.3
2002	147.7	148.3	148.7	147.8	147.6	149.0	149.3	150.2	149.6	150.3	151.8	154.1	149.5
2003	152.4	152.8	153.2	153.4	153.2	154.6	155.3	155.8	154.4	155.1	155.1	155.4	154.2
Professional and business services													
1990	167.8	170.5	172.7	174.3	177.2	181.5	182.8	185.4	183.6	182.3	182.4	181.3	178.4
1991	181.0	182.0	184.5	191.8	192.5	195.8	194.1	195.3	194.3	196.0	196.5	196.5	191.6
1992	190.1	191.4	193.0	196.6	198.1	201.1	202.6	202.9	202.6	204.3	203.1	204.8	199.2
1993	202.4	204.7	208.2	210.5	210.8	215.3	217.0	218.8	214.4	216.5	215.2	216.2	212.5
1994	209.7	212.1	216.7	220.7	223.9	228.1	227.5	229.0	228.3	229.5	230.5	232.8	224.1
1995	225.2	226.2	229.8	233.6	237.1	242.6	242.2	246.3	246.5	246.2	245.4	247.2	239.0
1996	237.8	236.7	239.4	245.6	251.6	257.0	257.4	261.3	259.4	259.7	258.5	260.6	252.1
1997	253.2	257.5	260.6	262.6	268.1	273.8	276.0	279.1	280.0	278.0	276.8	277.2	270.2
1998	265.2	267.1	270.4	274.4	276.9	281.8	285.1	286.6	284.1	286.8	285.0	287.2	279.2
1999	280.9	284.9	287.4	295.6	295.7	302.0	304.4	305.2	303.1	305.5	304.4	307.7	298.1
2000	298.7	299.6	304.7	309.6	313.1	319.2	322.2	324.5	324.2	322.8	321.3	322.0	315.2
2001	307.5	309.3	311.6	312.8	313.6	316.3	314.0	313.0	306.6	302.4	297.3	296.5	308.4
2002	284.6	287.0	288.8	293.4	296.0	297.7	295.6	298.7	294.7	291.7	289.5	289.1	292.2
2003	278.7	279.7	280.4	284.4	286.4	291.2	291.5	294.2	290.4	288.2	286.6	285.9	286.5
Educational and health services													
1990	127.4	128.8	129.7	130.0	130.4	131.0	130.2	131.9	132.2	133.1	134.4	135.0	131.1
1991	133.8	135.5	136.1	136.4	137.0	137.4	137.2	138.2	139.3	139.7	140.4	141.5	137.7
1992	140.6	142.0	143.1	143.4	143.8	144.0	143.8	144.6	146.2	147.6	148.5	149.5	144.7
1993	147.4	148.6	149.2	149.5	149.4	149.7	149.2	150.2	152.0	151.6	152.6	153.9	150.3
1994	152.8	155.6	156.0	155.9	156.6	157.2	156.5	157.8	159.4	158.9	160.5	161.9	157.4
1995	160.1	163.2	164.6	164.9	165.4	166.1	164.6	165.5	166.7	167.1	168.2	168.7	165.4
1996	167.7	169.5	170.3	169.3	169.4	169.2	168.7	170.0	171.2	174.5	176.3	177.7	171.2
1997	176.2	178.6	178.5	176.7	177.9	177.5	174.5	176.0	177.9	178.8	182.6	183.2	178.2
1998	181.5	183.4	184.1	184.2	184.0	183.8	180.4	181.4	182.1	182.5	183.4	184.2	182.9
1999	184.2	186.7	186.6	187.6	186.9	186.8	184.8	185.6	186.7	188.0	188.9	189.7	186.9
2000	187.4	189.3	190.1	191.3	191.8	193.0	192.1	193.4	194.6	195.2	196.9	198.0	192.8
2001	196.1	198.0	198.7	199.1	200.0	200.5	199.7	201.5	201.3	203.8	204.9	206.2	200.8
2002	204.2	205.7	206.4	208.0	208.7	208.4	207.7	209.1	209.7	210.2	211.4	212.0	208.5
2003	209.8	211.1	211.7	212.5	212.9	213.0	212.3	213.0	213.5	216.6	217.1	218.3	213.5

Employment by Industry: Colorado—*Continued*

(Numbers in thousands. Not seasonally adjusted.)

Industry	January	February	March	April	May	June	July	August	September	October	November	December	Annual Average
STATEWIDE—*Continued*													
Leisure and hospitality													
1990	163.4	164.2	167.4	165.5	159.9	171.6	174.4	176.9	168.9	160.0	161.7	170.0	166.9
1991	167.3	168.3	170.1	165.6	160.0	172.2	176.3	177.2	169.3	160.9	163.6	173.9	168.7
1992	172.4	174.5	177.7	175.1	169.9	182.8	189.4	191.5	182.6	175.5	176.2	186.2	179.4
1993	185.6	187.7	190.9	190.4	181.2	194.4	198.5	199.9	192.5	183.9	185.1	198.3	190.7
1994	196.3	197.8	200.7	200.8	191.7	206.2	212.7	213.6	204.9	196.9	199.0	213.0	202.8
1995	209.2	211.4	215.8	212.9	206.3	223.3	226.4	227.5	217.3	205.3	207.6	218.9	215.2
1996	215.2	217.0	221.8	218.9	211.4	225.2	229.6	231.8	222.3	210.6	212.8	225.0	220.1
1997	221.4	224.1	227.2	222.5	216.3	232.9	239.2	240.5	228.8	217.3	218.5	230.7	226.6
1998	227.0	230.0	231.5	226.9	221.3	236.8	241.1	242.4	232.0	222.8	224.6	236.1	231.0
1999	234.6	237.5	239.6	236.3	229.0	245.3	250.0	250.0	240.4	230.9	229.5	239.1	238.5
2000	237.5	240.5	245.6	242.3	236.6	254.0	258.9	259.5	248.5	238.0	240.5	250.1	246.0
2001	246.2	247.4	251.2	246.3	239.4	257.0	259.9	260.3	247.9	233.8	233.7	243.6	247.2
2002	242.2	243.4	246.1	245.2	240.3	256.9	259.6	260.0	248.7	237.2	236.0	248.5	247.0
2003	243.8	242.8	244.8	241.2	236.4	251.9	255.9	257.9	246.9	237.1	237.8	249.8	245.5
Other services													
1990	54.6	55.1	55.4	55.4	55.6	56.8	56.9	57.2	56.1	56.1	56.2	56.3	55.9
1991	56.1	56.2	56.4	56.2	56.4	57.5	57.1	57.4	57.0	57.3	57.5	57.9	56.9
1992	57.3	57.4	57.4	57.3	57.8	58.8	58.9	58.6	57.5	57.8	57.7	58.3	57.9
1993	58.1	58.6	59.1	59.1	59.2	60.6	61.6	61.6	60.9	61.0	61.4	62.7	60.3
1994	62.1	62.8	63.5	63.6	64.3	65.5	66.0	65.9	65.4	65.1	65.3	66.5	64.7
1995	65.7	66.2	67.0	66.7	67.4	69.3	69.8	70.2	69.7	69.6	70.0	70.9	68.5
1996	70.7	71.2	72.1	71.9	72.6	74.1	73.4	74.0	72.8	72.8	73.0	74.0	72.7
1997	74.2	74.5	75.3	74.7	75.4	76.9	77.3	77.1	76.0	75.5	75.2	76.0	75.7
1998	76.2	76.6	76.8	76.3	76.8	78.3	78.9	78.7	77.7	76.8	76.8	77.7	77.3
1999	78.2	78.1	78.0	78.7	78.3	80.4	80.7	80.0	79.0	78.4	78.7	79.5	79.0
2000	79.2	79.0	80.0	79.1	79.6	81.7	81.8	81.6	80.4	79.8	79.6	80.5	80.2
2001	82.6	82.7	83.4	83.3	83.6	85.5	85.2	85.2	83.7	83.1	83.0	83.7	83.8
2002	84.7	84.7	85.3	85.4	85.5	87.1	87.3	86.8	85.3	84.6	84.9	85.1	85.6
2003	85.7	85.2	85.2	85.5	85.7	87.3	87.2	86.7	85.1	85.3	85.4	85.4	85.8
Government													
1990	267.8	279.1	281.2	282.6	286.0	280.2	259.7	257.1	275.5	282.5	286.5	283.7	276.8
1991	275.2	284.8	286.4	287.8	289.9	285.2	267.5	264.1	282.8	292.2	293.0	291.1	283.3
1992	281.8	292.1	294.5	294.2	297.0	292.1	274.3	274.0	291.5	300.6	301.3	299.2	291.0
1993	288.9	299.8	301.6	303.1	303.9	296.7	280.3	279.4	294.2	304.3	304.7	303.1	296.7
1994	291.8	302.3	303.5	306.1	305.8	298.7	280.9	282.4	298.9	307.2	307.7	305.8	299.3
1995	294.1	305.5	308.0	307.8	309.5	303.5	286.0	287.7	305.5	312.0	312.8	311.6	303.7
1996	299.8	311.0	313.8	313.8	316.4	308.5	290.8	290.8	309.3	316.3	318.1	316.3	308.7
1997	308.0	316.7	318.7	319.3	321.8	315.3	299.3	296.6	316.3	324.7	325.8	324.4	315.6
1998	315.1	323.5	325.2	325.6	328.8	321.3	307.4	304.4	322.5	330.4	332.4	331.4	322.3
1999	320.1	330.0	331.6	332.5	335.0	327.7	312.2	310.8	329.6	336.4	336.8	337.6	328.4
2000	323.8	335.4	340.7	341.5	349.1	337.6	321.2	322.6	337.8	343.9	345.3	345.3	337.0
2001	332.1	344.1	345.0	345.3	348.6	344.1	328.2	330.2	347.5	353.4	355.8	355.1	344.1
2002	344.1	354.9	358.2	358.2	362.3	355.7	338.7	340.5	356.5	364.8	365.9	364.7	355.4
2003	350.5	360.5	362.5	361.2	366.2	355.6	337.9	338.7	356.0	364.8	364.6	362.7	356.8
Federal government													
1990	55.7	55.6	56.4	58.0	59.8	58.9	59.5	57.9	57.0	56.1	55.6	56.8	57.2
1991	55.6	55.3	55.4	56.3	56.9	58.5	59.2	58.8	58.2	57.8	57.6	58.1	57.3
1992	57.5	57.4	57.3	57.7	58.2	59.5	60.0	60.0	59.7	59.3	58.9	59.6	58.7
1993	59.0	59.0	58.9	59.2	59.6	60.8	61.0	61.0	60.6	60.4	59.9	61.0	60.0
1994	59.5	59.3	59.2	59.6	59.5	59.9	60.0	59.4	59.0	57.7	57.4	58.7	59.1
1995	56.8	56.6	56.6	56.7	56.9	57.5	57.7	57.7	57.5	56.6	55.9	56.8	56.9
1996	55.1	55.0	54.9	55.0	55.2	55.6	55.5	55.3	54.9	54.3	54.0	55.6	55.0
1997	54.0	53.9	53.8	53.9	54.0	54.7	54.8	54.6	54.4	54.0	54.1	55.4	54.3
1998	53.7	53.5	53.4	53.7	54.2	55.0	55.2	55.5	55.0	54.3	54.8	55.9	54.5
1999	53.9	53.5	53.5	53.7	53.8	54.9	54.9	54.9	54.4	53.8	53.4	54.6	54.1
2000	53.7	53.5	55.5	54.9	60.7	55.2	56.6	54.6	53.5	52.7	52.4	53.7	54.8
2001	52.6	51.9	52.0	52.0	52.5	53.9	54.2	53.8	53.6	52.8	52.4	53.2	52.9
2002	52.7	51.6	52.0	51.8	52.4	53.9	54.0	53.5	53.5	53.7	54.0	55.2	53.2
2003	53.2	53.1	53.3	53.1	53.6	54.4	54.5	54.1	53.8	54.0	53.5	54.7	53.8
State government													
1990	59.6	66.8	67.8	68.0	67.2	61.0	57.4	57.6	65.9	68.9	70.3	69.0	64.9
1991	63.2	70.4	71.4	71.1	70.5	62.4	61.3	60.0	68.4	72.0	72.4	71.0	67.8
1992	63.9	70.9	72.1	71.8	71.2	63.5	61.4	61.4	69.5	74.2	73.2	73.1	68.8
1993	65.7	73.4	74.4	75.3	74.1	64.3	63.4	63.4	70.7	75.0	75.2	74.1	70.8
1994	66.4	73.8	74.7	75.3	74.3	64.7	63.3	63.8	73.0	75.4	75.7	74.6	71.3
1995	66.9	74.7	75.8	75.5	74.9	66.2	63.6	64.4	73.5	76.5	76.8	75.7	72.0
1996	67.6	75.3	76.7	76.4	75.9	65.7	63.9	65.1	74.0	76.9	77.4	76.2	72.6
1997	71.2	76.7	77.3	76.9	76.8	67.3	66.4	66.5	76.5	79.7	79.6	78.5	74.5
1998	72.7	78.2	79.1	78.9	78.5	68.8	68.8	67.6	76.9	80.7	80.5	79.8	75.9
1999	72.4	79.4	80.6	80.7	80.8	69.4	68.5	68.8	79.1	82.2	81.9	81.9	77.1
2000	71.3	80.5	82.3	81.8	81.5	72.2	67.5	71.0	81.4	84.1	84.7	85.4	78.6
2001	74.5	84.1	83.1	82.7	82.5	73.7	70.8	71.8	82.0	84.4	85.8	85.1	80.0
2002	74.8	84.6	86.2	85.3	85.6	75.6	72.7	73.5	83.5	86.8	87.4	86.5	81.9
2003	76.3	84.3	85.4	84.4	84.6	71.8	69.8	70.7	81.7	85.5	85.6	84.8	80.4

Employment by Industry: Colorado—*Continued*

(Numbers in thousands. Not seasonally adjusted.)

Industry	January	February	March	April	May	June	July	August	September	October	November	December	Annual Average
STATEWIDE—*Continued*													
Local government													
1990	152.5	156.7	157.0	156.6	159.0	160.3	142.8	141.6	152.6	157.5	160.6	157.9	154.5
1991	156.4	159.1	159.6	160.4	162.5	164.3	147.0	145.3	156.2	162.4	163.0	162.0	158.1
1992	160.4	163.8	165.1	164.7	167.6	169.1	152.9	152.6	162.3	167.1	169.2	166.5	163.4
1993	164.2	167.4	168.3	168.6	170.2	171.6	155.9	155.0	162.9	168.9	169.6	168.0	165.9
1994	165.9	169.2	169.6	171.2	172.0	174.1	157.6	159.2	166.9	174.1	174.6	172.5	168.9
1995	170.4	174.2	175.6	175.6	177.7	179.8	164.7	165.6	174.5	178.9	180.1	179.1	174.7
1996	177.1	180.7	182.2	182.4	185.3	187.2	171.4	170.4	180.4	185.1	186.7	184.5	181.1
1997	182.8	186.1	187.6	188.5	191.0	193.3	178.1	175.5	185.4	191.0	192.1	190.5	186.8
1998	188.7	191.8	192.7	193.0	196.1	197.5	183.4	181.3	190.6	195.4	197.1	195.7	191.9
1999	193.8	197.1	197.5	198.1	200.4	203.4	188.8	187.1	196.1	200.4	201.5	201.1	197.1
2000	198.8	201.4	202.9	204.8	206.9	210.2	197.1	197.0	202.9	207.1	208.2	206.2	203.6
2001	205.0	208.1	209.9	210.6	213.6	216.5	203.2	204.6	211.9	216.2	217.6	216.8	211.2
2002	216.6	218.7	220.0	221.1	224.3	226.2	212.0	213.5	219.5	224.3	224.5	223.0	220.3
2003	221.0	223.1	223.8	223.7	228.0	229.4	213.6	213.9	220.5	225.3	225.5	223.2	222.6
BOULDER-LONGMONT													
Total nonfarm													
1990	113.8	115.6	116.3	116.1	117.5	118.0	116.6	117.2	118.9	118.7	121.0	120.1	117.4
1991	117.3	119.1	119.6	120.2	121.7	122.3	120.2	120.6	123.7	124.7	125.0	125.6	121.6
1992	122.6	123.7	124.8	126.1	127.9	127.7	126.3	124.9	128.6	130.2	131.1	131.7	127.1
1993	129.2	130.9	132.2	133.1	134.5	134.6	134.1	133.3	135.8	137.8	138.3	139.0	134.4
1994	134.7	137.0	138.4	139.6	141.9	142.7	141.8	142.2	145.4	145.4	147.0	148.1	142.0
1995	141.6	143.8	145.4	145.1	145.8	146.8	144.7	144.9	147.5	149.5	150.2	151.6	146.4
1996	145.3	147.7	149.2	149.4	150.7	150.1	148.6	149.0	151.4	153.0	154.3	154.9	150.3
1997	150.3	152.8	154.7	155.6	157.2	157.6	156.8	157.3	159.5	162.6	162.8	164.1	157.6
1998	157.4	160.3	162.1	162.3	163.8	163.4	162.8	162.9	165.6	166.9	167.5	168.6	163.6
1999	163.8	167.3	168.0	169.9	171.0	170.8	170.7	171.0	173.2	176.0	176.5	178.3	171.4
2000	173.2	176.7	179.9	179.9	182.1	182.0	181.7	185.5	189.2	191.7	193.8	195.4	184.3
2001	189.0	191.0	192.5	191.6	191.4	191.1	188.1	187.0	189.2	189.1	188.3	187.6	189.7
2002	181.8	182.8	184.3	184.5	185.8	184.5	180.6	180.0	182.4	182.5	182.1	181.7	182.8
2003	155.8	155.9	156.3	156.5	157.4	156.6	154.4	153.7	156.8	158.4	158.4	158.8	156.6
Total private													
1990	91.5	92.2	92.8	93.4	94.5	96.2	96.4	97.3	96.6	96.1	96.9	97.2	95.0
1991	94.2	94.9	95.1	95.8	97.2	99.3	99.3	100.1	99.9	100.0	100.4	101.0	98.1
1992	98.3	99.0	99.7	101.4	102.7	104.1	104.3	103.8	104.1	104.7	105.5	106.2	102.8
1993	105.2	105.7	106.8	107.7	108.7	110.5	111.6	111.6	110.9	112.0	112.4	113.0	109.7
1994	110.2	111.1	112.4	113.5	115.5	118.1	118.6	119.7	120.0	119.0	120.6	121.8	116.7
1995	116.7	117.6	118.9	118.8	119.2	121.5	121.9	122.5	122.4	123.3	123.9	125.4	121.0
1996	120.8	121.5	122.6	123.0	123.8	125.5	125.2	126.5	126.2	126.5	127.7	128.6	124.8
1997	125.5	126.6	128.1	128.9	130.1	132.5	133.1	134.3	133.7	135.1	135.7	137.2	131.7
1998	132.1	133.5	134.9	135.4	136.2	138.4	139.1	139.8	139.6	139.4	140.1	141.5	137.5
1999	138.3	140.2	140.9	142.5	143.3	145.6	146.5	146.8	146.4	147.9	148.6	150.5	144.8
2000	147.1	149.2	151.8	152.2	153.7	156.3	158.0	160.8	161.7	163.5	165.6	167.3	157.3
2001	162.2	162.9	163.7	163.1	162.5	164.1	162.8	161.8	160.8	159.6	158.7	158.2	161.7
2002	153.1	153.4	154.2	154.6	155.6	156.3	154.5	154.1	152.8	151.8	151.5	151.3	153.6
2003	126.8	126.6	126.8	127.1	127.9	129.4	129.0	129.2	128.4	128.9	128.7	129.2	128.2
Goods-producing													
1990	30.9	31.0	31.2	30.9	31.0	31.6	31.9	32.0	31.7	31.7	31.8	31.6	31.4
1991	31.3	31.5	31.3	31.0	31.3	31.7	31.6	31.4	31.3	31.4	31.3	31.2	31.3
1992	31.0	31.3	31.4	32.2	32.4	32.9	33.0	32.2	32.1	32.0	32.1	32.1	32.0
1993	32.0	32.1	32.1	32.3	32.6	33.0	33.4	33.5	33.3	33.2	33.2	33.2	32.8
1994	33.1	32.5	32.7	32.4	33.0	33.4	33.6	33.8	33.9	33.9	34.2	34.0	33.4
1995	32.8	32.9	33.2	33.3	33.4	33.9	33.8	33.9	33.8	33.9	33.9	34.0	33.6
1996	33.5	33.1	33.5	33.5	33.8	34.4	34.5	34.7	34.6	34.5	34.5	34.5	34.1
1997	33.4	33.6	33.9	34.1	34.6	35.3	35.5	36.0	35.6	36.0	36.3	36.4	35.1
1998	35.6	36.1	36.6	36.8	37.0	37.6	38.2	38.1	37.7	37.4	37.4	37.6	37.2
1999	37.0	37.6	37.9	37.3	37.5	38.0	37.9	37.5	37.2	37.0	36.8	36.7	37.4
2000	36.8	37.1	37.4	37.3	37.5	38.0	38.2	38.3	38.1	38.0	38.0	38.3	37.8
2001	37.5	37.5	37.7	37.5	37.2	37.8	37.5	37.1	36.4	36.2	35.6	35.2	36.9
2002	34.2	33.9	34.2	34.1	34.1	34.2	34.0	33.6	33.0	32.6	32.1	31.9	33.5
2003	26.8	26.6	26.3	26.3	26.6	27.0	26.8	26.8	26.5	26.5	26.4	26.5	26.6
Construction and mining													
1990	3.4	3.4	3.5	3.6	3.8	4.1	4.1	4.2	4.1	4.1	4.1	4.0	3.8
1991	3.6	3.7	3.7	3.8	4.0	4.3	4.5	4.6	4.5	4.5	4.4	4.3	4.1
1992	4.0	4.1	4.0	4.3	4.4	4.7	4.8	4.7	4.7	4.7	4.7	4.7	4.4
1993	4.6	4.7	4.8	4.9	5.2	5.5	5.9	6.0	5.8	5.9	5.8	5.7	5.4
1994	5.4	5.3	5.4	5.5	5.9	6.2	6.4	6.4	6.3	6.3	6.3	6.1	6.0
1995	5.8	5.8	5.9	5.9	6.0	6.3	6.4	6.4	6.2	6.3	6.2	6.2	6.1
1996	5.8	5.9	6.0	6.1	6.4	6.8	6.7	6.8	6.7	6.7	6.7	6.6	6.4
1997	6.0	6.1	6.2	6.3	6.6	6.8	6.9	7.1	6.9	7.0	6.7	6.9	6.6
1998	6.5	6.9	7.1	7.3	7.5	7.8	8.0	7.9	7.9	7.8	7.7	7.8	7.5
1999	7.2	7.5	7.7	7.7	7.9	8.2	8.4	8.5	8.4	8.3	8.2	8.1	8.0
2000	7.9	8.1	8.3	8.2	8.4	8.7	8.8	8.9	8.6	8.5	8.5	8.4	8.4
2001	8.1	8.0	8.3	8.4	8.4	8.8	8.9	8.9	8.6	8.6	8.3	8.1	8.5
2002	7.6	7.5	7.7	8.0	8.1	8.3	8.3	8.3	8.0	8.0	7.8	7.6	7.9
2003	6.4	6.3	6.3	6.3	6.6	6.9	6.9	6.9	6.7	6.6	6.5	6.4	6.6

Employment by Industry: Colorado—*Continued*

(Numbers in thousands. Not seasonally adjusted.)

Industry	January	February	March	April	May	June	July	August	September	October	November	December	Annual Average
BOULDER-LONGMONT *—Continued*													
Manufacturing													
1990	27.5	27.6	27.7	27.3	27.2	27.5	27.8	27.8	27.6	27.6	27.7	27.6	27.5
1991	27.7	27.8	27.6	27.2	27.3	27.4	27.1	26.8	26.8	26.9	26.9	26.9	27.2
1992	27.0	27.2	27.4	27.9	28.0	28.2	28.2	27.5	27.4	27.3	27.4	27.4	27.5
1993	27.4	27.4	27.3	27.4	27.4	27.5	27.5	27.5	27.5	27.3	27.4	27.5	27.4
1994	27.7	27.2	27.3	26.9	27.1	27.2	27.2	27.4	27.6	27.6	27.9	27.9	27.4
1995	27.0	27.1	27.3	27.4	27.4	27.6	27.4	27.5	27.6	27.6	27.7	27.8	27.5
1996	27.7	27.2	27.5	27.4	27.4	27.6	27.8	27.9	27.9	27.8	27.8	27.9	27.7
1997	27.4	27.5	27.7	27.8	28.0	28.5	28.6	28.9	28.7	29.0	29.6	29.5	28.4
1998	29.1	29.2	29.5	29.5	29.5	29.8	30.2	30.2	29.8	29.6	29.7	29.8	29.7
1999	29.8	30.1	30.2	29.6	29.6	29.8	29.5	29.0	28.8	28.7	28.6	28.6	29.4
2000	28.9	29.0	29.1	29.1	29.1	29.3	29.4	29.4	29.5	29.5	29.5	29.9	29.3
2001	29.4	29.5	29.4	29.1	28.8	29.0	28.6	28.2	27.8	27.6	27.3	27.1	28.5
2002	26.6	26.4	26.5	26.1	26.0	25.9	25.7	25.3	25.0	24.6	24.3	24.3	25.6
2003	20.4	20.3	20.0	20.0	20.0	20.1	19.9	19.9	19.8	19.9	19.9	20.1	20.0
Service-providing													
1990	82.9	84.6	85.1	85.2	86.5	86.4	84.7	85.2	87.2	87.0	89.2	88.5	86.0
1991	86.0	87.6	88.3	89.2	90.4	90.6	88.6	89.2	92.4	93.3	93.7	94.4	90.3
1992	91.6	92.4	93.4	93.9	95.5	94.8	93.3	92.7	96.5	98.2	99.0	99.6	95.0
1993	97.2	98.8	100.1	100.8	101.9	101.6	100.7	99.8	102.5	104.6	105.1	105.8	101.6
1994	101.6	104.5	105.7	107.2	108.9	109.3	108.2	108.4	111.5	111.5	112.8	114.1	108.6
1995	108.8	110.9	112.2	111.8	112.4	112.9	110.9	111.0	113.7	115.6	116.3	117.6	112.8
1996	111.8	114.6	115.7	115.9	116.9	115.7	114.1	114.3	116.8	118.5	119.8	120.4	116.2
1997	116.9	119.2	120.8	121.5	122.6	122.3	121.3	121.3	123.9	126.6	126.5	127.7	122.6
1998	121.8	124.2	125.5	125.5	126.8	125.8	124.6	124.8	127.9	129.5	130.1	131.0	126.5
1999	126.8	129.7	130.1	132.6	133.5	132.8	132.8	133.5	136.0	139.0	139.7	141.6	134.0
2000	136.4	139.6	142.5	142.6	144.6	144.0	143.5	147.2	151.1	153.7	155.8	157.1	146.5
2001	151.5	153.5	154.8	154.1	154.2	153.3	150.6	149.9	152.8	152.9	152.7	152.4	152.7
2002	147.6	148.9	150.1	150.4	151.7	150.3	146.6	146.4	149.4	149.9	150.0	149.8	149.3
2003	129.0	129.3	130.0	130.2	130.8	129.6	127.6	126.9	130.3	131.9	132.0	132.3	130.0
Trade, transportation, and utilities													
1990	16.5	16.2	16.3	16.5	16.8	17.0	16.9	17.0	17.4	17.2	17.9	18.2	16.9
1991	17.1	16.8	16.8	16.9	16.9	17.3	17.2	17.3	17.4	17.5	17.9	18.3	17.2
1992	17.5	17.4	17.4	17.5	17.8	17.9	17.9	18.0	18.2	18.7	19.0	19.4	18.0
1993	18.9	18.9	19.1	19.1	19.2	19.4	19.3	19.4	19.3	19.7	20.2	20.6	19.4
1994	19.4	19.6	19.6	19.7	20.1	20.5	20.6	21.0	21.0	21.1	21.7	22.5	20.6
1995	21.1	20.8	21.0	21.3	21.3	21.7	21.9	22.0	22.2	22.3	23.0	23.6	21.9
1996	22.5	22.5	22.6	22.6	22.9	22.8	22.9	23.1	23.2	23.3	24.3	24.6	23.1
1997	23.4	23.3	23.3	23.0	23.2	23.3	23.3	23.4	23.6	23.7	24.1	25.0	23.6
1998	23.2	23.2	23.3	23.2	23.2	23.5	23.5	23.6	23.6	23.7	24.5	25.0	23.6
1999	23.5	23.6	23.7	23.6	23.8	24.1	24.2	24.3	24.2	24.6	25.2	26.0	24.2
2000	24.5	24.6	24.8	25.1	25.3	25.7	26.2	27.7	28.2	29.4	30.5	31.4	27.0
2001	29.5	29.0	28.9	28.7	28.8	29.2	28.8	28.6	28.9	28.8	29.4	30.0	29.1
2002	28.0	28.1	28.2	28.2	28.4	28.7	28.2	28.0	27.8	27.7	28.2	28.4	28.2
2003	22.6	22.3	22.3	22.4	22.5	22.8	22.7	22.9	22.9	23.3	23.6	23.8	22.8
Wholesale trade													
1990	2.8	2.8	2.9	2.8	2.8	2.9	2.9	3.0	3.0	3.0	3.1	3.1	2.9
1991	3.0	3.0	3.0	3.0	3.0	3.1	3.1	3.0	3.0	3.0	3.1	3.1	3.0
1992	3.1	3.2	3.2	3.0	3.0	3.1	3.1	3.1	3.1	3.2	3.2	3.3	3.1
1993	3.4	3.4	3.5	3.4	3.4	3.4	3.5	3.5	3.5	3.4	3.5	3.6	3.5
1994	3.5	3.6	3.6	3.7	3.8	3.9	3.9	4.0	4.0	4.0	4.1	4.2	3.9
1995	4.1	4.2	4.3	4.3	4.3	4.4	4.4	4.4	4.5	4.5	4.6	4.6	4.4
1996	4.5	4.5	4.6	4.6	4.7	4.7	4.7	4.7	4.7	4.7	4.8	4.7	4.7
1997	4.6	4.8	4.8	4.8	4.9	5.0	5.0	5.0	5.1	5.2	5.2	5.2	5.0
1998	5.0	5.1	5.2	5.2	5.1	5.2	5.2	5.2	5.2	5.2	5.3	5.2	5.2
1999	5.1	5.1	5.2	5.1	5.1	5.1	5.2	5.2	5.2	5.2	5.2	5.3	5.2
2000	5.3	5.3	5.4	5.5	5.6	5.7	5.7	5.9	5.9	6.0	6.0	6.1	5.7
2001	6.0	6.1	6.0	6.0	6.0	6.0	5.9	5.9	5.9	5.7	5.6	5.6	5.9
2002	5.5	5.6	5.6	5.6	5.6	5.6	5.6	5.5	5.4	5.3	5.2	5.2	5.5
2003	4.7	4.7	4.8	4.8	4.8	4.9	4.9	4.9	4.9	5.1	5.1	5.1	4.9
Retail trade													
1990	12.3	12.0	12.0	12.2	12.5	12.6	12.5	12.5	12.7	12.5	13.0	13.3	12.5
1991	12.6	12.4	12.3	12.3	12.4	12.6	12.5	12.7	12.8	12.9	13.2	13.6	12.6
1992	12.9	12.6	12.7	13.0	13.3	13.3	13.3	13.4	13.6	14.0	14.3	14.6	13.4
1993	14.0	14.0	14.0	14.1	14.2	14.3	14.1	14.2	14.2	14.6	15.0	15.3	14.3
1994	14.2	14.3	14.3	14.4	14.7	15.0	15.2	15.5	15.5	15.7	16.2	16.9	15.2
1995	15.7	15.4	15.5	15.7	15.7	15.9	16.1	16.1	16.2	16.2	16.7	17.2	16.0
1996	16.3	16.2	16.2	16.2	16.4	16.3	16.4	16.5	16.7	16.8	17.6	18.0	16.6
1997	17.0	16.7	16.7	16.4	16.5	16.5	16.5	16.7	16.8	16.8	17.2	18.1	16.8
1998	16.6	16.6	16.7	16.5	16.6	16.8	16.8	16.9	16.9	17.0	17.6	18.2	16.9
1999	16.9	17.0	17.0	17.0	17.2	17.4	17.4	17.5	17.4	17.8	18.3	18.9	17.5
2000	17.5	17.6	17.7	17.8	17.9	18.1	18.5	19.8	20.3	21.3	22.4	23.1	19.3
2001	21.3	20.8	20.8	20.7	20.8	21.2	20.9	20.7	21.0	21.1	21.8	22.3	21.1
2002	20.6	20.5	20.6	20.6	20.8	21.0	20.6	20.5	20.4	20.4	20.9	21.1	20.7
2003	15.9	15.6	15.5	15.5	15.7	15.8	15.7	15.9	15.9	16.1	16.3	16.6	15.9

Employment by Industry: Colorado—*Continued*

(Numbers in thousands. Not seasonally adjusted.)

Industry	January	February	March	April	May	June	July	August	September	October	November	December	Annual Average
BOULDER-LONGMONT *—Continued*													
Transportation and utilities													
1990	1.4	1.4	1.4	1.5	1.5	1.5	1.5	1.5	1.7	1.7	1.8	1.8	1.5
1991	1.5	1.4	1.5	1.6	1.5	1.6	1.6	1.6	1.6	1.6	1.6	1.6	1.5
1992	1.5	1.6	1.5	1.5	1.5	1.5	1.5	1.5	1.5	1.5	1.5	1.5	1.5
1993	1.5	1.5	1.6	1.6	1.6	1.7	1.7	1.7	1.6	1.7	1.7	1.7	1.6
1994	1.7	1.7	1.7	1.6	1.6	1.6	1.5	1.5	1.5	1.4	1.4	1.4	1.6
1995	1.3	1.2	1.2	1.3	1.3	1.4	1.4	1.5	1.5	1.6	1.7	1.8	1.4
1996	1.7	1.8	1.8	1.8	1.8	1.8	1.8	1.9	1.8	1.8	1.9	1.9	1.8
1997	1.8	1.8	1.8	1.8	1.8	1.8	1.8	1.7	1.7	1.7	1.7	1.7	1.8
1998	1.6	1.5	1.4	1.5	1.5	1.5	1.5	1.5	1.5	1.5	1.6	1.6	1.5
1999	1.5	1.5	1.5	1.5	1.5	1.6	1.6	1.6	1.6	1.6	1.7	1.8	1.6
2000	1.7	1.7	1.7	1.8	1.8	1.9	2.0	2.0	2.0	2.1	2.1	2.2	1.9
2001	2.2	2.1	2.1	2.0	2.0	2.0	2.0	2.0	2.0	2.0	2.0	2.1	2.0
2002	1.9	2.0	2.0	2.0	2.0	2.1	2.0	2.0	2.0	2.0	2.1	2.1	2.0
2003	2.0	2.0	2.0	2.1	2.0	2.1	2.1	2.1	2.1	2.1	2.2	2.1	2.1
Information													
1990	3.1	3.1	3.1	3.1	3.2	3.3	3.3	3.4	3.5	3.4	3.5	3.5	3.2
1991	3.0	3.1	3.1	3.2	3.3	3.3	4.1	4.4	4.5	4.6	4.6	4.6	3.8
1992	4.4	4.5	4.5	4.5	4.6	4.6	4.6	4.7	4.7	4.6	4.8	4.8	4.6
1993	5.3	5.4	5.4	5.5	5.5	5.6	5.7	5.6	5.6	5.6	5.7	5.7	5.6
1994	5.9	6.0	6.0	7.4	7.5	7.7	7.8	7.9	8.1	8.0	8.2	8.2	7.4
1995	7.6	8.0	8.0	7.8	7.8	7.9	8.0	7.9	7.9	8.0	8.2	8.3	8.0
1996	8.1	8.2	8.1	8.2	8.3	8.2	8.4	8.5	8.5	8.6	8.7	8.8	8.4
1997	8.7	8.8	9.0	9.1	9.1	9.3	9.4	9.4	9.3	9.5	9.5	9.6	9.2
1998	9.5	9.7	10.0	9.6	9.7	10.0	10.0	10.2	10.3	10.5	10.5	10.7	10.1
1999	11.2	11.6	11.5	11.9	11.9	12.1	12.7	12.9	13.0	13.2	13.2	13.7	12.4
2000	13.6	14.0	14.8	14.6	14.8	15.0	15.5	15.7	16.0	16.2	16.5	16.7	15.3
2001	16.0	16.1	16.1	15.8	15.5	15.4	15.0	14.8	14.5	14.3	14.2	13.8	15.1
2002	13.7	13.5	13.5	13.4	13.3	13.3	12.9	12.8	12.6	12.6	12.6	12.5	13.1
2003	10.0	9.9	10.0	9.9	9.9	9.9	9.9	9.8	9.8	10.0	10.0	9.9	9.9
Financial activities													
1990	4.6	4.5	4.6	4.7	4.7	4.8	4.7	4.8	4.7	4.7	4.6	4.6	4.6
1991	4.5	4.5	4.6	4.6	4.7	4.8	4.7	4.8	4.7	4.7	4.7	4.8	4.6
1992	4.7	4.8	4.9	4.9	4.9	5.0	5.0	5.1	5.1	4.9	5.0	5.1	4.9
1993	5.1	5.1	5.2	5.3	5.3	5.4	5.4	5.5	5.5	5.6	5.7	5.8	5.4
1994	5.6	5.7	5.7	5.7	5.8	5.9	5.9	5.9	5.9	5.7	5.8	5.8	5.8
1995	5.7	5.7	5.8	5.8	5.7	5.8	5.9	5.9	5.9	5.9	5.9	6.0	5.8
1996	5.8	5.9	5.9	5.9	5.9	6.0	6.0	6.0	6.0	6.0	5.9	6.1	6.0
1997	6.3	6.4	6.4	6.5	6.6	6.7	6.7	6.8	6.7	6.7	6.7	6.9	6.6
1998	6.6	6.7	6.8	7.0	7.1	7.2	7.2	7.2	7.2	7.2	7.3	7.3	7.1
1999	7.4	7.5	7.6	7.5	7.6	7.7	7.7	7.7	7.6	7.7	7.7	7.8	7.6
2000	7.6	7.7	7.8	7.8	7.8	8.0	7.9	8.0	7.9	7.9	7.9	8.0	7.9
2001	8.0	8.0	8.1	8.3	8.3	8.4	8.4	8.4	8.4	8.5	8.5	8.6	8.3
2002	8.2	8.2	8.2	8.2	8.3	8.3	8.3	8.3	8.3	8.4	8.4	8.4	8.3
2003	7.3	7.4	7.4	7.3	7.4	7.5	7.6	7.6	7.5	7.5	7.6	7.6	7.5
Professional and business services													
1990	13.9	14.3	14.2	14.3	14.4	14.5	14.8	14.9	14.4	14.4	14.4	14.6	14.4
1991	14.3	14.3	14.4	15.1	15.3	15.7	15.5	15.7	15.7	15.8	16.0	16.2	15.3
1992	15.6	15.5	15.8	16.3	16.3	16.5	16.6	16.6	16.7	17.4	17.6	18.1	16.5
1993	17.4	17.3	17.6	17.8	18.0	18.3	18.6	18.5	18.4	18.7	18.5	18.7	18.2
1994	18.3	18.7	19.2	19.5	19.5	20.0	20.0	20.0	20.0	19.6	19.8	20.2	19.6
1995	19.6	20.0	20.1	20.0	20.0	20.2	20.7	20.7	20.6	21.0	21.1	21.4	20.5
1996	20.5	20.9	21.0	21.2	21.1	21.6	21.5	21.6	21.5	22.0	22.1	22.3	21.4
1997	21.9	22.3	22.7	23.4	23.4	23.9	24.1	24.4	24.4	25.2	25.3	25.3	23.9
1998	24.7	24.7	25.0	25.4	25.3	25.7	25.6	26.0	26.2	26.8	26.6	26.9	25.7
1999	26.1	25.6	25.9	27.3	27.2	27.7	27.8	28.0	28.2	28.9	29.1	29.6	27.6
2000	29.1	29.4	30.1	30.6	30.9	31.3	31.7	32.1	32.6	33.0	33.3	33.3	31.5
2001	33.2	33.4	33.6	33.6	33.0	32.9	32.8	32.7	32.3	32.1	31.2	30.8	32.6
2002	30.3	30.5	30.8	31.0	31.2	31.1	30.6	30.9	30.7	30.7	30.5	30.5	30.7
2003	24.8	25.0	25.0	25.3	25.1	25.4	25.3	25.5	25.4	25.5	25.2	25.6	25.3
Educational and health services													
1990	8.1	8.3	8.3	8.6	8.7	8.7	8.6	8.7	8.7	8.9	9.0	9.1	8.6
1991	9.1	9.3	9.3	9.4	9.5	9.6	9.4	9.5	9.5	9.7	9.7	9.8	9.4
1992	9.6	9.8	9.8	10.0	10.0	10.0	10.0	10.1	10.2	10.3	10.4	10.4	10.0
1993	10.4	10.5	10.6	10.7	10.7	10.7	10.7	10.7	10.8	11.0	11.0	11.1	10.7
1994	10.8	11.0	11.1	11.0	11.1	11.2	11.2	11.3	11.5	11.6	11.7	11.8	11.3
1995	11.5	11.6	11.7	11.5	11.6	11.6	11.5	11.5	11.7	12.1	12.2	12.3	11.7
1996	11.9	12.1	12.2	12.2	12.2	12.2	12.0	12.0	12.1	12.3	12.4	12.5	12.2
1997	12.5	12.6	12.7	12.7	12.7	12.7	12.6	12.7	12.9	13.0	13.1	13.2	12.8
1998	12.8	13.0	13.0	13.3	13.4	13.4	13.2	13.3	13.5	13.1	13.2	13.3	13.2
1999	13.3	13.8	13.7	14.0	14.0	14.0	14.0	14.0	14.1	14.3	14.4	14.5	14.0
2000	14.0	14.3	14.4	14.6	14.6	14.8	14.8	14.9	15.0	15.3	15.3	15.3	14.8
2001	15.0	15.3	15.3	15.3	15.5	15.5	15.4	15.5	15.6	15.8	15.9	15.9	15.5
2002	15.5	15.7	15.6	15.7	15.8	15.7	15.5	15.6	15.6	15.7	15.8	15.8	15.7
2003	15.5	15.5	15.6	15.7	15.8	15.9	15.6	15.6	15.7	16.0	16.0	16.1	15.8

Employment by Industry: Colorado—*Continued*

(Numbers in thousands. Not seasonally adjusted.)

Industry	January	February	March	April	May	June	July	August	September	October	November	December	Annual Average
BOULDER-LONGMONT *—Continued*													
Leisure and hospitality													
1990	10.4	10.7	11.0	11.2	11.7	12.2	12.1	12.4	12.1	11.8	11.6	11.5	11.5
1991	10.9	11.4	11.5	11.5	12.1	12.7	12.6	12.7	12.6	12.1	12.0	12.0	12.0
1992	11.4	11.6	11.8	11.8	12.4	12.8	12.9	12.8	12.9	12.5	12.4	12.1	12.2
1993	11.9	12.2	12.5	12.7	13.0	13.6	13.8	13.8	13.5	13.5	13.4	13.2	13.1
1994	12.4	12.9	13.3	13.0	13.6	14.4	14.5	14.7	14.6	14.2	14.3	14.3	13.9
1995	13.5	13.7	14.1	14.1	14.4	15.2	14.8	15.3	15.1	14.8	14.6	14.7	14.5
1996	13.6	13.8	14.2	14.3	14.5	15.0	14.8	15.4	15.2	14.7	14.7	14.7	14.6
1997	14.1	14.4	14.8	14.8	15.3	15.9	16.1	16.2	15.9	15.7	15.4	15.5	15.3
1998	14.5	14.8	15.0	14.9	15.3	15.7	16.0	16.0	15.8	15.3	15.2	15.3	15.3
1999	14.6	15.2	15.3	15.5	15.9	16.5	16.7	16.9	16.7	16.9	16.8	16.8	16.2
2000	16.2	16.7	17.1	16.7	17.3	17.8	18.1	18.6	18.5	18.3	18.7	18.8	17.7
2001	17.7	18.2	18.6	18.5	18.8	19.3	19.3	19.1	19.2	18.4	18.4	18.4	18.7
2002	17.6	17.8	17.9	18.2	18.7	19.1	19.1	19.1	19.0	18.4	18.2	18.1	18.4
2003	14.7	14.8	15.1	15.1	15.4	15.7	15.8	15.8	15.4	15.0	14.8	14.7	15.2
Other services													
1990	4.0	4.1	4.1	4.1	4.0	4.1	4.1	4.1	4.1	4.0	4.1	4.1	4.0
1991	4.0	4.0	4.1	4.1	4.1	4.2	4.2	4.3	4.2	4.2	4.2	4.1	4.1
1992	4.1	4.1	4.1	4.2	4.3	4.4	4.3	4.3	4.2	4.3	4.2	4.2	4.2
1993	4.2	4.2	4.3	4.3	4.4	4.5	4.7	4.6	4.5	4.7	4.7	4.7	4.5
1994	4.7	4.7	4.8	4.8	4.9	5.0	5.0	5.1	5.0	4.9	4.9	5.0	4.9
1995	4.9	4.9	5.0	5.0	5.0	5.2	5.3	5.3	5.2	5.3	5.0	5.1	5.1
1996	4.9	5.0	5.1	5.1	5.1	5.3	5.1	5.2	5.1	5.1	5.1	5.1	5.1
1997	5.2	5.2	5.3	5.3	5.2	5.4	5.4	5.4	5.3	5.3	5.3	5.3	5.3
1998	5.2	5.3	5.2	5.2	5.2	5.3	5.4	5.4	5.3	5.4	5.4	5.4	5.3
1999	5.2	5.3	5.3	5.4	5.4	5.5	5.5	5.5	5.4	5.3	5.4	5.4	5.4
2000	5.3	5.4	5.4	5.5	5.5	5.7	5.6	5.5	5.4	5.4	5.4	5.5	5.5
2001	5.3	5.4	5.4	5.4	5.4	5.6	5.6	5.6	5.5	5.5	5.5	5.5	5.5
2002	5.6	5.7	5.8	5.8	5.8	5.9	5.9	5.8	5.8	5.7	5.7	5.7	5.8
2003	5.1	5.1	5.1	5.1	5.2	5.2	5.3	5.2	5.2	5.1	5.1	5.0	5.1
Government													
1990	22.3	23.4	23.5	22.7	23.0	21.8	20.2	19.9	22.3	22.6	24.1	22.9	22.3
1991	23.1	24.2	24.5	24.4	24.5	23.0	20.9	20.5	23.8	24.7	24.6	24.6	23.5
1992	24.3	24.7	25.1	24.7	25.2	23.6	22.0	21.1	24.5	25.5	25.6	25.5	24.3
1993	24.0	25.2	25.4	25.4	25.8	24.1	22.5	21.7	24.9	25.8	25.9	26.0	24.7
1994	24.5	25.9	26.0	26.1	26.4	24.6	23.2	22.5	25.4	26.4	26.4	26.3	25.3
1995	24.9	26.2	26.5	26.3	26.6	25.3	22.8	22.4	25.1	26.2	26.3	26.2	25.4
1996	24.5	26.2	26.6	26.4	26.9	24.6	23.4	22.5	25.2	26.5	26.6	26.3	25.5
1997	24.8	26.2	26.6	26.7	27.1	25.1	23.7	23.0	25.8	27.5	27.1	26.9	25.9
1998	25.3	26.8	27.2	26.9	27.6	25.0	23.7	23.1	26.0	27.5	27.4	27.1	26.1
1999	25.5	27.1	27.1	27.4	27.7	25.2	24.2	24.2	26.8	28.1	27.9	27.8	26.6
2000	26.1	27.5	28.1	27.7	28.4	25.7	23.7	24.7	27.5	28.2	28.2	28.1	27.0
2001	26.8	28.1	28.8	28.5	28.9	27.0	25.3	25.2	28.4	29.5	29.6	29.4	28.0
2002	28.7	29.4	30.1	29.9	30.2	28.2	26.1	25.9	29.6	30.7	30.6	30.4	29.2
2003	29.0	29.3	29.5	29.4	29.5	27.2	25.4	24.5	28.4	29.5	29.7	29.6	28.4
Federal government													
1990	2.6	2.6	2.6	2.8	2.8	2.7	2.8	2.7	2.6	2.6	2.6	2.7	2.6
1991	2.6	2.6	2.6	2.6	2.6	2.7	2.7	2.6	2.6	2.6	2.6	2.6	2.6
1992	2.7	2.7	2.7	2.7	2.7	2.7	2.7	2.7	2.7	2.7	2.7	2.7	2.7
1993	2.7	2.7	2.7	2.7	2.7	2.7	2.7	2.7	2.7	2.7	2.7	2.8	2.7
1994	2.7	2.7	2.7	2.8	2.8	2.7	2.8	2.8	2.8	2.7	2.7	2.7	2.7
1995	2.7	2.7	2.7	2.7	2.7	2.7	2.7	2.7	2.7	2.7	2.7	2.7	2.7
1996	2.6	2.6	2.6	2.6	2.6	2.6	2.7	2.6	2.6	2.6	2.6	2.6	2.6
1997	2.6	2.6	2.6	2.7	2.6	2.7	2.7	2.7	2.6	2.6	2.6	2.6	2.6
1998	2.7	2.6	2.7	2.6	2.7	2.7	2.7	2.7	2.7	2.7	2.7	2.7	2.7
1999	2.7	2.7	2.7	2.7	2.7	2.7	2.7	2.7	2.7	2.7	2.7	2.7	2.7
2000	2.7	2.7	2.7	2.7	3.0	2.7	2.8	2.7	2.6	2.6	2.6	2.7	2.7
2001	2.7	2.7	2.7	2.7	2.6	2.7	2.7	2.7	2.6	2.6	2.6	2.6	2.7
2002	2.6	2.6	2.6	2.6	2.6	2.7	2.7	2.7	2.6	2.7	2.6	2.7	2.6
2003	2.6	2.6	2.6	2.6	2.6	2.6	2.7	2.6	2.6	2.6	2.6	2.6	2.6
State government													
1990	10.5	11.3	11.4	10.3	10.3	9.0	8.5	8.5	10.2	10.2	10.5	10.5	10.1
1991	10.9	11.8	12.1	11.9	11.8	9.9	9.0	8.9	11.3	11.9	12.0	12.0	11.1
1992	11.6	11.9	12.2	11.9	11.9	10.0	9.6	8.9	11.5	12.1	12.2	12.3	11.3
1993	10.9	11.9	12.0	11.9	12.1	10.0	9.7	9.1	11.7	12.2	12.3	12.4	11.4
1994	11.1	12.2	12.3	12.2	12.3	10.2	10.0	9.5	11.7	12.4	12.4	12.5	11.6
1995	11.2	12.3	12.4	12.3	12.3	10.6	9.9	9.4	11.4	12.2	12.4	12.5	11.6
1996	10.9	12.3	12.5	12.3	12.6	9.8	9.8	9.4	11.3	12.2	12.4	12.3	11.5
1997	11.0	12.2	12.4	12.2	12.5	9.8	9.8	9.5	11.5	12.8	12.5	12.5	11.6
1998	11.0	12.4	12.6	12.4	12.8	9.8	9.9	9.5	11.5	12.7	12.5	12.4	11.6
1999	10.9	12.2	12.2	12.6	12.6	9.7	9.7	9.5	11.6	12.7	12.5	12.5	11.6
2000	11.0	12.1	12.7	12.3	12.5	9.8	8.8	10.2	12.2	12.8	12.8	12.8	11.7
2001	11.3	12.4	13.0	12.6	12.8	10.6	10.2	10.2	12.6	13.2	13.2	13.2	12.1
2002	12.4	12.9	13.5	13.2	13.3	11.1	10.8	10.7	13.3	13.8	13.8	13.8	12.7
2003	13.4	13.6	13.7	13.5	13.4	11.0	10.6	10.3	12.9	13.5	13.5	13.5	12.7

Employment by Industry: Colorado—*Continued*

(Numbers in thousands. Not seasonally adjusted.)

Industry	January	February	March	April	May	June	July	August	September	October	November	December	Annual Average
BOULDER-LONGMONT —*Continued*													
Local government													
1990	9.2	9.5	9.5	9.6	9.9	10.1	8.9	8.7	9.5	9.8	11.0	9.7	9.6
1991	9.6	9.8	9.8	9.9	10.1	10.4	9.2	9.0	9.9	10.2	10.0	10.0	9.8
1992	10.0	10.1	10.2	10.1	10.6	10.9	9.7	9.5	10.3	10.7	10.7	10.5	10.2
1993	10.4	10.6	10.7	10.8	11.0	11.4	10.1	9.9	10.5	10.9	10.9	10.8	10.7
1994	10.7	11.0	11.0	11.1	11.3	11.7	10.4	10.2	10.9	11.3	11.3	11.1	11.0
1995	11.0	11.2	11.4	11.3	11.6	12.0	10.2	10.3	11.0	11.3	11.2	11.0	11.1
1996	11.0	11.3	11.5	11.5	11.7	12.2	10.9	10.5	11.3	11.7	11.6	11.4	11.4
1997	11.2	11.4	11.6	11.8	12.0	12.6	11.2	10.8	11.7	12.1	12.0	11.8	11.7
1998	11.6	11.8	11.9	11.9	12.1	12.5	11.1	10.9	11.8	12.1	12.2	12.0	11.8
1999	11.9	12.2	12.2	12.1	12.4	12.8	11.8	12.0	12.5	12.7	12.7	12.6	12.3
2000	12.4	12.7	12.7	12.7	12.9	13.2	12.1	11.8	12.7	12.8	12.8	12.6	12.6
2001	12.8	13.0	13.1	13.2	13.5	13.7	12.4	12.3	13.2	13.7	13.8	13.6	13.2
2002	13.7	13.9	14.0	14.1	14.3	14.4	12.6	12.5	13.7	14.2	14.2	13.9	13.8
2003	13.0	13.1	13.2	13.3	13.5	13.6	12.1	11.6	12.9	13.4	13.6	13.5	13.1
COLORADO SPRINGS													
Total nonfarm													
1990	150.3	150.2	151.4	152.7	155.5	158.1	156.3	157.2	155.9	156.7	157.7	156.8	154.9
1991	152.5	151.7	153.5	154.9	157.7	160.6	161.1	160.3	159.6	160.6	162.8	162.9	158.1
1992	159.5	159.6	160.6	162.2	165.5	168.1	167.8	168.1	168.9	170.4	171.1	171.3	166.0
1993	166.9	167.5	169.7	173.2	175.8	178.0	178.3	178.4	178.7	179.9	181.5	183.4	175.9
1994	174.9	176.2	177.6	181.6	185.0	188.4	187.0	188.0	188.8	190.0	192.1	193.5	185.2
1995	187.7	189.3	191.2	191.5	195.0	199.4	197.9	200.2	201.8	202.8	204.8	206.6	197.3
1996	199.8	200.7	202.7	204.8	208.8	211.6	209.4	211.3	211.2	210.5	212.6	214.8	208.1
1997	208.8	210.8	212.6	214.1	216.9	219.6	219.4	219.4	219.9	221.3	222.6	224.0	217.5
1998	219.0	219.3	220.1	221.7	224.6	227.3	226.8	225.3	224.4	225.5	226.2	227.4	224.0
1999	225.7	227.9	229.0	231.2	234.2	237.1	237.5	236.7	237.1	237.1	238.1	239.5	234.3
2000	233.2	234.2	236.4	238.7	242.1	246.2	245.4	246.0	245.8	246.4	247.5	248.2	242.5
2001	243.5	243.2	244.0	244.5	246.8	249.6	246.3	245.6	243.1	242.2	242.1	242.5	244.5
2002	236.1	236.7	238.2	238.7	242.4	244.0	241.1	241.7	240.9	240.3	240.3	240.2	240.1
2003	233.7	233.8	234.5	236.3	238.6	240.5	238.6	239.0	239.9	239.5	239.0	239.5	237.7
Total private													
1990	121.8	121.3	122.2	124.0	126.3	129.0	128.8	130.1	128.5	128.1	128.7	127.9	126.3
1991	124.2	123.1	124.2	125.4	128.0	130.5	130.9	131.9	131.6	131.8	133.0	132.8	128.9
1992	129.3	129.1	130.0	131.7	134.7	137.2	138.8	139.7	139.6	140.1	140.4	140.7	135.9
1993	135.9	136.3	138.1	141.6	143.9	146.0	148.2	148.6	147.9	148.2	149.7	151.4	144.6
1994	143.4	144.0	145.8	148.8	151.9	155.6	156.4	157.3	156.6	156.5	158.4	159.9	152.8
1995	155.0	155.9	157.5	158.4	161.8	166.3	166.8	168.6	168.8	168.9	170.6	172.4	164.2
1996	166.4	167.0	168.5	170.7	174.4	177.4	177.0	179.4	177.9	176.2	177.8	179.9	174.3
1997	174.5	176.1	177.6	179.1	181.7	184.5	186.0	186.6	185.7	185.8	186.7	188.1	182.7
1998	183.8	183.5	184.0	185.7	188.4	191.2	191.9	191.4	189.3	188.8	189.1	190.1	188.1
1999	189.6	190.9	192.0	194.2	197.0	200.4	201.3	201.5	200.5	199.6	200.2	201.2	197.4
2000	196.4	196.4	198.4	200.2	202.9	207.6	209.1	210.3	209.2	208.2	208.9	210.1	204.8
2001	205.5	204.5	205.2	205.9	207.9	210.7	209.5	208.2	204.5	202.6	202.0	202.3	205.7
2002	196.8	196.7	197.7	198.3	201.6	203.7	203.3	203.9	201.3	199.4	199.1	199.0	200.1
2003	193.1	192.6	193.0	195.3	197.2	199.6	200.0	200.6	199.5	198.4	197.5	198.0	197.1
Goods-producing													
1990	26.6	26.0	26.2	26.4	26.8	27.2	27.2	27.3	27.2	27.3	27.2	26.9	26.8
1991	26.0	25.0	25.1	25.4	25.8	26.2	26.4	26.6	26.8	26.8	26.6	26.3	26.0
1992	25.8	25.4	25.4	25.4	26.1	26.5	26.9	27.1	27.3	27.9	28.3	28.1	26.6
1993	27.8	27.5	27.9	28.6	28.8	29.1	29.8	29.9	29.8	30.0	30.3	30.4	29.1
1994	29.3	29.1	29.1	30.0	30.5	31.2	31.5	31.4	31.4	31.7	31.8	31.8	30.7
1995	31.7	32.0	32.2	32.4	32.9	33.6	33.5	33.7	33.9	34.2	34.6	35.2	33.3
1996	33.8	34.2	34.4	34.5	34.8	35.0	35.1	35.9	35.5	35.6	35.9	36.1	35.0
1997	35.2	35.5	35.7	35.7	36.3	36.5	37.5	37.6	37.7	37.9	37.7	38.0	36.8
1998	37.6	37.6	37.8	37.8	38.1	38.4	38.4	37.7	37.4	37.7	37.3	37.4	37.8
1999	37.2	37.6	37.4	38.3	38.7	39.1	39.5	39.3	38.9	38.7	38.6	38.4	38.5
2000	38.0	38.3	38.6	39.0	39.9	40.6	41.7	42.2	42.2	42.4	42.4	42.9	40.7
2001	42.3	42.0	42.3	42.2	42.3	42.3	41.9	41.2	40.1	39.9	38.8	38.5	41.2
2002	37.2	36.9	37.0	37.3	37.8	38.3	38.3	38.1	37.4	37.0	36.3	36.3	37.3
2003	35.5	35.1	35.1	35.5	35.8	36.1	35.9	35.6	35.3	35.5	35.1	35.1	35.5
Construction and mining													
1990	6.0	5.8	6.0	6.2	6.5	6.9	7.0	7.0	6.6	6.7	6.5	6.3	6.4
1991	5.6	5.6	5.8	6.1	6.6	6.9	7.2	7.2	7.1	7.3	7.3	7.1	6.6
1992	6.5	6.5	6.6	7.0	7.5	7.9	8.1	8.1	8.2	8.4	8.5	8.2	7.6
1993	7.7	7.8	8.1	8.6	8.8	9.0	9.3	9.2	9.0	9.2	9.2	9.1	8.7
1994	8.3	8.3	8.6	9.1	9.3	9.9	10.1	10.1	10.1	9.8	9.8	9.6	9.4
1995	9.1	9.1	9.5	9.7	10.0	10.5	10.6	10.7	10.6	10.6	10.6	10.8	10.1
1996	10.3	10.5	11.0	11.5	12.0	12.4	12.3	12.5	12.1	11.9	11.9	11.8	11.6
1997	11.1	11.4	11.7	11.9	12.2	12.3	12.7	12.7	12.7	12.5	12.1	12.2	12.1
1998	12.1	12.1	12.4	12.8	13.1	13.5	13.8	13.2	13.2	13.1	12.6	12.5	12.9
1999	12.3	12.4	12.7	13.5	13.7	14.3	14.6	14.6	14.3	14.2	14.1	14.1	13.7
2000	13.6	13.8	14.2	14.4	15.0	15.5	16.2	16.5	16.4	16.4	16.3	16.4	15.4
2001	15.9	15.8	16.0	15.9	16.3	16.6	16.4	16.3	15.7	15.7	15.3	15.1	15.9
2002	14.4	14.5	14.7	14.9	15.3	15.8	15.9	15.9	15.4	15.2	14.8	14.6	15.1
2003	14.4	14.2	14.4	14.6	15.0	15.3	15.4	15.2	15.2	15.3	14.8	14.6	14.9

Employment by Industry: Colorado—*Continued*

(Numbers in thousands. Not seasonally adjusted.)

Industry	January	February	March	April	May	June	July	August	September	October	November	December	Annual Average
COLORADO SPRINGS *—Continued*													
Manufacturing													
1990	20.6	20.2	20.2	20.2	20.3	20.3	20.2	20.3	20.6	20.6	20.7	20.6	20.4
1991	20.4	19.4	19.3	19.3	19.2	19.3	19.2	19.4	19.7	19.5	19.3	19.2	19.4
1992	19.3	18.9	18.8	18.4	18.6	18.6	18.8	19.0	19.1	19.5	19.8	19.9	19.0
1993	20.1	19.7	19.8	20.0	20.0	20.1	20.5	20.7	20.8	20.8	21.1	21.3	20.4
1994	21.0	20.8	20.5	20.9	21.2	21.3	21.4	21.3	21.3	21.9	22.0	22.2	21.3
1995	22.6	22.9	22.7	22.7	22.9	23.1	22.9	23.0	23.3	23.6	24.0	24.4	23.1
1996	23.5	23.7	23.4	23.0	22.8	22.6	22.8	23.4	23.4	23.7	24.0	24.3	23.3
1997	24.1	24.1	24.0	23.8	24.1	24.2	24.8	24.9	25.0	25.4	25.6	25.8	24.7
1998	25.5	25.5	25.4	25.0	25.0	24.9	24.6	24.5	24.2	24.6	24.7	24.9	24.9
1999	24.9	25.2	24.7	24.8	25.0	24.8	24.9	24.7	24.6	24.5	24.5	24.3	24.7
2000	24.4	24.5	24.4	24.6	24.9	25.1	25.5	25.7	25.8	26.0	26.1	26.5	25.3
2001	26.4	26.2	26.3	26.3	26.0	25.7	25.5	24.9	24.4	24.2	23.5	23.4	25.2
2002	22.8	22.4	22.3	22.4	22.5	22.5	22.4	22.2	22.0	21.8	21.5	21.7	22.2
2003	21.1	20.9	20.7	20.9	20.8	20.8	20.5	20.4	20.1	20.2	20.3	20.5	20.6
Service-providing													
1990	123.7	124.2	125.2	126.3	128.7	130.9	129.1	129.9	128.7	129.4	130.5	129.9	128.0
1991	126.5	126.7	128.4	129.5	131.9	134.4	134.7	133.7	132.8	133.8	136.2	136.6	132.1
1992	133.7	134.2	135.2	136.8	139.4	141.6	140.9	141.0	141.6	142.5	142.8	143.2	139.4
1993	139.1	140.0	141.8	144.6	147.0	148.9	148.5	148.5	148.9	149.9	151.2	153.0	146.7
1994	145.6	147.1	148.5	151.6	154.5	157.2	155.5	156.6	157.4	158.3	160.3	161.7	154.5
1995	156.0	157.3	159.0	159.1	162.1	165.8	164.4	166.5	167.9	168.6	170.2	171.4	164.0
1996	166.0	166.5	168.3	170.3	174.0	176.6	174.3	175.4	175.7	174.9	176.7	178.7	173.1
1997	173.6	175.3	176.9	178.4	180.6	183.1	181.9	181.8	182.2	183.4	184.9	186.0	180.7
1998	181.4	181.7	182.3	183.9	186.5	188.9	188.4	187.6	187.0	187.8	188.9	190.0	186.2
1999	188.5	190.3	191.6	192.9	195.5	198.0	198.0	197.4	198.2	198.4	199.5	201.1	195.8
2000	195.2	195.9	197.8	199.7	202.2	205.6	203.7	203.8	203.6	204.0	205.1	205.3	201.8
2001	201.2	201.2	201.7	202.3	204.5	207.3	204.4	204.4	203.0	202.3	203.3	204.0	203.3
2002	198.9	199.8	201.2	201.4	204.6	205.7	202.8	203.6	203.5	203.3	204.0	203.9	202.7
2003	198.2	198.7	199.4	200.8	202.8	204.4	202.7	203.4	204.6	204.0	203.9	204.4	202.3
Trade, transportation, and utilities													
1990	25.4	25.0	25.1	25.5	25.7	26.1	26.2	26.5	26.1	26.0	26.7	26.9	25.9
1991	25.6	25.2	25.0	24.9	25.4	25.6	25.9	26.2	25.8	26.2	26.9	27.1	25.8
1992	25.7	25.4	25.6	25.9	26.4	26.8	27.1	27.2	27.2	27.4	27.9	28.4	26.7
1993	25.9	25.8	26.2	26.7	27.2	27.5	27.8	28.0	27.8	28.2	29.0	29.5	27.4
1994	27.7	27.4	27.6	27.9	28.5	29.1	29.4	29.7	29.5	29.7	30.7	31.3	29.0
1995	29.4	29.2	29.4	29.5	30.1	30.7	30.8	31.6	32.1	32.6	33.7	34.6	31.1
1996	33.1	32.9	33.0	33.5	34.3	34.6	34.8	35.5	35.5	35.4	36.2	36.9	34.6
1997	34.6	34.2	34.3	34.9	35.6	35.9	35.9	36.4	36.3	36.7	37.3	37.9	35.8
1998	35.8	34.6	34.2	33.9	34.2	34.7	34.8	34.8	34.5	35.2	36.0	36.5	34.9
1999	35.3	35.1	35.3	35.5	35.9	36.6	36.9	37.1	36.9	36.8	37.8	38.6	36.5
2000	36.7	36.5	36.6	37.0	37.3	37.4	37.7	38.0	38.1	38.7	39.6	39.9	37.8
2001	38.3	37.7	37.7	37.7	38.0	38.6	38.6	38.5	38.1	38.1	39.2	39.6	38.3
2002	37.6	37.1	37.2	37.3	37.8	38.1	38.0	38.3	38.3	38.1	38.9	39.4	38.0
2003	37.2	36.6	36.6	37.1	37.3	37.4	37.4	37.6	37.8	37.9	38.2	38.6	37.5
Wholesale trade													
1990	3.8	3.8	3.9	3.9	3.8	3.9	3.9	3.9	3.8	3.8	3.9	3.9	3.8
1991	3.8	3.8	3.8	3.7	3.7	3.8	3.9	3.9	3.9	3.9	4.0	4.0	3.8
1992	4.0	4.1	4.1	4.1	4.1	4.2	4.2	4.2	4.2	4.2	4.2	4.2	4.1
1993	4.2	4.2	4.3	4.4	4.5	4.5	4.4	4.5	4.5	4.5	4.5	4.6	4.4
1994	4.5	4.5	4.5	4.7	4.8	4.9	4.9	4.9	4.9	4.9	5.0	5.0	4.7
1995	4.6	4.7	4.7	4.4	4.5	4.5	4.5	4.5	4.5	4.5	4.6	4.7	4.5
1996	4.6	4.6	4.7	4.7	4.7	4.8	4.9	5.0	5.0	5.1	5.1	5.2	4.8
1997	4.9	5.0	5.1	5.3	5.4	5.4	5.4	5.7	5.7	5.8	5.7	5.8	5.4
1998	5.7	5.7	5.7	5.6	5.6	5.7	5.7	5.7	5.7	5.9	5.8	5.8	5.7
1999	5.9	5.9	5.9	5.9	5.9	6.0	6.0	6.0	6.0	6.0	6.0	6.1	6.0
2000	6.0	6.0	6.1	6.1	6.2	6.3	6.4	6.4	6.4	6.4	6.4	6.3	6.3
2001	6.3	6.4	6.4	6.3	6.3	6.4	6.4	6.3	6.3	6.3	6.4	6.4	6.4
2002	6.2	6.2	6.2	6.1	6.1	6.1	6.1	6.2	6.2	6.1	6.1	6.2	6.2
2003	5.9	5.8	5.8	5.9	5.9	5.9	5.9	5.8	5.8	5.7	5.6	5.6	5.8
Retail trade													
1990	18.6	18.2	18.2	18.5	18.8	19.0	19.1	19.4	19.2	19.0	19.6	19.7	18.9
1991	18.7	18.3	18.2	18.2	18.6	18.7	18.9	19.2	18.9	19.2	19.7	19.9	18.8
1992	18.6	18.2	18.3	18.6	19.0	19.2	19.4	19.6	19.6	19.8	20.3	20.7	19.2
1993	18.3	18.3	18.6	18.9	19.2	19.4	19.8	19.9	19.7	20.1	20.8	21.1	19.5
1994	19.4	19.0	19.2	19.4	19.8	20.2	20.5	20.8	20.7	21.0	21.9	22.4	20.3
1995	21.1	20.9	21.0	21.2	21.5	21.8	21.8	22.4	22.8	23.2	24.0	24.7	22.2
1996	23.3	23.0	22.9	23.1	23.8	23.9	24.0	24.5	24.5	24.6	25.3	25.8	24.0
1997	24.0	23.4	23.5	23.9	24.4	24.7	24.7	24.9	24.9	25.3	26.1	26.7	24.7
1998	25.2	24.8	24.8	24.7	25.0	25.3	25.5	25.5	25.2	25.6	26.6	27.0	25.4
1999	25.9	25.7	25.8	26.0	26.3	26.8	26.9	27.1	27.0	27.0	28.0	28.6	26.8
2000	27.0	26.7	26.7	26.9	27.2	27.2	27.3	27.5	27.6	28.3	29.2	29.6	27.6
2001	27.9	27.3	27.3	27.4	27.6	28.0	27.9	27.9	27.6	27.6	28.6	29.0	27.8
2002	27.3	26.8	26.9	27.1	27.5	27.8	27.6	27.8	27.9	28.0	28.7	29.2	27.7
2003	27.3	26.9	26.9	27.2	27.4	27.4	27.4	27.8	27.9	28.1	28.4	28.8	27.6

Employment by Industry: Colorado—*Continued*

(Numbers in thousands. Not seasonally adjusted.)

Industry	January	February	March	April	May	June	July	August	September	October	November	December	Annual Average
COLORADO SPRINGS *—Continued*													
Transportation and utilities													
1990	3.0	3.0	3.0	3.1	3.1	3.2	3.2	3.2	3.1	3.2	3.2	3.3	3.1
1991	3.1	3.1	3.0	3.0	3.1	3.1	3.1	3.1	3.0	3.1	3.2	3.2	3.0
1992	3.1	3.1	3.2	3.2	3.3	3.4	3.5	3.4	3.4	3.4	3.4	3.5	3.3
1993	3.4	3.3	3.3	3.4	3.5	3.6	3.6	3.6	3.6	3.6	3.7	3.8	3.5
1994	3.8	3.9	3.9	3.8	3.9	4.0	4.0	4.0	3.9	3.8	3.8	3.9	3.8
1995	3.7	3.6	3.7	3.9	4.1	4.4	4.5	4.7	4.8	4.9	5.1	5.2	4.3
1996	5.2	5.3	5.4	5.7	5.8	5.9	5.9	6.0	6.0	5.7	5.8	5.9	5.7
1997	5.7	5.8	5.7	5.7	5.8	5.8	5.8	5.8	5.7	5.6	5.5	5.4	5.7
1998	4.9	4.1	3.7	3.6	3.6	3.7	3.6	3.6	3.6	3.7	3.6	3.7	3.8
1999	3.5	3.5	3.6	3.6	3.7	3.8	4.0	4.0	3.9	3.8	3.8	3.9	3.8
2000	3.7	3.8	3.8	4.0	3.9	3.9	4.0	4.1	4.1	4.0	4.0	4.0	3.9
2001	4.1	4.0	4.0	4.0	4.1	4.2	4.3	4.3	4.2	4.2	4.2	4.2	4.2
2002	4.1	4.1	4.1	4.1	4.2	4.2	4.3	4.3	4.2	4.0	4.1	4.0	4.1
2003	4.0	3.9	3.9	4.0	4.0	4.1	4.1	4.0	4.1	4.1	4.2	4.2	4.1
Information													
1990	4.9	5.0	5.0	5.0	5.1	5.0	5.0	5.0	4.9	5.0	4.9	4.9	4.9
1991	5.4	5.4	5.4	5.1	5.0	5.2	5.3	5.2	5.2	5.0	5.0	5.0	5.1
1992	5.1	5.2	5.4	5.4	5.5	5.5	5.5	5.5	5.3	5.4	5.4	5.5	5.3
1993	5.3	5.2	5.3	5.5	5.5	5.6	5.8	5.8	5.7	5.7	5.7	5.8	5.5
1994	5.6	6.0	6.2	6.3	6.3	6.3	6.3	6.4	6.3	6.3	6.5	6.6	6.2
1995	6.2	6.3	6.5	6.5	6.5	6.6	6.7	6.8	6.8	6.8	7.0	7.2	6.6
1996	7.2	7.2	7.2	6.9	6.9	7.1	7.0	7.0	6.8	7.0	7.0	7.2	7.0
1997	7.0	7.0	7.0	7.2	7.2	7.3	7.2	7.3	7.3	7.3	7.5	7.5	7.2
1998	8.2	8.4	8.4	8.3	8.6	8.2	8.7	8.5	9.3	9.4	9.5	9.3	8.7
1999	9.8	9.6	9.7	9.8	9.9	10.1	10.1	10.2	11.0	11.2	11.4	11.5	10.4
2000	11.8	11.5	11.7	11.8	11.9	12.4	12.4	12.4	12.6	12.7	12.9	12.9	12.3
2001	15.2	14.8	14.3	14.2	14.0	14.3	14.1	14.0	13.9	13.9	14.0	14.0	14.2
2002	13.9	13.3	13.2	13.0	12.9	12.7	12.0	11.7	11.6	11.5	11.6	11.0	12.4
2003	10.9	10.7	10.5	10.5	10.4	10.4	10.3	10.1	10.2	10.2	10.3	10.3	10.4
Financial activities													
1990	8.8	8.8	8.8	9.0	9.1	8.9	8.8	8.8	8.7	8.8	8.9	8.9	8.8
1991	8.8	8.8	8.9	8.9	8.9	8.9	8.9	8.9	8.8	8.9	8.9	9.0	8.8
1992	9.1	9.1	9.2	9.3	9.3	9.3	9.3	9.4	9.4	9.3	9.4	9.5	9.3
1993	9.5	9.5	9.7	10.1	10.2	10.4	10.4	10.4	10.4	10.5	10.5	10.8	10.2
1994	10.0	10.0	10.1	10.4	10.4	10.6	10.6	10.7	10.7	10.6	10.7	10.9	10.4
1995	10.6	10.7	10.8	10.8	10.9	11.1	11.1	11.2	11.3	11.3	11.4	11.6	11.0
1996	11.3	11.4	11.5	11.5	11.8	11.8	11.8	12.0	12.0	12.1	12.2	12.4	11.8
1997	12.4	12.6	12.7	12.8	12.9	13.0	12.9	12.9	12.9	13.1	13.3	13.4	12.9
1998	13.1	13.3	13.4	14.0	14.0	14.1	14.2	14.4	14.3	14.5	14.6	14.6	14.0
1999	14.8	14.8	14.9	15.1	15.2	15.3	15.0	14.9	14.9	15.0	15.1	15.3	15.0
2000	15.2	15.3	15.1	15.2	15.4	15.4	15.3	15.2	15.2	15.4	15.4	15.7	15.3
2001	14.7	14.9	15.1	15.2	15.3	15.4	15.5	15.5	15.5	15.5	15.7	15.8	15.3
2002	15.9	16.0	16.1	16.0	16.2	16.3	16.3	16.4	16.4	16.4	16.6	16.7	16.3
2003	16.4	16.6	16.7	16.7	16.8	16.9	16.9	17.0	16.9	16.7	17.1	17.4	16.8
Professional and business services													
1990	16.5	16.5	16.4	16.9	17.1	17.5	17.4	17.7	17.6	18.1	18.2	17.8	17.3
1991	17.7	17.8	17.9	18.3	18.5	18.8	18.5	18.8	19.0	19.9	20.5	20.6	18.8
1992	19.5	19.5	19.4	19.9	20.1	20.7	21.0	21.3	21.9	22.4	22.0	21.9	20.8
1993	21.8	22.1	22.6	23.4	23.8	23.9	24.3	24.3	24.4	24.9	25.4	26.0	23.9
1994	23.9	24.1	24.5	25.3	26.1	26.6	26.3	26.8	26.8	26.7	27.1	27.4	25.9
1995	26.8	26.9	27.1	26.4	26.7	27.7	28.8	29.3	29.7	30.3	30.3	30.2	28.3
1996	27.7	27.7	28.0	29.7	30.1	31.1	30.8	31.2	30.9	29.9	30.3	30.9	29.8
1997	30.6	31.2	31.8	31.9	32.1	32.8	33.6	33.2	33.5	33.9	34.2	34.2	32.8
1998	33.5	33.5	33.8	35.0	35.2	35.7	35.9	35.7	34.8	34.6	34.6	35.0	34.8
1999	36.4	36.9	37.5	38.1	38.0	38.3	39.2	39.4	38.5	38.7	38.3	38.4	38.1
2000	37.9	37.4	37.9	38.0	38.2	38.7	39.1	39.2	39.3	38.7	38.5	38.4	38.4
2001	35.4	35.0	35.2	35.1	35.2	35.5	34.9	34.7	34.0	33.7	33.4	33.2	34.6
2002	32.5	32.8	33.3	32.9	33.1	33.1	33.4	33.9	33.4	33.2	33.2	33.1	33.2
2003	32.3	32.7	32.6	33.2	33.1	33.3	33.9	34.5	34.3	34.3	33.8	33.6	33.5
Educational and health services													
1990	15.2	15.3	15.5	15.7	15.8	16.0	15.9	16.1	16.0	16.2	16.4	16.5	15.8
1991	16.2	16.6	16.8	17.0	17.2	17.3	17.0	17.3	17.5	17.5	17.6	17.7	17.1
1992	17.9	18.2	18.3	18.3	18.5	18.5	18.5	18.6	19.0	18.8	18.9	19.0	18.5
1993	18.5	18.8	18.7	18.9	19.1	19.1	19.1	19.0	19.6	19.5	19.6	19.6	19.1
1994	19.0	19.2	19.3	19.0	19.2	19.4	19.5	19.5	20.0	20.1	20.3	20.5	19.5
1995	19.8	20.1	20.2	20.6	20.9	20.8	20.4	20.6	20.8	20.7	21.0	20.6	20.5
1996	20.9	21.1	21.3	21.1	21.5	21.3	20.9	21.3	21.7	21.7	22.0	22.1	21.4
1997	21.7	22.1	22.2	22.1	22.0	22.0	21.6	21.7	21.9	22.0	22.1	22.3	22.0
1998	21.8	21.9	21.9	21.5	21.6	21.4	21.2	21.5	21.4	20.9	20.9	21.0	21.4
1999	20.7	21.1	20.9	20.7	20.7	20.6	20.3	20.5	20.7	20.9	20.8	21.0	20.7
2000	20.1	20.4	20.7	20.9	20.0	21.0	20.9	21.3	21.2	21.0	21.2	21.3	20.8
2001	21.2	21.5	21.4	21.5	21.7	21.6	21.7	22.0	22.0	22.1	22.2	22.3	21.8
2002	21.8	22.2	22.2	22.4	22.5	22.3	22.2	22.6	22.7	22.8	22.8	22.8	22.4
2003	22.4	22.6	22.7	22.8	22.9	22.9	22.8	22.9	23.1	23.1	23.2	23.3	22.9

Employment by Industry: Colorado—*Continued*

(Numbers in thousands. Not seasonally adjusted.)

Industry	January	February	March	April	May	June	July	August	September	October	November	December	Annual Average
COLORADO SPRINGS *—Continued*													
Leisure and hospitality													
1990	17.0	17.2	17.7	18.1	19.2	20.6	20.6	21.0	20.5	19.2	18.8	18.4	19.0
1991	17.3	17.1	17.7	18.5	19.8	21.0	21.3	21.3	20.6	19.4	19.2	18.6	19.3
1992	17.8	17.9	18.4	19.1	20.3	21.3	21.8	21.9	21.0	20.2	19.8	19.5	19.9
1993	18.6	18.8	19.1	19.7	20.5	21.4	22.0	22.1	21.3	20.5	20.2	20.1	20.3
1994	19.1	19.3	20.1	21.0	21.8	23.1	23.4	23.3	22.5	21.9	21.7	21.7	21.5
1995	20.9	21.2	21.5	22.5	23.9	25.5	25.3	25.3	24.2	23.0	23.1	23.4	23.3
1996	22.7	22.7	23.2	23.7	25.1	26.3	26.5	26.4	25.6	24.5	24.2	24.2	24.5
1997	23.0	23.2	23.5	24.2	25.2	26.3	26.6	26.7	25.5	24.2	23.9	24.0	24.7
1998	23.0	23.2	23.5	24.1	25.5	27.2	27.2	27.2	26.1	25.1	24.8	24.7	25.1
1999	23.8	24.1	24.4	24.8	26.6	28.0	27.6	27.6	27.0	25.9	25.7	25.4	25.9
2000	24.1	24.3	24.9	25.5	27.1	28.5	28.6	28.6	27.3	26.3	25.7	25.7	26.4
2001	25.0	25.1	25.6	26.3	27.6	28.8	28.6	28.3	27.1	25.9	25.2	25.3	26.6
2002	24.3	24.7	24.9	25.6	27.3	28.5	28.7	28.6	27.6	26.6	25.9	25.9	26.6
2003	24.6	24.5	24.9	25.7	26.9	28.2	28.5	28.8	28.1	27.1	26.1	26.0	26.6
Other services													
1990	7.4	7.5	7.5	7.4	7.5	7.7	7.7	7.7	7.5	7.5	7.6	7.6	7.5
1991	7.2	7.2	7.4	7.3	7.4	7.5	7.6	7.6	7.9	8.1	8.3	8.5	7.6
1992	8.4	8.4	8.3	8.4	8.5	8.6	8.7	8.7	8.5	8.7	8.7	8.8	8.5
1993	8.5	8.6	8.6	8.7	8.8	9.0	9.0	9.1	8.9	8.9	9.0	9.2	8.8
1994	8.8	8.9	8.9	8.9	9.1	9.3	9.4	9.5	9.4	9.5	9.6	9.7	9.2
1995	9.6	9.5	9.8	9.7	9.9	10.3	10.2	10.1	10.0	10.0	9.5	9.6	9.8
1996	9.7	9.8	9.9	9.8	9.9	10.2	10.1	10.1	9.9	10.0	10.0	10.1	9.9
1997	10.0	10.3	10.4	10.3	10.4	10.7	10.7	10.8	10.6	10.7	10.7	10.8	10.5
1998	10.8	11.0	11.0	11.1	11.2	11.5	11.5	11.6	11.5	11.4	11.4	11.6	11.3
1999	11.6	11.7	11.9	11.9	12.0	12.4	12.7	12.5	12.6	12.4	12.5	12.6	12.2
2000	12.6	12.7	12.9	12.8	13.1	13.6	13.4	13.4	13.3	13.0	13.2	13.3	13.1
2001	13.4	13.5	13.6	13.7	13.8	14.2	14.2	14.0	13.8	13.5	13.5	13.6	13.7
2002	13.6	13.7	13.8	13.8	14.0	14.4	14.4	14.3	13.9	13.8	13.8	13.8	13.9
2003	13.8	13.8	13.9	13.8	14.0	14.4	14.3	14.1	13.8	13.6	13.7	13.7	13.9
Government													
1990	28.5	28.9	29.2	28.7	29.2	29.1	27.5	27.1	27.4	28.6	29.0	28.9	28.5
1991	28.3	28.6	29.3	29.5	29.7	30.1	30.2	28.4	28.0	28.8	29.8	30.1	29.2
1992	30.2	30.5	30.6	30.5	30.8	30.9	29.0	28.4	29.3	30.3	30.7	30.6	30.1
1993	31.0	31.2	31.6	31.6	31.9	32.0	30.1	29.8	30.8	31.7	31.8	32.0	31.2
1994	31.5	32.2	31.8	32.8	33.1	32.8	30.6	30.7	32.2	33.5	33.7	33.6	32.3
1995	32.7	33.4	33.7	33.1	33.2	33.1	31.1	31.6	33.0	33.9	34.2	34.2	33.1
1996	33.4	33.7	34.2	34.1	34.4	34.2	32.4	31.9	33.3	34.3	34.8	34.9	33.8
1997	34.3	34.7	35.0	35.0	35.2	35.1	33.4	32.8	34.2	35.5	35.9	35.9	34.8
1998	35.2	35.8	36.1	36.0	36.2	36.1	34.9	33.9	35.1	36.7	37.1	37.3	35.9
1999	36.1	37.0	37.0	37.0	37.2	36.7	36.2	35.2	36.6	37.5	37.9	38.3	36.9
2000	36.8	37.8	38.0	38.5	39.2	38.6	36.3	35.7	36.6	38.2	38.6	38.1	37.7
2001	38.0	38.7	38.8	38.6	38.9	38.9	36.8	37.4	38.6	39.6	40.1	40.2	38.7
2002	39.3	40.0	40.5	40.4	40.8	40.3	37.8	37.8	39.6	40.9	41.2	41.2	40.0
2003	40.6	41.2	41.5	41.0	41.4	40.9	38.6	38.4	40.4	41.1	41.5	41.5	40.7
Federal government													
1990	10.0	9.9	10.0	9.8	10.0	10.0	10.1	9.9	9.8	9.7	9.7	9.7	9.8
1991	9.4	9.4	9.4	9.7	9.8	9.9	10.0	10.0	10.0	9.8	9.8	9.8	9.7
1992	9.7	9.6	9.6	9.7	9.7	9.7	9.6	9.6	9.5	9.5	9.5	9.5	9.6
1993	9.5	9.4	9.4	9.5	9.6	9.7	9.7	9.7	9.7	9.7	9.7	9.7	9.6
1994	10.1	10.0	10.0	10.2	10.3	10.4	10.5	10.5	10.5	10.5	10.5	10.5	10.3
1995	10.4	10.3	10.3	9.9	9.9	10.0	10.1	10.1	10.1	10.0	10.0	10.1	10.1
1996	9.9	9.8	9.9	9.9	10.0	10.2	10.3	10.3	10.3	10.3	10.3	10.4	10.1
1997	10.3	10.2	10.2	10.2	10.2	10.3	10.3	10.4	10.3	10.3	10.3	10.4	10.3
1998	10.1	10.1	10.1	10.2	10.2	10.4	10.5	10.5	10.3	10.3	10.3	10.5	10.3
1999	10.2	10.2	10.2	10.2	10.2	10.4	10.6	10.5	10.4	10.3	10.3	10.6	10.3
2000	10.3	10.4	10.5	10.5	11.2	10.9	11.0	10.8	10.4	10.3	10.3	10.4	10.6
2001	10.2	10.1	10.1	10.2	10.2	10.4	10.6	10.5	10.3	10.3	10.4	10.5	10.3
2002	10.3	10.2	10.2	10.2	10.2	10.3	10.3	10.3	10.1	10.3	10.3	10.5	10.3
2003	10.4	10.4	10.4	10.4	10.4	10.4	10.4	10.3	10.2	10.1	10.2	10.3	10.3
State government													
1990	2.3	2.6	2.7	2.7	2.8	2.5	2.2	2.3	2.6	2.7	2.8	2.6	2.5
1991	2.4	2.7	2.8	2.7	2.8	2.7	2.3	2.3	2.7	2.7	2.8	2.8	2.6
1992	2.6	2.8	2.8	2.8	2.8	2.7	2.4	2.4	2.8	2.8	2.8	2.8	2.7
1993	2.7	2.8	2.9	2.8	2.9	2.7	2.5	2.5	2.8	2.8	2.9	2.9	2.7
1994	2.6	3.1	3.1	3.1	3.1	2.7	2.6	2.6	3.1	3.2	3.1	3.1	2.9
1995	2.6	3.1	3.2	3.1	3.1	2.8	2.6	2.5	3.0	3.2	3.2	3.1	2.9
1996	2.7	3.1	3.2	3.1	3.2	2.6	2.6	2.6	3.1	3.2	3.2	3.2	2.9
1997	2.8	3.2	3.2	3.2	3.3	2.7	2.7	2.7	3.2	3.4	3.4	3.4	3.1
1998	2.9	3.3	3.4	3.4	3.4	2.8	2.8	2.7	3.0	3.5	3.5	3.5	3.2
1999	2.9	3.5	3.5	3.5	3.5	2.8	2.9	2.8	3.7	3.6	3.7	3.7	3.3
2000	3.0	3.6	3.7	3.8	3.7	3.2	2.7	2.9	3.7	3.8	3.9	3.9	3.5
2001	3.5	4.0	3.7	3.7	3.7	3.3	3.0	3.1	3.8	3.9	3.9	3.9	3.6
2002	3.2	3.8	4.0	3.9	4.0	3.3	3.1	3.1	3.8	4.0	4.1	3.8	3.7
2003	3.4	3.8	3.9	3.9	3.9	3.4	3.0	3.0	3.8	3.9	3.9	3.9	3.7

Employment by Industry: Colorado—*Continued*

(Numbers in thousands. Not seasonally adjusted.)

Industry	January	February	March	April	May	June	July	August	September	October	November	December	Annual Average
COLORADO SPRINGS *—Continued*													
Local government													
1990	16.1	16.4	16.5	16.2	16.4	16.6	15.2	14.9	15.0	16.3	16.5	16.7	16.0
1991	16.4	17.2	17.3	17.3	17.6	17.7	16.1	15.7	16.1	17.2	17.5	17.3	16.9
1992	17.9	18.1	18.2	18.1	18.3	18.4	17.0	16.4	17.0	18.1	18.4	18.2	17.8
1993	18.9	18.9	19.3	19.2	19.4	19.6	17.9	17.6	18.3	19.1	19.2	19.3	18.8
1994	18.8	19.1	18.7	19.5	19.7	19.7	17.5	17.6	18.6	19.8	20.1	20.0	19.0
1995	19.7	20.0	20.2	20.1	20.2	20.3	18.4	19.0	19.9	20.7	21.0	21.0	20.0
1996	20.8	20.8	21.1	21.1	21.2	21.4	19.5	19.0	19.9	20.8	21.3	21.3	20.6
1997	21.2	21.3	21.6	21.6	21.7	22.1	20.4	19.7	20.7	21.8	22.2	22.1	21.4
1998	22.2	22.4	22.6	22.4	22.6	22.9	21.6	20.7	21.8	22.9	23.3	23.3	22.4
1999	23.0	23.3	23.3	23.3	23.5	23.5	22.7	21.9	22.5	23.6	23.9	24.0	23.2
2000	23.5	23.8	23.8	24.2	24.3	24.5	22.6	22.0	22.5	24.1	24.4	23.8	23.6
2001	24.3	24.6	25.0	24.7	25.0	25.2	23.2	23.8	24.5	25.4	25.8	25.8	24.8
2002	25.8	26.0	26.3	26.3	26.6	26.7	24.4	24.4	25.7	26.6	26.8	26.9	26.0
2003	26.8	27.0	27.2	26.7	27.1	27.1	25.2	25.1	26.4	27.1	27.4	27.3	26.7
DENVER													
Total nonfarm													
1990	813.7	819.4	824.6	830.3	844.8	853.3	841.7	848.2	852.2	849.3	854.0	855.7	840.6
1991	831.0	834.6	839.0	842.8	851.7	861.6	851.7	854.0	858.6	859.2	862.7	866.3	851.1
1992	845.8	851.3	856.5	864.7	873.8	880.1	876.6	879.6	883.2	884.6	886.8	890.3	872.7
1993	871.5	879.2	886.9	898.7	904.8	915.7	911.1	914.0	917.0	921.1	922.7	930.5	906.1
1994	908.7	914.9	921.2	932.2	939.9	950.2	945.2	950.5	954.9	957.2	964.1	974.7	942.8
1995	947.5	956.5	965.5	967.9	978.4	990.5	982.6	987.9	993.9	991.7	996.3	1006.7	980.4
1996	977.7	983.6	993.6	998.4	1011.0	1022.1	1010.7	1020.9	1024.8	1025.1	1034.9	1040.3	1011.9
1997	1019.1	1027.2	1034.8	1041.4	1053.4	1065.5	1059.9	1064.8	1069.0	1071.7	1076.9	1086.5	1055.8
1998	1060.5	1067.6	1076.2	1082.2	1094.3	1104.7	1102.9	1105.2	1107.1	1111.4	1116.9	1126.5	1096.2
1999	1100.0	1110.9	1115.8	1126.1	1136.8	1148.3	1144.1	1144.2	1146.5	1150.4	1156.9	1167.6	1137.3
2000	1139.8	1148.7	1159.3	1166.7	1180.0	1192.9	1188.9	1194.5	1196.0	1193.4	1198.9	1207.1	1180.5
2001	1172.3	1175.8	1180.5	1181.9	1189.0	1199.2	1186.0	1185.8	1178.0	1167.6	1165.5	1163.6	1178.8
2002	1126.9	1130.0	1134.5	1144.2	1154.1	1161.3	1150.1	1154.3	1148.0	1144.9	1147.8	1149.2	1145.4
2003	1135.4	1134.5	1133.8	1138.2	1147.1	1154.3	1146.2	1150.8	1145.5	1143.5	1143.5	1142.5	1142.9
Total private													
1990	689.3	689.8	694.5	698.3	710.5	720.0	719.4	726.3	721.0	716.5	719.6	722.4	710.6
1991	701.6	701.8	705.9	708.9	716.8	726.7	725.6	729.5	725.6	723.0	726.3	730.8	718.5
1992	713.2	714.6	719.1	727.2	735.3	743.0	746.7	748.8	745.3	746.2	747.9	752.3	736.6
1993	735.0	738.6	746.0	756.8	762.8	774.5	778.6	781.8	779.1	779.8	781.7	789.9	767.0
1994	772.3	774.8	780.7	790.7	798.6	809.5	812.9	817.6	815.9	816.3	823.0	833.8	803.8
1995	812.0	816.1	824.4	827.3	837.6	850.1	848.8	853.7	852.4	849.9	854.3	864.3	840.9
1996	840.9	842.5	851.3	856.3	868.0	879.9	876.8	886.6	883.2	881.6	890.4	896.2	871.1
1997	877.5	882.5	889.5	896.4	908.0	920.9	921.9	928.0	924.2	924.4	928.8	938.3	911.7
1998	916.2	920.2	928.3	933.6	944.7	956.4	961.4	964.8	959.5	962.0	966.2	975.3	949.0
1999	954.0	961.0	965.2	974.7	984.5	997.6	1001.7	1001.9	996.6	999.6	1005.7	1015.3	988.1
2000	992.2	997.2	1006.2	1012.9	1023.1	1038.9	1041.5	1045.4	1041.1	1038.8	1043.2	1050.4	1027.5
2001	1020.0	1019.7	1025.0	1025.7	1031.8	1042.2	1034.1	1032.9	1019.3	1008.5	1004.7	1003.0	1022.2
2002	969.6	969.5	972.6	982.0	990.7	999.0	993.2	995.9	985.9	981.1	983.2	985.0	984.0
2003	976.0	971.9	970.7	975.0	982.0	990.7	989.4	993.1	983.8	980.1	979.9	979.5	981.0
Goods-producing													
1990	120.1	119.4	119.9	121.2	123.9	126.0	126.5	127.6	126.3	125.4	124.6	123.4	123.6
1991	120.0	119.7	120.0	120.4	121.7	123.7	124.3	125.6	124.8	124.3	123.6	122.6	122.5
1992	119.4	120.0	121.0	123.6	125.2	127.3	128.5	128.6	128.2	128.8	127.5	125.5	125.3
1993	122.2	123.3	125.7	127.3	129.7	132.2	134.9	136.0	135.6	136.4	134.6	134.0	130.9
1994	131.3	130.1	130.8	132.2	133.5	136.4	137.7	138.6	138.6	139.0	139.0	139.3	135.5
1995	136.4	137.0	138.4	138.3	139.8	142.0	143.1	143.9	144.0	143.4	143.1	142.5	140.9
1996	139.4	140.3	142.8	143.4	146.1	148.9	148.7	149.8	148.9	149.2	150.4	149.2	146.4
1997	145.4	147.0	149.1	150.7	153.5	156.5	156.8	157.1	156.9	158.2	155.8	156.5	153.6
1998	153.6	156.2	158.1	159.0	161.2	164.4	166.0	166.4	165.7	165.4	164.7	164.2	162.0
1999	160.9	162.8	164.6	167.2	168.2	171.5	172.0	171.9	171.2	172.0	171.7	171.0	168.7
2000	168.6	171.1	174.2	174.6	177.0	180.6	181.0	181.6	181.1	180.8	179.0	178.5	177.3
2001	174.0	174.2	175.5	175.4	176.8	178.6	177.1	176.8	174.7	171.2	167.8	164.5	173.9
2002	159.0	159.6	161.3	163.0	165.3	166.7	166.0	165.7	163.1	161.9	159.2	156.7	162.3
2003	156.1	154.7	154.2	154.4	156.3	158.3	157.9	157.5	155.3	155.3	153.9	151.3	155.4
Natural resources and mining													
1990	8.8	8.8	8.8	9.0	9.0	9.2	9.0	8.9	8.7	8.5	8.6	8.5	8.8
1991	8.3	8.3	8.2	8.0	8.0	8.1	8.1	8.2	8.0	8.0	8.0	8.0	8.1
1992	7.5	7.4	7.3	7.2	7.1	7.1	7.0	7.0	6.9	7.0	7.0	7.1	7.1
1993	7.0	6.9	6.8	6.7	6.8	6.8	6.9	6.9	6.9	6.9	7.0	7.1	6.8
1994	7.0	6.9	6.8	6.8	6.8	6.8	6.5	6.5	6.6	6.6	6.7	6.8	6.7
1995	6.7	6.4	6.2	6.0	5.9	6.0	6.2	6.1	6.0	6.0	6.0	5.9	6.1
1996	5.7	5.7	5.9	5.8	5.8	5.8	5.6	5.6	5.5	5.5	5.6	5.6	5.6
1997	5.8	5.9	5.9	5.8	5.8	6.0	6.1	6.1	6.1	6.2	6.1	6.2	6.0
1998	6.2	6.3	6.3	6.1	6.2	6.3	6.2	6.1	6.1	6.0	5.9	5.9	6.1
1999	5.5	5.5	5.6	5.4	5.3	5.2	5.1	5.0	5.0	5.1	5.1	5.2	5.2
2000	5.0	5.0	5.0	5.1	5.1	5.2	5.3	5.3	5.3	5.2	5.2	5.2	5.1
2001	5.0	5.1	5.1	5.2	5.3	5.4	5.3	5.3	5.3	5.3	5.3	5.3	5.2
2002	5.1	5.0	5.0	5.0	5.1	5.0	5.1	5.0	5.0	5.0	4.9	4.9	5.0
2003	4.9	4.8	4.8	4.9	4.9	4.9	5.0	5.0	5.0	5.0	5.1	5.1	5.0

Employment by Industry: Colorado—*Continued*

(Numbers in thousands. Not seasonally adjusted.)

Industry	January	February	March	April	May	June	July	August	September	October	November	December	Annual Average
DENVER—*Continued*													
Construction													
1990	29.7	29.1	29.4	30.5	32.5	34.1	35.1	36.4	35.8	35.8	35.3	34.3	33.1
1991	31.6	31.7	32.2	34.0	35.3	36.9	37.7	38.6	38.1	39.0	38.4	37.2	35.8
1992	35.2	35.9	36.8	39.3	41.3	43.0	44.3	44.8	44.7	45.2	44.1	42.1	41.3
1993	39.2	40.4	42.9	44.7	47.4	49.2	51.8	52.8	52.7	53.1	51.3	50.5	48.0
1994	48.3	47.7	48.6	49.9	50.8	52.9	54.0	54.5	54.2	54.5	54.0	53.7	51.9
1995	50.7	51.1	52.3	52.4	53.6	55.2	56.0	56.7	56.7	56.2	55.7	55.1	54.3
1996	52.5	53.3	55.0	56.1	58.2	60.3	60.7	61.6	61.0	60.5	60.5	59.0	58.2
1997	55.2	56.7	58.6	60.2	62.5	64.5	65.0	65.1	65.0	65.4	63.1	63.6	62.0
1998	61.7	63.3	65.4	67.1	69.0	71.5	73.1	73.8	73.8	73.5	73.0	72.8	69.8
1999	70.7	72.6	74.5	77.1	78.2	81.3	82.2	82.2	81.5	82.4	82.1	81.3	78.8
2000	79.7	82.0	84.8	86.1	88.6	91.5	91.8	92.5	92.3	92.2	90.7	90.1	88.5
2001	87.7	87.9	89.6	90.6	92.0	94.2	93.8	94.1	93.0	90.7	88.0	85.3	90.6
2002	81.6	82.5	84.2	86.4	88.6	90.0	89.5	89.5	87.3	86.2	84.2	81.9	86.0
2003	78.9	77.9	77.8	78.3	80.3	82.3	82.2	82.1	80.3	80.1	78.5	76.2	79.6
Manufacturing													
1990	81.6	81.5	81.7	81.7	82.4	82.7	82.4	82.3	81.8	81.1	80.7	80.6	81.7
1991	80.1	79.7	79.6	78.4	78.4	78.7	78.5	78.8	78.7	77.3	77.2	77.4	78.5
1992	76.7	76.7	76.9	77.1	76.8	77.2	77.2	76.8	76.6	76.6	76.4	76.3	76.7
1993	76.0	76.0	76.0	75.9	75.5	76.2	76.2	76.3	76.0	76.4	76.3	76.4	76.1
1994	76.0	75.5	75.4	75.5	75.9	76.7	77.2	77.6	77.8	77.9	78.3	78.8	76.8
1995	79.0	79.5	79.9	79.9	80.3	80.8	80.9	81.1	81.3	81.2	81.4	81.5	80.5
1996	81.2	81.3	81.9	81.5	82.1	82.8	82.4	82.6	82.4	83.2	84.3	84.6	82.5
1997	84.4	84.4	84.6	84.7	85.2	86.0	85.7	85.9	85.8	86.6	86.6	86.7	85.5
1998	85.7	86.6	86.4	85.8	86.0	86.6	86.7	86.5	85.8	85.9	85.8	85.5	86.1
1999	84.7	84.7	84.5	84.7	84.7	85.0	84.7	84.7	84.7	84.5	84.5	84.5	84.6
2000	83.9	84.1	84.4	83.4	83.3	83.9	83.9	83.8	83.5	83.4	83.1	83.2	83.6
2001	81.3	81.2	80.8	79.6	79.5	79.0	78.0	77.4	76.4	75.2	74.5	73.9	78.1
2002	72.3	72.1	72.1	71.6	71.6	71.7	71.4	71.2	70.8	70.7	70.1	69.9	71.3
2003	72.3	72.0	71.6	71.2	71.1	71.1	70.7	70.4	70.0	70.2	70.3	70.0	70.9
Service-providing													
1990	693.6	700.0	704.7	709.1	720.9	727.3	715.2	720.6	725.9	723.9	729.4	732.3	716.9
1991	711.0	714.9	719.0	722.4	730.0	737.9	727.4	728.4	733.8	734.9	739.1	743.7	728.5
1992	726.4	731.3	735.5	741.1	748.6	752.8	748.1	751.0	755.0	755.8	759.3	764.8	747.4
1993	749.3	755.9	761.2	771.4	775.1	783.5	776.2	778.0	781.4	784.7	788.1	796.5	775.1
1994	777.4	784.8	790.4	800.0	806.4	813.8	807.5	811.9	816.3	818.2	825.1	835.4	807.2
1995	811.1	819.5	827.1	829.6	838.6	848.5	839.5	844.0	849.9	848.3	853.2	864.2	839.4
1996	838.3	843.3	850.8	855.0	864.9	873.2	862.0	871.1	875.9	875.9	884.5	891.1	865.5
1997	873.7	880.2	885.7	890.7	899.9	909.0	903.1	907.7	912.1	913.5	921.1	930.0	902.2
1998	906.9	911.4	918.1	923.2	933.1	940.3	936.9	938.8	941.4	946.0	952.2	962.3	934.2
1999	939.1	948.1	951.2	958.9	968.6	976.8	972.1	972.3	975.3	978.4	985.2	996.6	968.5
2000	971.2	977.6	985.1	992.1	1003.0	1012.3	1007.9	1012.9	1014.9	1012.6	1019.9	1028.6	1003.1
2001	998.3	1001.6	1005.0	1006.5	1012.2	1020.6	1008.9	1009.0	1003.3	996.4	997.7	999.1	1004.9
2002	967.9	970.4	973.2	981.2	988.8	994.6	984.1	988.6	984.9	983.0	988.6	992.5	983.2
2003	979.3	979.8	979.6	983.8	990.8	996.0	988.3	993.3	990.2	988.2	989.6	991.2	987.5
Trade, transportation, and utilities													
1990	179.1	176.7	176.9	177.2	179.5	180.4	179.7	181.4	181.5	182.3	185.8	188.9	180.7
1991	179.9	177.2	177.4	177.2	178.7	179.6	179.4	180.5	180.7	182.4	185.8	188.6	180.6
1992	182.2	179.9	180.2	181.4	182.9	183.7	184.7	184.6	184.8	186.0	189.0	193.0	184.3
1993	184.5	183.7	184.1	186.6	187.2	188.8	190.0	190.5	190.8	193.6	197.5	201.5	189.9
1994	193.5	192.7	192.7	195.8	196.7	197.7	199.5	200.2	201.0	201.6	206.0	212.0	199.1
1995	202.0	200.9	201.6	201.8	203.8	204.8	205.8	206.4	207.2	209.6	214.6	220.3	206.5
1996	211.6	209.2	209.4	208.3	211.1	211.6	210.4	213.7	214.0	213.2	219.5	224.4	213.0
1997	216.1	214.1	214.3	214.9	215.9	216.4	217.2	217.9	217.0	219.1	224.6	230.4	218.1
1998	221.5	219.4	219.0	219.2	221.7	222.8	222.8	223.8	223.1	225.8	230.8	235.6	223.7
1999	227.2	226.7	226.0	226.6	228.5	229.8	230.9	231.1	231.1	232.7	239.1	245.2	231.2
2000	234.6	234.6	233.9	235.1	237.0	238.9	238.8	239.7	239.0	241.0	247.8	252.5	239.4
2001	242.9	240.1	240.3	239.4	240.6	242.3	241.1	240.6	239.2	239.0	242.0	243.0	240.9
2002	231.3	228.8	228.8	230.0	232.3	234.3	233.3	233.2	231.5	232.0	237.4	240.5	232.8
2003	234.2	231.7	230.5	229.0	229.2	229.9	229.6	230.4	230.1	229.5	232.5	234.7	230.9
Wholesale trade													
1990	52.3	52.4	52.5	52.3	53.1	53.2	52.6	52.8	52.8	53.1	53.3	53.0	52.7
1991	51.4	51.5	51.6	51.0	51.3	51.7	51.7	51.7	51.7	51.9	52.0	52.3	51.6
1992	51.8	52.2	52.6	52.9	53.3	53.6	53.9	53.7	53.7	53.7	53.8	54.0	53.2
1993	53.2	53.6	53.9	54.1	54.4	54.8	55.1	54.8	54.8	55.1	55.2	55.8	54.5
1994	55.0	55.5	55.7	55.3	55.7	56.4	56.7	56.9	57.0	56.6	57.2	57.9	56.3
1995	57.1	57.6	58.0	57.8	57.9	58.2	58.3	58.1	58.1	58.3	58.3	58.7	58.0
1996	57.7	58.0	58.4	58.1	58.5	59.0	58.7	59.3	59.2	59.5	60.0	60.5	58.9
1997	60.1	60.5	60.6	60.5	60.7	60.9	61.2	61.3	60.8	61.2	61.4	61.7	60.9
1998	61.5	62.0	62.4	62.0	62.9	63.2	62.6	62.6	62.4	63.3	63.3	63.8	62.6
1999	63.4	64.0	63.7	63.4	63.6	63.9	64.2	64.1	64.0	64.1	64.3	64.9	63.9
2000	65.2	66.6	67.1	67.9	68.4	68.8	68.2	67.6	67.4	68.1	68.4	68.8	67.7
2001	68.7	69.3	69.5	69.0	68.7	68.8	68.4	68.1	67.4	67.0	66.7	66.6	68.2
2002	65.2	65.1	65.1	64.9	65.0	65.0	64.7	64.3	63.8	63.7	63.5	63.6	64.5
2003	63.5	63.2	63.1	62.9	62.8	62.9	62.6	62.4	62.4	62.0	61.4	61.4	62.6

Employment by Industry: Colorado—*Continued*

(Numbers in thousands. Not seasonally adjusted.)

Industry	January	February	March	April	May	June	July	August	September	October	November	December	Annual Average
DENVER—*Continued*													
Retail trade													
1990	88.4	85.7	85.6	86.1	87.3	88.0	87.7	89.0	89.1	89.5	92.4	94.9	88.6
1991	89.0	86.2	86.2	86.5	87.6	88.0	87.8	88.7	88.7	90.0	93.1	95.3	88.9
1992	90.2	87.5	87.0	87.8	88.8	89.1	89.5	89.4	89.5	90.3	93.2	96.4	89.8
1993	89.9	88.7	88.6	90.6	90.7	91.8	91.9	92.8	92.4	94.5	98.0	101.5	92.6
1994	95.1	93.5	93.3	95.3	96.7	97.2	98.2	99.0	99.7	101.2	105.1	109.4	98.6
1995	102.1	100.3	100.3	100.7	102.1	102.9	103.3	103.8	104.2	105.8	110.3	114.9	104.2
1996	107.6	104.8	104.4	104.0	106.5	106.7	105.6	107.9	108.5	108.1	113.0	116.4	107.7
1997	109.6	107.2	107.1	107.4	108.4	108.9	109.3	109.8	109.6	111.2	115.6	120.4	110.3
1998	113.3	111.0	110.7	110.5	112.0	112.9	113.0	113.6	112.7	114.6	118.4	122.3	113.7
1999	115.7	114.4	114.1	114.9	116.3	117.8	118.0	118.0	117.8	119.3	124.4	129.0	118.3
2000	119.4	118.0	117.3	117.0	118.3	119.7	119.6	121.1	120.4	121.7	126.8	130.9	120.8
2001	121.4	118.3	118.3	117.9	119.0	120.4	119.3	118.9	118.6	119.4	123.5	125.3	120.0
2002	117.3	114.7	115.0	116.0	117.6	119.3	118.5	118.6	117.4	117.9	123.0	125.7	118.4
2003	120.7	118.7	117.7	117.5	118.4	119.4	118.9	119.9	119.8	119.2	122.3	124.6	119.8
Transportation and utilities													
1990	38.4	38.6	38.8	38.8	39.1	39.2	39.4	39.6	39.6	39.7	40.1	41.0	39.3
1991	39.5	39.5	39.6	39.7	39.8	39.9	39.9	40.1	40.3	40.5	40.7	41.0	40.0
1992	40.2	40.2	40.6	40.7	40.8	41.0	41.3	41.5	41.6	42.0	42.0	42.6	41.2
1993	41.4	41.4	41.6	41.9	42.1	42.2	43.0	42.9	43.6	44.0	44.3	44.2	42.7
1994	43.4	43.7	43.7	45.2	44.3	44.1	44.6	44.3	44.3	43.8	43.7	44.7	44.1
1995	42.8	43.0	43.3	43.3	43.8	43.7	44.2	44.5	44.9	45.5	46.0	46.7	44.3
1996	46.3	46.4	46.6	46.2	46.1	45.9	46.1	46.5	46.3	45.6	46.5	47.5	46.3
1997	46.4	46.4	46.6	47.0	46.8	46.6	46.7	46.8	46.6	46.7	47.6	48.3	46.8
1998	46.7	46.4	45.9	46.7	46.8	46.7	47.2	47.6	48.0	47.9	49.1	49.5	47.3
1999	48.1	48.3	48.2	48.3	48.6	48.1	48.7	49.0	49.3	49.3	50.4	51.3	48.9
2000	50.0	50.0	49.5	50.2	50.3	50.4	51.0	51.0	51.2	51.2	52.6	52.8	50.8
2001	52.8	52.5	52.5	52.5	52.9	53.1	53.4	53.6	53.2	52.6	51.8	51.1	52.7
2002	48.8	49.0	48.7	49.1	49.7	50.0	50.1	50.3	50.3	50.4	50.9	51.2	49.9
2003	50.0	49.8	49.7	48.6	48.0	47.6	48.1	48.1	47.9	48.3	48.8	48.7	48.6
Information													
1990	34.8	35.0	34.5	33.9	34.1	34.3	34.7	34.6	34.5	33.5	33.8	33.7	34.2
1991	34.3	34.3	34.8	34.6	35.1	35.2	34.7	34.9	34.8	34.7	34.9	35.2	34.7
1992	34.3	34.3	34.4	34.2	34.3	34.5	34.9	34.9	34.9	34.8	34.8	35.1	34.6
1993	35.1	35.2	35.0	35.1	35.3	35.8	35.9	35.8	35.8	36.6	36.8	37.2	35.8
1994	37.6	37.9	38.2	38.5	38.9	39.6	40.2	40.5	40.6	40.7	41.6	42.3	39.7
1995	42.4	42.9	43.1	43.0	42.8	43.2	43.4	43.5	43.5	43.3	43.5	44.3	43.2
1996	43.4	43.8	43.9	44.9	45.3	45.5	45.5	45.6	46.0	46.3	47.1	47.0	45.3
1997	48.0	48.1	47.9	48.6	49.0	49.8	50.2	51.4	50.9	52.4	54.3	54.3	50.4
1998	56.0	55.6	56.8	57.2	57.8	57.9	58.7	58.9	59.4	60.0	60.7	61.7	58.3
1999	62.0	62.2	62.6	62.8	63.6	63.7	65.6	65.9	66.0	66.3	67.0	67.4	64.5
2000	67.0	67.6	68.4	69.2	69.4	70.1	71.0	71.2	71.1	71.1	71.0	71.4	69.8
2001	71.1	71.0	70.6	69.5	69.1	68.8	66.8	66.1	65.0	63.6	63.2	62.4	67.3
2002	60.8	60.5	59.8	59.1	58.1	57.8	56.8	56.5	55.8	55.5	55.5	55.2	57.6
2003	56.0	55.7	55.3	54.7	54.5	54.3	54.2	54.1	53.8	53.7	53.8	53.7	54.5
Financial activities													
1990	64.4	64.9	65.7	66.2	66.7	67.0	66.7	66.9	66.5	66.1	66.1	66.3	66.1
1991	65.3	65.4	65.9	65.8	65.9	66.9	67.3	67.3	66.8	66.5	66.7	67.6	66.4
1992	67.1	67.6	68.0	67.9	68.4	69.2	69.2	69.3	69.0	69.3	69.4	70.1	68.7
1993	69.8	70.3	70.8	71.6	72.0	73.0	73.3	73.6	73.8	73.9	74.2	75.3	72.6
1994	75.2	75.7	76.2	76.0	76.2	76.9	76.8	76.9	76.6	76.6	76.7	77.6	76.4
1995	76.5	76.7	76.9	77.4	78.0	78.9	78.6	79.1	79.4	80.1	80.5	81.4	78.6
1996	79.8	80.5	81.2	82.5	83.2	84.2	83.5	84.3	83.8	84.2	84.6	85.6	83.1
1997	83.7	84.3	85.2	85.9	86.7	87.8	87.9	88.5	88.5	89.5	89.7	91.2	87.4
1998	90.1	90.8	91.4	91.1	91.8	92.8	93.7	94.1	93.9	93.9	94.2	95.0	92.7
1999	94.0	95.1	95.2	95.9	96.1	97.1	97.2	96.9	95.8	96.0	96.3	96.9	96.0
2000	94.8	95.2	95.8	95.3	95.7	96.5	96.7	96.8	96.5	96.4	96.6	97.5	96.1
2001	93.9	94.5	95.1	95.3	95.7	96.4	95.6	95.2	94.4	94.4	94.3	94.7	95.0
2002	93.3	93.7	93.7	93.3	93.7	94.5	94.4	95.0	94.9	95.7	96.5	97.2	94.7
2003	97.0	97.3	97.4	98.0	98.5	99.2	99.5	99.9	99.3	100.1	101.1	101.2	99.0
Professional and business services													
1990	120.1	121.6	123.4	123.4	126.1	128.3	128.9	130.9	130.3	129.3	129.5	129.2	126.7
1991	126.5	127.9	129.3	131.2	131.7	133.5	133.3	134.1	133.5	133.4	133.1	133.2	131.7
1992	129.9	130.8	131.7	133.5	134.4	135.5	136.0	136.6	136.2	136.1	135.4	136.5	134.3
1993	134.7	135.9	138.1	140.0	139.8	142.8	142.4	142.9	141.9	141.0	139.7	140.8	140.0
1994	138.3	139.8	142.6	144.5	146.3	148.3	148.2	149.5	149.5	149.4	149.9	150.6	146.4
1995	147.6	149.0	151.5	152.5	155.2	157.5	155.8	158.2	158.8	157.3	156.9	158.2	154.8
1996	152.2	153.3	155.8	157.7	158.8	161.7	162.2	164.7	164.2	163.9	163.1	163.1	160.0
1997	159.1	161.7	163.2	164.7	167.0	170.0	169.9	172.6	173.3	169.4	169.3	169.6	167.4
1998	163.3	164.2	166.8	169.4	170.2	172.8	175.4	176.4	175.4	177.1	176.2	177.8	172.0
1999	172.5	174.4	175.8	179.4	180.7	183.5	184.8	185.5	184.8	186.1	185.5	188.1	181.7
2000	184.7	184.9	187.4	190.3	192.2	195.2	195.6	196.8	197.0	196.1	195.7	196.6	192.7
2001	188.4	189.3	190.0	191.7	191.7	192.8	191.8	191.2	187.4	184.0	181.5	181.9	188.5
2002	173.5	174.4	175.0	178.1	179.2	179.8	178.2	179.9	177.8	175.8	174.8	174.9	176.8
2003	173.5	173.5	173.7	175.7	176.6	178.8	178.6	180.2	178.0	174.8	173.1	172.9	175.8

Employment by Industry: Colorado—*Continued*

(Numbers in thousands. Not seasonally adjusted.)

Industry	January	February	March	April	May	June	July	August	September	October	November	December	Annual Average
DENVER—*Continued*													
Educational and health services													
1990	70.1	70.7	71.1	70.9	71.6	71.7	71.2	72.1	72.9	73.1	73.8	74.0	71.9
1991	72.5	73.4	73.7	73.9	74.6	74.9	74.7	75.2	75.8	75.7	76.0	76.5	74.7
1992	75.6	76.3	77.0	77.3	77.4	77.6	77.8	78.2	79.0	79.5	79.9	80.1	77.9
1993	79.0	79.6	79.9	80.2	80.2	80.2	80.1	80.7	81.3	80.6	81.0	81.7	80.3
1994	80.7	81.6	81.7	81.8	82.1	82.5	82.1	83.1	83.8	85.0	85.7	86.1	83.0
1995	85.3	86.4	87.2	86.7	87.0	87.3	86.7	87.1	87.4	87.6	87.8	88.3	87.0
1996	87.9	88.5	88.9	88.9	89.4	89.6	88.4	89.4	89.9	92.4	93.3	93.6	90.0
1997	94.6	95.9	96.3	96.5	96.7	96.7	96.5	97.0	97.6	98.6	98.8	99.0	97.0
1998	97.8	98.7	99.6	99.8	99.8	99.4	98.5	98.4	98.5	99.2	99.5	99.7	99.0
1999	98.1	99.6	99.5	99.8	100.2	100.2	99.0	99.2	99.6	100.3	100.6	100.8	99.7
2000	99.6	100.3	100.4	101.2	101.5	102.5	102.2	102.9	103.5	103.5	104.3	105.0	102.2
2001	104.1	105.0	105.5	105.6	106.0	106.1	105.8	106.5	106.2	108.0	108.6	108.8	106.4
2002	107.8	108.4	108.8	109.6	109.7	109.5	109.4	110.0	110.2	110.7	111.2	111.5	109.7
2003	111.0	111.8	111.9	112.7	112.9	112.8	112.7	112.9	113.1	114.8	115.4	115.9	113.2
Leisure and hospitality													
1990	69.3	70.0	71.3	73.3	76.1	79.2	78.6	79.5	76.3	74.0	73.2	74.1	74.5
1991	70.4	71.1	71.9	72.7	75.6	78.9	78.4	78.3	76.0	72.7	72.7	73.6	74.3
1992	71.7	72.5	73.6	75.9	78.8	81.0	81.6	82.5	79.9	78.5	78.7	78.6	77.7
1993	76.4	77.3	78.8	82.1	84.4	86.8	86.6	87.0	84.9	82.7	82.7	83.6	82.7
1994	80.5	81.5	82.5	85.8	88.2	90.7	91.1	91.6	89.2	87.5	87.5	88.8	87.0
1995	85.4	86.7	88.9	90.8	93.7	98.4	97.3	97.2	93.4	89.7	89.4	90.4	91.7
1996	87.6	88.2	90.0	91.3	94.1	97.9	97.9	98.6	96.4	92.5	92.3	93.0	93.3
1997	90.0	91.0	92.7	94.1	97.7	101.7	101.7	101.8	98.8	96.0	95.2	96.0	96.3
1998	92.2	93.6	94.6	96.3	99.9	103.4	103.4	104.0	101.2	98.5	98.1	98.9	98.6
1999	96.5	97.7	99.0	100.3	104.2	108.0	108.3	107.9	105.0	103.5	102.6	102.6	102.9
2000	99.7	100.6	102.7	104.5	107.3	111.1	112.0	112.3	109.3	106.5	105.5	105.3	106.4
2001	102.4	102.9	104.8	105.7	108.5	113.1	112.1	112.6	109.0	105.1	104.0	104.3	107.0
2002	100.4	100.6	101.5	105.0	108.4	111.9	110.5	111.1	108.7	106.0	104.9	105.3	106.2
2003	104.3	103.7	104.3	106.9	110.2	113.0	112.7	114.0	110.9	108.3	106.8	106.4	108.5
Other services													
1990	31.4	31.5	31.7	32.2	32.5	33.1	33.1	33.3	32.7	32.8	32.8	32.8	32.4
1991	32.7	32.8	32.9	33.1	33.5	34.0	33.5	33.6	33.2	33.3	33.5	33.5	33.3
1992	33.0	33.2	33.2	33.4	33.9	34.2	34.0	34.1	33.3	33.2	33.2	33.4	33.5
1993	33.3	33.3	33.6	33.9	34.2	34.9	35.4	35.3	35.0	35.0	35.2	35.8	34.5
1994	35.2	35.5	36.0	36.1	36.7	37.4	37.3	37.2	36.6	36.5	36.6	37.1	36.5
1995	36.4	36.5	36.8	36.8	37.3	38.0	38.1	38.3	38.7	38.9	38.5	38.9	37.7
1996	39.0	38.7	39.3	39.3	40.0	40.5	40.2	40.5	40.0	39.9	40.1	40.3	39.8
1997	40.6	40.4	40.8	41.0	41.5	42.0	41.7	41.7	41.2	41.2	41.1	41.3	41.2
1998	41.7	41.7	42.0	41.6	42.3	42.9	42.9	42.8	42.3	42.1	42.0	42.4	42.2
1999	42.8	42.5	42.5	42.7	43.0	43.8	43.9	43.5	43.1	42.7	42.9	43.3	43.0
2000	43.2	42.9	43.4	42.7	43.0	44.0	44.2	44.1	43.6	43.4	43.3	43.6	43.4
2001	43.2	42.7	43.2	43.1	43.4	44.1	43.8	43.9	43.4	43.2	43.3	43.4	43.4
2002	43.5	43.5	43.7	43.9	44.0	44.5	44.6	44.5	43.9	43.5	43.7	43.7	43.9
2003	43.9	43.5	43.4	43.6	43.8	44.4	44.2	44.1	43.3	43.6	43.3	43.4	43.7
Government													
1990	124.4	129.6	130.1	132.0	134.3	133.3	122.3	121.9	131.2	132.8	134.4	133.3	129.9
1991	129.4	132.8	133.1	133.9	134.9	134.9	126.1	124.5	133.0	136.2	136.4	135.5	132.5
1992	132.6	136.7	137.4	137.5	138.5	137.1	129.9	130.8	137.9	138.4	138.9	138.0	136.1
1993	136.5	140.6	140.9	141.9	142.0	141.2	132.5	132.2	137.9	141.3	141.0	140.6	139.0
1994	136.4	140.1	140.5	141.5	141.3	140.7	132.3	132.9	139.0	140.9	141.1	140.9	138.9
1995	135.5	140.4	141.1	140.6	140.8	140.4	133.8	134.2	141.5	141.8	142.0	142.4	139.5
1996	136.8	141.1	142.3	142.1	143.0	142.2	133.9	134.3	141.6	143.5	144.5	144.1	140.7
1997	141.6	144.7	145.3	145.0	145.4	144.6	138.0	136.8	144.8	147.3	148.1	148.2	144.1
1998	144.3	147.4	147.9	148.6	149.6	148.3	141.5	140.4	147.6	149.4	150.7	151.2	147.2
1999	146.0	149.9	150.6	151.4	152.3	150.7	142.4	142.3	149.9	150.8	151.2	152.3	149.1
2000	147.6	151.5	153.1	153.8	156.9	154.0	147.4	149.1	154.9	154.6	155.7	156.7	152.9
2001	152.3	156.1	155.5	156.2	157.2	157.0	151.9	152.9	158.7	159.1	160.8	160.6	156.5
2002	157.3	160.5	161.9	162.2	163.4	162.3	156.9	158.4	162.1	163.8	164.6	164.2	161.5
2003	159.4	162.6	163.1	163.2	165.1	163.6	156.8	157.7	161.7	163.4	163.6	163.0	161.9
Federal government													
1990	33.2	33.2	33.5	33.7	35.3	34.7	34.9	34.4	34.1	34.0	34.0	34.7	34.1
1991	34.5	34.2	34.2	34.7	34.8	35.2	35.7	35.5	35.4	35.4	35.5	36.0	35.0
1992	35.7	35.6	35.6	35.7	35.8	36.1	36.6	36.6	36.6	36.8	36.8	37.5	36.2
1993	37.0	37.0	37.0	37.2	37.2	37.3	37.1	37.1	36.9	36.8	36.8	37.8	37.1
1994	36.6	36.4	36.3	36.3	35.8	35.6	35.2	34.4	34.1	33.6	33.7	35.0	35.2
1995	33.5	33.4	33.4	32.8	32.6	32.6	32.4	32.5	32.6	32.1	32.1	33.5	32.7
1996	31.6	31.5	31.4	31.3	31.2	31.1	30.8	30.6	30.6	30.3	30.3	31.7	31.0
1997	31.2	31.2	31.1	31.0	30.7	30.9	30.9	30.5	30.6	30.8	31.1	32.3	31.0
1998	31.1	30.9	30.8	30.9	30.9	30.9	30.9	30.9	30.7	30.7	31.1	32.6	31.0
1999	31.0	30.7	30.6	30.7	30.4	30.6	30.3	30.5	30.1	30.0	30.1	31.1	30.5
2000	30.8	30.4	30.6	30.6	33.1	30.2	30.3	29.6	29.5	29.2	29.3	30.3	30.3
2001	29.8	29.2	29.2	29.2	29.1	29.4	29.3	29.2	29.2	29.0	29.0	29.8	29.3
2002	29.7	28.9	29.1	28.9	28.9	29.2	29.2	29.1	29.3	29.7	30.2	31.2	29.5
2003	29.8	29.7	29.7	29.6	29.6	29.7	29.5	29.4	29.4	29.3	29.2	30.1	29.6

Employment by Industry: Colorado—*Continued*

(Numbers in thousands. Not seasonally adjusted.)

Industry	January	February	March	April	May	June	July	August	September	October	November	December	Annual Average
DENVER—*Continued*													
State government													
1990	22.6	25.6	25.7	27.9	27.4	26.2	24.8	25.2	27.8	28.3	28.7	27.9	26.5
1991	24.9	27.5	27.6	27.6	27.4	25.2	25.8	25.1	27.0	27.8	27.8	26.9	26.7
1992	24.9	27.6	27.8	27.8	27.5	24.8	25.9	26.1	27.7	26.4	26.4	26.0	26.5
1993	26.2	28.8	29.1	29.5	28.9	27.1	27.1	26.6	27.8	28.8	28.5	27.9	28.0
1994	25.8	28.4	28.5	28.9	28.2	26.5	26.5	26.2	29.0	28.4	28.9	28.3	27.8
1995	25.9	29.1	29.3	29.1	28.6	27.1	26.9	26.6	29.6	29.6	29.6	28.9	28.3
1996	26.5	29.3	29.9	29.7	29.3	27.7	27.3	27.2	29.7	30.1	30.3	29.7	28.8
1997	28.4	30.2	30.4	30.2	29.8	27.9	28.0	27.8	30.7	31.2	31.4	30.7	29.7
1998	28.9	31.0	31.3	31.4	30.8	28.7	29.0	28.0	31.2	31.6	31.7	31.2	30.4
1999	28.3	31.5	31.9	32.0	32.2	28.8	28.8	28.6	31.5	32.0	31.9	32.0	30.7
2000	28.4	31.8	32.5	32.3	32.2	30.0	28.5	29.5	33.2	33.3	33.6	34.2	31.6
2001	30.6	34.0	32.5	32.5	32.4	30.3	29.7	29.6	32.7	32.6	33.6	33.2	32.0
2002	29.6	33.1	33.7	33.4	33.6	30.6	30.0	29.7	32.4	32.8	33.1	32.6	32.1
2003	29.3	32.3	32.8	32.4	32.5	29.6	29.0	28.8	31.4	32.2	32.2	32.1	31.2
Local government													
1990	68.6	70.8	70.9	70.4	71.6	72.4	62.6	62.3	69.3	70.5	71.7	70.7	69.3
1991	70.0	71.1	71.3	71.6	72.7	74.5	64.6	63.9	70.6	73.0	73.1	72.6	70.7
1992	72.0	73.5	74.0	74.0	75.2	76.2	67.4	68.1	73.6	75.2	75.7	74.5	73.2
1993	73.3	74.8	74.8	75.2	75.9	76.8	68.3	68.5	73.2	75.7	75.7	74.9	73.9
1994	74.0	75.3	75.7	76.3	77.3	78.6	70.6	72.3	75.9	78.9	78.5	77.6	75.9
1995	76.1	77.9	78.4	78.7	79.6	80.7	74.5	75.1	79.3	80.1	80.3	80.0	78.3
1996	78.7	80.3	81.0	81.1	82.5	83.4	75.8	76.5	81.3	83.1	83.9	82.7	80.8
1997	82.0	83.3	83.8	83.8	84.9	85.8	79.1	78.5	83.5	85.3	85.6	85.2	83.4
1998	84.3	85.5	85.8	86.3	87.9	88.7	81.6	81.5	85.7	87.1	87.9	87.4	85.8
1999	86.7	87.7	88.1	88.7	89.7	91.3	83.3	83.2	88.3	88.8	89.2	89.2	87.8
2000	88.4	89.3	90.0	90.9	91.6	93.8	88.6	90.0	92.2	92.1	92.8	92.2	90.9
2001	91.9	92.9	93.8	94.5	95.7	97.3	92.9	94.1	96.8	97.5	98.2	97.6	95.3
2002	98.0	98.5	99.1	99.9	100.9	102.5	97.7	99.6	100.4	101.3	101.3	100.4	100.0
2003	100.3	100.6	100.6	101.2	103.0	104.3	98.3	99.5	100.9	101.9	102.2	100.8	101.1

Average Weekly Hours by Industry: Colorado

(Not seasonally adjusted.)

Industry	January	February	March	April	May	June	July	August	September	October	November	December	Annual Average
STATEWIDE													
Construction													
2001	39.2	37.6	38.1	36.0	41.1	41.3	41.4	41.5	42.2	41.8	41.6	40.7	40.3
2002	40.0	40.4	38.7	41.2	41.1	41.5	41.5	42.2	40.6	41.3	39.9	39.7	40.7
2003	39.5	38.0	39.1	40.0	40.1	40.9	39.9	39.4	38.1	38.1	38.5	37.0	39.1
Manufacturing													
2001	40.6	40.7	40.9	39.7	40.4	41.5	41.3	41.0	41.8	41.0	40.0	39.9	40.7
2002	39.9	40.1	39.9	39.5	40.7	41.4	41.2	40.4	39.8	41.2	42.0	41.3	40.6
2003	39.6	41.1	40.2	39.4	39.8	39.1	40.3	40.9	40.9	41.2	40.9	40.7	40.4
DENVER													
Construction													
2001	39.6	37.8	38.7	35.1	40.0	40.5	40.9	41.2	41.8	41.9	41.5	40.1	40.0
2002	38.6	39.8	38.1	40.0	40.4	41.8	41.5	41.6	40.8	41.9	40.0	39.9	40.4
2003	[1]39.0	39.0	38.9	39.9	39.9	40.7	39.7	40.2	39.7	38.9	39.1	39.2	[1]39.5
Manufacturing													
2001	40.5	40.9	41.4	39.3	38.8	40.7	40.4	40.4	40.8	40.0	39.7	39.6	40.2
2002	39.0	40.0	39.4	38.5	40.4	40.9	39.6	39.4	39.5	40.6	40.6	38.4	39.7
2003	[1]38.3	40.3	39.6	40.1	40.2	40.3	40.2	40.8	40.9	41.6	40.9	39.9	[1]40.3

Average Hourly Earnings by Industry: Colorado

(Dollars, not seasonally adjusted.)

Industry	January	February	March	April	May	June	July	August	September	October	November	December	Annual Average
STATEWIDE													
Construction													
2001	17.32	17.39	17.32	17.35	17.33	17.29	17.11	17.29	17.33	17.29	17.38	17.45	17.32
2002	17.65	17.71	17.66	17.61	17.49	17.58	17.48	17.92	18.24	17.83	18.25	18.37	17.81
2003	18.18	18.58	18.36	18.33	18.55	18.40	18.44	18.68	18.71	18.56	18.85	18.89	18.54
Manufacturing													
2001	14.45	14.62	14.65	14.56	14.66	14.43	14.66	14.74	14.69	14.93	15.00	15.41	14.72
2002	15.32	15.30	15.42	15.40	15.61	15.48	15.44	15.30	15.43	15.29	15.29	16.02	15.44
2003	16.09	16.04	16.30	17.23	17.11	17.14	17.44	17.34	17.25	16.89	16.84	16.86	16.89
DENVER													
Construction													
2001	17.37	17.24	17.37	17.73	17.70	17.86	17.69	17.86	17.97	17.82	17.71	17.94	17.70
2002	18.18	18.25	18.23	18.26	18.01	17.97	18.42	18.77	18.64	18.27	19.09	19.06	18.43
2003	18.72	18.97	19.09	18.93	19.29	19.25	19.40	19.70	19.66	19.45	19.71	19.40	19.30
Manufacturing													
2001	15.20	15.14	15.30	15.20	15.32	14.77	15.13	15.31	15.14	15.32	15.54	15.76	15.25
2002	15.78	15.77	15.65	15.81	15.89	15.90	15.90	15.66	15.46	15.48	15.59	15.89	15.73
2003	15.92	15.74	15.77	15.33	15.52	16.07	16.10	15.96	15.87	15.74	16.04	16.35	15.87

Average Weekly Earnings by Industry: Colorado

(Dollars, not seasonally adjusted.)

Industry	January	February	March	April	May	June	July	August	September	October	November	December	Annual Average
STATEWIDE													
Construction													
2001	678.94	653.86	659.89	624.60	712.26	714.08	708.35	717.54	731.33	722.72	723.01	710.22	698.00
2002	706.00	715.48	683.44	725.53	718.84	729.57	725.42	756.22	740.54	736.38	728.18	729.29	724.87
2003	718.11	706.04	717.88	733.20	743.86	752.56	735.76	735.99	712.85	707.14	725.73	698.93	724.91
Manufacturing													
2001	586.67	595.03	599.19	578.03	592.26	598.85	605.46	604.34	614.04	612.13	600.00	614.86	599.10
2002	611.27	613.53	615.26	608.30	635.33	640.87	636.13	618.12	614.11	629.95	642.18	661.63	626.86
2003	637.16	659.24	655.26	678.86	680.98	670.17	702.83	709.21	705.53	695.87	688.76	686.20	682.36
DENVER													
Construction													
2001	687.85	651.67	672.22	622.32	708.00	723.33	723.52	735.83	751.15	746.66	734.97	719.39	708.00
2002	701.75	726.35	694.56	730.40	727.60	751.15	764.43	780.83	760.51	765.51	763.60	760.49	744.57
2003	730.08	739.83	742.60	755.31	769.67	783.48	770.18	791.94	780.50	756.61	770.66	760.48	762.35
Manufacturing													
2001	615.60	619.23	633.42	597.36	594.42	601.14	611.25	618.52	617.71	612.80	616.94	624.10	613.05
2002	615.42	630.80	616.61	608.69	641.96	650.31	629.64	617.00	610.67	628.49	632.95	610.18	624.48
2003	609.74	634.32	624.49	614.73	623.90	647.62	647.22	651.17	649.08	654.78	656.04	652.37	639.56

CONNECTICUT AT A GLANCE

(Population and total nonfarm employment numbers in thousands)

Population, Census 2000:	3,405.6
Total nonfarm employment, 2003:	1,643.2
Change in total nonfarm employment	
(Number)	
1990–2003:	19.7
1990–2001:	57.6
2001–2003:	-37.9
(Compound annual rate of change)	
1990–2003:	0.1%
1990–2001:	0.3%
2001–2003:	-1.1%
Unemployment rate	
1990:	4.9%
2001:	3.1%
2003:	5.5%

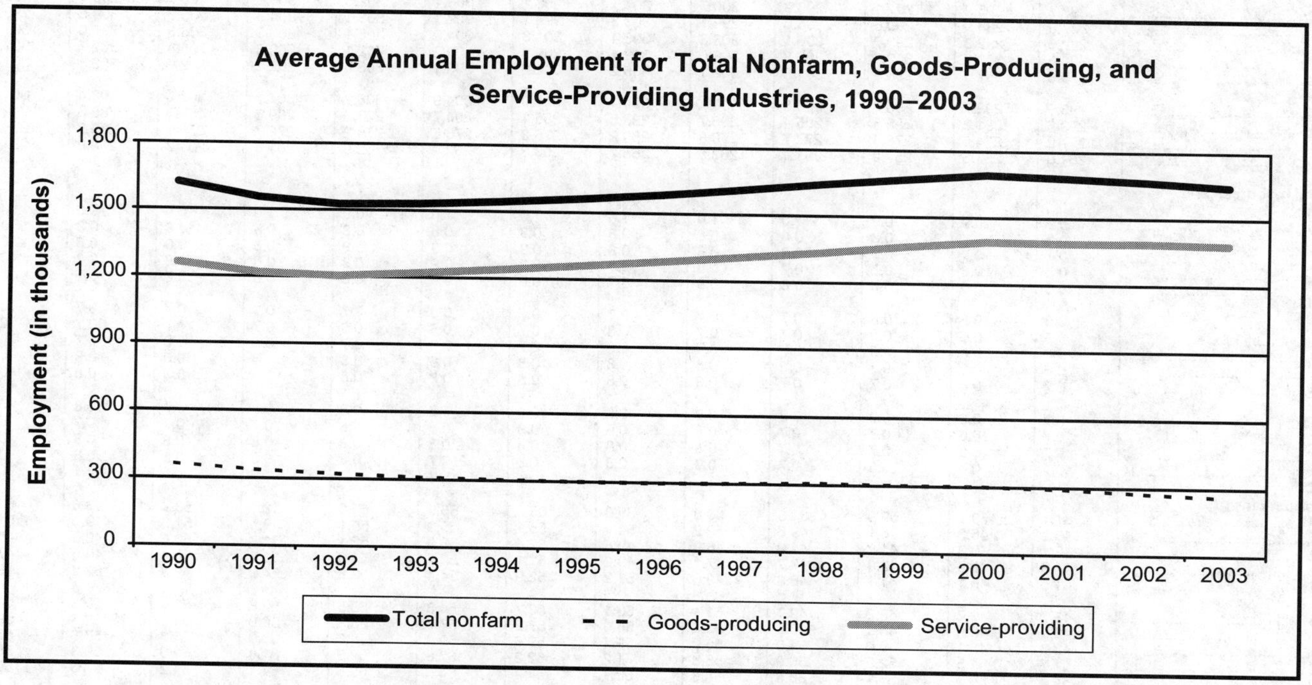

Nonfarm payroll employment experienced widespread declines in both the 1990–1991 and 2001 recessions, particularly in the earlier contraction. From 1990 to 2003, total employment increased only by 1.2 percent. During this period, employment in the goods-producing sector dropped by nearly 100,000, or 27.6 percent. Jobs in the service-providing sector, after declining in the early 1990s, rose steadily before easing after 2000.

Employment by Industry: Connecticut

(Numbers in thousands. Not seasonally adjusted.)

Industry	January	February	March	April	May	June	July	August	September	October	November	December	Annual Average
STATEWIDE													
Total nonfarm													
1990	1625.6	1617.7	1628.8	1626.2	1637.9	1650.1	1616.6	1608.3	1624.9	1614.4	1615.7	1616.1	1623.5
1991	1561.2	1547.3	1556.7	1560.9	1566.9	1576.5	1538.9	1531.8	1550.3	1553.8	1557.5	1560.9	1555.2
1992	1511.3	1507.3	1515.3	1521.2	1531.4	1540.3	1521.9	1513.2	1531.6	1535.8	1540.8	1544.9	1526.2
1993	1511.8	1515.0	1518.7	1522.1	1534.5	1541.7	1519.9	1512.9	1537.2	1546.4	1553.7	1560.2	1531.1
1994	1502.8	1503.3	1515.9	1537.0	1548.7	1560.3	1539.1	1535.6	1559.5	1568.1	1575.6	1579.2	1543.7
1995	1532.8	1539.3	1552.3	1553.9	1563.5	1571.8	1550.3	1549.0	1571.1	1574.3	1586.7	1593.4	1561.5
1996	1533.0	1547.0	1558.0	1572.0	1587.3	1600.1	1570.6	1575.3	1593.4	1612.0	1624.2	1630.8	1583.6
1997	1571.9	1580.1	1592.2	1603.9	1614.8	1626.7	1600.5	1598.6	1626.6	1634.5	1643.5	1656.6	1612.4
1998	1601.6	1612.6	1624.5	1630.4	1643.1	1658.3	1641.7	1634.8	1653.3	1662.1	1673.6	1685.2	1643.4
1999	1632.5	1639.1	1650.9	1663.1	1668.4	1683.3	1667.5	1663.3	1679.5	1682.7	1692.6	1706.4	1669.1
2000	1655.0	1661.5	1675.9	1687.0	1700.9	1713.0	1695.5	1685.8	1703.4	1704.2	1712.1	1723.8	1693.1
2001	1665.2	1661.0	1667.3	1677.0	1690.4	1699.4	1676.5	1669.7	1683.4	1687.9	1694.2	1701.2	1681.1
2002	1648.1	1648.7	1657.5	1670.2	1679.9	1687.0	1655.0	1652.0	1663.3	1665.2	1673.1	1678.2	1664.9
2003	1630.9	1626.0	1630.8	1642.2	1654.3	1660.1	1632.9	1630.6	1643.6	1648.5	1657.7	1660.9	1643.2
Total private													
1990	1416.2	1405.3	1414.7	1412.2	1421.1	1435.4	1419.6	1414.9	1417.0	1401.9	1399.1	1400.4	1413.1
1991	1351.0	1334.5	1342.7	1346.7	1353.6	1365.3	1346.9	1342.4	1348.6	1344.5	1345.3	1350.0	1347.6
1992	1305.6	1296.7	1303.1	1307.8	1317.4	1330.1	1327.1	1322.1	1328.6	1326.6	1328.1	1333.5	1318.8
1993	1305.5	1301.3	1303.2	1307.4	1319.4	1331.0	1321.4	1319.0	1328.9	1331.6	1333.7	1342.9	1320.4
1994	1294.4	1287.2	1296.7	1316.3	1327.5	1342.1	1332.7	1332.4	1341.2	1344.8	1348.0	1355.2	1326.5
1995	1315.2	1314.7	1325.2	1328.9	1340.1	1353.3	1342.2	1343.5	1350.2	1350.2	1358.3	1365.9	1340.6
1996	1316.8	1321.6	1331.9	1343.5	1360.9	1377.9	1361.6	1369.2	1373.3	1381.9	1391.9	1399.4	1360.8
1997	1349.3	1349.5	1360.8	1374.0	1386.9	1402.9	1387.5	1388.7	1399.3	1404.9	1411.5	1425.9	1386.7
1998	1380.0	1383.2	1392.2	1399.8	1414.4	1432.7	1427.6	1424.3	1424.0	1427.5	1434.9	1447.1	1415.6
1999	1404.2	1402.9	1412.0	1423.1	1430.5	1448.5	1444.9	1443.2	1442.7	1442.5	1449.8	1463.7	1434.0
2000	1417.6	1417.2	1428.6	1439.8	1450.2	1470.4	1466.4	1460.6	1463.3	1459.3	1465.5	1477.1	1451.3
2001	1423.4	1414.3	1420.0	1429.8	1443.3	1456.8	1449.0	1443.1	1438.9	1436.7	1438.7	1446.0	1436.7
2002	1399.4	1393.8	1401.7	1415.6	1425.7	1436.9	1423.9	1418.1	1416.5	1413.6	1417.8	1423.7	1415.6
2003	1380.6	1373.4	1377.6	1390.7	1402.9	1413.7	1405.0	1399.8	1400.0	1400.6	1406.2	1410.8	1396.8
Goods-producing													
1990	366.1	362.8	363.8	365.3	365.8	367.3	363.3	361.3	362.3	356.5	353.5	349.5	361.4
1991	337.9	332.5	333.2	339.6	339.5	342.7	334.9	335.4	340.2	339.4	337.3	333.3	337.1
1992	322.0	319.5	319.9	320.5	322.6	326.0	324.1	323.5	326.1	322.2	320.8	318.5	322.1
1993	310.7	308.7	307.6	308.5	309.7	312.5	310.0	310.2	314.2	311.8	310.0	308.6	310.2
1994	296.2	293.7	295.1	300.8	303.7	306.6	304.6	306.2	309.4	308.9	308.2	307.2	303.3
1995	297.7	295.2	297.1	298.9	300.7	304.1	298.1	300.1	302.5	300.9	300.7	299.4	299.6
1996	287.9	288.9	290.6	295.0	299.1	303.3	298.1	302.1	303.1	304.3	305.0	304.2	298.4
1997	292.6	292.8	293.7	300.1	303.3	308.4	301.3	304.9	306.1	306.6	306.8	306.0	301.8
1998	300.3	300.2	302.2	306.3	308.0	312.1	309.6	309.2	312.1	309.6	308.4	307.7	307.1
1999	299.5	297.5	298.5	301.6	302.1	305.2	302.2	303.1	303.5	302.7	302.9	303.4	301.8
2000	293.9	292.7	295.6	298.8	300.7	304.4	304.0	304.[illegible]	306.2	304.1	303.8	303.4	301.0
2001	293.5	291.3	292.5	295.4	296.7	298.5	295.1	294.7	292.8	289.6	287.3	285.8	292.8
2002	277.2	274.5	275.5	277.7	278.8	280.2	276.3	276.6	275.2	272.7	270.9	268.5	275.3
2003	261.0	257.3	257.9	261.4	263.6	265.7	263.3	263.7	262.9	261.8	261.2	258.9	261.6
Natural resources and mining													
1990	0.9	0.9	0.9	1.0	1.0	1.0	1.0	1.0	0.9	1.0	0.9	0.9	0.9
1991	0.8	0.7	0.8	0.8	0.8	0.8	0.8	0.8	0.8	0.8	0.8	0.8	0.7
1992	0.7	0.7	0.7	0.8	0.8	0.8	0.9	0.9	0.9	0.8	0.9	0.8	0.8
1993	0.6	0.6	0.7	0.7	0.8	0.8	0.8	0.9	0.8	0.8	0.8	0.8	0.7
1994	0.6	0.6	0.6	0.8	0.8	0.7	0.8	0.8	0.8	0.8	0.8	0.7	0.7
1995	0.6	0.5	0.6	0.7	0.7	0.7	0.7	0.8	0.7	0.7	0.7	0.7	0.6
1996	0.5	0.6	0.6	0.7	0.7	0.8	0.7	0.8	0.8	0.7	0.7	0.7	0.6
1997	0.6	0.6	0.6	0.7	0.7	0.8	0.7	0.7	0.7	0.8	0.8	0.7	0.7
1998	0.6	0.6	0.7	0.8	0.8	0.8	0.8	0.8	0.8	0.8	0.8	0.8	0.7
1999	0.7	0.6	0.7	0.7	0.8	0.8	0.8	0.8	0.8	0.8	0.8	0.8	0.7
2000	0.7	0.6	0.7	0.8	0.8	0.8	0.9	0.8	0.8	0.8	0.8	0.8	0.7
2001	0.7	0.6	0.7	0.7	0.8	0.8	0.8	0.8	0.8	0.7	0.7	0.7	0.7
2002	0.7	0.6	0.7	0.7	0.8	0.8	0.8	0.8	0.8	0.8	0.8	0.8	0.8
2003	0.7	0.6	0.6	0.7	0.7	0.8	0.8	0.7	0.8	0.8	0.8	0.8	0.7
Construction													
1990	61.1	59.2	59.9	61.5	63.8	65.3	65.9	65.9	65.3	62.1	59.9	56.6	62.2
1991	48.2	45.3	46.1	49.6	52.2	54.4	55.1	55.9	55.1	53.5	51.8	49.0	51.3
1992	42.1	40.3	41.2	44.0	46.9	49.8	52.4	53.0	52.1	51.8	50.6	48.6	47.7
1993	44.3	42.9	42.8	43.7	47.1	49.2	51.1	52.4	51.8	50.7	50.1	49.0	47.9
1994	41.5	40.1	41.1	46.8	49.5	51.2	52.9	54.4	53.6	54.0	53.3	52.0	49.2
1995	45.7	43.7	45.2	49.1	51.1	53.1	53.7	54.3	53.5	52.8	52.6	50.5	50.4
1996	42.9	42.9	45.0	50.0	53.3	56.0	57.2	57.7	56.8	56.8	56.3	54.6	52.4
1997	48.3	48.1	49.0	54.0	56.9	59.4	59.6	59.9	59.6	59.0	58.3	57.6	55.8
1998	51.7	51.5	52.5	56.9	58.8	61.2	62.2	62.8	62.2	61.4	61.0	60.3	58.5
1999	54.9	54.3	55.1	58.8	60.6	62.7	64.2	64.5	63.6	64.1	64.2	63.5	60.8
2000	58.1	57.1	59.9	62.9	65.0	67.0	68.0	68.5	68.0	67.3	67.1	66.0	64.5
2001	59.1	58.3	59.6	64.2	66.7	68.5	69.8	70.0	68.8	67.6	66.6	65.1	65.4
2002	59.4	58.5	59.9	63.3	65.0	66.4	66.8	66.7	65.5	64.5	63.7	61.3	63.4
2003	56.2	54.3	55.2	59.0	62.2	63.8	65.6	65.9	65.0	64.1	63.5	61.1	61.3

Employment by Industry: Connecticut—*Continued*

(Numbers in thousands. Not seasonally adjusted.)

Industry	January	February	March	April	May	June	July	August	September	October	November	December	Annual Average
STATEWIDE—*Continued*													
Manufacturing													
1990	304.1	302.7	303.0	302.8	301.0	301.0	296.4	294.4	296.1	293.4	292.7	292.0	298.3
1991	288.9	286.5	286.3	289.2	286.5	287.5	279.0	278.7	284.3	285.1	284.7	283.5	285.0
1992	279.2	278.5	278.0	275.7	274.9	275.4	270.8	269.6	273.1	269.6	269.3	269.1	273.6
1993	265.8	265.2	264.1	264.1	261.8	262.5	258.1	256.9	261.6	260.3	259.1	258.8	261.5
1994	254.1	253.0	253.4	253.2	253.4	254.7	250.9	251.0	255.0	254.1	254.1	254.5	253.4
1995	251.4	251.0	251.3	249.1	248.9	250.3	243.7	245.0	248.3	247.4	247.4	248.2	248.5
1996	244.5	245.4	245.0	244.3	245.1	246.5	240.2	243.6	245.5	246.8	248.0	248.9	245.3
1997	243.7	244.1	244.1	245.4	245.7	248.2	241.0	244.3	245.8	246.8	247.7	247.7	245.3
1998	248.0	248.1	249.0	248.6	248.4	250.1	246.6	245.6	249.1	247.4	246.6	246.6	247.8
1999	243.9	242.6	242.7	242.1	240.7	241.7	237.2	237.8	239.1	237.8	237.9	239.1	240.2
2000	235.1	235.0	235.0	235.1	234.9	236.6	235.1	235.6	237.4	236.0	235.9	236.6	235.6
2001	233.7	232.4	232.2	230.5	229.2	229.2	224.5	223.9	223.2	221.3	220.0	220.0	226.7
2002	217.1	215.4	214.9	213.7	213.0	213.0	208.7	209.1	208.9	207.4	206.4	206.4	211.2
2003	204.1	202.4	202.1	201.7	200.7	201.1	196.9	197.1	197.1	196.9	196.9	197.0	199.5
Service-providing													
1990	1259.5	1254.9	1265.0	1260.9	1272.1	1282.8	1253.3	1247.0	1262.6	1257.9	1262.2	1266.6	1262.0
1991	1223.3	1214.8	1223.5	1221.3	1227.4	1233.8	1204.0	1196.4	1210.1	1214.4	1220.2	1227.6	1218.0
1992	1189.3	1187.8	1195.4	1200.7	1208.8	1214.3	1197.8	1189.7	1205.5	1213.6	1220.0	1226.4	1204.1
1993	1201.1	1206.3	1211.1	1213.6	1224.8	1229.2	1209.9	1202.7	1223.0	1234.6	1243.7	1251.6	1220.9
1994	1206.6	1209.6	1220.8	1236.2	1245.0	1253.7	1234.5	1229.4	1250.1	1259.2	1267.4	1272.0	1240.3
1995	1235.1	1244.1	1255.2	1255.0	1262.8	1267.7	1252.2	1248.9	1268.6	1273.4	1286.0	1294.0	1261.9
1996	1245.1	1258.1	1267.4	1277.0	1288.2	1296.8	1272.5	1273.2	1290.3	1307.7	1319.2	1326.6	1285.1
1997	1279.3	1287.3	1298.5	1303.8	1311.5	1318.3	1299.2	1293.7	1320.5	1327.9	1336.7	1350.6	1310.6
1998	1301.3	1312.4	1322.3	1324.1	1335.1	1346.2	1332.1	1325.6	1341.2	1352.5	1365.2	1377.5	1336.2
1999	1333.0	1341.6	1352.4	1361.5	1366.3	1378.1	1365.3	1360.2	1376.0	1380.0	1389.7	1403.0	1367.2
2000	1361.1	1368.8	1380.3	1388.2	1400.2	1408.6	1391.5	1380.9	1397.2	1400.1	1408.3	1420.4	1392.1
2001	1371.7	1369.7	1374.8	1381.6	1393.7	1400.9	1381.4	1375.0	1390.6	1398.3	1406.9	1415.4	1388.3
2002	1370.9	1374.2	1382.0	1392.5	1401.1	1406.8	1378.7	1375.4	1388.1	1392.5	1402.2	1409.7	1389.5
2003	1369.9	1368.7	1372.9	1380.8	1390.7	1394.4	1369.6	1366.9	1380.7	1386.7	1396.5	1402.0	1381.7
Trade, transportation, and utilities													
1990	325.8	317.1	318.1	314.6	316.2	318.6	311.4	310.7	313.3	312.1	315.7	320.1	316.1
1991	306.1	295.4	296.8	295.8	297.7	298.5	293.1	292.5	295.6	295.9	301.4	307.0	297.9
1992	293.6	288.1	289.2	285.8	288.2	289.6	284.8	284.0	287.4	290.8	296.6	302.4	290.0
1993	290.5	286.1	285.3	282.7	285.6	288.1	282.3	282.0	286.6	290.3	295.9	302.4	288.1
1994	287.8	282.3	283.2	286.3	289.2	292.4	286.7	286.3	291.6	296.2	301.1	305.7	290.7
1995	295.0	290.9	292.7	288.7	290.9	293.6	289.9	290.0	294.1	297.6	304.7	309.8	294.8
1996	297.5	294.5	294.3	294.1	296.3	298.7	294.6	294.9	298.9	301.9	309.0	315.1	299.1
1997	299.1	294.9	295.8	296.1	299.1	301.9	297.3	296.7	304.7	308.8	314.6	321.6	302.5
1998	306.0	303.4	304.8	302.7	306.4	308.9	304.5	304.1	308.5	311.0	318.1	324.7	308.5
1999	310.8	306.7	308.0	307.9	308.2	311.2	306.8	307.9	310.8	315.8	322.3	329.4	312.1
2000	314.8	311.6	313.0	314.5	316.1	318.4	313.1	312.2	316.9	319.5	326.7	333.2	317.5
2001	314.2	306.4	307.0	308.8	311.5	313.6	309.5	307.8	310.0	313.6	318.9	324.7	312.2
2002	309.4	303.8	305.4	307.7	309.7	312.7	305.9	304.3	308.6	308.2	314.3	320.4	309.2
2003	306.3	300.9	302.5	301.7	304.3	307.2	301.3	300.1	304.6	304.9	310.8	316.4	305.1
Wholesale trade													
1990	74.7	74.0	74.0	72.8	72.8	72.8	72.7	72.4	71.8	70.7	70.3	70.1	72.4
1991	69.6	69.0	68.8	68.9	68.3	68.5	67.7	67.7	67.8	67.7	67.8	68.0	68.3
1992	66.6	66.5	66.7	66.0	65.9	66.4	64.6	64.3	64.1	64.7	64.3	64.6	65.3
1993	64.9	64.6	64.7	63.3	63.5	64.1	64.0	63.9	64.0	63.4	63.2	63.5	63.9
1994	61.2	60.9	61.4	62.5	62.7	63.2	62.8	62.6	63.3	63.2	63.2	63.5	62.5
1995	63.0	63.2	63.6	63.3	63.5	63.9	63.7	63.6	64.0	64.1	64.2	64.5	63.7
1996	64.1	64.5	65.0	64.5	63.9	64.1	63.7	63.8	63.7	64.0	64.6	64.7	64.2
1997	63.5	63.7	64.1	64.6	65.0	65.2	64.7	64.7	64.9	65.1	65.3	65.7	64.7
1998	64.4	64.9	65.6	66.5	66.5	67.3	67.0	66.8	67.1	66.8	66.8	67.1	66.4
1999	65.4	65.3	65.8	66.1	65.8	66.3	65.9	65.9	66.3	66.3	66.6	67.1	66.0
2000	66.9	67.0	67.3	68.1	68.5	68.7	68.4	68.2	68.5	68.4	68.9	69.3	68.1
2001	67.0	67.1	67.3	67.9	68.1	68.2	67.7	67.2	66.9	67.2	66.8	67.2	67.4
2002	65.9	65.5	65.7	66.1	66.3	66.4	66.3	66.2	66.0	65.8	65.8	66.2	66.0
2003	65.3	65.0	65.4	65.4	65.5	66.0	65.7	65.5	65.3	65.2	65.3	65.5	65.4
Retail trade													
1990	202.0	194.9	194.9	192.8	194.0	195.8	191.8	191.5	192.0	192.2	196.3	200.3	194.8
1991	188.0	179.9	180.1	178.5	180.6	181.2	179.8	179.8	180.1	179.8	185.4	190.4	181.9
1992	179.4	175.3	174.8	173.2	174.3	175.0	174.7	174.5	174.9	177.2	183.5	188.4	177.1
1993	177.4	173.6	172.4	172.2	173.7	175.0	172.1	172.4	173.6	176.5	182.3	188.3	175.7
1994	177.8	172.7	172.9	175.0	177.0	179.4	176.5	176.7	178.2	181.6	187.3	191.6	178.8
1995	182.8	178.5	179.4	176.2	177.8	180.0	178.5	179.6	180.2	183.2	190.3	195.2	181.8
1996	184.1	180.3	179.5	179.6	181.7	183.7	183.0	184.0	184.5	186.4	192.9	199.2	184.9
1997	187.5	183.1	183.5	182.7	184.9	187.1	185.8	188.0	189.7	192.4	198.2	204.5	188.9
1998	191.7	188.3	188.9	186.5	189.0	191.0	189.4	189.6	190.0	192.3	198.9	205.3	191.7
1999	194.1	190.0	190.8	190.8	190.5	192.8	191.8	194.0	193.0	196.4	202.9	209.5	194.7
2000	196.4	192.9	194.4	194.5	195.7	197.8	194.8	195.0	195.7	197.3	204.2	210.6	197.4
2001	195.6	188.6	189.4	190.0	192.3	194.6	193.6	193.8	193.0	195.3	201.4	206.8	194.5
2002	194.9	189.5	191.1	192.0	193.7	196.5	193.2	192.9	192.8	192.0	198.2	204.0	194.2
2003	192.1	187.3	188.2	187.8	189.9	191.9	190.0	190.1	190.1	189.7	195.6	200.8	191.1

Employment by Industry: Connecticut—*Continued*

(Numbers in thousands. Not seasonally adjusted.)

Industry	January	February	March	April	May	June	July	August	September	October	November	December	Annual Average
STATEWIDE—*Continued*													
Transportation and utilities													
1990	49.1	48.2	49.2	49.0	49.4	50.0	46.9	46.8	49.5	49.2	49.1	49.7	48.8
1991	48.5	46.5	47.9	48.4	48.8	48.8	45.6	45.0	47.7	48.4	48.2	48.6	47.7
1992	47.6	46.3	47.7	46.6	48.0	48.2	45.5	45.2	48.4	48.9	48.8	49.4	47.5
1993	48.2	47.9	48.2	47.2	48.4	49.0	46.2	45.7	49.0	50.4	50.4	50.6	48.4
1994	48.8	48.7	48.9	48.8	49.5	49.8	47.4	47.0	50.1	51.4	50.6	50.6	49.3
1995	49.2	49.2	49.7	49.2	49.6	49.7	47.7	46.8	49.9	50.3	50.2	50.1	49.3
1996	49.3	49.7	49.8	50.0	50.7	50.9	47.9	47.1	50.7	51.5	51.5	51.2	50.0
1997	48.1	48.1	48.2	48.8	49.2	49.6	46.8	44.0	50.1	51.3	51.1	51.4	48.8
1998	49.9	50.2	50.3	49.7	50.9	50.6	48.1	47.7	51.4	51.9	52.4	52.3	50.4
1999	51.3	51.4	51.4	51.0	51.9	52.1	49.1	48.0	51.5	53.1	52.8	52.8	51.3
2000	51.5	51.7	51.3	51.9	51.9	51.9	49.9	49.0	52.7	53.8	53.6	53.3	51.8
2001	51.6	50.7	50.3	50.9	51.1	50.8	48.2	46.8	50.1	51.1	50.7	50.7	50.3
2002	48.6	48.8	48.6	49.6	49.7	49.8	46.4	45.2	49.8	50.4	50.3	50.2	49.0
2003	48.9	48.6	48.9	48.5	48.9	49.3	45.6	44.5	49.2	50.0	49.9	50.1	48.5
Information													
1990	43.2	43.0	43.3	42.7	42.5	43.1	42.0	41.8	41.3	41.2	40.9	41.0	42.1
1991	41.6	41.3	41.2	40.0	40.0	40.0	39.9	39.5	39.5	39.4	39.3	39.7	40.1
1992	39.1	39.1	39.3	39.1	39.0	39.4	39.6	39.7	39.7	39.6	39.7	39.8	39.4
1993	39.7	39.8	39.7	39.2	39.1	39.5	39.4	39.4	39.5	39.9	40.2	40.3	39.6
1994	39.9	39.6	39.7	40.1	40.3	40.7	40.7	40.7	40.5	40.5	40.8	41.0	40.3
1995	41.0	41.0	41.2	41.5	41.6	41.9	41.4	41.5	41.3	42.1	41.6	42.0	41.5
1996	41.3	41.9	42.3	42.8	43.2	43.9	43.1	43.6	43.8	44.1	44.7	44.7	43.2
1997	44.2	44.5	44.8	44.8	44.7	45.0	44.6	44.8	44.9	43.8	43.8	44.1	44.5
1998	44.1	44.1	44.4	44.4	44.7	45.1	44.9	44.9	39.3	45.1	45.1	45.4	44.2
1999	44.4	44.3	44.3	44.2	44.2	44.4	44.8	44.8	44.6	45.0	45.4	45.7	44.6
2000	45.2	45.4	45.7	45.5	45.8	46.5	46.9	47.0	47.0	47.1	47.4	47.6	46.4
2001	46.3	46.4	46.0	45.3	45.1	45.1	44.2	44.2	43.6	43.2	43.3	43.3	44.7
2002	42.2	41.9	41.8	41.5	41.4	41.5	41.0	40.7	40.2	40.0	39.9	40.0	41.0
2003	40.1	39.9	39.8	39.6	39.6	39.8	39.7	39.6	39.1	38.8	38.8	39.0	39.5
Financial activities													
1990	153.5	153.7	154.1	153.2	154.0	155.3	155.7	155.4	153.3	151.6	150.2	151.1	153.4
1991	151.3	150.2	150.3	148.9	149.1	150.7	149.7	149.5	147.9	147.2	147.1	147.8	149.1
1992	142.2	141.8	142.3	143.2	143.7	144.6	144.9	143.8	142.5	141.4	141.1	141.9	142.7
1993	140.9	140.6	141.1	140.1	139.9	141.3	141.2	141.1	140.3	139.1	138.8	139.3	140.3
1994	136.8	136.2	135.9	136.5	136.6	137.4	136.1	135.9	135.4	133.5	133.4	133.8	135.6
1995	130.0	130.0	130.2	131.2	131.7	133.2	134.8	135.1	134.7	132.0	132.5	133.1	132.3
1996	127.9	128.7	128.9	128.2	128.3	129.4	128.8	129.0	127.3	128.6	129.0	129.0	128.5
1997	126.9	128.0	128.4	128.8	129.6	129.9	130.3	131.0	130.8	131.9	132.1	133.9	130.1
1998	133.1	133.5	134.7	133.9	134.4	136.7	139.8	140.3	139.2	138.7	139.2	140.3	136.9
1999	139.3	139.1	139.2	140.2	140.4	142.2	142.5	142.3	141.4	140.7	140.9	141.8	140.8
2000	141.2	141.2	141.8	141.5	142.1	144.2	145.1	145.3	143.9	143.0	143.0	144.1	143.0
2001	142.1	141.8	142.1	142.0	142.5	144.1	144.8	144.9	143.1	142.3	142.4	143.2	142.9
2002	142.8	142.1	142.1	141.4	142.1	143.4	143.9	143.8	142.5	141.8	142.5	143.1	142.6
2003	142.4	141.7	141.7	142.7	143.5	144.9	145.4	144.9	143.3	143.1	143.5	143.7	143.4
Professional and business services													
1990	168.1	168.9	171.4	169.5	170.8	174.1	172.1	172.5	171.9	170.4	169.8	169.6	170.7
1991	165.3	165.2	167.3	166.3	166.0	167.6	166.0	165.2	164.7	164.0	163.3	163.8	165.3
1992	160.2	160.4	161.9	165.1	164.6	165.9	165.4	165.2	165.1	165.0	163.7	163.2	163.8
1993	162.7	162.8	164.0	164.7	166.3	167.9	167.5	167.1	167.6	168.1	167.8	168.2	166.2
1994	163.5	164.6	166.7	170.4	171.0	173.3	172.3	173.0	173.8	175.6	175.5	175.5	171.2
1995	169.5	171.9	173.9	176.6	177.7	179.2	177.7	179.1	179.9	178.3	179.8	180.3	176.9
1996	175.6	179.7	182.3	186.0	187.9	190.2	187.9	190.6	191.0	193.0	194.4	194.4	187.7
1997	185.2	187.2	189.3	193.2	193.9	196.5	196.0	196.0	196.9	197.4	198.3	200.2	194.1
1998	195.7	196.9	199.5	203.1	203.4	206.5	205.3	205.8	206.4	207.2	208.0	209.4	203.9
1999	203.1	203.4	206.2	209.8	210.3	214.8	214.8	215.4	215.5	214.5	215.0	216.7	211.6
2000	207.7	208.9	211.6	214.4	216.1	220.9	219.7	219.5	219.4	217.6	217.2	218.0	215.9
2001	207.3	204.7	206.6	209.6	214.4	215.2	212.4	212.1	211.7	209.3	207.8	207.4	209.9
2002	197.7	197.7	200.7	203.2	203.9	206.2	203.3	204.1	203.4	201.6	201.2	201.0	202.0
2003	193.5	193.4	194.4	197.0	197.3	198.7	196.6	197.7	198.1	196.5	196.4	196.0	196.3
Educational and health services													
1990	192.9	193.7	194.9	196.6	197.2	197.1	195.4	195.1	200.1	201.5	203.1	203.9	197.6
1991	203.6	205.8	207.7	207.0	207.3	206.1	202.1	201.0	205.0	206.3	206.6	207.3	205.4
1992	205.9	204.5	205.3	205.6	206.2	206.2	206.7	205.3	210.8	211.8	212.6	213.9	207.9
1993	210.6	212.4	213.7	215.9	217.3	215.4	211.8	211.1	216.1	220.1	220.3	221.9	215.5
1994	217.0	217.6	219.6	221.3	221.9	220.8	218.0	216.5	221.1	224.6	225.1	227.3	220.9
1995	223.5	226.1	227.8	224.7	225.4	224.3	222.3	220.5	225.3	228.0	228.8	230.1	225.5
1996	224.1	226.9	227.3	228.6	230.1	230.1	228.2	228.5	233.0	233.0	234.7	236.2	230.0
1997	231.6	234.9	235.8	235.3	234.8	233.6	231.1	229.6	233.9	236.1	237.1	239.3	234.4
1998	234.2	237.4	236.5	236.3	237.4	238.0	236.4	234.2	238.5	240.2	241.6	242.7	237.7
1999	238.4	241.5	243.1	241.2	242.0	241.3	241.7	240.1	243.6	243.6	245.4	247.1	242.4
2000	243.4	245.6	246.7	246.3	245.7	244.5	244.2	240.6	244.6	245.7	247.0	248.8	245.2
2001	248.3	252.0	252.0	251.7	248.5	249.8	249.4	247.5	254.7	257.5	259.6	260.8	252.7
2002	255.1	258.9	258.9	260.3	259.6	257.1	255.9	253.7	259.4	264.4	266.5	266.9	259.7
2003	261.1	264.3	263.0	265.0	264.3	260.8	259.0	256.1	261.5	266.6	268.2	268.6	263.2

Employment by Industry: Connecticut—*Continued*

(Numbers in thousands. Not seasonally adjusted.)

Industry	January	February	March	April	May	June	July	August	September	October	November	December	Annual Average
STATEWIDE—*Continued*													
Leisure and hospitality													
1990	102.3	101.7	104.1	106.2	110.5	114.7	114.3	113.3	111.4	106.6	104.3	104.2	107.8
1991	93.2	93.0	95.3	99.4	103.9	108.3	108.3	107.8	105.1	102.1	100.2	100.3	101.4
1992	93.7	94.5	96.0	98.3	102.2	106.1	107.6	107.3	104.5	101.8	99.1	98.6	100.8
1993	95.3	95.1	95.4	99.8	105.1	109.1	110.5	110.2	107.2	104.4	102.4	103.4	103.1
1994	96.4	95.9	99.2	103.8	107.9	112.9	114.7	114.5	111.1	106.9	105.0	105.4	106.1
1995	101.2	101.2	103.9	108.8	113.1	117.0	117.9	117.4	113.3	111.8	110.4	110.7	110.5
1996	103.5	104.1	106.3	109.9	115.3	120.5	119.4	119.4	115.4	118.0	115.7	116.4	113.6
1997	109.9	110.4	112.3	116.4	121.8	127.3	126.6	125.9	122.2	118.7	117.0	118.3	118.9
1998	107.6	108.4	110.4	113.4	119.9	124.4	126.1	125.3	120.2	115.7	114.4	116.1	116.8
1999	108.9	110.3	111.9	117.6	122.6	128.1	130.2	128.5	122.9	119.6	117.4	118.6	119.7
2000	111.9	112.1	114.2	118.2	122.9	129.6	130.9	129.3	124.1	120.9	119.0	120.3	121.1
2001	111.0	111.0	112.7	115.8	122.9	127.7	129.7	128.6	121.2	118.9	116.9	118.0	119.5
2002	112.9	113.0	115.0	120.8	126.4	131.4	133.5	131.6	125.2	122.9	120.2	121.0	122.8
2003	114.7	114.6	116.4	121.5	128.0	133.2	136.0	134.6	128.6	126.7	124.7	125.4	125.4
Other services													
1990	64.3	64.4	65.0	64.1	64.1	65.2	65.4	64.8	63.4	62.0	61.6	61.0	63.7
1991	52.0	51.1	50.9	49.7	50.1	51.4	52.9	51.5	50.6	50.2	50.1	50.8	50.9
1992	48.9	48.8	49.2	50.2	50.9	52.3	54.0	53.3	52.5	54.0	54.5	55.2	51.9
1993	55.1	55.8	56.4	56.5	56.4	57.2	58.7	57.9	57.4	57.9	58.3	58.8	57.2
1994	56.8	57.3	57.3	57.1	56.9	58.0	59.6	59.3	58.3	58.6	58.9	59.3	58.1
1995	57.3	58.4	58.4	58.5	59.0	60.0	60.1	59.8	59.1	59.5	59.8	60.5	59.2
1996	59.0	56.9	59.9	58.9	60.7	61.8	61.5	61.1	60.8	59.0	59.4	59.4	59.8
1997	59.8	56.8	60.7	59.3	59.7	60.3	60.3	59.8	59.8	61.6	61.8	62.5	60.2
1998	59.0	59.3	59.7	59.7	60.2	61.0	61.0	60.5	59.8	60.0	60.1	60.8	60.0
1999	59.8	60.1	60.8	60.6	60.7	61.3	61.9	61.1	60.4	60.6	60.5	61.0	60.7
2000	59.5	59.7	60.0	60.6	60.8	61.9	62.5	61.8	61.2	61.4	61.4	61.7	61.0
2001	60.7	60.7	61.1	61.2	61.7	62.8	63.9	63.3	61.8	62.3	62.5	62.8	62.1
2002	62.1	61.9	62.3	63.0	63.8	64.4	64.1	63.3	62.0	62.0	62.3	62.8	62.8
2003	61.5	61.3	61.9	61.8	62.3	63.4	63.7	63.1	61.9	62.2	62.6	62.8	62.4
Government													
1990	209.4	212.4	214.1	214.0	216.8	214.7	197.0	193.4	207.9	212.5	216.6	215.7	210.3
1991	210.2	212.8	214.0	214.2	213.3	211.2	192.0	189.4	201.7	209.3	212.2	210.9	207.6
1992	205.7	210.6	212.2	213.4	214.0	210.2	194.8	191.1	203.0	209.2	212.7	211.4	207.3
1993	206.3	213.7	215.5	214.7	215.1	210.7	198.5	193.9	208.3	214.8	220.0	217.3	210.7
1994	208.4	216.1	219.2	220.7	221.2	218.2	206.4	203.2	218.3	223.3	227.6	224.0	217.2
1995	217.6	224.6	227.1	225.0	223.4	218.5	208.1	205.5	220.9	224.1	228.4	227.5	220.8
1996	216.2	225.4	226.1	228.5	226.4	222.2	209.0	206.1	220.1	230.1	232.3	231.4	222.8
1997	222.6	230.6	231.4	229.9	227.9	223.8	213.0	209.9	227.3	229.6	232.0	230.7	225.7
1998	221.6	229.4	232.3	230.6	228.7	225.6	214.1	210.5	229.3	234.6	238.7	238.1	227.7
1999	228.3	236.2	238.9	240.0	237.9	234.8	222.6	220.1	236.8	240.2	242.8	242.7	235.1
2000	237.4	244.3	247.3	247.2	250.7	242.6	229.1	225.2	240.1	244.9	246.6	246.7	241.8
2001	241.8	246.7	247.3	247.2	247.1	242.6	227.5	226.6	244.5	251.2	255.5	255.2	244.4
2002	248.7	254.9	255.8	254.6	254.2	250.1	231.1	233.9	246.8	251.6	255.3	254.5	249.3
2003	250.3	252.6	253.2	251.5	251.4	246.4	227.9	230.8	243.6	247.9	251.5	250.1	246.4
Federal government													
1990	25.1	25.0	25.4	26.1	29.6	28.2	27.3	25.7	26.0	25.3	25.2	25.3	26.1
1991	24.6	24.5	24.4	24.4	24.3	24.5	23.3	23.2	23.1	24.8	24.8	25.3	24.2
1992	25.2	25.0	25.0	25.1	24.9	24.9	24.9	24.9	25.0	25.4	25.1	25.7	25.0
1993	24.4	24.4	24.4	24.5	24.5	24.6	24.7	24.7	24.6	24.6	24.6	25.5	24.6
1994	24.1	24.1	24.1	24.3	24.3	24.3	24.3	24.2	24.1	24.0	23.9	24.3	24.1
1995	23.7	23.9	23.9	24.0	24.0	24.1	24.0	24.0	23.9	23.7	23.8	24.4	23.9
1996	23.5	23.5	23.6	23.7	23.6	23.7	23.4	23.5	23.3	23.1	23.2	23.9	23.5
1997	22.9	22.6	22.5	22.7	22.6	22.7	22.6	22.6	22.4	22.3	22.4	23.0	22.6
1998	22.1	22.1	22.1	22.1	22.2	22.2	22.3	22.3	22.2	22.5	22.7	23.4	22.3
1999	22.4	22.3	22.7	22.4	22.1	22.2	22.3	22.3	22.1	22.2	22.0	22.8	22.3
2000	22.6	22.6	23.3	24.1	28.6	25.5	25.0	22.4	21.7	21.9	21.7	22.2	23.4
2001	21.8	21.6	21.8	21.6	21.6	21.6	21.8	21.6	21.5	21.4	21.3	21.7	21.6
2002	21.4	21.2	21.2	21.1	21.0	21.3	21.1	21.3	21.2	21.4	21.2	21.4	21.2
2003	21.3	21.1	21.1	21.0	20.8	20.9	20.9	20.9	20.8	20.8	20.7	20.9	20.9
State government													
1990	65.3	67.8	67.8	68.1	66.3	64.4	64.8	64.1	65.7	68.3	69.0	69.0	66.7
1991	66.8	69.2	69.2	69.9	68.3	65.2	64.2	63.2	64.4	66.6	65.9	65.9	66.5
1992	63.1	65.8	65.3	67.1	66.3	62.7	60.7	60.7	62.0	64.8	65.3	64.8	64.0
1993	63.1	68.5	68.3	69.3	68.0	63.3	62.2	61.3	64.2	67.4	68.3	66.7	65.8
1994	61.9	68.8	69.8	70.0	69.1	64.3	64.2	63.7	67.1	71.0	71.8	69.9	67.6
1995	65.4	72.2	72.6	72.1	69.1	65.3	65.1	64.4	68.9	70.5	71.9	70.5	69.0
1996	63.5	70.5	69.9	71.5	67.4	64.4	61.6	61.2	66.2	68.3	68.7	67.3	66.7
1997	61.4	68.4	68.7	68.0	64.4	60.6	59.3	58.9	64.8	66.8	67.2	65.2	64.4
1998	59.2	65.2	66.5	67.2	63.3	61.2	59.7	59.1	64.0	68.2	69.9	68.4	64.3
1999	61.5	67.5	68.5	70.2	66.8	64.2	62.8	63.5	67.1	70.2	71.0	69.8	66.9
2000	64.5	70.0	71.4	71.7	69.7	65.8	65.0	64.4	68.6	71.7	72.0	71.2	68.8
2001	67.4	71.3	71.2	72.0	70.2	66.5	65.9	65.3	68.4	72.0	72.8	72.3	69.6
2002	67.4	73.0	72.8	73.5	71.6	67.3	66.3	65.7	69.2	71.6	72.2	71.6	70.2
2003	67.3	70.0	69.5	68.5	66.5	62.3	62.0	61.5	65.5	67.3	68.0	67.3	66.3

Employment by Industry: Connecticut—*Continued*

(Numbers in thousands. Not seasonally adjusted.)

Industry	January	February	March	April	May	June	July	August	September	October	November	December	Annual Average
STATEWIDE—*Continued*													
Local government													
1990	119.0	119.6	120.9	119.8	120.9	122.1	104.9	103.6	116.2	118.9	122.4	121.4	117.4
1991	118.8	119.1	120.4	119.9	120.7	121.5	104.5	103.0	114.2	117.9	121.5	119.7	116.7
1992	117.4	119.8	121.9	121.2	122.8	122.6	109.2	105.5	116.0	119.0	122.3	120.9	118.2
1993	118.8	120.8	122.8	120.9	122.6	122.8	111.6	107.9	119.5	122.8	127.1	125.1	120.2
1994	122.4	123.2	125.3	126.4	127.8	129.6	117.9	115.3	127.1	128.3	131.9	129.8	125.4
1995	128.5	128.5	130.6	128.9	130.3	129.1	119.0	117.1	128.1	129.9	132.7	132.6	127.9
1996	129.2	131.4	132.6	133.3	135.4	134.1	124.0	121.4	130.6	138.7	140.4	140.2	132.6
1997	138.3	139.6	140.2	139.2	140.9	140.5	131.1	128.4	140.1	140.5	142.4	142.5	138.6
1998	140.3	142.1	143.7	141.3	143.2	142.2	132.1	129.1	143.1	143.9	146.1	146.3	141.1
1999	144.4	146.4	147.7	147.4	149.0	148.4	137.5	134.3	147.6	147.8	149.8	150.1	145.8
2000	150.3	151.7	152.6	151.4	152.4	151.3	139.1	138.4	149.8	151.3	152.9	153.3	149.5
2001	152.6	153.8	154.3	153.6	155.3	154.5	139.8	139.7	154.6	157.8	161.4	161.2	153.2
2002	159.9	160.7	161.8	160.0	161.6	161.5	143.7	146.9	156.4	158.6	161.9	161.5	157.9
2003	161.7	161.5	162.6	162.0	164.1	163.2	145.0	148.4	157.3	159.8	162.8	161.9	159.2
BRIDGEPORT-MILFORD													
Total nonfarm													
1990	193.8	191.8	193.1	192.0	194.0	196.3	190.4	189.4	191.2	190.3	191.6	191.3	192.1
1991	182.9	180.3	182.0	182.4	182.8	183.2	178.0	178.4	181.0	182.7	183.3	182.6	181.6
1992	176.3	175.4	176.2	175.3	176.6	177.4	174.5	174.1	175.2	176.1	177.0	177.3	175.9
1993	174.0	173.0	173.8	174.6	176.2	176.8	175.6	175.1	175.6	176.8	178.0	178.9	175.7
1994	173.5	171.9	173.7	176.7	178.4	179.6	177.6	177.8	179.9	181.0	182.7	183.9	178.0
1995	177.0	176.9	178.9	178.1	179.1	180.5	177.6	177.8	178.8	179.6	180.9	181.2	178.8
1996	174.3	175.6	177.3	179.5	180.9	181.5	178.2	178.8	180.2	182.4	184.1	185.2	179.8
1997	179.5	179.2	180.9	182.3	184.3	186.3	182.6	182.8	186.0	187.3	188.7	191.3	184.2
1998	184.4	185.0	186.7	184.7	186.7	187.4	184.8	184.0	186.6	187.1	188.0	189.7	186.2
1999	183.0	184.0	184.8	186.7	188.4	188.8	187.2	186.8	187.5	188.4	189.8	191.2	187.2
2000	183.6	183.4	185.1	186.6	188.0	189.5	186.9	185.7	188.3	189.0	190.2	190.7	187.2
2001	185.3	184.7	185.7	186.5	187.9	187.9	185.3	184.8	185.8	187.4	187.6	188.3	186.4
2002	183.2	183.1	185.0	186.7	188.0	188.4	184.4	184.2	185.7	186.9	187.7	188.3	186.0
2003	183.3	183.2	184.2	184.6	186.2	186.5	182.6	182.3	183.2	185.1	185.8	186.4	184.5
Total private													
1990	173.5	171.4	172.6	171.7	173.2	175.0	172.5	172.0	172.0	170.4	171.4	171.3	172.2
1991	163.4	160.6	162.3	162.6	163.1	163.6	161.4	161.9	162.3	163.3	163.9	163.4	162.6
1992	157.6	156.5	157.2	156.3	157.3	158.3	156.2	156.2	157.1	157.9	158.5	158.7	157.3
1993	155.7	154.6	155.0	155.6	157.1	157.6	157.1	157.0	157.2	157.6	158.5	160.1	156.9
1994	154.6	152.9	154.4	156.7	158.2	159.2	157.9	158.5	160.0	160.9	162.4	163.4	158.2
1995	157.7	157.8	159.1	158.6	159.2	160.4	158.2	158.6	159.6	159.8	160.9	161.1	159.2
1996	155.0	155.9	157.5	159.4	160.6	161.8	159.0	160.2	160.6	161.5	163.0	164.0	159.8
1997	159.1	158.5	160.2	161.5	163.4	165.3	162.9	163.2	165.2	166.5	167.7	170.3	163.6
1998	163.1	163.2	164.8	163.5	165.4	166.9	165.5	164.8	165.8	166.0	166.7	168.4	165.3
1999	162.2	162.8	163.4	165.4	166.9	167.1	166.1	166.1	166.9	167.1	168.4	169.8	166.0
2000	162.6	162.1	163.7	165.9	166.8	168.1	166.6	165.8	167.5	167.7	168.8	169.2	166.2
2001	163.8	163.1	164.1	164.9	166.2	166.4	164.8	164.3	163.5	165.1	165.2	166.0	164.8
2002	160.9	160.8	162.5	164.0	165.2	165.4	163.6	163.5	163.8	164.6	165.1	165.7	163.8
2003	160.7	160.5	161.4	162.1	163.3	163.4	161.8	161.4	161.2	162.8	163.2	163.9	162.1
Goods-producing													
1990	55.9	55.1	55.4	55.2	55.5	55.6	55.6	54.6	54.7	53.1	53.2	52.6	54.7
1991	49.2	48.0	48.3	48.7	48.5	48.7	47.2	47.5	48.7	48.7	48.3	47.6	48.2
1992	46.0	45.9	46.3	45.9	45.9	46.3	45.6	46.0	46.1	45.6	45.5	45.2	45.8
1993	44.7	44.0	44.1	44.2	44.5	44.8	44.6	44.9	45.1	44.8	44.7	44.7	44.5
1994	42.6	42.4	42.4	43.4	43.8	44.3	43.7	44.5	44.7	44.6	44.5	44.8	43.8
1995	43.2	43.0	43.1	43.4	43.2	43.7	42.5	42.9	43.2	42.8	42.6	42.2	42.9
1996	41.0	41.5	41.6	41.9	42.0	42.5	41.7	42.3	42.2	42.2	42.3	42.2	41.9
1997	41.4	41.2	41.6	42.2	42.6	43.5	42.3	43.0	43.0	43.0	42.8	42.7	42.4
1998	41.7	41.6	41.7	41.7	42.0	42.6	42.0	42.0	42.0	41.7	41.6	41.5	41.8
1999	40.3	40.3	40.2	41.0	41.0	41.3	40.8	41.1	41.4	40.7	40.8	40.9	40.8
2000	39.4	39.2	39.6	39.9	40.2	40.8	40.4	40.3	40.5	40.2	40.2	39.9	40.0
2001	39.6	39.4	39.6	39.8	40.0	40.2	39.5	39.6	39.6	38.7	38.4	38.4	39.4
2002	37.5	37.4	37.7	37.9	37.9	38.2	37.6	37.8	37.7	37.3	37.1	36.8	37.6
2003	36.3	35.9	35.9	36.3	36.5	36.7	36.3	36.4	36.3	35.9	35.9	35.9	36.2
Construction and mining													
1990	7.1	6.8	6.9	7.0	7.3	7.4	7.3	7.4	7.2	6.9	6.7	6.3	7.0
1991	5.3	5.1	5.3	5.8	6.1	6.1	6.0	6.1	5.9	5.7	5.4	5.1	5.6
1992	4.7	4.5	4.7	4.6	4.8	5.0	5.3	5.3	5.2	5.3	5.1	5.1	4.9
1993	4.8	4.6	4.6	4.6	5.0	5.2	5.4	5.6	5.4	5.2	5.1	5.0	5.0
1994	4.2	4.1	4.2	4.8	5.1	5.3	5.6	5.7	5.6	5.6	5.7	5.7	5.1
1995	5.0	4.8	4.9	5.3	5.5	5.8	5.9	5.9	5.9	5.6	5.5	5.2	5.4
1996	4.6	4.7	4.8	5.3	5.6	6.0	6.1	6.1	6.0	6.0	5.9	5.8	5.5
1997	5.3	5.2	5.5	6.0	6.4	6.9	6.9	7.0	6.8	6.7	6.6	6.6	6.3
1998	5.8	5.7	5.8	6.1	6.3	6.7	6.8	6.8	6.7	6.8	6.7	6.6	6.4
1999	5.9	6.0	5.9	6.3	6.5	6.8	6.9	7.0	6.9	6.8	6.8	6.8	6.5
2000	6.1	5.9	6.3	6.8	7.0	7.2	7.3	7.3	7.2	7.3	7.2	7.0	6.8
2001	6.3	6.2	6.5	7.1	7.4	7.6	7.8	7.9	7.7	7.4	7.3	7.2	7.2
2002	6.6	6.6	6.8	7.0	7.1	7.3	7.4	7.5	7.4	7.2	7.1	6.9	7.1
2003	6.4	6.2	6.3	6.7	7.0	7.1	7.2	7.3	7.2	7.0	6.9	6.9	6.9

Employment by Industry: Connecticut—*Continued*

(Numbers in thousands. Not seasonally adjusted.)

Industry	January	February	March	April	May	June	July	August	September	October	November	December	Annual Average
BRIDGEPORT-MILFORD *—Continued*													
Manufacturing													
1990	48.8	48.3	48.5	48.2	48.2	48.2	48.3	47.2	47.5	46.2	46.5	46.3	47.6
1991	43.9	42.9	43.0	42.9	42.4	42.6	41.2	41.4	42.8	43.0	42.9	42.5	42.6
1992	41.3	41.4	41.6	41.3	41.1	41.3	40.3	40.7	40.9	40.3	40.4	40.1	40.8
1993	39.9	39.4	39.5	39.6	39.5	39.6	39.2	39.3	39.7	39.6	39.6	39.7	39.5
1994	38.4	38.3	38.2	38.6	38.7	39.0	38.1	38.8	39.1	39.0	38.8	39.1	38.6
1995	38.2	38.2	38.2	38.1	37.7	37.9	36.6	37.0	37.3	37.2	37.1	37.0	37.5
1996	36.4	36.8	36.8	36.6	36.4	36.5	35.6	36.2	36.2	36.2	36.4	36.4	36.3
1997	36.1	36.0	36.1	36.2	36.2	36.6	35.4	36.0	36.2	36.3	36.2	36.1	36.1
1998	35.9	35.9	35.9	35.6	35.7	35.9	35.2	35.2	35.3	34.9	34.9	34.9	35.4
1999	34.4	34.3	34.3	34.7	34.5	34.5	33.9	34.1	34.5	33.9	34.0	34.1	34.2
2000	33.3	33.3	33.3	33.1	33.2	33.6	33.1	33.0	33.3	32.9	33.0	32.9	33.1
2001	33.3	33.2	33.1	32.7	32.6	32.6	31.7	31.7	31.9	31.3	31.1	31.2	32.2
2002	30.9	30.8	30.9	30.9	30.8	30.9	30.2	30.3	30.3	30.1	30.0	29.9	30.5
2003	29.9	29.7	29.6	29.6	29.5	29.6	29.1	29.1	29.1	28.9	29.0	29.0	29.3
Service-providing													
1990	137.9	136.7	137.7	136.8	138.5	140.7	134.8	134.8	136.5	137.2	138.4	138.7	137.3
1991	133.7	132.3	133.7	133.7	134.3	134.5	130.8	130.9	132.3	134.0	135.0	135.0	133.3
1992	130.3	129.5	129.9	129.4	130.7	131.1	128.9	128.1	129.1	130.5	131.5	132.1	130.0
1993	129.3	129.0	129.7	130.4	131.7	132.0	131.0	130.2	130.5	132.0	133.3	134.2	131.1
1994	130.9	129.5	131.3	133.3	134.6	135.3	133.9	133.3	135.2	136.4	138.2	139.1	134.2
1995	133.8	133.9	135.8	134.7	135.9	136.8	135.1	134.9	135.6	136.8	138.3	139.0	135.8
1996	133.3	134.1	135.7	137.6	138.9	139.0	136.5	136.5	138.0	140.2	141.8	143.0	137.8
1997	138.1	138.0	139.3	140.1	141.7	142.8	140.3	139.8	143.0	144.3	145.9	148.6	141.8
1998	142.7	143.4	145.0	143.0	144.7	144.8	142.8	142.0	144.6	145.4	146.4	148.2	144.4
1999	142.7	143.7	144.6	145.7	147.4	147.5	146.4	145.7	146.1	147.7	149.0	150.3	146.4
2000	144.2	144.2	145.5	146.7	147.8	148.7	146.5	145.4	147.8	148.8	150.0	150.8	147.2
2001	145.7	145.3	146.1	146.7	147.9	147.7	145.8	145.2	146.2	148.7	149.2	149.9	147.0
2002	145.7	145.7	147.3	148.8	150.1	150.2	146.8	146.4	148.0	149.6	150.6	151.5	148.4
2003	147.0	147.3	148.3	148.3	149.7	149.8	146.3	145.9	146.9	149.2	149.9	150.5	148.3
Trade, transportation, and utilities													
1990	40.6	39.4	39.4	38.5	38.7	39.5	38.7	39.1	39.5	38.8	39.5	39.8	39.2
1991	38.6	37.4	37.5	37.2	37.4	37.3	36.7	37.1	37.0	37.6	38.7	39.1	37.6
1992	36.7	35.5	35.3	35.5	35.8	35.9	35.2	35.2	35.7	36.1	36.9	37.8	35.9
1993	36.1	35.5	35.3	34.9	35.4	35.5	35.0	34.8	35.0	35.4	36.3	37.1	35.5
1994	36.1	35.1	35.2	35.5	35.8	36.0	35.2	35.3	35.8	36.5	37.4	37.7	35.9
1995	36.3	36.0	36.2	36.0	36.2	36.6	35.9	35.6	36.4	37.0	37.8	38.3	36.5
1996	36.8	36.2	36.1	36.8	37.0	37.0	36.2	36.1	36.3	36.6	37.7	38.3	36.7
1997	37.0	36.3	36.5	37.0	37.5	37.7	37.2	36.6	37.8	38.4	39.4	40.3	37.6
1998	37.8	37.1	37.3	37.9	38.4	38.1	37.6	37.3	38.0	38.2	38.8	39.7	38.0
1999	37.9	37.3	37.4	37.7	37.8	37.8	36.9	37.0	37.8	38.2	39.0	39.9	37.8
2000	38.0	37.5	37.7	38.5	38.6	38.5	37.5	37.0	37.9	38.3	39.3	39.9	38.2
2001	37.7	36.4	36.4	36.4	36.6	36.8	36.4	36.2	36.0	36.4	37.0	37.7	36.7
2002	37.1	36.2	36.6	37.0	37.3	37.6	36.9	36.6	37.0	36.9	37.7	38.2	37.1
2003	36.6	36.0	36.2	35.8	36.1	36.4	35.7	35.5	35.6	35.6	36.2	36.8	36.0
Wholesale trade													
1990	8.6	8.6	8.5	8.4	8.4	8.4	8.4	8.5	8.5	8.3	8.3	8.2	8.4
1991	8.1	8.2	8.2	8.4	8.4	8.3	8.4	8.5	8.4	8.4	8.5	8.6	8.3
1992	7.9	7.9	7.9	8.0	8.0	8.1	8.0	7.9	8.0	8.0	8.1	8.1	7.9
1993	8.1	8.1	8.0	7.8	7.8	7.9	7.9	7.8	7.7	7.7	7.7	7.7	7.8
1994	7.5	7.3	7.3	7.3	7.2	7.3	7.3	7.3	7.4	7.4	7.4	7.4	7.3
1995	7.3	7.3	7.3	7.3	7.3	7.4	7.3	7.2	7.4	7.4	7.4	7.4	7.3
1996	7.3	7.3	7.4	7.5	7.5	7.4	7.4	7.4	7.3	7.2	7.4	7.4	7.3
1997	7.3	7.3	7.5	7.7	7.7	7.7	7.9	7.9	7.9	7.9	8.0	8.0	7.7
1998	7.9	7.9	7.9	7.9	8.0	8.0	8.0	7.9	7.9	7.9	7.9	8.0	7.9
1999	7.8	7.8	7.8	7.9	7.9	7.9	7.7	7.7	7.8	7.9	7.9	7.9	7.8
2000	8.0	8.0	8.0	8.1	8.1	8.1	8.0	7.9	7.9	7.6	7.7	7.7	7.9
2001	7.5	7.4	7.4	7.3	7.3	7.2	7.2	7.2	7.1	7.2	7.2	7.2	7.3
2002	7.3	7.1	7.3	7.2	7.2	7.2	7.2	7.2	7.1	7.1	7.1	7.1	7.2
2003	7.2	7.1	7.1	7.0	7.0	7.1	7.1	7.1	7.0	7.0	7.0	7.0	7.1
Retail trade													
1990	26.4	25.3	25.2	24.5	24.5	25.1	24.7	24.9	25.0	24.6	25.2	25.6	25.0
1991	24.2	23.0	23.0	22.5	22.7	22.6	22.6	23.0	22.7	22.8	23.6	23.9	23.0
1992	22.9	22.1	22.0	22.1	22.2	22.3	22.0	22.2	22.1	22.3	23.0	23.8	22.4
1993	22.3	21.7	21.6	21.3	21.6	21.6	21.3	21.4	21.3	21.6	22.5	23.3	21.7
1994	22.3	21.6	21.7	22.1	22.4	22.5	21.9	22.1	22.1	22.5	23.5	23.9	22.3
1995	22.8	22.4	22.6	22.0	22.3	22.5	22.1	22.1	22.3	22.7	23.5	24.2	22.6
1996	23.1	22.5	22.3	22.5	22.7	22.8	22.4	22.5	22.4	22.7	23.7	24.4	22.8
1997	23.3	22.7	22.7	22.9	23.3	23.4	23.1	23.1	23.3	23.9	24.8	25.8	23.5
1998	24.2	23.5	23.7	23.7	23.9	24.1	23.9	23.8	24.1	24.2	24.9	25.7	24.1
1999	24.1	23.5	23.6	23.7	23.7	23.7	23.5	23.7	23.9	24.3	25.1	26.0	24.0
2000	24.0	23.6	23.8	24.1	24.2	24.1	23.6	23.4	23.8	24.4	25.4	26.0	24.2
2001	24.1	23.1	23.1	23.1	23.2	23.5	23.4	23.4	23.1	23.3	24.0	24.8	23.5
2002	24.3	23.6	23.8	24.1	24.4	24.6	24.3	24.2	24.2	24.0	24.8	25.4	24.3
2003	23.7	23.2	23.3	23.3	23.5	23.7	23.4	23.3	23.3	23.2	23.9	24.5	23.5

Employment by Industry: Connecticut—*Continued*

(Numbers in thousands. Not seasonally adjusted.)

Industry	January	February	March	April	May	June	July	August	September	October	November	December	Annual Average
BRIDGEPORT-MILFORD *—Continued*													
Transportation and utilities													
1990	5.6	5.5	5.7	5.6	5.8	6.0	5.6	5.7	6.0	5.9	6.0	6.0	5.7
1991	6.3	6.2	6.3	6.3	6.3	6.4	5.7	5.6	5.9	6.4	6.6	6.6	6.2
1992	5.9	5.5	5.4	5.4	5.6	5.5	5.2	5.1	5.6	5.8	5.8	5.9	5.5
1993	5.7	5.7	5.7	5.8	6.0	6.0	5.8	5.6	6.0	6.1	6.1	6.1	5.8
1994	6.3	6.2	6.2	6.1	6.2	6.2	6.0	5.9	6.3	6.6	6.5	6.4	6.2
1995	6.2	6.3	6.3	6.7	6.6	6.7	6.5	6.3	6.7	6.9	6.9	6.7	6.5
1996	6.4	6.4	6.4	6.8	6.8	6.8	6.4	6.2	6.6	6.7	6.6	6.5	6.5
1997	6.4	6.3	6.3	6.4	6.5	6.6	6.2	5.6	6.6	6.6	6.6	6.5	6.3
1998	5.7	5.7	5.7	6.3	6.5	6.0	5.7	5.6	6.0	6.1	6.0	6.0	5.9
1999	6.0	6.0	6.0	6.1	6.2	6.2	5.7	5.6	6.1	6.0	6.0	6.0	5.9
2000	6.0	5.9	5.9	6.3	6.3	6.3	5.9	5.7	6.2	6.3	6.2	6.2	6.1
2001	6.1	5.9	5.9	6.0	6.1	6.1	5.8	5.6	5.8	5.9	5.8	5.7	5.9
2002	5.5	5.5	5.5	5.7	5.7	5.8	5.4	5.2	5.7	5.8	5.8	5.7	5.6
2003	5.7	5.7	5.8	5.5	5.6	5.6	5.2	5.1	5.3	5.4	5.3	5.3	5.5
Information													
1990	4.1	4.2	4.2	4.2	4.2	4.3	4.3	4.2	4.2	4.2	4.2	4.1	4.2
1991	4.3	4.2	4.3	4.2	4.1	4.2	4.2	4.2	4.1	4.2	4.2	4.2	4.2
1992	4.1	4.1	4.2	4.3	4.3	4.4	4.3	4.2	4.2	4.1	4.2	4.2	4.2
1993	4.3	4.3	4.3	4.4	4.3	4.4	4.5	4.5	4.3	4.3	4.5	4.6	4.3
1994	4.6	4.5	4.5	4.8	5.0	5.1	5.0	4.9	4.9	4.9	5.0	5.1	4.8
1995	5.1	5.1	4.8	4.5	4.4	4.5	4.4	4.5	4.4	4.4	4.3	4.3	4.5
1996	4.1	4.2	4.3	4.6	4.6	4.7	4.6	4.6	4.5	4.5	4.5	4.6	4.4
1997	4.7	4.7	4.8	4.8	4.8	4.9	4.9	5.0	4.8	4.8	4.6	4.7	4.7
1998	5.0	4.9	5.0	4.8	4.7	4.8	4.8	4.8	4.7	4.7	4.7	4.7	4.8
1999	4.4	4.3	4.4	4.3	4.4	4.4	4.4	4.3	4.2	4.4	4.4	4.4	4.3
2000	4.4	4.4	4.4	4.4	4.4	4.5	4.6	4.6	4.5	4.5	4.5	4.5	4.4
2001	4.3	4.3	4.3	4.3	4.2	4.3	4.3	4.3	4.1	4.1	4.2	4.2	4.2
2002	4.6	4.6	4.5	4.5	4.6	4.6	4.5	4.5	4.4	4.3	4.3	4.4	4.5
2003	4.4	4.4	4.4	4.4	4.4	4.4	4.3	4.3	4.2	4.2	4.2	4.2	4.3
Financial activities													
1990	13.7	13.6	13.7	13.5	13.5	13.5	13.1	13.1	12.9	12.9	12.9	12.9	13.2
1991	12.7	12.6	12.6	12.5	12.5	12.7	12.3	12.2	12.1	12.2	12.2	12.0	12.3
1992	12.4	12.3	12.3	11.6	11.6	11.7	11.5	11.4	11.4	11.5	11.5	11.5	11.7
1993	11.6	11.5	11.6	11.6	11.7	11.8	12.0	12.0	11.9	11.8	11.8	11.9	11.7
1994	11.2	11.1	11.1	11.0	11.0	11.2	11.0	10.9	11.0	10.7	10.8	10.8	10.9
1995	10.6	10.5	10.6	9.9	9.9	10.0	10.0	10.1	10.0	9.9	10.0	10.0	10.1
1996	9.8	9.8	10.0	9.9	10.0	10.1	10.2	10.3	10.2	10.0	10.0	10.1	10.0
1997	9.9	9.9	9.8	10.3	10.4	10.4	10.6	10.6	10.6	10.5	10.5	10.6	10.3
1998	10.3	10.2	10.5	10.3	10.4	10.7	11.1	11.1	10.9	10.9	11.0	11.2	10.7
1999	11.5	11.5	11.5	12.0	12.2	12.4	12.7	12.8	12.7	12.8	12.9	13.0	12.3
2000	12.9	12.8	12.9	12.8	12.9	13.1	13.1	13.0	13.0	12.8	12.8	12.9	12.9
2001	12.6	12.5	12.6	12.6	12.5	12.6	12.4	12.3	12.1	12.0	12.0	12.0	12.4
2002	11.8	11.7	11.7	11.8	11.9	12.2	12.4	12.6	12.7	12.9	13.2	13.4	12.4
2003	13.2	13.3	13.4	13.2	13.3	13.3	13.3	13.4	13.5	13.7	13.8	13.9	13.4
Professional and business services													
1990	18.9	18.9	19.1	19.1	19.4	20.0	19.2	19.1	19.0	19.3	19.4	19.6	19.2
1991	18.7	18.6	19.3	19.6	19.6	19.8	20.0	20.0	19.9	19.8	19.9	19.8	19.5
1992	18.8	18.9	19.1	19.2	19.1	19.2	19.2	19.1	19.2	19.4	19.3	19.1	19.1
1993	18.5	18.6	18.6	18.8	18.7	18.7	18.5	18.4	18.5	18.7	18.6	18.5	18.5
1994	18.2	18.0	18.4	18.7	18.8	18.7	19.3	19.3	19.7	20.3	20.5	20.6	19.2
1995	19.5	19.6	20.1	19.9	20.1	20.2	19.9	20.0	20.2	20.4	20.5	20.6	20.0
1996	19.5	19.8	20.4	21.8	22.0	22.5	21.1	21.8	22.2	23.1	23.2	23.2	21.7
1997	21.2	21.3	21.6	22.5	22.9	23.3	22.7	23.1	23.9	23.9	24.3	24.7	22.9
1998	22.6	23.2	23.6	22.6	22.9	23.3	22.9	22.9	23.4	23.8	24.0	24.1	23.2
1999	22.8	23.1	23.4	22.9	22.9	22.8	22.7	22.7	22.6	22.9	22.9	22.8	22.8
2000	21.7	21.6	22.0	22.4	22.2	22.5	22.4	22.5	22.8	23.0	23.0	22.7	22.4
2001	22.2	21.9	22.1	22.0	22.3	22.6	21.8	21.9	21.9	22.3	22.0	21.8	22.1
2002	20.4	20.5	20.8	21.1	21.2	21.2	20.6	20.8	20.9	21.0	20.8	20.8	20.8
2003	19.7	19.8	19.9	20.2	20.1	20.2	19.7	19.8	19.8	19.9	19.8	19.8	19.9
Educational and health services													
1990	21.8	21.8	22.2	22.5	22.7	22.5	22.3	22.4	22.8	23.5	23.7	23.9	22.6
1991	22.9	23.0	23.4	23.2	23.3	22.8	22.8	22.7	22.8	23.4	23.4	23.5	23.1
1992	23.1	23.2	23.4	23.2	23.5	23.2	22.9	22.8	23.3	24.1	24.0	23.9	23.3
1993	23.6	23.7	24.1	23.8	24.0	23.5	23.4	23.5	23.8	24.4	24.3	24.8	23.9
1994	24.2	24.3	24.8	25.0	25.2	24.8	24.5	24.4	25.0	25.6	25.8	26.1	24.9
1995	25.4	25.7	26.1	26.0	26.0	25.7	26.2	26.1	26.7	26.6	27.0	26.9	26.2
1996	26.0	26.3	26.6	26.0	26.1	25.9	26.1	26.1	26.5	26.6	26.9	27.2	26.3
1997	26.9	27.2	27.4	26.1	26.1	26.1	26.1	25.9	26.3	27.2	27.5	28.4	26.7
1998	27.7	28.1	28.2	27.3	27.3	27.3	26.7	26.4	27.1	27.8	27.8	28.1	27.4
1999	27.4	28.1	28.2	28.8	28.9	28.3	28.5	28.2	28.8	29.2	29.5	29.7	28.6
2000	28.4	28.8	29.0	29.2	29.1	28.7	28.6	28.5	29.3	29.9	30.2	30.2	29.1
2001	29.3	30.4	30.6	30.7	30.6	29.5	29.7	29.5	30.1	31.6	31.6	31.8	30.5
2002	30.3	31.3	31.9	31.8	31.7	30.8	30.7	30.3	31.0	32.4	32.5	32.5	31.4
2003	31.4	31.9	32.2	32.3	32.2	31.3	31.3	31.0	31.6	33.1	33.3	33.2	32.1

Employment by Industry: Connecticut—*Continued*

(Numbers in thousands. Not seasonally adjusted.)

Industry	January	February	March	April	May	June	July	August	September	October	November	December	Annual Average
BRIDGEPORT-MILFORD —*Continued*													
Leisure and hospitality													
1990	11.6	11.5	11.7	11.9	12.4	12.8	12.4	12.5	12.3	12.1	12.1	12.0	12.1
1991	10.9	10.8	11.0	11.3	11.8	12.1	12.2	12.2	12.0	11.7	11.5	11.5	11.5
1992	10.9	11.0	10.9	11.0	11.4	11.7	11.4	11.4	11.3	11.1	11.0	10.8	11.1
1993	10.6	10.7	10.6	11.4	12.0	12.3	12.3	12.2	12.1	11.8	11.8	12.0	11.6
1994	11.3	11.2	11.5	11.9	12.3	12.7	12.7	12.7	12.7	12.0	12.0	11.9	12.0
1995	11.7	11.9	12.1	12.6	13.1	13.3	12.9	13.0	12.5	12.4	12.5	12.5	12.5
1996	11.6	11.9	12.2	12.2	12.6	12.8	12.7	12.6	12.4	12.3	12.1	12.1	12.2
1997	11.7	11.6	12.1	12.3	12.7	12.9	12.7	12.6	12.4	12.3	12.1	12.3	12.3
1998	11.6	11.7	12.0	12.4	13.1	13.3	13.6	13.5	13.0	12.4	12.3	12.5	12.6
1999	11.6	11.8	11.9	12.2	13.1	13.4	13.3	13.2	12.7	12.3	12.3	12.4	12.5
2000	11.4	11.4	11.7	12.2	12.9	13.3	13.2	13.1	12.8	12.3	12.2	12.4	12.4
2001	11.6	11.7	12.0	12.5	13.4	13.6	13.8	13.6	12.9	13.2	13.2	13.2	12.9
2002	12.4	12.3	12.5	13.0	13.7	13.9	14.1	14.1	13.4	13.1	12.8	12.9	13.2
2003	12.4	12.5	12.7	13.2	14.0	14.3	14.5	14.4	13.7	13.9	13.5	13.6	13.6
Other services													
1990	6.9	6.9	6.9	6.8	6.8	6.8	6.9	7.0	6.6	6.5	6.4	6.4	6.7
1991	6.1	6.0	5.9	5.9	5.9	6.0	6.0	6.0	5.7	5.7	5.7	5.7	5.8
1992	5.6	5.6	5.7	5.6	5.7	5.9	6.1	6.1	5.9	6.0	6.1	6.2	5.8
1993	6.3	6.3	6.4	6.5	6.5	6.6	6.8	6.7	6.5	6.4	6.5	6.5	6.5
1994	6.4	6.3	6.5	6.4	6.3	6.4	6.5	6.5	6.2	6.3	6.4	6.4	6.3
1995	5.9	6.0	6.1	6.3	6.3	6.4	6.4	6.4	6.2	6.3	6.2	6.3	6.2
1996	6.2	6.2	6.3	6.2	6.3	6.3	6.4	6.4	6.3	6.2	6.3	6.3	6.2
1997	6.3	6.3	6.4	6.3	6.4	6.5	6.4	6.4	6.4	6.4	6.5	6.6	6.4
1998	6.4	6.4	6.5	6.5	6.6	6.8	6.8	6.8	6.7	6.5	6.5	6.6	6.5
1999	6.3	6.4	6.4	6.5	6.6	6.7	6.8	6.8	6.7	6.6	6.6	6.7	6.5
2000	6.4	6.4	6.4	6.5	6.5	6.7	6.8	6.8	6.7	6.7	6.6	6.7	6.6
2001	6.5	6.5	6.5	6.6	6.6	6.8	6.9	6.9	6.8	6.8	6.8	6.9	6.7
2002	6.8	6.8	6.8	6.9	6.9	6.9	6.8	6.8	6.7	6.7	6.7	6.7	6.8
2003	6.7	6.7	6.7	6.7	6.7	6.8	6.7	6.6	6.5	6.5	6.5	6.5	6.6
Government													
1990	20.3	20.4	20.5	20.3	20.8	21.3	17.9	17.4	19.2	19.9	20.2	20.0	19.8
1991	19.5	19.7	19.7	19.8	19.7	19.6	16.6	16.5	18.7	19.4	19.4	19.2	18.9
1992	18.7	18.9	19.0	19.0	19.3	19.1	18.3	17.9	18.1	18.2	18.5	18.6	18.6
1993	18.3	18.4	18.8	19.0	19.1	19.2	18.5	18.1	18.4	19.2	19.5	18.8	18.7
1994	18.9	19.0	19.3	20.0	20.2	20.4	19.7	19.3	19.9	20.1	20.3	20.5	19.8
1995	19.3	19.1	19.8	19.5	19.9	20.1	19.4	19.2	19.2	19.8	20.0	20.1	19.6
1996	19.3	19.7	19.8	20.1	20.3	19.7	19.2	18.6	19.6	20.9	21.1	21.2	19.9
1997	20.4	20.7	20.7	20.8	20.9	21.0	19.7	19.6	20.8	20.8	21.0	21.0	20.6
1998	21.3	21.8	21.9	21.2	21.3	20.5	19.3	19.2	20.8	21.1	21.3	21.3	20.9
1999	20.8	21.2	21.4	21.3	21.5	21.7	21.1	20.7	20.6	21.3	21.4	21.4	21.2
2000	21.0	21.3	21.4	20.7	21.2	21.4	20.3	19.9	20.8	21.3	21.4	21.5	21.0
2001	21.5	21.6	21.6	21.6	21.7	21.5	20.5	20.5	22.3	22.3	22.4	22.3	21.7
2002	22.3	22.3	22.5	22.7	22.8	23.0	20.8	20.7	21.9	22.3	22.6	22.6	22.2
2003	22.6	22.7	22.8	22.5	22.9	23.1	20.8	20.9	22.0	22.3	22.6	22.5	22.3
Federal government													
1995	2.0	1.9	2.0	1.9	1.9	1.9	1.9	1.9	1.9	1.9	1.9	2.0	1.9
1996	1.9	1.9	1.9	2.0	2.0	2.0	2.0	2.0	2.0	2.0	2.1	2.2	2.0
1997	2.2	2.2	2.2	2.2	2.2	2.2	2.2	2.2	2.2	2.2	2.2	2.2	2.2
1998	2.1	2.2	2.1	2.2	2.2	2.2	2.1	2.1	2.1	2.1	2.2	2.2	2.1
1999	2.1	2.1	2.1	2.1	2.1	2.1	2.2	2.2	2.1	2.2	2.1	2.2	2.1
2000	2.1	2.1	2.2	2.1	2.5	2.4	2.3	2.2	2.1	2.1	2.1	2.1	2.1
2001	2.0	2.0	2.0	2.0	2.0	2.0	2.0	2.0	2.0	2.0	2.0	2.0	2.0
2002	2.0	2.0	2.0	2.0	2.0	2.0	2.0	2.0	2.0	2.0	1.9	1.9	2.0
2003	1.9	1.9	1.9	1.9	1.9	1.9	1.9	1.9	1.9	1.9	1.8	1.8	1.9
State government													
2001	3.5	3.5	3.5	3.5	3.5	3.5	3.5	3.5	3.5	3.6	3.5	3.5	3.5
2002	3.5	3.5	3.5	3.5	3.5	3.5	3.4	3.3	3.3	3.5	3.5	3.5	3.5
2003	3.5	3.5	3.4	3.3	3.3	3.3	3.2	3.2	3.1	3.2	3.2	3.2	3.3
Local government													
2001	16.0	16.1	16.1	16.1	16.2	16.0	15.0	15.0	16.8	16.7	16.9	16.8	16.1
2002	16.8	16.8	17.0	17.2	17.3	17.5	15.4	15.4	16.6	16.8	17.2	17.2	16.8
2003	17.2	17.3	17.5	17.3	17.7	17.9	15.7	15.8	17.0	17.2	17.6	17.5	17.1
HARTFORD													
Total nonfarm													
1990	640.6	641.5	645.7	645.3	646.1	647.0	631.8	626.8	639.2	639.2	637.9	637.8	639.9
1991	613.9	611.9	613.9	612.5	611.5	611.9	595.4	594.2	604.0	606.5	609.5	608.8	607.8
1992	586.0	584.4	586.3	585.8	589.9	590.8	584.6	580.4	590.3	592.3	595.1	594.0	588.3
1993	579.6	582.6	581.7	582.9	588.4	588.4	579.5	576.9	586.7	589.4	593.8	595.7	585.4
1994	574.6	574.3	579.5	584.3	587.9	588.8	585.6	582.3	590.7	594.5	597.7	597.6	586.4
1995	577.6	579.1	582.9	583.0	585.2	586.3	579.1	577.6	586.5	588.5	593.1	595.0	584.4
1996	571.1	578.6	583.0	587.1	591.4	594.2	584.6	586.5	595.3	599.5	604.7	606.5	590.2
1997	586.8	587.7	595.8	596.7	599.8	599.9	590.5	589.9	600.1	606.3	608.3	611.5	597.7
1998	589.1	595.7	601.1	601.5	606.1	606.7	600.5	598.0	603.9	611.4	615.3	618.3	603.9
1999	600.7	606.4	611.2	611.2	613.4	614.0	609.3	607.7	611.8	618.5	622.6	627.4	612.8
2000	608.1	613.0	618.7	620.5	623.3	622.5	618.0	612.0	618.9	622.4	625.3	629.0	619.3
2001	611.7	611.3	613.9	615.6	616.6	617.3	609.6	606.3	611.1	613.9	617.1	618.2	613.6
2002	603.2	604.7	607.2	608.6	611.4	611.1	601.5	597.6	604.2	605.0	608.3	609.1	606.0
2003	594.8	592.1	592.8	597.4	600.4	599.5	590.5	587.2	594.1	597.3	600.6	598.7	595.5

Employment by Industry: Connecticut—*Continued*

(Numbers in thousands. Not seasonally adjusted.)

Industry	January	February	March	April	May	June	July	August	September	October	November	December	Annual Average
HARTFORD—*Continued*													
Total private													
1990	547.4	544.2	547.7	547.1	549.6	553.1	545.7	541.9	545.9	541.9	538.4	538.4	545.1
1991	520.0	513.2	514.8	513.4	514.1	518.1	507.5	505.9	510.6	509.0	510.0	510.5	512.2
1992	496.2	491.9	493.2	492.2	496.4	499.8	497.8	494.5	500.0	498.9	500.2	501.1	496.8
1993	491.2	489.8	488.4	490.2	495.6	498.7	493.0	490.7	497.5	496.8	499.7	502.6	494.5
1994	486.4	481.3	485.1	490.0	494.0	497.4	494.2	491.4	495.0	497.4	498.0	500.0	492.5
1995	486.0	483.3	486.3	486.6	490.8	494.4	490.4	489.7	493.2	493.3	495.8	498.1	490.6
1996	480.4	482.1	485.7	489.5	496.2	500.6	495.5	497.9	501.1	503.2	507.4	509.7	495.7
1997	492.4	493.6	497.8	500.9	505.8	508.6	503.1	503.0	507.1	511.1	512.4	516.7	504.3
1998	500.1	501.5	505.4	506.2	512.1	516.0	513.1	511.5	512.3	514.9	516.7	520.3	510.8
1999	507.9	508.7	512.2	512.3	514.9	519.8	517.5	516.6	516.7	518.5	521.2	526.3	516.0
2000	511.7	512.0	516.0	517.9	519.9	524.8	523.9	520.2	521.0	521.6	523.4	527.4	519.9
2001	513.1	509.5	511.7	513.1	515.1	519.8	517.9	515.2	512.2	511.6	512.7	514.1	513.8
2002	503.0	500.4	502.7	504.4	508.0	511.5	507.7	504.7	503.3	501.5	503.0	504.2	504.5
2003	493.9	489.2	490.2	495.3	499.7	502.2	499.3	497.0	496.1	495.9	497.3	498.5	496.2
Goods-producing													
1990	135.6	133.9	134.9	136.8	136.7	137.5	134.8	133.2	134.8	133.8	131.8	130.0	134.4
1991	126.9	124.7	124.7	126.8	126.1	127.1	122.5	122.7	124.3	124.3	123.4	122.1	124.6
1992	118.2	116.8	115.8	115.0	116.5	117.8	117.0	115.7	117.6	116.3	115.5	114.1	116.3
1993	113.0	112.7	111.3	111.4	112.3	113.2	111.6	110.3	113.1	112.4	112.1	111.5	112.0
1994	106.8	104.8	105.5	107.5	108.8	109.1	109.2	108.5	110.1	110.6	110.2	109.4	108.3
1995	105.3	103.4	103.2	103.5	104.5	105.8	103.2	103.5	104.7	104.9	105.0	104.0	104.2
1996	99.7	99.9	100.9	104.1	105.8	107.3	105.4	106.7	107.7	108.3	109.3	108.9	105.3
1997	104.0	104.0	104.6	107.7	109.5	110.5	108.6	109.0	110.1	110.6	110.1	110.4	108.2
1998	106.9	107.0	108.0	110.2	111.0	112.3	111.2	110.8	111.9	111.4	111.0	110.7	110.2
1999	107.5	107.0	107.7	109.4	109.9	110.9	109.1	109.1	109.4	109.5	109.6	109.8	109.0
2000	106.2	105.9	107.2	109.0	109.5	110.7	110.8	110.8	111.5	111.2	111.2	111.0	109.5
2001	107.5	106.5	106.8	107.5	107.8	108.4	107.3	107.1	106.4	105.5	104.7	104.4	106.7
2002	101.0	99.7	100.3	101.2	101.7	102.4	101.3	101.2	100.6	99.7	99.1	98.1	100.5
2003	95.0	93.3	93.5	94.8	95.6	96.2	95.6	95.5	95.0	93.9	93.0	92.8	94.5
Construction and mining													
1990	24.0	23.1	23.7	24.7	25.5	26.0	26.4	26.3	26.0	24.6	23.8	22.3	24.7
1991	18.5	17.2	17.7	18.8	20.0	20.7	20.9	21.1	20.8	20.4	19.6	18.4	19.5
1992	15.5	14.9	15.3	16.8	18.0	18.9	19.9	20.1	19.8	19.9	19.4	18.4	18.0
1993	16.5	16.1	16.1	17.0	18.8	19.5	20.1	20.5	20.4	20.2	20.1	19.5	18.7
1994	16.1	15.3	15.6	18.6	19.6	20.1	21.0	21.5	21.3	21.6	21.1	20.5	19.3
1995	17.6	16.6	17.0	18.0	18.9	20.0	19.7	20.2	19.8	19.9	19.8	18.8	18.8
1996	15.3	15.2	16.0	18.7	20.0	21.0	21.7	21.8	21.6	21.3	21.1	20.1	19.4
1997	17.7	17.5	17.5	19.2	20.6	21.1	21.0	21.1	20.9	20.9	20.4	20.1	19.8
1998	17.9	17.8	18.2	19.8	20.5	21.2	21.5	21.8	21.5	21.2	21.2	21.0	20.3
1999	18.8	18.5	18.9	20.6	21.4	22.2	22.7	22.9	22.7	22.8	22.9	22.5	21.4
2000	20.6	20.3	21.3	22.6	23.3	24.1	24.4	24.7	24.5	24.1	24.1	23.7	23.1
2001	21.4	21.0	21.5	22.8	23.8	24.3	24.4	24.5	24.0	23.7	23.1	22.6	23.1
2002	20.8	20.4	20.9	22.2	22.9	23.4	23.6	23.6	23.1	22.8	22.4	21.6	22.3
2003	19.7	18.9	19.1	20.5	21.6	22.1	22.3	22.3	21.8	21.6	21.2	20.7	21.0
Manufacturing													
1990	111.6	110.8	111.2	112.1	111.2	111.5	108.4	106.9	108.8	109.2	108.0	107.7	109.7
1991	108.4	107.5	107.0	108.0	106.1	106.4	101.6	101.6	103.5	103.9	103.8	103.7	105.1
1992	102.7	101.9	100.5	98.2	98.5	98.9	97.1	95.6	97.8	96.4	96.1	95.7	98.2
1993	96.5	96.6	95.2	94.4	93.5	93.7	91.5	89.8	92.7	92.2	92.0	92.0	93.3
1994	90.7	89.5	89.9	88.9	89.2	89.0	88.2	87.0	88.8	89.0	89.1	88.9	89.0
1995	87.7	86.8	86.2	85.5	85.6	85.8	83.5	83.3	84.9	85.0	85.2	85.2	85.3
1996	84.4	84.7	84.9	85.4	85.8	86.3	83.7	84.9	86.1	87.0	88.2	88.8	85.8
1997	86.3	86.5	87.1	88.5	88.9	89.4	87.6	87.9	89.2	89.7	89.7	90.3	88.4
1998	89.0	89.2	89.8	90.4	90.5	91.1	89.7	89.0	90.4	90.2	89.8	89.7	89.9
1999	88.7	88.5	88.8	88.8	88.5	88.7	86.4	86.2	86.7	86.7	86.7	87.3	87.6
2000	85.6	85.6	85.9	86.4	86.2	86.6	86.4	86.1	87.0	87.1	87.1	87.3	86.4
2001	86.1	85.5	85.3	84.7	84.0	84.1	82.9	82.6	82.4	81.8	81.6	81.8	83.6
2002	80.2	79.3	79.4	79.0	78.8	79.0	77.7	77.6	77.5	76.9	76.7	76.5	78.2
2003	75.3	74.4	74.4	74.3	74.0	74.1	73.3	73.2	73.2	72.3	71.8	72.1	73.5
Service-providing													
1990	505.0	507.6	510.8	508.5	509.4	509.5	497.0	493.6	504.4	505.4	506.1	507.8	505.4
1991	487.0	487.2	489.2	485.7	485.4	484.8	472.9	471.5	479.7	482.2	486.1	486.7	483.2
1992	467.8	467.6	470.5	470.8	473.4	473.0	467.6	464.7	472.7	476.0	479.6	479.9	471.9
1993	466.6	469.9	470.4	471.5	476.1	475.2	467.9	466.6	473.6	477.0	481.7	484.2	473.3
1994	467.8	469.5	474.0	476.8	479.1	479.7	476.4	473.8	480.6	483.9	487.5	488.2	478.1
1995	472.3	475.7	479.7	479.5	480.7	480.5	475.9	474.1	481.8	483.6	488.1	491.0	480.2
1996	471.4	478.7	482.1	483.0	485.6	486.9	479.2	479.8	487.6	491.2	495.4	497.6	484.8
1997	482.8	483.7	491.2	489.0	490.3	489.4	481.9	480.9	490.0	495.7	498.2	501.1	489.5
1998	482.2	488.7	493.1	491.3	495.1	494.4	489.3	487.2	492.0	500.0	504.3	507.6	493.7
1999	493.2	499.4	503.5	501.8	503.5	503.1	500.2	498.6	502.4	509.0	513.0	517.6	503.7
2000	501.9	507.1	511.5	511.5	513.8	511.8	507.2	501.2	507.4	511.2	514.1	518.0	509.7
2001	504.2	504.8	507.1	508.1	508.8	508.9	502.3	499.2	504.7	508.4	512.4	513.8	506.9
2002	502.2	505.0	506.9	507.4	509.7	508.7	500.2	496.4	503.6	505.3	509.2	511.0	505.5
2003	499.8	498.8	499.3	502.6	504.8	503.3	494.9	491.7	499.1	503.4	507.6	505.9	500.9

Employment by Industry: Connecticut—*Continued*

(Numbers in thousands. Not seasonally adjusted.)

Industry	January	February	March	April	May	June	July	August	September	October	November	December	Annual Average
HARTFORD—*Continued*													
Trade, transportation, and utilities													
1990	120.8	118.2	118.8	117.7	118.0	118.5	115.3	114.7	116.5	116.9	117.4	118.7	117.6
1991	113.0	109.0	109.3	107.9	108.7	108.9	106.7	106.4	108.4	108.4	110.3	112.6	109.1
1992	108.0	106.0	105.7	104.7	105.9	106.3	103.7	103.3	104.9	105.4	108.0	109.4	105.9
1993	106.4	104.8	104.2	102.9	103.9	104.8	103.3	103.4	105.4	106.0	108.0	110.1	105.2
1994	105.0	102.5	103.2	103.9	105.2	106.5	104.8	104.4	106.2	108.2	109.3	110.5	105.8
1995	109.3	107.6	107.1	105.2	106.1	106.7	104.9	105.1	106.6	107.5	109.7	111.0	107.2
1996	106.4	105.6	106.2	105.4	106.8	107.4	106.8	107.3	109.6	110.2	112.4	114.1	108.1
1997	108.8	107.5	108.4	108.5	109.6	110.4	108.4	108.6	110.8	112.6	113.7	115.6	110.2
1998	108.3	107.6	108.2	107.3	108.9	109.5	107.7	107.6	109.0	110.1	111.9	113.5	109.1
1999	109.1	108.0	108.5	107.6	108.3	109.2	107.7	108.3	109.5	111.6	113.8	115.6	109.7
2000	110.3	109.2	109.7	108.8	109.0	109.2	107.2	106.6	108.1	109.3	111.4	113.1	109.3
2001	107.7	105.6	106.2	107.0	107.4	107.4	106.0	104.9	106.3	107.0	109.0	109.9	107.0
2002	106.8	105.2	105.6	105.7	105.9	106.7	104.4	103.8	105.0	104.3	105.9	107.3	105.6
2003	103.7	102.1	102.3	102.5	103.1	103.8	101.8	101.1	102.5	102.4	104.1	105.1	102.9
Wholesale trade													
1990	26.9	26.7	26.6	26.1	26.0	25.9	25.9	25.7	25.4	25.2	24.9	24.8	25.8
1991	24.3	23.9	23.8	23.1	23.1	23.2	22.8	22.8	22.9	23.3	23.3	23.4	23.3
1992	23.1	22.9	22.8	23.0	23.0	23.3	22.8	22.6	22.7	22.5	22.2	22.3	22.7
1993	22.3	22.3	22.4	21.6	21.8	22.0	22.1	22.1	22.1	22.1	22.0	22.2	22.0
1994	21.3	21.1	21.4	21.8	22.1	22.3	22.2	22.2	22.4	22.4	22.3	22.3	21.9
1995	23.1	23.1	22.9	22.4	22.5	22.7	22.5	22.5	22.5	22.5	22.4	22.5	22.6
1996	22.4	22.5	22.9	22.9	23.0	23.1	23.0	23.1	23.4	23.8	24.0	23.9	23.1
1997	23.5	23.5	23.9	24.4	24.6	24.7	24.6	24.4	24.6	24.5	24.4	24.5	24.3
1998	23.6	23.6	24.0	24.5	24.4	24.7	24.7	24.6	24.6	24.5	24.3	24.3	24.3
1999	23.7	23.6	23.8	23.7	23.6	23.8	23.9	23.9	23.9	23.9	24.1	24.3	23.8
2000	24.2	24.2	24.3	24.0	23.9	23.8	23.8	23.7	23.7	23.7	23.8	24.0	23.9
2001	23.7	23.7	23.8	23.6	23.5	23.5	23.3	23.0	22.9	23.1	23.0	23.0	23.3
2002	22.7	22.6	22.6	22.5	22.5	22.5	22.4	22.4	22.3	22.2	22.2	22.4	22.4
2003	22.3	22.2	22.4	22.5	22.5	22.6	22.6	22.6	22.5	22.4	22.4	22.6	22.5
Retail trade													
1990	72.5	70.6	70.7	70.2	70.4	70.9	68.8	68.5	69.5	70.1	71.1	72.4	70.4
1991	67.4	64.7	64.6	63.5	64.1	64.2	63.5	63.5	64.1	63.5	65.6	67.6	64.6
1992	64.5	63.1	62.6	61.4	61.9	61.8	60.7	60.6	61.1	61.7	64.6	65.9	62.4
1993	63.2	61.8	61.0	60.8	61.0	61.4	60.9	61.1	62.0	62.3	64.3	66.1	62.1
1994	62.3	60.3	60.5	60.8	61.5	62.4	61.6	61.5	62.1	63.8	65.2	66.4	62.3
1995	64.7	63.1	62.7	62.1	62.6	63.1	62.2	62.7	63.1	64.1	66.4	67.5	63.6
1996	63.4	62.3	62.3	61.6	62.6	63.1	63.6	64.1	64.8	65.1	66.9	68.8	64.0
1997	65.1	63.7	64.1	63.5	64.2	64.9	64.0	64.8	65.5	66.6	67.8	69.5	65.3
1998	63.8	62.9	63.0	62.3	63.4	63.7	62.8	62.9	62.8	63.7	65.5	67.1	63.6
1999	64.0	63.0	63.1	62.7	63.0	63.6	63.1	64.2	63.9	65.2	67.3	69.0	64.3
2000	64.5	63.5	63.8	62.9	63.2	63.6	62.3	62.2	62.2	62.7	64.8	66.4	63.5
2001	62.6	61.0	61.6	62.5	63.0	63.2	62.8	62.7	62.6	62.8	64.9	65.8	63.0
2002	63.8	62.5	63.0	63.0	63.2	64.0	63.1	63.0	62.7	61.9	63.6	65.0	63.2
2003	61.8	60.5	60.5	60.5	61.0	61.5	60.6	60.5	60.3	60.3	62.0	62.9	61.0
Transportation and utilities													
1990	21.4	20.9	21.5	21.4	21.6	21.7	20.6	20.5	21.6	21.6	21.4	21.5	21.3
1991	21.3	20.4	20.9	21.3	21.5	21.5	20.4	20.1	21.4	21.6	21.4	21.6	21.1
1992	20.4	20.0	20.3	20.3	21.0	21.2	20.2	20.1	21.1	21.2	21.2	21.2	20.6
1993	20.9	20.7	20.8	20.5	21.1	21.4	20.3	20.2	21.3	21.6	21.7	21.8	21.0
1994	21.4	21.1	21.3	21.3	21.6	21.8	21.0	20.7	21.7	22.0	21.8	21.8	21.4
1995	21.5	21.4	21.5	20.7	21.0	20.9	20.2	19.9	21.0	20.9	20.9	21.0	20.9
1996	20.6	20.8	21.0	20.9	21.2	21.2	20.2	20.1	21.4	21.3	21.5	21.4	20.9
1997	20.2	20.3	20.4	20.6	20.8	20.8	19.8	19.4	20.7	21.5	21.5	21.6	20.6
1998	20.9	21.1	21.2	20.5	21.1	21.1	20.2	20.1	21.6	21.9	22.1	22.1	21.1
1999	21.4	21.4	21.6	21.2	21.7	21.8	20.7	20.2	21.7	22.5	22.4	22.3	21.5
2000	21.6	21.5	21.6	21.9	21.9	21.8	21.1	20.7	22.2	22.9	22.8	22.7	21.8
2001	21.4	20.9	20.8	20.9	20.9	20.7	19.9	19.2	20.8	21.1	21.1	21.1	20.7
2002	20.3	20.1	20.0	20.2	20.2	20.2	18.9	18.4	20.0	20.2	20.1	19.9	19.9
2003	19.6	19.4	19.4	19.5	19.6	19.7	18.6	18.0	19.7	19.7	19.7	19.6	19.4
Information													
1990	12.1	12.1	12.2	12.1	12.0	12.1	12.3	12.2	12.1	12.2	12.0	11.9	12.1
1991	12.0	11.9	11.9	11.7	11.7	11.6	11.5	11.4	11.5	11.4	11.4	11.5	11.6
1992	11.2	11.1	11.1	11.1	11.1	11.1	11.8	11.8	11.8	11.6	11.6	11.5	11.4
1993	11.3	11.5	11.3	11.3	11.3	11.4	11.2	11.2	11.4	11.4	11.5	11.5	11.3
1994	11.6	11.5	11.4	11.8	12.0	12.1	12.1	12.0	12.0	12.0	12.0	12.1	11.8
1995	11.8	11.9	11.9	12.6	12.6	12.8	12.8	12.9	12.9	13.0	13.0	13.0	12.6
1996	12.9	13.1	13.3	13.1	13.3	13.6	13.3	13.5	13.6	13.9	14.1	14.1	13.4
1997	14.0	14.1	14.2	14.1	14.0	14.0	13.8	14.0	14.1	13.3	12.5	12.6	13.7
1998	12.3	12.4	12.5	12.1	12.2	12.3	11.8	11.8	10.7	12.3	12.3	12.4	12.0
1999	11.8	11.9	11.9	12.7	12.8	12.7	12.8	13.0	13.0	13.2	13.3	13.3	12.7
2000	13.3	13.4	13.5	13.6	13.7	13.8	14.0	14.0	14.0	14.0	14.1	14.1	13.7
2001	13.6	13.7	13.5	13.2	13.1	13.1	12.8	12.8	12.6	12.4	12.5	12.3	13.0
2002	12.2	12.1	12.0	12.1	12.1	12.2	12.1	12.1	11.9	11.9	11.8	11.9	12.0
2003	12.0	11.9	12.0	11.9	11.8	12.0	11.9	11.9	11.7	11.7	11.7	11.5	11.8

Employment by Industry: Connecticut—*Continued*

(Numbers in thousands. Not seasonally adjusted.)

Industry	January	February	March	April	May	June	July	August	September	October	November	December	Annual Average
HARTFORD—*Continued*													
Financial activities													
1990	88.1	88.4	88.6	88.2	89.0	90.0	90.8	90.4	88.9	87.7	86.3	87.1	88.6
1991	87.6	86.7	86.7	85.3	85.2	86.2	85.6	85.7	84.8	84.1	84.4	82.6	85.4
1992	79.7	79.0	81.5	82.5	82.7	82.9	83.7	82.6	82.0	81.1	80.9	81.1	81.6
1993	81.2	80.6	80.6	79.4	79.5	80.3	80.1	79.7	79.5	78.0	78.1	78.3	79.6
1994	77.2	76.5	76.4	76.0	76.0	76.2	75.6	75.2	74.8	73.8	73.8	74.1	75.4
1995	68.4	68.2	71.3	72.6	72.8	73.6	75.0	75.0	74.8	72.3	72.4	72.5	72.4
1996	70.0	68.6	68.7	67.5	67.8	67.8	68.3	68.1	67.0	67.2	67.7	66.9	67.9
1997	66.9	67.6	68.2	66.2	66.7	66.6	66.4	66.9	66.9	68.2	70.2	70.9	67.6
1998	69.4	69.7	70.1	69.4	69.5	70.3	72.5	72.5	72.1	72.3	72.4	72.7	71.0
1999	72.8	72.9	72.9	72.1	72.0	72.6	72.9	72.7	72.1	72.0	72.0	72.4	72.4
2000	72.3	72.3	72.8	72.4	72.5	73.3	73.5	73.5	72.7	72.5	72.5	72.9	72.7
2001	73.1	72.8	72.9	72.8	73.0	73.9	74.2	74.0	73.1	72.5	72.4	72.7	73.1
2002	73.0	72.6	72.6	72.0	72.2	72.9	73.0	72.7	72.1	71.6	71.8	71.7	72.4
2003	72.0	71.5	71.3	72.3	72.5	73.3	73.4	73.1	72.5	72.0	72.2	72.1	72.4
Professional and business services													
1990	56.0	56.3	57.2	55.7	56.8	56.5	56.1	56.5	56.7	55.2	55.7	55.1	56.1
1991	53.4	53.2	53.6	52.7	52.5	53.0	52.0	51.6	51.5	51.3	51.1	51.1	52.2
1992	50.5	50.5	50.8	51.1	51.1	51.5	51.5	51.3	51.5	51.2	50.7	50.4	51.0
1993	49.6	49.3	50.0	50.0	50.6	51.0	51.2	51.2	51.5	51.2	51.5	51.4	50.7
1994	50.0	50.3	50.8	51.8	51.7	52.5	52.1	52.1	52.1	52.1	51.9	51.9	51.6
1995	51.2	51.8	51.9	53.0	53.3	53.3	53.0	53.3	53.5	53.6	54.1	54.2	53.0
1996	53.2	54.5	55.2	56.1	56.8	57.4	57.0	57.7	57.9	58.6	58.8	58.9	56.8
1997	56.2	56.8	57.5	58.7	58.7	59.1	59.9	59.3	59.3	60.2	60.1	60.6	58.8
1998	60.7	60.9	61.8	62.9	63.1	63.8	63.9	63.6	63.7	63.6	63.7	64.2	62.9
1999	63.0	63.1	64.1	64.3	63.9	65.6	66.4	66.3	66.0	65.8	65.8	66.7	65.0
2000	64.8	64.8	65.2	66.0	65.8	67.3	67.0	66.8	66.4	66.3	66.2	66.4	66.0
2001	64.3	63.7	64.2	64.9	64.6	65.2	64.5	64.5	63.8	64.3	64.0	63.7	64.3
2002	61.2	61.2	62.3	62.5	62.7	63.3	62.8	62.5	62.4	62.0	62.2	62.1	62.3
2003	60.1	59.8	60.0	61.1	61.2	61.4	60.9	60.7	60.5	60.8	61.0	60.9	60.7
Educational and health services													
1990	69.8	69.9	70.3	71.4	71.3	71.7	70.1	70.0	71.8	72.4	72.7	73.1	71.2
1991	72.5	73.1	73.8	73.1	73.1	73.1	71.5	71.1	72.6	73.0	72.9	73.6	72.7
1992	73.9	73.3	73.3	72.8	73.1	73.1	73.1	73.0	75.6	75.9	76.1	76.7	74.1
1993	73.8	74.5	74.6	77.5	78.6	77.9	76.1	75.8	77.3	78.8	79.4	80.1	77.0
1994	77.8	77.9	78.8	79.1	79.6	79.2	78.8	78.2	79.3	80.3	80.7	81.5	79.2
1995	80.4	80.8	81.1	79.3	79.8	79.7	79.0	78.2	79.4	80.2	80.5	81.3	79.9
1996	78.3	79.9	80.1	80.9	82.2	82.0	81.2	81.4	82.9	82.9	83.4	84.3	81.6
1997	82.5	83.7	84.4	84.0	84.1	83.4	82.6	82.4	83.4	83.9	84.0	84.0	83.5
1998	82.2	83.1	83.5	82.1	83.0	83.0	82.0	81.8	82.2	83.0	83.4	84.1	82.7
1999	82.4	83.4	84.2	82.6	82.9	82.8	82.5	81.9	82.6	82.6	83.4	84.4	82.9
2000	83.0	84.1	84.9	83.9	83.6	83.5	84.2	82.5	83.4	83.9	84.3	85.3	83.8
2001	85.1	85.6	85.8	84.9	84.0	85.5	85.7	85.2	85.6	86.3	87.2	88.0	85.7
2002	87.1	87.7	87.9	87.2	87.8	87.2	86.6	86.0	86.9	87.9	88.7	89.1	87.5
2003	88.0	87.9	87.8	88.3	88.6	87.8	87.2	86.5	87.5	88.4	89.2	89.8	88.1
Leisure and hospitality													
1990	39.3	39.7	39.9	39.9	40.8	41.4	40.9	40.0	40.9	40.0	39.1	39.3	40.1
1991	34.7	35.0	35.4	36.8	37.5	38.3	37.4	37.2	37.8	36.9	36.9	37.1	36.7
1992	35.4	36.1	35.9	35.7	36.5	36.9	36.7	36.8	36.7	36.9	36.7	37.0	36.4
1993	34.9	35.0	34.9	36.1	37.7	38.1	37.7	37.6	37.6	37.3	37.1	37.7	36.8
1994	36.1	36.1	37.3	38.0	38.8	39.6	39.5	39.3	38.8	38.5	38.1	38.4	38.2
1995	37.6	37.5	37.8	38.4	39.5	40.0	40.2	39.6	39.1	39.5	38.7	39.4	38.9
1996	37.6	38.0	38.6	39.8	40.8	42.0	40.8	40.6	39.9	39.9	39.5	40.1	39.8
1997	38.3	38.2	38.6	39.4	40.7	41.9	40.9	40.4	40.1	39.8	39.2	39.8	39.7
1998	37.8	38.2	38.5	39.1	41.1	41.7	41.2	40.8	40.2	39.4	39.2	39.7	39.7
1999	38.4	39.3	39.5	40.4	42.0	42.9	43.0	42.3	41.4	40.8	40.3	40.9	40.9
2000	39.1	39.5	39.8	41.1	42.7	43.7	43.8	42.9	42.0	41.3	40.6	41.4	41.4
2001	38.7	38.5	38.9	39.1	41.4	42.2	42.7	42.3	40.5	39.5	38.7	38.8	40.1
2002	37.7	37.9	37.7	39.5	41.2	42.4	43.1	42.5	40.8	40.4	39.7	40.1	40.3
2003	39.8	39.4	39.8	40.9	43.2	43.7	43.9	43.8	42.4	42.5	41.8	41.9	41.9
Other services													
1990	25.7	25.7	25.8	25.3	25.0	25.4	25.4	24.9	24.2	23.7	23.4	23.2	24.8
1991	19.9	19.6	19.4	19.1	19.3	19.9	20.3	19.8	19.7	19.6	19.6	19.9	19.6
1992	19.3	19.1	19.1	19.3	19.5	20.2	20.3	20.0	19.9	20.5	20.7	20.9	19.9
1993	21.0	21.4	21.5	21.6	21.7	22.0	21.8	21.5	21.7	21.7	22.0	22.0	21.6
1994	21.9	21.7	21.7	21.9	21.9	22.2	22.1	21.7	21.7	21.9	22.0	22.1	21.9
1995	22.0	22.1	22.0	22.0	22.2	22.5	22.3	22.1	22.2	22.3	22.4	22.7	22.2
1996	22.3	22.5	22.7	22.6	22.7	23.1	22.7	22.6	22.5	22.2	22.2	22.4	22.5
1997	21.7	21.7	21.9	22.3	22.5	22.7	22.5	22.4	22.4	22.5	22.6	22.8	22.3
1998	22.5	22.6	22.8	23.1	23.3	23.1	22.8	22.6	22.5	22.8	22.8	23.0	22.8
1999	22.9	23.1	23.4	23.2	23.1	23.1	23.1	23.0	22.7	23.0	23.0	23.2	23.0
2000	22.7	22.8	22.9	23.1	23.1	23.3	23.4	23.1	22.9	23.1	23.1	23.2	23.0
2001	23.1	23.1	23.4	23.7	23.8	24.1	24.7	24.4	23.9	24.1	24.2	24.3	23.9
2002	24.0	24.0	24.3	24.2	24.4	24.4	24.4	23.9	23.6	23.7	23.8	23.9	24.1
2003	23.3	23.3	23.5	23.5	23.7	24.0	24.6	24.4	24.0	24.2	24.3	24.4	23.9

Employment by Industry: Connecticut—*Continued*

(Numbers in thousands. Not seasonally adjusted.)

Industry	January	February	March	April	May	June	July	August	September	October	November	December	Annual Average
HARTFORD—*Continued*													
Government													
1990	93.2	97.3	98.0	98.2	96.5	93.9	86.1	84.9	93.3	97.3	99.5	99.4	94.8
1991	93.9	98.7	99.1	99.1	97.4	93.8	87.9	88.3	93.4	97.5	99.5	98.3	95.5
1992	89.8	92.5	93.1	93.6	93.5	91.0	86.8	85.9	90.3	93.4	94.9	92.9	91.4
1993	88.4	92.8	93.3	92.7	92.8	89.7	86.5	86.2	89.2	92.6	94.1	93.1	90.9
1994	88.2	93.0	94.4	94.3	93.9	91.4	91.4	90.9	95.7	97.1	99.7	97.6	93.9
1995	91.6	95.8	96.6	96.4	94.4	91.9	88.7	87.9	93.3	95.2	97.3	96.9	93.8
1996	90.7	96.5	97.3	97.6	95.2	93.6	89.1	88.6	94.2	96.3	97.3	96.8	94.4
1997	94.4	94.1	98.0	95.8	94.0	91.3	87.4	86.9	93.0	95.2	95.9	94.8	93.4
1998	89.0	94.2	95.7	95.3	94.0	90.7	87.4	86.5	91.6	96.5	98.6	98.0	93.1
1999	92.8	97.7	99.0	98.9	98.5	94.2	91.8	91.1	95.1	100.0	101.4	101.1	96.8
2000	96.4	101.0	102.7	102.6	103.4	97.7	94.1	91.8	97.9	100.8	101.9	101.6	99.3
2001	98.6	101.8	102.2	102.5	101.5	97.5	91.7	91.1	98.9	102.3	104.4	104.1	99.7
2002	100.2	104.3	104.5	104.2	103.4	99.6	93.8	92.9	100.9	103.5	105.3	104.9	101.5
2003	100.9	102.9	102.6	102.1	100.7	97.3	91.2	90.2	98.0	101.4	103.3	100.2	99.2
Federal government													
1995	8.8	8.7	8.8	8.7	8.7	8.8	8.7	8.7	8.7	8.6	8.6	8.9	8.7
1996	8.5	8.5	8.5	8.6	8.5	8.5	8.4	8.4	8.3	8.3	8.3	8.6	8.4
1997	8.1	8.0	8.0	8.1	8.1	8.2	8.1	8.1	8.0	8.0	8.0	8.3	8.0
1998	8.0	8.0	8.0	8.0	8.0	8.0	8.0	8.0	8.0	7.9	8.0	8.4	8.0
1999	8.0	7.9	7.9	7.9	7.8	7.9	7.9	8.0	7.8	7.9	7.8	8.1	7.9
2000	7.9	7.9	8.1	8.4	9.9	8.7	8.7	7.8	7.5	7.4	7.3	7.6	8.1
2001	7.4	7.3	7.3	7.3	7.3	7.3	7.3	7.3	7.2	7.2	7.2	7.3	7.3
2002	7.2	7.1	7.1	7.1	7.1	7.2	7.2	7.3	7.4	7.4	7.3	7.4	7.2
2003	7.3	7.3	7.2	7.2	7.1	7.2	7.2	7.2	7.3	7.3	7.3	7.4	7.3
State government													
1995	40.5	44.6	45.1	45.3	43.0	40.3	40.0	39.6	43.1	44.4	45.5	44.6	43.0
1996	40.0	45.0	45.4	45.6	42.6	40.9	39.1	38.9	43.1	44.9	45.1	44.1	42.8
1997	43.0	42.3	45.8	44.4	42.0	38.8	37.7	37.6	42.0	43.2	43.3	41.8	41.8
1998	37.5	42.2	43.0	43.3	41.1	38.2	37.6	37.4	39.9	43.4	44.8	43.7	41.0
1999	39.7	44.2	44.9	44.9	43.9	40.0	40.8	40.6	43.3	45.8	46.5	45.6	43.3
2000	41.4	45.5	46.7	46.9	45.7	42.0	41.7	41.2	44.3	46.6	46.9	46.2	44.5
2001	43.7	46.6	46.5	47.1	45.6	42.2	41.7	41.3	44.3	46.8	47.6	47.2	45.1
2002	43.8	47.7	47.6	48.0	46.4	43.1	42.8	42.0	45.0	47.5	48.2	47.7	45.8
2003	44.2	45.9	45.7	45.3	43.5	39.9	39.7	38.9	41.6	44.0	44.7	41.7	42.9
Local government													
1995	42.3	42.6	42.7	42.4	42.7	42.8	40.0	39.6	41.5	42.2	43.2	43.4	42.1
1996	42.1	42.9	43.5	43.4	44.1	44.1	41.5	41.2	42.8	43.1	43.9	44.1	43.0
1997	43.4	43.7	44.2	43.3	43.9	44.3	41.6	41.2	43.0	43.9	44.6	44.7	43.4
1998	43.5	44.0	44.7	44.0	44.9	44.5	41.7	41.0	43.6	45.1	45.8	45.9	44.0
1999	45.0	45.6	46.3	46.1	46.8	46.3	43.1	42.4	43.9	46.3	47.1	47.4	45.5
2000	47.1	47.6	48.0	47.4	47.8	47.0	43.8	42.9	46.2	46.9	47.7	47.8	46.6
2001	47.5	47.9	48.4	48.1	48.6	48.0	42.7	42.5	47.4	48.3	49.6	49.6	47.4
2002	49.2	49.5	49.8	49.1	49.9	49.3	43.8	43.6	48.5	48.6	49.8	49.8	48.4
2003	49.4	49.7	49.7	49.6	50.1	50.2	44.3	44.1	49.1	50.1	51.3	51.1	49.1
NEW HAVEN-MERIDEN													
Total nonfarm													
1990	253.3	253.2	255.1	254.3	256.9	259.4	254.3	253.0	255.9	252.7	253.7	253.3	254.5
1991	241.5	241.7	242.3	243.6	243.6	243.3	238.2	236.5	240.8	242.8	243.4	243.1	241.7
1992	233.3	232.4	233.5	235.7	237.4	238.1	237.3	235.7	238.1	240.5	240.4	241.2	236.9
1993	233.4	233.8	234.6	238.1	238.9	238.6	236.7	236.5	239.6	242.6	243.5	244.9	238.4
1994	231.9	232.6	235.0	239.0	238.1	239.6	238.9	239.4	240.9	243.1	244.2	243.8	238.8
1995	235.2	238.2	238.6	241.7	242.0	242.9	240.2	240.2	242.2	242.9	243.4	244.7	241.0
1996	237.8	238.2	241.0	241.9	244.7	246.6	242.8	243.8	245.3	250.0	251.8	251.5	244.6
1997	243.1	245.3	245.3	250.0	249.4	250.3	248.7	247.1	250.4	253.2	254.5	255.3	249.3
1998	248.9	251.2	251.1	255.3	255.0	257.7	256.4	255.1	256.9	261.6	263.7	264.5	256.4
1999	253.2	255.7	257.0	258.4	256.8	258.7	258.6	259.0	260.6	261.2	263.0	264.0	258.8
2000	258.2	260.3	261.7	263.6	265.4	265.9	265.0	262.5	264.5	264.2	265.9	268.2	263.7
2001	256.2	256.5	256.4	259.5	261.2	263.5	257.2	257.2	260.5	261.2	263.0	264.2	259.7
2002	255.2	257.5	257.6	262.1	262.8	264.8	258.1	257.9	261.3	261.8	263.8	264.2	260.6
2003	254.5	255.6	255.6	257.0	257.5	257.0	252.4	249.9	254.1	257.5	259.5	259.2	255.8
Total private													
1990	220.9	220.9	222.6	222.0	223.9	227.1	223.6	222.9	224.0	220.2	220.3	220.3	222.3
1991	209.0	209.9	210.1	211.7	211.4	211.4	208.5	207.5	210.2	211.1	211.0	211.4	210.2
1992	201.9	201.1	201.9	204.0	205.5	206.8	205.7	204.9	206.5	206.9	206.6	208.2	205.0
1993	202.0	201.7	202.3	206.2	207.2	207.4	205.8	206.1	208.3	211.7	212.1	214.0	207.0
1994	201.9	202.0	204.0	207.8	207.3	208.9	208.5	209.4	210.3	212.3	212.9	213.4	208.2
1995	205.3	206.8	206.9	210.5	211.0	212.6	209.7	210.1	211.5	211.8	211.9	213.3	210.1
1996	207.6	206.9	209.5	210.4	213.4	215.8	212.5	213.5	215.0	218.8	220.3	220.2	213.6
1997	212.4	213.8	213.7	218.5	217.9	218.9	218.2	217.0	219.7	221.9	222.6	223.7	218.1
1998	217.9	219.6	219.2	223.6	223.5	226.4	225.9	225.1	225.5	229.0	230.6	231.7	224.8
1999	221.4	222.9	224.0	225.4	224.3	226.3	226.0	226.7	228.0	227.6	228.9	229.8	225.9
2000	223.8	225.1	226.1	227.6	228.8	229.7	229.3	227.9	229.9	229.2	230.7	232.7	228.4
2001	220.9	221.0	220.9	224.1	225.8	227.9	224.4	224.4	227.1	226.9	227.6	228.9	225.0
2002	220.7	222.5	222.6	226.9	227.6	229.2	226.7	226.6	228.1	227.4	228.4	228.8	226.3
2003	219.9	221.2	221.1	222.8	223.3	224.2	222.1	219.9	221.6	224.0	225.3	225.1	222.5

Employment by Industry: Connecticut—*Continued*

(Numbers in thousands. Not seasonally adjusted.)

Industry	January	February	March	April	May	June	July	August	September	October	November	December	Annual Average
HEW HAVEN-MERIDEN *—Continued*													
Goods-producing													
1990	48.2	47.9	48.3	49.4	49.9	50.0	49.6	49.4	49.3	48.1	47.8	47.2	48.7
1991	46.3	46.1	46.3	46.2	46.5	46.8	46.2	46.1	46.5	46.4	46.2	46.0	46.3
1992	44.7	44.1	44.3	44.5	45.0	45.8	45.8	45.8	45.9	45.6	45.4	45.4	45.1
1993	43.4	42.9	43.0	43.7	43.8	44.0	43.8	44.0	44.2	44.3	44.0	44.2	43.7
1994	41.6	40.9	41.4	42.5	42.6	43.1	42.9	43.2	43.1	43.0	43.0	42.9	42.5
1995	41.6	41.4	42.0	43.3	43.8	44.6	43.8	43.8	44.0	43.5	43.3	43.1	43.1
1996	42.1	41.6	42.0	41.9	42.9	43.6	43.4	44.3	44.3	44.8	45.0	45.0	43.4
1997	43.2	43.8	43.1	45.0	45.7	46.2	45.0	45.7	45.5	45.8	45.9	45.5	45.0
1998	44.8	44.7	45.4	46.2	46.4	47.2	46.8	46.7	47.6	47.6	47.3	47.2	46.4
1999	45.4	45.2	45.5	45.4	45.2	45.6	45.6	45.6	45.4	45.1	45.1	45.1	45.3
2000	44.5	44.6	45.0	44.9	45.3	46.0	46.6	46.7	46.9	46.4	46.1	46.1	45.7
2001	44.3	43.9	44.4	45.2	45.3	45.8	45.7	45.4	45.6	44.9	44.6	44.2	44.9
2002	42.7	42.5	42.7	43.0	43.3	43.6	43.1	43.1	42.8	42.1	42.0	41.5	42.7
2003	40.3	40.0	40.0	40.6	41.1	41.5	41.5	41.3	40.7	40.4	40.5	40.0	40.7
Construction and mining													
1990	10.1	10.0	10.1	10.4	10.7	10.8	11.0	11.0	10.9	9.9	9.6	8.9	10.2
1991	7.6	7.3	7.3	7.9	8.3	8.5	8.7	8.8	8.6	8.2	8.0	7.8	8.0
1992	7.1	6.9	6.9	7.2	7.6	8.2	8.6	8.7	8.5	8.4	8.2	8.0	7.8
1993	7.4	7.1	7.0	7.1	7.5	7.7	7.9	8.0	7.9	7.8	7.9	7.9	7.6
1994	6.7	6.4	6.5	7.3	7.7	8.0	8.1	8.4	8.0	7.9	7.9	7.7	7.5
1995	6.8	6.6	6.8	8.0	8.3	8.7	9.1	9.1	8.9	8.6	8.5	8.1	8.1
1996	7.3	7.0	7.3	7.4	8.0	8.3	8.6	8.7	8.6	8.2	8.3	8.1	7.9
1997	7.4	7.5	7.5	8.7	9.2	9.6	9.8	9.9	9.7	9.7	9.6	9.5	9.0
1998	8.6	8.6	9.0	9.4	9.8	10.3	10.6	10.7	10.6	10.4	10.2	10.0	9.8
1999	8.8	8.7	9.0	9.5	9.8	10.1	10.6	10.6	10.4	10.4	10.4	10.3	9.8
2000	9.6	9.5	9.9	10.2	10.7	11.1	11.1	11.2	11.1	10.8	10.6	10.4	10.5
2001	9.2	9.1	9.5	10.6	10.9	11.2	11.3	11.3	11.2	10.8	10.8	10.5	10.5
2002	9.4	9.4	9.7	10.4	10.8	11.0	11.0	11.1	10.9	10.6	10.6	10.0	10.4
2003	9.1	8.9	9.1	9.6	10.2	10.5	10.6	10.7	10.4	10.1	10.1	9.6	9.9
Manufacturing													
1990	38.1	37.9	38.2	39.0	39.2	39.2	38.6	38.4	38.4	38.2	38.2	38.3	38.4
1991	38.7	38.8	39.0	38.3	38.2	38.3	37.5	37.3	37.9	38.2	38.2	38.2	38.2
1992	37.6	37.2	37.4	37.3	37.4	37.6	37.2	37.1	37.4	37.2	37.2	37.4	37.3
1993	36.0	35.8	36.0	36.6	36.3	36.3	35.9	36.0	36.3	36.5	36.1	36.3	36.1
1994	34.9	34.5	34.9	35.2	34.9	35.1	34.8	34.8	35.1	35.1	35.1	35.2	34.9
1995	34.8	34.8	35.2	35.3	35.5	35.9	34.7	34.7	35.1	34.9	34.8	35.0	35.0
1996	34.8	34.6	34.7	34.5	34.9	35.3	34.8	35.6	35.7	36.6	36.7	36.9	35.4
1997	35.8	36.3	35.6	36.3	36.5	36.6	35.2	35.8	35.8	36.1	36.3	36.0	36.0
1998	36.2	36.1	36.4	36.8	36.6	36.9	36.2	36.0	37.0	37.2	37.1	37.2	36.6
1999	36.6	36.5	36.5	35.9	35.4	35.5	35.0	35.0	35.0	34.7	34.7	34.8	35.4
2000	34.9	35.1	35.1	34.7	34.6	34.9	35.5	35.5	35.8	35.6	35.5	35.7	35.2
2001	35.1	34.8	34.9	34.6	34.4	34.6	34.4	34.1	34.4	34.1	33.8	33.7	34.4
2002	33.3	33.1	33.0	32.6	32.5	32.6	32.1	32.0	31.9	31.5	31.4	31.5	32.3
2003	31.2	31.1	30.9	31.0	30.9	31.0	30.9	30.6	30.3	30.3	30.4	30.4	30.8
Service-providing													
1990	205.1	205.3	206.8	204.9	207.0	209.4	204.7	203.6	206.6	204.6	205.9	206.1	205.8
1991	195.2	195.6	196.0	197.4	197.1	196.5	192.0	190.4	194.3	196.4	197.2	197.1	195.4
1992	188.6	188.3	189.2	191.2	192.4	192.3	191.5	189.9	192.2	194.9	195.0	195.8	191.7
1993	190.0	190.9	191.6	194.4	195.1	194.6	192.9	192.5	195.4	198.3	199.5	200.7	194.6
1994	190.3	191.7	193.6	196.5	195.5	196.5	196.0	196.2	197.8	200.1	201.2	200.9	196.3
1995	193.6	196.8	196.6	198.4	198.2	198.3	196.4	196.4	198.2	199.4	200.1	201.6	197.8
1996	195.7	196.6	199.0	200.0	201.8	203.0	199.4	199.5	201.0	205.2	206.8	206.5	201.2
1997	199.9	201.5	202.2	205.0	203.7	204.1	203.7	201.4	204.9	207.4	208.6	209.8	204.3
1998	204.1	206.5	205.7	209.1	208.6	210.5	209.6	208.4	209.3	214.0	216.4	217.3	209.9
1999	207.8	210.5	211.5	213.0	211.6	213.1	213.0	213.4	215.2	216.1	217.9	218.9	213.5
2000	213.7	215.7	216.7	218.7	220.1	219.9	218.4	215.8	217.6	217.8	219.8	222.1	218.0
2001	211.9	212.6	212.0	214.3	215.9	217.7	211.5	211.8	214.9	216.3	218.4	220.0	214.8
2002	212.5	215.0	214.9	219.1	219.5	221.2	215.0	214.8	218.5	219.7	221.8	222.7	217.9
2003	214.2	215.6	215.6	216.4	216.4	215.5	210.9	208.6	213.4	217.1	219.0	219.2	215.2
Trade, transportation, and utilities													
1990	50.8	49.6	49.8	48.8	49.4	50.0	48.7	48.3	48.4	48.0	48.5	48.8	49.0
1991	45.9	45.0	45.2	45.3	45.6	45.2	43.9	43.7	44.3	44.4	45.0	45.7	44.9
1992	43.0	42.2	42.4	42.4	43.0	43.0	42.1	42.2	42.1	43.0	43.5	44.3	42.7
1993	42.6	41.8	42.1	42.5	43.0	42.9	42.1	42.0	42.7	43.4	44.1	44.7	42.8
1994	41.7	41.3	41.8	42.3	42.6	42.9	42.5	42.6	42.8	43.5	44.0	44.4	42.7
1995	42.0	41.4	42.0	41.9	42.2	42.4	41.9	42.0	42.5	43.2	43.9	44.4	42.4
1996	43.4	43.1	43.0	42.9	42.8	43.1	42.2	42.2	42.7	43.6	44.5	45.4	43.2
1997	43.2	43.2	42.9	43.4	43.8	44.3	43.9	43.7	44.7	44.8	45.6	46.5	44.1
1998	44.8	44.9	45.4	44.9	45.7	46.3	45.6	45.8	46.6	46.6	47.5	48.6	46.0
1999	45.5	45.5	45.7	45.6	45.4	45.9	45.3	45.6	45.9	45.9	46.8	47.6	45.8
2000	46.0	45.6	46.1	46.1	46.2	46.3	46.0	46.0	46.6	46.8	47.5	48.5	46.4
2001	45.1	44.3	44.4	45.0	45.6	46.2	45.0	45.1	45.7	46.4	47.2	48.2	45.7
2002	46.4	45.8	46.1	46.6	47.0	47.4	46.6	46.3	47.3	47.4	48.2	49.1	47.0
2003	47.0	46.0	46.3	46.1	46.4	46.6	46.2	44.9	45.4	45.4	46.2	46.8	46.1

Employment by Industry: Connecticut—*Continued*

(Numbers in thousands. Not seasonally adjusted.)

Industry	January	February	March	April	May	June	July	August	September	October	November	December	Annual Average
NEW HAVEN-MERIDEN *—Continued*													
Wholesale trade													
1990	13.7	13.7	13.7	13.4	13.5	13.6	13.5	13.3	13.2	12.7	12.6	12.6	13.2
1991	12.1	12.2	12.1	12.2	12.2	12.2	12.1	12.1	12.2	12.0	12.0	12.0	12.1
1992	11.7	11.6	11.7	11.5	11.6	11.6	11.3	11.4	11.3	11.3	11.3	11.4	11.4
1993	11.1	11.0	11.0	11.1	11.1	11.2	11.1	11.0	11.0	11.1	11.1	11.1	11.0
1994	10.4	10.4	10.6	11.0	11.0	11.1	11.0	10.9	10.9	10.9	10.9	10.9	10.8
1995	10.5	10.4	10.7	10.7	10.6	10.7	10.7	10.8	10.8	10.9	10.9	10.9	10.7
1996	10.7	10.8	10.8	10.6	10.0	10.0	9.7	9.7	9.8	9.9	9.9	10.1	10.1
1997	10.0	10.2	10.1	10.3	10.4	10.5	10.6	10.6	10.7	10.9	10.9	11.0	10.5
1998	10.7	11.0	11.2	11.2	11.2	11.4	11.3	11.2	11.3	11.3	11.4	11.4	11.2
1999	11.1	11.3	11.3	11.1	11.1	11.2	10.9	11.0	11.1	11.0	11.0	11.1	11.1
2000	11.2	11.2	11.4	11.3	11.4	11.4	11.4	11.4	11.5	11.4	11.4	11.5	11.3
2001	11.1	11.1	11.1	11.2	11.3	11.3	10.8	10.8	10.7	10.7	10.6	10.7	11.0
2002	10.4	10.3	10.3	10.2	10.3	10.3	10.3	10.3	10.4	10.4	10.4	10.5	10.3
2003	10.3	10.2	10.2	10.3	10.4	10.4	10.3	10.3	10.5	10.4	10.4	10.4	10.3
Retail trade													
1990	31.0	30.1	30.0	29.3	29.7	30.2	29.4	29.3	29.0	28.9	29.5	29.8	29.6
1991	27.6	27.0	27.1	27.2	27.5	27.3	26.6	26.5	26.5	26.7	27.4	28.0	27.1
1992	25.4	24.8	24.8	25.1	25.4	25.5	25.2	25.2	24.8	25.5	26.0	26.7	25.3
1993	25.2	24.6	24.8	25.2	25.5	25.4	25.0	25.0	25.1	25.5	26.2	26.7	25.3
1994	24.9	24.4	24.7	25.1	25.2	25.5	25.4	25.6	25.5	26.0	26.6	26.9	25.4
1995	25.3	24.9	25.0	25.0	25.3	25.4	25.2	25.4	25.4	25.9	26.7	27.3	25.5
1996	26.6	26.2	26.0	26.1	26.6	26.8	26.6	26.8	26.6	27.1	28.0	28.7	26.8
1997	27.2	26.9	26.7	26.8	27.1	27.4	27.3	27.3	27.4	27.3	28.1	28.9	27.3
1998	27.5	27.2	27.5	27.4	27.9	28.2	28.1	28.4	28.5	28.4	29.2	30.3	28.2
1999	27.9	27.5	27.7	27.7	27.6	27.9	28.0	28.3	28.1	28.1	29.0	29.7	28.1
2000	28.2	27.8	28.2	28.1	28.2	28.3	28.2	28.3	28.3	28.5	29.3	30.1	28.4
2001	27.5	26.7	26.9	27.1	27.5	27.9	27.6	27.8	28.0	28.5	29.3	30.1	27.9
2002	28.6	28.0	28.3	28.6	28.9	29.3	29.0	28.9	29.0	29.0	29.8	30.6	29.0
2003	28.9	28.1	28.3	28.1	28.3	28.5	28.4	27.4	27.3	27.5	28.3	28.8	28.2
Transportation and utilities													
1990	6.1	5.8	6.1	6.1	6.2	6.2	5.8	5.7	6.2	6.4	6.4	6.4	6.1
1991	6.2	5.8	6.0	5.9	5.9	5.7	5.2	5.1	5.6	5.7	5.6	5.7	5.7
1992	5.9	5.8	5.9	5.8	6.0	5.9	5.6	5.6	6.0	6.2	6.2	6.2	5.9
1993	6.3	6.2	6.3	6.2	6.4	6.3	6.0	6.0	6.6	6.8	6.8	6.9	6.4
1994	6.4	6.5	6.5	6.2	6.4	6.3	6.1	6.1	6.4	6.6	6.5	6.6	6.3
1995	6.2	6.1	6.3	6.2	6.3	6.3	6.0	5.8	6.3	6.4	6.3	6.2	6.2
1996	6.1	6.1	6.2	6.2	6.2	6.3	5.9	5.7	6.3	6.6	6.6	6.6	6.2
1997	6.0	6.1	6.1	6.3	6.3	6.4	6.0	5.8	6.6	6.6	6.6	6.6	6.2
1998	6.6	6.7	6.7	6.3	6.6	6.7	6.2	6.2	6.8	6.9	6.9	6.9	6.6
1999	6.5	6.7	6.7	6.8	6.7	6.8	6.4	6.3	6.7	6.8	6.8	6.8	6.6
2000	6.6	6.6	6.5	6.7	6.6	6.6	6.4	6.3	6.8	6.9	6.8	6.9	6.6
2001	6.5	6.5	6.4	6.7	6.8	7.0	6.6	6.5	7.0	7.2	7.3	7.4	6.8
2002	7.4	7.5	7.5	7.8	7.8	7.8	7.3	7.1	7.9	8.0	8.0	8.0	7.7
2003	7.8	7.7	7.8	7.7	7.7	7.7	7.5	7.2	7.6	7.5	7.5	7.6	7.6
Information													
1990	11.7	11.6	11.9	11.4	11.5	11.9	10.7	10.7	10.4	10.2	10.2	10.3	11.0
1991	10.4	10.5	10.4	9.9	9.9	9.9	9.9	9.7	9.7	9.8	9.6	9.7	9.9
1992	9.6	9.6	9.6	9.5	9.6	9.8	9.7	9.8	9.8	9.7	9.7	9.8	9.6
1993	9.6	9.6	9.6	9.5	9.6	9.6	9.7	9.8	9.7	9.8	9.9	9.8	9.6
1994	9.5	9.2	9.3	9.0	9.0	9.1	9.4	9.5	9.5	9.6	9.7	9.6	9.3
1995	9.6	9.5	9.6	9.0	9.1	9.1	8.7	8.8	8.7	8.8	8.4	8.6	8.9
1996	8.5	8.6	8.8	9.1	9.2	9.4	9.2	9.3	9.4	9.6	9.6	9.4	9.1
1997	9.0	9.2	9.0	9.1	9.1	9.2	9.3	9.3	9.4	9.3	9.3	9.3	9.2
1998	9.5	9.4	9.5	9.5	9.6	9.7	9.8	9.9	7.2	9.8	9.8	9.8	9.4
1999	9.8	9.7	9.7	9.4	9.3	9.3	9.2	9.1	9.1	9.1	9.1	9.2	9.3
2000	9.5	9.5	9.6	9.3	9.4	9.6	9.9	10.0	10.0	10.2	10.3	10.2	9.7
2001	10.2	10.2	10.1	9.9	9.9	9.8	9.8	9.8	9.8	9.7	9.8	9.9	9.9
2002	9.8	9.8	9.7	9.6	9.5	9.5	9.3	9.3	9.2	9.2	9.1	9.1	9.4
2003	9.0	9.0	9.0	8.9	8.9	9.0	9.2	9.1	9.2	9.1	9.1	9.4	9.1
Financial activities													
1990	17.7	17.8	17.9	17.6	17.7	17.9	17.9	17.8	17.5	17.2	17.2	17.3	17.6
1991	16.9	16.9	16.9	17.0	16.9	16.8	16.6	16.6	16.2	16.3	16.1	16.0	16.6
1992	15.7	15.5	15.7	15.7	15.9	16.1	16.1	16.1	15.8	15.7	15.7	15.8	15.8
1993	15.3	15.4	15.5	15.3	15.5	15.6	15.5	15.6	15.4	15.4	15.4	15.3	15.4
1994	14.9	14.8	14.9	15.0	15.0	15.1	15.1	15.2	14.8	14.8	14.7	14.7	14.9
1995	14.6	14.5	14.5	14.4	14.4	14.7	14.4	14.5	14.3	14.1	14.1	14.2	14.3
1996	14.3	14.4	14.5	14.3	14.4	14.6	13.9	13.9	13.7	14.8	14.7	14.8	14.3
1997	13.7	14.0	13.9	13.5	13.6	13.8	13.8	13.7	13.7	13.9	13.8	14.0	13.7
1998	14.2	14.1	14.3	14.2	14.3	14.8	14.6	14.7	14.5	14.4	14.5	14.6	14.4
1999	13.8	13.8	13.9	13.6	13.5	13.6	13.5	13.4	13.3	13.1	13.1	13.3	13.4
2000	13.4	13.4	13.5	13.4	13.5	13.6	13.7	13.7	13.5	13.4	13.5	13.6	13.5
2001	13.4	13.4	13.4	13.5	13.6	13.7	13.9	14.0	13.9	13.9	13.9	14.1	13.7
2002	13.6	13.5	13.6	13.6	13.7	13.9	14.1	14.1	13.9	13.9	13.9	14.0	13.8
2003	13.7	13.7	13.7	13.7	13.8	13.9	13.9	13.8	13.7	13.9	13.9	13.9	13.8

Employment by Industry: Connecticut—*Continued*

(Numbers in thousands. Not seasonally adjusted.)

Industry	January	February	March	April	May	June	July	August	September	October	November	December	Annual Average
NEW HAVEN-MERIDEN *—Continued*													
Professional and business services													
1990	22.5	22.7	23.2	22.0	22.5	23.3	23.8	23.9	23.4	23.0	22.9	22.9	23.0
1991	21.5	21.7	22.0	22.5	22.2	22.4	22.4	22.3	22.2	21.9	21.9	21.9	22.0
1992	20.5	20.5	20.8	22.3	22.5	22.5	22.4	22.4	22.3	22.0	21.7	22.0	21.8
1993	22.2	22.2	22.4	23.0	23.5	23.5	23.0	23.4	23.0	23.5	23.6	23.8	23.0
1994	22.7	22.9	23.5	24.1	24.4	24.6	24.3	25.0	24.7	24.9	24.9	24.8	24.2
1995	23.6	23.9	23.9	24.9	24.6	25.0	24.8	25.3	25.2	24.5	24.5	24.7	24.5
1996	24.4	25.1	25.6	25.7	26.0	26.6	25.6	26.1	25.9	26.3	26.4	26.4	25.8
1997	25.0	25.6	25.6	26.8	26.5	26.8	27.1	26.8	26.7	27.2	27.1	27.3	26.5
1998	26.7	26.5	26.7	27.3	26.9	27.4	27.4	27.4	27.1	27.2	27.5	27.7	27.1
1999	26.7	26.5	26.6	28.5	28.9	29.5	29.2	30.2	29.8	29.7	30.0	30.5	28.8
2000	28.2	29.0	29.4	29.0	29.8	30.5	29.6	29.9	29.8	28.8	29.3	29.8	29.4
2001	27.6	27.4	28.0	27.7	28.7	28.9	28.1	28.4	29.1	27.3	27.3	27.8	28.0
2002	26.7	26.7	27.3	27.1	27.4	28.4	27.8	28.5	28.7	27.5	27.7	27.8	27.6
2003	25.9	26.1	26.0	25.7	25.7	25.9	25.5	25.9	26.5	26.3	26.1	25.8	26.0
Educational and health services													
1990	48.2	49.1	48.4	49.0	47.9	47.7	46.8	46.6	48.9	49.2	49.5	49.7	48.4
1991	48.2	50.0	49.1	50.7	49.2	48.5	46.9	46.8	49.9	51.0	51.2	51.2	49.3
1992	49.8	50.4	49.7	49.8	48.9	48.3	47.6	47.1	49.4	50.2	50.2	50.5	49.3
1993	49.1	49.8	48.9	50.7	49.8	49.1	48.2	48.2	50.7	52.5	52.6	53.1	50.2
1994	51.1	51.7	51.5	53.2	51.8	51.0	49.8	49.2	51.9	54.0	54.0	54.1	51.9
1995	52.6	54.0	52.8	53.7	52.7	51.6	51.1	50.6	53.0	54.3	54.3	54.9	52.9
1996	53.1	54.7	53.4	54.4	53.6	52.8	52.8	52.1	54.4	55.7	56.0	55.4	54.0
1997	53.8	56.4	54.0	56.4	54.5	53.0	53.2	52.1	54.8	56.0	56.1	56.1	54.7
1998	54.0	56.0	53.3	56.1	54.2	53.4	53.8	52.8	55.9	57.1	57.8	57.4	55.1
1999	55.5	57.2	56.8	57.1	55.6	55.0	55.6	55.6	58.3	58.9	59.2	58.5	56.9
2000	57.7	58.0	57.2	58.9	58.0	55.7	55.4	53.8	56.0	57.1	57.3	57.7	56.9
2001	55.5	56.7	55.3	56.8	55.5	55.5	54.0	53.7	56.5	58.1	58.4	58.2	56.2
2002	56.6	59.0	57.2	60.1	58.8	57.8	57.1	56.8	58.9	60.4	60.9	60.5	58.7
2003	58.8	60.8	59.9	60.8	59.8	58.4	56.7	55.7	57.9	60.8	61.5	61.1	59.4
Leisure and hospitality													
1990	14.7	14.7	15.4	15.8	16.6	17.3	17.1	17.0	16.7	15.4	15.1	15.1	15.9
1991	12.8	12.8	13.2	13.8	14.6	15.2	15.5	15.6	14.8	14.7	14.4	14.3	14.3
1992	12.7	13.0	13.4	13.7	14.4	15.0	14.9	14.8	14.5	13.8	13.4	13.3	13.9
1993	13.0	13.2	13.7	14.2	15.1	15.5	15.4	15.4	14.9	14.7	14.3	14.5	14.4
1994	12.9	13.0	13.7	14.6	15.3	16.1	16.2	16.3	15.3	14.4	14.4	14.5	14.7
1995	13.6	13.6	14.1	15.1	15.9	16.8	16.8	16.8	15.8	15.3	15.2	15.1	15.3
1996	13.8	13.9	13.9	14.8	15.8	16.8	16.5	16.7	15.7	15.4	15.3	15.2	15.3
1997	14.0	14.3	14.6	15.5	16.1	17.0	17.2	17.3	16.2	15.6	15.5	15.7	15.7
1998	14.9	15.0	15.5	16.1	17.0	17.9	18.3	18.3	17.1	16.7	16.6	16.6	16.6
1999	15.3	15.5	16.1	16.5	16.9	17.9	18.0	17.8	16.9	16.4	16.2	16.2	16.6
2000	15.2	15.6	15.9	16.5	17.1	18.4	18.4	18.3	17.4	16.9	17.0	17.1	16.9
2001	15.4	15.6	15.8	16.4	17.4	18.0	17.9	18.0	16.7	16.7	16.4	16.5	16.7
2002	15.0	15.3	16.0	16.9	17.7	18.3	18.6	18.4	17.4	17.0	16.7	16.8	17.0
2003	15.4	15.8	16.2	17.3	17.7	18.7	18.8	18.9	18.1	18.1	18.0	17.8	17.6
Other services													
1990	7.1	7.5	7.7	8.0	8.4	9.0	9.0	9.2	9.4	9.1	9.1	9.0	8.5
1991	7.0	6.9	7.0	6.3	6.5	6.6	7.1	6.7	6.6	6.6	6.6	6.6	6.7
1992	5.9	5.8	6.0	6.1	6.2	6.3	7.1	6.7	6.7	6.9	7.0	7.1	6.4
1993	6.8	6.8	7.1	7.3	6.9	7.2	8.1	7.7	7.7	8.1	8.2	8.6	7.5
1994	7.5	8.2	7.9	7.1	6.6	7.0	8.3	8.4	8.2	8.1	8.2	8.4	7.8
1995	7.7	8.5	8.0	8.2	8.3	8.4	8.2	8.3	8.0	8.1	8.2	8.3	8.1
1996	8.0	5.5	8.3	7.3	8.7	8.9	8.9	8.9	8.9	8.6	8.8	8.6	8.2
1997	10.5	7.3	10.6	8.8	8.6	8.6	8.7	8.4	8.7	9.3	9.3	9.3	9.0
1998	9.0	9.0	9.1	9.3	9.4	9.7	9.6	9.5	9.5	9.6	9.6	9.8	9.4
1999	9.4	9.5	9.7	9.3	9.5	9.5	9.6	9.4	9.3	9.4	9.4	9.4	9.4
2000	9.3	9.4	9.4	9.5	9.5	9.6	9.7	9.5	9.7	9.6	9.7	9.7	9.5
2001	9.4	9.5	9.5	9.6	9.8	10.0	10.0	10.0	9.8	9.9	10.0	10.0	9.8
2002	9.9	9.9	10.0	10.0	10.2	10.3	10.1	10.1	9.9	9.9	9.9	10.0	10.0
2003	9.8	9.8	10.0	9.7	9.9	10.2	10.3	10.3	10.1	10.0	10.0	10.3	10.0
Government													
1990	32.4	32.3	32.5	32.3	33.0	32.3	30.7	30.1	31.9	32.5	33.4	33.0	32.2
1991	32.5	31.8	32.2	31.9	32.2	31.9	29.7	29.0	30.6	31.7	32.4	31.7	31.4
1992	31.4	31.3	31.6	31.7	31.9	31.3	31.6	30.8	31.6	33.6	33.8	33.0	31.9
1993	31.4	32.1	32.3	31.9	31.7	31.2	30.9	30.4	31.3	30.9	31.4	30.9	31.3
1994	30.0	30.6	31.0	31.2	30.8	30.7	30.4	30.0	30.6	30.8	31.3	30.4	30.6
1995	29.9	31.4	31.7	31.2	31.0	30.3	30.5	30.1	30.7	31.1	31.5	31.4	30.9
1996	30.2	31.3	31.5	31.5	31.3	30.8	30.3	30.3	30.3	31.2	31.5	31.3	30.9
1997	30.7	31.5	31.6	31.5	31.5	31.4	30.5	30.1	30.7	31.3	31.9	31.6	31.1
1998	31.0	31.6	31.9	31.7	31.5	31.3	30.5	30.0	31.4	32.6	33.1	32.8	31.6
1999	31.8	32.8	33.0	33.0	32.5	32.4	32.6	32.3	32.6	33.6	34.1	34.2	32.9
2000	34.4	35.2	35.6	36.0	36.6	36.2	35.7	34.6	34.6	35.0	35.2	35.5	35.3
2001	35.3	35.5	35.5	35.4	35.4	35.6	32.8	32.8	33.4	34.3	35.4	35.3	34.7
2002	34.5	35.0	35.0	35.2	35.2	35.6	31.4	31.3	33.2	34.4	35.4	35.4	34.3
2003	34.6	34.4	34.5	34.2	34.2	32.8	30.3	30.0	32.5	33.5	34.2	34.1	33.3

Employment by Industry: Connecticut—*Continued*

(Numbers in thousands. Not seasonally adjusted.)

Industry	January	February	March	April	May	June	July	August	September	October	November	December	Annual Average
NEW HAVEN-MERIDEN —*Continued*													
Federal government													
1990	5.2	5.2	5.2	5.2	5.8	5.5	5.5	5.4	5.1	5.1	5.1	5.1	5.2
1991	5.0	5.0	5.0	5.0	5.0	5.1	5.0	5.1	5.1	5.1	5.2	5.3	5.0
1992	5.2	5.2	5.2	5.3	5.2	5.3	5.3	5.3	5.4	5.6	5.5	5.7	5.3
1993	5.3	5.3	5.3	5.2	5.2	5.3	5.3	5.4	5.3	5.4	5.4	5.6	5.3
1994	5.3	5.3	5.3	5.4	5.4	5.4	5.4	5.4	5.4	5.4	5.4	5.6	5.3
1995	5.4	5.5	5.4	5.5	5.5	5.5	5.5	5.5	5.5	5.5	5.6	5.7	5.5
1996	5.5	5.5	5.5	5.6	5.5	5.6	5.5	5.5	5.6	5.6	5.7	6.0	5.5
1997	5.7	5.7	5.7	5.7	5.7	5.7	5.7	5.7	5.7	5.6	5.7	5.8	5.7
1998	5.5	5.5	5.5	5.5	5.5	5.5	5.5	5.5	5.5	5.5	5.6	5.9	5.5
1999	5.6	5.6	5.5	5.6	5.5	5.6	5.6	5.6	5.6	5.5	5.5	5.8	5.5
2000	5.8	5.8	5.8	6.3	7.4	6.8	6.6	5.9	5.8	5.8	5.8	6.0	6.1
2001	5.8	5.8	5.8	5.8	5.8	5.8	5.8	5.8	5.7	5.8	5.8	5.8	5.8
2002	5.7	5.7	5.7	5.7	5.7	5.7	5.6	5.6	5.6	5.6	5.6	5.7	5.7
2003	5.6	5.6	5.6	5.6	5.6	5.6	5.6	5.5	5.5	5.5	5.4	5.5	5.6
State government													
2001	7.3	7.3	7.3	7.2	7.2	7.3	7.3	7.4	7.1	7.3	7.3	7.3	7.3
2002	7.1	7.4	7.3	7.3	7.3	7.1	6.9	6.9	6.9	7.1	7.3	7.2	7.2
2003	7.0	6.8	6.7	6.6	6.6	6.6	6.6	6.7	6.7	6.7	6.7	6.7	6.7
Local government													
2001	22.2	22.4	22.4	22.4	22.4	22.5	19.7	19.6	20.6	21.2	22.3	22.2	21.7
2002	21.7	21.9	22.0	22.2	22.2	22.8	18.9	18.8	20.7	21.7	22.5	22.5	21.5
2003	22.0	22.0	22.2	22.0	22.0	20.6	18.1	17.8	20.3	21.3	22.1	21.9	21.0
NEW LONDON-NORWICH													
Total nonfarm													
1995	127.9	127.8	129.4	130.1	131.6	133.6	134.0	134.2	132.9	131.7	132.6	132.5	131.5
1996	128.1	128.0	129.4	131.3	133.9	136.1	133.9	133.8	131.7	135.0	134.8	135.2	132.6
1997	132.4	131.9	132.5	134.2	136.2	139.2	139.0	138.8	137.5	137.2	137.5	138.1	136.2
1998	134.8	134.6	136.0	135.2	137.5	139.9	140.0	139.8	138.2	137.5	138.3	138.9	137.5
1999	136.6	137.0	138.1	138.9	140.6	143.0	142.6	142.9	141.1	141.1	140.8	141.9	140.3
2000	137.6	137.5	138.8	140.7	142.5	144.1	143.8	142.9	140.4	140.5	140.4	141.0	140.8
2001	138.9	137.9	138.7	139.8	141.8	144.1	144.7	145.1	145.2	145.7	145.8	146.4	142.8
2002	143.1	142.3	143.4	143.5	145.0	146.4	146.0	146.3	145.6	143.9	144.1	144.1	144.5
2003	142.4	141.2	142.0	143.4	146.5	148.7	148.4	148.0	147.4	145.8	145.8	145.4	145.4
Total private													
1995	98.6	98.3	99.8	100.5	101.8	103.4	103.3	103.6	102.6	101.2	101.3	101.2	101.3
1996	97.8	97.3	98.6	99.8	102.1	104.3	102.5	102.6	101.0	100.4	100.2	100.7	100.6
1997	97.7	97.0	98.0	99.9	101.7	104.2	103.4	103.4	102.1	101.9	102.1	102.7	101.1
1998	99.8	99.3	100.6	100.1	102.3	104.5	104.5	104.4	102.8	101.6	102.0	102.7	102.0
1999	100.4	100.5	101.4	102.3	103.7	106.1	106.1	106.3	104.7	103.5	103.0	104.0	103.5
2000	100.4	100.1	100.9	102.7	103.9	105.9	105.6	105.3	103.2	102.3	102.6	103.2	103.0
2001	100.6	99.5	100.1	101.7	103.5	105.8	106.2	106.5	104.8	103.5	103.3	104.1	103.3
2002	100.9	100.3	101.3	102.6	104.3	105.9	105.4	105.8	104.2	103.0	103.0	103.2	103.3
2003	100.4	99.5	100.0	101.5	104.0	106.2	106.2	106.1	105.0	104.1	104.0	104.2	103.4
Goods-producing													
1995	30.7	30.4	30.8	31.0	31.0	30.9	30.3	30.6	30.6	30.3	30.5	30.2	30.6
1996	28.9	28.6	29.0	29.6	29.9	30.1	29.3	29.2	28.8	29.0	28.4	28.2	29.0
1997	27.3	26.8	27.0	27.7	27.6	28.5	27.8	28.3	27.7	27.7	27.7	27.9	27.6
1998	27.0	26.9	27.1	27.7	27.9	28.1	28.3	28.8	28.3	28.0	28.1	28.1	27.8
1999	27.5	27.2	27.3	27.6	27.9	28.1	27.6	28.0	27.5	27.3	27.3	27.4	27.5
2000	26.6	26.5	26.5	27.4	27.5	27.7	27.4	27.7	27.4	27.3	27.3	27.3	27.2
2001	27.4	27.1	27.1	27.1	27.3	27.2	27.0	27.1	26.2	25.9	25.6	25.6	26.7
2002	24.9	24.7	24.7	24.6	24.7	24.6	24.2	24.4	24.3	24.2	24.0	23.9	24.4
2003	23.8	23.4	23.5	23.7	24.0	24.3	24.3	24.2	24.2	24.0	24.0	23.9	23.9
Construction and mining													
1995	3.7	3.6	3.8	4.2	4.4	4.0	4.0	4.1	4.1	4.0	4.3	4.1	4.0
1996	3.4	3.4	3.8	4.1	4.4	4.5	4.3	4.4	4.4	4.8	4.7	4.5	4.2
1997	3.9	3.9	4.1	4.5	4.5	4.8	4.6	4.8	4.9	4.9	4.8	4.8	4.5
1998	4.1	4.1	4.1	4.4	4.6	4.7	4.7	4.7	4.7	4.7	4.7	4.7	4.5
1999	4.6	4.6	4.6	4.7	5.0	5.0	5.0	4.9	4.7	4.8	4.8	4.8	4.7
2000	4.2	4.2	4.3	5.0	5.2	5.2	5.4	5.4	5.4	5.4	5.5	5.5	5.0
2001	5.2	5.2	5.2	5.1	5.3	5.5	5.6	5.7	5.6	5.4	5.3	5.1	5.4
2002	4.7	4.7	4.8	4.6	4.7	4.7	4.7	4.7	4.7	4.7	4.6	4.4	4.7
2003	4.1	4.0	4.1	4.3	4.6	4.9	4.9	4.9	4.9	4.8	4.7	4.6	4.6
Manufacturing													
1995	27.0	26.8	27.0	26.8	26.6	26.9	26.3	26.5	26.5	26.3	26.2	26.1	26.5
1996	25.5	25.2	25.2	25.5	25.5	25.6	25.0	24.8	24.4	24.2	23.7	23.7	24.8
1997	23.4	22.9	22.9	23.2	23.1	23.7	23.2	23.5	22.8	22.8	22.9	23.1	23.1
1998	22.9	22.8	23.0	23.3	23.3	23.4	23.6	24.1	23.6	23.3	23.4	23.4	23.3
1999	22.9	22.6	22.7	22.9	22.9	23.1	22.6	23.1	22.8	22.5	22.5	22.6	22.7
2000	22.4	22.3	22.2	22.4	22.3	22.5	22.0	22.3	22.0	21.9	21.8	21.8	22.1
2001	22.2	21.9	21.9	22.0	22.0	21.7	21.4	21.4	20.6	20.5	20.3	20.5	21.4
2002	20.2	20.0	19.9	20.0	20.0	19.9	19.5	19.7	19.6	19.5	19.4	19.5	19.8
2003	19.7	19.4	19.4	19.4	19.4	19.4	19.4	19.3	19.3	19.2	19.3	19.3	19.4

Employment by Industry: Connecticut—*Continued*

(Numbers in thousands. Not seasonally adjusted.)

Industry	January	February	March	April	May	June	July	August	September	October	November	December	Annual Average
NEW LONDON-NORWICH *—Continued*													
Service-providing													
1995	97.2	97.4	98.6	99.1	100.6	102.7	103.7	103.6	102.3	101.4	102.1	102.3	100.9
1996	99.2	99.4	100.4	101.7	104.0	106.0	104.6	104.6	102.9	106.0	106.4	107.0	103.5
1997	105.1	105.1	105.5	106.5	108.6	110.7	111.2	110.5	109.8	109.5	109.8	110.2	108.5
1998	107.8	107.7	108.9	107.5	109.6	111.8	111.7	111.0	109.9	109.5	110.2	110.8	109.7
1999	109.1	109.8	110.8	111.3	112.7	114.9	115.0	114.9	113.6	113.8	113.5	114.5	112.8
2000	111.0	111.0	112.3	113.3	115.0	116.4	116.4	115.2	113.0	113.2	113.1	113.7	113.6
2001	111.5	110.8	111.6	112.7	114.5	116.9	117.7	118.0	119.0	119.8	120.2	120.8	116.1
2002	118.2	117.6	118.7	118.9	120.3	121.8	121.8	121.9	121.3	119.7	120.1	120.2	120.0
2003	118.6	117.8	118.5	119.7	122.5	124.4	124.1	123.8	123.2	121.8	121.8	121.5	121.5
Trade, transportation, and utilities													
1995	21.6	21.3	21.4	21.2	21.4	21.8	21.9	22.0	22.1	21.8	22.0	22.3	21.7
1996	21.7	21.4	21.4	21.1	21.6	22.0	21.2	21.3	21.1	21.8	22.4	22.9	21.6
1997	22.0	21.7	21.9	21.9	22.2	22.7	22.6	22.6	22.6	23.0	23.7	23.9	22.5
1998	23.4	23.2	23.2	22.5	22.8	23.1	23.1	23.1	23.2	23.0	23.6	24.0	23.1
1999	23.5	23.3	23.5	22.9	23.2	23.4	23.6	23.8	23.7	23.9	24.2	24.6	23.6
2000	23.5	23.2	23.5	23.8	23.9	24.3	23.8	23.8	23.6	23.6	24.3	24.7	23.8
2001	24.1	23.5	23.4	23.7	24.0	24.3	24.2	24.5	24.4	23.9	24.5	24.9	24.1
2002	23.6	23.1	23.4	23.6	23.9	24.4	24.3	24.5	24.7	24.4	25.0	25.6	24.2
2003	23.9	23.6	23.6	23.6	24.2	24.6	24.4	24.5	24.8	24.8	25.3	25.8	24.4
Wholesale trade													
1995	2.0	2.0	2.0	2.1	2.1	2.1	2.2	2.2	2.2	2.2	2.1	2.2	2.1
1996	2.2	2.2	2.2	2.0	2.0	2.1	2.0	2.0	2.0	2.0	2.0	2.0	2.0
1997	2.0	2.0	2.0	2.0	2.0	2.1	2.1	2.0	2.0	2.0	2.0	1.9	2.0
1998	1.9	1.9	2.0	1.9	2.0	2.0	1.9	1.9	1.9	1.9	1.9	1.9	1.9
1999	1.9	1.9	1.9	1.9	2.0	2.0	2.0	2.0	2.0	2.0	2.0	2.0	1.9
2000	2.0	2.0	2.1	2.3	2.3	2.3	2.3	2.3	2.2	2.2	2.2	2.1	2.1
2001	2.2	2.2	2.2	2.2	2.3	2.3	2.3	2.3	2.3	2.2	2.2	2.2	2.2
2002	2.3	2.3	2.3	2.3	2.3	2.3	2.3	2.3	2.3	2.3	2.3	2.3	2.3
2003	2.2	2.2	2.2	2.2	2.3	2.3	2.3	2.3	2.3	2.3	2.3	2.3	2.3
Retail trade													
1995	15.4	15.2	15.3	14.8	15.0	15.4	15.5	15.7	15.6	15.3	15.7	15.9	15.4
1996	15.2	14.9	14.9	14.8	15.2	15.5	15.1	15.2	14.9	15.4	16.0	16.5	15.3
1997	15.8	15.5	15.7	15.6	15.9	16.2	16.2	16.3	16.2	16.5	17.2	17.5	16.2
1998	16.9	16.6	16.5	15.9	16.0	16.2	16.5	16.5	16.4	16.3	16.9	17.3	16.5
1999	16.7	16.4	16.6	16.5	16.6	16.8	17.0	17.3	17.1	17.2	17.6	18.1	16.9
2000	17.0	16.7	16.9	16.9	17.0	17.3	16.9	17.0	16.8	16.8	17.6	18.1	17.0
2001	17.0	16.6	16.6	16.8	17.0	17.4	17.4	17.8	17.6	17.6	18.3	18.7	17.4
2002	17.4	16.9	17.1	17.2	17.5	17.9	18.0	18.2	18.1	17.8	18.4	19.0	17.8
2003	17.5	17.2	17.2	17.2	17.7	18.0	18.1	18.3	18.2	18.2	18.7	19.2	18.0
Transportation and utilities													
1995	4.2	4.1	4.1	4.3	4.3	4.3	4.2	4.1	4.3	4.3	4.2	4.2	4.2
1996	4.3	4.3	4.3	4.3	4.4	4.4	4.1	4.1	4.2	4.4	4.4	4.4	4.3
1997	4.2	4.2	4.2	4.3	4.3	4.4	4.3	4.3	4.4	4.5	4.5	4.5	4.3
1998	4.6	4.7	4.7	4.7	4.8	4.9	4.7	4.7	4.9	4.8	4.8	4.8	4.7
1999	4.9	5.0	5.0	4.5	4.6	4.6	4.6	4.5	4.6	4.7	4.6	4.5	4.6
2000	4.5	4.5	4.5	4.6	4.6	4.7	4.6	4.5	4.6	4.6	4.5	4.5	4.5
2001	4.9	4.7	4.6	4.7	4.7	4.6	4.5	4.4	4.5	4.1	4.0	4.0	4.5
2002	3.9	3.9	4.0	4.1	4.1	4.2	4.0	4.0	4.3	4.3	4.3	4.3	4.1
2003	4.2	4.2	4.2	4.2	4.2	4.3	4.0	3.9	4.3	4.3	4.3	4.3	4.2
Information													
1995	2.4	2.4	2.4	2.6	2.6	2.5	2.5	2.4	2.4	2.4	2.4	2.4	2.4
1996	2.5	2.5	2.5	2.4	2.4	2.5	2.5	2.5	2.5	2.5	2.6	2.6	2.5
1997	2.7	2.8	2.8	2.8	2.8	2.8	2.8	2.6	2.6	2.6	2.7	2.7	2.7
1998	2.7	2.7	2.8	2.6	2.6	2.6	2.6	2.6	2.2	2.7	2.6	2.6	2.6
1999	2.6	2.6	2.6	2.6	2.6	2.5	2.5	2.4	2.4	2.4	2.5	2.5	2.5
2000	2.4	2.4	2.4	2.5	2.5	2.4	2.5	2.5	2.5	2.5	2.5	2.5	2.4
2001	2.6	2.5	2.5	2.5	2.5	2.6	2.6	2.6	2.6	2.6	2.6	2.6	2.6
2002	2.5	2.5	2.5	2.5	2.5	2.5	2.5	2.5	2.5	2.4	2.5	2.4	2.5
2003	2.5	2.5	2.4	2.4	2.4	2.4	2.4	2.4	2.3	2.3	2.4	2.4	2.4
Financial activities													
1995	3.5	3.5	3.5	3.4	3.5	3.5	3.6	3.6	3.5	3.5	3.5	3.5	3.5
1996	3.5	3.5	3.5	3.5	3.6	3.6	3.7	3.6	3.6	3.5	3.6	3.6	3.5
1997	3.6	3.6	3.6	3.8	3.9	4.0	4.0	3.9	3.9	4.0	3.9	4.0	3.8
1998	3.9	3.9	4.0	3.8	3.8	3.9	3.9	3.8	3.8	3.8	3.8	3.9	3.8
1999	4.0	4.0	4.0	4.0	4.0	4.0	4.1	4.1	4.1	4.1	4.1	4.0	4.0
2000	3.8	3.8	3.7	3.7	3.7	3.8	3.8	3.8	3.7	3.7	3.7	3.6	3.7
2001	3.6	3.6	3.6	3.6	3.6	3.7	3.8	3.7	3.6	3.6	3.6	3.6	3.6
2002	3.7	3.6	3.6	3.7	3.7	3.7	3.8	3.8	3.7	3.6	3.7	3.7	3.7
2003	3.5	3.5	3.5	3.5	3.6	3.6	3.7	3.8	3.7	3.7	3.8	3.8	3.6

Employment by Industry: Connecticut—*Continued*

(Numbers in thousands. Not seasonally adjusted.)

Industry	January	February	March	April	May	June	July	August	September	October	November	December	Annual Average
NEW LONDON-NORWICH *—Continued*													
Professional and business services													
1995	8.6	8.7	8.9	9.0	8.9	9.2	9.0	9.1	9.1	8.9	9.0	8.9	8.9
1996	9.0	8.9	9.2	9.3	9.4	9.5	9.2	9.2	9.1	8.9	9.0	8.9	9.1
1997	9.1	9.0	9.2	9.9	10.0	9.9	9.7	9.6	9.5	9.6	9.6	9.7	9.5
1998	9.7	9.5	9.6	10.0	9.9	10.1	9.7	9.5	9.5	9.6	9.7	9.8	9.7
1999	9.6	9.6	9.6	9.9	9.7	10.1	9.9	9.9	9.9	9.6	9.5	9.8	9.7
2000	9.5	9.5	9.6	9.6	9.6	9.8	9.7	9.6	9.5	9.5	9.4	9.6	9.5
2001	9.4	9.4	9.6	10.0	10.2	10.6	10.7	10.7	11.1	10.9	10.8	10.9	10.4
2002	10.8	10.8	10.9	11.2	11.1	11.3	10.9	10.8	10.6	10.8	10.7	10.6	10.9
2003	10.7	10.6	10.8	11.0	11.0	11.2	10.8	10.8	10.7	10.7	10.6	10.5	10.8
Educational and health services													
1995	16.0	16.2	16.4	16.2	16.5	16.2	15.8	15.7	15.9	16.2	16.3	16.4	16.1
1996	16.0	16.2	16.2	16.6	16.6	16.6	16.0	16.0	16.3	16.6	16.9	17.1	16.4
1997	16.4	16.7	16.8	17.8	17.8	17.7	17.3	17.1	17.9	18.1	18.2	18.2	17.5
1998	17.6	17.6	17.8	17.1	17.5	17.4	16.9	16.7	17.3	17.2	17.4	17.4	17.3
1999	17.3	17.7	17.9	17.8	17.7	17.7	17.5	17.3	17.8	17.8	17.8	17.9	17.6
2000	17.8	18.1	18.1	18.1	18.0	17.8	17.5	17.4	17.7	17.8	18.1	18.1	17.8
2001	17.5	17.7	17.8	17.8	17.7	17.7	17.5	17.4	18.0	18.3	18.3	18.4	17.8
2002	18.1	18.5	18.5	18.5	18.5	18.4	18.0	18.0	18.4	18.6	18.8	18.9	18.4
2003	18.7	18.8	18.9	19.0	19.1	19.0	18.6	18.4	18.8	19.1	19.2	19.2	18.9
Leisure and hospitality													
1995	10.7	10.7	11.2	11.8	12.6	13.9	14.6	14.6	13.4	12.5	12.0	11.8	12.4
1996	10.6	10.5	11.1	11.5	12.7	14.0	14.7	14.9	13.8	12.7	11.8	11.9	12.5
1997	11.3	11.2	11.5	11.9	13.2	14.4	14.9	15.0	13.6	12.7	12.1	12.0	12.8
1998	11.4	11.4	11.9	12.2	13.6	15.0	15.6	15.5	14.2	13.1	12.6	12.6	13.2
1999	11.7	11.9	12.2	13.2	14.3	15.9	16.5	16.4	14.9	14.0	13.3	13.4	13.9
2000	12.5	12.3	12.8	13.3	14.3	15.7	16.4	16.1	14.5	13.6	13.0	13.1	13.9
2001	12.0	11.8	12.2	13.0	14.1	15.5	16.2	16.3	14.7	14.1	13.7	13.8	14.0
2002	13.0	12.9	13.5	14.3	15.6	16.7	17.5	17.6	15.8	14.8	14.1	13.9	15.0
2003	13.1	12.9	13.1	14.2	15.5	16.8	17.7	17.7	16.2	15.2	14.4	14.3	15.1
Other services													
1995	5.1	5.1	5.2	5.3	5.3	5.4	5.6	5.6	5.6	5.6	5.6	5.7	5.4
1996	5.6	5.7	5.7	5.8	5.9	6.0	5.9	5.9	5.8	5.4	5.5	5.5	5.7
1997	5.3	5.2	5.2	4.1	4.2	4.2	4.3	4.3	4.3	4.2	4.2	4.3	4.4
1998	4.1	4.1	4.2	4.2	4.2	4.3	4.4	4.4	4.3	4.2	4.2	4.3	4.2
1999	4.2	4.2	4.3	4.3	4.3	4.4	4.4	4.4	4.4	4.4	4.3	4.4	4.3
2000	4.3	4.3	4.3	4.3	4.4	4.4	4.5	4.4	4.3	4.3	4.3	4.3	4.3
2001	4.0	3.9	3.9	4.0	4.1	4.2	4.2	4.2	4.2	4.2	4.2	4.3	4.1
2002	4.3	4.2	4.2	4.2	4.3	4.3	4.2	4.2	4.2	4.2	4.2	4.2	4.2
2003	4.2	4.2	4.2	4.1	4.2	4.3	4.3	4.3	4.3	4.3	4.3	4.3	4.3
Government													
1995	29.3	29.5	29.6	29.6	29.8	30.2	30.7	30.6	30.3	30.5	31.3	31.3	30.2
1996	30.3	30.7	30.8	31.5	31.8	31.8	31.4	31.2	30.7	34.6	34.6	34.5	31.9
1997	34.7	34.9	34.5	34.3	34.5	35.0	35.6	35.4	35.4	35.3	35.4	35.4	35.0
1998	35.0	35.3	35.4	35.1	35.2	35.4	35.5	35.4	35.4	35.9	36.3	36.2	35.5
1999	36.2	36.5	36.7	36.6	36.9	36.9	36.5	36.6	36.4	37.6	37.8	37.9	36.8
2000	37.2	37.4	37.9	38.0	38.6	38.2	38.2	37.6	37.2	38.2	37.8	37.8	37.8
2001	38.3	38.4	38.6	38.1	38.3	38.3	38.5	38.6	40.4	42.2	42.5	42.3	39.5
2002	42.2	42.0	42.1	40.9	40.7	40.5	40.6	40.5	41.4	40.9	41.1	40.9	41.2
2003	42.0	41.7	42.0	41.9	42.5	42.5	42.2	41.9	42.4	41.7	41.8	41.2	42.0
Federal government													
1995	4.0	4.0	3.9	3.9	3.9	3.9	3.9	3.9	3.9	3.9	3.9	3.9	3.9
1996	3.8	3.8	3.8	3.7	3.7	3.7	3.5	3.6	3.4	3.2	3.2	3.0	3.5
1997	3.0	3.0	2.8	2.8	2.8	2.8	2.8	2.8	2.8	2.7	2.7	2.7	2.8
1998	2.7	2.7	2.7	2.7	2.7	2.8	2.8	2.8	2.7	2.8	2.8	2.8	2.7
1999	2.8	2.7	2.7	2.7	2.7	2.8	2.8	2.8	2.7	2.8	2.8	2.8	2.7
2000	2.9	2.9	3.2	3.1	3.4	3.2	3.1	2.8	2.7	2.9	2.8	2.8	2.9
2001	2.9	2.9	3.1	2.8	2.8	2.8	2.9	2.9	2.9	2.9	2.9	2.9	2.9
2002	2.9	2.9	2.9	2.9	2.9	2.9	2.9	2.9	2.9	2.9	2.9	2.9	2.9
2003	3.0	3.0	2.9	2.9	2.9	2.9	2.6	2.6	2.5	2.5	2.5	2.5	2.7
State government													
1995	4.5	4.5	4.5	4.5	4.5	4.5	4.5	4.4	4.4	4.5	4.5	4.5	4.5
1996	4.5	4.5	4.5	4.6	4.6	4.6	4.5	4.5	4.5	4.6	4.6	4.5	4.5
1997	4.4	4.4	4.4	4.3	4.3	4.2	4.1	4.1	4.1	4.1	4.2	4.1	4.2
1998	20.1	20.3	20.6	20.5	20.7	21.0	21.6	21.6	21.3	21.5	22.3	22.3	21.1
1999	21.7	22.2	22.3	23.1	23.4	23.3	23.3	23.1	22.8	27.4	27.3	27.4	23.9
2000	27.8	27.8	27.7	27.6	27.8	28.3	28.8	28.6	28.6	28.4	28.4	28.4	28.1
2001	28.2	28.3	28.4	28.2	28.3	28.5	28.6	28.6	28.6	29.0	29.3	29.3	28.6
2002	29.2	29.6	29.7	29.6	29.9	29.8	29.4	29.4	29.4	30.4	30.7	30.7	29.8
2003	30.0	30.0	30.2	30.4	30.7	30.5	30.7	30.3	30.0	30.7	30.5	30.5	30.3
Local government													
2001	30.9	31.0	31.0	30.8	31.0	31.0	31.1	31.3	33.1	34.8	35.1	34.9	32.2
2002	34.8	34.6	34.7	33.4	33.2	33.0	33.2	33.1	34.0	33.4	33.6	33.5	33.7
2003	34.6	34.3	34.7	34.7	35.3	35.4	35.5	35.2	35.8	35.1	35.1	34.6	35.0

Employment by Industry: Connecticut—*Continued*

(Numbers in thousands. Not seasonally adjusted.)

Industry	January	February	March	April	May	June	July	August	September	October	November	December	Annual Average
STAMFORD													
Total nonfarm													
1990	189.6	187.9	189.2	188.8	190.7	193.8	190.9	190.5	189.6	188.4	188.8	189.7	189.8
1991	180.9	178.3	180.5	181.2	183.2	185.7	184.3	183.1	181.5	181.4	180.6	182.4	181.9
1992	176.4	174.8	176.2	177.6	179.5	182.3	181.9	180.4	180.0	180.3	180.1	181.6	179.2
1993	179.3	178.6	179.6	180.3	183.0	186.7	186.2	184.8	183.8	185.3	185.8	188.8	183.5
1994	179.9	179.5	181.3	183.5	185.8	188.8	186.7	185.6	185.9	186.9	187.7	190.1	185.1
1995	184.6	183.9	186.8	187.0	189.3	192.2	192.1	191.6	191.9	192.3	195.5	197.3	190.3
1996	189.2	189.4	192.5	193.3	195.2	199.0	197.6	197.7	197.0	198.9	200.8	203.2	196.1
1997	194.6	194.6	197.3	200.0	202.0	205.4	203.8	202.9	202.5	203.3	204.6	207.2	201.5
1998	200.3	201.2	203.2	204.3	206.4	209.9	208.7	206.3	206.1	205.2	206.9	209.1	205.6
1999	205.2	204.6	205.4	207.9	209.0	212.2	212.6	209.9	208.6	209.3	208.9	210.5	208.6
2000	204.2	204.0	205.9	208.2	210.6	214.0	214.2	212.0	211.4	211.0	210.8	213.3	209.9
2001	204.4	202.4	202.5	204.3	206.9	209.5	209.1	206.7	205.3	204.4	204.1	204.8	205.4
2002	198.2	196.7	198.2	198.8	199.8	201.8	199.3	196.6	196.1	196.7	197.6	198.5	198.2
2003	193.2	191.8	192.2	194.6	196.6	199.1	197.5	195.2	196.1	196.6	197.6	197.9	195.7
Total private													
1990	172.5	170.7	171.9	171.5	173.1	176.2	174.8	174.7	173.0	171.7	171.6	172.4	172.8
1991	164.0	161.3	163.4	164.0	166.0	168.3	168.6	167.7	165.2	164.8	163.8	165.4	165.2
1992	160.0	158.2	159.5	160.7	162.5	165.2	166.0	165.1	164.0	164.0	163.4	164.7	162.7
1993	162.9	162.0	162.8	163.7	166.2	169.6	169.7	169.0	167.2	168.4	168.7	171.6	166.8
1994	163.8	163.1	164.8	166.8	168.8	171.7	170.3	169.8	169.1	169.9	170.5	173.0	168.4
1995	167.8	166.9	169.4	169.7	171.9	174.7	175.0	175.1	174.9	175.0	177.7	179.9	173.1
1996	172.2	172.1	175.0	175.6	177.5	181.1	180.0	180.7	180.0	181.4	182.8	185.3	178.6
1997	177.5	177.3	179.7	182.1	184.3	187.7	186.4	185.9	185.1	185.5	186.6	189.1	183.9
1998	182.8	183.4	185.2	186.2	188.5	191.7	191.1	189.3	188.8	187.5	188.9	190.8	187.8
1999	187.1	186.3	187.1	189.4	190.5	193.6	194.6	192.4	190.7	190.9	190.2	191.8	190.3
2000	185.8	185.5	187.2	189.4	191.2	194.8	196.0	194.3	192.8	192.4	192.0	194.4	191.3
2001	185.8	183.7	183.9	185.5	187.9	190.1	190.8	188.8	186.0	185.4	184.8	185.4	186.5
2002	179.1	177.5	178.9	179.4	180.3	182.2	182.2	179.9	177.6	177.7	178.2	179.2	179.4
2003	174.0	172.8	173.2	175.7	177.6	179.9	180.4	178.8	177.7	177.7	178.6	179.1	177.1
Goods-producing													
1990	29.8	29.5	29.5	29.2	29.3	29.4	29.4	29.5	29.3	28.2	28.1	28.0	29.1
1991	26.1	25.7	26.0	26.5	27.0	27.5	27.9	27.9	27.5	27.7	27.4	27.2	27.0
1992	26.6	26.2	26.3	26.5	26.7	27.2	27.2	27.2	27.0	26.5	26.2	26.1	26.6
1993	25.1	24.9	25.1	25.0	25.3	25.9	26.0	25.8	25.6	25.2	25.1	25.1	25.3
1994	23.4	23.2	23.3	23.3	23.6	23.9	23.5	23.5	23.5	23.1	23.0	23.3	23.3
1995	22.3	22.1	22.4	22.5	22.8	23.2	23.3	23.6	23.6	23.6	23.9	23.7	23.0
1996	22.3	22.4	22.7	22.0	22.5	23.1	22.2	22.8	22.9	23.0	23.2	23.2	22.6
1997	22.6	22.5	22.8	22.3	22.5	23.0	23.2	23.4	23.1	23.3	23.3	22.8	22.9
1998	22.7	22.8	23.1	22.5	22.9	23.2	22.9	22.7	22.4	22.3	22.0	21.8	22.6
1999	21.4	21.4	21.2	21.7	21.7	22.1	22.4	22.2	22.2	22.2	22.0	21.9	21.8
2000	21.0	20.9	21.2	21.4	21.6	21.7	21.5	21.5	21.4	21.2	21.0	21.0	21.2
2001	19.8	19.8	19.8	20.3	20.5	20.5	20.2	20.2	20.0	19.8	19.7	19.3	20.0
2002	18.7	18.5	18.6	18.8	18.8	18.9	18.5	18.4	18.3	18.3	18.1	17.9	18.5
2003	16.8	16.8	16.7	16.9	17.2	17.3	17.0	16.9	16.6	16.5	16.4	16.4	16.8
Construction and mining													
1990	6.1	6.0	6.0	6.1	6.4	6.9	6.8	6.7	6.6	6.0	5.8	5.6	6.2
1991	4.7	4.4	4.5	5.0	5.3	5.7	5.7	5.7	5.5	5.2	5.1	5.0	5.1
1992	4.4	4.2	4.3	4.5	4.8	5.2	5.3	5.3	5.2	5.1	4.9	4.8	4.8
1993	4.6	4.5	4.6	4.6	4.9	5.2	5.3	5.2	5.0	4.9	4.8	4.8	4.8
1994	4.1	4.0	4.1	4.6	4.9	5.1	5.3	5.4	5.2	5.1	5.0	5.1	4.8
1995	4.5	4.3	4.5	4.9	5.0	5.3	5.3	5.3	5.2	5.2	5.4	5.2	5.0
1996	4.3	4.4	4.6	5.0	5.4	5.9	5.9	5.8	5.7	5.7	5.8	5.7	5.3
1997	5.2	5.1	5.3	5.6	5.8	6.2	6.4	6.2	6.3	6.0	5.9	5.9	5.8
1998	5.4	5.4	5.6	5.9	6.1	6.4	6.4	6.4	6.2	6.3	6.2	6.1	6.0
1999	5.6	5.5	5.5	6.1	6.2	6.5	6.6	6.5	6.4	6.4	6.4	6.3	6.1
2000	5.8	5.7	6.0	6.2	6.4	6.5	6.6	6.6	6.5	6.4	6.4	6.2	6.2
2001	5.5	5.4	5.5	6.0	6.2	6.3	6.6	6.6	6.4	6.4	6.3	6.1	6.1
2002	5.7	5.6	5.8	6.2	6.3	6.5	6.6	6.4	6.3	6.3	6.2	6.0	6.2
2003	5.5	5.4	5.4	5.9	6.2	6.3	6.3	6.2	6.1	6.0	5.9	6.0	5.9
Manufacturing													
1990	23.7	23.5	23.5	23.1	22.9	22.5	22.6	22.8	22.7	22.2	22.3	22.4	22.8
1991	21.4	21.3	21.5	21.5	21.7	21.8	22.2	22.2	22.0	22.5	22.3	22.2	21.8
1992	22.2	22.0	22.0	22.0	21.9	22.0	21.9	21.9	21.8	21.4	21.3	21.3	21.8
1993	20.5	20.4	20.5	20.4	20.4	20.7	20.7	20.6	20.6	20.3	20.3	20.3	20.4
1994	19.3	19.2	19.2	18.7	18.7	18.8	18.2	18.1	18.3	18.0	18.0	18.2	18.5
1995	17.8	17.8	17.9	17.6	17.8	17.9	18.0	18.3	18.4	18.4	18.5	18.5	18.0
1996	18.0	18.0	18.1	17.0	17.1	17.2	16.3	17.0	17.2	17.3	17.4	17.5	17.3
1997	17.4	17.4	17.5	16.7	16.7	16.8	16.8	17.2	16.8	17.3	17.4	16.9	17.0
1998	17.3	17.4	17.5	16.6	16.8	16.8	16.5	16.3	16.2	16.0	15.8	15.7	16.5
1999	15.8	15.9	15.7	15.6	15.5	15.6	15.8	15.7	15.8	15.8	15.6	15.6	15.7
2000	15.2	15.2	15.2	15.2	15.2	15.2	14.9	14.9	14.9	14.8	14.6	14.8	15.0
2001	14.3	14.4	14.3	14.3	14.3	14.2	13.6	13.6	13.6	13.4	13.4	13.2	13.9
2002	13.0	12.9	12.8	12.6	12.5	12.4	11.9	12.0	12.0	12.0	11.9	11.9	12.3
2003	11.3	11.4	11.3	11.0	11.0	11.0	10.7	10.7	10.5	10.5	10.5	10.4	10.9

Employment by Industry: Connecticut—*Continued*

(Numbers in thousands. Not seasonally adjusted.)

Industry	January	February	March	April	May	June	July	August	September	October	November	December	Annual Average
STAMFORD—*Continued*													
Service-providing													
1990	159.8	158.4	159.7	159.6	161.4	164.4	161.5	161.0	160.3	160.2	160.7	161.7	160.7
1991	154.8	152.6	154.5	154.7	156.2	158.2	156.4	155.2	154.0	153.7	153.2	155.2	154.8
1992	149.8	148.6	149.9	151.1	152.8	155.1	154.7	153.2	153.0	153.8	153.9	155.5	152.6
1993	154.2	153.7	154.5	155.3	157.7	160.8	160.2	159.0	158.2	160.1	160.7	163.7	158.1
1994	156.5	156.3	158.0	160.2	162.2	164.9	163.2	162.1	162.4	163.8	164.7	166.8	161.7
1995	162.3	161.8	164.4	164.5	166.5	169.0	168.8	168.0	168.3	168.7	171.6	173.6	167.2
1996	166.9	167.0	169.8	171.3	172.7	175.9	175.4	174.9	174.1	175.9	177.6	180.0	173.4
1997	172.0	172.1	174.5	177.7	179.5	182.4	180.6	179.5	179.4	180.0	181.3	184.4	178.6
1998	177.6	178.4	180.1	181.8	183.5	186.7	185.8	183.6	183.7	182.9	184.9	187.3	183.0
1999	183.8	183.2	184.2	186.2	187.3	190.1	190.2	187.7	186.4	187.1	186.9	188.6	186.8
2000	183.2	183.1	184.7	186.8	189.0	192.3	192.7	190.5	190.0	189.8	189.8	192.3	188.6
2001	184.6	182.6	182.7	184.0	186.4	189.0	188.9	186.5	185.3	184.6	184.4	185.5	185.4
2002	179.5	178.2	179.6	180.0	181.0	182.9	180.8	178.2	177.8	178.4	179.5	180.6	179.7
2003	176.4	175.0	175.5	177.7	179.4	181.8	180.5	178.3	179.5	180.1	181.2	181.5	178.9
Trade, transportation, and utilities													
1990	40.3	39.1	39.3	38.9	39.3	39.4	39.1	38.9	38.9	38.9	39.1	39.8	39.2
1991	37.5	36.0	36.2	36.2	36.3	36.6	36.2	36.0	35.8	35.8	36.3	37.4	36.3
1992	36.0	35.5	35.6	35.4	35.7	35.9	35.4	35.2	35.5	36.0	36.6	37.4	35.8
1993	35.7	35.3	35.1	34.9	35.6	36.4	35.3	35.0	35.2	36.1	36.8	38.5	35.8
1994	36.9	36.2	36.6	36.0	36.4	36.9	35.4	35.3	35.5	36.4	37.1	38.5	36.4
1995	36.6	35.7	36.2	35.0	35.4	36.0	35.8	35.6	35.9	36.3	37.2	38.5	36.1
1996	36.9	36.1	36.7	36.7	36.8	37.3	37.0	36.7	36.9	37.5	38.2	39.4	37.1
1997	36.9	36.3	36.5	37.0	37.5	37.9	37.2	37.2	38.0	38.2	38.9	40.0	37.6
1998	38.4	37.8	38.0	37.4	37.8	38.5	37.9	37.5	37.8	38.0	39.4	40.5	38.2
1999	39.1	38.5	38.6	37.8	38.0	38.5	37.7	37.6	37.7	38.2	38.6	39.7	38.3
2000	37.8	37.6	37.8	37.5	37.8	38.5	38.2	37.8	38.0	38.2	38.7	39.9	38.1
2001	38.0	36.8	36.5	36.5	37.0	37.3	37.1	36.8	36.6	37.4	37.5	38.2	37.1
2002	35.9	35.2	35.5	35.3	35.6	35.9	35.1	34.5	34.8	34.8	35.6	36.4	35.4
2003	34.5	33.7	33.9	34.2	34.6	34.7	34.7	34.1	34.3	34.2	35.0	36.0	34.5
Wholesale trade													
1990	10.5	10.4	10.5	10.2	10.2	10.3	10.2	10.2	10.1	10.0	9.9	10.0	10.2
1991	10.1	10.0	10.1	10.1	9.9	10.0	9.9	9.8	9.7	9.7	9.7	9.8	9.9
1992	9.8	9.8	9.9	9.4	9.5	9.5	9.1	9.1	9.1	9.3	9.3	9.3	9.4
1993	9.3	9.3	9.3	8.9	9.0	9.1	9.0	9.0	9.0	8.9	8.9	9.0	9.0
1994	8.6	8.6	8.9	8.4	8.4	8.4	8.4	8.3	8.4	8.4	8.4	8.5	8.4
1995	8.2	8.2	8.4	8.3	8.4	8.5	8.5	8.5	8.6	8.5	8.5	8.6	8.4
1996	8.5	8.4	8.5	8.5	8.5	8.6	8.5	8.5	8.4	8.5	8.5	8.6	8.5
1997	8.1	8.1	8.1	8.1	8.2	8.2	7.9	7.9	7.9	8.0	8.1	8.1	8.0
1998	7.9	7.9	7.9	8.3	8.2	8.4	8.3	8.3	8.4	8.3	8.4	8.5	8.2
1999	8.2	8.3	8.3	8.1	8.2	8.3	8.1	8.1	8.1	8.2	8.2	8.2	8.1
2000	8.0	8.1	8.1	8.0	8.1	8.2	8.1	8.1	8.0	8.0	8.1	8.2	8.0
2001	8.1	8.1	8.1	8.2	8.3	8.3	8.3	8.3	8.3	8.3	8.4	8.4	8.3
2002	8.1	8.0	8.1	7.9	7.9	7.9	7.8	7.8	7.8	7.8	7.8	7.8	7.9
2003	7.5	7.4	7.4	7.4	7.4	7.4	7.5	7.4	7.4	7.4	7.4	7.4	7.4
Retail trade													
1990	24.7	23.6	23.7	23.6	24.0	23.9	24.1	24.0	23.8	23.9	24.2	24.8	24.0
1991	22.9	21.7	21.8	21.9	22.1	22.3	22.1	22.0	21.9	21.9	22.4	23.3	22.1
1992	21.9	21.4	21.3	21.4	21.5	21.7	21.8	21.6	21.6	21.9	22.5	23.2	21.8
1993	21.7	21.3	21.1	21.3	21.8	22.4	21.7	21.5	21.4	22.2	22.9	24.4	21.9
1994	23.5	22.8	22.8	23.0	23.3	23.8	22.6	22.6	22.5	23.2	23.9	25.1	23.2
1995	23.7	22.8	23.1	22.1	22.4	22.8	22.9	22.7	22.7	23.0	23.9	25.0	23.0
1996	23.5	22.7	23.2	23.2	23.2	23.6	23.5	23.2	23.2	23.7	24.3	25.4	23.5
1997	23.8	23.2	23.4	23.8	24.1	24.4	24.3	24.5	24.7	24.8	25.4	26.4	24.4
1998	25.0	24.4	24.5	23.8	24.2	24.6	24.5	24.2	24.2	24.4	25.4	26.4	24.6
1999	25.2	24.6	24.7	24.3	24.3	24.7	24.5	24.5	24.3	24.7	25.2	26.3	24.7
2000	24.9	24.5	24.8	24.7	24.9	25.4	25.4	25.1	25.1	25.1	25.6	26.6	25.1
2001	25.2	23.9	23.7	23.7	24.1	24.4	24.4	24.2	23.7	24.5	24.5	25.2	24.3
2002	23.3	22.7	22.9	22.8	23.1	23.4	23.0	22.6	22.6	22.5	23.3	24.1	23.0
2003	22.6	22.0	22.1	22.4	22.8	22.9	23.0	22.6	22.5	22.4	23.2	24.0	22.7
Transportation and utilities													
1990	5.1	5.1	5.1	5.1	5.1	5.2	4.8	4.7	5.0	5.0	5.0	5.0	5.0
1991	4.5	4.3	4.3	4.2	4.3	4.3	4.2	4.2	4.2	4.2	4.2	4.3	4.2
1992	4.3	4.3	4.4	4.6	4.7	4.7	4.5	4.5	4.8	4.8	4.8	4.9	4.6
1993	4.7	4.7	4.7	4.7	4.8	4.9	4.6	4.5	4.8	5.0	5.0	5.1	4.7
1994	4.8	4.8	4.9	4.6	4.7	4.7	4.4	4.4	4.6	4.8	4.8	4.9	4.7
1995	4.7	4.7	4.7	4.6	4.6	4.7	4.4	4.4	4.6	4.8	4.8	4.9	4.6
1996	4.9	5.0	5.0	5.0	5.1	5.1	5.0	5.0	5.3	5.3	5.4	5.4	5.1
1997	5.0	5.0	5.0	5.1	5.2	5.3	5.0	4.8	5.4	5.4	5.4	5.5	5.1
1998	5.5	5.5	5.6	5.3	5.4	5.5	5.1	5.0	5.2	5.3	5.6	5.6	5.3
1999	5.7	5.6	5.6	5.4	5.5	5.5	5.1	5.0	5.3	5.3	5.2	5.2	5.3
2000	4.9	5.0	4.9	4.8	4.8	4.9	4.7	4.6	4.9	5.1	5.0	5.1	4.8
2001	4.7	4.8	4.7	4.6	4.6	4.6	4.4	4.3	4.6	4.6	4.6	4.6	4.6
2002	4.5	4.5	4.5	4.6	4.6	4.6	4.3	4.1	4.4	4.5	4.5	4.5	4.5
2003	4.4	4.3	4.4	4.4	4.4	4.4	4.2	4.1	4.4	4.4	4.4	4.6	4.4

Employment by Industry: Connecticut—*Continued*

(Numbers in thousands. Not seasonally adjusted.)

Industry	January	February	March	April	May	June	July	August	September	October	November	December	Annual Average
STAMFORD—*Continued*													
Information													
1990	7.2	7.2	7.2	7.0	6.9	7.1	7.0	7.0	6.8	6.8	6.7	6.8	6.9
1991	6.8	6.7	6.7	6.4	6.4	6.4	6.4	6.3	6.3	6.3	6.3	6.4	6.4
1992	6.2	6.2	6.3	6.3	6.3	6.4	6.4	6.5	6.4	6.4	6.4	6.4	6.3
1993	6.6	6.6	6.6	6.3	6.3	6.5	6.5	6.5	6.4	6.8	6.8	6.8	6.5
1994	6.6	6.6	6.7	6.8	6.9	6.9	6.8	6.7	6.5	6.4	6.5	6.6	6.6
1995	6.7	6.7	6.8	7.1	7.2	7.4	7.4	7.4	7.4	7.6	7.7	7.9	7.2
1996	7.8	7.8	7.9	8.1	8.1	8.2	8.1	8.2	8.3	8.3	8.4	8.5	8.1
1997	8.4	8.5	8.6	8.6	8.6	8.7	8.5	8.5	8.4	8.7	8.7	8.8	8.5
1998	8.8	8.9	8.9	8.9	8.9	8.9	9.2	9.1	8.9	9.1	9.1	9.2	8.9
1999	9.1	9.1	9.1	9.0	9.0	9.2	9.0	9.0	9.1	9.1	9.2	9.2	9.0
2000	9.0	9.0	9.1	9.2	9.2	9.3	9.5	9.4	9.3	9.3	9.4	9.5	9.2
2001	9.2	9.3	9.2	9.1	9.0	8.9	8.4	8.4	8.3	8.2	8.1	8.1	8.7
2002	7.3	7.2	7.1	7.0	6.9	6.8	6.8	6.7	6.6	6.6	6.6	6.6	6.9
2003	6.6	6.5	6.6	6.5	6.5	6.6	6.5	6.5	6.5	6.5	6.5	6.5	6.5
Financial activities													
1990	19.9	20.0	20.1	19.9	19.9	20.3	20.2	20.3	20.0	19.9	20.0	20.0	20.0
1991	19.3	19.2	19.4	19.4	19.7	19.9	20.2	20.2	19.9	19.8	19.5	19.9	19.7
1992	18.0	18.0	18.1	18.5	18.7	19.0	18.7	18.7	18.5	18.7	18.7	19.0	18.5
1993	18.7	18.7	18.8	19.2	19.3	19.7	19.9	19.7	19.4	19.7	19.8	20.0	19.4
1994	19.7	19.6	19.7	20.1	20.2	20.5	20.4	20.5	20.5	20.4	20.4	20.7	20.2
1995	20.4	20.3	20.4	20.4	20.6	21.1	21.2	21.2	21.3	21.4	21.8	21.9	21.0
1996	22.2	22.4	22.5	22.2	22.0	22.5	22.2	22.3	21.9	22.0	22.0	22.4	22.2
1997	21.9	22.0	22.2	22.8	23.0	23.5	23.3	23.2	23.0	23.5	23.8	24.4	23.0
1998	23.7	24.2	24.4	24.6	24.8	25.1	25.3	25.3	25.2	25.0	25.1	25.3	24.8
1999	24.8	24.9	25.0	25.5	25.7	26.2	26.6	26.5	26.3	26.4	26.2	26.2	25.8
2000	26.0	26.0	26.2	26.3	26.6	26.9	27.2	27.3	27.0	27.2	27.3	27.7	26.8
2001	26.7	26.9	26.8	26.8	26.9	27.1	27.2	27.4	27.2	27.0	27.2	27.2	27.0
2002	27.0	27.2	27.2	26.9	27.0	27.2	27.3	27.3	26.9	26.9	26.9	27.2	27.1
2003	26.7	26.6	26.5	26.8	26.9	27.2	27.3	27.1	27.0	27.3	27.3	27.5	27.0
Professional and business services													
1990	37.8	37.8	37.9	38.2	38.5	39.5	38.5	38.5	38.3	38.9	38.8	38.8	38.4
1991	37.7	37.3	37.9	38.2	38.6	38.7	39.0	38.9	38.3	38.0	37.4	37.4	38.1
1992	37.1	36.6	37.1	37.2	37.5	37.7	37.6	37.6	37.3	37.8	37.5	37.5	37.3
1993	38.3	38.3	38.6	39.1	39.5	40.3	40.5	40.0	39.7	40.3	40.1	40.6	39.6
1994	38.9	39.3	39.6	40.8	41.4	42.1	41.6	41.7	41.7	42.8	42.8	42.4	41.2
1995	41.7	41.9	42.5	42.9	43.4	43.8	43.8	43.8	44.0	44.1	44.4	44.7	43.4
1996	42.3	42.8	43.7	44.3	44.7	45.2	45.6	46.0	45.8	46.5	46.9	47.2	45.0
1997	44.9	45.0	45.8	47.2	47.7	48.5	48.2	48.5	48.3	47.8	47.9	48.4	47.3
1998	46.4	46.7	47.4	49.0	49.2	50.1	49.7	49.9	50.1	49.6	49.7	49.8	48.9
1999	49.0	48.9	49.4	50.3	50.6	51.2	51.2	50.7	50.4	50.4	50.0	50.2	50.1
2000	48.8	49.0	49.8	50.4	50.9	51.9	52.1	51.8	51.7	50.8	50.4	50.6	50.6
2001	48.4	47.3	47.5	48.0	49.0	49.0	49.3	48.7	48.0	47.4	46.6	46.2	48.0
2002	44.7	44.3	44.8	44.9	44.8	45.2	44.9	44.8	44.5	44.5	44.5	44.3	44.7
2003	43.9	43.9	43.7	45.0	45.1	45.3	44.8	45.1	45.6	45.3	45.5	44.8	44.8
Educational and health services													
1990	17.2	17.2	17.3	17.5	17.7	17.9	17.7	17.7	17.9	18.2	18.3	18.4	17.7
1991	18.1	18.2	18.4	18.0	18.0	17.9	17.5	17.4	17.5	17.6	17.7	17.7	17.8
1992	17.6	17.6	17.6	17.8	17.8	18.0	18.4	18.2	18.4	18.4	18.5	18.7	18.0
1993	18.9	19.0	19.2	19.2	19.3	18.4	18.7	19.5	19.6	19.5	19.5	19.7	19.2
1994	19.2	19.2	19.4	19.4	19.3	19.4	19.8	19.6	19.9	19.9	20.0	20.4	19.6
1995	19.8	20.0	20.2	20.0	20.0	20.0	19.8	20.1	19.9	20.1	20.2	20.3	20.0
1996	19.8	19.7	19.9	20.2	20.3	20.6	20.4	20.4	20.8	21.0	21.0	21.1	20.4
1997	20.8	20.9	21.2	21.6	21.6	21.5	21.2	20.8	21.1	21.1	21.2	21.3	21.1
1998	20.7	20.9	20.9	21.0	21.2	21.2	21.0	20.4	21.0	20.9	21.1	21.1	20.9
1999	20.9	20.9	20.9	21.0	21.0	21.1	21.3	20.9	20.9	20.7	20.7	20.9	20.9
2000	21.1	21.1	20.9	21.3	21.3	21.4	21.6	21.2	21.3	21.5	21.4	21.6	21.3
2001	20.9	20.9	21.0	21.1	20.8	21.3	21.8	21.4	21.4	21.5	21.6	21.7	21.3
2002	22.1	22.0	22.1	22.2	22.2	22.3	22.8	22.3	22.2	22.3	22.4	22.5	22.3
2003	22.3	22.2	22.2	22.1	22.2	22.3	22.9	22.6	22.5	22.7	22.9	22.8	22.5
Leisure and hospitality													
1990	13.0	12.5	13.1	13.6	14.2	15.2	15.3	15.4	14.8	14.0	13.9	13.9	14.0
1991	12.2	11.9	12.5	13.0	13.6	14.8	14.6	14.3	13.5	13.3	12.9	13.1	13.3
1992	12.2	11.8	12.2	12.6	13.2	14.3	15.2	14.8	14.1	13.5	12.7	12.7	13.2
1993	12.6	12.1	12.2	12.9	13.7	15.0	15.3	15.2	14.2	13.7	13.5	13.7	13.6
1994	12.2	12.1	12.6	13.3	13.8	14.7	15.3	15.1	14.3	13.6	13.5	13.7	13.6
1995	13.1	12.9	13.5	14.5	15.1	15.6	15.9	15.7	15.3	14.6	15.1	15.3	14.7
1996	13.6	13.5	14.1	14.6	15.5	16.3	16.7	16.5	15.7	15.5	15.4	15.7	15.2
1997	14.4	14.4	14.8	14.8	15.5	16.5	16.5	16.1	15.3	14.9	14.7	15.2	15.2
1998	14.0	14.0	14.4	15.0	15.8	16.5	16.8	16.4	15.6	14.7	14.6	15.1	15.2
1999	14.8	14.6	14.9	15.9	16.3	17.1	17.8	17.2	16.1	15.7	15.4	15.6	15.9
2000	14.3	14.1	14.4	15.3	15.7	16.9	17.3	16.9	16.0	16.0	15.6	15.8	15.6
2001	14.4	14.2	14.5	14.9	15.8	16.9	17.2	16.6	15.5	15.0	15.0	15.5	15.5
2002	14.5	14.2	14.7	15.5	16.0	16.9	17.5	16.8	15.6	15.5	15.2	15.3	15.6
2003	14.5	14.4	14.8	15.4	16.2	17.5	17.9	17.4	16.4	16.3	16.1	16.1	16.1

Employment by Industry: Connecticut—*Continued*

(Numbers in thousands. Not seasonally adjusted.)

Industry	January	February	March	April	May	June	July	August	September	October	November	December	Annual Average
STAMFORD—*Continued*													
Service-providing													
1990	159.8	158.4	159.7	159.6	161.4	164.4	161.5	161.0	160.3	160.2	160.7	161.7	160.7
1991	154.8	152.6	154.5	154.7	156.2	158.2	156.4	155.2	154.0	153.7	153.2	155.2	154.8
1992	149.8	148.6	149.9	151.1	152.8	155.1	154.7	153.2	153.0	153.8	153.9	155.5	152.6
1993	154.2	153.7	154.5	155.3	157.7	160.8	160.2	159.0	158.2	160.1	160.7	163.7	158.1
1994	156.5	156.3	158.0	160.2	162.2	164.9	163.2	162.1	162.4	163.8	164.7	166.8	161.7
1995	162.3	161.8	164.4	164.5	166.5	169.0	168.8	168.0	168.3	168.7	171.6	173.6	167.2
1996	166.9	167.0	169.8	171.3	172.7	175.9	175.4	174.9	174.1	175.9	177.6	180.0	173.4
1997	172.0	172.1	174.5	177.7	179.5	182.4	180.6	179.5	179.4	180.0	181.3	184.4	178.6
1998	177.6	178.4	180.1	181.8	183.5	186.7	185.8	183.6	183.7	182.9	184.9	187.3	183.0
1999	183.8	183.2	184.2	186.2	187.3	190.1	190.2	187.7	186.4	187.1	186.9	188.6	186.8
2000	183.2	183.1	184.7	186.8	189.0	192.3	192.7	190.5	190.0	189.8	189.8	192.3	188.6
2001	184.6	182.6	182.7	184.0	186.4	189.0	188.9	186.5	185.3	184.6	184.4	185.5	185.4
2002	179.5	178.2	179.6	180.0	181.0	182.9	180.8	178.2	177.8	178.4	179.5	180.6	179.7
2003	176.4	175.0	175.5	177.7	179.4	181.8	180.5	178.3	179.5	180.1	181.2	181.5	178.9
Trade, transportation, and utilities													
1990	40.3	39.1	39.3	38.9	39.3	39.4	39.1	38.9	38.9	38.9	39.1	39.8	39.2
1991	37.5	36.0	36.2	36.2	36.3	36.6	36.2	36.0	35.8	35.8	36.3	37.4	36.3
1992	36.0	35.5	35.6	35.4	35.7	35.9	35.4	35.2	35.5	36.0	36.6	37.4	35.8
1993	35.7	35.3	35.1	34.9	35.6	36.4	35.3	35.0	35.2	36.1	36.8	38.5	35.8
1994	36.9	36.2	36.6	36.0	36.4	36.9	35.4	35.3	35.5	36.4	37.1	38.5	36.4
1995	36.6	35.7	36.2	35.0	35.4	36.0	35.8	35.6	35.9	36.3	37.2	38.5	36.1
1996	36.9	36.1	36.7	36.7	36.8	37.3	37.0	36.7	36.9	37.5	38.2	39.4	37.1
1997	36.9	36.3	36.5	37.0	37.5	37.9	37.2	37.2	38.0	38.2	38.9	40.0	37.6
1998	38.4	37.8	38.0	37.4	37.8	38.5	37.9	37.5	37.8	38.0	39.4	40.5	38.2
1999	39.1	38.5	38.6	37.8	38.0	38.5	37.7	37.6	37.7	38.2	38.6	39.7	38.3
2000	37.8	37.6	37.8	37.5	37.8	38.5	38.2	37.8	38.0	38.2	38.7	39.9	38.1
2001	38.0	36.8	36.5	36.5	37.0	37.3	37.1	36.8	36.6	37.4	37.5	38.2	37.1
2002	35.9	35.2	35.5	35.3	35.6	35.9	35.1	34.5	34.8	34.8	35.6	36.4	35.4
2003	34.5	33.7	33.9	34.2	34.6	34.7	34.7	34.1	34.3	34.2	35.0	36.0	34.5
Wholesale trade													
1990	10.5	10.4	10.5	10.2	10.2	10.3	10.2	10.2	10.1	10.0	9.9	10.0	10.2
1991	10.1	10.0	10.1	10.1	9.9	10.0	9.9	9.8	9.7	9.7	9.7	9.8	9.9
1992	9.8	9.8	9.9	9.4	9.5	9.5	9.1	9.1	9.1	9.3	9.3	9.3	9.4
1993	9.3	9.3	9.3	8.9	9.0	9.1	9.0	9.0	9.0	8.9	8.9	9.0	9.0
1994	8.6	8.6	8.9	8.4	8.4	8.4	8.4	8.3	8.4	8.4	8.4	8.5	8.4
1995	8.2	8.2	8.4	8.3	8.4	8.5	8.5	8.5	8.6	8.5	8.5	8.6	8.4
1996	8.5	8.4	8.5	8.5	8.5	8.6	8.5	8.5	8.4	8.5	8.5	8.6	8.5
1997	8.1	8.1	8.1	8.1	8.2	8.2	7.9	7.9	7.9	8.0	8.1	8.1	8.0
1998	7.9	7.9	7.9	8.3	8.2	8.4	8.3	8.3	8.4	8.3	8.4	8.5	8.2
1999	8.2	8.3	8.3	8.1	8.2	8.3	8.1	8.1	8.1	8.2	8.2	8.2	8.1
2000	8.0	8.1	8.1	8.0	8.1	8.2	8.1	8.1	8.0	8.0	8.1	8.2	8.0
2001	8.1	8.1	8.1	8.2	8.3	8.3	8.3	8.3	8.3	8.3	8.4	8.4	8.3
2002	8.1	8.0	8.1	7.9	7.9	7.9	7.8	7.8	7.8	7.8	7.8	7.8	7.9
2003	7.5	7.4	7.4	7.4	7.4	7.4	7.5	7.4	7.4	7.4	7.4	7.4	7.4
Retail trade													
1990	24.7	23.6	23.7	23.6	24.0	23.9	24.1	24.0	23.8	23.9	24.2	24.8	24.0
1991	22.9	21.7	21.8	21.9	22.1	22.3	22.1	22.0	21.9	21.9	22.4	23.3	22.1
1992	21.9	21.4	21.3	21.4	21.5	21.7	21.8	21.6	21.6	21.9	22.5	23.2	21.8
1993	21.7	21.3	21.1	21.3	21.8	22.4	21.7	21.5	21.4	22.2	22.9	24.4	21.9
1994	23.5	22.8	22.8	23.0	23.3	23.8	22.6	22.6	22.5	23.2	23.9	25.1	23.2
1995	23.7	22.8	23.1	22.1	22.4	22.8	22.9	22.7	22.7	23.0	23.9	25.0	23.0
1996	23.5	22.7	23.2	23.2	23.2	23.6	23.5	23.2	23.2	23.7	24.3	25.4	23.5
1997	23.8	23.2	23.4	23.8	24.1	24.4	24.3	24.5	24.7	24.8	25.4	26.4	24.4
1998	25.0	24.4	24.5	23.8	24.2	24.6	24.5	24.2	24.2	24.4	25.4	26.4	24.6
1999	25.2	24.6	24.7	24.3	24.3	24.7	24.5	24.5	24.3	24.7	25.2	26.3	24.7
2000	24.9	24.5	24.8	24.7	24.9	25.4	25.4	25.1	25.1	25.1	25.6	26.6	25.1
2001	25.2	23.9	23.7	23.7	24.1	24.4	24.4	24.2	23.7	24.5	24.5	25.2	24.3
2002	23.3	22.7	22.9	22.8	23.1	23.4	23.0	22.6	22.6	22.5	23.3	24.1	23.0
2003	22.6	22.0	22.1	22.4	22.8	22.9	23.0	22.6	22.5	22.4	23.2	24.0	22.7
Transportation and utilities													
1990	5.1	5.1	5.1	5.1	5.1	5.2	4.8	4.7	5.0	5.0	5.0	5.0	5.0
1991	4.5	4.3	4.3	4.2	4.3	4.3	4.2	4.2	4.2	4.2	4.2	4.3	4.2
1992	4.3	4.3	4.4	4.6	4.7	4.7	4.5	4.5	4.8	4.8	4.8	4.9	4.6
1993	4.7	4.7	4.7	4.7	4.8	4.9	4.6	4.5	4.8	5.0	5.0	5.1	4.7
1994	4.8	4.8	4.9	4.6	4.7	4.7	4.4	4.4	4.6	4.8	4.8	4.9	4.7
1995	4.7	4.7	4.7	4.6	4.6	4.7	4.4	4.4	4.6	4.8	4.8	4.9	4.6
1996	4.9	5.0	5.0	5.0	5.1	5.1	5.0	5.0	5.3	5.3	5.4	5.4	5.1
1997	5.0	5.0	5.0	5.1	5.2	5.3	5.0	4.8	5.4	5.4	5.4	5.5	5.1
1998	5.5	5.5	5.6	5.3	5.4	5.5	5.1	5.0	5.2	5.3	5.6	5.6	5.3
1999	5.7	5.6	5.6	5.4	5.5	5.5	5.1	5.0	5.3	5.3	5.2	5.2	5.3
2000	4.9	5.0	4.9	4.8	4.8	4.9	4.7	4.6	4.9	5.1	5.0	5.1	4.8
2001	4.7	4.8	4.7	4.6	4.6	4.6	4.4	4.3	4.6	4.6	4.6	4.6	4.6
2002	4.5	4.5	4.5	4.6	4.6	4.6	4.3	4.1	4.4	4.5	4.5	4.5	4.5
2003	4.4	4.3	4.4	4.4	4.4	4.4	4.2	4.1	4.4	4.4	4.4	4.6	4.4

Employment by Industry: Connecticut—*Continued*

(Numbers in thousands. Not seasonally adjusted.)

Industry	January	February	March	April	May	June	July	August	September	October	November	December	Annual Average
STAMFORD—*Continued*													
Information													
1990	7.2	7.2	7.2	7.0	6.9	7.1	7.0	7.0	6.8	6.8	6.7	6.8	6.9
1991	6.8	6.7	6.7	6.4	6.4	6.4	6.4	6.3	6.3	6.3	6.3	6.4	6.4
1992	6.2	6.2	6.3	6.3	6.3	6.4	6.4	6.5	6.4	6.4	6.4	6.4	6.3
1993	6.6	6.6	6.6	6.3	6.3	6.5	6.5	6.5	6.4	6.8	6.8	6.8	6.5
1994	6.6	6.6	6.7	6.8	6.9	6.9	6.8	6.7	6.5	6.4	6.5	6.6	6.6
1995	6.7	6.7	6.8	7.1	7.2	7.4	7.4	7.4	7.4	7.6	7.7	7.9	7.2
1996	7.8	7.8	7.9	8.1	8.1	8.2	8.1	8.2	8.3	8.3	8.4	8.5	8.1
1997	8.4	8.5	8.6	8.6	8.6	8.7	8.5	8.5	8.4	8.7	8.7	8.8	8.5
1998	8.8	8.9	8.9	8.9	8.9	8.9	9.2	9.1	8.9	9.1	9.1	9.2	8.9
1999	9.1	9.1	9.1	9.0	9.0	9.2	9.0	9.0	9.1	9.1	9.2	9.2	9.0
2000	9.0	9.0	9.1	9.2	9.2	9.3	9.5	9.4	9.3	9.3	9.4	9.5	9.2
2001	9.2	9.3	9.2	9.1	9.0	8.9	8.4	8.4	8.3	8.2	8.1	8.1	8.7
2002	7.3	7.2	7.1	7.0	6.9	6.8	6.8	6.7	6.6	6.6	6.6	6.6	6.9
2003	6.6	6.5	6.6	6.5	6.5	6.6	6.5	6.5	6.5	6.5	6.5	6.5	6.5
Financial activities													
1990	19.9	20.0	20.1	19.9	19.9	20.3	20.2	20.3	20.0	19.9	20.0	20.0	20.0
1991	19.3	19.2	19.4	19.4	19.7	19.9	20.2	20.2	19.9	19.8	19.5	19.9	19.7
1992	18.0	18.0	18.1	18.5	18.7	19.0	18.7	18.7	18.5	18.7	18.7	19.0	18.5
1993	18.7	18.7	18.8	19.2	19.3	19.7	19.9	19.7	19.4	19.7	19.8	20.0	19.4
1994	19.7	19.6	19.7	20.1	20.2	20.5	20.4	20.5	20.5	20.4	20.4	20.7	20.2
1995	20.4	20.3	20.4	20.4	20.6	21.1	21.2	21.2	21.3	21.4	21.8	21.9	21.0
1996	22.2	22.4	22.5	22.2	22.0	22.5	22.2	22.3	21.9	22.0	22.0	22.4	22.2
1997	21.9	22.0	22.2	22.8	23.0	23.5	23.3	23.2	23.0	23.5	23.8	24.4	23.0
1998	23.7	24.2	24.4	24.6	24.8	25.1	25.3	25.3	25.2	25.0	25.1	25.3	24.8
1999	24.8	24.9	25.0	25.5	25.7	26.2	26.6	26.5	26.3	26.4	26.2	26.2	25.8
2000	26.0	26.0	26.2	26.3	26.6	26.9	27.2	27.3	27.0	27.2	27.3	27.7	26.8
2001	26.7	26.9	26.8	26.8	26.9	27.1	27.2	27.4	27.2	27.0	27.2	27.2	27.0
2002	27.0	27.2	27.2	26.9	27.0	27.2	27.3	27.3	26.9	26.9	26.9	27.2	27.1
2003	26.7	26.6	26.5	26.8	26.9	27.2	27.3	27.1	27.0	27.3	27.3	27.5	27.0
Professional and business services													
1990	37.8	37.8	37.9	38.2	38.5	39.5	38.5	38.5	38.3	38.9	38.8	38.8	38.4
1991	37.7	37.3	37.9	38.2	38.6	38.7	39.0	38.9	38.3	38.0	37.4	37.4	38.1
1992	37.1	36.6	37.1	37.2	37.5	37.7	37.6	37.6	37.3	37.8	37.5	37.5	37.3
1993	38.3	38.3	38.6	39.1	39.5	40.3	40.5	40.0	39.7	40.3	40.1	40.6	39.6
1994	38.9	39.3	39.6	40.8	41.4	42.1	41.6	41.7	41.7	42.8	42.8	42.4	41.2
1995	41.7	41.9	42.5	42.9	43.4	43.8	43.8	43.8	44.0	44.1	44.4	44.7	43.4
1996	42.3	42.8	43.7	44.3	44.7	45.2	45.6	46.0	45.8	46.5	46.9	47.2	45.0
1997	44.9	45.0	45.8	47.2	47.7	48.5	48.2	48.5	48.3	47.8	47.9	48.4	47.3
1998	46.4	46.7	47.4	49.0	49.2	50.1	49.7	49.9	50.1	49.6	49.7	49.8	48.9
1999	49.0	48.9	49.4	50.3	50.6	51.2	51.2	50.7	50.4	50.4	50.0	50.2	50.1
2000	48.8	49.0	49.8	50.4	50.9	51.9	52.1	51.8	51.7	50.8	50.4	50.6	50.6
2001	48.4	47.3	47.5	48.0	49.0	49.0	49.3	48.7	48.0	47.4	46.6	46.2	48.0
2002	44.7	44.3	44.8	44.9	44.8	45.2	44.9	44.8	44.5	44.5	44.5	44.3	44.7
2003	43.9	43.9	43.7	45.0	45.1	45.3	44.8	45.1	45.6	45.3	45.5	44.8	44.8
Educational and health services													
1990	17.2	17.2	17.3	17.5	17.7	17.9	17.7	17.7	17.9	18.2	18.3	18.4	17.7
1991	18.1	18.2	18.4	18.0	18.0	17.9	17.5	17.4	17.5	17.6	17.7	17.7	17.8
1992	17.6	17.6	17.6	17.8	17.8	18.0	18.4	18.2	18.4	18.4	18.5	18.7	18.0
1993	18.9	19.0	19.2	19.2	19.3	18.4	18.7	19.5	19.6	19.5	19.5	19.7	19.2
1994	19.2	19.2	19.4	19.4	19.3	19.4	19.8	19.6	19.9	19.9	20.0	20.4	19.6
1995	19.8	20.0	20.2	20.0	20.0	20.0	19.8	20.1	19.9	20.1	20.2	20.3	20.0
1996	19.8	19.7	19.9	20.2	20.3	20.6	20.4	20.4	20.8	21.0	21.0	21.1	20.4
1997	20.8	20.9	21.2	21.6	21.6	21.5	21.2	20.8	21.1	21.1	21.2	21.3	21.1
1998	20.7	20.9	20.9	21.0	21.2	21.2	21.0	20.4	21.0	20.9	21.1	21.1	20.9
1999	20.9	20.9	20.9	21.0	21.0	21.1	21.3	20.9	20.9	20.7	20.7	20.9	20.9
2000	21.1	21.1	20.9	21.3	21.3	21.4	21.6	21.2	21.3	21.5	21.4	21.6	21.3
2001	20.9	20.9	21.0	21.1	20.8	21.3	21.8	21.4	21.4	21.5	21.6	21.7	21.3
2002	22.1	22.0	22.1	22.2	22.2	22.3	22.8	22.3	22.2	22.3	22.4	22.5	22.3
2003	22.3	22.2	22.2	22.1	22.2	22.3	22.9	22.6	22.5	22.7	22.9	22.8	22.5
Leisure and hospitality													
1990	13.0	12.5	13.1	13.6	14.2	15.2	15.3	15.4	14.8	14.0	13.9	13.9	14.0
1991	12.2	11.9	12.5	13.0	13.6	14.8	14.6	14.3	13.5	13.3	12.9	13.1	13.3
1992	12.2	11.8	12.2	12.6	13.2	14.3	15.2	14.8	14.1	13.5	12.7	12.7	13.2
1993	12.6	12.1	12.2	12.9	13.7	15.0	15.3	15.2	14.2	13.7	13.5	13.7	13.6
1994	12.2	12.1	12.6	13.3	13.8	14.7	15.3	15.1	14.3	13.6	13.5	13.7	13.6
1995	13.1	12.9	13.5	14.5	15.1	15.6	15.9	15.7	15.3	14.6	15.1	15.3	14.7
1996	13.6	13.5	14.1	14.6	15.5	16.3	16.7	16.5	15.7	15.5	15.4	15.7	15.2
1997	14.4	14.4	14.8	14.8	15.5	16.5	16.5	16.1	15.3	14.9	14.7	15.2	15.2
1998	14.0	14.0	14.4	15.0	15.8	16.5	16.8	16.4	15.6	14.7	14.6	15.1	15.2
1999	14.8	14.6	14.9	15.9	16.3	17.1	17.8	17.2	16.1	15.7	15.4	15.6	15.9
2000	14.3	14.1	14.4	15.3	15.7	16.9	17.3	16.9	16.0	16.0	15.6	15.8	15.6
2001	14.4	14.2	14.5	14.9	15.8	16.9	17.2	16.6	15.5	15.0	15.0	15.5	15.5
2002	14.5	14.2	14.7	15.5	16.0	16.9	17.5	16.8	15.6	15.5	15.2	15.3	15.6
2003	14.5	14.4	14.8	15.4	16.2	17.5	17.9	17.4	16.4	16.3	16.1	16.1	16.1

Employment by Industry: Connecticut—*Continued*

(Numbers in thousands. Not seasonally adjusted.)

Industry	January	February	March	April	May	June	July	August	September	October	November	December	Annual Average
STAMFORD—*Continued*													
Other services													
1990	7.3	7.4	7.5	7.2	7.3	7.4	7.6	7.4	7.0	6.8	6.7	6.7	7.1
1991	6.3	6.3	6.3	6.3	6.4	6.5	6.8	6.7	6.4	6.3	6.3	6.3	6.4
1992	6.3	6.3	6.3	6.4	6.6	6.7	7.1	6.9	6.8	6.7	6.8	6.9	6.6
1993	7.0	7.1	7.2	7.1	7.2	7.4	7.5	7.3	7.1	7.1	7.1	7.2	7.1
1994	6.9	6.9	6.9	7.1	7.2	7.3	7.5	7.4	7.2	7.3	7.2	7.4	7.1
1995	7.2	7.3	7.4	7.3	7.4	7.6	7.8	7.7	7.5	7.3	7.4	7.6	7.4
1996	7.3	7.4	7.5	7.5	7.6	7.9	7.8	7.8	7.7	7.6	7.7	7.8	7.6
1997	7.6	7.7	7.8	7.8	7.9	8.1	8.3	8.2	7.9	8.0	8.1	8.2	7.9
1998	8.1	8.1	8.1	7.8	7.9	8.2	8.3	8.0	7.8	7.9	7.9	8.0	8.0
1999	8.0	8.0	8.0	8.2	8.2	8.2	8.6	8.3	8.0	8.2	8.1	8.1	8.1
2000	7.8	7.8	7.8	8.0	8.1	8.2	8.6	8.4	8.1	8.2	8.2	8.3	8.1
2001	8.4	8.5	8.6	8.8	8.9	9.1	9.6	9.3	9.0	9.1	9.1	9.2	9.0
2002	8.9	8.9	8.9	8.8	9.0	9.0	9.3	9.1	8.7	8.8	8.9	9.0	8.9
2003	8.7	8.7	8.8	8.8	8.9	9.0	9.3	9.1	8.8	8.9	8.9	9.0	8.9
Government													
1990	17.1	17.2	17.3	17.3	17.6	17.6	16.1	15.8	16.6	16.7	17.2	17.3	16.9
1991	16.9	17.0	17.1	17.2	17.2	17.4	15.7	15.4	16.3	16.6	16.8	17.0	16.7
1992	16.4	16.6	16.7	16.9	17.0	17.1	15.9	15.3	16.0	16.3	16.7	16.9	16.4
1993	16.4	16.6	16.8	16.6	16.8	17.1	16.5	15.8	16.6	16.9	17.1	17.2	16.7
1994	16.1	16.4	16.5	16.7	17.0	17.1	16.4	15.8	16.8	17.0	17.2	17.1	16.6
1995	16.8	17.0	17.4	17.3	17.4	17.5	17.1	16.5	17.0	17.3	17.8	17.4	17.2
1996	17.0	17.3	17.5	17.7	17.7	17.9	17.6	17.0	17.0	17.5	18.0	17.9	17.5
1997	17.1	17.3	17.6	17.9	17.7	17.7	17.4	17.0	17.4	17.8	18.0	18.1	17.5
1998	17.5	17.8	18.0	18.1	17.9	18.2	17.6	17.0	17.3	17.7	18.0	18.3	17.7
1999	18.1	18.3	18.3	18.5	18.5	18.6	18.0	17.5	17.9	18.4	18.7	18.7	18.2
2000	18.4	18.5	18.7	18.8	19.4	19.2	18.2	17.7	18.6	18.6	18.8	18.9	18.6
2001	18.6	18.7	18.6	18.8	19.0	19.4	18.3	17.9	19.3	19.0	19.3	19.4	18.9
2002	19.1	19.2	19.3	19.4	19.5	19.6	17.1	16.7	18.5	19.0	19.4	19.3	18.8
2003	19.2	19.0	19.0	18.9	19.0	19.2	17.1	16.4	18.4	18.9	19.0	18.8	18.6
Federal government													
1990	2.1	2.1	2.1	2.2	2.4	2.3	2.4	2.2	2.1	2.1	2.1	2.1	2.1
1991	2.1	2.1	2.1	2.0	2.0	2.0	2.0	2.0	2.0	2.0	1.9	2.0	2.0
1992	2.0	2.0	2.0	2.0	2.0	2.0	1.9	1.9	1.9	1.9	1.9	2.0	1.9
1993	1.9	1.9	1.9	1.9	1.8	1.9	1.9	1.9	1.9	1.9	1.9	2.0	1.9
1994	1.9	1.9	1.9	1.9	1.9	1.9	1.9	1.9	1.9	1.9	1.9	2.0	1.9
1995	1.9	1.9	1.9	1.9	1.9	1.9	1.9	1.9	1.9	1.9	1.9	2.0	1.9
1996	1.9	1.9	1.9	1.9	1.9	1.9	1.8	1.8	1.8	1.8	1.8	2.0	1.8
1997	1.9	1.9	1.9	1.9	1.9	1.9	1.9	1.9	1.9	1.9	1.9	2.0	1.9
1998	1.9	1.9	1.9	1.9	1.9	1.9	1.9	1.9	1.9	1.9	1.9	2.1	1.9
1999	2.0	2.0	1.9	2.0	1.9	1.9	1.9	1.9	1.9	1.9	1.9	2.0	1.9
2000	2.0	1.9	2.0	2.1	2.6	2.2	1.9	1.9	1.9	1.8	1.8	1.9	2.0
2001	1.8	1.8	1.8	1.8	1.8	1.8	1.8	1.8	1.8	1.8	1.8	1.9	1.8
2002	1.8	1.8	1.8	1.8	1.7	1.7	1.7	1.7	1.7	1.7	1.7	1.8	1.7
2003	1.7	1.7	1.7	1.7	1.7	1.7	1.7	1.7	1.7	1.7	1.7	1.7	1.7
State government													
2001	1.6	1.6	1.6	1.6	1.6	1.6	1.5	1.4	1.4	1.6	1.6	1.6	1.6
2002	1.6	1.6	1.6	1.6	1.6	1.6	1.4	1.4	1.4	1.6	1.6	1.6	1.6
2003	1.6	1.6	1.5	1.5	1.5	1.5	1.3	1.3	1.3	1.5	1.5	1.5	1.5
Local government													
2001	15.2	15.3	15.2	15.4	15.6	16.0	15.0	14.7	16.1	15.6	15.9	15.9	15.5
2002	15.7	15.8	15.9	16.0	16.2	16.3	14.0	13.6	15.4	15.7	16.1	15.9	15.6
2003	15.9	15.7	15.8	15.7	15.8	16.0	14.1	13.4	15.4	15.7	15.8	15.6	15.4

Average Weekly Hours by Industry: Connecticut

(Not seasonally adjusted.)

Industry	January	February	March	April	May	June	July	August	September	October	November	December	Annual Average
STATEWIDE													
Construction													
2001	39.0	39.1	39.0	38.4	40.4	40.4	40.1	40.2	39.7	40.1	39.2	38.7	39.6
2002	38.4	39.0	39.6	40.0	40.0	40.4	40.9	40.8	40.1	40.2	39.2	39.7	39.9
2003	39.2	38.8	39.7	38.4	40.3	39.7	40.3	40.4	40.1	40.0	39.0	39.4	39.7
Manufacturing													
2001	42.1	41.6	42.0	40.9	41.7	41.7	41.5	41.5	42.1	42.3	41.9	40.9	41.7
2002	41.8	41.3	41.5	41.6	41.4	42.1	41.0	41.4	42.0	41.8	41.9	41.9	41.6
2003	41.6	41.1	41.3	41.3	41.2	41.1	40.5	40.8	41.9	41.8	42.3	42.5	41.4
BRIDGEPORT-MILFORD													
Manufacturing													
2001	40.4	40.0	40.8	40.2	41.5	42.0	40.9	41.1	41.7	43.0	42.3	41.7	41.3
2002	42.1	40.7	42.2	41.6	42.0	42.6	40.7	41.2	41.8	41.6	42.2	40.6	41.6
2003	41.3	40.5	40.5	40.0	40.6	39.9	39.9	39.7	39.8	39.6	40.5	42.5	40.4
HARTFORD													
Manufacturing													
2001	43.7	43.3	43.7	41.4	42.7	42.8	42.2	42.1	42.5	42.9	43.0	39.4	42.5
2002	41.9	41.3	40.7	41.3	41.2	42.3	41.9	42.4	42.8	42.2	42.6	43.4	42.0
2003	42.5	42.1	42.9	42.8	43.0	42.4	41.3	41.3	43.0	42.2	42.6	43.2	42.5
NEW HAVEN-MERIDEN													
Manufacturing													
2001	42.3	42.8	43.0	42.9	43.3	42.4	41.9	42.9	42.6	42.1	41.9	42.4	42.6
2002	43.5	43.4	43.7	43.3	43.0	43.3	42.7	43.1	43.2	43.7	43.7	43.8	43.4
2003	42.5	40.9	42.4	42.8	42.8	43.3	42.0	41.5	41.2	41.0	41.7	43.1	42.1
NEW LONDON-NORWICH													
Manufacturing													
2001	42.3	41.2	43.2	41.5	41.3	42.5	41.3	40.6	42.7	42.8	41.8	42.2	41.9
2002	42.1	40.9	42.0	41.8	41.5	41.9	41.2	40.6	41.6	42.2	41.3	42.1	41.6
2003	42.0	40.2	42.1	41.3	41.5	41.6	41.3	41.0	42.0	42.4	42.2	42.0	41.6

Average Hourly Earnings by Industry: Connecticut

(Dollars, not seasonally adjusted.)

Industry	January	February	March	April	May	June	July	August	September	October	November	December	Annual Average
STATEWIDE													
Construction													
2001	21.59	21.38	21.68	21.82	22.03	22.11	21.96	22.18	22.26	22.30	21.90	22.12	21.96
2002	22.35	22.00	22.00	21.93	22.01	22.19	22.38	22.65	22.31	22.26	22.22	22.15	22.21
2003	22.54	22.52	22.54	22.57	22.59	22.82	22.96	22.50	22.85	22.72	22.92	22.84	22.71
Manufacturing													
2001	16.05	16.16	16.31	16.40	16.30	16.34	16.54	16.50	16.56	16.68	16.75	16.46	16.42
2002	16.99	16.91	17.14	17.21	17.09	17.18	17.26	17.22	17.44	17.45	17.37	17.67	17.24
2003	17.25	17.42	17.73	17.58	17.68	17.74	17.89	17.79	17.97	17.95	17.94	18.02	17.74
BRIDGEPORT-MILFORD													
Manufacturing													
2001	15.45	15.25	15.16	15.75	15.01	15.32	15.18	15.20	15.55	15.32	15.97	16.05	15.43
2002	16.34	16.00	16.84	16.97	16.95	17.33	17.58	17.47	17.82	18.24	18.35	18.95	17.36
2003	17.90	18.06	18.29	18.18	18.66	18.71	19.24	18.75	19.44	19.18	19.39	19.68	18.79
HARTFORD													
Manufacturing													
2001	16.82	16.98	17.29	17.29	17.25	17.20	17.76	17.54	17.30	17.50	17.56	16.96	17.28
2002	17.65	17.72	17.90	17.93	17.87	17.89	17.95	17.86	17.89	17.96	18.00	18.48	17.93
2003	17.92	18.25	18.61	18.20	18.80	18.63	19.05	18.91	19.19	19.06	18.94	19.47	18.75
NEW HAVEN-MERIDEN													
Manufacturing													
2001	16.54	16.66	16.89	17.01	17.06	17.13	17.49	17.90	17.91	17.81	17.62	17.30	17.27
2002	17.79	17.46	17.81	17.62	17.44	17.36	17.54	17.22	17.37	16.79	16.72	17.12	17.36
2003	17.45	17.12	17.27	17.31	17.09	17.27	17.09	16.69	16.08	16.17	15.64	16.14	16.78
NEW LONDON-NORWICH													
Manufacturing													
2001	16.71	16.60	16.85	17.14	17.08	16.92	17.18	17.05	16.98	17.26	17.21	17.18	17.01
2002	17.47	17.29	17.32	17.35	17.61	17.83	18.12	17.88	17.92	17.95	17.95	17.51	17.68
2003	17.34	17.81	17.49	17.58	17.71	17.81	17.93	18.04	18.17	18.14	18.07	18.25	17.87

Average Weekly Earnings by Industry: Connecticut

(Dollars, not seasonally adjusted.)

Industry	January	February	March	April	May	June	July	August	September	October	November	December	Annual Average
STATEWIDE													
Construction													
2001	842.01	835.96	845.52	837.89	890.01	893.24	880.60	891.64	883.72	894.23	858.48	856.04	869.62
2002	858.24	858.00	871.20	877.20	880.40	896.48	915.34	924.12	894.63	894.85	871.02	879.36	886.18
2003	883.57	873.78	894.84	866.69	910.38	905.95	925.29	909.00	916.29	908.80	893.88	899.90	901.59
Manufacturing													
2001	675.71	672.26	685.02	670.76	679.71	681.38	686.41	684.75	697.18	705.56	701.83	673.21	684.71
2002	710.18	698.38	711.31	715.94	707.53	723.28	707.66	712.91	732.48	729.41	727.80	740.37	717.18
2003	717.60	715.96	732.25	726.05	728.42	729.11	724.55	725.83	752.94	750.31	758.86	765.85	734.44
BRIDGEPORT-MILFORD													
Manufacturing													
2001	624.18	610.00	618.53	633.15	622.92	643.44	620.86	624.72	648.44	658.76	675.53	669.29	637.26
2002	687.91	651.20	710.65	705.95	711.90	738.26	715.51	719.76	744.88	758.78	774.37	769.37	722.18
2003	739.27	731.43	740.75	727.20	757.60	746.53	767.68	744.38	773.71	759.53	785.30	836.40	759.12
HARTFORD													
Manufacturing													
2001	735.03	735.23	755.57	715.81	736.58	736.16	749.47	738.43	735.25	750.75	755.08	668.22	734.40
2002	739.54	731.84	728.53	740.51	736.24	756.75	752.11	757.26	765.69	757.91	766.80	802.03	753.06
2003	761.60	768.33	798.37	778.96	808.40	789.91	786.77	780.98	825.17	804.33	806.84	841.10	796.88
NEW HAVEN-MERIDEN													
Manufacturing													
2001	699.64	713.05	726.27	729.73	738.70	726.31	732.83	767.91	762.97	749.80	738.28	733.52	735.70
2002	773.87	757.76	778.30	762.95	749.92	751.69	748.96	742.18	750.38	733.72	730.66	749.86	753.42
2003	741.63	700.21	732.25	740.87	731.45	747.79	717.78	692.64	662.50	662.97	652.19	695.63	706.44
NEW LONDON-NORWICH													
Manufacturing													
2001	706.83	683.92	727.92	711.31	705.40	719.10	709.53	692.23	725.05	738.73	719.38	725.00	712.72
2002	735.49	707.16	727.44	725.23	730.82	747.08	746.54	725.93	745.47	757.49	741.34	737.17	735.49
2003	728.28	715.96	736.33	726.05	734.97	740.90	740.51	739.64	763.14	769.14	762.55	766.50	743.39

DELAWARE AT A GLANCE

(Population and total nonfarm employment numbers in thousands)

Population, Census 2000:	783.6
Total nonfarm employment, 2003:	413.6
Change in total nonfarm employment	
(Number)	
1990–2003:	66.2
1990–2001:	72.0
2001–2003:	-5.8
(Compound annual rate of change)	
1990–2003:	1.4%
1990–2001:	1.7%
2001–2003:	-0.7%
Unemployment rate	
1990:	4.2%
2001:	3.5%
2003:	4.0%

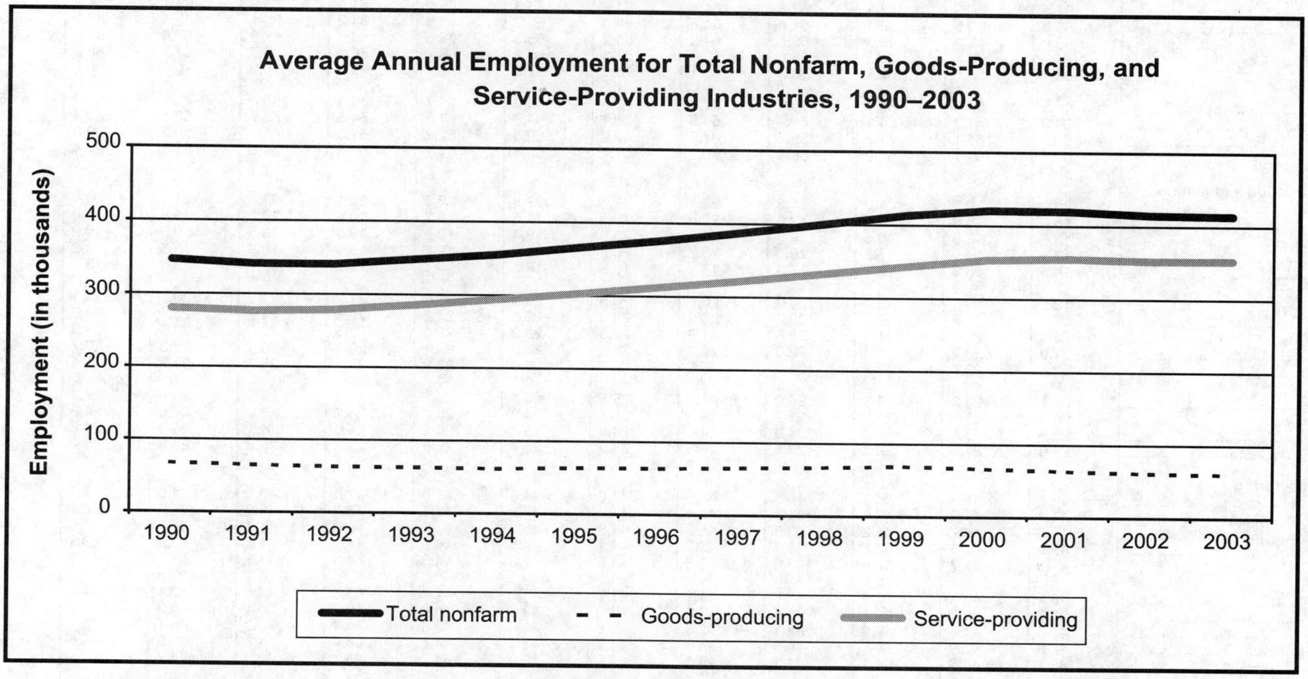

The 1990–1991 recession caused nonfarm payroll employment to dip early in the decade, which was followed by a long expansion that ended with the 2001 recession. With a relatively small goods-producing sector in Delaware, these trends reflected patterns in the private service-providing sector. In 2003, professional and business services employed 59,000, which was down considerably from 2000. However, it remains one of Delaware's leading sectors of employment.

Employment by Industry: Delaware

(Numbers in thousands. Not seasonally adjusted.)

Industry	January	February	March	April	May	June	July	August	September	October	November	December	Annual Average
STATEWIDE													
Total nonfarm													
1990	335.2	341.4	345.4	346.8	351.7	355.0	350.7	352.7	351.0	348.3	345.4	346.2	347.4
1991	338.0	332.4	341.6	336.1	346.2	349.7	344.6	340.5	341.3	343.5	343.7	343.8	341.7
1992	331.8	329.7	333.0	339.8	344.6	348.4	345.4	345.2	342.8	341.2	346.6	347.4	341.3
1993	336.3	337.3	339.1	346.3	350.7	355.1	353.7	353.0	354.1	351.2	352.7	354.9	348.7
1994	341.8	341.4	345.7	350.9	356.1	361.8	358.0	361.9	361.5	361.2	364.3	365.7	355.8
1995	353.8	354.5	359.0	362.6	366.7	369.9	369.1	372.2	371.4	370.4	371.9	374.0	366.2
1996	355.7	363.8	366.1	375.2	381.5	386.1	381.0	379.9	379.5	379.6	382.8	384.6	376.3
1997	372.5	373.8	378.7	383.5	388.2	394.8	391.1	393.8	392.4	391.7	395.0	399.4	387.9
1998	386.0	386.2	390.9	396.0	400.6	406.8	403.5	407.2	406.7	403.0	405.2	410.4	400.2
1999	396.5	398.4	404.2	410.2	413.4	418.1	416.7	418.8	416.1	417.9	421.3	423.5	412.9
2000	407.0	408.9	415.2	417.8	421.2	426.6	425.8	423.5	422.4	421.8	424.1	425.9	420.0
2001	410.9	412.3	419.7	419.8	422.9	427.2	422.9	421.5	417.9	417.8	419.9	419.8	419.4
2002	403.5	405.1	407.9	411.6	417.3	419.3	418.6	417.9	419.5	415.8	418.3	418.9	414.5
2003	403.1	400.4	404.6	409.6	415.6	421.3	417.2	417.2	418.6	417.9	418.9	418.6	413.6
Total private													
1990	288.5	292.9	296.4	297.6	302.2	307.1	304.5	307.7	304.5	299.5	296.3	297.4	299.5
1991	290.2	284.1	292.3	286.7	296.7	301.4	298.0	295.2	295.9	295.2	294.7	294.6	293.7
1992	283.2	281.4	283.6	289.9	295.5	299.5	298.3	298.6	296.2	291.9	296.6	297.5	292.6
1993	288.0	287.7	288.6	295.6	300.3	304.9	306.1	305.8	305.2	301.0	301.8	303.5	299.0
1994	292.6	291.0	294.6	299.6	304.8	311.2	309.0	312.9	312.8	310.6	313.0	313.7	305.4
1995	303.5	303.9	307.6	311.0	315.1	318.9	319.6	323.0	322.1	319.7	320.1	321.6	315.5
1996	304.9	312.1	313.0	321.7	327.8	333.1	330.4	329.3	328.3	326.7	329.1	330.5	323.9
1997	320.4	320.7	324.6	329.5	333.9	341.2	339.6	342.1	341.1	338.4	340.9	344.7	334.7
1998	332.7	332.2	335.9	340.8	345.3	352.2	350.7	354.3	353.2	348.5	349.6	354.4	345.8
1999	342.2	344.0	348.4	354.0	357.3	363.4	362.9	365.9	362.4	362.2	364.6	366.6	357.8
2000	352.7	353.2	357.7	360.0	362.9	369.4	368.9	368.8	367.2	365.3	366.4	368.1	363.3
2001	354.7	355.3	361.5	361.3	364.8	370.3	366.4	366.8	363.2	361.2	362.4	362.1	362.5
2002	347.8	348.1	350.2	353.7	359.6	363.1	363.8	364.5	362.0	357.2	359.0	359.9	357.4
2003	346.4	343.1	346.9	351.4	357.0	364.1	362.4	363.5	360.9	358.9	359.9	359.2	356.1
Goods-producing													
1990	62.3	66.8	67.7	67.8	68.9	69.7	67.4	70.8	69.9	68.6	65.1	64.8	67.4
1991	65.3	59.8	65.9	61.1	67.4	67.2	67.1	66.2	64.6	66.3	65.2	64.1	65.0
1992	60.9	60.6	60.7	62.9	64.7	64.9	64.4	64.8	64.2	60.2	64.0	63.6	62.9
1993	61.4	61.2	61.0	62.7	64.0	64.4	64.4	64.2	63.9	62.9	62.4	61.7	62.8
1994	59.1	58.0	58.9	60.6	61.6	62.5	60.8	64.0	64.0	63.8	64.1	63.7	61.7
1995	61.4	60.9	62.3	63.8	64.7	61.9	63.3	65.0	64.5	65.2	64.1	64.3	63.4
1996	55.8	60.5	58.1	64.6	64.8	66.0	65.3	63.8	64.2	65.1	65.4	65.1	63.2
1997	63.4	62.3	63.0	63.7	64.2	65.1	65.3	66.5	66.9	67.6	67.6	68.4	65.3
1998	64.7	63.8	65.5	66.6	67.0	67.9	66.2	68.7	68.2	67.7	67.1	68.3	66.8
1999	66.4	66.5	67.4	68.9	69.1	70.0	67.9	70.1	69.6	70.0	70.0	69.8	68.8
2000	64.3	64.8	66.1	66.3	67.0	68.3	66.5	66.7	66.4	66.8	65.8	65.4	66.2
2001	60.9	61.3	64.1	64.4	64.8	66.1	64.8	64.8	64.5	63.7	63.8	63.3	63.9
2002	60.5	61.1	61.2	59.7	61.8	62.2	62.3	62.2	61.9	61.1	60.8	60.8	61.3
2003	57.5	57.1	57.9	58.6	60.2	61.7	60.4	61.1	61.3	61.6	61.5	60.4	59.9
Construction and mining													
1990	20.2	20.5	21.3	21.8	22.4	22.7	22.8	22.8	22.1	21.5	21.1	20.4	21.6
1991	18.0	18.0	18.7	19.6	20.0	19.5	19.6	19.2	19.4	20.1	18.8	18.0	19.0
1992	16.3	15.9	16.5	19.0	20.5	20.3	19.4	19.6	19.3	19.5	19.5	19.2	18.7
1993	17.5	17.4	17.5	19.6	20.7	20.3	19.9	19.7	19.5	18.7	18.5	18.2	18.9
1994	16.0	15.3	16.1	17.6	18.3	18.9	19.5	19.7	19.7	19.7	20.0	19.8	18.3
1995	18.2	17.6	18.7	20.0	20.6	20.2	20.1	20.6	21.2	21.8	20.7	20.1	19.9
1996	17.1	17.9	19.0	20.2	20.9	22.0	22.8	23.2	23.5	24.7	25.1	24.7	21.7
1997	22.1	20.9	21.0	21.6	21.9	22.3	22.9	23.0	22.5	22.6	22.5	23.3	22.2
1998	21.9	20.9	21.0	22.0	22.3	23.0	23.8	24.1	23.8	23.4	23.3	23.7	22.7
1999	22.3	22.7	23.3	24.8	25.0	25.4	25.9	25.9	25.5	25.7	25.3	25.4	24.7
2000	24.1	23.2	24.5	24.9	24.8	25.5	25.1	25.1	24.9	25.5	24.5	24.2	24.6
2001	23.0	23.1	23.6	23.9	24.4	25.4	24.8	25.2	25.1	25.0	25.5	24.9	24.5
2002	23.4	23.1	23.2	24.0	24.4	24.9	25.3	25.1	24.6	24.1	24.0	24.2	24.2
2003	23.0	21.6	22.2	23.4	24.3	24.9	25.4	25.5	25.2	25.3	25.3	25.2	24.3
Manufacturing													
1990	42.1	46.3	46.4	46.0	46.5	47.0	44.6	48.0	47.8	47.1	44.0	44.4	45.8
1991	47.3	41.8	47.2	41.5	47.4	47.7	47.5	47.0	45.2	46.2	46.4	46.1	45.9
1992	44.6	44.7	44.2	43.9	44.2	44.6	45.0	45.2	44.9	40.7	44.5	44.4	44.2
1993	43.9	43.8	43.5	43.1	43.3	44.1	44.5	44.5	44.4	44.2	43.9	43.5	43.8
1994	43.1	42.7	42.8	43.0	43.3	43.6	41.3	44.3	44.3	44.1	44.1	43.9	43.3
1995	43.2	43.3	43.6	43.8	44.1	41.7	43.2	44.4	43.3	43.4	43.4	44.2	43.4
1996	38.7	42.6	39.1	44.4	43.9	44.0	42.5	40.6	40.7	40.4	40.3	40.4	41.4
1997	41.3	41.4	42.0	42.1	42.3	42.8	42.4	43.5	44.4	45.0	45.1	45.1	43.1
1998	42.8	42.9	44.5	44.6	44.7	44.9	42.4	44.6	44.4	44.3	43.8	44.6	44.0
1999	44.1	43.8	44.1	44.1	44.1	44.6	42.0	44.2	44.1	44.3	44.7	44.4	44.0
2000	40.2	41.6	41.6	41.4	42.2	42.8	41.4	41.6	41.5	41.3	41.3	41.2	41.5
2001	37.9	38.2	40.5	40.5	40.4	40.7	40.0	39.6	39.4	38.7	38.3	38.4	39.4
2002	37.1	38.0	38.0	35.7	37.4	37.3	37.0	37.1	37.3	37.0	36.8	36.6	37.1
2003	34.5	35.5	35.7	35.2	35.9	36.8	35.0	35.6	36.1	36.3	36.2	35.2	35.7

Employment by Industry: Delaware—*Continued*

(Numbers in thousands. Not seasonally adjusted.)

Industry	January	February	March	April	May	June	July	August	September	October	November	December	Annual Average
STATEWIDE—*Continued*													
Service-providing													
1990	272.9	274.6	277.7	279.0	282.8	285.3	283.3	281.9	281.1	279.7	280.3	281.4	280.0
1991	272.7	272.6	275.7	275.0	278.8	282.5	277.5	274.3	276.7	277.2	278.5	279.7	276.7
1992	270.9	269.1	272.3	276.9	279.9	283.5	281.0	280.4	278.6	281.0	282.6	283.8	278.3
1993	274.9	276.1	278.1	283.6	286.7	290.7	289.3	288.8	290.2	288.3	290.3	293.2	285.8
1994	282.7	283.4	286.8	290.3	294.5	299.3	297.2	297.9	297.5	297.4	300.2	302.0	294.1
1995	292.4	293.6	296.7	298.8	302.0	308.0	305.8	307.2	306.9	305.2	307.8	309.7	302.8
1996	299.9	303.3	308.0	310.6	316.7	320.1	315.7	316.1	315.3	314.5	317.4	319.5	313.0
1997	309.1	311.5	315.7	319.8	324.0	329.7	325.8	327.3	325.5	324.1	327.4	331.0	322.5
1998	321.3	322.4	325.4	329.4	333.6	338.9	337.3	338.5	338.5	335.3	338.1	342.1	333.4
1999	330.1	331.9	336.8	341.3	344.3	348.1	348.8	348.7	346.5	347.9	351.3	353.7	344.1
2000	342.7	344.1	349.1	351.5	354.2	358.3	359.3	356.8	356.0	355.0	358.3	360.5	353.8
2001	350.0	351.0	355.6	355.4	358.1	361.1	358.1	356.7	353.4	354.1	356.1	356.5	355.5
2002	343.0	344.0	346.7	351.9	355.5	357.1	356.3	355.7	357.6	354.7	357.5	358.1	353.2
2003	345.6	343.3	346.7	351.0	355.4	359.6	356.8	356.1	357.3	356.3	357.4	358.2	353.6
Trade, transportation, and utilities													
1990	67.5	65.7	66.5	66.6	66.9	67.7	67.6	67.5	67.6	67.4	68.7	69.7	67.4
1991	65.5	64.4	64.4	64.4	65.0	66.4	64.7	64.1	65.8	64.9	66.1	67.6	65.2
1992	64.0	63.0	63.1	63.7	64.3	65.4	64.3	64.3	64.5	65.7	67.2	68.3	64.8
1993	64.7	63.6	63.7	64.9	65.7	66.2	66.6	66.6	67.2	67.7	69.3	70.9	66.4
1994	66.6	65.7	66.5	67.4	68.3	69.1	68.6	68.5	68.5	69.3	71.5	72.9	68.5
1995	68.8	67.9	68.6	69.1	70.0	71.2	70.8	71.1	71.4	71.7	73.1	74.0	70.6
1996	69.9	69.3	69.8	70.3	71.7	72.5	71.8	71.4	71.2	72.0	73.6	75.3	71.5
1997	70.8	70.1	70.5	71.4	72.3	73.3	71.7	71.8	72.2	72.9	75.0	76.9	72.4
1998	72.5	71.5	72.0	72.8	73.8	74.7	74.3	75.0	76.2	76.2	78.0	79.5	74.7
1999	75.1	74.2	75.6	76.6	77.6	78.8	78.7	79.0	78.5	79.2	81.1	82.3	78.0
2000	77.4	76.6	76.7	77.9	78.5	79.7	79.6	79.4	79.5	79.4	80.9	83.0	79.0
2001	76.7	76.0	76.6	75.3	75.7	77.0	76.3	76.2	76.1	77.2	78.3	79.4	76.7
2002	74.9	74.2	75.1	75.4	76.9	77.8	77.8	77.7	77.9	77.3	79.0	80.4	77.0
2003	76.1	75.1	76.2	76.9	78.0	79.2	78.8	79.1	78.8	78.6	80.2	80.9	78.2
Wholesale trade													
1990	11.7	11.5	11.6	11.6	11.7	11.7	11.9	11.8	11.9	11.7	11.7	11.7	11.7
1991	11.7	11.5	11.4	11.4	11.3	11.6	11.4	11.3	11.5	11.2	11.2	11.1	11.3
1992	11.0	11.0	11.1	11.0	11.0	11.1	10.9	10.9	10.9	11.0	10.9	10.9	10.9
1993	10.9	10.9	10.9	11.0	11.0	11.1	11.3	11.3	11.2	11.2	11.2	11.2	11.1
1994	11.1	11.1	11.2	11.3	11.3	11.3	11.6	11.5	11.6	11.5	11.7	11.8	11.4
1995	11.5	11.6	11.8	11.9	12.0	12.2	12.0	11.9	11.8	11.6	11.6	11.7	11.8
1996	11.8	11.9	12.0	12.0	12.1	12.2	12.1	11.9	12.0	12.1	11.8	11.9	11.9
1997	11.8	11.9	11.9	12.0	12.1	12.2	12.1	12.0	12.0	12.0	12.1	12.1	12.0
1998	12.2	12.2	12.2	12.4	12.4	12.5	12.4	12.4	12.3	12.3	12.3	12.4	12.3
1999	12.2	12.2	12.3	12.4	12.5	12.6	12.5	12.6	12.5	12.5	12.6	12.7	12.4
2000	12.7	12.8	12.9	13.3	13.2	13.3	13.4	13.5	13.5	13.6	13.6	13.7	13.2
2001	13.4	13.5	13.6	13.3	13.3	13.4	13.3	13.3	13.3	13.4	13.3	13.4	13.4
2002	13.3	13.2	13.6	13.5	13.7	13.8	13.8	13.9	13.8	13.7	13.6	13.7	13.6
2003	13.6	13.6	13.9	14.1	14.3	14.3	14.4	14.5	14.6	14.4	14.5	14.4	14.2
Retail trade													
1990	43.7	42.3	42.5	42.7	43.0	43.6	43.8	44.1	43.6	43.6	45.0	46.0	43.6
1991	42.2	41.2	41.1	41.4	42.1	42.9	42.0	42.0	42.5	42.0	43.3	44.5	42.2
1992	41.3	40.5	40.4	41.1	41.7	42.5	42.3	42.5	42.1	42.8	44.4	45.4	42.2
1993	42.0	41.1	40.8	41.5	42.3	42.6	43.1	43.1	43.0	43.5	44.8	46.3	42.8
1994	42.3	41.2	41.6	42.4	43.4	44.4	44.1	44.2	44.0	44.8	47.0	48.2	43.9
1995	44.8	43.9	44.2	44.4	45.2	46.0	46.3	47.0	47.0	47.4	48.9	49.9	46.2
1996	46.3	45.2	45.6	45.8	46.8	47.6	47.5	47.5	47.0	47.4	49.4	51.0	47.2
1997	47.3	46.3	46.7	47.1	47.6	48.2	47.5	47.6	47.3	47.7	49.4	51.1	47.8
1998	46.9	45.5	45.8	46.4	47.4	48.2	48.4	48.8	49.4	49.4	51.2	52.7	48.3
1999	48.9	47.7	48.9	49.5	50.2	51.2	51.7	51.8	51.0	51.9	53.7	54.9	50.9
2000	50.3	49.4	49.4	50.2	50.9	52.2	52.2	51.9	51.7	51.5	53.1	55.0	51.4
2001	50.4	49.7	50.1	49.1	49.6	50.7	50.4	50.6	50.2	50.7	52.1	53.3	50.6
2002	49.6	48.7	49.3	49.7	50.7	51.7	51.9	51.9	51.6	51.0	52.8	54.2	51.1
2003	50.0	49.0	49.8	50.5	51.3	52.5	52.5	52.9	51.9	51.7	53.1	54.1	51.6
Transportation and utilities													
1990	12.1	11.9	12.4	12.3	12.2	12.4	11.9	11.6	12.1	12.1	12.0	12.0	12.0
1991	11.6	11.7	11.9	11.6	11.6	11.9	11.3	10.8	11.8	11.7	11.6	12.0	11.6
1992	11.7	11.5	11.6	11.6	11.6	11.8	11.1	10.9	11.5	11.9	11.9	12.0	11.5
1993	11.8	11.6	12.0	12.4	12.4	12.5	12.2	12.2	13.0	13.0	13.3	13.4	12.4
1994	13.2	13.4	13.7	13.7	13.6	13.4	12.9	12.8	12.9	13.0	12.8	12.9	13.1
1995	12.5	12.4	12.6	12.8	12.8	13.0	12.5	12.2	12.6	12.7	12.6	12.4	12.5
1996	11.8	12.2	12.2	12.5	12.8	12.7	12.2	12.0	12.2	12.5	12.4	12.4	12.3
1997	11.7	11.9	11.9	12.3	12.6	12.9	12.1	12.2	12.9	13.2	13.5	13.7	12.5
1998	13.4	13.8	14.0	14.0	14.0	14.0	13.5	13.8	14.5	14.5	14.5	14.4	14.0
1999	14.0	14.3	14.4	14.7	14.9	15.0	14.5	14.6	15.0	14.8	14.8	14.7	14.6
2000	14.4	14.4	14.4	14.4	14.4	14.2	14.0	14.0	14.3	14.3	14.2	14.3	14.2
2001	12.9	12.8	12.9	12.9	12.8	12.9	12.6	12.3	12.6	13.1	12.9	12.7	12.8
2002	12.0	12.3	12.2	12.2	12.6	12.3	12.1	11.9	12.5	12.6	12.6	12.5	12.3
2003	12.5	12.5	12.5	12.3	12.4	12.4	11.9	11.7	12.3	12.5	12.6	12.4	12.3

Employment by Industry: Delaware—*Continued*

(Numbers in thousands. Not seasonally adjusted.)

Industry	January	February	March	April	May	June	July	August	September	October	November	December	Annual Average
STATEWIDE—*Continued*													
Information													
1990	4.9	5.0	5.0	5.0	5.0	5.1	5.1	5.1	5.0	4.9	4.9	4.9	4.9
1991	4.7	4.6	4.5	4.4	4.4	4.4	4.3	4.3	4.3	4.1	4.2	4.2	4.3
1992	4.0	4.1	4.0	4.0	4.1	4.1	4.1	4.1	4.0	4.1	4.1	4.1	4.0
1993	4.0	3.9	3.9	4.0	4.0	4.1	4.1	4.1	4.1	4.1	4.3	4.4	4.0
1994	4.5	4.5	4.5	4.5	4.6	4.7	4.8	4.9	4.9	4.8	4.9	4.9	4.7
1995	5.3	5.4	5.5	4.9	5.0	5.1	5.1	5.2	5.1	5.2	5.1	5.1	5.1
1996	5.1	5.1	5.1	5.3	5.3	5.3	5.3	5.3	5.3	5.5	5.5	5.7	5.3
1997	5.6	5.8	5.7	5.7	6.0	7.0	7.0	7.1	7.0	6.9	7.0	7.1	6.4
1998	7.0	7.2	7.2	7.2	7.3	7.4	7.4	7.5	7.5	7.3	7.4	7.4	7.3
1999	7.6	7.8	7.8	7.7	7.8	7.9	7.9	8.0	8.0	7.9	8.0	8.1	7.8
2000	8.1	8.3	8.4	8.0	8.1	8.1	8.3	7.6	8.3	8.1	8.2	8.2	8.1
2001	8.0	8.0	8.1	8.1	8.1	8.2	8.2	8.2	8.1	7.9	8.0	8.0	8.1
2002	7.8	7.8	7.8	7.7	7.7	7.8	7.8	7.9	7.7	7.6	7.7	7.6	7.7
2003	7.5	7.5	7.5	7.4	7.4	7.4	7.4	7.5	7.3	7.2	7.3	7.3	7.4
Financial activities													
1990	26.6	26.8	26.8	26.9	27.5	27.9	28.1	28.2	27.9	27.2	27.1	27.3	27.3
1991	29.1	29.3	29.2	29.1	29.4	29.9	29.8	29.8	29.9	29.8	29.8	29.9	29.5
1992	29.8	30.0	30.2	30.0	30.3	30.7	30.6	30.7	30.5	30.2	30.3	30.4	30.3
1993	30.0	30.3	30.6	31.0	31.3	31.7	32.1	32.3	32.4	31.7	31.8	31.9	31.4
1994	31.4	31.6	31.9	31.8	32.3	33.0	33.2	33.5	33.5	33.3	33.2	33.2	32.6
1995	33.0	33.2	33.7	33.5	33.8	34.3	34.2	34.5	34.5	34.0	34.0	34.2	33.9
1996	33.8	34.2	34.7	34.9	35.1	35.3	35.4	35.7	35.5	35.2	35.3	35.5	35.0
1997	35.0	35.2	35.6	35.8	36.0	36.9	36.7	37.1	36.8	36.3	36.6	36.9	36.2
1998	37.7	38.0	37.6	37.1	37.5	38.3	38.3	38.4	37.9	38.1	38.4	38.9	38.0
1999	38.7	38.9	39.0	38.6	38.4	39.2	39.8	39.8	39.3	39.3	39.4	39.5	39.1
2000	38.8	39.0	38.9	38.7	38.8	39.3	39.4	39.6	39.1	38.9	39.2	39.4	39.0
2001	39.4	39.5	39.7	40.0	40.0	40.3	40.6	40.5	39.8	38.5	38.3	38.1	39.6
2002	38.8	38.7	38.9	39.1	38.9	38.9	39.2	39.0	38.4	38.0	38.1	38.0	38.7
2003	45.5	45.3	45.2	45.6	45.6	45.8	46.5	46.0	45.3	44.9	44.9	44.9	45.5
Professional and business services													
1990	59.0	59.5	60.2	60.2	60.5	60.8	60.6	60.1	59.5	58.9	58.7	58.9	59.7
1991	56.4	56.1	57.1	55.5	55.8	56.2	55.7	55.1	55.5	55.7	55.4	55.0	55.7
1992	53.2	52.4	53.0	53.9	54.1	54.2	55.2	55.5	55.4	54.9	55.0	55.4	54.3
1993	53.9	54.5	54.8	55.7	55.8	56.7	56.5	56.4	56.2	55.1	55.4	55.7	55.5
1994	54.3	54.9	55.4	55.8	56.1	56.5	56.1	56.7	57.3	56.8	57.1	57.6	56.2
1995	56.1	57.1	57.0	57.4	57.4	58.1	58.7	59.7	59.6	59.9	60.4	60.9	58.5
1996	59.3	60.5	61.3	60.7	62.1	63.3	62.6	63.0	63.2	62.1	62.8	62.7	61.9
1997	61.4	62.2	63.3	64.3	64.1	65.1	65.1	65.6	65.8	64.9	64.9	65.5	64.3
1998	63.9	64.0	64.8	66.4	66.7	68.6	69.1	69.2	69.0	67.4	67.7	68.5	67.1
1999	65.2	66.7	67.7	68.5	68.7	69.4	70.1	70.3	70.0	70.7	71.4	72.7	69.2
2000	72.3	72.2	73.3	72.9	72.5	73.5	74.0	74.3	74.3	74.0	74.5	74.7	73.5
2001	73.8	73.8	74.5	73.2	73.4	73.5	72.0	72.7	72.1	72.5	73.3	72.9	73.1
2002	68.9	68.5	68.0	68.4	68.6	67.9	68.4	68.8	68.7	68.3	68.5	69.1	68.5
2003	59.1	57.9	58.2	58.4	58.8	59.2	59.0	58.9	59.4	59.5	59.6	59.9	59.0
Educational and health services													
1990	31.9	32.3	32.7	32.5	32.7	32.9	32.7	33.1	33.6	33.6	33.7	33.9	32.9
1991	33.6	34.1	34.3	33.9	34.1	34.1	34.3	34.0	34.8	34.9	35.3	35.4	34.4
1992	35.2	35.1	35.4	35.9	36.1	36.0	35.8	35.6	35.8	36.5	36.6	36.6	35.8
1993	36.2	36.5	36.5	37.1	37.0	36.9	37.0	37.0	37.6	38.0	38.0	38.2	37.1
1994	38.1	38.1	38.2	38.5	38.8	38.6	38.5	38.6	39.1	39.6	39.9	39.7	38.8
1995	39.1	39.5	39.6	39.7	39.8	39.8	39.4	39.8	40.1	40.2	40.6	40.2	39.8
1996	40.0	40.7	41.1	40.9	41.3	41.1	40.1	40.0	40.7	41.0	41.2	41.3	40.7
1997	40.8	41.1	41.3	41.7	42.0	41.9	41.4	41.7	42.0	42.1	42.6	42.8	41.7
1998	42.2	42.5	42.9	42.7	42.9	42.7	42.4	42.4	42.9	43.2	43.5	43.7	42.8
1999	42.8	43.1	43.5	43.8	43.9	43.8	43.6	43.7	44.3	44.7	45.1	45.0	43.9
2000	44.5	44.9	45.3	45.4	45.2	45.3	45.4	45.6	46.1	46.0	46.4	46.6	45.5
2001	46.4	46.9	47.3	47.3	47.4	47.4	46.7	47.0	47.6	48.3	48.3	48.3	47.4
2002	47.6	48.0	48.2	48.6	48.8	48.6	48.1	48.7	49.2	49.3	49.6	49.7	48.7
2003	49.7	49.6	50.0	50.1	50.2	50.3	48.9	49.2	49.9	50.1	50.2	50.3	49.9
Leisure and hospitality													
1990	24.8	25.2	25.9	27.0	28.9	30.8	31.0	30.9	29.4	27.1	26.4	26.1	27.7
1991	24.0	24.1	25.1	26.5	28.5	30.9	30.1	29.8	29.3	27.6	26.9	26.6	27.4
1992	24.3	24.4	25.4	27.4	29.7	31.8	31.3	31.2	29.6	27.9	27.0	26.7	28.0
1993	25.5	25.5	25.8	27.7	29.9	32.2	32.7	32.5	31.3	28.9	28.0	28.0	29.0
1994	26.0	25.6	26.4	28.0	29.9	33.2	33.6	33.4	32.4	29.9	29.2	28.5	29.6
1995	26.9	26.9	27.7	29.4	31.1	34.7	34.4	34.1	33.5	30.2	29.4	29.4	30.6
1996	27.7	28.2	29.2	31.2	33.5	35.1	35.4	35.5	34.1	31.6	31.0	30.6	31.9
1997	29.2	29.7	30.7	31.9	34.1	36.4	36.9	36.8	35.3	32.8	32.2	32.0	33.1
1998	30.1	30.4	31.0	32.9	34.8	36.8	37.4	37.4	35.9	33.1	32.1	32.5	33.7
1999	31.1	31.3	31.7	34.0	35.8	37.8	38.5	38.6	36.6	34.8	33.9	33.4	34.7
2000	31.8	31.9	33.3	35.0	37.0	39.1	39.7	39.5	37.6	35.6	34.9	34.4	35.8
2001	32.4	32.7	33.9	35.8	38.1	39.9	40.4	40.0	37.8	35.8	35.1	34.7	36.4
2002	32.4	32.6	33.7	37.0	38.9	41.5	42.0	42.0	40.4	37.3	37.1	36.0	37.6
2003	33.3	33.0	34.2	36.6	38.8	42.1	42.7	42.9	40.6	38.7	38.0	37.1	38.2

Employment by Industry: Delaware—*Continued*

(Numbers in thousands. Not seasonally adjusted.)

Industry	January	February	March	April	May	June	July	August	September	October	November	December	Annual Average
STATEWIDE—*Continued*													
Other services													
1990	11.5	11.6	11.6	11.6	11.8	12.2	12.0	12.0	11.6	11.8	11.7	11.8	11.7
1991	11.6	11.7	11.8	11.8	12.1	12.3	12.0	11.9	11.7	11.9	11.8	11.8	11.8
1992	11.8	11.8	11.8	12.1	12.2	12.4	12.6	12.4	12.2	12.4	12.4	12.4	12.2
1993	12.3	12.2	12.3	12.5	12.6	12.7	12.7	12.7	12.5	12.6	12.6	12.7	12.5
1994	12.6	12.6	12.8	13.0	13.2	13.6	13.4	13.3	13.1	13.1	13.1	13.2	13.0
1995	12.9	13.0	13.2	13.2	13.3	13.8	13.7	13.6	13.4	13.3	13.4	13.5	13.3
1996	13.3	13.6	13.7	13.8	14.0	14.5	14.5	14.6	14.1	14.2	14.3	14.3	14.0
1997	14.2	14.3	14.5	15.0	15.2	15.5	15.5	15.5	15.1	14.9	15.0	15.1	14.9
1998	14.6	14.8	14.9	15.1	15.3	15.8	15.6	15.7	15.6	15.5	15.4	15.6	15.3
1999	15.3	15.5	15.7	15.9	16.0	16.5	16.4	16.4	16.1	15.6	15.7	15.8	15.9
2000	15.5	15.5	15.7	15.8	15.8	16.1	16.0	16.1	15.9	16.5	16.5	16.4	15.9
2001	17.1	17.1	17.3	17.2	17.3	17.9	17.4	17.4	17.2	17.3	17.3	17.4	17.3
2002	16.9	17.2	17.3	17.8	18.0	18.4	18.2	18.2	17.8	18.3	18.2	18.3	17.9
2003	17.7	17.6	17.7	17.8	18.0	18.4	18.7	18.9	18.4	18.3	18.2	18.4	18.2
Government													
1990	46.7	48.5	49.0	49.2	49.5	47.9	46.2	45.0	46.5	48.8	49.1	48.8	47.9
1991	47.8	48.3	49.3	49.4	49.5	48.3	46.6	45.3	45.4	48.3	49.0	49.2	48.0
1992	48.6	48.3	49.4	49.9	49.1	48.9	47.1	46.6	46.6	49.3	50.0	49.9	48.6
1993	48.3	49.6	50.5	50.7	50.4	50.2	47.6	47.2	48.9	50.2	50.9	51.4	49.6
1994	49.2	50.4	51.1	51.3	51.3	50.6	49.0	49.0	48.7	50.6	51.3	52.0	50.3
1995	50.3	50.6	51.4	51.6	51.6	51.0	49.5	49.2	49.3	50.7	51.8	52.4	50.7
1996	50.8	51.7	53.1	53.5	53.7	53.0	50.6	50.6	51.2	52.9	53.7	54.1	52.4
1997	52.1	53.1	54.1	54.0	54.3	53.6	51.5	51.7	51.3	53.3	54.1	54.7	53.1
1998	53.3	54.0	55.0	55.2	55.3	54.6	52.8	52.9	53.5	54.5	55.6	56.0	54.3
1999	54.3	54.4	55.8	56.2	56.1	54.7	53.8	52.9	53.7	55.7	56.7	56.9	55.1
2000	54.3	55.7	57.5	57.8	58.3	57.2	56.9	54.7	55.2	56.5	57.7	57.8	56.6
2001	56.2	57.0	58.2	58.5	58.1	56.9	56.5	54.7	54.7	56.6	57.5	57.7	56.9
2002	55.7	57.0	57.7	57.9	57.7	56.2	54.8	53.4	57.5	58.6	59.3	59.0	57.1
2003	56.7	57.3	57.7	58.2	58.6	57.2	54.8	53.6	57.6	59.0	59.0	59.4	57.4
Federal government													
1990	5.8	5.9	5.9	6.3	6.5	6.6	6.6	6.0	5.9	5.9	5.8	5.9	6.0
1991	5.9	5.9	6.0	5.9	5.9	6.0	6.0	6.0	5.9	5.8	5.9	5.9	5.9
1992	6.0	5.9	5.9	5.9	5.9	5.9	6.0	5.9	5.9	5.9	5.9	5.9	5.9
1993	5.8	5.8	5.8	5.9	5.9	5.9	5.9	5.9	5.8	5.9	5.9	6.2	5.8
1994	5.9	5.9	5.9	5.9	5.9	5.9	5.9	5.9	5.9	5.9	5.9	6.0	5.9
1995	5.9	5.8	5.8	5.9	5.9	5.9	6.0	5.9	5.9	5.8	5.8	6.0	5.8
1996	5.8	5.6	5.7	5.8	5.8	5.8	5.8	5.8	5.8	5.7	5.8	5.9	5.7
1997	5.6	5.5	5.5	5.5	5.5	5.5	5.4	5.5	5.4	5.4	5.5	5.7	5.5
1998	5.4	5.4	5.4	5.4	5.4	5.4	5.5	5.5	5.4	5.3	5.4	5.7	5.4
1999	5.3	5.3	5.4	5.4	5.4	5.4	5.4	5.4	5.3	5.4	5.6	5.7	5.4
2000	5.5	5.7	5.8	5.8	6.7	6.3	6.4	5.7	5.5	5.5	5.5	5.6	5.8
2001	5.6	5.6	5.6	5.5	5.5	5.6	5.6	5.6	5.5	5.5	5.6	5.6	5.6
2002	5.5	5.5	5.5	5.5	5.4	5.5	5.5	5.5	5.4	5.4	5.4	5.4	5.5
2003	5.4	5.4	5.3	5.2	5.2	5.2	5.4	5.4	5.4	5.4	5.4	5.4	5.3
State government													
1990	22.9	24.4	24.7	24.6	24.8	22.7	22.9	22.5	23.5	25.0	24.9	24.5	23.9
1991	23.6	24.0	24.7	24.6	24.7	23.2	22.9	22.0	22.3	24.0	24.3	24.2	23.7
1992	23.4	23.4	24.3	24.5	24.2	23.3	22.5	22.6	22.5	24.2	24.3	24.1	23.6
1993	22.8	23.8	24.6	24.6	24.5	23.9	22.8	22.8	24.4	24.9	25.1	25.0	24.1
1994	23.3	24.4	24.9	24.9	25.2	24.1	23.3	23.4	24.1	24.9	25.2	25.5	24.4
1995	24.1	24.3	24.9	25.1	25.4	24.3	24.1	24.1	24.9	25.2	25.7	25.9	24.8
1996	24.8	25.7	26.7	26.9	27.0	25.8	25.8	25.9	26.1	26.3	26.5	26.5	26.1
1997	25.2	26.0	26.9	27.0	27.3	26.1	26.3	26.3	26.4	26.7	27.0	27.1	26.5
1998	25.9	26.4	27.3	27.7	28.1	26.9	27.0	27.2	27.4	27.6	27.9	27.9	27.2
1999	26.6	26.6	27.7	28.1	28.1	26.3	26.7	26.7	27.3	28.0	28.5	28.5	27.4
2000	26.2	27.4	29.1	29.3	29.1	28.1	28.2	27.5	28.0	28.8	29.5	29.5	28.3
2001	27.9	28.5	29.6	30.2	29.9	28.3	28.3	27.6	28.0	28.8	29.2	29.4	28.8
2002	27.8	28.8	29.1	29.7	29.4	28.4	28.4	27.7	29.5	30.5	31.1	30.7	29.3
2003	28.5	29.2	29.4	30.1	30.3	28.8	28.4	27.6	29.5	30.5	30.4	30.7	29.5
Local government													
1990	18.0	18.2	18.4	18.3	18.2	18.6	16.7	16.5	17.1	17.9	18.4	18.4	17.8
1991	18.3	18.4	18.6	18.9	18.9	19.1	17.7	17.3	17.2	18.5	18.8	19.1	18.4
1992	19.2	19.0	19.2	19.5	19.0	19.7	18.6	18.1	18.2	19.2	19.8	19.9	19.1
1993	19.7	20.0	20.1	20.2	20.0	20.4	18.9	18.5	18.7	19.4	19.9	20.2	19.6
1994	20.0	20.1	20.3	20.5	20.2	20.6	19.8	19.7	18.7	19.8	20.2	20.5	20.0
1995	20.3	20.5	20.7	20.6	20.3	20.8	19.4	19.2	18.5	19.7	20.3	20.5	20.0
1996	20.2	20.4	20.7	20.8	20.9	21.4	19.0	18.9	19.3	20.9	21.4	21.7	20.4
1997	21.3	21.6	21.7	21.5	21.5	22.0	19.8	19.9	19.5	21.2	21.6	21.9	21.1
1998	22.0	22.2	22.3	22.1	21.8	22.3	20.3	20.2	20.7	21.6	22.3	22.4	21.6
1999	22.4	22.5	22.7	22.7	22.6	23.0	21.7	20.8	21.1	22.3	22.6	22.7	22.2
2000	22.6	22.6	22.6	22.7	22.5	22.8	22.3	21.5	21.7	22.2	22.7	22.7	22.4
2001	22.7	22.9	23.0	22.8	22.7	23.0	22.6	21.5	21.2	22.3	22.7	22.7	22.5
2002	22.4	22.7	23.1	22.7	22.9	22.3	20.9	20.2	22.6	22.7	22.8	22.9	22.4
2003	22.8	22.7	23.0	22.9	23.1	23.2	21.0	20.6	22.7	23.1	23.2	23.3	22.6

Employment by Industry: Delaware—*Continued*

(Numbers in thousands. Not seasonally adjusted.)

Industry	January	February	March	April	May	June	July	August	September	October	November	December	Annual Average
DOVER													
Total nonfarm													
1993	46.0	46.0	45.6	46.8	47.5	48.2	46.7	47.0	47.7	46.7	47.6	48.0	46.9
1994	46.7	45.8	46.8	48.0	48.8	49.6	48.9	48.8	50.2	50.5	51.1	51.2	48.8
1995	49.8	49.1	50.1	50.1	50.7	51.7	50.0	50.4	51.1	51.2	51.7	52.2	50.6
1996	50.0	50.1	50.7	51.8	52.4	53.0	51.8	52.3	52.3	52.4	53.2	52.9	51.9
1997	50.6	50.2	51.2	51.1	52.1	52.1	50.9	51.5	51.5	52.2	52.3	52.2	51.4
1998	51.7	51.0	51.6	52.9	53.1	53.4	53.2	53.2	53.4	53.8	54.4	55.4	53.0
1999	53.7	53.8	54.5	54.5	54.5	54.6	54.5	54.0	54.3	55.4	55.8	56.4	54.6
2000	54.2	53.7	55.3	56.1	55.9	56.6	55.8	55.7	55.9	55.4	55.5	55.7	55.4
2001	55.0	54.9	55.7	55.5	55.8	55.7	54.8	54.7	54.6	55.3	55.9	55.4	55.3
2002	54.0	54.1	55.1	57.3	57.9	57.3	57.4	57.4	58.3	58.7	58.8	58.5	57.1
2003	56.9	56.7	57.3	58.7	59.4	59.6	58.9	58.3	59.0	59.5	60.1	59.8	58.7
Total private													
1993	33.0	33.0	32.5	33.5	34.1	34.9	33.8	34.1	34.6	33.6	34.2	34.5	33.8
1994	33.4	32.7	33.3	33.8	34.5	35.3	34.8	34.8	36.1	36.1	36.5	36.6	34.8
1995	35.0	34.8	35.4	35.5	36.0	37.1	35.9	36.3	37.1	36.8	37.2	37.5	36.2
1996	35.8	35.9	36.2	36.8	37.4	37.9	37.4	37.7	37.8	37.7	38.2	37.8	37.2
1997	35.9	35.6	36.2	36.1	36.8	36.9	36.1	36.3	37.1	37.3	37.3	37.2	36.5
1998	36.5	36.1	36.3	37.4	37.5	37.8	37.6	37.7	38.2	38.1	38.2	39.1	37.5
1999	37.9	38.2	38.5	38.3	38.6	38.9	38.7	38.5	39.1	39.7	39.7	40.5	38.8
2000	38.6	38.2	39.2	39.5	39.4	40.0	39.5	39.7	40.1	39.9	39.9	40.0	39.5
2001	38.8	38.6	39.3	39.3	39.8	39.7	39.1	39.1	39.3	39.7	40.4	39.9	39.4
2002	38.6	38.4	39.0	40.4	40.9	40.7	40.8	41.2	41.4	41.4	41.6	41.4	40.5
2003	39.7	39.5	39.9	41.0	41.5	42.1	42.1	42.0	42.3	42.4	43.0	42.9	41.5
Goods-producing													
1993	7.8	8.0	7.7	8.1	8.2	8.5	8.2	8.3	8.2	8.0	8.0	7.8	8.0
1994	7.5	7.3	7.5	7.6	7.9	8.0	8.3	8.4	8.5	8.5	8.6	8.5	8.0
1995	8.1	8.0	8.2	8.2	8.4	8.5	8.0	8.7	8.6	8.8	8.7	8.7	8.4
1996	7.9	7.8	8.0	8.3	8.5	8.7	8.9	8.9	8.7	8.3	8.3	8.0	8.3
1997	7.7	7.6	7.8	7.7	7.8	8.0	7.8	7.8	7.9	8.1	8.1	8.0	7.8
1998	8.0	7.8	7.7	8.2	8.2	8.4	8.5	8.6	8.4	8.4	7.9	8.7	8.2
1999	8.3	8.2	8.2	8.4	8.4	8.5	8.5	8.5	8.5	8.6	8.6	8.8	8.4
2000	8.3	8.1	8.4	8.6	8.5	8.6	8.6	8.8	8.8	8.9	8.8	8.9	8.6
2001	8.4	8.3	8.4	8.4	8.5	8.6	8.3	8.3	8.2	8.3	8.3	8.3	8.4
2002	8.0	7.9	8.0	8.0	8.1	8.2	8.2	8.2	8.1	8.1	8.1	8.0	8.1
2003	7.7	7.4	7.7	7.7	7.8	7.8	7.7	7.8	8.0	8.0	8.1	8.2	7.8
Construction and mining													
1993	2.0	2.1	2.0	2.4	2.5	2.6	2.5	2.5	2.4	2.2	2.2	2.1	2.2
1994	1.9	1.8	1.9	2.1	2.3	2.3	2.5	2.5	2.5	2.5	2.5	2.5	2.2
1995	2.2	2.1	2.3	2.3	2.4	2.4	2.5	2.6	2.5	2.5	2.4	2.3	2.3
1996	2.0	2.0	2.1	2.2	2.3	2.4	2.5	2.5	2.4	2.3	2.4	2.3	2.2
1997	2.1	2.1	2.2	2.3	2.3	2.4	2.4	2.3	2.4	2.4	2.4	2.4	2.3
1998	2.3	2.2	2.2	2.5	2.5	2.6	2.7	2.8	2.7	2.6	2.6	2.6	2.5
1999	2.4	2.3	2.4	2.5	2.6	2.6	2.6	2.7	2.6	2.6	2.6	2.7	2.5
2000	2.4	2.3	2.5	2.6	2.6	2.6	2.7	2.7	2.7	2.8	2.7	2.8	2.6
2001	2.5	2.5	2.6	2.6	2.7	2.8	2.8	2.8	2.7	2.8	2.8	2.8	2.7
2002	2.7	2.6	2.7	2.8	2.8	2.9	3.0	3.0	3.0	3.0	3.0	2.9	2.9
2003	2.8	2.6	2.8	2.9	3.0	3.0	3.0	2.9	3.1	3.1	3.1	3.3	3.0
Manufacturing													
1993	5.8	5.9	5.7	5.7	5.7	5.9	5.7	5.8	5.8	5.8	5.8	5.7	5.7
1994	5.6	5.5	5.6	5.5	5.6	5.7	5.8	5.9	6.0	6.0	6.1	6.0	5.7
1995	5.9	5.9	5.9	5.9	6.0	6.1	5.5	6.1	6.1	6.3	6.3	6.4	6.0
1996	5.9	5.8	5.9	6.1	6.2	6.3	6.4	6.4	6.3	6.0	5.9	5.7	6.0
1997	5.6	5.5	5.6	5.4	5.5	5.6	5.4	5.5	5.5	5.7	5.7	5.6	5.5
1998	5.7	5.6	5.5	5.7	5.7	5.8	5.8	5.8	5.7	5.8	5.3	6.1	5.7
1999	5.9	5.9	5.8	5.9	5.8	5.9	5.9	5.8	5.9	6.0	6.0	6.1	5.9
2000	5.9	5.8	5.9	6.0	5.9	6.0	5.9	6.1	6.1	6.1	6.1	6.1	5.9
2001	5.9	5.8	5.8	5.8	5.8	5.8	5.5	5.5	5.5	5.5	5.5	5.5	5.7
2002	5.3	5.3	5.3	5.2	5.3	5.3	5.2	5.2	5.1	5.1	5.1	5.1	5.2
2003	4.9	4.8	4.9	4.8	4.8	4.8	4.7	4.9	4.9	4.9	5.0	4.9	4.9
Service-providing													
1993	38.2	38.0	37.9	38.7	39.3	39.7	38.5	38.7	39.5	38.7	39.6	40.2	38.9
1994	39.2	38.5	39.3	40.4	40.9	41.6	40.6	40.4	41.7	42.0	42.5	42.7	40.8
1995	41.7	41.1	41.9	41.9	42.3	43.2	42.0	41.7	42.5	42.4	43.0	43.5	42.2
1996	42.1	42.3	42.7	43.5	43.9	44.3	42.9	43.4	43.6	44.1	44.9	44.9	43.5
1997	42.9	42.6	43.4	43.4	44.3	44.1	43.1	43.7	43.6	44.1	44.2	44.2	43.6
1998	43.7	43.2	43.9	44.7	44.9	45.0	44.7	44.6	45.0	45.4	46.5	46.7	44.8
1999	45.4	45.6	46.3	46.1	46.1	46.1	46.0	45.5	45.8	46.8	47.2	47.6	46.2
2000	45.9	45.6	46.9	47.5	47.4	48.0	47.2	46.9	47.1	46.5	46.7	46.8	46.8
2001	46.6	46.6	47.3	47.1	47.3	47.1	46.5	46.4	46.4	47.0	47.6	47.1	46.9
2002	46.0	46.2	47.1	49.3	49.8	49.1	49.2	49.2	50.2	50.6	50.7	50.5	49.0
2003	49.2	49.3	49.6	51.0	51.6	51.8	51.2	50.5	51.0	51.5	52.0	51.6	50.9

Employment by Industry: Delaware—*Continued*

(Numbers in thousands. Not seasonally adjusted.)

Industry	January	February	March	April	May	June	July	August	September	October	November	December	Annual Average
DOVER—*Continued*													
Trade, transportation, and utilities													
1993	9.9	9.7	9.5	9.7	9.9	9.9	9.7	9.8	10.0	10.0	10.4	10.8	9.9
1994	10.0	9.6	9.7	9.8	10.2	10.4	10.2	10.1	10.5	10.6	11.0	11.3	10.2
1995	10.5	10.4	10.5	10.3	10.4	10.5	10.3	10.3	10.6	10.7	11.1	11.3	10.5
1996	10.5	10.5	10.4	10.5	10.5	10.6	10.3	10.4	10.7	11.0	11.4	11.4	10.6
1997	10.4	10.1	10.2	10.1	10.3	10.2	10.0	10.0	10.4	10.6	10.6	10.7	10.3
1998	10.2	9.9	9.8	9.9	9.9	10.0	9.9	9.9	10.3	10.3	10.7	10.8	10.1
1999	10.2	10.1	10.1	10.1	10.2	10.3	10.1	10.1	10.5	10.9	11.2	11.5	10.4
2000	10.4	10.1	10.2	10.4	10.3	10.5	10.2	10.2	10.3	9.9	10.0	10.1	10.2
2001	9.8	9.5	9.7	9.4	9.5	9.5	9.3	9.2	9.5	9.5	9.8	9.9	9.6
2002	9.8	9.6	9.6	9.8	10.0	9.9	9.9	9.8	10.0	10.1	10.3	10.5	9.9
2003	10.4	10.5	10.7	10.8	10.8	10.8	10.8	10.7	10.8	10.8	11.0	11.1	10.8
Wholesale trade													
1993	0.7	0.7	0.7	0.7	0.8	0.8	0.8	0.8	0.8	0.7	0.7	0.7	0.7
1994	0.7	0.7	0.7	0.7	0.8	0.8	0.8	0.8	0.8	0.8	0.8	0.8	0.7
1995	0.8	0.8	0.8	0.8	0.8	0.8	0.9	0.8	0.8	0.8	0.8	0.8	0.8
1996	1.0	1.0	1.0	1.0	1.0	1.0	1.0	1.0	1.0	1.0	1.0	1.0	1.0
1997	0.9	0.9	0.9	0.9	1.0	1.0	1.0	1.0	1.0	1.0	1.0	0.9	0.9
1998	0.9	0.9	0.9	0.9	0.9	0.9	0.9	0.9	0.9	0.9	0.9	0.9	0.9
1999	0.9	0.9	0.9	0.9	0.9	1.0	0.9	0.9	0.9	0.9	0.9	1.0	0.9
2000	1.0	0.9	1.0	1.0	0.9	1.0	1.0	1.0	1.0	1.0	1.0	1.0	0.9
2001	1.2	1.2	1.3	1.2	1.2	1.3	1.2	1.2	1.2	1.2	1.2	1.3	1.2
2002	1.4	1.4	1.4	1.4	1.5	1.5	1.5	1.5	1.5	1.5	1.5	1.5	1.5
2003	1.6	1.6	1.6	1.7	1.7	1.7	1.7	1.7	1.7	1.7	1.7	1.7	1.7
Retail trade													
1993	7.9	7.7	7.5	7.6	7.7	7.7	7.6	7.7	7.7	7.8	8.2	8.5	7.8
1994	7.7	7.3	7.4	7.5	7.8	8.0	7.9	7.9	8.1	8.2	8.6	8.9	7.9
1995	8.2	8.1	8.2	8.1	8.2	8.3	8.2	8.3	8.4	8.5	8.9	9.1	8.3
1996	8.2	8.1	8.0	8.1	8.1	8.2	8.0	8.1	8.2	8.5	9.0	9.0	8.2
1997	8.2	7.9	8.0	7.8	7.9	7.7	7.7	7.7	7.9	8.1	8.1	8.3	7.9
1998	7.7	7.4	7.3	7.4	7.4	7.5	7.5	7.5	7.7	7.7	8.1	8.2	7.6
1999	7.7	7.5	7.5	7.4	7.5	7.6	7.6	7.6	7.8	8.2	8.5	8.7	7.8
2000	7.7	7.5	7.5	7.6	7.6	7.7	7.5	7.5	7.5	7.0	7.1	7.3	7.4
2001	7.1	6.8	6.8	6.6	6.7	6.7	6.7	6.7	6.8	6.8	7.1	7.2	6.8
2002	7.0	6.8	6.8	7.0	7.1	7.1	7.1	7.1	7.1	7.1	7.3	7.5	7.1
2003	7.3	7.4	7.6	7.6	7.6	7.7	7.7	7.7	7.7	7.6	7.8	7.9	7.6
Transportation and utilities													
1993	1.3	1.3	1.3	1.4	1.4	1.4	1.3	1.3	1.5	1.5	1.5	1.6	1.4
1994	1.6	1.6	1.6	1.6	1.6	1.6	1.5	1.4	1.6	1.6	1.6	1.6	1.5
1995	1.5	1.5	1.5	1.4	1.4	1.4	1.2	1.2	1.4	1.4	1.4	1.4	1.3
1996	1.3	1.4	1.4	1.4	1.4	1.4	1.3	1.3	1.5	1.5	1.4	1.4	1.3
1997	1.3	1.3	1.3	1.4	1.4	1.5	1.3	1.3	1.5	1.5	1.5	1.5	1.4
1998	1.6	1.6	1.6	1.6	1.6	1.6	1.5	1.5	1.7	1.7	1.7	1.7	1.6
1999	1.6	1.7	1.7	1.8	1.8	1.7	1.6	1.6	1.8	1.8	1.8	1.8	1.7
2000	1.7	1.7	1.7	1.8	1.8	1.8	1.7	1.7	1.8	1.9	1.9	1.8	1.7
2001	1.5	1.5	1.6	1.6	1.6	1.5	1.4	1.3	1.5	1.5	1.5	1.4	1.5
2002	1.4	1.4	1.4	1.4	1.4	1.3	1.3	1.2	1.4	1.5	1.5	1.5	1.4
2003	1.5	1.5	1.5	1.5	1.5	1.4	1.4	1.3	1.4	1.5	1.5	1.5	1.5
Information													
1993	0.7	0.7	0.7	0.7	0.7	0.7	0.7	0.7	0.7	0.7	0.7	0.7	0.7
1994	0.6	0.6	0.6	0.7	0.7	0.7	0.7	0.7	0.7	0.7	0.7	0.7	0.6
1995	0.7	0.7	0.7	0.7	0.7	0.7	0.7	0.7	0.7	0.7	0.7	0.7	0.7
1996	0.7	0.7	0.7	0.8	0.8	0.8	0.9	0.9	0.8	0.8	0.9	0.9	0.8
1997	0.9	0.9	0.9	0.9	0.9	0.9	0.9	0.9	0.9	0.9	0.9	0.9	0.9
1998	0.9	0.9	0.8	0.9	0.9	0.9	0.8	0.8	0.8	0.8	0.8	0.8	0.8
1999	0.8	0.8	0.9	0.9	0.9	0.9	0.9	0.9	0.9	0.9	0.9	0.9	0.8
2000	1.0	1.0	1.0	0.7	0.7	0.7	0.7	0.6	0.7	0.8	0.8	0.8	0.7
2001	0.7	0.7	0.7	0.7	0.7	0.7	0.7	0.7	0.6	0.7	0.7	0.7	0.7
2002	0.7	0.6	0.7	0.6	0.7	0.6	0.6	0.6	0.6	0.6	0.6	0.6	0.6
2003	0.7	0.7	0.7	0.7	0.7	0.7	0.7	0.7	0.6	0.6	0.7	0.6	0.7
Financial activities													
1993	1.7	1.7	1.7	1.8	1.8	1.8	1.8	1.8	1.9	1.8	1.8	1.9	1.7
1994	1.8	1.8	1.8	1.9	1.9	1.9	2.0	2.0	2.0	2.0	2.0	2.0	1.9
1995	2.0	2.0	2.1	2.5	2.5	2.6	2.6	2.6	2.6	2.6	2.6	2.6	2.4
1996	2.6	2.6	2.6	2.7	2.7	2.8	2.7	2.7	2.7	2.7	2.7	2.7	2.6
1997	2.5	2.5	2.5	2.5	2.5	2.5	2.4	2.4	2.4	2.4	2.4	2.4	2.4
1998	2.5	2.5	2.5	2.5	2.5	2.5	2.5	2.5	2.5	2.5	2.5	2.6	2.5
1999	2.5	2.6	2.6	2.5	2.4	2.4	2.5	2.5	2.5	2.4	2.4	2.4	2.4
2000	2.4	2.4	2.4	2.3	2.3	2.3	2.3	2.3	2.3	2.4	2.4	2.5	2.3
2001	2.4	2.4	2.4	2.5	2.5	2.5	2.5	2.5	2.6	2.6	2.6	2.6	2.5
2002	2.6	2.6	2.6	2.6	2.6	2.5	2.5	2.5	2.5	2.5	2.6	2.6	2.6
2003	2.6	2.6	2.6	2.5	2.5	2.5	2.6	2.6	2.6	2.6	2.6	2.6	2.6

Employment by Industry: Delaware—*Continued*

(Numbers in thousands. Not seasonally adjusted.)

Industry	January	February	March	April	May	June	July	August	September	October	November	December	Annual Average
DOVER—*Continued*													
Professional and business services													
1993	2.4	2.4	2.4	2.5	2.6	2.7	2.7	2.7	2.8	2.4	2.5	2.5	2.5
1994	2.8	3.0	3.0	2.9	2.7	2.8	2.5	2.6	2.8	2.8	2.7	2.6	2.7
1995	2.4	2.4	2.5	2.5	2.5	2.6	2.6	2.5	2.5	2.5	2.5	2.6	2.5
1996	2.4	2.5	2.6	2.5	2.6	2.8	2.6	2.6	2.7	2.6	2.6	2.6	2.5
1997	2.3	2.3	2.3	2.3	2.3	2.4	2.2	2.2	2.3	2.3	2.3	2.3	2.2
1998	2.5	2.5	2.8	3.1	3.1	3.0	3.2	3.1	3.1	3.0	3.1	3.1	2.9
1999	3.1	3.2	3.3	2.8	2.9	2.9	2.9	2.9	2.9	2.9	2.7	2.9	2.9
2000	2.9	2.9	3.1	3.2	3.2	3.4	3.2	3.2	3.3	3.3	3.2	3.2	3.1
2001	3.5	3.7	3.9	3.7	3.6	3.6	3.5	3.7	3.9	4.1	4.4	3.8	3.8
2002	3.6	3.6	3.7	3.9	3.9	4.0	3.8	4.0	4.2	4.3	3.9	3.9	3.9
2003	3.7	3.7	3.4	3.7	3.7	3.6	3.7	3.7	3.8	3.7	3.6	3.6	3.7
Educational and health services													
1993	4.4	4.4	4.4	4.5	4.6	4.5	4.5	4.5	4.7	4.6	4.6	4.6	4.5
1994	4.5	4.5	4.5	4.7	4.7	4.6	4.6	4.6	4.8	5.0	5.0	5.0	4.7
1995	4.8	4.9	4.9	4.8	4.9	4.9	4.9	4.9	4.9	5.0	5.1	5.1	4.9
1996	5.0	5.2	5.2	5.1	5.2	5.1	5.1	5.1	5.1	5.2	5.2	5.2	5.1
1997	5.2	5.3	5.3	5.3	5.4	5.3	5.2	5.3	5.4	5.4	5.5	5.4	5.3
1998	5.3	5.4	5.5	5.5	5.5	5.4	5.4	5.4	5.6	5.7	5.8	5.7	5.5
1999	5.7	5.8	5.9	5.8	5.8	5.7	5.8	5.7	5.8	5.8	5.8	5.9	5.7
2000	5.8	5.9	6.0	6.1	6.1	6.0	6.0	6.2	6.2	6.2	6.2	6.2	6.0
2001	6.5	6.5	6.6	6.6	6.7	6.6	6.6	6.6	6.5	6.6	6.6	6.6	6.6
2002	6.5	6.7	6.7	6.7	6.7	6.8	6.9	7.1	7.0	7.0	7.1	7.0	6.9
2003	7.0	7.0	7.1	7.1	7.1	7.1	7.0	6.9	7.0	7.1	7.3	7.2	7.1
Leisure and hospitality													
1993	4.3	4.3	4.3	4.4	4.5	5.0	4.4	4.5	4.5	4.3	4.4	4.4	4.4
1994	4.4	4.2	4.4	4.4	4.6	5.1	4.7	4.6	5.0	4.6	4.6	4.6	4.6
1995	4.6	4.5	4.6	4.6	4.7	5.4	4.9	4.7	5.3	4.6	4.6	4.6	4.7
1996	4.8	4.7	4.8	5.0	5.1	5.1	4.9	5.1	5.1	5.1	5.1	5.0	4.9
1997	4.9	5.0	5.2	5.3	5.5	5.5	5.5	5.6	5.7	5.5	5.4	5.4	5.3
1998	5.0	5.0	5.1	5.2	5.3	5.4	5.2	5.3	5.3	5.3	5.3	5.3	5.2
1999	5.1	5.3	5.3	5.6	5.8	6.0	5.8	5.7	5.8	6.0	5.9	5.9	5.6
2000	5.7	5.7	6.0	6.1	6.2	6.4	6.4	6.3	6.4	6.2	6.3	6.1	6.1
2001	5.5	5.5	5.6	5.9	6.2	6.1	6.2	6.2	6.1	6.0	6.1	6.1	6.0
2002	5.4	5.4	5.6	6.7	6.8	6.6	6.7	6.8	6.8	6.6	6.8	6.6	6.4
2003	5.5	5.5	5.6	6.3	6.6	7.4	7.4	7.3	7.3	7.3	7.4	7.3	6.7
Other services													
1993	1.8	1.8	1.8	1.8	1.8	1.8	1.8	1.8	1.8	1.8	1.8	1.8	1.8
1994	1.8	1.7	1.8	1.8	1.8	1.8	1.8	1.8	1.8	1.9	1.9	1.9	1.8
1995	1.9	1.9	1.9	1.9	1.9	1.9	1.9	1.9	1.9	1.9	1.9	1.9	1.9
1996	1.9	1.9	1.9	1.9	2.0	2.0	2.0	2.0	2.0	2.0	2.0	2.0	1.9
1997	2.0	1.9	2.0	2.0	2.1	2.1	2.1	2.1	2.1	2.1	2.1	2.1	2.0
1998	2.1	2.1	2.1	2.1	2.1	2.2	2.1	2.1	2.2	2.1	2.1	2.1	2.1
1999	2.2	2.2	2.2	2.2	2.2	2.2	2.2	2.2	2.2	2.2	2.2	2.2	2.2
2000	2.1	2.1	2.1	2.1	2.1	2.1	2.1	2.1	2.1	2.2	2.2	2.2	2.1
2001	2.0	2.0	2.0	2.1	2.1	2.1	2.0	1.9	1.9	1.9	1.9	1.9	2.0
2002	2.0	2.0	2.1	2.1	2.1	2.1	2.2	2.2	2.2	2.2	2.2	2.2	2.1
2003	2.1	2.1	2.1	2.2	2.3	2.2	2.2	2.3	2.2	2.3	2.3	2.3	2.2
Government													
1993	13.0	13.0	13.1	13.3	13.4	13.3	12.9	12.9	13.1	13.1	13.4	13.5	13.1
1994	13.3	13.1	13.5	14.2	14.3	14.3	14.1	14.0	14.1	14.4	14.6	14.6	14.0
1995	14.8	14.3	14.7	14.6	14.7	14.6	14.1	14.1	14.0	14.4	14.5	14.7	14.4
1996	14.2	14.2	14.5	15.0	15.0	15.1	14.4	14.6	14.5	14.7	15.0	15.1	14.6
1997	14.7	14.6	15.0	15.0	15.3	15.2	14.8	15.2	14.4	14.9	15.0	15.0	14.9
1998	15.2	14.9	15.3	15.5	15.6	15.6	15.6	15.5	15.2	15.7	16.2	16.3	15.5
1999	15.8	15.6	16.0	16.2	15.9	15.7	15.8	15.5	15.2	15.7	16.1	15.9	15.7
2000	15.6	15.5	16.1	16.6	16.5	16.6	16.3	16.0	15.8	15.5	15.6	15.7	15.9
2001	16.2	16.3	16.4	16.2	16.0	16.0	15.7	15.6	15.3	15.6	15.5	15.5	15.9
2002	15.4	15.7	16.1	16.9	17.0	16.6	16.6	16.2	16.9	17.3	17.2	17.1	16.6
2003	17.2	17.2	17.4	17.7	17.9	17.5	16.8	16.3	16.7	17.1	17.1	16.9	17.2
Federal government													
1993	2.1	2.1	2.1	2.2	2.2	2.2	2.2	2.2	2.1	2.1	2.2	2.2	2.1
1994	2.1	2.1	2.1	2.2	2.2	2.2	2.2	2.2	2.2	2.1	2.1	2.1	2.1
1995	2.1	2.0	2.0	2.1	2.1	2.0	2.1	2.0	2.0	2.0	1.9	1.9	2.0
1996	1.9	1.9	1.9	2.0	2.0	2.0	2.0	2.0	2.1	2.0	2.0	2.0	1.9
1997	1.8	1.8	1.8	1.8	1.8	1.8	1.8	1.8	1.8	1.7	1.7	1.7	1.7
1998	1.8	1.8	1.8	1.7	1.7	1.8	1.8	1.8	1.7	1.7	1.7	1.7	1.7
1999	1.7	1.7	1.7	1.7	1.7	1.7	1.8	1.8	1.7	1.7	1.7	1.7	1.7
2000	1.7	1.7	1.7	1.7	1.9	1.9	1.9	1.8	1.7	1.7	1.7	1.7	1.7
2001	1.7	1.7	1.7	1.7	1.7	1.8	1.8	1.8	1.7	1.7	1.7	1.7	1.7
2002	1.7	1.6	1.7	1.6	1.6	1.7	1.7	1.7	1.7	1.7	1.7	1.7	1.7
2003	1.7	1.7	1.6	1.6	1.6	1.6	1.7	1.7	1.6	1.6	1.6	1.6	1.6

Employment by Industry: Delaware—*Continued*

(Numbers in thousands. Not seasonally adjusted.)

Industry	January	February	March	April	May	June	July	August	September	October	November	December	Annual Average
DOVER—*Continued*													
State government													
1993	6.9	6.9	7.0	7.0	7.1	7.0	7.2	7.2	7.3	7.1	7.2	7.2	7.0
1994	7.1	7.0	7.3	7.9	8.0	8.0	8.3	8.3	8.2	8.3	8.3	8.3	7.9
1995	8.4	8.0	8.3	8.2	8.3	8.2	8.2	8.3	8.2	8.2	8.3	8.4	8.2
1996	8.1	8.1	8.3	8.6	8.6	8.6	8.6	8.7	8.5	8.5	8.7	8.7	8.5
1997	8.6	8.5	8.8	8.9	9.1	9.0	9.1	9.1	8.9	9.0	9.0	8.9	8.9
1998	9.1	8.7	9.1	9.3	9.5	9.4	9.5	9.5	9.4	9.8	10.0	10.0	9.4
1999	9.6	9.4	9.7	10.0	9.7	9.5	9.8	9.7	9.6	9.7	9.8	9.7	9.6
2000	9.4	9.3	9.7	10.2	10.0	10.0	9.9	9.8	9.9	9.2	9.2	9.2	9.6
2001	9.8	9.8	9.9	9.7	9.6	9.4	9.3	9.3	9.4	9.3	9.1	9.0	9.5
2002	9.2	9.5	9.8	10.6	10.7	10.5	10.6	10.4	10.7	11.0	10.9	10.8	10.4
2003	10.8	10.9	11.1	11.4	11.5	11.3	10.8	10.4	10.5	10.8	10.7	10.5	10.9
Local government													
1993	4.0	4.0	4.0	4.1	4.1	4.1	3.5	3.5	3.7	3.9	4.0	4.1	3.9
1994	4.1	4.0	4.1	4.1	4.1	4.1	3.6	3.5	3.7	4.0	4.2	4.2	3.9
1995	4.3	4.3	4.4	4.3	4.3	4.4	3.8	3.8	3.8	4.2	4.3	4.4	4.1
1996	4.2	4.2	4.3	4.4	4.4	4.5	3.8	3.9	3.9	4.2	4.3	4.4	4.2
1997	4.3	4.3	4.4	4.3	4.4	4.4	3.9	4.3	3.7	4.2	4.3	4.4	4.2
1998	4.3	4.4	4.4	4.5	4.4	4.4	4.3	4.2	4.1	4.2	4.5	4.6	4.3
1999	4.5	4.5	4.6	4.5	4.5	4.5	4.2	4.0	3.9	4.3	4.6	4.5	4.3
2000	4.5	4.5	4.7	4.7	4.6	4.7	4.5	4.4	4.2	4.6	4.7	4.8	4.5
2001	4.7	4.8	4.8	4.8	4.7	4.8	4.6	4.5	4.2	4.6	4.7	4.8	4.7
2002	4.5	4.6	4.6	4.7	4.7	4.4	4.3	4.1	4.5	4.6	4.6	4.6	4.5
2003	4.7	4.6	4.7	4.7	4.8	4.6	4.3	4.2	4.6	4.7	4.8	4.8	4.6
WILMINGTON													
Total nonfarm													
1990	267.2	271.2	275.3	275.6	277.4	278.2	272.2	274.6	274.5	275.2	274.0	274.2	274.1
1991	265.7	260.4	269.2	261.7	269.7	269.7	265.8	262.6	264.2	268.5	268.8	268.8	266.2
1992	259.8	257.9	259.9	263.4	266.1	265.7	263.3	263.1	262.3	263.8	269.6	270.7	263.8
1993	262.5	263.2	264.2	269.2	271.7	271.9	272.5	271.8	273.8	274.0	276.2	278.4	270.7
1994	268.2	268.2	271.0	274.5	276.8	278.4	273.5	277.0	278.2	279.8	282.9	284.8	276.1
1995	276.1	276.6	278.9	281.8	284.2	282.5	282.7	283.3	284.4	287.2	288.9	290.3	283.0
1996	275.1	283.0	283.3	290.3	294.2	295.8	291.0	289.4	292.3	293.9	296.9	298.9	290.3
1997	291.3	292.5	295.8	298.9	300.8	304.3	300.6	303.2	304.4	305.2	308.1	313.0	301.5
1998	302.5	302.5	306.7	308.8	311.6	314.4	310.8	313.1	314.9	314.3	316.2	321.2	311.4
1999	310.9	312.6	316.3	320.7	322.2	323.2	320.0	322.4	322.1	325.2	328.6	330.8	321.2
2000	319.0	320.6	326.1	326.8	327.7	330.5	327.2	325.0	327.1	330.0	332.8	335.4	327.3
2001	319.4	322.2	327.2	326.7	327.9	328.5	323.3	322.7	322.8	324.9	326.5	327.8	325.0
2002	315.3	317.4	319.3	318.7	322.2	321.2	317.5	316.6	320.6	320.0	323.2	324.9	319.7
2003	312.2	311.2	313.8	315.9	319.4	321.1	318.1	317.7	320.5	322.1	324.7	325.4	318.5
Total private													
1990	234.1	236.9	240.5	240.6	242.4	245.4	240.3	243.4	242.3	240.6	239.1	239.6	240.4
1991	231.9	226.2	234.0	227.1	234.6	235.8	232.5	230.1	232.6	233.9	233.8	233.9	232.2
1992	225.4	223.7	224.9	228.0	231.4	231.5	229.6	229.8	229.7	228.5	233.9	235.1	229.2
1993	228.4	227.8	228.0	232.9	235.8	236.3	237.8	237.7	238.2	237.3	239.2	241.1	235.0
1994	232.7	232.1	233.7	237.7	240.0	242.6	239.6	243.2	243.8	244.7	247.4	248.7	240.5
1995	241.0	241.2	242.8	245.3	247.5	246.6	248.6	249.4	249.6	250.8	251.7	252.9	247.2
1996	239.2	246.2	245.4	252.6	256.3	258.9	255.2	253.8	255.8	256.0	258.4	260.1	253.1
1997	253.7	254.3	256.9	260.3	262.2	266.5	264.4	266.9	267.5	266.8	269.2	273.6	263.5
1998	264.0	263.3	266.8	269.0	271.7	275.6	273.6	276.3	276.7	275.3	276.6	281.1	272.5
1999	271.9	273.4	276.0	280.1	281.3	284.6	282.4	285.4	283.6	285.1	287.9	289.8	281.7
2000	279.8	280.0	284.1	284.5	284.9	288.4	286.6	286.7	286.8	287.6	289.5	291.5	285.8
2001	278.0	279.1	283.8	283.5	285.1	287.1	283.6	284.3	282.3	282.4	283.2	284.3	283.1
2002	274.3	274.7	276.0	276.2	279.9	280.1	279.8	279.9	279.3	277.7	280.0	281.9	278.3
2003	271.0	268.7	271.0	273.7	277.0	279.4	279.4	279.5	278.1	278.6	281.3	281.6	276.6
Goods-producing													
1990	47.4	48.1	49.1	49.7	50.2	50.7	47.9	51.1	50.8	50.0	46.8	46.5	49.0
1991	47.4	41.9	48.0	42.8	48.8	48.6	47.6	45.9	47.9	48.1	47.2	46.3	46.7
1992	44.1	43.4	43.2	44.7	46.0	45.7	44.9	45.2	45.0	41.6	45.5	45.3	44.5
1993	43.7	43.3	43.1	44.4	45.3	45.4	45.6	45.3	45.3	44.4	44.1	43.7	44.4
1994	41.4	40.8	41.1	42.7	43.2	43.8	41.5	44.7	44.7	44.1	44.3	44.2	43.0
1995	42.5	42.1	43.0	44.1	44.9	41.9	44.1	44.6	44.1	44.6	43.6	44.0	43.6
1996	36.4	41.1	38.3	44.3	45.2	46.3	45.2	44.8	44.4	45.7	46.1	46.2	43.6
1997	45.0	44.2	44.4	45.1	45.5	46.4	46.7	48.0	48.5	48.7	48.6	49.7	46.7
1998	47.1	45.1	46.9	47.4	47.9	48.7	45.3	49.2	48.8	48.3	48.2	48.8	47.6
1999	47.4	47.4	48.1	51.2	51.9	52.7	48.5	50.9	50.4	50.8	51.9	50.8	50.1
2000	46.9	46.2	47.1	47.1	46.7	47.8	46.8	47.1	46.9	47.4	46.5	46.2	46.8
2001	41.2	41.3	44.2	44.6	44.9	45.8	45.0	45.1	44.7	44.4	44.4	43.8	44.1
2002	42.0	42.8	42.9	41.5	43.3	43.6	43.7	43.3	43.2	42.4	42.2	42.3	42.8
2003	39.6	39.7	40.0	40.7	41.9	43.2	42.9	42.3	41.6	42.0	42.1	41.0	41.4

Employment by Industry: Delaware—*Continued*

(Numbers in thousands. Not seasonally adjusted.)

Industry	January	February	March	April	May	June	July	August	September	October	November	December	Annual Average
WILMINGTON—*Continued*													
Construction and mining													
1990	15.2	15.6	16.4	16.9	17.2	17.5	17.5	17.5	17.0	16.5	16.2	15.6	16.5
1991	13.6	13.6	14.1	14.9	15.2	14.7	15.0	14.9	14.9	15.5	14.3	13.5	14.5
1992	12.3	11.9	12.3	14.1	15.5	15.1	14.4	14.5	14.5	14.7	14.7	14.3	14.0
1993	12.9	12.7	12.8	14.5	15.2	15.0	14.9	14.8	14.7	14.0	13.9	13.5	14.0
1994	11.7	11.2	11.6	13.1	13.6	14.1	14.5	14.6	14.7	14.7	14.8	14.7	13.6
1995	13.3	12.8	13.7	14.8	15.5	15.2	15.2	15.4	15.9	16.5	15.6	15.1	14.9
1996	12.5	13.2	14.1	15.1	15.9	16.9	17.6	18.0	18.4	19.5	19.8	19.5	16.7
1997	17.1	16.1	16.0	16.3	16.5	17.0	17.6	17.7	17.2	17.1	17.0	17.8	16.9
1998	16.5	15.5	15.6	16.2	16.4	17.0	17.9	17.9	17.6	17.3	17.2	17.6	16.8
1999	16.4	16.7	17.2	18.2	18.2	18.6	19.3	19.4	19.1	19.4	20.5	19.2	18.5
2000	18.2	17.5	18.4	18.6	18.7	19.3	18.8	19.0	19.0	19.4	18.5	18.1	18.6
2001	17.0	17.1	17.5	17.9	18.4	19.1	18.8	19.3	19.2	19.2	19.6	18.9	18.5
2002	17.9	17.8	17.9	18.5	18.8	19.2	19.4	19.1	18.7	18.1	18.0	18.3	18.5
2003	17.2	16.1	16.5	17.4	18.2	18.7	18.9	19.1	18.6	18.7	18.7	18.6	18.1
Manufacturing													
1990	32.2	32.5	32.7	32.8	33.0	33.2	30.4	33.6	33.8	33.5	30.6	30.9	32.4
1991	33.8	28.3	33.9	27.9	33.6	33.9	32.6	31.0	33.0	32.6	32.9	32.8	32.1
1992	31.8	31.5	30.9	30.6	30.5	30.6	30.5	30.7	30.5	26.9	30.8	31.0	30.5
1993	30.8	30.6	30.3	29.9	30.1	30.4	30.7	30.5	30.6	30.4	30.2	30.2	30.3
1994	29.7	29.6	29.5	29.6	29.6	29.7	27.0	30.1	30.0	29.4	29.5	29.5	29.4
1995	29.2	29.3	29.3	29.3	29.4	26.7	28.9	29.2	28.2	28.1	28.0	28.9	28.7
1996	23.9	27.9	24.2	29.2	29.3	29.4	27.6	26.8	26.0	26.2	26.3	26.7	26.9
1997	27.9	28.1	28.4	28.8	29.0	29.4	29.1	30.3	31.3	31.6	31.6	31.9	29.7
1998	30.6	29.6	31.3	31.2	31.5	31.7	27.4	31.3	31.2	31.0	31.0	31.2	30.7
1999	31.0	30.7	30.9	33.0	33.7	34.1	29.2	31.5	31.3	31.4	31.4	31.6	31.6
2000	28.7	28.7	28.7	28.5	28.0	28.5	28.0	28.1	27.9	28.0	28.0	28.1	28.2
2001	24.2	24.2	26.7	26.7	26.5	26.7	26.2	25.8	25.5	25.2	24.8	24.9	25.6
2002	24.1	25.0	25.0	23.0	24.5	24.4	24.3	24.2	24.5	24.3	24.2	24.0	24.3
2003	22.4	23.6	23.5	23.3	23.7	24.5	24.0	23.2	23.0	23.3	23.4	22.4	23.4
Service-providing													
1990	219.8	223.1	226.2	225.9	227.2	227.5	224.3	223.5	223.7	225.2	227.2	227.7	225.1
1991	218.3	218.5	221.2	218.9	220.9	221.1	218.2	216.7	216.3	220.4	221.6	222.5	219.5
1992	215.7	214.5	216.7	218.7	220.1	220.0	218.4	217.9	217.3	222.2	224.1	225.4	219.2
1993	218.8	219.9	221.1	224.8	226.4	226.5	226.9	226.5	228.5	229.6	232.1	234.7	226.3
1994	226.8	227.4	229.9	231.8	233.6	234.6	232.0	232.3	233.5	235.7	238.6	240.6	233.0
1995	233.6	234.5	235.9	237.7	239.3	240.6	238.6	238.7	240.3	242.6	245.3	246.3	239.4
1996	238.7	241.9	245.0	246.0	249.0	249.5	245.8	244.6	247.9	248.2	250.8	252.7	246.6
1997	246.3	248.3	251.4	253.8	255.3	257.9	253.9	255.2	255.9	256.5	259.5	263.3	254.7
1998	255.4	257.4	259.8	261.4	263.7	265.7	265.5	263.9	266.1	266.0	268.0	272.4	263.7
1999	263.5	265.2	268.2	269.5	270.3	270.5	271.5	271.5	271.7	274.4	276.7	280.0	271.0
2000	272.1	274.4	279.0	279.7	281.0	282.7	280.4	277.9	280.2	282.6	286.3	289.2	280.4
2001	278.2	280.9	283.0	282.1	283.0	282.7	278.3	277.6	278.1	280.5	282.1	284.0	280.9
2002	273.3	274.6	276.4	277.2	278.9	277.6	273.8	273.3	277.4	277.6	281.0	282.6	277.0
2003	272.6	271.5	273.8	275.2	277.5	277.9	275.2	275.4	278.9	280.1	282.6	284.4	277.1
Trade, transportation, and utilities													
1990	52.5	51.8	52.6	51.6	51.5	52.1	51.4	51.4	51.7	52.0	53.5	54.2	52.1
1991	50.9	50.0	50.1	49.9	50.0	50.2	49.0	48.6	49.6	49.5	50.3	51.4	49.9
1992	48.6	47.8	47.6	47.6	47.9	48.1	47.2	47.1	47.5	49.2	50.6	51.7	48.4
1993	49.3	48.2	48.3	49.1	49.4	49.0	49.3	49.4	50.2	51.1	52.6	54.0	49.9
1994	50.8	50.1	50.4	51.1	51.3	51.3	50.9	50.8	51.0	52.3	54.2	55.6	51.6
1995	52.3	51.3	51.6	52.2	52.7	53.1	52.8	52.7	53.0	53.8	55.1	55.6	53.0
1996	52.8	52.2	52.7	52.9	53.6	53.7	53.0	52.2	52.9	53.7	54.8	56.1	53.3
1997	53.3	52.8	53.0	53.7	53.8	54.1	52.5	52.6	53.1	53.9	55.5	57.2	53.7
1998	53.7	53.3	53.8	54.2	54.7	55.0	55.1	55.2	56.2	56.8	58.2	59.4	55.4
1999	56.2	55.6	56.5	56.6	56.8	57.3	57.6	57.9	57.5	57.7	59.3	60.9	57.4
2000	57.2	56.9	57.2	58.1	58.6	59.3	58.5	58.5	59.0	59.4	61.0	62.9	58.8
2001	59.3	59.3	59.6	58.4	58.4	59.0	58.1	58.2	58.2	59.6	60.4	61.6	59.2
2002	57.7	57.1	57.8	57.7	58.5	58.9	58.4	58.6	59.0	58.9	60.4	61.8	58.7
2003	57.6	56.8	57.4	58.0	58.6	58.8	58.5	58.1	58.3	58.6	60.2	61.3	58.5
Wholesale trade													
1990	9.2	9.2	9.2	9.3	9.3	9.4	9.4	9.3	9.4	9.2	9.4	9.3	9.3
1991	9.2	9.0	8.9	8.9	8.7	8.7	8.6	8.5	8.6	8.4	8.3	8.3	8.6
1992	8.3	8.3	8.4	8.1	8.2	8.2	8.0	8.0	8.0	8.1	8.1	8.0	8.1
1993	8.1	8.1	8.0	8.3	8.2	8.2	8.4	8.4	8.3	8.4	8.4	8.4	8.2
1994	8.4	8.4	8.5	8.5	8.5	8.5	8.7	8.6	8.6	8.6	8.8	8.9	8.5
1995	8.7	8.7	8.8	9.0	9.1	9.2	9.0	8.9	8.8	8.7	8.7	8.8	8.8
1996	8.8	8.9	9.0	9.0	9.0	9.1	8.9	8.8	9.0	9.1	8.8	8.8	8.9
1997	8.8	8.9	8.9	9.1	9.1	9.2	9.1	9.0	9.0	9.0	9.0	9.1	9.0
1998	9.2	9.3	9.5	9.6	9.5	9.6	9.6	9.5	9.4	9.5	9.4	9.4	9.4
1999	9.3	9.4	9.5	9.5	9.5	9.5	9.5	9.6	9.5	9.4	9.5	9.7	9.4
2000	9.6	9.7	9.9	10.4	10.3	10.5	10.5	10.6	10.6	10.8	10.8	10.9	10.3
2001	11.6	11.9	12.0	11.6	11.6	11.6	11.6	11.6	11.6	11.8	11.6	11.7	11.7
2002	11.4	11.4	11.8	11.7	11.8	11.9	11.9	12.0	11.9	11.8	11.8	11.8	11.8
2003	11.5	11.6	11.9	12.1	12.3	12.2	12.3	12.4	12.3	12.2	12.3	12.3	12.1

Employment by Industry: Delaware—*Continued*

(Numbers in thousands. Not seasonally adjusted.)

Industry	January	February	March	April	May	June	July	August	September	October	November	December	Annual Average
WILMINGTON—*Continued*													
Retail trade													
1990	33.1	32.4	32.7	31.7	31.7	32.0	31.8	32.1	32.0	32.3	33.7	34.5	32.5
1991	31.7	30.8	30.8	30.9	31.1	31.2	30.5	30.6	30.8	30.9	32.0	32.7	31.1
1992	30.2	29.7	29.3	29.6	29.8	29.9	29.7	29.8	29.8	30.9	32.4	33.3	30.3
1993	31.1	30.2	30.0	30.3	30.7	30.4	30.7	30.8	31.1	31.8	33.0	34.3	31.2
1994	31.4	30.6	30.7	31.2	31.5	31.7	31.4	31.5	31.7	32.8	34.7	35.8	32.0
1995	33.2	32.2	32.3	32.4	32.7	32.8	33.0	33.3	33.6	34.3	35.7	36.4	33.4
1996	33.7	32.7	33.1	33.0	33.5	33.7	33.5	33.0	33.4	33.8	35.3	36.7	33.7
1997	34.3	33.6	33.8	34.2	34.2	34.3	33.4	33.6	33.8	34.3	35.8	37.3	34.3
1998	34.2	33.4	33.7	33.9	34.5	34.7	35.0	35.1	35.9	36.3	37.8	39.1	35.3
1999	36.3	35.3	36.0	35.9	36.0	36.3	36.9	37.0	36.6	37.1	38.5	39.9	36.8
2000	36.7	36.3	36.4	36.9	37.5	38.2	37.6	37.5	37.7	38.0	39.6	41.3	37.8
2001	36.6	36.3	36.6	35.7	35.8	36.3	35.7	36.0	35.9	36.8	38.1	39.3	36.6
2002	36.2	35.5	35.8	35.7	36.2	36.6	36.3	36.5	36.6	36.6	38.1	39.5	36.6
2003	36.0	35.1	35.4	35.9	36.3	36.7	36.5	36.2	36.0	36.3	37.7	39.0	36.4
Transportation and utilities													
1990	10.2	10.2	10.7	10.6	10.5	10.7	10.2	10.0	10.3	10.5	10.4	10.4	10.3
1991	10.0	10.2	10.4	10.1	10.2	10.3	9.9	9.5	10.2	10.2	10.0	10.4	10.1
1992	10.1	9.8	9.9	9.9	9.9	10.0	9.5	9.3	9.7	10.2	10.1	10.4	9.9
1993	10.1	9.9	10.3	10.5	10.5	10.4	10.2	10.2	10.8	10.9	11.2	11.3	10.5
1994	11.0	11.1	11.2	11.4	11.3	11.1	10.8	10.7	10.7	10.9	10.7	10.9	10.9
1995	10.4	10.4	10.5	10.8	10.9	11.1	10.8	10.5	10.6	10.8	10.7	10.4	10.6
1996	10.3	10.6	10.6	10.9	11.1	10.9	10.6	10.4	10.5	10.8	10.7	10.6	10.6
1997	10.2	10.3	10.3	10.4	10.5	10.6	10.0	10.0	10.3	10.6	10.7	10.8	10.3
1998	10.3	10.6	10.6	10.7	10.7	10.7	10.5	10.6	10.9	11.0	11.0	10.9	10.7
1999	10.6	10.9	11.0	11.2	11.3	11.5	11.2	11.3	11.4	11.2	11.3	11.3	11.1
2000	10.9	10.9	10.9	10.8	10.8	10.6	10.4	10.4	10.7	10.6	10.6	10.7	10.6
2001	11.1	11.1	11.0	11.1	11.0	11.1	10.8	10.6	10.7	11.0	10.7	10.6	10.9
2002	10.1	10.2	10.2	10.3	10.5	10.4	10.2	10.1	10.5	10.5	10.5	10.5	10.3
2003	10.1	10.1	10.1	10.0	10.0	9.9	9.7	9.5	10.0	10.1	10.2	10.0	10.0
Information													
1990	3.5	3.6	3.6	3.7	3.7	3.8	3.8	3.8	3.8	3.7	3.6	3.6	3.6
1991	3.4	3.3	3.3	3.2	3.2	3.1	3.1	3.1	3.0	2.9	3.0	2.9	3.1
1992	2.9	2.9	2.9	2.9	2.9	3.0	2.9	2.9	2.9	2.9	2.9	2.9	2.9
1993	2.8	2.8	2.8	2.8	2.8	2.9	3.0	3.0	2.9	3.0	3.1	3.2	2.9
1994	3.4	3.4	3.4	3.4	3.5	3.6	3.6	3.7	3.7	3.6	3.7	3.7	3.5
1995	4.1	4.2	4.2	3.7	3.7	3.8	3.8	3.9	3.9	3.9	3.9	3.9	3.9
1996	3.9	4.0	4.0	4.1	4.0	4.0	4.0	4.0	4.1	4.2	4.2	4.3	4.0
1997	4.3	4.5	4.4	4.4	4.6	5.6	5.6	5.7	5.6	5.5	5.7	5.8	5.1
1998	5.7	5.8	5.9	5.8	5.9	6.0	6.1	6.0	6.1	5.9	6.0	6.0	5.9
1999	6.3	6.5	6.5	6.3	6.4	6.4	6.5	6.6	6.6	6.5	6.5	6.6	6.4
2000	6.7	6.9	7.1	7.0	7.0	7.0	7.1	6.6	7.1	7.0	7.1	7.1	6.9
2001	7.1	7.2	7.2	7.1	7.1	7.2	7.2	7.2	7.1	7.0	7.0	7.0	7.1
2002	6.8	6.9	6.9	6.8	6.8	6.8	6.9	6.9	6.8	6.7	6.8	6.7	6.8
2003	6.6	6.6	6.6	6.5	6.5	6.5	6.5	6.6	6.5	6.5	6.6	6.5	6.5
Financial activities													
1990	22.8	23.3	23.3	23.6	23.9	24.2	24.2	24.2	23.9	23.5	23.5	23.7	23.6
1991	25.3	25.5	25.5	25.1	25.3	25.6	25.5	25.6	25.4	25.5	25.6	25.8	25.4
1992	25.8	26.0	26.1	25.8	26.1	26.4	26.0	26.2	26.2	26.0	26.1	26.2	26.0
1993	25.9	26.0	26.3	26.5	26.9	27.2	27.7	27.9	28.0	27.5	27.7	27.7	27.1
1994	27.5	27.7	27.8	27.7	28.0	28.6	28.7	28.9	29.0	29.0	29.0	28.9	28.4
1995	28.6	29.0	29.1	28.8	28.9	29.2	28.9	29.0	29.0	28.8	28.9	28.9	28.9
1996	28.6	28.9	29.1	29.3	29.4	29.4	29.3	29.5	29.6	29.4	29.5	29.5	29.2
1997	29.4	29.6	30.0	30.1	30.4	31.0	30.9	31.3	31.3	30.8	31.1	31.4	30.6
1998	32.1	32.6	32.2	31.6	32.2	32.9	33.0	32.9	32.6	33.0	33.1	33.7	32.6
1999	33.7	33.7	33.8	32.9	32.7	33.2	33.8	33.8	33.5	33.6	33.5	33.9	33.5
2000	33.1	33.4	33.3	33.1	33.1	33.5	33.3	33.6	33.4	33.4	33.8	33.8	33.4
2001	33.5	33.7	33.7	34.0	34.0	33.9	34.1	34.1	33.6	32.5	32.3	32.2	33.5
2002	33.1	32.9	33.1	33.0	33.0	32.6	32.9	32.6	32.3	32.1	32.2	32.3	32.7
2003	39.7	39.5	39.4	39.2	39.2	39.1	39.4	39.9	39.9	39.7	39.8	39.6	39.5
Professional and business services													
1990	54.3	55.3	56.0	56.7	56.8	57.1	56.8	56.6	56.1	55.6	55.7	55.6	56.0
1991	51.6	51.5	52.4	51.8	51.9	52.1	51.6	51.4	51.0	51.9	51.4	51.1	51.6
1992	49.2	48.6	49.2	49.8	50.2	49.8	50.8	51.1	51.0	50.9	50.9	51.4	50.2
1993	49.7	50.5	50.4	51.3	51.3	51.9	51.7	51.9	51.4	50.8	51.2	51.5	51.1
1994	49.9	50.5	50.8	51.3	51.5	51.8	51.5	52.1	52.4	52.2	52.6	53.1	51.6
1995	52.0	53.0	52.5	53.0	53.1	53.3	54.3	54.8	55.0	55.4	55.8	56.1	54.0
1996	54.8	56.0	56.5	56.2	57.1	57.7	57.2	57.2	58.0	57.0	57.6	57.7	56.9
1997	56.7	57.6	58.7	59.6	59.3	59.7	59.7	60.2	60.2	60.0	60.1	60.7	59.3
1998	58.7	58.9	59.9	61.0	61.2	62.1	63.0	62.8	62.9	61.9	62.1	63.2	61.4
1999	60.0	61.4	62.0	62.7	62.4	63.0	63.9	64.1	63.9	65.3	65.7	66.0	63.3
2000	66.0	66.1	67.4	66.6	66.1	66.8	67.1	66.9	66.7	66.6	66.9	67.3	66.7
2001	65.4	65.2	65.6	65.1	65.1	64.9	63.8	64.2	63.8	64.2	64.7	65.2	64.8
2002	62.3	62.1	61.3	61.5	61.4	60.6	61.0	61.2	60.9	61.0	61.8	62.4	61.5
2003	52.9	51.8	52.1	52.6	52.9	53.0	52.9	52.9	52.5	52.6	53.4	53.8	52.8

Employment by Industry: Delaware—*Continued*

(Numbers in thousands. Not seasonally adjusted.)

Industry	January	February	March	April	May	June	July	August	September	October	November	December	Annual Average
WILMINGTON—*Continued*													
Educational and health services													
1990	25.6	26.1	26.4	25.2	25.3	25.6	25.5	25.6	26.0	26.1	26.4	26.5	25.8
1991	25.9	26.2	26.4	25.9	26.0	26.0	26.2	26.2	26.6	26.7	27.0	27.1	26.3
1992	27.0	27.1	27.3	27.7	27.8	27.6	27.2	27.0	27.2	27.9	28.1	28.1	27.5
1993	28.1	28.3	28.2	28.6	28.6	28.4	28.5	28.4	28.9	29.5	29.5	29.8	28.7
1994	30.2	30.3	30.3	30.7	30.9	30.7	30.5	30.4	30.9	31.5	31.7	31.6	30.8
1995	31.1	31.2	31.3	31.6	31.6	31.5	31.1	31.2	31.8	32.0	32.2	32.0	31.5
1996	31.9	32.4	32.5	32.5	32.7	32.6	31.7	31.5	32.3	32.5	32.7	32.7	32.3
1997	32.2	32.4	32.6	32.8	33.0	32.9	32.7	32.8	33.0	33.2	33.5	33.7	32.9
1998	33.3	33.5	33.8	33.6	33.6	33.6	33.6	33.2	33.4	33.6	33.7	34.0	33.5
1999	33.4	33.6	33.8	33.9	33.9	33.9	34.2	34.1	34.5	34.8	34.9	35.2	34.1
2000	34.8	35.2	35.5	35.4	35.5	35.5	35.4	35.5	35.9	35.8	36.3	36.4	35.6
2001	35.3	35.7	36.1	35.9	36.1	36.2	36.0	36.2	36.2	36.6	36.8	36.9	36.2
2002	36.3	36.7	36.9	37.0	37.2	37.3	36.8	37.2	37.4	37.5	37.7	37.9	37.2
2003	37.8	37.7	38.0	38.1	38.2	38.2	38.1	38.4	38.6	38.8	39.0	39.2	38.3
Leisure and hospitality													
1990	19.2	19.7	20.4	20.9	21.6	22.2	21.3	21.3	20.9	20.3	20.2	20.1	20.6
1991	18.2	18.5	19.0	19.2	19.9	20.5	20.0	19.9	20.0	19.9	20.0	20.0	19.5
1992	18.5	18.7	19.3	20.0	20.9	21.2	20.8	20.7	20.4	20.3	20.1	19.9	20.0
1993	19.3	19.2	19.4	20.6	21.7	21.8	22.2	22.0	21.9	21.2	21.2	21.3	20.9
1994	19.7	19.5	19.9	20.7	21.4	22.3	22.5	22.3	22.0	21.8	21.7	21.4	21.2
1995	20.4	20.3	20.9	21.7	22.3	23.2	23.0	22.8	22.6	22.0	21.9	22.1	21.9
1996	20.5	21.1	21.7	22.7	23.6	24.1	23.7	23.5	23.7	22.5	22.5	22.6	22.6
1997	21.7	22.0	22.4	22.9	23.7	24.8	24.3	24.3	24.1	23.1	23.0	23.3	23.3
1998	22.0	22.5	22.6	23.6	24.3	25.1	25.2	24.9	24.6	23.7	23.3	23.8	23.8
1999	23.0	23.1	23.2	24.2	24.9	25.4	25.2	25.4	24.7	24.4	24.1	24.2	24.3
2000	23.0	23.1	24.1	24.9	25.6	25.9	26.0	26.0	25.4	25.1	24.9	24.9	24.9
2001	23.3	23.8	24.4	25.5	26.5	26.7	26.3	26.2	25.8	25.1	24.6	24.6	25.2
2002	23.3	23.2	23.9	25.5	26.4	26.8	26.8	26.8	26.6	25.5	25.5	25.0	25.4
2003	23.9	23.7	24.5	25.5	26.4	27.0	27.2	27.2	26.8	26.7	26.7	26.5	26.0
Other services													
1990	8.8	9.0	9.1	9.2	9.4	9.7	9.4	9.4	9.1	9.4	9.4	9.4	9.2
1991	9.2	9.3	9.3	9.2	9.5	9.7	9.5	9.4	9.1	9.4	9.3	9.3	9.3
1992	9.3	9.2	9.3	9.5	9.6	9.7	9.8	9.6	9.5	9.7	9.7	9.6	9.5
1993	9.6	9.5	9.5	9.6	9.8	9.7	9.8	9.8	9.6	9.8	9.8	9.9	9.7
1994	9.8	9.8	10.0	10.1	10.2	10.5	10.4	10.3	10.1	10.2	10.2	10.2	10.1
1995	10.0	10.1	10.2	10.2	10.3	10.6	10.6	10.4	10.2	10.3	10.3	10.3	10.2
1996	10.3	10.5	10.6	10.6	10.7	11.1	11.1	11.1	10.8	11.0	11.0	11.0	10.8
1997	11.1	11.2	11.4	11.7	11.9	12.0	12.0	12.0	11.7	11.6	11.7	11.8	11.6
1998	11.4	11.6	11.7	11.8	11.9	12.2	12.3	12.1	12.1	12.1	12.0	12.2	11.9
1999	11.9	12.1	12.1	12.3	12.3	12.7	12.7	12.6	12.5	12.0	12.0	12.2	12.2
2000	12.1	12.2	12.4	12.3	12.3	12.6	12.4	12.5	12.4	12.9	13.0	12.9	12.5
2001	12.9	12.9	13.0	12.9	13.0	13.4	13.1	13.1	12.9	13.0	13.0	13.0	13.0
2002	12.8	13.0	13.2	13.2	13.3	13.5	13.3	13.3	13.1	13.6	13.4	13.5	13.3
2003	12.9	12.9	13.0	13.1	13.3	13.6	13.9	14.1	13.9	13.7	13.5	13.7	13.5
Government													
1990	33.1	34.3	34.8	35.0	35.0	32.8	31.9	31.2	32.2	34.6	34.9	34.6	33.7
1991	33.8	34.2	35.2	34.6	35.1	33.9	33.3	32.5	31.6	34.6	35.0	34.9	34.0
1992	34.4	34.2	35.0	35.4	34.7	34.2	33.7	33.3	32.6	35.3	35.7	35.6	34.5
1993	34.1	35.4	36.2	36.3	35.9	35.6	34.7	34.1	35.6	36.7	37.0	37.3	35.7
1994	35.5	36.1	37.3	36.8	36.8	35.8	33.9	33.8	34.4	35.1	35.5	36.1	35.5
1995	35.1	35.4	36.1	36.5	36.7	35.9	34.1	33.9	34.8	36.4	37.2	37.4	35.7
1996	35.9	36.8	37.9	37.7	37.9	36.9	35.8	35.6	36.5	37.9	38.5	38.8	37.1
1997	37.6	38.2	38.9	38.6	38.6	37.8	36.2	36.3	36.9	38.4	38.9	39.4	37.9
1998	38.5	39.2	39.9	39.8	39.9	38.8	37.2	36.8	38.2	39.0	39.6	40.1	38.9
1999	39.0	39.2	40.3	40.6	40.9	38.6	37.6	37.0	38.5	40.1	40.7	41.0	39.4
2000	39.2	40.6	42.0	42.3	42.8	42.1	40.6	38.3	40.3	42.4	43.3	43.9	41.4
2001	41.4	43.1	43.4	43.2	42.8	41.4	39.7	38.4	40.5	42.5	43.3	43.5	41.9
2002	41.0	42.7	43.3	42.5	42.3	41.1	37.7	36.7	41.3	42.3	43.2	43.0	41.4
2003	41.2	42.5	42.8	42.2	42.4	41.7	38.7	38.2	42.4	43.5	43.4	43.8	41.9
Federal government													
1990	4.6	4.6	4.7	4.9	5.0	5.0	5.1	4.7	4.7	4.7	4.7	4.7	4.7
1991	4.7	4.7	4.7	4.7	4.7	4.7	4.7	4.7	4.7	4.7	4.8	4.9	4.7
1992	4.8	4.8	4.8	4.8	4.8	4.8	5.0	5.0	5.0	5.0	4.9	5.0	4.8
1993	4.9	4.9	4.9	4.9	4.9	4.9	5.0	5.0	5.1	5.1	5.1	5.4	5.0
1994	5.1	5.1	5.1	5.0	5.0	4.9	5.0	5.0	4.9	4.9	4.9	5.2	5.0
1995	4.9	4.9	4.9	5.0	5.0	5.1	5.1	5.1	5.0	5.4	5.4	5.5	5.1
1996	5.0	4.9	4.9	5.0	4.9	5.0	4.9	4.9	4.9	4.9	5.0	5.2	4.9
1997	4.9	4.9	4.8	4.8	4.8	4.8	4.8	4.8	4.8	4.8	4.9	5.1	4.8
1998	4.9	4.9	4.9	4.9	4.9	4.9	4.9	4.9	4.8	5.0	5.0	5.2	4.9
1999	4.9	4.9	4.9	4.9	4.9	4.9	4.9	4.9	4.9	4.9	4.9	5.1	4.9
2000	4.9	5.1	5.1	5.3	6.0	6.4	6.3	6.0	6.1	6.3	6.5	6.8	5.9
2001	6.6	6.6	6.6	6.6	6.6	6.6	6.6	6.6	6.6	6.7	6.7	6.7	6.6
2002	6.7	6.8	6.8	6.8	6.8	6.8	6.8	6.8	6.8	6.8	6.8	6.8	6.8
2003	6.8	6.8	6.8	6.5	6.5	6.5	6.6	6.7	6.7	6.7	6.7	6.7	6.7

Employment by Industry: Delaware—*Continued*

(Numbers in thousands. Not seasonally adjusted.)

Industry	January	February	March	April	May	June	July	August	September	October	November	December	Annual Average
WILMINGTON—*Continued*													
State government													
1990	14.7	15.8	16.1	16.1	16.1	13.8	14.0	13.7	14.6	16.2	16.2	16.0	15.2
1991	15.3	15.5	16.3	15.6	16.2	15.1	14.1	13.8	13.9	15.8	16.0	15.9	15.2
1992	15.3	15.2	15.9	16.1	15.7	14.9	13.9	14.0	13.9	15.9	15.9	15.7	15.2
1993	14.5	15.6	16.3	16.4	16.1	15.6	14.3	14.1	16.0	16.4	16.5	16.4	15.6
1994	15.2	15.8	16.7	16.3	16.3	15.3	14.3	14.3	15.1	15.1	15.3	15.4	15.4
1995	14.8	14.9	15.6	15.9	16.2	15.1	14.5	14.5	15.5	16.0	16.5	16.7	15.5
1996	15.8	16.6	17.5	17.1	17.3	15.9	16.2	16.2	16.7	17.0	17.1	17.1	16.7
1997	16.4	16.9	17.5	17.3	17.3	16.3	16.4	16.6	16.8	17.3	17.4	17.5	16.9
1998	16.8	17.4	17.9	17.9	18.0	16.8	16.8	16.9	17.3	17.5	17.7	17.9	17.4
1999	17.1	16.9	17.9	18.1	18.3	16.0	16.2	15.9	16.6	18.0	18.3	18.3	17.3
2000	16.6	17.7	19.2	19.2	19.1	18.0	18.0	16.6	17.1	19.0	19.4	19.6	18.2
2001	18.0	19.5	19.7	19.7	19.5	18.1	18.1	17.5	18.1	19.2	19.7	19.9	18.9
2002	17.7	18.9	19.2	18.8	18.6	17.9	16.8	16.4	17.7	18.4	19.1	18.9	18.2
2003	17.3	18.4	18.6	18.3	18.5	17.9	17.3	17.0	18.7	19.5	19.3	19.7	18.4
Local government													
1990	13.8	13.9	14.0	14.0	13.9	13.9	12.8	12.8	12.8	13.6	13.9	13.9	13.6
1991	13.9	13.9	14.1	14.2	14.1	14.2	14.4	14.1	12.9	14.0	14.3	14.2	14.0
1992	14.3	14.2	14.3	14.5	14.2	14.5	14.8	14.3	13.7	14.4	14.9	14.9	14.4
1993	14.7	14.9	15.0	15.0	14.9	15.1	15.4	15.0	14.5	15.2	15.4	15.5	15.0
1994	15.2	15.2	15.5	15.5	15.5	15.6	14.6	14.5	14.4	15.1	15.3	15.5	15.1
1995	15.4	15.6	15.6	15.6	15.5	15.7	14.5	14.3	14.3	15.0	15.3	15.2	15.1
1996	15.1	15.3	15.5	15.6	15.7	16.0	14.7	14.5	14.9	16.0	16.4	16.5	15.5
1997	16.3	16.4	16.6	16.5	16.5	16.7	15.0	14.9	15.3	16.3	16.6	16.8	16.1
1998	16.8	16.9	17.1	17.0	17.0	17.1	15.5	15.0	16.1	16.5	16.9	17.0	16.5
1999	17.0	17.4	17.5	17.6	17.7	17.7	16.5	16.2	17.0	17.2	17.5	17.6	17.2
2000	17.7	17.8	17.7	17.8	17.7	17.7	16.3	15.7	17.1	17.1	17.4	17.5	17.2
2001	16.8	17.0	17.1	16.9	16.7	16.7	15.0	14.3	15.8	16.6	16.9	16.9	16.4
2002	16.6	17.0	17.3	16.9	16.9	16.4	14.1	13.5	16.8	17.1	17.3	17.3	16.4
2003	17.1	17.3	17.4	17.4	17.4	17.3	14.8	14.5	17.0	17.3	17.4	17.4	16.9

Average Weekly Hours by Industry: Delaware

(Not seasonally adjusted.)

Industry	January	February	March	April	May	June	July	August	September	October	November	December	Annual Average
STATEWIDE													
Manufacturing													
2001	39.5	39.3	38.6	38.1	39.2	40.2	40.8	40.5	39.9	40.5	39.2	40.9	39.7
2002	38.5	38.5	39.3	39.2	40.5	41.3	41.1	41.5	40.5	39.3	40.1	40.4	40.0
2003	39.4	40.0	39.8	39.5	39.8	41.4	40.7	40.8	40.5	40.6	40.4	40.4	40.3
WILMINGTON													
Manufacturing													
2001	38.0	41.1	40.2	38.0	40.4	40.6	41.8	40.5	39.7	41.2	41.0	42.6	40.4
2002	39.1	40.6	40.8	42.0	41.8	42.3	41.4	41.6	41.9	41.3	41.5	41.2	41.3
2003	40.6	41.4	40.6	40.2	39.0	40.4	40.4	40.1	40.2	40.8	40.5	40.5	40.4

Average Hourly Earnings by Industry: Delaware

(Dollars, not seasonally adjusted.)

Industry	January	February	March	April	May	June	July	August	September	October	November	December	Annual Average
STATEWIDE													
Manufacturing													
2001	16.02	16.13	17.02	16.88	16.38	16.71	16.89	16.86	16.89	16.35	16.37	16.17	16.56
2002	16.01	16.38	16.40	16.68	16.26	16.29	16.47	16.76	16.84	16.87	17.07	17.22	16.60
2003	16.83	16.74	16.85	16.51	16.41	16.63	16.98	17.03	17.18	17.33	17.22	17.04	16.90
WILMINGTON													
Manufacturing													
2001	18.99	18.70	19.44	19.69	19.48	19.83	20.12	20.18	20.21	20.02	20.33	20.24	19.78
2002	19.99	20.16	19.86	19.77	19.63	19.96	20.15	20.44	20.40	20.58	20.59	20.75	20.19
2003	20.79	20.83	20.48	20.56	20.41	20.44	20.91	20.78	21.13	21.24	21.31	21.36	20.84

Average Weekly Earnings by Industry: Delaware

(Dollars, not seasonally adjusted.)

Industry	January	February	March	April	May	June	July	August	September	October	November	December	Annual Average
STATEWIDE													
Manufacturing													
2001	632.79	633.91	656.97	643.13	642.10	671.74	689.11	682.83	673.91	662.18	641.70	661.35	657.43
2002	616.39	630.63	644.52	653.86	658.53	672.78	676.92	695.54	682.02	662.99	684.51	695.69	664.00
2003	663.10	669.60	670.63	652.15	653.12	688.48	691.09	694.82	695.79	703.60	695.69	688.42	681.07
WILMINGTON													
Manufacturing													
2001	721.62	768.57	781.49	748.22	786.99	805.10	841.02	817.29	802.34	824.82	833.53	862.22	799.11
2002	781.61	818.50	810.29	830.34	820.53	844.31	834.21	850.30	854.76	849.95	854.49	854.90	833.85
2003	844.07	862.36	831.49	826.51	795.99	825.78	844.76	833.28	849.43	866.59	863.06	865.08	841.94

DISTRICT OF COLUMBIA AT A GLANCE

(Population and total nonfarm employment numbers in thousands)

Population, Census 2000:	572.1
Total nonfarm employment, 2003:	664.6
Change in total nonfarm employment	
(Number)	
1990–2003:	-21.4
1990–2001:	-32.3
2001–2003:	10.9
(Compound annual rate of change)	
1990–2003:	-0.2%
1990–2001:	-0.4%
2001–2003:	0.8%
Unemployment rate	
1990:	6.0%
2001:	6.2%
2003:	7.2%

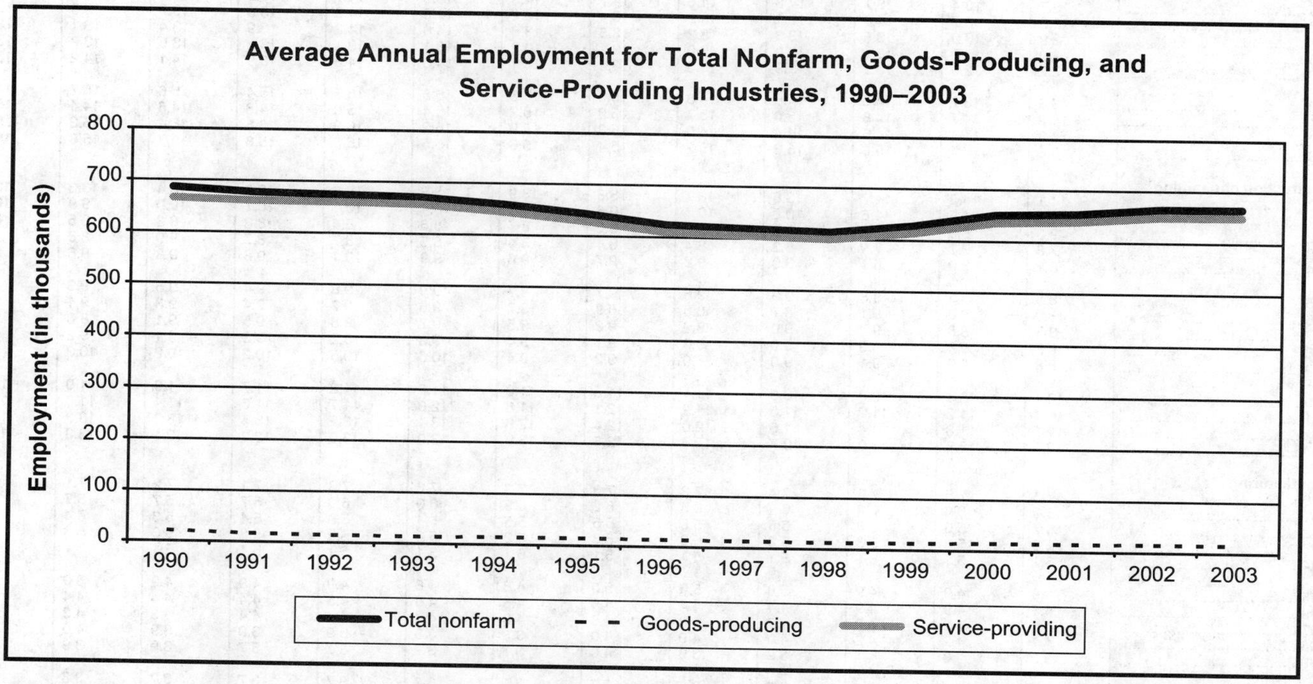

Total nonfarm payroll employment declined during much of the 1990s until private sector employment rebounded in 1998. The federal government, the largest employer in the District, shed jobs throughout the decade, but posted moderate gains following the 2001 recession. In 2003, the federal government provided 29 percent of employment. Overall, more than 97 percent of jobs are in the service-producing sector. (The unemployment rate and population data apply only to residents of the District, while the employment data includes workers who reside in the neighboring states of Maryland and Virginia.)

Employment by Industry: District of Columbia

(Numbers in thousands. Not seasonally adjusted.)

Industry	January	February	March	April	May	June	July	August	September	October	November	December	Annual Average
STATEWIDE													
Total nonfarm													
1990	677.1	682.3	688.5	684.2	688.7	695.0	697.5	684.8	686.6	681.0	682.0	685.0	686.0
1991	672.0	674.7	677.1	673.8	677.9	684.0	683.9	675.5	678.0	673.9	677.8	678.3	677.2
1992	666.5	666.4	671.3	673.9	676.6	679.7	687.5	670.0	672.1	672.8	672.0	675.2	673.6
1993	667.7	667.1	671.0	671.3	674.0	675.2	682.8	661.5	667.8	666.4	668.7	670.4	670.3
1994	649.0	651.9	656.3	663.4	664.8	669.0	673.1	653.9	657.8	655.2	655.1	655.3	658.7
1995	634.9	639.5	641.8	644.3	645.2	647.9	656.3	637.3	641.9	641.0	640.4	640.7	642.6
1996	615.5	626.7	629.5	620.4	619.8	622.1	634.3	619.0	622.1	621.0	622.4	623.7	623.0
1997	607.1	612.7	616.5	614.3	612.9	617.4	637.1	620.6	623.6	619.3	618.7	621.2	618.4
1998	603.5	610.7	612.3	612.2	612.4	616.9	622.6	611.6	613.8	614.8	615.0	617.0	613.5
1999	604.2	610.6	613.0	621.4	622.7	627.8	639.8	629.1	632.3	640.9	642.7	644.3	627.4
2000	628.8	634.5	638.9	643.9	644.0	652.1	661.5	656.6	654.0	659.0	662.9	667.2	650.2
2001	640.7	641.9	647.1	647.2	649.9	654.6	662.6	662.9	656.7	661.1	659.3	659.8	653.7
2002	648.3	653.3	660.3	662.6	660.9	664.8	674.4	669.9	666.9	667.4	670.9	671.1	664.2
2003	656.9	659.0	665.2	664.0	663.8	664.2	672.0	661.6	663.8	667.7	667.8	669.2	664.6
Total private													
1990	401.2	407.0	411.9	409.3	411.7	413.4	407.8	409.1	410.7	406.7	407.7	408.4	408.7
1991	394.6	397.9	399.4	396.9	399.4	399.4	393.7	392.9	396.1	392.3	395.0	394.8	396.0
1992	383.1	385.2	388.0	390.4	392.2	391.7	387.1	383.9	386.1	389.0	387.4	389.9	387.8
1993	379.4	381.1	384.6	384.0	385.8	384.8	381.9	379.1	385.8	389.4	391.6	393.0	385.0
1994	375.1	379.4	382.9	389.8	391.7	394.3	390.6	388.8	391.4	391.1	391.9	392.1	388.2
1995	377.3	382.1	384.9	387.9	389.9	393.0	389.2	386.3	390.7	389.2	390.4	391.6	387.7
1996	370.3	382.1	385.0	378.4	378.4	380.3	386.0	384.3	388.3	384.7	385.9	387.1	382.5
1997	372.7	378.9	383.9	380.7	379.4	382.9	390.7	387.8	393.0	390.4	390.2	392.5	385.2
1998	376.0	384.6	386.9	385.7	386.0	389.6	388.0	385.1	390.6	393.2	392.9	394.6	387.7
1999	383.0	390.0	392.2	402.3	401.6	404.7	408.0	406.0	410.5	417.9	420.9	422.0	404.9
2000	407.1	413.1	417.4	422.3	420.1	426.3	428.8	427.3	430.6	438.2	441.2	443.5	426.3
2001	419.7	423.3	427.2	427.2	428.6	428.8	427.8	428.1	427.4	431.4	430.8	429.9	427.5
2002	418.0	424.2	430.5	433.8	431.4	432.3	434.3	432.3	435.0	438.2	440.5	439.9	432.5
2003	427.3	429.4	434.2	433.6	432.9	431.6	433.1	429.3	433.1	437.9	439.0	439.0	433.4
Goods-producing													
1990	21.6	21.8	22.2	21.2	21.0	21.1	21.2	21.0	21.1	20.6	20.6	20.4	21.1
1991	18.7	18.5	18.5	17.0	17.0	16.8	16.2	16.4	16.1	15.8	15.7	15.6	16.8
1992	14.7	14.4	14.5	14.5	14.7	14.7	14.2	14.0	13.9	13.7	13.6	13.9	14.2
1993	13.1	13.0	13.2	13.6	13.7	13.7	13.6	13.7	14.0	14.0	14.2	14.1	13.6
1994	13.3	13.1	13.5	14.1	14.3	14.8	14.7	15.0	15.2	14.9	14.9	14.7	14.3
1995	13.7	13.4	13.7	14.3	14.6	14.7	14.5	14.7	14.7	14.3	14.4	14.3	14.2
1996	12.8	13.7	14.0	13.1	13.2	13.4	14.2	14.3	14.2	13.8	13.7	13.5	13.6
1997	12.9	13.0	13.5	13.3	13.2	13.5	13.8	14.0	14.2	13.9	13.4	13.1	13.4
1998	12.9	13.0	13.1	13.0	13.0	13.1	13.2	13.1	13.1	13.2	13.0	13.2	13.0
1999	12.7	12.9	13.2	12.9	12.8	13.2	14.1	14.3	14.2	13.9	14.1	14.2	13.5
2000	13.8	13.7	14.5	14.6	14.8	15.0	15.3	15.5	15.5	15.4	15.6	15.7	14.9
2001	14.9	14.7	14.8	15.0	15.4	15.6	15.2	15.4	15.0	14.8	14.6	14.4	15.0
2002	14.3	14.4	14.6	14.4	14.9	15.3	15.9	16.2	16.3	16.5	16.4	16.3	15.5
2003	15.6	15.4	15.8	15.3	15.2	15.4	15.6	15.5	15.5	15.8	15.7	15.8	15.6
Construction and mining													
1990	14.1	14.3	14.7	13.8	13.7	13.8	13.9	13.8	13.8	13.5	13.4	13.3	13.8
1991	11.8	11.6	11.6	10.8	10.7	10.6	10.3	10.4	10.1	10.1	10.0	9.9	10.6
1992	9.0	8.9	9.0	9.0	9.2	9.2	8.7	8.6	8.4	8.3	8.3	8.5	8.7
1993	7.8	7.7	7.9	8.3	8.4	8.4	8.4	8.5	8.7	8.7	8.9	8.8	8.3
1994	8.2	8.0	8.4	9.0	9.2	9.7	9.6	9.9	10.1	9.8	9.8	9.6	9.2
1995	8.8	8.5	8.8	9.3	9.6	9.7	9.7	9.9	9.8	9.4	9.5	9.3	9.3
1996	8.0	8.8	9.1	8.7	8.8	8.9	9.7	9.8	9.7	9.4	9.3	9.1	9.1
1997	8.7	8.8	9.2	9.0	8.9	9.2	9.5	9.7	9.8	9.5	9.1	8.8	9.1
1998	8.8	8.8	8.9	9.0	9.0	9.1	9.4	9.3	9.2	9.3	9.1	9.2	9.0
1999	8.8	8.9	9.1	9.0	8.9	9.2	10.4	10.6	10.5	10.2	10.2	10.3	9.6
2000	10.1	10.1	10.8	10.9	11.1	11.3	11.6	11.8	11.8	11.7	11.9	11.9	11.2
2001	11.4	11.2	11.2	11.5	11.9	12.1	11.8	12.0	11.7	11.6	11.4	11.3	11.6
2002	11.1	11.3	11.4	11.5	12.0	12.4	12.8	13.1	13.2	13.4	13.3	13.3	12.4
2003	13.0	12.8	13.2	12.7	12.6	12.8	13.0	13.0	13.0	13.2	13.1	13.3	13.0
Manufacturing													
1990	7.5	7.5	7.5	7.4	7.3	7.3	7.3	7.2	7.3	7.1	7.2	7.1	7.3
1991	6.9	6.9	6.9	6.2	6.3	6.2	5.9	6.0	6.0	5.7	5.7	5.7	6.2
1992	5.7	5.5	5.5	5.5	5.5	5.5	5.5	5.4	5.5	5.4	5.3	5.4	5.4
1993	5.3	5.3	5.3	5.3	5.3	5.3	5.2	5.2	5.3	5.3	5.3	5.3	5.2
1994	5.1	5.1	5.1	5.1	5.1	5.1	5.1	5.1	5.1	5.1	5.1	5.1	5.1
1995	4.9	4.9	4.9	5.0	5.0	5.0	4.8	4.8	4.9	4.9	4.9	5.0	4.9
1996	4.8	4.9	4.9	4.4	4.4	4.5	4.5	4.5	4.5	4.4	4.4	4.4	4.5
1997	4.2	4.2	4.3	4.3	4.3	4.3	4.3	4.3	4.4	4.4	4.3	4.3	4.3
1998	4.1	4.2	4.2	4.0	4.0	4.0	3.8	3.8	3.9	3.9	3.9	4.0	3.9
1999	3.9	4.0	4.1	3.9	3.9	4.0	3.7	3.7	3.7	3.7	3.9	3.9	3.8
2000	3.7	3.6	3.7	3.7	3.7	3.7	3.7	3.7	3.7	3.7	3.7	3.8	3.7
2001	3.5	3.5	3.6	3.5	3.5	3.5	3.4	3.4	3.3	3.2	3.2	3.1	3.4
2002	3.2	3.1	3.2	2.9	2.9	2.9	3.1	3.1	3.1	3.1	3.1	3.0	3.1
2003	2.6	2.6	2.6	2.6	2.6	2.6	2.6	2.5	2.5	2.6	2.6	2.5	2.6

Employment by Industry: District of Columbia—*Continued*

(Numbers in thousands. Not seasonally adjusted.)

Industry	January	February	March	April	May	June	July	August	September	October	November	December	Annual Average
STATEWIDE—*Continued*													
Service-providing													
1990	655.5	660.5	666.3	663.0	667.7	673.9	676.3	663.8	665.5	660.4	661.4	664.6	664.9
1991	653.3	656.2	658.6	656.8	660.9	667.2	667.7	659.1	661.9	658.1	662.1	662.7	660.3
1992	651.8	652.0	656.8	659.4	661.9	665.0	673.3	656.0	658.2	659.1	658.4	661.3	659.4
1993	654.6	654.1	657.8	657.7	660.3	661.5	669.2	647.8	653.8	652.4	654.5	656.3	656.6
1994	635.7	638.8	642.8	649.3	650.5	654.2	658.4	638.9	642.6	640.3	640.2	640.6	644.3
1995	621.2	626.1	628.1	630.0	630.6	633.2	641.8	622.6	627.2	626.7	626.0	626.4	628.3
1996	602.7	613.0	615.5	607.3	606.6	608.7	620.1	604.7	607.9	607.2	608.7	610.2	609.3
1997	594.2	599.7	603.0	601.0	599.7	603.9	623.3	606.6	609.4	605.4	605.3	608.1	604.9
1998	590.6	597.7	599.2	599.2	599.4	603.8	609.4	598.5	600.7	601.6	602.0	603.8	600.4
1999	591.5	597.7	599.8	608.5	609.9	614.6	625.7	614.8	618.1	627.0	628.6	630.1	613.8
2000	615.0	620.8	624.4	629.3	629.2	637.1	646.2	641.1	638.5	643.6	647.3	651.5	635.3
2001	625.8	627.2	632.3	632.2	634.5	639.0	647.4	647.5	641.7	646.3	644.7	645.4	638.7
2002	634.0	638.9	645.7	648.2	646.0	649.5	658.5	653.7	650.6	650.9	654.5	654.8	648.8
2003	641.3	643.6	649.4	648.7	648.6	648.8	656.4	646.1	648.3	651.9	652.1	653.4	649.1
Trade, transportation, and utilities													
1990	44.7	45.2	45.6	45.0	45.2	45.3	44.2	44.4	44.2	43.9	44.4	45.2	44.7
1991	42.8	42.6	42.6	42.2	42.4	42.5	41.9	41.9	41.9	41.7	42.1	42.5	42.2
1992	39.9	39.5	39.4	39.4	39.5	39.4	38.8	38.2	38.3	38.2	38.2	38.8	38.9
1993	36.9	36.7	36.8	36.5	36.7	36.8	36.3	36.0	36.1	36.6	37.2	37.7	36.6
1994	34.8	34.8	35.0	35.3	35.4	35.7	34.5	34.4	34.3	34.6	35.2	35.7	34.9
1995	33.6	33.5	33.2	33.4	33.3	33.8	32.9	32.8	32.9	33.4	34.0	34.7	33.4
1996	32.6	32.8	33.0	31.4	31.2	31.6	31.4	31.1	31.0	30.7	31.4	31.9	31.6
1997	29.8	29.9	30.0	29.6	29.3	29.7	29.9	29.7	30.0	30.2	30.3	30.6	29.9
1998	28.4	28.6	28.8	28.1	28.0	28.4	28.2	28.1	28.6	28.9	29.2	30.1	28.6
1999	27.6	27.8	27.8	29.6	29.4	29.7	30.1	30.1	30.2	30.2	30.7	31.6	29.5
2000	29.2	29.3	29.3	29.1	29.1	29.7	29.0	28.9	29.3	29.6	30.4	31.2	29.5
2001	28.2	27.8	28.0	27.7	27.9	28.3	27.7	28.0	28.1	28.3	28.5	28.8	28.1
2002	27.5	27.7	27.4	27.6	27.7	28.0	27.9	27.6	27.7	27.9	28.4	29.0	27.9
2003	27.5	27.3	27.7	27.7	27.8	28.3	27.6	27.9	27.7	27.8	28.2	28.7	27.9
Wholesale trade													
1990	6.5	6.6	6.6	6.6	6.7	6.6	6.6	6.6	6.5	6.4	6.3	6.4	6.5
1991	6.0	6.0	6.0	6.0	6.0	6.0	5.8	5.8	5.8	5.7	5.7	5.7	5.8
1992	5.5	5.6	5.6	5.8	5.7	5.8	5.8	5.7	5.7	5.7	5.6	5.6	5.6
1993	5.4	5.3	5.4	5.3	5.2	5.2	5.1	4.9	4.9	4.9	4.8	4.8	5.1
1994	4.5	4.5	4.5	4.5	4.5	4.5	4.4	4.4	4.3	4.2	4.3	4.3	4.4
1995	4.2	4.2	4.3	4.2	4.2	4.2	4.2	4.2	4.2	4.1	4.2	4.3	4.2
1996	4.3	4.3	4.3	4.1	4.1	4.1	4.1	4.2	4.1	4.0	4.1	4.0	4.1
1997	4.1	4.2	4.1	4.0	4.0	4.1	4.2	4.2	4.2	4.1	4.1	4.1	4.1
1998	3.9	3.9	3.9	4.1	4.0	4.1	4.0	3.9	4.0	4.0	4.0	4.0	3.9
1999	3.9	4.0	4.0	4.4	4.4	4.4	4.4	4.4	4.4	4.5	4.6	4.7	4.3
2000	4.5	4.5	4.5	4.4	4.4	4.4	4.3	4.3	4.3	4.4	4.4	4.5	4.4
2001	4.3	4.3	4.3	4.3	4.3	4.4	4.5	4.5	4.5	4.4	4.3	4.4	4.4
2002	4.1	4.2	4.2	4.2	4.2	4.3	4.5	4.4	4.5	4.5	4.5	4.6	4.4
2003	4.5	4.5	4.5	4.4	4.5	4.5	4.5	4.5	4.4	4.4	4.3	4.4	4.5
Retail trade													
1990	25.7	26.0	26.2	25.7	25.6	25.7	24.8	24.9	24.9	24.9	25.5	26.2	25.5
1991	23.9	23.6	23.6	22.8	22.8	22.9	22.4	22.4	22.5	22.5	22.9	23.4	22.9
1992	21.7	21.3	21.4	21.3	21.5	21.6	21.1	20.8	21.0	20.8	21.1	21.8	21.2
1993	20.3	20.2	20.0	19.9	20.1	20.1	19.7	19.5	19.6	20.1	20.7	21.2	20.1
1994	19.8	19.6	19.7	20.0	20.1	20.3	19.5	19.3	19.5	19.9	20.3	20.7	19.8
1995	19.2	19.3	19.2	19.6	19.6	19.7	19.1	19.0	19.2	19.3	19.7	20.3	19.4
1996	18.9	19.0	19.0	18.2	18.0	18.3	18.6	18.3	18.5	18.2	18.8	19.2	18.5
1997	17.7	17.6	17.8	17.6	17.5	17.6	17.7	17.6	18.0	18.2	18.5	18.6	17.8
1998	16.9	16.9	17.0	16.4	16.5	16.7	16.6	16.5	16.8	17.3	17.8	18.4	16.9
1999	16.6	16.6	16.6	17.6	17.6	17.8	17.5	17.4	17.7	17.8	18.2	18.8	17.5
2000	17.0	16.9	17.1	16.8	16.9	17.3	17.0	17.0	17.5	17.7	18.4	18.8	17.3
2001	17.3	17.0	17.1	16.7	16.9	17.0	16.6	16.9	17.0	17.5	17.9	18.1	17.2
2002	17.3	17.2	17.0	17.0	17.1	17.2	17.0	16.8	16.9	17.0	17.5	18.0	17.2
2003	16.7	16.6	16.7	16.8	16.8	17.3	16.8	17.0	17.1	17.2	17.7	18.1	17.1
Transportation and utilities													
1990	12.5	12.6	12.8	12.7	12.9	13.0	12.8	12.9	12.8	12.6	12.6	12.6	12.7
1991	12.9	13.0	13.0	13.4	13.6	13.6	13.7	13.7	13.6	13.5	13.5	13.4	13.4
1992	12.7	12.6	12.4	12.3	12.3	12.0	11.9	11.7	11.6	11.7	11.5	11.4	12.0
1993	11.2	11.2	11.4	11.3	11.4	11.5	11.5	11.6	11.6	11.6	11.7	11.7	11.4
1994	10.5	10.7	10.8	10.8	10.8	10.9	10.6	10.7	10.5	10.5	10.6	10.7	10.6
1995	10.2	10.0	9.7	9.6	9.5	9.9	9.6	9.6	9.5	10.0	10.1	10.1	9.8
1996	9.4	9.5	9.7	9.1	9.1	9.2	8.7	8.6	8.4	8.5	8.5	8.7	8.9
1997	8.0	8.1	8.1	8.0	7.8	8.0	8.0	7.9	7.8	7.9	7.7	7.9	7.9
1998	7.6	7.8	7.9	7.6	7.5	7.6	7.6	7.7	7.8	7.6	7.4	7.7	7.6
1999	7.1	7.2	7.2	7.6	7.4	7.5	8.2	8.3	8.1	7.9	7.9	8.1	7.7
2000	7.7	7.9	7.7	7.9	7.8	8.0	7.7	7.6	7.5	7.5	7.6	7.9	7.7
2001	6.6	6.5	6.6	6.7	6.7	6.9	6.6	6.6	6.6	6.4	6.3	6.3	6.6
2002	6.1	6.3	6.2	6.4	6.4	6.5	6.4	6.4	6.3	6.4	6.4	6.4	6.4
2003	6.3	6.2	6.5	6.5	6.5	6.5	6.3	6.4	6.2	6.2	6.2	6.2	6.3

Employment by Industry: District of Columbia—*Continued*

(Numbers in thousands. Not seasonally adjusted.)

Industry	January	February	March	April	May	June	July	August	September	October	November	December	Annual Average
STATEWIDE—*Continued*													
Information													
1990	25.5	25.6	25.8	25.8	25.9	26.2	26.1	26.2	26.2	25.7	25.8	26.0	25.9
1991	25.1	25.3	25.3	25.1	25.2	25.0	25.0	25.0	25.0	24.8	25.0	25.0	25.0
1992	23.9	23.8	24.1	24.3	24.4	24.5	24.5	24.6	24.6	24.6	24.7	25.0	24.4
1993	24.1	24.2	24.3	24.0	24.1	23.8	23.4	23.4	23.4	23.3	23.4	23.5	23.7
1994	23.0	23.1	23.3	23.1	23.1	23.6	23.0	23.0	23.0	22.7	22.9	23.1	23.0
1995	22.9	23.1	23.4	23.4	23.8	24.2	23.9	24.1	24.2	24.8	24.9	25.1	23.9
1996	24.0	24.3	24.5	24.1	24.0	24.8	24.3	24.3	24.3	24.1	24.3	24.5	24.2
1997	23.9	24.1	24.4	24.0	24.2	24.4	24.4	24.5	24.8	23.7	23.6	23.8	24.1
1998	22.8	23.1	23.1	22.9	22.9	22.9	22.3	22.4	22.5	22.7	22.6	22.8	22.7
1999	22.7	22.8	22.8	23.2	23.3	24.3	24.3	24.3	24.3	24.1	24.5	24.6	23.7
2000	24.2	24.4	24.6	24.7	24.6	25.5	25.8	26.0	26.1	25.9	26.1	26.4	25.3
2001	25.3	25.5	25.5	25.8	25.8	25.8	25.5	26.3	26.0	26.0	26.0	26.1	25.8
2002	25.7	25.6	26.0	25.7	25.7	25.8	25.3	25.3	25.1	24.6	24.7	24.7	25.4
2003	25.0	25.3	25.4	24.5	24.7	24.5	24.7	24.7	24.7	24.1	24.3	24.1	24.7
Financial activities													
1990	33.2	33.3	33.3	33.2	33.5	33.8	34.2	34.4	34.0	32.8	32.9	32.8	33.4
1991	33.7	32.7	32.9	31.9	32.3	31.8	32.1	32.0	31.6	31.4	31.1	30.8	32.0
1992	31.2	31.3	31.2	30.2	30.5	30.6	29.8	29.5	29.2	29.6	29.1	29.2	30.1
1993	29.3	28.8	29.5	28.9	28.8	29.0	29.0	28.9	28.9	29.7	29.7	30.3	29.2
1994	29.0	29.1	29.3	29.8	29.7	29.9	30.0	30.0	29.7	29.4	29.5	29.6	29.5
1995	29.3	29.2	29.3	29.3	29.3	29.6	29.3	29.2	29.0	29.5	29.4	29.5	29.3
1996	29.0	29.6	29.2	27.9	27.7	27.9	28.4	28.6	28.3	27.3	27.4	27.8	28.2
1997	28.4	28.1	28.7	28.1	28.2	28.4	28.6	27.7	27.7	28.5	28.6	28.8	28.3
1998	27.7	28.0	28.7	27.9	28.0	28.3	29.4	29.5	29.6	29.7	30.0	30.1	28.9
1999	30.2	30.6	30.4	29.8	30.4	30.8	31.3	31.4	31.6	32.3	32.9	33.6	31.2
2000	32.6	32.8	33.1	32.7	32.4	32.8	33.4	33.6	33.6	33.8	34.0	34.7	33.2
2001	30.4	30.4	30.5	31.0	31.0	31.1	31.5	31.5	31.2	31.3	31.2	31.5	31.1
2002	30.4	30.6	30.9	30.3	30.3	30.6	31.0	31.2	31.0	31.2	31.3	31.3	30.8
2003	30.8	30.8	30.8	31.3	31.4	31.3	31.1	30.8	30.7	31.0	31.0	31.1	31.0
Professional and business services													
1990	107.0	108.8	110.7	109.8	111.1	112.7	110.7	110.9	110.3	108.2	108.0	108.6	109.7
1991	105.9	107.0	107.5	106.9	107.5	108.8	108.9	108.4	107.9	107.3	107.4	107.7	107.6
1992	105.8	106.0	107.0	107.4	107.8	109.2	109.0	107.6	107.6	108.8	108.7	109.4	107.8
1993	105.2	106.2	106.9	107.1	107.9	109.7	108.8	108.4	108.7	110.8	110.6	111.5	108.4
1994	106.6	107.8	108.6	110.7	112.2	114.4	112.8	112.7	111.8	111.1	111.4	112.1	111.0
1995	108.2	109.7	110.4	110.6	111.0	113.0	111.8	111.7	110.7	111.2	111.8	112.4	111.0
1996	106.7	109.4	109.7	106.7	106.7	109.4	115.1	114.3	113.6	112.3	113.1	114.0	110.9
1997	111.3	112.5	114.2	111.4	111.5	114.3	116.7	115.6	116.5	119.0	118.4	119.4	115.0
1998	113.7	116.4	117.0	117.2	117.0	120.0	118.4	117.4	117.8	121.2	120.4	121.3	118.1
1999	116.5	119.5	120.2	123.9	124.0	126.1	127.2	126.6	125.8	129.9	130.4	131.5	125.1
2000	125.7	127.8	128.2	130.0	130.4	133.2	134.8	134.0	134.3	138.5	139.3	140.5	133.0
2001	135.9	137.3	138.4	137.6	138.0	140.8	140.2	139.5	137.4	139.9	139.9	140.1	138.8
2002	135.2	136.2	137.5	139.3	139.1	141.1	141.2	140.2	139.5	139.6	140.0	140.5	139.1
2003	137.7	137.9	138.8	139.8	140.3	141.5	142.7	141.7	141.3	142.3	143.0	143.6	140.9
Educational and health services													
1990	79.4	80.7	81.3	81.3	80.8	79.7	78.6	80.2	81.9	82.5	83.0	82.4	80.9
1991	80.0	82.4	82.6	83.7	83.6	82.0	79.3	79.9	83.0	81.0	82.5	82.4	81.8
1992	79.7	81.7	82.0	83.7	82.8	80.3	79.6	79.7	81.8	82.3	82.7	82.9	81.6
1993	81.4	82.2	82.7	81.6	81.0	78.3	79.4	78.2	82.7	82.0	83.4	83.0	81.3
1994	79.8	81.8	82.2	83.0	82.1	79.7	80.6	79.5	83.7	84.3	83.6	83.3	81.9
1995	78.1	80.5	80.9	81.5	80.5	79.8	81.7	79.3	84.5	80.2	80.2	79.9	80.5
1996	75.7	79.8	80.7	82.8	82.6	79.1	77.9	78.0	82.3	82.2	81.9	82.2	80.4
1997	78.2	81.5	82.4	84.2	82.6	80.6	84.9	85.1	86.8	82.7	83.8	84.9	83.1
1998	82.4	85.9	85.3	85.3	85.3	84.2	86.1	85.4	88.6	86.8	87.1	87.0	85.7
1999	86.4	87.9	87.5	90.8	89.0	86.2	84.6	84.7	88.9	89.6	89.2	88.3	87.7
2000	88.3	90.1	90.8	91.9	89.4	89.7	90.8	90.9	91.8	94.1	95.3	95.1	91.5
2001	84.5	85.5	86.2	86.6	86.1	81.5	83.0	83.3	86.3	87.7	86.8	85.7	85.3
2002	86.9	89.7	92.1	92.1	88.5	85.6	86.3	86.5	89.5	92.2	93.5	92.4	89.6
2003	88.3	89.7	90.7	89.1	86.8	84.2	86.0	84.6	88.4	90.9	90.9	90.0	88.3
Leisure and hospitality													
1990	45.3	46.8	47.8	47.5	48.5	48.5	46.9	46.4	47.2	47.4	47.1	47.0	47.2
1991	43.8	44.4	44.8	44.9	46.1	46.9	44.5	43.9	45.0	44.6	45.1	44.7	44.8
1992	42.3	42.5	43.4	44.2	45.5	45.5	43.5	43.4	43.9	44.3	43.4	43.3	43.7
1993	42.2	42.8	43.4	44.4	45.6	45.4	43.0	42.7	43.9	44.9	45.1	44.6	44.0
1994	41.3	42.0	43.1	45.1	45.9	46.4	45.3	45.1	45.0	45.9	46.0	45.1	44.6
1995	43.7	44.6	45.5	46.6	48.2	48.3	45.8	45.8	46.1	47.3	47.1	46.5	46.2
1996	42.2	44.6	45.6	45.4	46.0	46.3	45.9	45.4	46.7	45.6	45.9	44.4	45.3
1997	41.1	42.3	42.9	42.8	42.9	43.6	44.1	43.4	45.1	43.9	43.6	43.4	43.2
1998	41.2	42.1	42.9	43.3	44.0	44.4	41.7	40.7	42.0	41.9	41.7	41.0	42.2
1999	39.2	39.9	41.5	43.1	43.7	45.1	45.5	44.6	46.1	46.9	47.7	46.5	44.1
2000	43.3	44.5	46.0	48.2	48.5	49.1	48.4	47.5	48.8	50.0	50.4	50.1	47.9
2001	45.9	47.6	48.6	48.0	48.6	49.1	48.9	48.3	47.7	46.7	47.0	46.2	47.7
2002	43.4	44.9	46.7	48.3	49.2	49.5	49.6	48.5	49.3	49.9	49.9	49.3	48.2
2003	47.4	47.7	49.2	50.2	50.7	50.2	49.2	48.4	49.2	50.3	50.4	49.8	49.4

Employment by Industry: District of Columbia—*Continued*

(Numbers in thousands. Not seasonally adjusted.)

Industry	January	February	March	April	May	June	July	August	September	October	November	December	Annual Average
STATEWIDE—*Continued*													
Other services													
1990	44.5	44.8	45.2	45.5	45.7	46.1	45.9	45.6	45.8	45.6	45.9	46.0	45.5
1991	44.6	45.0	45.2	45.2	45.3	45.6	45.8	45.4	45.6	45.7	46.1	46.1	45.4
1992	45.6	46.0	46.4	46.7	47.0	47.5	47.7	46.9	46.8	47.5	47.0	47.4	46.8
1993	47.2	47.2	47.8	47.9	48.0	48.1	48.4	47.8	48.1	48.1	48.0	48.3	47.9
1994	47.3	47.7	47.9	48.7	49.0	49.8	49.7	49.1	48.7	48.2	48.4	48.5	48.5
1995	47.8	48.1	48.5	48.8	49.2	49.6	49.3	48.7	48.6	48.5	48.6	49.2	48.7
1996	47.3	47.9	48.3	47.0	47.0	47.8	48.8	48.3	47.9	48.7	48.2	48.8	48.0
1997	47.1	47.5	47.8	47.3	47.5	48.4	48.3	47.8	47.9	48.5	48.5	48.5	47.9
1998	46.9	47.5	48.0	48.0	47.8	48.3	48.7	48.5	48.4	48.8	48.9	49.1	48.2
1999	47.7	48.6	48.8	49.0	49.0	49.3	50.9	50.0	49.4	51.0	51.4	51.7	49.7
2000	50.0	50.5	50.9	51.1	50.9	51.3	51.3	50.9	51.2	50.9	50.1	49.8	50.7
2001	54.6	54.5	55.2	55.5	55.8	56.6	55.8	55.8	55.7	56.7	56.8	57.1	55.8
2002	54.6	55.1	55.3	56.1	56.0	56.4	57.1	56.8	56.6	56.3	56.3	56.4	56.1
2003	55.0	55.3	55.8	55.7	56.0	56.2	56.2	55.7	55.6	55.7	55.5	55.9	55.7
Government													
1990	275.9	275.3	276.6	274.9	277.0	281.6	289.7	275.7	275.9	274.3	274.3	276.6	277.3
1991	277.4	276.8	277.7	276.9	278.5	284.6	290.2	282.6	281.9	281.6	282.8	283.5	281.2
1992	283.4	281.2	283.3	283.5	284.4	288.0	300.4	286.1	286.0	283.8	284.6	285.3	285.8
1993	288.3	286.0	286.4	287.3	288.2	290.4	300.9	282.4	282.0	277.0	277.1	277.4	285.2
1994	273.9	272.5	273.4	273.6	273.1	274.7	282.5	265.1	266.4	264.1	263.2	263.2	270.4
1995	257.6	257.4	256.9	256.4	255.3	254.9	267.1	251.0	251.2	251.8	250.0	249.1	254.8
1996	245.2	244.6	244.5	242.0	241.4	241.8	248.3	234.7	233.8	236.3	236.5	236.6	240.4
1997	234.4	233.8	232.6	233.6	233.5	234.5	246.4	232.8	230.6	228.9	228.5	228.7	233.1
1998	227.5	226.1	225.4	226.5	226.4	227.3	234.6	226.5	223.2	221.6	222.1	222.4	225.8
1999	221.2	220.6	220.8	219.1	221.1	223.1	231.8	223.1	221.8	223.0	221.8	222.3	222.4
2000	221.7	221.4	221.5	221.6	223.9	225.8	232.7	229.3	223.4	220.8	221.7	223.7	223.9
2001	221.0	218.6	219.9	220.0	221.3	225.8	234.8	234.8	229.3	229.7	228.5	229.9	226.1
2002	230.3	229.1	229.8	228.8	229.5	232.5	240.1	237.6	231.9	229.2	230.4	231.2	231.7
2003	229.6	229.6	231.0	230.4	230.9	232.6	238.9	232.3	230.7	229.8	228.8	230.2	231.2
Federal government													
1990	220.2	218.9	219.5	217.8	219.8	224.6	223.6	221.7	220.0	217.9	217.2	219.0	220.0
1991	220.4	219.7	220.6	220.2	222.1	228.5	230.7	229.2	226.9	226.7	227.3	228.0	225.0
1992	228.8	227.6	228.1	228.0	229.2	232.9	235.2	233.6	231.2	228.9	228.9	229.1	230.1
1993	233.1	230.2	230.4	231.2	232.2	234.9	233.9	232.1	229.1	224.7	223.9	224.1	229.9
1994	221.7	219.9	220.3	220.4	220.1	221.7	217.9	215.9	214.7	212.7	211.5	211.8	217.3
1995	208.0	207.5	207.5	207.2	207.0	208.8	209.4	207.5	205.1	206.0	203.5	202.8	206.6
1996	199.4	198.8	198.8	196.0	195.8	197.1	195.0	193.2	191.2	194.0	193.4	193.7	195.5
1997	191.7	190.8	190.5	191.8	191.8	193.0	193.4	194.3	191.7	190.6	189.8	189.9	191.6
1998	188.8	187.2	186.3	187.2	187.1	188.2	188.5	187.5	185.4	184.3	184.3	184.4	186.6
1999	183.6	182.7	182.6	180.8	182.1	185.0	186.3	184.4	182.9	183.6	183.1	183.7	183.4
2000	183.6	182.7	182.7	182.8	184.9	186.8	186.9	183.7	182.2	181.8	182.1	183.0	183.6
2001	182.2	179.9	180.9	180.8	182.0	185.7	188.3	188.8	189.3	188.8	189.1	190.5	185.5
2002	191.6	190.6	191.2	190.2	191.0	193.9	195.9	193.4	193.1	192.6	192.4	193.1	192.4
2003	191.9	191.2	192.6	192.5	193.3	195.2	195.6	193.3	192.9	192.7	191.4	192.5	192.9
WASHINGTON MSA													
Total nonfarm													
1990	2307.5	2316.4	2336.4	2333.7	2356.7	2383.7	2364.9	2351.3	2357.2	2337.1	2340.9	2348.7	2344.5
1991	2271.9	2272.8	2283.4	2280.3	2299.6	2321.1	2296.5	2284.9	2296.0	2287.4	2300.6	2306.7	2291.7
1992	2246.7	2245.2	2264.1	2276.9	2299.5	2314.2	2291.1	2282.2	2297.0	2306.6	2314.6	2331.0	2289.0
1993	2279.1	2287.4	2296.9	2312.6	2337.8	2356.2	2347.9	2320.7	2342.6	2351.0	2366.8	2382.6	2331.8
1994	2309.5	2312.2	2339.9	2360.5	2381.1	2405.4	2396.8	2375.7	2395.9	2399.2	2413.6	2427.9	2376.4
1995	2359.0	2366.6	2390.5	2390.2	2406.2	2431.4	2416.5	2396.2	2413.6	2416.9	2428.6	2441.1	2404.7
1996	2346.3	2380.1	2404.4	2403.3	2423.6	2449.8	2445.5	2431.8	2443.3	2449.3	2466.7	2480.8	2427.0
1997	2418.4	2429.3	2455.6	2459.1	2476.3	2500.3	2504.4	2486.0	2505.5	2507.3	2521.7	2541.9	2483.8
1998	2470.5	2487.2	2509.4	2519.6	2542.8	2570.3	2570.8	2561.2	2574.1	2582.2	2601.5	2622.3	2550.9
1999	2548.0	2566.1	2586.7	2617.5	2633.4	2660.6	2654.6	2648.4	2674.0	2695.9	2712.4	2730.9	2644.0
2000	2663.7	2676.2	2713.1	2728.1	2749.4	2782.1	2771.1	2760.1	2786.6	2803.6	2823.2	2843.7	2758.4
2001	2749.2	2757.5	2781.3	2777.8	2797.9	2825.5	2789.5	2789.8	2790.8	2800.8	2807.3	2818.1	2790.5
2002	2743.7	2754.6	2779.6	2805.7	2819.6	2839.8	2806.5	2812.7	2820.4	2823.6	2838.6	2847.0	2807.7
2003	2776.8	2775.8	2800.8	2796.0	2816.4	2839.0	2836.3	2833.3	2844.0	2852.8	2865.1	2863.7	2825.0
Total private													
1990	1703.8	1710.3	1727.9	1727.1	1741.5	1762.9	1750.3	1753.7	1745.5	1722.3	1724.2	1728.1	1733.1
1991	1656.3	1653.1	1661.2	1659.2	1673.5	1689.3	1676.3	1676.3	1673.2	1658.4	1668.1	1672.5	1668.1
1992	1619.9	1616.2	1630.7	1643.9	1661.3	1674.8	1669.1	1666.2	1665.7	1671.1	1675.0	1690.5	1657.0
1993	1644.2	1648.7	1656.2	1671.8	1693.4	1711.5	1708.4	1705.9	1709.9	1717.3	1730.1	1745.9	1695.2
1994	1685.0	1684.6	1709.1	1729.5	1748.5	1771.7	1772.7	1772.3	1774.0	1774.0	1786.4	1800.8	1750.7
1995	1746.2	1748.1	1771.3	1779.7	1794.9	1818.1	1806.7	1806.5	1808.4	1806.2	1819.0	1832.7	1794.8
1996	1747.3	1777.6	1800.6	1802.4	1821.0	1847.7	1855.2	1858.2	1857.3	1856.5	1871.7	1886.2	1831.8
1997	1834.0	1841.7	1865.3	1869.7	1886.6	1910.6	1924.4	1924.2	1924.7	1922.8	1935.5	1957.5	1899.7
1998	1892.4	1907.4	1927.6	1937.0	1957.4	1984.8	1989.9	1990.8	1992.2	1998.0	2012.5	2031.7	1968.4
1999	1965.0	1978.5	1995.8	2027.4	2041.4	2067.8	2075.0	2081.1	2078.9	2097.7	2113.0	2130.0	2054.3
2000	2069.4	2080.4	2112.1	2127.6	2141.8	2177.4	2186.2	2187.3	2188.0	2201.3	2216.5	2233.4	2160.1
2001	2149.5	2157.1	2176.6	2172.9	2190.8	2214.3	2204.2	2204.3	2181.4	2183.9	2188.6	2196.4	2185.0
2002	2128.1	2136.1	2155.8	2183.3	2194.6	2213.5	2207.0	2204.0	2196.6	2194.8	2206.7	2213.5	2186.2
2003	2153.9	2148.8	2170.7	2168.4	2185.8	2207.6	2223.2	2220.6	2216.0	2216.0	2226.0	2223.7	2196.7

Employment by Industry: District of Columbia—*Continued*

(Numbers in thousands. Not seasonally adjusted.)

Industry	January	February	March	April	May	June	July	August	September	October	November	December	Annual Average
WASHINGTON MSA *—Continued*													
Goods-producing													
1990	228.4	229.4	231.6	229.6	230.7	232.3	229.7	228.2	225.5	220.4	216.9	212.6	226.2
1991	194.6	192.1	192.0	191.3	193.7	195.9	194.2	194.7	191.8	189.9	187.7	184.9	191.9
1992	175.8	173.6	176.0	178.2	181.3	184.0	183.0	182.9	182.4	182.9	181.6	181.4	180.2
1993	172.7	173.7	174.7	178.8	182.2	185.1	186.4	186.9	187.2	188.1	187.9	187.5	182.6
1994	177.7	176.4	181.3	189.5	193.5	197.5	201.9	201.9	201.8	202.2	202.2	202.0	193.9
1995	194.8	192.4	196.8	199.4	201.5	204.4	203.4	205.0	205.2	204.7	204.0	202.9	201.2
1996	186.2	194.2	199.0	200.6	204.0	209.5	212.0	213.2	213.1	213.0	213.3	212.2	205.8
1997	205.6	205.5	209.1	210.5	211.9	214.6	216.5	217.9	217.3	216.9	214.9	214.2	212.9
1998	207.7	208.2	209.9	214.2	216.5	220.6	223.1	224.3	224.2	224.7	223.3	223.5	218.3
1999	215.4	215.7	217.6	223.9	225.8	228.3	229.4	230.8	230.5	230.2	230.1	231.0	225.7
2000	225.7	226.6	232.6	233.8	236.2	240.9	244.0	244.8	245.2	244.3	243.9	243.9	238.4
2001	238.9	240.1	243.7	246.2	249.4	252.9	252.0	253.0	251.1	248.3	247.1	245.3	247.3
2002	238.1	239.0	241.8	244.4	247.2	249.3	248.8	249.2	246.7	244.9	243.7	241.7	244.6
2003	235.4	234.6	237.9	236.8	240.4	243.4	246.8	247.8	246.7	245.6	246.4	244.4	242.2
Construction and mining													
1990	145.9	146.6	149.6	147.7	148.7	150.0	146.9	146.0	143.5	138.6	135.0	130.7	144.1
1991	114.2	111.4	111.5	112.7	114.5	116.5	115.5	116.1	114.2	111.8	109.7	107.3	112.9
1992	99.5	98.2	100.1	102.4	105.2	107.6	107.6	107.6	107.2	107.0	105.8	105.3	104.4
1993	97.6	98.3	99.0	102.4	105.7	108.3	110.8	111.3	111.0	111.6	111.2	111.0	106.5
1994	101.8	100.5	104.8	111.0	114.8	118.6	122.7	124.1	123.6	122.9	122.5	122.0	115.7
1995	114.9	112.5	116.2	119.2	121.0	123.4	122.8	123.9	123.8	123.1	122.5	121.3	120.3
1996	106.4	113.1	117.7	120.4	123.4	127.5	130.3	131.6	131.0	131.2	131.0	129.9	124.4
1997	122.2	121.9	125.0	127.1	129.6	131.8	133.7	134.3	133.7	133.3	131.7	130.7	129.5
1998	124.1	124.5	125.8	130.6	132.5	135.8	138.8	139.8	139.4	139.6	138.2	138.4	133.9
1999	131.3	133.0	134.5	140.4	142.2	145.4	146.7	148.0	147.7	147.2	147.0	147.2	142.5
2000	142.4	142.9	148.5	150.4	152.6	156.2	159.0	160.0	160.2	159.3	159.6	159.3	154.2
2001	154.8	156.2	160.1	163.3	166.6	170.1	170.0	171.2	169.7	168.5	167.5	165.8	165.3
2002	160.1	161.3	163.9	167.9	170.8	173.1	173.4	174.3	172.1	171.3	170.6	168.5	168.9
2003	162.4	161.5	165.3	165.7	169.4	172.1	175.8	177.2	176.3	175.2	175.5	173.5	170.8
Manufacturing													
1990	82.5	82.8	82.0	81.9	82.0	82.3	82.8	82.2	82.0	81.8	81.9	81.9	82.1
1991	80.4	80.7	80.5	78.6	79.2	79.4	78.7	78.6	77.6	78.1	78.0	77.6	78.9
1992	76.3	75.4	75.9	75.8	76.1	76.4	75.4	75.3	75.2	75.9	75.8	76.1	75.8
1993	75.1	75.4	75.7	76.4	76.5	76.8	75.6	75.6	76.2	76.5	76.7	76.5	76.0
1994	75.9	75.9	76.5	78.5	78.7	78.9	79.2	77.8	78.2	79.3	79.7	80.0	78.2
1995	79.9	79.9	80.6	80.2	80.5	81.0	80.6	81.1	81.4	81.6	81.5	81.6	80.8
1996	79.8	81.1	81.3	80.2	80.6	82.0	81.7	81.6	82.1	81.8	82.3	82.3	81.4
1997	83.4	83.6	84.1	83.4	82.3	82.8	82.8	83.6	83.6	83.6	83.2	83.5	83.3
1998	83.6	83.7	84.1	83.6	84.0	84.8	84.3	84.5	84.8	85.1	85.1	85.1	84.3
1999	84.1	82.7	83.1	83.5	83.6	82.9	82.7	82.8	82.8	83.0	83.1	83.8	83.1
2000	83.3	83.7	84.1	83.4	83.6	84.7	85.0	84.8	85.0	85.0	84.3	84.6	84.2
2001	84.1	83.9	83.6	82.9	82.8	82.8	82.0	81.8	81.4	79.8	79.6	79.5	82.0
2002	78.0	77.7	77.9	76.5	76.4	76.2	75.4	74.9	74.6	73.6	73.1	73.2	75.6
2003	73.0	73.1	72.6	71.1	71.0	71.3	71.0	70.6	70.4	70.4	70.9	70.9	71.4
Service-providing													
1990	2079.1	2087.0	2104.8	2104.1	2126.0	2151.4	2135.2	2123.1	2131.7	2116.7	2124.0	2136.1	2118.2
1991	2077.3	2080.7	2091.4	2089.0	2105.9	2125.2	2102.3	2090.2	2104.2	2097.5	2112.9	2121.8	2099.8
1992	2070.9	2071.6	2088.1	2098.7	2118.2	2130.2	2108.1	2099.3	2114.6	2123.7	2133.0	2149.6	2108.8
1993	2106.4	2113.7	2122.2	2133.8	2155.6	2171.1	2161.5	2133.8	2155.4	2162.9	2178.9	2195.1	2149.2
1994	2131.8	2135.8	2158.6	2171.0	2187.6	2207.9	2194.9	2173.8	2194.1	2197.0	2211.4	2225.9	2182.4
1995	2164.2	2174.2	2193.7	2190.8	2204.7	2227.0	2213.1	2191.2	2208.4	2212.2	2224.6	2238.2	2203.5
1996	2160.1	2185.9	2205.4	2202.7	2219.6	2240.3	2233.5	2218.6	2230.2	2236.3	2253.4	2268.6	2221.2
1997	2212.8	2223.8	2246.5	2248.6	2264.4	2285.7	2287.9	2268.1	2288.2	2290.4	2306.8	2327.7	2270.9
1998	2262.8	2279.0	2299.5	2305.4	2326.3	2349.7	2347.7	2336.9	2349.9	2357.5	2378.2	2398.8	2332.6
1999	2332.6	2350.4	2369.1	2393.6	2407.6	2432.3	2425.2	2417.6	2443.5	2465.7	2482.3	2499.9	2418.3
2000	2438.0	2449.6	2480.5	2494.3	2513.2	2541.2	2527.1	2515.3	2541.4	2559.3	2579.3	2599.8	2519.9
2001	2510.3	2517.4	2537.6	2531.6	2548.5	2572.6	2537.5	2536.8	2539.7	2552.5	2560.2	2572.8	2543.1
2002	2505.6	2515.6	2537.8	2561.3	2572.4	2590.5	2557.7	2563.5	2573.7	2578.7	2594.9	2605.3	2563.1
2003	2541.4	2541.2	2562.9	2559.2	2576.0	2595.6	2589.5	2585.5	2597.3	2607.2	2618.7	2619.3	2582.8
Trade, transportation, and utilities													
1990	373.9	370.4	372.7	372.4	375.7	379.0	373.8	375.2	374.4	373.0	378.8	385.9	375.4
1991	360.8	354.2	356.1	352.0	354.3	356.6	355.0	356.0	356.0	353.2	360.6	368.3	356.9
1992	345.7	338.9	339.0	340.8	343.9	346.2	344.6	343.8	343.1	346.3	353.1	365.0	345.8
1993	349.1	344.5	343.6	345.0	350.7	353.7	354.1	354.0	353.9	359.4	368.8	381.1	354.8
1994	359.6	353.2	357.2	359.0	362.2	366.0	364.3	364.2	365.0	368.0	377.4	387.7	365.3
1995	367.7	361.0	363.0	362.8	364.1	367.1	361.6	362.8	363.6	368.5	377.8	385.8	367.1
1996	360.8	360.5	361.6	357.2	360.4	366.9	366.2	367.8	367.5	370.8	381.1	392.8	367.8
1997	370.3	364.1	366.1	363.9	367.9	372.1	370.7	372.1	373.0	377.5	388.1	396.9	373.5
1998	373.7	369.0	370.8	368.3	372.0	376.6	376.3	377.8	379.4	384.6	395.6	405.2	379.1
1999	380.0	376.1	379.7	384.1	386.5	390.6	389.9	390.7	390.7	395.5	405.1	414.5	390.2
2000	389.1	385.4	388.2	386.9	390.1	395.0	394.3	395.4	395.9	402.4	413.8	425.3	396.8
2001	399.4	393.0	394.6	392.6	396.8	401.7	399.5	400.1	397.9	400.3	409.2	415.6	400.1
2002	393.3	388.0	389.7	392.9	396.0	400.4	398.6	398.1	397.5	400.4	408.3	416.9	398.3
2003	393.2	388.3	390.5	388.0	391.5	396.1	397.9	399.3	398.5	399.3	404.6	408.2	396.3

Employment by Industry: District of Columbia—*Continued*

(Numbers in thousands. Not seasonally adjusted.)

Industry	January	February	March	April	May	June	July	August	September	October	November	December	Annual Average
WASHINGTON MSA —*Continued*													
Wholesale trade													
1990	63.2	63.1	63.3	63.4	63.6	63.8	63.8	63.9	63.5	62.7	62.5	62.6	63.2
1991	59.7	59.6	59.8	60.2	60.0	60.2	59.9	59.4	59.2	58.3	58.3	58.3	59.4
1992	57.0	56.8	57.1	57.1	57.2	57.5	57.4	57.3	57.0	57.1	56.8	57.8	57.1
1993	56.7	56.8	57.2	57.6	57.8	58.0	57.9	57.8	57.8	57.4	57.3	57.9	57.5
1994	58.2	58.3	58.7	59.2	59.6	60.2	60.1	59.8	59.8	59.3	59.6	60.1	59.4
1995	59.0	59.1	59.7	59.9	59.5	60.2	59.4	59.6	59.5	60.1	60.3	60.7	59.7
1996	59.2	60.3	60.6	59.2	59.1	59.9	60.1	60.2	59.8	60.0	60.1	60.2	59.8
1997	59.7	60.0	60.5	60.7	61.2	61.8	61.3	61.5	61.3	60.9	61.2	61.5	60.9
1998	58.9	59.2	59.6	60.1	60.1	60.5	61.2	61.1	60.7	61.0	61.2	61.6	60.4
1999	60.8	61.0	61.3	62.7	62.9	63.2	63.1	63.0	62.9	63.4	63.8	64.2	62.6
2000	62.6	63.1	63.5	63.2	63.6	64.1	64.2	64.2	64.1	65.6	65.9	66.5	64.2
2001	67.1	67.1	67.6	67.7	67.6	68.0	67.9	67.7	67.1	66.7	67.0	67.0	67.4
2002	66.6	66.5	66.6	67.5	67.7	68.0	67.6	67.5	67.0	67.6	67.9	68.2	67.4
2003	67.4	67.4	67.6	66.2	66.5	66.5	67.4	67.3	66.8	66.9	67.3	67.8	67.1
Retail trade													
1990	250.6	244.9	246.2	245.4	247.7	249.7	245.2	246.3	245.3	245.2	250.7	257.3	247.8
1991	237.3	230.6	232.3	227.5	229.2	230.5	228.7	230.5	230.3	229.5	236.2	243.3	232.1
1992	224.4	218.1	218.0	219.2	221.6	222.9	221.6	220.7	220.8	223.5	230.6	240.6	223.5
1993	228.0	223.5	222.5	222.6	226.9	228.7	227.9	227.7	227.2	231.8	241.0	251.9	229.9
1994	233.8	227.5	230.1	231.6	234.0	236.9	235.0	235.4	236.9	240.2	249.7	259.7	237.5
1995	242.8	236.3	237.6	237.6	239.5	241.1	238.0	239.5	240.8	242.8	252.1	260.6	242.3
1996	240.9	238.8	239.8	238.1	240.8	245.5	244.9	246.3	246.1	247.4	257.6	268.1	246.1
1997	249.5	243.2	245.1	242.9	245.4	248.0	247.0	247.9	248.9	252.2	262.6	272.5	250.4
1998	250.8	246.0	247.0	243.4	246.3	249.6	247.8	249.6	251.8	255.7	266.6	274.9	252.4
1999	253.3	249.1	251.6	253.4	255.2	258.0	256.4	257.4	257.7	260.1	269.8	278.7	258.3
2000	256.7	252.8	254.9	254.1	256.7	260.2	259.7	260.9	261.9	264.7	276.0	286.8	262.1
2001	261.7	255.5	256.6	254.1	257.7	261.7	260.1	261.0	260.1	263.2	272.9	280.2	262.1
2002	260.1	255.0	256.7	257.5	260.0	263.3	261.2	260.8	261.3	263.1	270.6	279.1	262.4
2003	258.3	253.9	255.4	255.8	258.5	262.7	262.0	263.5	263.8	265.8	270.3	273.7	262.0
Transportation and utilities													
1990	60.1	62.4	63.2	63.6	64.4	65.5	64.8	65.0	65.6	65.1	65.6	66.0	64.2
1991	63.8	64.0	64.0	64.3	65.1	65.9	66.4	66.1	66.5	65.4	66.1	66.7	65.3
1992	64.3	64.0	63.9	64.5	65.1	65.8	65.6	65.8	65.3	65.7	65.7	66.6	65.1
1993	64.4	64.2	63.9	64.8	66.0	67.0	68.3	68.5	68.9	70.2	70.5	71.3	67.3
1994	67.6	67.4	68.4	68.2	68.6	68.9	69.2	69.0	68.3	68.5	68.1	67.9	68.3
1995	65.9	65.6	65.7	65.3	65.1	65.8	64.2	63.7	63.3	65.6	65.4	64.5	65.0
1996	60.7	61.4	61.2	59.9	60.5	61.5	61.2	61.3	61.6	63.4	63.4	64.5	61.7
1997	61.1	60.9	60.5	60.3	61.3	62.3	62.4	62.7	62.8	64.4	64.3	62.9	62.1
1998	64.0	63.8	64.2	64.8	65.6	66.5	67.3	67.1	66.9	67.9	67.8	68.7	66.2
1999	65.9	66.0	66.8	68.0	68.4	69.4	70.4	70.3	70.1	72.0	71.5	71.6	69.2
2000	69.8	69.5	69.8	69.6	69.8	70.7	70.4	70.3	69.9	72.1	71.9	72.0	70.4
2001	70.6	70.4	70.4	70.8	71.5	72.0	71.5	71.4	70.7	70.4	69.3	68.4	70.6
2002	66.6	66.5	66.4	67.9	68.3	69.1	69.8	69.8	69.2	69.7	69.8	69.6	68.6
2003	67.5	67.0	67.5	66.0	66.5	66.9	68.5	68.5	67.9	66.6	67.0	66.7	67.2
Information													
1990	92.4	92.6	93.1	93.4	93.3	94.3	94.9	94.7	93.9	93.4	93.7	93.9	93.6
1991	93.1	93.4	93.2	92.8	92.7	92.9	91.6	89.0	86.6	85.8	86.0	85.3	90.2
1992	85.4	85.5	85.5	85.4	85.4	85.9	86.8	86.8	86.4	87.3	87.2	85.6	86.1
1993	84.3	84.6	84.8	84.6	84.9	85.8	85.2	85.3	85.0	85.1	85.4	82.8	84.8
1994	82.5	81.2	82.1	83.5	85.3	86.5	86.9	87.1	86.8	86.0	86.7	86.2	85.0
1995	86.8	87.6	88.8	89.9	91.1	92.5	91.5	92.3	92.5	92.0	92.6	93.8	90.9
1996	92.8	93.8	94.7	94.8	95.7	97.3	97.2	97.6	97.5	96.5	97.7	98.3	96.1
1997	97.3	98.5	99.3	99.5	100.4	101.6	101.4	101.7	101.6	100.9	101.5	103.6	100.6
1998	102.2	103.0	103.3	104.0	105.0	106.3	105.6	106.2	106.2	105.9	106.5	108.0	105.1
1999	107.0	107.9	108.2	109.8	110.5	113.2	114.0	115.0	115.6	117.3	118.4	119.4	113.0
2000	119.6	121.2	122.6	124.3	126.0	128.8	129.5	130.0	131.5	134.3	134.9	136.3	128.2
2001	136.6	137.2	137.1	135.6	135.6	134.5	133.1	133.0	131.5	129.3	127.9	127.7	133.3
2002	122.2	121.3	121.1	120.0	119.8	119.4	117.0	116.2	114.5	113.0	113.4	112.9	117.6
2003	112.3	112.6	112.7	110.7	111.2	111.5	111.8	111.7	110.9	109.6	110.3	110.1	111.3
Financial activities													
1990	136.6	137.1	137.9	136.9	137.9	139.6	140.0	140.8	139.2	137.2	137.2	137.8	138.1
1991	135.2	132.3	132.5	132.3	133.3	133.8	133.6	133.6	132.9	130.6	130.4	130.7	132.6
1992	127.4	127.3	127.9	127.2	128.4	129.4	128.7	128.5	127.7	127.6	127.6	128.5	128.0
1993	127.1	126.9	127.9	127.6	128.5	130.4	132.0	132.1	131.6	133.4	134.1	135.5	130.5
1994	133.3	134.0	135.3	135.8	136.0	136.8	136.1	136.4	135.1	133.9	134.2	135.0	135.1
1995	131.6	131.5	132.1	131.0	131.5	133.0	131.9	132.0	131.7	130.7	131.1	132.1	131.6
1996	129.5	131.3	132.2	130.5	130.9	132.9	133.6	134.4	133.2	132.3	132.9	133.9	132.3
1997	134.2	134.2	135.3	133.9	135.6	136.7	138.4	138.5	137.9	138.3	138.8	140.9	136.8
1998	136.5	137.3	138.6	139.2	140.7	142.9	143.9	144.4	143.8	144.2	144.5	146.0	141.8
1999	143.8	145.0	145.6	145.4	146.4	147.9	148.0	148.4	147.3	147.1	147.5	148.6	146.7
2000	146.2	146.6	147.7	146.9	147.3	149.0	150.0	149.9	149.2	149.1	149.8	151.7	148.6
2001	147.1	147.6	148.5	148.9	149.7	151.3	151.6	151.5	150.0	149.9	150.4	151.6	149.8
2002	149.9	150.9	151.2	151.5	152.0	153.6	154.0	154.5	153.7	154.4	155.3	156.4	153.1
2003	155.5	155.5	156.2	156.4	157.5	159.1	160.7	160.6	159.2	160.3	160.5	161.6	158.6

Employment by Industry: District of Columbia—*Continued*

(Numbers in thousands. Not seasonally adjusted.)

Industry	January	February	March	April	May	June	July	August	September	October	November	December	Annual Average
WASHINGTON MSA —*Continued*													
Professional and business services													
1990	374.8	378.2	384.5	384.1	386.3	391.6	389.2	390.2	387.8	380.5	379.4	379.1	383.8
1991	370.0	372.6	376.5	374.5	375.4	378.6	377.4	377.8	377.2	378.8	378.9	378.9	376.3
1992	375.1	375.8	381.3	384.7	385.7	390.9	393.2	391.0	392.0	394.6	394.3	397.5	388.0
1993	388.8	391.7	394.8	399.7	402.6	407.7	405.0	404.3	405.2	407.8	408.7	411.8	402.3
1994	398.4	401.5	405.4	407.5	410.0	417.2	415.9	417.8	417.9	417.5	419.2	421.7	412.5
1995	411.9	415.1	423.0	424.5	427.7	434.0	433.7	434.5	432.6	433.9	437.0	440.8	429.0
1996	426.9	428.7	436.4	438.3	441.3	445.4	452.8	454.1	451.4	453.7	455.1	456.8	445.0
1997	448.4	451.8	459.9	460.5	463.7	471.8	477.0	476.6	476.1	478.7	479.5	484.1	469.0
1998	476.2	482.5	491.0	489.6	493.5	501.8	503.9	504.6	502.9	505.3	506.8	511.7	497.4
1999	505.3	512.4	518.0	526.0	528.3	537.8	540.4	543.5	541.7	547.6	549.3	554.1	533.7
2000	546.1	551.1	561.0	564.1	565.7	576.6	578.9	580.0	580.9	584.3	585.6	591.6	572.1
2001	579.3	583.8	588.7	584.3	584.9	591.9	588.3	588.0	580.3	583.1	582.1	584.6	584.9
2002	565.7	569.2	574.0	585.7	586.1	590.2	590.0	589.1	585.9	584.8	585.7	587.8	582.9
2003	577.3	577.4	581.9	580.2	582.1	587.7	599.0	599.6	597.6	597.4	598.8	595.0	589.5
Educational and health services													
1990	208.6	210.7	212.1	212.0	212.7	212.7	210.8	212.8	216.4	217.9	219.5	219.5	213.8
1991	215.1	218.7	219.0	221.0	222.0	220.8	215.9	217.0	222.8	220.9	223.4	223.7	220.0
1992	220.0	222.9	224.2	225.7	225.6	222.8	220.8	220.6	224.7	228.2	228.6	229.9	224.5
1993	226.5	228.9	230.2	229.3	229.3	227.3	226.9	225.6	232.6	233.2	235.6	236.4	230.1
1994	231.7	235.1	237.8	237.1	237.2	234.9	234.5	233.2	240.5	243.6	243.8	244.4	237.8
1995	236.8	241.3	243.3	243.6	243.1	242.7	243.0	239.4	247.5	244.8	245.4	246.1	243.0
1996	236.4	246.0	247.6	249.8	250.4	247.6	244.6	244.2	250.8	252.8	254.0	255.2	248.2
1997	249.8	255.0	257.9	259.0	256.9	254.8	260.5	259.8	263.8	261.8	264.4	267.5	259.2
1998	263.0	269.2	271.1	270.7	271.0	269.8	271.2	268.5	275.0	277.5	280.1	281.0	272.3
1999	273.0	275.9	277.0	281.0	279.5	277.3	276.4	277.0	283.2	290.0	292.0	291.3	281.1
2000	282.1	286.6	289.2	292.2	290.4	291.7	293.6	292.9	295.4	298.7	301.6	296.1	292.5
2001	278.8	282.3	284.3	284.3	284.7	281.3	280.0	279.8	284.0	288.5	288.6	288.7	283.8
2002	289.5	294.5	297.9	300.0	297.1	294.6	289.1	289.1	297.5	303.0	305.6	304.7	296.9
2003	298.2	300.1	303.3	301.9	300.3	297.9	293.2	291.0	299.7	302.4	304.3	302.4	299.6
Leisure and hospitality													
1990	174.9	177.5	180.8	183.5	188.7	195.6	195.3	195.1	191.9	183.5	181.9	182.2	185.9
1991	174.5	176.4	177.9	180.6	186.0	192.9	190.2	189.6	187.1	180.9	181.6	180.2	183.1
1992	171.6	172.2	175.5	180.0	188.2	191.4	188.2	189.5	186.5	180.3	179.4	178.4	181.7
1993	172.9	175.0	176.0	182.2	189.9	194.4	191.8	191.2	188.0	184.3	183.8	183.6	184.4
1994	175.9	176.4	181.8	188.4	194.8	201.0	200.9	200.2	196.0	192.3	191.8	192.1	190.9
1995	186.6	188.2	192.2	195.8	202.3	209.3	206.7	206.1	201.3	197.7	197.0	196.3	198.2
1996	183.3	189.5	193.9	197.2	203.2	210.9	210.8	208.9	206.3	199.0	198.8	197.1	199.9
1997	190.2	193.4	197.2	202.0	208.4	215.3	215.2	213.6	211.5	204.8	204.1	204.8	205.0
1998	190.3	194.6	198.6	204.3	211.5	218.3	216.5	215.6	211.7	206.3	205.5	205.4	206.5
1999	192.2	196.0	199.2	206.4	213.0	220.2	222.4	221.7	216.9	215.2	215.5	215.3	211.1
2000	207.9	209.2	215.7	222.8	229.0	237.0	236.8	236.0	231.5	227.7	226.0	226.1	225.4
2001	212.7	215.9	221.1	222.2	229.4	238.1	237.0	236.5	226.2	224.9	223.7	222.5	225.9
2002	211.8	214.5	220.2	227.2	234.5	242.4	243.1	242.5	237.2	232.2	232.4	230.0	230.7
2003	222.1	220.0	225.7	232.7	240.4	247.6	248.4	246.7	240.9	240.2	240.1	240.5	237.1
Other services													
1990	114.2	114.4	115.2	115.2	116.2	117.8	116.6	116.7	116.4	116.4	116.8	117.1	116.0
1991	113.0	113.4	114.0	114.7	116.1	117.8	118.4	118.6	118.8	118.3	119.5	120.5	116.9
1992	118.9	120.0	121.3	121.9	122.8	124.2	123.8	123.1	122.9	123.9	123.2	124.2	122.5
1993	122.8	123.4	124.2	124.6	125.3	127.1	127.0	126.5	126.4	126.0	125.8	127.2	125.5
1994	125.9	126.8	128.2	128.7	129.5	131.8	132.2	131.5	130.9	130.5	131.1	131.7	129.9
1995	130.0	131.0	132.1	132.7	133.6	135.1	134.9	134.4	134.0	133.9	134.1	134.9	133.3
1996	131.4	133.6	135.2	134.0	135.1	137.2	138.0	138.0	137.5	138.4	138.8	139.9	136.4
1997	138.2	139.2	140.5	140.4	141.8	143.7	144.7	144.0	143.5	143.9	144.2	145.5	142.4
1998	142.8	143.6	144.3	146.7	147.2	148.5	149.4	149.4	149.0	149.5	150.2	150.9	147.6
1999	148.3	149.5	150.5	150.8	151.4	152.5	154.5	154.0	153.0	154.8	155.1	155.8	152.5
2000	152.7	153.7	155.1	156.6	157.1	158.4	159.1	158.3	158.4	160.5	160.9	162.4	157.7
2001	156.7	157.2	158.6	158.8	160.3	162.6	162.7	162.4	160.4	159.6	159.6	160.4	159.9
2002	157.6	158.7	159.9	161.6	161.9	163.6	166.4	165.3	163.6	162.1	162.3	163.1	162.2
2003	159.9	160.3	162.5	161.7	162.4	164.3	165.4	163.9	162.5	161.2	161.0	161.5	162.2
Government													
1990	603.7	606.1	608.5	606.6	615.2	620.8	614.6	597.6	611.7	614.8	616.7	620.6	611.4
1991	615.6	619.7	622.2	621.1	626.1	631.8	620.2	608.6	622.8	629.0	632.5	634.2	623.6
1992	626.8	629.0	633.4	633.0	638.2	639.4	622.0	616.0	631.3	635.5	639.6	640.5	632.0
1993	634.9	638.7	640.7	640.8	644.4	644.7	639.5	614.8	632.7	633.7	636.7	636.7	636.5
1994	624.5	627.6	630.8	631.0	632.6	633.7	624.1	603.4	621.9	625.2	627.2	627.1	625.7
1995	612.8	618.5	619.2	610.5	611.3	613.3	609.8	589.7	605.2	610.7	609.6	608.4	609.9
1996	599.0	602.5	603.8	600.9	602.6	602.1	590.3	573.6	586.0	592.8	595.0	594.6	595.2
1997	584.4	587.6	590.3	589.4	589.7	589.7	580.0	561.8	580.8	584.5	586.2	584.4	584.0
1998	578.1	579.8	581.8	582.6	585.4	585.5	580.9	570.4	581.9	584.2	589.0	590.6	582.5
1999	583.0	587.6	590.9	590.1	592.0	592.8	579.6	567.3	595.1	598.2	599.4	600.9	589.7
2000	594.3	595.8	601.0	600.5	607.6	604.7	584.9	572.8	598.6	602.3	606.7	610.3	598.2
2001	599.7	600.4	604.7	604.9	607.1	611.2	585.3	585.5	609.4	616.9	618.7	621.7	605.5
2002	615.6	618.5	623.8	622.4	625.0	626.3	599.5	608.7	623.8	628.8	631.9	633.5	621.5
2003	622.9	627.0	630.1	627.6	630.6	631.4	613.1	612.7	628.0	636.8	639.1	640.0	628.3

Employment by Industry: District of Columbia—*Continued*

(Numbers in thousands. Not seasonally adjusted.)

Industry	January	February	March	April	May	June	July	August	September	October	November	December	Annual Average
WASHINGTON MSA *—Continued*													
Federal government													
1990	372.1	370.4	371.1	368.9	374.2	381.4	380.7	376.1	373.8	369.7	369.0	372.5	373.3
1991	374.0	373.2	374.2	375.2	378.8	388.0	390.9	388.2	384.5	384.9	385.4	387.6	382.0
1992	387.6	386.5	387.7	388.5	391.0	396.4	397.8	395.3	392.0	388.3	387.8	389.4	390.6
1993	392.4	389.1	389.7	390.8	392.5	396.4	396.6	393.9	389.8	384.7	383.8	385.6	390.4
1994	381.2	379.0	378.8	378.2	378.1	380.9	377.9	375.1	371.7	369.3	367.8	368.8	375.5
1995	364.2	363.3	363.1	362.1	362.3	364.9	366.5	363.5	359.7	360.6	357.2	357.4	362.0
1996	351.7	351.3	350.9	348.2	348.4	351.2	349.5	347.7	344.1	346.4	346.0	346.8	348.5
1997	341.9	339.7	340.2	341.1	340.8	342.7	343.9	344.5	339.1	337.4	336.4	337.0	340.3
1998	334.2	331.8	331.0	332.0	333.0	335.2	337.2	336.3	332.6	331.2	331.5	332.4	333.2
1999	331.0	329.3	329.3	328.4	329.5	333.7	338.5	337.3	334.3	332.4	332.0	333.6	332.4
2000	332.4	331.2	331.9	332.5	338.6	339.7	338.0	334.1	328.8	329.3	329.7	331.5	333.1
2001	331.1	327.1	327.7	328.0	329.4	335.0	338.9	336.5	336.0	335.2	335.6	337.6	333.2
2002	338.1	336.3	337.3	337.1	338.7	343.6	347.0	344.0	342.5	342.5	342.2	344.2	341.1
2003	341.7	340.4	341.9	340.4	341.5	344.9	349.3	346.5	345.8	346.7	345.1	346.6	344.2
State government													
1992	80.8	81.5	83.1	84.5	84.0	81.8	78.8	79.0	81.3	84.6	86.0	86.6	82.6
1993	83.0	86.1	86.8	86.8	86.8	85.2	93.4	77.4	83.0	84.5	85.5	84.5	85.2
1994	81.3	83.9	85.0	85.8	86.0	84.3	93.0	78.0	82.8	84.0	84.5	83.2	84.3
1995	79.1	81.7	81.8	78.7	77.8	76.8	85.6	71.8	77.2	77.4	78.5	77.0	78.6
1996	74.3	75.6	76.2	77.2	76.6	74.6	81.2	69.6	73.6	73.6	74.3	73.1	74.9
1997	70.7	72.6	73.1	71.5	71.0	69.7	80.9	66.3	69.2	69.1	70.1	68.3	71.0
1998	68.1	68.9	70.3	70.6	69.2	68.4	75.1	68.5	70.1	70.6	71.7	71.8	70.2
1999	70.2	72.2	74.2	75.3	74.6	71.1	74.8	68.3	73.9	76.6	75.5	74.4	73.4
2000	71.4	73.0	75.4	74.2	73.9	70.4	76.6	76.5	76.7	76.9	78.0	79.1	75.1
2001	72.9	74.5	76.6	76.7	75.7	73.0	77.0	77.0	73.3	77.7	76.3	76.3	75.6
2002	73.7	75.2	78.5	77.4	76.2	72.7	75.9	76.5	75.1	76.3	77.5	77.8	76.1
2003	72.0	76.0	77.6	75.5	75.5	72.1	74.4	70.1	71.5	73.5	74.1	74.6	73.9
Local government													
1992	158.4	161.0	162.6	160.0	163.2	161.2	145.4	141.7	158.0	162.6	165.8	164.5	158.7
1993	159.5	163.5	164.2	163.2	165.1	163.1	149.5	143.5	159.9	164.5	167.4	166.6	160.8
1994	162.0	164.7	167.0	167.0	168.5	168.5	153.2	150.3	167.4	171.9	174.9	175.1	165.8
1995	169.5	173.5	174.3	169.7	171.2	171.6	157.7	154.4	168.3	172.7	173.9	174.0	169.2
1996	173.0	175.6	176.7	175.5	177.6	176.3	159.6	156.3	168.3	172.8	174.7	174.7	171.7
1997	171.8	175.3	177.0	176.8	177.9	177.3	155.2	151.0	172.5	178.0	179.7	179.1	172.6
1998	175.8	179.1	180.5	180.0	183.2	181.9	168.6	165.6	179.2	182.4	185.8	186.4	179.0
1999	181.8	186.1	187.4	186.4	187.9	188.0	166.3	161.7	186.9	189.2	191.9	192.9	183.8
2000	190.5	191.6	193.7	193.8	195.1	194.6	170.3	162.2	193.1	196.1	199.0	199.7	189.9
2001	195.7	198.8	200.4	200.2	202.0	203.2	169.4	172.0	200.1	204.0	206.8	207.8	196.7
2002	203.8	207.0	208.0	207.9	210.1	210.0	176.6	188.2	206.2	210.0	212.2	211.5	204.3
2003	209.2	210.6	210.6	211.7	213.6	214.4	189.4	196.1	210.7	216.6	219.9	218.8	210.1

Average Weekly Hours by Industry: District of Columbia

(Not seasonally adjusted.)

Industry	January	February	March	April	May	June	July	August	September	October	November	December	Annual Average
WASHINGTON MSA													
Manufacturing													
2001	37.5	36.9	37.5	37.7	37.5	38.5	38.1	38.1	37.5	37.8	37.6	37.5	37.7
2002	36.8	37.3	37.0	37.7	37.1	37.7	37.4	38.0	37.4	37.0	38.6	38.5	37.5
2003	38.1	37.3	38.5	38.3	36.9	38.2	37.6	38.7	39.2	39.3	38.7	38.8	38.3

Average Hourly Earnings by Industry: District of Columbia

(Dollars, not seasonally adjusted.)

Industry	January	February	March	April	May	June	July	August	September	October	November	December	Annual Average
WASHINGTON MSA													
Manufacturing													
2001	15.25	14.70	14.92	15.03	15.01	15.09	14.97	15.26	15.29	15.20	15.36	15.63	15.14
2002	15.28	15.44	15.19	15.03	15.02	15.25	15.56	15.64	15.51	15.34	15.54	15.85	15.39
2003	15.99	15.92	16.21	16.15	15.61	15.37	15.66	15.50	15.58	15.85	15.98	15.77	15.80

Average Weekly Earnings by Industry: District of Columbia

(Dollars, not seasonally adjusted.)

Industry	January	February	March	April	May	June	July	August	September	October	November	December	Annual Average
WASHINGTON MSA													
Manufacturing													
2001	571.88	542.43	559.50	566.63	562.88	580.97	570.36	581.41	573.38	574.56	577.54	586.13	570.78
2002	562.30	575.91	562.03	566.63	557.24	574.93	581.94	594.32	580.07	567.58	599.84	610.23	577.13
2003	609.22	593.82	624.09	618.55	576.01	587.13	588.82	599.85	610.74	622.91	618.43	611.88	605.14

FLORIDA AT A GLANCE

(Population and total nonfarm employment numbers in thousands)

Population, Census 2000:	15,982.4
Total nonfarm employment, 2003:	7,285.5
Change in total nonfarm employment	
(Number)	
1990–2003:	1,898.1
1990–2001:	1,783.3
2001–2003:	114.8
(Compound annual rate of change)	
1990–2003:	2.3%
1990–2001:	2.6%
2001–2003:	0.8%
Unemployment rate	
1990:	6.3%
2001:	4.6%
2003:	5.3%

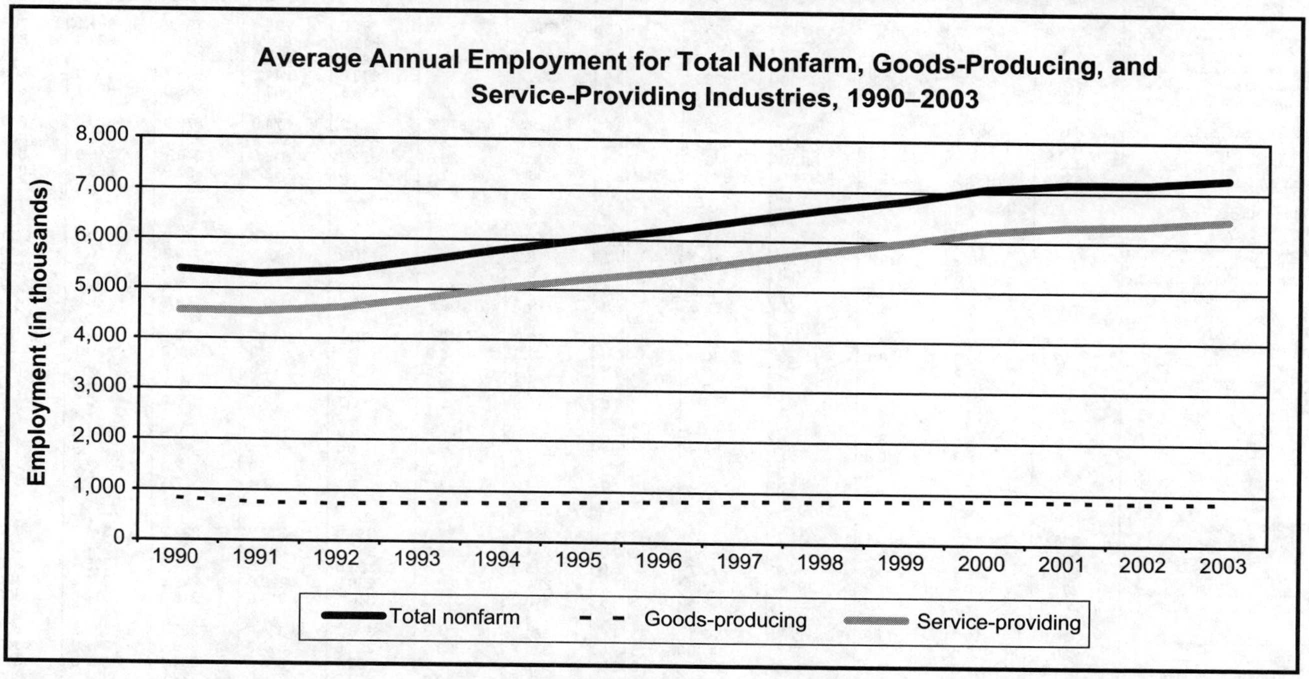

Total nonfarm payroll employment reflected the cyclical fluctuations of the national economy, dipping in 1991 and rebounding strongly through the rest of the decade before slowing substantially in 2001. Stronger growth resumed in 2003, as employment in the service-providing sector moved upward. Professional and business services employment increased from 10.5 percent of total employment in 1990 to 17.3 percent in 2003, adding nearly 700,000 jobs over that period. Manufacturing employment continued to decline and by 2003 was down 20 percent from 1990.

Employment by Industry: Florida

(Numbers in thousands. Not seasonally adjusted.)

Industry	January	February	March	April	May	June	July	August	September	October	November	December	Annual Average
STATEWIDE													
Total nonfarm													
1990	5334.7	5393.0	5448.0	5418.7	5430.4	5422.3	5304.1	5311.5	5362.9	5373.5	5414.0	5435.9	5387.4
1991	5301.8	5323.2	5355.6	5316.9	5318.3	5294.5	5193.0	5207.0	5260.3	5271.7	5332.5	5357.7	5294.3
1992	5277.2	5312.7	5390.8	5357.0	5363.3	5353.4	5267.0	5257.6	5345.9	5398.5	5462.3	5516.7	5358.5
1993	5434.6	5507.8	5557.9	5587.0	5580.4	5580.8	5492.8	5491.9	5576.3	5625.4	5678.8	5743.3	5571.4
1994	5657.7	5724.9	5788.2	5799.0	5801.8	5806.5	5708.5	5713.7	5828.1	5836.3	5947.3	5980.1	5799.3
1995	5882.1	5956.1	6019.7	5986.4	6001.1	6003.1	5877.8	5893.1	6009.9	6026.6	6114.5	6182.5	5996.0
1996	6056.0	6132.1	6222.0	6161.2	6180.7	6170.7	6063.5	6091.7	6200.4	6230.3	6312.2	6379.0	6183.3
1997	6286.9	6341.9	6400.6	6399.8	6415.9	6409.2	6310.8	6333.8	6450.0	6474.9	6536.7	6612.1	6414.3
1998	6529.9	6589.4	6639.6	6609.5	6619.7	6629.5	6529.6	6532.5	6641.7	6702.5	6769.8	6843.6	6636.4
1999	6704.1	6783.6	6836.6	6820.1	6827.0	6840.7	6706.9	6717.6	6817.3	6874.2	6956.6	7039.6	6827.0
2000	6930.5	6992.9	7072.4	7056.6	7090.3	7040.7	6974.8	7080.9	7115.9	7129.3	7208.1	7273.5	7080.5
2001	7107.7	7178.7	7240.5	7205.7	7209.5	7146.1	7057.0	7158.1	7158.8	7149.8	7198.0	7239.0	7170.7
2002	7100.1	7155.9	7217.4	7197.4	7209.3	7127.4	7048.0	7154.5	7165.3	7195.2	7264.2	7321.5	7179.7
2003	7187.8	7243.5	7298.9	7279.7	7294.4	7216.2	7167.6	7275.4	7298.7	7331.1	7392.2	7440.2	7285.5
Total private													
1990	4505.2	4550.5	4594.4	4563.1	4560.7	4569.7	4506.5	4522.5	4508.5	4503.0	4539.0	4565.7	4540.7
1991	4440.8	4453.7	4481.3	4444.3	4441.7	4433.9	4386.7	4404.0	4399.5	4400.7	4452.3	4481.9	4435.0
1992	4411.9	4439.5	4481.3	4480.6	4484.7	4485.3	4450.8	4454.5	4463.6	4510.5	4569.8	4628.7	4488.4
1993	4559.6	4619.5	4664.5	4691.3	4690.0	4700.6	4662.9	4674.7	4690.9	4719.1	4770.8	4833.6	4689.7
1994	4757.1	4811.2	4868.7	4877.8	4884.7	4898.8	4857.5	4878.6	4903.7	4905.1	4974.1	5047.8	4888.7
1995	4964.9	5023.6	5079.9	5050.1	5065.7	5081.5	5021.6	5051.7	5078.9	5094.2	5176.8	5243.8	5077.7
1996	5128.5	5191.7	5251.8	5219.5	5240.6	5245.9	5205.2	5242.2	5262.0	5285.4	5359.9	5426.6	5254.9
1997	5339.2	5387.1	5444.2	5444.8	5459.9	5466.0	5433.4	5465.9	5498.9	5512.9	5571.2	5642.9	5472.2
1998	5565.3	5619.9	5665.6	5642.3	5651.8	5676.9	5639.6	5659.0	5678.2	5729.0	5791.2	5860.9	5681.6
1999	5738.4	5805.6	5854.8	5839.9	5847.6	5876.6	5811.3	5836.1	5844.1	5885.7	5959.8	6037.1	5861.4
2000	5938.9	5991.4	6062.7	6042.0	6056.2	6092.4	6042.1	6075.2	6106.0	6111.1	6182.7	6244.4	6078.8
2001	6093.0	6150.5	6206.2	6170.5	6172.9	6177.3	6104.1	6124.9	6119.6	6108.1	6150.2	6189.8	6147.2
2002	6066.2	6111.7	6168.6	6148.1	6155.6	6149.5	6084.0	6106.3	6108.7	6133.2	6199.4	6254.0	6140.4
2003	6135.1	6180.0	6231.8	6214.5	6221.8	6221.6	6186.3	6212.3	6229.0	6255.4	6312.1	6359.7	6230.0
Goods-producing													
1990	852.3	854.1	856.9	843.3	844.3	845.8	833.9	833.8	827.0	816.2	808.8	799.7	834.6
1991	769.0	763.6	763.4	754.5	755.8	755.2	744.6	750.9	749.0	743.9	745.6	739.6	752.9
1992	724.1	723.3	727.9	728.3	732.1	734.9	735.0	736.0	742.0	752.7	757.3	760.4	737.8
1993	745.0	752.9	757.3	757.7	760.5	764.3	758.2	759.9	761.2	763.9	764.1	767.8	759.4
1994	748.7	754.7	759.4	759.3	764.6	771.8	768.9	773.3	777.9	772.3	777.4	782.6	767.5
1995	772.2	778.3	784.8	783.8	786.9	791.5	784.7	789.6	794.2	792.4	798.2	801.1	788.1
1996	796.2	805.7	811.5	807.5	813.5	816.6	805.5	812.3	813.6	821.4	825.2	825.9	812.9
1997	817.8	819.7	823.6	819.8	822.7	824.7	820.2	826.2	827.9	832.3	835.3	842.2	826.0
1998	826.6	832.3	836.8	831.0	833.7	839.6	835.4	836.9	840.0	844.6	846.7	852.2	838.0
1999	834.5	841.8	846.1	843.1	845.8	850.9	843.5	845.6	846.1	853.6	856.0	862.1	847.4
2000	851.7	859.3	867.6	861.1	866.1	875.8	872.3	875.6	881.2	874.9	876.9	879.6	870.2
2001	865.2	867.3	870.1	862.8	863.8	867.9	859.9	862.8	859.8	857.9	857.1	856.7	862.6
2002	838.0	839.0	842.1	837.4	840.0	841.5	832.8	839.8	839.2	843.0	846.1	846.9	840.5
2003	832.9	836.5	839.7	834.0	838.4	842.1	836.3	841.1	845.0	852.1	852.2	853.5	842.0
Natural resources and mining													
1990	11.2	11.2	11.2	11.1	11.0	11.0	11.2	11.2	11.0	11.0	10.8	10.7	11.1
1991	10.6	10.4	10.4	10.2	10.1	10.1	10.2	10.1	10.2	10.5	10.3	10.3	10.3
1992	9.8	9.6	9.7	9.8	9.8	9.7	9.7	9.6	9.6	9.9	9.8	9.8	9.7
1993	9.5	9.5	9.5	9.5	9.5	9.5	9.4	9.3	9.3	9.3	9.4	9.4	9.4
1994	9.6	9.7	9.8	9.7	9.8	9.8	9.7	9.7	9.6	9.6	9.6	9.6	9.7
1995	9.8	9.9	9.9	10.0	10.0	10.0	10.0	10.0	10.1	10.0	10.1	10.2	10.0
1996	10.0	10.0	10.1	9.9	10.0	10.0	9.9	9.9	10.0	9.9	9.9	10.1	10.0
1997	9.8	9.8	9.7	9.5	9.5	9.5	9.4	9.5	9.6	9.4	9.4	9.5	9.6
1998	9.3	9.3	9.4	9.5	9.6	9.6	9.5	9.5	9.6	9.6	9.7	9.7	9.5
1999	9.1	9.1	9.0	8.7	8.7	8.8	8.8	8.9	8.7	9.0	8.9	8.8	8.9
2000	8.8	8.8	8.9	8.6	8.7	8.8	8.6	8.6	8.7	8.8	8.6	8.6	8.7
2001	8.3	8.3	8.3	8.2	8.3	8.2	8.1	7.9	7.9	7.7	7.6	7.6	8.0
2002	7.3	7.4	7.3	7.3	7.3	7.3	7.2	7.2	7.1	7.0	7.0	7.0	7.2
2003	7.1	7.0	7.0	7.0	7.2	7.2	7.2	7.3	7.4	7.4	7.5	7.5	7.2
Construction													
1990	346.0	347.5	350.1	342.7	342.1	344.1	339.5	339.0	334.9	329.7	322.7	314.7	337.8
1991	295.8	292.0	292.2	287.6	289.0	289.0	284.9	288.0	285.6	282.4	281.5	277.4	287.1
1992	267.1	266.2	269.0	269.9	272.7	275.0	275.8	277.6	282.5	292.5	294.7	295.9	278.2
1993	284.1	288.6	291.2	292.0	293.6	297.3	296.0	296.7	298.0	299.3	299.6	301.8	294.9
1994	289.7	294.0	299.0	299.7	303.5	308.8	310.0	313.0	316.1	313.0	315.8	318.8	306.8
1995	310.2	313.0	317.3	317.9	320.1	324.3	321.7	324.6	326.7	324.9	328.1	329.2	321.5
1996	330.0	336.0	340.5	337.4	341.0	343.6	334.7	338.4	338.8	347.3	348.9	347.9	340.4
1997	341.3	341.8	346.0	346.5	349.3	352.8	352.0	355.2	358.1	363.5	364.1	367.3	353.2
1998	354.2	358.1	362.2	362.9	364.6	369.0	371.4	372.2	373.7	378.0	378.5	383.0	369.0
1999	370.6	375.1	378.8	378.8	380.5	384.7	382.4	384.0	385.1	390.2	391.2	394.9	383.0
2000	392.0	396.5	402.1	397.6	401.4	408.5	407.9	411.1	415.8	413.0	414.7	416.6	406.4
2001	411.3	414.1	417.5	414.8	417.5	423.6	423.6	427.3	427.3	429.5	430.4	429.8	422.2
2002	418.7	419.8	422.6	421.3	424.8	426.5	423.1	429.7	430.4	436.3	438.9	439.6	427.6
2003	430.4	434.8	438.2	437.1	441.9	446.3	445.3	448.7	452.3	457.1	458.1	460.8	445.9

Employment by Industry: Florida—*Continued*

(Numbers in thousands. Not seasonally adjusted.)

Industry	January	February	March	April	May	June	July	August	September	October	November	December	Annual Average
STATEWIDE—*Continued*													
Manufacturing													
1990	495.1	495.4	495.6	489.5	491.2	490.7	483.2	483.6	481.1	475.5	475.3	474.3	485.8
1991	462.6	461.2	460.8	456.7	456.7	456.1	449.5	452.8	453.2	451.0	453.8	451.9	455.5
1992	447.2	447.5	449.2	448.6	449.6	450.2	449.5	448.8	449.9	450.3	452.8	454.7	449.8
1993	451.4	454.8	456.6	456.2	457.4	457.5	452.8	453.9	453.9	455.3	455.1	456.6	455.1
1994	449.4	451.0	450.6	449.9	451.3	453.2	449.2	450.6	452.2	449.7	452.0	454.2	451.1
1995	452.2	455.4	457.6	455.9	456.8	457.2	453.0	455.0	457.4	457.5	460.0	461.7	456.6
1996	456.2	459.7	460.9	460.2	462.5	463.0	460.9	464.0	464.8	464.2	466.4	467.9	462.5
1997	466.7	468.1	467.9	463.8	463.9	462.4	458.8	461.5	460.2	459.4	461.8	465.4	463.3
1998	463.1	464.9	465.2	458.6	459.5	461.0	454.5	455.2	456.7	457.0	458.5	459.5	459.5
1999	454.8	457.6	458.3	455.6	456.6	457.4	452.3	452.7	452.3	454.4	455.9	458.4	455.5
2000	450.9	454.0	456.6	454.9	456.0	458.5	455.8	455.9	456.7	453.1	453.6	454.4	455.0
2001	445.6	444.9	444.3	439.8	438.0	436.1	428.2	427.6	424.6	420.7	419.1	419.3	432.3
2002	412.0	411.8	412.2	408.8	407.9	407.7	402.5	402.9	401.7	399.7	400.2	400.3	405.6
2003	395.4	394.7	394.5	389.9	389.3	388.6	383.8	385.1	385.3	387.6	386.6	385.2	388.8
Service-providing													
1990	4482.4	4538.9	4591.1	4575.4	4586.1	4576.5	4470.2	4477.7	4535.9	4557.3	4605.2	4636.2	4552.7
1991	4532.8	4559.6	4592.2	4562.4	4562.5	4539.3	4448.4	4456.1	4511.3	4527.8	4586.9	4618.1	4541.4
1992	4553.1	4589.4	4662.9	4628.7	4631.2	4618.5	4532.0	4521.6	4603.9	4645.8	4705.0	4756.3	4620.7
1993	4689.6	4754.9	4800.6	4829.3	4819.9	4816.5	4734.6	4732.0	4815.1	4861.5	4914.7	4975.5	4812.0
1994	4909.0	4970.2	5028.8	5039.7	5037.2	5034.7	4939.6	4940.4	5050.2	5064.0	5169.9	5197.5	5031.7
1995	5109.9	5177.8	5234.9	5202.6	5214.2	5211.6	5093.1	5103.5	5215.7	5234.2	5316.3	5381.4	5207.9
1996	5259.8	5326.4	5410.5	5353.7	5367.2	5354.1	5258.0	5279.4	5386.8	5408.9	5487.0	5553.1	5370.4
1997	5469.1	5522.2	5577.0	5580.0	5593.2	5584.5	5490.6	5507.6	5622.1	5642.6	5701.4	5769.9	5588.3
1998	5703.3	5757.1	5802.8	5778.5	5786.0	5789.9	5694.2	5695.6	5801.7	5857.9	5923.1	5991.4	5798.5
1999	5869.6	5941.8	5990.5	5977.0	5981.2	5989.8	5863.4	5872.0	5971.2	6020.6	6100.6	6177.5	5979.6
2000	6078.8	6133.6	6204.8	6195.5	6224.2	6164.9	6102.5	6205.3	6234.7	6254.4	6331.2	6393.9	6210.3
2001	6242.5	6311.4	6370.4	6342.9	6345.7	6278.2	6197.1	6295.3	6299.0	6291.9	6340.9	6382.3	6308.1
2002	6262.1	6316.9	6375.3	6360.0	6369.3	6285.9	6215.2	6314.7	6326.1	6352.2	6418.1	6474.6	6339.2
2003	6354.9	6407.0	6459.2	6445.7	6456.0	6374.1	6331.3	6434.3	6453.7	6479.0	6540.0	6586.7	6443.5
Trade, transportation, and utilities													
1990	1197.6	1194.9	1201.4	1196.2	1197.2	1199.5	1184.9	1190.1	1187.5	1196.6	1218.6	1243.1	1200.6
1991	1184.4	1171.9	1175.3	1169.3	1170.5	1169.2	1159.8	1163.3	1165.0	1174.5	1197.9	1218.3	1176.6
1992	1162.7	1163.2	1167.4	1167.9	1169.2	1170.5	1163.9	1165.7	1167.1	1182.5	1213.8	1245.0	1178.2
1993	1194.2	1201.7	1208.8	1213.0	1210.4	1213.9	1205.2	1208.4	1213.9	1229.5	1258.2	1290.9	1220.6
1994	1239.2	1242.1	1250.0	1248.8	1251.7	1253.1	1242.3	1253.0	1262.8	1272.0	1307.2	1340.1	1263.5
1995	1290.5	1293.8	1301.1	1288.9	1292.4	1294.9	1281.9	1291.4	1303.4	1314.9	1349.1	1385.0	1307.2
1996	1323.1	1324.9	1334.1	1319.7	1325.3	1324.5	1321.9	1331.2	1334.5	1343.1	1379.3	1412.5	1339.5
1997	1360.0	1357.1	1363.8	1367.5	1370.2	1368.2	1347.8	1346.5	1362.6	1386.7	1411.5	1450.7	1374.3
1998	1401.5	1398.1	1405.5	1398.4	1399.8	1405.6	1405.3	1411.1	1421.2	1444.4	1475.2	1505.4	1422.6
1999	1441.3	1439.4	1446.4	1437.4	1436.2	1439.2	1431.9	1438.6	1443.6	1459.5	1497.6	1530.8	1453.5
2000	1482.0	1480.9	1489.1	1481.3	1486.0	1493.0	1477.4	1488.1	1492.4	1498.0	1535.3	1566.4	1497.5
2001	1495.9	1491.5	1501.4	1490.7	1488.2	1484.4	1471.9	1476.9	1476.7	1479.3	1505.9	1528.7	1490.9
2002	1476.5	1467.4	1474.6	1467.3	1468.4	1462.9	1451.3	1457.6	1458.5	1465.5	1492.5	1521.4	1472.0
2003	1462.2	1454.8	1457.4	1452.2	1453.5	1448.8	1446.9	1449.8	1454.2	1460.5	1489.6	1519.4	1462.4
Wholesale trade													
1990	246.5	248.2	249.2	249.1	249.6	250.0	247.9	249.3	249.7	248.9	249.4	249.6	248.9
1991	242.9	242.4	243.4	241.4	242.0	241.3	239.9	241.0	241.6	243.2	244.9	246.2	242.5
1992	240.5	241.3	242.5	242.8	243.5	244.2	243.7	243.5	244.0	247.2	249.3	251.2	244.4
1993	247.5	249.8	252.1	251.9	252.7	253.5	252.5	253.2	253.9	255.6	257.7	259.5	253.3
1994	254.1	256.0	258.0	259.6	260.1	260.7	259.5	260.7	262.7	263.3	265.5	267.1	260.6
1995	265.3	267.9	270.5	268.9	270.1	270.9	268.0	270.1	272.0	273.0	274.7	276.8	270.6
1996	271.6	274.4	276.3	273.9	275.5	275.9	275.2	276.7	277.5	279.1	281.8	284.1	276.8
1997	283.0	285.4	286.8	288.3	289.9	290.1	287.8	288.5	291.2	293.1	295.7	298.7	289.8
1998	294.9	298.3	300.4	297.1	298.8	299.7	298.7	299.8	300.5	303.7	305.1	306.0	300.3
1999	299.7	301.9	303.4	303.1	303.1	303.2	301.8	301.9	302.5	304.5	306.3	309.7	303.4
2000	308.0	309.2	312.3	311.1	312.7	314.6	313.1	314.2	316.5	315.6	316.9	319.5	313.6
2001	312.0	313.8	315.6	314.7	314.7	313.7	311.0	311.4	311.6	311.3	311.4	312.9	312.8
2002	310.4	311.7	312.5	310.5	312.0	311.6	310.2	311.1	311.8	312.9	314.8	316.7	312.2
2003	311.9	312.8	313.3	312.7	312.8	312.4	311.1	311.8	312.9	313.8	315.3	317.2	313.2
Retail trade													
1990	761.9	756.3	759.1	753.7	754.1	754.3	744.3	747.0	743.7	752.7	773.0	793.1	757.7
1991	748.3	741.4	743.6	737.0	736.2	735.0	726.1	727.6	728.3	735.1	758.4	778.1	741.2
1992	731.5	729.3	730.0	729.8	731.0	730.6	726.0	728.2	729.1	739.1	767.3	792.2	738.6
1993	749.2	752.4	755.3	757.7	754.5	756.3	750.3	752.9	757.2	770.4	795.0	820.5	764.3
1994	777.5	777.6	781.5	780.4	780.2	781.9	772.3	780.1	788.2	797.5	828.8	853.8	791.6
1995	812.8	812.1	814.6	805.2	807.0	809.4	800.1	806.3	814.8	824.6	854.7	882.4	820.3
1996	834.0	830.0	835.3	826.3	829.2	827.7	826.1	832.8	835.0	842.5	873.2	898.6	840.8
1997	853.0	845.1	848.8	851.3	852.6	850.4	833.5	839.1	843.3	862.5	883.1	912.7	856.2
1998	874.6	866.0	870.8	867.2	865.8	870.3	871.5	875.5	882.9	897.1	923.3	947.5	884.4
1999	901.3	896.4	900.9	895.2	894.2	897.1	891.1	896.5	901.4	912.4	945.4	970.1	908.5
2000	930.1	927.5	931.7	925.4	928.4	933.5	919.8	928.9	929.6	936.7	970.3	992.8	937.9
2001	940.5	934.2	941.3	930.7	929.2	926.9	917.5	921.8	921.7	926.0	953.0	969.7	934.3
2002	929.0	919.0	923.6	918.5	919.0	914.9	905.1	910.7	911.5	917.7	941.8	965.2	923.0
2003	918.5	911.1	913.0	909.4	911.7	909.1	908.5	911.1	915.3	920.7	946.1	970.8	920.4

Employment by Industry: Florida—*Continued*

(Numbers in thousands. Not seasonally adjusted.)

Industry	January	February	March	April	May	June	July	August	September	October	November	December	Annual Average
STATEWIDE—*Continued*													
Transportation and utilities													
1990	189.2	190.4	193.1	193.4	193.5	195.2	192.7	193.8	194.1	195.0	196.2	200.4	193.9
1991	193.2	188.1	188.3	190.9	192.3	192.9	193.8	194.7	195.1	196.2	194.6	194.0	192.8
1992	190.7	192.6	194.9	195.3	194.7	195.7	194.2	194.0	194.0	196.2	197.2	201.6	195.0
1993	197.5	199.5	201.4	203.4	203.2	204.1	202.4	202.3	202.8	203.5	205.5	210.9	203.0
1994	207.6	208.5	210.5	208.8	211.4	210.5	210.5	212.2	211.9	211.2	212.9	219.2	211.2
1995	212.4	213.8	216.0	214.8	215.3	214.6	213.8	215.0	216.6	217.3	219.7	225.8	216.2
1996	217.5	220.5	222.5	219.5	220.6	220.9	220.6	221.7	222.0	221.5	224.3	229.8	221.7
1997	224.0	226.6	228.2	227.9	227.7	227.7	226.5	218.9	228.1	231.1	232.7	239.3	228.2
1998	232.0	233.8	234.3	234.1	235.2	235.6	235.1	235.8	237.8	243.6	246.8	251.9	238.0
1999	240.3	241.1	242.1	239.1	238.9	238.9	239.0	240.2	239.7	242.6	245.9	251.0	241.6
2000	243.9	244.2	245.1	244.8	244.9	244.9	244.5	245.0	246.3	245.7	248.1	254.1	246.0
2001	243.4	243.5	244.5	245.3	244.3	243.8	243.4	243.7	243.4	242.0	241.5	246.1	243.7
2002	237.1	236.7	238.5	238.3	237.4	236.4	236.0	235.8	235.2	234.9	235.9	239.5	236.8
2003	231.8	230.9	231.1	230.1	229.0	227.3	227.3	226.9	226.0	226.0	228.2	231.4	228.8
Information													
1990	131.7	132.0	131.8	131.9	132.1	132.8	132.7	132.7	132.5	133.2	134.0	134.9	132.6
1991	132.8	132.3	132.3	131.6	132.3	133.3	134.2	134.0	133.9	132.0	132.9	133.4	132.9
1992	131.5	131.3	132.5	130.5	131.1	131.5	132.2	132.0	132.0	131.8	132.7	134.3	131.9
1993	132.5	133.3	134.9	133.8	133.8	134.9	135.3	135.3	135.5	135.1	135.5	136.4	134.6
1994	136.1	136.3	137.2	137.3	137.9	139.4	140.9	141.5	141.9	140.3	141.5	142.1	139.3
1995	139.4	140.3	141.9	140.3	141.5	143.7	142.1	143.0	143.8	142.1	143.4	145.5	142.2
1996	142.2	142.8	144.9	144.7	146.4	147.7	146.2	146.9	147.9	145.8	147.3	148.8	145.9
1997	147.8	149.5	150.9	149.5	153.7	152.4	152.5	155.3	154.9	152.7	154.0	156.4	152.4
1998	158.7	160.3	161.5	161.5	163.9	165.8	165.0	165.2	166.8	167.1	169.0	170.8	164.6
1999	175.0	177.4	176.2	174.5	177.0	179.9	177.3	178.1	179.8	180.0	182.8	185.3	178.6
2000	180.9	182.1	185.5	182.3	183.9	187.4	189.0	190.5	192.2	192.0	193.6	195.5	187.9
2001	191.1	192.1	192.7	190.9	190.8	190.5	188.3	187.2	185.3	183.4	183.4	184.1	188.3
2002	181.1	180.6	180.8	178.6	178.9	178.4	176.9	176.3	175.4	174.8	175.4	176.0	177.8
2003	172.3	172.6	173.0	169.9	170.7	170.7	171.0	171.2	172.6	172.9	171.9	172.6	171.8
Financial activities													
1990	368.5	372.8	375.1	376.9	378.3	380.2	377.4	379.1	377.4	375.2	375.4	376.7	376.0
1991	365.8	366.2	367.0	364.3	365.2	365.8	363.4	364.6	362.5	362.2	362.5	363.7	364.4
1992	363.7	365.3	366.1	365.3	366.6	367.6	366.8	366.1	363.8	366.9	367.3	370.4	366.3
1993	366.2	369.1	370.5	370.4	371.1	373.1	375.3	376.1	375.0	376.8	378.2	381.5	373.6
1994	381.4	383.6	386.5	385.9	385.9	388.1	387.8	388.3	387.6	385.8	386.9	390.6	386.5
1995	388.1	391.1	393.9	391.3	391.6	394.2	392.7	393.8	394.6	390.9	394.1	396.6	392.7
1996	391.5	394.6	397.0	396.0	399.3	401.3	401.1	404.4	403.9	404.5	406.1	410.7	400.8
1997	402.0	404.7	408.5	411.4	414.2	415.6	416.7	418.0	418.7	414.2	415.8	420.9	413.3
1998	432.0	435.2	438.0	436.1	436.8	439.0	443.8	443.1	441.9	443.4	443.6	448.3	440.1
1999	445.2	448.7	450.8	448.4	449.1	451.8	454.4	454.8	450.5	453.6	455.2	459.5	451.8
2000	454.0	455.7	460.1	459.6	461.8	467.9	463.7	464.9	465.6	465.4	466.9	470.1	463.0
2001	460.1	463.4	467.2	468.8	469.5	472.9	471.4	472.7	471.2	470.6	471.3	473.1	469.3
2002	469.5	471.7	473.3	471.8	472.7	474.9	475.5	476.8	475.5	476.5	479.3	481.7	474.9
2003	475.9	477.7	479.7	481.5	483.3	485.9	487.6	488.4	487.8	486.8	488.1	488.8	484.3
Professional and business services													
1990	545.6	556.1	564.5	563.2	563.9	569.6	562.0	566.7	566.7	569.5	573.0	570.8	564.3
1991	565.5	571.4	574.7	567.6	566.5	566.9	565.1	569.5	569.1	568.1	574.6	575.7	569.5
1992	583.4	587.5	593.2	593.6	592.6	592.4	584.2	582.7	587.7	595.5	597.0	603.6	591.1
1993	610.7	618.3	623.0	645.0	644.3	647.1	641.8	645.5	650.7	661.1	664.9	671.2	643.6
1994	672.9	685.3	696.3	708.0	710.9	716.4	712.3	715.3	717.9	728.3	734.2	746.9	712.0
1995	734.8	747.3	757.0	762.9	771.2	776.0	766.2	779.4	778.9	794.4	807.9	814.3	774.1
1996	794.9	813.0	827.5	832.3	838.9	840.5	850.3	861.2	870.3	871.7	884.5	893.7	848.2
1997	882.6	898.0	915.8	926.4	930.6	942.5	952.3	964.7	971.7	980.0	989.6	991.4	945.4
1998	972.6	990.8	1000.6	1007.5	1011.2	1021.7	1007.5	1017.7	1022.3	1035.9	1047.4	1060.8	1016.3
1999	1046.8	1071.9	1088.4	1099.3	1103.4	1115.7	1096.6	1107.2	1110.2	1128.6	1136.7	1154.5	1104.9
2000	1141.1	1155.6	1174.9	1170.6	1175.0	1183.0	1173.6	1186.0	1197.3	1193.4	1203.3	1211.4	1180.4
2001	1191.5	1215.2	1227.5	1218.2	1218.5	1220.2	1204.9	1210.4	1208.9	1205.6	1207.1	1207.7	1211.3
2002	1185.3	1206.7	1220.9	1221.9	1223.0	1220.5	1209.4	1204.8	1206.2	1210.7	1222.7	1229.6	1213.5
2003	1211.4	1229.7	1246.5	1253.9	1254.6	1257.0	1259.3	1264.1	1269.5	1274.8	1284.5	1285.1	1257.5
Educational and health services													
1990	560.4	566.1	570.1	569.3	571.7	572.7	565.0	570.4	579.1	584.2	588.7	591.8	574.1
1991	588.6	594.6	596.1	600.1	602.8	601.3	596.5	599.8	607.0	611.6	617.5	618.5	602.8
1992	613.1	618.5	623.7	629.5	631.2	629.4	625.7	628.3	635.3	640.6	644.9	649.9	630.8
1993	642.3	650.1	655.4	658.1	660.4	660.9	656.7	659.0	669.4	675.8	680.5	684.3	662.7
1994	676.1	684.9	691.8	695.5	698.6	698.6	693.4	697.3	709.5	710.1	716.0	720.1	699.3
1995	715.9	725.3	732.0	726.1	728.6	728.7	718.0	721.4	733.2	737.2	743.9	749.4	729.9
1996	726.6	733.4	737.4	734.9	737.8	736.5	730.0	733.1	741.0	743.8	749.1	751.7	737.9
1997	745.2	751.4	757.1	756.9	759.2	759.0	751.8	756.7	766.1	767.5	772.9	777.1	760.0
1998	772.2	780.0	784.4	776.4	778.8	776.6	769.0	773.1	779.1	783.2	785.9	788.9	779.0
1999	778.4	785.3	790.7	781.8	783.5	782.2	774.4	778.9	785.0	788.1	793.7	797.2	784.9
2000	789.0	796.7	803.6	800.3	802.5	803.3	798.8	805.6	815.0	818.3	823.6	828.8	807.1
2001	811.9	820.6	825.6	826.7	830.0	832.2	822.7	830.4	839.0	844.0	848.7	854.8	832.2
2002	838.0	845.8	853.4	850.3	853.6	852.3	842.4	851.8	860.1	866.4	872.5	876.8	855.3
2003	868.3	878.6	884.4	882.5	885.7	883.4	875.0	883.3	892.0	895.2	898.3	900.2	885.6

Employment by Industry: Florida—*Continued*

(Numbers in thousands. Not seasonally adjusted.)

Industry	January	February	March	April	May	June	July	August	September	October	November	December	Annual Average
STATEWIDE—*Continued*													
Leisure and hospitality													
1990	626.7	649.5	667.3	656.4	647.4	642.2	625.6	624.6	614.0	604.9	616.4	624.0	633.2
1991	611.0	629.0	645.6	630.9	622.3	615.6	598.7	596.8	589.1	584.5	596.3	605.5	610.4
1992	605.6	621.4	640.0	634.6	630.1	625.9	610.9	612.0	604.9	607.8	622.6	629.1	620.4
1993	633.2	655.7	674.5	672.4	668.9	663.7	647.7	648.4	642.9	633.9	645.7	656.0	653.5
1994	659.4	679.1	700.4	696.0	688.5	683.5	665.0	664.1	660.1	649.4	663.0	675.5	673.6
1995	676.0	697.4	716.6	704.6	700.5	698.4	683.5	680.9	677.2	669.7	686.2	697.0	690.6
1996	700.7	720.4	740.9	728.9	722.5	721.4	695.2	697.5	695.1	698.1	709.8	722.8	712.7
1997	722.4	743.0	759.0	746.7	741.6	735.0	722.6	727.1	725.4	709.7	721.5	731.8	732.1
1998	731.8	751.0	763.9	758.9	754.1	753.5	739.8	738.8	733.9	735.5	747.9	758.0	747.3
1999	743.3	764.6	777.9	779.2	775.4	777.0	755.2	754.8	750.4	741.4	754.9	762.9	761.4
2000	754.5	773.0	790.6	795.4	787.8	786.7	773.4	771.5	767.9	773.3	787.3	795.9	779.8
2001	784.4	805.0	823.6	815.8	813.9	807.9	786.5	785.6	779.5	768.7	776.0	782.2	794.0
2002	774.6	794.7	814.0	814.4	811.1	809.4	788.1	790.5	784.8	784.4	796.6	806.1	797.4
2003	797.6	812.6	830.6	825.0	818.2	814.3	793.9	797.2	792.5	796.0	807.2	817.1	808.5
Other services													
1990	222.4	225.0	227.3	225.9	225.8	226.9	225.0	225.1	224.3	223.2	224.1	224.7	224.9
1991	223.7	224.7	226.9	226.0	226.3	226.6	224.4	225.1	223.9	223.9	225.0	227.2	225.3
1992	227.8	229.0	230.5	230.9	231.8	233.1	232.1	231.7	230.8	232.7	234.2	236.0	231.7
1993	235.5	238.4	240.1	240.9	240.6	242.7	242.7	242.1	242.3	243.0	243.7	245.5	241.4
1994	243.3	245.2	247.1	247.0	246.6	247.9	246.9	245.8	246.0	246.9	247.9	249.9	246.7
1995	248.0	250.1	252.6	252.2	253.0	254.1	252.5	252.2	253.6	252.6	254.0	254.9	252.4
1996	253.3	256.9	258.5	255.5	256.9	257.4	255.0	255.6	255.7	257.0	258.6	260.5	256.7
1997	261.4	263.7	265.5	266.6	267.7	268.6	269.5	271.4	271.6	269.8	270.6	272.4	268.2
1998	269.9	272.2	274.9	272.5	273.5	275.1	273.8	273.1	273.0	274.9	275.5	276.5	273.7
1999	273.9	276.5	278.3	276.2	277.2	279.9	278.0	278.1	278.5	280.9	282.9	284.8	278.8
2000	285.7	288.1	291.3	291.4	293.1	295.3	293.9	293.0	294.4	295.8	295.8	296.7	292.9
2001	292.9	295.4	298.1	296.6	298.2	301.3	298.5	298.9	299.2	298.6	300.7	302.5	298.4
2002	303.2	305.8	309.5	306.4	307.9	309.6	307.6	308.7	309.0	311.9	314.3	315.5	309.1
2003	314.5	317.5	320.5	315.5	317.4	319.4	316.3	317.2	315.4	317.1	320.3	323.0	317.8
Government													
1990	829.5	842.5	853.6	855.6	869.7	852.6	797.6	789.0	854.4	870.5	875.0	870.2	846.6
1991	861.0	869.5	874.3	872.6	876.6	860.6	806.3	803.0	860.8	871.0	880.2	875.8	859.3
1992	865.3	873.2	909.5	876.4	878.6	868.1	816.2	803.1	882.3	888.0	892.5	888.0	870.1
1993	875.0	888.3	893.4	895.7	890.4	880.2	829.9	817.2	885.4	906.3	908.0	909.7	881.6
1994	900.6	913.7	919.5	921.2	917.1	907.7	851.0	835.1	924.4	931.2	973.2	932.3	910.5
1995	917.2	932.5	939.8	936.3	935.4	921.6	856.2	841.4	931.0	932.4	937.7	938.7	918.3
1996	927.5	940.4	970.2	941.7	940.1	924.8	858.3	849.5	938.4	944.9	952.3	952.4	928.3
1997	947.7	954.8	956.4	955.0	956.0	943.2	877.4	867.9	951.1	962.0	965.5	969.2	942.1
1998	964.6	969.5	974.0	967.2	967.9	952.6	890.0	873.5	963.5	973.5	978.6	982.7	954.8
1999	965.7	978.0	981.8	980.2	979.4	964.1	895.6	881.5	973.2	988.5	996.8	1002.5	965.6
2000	991.6	1001.5	1009.7	1014.6	1034.1	948.3	932.7	1005.7	1009.9	1018.2	1025.4	1029.1	1001.7
2001	1014.7	1028.2	1034.3	1035.2	1036.6	968.8	952.9	1033.2	1039.2	1041.7	1047.8	1049.2	1023.4
2002	1033.9	1044.2	1048.8	1049.3	1053.7	977.9	964.0	1048.2	1056.6	1062.0	1064.8	1067.5	1039.2
2003	1052.7	1063.5	1067.1	1065.2	1072.6	994.6	981.3	1063.1	1069.7	1075.7	1080.1	1080.5	1055.5
Federal government													
1990	121.4	121.2	124.0	129.2	139.3	131.5	132.8	124.6	122.6	122.6	122.6	123.9	126.3
1991	122.3	122.0	122.1	121.9	122.4	123.0	122.4	122.3	122.3	122.6	123.3	125.0	122.6
1992	123.7	123.1	123.1	123.1	123.0	123.0	122.9	122.7	122.6	122.7	122.2	124.3	123.0
1993	121.5	121.1	121.4	120.9	121.3	121.4	122.0	122.0	121.5	121.9	122.2	124.7	121.8
1994	122.0	121.7	121.5	121.5	121.0	121.0	120.5	120.2	120.2	120.4	120.4	123.3	121.1
1995	119.1	118.9	118.8	119.0	118.8	119.3	119.9	120.1	120.2	120.3	120.5	122.9	119.8
1996	119.6	119.3	119.3	120.2	119.8	119.8	119.4	119.5	119.4	119.3	120.3	123.1	119.9
1997	120.0	119.8	119.8	120.1	120.1	120.1	120.0	120.2	120.3	120.0	120.8	123.4	120.3
1998	119.8	119.4	119.5	120.0	120.2	120.1	120.1	120.0	119.8	120.2	121.1	124.2	120.4
1999	120.7	121.9	121.6	120.7	119.7	119.8	119.6	119.6	119.4	119.4	120.0	122.6	120.4
2000	120.1	120.9	123.3	127.1	147.4	127.4	127.8	122.8	119.8	120.1	120.6	122.7	125.0
2001	121.6	121.1	121.4	121.0	121.2	121.9	122.4	122.3	122.2	121.2	121.4	123.3	121.7
2002	120.7	120.2	120.5	120.4	120.3	121.6	120.8	121.5	122.6	124.7	125.3	128.3	122.2
2003	126.7	126.0	125.9	126.3	126.3	126.4	126.2	125.7	125.3	125.4	124.7	126.7	126.0
State government													
1990	168.9	173.7	175.1	175.9	176.2	173.5	171.2	172.1	177.8	179.6	181.8	181.1	175.5
1991	176.4	179.9	180.8	181.3	184.3	173.4	173.2	174.0	179.0	181.9	183.1	181.1	179.0
1992	177.5	180.4	180.6	180.5	182.7	171.8	173.9	172.9	177.4	184.7	184.5	183.8	179.2
1993	180.6	185.1	186.7	189.0	185.0	179.1	183.4	182.2	185.2	192.5	191.0	191.0	185.9
1994	187.2	191.2	193.4	195.6	192.6	185.6	188.7	186.6	197.7	198.0	197.5	198.0	192.6
1995	192.3	197.9	202.3	200.5	199.2	191.0	192.3	191.7	200.8	200.4	201.5	201.2	197.5
1996	195.6	200.1	204.0	201.8	201.2	191.6	193.9	197.0	198.5	201.4	202.2	202.5	199.1
1997	203.8	203.0	204.0	204.3	203.7	194.4	196.8	200.0	202.6	206.5	206.9	206.8	202.7
1998	207.7	206.6	207.6	207.5	207.0	196.7	201.3	199.1	203.8	206.9	208.1	209.0	205.1
1999	203.4	207.7	209.1	209.4	209.6	198.7	203.9	202.1	206.2	210.0	211.8	213.8	207.1
2000	206.0	211.5	212.9	213.1	213.4	205.8	202.6	204.1	209.2	213.9	214.7	216.6	210.3
2001	207.7	214.0	215.7	215.4	215.1	207.1	204.0	204.8	208.7	213.4	217.0	213.8	211.3
2002	206.2	211.5	212.1	211.5	214.3	199.4	199.9	201.7	206.8	211.5	215.1	212.5	208.5
2003	206.9	212.4	213.8	213.8	217.5	202.2	203.0	202.5	207.2	214.6	213.5	213.3	210.1

Employment by Industry: Florida—*Continued*

(Numbers in thousands. Not seasonally adjusted.)

Industry	January	February	March	April	May	June	July	August	September	October	November	December	Annual Average
STATEWIDE—*Continued*													
Local government													
1990	539.2	547.6	554.5	550.5	554.2	547.6	493.6	492.3	554.0	568.3	570.6	565.2	544.8
1991	562.3	567.6	571.4	569.4	569.9	564.2	510.7	506.7	559.5	566.5	573.8	569.7	557.6
1992	564.1	569.7	605.8	572.8	572.9	573.3	519.4	507.5	582.3	580.6	585.8	579.9	567.8
1993	572.9	582.1	585.3	585.8	584.1	579.7	524.5	513.0	578.7	591.9	594.8	594.0	573.9
1994	591.4	600.8	604.6	604.1	603.5	601.1	541.8	528.3	606.5	612.8	655.3	611.0	596.7
1995	605.8	615.7	618.7	616.8	617.4	611.3	544.0	529.6	610.0	611.7	615.7	614.6	600.9
1996	612.3	621.0	646.9	619.7	619.1	613.4	545.0	533.0	620.5	624.2	629.8	626.8	609.3
1997	623.9	632.0	632.6	630.6	632.2	628.7	560.6	547.7	628.2	635.5	637.8	639.0	619.0
1998	637.1	643.5	646.9	639.7	640.7	635.8	568.6	554.4	639.9	646.4	649.4	649.5	629.3
1999	641.6	648.4	651.1	650.1	650.1	645.6	572.1	559.8	647.6	659.1	665.0	666.1	638.1
2000	665.5	669.1	673.5	674.4	673.3	615.1	602.3	678.8	680.9	684.2	690.1	689.8	666.4
2001	685.4	693.1	697.2	698.8	700.3	639.8	626.5	706.1	708.3	707.1	709.4	712.1	690.3
2002	707.0	712.5	716.2	717.4	719.1	656.9	643.3	725.0	727.2	725.8	724.4	726.7	708.5
2003	719.1	725.1	727.4	725.1	728.8	666.0	652.1	734.9	737.2	735.7	741.9	740.5	719.5
FORT LAUDERDALE-HOLLYWOOD-POMPANO BEACH													
Total nonfarm													
1990	512.9	517.0	524.5	515.4	515.6	515.3	503.5	504.0	508.5	516.5	517.9	523.1	514.5
1991	508.8	510.5	512.8	507.5	505.9	503.9	490.9	492.3	497.8	500.9	507.8	513.4	504.3
1992	503.9	508.2	515.6	509.0	510.5	510.3	500.3	499.9	512.3	522.3	529.6	538.3	513.3
1993	525.6	534.9	540.2	540.8	539.1	540.8	529.5	529.9	539.7	546.2	552.3	562.3	540.1
1994	550.7	556.8	563.5	563.1	565.1	566.3	555.1	558.1	566.7	566.9	579.5	585.2	564.7
1995	574.6	580.8	588.4	582.6	583.2	584.7	571.1	573.5	585.7	588.2	597.2	605.9	584.6
1996	596.0	602.5	611.7	604.5	606.6	606.9	595.2	599.3	609.2	610.4	619.7	627.0	607.4
1997	616.0	621.0	626.0	623.0	625.8	626.9	615.0	618.1	629.8	630.2	636.7	645.7	626.1
1998	634.1	638.9	644.2	635.8	635.7	637.4	627.1	628.5	638.2	644.5	649.9	659.5	639.4
1999	647.1	653.8	657.8	649.4	651.6	653.0	639.5	640.1	647.9	654.2	662.4	674.9	652.6
2000	660.4	665.3	672.9	674.7	680.2	682.4	672.1	674.1	687.3	689.3	698.9	709.7	680.6
2001	694.3	700.8	706.1	700.7	703.0	705.4	689.5	690.2	700.8	697.9	704.0	711.6	700.3
2002	698.2	700.1	708.1	705.7	705.8	706.4	695.2	696.0	708.2	707.3	716.6	725.1	706.1
2003	711.6	716.1	720.3	714.2	715.4	717.6	704.8	706.0	717.6	719.5	727.1	734.3	717.0
Total private													
1990	446.4	449.1	452.7	446.3	444.3	444.5	438.2	439.8	439.8	443.8	447.1	451.6	445.3
1991	437.6	438.1	439.9	434.6	432.4	430.8	423.6	425.5	426.5	428.2	434.7	439.9	432.6
1992	431.4	434.8	438.3	434.6	435.7	435.8	431.5	432.5	438.4	448.3	455.6	463.8	440.0
1993	451.9	459.6	463.9	464.7	463.0	464.4	459.1	460.6	463.4	469.7	475.4	484.8	465.0
1994	473.5	477.9	483.7	483.6	485.3	486.2	480.8	484.7	486.1	487.1	494.8	504.0	485.6
1995	495.7	499.9	506.5	501.5	501.8	503.4	495.7	499.7	504.3	507.0	515.8	523.8	504.5
1996	514.0	520.1	525.8	521.9	523.6	523.8	518.3	523.7	525.8	527.8	536.4	543.0	525.3
1997	532.4	537.0	541.8	538.5	541.0	541.8	536.3	540.6	544.4	545.0	550.9	559.5	542.4
1998	548.2	552.9	557.6	550.7	550.3	552.4	548.0	551.1	553.2	560.0	565.0	574.8	555.3
1999	562.4	568.4	572.5	564.1	566.0	567.6	559.3	561.1	561.4	567.6	575.2	586.8	567.7
2000	573.1	577.5	584.1	582.4	585.9	589.9	585.6	589.6	594.3	596.7	606.0	615.8	590.1
2001	602.0	608.0	612.4	606.7	608.4	610.7	601.1	603.2	605.0	603.1	608.9	615.7	607.1
2002	602.7	604.5	610.4	609.8	609.2	610.0	605.1	607.6	610.5	609.9	619.1	625.9	610.4
2003	612.8	616.6	619.8	615.2	615.8	618.0	611.9	614.9	617.2	619.7	626.7	633.6	618.5
Goods-producing													
1990	77.3	77.6	77.9	77.6	78.1	78.6	77.9	78.2	77.3	78.0	77.2	76.0	77.6
1991	71.2	70.8	70.0	68.2	68.0	67.5	67.2	67.9	67.8	67.1	66.9	66.1	68.2
1992	63.6	64.6	64.8	65.1	65.5	66.2	66.4	67.0	68.7	70.4	70.9	71.1	67.0
1993	68.7	70.4	70.8	72.5	72.7	73.6	73.2	73.6	74.3	74.8	75.1	75.9	72.9
1994	72.0	73.6	74.0	74.9	75.8	76.5	76.9	77.8	78.0	77.1	77.1	77.6	75.9
1995	75.7	77.1	77.8	77.3	77.7	78.4	77.4	78.0	79.2	79.8	79.7	80.0	78.1
1996	76.7	78.1	78.5	78.4	79.2	80.1	78.4	79.5	80.0	80.2	80.8	80.9	79.2
1997	77.8	78.6	79.4	77.7	78.1	78.5	79.0	79.6	80.2	80.2	80.1	80.4	79.1
1998	77.4	78.0	78.6	77.1	77.3	77.9	77.3	77.7	78.2	78.1	77.8	78.4	77.8
1999	76.1	77.3	77.9	78.5	79.3	79.9	79.0	79.0	79.5	80.2	80.1	80.1	78.9
2000	78.7	79.3	80.0	81.1	82.3	82.6	82.6	83.0	83.6	83.9	84.1	84.3	82.1
2001	83.1	82.8	82.9	82.6	82.8	83.4	81.9	81.8	81.7	81.0	80.4	80.4	82.0
2002	77.6	77.0	77.3	77.1	77.0	77.2	76.0	76.5	76.6	76.5	76.2	75.7	76.7
2003	74.4	74.9	75.0	74.3	74.9	75.3	75.8	76.0	76.3	76.5	76.1	76.3	75.5
Construction and mining													
1990	34.7	34.7	34.9	34.5	34.7	35.2	34.7	34.6	34.0	35.1	34.6	33.6	34.6
1991	30.9	30.3	29.6	28.4	28.5	28.0	28.1	28.5	28.2	27.9	27.8	27.3	28.6
1992	25.7	26.1	26.2	26.5	26.8	27.1	27.4	27.9	29.2	30.9	31.1	31.3	28.0
1993	30.3	31.3	31.6	32.3	32.4	33.0	32.7	32.9	33.1	33.1	33.4	33.8	32.4
1994	31.7	32.4	32.9	33.3	33.9	34.5	34.8	35.4	35.3	34.9	34.7	35.0	34.0
1995	34.3	35.2	35.8	35.5	35.6	36.2	35.6	35.8	36.3	36.6	36.4	36.4	35.8
1996	34.4	35.2	35.7	35.7	36.3	37.0	36.0	36.7	36.8	37.3	37.4	37.3	36.3
1997	36.0	36.3	36.8	35.9	36.2	36.5	36.9	37.4	37.7	38.2	38.1	38.3	37.0
1998	36.7	36.9	37.3	37.2	37.3	37.8	38.0	38.4	38.6	39.0	38.9	39.6	37.9
1999	38.4	39.1	39.8	40.6	41.2	41.5	41.0	41.2	41.5	42.3	42.3	42.4	40.9
2000	41.2	41.6	42.2	43.6	44.0	44.2	44.3	44.9	45.6	46.0	46.5	47.0	44.3
2001	45.6	45.2	45.4	45.2	45.7	46.2	45.7	45.9	45.8	45.6	45.2	45.1	45.5
2002	43.5	43.1	43.5	43.4	43.4	43.6	42.9	43.6	43.7	43.8	43.6	43.1	43.4
2003	42.6	43.2	43.3	43.0	43.6	44.0	44.4	45.0	45.4	45.5	45.3	45.6	44.2

Employment by Industry: Florida—*Continued*

(Numbers in thousands. Not seasonally adjusted.)

Industry	January	February	March	April	May	June	July	August	September	October	November	December	Annual Average
FORT LAUDERDALE-HOLLYWOOD-POMPANO BEACH—*Continued*													
Manufacturing													
1990	42.6	42.9	43.0	43.1	43.4	43.4	43.2	43.6	43.3	42.9	42.6	42.4	43.0
1991	40.3	40.5	40.4	39.8	39.5	39.5	39.1	39.4	39.6	39.2	39.1	38.8	39.6
1992	37.9	38.5	38.6	38.6	38.7	39.1	39.0	39.1	39.5	39.5	39.8	39.8	39.0
1993	38.4	39.1	39.2	40.2	40.3	40.6	40.5	40.7	41.2	41.7	41.7	42.1	40.4
1994	40.3	41.2	41.1	41.6	41.9	42.0	42.1	42.4	42.7	42.2	42.4	42.6	41.8
1995	41.4	41.9	42.0	41.8	42.1	42.2	41.8	42.2	42.9	43.2	43.3	43.6	42.3
1996	42.3	42.9	42.8	42.7	42.9	43.1	42.4	42.8	43.2	42.9	43.4	43.6	42.9
1997	41.8	42.3	42.6	41.8	41.9	42.0	42.1	42.2	42.5	42.0	42.0	42.1	42.1
1998	40.7	41.1	41.3	39.9	40.0	40.1	39.3	39.3	39.6	39.1	38.9	38.8	39.8
1999	37.7	38.2	38.1	37.9	38.1	38.4	38.0	37.8	38.0	37.9	37.8	37.7	37.9
2000	37.5	37.7	37.8	37.5	38.3	38.4	38.3	38.1	38.0	37.9	37.6	37.3	37.9
2001	37.5	37.6	37.5	37.4	37.1	37.2	36.2	35.9	35.9	35.4	35.2	35.3	36.5
2002	34.1	33.9	33.8	33.7	33.6	33.6	33.1	32.9	32.9	32.7	32.6	32.6	33.3
2003	31.8	31.7	31.7	31.3	31.3	31.3	31.4	31.0	30.9	31.0	30.8	30.7	31.2
Service-providing													
1990	435.6	439.4	446.6	437.8	437.5	436.7	425.6	425.8	431.2	438.5	440.7	447.1	436.8
1991	437.6	439.7	442.8	439.3	437.9	436.4	423.7	424.4	430.0	433.8	440.9	447.3	436.1
1992	440.3	443.6	450.8	443.9	445.0	444.1	433.9	432.9	443.6	451.9	458.7	467.2	446.3
1993	456.9	464.5	469.4	468.3	466.4	467.2	456.3	456.3	465.4	471.4	477.2	486.4	467.1
1994	478.7	483.2	489.5	488.2	489.3	489.8	478.2	480.3	488.7	489.8	502.4	507.6	488.8
1995	498.9	503.7	510.6	505.3	505.5	506.3	493.7	495.5	506.5	508.4	517.5	525.9	506.4
1996	519.3	524.4	533.2	526.1	527.4	526.8	516.8	519.8	529.2	530.2	538.9	546.1	528.1
1997	538.2	542.4	546.6	545.3	547.7	548.4	536.0	538.5	549.6	550.0	556.6	565.3	547.0
1998	556.7	560.9	565.6	558.7	558.4	559.5	549.8	550.8	560.0	566.4	572.1	581.1	561.6
1999	571.0	576.5	579.9	570.9	572.3	573.1	560.5	561.1	568.4	574.0	582.3	594.8	573.7
2000	581.7	586.0	592.9	593.6	597.9	599.8	589.5	591.1	603.7	605.4	614.8	625.4	598.5
2001	611.2	618.0	623.2	618.1	620.2	622.0	607.6	608.4	619.1	616.9	623.6	631.2	618.2
2002	620.6	623.1	630.8	628.6	628.8	629.2	619.2	619.5	631.6	630.8	640.4	649.4	629.3
2003	637.2	641.2	645.3	639.9	640.5	642.3	629.0	630.0	641.3	643.0	651.0	658.0	641.6
Trade, transportation, and utilities													
1990	118.4	117.4	117.9	117.3	116.9	116.7	115.4	115.4	115.2	118.4	120.1	123.2	117.6
1991	117.2	115.8	115.4	116.0	115.6	115.7	114.9	115.2	115.4	116.5	119.7	123.4	116.7
1992	118.8	117.9	117.9	117.3	117.1	117.6	115.3	115.1	116.0	117.6	121.7	125.8	118.1
1993	121.1	121.5	121.6	123.4	123.2	123.2	120.9	121.0	121.8	124.4	127.6	131.7	123.4
1994	125.1	124.5	125.9	126.8	127.2	127.6	126.0	127.3	128.2	130.8	134.2	137.7	128.4
1995	131.9	131.5	132.8	131.9	132.4	133.0	132.0	132.7	133.7	136.3	140.4	144.6	134.4
1996	138.2	137.4	138.1	136.6	137.1	136.8	136.4	137.3	137.5	138.9	142.9	146.7	138.6
1997	142.3	141.2	142.2	142.8	142.5	142.4	140.8	140.3	142.2	143.7	147.6	151.9	143.3
1998	145.7	144.9	145.1	146.3	145.7	146.2	146.0	146.6	147.5	149.7	153.1	157.0	147.8
1999	151.2	152.1	152.0	150.5	150.3	150.7	148.6	148.6	148.8	152.0	155.9	161.2	151.8
2000	154.1	154.2	154.3	155.1	154.3	154.7	153.2	154.0	153.8	155.3	159.5	163.7	155.5
2001	156.2	156.3	157.3	155.5	155.4	155.5	154.5	154.7	155.0	155.2	158.5	161.8	156.3
2002	156.1	154.9	155.5	154.9	155.1	155.1	153.5	154.8	155.6	155.6	159.2	162.7	156.1
2003	155.3	154.2	154.3	153.2	153.4	153.8	152.1	153.6	153.7	153.8	157.0	160.3	154.6
Wholesale trade													
1990	25.9	26.0	26.1	26.7	26.7	26.6	26.5	26.6	26.6	27.0	26.9	27.0	26.5
1991	26.8	26.7	26.7	26.7	26.7	26.6	26.1	26.0	26.0	25.9	26.0	26.2	26.3
1992	25.2	25.5	25.6	25.8	26.0	26.0	25.8	25.8	26.0	26.4	26.6	26.8	25.9
1993	26.5	27.0	27.2	27.6	27.8	27.8	27.8	27.6	27.7	28.0	28.2	28.4	27.6
1994	27.4	27.6	27.9	28.4	28.4	28.5	28.6	28.4	28.7	28.9	29.1	29.3	28.4
1995	29.3	29.5	30.0	29.8	29.9	30.1	29.9	30.0	30.3	30.7	30.9	31.1	30.1
1996	30.6	30.9	31.1	30.6	30.7	30.7	30.4	30.6	30.9	31.0	31.2	31.2	30.8
1997	31.3	31.5	31.8	32.6	32.6	32.7	32.7	32.8	33.1	32.9	33.2	33.4	32.5
1998	33.0	33.1	33.3	33.9	34.0	34.0	33.7	33.7	33.8	34.2	34.4	34.4	33.7
1999	33.4	34.0	34.1	34.2	34.3	34.3	34.2	34.2	34.4	34.7	34.9	35.7	34.3
2000	34.6	34.9	34.9	36.4	36.3	36.7	37.0	37.2	37.5	37.4	37.5	38.1	36.5
2001	38.6	39.1	39.4	39.4	39.5	39.8	39.5	39.4	39.5	39.5	39.6	39.8	39.4
2002	39.7	39.8	39.9	40.0	40.1	40.3	40.2	40.5	40.5	40.5	40.7	40.9	40.3
2003	39.7	39.7	39.8	39.4	39.1	39.2	38.7	38.9	38.9	39.1	39.3	39.3	39.3
Retail trade													
1990	82.2	81.0	81.1	80.4	80.2	80.1	78.7	78.6	78.4	80.3	82.0	84.3	80.6
1991	79.2	78.0	77.5	77.7	77.1	77.4	77.9	78.1	78.3	78.9	81.7	84.5	78.8
1992	80.8	79.1	78.9	78.3	78.1	78.5	77.3	77.3	77.8	78.7	82.3	85.9	79.4
1993	81.1	80.7	80.7	82.0	81.7	81.6	80.4	80.4	81.0	83.2	85.7	89.2	82.3
1994	83.6	82.9	83.5	83.9	84.2	84.6	83.0	84.2	84.8	86.9	89.8	92.7	85.3
1995	87.2	86.6	87.0	86.0	86.4	86.9	85.8	86.4	87.2	89.0	92.4	95.3	88.0
1996	90.6	89.1	89.3	88.7	89.2	89.0	89.1	89.6	89.7	91.3	94.5	97.5	90.6
1997	92.8	91.3	91.6	92.7	92.7	92.5	91.5	92.0	92.9	94.2	97.2	100.5	93.4
1998	95.9	94.7	95.2	95.5	95.1	95.2	95.6	96.2	96.8	98.4	100.9	103.8	96.9
1999	99.3	99.4	99.0	97.3	97.1	97.5	95.7	95.6	95.7	97.7	101.2	105.4	98.4
2000	100.1	100.0	100.2	99.0	98.7	99.2	97.3	98.0	97.6	99.2	102.8	105.8	99.8
2001	98.8	98.4	99.1	97.6	97.5	97.3	96.3	96.6	96.7	97.1	100.0	102.6	98.1
2002	98.1	96.9	97.2	96.6	96.7	96.6	94.9	95.8	96.4	96.1	98.9	101.7	97.2
2003	96.6	95.6	95.7	94.9	95.6	95.7	94.6	95.9	96.2	96.1	98.8	101.6	96.4

Employment by Industry: Florida—*Continued*

(Numbers in thousands. Not seasonally adjusted.)

Industry	January	February	March	April	May	June	July	August	September	October	November	December	Annual Average
FORT LAUDERDALE-HOLLYWOOD-POMPANO BEACH—*Continued*													
Transportation and utilities													
1990	10.3	10.4	10.7	10.2	10.0	10.0	10.2	10.2	10.2	11.1	11.2	11.9	10.5
1991	11.2	11.1	11.2	11.6	11.8	11.7	10.9	11.1	11.1	11.7	12.0	12.7	11.5
1992	12.8	13.3	13.4	13.2	13.0	13.1	12.2	12.0	12.2	12.5	12.8	13.1	12.8
1993	13.5	13.8	13.7	13.8	13.7	13.8	12.7	13.0	13.1	13.2	13.7	14.1	13.5
1994	14.1	14.0	14.5	14.5	14.6	14.5	14.4	14.7	14.7	15.0	15.3	15.7	14.6
1995	15.4	15.4	15.8	16.1	16.1	16.0	16.3	16.3	16.2	16.6	17.1	18.2	16.2
1996	17.0	17.4	17.7	17.3	17.2	17.1	16.9	17.1	16.9	16.6	17.2	18.0	17.2
1997	18.2	18.4	18.8	17.5	17.2	17.2	16.6	15.5	16.2	16.6	17.2	18.0	17.2
1998	16.8	17.1	16.6	16.9	16.6	17.0	16.7	16.7	16.9	17.1	17.8	18.8	17.0
1999	18.5	18.7	18.9	19.0	18.9	18.9	18.7	18.8	18.7	19.6	19.8	20.1	19.0
2000	19.4	19.3	19.2	19.7	19.3	18.8	18.9	18.8	18.7	18.7	19.2	19.8	19.2
2001	18.8	18.8	18.8	18.5	18.4	18.4	18.7	18.7	18.8	18.6	18.9	19.4	18.7
2002	18.3	18.2	18.4	18.3	18.3	18.2	18.4	18.5	18.7	19.0	19.6	20.1	18.7
2003	19.0	18.9	18.8	18.9	18.7	18.9	18.8	18.8	18.6	18.6	18.9	19.4	18.9
Information													
1990	12.7	12.7	12.7	12.6	12.7	12.7	12.7	12.7	13.5	12.5	12.6	12.6	12.7
1991	12.3	12.2	12.2	11.8	11.9	12.0	12.1	12.0	11.9	11.7	11.9	11.9	11.9
1992	12.3	12.2	12.2	12.3	12.3	12.4	12.3	12.3	12.4	12.4	12.5	12.6	12.3
1993	12.5	12.6	12.6	12.9	12.9	13.0	13.1	13.1	13.0	13.1	13.1	13.2	12.9
1994	13.1	13.2	13.3	13.6	13.6	13.7	13.8	13.7	13.6	13.6	13.7	13.9	13.5
1995	13.8	13.9	14.0	14.0	14.1	14.2	14.2	14.1	14.1	14.0	14.0	14.3	14.0
1996	14.5	14.7	14.9	15.1	15.5	15.5	15.1	15.2	15.4	15.5	15.5	15.8	15.2
1997	15.6	15.6	15.6	15.7	15.9	16.0	15.9	16.2	16.2	16.1	16.4	16.5	15.9
1998	16.6	17.0	17.0	17.1	17.3	17.4	17.5	17.6	17.5	17.3	17.1	17.2	17.2
1999	17.1	17.5	17.5	18.1	18.5	19.1	18.9	18.9	19.0	18.8	19.0	19.2	18.4
2000	19.0	18.8	19.3	19.5	19.7	20.5	20.6	20.8	20.9	20.3	20.4	20.8	20.1
2001	21.4	21.6	21.8	21.8	22.0	22.1	21.4	21.5	21.2	21.3	21.2	21.4	21.5
2002	20.7	20.5	20.5	20.4	20.5	20.6	20.3	20.1	20.0	19.9	19.8	20.0	20.3
2003	19.7	19.7	19.9	19.4	19.5	19.6	19.4	19.5	19.3	19.0	19.1	19.3	19.5
Financial activities													
1990	45.9	46.0	46.1	45.4	45.4	45.5	45.9	46.1	46.0	46.1	46.0	46.4	45.9
1991	45.1	45.2	45.2	43.0	43.0	42.7	42.8	43.0	42.8	43.8	43.9	44.1	43.7
1992	43.6	44.1	44.2	43.6	43.9	43.7	44.0	44.0	44.0	44.6	44.6	45.2	44.1
1993	43.7	43.9	44.3	44.4	44.6	45.0	45.4	45.6	45.8	46.4	46.7	47.5	45.2
1994	46.6	47.0	47.5	47.7	47.9	48.3	48.4	48.5	48.5	47.8	48.1	48.7	47.9
1995	49.3	49.6	49.4	48.2	47.9	48.5	48.0	48.5	48.9	47.9	48.8	48.9	48.6
1996	49.8	50.4	51.4	51.7	52.2	52.6	52.0	52.9	52.7	52.8	53.2	53.6	52.1
1997	52.7	52.9	53.0	53.8	54.1	54.1	53.9	54.5	54.5	55.0	55.2	56.3	54.1
1998	55.9	56.3	56.7	56.3	56.6	56.8	57.1	56.9	56.5	57.2	57.0	57.5	56.7
1999	56.5	54.8	54.7	54.0	54.1	54.6	54.4	54.6	54.2	54.1	54.2	54.9	54.5
2000	54.4	54.7	55.1	54.8	54.8	55.2	55.0	55.2	55.3	55.0	55.2	55.9	55.1
2001	54.1	54.6	55.0	55.3	55.4	55.7	55.1	55.2	55.1	55.4	55.6	55.6	55.1
2002	55.6	55.8	56.1	56.4	56.6	56.5	56.7	57.0	56.9	57.4	57.8	57.9	56.7
2003	56.9	57.0	57.2	57.5	57.7	57.8	58.1	58.4	58.2	58.4	58.3	58.3	57.8
Professional and business services													
1990	56.1	56.9	58.2	55.3	55.7	56.2	55.3	55.9	56.5	56.3	56.7	56.7	56.3
1991	56.1	55.5	56.4	56.7	56.7	56.9	55.7	55.8	56.5	56.0	56.7	56.9	56.3
1992	56.8	57.8	59.0	58.7	59.3	58.9	57.9	58.2	59.7	62.0	62.2	63.9	59.5
1993	62.7	64.5	65.7	64.7	64.0	64.6	64.1	65.0	65.1	66.3	66.3	67.6	65.0
1994	67.9	68.6	69.7	69.7	70.0	70.0	69.7	70.1	70.1	70.0	70.6	71.9	69.8
1995	70.9	71.1	72.4	73.4	73.8	74.1	73.5	75.0	75.5	76.2	77.5	78.4	74.3
1996	77.9	79.4	80.4	80.1	80.4	80.4	81.5	82.7	83.4	82.9	83.7	83.4	81.3
1997	81.9	83.1	85.1	84.3	85.6	86.6	86.6	87.5	88.2	85.2	85.4	86.4	85.4
1998	87.2	88.5	89.9	89.1	89.2	90.2	89.8	91.7	92.1	94.9	94.9	96.8	91.1
1999	95.8	97.5	98.2	95.4	95.2	94.9	94.7	96.0	96.0	97.8	98.1	100.6	96.6
2000	98.2	98.9	100.9	100.4	102.2	104.1	104.8	106.1	108.7	109.8	111.8	113.5	105.0
2001	114.8	117.1	117.9	116.4	116.1	117.4	116.8	117.4	117.8	117.3	118.4	119.0	117.2
2002	117.7	118.4	120.4	121.7	120.7	122.3	123.7	122.6	123.8	122.6	126.2	127.2	122.3
2003	125.6	127.6	127.9	127.8	127.2	127.6	126.9	126.7	128.0	128.1	130.4	131.3	127.9
Educational and health services													
1990	49.1	49.7	50.0	50.4	50.2	50.8	50.0	50.2	50.8	51.3	51.5	51.9	50.4
1991	51.5	51.9	52.5	53.1	53.1	53.2	51.9	52.5	52.9	53.9	54.4	54.7	52.9
1992	53.6	54.7	55.3	55.0	55.8	56.0	54.7	55.1	55.8	57.0	57.9	58.1	55.7
1993	57.4	57.9	57.8	58.0	58.1	58.7	57.4	57.7	58.4	58.6	58.6	58.7	58.1
1994	58.4	58.7	59.4	60.0	60.5	61.0	59.6	60.3	61.0	60.7	61.8	62.4	60.3
1995	61.9	63.0	64.2	63.8	64.0	64.4	62.4	63.0	63.9	64.9	65.1	65.5	63.8
1996	64.6	65.6	66.4	65.1	65.2	65.2	64.3	65.0	65.0	65.6	66.1	66.1	65.3
1997	65.6	66.3	66.7	67.3	67.5	68.0	67.5	68.3	69.0	69.6	70.3	70.7	68.0
1998	69.5	70.7	70.8	68.0	68.0	68.5	67.1	67.2	67.7	68.4	68.7	69.2	68.6
1999	68.3	69.0	69.9	68.9	69.7	70.3	69.2	69.9	69.8	70.6	71.7	72.4	69.9
2000	70.4	71.2	72.2	71.5	72.3	72.6	71.4	72.1	72.9	72.8	73.4	74.3	72.3
2001	71.5	72.4	73.2	72.9	73.9	74.7	72.8	73.7	75.4	75.1	75.9	77.0	74.0
2002	75.4	76.0	77.3	76.5	77.1	77.3	75.8	76.9	77.5	77.1	77.6	78.2	76.9
2003	77.7	78.5	79.0	78.6	78.9	79.7	78.1	79.2	79.9	80.9	81.3	81.8	79.5

Employment by Industry: Florida—*Continued*

(Numbers in thousands. Not seasonally adjusted.)

Industry	January	February	March	April	May	June	July	August	September	October	November	December	Annual Average
FORT LAUDERDALE-HOLLYWOOD-POMPANO BEACH—*Continued*													
Leisure and hospitality													
1990	63.3	64.9	65.7	63.5	61.3	60.1	57.4	57.8	56.9	57.5	59.4	61.1	60.7
1991	60.7	62.9	64.2	62.0	60.2	59.0	55.9	55.9	55.9	55.9	57.7	59.2	59.1
1992	59.3	59.8	61.0	58.8	57.9	56.9	57.4	57.3	58.0	60.2	61.3	62.4	59.1
1993	61.6	64.3	66.2	63.8	62.5	61.2	60.1	59.8	59.8	60.8	62.8	64.9	62.3
1994	65.4	67.1	68.5	65.5	64.9	63.5	61.3	61.9	61.3	61.7	63.8	66.0	64.2
1995	66.2	67.5	69.4	66.8	65.6	64.5	62.3	62.5	62.4	61.3	63.5	65.1	64.7
1996	65.2	66.5	67.8	66.5	65.6	64.9	63.1	63.6	64.1	63.6	65.5	67.2	65.3
1997	67.7	70.2	70.9	67.4	67.6	66.3	63.8	64.1	64.6	64.9	66.9	68.6	66.9
1998	67.2	68.6	69.6	67.3	66.6	65.7	63.6	63.7	63.7	64.4	66.3	68.4	66.2
1999	67.4	69.7	71.6	69.0	69.0	68.2	65.1	64.6	64.5	64.1	66.1	68.2	67.2
2000	68.2	70.0	71.6	69.5	69.6	69.0	67.5	67.6	68.1	68.7	70.5	72.2	69.4
2001	70.5	72.8	73.9	72.4	73.3	72.6	70.0	70.6	70.5	70.1	71.1	72.6	71.7
2002	71.6	73.3	74.2	74.1	73.4	72.3	70.3	70.7	70.8	71.5	72.6	74.1	72.4
2003	73.7	74.8	76.3	74.8	74.4	73.9	71.6	71.5	72.1	72.9	74.0	75.5	73.8
Other services													
1990	23.6	23.9	24.2	24.2	24.0	23.9	23.6	23.5	23.6	23.7	23.6	23.7	23.7
1991	23.5	23.8	24.0	23.8	23.9	23.8	23.1	23.2	23.3	23.3	23.5	23.6	23.5
1992	23.4	23.7	23.9	23.8	23.9	24.1	23.5	23.5	23.8	24.1	24.5	24.7	23.9
1993	24.2	24.5	24.9	25.0	25.0	25.1	24.9	24.8	25.2	25.3	25.2	25.3	24.9
1994	25.0	25.2	25.4	25.4	25.4	25.6	25.1	25.1	25.4	25.4	25.5	25.8	25.3
1995	26.0	26.2	26.5	26.1	26.3	26.3	25.9	25.9	26.6	26.6	26.8	27.0	26.3
1996	27.1	28.0	28.3	28.4	28.4	28.3	27.5	27.5	27.7	28.3	28.7	29.3	28.1
1997	28.8	29.1	28.9	29.5	29.7	29.9	28.8	30.1	29.5	30.3	29.0	28.7	29.3
1998	28.7	28.9	29.9	29.5	29.6	29.7	29.6	29.7	30.0	30.0	30.1	30.3	29.6
1999	30.0	30.5	30.7	29.7	29.9	29.9	29.4	29.5	29.6	30.0	30.1	30.2	29.9
2000	30.1	30.4	30.7	30.5	30.7	31.2	30.5	30.8	31.0	30.9	31.1	31.1	30.8
2001	30.4	30.4	30.4	29.8	29.5	29.3	28.6	28.3	28.3	27.7	27.8	27.9	29.0
2002	28.0	28.6	29.1	28.7	28.8	28.7	28.8	29.0	29.3	29.3	29.7	30.1	29.0
2003	29.5	29.9	30.2	29.6	29.8	30.3	29.9	30.0	29.7	30.1	30.5	30.8	30.0
Government													
1990	66.5	67.9	71.8	69.1	71.3	70.8	65.3	64.2	68.7	72.7	70.8	71.5	69.2
1991	71.2	72.4	72.9	72.9	73.5	73.1	67.3	66.8	71.3	72.7	73.1	73.5	71.7
1992	72.5	73.4	77.3	74.4	74.8	74.5	68.8	67.4	73.9	74.0	74.0	74.5	73.2
1993	73.7	75.3	76.3	76.1	76.1	76.4	70.4	69.3	76.3	76.5	76.9	77.5	75.0
1994	77.2	78.9	79.8	79.5	79.8	80.1	74.3	73.4	80.6	79.8	84.7	81.2	79.1
1995	78.9	80.9	81.9	81.1	81.4	81.3	75.4	73.8	81.4	81.2	81.4	82.1	80.0
1996	82.0	82.4	85.9	82.6	83.0	83.1	76.9	75.6	83.4	82.6	83.3	84.0	82.0
1997	83.6	84.0	84.2	84.5	84.8	85.1	78.7	77.5	85.4	85.2	85.8	86.2	83.7
1998	85.9	86.0	86.6	85.1	85.4	85.0	79.1	77.4	85.0	84.5	84.9	84.7	84.1
1999	84.7	85.4	85.3	85.3	85.6	85.4	80.2	79.0	86.5	86.6	87.2	88.1	84.9
2000	87.3	87.8	88.8	92.3	94.3	92.5	86.5	84.5	93.0	92.6	92.9	93.9	90.5
2001	92.3	92.8	93.7	94.0	94.6	94.7	88.4	87.0	95.8	94.8	95.1	95.9	93.2
2002	95.5	95.6	97.7	95.9	96.6	96.4	90.1	88.4	97.7	97.4	97.5	99.2	95.7
2003	98.8	99.5	100.5	99.0	99.6	99.6	92.9	91.1	100.4	99.8	100.4	100.7	98.5
Federal government													
1990	5.9	5.9	6.1	6.5	7.9	7.1	7.1	6.2	5.9	5.9	5.8	5.9	6.3
1991	5.9	5.9	5.9	6.1	6.1	6.1	6.2	6.2	6.3	6.3	6.3	6.4	6.1
1992	6.3	6.3	6.3	6.3	6.3	6.2	6.2	6.2	6.2	6.2	6.2	6.3	6.2
1993	6.2	6.1	6.2	6.3	6.3	6.3	6.4	6.4	6.4	6.5	6.6	6.8	6.3
1994	6.7	6.6	6.6	6.6	6.6	6.6	6.6	6.7	6.7	6.7	6.8	7.0	6.6
1995	6.8	6.8	6.8	6.8	6.8	6.8	6.8	6.8	6.8	6.8	6.8	7.0	6.8
1996	6.8	6.8	6.9	6.9	6.9	6.9	6.8	6.9	6.9	6.9	6.9	7.1	6.8
1997	7.0	7.0	7.0	7.0	7.0	7.0	7.0	7.1	7.1	7.1	7.2	7.3	7.0
1998	7.0	7.0	7.0	7.1	7.1	7.0	7.0	7.0	7.0	7.1	7.1	7.2	7.0
1999	7.2	7.5	7.2	7.2	7.1	7.2	7.2	7.3	7.3	7.4	7.4	7.6	7.3
2000	7.4	7.4	7.5	8.3	10.0	8.0	8.0	7.4	7.3	7.3	7.3	7.4	7.8
2001	7.3	7.3	7.3	7.2	7.2	7.2	7.3	7.3	7.3	7.3	7.3	7.4	7.2
2002	7.3	7.2	7.3	7.2	7.2	7.2	7.3	7.2	7.4	7.8	7.7	7.9	7.4
2003	7.9	7.9	7.9	7.9	7.8	7.8	7.7	7.7	7.6	7.6	7.6	7.6	7.8
State government													
1990	6.6	6.7	6.7	6.8	7.0	7.1	7.1	7.1	7.3	7.3	7.4	7.4	7.0
1991	7.3	7.3	7.3	7.3	7.5	7.3	7.3	7.3	7.3	7.3	7.4	7.3	7.3
1992	7.3	7.3	7.3	7.3	7.5	7.3	7.3	7.2	7.2	7.4	7.3	7.3	7.3
1993	7.3	7.4	7.4	7.5	7.5	7.6	7.6	7.5	7.5	7.6	7.6	7.6	7.5
1994	7.6	7.7	7.7	7.8	7.8	7.8	8.0	7.9	8.0	7.9	7.7	7.6	7.7
1995	7.6	7.6	7.8	7.8	7.8	7.8	7.8	7.8	7.9	7.9	7.8	7.9	7.7
1996	7.9	7.8	8.0	7.9	8.0	7.8	7.9	8.0	7.9	7.9	7.9	7.9	7.9
1997	8.1	8.0	8.0	8.1	8.1	8.0	8.1	8.1	8.0	8.1	8.2	8.2	8.0
1998	8.3	8.1	8.2	8.1	8.1	8.0	8.1	7.9	7.9	7.9	7.9	7.2	7.9
1999	7.1	7.2	7.2	7.3	7.3	7.2	7.4	7.3	7.3	7.4	7.4	7.5	7.3
2000	7.4	7.4	7.5	7.5	7.6	7.7	7.7	7.6	7.7	7.8	7.7	7.8	7.6
2001	7.6	7.7	7.7	7.7	7.7	7.7	7.6	7.5	7.5	7.6	7.7	7.6	7.6
2002	7.4	7.4	7.5	7.4	7.6	7.3	7.3	7.1	7.1	7.2	7.3	7.3	7.3
2003	7.1	7.2	7.3	7.2	7.3	7.1	7.1	6.8	6.8	7.0	6.8	6.8	7.0

Employment by Industry: Florida—*Continued*

(Numbers in thousands. Not seasonally adjusted.)

Industry	January	February	March	April	May	June	July	August	September	October	November	December	Annual Average
FORT LAUDERDALE-HOLLYWOOD-POMPANO BEACH—*Continued*													
Local government													
1990	54.0	55.3	59.0	55.8	56.4	56.6	51.1	50.9	55.5	59.5	57.6	58.2	55.8
1991	58.0	59.2	59.7	59.5	59.9	59.7	53.8	53.3	57.7	59.1	59.4	59.8	58.2
1992	58.9	59.8	63.7	60.8	61.0	61.0	55.3	54.0	60.5	60.4	60.5	60.9	59.7
1993	60.2	61.8	62.7	62.3	62.3	62.5	56.4	55.4	62.4	62.4	62.7	63.1	61.1
1994	62.9	64.6	65.5	65.1	65.4	65.7	59.7	58.8	65.9	65.2	70.2	66.6	64.6
1995	64.5	66.5	67.3	66.5	66.8	66.7	60.8	59.2	66.7	66.5	66.8	67.2	65.4
1996	67.3	67.8	71.0	67.8	68.1	68.4	62.2	60.7	68.6	67.8	68.5	69.0	67.2
1997	68.5	69.0	69.2	69.4	69.7	70.1	63.6	62.3	70.3	70.0	70.4	70.7	68.6
1998	70.6	70.9	71.4	69.9	70.2	70.0	64.0	62.5	70.1	69.5	69.9	70.3	69.1
1999	70.4	70.7	70.9	70.8	71.2	71.0	65.6	64.4	71.9	71.8	72.4	73.0	70.3
2000	72.5	73.0	73.8	76.5	76.7	76.8	70.8	69.5	78.0	77.5	77.9	78.7	75.1
2001	77.4	77.8	78.7	79.1	79.7	79.8	73.5	72.2	81.0	79.9	80.1	80.9	78.3
2002	80.8	81.0	82.9	81.3	81.8	81.9	75.5	74.1	83.2	82.4	82.5	84.0	81.0
2003	83.8	84.4	85.3	83.9	84.5	84.7	78.1	76.6	86.0	85.2	86.0	86.3	83.7
JACKSONVILLE													
Total nonfarm													
1990	415.9	418.0	422.0	424.5	428.3	427.5	423.3	422.7	425.2	425.6	426.1	426.8	423.8
1991	415.4	415.7	419.2	419.3	422.9	422.6	417.2	420.2	421.0	419.4	421.3	422.6	419.7
1992	415.0	416.0	422.0	420.2	422.9	423.8	422.2	421.2	424.5	429.3	430.3	433.5	423.4
1993	424.6	428.9	433.3	438.5	440.9	439.6	436.1	435.3	442.6	445.0	447.1	451.6	438.6
1994	444.5	447.6	451.6	453.6	457.9	460.1	457.0	458.7	467.4	466.9	472.4	475.3	459.4
1995	466.0	472.4	476.8	478.4	482.7	483.7	479.5	480.2	486.4	489.3	493.8	497.3	482.2
1996	484.6	489.1	494.0	491.7	494.8	493.0	487.9	490.7	497.8	498.2	502.8	508.4	494.4
1997	496.0	500.0	503.9	505.6	510.9	509.3	506.0	507.0	514.7	514.3	516.8	522.5	508.9
1998	516.2	522.0	526.7	520.8	524.4	524.7	518.8	518.8	526.1	530.1	536.3	541.5	525.5
1999	524.1	530.3	533.7	535.4	536.7	538.4	532.1	533.1	539.8	546.7	551.7	558.6	538.3
2000	547.5	550.4	555.1	558.1	562.3	560.0	555.6	563.0	563.0	565.6	566.7	570.5	559.8
2001	550.0	556.3	562.6	564.2	565.0	561.9	556.7	567.4	565.7	561.7	562.6	563.9	561.5
2002	551.6	553.3	558.6	558.8	560.5	554.5	547.2	555.0	552.5	553.8	557.0	559.2	555.2
2003	550.8	553.1	557.8	557.2	559.7	556.1	554.5	562.0	562.0	563.7	568.2	571.0	559.7
Total private													
1990	353.1	354.9	357.9	359.7	361.9	364.6	361.7	362.1	361.6	360.4	360.4	361.4	359.9
1991	350.9	351.2	354.4	354.8	358.4	359.4	357.2	359.9	358.7	356.3	357.9	358.8	356.4
1992	352.5	353.2	357.0	357.8	360.3	362.5	363.6	363.7	363.3	366.7	368.1	370.6	361.6
1993	362.6	366.5	370.7	375.4	377.5	379.5	377.8	378.2	380.3	381.2	383.1	387.1	376.6
1994	380.4	383.5	387.5	389.2	393.0	397.7	397.5	400.3	403.5	401.7	404.5	409.4	395.6
1995	400.9	406.7	410.9	411.4	415.4	419.2	418.7	420.6	421.4	422.0	426.3	429.2	416.8
1996	417.5	421.0	424.8	424.6	427.8	429.0	427.8	431.1	432.1	431.7	435.4	439.9	428.5
1997	429.4	432.4	436.5	438.0	442.8	444.0	445.4	447.0	448.7	448.7	451.0	455.9	443.3
1998	449.6	453.8	458.8	453.8	456.4	459.4	458.5	458.9	460.1	462.8	468.5	473.5	459.5
1999	458.4	463.4	466.6	467.7	468.9	473.6	472.0	473.8	474.6	479.3	483.3	490.3	472.6
2000	481.4	483.4	487.9	490.6	493.0	497.0	493.8	495.9	496.1	497.9	499.0	502.5	493.2
2001	483.4	488.3	494.4	495.5	496.1	498.1	494.1	498.5	497.0	493.1	493.6	494.4	493.8
2002	484.0	485.0	490.3	490.0	491.4	490.5	484.8	486.2	483.9	484.7	487.3	489.1	487.3
2003	481.5	483.7	488.4	487.5	489.2	489.8	489.9	491.3	491.4	492.1	496.4	498.4	490.0
Goods-producing													
1990	63.3	63.9	64.2	63.7	63.4	64.3	63.5	62.8	62.4	60.9	59.7	59.3	62.6
1991	57.9	57.5	58.3	58.3	59.5	59.6	58.4	59.1	58.4	58.7	58.0	57.4	58.4
1992	55.5	55.4	56.2	56.4	57.0	57.8	58.3	58.2	58.0	57.8	58.2	58.2	57.2
1993	56.9	57.2	57.8	58.1	58.3	58.0	57.7	57.8	58.2	58.1	58.0	58.0	57.8
1994	56.3	57.0	57.9	58.6	59.0	60.0	60.2	60.5	60.9	61.1	61.3	62.0	59.5
1995	61.2	62.0	62.9	62.8	63.4	64.2	64.3	64.5	64.5	63.9	64.4	64.7	63.5
1996	63.2	64.3	64.8	64.6	65.1	65.2	64.1	64.7	64.8	64.8	65.0	65.3	64.6
1997	64.9	65.2	66.0	66.8	67.8	67.9	68.9	69.5	69.2	68.7	69.1	69.3	67.7
1998	68.1	68.8	69.8	68.0	68.4	69.0	68.9	68.7	69.3	69.5	70.3	70.5	69.1
1999	67.6	69.0	69.0	69.2	69.4	69.8	69.7	69.7	69.7	69.4	69.5	70.5	69.3
2000	69.9	70.5	71.3	71.2	71.5	72.5	72.5	72.3	72.4	71.9	71.1	71.6	71.6
2001	68.0	68.7	68.9	68.9	68.6	69.3	69.4	69.0	68.4	68.4	68.3	68.1	68.6
2002	67.3	67.3	67.9	67.2	68.0	68.5	67.9	68.0	67.9	68.6	69.3	69.4	68.1
2003	68.7	69.3	70.0	68.8	69.2	69.9	70.2	69.4	69.4	69.6	69.0	69.3	69.4
Natural resources and mining													
1990	0.9	0.9	0.9	0.9	0.9	0.9	0.9	0.9	0.8	0.8	0.8	0.8	0.9
1991	0.8	0.8	0.8	0.5	0.5	0.5	0.5	0.5	0.5	0.5	0.5	0.5	0.6
1992	0.5	0.5	0.5	0.6	0.6	0.6	0.6	0.6	0.6	0.6	0.6	0.5	0.6
1993	0.5	0.5	0.5	0.5	0.5	0.5	0.5	0.5	0.5	0.5	0.5	0.5	0.5
1994	0.4	0.4	0.4	0.5	0.5	0.5	0.5	0.5	0.5	0.5	0.5	0.5	0.5
1995	0.5	0.5	0.5	0.5	0.5	0.5	0.5	0.5	0.5	0.5	0.5	0.5	0.5
1996	0.5	0.5	0.5	0.5	0.5	0.5	0.5	0.5	0.5	0.5	0.5	0.5	0.5
1997	0.5	0.5	0.5	0.5	0.5	0.5	0.5	0.5	0.5	0.5	0.5	0.5	0.5
1998	0.5	0.5	0.5	0.4	0.5	0.5	0.4	0.4	0.4	0.4	0.4	0.4	0.4
1999	0.4	0.4	0.4	0.4	0.4	0.4	0.5	0.5	0.5	0.5	0.5	0.5	0.5
2000	0.5	0.5	0.5	0.5	0.5	0.5	0.5	0.5	0.5	0.5	0.6	0.6	0.5
2001	0.5	0.5	0.5	0.4	0.5	0.5	0.5	0.5	0.5	0.5	0.6	0.6	0.5
2002	0.5	0.5	0.5	0.4	0.5	0.5	0.5	0.5	0.5	0.5	0.5	0.5	0.5
2003	0.5	0.5	0.5	0.5	0.5	0.5	0.5	0.5	0.5	0.5	0.5	0.5	0.5

Employment by Industry: Florida—*Continued*

(Numbers in thousands. Not seasonally adjusted.)

Industry	January	February	March	April	May	June	July	August	September	October	November	December	Annual Average
JACKSONVILLE—*Continued*													
Construction													
1990	26.4	27.0	27.4	27.0	26.7	27.1	26.5	26.3	26.1	25.4	24.0	23.8	26.1
1991	22.9	22.8	23.7	23.8	24.7	24.9	24.6	25.0	24.2	24.1	23.6	23.1	24.0
1992	22.2	22.4	22.8	22.7	23.1	23.7	24.2	24.1	23.5	23.6	23.7	23.5	23.3
1993	22.7	23.2	23.4	23.4	23.6	23.6	23.3	23.6	23.8	23.7	23.6	23.8	23.5
1994	22.6	23.0	23.7	24.5	24.6	25.0	24.9	25.1	25.4	25.5	25.7	26.1	24.7
1995	25.7	26.4	26.9	26.6	26.9	27.4	27.2	27.5	27.3	26.9	27.2	27.4	27.0
1996	27.2	27.9	28.3	28.4	28.7	28.8	27.7	28.2	28.0	28.3	28.5	28.7	28.2
1997	28.4	28.6	29.1	29.3	30.0	30.2	30.4	30.7	30.5	29.9	29.9	30.2	29.8
1998	29.3	29.8	30.4	29.7	29.8	30.1	30.1	30.1	30.2	30.5	30.8	31.1	30.2
1999	29.3	30.1	30.5	30.5	30.8	31.0	30.8	30.8	31.2	30.6	30.8	31.4	30.7
2000	30.6	30.9	31.6	31.4	31.6	32.2	32.3	32.3	32.6	32.4	32.1	32.4	31.9
2001	31.2	31.7	31.7	31.7	31.6	32.3	32.6	32.7	32.6	32.9	32.8	32.7	32.2
2002	32.1	32.0	32.7	32.6	33.4	33.8	33.3	33.5	33.6	34.2	34.8	35.0	33.4
2003	34.6	35.0	35.8	35.5	35.7	36.2	36.6	36.4	36.1	36.4	36.1	36.5	35.9
Manufacturing													
1990	36.0	36.0	35.9	35.8	35.8	36.3	36.1	35.6	35.5	34.7	34.9	34.7	35.6
1991	34.2	33.9	33.8	34.0	34.3	34.2	33.3	33.6	33.7	34.1	33.9	33.8	33.9
1992	32.8	32.5	32.9	33.1	33.3	33.5	33.5	33.5	33.9	33.6	33.9	34.2	33.3
1993	33.7	33.5	33.9	34.2	34.2	33.9	33.9	33.7	33.9	33.9	33.9	33.7	33.8
1994	33.3	33.6	33.8	33.6	33.9	34.5	34.8	34.9	35.0	35.1	35.1	35.4	34.4
1995	35.0	35.1	35.5	35.7	36.0	36.3	36.6	36.5	36.7	36.5	36.7	36.8	36.1
1996	35.5	35.9	36.0	35.7	35.9	35.9	35.9	36.0	36.3	36.0	36.0	36.1	35.9
1997	36.0	36.1	36.4	37.0	37.3	37.2	38.0	38.3	38.2	38.3	38.7	38.6	37.5
1998	38.3	38.5	38.9	37.9	38.1	38.4	38.4	38.2	38.7	38.6	39.1	39.0	38.5
1999	37.9	38.5	38.1	38.3	38.2	38.4	38.4	38.4	38.0	38.3	38.2	38.6	38.2
2000	38.8	39.1	39.2	39.3	39.4	39.8	39.7	39.5	39.3	39.0	38.4	38.6	39.2
2001	36.3	36.5	36.7	36.8	36.5	36.5	36.3	35.8	35.3	35.0	34.9	34.8	35.9
2002	34.7	34.8	34.7	34.2	34.1	34.2	34.1	34.0	33.8	33.9	34.0	33.9	34.2
2003	33.6	33.8	33.7	32.8	33.0	33.2	33.1	32.5	32.8	32.7	32.4	32.3	33.0
Service-providing													
1990	352.6	354.1	357.8	360.8	364.9	363.2	359.8	359.9	362.8	364.7	366.4	367.5	361.2
1991	357.5	358.2	360.9	361.0	363.4	363.0	358.8	361.1	362.6	360.7	363.3	365.2	361.3
1992	359.5	360.6	365.8	363.8	365.9	366.0	363.9	363.0	366.5	371.5	372.1	375.3	366.1
1993	367.7	371.7	375.5	380.4	382.6	381.6	378.4	377.5	384.4	386.9	389.1	393.6	380.7
1994	388.2	390.6	393.7	395.0	398.9	400.1	396.8	398.2	406.5	405.8	411.1	413.3	399.8
1995	404.8	410.4	413.9	415.6	419.3	419.5	415.2	415.7	421.9	425.4	429.4	432.6	418.6
1996	421.4	424.8	429.2	427.1	429.7	427.8	423.8	426.0	433.0	433.4	437.8	443.1	429.7
1997	431.1	434.8	437.9	438.8	443.1	441.4	437.1	437.5	445.5	445.6	447.7	453.2	441.1
1998	448.1	453.2	456.9	452.8	456.0	455.7	449.9	450.1	456.8	460.6	466.0	471.0	456.4
1999	456.5	461.3	464.7	466.2	467.3	468.6	462.4	463.4	470.1	477.3	482.2	488.1	469.0
2000	477.6	479.9	483.8	486.9	490.8	487.5	483.1	490.7	490.6	493.7	495.6	498.9	488.3
2001	482.0	487.6	493.7	495.3	496.4	492.6	487.3	498.4	497.3	493.3	494.3	495.8	492.8
2002	484.3	486.0	490.7	491.6	492.5	486.0	479.3	487.0	484.6	485.2	487.7	489.8	487.1
2003	482.1	483.8	487.8	488.4	490.5	486.2	484.3	492.6	492.6	494.1	499.2	501.7	490.3
Trade, transportation, and utilities													
1990	103.3	102.1	102.5	104.1	104.7	106.2	105.1	106.2	106.6	106.9	108.3	110.3	105.5
1991	104.7	103.9	104.5	104.6	105.4	106.0	104.2	104.7	105.4	105.7	107.5	108.5	105.4
1992	105.9	105.5	105.8	105.5	105.7	106.0	107.1	107.7	107.9	108.4	110.0	111.6	107.2
1993	106.1	106.7	107.5	107.7	108.0	108.8	108.2	108.5	108.7	110.2	111.7	114.8	108.9
1994	108.1	107.9	108.7	107.1	108.2	108.8	108.7	110.1	111.3	112.1	114.6	116.9	110.2
1995	112.0	112.9	113.0	112.4	113.5	113.7	113.1	113.5	114.6	116.0	118.1	120.8	114.4
1996	113.6	114.3	114.8	114.5	114.5	115.0	115.0	115.5	115.5	115.8	118.2	120.7	115.6
1997	115.3	115.8	116.4	117.1	117.7	117.7	117.4	116.3	118.2	119.1	119.1	124.4	117.8
1998	118.2	119.1	119.5	118.6	119.8	120.3	120.2	120.6	121.1	122.5	125.3	127.8	121.0
1999	120.4	121.7	122.6	121.2	121.3	122.0	121.9	122.3	123.3	125.3	128.0	131.0	123.4
2000	127.4	127.6	129.2	128.7	129.1	130.6	126.8	128.1	128.2	128.2	130.1	130.8	128.7
2001	125.0	124.0	125.2	124.5	124.5	124.5	123.5	124.7	124.5	123.7	125.2	127.1	124.7
2002	121.8	121.3	122.6	122.6	122.8	122.6	121.7	122.6	122.6	123.0	125.0	127.4	123.0
2003	123.1	122.3	123.0	122.8	123.2	122.5	122.8	123.5	124.4	125.9	127.6	129.8	124.2
Wholesale trade													
1990	21.7	21.8	22.0	21.8	21.7	22.0	22.4	22.3	22.2	21.9	21.8	21.7	21.9
1991	21.0	20.9	21.1	21.1	21.0	21.1	20.9	21.1	21.0	21.1	21.3	21.2	21.0
1992	21.1	21.1	21.2	21.2	21.2	21.2	21.2	21.3	21.3	21.4	21.4	21.5	21.2
1993	20.7	20.9	21.0	21.0	21.1	21.1	21.3	21.4	21.3	21.3	21.4	21.6	21.1
1994	21.3	21.4	21.4	21.2	21.3	21.5	21.1	21.3	21.5	21.5	21.7	21.9	21.4
1995	21.3	21.7	21.9	21.4	21.6	21.9	21.5	21.7	21.7	21.9	22.0	22.1	21.7
1996	21.6	22.0	22.0	22.1	22.2	22.2	22.2	22.3	22.2	22.3	22.3	22.6	22.1
1997	22.3	22.9	23.0	23.4	23.6	23.6	23.3	23.4	23.4	23.2	23.4	23.4	23.2
1998	23.6	24.1	24.4	23.7	23.9	24.2	24.3	24.2	24.2	24.4	24.6	24.8	24.2
1999	24.1	24.6	24.6	24.0	23.9	24.4	24.4	24.3	24.4	24.9	25.0	25.2	24.4
2000	26.0	26.2	26.6	26.1	26.2	26.2	26.3	26.2	26.0	26.2	26.4	26.5	26.2
2001	26.0	26.1	26.3	26.1	26.1	26.3	26.4	26.5	26.5	26.1	26.0	25.9	26.1
2002	25.0	25.2	25.3	25.5	25.6	25.9	25.8	26.0	26.1	26.3	26.5	26.8	25.8
2003	26.9	26.9	26.9	26.7	26.7	26.7	26.9	27.0	27.1	27.8	28.1	28.1	27.2

Employment by Industry: Florida—*Continued*

(Numbers in thousands. Not seasonally adjusted.)

Industry	January	February	March	April	May	June	July	August	September	October	November	December	Annual Average
JACKSONVILLE—*Continued*													
Retail trade													
1990	57.4	56.7	56.7	57.7	58.6	59.0	58.4	59.1	59.1	59.3	60.9	62.6	58.7
1991	59.0	58.4	58.4	58.0	58.4	58.6	57.3	57.7	58.2	58.7	60.2	61.3	58.6
1992	58.9	58.0	58.0	57.9	57.9	58.2	59.1	59.5	59.6	59.8	61.5	62.8	59.2
1993	59.6	59.4	60.0	60.1	60.3	60.7	60.6	60.8	61.1	61.5	62.9	65.0	61.0
1994	59.3	59.1	59.5	58.7	59.1	59.7	59.8	60.6	61.5	61.9	64.0	65.5	60.7
1995	62.2	62.2	62.0	62.1	62.7	63.0	62.9	63.3	63.7	64.5	66.6	68.6	63.6
1996	63.6	63.2	63.7	63.6	63.7	63.5	64.0	64.4	64.1	63.9	66.0	67.8	64.2
1997	63.6	63.4	64.1	63.0	63.4	63.5	64.0	64.3	64.2	65.1	64.4	68.8	64.3
1998	64.3	64.1	65.4	64.0	64.4	64.7	64.7	65.0	65.4	66.3	68.5	70.5	65.6
1999	65.1	65.5	66.3	65.4	66.0	66.2	66.1	66.3	66.6	67.6	70.3	72.5	66.9
2000	68.5	68.6	69.8	69.5	69.8	70.6	68.0	69.1	69.1	69.4	71.2	72.5	69.7
2001	67.3	66.5	67.2	66.5	66.8	66.7	66.1	66.5	66.3	66.2	67.9	69.0	66.9
2002	66.3	65.8	66.7	66.8	67.3	67.5	66.9	67.3	67.2	67.4	69.0	70.5	67.4
2003	67.8	67.1	67.4	67.0	67.4	67.6	67.9	68.2	68.4	69.3	70.9	72.5	68.5
Transportation and utilities													
1990	24.2	23.6	23.8	24.6	24.4	25.2	24.3	24.8	25.3	25.7	25.6	26.0	24.7
1991	24.7	24.6	25.0	25.5	26.0	26.3	26.0	25.9	26.2	25.9	26.0	26.0	25.6
1992	25.9	26.4	26.6	26.4	26.6	26.6	26.8	26.9	27.0	27.2	27.1	27.3	26.7
1993	25.8	26.4	26.5	26.6	26.6	27.0	26.3	26.3	26.3	27.4	27.4	28.2	26.7
1994	27.5	27.4	27.8	27.2	27.8	27.6	27.8	28.2	28.3	28.7	28.9	29.5	28.0
1995	28.5	29.0	29.1	28.9	29.2	28.8	28.7	28.5	29.2	29.6	29.5	30.1	29.0
1996	28.4	29.1	29.1	28.8	28.6	29.3	28.8	28.8	29.2	29.6	29.9	30.3	29.1
1997	29.4	29.5	29.3	30.7	30.7	30.6	30.1	28.6	30.6	30.8	31.3	32.2	30.3
1998	30.3	30.9	29.7	30.9	31.5	31.4	31.2	31.4	31.5	31.8	32.2	32.5	31.2
1999	31.2	31.6	31.7	31.8	31.4	31.4	31.4	31.7	32.3	32.8	32.7	33.3	31.9
2000	32.9	32.8	32.8	33.1	33.1	33.8	32.5	32.8	33.1	32.6	32.5	31.8	32.8
2001	31.7	31.4	31.7	31.9	31.6	31.5	31.0	31.7	31.7	31.4	31.3	32.2	31.5
2002	30.5	30.3	30.6	30.3	29.9	29.2	29.0	29.3	29.3	29.3	29.5	30.1	29.8
2003	28.4	28.3	28.7	29.1	29.1	28.2	28.0	28.3	28.9	28.8	28.6	29.2	28.6
Information													
1990	10.2	10.4	10.4	10.8	10.7	10.6	10.7	10.8	10.8	10.6	10.7	10.7	10.6
1991	10.2	10.2	10.3	10.4	10.3	10.4	10.2	10.3	10.3	10.2	10.2	10.2	10.2
1992	9.5	9.5	9.7	9.8	9.9	10.0	9.9	9.9	10.1	10.0	10.0	10.2	9.8
1993	9.4	9.6	9.6	9.7	9.7	9.9	9.8	9.9	10.1	10.2	10.2	10.3	9.8
1994	10.5	10.6	10.6	10.7	10.8	10.9	11.0	11.2	11.1	11.0	11.1	11.0	10.8
1995	10.8	11.0	11.0	10.7	10.9	11.2	11.0	11.2	10.9	11.2	11.6	12.0	11.1
1996	11.6	11.7	12.0	12.5	12.6	12.7	12.4	12.3	12.1	12.1	12.1	11.9	12.1
1997	11.6	11.7	11.7	12.2	12.3	12.3	12.2	13.0	13.0	13.0	12.8	12.7	12.3
1998	12.9	13.2	13.4	13.0	13.2	13.4	13.4	13.3	13.0	13.1	13.6	13.8	13.2
1999	13.1	13.4	13.3	14.0	14.3	14.5	14.2	14.3	14.3	15.0	15.2	15.4	14.2
2000	15.2	15.2	15.2	14.9	15.1	15.1	15.2	15.1	15.2	14.9	15.2	15.5	15.2
2001	14.9	14.9	14.9	14.8	14.6	14.5	14.4	14.1	14.0	13.6	13.5	13.4	14.2
2002	13.7	13.5	13.6	13.5	13.3	13.1	13.1	12.9	12.8	12.8	12.7	12.7	13.1
2003	12.5	12.6	12.6	12.5	12.5	12.4	12.5	12.3	12.5	12.5	12.8	12.8	12.5
Financial activities													
1990	39.6	39.5	39.8	39.7	40.0	40.5	40.8	41.1	41.3	41.1	41.4	41.4	40.5
1991	40.9	40.9	41.2	40.6	40.9	41.1	40.7	40.9	41.0	40.7	40.9	41.2	40.9
1992	41.6	41.7	41.8	41.8	42.3	42.6	42.3	42.3	42.3	43.2	43.3	43.6	42.4
1993	42.5	42.9	43.2	44.9	44.9	45.3	45.4	45.6	45.6	45.8	45.8	46.0	44.8
1994	46.8	46.8	47.0	46.8	47.1	47.3	47.6	47.9	47.8	47.7	48.1	48.5	47.4
1995	48.7	49.1	49.4	48.8	49.2	49.1	48.5	48.6	48.4	48.9	49.5	49.3	48.9
1996	48.3	48.7	48.9	48.8	49.0	48.9	48.1	48.5	48.4	48.6	48.4	48.8	48.6
1997	48.5	48.6	49.0	49.0	49.6	49.7	50.5	50.4	50.6	51.3	51.5	51.5	50.0
1998	51.6	51.9	52.4	52.7	52.4	52.2	53.6	53.6	53.7	54.9	54.7	55.7	53.2
1999	54.2	54.4	54.6	54.8	54.8	55.4	55.8	55.9	55.7	55.7	55.7	56.3	55.2
2000	55.6	55.6	55.7	56.3	56.6	57.0	56.9	56.5	56.2	56.3	56.4	56.8	56.3
2001	56.1	56.4	56.8	57.0	57.2	57.7	58.1	58.2	58.3	58.5	58.7	58.9	57.6
2002	58.4	57.8	57.7	57.7	57.6	57.5	57.4	57.3	57.0	57.1	57.2	57.2	57.5
2003	56.9	56.6	56.8	56.8	56.9	57.1	57.4	57.6	57.5	57.5	58.2	58.1	57.3
Professional and business services													
1990	36.5	37.1	37.5	38.3	40.2	41.1	40.3	39.8	39.5	40.3	39.5	39.5	39.1
1991	37.4	38.0	38.3	38.2	38.2	38.2	39.8	40.6	40.2	38.0	37.6	37.6	38.5
1992	37.6	38.5	39.7	37.5	37.7	38.2	38.8	38.7	38.8	40.4	39.9	40.1	38.8
1993	43.9	44.4	45.5	47.2	47.8	48.3	48.1	48.3	50.0	49.6	49.9	50.2	47.7
1994	50.2	50.9	51.9	52.3	53.7	55.7	55.4	55.9	57.2	56.0	56.1	56.9	54.3
1995	55.8	57.3	58.2	60.2	60.8	62.6	63.1	64.0	64.4	63.9	63.8	63.8	61.4
1996	64.7	65.0	66.0	66.3	67.1	67.5	70.1	71.4	72.3	71.6	71.8	72.2	68.8
1997	70.7	70.8	71.6	71.1	71.9	73.3	73.7	73.8	73.5	72.0	73.0	72.9	72.3
1998	75.7	76.4	76.9	76.2	75.9	76.6	75.6	76.4	76.5	75.7	76.1	77.2	76.2
1999	78.0	78.7	79.4	79.2	78.6	80.3	80.0	80.7	81.2	83.3	83.8	84.9	80.6
2000	83.1	83.4	84.3	86.2	86.2	87.0	90.3	91.2	91.5	94.8	94.0	94.7	88.9
2001	90.8	93.8	95.9	96.3	96.1	95.2	93.2	95.0	94.8	92.4	90.9	89.4	93.6
2002	87.5	88.8	90.0	89.8	89.1	87.3	84.9	84.3	83.4	82.7	81.5	80.4	85.8
2003	81.3	82.9	84.3	85.1	84.9	85.1	85.9	86.4	85.7	84.5	85.0	84.6	84.6

Employment by Industry: Florida—*Continued*

(Numbers in thousands. Not seasonally adjusted.)

Industry	January	February	March	April	May	June	July	August	September	October	November	December	Annual Average
JACKSONVILLE—*Continued*													
Educational and health services													
1990	42.2	42.9	43.2	42.7	42.6	42.7	42.3	42.4	43.0	43.9	44.1	43.8	42.9
1991	44.2	44.5	44.8	44.7	45.0	45.1	44.6	44.7	45.4	45.4	46.0	46.2	45.0
1992	45.8	45.5	45.7	46.4	46.4	46.5	46.2	46.2	46.5	47.4	47.4	47.5	46.4
1993	46.9	47.5	47.8	48.0	48.0	48.0	47.6	47.5	48.2	48.6	48.8	48.9	47.9
1994	49.7	50.2	50.2	50.6	50.7	51.1	50.4	50.6	51.3	51.3	51.3	51.6	50.7
1995	51.1	52.0	52.6	51.9	52.2	52.5	52.5	52.6	53.1	53.1	53.5	53.5	52.5
1996	52.2	52.4	52.4	51.9	52.6	52.7	52.9	53.0	53.2	53.2	53.3	53.7	52.7
1997	52.9	53.9	54.4	54.3	54.7	54.7	54.9	55.2	56.1	55.8	56.0	56.1	54.9
1998	57.0	57.2	58.2	56.3	56.7	56.9	56.3	56.1	57.1	57.9	58.0	58.2	57.1
1999	56.8	57.7	57.9	58.0	58.3	58.5	57.9	58.1	58.5	59.5	59.7	60.2	58.4
2000	59.4	59.6	59.8	59.3	59.6	59.7	58.3	58.7	59.0	58.5	58.7	59.1	59.1
2001	58.5	59.1	59.5	59.5	59.9	60.5	60.2	60.8	61.3	62.0	62.2	62.5	60.4
2002	62.0	62.3	62.7	62.7	63.0	63.1	62.6	63.0	63.1	63.3	63.5	63.7	62.9
2003	63.4	63.7	64.0	63.7	63.7	63.5	63.8	64.0	64.8	64.4	65.1	65.3	64.1
Leisure and hospitality													
1990	38.8	39.6	40.8	41.1	40.9	39.7	39.6	39.6	38.9	37.6	37.8	37.6	39.3
1991	36.8	37.3	38.1	39.2	40.1	39.9	40.0	40.4	38.9	38.3	38.6	38.7	38.8
1992	38.1	38.5	39.4	41.6	42.3	42.3	41.7	41.6	40.9	40.5	40.4	40.5	40.6
1993	38.8	39.9	40.8	41.3	42.4	42.5	42.0	41.8	40.9	39.9	40.0	40.1	40.8
1994	40.2	41.3	42.3	44.1	44.4	44.5	44.6	44.6	44.5	43.2	43.0	43.2	43.3
1995	42.4	43.4	44.7	44.9	45.5	46.0	46.0	46.0	45.4	44.9	45.1	45.0	44.9
1996	44.4	44.9	46.2	46.2	46.7	46.8	45.1	45.5	45.7	45.3	45.8	46.6	45.7
1997	44.8	45.4	46.4	46.5	47.4	46.9	46.0	46.8	46.2	47.0	47.4	47.2	46.5
1998	44.4	45.2	46.4	46.9	47.7	48.4	47.9	47.8	47.2	47.0	48.0	48.1	47.0
1999	46.0	46.4	47.4	49.1	49.8	50.3	49.5	49.8	49.3	48.4	48.7	49.2	48.6
2000	48.3	48.7	49.4	50.0	50.9	50.8	49.6	49.9	49.8	49.7	49.8	50.2	49.8
2001	47.3	48.2	49.8	51.1	51.8	52.3	51.2	52.4	51.7	50.5	50.8	51.2	50.7
2002	49.4	50.0	51.3	52.2	53.1	53.6	52.1	52.7	52.1	52.2	52.9	53.1	52.1
2003	50.5	51.0	52.2	52.5	53.3	53.4	51.7	52.3	51.4	52.0	52.6	52.3	52.1
Other services													
1990	19.2	19.4	19.5	19.3	19.4	19.5	19.4	19.4	19.1	19.1	18.9	18.8	19.2
1991	18.8	18.9	18.9	18.8	19.0	19.1	19.3	19.2	19.1	19.3	19.1	19.0	19.0
1992	18.5	18.6	18.7	18.8	19.0	19.1	19.3	19.1	18.8	19.0	18.9	18.9	18.8
1993	18.1	18.3	18.5	18.5	18.4	18.7	19.0	18.8	18.6	18.8	18.7	18.8	18.6
1994	18.6	18.8	18.9	19.0	19.1	19.4	19.6	19.5	19.4	19.3	19.0	19.3	19.1
1995	18.9	19.0	19.1	19.7	19.9	19.9	20.2	20.2	20.1	20.1	20.3	20.1	19.7
1996	19.5	19.7	19.7	19.8	20.2	20.2	20.1	20.2	20.1	20.3	20.8	20.7	20.1
1997	20.7	21.0	21.0	21.0	21.4	21.5	21.8	22.0	21.9	21.8	22.1	21.8	21.5
1998	21.7	22.0	22.2	22.1	22.3	22.6	22.6	22.4	22.2	22.2	22.5	22.2	22.2
1999	22.3	22.1	22.4	22.2	22.4	22.8	23.0	23.0	22.6	22.7	22.7	22.8	22.5
2000	22.5	22.8	23.0	24.0	24.0	24.3	24.2	24.1	23.8	23.6	23.7	23.8	23.7
2001	22.8	23.2	23.4	23.4	23.4	24.1	24.1	24.3	24.0	24.0	24.0	23.8	23.7
2002	23.9	24.0	24.5	24.3	24.5	24.8	25.1	25.4	25.0	25.0	25.2	25.2	24.7
2003	25.1	25.3	25.5	25.3	25.5	25.9	25.6	25.8	25.7	25.7	26.1	26.2	25.6
Government													
1990	62.8	63.1	64.1	64.8	66.4	62.9	61.6	60.6	63.6	65.2	65.7	65.4	63.8
1991	64.5	64.5	64.8	64.5	64.5	63.2	60.0	60.3	62.3	63.1	63.4	63.8	63.2
1992	62.5	62.8	65.0	62.4	62.6	61.3	58.6	57.5	61.2	62.6	62.2	62.9	61.8
1993	62.0	62.4	62.6	63.1	63.4	60.1	58.3	57.1	62.3	63.8	64.0	64.5	61.9
1994	64.1	64.1	64.1	64.4	64.9	62.4	59.5	58.4	63.9	65.2	67.9	65.9	63.7
1995	65.1	65.7	65.9	67.0	67.3	64.5	60.8	59.6	65.0	67.3	67.5	68.1	65.3
1996	67.1	68.1	69.2	67.1	67.0	64.0	60.1	59.6	65.7	66.5	67.4	68.5	65.8
1997	66.6	67.6	67.4	67.6	68.1	65.3	60.6	60.0	66.0	65.6	65.8	66.6	65.6
1998	66.6	68.2	67.9	67.0	68.0	65.3	60.3	59.9	66.0	67.3	67.8	68.0	66.0
1999	65.7	66.9	67.1	67.7	67.8	64.8	60.1	59.3	65.2	67.4	68.4	68.3	65.7
2000	66.1	67.0	67.2	67.5	69.3	63.0	61.8	67.1	66.9	67.7	67.7	68.0	66.6
2001	66.6	68.0	68.2	68.7	68.9	63.8	62.6	68.9	68.7	68.6	69.0	69.5	67.6
2002	67.6	68.3	68.3	68.8	69.1	64.0	62.4	68.8	68.6	69.1	69.7	70.1	67.9
2003	69.3	69.4	69.4	69.7	70.5	66.3	64.6	70.7	70.6	71.6	71.8	72.6	69.7
Federal government													
1990	18.2	18.2	18.9	19.7	20.9	20.0	20.1	19.3	19.1	19.6	19.6	19.9	19.4
1991	19.3	19.0	18.9	18.6	18.6	18.8	18.1	18.0	18.1	18.0	18.2	18.4	18.5
1992	18.1	17.8	17.8	17.7	17.6	17.6	17.6	17.5	17.4	17.5	17.5	17.7	17.6
1993	17.4	17.4	17.4	17.4	17.5	17.6	17.7	17.7	17.7	17.7	17.8	18.1	17.6
1994	17.9	17.8	17.8	17.9	17.8	17.8	17.9	17.9	17.9	18.1	18.1	18.7	17.9
1995	18.4	18.4	18.3	18.6	18.6	18.6	18.8	18.8	18.7	18.9	18.9	19.2	18.6
1996	18.8	18.8	18.8	19.0	18.9	18.9	18.9	18.9	18.9	18.9	19.0	19.4	18.9
1997	18.9	18.9	18.9	18.9	18.8	18.9	18.8	18.8	18.8	18.6	18.7	19.3	18.8
1998	18.6	18.6	18.6	18.5	18.6	18.6	18.5	18.4	18.4	18.4	18.7	19.1	18.5
1999	18.1	18.0	18.1	18.3	17.9	17.9	17.9	17.8	17.7	17.6	17.8	18.0	17.9
2000	17.5	17.6	17.6	17.6	19.2	17.6	17.8	17.5	17.3	17.5	17.6	17.9	17.7
2001	17.6	17.6	17.6	17.6	17.5	17.6	17.7	17.7	17.8	17.3	17.4	17.8	17.6
2002	17.3	17.3	17.3	17.5	17.5	17.6	17.6	17.6	17.6	17.9	18.0	18.5	17.6
2003	18.1	18.0	17.8	17.9	18.0	18.0	18.0	17.8	17.7	17.8	17.8	18.2	17.9

Employment by Industry: Florida—*Continued*

(Numbers in thousands. Not seasonally adjusted.)

Industry	January	February	March	April	May	June	July	August	September	October	November	December	Annual Average
JACKSONVILLE—*Continued*													
State government													
1990	8.1	8.3	8.4	8.4	8.4	8.4	8.1	8.0	8.5	8.5	8.5	8.4	8.3
1991	8.2	8.4	8.4	8.4	8.5	8.2	8.0	8.0	8.3	8.4	8.4	8.3	8.2
1992	8.0	8.2	8.1	8.2	8.3	8.0	8.0	7.8	8.2	8.4	8.4	8.4	8.1
1993	8.5	8.5	8.6	8.6	8.6	8.6	8.3	8.3	8.5	8.8	8.8	8.7	8.5
1994	8.7	8.8	8.8	8.9	8.9	8.6	8.6	8.5	9.0	9.0	9.1	9.1	8.8
1995	9.0	9.2	9.3	9.3	9.3	9.5	8.9	8.9	9.2	9.3	9.3	9.3	9.2
1996	9.2	9.3	9.4	9.4	9.5	9.0	9.1	9.1	9.3	9.4	9.5	9.5	9.3
1997	9.3	9.3	9.3	9.4	9.4	9.1	8.9	8.9	9.2	9.4	9.4	9.3	9.2
1998	9.4	9.4	9.5	9.4	9.4	9.1	8.8	8.8	9.3	9.3	9.4	9.4	9.2
1999	9.4	9.4	9.4	9.7	9.9	9.3	9.1	9.1	9.3	9.5	9.8	9.7	9.4
2000	9.4	9.6	9.6	9.7	9.8	10.0	9.3	9.2	9.5	10.3	9.7	9.7	9.7
2001	9.4	9.7	9.9	10.0	9.8	9.7	9.1	9.5	9.5	9.9	10.3	10.1	9.7
2002	9.7	9.7	9.7	9.7	9.8	9.1	8.8	9.3	9.4	9.6	9.8	9.6	9.5
2003	9.4	9.7	9.7	9.7	10.0	9.4	9.1	9.2	9.5	9.8	9.7	9.6	9.6
Local government													
1990	36.5	36.6	36.8	36.7	37.1	34.5	33.4	33.3	36.0	37.1	37.6	37.1	36.0
1991	37.0	37.1	37.5	37.5	37.4	36.2	33.9	34.3	35.9	36.7	36.8	37.1	36.4
1992	36.4	36.8	39.1	36.5	36.7	35.7	33.0	32.2	35.6	36.7	36.3	36.8	35.9
1993	36.1	36.5	36.6	37.1	37.3	33.9	32.3	31.1	36.1	37.3	37.4	37.7	35.7
1994	37.5	37.5	37.5	37.6	38.2	36.0	33.0	32.0	37.0	38.1	40.7	38.1	36.9
1995	37.7	38.1	38.3	39.1	39.4	36.4	33.1	31.9	37.1	39.1	39.3	39.6	37.4
1996	39.1	40.0	41.0	38.7	38.6	36.1	32.1	31.6	37.5	38.2	38.9	39.6	37.6
1997	38.4	39.4	39.2	39.3	39.9	37.3	32.9	32.3	38.0	37.6	37.7	38.0	37.5
1998	38.6	40.2	39.8	39.1	40.0	37.6	33.0	32.7	38.3	39.6	39.7	39.5	38.1
1999	38.2	39.5	39.6	39.7	40.0	37.6	33.1	32.4	38.2	40.3	40.8	40.6	38.3
2000	39.2	39.8	40.0	40.2	40.3	35.4	34.7	40.4	40.1	39.9	40.4	40.4	39.2
2001	39.6	40.7	40.7	41.1	41.6	36.5	35.8	41.7	41.4	41.4	41.3	41.6	40.2
2002	40.6	41.3	41.3	41.6	41.8	37.3	36.0	41.9	41.6	41.6	41.9	42.0	40.7
2003	41.8	41.7	41.9	42.1	42.5	38.9	37.5	43.7	43.4	44.0	44.3	44.8	42.2
MIAMI-HIALEAH													
Total nonfarm													
1990	877.4	883.9	892.8	883.9	889.9	886.8	865.9	865.6	878.6	879.7	884.5	887.6	881.3
1991	860.0	858.6	861.4	854.6	857.5	856.0	843.2	846.0	855.5	852.6	863.1	858.6	855.5
1992	844.2	848.0	858.4	856.9	857.8	858.2	845.4	842.3	855.7	865.7	873.2	882.6	857.3
1993	870.0	879.8	886.8	892.3	890.5	889.9	881.2	882.7	890.7	899.6	908.9	916.8	890.7
1994	896.0	905.6	912.6	908.7	909.9	909.2	897.4	896.6	910.1	912.8	925.4	933.1	909.7
1995	917.3	926.6	934.4	922.9	927.0	925.8	907.5	911.0	928.8	928.5	940.8	948.2	926.5
1996	926.6	934.6	946.1	931.6	936.8	937.2	918.3	921.3	938.5	943.2	953.9	964.2	937.6
1997	949.2	955.9	963.7	960.8	964.3	962.7	946.9	949.1	964.6	964.5	974.4	983.9	961.6
1998	966.1	970.8	978.8	969.6	972.8	973.2	959.8	958.6	974.4	985.2	994.5	1006.2	975.8
1999	974.2	982.5	987.3	982.2	983.4	986.5	971.5	971.8	988.2	993.4	1005.7	1018.2	987.0
2000	995.1	999.2	1006.3	1008.6	1014.7	1016.8	996.1	1000.0	1019.0	1020.5	1033.6	1044.5	1012.9
2001	1024.0	1032.2	1039.6	1030.9	1032.4	1033.6	1008.7	1008.1	1022.3	1017.9	1022.9	1027.9	1025.0
2002	1007.3	1014.6	1020.3	1012.7	1016.3	1013.9	987.7	986.8	1003.0	1004.3	1011.0	1016.4	1007.9
2003	999.5	1006.6	1010.5	1006.7	1007.4	1004.5	983.9	984.2	1003.6	1010.1	1014.4	1018.1	1004.1
Total private													
1990	757.6	763.0	769.9	760.1	761.9	764.8	752.0	754.9	754.8	753.0	760.1	763.5	759.6
1991	735.1	734.7	736.9	730.3	732.4	731.7	725.9	728.9	730.2	728.2	734.7	734.6	731.9
1992	720.5	723.5	729.0	731.5	732.6	732.8	724.1	722.5	720.5	732.5	742.5	754.3	730.5
1993	742.6	751.7	758.8	761.8	763.0	763.0	757.7	760.7	764.1	768.9	776.8	785.5	762.8
1994	765.8	773.9	779.8	773.8	776.1	775.8	768.9	771.1	777.4	778.3	786.9	797.8	777.1
1995	783.5	792.0	798.7	788.2	792.6	792.8	784.0	791.2	797.0	795.5	807.4	814.5	794.7
1996	792.7	801.5	809.3	796.9	803.5	804.8	794.7	800.5	805.4	809.5	819.5	829.2	805.6
1997	812.9	819.2	826.9	823.5	827.5	826.2	817.2	821.6	829.9	828.2	836.1	846.4	826.3
1998	826.2	832.3	839.0	830.8	833.8	835.5	827.4	830.1	837.7	845.9	855.0	866.1	838.3
1999	835.2	843.0	847.7	842.9	843.3	847.7	841.9	844.5	848.6	853.1	864.9	875.9	849.0
2000	851.7	856.7	863.0	863.1	866.1	871.3	863.4	869.3	876.0	873.5	885.6	895.4	869.6
2001	875.0	883.3	890.2	880.7	882.2	884.1	871.9	873.9	874.2	866.5	869.8	874.9	877.2
2002	856.2	862.5	867.5	859.8	862.3	861.6	848.9	850.3	852.1	852.5	857.1	862.7	857.8
2003	847.7	853.9	856.9	852.9	852.3	851.3	843.8	846.7	852.1	856.0	860.5	864.7	853.2
Goods-producing													
1990	133.0	133.8	135.1	131.9	131.6	131.6	127.6	127.8	127.1	124.9	124.1	123.2	129.3
1991	118.3	118.7	118.7	117.1	117.8	118.2	115.8	116.3	116.0	115.6	116.1	114.8	116.9
1992	110.3	110.9	111.9	112.9	113.9	114.3	112.1	111.5	114.3	117.6	119.3	120.0	114.0
1993	116.8	119.3	120.0	119.8	119.8	119.5	118.1	118.2	117.7	116.4	115.6	115.7	118.0
1994	112.7	114.1	115.1	114.3	115.0	115.5	114.6	114.3	114.9	113.1	113.0	113.4	114.1
1995	112.8	114.2	114.8	114.9	115.2	115.6	113.5	114.1	115.2	113.5	113.1	112.9	114.1
1996	112.1	114.2	115.5	112.1	112.5	112.8	112.0	112.8	112.7	113.6	113.6	114.0	113.1
1997	112.6	112.9	113.4	112.8	113.0	112.3	110.9	111.8	112.8	111.9	111.8	112.3	112.3
1998	110.5	111.5	112.2	111.3	111.4	112.2	110.1	109.9	110.4	110.9	110.9	111.1	111.0
1999	107.9	108.1	108.8	108.2	108.2	108.8	107.9	108.2	108.1	108.9	109.7	110.4	108.6
2000	107.8	108.1	109.2	106.9	107.3	108.0	105.6	105.8	106.0	105.3	105.6	105.4	106.8
2001	103.0	103.9	103.8	101.8	101.7	101.6	99.4	99.5	99.0	97.7	97.8	97.4	100.5
2002	95.4	96.6	96.7	95.3	96.0	96.5	95.1	95.0	95.3	95.5	95.6	96.1	95.8
2003	93.7	93.8	94.1	93.2	93.2	93.0	92.3	93.6	94.3	95.4	95.4	94.9	93.9

Employment by Industry: Florida—*Continued*

(Numbers in thousands. Not seasonally adjusted.)

Industry	January	February	March	April	May	June	July	August	September	October	November	December	Annual Average
MIAMI-HIALEAH—*Continued*													
Wholesale trade													
1990	59.8	60.4	60.9	61.8	62.2	62.3	61.1	61.6	62.2	62.0	62.3	62.4	61.5
1991	61.0	61.4	61.7	60.7	61.0	61.0	59.5	59.9	60.3	60.6	60.9	61.1	60.7
1992	58.9	59.2	59.5	60.3	60.5	60.6	60.7	60.6	60.2	60.9	61.2	61.3	60.3
1993	60.3	60.9	61.4	61.5	61.9	61.9	61.4	61.5	61.7	62.0	62.1	62.5	61.5
1994	60.9	61.6	62.3	61.7	62.0	61.9	61.4	61.5	61.7	61.2	61.8	62.5	61.7
1995	62.4	63.3	64.0	63.0	63.4	63.2	62.7	63.2	63.3	63.3	63.5	63.7	63.2
1996	63.3	63.9	64.5	63.7	64.2	64.6	63.7	64.2	64.6	65.1	65.7	66.2	64.4
1997	65.8	66.6	67.1	67.1	67.5	67.7	66.4	66.8	67.3	67.7	68.4	68.8	67.2
1998	66.0	66.7	67.4	67.0	67.6	67.6	67.6	67.8	68.1	68.6	68.6	69.1	67.6
1999	67.0	67.8	67.7	67.2	67.1	67.3	66.9	66.9	67.0	66.8	67.0	67.7	67.2
2000	66.7	66.9	67.6	68.2	68.6	68.9	68.6	68.7	69.3	68.9	69.6	70.4	68.5
2001	70.2	71.0	71.3	71.1	71.5	71.4	70.4	70.5	70.7	70.5	70.8	71.0	70.8
2002	70.0	70.4	70.9	69.6	70.0	70.1	69.3	69.5	69.4	69.6	69.5	69.8	69.8
2003	70.4	70.6	70.3	70.6	70.6	70.7	69.7	70.1	70.4	70.8	70.6	70.6	70.5
Retail trade													
1990	115.8	114.7	114.8	112.8	113.8	114.9	114.1	114.4	114.6	115.0	118.4	121.2	115.3
1991	111.9	110.9	111.1	109.6	111.1	110.9	109.8	110.6	111.0	110.3	112.8	115.7	111.3
1992	110.8	109.7	109.4	110.1	110.6	110.9	109.4	108.8	106.9	108.4	112.4	116.9	110.3
1993	112.0	111.6	112.2	111.5	111.4	111.6	110.6	111.5	112.4	114.8	118.6	122.3	113.3
1994	114.5	114.3	114.2	115.0	115.1	114.8	113.7	114.5	115.9	118.0	122.5	126.4	116.5
1995	118.7	118.3	118.4	115.4	115.7	116.0	114.7	116.7	117.6	118.2	121.8	126.4	118.1
1996	118.0	116.9	117.1	115.4	116.1	116.7	115.6	117.1	117.9	119.2	123.6	127.9	118.4
1997	119.5	118.2	118.5	118.6	119.5	119.1	118.6	119.8	120.9	122.2	125.2	129.2	120.7
1998	123.9	121.8	122.0	121.8	121.8	122.3	121.5	122.4	124.1	125.7	129.5	133.0	124.1
1999	125.2	124.4	124.7	124.4	124.8	125.8	126.6	127.1	127.2	129.1	133.3	136.4	127.4
2000	127.0	125.8	125.3	126.3	127.7	128.7	127.3	129.0	129.0	128.9	132.7	135.5	128.6
2001	127.3	126.0	126.9	125.2	124.5	124.4	123.3	124.4	124.5	123.7	127.0	129.0	125.5
2002	122.3	120.0	120.4	119.2	119.4	119.4	118.7	119.1	119.0	118.9	120.7	123.0	120.0
2003	116.5	115.6	115.7	116.1	116.3	116.1	116.3	116.5	116.6	116.9	119.8	122.1	117.0
Transportation and utilities													
1990	57.8	58.4	59.5	59.8	60.1	60.5	60.9	60.8	60.5	59.6	59.6	59.5	59.7
1991	59.3	55.2	54.0	54.1	54.0	54.1	54.5	54.7	54.7	54.2	53.9	49.7	54.3
1992	48.7	49.3	50.2	50.7	51.5	51.7	51.9	51.9	51.6	52.9	53.2	53.7	51.4
1993	53.4	53.7	54.0	54.9	55.7	55.3	55.8	55.8	55.6	56.2	56.1	56.4	55.2
1994	56.7	57.0	57.2	57.5	57.5	56.9	57.1	57.7	57.7	58.3	58.4	59.1	57.5
1995	58.1	58.9	59.7	59.6	59.9	59.9	59.9	60.3	60.8	60.6	61.2	62.2	60.0
1996	61.4	61.8	62.8	61.8	62.3	62.6	62.7	63.3	63.3	63.6	64.2	65.8	62.9
1997	64.8	65.2	65.8	65.2	65.4	65.4	65.6	64.1	66.3	66.5	67.1	68.8	65.8
1998	66.8	67.2	67.6	67.7	68.0	68.1	67.7	68.0	68.5	69.9	70.7	72.1	68.5
1999	69.7	70.0	70.4	70.3	70.4	70.8	71.5	71.8	71.8	73.2	74.0	75.0	71.5
2000	72.8	72.4	72.3	71.5	71.4	71.2	70.6	70.5	70.8	70.3	70.9	72.1	71.4
2001	70.3	70.5	71.2	70.7	70.3	70.1	70.6	70.3	69.6	69.0	68.0	68.1	69.8
2002	67.7	67.6	68.8	67.6	67.6	67.5	67.6	67.8	67.6	67.3	67.5	67.8	67.7
2003	66.9	67.0	66.7	65.8	65.2	65.2	64.6	64.4	64.5	64.2	64.5	65.0	65.3
Information													
1990	24.7	24.7	24.7	24.4	24.5	24.5	24.6	24.4	24.3	24.7	24.8	24.9	24.6
1991	25.3	25.0	24.6	24.3	24.9	25.7	25.8	25.7	25.5	25.4	25.5	25.4	25.2
1992	24.5	24.2	24.3	24.3	24.4	24.5	24.7	24.5	24.5	24.6	24.7	25.0	24.5
1993	25.1	25.1	25.6	24.8	25.1	25.2	25.5	25.4	25.3	24.8	25.1	25.1	25.1
1994	25.5	25.6	25.4	25.6	26.0	26.0	25.8	26.0	26.0	25.6	25.8	25.9	25.7
1995	25.3	25.4	25.4	24.8	24.8	25.1	25.0	25.1	25.3	24.8	24.8	25.0	25.0
1996	24.4	24.5	24.6	24.7	24.8	25.1	25.0	25.0	25.1	25.1	25.3	25.7	24.9
1997	25.4	25.7	26.0	25.6	26.1	26.5	26.2	26.4	26.6	26.3	26.4	26.8	26.1
1998	26.6	27.0	27.1	26.8	27.2	27.5	27.5	27.6	27.7	28.3	28.1	28.5	27.4
1999	28.3	28.6	28.9	28.0	28.3	28.6	28.3	28.4	28.7	29.1	29.6	29.6	28.7
2000	29.4	29.6	30.0	29.8	30.2	31.0	31.6	31.9	32.1	32.4	32.8	33.1	31.2
2001	33.1	33.4	33.9	33.6	33.9	33.8	33.3	33.3	33.0	32.5	32.3	32.6	33.2
2002	32.2	32.4	32.6	32.0	31.9	32.0	31.5	31.2	31.1	30.4	30.3	30.1	31.5
2003	29.0	28.7	28.7	28.5	28.5	28.4	28.7	28.5	28.7	27.9	27.6	27.9	28.4
Financial activities													
1990	70.7	71.3	71.9	71.5	71.4	72.0	71.2	71.6	71.6	70.3	70.1	70.1	71.1
1991	66.9	67.0	67.5	67.2	67.1	67.0	67.4	67.3	67.2	66.5	66.7	66.8	67.0
1992	64.8	64.9	65.0	64.2	64.4	64.6	64.4	64.1	63.8	63.9	63.8	64.5	64.3
1993	63.6	64.2	64.5	64.6	64.7	65.1	65.2	65.5	65.5	66.2	66.4	67.3	65.2
1994	66.6	67.0	67.4	66.9	67.1	67.1	67.3	67.2	67.2	67.1	67.3	67.8	67.1
1995	67.4	67.8	68.2	67.8	67.8	68.0	67.7	67.9	67.9	67.9	68.3	68.4	67.9
1996	64.8	65.5	65.9	66.7	67.3	67.4	66.4	66.6	66.5	67.3	67.3	67.7	66.6
1997	65.4	65.7	66.1	66.7	67.0	67.0	66.0	66.4	66.3	66.7	66.7	67.1	66.4
1998	66.4	66.6	67.2	65.6	65.3	65.5	65.5	65.5	65.4	66.0	66.0	66.5	65.9
1999	65.9	66.3	66.7	65.6	65.6	65.8	66.1	65.8	65.7	66.3	66.6	67.0	66.1
2000	66.3	66.6	66.5	66.1	65.9	66.9	65.8	66.0	66.1	65.8	65.9	66.3	66.2
2001	65.7	66.3	66.9	66.4	66.5	66.8	66.6	67.0	66.6	66.2	66.0	66.1	66.4
2002	66.4	66.9	67.3	66.7	66.6	66.6	66.8	67.1	67.0	67.1	67.2	67.4	66.9
2003	66.9	67.2	67.2	66.7	67.0	67.1	67.1	67.3	67.3	67.4	67.8	68.1	67.3

Employment by Industry: Florida—*Continued*

(Numbers in thousands. Not seasonally adjusted.)

Industry	January	February	March	April	May	June	July	August	September	October	November	December	Annual Average
MIAMI-HIALEAH—*Continued*													
Professional and business services													
1990	83.4	84.9	86.0	84.0	83.9	84.7	83.3	84.4	83.6	84.7	86.1	86.1	84.5
1991	82.0	82.7	83.6	83.1	83.3	83.2	83.6	84.0	83.9	83.5	84.3	85.3	83.5
1992	84.4	86.0	86.9	86.3	86.5	87.5	85.7	86.6	87.5	89.9	91.1	92.4	87.5
1993	92.4	93.9	95.2	96.9	97.0	97.7	95.5	96.3	97.4	99.4	100.6	101.9	97.0
1994	98.1	100.6	101.3	99.6	100.2	102.3	102.7	103.2	104.8	105.3	105.6	107.1	102.5
1995	105.0	107.0	109.0	107.3	108.0	109.0	109.4	111.6	112.4	112.3	115.4	115.3	110.1
1996	111.2	113.4	115.2	113.8	115.6	115.2	115.4	117.0	117.8	118.4	119.5	120.1	116.0
1997	116.8	118.5	120.1	117.9	119.1	119.6	116.8	118.0	120.8	121.3	122.0	123.7	119.5
1998	120.9	123.3	124.1	122.1	122.7	123.3	121.5	123.0	124.2	125.8	127.5	129.1	123.9
1999	122.3	125.0	125.0	126.9	126.8	127.1	127.8	128.6	130.1	130.7	132.1	134.7	128.0
2000	132.1	134.6	137.4	138.1	138.7	140.7	140.7	143.4	146.0	144.8	148.1	150.3	141.2
2001	149.0	152.0	153.1	151.8	152.8	154.6	151.2	151.7	152.9	151.6	151.7	152.5	152.0
2002	149.2	152.3	152.4	152.9	153.7	153.3	148.8	147.9	146.2	144.8	144.9	144.7	149.3
2003	143.0	145.5	146.2	146.5	146.6	147.5	146.8	147.8	147.9	148.8	148.0	147.0	146.8
Educational and health services													
1990	90.9	91.7	92.6	91.1	91.5	92.4	91.1	92.2	93.3	93.8	94.3	95.0	92.4
1991	93.1	94.5	95.5	95.7	96.3	96.4	96.9	96.8	98.5	99.1	100.2	100.3	96.9
1992	103.3	103.8	104.5	106.7	105.2	103.9	102.4	101.8	101.3	102.3	102.5	103.8	103.4
1993	102.3	103.6	104.8	105.0	105.1	105.0	106.2	106.6	108.0	109.5	110.3	110.9	106.4
1994	108.9	110.4	111.3	110.1	110.9	110.6	109.3	109.7	111.5	111.2	111.8	112.4	110.6
1995	111.7	112.7	113.4	113.7	114.5	114.6	112.9	113.3	115.1	115.6	116.4	116.5	114.2
1996	114.7	116.3	116.9	114.5	115.9	115.8	113.4	113.7	115.9	115.0	115.7	116.1	115.3
1997	116.7	118.0	119.4	119.3	120.1	119.9	117.1	117.9	120.4	119.2	119.5	120.0	118.9
1998	119.5	120.6	122.0	120.6	121.3	121.0	119.7	119.7	121.7	121.2	121.4	122.1	120.9
1999	120.2	121.3	122.3	120.6	121.1	121.6	118.6	119.0	120.4	120.4	121.0	121.8	120.6
2000	118.8	120.4	120.7	120.3	120.4	121.1	119.3	119.4	121.0	121.6	122.0	123.0	120.7
2001	119.4	121.2	122.1	122.1	122.9	123.1	122.7	122.1	123.7	124.1	124.6	125.7	122.8
2002	122.6	124.0	124.9	124.6	124.9	124.3	122.9	123.9	127.0	128.1	128.9	129.8	125.5
2003	127.9	129.6	130.4	129.9	129.5	129.0	127.9	127.3	130.8	131.3	132.5	132.8	129.9
Leisure and hospitality													
1990	85.3	86.4	87.5	85.6	85.6	84.3	81.3	81.1	81.1	81.7	84.1	84.6	84.0
1991	80.7	82.4	82.6	81.5	80.7	78.9	77.1	77.9	77.6	77.9	79.2	80.5	79.7
1992	79.5	80.0	81.7	80.0	79.5	78.6	76.7	76.8	74.4	76.0	78.1	79.9	78.4
1993	80.1	82.0	83.5	85.1	84.6	83.6	81.0	81.5	82.1	81.6	83.8	84.8	82.8
1994	83.2	84.5	86.5	84.1	83.2	81.7	78.1	78.3	79.0	79.8	81.7	83.9	82.0
1995	83.4	85.5	86.5	82.4	83.8	81.9	78.8	79.5	79.7	80.0	83.2	84.4	82.4
1996	83.7	85.3	87.0	84.8	85.0	84.6	80.4	80.7	81.5	82.1	84.3	85.1	83.7
1997	86.1	88.2	90.2	89.6	89.3	88.4	89.5	90.3	88.0	85.6	88.2	88.4	88.4
1998	85.4	87.1	88.4	87.4	87.5	87.3	85.7	85.5	86.9	88.8	91.4	93.3	87.8
1999	87.9	90.3	91.8	90.5	89.5	90.0	86.3	87.2	88.1	87.0	90.0	91.5	89.1
2000	88.9	90.2	91.8	93.4	93.1	92.0	91.1	92.1	92.9	92.4	95.0	96.2	92.4
2001	94.9	96.7	98.3	96.5	96.7	96.9	93.2	94.2	93.4	90.7	91.2	92.0	94.5
2002	89.8	91.5	92.7	91.4	91.5	91.0	87.4	88.0	88.5	89.5	90.9	92.2	90.4
2003	92.3	94.2	95.7	93.6	93.0	91.9	88.3	88.9	89.5	91.2	92.3	93.7	92.1
Other services													
1990	36.2	36.7	36.9	37.2	37.3	37.6	36.8	36.6	36.5	36.3	36.3	36.5	36.7
1991	36.6	36.9	37.6	37.0	36.2	36.3	35.5	35.7	35.5	35.1	35.1	35.0	36.0
1992	35.3	35.5	35.6	36.0	36.1	36.2	36.1	35.9	36.0	36.0	36.2	36.8	35.9
1993	36.6	37.4	37.6	37.7	37.7	38.1	38.4	38.4	38.4	38.0	38.2	38.6	37.9
1994	38.7	38.8	39.1	39.0	39.1	39.0	38.9	38.7	38.7	38.7	39.0	39.3	38.9
1995	38.7	38.9	39.3	39.3	39.5	39.5	39.4	39.5	39.7	39.3	39.7	39.7	39.3
1996	39.1	39.7	39.8	39.4	39.8	40.0	40.1	40.1	40.1	40.1	40.3	40.6	39.9
1997	39.8	40.2	40.3	40.7	40.5	40.3	40.1	40.1	40.5	40.8	40.8	41.3	40.4
1998	40.2	40.5	41.0	40.5	41.0	40.7	40.6	40.7	40.7	40.7	40.9	41.3	40.7
1999	40.8	41.2	41.4	41.2	41.5	41.9	41.9	41.5	41.5	41.6	41.6	41.8	41.4
2000	41.9	42.1	42.2	42.5	42.8	42.8	42.8	42.5	42.8	43.1	43.0	43.1	42.6
2001	42.1	42.3	42.7	41.5	41.4	41.4	41.2	40.9	40.8	40.5	40.4	40.5	41.3
2002	40.6	40.8	40.8	40.5	40.7	40.9	40.8	40.8	41.0	41.3	41.6	41.8	41.0
2003	41.1	41.7	41.9	42.0	42.4	42.4	42.1	42.3	42.1	42.1	42.0	42.6	42.1
Government													
1990	119.8	120.9	122.9	123.8	128.0	122.0	113.9	110.7	123.8	126.7	124.4	124.1	121.7
1991	124.9	123.9	124.5	124.3	125.1	124.3	117.3	117.1	125.3	124.4	128.4	124.0	123.6
1992	123.7	124.5	129.4	125.4	125.2	125.4	121.3	119.8	135.2	133.2	130.7	128.3	126.8
1993	127.4	128.1	128.0	130.5	127.5	126.9	123.5	122.0	126.6	130.7	132.1	131.3	127.8
1994	130.2	131.7	132.8	134.9	133.8	133.4	128.5	125.5	132.7	134.5	138.5	135.3	132.6
1995	133.8	134.6	135.7	134.7	134.4	133.0	123.5	119.8	131.8	133.0	133.4	133.7	131.7
1996	133.9	133.1	136.8	134.7	133.3	132.4	123.6	120.8	133.1	133.7	134.4	135.0	132.0
1997	136.3	136.7	136.8	137.3	136.8	136.5	129.7	127.5	134.7	136.3	138.3	137.5	135.3
1998	139.9	138.5	139.8	138.8	139.0	137.7	132.4	128.5	136.7	139.3	139.5	140.1	137.5
1999	139.0	139.5	139.6	139.3	140.1	138.8	129.6	127.3	139.6	140.3	140.8	142.3	138.0
2000	143.4	142.5	143.3	145.5	148.6	145.5	132.7	130.7	143.0	147.0	148.0	149.1	143.3
2001	149.0	148.9	149.4	150.2	150.2	149.5	136.8	134.2	148.1	151.4	153.1	153.0	147.8
2002	151.1	152.1	152.8	152.9	154.0	152.3	138.8	136.5	150.9	151.8	153.9	153.7	150.1
2003	151.8	152.7	153.6	153.8	155.1	153.2	140.1	137.5	151.5	154.1	153.9	153.4	150.9

Employment by Industry: Florida—*Continued*

(Numbers in thousands. Not seasonally adjusted.)

Industry	January	February	March	April	May	June	July	August	September	October	November	December	Annual Average
MIAMI-HIALEAH—*Continued*													
Federal government													
1990	18.8	18.8	19.0	20.0	21.2	19.9	20.4	19.3	19.1	19.1	19.0	19.1	19.4
1991	19.0	19.1	19.1	19.1	19.1	19.2	19.3	19.3	19.3	19.3	19.3	19.5	19.2
1992	19.3	19.3	19.4	19.3	19.3	19.3	19.2	19.2	19.4	19.6	19.1	19.1	19.2
1993	18.7	18.6	18.6	18.2	18.2	18.0	18.0	18.0	17.9	18.2	18.1	18.4	18.2
1994	18.1	18.1	18.1	18.1	18.1	18.1	18.0	18.0	18.0	18.0	17.9	18.3	18.0
1995	17.8	17.8	17.8	17.8	17.7	17.7	17.7	17.7	17.8	17.8	17.8	18.1	17.7
1996	17.8	17.8	17.8	17.9	17.8	17.8	18.0	18.0	18.1	18.0	18.1	18.3	17.9
1997	18.1	18.1	18.1	18.1	18.1	18.1	18.1	18.1	18.2	18.1	18.3	18.4	18.1
1998	18.3	18.2	18.3	18.4	18.4	18.3	18.4	18.4	18.4	18.3	18.3	18.6	18.3
1999	18.5	18.8	18.4	18.3	18.3	18.2	18.4	18.4	18.4	18.4	18.3	18.8	18.4
2000	18.5	18.7	18.8	19.9	22.6	19.8	19.5	19.6	18.5	18.3	18.3	18.4	19.2
2001	18.5	18.5	18.5	18.4	18.4	18.5	18.7	18.7	18.7	18.7	18.7	19.1	18.6
2002	18.6	18.6	18.6	18.6	18.7	18.8	18.8	18.8	18.7	19.3	19.8	20.5	19.0
2003	20.5	20.5	20.6	20.6	20.5	20.4	20.4	20.3	20.1	20.3	19.8	20.4	20.4
State government													
1990	13.9	14.3	14.5	14.5	14.5	14.1	14.0	14.2	14.6	14.7	14.8	14.9	14.4
1991	14.7	14.7	14.9	14.8	15.2	14.5	14.5	14.5	14.7	15.0	15.1	14.9	14.7
1992	14.8	14.7	14.8	14.8	15.0	14.4	14.6	14.5	14.3	15.5	15.4	15.5	14.8
1993	15.3	15.6	15.8	16.3	16.3	15.8	16.4	15.9	15.9	16.7	16.5	16.6	16.0
1994	16.2	16.3	16.6	17.2	17.1	16.4	16.4	16.5	17.2	17.3	17.1	17.1	16.7
1995	16.5	16.8	17.3	17.1	17.1	16.4	16.5	16.4	17.2	17.2	17.3	17.4	16.9
1996	17.2	17.1	17.5	17.5	17.5	16.6	16.9	16.9	17.1	17.5	17.6	17.8	17.2
1997	18.0	17.8	18.0	18.1	18.0	17.3	17.5	17.6	18.0	18.4	18.4	18.6	17.9
1998	18.8	18.6	18.7	18.6	18.7	17.8	18.1	17.8	18.2	18.3	18.5	18.5	18.3
1999	17.9	18.4	18.6	18.5	18.5	17.6	18.0	17.8	18.2	18.6	18.8	19.1	18.3
2000	18.2	19.0	19.3	19.4	19.6	19.2	19.0	19.0	19.5	19.7	20.0	20.2	19.3
2001	19.0	19.8	20.0	19.9	19.8	18.9	18.9	18.6	18.9	19.2	19.6	19.4	19.3
2002	18.4	19.0	19.1	19.1	19.2	18.0	17.9	17.8	18.4	18.6	19.0	18.9	18.6
2003	17.7	18.6	18.9	18.8	19.1	17.6	17.8	17.6	17.8	18.7	18.6	18.6	18.3
Local government													
1990	87.1	87.8	89.4	89.3	92.3	88.0	79.5	77.2	90.1	92.9	90.6	90.1	87.8
1991	91.2	90.1	90.5	90.4	90.8	90.6	83.5	83.3	91.3	90.1	94.0	89.6	89.6
1992	89.6	90.5	95.2	91.3	90.9	91.7	87.5	86.1	101.5	98.1	96.2	93.7	92.6
1993	93.4	93.9	93.6	96.0	93.0	93.1	89.1	88.1	92.8	95.8	97.5	96.3	93.5
1994	95.9	97.3	98.1	99.6	98.6	98.9	94.1	91.0	97.5	99.2	103.5	99.9	97.8
1995	99.5	100.0	100.6	99.8	99.6	98.9	89.3	85.7	96.8	98.0	98.3	98.2	97.0
1996	98.9	98.2	101.5	99.3	98.0	98.0	88.7	85.9	97.9	98.2	98.7	98.9	96.8
1997	100.2	100.8	100.7	101.1	100.7	101.1	94.1	91.8	98.5	99.8	101.6	100.5	99.2
1998	102.8	101.7	102.8	101.8	101.9	101.6	95.9	92.3	100.1	102.7	102.7	103.0	100.7
1999	102.6	102.3	102.6	102.5	103.3	103.0	93.2	91.1	103.0	103.3	103.7	104.4	101.2
2000	106.7	104.8	105.2	106.2	106.4	106.5	94.2	92.1	105.0	109.0	109.7	110.5	104.7
2001	111.5	110.6	110.9	111.9	112.0	112.1	99.2	96.9	110.5	113.5	114.8	114.5	109.8
2002	114.1	114.5	115.1	115.2	116.1	115.5	102.1	99.9	113.8	113.9	115.1	114.3	112.5
2003	113.6	113.6	114.1	114.4	115.5	115.2	101.9	99.6	113.6	115.1	115.5	114.4	112.2
ORLANDO													
Total nonfarm													
1990	596.4	606.3	612.1	610.5	614.5	618.7	610.0	609.3	611.6	609.0	614.0	614.3	610.5
1991	595.3	598.1	601.0	598.7	602.0	604.6	593.1	592.9	599.7	602.4	607.2	611.3	600.5
1992	603.5	607.1	615.8	615.3	618.5	621.3	614.9	615.2	623.2	625.1	630.7	636.2	618.9
1993	627.2	635.1	640.3	652.8	656.1	659.5	644.8	646.3	656.1	656.5	660.9	668.8	650.3
1994	663.1	669.1	676.4	683.0	684.1	687.5	675.8	679.1	691.0	686.7	698.5	703.6	683.1
1995	694.6	703.0	712.3	707.8	711.7	719.5	704.4	708.3	721.7	720.3	729.7	739.4	714.3
1996	721.5	733.4	743.7	741.2	746.5	753.1	739.4	746.5	761.4	762.1	769.7	779.3	749.8
1997	770.6	779.4	785.3	786.9	792.1	795.1	783.4	789.8	807.0	807.4	814.5	826.1	794.8
1998	813.3	823.6	830.7	829.9	831.7	837.0	829.6	831.2	847.3	853.3	859.4	867.2	837.8
1999	847.3	860.0	867.1	873.3	875.7	884.3	869.8	871.0	884.3	886.7	895.3	904.0	876.6
2000	888.8	899.3	906.8	905.7	910.9	908.0	898.6	910.6	916.5	916.4	923.8	930.7	909.7
2001	909.8	918.2	925.5	921.3	923.4	913.8	905.1	916.1	915.9	906.5	905.9	907.3	914.0
2002	890.2	900.0	907.0	904.5	907.8	899.4	893.7	906.4	907.6	912.3	920.5	927.2	906.4
2003	911.7	915.8	919.8	923.1	926.3	919.4	914.7	925.9	929.8	934.7	941.2	945.8	925.7
Total private													
1990	524.8	533.3	538.5	536.7	539.4	545.2	542.5	543.4	536.7	532.8	537.0	537.7	537.3
1991	519.3	521.0	523.4	521.5	524.1	527.6	523.3	524.3	523.1	524.2	528.6	532.7	524.4
1992	525.8	529.1	535.6	537.0	540.1	543.8	544.8	546.4	546.1	547.2	552.7	557.8	542.2
1993	550.6	557.2	561.7	573.9	577.7	581.6	573.5	575.6	577.2	576.6	580.8	588.1	572.8
1994	583.9	588.9	595.8	602.0	603.6	607.8	603.5	607.4	609.6	604.6	613.9	622.0	603.5
1995	614.7	622.2	630.9	626.4	631.1	639.5	632.0	636.3	640.2	638.9	647.7	657.2	634.7
1996	640.9	651.2	659.5	658.2	663.6	671.5	665.7	672.6	677.4	678.3	685.0	694.5	668.2
1997	686.7	694.8	700.7	702.8	707.2	711.2	707.5	713.7	721.1	720.1	726.9	737.7	710.8
1998	726.9	735.9	742.3	741.1	743.3	750.0	750.6	754.0	758.7	763.9	769.7	776.8	751.1
1999	759.1	770.2	776.6	782.2	784.9	794.4	788.9	791.7	793.3	794.7	803.0	811.3	787.5
2000	797.2	806.0	813.0	812.1	815.1	823.6	816.1	818.9	823.8	822.8	829.7	836.0	817.9
2001	816.2	822.5	828.1	823.7	826.0	826.1	819.5	820.4	818.8	807.4	805.9	807.0	818.4
2002	790.1	798.9	805.8	802.7	805.3	807.7	803.9	805.0	804.6	807.8	815.4	821.7	805.7
2003	807.3	810.7	814.6	817.5	820.2	824.7	821.9	822.2	825.0	828.4	834.4	839.5	822.2

Employment by Industry: Florida—*Continued*

(Numbers in thousands. Not seasonally adjusted.)

Industry	January	February	March	April	May	June	July	August	September	October	November	December	Annual Average
ORLANDO—*Continued*													
Goods-producing													
1990	93.5	93.9	93.9	92.4	92.1	91.9	90.1	89.8	88.0	87.2	87.1	85.7	90.4
1991	81.5	80.7	80.2	79.8	79.9	79.8	77.6	78.2	78.2	77.3	77.2	76.8	78.9
1992	74.8	74.6	75.1	75.5	76.1	76.3	76.7	76.6	76.7	76.9	76.8	77.3	76.1
1993	75.6	76.3	77.1	78.3	78.5	79.0	77.7	77.5	78.3	79.8	79.9	80.5	78.2
1994	79.3	79.7	80.3	80.1	80.0	80.5	80.3	80.9	81.2	80.7	81.8	82.4	80.6
1995	80.9	81.5	82.5	82.0	82.1	82.7	82.2	82.7	82.9	84.4	84.9	86.0	82.9
1996	86.4	88.3	89.1	89.7	90.4	91.2	89.3	89.9	90.6	91.9	92.1	92.9	90.1
1997	93.0	93.2	94.1	95.2	95.5	95.9	95.2	96.0	96.9	99.3	99.4	100.3	96.1
1998	99.1	100.3	101.6	100.9	101.7	102.1	101.6	101.6	102.1	103.2	103.4	104.5	101.8
1999	102.6	103.8	104.5	105.6	105.9	106.7	105.5	105.5	105.3	106.0	106.2	107.3	105.4
2000	105.6	106.5	106.7	106.8	107.3	108.0	106.9	107.1	107.3	105.5	106.0	106.4	106.7
2001	104.9	104.7	105.2	104.7	104.1	104.6	103.9	104.2	103.6	102.7	102.0	101.4	103.8
2002	100.6	101.1	101.5	100.6	100.8	100.5	100.1	101.0	101.2	102.1	102.4	103.0	101.2
2003	100.8	101.6	102.2	101.5	102.0	102.6	101.5	101.1	102.2	103.5	104.0	104.6	102.3
Natural resources and mining													
1990	0.4	0.4	0.4	0.4	0.5	0.5	0.5	0.5	0.5	0.4	0.4	0.4	0.4
1991	0.4	0.4	0.4	0.4	0.4	0.4	0.4	0.5	0.5	0.5	0.5	0.5	0.4
1992	0.4	0.4	0.4	0.5	0.4	0.5	0.5	0.4	0.4	0.4	0.4	0.4	0.4
1993	0.4	0.4	0.4	0.4	0.4	0.4	0.4	0.4	0.4	0.4	0.4	0.4	0.4
1994	0.4	0.4	0.4	0.4	0.4	0.4	0.4	0.4	0.4	0.4	0.4	0.4	0.4
1995	0.4	0.4	0.5	0.4	0.5	0.5	0.5	0.5	0.5	0.5	0.5	0.5	0.5
1996	0.5	0.5	0.5	0.5	0.5	0.5	0.5	0.5	0.5	0.5	0.5	0.5	0.5
1997	0.5	0.5	0.5	0.5	0.5	0.5	0.5	0.5	0.5	0.5	0.5	0.5	0.5
1998	0.5	0.5	0.5	0.5	0.5	0.5	0.5	0.5	0.5	0.5	0.5	0.5	0.5
1999	0.5	0.5	0.5	0.5	0.5	0.5	0.5	0.5	0.5	0.5	0.5	0.5	0.5
2000	0.5	0.5	0.5	0.5	0.5	0.5	0.5	0.4	0.5	0.5	0.5	0.4	0.5
2001	0.4	0.5	0.5	0.5	0.5	0.5	0.5	0.5	0.5	0.5	0.4	0.5	0.5
2002	0.4	0.5	0.5	0.5	0.5	0.5	0.5	0.5	0.5	0.5	0.5	0.5	0.5
2003	0.5	0.5	0.5	0.5	0.5	0.5	0.5	0.5	0.5	0.5	0.5	0.5	0.5
Construction													
1990	40.6	41.0	41.5	40.2	39.9	39.9	38.3	38.2	37.1	36.8	36.3	35.2	38.8
1991	32.9	32.3	31.9	32.0	32.3	32.4	31.5	31.8	31.6	30.9	30.8	30.2	31.7
1992	28.8	28.8	29.3	30.0	30.7	30.9	31.4	31.8	32.1	31.8	32.0	32.2	30.8
1993	30.7	31.0	31.6	32.4	32.6	32.9	33.0	33.2	33.9	34.4	34.4	34.8	32.9
1994	33.3	33.8	34.3	34.5	34.7	35.2	35.2	35.9	36.1	35.8	36.7	36.8	35.2
1995	35.7	36.0	36.5	36.6	36.8	37.3	37.0	37.4	37.6	38.0	38.3	38.7	37.2
1996	39.0	40.1	40.7	41.2	41.7	42.3	40.7	41.1	41.8	43.1	43.3	43.7	41.6
1997	43.3	43.5	44.0	44.4	44.9	45.2	44.9	45.5	46.1	47.8	47.9	48.5	45.5
1998	47.3	48.2	49.1	48.6	49.1	49.4	49.8	49.8	50.1	51.0	51.2	52.0	49.6
1999	50.4	51.0	51.5	53.1	53.4	54.1	53.3	53.4	53.2	54.1	54.1	54.8	53.0
2000	53.6	54.5	54.5	55.5	55.6	56.4	55.5	55.6	55.9	54.7	54.8	55.1	55.1
2001	54.5	54.4	54.9	54.6	54.5	55.3	55.6	56.1	56.0	55.8	55.7	55.4	55.2
2002	54.6	54.9	55.3	55.0	55.4	55.5	55.8	56.8	57.1	58.0	58.5	59.0	56.3
2003	57.4	58.2	58.7	58.9	59.3	59.9	59.7	59.4	60.5	62.0	62.6	63.0	60.0
Manufacturing													
1990	52.5	52.5	52.0	51.8	51.7	51.5	51.3	51.1	50.4	50.0	50.4	50.1	51.2
1991	48.2	48.0	47.9	47.4	47.2	47.0	45.7	45.9	46.1	45.9	45.9	46.1	46.7
1992	45.6	45.4	45.4	45.0	45.0	44.9	44.8	44.4	44.2	44.7	44.4	44.7	44.8
1993	44.5	44.9	45.1	45.5	45.5	45.7	44.3	43.9	44.0	45.0	45.1	45.3	44.9
1994	45.6	45.5	45.6	45.2	44.9	44.9	44.7	44.6	44.7	44.5	44.7	45.2	45.0
1995	44.8	45.1	45.5	45.0	44.8	44.9	44.7	44.8	44.8	45.9	46.1	46.8	45.2
1996	46.9	47.7	47.9	48.0	48.2	48.4	48.1	48.3	48.3	48.3	48.3	48.7	48.0
1997	49.2	49.2	49.6	50.3	50.1	50.2	49.8	50.0	50.3	51.0	51.0	51.3	50.1
1998	51.3	51.6	52.0	51.8	52.1	52.2	51.3	51.3	51.5	51.7	51.7	52.0	51.7
1999	51.7	52.3	52.5	52.0	52.0	52.1	51.7	51.6	51.6	51.4	51.6	52.0	51.9
2000	51.5	51.5	51.7	50.8	51.2	51.1	50.9	51.1	50.9	50.3	50.7	50.9	51.1
2001	50.0	49.8	49.8	49.6	49.1	48.8	47.8	47.6	47.1	46.4	45.9	45.5	48.1
2002	45.6	45.7	45.7	45.1	44.9	44.5	43.8	43.7	43.6	43.6	43.4	43.5	44.4
2003	42.9	42.9	43.0	42.1	42.2	42.2	41.3	41.2	41.2	41.0	40.9	41.1	41.8
Service-providing													
1990	502.9	512.4	518.2	518.1	522.4	526.8	519.9	519.5	523.6	521.8	526.9	528.6	520.0
1991	513.8	517.4	520.8	518.9	522.1	524.8	515.5	514.7	521.5	525.1	530.0	534.5	521.5
1992	528.7	532.5	540.7	539.8	542.4	545.0	538.2	538.6	546.5	548.2	553.9	558.9	542.7
1993	551.6	558.8	563.2	574.5	577.6	580.5	567.1	568.8	577.8	576.7	581.0	588.3	572.1
1994	583.8	589.4	596.1	602.9	604.1	607.0	595.5	598.2	609.8	606.0	616.7	621.2	602.5
1995	613.7	621.5	629.8	625.8	629.6	636.8	622.2	625.6	638.8	635.9	644.8	653.4	631.4
1996	635.1	645.1	654.6	651.5	656.1	661.9	650.1	656.6	670.8	670.2	677.6	686.4	659.6
1997	677.6	686.2	691.2	691.7	696.6	699.2	688.2	693.8	710.1	708.1	715.1	725.8	698.6
1998	714.2	723.3	729.1	729.0	730.0	734.9	728.0	729.6	745.2	750.1	756.0	762.7	736.0
1999	744.7	756.2	762.6	767.7	769.8	777.6	764.3	765.5	779.0	780.7	789.1	796.7	771.2
2000	783.2	792.8	800.1	798.9	803.6	800.0	791.7	803.5	809.2	810.9	817.8	824.3	803.0
2001	804.9	813.5	820.3	816.6	819.3	809.2	801.2	811.9	812.3	803.8	803.9	805.9	810.2
2002	789.6	798.9	805.5	803.9	807.0	798.9	793.6	805.4	806.4	810.2	818.1	824.2	805.1
2003	810.9	814.2	817.6	821.6	824.3	816.8	813.2	824.8	827.6	831.2	837.2	841.2	823.4

Employment by Industry: Florida—*Continued*

(Numbers in thousands. Not seasonally adjusted.)

Industry	January	February	March	April	May	June	July	August	September	October	November	December	Annual Average
ORLANDO—*Continued*													
Trade, transportation, and utilities													
1990	122.9	123.5	123.7	123.4	124.1	124.4	122.7	123.8	123.3	123.6	125.6	127.3	124.0
1991	121.9	120.8	121.0	121.1	121.5	121.7	120.6	121.0	121.3	122.3	124.6	127.0	122.0
1992	122.5	122.3	122.7	122.4	122.9	123.2	123.6	124.2	125.1	126.9	130.0	132.2	124.8
1993	127.7	128.4	128.7	130.2	130.6	131.8	130.2	130.4	131.2	132.3	135.6	138.6	131.3
1994	134.8	135.0	136.3	136.6	136.9	137.6	137.0	139.0	140.1	140.0	144.4	147.7	138.7
1995	142.8	142.0	143.7	143.0	144.2	144.8	143.5	144.8	146.1	146.6	149.6	152.9	145.3
1996	146.0	147.2	148.5	147.0	148.7	149.0	149.3	151.2	152.7	153.3	156.9	161.1	150.9
1997	155.0	154.9	155.8	158.6	159.1	159.1	158.4	158.5	162.0	159.5	162.2	166.8	159.1
1998	162.0	162.0	163.3	164.2	164.2	165.5	165.8	166.2	168.2	172.0	175.5	180.2	167.4
1999	172.1	171.5	172.1	170.8	171.1	172.8	172.0	172.6	174.5	178.3	182.3	186.1	174.7
2000	178.9	178.9	179.9	180.2	180.5	181.8	180.1	181.5	182.1	182.3	186.6	189.6	181.9
2001	181.3	180.3	181.0	180.8	180.8	180.4	180.0	180.2	179.9	178.0	179.9	181.6	180.3
2002	174.1	172.8	173.2	172.8	173.1	172.5	171.4	172.3	172.8	173.1	177.0	180.4	173.8
2003	174.3	173.2	173.4	172.5	172.2	172.2	172.0	172.5	173.7	173.8	177.4	181.0	174.0
Wholesale trade													
1990	28.5	28.9	28.8	29.0	28.9	29.0	29.0	29.1	29.0	28.8	28.8	28.6	28.8
1991	27.9	27.8	27.7	27.9	27.9	27.9	27.9	28.0	27.9	28.1	28.2	28.3	27.9
1992	28.8	28.9	29.0	29.0	28.6	28.8	28.8	28.8	28.9	29.2	29.3	29.4	28.9
1993	29.6	29.8	30.0	30.4	30.4	30.6	30.5	30.6	30.8	30.7	30.9	31.0	30.4
1994	30.6	31.0	31.3	32.0	32.0	31.9	32.1	32.6	32.8	32.9	33.3	33.0	32.1
1995	33.3	33.6	34.1	34.4	34.6	34.8	34.6	34.9	35.0	34.7	34.9	35.3	34.5
1996	34.0	34.5	33.9	33.6	34.2	34.4	35.0	35.2	36.0	36.0	36.1	36.5	34.9
1997	35.7	36.1	36.3	37.1	37.4	37.5	38.0	37.8	38.2	37.1	37.2	37.6	37.1
1998	36.8	37.2	37.5	38.1	38.2	38.4	38.3	38.3	38.4	38.9	38.9	39.1	38.1
1999	39.0	39.3	39.5	39.1	39.2	39.4	39.4	39.2	39.3	39.5	39.8	40.3	39.4
2000	40.2	40.6	40.9	42.5	42.8	43.3	43.5	43.7	43.9	43.7	43.8	44.1	42.8
2001	44.2	44.4	44.6	44.4	44.4	44.4	44.1	44.1	44.2	43.9	43.6	43.1	44.1
2002	42.1	42.1	42.2	41.9	41.9	41.6	41.4	41.4	41.5	41.6	41.7	41.6	41.8
2003	41.8	41.8	42.0	41.8	41.9	42.0	41.6	41.3	41.7	41.5	42.1	42.3	41.8
Retail trade													
1990	75.3	75.3	75.4	74.6	75.3	75.4	74.1	75.2	74.6	75.4	77.2	78.8	75.5
1991	75.0	74.2	74.4	73.0	73.2	73.0	72.2	72.5	72.8	73.7	75.7	77.6	73.9
1992	72.5	72.1	72.3	72.0	72.8	72.7	72.7	73.3	74.2	75.1	77.9	80.0	73.9
1993	76.1	76.5	76.5	77.3	77.6	78.1	77.2	77.4	77.9	79.1	82.0	84.5	78.3
1994	81.1	80.9	81.4	80.9	81.1	81.9	81.2	82.4	83.2	83.3	87.1	90.4	82.9
1995	86.6	86.1	86.9	86.3	87.2	87.8	86.7	87.6	88.4	89.8	92.3	94.8	88.3
1996	89.5	89.8	91.5	90.3	91.1	91.2	90.8	92.2	92.9	94.0	97.3	100.1	92.5
1997	94.9	94.2	94.7	96.0	96.1	96.1	94.8	96.5	97.8	96.2	98.4	101.3	96.4
1998	98.2	97.9	98.7	98.3	98.1	99.1	99.2	99.8	101.5	103.9	106.4	109.7	100.9
1999	103.8	102.9	103.3	103.2	103.3	104.9	104.1	104.8	106.6	109.1	112.6	115.0	106.1
2000	109.9	109.3	109.9	108.1	108.3	109.4	107.3	108.3	108.5	108.9	112.5	114.5	109.6
2001	106.8	105.9	106.4	106.0	106.2	106.2	106.3	106.6	106.3	105.7	108.1	109.7	106.6
2002	104.9	103.7	104.0	103.4	103.8	103.6	102.7	103.6	104.0	104.5	108.1	110.7	104.8
2003	105.8	105.1	105.2	104.8	104.7	104.8	104.9	105.8	106.2	106.7	109.0	111.6	106.2
Transportation and utilities													
1990	19.1	19.3	19.5	19.8	19.9	20.0	19.6	19.5	19.7	19.4	19.6	19.9	19.6
1991	19.0	18.8	18.9	20.2	20.4	20.8	20.5	20.5	20.6	20.5	20.7	21.1	20.1
1992	21.2	21.3	21.4	21.4	21.5	21.7	22.1	22.1	22.0	22.6	22.8	22.8	21.9
1993	22.0	22.1	22.2	22.5	22.6	23.1	22.5	22.4	22.5	22.5	22.7	23.1	22.5
1994	23.1	23.1	23.6	23.7	23.8	23.8	23.7	24.0	24.1	23.8	24.0	24.3	23.7
1995	22.9	22.3	22.7	22.3	22.4	22.2	22.2	22.3	22.7	22.1	22.4	22.8	22.4
1996	22.5	22.9	23.1	23.1	23.4	23.4	23.5	23.8	23.8	23.3	23.5	24.5	23.4
1997	24.4	24.6	24.8	25.5	25.6	25.5	25.6	24.2	26.0	26.2	26.6	27.9	25.5
1998	27.0	26.9	27.1	27.8	27.9	28.0	28.3	28.1	28.3	29.2	30.2	31.4	28.3
1999	29.3	29.3	29.3	28.5	28.6	28.5	28.5	28.6	28.6	29.7	29.9	30.8	29.1
2000	28.8	29.0	29.1	29.6	29.4	29.1	29.3	29.5	29.7	29.7	30.3	31.0	29.5
2001	30.3	30.0	30.0	30.4	30.2	29.8	29.6	29.5	29.4	28.4	28.2	28.8	29.5
2002	27.1	27.0	27.0	27.5	27.4	27.3	27.3	27.3	27.3	27.0	27.2	28.1	27.3
2003	26.7	26.3	26.2	25.9	25.6	25.4	25.5	25.4	25.8	25.6	26.3	27.1	26.0
Information													
1990	16.7	16.7	16.5	16.2	16.3	16.5	16.6	16.7	16.7	16.5	16.6	16.7	16.5
1991	16.4	16.3	16.4	16.5	16.6	16.7	17.3	17.3	17.5	17.1	17.2	17.4	16.8
1992	17.2	17.2	17.4	17.6	17.7	17.7	17.6	17.7	17.8	17.6	17.7	18.0	17.6
1993	17.9	17.9	18.0	18.1	17.9	18.1	18.1	18.1	18.3	18.1	18.2	18.4	18.0
1994	18.2	18.2	18.4	18.5	18.4	18.6	18.8	19.0	19.2	18.5	18.6	18.8	18.6
1995	18.9	18.9	19.3	19.2	19.4	19.7	19.5	19.7	19.8	19.7	20.1	20.4	19.5
1996	20.1	20.1	20.4	20.3	20.8	20.9	20.9	21.1	21.3	21.3	21.3	21.8	20.8
1997	21.7	21.9	22.3	22.4	22.6	22.8	22.2	22.5	22.4	21.6	21.6	21.9	22.1
1998	21.7	21.9	22.1	22.7	22.9	23.6	23.5	23.3	23.4	23.6	23.8	24.0	23.0
1999	23.5	24.0	23.9	24.5	24.8	24.9	25.1	25.3	25.4	25.1	25.5	25.4	24.8
2000	25.5	25.3	25.6	25.1	25.3	25.5	25.5	25.6	25.9	25.3	25.4	25.6	25.5
2001	25.2	25.3	25.1	24.9	25.1	25.1	25.0	24.9	24.8	24.6	24.8	25.0	24.9
2002	24.6	24.6	24.5	24.2	24.6	24.5	24.4	24.7	24.4	24.4	24.6	24.7	24.5
2003	24.4	24.9	24.8	24.5	25.0	25.0	24.9	25.0	25.1	25.1	25.1	24.9	24.9

Employment by Industry: Florida—*Continued*

(Numbers in thousands. Not seasonally adjusted.)

Industry	January	February	March	April	May	June	July	August	September	October	November	December	Annual Average
ORLANDO—*Continued*													
Financial activities													
1990	39.8	40.5	40.7	39.9	39.8	39.9	39.9	40.0	39.9	39.4	39.3	39.5	39.8
1991	39.5	39.7	39.2	39.9	40.3	40.4	40.5	40.7	40.4	40.0	39.9	39.9	40.0
1992	40.2	40.4	40.7	40.8	41.1	41.1	41.4	41.7	41.2	42.2	42.4	42.4	41.3
1993	42.1	42.7	42.9	43.3	43.7	43.9	44.3	44.4	44.1	44.6	45.0	45.4	43.8
1994	45.6	45.6	45.9	45.9	45.7	45.9	46.0	45.8	45.9	45.6	45.9	46.2	45.8
1995	46.0	46.8	47.0	46.2	46.5	46.9	46.8	47.6	47.5	46.8	47.0	47.2	46.8
1996	46.4	46.9	47.4	46.9	47.0	47.3	47.3	47.6	47.4	47.0	46.9	47.6	47.1
1997	46.7	47.2	47.6	49.0	49.1	49.1	49.5	49.3	49.6	49.3	49.6	50.2	48.8
1998	49.2	49.9	50.5	50.0	50.3	51.1	51.3	51.3	51.2	51.2	51.4	51.6	50.7
1999	51.1	51.8	52.2	53.4	53.3	53.5	54.0	54.3	53.7	53.9	54.0	54.7	53.3
2000	54.1	54.5	55.0	54.0	54.4	54.9	54.4	54.5	54.5	54.1	54.3	54.7	54.5
2001	53.3	53.4	53.7	54.4	54.4	54.9	54.7	54.9	54.6	53.9	54.0	54.3	54.2
2002	53.6	53.8	54.3	53.8	54.2	54.6	54.9	55.0	55.2	55.4	55.8	56.4	54.8
2003	56.0	56.4	56.7	56.4	56.4	57.0	57.0	57.5	57.5	57.9	58.1	58.1	57.1
Professional and business services													
1990	64.2	65.1	66.2	68.1	68.5	69.4	69.6	70.1	69.6	68.1	69.2	68.7	68.0
1991	68.6	69.1	69.5	69.1	69.1	69.2	69.1	68.9	69.3	70.3	71.4	71.1	69.5
1992	73.1	73.5	74.7	74.0	74.7	74.9	74.2	74.6	75.3	75.6	76.1	77.0	74.8
1993	79.5	80.1	80.4	84.3	85.9	85.6	84.5	86.2	86.4	86.2	86.5	87.3	84.4
1994	86.5	88.6	90.0	92.5	93.1	93.5	92.5	92.5	93.2	92.8	93.7	94.7	91.9
1995	96.2	98.8	99.8	98.8	100.4	100.9	100.2	100.8	102.4	102.1	103.7	104.6	100.7
1996	97.0	100.2	101.7	100.4	101.6	102.6	103.1	105.1	106.6	107.1	108.9	108.9	103.6
1997	108.2	110.7	110.0	107.9	109.3	109.8	109.4	111.7	112.2	111.7	113.4	115.2	110.7
1998	114.4	118.0	118.6	118.0	118.2	118.8	120.5	121.6	123.0	125.6	126.6	125.8	120.7
1999	123.3	125.8	127.8	130.0	130.2	132.3	131.1	132.7	132.7	133.5	135.6	136.5	131.0
2000	136.1	139.5	142.0	141.7	143.9	146.8	146.7	148.8	152.6	154.9	156.6	157.4	147.3
2001	154.7	157.3	159.2	156.5	157.3	155.0	154.3	154.6	154.1	153.3	152.3	152.0	155.0
2002	149.6	152.6	154.5	153.0	152.2	150.8	151.1	150.0	149.9	151.6	152.7	153.0	151.8
2003	150.7	150.3	150.2	153.8	154.2	154.7	155.9	155.8	156.0	156.2	157.4	156.9	154.3
Educational and health services													
1990	45.9	46.8	46.9	47.4	47.9	48.3	47.9	48.5	48.7	49.9	50.3	50.2	48.2
1991	50.1	50.4	50.7	50.7	51.2	51.4	50.9	51.4	51.9	52.6	52.8	53.2	51.4
1992	53.8	54.5	55.4	55.3	55.6	55.5	55.5	56.0	56.6	56.7	56.9	57.3	55.7
1993	56.0	56.9	57.5	60.0	60.4	60.5	59.8	60.2	61.0	61.6	61.9	62.5	59.8
1994	63.0	63.7	64.1	65.4	65.8	66.1	65.8	66.3	67.0	67.9	68.7	69.1	66.0
1995	69.2	69.9	70.5	70.3	70.5	71.0	68.8	69.5	70.5	70.9	72.0	72.6	70.4
1996	72.0	72.6	72.9	73.2	73.8	74.0	73.9	74.5	75.0	74.7	74.7	74.9	73.8
1997	76.1	76.7	77.7	77.7	78.3	78.6	78.5	79.2	80.2	80.9	81.6	81.9	78.9
1998	82.0	82.9	83.8	82.5	82.7	82.4	82.3	82.8	83.1	83.7	83.6	83.6	82.9
1999	81.9	82.5	83.0	82.7	82.9	82.7	83.4	84.0	84.3	84.6	84.7	84.7	83.5
2000	84.1	84.4	84.9	85.8	86.4	86.0	85.1	85.8	86.4	85.9	85.7	86.1	85.6
2001	84.2	85.0	85.6	86.3	86.7	86.8	86.4	87.6	88.3	88.8	89.1	89.2	86.9
2002	86.9	87.8	88.1	88.9	89.3	88.8	88.6	89.9	90.5	90.9	91.3	91.4	89.4
2003	91.5	92.0	92.1	92.6	93.3	93.1	93.1	94.0	94.8	95.3	95.1	95.2	93.5
Leisure and hospitality													
1990	118.1	122.8	126.2	124.7	126.1	129.9	130.9	129.6	125.8	123.6	124.4	125.0	125.5
1991	117.0	119.5	121.9	119.7	120.4	122.8	121.7	121.1	118.6	118.8	119.6	121.2	120.1
1992	117.9	120.2	123.1	125.0	125.2	128.0	128.6	128.4	126.3	124.1	125.6	126.3	124.8
1993	124.5	127.2	129.5	131.0	132.1	133.6	129.9	129.9	128.8	124.8	124.5	126.1	128.4
1994	127.4	128.7	131.2	133.2	133.8	135.4	132.8	133.8	132.9	128.9	130.4	132.4	131.7
1995	130.1	133.6	137.0	136.0	137.0	141.9	139.5	139.4	139.0	136.2	138.1	141.0	137.4
1996	140.5	142.9	146.2	147.2	147.5	152.4	148.2	149.4	149.7	148.9	149.8	152.7	147.9
1997	151.6	155.7	158.3	157.2	158.2	160.6	159.2	161.4	162.4	162.4	163.7	165.9	159.7
1998	163.1	165.5	166.9	166.9	167.3	169.9	168.9	170.7	171.1	167.5	168.3	169.6	167.9
1999	167.1	173.0	174.9	177.6	179.0	183.3	180.1	179.7	179.5	174.7	175.9	177.5	176.9
2000	173.6	177.4	179.4	178.6	177.3	180.5	178.0	176.4	175.6	174.8	175.4	176.4	177.0
2001	172.7	175.9	177.1	174.6	175.4	176.6	172.4	171.0	170.0	162.6	159.9	159.2	170.6
2002	156.2	161.3	164.6	164.7	166.0	170.7	168.0	166.4	164.7	164.4	165.5	166.9	165.0
2003	163.9	166.3	169.1	170.6	171.2	173.8	171.6	170.1	169.9	169.9	170.5	172.2	169.9
Other services													
1990	23.7	24.0	24.4	24.6	24.6	24.9	24.8	24.9	24.7	24.5	24.5	24.6	24.5
1991	24.3	24.5	24.5	24.7	25.1	25.6	25.6	25.7	25.9	25.8	25.9	26.1	25.3
1992	26.3	26.4	26.5	26.4	26.8	27.1	27.2	27.2	27.1	27.2	27.2	27.3	26.8
1993	27.3	27.7	27.6	28.7	28.6	29.1	29.0	28.9	29.1	29.2	29.2	29.3	28.6
1994	29.1	29.4	29.6	29.8	29.9	30.2	30.3	30.1	30.1	30.2	30.4	30.7	29.9
1995	30.6	30.7	31.1	30.9	31.0	31.6	31.5	31.8	32.0	32.2	32.3	32.5	31.5
1996	32.5	33.0	33.3	33.5	33.8	34.1	33.7	33.8	34.1	34.1	34.4	34.6	33.7
1997	34.4	34.5	34.9	34.8	35.1	35.3	35.1	35.1	35.4	35.4	35.4	35.5	35.0
1998	35.4	35.4	35.5	35.9	36.0	36.6	36.7	36.5	36.6	37.1	37.1	37.5	36.3
1999	37.5	37.8	38.2	37.6	37.7	38.2	37.7	37.6	37.9	38.6	38.8	39.1	38.1
2000	39.3	39.5	39.5	39.9	40.0	40.1	39.4	39.2	39.4	40.0	39.7	39.8	39.7
2001	39.9	40.6	41.2	41.5	42.2	42.7	42.8	43.0	43.5	43.5	43.9	44.3	42.4
2002	44.5	44.9	45.1	44.7	45.1	45.3	45.4	45.7	45.9	45.9	46.1	45.9	45.4
2003	45.7	46.0	46.1	45.6	45.9	46.3	45.9	46.2	45.8	46.7	46.8	46.6	46.1

Employment by Industry: Florida—*Continued*

(Numbers in thousands. Not seasonally adjusted.)

Industry	January	February	March	April	May	June	July	August	September	October	November	December	Annual Average
ORLANDO—*Continued*													
Government													
1990	71.6	73.0	73.6	73.8	75.1	73.5	67.5	65.9	74.9	76.2	77.0	76.6	73.2
1991	76.0	77.1	77.6	77.2	77.9	77.0	69.8	68.6	76.6	78.2	78.6	78.6	76.1
1992	77.7	78.0	80.2	78.3	78.4	77.5	70.1	68.8	77.1	77.9	78.0	78.4	76.7
1993	76.6	77.9	78.6	78.9	78.4	77.9	71.3	70.7	78.9	79.9	80.1	80.7	77.4
1994	79.2	80.2	80.6	81.0	80.5	79.7	72.3	71.7	81.4	82.1	84.6	81.6	79.5
1995	79.9	80.8	81.4	81.4	80.6	80.0	72.4	72.0	81.5	81.4	82.0	82.2	79.6
1996	80.6	82.2	84.2	83.0	82.9	81.6	73.7	73.9	84.0	83.8	84.7	84.8	81.6
1997	83.9	84.6	84.6	84.1	84.9	83.9	75.9	76.1	85.9	87.3	87.6	88.4	83.9
1998	86.4	87.7	88.4	88.8	88.4	87.0	79.0	77.2	88.6	89.4	89.7	90.4	86.7
1999	88.2	89.8	90.5	91.1	90.8	89.9	80.9	79.3	91.0	92.0	92.3	92.7	89.0
2000	91.6	93.3	93.8	93.6	95.8	84.4	82.5	91.7	92.7	93.6	94.1	94.7	91.8
2001	93.6	95.7	97.4	97.6	97.4	87.7	85.6	95.7	97.1	99.1	100.0	100.3	95.6
2002	100.1	101.1	101.2	101.8	102.5	91.7	89.8	101.4	103.0	104.5	105.1	105.5	100.6
2003	104.4	105.1	105.2	105.6	106.1	94.7	92.8	103.7	104.8	106.3	106.8	106.3	103.5
Federal government													
1990	10.1	10.0	10.1	10.3	11.4	10.8	10.8	10.3	10.2	10.2	10.2	10.5	10.4
1991	10.3	10.2	10.2	10.1	10.1	10.2	10.3	10.2	10.3	10.3	10.4	10.8	10.2
1992	10.5	10.4	10.4	10.4	10.3	10.5	10.5	10.5	10.5	10.6	10.6	11.3	10.5
1993	10.8	10.7	10.8	10.8	10.9	10.9	11.0	11.0	11.0	11.0	11.0	11.4	10.9
1994	11.0	10.9	10.9	10.9	10.8	10.8	10.6	10.6	10.6	10.3	10.3	10.7	10.7
1995	10.0	9.9	9.9	9.8	9.7	9.6	9.7	9.7	9.6	9.6	9.6	9.9	9.7
1996	9.2	9.1	9.1	9.2	9.2	9.2	9.2	9.3	9.3	9.3	9.6	10.1	9.3
1997	9.5	9.5	9.5	9.5	9.5	9.4	9.4	9.5	9.5	9.5	9.6	10.1	9.5
1998	9.4	9.4	9.4	9.5	9.5	9.4	9.4	9.4	9.3	9.6	9.6	10.0	9.4
1999	9.4	9.4	9.6	9.6	9.5	9.5	9.4	9.4	9.6	9.7	9.7	10.0	9.6
2000	9.7	9.8	9.9	10.2	12.4	10.4	10.5	10.0	9.7	9.8	9.8	10.2	10.2
2001	10.3	10.2	10.2	10.2	10.1	10.2	10.2	10.3	10.3	10.3	10.4	10.6	10.2
2002	10.0	10.0	10.0	10.0	9.8	9.9	10.0	10.7	10.7	11.0	11.1	11.6	10.4
2003	11.3	11.2	11.2	11.2	11.1	11.1	11.1	11.1	11.0	11.0	11.0	10.9	11.1
State government													
1990	10.3	11.1	11.2	11.1	11.2	11.0	10.8	10.9	11.5	11.5	11.9	11.9	11.2
1991	11.2	11.7	11.8	11.9	12.2	11.3	11.3	11.3	11.9	12.1	12.3	12.1	11.7
1992	11.5	12.0	12.0	12.0	12.2	11.2	11.3	11.1	11.8	12.4	12.3	12.2	11.8
1993	11.5	12.3	12.5	12.6	12.0	11.8	11.9	12.5	12.5	13.0	12.9	12.9	12.3
1994	12.1	12.8	13.0	13.2	12.7	12.3	12.5	12.3	13.5	13.6	13.6	13.6	12.9
1995	13.0	13.5	13.8	13.6	12.9	12.4	12.3	12.3	13.4	13.4	13.4	13.3	13.1
1996	12.2	13.2	13.5	13.4	13.4	12.4	12.5	12.6	13.3	13.6	13.7	13.7	13.1
1997	13.8	13.8	13.9	14.0	13.9	13.0	13.1	13.2	13.8	14.3	14.4	14.3	13.7
1998	14.0	14.4	14.5	14.5	14.4	13.5	13.6	13.3	14.2	14.5	14.6	14.8	14.1
1999	13.9	14.6	14.8	14.8	14.7	13.7	13.7	13.7	14.6	14.9	15.0	15.1	14.5
2000	14.3	15.0	15.1	15.1	15.1	14.2	13.9	14.1	14.9	15.3	15.4	15.6	14.8
2001	14.4	15.5	15.7	15.7	15.7	14.8	14.5	14.5	15.4	15.8	16.0	15.8	15.3
2002	15.0	15.7	15.6	15.6	16.0	14.6	14.6	14.8	15.8	16.1	16.4	16.2	15.5
2003	15.9	16.3	16.4	16.4	16.8	15.2	15.2	15.2	16.1	16.8	16.7	16.7	16.1
Local government													
1990	51.2	51.9	52.3	52.4	52.5	51.7	45.9	44.7	53.2	54.5	54.9	54.2	51.6
1991	54.5	55.2	55.6	55.2	55.6	55.5	48.2	47.1	54.4	55.8	55.9	55.7	54.0
1992	55.7	55.6	57.8	55.9	55.9	55.8	48.3	47.2	54.8	54.9	55.1	54.9	54.3
1993	54.3	54.9	55.3	55.5	55.5	55.2	48.4	47.2	55.4	55.9	56.2	56.4	54.1
1994	56.1	56.5	56.7	56.9	57.0	56.6	49.2	48.8	57.3	58.2	60.7	57.3	55.9
1995	56.9	57.4	57.7	58.0	58.0	58.0	50.4	50.0	58.5	58.4	59.0	59.0	56.7
1996	59.2	59.9	61.6	60.4	60.3	60.0	52.0	52.0	61.4	60.9	61.4	61.0	59.1
1997	60.6	61.3	61.2	60.6	61.5	61.5	53.4	53.4	62.6	63.5	63.6	64.0	60.6
1998	63.0	63.9	64.5	64.8	64.5	64.1	56.0	54.5	65.1	65.3	65.5	65.6	63.0
1999	64.9	65.8	66.1	66.7	66.6	66.7	57.8	56.2	66.8	67.4	67.6	67.6	65.0
2000	67.6	68.5	68.8	68.3	68.3	59.8	58.1	67.6	68.1	68.5	68.9	68.9	66.8
2001	68.9	70.0	71.5	71.7	71.6	62.7	60.9	70.9	71.4	73.0	73.6	73.9	70.0
2002	75.1	75.4	75.6	76.2	76.7	67.2	65.2	75.9	76.5	77.4	77.6	77.7	74.7
2003	77.2	77.6	77.6	78.0	78.2	68.4	66.5	77.4	77.7	78.5	79.1	78.7	76.2
SARASOTA													
Total nonfarm													
1990	181.8	184.9	185.2	184.7	184.5	183.4	178.8	178.6	182.5	183.3	186.0	186.2	183.3
1991	183.4	184.3	185.0	183.5	183.2	180.9	176.5	176.6	178.2	178.7	182.1	184.2	181.3
1992	184.0	185.1	188.0	186.5	185.8	183.9	179.6	179.0	182.3	184.3	188.0	190.2	184.7
1993	187.5	189.5	190.6	192.5	191.8	191.8	188.1	188.3	191.3	194.8	197.9	201.4	192.1
1994	197.3	198.9	201.8	202.5	200.6	200.2	198.0	198.6	202.0	202.3	209.0	211.8	201.9
1995	204.6	207.2	209.3	208.5	208.1	208.6	205.1	206.1	210.1	213.3	218.2	222.3	210.1
1996	218.3	221.1	226.8	226.4	227.3	227.7	228.4	229.8	236.1	235.5	242.4	246.3	230.5
1997	241.0	243.2	246.6	246.3	245.0	245.4	239.4	239.6	242.4	242.1	243.9	245.9	243.4
1998	244.1	246.2	247.8	246.5	246.3	244.9	241.4	241.3	244.8	250.7	253.6	257.0	247.0
1999	254.5	259.5	262.2	264.4	261.8	261.3	256.6	255.8	258.0	260.3	263.4	267.0	260.4
2000	266.0	268.6	271.6	272.9	272.9	272.4	268.6	272.1	272.2	274.4	277.4	279.7	272.4
2001	258.9	262.5	264.8	263.9	264.8	262.0	259.1	262.9	262.8	267.6	272.1	275.3	264.7
2002	269.5	273.5	277.4	279.4	278.0	274.8	272.6	276.4	276.9	278.3	280.3	282.5	276.6
2003	278.2	280.1	281.9	283.0	283.6	281.0	279.8	283.3	284.6	285.7	289.1	292.3	283.6

Employment by Industry: Florida—*Continued*

(Numbers in thousands. Not seasonally adjusted.)

Industry	January	February	March	April	May	June	July	August	September	October	November	December	Annual Average
SARASOTA—*Continued*													
Total private													
1990	159.5	161.3	162.4	161.4	160.6	159.6	156.9	157.4	157.2	158.4	160.3	162.3	159.7
1991	159.7	160.7	161.1	159.9	159.4	157.4	154.7	155.1	154.8	155.3	158.4	160.4	158.0
1992	160.3	161.4	162.2	162.7	162.0	160.1	157.7	157.4	158.1	159.8	162.9	166.2	160.9
1993	164.0	165.7	166.4	168.5	167.7	167.9	166.2	166.5	167.5	170.5	173.4	176.5	168.4
1994	173.0	174.1	176.8	176.8	175.6	175.6	175.4	176.1	176.6	177.5	181.8	186.4	177.1
1995	179.8	182.0	183.9	183.3	182.8	183.3	182.3	183.4	185.3	191.1	195.6	199.4	186.0
1996	196.0	198.4	201.6	203.6	204.4	204.8	207.7	209.5	212.5	211.7	217.9	222.6	207.5
1997	217.7	219.8	223.0	222.6	221.3	221.8	218.1	218.6	219.1	218.5	219.9	221.8	220.1
1998	220.4	222.3	223.7	222.3	222.2	221.0	219.7	219.9	221.1	226.7	229.3	232.4	223.4
1999	230.4	235.1	237.7	239.9	237.5	237.2	234.9	234.6	234.4	236.3	239.4	242.6	236.6
2000	241.7	244.1	247.0	248.2	247.5	249.9	246.4	247.8	248.1	250.0	252.7	254.8	248.2
2001	234.5	237.8	239.9	239.2	239.9	239.5	236.8	238.3	238.1	242.4	246.5	249.5	240.2
2002	244.2	247.8	251.6	253.7	252.1	251.4	249.4	250.8	251.1	252.4	254.1	256.3	251.2
2003	252.0	253.7	255.4	256.5	257.0	257.0	256.0	257.0	258.2	259.1	262.3	265.3	257.5
Goods-producing													
1990	31.4	31.1	31.2	30.4	30.3	30.2	29.6	29.7	30.0	29.0	29.1	29.1	30.0
1991	27.6	27.3	27.0	26.8	26.7	26.4	26.3	26.4	26.4	26.6	26.4	26.3	26.6
1992	26.2	25.7	25.6	25.2	25.5	25.3	25.0	25.0	25.4	25.4	25.4	25.7	25.4
1993	25.3	25.5	25.5	25.2	25.3	25.7	25.5	25.8	26.1	26.3	26.6	27.1	25.8
1994	26.9	26.8	26.9	27.7	27.8	28.2	28.4	28.6	28.7	28.7	28.9	29.3	28.0
1995	28.4	28.5	28.7	28.6	29.0	29.2	29.1	29.5	29.9	29.9	30.1	30.2	29.2
1996	30.7	31.1	31.2	31.7	31.8	32.2	33.2	33.5	33.8	33.5	34.1	34.3	32.5
1997	33.3	33.4	33.4	33.8	33.6	33.8	33.9	34.2	34.3	34.1	34.2	34.4	33.8
1998	34.7	35.1	35.3	34.8	34.8	35.0	35.3	35.3	35.8	36.5	36.7	36.9	35.5
1999	36.6	37.8	38.9	39.0	38.8	39.2	39.6	39.2	39.0	39.6	39.4	39.9	38.9
2000	38.5	38.7	39.1	39.9	39.5	39.4	38.8	38.3	38.3	38.0	37.9	38.0	38.7
2001	37.1	36.9	37.0	36.9	37.1	37.5	37.3	37.5	37.7	38.1	38.3	38.4	37.4
2002	38.1	38.4	38.3	38.1	38.3	38.3	38.2	38.7	38.4	38.3	38.3	38.5	38.3
2003	37.7	38.2	38.0	37.6	37.7	37.9	37.7	38.2	38.8	39.0	39.2	38.9	38.2
Construction and mining													
1990	13.2	12.9	13.0	12.4	12.4	12.6	12.4	12.5	12.6	12.2	12.2	12.1	12.5
1991	11.5	11.4	11.2	10.7	10.7	10.5	10.5	10.7	10.6	10.5	10.4	10.4	10.7
1992	10.2	9.6	9.7	9.1	9.4	9.4	9.3	9.3	9.6	9.6	9.6	9.7	9.5
1993	9.3	9.3	9.3	9.3	9.3	9.4	9.5	9.5	9.6	9.7	9.9	10.2	9.5
1994	9.8	9.7	9.7	9.8	9.8	10.0	10.0	10.1	10.1	10.1	10.1	10.2	9.9
1995	9.8	9.8	9.8	9.7	10.0	10.2	10.3	10.6	10.9	10.9	11.1	11.2	10.3
1996	11.9	12.0	12.1	12.1	12.0	12.4	13.1	13.1	13.3	13.0	13.2	13.2	12.6
1997	12.8	12.7	12.8	13.0	12.9	13.2	13.2	13.3	13.4	13.5	13.4	13.6	13.1
1998	13.8	13.8	13.9	13.7	13.6	13.9	14.4	14.5	14.8	15.2	15.1	15.3	14.3
1999	15.0	15.5	16.0	16.0	16.0	16.3	16.7	16.7	16.6	16.8	16.8	17.0	16.2
2000	16.5	16.8	17.0	17.4	17.4	17.5	17.3	17.2	17.1	17.2	17.2	17.4	17.2
2001	16.5	16.6	16.7	16.6	16.8	17.1	17.1	17.4	17.5	18.1	18.3	18.2	17.2
2002	18.2	18.4	18.4	18.3	18.6	18.7	18.7	19.0	18.9	19.2	19.3	19.5	18.8
2003	19.0	19.5	19.5	19.4	19.5	19.6	19.7	19.9	20.2	20.1	20.4	20.3	19.8
Manufacturing													
1990	18.2	18.2	18.2	18.0	17.9	17.6	17.2	17.2	17.4	16.8	16.9	17.0	17.5
1991	16.1	15.9	15.8	16.1	16.0	15.9	15.8	15.7	15.8	16.1	16.0	15.9	15.9
1992	16.0	16.1	15.9	16.1	16.1	15.9	15.7	15.7	15.8	15.8	15.8	16.0	15.9
1993	16.0	16.2	16.2	15.9	16.0	16.3	16.0	16.3	16.5	16.6	16.7	16.9	16.3
1994	17.1	17.1	17.2	17.9	18.0	18.2	18.4	18.5	18.6	18.6	18.8	19.1	18.1
1995	18.6	18.7	18.9	18.9	19.0	19.0	18.8	18.9	19.0	19.0	19.0	19.0	18.9
1996	18.8	19.1	19.1	19.6	19.8	19.8	20.1	20.4	20.5	20.5	20.9	21.1	19.9
1997	20.5	20.7	20.6	20.8	20.7	20.6	20.7	20.9	20.9	20.6	20.8	20.8	20.7
1998	20.9	21.3	21.4	21.1	21.2	21.1	20.9	20.8	21.0	21.3	21.6	21.6	21.1
1999	21.6	22.3	22.9	23.0	22.8	22.9	22.9	22.5	22.4	22.8	22.6	22.9	22.6
2000	22.0	21.9	22.1	22.5	22.1	21.9	21.5	21.1	21.2	20.8	20.7	20.6	21.5
2001	20.6	20.3	20.3	20.3	20.3	20.4	20.2	20.1	20.2	20.0	20.0	20.2	20.2
2002	19.9	20.0	19.9	19.8	19.7	19.6	19.5	19.7	19.5	19.1	19.0	19.0	19.6
2003	18.7	18.7	18.5	18.2	18.2	18.3	18.0	18.3	18.6	18.9	18.8	18.6	18.5
Service-providing													
1990	150.4	153.8	154.0	154.3	154.2	153.2	149.2	148.9	152.5	154.3	156.9	157.1	153.2
1991	155.8	157.0	158.0	156.7	156.5	154.5	150.2	150.2	151.8	152.1	155.7	157.9	154.7
1992	157.8	159.4	162.4	161.3	160.3	158.6	154.6	154.0	156.9	158.9	162.6	164.5	159.2
1993	162.2	164.0	165.1	167.3	166.5	166.1	162.6	162.5	165.2	168.5	171.3	174.3	166.3
1994	170.4	172.1	174.9	174.8	172.8	172.0	169.6	170.0	173.3	173.6	180.1	182.5	173.8
1995	176.2	178.7	180.6	179.9	179.1	179.4	176.0	176.6	180.2	183.4	188.1	192.1	180.8
1996	187.6	190.0	195.6	194.7	195.5	195.5	195.2	196.3	202.3	202.0	208.3	212.0	197.9
1997	207.7	209.8	213.2	212.5	211.4	211.6	205.5	205.4	208.1	208.0	209.7	211.5	209.5
1998	209.4	211.1	212.5	211.7	211.5	209.9	206.1	206.0	209.0	214.2	216.9	220.1	211.5
1999	217.9	221.7	223.3	225.4	223.0	222.1	217.0	216.6	219.0	220.7	224.0	227.1	221.4
2000	227.5	229.9	232.5	233.0	233.4	233.0	229.8	233.8	233.9	236.4	239.5	241.7	233.7
2001	221.8	225.6	227.8	227.0	227.7	224.5	221.8	225.4	225.1	229.5	233.8	236.9	227.2
2002	231.4	235.1	239.1	241.3	239.7	236.5	234.4	237.7	238.5	240.0	242.0	244.0	238.3
2003	240.5	241.9	243.9	245.4	245.9	243.1	242.1	245.1	245.8	246.7	249.9	253.4	245.3

Employment by Industry: Florida—*Continued*

(Numbers in thousands. Not seasonally adjusted.)

Industry	January	February	March	April	May	June	July	August	September	October	November	December	Annual Average
SARASOTA—*Continued*													
Trade, transportation, and utilities													
1990	37.6	37.6	37.7	37.7	37.4	36.9	36.3	36.3	36.2	37.0	38.0	38.9	37.3
1991	37.4	37.3	37.2	36.5	36.2	35.8	34.7	34.7	34.9	35.4	36.8	37.9	36.2
1992	36.6	36.5	36.5	36.1	35.8	35.5	34.8	34.8	35.1	35.8	37.4	38.7	36.1
1993	36.6	36.8	36.7	36.9	36.8	36.5	36.1	35.8	36.2	37.2	38.2	39.5	36.9
1994	37.9	38.1	38.4	39.1	38.9	38.7	38.3	38.7	39.0	39.6	41.4	42.8	39.2
1995	40.0	40.1	40.3	39.8	39.5	39.6	39.0	39.2	39.8	40.9	42.4	43.3	40.3
1996	41.0	41.2	41.4	41.2	41.9	41.4	42.0	42.5	43.1	44.2	46.4	47.8	42.8
1997	45.0	44.9	44.8	44.5	44.3	43.9	43.9	44.0	44.3	45.0	46.2	47.2	44.8
1998	45.7	46.3	46.4	45.8	45.7	44.9	44.7	44.6	44.7	46.1	47.5	48.5	45.9
1999	45.8	47.2	48.3	48.1	47.5	47.2	47.2	46.7	46.7	47.5	48.8	50.2	47.6
2000	48.6	48.8	48.8	49.4	49.1	48.8	47.7	48.0	47.9	48.6	50.3	51.1	48.9
2001	47.7	47.8	48.2	48.1	47.7	47.2	46.5	46.5	46.4	47.5	48.9	49.9	47.7
2002	48.3	48.0	48.3	48.0	47.7	47.4	46.8	47.0	47.3	47.5	48.8	49.9	47.9
2003	48.0	47.6	48.0	47.9	47.6	47.2	47.1	47.3	47.7	48.5	49.6	50.8	48.1
Wholesale trade													
1990	4.4	4.3	4.3	4.5	4.5	4.5	4.5	4.5	4.5	4.5	4.5	4.5	4.4
1991	4.5	4.4	4.4	4.2	4.2	4.2	4.2	4.2	4.2	4.2	4.3	4.2	4.2
1992	4.2	4.1	4.1	4.1	4.1	4.1	4.1	4.1	4.0	4.1	4.3	4.3	4.1
1993	4.2	4.3	4.2	4.4	4.4	4.5	4.5	4.5	4.5	4.8	4.8	4.9	4.5
1994	4.8	4.7	4.7	4.9	4.9	4.9	4.8	4.9	5.0	5.1	5.3	5.3	4.9
1995	5.0	5.1	5.1	5.0	5.0	5.0	5.0	4.9	5.0	5.1	5.3	5.2	5.0
1996	5.2	5.4	5.4	5.3	5.5	5.4	5.6	5.7	5.8	5.9	6.3	6.3	5.6
1997	6.0	5.9	5.9	5.9	6.0	5.9	5.9	5.9	6.0	6.0	6.1	6.2	5.9
1998	6.0	6.1	6.2	6.5	6.5	6.5	6.4	6.3	6.4	6.7	6.8	6.7	6.4
1999	6.2	6.4	6.5	6.8	6.9	6.6	6.7	6.6	6.7	6.9	7.0	7.0	6.6
2000	6.9	6.9	7.0	7.0	7.0	6.8	6.8	6.8	6.8	6.9	7.1	6.9	6.9
2001	6.6	6.6	6.7	7.0	7.0	6.9	6.8	6.9	6.8	7.1	7.2	7.2	6.8
2002	7.1	7.1	7.1	7.2	7.2	7.2	7.2	7.3	7.4	7.5	7.5	7.5	7.3
2003	7.2	7.2	7.4	7.4	7.4	7.3	7.3	7.3	7.4	7.5	7.5	7.5	7.4
Retail trade													
1990	30.2	30.2	30.3	30.2	29.9	29.4	28.9	28.9	28.7	29.5	30.5	31.2	29.8
1991	29.9	29.9	29.8	29.3	29.1	28.6	27.6	27.6	27.7	28.3	29.6	30.6	29.0
1992	29.3	29.4	29.3	29.0	28.7	28.4	27.9	27.9	28.3	28.8	30.1	31.4	29.0
1993	29.6	29.6	29.6	29.6	29.5	29.1	28.6	28.3	28.6	29.4	30.4	31.5	29.4
1994	30.3	30.5	30.8	31.2	31.1	30.9	30.7	31.0	31.1	31.4	33.0	34.3	31.3
1995	32.0	32.0	32.1	31.8	31.5	31.5	30.9	31.2	31.7	32.7	33.9	34.9	32.1
1996	32.8	32.7	32.9	32.8	33.3	32.9	33.3	33.7	34.1	35.2	37.0	38.3	34.0
1997	35.9	35.9	35.7	35.5	35.2	34.9	34.8	35.1	35.1	35.8	36.9	37.7	35.7
1998	36.6	37.0	37.0	36.0	35.9	35.2	35.1	35.1	35.1	36.1	37.4	38.3	36.2
1999	36.3	37.4	38.3	37.7	37.1	37.1	37.1	36.7	36.6	37.0	38.3	39.7	37.4
2000	38.3	38.5	38.4	39.0	38.8	38.7	37.6	37.8	37.7	38.4	39.9	40.7	38.7
2001	37.9	37.8	38.1	37.7	37.4	37.0	36.4	36.4	36.3	37.1	38.4	39.3	37.4
2002	38.0	37.7	38.0	37.6	37.3	37.0	36.4	36.6	36.7	36.9	38.1	39.1	37.5
2003	37.6	37.3	37.5	37.4	37.1	36.8	36.7	36.9	37.2	37.9	39.0	40.1	37.6
Transportation and utilities													
1990	3.0	3.1	3.1	3.0	3.0	3.0	2.9	2.9	3.0	3.0	3.0	3.2	3.0
1991	3.0	3.0	3.0	3.0	2.9	3.0	2.9	2.9	3.0	2.9	2.9	3.1	2.9
1992	3.1	3.0	3.1	3.0	3.0	3.0	2.8	2.8	2.8	2.9	3.0	3.0	2.9
1993	2.8	2.9	2.9	2.9	2.9	2.9	3.0	3.0	3.1	3.0	3.0	3.1	2.9
1994	2.8	2.9	2.9	3.0	2.9	2.9	2.8	2.8	2.9	3.1	3.1	3.2	2.9
1995	3.0	3.0	3.1	3.0	3.0	3.1	3.1	3.1	3.1	3.1	3.2	3.2	3.0
1996	3.0	3.1	3.1	3.1	3.1	3.1	3.1	3.1	3.2	3.1	3.1	3.2	3.1
1997	3.1	3.1	3.2	3.1	3.1	3.1	3.2	3.0	3.2	3.2	3.2	3.3	3.1
1998	3.1	3.2	3.2	3.3	3.3	3.2	3.2	3.2	3.2	3.3	3.3	3.5	3.2
1999	3.3	3.4	3.5	3.6	3.5	3.5	3.4	3.4	3.4	3.6	3.5	3.5	3.4
2000	3.4	3.4	3.4	3.4	3.3	3.3	3.3	3.4	3.4	3.3	3.3	3.5	3.4
2001	3.2	3.4	3.4	3.4	3.3	3.3	3.3	3.2	3.3	3.3	3.3	3.4	3.3
2002	3.2	3.2	3.2	3.2	3.2	3.2	3.2	3.1	3.2	3.1	3.2	3.3	3.2
2003	3.2	3.1	3.1	3.1	3.1	3.1	3.1	3.1	3.1	3.1	3.1	3.2	3.1
Information													
1990	3.7	3.7	3.7	3.6	3.6	3.7	3.6	3.6	3.6	3.5	3.5	3.5	3.6
1991	3.4	3.4	3.4	3.5	3.5	3.5	3.4	3.4	3.4	3.4	3.4	3.5	3.4
1992	3.6	3.5	3.5	3.4	3.4	3.4	3.6	3.5	3.5	3.4	3.4	3.5	3.4
1993	3.4	3.4	3.5	3.5	3.5	3.4	3.4	3.4	3.4	3.4	3.5	3.5	3.4
1994	3.2	3.2	3.2	3.3	3.3	3.4	3.4	3.3	3.4	3.3	3.4	3.4	3.3
1995	3.4	3.3	3.4	3.4	3.4	3.5	3.5	3.5	3.5	3.5	3.5	3.6	3.4
1996	3.3	3.3	3.4	3.3	3.3	3.3	3.4	3.4	3.5	3.4	3.4	3.5	3.3
1997	3.5	3.5	3.6	3.6	3.6	3.7	3.6	3.5	3.5	3.5	3.5	3.5	3.5
1998	3.6	3.7	3.7	3.7	3.7	3.7	3.6	3.6	3.7	3.8	3.8	3.9	3.7
1999	4.0	4.2	4.2	4.3	4.3	4.4	4.3	4.3	4.3	4.2	4.2	4.3	4.2
2000	4.3	4.2	4.3	4.4	4.3	4.4	4.6	4.6	4.5	4.5	4.5	4.5	4.4
2001	4.5	4.5	4.4	4.3	4.4	4.5	4.4	4.4	4.3	4.2	4.3	4.3	4.3
2002	4.3	4.3	4.3	4.3	4.3	4.3	4.3	4.2	4.2	4.3	4.3	4.3	4.3
2003	4.3	4.3	4.3	4.2	4.3	4.3	4.3	4.3	4.3	4.3	4.3	4.3	4.3

Employment by Industry: Florida—*Continued*

(Numbers in thousands. Not seasonally adjusted.)

Industry	January	February	March	April	May	June	July	August	September	October	November	December	Annual Average
SARASOTA—*Continued*													
Financial activities													
1990	8.8	9.0	8.9	9.0	9.1	9.1	9.2	9.3	9.3	9.3	9.4	9.4	9.1
1991	9.3	9.3	9.2	9.2	9.4	9.4	9.4	9.5	9.5	9.5	9.7	9.8	9.4
1992	9.7	10.7	11.1	11.2	11.2	11.1	11.1	11.1	11.0	11.1	11.1	11.3	10.9
1993	11.1	11.1	11.1	11.0	10.9	11.0	11.0	10.9	11.0	11.1	11.1	11.3	11.0
1994	11.2	11.2	11.3	11.6	11.5	11.6	11.7	11.7	11.8	11.7	11.7	11.9	11.5
1995	11.4	11.6	11.7	11.5	11.5	11.6	11.6	11.7	11.7	11.7	11.8	12.0	11.6
1996	11.1	11.2	11.4	11.4	11.6	11.8	11.8	11.9	12.1	12.1	12.3	12.5	11.7
1997	12.3	12.3	12.4	12.5	12.4	12.4	12.3	12.2	12.2	12.1	12.2	12.2	12.2
1998	12.2	12.5	12.6	13.0	12.9	12.9	12.8	12.8	12.7	12.6	12.6	12.7	12.6
1999	12.5	12.9	13.2	13.5	13.4	13.3	13.6	13.4	13.2	13.2	13.1	13.2	13.2
2000	12.9	12.9	13.0	13.3	13.5	13.6	13.2	13.0	12.9	13.0	13.0	13.0	13.1
2001	12.9	12.9	13.0	13.1	13.1	13.3	13.2	13.3	13.3	13.4	13.6	13.7	13.2
2002	13.7	13.7	13.7	13.6	13.5	13.7	13.7	13.8	13.7	13.7	13.8	14.0	13.7
2003	13.7	13.6	13.6	13.8	13.8	13.9	13.9	14.0	14.0	13.9	13.9	13.9	13.8
Professional and business services													
1990	27.3	27.7	28.2	28.3	28.3	28.4	27.8	27.7	27.9	28.9	29.3	29.6	28.2
1991	30.6	31.4	31.6	30.4	30.9	30.4	29.7	30.1	30.0	29.8	30.4	30.6	30.4
1992	30.9	31.3	31.4	32.3	32.2	31.9	31.5	31.3	31.5	32.1	32.5	33.3	31.8
1993	33.2	33.3	33.2	35.7	36.0	36.5	36.2	36.5	36.8	38.3	38.9	39.4	36.1
1994	38.4	38.9	40.0	36.5	36.8	36.6	37.2	37.5	37.6	37.6	38.5	39.7	37.9
1995	38.8	39.7	40.1	40.7	41.1	41.5	42.1	42.5	43.2	44.2	45.5	46.3	42.1
1996	46.1	46.6	48.7	51.0	51.6	51.9	53.8	54.5	55.3	52.5	54.1	55.6	51.8
1997	55.9	57.3	59.5	59.3	59.8	61.5	59.2	59.7	59.9	58.5	57.6	57.8	58.8
1998	56.6	55.7	55.9	56.4	57.2	57.8	57.1	57.6	58.1	60.3	60.6	61.8	57.9
1999	63.5	62.2	60.0	60.9	60.6	60.6	60.1	61.6	62.3	62.6	63.5	64.1	61.8
2000	66.7	67.8	69.0	67.0	67.6	69.9	71.1	72.9	73.1	73.2	73.5	74.1	70.5
2001	...	62.7	63.4	63.2	64.9	64.7	64.2	64.9	64.6	66.7	67.5	68.3	...
2002	66.1	69.0	71.6	75.1	74.1	73.3	73.0	73.0	73.2	73.3	71.7	71.0	72.0
2003	71.5	71.9	72.2	74.8	75.7	76.7	76.9	77.5	77.6	77.4	77.3	77.9	75.6
Educational and health services													
1990	19.7	20.1	20.3	20.2	20.4	20.6	20.1	20.3	20.4	20.9	20.8	21.0	20.4
1991	21.3	21.5	21.6	21.8	21.8	21.8	21.6	21.6	21.8	21.8	22.1	22.2	21.7
1992	22.3	22.5	22.6	22.7	22.8	22.8	22.6	22.7	22.8	22.7	22.9	23.2	22.7
1993	23.0	23.2	23.4	23.6	23.7	23.8	23.5	23.5	23.9	23.8	24.1	24.3	23.6
1994	23.5	23.6	23.8	24.9	24.8	24.9	24.7	24.8	25.1	25.5	25.9	26.3	24.8
1995	26.1	26.3	26.6	26.6	26.7	26.8	26.4	26.4	27.0	29.3	29.6	29.8	27.3
1996	29.0	29.2	29.5	29.9	30.1	30.2	30.2	30.5	31.5	32.3	32.8	33.1	30.6
1997	31.4	31.7	31.9	32.4	32.0	31.9	32.2	32.2	32.5	32.7	33.0	33.2	32.2
1998	33.1	33.7	33.9	33.4	33.3	33.1	33.4	33.3	33.8	33.9	34.1	34.1	33.5
1999	33.2	34.4	35.4	35.3	35.2	35.3	34.3	34.0	34.1	34.2	34.6	34.9	34.5
2000	34.0	34.4	34.7	35.2	34.9	35.4	34.5	34.7	35.2	35.6	35.9	36.0	35.0
2001	34.1	34.5	34.7	34.4	34.3	34.6	33.9	34.1	34.5	34.4	34.6	35.0	34.4
2002	34.3	34.4	34.7	34.7	34.9	35.0	34.9	35.4	35.8	36.2	36.7	37.0	35.3
2003	36.3	36.7	37.0	36.8	37.1	36.9	36.7	36.7	37.1	36.7	37.4	37.8	36.9
Leisure and hospitality													
1990	21.8	22.9	23.1	23.1	22.4	21.6	20.7	20.7	20.1	20.1	20.4	21.0	21.4
1991	20.7	21.2	21.7	21.6	20.8	20.0	19.6	19.4	18.8	19.0	19.5	20.1	20.2
1992	21.2	21.4	21.7	21.9	21.2	20.3	19.4	19.3	19.1	19.5	20.3	20.6	20.4
1993	21.4	22.4	22.9	22.4	21.5	21.0	20.6	20.7	20.2	20.4	21.1	21.5	21.3
1994	22.1	22.6	23.5	24.0	23.0	22.7	22.1	22.1	21.6	21.7	22.5	23.3	22.6
1995	22.8	23.5	24.0	23.6	22.5	22.0	21.5	21.5	21.0	22.2	23.2	24.6	22.7
1996	25.1	26.0	26.2	25.6	24.6	24.5	23.7	23.6	23.6	24.1	25.0	25.9	24.8
1997	26.4	26.7	27.3	26.4	25.5	24.5	23.2	23.0	22.5	22.8	23.5	23.7	24.6
1998	24.3	24.9	25.5	24.9	24.3	23.4	22.6	22.7	22.2	23.3	23.8	24.1	23.8
1999	24.4	25.7	26.7	27.4	26.5	26.0	24.9	24.6	24.1	24.3	25.2	25.3	25.4
2000	25.9	26.5	27.2	28.0	27.5	27.0	25.5	25.3	25.1	25.9	26.4	26.8	26.4
2001	26.6	27.3	28.0	28.0	27.2	26.4	26.0	26.2	25.9	26.7	27.8	28.3	27.0
2002	27.6	28.1	28.9	28.0	27.4	27.5	26.9	27.1	26.8	27.3	28.6	29.6	27.8
2003	28.6	29.3	30.2	29.5	28.9	28.3	27.7	27.3	27.1	27.6	28.9	29.9	28.6
Other services													
1990	9.2	9.2	9.3	9.1	9.1	9.1	9.6	9.8	9.7	9.7	9.8	9.8	9.4
1991	9.4	9.3	9.4	10.1	10.1	10.1	10.0	10.0	10.0	9.8	10.1	10.0	9.8
1992	9.8	9.8	9.8	9.9	9.9	9.8	9.7	9.7	9.7	9.8	9.9	9.9	9.8
1993	10.0	10.0	10.1	10.2	10.0	10.0	9.9	9.9	9.9	10.0	9.9	9.9	9.9
1994	9.8	9.7	9.7	9.7	9.5	9.5	9.6	9.4	9.4	9.4	9.5	9.7	9.5
1995	8.9	9.0	9.1	9.1	9.1	9.1	9.1	9.1	9.2	9.4	9.5	9.6	9.1
1996	9.7	9.8	9.8	9.5	9.5	9.5	9.6	9.6	9.6	9.6	9.8	9.9	9.6
1997	9.9	10.0	10.1	10.1	10.1	10.1	9.8	9.8	9.9	9.8	9.7	9.8	9.9
1998	10.2	10.4	10.4	10.3	10.3	10.2	10.2	10.0	10.1	10.2	10.2	10.4	10.2
1999	10.4	10.7	11.0	11.4	11.2	11.2	10.9	10.8	10.7	10.7	10.6	10.7	10.8
2000	10.8	10.8	10.9	11.0	11.1	11.4	11.0	11.0	11.1	11.2	11.2	11.3	11.1
2001	11.0	11.2	11.2	11.2	11.2	11.3	11.3	11.4	11.4	11.4	11.5	11.6	11.3
2002	11.8	11.9	11.8	11.9	11.9	11.9	11.6	11.6	11.7	11.8	11.9	12.0	11.8
2003	11.9	12.1	12.1	11.9	11.9	11.8	11.7	11.7	11.6	11.7	11.7	11.8	11.8

Employment by Industry: Florida—*Continued*

(Numbers in thousands. Not seasonally adjusted.)

Industry	January	February	March	April	May	June	July	August	September	October	November	December	Annual Average
SARASOTA—*Continued*													
Government													
1990	22.3	23.6	22.8	23.3	23.9	23.8	21.9	21.2	25.3	24.9	25.7	23.9	23.5
1991	23.7	23.6	23.9	23.6	23.8	23.5	21.8	21.5	23.4	23.4	23.7	23.8	23.3
1992	23.7	23.7	25.8	23.8	23.8	23.8	21.9	21.6	24.2	24.5	25.1	24.0	23.8
1993	23.5	23.8	24.2	24.0	24.1	23.9	21.9	21.8	23.8	24.3	24.5	24.9	23.7
1994	24.3	24.8	25.0	25.7	25.0	24.6	22.6	22.5	25.4	24.8	27.2	25.4	24.7
1995	24.8	25.2	25.4	25.2	25.3	25.3	22.8	22.7	24.8	22.2	22.6	22.9	24.1
1996	22.3	22.7	25.2	22.8	22.9	22.9	20.7	20.3	23.6	23.8	24.5	23.7	22.9
1997	23.3	23.4	23.6	23.7	23.7	23.6	21.3	21.0	23.3	23.6	24.0	24.1	23.2
1998	23.7	23.9	24.1	24.2	24.1	23.9	21.7	21.4	23.7	24.0	24.3	24.6	23.6
1999	24.1	24.4	24.5	24.5	24.3	24.1	21.7	21.2	23.6	24.0	24.0	24.4	23.7
2000	24.3	24.5	24.6	24.7	25.4	22.5	22.2	24.3	24.1	24.4	24.7	24.9	24.2
2001	24.4	24.7	24.9	24.7	24.9	22.5	22.3	24.6	24.7	25.2	25.6	25.8	24.5
2002	25.3	25.7	25.8	25.7	25.9	23.4	23.2	25.6	25.8	25.9	26.2	26.2	25.4
2003	26.2	26.4	26.5	26.5	26.6	24.0	23.8	26.3	26.4	26.6	26.8	27.0	26.1
Federal government													
1990	1.7	1.7	1.7	2.1	2.6	2.1	2.1	1.8	1.7	1.7	1.8	1.9	1.9
1991	1.8	1.8	1.8	1.8	1.8	1.7	1.7	1.7	1.7	1.7	1.8	2.0	1.7
1992	1.9	1.8	1.8	1.8	1.8	1.8	1.7	1.7	1.7	1.7	1.8	1.9	1.7
1993	1.7	1.8	1.8	1.7	1.8	1.8	1.8	1.8	1.8	1.8	1.8	2.0	1.8
1994	1.8	1.8	1.8	1.8	1.8	1.8	1.8	1.8	1.8	1.8	1.8	2.0	1.8
1995	1.9	1.9	1.9	1.9	1.9	1.9	1.9	1.9	1.9	1.9	1.9	2.1	1.9
1996	1.9	1.9	1.9	1.9	1.9	1.9	1.9	1.8	1.9	1.9	1.9	2.1	1.9
1997	1.9	1.9	1.9	1.9	1.9	1.9	1.9	1.9	1.9	1.9	2.0	2.1	1.9
1998	1.9	1.9	1.9	2.0	2.0	1.9	1.9	2.0	2.0	2.0	2.1	2.2	1.9
1999	2.1	2.2	2.1	2.1	2.0	2.1	2.0	2.0	2.0	2.0	2.0	2.1	2.0
2000	2.1	2.1	2.1	2.3	3.0	2.3	2.3	2.1	2.0	2.0	2.0	2.1	2.2
2001	2.0	2.0	2.0	2.0	2.0	2.0	2.0	2.0	2.0	2.0	2.0	2.1	2.0
2002	2.0	2.0	2.0	2.0	2.0	2.0	2.0	2.0	2.1	2.1	2.1	2.1	2.0
2003	2.1	2.1	2.1	2.1	2.0	2.0	2.0	2.0	2.0	2.0	2.0	2.1	2.0
State government													
1990	2.4	2.5	2.5	2.5	2.5	2.6	2.5	2.5	2.6	2.5	2.7	2.7	2.5
1991	2.6	2.5	2.6	2.7	2.7	2.5	2.5	2.5	2.6	2.6	2.6	2.5	2.5
1992	2.5	2.5	2.5	2.5	2.6	2.4	2.4	2.4	2.4	2.5	2.5	2.5	2.4
1993	2.5	2.5	2.6	2.6	2.6	2.4	2.4	2.5	2.6	2.7	2.7	2.7	2.5
1994	2.6	2.7	2.7	2.7	2.7	2.5	2.5	2.6	2.7	2.7	2.7	2.7	2.6
1995	2.7	2.7	2.8	2.7	2.8	2.7	2.6	2.6	2.7	2.7	2.7	2.7	2.7
1996	2.7	2.7	2.7	2.7	2.7	2.6	2.5	2.6	2.6	2.7	2.7	2.7	2.6
1997	2.7	2.6	2.6	2.7	2.7	2.6	2.5	2.6	2.6	2.7	2.7	2.7	2.6
1998	2.7	2.7	2.7	2.7	2.7	2.6	2.6	2.6	2.6	2.7	2.7	2.7	2.6
1999	2.7	2.7	2.7	2.7	2.7	2.3	2.3	2.2	2.2	2.2	2.2	2.2	2.4
2000	2.2	2.2	2.2	2.2	2.2	2.3	2.2	2.2	2.1	2.2	2.2	2.2	2.2
2001	2.2	2.2	2.2	2.2	2.2	2.2	2.2	2.1	2.1	2.3	2.3	2.3	2.2
2002	2.3	2.3	2.3	2.3	2.3	2.3	2.3	2.2	2.2	2.2	2.3	2.2	2.3
2003	2.3	2.3	2.3	2.3	2.3	2.3	2.3	2.2	2.2	2.3	2.2	2.2	2.3
Local government													
1990	18.2	19.4	18.6	18.7	18.8	19.1	17.3	16.9	21.0	20.7	21.2	19.3	19.1
1991	19.3	19.3	19.5	19.1	19.3	19.3	17.6	17.3	19.1	19.1	19.3	19.3	18.9
1992	19.3	19.4	21.5	19.5	19.4	19.6	17.8	17.5	20.1	20.3	20.8	19.6	19.5
1993	19.3	19.5	19.8	19.7	19.7	19.7	17.7	17.5	19.4	19.8	20.0	20.2	19.3
1994	19.9	20.3	20.5	21.2	20.5	20.3	18.3	18.1	20.9	20.3	22.7	20.7	20.3
1995	20.2	20.6	20.7	20.6	20.6	20.7	18.3	18.2	20.2	17.6	18.0	18.1	19.4
1996	17.7	18.1	20.6	18.2	18.3	18.4	16.3	15.9	19.1	19.2	19.9	18.9	18.3
1997	18.7	18.9	19.1	19.1	19.1	19.1	16.9	16.5	18.8	19.0	19.3	19.3	18.6
1998	19.1	19.3	19.5	19.5	19.4	19.4	17.2	16.8	19.1	19.3	19.5	19.7	18.9
1999	19.3	19.5	19.7	19.7	19.6	19.7	17.4	17.0	19.4	19.8	19.8	20.1	19.2
2000	20.0	20.2	20.3	20.2	20.2	17.9	17.7	20.0	20.0	20.2	20.5	20.6	19.8
2001	20.2	20.5	20.7	20.5	20.7	18.3	18.1	20.5	20.6	20.9	21.3	21.4	20.3
2002	21.0	21.4	21.5	21.4	21.6	19.1	18.9	21.4	21.5	21.6	21.8	21.9	21.1
2003	21.8	22.0	22.1	22.1	22.3	19.7	19.5	22.1	22.2	22.3	22.6	22.7	21.8
TALLAHASSEE													
Total nonfarm													
1990	122.2	124.7	125.7	125.9	126.5	125.6	123.1	122.5	126.7	127.5	129.3	128.5	125.6
1991	124.5	126.0	126.6	127.0	127.6	124.2	122.0	122.8	126.9	128.4	129.3	129.1	126.2
1992	125.7	128.0	129.3	128.6	128.5	125.8	125.2	125.2	129.1	131.3	132.1	132.1	128.4
1993	129.4	132.4	133.5	133.8	132.0	130.7	130.1	130.8	133.6	136.1	136.9	137.6	133.0
1994	134.0	136.6	138.1	138.4	137.4	135.9	135.1	134.8	141.1	142.8	144.5	144.3	138.5
1995	140.4	142.9	145.3	144.3	144.7	142.9	140.7	140.4	144.8	146.5	148.1	148.5	144.1
1996	142.1	144.2	146.7	145.6	145.4	142.5	141.9	142.3	145.7	146.4	147.3	148.0	144.8
1997	146.3	147.3	147.8	148.1	147.5	144.5	145.0	145.3	149.5	150.5	151.5	152.7	148.0
1998	150.1	151.3	152.2	152.6	152.3	149.3	149.3	149.3	152.6	154.4	155.4	157.0	152.1
1999	153.1	155.4	156.5	156.9	156.1	153.3	153.2	153.1	155.9	158.2	160.3	161.6	156.1
2000	157.4	159.4	160.5	161.5	161.3	158.1	155.8	157.7	160.0	160.1	162.3	162.9	159.7
2001	157.5	160.7	161.4	161.6	161.3	157.9	155.4	157.1	158.4	158.7	159.8	159.0	159.0
2002	155.7	158.8	158.9	158.2	158.1	153.2	152.9	154.8	156.5	158.9	160.7	160.3	157.3
2003	156.3	158.6	159.4	159.9	160.3	155.5	154.9	156.1	158.2	160.6	161.0	161.9	158.6

Employment by Industry: Florida—*Continued*

(Numbers in thousands. Not seasonally adjusted.)

Industry	January	February	March	April	May	June	July	August	September	October	November	December	Annual Average
TALLAHASSEE—*Continued*													
Total private													
1990	71.7	72.4	73.1	72.8	73.4	74.2	73.3	73.6	74.6	74.3	75.3	74.8	73.6
1991	72.3	72.5	72.5	72.9	72.9	73.0	72.6	73.5	74.0	74.3	74.8	74.9	73.3
1992	72.8	73.7	74.2	74.7	74.2	74.8	74.8	75.6	76.2	76.6	77.5	77.5	75.2
1993	76.1	77.3	78.0	78.3	77.7	78.1	78.2	78.4	79.9	79.9	80.7	81.2	78.6
1994	78.8	80.1	80.8	81.2	80.9	81.5	81.5	82.0	84.1	85.2	85.7	86.3	82.3
1995	83.8	84.7	85.9	85.4	86.1	87.2	86.1	86.6	87.3	88.2	89.5	89.9	86.7
1996	85.3	86.0	86.6	86.8	87.0	87.0	86.8	87.5	88.5	88.1	88.5	89.2	87.2
1997	87.7	88.4	88.8	89.3	89.0	88.9	89.6	90.3	92.1	92.0	92.6	93.7	90.2
1998	91.6	92.1	92.6	92.9	92.9	93.0	93.0	93.9	94.6	95.1	95.6	96.7	93.6
1999	94.5	95.2	95.9	96.7	96.2	96.5	96.0	96.1	97.1	98.2	99.5	100.3	96.8
2000	97.8	98.6	99.1	99.9	99.8	100.5	99.3	99.7	101.0	100.0	101.4	101.8	99.9
2001	98.2	99.9	100.1	100.2	100.1	100.1	98.5	98.7	99.1	98.5	98.6	98.5	99.2
2002	96.5	98.0	98.1	97.3	96.9	96.8	96.2	96.9	97.4	98.5	99.3	99.2	97.6
2003	96.5	97.5	97.9	98.6	98.3	98.3	97.6	98.0	98.7	99.4	100.0	101.0	98.5
Goods-producing													
1990	10.4	10.6	10.6	10.2	10.4	10.6	10.6	10.8	10.5	10.3	10.2	9.9	10.4
1991	9.7	9.8	9.7	9.9	10.0	9.9	9.7	10.1	9.8	9.8	9.7	9.9	9.8
1992	9.8	9.8	9.9	9.8	9.7	9.8	9.9	10.1	10.0	9.9	9.9	10.0	9.8
1993	9.8	10.1	10.2	10.1	9.9	10.0	9.7	9.6	9.6	9.4	9.3	9.4	9.7
1994	9.1	9.4	9.5	9.6	9.7	10.0	10.2	10.3	10.4	10.5	10.2	10.1	9.9
1995	10.0	10.1	10.3	10.4	10.4	10.6	10.3	10.4	10.3	10.4	10.5	10.5	10.3
1996	10.3	10.4	10.7	10.8	10.9	10.9	10.7	11.0	11.0	11.2	11.0	11.2	10.8
1997	11.0	11.1	11.1	11.1	11.1	11.0	11.0	10.9	11.0	10.9	10.8	10.8	10.9
1998	10.7	10.7	10.8	10.9	11.0	11.0	11.0	11.1	11.2	11.2	11.2	11.2	11.0
1999	11.1	11.2	11.3	11.1	11.0	11.2	11.0	11.0	10.9	11.1	11.1	11.2	11.1
2000	11.0	11.1	11.1	11.4	11.2	11.4	11.3	11.3	11.3	11.2	11.2	11.2	11.2
2001	10.4	10.6	10.6	10.5	10.5	10.5	10.3	10.3	10.2	10.3	10.2	10.0	10.3
2002	9.9	10.2	10.2	10.3	10.3	10.4	10.3	10.4	10.3	10.5	10.5	10.5	10.3
2003	10.4	10.5	10.4	10.7	10.9	11.0	11.0	11.1	11.2	11.2	11.2	11.3	10.9
Construction and mining													
1990	6.4	6.6	6.6	6.4	6.6	6.6	6.6	6.7	6.5	6.4	6.3	6.1	6.4
1991	6.0	6.1	6.1	6.3	6.4	6.3	6.1	6.4	6.1	6.1	6.0	6.2	6.1
1992	6.2	6.3	6.4	6.2	6.1	6.1	6.2	6.4	6.3	6.2	6.2	6.2	6.2
1993	6.0	6.2	6.3	6.2	6.0	6.0	5.8	5.7	5.6	5.4	5.3	5.4	5.8
1994	5.2	5.4	5.5	5.6	5.7	5.9	6.1	6.1	6.1	6.2	6.0	5.9	5.8
1995	5.8	5.8	6.0	6.1	6.1	6.2	6.0	6.1	6.1	6.0	6.0	5.9	6.0
1996	5.9	6.0	6.2	6.3	6.4	6.4	6.2	6.5	6.5	6.6	6.5	6.6	6.3
1997	6.5	6.5	6.5	6.6	6.6	6.5	6.4	6.4	6.4	6.4	6.3	6.4	6.4
1998	6.2	6.3	6.4	6.5	6.6	6.6	6.6	6.7	6.8	6.9	6.9	6.9	6.6
1999	6.7	6.8	6.8	6.7	6.6	6.8	6.6	6.6	6.5	6.7	6.7	6.8	6.6
2000	6.6	6.6	6.7	6.9	6.8	6.9	6.8	6.8	6.8	6.7	6.7	6.7	6.7
2001	6.4	6.6	6.6	6.5	6.6	6.6	6.5	6.5	6.4	6.6	6.6	6.4	6.5
2002	6.4	6.6	6.6	6.6	6.6	6.7	6.6	6.7	6.6	6.8	6.9	6.9	6.7
2003	6.9	6.9	6.8	7.1	7.3	7.4	7.4	7.5	7.5	7.6	7.6	7.7	7.3
Manufacturing													
1990	4.0	4.0	4.0	3.8	3.8	4.0	4.0	4.1	4.0	3.9	3.9	3.8	3.9
1991	3.7	3.7	3.6	3.6	3.6	3.6	3.6	3.7	3.7	3.7	3.7	3.7	3.6
1992	3.6	3.5	3.5	3.6	3.6	3.7	3.7	3.7	3.7	3.7	3.7	3.8	3.6
1993	3.8	3.9	3.9	3.9	3.9	4.0	3.9	3.9	4.0	4.0	4.0	4.0	3.9
1994	3.9	4.0	4.0	4.0	4.0	4.1	4.1	4.2	4.3	4.3	4.2	4.2	4.1
1995	4.2	4.3	4.3	4.3	4.3	4.4	4.3	4.3	4.2	4.4	4.5	4.6	4.3
1996	4.4	4.4	4.5	4.5	4.5	4.5	4.5	4.5	4.5	4.6	4.5	4.6	4.5
1997	4.5	4.6	4.6	4.5	4.5	4.5	4.6	4.5	4.6	4.5	4.5	4.4	4.5
1998	4.5	4.4	4.4	4.4	4.4	4.4	4.4	4.4	4.4	4.3	4.3	4.3	4.3
1999	4.4	4.4	4.5	4.4	4.4	4.4	4.4	4.4	4.4	4.4	4.4	4.4	4.4
2000	4.4	4.5	4.4	4.5	4.4	4.5	4.5	4.5	4.5	4.5	4.5	4.5	4.4
2001	4.0	4.0	4.0	4.0	3.9	3.9	3.8	3.8	3.8	3.7	3.6	3.6	3.8
2002	3.5	3.6	3.6	3.7	3.7	3.7	3.7	3.7	3.7	3.7	3.6	3.6	3.7
2003	3.5	3.6	3.6	3.6	3.6	3.6	3.6	3.6	3.7	3.6	3.6	3.6	3.6
Service-providing													
1990	111.8	114.1	115.1	115.7	116.1	115.0	112.5	111.7	116.2	117.2	119.1	118.6	115.2
1991	114.8	116.2	116.9	117.1	117.6	114.3	112.3	112.7	117.1	118.6	119.6	119.2	116.3
1992	115.9	118.2	119.4	118.8	118.8	116.0	115.3	115.1	119.1	121.4	122.2	122.1	118.5
1993	119.6	122.3	123.3	123.7	122.1	120.7	120.4	121.2	124.0	126.7	127.6	128.2	123.3
1994	124.9	127.2	128.6	128.8	127.7	125.9	124.9	124.5	130.7	132.3	134.3	134.2	128.6
1995	130.4	132.8	135.0	133.9	134.3	132.3	130.4	130.0	134.5	136.1	137.6	138.0	133.7
1996	131.8	133.8	136.0	134.8	134.5	131.6	131.2	131.3	134.7	135.2	136.3	136.8	134.0
1997	135.3	136.2	136.7	137.0	136.4	133.5	134.0	134.4	138.5	139.6	140.7	141.9	137.0
1998	139.4	140.6	141.4	141.7	141.3	138.3	138.3	138.2	141.4	143.2	144.2	145.8	141.1
1999	142.0	144.2	145.2	145.8	145.1	142.1	142.2	142.1	145.0	147.1	149.2	150.4	145.0
2000	146.4	148.3	149.4	150.1	150.1	146.7	144.5	146.4	148.7	148.9	151.1	151.7	148.5
2001	147.1	150.1	150.8	151.1	150.8	147.4	145.1	146.8	148.2	148.4	149.6	149.0	148.7
2002	145.8	148.6	148.7	147.9	147.8	142.8	142.6	144.4	146.2	148.4	150.2	149.8	146.9
2003	145.9	148.1	149.0	149.2	149.4	144.5	143.9	145.0	147.0	149.4	149.8	150.6	147.7

Employment by Industry: Florida—*Continued*

(Numbers in thousands. Not seasonally adjusted.)

Industry	January	February	March	April	May	June	July	August	September	October	November	December	Annual Average
TALLAHASSEE—*Continued*													
Trade, transportation, and utilities													
1990	19.6	19.5	19.4	19.2	19.3	19.5	19.3	19.3	19.8	19.5	20.1	20.3	19.5
1991	19.2	19.0	18.9	18.8	18.9	19.0	18.8	18.9	19.2	19.4	19.9	19.8	19.1
1992	18.8	18.7	18.6	18.4	18.5	18.7	18.8	19.1	19.2	19.4	19.9	20.1	19.0
1993	19.0	19.0	19.0	19.2	19.0	19.1	19.3	19.4	19.8	19.8	20.5	21.0	19.5
1994	20.2	20.2	20.1	20.1	20.1	20.3	20.3	20.5	21.2	21.2	21.7	22.3	20.6
1995	21.3	21.1	21.3	20.9	20.8	21.1	20.8	21.1	21.4	21.5	22.0	22.4	21.3
1996	21.0	20.9	20.8	20.9	20.9	20.9	21.0	21.2	21.3	21.3	21.7	22.2	21.1
1997	21.5	21.2	21.2	21.5	21.4	21.3	21.5	21.7	22.0	22.1	22.5	23.1	21.7
1998	22.4	22.1	22.1	22.2	22.3	22.5	22.5	22.8	23.1	23.1	23.8	24.6	22.7
1999	23.3	23.2	23.2	23.4	23.2	23.3	23.3	23.7	23.9	24.4	25.1	25.8	23.8
2000	24.5	24.4	24.2	24.1	24.0	24.1	23.8	23.9	24.2	24.1	24.6	25.3	24.2
2001	23.6	23.5	23.5	23.1	23.1	22.8	22.6	22.6	22.6	22.5	22.8	23.0	22.9
2002	22.5	22.3	22.2	21.7	21.8	21.7	21.6	21.8	22.0	22.3	22.5	23.1	22.1
2003	21.8	21.8	22.0	21.9	21.9	21.9	21.6	21.8	22.2	22.6	23.0	23.5	22.2
Wholesale trade													
1990	3.2	3.2	3.2	3.1	3.1	3.2	3.2	3.1	3.3	3.3	3.2	3.1	3.1
1991	3.0	3.0	3.0	3.0	3.1	3.2	3.0	3.0	3.1	3.3	3.3	3.1	3.0
1992	3.0	3.1	3.1	3.1	3.0	3.2	3.1	3.2	3.1	3.2	3.2	3.1	3.1
1993	3.1	3.1	3.1	3.1	3.1	3.1	3.2	3.1	3.1	3.1	3.0	3.0	3.0
1994	3.2	3.2	3.2	3.1	3.1	3.2	3.2	3.3	3.4	3.4	3.3	3.3	3.2
1995	3.3	3.3	3.3	3.3	3.4	3.5	3.4	3.4	3.4	3.5	3.3	3.4	3.3
1996	3.3	3.3	3.3	3.2	3.2	3.2	3.3	3.3	3.3	3.3	3.3	3.3	3.2
1997	3.3	3.3	3.3	3.3	3.3	3.3	3.3	3.3	3.3	3.4	3.3	3.2	3.3
1998	3.2	3.2	3.2	3.3	3.3	3.3	3.3	3.4	3.4	3.4	3.4	3.4	3.3
1999	3.3	3.4	3.4	3.3	3.4	3.4	3.5	3.6	3.6	3.7	3.7	3.7	3.5
2000	3.6	3.6	3.6	3.7	3.8	3.8	3.8	3.8	3.8	3.8	3.7	3.8	3.7
2001	3.8	3.8	3.8	3.7	3.7	3.6	3.6	3.5	3.5	3.3	3.2	3.2	3.5
2002	3.2	3.2	3.2	3.0	3.0	3.0	3.0	3.0	2.9	3.0	2.9	2.9	3.0
2003	2.8	2.8	2.9	2.9	2.9	2.9	2.9	2.9	2.9	3.0	3.0	2.9	2.9
Retail trade													
1990	15.0	14.9	14.8	14.7	14.8	14.9	14.8	14.8	15.1	14.9	15.5	15.8	15.0
1991	14.8	14.6	14.6	14.5	14.4	14.4	14.4	14.5	14.7	14.7	15.2	15.3	14.6
1992	14.3	14.1	14.0	13.9	14.1	14.0	14.3	14.5	14.6	14.7	15.3	15.5	14.4
1993	14.5	14.5	14.5	14.6	14.5	14.6	14.6	14.8	15.2	15.2	15.9	16.5	14.9
1994	15.5	15.5	15.4	15.4	15.4	15.5	15.5	15.6	16.1	16.1	16.7	17.3	15.8
1995	16.4	16.2	16.4	16.0	15.8	15.9	15.7	15.9	16.3	16.3	17.0	17.3	16.2
1996	16.1	15.9	15.8	16.0	16.1	16.1	16.0	16.2	16.3	16.3	16.7	17.2	16.2
1997	16.5	16.2	16.2	16.4	16.3	16.2	16.5	16.8	17.0	17.0	17.5	18.1	16.7
1998	17.5	17.2	17.2	17.2	17.2	17.4	17.4	17.6	17.9	17.8	18.5	19.2	17.6
1999	18.1	17.8	17.8	18.1	17.9	17.9	17.8	18.1	18.3	18.7	19.4	20.0	18.3
2000	19.0	18.9	18.7	18.5	18.3	18.4	18.1	18.2	18.5	18.5	19.1	19.6	18.6
2001	18.0	17.9	17.9	17.6	17.6	17.4	17.2	17.4	17.4	17.5	17.9	18.0	17.6
2002	17.4	17.2	17.2	16.9	17.0	16.9	16.7	16.9	17.3	17.5	17.8	18.4	17.3
2003	17.3	17.3	17.4	17.3	17.3	17.3	17.0	17.2	17.6	17.9	18.3	18.9	17.6
Transportation and utilities													
1990	1.4	1.4	1.4	1.4	1.4	1.4	1.3	1.4	1.4	1.3	1.4	1.4	1.3
1991	1.4	1.4	1.3	1.3	1.4	1.4	1.4	1.4	1.4	1.4	1.4	1.4	1.3
1992	1.5	1.5	1.5	1.4	1.4	1.5	1.4	1.4	1.5	1.5	1.4	1.5	1.4
1993	1.4	1.4	1.4	1.5	1.4	1.4	1.5	1.5	1.5	1.5	1.6	1.5	1.4
1994	1.5	1.5	1.5	1.6	1.6	1.6	1.6	1.6	1.7	1.7	1.7	1.7	1.6
1995	1.6	1.6	1.6	1.6	1.6	1.7	1.7	1.8	1.7	1.7	1.7	1.7	1.6
1996	1.6	1.7	1.7	1.7	1.6	1.6	1.7	1.7	1.7	1.7	1.7	1.7	1.6
1997	1.7	1.7	1.7	1.8	1.8	1.8	1.7	1.6	1.7	1.7	1.7	1.8	1.7
1998	1.7	1.7	1.7	1.7	1.8	1.8	1.8	1.8	1.8	1.9	1.9	2.0	1.8
1999	1.9	2.0	2.0	2.0	1.9	2.0	2.0	2.0	2.0	2.0	2.0	2.1	1.9
2000	1.9	1.9	1.9	1.9	1.9	1.9	1.9	1.9	1.9	1.8	1.8	1.9	1.8
2001	1.8	1.8	1.8	1.8	1.8	1.8	1.8	1.7	1.7	1.7	1.7	1.8	1.7
2002	1.9	1.9	1.8	1.8	1.8	1.8	1.9	1.9	1.8	1.8	1.8	1.8	1.8
2003	1.7	1.7	1.7	1.7	1.7	1.7	1.7	1.7	1.7	1.7	1.7	1.7	1.7
Information													
1990	3.6	3.6	3.6	3.7	3.7	3.8	3.7	3.7	3.8	3.8	3.8	3.8	3.7
1991	3.6	3.6	3.6	3.6	3.6	3.7	3.7	3.7	3.7	3.8	3.8	3.8	3.6
1992	3.6	3.6	3.6	3.7	3.6	3.7	3.7	3.6	3.6	3.7	3.7	3.7	3.6
1993	3.6	3.7	3.6	3.6	3.6	3.6	3.7	3.7	3.7	3.6	3.6	3.6	3.6
1994	3.5	3.5	3.5	3.5	3.5	3.5	3.5	3.2	3.3	3.3	3.3	3.3	3.4
1995	3.2	3.2	3.2	3.3	3.3	3.3	3.3	3.3	3.4	3.4	3.5	3.5	3.3
1996	3.3	3.3	3.3	3.3	3.3	3.4	3.5	3.4	3.6	3.5	3.7	3.7	3.4
1997	3.6	3.6	3.7	3.7	3.7	3.7	3.8	3.8	3.8	3.8	3.8	3.9	3.7
1998	4.0	4.0	4.0	4.1	4.2	4.2	4.1	4.1	4.2	4.3	4.2	4.3	4.1
1999	4.2	4.3	4.4	4.5	4.4	4.5	4.5	4.6	4.7	4.6	4.7	4.6	4.5
2000	4.6	4.7	4.7	4.7	4.8	4.9	4.8	4.8	4.8	4.7	4.8	4.8	4.7
2001	4.9	5.0	5.0	4.8	4.8	4.7	4.5	4.3	4.2	4.0	3.9	3.8	4.4
2002	4.0	4.0	4.0	4.0	3.9	3.9	3.9	3.9	3.8	3.7	3.7	3.7	3.9
2003	3.7	3.7	3.7	3.7	3.8	3.8	3.8	3.7	3.8	3.8	3.8	3.8	3.8

Employment by Industry: Florida—*Continued*

(Numbers in thousands. Not seasonally adjusted.)

Industry	January	February	March	April	May	June	July	August	September	October	November	December	Annual Average
TALLAHASSEE—*Continued*													
Financial activities													
1990	5.5	5.5	5.5	5.6	5.6	5.7	5.7	5.6	5.6	5.7	5.7	5.7	5.6
1991	5.5	5.5	5.5	5.2	5.2	5.2	5.3	5.3	5.4	5.4	5.5	5.5	5.3
1992	5.3	5.3	5.3	5.6	5.5	5.6	5.6	5.6	5.6	5.5	5.6	5.6	5.5
1993	5.4	5.5	5.5	5.5	5.6	5.6	5.6	5.6	5.6	5.8	5.8	5.8	5.6
1994	5.4	5.4	5.5	5.6	5.5	5.5	5.5	5.5	5.5	5.6	5.6	5.6	5.5
1995	5.4	5.4	5.5	5.6	5.6	5.7	5.7	5.7	5.7	5.7	5.8	5.8	5.6
1996	5.5	5.4	5.5	5.7	5.8	5.7	5.8	5.8	5.9	5.9	5.9	5.9	5.7
1997	5.7	5.8	5.8	5.8	5.8	5.8	6.0	6.1	6.2	6.3	6.2	6.2	5.9
1998	6.2	6.3	6.3	6.5	6.5	6.5	6.5	6.6	6.5	6.5	6.5	6.6	6.4
1999	6.6	6.5	6.6	6.6	6.6	6.6	6.6	6.6	6.6	6.6	6.6	6.7	6.6
2000	6.5	6.6	6.7	6.7	6.7	6.8	6.6	6.6	6.6	6.6	6.8	6.8	6.6
2001	6.5	6.6	6.7	6.5	6.5	6.6	6.6	6.6	6.5	6.6	6.5	6.6	6.5
2002	6.6	6.7	6.7	7.0	7.0	7.1	7.1	7.2	7.1	7.4	7.4	7.4	7.1
2003	7.0	7.1	7.1	7.3	7.3	7.3	7.1	7.2	7.2	7.1	7.1	7.1	7.2
Professional and business services													
1990	8.2	8.3	8.5	8.6	8.7	8.7	8.7	8.8	8.9	8.8	9.0	9.0	8.6
1991	8.8	9.0	9.0	9.1	9.1	9.1	8.8	9.0	8.9	9.0	9.0	9.0	8.9
1992	8.9	9.1	9.2	9.4	9.4	9.4	9.3	9.4	9.4	9.4	9.4	9.4	9.3
1993	9.9	10.2	10.3	10.4	10.3	10.4	10.6	10.7	10.8	11.1	11.0	11.0	10.5
1994	10.9	11.1	11.4	11.3	11.4	11.3	11.7	11.9	12.0	12.1	12.1	12.4	11.6
1995	12.4	12.6	12.8	12.6	13.0	13.2	13.2	13.2	13.3	13.8	13.9	14.1	13.1
1996	13.2	13.5	13.6	13.6	13.7	13.5	13.8	13.9	14.0	13.7	13.8	13.7	13.6
1997	13.6	13.8	13.8	13.9	13.8	13.9	14.2	14.4	14.6	14.3	14.2	14.5	14.0
1998	13.8	13.9	14.2	14.6	14.4	14.3	14.6	14.7	14.6	15.1	15.1	15.2	14.5
1999	15.1	15.2	15.6	15.6	15.5	15.7	15.6	15.7	15.8	16.2	16.6	16.8	15.7
2000	16.7	16.6	16.8	17.2	17.5	17.3	17.0	17.4	17.7	17.2	17.4	17.3	17.1
2001	17.2	18.0	17.9	18.5	18.7	18.8	18.1	18.5	18.5	18.1	18.3	18.2	18.2
2002	17.6	18.3	18.3	17.9	17.7	17.7	17.4	17.5	17.4	17.3	17.7	17.5	17.7
2003	17.2	17.6	17.7	17.9	17.8	17.7	17.5	17.7	17.3	17.5	17.4	17.3	17.6
Educational and health services													
1990	10.8	10.9	11.1	11.0	11.1	11.1	11.0	11.2	11.3	11.4	11.5	11.5	11.1
1991	11.3	11.4	11.5	11.7	11.8	11.7	11.8	12.0	12.0	12.1	12.1	12.1	11.7
1992	11.9	12.1	12.2	12.4	12.4	12.4	12.5	12.6	12.6	12.6	12.6	12.6	12.4
1993	12.8	12.8	12.9	13.0	13.0	13.1	13.0	13.0	13.1	13.0	13.2	13.2	13.0
1994	13.0	13.2	13.2	13.2	13.2	13.4	13.1	13.2	13.3	13.5	13.6	13.8	13.3
1995	13.4	13.6	13.8	13.7	13.9	14.1	14.0	14.0	14.0	14.2	14.4	14.4	13.9
1996	13.6	13.7	13.8	13.9	13.9	13.9	13.8	13.8	13.9	13.9	14.0	14.0	13.8
1997	14.1	14.3	14.4	14.3	14.3	14.4	14.3	14.5	14.6	14.8	15.1	15.2	14.5
1998	14.8	14.9	15.0	14.9	15.0	15.0	15.0	15.1	15.2	15.2	15.1	15.3	15.0
1999	15.3	15.3	15.3	15.6	15.7	15.7	15.8	15.4	15.5	15.7	15.8	16.0	15.5
2000	15.7	15.8	16.1	16.0	16.1	16.2	16.4	16.5	16.6	16.6	16.8	16.9	16.3
2001	16.1	16.3	16.3	16.4	16.3	16.4	16.2	16.2	16.1	16.2	16.2	16.2	16.2
2002	15.9	15.9	16.0	15.8	15.8	15.8	15.7	15.9	15.9	16.2	16.2	16.2	15.9
2003	16.2	16.3	16.4	16.2	16.1	16.1	16.4	16.1	16.1	16.0	16.1	16.4	16.2
Leisure and hospitality													
1990	8.2	8.5	8.8	8.9	8.9	9.0	8.7	8.6	9.0	9.0	9.0	8.7	8.7
1991	8.5	8.5	8.6	8.9	8.6	8.6	8.8	8.7	9.2	8.9	8.9	8.9	8.7
1992	8.3	8.8	9.1	9.3	9.0	8.9	8.8	9.0	9.5	9.7	9.9	9.7	9.1
1993	9.4	9.7	10.2	10.1	10.0	9.9	9.9	9.9	10.7	10.5	10.5	10.5	10.1
1994	10.0	10.5	10.7	11.1	10.6	10.5	10.3	10.4	11.4	11.7	11.9	11.7	10.9
1995	10.9	11.4	11.5	11.5	11.6	11.7	11.4	11.5	11.8	11.7	11.8	11.6	11.5
1996	11.1	11.4	11.4	11.6	11.5	11.7	11.1	11.3	11.6	11.5	11.3	11.4	11.4
1997	11.0	11.4	11.6	11.7	11.6	11.5	11.2	11.3	12.2	12.0	12.2	12.2	11.6
1998	11.7	12.0	12.0	11.9	11.6	11.6	11.4	11.6	11.9	11.9	11.9	11.8	11.7
1999	11.3	11.8	11.8	12.1	11.9	11.6	11.4	11.3	11.8	11.7	11.7	11.2	11.6
2000	11.0	11.5	11.5	11.8	11.5	11.7	11.3	11.1	11.7	11.5	11.7	11.3	11.4
2001	11.6	11.9	12.1	12.4	12.3	12.3	12.4	12.3	13.0	12.9	12.8	12.7	12.3
2002	12.0	12.5	12.6	12.6	12.4	12.2	12.3	12.4	13.1	13.2	13.5	13.1	12.7
2003	12.6	12.9	13.0	13.3	12.9	12.8	12.7	12.8	13.4	13.6	13.8	13.9	13.1
Other services													
1990	5.4	5.5	5.6	5.6	5.7	5.8	5.6	5.6	5.7	5.8	6.0	5.9	5.6
1991	5.7	5.7	5.7	5.7	5.7	5.8	5.7	5.8	5.8	5.9	5.9	5.9	5.7
1992	6.2	6.3	6.3	6.1	6.1	6.3	6.2	6.2	6.3	6.4	6.5	6.4	6.2
1993	6.2	6.3	6.3	6.4	6.3	6.4	6.4	6.5	6.6	6.7	6.8	6.7	6.4
1994	6.7	6.8	6.9	6.8	6.9	7.0	6.9	7.0	7.0	7.3	7.3	7.1	6.9
1995	7.2	7.3	7.5	7.4	7.5	7.5	7.4	7.4	7.4	7.5	7.6	7.6	7.4
1996	7.3	7.4	7.5	7.0	7.0	7.0	7.1	7.1	7.2	7.1	7.1	7.1	7.1
1997	7.2	7.2	7.2	7.3	7.3	7.3	7.6	7.6	7.7	7.8	7.8	7.8	7.4
1998	8.0	8.2	8.2	7.8	7.9	7.9	7.9	7.9	7.9	7.8	7.8	7.7	7.9
1999	7.6	7.7	7.7	7.8	7.9	7.9	7.8	7.8	7.9	7.9	7.9	8.0	7.8
2000	7.8	7.9	8.0	8.0	8.0	8.1	8.1	8.1	8.1	8.1	8.1	8.2	8.0
2001	7.9	8.0	8.0	8.0	7.9	8.0	7.8	7.9	8.0	7.9	7.9	8.0	7.9
2002	8.0	8.1	8.1	8.0	8.0	8.0	7.9	7.8	7.8	7.9	7.8	7.7	7.9
2003	7.6	7.6	7.6	7.6	7.6	7.7	7.5	7.6	7.5	7.6	7.6	7.7	7.6

Employment by Industry: Florida—*Continued*

(Numbers in thousands. Not seasonally adjusted.)

Industry	January	February	March	April	May	June	July	August	September	October	November	December	Annual Average
TALLAHASSEE—*Continued*													
Government													
1990	50.5	52.3	52.6	53.1	53.1	51.4	49.8	48.9	52.1	53.2	54.0	53.7	52.0
1991	52.2	53.5	54.1	54.1	54.7	51.2	49.4	49.3	52.9	54.1	54.5	54.2	52.8
1992	52.9	54.3	55.1	53.9	54.3	51.0	50.4	49.6	52.9	54.7	54.6	54.6	53.1
1993	53.3	55.1	55.5	55.5	54.3	52.6	51.9	52.4	53.7	56.2	56.2	56.4	54.4
1994	55.2	56.5	57.3	57.2	56.5	54.4	53.6	52.8	57.0	57.6	58.8	58.0	56.2
1995	56.6	58.2	59.4	58.9	58.6	55.7	54.6	53.8	57.5	58.3	58.6	58.6	57.4
1996	56.8	58.2	60.1	58.8	58.4	55.5	55.1	54.8	57.2	58.3	58.8	58.8	57.5
1997	58.6	58.9	59.0	58.8	58.5	55.6	55.4	55.0	57.4	58.5	58.9	59.0	57.8
1998	58.5	59.2	59.6	59.7	59.4	56.3	56.3	55.4	58.0	59.3	59.8	60.3	58.4
1999	58.6	60.2	60.6	60.2	59.9	56.8	57.2	57.0	58.8	60.0	60.8	61.3	59.2
2000	59.6	60.8	61.4	61.6	61.5	57.6	56.5	58.0	59.0	60.1	60.9	61.1	59.8
2001	59.3	60.8	61.3	61.4	61.2	57.8	56.9	58.4	59.3	60.2	61.2	60.5	59.8
2002	59.2	60.8	60.8	60.9	61.2	56.4	56.7	57.9	59.1	60.4	61.4	61.1	59.7
2003	59.8	61.1	61.5	61.3	62.0	57.2	57.3	58.1	59.5	61.2	61.0	60.9	60.1
Federal government													
1990	1.6	1.7	1.7	1.9	1.9	1.9	1.9	1.7	1.7	1.6	1.6	1.6	1.7
1991	1.6	1.6	1.6	1.6	1.7	1.7	1.7	1.7	1.7	1.7	1.7	1.7	1.6
1992	1.7	1.7	1.7	1.7	1.7	1.8	1.8	1.8	1.8	1.7	1.7	1.7	1.7
1993	1.7	1.7	1.7	1.7	1.7	1.8	1.8	1.8	1.7	1.8	1.7	1.8	1.7
1994	1.8	1.8	1.8	1.8	1.8	1.8	1.8	1.8	1.8	1.8	1.8	1.8	1.8
1995	1.8	1.8	1.8	1.8	1.8	1.8	1.8	1.8	1.8	1.8	1.8	1.8	1.8
1996	1.8	1.8	1.8	1.8	1.8	1.8	1.8	1.8	1.8	1.8	1.8	1.8	1.8
1997	1.8	1.8	1.8	1.8	1.8	1.8	1.8	1.8	1.8	1.8	1.8	1.8	1.8
1998	1.8	1.8	1.8	1.8	1.8	1.9	1.8	1.8	1.8	1.8	1.8	1.8	1.8
1999	1.8	1.8	1.9	1.8	1.8	1.8	1.8	1.8	1.8	1.8	1.8	1.8	1.8
2000	1.8	1.9	2.0	2.0	2.4	2.0	2.0	1.9	1.8	1.8	1.8	1.8	1.9
2001	1.8	1.8	1.8	1.8	1.8	1.8	1.8	1.8	1.8	1.8	1.8	1.8	1.8
2002	1.8	1.8	1.8	1.8	1.8	1.8	1.8	1.8	1.9	1.9	1.9	2.0	1.8
2003	1.9	1.9	1.9	1.8	1.9	1.9	1.9	1.9	1.9	1.9	1.9	1.9	1.9
State government													
1990	37.4	38.8	39.0	39.4	39.2	38.0	37.7	37.6	39.1	39.8	40.4	40.2	38.8
1991	38.8	39.9	40.4	40.3	40.7	37.5	37.3	37.7	39.5	40.3	40.6	40.2	39.4
1992	39.2	40.2	40.5	40.2	40.4	37.4	38.0	37.7	39.5	41.1	40.8	40.8	39.6
1993	39.4	41.0	41.5	41.8	40.2	38.6	39.3	40.3	40.0	42.2	42.1	42.1	40.7
1994	40.9	42.0	42.8	42.9	42.0	39.8	40.4	40.3	42.7	43.0	43.1	43.3	41.9
1995	41.9	43.2	44.3	44.0	43.4	40.7	41.2	40.9	42.9	43.1	43.3	43.4	42.6
1996	41.7	42.9	44.1	43.8	43.2	40.5	41.4	41.7	42.3	43.1	43.4	43.6	42.6
1997	43.4	43.5	43.7	43.7	43.3	40.6	41.6	41.7	42.4	43.6	43.8	43.9	42.9
1998	43.7	44.0	44.5	44.5	44.5	41.4	42.6	42.3	43.2	44.3	44.6	45.1	43.7
1999	43.5	44.9	45.3	45.3	45.3	42.4	44.0	43.8	44.1	45.2	45.6	46.2	44.6
2000	44.4	45.6	46.1	46.0	45.9	43.5	42.6	43.0	44.0	45.0	45.5	45.8	44.7
2001	44.0	45.4	45.9	45.9	45.9	43.7	43.0	43.2	44.0	45.0	46.0	45.4	44.7
2002	44.0	45.5	45.6	45.6	46.0	42.3	42.8	42.8	43.8	45.1	46.0	45.5	44.6
2003	44.3	45.4	45.9	45.8	46.5	42.9	43.1	42.7	44.0	45.8	45.5	45.5	44.8
Local government													
1990	11.5	11.8	11.9	11.8	12.0	11.5	10.2	9.6	11.3	11.8	12.0	11.9	11.4
1991	11.8	12.0	12.1	12.2	12.3	12.0	10.4	9.9	11.7	12.1	12.2	12.3	11.7
1992	12.0	12.4	12.9	12.0	12.2	11.8	10.6	10.1	11.6	11.9	12.1	12.1	11.8
1993	12.2	12.4	12.3	12.0	12.4	12.2	10.8	10.3	12.0	12.2	12.4	12.5	11.9
1994	12.5	12.7	12.7	12.5	12.7	12.8	11.4	10.7	12.5	12.8	13.9	12.9	12.5
1995	12.9	13.2	13.3	13.1	13.4	13.2	11.6	11.1	12.8	13.4	13.5	13.4	12.9
1996	13.3	13.5	14.2	13.2	13.4	13.2	11.9	11.3	13.1	13.4	13.6	13.4	13.1
1997	13.4	13.6	13.5	13.3	13.4	13.2	12.0	11.5	13.2	13.1	13.3	13.3	13.0
1998	13.0	13.4	13.3	13.4	13.1	13.0	11.9	11.3	13.0	13.2	13.4	13.4	12.9
1999	13.3	13.5	13.4	13.1	12.8	12.6	11.4	11.4	12.9	13.0	13.4	13.3	12.8
2000	13.4	13.3	13.3	13.6	13.2	12.1	11.9	13.1	13.2	13.3	13.6	13.5	13.1
2001	13.5	13.6	13.6	13.7	13.5	12.3	12.1	13.4	13.5	13.4	13.4	13.3	13.2
2002	13.4	13.5	13.4	13.5	13.4	12.3	12.1	13.3	13.4	13.4	13.5	13.6	13.2
2003	13.6	13.8	13.7	13.7	13.6	12.4	12.3	13.5	13.6	13.5	13.6	13.5	13.4
TAMPA-ST. PETERSBURG-CLEARWATER													
Total nonfarm													
1990	870.1	879.9	887.3	885.1	885.5	885.4	865.1	874.7	880.7	878.4	885.4	887.7	880.4
1991	859.8	864.3	869.4	860.1	860.3	855.5	838.3	842.2	852.2	857.3	866.0	871.9	858.1
1992	853.9	858.6	867.1	865.6	869.2	868.1	853.9	853.1	868.4	871.5	885.3	889.9	867.0
1993	875.1	887.2	894.8	898.6	901.0	903.9	892.8	895.6	910.4	917.7	928.0	938.9	903.6
1994	928.1	941.0	950.2	955.9	958.5	959.6	946.4	945.6	963.3	966.8	983.9	988.2	957.2
1995	973.1	984.5	993.9	994.0	996.4	995.2	976.9	980.7	995.9	997.8	1012.7	1023.5	993.7
1996	999.4	1014.6	1030.7	1016.6	1019.3	1017.7	1004.9	1008.0	1022.8	1031.8	1044.8	1053.9	1022.0
1997	1038.3	1049.8	1059.4	1062.0	1063.3	1064.5	1057.2	1062.6	1078.7	1086.6	1097.1	1108.1	1068.9
1998	1094.5	1108.2	1112.3	1108.3	1112.7	1116.5	1100.6	1101.7	1114.0	1126.9	1137.5	1145.0	1114.8
1999	1122.8	1139.1	1147.6	1146.3	1150.7	1154.6	1135.2	1136.0	1149.3	1162.0	1174.5	1184.1	1150.1
2000	1176.8	1192.7	1212.5	1210.8	1216.6	1205.3	1192.8	1208.6	1214.8	1215.2	1227.8	1236.6	1209.2
2001	1197.2	1210.2	1220.1	1217.6	1218.5	1208.6	1196.1	1210.1	1209.1	1212.5	1220.3	1226.2	1212.2
2002	1199.2	1212.5	1220.2	1220.4	1221.0	1204.4	1194.0	1206.7	1206.8	1210.0	1222.6	1228.0	1212.2
2003	1205.4	1213.7	1224.1	1228.4	1230.8	1218.8	1214.5	1225.6	1229.5	1234.0	1239.8	1243.3	1225.7

Employment by Industry: Florida—*Continued*

(Numbers in thousands. Not seasonally adjusted.)

Industry	January	February	March	April	May	June	July	August	September	October	November	December	Annual Average
TAMPA-ST. PETERSBURG-CLEARWATER—*Continued*													
Total private													
1990	755.6	764.2	770.8	768.1	768.1	769.1	758.4	763.0	762.5	759.3	764.9	769.1	764.4
1991	743.3	745.7	750.5	741.9	741.7	739.8	730.9	734.5	735.0	738.1	746.1	751.6	741.5
1992	735.6	739.2	744.8	745.9	748.5	748.8	742.1	742.7	745.4	749.7	759.4	765.9	747.3
1993	753.9	762.7	770.5	774.9	777.0	781.2	777.5	781.8	786.2	791.2	801.0	811.1	780.7
1994	802.1	812.6	822.1	826.9	829.8	832.0	826.1	827.1	831.3	834.7	843.9	856.3	828.7
1995	843.9	852.4	861.4	862.0	864.7	864.5	854.7	860.0	863.3	865.1	879.4	889.3	863.3
1996	868.3	880.7	891.4	884.3	887.2	887.2	881.6	885.8	888.9	896.3	909.2	919.7	890.0
1997	906.1	915.6	925.4	928.3	930.3	932.5	933.5	939.4	945.4	949.1	961.3	971.6	936.5
1998	959.9	972.3	976.1	973.0	977.9	982.9	975.0	977.6	978.4	989.5	998.9	1006.6	980.6
1999	989.1	1002.5	1010.8	1010.7	1015.2	1020.1	1009.3	1011.5	1013.1	1023.9	1033.0	1042.2	1015.1
2000	1035.0	1050.3	1069.3	1065.9	1069.3	1072.1	1061.0	1067.3	1070.7	1069.2	1080.0	1088.7	1066.6
2001	1051.5	1062.7	1071.8	1069.5	1069.7	1070.8	1059.9	1063.2	1061.0	1062.8	1070.6	1075.6	1065.7
2002	1052.2	1063.7	1071.1	1071.3	1072.9	1067.9	1058.8	1060.4	1058.8	1060.4	1072.0	1076.3	1065.5
2003	1058.1	1064.4	1075.0	1080.1	1082.0	1081.9	1078.7	1079.4	1081.9	1083.5	1087.6	1091.5	1078.7
Goods-providing													
1990	130.3	130.9	130.7	129.5	130.1	130.5	128.5	129.3	128.9	127.0	125.3	124.1	128.7
1991	118.4	117.5	117.4	115.7	115.6	116.2	114.7	115.6	115.8	115.0	115.0	114.4	115.9
1992	111.5	111.3	112.3	112.6	113.0	113.1	113.3	112.7	113.2	113.1	113.6	114.0	112.8
1993	115.2	115.6	116.5	115.8	116.3	117.4	118.6	118.3	118.5	117.9	118.3	118.1	117.2
1994	117.5	117.0	117.0	117.0	117.2	119.0	118.5	119.3	120.0	119.9	119.9	121.3	118.6
1995	120.9	121.2	122.6	122.6	122.6	123.1	122.6	123.8	124.7	124.2	125.2	126.1	123.3
1996	125.0	126.4	127.4	126.5	127.8	128.4	127.7	128.7	128.9	130.0	130.4	131.7	128.2
1997	130.0	131.1	131.9	133.6	134.8	136.2	135.9	136.5	137.5	136.7	137.1	138.3	134.9
1998	138.5	139.5	139.4	137.6	138.2	139.3	138.3	138.6	138.6	138.9	139.4	139.9	138.8
1999	138.1	139.5	140.0	139.5	140.5	142.0	141.6	141.7	141.4	142.2	142.7	143.8	141.0
2000	143.5	145.2	147.4	146.4	147.3	150.0	148.1	148.7	149.2	146.7	147.3	147.0	147.2
2001	141.8	142.0	142.4	141.7	142.0	142.6	142.0	142.3	141.4	140.6	141.1	141.0	141.7
2002	138.2	138.1	138.2	138.0	138.4	139.3	139.0	140.3	140.8	140.8	141.0	140.6	139.4
2003	136.9	137.8	137.7	136.9	137.5	137.8	136.8	137.8	139.5	140.4	140.7	140.3	138.3
Natural resources and mining													
1990	0.7	0.7	0.7	0.6	0.6	0.6	0.6	0.6	0.6	0.6	0.6	0.6	0.6
1991	0.6	0.5	0.5	0.5	0.5	0.5	0.5	0.5	0.5	0.5	0.5	0.5	0.5
1992	0.5	0.5	0.5	0.5	0.5	0.5	0.5	0.5	0.5	0.4	0.4	0.4	0.5
1993	0.5	0.5	0.5	0.5	0.5	0.5	0.5	0.5	0.5	0.5	0.5	0.5	0.5
1994	0.5	0.5	0.5	0.5	0.5	0.5	0.5	0.5	0.5	0.5	0.5	0.5	0.5
1995	0.5	0.5	0.5	0.5	0.5	0.4	0.4	0.4	0.4	0.4	0.4	0.4	0.4
1996	0.4	0.4	0.4	0.4	0.4	0.4	0.4	0.5	0.4	0.5	0.5	0.5	0.4
1997	0.5	0.4	0.4	0.4	0.4	0.4	0.4	0.4	0.4	0.5	0.5	0.5	0.4
1998	0.5	0.4	0.4	0.4	0.4	0.4	0.4	0.4	0.5	0.4	0.4	0.5	0.4
1999	0.4	0.5	0.5	0.5	0.4	0.4	0.5	0.5	0.5	0.5	0.5	0.5	0.5
2000	0.5	0.5	0.5	0.5	0.5	0.5	0.5	0.5	0.5	0.5	0.5	0.5	0.5
2001	0.5	0.5	0.5	0.5	0.5	0.5	0.5	0.5	0.5	0.5	0.5	0.5	0.5
2002	0.5	0.5	0.5	0.5	0.5	0.5	0.5	0.5	0.5	0.5	0.5	0.5	0.5
2003	0.5	0.5	0.5	0.5	0.5	0.5	0.5	0.5	0.5	0.5	0.5	0.5	0.5
Construction													
1990	49.0	49.0	49.2	48.8	49.0	49.2	49.0	49.6	49.6	49.1	48.0	47.3	48.9
1991	43.6	42.9	42.9	42.6	42.3	42.6	42.1	42.5	42.5	41.8	41.4	41.0	42.4
1992	39.3	39.3	40.0	40.5	40.8	41.2	41.0	40.7	40.6	41.8	41.6	41.6	40.7
1993	42.9	43.0	43.4	43.4	43.5	44.0	44.8	44.8	45.2	44.7	45.0	44.8	44.1
1994	44.8	44.2	43.8	44.1	44.1	45.3	45.6	46.1	46.7	46.8	47.0	47.8	45.5
1995	46.8	47.1	48.2	48.4	48.3	48.7	48.7	49.4	49.7	49.2	50.2	50.7	48.8
1996	50.7	51.7	52.8	52.4	53.3	53.7	53.0	53.5	54.0	55.2	55.5	56.0	53.5
1997	55.2	55.4	55.8	56.7	56.8	57.5	57.9	58.3	58.6	58.4	58.5	58.9	57.3
1998	56.9	57.6	57.6	57.6	58.3	58.7	58.4	58.6	58.2	58.6	58.7	59.1	58.2
1999	57.0	57.3	57.8	57.2	57.9	58.6	58.1	58.2	58.1	58.7	58.6	59.4	58.1
2000	58.6	59.6	60.9	61.0	61.6	63.4	62.1	62.5	62.9	62.0	62.6	62.5	61.6
2001	59.2	59.7	60.2	60.5	61.2	61.9	62.3	62.4	62.4	61.9	62.7	62.8	61.4
2002	61.2	61.6	61.6	61.8	62.6	62.9	63.0	64.1	64.7	65.2	65.6	65.4	63.3
2003	63.3	64.3	64.5	64.3	65.2	65.7	65.7	67.1	68.1	69.0	69.4	69.2	66.3
Manufacturing													
1990	80.6	81.2	80.8	80.1	80.5	80.7	78.9	79.1	78.7	77.3	76.7	76.2	79.2
1991	74.2	74.1	74.0	72.6	72.8	73.1	72.1	72.6	72.8	72.7	73.1	72.9	73.0
1992	71.7	71.5	71.8	71.6	71.7	71.4	71.8	71.5	72.1	70.9	71.6	72.0	71.6
1993	71.8	72.1	72.6	71.9	72.3	72.9	73.3	73.0	72.8	72.7	72.8	72.8	72.5
1994	72.2	72.3	72.7	72.4	72.6	73.2	72.4	72.7	72.8	72.6	72.4	73.0	72.6
1995	73.6	73.6	73.9	73.7	73.8	74.0	73.5	74.0	74.6	74.6	74.6	75.0	74.0
1996	73.9	74.3	74.2	73.7	74.1	74.3	74.3	74.7	74.5	74.3	74.4	75.2	74.3
1997	74.3	75.3	75.7	76.5	77.6	78.3	77.6	77.8	78.5	77.8	78.1	78.9	77.2
1998	81.1	81.5	81.4	79.6	79.5	80.2	79.5	79.6	79.9	79.9	80.3	80.3	80.2
1999	80.7	81.7	81.7	81.8	82.2	83.0	83.0	83.0	82.8	83.0	83.6	83.9	82.5
2000	84.4	85.1	86.0	84.9	85.2	86.1	85.5	85.7	85.8	84.2	84.2	84.0	85.1
2001	82.1	81.8	81.7	80.7	80.3	80.2	79.2	79.4	78.5	78.2	77.9	77.7	79.8
2002	76.5	76.0	76.1	75.7	75.3	75.9	75.5	75.7	75.6	75.1	74.9	74.7	75.6
2003	73.1	73.0	72.7	72.1	71.8	71.6	70.6	70.2	70.9	70.9	70.8	70.6	71.5

Employment by Industry: Florida—*Continued*

(Numbers in thousands. Not seasonally adjusted.)

Industry	January	February	March	April	May	June	July	August	September	October	November	December	Annual Average
TAMPA-ST. PETERSBURG-CLEARWATER—*Continued*													
Service-providing													
1990	739.8	749.0	756.6	755.6	755.4	754.9	736.6	745.4	751.8	751.4	760.1	763.6	751.6
1991	741.4	746.8	752.0	744.4	744.7	739.3	723.6	726.6	736.4	742.3	751.0	757.5	742.1
1992	742.4	747.3	754.8	753.0	756.2	755.0	740.6	740.4	755.2	758.4	771.7	775.9	754.2
1993	759.9	771.6	778.3	782.8	784.7	786.5	774.2	777.3	791.9	799.8	809.7	820.8	786.4
1994	810.6	824.0	833.2	838.9	841.3	840.6	827.9	826.3	843.3	846.9	864.0	866.9	838.6
1995	852.2	863.3	871.3	871.4	873.8	872.1	854.3	856.9	871.2	873.6	887.5	897.4	870.4
1996	874.4	888.2	903.3	890.1	891.5	889.3	877.2	879.3	893.9	901.8	914.4	922.2	893.8
1997	908.3	918.7	927.5	928.4	928.5	928.3	921.3	926.1	941.2	949.9	960.0	969.8	934.0
1998	956.0	968.7	972.9	970.7	974.5	977.2	962.3	963.1	975.4	988.0	998.1	1005.1	976.0
1999	984.7	999.6	1007.6	1006.8	1010.2	1012.6	993.6	994.3	1007.9	1019.8	1031.8	1040.3	1009.1
2000	1033.3	1047.5	1065.1	1064.4	1069.3	1055.3	1044.7	1059.9	1065.6	1068.5	1080.5	1089.6	1062.0
2001	1055.4	1068.2	1077.7	1075.9	1076.5	1066.0	1054.1	1067.8	1067.7	1071.9	1079.2	1085.2	1070.4
2002	1061.0	1074.4	1082.0	1082.4	1082.6	1065.1	1055.0	1066.4	1066.0	1069.2	1081.6	1087.4	1072.8
2003	1068.5	1075.9	1086.4	1091.5	1093.3	1081.0	1077.7	1087.8	1090.0	1093.6	1099.1	1103.0	1087.3
Trade, transportation, and utilities													
1990	200.0	199.8	201.1	200.3	200.6	200.2	197.2	198.2	197.1	197.2	201.0	206.2	199.9
1991	194.4	193.1	193.6	194.6	194.7	193.9	191.4	192.1	191.8	194.1	198.5	201.6	194.4
1992	192.2	192.7	193.5	192.9	193.6	192.8	190.7	190.5	190.7	193.3	198.6	201.7	193.6
1993	189.8	191.1	192.5	192.5	192.3	193.5	191.8	192.9	194.1	196.4	200.6	204.6	194.3
1994	197.7	198.8	200.1	200.0	201.1	200.4	199.1	200.3	201.6	203.9	209.0	212.8	202.0
1995	205.9	206.1	206.7	205.9	206.2	205.9	203.0	204.8	205.6	207.9	213.6	218.2	207.4
1996	208.4	208.9	209.6	206.7	208.1	207.5	206.7	207.6	208.2	209.7	216.0	220.3	209.8
1997	213.2	213.4	214.1	216.4	216.9	216.3	214.6	214.8	216.3	221.8	226.1	231.8	217.9
1998	224.9	225.0	225.9	223.3	223.8	225.0	224.0	223.8	224.6	228.2	232.2	236.3	226.4
1999	224.0	225.6	227.5	226.8	226.5	226.8	225.8	226.1	226.3	228.1	233.3	237.0	227.8
2000	232.7	233.7	236.6	233.9	235.2	236.5	233.3	235.3	235.4	236.0	242.3	245.8	236.4
2001	229.7	229.1	229.9	226.9	226.8	226.4	224.0	224.4	224.6	225.9	230.8	233.8	227.6
2002	227.1	225.4	225.5	224.1	224.3	222.0	220.0	221.5	219.9	221.1	223.9	227.6	223.5
2003	217.1	215.8	215.8	215.1	216.0	214.7	214.4	214.5	215.2	215.8	219.1	223.5	216.4
Wholesale trade													
1990	42.8	43.2	43.4	43.1	43.4	43.3	42.9	43.1	42.9	42.5	42.6	42.9	43.0
1991	42.6	42.6	42.7	42.2	42.4	42.2	41.8	41.9	41.9	41.9	42.3	42.6	42.2
1992	41.8	42.1	42.3	41.9	42.3	42.3	42.1	41.8	41.8	42.3	42.7	43.1	42.2
1993	41.4	41.7	42.1	41.3	41.7	41.8	41.4	41.9	42.2	42.5	42.9	43.3	42.0
1994	43.3	43.8	44.1	44.5	44.9	45.0	45.3	45.5	45.7	45.8	45.9	46.3	45.0
1995	46.1	46.5	46.9	47.3	47.5	47.7	47.1	47.6	47.8	47.7	48.0	48.3	47.3
1996	46.5	46.1	46.3	45.4	45.9	46.1	45.3	45.7	45.7	45.7	46.4	46.7	45.9
1997	46.8	47.4	47.6	47.9	48.4	48.5	48.1	48.4	48.4	48.5	48.9	49.5	48.2
1998	50.0	49.6	49.7	50.1	50.5	50.6	50.5	50.6	50.4	50.8	50.7	50.8	50.3
1999	50.2	50.7	50.9	50.8	50.9	51.2	50.5	50.3	50.4	50.6	50.7	51.3	50.7
2000	51.7	51.9	52.6	52.8	53.3	54.0	52.8	53.0	53.4	53.7	54.3	54.7	53.2
2001	53.0	53.0	53.1	52.6	52.3	51.9	51.3	51.3	51.1	51.2	51.0	51.4	51.9
2002	51.4	51.4	51.4	50.9	51.2	50.7	50.2	50.2	50.0	49.9	49.9	50.0	50.6
2003	48.3	48.4	48.1	48.2	48.3	48.3	47.9	47.9	48.1	47.5	47.7	48.3	48.1
Retail trade													
1990	127.1	126.2	126.9	126.0	125.9	125.4	123.4	123.9	123.0	123.6	127.0	130.6	125.7
1991	120.8	119.7	120.2	121.6	121.5	120.9	119.0	119.5	119.1	120.9	124.7	126.9	121.2
1992	118.7	118.5	118.8	119.1	119.4	118.7	117.0	117.5	117.7	119.0	123.8	126.8	119.5
1993	117.3	118.1	118.5	119.2	118.4	119.3	118.2	118.8	119.3	120.7	124.1	127.7	119.9
1994	121.4	121.7	122.5	122.0	122.6	122.2	120.9	121.9	122.8	124.4	129.2	132.6	123.6
1995	127.3	127.1	127.4	126.4	126.4	126.2	124.5	125.5	126.3	128.5	133.6	137.0	128.0
1996	130.3	130.6	131.2	129.4	130.0	129.5	129.6	130.2	130.8	132.1	137.4	140.6	131.8
1997	134.2	133.4	133.6	135.2	135.4	134.8	133.5	134.0	134.3	139.7	143.5	147.7	136.6
1998	140.3	139.7	140.5	137.7	137.6	138.6	138.3	138.1	138.9	141.6	145.5	148.6	140.4
1999	138.8	139.4	139.9	140.7	140.3	140.5	140.1	140.5	141.0	141.7	146.2	149.5	141.5
2000	145.2	145.7	147.1	144.7	145.2	145.6	143.3	145.0	144.8	146.1	151.2	153.9	146.5
2001	142.5	141.8	142.5	140.2	140.3	140.3	138.9	139.4	140.0	141.5	146.6	148.6	141.8
2002	143.0	141.3	141.8	140.7	140.8	139.1	137.7	139.2	138.4	139.7	142.8	146.2	140.9
2003	138.6	137.3	137.5	137.0	137.8	136.9	137.2	137.2	138.0	139.4	142.5	145.8	138.8
Transportation and utilities													
1990	30.1	30.4	30.8	31.2	31.3	31.5	30.9	31.2	31.2	31.1	31.4	32.7	31.1
1991	31.0	30.8	30.7	30.8	30.8	30.8	30.6	30.7	30.8	31.3	31.5	32.1	30.9
1992	31.7	32.1	32.4	31.9	31.9	31.8	31.6	31.2	31.2	32.0	32.1	31.8	31.8
1993	31.1	31.3	31.9	32.0	32.2	32.4	32.2	32.2	32.6	33.2	33.6	33.6	32.3
1994	33.0	33.3	33.5	33.5	33.6	33.2	32.9	32.9	33.1	33.7	33.9	33.9	33.3
1995	32.5	32.5	32.4	32.2	32.3	32.0	31.4	31.7	31.5	31.7	32.0	32.9	32.0
1996	31.6	32.2	32.1	31.9	32.2	31.9	31.8	31.7	31.7	31.9	32.2	33.0	32.0
1997	32.2	32.6	32.9	33.3	33.1	33.0	33.0	32.4	33.6	33.6	33.7	34.6	33.1
1998	34.6	35.7	35.7	35.5	35.7	35.8	35.2	35.1	35.3	35.8	36.0	36.9	35.6
1999	35.0	35.5	36.7	35.3	35.3	35.1	35.2	35.3	34.9	35.8	36.4	36.2	35.5
2000	35.8	36.1	36.9	36.4	36.7	36.9	37.2	37.3	37.2	36.2	36.8	37.2	36.7
2001	34.2	34.3	34.3	34.1	34.2	34.2	33.8	33.7	33.5	33.2	33.2	33.8	33.8
2002	32.7	32.7	32.3	32.5	32.3	32.2	32.1	32.1	31.5	31.5	31.2	31.4	32.0
2003	30.2	30.1	30.2	29.9	29.9	29.5	29.3	29.4	29.1	28.9	28.9	29.4	29.6

Employment by Industry: Florida—*Continued*

(Numbers in thousands. Not seasonally adjusted.)

Industry	January	February	March	April	May	June	July	August	September	October	November	December	Annual Average
TAMPA-ST. PETERSBURG-CLEARWATER—*Continued*													
Information													
1990	27.2	27.1	26.7	26.3	26.4	26.7	26.4	26.5	26.5	26.5	26.6	26.3	26.6
1991	26.6	26.5	26.7	26.8	26.9	26.9	26.9	27.2	27.2	27.2	27.4	27.6	26.9
1992	27.5	27.6	27.5	27.4	27.6	27.9	27.9	27.8	27.9	27.8	28.1	28.2	27.7
1993	27.6	27.6	27.6	27.5	27.6	27.6	27.8	27.6	27.9	27.7	27.8	28.1	27.7
1994	27.9	27.8	28.1	28.4	28.5	29.0	28.9	28.9	29.1	28.0	29.3	29.9	28.6
1995	28.8	29.0	29.8	29.8	30.1	30.8	29.9	30.2	30.8	29.9	30.2	30.6	29.9
1996	29.4	29.6	30.0	28.7	28.8	29.0	28.4	28.8	29.5	28.6	29.0	29.3	29.0
1997	29.9	30.3	30.6	31.4	32.2	32.5	32.4	32.8	32.6	31.2	31.8	32.7	31.7
1998	33.3	33.9	34.1	33.8	34.3	34.8	34.0	34.2	34.5	35.9	36.4	36.5	34.6
1999	37.8	38.2	38.1	37.6	37.9	38.2	37.3	37.3	37.7	37.1	37.5	38.6	37.7
2000	38.1	38.4	39.1	38.4	38.7	39.7	39.5	39.8	40.3	41.0	41.5	41.7	39.7
2001	40.5	40.5	40.5	40.1	39.7	39.3	39.0	38.3	37.5	37.5	37.3	36.6	38.9
2002	36.7	36.3	36.5	36.1	36.0	35.6	35.4	35.3	35.4	35.2	35.7	35.6	35.8
2003	35.1	34.9	35.0	35.0	34.9	34.7	34.8	34.7	34.7	34.7	33.6	33.7	34.7
Financial activities													
1990	64.5	65.0	65.2	65.7	66.1	66.2	66.5	66.8	66.5	65.8	66.2	66.6	65.9
1991	63.2	63.4	63.3	62.7	62.9	62.9	62.5	62.2	61.6	61.8	61.7	61.9	62.5
1992	61.1	61.3	60.3	60.4	60.7	60.8	60.2	59.8	59.7	59.9	59.9	60.5	60.3
1993	59.8	60.4	60.1	59.3	59.7	60.2	60.6	60.9	61.4	61.1	61.7	62.4	60.6
1994	64.7	65.5	65.9	66.5	66.5	66.8	67.1	67.0	66.7	67.3	67.6	68.6	66.6
1995	68.0	68.1	68.1	69.6	69.0	69.0	69.9	69.5	69.2	68.6	69.4	70.2	69.0
1996	68.0	68.3	69.7	69.5	69.9	70.4	70.3	71.0	71.2	71.7	72.2	73.0	70.4
1997	71.5	72.0	72.6	73.9	74.4	75.0	75.1	75.8	76.0	77.1	77.8	80.0	75.1
1998	79.8	81.0	81.3	81.1	81.7	81.9	81.7	81.8	81.9	83.3	83.8	85.5	82.0
1999	85.1	86.1	86.4	86.0	86.6	87.0	87.8	88.1	88.4	88.5	88.5	89.4	87.3
2000	88.9	89.4	90.3	91.1	91.2	91.1	91.0	91.1	91.3	91.2	91.8	92.1	90.9
2001	90.6	91.4	92.1	92.5	92.4	92.6	91.5	91.7	91.2	91.0	91.1	91.2	91.6
2002	90.6	91.6	91.6	91.2	91.3	91.7	92.0	92.2	91.8	92.1	92.7	93.2	91.8
2003	92.2	92.9	93.0	93.3	93.9	94.3	94.8	95.0	95.1	94.5	94.5	94.2	94.0
Professional and business services													
1990	104.3	106.8	108.4	109.0	108.3	110.2	109.1	110.6	110.8	112.1	112.9	110.0	109.3
1991	108.5	109.5	110.9	108.7	108.8	108.9	109.2	110.7	110.6	112.1	112.4	113.2	110.2
1992	111.6	110.3	111.2	113.3	114.1	114.6	115.8	116.1	116.3	117.3	118.6	120.2	114.9
1993	120.1	122.0	124.2	132.7	133.3	135.1	133.7	134.9	135.2	142.3	143.7	145.9	133.5
1994	143.8	146.1	148.3	152.7	154.0	153.9	151.2	151.4	151.6	152.7	152.9	156.4	151.2
1995	154.4	157.4	159.2	161.9	165.0	165.2	160.8	163.2	164.2	166.7	169.8	171.3	163.2
1996	168.4	172.2	175.1	175.7	175.7	176.6	179.2	179.5	180.8	183.2	187.0	189.0	178.5
1997	191.7	194.0	198.0	196.4	195.9	198.1	206.2	209.2	212.0	212.7	216.9	214.4	203.7
1998	208.4	213.0	213.9	215.9	218.5	220.5	219.9	223.0	222.9	227.3	231.1	230.7	220.4
1999	230.9	235.0	238.3	241.1	244.3	247.0	241.0	243.8	244.7	252.5	254.2	255.1	243.9
2000	256.4	262.3	269.0	268.7	270.7	269.9	268.2	272.3	274.2	274.7	275.6	279.5	270.1
2001	272.0	278.5	280.9	281.9	281.2	282.8	279.2	281.4	281.4	281.0	282.2	282.7	280.4
2002	276.3	284.0	285.8	288.1	288.0	285.4	283.3	279.4	278.3	278.0	283.9	282.5	282.8
2003	284.1	287.7	294.1	300.5	300.2	301.4	300.8	298.9	298.6	298.6	298.9	296.8	296.7
Educational and health services													
1990	101.8	103.2	103.9	104.1	104.5	104.7	104.2	104.8	106.0	105.8	106.5	107.5	104.7
1991	106.8	107.7	108.3	107.3	108.0	107.9	106.4	106.9	108.2	109.2	110.6	111.3	108.2
1992	111.8	112.8	113.4	115.2	114.8	115.0	114.6	114.9	116.3	116.7	117.3	118.1	115.0
1993	116.6	117.9	118.9	119.1	119.4	120.2	120.2	120.7	122.6	122.2	123.2	124.4	120.4
1994	121.6	123.7	125.5	126.7	127.2	128.0	128.6	129.0	131.1	132.1	133.1	133.8	128.3
1995	132.8	134.0	135.0	133.2	133.3	133.8	133.3	134.1	135.2	134.2	135.4	136.1	134.2
1996	131.4	132.6	134.1	134.7	134.7	134.2	132.3	132.9	133.9	134.1	135.0	135.7	133.8
1997	131.5	132.9	133.8	134.1	134.5	134.5	132.9	133.8	135.2	132.6	134.1	135.5	133.7
1998	134.9	136.7	136.6	134.9	135.4	135.6	134.0	134.5	134.6	134.6	134.5	135.4	135.1
1999	132.7	134.6	135.5	133.3	134.1	133.6	132.8	132.8	134.0	134.8	135.6	136.2	134.1
2000	134.4	135.9	136.7	136.6	135.1	134.1	133.4	134.1	135.2	134.8	135.7	136.0	135.2
2001	132.4	133.4	134.5	134.8	135.0	135.5	133.8	135.1	136.2	136.8	137.6	138.8	135.3
2002	134.6	135.7	137.2	137.6	138.4	138.1	136.9	138.2	139.1	140.1	141.5	142.1	138.3
2003	138.9	140.2	141.5	142.2	142.7	142.2	141.1	142.5	143.4	143.4	144.3	144.9	142.3
Leisure and hospitality													
1990	90.2	93.6	96.6	95.3	94.3	92.8	89.1	89.4	89.3	87.7	89.2	91.0	91.5
1991	88.7	91.3	93.5	89.9	88.3	86.4	83.3	83.5	83.7	82.8	84.4	85.5	86.7
1992	83.4	86.4	89.5	87.1	87.5	87.0	82.1	83.5	83.8	84.3	85.7	85.4	85.4
1993	87.4	90.4	92.8	90.1	90.7	89.4	86.8	88.4	88.4	85.6	87.4	88.9	88.8
1994	91.0	95.5	98.6	97.1	96.8	96.1	93.9	92.6	92.4	91.6	93.0	94.0	94.3
1995	94.4	97.3	100.3	99.2	98.4	96.5	95.2	94.3	93.7	93.6	95.6	96.4	96.2
1996	97.6	102.0	104.7	102.5	102.1	100.8	96.6	96.9	96.1	98.9	99.3	100.2	99.8
1997	98.2	101.2	103.4	101.8	100.6	98.7	95.3	95.6	94.8	95.8	96.5	97.6	98.2
1998	98.6	101.2	102.8	104.5	104.1	103.5	101.0	99.9	99.6	99.0	99.2	100.1	101.1
1999	98.2	100.7	102.0	103.7	102.2	102.2	100.0	99.0	97.9	97.7	98.2	98.8	100.0
2000	97.8	101.7	105.9	107.0	106.9	106.3	103.4	102.2	101.2	100.9	101.8	102.6	103.1
2001	101.6	104.8	107.9	107.8	108.1	106.2	105.7	105.3	104.0	105.2	105.2	105.8	105.6
2002	102.9	106.3	109.7	110.0	110.0	108.7	105.3	106.5	106.5	105.3	105.3	106.4	106.9
2003	105.7	107.1	110.1	109.4	108.8	108.4	108.0	107.8	107.3	107.7	108.0	109.1	108.1

Employment by Industry: Florida—*Continued*

(Numbers in thousands. Not seasonally adjusted.)

Industry	January	February	March	April	May	June	July	August	September	October	November	December	Annual Average
TAMPA-ST. PETERSBURG-CLEARWATER—*Continued*													
Other services													
1990	37.3	37.8	38.2	37.9	37.8	37.8	37.4	37.4	37.4	37.2	37.2	37.4	37.5
1991	36.7	36.7	36.8	36.2	36.5	36.7	36.5	36.3	36.1	35.9	36.1	36.1	36.3
1992	36.5	36.8	37.1	37.0	37.2	37.6	37.5	37.4	37.5	37.3	37.6	37.8	37.2
1993	37.4	37.7	37.9	37.9	37.7	37.8	38.0	38.1	38.1	38.0	38.3	38.7	37.9
1994	37.9	38.2	38.6	38.5	38.5	38.8	38.8	38.6	38.8	39.2	39.1	39.5	38.7
1995	38.7	39.3	39.7	39.8	40.1	40.2	40.0	40.1	39.9	40.0	40.2	40.4	39.8
1996	40.1	40.7	40.8	40.0	40.1	40.3	40.4	40.4	40.3	40.1	40.3	40.5	40.3
1997	40.1	40.7	41.0	40.7	41.0	41.2	41.1	40.9	41.0	41.2	41.0	41.3	40.9
1998	41.5	42.0	42.1	41.9	41.9	42.3	42.1	41.8	41.7	42.3	42.3	42.2	42.0
1999	42.3	42.8	43.0	42.7	43.1	43.3	43.0	42.7	42.7	43.0	43.0	43.3	42.9
2000	43.2	43.7	44.3	43.8	44.2	44.5	44.1	43.8	43.9	43.9	44.0	44.0	44.0
2001	42.9	43.0	43.6	43.8	44.5	45.4	44.7	44.7	44.7	44.8	45.3	45.7	44.4
2002	45.8	46.3	46.6	46.2	46.5	47.1	46.9	47.0	47.0	47.8	48.0	48.3	47.0
2003	48.1	48.0	47.8	47.7	48.0	48.4	48.0	48.2	48.1	48.4	48.5	49.0	48.2
Government													
1990	114.5	115.7	116.5	117.0	117.4	116.3	106.7	111.7	118.2	119.1	120.5	118.6	116.0
1991	116.5	118.6	118.9	118.2	118.6	115.7	107.4	107.7	117.2	119.2	119.9	120.3	116.5
1992	118.3	119.4	122.3	119.7	120.7	119.3	111.8	110.4	123.0	121.8	125.9	124.0	119.7
1993	121.2	124.5	124.3	123.7	124.0	122.7	115.3	113.8	124.2	126.5	127.0	127.8	122.9
1994	126.0	128.4	128.1	129.0	128.7	127.6	120.3	118.5	132.0	132.1	140.0	131.9	128.5
1995	129.2	132.1	132.5	132.0	131.7	130.7	122.2	120.7	132.6	132.7	133.3	134.2	130.3
1996	131.1	133.9	139.3	132.3	132.1	130.5	123.3	122.2	133.9	135.5	135.6	134.2	131.9
1997	132.2	134.2	134.0	133.7	133.0	132.0	123.7	123.2	133.3	137.5	135.8	136.5	132.4
1998	134.6	135.9	136.2	135.3	134.8	133.6	125.6	124.1	135.6	137.4	138.6	138.4	134.1
1999	133.7	136.6	136.8	135.6	135.5	134.5	125.9	124.5	136.2	138.1	141.5	141.9	135.0
2000	141.8	142.4	143.2	144.9	147.3	133.2	131.8	141.3	144.1	146.0	147.8	147.9	142.6
2001	145.7	147.5	148.3	148.1	148.8	137.8	136.2	146.9	148.1	149.7	149.7	150.6	146.4
2002	147.0	148.8	149.1	149.1	148.1	136.5	135.2	146.3	148.0	149.6	150.6	151.7	146.7
2003	147.3	149.3	149.1	148.3	148.8	136.9	135.8	146.2	147.6	150.5	152.2	151.8	147.0
Federal government													
1990	17.6	17.6	17.9	18.7	19.1	18.5	18.9	18.1	17.8	17.8	17.8	18.1	18.1
1991	17.8	17.9	17.9	17.9	18.0	18.1	18.1	18.2	18.2	18.2	18.3	18.7	18.1
1992	18.5	18.3	18.2	18.2	18.3	18.2	18.2	18.2	18.2	18.0	18.0	18.4	18.2
1993	18.1	18.0	17.9	18.0	18.0	18.1	18.2	18.2	18.1	18.0	18.1	18.6	18.1
1994	18.1	18.0	18.0	17.9	17.8	17.7	17.7	17.5	17.4	17.4	17.5	18.3	17.7
1995	17.4	17.3	17.2	17.3	17.2	17.4	17.8	17.8	17.8	17.7	17.8	18.4	17.5
1996	17.6	17.5	17.6	17.7	17.7	17.7	17.7	17.7	17.6	17.7	17.8	18.7	17.7
1997	17.8	17.8	17.8	17.8	17.8	17.8	17.9	18.0	18.0	18.1	18.3	18.8	17.9
1998	18.0	18.0	18.0	18.1	18.1	18.1	18.1	18.1	18.1	18.3	18.5	19.0	18.2
1999	18.4	18.7	18.4	18.7	18.4	18.3	18.1	18.2	18.2	18.1	18.2	18.7	18.3
2000	18.3	18.4	18.6	19.3	22.7	19.2	19.2	18.7	18.4	18.5	18.6	19.2	19.1
2001	18.8	18.8	18.8	18.7	18.7	18.9	18.8	18.8	18.8	18.8	18.8	19.2	18.8
2002	18.7	18.6	18.7	18.7	18.7	18.8	18.5	18.9	19.3	19.4	19.3	19.9	19.0
2003	19.5	19.4	19.4	19.5	19.5	19.4	19.3	19.4	19.3	19.4	19.3	19.7	19.4
State government													
1990	18.8	19.0	19.2	19.2	19.3	19.0	18.3	18.4	19.4	19.4	19.7	19.8	19.1
1991	19.3	19.6	19.6	19.6	19.9	18.4	18.4	18.6	19.6	19.8	20.0	19.8	19.3
1992	19.5	19.8	19.6	19.7	20.1	18.5	18.8	18.7	19.4	20.1	19.9	19.9	19.5
1993	19.9	20.3	20.3	20.5	20.2	19.0	19.3	19.8	20.2	20.7	20.5	20.6	20.1
1994	20.3	20.7	20.8	21.0	20.9	19.7	20.2	20.2	21.5	21.4	21.1	21.3	20.7
1995	20.7	21.3	21.7	21.4	21.5	20.0	20.3	20.4	21.5	21.6	21.6	21.6	21.1
1996	21.3	21.7	22.0	21.8	21.9	20.3	20.7	21.5	21.5	21.7	21.8	21.7	21.4
1997	21.9	21.9	21.9	22.0	22.1	20.7	21.0	22.0	21.9	22.3	22.4	22.3	21.8
1998	22.7	22.5	22.4	22.3	22.3	20.8	21.5	21.5	21.8	22.2	22.4	22.6	22.0
1999	21.9	22.5	22.6	22.6	22.5	21.1	22.0	21.8	22.4	22.9	23.1	23.3	22.3
2000	22.3	22.9	23.1	22.9	23.0	21.9	21.6	22.0	22.5	23.0	23.1	23.4	22.6
2001	22.5	22.9	23.0	22.8	22.7	21.6	21.2	21.8	22.1	22.7	23.1	22.9	22.4
2002	22.0	22.5	22.6	22.5	22.6	20.9	21.0	21.6	22.1	22.6	23.0	22.6	22.2
2003	22.1	22.7	22.7	22.7	22.9	21.1	21.2	21.5	22.1	23.0	22.8	22.7	22.3
Local government													
1990	78.1	79.1	79.4	79.1	79.0	78.8	69.5	75.2	81.0	81.9	83.0	80.7	78.7
1991	79.4	81.1	81.4	80.7	80.7	79.2	70.9	70.9	79.4	81.2	81.6	81.8	79.0
1992	80.3	81.3	84.5	81.8	82.3	82.6	74.8	73.5	85.4	83.7	88.0	85.7	81.9
1993	83.2	86.2	86.1	85.2	85.8	85.6	77.8	75.8	85.9	87.8	88.4	88.6	84.7
1994	87.6	89.7	89.3	90.1	90.0	90.2	82.4	80.8	93.1	93.3	101.4	92.3	90.0
1995	91.1	93.5	93.6	93.3	93.0	93.3	84.1	82.5	93.3	93.4	93.9	94.2	91.6
1996	92.2	94.7	99.7	92.8	92.5	92.5	84.9	83.0	94.8	96.1	96.0	93.8	92.7
1997	92.5	94.5	94.3	93.9	93.1	93.5	84.8	83.2	93.4	97.1	95.1	95.4	92.5
1998	93.9	95.4	95.8	94.9	94.4	94.7	86.0	84.5	95.7	96.9	97.7	96.8	93.8
1999	93.4	95.4	95.8	94.3	94.6	95.1	85.8	84.5	95.6	97.1	100.2	99.9	94.3
2000	101.2	101.1	101.5	102.7	101.6	92.1	91.0	100.6	103.2	104.5	106.1	105.3	100.9
2001	104.4	105.8	106.5	106.6	107.4	97.3	96.2	106.3	107.2	108.2	107.8	108.5	105.1
2002	106.3	107.7	107.8	107.9	106.8	96.8	95.7	105.8	106.6	107.6	108.3	109.2	105.5
2003	105.7	107.2	107.0	106.1	106.4	96.4	95.3	105.3	106.2	108.1	110.1	109.4	105.3

Employment by Industry: Florida—*Continued*

(Numbers in thousands. Not seasonally adjusted.)

Industry	January	February	March	April	May	June	July	August	September	October	November	December	Annual Average
WEST PALM BEACH-BOCA RATON-DEL RAY BEACH													
Total nonfarm													
1990	364.1	367.6	369.1	363.7	361.5	356.5	346.8	348.3	352.3	356.2	363.4	368.1	359.8
1991	361.5	362.3	363.9	357.4	355.7	351.4	341.0	341.8	346.3	347.8	357.5	362.6	354.1
1992	357.8	359.2	363.9	356.7	354.6	350.5	341.8	340.0	347.8	354.8	362.5	370.2	354.9
1993	364.9	368.8	371.2	369.4	367.8	366.3	359.3	358.4	366.3	374.4	381.0	385.9	369.4
1994	381.7	387.3	391.3	387.9	386.8	384.8	373.3	374.1	382.6	385.8	397.8	398.7	386.0
1995	393.6	399.9	403.4	398.5	398.5	397.3	385.8	386.9	396.3	401.0	410.7	416.2	399.0
1996	411.3	416.9	422.1	416.1	415.1	412.6	405.0	406.5	414.1	420.2	429.5	437.3	417.2
1997	430.1	434.9	438.3	436.3	435.4	433.6	426.2	428.8	436.8	444.5	452.7	461.7	438.2
1998	454.6	459.6	463.8	455.5	455.6	454.5	443.5	444.8	452.2	459.7	467.7	475.9	457.2
1999	465.9	471.6	474.2	469.4	468.4	467.3	456.6	457.5	463.9	470.5	479.1	488.0	469.3
2000	483.0	488.7	493.8	490.5	490.7	486.3	483.7	492.8	497.5	500.4	511.9	519.0	494.9
2001	512.1	515.7	519.6	515.7	513.3	505.1	498.1	506.6	508.9	513.2	521.2	528.0	513.1
2002	522.4	522.9	528.1	523.8	523.5	516.6	508.3	515.8	517.6	522.3	530.7	538.3	522.5
2003	526.8	528.9	531.7	529.3	527.6	519.6	513.8	521.3	525.1	528.4	535.2	542.0	527.5
Total private													
1990	318.4	321.2	322.3	316.4	313.7	309.3	302.8	304.9	305.6	308.9	315.6	320.1	313.2
1991	313.9	314.7	315.8	309.3	307.6	304.6	297.2	297.7	298.9	300.6	309.4	314.5	307.0
1992	310.2	311.5	313.6	308.8	306.4	303.0	297.7	297.1	301.2	307.9	315.1	322.5	307.9
1993	317.8	321.7	323.5	321.3	319.6	318.3	314.3	314.9	317.3	323.9	331.8	338.1	321.8
1994	333.5	338.1	341.3	337.8	336.9	335.1	327.6	329.5	332.5	334.8	343.2	349.4	336.6
1995	343.6	348.4	351.3	346.5	346.3	345.5	338.0	339.8	343.6	348.3	357.4	365.1	347.8
1996	359.4	363.6	366.1	362.3	361.5	359.7	356.1	358.2	361.0	367.0	375.5	383.1	364.4
1997	376.3	380.1	383.7	381.4	380.5	379.5	376.3	379.5	382.3	390.5	397.3	406.2	384.4
1998	400.4	404.6	408.8	400.2	400.2	399.9	393.0	395.3	397.5	404.7	412.0	420.8	403.1
1999	411.4	415.4	417.9	412.8	411.8	411.3	405.1	406.9	408.1	414.3	422.1	431.5	414.0
2000	427.0	431.2	435.8	432.3	431.7	433.1	431.1	435.2	439.9	442.6	453.5	461.2	437.9
2001	454.8	456.8	460.4	456.7	454.2	451.3	445.4	448.5	450.1	453.2	461.1	467.9	455.0
2002	461.1	461.5	466.4	462.0	461.5	460.5	452.9	454.3	455.0	459.3	467.3	474.7	461.4
2003	463.7	465.3	468.1	465.6	463.5	461.7	456.4	457.9	460.8	463.4	470.1	477.4	464.5
Goods-producing													
1990	60.8	60.1	59.4	58.3	57.9	57.7	57.1	57.8	57.9	57.2	56.9	55.9	58.0
1991	53.1	52.7	52.0	50.6	51.2	51.0	50.4	51.2	50.8	50.7	51.2	50.2	51.2
1992	49.6	49.0	48.6	47.1	47.2	47.3	47.6	47.7	48.7	50.7	51.2	51.4	48.8
1993	49.0	49.2	49.0	48.6	49.3	49.8	48.6	49.3	49.5	50.6	50.9	51.2	49.5
1994	49.2	49.2	49.5	48.1	48.6	49.2	47.9	48.9	49.6	49.8	50.8	51.1	49.3
1995	50.2	50.7	51.1	49.9	50.5	50.9	50.1	51.1	51.7	52.0	53.5	53.6	51.2
1996	52.4	52.6	52.4	51.6	52.1	52.0	51.2	52.0	52.6	53.7	54.3	54.6	52.6
1997	52.3	52.5	52.9	53.2	54.0	54.0	54.2	55.3	56.1	57.3	58.1	58.4	54.8
1998	56.9	57.3	57.8	56.8	57.7	58.3	56.8	57.3	57.6	58.9	59.1	59.9	57.8
1999	58.5	58.8	59.3	59.8	59.4	59.4	58.2	59.0	58.9	60.9	61.2	61.9	59.6
2000	60.6	61.4	62.1	61.3	61.6	61.4	60.6	61.3	61.9	61.7	62.4	62.8	61.6
2001	60.7	60.8	60.9	59.7	59.6	59.5	58.9	60.0	60.2	60.9	61.0	61.5	60.3
2002	60.0	59.4	59.3	58.6	58.8	58.4	57.4	58.1	58.3	58.0	58.5	58.7	58.6
2003	56.9	56.5	56.3	56.2	56.1	56.5	56.2	56.8	57.5	57.4	57.3	57.2	56.7
Construction and mining													
1990	29.4	28.7	28.5	27.6	27.4	27.6	27.5	27.8	28.0	27.2	26.6	25.3	27.6
1991	22.7	22.2	21.8	21.1	21.3	21.4	21.1	21.4	21.2	20.9	21.0	20.5	21.3
1992	20.0	19.6	19.5	19.1	19.3	19.6	19.7	19.9	20.7	22.1	22.1	22.2	20.3
1993	20.7	20.7	20.9	21.1	21.7	22.2	22.1	22.3	22.4	22.9	22.8	22.9	21.8
1994	21.5	21.5	21.7	21.6	22.0	22.7	22.3	22.9	23.4	23.4	23.5	23.9	22.5
1995	23.6	23.8	24.1	23.9	24.4	24.8	24.6	24.8	25.0	25.0	25.6	25.6	24.6
1996	25.2	25.2	25.2	25.2	25.4	25.7	25.5	25.4	25.7	26.4	26.2	26.0	25.5
1997	25.2	25.4	25.7	25.6	26.4	26.9	26.8	27.3	27.7	28.2	28.4	28.5	26.8
1998	27.5	27.7	27.9	28.3	28.6	29.1	29.2	29.0	29.1	30.0	30.0	30.4	28.9
1999	28.5	28.6	28.9	29.0	29.3	29.6	29.5	29.7	29.8	30.8	31.1	31.5	29.6
2000	30.8	31.4	31.9	32.1	32.6	32.8	32.9	33.2	33.6	33.7	33.9	34.3	32.8
2001	33.7	34.1	34.3	33.8	34.1	34.7	34.7	35.3	35.5	36.1	36.0	36.0	34.8
2002	35.3	34.9	34.9	34.7	35.1	35.3	35.1	35.5	35.6	35.6	35.5	35.5	35.3
2003	34.6	34.3	34.2	34.4	34.8	35.5	35.6	36.0	36.3	36.3	36.1	35.9	35.3
Manufacturing													
1990	31.4	31.4	30.9	30.7	30.5	30.1	29.6	30.0	29.9	30.0	30.3	30.6	30.4
1991	30.4	30.5	30.2	29.5	29.9	29.6	29.3	29.8	29.6	29.8	30.2	29.7	29.8
1992	29.6	29.4	29.1	28.0	27.9	27.7	27.9	27.8	28.0	28.6	29.1	29.2	28.5
1993	28.3	28.5	28.1	27.5	27.6	27.6	26.5	27.0	27.1	27.7	28.1	28.3	27.6
1994	27.7	27.7	27.8	26.5	26.6	26.5	25.6	26.0	26.2	26.4	27.3	27.2	26.7
1995	26.6	26.9	27.0	26.0	26.1	26.1	25.5	26.3	26.7	27.0	27.9	28.0	26.6
1996	27.2	27.4	27.2	26.4	26.7	26.3	25.7	26.6	26.9	27.3	28.1	28.6	27.0
1997	27.1	27.1	27.2	27.6	27.6	27.1	27.4	28.0	28.4	29.1	29.7	29.9	28.0
1998	29.4	29.6	29.9	28.5	29.1	29.2	27.6	28.3	28.5	28.9	29.1	29.5	28.9
1999	30.0	30.2	30.4	30.8	30.1	29.8	28.7	29.3	29.1	30.1	30.1	30.4	29.9
2000	29.8	30.0	30.2	29.2	29.0	28.6	27.7	28.1	28.3	28.0	28.5	28.5	28.8
2001	27.0	26.7	26.6	25.9	25.5	24.8	24.2	24.7	24.7	24.8	25.0	25.5	25.4
2002	24.7	24.5	24.4	23.9	23.7	23.1	22.3	22.6	22.7	22.4	23.0	23.2	23.4
2003	22.3	22.2	22.1	21.8	21.3	21.0	20.6	20.8	21.2	21.1	21.2	21.3	21.4

Employment by Industry: Florida—*Continued*

(Numbers in thousands. Not seasonally adjusted.)

Industry	January	February	March	April	May	June	July	August	September	October	November	December	Annual Average
WEST PALM BEACH-BOCA RATON-DELRAY BEACH *—Continued*													
Service-providing													
1990	303.3	307.5	309.7	305.4	303.6	298.8	289.7	290.5	294.4	299.0	306.5	312.2	301.7
1991	308.4	309.6	311.9	306.8	304.5	300.4	290.6	290.6	295.5	297.1	306.3	312.4	302.8
1992	308.2	310.2	315.3	309.6	307.4	303.2	294.2	292.3	299.1	304.1	311.3	318.8	306.1
1993	315.9	319.6	322.2	320.8	318.5	316.5	310.7	309.1	316.8	323.8	330.1	334.7	319.8
1994	332.5	338.1	341.8	339.8	338.2	335.6	325.4	325.2	333.0	336.0	347.0	347.6	336.6
1995	343.4	349.2	352.3	348.6	348.0	346.4	335.7	335.8	344.6	349.0	357.2	362.6	347.7
1996	358.9	364.3	369.7	364.5	363.0	360.6	353.8	354.5	361.5	366.5	375.2	382.7	364.6
1997	377.8	382.4	385.4	383.1	381.4	379.6	372.0	373.5	380.7	387.2	394.6	403.3	383.4
1998	397.7	402.3	406.0	398.7	397.9	396.2	386.7	387.5	394.6	400.8	408.6	416.0	399.4
1999	407.4	412.8	414.9	409.6	409.0	407.9	398.4	398.5	405.0	409.6	417.9	426.1	409.7
2000	422.4	427.3	431.7	429.2	429.1	424.9	423.1	431.5	435.6	438.7	449.5	456.2	433.3
2001	451.4	454.9	458.7	456.0	453.7	445.6	439.2	446.6	448.7	452.3	460.2	466.5	452.8
2002	462.4	463.5	468.8	465.2	464.7	458.2	450.9	457.7	459.3	464.3	472.2	479.6	463.9
2003	469.9	472.4	475.4	473.1	471.5	463.1	457.6	464.5	467.6	471.0	477.9	484.8	470.7
Trade, transportation, and utilities													
1990	74.2	74.2	74.2	74.1	73.8	73.1	70.8	71.4	71.7	73.6	75.8	78.8	73.8
1991	76.3	75.6	75.3	74.1	73.8	73.1	70.9	71.0	71.3	72.2	75.1	77.2	73.8
1992	74.4	74.2	74.3	72.8	72.5	72.1	70.6	70.3	71.2	72.6	75.3	78.3	73.2
1993	74.6	75.0	75.1	74.8	74.0	73.5	73.0	73.0	74.1	75.1	78.1	80.5	75.0
1994	77.0	77.4	77.7	76.5	76.3	75.5	73.3	74.0	74.9	76.2	78.7	80.7	76.5
1995	77.6	77.9	78.2	77.3	76.9	76.8	75.5	75.7	76.7	78.7	81.1	83.7	78.0
1996	80.8	80.7	81.1	80.3	80.2	79.9	79.9	80.6	81.2	82.8	85.7	88.7	81.8
1997	85.4	85.1	85.9	84.4	84.3	83.8	83.0	83.0	84.5	86.9	89.7	93.4	85.7
1998	90.7	90.0	91.1	87.7	87.6	87.6	87.4	87.9	88.4	89.9	92.0	95.6	89.6
1999	91.0	90.7	91.2	89.9	90.8	90.4	88.9	89.2	89.8	92.2	95.5	99.0	91.5
2000	94.3	94.4	94.9	93.7	94.0	94.6	92.7	93.5	93.6	95.2	99.1	101.8	95.2
2001	98.6	98.3	98.6	98.3	98.2	97.1	96.1	96.6	97.1	98.1	100.9	103.7	98.4
2002	100.2	99.6	100.2	99.6	99.2	98.7	97.7	98.0	99.0	99.6	102.8	105.9	100.0
2003	101.2	100.5	100.3	99.8	99.9	98.9	98.0	98.2	98.7	99.4	102.6	105.7	100.3
Wholesale trade													
1990	10.7	10.7	10.7	10.7	10.7	10.6	10.3	10.5	10.6	10.7	10.6	10.7	10.6
1991	10.7	10.6	10.6	10.5	10.5	10.5	10.5	10.6	10.6	10.7	10.8	11.0	10.6
1992	10.8	10.8	10.9	11.1	11.0	11.0	11.1	11.1	11.3	11.2	11.4	11.6	11.1
1993	11.7	11.9	12.0	11.8	11.8	11.8	12.0	12.1	12.2	12.1	12.3	12.5	12.0
1994	12.5	12.5	12.6	12.6	12.7	12.6	12.4	12.6	12.8	13.2	13.3	13.2	12.7
1995	13.3	13.5	13.6	13.5	13.4	13.6	13.4	13.5	13.7	14.0	14.2	14.4	13.6
1996	14.2	14.2	14.3	14.3	14.3	14.3	14.3	14.4	14.6	15.0	15.2	15.4	14.5
1997	15.3	15.5	15.7	15.3	15.3	15.4	15.2	15.3	15.7	16.1	16.4	16.6	15.6
1998	16.4	16.6	16.9	16.1	16.2	16.3	16.0	16.1	16.1	16.2	16.3	16.6	16.3
1999	16.2	16.4	16.3	15.9	16.0	15.9	15.5	15.6	15.8	16.1	16.4	16.8	16.0
2000	16.5	16.6	16.8	16.8	17.2	17.3	16.9	17.1	17.2	17.4	17.5	17.7	17.1
2001	18.3	18.4	18.5	18.9	19.0	18.4	18.9	19.1	19.1	19.5	19.9	20.2	19.0
2002	19.9	20.1	20.3	20.2	20.2	19.6	20.0	20.1	20.1	20.4	21.1	21.5	20.3
2003	20.9	21.1	21.2	21.0	20.9	20.3	20.4	20.4	20.4	20.6	21.1	21.5	20.8
Retail trade													
1990	55.3	55.1	55.1	54.9	54.6	54.1	52.4	52.4	52.5	53.9	56.1	58.7	54.5
1991	56.6	55.9	55.6	54.6	54.3	53.6	52.1	52.1	52.5	53.4	56.0	57.8	54.5
1992	55.0	54.8	54.7	53.3	53.1	52.8	51.3	51.0	51.6	52.7	55.1	57.8	53.6
1993	54.6	54.7	54.7	54.5	53.8	53.4	52.7	52.6	53.5	54.4	57.0	59.2	54.5
1994	56.0	56.3	56.6	55.5	55.2	54.7	52.6	53.3	54.0	54.7	57.3	59.4	55.4
1995	56.2	56.3	56.5	55.8	55.5	55.2	54.3	54.4	55.2	56.7	58.8	61.0	56.3
1996	58.6	58.6	58.8	57.9	57.6	57.3	57.1	57.6	57.8	58.6	61.4	63.9	58.7
1997	61.1	60.7	61.2	60.2	60.2	59.6	58.9	59.1	59.9	61.6	64.2	67.3	61.1
1998	65.2	64.3	65.2	62.8	62.5	62.4	62.5	62.9	63.3	64.5	66.8	69.5	64.3
1999	65.7	65.3	66.0	65.1	65.8	65.5	64.3	64.5	64.9	66.6	69.7	72.5	66.3
2000	68.3	68.1	68.4	67.3	67.2	67.7	66.0	66.7	66.6	67.8	71.5	73.8	68.3
2001	70.3	69.9	70.1	69.4	69.2	68.6	67.1	67.4	67.8	68.5	70.8	72.7	69.3
2002	69.7	68.8	69.1	68.5	68.0	67.9	66.7	67.1	68.1	68.6	71.0	73.5	68.9
2003	69.8	68.9	68.7	68.5	68.6	68.3	67.2	67.5	68.0	68.5	70.9	73.4	69.0
Transportation and utilities													
1990	8.2	8.4	8.4	8.5	8.5	8.4	8.1	8.5	8.6	9.0	9.1	9.4	8.5
1991	9.0	9.1	9.1	9.0	9.0	9.0	8.3	8.3	8.2	8.1	8.3	8.4	8.6
1992	8.6	8.6	8.7	8.4	8.4	8.3	8.2	8.2	8.3	8.7	8.8	8.9	8.5
1993	8.3	8.4	8.4	8.5	8.4	8.3	8.3	8.3	8.4	8.6	8.8	8.8	8.4
1994	8.5	8.6	8.5	8.4	8.4	8.2	8.3	8.1	8.1	8.3	8.1	8.1	8.3
1995	8.1	8.1	8.1	8.0	8.0	8.0	7.8	7.8	7.8	8.0	8.1	8.3	8.0
1996	8.0	7.9	8.0	8.1	8.3	8.3	8.5	8.6	8.8	9.2	9.1	9.4	8.5
1997	9.0	8.9	9.0	8.9	8.8	8.8	8.9	8.6	8.9	9.2	9.1	9.5	8.9
1998	9.1	9.1	9.0	8.8	8.9	8.9	8.9	8.9	9.0	9.2	8.9	9.5	9.0
1999	9.1	9.0	8.9	8.9	9.0	9.0	9.1	9.1	9.1	9.5	9.4	9.7	9.1
2000	9.5	9.7	9.7	9.6	9.6	9.6	9.8	9.7	9.8	10.0	10.1	10.3	9.8
2001	10.0	10.0	10.0	10.0	10.0	10.1	10.1	10.1	10.2	10.1	10.2	10.8	10.1
2002	10.6	10.7	10.8	10.9	11.0	11.2	11.0	10.8	10.8	10.6	10.7	10.9	10.8
2003	10.5	10.5	10.4	10.3	10.4	10.3	10.4	10.3	10.3	10.3	10.6	10.8	10.4

Employment by Industry: Florida—*Continued*

(Numbers in thousands. Not seasonally adjusted.)

Industry	January	February	March	April	May	June	July	August	September	October	November	December	Annual Average
WEST PALM BEACH-BOCA RATON-DELRAY BEACH *—Continued*													
Information													
1990	9.1	9.2	9.2	9.1	9.1	9.1	9.1	9.2	9.2	9.2	9.4	9.6	9.2
1991	9.4	9.3	9.3	9.4	9.4	9.5	9.5	9.4	9.4	9.1	9.1	9.2	9.3
1992	9.3	9.4	9.4	9.4	9.5	9.4	9.5	9.4	9.4	9.4	9.4	9.6	9.4
1993	9.3	9.4	9.4	9.3	9.3	9.5	9.4	9.6	9.5	9.5	9.5	9.6	9.4
1994	9.4	9.5	9.6	9.4	9.4	9.4	9.4	9.4	9.3	9.3	9.3	9.4	9.4
1995	9.3	9.3	9.4	9.3	9.3	9.4	9.2	9.3	9.3	9.2	9.3	9.5	9.3
1996	9.4	9.5	9.6	9.4	9.6	9.6	9.6	9.6	9.7	9.5	9.6	9.8	9.5
1997	9.8	9.7	9.7	9.8	10.0	9.9	9.8	10.1	10.1	9.9	10.0	10.0	9.9
1998	9.8	10.0	10.0	9.7	9.9	9.9	9.7	9.9	10.0	10.1	10.2	10.4	9.9
1999	10.4	10.5	10.5	10.2	10.5	10.9	11.1	11.0	11.2	11.0	11.1	11.2	10.8
2000	11.4	11.6	11.8	11.7	11.7	12.0	12.7	12.9	13.2	12.9	13.0	13.3	12.4
2001	13.2	13.3	13.3	13.1	13.0	12.9	12.7	12.7	12.5	12.4	12.5	12.5	12.8
2002	12.2	12.3	12.3	12.0	11.9	11.9	11.7	11.6	11.5	11.5	11.5	11.6	11.8
2003	11.2	11.2	11.4	11.1	11.1	11.2	11.1	11.1	11.2	11.1	11.1	11.3	11.2
Financial activities													
1990	26.2	26.3	26.3	26.4	26.3	26.3	25.5	25.5	25.4	25.6	25.6	25.7	25.9
1991	25.4	25.4	25.3	25.3	25.2	25.4	25.0	24.9	25.0	24.7	24.9	25.1	25.1
1992	25.0	24.9	25.2	25.1	25.3	25.2	25.1	25.1	25.2	25.4	25.5	25.8	25.2
1993	25.4	25.5	25.7	25.1	25.2	25.3	26.1	26.3	26.3	26.6	26.8	27.2	25.9
1994	27.1	27.4	27.5	27.4	27.4	27.5	27.5	27.5	27.5	27.6	27.6	27.8	27.4
1995	27.1	27.3	27.5	27.7	27.7	27.8	27.6	27.7	27.7	27.8	28.1	28.7	27.7
1996	28.0	28.2	28.3	28.7	28.7	29.2	29.6	29.7	29.7	29.8	29.9	30.4	29.1
1997	29.9	30.3	30.8	31.3	31.7	31.5	32.1	31.7	32.0	32.4	32.7	33.0	31.6
1998	33.0	33.3	33.5	33.4	33.7	33.8	33.2	33.4	33.3	34.1	34.2	34.7	33.6
1999	34.5	35.0	34.9	33.8	34.2	34.4	34.7	34.7	34.1	34.5	34.8	35.1	34.5
2000	35.0	35.1	35.4	35.9	35.8	36.6	36.5	36.7	36.9	36.8	37.1	37.4	36.3
2001	37.0	37.2	37.5	37.3	37.4	37.7	37.9	38.0	38.1	38.3	38.7	39.1	37.8
2002	38.6	38.7	38.8	38.5	38.5	38.7	38.6	38.8	38.8	38.6	38.9	39.1	38.7
2003	38.4	38.6	38.7	38.8	38.9	39.0	38.8	38.5	39.1	39.0	39.2	39.6	38.9
Professional and business services													
1990	39.9	40.8	41.2	39.7	39.8	39.4	39.6	39.8	40.0	40.3	40.8	40.6	40.1
1991	39.7	40.1	40.6	39.2	38.8	38.8	37.7	37.8	38.1	38.8	39.8	40.5	39.1
1992	40.7	41.0	41.4	41.8	41.2	41.3	40.9	41.0	41.5	42.3	42.2	42.8	41.5
1993	43.9	44.5	44.8	46.8	45.8	46.3	46.3	46.4	46.9	47.9	48.5	48.9	46.4
1994	50.3	51.2	52.1	53.6	53.6	53.5	53.0	53.2	53.5	53.4	54.5	55.2	53.0
1995	54.8	55.6	56.0	55.2	56.1	56.2	55.9	56.5	56.9	57.0	57.5	58.7	56.3
1996	57.1	58.0	58.9	60.7	60.8	60.7	61.6	61.9	62.2	62.0	63.3	63.7	60.9
1997	63.5	64.5	66.0	66.0	64.9	66.5	65.8	67.0	67.6	69.6	69.2	70.8	66.7
1998	71.3	73.0	74.0	73.3	73.1	73.8	73.0	74.2	75.2	76.5	77.7	77.9	74.4
1999	76.8	77.6	78.3	78.6	77.9	79.1	79.7	79.8	80.3	81.3	82.1	83.8	79.6
2000	83.3	83.8	85.4	86.7	86.9	88.6	90.6	92.2	94.2	94.5	96.0	97.3	90.0
2001	97.2	96.7	97.6	97.2	96.2	96.6	96.1	96.5	96.4	96.9	96.9	97.4	96.8
2002	95.3	94.0	97.1	96.6	97.3	97.7	97.1	96.3	94.8	96.1	96.6	98.1	96.4
2003	96.7	97.0	98.8	98.5	97.9	98.6	98.8	99.3	99.4	99.1	99.0	100.5	98.6
Educational and health services													
1990	40.1	40.8	41.3	41.5	42.0	41.9	40.6	41.1	41.8	42.5	43.1	43.4	41.6
1991	43.1	43.5	44.1	44.3	44.4	44.6	43.8	44.0	44.6	44.9	45.2	45.8	44.3
1992	45.2	45.7	46.1	45.8	45.9	45.8	45.1	45.5	46.3	46.7	47.3	47.8	46.1
1993	48.0	48.4	48.9	48.8	49.5	49.0	48.4	48.6	48.8	50.0	50.6	51.1	49.1
1994	50.6	51.2	51.8	51.6	52.1	52.3	51.9	52.3	53.0	52.8	53.3	53.9	52.2
1995	53.6	54.6	55.1	54.7	54.9	55.2	53.7	53.9	54.8	55.7	56.7	57.4	55.0
1996	56.4	57.3	57.7	57.2	57.3	57.8	56.9	57.2	57.6	58.8	59.4	59.9	57.7
1997	58.7	59.0	59.6	59.3	59.7	59.6	59.7	60.1	60.0	61.3	61.4	62.1	60.0
1998	62.0	62.6	63.4	61.8	62.0	62.0	60.7	61.1	61.5	61.4	62.1	62.7	61.9
1999	62.4	63.2	63.7	63.5	62.9	62.8	61.9	62.3	62.5	61.3	61.6	62.5	62.5
2000	63.8	64.5	64.7	63.2	63.1	63.0	62.5	63.0	63.4	63.7	64.3	64.6	63.7
2001	63.9	64.6	64.8	65.1	65.5	65.3	65.0	66.4	67.2	68.1	68.8	69.3	66.1
2002	69.9	71.1	71.6	71.3	71.4	72.2	70.3	71.1	71.6	72.2	72.5	73.0	71.5
2003	71.9	72.7	73.1	73.0	73.3	73.0	71.9	72.8	73.3	74.1	74.4	74.9	73.2
Leisure and hospitality													
1990	48.9	50.4	51.1	48.2	46.0	43.2	41.7	41.8	41.5	42.4	45.5	47.5	45.6
1991	47.8	49.0	50.0	47.7	46.2	43.8	41.3	40.8	41.4	41.6	45.1	47.4	45.1
1992	47.1	48.3	49.5	48.0	46.3	43.6	40.6	40.0	40.9	42.7	45.8	48.0	45.0
1993	48.7	50.6	51.4	49.0	47.7	46.1	43.8	43.2	43.7	45.3	48.2	50.1	47.3
1994	50.5	52.5	53.3	51.6	50.2	48.5	45.3	44.9	45.4	46.3	49.2	51.1	49.0
1995	50.5	52.4	53.3	51.8	50.3	48.7	45.7	45.4	46.3	47.2	50.1	52.0	49.4
1996	54.0	55.9	56.7	53.4	51.9	49.8	47.1	47.1	48.0	50.0	52.7	55.2	51.8
1997	55.6	57.8	57.5	56.2	54.7	53.4	50.6	51.2	51.0	52.1	55.1	57.0	54.3
1998	55.5	56.9	57.4	56.2	55.0	53.5	51.5	50.8	50.6	52.7	55.3	57.7	54.4
1999	56.3	58.1	58.3	55.3	54.8	52.9	49.6	49.9	50.3	51.5	54.0	55.9	53.9
2000	56.3	58.1	59.0	57.4	56.0	54.4	53.4	53.5	54.3	55.3	58.7	61.0	56.5
2001	61.2	62.7	64.4	62.7	61.0	58.9	56.1	55.8	56.1	56.1	59.5	61.4	59.6
2002	61.6	62.8	63.4	62.0	61.1	59.7	57.1	57.3	57.8	59.4	62.0	63.5	60.6
2003	62.6	63.6	64.0	63.2	61.3	59.5	57.0	56.7	57.2	58.5	61.3	62.6	60.6

Employment by Industry: Florida—*Continued*

(Numbers in thousands. Not seasonally adjusted.)

Industry	January	February	March	April	May	June	July	August	September	October	November	December	Annual Average
WEST PALM BEACH-BOCA RATON-DELRAY BEACH —*Continued*													
Other services													
1990	19.2	19.4	19.6	19.1	18.8	18.6	18.4	18.3	18.1	18.1	18.5	18.6	18.7
1991	19.1	19.1	19.2	18.7	18.6	18.4	18.6	18.6	18.3	18.6	19.0	19.1	18.7
1992	18.9	19.0	19.1	18.8	18.5	18.3	18.3	18.1	18.0	18.1	18.4	18.8	18.5
1993	18.9	19.1	19.2	18.9	18.8	18.8	18.7	18.5	18.5	18.9	19.2	19.5	18.9
1994	19.4	19.7	19.8	19.6	19.3	19.2	19.3	19.3	19.3	19.4	19.8	20.2	19.5
1995	20.5	20.6	20.7	20.6	20.6	20.5	20.3	20.2	20.2	20.7	21.1	21.5	20.6
1996	21.3	21.4	21.4	21.0	20.9	20.7	20.2	20.1	20.0	20.4	20.6	20.8	20.7
1997	21.1	21.2	21.3	21.2	21.2	20.8	21.1	21.1	21.0	21.0	21.1	21.5	21.1
1998	21.2	21.5	21.6	21.3	21.2	21.0	20.7	20.7	20.9	21.1	21.4	21.9	21.2
1999	21.5	21.5	21.7	21.7	21.3	21.4	21.0	21.0	21.0	21.6	21.8	22.1	21.4
2000	22.3	22.3	22.5	22.4	22.6	22.5	22.1	22.1	22.4	22.5	22.9	23.0	22.5
2001	23.0	23.2	23.3	23.3	23.3	23.3	22.6	22.5	22.5	22.4	22.8	23.0	22.9
2002	23.3	23.6	23.7	23.4	23.3	23.2	23.0	23.1	23.2	23.9	24.5	24.8	23.6
2003	24.8	25.2	25.5	25.0	25.0	25.0	24.6	24.5	24.4	24.8	25.2	25.6	25.0
Government													
1990	45.7	46.4	46.8	47.3	47.8	47.2	44.0	43.4	46.7	47.3	47.8	48.0	46.5
1991	47.6	47.6	48.1	48.1	48.1	46.8	43.8	44.1	47.4	47.2	48.1	48.1	47.0
1992	47.6	47.7	50.3	47.9	48.2	47.5	44.1	42.9	46.6	46.9	47.4	47.7	47.0
1993	47.1	47.1	47.7	48.1	48.2	48.0	45.0	43.5	49.0	50.5	49.2	47.8	47.6
1994	48.2	49.2	50.0	50.1	49.9	49.7	45.7	44.6	50.1	51.0	54.6	49.3	49.3
1995	50.0	51.5	52.1	52.0	52.2	51.8	47.8	47.1	52.7	52.7	53.3	51.1	51.1
1996	51.9	53.3	56.0	53.8	53.6	52.9	48.9	48.3	53.1	53.2	54.0	54.2	52.7
1997	53.8	54.8	54.6	54.9	54.9	54.1	49.9	49.3	54.5	54.0	55.4	55.5	53.8
1998	54.2	55.0	55.0	55.3	55.4	54.6	50.5	49.5	54.7	55.0	55.7	55.1	54.1
1999	54.5	56.2	56.3	56.6	56.6	56.0	51.5	50.6	55.8	56.2	57.0	56.5	55.3
2000	56.0	57.5	58.0	58.2	59.0	53.2	52.6	57.6	57.6	57.8	58.4	57.8	57.0
2001	57.3	58.9	59.2	59.0	59.1	53.8	52.7	58.1	58.8	60.0	60.1	60.1	58.0
2002	61.3	61.4	61.7	61.8	62.0	56.1	55.4	61.5	62.6	63.0	63.4	63.6	61.2
2003	63.1	63.6	63.6	63.7	64.1	57.9	57.4	63.4	64.3	65.0	65.1	64.6	63.0
Federal government													
1990	4.1	4.1	4.3	4.6	5.2	4.8	5.0	4.1	4.0	4.0	3.9	4.0	4.3
1991	4.0	3.9	3.9	3.9	3.9	3.9	4.0	3.9	3.9	3.9	4.0	4.1	3.9
1992	4.0	4.0	4.0	4.0	4.0	3.9	4.0	3.9	3.9	3.9	4.0	4.2	3.9
1993	3.9	3.9	3.9	3.9	3.9	3.9	4.0	4.0	4.0	4.0	4.1	4.3	3.9
1994	4.1	4.1	4.1	4.1	4.1	4.1	4.1	4.1	4.1	4.5	4.5	4.8	4.2
1995	4.7	4.7	4.8	4.8	5.0	5.2	5.3	5.5	5.6	5.6	5.7	5.8	5.2
1996	5.6	5.6	5.6	5.6	5.7	5.6	5.6	5.6	5.6	5.7	5.8	6.0	5.6
1997	5.7	5.8	5.7	5.7	5.7	5.6	5.6	5.6	5.7	5.7	5.9	6.0	5.7
1998	5.7	5.7	5.7	5.8	5.8	5.7	5.7	5.7	5.7	5.7	5.7	5.9	5.7
1999	5.6	5.7	5.6	5.6	5.6	5.6	5.5	5.5	5.5	5.5	5.6	5.8	5.5
2000	5.7	5.6	5.7	5.9	6.7	5.9	6.0	5.6	5.6	5.6	5.6	5.8	5.8
2001	5.8	5.7	5.7	5.5	5.4	5.2	5.1	4.9	4.7	4.6	4.4	4.3	5.1
2002	5.7	5.6	5.7	5.6	5.6	5.7	5.6	5.7	5.7	5.8	5.8	6.0	5.7
2003	5.9	5.9	5.8	5.8	5.8	5.8	5.8	5.8	5.7	5.8	5.7	5.7	5.8
State government													
1990	7.0	7.2	7.3	7.3	7.2	7.1	7.1	7.1	7.3	7.7	7.8	7.8	7.3
1991	7.5	7.7	7.7	7.8	7.9	7.4	7.4	7.4	7.5	7.7	7.8	7.7	7.6
1992	7.6	7.6	7.7	7.6	7.7	7.2	7.4	7.3	7.5	7.8	7.9	7.8	7.5
1993	7.6	7.7	7.9	8.1	8.0	7.5	8.0	7.5	7.9	8.2	8.1	8.1	7.8
1994	7.7	8.0	8.2	8.3	8.1	7.6	7.8	7.7	8.3	8.4	8.3	8.3	8.0
1995	8.0	8.2	8.5	8.3	8.3	7.7	7.7	7.7	8.3	8.4	8.4	8.4	8.1
1996	8.2	8.3	8.5	8.4	8.4	7.8	7.9	8.2	8.2	8.4	8.5	8.4	8.2
1997	8.6	8.5	8.5	8.6	8.6	7.9	8.0	8.2	8.4	8.7	8.7	8.7	8.4
1998	8.8	8.7	8.7	8.7	8.7	7.9	8.1	8.0	8.2	8.5	8.6	8.7	8.4
1999	8.4	8.6	8.7	8.7	8.7	7.9	8.1	8.0	8.2	8.6	8.6	8.8	8.4
2000	8.4	8.7	8.8	8.8	8.8	8.3	8.3	8.3	8.6	8.9	8.9	9.0	8.7
2001	8.6	8.8	8.9	8.8	8.8	8.3	8.1	8.1	8.5	8.8	9.0	8.9	8.6
2002	8.6	8.6	8.7	8.7	8.9	7.8	8.0	8.1	8.6	8.8	9.0	8.9	8.6
2003	8.6	8.9	8.9	9.0	9.2	8.1	8.3	8.2	8.7	9.0	9.0	9.0	8.7
Local government													
1990	34.6	35.1	35.2	35.4	35.4	35.3	31.9	32.2	35.4	35.6	36.1	36.2	34.8
1991	36.1	36.0	36.5	36.4	36.3	35.5	32.4	32.8	36.0	35.6	36.3	36.3	35.5
1992	36.0	36.1	38.6	36.3	36.5	36.4	32.7	31.7	35.2	35.2	35.5	35.7	35.4
1993	35.6	35.5	35.9	36.1	36.3	36.6	33.0	32.0	37.1	38.3	37.0	35.4	35.7
1994	36.4	37.1	37.7	37.7	37.7	38.0	33.8	32.8	37.7	38.1	41.8	36.2	37.0
1995	37.3	38.6	38.8	38.9	38.9	38.9	34.8	33.9	38.8	38.7	39.2	36.9	37.8
1996	38.1	39.4	41.9	39.8	39.5	39.5	35.4	34.5	39.3	39.1	39.7	39.8	38.8
1997	39.5	40.5	40.4	40.6	40.6	40.6	36.3	35.5	40.4	39.6	40.8	40.8	39.6
1998	39.7	40.6	40.6	40.8	40.9	41.0	36.7	35.8	40.8	40.8	41.4	40.5	39.9
1999	40.5	41.9	42.0	42.3	42.3	42.5	37.9	37.1	42.1	42.1	42.8	41.9	41.2
2000	41.9	43.2	43.5	43.5	43.5	39.0	38.3	43.7	43.4	43.3	43.9	43.0	42.5
2001	42.9	44.4	44.6	44.7	44.9	40.3	39.5	45.1	45.6	46.6	46.7	46.9	44.3
2002	47.0	47.2	47.3	47.5	47.5	42.6	41.8	47.7	48.3	48.4	48.6	48.7	46.9
2003	48.6	48.8	48.9	48.9	49.1	44.0	43.3	49.4	49.9	50.2	50.4	49.9	48.5

Average Weekly Earnings by Industry: Florida

(Dollars, not seasonally adjusted.)

Industry	January	February	March	April	May	June	July	August	September	October	November	December	Annual Average
STATEWIDE													
Manufacturing													
2001	514.11	509.49	509.04	494.79	500.75	514.81	508.99	517.30	503.14	517.34	537.06	558.52	514.81
2002	545.96	538.48	552.93	549.44	550.57	548.36	544.33	563.22	567.51	560.56	593.78	600.48	559.93
2003	598.55	585.62	585.31	573.66	565.60	572.27	568.90	568.99	579.34	572.27	580.68	582.62	577.69

Average Hourly Earnings by Industry: Florida

(Dollars, not seasonally adjusted.)

Industry	January	February	March	April	May	June	July	August	September	October	November	December	Annual Average
STATEWIDE													
Manufacturing													
2001	12.57	12.58	12.60	12.59	12.55	12.68	12.63	12.71	12.61	12.68	12.91	13.08	12.68
2002	13.03	13.07	13.01	13.02	13.14	13.15	13.18	13.41	13.48	13.54	13.65	13.90	13.30
2003	14.15	14.01	14.07	13.89	14.14	14.13	14.33	13.98	13.96	14.13	14.06	14.28	14.09

Average Weekly Hours by Industry: Florida

(Not seasonally adjusted.)

Industry	January	February	March	April	May	June	July	August	September	October	November	December	Annual Average
STATEWIDE													
Manufacturing													
2001	40.9	40.5	40.4	39.3	39.9	40.6	40.3	40.7	39.9	40.8	41.6	42.7	40.6
2002	41.9	41.2	42.5	42.2	41.9	41.7	41.3	42.0	42.1	41.4	43.5	43.2	42.1
2003	42.3	41.8	41.6	41.3	40.0	40.5	39.7	40.7	41.5	40.5	41.3	40.8	41.0

GEORGIA AT A GLANCE

(Population and total nonfarm employment numbers in thousands)

Population, Census 2000:	8,186.5
Total nonfarm employment, 2003:	3,859.8
Change in total nonfarm employment	
(Number)	
1990–2003:	868.0
1990–2001:	951.4
2001–2003:	-83.4
(Compound annual rate of change)	
1990–2003:	2.0%
1990–2001:	2.5%
2001–2003:	-1.1%
Unemployment rate	
1990:	5.2%
2001:	4.0%
2003:	4.7%

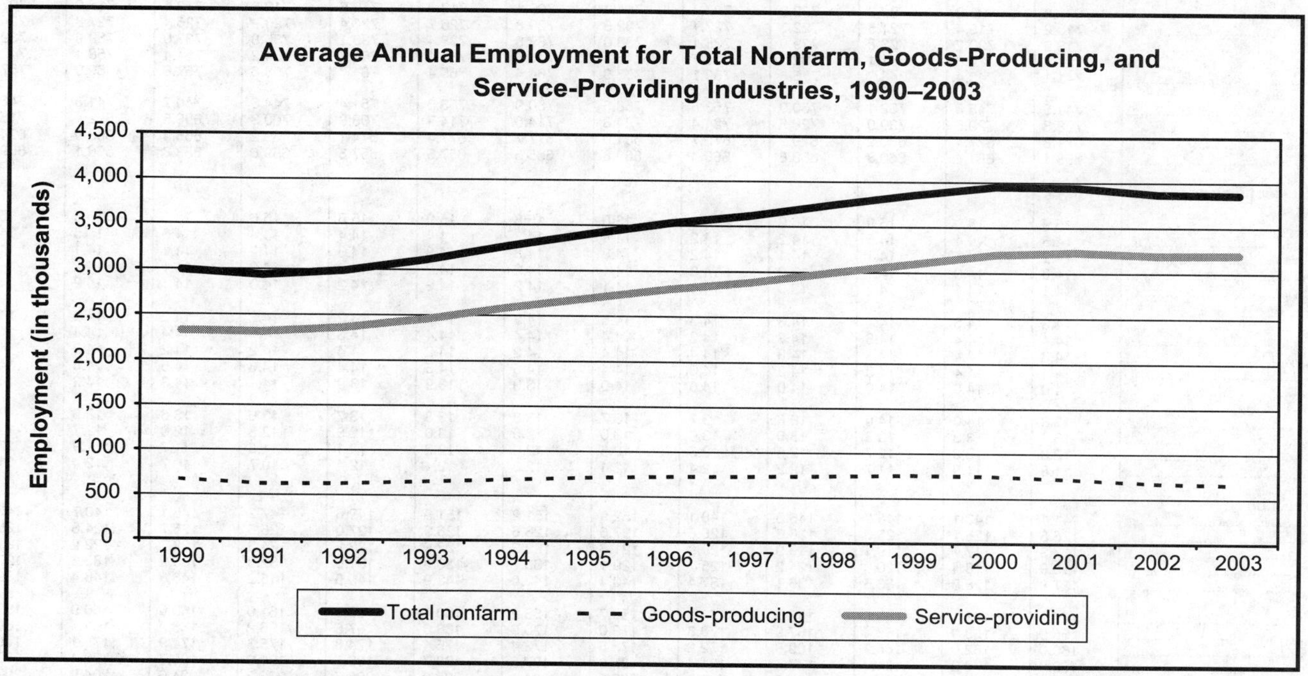

As the 1990s began, nonfarm payroll employment was sluggish. It rebounded robustly and expanded through 2001, when the recession caused the number of nonfarm jobs to fall. Jobs in the goods-producing sector were more sharply affected by the recession, particularly those in manufacturing. The number of jobs in the service-providing sector was stagnant over the 2000–2003 period due to a weakness in retail trade, information, and professional and business service industries.

Employment by Industry: Georgia

(Numbers in thousands. Not seasonally adjusted.)

Industry	January	February	March	April	May	June	July	August	September	October	November	December	Annual Average
STATEWIDE													
Total nonfarm													
1990	2938.9	2951.1	2980.0	2979.7	3000.0	3024.6	2999.0	3010.7	3012.8	2994.8	3004.6	3005.2	2991.8
1991	2918.3	2908.7	2924.8	2923.7	2943.8	2961.4	2928.6	2937.8	2944.0	2939.3	2953.7	2966.6	2937.6
1992	2906.4	2912.4	2940.4	2957.2	2979.5	2995.0	2991.2	2999.8	3013.3	3035.4	3048.8	3066.7	2987.2
1993	3003.1	3024.0	3042.1	3073.2	3088.7	3108.5	3112.4	3124.2	3141.1	3176.5	3196.3	3220.5	3109.2
1994	3153.3	3174.3	3203.6	3228.7	3247.3	3272.7	3257.9	3282.2	3305.4	3324.4	3359.8	3382.1	3266.0
1995	3309.1	3327.0	3360.3	3370.7	3393.7	3425.6	3382.5	3414.9	3436.5	3442.7	3470.1	3495.0	3402.3
1996	3416.9	3448.4	3482.2	3495.3	3529.4	3559.4	3582.4	3540.6	3541.4	3552.4	3578.3	3601.0	3527.3
1997	3517.7	3539.5	3572.7	3579.5	3606.4	3624.0	3596.0	3618.9	3646.8	3662.2	3686.8	3721.9	3614.4
1998	3639.0	3660.6	3694.0	3698.2	3730.5	3757.6	3730.3	3759.1	3777.4	3790.5	3815.3	3837.2	3740.8
1999	3731.7	3763.3	3791.1	3829.8	3856.2	3881.2	3848.2	3872.6	3891.4	3904.6	3929.3	3955.2	3854.6
2000	3851.6	3880.3	3922.3	3925.6	3958.4	3971.6	3944.4	3970.6	3978.7	3982.0	3994.0	4012.1	3949.3
2001	3931.3	3945.2	3971.8	3951.7	3958.3	3962.4	3915.3	3947.1	3939.0	3929.7	3933.0	3934.7	3943.2
2002	3816.3	3833.3	3860.3	3870.6	3885.1	3895.3	3841.1	3875.6	3874.5	3881.8	3896.8	3903.3	3869.5
2003	3814.1	3827.6	3847.6	3843.4	3855.3	3851.8	3832.8	3873.3	3882.4	3893.3	3896.3	3899.8	3859.8
Total private													
1990	2412.4	2421.5	2445.1	2446.8	2459.3	2485.2	2474.7	2489.0	2487.1	2459.4	2467.2	2470.9	2459.9
1991	2385.2	2371.2	2384.9	2384.0	2400.5	2417.7	2399.5	2410.0	2415.1	2400.1	2413.3	2430.2	2401.0
1992	2373.5	2377.3	2399.6	2421.2	2440.6	2456.8	2465.7	2473.9	2482.1	2489.6	2500.0	2521.2	2450.1
1993	2460.5	2477.2	2492.5	2524.7	2538.4	2560.6	2578.9	2590.7	2601.2	2615.6	2634.1	2658.8	2561.1
1994	2594.7	2611.5	2639.0	2661.6	2681.4	2707.9	2707.4	2732.4	2750.4	2749.9	2781.4	2806.5	2702.0
1995	2738.9	2753.9	2784.7	2794.6	2816.3	2847.0	2831.6	2862.8	2875.5	2867.2	2893.4	2918.2	2832.0
1996	2848.0	2875.6	2907.4	2921.3	2953.8	2986.0	3027.1	2989.8	2980.5	2978.0	3001.4	3024.6	2957.8
1997	2945.2	2962.8	2994.0	3000.2	3024.5	3044.1	3037.5	3057.0	3074.2	3075.4	3098.6	3131.8	3037.1
1998	3054.6	3072.3	3105.2	3111.0	3142.2	3170.6	3163.9	3187.1	3192.5	3198.6	3218.9	3241.3	3154.9
1999	3140.6	3167.3	3197.5	3238.1	3263.5	3295.3	3280.2	3302.4	3303.1	3307.6	3329.3	3354.6	3265.0
2000	3259.3	3283.4	3321.2	3324.5	3346.0	3374.3	3367.0	3385.3	3383.8	3381.4	3391.1	3407.8	3352.1
2001	3330.6	3338.6	3362.4	3342.1	3346.7	3355.4	3329.1	3339.9	3322.8	3308.0	3308.2	3311.3	3332.9
2002	3199.1	3213.6	3234.6	3243.9	3256.8	3275.9	3242.2	3253.9	3241.1	3246.8	3259.3	3268.8	3244.7
2003	3181.1	3189.6	3208.1	3204.6	3218.9	3228.4	3228.1	3250.3	3248.5	3254.5	3256.6	3259.4	3227.3
Goods-producing													
1990	663.4	666.1	672.0	673.7	675.6	684.2	673.4	674.8	670.8	662.0	657.2	650.8	668.7
1991	625.6	620.9	623.2	619.0	622.0	626.2	621.5	624.5	626.4	624.6	624.5	624.9	623.6
1992	614.6	613.1	618.4	621.9	625.3	630.0	630.2	629.6	633.7	633.8	632.5	634.0	626.4
1993	634.0	636.8	640.6	645.1	648.4	654.8	658.9	659.2	661.7	661.0	662.1	665.2	652.3
1994	656.4	659.3	664.7	667.9	672.6	681.1	682.2	690.1	693.8	693.4	697.8	700.4	680.0
1995	693.8	695.2	703.3	702.9	707.4	714.4	706.1	713.9	713.6	712.8	713.1	716.2	707.7
1996	710.2	715.4	721.5	722.5	727.1	732.8	729.8	726.7	726.4	726.9	726.4	727.8	724.5
1997	718.0	720.2	723.8	729.9	735.1	738.0	732.8	738.4	738.1	735.8	737.0	739.9	732.3
1998	721.8	724.8	731.1	732.0	739.7	746.4	746.0	752.1	752.7	754.2	754.4	758.4	742.8
1999	741.1	743.4	748.3	755.6	759.7	767.9	764.4	765.4	764.7	758.6	757.6	760.0	757.2
2000	741.5	745.3	752.1	750.9	753.5	758.5	750.9	753.6	751.4	744.6	740.7	741.3	748.7
2001	728.8	729.5	730.0	726.5	724.4	724.8	714.0	714.7	708.9	700.3	693.5	692.4	715.6
2002	671.8	677.4	680.2	679.2	679.7	681.0	677.7	677.4	674.1	669.2	666.4	663.9	674.8
2003	658.1	661.4	660.8	658.6	660.4	660.8	655.5	657.5	657.8	659.6	658.8	658.1	659.0
Natural resources and mining													
1990	15.9	15.9	15.9	16.0	15.9	16.0	15.8	15.9	15.8	15.6	15.5	15.5	15.8
1991	14.6	14.4	14.5	14.2	14.2	14.4	14.3	14.4	14.4	14.4	14.5	14.5	14.4
1992	14.2	14.1	14.1	14.1	14.2	14.3	14.3	14.3	14.3	14.2	14.1	14.1	14.2
1993	14.0	14.0	14.1	13.9	14.0	14.1	14.2	14.2	14.2	14.2	14.1	14.2	14.1
1994	14.1	14.1	14.2	13.9	14.0	14.1	14.2	14.2	14.2	14.0	14.1	14.2	14.1
1995	14.3	14.3	14.4	14.3	14.3	14.5	14.2	14.2	14.2	14.2	14.2	14.3	14.3
1996	14.4	14.4	14.5	14.3	14.3	14.4	14.4	14.4	14.3	14.4	14.4	14.4	14.4
1997	14.3	14.4	14.4	14.3	14.4	14.4	14.2	14.2	14.4	14.2	14.2	14.3	14.3
1998	14.4	14.4	14.3	14.2	14.3	14.4	14.5	14.5	14.4	14.6	14.5	14.6	14.4
1999	14.0	14.0	14.0	14.0	14.0	14.0	13.9	13.9	13.9	14.1	14.3	14.2	14.0
2000	13.8	14.0	14.0	13.6	13.7	13.7	13.8	13.8	13.7	13.6	13.6	13.6	13.7
2001	13.4	13.3	13.3	13.0	13.0	13.0	12.9	13.0	12.8	12.8	12.8	12.7	12.9
2002	12.6	12.6	12.7	12.5	12.5	12.5	12.0	12.2	12.1	11.8	11.7	11.9	12.3
2003	11.8	11.9	11.7	12.2	12.4	12.4	12.3	12.4	12.4	10.7	10.7	12.4	11.9
Construction													
1990	141.1	143.1	146.2	146.3	148.1	152.9	151.2	151.9	149.6	147.2	145.1	140.7	147.0
1991	126.5	125.1	125.3	126.6	126.6	127.6	126.6	126.9	127.0	126.5	125.7	124.8	126.3
1992	117.3	117.7	119.1	119.9	120.9	121.8	122.3	122.9	123.2	124.3	122.7	122.2	121.2
1993	115.9	118.4	120.8	124.2	125.7	129.1	130.7	130.9	131.6	132.8	133.2	133.8	127.3
1994	127.8	128.8	133.5	136.1	137.4	140.4	142.0	143.9	145.5	145.2	146.8	146.4	139.5
1995	140.9	141.1	145.5	148.1	152.1	156.7	158.2	160.4	160.5	161.0	160.6	160.9	153.8
1996	155.9	158.9	163.4	167.9	170.8	173.0	170.9	168.0	167.5	166.2	166.2	165.5	166.2
1997	160.0	162.0	164.7	169.5	172.2	173.5	172.4	175.4	174.8	175.3	174.9	175.1	170.8
1998	169.3	170.2	174.2	177.5	181.4	185.6	187.5	188.7	189.5	191.0	190.7	192.4	183.2
1999	187.3	189.8	192.9	198.5	201.5	206.6	204.1	205.9	205.7	205.2	204.6	204.9	200.6
2000	195.4	197.9	202.9	202.6	204.6	208.8	208.1	208.3	208.3	206.8	204.5	204.8	204.4
2001	198.3	199.9	201.6	204.5	206.5	208.7	208.4	208.4	206.1	205.2	202.9	201.7	204.3
2002	193.3	195.9	197.2	196.4	197.1	198.1	197.4	197.6	196.3	194.7	194.0	192.5	195.9
2003	188.5	190.0	191.7	191.2	193.1	194.7	196.9	197.9	198.9	202.3	201.0	199.0	195.4

Employment by Industry: Georgia—*Continued*

(Numbers in thousands. Not seasonally adjusted.)

Industry	January	February	March	April	May	June	July	August	September	October	November	December	Annual Average
STATEWIDE—*Continued*													
Manufacturing													
1990	506.4	507.1	509.9	511.4	511.6	515.3	506.4	507.0	505.4	499.2	496.6	494.6	505.9
1991	484.5	481.4	483.4	478.2	481.2	484.2	480.6	483.2	485.0	483.7	484.3	485.6	482.9
1992	483.1	481.3	485.2	487.9	490.2	493.9	493.6	492.4	496.2	495.3	495.7	497.7	491.0
1993	504.1	504.4	505.7	507.0	508.7	511.6	514.0	514.1	515.9	514.0	514.8	517.2	511.0
1994	514.5	516.4	517.0	517.9	521.2	526.6	526.0	532.0	534.1	534.2	536.9	539.8	526.4
1995	538.6	539.8	543.4	540.5	541.0	543.2	533.7	539.3	538.9	537.6	538.3	541.0	539.6
1996	539.9	542.1	543.6	540.3	542.0	545.4	544.5	544.3	544.6	546.3	545.8	547.9	543.9
1997	543.7	543.8	544.7	546.1	548.5	550.1	546.2	548.8	548.9	546.3	547.9	550.5	547.1
1998	538.1	540.2	542.6	540.3	544.0	546.4	544.0	548.9	548.8	548.6	549.2	551.4	545.2
1999	539.8	539.6	541.4	543.1	544.2	547.3	546.4	545.6	545.1	539.3	538.7	540.9	542.6
2000	532.3	533.4	535.2	534.7	535.2	536.0	529.0	531.5	529.4	524.2	522.6	522.9	530.5
2001	517.1	516.3	515.1	509.0	504.9	503.1	492.7	493.3	490.0	482.3	477.8	478.0	498.3
2002	465.9	468.9	470.3	470.3	470.1	470.4	468.3	467.6	465.7	462.7	460.7	459.5	466.7
2003	457.8	459.5	457.4	455.2	454.9	453.7	446.3	447.2	446.5	446.6	447.1	446.7	451.6
Service-providing													
1990	2275.5	2285.0	2308.0	2306.0	2324.4	2340.4	2325.6	2335.9	2342.0	2332.8	2347.4	2354.4	2323.1
1991	2292.7	2287.8	2301.6	2304.7	2321.8	2335.2	2307.1	2313.3	2317.6	2314.7	2329.2	2341.7	2314.0
1992	2291.8	2299.3	2322.0	2335.3	2354.2	2365.0	2361.0	2370.2	2379.6	2401.6	2416.3	2432.7	2360.8
1993	2369.1	2387.2	2401.5	2428.1	2440.3	2453.7	2453.5	2465.0	2479.4	2515.5	2534.2	2555.3	2456.9
1994	2496.9	2515.0	2538.9	2560.8	2574.7	2591.6	2575.7	2592.1	2611.6	2631.0	2662.0	2681.7	2586.0
1995	2615.3	2631.8	2657.0	2667.8	2686.3	2711.2	2676.4	2701.0	2722.9	2729.9	2757.0	2778.8	2694.6
1996	2706.7	2733.0	2760.7	2772.8	2802.3	2826.6	2852.6	2813.9	2815.0	2825.5	2851.9	2873.2	2802.9
1997	2799.7	2819.3	2848.9	2849.6	2871.3	2886.0	2863.2	2880.5	2908.7	2926.4	2949.8	2982.0	2882.1
1998	2917.2	2935.8	2962.9	2966.2	2990.8	3011.2	2984.3	3007.0	3024.7	3036.3	3060.9	3078.8	2998.0
1999	2990.6	3019.9	3042.8	3074.2	3096.5	3113.3	3083.8	3107.2	3126.7	3146.0	3171.7	3195.2	3097.3
2000	3110.1	3135.0	3170.2	3174.7	3204.9	3213.1	3193.5	3217.0	3227.3	3237.4	3253.3	3270.8	3200.6
2001	3202.5	3215.7	3241.8	3225.2	3233.9	3237.6	3201.3	3232.4	3230.1	3229.4	3239.5	3242.3	3227.6
2002	3144.5	3155.9	3180.1	3191.4	3205.4	3214.3	3163.4	3198.2	3200.4	3212.6	3230.4	3239.4	3194.7
2003	3156.0	3166.2	3186.8	3184.8	3194.9	3191.0	3177.3	3215.8	3224.6	3233.7	3237.5	3241.7	3200.9
Trade, transportation, and utilities													
1990	659.1	656.5	660.1	659.4	662.8	668.7	672.0	676.7	678.6	674.7	683.9	693.6	670.5
1991	650.9	638.3	637.8	636.3	641.6	644.0	640.7	644.3	647.2	645.3	656.2	668.1	645.9
1992	644.5	640.4	643.1	645.9	651.2	654.5	652.7	655.5	658.2	662.5	672.6	687.4	655.7
1993	652.9	650.7	652.8	658.4	660.3	664.8	671.5	675.3	679.1	691.4	704.3	719.2	673.4
1994	686.1	683.9	688.4	694.8	700.5	705.6	704.3	708.8	714.9	718.1	733.8	750.9	707.5
1995	715.6	710.4	716.0	718.3	723.5	729.5	729.2	735.2	740.7	742.6	759.5	773.6	732.8
1996	739.3	737.4	742.8	740.4	749.2	758.9	766.8	762.9	760.2	766.9	783.0	798.8	758.9
1997	764.8	760.0	768.3	763.4	769.0	773.3	773.1	772.5	781.8	789.8	805.4	823.7	778.8
1998	791.6	786.7	791.8	788.5	794.7	801.1	801.8	808.3	813.0	819.0	834.5	847.8	806.6
1999	806.5	806.7	813.2	821.6	827.7	835.1	835.3	842.9	842.8	849.2	863.9	878.3	835.3
2000	839.4	841.0	849.5	851.2	854.8	858.6	852.7	858.8	858.6	864.9	877.8	889.2	858.0
2001	856.6	850.6	855.4	845.5	847.1	848.0	848.1	848.8	847.9	848.7	859.0	865.2	851.7
2002	827.0	822.1	825.9	825.7	829.0	832.4	824.8	826.0	825.3	836.1	850.1	862.8	832.3
2003	819.1	814.0	818.7	814.2	818.2	819.0	819.4	823.1	823.6	826.3	836.2	841.9	822.8
Wholesale trade													
1990	167.4	167.9	168.9	164.5	164.7	166.4	170.7	171.2	171.8	170.5	170.0	170.0	168.7
1991	157.9	156.6	156.5	161.4	161.7	161.9	161.3	161.2	161.8	161.0	160.8	160.9	160.3
1992	160.1	159.9	160.3	161.0	161.6	162.7	162.1	162.5	162.5	164.2	163.2	163.4	162.0
1993	158.5	159.0	159.5	159.4	159.7	160.1	162.9	162.5	162.8	163.1	163.2	164.3	161.3
1994	160.1	161.2	161.9	163.5	164.0	165.4	165.8	166.4	167.9	168.1	168.7	170.0	165.3
1995	167.5	168.6	170.0	171.3	172.2	173.8	174.1	175.2	176.8	175.7	176.4	177.3	173.2
1996	176.5	178.2	179.5	177.8	179.1	180.9	182.8	181.4	181.9	183.4	184.0	185.2	180.9
1997	183.8	185.3	187.0	186.1	187.4	188.6	188.8	190.2	191.3	193.1	194.1	195.2	189.2
1998	194.2	194.5	195.7	194.6	195.8	197.3	198.3	199.1	200.0	201.0	201.4	201.5	197.8
1999	199.9	201.1	202.3	204.3	205.5	207.0	206.4	207.9	207.7	207.4	207.3	208.1	205.4
2000	206.3	207.8	209.5	210.2	211.1	212.4	211.2	212.0	211.7	212.3	211.6	211.8	210.7
2001	211.7	211.8	212.5	209.8	209.5	210.4	211.7	211.0	210.2	209.6	208.1	207.0	210.2
2002	203.9	204.0	205.3	205.2	205.1	205.6	204.2	203.9	203.0	205.6	204.7	204.7	204.6
2003	204.1	204.1	205.8	204.5	205.1	205.0	205.2	205.4	205.4	207.1	206.4	206.9	205.4
Retail trade													
1990	354.6	350.2	351.7	352.4	355.0	357.7	355.5	357.7	358.9	357.4	367.1	375.5	357.8
1991	349.5	341.4	342.9	338.0	341.4	342.9	340.0	342.2	343.0	340.8	351.7	361.0	344.6
1992	340.0	335.8	337.5	341.1	344.9	346.8	344.2	346.4	348.3	349.8	361.5	374.7	347.6
1993	350.2	347.9	348.7	353.8	354.5	357.2	358.8	361.9	363.8	373.6	385.8	398.9	362.9
1994	373.5	369.2	371.4	375.2	379.3	383.3	380.4	384.5	390.6	389.9	404.9	420.8	385.3
1995	393.5	388.2	391.3	393.2	398.2	402.3	400.1	405.4	410.2	410.9	427.6	441.4	405.2
1996	414.0	410.1	414.7	415.2	421.4	427.4	430.7	429.0	426.4	427.8	443.5	457.5	426.5
1997	429.3	422.5	427.5	424.8	427.9	430.5	428.1	431.8	433.5	437.3	452.0	468.3	434.5
1998	438.7	433.9	435.9	433.6	437.4	441.3	437.8	441.0	443.5	446.1	460.2	472.1	443.5
1999	438.1	436.1	440.3	443.4	447.8	453.2	452.9	458.2	458.8	462.0	476.8	489.8	454.8
2000	455.6	455.8	461.3	459.9	462.6	464.6	460.2	464.3	464.1	467.3	481.2	492.3	465.8
2001	464.6	459.0	463.2	455.7	457.2	457.1	454.3	456.1	456.7	456.0	470.4	477.7	460.6
2002	449.6	444.7	447.9	445.6	448.1	449.6	445.7	446.9	448.2	448.8	462.7	474.5	451.0
2003	440.7	436.1	438.6	437.6	440.5	441.1	440.8	443.7	443.9	444.8	454.7	458.6	443.4

Employment by Industry: Georgia—*Continued*

(Numbers in thousands. Not seasonally adjusted.)

Industry	January	February	March	April	May	June	July	August	September	October	November	December	Annual Average
STATEWIDE—*Continued*													
Transportation and utilities													
1990	137.1	138.4	139.5	142.5	143.1	144.6	145.8	147.8	147.9	146.8	146.8	148.1	144.0
1991	143.5	140.3	138.4	136.9	138.5	139.2	139.4	140.9	142.4	143.5	143.7	146.2	141.1
1992	144.4	144.7	145.3	143.8	144.7	145.0	146.4	146.6	147.4	148.5	147.9	149.3	146.2
1993	144.2	143.8	144.6	145.2	146.1	147.5	149.8	150.9	152.5	154.7	155.3	156.0	149.2
1994	152.5	153.5	155.1	156.1	157.2	156.9	158.1	157.9	156.4	160.1	160.2	160.1	157.0
1995	154.6	153.6	154.7	153.8	153.1	153.4	155.0	154.6	153.7	156.0	155.5	154.9	154.4
1996	148.8	149.1	148.6	147.4	148.7	150.6	153.3	152.5	151.9	155.7	155.5	156.1	151.5
1997	151.7	152.2	153.8	152.5	153.7	154.2	156.2	150.5	157.0	159.4	159.3	160.2	155.1
1998	158.7	158.3	160.2	160.3	161.5	162.5	165.7	168.2	169.5	171.9	172.9	174.2	165.3
1999	168.5	169.5	170.6	173.9	174.4	174.9	176.0	176.8	176.3	179.8	179.8	180.4	175.1
2000	177.5	177.4	178.7	181.1	181.1	181.6	181.3	182.5	182.8	185.3	185.0	185.1	181.6
2001	180.3	179.8	179.7	180.0	180.4	180.5	182.1	181.7	181.0	183.1	180.5	180.5	180.8
2002	173.5	173.4	172.7	174.9	175.8	177.2	174.9	175.2	174.1	181.7	182.7	183.6	176.6
2003	174.3	173.8	174.3	172.1	172.6	172.9	173.4	174.0	174.3	174.4	175.1	176.4	174.0
Information													
1990	83.9	83.7	84.2	85.3	85.3	86.8	88.5	88.8	88.5	87.7	88.5	88.6	86.7
1991	89.2	88.0	88.8	88.2	88.1	89.5	84.4	84.1	84.3	87.7	88.6	88.1	87.4
1992	87.8	88.3	91.6	91.9	92.0	93.5	94.0	93.7	94.0	93.8	93.7	94.2	92.4
1993	92.1	92.4	93.2	93.8	94.0	95.1	95.2	96.0	96.3	96.6	97.3	98.3	95.0
1994	96.4	96.4	96.8	97.2	98.4	100.1	100.7	101.5	102.1	102.1	103.5	103.9	99.9
1995	103.7	104.2	105.5	104.8	105.6	107.0	104.7	106.2	106.7	109.0	109.4	110.9	106.5
1996	109.7	108.9	109.4	111.8	112.8	113.9	116.1	115.1	114.8	115.4	116.7	117.5	113.5
1997	116.2	117.9	118.3	117.6	119.1	120.0	121.3	122.6	122.3	121.7	122.6	123.9	120.3
1998	122.8	123.8	124.5	123.5	124.7	124.9	126.2	126.6	126.3	126.2	128.2	129.1	125.6
1999	127.9	128.7	129.9	131.2	133.0	134.4	134.5	136.1	136.6	138.0	140.6	143.7	134.6
2000	140.5	140.9	140.6	139.7	140.9	143.5	143.8	145.2	145.1	146.2	147.1	148.5	143.5
2001	144.8	145.5	146.0	145.1	145.0	145.6	143.6	142.9	141.9	141.7	142.2	141.9	143.8
2002	135.0	134.9	133.5	132.6	132.5	132.0	131.6	131.1	129.8	130.8	128.9	128.9	131.8
2003	130.3	129.4	127.3	126.1	125.7	126.3	125.8	126.4	125.2	126.9	127.1	127.5	127.0
Financial activities													
1990	155.9	156.4	157.6	156.9	157.3	158.4	157.9	158.5	157.8	157.2	157.4	158.3	157.5
1991	153.9	153.7	154.5	153.6	155.0	157.0	156.5	156.9	155.9	153.3	153.7	155.1	154.9
1992	154.1	153.7	153.9	154.3	154.8	155.5	157.3	157.2	156.4	156.8	157.1	158.0	155.8
1993	156.7	157.4	158.2	158.5	158.8	159.6	163.3	163.2	163.4	161.0	161.5	162.6	160.4
1994	163.9	164.4	165.2	166.2	166.9	168.5	170.5	171.0	170.8	169.5	169.7	171.2	168.2
1995	169.6	170.6	171.2	170.6	170.9	172.7	173.5	174.5	174.6	173.2	173.8	175.3	172.5
1996	175.2	176.8	178.3	179.1	179.5	181.7	183.6	182.6	182.0	182.0	182.5	184.3	180.6
1997	182.0	183.0	184.2	184.0	185.7	186.7	188.3	189.5	189.3	189.0	190.4	192.9	187.1
1998	195.5	194.8	197.4	197.1	198.0	199.7	201.6	201.6	200.2	200.9	201.0	202.6	199.2
1999	199.8	200.9	201.6	203.0	204.2	205.5	206.1	207.0	205.4	206.2	206.5	208.1	204.5
2000	206.0	206.7	207.4	210.2	210.9	212.5	210.8	210.8	209.2	208.6	208.8	210.4	209.4
2001	206.8	207.1	208.0	210.7	210.9	211.6	214.1	214.5	213.2	213.4	213.4	213.8	211.4
2002	212.2	211.6	211.4	211.5	212.3	213.1	212.7	213.4	212.0	213.7	214.0	215.3	212.8
2003	213.1	213.0	214.6	214.8	216.3	217.7	218.8	219.6	219.3	217.9	217.5	217.6	216.7
Professional and business services													
1990	290.3	295.0	298.1	292.1	293.7	297.3	298.0	299.9	299.6	292.1	293.2	292.3	295.1
1991	289.4	290.7	293.0	296.0	296.5	300.7	299.7	301.1	303.1	301.7	302.3	305.0	298.3
1992	293.6	298.7	302.2	305.8	307.4	309.5	314.1	317.7	319.4	321.3	321.7	324.7	311.3
1993	317.5	322.7	323.4	332.4	335.5	340.6	341.6	346.2	347.7	353.4	354.7	357.7	339.5
1994	349.6	357.1	364.0	366.8	370.0	375.0	376.2	382.9	387.1	386.1	391.6	391.8	374.9
1995	381.6	390.3	395.2	395.2	400.5	407.0	402.6	411.9	414.9	411.5	414.9	415.8	403.5
1996	399.6	411.5	417.7	424.0	432.2	439.3	461.0	445.2	441.9	437.9	441.3	443.0	432.9
1997	430.8	437.9	445.5	443.0	446.7	453.0	452.9	460.7	466.8	470.2	471.2	476.5	454.6
1998	463.8	472.9	479.7	485.2	492.1	501.6	496.9	502.1	503.0	503.8	504.6	506.6	492.7
1999	494.9	505.3	511.9	521.3	522.7	532.7	524.0	529.2	530.0	529.9	532.1	533.4	522.3
2000	524.9	531.3	537.8	529.5	533.0	541.0	539.7	543.8	545.4	540.3	539.5	541.6	537.3
2001	527.0	528.5	531.6	529.6	528.1	528.8	526.8	531.8	527.3	526.3	522.0	522.1	527.4
2002	503.2	509.0	511.2	515.6	517.4	518.9	518.6	522.8	519.7	518.2	518.5	516.9	515.8
2003	483.4	488.1	491.0	487.7	486.2	489.4	493.8	500.0	500.1	502.2	500.4	501.8	493.7
Educational and health services													
1990	224.8	225.9	227.9	228.8	229.1	228.3	226.6	228.4	232.7	236.2	238.0	239.0	230.5
1991	241.2	243.6	245.7	243.4	243.8	241.5	242.7	243.6	246.0	244.8	245.1	245.9	243.9
1992	243.4	244.2	244.7	246.4	248.7	249.7	251.2	253.0	256.9	260.3	262.6	264.4	252.1
1993	260.4	264.6	267.2	269.6	269.6	268.6	269.6	270.7	274.9	276.7	278.1	279.2	270.8
1994	275.1	278.4	279.7	281.1	281.4	280.5	279.1	280.9	285.2	289.0	291.0	292.5	282.8
1995	284.8	288.9	291.2	294.2	294.6	294.2	292.2	295.0	300.3	302.9	305.0	306.3	295.8
1996	304.3	309.2	311.2	310.8	311.0	306.8	306.3	305.0	310.4	314.7	316.1	317.3	310.3
1997	310.8	314.6	316.1	315.8	316.0	314.7	313.2	315.7	322.0	326.0	327.9	329.1	318.5
1998	322.9	328.1	330.3	332.0	330.9	328.8	327.4	330.6	335.6	338.7	339.5	339.2	332.0
1999	329.4	334.1	335.4	339.6	339.3	336.1	333.4	336.1	341.6	346.0	347.7	346.4	338.8
2000	336.9	341.2	342.9	345.0	345.9	345.8	344.5	347.7	351.3	355.1	356.1	355.6	347.3
2001	349.5	352.5	355.3	357.0	357.4	358.1	355.3	359.5	363.3	366.9	368.4	368.7	359.3
2002	362.0	365.8	369.9	370.2	371.1	370.4	368.2	373.5	375.5	377.6	379.7	379.6	372.0
2003	380.5	383.8	385.9	386.0	387.9	385.8	383.3	388.2	389.8	390.9	392.7	390.6	387.1

Employment by Industry: Georgia—*Continued*

(Numbers in thousands. Not seasonally adjusted.)

Industry	January	February	March	April	May	June	July	August	September	October	November	December	Annual Average
STATEWIDE—*Continued*													
Leisure and hospitality													
1990	231.9	234.1	240.3	244.9	249.0	253.4	251.3	254.4	251.5	243.1	242.6	242.0	244.9
1991	230.4	230.7	235.9	241.6	246.9	251.3	247.4	248.8	245.9	236.9	237.4	237.5	240.9
1992	230.5	233.8	239.8	248.2	253.9	256.0	256.1	257.9	254.5	252.8	252.1	250.4	248.8
1993	240.2	245.4	249.2	258.1	262.9	266.9	267.7	269.8	267.6	265.1	265.5	266.1	260.4
1994	257.3	261.1	268.5	274.9	278.9	283.0	280.0	283.2	282.1	277.1	279.2	280.6	275.5
1995	275.6	279.4	286.0	291.7	295.9	301.9	302.8	305.2	303.2	294.2	296.0	297.2	294.1
1996	287.4	291.9	300.2	305.7	313.5	321.8	333.5	322.8	315.2	304.7	305.5	305.3	309.0
1997	293.4	298.4	305.9	313.2	318.8	323.1	320.4	321.8	318.2	308.1	309.0	309.5	311.7
1998	300.6	304.3	312.4	315.1	323.1	327.7	324.0	326.6	322.6	316.7	317.9	317.6	317.4
1999	303.5	309.3	317.0	323.3	332.0	336.6	334.3	336.7	332.4	327.8	327.6	329.2	325.8
2000	315.1	318.6	328.6	331.4	336.7	340.1	343.4	342.8	338.1	333.9	332.2	329.5	332.5
2001	317.7	322.1	329.2	338.0	343.2	346.6	340.9	342.1	336.2	335.0	334.1	332.0	334.7
2002	318.1	322.3	331.2	339.8	345.0	357.5	343.4	344.3	339.7	335.3	335.1	335.9	337.3
2003	331.8	334.6	342.7	348.4	353.1	356.3	356.3	359.3	355.7	354.5	349.9	350.9	349.5
Other services													
1990	103.1	103.8	104.9	105.7	106.5	108.1	107.0	107.5	107.6	106.4	106.4	106.3	106.1
1991	104.6	105.3	106.0	105.9	106.6	107.5	106.6	106.7	106.3	105.8	105.5	105.6	106.0
1992	105.0	105.1	105.9	106.8	107.3	108.1	110.1	109.3	109.0	108.3	107.7	108.1	107.6
1993	106.7	107.2	107.9	108.8	108.9	110.2	111.1	110.3	110.5	110.4	110.6	110.5	109.4
1994	109.9	110.9	111.7	112.7	112.7	114.1	114.4	114.0	114.4	114.6	114.8	115.2	113.3
1995	114.2	114.9	116.3	116.9	117.9	120.3	120.5	120.9	121.5	121.0	121.7	122.9	119.1
1996	122.3	124.5	126.3	127.0	128.5	130.8	130.0	129.5	129.6	129.5	129.9	130.6	128.2
1997	129.2	130.8	131.9	133.3	134.1	135.3	135.5	135.8	135.7	134.8	135.1	136.3	134.0
1998	135.6	136.9	138.0	137.6	139.0	140.4	140.0	139.2	139.1	139.1	138.8	140.0	138.6
1999	137.5	138.9	140.2	142.5	144.9	147.0	148.2	149.0	149.6	151.9	153.3	155.5	146.5
2000	155.0	158.4	162.3	166.6	170.3	174.3	181.2	182.6	184.7	187.8	188.9	191.7	175.3
2001	199.4	202.8	206.9	189.7	190.6	191.9	186.3	185.6	184.1	175.7	175.6	175.2	188.6
2002	169.8	170.5	171.3	169.3	169.8	170.6	165.2	165.4	165.0	165.9	166.6	165.5	167.9
2003	164.8	165.3	167.1	168.8	171.1	173.1	175.2	176.2	177.0	176.2	174.0	171.0	171.7
Government													
1990	526.5	529.6	534.9	532.9	540.7	539.4	524.3	521.7	525.7	535.4	537.4	534.3	531.9
1991	533.1	537.5	539.9	539.7	543.3	543.7	529.1	527.8	528.9	539.2	540.4	536.4	536.6
1992	532.9	535.1	540.8	536.0	538.9	538.2	525.5	525.9	531.2	545.8	548.8	545.5	537.1
1993	542.6	546.8	549.6	548.5	550.3	547.9	533.5	533.5	539.9	560.9	562.2	561.7	548.1
1994	558.6	562.8	564.6	567.1	565.9	564.8	550.5	549.8	555.0	574.5	578.4	575.6	564.0
1995	570.2	573.1	575.6	576.1	577.4	578.6	550.9	552.1	561.0	575.5	576.7	576.8	570.3
1996	568.9	572.8	574.8	574.0	575.6	573.4	555.3	550.8	560.9	574.4	576.9	576.4	569.5
1997	572.5	576.7	578.7	579.3	581.9	579.9	558.5	561.9	572.6	586.8	588.2	590.1	577.3
1998	584.4	588.3	588.8	587.2	588.3	587.0	566.4	572.0	584.9	591.9	596.4	595.9	586.0
1999	591.1	596.0	593.6	591.7	592.7	585.9	568.0	570.2	588.3	597.0	600.0	600.6	589.6
2000	592.3	596.9	601.1	601.1	612.4	597.3	577.4	585.3	594.9	600.6	602.9	604.3	597.2
2001	600.7	606.6	609.4	609.6	611.6	607.0	586.2	607.2	616.2	621.7	624.8	623.4	610.3
2002	617.2	619.7	625.7	626.7	628.3	619.4	598.9	621.7	633.4	635.0	637.5	634.5	624.8
2003	633.0	638.0	639.5	638.8	636.4	623.4	604.7	623.0	633.9	638.8	639.7	640.4	632.5
Federal government													
1990	101.6	102.1	105.1	103.9	109.1	108.2	106.8	102.8	102.1	101.4	100.5	101.0	103.7
1991	99.9	100.9	101.1	101.7	101.8	102.4	102.4	102.5	102.5	101.7	101.5	101.9	101.7
1992	101.7	102.1	102.2	102.0	102.1	102.6	102.4	102.4	102.1	101.3	100.6	101.5	101.9
1993	101.0	101.6	101.9	100.8	100.1	99.9	100.4	100.4	99.2	98.5	98.2	99.3	100.1
1994	98.7	99.5	100.0	100.6	99.5	99.5	99.5	99.3	99.3	98.4	97.7	98.6	99.2
1995	97.1	97.4	97.3	97.5	97.1	97.3	96.5	96.5	96.3	95.8	95.1	96.1	96.7
1996	94.3	94.6	94.9	95.4	94.5	94.8	94.7	94.4	94.1	93.6	93.5	94.6	94.5
1997	93.9	94.5	95.1	95.0	94.4	94.1	94.1	93.9	93.5	93.0	93.2	94.8	94.1
1998	92.5	93.6	94.2	94.5	93.6	92.3	93.5	93.5	93.2	93.1	93.3	94.4	93.5
1999	92.9	93.7	94.0	94.8	94.8	93.7	93.5	93.9	93.8	94.0	93.8	95.0	94.0
2000	94.1	95.5	98.9	99.8	110.3	99.8	99.6	95.9	94.2	94.0	94.4	95.8	97.7
2001	95.3	95.8	96.1	96.5	96.6	96.8	96.2	95.5	95.0	94.8	95.3	96.0	95.8
2002	94.7	96.0	96.5	96.2	95.9	96.7	95.6	95.3	95.1	94.5	95.2	95.6	95.6
2003	95.1	95.6	95.6	95.9	95.3	94.6	94.0	93.6	93.7	94.0	93.4	94.5	94.6
State government													
1990	129.9	131.5	132.0	131.2	132.2	131.1	127.8	127.0	124.3	131.5	131.5	129.6	130.0
1991	131.3	132.2	133.1	132.4	134.0	133.1	132.2	132.0	126.6	131.8	131.5	129.0	131.6
1992	130.2	131.0	131.4	132.6	133.5	133.0	130.3	130.4	127.9	136.5	137.1	136.3	132.5
1993	135.5	136.7	137.2	138.2	139.0	137.4	133.6	133.7	131.4	142.7	143.9	142.8	137.7
1994	141.3	143.4	143.8	144.3	145.5	144.5	139.6	140.9	138.3	148.9	149.8	148.4	144.1
1995	146.3	148.1	148.9	148.8	149.5	149.7	143.6	143.7	139.5	149.4	149.8	148.0	147.1
1996	146.0	147.9	147.7	148.1	148.8	148.1	144.8	144.7	142.5	149.4	149.2	148.5	147.1
1997	145.3	147.3	146.9	148.0	148.5	148.4	145.7	146.7	144.6	151.7	152.2	151.1	148.0
1998	149.4	151.2	151.2	148.7	149.0	147.7	146.3	148.9	149.7	151.6	152.2	151.3	149.8
1999	149.6	152.1	151.5	152.4	149.4	145.6	149.7	149.8	154.6	155.7	154.0	152.8	151.4
2000	147.1	149.4	148.6	149.6	148.3	144.9	143.3	145.5	148.0	149.0	149.7	149.0	147.7
2001	147.7	150.2	150.7	151.1	150.0	146.6	146.5	149.2	151.3	152.9	153.2	152.0	150.1
2002	150.4	152.7	153.1	153.0	152.5	147.9	147.6	149.9	153.8	156.0	155.6	155.7	152.4
2003	154.2	156.7	156.6	157.7	154.3	150.5	149.4	151.0	155.3	155.2	155.4	155.7	154.3

Employment by Industry: Georgia—*Continued*

(Numbers in thousands. Not seasonally adjusted.)

Industry	January	February	March	April	May	June	July	August	September	October	November	December	Annual Average
STATEWIDE—*Continued*													
Local government													
1990	295.0	296.0	297.8	297.8	299.4	300.1	289.7	291.9	299.3	302.5	305.4	303.7	298.2
1991	301.9	304.4	305.7	305.6	307.5	308.2	294.5	293.3	299.8	305.7	307.4	305.5	303.3
1992	301.0	302.0	307.2	301.4	303.3	302.6	292.8	293.1	301.2	308.0	311.1	307.7	302.6
1993	306.1	308.5	310.5	309.5	311.2	310.6	299.5	299.4	309.3	319.7	320.1	319.6	310.3
1994	318.6	319.9	320.8	322.2	320.9	320.8	311.4	309.6	317.4	327.2	330.9	328.6	320.7
1995	326.8	327.6	329.4	329.8	330.8	331.6	310.8	311.9	325.2	330.3	331.8	332.7	326.6
1996	328.6	330.3	332.2	330.5	332.3	330.5	315.8	311.7	324.3	331.4	334.2	333.3	327.9
1997	333.3	334.9	336.7	336.3	339.0	337.4	318.7	321.3	334.5	342.1	342.8	344.2	335.1
1998	342.5	343.5	343.4	344.0	345.7	347.0	326.6	329.6	342.0	347.2	350.9	350.2	342.7
1999	348.6	350.2	348.1	344.5	348.5	346.6	324.8	326.5	339.9	347.3	352.2	352.8	344.2
2000	351.1	352.0	353.6	351.7	353.8	352.6	334.5	343.9	352.7	357.6	358.8	359.5	351.8
2001	357.7	360.6	362.6	362.0	365.0	363.6	343.5	362.5	369.9	374.0	376.3	375.4	364.4
2002	372.1	371.0	376.1	377.5	379.9	374.8	355.7	376.5	384.5	384.5	386.7	383.2	376.9
2003	383.7	385.7	387.3	385.2	386.8	378.3	361.3	378.4	384.9	389.6	390.9	390.2	383.5
ATLANTA													
Total nonfarm													
1990	1498.7	1505.1	1519.5	1516.6	1526.0	1541.1	1535.2	1542.3	1543.4	1532.6	1541.7	1543.3	1528.8
1991	1496.4	1489.4	1494.9	1491.7	1501.9	1513.1	1508.1	1510.8	1510.2	1513.1	1520.7	1529.6	1506.7
1992	1499.5	1502.3	1517.7	1530.2	1543.4	1552.1	1555.1	1561.0	1565.5	1579.3	1589.3	1602.5	1549.8
1993	1572.6	1586.3	1592.7	1614.3	1625.7	1637.6	1639.7	1647.6	1649.5	1672.9	1685.6	1700.4	1635.4
1994	1669.1	1682.8	1697.2	1709.0	1719.0	1732.4	1733.3	1744.0	1756.1	1765.1	1786.8	1801.7	1733.0
1995	1757.1	1771.3	1787.0	1793.4	1803.6	1822.2	1813.1	1829.8	1838.8	1847.7	1862.5	1879.0	1817.1
1996	1832.2	1853.2	1871.4	1881.7	1903.1	1924.0	1951.5	1914.8	1907.6	1916.8	1933.5	1948.8	1903.2
1997	1898.4	1914.3	1934.5	1937.3	1953.2	1964.2	1952.7	1961.6	1973.7	1986.9	2005.0	2026.9	1959.1
1998	1977.5	1995.4	2012.5	2014.5	2030.2	2044.0	2041.5	2057.6	2064.4	2076.9	2093.3	2106.1	2042.8
1999	2050.0	2069.6	2082.1	2104.3	2124.1	2140.6	2125.5	2139.1	2149.7	2162.3	2176.1	2192.4	2126.3
2000	2130.2	2144.0	2165.8	2162.7	2178.9	2190.0	2178.5	2192.5	2195.3	2206.0	2215.9	2226.2	2182.2
2001	2172.5	2183.6	2198.6	2201.2	2203.5	2207.3	2183.6	2199.3	2190.9	2187.1	2188.2	2188.9	2192.0
2002	2139.0	2143.3	2159.2	2164.5	2173.5	2175.1	2155.6	2172.8	2174.0	2179.8	2189.3	2196.1	2168.5
2003	2129.1	2139.8	2150.8	2151.1	2157.3	2153.2	2148.2	2170.8	2172.2	2174.0	2177.8	2179.3	2158.6
Total private													
1990	1274.4	1279.2	1291.6	1287.9	1294.0	1308.5	1310.4	1317.2	1315.6	1301.1	1307.8	1310.8	1299.9
1991	1266.2	1256.4	1261.1	1258.8	1267.7	1278.3	1278.0	1281.4	1282.6	1278.9	1286.1	1297.7	1274.4
1992	1270.9	1272.2	1283.7	1300.6	1312.0	1320.7	1331.1	1335.5	1339.1	1344.6	1354.0	1368.1	1319.4
1993	1340.1	1351.2	1356.0	1377.0	1387.7	1400.2	1409.0	1416.4	1418.1	1431.0	1444.1	1459.5	1399.2
1994	1428.6	1440.1	1454.2	1462.5	1475.3	1490.0	1496.7	1508.5	1516.6	1518.3	1538.7	1553.7	1490.3
1995	1512.0	1524.5	1539.3	1543.8	1555.3	1573.0	1573.3	1588.4	1593.9	1597.0	1610.7	1627.0	1569.9
1996	1583.6	1602.3	1620.0	1629.5	1649.8	1671.0	1707.5	1672.6	1663.0	1663.5	1679.3	1694.2	1653.0
1997	1645.6	1658.9	1677.3	1680.4	1694.9	1707.7	1706.0	1715.8	1725.0	1729.5	1745.5	1766.2	1704.4
1998	1720.6	1736.2	1751.8	1756.7	1772.8	1788.2	1792.1	1804.7	1806.3	1814.2	1827.9	1840.6	1784.3
1999	1787.0	1804.1	1819.6	1843.9	1863.2	1883.6	1873.9	1887.7	1888.8	1896.4	1912.3	1927.3	1865.7
2000	1867.3	1878.6	1898.8	1895.9	1907.2	1925.6	1922.9	1933.2	1930.7	1938.1	1946.7	1956.0	1916.8
2001	1902.5	1910.2	1923.7	1926.7	1927.7	1934.1	1921.2	1924.8	1912.2	1905.7	1904.7	1906.6	1916.6
2002	1860.7	1866.5	1877.5	1880.4	1889.2	1895.8	1887.1	1891.4	1885.9	1890.3	1897.8	1907.6	1885.9
2003	1840.0	1849.7	1859.0	1859.8	1868.0	1873.0	1875.7	1888.1	1883.2	1881.8	1885.7	1886.2	1870.9
Goods-producing													
1990	246.8	247.8	251.2	250.5	251.4	254.7	253.6	252.9	251.0	248.1	245.4	242.9	249.7
1991	231.3	230.1	231.6	229.8	230.0	232.4	232.2	233.3	233.9	233.4	232.6	233.0	232.0
1992	228.4	226.5	229.5	235.0	236.6	238.8	240.0	239.1	242.0	242.4	242.1	243.0	237.0
1993	248.5	249.9	250.1	252.0	253.9	255.9	258.8	258.9	258.5	259.2	260.0	261.5	255.6
1994	259.2	260.8	262.7	263.5	265.7	269.2	270.3	272.8	274.6	275.7	277.8	279.7	269.3
1995	277.1	278.6	282.0	281.7	283.5	286.7	287.3	290.0	290.4	291.7	291.1	292.6	286.1
1996	290.0	291.9	295.1	295.6	297.1	299.8	299.4	296.8	296.9	298.6	298.4	298.3	296.5
1997	292.6	294.5	296.6	298.2	301.0	303.2	301.9	304.7	304.9	304.5	304.7	305.5	301.0
1998	290.8	292.1	294.8	294.3	296.9	300.1	303.1	305.0	305.6	307.6	307.8	308.9	300.6
1999	300.7	302.4	304.5	311.2	314.3	318.2	316.3	318.5	319.9	319.1	318.9	319.7	313.6
2000	309.4	310.7	314.6	313.7	314.9	318.3	315.6	319.1	318.9	318.6	317.1	316.9	315.7
2001	309.5	311.2	312.0	309.4	308.7	310.4	305.7	306.8	303.4	300.5	296.5	295.1	305.7
2002	283.8	287.3	288.8	288.0	287.8	288.7	289.1	287.1	286.9	287.2	286.0	284.4	287.1
2003	282.6	285.1	286.4	285.6	287.6	288.2	287.9	289.3	288.5	291.9	291.2	288.1	287.7
Natural resources and mining													
1990	1.9	1.9	1.9	1.9	1.9	1.9	1.9	1.9	1.9	1.8	1.8	1.8	1.9
1991	1.8	1.7	1.7	1.6	1.6	1.6	1.6	1.6	1.6	1.7	1.7	1.7	1.7
1992	1.6	1.6	1.6	1.6	1.6	1.6	1.6	1.6	1.6	1.6	1.6	1.6	1.6
1993	1.6	1.6	1.6	1.6	1.6	1.6	1.6	1.6	1.6	1.6	1.6	1.6	1.6
1994	1.6	1.6	1.6	1.6	1.6	1.6	1.6	1.7	1.7	1.6	1.6	1.6	1.6
1995	1.6	1.7	1.6	1.7	1.7	1.7	1.7	1.7	1.7	1.8	1.7	1.8	1.7
1996	1.8	1.7	1.8	1.7	1.7	1.7	1.7	1.7	1.7	1.7	1.7	1.7	1.7
1997	1.7	1.7	1.7	1.8	1.8	1.8	1.7	1.7	1.7	1.7	1.7	1.7	1.7
1998	1.7	1.7	1.7	1.7	1.7	1.8	1.8	1.8	1.8	1.9	1.9	1.9	1.8
1999	1.9	1.9	1.9	2.0	2.0	2.0	1.9	1.9	1.9	2.0	2.0	2.0	2.0
2000	1.9	1.9	1.9	1.8	1.8	1.9	1.9	1.9	1.9	2.0	2.0	2.0	1.9
2001	2.0	2.0	2.0	1.9	1.9	1.9	1.9	1.9	1.8	1.9	1.9	1.8	1.9
2002	1.9	1.9	1.9	1.9	1.9	1.9	1.9	2.0	1.9	1.9	1.8	1.8	1.9
2003	1.7	1.7	1.7	1.9	1.9	1.8	1.8	1.8	1.8	1.8	1.8	1.9	1.8

Employment by Industry: Georgia—*Continued*

(Numbers in thousands. Not seasonally adjusted.)

Industry	January	February	March	April	May	June	July	August	September	October	November	December	Annual Average
ATLANTA—*Continued*													
Construction													
1990	70.9	71.4	73.0	73.0	73.7	76.0	75.9	75.9	75.2	74.3	72.5	71.1	73.6
1991	64.0	63.4	63.8	65.0	64.8	66.2	66.5	66.8	66.9	66.2	65.6	65.4	65.4
1992	61.9	62.2	62.4	63.2	64.0	64.7	65.3	65.4	66.3	66.0	66.0	66.2	64.5
1993	62.8	64.3	64.9	66.7	68.1	69.2	70.4	70.1	69.9	70.8	71.1	71.4	68.3
1994	68.6	69.2	71.3	72.4	73.5	75.4	75.7	76.8	77.9	78.2	79.0	79.7	74.8
1995	76.7	77.0	79.5	81.6	83.0	85.2	86.2	87.6	88.1	89.8	89.4	89.7	84.5
1996	86.4	88.1	90.7	93.6	95.0	96.7	94.2	92.9	93.0	93.2	93.3	92.8	92.5
1997	89.2	90.4	92.2	94.0	95.7	96.7	96.5	98.2	98.5	98.3	98.1	98.1	95.5
1998	94.8	95.8	98.3	99.9	101.6	103.9	105.3	106.1	106.8	108.5	108.0	108.7	103.1
1999	105.6	107.5	109.3	113.4	115.3	117.9	117.3	118.3	119.2	118.9	118.7	118.4	115.0
2000	112.9	114.0	117.2	118.6	120.1	122.5	123.3	123.5	123.9	123.5	122.2	121.7	120.3
2001	117.8	118.9	120.1	121.5	122.0	123.4	123.4	123.1	121.7	121.4	119.6	118.5	120.9
2002	114.6	115.6	116.8	116.3	116.1	116.3	116.8	116.8	116.0	116.2	115.4	114.6	116.0
2003	111.2	111.8	113.0	113.1	114.1	115.2	116.3	117.3	117.5	120.4	119.3	117.7	115.6
Manufacturing													
1990	174.0	174.5	176.3	175.6	175.8	176.8	175.8	175.1	173.9	172.0	171.1	170.0	174.2
1991	165.5	165.0	166.1	163.2	163.6	164.6	164.1	164.9	165.4	165.5	165.3	165.9	164.9
1992	164.9	162.7	165.5	170.2	171.0	172.5	173.1	172.1	174.1	174.8	174.5	175.2	170.9
1993	184.1	184.0	183.6	183.7	184.2	185.1	186.8	187.2	187.0	186.8	187.3	188.5	185.7
1994	189.0	190.0	189.8	189.5	190.6	192.2	193.0	194.3	195.0	195.9	197.2	198.4	192.9
1995	198.8	199.9	200.9	198.4	198.8	199.8	199.4	200.7	200.6	200.1	200.0	201.1	199.9
1996	201.8	202.1	202.6	200.3	200.4	201.4	203.5	202.2	202.2	203.7	203.4	203.8	202.3
1997	201.7	202.4	202.7	202.4	203.5	204.7	203.7	204.8	204.7	204.5	204.9	205.7	203.8
1998	194.3	194.6	194.8	192.7	193.6	194.4	196.0	197.1	197.0	197.2	197.9	198.3	195.7
1999	193.2	193.0	193.3	195.8	197.0	198.3	197.1	198.3	198.8	198.2	198.2	199.3	196.7
2000	194.6	194.8	195.5	193.3	193.0	193.9	190.4	193.7	193.1	193.1	192.9	193.2	193.5
2001	189.7	190.3	189.9	186.0	184.8	185.1	180.4	181.8	179.9	177.2	175.0	174.8	182.9
2002	167.3	169.8	170.1	169.8	169.8	170.5	170.4	168.3	169.0	169.1	168.8	168.0	169.2
2003	169.7	171.6	171.7	170.6	171.6	171.2	169.8	170.2	169.2	169.7	170.1	168.5	170.3
Service-providing													
1990	1251.9	1257.3	1268.3	1266.1	1274.6	1286.4	1281.6	1289.4	1292.4	1284.5	1296.3	1300.4	1279.1
1991	1265.1	1259.3	1263.3	1261.9	1271.9	1280.7	1275.9	1277.5	1276.3	1279.7	1288.1	1296.6	1274.7
1992	1271.1	1275.8	1288.2	1295.2	1306.8	1313.3	1315.1	1321.9	1323.5	1336.9	1347.2	1359.5	1312.9
1993	1324.1	1336.4	1342.6	1362.3	1371.8	1381.7	1380.9	1388.7	1391.0	1413.7	1425.6	1438.9	1379.8
1994	1409.9	1422.0	1434.5	1445.5	1453.3	1463.2	1463.0	1471.2	1481.5	1489.4	1509.0	1522.0	1463.7
1995	1480.0	1492.7	1505.0	1511.7	1520.1	1535.5	1525.8	1539.8	1548.4	1556.0	1571.4	1586.4	1531.1
1996	1542.2	1561.3	1576.3	1586.1	1606.0	1624.2	1652.1	1618.0	1610.7	1618.2	1635.1	1650.5	1606.7
1997	1605.8	1619.8	1637.9	1639.1	1652.2	1661.0	1650.8	1656.9	1668.8	1682.4	1700.3	1721.4	1658.0
1998	1686.7	1703.3	1717.7	1720.2	1733.3	1743.9	1738.4	1752.6	1758.8	1769.3	1785.5	1797.2	1742.2
1999	1749.3	1767.2	1777.6	1793.1	1809.8	1822.4	1809.2	1820.6	1829.8	1843.2	1857.2	1872.7	1812.7
2000	1820.8	1833.3	1851.2	1849.0	1864.0	1871.7	1862.9	1873.4	1876.4	1887.4	1898.8	1909.3	1866.5
2001	1863.0	1872.4	1886.6	1891.8	1894.8	1896.9	1877.9	1892.5	1887.5	1886.6	1891.7	1893.8	1886.2
2002	1855.2	1856.0	1870.4	1876.5	1885.7	1886.4	1866.5	1885.7	1887.1	1892.6	1903.3	1911.7	1881.4
2003	1846.5	1854.7	1864.4	1865.5	1869.7	1865.0	1860.3	1881.5	1883.7	1882.1	1886.6	1891.2	1870.9
Trade, transportation, and utilities													
1990	372.2	371.1	371.4	371.2	372.3	375.2	379.6	383.6	384.3	383.8	389.4	394.3	379.0
1991	375.3	366.9	363.8	362.4	364.6	365.4	366.6	367.7	368.3	367.7	374.8	382.4	368.8
1992	373.9	371.2	371.5	373.2	375.4	376.9	376.5	377.9	377.8	380.6	388.1	397.6	378.4
1993	376.6	375.0	375.9	379.2	380.6	382.7	386.6	388.3	389.0	397.7	406.3	415.4	387.8
1994	401.3	399.5	400.0	399.4	404.5	408.1	408.3	410.6	413.2	416.3	426.4	437.2	410.4
1995	416.2	414.0	416.7	417.8	419.7	423.5	425.0	427.9	430.2	435.6	445.4	454.8	427.2
1996	436.7	435.7	438.2	436.6	441.9	447.2	452.5	448.8	446.2	450.1	461.1	471.0	447.2
1997	453.2	450.2	454.8	451.1	454.1	456.7	457.8	456.6	461.9	467.7	477.9	490.1	461.0
1998	474.0	470.9	474.9	472.3	474.4	477.8	481.0	485.4	487.0	490.9	501.6	510.0	483.4
1999	487.2	486.7	489.8	494.6	498.8	503.2	504.6	509.6	508.9	513.9	523.5	534.0	504.6
2000	510.1	510.2	514.7	514.8	516.4	518.7	515.3	518.4	517.3	524.9	534.4	542.0	519.8
2001	521.4	518.1	521.3	515.5	515.3	515.8	516.3	515.7	514.7	514.0	519.8	523.0	517.5
2002	505.0	500.4	502.8	501.1	503.8	505.1	499.5	500.4	499.5	504.1	513.0	521.1	504.7
2003	492.3	489.1	490.2	487.2	489.2	489.2	489.6	492.1	491.6	491.7	498.6	502.9	492.0
Wholesale trade													
1990	108.5	108.9	107.1	106.2	106.2	107.2	109.7	112.5	112.6	111.9	111.7	111.9	109.5
1991	110.3	110.4	109.8	108.9	109.0	108.9	109.1	108.8	108.2	108.2	108.3	108.8	109.1
1992	109.1	109.0	108.8	109.7	109.8	110.1	109.8	110.1	109.3	110.5	110.2	110.8	109.8
1993	106.7	106.9	107.1	107.9	107.9	107.9	110.2	109.7	109.3	109.2	109.7	110.6	108.6
1994	108.8	109.4	109.5	110.2	110.5	111.3	111.5	111.8	112.2	112.8	113.3	114.2	111.3
1995	113.7	114.7	115.3	116.8	117.1	118.1	118.8	119.3	119.5	119.5	119.9	120.8	117.8
1996	120.1	121.4	122.0	120.4	121.2	122.1	123.4	122.4	122.4	123.9	124.5	125.5	122.4
1997	125.7	127.0	128.5	127.7	128.5	129.0	129.2	130.3	130.3	131.9	133.2	133.8	129.6
1998	133.1	133.6	134.9	134.4	134.6	135.4	136.2	137.0	137.0	137.8	138.7	138.9	136.0
1999	137.7	138.2	139.0	140.7	141.6	142.8	141.9	143.4	142.9	142.3	142.9	143.9	141.4
2000	142.4	143.4	144.4	144.3	144.8	145.5	145.2	145.6	144.8	145.7	145.8	146.0	144.8
2001	144.9	144.9	145.5	143.3	142.8	143.3	144.0	143.0	142.1	141.4	140.5	139.3	142.9
2002	142.6	142.3	143.0	142.3	143.1	141.8	140.6	140.2	139.1	140.8	140.4	140.7	141.4
2003	137.1	137.0	137.4	136.5	136.7	136.7	136.8	136.5	135.9	135.7	135.6	136.8	136.6

Employment by Industry: Georgia—*Continued*

(Numbers in thousands. Not seasonally adjusted.)

Industry	January	February	March	April	May	June	July	August	September	October	November	December	Annual Average
ATLANTA—*Continued*													
Retail trade													
1990	178.7	176.2	177.3	175.5	176.7	177.7	177.8	178.0	178.4	179.0	184.8	188.7	179.1
1991	174.7	169.8	170.1	168.3	169.7	170.0	169.5	170.1	170.3	169.4	176.3	181.6	171.7
1992	172.0	169.3	169.5	170.8	172.4	173.3	172.7	173.6	174.3	175.5	183.2	191.5	174.8
1993	177.7	176.2	176.4	178.5	179.0	180.5	180.7	182.2	182.8	190.2	197.6	205.5	183.9
1994	193.9	190.9	190.6	190.2	192.6	195.8	194.8	197.0	200.5	200.2	209.5	219.6	198.0
1995	202.8	200.0	201.3	201.3	203.7	206.3	205.6	208.7	211.6	214.2	224.1	232.9	209.4
1996	218.8	216.4	219.0	218.8	222.1	225.5	227.6	225.9	223.9	224.3	234.7	243.5	225.0
1997	228.3	223.5	225.3	223.1	224.7	226.3	226.0	228.1	229.1	231.8	240.7	251.6	229.9
1998	236.2	232.9	234.2	231.7	233.3	235.3	234.6	236.6	237.4	238.9	247.8	255.3	237.9
1999	237.2	235.3	237.1	238.0	240.9	243.9	244.7	248.0	248.1	251.6	260.7	269.3	246.2
2000	247.7	246.9	249.9	248.6	249.8	251.3	247.9	249.8	249.3	254.2	263.2	270.4	252.4
2001	255.4	252.4	255.2	251.6	251.8	251.8	249.9	250.6	251.0	250.6	259.6	264.3	253.7
2002	247.8	244.1	245.8	243.1	244.4	245.4	242.9	243.4	244.1	245.7	254.6	262.3	247.0
2003	239.6	236.7	237.7	237.3	239.1	239.3	238.7	241.0	241.0	240.7	247.0	250.0	240.7
Transportation and utilities													
1990	85.0	86.0	87.0	89.5	89.4	90.3	92.1	93.1	93.3	92.9	92.9	93.7	90.4
1991	90.3	86.7	83.9	85.2	85.9	86.5	88.0	88.8	89.8	90.1	90.2	92.0	88.1
1992	92.8	92.9	93.2	92.7	93.2	93.5	94.0	94.2	94.2	94.6	94.7	95.3	93.8
1993	92.2	91.9	92.4	92.8	93.7	94.3	95.7	96.4	96.9	98.3	99.0	99.3	95.2
1994	98.6	99.2	99.9	99.0	101.4	101.0	102.0	101.8	100.5	103.3	103.6	103.4	101.1
1995	99.7	99.3	100.1	99.7	98.9	99.1	100.6	99.9	99.1	101.9	101.4	101.1	100.1
1996	97.8	97.9	97.2	97.4	98.6	99.6	101.5	100.5	99.9	101.9	101.9	102.0	99.7
1997	99.2	99.7	101.0	100.3	100.9	101.4	102.6	98.2	102.5	104.0	104.0	104.7	101.5
1998	104.7	104.4	105.8	106.2	106.5	107.1	110.2	111.8	112.6	114.2	115.1	115.8	109.5
1999	112.3	113.2	113.7	115.9	116.3	116.5	118.0	118.2	117.9	120.0	119.9	120.8	116.9
2000	120.0	119.9	120.4	121.9	121.8	121.9	122.2	123.0	123.2	125.0	125.4	125.6	122.5
2001	121.1	120.8	120.6	120.6	120.7	120.7	122.4	122.1	121.6	122.0	119.7	119.4	120.9
2002	114.6	114.0	114.0	115.7	116.3	117.9	116.0	116.8	116.3	117.6	118.0	118.1	116.3
2003	115.6	115.4	115.1	113.4	113.4	113.2	114.1	114.6	114.7	115.3	116.0	116.1	114.7
Information													
1990	62.2	62.0	62.5	62.9	62.6	63.6	65.7	65.4	65.3	64.6	65.0	65.2	63.9
1991	66.2	65.0	65.7	63.7	64.1	65.0	61.9	62.1	62.4	65.8	65.9	65.6	64.5
1992	64.6	65.2	68.1	70.2	70.8	71.5	72.1	71.8	71.9	71.5	71.8	72.4	70.2
1993	71.0	71.2	71.7	72.5	72.7	73.9	73.6	74.1	74.2	73.9	74.4	75.4	73.2
1994	68.7	68.9	72.3	74.8	75.6	77.0	77.3	77.8	78.2	78.4	79.3	79.7	75.7
1995	80.1	80.6	81.7	81.1	81.6	82.3	80.4	81.7	82.2	83.8	83.7	85.2	82.0
1996	84.3	83.6	83.9	86.1	86.8	87.7	89.9	88.6	88.3	89.1	90.0	91.0	87.4
1997	89.7	90.7	91.0	91.1	91.6	92.4	93.8	94.8	94.6	93.2	94.1	94.9	92.7
1998	94.7	95.6	96.2	95.5	96.6	96.8	96.3	96.5	96.1	96.6	97.8	98.6	96.4
1999	98.0	98.5	99.1	100.3	101.6	102.6	103.4	104.6	105.0	104.3	106.1	107.7	102.6
2000	106.2	106.4	108.0	107.3	108.1	110.0	109.9	110.7	110.6	111.6	112.2	113.5	109.5
2001	111.0	111.8	112.3	111.7	111.4	111.6	110.0	109.3	108.4	107.7	107.4	107.4	110.0
2002	106.7	105.8	106.8	103.6	103.0	103.0	102.5	101.9	100.9	100.9	100.3	100.2	103.0
2003	98.0	98.2	98.2	97.6	96.9	97.3	97.2	97.5	96.6	97.1	97.5	97.7	97.5
Financial activities													
1990	95.6	96.2	96.9	96.6	96.6	97.0	96.6	96.7	96.3	96.3	96.5	96.7	96.5
1991	93.9	93.7	94.2	94.7	95.9	97.6	97.7	97.7	97.0	95.4	95.8	96.7	95.9
1992	97.0	96.6	96.4	97.5	98.0	98.3	100.0	100.1	99.5	100.2	100.5	100.9	98.8
1993	100.5	101.3	101.6	102.5	102.9	103.4	106.0	106.0	106.1	104.3	104.8	105.3	103.7
1994	108.4	108.7	108.9	109.6	110.0	110.8	112.3	112.6	112.4	111.7	111.7	112.3	110.8
1995	111.4	112.3	110.6	110.0	110.2	111.2	111.9	112.2	112.2	111.8	111.9	112.7	111.5
1996	113.2	114.5	115.3	118.4	118.3	119.4	120.6	119.8	119.5	120.2	120.5	121.7	118.5
1997	120.0	120.9	121.8	122.2	123.2	123.9	124.6	125.3	125.1	125.0	126.0	127.6	123.8
1998	128.8	129.2	131.1	132.1	132.5	133.4	135.3	136.0	135.1	134.9	135.0	136.1	133.3
1999	134.4	135.3	135.6	137.1	138.1	139.1	139.2	140.0	138.8	138.9	139.2	140.2	138.0
2000	138.0	138.4	138.7	140.7	141.2	142.0	141.9	142.1	140.4	141.0	141.1	142.1	140.6
2001	141.4	141.6	142.2	143.6	143.7	144.0	145.8	145.9	145.1	144.7	144.9	146.4	144.1
2002	145.5	145.2	144.9	145.3	145.6	145.9	145.6	146.0	144.9	147.3	147.0	149.4	146.1
2003	146.5	147.0	147.6	147.7	148.6	149.3	149.5	150.0	149.7	147.7	146.5	146.2	148.0
Professional and business services													
1990	200.6	203.4	204.9	199.3	201.0	204.2	203.1	203.9	203.9	198.0	199.4	198.0	201.6
1991	194.2	194.3	195.8	199.0	200.0	202.7	203.3	203.9	205.3	205.2	205.8	208.1	201.5
1992	198.3	201.8	203.8	205.3	207.0	208.0	213.0	215.7	217.3	219.2	219.9	221.9	210.9
1993	216.7	220.7	220.3	227.1	230.0	233.8	233.2	236.8	238.1	242.3	244.3	246.4	232.5
1994	239.4	245.7	249.1	253.4	254.9	256.9	260.1	264.0	266.7	266.7	270.9	270.8	258.2
1995	263.8	269.5	273.2	274.2	277.7	281.4	279.8	285.2	286.3	285.6	287.7	287.9	279.4
1996	274.1	283.4	287.9	293.3	299.3	304.0	322.2	306.2	302.7	301.7	304.4	305.9	298.8
1997	295.0	299.9	305.0	304.5	307.4	311.3	310.7	315.7	319.2	323.9	325.2	328.5	312.2
1998	321.2	331.5	331.6	337.6	342.0	348.0	346.0	349.5	350.4	353.1	353.9	354.5	343.3
1999	347.8	354.5	357.5	363.7	365.5	372.5	364.8	368.4	368.5	370.5	372.3	372.7	364.9
2000	365.8	369.4	372.1	367.1	369.5	375.6	376.5	379.0	380.2	378.9	378.6	380.2	374.4
2001	366.7	369.0	370.9	367.7	365.8	366.5	364.7	367.3	363.8	362.9	359.6	359.8	365.3
2002	353.1	356.6	356.3	358.4	360.3	360.9	361.7	363.6	362.4	362.9	361.7	361.1	359.9
2003	330.6	335.5	334.6	336.4	334.3	335.6	338.7	342.2	341.6	343.3	341.0	341.4	337.9

Employment by Industry: Georgia—*Continued*

(Numbers in thousands. Not seasonally adjusted.)

Industry	January	February	March	April	May	June	July	August	September	October	November	December	Annual Average
ATLANTA—*Continued*													
Educational and health services													
1990	111.5	112.0	113.5	114.7	114.5	114.2	113.3	113.9	115.9	117.5	120.0	122.2	115.3
1991	120.4	121.8	122.7	121.1	121.2	120.2	121.0	121.1	122.3	121.9	121.9	122.3	121.5
1992	122.4	122.9	123.1	124.1	125.2	125.8	127.1	127.7	129.6	131.8	133.0	134.0	127.2
1993	131.5	134.1	135.3	136.9	137.2	137.0	137.8	138.1	139.9	141.3	141.9	142.4	137.8
1994	142.1	143.8	144.2	143.5	143.9	143.8	143.3	143.9	146.2	147.9	149.3	149.8	145.1
1995	144.1	146.7	148.2	149.6	150.5	150.6	150.5	151.4	154.1	155.0	155.8	157.2	151.1
1996	154.1	157.4	158.4	157.9	158.3	158.4	157.4	155.9	159.7	161.7	162.7	163.4	158.8
1997	161.0	163.8	164.6	164.9	165.0	163.8	162.5	163.0	166.4	168.9	170.1	170.7	165.4
1998	165.4	168.5	170.4	171.6	171.6	170.2	169.9	170.2	173.0	174.2	174.6	174.6	171.2
1999	170.2	173.4	175.0	177.2	177.5	175.6	174.5	174.0	176.8	179.8	182.3	182.3	176.6
2000	176.5	179.0	180.0	181.1	181.4	181.3	179.7	180.5	182.6	186.0	187.1	186.5	181.8
2001	184.3	186.3	187.8	189.5	190.1	190.1	189.0	190.4	192.4	194.6	195.6	196.2	190.5
2002	193.5	196.1	197.8	199.4	200.8	201.5	201.7	205.2	206.8	209.6	212.3	213.2	203.2
2003	209.3	211.6	213.0	212.6	213.8	212.3	211.4	214.1	214.7	213.4	215.6	214.8	213.1
Leisure and hospitality													
1990	128.6	129.5	133.3	134.1	136.7	139.7	139.2	141.0	139.2	134.1	133.3	132.9	135.1
1991	126.5	125.9	128.3	129.8	133.5	136.2	136.3	136.7	134.7	131.4	131.4	131.5	131.9
1992	127.9	129.7	132.6	135.7	139.2	141.2	140.4	141.6	139.8	138.2	138.2	137.4	136.8
1993	135.3	138.8	140.6	145.7	149.2	151.7	150.7	152.3	150.6	150.3	150.1	150.6	147.2
1994	146.7	149.3	153.5	154.2	156.7	159.5	160.1	161.8	160.3	156.6	158.1	158.9	156.3
1995	154.6	157.4	160.8	162.6	164.8	168.7	169.5	170.9	169.4	164.6	165.8	166.5	164.6
1996	161.5	164.6	169.1	169.2	174.9	180.3	191.6	183.1	176.6	168.5	168.5	168.6	173.0
1997	160.7	164.4	168.3	172.6	176.5	179.7	177.5	178.3	175.9	169.8	170.8	171.7	172.2
1998	168.3	169.8	173.5	175.3	180.1	182.5	180.9	182.7	180.0	177.6	178.1	178.1	177.2
1999	170.4	174.2	178.5	179.6	185.9	189.6	187.6	188.5	186.8	185.5	185.0	184.9	183.0
2000	177.4	179.6	184.5	185.5	189.5	192.6	196.1	195.8	193.5	191.3	190.5	188.6	188.7
2001	181.9	185.2	189.6	194.0	197.5	200.1	195.3	195.7	192.1	191.6	191.4	189.6	192.0
2002	180.7	182.9	187.7	192.2	195.8	198.3	196.1	196.4	194.1	191.3	190.8	192.2	191.5
2003	188.6	190.7	195.6	199.6	203.6	206.2	205.9	207.1	205.1	202.2	201.2	202.1	200.7
Other services													
1990	56.9	57.2	57.9	58.6	58.9	59.9	59.3	59.8	59.7	58.7	58.8	58.6	58.7
1991	58.4	58.7	59.0	58.3	58.4	58.8	59.0	58.9	58.7	58.1	57.9	58.1	58.5
1992	58.4	58.3	58.7	59.6	59.8	60.2	62.0	61.6	61.2	60.7	60.4	60.9	60.2
1993	60.0	60.2	60.5	61.1	61.2	61.8	62.3	61.9	61.7	62.0	62.3	62.5	61.5
1994	62.8	63.4	63.5	64.1	64.0	64.7	65.0	65.0	65.0	65.0	65.2	65.3	64.4
1995	64.7	65.4	66.1	66.8	67.3	68.6	68.9	69.1	69.1	68.9	69.3	70.1	67.9
1996	69.7	71.2	72.1	72.4	73.2	74.2	73.9	73.4	73.1	73.6	73.7	74.3	72.9
1997	73.4	74.5	75.2	75.8	76.1	76.7	77.2	77.4	77.0	76.5	76.7	77.2	76.1
1998	77.4	78.6	79.3	78.0	78.7	79.4	79.6	79.4	79.1	79.3	79.1	79.8	79.0
1999	78.3	79.1	79.6	80.2	81.5	82.8	83.5	84.1	84.1	84.4	85.0	85.8	82.4
2000	83.9	84.9	86.2	85.7	86.2	87.1	87.9	87.6	87.2	85.8	85.7	86.2	86.2
2001	86.3	87.0	87.6	95.3	95.2	95.6	94.4	93.7	92.3	89.7	89.5	89.1	91.3
2002	92.4	92.2	92.4	92.4	92.1	92.4	90.9	90.8	90.4	87.0	86.7	86.0	90.5
2003	92.1	92.5	93.4	93.1	94.0	94.9	95.5	95.8	95.4	94.5	94.1	93.0	94.0
Government													
1990	224.3	225.9	227.9	228.7	232.0	232.6	224.8	225.1	227.8	231.5	233.9	232.5	228.9
1991	230.2	233.0	233.8	232.9	234.2	234.8	230.1	229.4	227.6	234.2	234.6	231.9	232.2
1992	228.6	230.1	234.0	229.6	231.4	231.4	224.0	225.5	226.4	234.7	235.3	234.4	230.5
1993	232.5	235.1	236.7	237.3	238.0	237.4	230.7	231.2	231.4	241.9	241.5	240.9	236.2
1994	240.5	242.7	243.0	246.5	243.7	242.4	236.6	235.5	239.5	246.8	248.1	248.0	242.8
1995	245.1	246.8	247.7	249.6	248.3	249.2	239.8	241.4	244.9	250.7	251.8	252.0	247.3
1996	248.6	250.9	251.4	252.2	253.3	253.0	244.0	242.2	244.6	253.3	254.2	254.6	250.2
1997	252.8	255.4	257.2	256.9	258.3	256.5	246.7	245.8	248.7	257.4	259.5	260.7	254.7
1998	256.9	259.2	260.7	257.8	257.4	255.8	249.4	252.9	258.1	262.7	265.4	265.5	258.5
1999	263.0	265.5	262.5	260.4	260.9	257.0	251.6	251.4	260.9	265.9	263.8	265.1	260.7
2000	262.9	265.4	267.0	266.8	271.7	264.4	255.6	259.3	264.6	267.9	269.2	270.2	265.4
2001	270.0	273.4	274.9	274.5	275.8	273.2	262.4	274.5	278.7	281.4	283.5	282.3	275.3
2002	278.3	276.8	281.7	284.1	284.3	279.3	268.5	281.4	288.1	289.5	291.5	288.5	282.7
2003	289.1	290.1	291.8	291.3	289.3	280.2	272.5	282.7	289.0	292.2	292.1	293.1	287.8
Federal government													
1990	44.7	45.2	45.7	45.6	47.3	47.9	46.8	45.4	45.1	45.8	45.4	46.1	45.9
1991	45.5	46.5	46.7	47.1	46.8	47.0	46.9	47.0	46.8	46.4	46.2	46.7	46.6
1992	47.2	47.8	47.9	48.1	48.2	47.9	47.6	47.5	47.8	47.3	46.9	47.9	47.7
1993	47.5	48.3	48.6	48.8	48.4	48.1	48.1	48.5	47.4	47.7	47.7	47.5	48.1
1994	47.9	48.8	48.9	50.6	47.4	47.5	47.3	47.4	47.2	47.0	47.2	47.9	47.9
1995	47.2	48.1	47.8	49.5	47.5	47.1	46.8	46.9	46.7	46.8	46.9	47.6	47.4
1996	47.2	48.0	47.9	48.7	48.0	47.9	47.8	47.3	47.0	46.7	46.8	47.8	47.6
1997	47.4	48.0	48.6	48.9	48.0	47.6	47.3	47.1	46.7	46.6	47.2	48.7	47.7
1998	46.0	47.3	47.8	47.8	47.2	45.9	44.8	44.9	44.7	44.7	45.0	45.9	46.0
1999	44.9	45.9	46.1	46.4	46.0	45.5	45.5	45.8	46.1	46.1	45.2	46.1	45.8
2000	45.5	46.7	47.6	49.0	53.6	49.0	48.2	46.2	45.4	45.3	45.6	46.7	47.4
2001	46.8	47.5	47.8	48.0	47.9	47.8	47.6	47.1	46.8	46.5	46.7	47.1	47.3
2002	46.0	46.1	46.6	46.6	46.2	46.3	46.5	46.1	46.0	47.3	47.8	47.9	46.6
2003	46.9	47.6	47.4	48.1	47.4	46.6	46.6	46.0	45.9	46.1	45.5	46.0	46.7

Employment by Industry: Georgia—*Continued*

(Numbers in thousands. Not seasonally adjusted.)

Industry	January	February	March	April	May	June	July	August	September	October	November	December	Annual Average
ATLANTA—*Continued*													
State government													
1990	47.4	47.7	48.0	48.2	48.8	49.0	47.3	47.6	46.1	47.8	48.3	47.6	47.8
1991	48.0	48.2	48.3	47.5	48.1	47.6	47.5	47.7	44.4	47.6	47.4	46.7	47.4
1992	45.9	46.4	46.5	47.0	47.6	47.5	46.1	46.1	43.4	48.9	49.2	48.7	46.9
1993	48.3	48.8	49.2	49.6	49.9	49.7	49.5	49.8	45.7	51.8	52.1	51.7	49.7
1994	50.7	51.5	51.7	51.5	51.1	50.0	49.7	50.2	46.7	53.9	54.1	53.6	51.2
1995	52.3	52.9	53.4	53.5	53.9	53.9	53.0	53.6	51.6	54.9	55.1	54.1	53.5
1996	52.6	53.3	53.5	53.5	53.9	53.7	52.1	52.7	50.7	55.1	54.8	54.8	53.4
1997	52.5	53.8	53.7	53.6	54.0	54.0	52.7	52.7	50.1	55.3	55.5	55.0	53.6
1998	54.6	55.3	55.2	52.8	52.8	52.5	51.3	52.4	53.3	53.9	54.3	53.9	53.5
1999	53.3	54.3	53.7	54.5	52.9	50.3	54.9	54.8	57.4	57.9	54.4	54.1	54.4
2000	53.3	54.5	54.4	54.2	53.6	50.5	52.0	52.5	53.9	54.5	54.7	54.5	53.6
2001	54.3	55.5	55.7	55.6	55.1	52.3	52.9	54.4	55.3	56.0	56.3	56.2	54.9
2002	56.0	57.0	57.5	57.4	56.9	53.9	54.0	54.8	57.5	57.8	58.2	58.3	56.6
2003	58.5	59.2	59.2	59.1	56.8	54.6	55.3	55.5	58.3	58.4	58.5	58.9	57.7
Local government													
1990	132.2	133.0	134.2	134.9	135.9	135.7	130.7	132.1	136.6	137.9	140.2	138.8	135.2
1991	136.7	138.3	138.8	138.3	139.3	140.2	135.7	134.7	136.4	140.2	141.0	138.5	138.2
1992	135.5	135.9	139.6	134.5	135.6	136.0	130.3	131.9	135.2	138.5	139.2	137.8	135.8
1993	136.7	138.0	138.9	138.9	139.7	139.6	133.1	132.9	138.3	142.4	141.7	141.7	138.5
1994	141.9	142.4	142.4	144.4	145.2	144.9	139.6	137.9	145.6	145.9	146.8	146.5	143.6
1995	145.6	145.8	146.5	146.6	146.9	148.2	140.0	140.9	146.6	149.0	149.8	150.3	146.4
1996	148.8	149.6	150.0	150.0	151.4	151.4	144.1	142.2	146.9	151.5	152.6	152.0	149.2
1997	152.9	153.6	154.9	154.4	156.3	154.9	146.7	146.0	151.9	155.5	156.8	157.0	153.4
1998	156.3	156.6	157.7	157.2	157.4	157.4	153.3	155.6	160.1	164.1	166.1	165.7	159.0
1999	164.8	165.3	162.7	159.5	162.0	161.2	151.2	150.8	157.4	161.9	164.2	164.9	160.5
2000	164.1	164.2	165.0	163.6	164.5	164.9	155.4	160.6	165.3	168.1	168.9	169.0	164.5
2001	168.9	170.4	171.4	170.9	172.8	173.1	161.9	173.0	176.6	178.9	180.5	179.0	173.1
2002	176.3	173.7	177.6	180.1	181.2	179.1	168.0	180.5	184.6	184.4	185.5	182.3	179.4
2003	183.7	183.3	185.2	184.1	185.1	179.0	170.6	181.2	184.8	187.7	188.1	188.2	183.4
MACON-WARNER ROBINS													
Total nonfarm													
1990	127.4	127.6	128.5	130.3	132.0	132.2	130.1	130.3	130.9	129.9	129.6	129.5	129.9
1991	126.2	125.9	126.6	126.5	127.4	127.9	125.6	125.7	126.3	126.7	127.0	127.2	126.6
1992	125.3	125.0	126.1	127.7	127.9	128.6	128.5	128.7	128.9	129.4	130.3	131.1	128.1
1993	129.3	129.8	130.5	131.1	131.4	132.0	131.2	131.4	132.4	132.7	133.5	134.0	131.6
1994	132.8	133.2	134.1	136.6	136.7	137.4	134.9	136.2	138.5	138.5	140.0	140.2	136.6
1995	138.0	138.2	139.8	140.4	140.7	141.9	140.1	140.7	143.0	141.2	142.3	143.2	140.8
1996	140.5	141.8	142.9	144.2	145.6	146.7	146.2	144.1	145.1	145.3	146.7	147.2	144.7
1997	144.8	146.0	147.1	147.5	148.2	148.6	146.3	147.2	147.4	147.6	148.3	149.1	147.3
1998	146.4	146.2	147.1	147.6	147.7	148.9	147.9	148.2	148.7	148.5	148.7	149.2	147.9
1999	147.1	147.9	148.5	150.6	150.2	150.2	148.4	149.3	150.3	149.8	151.5	151.7	149.6
2000	148.6	149.7	151.1	149.8	149.9	149.6	148.3	148.6	147.4	148.0	148.6	149.7	149.1
2001	144.9	144.7	145.8	146.8	147.3	147.6	145.3	147.4	147.4	148.3	148.8	149.7	147.0
2002	145.9	146.0	147.4	147.1	147.5	148.0	146.2	147.7	148.0	148.5	149.0	149.5	147.6
2003	147.6	147.4	149.0	148.9	149.4	149.7	149.7	150.0	150.4	151.4	151.7	152.0	149.8
Total private													
1990	91.7	91.8	92.4	94.3	95.5	95.9	94.8	95.1	95.1	94.1	94.0	94.3	94.1
1991	91.4	91.1	91.8	91.6	92.3	92.8	91.9	91.9	91.5	91.5	91.7	92.0	91.8
1992	90.0	89.7	90.6	92.1	92.2	93.0	93.5	93.7	93.6	93.5	94.0	95.3	92.6
1993	93.5	93.9	94.6	95.8	96.3	96.8	96.9	97.0	97.1	97.4	98.0	98.5	96.3
1994	97.1	97.5	98.3	100.7	100.9	101.6	100.1	101.6	102.9	102.7	103.7	104.3	101.0
1995	102.3	102.4	103.9	104.6	104.8	106.0	105.5	106.2	107.6	105.7	106.7	107.6	105.3
1996	108.3	109.4	110.5	111.4	112.7	113.8	114.3	112.2	112.4	111.9	113.4	113.9	112.0
1997	111.8	112.9	113.9	114.4	114.8	115.1	114.1	114.8	114.1	114.2	115.0	115.5	114.2
1998	113.0	112.8	113.8	113.5	113.6	114.7	115.5	115.9	115.8	115.2	115.4	115.9	114.6
1999	113.9	114.5	115.1	117.1	116.8	116.9	115.9	116.1	116.9	116.1	118.2	118.4	116.3
2000	115.8	116.8	118.1	116.6	116.3	116.5	116.0	115.7	114.7	114.5	115.2	116.0	116.0
2001	111.5	111.2	111.7	112.8	113.2	113.7	112.1	113.1	112.6	113.1	113.6	114.3	112.7
2002	111.8	111.8	112.9	112.7	113.0	113.9	112.8	113.3	113.0	113.1	113.9	114.5	113.1
2003	112.7	112.1	113.7	113.8	114.3	114.8	115.3	115.6	115.5	116.1	116.5	116.8	114.8
Goods-producing													
1990	24.0	23.7	23.9	24.8	25.2	25.3	24.9	24.9	24.9	24.4	23.9	23.8	24.5
1991	23.3	23.1	23.4	22.7	22.8	22.9	22.7	22.5	22.4	22.8	22.8	22.7	22.8
1992	22.4	22.6	22.7	22.9	22.8	23.1	23.0	22.9	23.0	22.9	22.8	23.0	22.8
1993	22.7	22.7	22.9	23.1	23.1	23.3	23.0	23.3	23.4	23.2	23.1	23.0	23.1
1994	23.1	23.2	23.3	23.7	23.8	24.0	23.9	24.5	24.7	24.6	24.7	24.7	24.0
1995	24.5	24.4	24.8	24.7	24.7	25.1	24.9	25.1	25.6	24.8	24.9	25.0	24.9
1996	24.9	25.2	25.4	25.7	25.8	26.1	25.7	25.6	25.9	25.8	25.9	26.0	25.7
1997	26.0	26.2	26.2	26.2	26.3	26.4	26.4	26.2	26.2	26.2	25.9	26.0	26.2
1998	25.7	25.3	25.6	25.0	25.3	25.4	25.5	25.7	25.7	25.6	25.5	25.3	25.5
1999	24.9	24.8	24.7	25.2	24.9	25.4	25.1	24.9	24.9	24.6	24.8	24.5	24.9
2000	24.1	24.0	24.1	23.5	23.5	23.5	23.5	23.3	23.1	22.9	23.2	23.3	23.5
2001	23.2	23.0	23.1	22.6	22.7	22.8	22.6	23.0	22.8	22.9	22.6	22.6	22.8
2002	22.1	22.3	22.4	22.1	22.1	22.3	22.2	22.1	21.9	21.6	21.2	21.2	22.0
2003	20.6	20.6	20.7	20.4	20.6	20.7	20.8	20.7	20.3	20.2	20.2	20.1	20.5

Employment by Industry: Georgia—*Continued*

(Numbers in thousands. Not seasonally adjusted.)

Industry	January	February	March	April	May	June	July	August	September	October	November	December	Annual Average
MACON-WARNER ROBINS *—Continued*													
Construction and mining													
1990	6.7	6.6	6.7	6.8	7.0	7.0	6.6	6.5	6.4	6.1	5.9	6.0	6.5
1991	5.4	5.3	5.5	5.7	5.8	5.9	5.6	5.6	5.6	5.6	5.7	5.8	5.6
1992	5.5	5.5	5.5	5.6	5.6	5.6	5.5	5.4	5.4	5.3	5.3	5.4	5.5
1993	5.3	5.3	5.3	5.4	5.5	5.6	5.6	5.7	5.7	5.6	5.6	5.7	5.5
1994	5.7	5.7	5.8	5.9	6.0	6.1	6.2	6.2	6.2	6.4	6.5	6.5	6.1
1995	6.4	6.4	6.6	6.5	6.5	6.7	6.7	6.7	6.8	6.6	6.7	6.8	6.6
1996	6.9	6.9	7.0	7.3	7.4	7.5	7.5	7.3	7.3	7.1	7.1	7.2	7.2
1997	7.3	7.4	7.4	7.3	7.3	7.3	7.3	7.2	7.2	7.2	7.1	7.3	7.3
1998	7.0	7.0	7.1	7.0	7.2	7.2	7.4	7.4	7.4	7.3	7.4	7.3	7.2
1999	7.3	7.2	7.2	7.8	7.7	8.0	7.9	7.7	7.6	7.6	7.6	7.6	7.6
2000	7.3	7.3	7.4	7.0	7.0	7.0	7.0	6.9	6.7	6.6	6.6	6.6	7.0
2001	6.5	6.4	6.4	6.4	6.5	6.6	6.6	6.7	6.6	6.4	6.3	6.4	6.4
2002	6.4	6.4	6.5	6.3	6.4	6.5	6.6	6.5	6.3	6.0	6.0	6.1	6.3
2003	6.1	6.1	6.2	6.0	6.2	6.2	6.3	6.4	6.2	6.1	6.1	6.1	6.2
Manufacturing													
1990	17.3	17.1	17.2	18.0	18.2	18.3	18.3	18.4	18.5	18.3	18.0	17.8	18.0
1991	17.9	17.8	17.9	17.0	17.0	17.0	17.1	16.9	16.8	17.2	17.1	16.9	17.2
1992	16.9	17.1	17.2	17.3	17.2	17.5	17.5	17.5	17.6	17.6	17.5	17.6	17.4
1993	17.4	17.4	17.6	17.7	17.6	17.7	17.4	17.6	17.7	17.6	17.5	17.3	17.5
1994	17.4	17.5	17.5	17.8	17.8	17.9	17.7	18.3	18.5	18.2	18.2	18.2	17.9
1995	18.1	18.0	18.2	18.2	18.2	18.4	18.2	18.4	18.8	18.2	18.2	18.2	18.3
1996	18.0	18.3	18.4	18.4	18.4	18.6	18.2	18.3	18.6	18.7	18.8	18.8	18.5
1997	18.7	18.8	18.8	18.9	19.0	19.1	19.1	19.0	19.0	19.0	18.8	18.7	18.9
1998	18.7	18.3	18.5	18.0	18.1	18.2	18.1	18.3	18.3	18.3	18.1	18.0	18.2
1999	17.6	17.6	17.5	17.4	17.2	17.4	17.2	17.2	17.3	17.0	17.2	16.9	17.3
2000	16.8	16.7	16.7	16.5	16.5	16.5	16.5	16.4	16.4	16.3	16.6	16.7	16.6
2001	16.7	16.6	16.7	16.2	16.2	16.2	16.0	16.3	16.2	16.5	16.3	16.2	16.3
2002	15.7	15.9	15.9	15.8	15.7	15.8	15.6	15.6	15.6	15.6	15.2	15.1	15.6
2003	14.5	14.5	14.5	14.4	14.4	14.5	14.5	14.3	14.1	14.1	14.1	14.0	14.3
Service-providing													
1990	103.4	103.9	104.6	105.5	106.8	106.9	105.2	105.4	106.0	105.5	105.7	105.7	105.4
1991	102.9	102.8	103.2	103.8	104.6	105.0	102.9	103.2	103.9	103.9	104.2	104.5	103.7
1992	102.9	102.4	103.4	104.8	105.1	105.5	105.5	105.8	105.9	106.5	107.5	108.1	105.3
1993	106.6	107.1	107.6	108.0	108.3	108.7	108.2	108.1	109.0	109.5	110.4	111.0	108.5
1994	109.7	110.0	110.8	112.9	112.9	113.4	111.0	111.7	113.8	113.9	115.3	115.5	112.6
1995	113.5	113.8	115.0	115.7	116.0	116.8	115.2	115.6	117.4	116.4	117.4	118.2	115.9
1996	115.6	116.6	117.5	118.5	119.8	120.6	120.5	118.5	119.2	119.5	120.8	121.2	119.0
1997	118.8	119.8	120.9	121.3	121.9	122.2	119.9	121.0	121.2	121.4	122.4	123.1	121.2
1998	120.7	120.9	121.5	122.6	122.4	123.5	122.4	122.5	123.0	122.9	123.2	123.9	122.5
1999	122.2	123.1	123.8	125.4	125.3	124.8	123.3	124.4	125.4	125.2	126.7	127.2	124.7
2000	124.5	125.7	127.0	126.3	126.4	126.1	124.8	125.3	124.3	125.1	125.4	126.4	125.6
2001	121.7	121.7	122.7	124.2	124.6	124.8	122.7	124.4	124.6	125.4	126.2	127.1	124.1
2002	123.8	123.7	125.0	125.0	125.4	125.7	124.0	125.6	126.1	126.9	127.8	128.3	125.6
2003	127.0	126.8	128.3	128.5	128.8	129.0	128.9	129.3	130.1	131.2	131.5	131.9	129.3
Trade, transportation, and utilities													
1990	23.2	23.1	23.2	23.1	23.3	23.5	23.5	23.5	23.3	23.0	23.5	23.9	23.3
1991	23.0	22.8	22.9	22.0	22.2	22.2	22.1	22.3	22.3	22.8	23.4	23.8	22.7
1992	22.4	22.1	22.3	22.7	22.8	23.0	23.0	23.2	23.1	23.2	24.0	24.8	23.1
1993	23.4	23.3	23.4	23.0	23.1	23.3	23.2	23.4	23.2	23.6	24.2	24.8	23.5
1994	24.2	24.0	24.1	24.4	24.7	24.8	24.2	24.4	24.8	24.8	25.6	26.2	24.7
1995	25.1	24.7	25.0	25.3	25.5	25.5	25.4	25.7	26.0	25.7	26.3	27.0	25.6
1996	25.2	25.0	25.2	25.4	25.6	25.7	25.9	25.5	25.4	25.2	26.1	26.6	25.6
1997	25.3	25.4	25.7	25.3	25.3	25.2	24.9	25.0	24.8	25.3	26.3	26.9	25.5
1998	25.2	24.8	24.7	25.1	25.3	25.3	25.3	25.6	25.6	25.6	26.1	26.7	25.4
1999	25.4	25.4	25.6	25.9	26.2	26.6	26.4	26.5	26.7	26.7	27.7	28.2	26.4
2000	26.0	26.2	26.5	26.6	26.6	26.6	26.5	26.5	26.4	26.3	27.0	27.5	26.6
2001	26.1	25.7	25.8	25.8	25.8	25.9	26.2	26.5	26.6	26.5	27.0	27.5	26.2
2002	26.0	25.7	25.9	26.1	26.2	26.1	26.0	26.0	25.9	26.1	26.9	27.5	26.2
2003	25.4	25.3	25.5	25.4	25.6	25.7	25.7	25.7	25.7	26.1	26.6	26.9	25.8
Wholesale trade													
1990	4.2	4.2	4.2	4.0	4.0	4.1	4.1	4.0	4.0	3.9	3.9	3.9	4.0
1991	4.1	4.1	4.1	3.6	3.6	3.7	3.7	3.7	3.7	4.1	4.1	4.1	3.9
1992	4.0	4.0	4.1	4.0	4.0	4.0	4.0	4.1	4.1	4.2	4.2	4.2	4.1
1993	3.8	3.9	3.9	3.3	3.3	3.2	3.2	3.2	3.2	3.2	3.3	3.3	3.4
1994	3.3	3.3	3.3	3.3	3.3	3.3	3.3	3.2	3.3	3.3	3.3	3.3	3.3
1995	3.2	3.2	3.3	3.3	3.3	3.3	3.3	3.3	3.4	3.3	3.3	3.4	3.3
1996	3.4	3.4	3.4	3.6	3.6	3.6	3.7	3.6	3.6	3.4	3.4	3.4	3.5
1997	3.3	3.4	3.4	3.5	3.5	3.5	3.5	3.5	3.5	3.5	3.5	3.5	3.5
1998	3.5	3.4	3.4	3.4	3.5	3.5	3.5	3.5	3.5	3.6	3.6	3.6	3.5
1999	3.4	3.4	3.4	3.6	3.6	3.6	3.6	3.5	3.6	3.5	3.6	3.6	3.5
2000	3.5	3.5	3.6	3.5	3.5	3.5	3.6	3.6	3.6	3.6	3.6	3.6	3.6
2001	3.4	3.5	3.4	3.5	3.5	3.4	3.5	3.5	3.4	3.3	3.4	3.4	3.4
2002	3.4	3.5	3.4	3.4	3.4	3.4	3.4	3.4	3.4	3.5	3.6	3.6	3.5
2003	3.5	3.4	3.5	3.4	3.4	3.5	3.5	3.5	3.5	3.5	3.5	3.5	3.5

Employment by Industry: Georgia—*Continued*

(Numbers in thousands. Not seasonally adjusted.)

Industry	January	February	March	April	May	June	July	August	September	October	November	December	Annual Average
MACON-WARNER ROBINS —*Continued*													
Retail trade													
1990	15.8	15.7	15.8	15.9	16.1	16.1	16.1	16.2	16.0	15.9	16.4	16.8	16.1
1991	15.8	15.6	15.6	15.1	15.3	15.2	14.9	15.1	15.1	15.2	15.9	16.4	15.4
1992	15.2	14.9	15.0	15.4	15.5	15.6	15.5	15.6	15.5	15.5	16.3	17.0	15.6
1993	16.1	15.9	15.9	16.2	16.2	16.5	16.4	16.6	16.3	16.7	17.3	17.9	16.5
1994	17.1	16.9	17.0	17.2	17.4	17.5	16.9	17.2	17.5	17.4	18.2	18.8	17.4
1995	17.9	17.4	17.6	18.0	18.3	18.4	18.3	18.6	18.8	18.6	19.3	19.9	18.4
1996	18.2	17.9	18.1	18.4	18.5	18.6	18.6	18.4	18.3	18.3	19.1	19.8	18.5
1997	18.6	18.5	18.8	18.4	18.3	18.3	18.0	18.2	17.9	18.2	19.2	19.8	18.5
1998	18.2	17.9	17.8	18.0	18.1	18.1	17.8	18.0	18.0	17.9	18.4	18.9	18.1
1999	17.9	17.9	18.1	18.1	18.3	18.7	18.7	18.9	19.0	18.8	19.7	20.3	18.7
2000	18.5	18.7	18.8	18.9	18.9	18.9	18.8	18.9	18.8	18.9	19.5	19.9	19.0
2001	18.5	18.0	18.1	18.0	18.1	18.2	18.4	18.7	19.0	18.9	19.3	19.7	18.5
2002	18.4	18.1	18.4	18.3	18.4	18.3	18.2	18.3	18.3	18.3	19.0	19.6	18.5
2003	18.0	17.9	18.1	18.1	18.2	18.3	18.2	18.2	18.2	18.6	18.9	19.2	18.3
Transportation and utilities													
1990	3.2	3.2	3.2	3.2	3.2	3.3	3.3	3.3	3.3	3.2	3.2	3.2	3.2
1991	3.1	3.1	3.2	3.3	3.3	3.3	3.5	3.5	3.5	3.5	3.4	3.3	3.3
1992	3.2	3.2	3.2	3.3	3.3	3.4	3.5	3.5	3.5	3.5	3.5	3.6	3.4
1993	3.5	3.5	3.6	3.5	3.6	3.6	3.6	3.6	3.7	3.7	3.6	3.6	3.6
1994	3.8	3.8	3.8	3.9	4.0	4.0	4.0	4.0	4.0	4.1	4.1	4.1	4.0
1995	4.0	4.1	4.1	4.0	3.9	3.8	3.8	3.8	3.8	3.8	3.7	3.7	3.9
1996	3.6	3.7	3.7	3.4	3.5	3.5	3.6	3.5	3.5	3.5	3.6	3.4	3.5
1997	3.4	3.5	3.5	3.4	3.5	3.4	3.4	3.3	3.4	3.6	3.6	3.6	3.5
1998	3.5	3.5	3.5	3.7	3.7	3.7	4.0	4.1	4.1	4.1	4.1	4.2	3.9
1999	4.1	4.1	4.1	4.2	4.3	4.3	4.1	4.1	4.1	4.4	4.4	4.3	4.2
2000	4.0	4.0	4.1	4.2	4.2	4.2	4.1	4.0	4.0	3.8	3.9	4.0	4.0
2001	4.2	4.2	4.3	4.3	4.2	4.3	4.3	4.3	4.2	4.3	4.3	4.4	4.2
2002	4.2	4.1	4.1	4.4	4.4	4.4	4.4	4.3	4.2	4.3	4.3	4.3	4.3
2003	3.9	4.0	3.9	3.9	4.0	3.9	4.0	4.0	4.0	4.0	4.2	4.2	4.0
Information													
1990	2.4	2.4	2.4	2.3	2.3	2.3	2.3	2.3	2.3	2.3	2.3	2.3	2.3
1991	2.3	2.3	2.3	2.3	2.3	2.3	2.3	2.3	2.3	2.3	2.3	2.3	2.3
1992	2.4	2.4	2.4	2.3	2.3	2.3	2.4	2.4	2.4	2.6	2.6	2.6	2.4
1993	2.7	2.7	2.7	2.7	2.7	2.7	2.7	2.7	2.6	2.7	2.7	2.7	2.7
1994	2.6	2.6	2.6	2.6	2.6	2.6	2.5	2.5	2.5	2.5	2.5	2.6	2.6
1995	2.5	2.6	2.6	2.5	2.5	2.5	2.5	2.5	2.6	2.6	2.6	2.6	2.6
1996	2.5	2.5	2.6	2.5	2.6	2.6	2.6	2.6	2.6	2.6	2.6	2.6	2.6
1997	2.6	2.6	2.6	2.6	2.7	2.7	2.6	2.6	2.6	2.7	2.7	2.7	2.6
1998	2.7	2.7	2.6	2.6	2.6	2.6	2.6	2.6	2.6	2.5	2.5	2.5	2.6
1999	2.4	2.4	2.4	2.5	2.5	2.5	2.4	2.4	2.3	2.3	2.4	2.4	2.4
2000	2.5	2.5	2.5	2.4	2.4	2.5	2.6	2.6	2.6	2.7	2.7	2.7	2.6
2001	2.6	2.6	2.6	2.7	2.7	2.8	2.7	2.8	2.8	2.7	2.7	2.8	2.7
2002	2.7	2.7	2.8	2.8	2.8	2.8	2.7	2.7	2.6	2.6	2.6	2.6	2.7
2003	2.8	2.7	2.7	2.8	2.8	2.8	2.8	2.8	2.8	2.8	2.8	2.8	2.8
Financial activities													
1990	7.3	7.3	7.3	7.5	7.6	7.6	7.3	7.3	7.3	7.3	7.3	7.3	7.4
1991	7.5	7.5	7.6	7.7	7.8	7.8	8.2	8.3	8.3	7.4	7.4	7.4	7.7
1992	7.4	7.3	7.4	7.5	7.5	7.5	7.5	7.5	7.6	7.5	7.5	7.6	7.5
1993	7.5	7.5	7.5	7.6	7.6	7.6	7.7	7.6	7.5	7.5	7.5	7.5	7.6
1994	7.5	7.5	7.5	7.9	7.8	7.9	7.9	7.9	7.9	8.0	8.0	8.1	7.8
1995	8.0	8.0	8.1	8.1	8.1	8.1	8.1	8.2	8.2	8.2	8.2	8.2	8.1
1996	7.9	8.0	8.1	7.9	8.0	8.0	8.1	8.0	8.0	7.9	8.0	8.0	8.0
1997	8.0	8.1	8.2	8.4	8.6	8.6	8.4	8.5	8.4	8.5	8.5	8.6	8.4
1998	8.9	8.9	8.9	8.9	9.0	9.1	9.1	9.2	9.2	9.2	9.2	9.3	9.1
1999	9.1	9.2	9.1	9.2	9.1	9.2	9.1	9.1	9.3	9.5	9.7	9.8	9.3
2000	10.0	10.1	10.3	10.2	10.2	10.2	10.1	10.0	9.8	9.7	9.6	9.6	10.0
2001	9.3	9.4	9.5	9.6	9.6	9.5	9.2	9.0	9.0	9.1	9.0	9.1	9.2
2002	9.1	9.2	9.2	9.0	9.0	9.1	9.1	9.3	9.3	9.4	9.6	9.7	9.3
2003	9.6	9.7	9.8	9.9	10.0	10.0	10.4	10.4	10.4	10.5	10.6	10.6	10.2
Professional and business services													
1990	8.2	8.5	8.5	9.4	9.4	9.3	9.6	9.7	9.7	10.0	9.8	9.8	9.3
1991	8.6	8.6	8.6	9.0	9.0	9.2	9.1	9.1	8.8	9.1	9.0	9.0	8.9
1992	8.9	8.9	9.0	9.2	9.2	9.2	9.6	9.7	9.9	9.3	9.0	9.2	9.3
1993	9.1	9.4	9.6	10.7	10.9	11.0	11.0	10.7	10.9	10.9	10.6	10.6	10.5
1994	10.3	10.5	10.8	11.8	11.8	11.9	12.0	12.2	12.5	12.1	12.2	11.9	11.7
1995	11.8	12.0	12.4	12.7	12.6	12.9	12.7	12.7	12.6	12.7	12.7	12.8	12.6
1996	12.6	12.9	12.9	13.3	13.6	14.0	14.6	14.0	13.8	13.5	13.6	13.4	13.5
1997	13.1	13.4	13.6	14.4	14.4	14.7	14.5	14.8	14.8	14.2	14.2	14.1	14.2
1998	13.6	13.9	14.2	14.0	14.1	14.4	14.7	14.8	14.6	14.4	14.3	14.4	14.3
1999	14.8	15.0	15.0	15.8	15.5	15.5	15.3	15.2	15.2	15.3	15.4	15.4	15.3
2000	16.0	16.4	16.7	15.9	15.6	15.9	15.7	15.5	15.5	15.0	15.0	15.4	15.7
2001	14.7	14.6	14.8	15.2	15.3	15.4	14.9	14.8	14.5	14.9	15.1	15.2	14.9
2002	15.2	15.2	15.4	15.1	15.2	15.5	15.1	15.1	15.1	15.1	15.0	15.1	15.2
2003	15.2	15.0	15.5	15.4	15.6	15.8	15.8	16.1	16.2	16.7	16.4	16.3	15.8

Employment by Industry: Georgia—*Continued*

(Numbers in thousands. Not seasonally adjusted.)

Industry	January	February	March	April	May	June	July	August	September	October	November	December	Annual Average
MACON-WARNER ROBINS *—Continued*													
Educational and health services													
1990	11.8	11.9	12.0	12.0	12.1	12.1	11.8	11.9	12.1	12.2	12.3	12.3	12.0
1991	12.1	12.2	12.2	12.5	12.4	12.3	12.1	12.1	12.3	12.1	12.1	12.1	12.2
1992	12.0	11.9	11.9	12.0	12.0	12.1	11.9	12.0	12.1	12.6	12.7	12.6	12.2
1993	12.5	12.6	12.8	13.1	13.1	13.0	12.9	12.9	13.1	13.2	13.2	13.2	13.0
1994	13.1	13.3	13.3	13.4	13.3	13.3	13.0	13.2	13.5	13.6	13.7	13.6	13.4
1995	13.5	13.7	13.7	13.8	13.7	13.7	13.6	13.6	14.0	14.0	14.1	14.0	13.8
1996	17.7	18.0	18.1	18.1	18.1	18.2	18.1	17.9	18.2	18.6	18.6	18.6	18.2
1997	18.3	18.4	18.4	18.2	18.1	18.1	17.7	18.0	18.4	18.8	18.9	18.8	18.3
1998	18.1	18.2	18.2	19.2	18.3	18.8	19.2	18.8	19.3	19.5	19.5	19.4	18.9
1999	18.9	19.1	19.3	19.0	18.9	18.2	18.0	18.5	19.1	18.6	18.9	18.5	18.8
2000	18.3	18.3	18.5	18.2	18.2	18.2	18.0	18.3	18.2	18.5	18.5	18.5	18.3
2001	17.6	17.7	17.6	18.0	18.0	18.1	17.8	18.1	18.4	18.5	18.5	18.4	18.0
2002	18.4	18.5	18.5	18.8	18.8	18.9	18.7	19.0	19.4	19.6	19.8	19.6	19.0
2003	19.8	19.9	20.0	20.6	20.5	20.5	20.4	20.6	20.9	20.9	20.9	21.0	20.5
Leisure and hospitality													
1990	10.5	10.6	10.7	10.8	11.1	11.2	11.0	11.1	11.0	10.5	10.5	10.5	10.8
1991	10.2	10.2	10.3	10.9	11.2	11.4	10.7	10.7	10.5	10.4	10.2	10.2	10.6
1992	10.1	10.1	10.4	10.8	10.9	11.0	11.1	11.1	10.7	10.8	10.8	10.8	10.7
1993	10.9	11.0	11.0	10.8	11.0	11.1	11.5	11.6	11.6	11.5	11.9	11.9	11.3
1994	11.6	11.7	11.9	12.1	12.2	12.3	11.7	12.0	12.1	12.3	12.3	12.4	12.1
1995	12.1	12.2	12.4	12.6	12.8	13.1	13.2	13.3	13.3	12.5	12.7	12.7	12.7
1996	12.4	12.6	12.9	13.2	13.6	13.7	13.7	13.2	13.1	13.0	13.3	13.4	13.2
1997	13.2	13.4	13.8	13.8	13.9	13.8	14.0	14.1	13.4	13.0	13.0	12.9	13.5
1998	13.2	13.3	13.9	13.2	13.5	13.6	13.6	13.7	13.4	13.0	13.0	13.0	13.4
1999	13.0	13.1	13.5	14.0	14.2	13.9	13.9	13.9	13.8	13.4	13.5	13.8	13.7
2000	13.1	13.4	13.6	14.0	14.1	13.9	13.9	13.9	13.5	13.7	13.6	13.4	13.7
2001	12.5	12.7	12.8	13.1	13.3	13.4	13.1	13.4	13.0	13.1	13.3	13.3	13.0
2002	12.9	12.8	13.2	13.4	13.5	13.7	13.3	13.4	13.2	13.3	13.3	13.3	13.3
2003	13.8	13.5	13.9	13.8	13.7	13.7	13.7	13.7	13.6	13.2	13.3	13.4	13.6
Other services													
1990	4.3	4.3	4.4	4.4	4.5	4.6	4.4	4.4	4.5	4.4	4.4	4.4	4.4
1991	4.4	4.4	4.5	4.5	4.6	4.7	4.7	4.6	4.6	4.6	4.5	4.5	4.6
1992	4.4	4.4	4.5	4.7	4.7	4.8	5.0	4.9	4.8	4.6	4.6	4.7	4.7
1993	4.7	4.7	4.7	4.8	4.8	4.8	4.9	4.8	4.8	4.8	4.8	4.8	4.8
1994	4.7	4.7	4.8	4.8	4.7	4.8	4.9	4.9	4.9	4.8	4.7	4.8	4.8
1995	4.8	4.8	4.9	4.9	4.9	5.1	5.1	5.1	5.3	5.2	5.2	5.3	5.1
1996	5.1	5.2	5.3	5.3	5.4	5.5	5.6	5.4	5.4	5.3	5.3	5.3	5.3
1997	5.3	5.4	5.4	5.5	5.5	5.6	5.6	5.6	5.5	5.5	5.5	5.5	5.5
1998	5.6	5.7	5.7	5.5	5.5	5.5	5.5	5.5	5.4	5.4	5.3	5.3	5.5
1999	5.4	5.5	5.5	5.5	5.5	5.6	5.7	5.6	5.6	5.7	5.8	5.8	5.6
2000	5.8	5.9	5.9	5.8	5.7	5.7	5.7	5.6	5.6	5.7	5.6	5.6	5.7
2001	5.5	5.5	5.5	5.8	5.8	5.8	5.6	5.5	5.5	5.4	5.4	5.4	5.5
2002	5.4	5.4	5.5	5.4	5.4	5.5	5.7	5.7	5.6	5.4	5.5	5.5	5.5
2003	5.5	5.4	5.6	5.5	5.5	5.6	5.7	5.6	5.6	5.7	5.7	5.7	5.6
Government													
1990	35.7	35.8	36.1	36.0	36.5	36.3	35.3	35.2	35.8	35.8	35.6	35.2	35.8
1991	34.8	34.8	34.8	34.9	35.1	35.1	33.7	33.8	34.8	35.2	35.3	35.2	34.8
1992	35.3	35.3	35.5	35.6	35.7	35.6	35.0	35.0	35.3	35.9	36.3	35.8	35.5
1993	35.8	35.9	35.9	35.3	35.1	35.2	34.3	34.4	35.3	35.3	35.5	35.5	35.3
1994	35.7	35.7	35.8	35.9	35.8	35.8	34.8	34.6	35.6	35.8	36.3	35.9	35.6
1995	35.7	35.8	35.9	35.8	35.9	35.9	34.6	34.5	35.4	35.5	35.6	35.6	35.5
1996	32.2	32.4	32.4	32.8	32.9	32.9	31.9	31.9	32.7	33.4	33.3	33.3	32.7
1997	33.0	33.1	33.2	33.1	33.4	33.5	32.2	32.4	33.3	33.4	33.3	33.6	33.1
1998	33.4	33.4	33.3	34.1	34.1	34.2	32.4	32.3	32.9	33.3	33.3	33.3	33.3
1999	33.2	33.4	33.4	33.5	33.4	33.3	32.5	33.2	33.4	33.7	33.3	33.3	33.3
2000	32.8	32.9	33.0	33.2	33.6	33.1	32.3	32.9	32.7	33.5	33.4	33.7	33.1
2001	33.4	33.5	34.1	34.0	34.1	33.9	33.2	34.3	34.8	35.2	35.2	35.4	34.2
2002	34.1	34.2	34.5	34.4	34.5	34.1	33.4	34.4	35.0	35.4	35.1	35.0	34.5
2003	34.9	35.3	35.3	35.1	35.1	34.9	34.4	34.4	34.9	35.3	35.2	35.2	35.0
Federal government													
1990	17.6	17.6	17.7	17.6	18.0	17.7	17.6	17.3	17.4	17.0	16.7	16.4	17.4
1991	16.1	16.0	15.9	16.0	16.0	15.9	15.9	15.9	15.9	15.9	15.9	15.9	15.9
1992	15.9	15.9	15.9	16.0	16.0	16.0	16.0	15.9	15.8	15.8	15.9	15.8	15.9
1993	15.8	15.7	15.7	14.9	14.7	14.8	14.8	14.9	14.8	14.7	14.8	14.8	15.0
1994	14.9	14.9	14.9	14.8	14.7	14.7	14.7	14.6	14.5	14.5	14.5	14.5	14.7
1995	14.0	13.9	13.9	13.9	13.9	13.9	13.9	13.8	13.7	13.6	13.6	13.6	13.8
1996	13.5	13.5	13.4	13.4	13.4	13.4	13.4	13.4	13.3	13.3	13.3	13.3	13.4
1997	13.1	13.1	13.1	13.0	13.1	13.1	13.1	13.1	13.1	13.1	13.2	13.3	13.1
1998	13.2	13.1	13.0	13.1	13.1	13.1	13.2	13.1	13.2	13.3	13.4	13.4	13.2
1999	13.2	13.2	13.3	13.3	13.4	13.4	13.5	13.6	13.6	13.6	13.9	14.0	13.5
2000	13.8	13.8	13.8	13.9	14.2	13.9	13.9	14.0	13.7	13.9	14.0	14.1	13.9
2001	14.1	13.9	14.1	14.1	14.2	14.3	14.3	14.4	14.4	14.6	14.7	14.8	14.3
2002	14.0	14.0	14.0	14.1	14.1	14.1	14.1	14.1	14.1	14.0	14.0	14.1	14.1
2003	14.5	14.4	14.4	14.3	14.3	14.2	14.2	14.2	14.3	14.3	14.4	14.4	14.3

Employment by Industry: Georgia—*Continued*

(Numbers in thousands. Not seasonally adjusted.)

Industry	January	February	March	April	May	June	July	August	September	October	November	December	Annual Average
SAVANNAH													
Total nonfarm													
1990	112.0	113.0	112.8	114.1	115.2	117.8	117.5	117.9	117.7	116.4	116.9	117.0	115.7
1991	113.6	113.1	113.5	113.3	112.9	113.8	113.8	114.1	114.2	113.5	115.2	115.9	113.9
1992	114.5	114.8	116.0	116.1	116.7	117.1	117.0	117.2	118.0	119.2	119.4	120.0	117.2
1993	116.0	116.3	117.4	117.8	118.5	118.9	120.2	120.0	120.3	120.9	121.6	121.9	119.2
1994	119.7	120.2	121.3	122.3	123.7	123.8	121.4	121.9	122.3	124.4	125.8	126.3	122.8
1995	123.8	123.9	125.3	125.0	126.4	127.6	125.8	126.6	127.1	126.8	127.7	128.4	126.2
1996	125.6	127.0	128.1	128.7	129.8	129.9	128.9	129.0	128.8	128.1	129.3	129.7	128.6
1997	129.0	129.2	130.9	131.7	132.2	131.4	130.9	131.3	132.3	132.5	133.0	134.3	131.6
1998	130.9	131.7	131.6	132.4	133.0	133.6	133.3	134.1	134.0	133.9	135.7	136.9	133.4
1999	133.1	133.4	134.4	136.0	136.4	136.1	135.3	136.4	135.5	135.9	137.1	138.3	135.7
2000	134.5	135.7	137.0	137.3	138.1	138.0	136.0	136.8	137.1	136.3	137.2	137.9	136.8
2001	134.6	134.8	136.0	136.6	137.4	137.0	136.7	138.4	137.6	137.4	137.1	137.2	136.7
2002	134.3	135.9	137.4	138.6	139.7	139.3	138.0	138.2	138.4	139.0	140.4	141.3	138.4
2003	136.7	136.7	138.1	138.3	138.5	138.7	139.1	140.7	141.4	142.6	142.6	142.9	139.7
Total private													
1990	94.1	95.0	94.6	96.1	96.9	99.6	99.3	100.5	100.0	98.7	99.2	99.2	97.8
1991	95.8	95.1	95.2	95.3	94.8	95.7	95.5	96.2	95.9	95.1	96.6	97.1	95.7
1992	95.5	95.7	96.9	96.8	97.4	97.8	98.2	98.3	98.7	99.7	99.8	100.5	97.9
1993	96.4	96.7	97.7	97.9	98.7	99.2	101.0	101.1	100.8	101.1	101.7	102.1	99.5
1994	99.8	100.2	101.2	102.2	103.6	103.5	101.7	102.3	102.3	103.8	105.5	106.3	102.7
1995	103.0	102.9	104.1	104.0	105.3	106.6	105.5	106.1	106.4	106.1	107.0	107.8	105.4
1996	104.9	106.2	107.3	107.7	108.8	109.2	108.7	108.7	108.2	107.4	108.2	109.0	107.9
1997	108.0	108.1	109.8	110.7	111.1	110.5	110.8	111.2	111.7	111.6	112.7	113.6	110.8
1998	110.2	110.9	110.8	111.3	111.9	112.7	113.1	113.7	113.4	113.7	114.9	116.0	112.7
1999	112.2	112.3	113.3	115.2	115.9	116.2	115.7	116.3	115.2	115.5	116.8	118.2	115.2
2000	114.4	115.2	116.3	116.8	117.1	117.6	116.9	117.0	117.1	116.3	117.1	117.6	116.6
2001	114.3	114.1	115.3	115.9	116.8	116.7	117.1	117.9	116.8	116.9	116.5	116.6	116.2
2002	114.1	115.4	116.7	118.0	118.8	119.0	118.1	117.7	117.9	118.2	119.6	120.5	117.8
2003	116.1	115.7	117.2	117.2	117.7	118.1	118.6	119.6	120.2	121.3	121.4	121.5	118.7
Goods-producing													
1990	25.3	25.8	25.3	25.9	26.1	28.0	28.4	28.6	28.1	27.8	27.7	27.0	27.0
1991	26.1	25.5	25.0	25.0	24.2	24.3	23.7	23.5	23.3	23.3	23.7	23.5	24.3
1992	23.0	22.7	22.7	22.7	22.7	22.9	23.3	23.3	23.5	23.5	23.6	23.6	23.1
1993	22.7	22.6	22.9	23.0	23.2	23.4	23.8	23.8	23.8	23.5	23.4	23.4	23.3
1994	23.3	22.9	22.8	23.0	23.1	23.2	23.2	23.1	23.1	23.1	23.6	23.7	23.2
1995	23.3	23.2	23.3	22.8	22.9	23.3	23.2	23.3	23.3	23.5	23.5	23.8	23.3
1996	23.9	24.0	24.1	23.6	23.8	23.9	23.7	23.9	24.0	23.7	23.6	23.7	23.8
1997	24.1	23.9	24.2	24.9	24.6	24.6	24.9	25.2	25.1	25.0	25.4	25.6	24.8
1998	25.5	25.3	25.3	24.8	25.0	25.2	25.3	25.6	25.5	25.1	25.4	26.0	25.3
1999	24.2	24.4	24.5	25.4	25.4	25.7	25.6	25.4	25.1	24.6	24.8	25.1	25.0
2000	25.0	25.1	25.3	24.9	24.8	25.1	25.0	24.7	24.7	24.6	24.5	24.7	24.9
2001	23.9	24.0	24.1	24.3	24.6	24.8	25.0	24.9	24.7	24.4	23.6	23.4	24.3
2002	23.3	23.4	23.6	23.0	23.0	22.9	22.7	22.4	22.4	22.3	22.1	22.2	22.8
2003	22.4	22.4	22.3	22.1	22.0	21.9	21.1	21.8	21.9	22.0	21.9	21.9	22.0
Construction and mining													
1990	8.8	9.2	8.9	9.2	9.5	11.1	11.5	11.7	11.3	11.0	10.9	10.2	10.3
1991	9.6	9.0	8.6	9.0	8.4	8.3	7.6	7.3	6.9	6.8	7.1	6.9	8.0
1992	6.5	6.3	6.3	6.4	6.4	6.6	6.7	6.8	6.8	6.8	6.8	6.8	6.6
1993	6.0	6.0	6.2	6.2	6.2	6.3	6.5	6.7	6.8	6.7	6.9	6.9	6.5
1994	7.0	6.7	6.7	6.8	6.8	6.9	7.1	7.0	7.0	6.9	7.2	7.2	6.9
1995	7.1	7.0	7.2	6.7	6.8	7.1	6.9	7.0	7.0	7.4	7.3	7.5	7.1
1996	7.8	7.8	7.9	8.1	7.8	7.8	7.8	7.6	7.6	7.6	7.5	7.4	7.7
1997	7.4	7.4	7.5	8.4	8.1	7.9	7.9	8.1	8.0	8.0	8.2	8.3	7.9
1998	7.9	7.8	7.8	7.8	7.9	7.9	8.0	8.1	8.0	8.0	8.2	8.4	8.0
1999	8.0	8.2	8.3	8.2	8.3	8.4	8.0	8.0	7.9	8.0	8.2	8.4	8.2
2000	8.1	8.3	8.4	8.3	8.3	8.6	8.6	8.5	8.5	8.5	8.5	8.7	8.4
2001	7.9	8.1	8.3	8.7	9.0	9.2	9.3	9.3	9.2	9.0	8.2	8.2	8.6
2002	8.4	8.5	8.7	8.5	8.4	8.4	8.2	8.1	8.2	8.2	8.2	8.2	8.3
2003	8.4	8.5	8.4	8.5	8.5	8.5	8.4	8.4	8.5	8.5	8.5	8.4	8.5
Manufacturing													
1990	16.5	16.6	16.4	16.7	16.6	16.9	16.9	16.9	16.8	16.8	16.8	16.8	16.7
1991	16.5	16.5	16.4	16.0	15.8	16.0	16.1	16.2	16.4	16.5	16.6	16.6	16.3
1992	16.5	16.4	16.4	16.3	16.3	16.3	16.6	16.5	16.7	16.7	16.8	16.8	16.5
1993	16.7	16.6	16.7	16.8	17.0	17.1	17.3	17.1	17.0	16.8	16.5	16.5	16.8
1994	16.3	16.2	16.1	16.2	16.3	16.3	16.1	16.1	16.1	16.2	16.4	16.5	16.2
1995	16.2	16.2	16.1	16.1	16.1	16.2	16.3	16.3	16.3	16.1	16.2	16.3	16.2
1996	16.1	16.2	16.2	15.5	16.0	16.1	15.9	16.3	16.4	16.1	16.1	16.3	16.1
1997	16.7	16.5	16.7	16.5	16.5	16.7	17.0	17.1	17.1	17.0	17.2	17.3	16.9
1998	17.6	17.5	17.5	17.0	17.1	17.3	17.3	17.5	17.5	17.1	17.2	17.6	17.4
1999	16.2	16.2	16.2	17.2	17.1	17.3	17.6	17.4	17.2	16.6	16.6	16.7	16.9
2000	16.9	16.8	16.9	16.6	16.5	16.5	16.4	16.2	16.2	16.1	16.0	16.0	16.4
2001	16.0	15.9	15.8	15.6	15.6	15.6	15.7	15.6	15.5	15.4	15.4	15.2	15.6
2002	14.9	14.9	14.9	14.5	14.6	14.5	14.5	14.3	14.2	14.1	13.9	14.0	14.4
2003	14.0	13.9	13.9	13.6	13.5	13.4	12.7	13.4	13.4	13.5	13.4	13.5	13.5

Employment by Industry: Georgia—*Continued*

(Numbers in thousands. Not seasonally adjusted.)

Industry	January	February	March	April	May	June	July	August	September	October	November	December	Annual Average
SAVANNAH—*Continued*													
Service-providing													
1990	86.7	87.2	87.5	88.2	89.1	89.8	89.1	89.3	89.6	88.6	89.2	90.0	88.7
1991	87.5	87.6	88.5	88.3	88.7	89.5	90.1	90.6	90.9	90.2	91.5	92.4	89.7
1992	91.5	92.1	93.3	93.4	94.0	94.2	93.7	93.9	94.5	95.7	95.8	96.4	94.0
1993	93.3	93.7	94.5	94.8	95.3	95.5	96.4	96.2	96.5	97.4	98.2	98.5	95.9
1994	96.4	97.3	98.5	99.3	100.6	100.6	98.2	98.8	99.2	101.3	102.2	102.6	99.6
1995	100.5	100.7	102.0	102.2	103.5	104.3	102.6	103.3	103.8	103.3	104.2	104.6	102.9
1996	101.7	103.0	104.0	105.1	106.0	106.0	105.2	105.1	104.8	104.4	105.7	106.0	104.8
1997	104.9	105.3	106.7	106.8	107.6	106.8	106.0	106.1	107.2	107.5	107.6	108.7	106.8
1998	105.4	106.4	106.3	107.6	108.0	108.4	108.0	108.5	108.5	108.8	110.3	110.9	108.1
1999	108.9	109.0	109.9	110.6	111.0	110.4	109.7	111.0	110.4	111.3	112.3	113.2	110.6
2000	109.5	110.6	111.7	112.4	113.3	112.9	111.0	112.1	112.4	111.7	112.7	113.2	112.0
2001	110.7	110.8	111.9	112.3	112.8	112.2	111.7	113.5	112.9	113.0	113.5	113.8	112.4
2002	111.0	112.5	113.8	115.6	116.7	116.4	115.3	115.8	116.0	116.7	118.3	119.1	115.6
2003	114.3	114.3	115.8	116.2	116.5	116.8	118.0	118.9	119.5	120.6	120.7	121.0	117.7
Trade, transportation, and utilities													
1990	26.0	25.8	25.5	26.5	26.6	27.0	26.7	27.4	27.6	27.1	27.6	28.3	26.8
1991	26.3	25.7	25.7	25.6	26.0	26.2	25.9	26.7	26.5	26.9	27.9	28.5	26.5
1992	27.6	27.6	27.6	27.4	27.4	27.4	27.5	27.7	27.9	28.5	28.5	29.3	27.9
1993	27.2	27.0	27.3	26.9	27.0	27.3	27.8	27.8	27.6	28.1	28.7	29.3	27.7
1994	27.8	27.8	28.2	27.7	28.2	28.1	27.7	28.0	28.1	28.6	29.4	30.1	28.3
1995	28.5	27.9	28.2	28.2	28.5	28.9	28.6	28.8	28.9	29.1	29.7	30.2	28.8
1996	28.1	28.1	28.3	28.9	28.9	29.3	28.7	28.7	28.3	28.9	29.5	30.3	28.8
1997	28.5	28.1	28.6	28.5	28.7	28.6	28.6	28.4	28.7	29.1	29.7	30.3	28.8
1998	28.1	27.7	27.6	27.8	28.0	28.5	28.6	28.6	28.3	28.7	29.4	30.0	28.4
1999	29.0	28.5	28.7	29.2	29.3	29.4	29.1	29.3	29.0	29.9	30.9	31.2	29.5
2000	29.5	29.5	30.0	29.9	30.0	30.0	29.7	30.1	29.8	30.2	30.7	31.3	30.1
2001	29.9	29.4	29.6	29.1	29.6	29.4	29.8	29.8	29.5	30.0	30.2	30.9	29.7
2002	28.3	29.3	29.4	29.8	30.0	30.4	30.3	30.3	30.5	30.2	30.9	31.9	30.1
2003	30.1	29.9	30.4	29.7	29.9	30.1	30.2	30.2	30.5	30.8	30.7	31.0	30.3
Wholesale trade													
1990	4.6	4.6	4.5	4.5	4.5	4.5	4.5	4.5	4.5	4.4	4.4	4.4	4.5
1991	4.2	4.2	4.2	4.2	4.2	4.2	4.2	4.2	4.2	4.2	4.2	4.2	4.2
1992	4.2	4.2	4.2	4.3	4.3	4.3	4.3	4.3	4.3	4.3	4.2	4.2	4.3
1993	4.1	4.1	4.2	4.1	4.2	4.2	4.2	4.2	4.2	4.3	4.3	4.3	4.2
1994	4.2	4.2	4.2	4.1	4.1	4.2	4.1	4.1	4.1	4.1	4.2	4.2	4.2
1995	4.2	4.1	4.2	4.1	4.1	4.1	4.1	4.1	4.2	4.2	4.2	4.2	4.2
1996	4.0	4.0	4.1	4.1	4.1	4.2	4.2	4.2	4.2	4.2	4.2	4.2	4.1
1997	4.2	4.2	4.2	4.1	4.2	4.2	4.2	4.2	4.2	4.2	4.1	4.2	4.2
1998	3.9	3.9	3.9	3.9	3.9	4.0	4.1	4.1	4.0	4.1	4.1	4.1	4.0
1999	4.2	4.2	4.2	4.2	4.2	4.2	4.3	4.3	4.3	4.3	4.3	4.3	4.3
2000	4.4	4.4	4.5	4.6	4.7	4.7	4.5	4.6	4.5	4.4	4.4	4.4	4.5
2001	4.5	4.5	4.6	4.5	4.5	4.5	4.6	4.6	4.5	4.4	4.4	4.5	4.5
2002	4.4	4.4	4.5	4.6	4.6	4.6	4.6	4.6	4.6	4.7	4.8	4.8	4.6
2003	4.8	4.9	4.9	4.9	4.9	5.0	5.0	5.0	5.0	5.0	5.0	5.0	5.0
Retail trade													
1990	14.7	14.3	14.3	14.9	14.9	15.2	14.8	15.1	15.5	15.5	16.1	16.7	15.2
1991	14.3	13.8	13.8	14.1	14.2	14.4	14.4	15.0	14.7	14.8	15.6	16.1	14.6
1992	15.0	14.8	14.8	14.8	14.9	15.0	15.1	15.2	15.5	15.7	16.2	16.7	15.3
1993	15.1	15.0	15.1	15.6	15.6	15.8	15.9	16.0	15.8	15.8	16.5	17.2	15.8
1994	15.9	15.7	15.9	16.1	16.3	16.4	16.0	16.3	16.5	16.5	17.1	17.9	16.4
1995	16.3	16.0	16.1	16.4	16.7	17.0	16.6	16.7	16.8	16.9	17.7	18.2	16.8
1996	16.7	16.7	16.8	17.0	17.1	17.4	16.6	16.8	16.6	16.7	17.4	18.0	17.0
1997	16.5	16.2	16.4	16.6	16.7	16.7	16.5	16.6	16.6	16.8	17.5	18.2	16.8
1998	16.7	16.5	16.4	16.6	16.8	17.2	16.9	17.0	17.0	17.2	17.9	18.5	17.1
1999	17.2	17.0	17.1	17.4	17.5	17.6	17.4	17.6	17.4	17.6	18.3	18.9	17.6
2000	17.5	17.5	17.5	17.4	17.4	17.4	17.3	17.5	17.5	17.7	18.2	18.9	17.7
2001	17.4	17.0	17.3	17.1	17.3	17.2	17.3	17.2	17.2	17.2	17.7	18.0	17.3
2002	16.9	17.1	16.8	17.3	17.4	17.6	17.5	17.4	17.6	17.7	18.0	18.8	17.5
2003	17.4	17.3	17.3	17.1	17.3	17.3	17.5	17.5	17.5	17.8	17.8	18.0	17.5
Transportation and utilities													
1990	6.7	6.9	6.7	7.1	7.2	7.3	7.4	7.8	7.6	7.2	7.1	7.2	7.2
1991	7.8	7.7	7.7	7.3	7.6	7.6	7.3	7.5	7.6	7.9	8.1	8.2	7.7
1992	8.4	8.6	8.6	8.3	8.2	8.1	8.1	8.2	8.1	8.5	8.1	8.4	8.3
1993	8.0	7.9	8.0	7.2	7.2	7.3	7.7	7.6	7.6	8.0	7.9	7.8	7.7
1994	7.7	7.9	8.1	7.5	7.8	7.5	7.6	7.6	7.5	8.0	8.1	8.0	7.8
1995	8.0	7.8	7.9	7.7	7.7	7.8	7.9	8.0	7.9	8.0	7.8	7.8	7.9
1996	7.4	7.4	7.4	7.8	7.7	7.7	7.9	7.7	7.5	8.0	7.9	8.1	7.7
1997	7.8	7.7	8.0	7.8	7.8	7.7	7.9	7.6	7.9	8.1	8.1	7.9	7.9
1998	7.5	7.3	7.3	7.3	7.3	7.3	7.6	7.5	7.3	7.4	7.4	7.4	7.4
1999	7.6	7.3	7.4	7.6	7.6	7.6	7.4	7.4	7.3	8.0	8.3	8.0	7.6
2000	7.6	7.6	8.0	7.9	7.9	7.9	7.9	8.0	7.8	8.1	8.1	8.0	7.9
2001	8.0	7.9	7.7	7.5	7.8	7.7	7.9	8.0	7.8	8.4	8.1	8.4	7.9
2002	7.0	7.8	8.1	7.9	8.0	8.2	8.2	8.3	8.3	7.8	8.1	8.3	8.0
2003	7.9	7.7	8.2	7.7	7.7	7.8	7.7	7.7	8.0	8.0	7.9	8.0	7.9

Employment by Industry: Georgia—*Continued*

(Numbers in thousands. Not seasonally adjusted.)

Industry	January	February	March	April	May	June	July	August	September	October	November	December	Annual Average
SAVANNAH—*Continued*													
Information													
1990	1.9	1.9	1.9	1.9	1.9	2.0	2.0	2.0	2.0	2.0	2.0	2.0	2.0
1991	2.0	2.0	2.0	1.9	1.9	1.9	1.9	1.9	1.9	1.8	1.9	1.9	1.9
1992	1.8	1.8	1.9	1.9	1.9	1.9	1.9	1.9	1.9	2.0	2.0	2.0	1.9
1993	2.0	2.0	2.0	2.0	2.0	2.0	2.2	2.2	2.1	2.1	2.2	2.2	2.1
1994	2.2	2.2	2.2	2.1	2.1	2.2	2.2	2.2	2.2	2.2	2.2	2.2	2.2
1995	2.1	2.1	2.2	2.1	2.2	2.2	2.2	2.2	2.1	2.1	2.1	2.0	2.1
1996	2.0	2.0	2.0	2.0	2.1	2.1	2.1	2.1	2.1	2.0	2.0	2.0	2.0
1997	2.0	2.0	2.0	2.0	2.0	2.0	2.1	2.0	1.9	2.0	1.9	2.0	2.0
1998	1.8	1.8	1.7	1.9	1.9	1.9	2.0	2.0	2.0	2.0	2.0	2.1	1.9
1999	2.0	2.0	2.0	2.1	2.2	2.2	2.3	2.3	2.3	2.2	2.2	2.2	2.2
2000	2.2	2.2	2.3	2.1	2.2	2.2	2.4	2.4	2.4	2.4	2.4	2.4	2.3
2001	2.4	2.4	2.4	2.4	2.4	2.5	2.4	2.5	2.4	2.4	2.5	2.5	2.4
2002	2.5	2.5	2.6	2.5	2.4	2.3	2.2	2.2	2.1	2.1	2.1	2.1	2.3
2003	2.0	1.9	1.9	1.9	1.9	2.0	2.0	1.9	1.9	1.9	1.9	1.9	1.9
Financial activities													
1990	4.8	4.8	4.8	4.7	4.7	4.6	4.6	4.6	4.6	4.4	4.5	4.6	4.6
1991	4.7	4.7	4.7	4.8	4.7	4.8	4.8	4.8	4.8	4.9	4.8	4.8	4.8
1992	4.7	4.6	4.7	4.6	4.6	4.6	4.6	4.6	4.5	4.6	4.6	4.7	4.6
1993	4.6	4.6	4.6	4.5	4.5	4.5	4.6	4.6	4.5	4.5	4.5	4.5	4.5
1994	4.4	4.5	4.5	4.4	4.5	4.5	4.6	4.6	4.6	4.6	4.7	4.8	4.6
1995	4.7	4.7	4.7	4.7	4.7	4.8	4.7	4.7	4.7	4.7	4.6	4.7	4.7
1996	4.5	4.6	4.6	4.5	4.6	4.6	4.6	4.6	4.6	4.7	4.7	4.8	4.6
1997	4.7	4.6	4.7	4.5	4.6	4.7	4.9	4.9	4.9	4.8	4.8	4.9	4.8
1998	5.0	4.9	4.8	5.0	5.0	5.1	5.0	5.0	5.0	5.0	4.9	5.0	5.0
1999	5.1	5.1	5.1	5.1	5.1	5.2	5.0	5.0	5.0	5.2	5.2	5.3	5.1
2000	5.2	5.2	5.2	5.2	5.2	5.3	5.1	5.2	5.2	5.1	5.2	5.1	5.2
2001	4.9	4.9	5.0	5.3	5.2	5.3	5.7	5.7	5.6	5.9	5.9	5.9	5.4
2002	5.4	5.3	5.4	5.4	5.5	5.6	5.8	5.7	5.7	5.5	5.6	5.7	5.6
2003	5.5	5.5	5.5	5.8	6.0	6.2	6.3	6.4	6.5	6.5	6.5	6.5	6.1
Professional and business services													
1990	7.4	7.5	7.6	7.4	7.3	7.8	7.3	7.3	7.3	7.0	6.9	6.9	7.3
1991	6.8	6.9	6.9	7.4	7.3	7.5	7.5	7.6	7.7	7.6	7.6	7.7	7.4
1992	8.6	8.9	9.2	9.1	9.0	9.1	9.1	9.1	9.2	9.2	9.2	9.3	9.1
1993	8.9	9.0	8.9	9.3	9.4	9.3	9.6	9.6	9.9	10.1	9.9	9.8	9.5
1994	9.9	10.1	10.5	10.8	10.9	11.0	10.6	10.8	10.5	10.9	10.9	10.6	10.6
1995	10.3	10.6	10.8	10.6	11.1	11.5	10.9	11.1	11.2	10.1	10.1	10.1	10.7
1996	10.2	10.7	10.9	11.0	11.3	11.6	11.6	11.8	11.9	11.2	11.3	11.4	11.2
1997	11.6	11.9	12.2	12.1	12.0	11.9	12.0	12.4	12.6	12.4	12.5	12.4	12.2
1998	12.1	12.4	12.5	12.4	12.3	12.6	12.7	12.7	12.7	12.6	12.7	12.9	12.6
1999	12.5	12.5	12.7	12.4	12.5	12.7	13.3	13.5	13.5	13.2	13.2	13.7	13.0
2000	12.9	12.7	12.9	12.9	12.6	12.8	12.2	12.1	12.4	11.8	12.0	12.2	12.5
2001	12.6	12.3	12.4	12.7	12.4	12.5	12.7	13.0	13.0	13.0	13.2	13.2	12.7
2002	13.7	13.8	13.9	14.4	14.4	14.5	14.7	14.7	14.8	14.8	15.0	14.8	14.5
2003	13.1	13.1	13.5	13.7	13.6	13.8	14.6	14.8	15.1	15.8	15.9	15.8	14.4
Educational and health services													
1990	13.2	13.4	13.4	13.1	13.2	13.1	13.3	13.5	13.6	14.1	14.2	14.3	13.5
1991	14.5	14.7	14.8	14.3	14.2	14.2	15.1	15.2	15.2	14.9	14.9	14.9	14.7
1992	14.2	14.3	14.3	14.1	14.4	14.4	14.5	14.5	14.6	14.8	14.9	14.8	14.5
1993	14.5	14.7	14.9	14.8	14.9	14.8	14.8	14.9	15.1	15.3	15.4	15.3	15.0
1994	15.0	15.3	15.2	15.5	15.7	15.6	14.9	15.0	15.2	16.0	16.1	16.0	15.5
1995	15.5	15.7	15.7	15.8	15.8	15.7	15.6	15.6	15.9	16.3	16.7	16.5	15.9
1996	16.4	16.7	16.7	16.6	16.5	15.9	16.2	16.1	16.0	16.4	16.5	16.3	16.4
1997	16.5	16.7	16.8	16.9	17.0	16.6	16.6	16.6	16.7	17.1	17.2	17.1	16.8
1998	16.9	17.6	17.4	17.1	17.0	16.7	17.0	17.1	17.2	17.9	18.0	17.8	17.3
1999	17.2	17.4	17.4	17.6	17.7	17.5	17.2	17.3	17.4	17.8	17.7	17.6	17.5
2000	16.8	17.4	17.2	17.8	17.8	17.8	17.6	17.7	18.1	18.3	18.4	18.2	17.8
2001	16.9	17.1	17.4	17.3	17.3	17.2	16.9	17.1	17.2	17.4	17.5	17.0	17.2
2002	17.2	17.1	17.3	17.8	17.9	17.9	17.7	17.8	18.2	18.7	19.0	19.0	18.0
2003	19.3	19.3	19.3	19.4	19.5	19.4	19.1	19.2	19.3	19.3	19.6	19.5	19.4
Leisure and hospitality													
1990	11.2	11.5	11.7	12.2	12.6	12.5	12.5	12.6	12.3	12.0	12.0	11.8	12.1
1991	11.2	11.4	11.8	12.0	12.1	12.3	12.1	12.1	12.1	11.3	11.3	11.3	11.8
1992	11.3	11.5	12.1	12.6	12.9	12.9	12.9	12.8	12.7	12.6	12.5	12.4	12.4
1993	12.0	12.3	12.6	12.8	13.1	13.2	13.4	13.4	13.1	12.9	12.9	12.9	12.9
1994	12.6	12.7	13.1	13.9	14.3	14.1	13.7	13.9	13.9	13.7	13.8	14.0	13.6
1995	13.8	13.9	14.3	14.9	15.2	15.3	15.3	15.4	15.3	15.3	15.3	15.5	15.0
1996	14.8	15.0	15.5	15.9	16.3	16.4	16.4	16.1	15.9	15.1	15.2	15.1	15.6
1997	15.2	15.4	15.8	16.3	16.6	16.6	16.2	16.2	16.2	15.6	15.5	15.6	15.9
1998	15.3	15.6	15.9	16.7	17.1	17.1	16.8	17.1	17.0	16.6	16.7	16.4	16.5
1999	16.2	16.3	16.8	17.3	17.5	17.3	17.0	17.3	16.7	16.4	16.5	16.7	16.8
2000	16.4	16.6	16.9	17.4	17.6	17.5	18.1	18.0	17.6	17.1	17.1	16.9	17.3
2001	16.1	16.4	16.7	16.8	17.3	17.2	17.1	17.3	17.0	16.7	16.6	16.7	16.8
2002	16.5	16.8	17.3	17.8	18.1	18.0	17.5	17.4	16.9	16.8	17.0	16.9	17.3
2003	16.6	16.6	17.1	17.5	17.7	17.6	18.2	18.1	17.9	18.0	17.9	17.9	17.6

Employment by Industry: Georgia—*Continued*

(Numbers in thousands. Not seasonally adjusted.)

Industry	January	February	March	April	May	June	July	August	September	October	November	December	Annual Average
SAVANNAH—*Continued*													
Other services													
1990	4.3	4.3	4.4	4.4	4.5	4.6	4.5	4.5	4.5	4.3	4.3	4.3	4.4
1991	4.2	4.2	4.3	4.3	4.4	4.5	4.5	4.4	4.4	4.4	4.5	4.5	4.4
1992	4.3	4.3	4.4	4.4	4.5	4.6	4.4	4.4	4.4	4.5	4.5	4.4	4.4
1993	4.5	4.5	4.5	4.6	4.6	4.7	4.8	4.8	4.7	4.6	4.7	4.7	4.6
1994	4.6	4.7	4.7	4.8	4.8	4.8	4.8	4.7	4.7	4.7	4.8	4.9	4.8
1995	4.8	4.8	4.9	4.9	4.9	4.9	5.0	5.0	5.0	5.0	5.0	5.0	4.9
1996	5.0	5.1	5.2	5.2	5.3	5.4	5.4	5.4	5.4	5.4	5.4	5.4	5.3
1997	5.4	5.5	5.5	5.5	5.6	5.5	5.5	5.5	5.6	5.6	5.7	5.7	5.6
1998	5.5	5.6	5.6	5.6	5.6	5.6	5.7	5.6	5.7	5.8	5.8	5.8	5.7
1999	6.0	6.1	6.1	6.1	6.2	6.2	6.2	6.2	6.2	6.2	6.3	6.4	6.2
2000	6.4	6.5	6.5	6.6	6.9	6.9	6.8	6.8	6.9	6.8	6.8	6.8	6.7
2001	7.6	7.6	7.7	8.0	8.0	7.8	7.5	7.6	7.4	7.1	7.0	7.0	7.5
2002	7.2	7.2	7.2	7.3	7.5	7.4	7.2	7.2	7.3	7.8	7.9	7.9	7.4
2003	7.1	7.0	7.2	7.1	7.1	7.1	7.1	7.2	7.1	7.0	7.0	7.0	7.1
Government													
1990	17.9	18.0	18.2	18.0	18.3	18.2	18.2	17.4	17.7	17.7	17.7	17.8	17.9
1991	17.8	18.0	18.3	18.0	18.1	18.1	18.3	17.9	18.3	18.4	18.6	18.8	18.2
1992	19.0	19.1	19.1	19.3	19.3	19.3	18.8	18.9	19.3	19.5	19.6	19.5	19.2
1993	19.6	19.6	19.7	19.9	19.8	19.7	19.2	18.9	19.5	19.8	19.9	19.8	19.6
1994	19.9	20.0	20.1	20.1	20.1	20.3	19.7	19.6	20.0	20.6	20.3	20.0	20.1
1995	20.8	21.0	21.2	21.0	21.1	21.0	20.3	20.5	20.7	20.7	20.7	20.6	20.8
1996	20.7	20.8	20.8	21.0	21.0	20.7	20.2	20.3	20.6	20.7	21.1	20.7	20.7
1997	21.0	21.1	21.1	21.0	21.1	20.9	20.1	20.1	20.6	20.9	20.3	20.7	20.7
1998	20.7	20.8	20.8	21.1	21.1	20.9	20.2	20.4	20.6	20.2	20.8	20.9	20.7
1999	20.9	21.1	21.1	20.8	20.5	19.9	19.6	20.1	20.3	20.4	20.3	20.1	20.4
2000	20.1	20.5	20.7	20.5	21.0	20.4	19.1	19.8	20.0	20.0	20.1	20.3	20.2
2001	20.3	20.7	20.7	20.7	20.6	20.3	19.6	20.5	20.8	20.5	20.6	20.6	20.4
2002	20.2	20.5	20.7	20.6	20.9	20.3	19.9	20.5	20.5	20.8	20.8	20.8	20.5
2003	20.6	21.0	20.9	21.1	20.8	20.6	20.5	21.1	21.2	21.3	21.2	21.4	21.0
Federal government													
1990	2.8	2.8	2.9	3.0	3.3	3.1	3.0	2.8	2.7	2.7	2.7	2.7	2.9
1991	2.7	2.7	2.7	2.7	2.7	2.7	2.8	2.8	2.8	2.8	2.8	2.8	2.8
1992	2.9	2.9	2.9	2.9	2.9	2.9	2.9	2.9	3.0	2.9	2.9	2.9	2.9
1993	2.8	2.8	2.8	2.8	2.8	2.8	2.8	2.8	2.8	2.8	2.8	2.9	2.8
1994	2.9	2.8	2.8	2.9	2.9	2.9	2.9	2.9	2.9	2.9	2.9	2.9	2.9
1995	2.9	2.9	2.9	3.0	3.0	3.0	3.0	3.0	3.0	3.0	3.0	3.0	3.0
1996	3.0	3.0	3.0	3.0	3.0	3.0	3.0	3.0	3.0	3.0	3.0	3.0	3.0
1997	3.2	3.1	3.1	2.9	2.9	2.9	2.9	2.9	2.9	2.9	2.8	2.9	3.0
1998	2.8	2.8	2.8	2.8	2.8	2.8	2.8	2.8	2.8	2.7	2.7	2.8	2.8
1999	2.7	2.7	2.7	2.7	2.7	2.7	2.7	2.7	2.7	2.7	2.7	2.7	2.7
2000	2.8	2.8	3.0	2.9	3.4	3.0	3.0	2.8	2.8	2.8	2.8	2.8	2.9
2001	2.7	2.7	2.7	2.7	2.7	2.8	2.8	2.7	2.7	2.7	2.7	2.7	2.7
2002	2.5	2.6	2.6	2.6	2.7	2.7	2.6	2.6	2.6	2.7	2.6	2.7	2.6
2003	2.7	2.7	2.7	2.7	2.7	2.7	2.7	2.7	2.7	2.7	2.7	2.8	2.7

Average Weekly Hours by Industry: Georgia

(Not seasonally adjusted.)

Industry	January	February	March	April	May	June	July	August	September	October	November	December	Annual Average
STATEWIDE													
Manufacturing													
2001	39.8	38.9	40.3	39.2	40.0	40.4	40.7	41.5	41.6	41.2	40.5	40.8	40.4
2002	41.0	40.0	41.1	40.6	40.8	41.3	39.9	41.0	41.4	41.2	41.1	41.4	40.9
2003	39.9	40.2	40.3	39.8	40.1	40.6	39.9	38.9	39.3	38.9	39.6	39.8	39.8
ATLANTA													
Manufacturing													
2001	40.2	39.2	39.4	39.1	40.5	40.1	41.6	43.0	42.0	40.2	39.8	40.4	40.4
2002	39.0	38.5	40.8	39.2	39.6	40.8	39.2	39.4	39.7	40.1	39.1	40.1	39.6
2003	37.9	38.9	38.9	38.6	38.0	38.8	38.6	35.0	36.2	36.3	38.9	38.1	37.9

Average Hourly Earnings by Industry: Georgia

(Dollars, not seasonally adjusted.)

Industry	January	February	March	April	May	June	July	August	September	October	November	December	Annual Average
STATEWIDE													
Manufacturing													
2001	11.98	12.16	12.05	12.08	12.22	12.49	12.57	12.76	12.82	12.77	12.77	13.42	12.50
2002	13.24	13.50	13.21	13.11	13.16	13.22	12.92	12.94	13.45	13.64	13.88	14.34	13.38
2003	13.88	13.95	13.87	13.83	14.20	14.09	14.02	13.78	13.84	14.57	14.25	14.67	14.08
ATLANTA													
Manufacturing													
2001	13.37	13.51	13.56	13.63	13.54	13.87	13.65	14.00	14.31	14.44	14.76	15.46	13.99
2002	15.12	15.43	15.54	15.32	14.88	15.11	15.01	14.98	15.41	15.27	15.59	15.71	15.28
2003	15.33	15.31	15.14	15.28	15.41	15.16	15.04	14.70	15.06	15.46	13.93	15.85	15.14

Average Weekly Earnings by Industry: Georgia

(Dollars, not seasonally adjusted.)

Industry	January	February	March	April	May	June	July	August	September	October	November	December	Annual Average
STATEWIDE													
Manufacturing													
2001	476.80	473.02	485.62	473.54	488.80	504.60	511.60	529.54	533.31	526.12	517.19	547.54	505.00
2002	542.84	540.00	542.93	532.27	536.93	545.99	515.51	530.54	556.83	561.97	570.47	593.68	547.24
2003	553.81	560.79	558.96	550.43	569.42	572.05	559.40	536.04	543.91	566.77	564.30	583.87	560.38
ATLANTA													
Manufacturing													
2001	537.47	529.59	534.26	532.93	548.37	556.19	567.84	602.00	601.02	580.49	587.45	624.58	565.20
2002	589.68	594.06	634.03	600.54	589.25	616.49	588.39	590.21	611.78	612.33	609.57	629.97	605.09
2003	581.01	595.56	588.95	589.81	585.58	588.21	580.54	514.50	545.17	561.20	541.88	603.89	573.81

HAWAII AT A GLANCE

(Population and total nonfarm employment numbers in thousands)

Population, Census 2000:	1,211.5
Total nonfarm employment, 2003:	567.3
Change in total nonfarm employment	
(Number)	
1990–2003:	38.9
1990–2001:	26.6
2001–2003:	12.3
(Compound annual rate of change)	
1990–2003:	0.5%
1990–2001:	0.4%
2001–2003:	1.1%
Unemployment rate	
1990:	2.4%
2001:	4.3%
2003:	3.9%

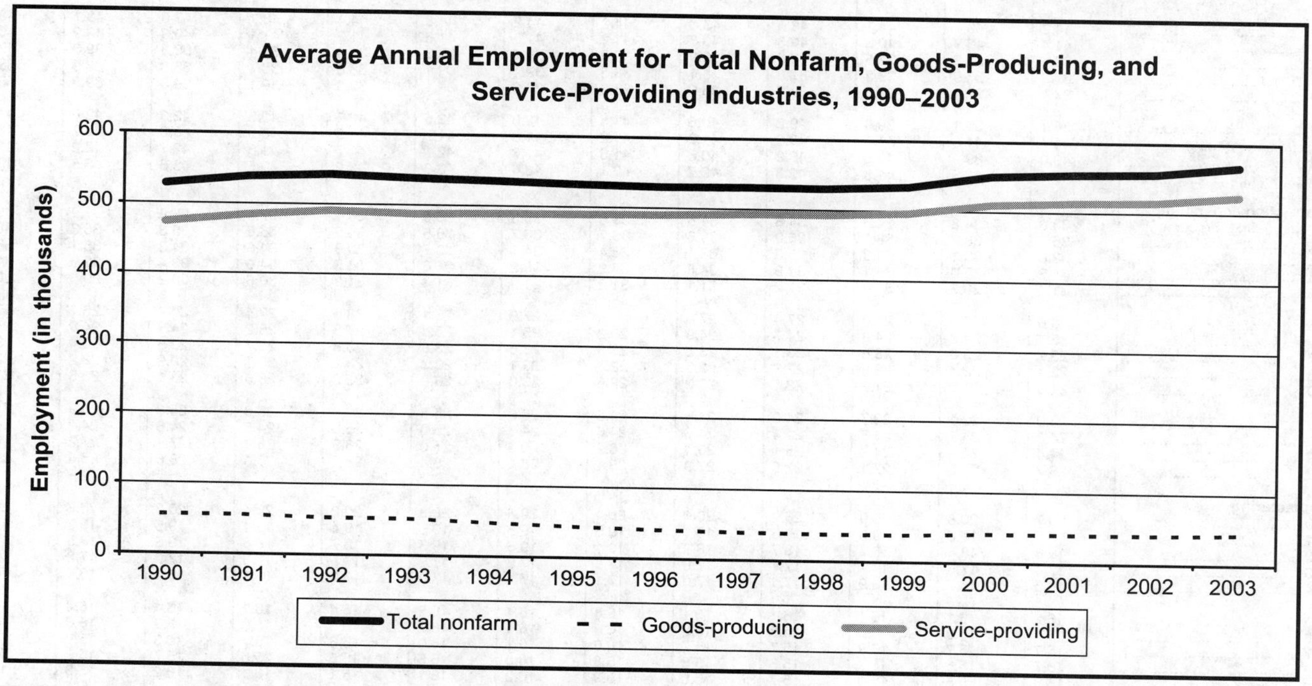

The changes in nonfarm payroll employment in Hawaii between 1990 and 2003 were quite different from most other states. Total employment rose during the 1990–1991 recession, primarily due to growth in the service-providing sector, which accounts for approximately 90 percent of employment in Hawaii. Professional and business services and educational and health services experienced substantial growth in employment from 1990 to 2003. Leisure and hospitality remained flat during this period, but is still one of Hawaii's dominant industries, employing close to 100,000 people in 2003.

Employment by Industry: Hawaii

(Numbers in thousands. Not seasonally adjusted.)

Industry	January	February	March	April	May	June	July	August	September	October	November	December	Annual Average
STATEWIDE													
Total nonfarm													
1990	513.4	521.6	525.1	525.6	528.7	531.5	527.8	528.1	521.7	532.4	540.5	544.9	528.4
1991	536.3	537.9	539.5	535.2	537.4	539.3	537.7	538.4	532.0	539.0	545.5	551.2	539.1
1992	539.7	543.1	546.4	544.3	544.8	545.0	542.2	540.6	533.4	539.3	544.0	551.0	542.8
1993	535.5	540.8	543.8	543.1	544.1	543.2	536.2	532.9	527.2	535.6	538.7	544.5	538.8
1994	530.6	535.5	539.8	538.3	536.4	539.5	533.0	531.2	527.3	534.3	540.8	546.7	536.1
1995	531.7	536.5	539.8	535.1	536.6	537.2	529.0	526.7	522.5	527.2	533.5	538.8	532.8
1996	525.1	533.0	535.7	529.6	532.6	532.1	527.7	527.7	522.4	527.7	534.0	541.2	530.7
1997	528.9	533.4	536.4	532.3	533.8	534.2	526.8	529.1	523.5	528.2	533.4	539.2	531.6
1998	526.1	530.2	533.2	532.1	533.8	533.0	527.1	529.1	527.1	529.1	534.7	539.9	531.3
1999	523.3	528.6	532.9	533.1	534.6	536.5	530.3	534.5	532.7	538.2	544.5	551.1	535.0
2000	535.1	542.9	548.8	548.3	552.2	556.3	547.6	548.2	552.3	555.3	561.9	567.4	551.4
2001	546.9	557.4	561.2	556.1	557.5	562.9	552.5	554.6	555.5	548.1	551.9	555.5	555.0
2002	541.9	549.4	554.0	547.9	558.0	564.7	553.2	554.2	557.3	560.7	566.9	573.4	556.8
2003	559.6	564.5	567.9	562.6	568.0	569.0	560.8	562.0	564.5	570.9	576.1	581.1	567.3
Total private													
1990	412.2	416.7	417.2	416.8	418.2	423.9	425.4	426.0	424.3	427.3	431.3	434.6	422.8
1991	428.8	428.1	428.1	424.3	425.5	429.6	433.1	433.2	431.5	430.1	433.1	437.0	430.2
1992	429.4	430.1	431.7	429.7	430.0	432.3	436.0	434.3	431.6	429.2	430.5	435.4	431.7
1993	425.5	427.4	428.2	427.4	427.2	429.9	430.1	426.8	425.6	425.0	425.5	428.8	427.3
1994	421.2	421.4	423.8	422.3	422.0	424.6	425.8	424.2	424.7	423.2	426.9	430.8	424.2
1995	420.1	420.9	422.7	418.2	419.5	422.8	422.6	422.0	421.5	418.9	422.2	425.9	421.4
1996	417.6	419.7	421.0	415.6	417.3	419.4	421.1	421.2	420.9	418.8	421.8	427.5	420.2
1997	418.4	419.8	422.2	418.3	418.2	420.1	420.3	420.6	419.0	417.3	420.2	424.5	419.9
1998	415.0	416.7	418.1	417.3	418.1	419.3	420.0	420.6	419.6	417.9	421.5	425.0	419.1
1999	412.9	415.2	418.3	418.6	419.8	422.5	422.8	423.8	423.8	425.5	429.3	434.6	422.2
2000	424.5	427.8	431.4	431.2	432.6	438.6	437.9	439.1	442.0	441.2	445.3	449.3	436.7
2001	438.8	441.3	444.1	440.9	442.7	445.6	443.7	444.8	443.5	432.6	432.8	435.5	440.5
2002	427.3	430.3	433.4	433.4	436.5	440.7	441.2	441.9	443.0	441.9	446.0	450.9	438.9
2003	440.7	442.9	445.5	443.6	445.6	447.9	446.9	448.9	450.2	451.2	454.8	458.9	448.1
Goods-producing													
1990	54.3	55.1	55.5	54.5	54.9	56.0	56.1	56.3	56.3	57.4	57.2	57.5	55.9
1991	55.7	55.5	55.7	55.3	55.6	56.2	56.3	56.0	55.3	55.0	54.8	54.6	55.5
1992	52.2	51.9	52.0	51.7	51.8	52.5	53.7	53.0	51.7	52.9	53.3	53.6	52.5
1993	52.0	52.6	52.8	52.5	52.4	52.8	53.0	52.3	52.0	51.3	50.6	49.8	52.0
1994	47.5	47.4	47.9	48.3	48.1	48.3	48.4	48.4	48.2	47.2	46.6	45.9	47.6
1995	44.2	43.7	44.1	43.5	43.6	44.2	44.2	44.6	44.4	43.7	43.6	43.1	43.9
1996	41.4	40.7	40.8	40.5	40.8	41.2	41.5	41.6	41.2	41.1	40.0	40.9	40.9
1997	39.4	39.3	39.5	38.8	38.9	39.3	39.7	39.8	39.4	39.4	39.3	39.3	39.3
1998	37.8	37.9	38.2	37.8	38.1	38.5	39.1	39.1	38.8	38.7	38.6	38.9	38.4
1999	37.4	37.4	37.5	37.8	38.0	38.5	39.2	39.1	39.3	39.1	39.3	39.8	38.5
2000	39.1	39.1	39.9	40.2	40.6	41.3	42.0	42.5	42.7	42.3	42.3	42.6	41.2
2001	41.4	41.3	41.4	40.9	41.2	41.2	41.3	41.6	41.5	40.5	40.6	40.7	41.1
2002	40.0	39.9	40.6	40.2	40.6	41.6	41.8	42.1	41.7	41.8	42.1	42.2	41.2
2003	41.4	41.5	41.8	42.3	42.7	43.1	43.0	43.3	43.2	43.5	43.6	43.5	42.7
Construction and mining													
1990	33.6	34.3	34.6	34.3	34.8	35.6	35.6	36.0	36.1	37.0	36.9	37.2	35.5
1991	36.1	35.9	36.1	36.0	36.5	36.7	36.7	36.5	35.9	35.6	35.3	35.3	36.0
1992	33.6	33.1	33.3	33.0	33.1	33.4	34.1	33.7	33.0	34.3	34.8	35.1	33.7
1993	34.6	35.0	35.1	34.8	34.8	34.9	35.2	34.6	34.5	34.0	33.4	32.6	34.4
1994	31.0	30.7	31.0	31.2	31.1	31.2	31.3	31.4	31.2	30.6	30.2	29.5	30.8
1995	28.0	27.6	28.0	27.4	27.5	27.9	27.8	28.1	28.0	27.4	27.2	26.7	27.6
1996	25.4	24.8	24.8	24.7	24.9	25.2	25.1	25.4	25.3	25.2	24.1	24.9	24.9
1997	23.7	23.6	23.6	23.1	23.2	23.3	23.6	23.8	23.8	23.7	23.5	23.4	23.5
1998	22.1	22.4	22.5	22.3	22.5	22.7	23.1	23.3	23.2	23.1	22.9	23.2	22.7
1999	21.9	21.9	21.9	22.1	22.2	22.6	23.0	23.0	23.2	23.0	23.1	23.5	22.6
2000	23.0	23.1	23.7	24.0	24.4	24.8	25.5	25.8	26.0	25.6	25.6	25.9	24.7
2001	24.8	24.7	24.8	24.4	24.6	24.6	24.8	25.0	25.0	24.5	24.6	24.7	24.7
2002	24.4	24.3	24.9	25.1	25.4	26.2	26.6	27.0	26.8	26.9	27.1	27.2	26.0
2003	26.7	26.8	27.1	27.5	27.9	28.1	28.1	28.4	28.4	28.6	28.6	28.4	27.9
Manufacturing													
1990	20.7	20.8	20.9	20.2	20.1	20.4	20.5	20.3	20.2	20.4	20.3	20.3	20.4
1991	19.6	19.6	19.6	19.3	19.1	19.5	19.6	19.5	19.4	19.4	19.5	19.3	19.4
1992	18.6	18.8	18.7	18.7	18.7	19.1	19.6	19.3	18.7	18.6	18.5	18.5	18.8
1993	17.4	17.6	17.7	17.7	17.6	17.9	17.8	17.7	17.5	17.3	17.2	17.2	17.5
1994	16.5	16.7	16.9	17.1	17.0	17.1	17.1	17.0	17.0	16.6	16.4	16.4	16.8
1995	16.2	16.1	16.1	16.1	16.1	16.3	16.4	16.5	16.4	16.3	16.4	16.4	16.2
1996	16.0	15.9	16.0	15.8	15.9	16.0	16.4	16.2	15.9	15.9	15.9	16.0	15.9
1997	15.7	15.7	15.9	15.7	15.7	16.0	16.1	16.0	15.6	15.7	15.8	15.9	15.8
1998	15.7	15.5	15.7	15.5	15.6	15.8	16.0	15.8	15.6	15.6	15.7	15.7	15.6
1999	15.5	15.5	15.6	15.7	15.8	15.9	16.2	16.1	16.1	16.1	16.2	16.3	15.9
2000	16.1	16.0	16.2	16.2	16.2	16.5	16.5	16.7	16.7	16.7	16.7	16.7	16.4
2001	16.6	16.6	16.6	16.5	16.6	16.6	16.5	16.6	16.5	16.0	16.0	16.0	16.4
2002	15.6	15.6	15.7	15.1	15.2	15.4	15.2	15.1	14.9	14.9	15.0	15.0	15.2
2003	14.7	14.7	14.7	14.8	14.8	15.0	14.9	14.9	14.8	14.9	15.0	15.1	14.9

Employment by Industry: Hawaii—*Continued*

(Numbers in thousands. Not seasonally adjusted.)

Industry	January	February	March	April	May	June	July	August	September	October	November	December	Annual Average
STATEWIDE—*Continued*													
Service-providing													
1990	459.1	466.5	469.6	471.1	473.8	475.5	471.7	471.8	465.4	475.0	483.3	487.4	472.5
1991	480.6	482.4	483.8	479.9	481.8	483.1	481.4	482.4	476.7	484.0	490.7	496.6	483.6
1992	487.5	491.2	494.4	492.6	493.0	492.5	488.5	487.6	481.7	486.4	490.7	497.4	490.3
1993	483.5	488.2	491.0	490.6	491.7	490.4	483.2	480.6	475.2	484.3	488.1	494.7	486.8
1994	483.1	488.1	491.9	490.0	488.3	491.2	484.6	482.8	479.1	487.1	494.2	500.8	488.4
1995	487.5	492.8	495.7	491.6	493.0	493.0	484.8	482.1	478.1	483.5	489.9	495.7	488.9
1996	483.7	492.3	494.9	489.1	491.8	490.9	486.2	486.1	481.2	486.6	494.0	500.3	489.8
1997	489.7	494.1	496.9	493.5	494.9	494.9	487.1	489.3	484.1	488.8	494.1	499.9	492.3
1998	488.3	492.3	495.0	494.3	495.7	494.5	488.0	490.0	488.3	490.4	496.1	501.0	492.8
1999	485.9	491.2	495.4	495.3	496.6	498.0	491.1	495.4	493.4	499.1	505.2	511.3	496.4
2000	496.0	503.8	508.9	508.1	511.6	515.0	505.6	505.7	509.6	513.0	519.6	524.8	510.1
2001	505.5	516.1	519.8	515.2	516.3	521.7	511.2	513.0	514.0	507.6	511.3	514.8	513.9
2002	501.9	509.5	513.4	507.7	517.4	523.1	511.4	512.1	515.6	518.9	524.8	531.2	515.6
2003	518.2	523.0	526.1	520.3	525.3	525.9	517.8	518.7	521.3	527.4	532.5	537.6	524.5
Trade, transportation, and utilities													
1990	110.7	111.2	111.2	111.0	111.5	113.1	113.9	113.4	113.2	113.8	115.4	117.0	113.0
1991	114.4	113.7	113.0	111.7	112.2	113.3	114.4	113.9	113.6	113.9	115.4	118.0	114.0
1992	114.7	114.3	114.5	113.7	114.0	114.8	115.1	114.3	114.4	113.5	114.4	116.7	114.5
1993	112.5	112.3	111.9	112.1	112.1	113.7	114.5	113.2	112.9	113.4	114.4	116.8	113.3
1994	112.4	111.4	111.6	111.5	111.6	112.0	112.3	112.2	112.3	112.5	115.2	117.6	112.7
1995	113.3	112.4	112.6	111.4	112.2	113.2	113.2	113.3	113.0	112.9	114.5	116.7	113.2
1996	112.9	112.0	111.8	110.3	110.5	111.2	111.3	111.0	110.8	109.9	112.1	114.3	111.5
1997	112.3	111.1	111.3	110.2	109.8	110.0	109.7	109.2	109.3	109.2	110.3	111.8	110.3
1998	109.2	108.2	107.8	107.3	107.4	107.7	107.1	106.9	107.4	107.2	108.7	110.3	107.9
1999	106.3	105.6	105.9	106.2	106.5	107.2	107.1	107.6	108.1	108.9	111.0	112.8	107.7
2000	109.3	109.1	109.1	108.5	108.8	110.3	110.4	110.9	111.3	111.6	114.1	115.6	110.8
2001	112.3	111.7	111.9	111.2	111.5	112.2	111.8	112.0	111.6	108.9	107.6	109.2	111.0
2002	105.5	104.8	104.9	105.0	105.5	106.5	107.0	107.3	107.1	107.5	109.0	111.0	106.8
2003	107.4	107.0	106.8	106.3	106.4	107.1	107.2	107.6	107.8	108.4	110.5	112.9	108.0
Wholesale trade													
1990	17.3	17.5	17.5	17.4	17.5	17.7	17.8	17.7	17.7	17.7	17.7	17.8	17.6
1991	17.4	17.4	17.3	17.3	17.3	17.4	17.5	17.5	17.4	17.5	17.5	17.5	17.4
1992	17.1	17.0	17.0	17.1	17.1	17.2	17.4	17.3	17.1	16.9	17.0	17.1	17.1
1993	17.0	17.0	16.9	17.0	16.9	16.9	16.9	16.8	16.7	16.5	16.7	16.7	16.8
1994	16.4	16.3	16.4	16.4	16.4	16.5	16.5	16.5	16.4	16.4	16.3	16.5	16.4
1995	16.3	16.3	16.3	16.3	16.3	16.4	16.1	16.1	16.1	16.0	16.0	16.1	16.1
1996	16.0	16.0	16.0	15.9	15.9	16.0	16.0	16.0	15.9	15.8	15.8	15.9	15.9
1997	15.6	15.6	15.6	15.6	15.6	15.7	15.7	15.8	15.8	15.8	15.8	16.0	15.7
1998	15.7	15.8	15.8	15.9	15.9	15.9	15.8	15.8	15.9	15.9	15.9	16.0	15.8
1999	15.6	15.5	15.6	15.7	15.7	15.7	15.7	15.8	15.8	15.9	15.9	16.1	15.7
2000	16.0	16.0	16.1	16.0	16.0	16.3	16.3	16.4	16.4	16.4	16.5	16.5	16.2
2001	16.4	16.4	16.4	16.4	16.5	16.6	16.5	16.6	16.5	16.3	16.2	16.4	16.4
2002	16.1	16.1	16.2	16.2	16.3	16.4	16.5	16.5	16.5	16.6	16.7	16.9	16.4
2003	16.5	16.5	16.6	16.7	16.7	16.8	16.8	16.8	16.8	16.9	16.9	17.0	16.8
Retail trade													
1990	66.4	66.2	66.3	66.0	66.4	67.3	67.7	67.3	66.9	67.4	68.7	70.0	67.2
1991	68.1	67.3	67.1	66.0	66.2	66.6	67.5	67.2	66.9	66.9	68.2	70.3	67.4
1992	68.4	67.7	67.8	67.1	67.2	67.6	67.9	67.4	67.4	67.1	67.9	70.0	67.7
1993	66.3	66.1	66.1	66.4	66.5	67.9	68.4	67.5	67.0	67.2	68.6	70.9	67.4
1994	67.3	66.2	66.2	66.0	66.0	66.3	67.0	67.0	66.9	67.7	70.2	72.1	67.4
1995	68.8	67.8	67.9	66.9	67.4	68.0	68.6	68.8	68.5	68.8	70.3	72.1	68.6
1996	69.0	68.1	68.0	67.1	67.1	67.5	67.6	67.2	67.1	66.0	68.0	69.8	67.7
1997	67.9	67.2	67.3	66.6	66.0	66.1	65.7	65.4	65.4	65.4	66.4	67.7	66.4
1998	65.6	64.7	64.2	63.7	63.6	63.8	63.7	63.6	64.0	63.9	65.5	67.1	64.5
1999	64.0	63.3	63.4	63.5	63.4	63.9	64.0	64.3	64.7	65.3	67.2	68.6	64.6
2000	65.8	65.3	65.1	64.6	64.9	65.6	65.9	66.3	66.3	66.7	68.8	70.2	66.3
2001	67.2	66.5	66.5	65.9	65.9	66.3	66.1	66.3	66.0	64.9	65.3	66.7	66.1
2002	63.8	63.0	62.9	62.8	63.0	63.7	64.1	64.1	63.9	64.1	65.3	67.1	64.0
2003	64.0	63.4	63.1	62.8	63.0	63.8	64.1	64.3	64.3	64.8	66.7	68.8	64.4
Transportation and utilities													
1990	27.0	27.5	27.4	27.6	27.6	28.1	28.4	28.4	28.6	28.7	29.0	29.2	28.1
1991	28.9	29.0	28.6	28.4	28.7	29.3	29.4	29.2	29.3	29.5	29.7	30.2	29.2
1992	29.2	29.6	29.7	29.5	29.7	30.0	29.8	29.6	29.9	29.5	29.5	29.6	29.6
1993	29.2	29.2	28.9	28.7	28.7	28.9	29.2	28.9	29.2	29.7	29.1	29.2	29.0
1994	28.7	28.9	29.0	29.1	29.2	29.2	28.8	28.7	29.0	28.4	28.7	29.0	28.8
1995	28.2	28.3	28.4	28.2	28.5	28.8	28.5	28.4	28.4	28.1	28.2	28.5	28.3
1996	27.9	27.9	27.8	27.3	27.5	27.7	27.7	27.8	27.8	28.1	28.3	28.6	27.8
1997	28.1	28.3	28.4	28.0	28.2	28.2	28.3	28.0	28.1	28.0	28.1	28.1	28.1
1998	27.9	27.7	27.8	27.7	27.9	28.0	27.6	27.5	27.5	27.4	27.3	27.2	27.6
1999	26.7	26.8	26.9	27.0	27.4	27.6	27.4	27.5	27.6	27.7	27.9	28.1	27.3
2000	27.5	27.8	27.9	27.9	27.9	28.4	28.2	28.2	28.6	28.5	28.8	28.9	28.2
2001	28.7	28.8	29.0	28.9	29.1	29.3	29.2	29.1	29.1	27.7	26.1	26.1	28.4
2002	25.6	25.7	25.8	26.0	26.2	26.4	26.4	26.7	26.7	26.8	27.0	27.0	26.4
2003	26.9	27.1	27.1	26.8	26.7	26.5	26.3	26.5	26.7	26.7	26.9	27.1	26.8

Employment by Industry: Hawaii—*Continued*

(Numbers in thousands. Not seasonally adjusted.)

Industry	January	February	March	April	May	June	July	August	September	October	November	December	Annual Average
STATEWIDE—*Continued*													
Information													
1990	9.5	9.6	9.6	9.8	9.8	9.8	9.8	9.8	9.8	9.9	9.9	10.1	9.7
1991	9.7	9.8	9.8	9.9	9.8	9.8	9.8	9.4	9.8	9.8	9.8	10.0	9.7
1992	10.1	10.4	10.4	9.6	9.7	9.8	10.4	10.4	10.6	10.6	10.4	10.5	10.2
1993	10.4	10.0	10.3	9.9	10.0	9.8	10.0	9.9	9.8	9.6	9.7	9.8	9.9
1994	9.9	10.1	10.6	10.3	10.1	9.9	10.1	10.3	10.3	10.8	10.9	11.1	10.3
1995	10.2	10.3	10.7	10.1	10.2	10.4	10.4	10.4	10.4	10.3	10.5	10.4	10.3
1996	10.5	10.7	10.7	10.5	10.7	10.5	10.3	10.4	10.4	11.1	11.2	11.5	10.7
1997	10.6	10.6	10.6	11.0	11.1	11.5	11.5	11.5	11.3	11.0	11.0	11.1	11.0
1998	11.0	11.1	11.1	11.5	11.4	11.5	11.5	11.7	11.6	11.7	11.7	11.9	11.4
1999	11.0	11.2	11.4	11.2	11.3	11.6	11.7	11.8	11.9	11.6	11.7	12.2	11.5
2000	11.5	11.5	11.7	12.4	12.3	12.7	12.0	12.5	13.3	12.9	12.4	12.1	12.2
2001	12.1	12.1	12.4	11.8	12.1	11.9	11.7	11.9	11.5	11.5	11.7	11.6	11.9
2002	11.7	11.7	11.6	11.5	11.5	11.3	11.2	11.3	12.0	11.1	11.1	11.7	11.5
2003	10.8	10.9	10.9	10.5	11.2	10.9	10.0	10.0	9.9	9.9	10.0	10.0	10.4
Financial activities													
1990	30.4	30.7	31.0	30.8	30.9	31.3	31.5	31.5	31.4	31.2	31.3	31.4	31.1
1991	31.3	31.2	31.5	31.2	31.4	31.5	31.3	31.5	31.3	31.2	31.4	31.4	31.4
1992	30.6	30.6	30.8	30.7	30.7	30.8	31.1	31.1	31.1	31.2	31.2	31.5	30.9
1993	31.5	31.7	31.9	32.2	32.2	32.1	32.5	32.5	32.4	32.0	32.3	32.4	32.1
1994	32.5	32.7	32.7	31.7	31.6	31.8	31.8	31.8	31.9	31.4	31.4	31.4	31.8
1995	30.9	31.0	31.1	30.8	30.8	30.9	30.6	31.1	30.9	30.7	30.8	30.7	30.8
1996	30.5	30.8	30.9	30.5	30.6	30.6	30.5	30.6	30.7	30.1	30.4	30.6	30.5
1997	30.3	30.5	30.7	30.1	30.1	30.1	30.0	30.0	30.1	29.6	29.7	30.2	30.1
1998	29.9	29.7	30.0	29.9	29.9	30.0	30.3	30.3	30.2	30.0	30.2	30.4	30.0
1999	29.8	30.0	30.1	30.1	30.0	30.2	29.8	29.7	29.6	29.5	29.5	29.6	29.8
2000	29.1	29.3	29.4	29.2	29.3	29.5	29.6	29.7	29.6	29.6	29.5	29.8	29.4
2001	28.1	28.2	28.4	28.2	28.2	28.3	28.1	28.1	28.0	27.6	27.6	27.7	28.0
2002	27.2	27.3	27.6	27.4	27.6	27.8	27.8	27.8	27.8	27.9	28.1	28.4	27.7
2003	27.7	27.9	28.1	28.0	28.2	28.5	28.6	28.7	28.7	28.5	28.5	28.6	28.3
Professional and business services													
1990	48.2	49.1	49.9	49.2	49.2	50.1	50.0	50.5	50.2	50.7	50.6	50.8	49.8
1991	50.6	50.8	50.5	50.5	50.1	50.7	50.8	50.7	50.9	50.6	51.1	51.2	50.7
1992	50.5	50.9	51.3	51.7	51.1	51.3	51.9	52.0	51.6	51.8	51.5	52.3	51.4
1993	51.4	51.6	52.0	51.9	51.1	51.6	51.6	51.3	51.3	51.5	51.5	52.3	51.5
1994	52.0	52.1	52.4	52.7	52.4	52.9	52.5	52.8	52.7	52.7	52.9	53.8	52.6
1995	53.0	53.7	54.0	53.4	53.5	53.7	53.9	53.6	53.5	53.3	53.8	54.4	53.6
1996	54.5	55.3	55.7	55.0	55.0	55.5	55.8	55.6	56.0	55.5	55.8	56.7	55.5
1997	55.9	56.4	57.0	56.4	55.7	56.1	56.2	56.0	56.4	55.9	56.4	57.1	56.3
1998	55.8	56.2	56.8	56.4	56.0	56.4	56.6	56.8	56.4	55.8	56.3	56.7	56.3
1999	56.1	56.4	57.3	57.0	57.5	57.5	57.9	58.3	58.4	59.2	59.2	60.6	57.9
2000	59.3	59.8	60.6	60.7	60.7	61.4	61.6	61.7	62.4	62.5	63.0	63.7	61.4
2001	62.3	63.1	63.9	63.3	63.8	64.7	64.4	64.9	64.8	63.5	64.1	64.4	63.9
2002	63.5	64.9	65.4	65.9	66.5	67.5	67.8	68.6	68.8	68.8	68.6	70.6	67.2
2003	69.0	68.6	69.2	68.9	68.8	69.6	69.3	70.1	70.5	70.2	70.4	70.7	69.6
Educational and health services													
1990	45.0	45.6	46.0	45.9	46.3	46.6	47.3	46.9	47.0	47.6	48.1	48.2	46.7
1991	47.6	48.1	49.0	48.1	48.1	48.4	49.3	48.8	48.7	49.5	50.0	50.0	48.8
1992	49.4	49.9	50.3	50.2	50.5	50.6	51.0	50.4	50.7	50.7	50.9	51.1	50.4
1993	50.6	51.4	51.6	51.3	51.5	51.6	52.0	51.1	51.6	51.8	52.1	52.5	51.5
1994	51.7	52.0	52.4	52.3	52.4	52.5	52.8	51.2	51.8	52.5	52.9	53.0	52.2
1995	52.0	52.5	52.6	52.2	53.2	52.6	52.8	51.3	52.3	52.4	52.7	53.3	52.4
1996	52.0	52.8	53.4	52.8	53.4	52.9	53.9	53.2	53.1	53.7	54.5	54.4	53.3
1997	53.8	54.3	55.1	54.6	55.7	55.5	56.3	56.5	55.5	55.8	56.5	56.9	55.5
1998	55.4	56.4	56.5	57.0	57.6	57.3	58.1	58.0	57.6	57.9	58.6	58.9	57.4
1999	56.9	57.9	58.0	58.4	58.7	58.6	59.0	58.9	58.3	58.8	59.4	59.6	58.5
2000	58.2	59.4	59.9	59.4	59.7	60.7	60.0	59.1	60.0	60.0	60.9	61.5	59.9
2001	59.9	61.0	61.4	61.4	61.8	62.2	62.1	61.5	62.0	62.0	63.0	63.2	61.8
2002	61.5	62.6	62.9	63.0	63.4	63.5	63.5	62.5	63.7	63.8	65.0	64.4	63.3
2003	63.1	64.6	65.2	64.9	65.2	64.9	65.1	64.7	65.9	66.5	67.1	67.2	65.4
Leisure and hospitality													
1990	94.9	96.1	94.3	96.0	96.0	96.8	96.8	97.6	96.7	96.7	98.9	99.6	96.7
1991	99.6	99.0	98.3	97.5	98.1	99.3	100.5	101.9	101.0	99.4	99.6	100.8	99.6
1992	101.1	101.0	101.3	100.9	101.0	101.0	101.0	101.3	99.9	97.1	97.5	98.4	100.1
1993	96.0	96.4	96.2	95.7	96.2	96.4	94.4	94.5	93.8	93.6	93.1	93.3	94.9
1994	93.8	94.0	94.5	93.8	94.0	95.1	95.9	95.7	95.5	94.5	95.1	96.2	94.8
1995	95.1	95.6	95.7	95.1	94.3	95.9	95.5	95.8	95.4	94.0	94.7	95.6	95.2
1996	94.3	95.6	95.9	94.4	94.6	95.5	95.8	96.7	96.7	95.6	96.1	97.2	95.7
1997	95.4	96.0	96.2	95.4	95.1	95.5	95.1	95.8	95.3	94.8	95.4	96.3	95.5
1998	94.8	95.6	96.1	95.6	95.9	95.9	95.5	95.9	95.8	94.8	95.6	96.2	95.6
1999	94.4	95.2	96.4	96.0	96.0	96.9	96.4	96.6	96.3	96.5	97.3	98.1	96.3
2000	96.7	97.7	98.8	98.8	99.2	100.5	100.3	100.6	100.7	100.2	100.6	101.5	99.6
2001	99.5	100.5	101.0	100.4	100.5	101.1	100.4	101.1	100.4	95.3	94.9	95.3	99.2
2002	94.7	95.8	96.8	96.8	97.7	98.7	98.3	98.5	98.0	97.2	98.2	98.6	97.4
2003	97.8	98.5	99.5	98.5	98.9	99.5	99.6	100.2	99.9	100.0	100.1	101.4	99.5

Employment by Industry: Hawaii—*Continued*

(Numbers in thousands. Not seasonally adjusted.)

Industry	January	February	March	April	May	June	July	August	September	October	November	December	Annual Average
STATEWIDE—*Continued*													
Other services													
1990	19.2	19.3	19.7	19.6	19.6	20.2	20.0	20.0	19.7	20.0	19.9	20.0	19.7
1991	19.9	20.0	20.3	20.1	20.2	20.4	20.7	21.0	20.9	20.7	21.0	21.0	20.5
1992	20.8	21.1	21.1	21.2	21.2	21.5	21.8	21.8	21.6	21.4	21.3	21.5	21.3
1993	21.1	21.4	21.5	21.8	21.7	21.9	22.1	22.0	21.8	21.8	21.8	21.9	21.7
1994	21.4	21.7	21.7	21.7	21.8	22.1	22.0	21.8	22.0	21.6	21.9	21.8	21.7
1995	21.4	21.7	21.9	21.7	21.7	21.9	22.0	21.9	21.6	21.6	21.6	21.7	21.7
1996	21.5	21.8	21.8	21.6	21.7	22.0	22.0	22.1	22.0	21.8	21.7	21.9	21.8
1997	21.3	21.6	21.8	21.8	21.8	22.0	21.7	21.8	21.7	21.6	21.6	21.8	21.7
1998	21.1	21.6	21.6	21.8	21.8	22.0	21.8	21.9	21.8	21.8	21.8	21.7	21.7
1999	21.0	21.5	21.7	21.9	21.8	22.0	21.7	21.8	21.9	21.9	21.9	21.9	21.7
2000	21.3	21.9	22.0	22.0	22.0	22.2	22.0	22.1	22.0	22.1	22.5	22.5	22.0
2001	23.2	23.4	23.7	23.7	23.6	24.0	23.9	23.7	23.7	23.3	23.3	23.4	23.6
2002	23.2	23.3	23.6	23.6	23.7	23.8	23.8	23.8	23.9	23.8	23.9	24.0	23.7
2003	23.5	23.9	24.0	24.2	24.2	24.3	24.1	24.3	24.3	24.2	24.6	24.6	24.2
Government													
1990	101.2	104.9	107.9	108.8	110.5	107.6	102.4	102.1	97.4	105.1	109.2	110.3	105.6
1991	107.5	109.8	111.4	110.9	111.9	109.7	104.6	105.2	100.5	108.9	112.4	114.2	108.9
1992	110.3	113.0	114.7	114.6	114.8	112.7	106.2	106.3	101.8	110.1	113.5	115.4	111.1
1993	110.0	113.4	115.6	115.7	116.9	113.3	106.1	106.1	101.6	110.6	113.2	115.7	111.5
1994	109.4	114.1	116.0	116.0	114.4	114.9	107.2	107.0	102.6	111.1	113.9	115.9	111.8
1995	111.6	115.6	117.1	116.9	117.1	114.4	106.4	104.7	101.0	108.3	111.3	112.9	111.4
1996	107.5	113.3	114.7	114.0	115.3	112.7	106.6	106.5	101.5	108.9	112.2	113.7	110.5
1997	110.7	113.6	114.2	114.0	115.6	114.1	106.5	108.5	104.5	110.9	113.2	114.7	111.7
1998	111.1	113.5	115.1	114.8	115.7	113.7	107.1	108.5	107.5	111.2	113.2	114.9	112.1
1999	110.4	113.4	114.6	114.5	114.8	114.0	107.5	110.7	108.9	112.7	115.2	116.5	112.7
2000	110.6	115.1	117.4	117.1	119.6	117.7	109.7	109.1	110.3	114.1	116.6	118.1	114.6
2001	108.1	116.1	117.1	115.2	114.8	117.3	108.8	109.8	112.0	115.5	119.1	120.0	114.5
2002	114.6	119.1	120.6	114.5	121.5	124.0	112.0	112.3	114.3	118.8	120.9	122.5	117.9
2003	118.9	121.6	122.4	119.0	122.4	121.1	113.9	113.1	114.3	119.7	121.3	122.2	119.2
Federal government													
1990	33.9	33.8	33.9	34.5	35.4	35.0	34.4	34.1	33.7	33.7	33.8	33.6	34.1
1991	33.6	33.3	33.3	33.4	33.4	33.7	34.5	34.5	34.3	34.2	33.9	34.3	33.8
1992	33.8	33.6	33.5	33.6	33.4	33.6	33.2	33.1	32.9	32.9	32.8	32.9	33.2
1993	31.8	31.7	31.8	31.9	32.0	32.0	31.9	32.0	31.8	31.6	31.5	31.9	31.8
1994	31.5	31.3	31.2	31.5	31.6	31.6	31.3	31.2	31.2	30.9	30.9	31.1	31.2
1995	31.1	31.0	30.9	31.3	31.1	31.3	31.3	31.1	31.1	30.8	30.7	31.1	31.0
1996	31.3	31.3	31.2	31.0	30.7	30.7	31.7	31.5	31.5	30.7	30.8	31.1	31.1
1997	30.7	30.5	30.5	30.5	30.8	31.0	30.9	30.9	30.5	30.5	30.5	31.0	30.6
1998	30.4	30.3	30.3	30.3	30.3	30.6	30.4	30.4	30.4	30.2	30.3	30.8	30.3
1999	30.2	30.1	30.0	30.1	29.9	30.4	30.7	30.6	30.2	30.2	30.4	30.9	30.3
2000	30.3	30.3	31.0	31.2	32.6	31.8	31.8	30.8	30.2	30.2	30.5	30.9	30.9
2001	29.9	29.9	29.9	29.9	30.0	30.4	30.5	30.4	30.2	29.9	30.0	30.1	30.1
2002	30.0	30.1	30.2	30.1	30.1	30.5	30.8	30.7	30.7	31.3	31.7	32.0	30.7
2003	31.7	31.6	31.5	31.2	31.3	31.7	32.1	31.7	31.6	31.7	31.6	32.2	31.7
State government													
1990	53.5	57.2	60.0	60.3	61.0	58.4	52.3	52.2	49.5	57.2	61.0	62.3	57.0
1991	59.6	62.1	63.7	63.1	64.0	61.4	54.1	54.6	51.6	60.1	63.8	65.1	60.2
1992	62.0	64.7	66.4	66.2	66.6	64.1	56.7	56.6	53.3	61.9	65.4	67.1	62.5
1993	63.1	66.5	68.6	68.5	69.6	66.0	57.7	57.8	54.9	63.6	66.3	68.3	64.2
1994	62.5	67.5	69.4	69.1	67.4	67.9	59.2	59.1	55.9	64.9	67.6	69.3	64.9
1995	64.1	68.5	70.0	69.4	69.8	66.8	57.6	56.2	53.6	61.3	64.3	65.6	63.9
1996	60.0	65.7	67.1	66.7	68.3	65.6	57.0	57.1	53.5	61.8	64.9	66.1	62.8
1997	63.6	66.7	67.3	67.1	68.4	66.5	57.6	59.6	56.9	64.0	66.2	67.2	64.2
1998	64.3	66.8	68.3	68.0	68.9	66.4	58.2	59.8	60.1	64.5	66.4	67.6	64.9
1999	63.8	66.9	68.2	68.0	68.5	67.2	58.8	62.1	62.3	66.2	68.4	69.1	65.7
2000	64.0	68.4	70.1	69.5	70.6	69.2	59.8	60.5	63.7	67.4	69.5	70.6	66.9
2001	61.5	69.5	70.4	68.5	68.1	69.8	60.1	61.2	65.1	68.7	72.0	72.7	67.3
2002	67.6	72.0	73.4	67.4	74.5	76.3	63.4	63.8	66.7	70.7	72.3	73.6	70.1
2003	70.3	73.2	74.0	70.9	74.2	72.4	64.0	63.7	67.2	71.1	72.8	73.0	70.6
Local government													
1990	13.8	13.9	14.0	14.0	14.1	14.2	15.7	15.8	14.2	14.2	14.4	14.4	14.3
1991	14.3	14.4	14.4	14.4	14.5	14.6	16.0	16.1	14.6	14.6	14.7	14.8	14.7
1992	14.5	14.7	14.8	14.8	14.8	15.0	16.3	16.6	15.6	15.3	15.3	15.4	15.2
1993	15.1	15.2	15.2	15.3	15.3	15.3	16.5	16.3	14.9	15.4	15.4	15.5	15.4
1994	15.4	15.3	15.4	15.4	15.4	15.4	16.7	16.7	15.5	15.3	15.4	15.5	15.6
1995	16.4	16.1	16.2	16.2	16.2	16.3	17.5	17.4	16.3	16.2	16.3	16.2	16.4
1996	16.2	16.3	16.4	16.3	16.3	16.4	17.9	17.9	16.5	16.4	16.5	16.5	16.6
1997	16.4	16.4	16.4	16.4	16.4	16.6	18.0	18.0	17.1	16.4	16.5	16.5	16.7
1998	16.4	16.4	16.5	16.5	16.5	16.7	18.5	18.3	17.0	16.5	16.5	16.5	16.8
1999	16.4	16.4	16.4	16.4	16.4	16.4	18.0	18.0	16.4	16.3	16.4	16.5	16.6
2000	16.3	16.4	16.3	16.4	16.4	16.7	18.1	17.8	16.4	16.5	16.6	16.6	16.7
2001	16.7	16.7	16.8	16.8	16.7	17.1	18.2	18.2	16.7	16.9	17.1	17.2	17.1
2002	17.0	17.0	17.0	17.0	16.9	17.2	17.8	17.8	16.9	16.8	16.9	16.9	17.1
2003	16.9	16.8	16.9	16.9	16.9	17.0	17.8	17.7	15.5	16.9	16.9	17.0	16.9

Employment by Industry: Hawaii—*Continued*

(Numbers in thousands. Not seasonally adjusted.)

Industry	January	February	March	April	May	June	July	August	September	October	November	December	Annual Average
HONOLULU													
Total nonfarm													
1990	399.4	406.1	408.3	409.3	411.9	413.4	409.9	409.6	404.6	413.8	419.4	422.4	410.7
1991	414.6	416.6	417.3	413.7	414.6	416.4	413.4	413.0	408.4	414.8	419.9	424.4	415.5
1992	413.9	417.9	420.6	418.6	419.1	419.2	416.2	415.0	410.4	417.7	421.1	426.4	418.0
1993	413.1	417.1	419.3	418.2	419.4	418.8	411.0	408.8	405.3	412.2	414.3	420.0	414.8
1994	407.8	412.3	415.9	414.0	412.4	414.3	406.8	406.1	403.4	410.4	415.3	420.0	411.6
1995	406.8	411.7	414.7	410.6	412.3	412.0	404.0	402.1	399.6	403.8	408.8	412.7	408.3
1996	401.3	408.1	410.3	404.6	407.3	406.6	401.0	400.3	397.2	401.7	407.0	411.1	404.7
1997	401.2	404.8	407.2	404.4	406.7	407.2	398.2	400.3	396.8	401.1	405.4	409.6	403.6
1998	399.0	402.4	404.4	402.1	403.1	402.2	395.1	397.1	396.9	398.7	403.0	406.9	400.9
1999	392.3	396.7	399.8	400.8	402.2	403.9	396.2	399.8	400.3	403.8	408.5	413.7	401.5
2000	399.1	406.3	409.8	409.6	412.9	416.1	407.6	409.0	413.1	415.3	420.3	424.5	412.0
2001	405.9	415.2	417.9	413.0	414.3	419.1	409.3	410.6	412.3	408.3	410.7	413.4	412.5
2002	401.8	408.3	411.0	405.0	414.7	419.6	408.0	409.0	413.0	416.5	421.3	426.2	412.9
2003	414.3	418.8	421.0	416.5	421.3	421.0	413.2	414.0	416.5	422.3	426.8	430.3	419.7
Total private													
1990	315.1	318.3	317.9	318.0	319.1	323.3	325.1	325.2	324.4	326.4	328.2	330.3	322.6
1991	325.2	325.1	324.5	321.3	322.1	325.8	327.7	326.9	326.6	325.3	327.4	330.4	325.6
1992	323.3	324.8	326.1	324.3	324.8	326.5	329.9	328.8	328.3	328.0	328.5	332.3	327.1
1993	324.1	324.8	325.3	323.9	324.2	326.6	325.6	323.4	323.5	322.7	322.5	326.0	324.4
1994	319.6	319.7	321.8	319.9	319.8	321.3	321.3	320.9	321.6	320.8	323.4	326.3	321.4
1995	316.8	317.9	319.6	315.9	317.4	319.7	319.0	318.5	318.9	316.7	319.0	321.5	318.4
1996	315.0	316.4	317.4	312.7	314.4	315.7	315.7	315.3	316.2	314.1	316.5	319.6	315.8
1997	312.3	313.1	314.9	312.5	313.2	315.0	313.3	313.6	313.1	311.8	314.0	317.0	313.7
1998	309.5	310.7	311.3	309.8	309.7	310.7	310.0	310.6	310.6	309.5	311.9	314.4	310.7
1999	303.7	305.2	307.3	308.5	309.8	311.9	311.2	312.0	313.1	313.3	316.1	319.9	311.0
2000	310.8	313.8	315.9	315.7	317.3	321.8	320.7	322.5	324.9	324.0	326.8	329.6	320.3
2001	320.4	322.2	324.1	321.0	322.7	325.2	323.3	323.7	323.1	316.2	315.6	317.3	321.2
2002	310.7	313.0	314.5	314.6	317.4	319.9	319.9	320.3	322.2	321.6	324.8	328.2	318.9
2003	319.6	321.5	323.2	322.0	323.6	324.3	323.3	324.9	326.0	326.9	329.9	332.6	324.8
Goods-producing													
1990	40.9	41.3	41.6	40.8	41.1	41.9	41.9	41.9	41.9	42.7	42.6	42.6	41.7
1991	41.3	41.1	41.2	40.7	41.2	41.3	41.5	41.2	40.9	40.8	40.6	40.7	41.0
1992	39.3	39.0	39.2	39.2	39.2	39.5	40.1	39.7	39.0	39.2	39.5	39.7	39.4
1993	38.4	39.0	39.0	38.8	38.9	39.0	39.2	38.9	38.8	38.4	37.9	37.5	38.7
1994	36.0	35.9	36.5	36.7	36.6	36.6	36.7	36.9	36.7	36.1	35.8	35.3	36.3
1995	33.8	33.6	34.0	33.4	33.4	33.7	33.6	33.9	33.9	33.4	33.2	32.9	33.6
1996	31.6	31.1	31.1	30.8	31.2	31.1	31.2	31.3	31.2	31.1	30.4	31.1	31.1
1997	30.2	30.1	30.2	29.7	29.8	30.1	30.1	30.4	30.1	30.1	29.9	29.7	30.0
1998	28.7	29.0	29.1	28.7	28.9	29.0	29.3	29.3	29.2	29.3	29.0	29.3	29.1
1999	28.1	28.0	28.2	28.4	28.4	28.8	29.2	29.3	29.5	29.1	29.3	29.7	28.8
2000	28.7	28.8	29.4	29.5	29.9	30.3	30.6	31.0	31.2	31.0	30.8	31.0	30.1
2001	30.1	30.1	30.0	29.8	29.9	30.1	30.0	30.1	29.9	29.2	29.1	29.2	29.8
2002	28.7	28.6	29.1	28.9	29.2	30.0	30.1	30.3	30.0	29.9	30.1	30.2	29.6
2003	29.6	29.7	30.2	30.3	30.7	30.9	30.8	31.1	31.2	31.7	31.6	31.3	30.8
Construction and mining													
1990	25.4	25.9	26.3	25.7	26.2	26.7	26.7	26.9	27.0	27.7	27.7	27.9	26.6
1991	26.8	26.7	26.9	26.8	27.3	27.3	27.5	27.4	27.0	26.9	26.7	26.9	27.0
1992	25.7	25.4	25.7	25.6	25.6	25.8	26.4	26.2	25.7	25.9	26.2	26.2	25.9
1993	25.6	26.0	25.9	25.6	25.7	25.8	26.2	26.0	25.9	25.6	25.1	24.8	25.7
1994	23.5	23.4	23.8	23.9	23.8	23.8	24.0	24.2	24.0	23.5	23.2	22.6	23.6
1995	21.4	21.2	21.6	21.0	21.0	21.3	21.2	21.4	21.4	20.9	20.7	20.3	21.1
1996	19.2	18.8	18.8	18.8	18.9	19.0	18.9	18.9	18.9	19.0	18.2	18.9	18.9
1997	18.1	18.0	18.0	17.7	17.8	17.9	18.0	18.3	18.1	18.1	17.9	17.7	18.0
1998	16.8	17.0	17.2	16.9	17.0	17.1	17.3	17.4	17.3	17.3	17.0	17.2	17.1
1999	16.2	16.1	16.2	16.2	16.2	16.6	16.8	16.8	16.9	16.6	16.7	17.0	16.5
2000	16.4	16.5	16.8	17.0	17.3	17.6	17.9	18.1	18.2	18.0	17.9	18.1	17.4
2001	17.3	17.2	17.2	16.9	17.0	17.1	17.1	17.2	17.0	16.7	16.6	16.7	17.0
2002	16.5	16.5	16.9	17.1	17.4	18.1	18.4	18.7	18.5	18.5	18.7	18.7	17.8
2003	18.3	18.4	18.8	19.0	19.3	19.4	19.5	19.7	19.7	20.1	19.9	19.6	19.3
Manufacturing													
1990	15.5	15.4	15.3	15.1	14.9	15.2	15.2	15.0	14.9	15.0	14.9	14.7	15.0
1991	14.5	14.4	14.3	13.9	13.9	14.0	14.0	13.8	13.9	13.9	13.9	13.8	14.0
1992	13.6	13.6	13.5	13.6	13.6	13.7	13.7	13.5	13.3	13.3	13.3	13.3	13.5
1993	12.8	13.0	13.1	13.2	13.2	13.2	13.0	12.9	12.9	12.8	12.8	12.7	13.0
1994	12.5	12.5	12.7	12.8	12.8	12.8	12.7	12.7	12.7	12.6	12.6	12.7	12.7
1995	12.4	12.4	12.4	12.4	12.4	12.4	12.4	12.5	12.5	12.5	12.5	12.6	12.5
1996	12.4	12.3	12.3	12.0	12.3	12.1	12.3	12.4	12.3	12.1	12.2	12.2	12.2
1997	12.1	12.1	12.2	12.0	12.0	12.2	12.1	12.1	12.0	12.0	12.0	12.0	12.1
1998	11.9	12.0	11.9	11.8	11.9	11.9	12.0	11.9	11.9	12.0	12.0	12.1	11.9
1999	11.9	11.9	12.0	12.2	12.2	12.2	12.4	12.5	12.6	12.5	12.6	12.7	12.3
2000	12.3	12.3	12.6	12.5	12.6	12.7	12.7	12.9	13.0	13.0	12.9	12.9	12.7
2001	12.8	12.9	12.8	12.9	12.9	13.0	12.9	12.9	12.9	12.5	12.5	12.5	12.8
2002	12.2	12.1	12.2	11.8	11.8	11.9	11.7	11.6	11.5	11.4	11.4	11.5	11.8
2003	11.3	11.3	11.4	11.3	11.4	11.5	11.3	11.4	11.5	11.6	11.7	11.7	11.5

Employment by Industry: Hawaii—*Continued*

(Numbers in thousands. Not seasonally adjusted.)

Industry	January	February	March	April	May	June	July	August	September	October	November	December	Annual Average
HONOLULU—*Continued*													
Service-providing													
1990	358.5	364.8	366.7	368.5	370.8	371.5	368.0	367.7	362.7	371.1	376.8	379.8	368.9
1991	373.3	375.5	376.1	373.0	373.4	375.1	371.9	371.8	367.5	374.0	379.3	383.7	374.5
1992	374.6	378.9	381.4	379.4	379.9	379.7	376.1	375.3	371.4	378.5	381.6	386.7	378.6
1993	374.7	378.1	380.3	379.4	380.5	379.8	371.8	369.9	366.5	373.8	376.4	382.5	376.1
1994	371.7	376.3	379.2	377.3	375.8	377.7	370.1	369.2	366.7	374.3	379.5	384.7	375.2
1995	37.3	378.1	380.7	377.2	378.9	378.3	370.4	368.2	365.7	370.4	375.6	379.8	346.7
1996	369.7	377.0	379.2	373.8	376.1	375.5	369.8	369.0	366.0	370.6	376.6	380.0	373.6
1997	371.0	374.7	377.0	374.7	376.9	377.1	368.1	369.9	366.7	371.0	375.5	379.9	373.5
1998	370.3	373.4	375.3	373.4	374.2	373.2	365.8	367.8	367.7	369.4	374.0	377.6	371.8
1999	364.2	368.7	371.6	372.4	373.8	375.1	367.0	370.5	370.8	374.7	379.2	384.0	372.7
2000	370.4	377.5	380.4	380.1	383.0	385.8	377.0	378.0	381.9	384.3	389.5	393.5	381.8
2001	375.8	385.1	387.9	383.2	384.4	389.0	379.3	380.5	382.4	379.1	381.6	384.2	382.7
2002	373.1	379.7	381.9	376.1	385.5	389.6	377.9	378.7	383.0	386.6	391.2	396.0	383.3
2003	384.7	389.1	390.8	386.2	390.6	390.1	382.4	382.9	385.3	390.6	395.2	399.0	388.9
Trade, transportation, and utilities													
1990	85.0	85.3	85.3	85.3	85.7	86.7	87.7	87.1	86.9	87.5	88.8	90.1	86.7
1991	87.4	86.9	86.2	85.1	85.3	86.4	87.2	86.6	86.5	86.3	88.0	89.8	86.8
1992	86.8	86.7	86.9	86.1	86.4	87.0	87.4	87.0	87.2	87.3	87.8	89.5	87.2
1993	86.1	85.4	85.0	84.9	85.0	86.1	86.6	85.7	85.6	85.9	86.8	88.8	86.0
1994	85.1	84.3	84.4	84.1	84.2	84.3	84.8	84.7	84.7	84.5	86.4	88.3	85.0
1995	85.1	84.8	85.1	84.0	84.3	85.1	85.5	85.4	85.2	85.5	86.8	88.5	85.4
1996	85.0	84.4	84.3	83.3	83.7	84.0	83.8	83.4	83.2	82.7	84.2	85.9	84.0
1997	83.6	83.1	83.3	82.2	82.3	82.6	82.4	82.0	82.0	81.7	82.7	84.4	82.7
1998	81.9	81.0	80.4	79.8	79.6	79.9	79.1	79.0	79.3	79.3	80.4	81.6	80.1
1999	77.9	77.4	77.3	78.2	78.4	79.0	79.0	79.4	79.8	80.2	82.0	83.4	79.3
2000	80.4	80.3	80.1	79.6	79.8	80.9	81.1	81.5	81.7	81.7	84.0	84.8	81.3
2001	82.3	81.7	81.8	81.1	81.3	81.8	81.7	81.7	81.5	79.1	77.9	79.0	80.9
2002	75.9	75.3	75.1	75.3	75.8	76.3	76.6	76.8	76.7	76.9	78.2	79.6	76.5
2003	76.6	76.3	76.1	75.7	75.7	76.1	76.3	76.5	76.5	76.7	78.2	80.3	76.8
Wholesale trade													
1990	14.6	14.7	14.8	14.7	14.8	14.9	15.0	14.9	14.9	14.9	14.8	14.9	14.8
1991	14.5	14.6	14.5	14.4	14.4	14.5	14.6	14.6	14.5	14.6	14.6	14.6	14.5
1992	14.2	14.1	14.1	14.3	14.3	14.4	14.5	14.5	14.3	14.2	14.2	14.3	14.3
1993	14.3	14.2	14.2	14.2	14.1	14.2	14.2	14.1	14.0	13.8	14.0	14.1	14.1
1994	13.8	13.7	13.8	13.8	13.8	13.8	13.9	13.9	13.8	13.8	13.8	13.9	13.8
1995	13.6	13.7	13.7	13.6	13.7	13.7	13.5	13.4	13.4	13.4	13.4	13.5	13.6
1996	13.4	13.4	13.4	13.3	13.4	13.4	13.3	13.3	13.2	13.2	13.1	13.2	13.3
1997	13.0	13.0	13.0	13.1	12.9	13.0	13.1	13.1	13.3	13.1	13.1	13.4	13.1
1998	13.3	13.2	13.1	13.3	13.2	13.2	13.2	13.2	13.2	13.2	13.2	13.3	13.2
1999	12.9	12.8	12.9	13.0	13.0	13.0	13.0	13.1	13.1	13.1	13.1	13.3	13.0
2000	13.1	13.2	13.2	13.2	13.2	13.4	13.5	13.6	13.5	13.5	13.6	13.6	13.3
2001	13.5	13.6	13.6	13.5	13.6	13.7	13.6	13.7	13.6	13.4	13.4	13.5	13.6
2002	13.3	13.3	13.3	13.3	13.5	13.5	13.5	13.5	13.6	13.6	13.7	13.8	13.5
2003	13.5	13.6	13.6	13.7	13.7	13.7	13.8	13.8	13.8	13.9	13.9	14.0	13.8
Retail trade													
1990	49.6	49.4	49.5	49.3	49.6	50.1	50.5	50.1	49.8	50.3	51.4	52.4	50.1
1991	50.3	49.6	49.3	48.6	48.6	49.0	49.7	49.2	49.3	48.8	50.3	51.8	49.5
1992	50.1	49.6	49.7	48.9	49.1	49.4	49.7	49.3	49.6	49.9	50.5	51.9	49.8
1993	48.8	48.3	48.2	48.4	48.6	49.3	49.5	48.9	48.7	48.9	50.2	51.9	49.1
1994	49.0	48.2	48.2	47.8	47.8	48.0	48.7	48.7	48.7	49.0	50.6	52.1	48.9
1995	49.1	48.6	48.7	48.2	48.3	48.7	49.3	49.4	49.3	49.8	51.0	52.4	49.4
1996	50.0	49.0	49.0	48.5	48.5	48.7	48.7	48.3	48.2	47.4	48.8	50.2	48.8
1997	48.4	47.8	47.9	47.1	47.3	47.4	47.1	46.8	46.8	46.7	47.6	49.0	47.5
1998	46.7	46.1	45.6	44.9	44.7	44.9	44.4	44.4	44.8	44.9	46.0	47.3	45.4
1999	44.4	44.0	43.8	44.4	44.5	44.7	44.8	45.1	45.5	45.7	47.4	48.4	45.2
2000	46.1	45.7	45.4	45.0	45.2	45.7	46.0	46.2	46.3	46.3	48.2	48.8	46.2
2001	46.7	46.0	46.0	45.5	45.4	45.6	45.6	45.6	45.6	44.6	45.0	46.0	45.6
2002	43.7	43.0	42.7	42.7	42.9	43.2	43.6	43.6	43.5	43.6	44.6	46.0	43.6
2003	43.4	42.9	42.7	42.4	42.6	43.1	43.3	43.4	43.3	43.5	45.0	46.7	43.5
Transportation and utilities													
1990	20.8	21.2	21.0	21.3	21.3	21.7	22.2	22.1	22.2	22.3	22.6	22.8	21.7
1991	22.6	22.7	22.4	22.1	22.3	22.9	22.9	22.8	22.7	22.9	23.1	23.4	22.7
1992	22.5	23.0	23.1	22.9	23.0	23.2	23.2	23.2	23.3	23.2	23.1	23.2	23.1
1993	23.0	22.9	22.6	22.3	22.3	22.6	22.9	22.7	22.9	23.2	22.6	22.8	22.7
1994	22.2	22.3	22.3	22.5	22.6	22.5	22.2	22.1	22.2	21.7	22.0	22.3	22.2
1995	22.4	22.5	22.7	22.2	22.3	22.7	22.7	22.6	22.5	22.3	22.4	22.6	22.5
1996	22.1	22.0	21.9	21.5	21.8	21.9	21.8	21.8	21.8	22.1	22.3	22.5	22.0
1997	22.2	22.3	22.4	22.0	22.1	22.2	22.2	22.1	21.9	21.9	22.0	22.0	22.1
1998	21.9	21.7	21.7	21.6	21.7	21.8	21.5	21.4	21.3	21.2	21.2	21.0	21.5
1999	20.6	20.6	20.6	20.8	20.9	21.3	21.2	21.2	21.2	21.4	21.5	21.7	21.1
2000	21.2	21.4	21.5	21.4	21.4	21.8	21.6	21.7	21.9	21.9	22.2	22.4	21.7
2001	22.1	22.1	22.2	22.1	22.3	22.5	22.5	22.4	22.3	21.1	19.5	19.5	21.7
2002	18.9	19.0	19.1	19.3	19.4	19.6	19.5	19.7	19.6	19.7	19.9	19.8	19.5
2003	19.7	19.8	19.8	19.6	19.4	19.3	19.2	19.3	19.4	19.3	19.3	19.6	19.5

Employment by Industry: Hawaii—*Continued*

(Numbers in thousands. Not seasonally adjusted.)

Industry	January	February	March	April	May	June	July	August	September	October	November	December	Annual Average
HONOLULU—*Continued*													
Information													
1990	7.9	8.0	8.0	8.2	8.2	8.2	8.2	8.1	8.2	8.1	8.2	8.3	8.1
1991	7.9	8.0	8.0	8.1	8.1	8.1	8.1	8.0	8.1	8.1	8.1	8.2	8.0
1992	8.3	8.6	8.6	7.9	7.9	8.0	8.5	8.7	8.9	8.9	8.7	8.8	8.5
1993	8.6	8.2	8.4	8.2	8.2	8.0	8.2	8.2	8.1	7.9	7.9	8.1	8.2
1994	8.1	8.4	8.9	8.5	8.3	8.1	8.3	8.5	8.5	9.1	9.1	9.3	8.6
1995	8.3	8.4	8.8	8.2	8.3	8.5	8.6	8.6	8.6	8.4	8.5	8.6	8.5
1996	8.5	8.7	8.8	8.7	8.7	8.7	8.4	8.5	8.6	9.1	9.3	9.4	8.8
1997	8.6	8.5	8.5	8.8	8.8	9.2	9.2	9.3	9.0	9.0	9.0	9.0	8.9
1998	9.0	9.1	9.1	9.1	8.8	8.8	9.0	9.0	9.1	9.3	9.3	9.3	9.1
1999	8.9	8.9	8.9	9.0	9.0	9.3	9.3	9.3	9.4	9.4	9.4	9.7	9.2
2000	9.2	9.2	9.3	10.1	10.1	10.9	10.1	10.7	11.4	11.0	10.5	10.3	10.2
2001	10.2	10.2	10.4	9.8	10.2	10.0	9.8	10.0	9.7	9.7	9.8	9.7	10.0
2002	9.8	9.7	9.7	9.5	9.5	9.3	9.1	9.2	9.9	9.1	9.1	9.7	9.5
2003	8.9	9.0	9.0	8.8	9.4	9.2	8.3	8.2	8.2	8.2	8.2	8.2	8.6
Financial activities													
1990	24.3	24.5	24.5	24.5	24.7	24.8	25.3	25.3	25.2	25.1	25.1	25.1	24.8
1991	25.2	25.1	25.2	25.1	25.2	25.4	25.2	25.2	25.2	25.1	25.0	25.0	25.1
1992	24.6	24.7	24.8	24.7	24.7	24.7	25.0	25.0	25.1	25.3	25.3	25.6	25.0
1993	25.8	26.1	26.2	26.5	26.6	26.6	26.9	27.0	26.8	26.4	26.6	26.7	26.5
1994	26.9	27.0	26.9	26.1	26.0	26.1	26.0	26.0	26.1	25.8	25.8	25.8	26.2
1995	24.9	25.1	25.2	24.8	24.8	25.0	24.6	25.0	24.9	24.8	24.9	24.6	24.9
1996	24.6	24.8	24.9	24.3	24.4	24.5	24.3	24.4	24.4	24.1	24.3	24.4	24.5
1997	24.0	24.0	24.2	23.9	23.9	23.9	23.7	23.8	23.9	23.5	23.6	24.0	23.9
1998	23.8	23.8	23.8	23.8	23.7	23.9	24.1	24.2	24.1	24.0	24.1	24.3	24.0
1999	23.8	23.9	24.1	24.0	24.1	24.2	23.9	23.8	23.7	23.6	23.7	23.8	23.9
2000	23.3	23.4	23.4	23.3	23.4	23.6	23.6	23.7	23.6	23.6	23.5	23.7	23.5
2001	22.0	22.1	22.2	22.0	22.0	22.1	21.8	21.8	21.7	21.6	21.5	21.6	21.9
2002	21.1	21.2	21.4	21.3	21.5	21.6	21.6	21.5	21.5	21.6	21.7	21.8	21.5
2003	21.4	21.5	21.6	21.5	21.8	21.9	22.0	22.1	22.0	21.9	21.9	22.0	21.8
Professional and business services													
1990	41.4	42.2	42.8	42.5	42.4	43.2	43.1	43.5	43.2	43.5	43.2	43.6	42.8
1991	43.4	43.6	43.2	43.3	43.0	43.8	43.7	43.7	43.9	43.6	44.0	44.0	43.6
1992	43.0	43.4	43.6	43.9	43.4	43.7	44.4	44.5	44.0	44.2	43.9	44.6	43.9
1993	43.7	43.6	44.1	43.8	43.3	43.8	43.9	43.6	43.6	43.5	43.5	44.2	43.7
1994	44.0	43.9	44.2	44.7	44.3	44.7	44.7	44.9	44.7	44.9	45.2	45.7	44.7
1995	44.6	45.3	45.5	45.1	45.2	45.4	45.5	45.3	45.4	44.8	45.4	45.8	45.3
1996	45.6	46.1	46.5	45.8	45.7	46.1	46.6	46.6	46.9	46.1	46.4	46.9	46.3
1997	46.4	46.8	47.2	47.4	46.8	47.2	47.2	46.8	47.5	47.0	47.4	47.8	47.1
1998	46.7	46.9	47.5	47.2	46.8	47.1	46.9	47.2	46.7	46.0	46.5	46.8	46.9
1999	46.4	46.5	47.4	47.0	47.2	47.3	47.8	48.1	48.0	48.4	48.5	49.6	47.7
2000	48.1	48.6	49.3	49.5	49.5	50.1	50.3	50.5	51.0	51.2	51.6	52.1	50.1
2001	51.3	51.8	52.5	51.9	52.2	52.8	52.8	53.0	53.0	52.1	52.8	52.8	52.4
2002	52.4	53.5	53.7	54.0	54.5	55.3	55.7	56.3	56.4	56.4	56.5	58.1	55.2
2003	56.6	56.5	56.8	56.4	56.3	56.9	56.8	57.5	57.8	57.1	57.7	57.6	57.0
Educational and health services													
1990	38.1	38.6	38.8	38.7	39.0	39.3	39.4	39.2	39.5	40.2	40.6	40.7	39.3
1991	39.9	40.5	41.3	40.4	40.4	40.7	41.0	40.7	41.0	41.7	41.9	42.0	40.9
1992	41.1	41.7	42.2	42.0	42.3	42.3	42.4	41.8	42.6	42.5	42.7	43.1	42.2
1993	42.5	42.9	43.2	42.5	42.9	42.9	42.5	41.9	42.9	43.1	43.4	43.8	42.9
1994	42.5	42.9	43.2	42.8	43.0	43.1	42.6	41.7	42.5	42.8	43.1	43.1	42.8
1995	42.4	43.0	43.2	42.9	43.6	43.1	42.8	42.1	43.0	42.9	43.2	43.7	43.0
1996	42.7	43.4	43.7	43.0	43.4	43.0	43.3	42.5	43.0	43.4	44.2	43.9	43.3
1997	43.4	44.0	44.5	44.3	45.3	44.9	44.7	44.9	44.7	45.0	45.5	45.8	44.8
1998	45.1	45.6	45.8	46.0	46.4	46.3	46.4	46.4	46.5	46.8	47.3	47.5	46.3
1999	45.6	46.4	46.4	47.0	47.4	47.3	46.8	46.7	47.2	47.3	48.0	48.2	47.0
2000	46.8	47.9	48.4	47.9	48.1	48.2	47.7	47.5	48.3	48.2	48.9	49.4	48.1
2001	47.8	48.7	49.1	48.9	49.3	49.4	49.0	48.7	49.2	49.2	49.9	50.0	49.1
2002	48.6	49.7	49.8	50.0	50.4	50.2	50.1	49.6	50.6	50.9	52.0	51.2	50.3
2003	50.3	51.6	51.9	51.9	52.1	51.7	51.7	51.7	52.6	53.2	53.8	53.7	52.2
Leisure and hospitality													
1990	61.9	62.7	60.9	62.0	62.0	62.7	63.0	63.6	63.3	62.9	63.3	63.5	62.7
1991	63.8	63.6	63.0	62.3	62.5	63.4	64.1	64.4	64.1	62.8	62.8	63.7	63.3
1992	63.4	63.7	63.8	63.5	63.8	64.0	64.5	64.4	64.0	63.2	63.3	63.9	63.8
1993	61.9	62.3	62.0	61.6	61.8	62.5	60.4	60.3	60.0	59.8	58.8	59.2	60.9
1994	59.5	59.7	60.0	59.3	59.7	60.5	60.3	60.5	60.6	59.9	60.2	61.0	60.1
1995	60.4	60.0	60.0	59.7	60.0	61.0	60.4	60.3	60.3	59.2	59.3	59.7	60.0
1996	59.4	60.2	60.3	59.2	59.6	60.5	60.2	60.7	60.8	59.9	60.0	60.3	60.1
1997	59.1	59.3	59.5	58.8	58.9	59.6	58.8	58.9	58.8	58.3	58.7	59.1	59.0
1998	57.6	58.0	58.2	57.7	58.0	58.1	57.8	58.0	58.4	57.3	57.9	58.3	57.9
1999	56.3	57.0	57.7	57.3	57.7	58.3	57.8	58.0	58.1	57.7	57.7	58.2	57.7
2000	57.3	58.1	58.4	58.2	58.9	60.0	59.7	59.9	60.0	59.5	59.5	60.4	59.2
2001	58.2	58.9	59.3	58.6	58.9	59.8	59.1	59.5	59.2	56.7	56.0	56.3	58.4
2002	55.7	56.4	56.9	56.8	57.6	58.3	57.8	57.8	58.1	57.9	58.1	58.5	57.5
2003	57.5	57.9	58.5	58.1	58.3	58.3	58.2	58.6	58.5	58.9	59.0	60.0	58.5

Employment by Industry: Hawaii—*Continued*

(Numbers in thousands. Not seasonally adjusted.)

Industry	January	February	March	April	May	June	July	August	September	October	November	December	Annual Average
HONOLULU—*Continued*													
Other services													
1990	15.6	15.7	16.0	16.0	16.0	16.5	16.5	16.5	16.2	16.4	16.4	16.4	16.1
1991	16.3	16.3	16.4	16.3	16.4	16.7	16.9	17.1	16.9	16.9	17.0	17.0	16.6
1992	16.8	17.0	17.0	17.0	17.1	17.3	17.6	17.7	17.5	17.4	17.3	17.4	17.3
1993	17.1	17.3	17.4	17.6	17.5	17.7	17.9	17.8	17.7	17.7	17.6	17.7	17.6
1994	17.5	17.6	17.7	17.7	17.7	17.9	17.9	17.7	17.8	17.7	17.8	17.8	17.7
1995	17.3	17.7	17.8	17.8	17.8	17.9	18.0	17.9	17.6	17.7	17.7	17.7	17.7
1996	17.5	17.7	17.8	17.6	17.7	17.8	17.9	17.9	17.9	17.7	17.7	17.7	17.7
1997	17.0	17.3	17.5	17.4	17.4	17.4	17.4	17.5	17.3	17.4	17.4	17.3	17.4
1998	16.8	17.2	17.5	17.5	17.5	17.6	17.4	17.5	17.3	17.5	17.4	17.3	17.4
1999	16.7	17.1	17.3	17.6	17.6	17.7	17.4	17.4	17.5	17.6	17.5	17.3	17.4
2000	17.0	17.5	17.6	17.6	17.6	17.8	17.6	17.7	17.7	17.8	18.0	17.9	17.6
2001	18.5	18.7	18.8	18.9	18.9	19.2	19.1	18.9	18.9	18.6	18.6	18.7	18.8
2002	18.5	18.6	18.8	18.8	18.9	18.9	18.9	18.8	19.0	18.9	19.1	19.1	18.9
2003	18.7	19.0	19.1	19.3	19.3	19.3	19.2	19.2	19.2	19.2	19.5	19.5	19.2
Government													
1990	84.3	87.8	90.4	91.3	92.8	90.1	84.8	84.4	80.2	87.4	91.2	92.1	88.0
1991	89.4	91.5	92.8	92.4	92.5	90.6	85.7	86.1	81.8	89.5	92.5	94.0	89.9
1992	90.6	93.1	94.5	94.3	94.3	92.7	86.3	86.2	82.1	89.7	92.6	94.1	90.9
1993	89.0	92.3	94.0	94.3	95.2	92.2	85.4	85.4	81.8	89.5	91.8	94.0	90.4
1994	88.2	92.6	94.1	94.1	92.6	93.0	85.5	85.2	81.8	89.6	91.9	93.7	90.2
1995	90.0	93.8	95.1	94.7	94.9	92.3	85.0	83.6	80.7	87.1	89.8	91.2	89.9
1996	86.3	91.7	92.9	91.9	92.9	90.9	85.3	85.0	82.0	87.6	90.5	91.5	89.0
1997	88.9	91.7	92.3	91.9	93.5	92.2	84.9	86.7	83.7	89.3	91.4	92.6	89.9
1998	89.5	91.7	93.1	92.3	93.4	91.5	85.1	86.5	86.3	89.2	91.1	92.5	90.2
1999	88.6	91.5	92.5	92.3	92.4	92.0	85.0	87.8	87.1	90.5	92.4	93.8	90.5
2000	88.3	92.5	93.9	93.9	95.6	94.3	86.9	86.5	88.2	91.3	93.5	94.9	91.6
2001	85.5	93.0	93.8	92.0	91.6	93.9	86.0	86.9	89.2	92.1	95.1	96.1	91.3
2002	91.1	95.3	96.5	90.4	97.3	99.7	88.1	88.7	90.8	94.9	96.5	98.0	93.9
2003	94.7	97.3	97.8	94.5	97.7	96.7	89.9	89.1	90.5	95.4	96.9	97.7	94.9
Federal government													
1990	32.4	32.2	32.4	33.0	33.8	33.4	32.8	32.6	32.2	32.2	32.2	32.0	32.6
1991	32.1	31.8	31.7	31.8	31.8	32.1	32.8	32.9	32.7	32.6	32.3	32.6	32.2
1992	32.2	32.1	31.9	31.9	31.7	32.0	31.5	31.4	31.2	31.3	31.1	31.3	31.6
1993	30.1	30.0	30.0	30.3	30.3	30.3	30.1	30.3	30.1	29.9	29.8	30.2	30.1
1994	29.8	29.5	29.5	29.8	29.8	29.7	29.5	29.4	29.4	29.1	29.1	29.3	29.5
1995	29.3	29.2	29.2	29.5	29.3	29.5	29.4	29.2	29.3	28.9	28.9	29.3	29.3
1996	29.4	29.5	29.4	29.1	28.8	28.9	29.8	29.7	29.7	28.9	29.0	29.2	29.3
1997	28.8	28.7	28.7	28.7	29.0	29.2	29.2	29.1	28.7	28.7	28.7	29.2	28.9
1998	28.7	28.6	28.5	28.5	28.6	29.1	29.1	29.0	28.7	28.5	28.6	29.1	28.8
1999	28.5	28.3	28.3	28.4	28.1	28.7	29.0	28.8	28.5	28.4	28.6	29.0	28.6
2000	28.5	28.5	28.6	29.1	29.8	29.5	29.7	28.9	28.4	28.3	28.5	29.0	28.9
2001	28.0	28.0	28.0	28.0	28.1	28.5	28.6	28.4	28.2	28.0	28.0	28.2	28.2
2002	28.0	28.1	28.2	28.1	28.1	28.5	28.8	28.7	28.6	29.1	29.3	29.5	28.6
2003	29.2	29.1	28.9	28.7	28.7	29.1	29.6	29.2	29.1	29.2	29.1	29.7	29.1
State government													
1990	42.3	45.9	48.4	48.7	49.3	46.9	40.9	40.7	38.2	45.3	49.0	50.1	45.4
1991	47.5	49.8	51.2	50.6	50.7	48.4	41.6	41.9	39.1	46.9	50.1	51.3	47.4
1992	48.5	51.0	52.5	52.3	52.5	50.5	43.5	43.3	40.2	48.0	51.1	52.4	48.8
1993	48.7	52.0	53.6	53.6	54.5	51.5	43.8	43.7	41.4	49.3	51.6	53.4	49.8
1994	48.0	52.7	54.2	53.9	52.4	52.9	44.8	44.6	42.1	50.2	52.4	54.0	50.2
1995	49.3	53.4	54.7	54.0	54.4	51.7	43.6	42.5	40.3	47.0	49.7	50.8	49.3
1996	45.7	51.0	52.2	51.5	52.8	50.7	43.1	43.0	40.2	47.4	50.1	51.0	48.2
1997	48.8	51.7	52.3	51.9	53.2	51.6	43.3	45.1	43.0	49.1	51.2	51.9	49.4
1998	49.4	51.8	53.1	52.5	53.5	51.2	43.3	45.0	45.8	49.5	51.2	52.2	49.9
1999	48.8	51.9	52.9	52.6	53.0	52.0	43.6	46.6	47.4	51.0	52.5	53.4	50.5
2000	48.6	52.8	54.1	53.6	54.6	53.5	44.9	45.4	48.6	51.7	53.6	54.5	51.3
2001	46.1	53.6	54.3	52.5	52.1	53.9	44.9	46.1	49.6	52.6	55.4	56.1	51.4
2002	51.4	55.6	56.7	50.7	57.6	59.6	47.4	48.1	50.7	54.3	55.7	57.0	53.7
2003	54.0	56.8	57.4	54.3	57.5	56.1	48.4	48.1	51.4	54.8	56.4	56.5	54.3
Local government													
1990	9.6	9.7	9.6	9.6	9.7	9.8	11.1	11.1	9.8	9.9	10.0	10.0	9.9
1991	9.8	9.9	9.9	10.0	10.0	10.1	11.3	11.3	10.0	10.0	10.1	10.1	10.2
1992	9.9	10.0	10.1	10.1	10.1	10.2	11.3	11.5	10.7	10.4	10.4	10.4	10.4
1993	10.2	10.3	10.4	10.4	10.4	10.4	11.5	11.4	10.3	10.3	10.4	10.4	10.5
1994	10.4	10.4	10.4	10.4	10.4	10.4	11.2	11.2	10.3	10.3	10.4	10.4	10.5
1995	11.4	11.2	11.2	11.2	11.2	11.1	12.0	11.9	11.1	11.2	11.2	11.1	11.3
1996	11.2	11.2	11.3	11.3	11.3	11.3	12.4	12.3	11.3	11.3	11.4	11.3	11.5
1997	11.3	11.3	11.3	11.3	11.3	11.4	12.5	12.5	12.0	11.4	11.5	11.4	11.6
1998	11.4	11.3	11.5	11.3	11.3	11.2	12.7	12.5	11.8	11.2	11.3	11.2	11.6
1999	11.3	11.3	11.3	11.3	11.3	11.3	12.4	12.4	11.2	11.1	11.3	11.4	11.5
2000	11.2	11.2	11.2	11.2	11.2	11.3	12.3	12.2	11.2	11.3	11.4	11.4	11.4
2001	11.4	11.4	11.5	11.5	11.4	11.5	12.5	12.4	11.4	11.5	11.7	11.8	11.7
2002	11.7	11.6	11.6	11.6	11.6	11.6	11.9	11.9	11.5	11.5	11.5	11.5	11.6
2003	11.5	11.4	11.5	11.5	11.5	11.5	11.9	11.8	10.0	11.4	11.4	11.5	11.4

Average Weekly Hours by Industry: Hawaii

(Not seasonally adjusted.)

Industry	January	February	March	April	May	June	July	August	September	October	November	December	Annual Average
STATEWIDE													
Construction and mining													
2001	37.7	35.7	38.7	36.1	38.8	33.9	37.4	36.3	35.4	32.5	32.9	34.1	35.8
2002	36.1	36.7	38.9	39.2	36.4	35.1	38.6	37.1	39.1	38.2	34.3	39.1	37.4
2003	38.2	36.7	37.9	37.6	37.9	33.3	37.0	35.2	35.7	33.6	33.4	35.8	36.0
Manufacturing													
2001	34.5	36.0	35.9	37.0	36.1	35.6	36.6	36.4	35.3	35.7	36.5	36.8	36.0
2002	35.0	36.0	35.6	35.6	34.5	36.0	34.3	34.9	36.9	35.5	35.6	37.7	35.6
2003	34.8	36.4	35.8	35.4	36.8	36.9	36.2	37.9	37.4	38.9	40.8	38.9	37.2
Trade, transportation, and utilities													
2001	32.0	32.2	31.9	31.8	32.3	32.4	32.4	32.2	32.4	31.3	31.4	32.7	32.1
2002	31.9	32.5	32.2	32.0	32.4	32.9	32.5	32.1	32.6	31.4	31.4	32.5	32.2
2003	31.1	32.1	32.1	31.5	31.6	33.5	32.6	32.9	32.4	32.2	32.9	32.1	32.2
Wholesale trade													
2001	35.2	35.6	35.3	36.6	35.5	34.4	35.6	33.8	35.2	33.8	34.1	35.9	35.1
2002	35.9	35.7	36.2	36.2	35.4	36.4	36.5	35.1	36.6	34.8	34.7	37.2	35.9
2003	34.1	35.8	35.6	33.7	33.8	35.0	36.3	35.1	36.4	37.0	38.2	36.0	35.6
Retail trade													
2001	30.3	30.7	30.4	30.6	30.4	31.0	30.7	30.1	30.4	29.2	29.4	30.7	30.3
2002	30.1	30.5	30.4	30.1	30.6	31.4	31.2	31.0	31.4	30.1	29.8	31.0	30.6
2003	30.5	31.2	31.3	31.0	30.9	32.6	31.2	31.7	31.3	30.8	31.1	30.9	31.2
Information													
2001	39.9	38.8	39.1	39.0	37.2	38.7	38.0	36.7	36.0	35.1	35.3	34.9	37.4
2002	34.9	35.4	35.5	34.2	34.8	35.9	35.4	34.1	34.6	35.0	34.8	34.3	34.9
2003	33.7	32.4	32.8	32.2	32.9	34.1	33.0	33.0	33.7	33.8	34.9	33.8	33.4
Financial activities													
2001	35.7	36.1	36.9	35.8	33.6	33.9	34.9	33.0	34.7	33.6	34.2	36.3	34.9
2002	34.6	34.7	32.7	33.1	33.0	34.3	33.1	33.6	34.0	32.3	31.9	34.8	33.5
2003	33.9	35.2	34.5	33.2	33.2	35.0	33.4	36.0	33.5	34.3	35.3	33.1	34.2
HONOLULU													
Construction and mining													
2001	37.5	35.3	38.6	35.8	37.7	32.8	36.0	35.0	33.8	31.6	32.5	33.5	35.0
2002	37.3	39.6	42.3	41.2	38.1	36.3	39.5	36.8	38.2	37.9	34.1	39.3	38.3
2003	37.6	36.4	39.1	38.4	38.5	33.2	38.0	35.8	36.5	33.8	33.4	36.5	36.4
Manufacturing													
2001	35.3	37.0	36.5	37.4	36.9	34.9	37.0	36.0	34.9	35.4	36.3	36.6	36.2
2002	34.9	35.5	35.4	35.9	34.9	36.8	34.4	34.3	36.3	34.9	35.3	37.7	35.5
2003	34.7	36.5	35.7	35.1	37.1	36.7	35.5	36.3	36.0	36.0	38.6	36.7	36.3
Trade, transportation, and utilities													
2001	33.2	33.8	33.2	33.0	33.0	32.9	33.2	32.7	32.9	32.5	32.5	33.6	33.0
2002	32.8	33.2	33.5	33.1	33.4	34.3	33.9	33.8	34.5	33.1	33.1	34.5	33.6
2003	33.6	34.4	34.4	33.6	33.3	35.3	34.7	34.9	34.7	35.0	35.2	34.5	34.5
Wholesale trade													
2001	36.4	37.6	36.1	37.4	35.2	33.0	33.9	32.5	34.2	34.0	34.5	35.8	35.0
2002	36.6	36.5	37.5	36.9	36.5	37.4	36.9	35.4	37.1	35.0	35.0	38.2	36.6
2003	34.5	36.8	36.0	33.8	34.1	35.6	37.0	35.5	37.1	37.7	38.5	36.0	36.0
Retail trade													
2001	30.3	30.8	30.4	30.5	30.4	31.0	30.6	30.0	30.2	29.3	29.2	30.7	30.3
2002	29.6	29.9	30.3	30.2	30.6	31.5	31.0	31.0	31.5	29.9	29.3	30.9	30.5
2003	30.3	30.9	31.5	30.9	30.9	32.9	31.4	31.9	31.4	31.5	31.6	31.4	31.4
Information													
2001	40.7	40.1	40.0	39.8	36.8	37.7	37.3	35.9	36.0	35.2	35.4	34.8	37.6
2002	34.6	34.9	35.0	33.6	34.3	35.1	35.1	34.4	34.9	35.3	35.1	34.4	34.7
2003	33.9	32.4	32.6	32.0	32.7	34.0	33.0	32.9	33.9	34.6	35.2	34.4	33.5
Financial activities													
2001	37.5	37.4	37.8	39.8	37.0	37.4	39.3	37.2	38.8	37.1	37.5	39.5	38.0
2002	37.2	37.3	37.0	37.3	37.1	39.2	37.2	37.3	38.4	37.1	37.3	38.8	37.6
2003	36.6	39.0	38.1	36.9	37.3	39.6	37.4	37.9	36.4	36.9	38.6	35.9	37.5

Average Hourly Earnings by Industry: Hawaii

(Dollars, not seasonally adjusted.)

Industry	January	February	March	April	May	June	July	August	September	October	November	December	Annual Average
STATEWIDE													
Construction and mining													
2001	27.37	27.61	27.61	27.46	27.33	27.88	27.86	27.52	27.58	27.54	27.69	27.28	27.56
2002	26.83	26.48	27.17	26.78	26.75	27.07	27.61	27.66	28.60	28.30	27.47	28.17	27.45
2003	28.23	28.20	28.41	27.21	27.56	27.91	28.73	28.81	28.47	28.85	29.05	29.01	28.36
Manufacturing													
2001	12.83	12.78	12.87	12.96	12.98	13.17	13.49	13.19	13.23	13.44	13.65	13.61	13.18
2002	13.61	13.53	13.20	13.33	13.13	12.90	13.20	12.87	12.98	12.79	12.63	12.68	13.07
2003	12.50	12.38	12.49	12.63	13.36	13.09	13.37	13.05	13.15	12.84	12.73	13.13	12.90
Trade, transportation, and utilities													
2001	12.78	12.73	12.73	12.71	12.36	12.37	12.45	12.35	12.43	12.56	12.69	12.72	12.57
2002	12.94	12.83	12.83	12.74	12.79	12.98	13.01	13.03	13.06	13.15	13.35	13.35	13.01
2003	13.45	13.59	13.45	13.37	13.20	13.32	13.51	13.66	13.84	13.88	14.02	13.85	13.60
Wholesale trade													
2001	13.21	13.17	13.14	13.46	13.27	13.52	13.52	13.39	13.72	13.71	14.06	13.76	13.49
2002	13.73	13.79	13.78	13.12	13.24	13.51	13.51	13.60	13.78	13.65	14.43	14.43	13.72
2003	14.68	14.86	15.10	15.13	14.84	15.16	15.53	15.87	15.93	15.77	16.43	16.54	15.50
Retail trade													
2001	10.91	10.74	10.93	10.91	10.74	10.82	10.87	10.78	10.94	10.93	10.94	10.77	10.86
2002	11.15	11.02	10.97	10.95	10.92	10.97	10.85	10.86	10.86	10.92	11.00	11.03	10.96
2003	11.09	11.37	11.20	11.07	11.03	11.03	11.06	10.91	11.18	11.26	11.09	11.06	11.11
Information													
2001	18.99	19.05	19.28	18.90	18.54	18.23	18.16	18.33	18.94	19.07	18.77	19.11	18.78
2002	19.21	19.56	18.53	19.44	19.23	18.80	18.83	19.04	19.76	19.49	19.87	20.85	19.37
2003	20.39	20.04	19.86	19.98	19.87	19.88	19.41	19.47	19.62	19.97	19.80	19.98	19.85
Financial activities													
2001	14.88	14.81	14.86	15.41	15.11	15.00	15.47	15.19	15.19	15.38	15.33	16.02	15.22
2002	15.57	15.54	16.01	15.73	16.17	15.95	15.72	15.75	16.07	15.49	15.70	16.11	15.82
2003	15.95	16.47	16.54	16.30	16.49	16.42	15.81	16.10	16.20	16.01	16.00	15.87	16.18
HONOLULU													
Construction and mining													
2001	27.76	27.80	27.65	27.54	27.54	28.25	28.00	27.90	28.04	27.74	27.35	28.09	27.80
2002	28.18	27.97	28.70	27.97	28.01	28.14	28.80	28.43	28.99	28.89	27.73	28.51	28.38
2003	28.69	28.99	29.46	27.77	28.40	29.01	29.52	29.59	29.32	29.73	29.99	30.11	29.20
Manufacturing													
2001	12.72	12.68	12.80	12.87	12.79	12.99	12.94	12.95	12.99	13.32	13.41	13.49	12.99
2002	13.24	13.31	12.84	12.86	12.70	12.49	12.64	12.60	12.65	12.56	12.42	12.49	12.74
2003	12.47	12.42	12.59	12.47	13.54	13.12	13.41	13.23	13.25	13.65	13.51	13.72	13.13
Trade, transportation, and utilities													
2001	14.84	14.95	14.69	14.78	14.54	14.71	14.85	14.84	14.89	15.08	15.12	15.20	14.87
2002	15.51	15.53	15.66	15.42	15.49	15.72	15.79	16.01	15.94	16.12	16.46	16.02	15.81
2003	16.65	16.84	16.74	16.61	16.41	16.39	16.71	16.93	17.08	17.03	17.04	16.81	16.77
Wholesale trade													
2001	13.90	13.65	13.56	13.78	13.81	14.47	14.26	14.02	14.46	14.40	14.84	14.43	14.12
2002	14.24	14.42	14.35	13.50	13.64	13.94	13.90	14.16	14.29	14.07	14.86	14.81	14.19
2003	15.17	15.82	16.12	16.08	15.78	16.09	16.42	16.81	16.76	16.63	17.36	17.20	16.37
Retail trade													
2001	10.79	10.95	10.90	11.23	10.99	11.03	11.22	11.09	11.25	11.24	11.25	11.13	11.09
2002	11.49	11.24	11.23	11.31	11.15	11.17	11.06	11.12	11.16	11.16	11.22	11.11	11.20
2003	11.42	11.73	11.51	11.33	11.23	11.30	11.32	11.21	11.56	11.56	11.33	11.36	11.40
Information													
2001	19.25	19.37	19.64	19.19	18.49	18.16	18.05	18.19	18.92	19.04	18.73	19.17	18.87
2002	19.22	19.59	18.38	19.92	19.66	19.31	19.30	19.53	20.27	19.95	20.14	21.12	19.69
2003	20.16	20.39	20.17	20.32	20.17	20.17	19.53	19.73	19.92	20.17	19.97	20.12	20.07
Financial activities													
2001	15.40	15.45	15.21	15.49	15.38	15.25	15.63	15.38	15.47	15.54	15.39	16.17	15.48
2002	15.65	15.85	16.21	15.95	16.19	16.09	15.76	15.88	16.26	15.78	16.08	16.49	16.02
2003	16.69	17.04	17.12	16.75	16.97	17.06	16.38	16.60	16.61	16.15	16.18	16.16	16.64

Average Weekly Earnings by Industry: Hawaii

(Dollars, not seasonally adjusted.)

Industry	January	February	March	April	May	June	July	August	September	October	November	December	Annual Average
STATEWIDE													
Construction and mining													
2001	1031.85	985.68	1068.51	991.31	1060.40	945.13	1041.96	998.98	976.33	895.05	911.00	930.25	986.65
2002	968.56	971.82	1056.91	1049.78	973.70	950.16	1065.75	1026.19	1118.26	1081.06	942.22	1101.45	1026.63
2003	1078.39	1034.94	1076.74	1023.10	1044.52	929.40	1063.01	1014.11	1016.38	969.36	970.27	1038.56	1020.96
Manufacturing													
2001	442.64	460.08	462.03	479.52	468.58	468.85	493.73	480.12	467.02	479.81	498.23	500.85	474.48
2002	476.35	487.08	469.92	474.55	452.99	464.40	452.76	449.16	478.96	454.05	449.63	478.04	465.29
2003	435.00	450.63	447.14	447.10	491.65	483.02	483.99	494.60	491.81	499.48	519.38	510.76	479.88
Trade, transportation, and utilities													
2001	408.96	409.91	406.09	404.18	399.23	400.79	403.38	397.67	402.73	393.13	398.47	415.94	403.50
2002	412.79	416.98	413.13	407.68	414.40	427.04	422.83	418.26	425.76	412.91	419.19	433.88	418.92
2003	418.30	436.24	431.75	421.16	417.12	446.22	440.43	449.41	448.42	446.94	461.26	444.59	437.92
Wholesale trade													
2001	464.99	468.85	463.84	492.64	471.09	465.09	481.31	452.58	482.94	463.40	479.45	493.98	473.50
2002	492.91	492.30	498.84	474.94	468.70	491.76	493.12	477.36	504.35	475.02	500.72	536.80	492.55
2003	500.59	531.99	537.56	509.88	501.59	530.60	563.74	557.04	579.85	583.49	627.63	595.44	551.80
Retail trade													
2001	330.57	329.72	332.27	333.85	326.50	335.42	333.71	324.48	332.58	319.16	321.64	330.64	329.06
2002	335.62	336.11	333.49	329.60	334.15	344.46	338.52	336.66	341.00	328.69	327.80	341.93	335.38
2003	338.25	354.74	350.56	343.17	340.83	359.58	345.07	345.85	349.93	346.81	344.90	341.75	346.63
Information													
2001	757.70	739.14	753.85	737.10	689.69	705.50	690.08	672.71	681.84	669.36	662.58	666.94	702.37
2002	670.43	692.42	657.82	664.85	669.20	674.92	666.58	649.26	683.70	682.15	691.48	715.16	676.01
2003	687.14	649.30	651.41	643.36	653.72	677.91	640.53	642.51	661.19	674.99	691.02	675.32	662.99
Financial activities													
2001	531.22	534.64	548.33	551.68	507.70	508.50	539.90	501.27	527.09	516.77	524.29	581.53	531.18
2002	538.72	539.24	523.53	520.66	533.61	547.09	520.33	529.20	546.38	500.33	500.83	560.63	529.97
2003	540.71	579.74	570.63	541.16	547.47	574.70	528.05	579.60	542.70	549.14	564.80	525.30	553.36
HONOLULU													
Construction and mining													
2001	1041.00	981.34	1067.29	985.93	1038.26	926.60	1008.00	976.50	947.75	876.58	888.88	941.02	973.00
2002	1051.11	1107.61	1214.01	1152.36	1067.18	1021.48	1137.60	1046.22	1107.42	1094.93	945.59	1120.44	1086.95
2003	1078.74	1055.24	1151.89	1066.37	1093.40	963.13	1121.76	1059.32	1070.18	1004.87	1001.67	1099.02	1062.88
Manufacturing													
2001	449.02	469.16	467.20	481.34	471.95	453.35	478.78	466.20	453.35	471.53	486.78	493.73	470.24
2002	462.08	472.51	454.54	461.67	443.23	459.63	434.82	432.18	459.20	438.34	438.43	470.87	452.27
2003	432.71	453.33	449.46	437.70	502.33	481.50	476.06	480.25	477.00	491.40	521.49	503.52	476.62
Trade, transportation, and utilities													
2001	492.69	505.31	487.71	487.74	479.82	483.96	493.02	485.27	489.88	490.10	491.40	510.72	490.71
2002	508.73	515.60	524.61	510.40	517.37	539.20	535.28	541.14	549.93	533.57	544.83	552.69	531.22
2003	559.44	579.30	575.86	558.10	546.45	578.57	579.84	590.86	592.68	596.05	599.81	579.95	578.57
Wholesale trade													
2001	505.96	513.24	489.52	515.37	486.11	477.51	483.41	455.65	494.53	489.60	511.98	516.59	494.20
2002	521.18	526.33	538.13	498.15	497.86	521.36	512.91	501.26	530.16	492.45	520.10	565.74	519.35
2003	523.37	582.18	580.32	543.50	538.10	572.80	607.54	596.76	621.80	626.95	668.36	619.20	589.32
Retail trade													
2001	326.94	337.26	331.36	342.52	334.10	341.93	343.33	332.70	339.75	329.33	328.50	341.69	336.03
2002	340.10	336.08	340.27	341.56	341.19	351.86	342.86	344.72	351.54	333.68	328.75	343.30	341.60
2003	346.03	362.46	362.57	350.10	347.01	371.77	355.45	357.60	362.98	364.14	358.03	356.70	357.96
Information													
2001	783.48	776.74	785.60	763.76	680.43	684.63	673.27	653.02	681.12	670.21	663.04	667.12	709.51
2002	665.01	683.69	643.30	669.31	674.34	677.78	677.43	671.83	707.42	704.24	706.91	726.53	683.24
2003	683.42	660.64	657.54	650.24	659.56	685.78	644.49	649.12	675.29	697.88	702.94	692.13	672.35
Financial activities													
2001	577.50	577.83	574.94	616.50	569.06	570.35	614.26	572.14	600.24	576.53	577.13	638.72	588.24
2002	582.18	591.21	599.77	594.94	600.65	630.73	586.27	592.32	624.38	585.44	599.78	639.81	602.35
2003	610.85	664.56	652.27	618.08	632.98	675.58	612.61	629.14	604.60	595.94	624.55	580.14	624.00

IDAHO AT A GLANCE

(Population and total nonfarm employment numbers in thousands)

Population, Census 2000:	1,294.0
Total nonfarm employment, 2003:	571.8
Change in total nonfarm employment	
(Number)	
1990–2003:	186.8
1990–2001:	182.7
2001–2003:	4.1
(Compound annual rate of change)	
1990–2003:	3.1%
1990–2001:	3.6%
2001–2003:	0.4%
Unemployment rate	
1990:	5.5%
2001:	4.9%
2003:	5.3%

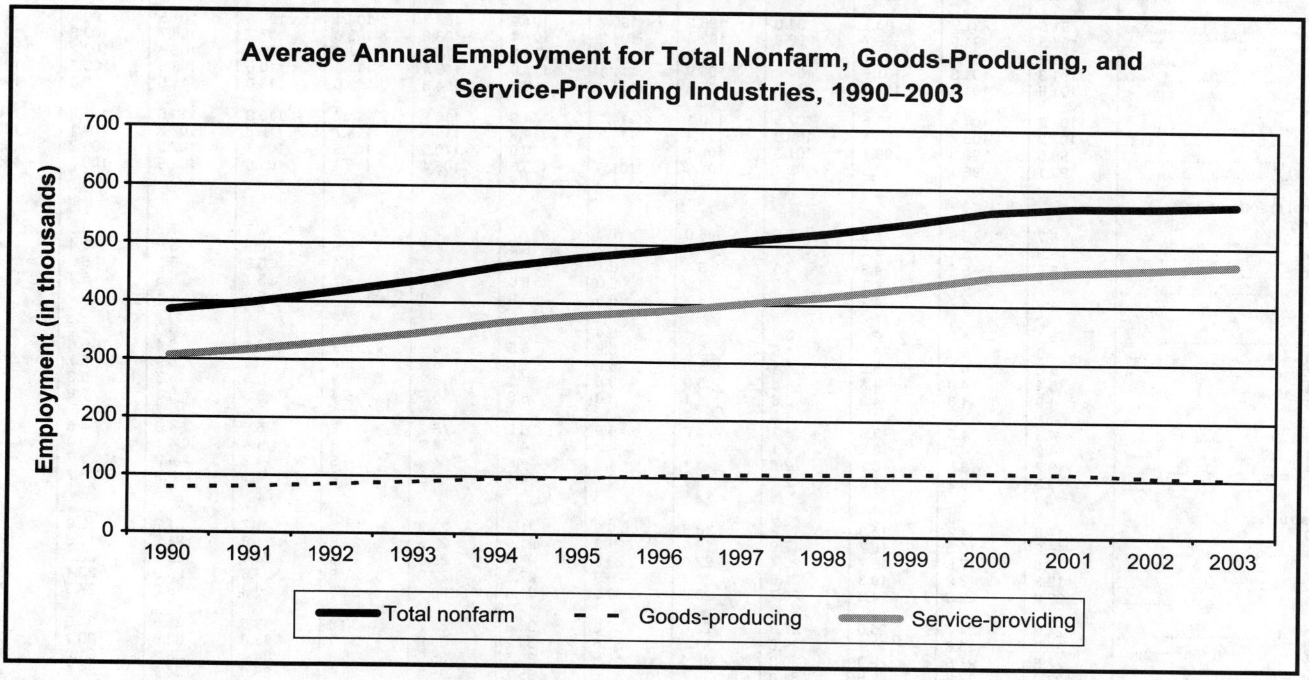

Nonfarm payroll employment grew steadily throughout the 1990s before slowing sharply in 2001, as growth in the service sector was offset by declines in the good-producing sector. From 1990 to 2003, employment in professional and business services more than doubled. Educational and health services also experienced rapid growth during this period, adding over 30,000 jobs. As a result, these service-producing industries became two of Idaho's leading employers.

Employment by Industry: Idaho

(Numbers in thousands. Not seasonally adjusted.)

Industry	January	February	March	April	May	June	July	August	September	October	November	December	Annual Average
STATEWIDE													
Total nonfarm													
1990	364.1	367.8	373.0	378.7	383.8	390.7	386.5	391.9	399.2	397.8	393.9	392.0	385.0
1991	379.4	382.5	385.6	390.0	396.0	403.4	400.7	404.3	411.0	409.9	408.0	405.9	398.1
1992	396.1	398.9	403.2	408.5	415.1	422.9	421.2	422.0	427.3	429.2	426.8	425.7	416.4
1993	413.5	417.3	420.0	427.0	433.9	440.8	441.2	443.9	451.2	451.5	448.6	449.1	436.5
1994	436.4	439.9	446.8	454.2	460.6	469.2	465.2	466.8	476.4	473.8	470.6	470.6	460.9
1995	456.9	461.3	467.6	469.6	474.8	484.1	478.8	482.3	490.5	489.7	486.9	485.6	477.3
1996	468.2	470.0	477.2	483.1	489.5	498.6	495.8	499.8	504.0	503.2	501.9	500.4	491.0
1997	485.8	488.2	493.7	499.5	506.2	514.4	511.5	515.5	521.8	518.7	517.0	517.3	507.5
1998	497.9	502.1	506.8	513.4	520.2	526.5	525.7	528.9	534.5	533.3	532.2	531.7	521.1
1999	513.7	517.3	523.5	530.3	536.4	547.0	545.4	547.1	553.1	552.1	551.1	549.7	538.9
2000	533.0	537.1	543.9	552.9	562.0	569.2	564.6	569.0	574.0	570.2	570.7	568.5	559.6
2001	549.3	553.7	561.0	565.2	571.1	578.9	572.3	576.3	578.0	572.5	568.7	565.6	567.7
2002	545.8	548.2	553.8	562.1	569.4	578.4	574.2	575.9	579.7	579.1	577.2	575.0	568.2
2003	555.3	556.5	561.2	566.1	572.3	581.2	575.0	578.4	582.6	579.7	576.8	576.3	571.8
Total private													
1990	286.5	288.2	291.9	295.8	300.2	308.3	310.3	315.2	315.9	313.0	309.8	308.5	303.6
1991	298.4	298.7	300.7	304.5	309.9	317.9	321.4	324.7	325.6	322.6	320.5	319.7	313.7
1992	310.8	312.1	315.3	319.5	325.9	333.3	337.1	338.4	338.7	337.5	335.6	335.6	328.3
1993	326.2	327.0	329.2	335.7	341.5	350.1	355.7	358.2	359.3	357.8	355.6	356.7	346.1
1994	347.1	347.7	353.6	359.8	365.4	375.2	379.5	381.3	381.6	376.2	374.2	374.3	368.0
1995	364.1	365.3	370.5	372.1	377.1	387.6	388.6	392.6	393.7	390.8	389.0	388.0	381.6
1996	374.2	373.8	379.6	384.9	391.2	400.8	404.4	407.8	405.6	402.9	401.6	401.3	394.0
1997	388.4	389.0	393.6	398.8	405.1	414.5	417.0	420.9	420.3	414.5	413.1	414.5	407.5
1998	397.0	398.6	402.1	411.1	417.5	424.7	428.0	431.5	430.9	427.4	426.1	426.6	418.5
1999	412.1	412.3	417.6	424.0	429.3	440.5	444.3	446.4	446.7	444.2	443.1	443.3	433.7
2000	428.0	429.3	435.2	441.8	447.0	458.3	460.5	465.8	465.8	459.4	460.1	458.6	450.8
2001	443.7	444.0	450.2	453.9	458.6	468.2	467.1	471.8	466.8	458.6	455.3	453.0	457.6
2002	436.4	436.2	440.6	448.8	454.9	464.1	467.4	470.3	467.7	464.6	462.5	461.1	456.2
2003	444.7	443.9	447.1	451.7	456.6	465.9	467.3	471.9	469.6	464.8	462.0	461.9	459.0
Goods-producing													
1990	71.6	72.5	73.2	74.4	77.4	80.7	81.6	83.1	84.1	83.4	81.1	78.4	78.5
1991	74.9	75.1	74.3	75.6	78.9	82.8	84.0	86.0	86.4	85.7	83.9	81.4	80.8
1992	78.5	78.6	79.0	81.3	84.6	87.6	89.8	90.1	89.9	89.9	88.2	86.5	85.3
1993	82.9	82.8	83.0	85.2	88.6	92.5	94.9	95.6	95.7	96.3	93.9	92.1	90.3
1994	88.0	87.6	89.9	92.6	95.5	99.8	101.8	102.2	103.0	100.6	98.2	96.5	96.3
1995	91.5	91.7	93.2	94.0	96.2	100.7	101.9	103.3	104.1	103.5	101.5	99.5	98.4
1996	95.3	94.9	96.7	98.8	102.3	105.9	107.4	108.8	108.0	107.7	106.7	103.8	103.0
1997	99.6	99.7	101.1	102.2	104.9	108.6	110.2	111.5	111.2	109.8	108.6	107.2	106.2
1998	101.3	101.3	101.9	104.4	106.9	110.1	111.6	112.4	111.2	110.0	108.5	106.7	107.2
1999	101.8	101.5	102.6	105.3	107.8	111.4	113.5	114.3	113.6	113.0	111.5	109.3	108.8
2000	104.6	104.4	105.6	107.5	110.1	114.1	114.9	115.9	115.4	113.9	113.5	111.2	110.9
2001	107.2	106.7	108.1	108.8	111.4	114.8	114.9	115.8	113.7	110.8	107.3	104.1	110.3
2002	99.5	98.3	99.1	101.3	105.1	108.3	110.0	110.5	109.5	108.7	107.3	105.2	105.2
2003	99.1	98.1	97.5	99.1	101.3	104.5	105.6	106.4	105.9	104.6	102.6	100.6	102.1
Natural resources and mining													
1990	6.7	6.6	5.8	5.2	6.0	7.0	7.7	7.9	7.8	7.7	7.2	6.5	6.8
1991	5.9	5.4	4.4	4.1	4.7	5.7	6.4	6.7	6.6	6.5	5.9	5.4	5.6
1992	5.5	5.2	4.3	4.5	5.4	6.1	6.4	6.2	6.1	5.9	5.5	5.0	5.5
1993	4.7	4.5	4.1	3.6	4.0	5.0	5.6	5.8	5.7	5.7	5.5	5.1	4.9
1994	4.8	4.7	4.2	4.0	4.7	5.5	5.9	5.9	6.0	5.8	5.5	5.3	5.2
1995	5.1	4.9	4.5	3.9	4.4	5.4	5.9	6.2	6.2	6.1	6.0	5.8	5.4
1996	5.3	5.3	4.9	4.5	5.0	5.8	6.5	6.8	6.7	6.6	6.4	6.0	5.8
1997	5.6	5.7	5.0	4.4	5.0	6.0	6.4	6.5	6.4	6.2	5.9	5.7	5.7
1998	5.1	4.9	4.3	4.3	5.0	5.6	6.1	6.2	5.9	5.8	5.5	5.3	5.3
1999	4.9	4.8	4.2	3.8	4.1	5.0	5.3	5.5	5.4	5.6	5.3	4.9	4.9
2000	4.6	4.5	3.9	3.7	4.2	4.9	5.2	5.2	5.2	5.0	4.8	4.6	4.7
2001	4.2	4.1	3.6	3.1	3.4	4.2	4.6	4.7	4.6	4.4	4.1	3.9	4.0
2002	3.7	3.6	3.2	2.7	3.1	4.0	4.3	4.3	4.3	4.2	4.0	3.7	3.7
2003	3.5	3.2	2.9	2.7	3.1	3.7	4.1	4.2	4.2	4.1	3.9	3.7	3.6
Construction													
1990	14.6	14.2	15.3	17.2	18.8	20.3	21.4	21.9	21.6	21.7	21.7	19.9	19.1
1991	16.2	16.5	16.7	17.9	19.4	21.3	21.5	22.5	22.5	21.8	21.2	19.6	19.8
1992	17.5	17.5	18.7	20.4	22.0	23.3	24.6	25.0	24.6	24.4	23.2	22.2	22.0
1993	19.3	18.9	19.3	21.6	24.1	25.9	27.3	27.9	27.8	27.6	26.9	25.4	24.3
1994	22.9	22.5	24.3	26.7	28.2	30.5	31.8	32.1	32.0	30.3	29.2	27.5	28.2
1995	24.3	24.7	26.0	27.8	29.6	32.2	32.9	33.7	33.8	32.6	31.6	30.0	29.9
1996	26.0	25.6	27.1	29.3	31.7	33.6	34.2	34.9	34.0	33.8	32.9	30.7	31.2
1997	27.5	27.5	29.0	30.3	32.4	34.2	35.5	35.9	35.3	34.4	33.3	31.9	32.3
1998	27.6	27.5	28.5	31.0	32.7	34.5	35.7	36.0	35.6	35.0	34.1	32.9	32.6
1999	29.6	29.0	30.4	33.0	34.8	37.0	38.1	38.7	38.4	38.1	37.1	35.5	35.0
2000	31.4	31.2	32.6	34.9	36.5	38.7	39.3	40.1	39.7	38.5	37.6	36.0	36.4
2001	33.2	32.8	34.6	36.8	38.9	41.0	41.5	42.3	41.1	39.6	37.8	35.2	37.9
2002	31.5	31.0	31.9	34.4	37.3	38.6	40.0	40.1	39.4	39.0	38.0	36.8	36.5
2003	32.3	32.0	32.7	34.6	36.7	38.5	39.4	40.1	39.6	38.8	37.7	36.1	36.5

Employment by Industry: Idaho—*Continued*

(Numbers in thousands. Not seasonally adjusted.)

Industry	January	February	March	April	May	June	July	August	September	October	November	December	Annual Average
STATEWIDE—*Continued*													
Manufacturing													
1990	50.3	51.7	52.1	52.0	52.6	53.4	52.5	53.3	54.7	54.0	52.2	52.0	52.6
1991	52.8	53.2	53.2	53.6	54.8	55.8	56.1	56.8	57.3	57.4	56.8	56.4	55.4
1992	55.5	55.9	56.0	56.4	57.2	58.2	58.8	58.9	59.2	59.6	59.5	59.3	57.9
1993	58.9	59.4	59.6	60.0	60.5	61.6	62.0	61.9	62.2	63.0	61.5	61.6	61.0
1994	60.3	60.4	61.4	61.9	62.6	63.8	64.1	64.2	65.0	64.5	63.5	63.7	63.0
1995	62.1	62.1	62.7	62.3	62.2	63.1	63.1	63.4	64.1	64.8	63.9	63.7	63.1
1996	64.0	64.0	64.7	65.0	65.6	66.5	66.7	67.1	67.3	67.3	67.4	67.1	66.1
1997	66.5	66.5	67.1	67.5	67.5	68.4	68.3	69.1	69.5	69.2	69.4	69.6	68.2
1998	68.6	68.9	69.1	69.1	69.2	70.0	69.8	70.2	69.7	69.2	68.9	68.5	69.3
1999	67.3	67.7	68.0	68.5	68.9	69.4	70.1	70.1	69.8	69.3	69.1	68.9	68.9
2000	68.6	68.7	69.1	68.9	69.4	70.5	70.4	70.6	70.5	70.4	71.1	70.6	69.9
2001	69.8	69.8	69.9	68.9	69.1	69.6	68.8	68.8	68.0	66.8	65.4	65.0	68.3
2002	64.3	63.7	64.0	64.2	64.7	65.7	65.7	66.1	65.8	65.5	65.3	64.7	64.9
2003	63.3	62.9	61.9	61.8	61.5	62.3	62.1	62.1	62.1	61.7	61.0	60.8	62.0
Service-providing													
1990	292.5	295.3	299.8	304.3	306.4	310.0	304.9	308.8	315.1	314.4	312.8	313.6	306.5
1991	304.5	307.4	311.3	314.4	317.1	320.6	316.7	318.3	324.6	324.2	324.1	324.5	317.3
1992	317.6	320.3	324.2	327.2	330.5	335.3	331.4	331.9	337.4	339.3	338.6	339.2	331.1
1993	330.6	334.5	337.0	341.8	345.3	348.3	346.3	348.3	355.5	355.2	354.7	357.0	346.2
1994	348.4	352.3	356.9	361.6	365.1	369.4	363.4	364.6	373.4	373.2	372.4	374.1	364.6
1995	365.4	369.6	374.4	375.6	378.6	383.4	376.9	379.0	386.4	386.2	385.4	386.1	378.9
1996	372.9	375.1	380.5	384.3	387.2	392.7	388.4	391.0	396.0	395.5	395.2	396.6	388.0
1997	386.2	388.5	392.6	397.3	401.3	405.8	401.3	404.0	410.6	408.9	408.4	410.1	401.3
1998	396.6	400.8	404.9	409.0	413.3	416.4	414.1	416.5	423.3	423.3	423.7	425.0	413.9
1999	411.9	415.8	420.9	425.0	428.6	435.6	431.9	432.8	439.5	439.1	439.6	440.4	430.1
2000	428.4	432.7	438.3	445.4	451.9	455.1	449.7	453.1	458.6	456.3	457.2	457.3	448.7
2001	442.1	447.0	452.9	456.4	459.7	464.1	457.4	460.5	464.3	461.7	461.4	461.5	457.4
2002	446.3	449.9	454.7	460.8	464.3	470.1	464.2	465.4	470.2	470.4	469.9	469.8	462.9
2003	456.2	458.4	463.7	467.0	471.0	476.7	469.4	472.0	476.7	475.1	474.2	475.7	469.7
Trade, transportation, and utilities													
1990	82.2	81.8	82.4	83.2	84.0	85.0	84.7	85.6	86.7	87.1	87.7	88.6	84.9
1991	83.8	82.9	83.1	84.4	85.8	86.4	87.1	87.2	88.6	89.3	90.1	90.7	86.6
1992	87.2	86.9	87.7	88.9	89.7	90.8	90.6	90.1	91.5	92.1	93.3	93.9	90.2
1993	90.0	89.5	89.7	91.3	92.4	93.5	94.1	94.4	95.8	96.7	98.1	99.6	93.8
1994	95.6	94.9	96.0	97.3	98.5	99.7	99.9	100.0	101.0	101.0	101.8	102.8	99.0
1995	98.5	98.0	98.7	99.1	100.2	101.9	101.5	102.0	103.2	104.5	105.9	106.6	101.7
1996	101.8	101.2	102.1	102.8	104.4	106.0	106.4	106.6	107.4	108.3	110.0	111.2	105.7
1997	105.2	104.8	105.4	106.9	107.8	108.9	107.9	107.5	108.7	107.8	108.7	109.6	107.4
1998	106.7	105.6	106.3	110.5	112.0	112.7	113.2	113.9	114.6	115.2	116.5	117.2	112.0
1999	113.3	112.4	113.7	114.3	115.1	118.4	118.9	117.6	118.7	119.5	121.2	121.7	117.1
2000	116.7	116.0	117.2	118.8	120.1	121.9	122.3	124.2	124.2	124.0	125.3	125.1	121.3
2001	116.0	115.1	115.9	116.4	117.3	118.4	116.7	117.1	117.3	116.8	118.0	118.4	116.9
2002	113.5	112.6	113.3	114.6	115.7	116.6	116.4	116.9	117.0	116.7	118.4	118.9	115.9
2003	113.8	113.0	113.9	114.3	115.1	116.2	115.4	116.3	116.2	116.2	117.7	118.3	115.5
Wholesale trade													
1990	18.5	18.4	18.5	18.5	18.4	18.4	18.4	18.3	19.0	19.1	18.9	18.9	18.6
1991	18.3	18.4	18.7	18.9	19.1	19.1	19.0	18.1	18.7	19.1	19.3	19.1	18.8
1992	19.5	19.6	20.0	20.2	20.2	20.3	20.0	19.1	19.7	19.9	20.0	19.7	19.9
1993	19.0	19.1	19.2	19.6	19.8	20.0	20.0	19.6	19.8	20.1	20.5	20.3	19.8
1994	21.5	21.5	22.0	22.6	22.6	22.8	22.5	22.0	22.5	22.4	22.5	22.6	22.3
1995	22.5	22.5	22.8	23.1	23.3	23.5	23.3	22.8	22.9	23.3	23.3	23.2	23.0
1996	22.9	23.1	23.4	23.6	23.6	23.8	24.0	23.6	23.8	24.0	24.3	24.5	23.7
1997	24.1	24.1	24.4	24.4	24.4	24.7	24.4	24.1	24.7	24.9	25.0	24.9	24.5
1998	24.3	24.3	24.6	24.6	24.7	24.9	24.5	24.6	24.6	24.8	24.7	24.7	24.6
1999	24.9	24.9	25.3	25.4	25.4	25.7	25.6	24.9	25.6	25.3	25.3	25.4	25.3
2000	25.1	25.1	25.4	25.7	25.8	26.0	25.9	25.8	26.1	25.9	25.9	25.9	25.7
2001	25.3	25.3	25.6	25.8	25.8	26.0	25.4	25.1	25.4	25.4	25.3	25.1	25.4
2002	24.4	24.6	24.8	25.0	25.1	25.3	25.1	24.9	25.2	25.0	25.2	24.9	25.0
2003	24.3	24.4	24.4	24.9	25.0	25.0	24.3	24.1	24.2	24.1	24.1	24.0	24.4
Retail trade													
1990	50.5	50.0	50.5	51.1	52.0	52.8	52.7	53.2	53.2	53.3	54.3	55.4	52.4
1991	51.1	50.1	50.1	51.2	52.3	52.9	53.6	54.4	54.8	55.0	56.0	56.6	53.2
1992	53.3	52.6	53.1	54.0	54.9	55.6	55.8	56.2	56.3	56.8	58.1	58.8	55.5
1993	56.1	55.4	55.6	56.7	57.5	58.1	58.4	58.8	59.1	59.6	60.7	62.1	58.2
1994	57.1	56.4	56.8	57.8	58.8	59.8	60.4	61.0	60.8	60.8	62.2	63.3	59.6
1995	60.2	59.6	60.0	60.3	61.1	62.3	62.0	62.9	63.3	63.8	65.5	66.3	62.3
1996	61.9	61.2	61.7	62.3	63.7	64.8	65.0	65.3	65.3	65.4	67.3	68.5	64.4
1997	63.4	63.1	63.5	65.0	65.8	66.4	65.9	65.5	65.5	64.1	65.3	66.3	65.0
1998	64.6	63.7	64.1	68.2	69.7	69.9	70.5	70.8	71.2	71.1	72.7	73.4	69.2
1999	69.8	69.0	69.7	70.3	71.0	73.6	74.2	73.5	73.6	74.2	76.1	76.7	72.6
2000	73.4	72.7	73.7	74.9	76.1	77.1	77.6	79.1	78.9	78.8	80.3	79.6	76.9
2001	71.8	71.1	71.5	71.8	72.6	73.3	72.4	72.8	72.6	72.3	73.8	74.5	72.5
2002	70.9	69.7	70.3	71.3	72.2	72.7	72.9	73.1	72.8	72.5	74.2	75.0	72.3
2003	70.8	70.1	70.9	71.2	71.9	72.7	72.6	73.3	73.0	72.8	74.5	75.2	72.4

Employment by Industry: Idaho—*Continued*

(Numbers in thousands. Not seasonally adjusted.)

Industry	January	February	March	April	May	June	July	August	September	October	November	December	Annual Average
STATEWIDE—*Continued*													
Transportation and utilities													
1990	13.2	13.4	13.4	13.6	13.6	13.8	13.6	14.1	14.5	14.7	14.5	14.3	13.9
1991	14.4	14.4	14.3	14.3	14.4	14.4	14.5	14.7	15.1	15.2	14.8	15.0	14.6
1992	14.4	14.7	14.6	14.7	14.6	14.9	14.8	14.8	15.5	15.4	15.2	15.4	14.9
1993	14.9	15.0	14.9	15.0	15.1	15.4	15.7	16.0	16.9	17.0	16.9	17.2	15.8
1994	17.0	17.0	17.2	16.9	17.1	17.1	17.0	17.0	17.7	17.8	17.1	16.9	17.2
1995	15.8	15.9	15.9	15.7	15.8	16.1	16.2	16.3	17.0	17.4	17.1	17.1	16.4
1996	17.0	16.9	17.0	16.9	17.1	17.4	17.4	17.7	18.3	18.9	18.4	18.2	17.6
1997	17.7	17.6	17.5	17.5	17.6	17.8	17.6	17.9	18.5	18.8	18.4	18.4	17.9
1998	17.8	17.6	17.6	17.7	17.6	17.9	18.2	18.5	18.8	19.3	19.1	19.1	18.3
1999	18.6	18.5	18.7	18.6	18.7	19.1	19.1	19.2	19.5	20.0	19.8	19.6	19.1
2000	18.2	18.2	18.1	18.2	18.2	18.8	18.8	19.3	19.2	19.3	19.1	19.6	18.8
2001	18.9	18.7	18.8	18.8	18.9	19.1	18.9	19.2	19.3	19.1	18.9	18.8	18.9
2002	18.2	18.3	18.2	18.3	18.4	18.6	18.4	18.9	19.0	19.2	19.0	19.0	18.6
2003	18.7	18.5	18.6	18.2	18.2	18.5	18.5	18.9	19.0	19.3	19.1	19.1	18.7
Information													
1990	7.4	7.4	7.4	7.5	7.6	7.7	7.6	8.1	7.7	7.5	7.5	7.5	7.6
1991	7.4	7.4	7.4	7.5	7.6	7.6	7.6	7.6	7.6	7.6	7.6	7.7	7.6
1992	7.5	7.5	7.6	7.6	7.6	7.7	7.7	7.8	7.8	7.8	7.8	7.8	7.7
1993	7.8	7.7	7.8	7.8	7.9	7.9	8.0	7.9	7.9	7.9	7.9	7.8	7.9
1994	7.7	7.7	7.7	7.8	7.9	8.0	8.0	8.0	8.1	7.9	8.0	8.0	7.9
1995	8.0	8.0	8.1	8.1	8.2	8.3	8.3	8.2	8.2	8.0	8.0	8.0	8.1
1996	7.9	7.8	7.9	7.9	8.0	8.2	8.3	8.3	8.2	7.9	7.9	8.0	8.0
1997	7.8	7.7	7.9	8.0	8.1	8.2	8.1	8.1	8.0	8.0	8.1	8.2	8.0
1998	8.4	8.4	8.4	8.7	8.9	8.9	8.7	8.7	8.8	8.9	8.9	9.0	8.7
1999	8.8	8.8	9.0	9.1	9.2	9.5	9.4	9.4	9.5	9.4	9.5	9.6	9.3
2000	9.3	9.4	9.7	9.4	9.6	9.8	9.8	9.8	9.8	9.7	9.7	9.8	9.7
2001	9.6	9.7	9.7	9.6	9.6	9.8	9.7	9.8	9.5	9.4	9.4	9.4	9.6
2002	9.2	9.1	9.1	9.2	9.3	9.3	9.1	9.1	9.1	9.1	9.3	9.3	9.2
2003	9.1	9.1	9.1	9.2	9.3	9.3	9.2	9.2	9.2	9.1	9.1	9.2	9.2
Financial activities													
1990	18.9	18.8	19.0	19.0	19.1	19.3	19.3	19.6	19.5	19.3	19.3	19.2	19.2
1991	18.9	18.7	18.7	18.6	18.9	19.1	19.4	19.3	19.2	19.1	19.0	19.2	19.0
1992	18.9	19.1	19.3	19.5	19.7	19.8	19.7	19.9	19.8	19.8	19.8	19.9	19.6
1993	20.0	20.1	20.3	20.6	20.6	20.8	20.9	21.0	21.1	21.2	21.2	21.4	20.8
1994	23.8	23.9	24.2	24.4	24.6	24.7	24.9	24.9	24.8	24.7	24.5	24.7	24.5
1995	26.0	25.5	26.5	26.7	27.1	26.7	27.0	27.2	26.9	26.7	26.8	26.7	26.7
1996	26.7	26.7	26.8	26.8	26.9	27.1	27.1	27.1	26.9	26.6	26.5	26.7	26.8
1997	26.8	26.5	26.6	26.6	26.9	27.0	26.8	27.0	26.9	26.8	27.0	27.3	26.9
1998	23.4	23.5	23.6	23.6	24.0	24.3	24.7	24.8	24.7	24.7	24.8	25.1	24.3
1999	24.9	24.9	25.2	25.4	25.4	25.6	25.6	25.7	25.3	25.2	25.3	25.3	25.3
2000	24.9	24.9	24.9	25.1	25.2	25.4	25.3	25.4	25.4	25.1	25.2	25.1	25.2
2001	24.2	24.2	24.5	24.8	24.9	25.2	25.4	25.7	25.2	25.1	25.1	25.4	24.9
2002	25.1	25.2	25.3	25.3	25.7	25.8	26.3	26.3	26.1	26.1	26.2	26.4	25.8
2003	26.1	26.1	26.3	26.5	26.8	27.2	27.5	27.6	27.4	27.2	27.2	27.4	26.9
Professional and business services													
1990	30.6	30.8	31.6	32.5	32.7	33.7	34.3	34.7	34.5	34.3	33.5	33.3	33.0
1991	33.8	34.2	35.9	36.6	36.4	37.3	37.0	37.7	37.5	37.3	37.1	37.0	36.5
1992	36.5	37.1	38.0	37.9	38.2	39.0	39.0	39.4	39.3	39.2	38.9	39.1	38.5
1993	38.3	38.8	39.2	40.5	41.0	42.0	42.2	43.1	42.7	41.8	41.7	42.1	41.1
1994	39.2	40.0	40.5	41.7	42.4	43.0	42.8	43.4	42.6	42.3	42.5	42.5	41.9
1995	40.1	41.0	41.6	42.1	42.4	43.1	42.9	43.6	43.4	43.6	43.2	42.9	42.5
1996	40.2	40.3	41.0	42.4	42.8	43.6	44.6	45.1	44.3	44.5	43.6	43.3	43.0
1997	42.5	42.6	43.8	45.4	46.8	48.3	49.4	50.7	50.2	49.5	49.4	49.6	47.4
1998	46.7	47.5	48.9	50.0	50.9	51.4	51.3	52.1	52.5	52.8	53.0	52.4	50.8
1999	50.0	50.2	51.6	52.5	54.0	55.2	55.5	57.3	58.0	57.7	57.6	58.1	54.8
2000	55.6	56.2	57.9	58.9	60.3	62.1	61.7	62.7	63.4	63.1	63.4	62.6	60.7
2001	64.0	63.9	65.8	66.7	68.2	69.4	69.1	71.1	69.6	68.5	68.1	67.1	67.6
2002	63.7	64.5	65.5	68.5	69.1	70.8	70.8	71.9	71.2	71.7	70.8	69.9	69.0
2003	66.2	67.0	68.2	69.4	70.1	71.6	70.9	72.4	72.3	71.9	71.3	71.1	70.2
Educational and health services													
1990	30.7	31.1	31.2	31.6	31.3	31.5	31.7	31.9	33.2	33.9	34.3	34.4	32.2
1991	34.0	34.5	34.8	34.7	34.2	34.1	34.0	34.1	35.1	35.4	35.6	35.7	34.7
1992	35.6	35.8	35.8	36.0	35.4	35.3	35.4	35.5	36.6	37.4	37.7	37.5	36.2
1993	36.9	37.3	37.3	37.8	37.3	36.9	37.0	37.2	38.3	38.8	39.0	39.1	37.7
1994	38.3	38.8	39.0	39.1	38.7	38.8	39.0	39.3	40.2	40.5	40.6	40.9	39.4
1995	41.3	41.3	41.4	41.3	40.9	41.2	40.7	41.2	42.6	42.8	43.3	43.2	41.8
1996	42.4	43.1	43.4	43.8	43.3	43.3	42.6	43.3	44.7	45.6	45.9	46.0	44.0
1997	45.7	46.2	46.4	46.7	46.2	46.4	45.7	46.2	47.2	48.3	48.7	48.8	46.9
1998	48.0	48.6	48.7	49.0	48.5	48.5	48.0	48.5	49.5	49.9	50.2	50.0	49.0
1999	49.5	50.1	50.0	50.5	50.0	50.3	49.0	49.4	50.9	51.4	51.8	51.5	50.4
2000	51.3	51.9	52.2	52.3	51.4	51.8	51.7	52.3	53.9	54.3	54.7	55.3	52.8
2001	54.9	55.8	56.2	57.0	55.7	56.1	56.0	56.6	58.1	58.5	59.1	59.6	56.9
2002	58.6	58.9	59.4	59.8	58.9	59.1	59.0	59.1	60.4	60.8	61.3	61.6	59.7
2003	61.3	61.4	61.7	62.2	61.6	61.8	61.8	62.0	63.6	64.2	64.4	64.6	62.6

Employment by Industry: Idaho—*Continued*

(Numbers in thousands. Not seasonally adjusted.)

Industry	January	February	March	April	May	June	July	August	September	October	November	December	Annual Average
STATEWIDE—*Continued*													
Leisure and hospitality													
1990	33.8	34.5	35.6	36.0	36.6	38.7	39.3	40.3	38.8	36.2	35.0	35.7	36.7
1991	34.6	34.8	35.4	35.9	36.8	39.2	40.5	41.2	40.0	37.5	36.6	37.0	37.5
1992	36.3	36.9	37.6	37.9	39.9	42.0	43.2	43.9	42.3	39.7	38.2	38.9	39.7
1993	38.4	38.6	39.3	39.7	40.7	43.4	45.0	45.4	44.4	41.8	40.5	41.3	41.5
1994	39.7	40.0	41.2	41.8	42.5	45.8	47.2	47.6	46.2	43.8	43.1	43.4	43.5
1995	43.4	44.4	45.4	45.1	46.3	49.7	50.0	50.7	49.2	45.8	44.5	45.2	46.6
1996	44.8	44.8	46.4	46.9	47.7	50.7	51.6	52.2	50.3	46.7	45.6	46.8	47.9
1997	46.0	46.4	47.1	47.7	48.9	51.4	52.9	53.6	52.0	48.3	46.7	47.7	49.1
1998	46.7	47.8	48.4	48.7	50.2	52.3	53.4	53.9	52.6	49.1	47.4	48.4	49.9
1999	47.1	47.6	48.5	49.9	50.5	52.7	54.5	54.7	53.2	50.7	48.9	50.4	50.7
2000	48.5	49.2	50.2	52.1	52.2	55.1	56.7	57.3	55.8	51.6	50.6	51.4	52.6
2001	50.0	50.6	51.7	52.3	53.2	55.9	56.8	57.2	55.3	51.7	50.6	51.3	53.0
2002	49.5	50.0	50.8	52.1	53.1	56.0	57.2	57.8	56.3	53.4	51.2	51.9	53.2
2003	51.4	51.4	52.4	52.9	54.2	57.0	58.2	59.1	56.6	53.4	51.6	52.6	54.2
Other services													
1990	11.3	11.3	11.5	11.6	11.5	11.7	11.8	11.9	11.4	11.3	11.4	11.4	11.5
1991	11.0	11.1	11.1	11.2	11.3	11.4	11.8	11.6	11.2	10.7	10.6	11.0	11.2
1992	10.3	10.2	10.3	10.4	10.8	11.1	11.7	11.7	11.5	11.6	11.7	12.0	11.1
1993	11.9	12.2	12.6	12.8	13.0	13.1	13.6	13.6	13.4	13.3	13.3	13.3	13.0
1994	14.8	14.8	15.1	15.1	15.3	15.4	15.9	15.9	15.7	15.4	15.5	15.5	15.4
1995	15.3	15.4	15.6	15.7	15.8	16.0	16.3	16.4	16.1	15.9	15.8	15.9	15.9
1996	15.1	15.0	15.3	15.5	15.8	16.0	16.4	16.4	15.8	15.6	15.4	15.5	15.7
1997	14.8	15.1	15.3	15.3	15.5	15.7	16.0	16.3	16.1	16.0	15.9	16.1	15.7
1998	15.8	15.9	15.9	16.2	16.1	16.5	17.1	17.2	17.0	16.8	16.8	17.8	16.6
1999	16.7	16.8	17.0	17.0	17.3	17.4	17.9	18.0	17.5	17.3	17.3	17.4	17.3
2000	17.1	17.3	17.5	17.7	18.1	18.1	18.1	18.2	17.9	17.7	17.7	18.1	17.8
2001	17.8	18.0	18.3	18.3	18.3	18.6	18.5	18.5	18.1	17.8	17.7	17.7	18.1
2002	17.3	17.6	18.1	18.0	18.0	18.2	18.6	18.7	18.1	18.1	18.0	17.9	18.1
2003	17.7	17.8	18.0	18.1	18.2	18.3	18.7	18.9	18.4	18.2	18.1	18.1	18.2
Government													
1990	77.6	79.6	81.1	82.9	83.6	82.4	76.2	76.7	83.3	84.8	84.1	83.5	81.3
1991	81.0	83.8	84.9	85.5	86.1	85.5	79.3	79.6	85.4	87.3	87.5	86.2	84.3
1992	85.3	86.8	87.9	89.0	89.2	89.6	84.1	83.6	88.6	91.7	91.2	90.1	88.1
1993	87.3	90.3	90.8	91.3	92.4	90.7	85.5	85.7	91.9	93.7	93.0	92.4	90.4
1994	89.3	92.2	93.2	94.4	95.2	94.0	85.7	85.5	94.8	97.6	96.4	96.3	92.9
1995	92.8	96.0	97.1	97.5	97.7	96.5	90.2	89.7	96.8	98.9	97.9	97.6	95.7
1996	94.0	96.2	97.6	98.2	98.3	97.8	91.4	92.0	98.4	100.3	100.3	99.1	97.0
1997	97.4	99.2	100.1	100.7	101.1	99.9	94.5	94.6	101.5	104.2	103.9	102.8	100.0
1998	100.9	103.5	104.7	102.3	102.7	101.8	97.7	97.4	103.6	105.9	106.1	105.1	102.6
1999	101.6	105.0	105.9	106.3	107.1	106.5	101.1	100.7	106.4	107.9	108.0	106.4	105.2
2000	105.0	107.8	108.7	111.1	115.0	110.9	104.1	103.2	108.2	110.8	110.6	109.9	108.8
2001	105.6	109.7	110.8	111.3	112.5	110.7	105.2	104.5	111.2	113.9	113.4	112.6	110.1
2002	109.4	112.0	113.2	113.3	114.5	114.3	106.8	105.6	112.0	114.5	114.7	113.9	112.0
2003	110.6	112.6	114.1	114.4	115.7	115.3	107.7	106.5	113.0	114.9	114.8	114.4	112.8
Federal government													
1990	11.6	11.3	11.8	13.3	13.5	14.8	14.5	14.0	13.7	13.1	12.6	12.4	13.1
1991	11.5	11.5	11.6	12.1	12.5	14.1	14.5	14.3	14.0	13.3	13.1	12.4	12.9
1992	12.0	12.1	12.3	12.8	13.3	14.5	15.1	15.0	14.6	13.8	13.2	12.8	13.5
1993	12.4	12.6	12.4	13.0	13.4	14.5	15.1	15.0	14.4	14.1	13.2	13.0	13.6
1994	12.4	12.4	12.6	13.3	13.7	14.7	14.6	14.6	14.1	14.0	12.8	12.5	13.5
1995	12.1	12.1	12.3	12.7	13.2	14.0	14.4	14.4	13.9	13.5	12.4	12.1	13.1
1996	11.8	11.9	11.9	12.6	13.0	13.8	14.0	14.0	13.7	13.1	12.7	12.4	12.9
1997	12.1	12.0	12.0	12.4	12.9	13.6	14.1	14.1	13.6	12.9	12.6	12.3	12.9
1998	12.1	11.9	12.1	12.2	12.7	13.4	14.0	14.2	13.5	12.8	12.6	12.2	12.8
1999	11.9	11.8	11.8	12.1	12.6	13.4	14.1	14.1	13.6	13.2	12.7	12.3	12.8
2000	12.0	12.0	12.3	13.7	17.4	15.3	14.6	14.4	13.4	13.1	12.9	12.5	13.6
2001	12.1	12.0	12.3	12.8	13.0	14.3	14.8	14.5	14.2	13.4	13.0	12.9	13.2
2002	12.3	12.1	12.3	12.8	13.0	14.5	15.4	15.0	14.5	13.7	13.5	13.5	13.6
2003	12.5	12.6	12.8	12.9	13.5	15.1	15.3	15.1	14.6	13.7	13.1	13.0	13.7
State government													
1990	20.0	22.1	22.7	22.8	22.7	20.8	20.6	21.7	23.3	23.9	23.2	22.7	22.2
1991	21.9	23.8	24.2	24.2	23.8	22.3	21.4	22.0	23.5	24.5	24.4	23.5	23.3
1992	23.3	24.2	24.5	25.0	24.2	23.3	23.2	23.1	24.7	25.6	24.9	24.6	24.2
1993	23.5	25.5	25.9	25.7	25.7	23.2	23.3	23.4	26.2	26.8	26.5	25.9	25.1
1994	23.9	26.1	26.5	26.4	26.2	24.0	24.1	24.0	26.4	27.7	27.1	27.1	25.8
1995	24.7	27.0	27.4	27.3	26.5	24.4	24.4	24.2	26.6	27.5	27.0	26.8	26.2
1996	23.7	25.4	26.0	25.7	24.6	23.5	23.7	24.5	26.1	26.9	26.6	26.1	25.2
1997	24.8	25.9	26.2	26.7	25.9	24.1	23.9	24.4	27.2	27.6	27.1	26.2	25.8
1998	25.5	27.3	27.5	27.7	27.0	25.6	25.4	25.2	27.5	28.7	28.3	28.0	27.0
1999	25.3	28.2	28.4	28.4	28.0	26.7	25.9	26.6	28.0	29.2	29.0	28.0	27.6
2000	27.0	28.7	28.8	29.1	28.6	26.8	26.8	27.1	28.4	29.7	29.3	29.1	28.3
2001	26.2	29.1	29.4	29.3	29.5	26.6	27.0	27.1	29.3	30.8	30.3	29.8	28.7
2002	28.0	29.5	29.8	29.5	29.8	28.4	26.7	26.5	28.6	29.9	29.6	29.2	28.8
2003	28.0	28.6	29.3	29.5	29.3	27.6	27.1	26.6	29.0	30.0	29.8	29.4	28.7

Employment by Industry: Idaho—*Continued*

(Numbers in thousands. Not seasonally adjusted.)

Industry	January	February	March	April	May	June	July	August	September	October	November	December	Annual Average
STATEWIDE—*Continued*													
Local government													
1990	46.0	46.2	46.6	46.8	47.4	46.8	41.1	41.0	46.3	47.8	48.3	48.4	46.1
1991	47.6	48.5	49.1	49.2	49.8	49.1	43.4	43.3	47.9	49.5	50.0	50.3	48.1
1992	50.0	50.5	51.1	51.2	51.7	51.8	45.8	45.5	49.3	52.3	53.1	52.7	50.4
1993	51.4	52.2	52.5	52.6	53.3	53.0	47.1	47.3	51.3	52.8	53.3	53.5	51.7
1994	53.0	53.7	54.1	54.7	55.3	55.3	47.0	46.9	54.3	55.9	56.5	56.7	53.6
1995	56.0	56.9	57.4	57.5	58.0	58.1	51.4	51.1	56.3	57.9	58.5	58.7	56.5
1996	58.5	58.9	59.7	59.9	60.7	60.5	53.7	53.5	58.6	60.3	61.0	60.6	58.8
1997	60.5	61.3	61.9	61.6	62.3	62.2	56.5	56.1	60.7	63.7	64.2	64.3	61.3
1998	63.3	64.3	65.1	62.4	63.0	62.8	58.3	58.0	62.6	64.4	65.2	64.9	62.9
1999	64.4	65.0	65.7	65.8	66.5	66.4	61.1	60.0	64.8	65.5	66.3	66.1	64.8
2000	66.0	67.1	67.6	68.3	69.0	68.8	62.7	61.7	66.4	68.0	68.4	68.3	66.9
2001	67.3	68.6	69.1	69.2	70.0	69.8	63.4	62.9	67.7	69.7	70.1	69.9	68.1
2002	69.1	70.4	71.1	71.0	71.7	71.4	64.7	64.1	68.9	70.9	71.6	71.2	69.7
2003	70.1	71.4	72.0	72.0	72.9	72.6	65.3	64.8	69.4	71.2	71.9	72.0	70.5
BOISE CITY													
Total nonfarm													
1990	128.5	130.4	132.4	134.1	136.0	137.0	135.1	137.6	138.7	139.5	139.4	139.4	135.6
1991	134.7	136.8	137.9	139.8	141.7	143.4	141.8	143.0	143.6	144.7	145.2	144.9	141.4
1992	142.2	143.4	145.0	147.5	149.4	151.1	150.4	151.5	152.3	154.8	155.0	155.0	149.8
1993	150.5	152.5	153.9	156.9	158.6	160.1	160.1	161.2	163.0	164.2	164.8	166.3	159.3
1994	161.8	163.9	167.0	169.6	171.2	173.3	169.2	170.6	173.5	174.4	174.9	174.8	170.3
1995	171.9	173.2	176.0	176.8	178.4	180.9	178.7	180.1	182.0	182.7	183.7	183.7	179.0
1996	178.6	179.5	182.2	184.7	186.0	188.3	185.7	187.0	188.0	189.8	190.0	190.2	185.8
1997	185.9	186.7	189.2	191.1	193.4	195.2	194.2	195.6	196.7	197.9	198.9	200.8	193.8
1998	194.2	196.3	198.8	200.7	202.4	204.4	203.4	203.7	206.0	207.3	207.3	207.9	202.7
1999	202.0	203.2	206.0	208.9	210.6	213.8	212.7	213.4	214.7	216.0	216.9	217.2	211.2
2000	211.4	213.8	217.6	223.3	226.3	228.9	229.2	230.8	232.3	231.7	233.1	232.2	225.8
2001	224.8	226.5	230.0	230.0	231.5	232.7	230.3	231.6	231.6	230.3	229.4	228.3	229.7
2002	221.1	222.4	224.8	226.8	229.3	230.6	229.0	230.3	231.4	232.2	231.7	231.3	228.4
2003	224.2	224.8	226.3	228.1	229.9	230.6	228.0	229.3	230.3	231.9	232.3	233.3	229.1
Total private													
1990	105.2	106.8	108.2	110.0	111.5	112.9	112.3	115.0	114.7	114.9	114.6	114.7	111.7
1991	110.6	111.9	112.6	114.5	116.6	118.3	118.1	119.4	119.1	119.0	119.4	119.3	116.5
1992	116.6	117.3	118.5	120.9	123.1	124.8	125.2	126.6	126.6	127.9	128.0	128.2	123.6
1993	124.3	125.5	126.7	129.7	131.5	133.4	134.6	135.6	136.2	136.9	137.5	139.0	132.5
1994	135.2	136.4	139.4	141.7	143.8	145.8	145.2	146.7	146.0	146.0	146.5	146.4	143.2
1995	144.4	144.7	147.3	148.1	150.2	152.6	152.0	153.6	154.0	153.9	154.9	155.1	150.9
1996	150.9	151.1	153.5	155.6	157.2	159.6	158.9	159.9	159.4	160.4	160.6	160.9	157.3
1997	156.9	157.1	159.4	161.2	163.5	165.9	166.1	167.5	167.4	167.5	168.7	170.2	164.2
1998	163.9	165.4	167.6	169.3	171.0	172.8	173.6	174.3	175.0	175.1	175.0	175.7	171.5
1999	170.1	170.9	173.6	176.2	177.8	181.0	181.6	182.5	182.8	183.0	183.8	184.2	178.9
2000	179.5	180.7	184.2	190.1	192.3	195.7	196.6	198.5	199.5	198.3	199.6	198.7	192.8
2001	191.6	192.0	195.1	195.0	196.2	197.9	196.7	198.2	196.7	194.3	193.5	192.4	194.9
2002	186.6	186.6	188.7	190.7	193.0	194.8	194.8	196.4	195.2	195.1	194.5	194.0	192.5
2003	188.3	188.3	189.5	191.1	192.7	194.2	193.9	195.4	195.1	195.9	196.2	197.0	193.1
Goods-producing													
1990	26.4	26.9	27.3	27.6	28.3	28.7	28.7	29.3	29.3	29.6	29.4	29.0	28.3
1991	28.0	28.6	28.4	29.1	30.0	30.6	30.7	31.1	31.1	31.1	31.2	30.8	30.0
1992	30.5	30.8	31.2	32.1	33.1	33.6	33.8	34.2	34.2	34.9	34.9	34.4	33.1
1993	33.3	33.7	33.9	35.1	35.9	36.9	37.5	37.8	37.9	38.3	38.4	38.5	36.4
1994	37.3	37.4	38.8	39.8	40.3	41.2	41.2	41.7	41.3	41.4	41.5	41.0	40.2
1995	40.7	40.9	41.6	41.6	42.1	43.3	43.1	43.7	43.9	43.6	43.7	43.4	42.6
1996	42.3	42.3	43.4	44.1	44.8	45.7	45.5	45.6	45.3	45.4	45.3	44.7	44.5
1997	43.6	43.9	44.8	45.0	45.5	46.5	47.3	47.3	47.2	47.6	47.8	47.8	46.1
1998	46.7	46.9	47.4	47.8	48.0	48.7	48.8	48.9	48.5	48.4	48.2	47.7	48.0
1999	46.6	46.7	47.5	48.6	48.9	49.9	50.2	50.5	50.0	49.9	49.8	49.3	48.9
2000	48.5	48.6	49.5	50.9	51.4	52.6	52.8	53.3	53.5	53.5	53.7	53.3	51.8
2001	50.8	50.9	51.6	51.0	51.1	51.7	51.6	51.5	50.8	49.9	48.7	47.8	50.6
2002	46.0	45.4	46.0	46.4	47.4	48.2	48.2	48.5	48.0	47.9	47.2	46.7	47.1
2003	45.0	44.9	44.1	44.7	45.0	45.6	45.7	45.9	45.7	45.9	45.8	45.5	45.3
Construction and mining													
1990	5.4	5.4	5.9	6.2	6.5	6.8	6.9	7.2	7.4	7.8	7.8	7.5	6.7
1991	6.0	6.3	6.4	6.8	7.2	7.7	7.9	8.1	8.1	8.0	7.9	7.8	7.3
1992	7.4	7.6	7.9	8.4	8.9	9.1	9.4	9.5	9.4	9.5	9.4	9.0	8.7
1993	7.9	8.0	8.2	9.1	9.7	10.2	10.7	10.9	10.9	11.0	11.0	10.8	9.8
1994	10.1	10.2	11.0	11.8	12.1	12.7	13.1	13.3	12.8	12.6	12.4	11.9	12.0
1995	11.2	11.5	11.9	12.5	12.9	13.7	13.6	13.9	13.8	13.4	13.4	13.0	12.9
1996	11.8	11.4	12.1	12.7	13.1	13.6	13.8	13.9	13.7	13.7	13.4	13.0	13.0
1997	12.0	12.3	13.0	12.8	13.2	13.8	14.4	14.4	14.1	14.2	14.1	13.8	13.5
1998	12.6	12.7	13.0	13.6	13.8	14.2	14.5	14.6	14.6	14.5	14.4	14.3	13.9
1999	13.6	13.5	14.1	14.8	15.2	15.8	16.2	16.3	16.3	16.3	16.1	15.7	15.3
2000	14.7	14.7	15.4	16.2	16.5	17.2	17.4	17.6	17.7	17.6	17.4	17.0	16.6
2001	15.7	15.7	16.4	16.6	16.8	17.3	17.4	17.5	17.3	17.2	16.7	16.0	16.7
2002	14.4	14.3	14.7	15.3	16.0	16.3	16.5	16.6	16.4	16.0	15.8	15.6	15.6
2003	14.2	14.3	14.6	15.1	15.5	16.1	16.1	16.4	16.3	16.3	16.1	15.8	15.6

Employment by Industry: Idaho—*Continued*

(Numbers in thousands. Not seasonally adjusted.)

Industry	January	February	March	April	May	June	July	August	September	October	November	December	Annual Average
BOISE CITY—*Continued*													
Manufacturing													
1990	21.0	21.5	21.4	21.4	21.8	21.9	21.8	22.1	21.9	21.8	21.6	21.5	21.6
1991	22.0	22.3	22.0	22.3	22.8	22.9	22.8	23.0	23.0	23.1	23.3	23.0	22.7
1992	23.1	23.2	23.3	23.7	24.2	24.5	24.4	24.7	24.8	25.4	25.5	25.4	24.3
1993	25.4	25.7	25.7	26.0	26.2	26.7	26.8	26.9	27.0	27.3	27.4	27.7	26.5
1994	27.2	27.2	27.8	28.0	28.2	28.5	28.1	28.4	28.5	28.8	29.1	29.1	28.2
1995	29.5	29.4	29.7	29.1	29.2	29.6	29.5	29.8	30.1	30.2	30.3	30.4	29.7
1996	30.5	30.9	31.3	31.4	31.7	32.1	31.7	31.7	31.6	31.7	31.9	31.7	31.5
1997	31.6	31.6	31.8	32.2	32.3	32.7	32.9	32.9	33.1	33.4	33.7	34.0	32.6
1998	34.1	34.2	34.4	34.2	34.2	34.5	34.3	34.3	33.9	33.9	33.8	33.4	34.1
1999	33.0	33.2	33.4	33.8	33.7	34.1	34.0	34.2	33.7	33.6	33.7	33.6	33.6
2000	33.8	33.9	34.1	34.7	34.9	35.4	35.4	35.7	35.8	35.9	36.3	36.3	35.1
2001	35.1	35.2	35.2	34.4	34.3	34.4	34.2	34.0	33.5	32.7	32.0	31.8	33.9
2002	31.6	31.1	31.3	31.1	31.4	31.9	31.7	31.9	31.6	31.9	31.4	31.1	31.5
2003	30.8	30.6	29.5	29.6	29.5	29.5	29.6	29.5	29.4	29.6	29.7	29.7	29.8
Service-providing													
1990	102.1	103.5	105.1	106.5	107.7	108.3	106.4	108.3	109.4	109.9	110.0	110.4	107.3
1991	106.7	108.2	109.5	110.7	111.7	112.8	111.1	111.9	112.5	113.6	114.0	114.1	111.4
1992	111.7	112.6	113.8	115.4	116.3	117.5	116.6	117.3	118.1	119.9	120.1	120.6	116.6
1993	117.2	118.8	120.0	121.8	122.7	123.2	122.6	123.4	125.1	125.9	126.4	127.8	122.9
1994	124.5	126.5	128.2	129.8	130.9	132.1	128.0	128.9	132.2	133.0	133.4	133.8	130.1
1995	131.2	132.3	134.4	135.2	136.3	137.6	135.6	136.4	138.1	139.1	140.0	140.3	136.3
1996	136.3	137.2	138.8	140.6	141.2	142.6	140.2	141.4	142.7	144.4	144.7	145.5	141.3
1997	142.3	142.8	144.4	146.1	147.9	148.7	146.9	148.3	149.5	150.3	151.1	153.0	147.6
1998	147.5	149.4	151.4	152.9	154.4	155.7	154.6	154.8	157.5	158.9	159.1	160.2	154.7
1999	155.4	156.5	158.5	160.3	161.7	163.9	162.5	162.9	164.7	166.1	167.1	167.9	162.2
2000	162.9	165.2	168.1	172.4	174.9	176.3	176.4	177.5	178.8	178.2	179.4	178.9	174.0
2001	174.0	175.6	178.4	179.0	180.4	181.0	178.7	180.1	180.8	180.4	180.7	180.5	179.1
2002	175.1	177.0	178.8	180.4	181.9	182.4	180.8	181.8	183.4	184.3	184.5	184.6	181.3
2003	179.2	179.9	182.2	183.4	184.9	185.0	182.3	183.4	184.6	186.0	186.5	187.8	183.8
Trade, transportation, and utilities													
1990	29.1	29.2	29.3	29.5	29.7	30.0	29.8	30.7	30.8	31.1	31.4	31.6	30.1
1991	29.0	28.8	28.8	29.1	29.4	29.7	29.7	30.0	30.2	30.4	30.5	30.7	29.6
1992	29.4	29.4	29.5	30.0	30.2	30.5	30.5	30.7	31.0	31.4	31.7	31.9	30.5
1993	30.4	30.2	30.3	30.8	30.9	31.1	31.2	31.6	31.9	32.9	33.3	34.0	31.5
1994	32.0	32.0	32.3	32.7	33.1	33.5	33.5	33.8	33.9	34.3	34.6	34.9	33.3
1995	33.7	33.1	33.5	33.5	34.0	34.3	34.0	34.3	34.8	35.4	36.0	36.1	34.3
1996	34.3	34.1	34.3	34.6	35.0	35.5	35.1	35.3	35.6	36.3	36.6	37.3	35.3
1997	35.9	35.5	35.6	35.9	36.3	36.8	36.5	36.7	36.9	37.1	37.8	38.3	36.6
1998	36.4	36.2	36.6	36.9	37.3	37.6	38.0	38.1	38.7	38.9	39.4	40.1	37.8
1999	38.3	38.2	38.6	39.1	39.4	40.2	40.2	40.4	40.8	41.3	41.9	42.3	40.0
2000	40.5	40.4	41.0	42.3	42.9	43.6	44.0	44.4	44.8	44.8	45.5	45.7	43.3
2001	44.1	44.0	44.4	45.0	45.0	45.6	44.8	44.9	45.1	45.0	45.6	45.7	44.9
2002	43.9	43.4	43.7	44.1	44.5	44.6	44.8	45.2	45.1	44.5	45.4	45.5	44.6
2003	43.5	43.1	43.5	43.7	44.0	44.0	43.7	44.0	44.1	44.2	45.0	45.3	44.0
Wholesale trade													
1990	6.7	6.7	6.7	6.7	6.6	6.7	6.8	7.1	7.1	7.1	7.0	6.9	6.8
1991	6.4	6.4	6.5	6.6	6.7	6.9	6.9	7.1	7.0	7.0	7.0	6.9	6.7
1992	6.7	6.8	6.8	7.0	7.0	7.1	7.3	7.2	7.1	7.1	7.1	7.0	7.0
1993	6.6	6.7	6.7	6.8	6.8	6.9	7.2	7.3	7.3	7.2	7.2	7.2	6.9
1994	7.0	7.0	7.1	7.2	7.3	7.4	7.5	7.6	7.5	7.5	7.5	7.5	7.3
1995	7.6	7.5	7.6	7.7	7.8	7.9	7.9	8.0	7.9	7.9	8.0	7.9	7.8
1996	7.8	7.9	8.0	7.9	7.9	8.0	8.1	8.2	8.2	8.1	8.1	8.1	8.0
1997	8.1	8.1	8.2	8.2	8.3	8.5	8.5	8.5	8.6	8.5	8.5	8.6	8.3
1998	8.3	8.3	8.4	8.4	8.5	8.6	8.7	8.7	8.7	8.7	8.6	8.5	8.5
1999	8.7	8.7	8.8	8.8	8.9	9.0	9.1	9.1	9.2	9.0	9.0	9.1	8.9
2000	9.2	9.2	9.3	9.5	9.6	9.7	9.8	9.8	9.9	9.9	9.8	9.8	9.6
2001	10.3	10.2	10.2	10.4	10.3	10.6	10.4	10.3	10.3	10.2	10.1	10.1	10.2
2002	9.8	9.9	9.9	10.1	10.1	10.3	10.4	10.5	10.5	10.3	10.3	10.2	10.2
2003	10.0	10.0	9.9	10.1	10.2	10.2	10.1	9.9	9.8	9.7	9.7	9.7	9.9
Retail trade													
1990	16.6	16.6	16.6	16.8	17.0	17.2	17.1	17.5	17.6	17.8	18.2	18.6	17.3
1991	16.6	16.3	16.3	16.5	16.7	16.8	16.9	17.0	17.0	17.3	17.6	17.8	16.9
1992	17.0	16.8	16.9	17.1	17.3	17.5	17.4	17.6	17.7	18.1	18.5	18.8	17.5
1993	17.8	17.5	17.6	18.0	18.1	18.2	18.0	18.2	18.4	19.4	19.9	20.5	18.4
1994	18.8	18.7	18.8	19.2	19.5	19.8	19.8	20.0	20.0	20.4	21.0	21.4	19.7
1995	20.1	19.7	19.9	19.9	20.3	20.6	20.4	20.6	20.9	21.3	22.1	22.3	20.6
1996	20.9	20.7	20.8	21.1	21.5	21.7	21.4	21.4	21.5	22.1	22.7	23.4	21.6
1997	22.1	21.7	21.7	22.0	22.3	22.5	22.3	22.4	22.3	22.5	23.3	23.7	22.4
1998	22.2	22.0	22.2	22.5	22.9	23.1	23.2	23.3	23.7	23.7	24.5	25.3	23.2
1999	23.5	23.3	23.5	23.9	24.1	24.7	24.7	24.9	25.0	25.5	26.3	26.6	24.6
2000	25.0	24.9	25.4	26.3	26.8	27.2	27.8	28.0	28.3	28.2	29.0	29.2	27.1
2001	26.8	26.8	27.1	27.2	27.3	27.6	27.1	27.3	27.4	27.4	28.2	28.3	27.3
2002	27.0	26.4	26.7	26.9	27.2	27.2	27.5	27.6	27.4	27.1	28.0	28.3	27.3
2003	26.5	26.1	26.6	26.6	26.8	26.9	26.8	27.2	27.3	27.4	28.3	28.6	27.1

Employment by Industry: Idaho—*Continued*

(Numbers in thousands. Not seasonally adjusted.)

Industry	January	February	March	April	May	June	July	August	September	October	November	December	Annual Average
BOISE CITY—*Continued*													
Transportation and utilities													
1990	5.8	5.9	6.0	6.0	6.1	6.1	5.9	6.1	6.1	6.2	6.2	6.1	6.0
1991	6.0	6.1	6.0	6.0	6.0	6.0	5.9	5.9	6.2	6.1	5.9	6.0	6.0
1992	5.7	5.8	5.8	5.9	5.9	5.9	5.8	5.9	6.2	6.2	6.1	6.1	5.9
1993	6.0	6.0	6.0	6.0	6.0	6.0	6.0	6.1	6.2	6.3	6.2	6.3	6.0
1994	6.2	6.3	6.4	6.3	6.3	6.3	6.2	6.2	6.4	6.4	6.1	6.0	6.2
1995	6.0	5.9	6.0	5.9	5.9	5.8	5.7	5.7	6.0	6.2	5.9	5.9	5.9
1996	5.6	5.5	5.5	5.6	5.6	5.8	5.6	5.7	5.9	6.1	5.8	5.8	5.7
1997	5.7	5.7	5.7	5.7	5.7	5.8	5.7	5.8	6.0	6.1	6.0	6.0	5.8
1998	5.9	5.9	6.0	6.0	5.9	5.9	6.1	6.1	6.3	6.5	6.3	6.3	6.1
1999	6.1	6.2	6.3	6.4	6.4	6.5	6.4	6.4	6.6	6.8	6.6	6.6	6.4
2000	6.3	6.3	6.3	6.5	6.5	6.7	6.4	6.6	6.6	6.7	6.7	6.7	6.5
2001	7.0	7.0	7.1	7.4	7.4	7.4	7.3	7.3	7.4	7.4	7.3	7.3	7.2
2002	7.1	7.1	7.1	7.1	7.2	7.1	6.9	7.1	7.2	7.1	7.1	7.0	7.1
2003	7.0	7.0	7.0	7.0	7.0	6.9	6.8	6.9	7.0	7.1	7.0	7.0	7.0
Information													
1990	2.8	2.9	2.8	2.9	2.9	3.0	3.0	3.0	3.0	3.0	3.0	3.0	2.9
1991	3.1	3.2	3.2	3.1	3.2	3.2	3.2	3.2	3.2	3.2	3.2	3.2	3.1
1992	3.2	3.2	3.2	3.3	3.2	3.3	3.3	3.2	3.2	3.2	3.2	3.2	3.2
1993	3.2	3.2	3.2	3.3	3.3	3.3	3.4	3.3	3.3	3.3	3.3	3.3	3.2
1994	3.2	3.2	3.3	3.3	3.3	3.3	3.3	3.3	3.3	3.3	3.3	3.3	3.2
1995	3.4	3.4	3.4	3.4	3.4	3.5	3.4	3.4	3.4	3.3	3.3	3.3	3.3
1996	3.2	3.1	3.1	3.1	3.2	3.2	3.1	3.2	3.2	3.2	3.2	3.2	3.1
1997	3.1	3.1	3.1	3.2	3.2	3.2	3.2	3.2	3.2	3.2	3.2	3.4	3.1
1998	3.4	3.4	3.4	3.5	3.4	3.5	3.4	3.4	3.4	3.5	3.5	3.5	3.4
1999	3.4	3.4	3.4	3.7	3.8	3.9	3.8	3.9	4.0	4.0	4.0	4.0	3.7
2000	3.8	3.9	3.9	4.0	4.1	4.2	4.2	4.2	4.2	4.2	4.2	4.2	4.0
2001	4.1	4.1	4.1	4.0	3.9	4.0	3.9	4.0	3.9	3.7	3.7	3.7	3.9
2002	3.7	3.7	3.7	3.7	3.7	3.8	3.7	3.7	3.7	3.8	3.9	3.9	3.8
2003	3.9	3.9	3.9	3.9	4.0	3.9	3.9	3.9	3.9	3.9	3.9	4.0	3.9
Financial activities													
1990	7.7	7.8	7.9	8.0	8.0	8.2	8.0	8.2	8.2	8.2	8.2	8.3	8.0
1991	7.8	7.8	7.9	7.9	8.0	8.0	8.1	8.1	8.0	8.0	8.0	8.1	7.9
1992	8.1	8.1	8.1	8.3	8.4	8.4	8.4	8.5	8.5	8.5	8.5	8.6	8.3
1993	8.7	8.7	8.8	8.8	8.9	9.0	9.0	9.0	9.0	9.2	9.2	9.4	8.9
1994	9.1	9.2	9.3	9.7	9.8	9.8	9.8	9.8	9.8	9.8	9.8	9.8	9.6
1995	9.6	9.7	9.8	9.8	9.8	9.9	9.9	10.0	9.9	9.9	9.9	9.9	9.8
1996	9.8	9.9	10.0	10.1	10.3	10.4	10.4	10.6	10.6	10.6	10.7	10.8	10.3
1997	10.9	11.0	11.2	11.2	11.2	11.3	11.2	11.3	11.2	11.2	11.3	11.4	11.2
1998	11.1	11.0	11.0	10.9	11.0	11.1	11.1	11.0	10.9	10.8	10.8	10.9	10.9
1999	10.7	10.6	10.6	10.8	10.8	10.9	11.0	11.1	11.1	11.1	11.2	11.2	10.9
2000	11.1	11.2	11.3	11.6	11.7	11.8	11.7	11.7	11.8	11.8	11.8	11.8	11.6
2001	11.3	11.3	11.5	11.5	11.6	11.7	11.8	11.8	11.7	11.5	11.6	11.7	11.5
2002	11.9	11.8	11.8	11.9	12.0	12.0	12.1	12.1	12.1	12.2	12.2	12.3	12.0
2003	12.1	12.1	12.2	12.3	12.4	12.6	12.6	12.6	12.6	12.5	12.6	12.7	12.4
Professional and business services													
1990	12.4	12.8	13.3	13.8	14.0	14.1	14.2	14.6	14.4	14.3	14.1	14.1	13.8
1991	13.9	14.3	14.7	15.3	15.6	16.0	15.6	16.0	15.8	16.1	16.2	16.2	15.4
1992	16.1	16.3	16.8	16.7	16.8	17.0	16.9	17.3	17.1	17.4	17.3	17.5	16.9
1993	16.7	17.1	17.5	18.2	18.4	18.7	18.7	19.2	18.9	18.4	18.7	19.1	18.3
1994	19.4	19.9	20.5	20.7	20.9	21.1	20.6	21.1	20.7	20.7	20.9	21.0	20.6
1995	20.7	20.9	21.7	21.9	22.4	22.3	22.7	23.2	23.0	23.3	23.3	23.4	22.4
1996	22.5	22.6	22.9	23.7	23.6	24.0	24.3	24.3	23.7	24.1	23.8	23.7	23.6
1997	22.8	22.7	23.4	23.9	24.2	24.7	24.6	25.5	25.2	25.0	25.1	25.4	24.3
1998	23.4	23.8	24.6	24.8	25.0	25.3	25.7	26.1	26.6	27.1	27.0	27.0	25.5
1999	25.9	26.1	27.0	27.6	27.9	28.6	28.7	28.9	29.1	28.9	28.9	29.2	28.0
2000	28.3	28.6	29.6	30.3	30.4	30.8	31.0	31.5	31.8	31.6	31.6	31.0	30.5
2001	31.5	31.2	31.9	31.7	31.8	31.9	31.7	32.7	31.8	31.8	31.3	30.8	31.6
2002	29.9	30.3	30.9	31.6	31.5	31.9	31.7	32.4	32.0	32.5	31.8	31.7	31.5
2003	30.4	30.7	31.5	31.5	31.8	32.2	32.1	32.7	32.6	33.3	32.6	32.8	32.0
Educational and health services													
1990	12.3	12.6	12.6	12.7	12.8	12.8	12.8	13.0	13.3	13.3	13.3	13.4	12.9
1991	13.3	13.5	13.7	13.6	13.7	13.7	13.8	13.8	13.9	13.7	13.8	13.7	13.6
1992	13.7	13.7	13.7	14.0	14.1	14.3	14.6	14.7	14.8	15.0	15.1	15.2	14.4
1993	15.0	15.4	15.5	15.6	15.6	15.6	15.6	15.7	15.9	16.0	15.9	16.0	15.6
1994	15.6	15.8	15.9	15.9	16.1	16.1	16.1	16.1	16.3	16.3	16.4	16.4	16.0
1995	16.3	16.5	16.7	16.8	16.8	17.0	17.0	17.1	17.4	17.5	17.7	17.8	17.0
1996	17.8	18.0	18.2	18.4	18.4	18.4	18.3	18.6	18.9	19.0	19.3	19.3	18.5
1997	19.2	19.4	19.6	19.9	20.1	20.2	20.0	20.3	20.5	20.8	20.9	21.1	20.1
1998	20.6	21.0	21.1	21.9	22.0	22.1	22.0	22.1	22.2	22.4	22.4	22.6	21.8
1999	22.0	22.3	22.3	21.8	21.9	22.0	21.9	22.1	22.5	22.7	22.8	22.8	22.2
2000	22.8	23.1	23.3	24.0	24.2	24.5	24.8	25.0	25.2	25.3	25.6	25.6	24.4
2001	24.7	24.9	25.2	25.3	25.4	25.4	25.4	25.7	26.1	26.1	26.3	26.5	25.5
2002	26.3	26.6	26.8	26.8	27.0	26.8	26.9	27.0	27.3	27.6	27.6	27.8	27.0
2003	27.7	27.9	27.9	28.3	28.4	28.3	28.3	28.4	28.9	29.2	29.4	29.7	28.5

Employment by Industry: Idaho—*Continued*

(Numbers in thousands. Not seasonally adjusted.)

Industry	January	February	March	April	May	June	July	August	September	October	November	December	Annual Average
BOISE CITY—*Continued*													
Leisure and hospitality													
1990	10.4	10.5	10.8	11.3	11.7	12.0	11.6	11.9	11.6	11.3	11.1	11.2	11.2
1991	11.1	11.3	11.5	11.9	12.3	12.6	12.5	12.7	12.5	12.2	12.2	12.0	12.0
1992	11.6	11.8	12.0	12.5	13.1	13.4	13.3	13.5	13.3	13.0	12.7	12.7	12.7
1993	12.3	12.3	12.5	12.9	13.4	13.7	13.9	13.8	14.0	13.5	13.4	13.4	13.2
1994	13.3	13.5	13.8	14.0	14.6	15.0	14.9	15.1	14.9	14.4	14.1	14.2	14.3
1995	14.0	14.2	14.5	14.9	15.5	16.1	15.7	15.7	15.4	14.7	14.7	14.9	15.0
1996	14.7	14.8	15.3	15.3	15.6	16.0	15.9	16.0	15.8	15.4	15.3	15.5	15.4
1997	15.0	15.1	15.3	15.7	16.5	16.7	16.8	16.7	16.7	16.1	16.0	16.2	16.0
1998	15.7	16.5	16.9	16.9	17.6	17.7	17.5	17.6	17.7	16.9	16.7	16.8	17.0
1999	16.1	16.4	16.9	17.5	18.0	18.3	18.4	18.1	17.9	17.8	17.9	18.1	17.6
2000	17.2	17.5	18.1	19.3	19.9	20.3	20.4	20.6	20.5	19.4	19.5	19.4	19.3
2001	18.3	18.7	19.3	19.5	20.3	20.7	20.7	20.8	20.6	19.6	19.7	19.5	19.8
2002	18.4	18.7	19.1	19.5	20.2	20.8	20.6	20.7	20.4	20.0	19.8	19.6	19.8
2003	19.2	19.2	19.7	20.0	20.4	20.8	20.8	21.1	20.6	20.2	20.2	20.2	20.2
Other services													
1990	4.1	4.1	4.2	4.2	4.1	4.1	4.2	4.3	4.1	4.1	4.1	4.1	4.1
1991	4.4	4.4	4.4	4.5	4.4	4.5	4.5	4.5	4.4	4.3	4.3	4.6	4.4
1992	4.0	4.0	4.0	4.0	4.2	4.3	4.4	4.5	4.5	4.5	4.6	4.7	4.3
1993	4.7	4.9	5.0	5.0	5.1	5.1	5.3	5.2	5.3	5.3	5.3	5.3	5.1
1994	5.3	5.4	5.5	5.6	5.7	5.8	5.8	5.8	5.8	5.8	5.9	5.8	5.6
1995	6.0	6.0	6.1	6.2	6.2	6.2	6.2	6.2	6.2	6.2	6.3	6.3	6.1
1996	6.3	6.3	6.3	6.3	6.3	6.4	6.3	6.3	6.3	6.4	6.4	6.4	6.3
1997	6.4	6.4	6.4	6.4	6.5	6.5	6.5	6.5	6.5	6.5	6.6	6.6	6.4
1998	6.6	6.6	6.6	6.6	6.7	6.8	7.1	7.1	7.0	7.1	7.0	7.1	6.8
1999	7.1	7.2	7.3	7.1	7.1	7.2	7.4	7.5	7.4	7.3	7.3	7.3	7.2
2000	7.3	7.4	7.5	7.7	7.7	7.9	7.7	7.8	7.7	7.7	7.7	7.7	7.6
2001	6.8	6.9	7.1	7.0	7.1	6.9	6.8	6.8	6.7	6.7	6.6	6.7	6.8
2002	6.5	6.7	6.7	6.7	6.7	6.7	6.8	6.8	6.6	6.6	6.6	6.5	6.7
2003	6.5	6.5	6.7	6.7	6.7	6.8	6.8	6.8	6.7	6.7	6.7	6.8	6.7
Government													
1990	23.3	23.6	24.2	24.1	24.5	24.1	22.8	22.6	24.0	24.6	24.8	24.7	23.9
1991	24.1	24.9	25.3	25.3	25.1	25.1	23.7	23.6	24.5	25.7	25.8	25.6	24.8
1992	25.6	26.1	26.5	26.6	26.3	26.3	25.2	24.9	25.7	26.9	27.0	26.8	26.1
1993	26.2	27.0	27.2	27.2	27.1	26.7	25.5	25.6	26.8	27.3	27.3	27.3	26.7
1994	26.6	27.5	27.6	27.9	27.4	27.5	24.0	23.9	27.5	28.4	28.4	28.4	27.0
1995	27.5	28.5	28.7	28.7	28.2	28.3	26.7	26.5	28.0	28.8	28.8	28.6	28.1
1996	27.7	28.4	28.7	29.1	28.8	28.7	26.8	27.1	28.6	29.4	29.4	29.3	28.5
1997	29.0	29.6	29.8	29.9	29.9	29.3	28.1	28.1	29.3	30.4	30.2	30.6	29.5
1998	30.3	30.9	31.2	31.4	31.4	31.6	29.8	29.4	31.0	32.2	32.3	32.2	31.1
1999	31.9	32.3	32.4	32.7	32.8	32.8	31.1	30.9	31.9	33.0	33.1	33.0	32.3
2000	31.9	33.1	33.4	33.2	34.0	33.2	32.6	32.3	32.8	33.4	33.5	33.5	33.0
2001	33.2	34.5	34.9	35.0	35.3	34.8	33.6	33.4	34.9	36.0	35.9	35.9	34.7
2002	34.5	35.8	36.1	36.1	36.3	35.8	34.2	33.9	36.2	37.1	37.2	37.3	35.9
2003	35.9	36.5	36.8	37.0	37.2	36.4	34.1	33.9	35.2	36.0	36.1	36.3	36.0
Federal government													
1990	4.3	4.3	4.3	4.5	4.7	4.8	4.7	4.6	4.5	4.5	4.5	4.5	4.5
1991	4.3	4.4	4.4	4.5	4.6	4.7	4.7	4.7	4.6	4.7	4.6	4.6	4.5
1992	4.6	4.6	4.6	4.8	4.8	4.9	5.0	5.0	5.0	4.9	4.9	5.0	4.8
1993	4.9	4.9	4.9	4.9	5.0	5.0	5.1	5.1	5.1	5.0	4.9	5.0	4.9
1994	4.9	4.8	4.8	4.9	4.9	5.0	5.0	5.0	5.0	4.9	4.8	4.9	4.9
1995	4.8	4.8	4.8	4.9	4.9	5.0	5.1	5.0	5.0	4.9	4.9	4.9	4.9
1996	4.7	4.7	4.7	4.8	4.8	4.9	4.8	4.9	4.8	4.8	4.8	4.8	4.7
1997	4.7	4.7	4.7	4.7	4.8	4.8	4.9	4.9	4.8	4.8	4.7	4.8	4.7
1998	4.7	4.7	4.8	4.8	4.9	4.9	4.9	4.9	4.9	4.9	4.8	4.9	4.8
1999	4.8	4.8	4.8	4.8	4.9	4.9	5.0	5.0	5.0	5.0	4.9	4.9	4.9
2000	4.9	4.9	4.9	5.0	6.0	5.2	5.3	5.4	5.1	5.1	5.1	5.1	5.1
2001	4.9	4.9	5.0	5.1	5.2	5.4	5.2	5.2	5.3	5.2	5.2	5.3	5.1
2002	5.1	5.1	5.1	5.2	5.3	5.6	5.4	5.4	5.4	5.4	5.4	5.6	5.3
2003	5.3	5.2	5.3	5.3	5.4	5.6	5.6	5.6	5.6	5.5	5.4	5.6	5.5
State government													
1990	9.1	9.4	9.8	9.6	9.6	9.1	9.1	9.2	9.9	9.9	9.9	9.8	9.5
1991	9.6	10.0	10.2	10.1	9.7	9.6	9.5	9.5	9.8	10.3	10.3	10.1	9.8
1992	10.1	10.5	10.7	10.6	10.1	9.9	9.9	9.8	10.3	10.6	10.5	10.5	10.2
1993	10.0	10.7	10.8	10.8	10.4	10.0	9.9	9.9	10.7	10.7	10.6	10.5	10.4
1994	10.0	10.8	10.8	10.9	10.3	10.1	10.1	10.1	10.9	11.0	10.9	10.8	10.5
1995	10.3	11.0	11.1	11.0	10.4	10.2	10.2	10.2	10.8	10.9	10.7	10.6	10.6
1996	9.8	10.5	10.5	10.8	10.4	10.2	10.0	10.1	10.8	10.9	10.8	10.7	10.4
1997	10.5	10.8	10.9	11.0	10.8	10.2	10.4	10.5	11.1	11.4	11.2	11.3	10.8
1998	11.2	11.6	11.7	11.8	11.5	11.6	11.4	11.0	11.9	12.2	12.0	12.0	11.6
1999	11.9	12.1	12.1	12.4	12.2	12.1	11.2	11.4	11.8	12.4	12.3	12.2	12.0
2000	11.3	12.3	12.4	12.1	11.8	11.7	12.0	12.2	12.3	12.1	12.0	11.9	12.0
2001	12.0	13.0	13.2	13.2	13.1	12.4	12.5	12.7	13.3	13.7	13.5	13.4	12.9
2002	12.2	13.2	13.3	13.3	13.3	12.4	12.4	12.5	14.0	14.3	14.0	13.9	13.3
2003	13.2	13.6	13.7	13.9	13.7	12.7	12.8	12.7	13.4	13.6	13.5	13.5	13.4

Employment by Industry: Idaho—*Continued*

(Numbers in thousands. Not seasonally adjusted.)

Industry	January	February	March	April	May	June	July	August	September	October	November	December	Annual Average
BOISE CITY—*Continued*													
Local government													
1990	9.9	9.9	10.1	10.0	10.2	10.2	9.0	8.8	9.6	10.2	10.4	10.4	9.8
1991	10.2	10.5	10.7	10.7	10.8	10.8	9.5	9.4	10.1	10.7	10.9	10.9	10.4
1992	10.9	11.0	11.2	11.2	11.4	11.5	10.3	10.1	10.4	11.4	11.6	11.3	11.0
1993	11.3	11.4	11.5	11.5	11.7	11.7	10.5	10.6	11.0	11.6	11.8	11.8	11.3
1994	11.7	11.9	12.0	12.1	12.2	12.4	8.9	8.8	11.6	12.5	12.7	12.7	11.6
1995	12.4	12.7	12.8	12.8	12.9	13.1	11.4	11.3	12.2	13.0	13.2	13.1	12.5
1996	13.2	13.2	13.5	13.5	13.6	13.6	12.0	12.1	13.0	13.7	13.8	13.8	13.2
1997	13.8	14.1	14.2	14.2	14.3	14.3	12.8	12.7	13.4	14.2	14.3	14.5	13.9
1998	14.4	14.6	14.7	14.8	15.0	15.1	13.5	13.5	14.2	15.1	15.5	15.3	14.6
1999	15.2	15.4	15.5	15.5	15.7	15.8	14.9	14.5	15.1	15.6	15.9	15.9	15.4
2000	15.7	15.9	16.1	16.1	16.2	16.3	15.3	14.7	15.4	16.2	16.4	16.5	15.9
2001	16.3	16.6	16.7	16.7	17.0	17.0	15.9	15.5	16.3	17.1	17.2	17.2	16.6
2002	17.2	17.5	17.7	17.6	17.7	17.8	16.4	16.0	16.8	17.4	17.8	17.8	17.3
2003	17.4	17.7	17.8	17.8	18.1	18.1	15.7	15.6	16.2	16.9	17.2	17.2	17.1

Average Weekly Hours by Industry: Idaho

(Not seasonally adjusted.)

Industry	January	February	March	April	May	June	July	August	September	October	November	December	Annual Average
STATEWIDE													
Manufacturing													
2001	39.2	39.2	39.4	39.1	39.0	38.6	38.5	38.5	39.7	39.3	39.0	39.6	39.1
2002	38.4	37.8	38.8	38.8	39.4	39.6	38.4	37.9	42.0	40.6	40.6	42.3	39.6
2003	39.1	38.8	40.9	40.5	42.4	43.6	42.1	42.1	41.6	41.0	41.7	41.4	41.3

Average Hourly Earnings by Industry: Idaho

(Dollars, not seasonally adjusted.)

Industry	January	February	March	April	May	June	July	August	September	October	November	December	Annual Average
STATEWIDE													
Manufacturing													
2001	13.72	13.78	13.42	13.63	13.78	13.58	13.83	13.93	14.20	14.13	14.29	14.00	13.85
2002	14.14	14.06	13.77	13.84	13.87	13.90	13.84	13.79	13.83	13.58	13.48	13.53	13.80
2003	13.56	13.78	13.58	13.51	13.74	13.79	13.84	13.94	13.94	13.73	13.49	13.69	13.72

Average Weekly Earnings by Industry: Idaho

(Dollars, not seasonally adjusted.)

Industry	January	February	March	April	May	June	July	August	September	October	November	December	Annual Average
STATEWIDE													
Manufacturing													
2001	537.82	540.18	528.75	532.93	537.42	524.19	532.46	536.31	563.74	555.31	557.31	554.40	541.54
2002	542.98	531.47	534.28	536.99	546.48	550.44	531.46	522.64	580.86	551.35	547.29	572.32	546.48
2003	530.20	534.66	555.42	547.16	582.58	601.24	582.66	586.87	579.90	562.93	562.53	566.77	566.64

ILLINOIS AT A GLANCE

(Population and total nonfarm employment numbers in thousands)

Population, Census 2000:	12,419.3
Total nonfarm employment, 2003:	5,817.6
Change in total nonfarm employment	
(Number)	
1990–2003:	529.2
1990–2001:	706.8
2001–2003:	-177.6
(Compound annual rate of change)	
1990–2003:	0.7%
1990–2001:	1.1%
2001–2003:	-1.5%
Unemployment rate	
1990:	6.3%
2001:	5.4%
2003:	6.7%

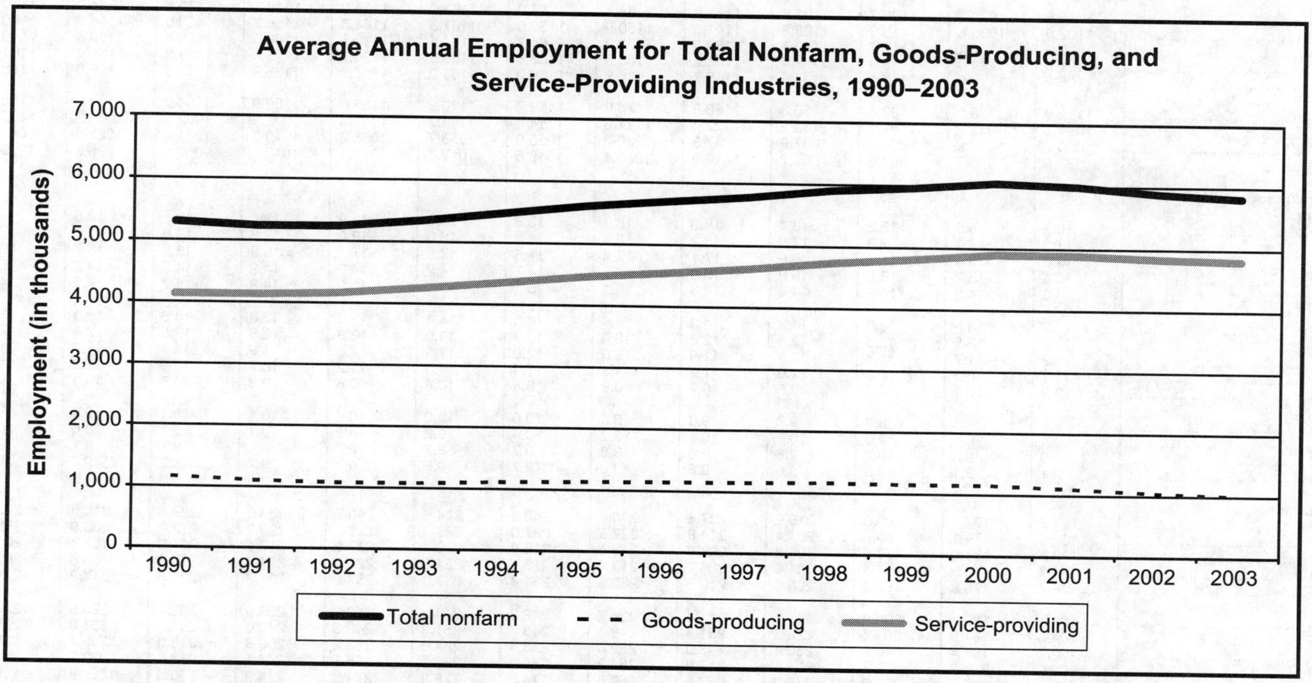

Nonfarm payroll employment experienced weakness at the beginning of the 1990s, but resumed steady growth until the onset of the 2001 recession. In 2003, employment remained below its peak in 2000, mainly due to the ongoing erosion of jobs in manufacturing industries, which employed nearly 200,000 fewer people than in 1990. Employment in the service-providing industries declined moderately in the 2001 recession. However, educational and health services and leisure and hospitality continued to add jobs during this period.

Employment by Industry: Illinois

(Numbers in thousands. Not seasonally adjusted.)

Industry	January	February	March	April	May	June	July	August	September	October	November	December	Annual Average
STATEWIDE													
Total nonfarm													
1990	5157.5	5176.7	5228.7	5252.8	5306.7	5352.6	5330.0	5337.3	5347.8	5321.8	5324.3	5324.6	5288.4
1991	5151.5	5144.3	5183.5	5224.1	5264.8	5283.9	5248.7	5238.7	5266.1	5257.2	5260.6	5254.8	5231.5
1992	5098.2	5109.9	5144.8	5186.0	5241.0	5276.5	5261.0	5261.5	5294.0	5306.0	5315.8	5322.7	5234.7
1993	5170.8	5194.8	5228.2	5293.1	5342.5	5367.6	5345.1	5352.7	5382.9	5414.0	5429.5	5444.1	5330.4
1994	5273.2	5300.3	5366.8	5426.4	5481.1	5524.8	5489.2	5500.4	5543.8	5529.1	5555.7	5564.6	5462.9
1995	5428.6	5465.6	5524.4	5563.4	5604.8	5652.8	5582.4	5599.4	5672.0	5654.9	5678.1	5691.8	5593.1
1996	5519.6	5542.3	5597.1	5642.0	5696.8	5739.6	5697.6	5724.6	5737.0	5745.8	5784.7	5788.4	5684.6
1997	5598.9	5624.7	5683.9	5726.1	5798.1	5826.7	5782.1	5793.5	5824.0	5836.7	5873.7	5896.6	5772.0
1998	5716.4	5745.6	5791.2	5851.5	5914.4	5947.4	5926.6	5935.5	5975.8	5971.9	5994.6	6012.4	5898.6
1999	5776.4	5821.8	5873.6	5934.6	5975.4	6018.7	5977.4	5983.2	5997.1	6028.1	6048.6	6066.5	5958.4
2000	5874.4	5906.8	5973.3	6025.9	6078.8	6124.8	6061.6	6080.5	6095.3	6092.5	6115.2	6108.5	6044.8
2001	5906.2	5930.3	5977.0	6016.0	6060.4	6093.1	6012.8	6012.3	6006.1	5976.5	5977.0	5974.4	5995.2
2002	5778.6	5781.4	5819.3	5875.3	5921.8	5948.7	5897.0	5910.8	5914.5	5914.1	5926.8	5918.3	5883.9
2003	5713.0	5712.1	5742.5	5801.2	5850.0	5878.2	5823.8	5827.3	5849.3	5868.6	5875.7	5869.2	5817.6
Total private													
1990	4413.1	4413.7	4452.0	4474.4	4524.1	4581.7	4586.8	4604.1	4588.2	4544.9	4543.4	4542.8	4522.4
1991	4389.9	4368.5	4400.3	4434.4	4476.9	4523.7	4505.6	4511.3	4503.4	4477.3	4470.8	4469.5	4460.9
1992	4333.4	4330.9	4356.3	4393.6	4454.8	4502.2	4524.8	4538.9	4524.9	4520.3	4518.0	4532.6	4460.8
1993	4406.9	4413.2	4441.3	4500.7	4544.3	4595.8	4606.4	4625.2	4621.6	4629.4	4635.3	4652.0	4556.0
1994	4508.7	4515.6	4569.1	4629.5	4680.5	4742.3	4733.7	4751.6	4762.8	4725.5	4745.7	4758.1	4676.9
1995	4645.8	4657.4	4711.1	4745.3	4788.5	4851.9	4835.1	4861.2	4866.1	4841.3	4855.2	4875.1	4794.5
1996	4730.0	4726.9	4771.8	4815.6	4870.4	4925.4	4919.1	4951.9	4934.3	4930.8	4955.3	4971.3	4875.2
1997	4806.0	4810.8	4863.6	4910.1	4969.9	5016.1	5003.7	5019.1	5020.4	5026.5	5046.2	5072.7	4963.7
1998	4918.4	4928.2	4963.8	5026.0	5085.5	5133.3	5142.2	5157.7	5156.0	5143.6	5157.5	5178.2	5082.5
1999	4973.7	4998.9	5041.0	5095.2	5136.9	5193.8	5177.6	5189.1	5170.2	5187.9	5204.6	5225.6	5132.8
2000	5057.8	5065.8	5123.3	5178.3	5216.7	5278.9	5251.7	5274.2	5261.9	5243.1	5258.7	5251.9	5205.1
2001	5079.7	5077.5	5120.1	5159.7	5196.0	5242.0	5187.6	5193.7	5158.0	5112.1	5108.0	5103.3	5144.8
2002	4932.8	4915.3	4946.8	4999.5	5040.3	5083.5	5069.0	5088.1	5064.3	5042.3	5049.9	5043.0	5022.9
2003	4865.9	4846.5	4874.2	4929.0	4975.4	5016.6	4996.9	5007.8	5006.5	5007.3	5010.4	5003.8	4961.7
Goods-producing													
1990	1128.4	1130.5	1139.6	1150.4	1167.3	1184.0	1178.6	1185.5	1176.8	1159.7	1149.7	1134.0	1157.0
1991	1081.1	1071.9	1078.5	1096.3	1110.9	1125.4	1120.7	1121.3	1120.5	1115.9	1103.3	1080.2	1102.1
1992	1028.6	1026.8	1033.3	1057.7	1076.6	1093.9	1104.9	1108.8	1104.8	1092.8	1082.7	1074.9	1073.8
1993	1038.8	1039.8	1046.7	1063.4	1078.2	1094.2	1097.8	1100.1	1098.9	1099.8	1096.9	1088.9	1078.6
1994	1054.3	1053.3	1073.3	1095.5	1116.1	1138.0	1126.6	1130.6	1134.5	1126.8	1125.2	1119.2	1107.7
1995	1086.6	1088.7	1105.3	1121.8	1133.2	1154.1	1147.0	1153.0	1154.0	1146.7	1140.8	1134.0	1130.4
1996	1102.0	1099.6	1113.3	1126.8	1141.6	1160.9	1159.5	1167.3	1161.5	1156.7	1153.0	1144.6	1140.5
1997	1099.9	1103.1	1118.7	1144.5	1160.3	1173.3	1164.7	1174.1	1172.5	1166.6	1160.4	1155.6	1149.4
1998	1121.0	1122.3	1128.0	1153.4	1168.2	1183.3	1183.8	1186.5	1184.7	1175.6	1168.2	1165.6	1161.7
1999	1108.2	1114.9	1117.1	1138.4	1148.7	1168.2	1166.0	1169.2	1167.9	1166.9	1162.5	1155.3	1148.6
2000	1112.9	1115.9	1132.6	1150.3	1160.8	1174.3	1169.7	1170.9	1166.6	1159.9	1154.2	1134.0	1150.1
2001	1091.1	1093.2	1102.0	1113.9	1122.0	1131.3	1114.4	1114.7	1106.3	1092.2	1082.5	1068.2	1102.7
2002	1020.9	1015.9	1023.0	1037.9	1047.3	1060.2	1055.9	1059.7	1055.8	1048.5	1041.8	1026.8	1041.1
2003	982.6	975.7	982.6	1000.7	1010.9	1020.4	1015.5	1017.7	1017.1	1013.5	1009.6	996.3	1003.6
Natural resources and mining													
1990	18.2	18.0	18.2	18.1	18.3	18.7	18.8	19.0	18.9	18.7	18.6	18.6	18.5
1991	17.3	17.1	17.3	17.9	18.2	18.4	18.4	18.3	18.0	17.8	17.8	17.3	17.8
1992	16.6	16.4	16.6	16.8	17.1	17.4	17.5	17.5	17.1	16.9	16.9	16.7	16.9
1993	16.0	15.7	15.8	15.9	16.0	15.9	14.7	14.2	14.2	14.2	14.2	14.2	15.0
1994	14.8	14.6	14.2	14.6	14.8	15.1	15.1	15.0	14.9	14.8	14.7	14.6	14.7
1995	13.7	13.5	13.9	14.2	14.3	14.4	14.3	14.1	13.9	13.8	13.6	13.3	13.9
1996	12.6	12.5	12.6	12.6	12.8	13.0	12.9	13.0	12.8	12.8	12.5	12.3	12.7
1997	11.7	11.7	11.8	12.1	11.9	12.0	12.0	11.9	11.8	11.8	11.7	11.6	11.8
1998	11.1	10.6	10.7	11.0	11.2	11.3	11.4	11.3	11.2	10.7	10.9	11.2	11.0
1999	10.2	10.1	10.4	10.5	10.7	10.9	10.8	10.8	10.8	10.8	10.5	10.5	10.5
2000	9.7	9.5	9.7	9.8	9.8	9.9	10.0	10.0	10.0	10.1	10.1	9.9	9.8
2001	9.4	9.4	9.8	10.0	10.1	10.2	10.4	10.2	10.2	10.1	10.1	10.0	10.0
2002	9.6	9.5	9.7	9.6	9.6	9.8	9.7	9.7	9.7	9.8	9.7	9.7	9.7
2003	9.1	9.1	9.3	9.6	9.6	9.8	9.7	9.8	9.7	9.7	9.7	9.7	9.6
Construction													
1990	197.9	197.9	203.8	215.9	227.6	236.2	242.2	244.6	240.7	233.9	229.1	216.4	223.8
1991	181.0	179.1	185.7	201.4	214.8	222.8	227.0	229.0	226.0	223.9	212.4	200.0	208.5
1992	176.8	174.0	178.6	191.8	204.0	213.4	218.9	220.4	217.9	217.1	207.8	199.7	201.7
1993	173.7	172.9	176.5	191.6	204.7	213.4	218.5	221.8	220.9	221.7	216.3	206.3	203.1
1994	178.7	175.6	188.2	205.6	219.9	230.5	234.4	237.3	237.8	231.3	225.8	217.2	215.1
1995	191.1	189.4	200.0	211.1	221.4	236.7	242.3	244.2	243.6	239.6	232.7	223.5	222.9
1996	194.3	191.9	201.4	220.5	231.4	242.7	248.6	251.9	248.3	246.0	241.2	231.0	229.1
1997	198.7	198.4	210.2	230.4	243.0	252.6	253.4	254.0	252.2	250.8	245.0	236.1	235.4
1998	206.6	206.2	209.7	235.1	247.9	257.2	265.0	267.1	265.5	264.1	258.9	253.7	244.7
1999	215.9	219.3	227.2	248.0	257.5	269.8	274.6	276.3	274.3	274.9	270.3	262.6	255.8
2000	234.8	234.6	248.2	266.1	276.3	285.2	287.1	289.7	286.6	284.7	279.6	263.8	269.7
2001	239.0	241.5	252.3	272.0	284.5	293.0	295.5	297.6	292.8	291.1	289.4	278.9	277.3
2002	246.4	244.1	251.4	268.3	278.9	289.5	295.2	298.3	296.4	295.4	289.9	276.9	277.6
2003	246.8	240.8	248.2	269.2	281.1	290.3	292.8	295.6	294.7	292.2	288.0	278.0	276.5

Employment by Industry: Illinois—*Continued*

(Numbers in thousands. Not seasonally adjusted.)

Industry	January	February	March	April	May	June	July	August	September	October	November	December	Annual Average
STATEWIDE—*Continued*													
Manufacturing													
1990	912.3	914.6	917.6	916.4	921.4	929.1	917.6	921.9	917.2	907.1	902.0	899.0	914.6
1991	882.8	875.7	875.5	877.0	877.9	884.2	875.3	874.0	876.5	874.2	873.1	862.9	875.7
1992	835.2	836.4	838.1	849.1	855.5	863.1	868.5	870.9	869.8	858.8	858.0	858.5	855.1
1993	849.1	851.2	854.4	855.9	857.5	864.9	864.6	864.1	863.8	863.9	866.4	868.4	860.3
1994	860.8	863.1	870.9	875.3	881.4	892.4	877.1	878.3	881.8	880.7	884.7	887.4	877.8
1995	881.8	885.8	891.4	896.5	897.5	903.0	890.4	894.7	896.5	893.3	894.5	897.2	893.5
1996	895.1	895.2	899.3	893.7	897.4	905.2	898.0	902.4	900.4	897.9	899.3	901.3	898.7
1997	889.5	893.0	896.7	902.0	905.4	908.7	899.3	908.2	908.5	904.0	903.7	907.9	902.2
1998	903.3	905.5	907.6	907.3	909.1	914.8	907.4	908.1	908.0	900.8	898.4	900.7	905.9
1999	882.1	885.5	879.5	879.9	880.5	887.5	880.6	882.1	882.8	881.2	881.7	882.2	882.1
2000	868.4	871.8	874.7	874.4	874.7	879.2	872.6	871.2	870.0	865.1	864.5	860.3	870.5
2001	842.7	842.3	839.9	831.9	827.4	828.1	808.5	806.9	803.3	791.0	783.0	779.3	815.4
2002	764.9	762.3	761.9	760.0	758.8	760.9	751.0	751.7	749.7	743.3	742.2	740.2	753.9
2003	726.7	725.8	725.1	721.9	720.2	720.3	713.0	712.3	712.7	711.6	711.9	708.6	717.5
Service-providing													
1990	4029.1	4046.2	4089.1	4102.4	4139.4	4168.6	4151.4	4151.8	4171.0	4162.1	4174.6	4190.6	4131.3
1991	4070.4	4072.4	4105.0	4127.8	4153.9	4158.5	4128.0	4117.4	4145.6	4141.3	4157.3	4174.6	4129.3
1992	4069.6	4083.1	4111.5	4128.3	4164.4	4182.6	4156.1	4152.7	4189.2	4213.2	4233.1	4247.8	4160.9
1993	4132.0	4155.0	4181.5	4229.7	4264.3	4273.4	4247.3	4252.6	4284.0	4314.2	4332.6	4355.2	4251.8
1994	4218.9	4247.0	4293.5	4330.9	4365.0	4386.8	4362.6	4369.8	4409.3	4402.3	4430.5	4445.4	4355.1
1995	4342.0	4376.9	4419.1	4441.6	4471.6	4498.7	4435.4	4446.4	4518.0	4508.2	4537.3	4557.8	4462.7
1996	4417.6	4442.7	4483.8	4515.2	4555.2	4578.7	4538.1	4557.3	4575.5	4589.1	4631.7	4643.8	4544.0
1997	4499.0	4521.6	4565.2	4581.6	4637.8	4653.4	4617.4	4619.4	4651.5	4670.1	4713.3	4741.0	4622.6
1998	4595.4	4623.3	4663.2	4698.1	4746.2	4764.1	4742.8	4749.0	4791.1	4796.3	4826.4	4846.8	4736.8
1999	4668.2	4706.9	4756.5	4796.2	4826.7	4850.5	4811.4	4814.0	4829.2	4861.2	4886.1	4911.2	4809.8
2000	4761.5	4790.9	4840.7	4875.6	4918.0	4950.5	4891.9	4909.6	4928.7	4932.6	4961.0	4974.5	4894.6
2001	4815.1	4837.1	4875.0	4902.1	4938.4	4961.8	4898.4	4897.6	4899.8	4884.3	4894.5	4906.2	4892.5
2002	4757.7	4765.5	4796.3	4837.4	4874.5	4888.5	4841.1	4851.1	4858.7	4865.6	4885.0	4891.5	4842.7
2003	4730.4	4736.4	4759.9	4800.5	4839.1	4857.8	4808.3	4809.6	4832.2	4855.1	4866.1	4872.9	4814.0
Trade, transportation, and utilities													
1990	1142.7	1129.3	1134.7	1131.4	1140.2	1151.5	1148.4	1151.1	1146.6	1147.5	1160.3	1176.0	1146.6
1991	1135.5	1115.3	1118.2	1113.0	1119.6	1125.6	1122.8	1125.9	1123.2	1121.3	1133.5	1150.9	1125.4
1992	1109.4	1097.3	1098.3	1094.3	1105.5	1112.1	1102.9	1105.2	1105.7	1129.4	1143.3	1162.7	1113.8
1993	1116.6	1106.9	1109.1	1119.2	1127.0	1136.7	1138.4	1141.2	1141.3	1156.9	1175.7	1194.4	1138.6
1994	1147.2	1137.9	1144.0	1147.2	1158.2	1168.1	1166.7	1171.8	1177.1	1182.9	1202.6	1218.7	1168.5
1995	1175.2	1163.9	1168.9	1168.1	1177.0	1186.3	1184.5	1189.8	1191.4	1200.7	1220.8	1237.0	1188.6
1996	1192.8	1178.1	1182.5	1174.9	1186.7	1196.4	1188.2	1194.6	1193.8	1209.8	1233.3	1252.2	1198.6
1997	1199.7	1182.5	1188.5	1190.7	1202.1	1210.6	1205.2	1193.7	1206.4	1219.0	1239.4	1260.0	1208.1
1998	1205.6	1190.6	1195.5	1193.0	1206.7	1213.3	1214.3	1216.5	1218.5	1228.3	1250.7	1266.8	1216.6
1999	1211.6	1202.8	1209.7	1213.8	1221.1	1230.9	1230.5	1230.8	1227.0	1240.4	1262.8	1281.7	1230.2
2000	1232.7	1220.7	1226.6	1231.2	1238.7	1246.8	1242.8	1249.5	1249.3	1256.9	1280.0	1295.7	1247.5
2001	1241.9	1225.7	1230.2	1233.2	1236.7	1242.1	1224.6	1223.5	1221.6	1217.4	1234.7	1246.2	1231.5
2002	1194.2	1176.7	1182.1	1186.3	1193.8	1198.7	1192.2	1195.6	1196.6	1200.7	1221.0	1235.1	1197.8
2003	1180.2	1168.0	1171.1	1173.6	1182.8	1188.5	1178.6	1183.6	1184.9	1192.1	1211.0	1227.1	1186.8
Wholesale trade													
1990	302.9	303.1	305.2	305.7	307.6	310.8	312.8	312.9	310.6	308.2	306.6	307.1	307.7
1991	300.1	299.1	299.8	299.9	300.3	302.8	303.2	302.2	299.4	294.7	294.0	293.8	299.1
1992	294.3	293.4	294.3	292.3	294.1	296.1	297.5	296.2	295.6	296.7	296.0	295.7	295.1
1993	291.3	291.6	293.0	294.4	295.9	298.9	299.3	298.7	296.9	297.5	297.2	297.7	296.0
1994	290.2	290.1	291.8	293.6	295.0	297.8	298.4	299.5	300.0	298.1	298.6	300.1	296.1
1995	299.4	300.9	303.6	304.8	306.0	309.7	308.1	308.3	307.0	306.3	304.9	306.5	305.4
1996	301.2	301.8	303.6	303.0	304.7	307.9	307.6	307.7	305.1	305.6	306.5	307.2	305.1
1997	301.1	301.5	304.0	305.7	307.4	310.5	309.6	309.8	308.0	308.9	309.1	310.5	307.1
1998	308.8	309.7	311.4	313.3	314.6	317.8	315.8	314.6	313.7	313.9	313.9	315.5	313.5
1999	311.5	312.9	314.4	316.0	317.2	319.3	320.6	319.3	318.2	318.3	318.1	319.3	317.0
2000	315.9	316.3	318.2	319.5	321.0	323.6	322.9	322.5	321.9	322.6	322.2	323.2	320.8
2001	316.8	316.5	317.6	319.8	319.8	320.7	317.7	316.9	315.9	313.1	311.9	311.8	316.5
2002	305.7	305.0	305.9	307.0	307.9	310.4	308.1	307.8	307.3	307.3	307.7	307.7	307.3
2003	303.6	303.2	304.2	304.4	305.5	306.7	307.4	306.9	305.0	303.6	303.0	303.8	304.8
Retail trade													
1990	613.3	598.6	599.2	596.5	601.2	608.5	606.5	608.9	604.2	607.1	620.9	635.6	608.3
1991	608.6	590.3	590.9	586.0	592.1	595.0	593.3	596.7	592.1	594.2	611.2	627.5	598.1
1992	591.3	580.9	580.0	577.9	585.3	589.3	575.6	578.6	575.1	598.8	613.5	631.1	589.7
1993	594.1	584.0	584.1	586.7	590.3	594.8	595.8	597.7	594.9	605.0	623.1	639.5	599.1
1994	602.8	592.2	593.9	597.4	603.6	611.3	611.2	616.1	618.7	624.8	645.2	661.3	614.8
1995	626.5	615.0	617.1	613.1	618.9	624.1	623.3	628.0	627.7	634.6	656.7	670.5	629.6
1996	637.3	622.3	623.3	615.0	623.9	629.2	625.1	630.1	629.0	640.1	663.1	681.0	634.9
1997	640.0	623.4	625.5	624.8	632.3	636.7	634.6	637.2	632.0	640.3	660.7	680.0	638.9
1998	633.8	618.2	620.2	614.9	624.5	628.1	629.8	631.0	630.8	639.5	663.7	678.3	634.4
1999	632.2	622.7	626.7	626.7	633.0	641.1	639.2	641.3	637.2	646.6	668.8	685.9	641.7
2000	644.4	632.8	636.2	637.2	642.2	648.6	645.7	650.4	648.3	654.0	676.8	690.7	650.6
2001	650.5	636.2	638.6	638.1	640.9	647.5	637.0	637.4	633.9	634.2	655.4	669.4	643.3
2002	630.4	615.4	620.3	620.9	626.9	632.2	628.2	629.8	628.2	630.9	651.4	665.7	631.7
2003	621.0	611.1	613.4	615.0	621.7	627.5	622.8	626.3	625.8	630.8	648.7	663.8	627.3

Employment by Industry: Illinois—*Continued*

(Numbers in thousands. Not seasonally adjusted.)

Industry	January	February	March	April	May	June	July	August	September	October	November	December	Annual Average
STATEWIDE—*Continued*													
Transportation and utilities													
1990	226.5	227.6	230.3	229.2	231.4	232.2	229.1	229.3	231.8	232.2	232.8	233.3	230.4
1991	226.8	225.9	227.5	227.1	227.2	227.8	226.3	227.0	231.7	232.4	228.3	229.6	228.1
1992	223.8	223.0	224.0	224.1	226.1	226.7	229.8	230.4	235.0	233.9	233.8	235.9	228.8
1993	231.2	231.3	232.0	238.1	240.8	243.0	243.3	244.8	249.5	254.4	255.4	257.2	243.4
1994	254.2	255.6	258.3	256.2	259.6	259.0	257.1	256.2	258.4	260.0	258.8	257.3	257.5
1995	249.3	248.0	248.2	250.2	252.1	252.5	253.1	253.5	256.7	259.8	259.2	260.0	253.5
1996	254.3	254.0	255.6	256.9	258.1	259.3	255.5	256.8	259.7	264.1	263.7	264.0	258.5
1997	258.6	257.6	259.0	260.2	262.4	263.4	261.0	246.7	266.4	269.8	269.6	269.5	262.0
1998	263.0	262.7	263.9	264.8	267.6	267.4	268.7	270.9	274.0	274.9	273.1	273.0	268.6
1999	267.9	267.2	268.6	271.1	270.9	270.5	270.7	270.2	271.6	275.5	275.9	276.5	271.3
2000	272.4	271.6	272.2	274.5	275.5	274.6	274.2	276.6	279.1	280.3	281.0	281.8	276.1
2001	274.6	273.0	274.0	275.3	276.0	273.9	269.9	269.2	271.8	270.1	267.4	265.0	271.7
2002	258.1	256.3	255.9	258.4	259.0	256.1	255.9	258.0	261.1	262.5	261.9	261.7	258.7
2003	255.6	253.7	253.5	254.2	255.6	254.3	248.4	250.4	254.1	257.7	259.3	259.5	254.7
Information													
1990	130.7	130.8	130.8	129.8	130.6	132.0	132.7	132.2	131.5	131.1	131.5	131.5	131.2
1991	133.6	133.1	133.1	131.3	131.3	133.3	134.0	133.3	132.4	133.6	132.6	133.2	132.9
1992	131.0	130.7	130.5	128.6	128.1	129.0	131.2	132.7	131.9	130.6	130.8	131.6	130.5
1993	129.9	131.2	131.8	130.5	130.8	132.1	133.1	133.6	134.1	134.3	135.1	135.3	132.6
1994	137.3	137.3	137.6	137.6	139.5	140.0	139.1	139.3	137.9	138.5	139.2	138.9	138.5
1995	139.7	140.1	140.4	137.2	138.3	140.0	138.1	138.3	138.4	137.6	139.1	139.5	138.8
1996	141.7	141.3	141.2	139.2	141.1	141.9	144.8	145.0	143.2	144.7	145.6	146.2	142.9
1997	145.2	145.0	145.7	145.8	146.8	147.6	148.2	149.0	147.8	148.3	148.8	150.3	147.3
1998	148.3	147.8	148.2	150.0	151.0	153.1	151.8	151.9	150.1	150.0	150.2	150.5	150.2
1999	149.3	148.5	148.4	147.2	147.1	146.8	147.2	146.9	147.0	147.3	149.1	149.9	147.8
2000	148.7	149.2	150.6	150.7	151.9	153.6	154.0	154.5	152.8	153.7	155.0	155.9	152.5
2001	153.9	154.3	154.8	155.1	155.6	157.4	155.5	155.0	152.8	150.8	151.0	151.5	154.0
2002	148.5	147.8	147.6	147.6	147.4	147.0	144.1	143.6	140.9	140.4	139.9	139.4	144.5
2003	136.4	136.3	135.2	135.5	135.7	136.1	135.5	134.9	133.6	133.4	133.6	133.4	135.0
Financial activities													
1990	369.0	369.8	371.3	370.5	373.2	378.6	381.4	380.9	377.3	372.7	372.6	374.4	374.3
1991	370.9	370.1	372.0	372.5	374.4	379.9	378.8	379.3	375.1	371.0	371.1	374.9	374.1
1992	371.1	371.1	371.9	370.4	373.4	378.1	384.6	384.8	379.9	374.1	374.3	377.1	375.9
1993	375.9	375.0	377.0	378.1	380.2	385.5	387.5	389.7	384.1	384.1	384.5	385.2	382.2
1994	373.5	374.1	376.0	376.9	378.5	384.2	383.0	383.4	378.7	373.7	373.8	376.2	377.6
1995	373.8	374.3	375.8	375.8	377.6	383.2	378.4	378.4	374.9	373.9	374.6	377.7	376.5
1996	370.8	371.2	373.4	381.9	384.6	390.0	390.7	391.4	386.7	385.9	387.3	390.3	383.6
1997	388.1	388.3	390.0	390.8	393.5	398.2	398.9	400.8	395.2	394.1	395.6	398.6	394.3
1998	396.9	399.0	400.1	402.5	400.8	405.9	403.0	402.6	397.6	397.9	398.9	402.8	400.6
1999	399.1	400.1	402.5	404.1	406.1	410.6	412.3	412.1	405.1	404.6	404.4	406.6	405.6
2000	403.0	402.8	402.6	402.1	402.7	407.4	406.2	406.8	402.1	402.8	403.1	407.6	404.1
2001	400.4	401.1	403.5	402.9	404.3	408.7	407.6	406.7	402.0	400.7	401.8	403.7	403.6
2002	398.7	398.3	399.1	398.2	399.4	403.3	402.7	402.9	400.1	400.2	401.3	403.7	400.7
2003	398.9	398.1	399.3	400.1	402.3	406.4	404.9	405.5	404.9	405.2	404.8	405.0	403.0
Professional and business services													
1990	551.4	555.5	564.8	567.9	572.2	581.5	589.0	592.8	590.4	578.2	574.8	570.4	574.0
1991	549.1	549.1	554.8	560.5	563.0	575.4	574.9	573.3	573.2	566.1	562.4	560.3	563.5
1992	552.0	555.4	560.0	569.9	577.8	585.5	598.2	602.9	598.1	586.2	585.1	581.2	579.3
1993	567.4	572.0	577.6	595.1	600.4	612.3	613.7	620.1	620.8	619.4	616.1	614.0	602.4
1994	592.5	599.2	609.1	627.2	630.6	642.4	653.8	657.1	657.7	645.4	644.5	643.2	633.5
1995	630.9	638.3	650.2	659.1	661.8	672.8	674.5	683.4	682.9	680.6	678.2	678.6	665.9
1996	644.8	649.8	659.7	679.6	687.2	695.4	701.6	714.2	712.7	706.8	709.2	708.3	689.1
1997	681.4	689.5	702.0	712.1	720.4	731.2	743.2	751.8	749.3	755.2	758.5	761.2	729.6
1998	733.5	740.3	750.1	764.5	774.4	786.3	799.1	809.0	811.9	804.6	803.4	803.8	781.7
1999	770.7	779.7	794.6	806.5	812.7	825.1	817.8	828.1	822.3	832.7	832.2	833.0	812.9
2000	794.7	802.3	817.5	834.1	838.6	854.2	850.2	860.2	858.3	851.3	848.7	842.9	837.7
2001	806.3	805.0	810.3	817.2	821.6	830.2	821.6	825.5	817.3	810.9	800.8	796.9	813.6
2002	764.0	762.5	766.0	782.4	785.4	791.9	795.4	803.5	799.0	791.9	788.1	779.4	784.1
2003	747.5	746.3	749.8	762.3	766.3	770.2	771.0	773.7	779.1	780.4	777.2	770.7	766.2
Educational and health services													
1990	525.5	529.1	533.7	531.8	534.6	532.3	531.0	532.7	544.0	549.5	552.7	554.1	537.5
1991	545.5	553.7	557.5	566.9	568.4	565.0	559.6	560.4	566.7	573.1	574.1	575.7	563.8
1992	568.6	573.4	576.6	576.8	578.3	577.2	578.3	578.7	587.7	591.4	592.0	593.3	581.0
1993	586.5	592.4	594.8	594.8	593.9	588.8	588.3	589.1	596.8	602.0	602.7	605.1	594.6
1994	593.8	600.4	603.2	603.2	603.0	600.3	597.7	600.0	613.1	607.1	613.0	613.3	604.0
1995	605.6	613.8	619.1	619.6	622.1	620.1	615.0	618.0	630.2	625.1	629.5	633.0	620.9
1996	625.0	631.6	634.5	634.6	634.1	630.1	627.7	628.0	637.0	644.6	648.7	650.4	635.5
1997	634.5	640.1	643.8	645.6	647.2	641.9	630.2	631.8	639.9	650.2	652.5	653.6	642.6
1998	648.7	656.0	661.2	662.7	664.6	658.3	653.9	655.2	665.5	667.7	670.2	672.1	661.3
1999	654.0	662.0	665.7	665.1	666.2	662.8	657.6	657.0	665.8	671.5	673.9	678.2	664.9
2000	671.6	676.6	680.0	681.5	682.9	684.2	673.8	675.4	683.8	684.3	689.0	690.4	681.1
2001	682.2	688.5	694.9	696.8	698.0	697.7	692.0	695.5	702.4	703.2	706.7	707.9	697.2
2002	699.8	706.1	709.9	711.1	713.9	710.3	703.0	705.0	712.8	716.0	719.4	720.5	710.7
2003	709.0	712.2	716.0	715.7	717.9	716.6	713.9	713.3	721.7	725.5	726.2	726.4	717.9

Employment by Industry: Illinois—*Continued*

(Numbers in thousands. Not seasonally adjusted.)

Industry	January	February	March	April	May	June	July	August	September	October	November	December	Annual Average
STATEWIDE—*Continued*													
Leisure and hospitality													
1990	362.3	365.2	373.2	388.2	401.3	413.1	415.4	417.4	411.7	396.9	392.1	391.3	394.0
1991	366.7	367.2	375.8	387.3	400.7	408.0	404.5	408.8	404.2	389.7	387.0	385.6	390.4
1992	366.0	369.3	377.6	389.9	407.7	416.2	411.3	413.8	405.2	404.4	399.1	399.0	396.6
1993	384.2	387.9	394.0	409.3	422.7	431.6	432.8	437.8	431.9	421.0	412.2	414.8	415.0
1994	397.0	399.4	409.0	424.5	437.3	448.0	445.7	449.0	443.7	432.6	429.2	428.3	428.6
1995	415.7	418.7	429.4	442.0	455.3	468.2	471.5	475.0	470.0	453.0	448.1	448.7	449.6
1996	429.6	431.2	440.5	452.3	467.5	479.6	476.3	480.6	470.9	455.3	450.6	450.4	457.0
1997	433.3	436.4	446.3	450.7	467.9	478.7	479.8	484.1	476.5	460.9	458.8	458.8	461.0
1998	433.3	439.2	445.5	464.7	482.8	492.3	496.5	497.1	489.1	480.1	476.2	476.5	472.7
1999	444.6	451.8	460.9	476.5	490.7	501.6	498.7	499.1	491.5	482.2	476.3	475.8	479.1
2000	454.1	457.1	469.7	483.6	496.1	509.4	506.9	508.6	501.5	489.5	483.5	479.5	486.6
2001	459.6	463.5	475.1	490.5	506.3	518.3	514.4	516.1	504.0	488.0	480.2	477.9	491.2
2002	459.7	460.6	469.9	486.1	502.6	515.0	515.6	517.6	508.1	494.9	488.0	486.7	492.1
2003	464.7	463.5	471.5	492.3	509.2	521.7	522.0	524.1	513.3	506.1	498.2	495.5	498.5
Other services													
1990	203.1	203.5	203.9	204.4	204.7	208.7	210.3	211.5	209.9	209.3	209.7	211.1	207.5
1991	207.5	208.1	210.4	206.6	208.6	211.1	210.3	209.0	208.1	206.6	206.8	208.7	208.4
1992	206.7	206.9	208.1	206.0	207.4	210.2	213.4	212.0	211.6	211.4	210.7	212.8	209.7
1993	207.6	208.0	210.3	210.3	211.1	214.6	214.8	213.6	213.7	211.9	212.1	214.3	211.8
1994	213.1	214.0	216.9	217.4	217.3	221.3	221.1	220.4	220.1	218.5	218.2	220.3	218.2
1995	218.3	219.6	222.0	221.7	223.2	227.2	226.1	225.3	224.3	223.7	224.1	226.6	223.5
1996	223.3	224.1	226.7	226.3	227.6	231.1	230.3	230.8	228.5	227.0	227.6	228.9	227.6
1997	223.9	225.9	228.6	229.9	231.7	234.6	233.5	233.8	232.8	232.2	232.2	234.6	231.1
1998	231.1	233.0	235.2	235.2	237.0	240.8	239.8	238.9	238.6	239.4	239.7	240.1	237.4
1999	236.2	239.1	242.1	243.6	244.3	247.8	247.5	245.9	243.6	242.3	243.4	245.1	243.4
2000	240.1	241.2	243.7	244.8	245.0	249.0	248.1	248.3	247.5	244.7	245.2	245.9	245.2
2001	244.3	246.2	249.3	250.1	251.5	256.3	257.5	256.7	251.6	248.9	250.3	251.0	251.1
2002	247.0	247.4	249.2	249.9	250.5	257.1	260.1	260.2	251.0	249.7	250.4	251.4	252.0
2003	246.6	246.4	248.7	248.8	250.3	256.7	255.5	255.0	251.9	251.1	249.8	249.4	250.9
Government													
1990	744.4	763.0	776.7	778.4	782.6	770.9	743.2	733.2	759.6	776.9	780.9	781.8	765.9
1991	761.6	775.8	783.2	789.7	787.9	760.2	743.1	727.4	762.7	779.9	789.8	785.3	770.5
1992	764.8	779.0	788.5	792.4	786.2	774.3	736.2	722.6	769.1	785.7	797.8	790.1	773.8
1993	763.9	781.6	786.9	792.4	798.2	771.8	738.7	727.5	761.3	784.6	794.2	792.1	774.4
1994	764.5	784.7	797.7	796.9	800.6	782.5	755.5	748.8	781.0	803.6	810.0	806.5	786.0
1995	782.8	808.2	813.3	818.1	816.3	800.9	747.3	738.2	805.9	813.6	822.9	816.7	798.6
1996	789.6	815.4	825.3	826.4	826.4	814.2	778.5	772.7	802.7	815.0	829.4	817.1	809.3
1997	792.9	813.9	820.3	816.0	828.2	810.6	778.4	774.4	803.6	810.2	827.5	823.9	808.3
1998	798.0	817.4	827.4	825.5	828.9	814.1	784.4	777.8	819.8	828.3	837.1	834.2	816.0
1999	802.7	822.9	832.6	839.4	838.5	824.9	799.8	794.1	826.9	840.2	844.0	840.9	825.5
2000	816.6	841.0	850.0	847.6	862.1	845.9	809.9	806.3	833.4	849.4	856.5	856.6	839.6
2001	826.5	852.8	856.9	856.3	864.4	851.1	825.2	818.6	848.1	864.4	869.0	871.1	850.4
2002	845.8	866.1	872.5	875.8	881.5	865.2	828.0	822.7	850.2	871.8	876.9	875.3	861.0
2003	847.1	865.6	868.3	872.2	874.6	861.6	826.9	819.5	842.8	861.3	865.3	865.4	855.9
Federal government													
1990	110.6	111.1	113.3	115.8	123.6	118.0	117.0	114.5	110.1	108.1	107.0	108.8	113.1
1991	106.8	106.7	105.9	106.5	106.7	107.4	107.3	107.3	108.4	105.6	105.8	108.6	106.9
1992	108.4	107.1	106.9	107.6	106.3	106.3	107.3	106.9	106.4	106.6	105.8	108.6	107.0
1993	105.2	104.8	104.4	104.1	103.8	104.1	103.2	103.2	102.9	102.5	103.5	107.7	104.1
1994	102.5	102.3	101.9	102.6	103.0	103.9	103.3	103.6	104.0	103.6	103.3	107.4	103.4
1995	103.8	103.6	103.1	102.6	102.5	103.2	102.9	102.6	102.3	102.1	102.5	105.5	103.0
1996	102.2	102.0	101.5	101.9	100.9	101.2	100.8	100.9	100.3	99.8	100.0	102.1	101.1
1997	99.0	98.7	98.2	97.8	97.4	97.5	97.3	97.5	97.1	96.6	97.1	100.1	97.8
1998	98.0	97.3	96.8	95.7	96.1	96.1	96.2	96.4	96.2	96.0	96.9	100.0	96.8
1999	96.7	96.3	96.4	98.2	96.6	96.2	96.3	95.8	95.3	95.5	96.2	99.6	96.5
2000	97.0	97.2	98.3	103.1	112.2	110.5	102.3	105.7	94.6	94.2	94.9	98.2	100.6
2001	94.7	94.3	94.1	93.4	93.3	93.6	94.4	94.7	94.0	92.8	93.0	94.9	93.9
2002	93.0	92.4	92.0	91.3	91.1	92.3	92.0	91.8	92.1	93.4	93.6	95.7	92.6
2003	93.8	93.4	92.1	92.7	92.3	92.1	92.0	91.5	91.2	92.5	92.5	94.6	92.6
State government													
1990	158.3	165.6	166.7	166.8	160.2	154.9	152.6	154.5	165.3	170.2	169.4	169.2	162.8
1991	165.9	169.3	170.7	170.4	165.4	153.6	152.6	154.3	162.1	165.7	166.4	164.1	163.3
1992	157.7	162.8	164.7	166.9	157.4	150.5	151.0	151.3	162.1	165.3	166.2	163.8	159.9
1993	158.6	165.4	166.2	165.3	161.8	148.1	153.4	155.7	160.1	166.1	166.4	165.6	161.0
1994	158.4	166.9	168.1	165.8	163.3	152.6	152.2	154.2	161.3	167.8	168.1	164.6	161.9
1995	155.6	167.9	168.1	167.2	164.0	150.3	150.4	151.7	161.6	165.6	166.0	162.3	160.8
1996	154.3	167.0	165.7	167.0	163.7	162.2	155.1	157.8	162.6	164.6	167.9	165.6	162.7
1997	157.4	166.7	167.0	158.1	166.7	152.8	151.7	154.6	161.2	156.3	166.6	166.6	160.4
1998	154.1	161.4	165.6	165.0	162.4	151.8	152.8	155.3	163.6	168.3	169.9	168.5	161.5
1999	156.4	162.7	166.9	168.0	165.6	155.0	156.2	159.0	168.0	171.1	172.3	169.7	164.2
2000	160.9	170.6	171.2	168.3	164.4	156.5	156.3	158.6	166.9	170.0	171.2	171.5	165.5
2001	163.0	172.1	172.6	172.6	170.4	158.1	159.2	161.2	170.6	175.3	176.3	174.6	168.8
2002	167.1	174.4	174.7	175.7	172.5	158.1	157.6	160.6	166.3	170.5	171.3	169.2	168.2
2003	158.4	162.7	162.8	164.9	161.8	151.2	152.0	153.7	159.5	163.3	164.3	163.3	159.8

Employment by Industry: Illinois—*Continued*

(Numbers in thousands. Not seasonally adjusted.)

Industry	January	February	March	April	May	June	July	August	September	October	November	December	Annual Average
STATEWIDE—*Continued*													
Local government													
1990	475.5	486.3	496.7	495.8	498.8	498.0	473.6	464.2	484.2	498.6	504.5	503.8	490.0
1991	488.9	499.8	506.6	512.8	515.8	499.2	483.2	465.8	492.2	508.6	517.6	512.6	500.2
1992	498.7	509.1	516.9	517.9	522.5	517.5	477.9	464.4	500.6	513.8	525.8	517.7	506.9
1993	500.1	511.4	516.3	523.0	532.6	519.6	482.1	468.6	498.3	516.0	524.3	518.8	509.2
1994	503.6	515.5	527.7	528.5	534.3	526.0	500.0	491.0	515.7	532.2	538.6	534.5	520.6
1995	523.4	536.7	542.1	548.3	549.8	547.4	494.0	483.9	542.0	545.9	554.4	548.9	534.7
1996	533.1	546.4	558.1	557.5	561.8	550.8	522.6	514.0	539.8	550.6	561.5	549.4	545.4
1997	536.5	548.5	555.1	560.1	564.1	560.3	529.4	522.3	545.3	557.3	563.8	557.2	549.9
1998	545.9	558.7	565.0	564.8	570.4	566.2	535.4	526.1	560.0	564.0	570.3	565.7	557.7
1999	549.6	563.9	569.3	573.2	576.3	573.7	547.3	539.3	563.6	573.6	575.5	571.6	564.7
2000	558.7	573.2	580.5	576.2	585.5	578.9	551.3	542.0	571.9	585.2	590.4	586.9	573.3
2001	568.8	586.4	590.2	590.3	600.7	599.4	571.6	562.7	583.5	596.3	599.7	601.6	587.6
2002	585.7	599.3	605.8	608.8	617.9	614.8	578.4	570.3	591.8	607.9	612.0	610.4	600.3
2003	594.9	609.5	613.4	614.6	620.5	618.3	582.9	574.3	592.1	605.5	608.5	607.5	603.5
CHAMPAIGN-URBANA-RANTOUL													
Total nonfarm													
1990	87.2	89.7	90.8	91.4	91.9	89.2	88.2	88.0	91.4	92.6	93.5	93.4	90.6
1991	88.1	91.0	92.6	92.5	94.6	89.7	88.6	88.2	90.9	94.3	94.7	93.7	91.5
1992	88.4	91.7	92.4	93.4	92.4	89.6	89.1	89.0	93.2	93.4	93.3	93.2	91.5
1993	87.1	91.6	91.4	91.9	92.0	90.5	88.7	88.5	90.8	94.4	94.1	93.6	91.2
1994	88.3	91.9	93.9	92.9	94.1	90.7	91.3	90.9	93.8	95.8	96.5	95.9	93.0
1995	89.0	92.2	93.6	95.3	95.2	92.1	93.3	94.0	95.8	97.9	98.3	98.0	94.5
1996	93.2	96.1	95.8	97.9	97.0	96.5	96.4	95.3	95.6	97.7	99.0	98.8	96.6
1997	93.3	96.7	98.0	97.9	98.2	95.5	94.4	94.2	95.1	99.3	99.6	99.4	96.8
1998	92.0	97.2	97.8	98.4	99.2	96.5	96.5	96.4	98.5	102.1	103.1	103.1	98.4
1999	95.4	100.1	101.1	103.6	102.9	99.4	100.3	100.4	102.2	104.8	102.6	104.9	101.4
2000	97.6	103.0	104.4	105.9	105.3	102.3	103.3	102.4	105.0	106.8	106.9	106.2	104.0
2001	99.9	104.5	105.0	105.9	106.2	103.0	102.4	102.7	104.8	107.2	107.9	107.1	104.7
2002	100.7	104.0	105.2	106.0	105.9	102.3	102.4	102.3	104.3	107.3	107.6	107.5	104.6
2003	101.0	103.5	105.4	106.3	106.4	102.6	101.9	102.1	102.6	106.0	106.6	107.2	104.3
Total private													
1990	54.0	54.0	54.4	55.3	55.7	56.2	56.7	57.0	57.2	56.3	56.9	56.8	55.8
1991	54.9	55.0	55.9	56.3	56.4	56.9	56.6	56.9	57.8	57.5	57.8	57.5	56.6
1992	55.1	55.7	55.7	56.6	56.8	57.0	57.1	57.7	58.0	58.1	58.1	58.2	57.0
1993	56.1	56.4	56.4	57.4	57.8	58.6	58.1	58.8	59.4	59.0	59.4	59.1	58.0
1994	57.6	57.9	58.4	58.8	60.0	59.8	61.0	61.4	61.6	60.6	60.9	61.4	59.9
1995	58.0	57.9	59.0	60.9	61.1	61.0	60.7	61.3	62.3	62.5	62.6	62.9	60.8
1996	60.9	61.2	61.0	62.2	62.5	62.4	62.5	63.3	63.2	63.7	63.5	63.5	62.4
1997	61.8	62.3	62.8	63.2	63.4	63.6	63.3	63.4	63.9	64.3	64.5	64.4	63.4
1998	62.1	63.0	62.7	63.8	64.1	64.6	65.2	65.5	65.7	66.9	67.3	67.7	64.8
1999	63.9	65.1	65.7	67.4	67.4	67.1	68.3	68.5	68.5	68.8	69.2	69.6	67.4
2000	66.8	67.5	68.4	69.4	69.9	70.0	70.7	70.5	70.7	70.6	70.5	70.1	69.5
2001	68.0	68.3	68.5	69.9	70.3	70.4	69.7	70.0	69.4	69.4	69.8	69.4	69.4
2002	67.0	66.8	67.5	68.6	68.6	68.3	68.3	68.5	69.3	69.1	69.2	69.4	68.4
2003	66.6	66.6	67.4	68.7	69.0	68.5	68.1	68.3	68.9	68.7	69.1	69.0	68.2
Goods-producing													
1990	11.4	11.6	11.8	11.9	12.1	12.3	12.5	12.4	12.3	11.7	11.8	11.7	11.9
1991	10.9	10.7	11.3	11.7	11.8	12.2	12.0	12.2	12.1	12.1	11.9	11.6	11.7
1992	10.8	11.1	11.4	11.6	11.8	12.0	12.0	12.3	12.0	11.9	11.7	11.6	11.6
1993	11.2	11.1	11.3	11.7	12.1	12.6	12.8	12.9	12.8	12.5	12.5	12.4	12.1
1994	11.9	12.0	12.4	12.9	13.4	13.6	13.8	13.9	13.8	13.3	13.3	13.3	13.1
1995	12.6	12.4	12.7	13.1	13.4	13.6	13.5	13.8	13.8	13.7	13.7	13.6	13.3
1996	13.0	13.1	13.2	13.7	14.0	14.2	14.1	14.3	14.1	14.0	13.8	13.7	13.7
1997	13.2	13.2	13.5	13.7	13.8	14.2	14.1	13.9	13.8	13.7	13.6	13.4	13.6
1998	13.2	13.2	12.9	13.4	13.6	14.2	13.9	14.1	13.8	13.9	13.7	13.7	13.6
1999	12.9	13.0	13.2	13.8	14.1	14.5	14.7	14.8	14.6	14.5	14.5	14.5	14.0
2000	13.8	13.8	14.2	14.6	14.9	15.3	15.3	15.3	15.1	15.0	14.9	14.6	14.7
2001	13.8	13.6	13.9	14.4	14.6	14.9	14.5	14.7	14.3	14.2	14.3	13.9	14.3
2002	13.3	13.0	13.3	13.8	14.1	14.4	14.7	14.7	14.7	14.4	14.3	14.3	14.1
2003	13.9	13.6	13.8	14.2	14.5	14.7	14.6	14.5	14.3	14.2	14.1	13.9	14.2
Construction and mining													
1990	2.2	2.2	2.3	2.5	2.6	2.8	2.8	2.8	2.6	2.5	2.6	2.5	2.5
1991	2.1	2.0	2.2	2.5	2.7	2.9	2.9	2.9	2.8	2.9	2.8	2.6	2.6
1992	2.2	2.2	2.3	2.5	2.6	2.8	2.8	3.0	2.9	2.7	2.6	2.4	2.5
1993	2.1	2.0	2.1	2.2	2.6	2.9	3.0	3.0	2.9	2.9	2.8	2.7	2.6
1994	2.2	2.2	2.4	2.6	2.9	3.1	3.3	3.3	3.2	3.0	3.0	2.9	2.8
1995	2.6	2.5	2.6	2.6	2.8	3.0	3.2	3.2	3.2	3.0	2.9	2.8	2.8
1996	2.5	2.4	2.5	2.9	3.2	3.4	3.5	3.6	3.4	3.3	3.2	3.0	3.0
1997	2.7	2.6	2.8	3.0	3.1	3.4	3.5	3.4	3.3	3.4	3.3	3.1	3.1
1998	3.0	3.0	3.0	3.4	3.6	4.0	4.1	4.1	3.8	3.9	3.7	3.6	3.6
1999	3.0	3.0	3.2	3.5	3.8	4.2	4.4	4.3	4.2	4.0	3.9	3.9	3.7
2000	3.4	3.3	3.5	3.6	3.8	4.1	4.1	4.1	4.0	4.0	3.9	3.6	3.7
2001	3.2	3.3	3.6	3.9	4.1	4.4	4.5	4.5	4.1	4.1	4.2	3.8	4.0
2002	3.4	3.2	3.3	3.7	3.9	4.2	4.4	4.4	4.3	4.2	4.0	3.9	3.9
2003	3.5	3.4	3.6	3.9	4.1	4.2	4.3	4.2	4.1	4.1	4.0	3.8	3.9

Employment by Industry: Illinois—*Continued*

(Numbers in thousands. Not seasonally adjusted.)

Industry	January	February	March	April	May	June	July	August	September	October	November	December	Annual Average
CHAMPAIGN-URBANA-RANTOUL—*Continued*													
Manufacturing													
1990	9.2	9.4	9.5	9.4	9.5	9.5	9.7	9.6	9.7	9.2	9.2	9.2	9.4
1991	8.8	8.7	9.1	9.2	9.1	9.3	9.1	9.3	9.3	9.2	9.1	9.0	9.1
1992	8.6	8.9	9.1	9.1	9.2	9.2	9.2	9.3	9.1	9.2	9.1	9.2	9.1
1993	9.1	9.1	9.2	9.5	9.5	9.7	9.8	9.9	9.9	9.6	9.7	9.7	9.5
1994	9.7	9.8	10.0	10.3	10.5	10.5	10.5	10.6	10.6	10.3	10.3	10.4	10.2
1995	10.0	9.9	10.1	10.5	10.6	10.6	10.3	10.6	10.6	10.7	10.8	10.8	10.4
1996	10.5	10.7	10.7	10.8	10.8	10.8	10.6	10.7	10.7	10.7	10.6	10.7	10.6
1997	10.5	10.6	10.7	10.7	10.7	10.8	10.6	10.5	10.5	10.3	10.3	10.3	10.5
1998	10.2	10.2	9.9	10.0	10.0	10.2	9.8	10.0	10.0	10.0	10.0	10.1	10.0
1999	9.9	10.0	10.0	10.3	10.3	10.3	10.3	10.5	10.4	10.5	10.6	10.6	10.3
2000	10.4	10.5	10.7	11.0	11.1	11.2	11.2	11.2	11.1	11.0	11.0	11.0	10.9
2001	10.6	10.3	10.3	10.5	10.5	10.5	10.0	10.2	10.2	10.1	10.1	10.1	10.3
2002	9.9	9.8	10.0	10.1	10.2	10.2	10.3	10.3	10.4	10.2	10.3	10.4	10.2
2003	10.4	10.2	10.2	10.3	10.4	10.5	10.3	10.3	10.2	10.1	10.1	10.1	10.3
Service-providing													
1990	75.8	78.1	79.0	79.5	79.8	76.9	75.7	75.6	79.1	80.9	81.7	81.7	78.6
1991	77.2	80.3	81.3	80.8	82.8	77.5	76.6	76.0	78.8	82.2	82.8	82.1	79.8
1992	77.6	80.6	81.0	81.8	80.6	77.6	77.1	76.7	81.2	81.5	81.6	81.6	79.9
1993	75.9	80.5	80.1	80.2	79.9	77.9	75.9	75.6	78.0	81.9	81.6	81.2	79.0
1994	76.4	79.9	81.5	80.0	80.7	77.1	77.5	77.0	80.0	82.5	83.2	82.6	79.8
1995	76.4	79.8	80.9	82.2	81.8	78.5	79.8	80.2	82.0	84.2	84.6	84.4	81.2
1996	80.2	83.0	82.6	84.2	83.0	82.3	82.3	81.0	81.5	83.7	85.2	85.1	82.8
1997	80.1	83.5	84.5	84.2	84.4	81.3	80.3	80.3	81.3	85.6	86.0	86.0	83.1
1998	78.8	84.0	84.9	85.0	85.6	82.3	82.6	82.3	84.7	88.2	89.4	89.4	84.7
1999	82.5	87.1	87.9	89.8	88.8	84.9	85.6	85.6	87.6	90.3	88.1	90.4	87.3
2000	83.8	89.2	90.2	91.3	90.4	87.0	88.0	87.1	89.9	91.8	92.0	91.6	89.3
2001	86.1	90.9	91.1	91.6	91.6	88.1	87.9	88.1	90.6	93.1	93.6	93.2	90.5
2002	87.4	91.0	91.9	92.2	91.8	87.9	87.7	87.6	89.6	92.9	93.3	93.2	90.5
2003	87.1	89.9	91.6	92.1	91.9	87.9	87.3	87.6	88.3	91.8	92.5	93.3	90.1
Trade, transportation, and utilities													
1990	13.9	13.6	13.5	13.9	14.1	14.3	14.4	14.4	14.4	14.4	14.7	14.8	14.2
1991	14.7	14.4	14.4	14.3	14.3	14.4	14.5	14.5	14.7	14.6	15.2	15.4	14.6
1992	14.7	14.5	14.3	14.2	14.2	14.2	14.1	14.2	14.3	14.6	15.0	15.3	14.4
1993	14.2	14.1	13.8	14.1	14.1	14.4	14.1	14.4	14.5	14.7	15.1	15.1	14.3
1994	14.4	14.1	14.1	14.0	14.1	14.2	14.4	14.6	14.5	14.5	14.8	15.2	14.4
1995	14.2	13.9	14.4	15.2	15.3	15.3	15.3	15.4	15.6	15.9	16.1	16.2	15.2
1996	15.6	15.3	15.2	15.1	15.0	15.1	15.2	15.6	15.7	16.0	16.2	16.3	15.5
1997	15.8	15.5	15.5	15.5	15.3	15.6	15.8	15.8	15.9	16.3	16.7	16.8	15.8
1998	16.1	15.9	15.6	16.2	16.1	16.1	16.6	16.6	16.6	17.0	17.4	17.6	16.4
1999	16.3	16.3	16.4	16.4	16.3	16.3	16.6	16.5	16.6	17.2	17.6	17.9	16.7
2000	16.8	16.7	16.9	17.3	17.2	17.2	17.5	17.4	17.6	17.4	17.7	18.0	17.3
2001	17.1	17.2	16.9	17.0	17.0	17.0	17.1	17.2	17.1	16.9	17.4	17.7	17.1
2002	17.0	16.7	16.7	16.8	16.7	16.9	16.7	16.9	17.0	17.1	17.4	17.8	17.0
2003	16.7	16.6	16.6	16.4	16.6	16.7	16.8	16.8	16.9	16.8	17.1	17.4	16.8
Wholesale trade													
1990	2.8	2.8	2.8	2.9	3.0	3.1	3.2	3.1	3.0	3.1	3.1	3.1	3.0
1991	3.1	3.1	3.1	3.1	3.1	3.2	3.3	3.1	3.2	3.1	3.1	3.0	3.1
1992	3.0	3.0	2.9	2.9	2.8	2.9	2.9	2.8	2.8	2.9	2.9	2.8	2.8
1993	2.8	2.8	2.8	2.9	2.8	3.0	2.9	2.9	2.8	2.9	2.9	2.8	2.8
1994	2.8	2.7	2.8	2.7	2.7	2.7	2.9	2.9	2.8	2.8	2.8	2.9	2.7
1995	2.7	2.6	2.7	2.8	2.7	2.8	2.9	2.8	2.9	2.9	2.9	2.9	2.8
1996	2.7	2.6	2.7	2.7	2.7	2.7	2.8	2.9	2.8	2.9	2.9	2.8	2.7
1997	2.7	2.6	2.6	2.7	2.6	2.7	2.7	2.7	2.8	2.9	2.9	2.9	2.7
1998	2.8	2.8	2.7	2.7	2.7	2.7	2.8	2.7	2.7	2.8	2.7	2.7	2.7
1999	2.5	2.5	2.5	2.5	2.5	2.6	2.7	2.6	2.6	2.7	2.7	2.7	2.5
2000	2.6	2.6	2.7	2.8	2.7	2.8	2.9	2.8	2.8	2.9	2.9	2.9	2.7
2001	2.8	2.9	2.9	2.9	2.9	3.0	3.1	3.0	3.0	3.0	3.1	3.1	3.0
2002	2.9	2.9	2.9	3.0	3.0	3.1	3.0	3.0	3.0	3.1	3.1	3.1	3.0
2003	3.0	3.0	3.0	3.0	3.0	3.1	3.1	3.1	3.1	3.1	3.1	3.1	3.1
Retail trade													
1990	9.4	9.1	9.0	9.3	9.4	9.5	9.4	9.5	9.6	9.6	9.8	10.0	9.4
1991	9.9	9.6	9.6	9.6	9.5	9.6	9.5	9.7	9.8	9.8	10.4	10.7	9.8
1992	9.9	9.7	9.6	9.5	9.6	9.5	9.4	9.5	9.6	9.8	10.2	10.6	9.7
1993	9.5	9.4	9.1	9.3	9.3	9.4	9.2	9.4	9.6	9.6	10.0	10.1	9.4
1994	9.6	9.3	9.2	9.2	9.3	9.4	9.5	9.7	9.7	9.7	10.0	10.3	9.5
1995	9.7	9.5	9.9	10.6	10.7	10.6	10.6	10.8	10.8	11.1	11.3	11.4	10.5
1996	11.1	10.8	10.6	10.5	10.4	10.5	10.5	10.6	10.7	11.0	11.1	11.3	10.7
1997	10.9	10.7	10.5	10.5	10.4	10.4	10.6	10.6	10.5	10.8	11.2	11.3	10.7
1998	10.7	10.5	10.3	10.8	10.7	10.7	11.1	11.1	11.1	11.4	11.9	12.1	11.0
1999	11.0	11.0	11.1	11.1	11.0	10.9	11.0	11.0	11.1	11.5	12.0	12.3	11.2
2000	11.3	11.1	11.1	11.4	11.4	11.3	11.5	11.4	11.6	11.4	11.8	12.1	11.4
2001	11.4	11.3	11.0	10.9	10.9	10.8	11.0	11.1	11.0	10.9	11.3	11.6	11.1
2002	10.9	10.6	10.6	10.5	10.5	10.6	10.5	10.6	10.7	10.8	11.0	11.3	10.7
2003	10.6	10.4	10.4	10.3	10.5	10.5	10.6	10.6	10.7	10.7	11.0	11.3	10.6

Employment by Industry: Illinois—*Continued*

(Numbers in thousands. Not seasonally adjusted.)

Industry	January	February	March	April	May	June	July	August	September	October	November	December	Annual Average
CHAMPAIGN-URBANA-RANTOUL—*Continued*													
Transportation and utilities													
1990	1.7	1.7	1.7	1.7	1.7	1.7	1.8	1.8	1.8	1.7	1.8	1.7	1.7
1991	1.7	1.7	1.7	1.6	1.7	1.6	1.7	1.7	1.7	1.7	1.7	1.7	1.6
1992	1.8	1.8	1.8	1.8	1.8	1.8	1.8	1.9	1.9	1.9	1.9	1.9	1.8
1993	1.9	1.9	1.9	1.9	2.0	2.0	2.0	2.1	2.1	2.2	2.2	2.2	2.0
1994	2.0	2.1	2.1	2.1	2.1	2.1	2.0	2.0	2.0	2.0	2.0	2.0	2.0
1995	1.8	1.8	1.8	1.8	1.9	1.9	1.8	1.8	1.9	1.9	1.9	1.9	1.8
1996	1.8	1.9	1.9	1.9	1.9	1.9	1.9	2.1	2.2	2.1	2.2	2.2	2.0
1997	2.2	2.2	2.4	2.3	2.3	2.5	2.5	2.5	2.6	2.6	2.6	2.6	2.4
1998	2.6	2.6	2.6	2.7	2.7	2.7	2.7	2.8	2.8	2.8	2.8	2.8	2.7
1999	2.8	2.8	2.8	2.8	2.8	2.8	2.9	2.9	2.9	3.0	2.9	2.9	2.8
2000	2.9	3.0	3.1	3.1	3.1	3.1	3.1	3.2	3.2	3.1	3.0	3.0	3.0
2001	2.9	3.0	3.0	3.2	3.2	3.2	3.0	3.1	3.1	3.0	3.0	3.0	3.1
2002	3.2	3.2	3.2	3.3	3.2	3.2	3.2	3.3	3.3	3.2	3.3	3.4	3.3
2003	3.1	3.2	3.2	3.1	3.1	3.1	3.1	3.1	3.1	3.0	3.0	3.0	3.1
Information													
1990	1.9	2.0	2.0	2.0	1.8	1.8	1.9	1.9	2.2	2.1	2.1	2.1	1.9
1991	2.2	2.2	2.2	2.2	1.9	2.0	2.0	2.0	2.2	2.2	2.2	2.1	2.1
1992	2.1	2.2	2.1	2.1	1.9	1.9	1.9	1.9	2.1	2.2	2.2	2.2	2.0
1993	2.1	2.2	2.1	2.3	2.1	2.1	2.0	2.1	2.2	2.3	2.3	2.2	2.1
1994	2.2	2.3	2.2	2.3	2.3	2.1	2.1	2.1	2.3	2.3	2.4	2.4	2.2
1995	2.3	2.4	2.4	2.4	2.3	2.2	2.2	2.2	2.4	2.4	2.5	2.5	2.3
1996	2.4	2.4	2.4	2.4	2.4	2.4	2.5	2.4	2.4	2.4	2.4	2.4	2.4
1997	2.5	2.5	2.5	2.5	2.5	2.5	2.3	2.3	2.3	2.5	2.4	2.5	2.4
1998	2.2	2.3	2.3	2.2	2.3	2.3	2.3	2.3	2.3	2.3	2.3	2.4	2.2
1999	2.3	2.3	2.4	2.5	2.5	2.5	2.4	2.4	2.4	2.4	2.4	2.4	2.4
2000	2.5	2.4	2.5	2.6	2.7	2.7	2.7	2.7	2.6	2.6	2.5	2.5	2.5
2001	2.4	2.5	2.5	2.7	2.8	2.8	2.9	2.8	2.7	2.5	2.6	2.6	2.7
2002	2.7	2.7	2.7	2.7	2.6	2.5	2.4	2.4	2.3	2.3	2.4	2.4	2.5
2003	2.3	2.3	2.3	3.0	2.7	2.4	2.4	2.3	2.2	2.2	2.3	2.3	2.4
Financial activities													
1990	3.5	3.4	3.5	3.3	3.4	3.4	3.6	3.6	3.4	3.4	3.4	3.4	3.4
1991	3.5	3.5	3.6	3.4	3.5	3.6	3.5	3.5	3.4	3.5	3.4	3.4	3.4
1992	3.4	3.5	3.5	3.6	3.6	3.7	3.7	3.8	3.6	3.6	3.6	3.6	3.6
1993	3.4	3.4	3.4	3.5	3.5	3.6	3.6	3.7	3.6	3.5	3.5	3.5	3.5
1994	3.5	3.5	3.5	3.6	3.7	3.8	3.8	3.9	3.7	3.6	3.6	3.6	3.6
1995	3.5	3.5	3.5	3.5	3.6	3.6	3.6	3.7	3.6	3.5	3.6	3.6	3.5
1996	3.7	3.6	3.6	3.7	3.8	3.8	3.9	4.0	3.8	3.9	3.8	3.8	3.7
1997	3.8	3.8	3.8	3.7	3.7	3.8	3.8	3.9	3.8	3.8	3.8	3.8	3.7
1998	3.8	3.9	3.9	4.1	4.1	4.2	4.1	4.2	4.1	4.1	4.2	4.3	4.0
1999	4.2	4.2	4.2	4.3	4.3	4.3	4.5	4.5	4.4	4.4	4.4	4.4	4.3
2000	4.3	4.4	4.4	4.4	4.5	4.5	4.5	4.6	4.4	4.4	4.4	4.4	4.4
2001	4.4	4.4	4.4	4.5	4.5	4.5	4.4	4.5	4.4	4.3	4.3	4.2	4.4
2002	4.2	4.2	4.2	4.2	4.2	4.1	4.2	4.2	4.1	4.0	3.9	3.9	4.1
2003	3.8	3.8	3.8	3.9	4.0	4.0	4.0	4.1	4.1	4.1	4.1	4.0	4.0
Professional and business services													
1990	4.7	4.6	4.6	4.7	4.7	4.9	4.8	4.8	4.7	4.6	4.7	4.7	4.7
1991	4.0	4.1	4.1	4.2	4.3	4.4	4.5	4.5	4.4	4.1	4.2	4.2	4.2
1992	4.0	4.0	4.0	4.1	4.0	4.3	4.4	4.4	4.4	4.4	4.2	4.3	4.2
1993	4.5	4.6	4.7	4.7	4.7	4.8	4.8	4.8	4.8	4.6	4.6	4.6	4.6
1994	4.5	4.7	4.7	4.7	4.8	4.9	5.5	5.5	5.4	5.2	5.1	5.0	5.0
1995	5.0	4.9	5.0	5.2	5.2	5.3	5.0	5.1	5.1	5.1	4.9	4.9	5.0
1996	4.8	4.9	4.8	4.9	4.8	4.8	5.1	5.3	5.1	5.1	5.0	5.0	4.9
1997	5.3	5.5	5.5	5.5	5.5	5.5	5.6	5.6	5.5	5.6	5.6	5.6	5.5
1998	5.7	5.7	5.8	5.8	5.9	6.1	6.2	6.3	6.3	6.5	6.6	6.8	6.1
1999	6.6	6.7	6.8	6.9	6.9	7.0	7.2	7.3	7.1	7.1	7.1	7.1	6.9
2000	6.9	6.9	7.1	7.1	7.1	7.3	7.3	7.3	7.3	7.4	7.3	7.3	7.1
2001	7.4	7.3	7.4	7.4	7.4	7.5	7.4	7.4	7.1	7.2	6.9	6.9	7.3
2002	6.5	6.5	6.6	6.7	6.7	6.7	6.5	6.5	6.5	6.6	6.5	6.4	6.6
2003	6.4	6.4	6.5	6.5	6.5	6.5	6.5	6.5	6.5	6.5	6.6	6.6	6.5
Educational and health services													
1990	9.5	9.4	9.4	9.5	9.6	9.7	9.7	9.8	9.8	9.9	10.0	10.0	9.6
1991	9.7	9.9	10.1	10.1	10.2	10.3	10.3	10.2	10.3	10.1	10.2	10.3	10.1
1992	10.0	10.1	10.1	10.1	10.1	10.2	10.3	10.2	10.1	10.0	10.0	9.9	10.0
1993	9.8	9.8	9.9	9.9	10.1	10.2	10.1	10.1	10.0	10.2	10.2	10.2	10.0
1994	10.2	10.2	10.3	10.2	10.2	10.3	10.3	10.2	10.2	10.2	10.2	10.3	10.2
1995	9.6	9.6	9.6	9.8	9.8	9.9	9.8	9.6	9.7	9.8	9.8	9.9	9.7
1996	9.9	10.0	10.0	10.1	10.1	10.1	10.1	10.0	10.0	10.1	10.1	10.2	10.0
1997	10.0	10.0	10.0	10.1	10.1	10.1	10.0	10.1	10.2	10.4	10.4	10.4	10.1
1998	10.1	10.2	10.2	10.1	10.0	10.1	10.2	10.1	10.2	10.4	10.4	10.4	10.2
1999	10.2	10.3	10.3	10.4	10.3	10.2	10.4	10.3	10.3	10.3	10.3	10.4	10.3
2000	10.3	10.5	10.6	10.5	10.5	10.5	10.6	10.6	10.5	10.6	10.6	10.6	10.5
2001	10.4	10.4	10.4	10.5	10.5	10.6	10.6	10.6	10.6	10.9	10.9	10.9	10.6
2002	10.8	10.9	10.9	11.0	11.0	11.0	10.8	10.8	10.9	11.0	10.9	10.9	10.9
2003	10.7	10.7	10.8	10.8	10.8	10.8	10.8	10.8	10.9	10.9	10.9	10.9	10.8

Employment by Industry: Illinois—*Continued*

(Numbers in thousands. Not seasonally adjusted.)

Industry	January	February	March	April	May	June	July	August	September	October	November	December	Annual Average
CHAMPAIGN-URBANA-RANTOUL—*Continued*													
Leisure and hospitality													
1990	6.8	7.0	7.2	7.5	7.5	7.2	7.2	7.5	7.9	7.7	7.7	7.6	7.4
1991	7.4	7.7	7.6	7.8	7.8	7.3	7.2	7.4	8.1	8.3	8.1	7.9	7.7
1992	7.5	7.7	7.7	8.3	8.5	8.0	8.0	8.2	8.8	8.7	8.7	8.6	8.2
1993	8.2	8.5	8.5	8.5	8.5	8.1	7.9	8.0	8.7	8.4	8.5	8.3	8.3
1994	8.1	8.3	8.4	8.4	8.7	8.1	8.2	8.4	8.8	8.7	8.7	8.8	8.4
1995	8.1	8.4	8.6	8.8	8.7	8.3	8.4	8.6	9.2	9.2	9.1	9.3	8.7
1996	8.7	9.0	8.9	9.4	9.5	9.1	8.7	8.8	9.2	9.3	9.3	9.2	9.0
1997	8.4	8.9	9.1	9.4	9.7	9.1	9.0	9.1	9.7	9.2	9.2	9.1	9.1
1998	8.2	9.0	9.2	9.1	9.2	8.7	9.0	9.0	9.6	9.8	9.8	9.6	9.1
1999	8.6	9.4	9.5	10.1	10.0	9.3	9.5	9.7	10.1	9.9	9.9	9.9	9.6
2000	9.3	9.9	9.8	9.9	10.0	9.5	9.7	9.6	10.2	10.2	10.1	9.7	9.8
2001	9.5	9.9	10.0	10.4	10.4	9.8	9.6	9.7	10.2	10.4	10.3	10.1	10.0
2002	9.4	9.7	10.0	10.3	10.2	9.4	9.7	9.8	10.7	10.6	10.7	10.5	10.1
2003	9.7	10.1	10.4	10.7	10.7	10.1	9.8	10.0	10.8	10.8	10.8	10.7	10.4
Other services													
1990	2.3	2.4	2.4	2.5	2.5	2.6	2.6	2.6	2.5	2.5	2.5	2.5	2.4
1991	2.5	2.5	2.6	2.6	2.6	2.7	2.6	2.6	2.6	2.6	2.6	2.6	2.5
1992	2.6	2.6	2.6	2.6	2.7	2.7	2.7	2.7	2.7	2.7	2.7	2.7	2.6
1993	2.7	2.7	2.7	2.7	2.7	2.8	2.8	2.8	2.8	2.8	2.7	2.8	2.7
1994	2.8	2.8	2.8	2.7	2.8	2.8	2.9	2.8	2.9	2.8	2.8	2.8	2.8
1995	2.7	2.8	2.8	2.9	2.8	2.8	2.9	2.9	2.9	2.9	2.9	2.9	2.8
1996	2.8	2.9	2.9	2.9	2.9	2.9	2.9	2.9	2.9	2.9	2.9	2.9	2.8
1997	2.8	2.9	2.9	2.8	2.8	2.8	2.7	2.7	2.7	2.8	2.8	2.8	2.7
1998	2.8	2.8	2.8	2.9	2.9	2.9	2.9	2.9	2.8	2.9	2.9	2.9	2.8
1999	2.8	2.9	2.9	3.0	3.0	3.0	3.0	3.0	3.0	3.0	3.0	3.0	2.9
2000	2.9	2.9	2.9	3.0	3.0	3.0	3.1	3.0	3.0	3.0	3.0	3.0	2.9
2001	3.0	3.0	3.0	3.1	3.1	3.3	3.2	3.2	3.1	3.1	3.1	3.1	3.1
2002	3.1	3.1	3.1	3.1	3.1	3.3	3.3	3.2	3.1	3.1	3.1	3.2	3.2
2003	3.1	3.1	3.2	3.2	3.2	3.3	3.2	3.3	3.2	3.2	3.2	3.2	3.2
Government													
1990	33.2	35.7	36.4	36.1	36.2	33.0	31.5	31.0	34.2	36.3	36.6	36.6	34.7
1991	33.2	36.0	36.7	36.2	38.2	32.8	32.0	31.3	33.1	36.8	36.9	36.2	34.9
1992	33.3	36.0	36.7	36.8	35.6	32.6	32.0	31.3	35.2	35.3	35.2	35.0	34.5
1993	31.0	35.2	35.0	34.5	34.2	31.9	30.6	29.7	31.4	35.4	34.7	34.5	33.1
1994	30.7	34.0	35.5	34.1	34.1	30.9	30.3	29.5	32.2	35.2	35.6	34.5	33.0
1995	31.0	34.3	34.6	34.4	34.1	31.1	32.6	32.7	33.5	35.4	35.7	35.1	33.7
1996	32.3	34.9	34.8	35.7	34.5	34.1	33.9	32.0	32.4	34.0	35.5	35.3	34.1
1997	31.5	34.4	35.2	34.7	34.8	31.9	31.1	30.8	31.2	35.0	35.1	35.0	33.3
1998	29.9	34.2	35.1	34.6	35.1	31.9	31.3	30.9	32.8	35.2	35.8	35.4	33.5
1999	31.5	35.0	35.4	36.2	35.5	32.3	32.0	31.9	33.7	36.0	33.4	35.3	34.0
2000	30.8	35.5	36.0	36.5	35.4	32.3	32.6	31.9	34.3	36.2	36.4	36.1	34.5
2001	31.9	36.2	36.5	36.0	35.9	32.6	32.7	32.7	35.4	37.8	38.1	37.7	35.3
2002	33.7	37.2	37.7	37.4	37.3	34.0	34.1	33.8	35.0	38.2	38.4	38.1	36.2
2003	34.4	36.9	38.0	37.6	37.4	34.1	33.8	33.8	33.7	37.3	37.5	38.2	36.1
Federal government													
2001	1.4	1.4	1.4	1.2	1.0	1.0	0.8	1.3	1.4	1.4	1.4	1.4	1.3
2002	1.4	1.4	1.4	1.4	1.4	1.4	1.4	1.4	1.4	1.4	1.4	1.4	1.4
2003	1.4	1.4	1.4	1.3	1.3	1.4	1.3	1.3	1.3	1.3	1.3	1.4	1.3
State government													
1990	23.1	25.1	25.8	25.7	25.4	22.9	22.5	22.1	24.3	26.4	26.5	26.4	24.6
1991	23.8	26.0	26.7	26.3	28.0	23.2	23.2	22.7	23.3	26.5	26.5	26.0	25.1
1992	23.8	26.0	26.7	26.9	25.6	23.0	23.1	22.6	25.6	25.6	25.6	25.5	25.0
1993	22.2	26.0	25.8	25.3	24.8	23.0	23.1	22.5	23.2	26.0	26.0	25.6	24.4
1994	22.4	25.3	26.1	25.5	25.4	22.3	22.6	22.2	23.7	26.3	26.1	25.4	24.4
1995	22.5	25.3	25.6	25.5	25.1	22.4	24.4	24.3	24.7	26.3	26.5	25.9	24.8
1996	23.6	25.7	25.6	26.6	25.3	25.4	25.5	23.5	23.6	24.9	26.2	26.1	25.1
1997	22.7	25.3	26.0	25.3	25.4	23.0	22.5	22.2	22.2	25.8	25.8	25.6	24.3
1998	21.0	24.9	25.7	25.2	25.5	22.7	22.5	22.1	23.5	25.7	26.1	25.7	24.2
1999	22.3	25.4	25.8	26.4	25.6	22.7	22.9	23.0	24.2	26.3	23.7	25.4	24.4
2000	21.6	25.8	26.2	26.5	25.2	22.7	23.3	22.8	24.8	26.1	26.3	26.1	24.7
2001	22.5	26.3	26.6	26.1	26.0	23.2	23.7	23.3	25.5	27.6	27.9	27.5	25.5
2002	24.1	27.2	27.6	27.2	26.9	24.0	24.4	24.1	25.1	28.1	28.2	27.9	26.2
2003	24.5	26.8	27.9	27.6	27.4	24.3	24.5	24.5	24.3	27.7	27.9	28.5	26.3

Employment by Industry: Illinois—*Continued*

(Numbers in thousands. Not seasonally adjusted.)

Industry	January	February	March	April	May	June	July	August	September	October	November	December	Annual Average
CHAMPAIGN-URBANA-RANTOUL—*Continued*													
Local government													
1990	7.2	7.7	7.8	7.4	7.7	7.1	6.1	6.0	7.0	7.1	7.3	7.4	7.1
1991	6.6	7.2	7.3	7.1	7.4	6.8	6.0	5.8	7.0	7.5	7.6	7.5	6.9
1992	6.7	7.3	7.3	7.2	7.3	6.9	6.2	6.1	7.0	7.2	7.2	7.2	6.9
1993	6.5	7.0	7.0	7.1	7.4	7.0	5.9	5.7	6.6	7.9	7.2	7.4	6.8
1994	6.8	7.2	7.9	7.1	7.2	7.1	6.2	5.8	7.0	7.5	8.1	7.6	7.1
1995	7.1	7.6	7.6	7.5	7.6	7.3	6.8	7.0	7.4	7.7	7.8	7.8	7.4
1996	7.3	7.8	7.8	7.8	7.9	7.4	7.1	7.2	7.5	7.8	8.0	7.9	7.6
1997	7.5	7.8	7.9	8.1	8.1	7.6	7.3	7.3	7.7	7.9	7.9	8.0	7.7
1998	7.5	7.9	8.0	8.1	8.3	7.8	7.5	7.5	7.9	8.2	8.3	8.3	7.9
1999	7.8	8.2	8.2	8.4	8.5	8.2	7.7	7.5	8.1	8.3	8.3	8.4	8.1
2000	7.8	8.3	8.4	8.5	8.6	8.1	7.8	7.6	8.2	8.7	8.6	8.6	8.2
2001	8.0	8.5	8.5	8.7	8.9	8.4	8.2	8.1	8.5	8.8	8.8	8.8	8.5
2002	8.2	8.6	8.7	8.8	9.0	8.6	8.3	8.3	8.5	8.7	8.8	8.8	8.6
2003	8.5	8.7	8.7	8.7	8.7	8.4	8.0	8.0	8.1	8.3	8.3	8.3	8.4
CHICAGO													
Total nonfarm													
1990	3639.4	3645.4	3672.4	3681.6	3721.6	3755.8	3741.1	3741.4	3752.4	3715.4	3718.4	3721.6	3708.9
1991	3611.7	3606.3	3628.8	3638.5	3670.2	3682.5	3663.4	3663.1	3672.7	3654.4	3657.5	3660.3	3650.8
1992	3564.4	3570.9	3585.1	3608.0	3647.5	3675.1	3680.6	3678.5	3688.2	3688.3	3691.8	3704.9	3648.6
1993	3610.3	3619.7	3638.6	3696.5	3739.0	3765.4	3758.5	3760.5	3761.3	3774.8	3780.0	3794.1	3724.9
1994	3681.7	3692.8	3726.2	3772.5	3809.7	3850.9	3849.7	3858.8	3873.0	3850.0	3872.4	3884.9	3810.2
1995	3799.5	3822.2	3857.4	3862.8	3899.6	3940.6	3922.7	3929.4	3967.8	3950.0	3964.8	3983.9	3908.4
1996	3866.4	3873.4	3906.9	3930.8	3973.0	4006.5	3985.9	4000.0	4001.9	4012.3	4034.8	4045.1	3969.8
1997	3921.1	3932.1	3970.4	3995.2	4046.5	4082.0	4058.0	4064.6	4081.1	4079.0	4103.5	4126.8	4038.4
1998	4007.5	4023.3	4048.7	4087.2	4131.2	4154.5	4147.9	4152.2	4176.6	4177.2	4190.8	4201.9	4124.9
1999	4068.8	4094.8	4122.9	4141.5	4170.3	4207.2	4192.5	4193.9	4199.4	4226.1	4243.8	4253.3	4176.2
2000	4113.1	4131.6	4172.5	4206.3	4247.3	4288.6	4255.4	4273.5	4272.2	4278.5	4295.7	4299.1	4236.2
2001	4162.6	4169.3	4197.7	4219.5	4253.7	4291.2	4242.1	4241.9	4222.6	4196.9	4194.1	4196.5	4215.7
2002	4059.2	4054.7	4075.9	4114.6	4145.1	4176.4	4157.4	4163.6	4145.7	4147.8	4157.4	4154.5	4129.4
2003	4011.4	4007.9	4026.8	4060.1	4096.0	4128.6	4110.0	4103.9	4109.4	4125.3	4124.8	4126.1	4085.9
Total private													
1990	3191.8	3191.2	3212.9	3224.3	3256.2	3293.8	3298.5	3310.2	3304.8	3260.1	3258.8	3261.3	3255.3
1991	3160.0	3146.6	3166.6	3174.4	3202.4	3228.8	3212.3	3222.5	3219.1	3191.9	3191.9	3192.9	3192.5
1992	3107.5	3108.5	3120.5	3143.0	3178.2	3205.9	3225.4	3234.7	3230.7	3222.9	3223.0	3235.7	3186.3
1993	3153.7	3157.0	3173.1	3229.3	3264.3	3292.8	3295.6	3305.1	3303.9	3307.8	3309.6	3321.8	3259.5
1994	3223.5	3226.6	3256.6	3297.0	3329.5	3370.7	3380.4	3394.2	3399.7	3373.5	3393.6	3405.3	3337.6
1995	3322.3	3334.9	3368.8	3373.5	3407.2	3447.2	3456.0	3473.7	3476.6	3458.6	3471.1	3490.0	3423.3
1996	3384.4	3382.9	3412.8	3434.4	3473.9	3510.6	3505.5	3525.1	3516.9	3521.8	3542.9	3557.6	3480.7
1997	3440.0	3442.4	3478.0	3503.9	3549.0	3584.4	3575.5	3584.5	3591.4	3586.4	3607.9	3631.6	3547.9
1998	3521.1	3529.0	3551.9	3591.4	3632.6	3658.1	3666.6	3676.5	3679.8	3680.5	3691.2	3702.4	3631.8
1999	3580.6	3597.9	3622.7	3640.9	3669.0	3708.0	3708.4	3714.7	3707.2	3728.5	3744.5	3758.3	3681.7
2000	3626.8	3632.8	3668.6	3705.5	3730.4	3770.8	3756.0	3773.0	3770.6	3772.2	3787.6	3790.2	3732.0
2001	3667.7	3661.4	3687.9	3712.1	3738.9	3775.2	3735.1	3740.1	3718.7	3683.3	3678.8	3679.5	3706.6
2002	3552.4	3538.7	3557.4	3593.0	3620.3	3650.1	3638.9	3649.9	3635.4	3625.5	3633.1	3629.8	3610.4
2003	3497.8	3484.7	3502.5	3536.6	3571.1	3603.2	3594.3	3596.3	3601.2	3603.8	3603.3	3605.0	3566.7
Goods-producing													
1990	772.2	774.8	779.6	783.5	793.3	802.1	800.8	803.3	799.6	784.9	777.8	768.5	786.7
1991	732.8	728.8	731.6	737.7	746.5	753.5	749.0	755.9	755.8	750.1	744.0	732.1	743.2
1992	698.8	698.1	700.9	712.8	721.4	730.9	736.9	741.4	741.0	733.6	729.7	724.5	722.5
1993	699.5	701.2	704.8	717.4	728.0	736.5	738.6	741.8	742.5	741.2	738.7	734.5	727.1
1994	704.5	704.5	715.7	728.1	740.7	753.5	754.3	760.5	762.6	757.4	759.1	756.7	741.5
1995	736.0	739.7	749.6	754.9	762.8	773.7	774.2	780.8	778.1	773.3	770.4	766.6	763.3
1996	739.4	739.1	746.6	753.1	761.6	770.7	769.7	774.5	771.6	770.6	768.9	764.1	760.8
1997	739.2	740.1	749.9	764.8	775.3	783.9	776.9	782.8	784.1	777.6	774.1	771.3	768.3
1998	749.8	752.1	754.3	769.6	776.2	780.9	782.9	782.6	783.3	780.2	777.9	774.9	772.1
1999	743.9	749.5	746.5	754.6	761.4	771.4	772.7	775.3	775.7	777.2	776.1	772.4	764.7
2000	742.6	744.3	755.1	765.3	769.7	775.5	773.2	777.3	776.3	775.5	774.1	764.8	766.1
2001	732.6	731.3	735.5	741.5	746.0	749.8	737.9	739.3	736.0	729.4	722.2	714.6	734.7
2002	682.9	679.3	683.6	693.3	698.0	704.0	699.2	701.9	700.5	698.2	694.3	685.9	693.4
2003	655.5	650.8	654.1	666.4	673.5	678.1	672.7	675.4	675.7	674.8	671.2	665.9	667.8
Natural resources and mining													
1990	2.2	2.2	2.2	2.4	2.5	2.5	2.6	2.6	2.6	2.5	2.5	2.4	2.4
1991	2.1	2.2	2.3	2.2	2.3	2.3	2.4	2.4	2.4	2.3	2.3	2.0	2.3
1992	1.9	2.0	2.1	2.1	2.2	2.3	2.3	2.3	2.3	2.2	2.2	2.1	2.2
1993	1.9	1.9	2.0	2.1	2.2	2.3	2.3	2.2	2.2	2.2	2.1	2.0	2.1
1994	1.8	1.7	1.9	2.0	2.1	2.2	2.1	2.1	2.1	2.0	2.0	1.9	2.0
1995	1.7	1.7	1.9	1.9	2.0	2.0	2.0	1.9	1.9	2.0	1.9	1.9	1.9
1996	1.7	1.7	1.8	1.8	1.8	1.9	1.8	1.9	1.8	1.8	1.8	1.7	1.8
1997	1.5	1.5	1.6	1.8	1.9	1.9	1.9	1.9	1.9	1.8	1.8	1.8	1.8
1998	1.6	1.6	1.7	1.8	1.9	1.9	1.9	1.9	1.9	2.0	1.9	1.9	1.8
1999	1.6	1.6	1.8	1.9	1.9	2.0	2.0	2.0	2.0	2.0	2.0	1.9	1.9
2000	1.7	1.7	1.8	1.9	1.9	2.0	2.0	2.0	2.0	2.1	2.0	2.0	1.9
2001	1.7	1.7	1.8	2.0	2.0	2.0	2.0	2.0	2.0	2.0	1.9	1.9	1.9
2002	1.7	1.7	1.9	1.9	1.9	2.0	2.0	2.0	2.0	1.9	1.9	1.9	1.9
2003	1.6	1.7	1.8	1.9	1.9	1.9	1.9	1.9	1.9	1.9	1.9	1.9	1.9

Employment by Industry: Illinois—*Continued*

(Numbers in thousands. Not seasonally adjusted.)

Industry	January	February	March	April	May	June	July	August	September	October	November	December	Annual Average
CHICAGO—*Continued*													
Construction													
1990	147.5	148.4	152.4	158.3	165.3	169.5	173.4	173.9	171.7	166.0	162.2	155.3	162.0
1991	135.7	133.0	135.9	144.3	152.3	156.2	160.2	161.6	160.0	157.5	151.5	143.7	149.3
1992	128.6	127.0	129.3	136.8	144.0	149.9	153.5	154.2	152.9	151.1	147.4	142.6	143.1
1993	126.0	125.5	127.6	137.6	145.3	149.4	152.8	154.1	154.0	154.8	152.1	146.9	143.8
1994	127.6	125.5	132.8	144.4	152.9	159.0	161.1	162.1	162.1	158.4	156.0	151.5	149.5
1995	135.2	135.3	141.0	146.8	153.9	162.1	167.0	168.9	168.3	167.2	163.5	158.4	155.6
1996	140.0	137.7	143.7	155.7	162.1	167.3	172.3	173.4	171.7	170.6	168.2	162.3	160.4
1997	141.8	142.2	148.6	159.8	168.0	174.1	174.4	175.4	175.8	173.5	171.0	165.7	164.2
1998	147.2	147.4	149.2	166.4	173.0	176.6	181.3	182.8	182.3	182.1	179.7	176.6	170.4
1999	157.8	160.3	164.7	175.9	182.2	188.8	192.3	194.0	193.6	195.1	193.8	189.8	182.4
2000	170.4	170.7	178.9	189.8	194.9	199.4	201.6	203.6	202.8	202.9	201.1	192.7	192.4
2001	172.6	174.0	179.9	192.6	200.2	204.9	206.8	208.4	206.6	206.2	204.9	200.0	196.4
2002	176.7	175.5	180.2	191.6	198.1	203.9	207.4	209.2	208.4	208.5	206.2	198.4	197.0
2003	178.5	175.0	179.0	193.2	201.7	206.6	207.9	209.8	209.5	208.3	203.8	200.8	197.8
Manufacturing													
1990	622.5	624.2	625.0	622.8	625.5	630.1	624.8	626.8	625.3	616.4	613.1	610.8	622.3
1991	595.0	593.6	593.4	591.2	591.9	595.0	586.4	591.9	593.4	590.3	590.2	586.4	591.6
1992	568.3	569.1	569.5	573.9	575.2	578.7	581.1	584.9	585.8	580.3	580.1	579.8	577.2
1993	571.6	573.8	575.2	577.7	580.5	584.8	583.5	585.5	586.3	584.2	584.5	585.6	581.1
1994	575.1	577.3	581.0	581.7	585.7	592.3	591.1	596.3	598.4	597.0	601.1	603.3	590.0
1995	599.1	602.7	606.7	606.2	606.9	609.6	605.2	610.0	607.9	604.1	605.0	606.3	605.8
1996	597.7	599.7	601.1	595.6	597.7	601.5	595.6	599.2	598.1	598.2	598.9	600.1	598.6
1997	595.9	596.4	599.7	603.2	605.4	607.9	600.6	605.5	606.4	602.3	601.3	603.8	602.4
1998	601.0	603.1	603.4	601.4	601.3	602.4	599.7	597.9	599.1	596.1	596.3	596.4	599.8
1999	584.5	587.6	580.0	576.8	577.3	580.6	578.4	579.3	580.1	580.1	580.3	580.7	580.5
2000	570.5	571.9	574.4	573.6	572.9	574.1	569.6	571.7	571.5	570.5	571.0	570.1	571.8
2001	558.3	555.6	553.8	546.9	543.8	542.9	529.1	528.9	527.4	521.2	515.4	512.7	536.3
2002	504.5	502.1	501.5	499.8	498.0	498.1	489.8	490.7	490.1	487.8	486.2	485.6	494.5
2003	475.4	474.1	473.3	471.3	469.9	469.6	462.9	463.7	464.3	464.6	465.5	463.2	468.2
Service-providing													
1990	2867.2	2870.6	2892.8	2898.1	2928.3	2953.7	2940.3	2938.1	2952.8	2930.5	2940.6	2953.1	2922.2
1991	2878.9	2877.5	2897.2	2900.8	2923.7	2929.0	2914.4	2907.2	2916.9	2904.3	2913.5	2928.2	2907.6
1992	2865.6	2872.8	2884.2	2895.2	2926.1	2944.2	2943.7	2937.1	2947.2	2954.7	2962.1	2980.4	2926.1
1993	2910.8	2918.5	2933.8	2979.1	3011.0	3028.9	3019.9	3018.7	3018.8	3033.6	3041.3	3059.6	2997.8
1994	2977.2	2988.3	3010.5	3044.4	3069.0	3097.4	3095.4	3098.3	3110.4	3092.6	3113.3	3128.2	3068.8
1995	3063.5	3082.5	3107.8	3107.9	3136.8	3166.9	3148.5	3148.6	3189.7	3176.7	3194.4	3217.3	3145.1
1996	3127.0	3134.3	3160.3	3177.7	3211.4	3235.8	3216.2	3225.5	3230.3	3241.7	3265.9	3281.0	3208.9
1997	3181.9	3192.0	3220.5	3230.4	3271.2	3298.1	3281.1	3281.8	3297.0	3301.4	3329.4	3355.5	3270.0
1998	3257.7	3271.2	3294.4	3317.6	3355.0	3373.6	3365.0	3369.6	3393.3	3397.0	3412.9	3427.0	3352.9
1999	3324.9	3345.3	3376.4	3386.9	3408.9	3435.8	3419.8	3418.6	3423.7	3448.9	3467.7	3480.9	3411.5
2000	3370.5	3387.3	3417.4	3441.0	3477.6	3513.1	3482.2	3496.2	3495.9	3503.0	3521.6	3534.3	3470.0
2001	3430.0	3438.0	3462.2	3478.0	3507.7	3541.4	3504.2	3502.6	3486.6	3467.5	3471.9	3481.9	3481.0
2002	3376.3	3375.4	3392.3	3421.3	3447.1	3472.4	3458.2	3461.7	3445.2	3449.6	3463.1	3468.6	3435.9
2003	3355.9	3357.1	3372.7	3393.7	3422.5	3450.5	3437.3	3428.5	3433.7	3450.5	3453.6	3460.2	3418.0
Trade, transportation, and utilities													
1990	821.0	810.0	811.8	806.8	812.2	819.1	817.6	818.4	813.8	811.9	821.1	832.2	816.3
1991	805.7	791.5	793.6	787.5	791.9	794.7	792.6	793.8	790.1	788.0	799.2	810.9	795.0
1992	780.6	772.6	772.0	772.3	778.0	782.1	776.9	778.0	780.6	795.5	805.6	820.4	784.6
1993	794.1	785.9	786.0	792.8	798.1	802.8	804.8	804.2	805.6	816.2	829.1	843.6	805.3
1994	810.6	803.7	806.6	808.8	816.8	823.9	824.9	828.3	831.1	835.4	850.1	863.9	825.3
1995	831.7	824.3	827.2	820.4	827.2	832.9	836.4	843.1	841.9	849.0	864.0	877.3	839.6
1996	850.4	839.8	842.7	830.9	839.7	846.3	837.8	842.9	842.9	855.2	872.5	888.3	849.1
1997	851.0	839.0	843.3	842.0	851.5	858.4	853.3	844.5	854.9	862.1	878.0	895.5	856.1
1998	857.4	847.0	849.4	840.7	850.1	855.7	856.9	857.6	858.5	867.9	883.3	894.9	860.0
1999	863.3	857.4	861.0	855.8	860.6	866.4	870.1	868.2	865.8	877.6	894.2	908.6	870.8
2000	871.2	864.3	867.0	870.1	874.2	880.4	879.6	885.2	884.9	892.2	909.7	922.1	883.4
2001	886.7	874.3	876.4	880.0	883.3	889.6	879.3	878.4	876.6	869.1	880.7	890.9	880.4
2002	852.6	839.9	842.5	845.3	849.5	853.3	848.7	850.3	850.3	853.3	868.2	879.0	852.7
2003	839.7	831.6	833.6	832.6	838.8	844.1	842.2	842.9	847.1	854.8	863.6	871.1	845.2
Wholesale trade													
1990	232.5	232.5	233.1	232.5	233.5	234.6	235.6	236.2	232.8	231.0	230.2	229.7	232.9
1991	223.9	223.2	224.1	224.5	225.3	226.5	225.7	225.4	224.1	221.4	221.5	221.1	223.9
1992	222.9	222.6	222.3	221.2	222.3	223.4	224.6	223.0	223.8	224.6	224.6	225.0	223.4
1993	220.8	221.1	221.6	222.6	222.8	222.6	222.9	220.8	220.4	220.6	220.4	220.7	221.4
1994	217.5	217.6	218.9	220.0	221.1	222.8	223.4	224.6	224.7	223.7	223.8	225.7	222.0
1995	224.6	225.9	227.5	228.0	228.9	230.7	230.4	231.6	230.1	230.0	229.5	231.3	229.0
1996	229.0	229.4	230.5	228.6	229.9	232.0	231.0	231.7	230.2	230.5	231.5	232.9	230.6
1997	228.5	229.3	231.1	231.5	233.1	235.4	234.4	235.0	233.6	233.6	234.4	236.1	233.0
1998	236.0	236.9	237.8	236.1	236.6	238.8	237.0	236.4	235.7	236.5	237.1	238.4	236.9
1999	237.2	238.3	238.8	236.9	237.5	239.5	240.9	240.1	239.4	239.1	239.5	240.8	239.0
2000	236.9	237.5	237.8	239.0	239.7	241.8	241.0	241.8	241.0	241.9	242.3	243.5	240.4
2001	242.2	241.9	242.0	245.1	246.4	248.4	248.3	248.0	247.2	243.3	242.2	242.9	244.8
2002	238.3	238.3	238.6	238.7	238.9	240.4	239.0	238.9	238.1	237.8	238.4	238.6	238.7
2003	236.2	236.3	237.1	235.9	236.8	237.7	237.8	237.1	235.7	235.3	235.6	235.8	236.4

Employment by Industry: Illinois—*Continued*

(Numbers in thousands. Not seasonally adjusted.)

Industry	January	February	March	April	May	June	July	August	September	October	November	December	Annual Average
CHICAGO—*Continued*													
Retail trade													
1990	423.6	411.9	411.4	408.0	411.2	415.9	414.8	415.4	412.8	413.1	422.7	433.4	416.2
1991	417.1	403.9	404.1	397.9	401.8	402.7	402.0	403.4	400.5	401.1	412.9	424.2	406.0
1992	399.7	392.7	391.8	393.1	396.9	399.0	390.1	392.2	390.8	406.4	416.3	429.1	399.8
1993	407.9	399.3	398.6	399.0	401.9	404.1	405.0	405.7	404.3	410.9	423.3	435.8	408.0
1994	410.5	402.6	402.6	404.1	408.3	413.5	414.5	417.5	419.6	423.9	438.9	451.4	417.3
1995	426.0	418.3	419.4	411.8	415.9	419.1	421.0	426.0	425.4	430.4	445.9	457.0	426.4
1996	434.3	423.6	424.2	414.0	420.0	423.6	419.2	423.0	423.0	431.5	448.3	462.3	428.9
1997	433.1	421.0	422.8	421.2	427.0	430.5	427.0	429.9	426.4	431.7	446.7	462.4	431.6
1998	428.8	417.7	418.3	409.3	416.1	419.5	420.4	420.9	421.0	428.3	444.5	455.2	425.0
1999	426.8	420.9	423.2	419.6	424.1	428.3	428.1	428.3	426.0	434.3	449.8	462.2	431.0
2000	432.9	426.0	428.4	428.2	430.6	434.8	434.8	438.3	437.2	441.8	457.7	467.8	438.2
2001	440.6	430.0	431.7	433.8	435.2	440.8	433.2	433.2	431.0	428.7	443.9	455.3	436.5
2002	426.8	415.7	419.0	419.2	423.3	427.4	424.2	425.0	424.3	426.8	441.9	452.7	427.2
2003	420.3	413.4	415.0	415.1	419.5	424.4	421.8	423.1	426.8	434.1	443.3	450.8	425.6
Transportation and utilities													
1990	164.9	165.6	167.3	166.3	167.5	168.6	167.2	166.8	168.2	167.8	168.2	169.1	167.3
1991	164.7	164.4	165.4	165.1	164.8	165.5	164.9	165.0	165.5	165.5	164.8	165.6	165.1
1992	158.0	157.3	157.9	158.0	158.8	159.7	162.2	162.8	166.0	164.5	164.7	166.3	161.4
1993	165.4	165.5	165.8	171.2	173.4	176.1	176.9	177.7	180.9	184.7	185.4	187.1	175.8
1994	182.6	183.5	185.1	184.7	187.4	187.6	187.0	186.2	186.8	187.8	187.4	186.8	186.1
1995	181.1	180.1	180.3	180.6	182.4	183.1	185.0	185.5	186.4	188.6	188.6	189.0	184.2
1996	187.1	186.8	188.0	188.3	189.8	190.7	187.6	188.2	189.7	193.2	192.7	193.1	189.6
1997	189.4	188.7	189.4	189.3	191.4	192.5	191.9	179.6	194.9	196.8	196.9	197.0	191.5
1998	192.6	192.4	193.3	195.3	197.4	197.4	199.5	200.3	201.8	203.1	201.7	201.3	198.0
1999	199.3	198.2	199.0	199.3	199.0	198.6	201.1	199.8	200.4	204.2	204.9	205.6	200.8
2000	201.4	200.8	200.8	202.9	203.9	203.8	203.8	205.1	206.7	208.5	209.7	210.8	204.9
2001	203.9	202.4	202.7	201.1	201.7	200.4	197.8	197.2	198.4	197.1	194.6	192.7	199.2
2002	187.5	185.9	184.9	187.4	187.3	185.5	185.5	186.4	187.9	188.7	187.9	187.7	186.9
2003	183.2	181.9	181.5	181.6	182.5	182.0	182.6	182.7	184.6	185.4	184.7	184.5	183.1
Information													
1990	97.0	97.1	97.1	96.5	97.4	98.5	97.9	99.0	98.6	97.3	97.7	97.7	97.7
1991	100.8	100.3	100.4	98.8	99.2	100.9	101.4	101.1	100.3	101.1	100.2	100.5	100.4
1992	98.1	97.8	97.6	98.1	98.4	99.7	99.7	99.3	98.7	99.2	98.8	99.2	98.7
1993	98.7	99.1	99.8	100.9	102.3	104.2	106.0	105.0	103.2	104.2	105.5	105.9	102.9
1994	104.0	103.8	104.1	105.5	105.6	106.6	106.0	106.0	104.6	105.1	105.6	105.3	105.2
1995	106.6	106.5	107.0	103.9	105.0	106.0	104.2	104.8	104.4	103.6	105.0	105.6	105.2
1996	106.9	107.1	107.2	104.1	105.6	106.1	108.1	108.2	107.8	109.1	109.6	110.0	107.5
1997	109.3	109.3	110.0	109.7	110.4	111.0	111.4	112.2	111.4	111.6	112.1	113.6	111.0
1998	112.1	111.3	111.7	110.0	109.4	110.3	111.3	111.0	109.9	110.0	109.0	108.0	110.3
1999	107.4	107.3	108.1	107.3	107.3	108.1	108.5	108.8	108.6	108.9	109.4	110.3	108.3
2000	110.1	110.5	111.5	111.4	112.1	113.6	113.5	113.7	113.2	113.9	114.5	115.1	112.8
2001	114.3	114.5	114.8	113.8	114.3	115.4	114.1	114.1	112.5	110.6	110.5	110.8	113.3
2002	108.0	107.4	107.2	106.7	106.9	106.9	104.7	104.3	102.7	102.5	102.0	101.7	105.1
2003	99.1	99.2	98.1	97.6	97.7	98.4	98.3	97.3	97.0	97.1	96.8	96.7	97.8
Financial activities													
1990	282.5	283.3	284.0	285.9	287.4	291.3	293.9	293.6	291.2	286.7	286.5	287.6	287.8
1991	284.8	284.3	285.9	287.1	288.3	291.5	291.1	291.7	289.2	285.2	285.1	287.6	287.7
1992	284.9	284.8	285.2	284.6	286.1	288.9	293.7	293.8	290.6	286.3	286.6	288.5	287.8
1993	287.4	287.1	288.3	290.9	292.7	293.1	294.1	292.0	286.8	285.2	284.6	283.8	288.8
1994	282.1	282.6	283.7	285.4	286.8	290.6	290.6	290.7	287.0	282.8	282.2	283.4	285.7
1995	281.8	282.4	283.4	281.8	283.1	287.0	286.6	287.1	283.8	282.4	282.8	285.4	284.0
1996	282.6	283.1	285.0	293.3	294.9	298.7	299.1	298.9	295.8	295.6	296.4	298.9	293.5
1997	297.4	298.5	300.1	301.2	303.1	306.7	307.2	308.5	304.4	302.9	304.0	306.2	303.4
1998	304.9	306.7	307.4	308.7	308.1	311.2	308.5	307.9	304.3	305.5	305.9	308.4	307.3
1999	307.1	307.3	308.9	308.6	310.3	313.0	315.4	315.0	310.5	310.4	310.3	311.2	310.7
2000	308.3	308.7	308.4	308.5	308.6	311.8	310.6	310.7	307.5	309.2	309.6	312.4	309.5
2001	312.4	313.3	315.3	315.7	316.6	319.8	319.1	318.6	314.9	313.7	314.5	316.1	315.8
2002	311.3	310.9	311.5	310.8	311.6	315.0	314.4	314.8	312.8	313.4	314.5	316.4	313.1
2003	312.2	312.2	313.1	313.6	314.9	318.4	318.7	318.0	319.7	319.3	319.4	319.3	316.6
Professional and business services													
1990	477.4	480.1	486.4	491.5	495.2	503.6	507.3	511.6	510.7	498.6	495.5	491.9	495.8
1991	477.4	476.2	480.5	483.7	485.2	494.0	491.3	491.8	493.2	486.2	482.0	479.3	485.1
1992	476.1	479.6	481.4	487.6	494.8	499.4	510.5	514.1	510.4	499.7	496.6	494.6	495.4
1993	481.6	484.4	488.5	509.1	514.7	523.8	524.3	529.9	527.6	527.9	524.2	522.2	513.2
1994	514.8	516.8	523.6	536.9	539.3	548.1	556.6	559.1	559.1	551.0	550.8	549.3	542.1
1995	536.5	543.1	551.1	556.2	560.8	570.2	575.8	573.1	581.0	579.5	577.6	579.5	565.4
1996	543.9	547.2	555.1	572.4	579.9	588.4	597.5	606.8	606.0	602.4	605.1	603.7	584.0
1997	575.0	579.9	588.7	598.4	606.5	616.1	623.3	630.2	628.7	632.3	636.1	638.4	612.8
1998	616.0	620.5	628.5	645.7	655.7	664.0	674.3	686.2	690.0	682.1	681.6	682.7	660.6
1999	657.8	663.1	674.1	687.7	692.2	702.4	697.5	706.4	703.8	712.6	712.9	712.2	693.6
2000	676.2	680.1	690.1	701.1	706.9	718.3	716.5	723.2	723.2	720.3	718.7	715.1	707.5
2001	681.5	679.1	682.4	685.5	690.2	697.7	687.0	690.1	684.6	679.1	670.5	667.1	682.9
2002	638.8	637.7	639.1	651.9	654.6	660.3	660.7	667.1	664.6	658.8	655.7	648.4	653.1
2003	620.5	618.5	621.4	630.8	635.0	638.4	638.6	638.8	642.9	640.2	637.8	639.3	633.5

Employment by Industry: Illinois—*Continued*

(Numbers in thousands. Not seasonally adjusted.)

Industry	January	February	March	April	May	June	July	August	September	October	November	December	Annual Average
CHICAGO—*Continued*													
Educational and health services													
1990	349.4	351.5	354.5	352.9	353.3	350.5	348.1	349.9	360.6	363.7	365.6	368.3	355.7
1991	362.1	368.4	371.2	374.7	375.5	371.2	367.0	367.3	373.0	376.4	377.3	377.8	371.8
1992	375.2	379.0	381.2	381.4	381.0	378.8	377.7	377.9	385.9	390.1	390.4	391.3	382.5
1993	386.4	391.1	392.3	393.5	393.1	388.2	384.2	386.4	395.2	399.8	400.0	401.0	392.6
1994	389.9	395.6	396.6	395.3	395.2	392.1	391.2	392.3	402.8	397.8	402.9	403.8	396.3
1995	397.9	403.8	407.8	407.0	409.4	406.2	404.5	407.2	415.3	411.4	414.6	417.5	408.6
1996	414.5	419.5	421.7	421.5	422.0	418.5	414.8	413.9	421.0	428.2	431.3	431.9	421.6
1997	419.4	423.9	426.4	429.2	430.1	425.3	419.7	420.3	427.5	431.7	434.2	434.9	426.9
1998	431.0	435.9	438.5	439.3	441.7	435.9	433.1	433.4	442.0	445.9	448.0	448.7	439.5
1999	435.1	440.8	443.3	439.7	440.9	437.2	434.1	432.3	440.5	445.1	447.5	449.0	440.5
2000	444.8	448.4	450.5	452.8	453.9	453.9	445.6	445.6	453.4	457.7	461.1	461.8	452.5
2001	461.6	466.4	471.8	472.9	473.4	474.6	469.8	472.4	477.7	478.2	481.5	481.7	473.5
2002	475.6	480.3	483.3	484.2	486.1	483.1	478.1	478.8	484.7	488.4	491.2	491.3	483.8
2003	483.7	486.2	489.4	488.9	490.7	490.9	489.0	488.7	491.2	494.7	496.2	496.3	490.5
Leisure and hospitality													
1990	248.7	250.6	254.3	262.4	270.9	279.1	281.5	282.2	279.2	267.5	264.4	264.1	267.1
1991	248.6	249.0	254.1	260.3	269.3	275.1	272.0	273.9	271.3	260.8	259.4	258.6	262.7
1992	248.4	250.7	255.5	261.5	273.2	279.2	280.1	281.2	274.5	269.5	266.6	267.0	267.3
1993	260.0	261.7	265.6	276.2	286.0	292.4	291.4	294.6	291.1	283.5	277.4	279.4	279.9
1994	267.1	268.9	274.2	284.5	292.6	300.5	300.4	301.9	297.7	290.5	289.2	287.8	287.9
1995	278.5	280.8	287.1	294.8	303.2	312.7	315.7	319.1	315.0	303.0	299.7	299.5	300.8
1996	289.6	289.6	295.4	300.1	310.4	319.9	316.8	317.9	311.6	301.5	299.4	299.9	304.3
1997	290.5	292.1	298.2	296.3	308.5	317.4	318.8	320.8	315.9	304.0	304.8	305.2	306.0
1998	285.3	289.3	294.4	311.0	324.1	330.3	329.9	328.8	323.3	319.0	315.2	315.1	313.8
1999	298.7	303.1	309.7	316.7	325.4	335.7	335.3	335.3	330.3	325.9	322.7	322.2	321.8
2000	305.5	307.6	315.6	324.9	333.5	342.6	341.9	342.2	337.3	330.8	327.0	325.6	327.9
2001	306.8	309.9	317.5	327.9	339.5	349.3	347.9	348.0	339.3	328.8	323.6	322.6	330.1
2002	310.3	310.4	316.3	326.5	338.9	349.4	350.9	350.2	343.5	335.4	331.1	330.6	332.8
2003	313.9	313.1	318.2	332.7	345.6	356.9	357.2	357.8	350.5	347.1	342.3	340.3	339.6
Other services													
1990	143.6	143.8	145.2	144.8	146.5	149.6	151.4	152.2	151.1	149.5	150.2	151.0	148.2
1991	147.8	148.1	149.3	144.6	146.5	147.9	147.9	147.0	146.2	144.1	144.7	146.1	146.7
1992	145.4	145.9	146.7	144.7	145.3	146.9	149.9	149.0	149.0	149.0	148.7	150.2	147.6
1993	146.0	146.5	147.8	148.5	149.4	151.8	152.2	151.2	151.9	149.8	150.1	151.4	149.7
1994	150.5	150.7	152.1	152.5	152.5	155.4	156.4	155.4	154.8	153.5	153.7	155.1	153.6
1995	153.3	154.3	155.6	154.5	155.7	158.5	158.6	158.5	157.1	156.4	157.0	158.6	156.5
1996	157.1	157.5	159.1	159.0	159.8	162.0	161.7	162.0	160.2	159.2	159.7	160.8	159.8
1997	158.2	159.6	161.4	162.3	163.6	165.6	164.9	165.2	164.5	164.2	164.6	166.5	163.4
1998	164.6	166.2	167.7	166.4	167.3	169.8	169.7	169.0	168.5	169.9	170.3	169.7	168.3
1999	167.3	169.4	171.1	170.5	170.9	173.8	174.8	173.4	172.0	170.8	171.4	172.4	171.5
2000	168.1	168.9	170.4	171.4	171.5	174.7	175.1	175.1	174.8	172.6	172.9	173.3	172.4
2001	171.8	172.6	174.2	174.8	175.6	179.0	180.0	179.2	177.1	174.4	175.3	175.7	175.8
2002	172.9	172.8	173.9	174.3	174.7	178.1	182.2	182.5	176.3	175.5	176.1	176.5	176.3
2003	173.2	173.1	174.6	174.0	174.9	178.0	177.6	177.4	177.1	175.8	176.0	176.1	175.7
Government													
1990	447.6	454.2	459.5	457.3	465.4	462.0	442.6	431.2	447.6	455.3	459.6	460.3	453.6
1991	451.7	459.7	462.2	464.1	467.8	453.7	451.1	440.6	453.6	462.5	465.6	467.4	458.3
1992	456.9	462.4	464.6	465.0	469.3	469.2	455.2	443.8	457.5	465.4	468.8	469.2	462.3
1993	456.6	462.7	465.5	467.2	474.7	472.6	462.9	455.4	457.4	467.0	470.4	472.3	465.4
1994	458.2	466.2	469.6	475.5	480.2	480.2	469.3	464.6	473.3	476.5	478.8	479.6	472.7
1995	477.2	487.3	488.6	489.3	492.4	493.4	466.7	455.7	491.2	491.4	493.7	493.9	485.1
1996	482.0	490.5	494.1	496.4	499.1	495.9	480.4	474.9	485.0	490.5	491.9	487.5	489.0
1997	481.1	489.7	492.4	491.3	497.5	497.6	482.5	480.1	489.7	492.6	495.6	495.2	490.4
1998	486.4	494.3	496.8	495.8	498.6	496.4	481.3	475.7	496.8	496.7	499.6	499.5	493.2
1999	488.2	496.9	500.2	500.6	501.3	499.2	484.1	479.2	492.2	497.6	499.3	495.0	494.5
2000	486.3	498.8	503.9	500.8	516.9	517.8	499.4	500.5	501.6	506.3	508.1	508.9	504.1
2001	494.9	507.9	509.8	507.4	514.8	516.0	507.0	501.8	503.9	513.6	515.3	517.0	509.1
2002	506.8	516.0	518.5	521.6	524.8	526.3	518.5	513.7	510.3	522.3	524.3	524.7	519.0
2003	513.6	523.2	524.3	523.5	524.9	525.4	515.7	507.6	508.2	521.5	521.5	521.1	519.2
Federal government													
1990	75.2	74.8	74.9	75.1	78.3	75.9	74.8	72.8	72.4	72.0	72.0	74.0	74.4
1991	72.2	72.0	71.7	71.9	72.1	72.4	72.1	72.1	73.1	72.1	72.3	74.0	72.3
1992	72.4	71.2	71.4	71.4	70.1	69.9	71.1	70.8	70.5	70.5	70.0	72.4	71.0
1993	69.9	69.5	69.5	69.2	69.2	69.4	69.7	69.7	69.5	69.4	70.4	74.1	70.0
1994	68.5	68.4	68.2	69.4	69.8	70.3	70.3	70.3	70.5	70.4	70.2	73.8	70.0
1995	70.3	70.1	70.1	69.8	69.8	70.4	69.3	69.2	69.1	69.2	69.5	72.3	69.9
1996	69.2	68.9	68.9	69.0	68.3	68.4	68.0	68.1	67.9	67.5	67.7	69.5	68.5
1997	68.1	68.0	67.7	67.7	67.5	67.5	67.3	67.5	67.4	67.0	67.3	70.0	67.8
1998	67.3	67.1	66.8	65.9	66.0	66.1	66.3	66.4	66.3	66.1	66.8	69.3	66.7
1999	66.3	66.2	66.4	66.3	66.4	66.4	65.3	64.1	64.3	64.1	64.4	66.6	65.6
2000	65.0	64.9	65.5	68.5	76.0	77.2	68.8	72.7	63.7	63.1	63.3	65.7	67.9
2001	62.7	62.6	62.5	62.1	62.0	62.0	62.3	62.7	62.3	61.3	61.1	62.7	62.2
2002	60.9	60.7	60.4	60.1	60.0	60.4	60.3	60.6	60.9	62.2	62.0	63.7	61.0
2003	62.1	62.0	60.8	61.6	61.3	61.3	61.1	59.7	59.3	61.0	61.1	62.8	61.2

Employment by Industry: Illinois—*Continued*

(Numbers in thousands. Not seasonally adjusted.)

Industry	January	February	March	April	May	June	July	August	September	October	November	December	Annual Average
CHICAGO—*Continued*													
State government													
1990	56.1	57.1	57.1	57.5	57.0	56.2	54.9	54.6	53.6	53.9	54.4	54.3	55.6
1991	54.9	55.8	55.6	55.7	55.4	55.2	54.5	54.7	54.8	55.6	55.6	55.6	55.3
1992	55.3	55.8	55.8	55.8	55.8	54.3	55.0	55.1	55.2	56.0	56.2	56.1	55.5
1993	54.6	54.9	55.0	54.7	56.3	55.5	57.2	58.1	59.4	58.5	58.7	58.6	56.8
1994	57.3	58.1	58.5	58.6	59.0	57.9	57.3	58.5	60.4	61.7	62.2	61.7	59.3
1995	59.3	61.9	61.4	61.3	60.6	57.2	60.6	60.4	60.6	61.1	61.4	60.9	60.6
1996	60.7	60.8	60.9	60.9	60.9	60.9	58.4	59.1	60.9	61.9	62.1	60.2	60.6
1997	60.3	62.0	62.0	60.7	62.4	61.6	60.1	61.7	62.6	60.5	62.4	62.0	61.5
1998	61.2	62.4	62.2	62.5	61.2	58.2	58.9	59.5	61.3	62.9	63.7	62.4	61.4
1999	61.4	62.0	62.5	62.3	60.9	57.6	54.5	55.4	57.5	58.5	58.9	57.1	59.1
2000	55.7	58.5	58.7	58.5	57.7	55.0	55.5	56.8	59.4	58.9	59.1	59.3	57.8
2001	58.0	60.0	60.3	60.5	59.7	57.3	57.7	58.5	56.5	60.2	60.5	59.7	59.1
2002	58.2	59.6	60.0	60.4	58.2	55.1	55.2	56.4	56.9	57.9	58.3	57.7	57.8
2003	55.5	56.4	56.6	55.6	53.0	50.4	50.3	50.8	54.6	56.3	56.1	55.3	54.2
Local government													
1990	316.3	322.3	327.5	324.7	330.1	329.9	312.9	303.8	321.6	329.4	333.2	332.0	323.6
1991	324.6	331.9	334.9	336.5	340.3	326.1	324.5	313.8	325.7	334.8	337.7	337.8	330.7
1992	329.2	335.4	337.4	337.8	343.4	345.0	329.1	317.9	331.8	338.9	342.6	340.7	335.8
1993	332.1	338.3	341.0	343.3	349.2	347.7	336.0	327.6	328.5	339.1	341.3	339.6	338.6
1994	332.4	339.7	342.9	347.5	351.4	352.0	341.7	335.8	342.4	344.4	346.4	344.1	343.4
1995	347.6	355.3	357.1	358.2	362.0	365.8	336.8	326.1	361.5	361.1	362.8	360.7	354.6
1996	352.1	360.8	364.3	366.5	369.9	366.6	354.0	347.7	356.2	361.1	362.1	357.8	359.9
1997	352.7	359.7	362.7	362.9	367.6	368.5	355.1	350.9	359.7	365.1	365.9	363.2	361.2
1998	357.9	364.8	367.8	367.4	371.4	372.1	356.1	349.8	369.2	367.7	369.1	367.8	365.1
1999	360.5	368.7	371.3	372.0	374.0	375.2	364.3	359.7	370.4	375.0	376.0	371.3	369.9
2000	365.6	375.4	379.7	373.8	383.2	385.6	375.1	371.0	378.5	384.3	385.7	383.9	378.5
2001	374.2	385.3	387.0	384.8	393.1	396.7	387.0	380.6	385.1	392.1	393.7	394.6	387.9
2002	387.7	395.7	398.1	401.1	406.6	410.8	403.0	396.7	392.5	402.2	404.0	403.3	400.1
2003	396.0	404.8	406.9	406.3	410.6	413.7	404.3	397.1	394.3	404.2	404.3	403.0	403.8
SPRINGFIELD													
Total nonfarm													
1990	103.7	103.3	104.5	105.7	107.5	110.0	108.9	115.2	109.7	109.2	109.4	110.1	108.1
1991	107.7	107.6	108.3	108.7	110.0	111.5	110.3	114.4	110.4	110.2	111.1	111.1	110.1
1992	106.2	106.0	106.7	107.0	107.8	108.6	108.3	117.0	108.7	108.9	108.8	109.1	108.5
1993	104.6	104.5	105.1	107.5	107.9	108.2	107.2	115.4	108.4	108.7	108.8	109.2	107.9
1994	105.8	106.1	107.3	108.7	110.2	110.5	110.0	114.5	111.0	110.6	111.4	111.2	109.7
1995	108.1	108.0	109.3	110.2	110.5	111.7	111.1	114.2	112.0	111.2	111.7	112.1	110.8
1996	109.9	109.3	110.1	111.3	111.7	112.8	111.1	118.1	111.6	112.3	112.2	112.8	111.9
1997	109.9	109.5	110.5	111.7	112.2	113.4	112.2	114.6	112.2	112.2	113.2	113.3	112.0
1998	111.0	111.8	112.2	113.4	114.3	115.6	114.0	119.3	113.8	114.2	114.6	115.1	114.1
1999	111.2	112.0	112.7	112.8	113.5	114.2	113.2	118.2	113.1	113.6	113.7	114.7	113.5
2000	111.6	111.8	113.3	115.2	116.3	117.0	115.6	121.8	115.0	114.8	115.2	115.5	115.2
2001	111.8	112.2	113.7	115.5	116.1	117.2	115.9	119.3	115.6	115.6	115.8	115.8	115.4
2002	112.6	112.6	113.4	114.5	115.3	115.8	115.0	117.7	114.2	113.2	113.3	113.7	114.3
2003	108.2	108.0	108.9	110.3	110.9	111.0	110.7	113.1	110.6	110.4	110.4	110.4	110.2
Total private													
1990	70.2	69.3	70.3	71.1	72.6	75.3	74.8	80.1	75.1	74.5	74.6	75.4	73.6
1991	73.2	73.1	74.0	74.2	75.2	76.9	76.6	79.8	76.3	75.7	76.6	76.7	75.6
1992	73.6	73.3	73.9	74.2	74.8	75.6	76.0	82.7	76.0	75.8	75.9	76.2	75.6
1993	72.1	71.9	72.4	74.4	74.7	75.3	75.3	80.0	75.6	75.5	75.6	76.0	74.9
1994	72.9	72.8	73.9	75.0	76.4	77.6	77.9	81.5	77.7	76.9	77.7	77.3	76.4
1995	74.8	74.3	75.4	76.2	76.5	78.2	78.5	80.6	78.6	77.7	78.1	78.4	77.2
1996	76.4	75.7	76.4	77.6	77.9	79.5	78.5	83.3	78.0	78.4	78.3	78.8	78.2
1997	76.2	75.7	76.7	77.9	78.4	79.7	79.3	79.6	78.8	78.6	79.3	79.4	78.3
1998	77.4	77.7	78.1	79.0	79.8	81.5	80.8	85.1	80.1	80.1	80.2	80.8	80.0
1999	77.8	78.2	78.8	78.9	79.9	81.1	81.5	85.6	81.1	81.0	81.0	82.1	80.5
2000	79.6	79.4	80.9	82.5	83.5	84.4	84.0	88.2	83.3	82.7	82.9	83.3	82.8
2001	80.2	79.8	81.1	82.6	83.1	84.0	83.8	86.6	83.2	82.5	82.5	82.6	82.7
2002	79.9	79.5	80.2	81.2	81.8	82.4	82.0	84.5	82.1	81.3	81.3	81.8	81.5
2003	78.8	78.1	78.9	80.2	80.7	80.7	80.9	83.0	81.0	80.4	80.4	80.5	80.3
Goods-producing													
1990	7.1	7.1	7.5	7.8	8.2	8.7	8.8	9.7	8.9	8.4	8.5	8.3	8.2
1991	7.3	7.3	7.7	8.7	8.9	9.3	9.3	9.5	8.9	8.8	8.6	8.3	8.5
1992	8.0	8.0	8.1	8.5	8.9	9.0	9.2	9.9	9.1	8.8	8.5	8.3	8.6
1993	7.6	7.6	7.6	8.2	8.5	8.5	8.6	9.4	9.2	9.1	8.9	8.8	8.5
1994	7.9	7.9	8.3	8.6	9.2	9.4	9.3	9.7	9.3	8.9	8.6	8.4	8.7
1995	7.8	7.8	8.1	8.7	8.9	9.3	9.5	9.7	9.6	9.2	9.0	8.8	8.8
1996	8.4	8.3	8.4	9.0	9.0	9.6	9.8	10.4	9.6	9.7	9.5	9.2	9.2
1997	8.3	8.4	8.5	9.1	9.1	9.4	9.6	9.5	9.4	9.3	9.0	8.8	9.0
1998	8.3	8.4	8.5	8.8	9.0	9.4	9.5	9.8	9.3	9.2	9.1	9.1	9.0
1999	9.1	9.4	9.5	9.7	9.8	10.0	10.0	10.4	9.9	9.9	9.7	9.8	9.7
2000	9.5	9.8	10.1	10.1	10.2	10.4	10.5	11.0	10.3	10.2	10.0	9.7	10.1
2001	8.7	8.8	9.3	9.7	10.1	10.4	10.5	10.6	10.4	9.9	9.6	9.3	9.8
2002	8.6	8.5	8.7	9.2	9.3	9.6	9.7	10.0	9.8	9.8	9.5	9.2	9.3
2003	8.3	8.1	8.5	9.0	8.9	8.9	8.9	8.8	9.0	9.0	8.8	8.5	8.7

Employment by Industry: Illinois—*Continued*

(Numbers in thousands. Not seasonally adjusted.)

Industry	January	February	March	April	May	June	July	August	September	October	November	December	Annual Average
SPRINGFIELD—*Continued*													
Construction and mining													
1990	2.9	2.9	3.2	3.5	3.9	4.4	4.4	5.0	4.5	4.2	4.3	4.0	3.9
1991	3.1	3.1	3.4	4.3	4.6	5.1	5.1	5.3	5.0	4.9	4.7	4.4	4.4
1992	4.0	4.0	4.1	4.4	4.8	5.0	5.0	5.4	4.9	4.7	4.4	4.2	4.5
1993	3.6	3.6	3.6	4.0	4.3	4.4	4.5	5.0	5.0	5.0	4.9	4.7	4.3
1994	3.9	3.9	4.2	4.4	4.9	5.2	5.1	5.3	5.1	4.7	4.3	4.2	4.6
1995	3.6	3.5	3.8	4.4	4.6	5.0	5.0	5.3	5.3	4.9	4.7	4.5	4.5
1996	4.1	4.0	4.2	4.7	4.8	5.3	5.5	5.8	5.3	5.3	5.1	4.8	4.9
1997	4.1	4.1	4.2	4.7	4.8	4.9	5.1	5.0	5.0	4.9	4.6	4.3	4.6
1998	3.8	3.9	4.0	4.5	4.7	5.0	5.1	5.2	5.0	4.9	4.8	4.8	4.6
1999	4.9	5.2	5.4	5.6	5.7	5.8	5.9	6.2	5.8	5.8	5.6	5.7	5.6
2000	5.5	5.8	6.0	5.9	6.1	6.2	6.3	6.7	6.2	6.1	5.9	5.6	6.0
2001	4.8	4.9	5.4	5.8	6.1	6.4	6.6	6.7	6.5	6.1	5.8	5.4	5.9
2002	4.8	4.7	4.8	5.3	5.4	5.7	5.8	6.1	6.0	6.0	5.8	5.5	5.5
2003	4.8	4.6	5.0	5.5	5.4	5.4	5.4	5.3	5.5	5.5	5.3	5.0	5.2
Manufacturing													
1990	4.2	4.2	4.3	4.3	4.3	4.3	4.4	4.7	4.4	4.2	4.2	4.3	4.3
1991	4.2	4.2	4.3	4.4	4.3	4.2	4.2	4.2	3.9	3.9	3.9	3.9	4.1
1992	4.0	4.0	4.0	4.1	4.1	4.0	4.2	4.5	4.2	4.1	4.1	4.1	4.1
1993	4.0	4.0	4.0	4.2	4.2	4.1	4.1	4.4	4.2	4.1	4.0	4.1	4.1
1994	4.0	4.0	4.1	4.2	4.3	4.2	4.2	4.4	4.2	4.2	4.3	4.2	4.1
1995	4.2	4.3	4.3	4.3	4.3	4.3	4.5	4.4	4.3	4.3	4.3	4.3	4.3
1996	4.3	4.3	4.2	4.3	4.2	4.3	4.3	4.6	4.3	4.4	4.4	4.4	4.3
1997	4.2	4.3	4.3	4.4	4.3	4.5	4.5	4.5	4.4	4.4	4.4	4.5	4.3
1998	4.5	4.5	4.5	4.3	4.3	4.4	4.4	4.6	4.3	4.3	4.3	4.3	4.3
1999	4.2	4.2	4.1	4.1	4.1	4.2	4.1	4.2	4.1	4.1	4.1	4.1	4.1
2000	4.0	4.0	4.1	4.2	4.1	4.2	4.2	4.3	4.1	4.1	4.1	4.1	4.1
2001	3.9	3.9	3.9	3.9	4.0	4.0	3.9	3.9	3.9	3.8	3.8	3.9	3.9
2002	3.8	3.8	3.9	3.9	3.9	3.9	3.9	3.9	3.8	3.8	3.7	3.7	3.8
2003	3.5	3.5	3.5	3.5	3.5	3.5	3.5	3.5	3.5	3.5	3.5	3.5	3.5
Service-providing													
1990	96.6	96.2	97.0	97.9	99.3	101.3	100.1	105.5	100.8	100.8	100.9	101.8	99.8
1991	100.4	100.3	100.6	100.0	101.1	102.2	101.0	104.9	101.5	101.4	102.5	102.8	101.5
1992	98.2	98.0	98.6	98.5	98.9	99.6	99.1	107.1	99.6	100.1	100.3	100.8	99.9
1993	97.0	96.9	97.5	99.3	99.4	99.7	98.6	106.0	99.2	99.6	99.9	100.4	99.4
1994	97.9	98.2	99.0	100.1	101.0	101.1	100.7	104.8	101.7	101.7	102.8	102.8	100.9
1995	100.3	100.2	101.2	101.5	101.6	102.4	101.6	104.5	102.4	102.0	102.7	103.3	101.9
1996	101.5	101.0	101.7	102.3	102.7	103.2	101.3	107.7	102.0	102.6	102.7	103.6	102.6
1997	101.6	101.1	102.0	102.6	103.1	104.0	102.6	105.1	102.8	102.9	104.2	104.5	103.0
1998	102.7	103.4	103.7	104.6	105.3	106.2	104.5	109.5	104.5	105.0	105.5	106.0	105.0
1999	102.1	102.6	103.2	103.1	103.7	104.2	103.2	107.8	103.2	103.7	104.0	104.9	103.8
2000	102.1	102.0	103.2	105.1	106.1	106.6	105.1	110.8	104.7	104.6	105.2	105.8	105.1
2001	103.1	103.4	104.4	105.8	106.0	106.8	105.4	108.7	105.2	105.7	106.2	106.5	105.6
2002	104.0	104.1	104.7	105.3	106.0	106.2	105.3	107.7	104.4	103.4	103.8	104.5	105.0
2003	99.9	99.9	100.4	101.3	102.0	102.1	101.8	104.3	101.6	101.4	101.6	101.9	101.5
Trade, transportation, and utilities													
1990	18.9	18.2	18.3	18.8	19.1	19.7	19.4	20.6	19.6	20.0	20.1	20.9	19.4
1991	20.2	20.0	20.2	20.2	20.6	20.7	20.5	21.7	20.8	20.7	21.5	21.6	20.7
1992	20.2	20.0	20.1	20.0	20.0	20.0	20.2	21.7	20.2	20.0	20.7	20.8	20.3
1993	19.6	19.4	19.5	19.8	19.8	19.7	19.9	20.9	19.9	20.1	20.5	20.8	19.9
1994	19.6	19.6	19.7	19.9	20.2	20.1	20.4	21.2	20.5	20.5	21.1	21.1	20.3
1995	20.1	19.7	19.7	19.9	19.8	20.0	20.1	20.6	20.3	20.1	20.5	20.8	20.1
1996	19.9	19.7	19.7	19.8	19.8	20.1	20.0	21.0	19.8	20.1	20.5	20.8	20.1
1997	19.7	19.4	19.3	18.9	18.8	18.9	18.8	18.5	18.7	18.5	19.0	19.3	18.9
1998	18.3	18.2	18.2	18.0	18.0	18.3	18.0	19.0	18.1	18.6	18.9	19.2	18.4
1999	18.0	17.8	17.8	18.1	18.2	18.4	18.3	19.1	18.4	18.5	19.0	19.3	18.4
2000	18.1	17.8	17.9	18.3	18.8	19.1	18.6	19.4	18.4	18.6	19.1	19.6	18.6
2001	18.5	17.8	17.8	17.8	17.8	17.8	17.5	18.1	17.7	18.0	18.6	18.7	18.0
2002	17.7	17.4	17.4	17.4	17.6	17.6	17.6	18.1	17.6	17.6	18.1	18.6	17.7
2003	17.4	17.1	17.1	17.5	17.6	17.7	17.8	18.3	17.8	17.8	18.1	18.5	17.7
Wholesale trade													
1990	3.4	3.4	3.4	3.5	3.5	3.8	3.7	4.0	3.8	3.9	3.9	3.9	3.6
1991	3.9	3.9	3.9	3.8	3.9	3.9	3.9	4.1	3.9	3.8	3.9	3.9	3.9
1992	4.0	3.9	4.0	3.9	3.9	3.9	3.9	4.3	3.9	3.9	3.8	3.8	3.9
1993	3.7	3.7	3.7	3.9	3.9	3.9	4.0	4.2	4.0	4.0	3.9	3.9	3.9
1994	3.7	3.7	3.8	3.9	4.0	4.0	4.2	4.3	4.2	4.2	4.2	4.2	4.0
1995	4.0	4.0	4.0	4.0	3.9	4.0	4.1	4.2	4.2	4.1	4.1	4.1	4.0
1996	3.9	3.9	3.9	4.0	4.0	4.1	4.1	4.4	4.2	4.2	4.2	4.2	4.0
1997	4.1	4.1	4.1	4.3	4.2	4.2	4.3	4.1	4.1	4.0	4.0	4.0	4.1
1998	3.9	3.9	3.9	4.0	3.9	4.0	3.8	4.0	3.8	4.0	3.9	3.9	3.9
1999	3.7	3.7	3.7	3.7	3.7	3.8	3.8	3.9	3.8	3.7	3.7	3.7	3.7
2000	3.7	3.7	3.7	3.6	3.6	3.7	3.6	3.8	3.6	3.6	3.5	3.6	3.6
2001	3.7	3.7	3.8	3.8	3.8	3.8	3.8	3.7	3.7	3.7	3.7	3.7	3.7
2002	3.6	3.6	3.6	3.6	3.6	3.7	3.7	3.7	3.7	3.7	3.7	3.7	3.7
2003	3.7	3.7	3.7	3.8	3.8	3.8	3.9	3.9	3.9	3.9	3.9	3.9	3.8

Employment by Industry: Illinois—*Continued*

(Numbers in thousands. Not seasonally adjusted.)

Industry	January	February	March	April	May	June	July	August	September	October	November	December	Annual Average
SPRINGFIELD—*Continued*													
Retail trade													
1990	12.6	11.9	12.0	12.3	12.5	12.8	12.7	13.4	12.6	12.9	13.0	13.8	12.7
1991	13.1	12.9	13.1	12.9	13.2	13.4	13.2	13.9	13.3	13.3	14.0	14.1	13.3
1992	12.6	12.5	12.5	12.5	12.5	12.6	12.7	13.6	12.6	12.4	13.2	13.3	12.7
1993	12.4	12.2	12.3	12.4	12.4	12.4	12.5	13.0	12.3	12.4	12.9	13.1	12.5
1994	12.2	12.1	12.1	12.2	12.3	12.4	12.4	13.0	12.4	12.3	12.9	13.0	12.4
1995	12.3	12.0	12.0	12.2	12.3	12.5	12.5	12.8	12.6	12.5	12.9	13.2	12.4
1996	12.5	12.4	12.4	12.5	12.6	12.8	12.7	13.2	12.5	12.7	13.2	13.5	12.7
1997	12.5	12.2	12.1	11.6	11.6	11.7	11.7	11.7	11.8	11.9	12.4	12.7	11.9
1998	11.8	11.6	11.6	11.4	11.5	11.8	11.8	12.4	11.7	11.9	12.4	12.7	11.8
1999	11.8	11.5	11.5	11.8	11.9	12.0	12.0	12.5	11.9	12.1	12.6	12.9	12.0
2000	11.8	11.6	11.6	12.1	12.6	12.9	12.5	12.9	12.2	12.4	13.0	13.4	12.4
2001	12.5	11.9	11.7	11.7	11.7	11.8	11.6	12.2	11.8	12.0	12.6	12.8	12.0
2002	12.0	11.7	11.7	11.7	11.9	11.9	11.9	12.4	11.8	11.8	12.3	12.7	12.0
2003	11.7	11.4	11.4	11.6	11.7	11.8	11.9	12.4	11.8	11.8	12.1	12.5	11.8
Transportation and utilities													
1990	2.9	2.9	2.9	3.0	3.1	3.1	3.0	3.2	3.2	3.2	3.2	3.2	3.0
1991	3.2	3.2	3.2	3.5	3.5	3.4	3.4	3.7	3.6	3.6	3.6	3.6	3.4
1992	3.6	3.6	3.6	3.6	3.6	3.5	3.6	3.8	3.7	3.7	3.7	3.7	3.6
1993	3.5	3.5	3.5	3.5	3.5	3.4	3.4	3.7	3.6	3.7	3.7	3.8	3.5
1994	3.7	3.8	3.8	3.8	3.9	3.7	3.8	3.9	3.9	4.0	4.0	3.9	3.8
1995	3.8	3.7	3.7	3.7	3.6	3.5	3.5	3.6	3.5	3.5	3.5	3.5	3.5
1996	3.5	3.4	3.4	3.3	3.2	3.2	3.2	3.4	3.1	3.2	3.1	3.1	3.2
1997	3.1	3.1	3.1	3.0	3.0	3.0	2.8	2.7	2.8	2.6	2.6	2.6	2.8
1998	2.6	2.7	2.7	2.6	2.6	2.5	2.4	2.6	2.6	2.7	2.6	2.6	2.6
1999	2.5	2.6	2.6	2.6	2.6	2.6	2.5	2.7	2.7	2.7	2.7	2.7	2.6
2000	2.6	2.5	2.6	2.6	2.6	2.5	2.5	2.7	2.6	2.6	2.6	2.6	2.5
2001	2.3	2.2	2.3	2.3	2.3	2.2	2.1	2.2	2.2	2.3	2.3	2.2	2.2
2002	2.1	2.1	2.1	2.1	2.1	2.0	2.0	2.0	2.1	2.1	2.1	2.2	2.1
2003	2.0	2.0	2.0	2.1	2.1	2.1	2.0	2.0	2.1	2.1	2.1	2.1	2.1
Information													
1990	2.6	2.6	2.5	2.5	2.6	2.7	2.6	2.8	2.6	2.6	2.5	2.6	2.6
1991	2.5	2.5	2.5	2.4	2.4	2.5	2.5	2.5	2.4	2.4	2.5	2.4	2.4
1992	2.4	2.4	2.4	2.4	2.4	2.3	2.4	2.6	2.4	2.4	2.4	2.4	2.4
1993	2.2	2.2	2.2	2.3	2.3	2.3	2.3	2.4	2.3	2.4	2.4	2.4	2.3
1994	2.4	2.4	2.4	2.5	2.5	2.5	2.5	2.5	2.5	2.5	2.5	2.4	2.4
1995	2.5	2.4	2.4	2.4	2.4	2.5	2.5	2.5	2.4	2.4	2.5	2.5	2.4
1996	2.5	2.5	2.5	2.6	2.6	2.6	2.7	2.9	2.7	2.7	2.7	2.7	2.6
1997	2.7	2.7	2.7	2.7	2.6	2.7	2.6	2.6	2.6	2.8	2.8	2.7	2.6
1998	2.7	2.7	2.6	2.8	2.9	2.9	2.9	3.0	2.9	2.9	2.9	2.9	2.8
1999	2.8	2.8	2.8	2.7	2.8	2.8	2.8	2.9	2.7	2.7	2.7	2.8	2.7
2000	2.7	2.7	2.8	2.8	2.8	2.9	2.9	3.0	2.9	3.0	3.0	3.0	2.8
2001	3.0	3.0	3.0	3.1	3.2	3.4	3.5	3.8	3.3	3.3	3.3	3.3	3.3
2002	3.3	3.3	3.3	3.3	3.4	3.4	3.4	3.8	3.3	3.3	3.3	3.3	3.4
2003	3.2	3.2	3.2	3.2	3.2	3.2	3.2	3.6	3.2	3.2	3.2	3.2	3.2
Financial activities													
1990	7.8	7.8	7.9	7.5	7.6	7.9	7.8	8.3	8.0	7.7	7.7	7.7	7.8
1991	8.0	7.9	8.0	7.9	7.9	8.0	8.0	8.2	8.0	8.0	8.1	8.2	8.0
1992	8.2	8.1	8.2	8.1	8.1	8.2	8.3	8.9	8.3	8.2	8.1	8.2	8.2
1993	7.9	7.9	8.0	8.0	8.0	8.1	8.1	8.5	8.1	8.3	8.3	8.3	8.1
1994	8.3	8.3	8.3	8.3	8.4	8.5	8.5	8.8	8.3	8.4	8.4	8.4	8.4
1995	8.3	8.2	8.3	8.2	8.1	8.2	7.9	8.0	7.8	8.0	8.0	8.0	8.0
1996	8.0	7.9	7.9	7.9	7.9	8.1	7.9	8.3	7.8	7.8	7.8	7.9	7.9
1997	7.7	7.6	7.8	7.8	7.8	7.9	7.8	7.8	7.8	7.8	7.8	7.9	7.7
1998	7.9	7.9	7.9	8.1	8.1	8.3	8.2	8.6	8.1	8.2	8.2	8.2	8.1
1999	8.1	8.1	8.1	8.1	8.1	8.2	8.0	8.3	7.9	7.8	7.8	7.9	8.0
2000	7.6	7.5	7.6	7.7	7.8	7.8	7.9	8.1	7.8	7.7	7.8	7.8	7.7
2001	7.8	7.7	7.7	7.6	7.6	7.7	7.7	7.7	7.6	7.7	7.7	7.8	7.7
2002	7.8	7.7	7.7	7.7	7.7	7.7	7.6	7.5	7.4	7.4	7.3	7.4	7.6
2003	7.5	7.4	7.4	7.4	7.5	7.5	7.6	7.5	7.5	7.5	7.5	7.5	7.5
Professional and business services													
1990	6.4	6.4	6.6	6.9	7.1	7.3	7.3	7.7	7.3	7.3	7.3	7.3	7.0
1991	7.3	7.3	7.3	7.3	7.4	7.6	7.4	7.7	7.6	7.5	7.5	7.6	7.4
1992	7.2	7.3	7.4	6.5	6.5	6.7	6.8	7.3	6.8	6.6	6.6	6.7	6.8
1993	6.6	6.5	6.6	6.6	6.5	6.6	6.3	6.6	6.4	6.5	6.6	6.7	6.5
1994	6.7	6.7	6.9	6.9	7.0	7.3	7.2	7.6	7.3	7.0	7.1	7.1	7.0
1995	7.2	7.2	7.3	7.4	7.4	7.7	7.5	7.7	7.5	7.6	7.7	7.7	7.4
1996	7.7	7.5	7.6	7.9	7.9	7.9	7.8	8.3	7.9	7.9	7.9	8.1	7.8
1997	8.4	8.3	8.4	8.8	8.9	9.1	9.0	9.1	9.1	9.4	9.5	9.5	8.9
1998	9.3	9.3	9.4	9.7	9.8	9.9	9.5	10.0	9.3	9.0	9.0	9.2	9.4
1999	9.0	9.1	9.1	9.0	9.0	9.1	9.5	10.0	9.6	9.4	9.3	9.5	9.3
2000	9.6	9.6	9.8	10.1	9.9	9.8	9.6	10.0	9.7	9.6	9.5	9.6	9.7
2001	9.6	9.9	10.2	10.7	10.6	10.4	10.4	10.6	10.4	10.2	10.4	10.4	10.3
2002	10.1	10.1	10.2	10.6	10.4	10.2	10.2	10.4	10.5	10.5	10.6	10.5	10.4
2003	10.4	10.4	10.7	10.8	10.8	10.8	10.7	10.6	10.6	10.6	10.6	10.6	10.6

Employment by Industry: Illinois—*Continued*

(Numbers in thousands. Not seasonally adjusted.)

Industry	January	February	March	April	May	June	July	August	September	October	November	December	Annual Average
SPRINGFIELD—*Continued*													
Educational and health services													
1990	13.4	13.3	13.4	13.2	13.4	13.9	13.7	14.5	13.8	13.8	13.8	13.9	13.6
1991	14.4	14.5	14.6	14.3	14.3	14.7	14.6	15.0	14.6	14.8	14.8	14.9	14.6
1992	14.9	14.8	14.9	14.9	14.8	14.9	15.4	16.7	15.6	15.4	15.4	15.4	15.2
1993	14.7	14.7	14.8	14.8	14.8	14.9	14.9	15.6	14.9	14.7	14.6	14.8	14.8
1994	14.1	14.0	14.1	14.2	14.3	14.4	14.5	15.0	14.4	14.6	14.8	14.7	14.4
1995	14.6	14.8	14.9	14.7	14.8	15.0	14.9	15.2	15.1	15.2	15.4	15.5	15.0
1996	15.3	15.1	15.2	15.1	15.1	15.2	14.8	15.5	14.9	15.1	15.1	15.3	15.1
1997	15.0	15.0	15.1	15.3	15.4	15.5	15.5	15.6	15.5	15.6	15.8	15.8	15.4
1998	16.0	16.1	16.2	15.7	15.7	15.9	16.1	16.6	16.0	16.4	16.3	16.4	16.1
1999	15.6	15.7	15.7	15.8	16.0	16.1	16.3	17.1	16.4	16.7	16.7	16.8	16.2
2000	16.7	16.6	16.8	17.2	17.3	17.3	17.4	18.1	17.3	17.2	17.1	17.2	17.1
2001	16.7	16.7	16.8	16.7	16.7	16.7	16.7	16.7	16.7	16.8	16.7	16.8	16.7
2002	16.6	16.6	16.7	16.7	16.7	16.7	16.5	16.5	16.7	16.6	16.6	16.7	16.6
2003	16.2	16.2	16.1	16.0	16.0	15.7	15.8	15.9	16.0	16.0	16.0	16.0	16.0
Leisure and hospitality													
1990	8.9	8.8	9.0	9.2	9.3	9.5	9.6	10.6	9.4	9.2	9.2	9.2	9.3
1991	8.2	8.1	8.2	8.0	8.3	8.6	8.7	9.5	8.5	8.0	8.1	8.1	8.3
1992	7.2	7.2	7.3	8.3	8.7	9.0	8.2	9.7	8.2	8.9	8.7	9.0	8.3
1993	8.3	8.4	8.5	9.2	9.3	9.7	9.6	10.8	9.3	8.9	8.8	8.8	9.1
1994	8.6	8.5	8.7	9.1	9.4	9.9	9.9	10.8	9.7	9.3	9.5	9.5	9.4
1995	8.7	8.7	9.1	9.3	9.5	9.9	10.4	11.2	10.2	9.4	9.3	9.3	9.5
1996	8.8	8.9	9.2	9.5	9.8	10.2	9.8	11.0	9.6	9.4	9.2	9.3	9.5
1997	8.8	8.7	9.2	9.7	10.1	10.5	10.3	10.8	10.0	9.6	9.8	9.8	9.7
1998	9.3	9.5	9.7	10.3	10.7	11.0	11.0	12.2	10.8	10.1	10.1	10.0	10.3
1999	9.6	9.6	10.0	9.9	10.3	10.7	10.9	11.9	10.5	10.2	10.0	10.1	10.3
2000	9.7	9.7	10.2	10.4	10.8	11.1	11.2	12.3	10.8	10.5	10.4	10.4	10.6
2001	9.8	9.8	10.1	10.7	10.8	11.2	11.1	12.8	10.8	10.3	10.0	10.0	10.6
2002	9.6	9.7	9.9	10.0	10.3	10.7	10.6	11.9	10.6	10.0	9.8	9.9	10.3
2003	9.7	9.6	9.7	10.1	10.5	10.6	10.6	11.9	10.5	10.0	9.9	9.9	10.3
Other services													
1990	5.1	5.1	5.1	5.2	5.3	5.6	5.6	5.9	5.5	5.5	5.5	5.5	5.4
1991	5.3	5.5	5.5	5.4	5.4	5.5	5.6	5.7	5.5	5.5	5.5	5.6	5.5
1992	5.5	5.5	5.5	5.5	5.4	5.5	5.5	5.9	5.4	5.5	5.5	5.4	5.5
1993	5.2	5.2	5.2	5.5	5.5	5.5	5.6	5.8	5.5	5.5	5.5	5.4	5.4
1994	5.3	5.4	5.5	5.5	5.4	5.5	5.6	5.9	5.7	5.7	5.7	5.7	5.5
1995	5.6	5.5	5.6	5.6	5.6	5.6	5.7	5.7	5.7	5.8	5.7	5.8	5.6
1996	5.8	5.8	5.9	5.8	5.8	5.8	5.7	5.9	5.7	5.7	5.6	5.5	5.7
1997	5.6	5.6	5.7	5.6	5.7	5.7	5.7	5.7	5.7	5.6	5.6	5.6	5.6
1998	5.6	5.6	5.6	5.6	5.6	5.8	5.6	5.9	5.6	5.7	5.7	5.8	5.6
1999	5.6	5.7	5.8	5.6	5.7	5.8	5.7	5.9	5.7	5.8	5.8	5.9	5.7
2000	5.7	5.7	5.7	5.9	5.9	6.0	5.9	6.3	6.1	5.9	6.0	6.0	5.9
2001	6.1	6.1	6.2	6.3	6.3	6.4	6.4	6.3	6.3	6.3	6.2	6.3	6.3
2002	6.2	6.2	6.3	6.3	6.4	6.5	6.4	6.3	6.2	6.1	6.1	6.2	6.3
2003	6.1	6.1	6.2	6.2	6.2	6.3	6.3	6.4	6.4	6.3	6.3	6.3	6.3
Government													
1990	33.5	34.0	34.2	34.6	34.9	34.7	34.1	35.1	34.6	34.7	34.8	34.7	34.4
1991	34.5	34.5	34.3	34.5	34.8	34.6	33.7	34.6	34.1	34.5	34.5	34.4	34.4
1992	32.6	32.7	32.8	32.8	33.0	33.0	32.3	34.3	32.7	33.1	32.9	32.9	32.9
1993	32.5	32.6	32.7	33.1	33.2	32.9	31.9	35.4	32.8	33.2	33.2	33.2	33.0
1994	32.9	33.3	33.4	33.7	33.8	32.9	32.1	33.0	33.3	33.7	33.7	33.9	33.3
1995	33.3	33.7	33.9	34.0	34.0	33.5	32.6	33.6	33.4	33.5	33.6	33.7	33.5
1996	33.5	33.6	33.7	33.7	33.8	33.3	32.6	34.8	33.6	33.9	33.9	34.0	33.7
1997	33.7	33.8	33.8	33.8	33.8	33.7	32.9	35.0	33.4	33.6	33.9	33.9	33.7
1998	33.6	34.1	34.1	34.4	34.5	34.1	33.2	34.2	33.7	34.1	34.4	34.3	34.0
1999	33.4	33.8	33.9	33.9	33.6	33.1	31.7	32.6	32.0	32.6	32.7	32.6	32.9
2000	32.0	32.4	32.4	32.7	32.8	32.6	31.6	33.6	31.7	32.1	32.3	32.2	32.3
2001	31.6	32.4	32.6	32.9	33.0	33.2	32.1	32.7	32.4	33.1	33.3	33.2	32.7
2002	32.7	33.1	33.2	33.3	33.5	33.4	33.0	33.2	32.1	31.9	32.0	31.9	32.8
2003	29.4	29.9	30.0	30.1	30.2	30.3	29.8	30.1	29.6	30.0	30.0	29.9	29.9
Federal government													
2001	2.3	2.2	2.2	2.2	2.2	2.2	2.2	2.2	2.2	2.2	2.2	2.2	2.2
2002	2.2	2.2	2.2	2.2	2.2	2.2	2.2	2.2	2.2	2.2	2.2	2.2	2.2
2003	2.2	2.2	2.2	2.2	2.2	2.2	2.2	2.2	2.1	2.2	2.2	2.2	2.2

Employment by Industry: Illinois—*Continued*

(Numbers in thousands. Not seasonally adjusted.)

Industry	January	February	March	April	May	June	July	August	September	October	November	December	Annual Average
SPRINGFIELD—*Continued*													
State government													
1990	22.9	22.9	22.9	23.0	23.0	23.3	23.6	24.7	23.6	23.4	23.4	23.4	23.3
1991	23.3	23.3	23.3	23.2	23.2	23.3	23.5	24.6	23.0	23.0	23.0	23.0	23.3
1992	21.5	21.4	21.4	21.4	21.4	21.5	21.7	23.9	21.7	21.8	21.6	21.6	21.7
1993	21.5	21.3	21.3	21.6	21.6	21.6	21.4	24.9	21.6	21.7	21.6	21.6	21.8
1994	21.4	21.6	21.6	21.7	21.8	21.6	21.6	22.8	21.7	21.7	21.7	21.7	21.7
1995	21.6	21.6	21.6	21.7	21.8	21.6	21.6	22.6	21.6	21.6	21.6	21.6	21.7
1996	21.6	21.7	21.6	21.6	21.6	21.6	21.6	23.8	21.6	21.6	21.6	21.6	21.7
1997	21.6	21.6	21.6	21.6	21.6	21.6	21.6	23.8	21.6	21.6	21.6	21.6	21.7
1998	21.6	21.6	21.6	21.8	21.8	21.6	21.6	22.7	21.6	21.6	21.6	21.6	21.7
1999	21.6	21.6	21.6	21.3	20.9	20.6	20.1	21.2	20.1	20.1	20.1	19.8	20.7
2000	19.7	19.7	19.7	19.7	19.7	19.7	19.6	21.8	19.2	19.2	19.3	19.1	19.7
2001	19.1	19.6	19.7	19.8	19.8	20.2	20.1	20.7	19.9	20.2	20.2	20.2	20.0
2002	20.0	20.1	20.1	20.3	20.4	20.3	20.8	21.1	19.6	19.1	19.2	19.1	20.0
2003	17.0	17.1	17.1	17.2	17.3	17.4	17.5	18.0	17.4	17.3	17.3	17.2	17.3
Local government													
1990	8.4	8.9	9.1	9.1	9.3	9.0	8.1	8.0	8.8	9.0	9.1	9.0	8.8
1991	8.9	8.9	8.7	9.0	9.3	9.0	7.9	7.7	8.7	9.2	9.1	9.0	8.7
1992	8.8	9.0	9.1	9.1	9.3	9.3	8.3	8.1	8.7	9.0	9.0	9.0	8.8
1993	8.7	9.0	9.1	9.2	9.4	9.0	8.2	8.2	8.9	9.2	9.3	9.3	8.9
1994	9.2	9.4	9.5	9.7	9.7	9.0	8.2	7.9	9.3	9.7	9.7	9.8	9.2
1995	9.4	9.8	10.0	10.0	10.0	9.7	8.8	8.8	9.6	9.7	9.8	9.8	9.6
1996	9.7	9.7	9.9	9.9	10.0	9.5	8.8	8.8	9.8	10.1	10.1	10.2	9.7
1997	9.9	10.0	10.0	10.0	10.1	9.9	9.2	9.1	9.7	9.9	10.1	10.1	9.8
1998	9.8	10.3	10.3	10.4	10.5	10.3	9.4	9.3	9.9	10.3	10.5	10.4	10.1
1999	9.6	10.0	10.1	10.4	10.5	10.3	9.4	9.2	9.7	10.3	10.4	10.5	10.0
2000	10.0	10.4	10.4	10.5	10.6	10.6	9.6	9.5	10.2	10.6	10.7	10.8	10.3
2001	10.2	10.6	10.7	10.9	11.0	10.8	9.8	9.8	10.3	10.7	10.9	10.8	10.5
2002	10.5	10.8	10.9	10.8	10.9	10.9	10.0	9.9	10.3	10.6	10.6	10.6	10.6
2003	10.2	10.6	10.7	10.7	10.7	10.7	10.1	9.9	10.1	10.5	10.5	10.5	10.4

Average Weekly Hours by Industry: Illinois

(Not seasonally adjusted.)

Industry	January	February	March	April	May	June	July	August	September	October	November	December	Annual Average
STATEWIDE													
Natural resources and mining													
2001	41.1	41.4	44.7	43.3	44.8	44.5	46.7	47.2	46.2	41.9	41.7	41.5	43.9
2002	38.7	38.2	40.6	39.2	38.7	39.6	39.4	40.6	40.6	41.9	41.4	41.0	40.0
2003	38.9	37.8	38.8	39.7	40.4	38.8	39.0	40.4	41.9	42.1	41.6	41.8	40.1
Construction													
2001	37.2	37.0	35.7	36.6	37.8	38.4	39.1	37.7	38.3	36.6	38.0	37.4	37.5
2002	36.3	36.4	36.8	35.9	36.3	36.8	38.1	37.5	38.9	38.9	38.2	37.9	37.4
2003	36.7	35.2	36.1	36.4	37.2	37.2	37.3	38.2	38.6	37.3	37.8	35.4	37.0
Manufacturing													
2001	41.2	40.9	40.7	39.3	41.0	41.2	40.8	41.2	41.7	41.0	41.2	41.7	41.0
2002	40.5	40.8	41.1	41.1	41.3	41.7	41.1	41.6	41.8	41.7	42.0	42.1	41.4
2003	40.6	40.5	40.4	40.1	40.5	40.6	39.6	40.6	41.0	40.7	41.1	41.6	40.6
Trade, transportation, and utilities													
2001	31.6	31.5	31.7	31.9	32.2	32.1	32.5	33.0	33.1	32.5	32.8	33.3	32.3
2002	32.0	32.4	32.8	32.8	33.4	33.7	33.3	32.9	33.2	32.8	32.2	33.1	32.9
2003	31.4	31.9	32.0	31.8	32.4	32.5	32.4	32.1	32.3	32.1	32.2	32.4	32.1
Wholesale trade													
2001	38.5	38.4	38.5	38.9	38.7	38.4	38.4	39.0	38.7	38.3	38.8	38.8	38.6
2002	38.2	38.3	38.6	38.6	39.4	39.8	39.1	39.1	39.7	39.6	39.0	39.5	39.1
2003	38.2	39.6	39.0	38.7	39.3	39.4	39.2	38.8	39.6	39.5	40.0	39.0	39.2
Retail trade													
2001	28.3	28.1	28.2	28.6	28.8	29.1	29.7	30.5	30.4	29.6	29.8	30.6	29.3
2002	29.0	29.7	30.0	30.2	30.4	31.2	31.3	30.6	30.4	29.9	29.6	30.7	30.3
2003	28.7	29.1	29.3	29.4	29.8	30.3	30.3	30.2	29.8	29.6	29.6	30.3	29.7
Transportation and utilities													
2001	31.7	31.8	32.4	31.8	32.7	32.2	32.4	31.5	32.6	32.3	33.0	33.3	32.3
2002	31.7	31.7	32.3	32.1	33.2	32.4	31.4	31.1	32.3	31.9	31.1	32.1	31.9
2003	30.0	29.5	30.1	29.3	30.7	29.9	29.5	28.8	30.0	29.8	29.9	30.3	29.8
Information													
2001	39.5	40.1	39.4	39.3	38.9	39.2	39.4	39.6	39.5	39.6	39.7	39.9	39.5
2002	39.7	40.1	39.7	39.6	39.4	39.1	39.2	38.6	37.6	37.8	37.6	37.1	38.8
2003	36.6	35.8	35.6	36.5	36.0	36.5	36.1	36.0	35.5	35.5	37.6	36.3	36.2
Financial activities													
2001	34.4	34.9	34.9	35.8	35.3	35.8	35.7	35.0	35.6	35.0	34.9	36.1	35.3
2002	34.6	35.0	35.1	35.0	35.3	36.0	35.1	35.4	35.9	35.8	35.3	36.2	35.4
2003	36.1	36.9	36.9	36.0	36.0	37.1	36.1	36.0	35.7	35.8	36.9	36.0	36.3
Professional and business services													
2001	34.0	34.4	34.6	35.3	34.9	34.6	34.4	34.4	34.9	34.7	34.9	35.0	34.7
2002	34.5	35.4	35.4	35.3	35.5	36.0	35.0	35.5	35.7	35.5	35.1	34.5	35.3
2003	33.8	34.5	34.6	34.3	34.7	35.0	34.0	34.4	33.9	34.3	34.4	33.4	34.3
Educational and health services													
2001	33.1	32.9	33.0	33.2	33.4	33.2	33.5	33.2	33.7	33.1	33.3	33.9	33.3
2002	33.5	33.4	33.6	33.5	33.6	34.2	33.3	33.1	34.0	33.1	33.2	33.4	33.5
2003	32.8	33.3	33.2	32.8	32.7	33.0	32.7	32.4	32.3	32.0	32.8	32.2	32.7
Leisure and hospitality													
2001	24.8	25.2	24.9	25.1	25.6	26.1	26.2	25.6	26.5	25.1	25.2	26.4	25.6
2002	25.0	25.4	25.5	25.6	25.9	26.8	26.1	26.0	25.7	25.6	25.4	25.5	25.7
2003	24.0	24.3	24.8	24.3	24.8	25.9	25.3	25.4	24.8	24.8	25.3	25.2	24.9
Other services													
2001	31.7	31.5	32.0	31.8	31.7	31.6	31.9	31.9	32.1	31.7	31.7	32.3	31.8
2002	31.4	31.1	31.3	31.4	32.1	32.9	31.5	31.6	32.2	31.4	31.2	32.0	31.7
2003	31.0	31.5	30.8	29.8	30.3	30.7	30.4	30.4	30.0	30.1	30.7	29.7	30.4
CHAMPAIGN-URBANA-RANTOUL													
Manufacturing													
2001	37.4	38.0	38.0	38.8	39.3	39.7	40.8	40.1	40.7	39.7	41.5	39.4	39.5
2002	39.2	39.8	41.4	40.4	40.9	40.4	40.0	41.3	41.8	40.9	40.5	39.9	40.5
2003	39.4	39.3	39.5	39.7	39.6	39.8	40.0	40.2	40.1	40.2	40.6	40.8	39.9
CHICAGO													
Manufacturing													
2001	41.8	41.7	41.5	39.7	41.7	41.8	41.7	42.0	42.2	41.8	42.1	42.8	41.7
2002	41.6	41.9	42.2	42.0	42.3	42.8	41.9	42.4	42.5	42.4	42.7	42.8	42.3
2003	41.1	41.2	40.9	40.4	40.6	40.8	39.9	40.2	40.7	40.8	41.0	41.3	40.7

Average Hourly Earnings by Industry: Illinois

(Dollars, not seasonally adjusted.)

Industry	January	February	March	April	May	June	July	August	September	October	November	December	Annual Average
STATEWIDE													
Natural resources and mining													
2001	18.02	18.34	18.45	18.84	18.52	18.80	18.83	18.91	18.43	19.34	18.75	18.27	18.64
2002	17.98	18.12	18.14	18.27	18.75	18.91	18.83	19.09	18.97	19.10	19.12	19.15	18.72
2003	19.04	19.11	18.96	19.20	19.40	19.60	19.85	19.90	19.95	20.07	20.07	20.01	19.62
Construction													
2001	25.00	25.43	24.88	24.72	25.15	25.09	25.16	25.31	25.53	25.50	25.58	25.86	25.28
2002	25.61	26.09	25.86	26.08	25.85	26.06	26.21	26.43	26.54	26.49	26.33	26.24	26.17
2003	25.82	25.94	26.20	26.08	26.15	26.39	26.60	26.70	26.97	26.94	26.90	26.83	26.49
Manufacturing													
2001	14.39	14.37	14.36	14.52	14.56	14.69	14.79	14.75	14.90	14.81	14.86	14.94	14.66
2002	14.91	14.77	14.81	14.84	14.90	14.98	15.04	14.99	15.18	15.11	15.13	15.17	14.99
2003	15.18	15.07	15.07	15.10	15.16	15.21	15.12	15.20	15.35	15.21	15.34	15.41	15.20
Trade, transportation, and utilities													
2001	13.51	13.68	13.66	13.69	13.55	13.47	13.52	13.68	13.76	13.89	13.82	13.76	13.66
2002	13.90	13.91	13.98	14.01	14.00	13.93	13.79	13.93	13.79	13.86	13.78	13.75	13.88
2003	13.83	13.90	13.82	13.78	13.69	13.69	13.66	13.70	13.72	13.71	13.65	13.51	13.72
Wholesale trade													
2001	15.80	15.81	15.82	15.92	15.81	15.58	15.79	15.75	15.79	16.08	16.02	16.07	15.85
2002	16.12	16.11	16.18	16.13	16.21	16.14	15.87	15.94	15.78	15.85	15.72	15.88	15.99
2003	15.73	15.74	15.59	15.50	15.48	15.53	15.40	15.52	15.60	15.69	15.66	15.64	15.59
Retail trade													
2001	10.73	10.97	11.07	10.99	10.88	10.86	10.84	10.95	11.10	11.10	11.17	11.06	10.97
2002	11.13	11.18	11.20	11.27	11.17	11.16	11.11	11.31	11.19	11.28	11.28	11.29	11.22
2003	11.35	11.35	11.28	11.26	11.20	11.21	11.16	11.21	11.18	11.08	11.13	10.98	11.19
Transportation and utilities													
2001	16.32	16.38	16.06	16.25	16.03	16.22	16.28	16.37	16.25	16.41	16.25	16.44	16.27
2002	16.48	16.40	16.61	16.65	16.64	16.69	16.80	16.89	16.58	16.62	16.74	16.64	16.64
2003	16.76	16.85	16.91	17.06	16.81	17.06	17.30	17.31	17.07	17.12	16.96	17.02	17.02
Information													
2001	18.26	18.20	18.45	18.57	18.65	18.70	18.72	18.83	19.04	19.19	19.01	19.07	18.72
2002	19.22	19.25	19.12	19.25	19.27	19.20	19.20	18.76	18.93	18.57	19.04	18.66	19.05
2003	18.71	18.94	19.10	19.09	19.30	19.30	19.30	19.16	19.42	19.45	19.48	19.50	19.23
Financial activities													
2001	15.82	15.95	15.95	15.99	15.95	15.87	15.97	15.98	16.09	16.14	16.22	16.26	16.02
2002	16.23	16.44	16.40	16.38	16.46	16.48	16.64	16.68	16.83	16.91	16.92	16.98	16.62
2003	17.11	17.34	17.28	17.17	16.99	17.14	17.26	17.33	17.34	17.36	17.31	17.35	17.25
Professional and business services													
2001	16.72	17.09	17.13	17.35	17.13	16.91	17.23	16.78	17.24	17.16	17.11	17.60	17.12
2002	17.40	17.78	17.72	17.68	17.44	17.52	17.39	17.40	17.33	17.29	17.49	17.71	17.51
2003	17.83	17.96	18.02	17.89	17.64	17.59	17.50	17.41	17.47	17.42	17.52	17.44	17.64
Educational and health services													
2001	13.93	13.94	13.92	14.05	13.94	14.00	14.17	14.18	14.34	14.34	14.36	14.33	14.13
2002	14.38	14.39	14.44	14.43	14.46	14.50	14.62	14.65	14.79	14.81	14.86	14.92	14.60
2003	14.86	14.94	14.93	14.96	14.99	15.03	15.11	15.14	15.17	15.22	15.24	15.27	15.07
Leisure and hospitality													
2001	8.29	8.39	8.39	8.32	8.49	8.51	8.54	8.51	8.47	8.58	8.49	8.61	8.47
2002	8.52	8.51	8.57	8.63	8.63	8.74	8.79	8.76	8.65	8.65	8.53	8.51	8.63
2003	8.49	8.43	8.44	8.44	8.54	8.49	8.51	8.51	8.60	8.58	8.58	8.62	8.52
Other services													
2001	13.31	13.41	13.40	13.42	13.52	13.43	13.63	13.67	13.66	13.72	13.55	13.65	13.53
2002	13.65	13.49	13.52	13.40	13.51	13.59	13.61	13.75	13.88	13.85	14.02	13.92	13.69
2003	13.88	13.97	14.17	14.13	14.12	14.22	14.12	14.14	14.11	14.09	14.17	14.17	14.11
CHAMPAIGN-URBANA-RANTOUL													
Manufacturing													
2001	13.19	13.13	13.30	13.26	13.36	13.35	13.31	13.35	13.59	13.45	13.58	13.56	13.37
2002	13.71	13.81	13.43	13.65	13.55	13.57	13.60	13.54	13.51	13.67	13.76	13.75	13.63
2003	13.93	13.89	14.02	13.91	13.87	13.97	13.91	13.96	14.00	13.98	13.97	14.01	13.95
CHICAGO													
Manufacturing													
2001	14.16	14.14	14.18	14.34	14.44	14.62	14.78	14.71	14.81	14.76	14.78	14.80	14.54
2002	14.80	14.70	14.68	14.72	14.75	14.76	14.74	14.76	14.78	14.79	14.78	14.78	14.75
2003	14.72	14.60	14.69	14.73	14.80	14.85	14.77	14.82	14.96	14.87	15.01	15.07	14.82

Average Weekly Earnings by Industry: Illinois

(Dollars, not seasonally adjusted.)

Industry	January	February	March	April	May	June	July	August	September	October	November	December	Annual Average
STATEWIDE													
Natural resources and mining													
2001	740.62	759.28	824.72	815.77	829.70	836.60	879.36	892.55	851.47	810.35	781.88	758.21	818.30
2002	695.83	692.18	736.48	716.18	725.63	748.84	741.90	775.05	770.18	800.29	791.57	785.15	748.80
2003	740.66	722.36	735.65	762.24	783.76	760.48	774.15	803.96	835.91	844.95	834.91	836.42	786.76
Construction													
2001	930.00	940.91	888.22	904.75	950.67	963.46	983.76	954.19	977.80	933.30	972.04	967.16	948.00
2002	929.64	949.68	951.65	936.27	938.36	959.01	998.60	991.13	1032.41	1030.46	1005.81	994.50	978.76
2003	947.59	913.09	945.82	949.31	972.78	981.71	992.18	1019.94	1041.04	1004.86	1016.82	949.78	980.13
Manufacturing													
2001	592.87	587.73	584.45	570.64	596.96	605.23	603.43	607.70	621.33	607.21	612.23	623.00	601.06
2002	603.86	602.62	608.69	609.92	615.37	624.67	618.14	623.58	634.52	630.09	635.46	638.66	620.59
2003	616.31	610.34	608.83	605.51	613.98	617.53	598.75	617.12	629.35	619.05	630.47	641.06	617.12
Trade, transportation, and utilities													
2001	426.92	430.92	433.02	436.71	436.31	432.39	439.40	451.44	455.46	451.43	453.30	458.21	441.22
2002	444.80	450.68	458.54	459.53	467.60	469.44	459.21	458.30	457.83	454.61	443.72	455.13	456.65
2003	434.26	443.41	442.24	438.20	443.56	444.93	442.58	439.77	443.16	440.09	439.53	437.72	440.41
Wholesale trade													
2001	608.30	607.10	609.07	619.29	611.85	598.27	606.34	614.25	611.07	615.86	621.58	623.52	611.81
2002	615.78	617.01	624.55	622.62	638.67	642.37	620.52	623.25	626.47	627.66	613.08	627.26	625.21
2003	600.89	623.30	608.01	599.85	608.36	611.88	603.68	602.18	617.76	619.76	626.40	609.96	611.13
Retail trade													
2001	303.66	308.26	312.17	314.31	313.34	316.03	321.95	333.98	337.44	328.56	332.87	338.44	321.42
2002	322.77	332.05	336.00	340.35	339.57	348.19	347.74	346.09	340.18	337.27	333.89	346.60	339.97
2003	325.75	330.29	330.50	331.04	333.76	339.66	338.15	338.54	333.16	327.97	329.45	332.69	332.34
Transportation and utilities													
2001	517.34	520.88	520.34	516.75	524.18	522.28	527.47	515.66	529.75	530.04	536.25	547.45	525.52
2002	522.42	519.88	536.50	534.47	552.45	540.76	527.52	525.28	535.53	530.18	520.61	534.14	530.82
2003	502.80	497.08	508.99	499.86	516.07	510.09	510.35	498.53	512.10	510.18	507.10	515.71	507.20
Information													
2001	721.27	729.82	726.93	729.80	725.49	733.04	737.57	745.67	752.08	759.92	754.70	760.89	739.44
2002	763.03	771.93	759.06	762.30	759.24	750.72	752.64	724.14	711.77	701.95	715.90	692.29	739.14
2003	684.79	678.05	679.96	696.79	694.80	704.45	696.73	689.76	689.41	690.48	732.45	707.85	696.13
Financial activities													
2001	544.21	556.66	556.66	572.44	563.04	568.15	570.13	559.30	572.80	564.90	566.08	586.99	565.51
2002	561.56	575.40	575.64	573.30	581.04	593.28	584.06	590.47	604.20	605.38	597.28	614.68	588.35
2003	617.67	639.85	637.63	618.12	611.64	635.89	623.09	623.88	619.04	621.49	638.74	624.60	626.18
Professional and business services													
2001	568.48	587.90	592.70	612.46	597.84	585.09	592.71	577.23	601.68	595.45	597.14	616.00	594.06
2002	600.30	629.41	627.29	624.10	619.12	630.72	608.65	617.70	618.68	613.80	613.90	611.00	618.10
2003	602.65	619.62	623.49	613.63	612.11	615.65	595.00	598.90	592.23	597.51	602.69	582.50	605.05
Educational and health services													
2001	461.08	458.63	459.36	466.46	465.60	464.80	474.70	470.78	483.26	474.65	478.19	485.79	470.53
2002	481.73	480.63	485.18	483.41	485.86	495.90	486.85	484.92	502.86	490.21	493.35	498.33	489.10
2003	487.41	497.50	495.68	490.69	490.17	495.99	494.10	490.54	489.99	487.04	499.87	491.69	492.79
Leisure and hospitality													
2001	205.59	211.43	208.91	208.83	217.34	222.11	223.75	217.86	224.46	215.36	213.95	227.30	216.83
2002	213.00	216.15	218.54	220.93	223.52	234.23	229.42	227.76	222.31	221.44	216.66	217.01	221.79
2003	203.76	204.85	209.31	205.09	211.79	219.89	215.30	216.15	213.28	212.78	217.07	217.22	212.15
Other services													
2001	421.93	422.42	428.80	426.76	428.58	424.39	434.80	436.07	438.49	434.92	429.54	440.90	430.25
2002	428.61	419.54	423.18	420.76	433.67	447.11	428.72	434.50	446.94	434.89	437.42	445.44	433.97
2003	430.28	440.06	436.44	421.07	427.84	436.55	429.25	429.86	423.30	424.11	435.02	420.85	428.94
CHAMPAIGN-URBANA-RANTOUL													
Manufacturing													
2001	493.31	498.94	505.40	514.49	525.05	530.00	543.05	535.34	553.11	533.97	563.57	534.26	528.12
2002	537.43	549.64	556.00	551.46	554.20	548.23	544.00	559.20	564.72	559.10	557.28	548.63	552.02
2003	548.84	545.88	553.79	552.23	549.25	556.01	556.40	561.19	561.40	562.00	567.18	571.61	556.61
CHICAGO													
Manufacturing													
2001	591.89	589.64	588.47	569.30	602.15	611.12	616.33	617.82	624.98	616.97	622.24	633.44	606.32
2002	615.68	615.93	619.50	618.24	623.93	631.73	617.61	625.82	628.15	627.10	631.11	632.58	623.93
2003	604.99	601.52	600.82	595.09	600.88	605.88	589.32	595.76	608.87	606.70	615.41	622.39	603.17

INDIANA AT A GLANCE

(Population and total nonfarm employment numbers in thousands)

Population, Census 2000:	6,080.5
Total nonfarm employment, 2003:	2,896.8
Change in total nonfarm employment	
(Number)	
1990–2003:	374.9
1990–2001:	411.5
2001–2003:	-36.6
(Compound annual rate of change)	
1990–2003:	1.1%
1990–2001:	1.4%
2001–2003:	-0.6%
Unemployment rate	
1990:	5.0%
2001:	4.2%
2003:	5.3%

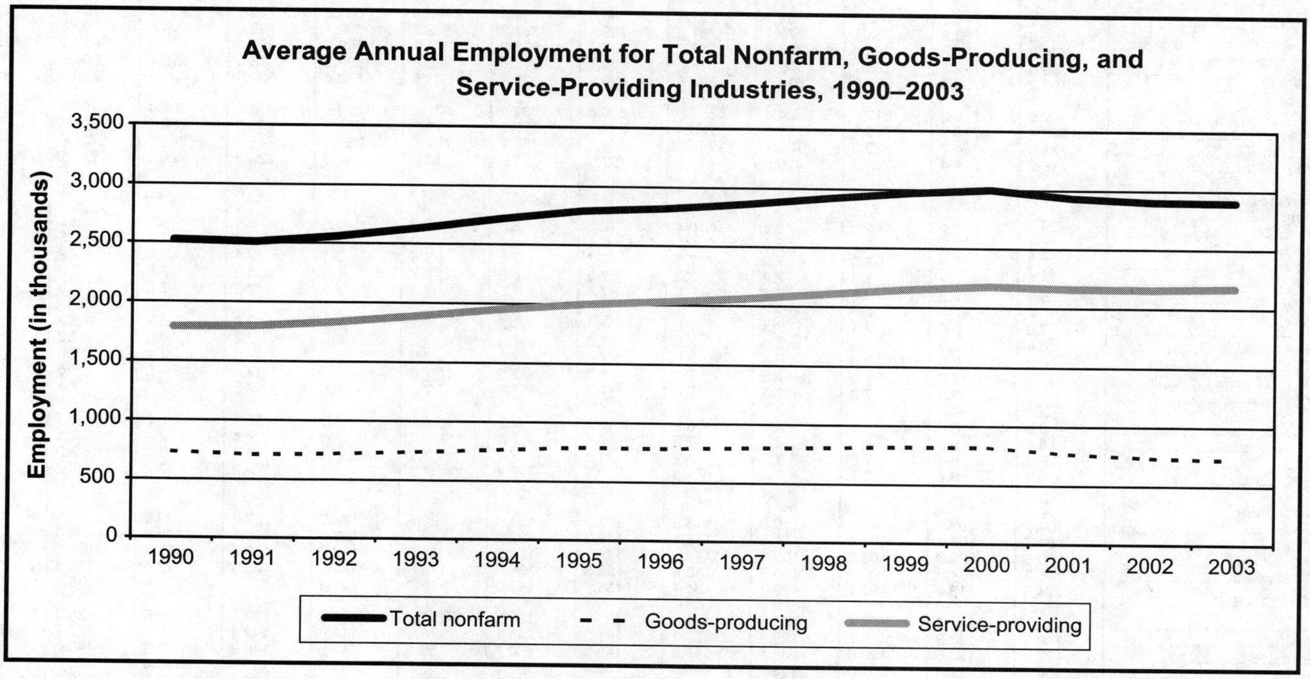

Employment in the goods-producing sector rose steadily throughout the 1990s, but fell off with the 2001 recession. From 2000 to 2003, employment in the manufacturing industry declined by over 90,000. In 2003, manufacturing employment represented 20 percent of total employment, down from over 24 percent in 1990. In the service-providing sector, the upward trend in employment in the 1990s slowed in 2001. However, educational and health services continued to experience high growth. From 2000 to 2003, employment increased 9.6 percent.

Employment by Industry: Indiana

(Numbers in thousands. Not seasonally adjusted.)

Industry	January	February	March	April	May	June	July	August	September	October	November	December	Annual Average
STATEWIDE													
Total nonfarm													
1990	2462.6	2469.7	2491.9	2501.2	2531.1	2537.0	2528.5	2543.7	2563.9	2551.9	2542.6	2538.8	2521.9
1991	2460.4	2455.3	2464.7	2496.5	2524.5	2520.9	2491.9	2510.0	2544.2	2538.8	2540.1	2540.6	2507.3
1992	2474.7	2483.8	2502.1	2539.7	2571.1	2567.0	2550.3	2561.9	2596.5	2600.3	2598.7	2604.8	2554.2
1993	2547.3	2557.0	2572.5	2609.0	2633.9	2636.5	2613.7	2625.7	2668.1	2677.6	2686.6	2695.2	2626.9
1994	2625.4	2640.8	2672.5	2688.2	2719.8	2714.1	2693.9	2711.9	2771.6	2756.3	2773.7	2784.4	2712.7
1995	2715.6	2733.8	2764.8	2780.1	2803.9	2789.5	2755.0	2769.7	2837.4	2822.1	2829.5	2836.6	2786.5
1996	2739.2	2758.3	2778.7	2808.5	2842.3	2823.8	2773.1	2802.8	2858.9	2854.6	2864.3	2867.9	2814.3
1997	2781.4	2802.1	2828.0	2857.4	2885.5	2866.9	2831.1	2841.6	2893.4	2898.7	2902.3	2913.2	2858.4
1998	2839.4	2855.6	2874.1	2913.8	2944.6	2934.4	2872.0	2900.9	2953.0	2961.5	2972.9	2984.3	2917.2
1999	2867.9	2903.3	2929.4	2973.4	3000.5	2987.3	2943.9	2951.4	3007.6	3013.7	3024.6	3035.9	2969.9
2000	2947.2	2957.5	2989.7	3016.3	3046.3	3024.0	2971.9	2986.0	3030.8	3014.3	3011.7	3005.0	3000.0
2001	2901.7	2915.7	2937.1	2959.2	2969.7	2949.5	2892.6	2918.5	2953.7	2938.8	2935.3	2928.8	2933.4
2002	2833.3	2847.0	2865.1	2893.0	2921.6	2907.8	2885.3	2912.7	2940.0	2932.8	2938.9	2933.2	2900.9
2003	2850.2	2849.4	2868.6	2896.1	2923.5	2900.0	2861.1	2890.7	2928.6	2934.1	2930.5	2928.4	2896.8
Total private													
1990	2089.4	2089.0	2110.1	2116.2	2144.4	2162.7	2167.8	2181.3	2181.8	2166.4	2156.7	2154.0	2143.3
1991	2083.8	2069.7	2078.0	2108.4	2138.2	2153.0	2143.8	2154.7	2158.6	2147.2	2147.0	2146.3	2127.3
1992	2090.0	2089.5	2110.4	2144.6	2178.6	2189.7	2190.7	2197.5	2202.3	2201.4	2199.5	2205.7	2166.6
1993	2157.6	2158.5	2173.8	2209.6	2237.3	2253.0	2251.0	2261.6	2271.0	2277.3	2284.5	2292.3	2235.6
1994	2227.0	2234.3	2264.7	2295.4	2328.1	2345.5	2338.2	2356.3	2372.1	2353.1	2368.5	2381.4	2322.0
1995	2322.8	2330.6	2360.4	2374.8	2404.3	2420.6	2402.1	2420.6	2434.5	2415.3	2422.1	2429.9	2394.8
1996	2345.6	2352.6	2371.8	2401.9	2438.4	2447.9	2430.1	2457.9	2457.5	2450.2	2459.5	2466.9	2423.3
1997	2392.0	2400.5	2426.1	2454.8	2483.3	2487.3	2477.9	2489.7	2493.3	2492.7	2495.3	2504.8	2466.4
1998	2440.4	2447.1	2465.6	2504.0	2535.3	2548.0	2519.7	2539.8	2544.6	2547.3	2557.5	2567.2	2518.0
1999	2471.7	2491.7	2516.1	2559.2	2581.5	2595.7	2585.8	2592.4	2593.5	2596.3	2606.3	2617.0	2567.2
2000	2535.5	2538.7	2567.4	2592.5	2615.4	2627.4	2601.1	2612.3	2608.1	2596.7	2593.4	2588.4	2589.7
2001	2492.4	2492.9	2511.4	2534.7	2549.6	2559.3	2532.2	2543.9	2534.1	2514.2	2510.6	2505.3	2523.4
2002	2423.8	2423.0	2441.2	2466.4	2496.5	2514.7	2508.5	2521.3	2512.2	2498.3	2503.0	2498.0	2483.9
2003	2427.5	2418.3	2434.6	2464.0	2490.4	2497.0	2482.2	2497.4	2495.7	2495.6	2493.7	2492.2	2474.1
Goods-producing													
1990	713.2	714.9	723.1	727.9	738.1	746.9	749.1	752.8	751.6	742.5	727.5	719.8	733.9
1991	698.4	688.5	686.8	702.4	714.5	722.6	722.4	728.0	728.0	724.1	718.9	714.5	712.4
1992	693.7	694.3	701.9	713.7	724.8	733.3	734.7	738.6	739.5	733.1	728.8	728.7	722.0
1993	715.0	713.9	718.3	729.6	738.4	746.3	747.9	752.0	754.9	752.8	754.0	751.6	739.5
1994	729.3	731.3	742.2	753.2	764.3	772.8	771.9	782.1	786.2	780.5	783.4	785.3	765.2
1995	772.1	774.3	782.5	782.1	791.3	798.0	794.0	799.9	801.8	793.7	791.5	789.1	789.1
1996	762.5	763.9	768.1	779.4	791.8	799.7	787.3	802.2	802.1	798.6	794.5	792.6	786.8
1997	774.2	777.3	783.9	795.8	805.2	809.0	805.2	811.0	809.3	808.0	805.2	802.9	798.9
1998	789.9	792.2	795.1	809.2	818.2	824.7	810.0	820.8	822.2	813.0	810.2	808.8	809.5
1999	792.8	797.9	802.6	814.5	820.6	828.9	829.4	831.8	832.1	832.9	831.3	830.0	820.4
2000	809.5	810.2	817.6	824.4	830.2	836.8	830.5	832.9	826.5	815.9	808.4	799.1	820.1
2001	770.4	770.9	773.1	779.1	783.4	786.6	777.0	778.7	770.7	759.6	753.7	746.6	770.8
2002	723.6	724.0	729.0	735.7	744.1	754.3	753.2	757.8	752.9	745.6	742.7	734.6	741.5
2003	716.2	712.4	715.9	720.9	728.1	732.5	725.3	734.3	730.6	729.2	726.3	723.1	724.6
Natural resources and mining													
1990	7.9	7.9	8.0	8.2	8.4	8.5	8.5	8.6	8.5	8.5	8.5	8.4	8.3
1991	8.1	7.9	7.9	7.9	8.1	8.1	8.1	7.9	7.9	7.8	7.6	7.5	7.9
1992	7.2	7.2	7.3	7.5	7.6	7.7	7.5	7.5	7.4	7.4	7.4	7.2	7.4
1993	6.9	6.9	7.0	7.2	7.3	7.5	6.8	6.7	6.6	6.5	6.6	7.2	6.9
1994	6.9	6.9	7.0	7.3	7.5	7.6	7.5	7.5	7.5	7.5	7.5	7.3	7.3
1995	7.0	6.9	7.1	7.3	7.3	7.4	7.2	7.1	7.0	7.0	6.9	6.9	7.0
1996	6.4	6.3	6.6	6.9	7.0	7.2	7.1	7.2	7.2	7.3	7.3	7.2	6.9
1997	6.9	6.9	7.0	7.4	7.6	7.6	7.8	7.8	7.8	7.7	7.7	7.6	7.4
1998	7.4	7.3	7.3	7.5	7.6	7.7	7.6	7.6	7.6	7.6	7.6	7.6	7.5
1999	7.1	7.2	7.3	7.5	7.6	7.7	7.6	7.5	7.5	7.5	7.4	7.4	7.4
2000	6.5	6.5	6.6	6.8	6.9	6.9	6.9	6.9	6.9	6.8	6.8	6.7	6.7
2001	6.4	6.5	6.7	7.1	7.2	7.3	7.4	7.4	7.4	7.4	7.3	7.1	7.1
2002	6.8	6.9	7.0	7.2	7.2	7.3	7.2	7.2	7.2	7.1	7.0	7.0	7.1
2003	6.6	6.7	6.7	7.0	7.0	7.1	7.2	7.2	7.3	7.3	7.2	7.2	7.0
Construction													
1990	104.5	103.1	106.9	110.5	115.9	121.0	124.8	126.6	124.9	122.2	120.8	116.8	116.5
1991	104.7	103.9	106.8	111.5	116.4	119.8	122.0	123.4	120.6	119.8	115.8	112.0	114.7
1992	100.6	99.0	102.8	109.2	114.4	118.1	123.6	124.2	122.7	120.9	117.7	115.9	114.0
1993	105.2	104.2	106.5	114.3	118.6	122.3	126.5	126.8	125.1	125.5	123.4	119.3	118.1
1994	114.5	113.6	120.1	129.2	134.1	138.7	142.0	142.7	141.3	141.2	137.6	135.1	132.5
1995	123.7	122.5	128.1	126.3	131.4	138.1	137.7	138.0	135.6	132.2	129.5	126.5	130.8
1996	113.3	113.9	119.7	129.2	136.1	141.3	144.1	145.6	143.8	142.8	141.1	137.7	134.0
1997	123.2	123.5	129.8	138.1	143.9	148.3	150.1	150.3	147.3	146.9	144.6	140.7	140.5
1998	130.1	129.8	131.3	143.0	149.3	153.4	155.2	153.2	151.8	151.6	148.4	146.1	145.2
1999	128.9	131.6	135.8	146.5	150.2	154.6	157.9	157.3	155.3	156.2	153.6	150.2	148.1
2000	137.7	136.5	144.0	150.8	155.0	158.8	158.9	159.0	156.1	151.4	148.2	142.4	149.9
2001	130.6	132.1	138.2	146.3	152.2	156.7	157.3	158.5	154.8	153.0	152.4	147.5	148.3
2002	134.4	133.5	137.0	142.9	147.9	152.3	155.2	155.1	152.6	149.5	148.1	143.6	146.0
2003	131.7	128.5	133.0	141.8	147.9	149.8	152.2	153.6	151.3	151.7	149.3	146.2	144.8

Employment by Industry: Indiana—*Continued*

(Numbers in thousands. Not seasonally adjusted.)

Industry	January	February	March	April	May	June	July	August	September	October	November	December	Annual Average
STATEWIDE—*Continued*													
Manufacturing													
1990	600.8	603.9	608.2	609.2	613.8	617.4	615.8	617.6	618.2	611.8	598.2	594.6	609.1
1991	585.6	576.7	572.1	583.0	590.0	594.7	592.3	596.7	599.5	596.5	595.5	595.0	589.8
1992	585.9	588.1	591.8	597.0	602.8	607.5	603.6	606.9	609.4	604.8	603.7	605.6	600.5
1993	602.9	602.8	604.8	608.1	612.5	616.5	614.6	618.5	623.2	620.8	624.0	625.1	614.4
1994	607.9	610.8	615.1	616.7	622.7	626.5	622.4	631.9	637.4	631.8	638.3	642.9	625.3
1995	641.4	644.9	647.3	648.5	652.6	652.5	649.1	654.8	659.2	654.5	655.1	655.7	651.3
1996	642.8	643.7	641.8	643.3	648.7	651.2	636.1	649.4	651.1	648.5	646.1	647.7	645.8
1997	644.1	646.9	647.1	650.3	653.7	653.1	647.3	652.9	654.2	653.4	652.9	654.6	650.8
1998	652.4	655.1	656.5	658.7	661.3	663.6	647.2	660.0	662.8	653.8	654.2	655.1	656.7
1999	656.8	659.1	659.5	660.5	662.8	666.6	663.9	667.0	669.3	669.2	670.3	672.4	664.7
2000	665.3	667.2	667.0	666.8	668.3	671.1	664.7	667.0	663.5	657.7	653.4	650.0	663.5
2001	633.4	632.3	628.2	625.7	624.0	622.6	612.3	612.8	608.5	599.2	594.0	592.0	615.4
2002	582.4	583.6	585.0	585.6	589.0	594.7	590.8	595.5	593.1	589.0	587.6	584.0	588.4
2003	577.9	577.2	576.2	572.1	573.2	575.6	565.9	573.5	572.0	570.2	569.8	569.7	572.8
Service-providing													
1990	1749.4	1754.8	1768.8	1773.3	1793.0	1790.1	1779.4	1790.9	1812.3	1809.4	1815.1	1819.0	1787.9
1991	1762.0	1766.8	1777.9	1794.1	1810.0	1798.3	1769.5	1782.0	1816.2	1814.7	1821.2	1826.1	1794.9
1992	1781.0	1789.5	1800.2	1826.0	1846.3	1833.7	1815.6	1823.3	1857.0	1867.2	1869.9	1876.1	1832.1
1993	1832.3	1843.1	1854.2	1879.4	1895.5	1890.2	1865.8	1873.7	1913.2	1924.8	1932.6	1943.6	1887.3
1994	1896.1	1909.5	1930.3	1935.0	1955.5	1941.3	1922.0	1929.8	1985.4	1975.8	1990.3	1999.1	1947.5
1995	1943.5	1959.5	1982.3	1998.0	2012.6	1991.5	1961.0	1969.8	2035.6	2028.4	2038.0	2047.5	1997.3
1996	1976.7	1994.4	2010.6	2029.1	2050.5	2024.1	1985.8	2000.6	2056.8	2056.0	2069.8	2075.3	2027.4
1997	2007.2	2024.8	2044.1	2061.6	2080.3	2057.9	2025.9	2030.6	2084.1	2090.7	2097.1	2110.3	2059.5
1998	2049.5	2063.4	2079.0	2104.6	2126.4	2109.7	2062.0	2080.1	2130.8	2148.5	2162.7	2175.5	2107.6
1999	2075.1	2105.4	2126.8	2158.9	2179.9	2158.4	2114.5	2119.6	2175.5	2180.8	2193.3	2205.9	2149.5
2000	2137.7	2147.3	2172.1	2191.9	2216.1	2187.2	2141.4	2153.1	2204.3	2198.4	2203.3	2205.9	2179.8
2001	2131.3	2144.8	2164.0	2180.1	2186.3	2162.9	2115.6	2139.8	2183.0	2179.2	2181.6	2182.2	2162.6
2002	2109.7	2123.0	2136.1	2157.3	2177.5	2153.5	2132.1	2154.9	2187.1	2187.2	2196.2	2198.6	2159.4
2003	2134.0	2137.0	2152.7	2175.2	2195.4	2167.5	2135.8	2156.4	2198.0	2204.9	2204.2	2205.3	2172.2
Trade, transportation, and utilities													
1990	523.4	517.9	520.1	518.6	524.3	526.4	528.7	533.0	532.4	532.1	541.2	545.9	528.6
1991	519.9	512.5	513.2	517.3	524.4	525.1	523.8	525.2	524.6	522.2	531.1	535.7	522.9
1992	514.8	509.9	511.7	516.1	523.7	525.1	524.4	526.5	527.3	531.5	538.2	545.4	524.5
1993	521.9	517.5	519.5	525.4	532.0	534.0	535.3	537.1	538.5	543.5	554.2	562.0	535.0
1994	537.9	534.4	540.5	545.9	555.4	558.8	555.6	559.5	563.7	561.7	574.1	582.6	555.8
1995	559.4	554.8	561.3	566.0	573.4	576.5	574.9	578.1	582.3	581.7	592.5	600.4	575.1
1996	573.2	566.8	569.0	572.6	579.6	579.7	577.0	579.9	579.9	580.4	593.9	602.1	579.5
1997	578.8	572.6	577.5	581.2	587.7	587.6	583.9	582.6	584.9	591.3	600.7	609.9	586.5
1998	583.7	576.9	579.6	587.4	595.2	598.2	594.1	596.0	597.2	603.4	617.0	625.8	596.2
1999	589.6	588.2	594.0	602.6	606.8	608.0	606.3	606.1	606.0	608.5	619.1	628.1	605.2
2000	606.0	600.9	606.7	609.9	614.6	616.6	614.6	615.6	614.1	621.0	630.8	638.2	615.7
2001	602.0	594.3	596.1	599.2	602.4	604.6	599.0	599.4	596.2	595.6	604.0	608.0	600.1
2002	579.0	572.6	574.5	575.9	581.1	584.0	582.7	583.2	580.7	579.3	590.8	595.6	581.6
2003	568.8	561.7	564.6	570.3	573.8	575.4	572.6	572.8	573.4	574.0	581.0	583.1	572.6
Wholesale trade													
1990	104.9	105.0	105.5	105.0	105.6	106.3	107.1	107.0	106.6	108.1	109.5	109.3	106.6
1991	106.2	106.1	106.4	107.5	108.7	108.6	107.3	106.8	106.7	106.2	106.3	106.3	106.9
1992	104.4	104.3	104.8	106.0	107.0	107.4	108.2	107.7	106.9	108.0	107.3	107.6	106.6
1993	104.2	104.6	105.2	106.3	107.5	107.6	107.2	106.7	106.9	107.2	107.2	107.4	106.5
1994	105.4	105.7	106.7	107.5	108.6	109.3	108.6	108.9	109.2	109.4	109.7	110.3	108.2
1995	108.9	109.6	111.0	112.4	113.4	113.9	113.6	113.7	114.1	113.3	113.2	114.1	112.6
1996	111.9	112.9	113.6	114.4	115.3	115.5	114.9	114.8	114.6	115.1	115.6	116.2	114.5
1997	114.3	114.8	116.1	117.5	118.4	118.5	118.3	118.0	118.3	118.1	118.3	118.7	117.4
1998	117.8	118.5	119.7	121.2	122.3	122.6	121.1	120.7	121.2	121.7	121.6	122.1	120.8
1999	119.3	120.1	120.8	123.3	123.5	123.9	123.3	122.9	122.9	123.6	123.6	124.6	122.6
2000	123.5	123.9	125.2	125.4	126.1	126.9	126.6	126.5	125.9	125.9	125.7	125.5	125.5
2001	123.7	123.6	124.1	123.8	124.1	124.5	123.8	123.4	122.8	122.4	121.8	121.7	123.3
2002	119.7	119.3	119.3	120.0	120.6	121.1	120.5	119.9	119.2	118.5	118.3	118.3	119.6
2003	117.6	117.3	117.4	117.7	118.3	118.8	118.3	118.0	117.4	118.2	117.9	117.9	117.9
Retail trade													
1990	309.0	302.9	303.9	302.9	306.7	307.1	308.6	311.9	311.5	310.4	318.3	322.9	309.6
1991	304.1	297.2	296.9	300.2	304.7	304.9	304.9	306.2	306.0	305.2	313.9	318.3	305.2
1992	301.8	296.9	297.5	298.3	303.2	303.6	301.3	303.1	303.5	308.6	315.9	322.8	304.7
1993	305.8	301.2	301.8	304.4	307.7	308.8	309.0	310.8	311.0	314.2	324.0	330.7	310.7
1994	311.8	307.2	310.6	315.5	322.0	324.8	322.7	326.5	329.7	327.8	339.7	347.6	323.8
1995	329.7	324.6	329.2	330.2	335.7	337.7	335.6	338.9	342.3	342.8	353.9	361.2	338.4
1996	340.0	332.9	333.4	335.5	340.5	341.1	339.0	340.9	341.3	340.7	353.4	360.8	341.6
1997	343.4	336.1	338.4	339.9	344.8	344.8	342.8	343.8	342.8	348.5	358.0	365.1	345.7
1998	342.9	337.2	337.7	341.7	346.7	348.5	346.4	346.9	346.8	351.8	364.7	372.2	348.6
1999	345.0	341.8	345.8	350.4	353.6	354.9	352.5	352.3	352.2	352.8	363.4	370.5	352.9
2000	353.3	347.9	351.4	353.2	357.1	358.1	354.9	355.4	354.8	359.5	371.8	378.6	358.0
2001	351.8	344.9	345.4	346.5	349.4	350.8	346.0	345.8	344.6	346.1	355.7	358.8	348.8
2002	338.8	333.7	335.8	336.3	340.5	342.8	340.7	340.6	339.1	337.7	348.4	353.8	340.7
2003	331.1	325.4	327.8	331.2	334.7	336.3	333.4	333.8	335.1	333.5	340.3	342.9	333.8

Employment by Industry: Indiana—*Continued*

(Numbers in thousands. Not seasonally adjusted.)

Industry	January	February	March	April	May	June	July	August	September	October	November	December	Annual Average
STATEWIDE—*Continued*													
Transportation and utilities													
1990	109.5	110.0	110.7	110.7	112.0	113.0	113.0	114.1	114.3	113.6	113.4	113.7	112.3
1991	109.6	109.2	109.9	109.6	111.0	111.6	111.6	112.2	111.9	110.8	110.9	111.1	110.7
1992	108.6	108.7	109.4	111.8	113.5	114.1	114.9	115.7	116.4	114.9	115.0	115.0	113.1
1993	111.9	111.7	112.5	114.7	116.8	117.6	119.1	119.6	120.6	122.1	123.0	123.9	117.7
1994	120.7	121.5	123.2	122.9	124.8	124.7	124.3	124.1	124.8	124.5	124.7	124.7	123.7
1995	120.8	120.6	121.1	123.4	124.3	124.9	125.7	125.5	125.9	125.6	125.4	125.1	124.0
1996	121.3	121.0	122.0	122.7	123.8	123.1	123.1	124.2	124.0	124.6	124.9	125.1	123.3
1997	121.1	121.7	123.0	123.8	124.5	124.3	122.8	120.8	123.8	124.7	124.4	126.1	123.4
1998	123.0	121.2	122.2	124.5	126.2	127.1	126.6	128.4	129.2	129.9	130.7	131.5	126.7
1999	125.3	126.3	127.4	128.9	129.7	129.2	130.5	130.9	130.9	132.1	132.1	133.0	129.6
2000	129.2	129.1	130.1	131.3	131.4	131.6	133.1	133.7	133.4	135.6	133.3	134.1	132.1
2001	126.5	125.8	126.6	128.9	128.9	129.3	129.2	130.2	128.8	127.1	126.5	127.5	127.9
2002	120.5	119.6	119.4	119.6	120.0	120.1	121.5	122.7	122.4	123.1	124.1	123.5	121.4
2003	120.1	119.0	119.4	121.4	120.8	120.3	120.9	121.0	120.9	122.3	122.8	122.3	120.9
Information													
1990	45.0	44.9	44.9	45.0	45.3	45.6	45.6	45.4	45.0	43.3	43.2	43.3	44.7
1991	43.1	42.9	42.6	42.4	42.6	42.9	43.3	43.2	42.9	42.8	42.9	43.3	42.9
1992	41.9	41.9	42.0	42.2	42.3	42.5	42.9	42.7	42.4	42.4	42.3	42.5	42.3
1993	41.9	42.1	42.3	42.0	42.2	42.6	43.3	43.1	42.3	42.3	42.5	42.6	42.4
1994	41.6	41.7	41.9	41.7	41.9	42.4	42.9	42.3	42.1	41.9	42.0	42.5	42.0
1995	41.5	41.9	42.4	41.1	41.6	42.1	41.6	41.4	41.8	41.0	41.5	41.8	41.6
1996	40.7	41.0	41.3	40.9	41.4	41.8	41.9	42.3	42.4	43.7	43.9	44.8	42.1
1997	43.8	44.1	44.3	44.2	44.5	44.8	44.2	44.4	44.1	42.9	43.1	43.6	44.0
1998	44.2	44.4	44.5	44.4	45.0	45.3	45.1	45.3	45.1	44.8	45.0	45.5	44.8
1999	44.5	44.6	45.0	45.2	45.9	46.2	45.5	45.6	45.6	46.0	45.9	46.1	45.5
2000	45.6	45.8	46.3	45.3	45.9	46.6	46.0	46.3	46.0	45.6	46.1	46.2	45.9
2001	45.5	45.3	45.6	45.0	45.2	45.3	45.0	44.6	44.0	43.6	43.8	43.9	44.7
2002	42.9	42.6	42.9	42.5	42.8	43.1	42.8	42.8	42.1	41.7	41.9	41.8	42.5
2003	41.0	40.7	41.1	40.6	41.2	41.6	41.3	41.6	40.8	40.7	40.8	41.2	41.1
Financial activities													
1990	127.9	128.1	129.0	128.5	129.6	131.3	131.7	131.8	130.9	129.8	129.8	130.3	129.8
1991	128.1	128.0	128.8	129.5	131.0	133.0	131.9	131.9	130.9	129.6	129.6	130.2	130.2
1992	128.9	128.9	129.9	130.7	132.3	133.1	132.0	131.5	130.4	130.0	129.6	130.4	130.6
1993	130.6	130.7	131.7	135.2	136.1	137.4	137.1	137.0	136.8	135.9	133.8	134.7	134.7
1994	133.6	133.8	134.7	136.4	137.9	139.6	139.0	138.9	137.9	136.8	137.1	138.1	136.9
1995	134.0	134.4	135.4	136.8	138.1	140.0	137.2	137.8	136.9	136.2	135.7	137.4	136.6
1996	135.8	136.2	137.4	139.5	141.2	142.1	141.1	141.5	140.7	139.5	139.8	140.6	139.6
1997	139.5	139.6	140.6	141.7	143.0	144.4	145.3	145.5	144.5	144.5	144.4	145.7	143.2
1998	142.8	142.5	143.3	143.5	144.8	146.1	147.0	146.8	145.5	144.7	144.2	145.2	144.7
1999	143.5	143.4	143.9	145.5	146.7	147.7	147.1	146.9	145.0	144.9	144.7	145.9	145.4
2000	144.1	143.8	144.2	144.4	145.4	146.8	146.0	145.7	144.4	143.6	143.6	144.6	144.7
2001	142.0	142.2	142.8	143.6	144.3	146.0	144.6	144.0	141.8	140.8	140.8	141.5	142.9
2002	139.2	138.9	138.9	138.8	139.8	141.1	141.5	141.6	140.3	139.8	140.1	140.8	140.1
2003	139.5	139.5	140.2	140.6	142.0	143.3	142.9	142.6	141.2	140.6	140.6	140.7	141.1
Professional and business services													
1990	148.4	149.4	152.1	152.9	154.3	156.1	157.1	158.2	159.1	160.5	157.6	156.6	155.1
1991	151.6	152.6	154.5	156.3	157.4	159.0	158.8	160.1	161.7	160.4	158.9	157.2	157.3
1992	156.7	156.9	161.0	166.4	169.0	169.4	169.2	169.4	170.1	169.1	167.2	166.7	165.9
1993	166.0	167.5	170.7	174.8	177.1	179.9	177.8	181.6	183.0	185.3	185.6	185.0	177.8
1994	181.9	185.9	189.5	194.7	196.6	199.4	202.0	203.7	207.0	203.2	203.7	202.2	197.4
1995	199.0	202.4	206.1	206.8	208.7	211.8	208.0	213.2	216.0	213.9	213.1	212.0	209.2
1996	203.5	206.1	208.5	213.9	217.8	217.7	217.2	219.6	219.1	219.1	217.5	215.9	214.6
1997	207.0	209.5	214.4	220.9	221.5	221.2	225.1	227.7	228.7	228.9	228.5	229.4	221.9
1998	222.2	225.7	230.5	237.6	238.8	241.5	242.7	246.1	247.2	250.2	250.7	250.1	240.2
1999	238.9	243.3	248.5	255.6	256.2	258.8	258.7	260.6	260.8	259.4	261.5	262.0	255.3
2000	248.5	249.8	254.7	260.4	262.8	265.5	260.9	263.2	263.9	260.3	258.8	255.8	258.7
2001	241.6	242.2	246.1	250.3	251.7	253.8	252.1	256.2	252.7	251.9	249.6	247.6	249.7
2002	239.4	240.8	244.8	251.4	255.8	258.2	259.1	261.7	260.2	258.9	257.9	256.3	253.7
2003	246.5	246.5	248.2	252.2	254.9	256.0	255.1	258.2	259.5	261.6	259.5	258.9	254.8
Educational and health services													
1990	242.1	243.1	244.5	246.0	246.7	246.6	245.2	246.9	252.0	254.3	255.3	255.7	248.2
1991	252.4	254.5	255.3	256.9	257.4	255.9	255.3	256.0	261.5	264.5	265.0	265.6	258.3
1992	263.5	265.1	265.8	269.1	270.8	268.3	268.8	268.3	273.7	279.3	279.6	279.7	271.0
1993	278.4	280.4	281.1	284.4	284.0	281.9	281.3	281.0	287.2	291.8	291.4	292.5	284.6
1994	290.2	292.6	293.7	295.0	294.7	290.4	289.6	290.1	296.8	298.4	298.5	299.2	294.1
1995	295.3	298.6	300.4	302.2	301.7	298.6	296.0	296.7	303.9	305.6	307.0	306.9	301.0
1996	301.7	305.9	308.0	308.6	308.2	304.5	306.2	307.7	315.1	316.1	318.3	318.9	309.9
1997	313.1	317.2	318.7	317.6	317.5	313.9	309.7	310.6	317.7	320.7	321.4	321.6	316.6
1998	317.8	321.2	322.1	323.2	322.9	319.2	313.3	314.2	321.5	326.3	327.9	328.4	321.5
1999	319.0	323.8	324.8	327.6	326.5	322.0	319.2	319.9	327.2	332.9	334.6	335.4	326.0
2000	326.3	329.9	331.7	332.9	333.0	326.2	320.8	323.4	332.2	334.1	334.8	335.7	330.0
2001	335.6	338.4	340.0	341.8	337.0	330.0	327.7	330.2	346.3	346.7	348.3	349.1	339.3
2002	345.2	347.3	348.4	349.4	348.6	344.1	342.7	344.5	353.5	355.7	357.2	357.8	349.5
2003	357.5	359.6	360.8	363.4	363.6	356.0	354.0	355.9	366.0	366.9	367.5	367.6	361.6

Employment by Industry: Indiana—*Continued*

(Numbers in thousands. Not seasonally adjusted.)

Industry	January	February	March	April	May	June	July	August	September	October	November	December	Annual Average
STATEWIDE—*Continued*													
Leisure and hospitality													
1990	195.6	196.6	201.5	202.6	211.0	213.6	214.4	216.9	214.8	207.3	205.4	205.8	207.1
1991	194.7	194.8	200.0	206.2	213.0	215.6	210.9	212.8	211.7	206.1	203.1	202.1	205.9
1992	194.2	195.9	200.8	208.8	217.2	218.7	217.9	219.6	217.9	215.1	213.2	211.2	210.8
1993	202.6	205.0	209.0	217.4	226.2	228.8	226.5	228.2	226.5	223.2	220.6	220.8	219.5
1994	211.9	213.1	218.7	224.7	232.9	236.5	233.2	235.8	234.3	226.4	225.4	226.4	226.6
1995	218.6	220.4	227.0	234.4	243.4	246.3	244.9	247.9	246.2	238.2	235.7	236.5	236.6
1996	224.3	228.0	233.5	240.8	251.0	254.6	252.7	257.8	251.5	246.9	246.1	246.1	244.4
1997	232.5	236.5	242.1	247.7	257.0	259.0	258.2	261.6	258.3	250.6	247.1	246.1	249.7
1998	235.9	239.5	244.9	252.8	263.8	265.6	260.6	264.2	259.6	257.8	255.9	256.3	254.7
1999	239.5	244.7	250.9	260.8	270.9	275.0	271.5	273.2	268.9	263.8	261.7	261.6	261.8
2000	249.4	251.3	257.8	266.2	274.0	278.6	273.6	276.3	272.4	268.5	263.4	261.1	266.0
2001	249.0	252.5	259.5	267.1	276.0	282.0	277.6	281.9	275.2	269.7	264.2	262.2	268.1
2002	250.5	252.1	257.1	266.2	276.3	280.9	278.7	282.1	276.1	271.2	266.5	265.0	268.6
2003	253.9	253.2	258.4	270.0	279.9	284.2	283.4	285.4	278.7	277.4	272.8	272.6	272.5
Other services													
1990	93.8	94.1	94.9	94.7	95.1	96.2	96.0	96.3	96.0	96.6	96.7	96.6	95.5
1991	95.6	95.9	96.8	97.4	97.9	98.9	97.4	97.5	97.3	97.5	97.5	97.7	97.2
1992	96.3	96.6	97.3	97.6	98.5	99.3	100.8	100.9	101.0	100.9	100.6	101.1	99.2
1993	101.2	101.4	101.2	100.8	101.3	102.1	101.8	101.6	101.8	102.5	102.4	103.1	101.7
1994	100.6	101.5	103.5	103.8	104.4	105.6	104.0	103.9	104.1	104.2	104.3	105.1	103.7
1995	102.9	103.8	105.3	105.4	106.1	107.3	105.5	105.6	105.6	105.0	105.1	105.8	105.2
1996	103.9	104.7	106.0	106.2	107.4	107.8	106.7	106.9	106.7	105.9	105.5	105.9	106.1
1997	103.1	103.7	104.6	105.7	106.9	107.4	106.3	106.3	105.8	105.8	104.9	105.6	105.5
1998	103.9	104.7	105.6	105.9	106.6	107.4	106.9	106.4	106.3	107.1	106.6	107.1	106.2
1999	103.9	105.8	106.4	107.4	107.9	109.1	108.1	108.3	107.9	107.9	107.5	107.9	107.3
2000	106.1	107.0	108.4	109.0	109.5	110.3	108.7	108.9	108.6	107.7	107.5	107.7	108.2
2001	106.3	107.1	108.2	108.6	109.6	111.0	109.2	108.9	107.2	106.3	106.2	106.4	107.9
2002	104.0	104.7	105.6	106.5	108.0	109.0	107.8	107.6	106.4	106.1	105.9	106.1	106.5
2003	104.1	104.7	105.4	106.0	106.9	108.0	107.6	106.6	105.5	105.2	105.2	105.0	105.9
Government													
1990	373.2	380.7	381.8	385.0	386.7	374.3	360.7	362.4	382.1	385.5	385.9	384.8	378.5
1991	376.6	385.6	386.7	388.1	386.3	367.9	348.1	355.3	385.6	391.6	393.1	394.3	379.9
1992	384.7	394.3	391.7	395.1	392.5	377.3	359.6	364.4	394.2	398.9	399.2	399.1	387.5
1993	389.7	398.5	398.7	399.4	396.6	383.5	362.7	364.1	397.1	400.3	402.1	402.9	391.3
1994	398.4	406.5	407.8	392.8	391.7	368.6	355.7	355.6	399.5	403.2	405.2	403.0	390.6
1995	392.8	403.2	404.4	405.3	399.6	368.9	352.9	349.1	402.9	406.8	407.4	406.7	391.6
1996	393.6	405.7	406.9	406.6	403.9	375.9	343.0	344.9	401.4	404.4	404.8	401.0	391.0
1997	389.4	401.6	401.9	402.6	402.2	379.6	353.2	351.9	400.1	406.0	407.0	408.4	391.9
1998	399.0	408.5	408.5	409.8	409.3	386.4	352.3	361.1	408.4	414.2	415.4	417.1	399.1
1999	396.2	411.6	413.3	414.2	419.0	391.6	358.1	359.0	414.1	417.4	418.3	418.9	402.6
2000	411.7	418.8	422.3	423.8	430.9	396.6	370.8	373.7	422.7	417.6	418.3	416.6	410.3
2001	409.3	422.8	425.7	424.5	420.1	390.2	360.4	374.6	419.6	424.6	424.7	423.5	410.0
2002	409.5	424.0	423.9	426.6	425.1	393.1	376.8	391.4	427.8	434.5	435.9	435.2	417.0
2003	422.7	431.1	434.0	432.1	433.1	403.0	378.9	393.3	432.9	438.5	436.8	436.2	422.7
Federal government													
1990	46.1	46.1	46.6	49.2	52.4	49.4	49.1	47.8	47.1	45.7	45.6	45.8	47.5
1991	45.1	45.0	44.7	44.9	45.0	45.3	45.5	45.0	45.2	45.1	45.2	45.5	45.1
1992	45.1	44.9	42.4	44.9	44.9	45.0	45.2	44.9	44.7	44.7	44.1	44.5	44.6
1993	44.2	44.3	44.3	44.7	44.8	45.1	45.0	44.7	44.5	44.3	44.2	44.9	44.5
1994	44.1	44.0	43.9	43.7	43.6	43.7	43.5	43.1	42.7	42.3	42.2	42.8	43.3
1995	42.3	42.3	42.2	43.3	42.3	42.3	42.4	42.4	42.1	42.1	42.1	42.5	42.3
1996	41.5	41.5	41.4	41.3	40.9	40.7	40.2	39.9	39.3	38.5	38.4	38.9	40.2
1997	38.3	38.0	38.1	38.1	38.0	38.0	37.9	37.8	38.0	37.9	38.8	39.6	38.2
1998	38.8	38.7	38.6	38.6	38.7	38.7	38.5	38.3	38.6	39.4	40.3	40.8	39.0
1999	39.4	39.3	39.1	40.3	39.2	39.3	39.1	39.2	39.2	39.3	40.0	40.5	39.4
2000	39.9	41.4	42.6	45.6	50.5	50.1	45.6	45.6	39.6	39.2	39.0	39.8	43.2
2001	38.8	38.7	38.7	38.8	38.8	39.0	39.2	38.9	38.3	37.7	37.9	38.1	38.6
2002	37.4	36.8	36.8	37.0	37.1	37.5	37.3	36.9	36.7	37.4	37.4	37.6	37.2
2003	37.5	37.4	37.3	37.2	37.1	37.2	37.0	36.9	36.8	36.8	36.5	36.9	37.1
State government													
1990	100.9	104.3	103.4	104.2	99.1	91.9	94.4	93.5	103.9	104.5	104.3	101.9	100.5
1991	99.4	103.7	104.1	105.2	99.4	93.8	92.4	96.9	104.4	107.0	108.1	106.9	101.7
1992	103.1	108.7	108.4	108.9	101.9	97.6	96.6	96.8	109.1	110.7	110.8	109.8	105.2
1993	105.3	109.6	109.7	109.9	102.9	96.4	97.3	95.9	110.2	110.6	110.8	109.9	105.7
1994	110.0	114.8	114.8	110.4	105.5	95.1	97.9	100.0	110.0	110.9	111.1	107.8	107.3
1995	104.9	110.3	110.3	111.2	102.1	94.7	93.0	93.2	110.3	111.0	111.5	108.2	105.0
1996	105.7	110.6	110.2	111.4	104.2	94.1	92.9	93.5	108.8	109.3	108.4	102.3	104.2
1997	102.3	107.2	105.8	107.5	102.4	95.7	96.3	93.6	105.5	107.7	107.4	105.9	103.1
1998	103.2	107.7	107.1	108.7	103.5	96.6	90.8	94.3	107.5	109.0	109.0	108.1	103.7
1999	103.6	106.4	106.8	107.6	109.0	95.1	94.7	91.7	108.7	108.4	108.1	107.1	103.9
2000	105.5	108.3	109.4	109.2	107.4	96.1	95.5	94.5	114.7	109.7	111.0	107.4	105.7
2001	108.0	114.3	115.4	115.8	106.9	101.0	99.7	99.0	111.5	113.9	113.8	110.1	109.1
2002	106.6	113.0	112.2	115.4	109.3	101.7	103.0	101.0	116.4	119.1	119.6	117.2	111.2
2003	112.5	116.1	117.2	116.5	112.5	103.9	104.2	104.7	119.2	121.9	121.0	119.0	114.1

Employment by Industry: Indiana—*Continued*

(Numbers in thousands. Not seasonally adjusted.)

Industry	January	February	March	April	May	June	July	August	September	October	November	December	Annual Average
STATEWIDE—*Continued*													
Local government													
1990	226.3	230.4	231.8	231.6	235.2	232.9	217.2	221.1	231.2	235.3	236.0	237.1	230.5
1991	232.0	237.0	238.0	238.0	241.8	228.8	210.2	213.4	236.1	239.4	239.9	242.0	233.0
1992	236.5	240.7	240.9	241.3	245.7	234.7	217.8	222.7	240.4	243.5	244.3	244.8	237.7
1993	240.2	244.6	244.7	244.8	248.9	242.0	220.4	223.5	242.4	245.4	247.1	248.1	241.0
1994	244.3	247.7	249.1	238.7	242.6	229.8	214.3	212.5	246.8	250.0	251.9	252.4	240.0
1995	245.6	250.6	251.9	250.8	255.2	231.9	217.5	213.5	250.5	253.7	253.8	256.0	244.2
1996	246.4	253.6	255.3	253.9	258.8	241.1	209.9	211.5	253.3	256.6	258.0	259.8	246.5
1997	248.8	256.4	258.0	257.0	261.8	245.9	219.0	220.5	256.6	260.4	260.8	262.9	250.6
1998	257.0	262.1	262.8	262.5	267.1	251.1	223.0	228.5	262.3	265.8	266.1	268.2	256.3
1999	253.2	265.9	267.4	266.3	270.8	257.2	224.3	228.1	266.2	269.7	270.2	271.3	259.2
2000	266.3	269.1	270.3	269.0	273.0	250.4	229.7	233.6	268.4	268.7	268.3	269.4	261.3
2001	262.5	269.8	271.6	269.9	274.4	250.2	221.5	236.7	269.8	273.0	273.0	275.3	262.3
2002	265.5	274.2	274.9	274.2	278.7	253.9	236.5	253.5	274.7	278.0	278.9	280.4	268.6
2003	272.7	277.6	279.5	278.4	283.5	261.9	237.7	251.7	276.9	279.8	279.3	280.3	271.6
FORT WAYNE													
Total nonfarm													
1990	233.7	233.4	235.7	235.3	236.3	237.4	235.9	237.4	240.3	239.5	238.4	238.0	236.8
1991	229.5	227.9	229.1	232.9	235.8	236.0	235.1	237.0	239.7	239.2	239.5	238.5	235.0
1992	231.7	233.8	235.8	237.7	240.4	240.4	241.0	241.4	243.5	244.4	244.1	243.9	239.8
1993	239.6	240.0	241.7	244.5	246.4	246.5	245.4	244.8	247.4	247.6	248.7	249.2	245.2
1994	242.9	243.7	247.1	249.7	253.2	256.0	252.3	252.4	258.0	256.8	258.2	259.9	252.5
1995	253.7	255.4	258.0	259.4	262.7	261.4	257.0	258.8	264.6	262.6	263.1	264.2	260.1
1996	255.8	256.6	256.7	261.1	264.9	265.8	261.3	263.5	266.2	266.5	267.7	268.7	262.9
1997	261.6	262.2	263.5	267.1	270.7	271.0	268.2	269.0	272.7	273.9	273.4	274.7	269.0
1998	266.6	267.0	268.5	272.8	276.1	275.8	268.9	273.0	277.6	277.5	278.7	280.7	273.6
1999	268.7	270.2	271.8	275.2	276.4	275.8	274.9	275.1	279.0	278.8	279.1	280.5	275.5
2000	273.7	274.3	277.5	278.9	281.4	280.1	273.9	274.3	277.3	275.0	274.7	274.7	276.3
2001	269.8	269.4	271.2	272.7	275.6	272.8	267.5	269.8	273.5	271.5	271.6	271.2	271.4
2002	263.1	263.2	265.2	267.4	270.5	267.2	266.8	269.9	272.4	271.8	271.8	271.5	268.4
2003	263.0	262.1	263.1	264.9	267.3	262.8	260.0	262.5	263.6	264.9	264.9	265.0	263.7
Total private													
1990	210.2	209.4	211.6	211.3	212.2	214.2	213.4	213.4	216.3	215.0	213.8	215.5	213.0
1991	205.4	203.4	204.4	208.3	211.2	213.5	213.2	214.7	215.1	214.6	214.8	213.6	211.0
1992	207.5	209.0	210.9	212.9	215.6	217.4	218.6	218.7	218.9	219.4	219.0	218.7	215.6
1993	214.9	215.0	216.5	219.2	220.8	221.8	222.5	222.7	222.0	222.1	223.1	223.4	220.3
1994	217.9	218.1	221.3	223.8	227.1	230.8	230.4	230.9	232.3	230.7	232.3	233.9	227.5
1995	228.0	229.3	231.7	233.2	236.2	239.5	235.5	237.6	237.8	235.6	236.1	237.0	234.8
1996	229.6	229.7	229.6	234.0	237.5	240.1	238.8	240.2	239.8	239.5	240.3	241.1	236.7
1997	235.2	235.2	236.2	239.8	243.1	245.3	244.1	245.5	245.3	246.6	245.8	247.0	242.4
1998	239.8	239.7	241.3	245.7	248.5	251.1	246.7	250.0	250.1	249.9	251.0	252.7	247.2
1999	242.4	242.9	244.5	247.3	248.6	250.2	252.2	252.8	251.4	251.0	251.2	252.5	248.9
2000	246.6	246.7	249.4	250.6	252.5	253.5	251.1	251.7	250.0	247.4	247.0	246.9	249.5
2001	242.6	241.8	243.2	245.0	247.2	248.5	246.4	246.8	245.7	243.3	243.2	242.7	244.7
2002	235.8	234.9	236.8	239.9	242.3	244.5	243.6	245.8	244.3	243.1	243.2	242.8	241.4
2003	235.5	233.9	234.8	236.8	238.7	239.9	238.1	239.3	238.7	239.6	239.7	239.6	237.9
Goods-producing													
1990	73.2	72.7	73.6	74.1	74.4	75.3	75.0	75.0	76.0	75.1	71.4	71.5	73.9
1991	68.3	67.1	67.2	69.3	70.5	72.0	72.2	72.9	73.0	72.6	72.1	71.1	70.7
1992	68.3	69.8	70.6	70.7	72.3	73.6	74.2	74.1	74.1	73.7	73.2	72.7	72.3
1993	72.4	72.5	73.4	74.9	76.0	76.6	77.5	77.5	77.4	76.0	76.0	75.6	75.5
1994	75.2	75.3	76.3	77.0	78.2	79.5	78.9	79.5	80.3	79.9	80.0	80.7	78.4
1995	81.1	81.6	81.8	82.9	84.1	85.1	83.0	84.0	83.7	82.8	82.7	82.9	83.0
1996	80.7	80.5	80.2	81.5	82.7	84.3	83.8	84.7	84.5	84.7	84.5	84.2	83.0
1997	83.0	83.0	83.0	84.4	85.8	86.6	85.9	86.6	86.4	86.8	85.6	85.7	85.2
1998	84.2	84.7	84.8	85.7	86.5	87.8	86.1	87.4	87.3	86.6	86.2	86.2	86.1
1999	84.2	84.0	84.4	85.0	85.3	86.0	86.8	87.2	86.6	85.8	85.6	85.6	85.5
2000	84.7	85.0	85.4	86.6	87.8	88.2	86.1	85.7	84.4	82.7	81.4	81.0	84.9
2001	77.7	77.8	77.6	78.1	78.4	78.5	77.1	77.4	76.7	75.3	74.6	74.4	77.0
2002	72.4	72.2	72.8	73.9	74.7	75.8	75.2	76.5	76.1	75.8	74.9	74.6	74.6
2003	72.6	71.7	71.8	72.1	72.5	72.9	72.0	73.0	72.5	72.4	71.9	71.9	72.3
Construction and mining													
1990	9.7	9.5	9.7	10.0	10.4	11.1	11.2	11.3	11.2	10.8	10.7	10.4	10.5
1991	9.3	8.9	9.2	9.3	10.0	10.6	10.7	10.7	10.4	10.4	10.2	10.0	10.0
1992	9.2	8.9	9.2	9.5	10.0	10.5	11.0	10.9	10.5	10.3	10.0	9.9	10.0
1993	9.2	9.0	9.0	9.5	10.2	10.6	11.3	11.2	10.7	10.7	10.5	10.5	10.2
1994	9.6	9.3	9.7	10.4	11.1	11.8	12.1	11.9	11.7	11.4	11.4	11.5	11.0
1995	10.5	10.3	10.6	11.1	11.6	12.3	12.5	12.4	12.1	11.6	11.4	11.2	11.5
1996	10.3	10.1	10.4	11.3	11.9	12.8	12.7	12.8	12.5	12.5	12.2	11.9	11.8
1997	11.0	10.9	11.3	11.9	12.6	13.1	13.3	13.3	12.9	13.1	12.9	12.5	12.4
1998	11.5	11.4	11.5	12.3	12.7	13.4	13.6	13.8	13.6	13.5	13.2	13.0	12.8
1999	12.0	11.9	12.4	12.7	13.2	13.7	14.3	14.4	13.9	13.9	13.7	13.6	13.3
2000	12.5	12.4	13.1	13.8	14.4	14.9	14.8	14.9	14.6	14.0	13.9	13.4	13.9
2001	12.4	12.5	12.9	13.9	14.6	15.2	15.3	15.1	14.6	14.4	14.3	13.9	14.1
2002	13.0	12.7	12.9	13.4	13.9	14.4	14.7	14.7	14.5	14.4	14.2	13.9	13.9
2003	12.9	12.4	12.5	13.3	14.0	14.5	14.9	14.9	14.5	14.4	14.3	14.2	13.9

Employment by Industry: Indiana—*Continued*

(Numbers in thousands. Not seasonally adjusted.)

Industry	January	February	March	April	May	June	July	August	September	October	November	December	Annual Average
FORT WAYNE—*Continued*													
Manufacturing													
1990	63.5	63.2	63.9	64.1	64.0	64.2	63.8	63.7	64.8	64.3	60.7	61.1	63.4
1991	59.0	58.2	58.0	60.0	60.5	61.4	61.5	62.2	62.6	62.2	61.9	61.1	60.7
1992	59.1	60.9	61.4	61.2	62.3	63.1	63.2	63.2	63.6	63.4	63.2	62.8	62.3
1993	63.2	63.5	64.4	65.4	65.8	66.0	66.2	66.3	66.7	65.3	65.5	65.1	65.3
1994	65.6	66.0	66.6	66.6	67.1	67.7	66.8	67.6	68.6	68.5	68.6	69.2	67.4
1995	70.6	71.3	71.2	71.8	72.5	72.8	70.5	71.6	71.6	71.2	71.3	71.7	71.5
1996	70.4	70.4	69.8	70.2	70.8	71.5	71.1	71.9	72.0	72.2	72.3	72.3	71.2
1997	72.0	72.1	71.7	72.5	73.2	73.5	72.6	73.3	73.5	73.7	72.7	73.2	72.8
1998	72.7	73.3	73.3	73.4	73.8	74.4	72.5	73.6	73.7	73.1	73.0	73.2	73.3
1999	72.2	72.1	72.0	72.3	72.1	72.3	72.5	72.8	72.7	71.9	71.9	72.0	72.2
2000	72.2	72.6	72.3	72.8	73.4	73.3	71.3	70.8	69.8	68.7	67.5	67.6	71.0
2001	65.3	65.3	64.7	64.2	63.8	63.3	61.8	62.3	62.1	60.9	60.3	60.5	62.9
2002	59.4	59.5	59.9	60.5	60.8	61.4	60.5	61.8	61.6	61.4	60.7	60.7	60.7
2003	59.7	59.3	59.3	58.8	58.5	58.4	57.1	58.1	58.0	58.0	57.6	57.7	58.4
Service-providing													
1990	160.5	160.7	162.1	161.2	161.9	162.1	160.9	162.4	164.3	164.4	167.0	166.5	162.8
1991	161.2	160.8	161.9	163.6	165.3	164.0	162.9	164.1	166.7	166.6	167.4	167.4	164.3
1992	163.4	164.0	165.2	167.0	168.1	166.8	166.8	167.3	169.4	170.7	170.9	171.2	167.6
1993	167.2	167.5	168.3	169.6	170.4	169.9	167.9	167.3	170.0	171.6	172.7	173.6	169.7
1994	167.7	168.4	170.8	172.7	175.0	176.5	173.4	172.9	177.7	176.9	178.2	179.2	174.1
1995	172.6	173.8	176.2	176.5	178.6	176.3	174.0	174.8	180.9	179.8	180.4	181.3	177.1
1996	175.1	176.1	176.5	179.6	182.2	181.5	177.5	178.8	181.7	181.8	183.2	184.5	179.9
1997	178.6	179.2	180.5	182.7	184.9	184.4	182.3	182.4	186.3	187.1	187.8	189.0	183.8
1998	182.4	182.3	183.7	187.1	189.6	188.0	182.8	185.6	190.3	190.9	192.5	194.5	187.5
1999	184.5	186.2	187.4	190.2	191.1	189.8	188.1	187.9	192.4	193.0	193.5	194.9	189.9
2000	189.0	189.3	192.1	192.3	193.6	191.9	187.8	188.6	192.9	192.3	193.3	193.7	191.4
2001	192.1	191.6	193.6	194.6	197.2	194.3	190.4	192.4	196.8	196.2	197.0	196.8	194.4
2002	190.7	191.0	192.4	193.5	195.8	191.4	191.6	193.4	196.3	196.0	196.9	196.9	193.8
2003	190.4	190.4	191.3	192.8	194.8	189.9	188.0	189.5	191.1	192.5	193.0	193.1	191.4
Trade, transportation, and utilities													
1990	52.7	52.4	52.4	51.6	51.6	51.9	51.5	51.6	52.4	52.2	54.1	54.8	52.4
1991	51.4	50.7	50.6	51.9	52.3	52.2	52.1	52.3	52.0	51.5	52.9	53.2	51.9
1992	50.9	50.5	50.5	51.3	51.0	51.4	52.2	52.4	52.3	52.7	53.7	54.4	51.9
1993	51.7	51.1	50.9	50.8	50.1	50.4	50.2	49.8	49.1	49.4	50.2	51.0	50.4
1994	48.8	48.1	48.7	49.6	50.5	51.9	51.7	51.7	51.4	51.0	52.3	53.2	50.7
1995	51.0	51.0	51.7	51.8	52.3	53.1	52.9	52.9	53.0	53.1	54.0	54.7	52.6
1996	52.6	51.9	51.9	52.5	53.0	53.6	53.4	53.7	53.5	53.3	54.4	55.3	53.3
1997	53.7	53.0	53.2	53.7	54.2	54.6	54.6	54.5	54.3	55.0	55.8	56.9	54.5
1998	54.1	53.7	53.8	54.3	54.7	55.2	54.7	55.5	55.0	55.4	56.8	57.5	55.1
1999	54.5	54.0	54.4	55.2	55.9	56.2	56.8	57.1	56.7	57.3	58.2	59.3	56.3
2000	57.2	56.8	57.4	58.0	58.7	58.8	58.3	57.6	56.7	57.1	58.5	59.1	57.9
2001	57.1	56.3	56.3	56.6	57.1	57.6	57.1	57.4	57.5	57.1	58.1	58.2	57.2
2002	55.8	54.8	54.7	54.8	55.2	55.3	55.1	55.3	55.0	54.8	56.1	56.4	55.3
2003	54.0	53.4	53.2	53.7	53.8	54.3	54.0	54.1	53.9	54.4	55.4	55.7	54.2
Wholesale trade													
1990	11.7	11.8	11.8	11.6	11.6	11.8	11.9	11.7	12.0	12.2	12.3	12.3	11.9
1991	11.9	11.9	11.8	11.8	11.9	11.9	11.9	11.9	11.9	11.8	11.9	11.9	11.9
1992	11.7	11.8	11.7	12.4	11.7	11.8	11.9	11.8	11.8	11.7	11.7	11.8	11.8
1993	11.7	11.7	11.7	11.7	11.7	11.8	11.9	11.8	11.8	11.8	11.7	11.7	11.8
1994	11.6	11.6	11.7	11.9	12.0	12.1	12.3	12.3	12.2	12.2	12.3	12.4	12.1
1995	12.4	12.5	12.7	12.7	12.8	13.1	13.1	13.1	13.1	13.0	13.0	13.2	12.9
1996	13.1	13.1	13.2	13.2	13.3	13.5	13.4	13.3	13.3	13.4	13.5	13.5	13.3
1997	13.5	13.6	13.7	14.0	14.0	14.2	14.2	14.1	14.1	14.1	14.2	14.4	14.0
1998	14.4	14.5	14.6	14.5	14.6	14.8	14.6	14.6	14.7	15.0	15.0	15.0	14.7
1999	14.5	14.4	14.6	15.0	15.3	15.5	15.3	15.4	15.4	15.4	15.4	15.5	15.1
2000	15.5	15.6	15.9	16.3	16.3	16.4	16.2	16.0	15.9	15.9	15.9	15.9	16.0
2001	15.7	15.6	15.6	15.7	15.7	15.8	15.6	15.6	15.8	15.8	15.8	15.7	15.7
2002	15.7	15.4	15.5	15.4	15.3	15.2	15.1	15.0	14.9	14.3	14.4	14.3	15.0
2003	14.3	14.2	14.2	14.3	14.3	14.2	14.1	14.0	13.8	13.9	13.7	13.8	14.1
Retail trade													
1990	29.1	28.6	28.5	27.9	28.0	27.9	27.7	28.0	28.4	28.4	29.9	30.4	28.6
1991	28.2	27.6	27.6	27.5	27.6	27.5	27.4	27.5	27.2	27.5	29.0	29.4	27.8
1992	27.6	27.0	27.1	26.8	27.0	27.3	27.3	27.7	27.6	28.2	29.3	30.0	27.7
1993	27.8	27.2	27.0	26.9	26.0	26.2	26.2	26.5	26.1	26.8	27.7	28.5	26.9
1994	26.7	26.0	26.3	26.7	27.5	28.8	28.4	28.4	28.3	28.1	29.2	30.1	27.9
1995	28.2	28.0	28.4	28.3	28.6	29.0	28.8	28.8	28.9	29.3	30.2	30.7	28.9
1996	29.2	28.5	28.3	28.5	28.8	29.0	29.0	29.2	28.9	28.8	29.9	30.8	29.1
1997	29.4	28.7	28.7	28.8	29.1	29.4	29.5	29.6	29.2	30.1	30.9	31.7	29.6
1998	29.3	28.8	28.8	29.2	29.4	29.7	29.3	29.8	29.4	29.6	30.8	31.6	29.6
1999	29.6	29.1	29.3	29.4	29.7	29.9	29.8	30.0	29.7	30.4	31.2	32.2	30.0
2000	30.5	29.9	30.2	30.4	31.0	31.0	30.6	30.2	29.7	30.0	31.2	31.8	30.5
2001	30.4	29.7	29.7	29.8	30.2	30.1	29.6	29.6	29.5	29.5	30.5	30.8	30.0
2002	29.0	28.4	28.3	28.5	28.9	29.0	28.8	29.0	28.8	28.9	30.0	30.6	29.0
2003	28.6	28.1	28.1	28.5	28.7	29.2	29.0	29.2	29.0	29.3	30.4	30.7	29.1

Employment by Industry: Indiana—*Continued*

(Numbers in thousands. Not seasonally adjusted.)

Industry	January	February	March	April	May	June	July	August	September	October	November	December	Annual Average
FORT WAYNE—*Continued*													
Transportation and utilities													
1990	11.9	12.0	12.1	12.1	12.0	12.2	11.9	11.9	12.0	11.6	11.9	12.1	12.0
1991	11.3	11.2	11.2	12.6	12.8	12.8	12.8	12.9	12.9	12.2	12.0	11.9	12.2
1992	11.6	11.7	11.7	12.1	12.3	12.3	13.0	12.9	12.9	12.8	12.7	12.6	12.4
1993	12.2	12.2	12.2	12.2	12.4	12.4	12.1	11.5	11.2	10.8	10.8	10.8	11.7
1994	10.5	10.5	10.7	11.0	11.0	11.0	11.0	11.0	10.9	10.7	10.8	10.7	10.8
1995	10.4	10.5	10.6	10.8	10.9	11.0	11.0	11.0	11.0	10.8	10.8	10.8	10.8
1996	10.3	10.3	10.4	10.8	10.9	11.1	11.0	11.2	11.3	11.1	11.0	11.0	10.9
1997	10.8	10.7	10.8	10.9	11.1	11.0	10.9	10.8	11.0	10.8	10.7	10.8	10.9
1998	10.4	10.4	10.4	10.6	10.7	10.7	10.8	11.1	10.9	10.8	11.0	10.9	10.7
1999	10.4	10.5	10.5	10.8	10.9	10.8	11.7	11.7	11.6	11.5	11.6	11.6	11.1
2000	11.2	11.3	11.3	11.3	11.4	11.4	11.5	11.4	11.1	11.2	11.4	11.4	11.3
2001	11.0	11.0	11.0	11.1	11.2	11.7	11.9	12.2	12.2	11.8	11.8	11.7	11.6
2002	11.1	11.0	10.9	10.9	11.0	11.1	11.2	11.3	11.3	11.6	11.7	11.5	11.2
2003	11.1	11.1	10.9	10.9	10.8	10.9	10.9	10.9	11.1	11.2	11.3	11.2	11.0
Information													
1990	5.9	5.9	5.9	5.9	5.9	6.0	5.9	5.9	6.0	5.8	5.9	6.0	5.9
1991	5.7	5.7	5.8	5.7	5.7	5.8	5.8	5.8	5.8	5.9	5.9	5.9	5.8
1992	5.8	5.7	5.8	5.7	5.8	5.8	5.9	5.9	5.9	5.9	5.9	5.9	5.8
1993	5.7	5.7	5.7	5.7	5.6	5.7	5.8	5.7	5.7	5.7	5.7	5.8	5.7
1994	5.5	5.6	5.6	5.6	5.7	5.7	5.9	5.6	5.6	5.6	5.6	5.7	5.6
1995	5.4	5.5	5.5	5.3	5.4	5.6	5.4	5.3	5.5	5.3	5.4	5.3	5.4
1996	4.9	4.9	4.9	4.9	4.9	4.9	4.9	4.9	5.1	5.2	5.2	5.3	5.0
1997	5.1	5.2	5.2	5.3	5.3	5.5	5.2	5.3	5.4	4.3	4.3	4.4	5.0
1998	5.4	5.5	5.5	5.6	5.6	5.7	5.6	5.8	5.8	5.8	5.8	5.8	5.7
1999	5.6	5.6	5.6	5.8	5.9	6.0	5.6	5.6	5.7	5.6	5.6	5.7	5.7
2000	5.8	5.9	5.9	5.5	5.5	5.6	5.3	5.3	5.3	5.3	5.4	5.3	5.5
2001	5.4	5.3	5.5	5.3	5.3	5.3	5.2	5.2	5.1	5.1	5.2	5.2	5.3
2002	5.0	4.9	5.0	4.8	4.8	4.8	4.8	4.8	4.7	4.7	4.8	4.7	4.8
2003	4.4	4.4	4.5	4.4	4.5	4.5	4.5	4.4	4.4	4.4	4.3	4.3	4.4
Financial activities													
1990	14.6	14.7	14.9	14.9	15.0	15.2	15.2	15.0	15.1	15.0	15.1	15.3	15.0
1991	14.9	14.9	14.9	15.0	15.1	15.5	15.4	15.4	15.3	15.2	15.1	15.2	15.2
1992	14.8	14.7	14.7	14.8	14.8	14.7	14.4	14.3	14.2	14.0	13.9	14.0	14.4
1993	14.1	14.1	14.0	14.0	14.0	14.1	14.1	14.0	13.9	14.0	14.0	14.1	14.0
1994	14.0	14.0	14.1	14.4	14.7	15.1	15.2	15.2	15.1	15.2	15.2	15.3	14.8
1995	14.8	14.8	14.8	15.0	15.1	15.5	15.3	15.3	15.2	15.0	14.9	15.0	15.1
1996	14.9	14.9	14.9	15.2	15.4	15.8	15.9	15.8	15.5	15.4	15.4	15.7	15.4
1997	15.8	15.8	15.8	15.8	16.0	16.2	16.3	16.3	16.1	16.3	16.3	16.4	16.1
1998	16.3	15.9	15.9	16.2	16.2	16.4	16.4	16.4	16.2	15.8	15.4	15.3	16.0
1999	15.5	15.4	15.2	15.0	15.1	15.2	15.1	15.1	14.7	14.7	14.6	14.7	15.0
2000	14.8	14.7	14.9	15.2	15.3	15.3	15.2	15.1	15.0	15.0	15.1	15.3	15.1
2001	15.3	15.4	15.5	15.4	15.5	15.5	15.4	15.2	14.9	14.8	14.9	15.0	15.2
2002	14.6	14.5	14.7	14.8	14.8	14.9	14.7	14.7	14.6	14.5	14.5	14.6	14.7
2003	14.3	14.3	14.5	14.4	14.5	14.8	14.8	14.7	14.5	14.5	14.3	14.3	14.5
Professional and business services													
1990	13.8	13.9	14.4	14.4	14.6	14.9	14.8	15.2	15.3	15.3	15.2	15.0	14.7
1991	14.0	14.1	14.3	14.6	14.9	15.5	15.5	16.0	16.3	16.4	16.0	15.4	15.3
1992	15.6	15.8	16.4	17.1	17.4	17.7	17.4	17.5	17.7	17.5	16.9	16.4	17.0
1993	16.4	16.9	17.5	18.0	18.3	18.3	18.5	19.1	19.1	19.6	20.0	19.7	18.5
1994	18.4	19.0	19.8	19.7	20.3	20.8	20.9	21.4	21.6	21.3	21.3	20.9	20.5
1995	19.6	20.0	20.5	20.3	20.9	21.4	20.7	21.7	21.6	21.4	21.5	21.2	20.9
1996	19.5	20.2	19.9	20.7	21.3	21.4	20.8	20.9	20.8	21.1	20.8	20.5	20.7
1997	19.6	19.7	19.9	21.2	21.3	21.8	22.0	22.4	22.3	23.1	23.0	22.8	21.6
1998	20.8	20.6	21.2	23.1	23.5	24.3	23.7	24.3	24.6	25.0	25.6	26.1	23.6
1999	23.1	23.5	23.9	24.6	24.2	24.5	25.3	25.1	24.9	25.0	24.9	24.8	24.5
2000	22.7	22.4	23.1	24.1	24.3	24.5	25.0	25.1	24.6	23.5	23.1	22.7	23.8
2001	21.9	21.4	21.8	22.0	22.3	22.5	22.8	22.8	22.6	22.6	22.1	21.9	22.2
2002	20.8	20.8	21.3	22.2	22.7	23.3	23.6	24.0	23.4	22.9	22.8	22.5	22.5
2003	21.7	21.5	21.8	21.7	22.1	22.1	21.7	21.7	22.0	22.0	22.2	22.1	21.9
Educational and health services													
1990	23.2	23.2	23.3	23.3	23.3	23.3	23.5	23.4	24.1	24.3	24.6	24.9	23.7
1991	24.4	24.4	24.5	24.4	24.5	24.3	24.4	24.5	24.9	25.6	25.6	25.6	24.8
1992	25.5	25.7	25.8	25.7	26.0	25.9	26.1	26.0	26.3	26.8	26.7	26.7	26.1
1993	26.8	26.9	27.0	27.4	27.4	27.1	26.9	27.0	27.4	28.1	28.3	28.2	27.4
1994	27.6	27.9	28.0	28.3	28.2	27.9	27.9	27.8	28.1	28.0	28.1	28.1	28.0
1995	27.5	28.0	28.1	28.3	28.0	28.1	27.8	27.8	28.3	28.6	28.7	28.6	28.2
1996	28.1	28.3	28.4	28.6	28.7	28.6	28.6	28.8	29.2	29.4	29.6	29.4	28.8
1997	28.7	29.1	29.3	29.1	29.3	29.2	28.9	29.1	29.5	30.1	30.3	30.3	29.4
1998	29.9	30.1	30.4	30.3	30.7	30.3	29.5	29.7	30.2	30.6	30.7	31.0	30.3
1999	30.2	30.8	31.0	30.9	30.8	30.6	30.8	31.1	31.5	31.9	32.0	32.0	31.1
2000	31.5	32.0	32.2	29.5	28.3	28.1	29.2	30.9	32.4	33.0	33.0	33.0	31.1
2001	30.8	31.1	31.5	31.8	31.9	32.1	32.0	32.0	32.6	32.7	33.0	32.7	32.0
2002	32.6	33.0	33.2	33.3	33.2	33.2	33.2	33.5	34.0	34.1	34.1	34.1	33.5
2003	33.3	33.8	33.9	34.2	34.2	33.8	34.0	34.2	34.4	34.8	34.9	34.9	34.2

Employment by Industry: Indiana—*Continued*

(Numbers in thousands. Not seasonally adjusted.)

Industry	January	February	March	April	May	June	July	August	September	October	November	December	Annual Average
FORT WAYNE—*Continued*													
Leisure and hospitality													
1990	17.9	17.8	18.2	18.2	18.5	18.6	18.6	18.4	18.5	18.2	18.3	18.6	18.3
1991	17.6	17.4	17.9	18.2	18.9	18.7	18.4	18.4	18.6	18.2	18.0	18.0	18.2
1992	17.4	17.6	17.9	18.5	19.1	19.0	18.9	19.0	19.0	19.1	19.1	19.0	18.6
1993	18.3	18.2	18.4	18.8	19.6	19.7	19.6	19.7	19.6	19.4	19.1	19.0	19.1
1994	18.7	18.6	19.0	19.3	19.6	19.7	19.8	19.7	20.1	19.7	19.7	19.8	19.5
1995	18.7	18.4	19.1	19.4	20.0	20.2	20.2	20.4	20.4	19.4	18.9	19.1	19.5
1996	18.9	18.9	19.3	20.3	21.1	21.0	20.9	21.0	20.7	20.1	20.1	20.3	20.2
1997	19.2	19.3	19.6	20.2	20.8	21.1	20.8	21.0	21.0	20.7	20.2	20.2	20.3
1998	19.0	19.1	19.5	20.4	20.9	21.1	20.6	20.7	20.8	20.6	20.5	20.7	20.3
1999	19.4	19.7	20.1	20.8	21.5	21.6	21.7	21.6	21.5	20.8	20.5	20.6	20.8
2000	19.9	19.9	20.5	21.5	22.4	22.6	21.9	22.0	21.8	21.0	20.8	20.8	21.3
2001	21.4	21.5	22.0	22.7	23.5	23.7	23.6	23.7	23.4	22.8	22.5	22.5	22.8
2002	21.9	22.0	22.4	23.3	23.9	24.2	24.1	24.2	23.8	23.5	23.4	23.3	23.3
2003	22.2	21.8	22.1	23.3	24.0	24.3	24.0	24.2	24.1	24.2	23.9	23.8	23.5
Other services													
1990	8.9	8.8	8.9	8.9	8.9	9.0	8.9	8.9	8.9	9.1	9.2	9.4	9.0
1991	9.1	9.1	9.2	9.2	9.3	9.5	9.4	9.4	9.2	9.2	9.2	9.2	9.3
1992	9.2	9.2	9.2	9.1	9.2	9.3	9.5	9.5	9.4	9.7	9.6	9.6	9.4
1993	9.5	9.6	9.6	9.6	9.8	9.9	9.9	9.9	9.8	9.9	9.8	10.0	9.8
1994	9.7	9.6	9.8	9.9	9.9	10.2	10.1	10.0	10.1	10.0	10.1	10.2	10.0
1995	9.9	10.0	10.2	10.2	10.4	10.5	10.2	10.2	10.1	10.0	10.0	10.2	10.2
1996	10.0	10.1	10.1	10.3	10.4	10.5	10.5	10.4	10.5	10.3	10.3	10.4	10.3
1997	10.1	10.1	10.2	10.1	10.4	10.3	10.4	10.3	10.3	10.3	10.3	10.3	10.3
1998	10.1	10.1	10.2	10.1	10.4	10.3	10.1	10.2	10.2	10.1	10.0	10.1	10.2
1999	9.9	9.9	9.9	10.0	9.9	10.1	10.1	10.0	9.8	9.9	9.8	9.8	9.9
2000	10.0	10.0	10.0	10.2	10.2	10.4	10.1	10.0	9.8	9.8	9.7	9.7	10.0
2001	13.0	13.0	13.0	13.1	13.2	13.3	13.2	13.1	12.9	12.9	12.8	12.8	13.0
2002	12.7	12.7	12.7	12.8	13.0	13.0	12.9	12.8	12.7	12.8	12.6	12.6	12.8
2003	13.0	13.0	13.0	13.0	13.1	13.2	13.1	13.0	12.9	12.9	12.8	12.6	13.0
Government													
1990	23.5	24.0	24.1	24.0	24.1	23.2	22.5	24.0	24.0	24.5	24.6	22.5	23.8
1991	24.1	24.5	24.7	24.6	24.6	22.5	21.9	22.3	24.6	24.6	24.7	24.9	24.0
1992	24.2	24.8	24.9	24.8	24.8	23.0	22.4	22.7	24.6	25.0	25.1	25.2	24.3
1993	24.7	25.0	25.2	25.3	25.6	24.7	22.9	22.1	25.4	25.5	25.6	25.8	24.8
1994	25.0	25.6	25.8	25.9	26.1	25.2	21.9	21.5	25.7	26.1	25.9	26.0	25.1
1995	25.7	26.1	26.3	26.2	26.5	21.9	21.5	21.2	26.8	27.0	27.0	27.2	25.3
1996	26.2	26.9	27.1	27.1	27.4	25.7	22.5	23.3	26.4	27.0	27.4	27.6	26.2
1997	26.4	27.0	27.3	27.3	27.6	25.7	24.1	23.5	27.4	27.3	27.6	27.7	26.6
1998	26.8	27.3	27.2	27.1	27.6	24.7	22.2	23.0	27.5	27.6	27.7	28.0	26.4
1999	26.3	27.3	27.3	27.9	27.8	25.6	22.7	22.3	27.6	27.8	27.9	28.0	26.5
2000	27.1	27.6	28.1	28.3	28.9	26.6	22.8	22.6	27.3	27.6	27.7	27.8	26.9
2001	27.2	27.6	28.0	27.7	28.4	24.3	21.1	23.0	27.8	28.2	28.4	28.5	26.7
2002	27.3	28.3	28.4	27.5	28.2	22.7	23.2	24.1	28.1	28.7	28.6	28.7	27.0
2003	27.5	28.2	28.3	28.1	28.6	22.9	21.9	23.2	24.9	25.3	25.2	25.4	25.8
State government													
1990	3.6	3.8	3.7	3.7	3.6	3.6	3.6	3.5	3.6	3.8	3.9	3.8	3.7
1991	3.6	3.9	3.9	3.9	3.8	3.1	3.1	3.1	3.9	4.0	4.1	4.1	3.7
1992	4.0	4.4	4.4	4.4	4.2	3.6	3.6	3.7	4.2	4.4	4.4	4.4	4.1
1993	4.1	4.4	4.4	4.3	4.3	3.7	3.6	3.6	4.5	4.4	4.4	4.4	4.2
1994	4.0	4.3	4.4	4.3	4.3	3.7	3.5	3.8	4.2	4.3	4.3	4.2	4.1
1995	3.9	4.2	4.2	4.2	4.2	3.5	3.5	3.4	4.1	4.2	4.2	4.1	4.0
1996	3.8	4.2	4.2	4.2	4.1	3.5	3.7	3.5	3.8	4.2	4.2	4.2	4.0
1997	3.9	4.2	4.2	4.2	4.1	3.5	3.5	3.5	4.4	4.2	4.3	4.2	4.0
1998	4.0	4.2	4.2	4.3	4.2	3.5	3.5	3.5	4.7	4.3	4.3	4.3	4.1
1999	3.9	4.2	4.3	4.3	4.3	3.7	3.5	3.5	4.7	4.4	4.3	4.3	4.1
2000	4.0	4.3	4.4	4.7	4.3	3.6	3.5	3.5	4.5	4.4	4.4	4.3	4.2
2001	4.3	4.5	4.6	4.5	4.6	4.2	4.1	4.1	4.7	4.7	4.7	4.6	4.5
2002	4.3	4.7	4.7	4.5	4.6	3.9	4.0	4.2	4.5	4.8	4.8	4.7	4.5
2003	4.2	4.6	4.6	4.6	4.5	3.9	3.9	3.8	4.4	4.5	4.5	4.5	4.3
Local government													
1990	13.3	13.5	13.6	13.6	13.7	13.1	12.7	12.5	13.6	13.9	14.0	13.9	13.5
1991	13.8	14.0	14.0	14.0	14.1	12.8	12.6	12.6	14.0	13.8	13.9	13.9	13.6
1992	18.0	18.2	18.3	18.2	18.5	17.3	16.5	16.8	18.3	18.5	18.6	18.6	18.0
1993	18.5	18.5	18.7	18.8	19.2	18.9	17.1	16.3	18.8	19.0	19.1	19.3	18.5
1994	18.9	19.2	19.4	19.5	19.7	19.4	16.3	15.6	19.4	19.7	19.5	19.7	18.9
1995	19.6	19.8	20.0	19.9	20.3	16.3	15.4	15.1	20.1	20.2	20.2	20.5	19.0
1996	19.9	20.1	20.3	20.4	20.9	19.6	16.2	17.1	20.1	20.2	20.4	20.5	19.6
1997	19.6	19.9	20.1	20.1	20.5	19.3	17.7	17.1	20.1	20.2	20.4	20.5	19.6
1998	20.0	20.4	20.4	20.3	20.8	18.5	16.2	16.9	20.3	20.6	20.7	20.8	19.7
1999	19.7	20.5	20.6	20.6	21.1	19.4	16.8	16.3	20.3	20.9	20.9	21.0	19.8
2000	20.5	20.7	20.9	20.8	21.3	19.3	16.2	15.9	20.2	20.6	20.5	20.6	19.8
2001	20.2	20.5	20.8	20.6	21.2	17.5	14.4	16.3	20.5	20.9	21.0	21.1	19.6
2002	20.4	21.0	21.1	20.4	20.9	16.1	16.5	17.2	21.0	21.2	21.1	21.2	19.8
2003	20.6	21.0	21.1	20.9	21.5	16.5	15.5	16.9	18.0	18.3	18.2	18.4	18.9

Employment by Industry: Indiana—*Continued*

(Numbers in thousands. Not seasonally adjusted.)

Industry	January	February	March	April	May	June	July	August	September	October	November	December	Annual Average
GARY-HAMMOND													
Total nonfarm													
1990	241.8	241.7	243.0	242.5	245.6	248.2	246.0	246.0	250.8	249.5	250.3	251.5	246.4
1991	245.0	243.4	243.6	245.9	247.9	247.9	244.8	244.6	249.9	249.1	249.4	249.7	246.8
1992	239.6	239.4	239.7	243.6	246.5	246.5	245.2	245.6	250.8	249.0	249.1	250.3	245.4
1993	242.3	243.0	244.1	246.6	248.4	248.1	243.8	243.6	250.8	252.2	253.3	254.0	247.5
1994	242.4	243.6	246.0	249.6	251.9	251.9	248.8	250.3	254.8	253.1	252.7	252.9	249.8
1995	244.1	245.5	246.9	250.8	253.9	256.4	251.0	250.2	255.6	255.4	256.5	257.7	252.0
1996	250.1	250.5	252.8	255.7	260.2	261.8	258.9	259.1	262.9	261.6	263.3	264.7	258.5
1997	259.1	259.2	261.4	264.4	266.7	267.3	264.0	264.4	268.5	267.5	269.1	270.5	265.2
1998	260.9	262.2	261.9	268.1	272.3	274.2	268.9	268.8	271.2	270.7	271.4	272.0	268.6
1999	262.2	263.6	265.7	271.0	272.8	273.1	269.3	268.7	271.4	271.2	272.5	272.8	269.5
2000	263.6	263.4	266.8	269.0	271.1	269.2	262.8	263.0	267.2	265.6	266.1	266.1	266.2
2001	262.6	262.7	265.2	266.3	269.6	267.9	262.1	263.8	267.3	266.7	268.5	267.7	265.9
2002	253.9	253.7	254.9	256.9	260.7	259.4	256.3	259.4	263.5	262.1	262.9	263.5	258.9
2003	255.9	255.8	257.9	262.0	264.8	263.5	259.6	259.3	263.4	263.8	263.6	263.3	261.1
Total private													
1990	208.7	208.0	209.1	208.7	211.5	214.5	214.6	216.3	216.9	215.3	216.0	217.2	213.1
1991	211.3	209.1	209.2	211.4	213.1	213.7	213.5	215.1	215.9	214.4	214.6	214.5	213.0
1992	205.3	204.5	204.9	208.7	211.6	212.4	214.4	214.8	216.3	214.0	214.0	215.2	211.3
1993	208.0	208.0	209.0	211.9	213.5	214.7	215.3	216.0	216.4	217.4	218.4	218.9	214.0
1994	207.9	208.4	210.6	214.3	216.4	217.5	217.4	219.4	219.6	217.4	217.2	217.0	215.3
1995	209.8	210.4	211.7	215.4	218.2	221.0	219.2	220.0	220.1	218.9	220.0	221.1	217.2
1996	214.1	213.9	216.0	219.0	223.2	226.3	226.2	227.5	226.6	225.1	226.7	227.7	222.7
1997	222.8	222.3	224.7	227.6	229.7	230.8	230.2	230.9	230.2	229.6	230.9	232.0	228.5
1998	223.5	224.4	224.1	230.2	233.9	235.7	233.8	233.9	232.9	232.1	232.6	233.1	230.9
1999	224.4	225.0	227.1	231.8	233.8	234.9	233.2	233.5	232.8	232.7	234.0	234.5	231.5
2000	226.5	225.8	229.1	230.8	231.9	233.0	229.7	230.1	228.9	227.5	228.0	228.1	229.1
2001	224.8	224.3	226.5	228.0	230.8	231.6	228.7	229.6	229.2	228.6	230.3	229.3	228.5
2002	216.8	215.5	216.7	218.5	221.6	223.5	223.4	225.1	225.6	223.5	224.3	224.9	221.6
2003	218.4	217.4	219.3	223.6	226.2	225.8	224.8	224.6	225.1	225.5	225.0	224.6	223.4
Goods-producing													
1990	70.3	69.6	69.5	69.9	71.1	72.1	72.7	73.3	73.3	72.5	72.3	72.3	71.6
1991	70.2	68.7	68.5	69.6	70.2	70.1	71.5	72.2	71.7	71.2	70.2	69.6	70.3
1992	66.5	66.1	66.2	67.6	68.6	69.0	71.2	71.3	71.8	69.7	69.1	69.2	68.9
1993	65.6	65.4	66.0	67.3	67.5	68.1	68.1	68.6	68.2	68.7	69.0	68.0	67.5
1994	64.0	64.4	65.3	66.9	67.4	68.2	69.1	70.0	69.8	69.9	68.5	67.5	67.6
1995	65.6	65.6	65.5	66.9	67.8	69.8	68.8	68.3	67.8	67.3	67.2	67.5	67.3
1996	65.4	65.2	65.7	67.3	69.1	69.5	68.7	69.4	69.1	68.2	68.3	68.1	67.8
1997	66.1	65.9	66.6	67.6	67.8	68.7	68.6	69.2	68.7	67.9	68.8	68.3	67.9
1998	66.5	67.0	66.9	70.1	71.8	72.7	71.2	70.2	69.1	68.9	68.1	67.6	69.2
1999	65.6	65.7	66.3	66.7	67.2	67.6	67.0	66.9	66.3	66.8	66.9	65.8	66.6
2000	62.9	62.4	63.7	63.6	64.1	64.2	63.7	63.9	63.2	62.8	62.3	61.6	63.2
2001	59.1	58.9	59.8	59.8	60.6	60.9	59.8	60.3	60.1	59.8	60.5	58.8	59.9
2002	53.5	53.1	53.2	53.5	54.3	55.6	56.1	56.4	56.6	55.7	56.0	55.1	54.9
2003	53.6	53.5	54.4	56.0	56.3	56.1	56.0	56.3	56.3	56.6	55.7	55.1	55.5
Construction and mining													
1990	13.4	13.6	13.9	14.5	15.2	15.5	15.9	16.4	16.9	16.4	16.3	16.5	15.4
1991	14.9	15.5	15.8	16.1	16.5	15.8	17.0	17.9	17.5	17.3	16.3	15.9	16.4
1992	13.6	13.5	13.7	14.5	15.2	15.1	16.3	16.3	16.7	16.1	15.7	15.2	15.2
1993	13.0	13.0	13.6	15.4	15.3	15.5	15.5	15.8	15.6	16.1	16.1	15.3	15.0
1994	13.2	13.6	14.3	16.2	16.3	16.7	17.7	18.3	18.4	18.9	17.4	16.6	16.5
1995	14.7	14.7	14.6	15.8	16.3	17.8	17.0	16.4	15.9	15.7	15.6	15.7	15.9
1996	14.4	14.4	15.4	16.9	18.1	18.4	18.3	18.6	18.6	17.6	17.8	17.5	17.2
1997	16.1	16.0	16.8	17.8	17.9	18.5	18.8	18.8	18.4	18.1	18.8	18.4	17.9
1998	16.9	17.4	17.2	20.0	21.5	22.1	20.8	19.5	18.8	18.7	17.9	17.6	19.0
1999	16.2	16.4	16.9	17.8	18.0	18.2	17.8	17.7	17.3	18.0	18.3	17.3	17.5
2000	15.2	14.9	16.0	16.3	16.8	17.0	17.3	17.2	16.8	16.5	16.6	16.1	16.4
2001	14.8	15.2	15.9	16.3	17.4	17.6	17.1	17.6	17.5	17.7	18.6	17.7	17.0
2002	15.0	15.1	15.3	15.6	16.3	16.4	17.1	17.2	17.3	16.6	16.9	16.2	16.3
2003	14.9	14.9	16.0	17.1	18.1	17.7	18.0	18.4	18.6	19.0	18.1	17.6	17.4
Manufacturing													
1990	56.9	56.0	55.6	55.4	55.9	56.6	56.8	56.9	56.4	56.1	56.0	55.8	56.2
1991	55.3	53.2	52.7	53.5	53.7	54.3	54.5	54.3	54.2	53.9	53.9	53.7	53.9
1992	52.9	52.6	52.5	53.1	53.4	53.9	54.9	55.0	55.1	53.6	53.4	54.0	53.7
1993	52.6	52.4	52.4	51.9	52.2	52.6	52.6	52.8	52.6	52.6	52.9	52.7	52.5
1994	50.8	50.8	51.0	50.7	51.1	51.5	51.4	51.7	51.4	51.0	51.1	50.9	51.1
1995	50.9	50.9	50.9	51.1	51.5	52.0	51.8	51.9	51.9	51.6	51.6	51.8	51.5
1996	51.0	50.8	50.3	50.4	51.0	51.1	50.4	50.8	50.5	50.6	50.5	50.6	50.7
1997	50.0	49.9	49.8	49.8	49.9	50.2	49.8	50.4	50.3	49.8	50.0	49.9	50.0
1998	49.6	49.6	49.7	50.1	50.3	50.6	50.4	50.7	50.3	50.2	50.2	50.0	50.1
1999	49.4	49.3	49.4	48.9	49.2	49.4	49.2	49.2	49.0	48.8	48.6	48.5	49.1
2000	47.7	47.5	47.7	47.3	47.3	47.2	46.4	46.7	46.4	46.3	45.7	45.5	46.8
2001	44.3	43.7	43.9	43.5	43.2	43.3	42.7	42.7	42.6	42.1	41.9	41.1	42.9
2002	38.5	38.0	37.9	37.9	38.0	39.2	39.0	39.2	39.3	39.1	39.1	38.9	38.7
2003	38.7	38.6	38.4	38.9	38.2	38.4	38.0	37.9	37.7	37.6	37.6	37.5	38.1

Employment by Industry: Indiana—*Continued*

(Numbers in thousands. Not seasonally adjusted.)

Industry	January	February	March	April	May	June	July	August	September	October	November	December	Annual Average
GARY-HAMMOND *—Continued*													
Service-providing													
1990	171.5	172.1	173.5	172.6	174.5	176.1	173.3	172.7	177.5	177.0	178.0	179.2	174.8
1991	174.8	174.7	175.1	176.3	177.7	177.8	173.3	172.4	178.2	177.9	179.2	180.1	176.5
1992	173.1	173.3	173.5	176.0	177.9	177.5	174.0	174.3	179.0	179.3	180.0	181.1	176.6
1993	176.7	177.6	178.1	179.3	180.9	180.0	175.7	175.0	182.6	183.5	184.3	186.0	180.0
1994	178.4	179.2	180.7	182.7	184.5	183.7	179.7	180.3	185.0	183.2	184.2	185.4	182.3
1995	178.5	179.9	181.4	183.9	186.1	186.6	182.2	181.9	187.8	188.1	189.3	190.2	184.7
1996	184.7	185.3	187.1	188.4	191.1	192.3	190.2	189.7	193.8	193.4	195.0	196.6	190.6
1997	193.0	193.3	194.8	196.8	198.9	198.6	195.4	195.2	199.8	199.6	200.3	202.2	197.3
1998	194.4	195.2	195.0	198.0	200.5	201.5	197.7	198.6	202.1	201.8	203.3	204.4	199.4
1999	196.6	197.9	199.4	204.3	205.6	205.5	202.3	201.8	205.1	204.4	205.6	207.0	203.0
2000	200.7	201.0	203.1	205.4	207.0	205.0	199.1	199.1	204.0	202.8	203.8	204.5	203.0
2001	203.5	203.8	205.4	206.5	209.0	207.0	202.3	203.5	207.2	206.9	208.0	208.9	206.0
2002	200.4	200.6	201.7	203.4	206.4	203.8	200.2	203.0	206.9	206.4	206.9	208.4	204.0
2003	202.3	202.3	203.5	206.0	208.5	207.4	203.6	203.0	207.1	207.2	207.9	208.2	205.6
Trade, transportation, and utilities													
1990	55.0	54.5	54.7	54.2	54.6	55.2	55.2	56.0	55.9	56.2	57.1	57.9	55.5
1991	56.1	55.0	55.1	54.8	55.5	55.7	55.4	56.1	56.3	55.8	57.2	57.7	55.9
1992	54.1	53.2	53.4	53.4	53.7	54.1	53.7	53.8	53.7	53.8	54.8	55.6	53.9
1993	53.7	53.5	53.7	53.9	54.4	54.4	54.6	54.8	55.1	55.6	56.6	57.3	54.8
1994	52.2	52.1	52.4	52.9	53.6	53.8	53.9	54.6	54.4	53.9	55.2	55.8	53.7
1995	53.1	52.5	52.7	53.0	53.7	54.2	53.7	54.4	54.4	54.4	55.5	56.1	54.0
1996	53.8	53.1	53.3	53.6	54.3	54.4	54.4	54.8	54.3	54.6	56.1	57.0	54.5
1997	55.1	54.1	54.4	54.9	55.5	55.5	54.5	54.6	54.3	55.3	56.3	57.3	55.2
1998	53.5	53.0	52.5	53.5	54.2	55.1	55.2	55.9	55.6	55.6	57.0	57.8	54.9
1999	54.6	54.2	55.0	56.0	56.6	56.9	56.9	57.1	56.6	56.5	57.5	58.4	56.4
2000	56.4	55.6	56.2	56.2	56.8	57.4	57.1	57.2	56.9	56.7	57.9	58.6	56.9
2001	56.9	56.6	56.9	56.7	57.3	57.5	56.9	57.1	56.9	56.9	58.0	58.6	57.2
2002	55.2	54.2	54.6	54.6	55.1	55.2	54.9	55.1	54.9	54.8	55.9	56.7	55.1
2003	54.0	53.2	53.5	53.9	54.6	54.6	54.7	54.5	54.4	54.7	55.3	55.8	54.4
Wholesale trade													
1990	8.8	8.8	8.9	8.6	8.6	8.7	8.9	8.9	8.8	9.2	9.2	9.2	8.9
1991	9.1	8.9	8.9	8.9	8.9	9.0	9.0	9.2	9.1	9.3	9.4	9.4	9.1
1992	8.9	8.9	8.9	9.2	9.2	9.2	9.4	9.4	9.3	9.2	9.2	9.3	9.2
1993	9.1	9.1	9.2	9.2	9.3	9.3	9.4	9.4	9.4	9.1	9.2	9.4	9.3
1994	8.8	8.9	8.9	9.2	9.2	9.3	9.4	9.5	9.4	9.4	9.4	9.5	9.2
1995	9.3	9.3	9.3	9.3	9.4	9.4	9.4	9.5	9.4	9.3	9.3	9.3	9.4
1996	9.0	9.1	9.1	9.5	9.7	9.7	9.7	9.7	9.6	9.8	9.8	9.9	9.6
1997	9.7	9.7	9.8	9.9	10.0	10.0	10.1	10.1	10.1	10.1	10.2	10.2	10.0
1998	10.0	10.0	9.9	10.1	10.2	10.3	10.4	10.4	10.5	10.4	10.3	10.4	10.2
1999	10.3	10.4	10.4	10.6	10.7	10.7	10.8	10.8	10.8	10.7	10.7	10.9	10.7
2000	10.9	10.9	11.0	11.0	11.1	11.2	11.1	10.9	10.8	10.8	10.8	10.7	10.9
2001	10.6	10.6	10.6	10.4	10.5	10.4	10.4	10.5	10.4	10.2	10.1	10.1	10.4
2002	10.0	9.9	9.9	10.0	10.0	10.0	9.8	9.8	9.7	9.8	9.7	9.7	9.9
2003	9.7	9.6	9.6	9.7	9.7	9.7	9.7	9.7	9.7	9.7	9.6	9.6	9.7
Retail trade													
1990	31.5	31.1	31.3	31.1	31.5	31.8	31.7	32.3	32.2	32.0	32.8	33.6	31.9
1991	31.8	30.9	30.8	30.7	31.2	31.3	31.1	31.5	31.4	30.9	32.2	32.6	31.4
1992	30.7	29.9	29.9	30.1	30.3	30.6	30.0	30.1	30.0	30.5	31.3	32.2	30.5
1993	30.9	30.6	30.6	30.7	30.9	31.0	30.9	31.1	31.3	31.7	32.6	33.2	31.3
1994	30.2	30.0	30.1	30.3	30.8	31.0	31.2	31.7	31.4	31.3	32.5	33.0	31.1
1995	30.9	30.2	30.4	30.6	31.2	31.6	31.6	32.0	32.1	32.1	33.2	33.8	31.6
1996	31.8	30.9	30.9	30.9	31.4	31.5	31.6	32.0	31.7	31.7	33.2	34.1	31.8
1997	32.6	31.7	31.8	32.0	32.8	33.0	32.5	32.5	32.1	33.0	34.1	35.0	32.8
1998	32.2	31.7	31.3	31.7	32.2	32.8	32.9	33.4	33.0	33.2	34.6	35.5	32.9
1999	32.6	32.0	32.6	33.0	33.5	33.8	33.6	33.6	33.1	33.4	34.5	35.1	33.4
2000	33.3	32.5	32.9	32.9	33.4	33.7	33.5	33.6	33.5	33.5	34.8	35.6	33.6
2001	33.9	33.6	33.8	33.8	34.1	34.5	33.9	33.9	33.8	34.0	35.1	35.7	34.2
2002	33.0	32.2	32.5	32.5	32.9	33.2	32.9	33.0	32.8	32.5	33.8	34.6	33.0
2003	32.4	31.8	32.0	32.3	32.7	32.8	32.8	32.6	32.5	32.6	33.4	33.9	32.7
Transportation and utilities													
1990	14.7	14.6	14.5	14.5	14.5	14.7	14.6	14.8	14.9	15.0	15.1	15.1	14.8
1991	15.2	15.2	15.4	15.2	15.4	15.4	15.3	15.4	15.8	15.6	15.6	15.7	15.4
1992	14.5	14.4	14.6	14.1	14.2	14.3	14.3	14.3	14.4	14.1	14.3	14.1	14.3
1993	13.7	13.8	13.9	14.0	14.2	14.1	14.3	14.3	14.4	14.8	14.8	14.7	14.3
1994	13.2	13.2	13.4	13.4	13.6	13.5	13.3	13.4	13.6	13.2	13.3	13.3	13.4
1995	12.9	13.0	13.0	13.1	13.1	13.2	12.7	12.9	12.9	13.0	13.0	13.0	13.0
1996	13.0	13.1	13.3	13.2	13.2	13.2	13.1	13.1	13.0	13.1	13.1	13.0	13.1
1997	12.8	12.7	12.8	13.0	12.7	12.5	11.9	12.0	12.1	12.2	12.0	12.1	12.4
1998	11.3	11.3	11.3	11.7	11.8	12.0	11.9	12.1	12.1	12.0	12.1	11.9	11.8
1999	11.7	11.8	12.0	12.4	12.4	12.4	12.5	12.7	12.7	12.4	12.3	12.4	12.3
2000	12.2	12.2	12.3	12.3	12.3	12.5	12.5	12.7	12.6	12.4	12.3	12.3	12.4
2001	12.4	12.4	12.5	12.5	12.7	12.6	12.6	12.7	12.7	12.7	12.8	12.8	12.6
2002	12.2	12.1	12.2	12.1	12.2	12.0	12.2	12.3	12.4	12.5	12.4	12.4	12.3
2003	11.9	11.8	11.9	11.9	12.2	12.1	12.2	12.2	12.2	12.4	12.3	12.3	12.1

Employment by Industry: Indiana—*Continued*

(Numbers in thousands. Not seasonally adjusted.)

Industry	January	February	March	April	May	June	July	August	September	October	November	December	Annual Average
GARY-HAMMOND *—Continued*													
Information													
1990	2.9	2.9	3.0	3.0	3.0	3.1	3.1	3.0	3.0	3.1	3.0	3.1	3.0
1991	3.0	3.0	3.0	2.9	3.0	3.1	3.1	3.1	3.1	3.1	3.1	3.1	3.1
1992	3.0	3.0	3.0	3.0	3.0	3.0	2.8	2.8	2.8	2.9	3.0	3.0	2.9
1993	3.0	2.9	2.9	2.8	2.9	2.9	2.9	2.9	2.9	2.8	2.8	2.8	2.9
1994	2.8	2.7	2.8	2.8	2.8	2.8	2.8	2.8	2.8	2.7	2.7	2.7	2.8
1995	2.7	2.7	2.7	2.7	2.8	2.8	2.7	2.7	2.7	2.6	2.6	2.6	2.7
1996	2.6	2.6	2.7	2.6	2.7	2.7	2.7	2.7	2.7	2.7	2.7	2.8	2.7
1997	2.7	2.8	2.8	2.7	2.8	2.8	2.8	2.8	2.8	2.8	2.7	2.9	2.8
1998	2.9	2.9	2.9	2.9	3.0	3.0	3.1	3.0	3.0	2.9	3.0	3.0	3.0
1999	3.1	3.1	3.1	3.2	3.2	3.2	3.2	3.1	3.1	3.1	3.2	3.2	3.2
2000	3.3	3.3	3.3	3.2	3.2	3.3	3.2	3.2	3.2	3.1	3.1	3.1	3.2
2001	3.0	3.0	3.0	3.0	3.1	3.1	3.0	3.0	2.9	2.8	2.9	2.8	3.0
2002	2.8	2.8	2.8	2.8	2.8	2.8	2.8	2.9	2.8	2.7	2.7	2.7	2.8
2003	2.4	2.4	2.4	2.3	2.4	2.4	2.4	2.4	2.3	2.3	2.4	2.4	2.4
Financial activities													
1990	10.1	10.1	10.1	10.0	10.2	10.4	10.5	10.4	10.3	10.1	10.1	10.2	10.2
1991	10.0	9.9	10.0	10.1	10.2	10.4	10.2	10.1	10.3	10.1	10.2	10.2	10.1
1992	10.0	10.0	10.1	10.3	10.5	10.6	10.5	10.5	10.4	10.5	10.5	10.6	10.4
1993	10.7	10.7	10.8	10.8	10.9	11.1	11.3	11.2	11.2	11.0	11.0	11.1	11.0
1994	10.8	10.8	10.9	10.8	10.9	11.1	11.0	11.0	10.8	10.8	10.9	10.9	10.9
1995	10.4	10.4	10.5	10.6	10.6	10.8	10.8	10.9	10.6	10.6	10.5	10.6	10.6
1996	10.2	10.2	10.3	10.3	10.5	10.7	10.7	10.7	10.5	10.4	10.5	10.6	10.5
1997	10.4	10.3	10.4	10.4	10.5	10.6	10.6	10.7	10.4	10.4	10.3	10.5	10.5
1998	10.0	10.1	10.1	10.2	10.3	10.5	10.5	10.6	10.3	10.2	10.2	10.3	10.3
1999	10.2	10.2	10.1	10.2	10.2	10.4	10.4	10.4	10.1	10.1	10.1	10.1	10.2
2000	10.0	10.0	10.0	10.2	10.2	10.4	10.1	10.0	9.9	9.6	9.6	9.7	10.0
2001	10.7	10.5	10.7	10.7	10.8	11.0	10.9	10.8	10.6	10.5	10.6	10.7	10.7
2002	10.4	10.3	10.4	10.3	10.5	10.6	10.6	10.6	10.4	10.3	10.3	10.5	10.4
2003	10.5	10.5	10.6	10.6	10.9	10.9	10.9	10.8	10.7	10.6	10.6	10.6	10.7
Professional and business services													
1990	14.2	14.3	14.6	14.8	14.8	15.0	15.3	15.3	15.3	15.0	14.9	15.1	14.9
1991	15.0	15.2	15.3	15.4	15.3	15.3	14.9	15.0	15.2	15.1	15.0	14.8	15.1
1992	14.6	14.5	14.9	15.1	15.2	15.5	15.4	15.5	15.7	15.5	15.3	15.5	15.2
1993	15.1	15.1	15.3	15.3	15.4	15.5	16.0	16.0	15.9	15.9	15.9	16.3	15.6
1994	15.8	15.9	16.3	16.6	16.6	16.6	16.6	16.7	16.7	16.1	15.9	15.8	16.3
1995	15.9	16.3	16.6	17.1	17.3	17.4	17.3	17.4	17.3	17.2	17.2	17.1	17.0
1996	16.4	16.6	17.0	17.2	17.4	17.5	17.7	17.6	17.2	16.7	16.7	16.7	17.1
1997	17.2	17.4	17.8	18.2	18.3	18.5	18.5	18.6	18.6	18.1	17.7	18.0	18.1
1998	17.7	17.7	17.8	19.0	18.8	18.8	18.9	19.2	19.3	19.3	19.1	19.1	18.7
1999	18.8	18.9	19.0	19.2	19.3	19.6	19.5	19.4	19.6	19.5	19.4	19.7	19.3
2000	19.4	19.5	19.9	20.6	20.1	20.5	20.2	19.8	19.8	19.6	19.6	19.7	19.9
2001	19.7	19.6	19.8	20.3	20.6	20.8	20.6	20.6	20.5	20.5	20.5	20.4	20.3
2002	19.9	19.8	20.1	20.3	20.6	20.9	21.1	21.4	21.7	21.3	21.2	21.3	20.8
2003	21.1	20.9	20.9	21.6	21.8	21.6	21.1	21.0	21.5	21.6	21.5	21.4	21.3
Educational and health services													
1990	26.2	26.4	26.5	26.4	26.5	26.7	25.6	26.0	26.9	27.3	27.4	27.4	26.6
1991	27.2	27.5	27.2	27.8	27.3	27.3	27.1	27.1	28.1	28.3	28.3	28.5	27.6
1992	27.2	27.6	26.8	28.6	28.8	28.1	28.5	28.4	29.5	29.8	29.8	29.9	28.6
1993	29.5	29.8	29.2	30.1	29.6	29.3	29.1	29.1	29.9	30.7	30.6	30.7	29.8
1994	31.3	31.5	31.2	31.6	31.6	30.9	30.9	31.0	32.0	32.0	32.0	32.0	31.5
1995	30.8	31.4	31.5	32.1	32.1	31.5	31.3	31.4	32.6	33.1	33.5	33.6	32.1
1996	33.0	33.2	33.7	33.8	33.7	33.0	32.9	32.8	33.7	34.1	34.3	34.3	33.5
1997	33.9	34.3	34.3	34.6	34.5	34.0	33.4	33.3	34.3	34.6	34.8	34.8	34.2
1998	34.3	34.8	34.5	34.9	34.9	34.1	33.6	33.6	34.7	35.1	35.3	35.4	34.6
1999	33.5	33.8	33.8	35.6	35.3	34.6	33.7	34.0	34.9	35.2	35.4	35.5	34.6
2000	34.6	35.0	35.1	35.5	35.4	34.7	34.0	34.3	34.8	35.3	35.3	35.4	35.0
2001	35.1	35.4	35.3	35.7	35.6	34.8	34.3	34.6	35.5	35.8	35.9	36.0	35.3
2002	35.4	35.7	35.5	36.2	36.0	35.7	35.1	35.7	36.5	36.9	36.9	37.2	36.1
2003	36.6	36.9	36.8	37.5	37.5	36.6	36.4	36.0	37.0	37.0	37.1	37.0	36.9
Leisure and hospitality													
1990	19.6	19.7	20.1	19.9	20.7	21.3	21.4	21.5	21.3	20.3	20.3	20.3	20.5
1991	19.2	19.1	19.3	19.9	20.7	20.9	20.6	20.8	20.4	20.2	19.9	19.8	20.1
1992	19.3	19.4	19.7	20.1	21.0	21.2	21.3	21.4	21.2	20.8	20.4	20.2	20.5
1993	19.4	19.5	19.8	20.5	21.5	21.9	21.9	22.0	21.8	21.2	21.0	21.2	21.0
1994	20.0	19.9	20.3	21.2	22.0	22.4	21.8	22.0	21.7	20.8	20.7	20.8	21.1
1995	20.2	20.3	20.9	21.8	22.5	23.0	23.2	23.5	23.2	22.3	22.1	22.1	22.1
1996	21.3	21.5	21.8	22.7	23.9	26.8	27.5	27.9	27.5	27.0	26.7	26.6	25.1
1997	25.9	25.9	26.7	27.2	28.1	28.6	29.8	29.7	29.2	28.4	28.3	28.2	28.0
1998	26.9	27.1	27.5	27.8	28.9	29.4	29.3	29.4	29.0	28.2	28.1	28.0	28.3
1999	26.8	27.1	27.7	28.8	29.8	30.3	30.2	30.3	30.0	29.3	29.3	29.5	29.1
2000	27.8	27.8	28.6	29.2	29.7	30.1	29.3	29.5	29.0	28.5	28.4	28.2	28.8
2001	27.7	27.7	28.3	29.1	30.0	30.5	30.4	30.4	30.0	29.6	29.2	29.2	29.3
2002	27.5	27.4	27.8	28.4	29.6	30.1	30.3	30.5	30.3	29.3	28.8	28.8	29.1
2003	27.7	27.5	28.1	29.1	29.9	30.7	30.5	30.6	30.0	29.9	29.6	29.6	29.4

Employment by Industry: Indiana—*Continued*

(Numbers in thousands. Not seasonally adjusted.)

Industry	January	February	March	April	May	June	July	August	September	October	November	December	Annual Average
GARY-HAMMOND *—Continued*													
Other services													
1990	10.4	10.5	10.6	10.5	10.6	10.7	10.8	10.8	10.9	10.8	10.9	10.9	10.7
1991	10.6	10.7	10.8	10.9	10.9	10.9	10.7	10.7	10.8	10.6	10.7	10.8	10.8
1992	10.6	10.7	10.8	10.6	10.8	10.9	11.0	11.1	11.2	11.0	11.1	11.2	10.9
1993	11.0	11.1	11.3	11.2	11.3	11.5	11.4	11.4	11.4	11.5	11.5	11.5	11.3
1994	11.0	11.1	11.4	11.5	11.5	11.7	11.3	11.3	11.4	11.2	11.3	11.5	11.4
1995	11.1	11.2	11.3	11.2	11.4	11.5	11.4	11.4	11.5	11.4	11.4	11.5	11.4
1996	11.4	11.5	11.5	11.5	11.6	11.7	11.6	11.6	11.6	11.4	11.4	11.6	11.5
1997	11.5	11.6	11.7	12.0	12.2	12.1	12.0	12.0	11.9	12.1	12.0	12.0	11.9
1998	11.7	11.8	11.9	11.8	12.0	12.1	12.0	12.0	11.9	11.9	11.8	11.9	11.9
1999	11.8	12.0	12.1	12.1	12.2	12.3	12.3	12.3	12.2	12.2	12.2	12.3	12.2
2000	12.1	12.2	12.3	12.3	12.4	12.4	12.1	12.2	12.1	11.9	11.8	11.8	12.1
2001	12.6	12.6	12.7	12.7	12.8	13.0	12.8	12.8	12.7	12.7	12.7	12.8	12.7
2002	12.1	12.2	12.3	12.4	12.7	12.6	12.5	12.5	12.4	12.5	12.5	12.6	12.4
2003	12.5	12.5	12.6	12.6	12.8	12.9	12.8	13.0	12.9	12.8	12.8	12.7	12.7
Government													
1990	33.1	33.7	33.9	33.8	34.1	33.7	31.4	29.7	33.9	34.2	34.3	34.3	33.3
1991	33.7	34.3	34.4	34.5	34.8	34.2	31.3	29.5	34.0	34.7	34.8	35.2	33.8
1992	34.3	34.9	34.8	34.9	34.9	34.1	30.8	30.8	34.5	35.0	35.1	35.1	34.1
1993	34.3	35.0	35.1	34.7	34.9	33.4	28.5	27.6	34.4	34.8	34.9	35.1	33.6
1994	34.5	35.2	35.4	35.3	35.5	34.4	31.4	30.9	35.2	35.7	35.5	35.9	34.6
1995	34.3	35.1	35.2	35.4	35.7	35.4	31.8	30.2	35.5	36.5	36.5	36.6	34.9
1996	36.0	36.6	36.8	36.7	37.0	35.5	32.7	31.6	36.3	36.5	36.6	37.0	35.8
1997	36.3	36.9	36.7	36.8	37.0	36.5	33.8	33.5	38.3	37.9	38.2	38.5	36.7
1998	37.4	37.8	37.8	37.9	38.4	38.5	35.1	34.9	38.3	38.6	38.8	38.9	37.7
1999	37.8	38.6	38.6	39.2	39.0	38.2	36.1	35.2	38.6	38.5	38.5	38.3	38.1
2000	37.1	37.6	37.7	38.2	39.2	36.2	33.1	32.9	38.3	38.1	38.1	38.0	37.0
2001	37.8	38.4	38.7	38.3	38.8	36.3	33.4	34.2	38.1	38.1	38.2	38.4	37.4
2002	37.1	38.2	38.2	38.4	39.1	35.9	32.9	34.3	37.9	38.6	38.6	38.6	37.3
2003	37.5	38.4	38.6	38.4	38.6	37.7	34.8	34.7	38.3	38.3	38.6	38.7	37.7
Federal government													
1990	2.1	2.0	2.0	2.1	2.1	2.1	2.1	2.0	2.0	2.0	2.0	2.0	2.0
1991	2.0	2.0	2.0	2.0	2.0	2.0	2.0	2.0	2.0	2.0	2.0	2.0	2.0
1992	2.0	1.9	2.0	2.0	2.0	2.0	2.0	2.0	2.0	2.0	2.0	2.0	2.0
1993	2.0	1.9	1.9	1.9	2.0	2.0	2.0	2.0	2.0	2.0	2.0	2.2	2.0
1994	2.0	2.0	2.0	2.0	2.0	2.0	2.0	2.0	2.0	2.0	2.0	2.3	2.0
1995	2.0	2.0	2.0	2.0	2.1	2.1	2.1	2.1	2.1	2.5	2.8	2.9	2.2
1996	2.8	2.9	2.9	2.9	2.9	2.8	2.8	2.9	2.7	2.7	2.7	2.9	2.8
1997	2.8	2.7	2.6	2.6	2.6	2.6	2.6	2.5	2.7	2.8	3.0	3.2	2.7
1998	2.8	2.5	2.5	2.5	2.5	2.6	2.5	2.6	2.5	2.6	2.8	2.9	2.6
1999	2.5	2.5	2.4	2.9	2.4	2.4	2.4	2.4	2.4	2.3	2.5	2.6	2.5
2000	2.3	2.2	2.2	2.4	3.0	2.5	2.5	2.4	2.1	2.1	2.1	2.2	2.3
2001	2.1	2.1	2.1	2.1	2.2	2.2	2.2	2.2	2.2	2.1	2.1	2.2	2.2
2002	2.1	2.1	2.1	2.1	2.1	2.2	2.2	2.2	2.2	2.1	2.1	2.1	2.1
2003	2.0	2.0	2.0	2.0	2.0	2.1	2.1	2.1	2.1	2.0	2.0	2.0	2.0
State government													
1990	3.5	3.6	3.6	3.5	3.4	3.1	3.3	3.3	3.5	3.6	3.6	3.6	3.5
1991	3.4	3.6	3.7	3.7	3.5	3.3	3.3	3.3	3.6	3.8	3.8	3.7	3.6
1992	3.6	3.8	3.9	3.9	3.6	3.0	3.2	3.2	3.7	4.0	4.0	4.0	3.7
1993	3.7	4.0	4.0	4.0	3.6	3.0	3.3	3.1	3.9	4.0	4.1	4.0	3.7
1994	3.7	4.0	4.1	4.1	3.8	3.2	3.3	3.4	3.9	4.1	4.1	4.0	3.8
1995	3.6	4.0	4.1	4.1	4.0	3.2	3.0	3.1	4.0	4.1	4.1	3.9	3.8
1996	3.6	4.1	4.1	4.1	4.0	3.4	3.7	3.7	4.2	4.2	4.0	3.9	3.9
1997	3.9	4.1	4.1	4.2	3.9	3.1	4.2	4.1	4.6	4.3	4.2	4.1	4.1
1998	4.0	4.2	4.2	4.3	4.1	3.6	4.2	4.0	4.5	4.3	4.3	4.2	4.2
1999	3.9	4.2	4.2	4.3	4.1	3.7	4.2	4.1	4.5	4.3	4.2	4.2	4.2
2000	3.8	4.2	4.2	4.2	4.1	3.6	3.6	3.6	4.4	4.2	4.3	4.1	4.0
2001	4.1	4.4	4.5	4.4	4.4	4.3	4.4	4.4	4.5	4.5	4.5	4.4	4.4
2002	4.0	4.5	4.5	4.5	5.0	4.4	4.1	4.4	4.4	4.5	4.6	4.5	4.5
2003	4.1	4.5	4.5	4.4	4.2	3.8	3.8	3.7	4.1	4.2	4.3	4.2	4.2
Local government													
1990	27.5	28.0	28.3	28.2	28.6	28.5	26.0	24.3	28.3	28.6	28.7	28.8	27.8
1991	28.3	28.7	28.7	28.9	29.3	28.9	25.9	24.3	28.4	28.9	29.0	29.4	28.2
1992	28.7	29.2	28.9	29.0	29.3	29.1	25.6	25.6	28.8	29.0	29.1	29.1	28.5
1993	28.6	29.1	29.2	28.8	29.3	28.4	23.2	22.5	28.5	28.8	28.8	28.9	27.8
1994	28.8	29.2	29.3	29.2	29.7	29.2	26.1	25.5	29.3	29.6	29.4	29.6	28.7
1995	28.7	29.1	29.1	29.3	29.6	30.1	26.7	25.0	29.4	29.9	29.6	29.8	28.9
1996	29.6	29.6	29.8	29.7	30.1	29.3	26.2	25.0	29.4	29.6	29.9	30.2	29.0
1997	29.6	30.1	30.0	30.0	30.5	30.8	27.0	26.9	31.0	30.8	31.0	31.2	29.9
1998	30.6	31.1	31.1	31.1	31.8	32.3	28.4	28.3	31.3	31.7	31.7	31.8	30.9
1999	31.4	31.9	32.0	32.0	32.5	32.1	29.5	28.7	31.7	31.9	31.8	31.5	31.4
2000	31.0	31.2	31.3	31.6	32.1	30.1	27.0	26.9	31.8	31.8	31.7	31.7	30.7
2001	31.6	31.9	32.1	31.8	32.2	29.8	26.8	27.6	31.4	31.5	31.6	31.8	30.8
2002	31.0	31.6	31.6	31.8	32.0	29.3	26.6	27.7	31.3	32.0	31.9	32.0	30.7
2003	31.4	31.9	32.1	32.0	32.4	31.8	28.9	28.9	32.1	32.1	32.3	32.5	31.5

Employment by Industry: Indiana—*Continued*

(Numbers in thousands. Not seasonally adjusted.)

Industry	January	February	March	April	May	June	July	August	September	October	November	December	Annual Average
INDIANAPOLIS													
Total nonfarm													
1990	703.2	706.1	711.7	712.9	723.0	723.1	722.9	727.9	732.8	732.3	733.1	730.7	721.6
1991	710.5	709.3	712.1	720.7	727.4	726.8	717.5	722.7	727.4	725.5	728.4	730.5	721.6
1992	710.1	710.2	716.6	722.7	735.2	733.2	728.8	733.3	739.6	743.0	743.5	745.8	730.2
1993	726.0	727.1	731.5	742.4	752.6	756.2	748.5	751.5	759.5	765.0	768.0	771.4	750.0
1994	748.4	750.7	760.1	766.6	777.8	778.9	773.5	780.0	786.9	780.8	786.8	792.9	773.6
1995	773.7	778.9	787.9	790.8	800.6	799.6	788.0	796.7	811.4	807.9	810.9	815.0	796.8
1996	787.2	794.5	800.8	807.4	818.3	815.5	801.2	812.8	820.3	820.0	826.0	829.8	811.2
1997	803.1	809.1	818.5	824.7	833.7	831.1	827.7	829.4	836.9	840.1	842.5	850.7	829.0
1998	827.1	829.6	836.5	843.4	853.4	855.9	834.6	845.4	854.2	858.2	861.7	866.3	847.2
1999	836.0	846.3	854.3	865.7	873.8	878.7	873.1	876.2	882.9	885.7	890.4	895.2	871.5
2000	874.5	878.0	888.3	890.8	902.0	905.2	887.6	894.7	898.0	897.5	894.9	896.3	892.3
2001	877.7	879.6	888.7	896.0	903.7	904.7	890.5	900.8	899.2	894.8	893.5	893.6	893.6
2002	866.4	869.1	874.6	881.9	893.0	893.1	884.5	893.2	890.7	893.0	895.2	895.2	885.8
2003	871.0	870.2	875.9	885.4	895.8	893.0	888.3	896.1	895.7	897.1	893.8	893.6	888.0
Total private													
1990	599.2	600.9	606.1	607.2	617.1	620.2	623.2	626.7	627.5	626.3	626.5	624.4	617.1
1991	604.7	602.2	604.3	612.7	618.4	623.0	618.8	620.9	620.8	617.0	618.9	620.4	615.2
1992	601.2	599.9	606.1	612.9	624.6	626.5	627.9	628.2	629.5	631.8	632.4	634.5	621.3
1993	617.8	617.5	622.1	631.7	641.3	648.2	645.7	648.3	649.5	653.7	656.2	659.5	641.0
1994	637.4	638.7	647.4	655.9	666.9	672.9	670.6	675.4	675.4	669.6	674.6	680.6	663.8
1995	663.9	666.6	675.2	677.3	687.6	694.2	691.3	696.5	699.7	696.0	699.1	702.7	687.5
1996	678.4	682.4	688.7	696.0	707.1	710.7	704.6	715.2	712.3	712.5	719.0	723.2	704.2
1997	700.3	703.8	713.3	719.5	727.5	729.2	730.8	733.5	731.8	733.9	736.0	743.4	725.3
1998	720.8	721.8	728.7	735.6	745.0	751.5	741.7	749.8	746.1	749.0	752.6	756.8	741.6
1999	730.3	736.5	744.5	756.0	763.7	771.4	773.9	775.9	772.3	775.3	779.9	784.7	763.7
2000	764.6	767.2	776.8	779.8	788.9	796.9	788.7	790.9	786.3	786.6	783.3	784.4	782.9
2001	767.7	767.3	775.6	783.3	789.8	795.9	790.2	795.8	785.3	780.8	779.6	779.6	782.6
2002	756.0	754.7	759.9	767.1	777.3	782.6	779.2	782.6	775.4	775.4	777.2	777.1	772.0
2003	755.2	751.7	756.9	766.9	776.6	779.9	779.0	782.7	778.1	778.9	776.3	775.9	771.5
Goods-producing													
1990	152.5	155.1	156.6	157.3	159.2	160.6	161.9	162.7	163.1	161.8	159.7	157.6	159.0
1991	152.9	150.7	149.5	154.4	155.6	157.5	157.6	158.5	158.1	156.2	155.2	154.5	155.1
1992	149.0	148.2	149.7	151.5	153.8	154.7	156.6	157.2	157.4	156.0	155.3	155.3	153.7
1993	151.3	150.4	149.9	150.5	152.2	154.1	155.6	156.2	157.0	156.6	156.3	155.5	153.8
1994	149.0	148.6	151.0	151.9	154.4	156.8	156.5	158.3	158.6	156.8	156.7	157.3	154.7
1995	153.8	154.0	156.0	157.1	159.4	161.8	160.9	162.4	162.6	160.5	160.1	158.9	159.0
1996	153.5	154.5	155.9	157.9	160.2	162.4	158.6	164.1	163.8	163.2	162.6	162.2	159.9
1997	160.6	158.9	161.3	163.4	165.2	165.5	166.5	167.6	166.6	166.3	164.8	165.0	164.3
1998	161.2	161.4	162.1	163.9	166.3	168.1	164.0	168.2	168.2	162.8	161.7	161.4	164.1
1999	160.8	161.9	162.4	164.6	166.2	169.3	171.8	172.1	172.0	170.8	170.2	169.9	167.7
2000	167.6	167.9	169.7	171.1	172.7	175.6	175.7	176.1	174.9	172.7	171.2	169.8	172.1
2001	163.9	163.7	165.1	166.6	168.4	170.2	169.3	170.7	168.5	166.6	165.0	163.8	166.8
2002	158.9	157.9	158.9	160.1	162.5	164.7	164.8	165.4	163.8	162.1	161.4	160.0	161.7
2003	154.6	153.4	154.1	156.2	158.1	159.9	160.9	160.9	161.1	160.4	159.7	159.0	158.2
Natural resources and mining													
1990	0.5	0.5	0.6	0.6	0.6	0.6	0.6	0.6	0.6	0.6	0.6	0.6	0.6
1991	0.5	0.5	0.6	0.6	0.6	0.6	0.6	0.6	0.6	0.6	0.6	0.6	0.6
1992	0.6	0.6	0.6	0.6	0.7	0.6	0.6	0.6	0.6	0.6	0.6	0.6	0.6
1993	0.6	0.6	0.6	0.7	0.7	0.7	0.7	0.7	0.7	0.7	0.7	0.7	0.7
1994	0.6	0.6	0.7	0.7	0.7	0.8	0.7	0.7	0.7	0.7	0.7	0.7	0.7
1995	0.7	0.7	0.7	0.7	0.7	0.7	0.8	0.8	0.8	0.8	0.8	0.8	0.8
1996	0.7	0.7	0.7	0.8	0.8	0.8	0.8	0.8	0.8	0.8	0.8	0.8	0.8
1997	0.7	0.7	0.8	0.8	0.8	0.8	0.8	0.8	0.8	0.8	0.8	0.8	0.8
1998	0.7	0.7	0.7	0.7	0.7	0.7	0.7	0.7	0.7	0.7	0.7	0.7	0.7
1999	0.7	0.8	0.8	0.7	0.8	0.8	0.8	0.8	0.8	0.8	0.8	0.8	0.8
2000	0.7	0.7	0.7	0.8	0.8	0.8	0.8	0.8	0.8	0.8	0.8	0.8	0.8
2001	0.7	0.7	0.7	0.8	0.8	0.8	0.8	0.8	0.8	0.8	0.8	0.8	0.8
2002	0.8	0.8	0.8	0.8	0.8	0.8	0.8	0.8	0.8	0.8	0.8	0.8	0.8
2003	0.7	0.7	0.7	0.7	0.7	0.8	0.8	0.8	0.8	0.8	0.8	0.8	0.8
Construction													
1990	33.6	33.5	34.6	35.7	36.8	38.2	39.5	40.3	39.4	38.7	38.4	37.1	37.2
1991	34.1	33.5	34.1	35.7	36.9	38.2	38.6	39.1	38.2	37.3	36.1	35.1	36.4
1992	31.5	31.1	31.9	33.8	35.2	36.3	37.9	38.3	37.9	37.3	36.7	36.5	35.4
1993	33.6	33.4	33.6	35.5	36.7	37.5	39.1	38.8	38.5	38.5	38.0	37.3	36.7
1994	34.1	33.7	35.4	37.6	39.2	40.6	41.1	41.1	40.8	40.7	40.0	39.4	38.6
1995	36.0	35.8	37.5	38.6	39.9	42.0	42.3	42.7	41.9	40.9	40.3	39.3	39.8
1996	36.3	36.7	37.8	40.3	42.1	43.8	44.8	45.5	44.8	43.9	43.8	42.8	41.9
1997	39.6	39.2	41.0	43.3	44.9	45.8	46.7	46.7	45.4	45.3	44.3	43.5	43.8
1998	40.5	40.2	40.8	43.1	44.7	46.0	47.2	47.0	47.0	47.2	46.7	46.1	44.7
1999	40.8	41.4	42.4	45.4	47.2	48.7	50.0	49.9	49.6	49.6	48.9	48.2	46.8
2000	46.0	46.0	47.9	49.3	50.4	51.8	52.0	51.7	51.0	49.4	48.6	47.2	49.3
2001	45.5	46.2	47.9	49.9	51.4	52.9	53.6	54.0	53.1	52.0	51.4	50.5	50.7
2002	47.3	46.9	47.8	49.6	51.2	52.3	53.4	53.3	52.3	51.5	51.0	49.9	50.5
2003	46.1	45.1	46.1	48.7	50.3	51.6	52.7	52.7	53.2	52.5	52.0	51.4	50.2

Employment by Industry: Indiana—*Continued*

(Numbers in thousands. Not seasonally adjusted.)

Industry	January	February	March	April	May	June	July	August	September	October	November	December	Annual Average
INDIANAPOLIS—*Continued*													
Manufacturing													
1990	118.4	121.1	121.4	121.0	121.8	121.8	121.8	121.8	123.1	122.5	120.7	119.9	121.3
1991	118.3	116.7	114.8	118.1	118.1	118.7	118.4	118.8	119.3	118.3	118.5	118.8	118.1
1992	116.9	116.5	117.2	117.1	117.9	117.8	118.1	118.3	118.9	118.1	118.0	118.2	117.8
1993	117.1	116.4	115.7	114.3	114.8	115.9	115.8	116.7	117.8	117.4	117.6	117.5	116.4
1994	114.3	114.3	114.9	113.6	114.5	115.4	114.7	116.5	117.1	115.4	116.0	117.2	115.3
1995	117.1	117.5	117.8	117.8	118.8	119.1	117.8	118.9	119.9	118.8	119.0	118.8	118.4
1996	116.5	117.1	117.4	116.8	117.3	117.8	113.0	117.8	118.2	118.5	118.0	118.6	117.3
1997	120.3	119.0	119.5	119.3	119.5	118.9	119.0	120.1	120.4	120.2	119.7	120.7	119.7
1998	120.0	120.5	120.6	120.1	120.9	121.4	116.1	120.5	120.5	114.9	114.3	114.6	118.7
1999	119.3	119.7	119.2	118.5	118.2	119.8	121.0	121.4	121.6	120.4	120.5	120.9	120.0
2000	120.9	121.2	121.1	121.0	121.5	123.0	122.9	123.6	123.1	122.5	121.8	121.8	122.0
2001	117.7	116.8	116.5	115.9	116.2	116.5	114.9	115.9	114.6	113.8	112.8	112.5	115.3
2002	110.8	110.2	110.3	109.7	110.5	111.6	110.6	111.3	110.7	109.8	109.6	109.3	110.4
2003	107.8	107.6	107.3	106.8	107.1	107.5	107.4	107.4	107.1	107.1	106.9	106.8	107.2
Service-providing													
1990	550.7	551.0	555.1	555.6	563.8	562.5	561.0	565.2	569.7	570.5	573.4	573.1	562.6
1991	557.6	558.6	562.6	566.3	571.8	569.3	559.9	564.2	569.3	569.3	573.2	576.0	566.5
1992	561.1	562.0	566.9	571.2	581.4	578.5	572.2	576.1	582.2	587.0	588.2	590.5	576.4
1993	574.7	576.7	581.6	591.9	600.4	602.1	592.9	595.3	602.5	608.4	611.7	615.9	596.2
1994	599.4	602.1	609.1	614.7	623.4	622.1	617.0	621.7	628.3	624.0	630.1	635.6	619.0
1995	619.9	624.9	631.9	633.7	641.2	637.8	627.1	634.3	648.8	647.4	650.8	656.1	637.8
1996	633.7	640.0	644.9	649.5	658.1	653.1	642.6	648.7	656.5	656.8	663.4	667.6	651.2
1997	642.5	650.2	657.2	661.3	668.5	665.6	661.2	661.8	670.3	673.8	677.7	685.7	664.7
1998	665.9	668.2	674.4	679.5	687.1	687.8	670.6	677.2	686.0	695.4	700.0	704.9	683.1
1999	675.2	684.4	691.9	701.1	707.6	709.4	701.3	704.1	710.9	714.9	720.2	725.3	703.9
2000	706.9	710.1	718.6	719.7	729.3	729.6	711.9	718.6	723.1	724.8	723.7	726.5	720.2
2001	713.8	715.9	723.6	729.4	735.3	734.5	721.2	730.1	730.7	728.2	728.5	729.8	726.8
2002	707.5	711.2	715.7	721.8	730.5	728.4	719.7	727.8	726.9	730.9	733.8	735.2	724.1
2003	716.4	716.8	721.8	729.2	737.7	733.1	727.4	735.2	734.6	736.7	734.1	734.6	729.8
Trade, transportation, and utilities													
1990	159.4	157.4	158.2	157.0	158.9	158.9	160.4	161.5	161.5	162.2	164.9	165.9	160.5
1991	157.2	155.7	155.5	155.5	157.1	157.6	157.2	157.2	157.0	157.0	159.7	161.5	157.4
1992	155.1	154.0	154.4	154.5	157.4	158.1	156.6	156.9	157.8	162.1	164.7	167.3	158.2
1993	159.2	157.5	158.6	160.3	163.1	164.1	164.0	164.6	165.1	167.0	170.7	173.9	164.0
1994	166.5	165.7	167.5	168.8	172.5	173.6	172.7	174.2	174.9	174.8	179.4	182.7	172.8
1995	175.5	173.9	175.6	175.7	178.1	179.4	180.4	181.0	182.8	183.0	187.2	190.9	180.3
1996	182.2	181.3	181.6	181.8	183.8	184.4	183.7	184.7	184.5	185.1	190.3	193.9	184.8
1997	188.5	184.3	185.9	186.6	188.7	189.3	189.0	187.7	188.7	191.3	195.1	199.5	189.6
1998	191.6	188.6	189.5	191.0	193.7	195.3	193.6	194.2	194.4	197.5	202.1	205.7	194.8
1999	194.4	194.0	195.9	197.2	198.3	199.5	200.8	200.5	199.6	199.9	203.9	207.9	199.3
2000	203.9	203.3	204.9	203.2	204.5	205.3	206.3	205.7	204.9	208.2	210.8	214.8	206.3
2001	208.8	205.2	206.0	207.8	207.6	207.7	208.1	208.3	207.0	204.9	208.1	210.7	207.5
2002	200.6	198.6	199.1	199.9	201.0	201.7	200.7	200.7	200.0	199.3	203.6	205.8	200.9
2003	196.3	193.1	194.5	195.3	195.5	196.0	194.7	194.8	194.0	193.8	195.3	196.5	195.0
Wholesale trade													
1990	36.7	36.8	36.8	36.4	36.6	36.7	37.0	37.1	37.0	38.0	38.0	37.8	37.1
1991	36.6	36.7	36.8	37.0	37.2	37.4	36.8	36.7	36.6	36.7	36.8	37.0	36.9
1992	36.8	36.7	36.8	37.2	37.5	38.1	38.6	38.5	38.5	38.9	38.8	38.9	37.9
1993	38.5	38.7	39.0	39.3	39.5	39.4	39.5	39.4	39.6	40.0	40.1	40.6	39.5
1994	39.5	39.6	40.0	39.9	40.3	40.7	40.4	40.7	40.8	41.0	41.2	41.5	40.5
1995	41.0	41.2	41.6	42.1	42.5	42.9	42.8	42.8	42.9	43.0	43.0	43.4	42.4
1996	42.3	43.3	43.3	43.1	43.3	43.4	43.3	43.7	43.6	44.0	44.3	44.5	43.5
1997	44.3	44.0	44.3	44.7	44.9	45.1	45.1	45.1	45.4	45.3	45.6	45.7	45.0
1998	45.6	46.1	46.6	47.0	47.3	47.5	46.9	46.8	46.8	47.2	47.3	47.5	46.9
1999	46.9	47.3	47.5	47.9	47.9	48.2	48.5	48.4	48.4	48.5	48.8	49.2	48.1
2000	49.4	49.7	50.1	49.9	50.2	50.5	50.4	50.4	50.3	50.4	50.2	50.3	50.2
2001	50.6	50.5	50.6	50.6	50.6	50.7	50.6	50.5	50.2	50.2	50.0	50.0	50.4
2002	48.8	49.1	48.9	48.9	49.1	49.2	49.0	48.8	48.4	48.2	48.1	48.2	48.7
2003	47.9	47.8	47.8	47.6	47.7	47.9	47.7	47.8	47.7	47.4	47.3	47.4	47.7
Retail trade													
1990	89.1	86.9	87.4	87.1	88.4	88.3	89.4	90.1	90.2	89.7	92.4	93.7	89.4
1991	87.4	85.6	85.2	86.5	87.5	87.6	87.9	87.0	87.9	88.2	90.6	92.1	87.9
1992	87.0	85.9	86.0	85.1	86.9	86.9	87.3	87.6	88.1	90.1	92.8	94.9	88.2
1993	88.3	86.6	87.0	87.7	89.3	89.8	88.7	88.9	88.7	89.3	92.4	94.6	89.3
1994	89.2	88.0	88.7	90.6	92.8	93.5	92.9	94.3	94.8	94.0	98.2	100.8	93.2
1995	95.1	93.8	94.9	93.5	95.3	96.0	95.8	97.0	98.4	98.7	102.7	105.5	97.2
1996	99.2	97.4	97.4	97.4	98.8	99.1	98.3	98.6	98.7	98.6	103.0	106.0	99.4
1997	101.3	97.7	98.6	98.3	99.6	99.8	99.7	99.8	99.3	101.3	104.8	107.6	100.7
1998	100.9	99.1	99.1	99.2	100.8	101.5	100.9	100.7	100.8	103.0	107.3	110.0	101.9
1999	101.9	100.6	101.8	102.0	103.1	103.8	103.9	103.3	102.7	101.9	105.6	108.3	103.2
2000	104.7	103.6	104.5	103.6	104.7	105.5	104.6	104.7	104.1	106.8	110.0	112.7	105.8
2001	107.7	105.2	105.3	105.4	105.8	106.3	105.3	105.1	104.8	105.6	109.6	111.0	106.4
2002	105.0	103.5	104.3	104.0	105.0	105.7	104.4	104.2	104.0	103.2	106.8	109.0	104.9
2003	101.1	99.1	100.2	100.6	101.8	102.3	100.8	100.7	100.1	100.0	101.5	102.8	100.9

Employment by Industry: Indiana—*Continued*

(Numbers in thousands. Not seasonally adjusted.)

Industry	January	February	March	April	May	June	July	August	September	October	November	December	Annual Average
INDIANAPOLIS—*Continued*													
Transportation and utilities													
1990	33.6	33.7	34.0	33.5	33.9	33.9	34.0	34.3	34.3	34.5	34.5	34.4	34.1
1991	33.2	33.4	33.5	32.0	32.4	32.6	32.5	32.6	32.5	32.1	32.3	32.4	32.6
1992	31.3	31.4	31.6	32.2	33.0	33.1	30.7	30.8	31.2	33.1	33.1	33.5	32.1
1993	32.4	32.2	32.6	33.3	34.3	34.9	35.8	36.3	36.8	37.7	38.2	38.7	35.3
1994	37.8	38.1	38.8	38.3	39.4	39.4	39.4	39.2	39.3	39.8	40.0	40.4	39.2
1995	39.4	38.9	39.1	40.1	40.3	40.5	41.8	41.2	41.5	41.3	41.5	42.0	40.6
1996	40.7	40.6	40.9	41.3	41.7	41.9	42.1	42.4	42.2	42.5	43.0	43.4	41.9
1997	42.9	42.6	43.0	43.6	44.2	44.4	44.2	42.8	44.0	44.7	44.7	46.2	43.9
1998	45.1	43.4	43.8	44.8	45.6	46.3	45.8	46.7	46.8	47.3	47.5	48.2	45.9
1999	45.6	46.1	46.6	47.3	47.3	47.5	48.4	48.8	48.5	49.5	49.5	50.4	48.0
2000	49.8	50.0	50.3	49.7	49.6	49.3	51.3	50.6	50.5	51.0	50.6	51.8	50.4
2001	50.5	49.5	50.1	51.8	51.2	50.7	52.2	52.7	52.0	49.1	48.5	49.7	50.7
2002	46.8	46.0	45.9	47.0	46.9	46.8	47.3	47.7	47.6	47.9	48.7	48.6	47.3
2003	47.3	46.2	46.5	47.1	46.0	45.8	46.2	46.3	46.2	46.4	46.5	46.3	46.4
Information													
1990	16.2	16.1	16.1	16.1	16.4	16.5	16.5	16.4	16.3	15.5	15.5	15.5	16.1
1991	15.4	15.4	15.2	15.2	15.4	15.6	15.7	15.6	15.4	15.3	15.3	15.5	15.4
1992	15.1	15.3	15.3	15.5	15.5	15.5	14.3	14.2	14.0	15.4	15.2	15.2	15.0
1993	14.9	15.1	15.3	15.3	15.5	15.7	15.9	16.0	15.9	15.7	15.7	15.7	15.6
1994	15.3	15.2	15.4	15.3	15.3	15.8	16.0	15.8	15.6	15.6	15.7	15.8	15.6
1995	15.5	15.7	16.1	15.1	15.2	15.4	15.4	15.4	15.5	15.1	15.5	15.6	15.5
1996	15.4	15.5	15.7	15.3	15.6	15.9	16.1	16.3	16.2	17.7	17.7	18.1	16.3
1997	17.8	17.8	17.9	17.7	17.7	17.9	17.6	17.7	17.6	17.3	17.4	17.7	17.7
1998	17.5	17.5	17.5	17.3	17.4	17.6	17.5	17.5	17.3	17.3	17.3	17.5	17.4
1999	17.4	17.5	17.6	17.3	17.5	17.5	17.6	17.6	17.4	17.6	17.5	17.4	17.5
2000	17.4	17.5	17.8	17.3	17.4	17.8	17.9	18.1	17.8	17.9	18.0	18.1	17.8
2001	18.0	17.8	18.0	17.5	17.7	17.8	17.7	17.4	17.2	17.1	17.0	17.1	17.5
2002	16.8	16.7	16.9	16.7	16.9	17.1	16.9	16.9	16.7	16.6	16.5	16.5	16.8
2003	16.4	16.3	16.5	16.3	16.6	16.8	16.7	16.8	16.6	16.5	16.5	16.5	16.5
Financial activities													
1990	50.6	50.9	51.1	51.0	51.4	52.0	52.2	52.2	52.0	52.0	52.0	51.9	51.6
1991	50.9	51.0	51.3	51.6	52.0	52.7	52.1	52.2	51.7	51.2	51.4	51.5	51.6
1992	51.9	52.0	52.3	52.6	53.4	53.8	53.9	53.4	53.1	51.7	51.3	51.6	52.6
1993	52.0	52.2	52.7	56.0	56.5	57.1	56.5	56.4	56.4	56.3	56.0	56.2	55.4
1994	56.3	56.5	56.9	57.2	57.7	58.2	57.7	57.6	57.1	56.3	56.4	56.7	57.1
1995	54.8	54.9	55.6	55.5	56.0	57.0	54.9	55.1	55.0	55.1	55.2	55.7	55.4
1996	55.5	55.8	56.5	57.9	58.6	58.7	57.7	58.4	58.3	58.1	58.4	58.8	57.7
1997	59.1	58.6	59.3	59.7	60.3	61.0	62.2	62.5	62.3	62.4	62.4	62.9	61.1
1998	61.6	61.6	62.0	62.1	62.4	63.2	63.4	63.3	62.8	63.0	63.0	63.6	62.7
1999	62.7	62.8	63.5	64.0	64.4	65.0	65.4	65.4	64.7	64.4	64.4	65.1	64.3
2000	64.4	64.4	64.2	64.4	65.0	65.5	65.0	64.6	64.1	64.0	63.6	63.8	64.4
2001	63.2	63.4	63.5	64.1	64.3	65.1	64.4	64.0	63.3	62.6	62.7	63.1	63.6
2002	63.2	63.2	62.9	63.1	63.4	64.0	65.2	65.3	64.9	65.3	65.5	65.6	64.3
2003	65.2	65.3	65.5	65.8	66.2	66.7	67.2	67.4	66.9	67.0	67.2	67.2	66.5
Professional and business services													
1990	61.1	61.2	61.9	62.4	63.2	64.1	64.2	64.3	64.9	65.6	64.8	64.3	63.5
1991	62.9	63.2	64.0	64.4	64.5	65.1	65.2	66.0	66.6	65.5	65.3	65.2	64.8
1992	64.2	63.8	65.2	66.9	68.2	67.9	68.1	67.6	67.9	67.6	66.9	66.7	66.8
1993	65.8	66.1	67.3	68.3	69.2	70.8	70.5	70.9	71.6	73.3	73.1	72.9	70.0
1994	70.5	71.9	72.4	76.2	77.2	78.2	79.9	80.3	80.6	79.7	79.9	79.9	77.2
1995	79.3	80.9	82.0	82.6	83.5	84.7	84.8	86.5	87.5	87.6	86.7	86.7	84.4
1996	82.7	83.2	84.1	85.2	86.5	87.2	86.8	86.8	86.5	86.2	86.7	86.3	85.7
1997	85.5	85.4	87.3	89.7	89.5	89.3	91.2	91.8	91.9	92.3	92.7	94.0	90.1
1998	90.5	92.1	94.3	95.2	95.3	96.3	97.5	98.0	97.2	99.7	99.8	98.9	96.2
1999	95.5	96.7	98.9	102.7	103.2	103.8	104.3	105.0	105.0	106.2	107.1	107.1	103.0
2000	101.8	102.2	104.4	105.6	107.4	108.6	107.4	107.7	108.1	106.7	105.9	104.7	105.9
2001	107.8	108.7	111.0	113.1	113.2	114.0	113.3	114.3	111.5	111.5	110.5	109.0	111.5
2002	108.2	108.5	109.5	111.6	112.5	112.9	113.0	112.9	111.9	113.0	112.2	111.4	111.5
2003	108.6	108.7	108.9	111.6	113.6	114.1	114.3	113.8	112.1	113.5	112.9	112.2	112.0
Educational and health services													
1990	69.4	69.5	69.9	70.9	71.3	71.1	71.2	71.6	72.8	73.9	74.2	73.8	71.6
1991	72.9	73.8	74.4	74.6	74.9	74.5	74.6	74.6	76.0	76.7	76.9	76.9	75.1
1992	76.8	77.1	77.9	78.3	79.1	78.3	79.3	79.3	80.9	81.5	81.6	81.3	79.3
1993	80.9	81.5	81.8	82.7	82.9	82.5	81.8	81.8	83.6	84.7	84.8	84.8	82.8
1994	83.3	84.0	84.7	84.8	85.0	83.4	83.1	83.0	84.7	85.2	85.1	85.6	84.3
1995	85.7	86.9	87.2	87.3	87.3	86.4	86.1	86.1	88.0	87.8	88.2	88.2	87.1
1996	87.2	88.8	89.4	90.0	89.8	88.9	91.2	91.7	93.9	94.0	95.0	95.4	91.3
1997	84.9	94.6	95.1	94.3	94.3	93.5	91.9	92.3	94.2	95.9	95.9	96.1	93.6
1998	94.3	95.3	95.7	96.4	96.0	95.3	92.5	93.0	95.0	97.1	97.8	97.7	95.5
1999	95.8	97.2	97.6	98.5	98.2	96.9	97.5	97.2	99.2	102.0	102.7	103.1	98.8
2000	99.7	101.1	102.0	100.8	100.7	100.2	96.2	96.5	97.7	97.8	97.7	98.0	99.0
2001	96.9	97.9	98.3	98.5	98.8	97.7	97.5	98.5	101.0	100.6	101.3	101.7	99.1
2002	99.7	100.2	100.7	100.5	100.7	99.6	98.5	99.2	101.1	102.2	103.0	103.1	100.7
2003	102.7	103.3	103.8	104.2	104.1	102.0	103.0	102.6	104.6	105.4	104.8	104.9	103.8

Employment by Industry: Indiana—*Continued*

(Numbers in thousands. Not seasonally adjusted.)

Industry	January	February	March	April	May	June	July	August	September	October	November	December	Annual Average
INDIANAPOLIS—*Continued*													
Leisure and hospitality													
1990	60.2	60.7	62.1	62.4	66.5	66.6	66.4	67.4	66.5	64.4	64.3	64.5	64.3
1991	61.4	61.3	63.0	65.4	67.3	68.0	65.0	65.5	64.8	63.6	63.5	63.6	64.4
1992	60.2	60.4	62.0	64.5	67.7	68.6	68.5	68.9	67.8	67.1	67.1	66.7	65.8
1993	63.7	64.8	66.1	68.3	71.4	73.1	70.7	71.7	69.5	69.4	68.7	69.4	68.9
1994	66.5	66.5	68.5	70.4	73.4	75.0	73.4	74.9	72.9	70.2	70.3	71.2	71.1
1995	68.4	69.2	71.1	72.5	76.6	77.2	76.7	78.0	76.6	75.2	74.7	75.0	74.3
1996	70.7	71.9	73.7	76.1	80.5	80.7	78.2	80.7	77.1	76.3	76.5	76.7	76.6
1997	72.4	72.9	74.8	76.2	79.6	80.1	80.0	81.4	78.5	76.3	75.8	76.0	77.0
1998	72.4	73.3	75.3	77.4	81.5	82.6	80.3	82.9	78.9	78.6	77.9	78.8	78.3
1999	72.2	74.0	75.9	78.8	82.9	85.8	83.1	84.4	81.3	81.0	80.8	80.7	80.1
2000	76.5	77.2	79.7	83.4	87.0	89.3	86.0	88.0	85.3	85.5	82.5	81.6	83.5
2001	79.0	80.2	82.9	85.0	88.7	91.7	88.4	91.2	86.5	87.3	84.7	83.9	85.8
2002	78.8	79.5	81.5	84.3	88.8	90.5	88.3	90.6	86.2	86.2	84.2	84.0	85.2
2003	81.2	81.1	82.9	86.7	91.0	92.5	90.4	94.7	90.9	90.4	88.6	88.4	88.2
Other services													
1990	29.8	30.0	30.2	30.1	30.2	30.4	30.4	30.6	30.4	30.9	31.1	30.9	30.4
1991	31.1	31.1	31.4	31.6	31.6	32.0	31.4	31.3	31.2	31.5	31.6	31.7	31.5
1992	28.9	29.1	29.3	29.1	29.5	29.6	30.6	30.7	30.6	30.4	30.3	30.4	29.9
1993	30.0	29.9	30.4	30.3	30.5	30.8	30.7	30.7	30.4	30.7	30.9	31.1	30.5
1994	30.0	30.3	31.0	31.3	31.4	31.9	31.3	31.3	31.0	31.0	31.1	31.4	31.1
1995	30.9	31.1	31.6	31.5	31.5	32.3	32.1	32.0	31.7	31.7	31.5	31.7	31.6
1996	31.2	31.4	31.8	31.8	32.1	32.5	32.3	32.5	32.0	31.9	31.8	31.8	31.9
1997	31.5	31.3	31.7	31.9	32.2	32.6	32.4	32.5	32.0	32.1	31.9	32.2	32.0
1998	31.7	32.0	32.3	32.3	32.4	33.1	32.9	32.7	32.3	33.0	33.0	33.2	32.6
1999	31.5	32.4	32.7	32.9	33.0	33.6	33.4	33.7	33.1	33.4	33.3	33.5	33.0
2000	33.3	33.6	34.1	34.0	34.2	34.6	34.2	34.2	33.5	33.8	33.6	33.6	33.9
2001	30.1	30.4	30.8	30.7	31.1	31.7	31.5	31.4	30.3	30.2	30.3	30.3	30.7
2002	29.8	30.1	30.4	30.9	31.5	32.1	31.8	31.6	30.8	30.7	30.8	30.7	30.9
2003	30.2	30.5	30.7	30.8	31.5	31.9	31.8	31.7	31.9	31.9	31.3	31.2	31.3
Government													
1990	104.0	105.2	105.6	105.7	105.9	102.9	99.7	101.2	105.3	106.0	106.6	106.3	104.5
1991	105.8	107.1	107.8	108.0	109.0	103.8	98.7	101.8	106.6	108.5	109.5	110.1	106.4
1992	108.9	110.3	110.5	109.8	110.6	106.7	100.9	105.1	110.1	111.2	111.1	111.3	108.9
1993	108.2	109.6	109.4	110.7	111.3	108.0	102.8	103.2	110.0	111.3	111.8	111.9	109.0
1994	111.0	112.0	112.7	110.7	110.9	106.0	102.9	104.6	111.5	111.2	112.2	112.3	109.8
1995	109.8	112.3	112.7	113.5	113.0	105.4	96.7	100.2	111.7	111.9	111.8	112.3	109.3
1996	108.8	112.1	112.1	111.4	111.2	104.8	96.6	97.6	108.0	107.5	107.0	106.6	107.0
1997	102.8	105.3	105.2	105.2	106.2	101.9	96.9	95.9	105.1	106.2	106.5	107.3	103.7
1998	106.3	107.8	107.8	107.8	108.4	104.4	92.9	95.6	108.1	109.2	109.1	109.5	105.6
1999	105.7	109.8	109.8	109.7	110.1	107.3	99.2	100.3	110.6	110.4	110.5	110.5	107.8
2000	109.9	110.8	111.5	111.0	113.1	108.3	98.9	103.8	111.7	110.9	111.6	111.9	109.5
2001	110.0	112.3	113.1	112.7	113.9	108.8	100.3	105.0	113.9	114.0	113.9	114.0	111.0
2002	110.4	114.4	114.7	114.8	115.7	110.5	105.3	110.6	115.3	117.6	118.0	118.1	113.8
2003	115.8	118.5	119.0	118.5	119.2	113.1	109.3	113.4	117.6	118.2	117.5	117.7	116.5
Federal government													
1990	19.2	19.3	19.1	19.1	19.2	19.1	19.2	19.1	18.9	18.8	18.9	18.9	19.1
1991	18.8	18.8	18.9	19.0	19.0	19.1	19.2	18.9	19.0	18.9	19.0	19.2	19.0
1992	19.3	19.3	19.5	19.3	19.3	19.4	19.5	19.4	19.4	19.3	19.1	19.4	19.4
1993	19.2	19.2	19.2	19.2	19.2	19.2	19.3	19.0	18.9	19.1	19.1	19.5	19.2
1994	19.2	19.3	19.3	19.2	19.2	19.2	19.2	19.1	18.8	18.6	18.6	18.9	19.1
1995	19.4	19.2	19.1	19.9	19.1	19.0	18.9	18.9	18.8	18.6	18.4	18.7	19.0
1996	18.2	18.0	17.9	17.7	17.4	17.1	16.8	16.4	16.0	15.5	15.2	15.4	16.8
1997	15.0	14.9	14.9	14.8	14.8	14.8	14.8	14.8	14.9	14.8	15.2	15.3	14.9
1998	15.1	15.0	15.0	14.9	14.9	14.9	14.9	14.9	14.9	14.9	14.9	15.1	15.0
1999	14.9	14.9	14.9	15.1	15.0	15.1	15.1	15.2	15.2	15.1	15.3	15.4	15.1
2000	15.3	15.2	15.3	16.0	17.4	17.3	16.2	16.4	15.1	15.0	15.1	15.3	15.8
2001	14.9	14.9	14.9	14.9	14.9	15.0	15.0	14.9	14.9	14.9	14.9	15.0	14.9
2002	14.8	14.6	14.6	14.5	14.5	14.6	14.6	14.5	14.4	14.8	14.6	14.7	14.6
2003	14.6	14.5	14.5	14.4	14.4	14.4	14.3	14.3	14.2	14.3	14.2	14.3	14.4
State government													
1990	27.2	27.6	27.7	27.5	27.3	27.2	27.1	27.9	27.5	27.4	27.6	27.3	27.4
1991	27.7	28.0	28.3	28.6	28.6	26.9	26.8	27.9	27.3	28.4	29.0	29.2	28.1
1992	30.6	31.1	31.1	31.1	31.0	30.3	29.9	30.4	31.4	31.6	31.6	31.6	31.0
1993	29.9	30.3	30.4	31.7	31.1	30.4	30.2	30.3	31.3	31.3	31.5	31.4	30.8
1994	31.4	32.0	32.3	30.5	30.0	29.9	30.1	31.2	31.3	31.3	31.6	31.4	31.1
1995	30.3	30.9	31.1	31.4	30.9	30.3	26.6	30.6	31.3	30.9	31.1	30.9	30.5
1996	30.6	31.2	31.1	31.1	30.5	30.0	28.9	29.4	29.5	28.9	28.3	27.5	29.8
1997	27.0	26.9	26.6	27.0	26.9	25.5	25.3	26.7	26.6	26.9	26.8	26.7	26.6
1998	26.7	27.1	27.0	27.2	27.0	26.0	25.7	25.5	27.6	27.4	27.2	27.2	26.8
1999	26.6	27.3	27.3	27.5	27.3	26.4	26.5	25.3	28.1	27.6	27.4	27.1	27.0
2000	27.0	27.7	28.0	27.5	27.6	27.4	26.5	27.9	29.0	27.7	28.3	28.1	27.7
2001	27.5	27.7	28.0	28.1	28.3	27.7	26.7	27.6	28.5	27.8	27.8	27.3	27.8
2002	27.3	27.8	27.9	29.4	29.0	28.9	27.8	28.4	28.9	29.7	29.8	29.8	28.7
2003	29.6	30.4	30.6	30.7	30.2	29.6	29.8	30.4	29.7	29.7	29.5	29.5	30.0

Employment by Industry: Indiana—*Continued*

(Numbers in thousands. Not seasonally adjusted.)

Industry	January	February	March	April	May	June	July	August	September	October	November	December	Annual Average
INDIANAPOLIS—*Continued*													
Local government													
1990	51.1	51.7	52.1	52.2	52.8	49.9	47.0	47.9	52.2	53.0	53.2	53.2	51.4
1991	52.5	53.3	53.7	53.6	54.3	51.0	46.2	48.4	53.6	54.4	54.5	54.7	52.5
1992	59.0	59.9	59.9	59.4	60.3	57.0	51.5	55.3	59.3	60.3	60.4	60.3	58.6
1993	59.1	60.1	59.8	59.8	61.0	58.4	53.3	53.9	59.8	60.9	61.2	61.0	59.0
1994	60.4	60.7	61.1	61.0	61.7	56.9	53.6	54.3	61.4	61.3	62.0	62.0	59.7
1995	60.1	62.2	62.5	62.2	63.0	56.1	51.2	50.7	61.6	62.4	62.3	62.7	59.8
1996	60.0	62.9	63.1	62.6	63.3	57.7	50.9	51.8	62.5	63.1	63.5	63.7	60.4
1997	60.8	63.5	63.7	63.4	64.5	61.6	56.8	54.4	63.6	64.5	64.5	65.3	62.2
1998	64.5	65.7	65.8	65.7	66.5	63.5	52.3	55.2	65.6	66.9	67.0	67.2	63.8
1999	64.2	67.6	67.6	67.1	67.8	65.8	57.6	59.8	67.3	67.7	67.8	68.0	65.7
2000	67.6	67.9	68.2	67.5	68.1	63.6	56.2	59.5	67.6	68.2	68.2	68.5	65.9
2001	67.6	69.7	70.2	69.7	70.7	66.1	58.6	62.5	70.5	71.3	71.2	71.7	68.3
2002	68.3	72.0	72.2	70.9	72.2	67.0	62.9	67.7	72.0	73.1	73.6	73.6	70.5
2003	71.6	73.6	73.9	73.4	74.6	69.1	65.2	68.7	73.7	74.2	73.8	73.9	72.1
MUNCIE													
Total nonfarm													
1990	53.4	53.7	54.1	54.7	54.5	53.3	53.1	53.3	55.5	56.2	56.1	55.9	54.4
1991	53.9	53.7	53.8	54.4	55.2	52.9	51.8	51.9	55.0	55.6	56.0	55.6	54.1
1992	55.2	55.8	56.0	57.6	57.6	54.7	54.5	54.2	58.2	58.6	58.7	58.5	56.6
1993	56.3	56.6	56.5	57.3	58.1	55.6	54.6	54.4	58.9	59.1	59.1	59.1	57.1
1994	58.3	58.6	58.7	59.6	60.3	58.0	57.7	57.3	61.5	61.4	61.6	61.8	59.5
1995	60.0	60.3	60.8	61.9	63.0	60.4	59.9	59.9	63.4	62.9	62.5	62.0	61.4
1996	59.5	60.0	60.1	60.3	60.9	57.2	55.5	56.1	60.4	60.6	62.3	61.4	59.5
1997	58.7	59.8	60.3	60.8	61.5	56.9	55.4	55.6	60.8	61.4	61.6	61.7	59.5
1998	59.1	59.8	59.9	60.5	60.8	58.4	55.9	56.0	60.3	60.7	60.9	60.6	59.4
1999	57.5	58.8	59.1	60.5	60.6	58.1	56.0	56.1	59.0	59.5	59.8	59.7	58.7
2000	58.0	58.4	58.6	59.5	59.7	57.6	56.5	56.7	59.4	59.1	59.3	58.9	58.4
2001	57.3	58.1	58.3	59.6	60.0	57.7	56.1	56.5	59.6	58.8	59.1	59.1	58.4
2002	56.4	57.4	57.7	56.7	57.5	55.0	54.2	53.6	57.3	57.7	58.2	57.5	56.6
2003	55.2	55.6	55.9	56.6	57.2	54.9	54.1	54.1	56.2	56.7	56.8	56.3	55.8
Total private													
1990	41.4	41.2	41.7	42.3	42.3	42.8	42.9	43.1	43.3	43.3	43.2	43.2	42.5
1991	41.5	41.0	41.1	41.6	42.0	42.7	42.2	42.5	42.6	42.7	42.9	42.6	42.1
1992	43.0	42.6	43.0	44.5	44.6	44.8	45.2	44.9	45.2	45.3	45.3	45.3	44.4
1993	43.8	43.4	43.3	44.3	44.9	45.4	44.9	45.2	46.0	45.9	45.9	46.0	44.9
1994	45.5	45.3	45.6	46.5	47.1	47.8	48.1	48.2	48.5	48.4	48.6	48.7	47.3
1995	47.1	47.2	47.7	48.8	49.9	50.4	50.7	51.3	50.6	50.1	49.6	49.1	49.3
1996	47.2	47.2	47.3	47.5	48.1	48.4	47.7	48.2	47.7	47.8	48.7	48.5	47.8
1997	46.3	47.0	47.5	47.9	48.6	48.4	47.6	47.9	48.1	48.5	48.7	48.8	47.9
1998	46.6	46.9	47.0	47.7	47.9	48.4	47.1	47.0	47.6	47.8	48.1	47.7	47.4
1999	45.3	45.9	46.2	47.5	47.6	47.8	47.2	47.2	47.4	47.3	47.6	47.3	47.0
2000	46.3	46.2	46.4	47.2	47.1	47.8	47.6	47.8	47.9	47.2	47.2	47.0	47.1
2001	46.1	46.1	46.3	47.6	47.6	47.8	46.9	47.2	47.7	46.4	46.7	46.7	46.9
2002	44.6	44.9	45.2	44.2	44.6	44.9	44.4	44.8	44.9	44.7	45.1	44.5	44.7
2003	43.0	42.6	42.9	43.5	43.9	44.2	43.8	44.0	43.7	43.6	43.6	43.3	43.5
Goods-producing													
1990	11.9	11.9	12.1	12.3	12.4	12.7	12.8	12.8	12.8	12.7	12.6	12.5	12.4
1991	11.9	11.4	11.3	11.7	11.8	12.2	12.0	12.2	12.3	12.5	12.5	12.2	12.0
1992	12.3	12.3	12.3	12.6	12.7	12.8	13.1	12.8	12.9	12.8	12.7	12.5	12.6
1993	12.0	12.0	11.9	12.1	12.3	12.5	12.6	12.6	12.6	12.4	12.4	12.4	12.3
1994	12.2	12.2	12.4	12.6	12.9	13.1	13.3	13.3	13.2	13.2	13.1	13.2	12.8
1995	12.8	12.9	13.0	13.1	13.3	13.3	13.3	13.5	13.4	13.1	13.0	12.9	13.1
1996	12.6	12.7	12.9	13.0	13.2	13.3	13.3	13.4	13.1	13.1	13.2	13.1	13.0
1997	12.7	13.0	13.2	13.2	13.4	13.4	13.4	13.5	13.3	13.3	13.3	13.2	13.2
1998	12.6	12.6	12.5	12.5	12.5	12.4	11.9	11.8	11.8	12.2	12.1	11.9	12.2
1999	11.2	11.4	11.4	11.9	12.1	12.2	11.9	11.8	11.7	11.9	11.7	11.6	11.7
2000	11.4	11.5	11.5	11.8	11.9	12.3	12.1	12.1	12.0	11.8	11.6	11.1	11.7
2001	11.0	10.9	11.1	11.4	11.6	11.5	11.2	11.2	11.2	10.6	10.6	10.4	11.1
2002	10.1	10.1	10.1	10.4	10.6	10.8	10.8	10.8	10.8	10.6	10.6	10.3	10.5
2003	10.0	9.8	9.9	9.9	10.0	10.1	10.1	10.1	10.2	10.0	10.0	9.9	10.0
Construction and mining													
1990	1.8	1.8	1.8	1.9	1.9	2.1	2.2	2.2	2.1	2.1	2.1	2.1	2.0
1991	1.8	1.7	1.8	2.0	2.0	2.2	2.2	2.3	2.2	2.3	2.2	2.2	2.0
1992	2.0	1.9	1.9	2.1	2.1	2.2	2.4	2.4	2.4	2.3	2.2	2.0	2.1
1993	1.7	1.7	1.7	2.0	2.2	2.3	2.5	2.5	2.4	2.3	2.3	2.2	2.1
1994	2.0	1.9	2.1	2.3	2.5	2.6	2.7	2.8	2.7	2.6	2.5	2.5	2.4
1995	2.2	2.2	2.3	2.3	2.4	2.4	2.5	2.6	2.5	2.4	2.3	2.2	2.3
1996	2.0	2.0	2.2	2.3	2.5	2.6	2.8	2.8	2.6	2.5	2.5	2.4	2.4
1997	2.0	2.1	2.3	2.4	2.6	2.6	2.7	2.7	2.6	2.6	2.6	2.5	2.4
1998	2.1	2.2	2.1	2.3	2.4	2.6	2.6	2.5	2.5	2.5	2.5	2.4	2.3
1999	2.0	2.2	2.1	2.4	2.5	2.6	2.6	2.6	2.5	2.5	2.4	2.3	2.3
2000	2.1	2.1	2.2	2.4	2.5	2.7	2.7	2.7	2.6	2.6	2.4	2.2	2.4
2001	2.1	2.3	2.3	2.5	2.7	2.7	2.6	2.7	2.6	2.5	2.5	2.3	2.5
2002	2.0	1.9	1.9	2.1	2.3	2.4	2.4	2.4	2.4	2.3	2.3	2.2	2.2
2003	2.0	1.9	2.0	2.1	2.2	2.4	2.4	2.4	2.5	2.4	2.4	2.3	2.3

Employment by Industry: Indiana—*Continued*

(Numbers in thousands. Not seasonally adjusted.)

Industry	January	February	March	April	May	June	July	August	September	October	November	December	Annual Average
MUNCIE—*Continued*													
Manufacturing													
1990	10.1	10.1	10.3	10.4	10.5	10.6	10.6	10.6	10.7	10.6	10.5	10.4	10.4
1991	10.1	9.7	9.5	9.7	9.8	10.0	9.8	9.9	10.1	10.2	10.3	10.0	9.9
1992	10.3	10.4	10.4	10.5	10.6	10.6	10.7	10.4	10.5	10.5	10.5	10.5	10.4
1993	10.3	10.3	10.2	10.1	10.1	10.2	10.1	10.1	10.2	10.1	10.1	10.2	10.1
1994	10.2	10.3	10.3	10.3	10.4	10.5	10.6	10.5	10.5	10.6	10.6	10.7	10.4
1995	10.6	10.7	10.7	10.8	10.9	10.9	10.8	10.9	10.9	10.7	10.7	10.7	10.7
1996	10.6	10.7	10.7	10.7	10.7	10.7	10.5	10.6	10.5	10.6	10.7	10.7	10.6
1997	10.7	10.9	10.9	10.8	10.8	10.8	10.7	10.8	10.7	10.7	10.7	10.7	10.7
1998	10.5	10.4	10.4	10.2	10.1	9.8	9.3	9.3	9.3	9.7	9.6	9.5	9.8
1999	9.2	9.2	9.3	9.5	9.6	9.6	9.3	9.2	9.2	9.4	9.3	9.3	9.3
2000	9.3	9.4	9.3	9.4	9.4	9.6	9.4	9.4	9.4	9.2	9.2	8.9	9.3
2001	8.9	8.6	8.8	8.9	8.9	8.8	8.6	8.5	8.6	8.1	8.1	8.1	8.6
2002	8.1	8.2	8.2	8.3	8.3	8.4	8.4	8.4	8.4	8.3	8.3	8.1	8.3
2003	8.0	7.9	7.9	7.8	7.8	7.7	7.7	7.7	7.7	7.6	7.6	7.6	7.8
Service-providing													
1990	41.5	41.8	42.0	42.4	42.1	40.6	40.3	40.5	42.7	43.5	43.5	43.4	42.0
1991	42.0	42.3	42.5	42.7	43.4	40.7	39.8	39.7	42.7	43.1	43.5	43.4	42.1
1992	42.9	43.5	43.7	45.0	44.9	41.9	41.4	41.4	45.3	45.8	46.0	46.0	43.9
1993	44.3	44.6	44.6	45.2	45.8	43.1	42.0	41.8	46.3	46.7	46.7	46.7	44.8
1994	46.1	46.4	46.3	47.0	47.4	44.9	44.4	44.0	48.3	48.2	48.5	48.6	46.6
1995	47.2	47.4	47.8	48.8	49.7	47.1	46.6	46.4	50.0	49.8	49.5	49.1	48.2
1996	46.9	47.3	47.2	47.3	47.7	43.9	42.2	42.7	47.3	47.5	49.1	48.3	46.4
1997	46.0	46.8	47.1	47.6	48.1	43.5	42.0	42.1	47.5	48.1	48.3	48.5	46.3
1998	46.5	47.2	47.4	48.0	48.3	46.0	44.0	44.2	48.5	48.5	48.8	48.7	47.1
1999	46.3	47.4	47.7	48.6	48.5	45.9	44.1	44.3	47.3	47.6	48.1	48.1	46.9
2000	46.6	46.9	47.1	47.7	47.8	45.3	44.4	44.6	47.4	47.3	47.7	47.8	46.7
2001	46.3	47.2	47.2	48.2	48.4	46.2	44.9	45.3	48.4	48.2	48.5	48.7	47.3
2002	46.3	47.3	47.6	46.3	46.9	44.2	43.4	42.8	46.5	47.1	47.6	47.2	46.1
2003	45.2	45.8	46.0	46.7	47.2	44.8	44.0	44.0	46.0	46.7	46.8	46.4	45.8
Trade, transportation, and utilities													
1990	12.0	11.8	11.8	12.1	12.1	12.1	12.0	12.1	12.2	12.2	12.4	12.5	12.1
1991	11.9	11.8	11.8	11.8	12.0	12.1	12.0	11.9	12.0	11.9	12.1	12.3	11.9
1992	12.1	11.9	11.9	12.6	12.6	12.5	12.4	12.5	12.5	12.7	13.0	13.0	12.4
1993	12.1	11.9	11.8	12.2	12.5	12.6	12.4	12.5	12.6	12.8	13.2	13.3	12.4
1994	13.2	12.9	12.9	13.1	13.3	13.4	13.4	13.4	13.6	13.7	14.0	14.0	13.4
1995	13.4	13.3	13.5	14.2	14.8	15.1	15.6	15.8	15.1	15.0	14.7	14.5	14.5
1996	13.1	12.8	12.5	12.4	12.4	12.6	12.0	12.0	12.1	12.1	12.5	12.5	12.4
1997	11.7	11.6	11.7	11.7	11.9	11.9	11.5	11.6	12.0	12.1	12.3	12.5	11.8
1998	11.7	11.7	11.8	12.2	12.2	12.5	12.2	12.0	12.3	12.3	12.8	12.8	12.2
1999	12.0	12.0	12.1	12.2	12.3	12.3	11.9	12.1	12.2	12.2	12.7	12.7	12.2
2000	12.2	11.9	12.1	12.2	12.2	12.2	12.3	12.2	12.4	12.2	12.5	12.7	12.2
2001	12.3	12.2	12.3	12.6	12.4	12.6	12.2	12.2	12.4	12.2	12.6	12.5	12.4
2002	11.9	11.8	11.8	9.8	9.8	9.8	9.6	9.9	9.8	9.9	10.3	10.3	10.4
2003	9.7	9.5	9.4	9.6	9.6	9.6	9.3	9.2	9.1	9.2	9.3	9.3	9.4
Wholesale trade													
1990	1.4	1.4	1.4	1.5	1.5	1.5	1.5	1.5	1.5	1.5	1.5	1.5	1.4
1991	1.5	1.6	1.6	1.6	1.6	1.6	1.6	1.5	1.5	1.5	1.5	1.5	1.5
1992	1.5	1.5	1.5	1.6	1.6	1.6	1.6	1.6	1.5	1.4	1.5	1.4	1.5
1993	1.5	1.4	1.4	1.6	1.6	1.6	1.5	1.5	1.5	1.5	1.5	1.5	1.5
1994	1.5	1.5	1.5	1.6	1.6	1.6	1.6	1.6	1.6	1.5	1.5	1.5	1.5
1995	1.5	1.5	1.5	1.5	1.5	1.4	1.4	1.4	1.4	1.3	1.3	1.3	1.4
1996	1.3	1.3	1.3	1.3	1.3	1.3	1.3	1.3	1.3	1.3	1.3	1.3	1.3
1997	1.3	1.3	1.3	1.3	1.3	1.3	1.3	1.3	1.3	1.2	1.2	1.3	1.2
1998	1.2	1.3	1.3	1.3	1.3	1.4	1.3	1.3	1.3	1.3	1.3	1.3	1.3
1999	1.2	1.3	1.3	1.3	1.4	1.4	1.3	1.3	1.3	1.3	1.4	1.4	1.3
2000	1.4	1.4	1.4	1.4	1.4	1.4	1.4	1.3	1.4	1.3	1.3	1.3	1.3
2001	1.3	1.3	1.3	1.3	1.2	1.3	1.2	1.2	1.3	1.2	1.2	1.2	1.3
2002	1.3	1.3	1.3	1.3	1.3	1.3	1.3	1.3	1.3	1.3	1.3	1.3	1.3
2003	1.3	1.3	1.3	1.4	1.4	1.4	1.4	1.3	1.3	1.4	1.3	1.3	1.3
Retail trade													
1990	6.5	6.3	6.3	6.4	6.4	6.4	6.4	6.5	6.5	6.5	6.7	6.8	6.4
1991	6.4	6.2	6.1	6.2	6.3	6.4	6.4	6.4	6.5	6.3	6.5	6.7	6.3
1992	6.6	6.4	6.4	6.5	6.5	6.5	6.3	6.3	6.4	6.5	6.7	6.8	6.4
1993	6.4	6.3	6.2	6.5	6.7	6.7	6.6	6.7	6.7	6.7	7.0	6.9	6.6
1994	6.8	6.5	6.5	6.6	6.7	6.7	6.7	6.7	6.8	6.9	7.2	7.3	6.7
1995	7.0	6.8	6.9	7.3	7.7	7.6	7.5	7.6	7.7	7.7	7.9	8.0	7.4
1996	7.5	7.2	7.1	7.2	7.2	7.1	7.1	7.2	7.3	7.3	7.7	7.8	7.3
1997	7.4	7.2	7.2	7.2	7.3	7.3	7.1	7.1	7.4	7.5	7.7	7.8	7.3
1998	7.3	7.1	7.1	7.4	7.4	7.6	7.4	7.3	7.5	7.5	7.9	7.9	7.4
1999	7.4	7.2	7.2	7.2	7.2	7.2	7.1	7.2	7.3	7.3	7.7	7.7	7.3
2000	7.5	7.4	7.4	7.5	7.4	7.4	7.5	7.4	7.5	7.5	7.9	8.1	7.5
2001	7.8	7.6	7.6	7.7	7.7	7.7	7.6	7.6	7.7	7.6	8.0	8.0	7.7
2002	7.6	7.4	7.4	7.3	7.3	7.3	7.2	7.4	7.3	7.4	7.8	7.8	7.4
2003	7.3	7.1	7.0	7.0	7.0	7.0	6.9	6.9	6.7	6.7	6.9	6.9	7.0

Employment by Industry: Indiana—*Continued*

(Numbers in thousands. Not seasonally adjusted.)

Industry	January	February	March	April	May	June	July	August	September	October	November	December	Annual Average
MUNCIE—*Continued*													
Transportation and utilities													
1990	4.1	4.1	4.1	4.2	4.2	4.2	4.1	4.1	4.2	4.2	4.2	4.2	4.1
1991	4.0	4.0	4.1	4.0	4.1	4.1	4.0	4.0	4.0	4.1	4.1	4.1	4.0
1992	4.0	4.0	4.0	4.5	4.5	4.4	4.5	4.6	4.6	4.8	4.8	4.8	4.4
1993	4.2	4.2	4.2	4.1	4.2	4.3	4.3	4.3	4.4	4.6	4.7	4.9	4.3
1994	4.9	4.9	4.9	4.9	5.0	5.1	5.1	5.1	5.2	5.3	5.3	5.2	5.0
1995	4.9	5.0	5.1	5.4	5.6	6.1	6.7	6.8	6.0	6.0	5.5	5.2	5.6
1996	4.3	4.3	4.1	3.9	3.9	4.2	3.6	3.5	3.5	3.5	3.5	3.4	3.8
1997	3.0	3.1	3.2	3.2	3.3	3.3	3.1	3.2	3.3	3.4	3.4	3.4	3.2
1998	3.2	3.3	3.4	3.5	3.5	3.5	3.5	3.4	3.5	3.5	3.6	3.6	3.4
1999	3.4	3.5	3.6	3.7	3.7	3.7	3.5	3.6	3.6	3.6	3.6	3.6	3.5
2000	3.3	3.1	3.3	3.3	3.4	3.4	3.4	3.5	3.5	3.4	3.3	3.3	3.3
2001	3.2	3.3	3.4	3.6	3.5	3.6	3.4	3.4	3.4	3.4	3.4	3.3	3.4
2002	3.0	3.1	3.1	1.2	1.2	1.2	1.1	1.2	1.2	1.2	1.2	1.2	1.7
2003	1.1	1.1	1.1	1.2	1.2	1.2	1.0	1.0	1.1	1.1	1.1	1.1	1.1
Information													
1990	0.7	0.7	0.7	0.7	0.7	0.7	0.7	0.7	0.7	0.7	0.7	0.7	0.7
1991	0.7	0.6	0.6	0.7	0.7	0.7	0.7	0.7	0.7	0.7	0.7	0.7	0.6
1992	0.6	0.6	0.6	0.7	0.7	0.7	0.6	0.6	0.6	0.7	0.7	0.7	0.6
1993	0.7	0.7	0.7	0.7	0.7	0.7	0.7	0.7	0.7	0.7	0.7	0.7	0.7
1994	0.7	0.7	0.7	0.7	0.7	0.7	0.7	0.7	0.7	0.7	0.7	0.7	0.7
1995	0.7	0.6	0.7	0.6	0.7	0.7	0.6	0.6	0.6	0.6	0.6	0.6	0.6
1996	0.6	0.6	0.6	0.6	0.6	0.6	0.6	0.6	0.6	0.5	0.5	0.6	0.5
1997	0.6	0.6	0.6	0.5	0.6	0.5	0.5	0.5	0.5	0.6	0.6	0.6	0.5
1998	0.6	0.6	0.6	0.5	0.5	0.5	0.5	0.5	0.5	0.6	0.6	0.6	0.5
1999	0.5	0.5	0.5	0.6	0.6	0.7	0.6	0.6	0.6	0.7	0.7	0.7	0.6
2000	0.6	0.6	0.6	0.6	0.7	0.7	0.6	0.6	0.6	0.6	0.6	0.6	0.6
2001	0.5	0.5	0.5	0.5	0.5	0.5	0.5	0.5	0.5	0.5	0.6	0.6	0.5
2002	0.5	0.5	0.5	0.5	0.5	0.5	0.5	0.5	0.5	0.5	0.5	0.5	0.5
2003	0.5	0.5	0.5	0.5	0.5	0.5	0.5	0.5	0.4	0.4	0.5	0.5	0.5
Financial activities													
1990	1.8	1.8	1.8	1.8	1.8	1.8	1.8	1.8	1.8	1.8	1.8	1.8	1.8
1991	1.8	1.8	1.8	1.8	1.8	1.9	1.9	1.9	1.8	1.9	1.8	1.8	1.8
1992	1.9	1.9	2.0	2.0	2.0	2.0	2.0	2.0	2.0	2.0	2.0	2.0	1.9
1993	2.0	2.0	2.0	2.0	2.1	2.1	2.1	2.1	2.1	2.0	2.0	2.0	2.0
1994	2.0	2.0	2.0	2.0	2.0	2.0	2.0	2.0	2.0	2.0	2.0	2.0	2.0
1995	2.0	2.0	2.0	2.1	2.1	2.1	2.1	2.1	2.0	2.0	2.0	2.0	2.0
1996	2.0	2.0	2.0	2.0	2.1	2.1	2.0	2.0	2.0	2.0	2.0	2.0	2.0
1997	1.9	1.9	2.0	2.0	2.1	2.1	2.0	2.0	2.0	2.0	2.0	2.0	2.0
1998	2.0	2.0	2.0	2.0	2.1	2.1	2.1	2.1	2.1	2.1	2.1	2.1	2.0
1999	2.1	2.1	2.1	2.1	2.1	2.1	2.1	2.1	2.1	2.1	2.1	2.1	2.1
2000	2.1	2.1	2.1	2.1	2.1	2.1	2.1	2.2	2.1	2.1	2.1	2.1	2.1
2001	2.1	2.1	2.1	2.1	2.2	2.2	2.2	2.2	2.2	2.2	2.2	2.2	2.2
2002	2.1	2.1	2.1	2.2	2.2	2.2	2.2	2.2	2.2	2.1	2.1	2.1	2.2
2003	2.1	2.1	2.1	2.2	2.2	2.2	2.2	2.2	2.2	2.2	2.2	2.1	2.2
Professional and business services													
1990	2.8	2.7	2.8	2.5	2.5	2.6	2.7	2.7	2.8	2.9	2.8	2.8	2.7
1991	2.6	2.7	2.7	2.6	2.6	2.7	2.7	2.7	2.7	2.6	2.6	2.5	2.6
1992	2.7	2.5	2.5	2.6	2.6	2.6	2.7	2.7	2.7	2.8	2.7	2.6	2.6
1993	2.9	2.7	2.7	2.9	2.8	2.8	2.7	2.8	3.0	3.1	2.9	2.9	2.8
1994	2.9	2.9	2.9	3.1	3.1	3.1	3.0	3.0	3.1	2.9	2.9	2.8	2.9
1995	3.1	3.2	3.1	3.2	3.2	3.3	3.1	3.2	3.4	3.4	3.3	3.3	3.2
1996	3.3	3.4	3.4	3.5	3.5	3.5	3.5	3.8	3.6	3.6	3.7	3.6	3.5
1997	3.5	3.6	3.6	3.8	3.7	3.7	3.8	4.0	4.0	4.1	4.1	4.1	3.8
1998	3.6	3.6	3.6	3.8	3.7	3.8	3.7	3.9	4.0	4.0	4.0	3.8	3.7
1999	3.9	4.0	4.0	4.2	4.1	4.0	4.0	4.1	4.3	4.1	4.1	3.9	4.0
2000	3.9	3.9	3.9	4.1	3.9	4.0	4.0	4.1	4.1	4.0	3.9	4.0	3.9
2001	4.1	4.0	4.0	4.1	4.0	4.1	4.2	4.4	4.4	4.2	4.2	4.3	4.2
2002	3.8	3.9	4.2	4.4	4.3	4.4	4.2	4.4	4.4	4.3	4.2	4.1	4.2
2003	3.8	3.9	4.0	4.1	4.1	4.3	4.2	4.4	4.3	4.3	4.2	4.2	4.2
Educational and health services													
1990	5.8	5.8	5.9	6.0	6.0	6.1	6.1	6.1	6.1	6.2	6.2	6.2	6.0
1991	6.1	6.1	6.2	6.3	6.3	6.3	6.4	6.5	6.4	6.5	6.6	6.6	6.3
1992	6.8	6.8	6.9	7.0	7.0	7.1	7.3	7.3	7.3	7.3	7.3	7.4	7.1
1993	7.3	7.3	7.4	7.5	7.5	7.6	7.5	7.5	7.6	7.6	7.6	7.7	7.5
1994	7.5	7.6	7.6	7.8	7.8	8.0	8.2	8.2	8.2	8.4	8.4	8.4	8.0
1995	7.7	7.8	7.9	7.9	7.9	7.9	8.1	8.1	8.1	8.2	8.2	8.1	7.9
1996	8.2	8.3	8.4	8.4	8.5	8.5	8.8	8.7	8.8	8.8	9.0	9.0	8.6
1997	8.9	9.1	9.2	9.1	9.2	9.1	9.0	8.8	8.7	8.9	9.0	9.0	9.0
1998	8.9	9.0	9.1	9.1	9.2	9.3	9.1	9.1	9.2	9.1	9.1	9.1	9.1
1999	8.7	8.9	9.1	9.1	9.0	9.0	8.9	8.9	9.0	9.0	9.0	9.0	8.9
2000	9.1	9.0	9.1	9.1	9.0	9.3	9.3	9.3	9.3	9.3	9.3	9.4	9.2
2001	9.0	9.1	9.1	9.4	9.4	9.5	9.3	9.4	9.5	9.5	9.3	9.5	9.3
2002	9.4	9.5	9.5	9.8	9.9	10.0	10.0	9.9	10.0	10.2	10.3	10.2	9.9
2003	10.0	10.0	10.1	10.1	10.2	10.2	10.3	10.3	10.3	10.4	10.3	10.2	10.2

Employment by Industry: Indiana—*Continued*

(Numbers in thousands. Not seasonally adjusted.)

Industry	January	February	March	April	May	June	July	August	September	October	November	December	Annual Average
MUNCIE—*Continued*													
Leisure and hospitality													
1990	4.4	4.4	4.5	4.7	4.7	4.6	4.6	4.7	4.7	4.7	4.6	4.6	4.6
1991	4.4	4.4	4.6	4.5	4.6	4.6	4.4	4.5	4.6	4.5	4.5	4.4	4.5
1992	4.5	4.5	4.7	4.9	4.9	4.9	5.0	4.9	5.0	4.8	4.8	4.9	4.8
1993	4.6	4.6	4.6	4.7	4.8	4.8	4.7	4.7	5.1	5.0	4.9	4.8	4.7
1994	4.8	4.8	4.9	5.0	5.0	5.2	5.2	5.3	5.4	5.1	5.1	5.2	5.0
1995	5.1	5.1	5.2	5.4	5.5	5.6	5.5	5.6	5.6	5.4	5.4	5.4	5.4
1996	5.0	5.0	5.1	5.2	5.4	5.4	5.2	5.4	5.2	5.4	5.5	5.4	5.2
1997	4.8	5.0	5.0	5.3	5.4	5.4	5.2	5.3	5.4	5.3	5.2	5.2	5.2
1998	5.0	5.2	5.2	5.4	5.5	5.5	5.4	5.4	5.5	5.3	5.2	5.2	5.3
1999	4.8	4.8	4.9	5.2	5.2	5.3	5.6	5.4	5.3	5.2	5.2	5.2	5.1
2000	4.9	5.0	4.9	5.1	5.1	5.0	5.1	5.1	5.3	5.1	5.0	5.0	5.0
2001	4.9	5.0	5.0	5.2	5.2	5.2	5.1	5.1	5.3	5.1	5.1	5.1	5.1
2002	4.7	4.9	4.9	4.9	5.0	4.9	4.9	4.9	5.0	4.9	4.9	4.9	4.9
2003	4.8	4.7	4.8	5.0	5.1	5.1	5.1	5.2	5.1	5.0	5.0	5.0	5.0
Other services													
1990	2.0	2.1	2.1	2.2	2.1	2.2	2.2	2.2	2.2	2.1	2.1	2.1	2.1
1991	2.1	2.2	2.1	2.2	2.2	2.2	2.1	2.1	2.1	2.1	2.1	2.1	2.1
1992	2.1	2.1	2.1	2.1	2.1	2.2	2.1	2.1	2.2	2.2	2.1	2.2	2.1
1993	2.2	2.2	2.2	2.2	2.2	2.3	2.2	2.3	2.3	2.3	2.2	2.2	2.2
1994	2.2	2.2	2.2	2.2	2.3	2.3	2.3	2.3	2.3	2.4	2.4	2.4	2.2
1995	2.3	2.3	2.3	2.3	2.4	2.4	2.4	2.4	2.4	2.4	2.4	2.3	2.3
1996	2.4	2.4	2.4	2.4	2.4	2.4	2.3	2.3	2.3	2.3	2.3	2.3	2.3
1997	2.2	2.2	2.2	2.3	2.3	2.3	2.2	2.2	2.2	2.2	2.2	2.2	2.2
1998	2.2	2.2	2.2	2.2	2.2	2.3	2.2	2.2	2.2	2.2	2.2	2.2	2.2
1999	2.1	2.2	2.1	2.2	2.2	2.2	2.2	2.2	2.2	2.1	2.1	2.1	2.1
2000	2.1	2.2	2.2	2.2	2.2	2.2	2.1	2.2	2.1	2.1	2.2	2.1	2.1
2001	2.2	2.3	2.2	2.3	2.3	2.2	2.2	2.2	2.2	2.1	2.1	2.1	2.2
2002	2.1	2.1	2.1	2.2	2.3	2.3	2.2	2.2	2.2	2.2	2.2	2.1	2.2
2003	2.1	2.1	2.1	2.1	2.2	2.2	2.1	2.1	2.1	2.1	2.1	2.1	2.1
Government													
1990	12.0	12.5	12.4	12.4	12.2	10.5	10.2	10.2	12.2	12.9	12.9	12.7	11.9
1991	12.4	12.7	12.7	12.8	13.2	10.2	9.6	9.4	12.4	12.9	13.1	13.0	12.0
1992	12.2	13.2	13.0	13.1	13.0	9.9	9.3	9.3	13.0	13.3	13.4	13.2	12.1
1993	12.5	13.2	13.2	13.0	13.2	10.2	9.7	9.2	12.9	13.2	13.2	13.1	12.2
1994	12.8	13.3	13.1	13.1	13.2	10.2	9.6	9.1	13.0	13.0	13.0	13.1	12.2
1995	12.9	13.1	13.1	13.1	13.1	10.0	9.2	8.6	12.8	12.8	12.9	12.9	12.0
1996	12.3	12.8	12.8	12.8	12.8	8.8	7.8	7.9	12.7	12.8	13.6	12.9	11.6
1997	12.4	12.8	12.8	12.9	12.9	8.5	7.8	7.7	12.7	12.9	12.9	12.9	11.6
1998	12.5	12.9	12.9	12.8	12.9	10.0	8.8	9.0	12.7	12.9	12.8	12.9	11.9
1999	12.2	12.9	12.9	13.0	13.0	10.3	8.8	8.9	11.6	12.2	12.2	12.4	11.7
2000	11.7	12.2	12.2	12.3	12.6	9.8	8.9	8.9	11.5	11.9	12.1	11.9	11.3
2001	11.2	12.0	12.0	12.0	12.4	9.9	9.2	9.3	11.9	12.4	12.4	12.4	11.4
2002	11.8	12.5	12.5	12.5	12.9	10.1	9.8	8.8	12.4	13.0	13.1	13.0	11.9
2003	12.2	13.0	13.0	13.1	13.3	10.7	10.3	10.1	12.5	13.1	13.2	13.0	12.3
State government													
1990	7.5	7.8	7.8	7.8	7.5	5.9	5.8	6.0	7.7	8.1	8.1	7.9	7.3
1991	7.7	7.9	7.9	8.0	8.3	5.1	5.2	5.1	7.8	8.1	8.3	8.1	7.2
1992	7.5	8.2	8.2	8.3	8.1	5.0	5.0	4.5	8.3	8.4	8.5	8.3	7.3
1993	7.7	8.3	8.3	8.1	8.3	5.4	5.5	5.0	8.2	8.2	8.3	8.2	7.4
1994	8.1	8.2	8.2	8.2	8.2	5.3	5.5	5.0	8.2	8.2	8.1	8.2	7.4
1995	8.1	8.1	8.2	8.2	8.1	5.2	4.8	4.4	8.1	8.0	8.1	8.1	7.2
1996	7.9	8.1	8.1	8.1	8.1	4.2	3.8	3.7	8.1	8.1	8.1	8.1	7.0
1997	7.9	8.1	8.1	8.1	8.1	3.9	3.8	3.6	8.0	8.1	8.1	8.0	6.9
1998	7.9	8.0	8.1	8.1	8.1	5.3	4.9	5.0	8.0	8.1	8.0	8.0	7.2
1999	7.8	8.1	8.0	8.1	8.0	5.5	4.8	4.7	6.7	7.2	7.3	7.4	6.9
2000	6.7	7.2	7.2	7.1	7.3	4.9	4.9	4.7	6.8	7.1	7.3	7.1	6.5
2001	6.6	7.2	7.2	7.2	7.5	5.2	5.1	5.0	7.2	7.5	7.6	7.5	6.7
2002	6.9	7.6	7.6	7.6	7.9	5.5	5.4	4.2	7.5	8.0	8.2	8.0	7.0
2003	7.4	8.1	8.1	8.3	8.3	6.1	6.0	5.8	7.7	8.3	8.3	8.2	7.6
Local government													
1990	4.1	4.2	4.2	4.2	4.2	4.2	3.9	3.8	4.1	4.3	4.3	4.4	4.1
1991	4.3	4.4	4.4	4.4	4.5	4.6	4.0	3.9	4.2	4.4	4.4	4.4	4.3
1992	4.2	4.5	4.4	4.4	4.4	4.4	3.9	4.3	4.3	4.4	4.4	4.4	4.3
1993	4.3	4.5	4.4	4.5	4.5	4.4	3.8	3.7	4.3	4.5	4.5	4.5	4.3
1994	4.3	4.6	4.4	4.5	4.5	4.4	3.7	3.6	4.4	4.4	4.4	4.4	4.3
1995	4.4	4.5	4.5	4.5	4.5	4.4	3.9	3.8	4.3	4.3	4.4	4.4	4.3
1996	4.0	4.3	4.2	4.3	4.3	4.2	3.6	3.8	4.2	4.3	5.0	4.4	4.2
1997	4.0	4.3	4.3	4.4	4.4	4.2	3.6	3.7	4.2	4.4	4.4	4.4	4.1
1998	4.2	4.4	4.4	4.4	4.4	4.2	3.5	3.6	4.3	4.4	4.4	4.4	4.2
1999	4.0	4.5	4.5	4.5	4.5	4.3	3.6	3.8	4.4	4.5	4.5	4.6	4.3
2000	4.5	4.5	4.5	4.6	4.7	4.4	3.5	3.8	4.3	4.4	4.4	4.3	4.3
2001	4.2	4.4	4.4	4.4	4.5	4.3	3.7	3.9	4.3	4.5	4.4	4.5	4.3
2002	4.5	4.5	4.5	4.5	4.6	4.2	4.0	4.2	4.5	4.6	4.5	4.6	4.4
2003	4.4	4.5	4.5	4.4	4.6	4.2	3.9	3.9	4.4	4.4	4.5	4.4	4.3

Employment by Industry: Indiana—*Continued*

(Numbers in thousands. Not seasonally adjusted.)

Industry	January	February	March	April	May	June	July	August	September	October	November	December	Annual Average
SOUTH BEND-MISHAWAKA													
Total nonfarm													
1990	117.2	116.9	117.9	118.5	119.9	117.8	116.9	117.2	120.5	120.0	119.9	119.9	118.5
1991	116.0	115.5	116.4	117.5	118.8	117.0	115.2	115.4	119.0	118.4	118.9	118.6	117.2
1992	115.4	115.2	116.3	114.9	116.5	117.0	116.7	117.1	119.8	121.1	121.4	121.4	117.7
1993	118.4	118.6	119.1	120.3	121.8	119.3	117.0	117.7	123.8	125.3	126.2	126.7	121.1
1994	122.8	123.3	124.6	128.0	128.6	128.8	125.7	125.9	130.2	130.0	130.7	131.3	127.4
1995	128.3	128.5	130.1	130.3	131.4	132.9	129.0	129.8	132.0	131.6	132.2	133.3	130.7
1996	128.6	128.8	129.6	130.3	131.5	132.0	130.3	131.2	132.0	132.2	132.8	133.9	131.1
1997	130.3	130.8	132.3	133.1	134.9	135.4	133.9	134.0	134.9	137.0	137.9	138.2	134.3
1998	132.8	132.9	133.6	135.0	136.6	137.6	134.2	135.4	137.4	137.4	137.9	139.1	135.8
1999	133.4	134.5	135.8	137.4	137.7	138.3	135.3	136.2	137.3	137.8	138.4	139.1	136.7
2000	135.0	135.2	136.5	137.5	139.1	139.7	136.8	137.5	138.9	137.6	138.5	138.2	137.5
2001	133.0	132.9	133.7	134.5	135.3	135.2	132.2	133.3	134.1	134.0	134.1	133.8	133.8
2002	128.8	129.2	129.6	130.9	132.9	133.3	130.4	131.9	133.6	133.4	134.1	134.4	131.9
2003	129.2	129.6	130.4	131.2	132.4	132.7	131.3	131.2	132.1	132.5	133.6	133.3	131.6
Total private													
1990	105.6	105.0	105.8	106.5	107.6	105.7	105.1	105.6	108.5	107.9	107.7	107.8	106.5
1991	104.0	103.4	104.2	105.3	106.4	104.6	103.1	103.3	106.7	106.0	106.4	106.1	104.9
1992	103.0	102.5	103.6	102.2	103.8	104.7	104.4	104.6	107.2	108.2	108.6	108.6	105.1
1993	105.8	105.7	106.1	107.3	108.6	106.6	106.9	107.5	110.8	112.1	112.9	113.5	108.6
1994	110.1	110.5	111.5	115.1	115.7	116.3	115.7	116.1	117.4	117.0	117.6	118.2	115.1
1995	115.7	115.7	117.1	117.3	118.4	120.1	117.6	118.2	118.9	118.3	118.7	119.9	117.9
1996	115.8	115.7	116.4	116.9	118.2	118.7	118.3	119.0	118.7	118.7	119.4	120.3	118.0
1997	117.1	117.3	118.7	119.5	121.3	121.8	120.7	120.9	121.3	123.0	124.0	124.4	120.8
1998	119.2	119.0	119.7	121.1	122.6	123.7	121.9	122.6	123.4	123.3	123.9	125.1	122.1
1999	119.9	120.7	122.0	123.5	123.6	124.4	123.1	123.6	123.6	123.8	124.4	125.1	123.1
2000	121.4	121.3	122.4	123.3	124.7	125.2	124.0	124.8	124.6	123.6	124.2	124.1	123.6
2001	119.8	119.4	120.0	120.3	120.8	121.4	119.8	120.7	120.1	119.4	119.6	119.3	120.1
2002	115.0	114.7	115.0	116.1	117.9	118.6	118.1	119.0	119.2	118.6	119.3	119.4	117.6
2003	114.9	114.9	115.4	116.2	117.4	117.6	117.1	117.4	117.0	116.6	117.6	117.6	116.6
Goods-producing													
1990	27.6	27.1	27.4	27.3	27.7	27.3	26.9	27.2	27.7	27.7	27.4	27.1	27.3
1991	26.3	26.0	26.2	26.6	26.7	26.3	26.0	26.1	26.3	26.4	26.4	26.0	26.2
1992	25.1	24.8	25.0	24.9	25.3	26.0	26.1	26.3	26.7	26.6	26.6	26.4	25.8
1993	26.3	26.3	26.6	26.0	26.3	26.2	26.6	26.8	27.5	27.6	27.6	27.5	26.7
1994	26.6	26.5	26.9	28.4	28.5	29.2	29.4	29.5	29.6	29.6	29.6	29.6	28.6
1995	29.1	28.9	29.2	29.7	30.2	30.8	30.1	30.2	29.7	29.8	29.5	29.7	29.7
1996	28.8	28.3	28.6	29.3	29.6	29.8	29.9	29.9	29.6	29.6	29.6	29.8	29.4
1997	28.8	28.8	29.2	29.7	30.0	30.7	30.6	30.4	30.1	30.3	30.3	30.1	29.9
1998	29.5	29.4	29.5	30.0	30.4	31.0	31.0	31.1	31.0	30.3	30.2	30.4	30.3
1999	29.5	29.7	30.1	30.4	30.6	31.1	30.7	31.2	30.7	30.3	29.9	29.8	30.3
2000	29.2	29.4	29.6	29.5	30.0	30.5	30.1	30.3	29.9	29.5	29.2	28.8	29.6
2001	27.1	26.8	27.0	27.0	27.0	27.4	27.2	27.4	26.9	26.7	26.4	26.1	26.9
2002	25.2	25.2	25.3	25.5	26.1	26.3	26.3	26.3	25.9	25.6	25.5	25.5	25.7
2003	24.4	24.2	24.3	24.6	24.8	24.9	25.0	25.0	25.0	24.8	24.7	24.7	24.7
Construction and mining													
1990	5.5	5.4	5.5	5.6	5.9	6.1	6.1	6.2	6.1	6.2	6.3	6.1	5.9
1991	5.7	5.6	5.8	6.5	6.5	6.6	6.4	6.4	6.3	6.3	6.2	6.0	6.1
1992	5.4	5.3	5.5	5.6	5.9	6.4	6.6	6.8	6.7	6.4	6.4	6.3	6.1
1993	6.1	6.1	6.3	5.5	5.7	6.0	6.2	6.3	6.5	6.5	6.4	6.3	6.1
1994	5.7	5.5	5.7	6.6	6.6	6.9	7.2	7.1	7.1	6.8	6.6	6.4	6.5
1995	6.0	5.8	6.0	6.5	6.7	7.2	7.1	7.2	6.8	6.7	6.5	6.5	6.5
1996	6.2	5.9	6.2	7.0	7.1	7.3	7.6	7.6	7.4	7.3	7.3	7.3	7.0
1997	6.8	6.8	7.1	7.4	7.7	8.1	8.2	8.0	7.7	7.7	7.6	7.4	7.5
1998	6.9	6.8	6.8	7.2	7.6	7.8	8.0	8.0	7.8	7.5	7.4	7.4	7.4
1999	6.8	7.0	7.2	7.6	7.7	8.0	8.5	8.6	8.2	8.0	7.8	7.7	7.7
2000	7.3	7.3	7.5	7.5	7.7	8.1	8.2	8.2	8.0	7.8	7.6	7.3	7.7
2001	6.9	6.8	7.0	7.4	7.6	7.9	8.1	8.2	8.0	7.9	7.8	7.5	7.6
2002	6.9	6.7	6.8	7.0	7.3	7.4	7.5	7.4	7.1	6.8	6.7	6.6	7.0
2003	6.0	5.8	5.9	6.2	6.3	6.5	6.7	6.7	6.7	6.6	6.5	6.3	6.4
Manufacturing													
1990	22.1	21.7	21.9	21.7	21.8	21.2	20.8	21.0	21.6	21.5	21.1	21.0	21.4
1991	20.6	20.4	20.4	20.1	20.2	19.7	19.6	19.7	20.0	20.1	20.2	20.0	20.0
1992	19.7	19.5	19.5	19.3	19.4	19.6	19.5	19.5	20.0	20.2	20.2	20.1	19.7
1993	20.2	20.2	20.3	20.5	20.6	20.2	20.4	20.5	21.0	21.1	21.2	21.2	20.6
1994	20.9	21.0	21.2	21.8	21.9	22.3	22.2	22.4	22.5	22.8	23.0	23.2	22.1
1995	23.1	23.1	23.2	23.2	23.5	23.6	23.0	23.0	22.9	23.1	23.0	23.2	23.1
1996	22.6	22.4	22.4	22.3	22.5	22.5	22.3	22.3	22.2	22.3	22.3	22.5	22.3
1997	22.0	22.0	22.1	22.3	22.3	22.6	22.4	22.4	22.4	22.6	22.7	22.7	22.3
1998	22.6	22.6	22.7	22.8	22.8	23.2	23.0	23.1	23.2	22.8	22.8	23.0	22.8
1999	22.7	22.7	22.9	22.8	22.9	23.1	22.2	22.6	22.5	22.3	22.1	22.1	22.5
2000	21.9	22.1	22.1	22.0	22.3	22.4	21.9	22.1	21.9	21.7	21.6	21.5	21.9
2001	20.2	20.0	20.0	19.6	19.4	19.5	19.1	19.2	18.9	18.8	18.6	18.6	19.3
2002	18.3	18.5	18.5	18.5	18.8	18.9	18.8	18.9	18.8	18.8	18.8	18.9	18.7
2003	18.4	18.4	18.4	18.4	18.5	18.4	18.3	18.3	18.3	18.2	18.2	18.4	18.4

Employment by Industry: Indiana—*Continued*

(Numbers in thousands. Not seasonally adjusted.)

Industry	January	February	March	April	May	June	July	August	September	October	November	December	Annual Average
SOUTH BEND-MISHAWAKA *—Continued*													
Service-providing													
1990	89.6	89.8	90.5	91.2	92.2	90.5	90.0	90.0	92.8	92.3	92.5	92.8	91.1
1991	89.7	89.5	90.2	90.9	92.1	90.7	89.2	89.3	92.7	92.0	92.5	92.6	90.9
1992	90.3	90.4	91.3	90.0	91.2	91.0	90.6	90.8	93.1	94.5	94.8	95.0	91.9
1993	92.1	92.3	92.5	94.3	95.5	93.1	90.4	90.9	96.3	97.7	98.6	99.2	94.4
1994	96.2	96.8	97.7	99.6	100.1	99.6	96.3	96.4	100.6	100.4	101.1	101.7	98.8
1995	99.2	99.6	100.9	100.6	101.2	102.1	98.9	99.6	102.3	101.8	102.7	103.6	101.0
1996	99.8	100.5	101.0	101.0	101.9	102.2	100.4	101.3	102.4	102.6	103.2	104.1	101.7
1997	101.5	102.0	103.1	103.4	104.9	104.7	103.3	103.6	104.8	106.7	107.6	108.1	104.4
1998	103.3	103.5	104.1	105.0	106.2	106.6	103.2	104.3	106.4	107.1	107.7	108.7	105.5
1999	103.9	104.8	105.7	107.0	107.1	107.2	104.6	105.0	106.6	107.5	108.5	109.3	106.4
2000	105.8	105.8	106.9	108.0	109.1	109.2	106.7	107.2	109.0	108.1	109.3	109.4	107.8
2001	105.9	106.1	106.7	107.5	108.3	107.8	105.0	105.9	107.2	107.3	107.7	107.7	106.9
2002	103.6	104.0	104.3	105.4	106.8	107.0	104.1	105.6	107.7	107.8	108.6	108.9	106.2
2003	104.8	105.4	106.1	106.6	107.6	107.8	106.3	106.2	107.1	107.7	108.9	108.6	106.9
Trade, transportation, and utilities													
1990	27.8	27.5	27.4	27.9	28.1	27.5	27.4	27.4	28.2	28.0	28.4	28.7	27.8
1991	27.3	26.9	26.7	26.7	27.0	26.4	26.3	26.3	27.1	27.0	27.5	27.8	26.9
1992	26.5	25.8	26.1	25.7	25.9	25.9	25.7	25.8	26.5	27.1	27.4	27.7	26.3
1993	26.6	26.2	26.0	26.0	26.3	25.9	25.8	25.8	26.6	27.5	28.3	28.7	26.6
1994	27.4	27.2	27.3	27.9	28.3	28.3	27.7	27.7	27.8	27.8	28.4	29.0	27.9
1995	28.1	27.9	28.3	28.0	28.4	28.8	28.3	28.3	28.6	28.6	29.2	30.0	28.5
1996	28.3	27.8	27.8	28.1	28.5	28.8	28.4	28.6	28.3	28.6	29.4	30.0	28.5
1997	28.4	28.2	28.4	28.4	29.0	29.0	28.8	28.8	28.8	29.7	30.6	31.1	29.1
1998	29.3	28.8	28.9	29.1	29.4	29.4	29.2	29.6	29.3	29.8	30.5	31.0	29.5
1999	29.2	29.2	29.7	29.6	29.5	29.6	29.8	29.5	29.5	29.9	30.4	31.0	29.7
2000	29.6	29.0	29.2	29.6	30.0	30.0	29.8	30.1	29.9	30.1	30.9	31.3	29.9
2001	29.8	29.1	29.0	28.5	28.8	28.9	28.6	28.6	28.2	28.3	28.8	28.9	28.8
2002	27.6	27.1	27.1	26.9	27.3	27.6	27.8	27.8	27.8	27.7	28.3	28.7	27.6
2003	27.2	27.0	26.9	27.1	27.4	27.6	27.5	27.7	27.9	27.9	28.6	28.9	27.6
Wholesale trade													
1990	6.3	6.3	6.3	6.4	6.4	6.3	6.3	6.2	6.4	6.3	6.3	6.3	6.3
1991	6.4	6.4	6.4	6.4	6.4	6.1	6.1	6.1	6.3	6.4	6.4	6.4	6.3
1992	6.2	6.0	6.2	6.1	6.0	6.0	6.0	6.0	6.1	6.3	6.3	6.3	6.1
1993	6.2	6.1	6.0	6.0	6.0	5.9	5.7	5.7	5.8	6.1	6.1	6.1	5.9
1994	6.1	6.1	6.1	6.3	6.4	6.5	6.5	6.4	6.5	6.4	6.4	6.5	6.3
1995	6.5	6.6	6.7	6.5	6.6	6.7	6.5	6.5	6.5	6.4	6.4	6.5	6.5
1996	6.5	6.5	6.5	6.6	6.7	6.8	6.7	6.7	6.6	6.6	6.6	6.6	6.6
1997	6.5	6.6	6.7	6.7	6.8	6.8	6.8	6.8	6.8	6.8	6.9	6.9	6.7
1998	6.8	6.8	6.9	6.9	7.0	7.0	7.0	7.1	7.0	7.1	7.1	7.1	6.9
1999	7.0	7.0	7.1	7.1	7.2	7.3	7.4	7.3	7.3	7.3	7.3	7.3	7.2
2000	7.3	7.3	7.4	7.4	7.5	7.5	7.6	7.6	7.5	7.5	7.4	7.4	7.4
2001	7.6	7.6	7.6	7.5	7.6	7.7	7.6	7.5	7.4	7.3	7.3	7.3	7.5
2002	7.1	7.1	7.1	7.1	7.2	7.3	7.3	7.3	7.3	7.2	7.2	7.3	7.2
2003	7.2	7.2	7.2	7.2	7.2	7.2	7.2	7.2	7.2	7.2	7.2	7.2	7.2
Retail trade													
1990	17.2	16.8	16.7	16.9	17.0	16.6	16.5	16.6	17.0	17.0	17.4	17.7	16.9
1991	16.5	16.1	15.9	16.2	16.5	16.2	16.1	16.1	16.5	16.4	17.0	17.3	16.4
1992	16.2	15.8	15.8	15.6	15.8	15.8	15.6	15.8	16.2	16.7	17.0	17.3	16.1
1993	16.5	16.2	16.1	15.9	16.2	15.9	15.9	15.9	16.4	16.9	17.6	18.0	16.4
1994	16.7	16.4	16.5	16.7	16.9	16.8	16.4	16.5	16.5	16.6	17.2	17.8	16.7
1995	17.1	16.8	17.2	17.1	17.4	17.6	17.4	17.4	17.6	17.7	18.3	19.0	17.5
1996	17.4	16.9	16.8	16.9	17.1	17.3	17.1	17.3	17.1	17.3	18.1	18.7	17.3
1997	17.6	17.3	17.4	17.2	17.6	17.6	17.4	17.5	17.4	18.3	19.1	19.6	17.8
1998	17.9	17.5	17.5	17.6	17.8	17.8	17.6	17.9	17.7	18.1	18.8	19.2	17.9
1999	17.6	17.7	18.0	18.2	18.0	18.0	18.0	18.2	18.3	18.5	19.1	19.7	18.2
2000	18.4	17.9	18.1	18.3	18.6	18.5	18.2	18.5	18.4	18.7	19.6	20.1	18.6
2001	18.3	17.7	17.7	17.3	17.5	17.5	17.2	17.3	17.1	17.3	17.8	17.9	17.6
2002	16.9	16.4	16.4	16.2	16.5	16.6	16.8	16.8	16.8	16.8	17.4	17.7	16.8
2003	16.4	16.2	16.1	16.3	16.5	16.7	16.6	16.8	17.0	17.0	17.7	18.0	16.8
Transportation and utilities													
1990	4.3	4.4	4.4	4.6	4.7	4.6	4.6	4.6	4.8	4.7	4.7	4.7	4.5
1991	4.4	4.4	4.4	4.1	4.1	4.1	4.1	4.1	4.3	4.2	4.1	4.1	4.2
1992	4.1	4.0	4.1	4.0	4.1	4.1	4.1	4.0	4.2	4.1	4.1	4.1	4.0
1993	3.9	3.9	3.9	4.1	4.1	4.1	4.2	4.2	4.4	4.5	4.6	4.6	4.2
1994	4.6	4.7	4.7	4.9	5.0	5.0	4.8	4.8	4.8	4.8	4.8	4.7	4.8
1995	4.5	4.5	4.4	4.4	4.4	4.5	4.4	4.4	4.5	4.5	4.5	4.5	4.4
1996	4.4	4.4	4.5	4.6	4.7	4.7	4.6	4.6	4.6	4.7	4.7	4.7	4.6
1997	4.3	4.3	4.3	4.5	4.6	4.6	4.6	4.5	4.6	4.6	4.6	4.6	4.5
1998	4.6	4.5	4.5	4.6	4.6	4.6	4.6	4.6	4.6	4.6	4.6	4.7	4.5
1999	4.6	4.5	4.6	4.3	4.3	4.3	4.4	4.0	3.9	4.1	4.0	4.0	4.2
2000	3.9	3.8	3.7	3.9	3.9	4.0	4.0	4.0	4.0	3.9	3.9	3.8	3.9
2001	3.9	3.8	3.7	3.7	3.7	3.7	3.8	3.8	3.7	3.7	3.7	3.7	3.7
2002	3.6	3.6	3.6	3.6	3.6	3.7	3.7	3.7	3.7	3.7	3.7	3.7	3.7
2003	3.6	3.6	3.6	3.6	3.7	3.7	3.7	3.7	3.7	3.7	3.7	3.7	3.7

Employment by Industry: Indiana—*Continued*

(Numbers in thousands. Not seasonally adjusted.)

Industry	January	February	March	April	May	June	July	August	September	October	November	December	Annual Average
SOUTH BEND-MISHAWAKA *—Continued*													
Information													
1990	2.4	2.4	2.4	2.4	2.4	2.3	2.3	2.3	2.3	2.3	2.3	2.3	2.3
1991	2.3	2.2	2.2	2.2	2.2	2.2	2.2	2.2	2.2	2.2	2.1	2.2	2.2
1992	2.1	2.1	2.1	2.0	2.0	2.1	2.1	2.1	2.1	2.1	2.1	2.1	2.0
1993	2.1	2.1	2.1	2.1	2.2	2.1	2.2	2.2	2.2	2.2	2.2	2.2	2.1
1994	2.2	2.2	2.2	2.3	2.3	2.3	2.3	2.3	2.3	2.3	2.3	2.3	2.2
1995	2.3	2.4	2.4	2.3	2.3	2.4	2.4	2.4	2.3	2.3	2.3	2.4	2.3
1996	2.4	2.4	2.4	2.3	2.4	2.4	2.4	2.4	2.3	2.3	2.3	2.4	2.3
1997	2.4	2.4	2.3	2.3	2.3	2.3	2.3	2.3	2.2	2.3	2.3	2.4	2.3
1998	2.3	2.4	2.3	2.3	2.5	2.5	2.5	2.5	2.4	2.4	2.4	2.4	2.4
1999	2.3	2.3	2.3	2.5	2.4	2.5	2.5	2.5	2.4	2.4	2.5	2.5	2.4
2000	2.4	2.4	2.4	2.5	2.5	2.5	2.5	2.5	2.5	2.5	2.5	2.6	2.4
2001	2.4	2.4	2.4	2.4	2.3	2.3	2.3	2.3	2.3	2.2	2.3	2.3	2.3
2002	2.2	2.2	2.1	2.1	2.1	2.2	2.2	2.2	2.1	2.1	2.1	2.1	2.1
2003	2.1	2.0	2.0	2.0	2.0	2.1	2.1	2.1	2.0	2.0	2.1	2.1	2.1
Financial activities													
1990	6.8	6.9	6.9	6.8	6.9	6.9	6.9	6.9	7.0	6.7	6.7	6.8	6.8
1991	6.6	6.6	6.7	6.8	6.9	6.9	7.0	6.9	7.1	7.1	7.1	7.1	6.9
1992	7.0	7.0	7.1	6.7	6.9	6.9	6.9	6.9	6.9	6.8	6.9	6.9	6.9
1993	6.7	6.7	6.7	6.9	6.9	6.7	6.8	6.9	6.9	6.8	7.0	7.0	6.8
1994	6.8	6.9	6.9	7.0	7.1	7.2	7.3	7.3	7.2	7.0	7.0	7.1	7.0
1995	7.0	7.1	7.1	7.1	7.2	7.3	7.2	7.2	7.2	7.0	7.0	7.1	7.1
1996	7.3	7.4	7.4	7.3	7.4	7.5	7.4	7.4	7.2	7.1	7.2	7.2	7.3
1997	7.3	7.2	7.3	7.3	7.4	7.5	7.6	7.6	7.4	7.4	7.5	7.6	7.4
1998	7.6	7.6	7.6	7.5	7.6	7.7	7.7	7.8	7.8	7.7	7.6	7.7	7.6
1999	7.5	7.5	7.5	7.5	7.4	7.5	7.5	7.5	7.4	7.2	7.2	7.4	7.4
2000	7.3	7.3	7.4	7.3	7.3	7.4	7.4	7.3	7.2	7.2	7.1	7.1	7.2
2001	6.9	6.9	7.0	7.0	7.0	7.1	6.9	6.9	6.9	6.9	6.9	7.0	7.0
2002	6.8	6.8	6.8	6.9	6.9	7.0	6.9	7.0	6.9	6.9	6.9	7.0	6.9
2003	6.8	6.8	6.8	6.9	7.0	7.1	7.0	7.0	6.9	6.9	6.9	6.9	6.9
Professional and business services													
1990	7.4	7.4	7.5	7.6	7.6	7.5	7.7	7.7	7.9	7.6	7.4	7.4	7.5
1991	7.3	7.3	7.4	7.7	7.8	7.8	7.7	7.7	8.1	7.9	7.8	7.7	7.6
1992	7.6	7.7	8.0	8.1	8.5	8.6	8.7	8.5	8.8	9.3	9.4	9.4	8.5
1993	8.9	8.9	9.1	9.6	9.8	9.7	9.5	9.7	9.9	9.9	9.8	9.8	9.5
1994	9.5	9.7	10.0	10.4	10.4	10.4	10.5	10.4	10.4	10.3	10.3	10.2	10.2
1995	10.2	10.2	10.5	10.5	10.4	10.6	10.2	10.3	10.3	10.1	10.2	10.1	10.3
1996	10.0	10.2	10.4	10.3	10.7	10.5	10.5	10.8	10.7	10.7	10.6	10.6	10.5
1997	10.4	10.5	10.9	11.1	11.4	11.1	11.1	11.3	11.1	11.1	11.1	11.3	11.0
1998	10.1	10.3	10.4	10.4	10.4	10.6	10.7	10.8	10.8	10.5	10.4	10.6	10.5
1999	10.5	10.7	10.7	11.0	11.0	11.1	11.5	11.4	11.2	11.0	11.0	11.1	11.0
2000	10.8	10.9	11.1	10.9	11.0	11.0	11.6	11.6	11.7	11.4	11.5	11.5	11.2
2001	11.2	11.3	11.4	11.5	11.4	11.5	11.4	11.7	11.8	11.4	11.3	11.3	11.4
2002	10.6	10.7	10.7	11.2	11.3	11.4	11.7	12.0	12.2	12.3	12.4	12.5	11.6
2003	11.7	11.7	11.9	11.7	11.9	11.8	11.7	11.9	11.9	12.0	11.9	11.9	11.8
Educational and health services													
1990	18.5	18.7	18.9	19.1	19.0	18.4	18.0	18.2	19.3	19.5	19.5	19.6	18.8
1991	19.2	19.4	19.5	19.7	19.7	19.2	18.5	18.7	20.0	20.1	20.1	20.1	19.5
1992	20.1	20.3	20.3	20.0	20.0	19.9	19.8	19.7	20.6	21.1	21.1	21.2	20.3
1993	20.6	20.7	20.7	21.0	20.9	20.0	20.1	20.0	21.2	21.8	21.7	21.9	20.8
1994	22.2	22.3	22.4	22.8	22.4	22.0	21.8	22.0	23.1	23.1	23.2	23.1	22.5
1995	22.8	22.9	23.0	22.8	22.5	22.3	22.0	22.3	23.1	23.3	23.3	23.5	22.8
1996	22.8	23.1	23.2	22.8	22.4	22.2	22.4	22.5	23.3	23.5	23.6	23.6	22.9
1997	23.4	23.7	23.8	23.4	23.4	23.1	22.6	22.7	23.9	24.6	24.7	24.7	23.6
1998	24.1	24.2	24.4	24.9	25.1	25.1	23.4	23.4	24.8	25.6	25.7	25.9	24.7
1999	24.7	25.0	25.2	25.5	25.4	25.2	23.9	24.2	25.4	26.3	26.4	26.3	25.2
2000	25.9	26.0	26.1	26.5	26.5	26.4	25.4	25.8	26.2	26.3	26.4	26.4	26.1
2001	27.9	28.1	28.3	28.5	28.4	28.1	27.6	27.9	28.4	28.7	28.7	28.5	28.3
2002	28.3	28.5	28.5	28.5	28.9	28.6	28.0	28.3	29.1	29.2	29.3	29.1	28.7
2003	28.6	29.0	29.1	29.1	29.1	28.8	28.6	28.4	28.3	28.3	28.5	28.7	28.7
Leisure and hospitality													
1990	10.0	10.0	10.2	10.3	10.8	10.7	10.7	10.8	10.8	10.7	10.6	10.6	10.5
1991	9.8	9.8	10.2	10.4	10.8	10.5	10.3	10.3	10.5	10.1	10.1	10.0	10.2
1992	9.6	9.8	9.9	9.8	10.2	10.1	9.9	10.1	10.2	9.8	9.7	9.7	9.9
1993	9.2	9.4	9.5	10.2	10.7	10.5	10.4	10.6	10.8	10.6	10.6	10.8	10.2
1994	10.0	10.2	10.3	10.6	10.9	11.1	10.9	11.1	11.1	11.0	11.0	11.1	10.7
1995	10.6	10.6	10.9	11.2	11.7	12.0	11.6	11.7	11.8	11.4	11.4	11.4	11.3
1996	10.5	10.8	10.9	11.1	11.3	11.5	11.4	11.5	11.3	11.0	10.9	11.0	11.1
1997	10.8	10.9	11.2	11.5	11.9	12.0	11.7	11.8	11.7	11.6	11.6	11.4	11.5
1998	10.7	10.7	10.9	11.1	11.4	11.5	11.4	11.5	11.3	11.1	11.2	11.3	11.1
1999	10.6	10.6	10.8	11.2	11.5	11.5	11.3	11.4	11.0	10.8	11.1	11.3	11.0
2000	10.6	10.7	10.9	11.2	11.5	11.5	11.4	11.4	11.2	10.8	10.7	10.6	11.0
2001	9.8	10.1	10.1	10.6	11.0	11.1	10.9	11.1	10.9	10.5	10.6	10.7	10.6
2002	10.1	10.0	10.2	10.7	10.9	11.0	10.9	11.1	10.8	10.5	10.5	10.3	10.6
2003	10.0	10.1	10.3	10.7	11.1	11.2	11.1	11.2	10.9	11.2	11.3	10.9	10.8

Employment by Industry: Indiana—*Continued*

(Numbers in thousands. Not seasonally adjusted.)

Industry	January	February	March	April	May	June	July	August	September	October	November	December	Annual Average
SOUTH BEND-MISHAWAKA *—Continued*													
Other services													
1990	5.1	5.0	5.1	5.1	5.1	5.1	5.2	5.1	5.3	5.4	5.4	5.3	5.1
1991	5.2	5.2	5.3	5.2	5.3	5.3	5.1	5.1	5.4	5.2	5.3	5.2	5.2
1992	5.0	5.0	5.1	5.0	5.0	5.2	5.2	5.2	5.4	5.4	5.4	5.2	5.1
1993	5.4	5.4	5.4	5.5	5.5	5.5	5.5	5.5	5.7	5.7	5.7	5.6	5.5
1994	5.4	5.5	5.5	5.7	5.8	5.8	5.8	5.8	5.9	5.9	5.8	5.8	5.7
1995	5.6	5.7	5.7	5.7	5.7	5.9	5.8	5.8	5.9	5.8	5.8	5.7	5.7
1996	5.7	5.7	5.7	5.7	5.9	6.0	5.9	5.9	6.0	5.9	5.8	5.7	5.8
1997	5.6	5.6	5.6	5.8	5.9	6.1	6.0	6.0	6.1	6.0	5.9	5.8	5.8
1998	5.6	5.6	5.7	5.8	5.8	5.9	6.0	5.9	6.0	5.9	5.9	5.8	5.8
1999	5.6	5.7	5.7	5.8	5.8	5.9	5.9	5.9	6.0	5.9	5.9	5.7	5.8
2000	5.6	5.6	5.7	5.8	5.9	5.9	5.8	5.8	6.0	5.8	5.9	5.8	5.8
2001	4.7	4.7	4.8	4.8	4.9	5.0	4.9	4.8	4.7	4.7	4.6	4.5	4.8
2002	4.2	4.2	4.3	4.3	4.4	4.5	4.3	4.3	4.4	4.3	4.3	4.2	4.3
2003	4.1	4.1	4.1	4.1	4.1	4.1	4.1	4.1	4.1	4.0	4.0	3.9	4.1
Government													
1990	11.6	11.9	12.1	12.0	12.3	12.1	11.8	11.6	12.0	12.1	12.2	12.1	11.9
1991	12.0	12.1	12.2	12.2	12.4	12.4	12.1	12.1	12.3	12.4	12.5	12.5	12.2
1992	12.4	12.7	12.7	12.7	12.7	12.3	12.3	12.5	12.6	12.9	12.8	12.8	12.6
1993	12.6	12.9	13.0	13.0	13.2	12.7	10.1	10.2	13.0	13.2	13.3	13.2	12.5
1994	12.7	12.8	13.1	12.9	12.9	12.5	10.0	9.8	12.8	13.0	13.1	13.1	12.3
1995	12.6	12.8	13.0	13.0	13.0	12.8	11.4	11.6	13.1	13.3	13.5	13.4	12.7
1996	12.8	13.1	13.2	13.4	13.3	13.3	12.0	12.2	13.3	13.5	13.4	13.6	13.0
1997	13.2	13.5	13.6	13.6	13.6	13.6	13.2	13.1	13.6	14.0	13.9	13.8	13.5
1998	13.6	13.9	13.9	13.9	14.0	13.9	12.3	12.8	14.0	14.1	14.0	14.0	13.7
1999	13.5	13.8	13.8	13.9	14.1	13.9	12.2	12.6	13.7	14.0	14.0	14.0	13.6
2000	13.6	13.9	14.1	14.2	14.4	14.5	12.8	12.7	14.3	14.0	14.3	14.1	13.9
2001	13.2	13.5	13.7	14.2	14.5	13.8	12.4	12.6	14.0	14.6	14.5	14.5	13.8
2002	13.8	14.5	14.6	14.8	15.0	14.7	12.3	12.9	14.4	14.8	14.8	15.0	14.3
2003	14.3	14.7	15.0	15.0	15.0	15.1	14.2	13.8	15.1	15.4	15.6	15.3	14.9
Federal government													
1992	1.1	1.1	1.1	1.1	1.1	1.1	1.1	1.1	1.1	1.1	1.1	1.1	1.1
1993	1.1	1.1	1.1	1.1	1.1	1.1	1.1	1.1	1.1	1.1	1.1	1.1	1.1
1994	1.1	1.1	1.1	1.1	1.1	1.1	1.1	1.1	1.1	1.1	1.1	1.1	1.1
1995	1.1	1.1	1.1	1.1	1.1	1.1	1.1	1.1	1.1	1.1	1.2	1.2	1.1
1996	1.1	1.1	1.1	1.1	1.1	1.1	1.1	1.1	1.1	1.1	1.1	1.2	1.1
1997	1.2	1.2	1.2	1.2	1.2	1.2	1.2	1.2	1.2	1.2	1.2	1.2	1.2
1998	1.2	1.2	1.2	1.2	1.2	1.2	1.2	1.2	1.2	1.2	1.2	1.2	1.2
1999	1.2	1.2	1.2	1.2	1.2	1.2	1.2	1.2	1.2	1.2	1.2	1.3	1.2
2000	1.2	1.2	1.3	1.4	1.5	1.9	1.5	1.6	1.2	1.2	1.2	1.2	1.3
2001	1.2	1.2	1.2	1.2	1.2	1.2	1.2	1.2	1.2	1.2	1.2	1.2	1.2
2002	1.2	1.2	1.2	1.2	1.2	1.2	1.2	1.2	1.2	1.3	1.3	1.3	1.2
2003	1.3	1.2	1.2	1.2	1.2	1.2	1.2	1.2	1.2	1.2	1.2	1.2	1.2
State government													
1990	1.9	2.0	2.0	2.0	2.0	1.9	1.9	1.9	1.9	2.0	2.0	2.0	1.9
1991	2.0	1.9	2.0	2.2	2.1	2.0	2.0	2.1	2.1	2.1	2.2	2.1	2.0
1992	2.1	2.2	2.2	2.3	2.2	1.9	1.9	2.0	2.2	2.4	2.4	2.4	2.1
1993	2.2	2.3	2.4	2.4	2.4	1.9	1.9	1.9	2.3	2.4	2.5	2.4	2.2
1994	2.1	2.1	2.3	2.4	2.3	1.9	2.0	1.9	2.3	2.4	2.4	2.4	2.2
1995	2.0	2.1	2.3	2.3	2.2	1.9	1.8	2.0	2.3	2.4	2.5	2.4	2.1
1996	2.1	2.3	2.4	2.4	2.3	2.2	2.0	2.0	2.4	2.4	2.4	2.4	2.2
1997	2.2	2.4	2.4	2.4	2.4	2.2	2.0	2.1	2.3	2.5	2.5	2.5	2.3
1998	2.3	2.4	2.4	2.4	2.4	2.0	2.0	2.0	2.4	2.5	2.4	2.4	2.3
1999	2.1	2.2	2.2	2.3	2.3	1.9	1.8	1.8	2.2	2.3	2.3	2.2	2.1
2000	2.0	2.2	2.3	2.3	2.3	1.9	1.8	1.8	2.4	2.2	2.4	2.3	2.1
2001	2.0	2.1	2.2	2.3	2.5	1.9	1.8	1.8	2.1	2.5	2.4	2.4	2.2
2002	2.1	2.4	2.5	2.7	2.7	2.6	1.9	2.1	2.6	2.6	2.6	2.7	2.5
2003	2.3	2.6	2.7	2.8	2.6	2.6	2.6	2.5	2.8	2.8	2.9	2.6	2.7
Local government													
1990	8.5	8.8	8.9	8.9	9.2	9.1	8.8	8.6	9.0	9.1	9.1	9.0	8.9
1991	8.9	9.1	9.1	9.0	9.2	9.3	8.9	8.8	9.1	9.2	9.3	9.3	9.1
1992	9.2	9.4	9.4	9.3	9.4	9.3	9.3	9.4	9.3	9.4	9.3	9.3	9.3
1993	9.3	9.5	9.5	9.5	9.7	9.7	7.1	7.2	9.6	9.7	9.7	9.7	9.1
1994	9.5	9.6	9.7	9.4	9.5	9.5	6.9	6.8	9.4	9.5	9.6	9.6	9.0
1995	9.5	9.6	9.6	9.6	9.7	9.8	8.5	8.5	9.7	9.8	9.8	9.8	9.4
1996	9.6	9.7	9.7	9.9	9.9	10.0	8.9	9.1	9.8	10.0	9.9	10.0	9.7
1997	9.8	9.9	10.0	10.0	10.0	10.2	10.0	9.8	10.1	10.3	10.2	10.1	10.0
1998	10.1	10.3	10.3	10.3	10.4	10.7	9.1	9.6	10.4	10.4	10.4	10.4	10.2
1999	10.2	10.4	10.4	10.4	10.6	10.8	9.2	9.6	10.3	10.5	10.5	10.5	10.2
2000	10.4	10.5	10.5	10.5	10.6	10.7	9.5	9.3	10.7	10.6	10.7	10.6	10.3
2001	10.0	10.2	10.3	10.7	10.8	10.7	9.4	9.6	10.7	10.9	10.9	10.9	10.4
2002	10.5	10.9	10.9	10.9	11.1	10.9	9.2	9.6	10.6	10.9	10.9	11.0	10.6
2003	10.7	10.9	11.1	11.0	11.2	11.3	10.4	10.1	11.1	11.4	11.5	11.5	11.0

Average Weekly Hours by Industry: Indiana

(Not seasonally adjusted.)

Industry	January	February	March	April	May	June	July	August	September	October	November	December	Annual Average
STATEWIDE													
Construction													
2001	37.4	36.1	36.1	37.5	38.7	39.3	40.4	40.3	39.7	36.6	40.1	36.4	38.3
2002	37.0	37.8	38.1	37.1	36.8	40.7	41.1	40.0	40.4	39.8	38.5	38.6	38.9
2003	37.4	36.0	37.0	36.5	37.6	37.6	37.9	39.2	39.5	36.7	37.2	35.9	37.4
Manufacturing													
2001	40.9	40.6	40.6	39.5	41.1	41.1	40.5	41.5	41.5	41.3	41.5	42.2	41.0
2002	41.9	41.7	42.8	42.6	42.6	42.5	41.5	42.8	43.0	42.4	42.5	43.0	42.4
2003	42.3	42.0	41.9	41.7	41.7	41.7	40.9	42.0	42.9	42.1	42.4	42.9	42.1
Financial activities													
2001	36.7	35.9	35.8	36.2	36.3	36.6	37.0	36.8	36.6	36.3	36.4	36.7	36.5
2002	36.3	36.3	36.2	35.9	36.8	36.1	35.8	35.9	36.0	35.8	35.5	35.7	36.0
2003	35.5	35.4	35.5	35.2	35.7	35.9	35.8	35.7	35.7	35.7	35.6	35.7	35.6
FORT WAYNE													
Manufacturing													
2001	40.6	39.9	39.6	38.3	39.8	39.1	38.8	39.3	39.3	39.2	39.4	40.1	39.5
2002	38.9	38.7	40.1	40.1	39.3	40.3	39.6	42.7	42.8	42.5	41.2	43.0	40.7
2003	41.2	40.6	41.4	41.4	40.7	41.2	39.2	40.5	42.5	42.2	42.6	42.7	41.4
INDIANAPOLIS													
Manufacturing													
2001	40.6	41.5	40.5	40.6	40.7	40.7	41.2	41.1	41.1	41.2	41.1	41.1	40.9
2002	40.8	40.3	40.9	40.9	40.8	40.8	41.0	40.9	40.8	40.5	40.4	40.4	40.7
2003	40.4	39.9	39.8	39.7	39.9	39.7	39.9	39.8	39.7	39.6	39.7	39.7	39.8

Average Hourly Earnings by Industry: Indiana

(Dollars, not seasonally adjusted.)

Industry	January	February	March	April	May	June	July	August	September	October	November	December	Annual Average
STATEWIDE													
Construction													
2001	19.70	19.95	19.86	20.14	20.23	20.49	20.83	20.77	21.06	20.43	20.43	19.69	20.34
2002	19.63	19.65	19.71	19.50	19.69	19.78	19.64	19.20	19.52	20.03	20.08	20.51	19.74
2003	20.41	20.73	21.14	21.34	20.44	20.24	20.06	20.03	20.38	19.81	19.56	19.45	20.27
Manufacturing													
2001	16.09	16.16	16.05	16.34	16.23	16.37	16.40	16.54	16.58	16.71	16.80	16.90	16.42
2002	17.00	17.01	17.02	16.95	17.01	17.07	17.04	17.16	17.15	17.21	17.47	17.69	17.15
2003	17.66	17.78	17.74	17.74	17.84	17.86	17.67	17.90	17.86	17.89	18.00	18.15	17.84
Financial activities													
2001	12.58	13.16	13.34	13.27	13.33	13.23	13.26	13.27	13.38	13.44	13.54	13.50	13.27
2002	13.61	13.65	13.64	13.76	13.64	13.60	13.55	13.55	13.55	13.46	13.54	13.63	13.60
2003	13.75	13.68	13.75	13.79	13.80	13.67	13.70	13.75	13.71	13.68	13.70	13.69	13.72
FORT WAYNE													
Manufacturing													
2001	15.63	15.55	15.72	15.79	15.86	15.93	15.89	15.76	15.45	16.15	16.12	16.41	15.85
2002	16.44	16.45	16.44	16.30	16.11	16.11	16.17	16.50	16.43	16.30	16.39	16.82	16.37
2003	16.72	16.73	16.54	16.66	16.62	16.45	16.79	16.83	16.60	16.94	16.85	17.31	16.76
INDIANAPOLIS													
Manufacturing													
2001	18.33	18.39	18.38	18.65	18.43	18.60	18.24	18.24	18.24	18.24	18.25	18.25	18.35
2002	18.16	18.29	18.24	18.13	18.19	18.16	18.05	18.03	17.98	17.96	17.97	17.95	18.09
2003	18.04	18.22	18.27	18.29	18.28	18.42	18.28	18.34	18.32	18.31	18.31	18.30	18.28

Average Weekly Earnings by Industry: Indiana

(Dollars, not seasonally adjusted.)

Industry	January	February	March	April	May	June	July	August	September	October	November	December	Annual Average
STATEWIDE													
Construction													
2001	736.78	720.20	716.95	755.25	782.90	805.26	841.53	837.03	836.08	747.74	819.24	716.72	779.02
2002	726.31	742.77	750.95	723.45	724.59	805.05	807.20	768.00	788.61	797.19	773.08	791.69	767.89
2003	763.33	746.28	782.18	778.91	768.54	761.02	760.27	785.18	805.01	727.03	727.63	698.26	758.10
Manufacturing													
2001	658.08	656.10	651.63	645.43	667.05	672.81	664.20	686.41	688.07	690.12	697.20	713.18	673.22
2002	712.30	709.32	728.46	722.07	724.63	725.48	707.16	734.45	737.45	729.70	742.48	760.67	727.16
2003	747.02	746.76	743.31	739.76	743.93	744.76	722.70	751.80	766.19	753.17	763.20	778.64	751.06
Financial activities													
2001	461.69	472.44	477.57	480.37	483.88	484.22	490.62	488.34	489.71	487.87	492.86	495.45	484.36
2002	494.04	495.50	493.77	493.98	501.95	490.96	485.09	486.45	487.80	481.87	480.67	486.59	489.60
2003	488.13	484.27	488.13	485.41	492.66	490.75	490.46	490.88	489.45	488.38	487.72	488.73	488.43
FORT WAYNE													
Manufacturing													
2001	634.58	620.45	622.51	604.76	631.23	622.86	616.53	619.37	607.19	633.08	635.13	658.04	626.08
2002	639.52	636.62	659.24	653.63	633.12	649.23	640.33	704.55	703.20	692.75	675.27	723.26	666.26
2003	688.86	679.24	684.76	689.72	676.43	677.74	658.17	681.62	705.50	714.87	717.81	739.14	693.86
INDIANAPOLIS													
Manufacturing													
2001	744.20	763.19	744.39	757.19	750.10	757.02	751.49	749.66	749.66	751.49	750.08	750.08	750.52
2002	740.93	737.09	746.02	741.52	742.15	740.93	740.05	737.43	733.58	727.38	725.99	725.18	736.26
2003	728.82	726.98	727.15	726.11	729.37	731.27	729.37	729.93	727.30	725.08	726.91	726.51	727.54

IOWA AT A GLANCE

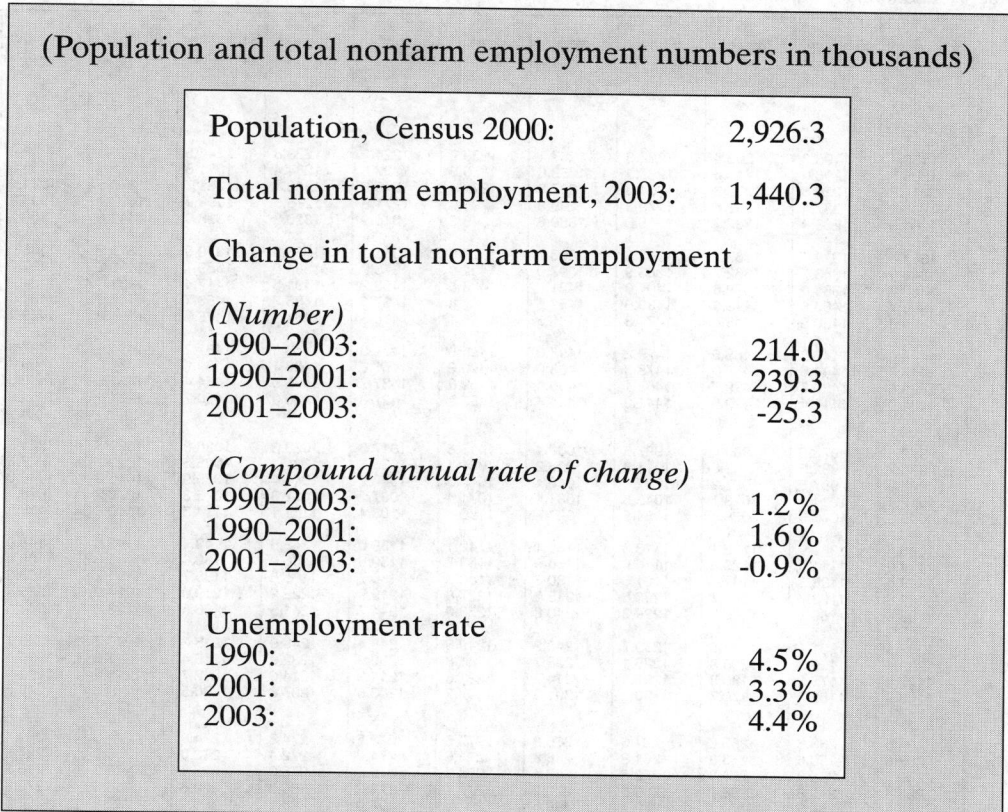

(Population and total nonfarm employment numbers in thousands)

Population, Census 2000:	2,926.3
Total nonfarm employment, 2003:	1,440.3
Change in total nonfarm employment	
(Number)	
1990–2003:	214.0
1990–2001:	239.3
2001–2003:	-25.3
(Compound annual rate of change)	
1990–2003:	1.2%
1990–2001:	1.6%
2001–2003:	-0.9%
Unemployment rate	
1990:	4.5%
2001:	3.3%
2003:	4.4%

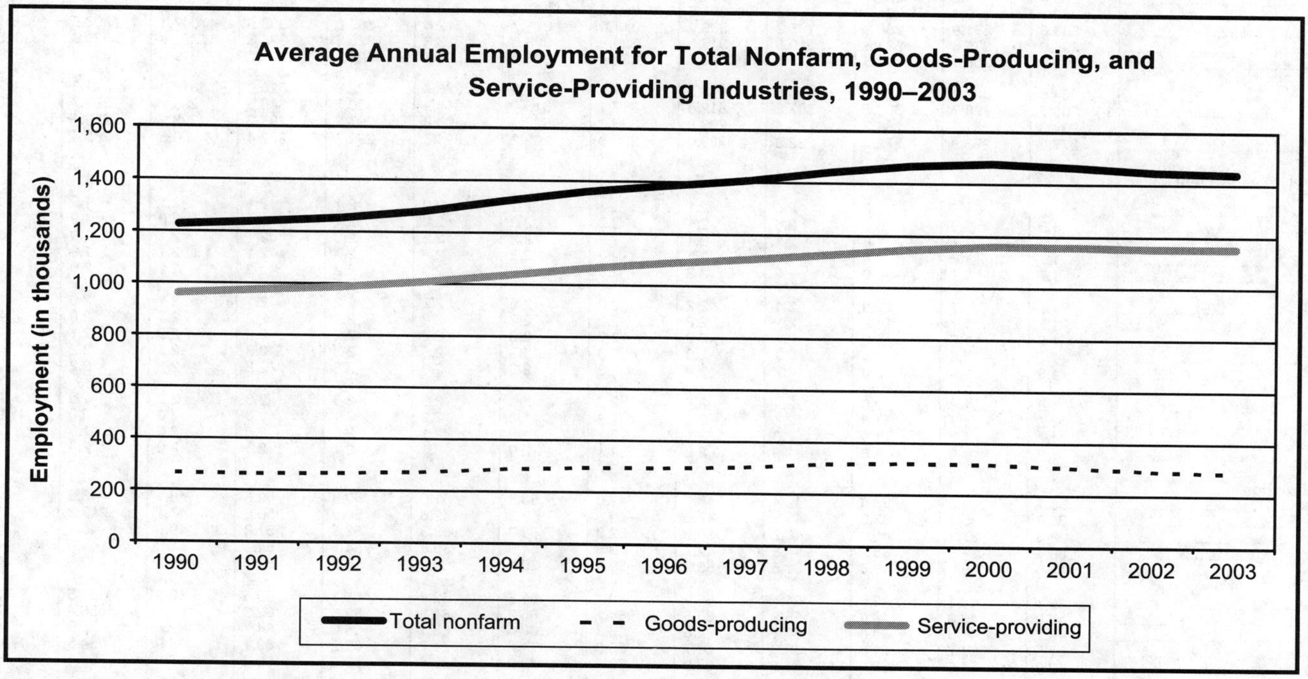

Nonfarm payroll employment gained throughout the 1990s before dropping somewhat following the 2001 recession, largely because of a decline in jobs in goods-producing industries. Most of the jobs created during the 1990s were in the service-providing sector, which stagnated during the early 2000s. Financial activities and educational and health services were the only two service-producing industries that experienced substantial gains from 2000 to 2003.

Employment by Industry: Iowa

(Numbers in thousands. Not seasonally adjusted.)

Industry	January	February	March	April	May	June	July	August	September	October	November	December	Annual Average
STATEWIDE													
Total nonfarm													
1990	1188.1	1195.3	1203.4	1222.6	1237.1	1239.9	1224.2	1223.8	1244.5	1245.8	1248.2	1243.5	1226.3
1991	1205.3	1206.0	1217.5	1237.3	1252.8	1256.3	1236.5	1234.4	1251.8	1253.5	1254.0	1252.4	1238.1
1992	1214.8	1220.3	1232.3	1254.3	1267.8	1272.4	1245.5	1246.1	1261.7	1270.5	1274.1	1271.2	1252.5
1993	1233.4	1237.4	1249.6	1273.3	1290.3	1298.7	1271.8	1275.6	1293.9	1303.7	1307.3	1307.5	1278.5
1994	1266.9	1268.9	1287.7	1315.0	1330.6	1345.3	1316.9	1320.2	1338.0	1342.6	1353.7	1353.1	1319.9
1995	1314.4	1319.7	1337.2	1353.6	1366.7	1377.8	1351.1	1355.5	1370.0	1378.9	1385.0	1386.7	1358.0
1996	1346.0	1343.7	1362.7	1383.9	1397.0	1402.0	1376.9	1381.0	1389.7	1403.5	1407.7	1407.2	1383.4
1997	1363.3	1364.0	1379.6	1401.0	1421.6	1428.6	1403.2	1401.5	1417.4	1431.3	1434.2	1438.4	1407.0
1998	1396.7	1400.6	1413.6	1439.0	1457.5	1467.8	1437.7	1438.7	1453.7	1465.9	1469.0	1473.1	1442.7
1999	1424.6	1430.5	1445.4	1474.3	1486.5	1495.1	1464.3	1461.5	1475.3	1484.2	1489.3	1492.2	1468.6
2000	1443.6	1446.8	1465.5	1479.2	1493.0	1495.9	1474.0	1473.8	1487.2	1494.5	1497.3	1490.7	1478.4
2001	1446.7	1444.5	1455.0	1475.3	1488.0	1490.3	1457.6	1458.1	1469.9	1468.0	1468.7	1464.8	1465.6
2002	1422.6	1420.8	1429.7	1453.1	1466.4	1469.6	1437.7	1435.6	1454.4	1457.5	1462.0	1458.6	1447.3
2003	1411.9	1411.4	1420.5	1441.3	1454.4	1455.7	1427.3	1430.9	1450.7	1461.1	1461.9	1456.4	1440.3
Total private													
1990	972.6	973.5	980.4	997.6	1009.4	1016.6	1017.5	1023.3	1028.8	1024.5	1024.5	1020.0	1007.3
1991	985.7	982.5	992.5	1011.8	1025.2	1031.7	1030.6	1031.1	1035.5	1029.7	1027.5	1026.3	1017.5
1992	993.8	997.8	1007.2	1027.4	1040.4	1045.3	1040.9	1044.4	1045.9	1045.9	1046.0	1043.6	1031.5
1993	1012.1	1014.3	1023.1	1045.8	1061.4	1071.4	1067.2	1072.3	1075.3	1076.2	1076.7	1077.3	1056.0
1994	1043.5	1043.5	1058.5	1084.5	1097.7	1110.4	1108.4	1111.1	1114.5	1110.6	1116.2	1117.0	1092.9
1995	1085.6	1087.9	1102.1	1118.3	1130.1	1142.1	1139.0	1143.6	1143.4	1143.6	1148.0	1149.6	1127.7
1996	1114.2	1111.0	1125.8	1146.0	1156.9	1163.8	1159.6	1166.9	1160.6	1165.6	1168.6	1167.9	1150.5
1997	1129.4	1128.3	1141.5	1161.6	1180.3	1188.8	1186.7	1185.6	1185.7	1191.2	1193.3	1196.2	1172.3
1998	1160.8	1162.7	1174.1	1198.6	1215.2	1227.8	1219.9	1222.2	1219.0	1224.9	1225.4	1228.9	1206.6
1999	1185.6	1189.4	1202.3	1229.3	1240.8	1253.0	1244.7	1241.5	1236.5	1238.8	1242.5	1245.1	1229.1
2000	1202.1	1201.1	1217.5	1230.7	1240.2	1249.6	1248.4	1249.6	1245.9	1246.7	1248.1	1241.6	1235.1
2001	1202.1	1196.3	1205.9	1225.1	1236.7	1241.8	1230.7	1232.9	1225.4	1217.6	1216.4	1214.1	1220.4
2002	1177.4	1172.5	1180.5	1203.4	1214.7	1221.6	1214.3	1214.0	1212.7	1209.2	1211.7	1208.3	1203.4
2003	1168.9	1162.7	1170.7	1190.7	1201.9	1207.7	1203.5	1207.6	1206.5	1210.6	1209.6	1205.0	1195.5
Goods-producing													
1990	254.6	253.8	253.2	261.3	266.8	272.3	273.5	274.8	274.8	271.9	269.4	262.8	265.7
1991	252.6	250.6	253.3	261.3	266.8	271.6	274.2	272.4	272.0	268.6	264.8	260.4	264.0
1992	249.7	252.0	254.8	262.8	268.4	274.4	275.3	275.9	273.1	270.9	270.2	264.7	266.0
1993	255.4	255.8	258.2	263.5	270.2	278.0	278.8	280.9	280.6	280.9	279.8	275.8	271.4
1994	265.4	264.3	270.3	280.7	286.6	294.8	296.0	295.4	293.9	292.5	292.3	288.8	285.0
1995	279.4	279.2	283.9	289.9	294.5	302.1	302.8	302.4	301.2	298.4	296.9	294.5	293.7
1996	282.3	279.6	284.3	293.3	296.6	302.2	301.8	302.1	301.8	300.9	299.2	295.6	294.9
1997	283.6	281.9	286.2	295.9	303.6	311.0	311.7	312.6	309.6	308.5	307.1	303.5	301.2
1998	295.0	295.6	298.8	310.8	317.9	326.2	328.6	329.3	325.5	325.3	322.8	320.6	316.3
1999	306.4	308.1	311.5	320.6	326.3	333.1	330.1	329.1	325.3	321.7	319.5	316.8	320.7
2000	304.9	303.4	310.2	316.1	321.0	327.2	327.9	326.7	322.8	320.9	318.0	311.3	317.5
2001	300.6	298.7	300.7	307.8	312.8	317.1	316.0	314.9	309.7	302.6	299.9	296.7	306.5
2002	284.3	281.7	284.2	293.4	298.8	303.3	302.3	300.8	297.3	295.2	293.9	289.1	293.7
2003	277.2	273.3	275.7	282.8	288.0	292.8	293.2	294.7	292.7	292.4	290.5	285.4	286.6
Natural resources and mining													
1990	1.6	1.6	1.8	2.0	2.1	2.1	2.1	2.2	2.1	2.1	2.1	1.9	1.9
1991	1.5	1.6	1.8	2.0	2.1	2.2	2.2	2.2	2.1	2.1	2.0	1.9	1.9
1992	1.6	1.7	1.9	2.1	2.1	2.2	2.2	2.2	2.2	2.1	2.1	1.9	2.0
1993	1.7	1.8	1.9	2.0	2.1	2.2	2.2	2.2	2.1	2.1	2.1	1.9	2.0
1994	1.7	1.7	2.0	2.2	2.2	2.3	2.3	2.3	2.2	2.2	2.2	2.0	2.1
1995	1.7	1.7	1.9	2.1	2.2	2.3	2.2	2.2	2.2	2.1	2.1	2.0	2.0
1996	1.7	1.7	1.9	2.2	2.2	2.2	2.2	2.2	2.2	2.2	2.1	2.0	2.0
1997	1.6	1.7	1.9	2.1	2.2	2.2	2.2	2.2	2.2	2.2	2.2	2.1	2.0
1998	1.7	1.8	1.9	2.2	2.2	2.3	2.3	2.3	2.3	2.3	2.3	2.2	2.1
1999	1.8	1.9	2.0	2.2	2.3	2.3	2.3	2.3	2.3	2.3	2.3	2.2	2.1
2000	1.8	1.8	2.0	2.1	2.2	2.3	2.3	2.3	2.3	2.3	2.2	1.9	2.1
2001	1.6	1.7	1.8	2.1	2.2	2.2	2.2	2.2	2.1	2.0	2.0	2.0	2.0
2002	1.7	1.7	1.9	2.0	2.1	2.1	1.9	2.1	2.0	2.0	2.0	1.9	2.0
2003	1.5	1.5	1.6	1.9	2.0	2.1	2.0	2.1	2.1	2.1	2.0	2.0	1.9
Construction													
1990	35.1	34.8	36.5	42.4	46.0	49.0	50.6	51.9	50.8	49.6	48.1	43.9	44.8
1991	36.6	35.5	37.6	43.8	47.6	50.9	52.3	52.6	50.9	50.0	47.1	43.2	45.6
1992	38.3	37.8	40.0	46.2	50.0	52.9	53.7	53.8	52.3	51.8	49.6	45.1	47.6
1993	38.4	37.7	38.9	44.3	49.7	53.8	54.8	55.6	54.7	54.4	53.0	49.0	48.6
1994	41.0	39.8	43.6	51.6	55.9	59.5	60.1	60.3	58.7	57.7	56.3	52.5	53.0
1995	45.1	44.1	46.4	51.4	55.0	60.1	61.5	62.4	61.1	60.5	58.9	55.5	55.1
1996	47.9	46.3	49.0	56.9	60.5	64.2	65.2	64.9	63.6	62.3	60.4	56.4	58.1
1997	48.1	47.5	50.6	57.1	62.6	66.7	68.4	68.1	66.0	64.7	62.6	58.9	60.1
1998	51.5	50.7	51.8	59.3	64.7	69.3	71.2	71.7	69.2	69.1	66.9	64.5	63.3
1999	53.8	54.5	56.8	64.5	68.9	73.6	73.5	72.9	70.1	69.2	67.4	64.1	65.7
2000	54.5	53.4	58.2	62.8	66.4	69.9	70.9	70.8	68.2	67.0	65.0	60.0	63.9
2001	53.4	52.6	54.1	61.0	66.6	70.4	71.5	71.9	69.4	68.5	67.4	63.7	64.2
2002	54.8	53.1	55.4	62.9	67.1	70.2	71.2	70.9	68.6	68.2	67.1	63.4	64.4
2003	55.2	52.5	54.6	61.7	66.5	69.4	71.1	72.0	70.4	70.0	68.6	64.1	64.7

Employment by Industry: Iowa—*Continued*

(Numbers in thousands. Not seasonally adjusted.)

Industry	January	February	March	April	May	June	July	August	September	October	November	December	Annual Average
STATEWIDE—*Continued*													
Manufacturing													
1990	217.9	217.4	214.9	216.9	218.7	221.2	220.8	220.7	221.9	220.2	219.2	217.0	218.9
1991	214.5	213.5	213.9	215.5	217.1	218.5	219.7	217.6	219.0	216.5	215.7	215.3	216.4
1992	209.8	212.5	212.9	214.5	216.3	219.3	219.4	219.9	218.6	217.0	218.5	217.7	216.3
1993	215.3	216.3	217.4	217.2	218.4	222.0	221.8	223.1	223.8	224.4	224.7	224.9	220.7
1994	222.7	222.8	224.7	226.9	228.5	233.0	233.6	232.8	233.0	232.6	233.8	234.3	229.8
1995	232.6	233.4	235.6	236.4	237.3	239.7	239.1	237.8	237.9	235.8	235.9	237.0	236.5
1996	232.7	231.6	233.4	234.2	233.9	235.8	234.4	235.0	236.0	236.4	236.7	237.2	234.7
1997	233.9	232.7	233.7	236.7	238.8	242.1	241.1	242.3	241.4	241.6	242.3	242.5	239.0
1998	241.8	243.1	245.1	249.3	251.0	254.6	255.1	255.3	254.0	253.9	253.6	253.9	250.8
1999	250.8	251.7	252.7	253.9	255.1	257.2	254.3	253.9	252.9	250.2	249.8	250.5	252.7
2000	248.6	248.2	250.0	251.2	252.4	255.0	254.7	253.6	252.3	251.6	250.8	249.4	251.4
2001	245.6	244.4	244.8	244.7	244.0	244.5	242.3	240.8	238.2	232.1	230.5	231.0	240.2
2002	227.8	226.9	226.9	228.5	229.6	231.0	229.2	227.8	226.7	225.0	224.8	223.8	227.3
2003	220.5	219.3	219.5	219.2	219.5	221.3	220.1	220.6	220.2	220.3	219.9	219.3	220.0
Service-providing													
1990	933.5	941.5	950.2	961.3	970.3	967.6	950.7	949.0	969.7	973.9	978.8	980.7	960.6
1991	952.7	955.4	964.2	976.0	986.0	984.7	962.3	962.0	979.8	984.9	989.2	992.0	974.1
1992	965.1	968.3	977.5	991.5	999.4	998.0	970.2	970.2	988.6	999.6	1003.9	1006.5	986.5
1993	978.0	981.6	991.4	1009.8	1020.1	1020.7	993.0	994.7	1013.3	1022.8	1027.5	1031.7	1007.0
1994	1001.5	1004.6	1017.4	1034.3	1044.0	1050.5	1020.9	1024.8	1044.1	1050.1	1061.4	1064.3	1034.8
1995	1035.0	1040.5	1053.3	1063.7	1072.2	1075.7	1048.3	1053.1	1068.8	1080.5	1088.1	1092.2	1064.2
1996	1063.7	1064.1	1078.4	1090.6	1100.4	1099.8	1075.1	1078.9	1087.9	1102.6	1108.5	1111.6	1088.4
1997	1079.7	1082.1	1093.4	1105.1	1118.0	1117.6	1091.5	1088.9	1107.8	1122.8	1127.1	1134.9	1105.7
1998	1101.7	1105.0	1114.8	1128.2	1139.6	1141.6	1109.1	1109.4	1128.2	1140.6	1146.2	1152.5	1126.4
1999	1118.2	1122.4	1133.9	1153.7	1160.2	1162.0	1134.2	1132.4	1150.0	1162.5	1169.8	1175.4	1147.8
2000	1138.7	1143.4	1155.3	1163.1	1172.0	1168.7	1146.1	1147.1	1164.4	1173.6	1179.3	1179.4	1160.9
2001	1146.1	1145.8	1154.3	1167.5	1175.2	1173.2	1141.6	1143.2	1160.2	1165.4	1168.8	1168.1	1159.1
2002	1138.3	1139.1	1145.5	1159.7	1167.6	1166.3	1135.4	1134.8	1157.1	1162.3	1168.1	1169.5	1153.6
2003	1134.7	1138.1	1144.8	1158.5	1166.4	1162.9	1134.1	1136.2	1158.0	1168.7	1171.4	1171.0	1153.7
Trade, transportation, and utilities													
1990	261.9	259.1	261.6	266.4	268.9	270.9	271.0	272.9	273.2	274.0	276.4	278.2	269.5
1991	266.2	261.9	263.7	267.8	270.9	272.5	273.0	273.5	272.7	273.0	275.9	277.8	270.7
1992	267.5	265.0	267.0	271.9	274.3	275.3	274.1	274.6	273.6	277.4	279.4	282.3	273.5
1993	270.5	268.2	270.1	275.4	278.9	281.0	282.4	283.4	281.4	283.2	285.8	288.3	279.0
1994	276.5	274.1	276.7	282.3	284.8	287.4	291.9	292.4	293.6	292.2	296.1	299.5	287.2
1995	288.0	285.6	288.0	290.8	293.9	295.0	296.5	298.2	296.8	297.5	302.1	304.6	294.7
1996	293.8	289.1	291.3	295.5	298.4	298.9	299.9	305.2	299.4	302.8	307.0	308.8	299.1
1997	297.5	293.1	295.3	299.5	304.7	304.5	305.7	302.9	304.3	306.6	311.3	315.5	303.4
1998	301.0	296.9	298.6	303.5	307.8	310.3	310.1	311.1	311.4	314.5	317.6	320.9	308.6
1999	306.4	301.7	304.1	310.0	312.0	313.6	318.4	317.4	315.0	317.9	322.0	325.1	313.6
2000	310.4	308.4	310.6	313.7	315.1	317.0	317.0	316.9	315.9	317.9	322.6	324.2	315.8
2001	310.8	306.3	306.9	310.3	312.6	313.2	311.9	312.8	310.5	309.7	314.7	315.4	311.3
2002	303.6	299.1	300.3	304.2	305.6	307.9	307.2	307.4	306.0	306.4	310.9	312.3	305.9
2003	299.5	295.7	297.6	301.3	304.2	304.3	304.9	304.9	303.4	304.8	307.6	309.1	303.1
Wholesale trade													
1990	61.2	61.0	61.8	64.0	64.1	64.2	64.3	64.7	65.0	65.5	63.9	63.6	63.6
1991	61.5	61.2	62.0	64.0	64.8	65.3	65.6	65.3	65.3	65.1	64.2	63.7	64.0
1992	62.2	62.1	62.9	64.9	65.1	65.0	64.9	64.8	64.1	66.3	65.1	64.9	64.3
1993	63.3	63.0	63.6	65.0	66.3	66.4	68.4	69.0	67.0	66.4	65.4	65.2	65.7
1994	62.9	63.0	63.9	66.3	66.0	66.4	70.0	69.1	68.8	66.9	66.2	66.1	66.3
1995	64.7	64.9	65.6	66.8	67.7	67.6	69.2	70.0	68.7	67.7	67.3	67.5	67.3
1996	65.6	65.3	66.4	67.8	68.3	68.4	67.8	71.7	67.9	69.1	68.4	67.9	67.8
1997	65.9	65.6	66.5	68.2	68.7	68.7	70.8	70.3	69.5	70.0	68.8	68.6	68.4
1998	67.6	67.3	67.8	69.2	69.8	70.2	72.2	70.2	70.4	70.0	69.2	69.0	69.4
1999	67.0	67.1	67.5	69.0	69.4	69.6	70.5	70.3	68.9	69.5	68.7	68.5	68.8
2000	66.4	66.3	67.5	68.8	68.7	69.2	70.6	69.2	68.8	68.5	67.7	67.4	68.2
2001	66.7	66.3	67.0	68.4	68.9	69.0	70.2	70.1	69.4	68.1	67.6	67.0	68.2
2002	65.8	65.4	65.5	66.9	66.8	67.3	68.8	68.0	67.3	67.0	66.5	66.0	66.8
2003	64.1	63.7	64.2	65.5	65.8	66.0	67.0	66.7	65.7	65.0	64.0	63.6	65.1
Retail trade													
1990	156.8	154.3	155.3	158.1	160.1	161.6	161.7	162.9	162.8	163.3	167.1	169.2	161.1
1991	161.2	157.4	157.8	159.5	161.3	162.1	162.5	163.2	162.3	163.0	166.8	168.9	162.1
1992	160.7	158.4	159.3	161.4	163.1	163.8	163.0	163.6	163.1	164.1	167.5	170.3	163.1
1993	162.1	160.0	161.0	163.8	165.7	167.1	166.0	166.4	166.4	167.9	171.7	174.6	166.0
1994	166.8	164.3	165.6	168.0	170.5	171.7	172.7	174.2	175.0	175.0	179.4	182.6	172.1
1995	173.1	170.3	171.6	172.9	174.9	175.9	175.7	176.6	176.6	177.8	182.7	184.8	176.0
1996	178.3	173.7	174.4	176.8	178.9	179.2	180.3	181.7	179.5	180.7	185.4	187.9	179.7
1997	180.4	176.4	177.4	178.3	182.7	182.3	181.6	181.8	181.5	182.6	188.4	192.5	182.1
1998	180.2	176.5	177.1	179.7	183.0	184.7	182.6	185.3	185.1	188.2	192.2	195.5	184.1
1999	183.5	178.6	180.1	183.3	184.5	185.8	190.1	189.0	188.4	190.2	195.0	198.4	187.2
2000	187.2	185.3	185.7	187.0	188.5	189.8	188.6	189.4	189.1	191.0	196.5	198.7	189.7
2001	187.7	183.6	183.3	185.1	186.6	186.8	185.0	185.6	184.4	184.8	190.1	191.5	186.2
2002	182.4	178.5	179.2	181.2	182.3	183.6	181.1	181.5	181.2	181.3	185.9	187.7	182.2
2003	179.0	175.8	176.6	178.8	181.0	181.3	180.5	180.5	180.3	182.0	185.5	187.5	180.7

Employment by Industry: Iowa—*Continued*

(Numbers in thousands. Not seasonally adjusted.)

Industry	January	February	March	April	May	June	July	August	September	October	November	December	Annual Average
STATEWIDE—*Continued*													
Transportation and utilities													
1990	43.9	43.8	44.5	44.3	44.7	45.1	45.0	45.3	45.4	45.2	45.4	45.4	44.8
1991	43.5	43.3	43.9	44.3	44.8	45.1	44.9	45.0	45.1	44.9	44.9	45.2	44.5
1992	44.6	44.5	44.8	45.6	46.1	46.5	46.2	46.2	46.4	47.0	46.8	47.1	45.9
1993	45.1	45.2	45.5	46.6	46.9	47.5	48.0	48.0	48.0	48.9	48.7	48.5	47.2
1994	46.8	46.8	47.2	48.0	48.3	49.3	49.2	49.1	49.8	50.3	50.5	50.8	48.8
1995	50.2	50.4	50.8	51.1	51.3	51.5	51.6	51.6	51.5	52.0	52.1	52.3	51.3
1996	49.9	50.1	50.5	50.9	51.2	51.3	51.8	51.8	52.0	53.0	53.2	53.0	51.5
1997	51.2	51.1	51.4	53.0	53.3	53.5	53.3	50.8	53.3	54.0	54.1	54.4	52.7
1998	53.2	53.1	53.7	54.6	55.0	55.4	55.3	55.6	55.9	56.3	56.2	56.4	55.0
1999	55.9	56.0	56.5	57.7	58.1	58.2	57.8	58.1	57.7	58.2	58.3	58.2	57.5
2000	56.8	56.8	57.4	57.9	57.9	58.0	57.8	58.3	58.0	58.4	58.4	58.1	57.8
2001	56.4	56.4	56.6	56.8	57.1	57.4	56.7	57.1	56.7	56.8	57.0	56.9	56.8
2002	55.4	55.2	55.6	56.1	56.5	57.0	57.3	57.9	57.5	58.1	58.5	58.6	57.0
2003	56.4	56.2	56.8	57.0	57.4	57.0	57.4	57.7	57.4	57.8	58.1	58.0	57.3
Information													
1990	29.8	30.1	30.2	29.6	29.6	29.6	29.8	30.0	30.0	30.1	30.2	30.1	29.9
1991	29.3	29.5	29.6	29.4	29.5	29.5	28.1	28.2	28.1	29.0	29.1	29.2	29.0
1992	28.3	28.5	28.8	29.0	29.3	29.3	28.4	28.4	28.2	28.3	28.5	28.8	28.6
1993	28.4	28.6	28.8	29.0	29.0	29.2	29.0	29.2	29.0	29.2	29.5	29.6	29.0
1994	29.4	29.6	29.8	30.0	30.3	30.6	31.0	31.2	31.1	31.3	32.4	33.0	30.8
1995	32.1	32.0	32.4	32.4	33.1	33.1	32.6	32.8	32.3	32.4	33.4	33.7	32.6
1996	32.7	32.9	33.1	33.6	33.9	33.8	33.9	33.6	33.5	34.4	34.8	35.2	33.7
1997	33.5	33.4	33.8	34.6	35.0	34.8	34.6	34.4	34.0	34.6	35.2	35.6	34.4
1998	34.8	34.7	35.0	35.7	36.0	36.2	35.7	35.4	34.9	35.8	36.8	37.1	35.6
1999	37.8	37.8	37.7	39.4	39.6	39.6	38.1	37.6	37.8	39.1	39.5	39.9	38.6
2000	39.8	39.7	40.2	40.6	40.8	41.3	40.5	40.0	39.7	39.9	40.6	41.2	40.3
2001	38.5	38.5	39.0	38.1	37.8	37.8	37.7	36.8	36.5	36.5	36.3	36.0	37.5
2002	35.6	35.6	35.4	35.5	35.6	35.6	34.8	34.7	34.4	34.4	34.7	34.5	35.1
2003	33.6	33.9	33.7	33.9	33.8	33.8	34.0	33.6	33.5	33.6	33.8	33.6	33.7
Financial activities													
1990	68.0	67.9	68.2	69.1	69.5	70.4	70.6	70.5	69.9	69.8	69.9	70.4	69.5
1991	70.1	69.9	70.6	70.6	71.1	72.4	72.5	72.7	72.2	71.1	71.3	72.1	71.3
1992	70.8	70.8	71.1	71.8	72.2	73.2	73.2	73.4	72.6	72.8	72.9	73.7	72.3
1993	72.1	72.0	72.5	74.0	74.2	75.2	75.4	75.4	74.7	74.7	74.8	75.5	74.2
1994	74.7	74.6	74.9	75.4	75.9	77.1	78.5	78.5	77.9	76.9	77.0	77.8	76.6
1995	76.5	76.3	76.5	77.0	77.2	78.4	78.9	79.1	78.3	78.0	78.3	79.3	77.8
1996	79.1	78.8	79.5	80.2	79.6	80.6	81.7	81.7	79.5	79.5	79.8	80.4	80.0
1997	79.2	79.1	79.5	79.7	80.3	81.6	82.5	82.9	82.0	83.0	83.4	84.2	81.4
1998	84.0	83.9	84.2	85.4	85.9	87.7	87.9	88.4	87.3	86.7	86.6	87.3	86.2
1999	87.8	87.9	88.4	88.3	88.6	90.0	90.3	90.1	88.8	88.9	89.1	90.0	89.0
2000	88.8	88.7	88.5	89.1	89.5	90.6	90.5	90.7	90.0	89.6	89.8	90.3	89.6
2001	90.0	89.8	90.4	90.8	91.5	93.0	93.2	93.1	92.6	92.6	93.1	94.1	92.0
2002	93.0	93.0	93.3	93.7	93.7	94.7	95.0	94.7	93.8	93.8	93.7	94.2	93.9
2003	94.2	94.2	94.2	94.4	94.9	95.7	95.9	96.1	95.5	95.7	96.5	97.0	95.4
Professional and business services													
1990	66.6	67.1	67.9	67.6	67.6	69.1	70.5	70.8	70.7	70.2	69.9	70.1	69.0
1991	68.4	68.9	69.2	70.3	70.4	71.5	71.8	71.2	71.7	71.4	71.4	71.8	70.6
1992	69.8	70.6	71.3	73.2	73.2	73.2	73.9	74.7	75.7	76.0	75.6	75.4	73.5
1993	74.9	75.8	77.2	78.7	79.5	81.1	80.4	81.2	81.4	82.7	82.8	82.4	79.8
1994	80.1	80.6	82.3	84.2	84.4	87.2	85.0	85.6	84.9	86.0	87.4	86.2	84.4
1995	84.9	86.0	87.8	88.3	87.8	89.9	89.5	90.4	90.5	90.9	91.5	91.8	89.1
1996	91.2	93.2	94.7	95.2	95.2	96.1	96.9	97.5	97.6	97.6	98.3	98.9	96.0
1997	96.0	97.9	98.6	98.7	98.7	100.5	100.9	100.6	100.2	102.3	102.3	102.4	99.9
1998	99.3	101.4	103.6	104.3	104.5	106.9	105.4	104.9	104.8	105.5	105.2	105.4	104.2
1999	100.8	102.4	104.5	107.5	107.3	109.7	108.7	107.8	107.7	107.8	108.3	108.3	106.7
2000	103.9	103.9	106.4	107.3	107.1	108.6	109.1	109.2	108.5	109.7	109.2	108.7	107.6
2001	107.3	106.2	106.7	108.8	109.1	109.1	106.9	108.3	106.8	107.4	105.6	105.4	107.3
2002	102.4	102.6	103.7	105.5	105.5	107.5	107.4	107.0	107.0	106.1	106.9	106.1	105.6
2003	102.3	102.2	102.5	105.7	104.7	106.1	106.2	107.3	106.4	106.5	106.0	105.9	105.2
Educational and health services													
1990	144.5	146.9	147.5	147.0	146.7	140.8	139.5	140.6	149.2	151.5	152.7	152.4	146.6
1991	150.3	152.7	153.3	152.9	152.8	146.8	144.5	145.4	153.6	156.7	157.5	157.5	152.0
1992	155.7	157.6	158.0	158.0	157.7	151.6	150.0	150.3	159.2	161.3	162.4	162.4	157.0
1993	159.7	161.5	162.0	162.5	162.0	155.9	152.8	152.7	161.6	162.4	163.0	163.9	160.0
1994	162.7	164.8	165.3	165.5	165.0	159.1	154.1	154.7	162.9	165.2	165.8	166.3	162.6
1995	164.9	167.2	167.8	168.6	166.6	163.2	158.6	159.1	165.5	172.4	173.5	174.3	166.8
1996	169.3	170.8	172.6	172.3	171.9	166.9	161.8	162.2	169.1	176.8	178.1	177.7	170.7
1997	174.1	176.1	178.1	178.4	177.4	172.6	167.7	167.9	174.6	180.9	181.7	182.1	175.9
1998	178.1	179.9	181.3	179.9	178.0	172.4	166.2	165.7	171.5	178.6	179.7	180.3	175.9
1999	176.6	179.1	180.6	181.2	179.9	175.8	169.7	169.9	175.8	181.1	182.7	183.2	177.9
2000	180.3	182.2	184.0	183.6	182.5	177.9	173.3	174.4	181.5	187.0	187.9	187.7	181.8
2001	183.8	185.5	187.9	188.9	187.3	182.0	176.4	177.5	184.9	190.0	190.4	190.7	185.4
2002	187.0	188.7	189.6	190.4	189.5	183.6	178.7	179.4	187.9	192.6	193.8	194.3	188.0
2003	189.9	191.9	193.1	192.1	190.7	185.6	180.3	180.6	188.9	194.4	195.0	194.8	189.8

Employment by Industry: Iowa—*Continued*

(Numbers in thousands. Not seasonally adjusted.)

Industry	January	February	March	April	May	June	July	August	September	October	November	December	Annual Average
STATEWIDE—*Continued*													
Leisure and hospitality													
1990	92.7	93.9	96.7	101.3	104.8	107.5	106.6	107.8	105.5	101.2	99.7	99.6	101.4
1991	93.3	93.6	96.9	103.4	107.2	110.7	110.1	111.3	109.1	103.9	101.4	100.9	103.4
1992	96.4	97.5	100.2	104.4	108.7	111.3	109.5	110.9	107.8	103.4	101.3	100.4	104.3
1993	96.5	97.6	99.3	106.6	111.2	114.2	111.9	113.3	110.4	106.5	104.0	104.6	106.3
1994	99.0	99.7	102.8	109.6	113.7	116.8	114.9	116.4	113.3	109.6	108.1	107.9	109.3
1995	103.8	105.3	108.9	114.4	120.1	122.7	122.9	124.4	121.8	116.8	114.9	115.5	115.9
1996	111.3	112.1	115.2	120.5	125.4	128.9	127.7	129.0	124.2	119.4	117.0	116.5	120.6
1997	111.6	112.9	115.5	120.2	125.6	128.4	129.0	130.2	126.9	121.1	118.4	118.6	121.5
1998	114.7	116.3	118.2	124.0	129.6	131.8	130.0	131.6	128.2	122.9	120.9	121.4	124.1
1999	115.0	117.1	119.6	125.9	130.5	133.9	132.5	133.0	129.7	125.5	124.3	124.6	125.9
2000	118.0	118.7	121.2	123.7	127.4	129.6	132.6	134.5	130.7	124.9	123.0	121.5	125.4
2001	115.3	115.5	118.1	123.9	129.0	132.2	131.7	132.8	128.4	122.7	120.4	119.6	124.1
2002	115.7	115.9	117.7	123.9	129.1	131.6	131.7	132.9	129.8	124.0	121.2	121.5	124.6
2003	116.6	116.0	118.0	124.2	129.3	132.6	132.3	133.7	129.6	127.0	124.1	123.1	125.5
Other services													
1990	54.5	54.7	55.1	55.3	55.5	56.0	56.0	55.9	55.5	55.8	56.3	56.4	55.5
1991	55.5	55.4	55.9	56.1	56.5	56.7	56.4	56.4	56.1	56.0	56.1	56.6	56.1
1992	55.6	55.8	56.0	56.3	56.6	57.0	56.5	56.2	55.7	55.8	55.7	55.9	56.0
1993	54.6	54.8	55.0	56.1	56.4	56.8	56.5	56.2	56.2	56.6	57.0	57.2	56.1
1994	55.7	55.8	56.4	56.8	57.0	57.4	57.0	56.9	56.9	56.9	57.1	57.5	56.7
1995	56.0	56.3	56.8	56.9	56.9	57.7	57.2	57.2	57.0	57.2	57.4	55.9	56.8
1996	54.5	54.5	55.1	55.4	55.9	56.4	55.9	55.6	55.5	54.2	54.4	54.8	55.1
1997	53.9	53.9	54.5	54.6	55.0	55.4	54.6	54.1	54.1	54.2	53.9	54.3	54.3
1998	53.9	54.0	54.4	55.0	55.5	56.3	56.0	55.8	55.4	55.6	55.8	55.9	55.3
1999	54.8	55.3	55.9	56.4	56.6	57.3	56.9	56.6	56.4	56.8	57.1	57.2	56.4
2000	56.0	56.1	56.4	56.6	56.8	57.4	57.5	57.2	56.8	56.8	57.0	56.7	56.7
2001	55.8	55.8	56.2	56.5	56.6	57.4	56.9	56.7	56.0	56.1	56.0	56.2	56.4
2002	55.8	55.9	56.3	56.8	56.9	57.4	57.2	57.1	56.5	56.7	56.6	56.3	56.6
2003	55.6	55.5	55.9	56.3	56.3	56.8	56.7	56.7	56.5	56.2	56.1	56.1	56.2
Government													
1990	215.5	221.8	223.0	225.0	227.7	223.3	206.7	200.5	215.7	221.3	223.7	223.5	218.9
1991	219.6	223.5	225.0	225.5	227.6	224.6	205.9	203.3	216.3	223.8	226.5	226.1	220.6
1992	221.0	222.5	225.1	226.9	227.4	227.1	204.6	201.7	215.8	224.6	228.1	227.6	221.0
1993	221.3	223.1	226.5	227.5	228.9	227.3	204.6	203.3	218.6	227.5	230.6	230.2	222.4
1994	223.4	225.4	229.2	230.5	232.9	234.9	208.5	209.1	223.5	232.0	237.5	236.1	226.9
1995	228.8	231.8	235.1	235.3	236.6	235.7	212.1	211.9	226.6	235.3	237.0	237.1	230.2
1996	231.8	232.7	236.9	237.9	240.1	238.2	217.3	214.1	229.1	237.9	239.1	239.3	232.8
1997	233.9	235.7	238.1	239.4	241.3	239.8	216.5	215.9	231.7	240.1	240.9	242.2	234.6
1998	235.9	237.9	239.5	240.4	242.3	240.0	217.8	216.5	234.7	241.0	243.6	244.2	236.1
1999	239.0	241.1	243.1	245.0	245.7	242.1	219.6	220.0	238.8	245.4	246.8	247.1	239.4
2000	241.5	245.7	248.0	248.5	252.8	246.3	225.6	224.2	241.3	247.8	249.2	249.1	243.3
2001	244.6	248.2	249.1	250.2	251.3	248.5	226.9	225.2	244.5	250.4	252.3	250.7	245.2
2002	245.2	248.3	249.2	249.7	251.7	248.0	223.4	221.6	241.7	248.3	250.3	250.3	244.0
2003	243.0	248.7	249.8	250.6	252.5	248.0	223.8	223.3	244.2	250.5	252.3	251.4	244.8
Federal government													
1990	20.6	20.5	21.5	21.6	23.2	21.8	21.5	20.7	20.2	19.7	20.0	20.3	20.9
1991	20.3	20.2	20.3	20.5	20.3	20.9	20.6	20.4	20.3	20.2	20.3	20.4	20.3
1992	20.6	20.3	20.3	20.5	20.1	20.4	20.5	20.4	20.1	20.2	19.9	20.2	20.2
1993	20.0	20.1	20.1	20.2	20.1	20.2	20.3	20.4	20.5	20.3	20.6	20.9	20.3
1994	20.5	20.5	20.5	20.7	20.5	20.6	20.5	20.6	20.6	20.6	20.6	21.3	20.6
1995	20.6	20.6	20.6	20.7	20.7	20.8	20.8	20.9	20.8	20.6	20.6	20.9	20.7
1996	20.4	20.4	20.5	21.0	21.0	21.1	21.1	21.2	21.0	20.7	20.7	21.2	20.8
1997	20.3	20.3	20.3	20.4	20.3	20.4	20.4	20.4	20.3	20.3	20.3	21.0	20.3
1998	20.2	20.0	20.0	19.9	20.0	20.0	20.0	20.1	20.0	20.1	20.3	20.7	20.1
1999	20.8	20.7	20.7	20.5	20.0	20.0	20.1	20.2	20.2	20.2	20.5	21.0	20.4
2000	20.4	20.1	21.4	20.8	23.9	22.1	21.7	21.4	19.4	19.5	19.6	20.0	20.8
2001	19.7	19.4	19.4	19.3	19.3	19.5	19.6	19.5	19.4	19.3	19.4	19.6	19.5
2002	19.4	19.1	19.2	19.0	19.1	19.5	19.6	19.3	19.2	19.2	19.4	19.6	19.3
2003	19.3	19.1	19.1	19.1	19.2	19.2	19.2	19.1	19.0	19.0	18.9	19.1	19.1
State government													
1990	59.3	63.6	63.2	63.1	62.5	57.1	56.6	57.2	59.9	61.2	61.7	61.6	60.5
1991	60.4	61.8	61.9	62.1	61.9	57.2	55.1	56.3	59.0	60.1	60.5	60.4	59.7
1992	59.0	58.7	60.4	61.0	60.4	55.4	54.5	55.2	58.3	60.0	60.3	60.6	58.6
1993	58.7	58.7	60.8	60.9	60.9	56.6	54.3	56.3	59.1	60.9	61.6	61.7	59.2
1994	59.1	59.8	62.0	62.4	62.2	58.0	55.0	58.5	59.7	62.0	62.6	62.2	60.2
1995	59.8	60.4	62.6	63.2	63.0	58.1	55.5	58.9	60.9	62.6	63.3	62.7	60.9
1996	60.5	60.8	63.0	63.6	63.2	57.9	56.8	58.2	60.6	63.2	63.2	63.1	61.1
1997	61.9	62.0	62.8	63.7	63.1	58.0	55.7	58.5	61.1	63.9	63.7	63.5	61.4
1998	62.1	62.1	63.0	63.9	63.1	57.7	55.9	58.0	62.3	63.6	64.2	64.2	61.6
1999	63.6	63.8	64.7	65.3	64.0	58.8	55.2	59.3	64.2	65.4	65.7	65.3	62.9
2000	63.5	65.9	65.8	66.6	65.5	59.8	58.5	61.1	65.9	66.5	66.6	66.0	64.3
2001	65.6	67.0	67.0	67.4	65.7	59.4	58.6	60.5	65.5	66.5	66.6	66.0	64.7
2002	64.2	65.1	65.1	65.4	64.4	59.0	56.9	58.6	63.6	64.9	65.0	64.9	63.1
2003	61.9	65.2	65.5	66.1	65.1	59.9	58.2	60.2	65.7	66.7	66.7	66.8	64.0

Employment by Industry: Iowa—*Continued*

(Numbers in thousands. Not seasonally adjusted.)

Industry	January	February	March	April	May	June	July	August	September	October	November	December	Annual Average
STATEWIDE—*Continued*													
Local government													
1990	135.6	137.7	138.3	140.3	142.0	144.4	128.6	122.6	135.6	140.4	142.0	141.6	137.4
1991	138.9	141.5	142.8	142.9	145.4	146.5	130.2	126.6	137.0	143.5	145.7	145.3	140.5
1992	141.4	143.5	144.4	145.4	146.9	151.3	129.6	126.1	137.4	144.4	147.9	146.8	142.0
1993	142.6	144.3	145.6	146.4	147.9	150.5	130.0	126.6	139.0	146.3	148.4	147.6	142.9
1994	143.8	145.1	146.7	147.4	150.2	156.3	133.0	130.0	143.2	149.4	154.3	152.6	146.0
1995	148.4	150.8	151.9	151.4	152.9	156.8	135.8	132.1	144.9	152.1	153.1	153.5	148.6
1996	150.9	151.5	153.4	153.3	155.9	159.2	139.4	134.7	147.5	154.0	155.2	155.0	150.8
1997	151.7	153.4	155.0	155.3	157.9	161.4	140.4	137.0	150.3	155.9	156.9	157.7	152.7
1998	153.6	155.8	156.5	156.6	159.2	162.3	141.9	138.4	152.4	157.3	159.1	159.3	154.3
1999	154.6	156.6	157.7	159.2	161.7	163.3	144.3	140.5	154.4	159.8	160.6	160.8	156.1
2000	157.6	159.7	160.8	161.1	163.4	164.4	145.4	141.7	156.0	161.8	163.0	163.1	158.1
2001	159.3	161.8	162.7	163.5	166.3	169.6	148.7	145.2	159.6	164.6	166.3	165.1	161.1
2002	161.6	164.1	164.9	165.3	168.2	169.5	146.9	143.7	158.9	164.2	165.9	165.8	161.6
2003	161.8	164.4	165.2	165.4	168.2	168.9	146.4	144.0	159.5	164.8	166.7	165.5	161.7
CEDAR RAPIDS													
Total nonfarm													
1990	92.6	92.9	92.2	93.4	94.3	95.4	93.5	94.1	95.4	95.0	95.6	95.5	94.1
1991	92.6	92.6	93.0	94.4	95.0	95.2	93.3	93.6	94.4	94.8	95.6	95.4	94.1
1992	93.9	94.7	94.9	95.7	96.4	96.9	94.9	95.4	97.2	97.8	98.2	98.7	96.2
1993	96.0	96.0	96.1	97.6	99.2	99.9	98.1	98.3	99.9	101.3	101.4	101.5	98.7
1994	98.9	99.0	100.4	102.3	103.3	104.9	102.8	102.8	104.1	105.9	107.2	108.0	103.3
1995	105.5	105.8	106.9	107.4	107.6	108.4	106.4	106.2	107.3	108.2	109.1	109.6	107.3
1996	106.8	107.2	108.7	108.3	108.8	110.4	107.8	107.6	109.7	111.6	112.3	111.8	109.2
1997	108.6	108.8	109.6	111.2	111.8	113.0	110.6	111.1	112.4	114.5	115.7	116.4	111.9
1998	112.9	113.6	114.8	115.5	115.4	117.7	115.1	116.4	118.2	118.4	119.4	120.6	116.5
1999	118.3	119.0	120.1	121.7	121.9	123.5	121.0	121.4	122.0	123.0	123.9	124.2	121.6
2000	122.3	121.8	123.8	123.6	124.1	126.0	124.0	125.0	125.4	127.1	127.8	128.0	124.9
2001	122.1	121.9	122.1	123.0	122.7	123.7	119.4	120.3	120.2	121.7	122.2	120.9	121.7
2002	117.7	117.4	118.1	119.9	119.9	120.2	116.7	117.2	118.1	119.7	120.7	119.6	118.8
2003	115.9	115.5	116.3	117.5	117.0	117.3	115.2	115.5	116.4	119.6	119.1	118.1	117.0
Total private													
1990	82.2	82.4	81.7	82.7	83.3	83.9	84.0	84.6	84.8	84.2	84.6	84.7	83.5
1991	81.9	81.7	82.1	83.4	83.8	83.6	83.5	83.9	83.7	83.8	84.6	84.4	83.3
1992	83.1	83.8	84.0	84.7	85.2	85.2	85.2	85.8	86.6	86.5	87.2	87.2	85.3
1993	85.1	85.1	85.2	86.6	87.9	88.4	88.5	88.9	89.2	89.9	90.3	90.2	87.9
1994	88.0	88.0	89.3	91.2	92.0	93.3	92.9	93.1	93.2	94.5	95.9	96.3	92.3
1995	94.7	94.6	95.6	96.1	96.2	96.8	95.9	96.1	95.7	96.9	97.7	98.3	96.2
1996	96.0	96.1	97.4	97.1	97.3	98.5	98.2	98.7	98.7	100.1	100.8	100.5	98.2
1997	97.6	97.6	98.2	99.7	100.1	101.2	101.5	101.7	102.3	102.9	104.2	104.8	100.9
1998	101.8	102.2	103.2	104.0	103.7	105.9	105.5	106.1	107.0	106.7	107.7	108.8	105.2
1999	106.8	107.4	108.5	109.9	110.0	111.4	111.1	110.6	110.3	111.0	111.9	112.2	110.0
2000	110.2	109.7	111.4	111.3	111.5	113.3	113.8	113.7	113.3	114.7	115.3	115.7	112.8
2001	109.8	109.5	109.6	110.5	110.0	110.9	109.1	109.6	108.0	109.0	109.4	108.4	109.5
2002	105.5	104.8	105.3	107.1	106.9	107.4	106.3	106.5	106.0	106.9	107.6	106.8	106.4
2003	103.5	102.8	103.5	104.6	103.9	104.2	104.6	104.6	104.2	106.8	106.3	105.5	104.5
Goods-producing													
1990	25.3	25.2	24.3	24.9	25.4	25.6	25.8	26.0	25.8	25.0	24.8	24.6	25.2
1991	23.9	23.8	23.8	24.3	24.7	24.7	25.0	25.2	25.1	24.4	24.4	24.2	24.4
1992	24.2	24.3	24.0	24.0	24.3	24.5	24.5	24.6	24.8	24.3	24.4	24.1	24.3
1993	23.6	23.5	23.4	23.6	24.2	24.4	24.8	24.9	24.9	24.7	24.7	24.3	24.2
1994	23.6	23.5	23.9	24.7	25.1	25.6	25.7	26.0	25.7	25.6	25.9	25.6	25.0
1995	25.1	25.1	25.4	25.4	25.7	26.0	26.0	25.9	25.7	25.9	26.0	25.9	25.6
1996	24.9	24.5	24.8	25.2	25.4	25.6	25.1	25.0	25.4	26.0	25.9	25.4	25.2
1997	24.2	24.4	24.5	24.7	25.1	25.5	25.7	26.5	26.7	27.0	27.0	26.8	25.6
1998	26.4	26.4	26.8	27.0	27.0	27.6	27.9	28.0	28.0	27.9	27.7	27.8	27.3
1999	26.9	27.1	27.2	27.7	27.7	28.1	28.0	28.2	27.9	27.5	27.6	27.2	27.5
2000	26.6	26.3	27.0	26.8	27.0	27.5	28.3	28.4	28.3	28.4	28.3	28.1	27.5
2001	27.3	27.4	27.3	27.4	27.6	28.0	27.8	27.9	26.9	26.7	26.5	26.2	27.3
2002	24.9	24.6	24.9	25.3	25.4	25.4	25.3	25.3	25.0	24.9	24.9	24.5	25.0
2003	23.7	23.4	23.7	23.8	23.9	24.1	24.8	24.9	24.6	24.6	23.9	23.5	24.1
Construction and mining													
1990	3.7	3.8	3.9	4.4	4.8	5.0	5.4	5.4	5.2	4.6	4.5	4.3	4.5
1991	3.8	3.8	3.9	4.5	4.8	5.0	5.1	5.2	5.2	5.0	4.8	4.6	4.6
1992	4.3	4.4	4.6	4.7	4.9	5.2	5.1	5.2	5.2	5.0	5.0	4.9	4.8
1993	4.4	4.3	4.4	4.5	4.9	5.2	5.5	5.6	5.5	5.3	5.2	5.0	4.9
1994	4.4	4.2	4.6	5.2	5.5	5.8	5.9	6.0	5.8	5.8	5.8	5.7	5.3
1995	5.3	5.2	5.3	5.4	5.6	5.8	5.8	5.8	5.7	6.0	6.0	5.8	5.6
1996	5.1	4.9	4.9	5.4	5.5	5.7	5.9	5.9	5.8	6.0	5.9	5.6	5.5
1997	4.6	4.5	4.6	5.2	5.5	5.7	5.8	5.7	5.8	5.8	5.7	5.6	5.3
1998	5.5	5.4	5.6	6.2	6.1	6.4	6.6	6.6	6.5	6.5	6.4	6.4	6.1
1999	5.6	5.7	5.8	6.3	6.5	6.9	7.0	7.0	6.8	7.0	7.0	6.6	6.5
2000	6.0	5.8	6.3	6.1	6.3	6.6	7.1	7.2	7.1	7.1	7.0	6.7	6.6
2001	6.4	6.4	6.5	6.9	7.2	7.5	7.6	7.7	7.5	7.5	7.5	7.3	7.2
2002	6.3	6.0	6.3	6.9	7.0	7.0	7.1	7.1	6.8	6.6	6.6	6.4	6.7
2003	5.8	5.5	5.9	6.3	6.3	6.5	7.1	7.2	7.1	7.1	6.4	5.9	6.4

Employment by Industry: Iowa—*Continued*

(Numbers in thousands. Not seasonally adjusted.)

Industry	January	February	March	April	May	June	July	August	September	October	November	December	Annual Average
CEDAR RAPIDS—*Continued*													
Manufacturing													
1990	21.6	21.4	20.4	20.5	20.6	20.6	20.4	20.6	20.6	20.4	20.3	20.3	20.6
1991	20.1	20.0	19.9	19.8	19.9	19.7	19.9	20.0	19.9	19.4	19.6	19.6	19.8
1992	19.9	19.9	19.4	19.3	19.4	19.3	19.4	19.4	19.6	19.3	19.4	19.2	19.4
1993	19.2	19.2	19.0	19.1	19.3	19.2	19.3	19.3	19.4	19.4	19.5	19.3	19.2
1994	19.2	19.3	19.3	19.5	19.6	19.8	19.8	20.0	19.9	19.8	20.1	19.9	19.6
1995	19.8	19.9	20.1	20.0	20.1	20.2	20.2	20.1	20.0	19.9	20.0	20.1	20.0
1996	19.8	19.6	19.9	19.8	19.9	19.9	19.2	19.1	19.6	20.0	20.0	19.8	19.7
1997	19.6	19.9	19.9	19.5	19.6	19.8	19.9	20.8	20.9	21.2	21.3	21.2	20.3
1998	20.9	21.0	21.2	20.8	20.9	21.2	21.3	21.4	21.5	21.4	21.3	21.4	21.1
1999	21.3	21.4	21.4	21.4	21.2	21.2	21.0	21.2	21.1	20.5	20.6	20.6	21.0
2000	20.6	20.5	20.7	20.7	20.7	20.9	21.2	21.2	21.2	21.3	21.3	21.4	20.9
2001	20.9	21.0	20.8	20.5	20.4	20.5	20.2	20.2	19.4	19.2	19.0	18.9	20.1
2002	18.6	18.6	18.6	18.4	18.4	18.4	18.2	18.2	18.2	18.3	18.3	18.1	18.4
2003	17.9	17.9	17.8	17.5	17.6	17.6	17.7	17.7	17.5	17.5	17.5	17.6	17.7
Service-providing													
1990	67.3	67.7	67.9	68.5	68.9	69.8	67.7	68.1	69.6	70.0	70.8	70.9	68.9
1991	68.7	68.8	69.2	70.1	70.3	70.5	68.3	68.4	69.3	70.4	71.2	71.2	69.7
1992	69.7	70.4	70.9	71.7	72.1	72.4	70.4	70.8	72.4	73.5	73.8	74.6	71.8
1993	72.4	72.5	72.7	74.0	75.0	75.5	73.3	73.4	75.0	76.6	76.7	77.2	74.5
1994	75.3	75.5	76.5	77.6	78.2	79.3	77.1	76.8	78.4	80.3	81.3	82.4	78.2
1995	80.4	80.7	81.5	82.0	81.9	82.4	80.4	80.3	81.6	82.3	83.1	83.7	81.6
1996	81.9	82.7	83.9	83.1	83.4	84.8	82.7	82.6	84.3	85.6	86.4	86.4	83.9
1997	84.4	84.4	85.1	86.5	86.7	87.5	84.9	84.6	85.7	87.5	88.7	89.6	86.3
1998	86.5	87.2	88.0	88.5	88.4	90.1	87.2	88.4	90.2	90.5	91.7	92.8	89.1
1999	91.4	91.9	92.9	94.0	94.2	95.4	93.0	93.2	94.1	95.5	96.3	97.0	94.0
2000	95.7	95.5	96.8	96.8	97.1	98.5	95.7	96.6	97.1	98.7	99.5	99.9	97.3
2001	94.8	94.5	94.8	95.6	95.1	95.7	91.6	92.4	93.3	95.0	95.7	94.7	94.4
2002	92.8	92.8	93.2	94.6	94.5	94.8	91.4	91.9	93.1	94.8	95.8	95.1	93.7
2003	92.2	92.1	92.6	93.7	93.1	93.2	90.4	90.6	91.8	95.0	95.2	94.6	92.9
Trade, transportation, and utilities													
1990	20.5	20.2	20.2	20.5	20.7	20.8	20.7	21.0	21.0	21.1	21.6	21.8	20.8
1991	20.9	20.5	20.5	20.4	20.7	20.5	20.8	20.9	20.9	20.8	21.2	21.4	20.7
1992	20.9	20.9	21.1	21.2	21.4	21.3	21.5	21.6	21.7	21.6	22.1	22.3	21.4
1993	21.5	21.2	21.3	21.8	22.1	22.1	22.1	22.3	22.3	22.4	22.6	22.8	22.0
1994	22.0	21.9	22.0	22.3	22.8	22.7	22.8	23.0	23.1	23.2	23.7	24.0	22.7
1995	23.8	23.7	23.8	23.6	23.6	23.7	23.6	23.7	23.5	23.8	24.1	24.5	23.7
1996	23.8	23.5	23.7	23.6	23.8	23.9	23.7	23.9	23.7	24.0	24.5	24.7	23.9
1997	24.1	23.6	23.8	24.1	24.4	24.3	24.4	24.2	24.5	24.4	25.3	25.7	24.4
1998	24.8	24.5	24.4	24.7	24.8	25.3	25.3	25.4	25.4	25.5	25.9	26.4	25.2
1999	25.9	25.3	25.5	26.0	26.3	26.6	27.1	27.0	26.7	26.7	27.1	27.6	26.4
2000	26.7	26.5	26.7	26.7	26.6	26.6	26.9	26.8	27.1	27.4	28.0	28.2	27.0
2001	26.6	26.0	25.9	25.9	25.8	26.0	25.8	25.7	25.7	25.9	26.6	26.4	26.0
2002	25.7	25.2	25.3	25.4	25.3	25.5	25.5	25.7	25.6	25.9	26.5	26.7	25.7
2003	25.0	24.7	24.7	24.7	24.9	24.8	24.9	24.8	24.8	24.9	25.8	26.1	25.0
Wholesale trade													
1990	3.8	3.8	3.8	3.9	3.9	3.9	4.0	4.0	4.0	4.0	4.0	4.0	3.9
1991	3.9	3.9	3.9	4.0	4.0	4.0	4.1	4.1	4.1	4.0	4.0	4.0	4.0
1992	3.9	3.9	3.9	3.9	4.0	4.0	4.0	4.0	4.0	4.0	4.0	4.0	3.9
1993	4.0	4.0	4.0	4.0	4.1	4.1	4.1	4.2	4.2	4.1	4.0	4.0	4.0
1994	4.0	4.1	4.1	4.1	4.2	4.2	4.2	4.2	4.3	4.2	4.2	4.2	4.1
1995	4.2	4.3	4.3	4.3	4.3	4.3	4.4	4.4	4.4	4.4	4.4	4.4	4.3
1996	4.4	4.3	4.4	4.4	4.4	4.4	4.4	4.4	4.4	4.4	4.4	4.4	4.3
1997	4.3	4.2	4.3	4.4	4.4	4.4	4.5	4.6	4.6	4.5	4.6	4.6	4.4
1998	4.5	4.6	4.6	4.6	4.5	4.6	4.7	4.7	4.7	4.6	4.6	4.6	4.6
1999	4.8	4.8	4.8	5.0	4.9	5.0	5.0	5.0	5.0	5.1	5.0	5.1	4.9
2000	4.9	4.9	4.9	5.1	5.1	5.1	5.4	5.3	5.3	5.2	5.2	5.2	5.1
2001	5.1	5.0	5.0	5.0	5.0	5.1	5.1	5.0	4.9	4.9	4.9	4.8	5.0
2002	4.8	4.7	4.7	4.8	4.7	4.8	4.7	4.7	4.6	4.6	4.6	4.6	4.7
2003	4.4	4.3	4.3	4.3	4.4	4.3	4.3	4.3	4.3	4.2	4.2	4.2	4.3
Retail trade													
1990	10.9	10.6	10.6	10.6	10.8	10.9	10.8	11.0	11.0	11.2	11.7	11.8	10.9
1991	11.2	10.8	10.8	10.6	10.8	10.6	10.7	10.8	10.8	10.8	11.2	11.4	10.8
1992	10.8	10.8	11.0	11.0	11.1	11.0	11.0	11.1	11.2	11.2	11.6	11.8	11.1
1993	11.2	10.9	11.0	11.1	11.2	11.2	11.1	11.2	11.2	11.4	11.8	12.0	11.2
1994	11.3	11.1	11.2	11.4	11.7	11.6	11.6	11.8	11.7	11.9	12.4	12.7	11.7
1995	12.3	12.1	12.2	12.1	12.2	12.3	12.3	12.4	12.3	12.6	12.9	13.3	12.4
1996	12.8	12.5	12.5	12.4	12.6	12.6	12.6	12.8	12.6	12.8	13.3	13.6	12.7
1997	13.1	12.7	12.8	12.9	13.2	13.1	13.1	13.0	13.1	13.2	13.8	14.2	13.1
1998	13.4	13.0	12.9	13.0	13.2	13.4	13.3	13.4	13.4	13.6	14.0	14.4	13.4
1999	13.7	13.2	13.3	13.6	13.9	14.2	14.6	14.4	14.2	14.2	14.7	15.1	14.0
2000	14.3	14.1	14.2	14.0	14.0	14.0	13.9	13.9	14.1	14.6	15.3	15.4	14.3
2001	14.5	14.1	14.1	14.0	14.0	14.0	13.8	13.7	13.7	13.9	14.4	14.4	14.1
2002	13.7	13.4	13.4	13.5	13.5	13.6	13.4	13.4	13.2	13.3	13.8	13.9	13.5
2003	13.4	13.1	13.0	13.3	13.4	13.4	13.5	13.4	13.4	13.7	14.4	14.6	13.6

Employment by Industry: Iowa—*Continued*

(Numbers in thousands. Not seasonally adjusted.)

Industry	January	February	March	April	May	June	July	August	September	October	November	December	Annual Average
CEDAR RAPIDS—*Continued*													
Transportation and utilities													
1990	5.8	5.8	5.8	6.0	6.0	6.0	5.9	6.0	6.0	5.9	5.9	6.0	5.9
1991	5.8	5.8	5.8	5.8	5.9	5.9	6.0	6.0	6.0	6.0	6.0	6.0	5.9
1992	6.2	6.2	6.2	6.3	6.3	6.3	6.5	6.5	6.5	6.4	6.5	6.5	6.3
1993	6.3	6.3	6.3	6.7	6.8	6.8	6.9	6.9	6.9	6.9	6.8	6.8	6.7
1994	6.7	6.7	6.7	6.8	6.9	6.9	7.0	7.0	7.1	7.1	7.1	7.1	6.9
1995	7.3	7.3	7.3	7.2	7.1	7.1	6.9	6.9	6.8	6.8	6.8	6.8	7.0
1996	6.6	6.7	6.8	6.8	6.8	6.9	6.7	6.7	6.7	6.8	6.8	6.7	6.7
1997	6.7	6.7	6.7	6.8	6.8	6.8	6.8	6.6	6.8	6.7	6.9	6.9	6.7
1998	6.9	6.9	6.9	7.1	7.1	7.3	7.3	7.3	7.3	7.3	7.3	7.4	7.1
1999	7.4	7.3	7.4	7.4	7.5	7.4	7.5	7.6	7.5	7.4	7.4	7.4	7.4
2000	7.5	7.5	7.6	7.6	7.5	7.5	7.6	7.6	7.7	7.6	7.5	7.6	7.5
2001	7.0	6.9	6.8	6.9	6.8	6.9	6.9	7.0	7.1	7.1	7.3	7.2	7.0
2002	7.2	7.1	7.2	7.1	7.1	7.1	7.4	7.6	7.8	8.0	8.1	8.2	7.5
2003	7.2	7.3	7.4	7.1	7.1	7.1	7.1	7.1	7.1	7.0	7.2	7.3	7.2
Information													
1990	3.2	3.2	3.2	3.3	3.3	3.4	3.4	3.5	3.4	3.3	3.3	3.2	3.3
1991	3.1	3.1	3.1	3.0	3.0	3.0	2.9	2.8	2.9	3.1	3.1	3.2	3.0
1992	3.0	3.2	3.2	3.2	3.3	3.2	3.1	3.2	3.2	3.2	3.2	3.3	3.1
1993	3.4	3.4	3.4	3.5	3.5	3.6	3.7	3.8	3.7	3.8	3.9	3.9	3.6
1994	4.0	4.0	4.1	4.0	4.0	4.2	4.9	4.9	5.0	4.6	4.7	4.8	4.4
1995	4.7	4.7	4.7	4.7	5.0	4.9	4.9	4.9	4.8	4.9	5.0	5.1	4.8
1996	5.1	5.2	5.3	5.3	5.4	5.6	5.7	5.7	5.7	5.7	5.7	5.7	5.5
1997	5.8	5.8	5.9	6.0	6.0	6.2	6.2	5.9	5.6	5.9	6.0	6.1	5.9
1998	5.8	5.8	5.8	5.7	5.7	5.7	6.4	6.5	6.5	6.6	6.9	6.9	6.1
1999	7.3	7.4	7.5	7.7	7.8	7.7	7.8	7.5	7.6	7.8	8.0	8.2	7.6
2000	8.3	8.3	8.3	8.8	8.8	9.0	8.8	8.6	8.4	8.4	8.5	8.7	8.5
2001	7.0	7.1	7.4	6.8	6.7	6.7	6.5	6.5	6.5	6.4	6.3	6.2	6.7
2002	6.1	6.1	6.1	6.3	6.3	6.3	6.0	5.9	5.8	6.0	6.0	5.8	6.1
2003	5.7	5.8	5.7	5.9	5.7	5.7	5.7	5.7	5.6	5.8	5.5	5.6	5.7
Financial activities													
1990	4.9	4.9	4.9	4.9	5.0	5.0	5.1	4.9	4.9	4.9	4.9	5.0	4.9
1991	4.8	4.9	4.9	5.2	5.2	5.2	5.2	5.3	5.2	5.3	5.3	5.3	5.1
1992	4.9	4.9	4.9	5.3	5.3	5.4	5.4	5.4	5.5	5.4	5.4	5.5	5.2
1993	5.1	5.1	5.2	5.5	5.7	5.7	5.7	5.6	5.7	5.6	5.7	5.7	5.5
1994	5.7	5.7	5.7	5.7	5.8	5.9	6.0	6.0	6.0	5.9	5.9	6.0	5.8
1995	6.0	6.0	6.0	5.9	5.9	6.1	6.0	6.0	5.9	5.9	6.0	6.0	5.9
1996	5.7	5.7	5.7	6.0	6.0	6.1	6.3	6.3	6.0	6.1	6.1	6.1	6.0
1997	6.0	6.0	6.0	6.2	6.2	6.3	6.5	6.5	6.5	6.3	6.4	6.5	6.2
1998	6.4	6.4	6.4	6.6	6.7	6.7	6.7	6.8	6.8	6.8	6.9	7.0	6.6
1999	7.1	7.2	7.2	7.3	7.4	7.6	7.6	7.6	7.5	7.5	7.4	7.5	7.4
2000	7.6	7.6	7.7	7.7	7.7	7.8	7.9	8.0	8.0	8.1	8.1	8.2	7.8
2001	8.1	8.2	8.2	8.3	8.4	8.5	8.5	8.6	8.5	8.4	8.5	8.5	8.4
2002	8.5	8.5	8.5	8.6	8.6	8.8	8.7	8.8	8.8	8.9	9.0	9.2	8.7
2003	9.0	9.0	9.1	9.1	9.2	9.2	9.2	9.1	9.2	9.2	9.3	9.2	9.2
Professional and business services													
1990	6.7	7.0	7.1	6.8	6.9	7.0	7.5	7.7	8.2	7.4	7.4	7.4	7.2
1991	7.1	7.2	7.2	7.2	7.4	7.6	7.3	7.4	7.3	7.3	7.6	7.5	7.3
1992	7.4	7.6	7.7	7.7	7.9	7.9	8.1	8.2	8.3	8.3	8.4	8.3	7.9
1993	8.1	8.3	8.2	8.2	8.5	8.8	9.1	9.2	9.2	9.1	9.2	9.2	8.7
1994	9.0	9.0	9.3	9.5	9.7	10.1	9.1	9.1	9.1	10.0	10.3	10.3	9.5
1995	9.9	9.9	10.1	10.9	10.7	10.9	10.8	10.9	11.1	10.6	10.9	11.3	10.6
1996	12.0	12.6	12.7	11.8	11.9	12.2	13.0	13.5	13.7	13.1	13.3	13.3	12.7
1997	12.7	12.9	12.7	12.7	12.9	13.1	13.5	13.6	13.6	13.5	13.8	14.0	13.2
1998	13.0	13.2	13.7	13.6	13.7	14.4	13.9	14.0	14.5	13.5	13.8	14.1	13.7
1999	13.3	13.5	14.0	13.5	13.6	13.9	13.9	13.6	13.9	13.4	13.7	13.6	13.6
2000	13.7	13.2	13.6	13.4	13.3	13.8	13.6	13.5	13.2	14.0	13.9	14.1	13.6
2001	13.7	13.4	13.1	13.9	13.6	13.4	13.0	13.3	13.1	13.3	13.2	13.0	13.3
2002	12.7	12.6	12.5	12.9	12.9	12.9	12.9	12.7	12.7	12.6	12.7	12.6	12.7
2003	12.0	11.9	12.0	12.3	11.9	12.0	12.0	12.1	12.1	11.8	11.4	11.1	11.9
Educational and health services													
1990	10.2	10.3	10.3	10.2	9.7	9.6	9.2	9.3	9.6	10.6	10.5	10.5	10.0
1991	10.5	10.6	10.7	10.6	10.0	9.8	9.7	9.7	10.0	11.0	11.0	10.9	10.3
1992	11.0	11.1	11.2	11.2	10.7	10.5	10.2	10.3	10.8	11.6	11.6	11.6	10.9
1993	11.6	11.8	11.8	11.7	11.1	10.8	10.3	10.3	10.8	11.8	11.8	11.8	11.3
1994	11.7	11.9	12.0	12.0	11.4	11.2	10.8	10.7	11.1	12.0	12.1	12.1	11.5
1995	12.0	12.1	12.2	12.0	11.4	11.3	11.0	11.0	11.3	12.6	12.5	12.6	11.8
1996	12.0	12.2	12.3	12.2	11.6	11.5	10.9	11.0	11.3	12.5	12.5	12.6	11.8
1997	12.4	12.5	12.5	12.6	12.0	12.0	11.5	11.4	11.9	12.8	12.8	12.7	12.2
1998	12.7	12.9	12.9	12.8	12.1	12.2	11.6	11.6	12.1	13.1	13.1	13.1	12.5
1999	13.4	13.6	13.7	13.7	13.1	13.0	12.3	12.3	12.6	13.7	13.7	13.9	13.2
2000	13.5	13.7	13.9	13.7	13.6	13.8	13.7	13.7	13.8	14.0	14.0	14.1	13.7
2001	13.8	14.0	14.1	14.1	13.5	13.4	13.0	13.0	13.2	14.3	14.4	14.3	13.8
2002	14.3	14.5	14.6	14.6	14.1	14.0	13.6	13.7	13.8	14.9	14.9	14.7	14.3
2003	14.7	14.8	14.7	14.7	14.0	13.9	13.6	13.6	13.7	16.7	16.8	16.6	14.8

Employment by Industry: Iowa—*Continued*

(Numbers in thousands. Not seasonally adjusted.)

Industry	January	February	March	April	May	June	July	August	September	October	November	December	Annual Average
CEDAR RAPIDS—*Continued*													
Leisure and hospitality													
1990	7.1	7.2	7.3	7.7	7.9	8.1	7.8	7.8	7.5	7.5	7.7	7.8	7.6
1991	7.2	7.2	7.5	8.2	8.3	8.3	8.0	8.1	7.9	7.5	7.5	7.5	7.7
1992	7.3	7.4	7.4	7.6	7.8	7.7	7.8	7.9	7.8	7.6	7.5	7.5	7.6
1993	7.3	7.3	7.4	7.8	8.2	8.3	8.1	8.1	8.0	7.9	7.8	7.9	7.8
1994	7.5	7.5	7.8	8.3	8.6	8.8	8.8	8.7	8.5	8.5	8.6	8.8	8.3
1995	8.5	8.4	8.6	8.9	9.1	9.0	8.8	8.8	8.6	8.4	8.3	8.3	8.6
1996	8.0	8.0	8.4	8.5	8.6	8.8	8.8	8.6	8.3	8.3	8.3	8.2	8.4
1997	8.0	8.0	8.3	8.8	8.9	9.1	9.0	9.1	9.0	8.6	8.5	8.5	8.6
1998	8.3	8.5	8.7	9.0	9.1	9.2	9.0	9.2	9.1	8.8	8.8	8.9	8.8
1999	8.3	8.6	8.7	9.3	9.4	9.6	9.6	9.6	9.4	9.4	9.4	9.2	9.2
2000	8.9	9.1	9.1	9.2	9.4	9.6	9.4	9.5	9.4	9.3	9.4	9.3	9.3
2001	8.6	8.7	8.8	9.3	9.6	9.9	9.5	9.6	9.3	9.2	9.1	9.2	9.2
2002	8.7	8.7	8.8	9.3	9.5	9.6	9.4	9.4	9.5	9.0	8.9	8.9	9.1
2003	8.7	8.6	8.9	9.3	9.6	9.7	9.5	9.6	9.5	9.1	8.9	8.8	9.2
Other services													
1990	4.3	4.4	4.4	4.4	4.4	4.4	4.5	4.4	4.4	4.4	4.4	4.4	4.4
1991	4.4	4.4	4.4	4.5	4.5	4.5	4.6	4.5	4.4	4.4	4.5	4.4	4.4
1992	4.4	4.4	4.5	4.5	4.5	4.7	4.6	4.6	4.5	4.5	4.6	4.6	4.5
1993	4.5	4.5	4.5	4.5	4.6	4.7	4.7	4.7	4.6	4.6	4.6	4.6	4.5
1994	4.5	4.5	4.5	4.7	4.6	4.8	4.8	4.7	4.7	4.7	4.7	4.7	4.6
1995	4.7	4.7	4.8	4.7	4.8	4.9	4.8	4.9	4.8	4.8	4.9	4.6	4.7
1996	4.5	4.4	4.5	4.5	4.6	4.8	4.7	4.7	4.6	4.4	4.5	4.5	4.5
1997	4.4	4.4	4.5	4.6	4.6	4.7	4.7	4.5	4.5	4.4	4.4	4.5	4.5
1998	4.4	4.5	4.5	4.6	4.6	4.8	4.7	4.6	4.6	4.5	4.6	4.6	4.5
1999	4.6	4.7	4.7	4.7	4.7	4.9	4.8	4.8	4.7	5.0	5.0	5.0	4.8
2000	4.9	5.0	5.1	5.0	5.1	5.2	5.2	5.2	5.1	5.1	5.1	5.0	5.0
2001	4.7	4.7	4.8	4.8	4.8	5.0	5.0	5.0	4.8	4.8	4.8	4.6	4.8
2002	4.6	4.6	4.6	4.7	4.8	4.9	4.9	5.0	4.8	4.7	4.7	4.4	4.7
2003	4.7	4.6	4.7	4.8	4.7	4.8	4.9	4.8	4.7	4.7	4.7	4.6	4.7
Government													
1990	10.4	10.5	10.5	10.7	11.0	11.5	9.5	9.5	10.6	10.8	11.0	10.8	10.5
1991	10.7	10.9	10.9	11.0	11.2	11.6	9.8	9.7	10.7	11.0	11.0	11.0	10.7
1992	10.8	10.9	10.9	11.0	11.2	11.7	9.7	9.6	10.6	11.3	11.0	11.5	10.8
1993	10.9	10.9	10.9	11.0	11.3	11.5	9.6	9.4	10.7	11.4	11.1	11.3	10.8
1994	10.9	11.0	11.1	11.1	11.3	11.6	9.9	9.7	10.9	11.4	11.3	11.7	10.9
1995	10.8	11.2	11.3	11.3	11.4	11.6	10.5	10.1	11.6	11.3	11.4	11.3	11.1
1996	10.8	11.1	11.3	11.2	11.5	11.9	9.6	8.9	11.0	11.5	11.5	11.3	10.9
1997	11.0	11.2	11.4	11.5	11.7	11.8	9.1	9.4	10.1	11.6	11.5	11.6	10.9
1998	11.1	11.4	11.6	11.5	11.7	11.8	9.6	10.3	11.2	11.7	11.7	11.8	11.2
1999	11.5	11.6	11.6	11.8	11.9	12.1	9.9	10.8	11.7	12.0	12.0	12.0	11.5
2000	12.1	12.1	12.4	12.3	12.6	12.7	10.2	11.3	12.1	12.4	12.5	12.3	12.0
2001	12.3	12.4	12.5	12.5	12.7	12.8	10.3	10.7	12.2	12.7	12.8	12.5	12.2
2002	12.2	12.6	12.8	12.8	13.0	12.8	10.4	10.7	12.1	12.8	13.1	12.8	12.3
2003	12.4	12.7	12.8	12.9	13.1	13.1	10.6	10.9	12.2	12.8	12.8	12.6	12.4
Federal government													
1990	1.1	1.1	1.1	1.1	1.1	1.2	1.2	1.2	1.1	1.1	1.1	1.1	1.1
1991	1.1	1.1	1.1	1.1	1.1	1.1	1.1	1.1	1.1	1.1	1.1	1.1	1.1
1992	1.1	1.1	1.1	1.1	1.1	1.1	1.1	1.1	1.1	1.2	1.1	1.1	1.1
1993	1.1	1.1	1.1	1.1	1.1	1.1	1.1	1.1	1.1	1.1	1.1	1.1	1.1
1994	1.1	1.1	1.1	1.1	1.1	1.1	1.1	1.1	1.1	1.1	1.1	1.1	1.1
1995	1.1	1.1	1.1	1.1	1.1	1.1	1.1	1.1	1.1	1.1	1.1	1.1	1.1
1996	1.1	1.1	1.1	1.1	1.1	1.1	1.1	1.1	1.1	1.1	1.1	1.1	1.1
1997	1.1	1.1	1.1	1.1	1.1	1.1	1.1	1.1	1.1	1.1	1.1	1.1	1.1
1998	1.1	1.1	1.1	1.0	1.0	1.0	1.1	1.1	1.1	1.1	1.1	1.1	1.0
1999	1.1	1.1	1.1	1.2	1.1	1.1	1.2	1.2	1.2	1.2	1.2	1.2	1.1
2000	1.2	1.2	1.3	1.3	1.5	1.5	1.3	1.4	1.2	1.2	1.2	1.2	1.2
2001	1.2	1.2	1.2	1.2	1.2	1.2	1.2	1.2	1.2	1.2	1.2	1.2	1.2
2002	1.2	1.2	1.2	1.2	1.2	1.2	1.2	1.2	1.1	1.2	1.2	1.2	1.2
2003	1.2	1.2	1.2	1.2	1.2	1.2	1.2	1.2	1.1	1.2	1.2	1.2	1.2
State government													
1990	0.6	0.6	0.6	0.7	0.7	0.7	0.6	0.6	0.6	0.6	0.6	0.6	0.6
1991	0.6	0.6	0.6	0.6	0.6	0.6	0.7	0.7	0.6	0.6	0.6	0.6	0.6
1992	0.6	0.6	0.6	0.6	0.6	0.6	0.6	0.6	0.6	0.6	0.6	0.6	0.6
1993	0.6	0.6	0.5	0.6	0.6	0.6	0.6	0.6	0.6	0.6	0.6	0.6	0.5
1994	0.6	0.6	0.6	0.6	0.6	0.6	0.6	0.6	0.6	0.6	0.6	0.6	0.6
1995	0.6	0.6	0.6	0.6	0.6	0.7	0.7	0.7	0.6	0.6	0.6	0.6	0.6
1996	0.6	0.6	0.6	0.6	0.6	0.6	0.7	0.6	0.6	0.6	0.6	0.6	0.6
1997	0.6	0.6	0.6	0.6	0.6	0.6	0.6	0.6	0.6	0.6	0.6	0.6	0.6
1998	0.6	0.6	0.6	0.6	0.6	0.6	0.6	0.6	0.6	0.6	0.6	0.6	0.6
1999	0.6	0.6	0.6	0.6	0.6	0.6	0.6	0.6	0.6	0.6	0.6	0.6	0.6
2000	0.6	0.6	0.6	0.6	0.6	0.6	0.7	0.7	0.6	0.6	0.6	0.6	0.6
2001	0.6	0.6	0.6	0.6	0.6	0.6	0.6	0.6	0.6	0.6	0.6	0.6	0.6
2002	0.6	0.6	0.6	0.6	0.6	0.6	0.5	0.5	0.5	0.5	0.6	0.6	0.6
2003	0.6	0.6	0.6	0.6	0.6	0.6	0.5	0.5	0.5	0.5	0.5	0.5	0.6

Employment by Industry: Iowa—*Continued*

(Numbers in thousands. Not seasonally adjusted.)

Industry	January	February	March	April	May	June	July	August	September	October	November	December	Annual Average
CEDAR RAPIDS—*Continued*													
Local government													
1990	8.7	8.8	8.8	8.9	9.2	9.6	7.7	7.7	8.9	9.1	9.3	9.1	8.8
1991	9.0	9.2	9.2	9.3	9.5	9.9	8.0	7.9	9.0	9.3	9.3	9.3	9.0
1992	9.1	9.2	9.2	9.3	9.5	10.0	8.0	7.9	8.9	9.5	9.3	9.8	9.1
1993	9.2	9.2	9.3	9.3	9.6	9.8	7.9	7.7	9.0	9.7	9.4	9.6	9.1
1994	9.2	9.3	9.4	9.4	9.6	9.9	8.2	8.0	9.2	9.7	9.6	10.0	9.2
1995	9.1	9.5	9.6	9.6	9.7	9.8	8.7	8.3	9.9	9.6	9.7	9.6	9.4
1996	9.1	9.4	9.6	9.5	9.8	10.2	7.8	7.2	9.3	9.8	9.8	9.6	9.2
1997	9.3	9.5	9.7	9.8	10.0	10.1	7.4	7.7	8.4	9.9	9.8	9.9	9.2
1998	9.4	9.7	9.9	9.9	10.1	10.2	7.9	8.6	9.5	10.0	10.0	10.1	9.6
1999	9.8	9.9	9.9	10.0	10.2	10.4	8.1	9.0	9.9	10.2	10.2	10.2	9.8
2000	10.3	10.3	10.5	10.4	10.5	10.6	8.2	9.2	10.3	10.6	10.7	10.5	10.1
2001	10.5	10.6	10.7	10.7	10.9	11.0	8.5	8.9	10.4	10.9	11.0	10.7	10.4
2002	10.4	10.8	11.0	11.0	11.2	11.0	8.7	9.0	10.5	11.0	11.3	11.0	10.6
2003	10.6	10.9	11.0	11.1	11.3	11.3	8.9	9.2	10.6	11.1	11.1	10.9	10.7
DES MOINES													
Total nonfarm													
1990	225.9	226.5	228.7	230.6	233.1	236.2	233.8	234.7	235.5	235.2	236.5	237.4	232.8
1991	229.7	229.5	232.5	233.7	237.0	240.0	236.1	236.1	236.4	237.3	237.4	238.6	235.3
1992	232.9	233.8	236.0	238.9	241.4	244.2	240.7	241.1	241.6	242.2	243.1	242.9	239.9
1993	236.3	236.1	239.1	242.4	246.0	249.4	241.8	244.6	246.2	248.5	249.7	251.1	244.2
1994	243.3	243.8	246.7	250.7	253.6	257.4	254.4	255.5	255.5	255.9	258.2	258.9	252.8
1995	252.2	253.3	256.7	258.9	261.8	265.6	261.8	264.4	263.6	266.3	268.3	269.4	261.8
1996	261.9	261.0	264.1	267.7	269.4	271.6	267.9	269.4	266.9	268.5	270.3	271.4	267.5
1997	263.4	263.4	266.2	268.4	271.9	274.9	272.7	273.0	271.7	273.2	274.9	276.4	270.8
1998	269.5	269.8	271.5	277.3	280.9	284.5	280.5	281.1	280.4	282.8	284.6	286.1	279.0
1999	278.8	279.6	282.3	285.9	288.4	291.1	286.9	286.3	285.2	286.4	287.7	289.9	285.7
2000	281.2	281.4	284.7	284.8	288.5	291.5	291.5	292.1	290.2	291.6	292.2	291.6	288.4
2001	283.9	283.2	285.2	287.9	291.7	295.3	288.8	289.7	288.6	289.2	289.9	289.5	288.6
2002	281.6	280.6	282.1	286.4	288.8	291.6	286.5	287.1	286.2	287.1	287.9	287.2	286.1
2003	280.3	279.0	280.1	284.4	287.3	290.1	285.5	287.0	287.0	290.5	288.8	288.6	285.7
Total private													
1990	194.5	194.4	196.3	198.4	200.7	203.5	203.5	204.8	203.9	203.4	204.1	204.7	201.0
1991	198.0	196.9	199.4	201.0	203.9	207.2	205.3	205.8	205.4	205.1	204.9	205.9	203.2
1992	200.7	201.0	203.0	206.1	208.4	211.3	209.9	210.7	210.4	209.8	210.3	210.1	207.6
1993	204.0	203.3	206.0	209.4	212.7	216.2	210.8	214.0	214.7	215.8	216.5	217.8	211.7
1994	211.2	211.0	213.6	217.6	220.4	224.0	223.0	223.3	223.5	222.5	224.3	224.5	219.9
1995	218.7	219.2	222.3	224.6	227.4	230.9	230.0	231.7	230.7	232.1	233.9	234.6	228.0
1996	227.3	226.3	228.9	232.7	234.2	236.0	235.0	235.8	233.2	233.6	235.2	235.7	232.8
1997	228.7	228.1	230.6	233.1	236.2	239.1	239.4	238.6	237.7	238.2	239.5	240.3	235.7
1998	234.4	234.5	236.1	242.4	245.5	248.9	247.3	248.1	246.2	247.6	248.9	250.1	244.1
1999	242.6	243.1	245.5	249.2	251.6	254.5	252.5	252.0	249.9	250.7	252.0	253.6	249.7
2000	245.5	245.2	248.3	248.5	251.2	254.1	256.5	257.4	255.1	255.5	255.9	254.9	252.3
2001	247.1	246.1	247.9	250.7	254.3	257.6	253.2	254.4	252.1	251.8	252.2	252.2	251.6
2002	244.5	243.3	244.8	248.9	251.2	254.1	251.5	252.3	250.3	250.3	251.1	250.0	249.4
2003	243.7	242.1	242.9	247.4	250.0	252.8	251.0	252.5	251.0	253.0	251.3	250.9	249.1
Goods-producing													
1990	29.1	29.1	29.6	31.1	31.8	32.4	32.6	33.1	32.9	32.4	32.2	31.3	31.4
1991	29.2	29.0	29.4	30.0	30.8	31.6	32.1	32.4	32.1	32.0	31.2	30.7	30.8
1992	29.3	29.4	30.0	30.9	31.5	32.5	32.6	32.7	32.6	32.7	32.3	31.1	31.4
1993	29.4	29.3	29.9	30.7	31.5	32.4	30.5	32.2	32.8	33.3	33.2	32.7	31.4
1994	31.0	30.6	31.4	33.3	33.8	34.6	34.9	33.1	33.4	33.3	33.0	32.6	32.9
1995	31.1	31.5	32.6	33.4	33.8	35.0	35.0	34.8	34.7	35.0	34.6	34.1	33.8
1996	32.6	32.3	32.9	34.5	34.1	34.9	35.1	35.1	34.9	34.6	34.0	33.4	34.0
1997	31.6	31.5	31.9	34.0	34.7	35.6	36.2	36.2	35.9	36.1	35.5	34.5	34.4
1998	32.5	32.9	32.9	34.7	34.6	35.6	36.6	36.6	36.4	36.1	36.0	36.0	35.0
1999	34.0	34.7	35.0	36.4	36.8	37.6	37.2	37.0	36.6	36.3	36.0	35.6	36.1
2000	33.2	33.0	34.4	35.0	35.7	36.6	36.7	36.7	36.1	35.6	35.4	33.9	35.1
2001	33.0	32.8	33.1	34.2	35.2	36.1	36.1	36.1	35.6	35.1	34.7	33.9	34.7
2002	32.0	31.7	32.1	33.9	34.6	35.3	35.2	35.1	34.6	34.6	34.4	33.4	33.9
2003	31.4	30.9	31.2	32.9	33.7	34.2	34.2	34.4	34.4	34.2	33.6	32.6	33.1
Natural resources and mining													
1990	0.2	0.2	0.2	0.2	0.2	0.2	0.2	0.2	0.2	0.2	0.2	0.2	0.2
1991	0.1	0.2	0.2	0.2	0.2	0.2	0.2	0.2	0.2	0.2	0.2	0.2	0.1
1992	0.2	0.2	0.2	0.2	0.2	0.3	0.2	0.2	0.2	0.2	0.2	0.2	0.2
1993	0.2	0.2	0.2	0.2	0.2	0.2	0.2	0.2	0.2	0.2	0.2	0.2	0.2
1994	0.2	0.2	0.2	0.3	0.3	0.3	0.3	0.3	0.3	0.2	0.2	0.2	0.2
1995	0.2	0.2	0.2	0.2	0.2	0.2	0.2	0.2	0.2	0.2	0.2	0.2	0.2
1996	0.2	0.2	0.2	0.2	0.2	0.2	0.2	0.2	0.2	0.2	0.2	0.2	0.2
1997	0.2	0.2	0.2	0.2	0.2	0.2	0.2	0.2	0.2	0.3	0.2	0.2	0.2
1998	0.2	0.2	0.2	0.2	0.2	0.2	0.3	0.3	0.3	0.3	0.3	0.3	0.2
1999	0.3	0.3	0.3	0.3	0.3	0.3	0.3	0.3	0.3	0.3	0.3	0.3	0.3
2000	0.2	0.2	0.3	0.2	0.2	0.3	0.3	0.3	0.3	0.3	0.3	0.2	0.2
2001	0.2	0.2	0.2	0.2	0.2	0.2	0.2	0.2	0.2	0.2	0.2	0.2	0.2
2002	0.2	0.2	0.3	0.3	0.3	0.3	0.2	0.2	0.2	0.2	0.2	0.2	0.2
2003	0.2	0.2	0.2	0.2	0.2	0.2	0.2	0.2	0.2	0.2	0.2	0.2	0.2

Employment by Industry: Iowa—*Continued*

(Numbers in thousands. Not seasonally adjusted.)

Industry	January	February	March	April	May	June	July	August	September	October	November	December	Annual Average
DES MOINES—*Continued*													
Construction													
1990	7.4	7.4	7.9	8.9	9.5	9.8	9.8	10.0	9.9	9.7	9.8	9.0	9.0
1991	7.4	7.2	7.6	8.2	8.8	9.5	10.0	10.2	9.9	9.9	9.2	8.6	8.8
1992	7.8	7.7	8.2	9.2	9.5	10.2	10.2	10.4	10.2	10.3	10.0	9.2	9.4
1993	7.8	7.7	8.0	8.6	9.4	10.0	10.1	10.4	10.4	10.5	10.4	9.7	9.4
1994	8.4	8.1	8.8	10.3	10.9	11.4	11.6	11.7	11.4	11.2	11.1	10.4	10.4
1995	9.1	9.0	9.5	10.2	10.6	11.5	11.9	12.0	11.8	11.7	11.5	10.7	10.7
1996	9.7	9.4	9.9	11.1	11.7	12.3	12.4	12.5	12.4	12.2	11.7	11.0	11.3
1997	10.1	10.1	10.6	11.6	12.2	12.8	13.2	13.1	12.8	12.7	12.3	11.5	11.9
1998	10.3	10.1	10.2	11.7	12.2	12.9	13.8	13.8	13.6	13.5	13.4	13.2	12.3
1999	11.9	12.4	12.7	13.7	14.1	14.8	14.5	14.5	14.2	14.2	14.0	13.6	13.7
2000	11.9	11.8	12.9	13.5	14.1	14.7	15.0	14.9	14.6	14.3	14.1	13.0	13.7
2001	12.0	11.8	12.1	13.4	14.3	15.1	15.4	15.5	15.2	14.8	14.5	13.8	14.0
2002	12.4	12.3	12.8	14.1	14.7	15.4	15.4	15.4	14.9	15.1	15.0	14.1	14.3
2003	12.7	12.2	12.5	13.9	14.7	15.2	15.4	15.6	15.5	15.3	15.1	14.4	14.4
Manufacturing													
1990	21.5	21.5	21.5	22.0	22.1	22.4	22.6	22.9	22.8	22.5	22.2	22.1	22.1
1991	21.7	21.6	21.6	21.6	21.8	21.9	21.9	22.0	22.0	21.9	21.8	21.9	21.8
1992	21.3	21.5	21.6	21.5	21.8	22.0	22.2	22.1	22.2	22.2	22.1	21.7	21.8
1993	21.4	21.4	21.7	21.9	21.9	22.2	20.2	21.6	22.2	22.6	22.6	22.8	21.8
1994	22.4	22.3	22.4	22.7	22.6	22.9	23.0	21.1	21.7	21.9	21.7	22.0	22.2
1995	21.8	22.3	22.9	23.0	23.0	23.3	22.9	22.6	22.7	23.1	22.9	23.2	22.8
1996	22.7	22.7	22.8	23.2	22.2	22.4	22.5	22.4	22.3	22.2	22.1	22.2	22.4
1997	21.3	21.2	21.1	22.2	22.3	22.6	22.8	22.9	22.9	23.1	23.0	22.8	22.3
1998	22.0	22.6	22.5	22.8	22.2	22.5	22.5	22.5	22.5	22.3	22.3	22.5	22.4
1999	21.8	22.0	22.0	22.4	22.4	22.5	22.4	22.2	22.1	21.8	21.7	21.7	22.0
2000	21.1	21.0	21.2	21.3	21.4	21.6	21.4	21.5	21.2	21.0	21.0	20.7	21.2
2001	20.8	20.8	20.8	20.6	20.7	20.8	20.5	20.4	20.2	20.1	20.0	19.9	20.5
2002	19.4	19.2	19.0	19.5	19.6	19.6	19.6	19.5	19.5	19.3	19.2	19.1	19.4
2003	18.5	18.5	18.5	18.8	18.8	18.8	18.6	18.6	18.7	18.7	18.3	18.0	18.6
Service-providing													
1990	196.8	197.4	199.1	199.5	201.3	203.8	201.2	201.6	202.6	202.8	204.3	206.1	201.3
1991	200.5	200.5	203.1	203.7	206.2	208.4	204.0	203.7	204.3	205.3	206.2	207.9	204.4
1992	203.6	204.4	206.0	208.0	209.9	211.7	208.1	208.4	209.0	209.5	210.8	211.8	208.4
1993	206.9	206.8	209.2	211.7	214.5	217.0	211.3	212.4	213.4	215.2	216.5	218.4	212.7
1994	212.3	213.2	215.3	217.4	219.8	222.8	219.5	222.4	222.1	222.6	225.2	226.3	219.9
1995	221.1	221.8	224.1	225.5	228.0	230.6	226.8	229.6	228.9	231.3	233.7	235.3	228.0
1996	229.3	228.7	231.2	233.2	235.3	236.7	232.8	234.3	232.0	233.9	236.3	238.0	233.4
1997	231.8	231.9	234.3	234.4	237.2	239.3	236.5	236.8	235.8	237.1	239.4	241.9	236.3
1998	237.0	236.9	238.6	242.6	246.3	248.9	243.9	244.5	244.0	246.7	248.6	250.1	244.0
1999	244.8	244.9	247.3	249.5	251.6	253.5	249.7	249.3	248.6	250.1	251.7	254.3	249.6
2000	248.0	248.4	250.3	249.8	252.8	254.9	254.8	255.4	254.1	256.0	256.8	257.7	253.2
2001	250.9	250.4	252.1	253.7	256.5	259.2	252.7	253.6	253.0	254.1	255.2	255.6	253.9
2002	249.6	248.9	250.0	252.5	254.2	256.3	251.3	252.0	251.6	252.5	253.5	253.8	252.2
2003	248.9	248.1	248.9	251.5	253.6	255.9	251.3	252.6	252.6	256.3	255.2	256.0	252.6
Trade, transportation, and utilities													
1990	54.8	54.2	54.3	54.6	55.0	55.8	55.9	56.1	55.9	56.3	57.2	58.0	55.6
1991	55.6	54.5	54.8	55.4	55.9	56.4	56.2	56.3	56.1	57.3	58.0	58.5	56.2
1992	56.7	56.1	56.4	57.6	57.8	58.5	58.3	58.2	58.0	57.8	58.7	59.3	57.7
1993	56.9	56.2	56.8	57.7	58.1	58.7	58.3	58.6	58.4	59.4	59.9	60.9	58.3
1994	59.3	58.7	59.0	59.5	60.0	60.7	61.5	62.0	62.8	63.2	63.9	64.7	61.2
1995	62.8	62.2	62.6	62.5	63.0	63.3	63.4	63.7	63.7	65.0	66.3	66.7	63.7
1996	63.3	61.9	62.1	63.1	63.2	63.2	63.7	64.0	63.6	64.6	65.8	66.4	63.7
1997	63.5	62.3	62.6	62.6	63.2	63.4	63.8	62.6	63.3	63.6	65.2	66.2	63.5
1998	63.5	63.0	63.3	64.7	65.5	65.9	66.0	66.0	66.0	67.2	68.5	69.2	65.7
1999	64.6	63.1	63.4	64.1	64.2	64.7	66.1	65.4	65.3	66.6	67.6	68.4	65.2
2000	64.9	64.9	64.9	64.8	65.1	65.7	66.0	66.3	66.0	67.3	68.5	68.9	66.1
2001	64.9	63.8	64.0	64.1	64.5	64.6	64.1	64.3	64.2	63.8	65.2	65.8	64.4
2002	62.9	61.9	61.9	62.4	62.6	63.2	62.3	62.2	62.0	62.3	63.6	63.8	62.6
2003	61.2	60.2	60.3	60.9	61.5	61.8	61.7	61.8	61.4	61.2	61.7	63.1	61.4
Wholesale trade													
1990	15.1	15.1	15.2	15.4	15.5	15.7	15.8	15.8	15.8	15.6	15.6	15.6	15.5
1991	15.2	15.1	15.2	15.4	15.6	15.6	15.7	15.6	15.7	15.6	15.5	15.5	15.4
1992	15.3	15.3	15.3	15.8	15.8	16.0	16.3	16.3	16.3	15.8	15.8	15.7	15.8
1993	15.5	15.4	15.5	15.8	15.8	16.0	16.0	16.1	15.9	16.0	15.9	16.0	15.8
1994	16.0	16.1	16.1	16.3	16.3	16.6	16.7	16.7	16.8	16.8	16.8	16.8	16.5
1995	16.9	16.9	16.9	17.0	17.2	17.3	17.2	17.4	17.3	17.4	17.4	17.6	17.2
1996	17.1	17.0	17.1	17.0	17.1	17.2	16.9	17.0	16.9	17.1	17.0	17.0	17.0
1997	16.8	16.8	16.9	16.9	16.9	17.2	17.3	17.2	17.3	17.0	17.1	17.2	17.0
1998	17.1	17.2	17.3	17.6	17.8	17.9	18.0	17.9	17.9	17.9	18.0	18.0	17.7
1999	17.9	18.0	18.0	18.0	18.1	18.2	18.2	18.0	17.8	18.1	18.0	18.2	18.0
2000	17.7	17.7	17.7	17.7	17.8	17.9	18.0	17.7	17.6	17.8	17.7	17.7	17.7
2001	17.6	17.5	17.6	17.5	17.5	17.6	17.4	17.3	17.4	17.1	17.0	17.1	17.4
2002	16.8	16.7	16.7	16.5	16.4	16.6	16.7	16.6	16.4	16.4	16.4	16.3	16.5
2003	16.0	15.9	15.9	16.0	16.1	16.3	16.4	16.3	16.1	16.1	15.7	16.2	16.1

Employment by Industry: Iowa—*Continued*

(Numbers in thousands. Not seasonally adjusted.)

Industry	January	February	March	April	May	June	July	August	September	October	November	December	Annual Average
DES MOINES—*Continued*													
Retail trade													
1990	29.3	28.7	28.7	28.9	29.1	29.6	29.5	29.6	29.4	29.9	30.7	31.5	29.5
1991	30.0	29.1	29.2	29.7	30.0	30.2	30.1	30.3	30.0	31.2	32.0	32.4	30.3
1992	30.6	30.0	30.3	30.8	31.0	31.4	31.2	31.2	31.2	31.5	32.4	33.1	31.2
1993	31.3	30.7	31.1	31.7	32.0	32.3	31.9	32.0	32.1	32.6	33.3	34.1	32.0
1994	33.1	32.4	32.6	32.8	33.2	33.5	34.0	34.6	35.2	35.3	36.1	36.8	34.1
1995	34.8	34.1	34.4	34.2	34.5	34.7	34.6	34.7	34.8	35.7	37.0	37.1	35.0
1996	34.9	33.7	33.7	34.5	34.5	34.4	34.9	35.1	34.8	35.1	36.4	37.1	34.9
1997	34.9	33.7	33.9	33.7	34.3	34.2	34.2	34.2	33.9	34.3	35.8	36.7	34.4
1998	34.5	33.9	34.1	34.6	35.2	35.4	35.3	35.3	35.2	36.3	37.5	38.2	35.4
1999	34.2	32.6	32.8	33.3	33.3	33.7	35.2	34.8	34.8	35.6	36.8	37.5	34.5
2000	34.9	34.9	35.0	34.7	35.0	35.4	35.5	36.1	35.9	36.6	37.9	38.4	35.8
2001	36.7	35.8	35.9	35.9	36.3	36.2	36.0	36.2	36.1	36.0	37.5	38.0	36.4
2002	35.8	35.1	35.1	35.6	35.9	36.2	35.0	35.0	35.1	35.3	36.6	37.0	35.6
2003	35.0	34.2	34.3	34.8	35.2	35.3	35.0	35.1	35.1	35.1	36.0	36.9	35.2
Transportation and utilities													
1990	10.4	10.4	10.4	10.3	10.4	10.5	10.6	10.7	10.7	10.8	10.9	10.9	10.5
1991	10.4	10.3	10.4	10.3	10.3	10.6	10.4	10.4	10.4	10.5	10.5	10.6	10.4
1992	10.8	10.8	10.8	11.0	11.0	11.1	10.8	10.7	10.5	10.5	10.5	10.5	10.7
1993	10.1	10.1	10.2	10.2	10.3	10.4	10.4	10.5	10.4	10.8	10.7	10.8	10.4
1994	10.2	10.2	10.3	10.4	10.5	10.6	10.8	10.7	10.8	11.1	11.0	11.1	10.6
1995	11.1	11.2	11.3	11.3	11.3	11.3	11.6	11.6	11.6	11.9	11.9	12.0	11.5
1996	11.3	11.2	11.3	11.6	11.6	11.6	11.9	11.9	11.9	12.4	12.4	12.3	11.7
1997	11.8	11.8	11.8	12.0	12.0	12.0	12.3	11.2	12.1	12.3	12.3	12.3	11.9
1998	11.9	11.9	11.9	12.5	12.5	12.6	12.7	12.8	12.9	13.0	13.0	13.0	12.5
1999	12.5	12.5	12.6	12.8	12.8	12.8	12.7	12.6	12.7	12.9	12.8	12.7	12.7
2000	12.3	12.3	12.2	12.4	12.3	12.4	12.5	12.5	12.5	12.9	12.9	12.8	12.5
2001	10.6	10.5	10.5	10.7	10.7	10.8	10.7	10.8	10.7	10.7	10.7	10.7	10.7
2002	10.3	10.1	10.1	10.3	10.3	10.4	10.6	10.6	10.5	10.6	10.6	10.5	10.4
2003	10.2	10.1	10.1	10.1	10.2	10.2	10.3	10.4	10.2	10.0	10.0	10.0	10.2
Information													
1990	8.9	8.9	8.9	8.7	8.7	8.7	8.7	8.7	8.8	9.0	8.9	8.8	8.8
1991	8.7	8.7	8.7	8.5	8.5	8.6	7.5	7.5	7.4	7.4	7.4	7.5	8.0
1992	7.4	7.4	7.6	7.7	7.6	7.7	7.7	7.6	7.5	7.4	7.4	7.4	7.5
1993	7.3	7.2	7.2	7.2	7.3	7.4	7.3	7.3	7.3	7.4	7.4	7.4	7.3
1994	7.2	7.2	7.2	7.3	7.3	7.5	7.4	7.5	7.5	7.8	8.0	8.2	7.5
1995	8.1	8.1	8.2	8.1	8.1	8.2	8.1	8.1	8.1	8.0	8.2	8.2	8.1
1996	8.0	8.0	8.0	8.1	8.2	8.1	8.1	8.0	8.0	8.1	8.4	8.5	8.1
1997	8.2	8.1	8.1	8.1	8.1	8.3	8.5	8.7	8.8	8.8	8.6	8.6	8.4
1998	8.8	8.7	8.7	8.7	8.8	8.9	8.6	8.5	8.4	8.6	8.9	8.9	8.7
1999	9.9	9.8	9.8	10.5	10.5	10.6	10.1	10.1	10.1	10.4	10.4	10.5	10.2
2000	10.3	10.2	10.3	10.2	10.3	10.4	10.4	10.3	10.4	10.5	10.5	10.6	10.3
2001	10.5	10.5	10.4	10.2	10.2	10.2	10.1	10.1	10.0	10.1	9.9	9.7	10.2
2002	9.8	9.7	9.6	9.4	9.4	9.5	9.4	9.4	9.4	9.4	9.5	9.4	9.5
2003	9.2	9.2	9.2	9.2	9.3	9.3	9.3	9.3	9.2	9.2	9.4	9.4	9.3
Financial activities													
1990	28.7	28.7	28.8	29.3	29.3	29.8	30.0	30.0	29.8	29.8	29.6	29.8	29.4
1991	29.9	29.9	30.2	29.7	29.9	30.6	30.7	30.8	30.8	30.1	30.2	30.5	30.2
1992	30.3	30.4	30.5	30.6	30.7	31.4	31.5	31.6	31.3	31.5	31.4	31.7	31.0
1993	31.2	31.1	31.4	31.8	31.8	32.3	32.5	32.4	32.3	32.4	32.5	32.8	32.0
1994	32.5	32.5	32.6	32.8	33.0	33.7	33.8	33.9	33.7	33.0	32.9	33.2	33.1
1995	32.5	32.5	32.6	32.9	32.8	33.5	33.8	33.9	33.6	33.6	33.6	34.2	33.2
1996	34.7	34.5	35.0	35.1	35.4	35.8	36.3	36.4	35.6	35.6	35.6	35.8	35.4
1997	35.4	35.3	35.7	35.6	35.9	36.6	37.2	37.3	36.9	38.1	38.2	38.4	36.7
1998	38.5	38.4	38.5	39.5	39.6	40.9	40.9	41.2	40.7	40.3	40.0	40.2	39.8
1999	40.9	41.1	41.2	41.0	41.0	41.4	41.4	41.2	40.9	41.1	41.3	41.7	41.1
2000	41.0	40.9	41.0	41.0	41.1	41.5	41.5	41.4	41.3	41.2	41.3	41.6	41.2
2001	42.2	42.1	42.4	42.7	42.8	43.7	43.4	43.2	43.2	43.3	43.7	44.0	43.1
2002	43.9	44.1	44.1	44.3	44.1	44.5	44.7	44.5	44.1	44.0	43.8	43.8	44.2
2003	44.0	44.1	44.2	44.1	44.3	44.7	44.9	45.0	44.9	45.0	45.5	45.4	44.7
Professional and business services													
1990	19.1	18.8	19.1	19.1	19.0	19.5	19.8	20.0	19.6	19.6	19.3	19.4	19.3
1991	19.0	18.8	19.0	19.6	19.8	20.1	20.8	20.5	21.0	20.7	20.1	20.4	19.9
1992	19.7	19.9	20.0	20.6	20.7	20.8	20.4	20.6	21.6	21.9	21.6	21.5	20.7
1993	21.6	21.7	21.8	21.9	22.2	23.1	22.4	23.2	23.8	23.8	23.5	23.6	22.7
1994	22.3	22.5	22.8	23.4	23.9	24.4	24.0	24.6	24.8	24.3	24.7	24.0	23.8
1995	23.9	24.0	24.3	24.6	24.9	25.4	25.4	26.0	26.0	26.4	26.4	26.2	25.2
1996	25.7	26.3	26.5	26.5	26.3	26.7	26.4	26.5	26.4	26.6	26.7	26.8	26.4
1997	26.5	26.6	27.0	27.3	27.5	27.9	27.2	27.1	27.2	27.6	27.6	27.6	27.2
1998	26.9	26.9	27.4	28.1	28.2	28.5	28.4	28.4	28.3	28.9	28.6	28.6	28.1
1999	27.5	27.7	28.4	29.2	29.3	29.9	29.3	29.3	29.2	29.4	29.3	29.6	29.0
2000	28.9	28.9	29.4	29.3	29.5	29.8	30.2	30.1	30.0	31.0	31.0	30.8	29.9
2001	30.4	30.5	30.5	30.8	31.2	31.4	30.5	30.9	30.7	30.7	30.4	30.4	30.7
2002	29.2	28.9	29.3	29.9	29.8	30.1	30.1	30.5	30.7	30.4	30.5	30.4	30.0
2003	29.3	29.3	29.4	30.1	29.9	30.5	30.5	31.1	30.8	30.9	30.6	30.4	30.2

Employment by Industry: Iowa—*Continued*

(Numbers in thousands. Not seasonally adjusted.)

Industry	January	February	March	April	May	June	July	August	September	October	November	December	Annual Average
DES MOINES—*Continued*													
Educational and health services													
1990	25.4	25.6	25.8	25.3	25.5	25.0	24.2	24.4	25.1	25.6	26.5	26.6	25.4
1991	26.2	26.5	26.8	26.7	26.9	26.4	25.4	25.5	26.3	26.5	27.3	27.4	26.4
1992	27.2	27.4	27.5	27.5	27.6	26.9	26.0	26.1	26.9	26.9	27.6	27.8	27.1
1993	27.3	27.4	27.9	27.7	27.8	27.2	26.0	25.9	26.9	27.0	27.7	27.9	27.2
1994	27.8	28.0	28.3	27.9	28.0	27.4	26.5	26.6	27.3	27.5	28.3	28.5	27.6
1995	28.1	28.4	28.8	28.8	29.1	28.9	27.5	27.7	28.8	29.1	29.9	30.3	28.7
1996	29.5	29.8	30.3	30.2	30.3	29.7	28.5	28.5	29.5	29.6	30.5	30.6	29.7
1997	30.2	30.5	30.9	30.6	30.7	30.0	29.5	29.5	30.4	30.0	31.0	31.2	30.3
1998	30.9	31.1	31.4	31.5	31.8	31.1	29.9	30.0	30.6	31.0	31.9	32.1	31.1
1999	31.8	32.2	32.5	32.2	32.4	31.8	30.6	30.7	31.1	30.8	31.7	31.8	31.6
2000	32.9	33.2	33.4	33.1	33.2	33.1	33.8	34.1	34.6	34.2	34.1	34.2	33.6
2001	33.0	33.4	33.9	34.1	34.1	34.1	32.1	32.3	32.8	34.3	34.1	34.1	33.5
2002	33.4	33.5	33.7	33.8	33.9	33.7	32.1	32.3	33.0	34.0	34.1	34.1	33.5
2003	34.3	34.1	34.0	34.5	34.5	34.3	32.5	32.4	33.2	36.8	36.7	36.6	34.5
Leisure and hospitality													
1990	16.9	17.4	18.0	18.6	19.5	20.2	20.3	20.5	19.8	18.6	18.2	18.5	18.8
1991	17.3	17.4	18.2	18.7	19.7	20.9	20.2	20.4	19.3	18.7	18.4	18.4	18.9
1992	17.7	18.0	18.6	18.9	20.1	20.9	20.8	21.3	20.0	19.3	18.9	18.9	19.4
1993	18.2	18.2	18.8	19.9	21.3	22.2	21.0	21.6	20.3	19.7	19.4	19.5	20.0
1994	18.5	18.8	19.4	20.5	21.5	22.6	22.0	22.7	21.1	20.4	20.4	20.2	20.6
1995	19.4	19.6	20.2	21.3	23.0	23.7	24.0	24.7	23.1	22.0	21.9	22.2	22.0
1996	21.2	21.2	21.7	22.7	24.1	24.9	24.4	24.8	22.8	22.2	22.0	22.0	22.8
1997	21.0	21.5	22.0	22.5	23.6	24.7	25.2	25.5	23.6	22.3	21.8	22.1	22.9
1998	21.7	21.9	22.2	23.3	25.0	25.8	24.9	25.4	23.9	23.3	22.7	23.0	23.5
1999	22.0	22.4	23.1	23.7	25.2	26.2	25.6	26.1	24.4	23.9	23.5	23.7	24.1
2000	22.2	22.0	22.8	22.9	24.0	24.6	25.5	26.2	24.5	23.4	22.7	22.6	23.6
2001	22.0	22.0	22.5	23.4	25.1	26.1	25.7	26.4	24.5	23.4	23.0	23.0	23.9
2002	22.1	22.2	22.7	23.8	25.3	26.0	25.9	26.5	25.0	23.9	23.5	23.7	24.2
2003	23.0	22.9	23.1	24.2	25.3	26.3	26.2	26.9	25.5	24.0	22.4	22.0	24.3
Other services													
1990	11.6	11.7	11.8	11.7	11.9	12.1	12.0	12.0	12.0	12.1	12.2	12.3	11.9
1991	12.1	12.1	12.3	12.4	12.4	12.6	12.4	12.4	12.4	12.4	12.3	12.5	12.3
1992	12.4	12.4	12.4	12.3	12.4	12.6	12.6	12.6	12.5	12.3	12.4	12.4	12.4
1993	12.1	12.2	12.2	12.5	12.7	12.9	12.8	12.8	12.9	12.8	12.9	13.0	12.6
1994	12.6	12.7	12.9	12.9	12.9	13.1	12.9	12.9	12.9	13.0	13.1	13.1	12.9
1995	12.8	12.9	13.0	13.0	12.7	12.9	12.8	12.8	12.7	13.0	13.0	12.7	12.8
1996	12.3	12.3	12.4	12.5	12.6	12.7	12.5	12.5	12.4	12.3	12.2	12.2	12.4
1997	12.3	12.3	12.4	12.4	12.5	12.6	11.8	11.7	11.6	11.7	11.6	11.7	12.0
1998	11.6	11.6	11.7	11.9	12.0	12.2	12.0	12.0	11.9	12.2	12.3	12.1	11.9
1999	11.9	12.1	12.1	12.1	12.2	12.3	12.2	12.2	12.3	12.2	12.2	12.3	12.1
2000	12.1	12.1	12.1	12.2	12.3	12.4	12.4	12.3	12.2	12.3	12.4	12.3	12.2
2001	11.1	11.0	11.1	11.2	11.2	11.4	11.2	11.1	11.1	11.1	11.2	11.3	11.2
2002	11.2	11.3	11.4	11.4	11.5	11.8	11.8	11.8	11.5	11.7	11.7	11.4	11.5
2003	11.3	11.4	11.5	11.5	11.5	11.7	11.7	11.6	11.6	11.7	11.4	11.4	11.5
Government													
1990	31.4	32.1	32.4	32.2	32.4	32.7	30.3	29.9	31.6	31.8	32.4	32.7	31.8
1991	31.7	32.6	33.1	32.7	33.1	32.8	30.8	30.3	31.0	32.2	32.5	32.7	32.1
1992	32.2	32.8	33.0	32.8	33.0	32.9	30.8	30.4	31.2	32.4	32.8	32.8	32.2
1993	32.3	32.8	33.1	33.0	33.3	33.2	31.0	30.6	31.5	32.7	33.2	33.3	32.5
1994	32.1	32.8	33.1	33.1	33.2	33.4	31.4	32.2	32.0	33.4	33.9	34.4	32.9
1995	33.5	34.1	34.4	34.3	34.4	34.7	31.8	32.7	32.9	34.2	34.4	34.8	33.8
1996	34.6	34.7	35.2	35.0	35.2	35.6	32.9	33.6	33.7	34.9	35.1	35.7	34.6
1997	34.7	35.3	35.6	35.3	35.7	35.8	33.3	34.4	34.0	35.0	35.4	36.1	35.0
1998	35.1	35.3	35.4	34.9	35.4	35.6	33.2	33.0	34.2	35.2	35.7	36.0	34.9
1999	36.2	36.5	36.8	36.7	36.8	36.6	34.4	34.3	35.3	35.7	35.7	36.3	35.9
2000	35.7	36.2	36.4	36.3	37.3	37.4	35.0	34.7	35.1	36.1	36.3	36.7	36.1
2001	36.8	37.1	37.3	37.2	37.4	37.7	35.6	35.3	36.5	37.4	37.7	37.3	36.9
2002	37.1	37.3	37.3	37.5	37.6	37.5	35.0	34.8	35.9	36.8	36.8	37.2	36.7
2003	36.6	36.9	37.2	37.0	37.3	37.3	34.5	34.5	36.0	37.5	37.5	37.7	36.7
Federal government													
1990	5.8	5.8	5.8	5.8	5.8	5.9	5.9	5.8	5.7	5.5	5.7	5.7	5.7
1991	5.7	5.8	5.8	5.8	5.8	5.8	5.9	5.8	5.8	5.8	5.8	5.9	5.8
1992	5.9	5.8	5.8	5.8	5.8	5.8	5.8	5.8	5.8	5.8	5.7	5.9	5.8
1993	5.7	5.7	5.7	5.8	5.8	5.8	5.9	5.9	5.9	5.8	5.9	6.2	5.8
1994	5.9	5.9	5.9	5.9	5.9	5.9	6.1	6.2	6.2	6.2	6.4	7.1	6.1
1995	6.4	6.4	6.4	6.5	6.4	6.5	6.4	6.4	6.4	6.3	6.3	6.7	6.4
1996	6.3	6.3	6.3	6.4	6.4	6.4	6.4	6.4	6.3	6.3	6.4	6.7	6.3
1997	6.1	6.1	6.1	6.1	6.1	6.1	6.0	6.1	6.1	6.1	6.2	6.6	6.1
1998	6.1	6.1	6.0	6.0	6.0	6.1	6.0	6.0	6.0	6.0	6.0	6.3	6.0
1999	6.7	6.7	6.7	6.3	5.9	5.9	5.9	5.9	5.9	5.8	5.9	6.2	6.1
2000	5.9	5.8	5.8	5.8	6.2	6.4	5.8	6.0	5.6	5.5	5.6	5.8	5.8
2001	5.7	5.6	5.6	5.6	5.6	5.6	5.6	5.6	5.6	5.6	5.6	5.7	5.6
2002	5.6	5.5	5.5	5.5	5.5	5.5	5.5	5.6	5.5	5.5	5.5	5.6	5.5
2003	5.6	5.5	5.4	5.5	5.4	5.4	5.5	5.3	5.3	5.4	5.3	5.4	5.4

Employment by Industry: Iowa—*Continued*

(Numbers in thousands. Not seasonally adjusted.)

Industry	January	February	March	April	May	June	July	August	September	October	November	December	Annual Average
DES MOINES—*Continued*													
State government													
1990	8.3	8.4	8.5	8.5	8.3	8.3	8.3	8.3	8.2	7.9	8.0	8.0	8.2
1991	8.3	8.4	8.4	8.5	8.6	8.2	8.2	8.1	7.9	7.7	7.7	7.7	8.1
1992	7.9	8.0	8.0	8.1	7.9	7.7	7.7	7.6	7.5	7.5	7.5	7.5	7.7
1993	7.7	7.8	7.9	7.8	7.8	7.6	7.5	7.5	7.4	7.4	7.4	7.4	7.6
1994	7.4	7.5	7.6	7.8	7.7	7.7	7.7	8.6	7.5	7.5	7.5	7.4	7.6
1995	7.7	7.8	7.9	8.0	7.9	7.9	7.9	8.9	7.7	7.7	7.7	7.8	7.9
1996	8.1	8.1	8.2	8.3	8.1	8.2	8.3	9.3	8.0	7.9	7.9	8.1	8.2
1997	8.1	8.3	8.3	8.3	8.3	8.2	8.3	9.4	8.1	8.0	8.0	8.1	8.2
1998	8.0	8.0	8.1	8.0	7.8	7.9	8.3	8.4	8.2	7.8	7.9	7.8	8.0
1999	8.3	8.4	8.5	8.4	8.3	8.3	8.4	8.5	8.4	8.1	8.0	8.1	8.3
2000	8.3	8.4	8.4	8.7	8.7	8.8	8.7	8.8	8.5	8.1	8.1	8.1	8.4
2001	8.7	8.8	8.8	8.8	8.7	8.8	8.7	8.7	8.5	8.3	8.2	8.2	8.6
2002	8.3	8.2	8.2	8.5	8.3	8.6	8.1	8.1	7.9	7.8	7.8	7.8	8.1
2003	8.0	8.0	8.1	8.3	8.2	8.3	8.3	8.3	8.2	8.2	8.2	8.2	8.2
Local government													
1990	17.3	17.9	18.1	17.9	18.3	18.5	16.1	15.8	17.7	18.4	18.7	19.0	17.8
1991	17.7	18.4	18.9	18.4	18.7	18.8	16.7	16.4	17.3	18.7	19.0	19.1	18.1
1992	18.4	19.0	19.2	18.9	19.3	19.4	17.3	17.0	17.9	19.1	19.6	19.4	18.7
1993	18.9	19.3	19.5	19.4	19.7	19.8	17.6	17.2	18.2	19.5	19.9	19.7	19.0
1994	18.8	19.4	19.6	19.4	19.6	19.8	17.6	17.4	18.3	19.7	20.0	19.9	19.1
1995	19.4	19.9	20.1	19.8	20.1	20.3	17.5	17.4	18.8	20.2	20.4	20.3	19.5
1996	20.2	20.3	20.7	20.3	20.7	21.0	18.2	17.9	19.4	20.7	20.8	20.9	20.0
1997	20.5	20.9	21.2	20.9	21.3	21.5	19.0	18.9	19.8	20.9	21.2	21.4	20.6
1998	21.0	21.2	21.3	20.9	21.6	21.6	18.9	18.6	20.0	21.4	21.8	21.9	20.8
1999	21.2	21.4	21.6	22.0	22.6	22.4	20.1	19.9	21.0	21.8	21.8	22.0	21.4
2000	21.5	22.0	22.2	21.8	22.4	22.2	20.5	19.9	21.0	22.5	22.6	22.8	21.7
2001	22.4	22.7	22.9	22.8	23.1	23.3	21.3	21.0	22.4	23.5	23.9	23.4	22.7
2002	23.2	23.6	23.6	23.5	23.8	23.4	21.4	21.1	22.5	23.5	23.5	23.8	23.1
2003	23.0	23.4	23.7	23.2	23.7	23.6	20.7	20.9	22.5	23.9	24.0	24.1	23.1
IOWA CITY													
Total nonfarm													
1990	55.1	55.6	55.9	56.8	56.8	55.6	53.4	55.2	55.9	57.4	58.0	57.4	56.0
1991	56.2	55.2	56.7	57.5	57.8	56.5	53.9	54.8	56.3	57.8	58.5	58.6	56.6
1992	56.9	55.8	58.0	58.6	58.8	57.3	55.8	56.3	56.6	57.9	58.7	59.0	57.4
1993	57.8	56.6	59.6	60.3	60.4	59.7	57.5	58.5	59.1	60.9	62.4	62.8	59.6
1994	60.6	59.5	62.0	62.9	63.4	62.4	59.3	60.8	61.9	62.9	64.2	64.4	62.0
1995	63.2	61.7	64.6	64.4	64.8	63.7	60.1	61.9	62.5	64.1	65.8	65.5	63.5
1996	63.4	61.8	64.5	65.3	65.7	64.0	61.6	62.1	63.4	65.9	66.7	66.3	64.2
1997	64.0	63.5	65.3	66.3	67.0	65.6	62.2	63.1	65.2	67.5	68.0	68.1	65.4
1998	66.5	66.3	68.1	69.2	69.9	68.2	64.7	65.9	68.0	70.4	71.7	71.8	68.3
1999	69.3	69.0	70.5	72.4	72.1	70.8	66.9	69.9	71.8	72.8	73.8	73.4	71.0
2000	70.9	72.4	73.3	73.5	73.5	71.2	69.1	70.3	73.2	73.6	74.5	73.9	72.4
2001	72.2	72.9	73.3	74.5	74.3	72.0	70.5	71.6	74.0	74.8	75.0	75.1	73.4
2002	72.9	73.7	74.5	75.1	75.3	73.3	71.6	72.3	75.3	76.1	77.5	77.4	74.6
2003	74.9	73.9	75.9	77.4	77.6	76.5	74.2	75.0	78.2	78.8	79.3	79.0	76.7
Total private													
1990	28.7	29.0	29.3	30.0	30.0	30.3	30.0	30.1	30.6	30.8	30.8	30.1	29.9
1991	28.9	29.2	29.7	30.5	30.8	30.9	30.3	30.4	31.1	31.5	31.6	31.5	30.5
1992	30.1	30.7	31.0	31.5	31.5	31.4	30.4	31.1	31.2	31.3	31.3	31.3	31.0
1993	30.4	31.1	31.7	32.6	32.4	32.9	32.7	32.7	33.1	33.4	34.0	34.1	32.5
1994	32.7	33.4	34.0	34.9	35.3	35.3	34.9	34.7	35.7	35.3	36.0	36.2	34.8
1995	35.3	35.6	36.3	36.1	36.5	36.6	35.7	35.9	36.4	36.3	37.1	37.0	36.2
1996	35.0	35.6	36.2	36.9	37.3	37.1	37.1	36.9	37.6	37.6	38.0	37.9	36.9
1997	36.0	36.4	37.2	37.9	38.7	38.6	38.2	38.2	38.8	38.8	39.2	39.4	38.1
1998	38.1	38.7	39.5	40.7	41.4	41.3	40.5	41.0	41.5	42.6	42.9	43.1	40.9
1999	40.9	41.3	41.9	43.2	43.2	43.6	43.3	43.1	43.9	43.9	44.5	44.5	43.1
2000	43.1	43.3	44.2	44.4	44.4	44.2	43.5	43.5	44.5	44.3	45.1	44.8	44.1
2001	43.7	44.1	44.5	45.7	45.5	45.4	45.0	45.2	45.4	45.7	45.8	46.1	45.2
2002	44.2	45.0	45.3	46.1	46.3	46.8	46.4	46.2	46.8	46.9	47.5	47.5	46.3
2003	45.4	45.9	46.0	47.1	47.5	47.3	47.3	47.1	47.9	48.0	47.9	47.9	47.1
Goods-producing													
1990	5.4	5.4	5.5	5.7	5.9	5.9	6.0	6.0	5.9	5.9	5.8	5.5	5.7
1991	5.3	5.2	5.4	5.6	6.0	6.2	6.3	6.2	6.2	6.2	6.1	5.9	5.8
1992	5.7	5.7	5.6	5.7	5.8	6.0	5.9	6.0	5.7	5.6	5.5	5.5	5.7
1993	5.3	5.4	5.4	5.6	5.7	6.0	6.1	6.0	5.9	5.8	5.9	5.9	5.7
1994	5.7	5.7	5.8	6.2	6.3	6.5	6.6	6.5	6.5	6.4	6.4	6.4	6.2
1995	6.3	6.2	6.3	6.3	6.4	6.6	6.7	6.6	6.5	6.5	6.5	6.4	6.4
1996	6.0	6.0	6.2	6.5	6.6	6.8	6.8	6.8	7.0	6.9	6.8	6.7	6.5
1997	6.5	6.4	6.5	6.6	6.8	7.0	7.0	7.1	7.0	6.9	6.8	6.8	6.7
1998	6.6	6.7	6.7	7.1	7.4	7.6	7.4	7.3	7.3	7.6	7.5	7.4	7.2
1999	7.2	7.4	7.5	7.6	7.8	8.0	8.0	8.0	8.1	7.9	7.8	7.7	7.7
2000	7.6	7.6	7.7	7.6	7.7	7.9	7.9	7.9	7.8	7.8	7.8	7.6	7.7
2001	7.6	7.6	7.6	7.9	8.1	8.3	8.1	8.2	8.1	7.9	7.7	7.8	7.9
2002	7.5	7.5	7.6	7.8	8.0	8.3	8.2	8.1	8.0	7.9	7.9	7.8	7.9
2003	7.5	7.4	7.4	7.8	8.0	8.1	8.3	8.4	8.3	8.2	8.1	7.9	8.0

Employment by Industry: Iowa—*Continued*

(Numbers in thousands. Not seasonally adjusted.)

Industry	January	February	March	April	May	June	July	August	September	October	November	December	Annual Average
IOWA CITY—*Continued*													
Construction and mining													
1990	1.3	1.3	1.4	1.6	1.8	1.8	1.9	1.9	1.7	1.7	1.6	1.5	1.6
1991	1.4	1.4	1.4	1.6	1.8	1.9	1.9	1.8	1.8	1.8	1.7	1.6	1.6
1992	1.5	1.5	1.5	1.6	1.7	1.9	1.8	1.8	1.7	1.7	1.6	1.6	1.6
1993	1.5	1.5	1.5	1.7	1.8	2.0	2.0	2.0	1.9	1.9	1.9	1.9	1.8
1994	1.7	1.7	1.8	2.0	2.1	2.3	2.3	2.3	2.3	2.2	2.1	2.1	2.0
1995	2.0	2.0	2.0	2.1	2.2	2.3	2.3	2.2	2.1	2.1	2.1	2.0	2.1
1996	1.7	1.7	1.8	2.1	2.2	2.3	2.3	2.3	2.3	2.3	2.2	2.1	2.1
1997	1.9	1.8	1.9	2.0	2.2	2.4	2.4	2.4	2.3	2.3	2.2	2.1	2.1
1998	1.9	2.0	2.0	2.3	2.5	2.7	2.5	2.6	2.5	2.5	2.5	2.3	2.3
1999	2.1	2.2	2.3	2.4	2.6	2.7	2.7	2.7	2.7	2.7	2.6	2.4	2.5
2000	2.3	2.3	2.4	2.3	2.4	2.6	2.7	2.7	2.5	2.6	2.6	2.5	2.4
2001	2.3	2.3	2.3	2.4	2.6	2.7	2.7	2.7	2.6	2.6	2.5	2.5	2.5
2002	2.4	2.3	2.4	2.6	2.8	3.0	3.0	2.9	2.8	2.7	2.7	2.6	2.7
2003	2.5	2.4	2.4	2.6	2.8	2.9	3.0	3.0	2.9	2.9	2.8	2.6	2.7
Manufacturing													
1990	4.1	4.1	4.1	4.1	4.1	4.1	4.1	4.1	4.2	4.2	4.2	4.0	4.1
1991	3.9	3.8	4.0	4.0	4.2	4.3	4.4	4.4	4.4	4.4	4.4	4.3	4.2
1992	4.2	4.2	4.1	4.1	4.1	4.1	4.1	4.2	4.0	3.9	3.9	3.9	4.0
1993	3.8	3.9	3.9	3.9	3.9	4.0	4.1	4.0	4.0	3.9	4.0	4.0	3.9
1994	4.0	4.0	4.0	4.2	4.2	4.2	4.3	4.2	4.2	4.2	4.3	4.3	4.1
1995	4.3	4.2	4.3	4.2	4.2	4.3	4.4	4.4	4.4	4.4	4.4	4.4	4.3
1996	4.3	4.3	4.4	4.4	4.4	4.5	4.5	4.5	4.7	4.6	4.6	4.6	4.4
1997	4.6	4.6	4.6	4.6	4.6	4.6	4.6	4.7	4.7	4.6	4.6	4.7	4.6
1998	4.7	4.7	4.7	4.8	4.9	4.9	4.9	4.7	4.8	5.1	5.0	5.1	4.8
1999	5.1	5.2	5.2	5.2	5.2	5.3	5.3	5.3	5.4	5.2	5.2	5.3	5.2
2000	5.3	5.3	5.3	5.3	5.3	5.3	5.2	5.2	5.3	5.2	5.2	5.1	5.2
2001	5.3	5.3	5.3	5.5	5.5	5.6	5.4	5.5	5.5	5.3	5.2	5.3	5.4
2002	5.1	5.2	5.2	5.2	5.2	5.3	5.2	5.2	5.2	5.2	5.2	5.2	5.2
2003	5.0	5.0	5.0	5.2	5.2	5.2	5.3	5.4	5.4	5.3	5.3	5.3	5.2
Service-providing													
1990	49.7	50.2	50.4	51.1	50.9	49.7	47.4	49.2	50.0	51.5	52.2	51.9	50.3
1991	50.9	50.0	51.3	51.9	51.8	50.3	47.6	48.6	50.1	51.6	52.4	52.7	50.7
1992	51.2	50.1	52.4	52.9	53.0	51.3	49.9	50.3	50.9	52.3	53.2	53.5	51.7
1993	52.5	51.2	54.2	54.7	54.7	53.7	51.4	52.5	53.2	55.1	56.5	56.9	53.8
1994	54.9	53.8	56.2	56.7	57.1	55.9	52.7	54.3	55.4	56.5	57.8	58.0	55.7
1995	56.9	55.5	58.3	58.1	58.4	57.1	53.4	55.3	56.0	57.6	59.3	59.1	57.0
1996	57.4	55.8	58.3	58.8	59.1	57.2	54.8	55.3	56.4	59.0	59.9	59.6	57.6
1997	57.5	57.1	58.8	59.7	60.2	58.6	55.2	56.0	58.2	60.6	61.2	61.3	58.7
1998	59.9	59.6	61.4	62.1	62.5	60.6	57.3	58.6	60.7	62.8	64.2	64.4	61.1
1999	62.1	61.6	63.0	64.8	64.3	62.8	58.9	61.9	63.7	64.9	66.0	65.7	63.3
2000	63.3	64.8	65.6	65.9	65.8	63.3	61.2	62.4	65.4	65.8	66.7	66.3	64.7
2001	64.6	65.3	65.7	66.6	66.2	63.7	62.4	63.4	65.9	66.9	67.3	67.3	65.4
2002	65.4	66.2	66.9	67.3	67.3	65.0	63.4	64.2	67.3	68.2	69.6	69.6	66.7
2003	67.4	66.5	68.5	69.6	69.6	68.4	65.9	66.6	69.9	70.6	71.2	71.1	68.8
Trade, transportation, and utilities													
1990	7.5	7.4	7.5	7.6	7.6	7.9	7.8	7.8	8.0	8.0	8.2	8.1	7.7
1991	7.7	7.7	7.8	8.0	7.9	8.0	8.0	8.0	8.2	8.2	8.3	8.4	8.0
1992	8.0	8.0	8.1	8.2	8.1	8.1	7.9	8.0	8.3	8.3	8.3	8.3	8.1
1993	8.0	7.9	8.0	8.1	8.1	8.2	8.2	8.3	8.5	8.5	8.6	8.6	8.2
1994	8.3	8.3	8.4	8.4	8.5	8.5	8.4	8.5	8.9	9.0	9.2	9.4	8.6
1995	9.3	9.3	9.3	9.0	9.1	9.1	9.2	9.2	9.4	9.2	9.4	9.6	9.2
1996	9.2	9.2	9.1	9.2	9.2	9.3	9.4	9.4	9.6	9.9	10.0	10.0	9.4
1997	9.5	9.5	9.5	9.7	9.9	9.9	9.8	9.7	9.9	10.0	10.2	10.4	9.8
1998	9.9	9.8	9.8	9.9	9.9	9.9	10.4	10.8	11.1	11.4	11.7	11.8	10.5
1999	10.9	10.6	10.6	10.9	11.0	11.1	11.7	11.8	11.9	11.9	12.2	12.4	11.4
2000	11.6	11.5	11.4	11.5	11.4	11.5	11.4	11.5	12.0	12.2	12.7	12.7	11.7
2001	12.3	12.3	12.2	12.5	12.3	12.4	12.5	12.4	12.6	12.8	13.2	13.3	12.6
2002	12.6	12.5	12.6	12.6	12.7	13.0	12.9	13.0	13.2	13.4	13.8	13.9	13.0
2003	13.2	13.2	13.3	13.4	13.6	13.6	13.7	13.7	13.7	13.8	13.9	14.0	13.6
Wholesale trade													
1990	1.0	1.0	1.0	1.0	1.0	1.1	1.1	1.1	1.2	1.1	1.1	1.0	1.0
1991	1.0	1.0	1.0	1.0	1.0	1.1	1.1	1.1	1.2	1.1	1.0	1.0	1.0
1992	1.0	1.0	1.0	1.0	1.0	1.0	1.0	1.0	1.0	1.0	1.0	1.0	1.0
1993	1.0	0.9	1.0	1.0	0.9	1.0	1.0	1.0	1.1	1.1	1.0	1.0	1.0
1994	1.0	1.0	1.0	1.0	1.0	1.0	1.1	1.1	1.2	1.0	1.0	1.0	1.0
1995	1.0	1.1	1.0	1.0	1.0	1.1	1.1	1.1	1.2	1.1	1.1	1.1	1.0
1996	1.0	1.0	1.0	1.1	1.1	1.1	1.1	1.1	1.2	1.2	1.1	1.1	1.0
1997	1.0	1.0	1.0	1.1	1.1	1.1	1.2	1.2	1.2	1.1	1.1	1.1	1.1
1998	1.1	1.1	1.1	1.2	1.2	1.2	1.3	1.3	1.3	1.2	1.2	1.2	1.2
1999	1.1	1.1	1.1	1.1	1.2	1.2	1.2	1.2	1.2	1.2	1.2	1.2	1.1
2000	1.1	1.1	1.2	1.1	1.1	1.1	1.2	1.1	1.1	1.1	1.1	1.1	1.1
2001	1.1	1.1	1.1	1.1	1.1	1.1	1.1	1.1	1.1	1.1	1.1	1.1	1.1
2002	1.1	1.1	1.1	1.1	1.1	1.1	1.1	1.1	1.1	1.1	1.1	1.1	1.1
2003	1.1	1.0	1.1	1.1	1.1	1.1	1.2	1.2	1.1	1.1	1.1	1.1	1.1

Employment by Industry: Iowa—*Continued*

(Numbers in thousands. Not seasonally adjusted.)

Industry	January	February	March	April	May	June	July	August	September	October	November	December	Annual Average
IOWA CITY—*Continued*													
Retail trade													
1990	5.2	5.1	5.2	5.3	5.3	5.4	5.4	5.4	5.5	5.5	5.7	5.7	5.3
1991	5.4	5.4	5.5	5.6	5.5	5.5	5.5	5.5	5.6	5.7	5.9	6.0	5.5
1992	5.6	5.6	5.7	5.8	5.7	5.7	5.6	5.7	5.9	5.9	5.9	5.9	5.7
1993	5.6	5.6	5.6	5.7	5.7	5.7	5.7	5.8	5.9	5.9	6.1	6.1	5.7
1994	5.8	5.8	5.9	5.9	6.0	6.0	6.0	6.0	6.3	6.5	6.6	6.8	6.1
1995	6.4	6.3	6.4	6.2	6.3	6.3	6.3	6.3	6.4	6.3	6.5	6.6	6.3
1996	6.4	6.4	6.3	6.3	6.3	6.4	6.5	6.6	6.6	6.8	7.0	7.0	6.5
1997	6.7	6.6	6.6	6.6	6.7	6.8	6.8	6.7	6.9	7.0	7.2	7.3	6.8
1998	6.9	6.8	6.8	6.8	6.8	6.8	7.3	7.7	7.9	8.2	8.5	8.7	7.4
1999	7.9	7.6	7.6	7.9	7.8	7.9	8.5	8.4	8.6	8.6	8.9	9.1	8.2
2000	8.4	8.3	8.1	8.2	8.1	8.1	8.0	8.1	8.6	8.8	9.3	9.3	8.4
2001	8.8	8.7	8.4	8.7	8.5	8.5	8.6	8.5	8.7	8.8	9.1	9.2	8.7
2002	8.5	8.4	8.4	8.4	8.4	8.4	8.3	8.3	8.5	8.6	8.9	9.0	8.5
2003	8.3	8.3	8.2	8.3	8.5	8.4	8.4	8.3	8.5	8.6	8.7	8.7	8.4
Transportation and utilities													
1990	1.3	1.3	1.3	1.3	1.3	1.4	1.3	1.3	1.3	1.4	1.4	1.4	1.3
1991	1.3	1.3	1.3	1.4	1.4	1.4	1.4	1.4	1.4	1.4	1.4	1.4	1.3
1992	1.4	1.4	1.4	1.4	1.4	1.4	1.3	1.3	1.4	1.4	1.4	1.4	1.3
1993	1.4	1.4	1.4	1.4	1.5	1.5	1.5	1.5	1.5	1.5	1.5	1.5	1.4
1994	1.5	1.5	1.5	1.5	1.5	1.5	1.3	1.4	1.4	1.5	1.6	1.6	1.4
1995	1.9	1.9	1.9	1.8	1.8	1.7	1.8	1.8	1.8	1.8	1.8	1.9	1.8
1996	1.8	1.8	1.8	1.8	1.8	1.8	1.8	1.7	1.8	1.9	1.9	1.9	1.8
1997	1.8	1.9	1.9	2.0	2.1	2.0	1.8	1.8	1.8	1.9	1.9	2.0	1.9
1998	1.9	1.9	1.9	1.9	1.9	1.9	1.8	1.8	1.9	2.0	2.0	1.9	1.9
1999	1.9	1.9	1.9	1.9	2.0	2.0	2.0	2.2	2.1	2.1	2.1	2.1	2.0
2000	2.1	2.1	2.1	2.2	2.2	2.3	2.2	2.3	2.3	2.3	2.3	2.3	2.2
2001	2.4	2.5	2.7	2.7	2.7	2.8	2.8	2.8	2.8	2.9	3.0	3.0	2.8
2002	3.0	3.0	3.1	3.1	3.2	3.5	3.5	3.6	3.6	3.7	3.8	3.8	3.4
2003	3.8	3.9	4.0	4.0	4.0	4.1	4.1	4.2	4.1	4.1	4.1	4.2	4.1
Information													
1990	1.3	1.4	1.5	1.5	1.4	1.2	1.2	1.2	1.3	1.4	1.5	1.3	1.3
1991	1.2	1.3	1.4	1.5	1.4	1.3	1.2	1.2	1.3	1.3	1.5	1.5	1.3
1992	1.3	1.5	1.6	1.5	1.6	1.4	1.2	1.3	1.2	1.2	1.2	1.2	1.3
1993	1.3	1.5	1.7	1.8	1.6	1.4	1.3	1.3	1.3	1.3	1.5	1.4	1.4
1994	1.4	1.6	1.7	2.0	2.0	1.8	1.7	1.6	1.6	1.6	2.0	2.0	1.7
1995	1.7	1.8	2.0	2.1	2.3	2.1	1.5	1.5	1.5	1.6	2.0	2.0	1.8
1996	1.7	1.9	2.1	2.4	2.5	2.2	2.1	1.7	1.6	1.7	2.1	2.0	2.0
1997	1.9	1.8	2.1	2.5	2.6	2.3	2.0	1.8	1.8	1.9	2.2	2.2	2.0
1998	2.1	2.2	2.4	3.0	3.1	2.9	2.1	1.9	1.7	2.0	2.3	2.4	2.3
1999	2.2	2.1	2.4	2.7	2.6	2.6	2.2	1.9	2.1	2.3	2.4	2.4	2.3
2000	2.5	2.4	2.8	2.8	2.8	2.7	2.3	2.0	1.9	2.1	2.2	2.4	2.4
2001	2.5	2.7	3.0	3.2	3.0	2.8	2.6	2.3	2.2	2.5	2.5	2.5	2.7
2002	2.5	2.7	2.9	3.0	3.0	3.0	2.8	2.6	2.5	2.5	2.5	2.5	2.7
2003	2.2	2.5	2.5	2.8	2.5	2.4	2.5	2.2	2.2	2.3	2.5	2.5	2.4
Financial activities													
1990	1.4	1.4	1.4	1.4	1.4	1.5	1.5	1.5	1.4	1.4	1.4	1.4	1.4
1991	1.4	1.4	1.4	1.5	1.5	1.5	1.5	1.6	1.5	1.5	1.5	1.5	1.4
1992	1.5	1.5	1.5	1.6	1.6	1.6	1.6	1.7	1.6	1.6	1.6	1.6	1.5
1993	1.6	1.5	1.5	1.5	1.6	1.6	1.6	1.7	1.6	1.6	1.6	1.6	1.5
1994	1.6	1.6	1.6	1.7	1.7	1.7	1.8	1.7	1.7	1.6	1.6	1.7	1.6
1995	1.6	1.6	1.6	1.7	1.7	1.7	1.7	1.8	1.7	1.7	1.7	1.7	1.6
1996	1.6	1.6	1.6	1.6	1.7	1.7	1.8	1.8	1.7	1.7	1.7	1.7	1.6
1997	1.7	1.7	1.7	1.8	1.8	1.9	1.9	1.9	1.8	1.8	1.9	1.9	1.8
1998	1.9	1.9	2.0	2.0	2.1	2.1	2.1	2.1	2.1	2.2	2.1	2.2	2.0
1999	2.3	2.3	2.3	2.4	2.5	2.6	2.6	2.6	2.6	2.4	2.4	2.5	2.4
2000	2.5	2.5	2.5	2.5	2.6	2.6	2.5	2.5	2.6	2.4	2.5	2.5	2.5
2001	2.5	2.4	2.4	2.4	2.4	2.4	2.5	2.4	2.4	2.5	2.5	2.6	2.5
2002	2.4	2.4	2.5	2.5	2.4	2.5	2.6	2.5	2.5	2.5	2.5	2.5	2.5
2003	2.5	2.5	2.4	2.5	2.6	2.6	2.6	2.7	2.6	2.6	2.6	2.7	2.6
Professional and business services													
1990	3.0	3.0	3.0	3.2	3.2	3.4	3.2	3.1	3.1	3.2	3.1	3.0	3.1
1991	3.0	3.0	3.0	3.2	3.2	3.2	3.0	3.0	3.0	3.3	3.2	3.4	3.1
1992	3.1	3.2	3.2	3.3	3.3	3.3	3.2	3.2	3.1	3.4	3.4	3.4	3.2
1993	3.5	3.6	3.8	4.1	4.0	4.3	4.3	4.2	4.2	4.5	4.5	4.6	4.1
1994	4.3	4.4	4.5	4.5	4.5	4.5	4.5	4.4	4.5	4.3	4.4	4.3	4.4
1995	4.2	4.3	4.5	4.5	4.4	4.6	4.3	4.4	4.4	4.3	4.4	4.3	4.3
1996	4.2	4.3	4.5	4.6	4.7	4.6	4.7	4.7	4.8	4.6	4.6	4.8	4.5
1997	4.3	4.5	4.7	4.5	4.6	4.8	4.7	4.8	4.8	4.9	4.9	4.9	4.7
1998	4.8	4.9	5.2	5.1	5.2	5.4	5.2	5.2	5.3	5.1	5.1	5.1	5.1
1999	4.9	5.1	5.2	5.2	5.1	5.3	5.1	5.0	5.0	5.0	5.2	5.1	5.1
2000	5.1	5.0	5.3	5.4	5.4	5.2	5.2	5.3	5.3	5.3	5.3	5.2	5.2
2001	5.5	5.6	5.8	5.7	5.8	5.8	5.7	6.0	5.9	5.9	5.8	5.8	5.8
2002	5.6	5.7	5.8	5.7	5.4	5.6	5.3	5.2	5.4	5.2	5.3	5.2	5.5
2003	4.9	5.1	4.9	4.9	4.8	4.8	4.7	4.6	5.0	4.9	4.7	4.8	4.8

Employment by Industry: Iowa—*Continued*

(Numbers in thousands. Not seasonally adjusted.)

Industry	January	February	March	April	May	June	July	August	September	October	November	December	Annual Average
IOWA CITY—*Continued*													
Educational and health services													
1990	4.0	4.1	4.1	4.1	4.1	4.0	3.8	3.9	4.1	4.3	4.3	4.3	4.0
1991	4.3	4.4	4.4	4.1	4.1	4.1	3.9	3.9	4.1	4.3	4.4	4.3	4.1
1992	4.6	4.6	4.7	4.7	4.6	4.6	4.4	4.4	4.6	4.7	4.8	4.8	4.6
1993	4.7	4.8	4.9	4.9	4.8	4.9	4.7	4.6	4.8	4.9	5.0	5.3	4.8
1994	5.2	5.3	5.3	5.3	5.3	5.3	5.1	5.2	5.3	5.4	5.4	5.5	5.3
1995	5.4	5.5	5.5	5.4	5.5	5.4	5.3	5.3	5.5	5.5	5.6	5.6	5.4
1996	5.4	5.5	5.6	5.5	5.4	5.3	5.1	5.2	5.4	5.5	5.5	5.5	5.4
1997	5.4	5.5	5.6	5.6	5.6	5.5	5.5	5.4	5.6	5.7	5.7	5.7	5.5
1998	5.6	5.7	5.7	5.8	5.7	5.7	5.5	5.5	5.6	5.9	5.9	5.9	5.7
1999	5.7	5.8	5.8	5.9	5.8	5.8	5.7	5.7	5.9	6.0	6.1	6.1	5.8
2000	6.0	6.1	6.2	6.2	6.2	6.2	5.9	5.9	6.2	6.2	6.2	6.2	6.1
2001	5.5	5.6	5.6	5.6	5.6	5.6	5.6	5.7	5.7	5.7	5.7	5.7	5.6
2002	5.6	5.7	5.5	5.9	6.1	6.1	6.2	6.4	6.6	6.8	6.9	7.1	6.2
2003	7.0	7.0	7.2	7.1	7.3	7.2	7.0	6.9	7.2	7.4	7.5	7.5	7.2
Leisure and hospitality													
1990	4.5	4.7	4.7	4.8	4.8	4.8	4.8	4.9	5.1	5.0	4.9	4.8	4.8
1991	4.4	4.6	4.7	4.9	5.0	4.9	4.7	4.8	5.1	5.0	4.9	4.8	4.8
1992	4.3	4.6	4.6	4.8	4.8	4.7	4.6	4.8	5.0	4.8	4.8	4.8	4.7
1993	4.4	4.8	4.8	4.9	4.9	4.8	4.8	4.9	5.1	5.1	5.1	4.9	4.8
1994	4.5	4.8	4.9	5.1	5.2	5.2	5.1	5.1	5.4	5.2	5.2	5.1	5.0
1995	5.0	5.2	5.3	5.3	5.3	5.2	5.2	5.3	5.6	5.7	5.7	5.7	5.3
1996	5.2	5.4	5.4	5.4	5.5	5.5	5.5	5.6	5.8	5.7	5.7	5.6	5.5
1997	5.1	5.4	5.5	5.6	5.8	5.6	5.7	5.9	6.3	6.0	5.9	5.9	5.7
1998	5.6	5.9	6.0	6.1	6.3	6.0	6.1	6.5	6.7	6.7	6.6	6.6	6.2
1999	6.0	6.3	6.3	6.7	6.6	6.4	6.2	6.3	6.5	6.6	6.6	6.5	6.4
2000	6.1	6.4	6.5	6.6	6.5	6.3	6.5	6.6	6.9	6.5	6.6	6.4	6.4
2001	6.0	6.1	6.1	6.5	6.5	6.3	6.2	6.4	6.7	6.5	6.5	6.5	6.4
2002	6.1	6.6	6.5	6.7	6.8	6.5	6.5	6.5	6.8	6.7	6.8	6.7	6.6
2003	6.3	6.4	6.5	6.8	6.9	6.7	6.6	6.7	7.1	7.0	6.8	6.7	6.7
Other services													
1990	1.6	1.6	1.6	1.7	1.6	1.6	1.7	1.7	1.7	1.6	1.6	1.7	1.6
1991	1.6	1.6	1.6	1.7	1.7	1.7	1.7	1.7	1.7	1.7	1.7	1.7	1.6
1992	1.6	1.6	1.7	1.7	1.7	1.7	1.6	1.7	1.7	1.7	1.7	1.7	1.6
1993	1.6	1.6	1.6	1.7	1.7	1.7	1.7	1.7	1.7	1.7	1.8	1.8	1.6
1994	1.7	1.7	1.8	1.7	1.8	1.8	1.7	1.7	1.8	1.8	1.8	1.8	1.7
1995	1.8	1.7	1.8	1.8	1.8	1.9	1.8	1.8	1.8	1.8	1.8	1.7	1.7
1996	1.7	1.7	1.7	1.7	1.7	1.7	1.7	1.7	1.7	1.6	1.6	1.6	1.6
1997	1.6	1.6	1.6	1.6	1.6	1.6	1.6	1.6	1.6	1.6	1.6	1.6	1.6
1998	1.6	1.6	1.7	1.7	1.7	1.7	1.7	1.7	1.7	1.7	1.7	1.7	1.6
1999	1.7	1.7	1.8	1.8	1.8	1.8	1.8	1.8	1.8	1.8	1.8	1.8	1.7
2000	1.7	1.8	1.8	1.8	1.8	1.8	1.8	1.8	1.8	1.8	1.8	1.8	1.7
2001	1.8	1.8	1.8	1.9	1.8	1.8	1.8	1.8	1.8	1.9	1.9	1.9	1.8
2002	1.9	1.9	1.9	1.9	1.9	1.8	1.9	1.9	1.8	1.9	1.8	1.8	1.9
2003	1.8	1.8	1.8	1.8	1.8	1.9	1.9	1.9	1.8	1.8	1.8	1.8	1.8
Government													
1990	26.4	26.6	26.6	26.8	26.8	25.3	23.4	25.1	25.3	26.6	27.2	27.3	26.1
1991	27.3	26.0	27.0	27.0	27.0	25.6	23.6	24.4	25.2	26.3	26.9	27.1	26.1
1992	26.8	25.1	27.0	27.1	27.3	25.9	25.4	25.2	25.4	26.6	27.4	27.7	26.4
1993	27.4	25.5	27.9	27.7	28.0	26.8	24.8	25.8	26.0	27.5	28.4	28.7	27.0
1994	27.9	26.1	28.0	28.0	28.1	27.1	24.4	26.1	26.2	27.6	28.2	28.2	27.1
1995	27.9	26.1	28.3	28.3	28.3	27.1	24.4	26.0	26.1	27.8	28.7	28.5	27.2
1996	28.4	26.2	28.3	28.4	28.4	26.9	24.5	25.2	25.8	28.3	28.7	28.4	27.2
1997	28.0	27.1	28.1	28.4	28.3	27.0	24.0	24.9	26.4	28.7	28.8	28.7	27.3
1998	28.4	27.6	28.6	28.5	28.5	26.9	24.2	24.9	26.5	27.8	28.8	28.7	27.4
1999	28.4	27.7	28.6	29.2	28.9	27.2	23.6	26.8	27.9	28.9	29.3	28.9	27.9
2000	27.8	29.1	29.1	29.1	29.1	27.0	25.6	26.8	28.7	29.3	29.4	29.1	28.3
2001	28.5	28.8	28.8	28.8	28.8	26.6	25.5	26.4	28.6	29.1	29.2	29.0	28.2
2002	28.7	28.7	29.2	29.0	29.0	26.5	25.2	26.1	28.5	29.2	30.0	29.9	28.3
2003	29.5	28.0	29.9	30.3	30.1	29.2	26.9	27.9	30.3	30.8	31.4	31.1	29.6
Federal government													
1990	1.6	1.6	1.6	1.6	1.7	1.7	1.7	1.7	1.6	1.6	1.6	1.6	1.6
1991	1.6	1.6	1.6	1.6	1.6	1.7	1.5	1.5	1.5	1.5	1.5	1.5	1.5
1992	1.5	1.6	1.6	1.6	1.6	1.6	1.6	1.6	1.6	1.6	1.6	1.6	1.5
1993	1.6	1.6	1.7	1.7	1.7	1.7	1.7	1.7	1.7	1.7	1.6	1.7	1.6
1994	1.7	1.7	1.7	1.7	1.7	1.7	1.7	1.7	1.7	1.7	1.6	1.7	1.6
1995	1.7	1.7	1.7	1.7	1.7	1.7	1.6	1.7	1.6	1.6	1.6	1.6	1.6
1996	1.7	1.7	1.7	1.7	1.6	1.6	1.6	1.6	1.6	1.6	1.6	1.6	1.6
1997	1.5	1.5	1.5	1.5	1.5	1.6	1.6	1.6	1.6	1.6	1.6	1.6	1.5
1998	1.6	1.6	1.6	1.6	1.6	1.6	1.6	1.6	1.6	1.6	1.6	1.6	1.6
1999	1.6	1.6	1.6	1.6	1.6	1.6	1.6	1.6	1.6	1.6	1.6	1.6	1.6
2000	1.6	1.6	1.6	1.6	1.8	1.7	1.7	1.7	1.6	1.6	1.6	1.6	1.6
2001	1.7	1.7	1.7	1.6	1.7	1.7	1.6	1.6	1.6	1.5	1.5	1.5	1.6
2002	1.6	1.6	1.7	1.6	1.7	1.7	1.6	1.6	1.6	1.6	1.6	1.6	1.6
2003	1.6	1.6	1.6	1.6	1.6	1.6	1.6	1.6	1.6	1.6	1.6	1.6	1.6

Employment by Industry: Iowa—*Continued*

(Numbers in thousands. Not seasonally adjusted.)

Industry	January	February	March	April	May	June	July	August	September	October	November	December	Annual Average
IOWA CITY—*Continued*													
State government													
1990	22.0	22.2	22.2	22.3	22.1	20.5	18.9	20.5	20.8	22.1	22.6	22.8	21.5
1991	22.8	21.5	22.4	22.5	22.4	20.6	19.1	19.8	20.6	21.6	22.1	22.4	21.4
1992	22.3	20.4	22.3	22.4	22.4	20.7	20.7	20.6	20.9	22.1	22.6	23.1	21.7
1993	22.7	20.8	23.0	22.8	23.0	21.7	19.9	20.9	21.3	22.5	23.3	23.7	22.1
1994	23.0	21.1	23.0	23.0	23.0	21.6	19.4	21.0	21.3	22.5	23.2	23.1	22.1
1995	22.9	21.0	23.1	23.2	23.1	21.8	19.6	21.1	21.4	22.6	23.5	23.3	22.2
1996	23.1	20.9	23.0	23.1	23.1	21.2	19.5	20.4	20.8	23.0	23.0	23.1	22.0
1997	22.9	22.0	22.8	23.1	23.0	21.2	19.5	20.4	21.0	23.1	23.0	23.1	22.0
1998	22.9	22.0	22.9	23.2	23.1	21.2	19.7	20.5	21.4	22.5	23.2	23.4	22.1
1999	23.2	22.4	23.2	23.6	23.4	21.6	18.4	21.8	22.7	23.4	23.7	23.5	22.5
2000	22.5	23.7	23.6	23.5	23.4	21.2	20.7	22.1	23.4	23.8	23.8	23.7	22.9
2001	23.1	23.2	23.2	23.3	23.1	20.7	20.6	21.5	23.1	23.5	23.6	23.5	22.7
2002	23.2	23.1	23.4	23.3	23.1	20.6	20.5	21.3	23.0	23.5	24.2	24.2	22.8
2003	23.9	22.2	24.2	24.5	24.3	23.2	22.1	23.1	24.7	25.0	25.1	25.2	24.0
Local government													
1990	2.8	2.8	2.8	2.9	3.0	3.1	2.8	2.9	2.9	2.9	3.0	2.9	2.9
1991	2.9	2.9	3.0	2.9	3.0	3.3	3.0	3.1	3.1	3.2	3.3	3.2	3.0
1992	3.0	3.1	3.1	3.1	3.3	3.6	3.1	3.0	2.9	2.9	3.2	3.0	3.1
1993	3.1	3.1	3.2	3.2	3.3	3.4	3.2	3.2	3.0	3.3	3.5	3.3	3.2
1994	3.2	3.3	3.3	3.3	3.4	3.8	3.3	3.4	3.2	3.4	3.4	3.4	3.3
1995	3.3	3.4	3.5	3.4	3.5	3.6	3.2	3.2	3.1	3.6	3.6	3.6	3.4
1996	3.6	3.6	3.6	3.6	3.7	4.1	3.4	3.2	3.4	3.7	4.1	3.7	3.6
1997	3.6	3.6	3.8	3.8	3.8	4.2	2.9	2.9	3.8	4.0	4.2	4.0	3.7
1998	3.9	4.0	4.1	3.7	3.8	4.1	2.9	2.8	3.5	3.7	4.0	3.7	3.6
1999	3.6	3.7	3.8	4.0	3.9	4.0	3.6	3.4	3.6	3.9	4.0	3.8	3.7
2000	3.7	3.8	3.9	4.0	3.9	4.1	3.2	3.0	3.7	3.9	4.0	3.8	3.7
2001	3.7	3.9	3.9	3.9	4.0	4.2	3.3	3.3	3.9	4.1	4.1	4.0	3.9
2002	3.9	4.0	4.1	4.1	4.2	4.2	3.1	3.2	3.9	4.1	4.2	4.1	3.9
2003	4.0	4.2	4.1	4.2	4.2	4.4	3.2	3.2	4.0	4.2	4.7	4.3	4.1
SIOUX CITY													
Total nonfarm													
1990	54.9	54.9	55.2	55.2	56.3	56.2	55.6	56.2	56.3	57.1	56.5	56.1	55.8
1991	55.9	56.1	56.2	57.2	57.7	57.8	56.5	56.4	57.2	57.2	57.2	56.8	56.8
1992	55.9	56.3	56.7	57.7	58.5	59.4	58.3	57.9	58.5	58.9	58.9	58.9	57.9
1993	57.6	57.9	58.3	59.5	60.2	60.4	59.9	60.1	60.6	61.1	61.3	61.4	59.8
1994	59.8	59.8	60.4	61.7	62.1	62.3	61.1	61.6	61.7	62.5	62.9	62.5	61.5
1995	61.1	61.5	62.4	63.1	63.8	64.0	64.2	64.5	64.0	64.5	64.8	64.8	63.5
1996	63.6	63.0	63.4	64.2	65.0	65.2	64.9	64.4	64.6	64.6	65.2	65.4	64.4
1997	63.6	63.1	63.6	64.4	65.8	65.9	65.1	64.7	65.6	66.0	66.8	67.1	65.1
1998	64.5	64.6	64.8	65.6	66.7	67.3	66.3	66.3	66.7	66.5	66.8	66.6	66.0
1999	65.0	65.2	65.8	66.9	67.3	67.5	66.0	66.3	66.9	67.1	66.7	67.0	66.4
2000	65.0	64.7	65.1	65.9	66.4	66.5	65.9	66.0	66.3	65.8	66.2	66.6	65.8
2001	63.5	63.3	63.9	66.2	67.0	67.3	65.4	65.3	65.7	65.3	65.4	65.1	65.3
2002	63.5	63.0	63.8	64.4	65.1	64.9	63.9	64.0	64.4	64.8	65.1	65.1	64.3
2003	61.8	61.3	61.4	62.4	62.6	62.5	61.7	61.1	62.0	62.5	62.6	61.9	62.0
Total private													
1990	48.4	48.3	48.5	48.3	49.2	49.3	49.3	49.9	49.9	50.5	49.8	49.5	49.2
1991	49.3	49.4	49.5	50.5	50.9	50.9	50.4	50.5	50.8	50.5	50.4	50.1	50.2
1992	49.3	49.6	49.9	50.9	51.6	52.2	52.0	51.7	51.9	52.1	52.0	52.1	51.2
1993	50.9	51.2	51.5	52.7	53.4	53.4	53.6	54.0	54.0	54.3	54.4	54.5	53.1
1994	53.0	53.0	53.6	54.8	55.1	55.3	54.9	55.4	54.9	55.6	55.8	55.5	54.7
1995	53.7	54.0	54.9	55.7	56.3	56.4	57.0	57.4	56.7	57.1	57.4	57.4	56.1
1996	56.3	55.6	56.0	56.8	57.5	57.6	57.9	57.5	57.2	57.1	57.6	57.8	57.0
1997	56.2	55.6	56.1	56.9	58.1	58.2	58.2	57.9	58.1	58.4	59.1	59.4	57.6
1998	56.8	56.9	57.0	57.8	58.9	59.3	59.1	59.2	59.0	58.8	59.0	58.8	58.3
1999	57.3	57.4	58.0	59.1	59.4	59.5	58.9	59.1	59.2	59.3	58.8	59.1	58.7
2000	57.1	56.7	57.0	57.8	57.9	58.6	58.5	58.6	58.4	57.9	58.3	58.6	57.9
2001	55.7	55.4	55.9	58.2	58.8	59.0	58.1	58.0	57.8	57.4	57.4	57.2	57.4
2002	55.6	55.1	55.8	56.3	57.0	57.2	56.7	56.8	56.5	56.8	57.0	57.0	56.5
2003	53.8	53.3	53.4	54.4	54.6	54.7	54.4	54.0	54.3	54.6	54.7	53.9	54.2
Goods-producing													
1990	12.7	12.8	12.5	12.5	13.2	13.4	13.7	13.8	13.5	13.5	13.2	12.7	13.1
1991	12.9	13.1	12.9	13.2	13.9	14.0	13.9	13.8	13.6	13.4	13.3	12.8	13.4
1992	12.7	12.9	12.9	13.4	14.0	14.3	14.6	14.4	14.2	14.0	13.9	13.6	13.7
1993	13.0	13.1	13.2	13.8	14.4	14.7	14.8	14.9	14.7	14.6	14.6	14.3	14.1
1994	13.7	13.9	14.0	14.8	15.1	15.4	15.5	15.5	15.1	15.2	15.2	14.7	14.8
1995	14.0	14.2	14.3	15.1	15.7	15.9	16.3	16.7	16.1	16.1	15.9	15.6	15.4
1996	15.3	15.1	15.0	15.6	16.3	16.5	17.1	16.9	16.6	16.5	16.6	16.4	16.1
1997	15.4	15.1	15.2	15.6	16.3	16.6	17.0	16.9	16.7	17.0	17.1	16.7	16.3
1998	15.8	16.0	15.9	16.3	17.0	17.4	17.7	17.7	17.3	16.7	16.8	16.3	16.7
1999	16.0	16.2	16.3	16.8	17.1	17.4	17.1	17.2	16.8	16.7	16.3	16.2	16.6
2000	15.4	15.4	15.2	15.6	16.1	16.7	16.9	16.8	16.4	16.5	16.5	16.2	16.1
2001	15.6	15.6	15.7	16.3	16.5	16.7	16.7	16.7	16.6	16.6	16.4	16.1	16.3
2002	15.4	15.4	15.5	15.6	16.0	16.1	16.1	16.2	16.1	16.2	16.1	16.0	15.9
2003	13.8	13.6	13.5	14.2	14.1	14.3	14.1	13.9	13.9	13.9	14.0	13.6	13.9

Employment by Industry: Iowa—*Continued*

(Numbers in thousands. Not seasonally adjusted.)

Industry	January	February	March	April	May	June	July	August	September	October	November	December	Annual Average
SIOUX CITY—*Continued*													
Construction and mining													
1990	1.8	1.8	1.9	2.1	2.5	2.6	2.7	2.8	2.7	2.7	2.5	2.2	2.3
1991	1.9	1.9	1.8	2.3	2.6	2.7	2.8	2.7	2.5	2.4	2.3	2.0	2.3
1992	1.8	1.9	1.9	2.3	2.6	2.9	3.2	2.9	2.8	2.6	2.4	2.1	2.4
1993	1.8	1.8	1.9	2.4	2.6	2.8	2.8	2.8	2.7	2.6	2.5	2.3	2.4
1994	1.9	1.9	2.1	2.6	2.8	3.0	3.2	3.1	3.0	3.0	2.9	2.5	2.6
1995	2.2	2.2	2.3	2.7	3.0	3.2	3.5	3.8	3.6	3.5	3.3	3.0	3.0
1996	2.6	2.6	2.6	3.2	3.4	3.6	4.1	3.8	3.9	3.8	3.8	3.4	3.4
1997	2.7	2.8	2.9	3.2	3.6	4.0	4.3	4.2	4.1	4.2	4.1	3.8	3.6
1998	3.1	3.2	3.1	3.5	3.9	4.2	4.4	4.4	4.3	3.1	3.0	2.8	3.5
1999	2.4	2.4	2.6	3.0	3.3	3.5	3.5	3.5	3.3	3.2	3.1	2.9	3.0
2000	2.3	2.3	2.5	2.8	3.2	3.2	3.2	3.2	3.1	3.0	2.9	2.7	2.8
2001	2.5	2.4	2.4	2.7	2.9	3.0	3.0	3.1	3.0	2.9	2.9	2.7	2.8
2002	2.3	2.3	2.4	2.5	2.9	3.0	3.0	3.0	3.0	3.2	3.1	3.1	2.8
2003	2.6	2.5	2.5	3.0	3.1	3.2	3.2	3.2	3.2	3.2	3.1	2.9	3.0
Manufacturing													
1990	10.9	11.0	10.6	10.4	10.7	10.8	11.0	11.0	10.8	10.8	10.7	10.5	10.7
1991	11.0	11.2	11.1	10.9	11.3	11.3	11.1	11.1	11.1	11.0	11.0	10.8	11.0
1992	10.9	11.0	11.0	11.1	11.4	11.4	11.4	11.5	11.4	11.4	11.5	11.5	11.2
1993	11.2	11.3	11.3	11.4	11.8	11.9	12.0	12.1	12.0	12.0	12.1	12.0	11.7
1994	11.8	12.0	11.9	12.2	12.3	12.4	12.3	12.4	12.1	12.2	12.3	12.2	12.1
1995	11.8	12.0	12.0	12.4	12.7	12.7	12.8	12.9	12.5	12.6	12.6	12.6	12.4
1996	12.7	12.5	12.4	12.4	12.9	12.9	13.0	13.1	12.7	12.7	12.8	13.0	12.7
1997	12.7	12.3	12.3	12.4	12.7	12.6	12.7	12.7	12.6	12.8	13.0	12.9	12.6
1998	12.7	12.8	12.8	12.8	13.1	13.2	13.3	13.3	13.0	13.6	13.8	13.5	13.1
1999	13.6	13.8	13.7	13.8	13.8	13.9	13.6	13.7	13.5	13.5	13.2	13.3	13.6
2000	13.1	13.1	12.7	12.8	12.9	13.5	13.7	13.6	13.3	13.5	13.6	13.5	13.2
2001	13.1	13.2	13.3	13.6	13.6	13.7	13.7	13.6	13.6	13.7	13.5	13.4	13.5
2002	13.1	13.1	13.1	13.1	13.1	13.1	13.1	13.2	13.1	13.0	13.0	12.9	13.1
2003	11.2	11.1	11.0	11.2	11.0	11.1	10.9	10.7	10.7	10.7	10.9	10.7	10.9
Service-providing													
1990	42.2	42.1	42.7	42.7	43.1	42.8	41.9	42.4	42.8	43.6	43.3	43.4	42.7
1991	43.0	43.0	43.3	44.0	43.8	43.8	42.6	42.6	43.6	43.8	43.9	44.0	43.4
1992	43.2	43.4	43.8	44.3	44.5	45.1	43.7	43.5	44.3	44.9	45.0	45.3	44.2
1993	44.6	44.8	45.1	45.7	45.8	45.7	45.1	45.2	45.9	46.5	46.7	47.1	45.6
1994	46.1	45.9	46.4	46.9	47.0	46.9	45.6	46.1	46.6	47.3	47.7	47.8	46.6
1995	47.1	47.3	48.1	48.0	48.1	48.1	47.9	47.8	47.9	48.4	48.9	49.2	48.0
1996	48.3	47.9	48.4	48.6	48.7	48.7	47.8	47.5	48.0	48.1	48.6	49.0	48.3
1997	48.2	48.0	48.4	48.8	49.5	49.3	48.1	47.8	48.9	49.0	49.7	50.4	48.8
1998	48.7	48.6	48.9	49.3	49.7	49.9	48.6	48.6	49.4	49.8	50.0	50.3	49.3
1999	49.0	49.0	49.5	50.1	50.2	50.1	48.9	49.1	50.1	50.4	50.4	50.8	49.8
2000	49.6	49.3	49.9	50.3	50.3	49.8	49.0	49.2	49.9	49.3	49.7	50.4	49.7
2001	47.9	47.7	48.2	49.9	50.5	50.6	48.7	48.6	49.1	48.7	49.0	49.0	49.0
2002	48.1	47.6	48.3	48.8	49.1	48.8	47.8	47.8	48.3	48.6	49.0	49.1	48.4
2003	48.0	47.7	47.9	48.2	48.5	48.2	47.6	47.2	48.1	48.6	48.6	48.3	48.1
Trade, transportation, and utilities													
1990	12.3	12.1	12.2	12.2	12.6	12.5	12.8	13.0	12.6	12.6	12.7	13.0	12.5
1991	12.5	12.3	12.3	12.7	12.9	13.0	13.0	13.1	12.6	12.6	12.9	13.1	12.7
1992	12.7	12.5	12.5	12.6	12.9	13.1	13.0	13.1	12.8	13.2	13.4	13.6	12.9
1993	13.1	12.9	12.9	13.1	13.5	13.6	13.5	13.6	13.2	13.7	13.8	14.1	13.4
1994	13.7	13.4	13.5	13.7	14.0	14.1	14.1	14.2	13.8	13.8	14.1	14.3	13.8
1995	13.6	13.4	13.7	13.7	14.1	14.1	14.3	14.3	13.8	14.0	14.4	14.5	13.9
1996	14.1	13.7	13.8	14.1	14.3	14.4	14.5	14.6	14.1	14.3	14.6	14.8	14.2
1997	14.2	13.9	13.9	14.1	14.5	14.5	14.7	14.5	14.3	14.2	14.5	14.9	14.3
1998	14.1	13.7	13.7	14.0	14.5	14.6	14.7	14.8	14.6	14.6	14.8	15.2	14.4
1999	14.2	14.0	14.1	14.3	14.5	14.5	14.7	14.7	14.5	14.8	15.0	15.2	14.5
2000	14.5	14.2	14.3	14.5	14.5	14.6	14.6	14.6	14.1	14.1	14.4	14.5	14.4
2001	14.4	14.2	14.3	14.6	14.8	14.9	14.7	14.5	14.2	14.5	14.8	14.8	14.6
2002	14.2	13.9	14.0	14.2	14.2	14.3	14.2	14.3	14.1	14.1	14.3	14.4	14.2
2003	13.7	13.4	13.5	13.7	13.8	13.7	14.0	14.0	13.8	13.9	13.9	13.8	13.8
Wholesale trade													
1990	2.5	2.5	2.5	2.5	2.6	2.6	2.7	2.7	2.6	2.6	2.6	2.6	2.5
1991	2.6	2.6	2.6	2.8	2.8	2.8	2.8	2.8	2.7	2.7	2.7	2.7	2.7
1992	2.7	2.7	2.7	2.7	2.8	2.8	2.8	2.8	2.7	2.7	2.7	2.7	2.7
1993	2.6	2.6	2.6	2.7	2.8	2.8	2.8	2.8	2.7	2.8	2.7	2.8	2.7
1994	2.8	2.8	2.8	2.8	2.9	2.9	2.9	3.0	2.9	2.9	2.8	2.8	2.8
1995	2.8	2.8	2.9	2.8	2.9	2.9	2.9	2.9	2.8	2.8	2.9	2.9	2.8
1996	2.9	2.8	2.9	2.9	3.0	3.0	3.0	3.0	2.9	2.9	2.9	2.9	2.9
1997	2.8	2.8	2.8	2.8	2.9	2.9	3.0	2.9	2.9	2.8	2.8	2.8	2.8
1998	2.7	2.7	2.8	2.8	2.9	2.9	2.9	2.9	2.8	2.8	2.8	2.9	2.8
1999	2.8	2.8	2.8	2.9	2.9	2.9	2.9	2.9	2.8	2.8	2.8	2.8	2.8
2000	2.8	2.8	2.8	2.9	2.9	2.9	3.0	2.9	2.8	2.8	2.9	2.8	2.8
2001	2.9	2.9	2.9	2.9	2.9	3.0	3.0	3.0	2.9	2.9	2.9	2.9	2.9
2002	2.9	2.8	2.8	2.8	2.8	2.9	2.9	2.9	2.9	2.9	2.9	2.9	2.9
2003	2.9	2.9	2.9	2.9	2.9	2.9	2.9	2.9	2.9	2.9	2.9	2.9	2.9

Employment by Industry: Iowa—*Continued*

(Numbers in thousands. Not seasonally adjusted.)

Industry	January	February	March	April	May	June	July	August	September	October	November	December	Annual Average
SIOUX CITY—*Continued*													
Retail trade													
1990	6.9	6.9	6.9	7.1	7.3	7.2	7.2	7.3	7.1	7.1	7.3	7.5	7.1
1991	7.2	7.0	7.0	7.1	7.2	7.3	7.2	7.3	6.9	7.0	7.3	7.5	7.1
1992	7.1	7.0	7.0	7.1	7.2	7.3	7.2	7.3	7.2	7.5	7.7	7.8	7.2
1993	7.5	7.3	7.3	7.5	7.7	7.8	7.7	7.8	7.6	7.8	8.0	8.2	7.6
1994	7.8	7.5	7.6	7.7	7.9	7.9	7.9	7.9	7.6	7.7	8.0	8.2	7.8
1995	7.7	7.5	7.6	7.7	7.9	7.9	8.0	8.1	7.8	7.9	8.2	8.3	7.8
1996	8.0	7.8	7.8	8.0	8.1	8.1	8.2	8.4	8.0	8.2	8.4	8.6	8.1
1997	8.2	8.0	8.0	8.1	8.4	8.4	8.5	8.5	8.3	8.3	8.6	8.9	8.3
1998	8.4	8.1	7.9	8.1	8.5	8.6	8.6	8.7	8.7	8.7	8.9	9.1	8.5
1999	8.2	8.0	8.1	8.1	8.3	8.3	8.6	8.6	8.5	8.7	8.9	9.1	8.4
2000	8.5	8.2	8.2	8.4	8.4	8.5	8.5	8.5	8.2	8.2	8.4	8.6	8.3
2001	8.4	8.2	8.2	8.3	8.5	8.6	8.4	8.4	8.2	8.3	8.6	8.6	8.4
2002	8.1	7.9	8.0	8.1	8.2	8.2	8.2	8.4	8.2	8.2	8.4	8.5	8.2
2003	8.0	7.7	7.8	7.9	8.0	8.0	8.3	8.2	8.0	8.1	8.1	8.1	8.0
Transportation and utilities													
1990	2.9	2.7	2.8	2.6	2.7	2.7	2.9	3.0	2.9	2.9	2.8	2.9	2.8
1991	2.7	2.7	2.7	2.8	2.9	2.9	3.0	3.0	3.0	2.9	2.9	2.9	2.8
1992	2.9	2.8	2.8	2.8	2.9	3.0	3.0	3.0	2.9	3.0	3.0	3.1	2.9
1993	3.0	3.0	3.0	2.9	3.0	3.0	3.0	3.0	2.9	3.1	3.1	3.1	3.0
1994	3.1	3.1	3.1	3.2	3.2	3.3	3.3	3.3	3.3	3.2	3.3	3.3	3.2
1995	3.1	3.1	3.2	3.2	3.3	3.3	3.4	3.3	3.2	3.3	3.3	3.3	3.2
1996	3.2	3.1	3.1	3.2	3.2	3.3	3.3	3.2	3.2	3.2	3.3	3.3	3.2
1997	3.2	3.1	3.1	3.2	3.2	3.2	3.2	3.1	3.1	3.1	3.1	3.2	3.1
1998	3.0	2.9	3.0	3.1	3.1	3.1	3.2	3.2	3.1	3.1	3.1	3.2	3.0
1999	3.2	3.2	3.2	3.3	3.3	3.3	3.2	3.2	3.2	3.3	3.3	3.3	3.2
2000	3.2	3.2	3.3	3.2	3.2	3.2	3.1	3.2	3.1	3.1	3.1	3.1	3.1
2001	3.1	3.1	3.2	3.4	3.4	3.3	3.3	3.1	3.1	3.3	3.3	3.3	3.2
2002	3.2	3.2	3.2	3.3	3.2	3.2	3.1	3.0	3.0	3.0	3.0	3.0	3.1
2003	2.8	2.8	2.8	2.9	2.9	2.8	2.8	2.9	2.9	2.9	2.9	2.8	2.9
Information													
1990	0.9	0.9	0.9	0.9	0.9	0.9	0.9	0.9	0.9	0.9	0.8	0.8	0.8
1991	0.8	0.8	0.8	0.8	0.8	0.8	0.9	0.9	0.9	0.9	0.9	0.8	0.8
1992	0.8	0.8	0.8	0.8	0.8	0.8	0.9	0.8	0.8	0.8	0.8	0.8	0.8
1993	0.8	0.8	0.8	0.8	0.8	0.8	0.8	0.8	0.8	0.8	0.8	0.8	0.8
1994	0.8	0.8	0.8	0.8	0.8	0.8	0.8	0.8	0.8	0.8	0.8	0.8	0.8
1995	0.8	0.8	0.8	0.8	0.8	0.8	0.8	0.8	0.8	0.8	0.8	0.8	0.8
1996	0.8	0.8	0.8	0.8	0.8	0.8	0.9	0.9	0.8	0.8	0.8	0.9	0.8
1997	0.9	0.9	0.9	0.9	1.0	1.0	1.0	1.0	0.9	0.9	1.0	1.0	0.9
1998	0.9	0.9	0.9	0.9	0.9	1.0	1.0	0.9	0.9	0.9	1.0	1.0	0.9
1999	0.9	0.9	1.0	0.9	1.0	1.0	1.0	1.0	1.0	1.0	1.0	1.0	0.9
2000	1.0	0.9	1.0	1.0	1.0	1.0	1.0	1.0	0.9	0.9	0.9	0.9	0.9
2001	0.9	0.9	0.9	0.9	0.9	0.9	0.9	0.9	0.9	0.9	0.9	0.9	0.9
2002	0.9	0.9	0.9	0.9	0.9	0.9	0.8	0.8	0.8	0.8	0.8	0.8	0.9
2003	0.8	0.8	0.8	0.8	0.8	0.8	0.8	0.8	0.8	0.8	0.8	0.8	0.8
Financial activities													
1990	2.5	2.5	2.5	2.5	2.5	2.5	2.5	2.5	2.5	2.5	2.4	2.5	2.4
1991	2.4	2.4	2.4	2.5	2.5	2.5	2.6	2.6	2.5	2.5	2.5	2.5	2.4
1992	2.4	2.4	2.4	2.5	2.6	2.7	2.7	2.6	2.6	2.5	2.6	2.7	2.5
1993	2.5	2.6	2.5	2.6	2.7	2.7	2.7	2.8	2.7	2.6	2.6	2.6	2.6
1994	2.6	2.6	2.6	2.6	2.7	2.7	2.6	2.7	2.6	2.6	2.6	2.6	2.6
1995	2.5	2.5	2.5	2.6	2.6	2.7	2.7	2.7	2.5	2.6	2.6	2.6	2.5
1996	2.6	2.5	2.5	2.5	2.6	2.7	2.6	2.6	2.6	2.6	2.6	2.6	2.5
1997	2.6	2.5	2.6	2.5	2.6	2.6	2.6	2.6	2.5	2.5	2.6	2.6	2.5
1998	2.5	2.6	2.5	2.5	2.6	2.6	2.6	2.7	2.6	2.7	2.7	2.7	2.6
1999	2.7	2.7	2.7	2.7	2.8	2.8	2.8	2.8	2.8	2.8	2.8	2.8	2.7
2000	2.8	2.8	2.7	2.7	2.7	2.7	2.7	2.7	2.6	2.6	2.6	2.7	2.6
2001	2.9	2.8	2.9	2.9	2.9	3.0	2.9	3.0	3.0	2.9	2.9	2.9	2.9
2002	2.8	2.8	2.8	2.8	2.8	2.9	2.9	2.9	2.9	2.9	2.9	2.9	2.9
2003	2.9	2.9	2.9	2.9	2.9	2.9	2.9	3.0	3.0	3.0	3.0	3.0	2.9
Professional and business services													
1990	3.6	3.6	3.7	3.5	3.6	3.8	3.8	3.9	3.8	4.2	4.1	4.0	3.8
1991	4.1	4.1	4.2	4.2	4.0	4.2	4.1	4.1	4.1	4.2	4.0	3.9	4.1
1992	3.9	4.0	4.0	4.3	4.5	4.5	4.4	4.3	4.2	4.2	4.0	4.1	4.2
1993	4.2	4.3	4.4	4.5	4.5	4.5	4.7	4.7	4.5	4.5	4.5	4.5	4.4
1994	4.4	4.4	4.5	4.4	4.5	4.5	4.4	4.5	4.2	4.4	4.4	4.4	4.4
1995	4.3	4.4	4.5	4.5	4.5	4.4	4.5	4.4	4.3	4.4	4.4	4.5	4.4
1996	4.4	4.3	4.4	4.4	4.4	4.4	4.5	4.4	4.2	4.2	4.3	4.3	4.3
1997	4.5	4.5	4.6	4.6	4.7	4.7	4.8	4.8	4.8	4.8	4.8	4.9	4.7
1998	4.7	4.7	4.8	4.7	4.8	4.8	4.7	4.7	4.5	4.7	4.6	4.6	4.6
1999	4.6	4.6	4.6	4.9	4.9	5.0	5.0	5.0	4.9	4.8	4.6	4.6	4.7
2000	4.4	4.4	4.5	4.8	4.8	5.0	4.9	5.0	5.0	4.7	4.6	4.7	4.7
2001	4.8	4.8	4.8	4.8	4.8	4.7	4.5	4.5	4.5	4.4	4.4	4.4	4.6
2002	4.3	4.2	4.4	4.4	4.6	4.7	4.5	4.5	4.3	4.5	4.7	4.7	4.5
2003	4.8	4.8	4.8	4.8	4.7	4.9	4.7	4.5	4.6	4.5	4.6	4.6	4.7

Employment by Industry: Iowa—*Continued*

(Numbers in thousands. Not seasonally adjusted.)

Industry	January	February	March	April	May	June	July	August	September	October	November	December	Annual Average
SIOUX CITY—*Continued*													
Educational and health services													
1990	9.7	9.7	9.8	9.8	9.1	8.7	8.3	8.4	9.5	9.6	9.6	9.5	9.3
1991	9.8	9.8	9.9	9.9	9.3	8.9	8.5	8.5	9.7	9.9	9.9	10.0	9.5
1992	10.1	10.2	10.3	10.4	9.6	9.3	9.0	9.0	10.1	10.2	10.2	10.2	9.8
1993	10.4	10.4	10.5	10.6	9.9	9.4	9.1	9.1	10.3	10.4	10.4	10.4	10.0
1994	10.5	10.6	10.7	10.7	9.9	9.6	9.3	9.4	10.4	10.7	10.6	10.6	10.2
1995	10.7	10.8	10.9	10.9	10.2	10.0	9.9	9.9	10.6	10.9	11.0	11.1	10.5
1996	11.1	11.2	11.2	11.2	10.5	10.2	9.9	9.8	10.8	10.9	11.0	11.1	10.7
1997	11.2	11.3	11.3	11.3	10.6	10.3	9.7	9.6	10.6	11.0	11.1	11.2	10.7
1998	11.1	11.2	11.2	11.3	10.6	10.4	10.0	9.9	11.0	11.3	11.3	11.3	10.8
1999	11.4	11.4	11.5	11.6	10.8	10.6	10.0	10.0	11.0	11.2	11.2	11.3	11.0
2000	11.3	11.3	11.4	11.4	10.7	10.5	10.1	10.2	11.3	11.2	11.2	11.3	10.9
2001	9.6	9.5	9.6	10.2	10.2	10.0	9.8	9.7	10.1	10.1	10.2	10.2	9.9
2002	10.0	10.0	10.0	10.0	9.9	9.7	9.7	9.6	10.0	10.1	10.1	10.1	9.9
2003	9.9	10.0	9.9	9.9	9.9	9.6	9.5	9.4	9.9	10.2	10.1	9.8	9.8
Leisure and hospitality													
1990	4.4	4.3	4.5	4.6	4.9	5.1	4.9	5.0	4.8	4.8	4.6	4.6	4.7
1991	4.4	4.5	4.6	4.8	5.1	5.1	5.0	5.1	5.0	4.6	4.6	4.6	4.7
1992	4.4	4.5	4.6	4.6	4.8	5.0	5.0	5.0	4.8	4.7	4.6	4.6	4.7
1993	4.5	4.7	4.8	4.9	5.1	5.2	5.5	5.6	5.3	5.2	5.1	5.2	5.0
1994	4.8	4.8	5.0	5.2	5.4	5.6	5.7	5.8	5.4	5.5	5.5	5.5	5.3
1995	5.2	5.3	5.6	5.5	5.8	5.9	5.9	6.0	6.0	5.7	5.6	5.7	5.6
1996	5.5	5.5	5.7	5.7	6.0	6.1	5.9	5.8	5.6	5.5	5.4	5.3	5.6
1997	5.1	5.1	5.3	5.6	6.0	6.1	6.0	6.1	5.9	5.7	5.6	5.7	5.6
1998	5.3	5.4	5.6	5.7	6.0	6.0	6.0	6.1	5.7	5.5	5.4	5.3	5.6
1999	5.2	5.3	5.4	5.5	5.9	5.9	6.0	6.0	5.8	5.7	5.6	5.6	5.6
2000	5.4	5.4	5.5	5.5	5.7	5.8	6.0	6.0	5.8	5.6	5.8	6.0	5.7
2001	5.8	5.9	5.9	6.1	6.4	6.5	6.3	6.3	6.1	6.0	5.8	5.9	6.1
2002	5.6	5.5	5.8	5.9	6.2	6.2	6.1	6.1	5.9	5.9	5.8	5.8	5.9
2003	5.6	5.5	5.7	5.8	6.1	6.2	6.1	6.1	5.9	6.0	5.9	5.9	5.9
Other services													
1990	2.3	2.4	2.4	2.3	2.4	2.4	2.4	2.4	2.3	2.4	2.4	2.4	2.3
1991	2.4	2.4	2.4	2.4	2.4	2.4	2.4	2.4	2.4	2.4	2.3	2.4	2.3
1992	2.3	2.3	2.4	2.3	2.4	2.5	2.4	2.5	2.4	2.5	2.5	2.5	2.4
1993	2.4	2.4	2.4	2.4	2.5	2.5	2.5	2.5	2.5	2.5	2.6	2.6	2.4
1994	2.5	2.5	2.5	2.6	2.7	2.6	2.5	2.5	2.6	2.6	2.6	2.6	2.5
1995	2.6	2.6	2.6	2.6	2.6	2.6	2.6	2.6	2.6	2.6	2.7	2.6	2.6
1996	2.5	2.5	2.6	2.5	2.6	2.5	2.5	2.5	2.5	2.3	2.3	2.4	2.4
1997	2.3	2.3	2.3	2.3	2.4	2.4	2.4	2.4	2.4	2.3	2.4	2.4	2.3
1998	2.4	2.4	2.4	2.4	2.5	2.5	2.4	2.4	2.4	2.4	2.4	2.4	2.4
1999	2.3	2.3	2.4	2.4	2.4	2.3	2.3	2.4	2.4	2.3	2.3	2.4	2.3
2000	2.3	2.3	2.4	2.3	2.4	2.3	2.3	2.3	2.3	2.3	2.3	2.3	2.3
2001	1.7	1.7	1.8	2.4	2.3	2.3	2.3	2.4	2.4	2.0	2.0	2.0	2.1
2002	2.4	2.4	2.4	2.5	2.4	2.4	2.4	2.4	2.4	2.3	2.3	2.3	2.4
2003	2.3	2.3	2.3	2.3	2.3	2.3	2.3	2.3	2.4	2.3	2.4	2.4	2.3
Government													
1990	6.5	6.6	6.7	6.9	7.1	6.9	6.3	6.3	6.4	6.6	6.7	6.6	6.6
1991	6.6	6.7	6.7	6.7	6.8	6.9	6.1	5.9	6.4	6.7	6.8	6.7	6.5
1992	6.6	6.7	6.8	6.8	6.9	7.2	6.3	6.2	6.6	6.8	6.9	6.8	6.7
1993	6.7	6.7	6.8	6.8	6.8	7.0	6.3	6.1	6.6	6.8	6.9	6.9	6.7
1994	6.8	6.8	6.8	6.9	7.0	7.0	6.2	6.2	6.8	6.9	7.1	7.0	6.7
1995	7.4	7.5	7.5	7.4	7.5	7.6	7.2	7.1	7.3	7.4	7.4	7.4	7.3
1996	7.3	7.4	7.4	7.4	7.5	7.6	7.0	6.9	7.4	7.5	7.6	7.6	7.3
1997	7.4	7.5	7.5	7.5	7.7	7.7	6.9	6.8	7.5	7.6	7.7	7.7	7.4
1998	7.7	7.7	7.8	7.8	7.8	8.0	7.2	7.1	7.7	7.7	7.8	7.8	7.6
1999	7.7	7.8	7.8	7.8	7.9	8.0	7.1	7.2	7.7	7.8	7.9	7.9	7.7
2000	7.9	8.0	8.1	8.1	8.5	7.9	7.4	7.4	7.9	7.9	7.9	8.0	7.9
2001	7.8	7.9	8.0	8.0	8.2	8.3	7.3	7.3	7.9	7.9	8.0	7.9	7.9
2002	7.9	7.9	8.0	8.1	8.1	7.7	7.2	7.2	7.9	8.0	8.1	8.1	7.9
2003	8.0	8.0	8.0	8.0	8.0	7.8	7.3	7.1	7.7	7.9	7.9	8.0	7.8
Federal government													
1990	0.9	0.9	1.0	1.1	1.2	1.0	1.0	0.9	0.9	0.9	0.9	0.9	0.9
1991	0.9	0.9	0.9	0.9	0.9	0.9	0.9	0.9	0.9	0.9	0.9	0.9	0.9
1992	0.9	0.9	0.9	0.9	0.9	1.0	0.9	1.0	0.9	0.9	0.9	0.9	0.9
1993	0.9	0.9	0.9	0.9	0.9	0.9	0.9	1.0	0.9	0.9	0.9	0.9	0.9
1994	0.9	0.9	0.9	0.9	0.9	0.9	0.9	0.9	0.9	0.9	0.9	1.0	0.9
1995	0.9	0.9	0.9	1.0	1.0	1.0	0.9	0.9	0.9	0.9	0.9	0.9	0.9
1996	0.9	0.9	0.9	0.9	0.9	0.9	0.9	0.9	0.9	0.9	0.9	0.9	0.9
1997	0.9	0.9	0.9	0.9	0.9	0.9	0.9	0.9	0.9	0.9	0.9	0.9	0.9
1998	0.9	0.9	0.9	0.9	0.9	0.9	0.9	0.9	0.9	0.9	0.9	0.9	0.9
1999	0.9	0.9	0.9	0.9	0.9	0.9	0.9	0.9	0.9	0.9	0.9	0.9	0.9
2000	1.0	1.0	1.0	1.0	1.2	1.0	1.0	1.0	0.9	0.9	0.9	0.9	0.9
2001	0.9	0.9	0.9	0.9	0.9	0.9	0.9	0.9	0.9	0.9	0.9	0.9	0.9
2002	0.9	0.9	0.9	0.9	0.9	0.9	0.9	0.9	0.9	0.9	1.0	1.0	0.9
2003	1.0	0.9	0.9	0.9	0.9	0.9	0.9	0.9	0.9	0.9	0.9	0.9	0.9

Employment by Industry: Iowa—*Continued*

(Numbers in thousands. Not seasonally adjusted.)

Industry	January	February	March	April	May	June	July	August	September	October	November	December	Annual Average
SIOUX CITY—*Continued*													
Local government													
1990	5.0	5.0	5.1	5.2	5.3	5.3	4.7	4.7	4.8	5.1	5.2	5.1	5.0
1991	5.1	5.2	5.2	5.2	5.3	5.4	4.5	4.3	4.9	5.2	5.3	5.2	5.0
1992	5.1	5.2	5.3	5.3	5.4	5.7	4.7	4.6	5.1	5.3	5.4	5.3	5.2
1993	5.2	5.3	5.3	5.3	5.4	5.5	4.8	4.5	5.1	5.3	5.4	5.4	5.2
1994	5.3	5.4	5.4	5.4	5.5	5.5	4.7	4.7	5.3	5.4	5.6	5.5	5.3
1995	5.9	6.1	6.1	5.9	5.9	6.0	5.7	5.6	5.8	5.9	5.9	6.0	5.9
1996	5.8	6.0	5.9	6.0	6.1	6.2	5.5	5.4	6.0	6.1	6.2	6.1	5.9
1997	6.0	6.1	6.1	6.1	6.3	6.3	5.5	5.4	6.1	6.2	6.3	6.3	6.0
1998	6.3	6.3	6.4	6.4	6.4	6.6	5.8	5.7	6.3	6.3	6.4	6.4	6.2
1999	6.2	6.4	6.4	6.4	6.5	6.6	5.7	5.8	6.3	6.4	6.4	6.5	6.3
2000	6.4	6.5	6.5	6.6	6.8	6.3	5.8	5.8	6.4	6.5	6.5	6.5	6.3
2001	6.4	6.5	6.6	6.6	6.8	6.9	5.9	5.9	6.5	6.5	6.6	6.5	6.5
2002	6.5	6.5	6.6	6.7	6.7	6.3	5.8	5.8	6.5	6.6	6.6	6.6	6.4
2003	6.5	6.6	6.6	6.6	6.6	6.4	5.9	5.7	6.3	6.5	6.5	6.6	6.4
WATERLOO-CEDAR FALLS													
Total nonfarm													
1990	59.1	59.7	60.5	61.6	62.0	60.6	59.5	60.5	63.0	63.9	64.2	63.9	61.5
1991	61.9	62.0	62.4	62.7	63.5	61.8	60.5	60.8	63.5	64.4	64.1	64.4	62.6
1992	62.4	62.8	63.2	63.7	64.3	62.4	62.1	62.4	65.0	64.7	65.1	65.9	63.6
1993	63.8	64.4	64.7	66.0	65.9	64.3	63.7	63.3	66.1	66.7	67.4	67.3	65.3
1994	64.6	65.0	65.8	66.6	67.5	65.6	64.4	65.1	67.2	67.8	68.8	68.4	66.4
1995	65.6	67.3	67.6	67.9	68.6	67.2	67.3	67.2	69.9	69.8	70.5	70.1	68.2
1996	67.5	68.1	68.8	69.5	70.3	68.1	67.3	67.4	69.6	70.6	71.3	71.2	69.1
1997	69.4	69.8	70.2	71.2	71.7	70.5	70.0	69.9	72.2	73.6	74.0	73.9	71.3
1998	72.1	72.6	72.9	74.2	74.5	73.0	71.3	71.8	73.5	74.8	74.7	74.4	73.3
1999	69.9	71.4	71.9	73.6	73.8	72.2	71.2	71.0	73.9	74.1	74.8	74.6	72.7
2000	71.7	72.1	72.6	73.5	73.8	72.4	72.3	72.4	74.6	75.5	75.8	75.1	73.4
2001	72.7	72.8	72.7	73.9	74.3	72.7	71.3	71.6	73.6	74.0	74.0	74.0	73.1
2002	71.7	72.3	72.5	73.0	73.7	72.3	71.4	71.2	73.1	73.9	74.4	74.2	72.8
2003	71.8	71.9	72.1	73.2	73.4	71.1	70.8	70.4	72.9	73.7	73.9	74.1	72.4
Total private													
1990	47.5	47.4	48.3	49.2	49.5	50.0	49.8	50.7	51.2	51.6	51.8	51.5	49.8
1991	49.6	49.4	49.9	50.3	50.9	51.1	50.7	50.7	51.5	51.9	51.5	51.9	50.7
1992	50.1	50.4	50.7	51.2	51.8	52.0	52.2	52.3	52.9	52.2	52.6	53.4	51.8
1993	51.7	51.9	52.1	53.4	53.4	53.8	53.8	53.1	54.0	54.1	54.7	54.7	53.3
1994	52.6	52.4	53.0	53.8	54.4	54.5	54.3	54.6	55.1	54.8	55.3	55.5	54.1
1995	53.5	54.3	54.6	54.9	55.5	56.1	56.7	56.6	57.1	56.8	57.4	57.1	55.8
1996	55.3	55.2	55.7	56.4	57.3	57.0	56.7	57.0	57.1	57.6	58.1	58.4	56.8
1997	56.7	56.9	57.3	58.2	58.8	59.5	59.7	59.5	59.6	60.2	60.7	60.8	58.9
1998	59.3	59.6	59.9	61.2	61.6	62.0	61.0	61.3	60.8	61.7	61.4	61.2	60.9
1999	57.1	58.4	58.8	60.6	60.9	61.3	60.7	60.7	61.2	61.1	61.6	61.4	60.3
2000	58.9	59.2	59.5	60.4	60.7	61.2	61.3	61.5	61.7	62.2	62.3	61.7	60.8
2001	59.8	59.5	59.4	60.7	61.3	61.6	60.9	61.0	61.2	61.0	60.8	61.0	60.7
2002	59.0	59.2	59.4	60.0	60.7	61.1	60.9	60.7	60.7	60.7	61.1	61.1	60.4
2003	58.9	58.7	59.0	59.9	60.2	60.0	60.5	60.1	60.6	60.8	61.0	61.1	60.1
Goods-producing													
1990	14.7	14.7	14.9	15.3	15.9	16.2	16.1	16.3	16.5	16.7	16.4	15.9	15.8
1991	15.4	15.4	15.5	15.9	16.2	16.5	16.5	16.5	16.5	16.3	16.0	16.0	16.0
1992	15.7	15.8	16.0	16.2	16.5	16.7	16.8	16.8	16.8	15.8	15.9	16.3	16.2
1993	15.9	15.9	15.9	16.1	16.2	16.5	16.7	16.4	16.6	16.4	16.5	16.3	16.2
1994	15.7	15.6	15.7	16.1	16.4	16.6	16.6	16.7	16.6	16.4	16.3	16.3	16.2
1995	15.8	16.1	16.1	16.5	16.9	17.2	17.4	17.4	17.4	17.1	17.0	16.8	16.8
1996	16.3	16.4	16.5	16.9	17.0	17.2	17.1	16.9	16.8	16.9	16.8	16.8	16.8
1997	16.3	16.5	16.7	17.2	17.5	17.9	17.9	17.7	17.4	17.7	17.6	17.6	17.3
1998	17.3	17.3	17.3	17.8	18.0	18.3	18.0	18.0	17.6	18.0	17.7	17.4	17.7
1999	15.3	16.5	16.6	17.2	17.5	17.7	17.5	17.5	17.6	17.0	17.0	16.8	17.0
2000	16.4	16.6	16.8	17.0	17.2	17.6	17.8	17.8	17.6	17.9	17.6	17.4	17.3
2001	17.0	17.1	17.2	17.4	17.7	18.0	17.9	17.9	17.6	17.4	17.3	17.2	17.5
2002	16.4	16.4	16.6	17.0	17.1	17.5	17.7	17.5	17.4	17.3	17.4	17.2	17.1
2003	16.7	16.5	16.5	16.7	16.8	17.1	17.1	16.9	16.8	16.9	16.8	16.6	16.8
Construction and mining													
1990	1.7	1.7	1.7	2.0	2.2	2.3	2.4	2.4	2.3	2.5	2.5	2.2	2.1
1991	1.9	1.8	2.0	2.1	2.4	2.5	2.6	2.6	2.7	2.5	2.3	2.2	2.3
1992	2.0	2.0	2.1	2.4	2.6	2.8	2.8	2.8	2.8	2.7	2.6	2.3	2.4
1993	2.0	1.9	1.9	2.1	2.5	2.7	2.8	2.7	2.7	2.7	2.7	2.5	2.4
1994	2.0	2.0	2.1	2.4	2.6	2.8	2.9	2.9	2.9	2.8	2.6	2.5	2.5
1995	2.1	2.1	2.2	2.5	2.7	2.9	3.0	3.0	3.0	2.8	2.7	2.5	2.6
1996	2.1	2.1	2.1	2.5	2.7	2.9	2.9	2.9	2.9	2.8	2.7	2.6	2.6
1997	2.2	2.2	2.3	2.7	3.0	3.1	3.1	3.0	2.9	2.9	2.8	2.7	2.7
1998	2.4	2.4	2.4	2.7	2.9	3.0	3.0	3.0	2.8	2.9	2.7	2.7	2.7
1999	2.2	2.3	2.3	2.8	3.0	3.2	3.1	3.1	3.1	3.0	2.9	2.7	2.8
2000	2.4	2.5	2.6	2.8	3.0	3.2	3.2	3.2	3.0	3.1	2.9	2.7	2.8
2001	2.4	2.4	2.5	2.7	3.0	3.2	3.1	3.1	3.0	2.9	2.8	2.7	2.8
2002	2.4	2.3	2.4	2.6	2.8	3.0	3.1	3.0	3.0	3.0	2.9	2.7	2.8
2003	2.4	2.3	2.4	2.6	2.9	3.1	3.1	3.1	3.0	3.0	2.9	2.7	2.8

Employment by Industry: Iowa—*Continued*

(Numbers in thousands. Not seasonally adjusted.)

Industry	January	February	March	April	May	June	July	August	September	October	November	December	Annual Average
WATERLOO-CEDAR FALLS *—Continued*													
Manufacturing													
1990	13.0	13.0	13.2	13.3	13.7	13.9	13.7	13.9	14.2	14.2	13.9	13.7	13.6
1991	13.5	13.6	13.5	13.8	13.8	14.0	13.9	13.9	13.8	13.8	13.7	13.8	13.7
1992	13.7	13.8	13.9	13.8	13.9	13.9	14.0	14.0	14.0	13.1	13.3	14.0	13.7
1993	13.9	14.0	14.0	14.0	13.7	13.8	13.9	13.7	13.9	13.7	13.8	13.8	13.8
1994	13.7	13.6	13.6	13.7	13.8	13.8	13.7	13.8	13.7	13.6	13.7	13.8	13.7
1995	13.7	14.0	13.9	14.0	14.2	14.3	14.4	14.4	14.4	14.3	14.3	14.3	14.1
1996	14.2	14.3	14.4	14.4	14.3	14.3	14.2	14.0	13.9	14.1	14.1	14.2	14.2
1997	14.1	14.3	14.4	14.5	14.5	14.8	14.8	14.7	14.5	14.8	14.8	14.9	14.5
1998	14.9	14.9	14.9	15.1	15.1	15.3	15.0	15.0	14.8	15.1	15.0	14.7	14.9
1999	13.1	14.2	14.3	14.4	14.5	14.5	14.4	14.4	14.5	14.0	14.1	14.1	14.2
2000	14.0	14.1	14.2	14.2	14.2	14.4	14.6	14.6	14.6	14.8	14.7	14.7	14.4
2001	14.6	14.7	14.7	14.7	14.7	14.8	14.8	14.8	14.6	14.5	14.5	14.5	14.7
2002	14.0	14.1	14.2	14.4	14.3	14.5	14.6	14.5	14.4	14.3	14.5	14.5	14.4
2003	14.3	14.2	14.1	14.1	13.9	14.0	14.0	13.8	13.8	13.9	13.9	13.9	14.0
Service-providing													
1990	44.4	45.0	45.6	46.3	46.1	44.4	43.4	44.2	46.5	47.2	47.8	48.0	45.7
1991	46.5	46.6	46.9	46.8	47.3	45.3	44.0	44.3	47.0	48.1	48.1	48.4	46.6
1992	46.7	47.0	47.2	47.5	47.8	45.7	45.3	45.6	48.2	48.9	49.2	49.6	47.3
1993	47.9	48.5	48.8	49.9	49.7	47.8	47.0	46.9	49.5	50.3	50.9	51.0	49.0
1994	48.9	49.4	50.1	50.5	51.1	49.0	47.8	48.4	50.6	51.4	52.5	52.1	50.1
1995	49.8	51.2	51.5	51.4	51.7	50.0	49.9	49.8	52.5	52.7	53.5	53.3	51.4
1996	51.2	51.7	52.3	52.6	53.3	50.9	50.2	50.5	52.8	53.7	54.5	54.4	52.3
1997	53.1	53.3	53.5	54.0	54.2	52.6	52.1	52.2	54.8	55.9	56.4	56.3	54.0
1998	54.8	55.3	55.6	56.4	56.5	54.7	53.3	53.8	55.9	56.8	57.0	57.0	55.5
1999	54.6	54.9	55.3	56.4	56.3	54.5	53.7	53.5	56.3	57.1	57.8	57.8	55.6
2000	55.3	55.5	55.8	56.5	56.6	54.8	54.5	54.6	57.0	57.6	58.2	57.7	56.1
2001	55.7	55.7	55.5	56.5	56.6	54.7	53.4	53.7	56.0	56.6	56.7	56.8	55.7
2002	55.3	55.9	55.9	56.0	56.6	54.8	53.7	53.7	55.7	56.6	57.0	57.0	55.7
2003	55.1	55.4	55.6	56.5	56.6	54.0	53.7	53.5	56.1	56.8	57.1	57.5	55.7
Trade, transportation, and utilities													
1990	11.2	11.0	11.2	11.3	11.4	11.5	11.4	11.8	11.9	11.8	12.1	12.2	11.5
1991	11.6	11.4	11.4	11.4	11.6	11.6	11.4	11.4	11.5	11.9	12.0	12.1	11.6
1992	11.2	11.1	11.1	11.2	11.4	11.4	11.4	11.3	11.4	11.6	11.7	12.0	11.4
1993	11.3	11.4	11.4	11.8	11.7	11.9	11.9	11.6	11.9	12.1	12.3	12.5	11.8
1994	11.7	11.7	11.8	11.8	12.1	12.1	12.0	12.1	12.2	12.3	12.5	12.7	12.0
1995	11.9	12.0	12.1	12.2	12.4	12.4	12.2	12.4	12.6	12.5	12.8	13.0	12.3
1996	12.3	12.1	12.2	12.2	12.4	12.4	12.6	12.8	12.7	12.8	13.1	13.4	12.5
1997	12.9	12.6	12.7	12.9	13.1	13.1	13.2	13.1	13.2	13.2	13.7	13.8	13.1
1998	13.1	12.9	12.9	13.5	13.6	13.7	13.4	13.5	13.6	13.8	13.9	14.2	13.5
1999	13.2	13.0	13.0	13.6	13.6	13.5	13.6	13.7	13.7	13.8	14.1	14.3	13.5
2000	13.5	13.4	13.4	13.7	13.8	14.0	13.7	13.7	13.9	14.2	14.5	14.5	13.8
2001	13.8	13.5	13.2	13.7	13.8	13.8	13.6	13.6	13.9	14.0	14.2	14.3	13.8
2002	13.6	13.5	13.5	13.5	13.6	13.6	13.3	13.3	13.4	13.6	13.9	14.0	13.6
2003	13.3	13.2	13.6	13.8	13.9	13.5	14.1	14.1	14.2	14.2	14.5	14.7	13.9
Wholesale trade													
1990	2.1	2.1	2.2	2.2	2.2	2.2	2.0	2.1	2.1	2.1	2.1	2.1	2.1
1991	2.1	2.1	2.1	2.1	2.1	2.1	2.0	2.0	2.0	2.1	2.0	2.0	2.0
1992	2.1	2.1	2.1	2.1	2.2	2.2	2.2	2.1	2.2	2.2	2.2	2.2	2.1
1993	2.2	2.1	2.1	2.2	2.2	2.3	2.2	2.2	2.2	2.3	2.3	2.3	2.2
1994	2.1	2.2	2.2	2.2	2.3	2.3	2.3	2.3	2.3	2.3	2.3	2.3	2.2
1995	2.2	2.3	2.3	2.3	2.4	2.5	2.4	2.4	2.4	2.4	2.5	2.5	2.3
1996	2.3	2.3	2.4	2.4	2.4	2.4	2.5	2.5	2.4	2.5	2.4	2.4	2.4
1997	2.3	2.3	2.4	2.4	2.5	2.5	2.5	2.5	2.5	2.5	2.5	2.5	2.4
1998	2.4	2.4	2.4	2.5	2.5	2.5	2.5	2.5	2.5	2.5	2.5	2.5	2.4
1999	2.4	2.4	2.5	2.6	2.6	2.6	2.5	2.5	2.5	2.5	2.5	2.6	2.5
2000	2.5	2.5	2.6	2.7	2.7	2.7	2.7	2.7	2.7	2.7	2.7	2.7	2.6
2001	2.6	2.6	2.6	2.7	2.7	2.7	2.7	2.7	2.7	2.7	2.7	2.7	2.7
2002	2.6	2.7	2.7	2.6	2.6	2.6	2.6	2.6	2.6	2.6	2.6	2.6	2.6
2003	2.5	2.5	2.5	2.5	2.5	2.5	2.6	2.6	2.6	2.5	2.5	2.5	2.5
Retail trade													
1990	7.9	7.7	7.8	7.9	8.0	8.0	8.1	8.4	8.5	8.5	8.8	8.9	8.2
1991	8.3	8.1	8.1	8.1	8.2	8.2	8.2	8.2	8.3	8.6	8.8	8.9	8.3
1992	7.9	7.8	7.8	7.9	8.0	8.0	8.0	8.0	8.0	8.2	8.3	8.5	8.0
1993	8.0	8.1	8.1	8.3	8.2	8.3	8.4	8.1	8.4	8.4	8.6	8.8	8.3
1994	8.3	8.2	8.3	8.3	8.5	8.4	8.4	8.5	8.6	8.7	8.9	9.1	8.5
1995	8.5	8.5	8.6	8.7	8.8	8.7	8.6	8.8	8.9	8.9	9.1	9.3	8.7
1996	8.8	8.6	8.6	8.6	8.8	8.8	8.8	8.9	8.9	8.9	9.3	9.5	8.8
1997	9.1	8.9	8.9	9.0	9.1	9.1	9.2	9.2	9.2	9.2	9.7	9.9	9.2
1998	9.2	9.0	9.0	9.4	9.5	9.6	9.4	9.5	9.5	9.8	9.9	10.2	9.5
1999	9.4	9.1	9.1	9.4	9.4	9.3	9.6	9.6	9.7	9.8	10.1	10.2	9.5
2000	9.6	9.5	9.3	9.4	9.5	9.7	9.6	9.5	9.7	10.0	10.3	10.3	9.7
2001	9.6	9.3	9.0	9.4	9.5	9.5	9.4	9.4	9.6	9.7	9.9	10.0	9.5
2002	9.4	9.2	9.1	9.2	9.2	9.2	9.0	9.0	9.2	9.3	9.6	9.7	9.3
2003	9.0	8.9	9.0	9.0	9.1	9.0	9.1	9.1	9.2	9.3	9.6	9.7	9.2

Employment by Industry: Iowa—*Continued*

(Numbers in thousands. Not seasonally adjusted.)

Industry	January	February	March	April	May	June	July	August	September	October	November	December	Annual Average
WATERLOO-CEDAR FALLS —*Continued*													
Transportation and utilities													
1990	1.2	1.2	1.2	1.2	1.2	1.3	1.3	1.3	1.3	1.2	1.2	1.2	1.2
1991	1.2	1.2	1.2	1.2	1.3	1.3	1.2	1.2	1.2	1.2	1.2	1.2	1.2
1992	1.2	1.2	1.2	1.2	1.2	1.2	1.2	1.2	1.2	1.2	1.2	1.3	1.2
1993	1.1	1.2	1.2	1.3	1.3	1.3	1.3	1.3	1.3	1.4	1.4	1.4	1.2
1994	1.3	1.3	1.3	1.3	1.3	1.4	1.3	1.3	1.3	1.3	1.3	1.3	1.3
1995	1.2	1.2	1.2	1.2	1.2	1.2	1.2	1.2	1.3	1.2	1.2	1.2	1.2
1996	1.2	1.2	1.2	1.2	1.2	1.2	1.3	1.4	1.4	1.4	1.4	1.5	1.3
1997	1.5	1.4	1.4	1.5	1.5	1.5	1.5	1.4	1.5	1.5	1.5	1.4	1.4
1998	1.5	1.5	1.5	1.6	1.6	1.6	1.5	1.5	1.6	1.5	1.5	1.5	1.5
1999	1.4	1.5	1.4	1.6	1.6	1.6	1.5	1.6	1.5	1.5	1.5	1.5	1.5
2000	1.4	1.4	1.5	1.6	1.6	1.6	1.4	1.5	1.5	1.5	1.5	1.5	1.5
2001	1.6	1.6	1.6	1.6	1.6	1.6	1.5	1.5	1.6	1.6	1.6	1.6	1.6
2002	1.6	1.6	1.7	1.7	1.8	1.8	1.7	1.7	1.6	1.7	1.7	1.7	1.7
2003	1.8	1.8	2.1	2.3	2.3	2.0	2.4	2.4	2.4	2.4	2.4	2.5	2.2
Information													
1990	0.9	1.0	0.9	0.9	1.0	1.0	1.0	1.0	1.0	1.0	1.0	1.0	0.9
1991	1.0	1.0	1.1	1.0	1.0	1.0	1.0	1.0	1.0	1.0	1.0	1.0	1.0
1992	1.0	1.0	1.0	0.9	0.9	0.9	0.9	0.9	0.9	0.9	0.9	0.9	0.9
1993	0.9	0.9	0.9	0.9	0.9	0.9	1.0	0.9	0.9	0.9	0.9	0.9	0.9
1994	0.9	1.0	0.9	1.0	1.0	1.0	1.0	1.0	1.0	0.9	1.0	1.0	0.9
1995	0.9	1.0	1.0	1.0	1.0	1.0	1.0	1.0	0.9	0.9	0.9	0.9	0.9
1996	0.9	0.9	0.9	0.9	1.0	0.9	0.9	1.0	1.0	1.0	1.1	1.0	0.9
1997	1.0	1.0	1.0	1.0	1.0	1.0	1.0	1.0	1.0	1.1	1.1	1.1	1.0
1998	1.1	1.1	1.1	1.2	1.2	1.2	1.2	1.2	1.1	1.1	1.1	1.1	1.1
1999	1.1	1.1	1.1	1.1	1.2	1.2	1.2	1.2	1.2	1.2	1.2	1.2	1.1
2000	1.2	1.2	1.1	1.2	1.2	1.2	1.2	1.2	1.2	1.2	1.2	1.2	1.1
2001	1.1	1.2	1.1	1.1	1.1	1.1	1.1	1.1	1.1	1.1	1.1	1.1	1.1
2002	1.0	1.0	1.0	1.0	1.0	1.0	1.0	1.0	1.0	1.0	1.0	1.0	1.0
2003	1.0	1.1	1.0	1.0	1.1	1.1	1.0	1.0	1.0	1.0	1.0	1.0	1.0
Financial activities													
1990	2.3	2.2	2.3	2.4	2.4	2.4	2.5	2.5	2.5	2.5	2.5	2.5	2.4
1991	2.4	2.4	2.5	2.5	2.6	2.6	2.6	2.6	2.7	2.7	2.7	2.8	2.5
1992	2.8	2.8	2.9	2.9	2.9	2.9	3.0	3.0	3.1	3.1	3.1	3.1	2.9
1993	3.1	3.1	3.1	3.1	3.1	3.1	3.1	3.1	3.1	3.1	3.1	3.1	3.1
1994	3.0	3.0	3.1	3.0	3.0	3.0	3.1	3.0	3.1	3.1	3.1	3.2	3.0
1995	3.1	3.2	3.2	3.2	3.1	3.1	3.3	3.3	3.3	3.3	3.4	3.4	3.2
1996	3.4	3.4	3.4	3.4	3.5	3.5	3.6	3.6	3.5	3.6	3.6	3.7	3.5
1997	3.6	3.6	3.6	3.5	3.5	3.6	3.6	3.7	3.6	3.6	3.7	3.7	3.6
1998	3.6	3.6	3.6	3.7	3.7	3.7	3.6	3.6	3.5	3.5	3.5	3.5	3.5
1999	3.4	3.4	3.4	3.5	3.4	3.5	3.5	3.4	3.4	3.4	3.4	3.4	3.4
2000	3.4	3.4	3.3	3.4	3.3	3.3	3.5	3.5	3.5	3.5	3.5	3.5	3.4
2001	3.5	3.5	3.5	3.5	3.5	3.5	3.6	3.7	3.7	3.6	3.6	3.7	3.6
2002	3.6	3.6	3.6	3.7	3.7	3.7	3.6	3.6	3.5	3.6	3.6	3.6	3.6
2003	3.6	3.6	3.6	3.6	3.6	3.7	3.7	3.6	3.6	3.6	3.6	3.6	3.6
Professional and business services													
1990	3.8	3.8	4.0	4.0	3.8	3.9	3.9	3.9	4.0	3.9	4.1	4.1	3.9
1991	3.8	3.8	3.9	3.9	4.0	3.9	4.0	3.8	3.9	4.0	4.0	4.1	3.9
1992	3.9	3.9	3.9	4.0	4.0	3.9	4.0	4.2	4.3	4.4	4.5	4.5	4.1
1993	4.3	4.4	4.6	4.8	4.7	4.7	4.7	4.7	4.9	5.0	5.2	5.1	4.7
1994	4.9	4.7	4.8	5.1	5.0	5.1	5.0	5.1	5.3	5.3	5.4	5.4	5.0
1995	5.3	5.3	5.3	5.0	4.8	5.3	5.7	5.5	5.6	5.7	5.8	5.7	5.4
1996	5.6	5.6	5.7	5.8	5.8	5.7	5.5	5.5	5.8	6.0	6.2	6.2	5.7
1997	6.0	6.2	6.1	6.3	6.4	6.5	6.6	6.4	6.7	6.8	6.8	6.9	6.4
1998	6.7	7.1	7.2	6.8	6.7	6.8	6.9	6.9	6.8	6.9	6.9	6.7	6.8
1999	6.6	6.7	6.7	6.7	6.6	6.6	6.6	6.5	6.5	6.7	6.9	6.8	6.6
2000	6.4	6.4	6.6	6.7	6.6	6.5	6.6	6.7	6.8	6.5	6.7	6.5	6.5
2001	6.2	6.0	6.1	6.4	6.4	6.4	6.3	6.3	6.3	6.4	6.2	6.2	6.3
2002	6.3	6.4	6.4	6.3	6.4	6.4	6.5	6.5	6.4	6.3	6.4	6.2	6.4
2003	5.9	5.8	5.8	5.9	5.8	5.8	5.9	5.8	5.9	6.1	6.2	6.3	5.9
Educational and health services													
1990	6.4	6.5	6.6	6.6	6.6	6.6	6.5	6.6	6.7	6.9	6.9	7.0	6.6
1991	6.8	6.9	6.9	6.9	6.9	7.0	6.8	6.8	7.0	7.3	7.2	7.3	6.9
1992	7.1	7.3	7.3	7.3	7.3	7.4	7.3	7.3	7.5	7.5	7.6	7.6	7.3
1993	7.6	7.6	7.6	7.6	7.6	7.6	7.6	7.6	7.7	7.7	7.8	7.9	7.6
1994	7.8	7.8	7.9	7.9	7.9	7.9	7.8	7.9	7.9	7.9	8.0	8.0	7.8
1995	8.0	8.1	8.1	8.1	8.2	8.1	7.9	8.0	8.1	8.2	8.3	8.3	8.1
1996	8.2	8.2	8.2	8.2	8.3	8.2	8.1	8.2	8.3	8.4	8.5	8.5	8.2
1997	8.5	8.5	8.6	8.6	8.7	8.6	8.7	8.8	8.8	8.9	8.9	8.9	8.7
1998	8.8	8.8	8.9	9.0	9.0	8.9	8.7	8.7	8.9	9.1	9.1	9.1	8.9
1999	8.9	9.0	9.1	9.2	9.3	9.3	9.1	9.3	9.4	9.5	9.5	9.5	9.2
2000	9.3	9.3	9.4	9.4	9.5	9.4	9.4	9.5	9.6	9.7	9.6	9.6	9.4
2001	9.4	9.4	9.5	9.7	9.7	9.6	9.3	9.4	9.5	9.5	9.5	9.6	9.5
2002	9.6	9.7	9.7	9.7	9.8	9.7	9.5	9.6	9.7	9.7	9.7	9.9	9.7
2003	9.7	9.6	9.6	9.7	9.7	9.6	9.6	9.6	9.8	9.9	9.9	10.0	9.7

Employment by Industry: Iowa—*Continued*

(Numbers in thousands. Not seasonally adjusted.)

Industry	January	February	March	April	May	June	July	August	September	October	November	December	Annual Average
WATERLOO-CEDAR FALLS *—Continued*													
Leisure and hospitality													
1990	5.3	5.3	5.4	5.7	5.4	5.4	5.4	5.6	5.5	5.7	5.7	5.7	5.5
1991	5.5	5.5	5.5	5.6	5.5	5.5	5.4	5.5	5.8	5.6	5.5	5.5	5.5
1992	5.4	5.4	5.5	5.5	5.5	5.5	5.5	5.6	5.7	5.6	5.6	5.7	5.5
1993	5.5	5.5	5.4	5.9	6.0	5.9	5.6	5.7	5.7	5.6	5.6	5.6	5.6
1994	5.5	5.5	5.7	5.8	5.9	5.7	5.7	5.7	5.8	5.7	5.7	5.6	5.6
1995	5.4	5.5	5.6	5.7	5.9	5.8	6.0	5.9	6.0	5.9	5.9	5.9	5.7
1996	5.6	5.6	5.8	5.9	6.1	6.0	5.8	5.9	5.8	5.9	5.8	5.8	5.8
1997	5.5	5.6	5.7	5.7	5.7	5.8	5.7	5.9	5.9	5.8	5.8	5.7	5.7
1998	5.7	5.8	5.9	6.1	6.2	6.2	6.2	6.3	6.2	6.2	6.1	6.1	6.0
1999	5.7	5.8	5.9	6.2	6.2	6.3	6.1	6.1	6.3	6.3	6.3	6.2	6.1
2000	5.7	5.9	5.9	5.9	6.0	6.0	6.0	6.1	6.0	6.0	6.0	5.9	5.9
2001	5.8	5.8	5.8	5.9	6.1	6.1	6.1	6.0	6.1	6.0	5.9	5.9	6.0
2002	5.7	5.7	5.7	5.8	6.2	6.2	6.4	6.4	6.4	6.3	6.2	6.3	6.1
2003	6.0	6.1	6.1	6.3	6.4	6.4	6.3	6.4	6.5	6.3	6.2	6.1	6.3
Other services													
1990	2.9	2.9	3.0	3.0	3.0	3.0	3.0	3.0	3.1	3.1	3.1	3.1	3.0
1991	3.1	3.0	3.1	3.1	3.1	3.0	3.0	3.1	3.1	3.1	3.1	3.1	3.0
1992	3.0	3.1	3.0	3.2	3.3	3.3	3.3	3.2	3.2	3.3	3.3	3.3	3.2
1993	3.1	3.1	3.2	3.2	3.2	3.2	3.2	3.1	3.2	3.3	3.3	3.3	3.2
1994	3.1	3.1	3.1	3.1	3.1	3.1	3.1	3.1	3.2	3.2	3.3	3.3	3.1
1995	3.1	3.1	3.2	3.2	3.2	3.2	3.2	3.1	3.2	3.2	3.3	3.1	3.1
1996	3.0	3.0	3.0	3.1	3.2	3.1	3.1	3.1	3.2	3.0	3.0	3.0	3.0
1997	2.9	2.9	2.9	3.0	2.9	3.0	3.0	2.9	3.0	3.1	3.1	3.1	2.9
1998	3.0	3.0	3.0	3.1	3.2	3.2	3.0	3.1	3.1	3.1	3.1	3.1	3.0
1999	2.9	2.9	3.0	3.1	3.1	3.2	3.1	3.0	3.1	3.2	3.2	3.2	3.0
2000	3.0	3.0	3.0	3.1	3.1	3.2	3.1	3.0	3.1	3.2	3.2	3.1	3.0
2001	3.0	3.0	3.0	3.0	3.0	3.1	3.0	3.0	3.0	3.0	3.0	3.0	3.0
2002	2.8	2.9	2.9	3.0	2.9	3.0	2.9	2.8	2.9	2.9	2.9	2.9	2.9
2003	2.7	2.8	2.8	2.9	2.9	2.8	2.8	2.7	2.8	2.8	2.8	2.8	2.8
Government													
1990	11.6	12.3	12.2	12.4	12.5	10.6	9.7	9.8	11.8	12.3	12.4	12.4	11.6
1991	12.3	12.6	12.5	12.4	12.6	10.7	9.8	10.1	12.0	12.5	12.6	12.5	11.8
1992	12.3	12.4	12.5	12.5	12.5	10.4	9.9	10.1	12.1	12.5	12.5	12.5	11.8
1993	12.1	12.5	12.6	12.6	12.5	10.5	9.9	10.2	12.1	12.6	12.7	12.6	11.9
1994	12.0	12.6	12.8	12.8	13.1	11.1	10.1	10.5	12.1	13.0	13.5	12.9	12.2
1995	12.1	13.0	13.0	13.0	13.1	11.1	10.6	10.6	12.8	13.0	13.1	13.0	12.3
1996	12.2	12.9	13.1	13.1	13.0	11.1	10.6	10.4	12.5	13.0	13.2	12.8	12.3
1997	12.7	12.9	12.9	13.0	12.9	11.0	10.3	10.4	12.6	13.4	13.3	13.1	12.3
1998	12.8	13.0	13.0	13.0	12.9	11.0	10.3	10.5	12.7	13.1	13.3	13.2	12.4
1999	12.8	13.0	13.1	13.0	12.9	10.9	10.5	10.3	12.7	13.0	13.2	13.2	12.3
2000	12.8	12.9	13.1	13.1	13.1	11.2	11.0	10.9	12.9	13.3	13.5	13.4	12.6
2001	12.9	13.3	13.3	13.2	13.0	11.1	10.4	10.6	12.4	13.0	13.2	13.0	12.5
2002	12.7	13.1	13.1	13.0	13.0	11.2	10.5	10.5	12.4	13.2	13.3	13.1	12.4
2003	12.9	13.2	13.1	13.3	13.2	11.1	10.3	10.3	12.3	12.9	12.9	13.0	12.4
Federal government													
2001	0.6	0.6	0.6	0.6	0.6	0.6	0.6	0.6	0.6	0.6	0.6	0.6	0.6
2002	0.6	0.6	0.6	0.5	0.5	0.6	0.6	0.5	0.5	0.6	0.6	0.6	0.6
2003	0.6	0.6	0.6	0.6	0.6	0.5	0.5	0.5	0.5	0.5	0.5	0.5	0.5
State government													
1990	4.7	5.0	4.9	5.0	4.9	3.0	2.9	3.2	4.9	5.1	5.2	5.1	4.4
1991	5.2	5.3	5.2	5.2	5.1	3.1	3.0	3.4	5.0	5.2	5.3	5.2	4.6
1992	5.2	5.1	5.2	5.2	5.0	3.1	3.0	3.3	5.0	5.2	5.2	5.2	4.6
1993	5.0	5.2	5.2	5.2	5.1	3.2	3.1	3.5	5.0	5.2	5.3	5.2	4.6
1994	4.7	5.2	5.3	5.2	5.1	3.4	3.2	3.6	4.6	5.4	5.5	5.3	4.7
1995	4.7	5.4	5.4	5.4	5.3	3.3	3.3	3.6	5.2	5.4	5.5	5.4	4.8
1996	4.8	5.4	5.5	5.4	5.3	3.5	3.3	3.6	5.3	5.6	5.7	5.5	4.9
1997	5.4	5.5	5.5	5.5	5.3	3.5	3.3	3.6	5.4	5.7	5.7	5.6	5.0
1998	5.5	5.6	5.6	5.6	5.4	3.5	3.3	3.7	5.5	5.7	5.8	5.7	5.0
1999	5.4	5.6	5.6	5.6	5.4	3.4	3.4	3.6	5.5	5.7	5.8	5.8	5.0
2000	5.5	5.8	5.8	5.8	5.6	3.7	3.6	3.9	5.9	6.0	6.1	6.0	5.3
2001	5.6	6.0	5.9	5.9	5.7	3.7	3.5	3.8	5.4	5.8	5.9	5.8	5.3
2002	5.6	5.8	5.8	5.7	5.5	3.6	3.4	3.7	5.4	5.8	5.8	5.7	5.2
2003	5.5	5.6	5.6	5.7	5.5	3.6	3.3	3.6	5.3	5.6	5.6	5.6	5.0
Local government													
1990	6.4	6.7	6.7	6.7	6.8	6.9	6.2	6.0	6.4	6.7	6.7	6.7	6.5
1991	6.5	6.7	6.8	6.7	6.9	7.0	6.2	6.1	6.4	6.7	6.7	6.7	6.6
1992	6.5	6.7	6.7	6.7	6.9	6.7	6.3	6.2	6.5	6.7	6.7	6.7	6.6
1993	6.5	6.7	6.8	6.8	6.8	6.7	6.2	6.1	6.5	6.8	6.8	6.8	6.6
1994	6.7	6.8	6.9	7.0	7.4	7.1	6.3	6.3	6.9	7.0	7.4	7.0	6.9
1995	6.8	7.0	7.0	7.0	7.2	7.2	6.7	6.4	7.0	7.0	7.0	7.0	6.9
1996	6.8	6.9	7.0	7.1	7.1	7.0	6.7	6.2	6.6	6.8	6.9	6.7	6.8
1997	6.7	6.8	6.8	6.9	7.0	6.9	6.4	6.2	6.6	7.1	7.0	6.9	6.7
1998	6.7	6.8	6.8	6.8	6.9	6.9	6.4	6.2	6.6	6.8	6.9	6.9	6.7
1999	6.8	6.8	6.9	6.8	6.9	6.9	6.5	6.1	6.6	6.7	6.8	6.8	6.7
2000	6.7	6.5	6.6	6.6	6.7	6.7	6.7	6.3	6.4	6.7	6.8	6.8	6.6
2001	6.7	6.7	6.8	6.7	6.7	6.8	6.3	6.2	6.4	6.6	6.7	6.6	6.6
2002	6.5	6.7	6.7	6.8	7.0	7.0	6.5	6.3	6.5	6.8	6.9	6.8	6.7
2003	6.8	7.0	6.9	7.0	7.1	7.0	6.5	6.2	6.5	6.8	6.8	6.9	6.8

Average Weekly Hours by Industry: Iowa

(Not seasonally adjusted.)

Industry	January	February	March	April	May	June	July	August	September	October	November	December	Annual Average
STATEWIDE													
Total private													
2001	32.9	32.5	32.6	32.5	33.1	33.7	34.1	34.1	33.4	33.6	33.4	33.6	33.3
2002	32.8	33.1	33.1	33.1	33.4	34.2	33.7	33.6	33.7	33.3	33.4	33.6	33.4
2003	32.7	32.7	32.8	32.4	32.9	33.6	33.2	33.5	33.1	33.1	33.3	32.5	33.0
Goods-producing													
2001	40.5	40.1	40.1	39.1	40.2	40.6	41.1	40.5	41.4	41.0	41.0	41.0	40.5
2002	40.2	40.4	40.3	40.4	40.4	40.8	40.3	40.7	41.2	41.2	41.2	41.0	40.7
2003	40.1	39.3	40.1	40.0	41.1	41.8	40.7	42.7	42.1	41.9	42.5	41.4	41.2
Natural resources and mining													
2001	40.0	40.3	41.0	44.6	45.4	45.1	47.4	41.9	44.5	43.3	43.5	41.0	44.1
2002	41.7	43.4	38.3	43.5	45.6	46.4	47.7	47.6	48.8	48.9	46.3	44.2	45.4
2003	42.9	42.1	44.4	45.5	50.8	51.8	50.1	51.3	49.7	50.9	49.8	41.6	48.0
Construction													
2001	37.7	36.5	36.6	37.9	39.5	39.4	42.9	40.5	41.1	39.7	38.9	36.9	39.2
2002	36.7	36.5	36.3	36.7	39.3	38.6	38.2	38.6	40.5	41.3	40.4	38.6	38.6
2003	37.6	36.0	37.9	38.5	40.0	41.0	39.5	42.3	40.2	41.3	39.9	36.4	39.4
Manufacturing													
2001	41.1	40.9	40.9	39.3	40.3	41.0	40.5	40.5	41.4	41.4	41.6	42.2	40.9
2002	41.0	41.4	41.3	41.5	40.7	41.5	41.0	41.4	41.4	41.1	41.5	41.7	41.3
2003	40.7	40.1	40.6	40.4	41.4	42.0	41.1	42.8	42.7	42.1	43.3	43.0	41.7
Trade, transportation, and utilities													
2001	31.1	30.5	30.8	31.4	31.9	31.9	32.5	32.6	31.7	31.9	31.8	31.6	31.6
2002	30.6	31.1	31.0	31.3	31.7	32.7	32.4	32.5	32.1	31.7	31.8	32.0	31.8
2003	30.9	31.2	31.2	31.1	31.2	32.2	32.0	31.8	31.4	31.6	31.4	31.1	31.4
Wholesale trade													
2001	37.3	37.1	37.1	37.4	38.5	37.9	37.5	37.7	37.9	39.5	39.3	36.8	37.8
2002	37.1	37.9	37.4	38.7	38.6	40.2	38.4	38.4	38.4	38.1	38.6	37.9	38.3
2003	37.5	36.9	37.7	36.8	37.8	38.2	37.2	36.9	37.8	38.9	38.4	37.1	37.6
Retail trade													
2001	26.6	26.2	26.6	27.4	28.0	28.6	28.8	29.3	27.9	27.2	27.4	27.9	27.7
2002	26.3	27.0	26.8	26.9	27.9	28.4	28.5	28.1	27.3	26.9	26.9	27.8	27.4
2003	26.2	26.7	26.7	26.8	27.4	28.3	28.2	28.2	27.4	27.2	27.4	27.1	27.3
Financial activities													
2001	34.9	36.3	35.3	36.2	34.5	40.0	40.9	40.3	41.0	39.5	40.4	41.5	38.4
2002	40.1	39.8	39.8	38.7	40.0	40.0	38.6	38.6	38.6	37.8	36.7	37.4	38.8
2003	36.9	37.5	36.8	36.0	36.2	36.9	36.4	36.7	36.0	36.5	36.4	35.0	36.4
DES MOINES													
Manufacturing													
2001	40.9	42.2	40.9	40.2	39.9	39.4	41.2	41.6	41.0	39.8	42.8	44.1	41.2
2002	43.6	46.2	45.3	44.2	44.3	43.9	38.0	42.8	42.1	41.9	43.0	44.6	43.3
2003	41.7	40.8	41.2	40.1	41.7	41.5	39.2	41.6	40.7	42.0	43.9	45.8	41.7

Average Hourly Earnings by Industry: Iowa

(Dollars, not seasonally adjusted.)

Industry	January	February	March	April	May	June	July	August	September	October	November	December	Annual Average
STATEWIDE													
Total private													
2001	12.68	12.67	12.69	12.82	12.72	12.72	12.93	12.72	12.97	12.92	13.06	13.00	12.83
2002	12.98	13.06	13.17	13.19	13.28	13.18	13.29	13.20	13.41	13.43	13.53	13.61	13.28
2003	13.28	13.32	13.34	13.43	13.37	13.25	13.35	13.50	13.56	13.49	13.65	13.64	13.43
Goods-producing													
2001	14.88	14.72	14.84	15.05	15.00	14.98	15.41	15.24	15.30	15.20	15.57	15.52	15.15
2002	15.54	15.44	15.69	15.64	15.87	15.83	15.92	15.97	16.11	16.06	16.20	16.42	15.90
2003	15.89	15.73	15.98	16.11	16.20	15.96	16.07	16.14	16.25	16.07	16.49	16.47	16.12
Natural resources and mining													
2001	12.75	12.52	12.10	12.72	13.11	13.12	13.84	14.13	15.29	14.25	14.00	14.06	13.58
2002	14.70	15.02	13.79	13.19	13.95	14.03	14.46	14.05	14.17	14.28	14.13	14.16	14.14
2003	13.91	14.14	14.46	14.54	15.21	15.10	14.94	15.13	15.22	15.21	15.09	14.77	14.89
Construction													
2001	16.46	16.50	16.47	16.72	16.69	16.54	16.84	16.73	17.25	16.85	17.58	17.89	16.89
2002	17.85	17.95	18.18	18.00	17.88	17.89	17.48	17.91	18.23	18.24	18.08	18.13	17.98
2003	18.09	18.23	18.40	17.62	17.69	17.09	16.95	17.34	17.61	17.44	17.53	17.37	17.56
Manufacturing													
2001	14.56	14.37	14.52	14.65	14.52	14.52	14.93	14.75	14.68	14.69	14.98	14.92	14.67
2002	15.02	14.90	15.15	15.05	15.28	15.22	15.44	15.37	15.44	15.36	15.62	15.96	15.32
2003	15.38	15.18	15.42	15.70	15.73	15.59	15.78	15.72	15.81	15.61	16.18	16.24	15.70
Trade, transportation, and utilities													
2001	11.76	11.98	11.90	12.02	11.92	11.91	11.82	11.73	12.03	12.02	12.09	11.95	11.93
2002	11.69	12.17	12.23	12.20	12.35	12.11	12.04	12.22	12.45	12.42	12.74	12.56	12.27
2003	12.28	12.52	12.53	12.77	12.47	12.47	12.63	12.71	12.62	12.53	12.50	12.51	12.55
Wholesale trade													
2001	13.27	13.44	13.57	13.59	13.25	13.52	13.38	13.31	13.44	13.53	13.30	13.62	13.43
2002	12.79	12.95	13.13	13.13	13.57	13.92	13.56	13.87	13.83	14.02	14.92	14.73	13.72
2003	13.89	14.12	14.25	14.44	14.21	14.79	15.10	15.36	15.04	14.79	14.86	15.04	14.66
Retail trade													
2001	10.21	10.25	10.34	10.38	10.27	10.36	10.31	9.97	10.44	10.56	10.58	10.41	10.34
2002	10.53	10.56	10.80	10.60	10.52	10.44	10.43	10.47	10.64	10.51	10.46	10.42	10.53
2003	10.52	10.58	10.62	10.68	10.49	10.47	10.47	10.56	10.56	10.53	10.55	10.67	10.56
Financial activities													
2001	14.18	13.93	14.18	14.59	14.46	14.69	14.96	14.69	15.10	15.29	15.07	14.89	14.70
2002	15.25	15.22	15.40	15.55	15.41	15.02	15.10	15.06	15.74	15.49	15.48	14.65	15.28
2003	14.57	15.05	15.25	15.14	15.18	14.83	14.96	15.22	15.17	15.17	15.18	15.07	15.06
DES MOINES													
Manufacturing													
2001	15.68	15.24	15.24	15.59	15.49	15.76	15.88	15.93	15.72	15.75	16.34	16.33	15.75
2002	16.05	15.67	15.70	15.44	15.89	15.84	16.03	16.24	16.16	16.53	16.54	18.75	16.23
2003	16.97	17.26	17.64	17.85	17.66	17.99	17.69	17.73	17.96	17.61	17.66	18.67	17.73

Average Weekly Earnings by Industry: Iowa

(Dollars, not seasonally adjusted.)

Industry	January	February	March	April	May	June	July	August	September	October	November	December	Annual Average
STATEWIDE													
Total private													
2001	417.17	411.78	413.69	416.65	421.03	428.66	440.91	433.75	433.20	434.11	436.20	436.80	427.24
2002	425.74	432.29	435.93	436.59	443.55	450.76	447.87	443.52	451.92	447.22	451.90	457.30	443.55
2003	434.26	435.56	437.55	435.13	439.87	445.20	443.22	452.25	448.84	446.52	454.55	443.30	443.19
Goods-producing													
2001	602.64	590.27	595.08	588.46	603.00	608.19	633.35	617.22	633.42	623.20	638.37	636.32	613.58
2002	624.71	623.78	632.31	631.86	641.15	645.86	641.58	649.98	663.73	661.67	667.44	673.22	647.13
2003	637.19	618.19	640.80	644.40	665.82	667.13	654.05	689.18	684.13	673.33	700.83	681.86	664.14
Natural resources and mining													
2001	510.00	504.56	496.10	567.31	595.19	591.71	656.02	592.05	680.41	617.03	609.00	576.46	598.88
2002	612.99	651.87	528.16	573.77	636.12	650.99	689.74	668.78	691.50	698.29	654.22	625.87	641.96
2003	596.74	595.29	642.02	661.57	772.67	782.18	748.49	776.17	756.43	774.19	751.48	614.43	714.72
Construction													
2001	620.54	602.25	602.80	633.69	659.26	651.68	722.44	677.57	708.98	668.95	683.86	660.14	662.09
2002	655.10	655.18	659.93	660.60	702.68	690.55	667.74	691.33	738.32	753.31	730.43	699.82	694.03
2003	680.18	656.28	697.36	678.37	707.60	700.69	669.53	733.48	707.92	720.27	699.45	632.27	691.86
Manufacturing													
2001	598.42	587.73	593.87	575.75	585.16	595.32	604.67	597.38	607.75	608.17	623.17	629.62	600.00
2002	615.82	616.86	625.70	624.58	621.90	631.63	633.04	636.32	639.22	631.30	648.23	665.53	632.72
2003	625.97	608.72	626.05	634.28	651.22	654.78	648.56	672.82	675.09	657.18	700.59	698.32	654.69
Trade, transportation, and utilities													
2001	365.74	365.39	366.52	377.43	380.25	379.93	384.15	382.40	381.35	383.44	384.46	377.62	376.99
2002	357.71	378.49	379.13	381.86	391.50	396.00	390.10	397.15	399.65	393.71	405.13	401.92	390.19
2003	379.45	390.62	390.94	397.15	389.06	401.53	404.16	404.18	396.27	395.95	392.50	389.06	394.07
Wholesale trade													
2001	494.97	498.62	503.45	508.27	510.13	512.41	501.75	501.79	509.38	534.44	522.69	501.22	507.65
2002	474.51	490.81	491.06	508.13	523.80	559.58	520.70	532.61	531.07	534.16	575.91	558.27	525.48
2003	520.88	521.03	537.23	531.39	537.14	564.98	561.72	566.78	568.51	575.33	570.62	557.98	551.22
Retail trade													
2001	271.59	268.55	275.04	284.41	287.56	296.30	296.93	292.12	291.28	287.23	289.89	290.44	286.42
2002	276.94	285.12	289.44	285.14	293.51	296.50	297.26	294.21	290.47	282.72	281.37	289.68	288.52
2003	275.62	282.49	283.55	286.22	287.43	296.30	295.25	297.79	289.34	286.42	289.07	289.16	288.29
Financial activities													
2001	494.88	505.66	500.55	528.16	498.87	587.60	611.86	592.01	619.10	603.96	608.83	617.94	564.48
2002	611.53	605.76	612.92	601.79	616.40	600.80	582.86	581.32	607.56	585.52	568.12	547.91	592.86
2003	537.63	564.38	561.20	545.04	549.52	547.23	544.54	558.57	546.12	553.71	552.55	527.45	548.18
DES MOINES													
Manufacturing													
2001	641.31	643.13	623.32	626.72	618.05	620.94	654.26	662.69	644.52	626.85	699.35	720.15	648.90
2002	699.78	723.95	711.21	682.45	703.93	695.38	609.14	695.07	680.34	692.61	711.22	836.25	702.76
2003	707.65	704.21	726.77	715.79	736.42	746.59	693.45	737.57	730.97	739.62	775.27	855.09	739.34

KANSAS AT A GLANCE

(Population and total nonfarm employment numbers in thousands)

Population, Census 2000:	2,688.4
Total nonfarm employment, 2003:	1,311.9
Change in total nonfarm employment	
(Number)	
1990–2003:	223.5
1990–2001:	259.3
2001–2003:	-35.8
(Compound annual rate of change)	
1990–2003:	1.4%
1990–2001:	2.0%
2001–2003:	-1.3%
Unemployment rate	
1990:	4.3%
2001:	4.3%
2003:	5.6%

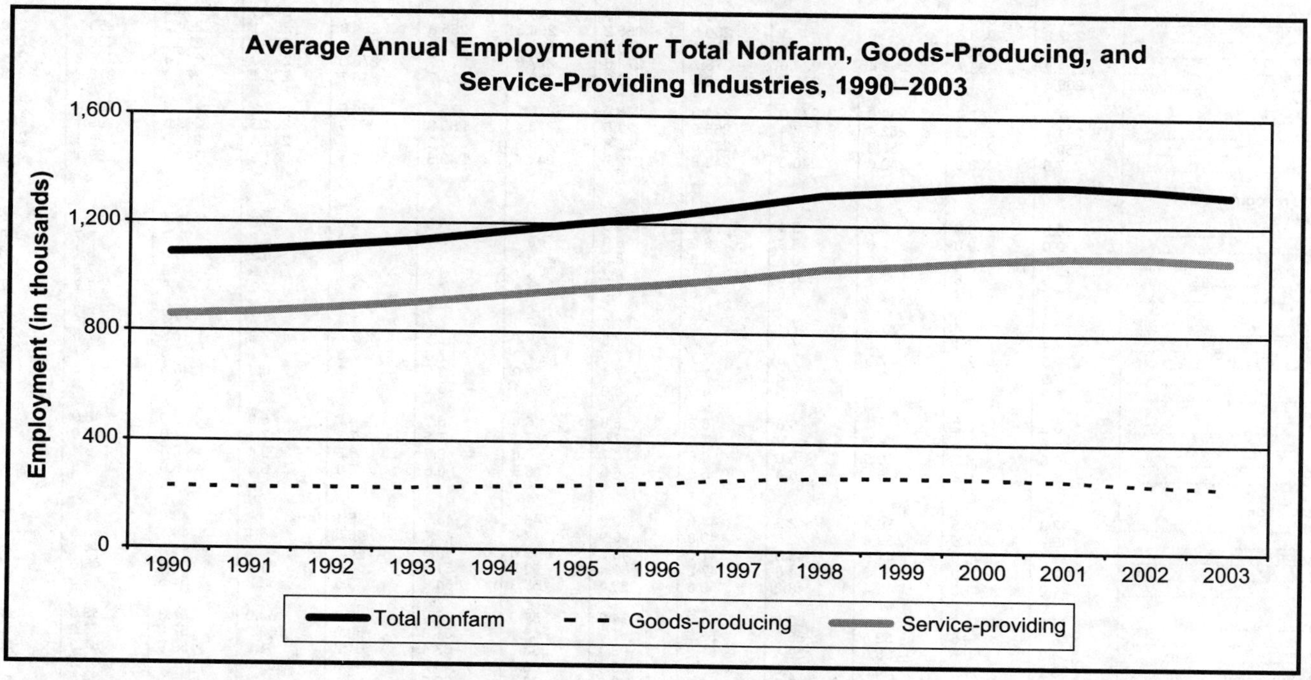

Nonfarm payroll employment rose steadily during the early 1990s, propelled by the growth in service-providing industries. In contrast, the growth of goods-producing jobs was soft early in the period, but subsequently strengthened. After 1998, growth slowed considerably, especially in the goods-producing sector, which declined 12 percent from 1998 to 2003. The construction industry is the only goods-producing industry with higher employment in 2003 than in 1990.

Employment by Industry: Kansas

(Numbers in thousands. Not seasonally adjusted.)

Industry	January	February	March	April	May	June	July	August	September	October	November	December	Annual Average
STATEWIDE													
Total nonfarm													
1990	1062.3	1070.3	1080.2	1091.8	1099.1	1101.9	1071.8	1078.0	1099.5	1098.2	1106.5	1102.3	1088.4
1991	1063.1	1070.4	1083.8	1098.7	1102.2	1101.5	1091.1	1091.2	1109.2	1109.3	1110.6	1113.5	1095.3
1992	1087.9	1093.8	1102.3	1123.8	1123.3	1122.2	1105.8	1110.0	1122.9	1125.6	1132.1	1130.4	1115.0
1993	1097.3	1108.1	1119.7	1137.7	1141.0	1148.2	1128.5	1124.9	1148.3	1145.8	1147.4	1153.4	1133.3
1994	1125.9	1133.5	1149.6	1162.0	1171.2	1179.5	1149.3	1160.2	1183.4	1184.6	1196.4	1194.0	1165.8
1995	1165.3	1176.6	1189.2	1197.4	1203.3	1208.8	1186.3	1188.4	1211.2	1212.9	1212.8	1224.7	1198.0
1996	1186.7	1198.6	1214.4	1229.8	1229.7	1238.4	1208.6	1214.9	1238.8	1245.2	1255.7	1259.3	1226.6
1997	1222.1	1233.7	1250.3	1267.7	1278.7	1280.5	1261.7	1261.1	1281.8	1288.2	1294.7	1300.8	1268.4
1998	1273.4	1285.1	1292.4	1314.0	1323.4	1326.2	1303.9	1304.2	1321.4	1329.9	1334.5	1338.8	1312.3
1999	1298.2	1308.3	1318.7	1330.7	1331.0	1336.8	1319.7	1312.8	1329.8	1340.5	1346.3	1352.3	1327.1
2000	1316.1	1318.8	1333.2	1349.6	1358.8	1364.1	1332.6	1331.4	1349.7	1358.2	1363.6	1362.5	1344.9
2001	1328.9	1331.9	1345.7	1355.5	1361.8	1364.3	1336.7	1332.5	1350.4	1354.1	1355.0	1355.1	1347.7
2002	1319.8	1318.6	1330.6	1344.4	1350.9	1353.6	1324.9	1323.6	1338.6	1334.9	1340.7	1339.7	1335.0
2003	1300.0	1300.8	1307.0	1314.1	1323.3	1323.5	1299.6	1293.7	1310.3	1319.8	1326.0	1324.3	1311.9
Total private													
1990	849.8	852.1	860.7	871.1	878.1	888.4	884.6	884.4	884.0	878.5	877.3	880.1	874.0
1991	848.1	850.1	860.0	870.0	876.7	885.4	888.6	889.8	889.8	885.7	885.4	887.2	876.4
1992	867.3	868.0	874.6	888.4	893.4	897.7	899.3	898.0	896.9	895.4	895.0	897.7	889.3
1993	872.7	877.8	885.0	899.6	905.3	914.7	914.3	915.7	917.1	912.2	913.0	918.4	903.8
1994	896.0	898.4	912.1	924.3	931.9	944.3	944.7	946.4	948.4	943.9	947.4	951.4	932.4
1995	931.3	936.4	946.2	952.9	959.5	970.0	968.2	972.1	974.4	972.3	971.0	982.2	961.3
1996	957.1	960.7	972.2	987.6	995.0	1003.0	1003.1	1006.2	1004.7	1004.0	1009.6	1014.7	993.1
1997	989.0	994.9	1007.4	1024.3	1034.5	1045.3	1045.3	1047.8	1049.7	1047.7	1052.4	1057.2	1033.0
1998	1036.6	1043.3	1047.7	1067.1	1074.7	1085.8	1082.3	1084.4	1082.2	1084.4	1087.8	1092.8	1072.4
1999	1061.8	1066.2	1072.7	1082.9	1085.6	1096.2	1099.3	1095.3	1093.2	1094.7	1098.2	1103.5	1087.5
2000	1076.8	1076.2	1085.5	1097.6	1102.5	1112.5	1106.5	1108.0	1109.3	1107.0	1109.5	1108.9	1100.0
2001	1083.8	1083.1	1093.0	1101.4	1106.9	1116.2	1107.7	1107.2	1102.6	1098.3	1097.6	1097.5	1099.6
2002	1069.3	1066.5	1074.6	1087.8	1092.0	1097.9	1092.3	1092.8	1089.6	1080.6	1084.3	1083.2	1084.2
2003	1049.4	1048.2	1051.3	1058.5	1065.0	1068.5	1068.3	1065.7	1064.2	1065.5	1069.1	1067.4	1061.8
Goods-producing													
1990	220.6	222.5	225.8	229.4	231.5	236.4	235.5	232.9	233.5	232.2	229.5	229.9	229.9
1991	216.1	218.1	222.0	224.8	226.4	229.7	232.0	231.6	231.1	231.6	229.6	228.6	226.8
1992	222.6	222.5	224.2	228.9	230.0	231.9	232.8	231.5	231.1	230.4	228.8	226.3	228.4
1993	216.9	218.3	220.3	224.7	226.7	231.3	232.1	232.5	231.8	231.4	229.0	227.5	226.8
1994	220.4	220.9	226.2	230.3	233.5	238.3	238.8	238.1	238.9	239.2	238.4	236.5	233.2
1995	230.9	233.2	236.3	238.2	239.6	243.3	243.6	243.6	244.1	244.3	236.6	243.0	239.7
1996	237.3	238.6	242.6	248.1	250.5	255.2	256.5	256.8	254.8	254.1	254.3	253.9	250.2
1997	250.2	252.7	257.4	262.6	265.5	270.6	271.0	271.2	269.9	270.4	270.3	268.5	265.0
1998	263.2	265.7	265.4	274.0	276.7	278.8	277.6	279.7	278.0	277.9	276.4	276.2	274.1
1999	269.6	271.0	272.6	275.6	276.5	280.2	280.9	278.7	276.7	275.1	274.0	273.2	275.3
2000	267.5	267.4	269.6	273.0	274.3	278.4	276.7	275.7	274.9	273.2	271.3	267.4	272.5
2001	261.4	259.6	263.4	267.4	268.5	271.5	270.4	269.8	266.9	264.5	263.0	259.1	265.5
2002	250.2	248.5	250.3	252.5	253.9	256.8	255.3	256.2	254.0	249.4	247.9	246.1	251.8
2003	237.8	238.9	240.0	240.0	242.8	242.7	244.4	243.5	242.1	241.3	240.9	239.1	241.1
Natural resources and mining													
1990	8.9	8.9	8.9	9.1	9.1	9.5	9.6	9.5	9.6	9.8	9.9	10.1	9.4
1991	9.0	9.0	9.0	8.9	8.9	8.9	9.1	9.1	8.9	8.8	8.7	8.7	8.9
1992	8.4	8.4	8.5	8.5	8.5	8.5	8.4	8.2	8.3	8.2	8.2	8.1	8.3
1993	7.8	7.8	7.7	8.0	8.1	8.2	8.1	8.2	8.1	7.9	7.9	7.8	7.9
1994	7.6	7.4	7.6	7.5	7.6	7.8	7.8	7.8	7.8	7.7	7.6	7.7	7.6
1995	7.4	7.4	7.5	7.4	7.5	7.5	7.5	7.5	7.4	7.4	7.4	7.4	7.4
1996	7.4	7.4	7.5	7.5	7.4	7.5	7.5	7.5	7.4	7.3	7.5	7.5	7.4
1997	7.5	7.5	7.5	7.8	7.7	7.9	7.8	7.8	7.8	7.7	7.6	7.7	7.7
1998	7.5	7.5	7.3	7.2	7.2	7.1	7.0	6.9	6.7	6.6	6.5	6.5	7.0
1999	6.2	6.1	6.2	5.9	6.0	6.0	6.1	6.0	6.1	6.1	6.1	6.3	6.1
2000	6.2	6.2	6.4	6.6	6.6	6.8	6.6	6.7	6.7	6.9	7.0	6.9	6.6
2001	6.6	6.6	6.7	6.8	7.0	7.1	7.1	7.3	7.3	7.1	7.0	7.0	7.0
2002	6.6	6.5	6.5	6.6	6.6	6.7	6.6	6.5	6.5	6.4	6.4	6.4	6.5
2003	6.2	6.2	6.3	6.4	6.5	6.6	6.5	6.6	6.6	6.6	6.6	6.5	6.5
Construction													
1990	37.9	37.5	39.4	42.2	44.0	46.8	46.6	46.5	45.1	44.5	43.6	41.9	43.0
1991	35.7	37.5	39.4	42.5	43.8	45.9	47.4	47.1	46.6	46.1	44.7	43.8	43.3
1992	39.6	40.0	41.6	45.5	47.0	48.3	49.6	49.6	48.9	48.3	46.8	44.5	45.8
1993	37.5	38.9	41.3	44.8	47.2	50.4	50.5	51.6	51.1	51.1	48.8	46.5	46.6
1994	41.2	41.2	45.4	48.2	50.6	53.4	55.3	54.8	53.5	52.8	51.3	48.8	49.7
1995	44.6	45.6	48.1	50.8	51.7	54.3	55.9	56.0	55.7	56.0	55.3	53.9	52.3
1996	48.5	49.5	52.5	56.8	58.5	61.0	62.1	61.8	60.0	59.0	57.8	56.6	57.0
1997	51.3	52.5	56.0	59.1	61.2	63.4	63.7	63.4	61.8	61.2	59.9	57.3	59.2
1998	53.2	54.8	54.5	61.0	62.8	65.1	66.3	66.2	64.5	64.0	62.5	62.2	61.4
1999	57.2	58.6	60.2	65.0	66.3	69.2	70.1	69.9	68.4	67.3	66.3	64.5	65.3
2000	60.5	60.3	62.2	65.9	67.1	69.7	69.8	69.8	68.7	67.0	64.6	61.4	65.6
2001	57.9	57.5	60.7	64.9	66.6	68.9	68.3	68.0	65.9	65.1	64.5	62.2	64.2
2002	58.2	57.6	59.5	62.4	64.1	66.4	67.2	66.7	65.2	64.3	63.5	62.4	63.1
2003	58.0	58.1	59.7	62.2	63.6	65.8	66.6	65.7	64.4	63.5	63.1	61.3	62.7

Employment by Industry: Kansas—*Continued*

(Numbers in thousands. Not seasonally adjusted.)

Industry	January	February	March	April	May	June	July	August	September	October	November	December	Annual Average
STATEWIDE—*Continued*													
Manufacturing													
1990	173.8	176.1	177.5	178.1	178.4	180.1	179.3	176.9	178.8	177.9	176.0	177.9	177.5
1991	171.4	171.6	173.6	173.4	173.7	174.9	175.5	175.4	175.6	176.7	176.2	176.1	174.5
1992	174.6	174.1	174.1	174.9	174.5	175.1	174.8	173.7	173.9	173.9	173.8	173.7	174.2
1993	171.6	171.6	171.3	171.9	171.4	172.7	173.5	172.7	172.6	172.4	172.3	173.2	172.2
1994	171.6	172.3	173.2	174.6	175.3	177.1	175.7	175.5	177.6	178.7	179.5	180.0	175.9
1995	178.9	180.2	180.7	180.0	180.4	181.5	180.2	180.1	181.0	180.9	173.9	181.7	179.9
1996	181.4	181.7	182.6	183.8	184.6	186.7	186.9	187.5	187.4	187.8	189.0	189.8	185.7
1997	191.4	192.7	193.9	195.7	196.6	199.3	199.5	200.0	200.3	201.5	202.8	203.5	198.1
1998	202.5	203.4	203.6	205.8	206.7	206.6	204.3	206.6	206.8	207.3	207.4	207.5	205.7
1999	206.2	206.3	206.2	204.7	204.2	205.0	204.7	202.8	202.2	201.7	201.6	202.4	204.0
2000	200.8	200.9	201.0	200.5	200.6	201.9	200.3	199.2	199.5	199.3	199.7	199.1	200.2
2001	196.9	195.5	196.0	195.7	194.9	195.5	195.0	194.5	193.7	192.3	191.5	189.9	194.3
2002	185.4	184.4	184.3	183.5	183.2	183.7	181.5	183.0	182.3	178.7	178.0	177.3	182.1
2003	173.6	174.6	174.0	171.4	172.7	170.3	171.3	171.2	171.1	171.2	171.2	171.3	172.0
Service-providing													
1990	841.7	847.8	854.4	862.4	867.6	865.5	836.3	845.1	866.0	866.0	877.0	872.4	858.5
1991	847.0	852.3	861.8	873.9	875.8	871.8	859.1	859.6	878.1	877.7	881.0	884.9	868.5
1992	865.3	871.3	878.1	894.9	893.3	890.3	873.0	878.5	891.8	895.2	903.3	904.1	886.5
1993	880.4	889.8	899.4	913.0	914.3	916.9	896.4	892.4	916.5	914.4	918.4	925.9	906.4
1994	905.5	912.6	923.4	931.7	937.7	941.2	910.5	922.1	944.5	945.4	958.0	957.5	932.5
1995	934.4	943.4	952.9	959.2	963.7	965.5	942.7	944.8	967.1	968.6	976.2	981.7	958.3
1996	949.4	960.0	971.8	981.7	979.2	983.2	952.1	958.1	984.0	991.1	1001.4	1005.4	976.4
1997	971.9	981.0	992.9	1005.1	1013.2	1009.9	990.7	989.9	1011.9	1017.8	1024.4	1032.3	1003.4
1998	1010.2	1019.4	1027.0	1040.0	1046.7	1047.4	1026.3	1024.5	1043.4	1052.0	1058.1	1062.6	1038.1
1999	1028.6	1037.3	1046.1	1055.1	1054.5	1056.6	1038.8	1034.1	1053.1	1065.4	1072.3	1079.1	1051.8
2000	1048.6	1051.4	1063.6	1076.6	1084.5	1085.7	1055.9	1055.7	1074.8	1085.0	1092.3	1095.1	1072.4
2001	1067.5	1072.3	1082.3	1088.1	1093.3	1092.8	1066.3	1062.7	1083.5	1089.6	1092.0	1096.0	1082.2
2002	1069.6	1070.1	1080.3	1091.9	1097.0	1096.8	1069.6	1067.4	1084.6	1085.5	1092.8	1093.6	1083.3
2003	1062.2	1061.9	1067.0	1074.1	1080.5	1080.8	1055.2	1050.2	1068.2	1078.5	1085.1	1085.2	1070.7
Trade, transportation, and utilities													
1990	240.7	238.5	240.4	240.5	242.5	245.0	244.3	244.5	244.4	243.1	245.3	247.0	243.0
1991	233.2	230.5	232.1	235.4	236.7	238.6	237.7	238.1	238.2	237.9	240.4	243.0	236.8
1992	232.8	230.8	231.9	234.6	235.6	236.6	237.5	237.3	237.0	237.9	240.5	243.4	236.3
1993	235.1	234.0	235.1	238.7	238.7	239.8	240.2	239.8	240.6	240.8	244.2	247.8	239.5
1994	239.4	239.0	241.1	242.7	244.7	247.2	247.6	248.3	249.1	250.0	254.3	257.9	246.7
1995	248.5	247.2	248.3	249.4	251.1	253.0	254.3	254.7	255.6	257.0	262.0	264.7	253.8
1996	254.6	252.7	254.6	256.4	257.9	258.9	258.2	258.8	258.8	260.9	265.5	268.5	258.8
1997	257.7	256.2	258.2	260.1	262.1	264.6	263.3	263.4	266.6	267.7	271.8	274.6	263.9
1998	265.6	264.8	265.4	267.8	270.3	272.2	270.3	270.0	270.5	273.5	278.2	281.5	270.8
1999	270.4	269.0	269.8	270.4	271.0	273.8	274.0	273.1	272.7	277.4	281.7	285.1	274.0
2000	273.6	271.4	272.3	273.8	274.5	276.8	273.8	274.8	274.7	275.8	280.5	282.6	275.4
2001	272.5	269.2	269.2	270.4	271.9	272.5	271.3	271.8	270.5	271.6	274.1	276.5	271.8
2002	266.6	262.8	263.1	266.4	267.4	268.7	266.0	266.0	265.6	265.9	269.4	271.0	266.6
2003	260.2	258.0	258.3	260.0	261.4	261.8	261.7	261.4	262.0	262.7	265.5	266.4	261.6
Wholesale trade													
1990	58.2	58.3	58.8	59.2	59.6	61.1	61.2	60.4	60.1	60.2	60.0	59.9	59.7
1991	55.7	55.7	56.1	56.8	56.9	58.3	57.9	57.5	57.0	56.5	56.1	56.2	56.7
1992	55.3	55.2	55.2	55.8	55.8	56.8	57.2	56.4	55.8	55.3	54.9	54.9	55.7
1993	55.3	55.5	55.9	56.8	57.1	57.8	57.9	57.1	56.9	57.1	56.9	57.0	56.7
1994	56.5	56.5	57.1	56.8	57.2	58.2	58.5	58.2	57.9	57.6	57.8	58.0	57.5
1995	57.3	57.5	57.8	57.9	58.3	59.2	59.7	58.8	58.3	58.2	58.3	58.5	58.3
1996	58.0	58.0	58.3	58.9	59.2	60.0	60.0	59.7	59.4	59.5	59.7	60.0	59.2
1997	59.7	59.9	60.5	60.8	61.3	62.4	62.6	61.9	61.6	61.3	61.3	61.3	61.2
1998	61.1	61.3	61.6	62.4	62.9	64.2	63.5	62.7	62.3	62.8	62.5	62.5	62.5
1999	62.3	62.0	62.2	62.3	62.3	63.6	63.8	62.9	62.5	62.1	61.7	61.9	62.5
2000	61.6	61.6	61.9	61.6	61.9	63.2	62.6	62.0	61.7	61.6	61.3	61.4	61.9
2001	61.4	61.2	61.3	61.5	61.9	62.8	62.5	61.7	61.1	61.3	60.9	61.1	61.6
2002	60.6	60.5	60.7	61.2	61.1	61.9	61.9	61.3	60.8	60.3	60.1	60.1	60.9
2003	58.8	58.6	58.6	58.5	58.6	59.4	59.5	58.8	58.4	58.2	58.0	57.8	58.6
Retail trade													
1990	136.6	134.3	134.8	134.9	136.1	136.8	136.2	137.3	137.2	137.2	139.5	140.7	136.8
1991	131.0	128.5	129.4	131.7	132.4	132.7	133.5	134.2	134.1	134.3	137.1	138.8	133.1
1992	131.9	130.0	129.8	131.8	132.5	132.4	133.4	134.0	134.4	135.9	139.2	141.5	133.9
1993	133.6	132.4	132.6	134.4	133.7	133.8	134.0	134.5	135.1	135.3	138.8	141.8	135.0
1994	135.6	135.0	136.1	137.8	138.7	139.7	140.0	140.9	141.7	142.2	146.3	149.6	140.3
1995	141.9	140.3	140.9	141.3	142.4	143.5	143.6	145.0	146.5	146.8	151.2	153.5	144.7
1996	145.2	143.4	144.8	145.2	146.2	146.5	146.3	147.2	147.3	148.2	152.7	155.6	147.3
1997	146.0	144.4	145.6	146.5	147.8	148.8	148.9	151.0	151.6	152.7	156.9	160.1	150.0
1998	152.6	151.5	151.8	153.6	155.4	156.4	153.9	154.1	154.2	156.5	161.6	165.5	155.6
1999	155.2	154.2	155.1	155.9	156.8	157.8	157.8	158.1	158.0	161.1	165.7	168.9	158.7
2000	157.9	155.9	156.4	156.7	157.3	158.5	156.6	157.8	157.8	158.2	163.5	165.5	158.5
2001	156.7	154.0	154.1	155.0	156.0	156.6	155.8	156.3	155.4	155.7	159.2	161.8	156.4
2002	153.9	150.7	150.9	152.6	153.5	154.1	152.1	152.2	152.2	152.6	156.3	158.0	153.3
2003	149.5	147.5	147.9	148.8	149.8	150.3	150.2	150.7	150.9	151.6	154.6	155.9	150.6

Employment by Industry: Kansas—*Continued*

(Numbers in thousands. Not seasonally adjusted.)

Industry	January	February	March	April	May	June	July	August	September	October	November	December	Annual Average
STATEWIDE—*Continued*													
Transportation and utilities													
1990	45.9	45.9	46.8	46.4	46.8	47.1	46.9	46.8	47.1	45.7	45.8	46.4	46.4
1991	46.5	46.3	46.6	46.9	47.4	47.6	46.3	46.4	47.1	47.1	47.2	48.0	46.9
1992	45.6	45.6	46.9	47.0	47.3	47.4	46.9	46.9	46.8	46.7	46.4	47.0	46.7
1993	46.2	46.1	46.6	47.5	47.9	48.2	48.3	48.2	48.6	48.4	48.5	49.0	47.7
1994	47.3	47.5	47.9	48.1	48.8	49.3	49.1	49.2	49.5	50.2	50.2	50.3	48.9
1995	49.3	49.4	49.6	50.2	50.4	50.3	51.0	50.9	50.8	52.0	52.5	52.7	50.7
1996	51.4	51.3	51.5	52.3	52.5	52.4	51.9	51.9	52.1	53.2	53.1	52.9	52.2
1997	52.0	51.9	52.1	52.8	53.0	53.4	51.8	50.5	53.4	53.7	53.6	53.2	52.6
1998	51.9	52.0	52.0	51.8	52.0	51.6	52.9	53.2	54.0	54.2	54.1	53.5	52.8
1999	52.9	52.8	52.5	52.2	51.9	52.4	52.4	52.1	52.2	54.2	54.3	54.3	52.9
2000	54.1	53.9	54.0	55.5	55.3	55.1	54.6	55.0	55.2	56.0	55.7	55.7	55.0
2001	54.4	54.0	53.8	53.9	54.0	53.1	53.0	53.8	54.0	54.6	54.0	53.6	53.9
2002	52.1	51.6	51.5	52.6	52.8	52.7	52.0	52.5	52.6	53.0	53.0	52.9	52.4
2003	51.9	51.9	51.8	52.7	53.0	52.1	52.0	51.9	52.7	52.9	52.9	52.7	52.4
Information													
1990	30.2	30.2	30.2	30.5	30.4	30.6	30.9	31.1	30.5	29.8	30.2	30.3	30.4
1991	30.8	30.3	30.5	30.3	30.2	30.4	30.4	30.4	30.0	29.5	29.8	30.0	30.2
1992	29.7	29.7	30.0	29.8	29.8	30.0	29.8	29.5	29.1	28.7	28.7	29.2	29.5
1993	29.9	30.2	30.5	30.7	30.7	31.1	31.2	31.2	30.8	30.6	30.8	31.1	30.7
1994	31.4	31.4	31.8	31.8	32.1	32.4	32.7	32.4	32.0	31.8	32.0	32.6	32.0
1995	32.5	32.5	32.9	33.0	33.3	33.6	33.5	33.5	33.4	32.9	33.3	33.9	33.1
1996	33.6	33.7	33.9	34.7	35.0	35.2	35.1	35.0	34.6	34.6	34.6	35.2	34.6
1997	35.2	35.8	36.4	36.8	37.4	37.6	37.6	37.4	36.3	36.5	36.6	37.3	36.7
1998	38.2	38.3	38.7	39.0	38.7	39.2	39.1	38.9	38.5	38.5	38.8	39.4	38.8
1999	41.2	41.5	41.7	41.7	41.7	42.2	43.4	43.8	43.3	43.9	44.2	44.8	42.8
2000	44.8	44.8	45.3	47.0	47.2	47.9	48.9	49.0	49.3	48.4	49.3	49.6	47.6
2001	51.7	52.1	52.3	51.8	51.5	52.4	51.8	51.8	51.4	50.8	51.0	51.4	51.7
2002	51.4	51.3	51.4	51.6	51.2	51.0	50.7	50.2	49.5	48.7	49.2	49.3	50.5
2003	48.8	48.1	48.0	47.4	47.1	47.3	46.9	45.7	46.0	46.1	46.5	46.7	47.1
Financial activities													
1990	59.1	59.1	59.2	59.9	60.1	60.9	60.8	60.5	59.7	59.6	59.4	59.5	59.8
1991	58.4	58.5	58.7	58.8	59.1	60.1	59.9	59.7	59.0	58.2	58.2	58.4	58.9
1992	58.1	58.3	58.3	58.7	59.1	59.6	59.6	59.4	58.6	58.8	58.6	58.9	58.8
1993	58.2	58.2	58.6	58.6	58.7	59.6	59.8	59.8	59.3	59.1	59.0	59.4	59.0
1994	59.1	59.0	59.0	58.7	58.9	59.4	59.7	59.7	59.1	58.4	58.5	58.8	59.0
1995	57.7	57.5	57.8	58.4	58.6	59.2	59.6	59.8	59.3	59.6	59.6	60.0	58.9
1996	59.0	59.0	59.4	59.6	59.8	60.4	60.6	61.0	60.4	60.4	60.3	60.8	60.0
1997	61.3	61.1	61.7	62.3	62.3	62.5	62.9	63.0	62.2	62.5	62.5	63.5	62.3
1998	63.2	63.3	63.6	63.8	63.8	64.7	65.2	65.1	64.5	64.9	64.9	65.1	64.3
1999	64.8	64.8	65.2	64.8	64.6	65.3	65.7	65.4	64.7	64.8	64.7	65.0	65.0
2000	64.7	64.7	64.5	65.0	65.5	66.1	66.3	66.4	65.9	65.8	65.6	66.6	65.6
2001	66.0	66.0	66.3	66.5	67.0	67.8	68.4	68.3	67.6	67.7	67.9	68.4	67.3
2002	68.2	68.4	68.8	68.4	68.7	69.0	69.5	69.3	68.8	69.0	69.3	69.6	68.9
2003	68.5	68.5	69.0	69.6	69.8	70.3	70.5	70.4	70.4	70.5	70.4	70.8	69.9
Professional and business services													
1990	74.4	75.2	76.3	77.3	77.4	77.9	77.6	78.2	77.9	77.4	77.1	76.9	76.9
1991	80.8	81.7	83.7	84.6	85.3	86.4	88.8	88.6	88.6	87.3	87.1	86.3	85.7
1992	85.7	86.5	87.9	90.2	90.2	91.3	92.1	92.5	92.4	90.9	90.3	91.2	90.1
1993	89.6	91.4	92.9	94.1	94.6	95.5	95.9	96.2	96.4	95.9	95.7	96.7	94.5
1994	93.4	94.1	96.4	99.8	99.2	101.4	102.9	103.1	103.7	101.9	101.7	102.3	99.9
1995	100.9	102.9	104.0	104.2	104.0	105.3	105.5	107.1	106.5	105.6	106.1	106.5	104.8
1996	104.6	106.3	108.5	110.6	110.9	111.4	112.8	113.7	113.4	113.7	114.2	115.0	111.2
1997	109.4	111.6	113.0	116.2	116.8	118.8	119.8	120.3	120.6	120.4	120.0	121.1	117.3
1998	119.2	120.9	122.1	123.7	123.2	127.0	127.0	126.7	125.7	127.3	126.5	126.7	124.7
1999	121.2	122.3	124.2	127.1	126.0	127.9	129.4	128.8	129.4	128.1	128.8	129.7	126.9
2000	127.1	126.3	129.5	129.7	129.9	131.8	129.3	130.3	130.2	131.1	131.0	131.3	129.8
2001	127.6	129.1	131.1	130.0	130.0	132.4	129.9	129.4	129.5	128.0	126.5	126.4	129.2
2002	123.4	124.3	126.3	129.1	128.4	129.6	130.1	129.7	129.1	126.2	127.0	126.7	127.5
2003	122.5	122.0	121.8	125.0	124.6	126.6	125.0	125.0	124.5	125.0	125.0	125.1	124.3
Educational and health services													
1990	102.3	103.3	103.7	105.0	105.6	104.8	104.2	105.1	106.6	106.6	107.1	107.3	105.1
1991	106.2	107.1	107.6	108.3	108.8	107.8	108.7	109.1	111.2	111.4	111.6	111.9	109.1
1992	112.3	113.1	113.8	114.1	114.5	113.8	113.8	113.6	115.7	116.2	116.4	116.8	114.5
1993	115.3	116.4	116.6	118.1	118.3	117.6	117.6	117.7	119.8	119.0	119.2	119.3	117.9
1994	119.3	120.1	121.1	121.4	121.6	120.6	120.3	120.7	122.1	122.1	122.6	123.0	121.2
1995	123.1	124.4	125.3	126.1	126.8	126.5	124.9	125.7	128.0	127.2	127.9	128.1	126.1
1996	127.3	128.2	128.9	129.9	130.2	129.4	129.1	129.5	132.0	131.8	132.8	133.1	130.1
1997	131.4	132.4	133.2	134.8	136.2	135.5	135.3	136.2	138.8	139.5	140.0	140.7	136.2
1998	138.5	139.5	140.2	141.0	141.5	140.9	141.0	141.3	143.1	143.1	144.4	144.8	141.6
1999	143.2	144.3	144.8	144.7	144.9	143.8	144.5	144.6	146.5	145.9	145.9	146.2	144.9
2000	144.8	145.5	146.2	146.9	147.3	146.4	147.3	147.8	150.4	150.6	151.3	151.7	148.0
2001	150.0	151.6	152.3	153.4	153.8	153.4	151.7	152.2	154.3	153.3	154.2	155.4	153.0
2002	154.2	155.1	155.9	157.8	158.4	157.1	155.8	156.3	158.7	159.0	159.5	159.6	157.3
2003	156.0	156.3	156.0	157.9	157.6	155.4	154.7	154.4	156.2	157.9	159.0	158.5	156.7

Employment by Industry: Kansas—*Continued*

(Numbers in thousands. Not seasonally adjusted.)

Industry	January	February	March	April	May	June	July	August	September	October	November	December	Annual Average
STATEWIDE—*Continued*													
Leisure and hospitality													
1990	82.3	83.0	84.5	87.4	89.3	91.0	89.6	90.7	90.1	88.7	87.8	88.0	87.7
1991	81.9	83.2	84.4	86.5	88.8	90.4	89.3	90.7	90.3	88.1	87.0	87.1	87.3
1992	84.7	85.7	86.9	90.2	92.2	92.4	91.7	92.4	91.4	90.0	89.5	89.4	89.7
1993	85.8	87.2	88.6	91.9	94.6	96.2	94.4	95.5	95.1	91.9	91.7	92.6	92.1
1994	89.8	90.6	92.9	95.5	97.7	100.3	98.5	100.0	99.3	96.1	95.5	95.8	96.0
1995	93.2	94.5	96.7	98.6	101.2	103.4	102.0	102.5	102.3	100.1	99.6	99.7	99.4
1996	96.0	97.0	98.9	102.3	104.6	106.3	104.8	105.3	104.6	102.2	101.5	101.8	102.1
1997	97.8	98.9	100.9	104.4	106.8	107.7	107.7	108.5	107.2	102.6	102.6	102.6	104.0
1998	100.2	101.9	103.3	107.5	110.2	112.2	112.1	112.6	111.6	109.0	108.4	108.5	108.1
1999	101.8	103.2	104.1	108.1	110.1	111.4	110.7	110.5	109.4	108.5	108.0	108.0	107.8
2000	103.1	104.5	106.4	110.8	112.1	113.3	112.2	112.0	111.6	109.8	108.4	107.5	109.3
2001	102.9	103.7	106.1	109.5	111.7	113.5	111.6	111.6	110.0	109.4	108.2	107.3	108.8
2002	103.0	103.7	106.0	108.9	110.9	111.8	111.8	112.3	110.6	109.5	109.2	108.0	108.8
2003	103.4	103.9	105.5	106.2	108.6	111.3	112.1	112.2	110.5	109.9	109.6	108.6	108.5
Other services													
1990	40.2	40.3	40.6	41.1	41.3	41.8	41.7	41.4	41.3	41.1	40.9	41.2	41.0
1991	40.7	40.7	41.0	41.3	41.4	42.0	41.8	41.6	41.4	41.7	41.7	41.9	41.4
1992	41.4	41.4	41.6	41.9	42.0	42.1	42.0	41.8	41.6	42.5	42.2	42.5	41.9
1993	41.9	42.1	42.4	42.8	43.0	43.6	43.1	43.0	43.3	43.5	43.4	44.0	43.0
1994	43.2	43.3	43.6	44.1	44.2	44.7	44.2	44.1	44.2	44.4	44.4	44.5	44.0
1995	44.5	44.2	44.9	45.0	44.9	45.7	44.8	45.2	45.2	45.6	45.9	46.3	45.1
1996	44.7	45.2	45.4	46.0	46.1	46.2	46.0	46.1	46.1	46.3	46.4	46.4	45.9
1997	46.0	46.2	46.6	47.1	47.4	48.0	47.7	47.8	48.1	48.1	48.6	48.9	47.5
1998	48.5	48.9	49.0	50.3	50.3	50.8	50.0	50.1	50.3	50.2	50.2	50.6	49.9
1999	49.6	50.1	50.3	50.5	50.8	51.6	50.7	50.4	50.5	51.0	50.9	51.5	50.7
2000	51.2	51.6	51.7	51.4	51.7	51.8	52.0	52.0	52.3	52.3	52.1	52.2	51.9
2001	51.7	51.8	52.3	52.4	52.5	52.7	52.6	52.3	52.4	53.0	52.7	53.0	52.5
2002	52.3	52.4	52.8	53.1	53.1	53.9	53.1	52.8	53.3	52.9	52.8	52.9	53.0
2003	52.2	52.5	52.7	52.4	53.1	53.1	53.0	53.1	52.5	52.1	52.2	52.2	52.6
Government													
1990	212.5	218.2	219.5	220.7	221.0	213.5	187.2	193.6	215.5	219.7	229.2	222.2	214.4
1991	215.0	220.3	223.8	228.7	225.5	216.1	202.5	201.4	219.4	223.6	225.2	226.3	218.9
1992	220.6	225.8	227.7	235.4	229.9	224.5	206.5	212.0	226.0	230.2	237.1	232.7	225.7
1993	224.6	230.3	234.7	238.1	235.7	233.5	214.2	209.2	231.2	233.6	234.4	235.0	229.5
1994	229.9	235.1	237.5	237.7	239.3	235.2	204.6	213.8	235.0	240.7	249.0	242.6	233.3
1995	234.0	240.2	243.0	244.5	243.8	238.8	218.1	216.3	236.8	240.6	241.8	242.5	236.7
1996	229.6	237.9	242.2	242.2	234.7	235.4	205.5	208.7	234.1	241.2	246.1	244.6	233.5
1997	233.1	238.8	242.9	243.4	244.2	235.2	216.4	213.3	232.1	240.5	242.3	243.6	235.5
1998	236.8	241.8	244.7	246.9	248.7	240.4	221.6	219.8	239.2	245.5	246.7	246.0	239.8
1999	236.4	242.1	246.0	247.8	245.4	240.6	220.4	217.5	236.6	245.8	248.1	248.8	239.6
2000	239.3	242.6	247.7	252.0	256.3	251.6	226.1	223.4	240.4	251.2	254.1	253.6	244.9
2001	245.1	248.8	252.7	254.1	254.9	248.1	229.0	225.3	247.8	255.8	257.4	257.6	248.1
2002	250.5	252.1	256.0	256.6	258.9	255.7	232.6	230.8	249.0	254.3	256.4	256.5	250.8
2003	250.6	252.6	255.7	255.6	258.3	255.0	231.3	228.0	246.1	254.3	256.9	256.9	250.1
Federal government													
1990	29.3	29.2	29.6	29.7	29.5	29.6	30.7	29.5	29.0	28.3	28.3	28.7	29.2
1991	28.2	28.1	28.2	28.6	29.0	29.3	29.2	29.2	29.0	28.9	29.0	29.4	28.8
1992	29.5	29.3	29.4	29.7	29.8	29.9	29.6	29.5	29.0	29.1	28.9	29.1	29.4
1993	28.6	28.6	28.7	29.2	29.3	29.6	30.6	30.8	30.3	29.7	29.4	29.7	29.5
1994	29.2	29.2	29.3	29.4	29.4	29.7	30.1	30.0	29.5	29.4	29.2	29.4	29.4
1995	29.1	29.2	29.4	29.3	29.1	29.1	28.9	28.7	28.3	28.4	27.8	27.7	28.7
1996	27.3	27.4	27.6	27.4	27.3	27.4	27.0	26.9	26.7	26.6	26.9	26.9	27.1
1997	27.0	26.8	26.8	26.8	26.9	26.9	26.9	26.9	26.8	26.4	26.6	26.8	26.8
1998	26.7	26.6	26.5	26.6	26.7	26.8	26.6	26.6	26.4	25.7	26.0	26.5	26.5
1999	25.9	26.0	25.9	26.2	25.7	25.8	25.9	25.9	25.8	26.1	26.3	26.5	26.0
2000	25.5	25.8	27.1	27.4	30.3	31.1	29.2	29.2	26.2	26.5	26.8	27.0	27.7
2001	26.3	26.2	26.1	26.2	26.4	26.7	26.7	26.5	26.3	26.3	26.5	26.9	26.4
2002	26.3	26.2	26.2	26.2	26.1	26.8	26.4	26.3	26.1	26.3	26.5	26.8	26.4
2003	26.2	26.2	26.1	26.2	26.3	26.4	26.2	26.2	25.9	25.9	26.0	26.3	26.2
State government													
2001	52.0	52.5	55.1	54.7	55.1	48.3	47.3	47.3	52.5	54.8	55.3	55.2	52.5
2002	53.1	52.1	54.6	55.3	55.6	51.1	47.4	47.3	52.4	54.6	54.8	55.0	52.8
2003	54.1	53.7	54.7	54.3	54.6	50.7	46.8	46.6	51.7	54.0	54.4	54.9	52.5
Local government													
2001	166.8	170.1	171.5	173.2	173.4	173.1	155.0	151.5	169.0	174.7	175.6	175.5	169.1
2002	171.1	173.8	175.2	175.1	177.2	177.8	158.8	157.2	170.5	173.4	175.1	174.7	171.7
2003	170.3	172.7	174.9	175.1	177.4	177.9	158.3	155.2	168.5	174.4	176.5	175.7	171.4

Employment by Industry: Kansas—*Continued*

(Numbers in thousands. Not seasonally adjusted.)

Industry	January	February	March	April	May	June	July	August	September	October	November	December	Annual Average
LAWRENCE													
Total nonfarm													
1990	35.3	36.7	36.5	37.4	37.6	35.8	34.8	36.5	38.3	38.4	38.3	38.1	36.9
1991	36.0	37.2	37.4	38.8	38.5	36.0	35.4	36.7	39.1	39.6	39.8	39.4	37.8
1992	38.2	39.4	39.4	40.4	40.2	37.2	36.2	38.5	40.9	40.8	41.3	40.5	39.4
1993	39.0	40.0	40.5	40.7	41.3	38.8	37.5	39.1	41.6	42.2	42.2	42.1	40.4
1994	40.8	41.0	41.6	42.4	42.3	39.4	39.1	41.2	43.0	44.3	44.4	43.9	41.9
1995	42.5	43.3	43.5	44.4	44.4	41.3	40.6	42.5	44.6	45.3	45.7	45.6	43.6
1996	41.0	44.0	44.8	45.4	45.8	41.6	41.6	42.3	44.4	45.4	46.5	46.1	44.0
1997	43.6	45.0	46.6	47.0	47.5	43.8	43.5	43.7	46.3	47.9	48.7	48.7	46.0
1998	45.9	46.7	47.6	48.5	48.9	45.4	45.2	45.3	48.3	49.5	49.8	49.9	47.6
1999	47.1	48.3	49.3	50.3	50.5	49.0	46.5	46.2	48.7	50.1	50.9	50.9	49.0
2000	48.0	49.3	50.5	50.2	50.3	48.6	46.3	46.1	48.7	52.1	52.9	52.7	49.6
2001	50.8	51.1	52.1	52.6	53.0	51.1	48.9	49.5	52.3	53.7	53.8	54.0	51.9
2002	51.5	51.3	52.7	52.1	52.4	50.6	48.2	48.6	51.5	52.0	52.5	52.4	51.3
2003	50.2	50.7	51.1	52.1	52.0	50.5	48.7	48.5	50.5	51.2	51.6	51.7	50.7
Total private													
1990	23.8	24.3	24.2	25.0	25.2	25.4	25.2	25.5	26.1	25.9	25.7	25.7	25.1
1991	24.0	24.6	24.7	25.8	25.8	25.8	25.7	25.9	26.9	26.9	27.0	26.7	25.8
1992	26.1	26.6	26.6	27.3	27.4	26.8	26.4	27.0	28.1	27.9	27.9	27.5	27.1
1993	26.5	26.8	27.1	27.5	28.2	27.8	27.5	27.7	28.6	28.8	28.7	28.8	27.8
1994	27.9	27.7	28.3	29.1	29.1	28.8	29.1	29.3	30.1	30.9	30.8	30.6	29.3
1995	29.7	30.0	30.1	30.6	30.9	30.3	30.2	30.4	31.3	31.9	32.3	32.2	30.8
1996	30.4	31.0	31.3	32.0	32.3	31.6	31.5	31.8	32.5	32.2	32.8	32.7	31.8
1997	31.2	31.9	33.0	33.5	33.9	33.8	33.0	33.3	33.9	34.4	34.8	34.9	33.5
1998	33.0	33.2	33.4	34.4	34.7	34.6	34.3	34.5	35.2	35.3	35.3	35.5	34.5
1999	33.5	34.5	34.7	35.4	35.8	35.7	35.3	35.0	35.6	35.7	35.8	36.0	35.3
2000	34.0	35.2	35.7	35.2	35.2	35.1	34.8	34.9	35.8	36.9	37.5	37.4	35.6
2001	36.0	36.6	36.8	37.3	37.7	37.1	37.1	37.4	38.0	38.4	38.3	38.5	37.4
2002	36.4	36.9	37.3	36.6	36.8	36.2	36.3	36.6	37.2	36.9	37.2	37.1	36.8
2003	35.3	35.7	35.7	36.9	36.6	36.2	36.1	36.1	36.2	36.2	36.5	36.4	36.2
Goods-producing													
1990	5.0	5.0	4.9	5.0	5.0	5.3	5.3	5.2	5.2	5.0	5.0	4.9	5.0
1991	4.7	4.8	4.8	5.0	5.0	5.2	5.3	5.2	5.3	5.2	5.2	5.2	5.0
1992	5.2	5.2	5.2	5.4	5.5	5.6	5.5	5.5	5.6	5.5	5.4	5.2	5.4
1993	4.9	4.8	5.0	5.1	5.2	5.3	5.4	5.4	5.5	5.4	5.5	5.3	5.2
1994	5.1	4.9	5.1	5.6	5.5	5.7	5.9	5.8	5.7	5.9	5.9	5.8	5.5
1995	5.6	5.6	5.7	5.8	5.8	5.8	5.9	5.8	5.8	5.8	5.8	5.8	5.7
1996	5.6	5.7	5.8	6.0	6.1	6.3	6.3	6.2	6.1	5.8	6.2	6.1	6.0
1997	5.8	5.8	6.1	6.2	6.3	6.5	6.3	6.3	6.2	6.3	6.3	6.1	6.2
1998	5.9	6.0	6.0	6.2	6.3	6.5	6.4	6.4	6.5	6.1	6.3	6.2	6.2
1999	6.1	6.2	6.2	6.5	6.6	6.8	6.7	6.6	6.4	6.6	6.5	6.5	6.5
2000	6.3	6.3	6.5	6.4	6.6	6.8	6.9	6.8	6.7	6.7	6.7	6.6	6.6
2001	6.0	6.0	6.2	6.5	6.6	6.6	6.6	6.6	6.5	6.4	6.3	6.1	6.4
2002	6.1	5.9	6.0	6.0	6.0	6.1	6.2	6.3	6.1	6.1	6.0	6.0	6.1
2003	5.9	5.8	5.8	5.9	6.0	6.1	6.1	6.1	6.1	6.1	6.1	6.0	6.0
Construction and mining													
1990	1.3	1.3	1.3	1.4	1.4	1.6	1.6	1.6	1.5	1.4	1.4	1.3	1.4
1991	1.1	1.2	1.3	1.5	1.5	1.6	1.7	1.6	1.6	1.4	1.4	1.4	1.4
1992	1.4	1.4	1.4	1.6	1.7	1.7	1.7	1.7	1.7	1.6	1.5	1.4	1.5
1993	1.3	1.3	1.4	1.6	1.7	1.7	1.8	1.8	1.8	1.8	1.8	1.6	1.6
1994	1.4	1.4	1.6	1.9	2.0	2.1	2.1	2.1	2.0	1.9	1.9	1.8	1.8
1995	1.7	1.7	1.8	1.9	1.9	2.0	2.1	2.0	2.0	1.9	1.9	1.9	1.9
1996	1.8	1.8	1.9	2.1	2.2	2.3	2.3	2.2	2.1	2.0	2.1	2.0	2.0
1997	1.8	1.8	2.0	2.2	2.3	2.4	2.3	2.3	2.2	2.2	2.2	2.0	2.1
1998	1.9	2.0	2.0	2.2	2.3	2.5	2.5	2.5	2.5	2.3	2.3	2.3	2.2
1999	2.1	2.2	2.2	2.6	2.7	2.8	2.7	2.7	2.6	2.6	2.5	2.5	2.5
2000	2.3	2.3	2.4	2.5	2.6	2.8	2.8	2.7	2.6	2.5	2.5	2.4	2.5
2001	2.2	2.2	2.4	2.7	2.8	2.9	2.9	2.9	2.8	2.7	2.7	2.5	2.6
2002	2.5	2.4	2.5	2.5	2.5	2.6	2.6	2.7	2.6	2.6	2.5	2.5	2.5
2003	2.4	2.4	2.4	2.5	2.6	2.7	2.7	2.7	2.7	2.7	2.7	2.6	2.6
Manufacturing													
1990	3.7	3.7	3.6	3.6	3.6	3.7	3.7	3.6	3.7	3.6	3.6	3.6	3.6
1991	3.6	3.6	3.5	3.5	3.5	3.6	3.6	3.6	3.7	3.8	3.8	3.8	3.6
1992	3.8	3.8	3.8	3.8	3.8	3.9	3.8	3.8	3.9	3.9	3.9	3.8	3.8
1993	3.6	3.5	3.6	3.5	3.5	3.6	3.6	3.6	3.7	3.6	3.7	3.7	3.6
1994	3.7	3.5	3.5	3.7	3.5	3.6	3.8	3.7	3.7	4.0	4.0	4.0	3.7
1995	3.9	3.9	3.9	3.9	3.9	3.8	3.8	3.8	3.8	3.9	3.9	3.9	3.8
1996	3.8	3.9	3.9	3.9	3.9	4.0	4.0	4.0	4.0	3.8	4.1	4.1	3.9
1997	4.0	4.0	4.1	4.0	4.0	4.1	4.0	4.0	4.0	4.1	4.1	4.1	4.0
1998	4.0	4.0	4.0	4.0	4.0	4.0	3.9	3.9	4.0	3.8	4.0	3.9	4.0
1999	4.0	4.0	4.0	3.9	3.9	4.0	4.0	3.9	3.8	4.0	4.0	4.0	4.0
2000	4.0	4.0	4.1	3.9	4.0	4.0	4.1	4.1	4.1	4.2	4.2	4.2	4.1
2001	3.8	3.8	3.8	3.8	3.8	3.7	3.7	3.7	3.7	3.7	3.6	3.6	3.7
2002	3.6	3.5	3.5	3.5	3.5	3.5	3.6	3.6	3.5	3.5	3.5	3.5	3.5
2003	3.5	3.4	3.4	3.4	3.4	3.4	3.4	3.4	3.4	3.4	3.4	3.4	3.4

Employment by Industry: Kansas—*Continued*

(Numbers in thousands. Not seasonally adjusted.)

Industry	January	February	March	April	May	June	July	August	September	October	November	December	Annual Average
LAWRENCE—*Continued*													
Service-providing													
1990	30.3	31.7	31.6	32.4	32.6	30.5	29.5	31.3	33.1	33.4	33.3	33.2	31.9
1991	31.3	32.4	32.6	33.8	33.5	30.8	30.1	31.5	33.8	34.4	34.6	34.2	32.7
1992	33.0	34.2	34.2	35.0	34.7	31.6	30.7	33.0	35.3	35.3	35.9	35.3	34.0
1993	34.1	35.2	35.5	35.6	36.1	33.5	32.1	33.7	36.1	36.8	36.7	36.8	35.1
1994	35.7	36.1	36.5	36.8	36.8	33.7	33.2	35.4	37.3	38.4	38.5	38.1	36.3
1995	36.9	37.7	37.8	38.6	38.6	35.5	34.7	36.7	38.8	39.5	39.9	39.8	37.8
1996	35.4	38.3	39.0	39.4	39.7	35.3	35.3	36.1	38.3	39.6	40.3	40.0	38.0
1997	37.8	39.2	40.5	40.8	41.2	37.3	37.2	37.4	40.1	41.6	42.4	42.6	39.8
1998	40.0	40.7	41.6	42.3	42.6	38.9	38.8	38.9	41.8	43.4	43.5	43.7	41.4
1999	41.0	42.1	43.1	43.8	43.9	42.2	39.8	39.6	42.3	43.5	44.4	44.4	42.5
2000	41.7	43.0	44.0	43.8	43.7	41.8	39.4	39.3	42.0	45.4	46.2	46.1	43.0
2001	44.8	45.1	45.9	46.1	46.4	44.5	42.3	42.9	45.8	47.3	47.5	47.9	45.5
2002	45.4	45.4	46.7	46.1	46.4	44.5	42.0	42.3	45.4	45.9	46.5	46.4	45.3
2003	44.3	44.9	45.3	46.2	46.0	44.4	42.6	42.4	44.4	45.1	45.5	45.7	44.7
Trade, transportation, and utilities													
1990	5.2	5.3	5.3	5.6	5.6	5.6	5.5	5.6	5.7	5.8	5.8	5.9	5.5
1991	5.6	5.7	5.7	5.8	5.6	5.5	5.6	5.6	5.9	6.1	6.1	6.2	5.7
1992	5.8	5.9	5.9	6.0	6.0	5.7	5.5	5.5	6.0	6.0	6.0	6.0	5.8
1993	5.9	6.0	6.0	5.9	6.1	5.9	5.9	5.9	6.2	6.4	6.5	6.7	6.1
1994	6.4	6.4	6.4	6.4	6.4	6.3	6.4	6.4	6.9	7.2	7.3	7.5	6.6
1995	7.0	6.9	6.9	7.1	7.1	6.8	6.8	6.9	7.2	7.4	7.8	7.9	7.1
1996	7.3	7.3	7.3	7.4	7.4	7.2	7.2	7.4	7.7	7.8	8.1	8.3	7.5
1997	7.7	7.7	7.6	7.6	7.8	7.7	7.5	7.7	7.8	8.1	8.3	8.3	7.8
1998	7.8	7.8	7.9	8.1	8.0	8.0	7.9	8.0	8.1	8.2	8.6	8.7	8.1
1999	8.1	8.3	8.5	8.7	8.6	8.5	8.3	8.2	8.7	8.7	8.7	8.8	8.5
2000	8.2	8.5	8.5	8.6	8.7	8.6	8.3	8.3	8.7	8.8	9.0	9.1	8.6
2001	8.1	8.1	8.2	8.4	8.6	8.4	8.2	8.5	8.6	8.5	8.7	8.8	8.4
2002	8.1	8.2	8.2	8.0	8.0	7.8	7.8	7.9	8.0	8.0	8.1	8.2	8.0
2003	7.7	7.7	7.7	8.0	8.0	7.9	7.9	7.9	7.9	8.0	8.2	8.3	7.9
Wholesale trade													
1990	0.8	0.8	0.8	0.9	0.9	1.0	1.0	1.0	1.0	1.0	1.0	1.0	0.9
1991	1.0	1.0	1.0	1.0	1.0	1.0	1.0	1.0	1.1	1.1	1.1	1.1	1.0
1992	1.0	1.0	1.0	1.0	1.1	1.0	0.9	0.9	1.0	0.9	0.9	0.9	0.9
1993	0.9	1.0	0.9	0.9	0.9	1.0	1.0	1.0	0.9	1.0	1.0	1.0	0.9
1994	1.0	1.0	1.0	1.0	1.0	0.9	0.9	0.9	0.9	1.0	1.0	1.0	0.9
1995	1.0	1.0	1.0	1.0	1.0	1.0	1.0	1.0	1.0	0.9	1.0	1.0	0.9
1996	1.0	1.0	1.0	1.0	1.0	1.0	1.0	1.0	1.0	1.0	1.0	1.0	1.0
1997	1.0	1.0	1.0	0.9	0.9	1.0	1.0	0.9	0.9	1.0	1.0	1.0	1.0
1998	1.0	1.0	1.0	1.0	1.0	1.0	1.0	0.9	0.9	0.9	1.0	0.9	1.0
1999	0.9	1.0	1.0	0.9	0.8	0.8	0.8	0.8	0.8	0.8	0.8	0.8	0.9
2000	0.8	0.8	0.8	0.8	0.8	0.8	0.8	0.8	0.8	0.8	0.8	0.8	0.8
2001	0.8	0.8	0.9	0.9	1.0	1.0	0.9	0.9	0.9	0.9	0.8	0.8	0.9
2002	0.8	0.9	0.9	0.8	0.8	0.8	0.8	0.8	0.8	0.8	0.8	0.8	0.8
2003	0.8	0.8	0.8	0.8	0.8	0.8	0.8	0.8	0.8	0.8	0.8	0.8	0.8
Retail trade													
1990	3.5	3.5	3.5	3.7	3.8	3.7	3.6	3.7	3.8	3.9	3.9	4.0	3.7
1991	3.7	3.8	3.8	3.9	3.7	3.6	3.7	3.7	3.9	4.0	4.0	4.1	3.8
1992	3.8	3.9	3.9	4.0	3.9	3.8	3.7	3.7	4.0	4.1	4.1	4.1	3.9
1993	4.0	4.0	4.1	4.1	4.2	3.9	3.9	3.9	4.2	4.2	4.3	4.5	4.1
1994	4.2	4.2	4.2	4.2	4.2	4.3	4.4	4.4	4.9	5.1	5.2	5.4	4.5
1995	5.0	4.9	5.0	5.1	5.1	5.0	5.0	5.1	5.4	5.7	6.0	6.1	5.2
1996	5.6	5.6	5.6	5.6	5.6	5.5	5.5	5.6	5.8	5.9	6.2	6.3	5.7
1997	5.8	5.7	5.6	5.7	5.9	5.7	5.6	5.8	5.9	6.1	6.3	6.3	5.9
1998	5.8	5.8	5.9	6.1	6.0	6.0	6.0	6.1	6.2	6.3	6.6	6.8	6.1
1999	6.2	6.3	6.5	6.8	6.8	6.7	6.5	6.4	6.8	6.9	6.9	7.0	6.7
2000	6.3	6.6	6.6	6.7	6.8	6.7	6.4	6.4	6.7	6.9	7.0	7.1	6.7
2001	6.4	6.4	6.4	6.4	6.4	6.3	6.2	6.3	6.3	6.2	6.4	6.5	6.4
2002	5.8	5.7	5.7	5.6	5.6	5.5	5.5	5.5	5.6	5.6	5.7	5.8	5.6
2003	5.4	5.4	5.4	5.7	5.7	5.7	5.7	5.7	5.7	5.8	6.0	6.1	5.7
Transportation and utilities													
1990	0.9	1.0	1.0	1.0	0.9	0.9	0.9	0.9	0.9	0.9	0.9	0.9	0.9
1991	0.9	0.9	0.9	0.9	0.9	0.9	0.9	0.9	0.9	1.0	1.0	1.0	0.9
1992	1.0	1.0	1.0	1.0	1.0	0.9	0.9	0.9	1.0	1.0	1.0	1.0	0.9
1993	1.0	1.0	1.0	0.9	1.0	1.0	1.0	1.0	1.1	1.2	1.2	1.2	1.0
1994	1.2	1.2	1.2	1.2	1.2	1.1	1.1	1.1	1.1	1.1	1.1	1.1	1.1
1995	1.0	1.0	0.9	1.0	1.0	0.8	0.8	0.8	0.8	0.8	0.8	0.8	0.8
1996	0.7	0.7	0.7	0.8	0.8	0.7	0.7	0.8	0.9	0.9	0.9	1.0	0.8
1997	0.9	1.0	1.0	1.0	1.0	1.0	0.9	1.0	1.0	1.0	1.0	1.0	1.0
1998	1.0	1.0	1.0	1.0	1.0	1.0	0.9	1.0	1.0	1.0	1.0	1.0	1.0
1999	1.0	1.0	1.0	1.0	1.0	1.0	1.0	1.0	1.1	1.0	1.0	1.0	1.0
2000	1.1	1.1	1.1	1.1	1.1	1.1	1.1	1.1	1.2	1.1	1.2	1.2	1.1
2001	0.9	0.9	0.9	1.1	1.2	1.1	1.1	1.3	1.4	1.4	1.5	1.5	1.2
2002	1.5	1.6	1.6	1.6	1.6	1.5	1.5	1.6	1.6	1.6	1.6	1.6	1.6
2003	1.5	1.5	1.5	1.5	1.5	1.4	1.4	1.4	1.4	1.4	1.4	1.4	1.4

Employment by Industry: Kansas—*Continued*

(Numbers in thousands. Not seasonally adjusted.)

Industry	January	February	March	April	May	June	July	August	September	October	November	December	Annual Average
LAWRENCE—*Continued*													
Information													
1990	1.8	1.8	1.8	1.8	1.8	1.9	1.9	1.8	1.8	1.9	1.8	1.9	1.8
1991	1.9	1.9	1.9	1.9	1.9	1.9	1.9	1.9	1.9	1.9	1.9	1.9	1.9
1992	1.9	1.9	1.9	2.0	1.9	1.9	2.0	2.0	2.1	2.1	2.1	2.0	1.9
1993	2.1	2.1	2.1	2.1	2.1	2.1	2.1	2.1	2.2	2.2	2.2	2.2	2.1
1994	2.2	2.2	2.2	2.2	2.2	2.2	2.2	2.2	2.2	2.2	2.2	2.2	2.2
1995	2.2	2.2	2.2	2.2	2.2	2.2	2.2	2.2	2.1	2.2	2.2	2.2	2.1
1996	2.1	2.1	2.2	2.2	2.1	2.1	2.1	2.2	2.2	2.2	2.2	2.2	2.1
1997	2.1	2.2	2.2	2.3	2.2	2.2	2.2	2.2	2.2	2.2	2.3	2.3	2.2
1998	2.2	2.2	2.2	2.2	2.2	2.2	2.2	2.2	2.2	2.2	2.2	2.3	2.2
1999	2.2	2.3	2.3	2.2	2.3	2.3	2.3	2.3	2.3	2.2	2.2	2.3	2.3
2000	2.3	2.3	2.3	2.2	2.2	2.2	2.2	2.2	2.2	2.4	2.4	2.4	2.3
2001	3.1	3.1	3.1	2.9	2.9	2.9	3.0	2.9	2.9	2.9	2.9	2.8	3.0
2002	2.8	2.7	2.7	2.6	2.6	2.6	2.6	2.6	2.6	2.2	2.2	2.2	2.5
2003	2.2	2.2	2.1	2.2	2.1	2.2	2.2	2.2	2.2	2.2	2.2	2.2	2.2
Financial activities													
1990	1.6	1.6	1.7	1.7	1.8	1.8	1.8	1.7	1.7	1.7	1.7	1.7	1.7
1991	1.6	1.6	1.6	1.6	1.6	1.6	1.6	1.6	1.6	1.7	1.7	1.6	1.6
1992	1.6	1.7	1.7	1.7	1.8	1.7	1.8	1.8	1.8	1.8	1.8	1.8	1.7
1993	1.8	1.8	1.8	1.8	1.8	1.8	1.8	1.8	1.8	1.8	1.7	1.8	1.7
1994	1.8	1.8	1.8	1.8	1.8	1.8	1.8	1.8	1.8	1.8	1.8	1.8	1.8
1995	1.8	1.8	1.8	1.8	1.8	1.8	1.8	1.9	1.9	1.9	2.0	1.9	1.8
1996	1.9	1.9	1.9	1.9	1.9	1.8	1.8	1.8	1.9	1.8	1.7	1.7	1.8
1997	1.7	1.7	1.8	1.8	1.8	1.8	1.9	2.0	2.0	1.9	1.9	1.9	1.9
1998	1.9	1.9	1.9	1.9	2.0	2.0	1.9	2.0	2.0	2.0	2.0	2.0	2.0
1999	2.0	2.0	1.9	1.9	1.9	1.9	1.9	1.8	1.8	1.8	1.9	2.0	1.9
2000	1.8	1.9	1.8	1.7	1.7	1.7	1.7	1.7	1.7	1.8	1.9	1.9	1.8
2001	1.8	1.6	1.5	1.5	1.6	1.6	1.7	1.7	1.6	1.6	1.6	1.6	1.6
2002	1.7	1.8	1.8	1.8	1.8	1.8	1.9	1.8	1.8	1.8	1.8	1.8	1.8
2003	1.7	1.7	1.7	1.8	1.8	1.8	1.8	1.8	1.8	1.8	1.8	1.8	1.8
Professional and business services													
1990	2.1	2.1	2.1	2.1	2.1	2.1	2.2	2.3	2.3	2.2	2.2	2.1	2.1
1991	1.8	1.9	2.0	2.4	2.6	2.7	2.7	2.6	2.7	2.4	2.4	2.4	2.3
1992	2.4	2.5	2.4	2.5	2.6	2.6	2.5	2.7	2.7	2.7	2.7	2.7	2.5
1993	2.4	2.4	2.4	2.5	2.7	2.8	2.6	2.5	2.5	2.6	2.4	2.5	2.5
1994	2.5	2.4	2.5	2.5	2.7	2.8	2.8	2.8	2.7	2.8	2.7	2.7	2.6
1995	2.6	2.7	2.7	2.7	2.7	2.7	2.7	2.7	2.7	2.7	2.8	2.8	2.7
1996	2.4	2.5	2.7	2.8	2.9	2.8	2.7	2.6	2.7	2.7	2.8	2.7	2.6
1997	2.7	2.8	3.1	3.3	3.4	3.4	3.3	3.2	3.3	3.3	3.4	3.8	3.3
1998	3.7	3.6	3.6	3.7	3.7	3.7	4.2	3.8	3.8	3.7	3.8	3.8	3.8
1999	3.8	3.8	4.0	4.2	4.2	4.2	4.3	4.2	4.2	4.1	4.2	4.3	4.1
2000	4.2	4.2	4.3	4.3	4.1	4.1	4.1	4.2	4.3	4.5	4.6	4.6	4.3
2001	4.8	5.0	4.9	4.5	4.6	4.6	4.6	4.4	4.4	4.5	4.3	4.4	4.6
2002	3.7	3.8	3.9	3.6	3.8	3.9	4.2	4.3	4.5	4.5	4.7	4.8	4.1
2003	4.4	4.4	4.6	5.0	4.7	4.6	4.7	4.8	4.7	4.7	4.7	4.7	4.7
Educational and health services													
1990	2.4	2.5	2.5	2.6	2.6	2.6	2.5	2.6	2.7	2.7	2.7	2.7	2.5
1991	2.5	2.6	2.6	2.7	2.7	2.7	2.7	2.6	2.8	2.9	2.9	2.8	2.7
1992	2.8	2.9	2.9	2.9	2.9	2.9	2.9	3.0	3.1	3.1	3.1	3.0	2.9
1993	2.9	3.1	3.1	3.1	3.2	3.1	3.1	3.2	3.3	3.3	3.3	3.3	3.1
1994	3.2	3.3	3.3	3.4	3.4	3.4	3.5	3.5	3.6	3.6	3.6	3.5	3.4
1995	3.5	3.6	3.6	3.6	3.6	3.6	3.5	3.6	3.9	4.0	3.9	3.8	3.6
1996	3.7	3.8	3.8	3.9	4.0	3.8	3.7	3.9	4.0	4.0	4.0	4.0	3.8
1997	3.9	4.0	4.1	4.1	4.2	4.1	4.0	4.1	4.4	4.4	4.4	4.4	4.2
1998	4.1	4.2	4.3	4.3	4.3	4.2	4.1	4.3	4.6	4.4	4.5	4.5	4.3
1999	4.3	4.5	4.4	4.4	4.4	4.3	4.3	4.4	4.5	4.5	4.5	4.5	4.4
2000	4.2	4.5	4.5	4.5	4.4	4.3	4.2	4.3	4.5	4.7	4.8	4.8	4.5
2001	4.5	4.6	4.7	5.0	5.0	4.9	4.9	5.0	5.2	5.6	5.4	5.7	5.0
2002	5.2	5.4	5.5	5.5	5.5	5.2	5.1	5.2	5.4	5.5	5.6	5.6	5.4
2003	5.4	5.5	5.4	5.6	5.5	5.4	5.3	5.3	5.4	5.5	5.6	5.6	5.5
Leisure and hospitality													
1990	3.3	3.5	3.5	3.7	3.8	3.7	3.7	3.8	4.1	4.0	3.9	3.9	3.7
1991	3.5	3.6	3.6	3.9	3.9	3.8	3.6	3.9	4.1	4.1	4.1	4.0	3.8
1992	3.8	3.9	3.9	4.1	4.1	4.0	3.9	4.0	4.1	4.0	4.1	4.1	4.0
1993	3.8	3.9	4.0	4.2	4.3	4.3	4.2	4.2	4.4	4.3	4.2	4.1	4.1
1994	3.9	4.0	4.2	4.3	4.3	4.0	4.0	4.1	4.4	4.5	4.4	4.3	4.2
1995	4.2	4.3	4.4	4.6	4.8	4.8	4.7	4.5	4.8	4.9	4.8	4.8	4.6
1996	4.4	4.7	4.7	4.8	4.9	4.8	5.0	4.9	5.0	4.9	4.9	4.8	4.8
1997	4.5	4.8	5.1	5.3	5.4	5.3	5.2	5.2	5.2	5.2	5.2	5.2	5.1
1998	4.8	4.9	4.9	5.2	5.4	5.4	5.1	5.2	5.3	6.1	5.2	5.2	5.2
1999	4.7	4.9	4.9	5.1	5.3	5.3	5.3	5.1	5.2	5.1	5.1	4.9	5.1
2000	4.5	4.9	5.1	5.1	5.2	5.1	5.1	5.1	5.1	5.2	5.2	5.1	5.1
2001	5.5	5.9	5.9	6.0	6.0	5.8	5.9	6.0	6.3	6.4	6.6	6.6	6.1
2002	6.0	6.3	6.4	6.5	6.5	6.3	6.1	6.1	6.2	6.2	6.2	6.0	6.2
2003	5.7	5.9	6.0	6.0	6.1	6.0	5.9	5.8	5.8	5.6	5.6	5.5	5.8

Employment by Industry: Kansas—*Continued*

(Numbers in thousands. Not seasonally adjusted.)

Industry	January	February	March	April	May	June	July	August	September	October	November	December	Annual Average
LAWRENCE—*Continued*													
Other services													
1990	2.4	2.5	2.4	2.5	2.5	2.4	2.3	2.5	2.6	2.6	2.6	2.6	2.4
1991	2.4	2.5	2.5	2.5	2.5	2.4	2.3	2.5	2.6	2.6	2.7	2.6	2.5
1992	2.6	2.6	2.7	2.7	2.6	2.4	2.3	2.5	2.7	2.7	2.7	2.7	2.6
1993	2.7	2.7	2.7	2.8	2.8	2.5	2.4	2.6	2.7	2.8	2.9	2.9	2.7
1994	2.8	2.7	2.8	2.9	2.8	2.6	2.5	2.7	2.8	2.9	2.9	2.8	2.7
1995	2.8	2.9	2.8	2.8	2.9	2.6	2.6	2.8	2.9	3.0	3.0	3.0	2.8
1996	3.0	3.0	2.9	3.0	3.0	2.8	2.7	2.8	2.9	3.0	2.9	2.9	2.9
1997	2.8	2.9	3.0	2.9	2.8	2.8	2.6	2.6	2.8	3.0	3.0	2.9	2.8
1998	2.6	2.6	2.6	2.8	2.8	2.6	2.5	2.6	2.7	2.6	2.7	2.8	2.7
1999	2.3	2.5	2.5	2.4	2.5	2.4	2.2	2.4	2.5	2.7	2.7	2.7	2.5
2000	2.5	2.6	2.7	2.4	2.3	2.3	2.3	2.3	2.6	2.8	2.9	2.9	2.6
2001	2.2	2.3	2.3	2.5	2.4	2.3	2.2	2.3	2.5	2.5	2.5	2.5	2.4
2002	2.8	2.8	2.8	2.6	2.6	2.5	2.4	2.4	2.6	2.6	2.6	2.5	2.6
2003	2.3	2.5	2.4	2.4	2.4	2.2	2.2	2.2	2.3	2.3	2.3	2.3	2.3
Government													
1990	11.5	12.4	12.3	12.4	12.4	10.4	9.6	11.0	12.2	12.5	12.6	12.4	11.8
1991	12.0	12.6	12.7	13.0	12.7	10.2	9.7	10.8	12.2	12.7	12.8	12.7	12.0
1992	12.1	12.8	12.8	13.1	12.8	10.4	9.8	11.5	12.8	12.9	13.4	13.0	12.2
1993	12.5	13.2	13.4	13.2	13.1	11.0	10.0	11.4	13.0	13.4	13.5	13.3	12.5
1994	12.9	13.3	13.3	13.3	13.2	10.6	10.0	11.9	12.9	13.4	13.6	13.3	12.6
1995	12.8	13.3	13.4	13.8	13.5	11.0	10.4	12.1	13.3	13.4	13.4	13.4	12.8
1996	10.6	13.0	13.5	13.4	13.5	10.0	10.1	10.5	11.9	13.2	13.7	13.4	12.2
1997	12.4	13.1	13.6	13.5	13.6	10.0	10.5	10.4	12.4	13.5	13.9	13.8	12.6
1998	12.9	13.5	14.2	14.1	14.2	10.8	10.9	10.8	13.1	14.2	14.5	14.4	13.1
1999	13.6	13.8	14.6	14.9	14.7	13.3	11.2	11.2	13.1	14.4	15.1	14.9	13.7
2000	14.0	14.1	14.8	15.0	15.1	13.5	11.5	11.2	12.9	15.2	15.4	15.3	14.0
2001	14.8	14.5	15.3	15.3	15.3	14.0	11.8	12.1	14.3	15.3	15.5	15.5	14.5
2002	15.1	14.4	15.4	15.5	15.6	14.4	11.9	12.0	14.3	15.1	15.3	15.3	14.5
2003	14.9	15.0	15.4	15.2	15.4	14.3	12.6	12.4	14.3	15.0	15.1	15.3	14.6
TOPEKA													
Total nonfarm													
1990	90.9	91.1	91.7	92.9	93.1	93.7	91.2	91.3	92.1	91.7	92.5	92.1	92.0
1991	89.7	90.2	91.0	92.4	91.9	92.3	91.8	91.4	91.6	91.3	91.2	91.9	91.3
1992	90.2	90.7	90.8	93.1	93.1	93.3	91.9	93.1	92.7	92.0	93.4	93.0	92.2
1993	90.9	91.5	93.3	93.9	93.9	95.3	93.9	94.2	95.2	95.0	95.5	95.5	94.0
1994	94.4	94.6	96.5	97.7	97.0	99.1	96.6	97.0	96.8	96.7	97.8	97.6	96.8
1995	96.2	96.2	97.4	98.6	99.0	100.0	97.9	98.9	98.9	98.8	99.6	100.1	98.4
1996	97.8	98.5	100.1	100.9	101.6	102.4	100.5	100.1	99.8	99.6	100.3	100.6	100.1
1997	97.2	98.6	99.2	99.6	99.4	100.8	99.6	100.1	99.7	100.1	100.2	100.7	99.6
1998	98.9	99.5	99.8	101.1	101.5	102.1	101.4	100.9	101.1	101.4	101.0	101.5	100.8
1999	99.2	100.1	100.8	101.9	101.4	102.2	100.2	99.8	101.0	101.2	102.1	102.1	101.0
2000	101.3	101.2	103.0	103.9	104.1	104.8	103.5	104.5	104.2	104.1	104.0	104.2	103.5
2001	102.5	102.8	103.8	108.6	108.9	109.3	105.6	106.2	106.8	106.2	107.1	106.9	106.2
2002	104.2	104.7	105.3	102.2	102.7	102.8	101.7	101.8	101.6	101.6	102.0	102.0	102.7
2003	99.3	98.5	99.5	101.1	101.6	100.6	100.1	100.0	99.6	100.2	100.3	100.1	100.1
Total private													
1990	69.1	68.8	69.3	70.3	70.3	71.2	70.2	69.8	69.7	69.4	69.4	69.8	69.7
1991	67.6	67.6	68.3	69.1	69.2	70.3	70.3	69.8	69.3	69.0	68.7	69.4	69.0
1992	67.9	68.1	68.0	69.5	70.3	70.7	70.6	70.6	70.1	69.4	69.9	70.1	69.6
1993	68.3	68.4	69.4	69.9	70.6	71.5	71.6	72.0	72.3	71.6	72.2	71.9	70.8
1994	71.2	71.0	72.4	73.3	73.2	74.7	73.8	73.6	73.3	73.1	73.5	74.0	73.0
1995	72.8	72.3	73.1	74.0	74.9	75.3	75.1	75.6	75.1	75.0	75.8	75.8	74.5
1996	74.2	74.5	76.0	77.0	77.3	77.9	77.3	76.7	76.3	76.0	76.2	77.0	76.3
1997	74.6	75.7	76.1	76.9	76.6	78.2	78.1	78.4	77.6	77.3	77.5	77.6	77.0
1998	76.3	76.9	77.0	78.6	79.0	79.7	79.8	79.7	78.8	79.0	78.7	79.2	78.5
1999	77.5	78.0	78.7	79.8	79.4	80.5	80.2	79.7	79.5	79.3	80.2	80.2	79.4
2000	79.6	79.2	80.7	81.9	82.0	82.7	83.1	83.6	82.5	82.0	81.8	82.0	81.7
2001	80.5	80.3	81.0	85.3	85.6	86.5	84.8	84.6	83.8	82.7	83.5	83.4	83.5
2002	82.0	81.6	82.4	79.0	79.3	79.2	79.2	78.9	78.2	78.4	78.8	78.8	79.7
2003	76.1	75.4	76.1	77.1	77.3	77.5	77.7	77.5	76.8	77.2	77.4	77.1	76.9
Goods-producing													
1990	10.7	10.6	10.8	11.4	11.5	11.7	11.7	11.4	11.4	11.3	11.0	10.9	11.2
1991	10.4	10.6	11.1	11.0	10.8	11.2	11.3	11.1	11.0	11.0	10.9	10.7	10.9
1992	10.2	10.5	10.4	10.7	11.0	11.2	11.1	11.1	11.0	10.8	10.8	10.8	10.8
1993	9.9	10.0	10.1	10.6	11.0	11.3	11.3	11.5	11.7	11.8	11.7	11.5	11.0
1994	11.1	11.2	11.8	12.2	12.4	12.8	12.8	12.8	12.8	12.7	12.7	12.6	12.3
1995	12.3	12.0	12.1	12.5	12.7	12.8	12.7	12.6	12.4	12.5	12.5	12.6	12.4
1996	12.3	12.6	12.9	13.3	13.6	13.8	13.2	12.9	12.7	12.3	12.4	12.5	12.8
1997	11.6	12.0	12.3	12.7	12.1	12.9	12.8	12.8	12.5	12.3	12.0	11.7	12.3
1998	11.4	11.7	11.4	12.5	12.7	13.0	13.0	13.0	12.8	13.1	12.7	12.7	12.5
1999	12.4	12.4	12.4	12.8	12.8	13.4	13.0	13.1	12.8	12.7	12.6	12.4	12.7
2000	12.1	12.0	12.4	12.8	12.8	13.0	13.1	13.3	13.1	12.7	12.2	12.0	12.6
2001	12.2	12.1	12.4	13.0	12.9	13.1	12.9	12.8	12.6	12.3	12.8	12.4	12.6
2002	11.8	11.6	11.8	11.8	12.2	12.2	12.2	12.2	12.1	11.9	11.8	11.6	11.9
2003	11.1	11.0	11.3	11.5	11.7	11.9	11.7	11.5	11.7	11.6	11.6	11.2	11.5

Employment by Industry: Kansas—*Continued*

(Numbers in thousands. Not seasonally adjusted.)

Industry	January	February	March	April	May	June	July	August	September	October	November	December	Annual Average
TOPEKA—*Continued*													
Construction and mining													
1990	3.4	3.2	3.4	3.7	3.8	4.0	4.0	3.8	3.9	3.7	3.4	3.3	3.6
1991	2.6	2.9	3.4	3.4	3.4	3.6	3.7	3.7	3.7	3.6	3.4	3.3	3.3
1992	2.8	3.0	3.1	3.4	3.6	3.7	3.8	3.8	3.8	3.7	3.5	3.2	3.4
1993	2.6	2.8	2.9	3.1	3.5	3.6	3.7	3.9	4.0	4.2	4.0	3.5	3.4
1994	3.3	3.3	3.8	4.1	4.4	4.6	4.6	4.5	4.4	4.3	4.3	4.1	4.1
1995	3.6	3.6	3.7	4.0	4.1	4.2	4.4	4.3	4.3	4.4	4.3	4.1	4.0
1996	3.7	3.8	4.1	4.6	4.9	4.9	4.9	5.0	4.9	4.7	4.7	4.6	4.5
1997	3.7	3.9	4.2	4.5	4.6	4.8	4.8	4.9	4.8	4.5	4.5	4.1	4.4
1998	3.8	3.9	3.7	4.6	4.9	5.1	5.3	5.4	5.3	5.6	5.2	5.0	4.8
1999	4.7	4.6	4.7	4.9	5.0	5.4	5.2	5.3	5.1	5.2	5.1	4.8	5.0
2000	4.3	4.3	4.5	5.0	5.0	5.2	5.4	5.6	5.4	5.1	4.8	4.4	4.9
2001	4.5	4.5	4.6	5.3	5.2	5.4	5.4	5.4	5.3	5.1	5.4	5.1	5.1
2002	4.6	4.6	4.8	4.9	5.3	5.2	5.3	5.3	5.2	5.0	5.0	4.8	5.0
2003	4.4	4.3	4.5	4.7	4.9	5.1	5.0	4.8	4.9	4.8	4.8	4.5	4.7
Manufacturing													
1990	7.3	7.4	7.4	7.7	7.7	7.7	7.7	7.6	7.5	7.6	7.6	7.6	7.5
1991	7.8	7.7	7.7	7.6	7.4	7.6	7.6	7.4	7.3	7.4	7.5	7.4	7.5
1992	7.4	7.5	7.3	7.3	7.4	7.5	7.3	7.3	7.2	7.1	7.3	7.6	7.3
1993	7.3	7.2	7.2	7.5	7.5	7.7	7.6	7.6	7.7	7.6	7.7	8.0	7.5
1994	7.8	7.9	8.0	8.1	8.0	8.2	8.2	8.3	8.4	8.4	8.4	8.5	8.1
1995	8.7	8.4	8.4	8.5	8.6	8.6	8.3	8.3	8.1	8.1	8.2	8.5	8.3
1996	8.6	8.8	8.8	8.7	8.7	8.9	8.3	7.9	7.8	7.6	7.7	7.9	8.3
1997	7.9	8.1	8.1	8.2	7.5	8.1	8.0	7.9	7.7	7.8	7.5	7.6	7.8
1998	7.6	7.8	7.7	7.9	7.8	7.9	7.7	7.6	7.5	7.5	7.5	7.7	7.6
1999	7.7	7.8	7.7	7.9	7.8	8.0	7.8	7.8	7.7	7.5	7.5	7.6	7.7
2000	7.8	7.7	7.9	7.8	7.8	7.8	7.7	7.7	7.7	7.6	7.4	7.6	7.7
2001	7.7	7.6	7.8	7.7	7.7	7.7	7.5	7.4	7.3	7.2	7.4	7.3	7.5
2002	7.2	7.0	7.0	6.9	6.9	7.0	6.9	6.9	6.9	6.9	6.8	6.8	6.9
2003	6.7	6.7	6.8	6.8	6.8	6.8	6.7	6.7	6.8	6.8	6.8	6.7	6.8
Service-providing													
1990	80.2	80.5	80.9	81.5	81.6	82.0	79.5	79.9	80.7	80.4	81.5	81.2	80.8
1991	79.3	79.6	79.9	81.4	81.1	81.1	80.5	80.3	80.6	80.3	80.3	81.2	80.4
1992	80.0	80.2	80.4	82.4	82.1	82.1	80.8	82.0	81.7	81.2	82.6	82.2	81.4
1993	81.0	81.5	83.2	83.3	82.9	84.0	82.6	82.7	83.5	83.2	83.8	84.0	82.9
1994	83.3	83.4	84.7	85.5	84.6	86.3	83.8	84.2	84.0	84.0	85.1	85.0	84.4
1995	83.9	84.2	85.3	86.1	86.3	87.2	85.2	86.3	86.5	86.3	87.1	87.5	85.9
1996	85.5	85.9	87.2	87.6	88.0	88.6	87.3	87.2	87.1	87.3	87.9	88.1	87.3
1997	85.6	86.6	86.9	86.9	87.3	87.9	86.8	87.3	87.2	87.8	88.2	89.0	87.2
1998	87.5	87.8	88.4	88.6	88.8	89.1	88.4	87.9	88.3	88.3	88.3	88.8	88.3
1999	86.8	87.7	88.4	89.1	88.6	88.8	87.2	86.7	88.2	88.5	89.5	89.7	88.2
2000	89.2	89.2	90.6	91.1	91.3	91.8	90.4	91.2	91.1	91.4	91.8	92.2	90.9
2001	90.3	90.7	91.4	95.6	96.0	96.2	92.7	93.4	94.2	93.9	94.3	94.5	93.6
2002	92.4	93.1	93.5	90.4	90.5	90.6	89.5	89.6	89.5	89.7	90.2	90.4	90.8
2003	88.2	87.5	88.2	89.6	89.9	88.7	88.4	88.5	87.9	88.6	88.7	88.9	88.6
Trade, transportation, and utilities													
1990	19.3	18.9	19.0	19.1	19.0	19.2	19.0	19.1	19.1	19.2	19.4	19.6	19.1
1991	17.9	17.5	17.4	17.6	17.7	17.9	17.3	17.3	17.1	17.9	18.1	18.6	17.6
1992	17.9	17.6	17.4	17.6	17.8	18.0	18.2	18.4	18.3	18.0	18.6	18.8	18.0
1993	18.1	17.9	18.1	18.2	18.1	18.3	18.7	18.8	18.8	19.0	19.4	19.6	18.5
1994	18.6	18.3	18.7	18.7	18.6	18.7	18.6	18.6	18.5	18.5	18.9	19.4	18.6
1995	18.6	18.3	18.8	18.6	18.9	18.9	18.9	18.9	18.9	19.0	19.5	19.4	18.8
1996	18.6	18.5	18.7	18.5	18.6	18.7	18.5	18.4	18.5	19.0	19.2	19.4	18.7
1997	18.5	18.8	18.6	18.3	18.4	18.6	18.5	18.8	18.6	18.8	19.3	19.4	18.7
1998	18.6	18.4	18.6	18.7	18.9	19.0	18.9	18.8	18.8	19.0	19.1	19.4	18.8
1999	18.2	18.3	18.3	18.5	18.5	19.0	18.9	18.7	19.3	19.1	19.6	19.6	18.8
2000	19.1	18.9	19.2	19.8	19.9	20.2	19.9	20.0	20.0	20.1	20.6	20.6	19.8
2001	20.4	20.2	20.3	20.3	20.6	20.9	20.5	20.4	20.3	20.2	20.3	20.7	20.4
2002	20.2	19.8	20.0	19.4	19.5	19.5	19.2	19.0	18.9	19.4	19.6	19.7	19.5
2003	18.7	18.6	18.7	19.0	19.1	19.0	19.2	19.3	19.1	19.1	19.2	19.1	19.0
Wholesale trade													
1990	3.1	3.1	3.1	3.1	3.1	3.1	3.2	3.3	3.3	3.4	3.4	3.4	3.2
1991	3.2	3.2	3.2	3.2	3.2	3.3	3.3	3.2	3.2	3.3	3.3	3.2	3.2
1992	3.2	3.2	3.1	3.2	3.2	3.3	3.2	3.2	3.2	3.2	3.2	3.2	3.2
1993	3.1	3.0	3.0	3.1	3.0	3.0	3.0	3.0	3.0	3.0	3.0	3.0	3.0
1994	2.9	2.9	2.9	2.7	2.6	2.6	2.6	2.5	2.5	2.5	2.5	2.5	2.6
1995	2.5	2.4	2.5	2.4	2.4	2.4	2.5	2.5	2.4	2.4	2.4	2.4	2.4
1996	2.4	2.4	2.4	2.4	2.4	2.4	2.4	2.3	2.4	2.4	2.4	2.4	2.3
1997	2.4	2.5	2.4	2.4	2.4	2.5	2.4	2.4	2.4	2.4	2.4	2.4	2.4
1998	2.7	2.7	2.7	2.6	2.6	2.6	2.6	2.6	2.5	2.5	2.5	2.5	2.5
1999	2.6	2.6	2.6	2.5	2.5	2.6	2.5	2.5	2.5	2.4	2.5	2.4	2.5
2000	2.5	2.5	2.5	2.7	2.6	2.7	2.6	2.7	2.7	2.7	2.7	2.7	2.6
2001	3.2	3.2	3.2	3.1	3.2	3.1	3.1	3.1	3.1	3.1	3.0	3.1	3.1
2002	3.1	3.1	3.1	2.7	2.8	2.8	2.9	2.9	2.9	3.1	3.1	3.2	3.0
2003	2.7	2.7	2.7	2.7	2.8	2.7	2.8	2.8	2.7	2.7	2.7	2.7	2.7

Employment by Industry: Kansas—*Continued*

(Numbers in thousands. Not seasonally adjusted.)

Industry	January	February	March	April	May	June	July	August	September	October	November	December	Annual Average
TOPEKA—*Continued*													
Retail trade													
1990	11.5	11.1	11.2	11.5	11.5	11.6	11.5	11.6	11.6	11.8	12.0	12.1	11.5
1991	10.3	9.8	9.7	9.9	10.0	10.1	10.1	10.2	10.0	10.1	10.3	10.8	10.1
1992	10.3	10.0	9.9	9.9	10.1	10.1	10.2	10.3	10.3	10.1	10.5	10.7	10.2
1993	10.1	9.9	10.0	9.9	9.8	9.9	10.2	10.2	10.1	10.2	10.6	10.8	10.1
1994	10.8	10.5	10.8	11.0	11.1	11.2	11.2	11.3	11.2	11.2	11.7	11.9	11.1
1995	11.6	11.5	11.9	11.8	12.0	12.2	12.1	12.1	12.1	12.2	12.6	12.6	12.0
1996	11.9	11.8	11.9	11.8	11.9	11.9	11.7	11.7	11.6	11.9	12.2	12.4	11.8
1997	11.7	11.8	11.7	11.6	11.7	11.7	11.8	11.9	11.8	12.0	12.5	12.7	11.9
1998	11.8	11.6	11.8	12.0	12.2	12.4	12.3	12.2	12.3	12.4	12.6	12.9	12.2
1999	11.8	11.8	11.9	12.2	12.2	12.5	12.6	12.4	12.9	12.9	13.2	13.3	12.4
2000	12.6	12.4	12.7	12.8	13.0	13.2	13.1	13.1	13.1	13.2	13.7	13.8	13.0
2001	13.1	12.9	13.0	13.1	13.3	13.7	13.3	13.2	13.1	13.1	13.3	13.6	13.2
2002	13.3	13.0	13.1	12.8	12.7	12.7	12.4	12.1	11.9	12.1	12.3	12.3	12.6
2003	11.6	11.4	11.5	11.7	11.7	11.7	11.8	11.9	11.8	11.8	11.9	11.9	11.7
Transportation and utilities													
1990	4.7	4.7	4.7	4.5	4.4	4.5	4.3	4.2	4.2	4.0	4.0	4.1	4.3
1991	4.4	4.5	4.5	4.5	4.5	4.5	3.9	3.9	3.9	4.5	4.5	4.6	4.3
1992	4.4	4.4	4.4	4.5	4.5	4.6	4.8	4.9	4.8	4.7	4.9	4.9	4.6
1993	4.9	5.0	5.1	5.2	5.3	5.4	5.5	5.6	5.7	5.8	5.8	5.8	5.4
1994	4.9	4.9	5.0	5.0	4.9	4.9	4.8	4.8	4.8	4.8	4.7	5.0	4.8
1995	4.5	4.4	4.4	4.4	4.5	4.3	4.3	4.3	4.4	4.4	4.5	4.4	4.4
1996	4.3	4.3	4.4	4.3	4.3	4.4	4.4	4.4	4.5	4.7	4.6	4.6	4.4
1997	4.4	4.5	4.5	4.3	4.3	4.4	4.3	4.5	4.4	4.4	4.4	4.3	4.3
1998	4.1	4.1	4.1	4.1	4.1	4.0	4.0	4.0	4.0	4.1	4.0	4.0	4.0
1999	3.8	3.9	3.8	3.8	3.8	3.9	3.8	3.8	3.9	3.8	3.9	3.9	3.8
2000	4.0	4.0	4.0	4.3	4.3	4.3	4.2	4.2	4.2	4.2	4.2	4.1	4.1
2001	4.1	4.1	4.1	4.1	4.1	4.1	4.1	4.1	4.1	4.0	4.0	4.0	4.1
2002	3.8	3.7	3.8	3.9	4.0	4.0	3.9	4.0	4.1	4.2	4.2	4.2	4.0
2003	4.4	4.5	4.5	4.6	4.6	4.6	4.6	4.6	4.6	4.6	4.6	4.5	4.6
Information													
1990	5.0	5.1	5.1	5.2	5.2	5.1	5.0	4.8	4.5	4.4	4.6	5.0	4.9
1991	4.8	4.9	4.9	4.9	4.8	4.7	4.6	4.4	4.2	4.0	4.2	4.4	4.5
1992	4.4	4.5	4.6	4.6	4.5	4.4	4.3	4.1	3.9	3.8	3.9	4.1	4.2
1993	4.3	4.3	4.4	4.5	4.4	4.3	4.2	4.1	3.9	3.8	3.9	4.0	4.1
1994	4.3	4.4	4.4	4.5	4.5	4.5	4.4	4.2	4.1	3.9	4.0	4.2	4.2
1995	4.3	4.3	4.4	4.6	4.6	4.5	4.4	4.5	4.4	4.0	4.1	4.2	4.3
1996	4.4	4.5	4.6	4.8	4.7	4.7	4.6	4.5	4.2	4.2	4.2	4.5	4.4
1997	4.5	4.7	4.8	4.9	4.9	4.8	4.6	4.4	4.2	4.2	4.2	4.4	4.5
1998	4.5	4.5	4.6	4.8	4.7	4.6	4.4	4.2	4.0	3.9	3.9	4.1	4.3
1999	4.3	4.4	4.5	4.6	4.5	4.3	4.4	4.3	4.1	3.9	4.1	4.2	4.3
2000	4.6	4.6	4.7	4.7	4.7	4.6	4.6	4.5	4.4	4.3	4.3	4.5	4.5
2001	4.5	4.5	4.6	5.2	5.2	5.1	4.9	4.8	4.6	4.4	4.6	4.7	4.8
2002	4.9	5.0	5.0	4.3	4.2	4.1	3.9	3.8	3.6	3.5	3.8	3.9	4.2
2003	3.9	3.9	4.0	4.1	4.0	4.0	4.1	3.7	3.6	3.7	3.9	4.0	3.9
Financial activities													
1990	6.5	6.5	6.5	6.6	6.6	6.7	6.7	6.7	6.6	6.6	6.6	6.5	6.5
1991	6.4	6.4	6.4	6.3	6.3	6.4	6.3	6.3	6.3	6.1	6.0	6.1	6.2
1992	6.1	6.1	6.1	6.2	6.2	6.2	6.2	6.1	6.1	6.1	6.1	6.1	6.1
1993	6.1	6.1	6.1	6.2	6.2	6.3	6.3	6.3	6.3	6.2	6.3	6.3	6.2
1994	6.3	6.3	6.3	6.4	6.3	6.4	6.4	6.4	6.4	6.3	6.3	6.3	6.3
1995	6.2	6.2	6.1	6.3	6.4	6.4	6.5	6.5	6.5	6.6	6.6	6.6	6.4
1996	6.4	6.3	6.4	6.5	6.5	6.6	6.6	6.7	6.7	6.8	6.8	6.8	6.5
1997	6.6	6.6	6.5	6.4	6.4	6.6	6.7	6.7	6.6	6.7	6.6	6.7	6.5
1998	6.6	6.6	6.6	6.7	6.7	6.8	6.8	6.8	6.7	6.7	6.6	6.6	6.6
1999	6.7	6.7	6.7	6.5	6.4	6.6	6.6	6.6	6.5	6.6	6.6	6.6	6.5
2000	6.5	6.5	6.6	6.9	6.9	7.0	7.1	7.3	7.2	7.2	6.9	7.3	6.9
2001	7.0	7.0	7.0	7.2	7.3	7.3	7.5	7.5	7.4	7.3	7.3	7.3	7.3
2002	7.2	7.2	7.4	6.8	6.9	6.9	6.8	6.5	6.6	6.6	6.6	6.6	6.8
2003	6.5	6.4	6.5	6.5	6.6	6.6	6.6	6.7	6.7	6.7	6.7	6.7	6.6
Professional and business services													
1990	6.8	6.7	6.7	6.6	6.4	6.5	6.4	6.3	6.4	6.4	6.4	6.3	6.4
1991	7.3	7.1	7.3	7.4	7.4	7.6	8.3	8.3	8.3	7.7	7.5	7.5	7.6
1992	7.3	7.3	7.3	7.5	7.5	7.5	7.6	7.6	7.6	7.3	7.2	7.2	7.4
1993	7.2	7.3	7.6	7.5	7.7	7.9	7.6	7.8	8.0	7.6	7.7	7.6	7.6
1994	7.7	7.8	8.0	8.0	7.9	8.2	7.8	7.8	7.8	8.0	7.9	7.9	7.9
1995	7.8	7.9	7.8	7.9	7.9	8.1	8.2	8.4	8.2	8.3	8.5	8.6	8.1
1996	8.3	8.3	8.6	8.8	8.8	8.8	9.4	9.3	9.3	8.8	8.6	8.7	8.8
1997	8.2	8.4	8.6	9.0	8.8	9.0	8.9	9.0	9.1	8.9	8.8	8.8	8.7
1998	8.8	9.1	9.3	9.4	9.2	9.6	9.5	9.6	9.4	9.5	9.4	9.5	9.3
1999	9.4	9.6	10.0	10.2	9.9	10.2	10.1	9.9	9.9	9.8	10.1	10.2	9.9
2000	9.9	9.9	10.2	9.5	9.4	9.5	9.5	9.9	9.9	10.0	9.6	9.6	9.7
2001	9.9	9.9	10.0	11.0	10.8	10.9	10.6	10.5	10.6	10.6	10.5	10.3	10.5
2002	9.7	9.8	9.9	9.2	8.9	8.7	9.2	9.3	9.1	9.1	9.1	9.2	9.3
2003	8.8	8.5	8.5	8.6	8.6	8.6	8.6	8.6	8.5	8.6	8.6	8.6	8.6

Employment by Industry: Kansas—*Continued*

(Numbers in thousands. Not seasonally adjusted.)

Industry	January	February	March	April	May	June	July	August	September	October	November	December	Annual Average
TOPEKA—*Continued*													
Educational and health services													
1990	10.8	10.9	11.0	10.9	11.0	11.0	10.9	10.9	11.2	11.2	11.2	11.2	11.0
1991	11.0	11.1	11.1	11.4	11.5	11.6	11.9	11.8	11.9	11.9	11.9	11.9	11.5
1992	11.7	11.7	11.8	11.8	12.0	12.0	12.0	11.9	12.1	12.0	12.0	11.9	11.9
1993	11.9	11.9	11.9	11.9	12.0	12.0	12.2	12.1	12.3	12.2	12.2	12.1	12.0
1994	12.1	12.0	12.1	12.3	12.2	12.3	12.3	12.2	12.4	12.5	12.5	12.4	12.2
1995	12.6	12.6	12.6	12.5	12.6	12.5	12.6	12.7	12.8	12.8	12.9	12.8	12.6
1996	12.9	13.0	13.2	13.4	13.2	13.3	13.1	13.1	13.3	13.4	13.5	13.5	13.2
1997	13.8	13.8	13.9	13.9	14.1	14.2	14.6	14.5	14.6	14.7	14.8	14.8	14.3
1998	14.7	14.8	14.8	14.6	14.7	14.4	14.9	15.0	14.8	14.9	15.0	15.0	14.8
1999	14.8	14.8	14.9	15.0	15.0	14.5	15.0	14.9	14.8	15.0	15.0	15.0	14.8
2000	15.1	15.1	15.1	15.1	15.1	15.1	15.4	15.6	15.7	15.7	15.6	15.7	15.3
2001	15.5	15.6	15.6	16.3	16.3	16.2	15.8	15.9	15.8	15.7	15.7	15.8	15.9
2002	15.5	15.5	15.5	15.5	15.5	15.4	15.4	15.5	15.5	15.7	15.7	15.7	15.5
2003	15.2	15.2	15.2	15.6	15.3	15.3	15.3	15.6	15.4	15.4	15.4	15.5	15.4
Leisure and hospitality													
1990	6.4	6.4	6.5	6.8	6.9	7.2	6.7	6.9	6.8	6.6	6.5	6.6	6.6
1991	6.0	6.1	6.3	6.6	6.8	6.9	6.6	6.7	6.6	6.5	6.3	6.4	6.4
1992	6.5	6.6	6.6	7.2	7.4	7.5	7.3	7.5	7.2	7.4	7.3	7.3	7.1
1993	6.9	7.0	7.2	7.1	7.3	7.4	7.3	7.5	7.4	7.0	7.0	6.9	7.1
1994	7.1	7.1	7.1	7.2	7.3	7.7	7.4	7.5	7.3	7.1	7.1	7.1	7.2
1995	6.9	7.0	7.2	7.5	7.7	7.9	7.7	7.9	7.8	7.6	7.5	7.4	7.5
1996	7.2	7.2	7.4	7.5	7.7	7.8	7.6	7.6	7.4	7.2	7.2	7.3	7.4
1997	7.1	7.1	7.2	7.4	7.5	7.6	7.6	7.8	7.6	7.2	7.3	7.3	7.3
1998	7.2	7.3	7.2	7.3	7.4	7.5	7.6	7.6	7.6	7.2	7.3	7.2	7.3
1999	7.0	7.1	7.1	7.6	7.7	7.8	7.5	7.6	7.5	7.5	7.5	7.5	7.4
2000	7.5	7.4	7.6	7.8	7.8	8.0	7.9	8.0	7.8	7.7	7.5	7.6	7.7
2001	7.4	7.4	7.5	7.7	7.8	8.1	7.8	7.9	7.8	7.5	7.5	7.4	7.7
2002	7.6	7.6	7.7	7.3	7.4	7.5	7.6	7.8	7.6	7.4	7.4	7.4	7.5
2003	7.2	7.1	7.2	7.3	7.4	7.5	7.6	7.5	7.3	7.4	7.3	7.3	7.3
Other services													
1990	3.6	3.7	3.7	3.7	3.7	3.8	3.8	3.7	3.7	3.7	3.7	3.7	3.7
1991	3.8	3.9	3.8	3.9	3.9	4.0	4.0	3.9	3.9	3.9	3.8	3.8	3.8
1992	3.8	3.8	3.8	3.9	3.9	3.9	3.9	3.9	3.9	4.0	4.0	3.9	3.8
1993	3.9	3.9	4.0	3.9	3.9	4.0	4.0	3.9	3.9	4.0	4.0	3.9	3.9
1994	4.0	3.9	4.0	4.0	4.0	4.1	4.1	4.1	4.0	4.1	4.1	4.1	4.0
1995	4.1	4.0	4.1	4.1	4.1	4.2	4.1	4.1	4.1	4.2	4.2	4.2	4.1
1996	4.1	4.1	4.2	4.2	4.2	4.2	4.3	4.2	4.2	4.3	4.3	4.3	4.2
1997	4.3	4.3	4.2	4.3	4.4	4.5	4.4	4.4	4.4	4.5	4.5	4.5	4.3
1998	4.5	4.5	4.5	4.6	4.7	4.8	4.7	4.7	4.7	4.7	4.7	4.7	4.6
1999	4.7	4.7	4.8	4.6	4.6	4.7	4.7	4.6	4.6	4.7	4.7	4.7	4.6
2000	4.8	4.8	4.9	5.3	5.4	5.3	5.6	5.0	4.4	4.3	5.1	4.7	4.9
2001	3.6	3.6	3.6	4.6	4.7	4.9	4.8	4.8	4.7	4.7	4.8	4.8	4.5
2002	5.1	5.1	5.1	4.7	4.7	4.9	4.9	4.8	4.8	4.8	4.8	4.7	4.9
2003	4.7	4.7	4.7	4.5	4.6	4.6	4.6	4.6	4.5	4.7	4.7	4.7	4.6
Government													
1990	21.8	22.3	22.4	22.6	22.8	22.5	21.0	21.5	22.4	22.3	23.1	22.3	22.2
1991	22.1	22.6	22.7	23.3	22.7	22.0	21.5	21.6	22.3	22.3	22.5	22.5	22.3
1992	22.3	22.6	22.8	23.6	22.8	22.6	21.3	22.5	22.6	22.6	23.5	22.9	22.6
1993	22.6	23.1	23.9	24.0	23.3	23.8	22.3	22.2	22.9	23.4	23.3	23.6	23.2
1994	23.2	23.6	24.1	24.4	23.8	24.4	22.8	23.4	23.5	23.6	24.3	23.6	23.7
1995	23.4	23.9	24.3	24.6	24.1	24.7	22.8	23.3	23.8	23.8	23.8	24.3	23.9
1996	23.6	24.0	24.1	23.9	24.3	24.5	23.2	23.4	23.5	23.6	24.1	23.6	23.8
1997	22.6	22.9	23.1	22.7	22.8	22.6	21.5	21.7	22.1	22.8	22.7	23.1	22.5
1998	22.6	22.6	22.8	22.5	22.5	22.4	21.6	21.2	22.3	22.4	22.3	22.3	22.2
1999	21.7	22.1	22.1	22.1	22.0	21.7	20.0	20.1	21.5	21.9	21.9	21.9	21.5
2000	21.7	22.0	22.3	22.0	22.1	22.1	20.4	20.9	21.7	22.1	22.2	22.2	21.8
2001	22.0	22.5	22.8	23.3	23.3	22.8	20.8	21.6	23.0	23.5	23.6	23.5	22.7
2002	22.2	23.1	22.9	23.2	23.4	23.6	22.5	22.9	23.4	23.2	23.2	23.2	23.1
2003	23.2	23.1	23.4	24.0	24.3	23.1	22.4	22.5	22.8	23.0	22.9	23.0	23.1
WICHITA													
Total nonfarm													
1990	238.9	239.3	240.4	242.5	243.7	243.7	241.5	243.0	245.3	246.0	248.2	246.7	243.2
1991	240.2	240.9	242.5	244.3	245.2	244.3	243.9	244.0	246.3	247.9	248.3	248.4	244.6
1992	245.6	246.1	247.1	249.0	249.0	249.2	247.3	246.2	250.2	250.8	251.3	252.8	248.7
1993	246.2	247.8	249.3	253.4	252.1	253.7	248.5	248.1	250.7	250.2	249.3	250.3	249.9
1994	245.3	246.4	249.3	251.7	252.9	254.7	251.1	250.8	254.9	254.5	256.8	256.9	252.1
1995	251.0	253.6	255.2	255.7	256.4	257.8	253.2	253.7	258.0	258.2	253.7	262.6	255.7
1996	257.0	258.5	261.4	264.3	265.7	265.4	263.4	262.8	266.2	267.2	270.7	270.4	264.4
1997	264.1	266.4	269.2	273.5	276.4	277.9	274.3	274.5	278.7	280.9	283.0	284.6	275.3
1998	280.3	282.0	283.5	286.7	288.0	289.2	284.6	283.8	287.6	289.0	289.5	291.3	286.3
1999	282.5	283.8	285.1	288.3	287.2	287.7	283.6	281.2	285.2	286.5	287.0	288.1	285.5
2000	282.6	282.7	284.5	286.9	288.6	290.7	279.7	280.2	287.1	288.6	289.4	290.0	285.9
2001	285.1	285.6	289.2	292.0	293.5	293.8	284.0	284.1	291.9	291.8	291.2	290.8	289.4
2002	285.0	282.4	285.5	283.8	283.8	283.5	278.8	279.1	280.1	279.5	280.8	281.2	282.0
2003	274.4	276.0	277.2	277.4	277.9	274.2	269.9	270.0	274.6	275.3	275.5	275.4	274.8

Employment by Industry: Kansas—*Continued*

(Numbers in thousands. Not seasonally adjusted.)

Industry	January	February	March	April	May	June	July	August	September	October	November	December	Annual Average
WICHITA—*Continued*													
Total private													
1990	210.2	210.0	211.2	212.9	214.0	216.0	216.1	216.4	216.2	216.2	217.0	216.8	214.4
1991	211.1	211.2	212.5	214.1	214.9	215.6	216.6	217.3	216.9	217.5	217.9	218.1	215.3
1992	215.4	215.2	216.3	217.1	217.9	218.7	219.8	219.2	219.0	218.9	219.3	220.5	218.1
1993	214.9	215.6	216.9	220.2	219.4	221.2	219.7	219.4	218.3	217.2	216.7	217.7	218.1
1994	213.0	213.5	216.3	218.8	219.8	221.6	221.1	221.3	222.1	220.7	221.6	222.8	219.3
1995	218.4	220.2	221.7	222.1	222.7	224.7	224.0	224.7	225.0	224.6	219.8	228.6	223.0
1996	224.1	224.9	227.4	230.3	231.6	233.1	233.5	233.7	233.8	233.7	235.2	236.5	231.4
1997	231.0	232.9	235.3	239.6	242.3	244.6	244.6	245.9	246.0	247.1	249.1	250.3	242.4
1998	246.9	248.2	249.5	252.2	253.2	255.3	254.9	254.8	254.4	255.1	255.3	257.0	253.1
1999	249.3	250.1	250.9	253.5	252.8	254.7	254.5	252.0	251.7	251.5	251.7	252.7	252.1
2000	248.2	247.8	248.8	251.2	252.1	254.4	252.1	252.3	252.6	252.7	253.1	253.8	251.6
2001	248.9	249.3	252.3	255.3	256.3	258.1	256.2	256.4	256.2	254.6	253.8	253.3	254.2
2002	248.0	246.0	248.1	246.5	246.1	246.9	245.4	244.6	243.4	242.1	242.9	243.0	245.3
2003	236.6	237.9	239.0	239.6	239.9	236.4	237.6	236.9	237.4	237.4	237.5	237.4	237.8
Goods-producing													
1990	74.0	73.9	74.0	73.8	74.3	74.8	75.2	74.8	74.9	75.5	75.5	75.2	74.6
1991	73.8	73.7	73.9	75.0	75.1	75.5	75.8	75.6	75.6	76.3	76.3	76.3	75.2
1992	74.9	74.6	74.5	74.9	75.1	75.0	75.3	74.2	74.5	74.4	74.1	73.8	74.6
1993	71.8	71.5	72.0	72.3	71.9	72.6	72.5	72.3	72.1	71.5	70.4	70.0	71.7
1994	68.4	68.1	68.7	69.5	69.9	70.5	71.4	70.5	71.2	71.2	70.9	70.7	70.0
1995	70.0	70.6	71.0	70.9	70.8	71.9	72.0	71.7	72.7	73.3	66.8	73.7	71.2
1996	72.8	73.2	74.2	75.3	75.9	77.3	78.2	78.7	79.5	79.5	80.2	80.2	77.0
1997	79.4	80.1	81.5	82.8	84.1	85.3	85.8	86.8	87.1	87.4	88.1	88.3	84.7
1998	86.9	87.6	88.1	89.6	89.8	90.3	90.5	90.3	90.1	90.1	89.9	90.1	89.4
1999	89.5	89.8	90.4	90.3	90.1	90.4	90.4	89.2	88.7	88.3	87.9	87.9	89.4
2000	86.4	86.3	86.8	87.4	87.6	88.6	87.6	87.9	87.4	87.3	87.3	87.2	87.3
2001	85.2	85.5	86.8	88.4	88.5	89.6	89.6	89.3	88.9	87.3	86.5	85.5	87.6
2002	83.4	81.5	81.7	80.8	80.3	80.6	80.8	80.1	79.2	78.2	77.4	77.2	80.1
2003	73.9	75.1	74.7	74.1	74.1	71.5	73.6	73.1	73.1	73.1	72.7	72.6	73.5
Natural resources and mining													
1990	1.6	1.6	1.6	1.7	1.7	1.7	1.6	1.6	1.6	1.8	1.8	1.9	1.6
1991	1.9	1.8	1.8	1.8	1.8	1.7	1.7	1.7	1.7	1.7	1.7	1.7	1.7
1992	1.5	1.5	1.5	1.5	1.5	1.5	1.5	1.4	1.4	1.4	1.4	1.4	1.4
1993	1.4	1.4	1.4	1.4	1.4	1.4	1.4	1.4	1.4	1.3	1.4	1.4	1.3
1994	1.3	1.3	1.2	1.2	1.2	1.2	1.3	1.3	1.3	1.2	1.2	1.2	1.2
1995	1.2	1.2	1.1	1.2	1.2	1.2	1.2	1.2	1.2	1.2	1.2	1.2	1.1
1996	1.2	1.2	1.2	1.2	1.2	1.2	1.2	1.2	1.2	1.2	1.2	1.2	1.2
1997	1.2	1.2	1.2	1.2	1.2	1.3	1.2	1.2	1.2	1.2	1.2	1.2	1.2
1998	1.2	1.2	1.1	1.1	1.1	1.1	1.1	1.1	1.0	1.0	1.0	1.0	1.1
1999	0.9	0.9	0.9	0.9	0.9	0.9	0.9	0.9	0.9	0.9	0.9	0.9	0.9
2000	0.9	0.9	0.9	1.1	1.1	1.1	1.1	1.1	1.1	1.2	1.2	1.2	1.1
2001	1.1	1.1	1.1	1.1	1.1	1.1	1.2	1.2	1.2	1.2	1.1	1.2	1.1
2002	1.0	1.0	1.0	1.0	1.0	0.9	0.9	0.9	0.9	0.9	0.9	0.9	0.9
2003	0.9	0.9	0.9	0.9	0.9	0.9	0.9	0.9	0.9	0.9	0.9	0.9	0.9
Construction													
1990	9.2	9.2	9.5	9.9	10.4	10.9	11.0	11.1	10.9	11.4	11.1	10.9	10.4
1991	9.5	9.8	10.2	11.5	11.7	12.0	12.2	12.1	12.0	11.9	12.0	12.1	11.4
1992	11.1	10.9	11.2	11.7	12.1	12.2	12.9	12.9	12.7	12.5	12.1	11.8	12.0
1993	10.3	10.5	11.0	11.8	12.1	12.9	13.2	13.7	13.6	13.5	12.7	12.3	12.3
1994	10.7	10.7	11.5	12.0	12.4	12.8	12.9	12.8	12.7	12.9	12.5	12.3	12.1
1995	11.1	11.2	11.6	12.0	12.1	12.8	13.1	13.2	13.2	13.5	13.8	13.7	12.6
1996	12.1	12.3	12.7	13.3	13.4	14.0	14.2	14.1	13.9	13.8	13.8	13.4	13.4
1997	12.4	12.6	13.2	13.8	14.3	14.6	14.8	15.0	14.7	14.5	14.2	13.9	14.0
1998	12.7	13.1	13.3	14.7	14.5	14.9	15.1	15.3	15.0	15.0	14.6	14.4	14.4
1999	13.5	13.7	14.0	14.9	14.9	15.5	15.7	15.6	15.2	14.9	14.7	14.4	14.8
2000	13.8	13.7	13.9	14.4	14.5	15.1	14.9	15.0	14.6	14.4	13.8	13.3	14.3
2001	12.7	12.7	13.3	14.8	15.2	15.8	15.6	15.5	15.3	14.8	14.6	14.4	14.6
2002	13.6	13.5	14.3	14.3	14.3	14.9	15.1	15.1	14.7	14.8	14.7	14.5	14.5
2003	13.6	13.8	14.2	14.8	15.0	15.3	15.5	15.4	15.1	15.2	14.9	14.8	14.8
Manufacturing													
1990	63.2	63.1	62.9	62.2	62.2	62.2	62.6	62.1	62.4	62.3	62.6	62.4	62.5
1991	62.4	62.1	61.9	61.7	61.6	61.8	61.9	61.8	61.9	62.7	62.6	62.5	62.0
1992	62.3	62.2	61.8	61.7	61.5	61.3	60.9	59.9	60.4	60.5	60.6	60.6	61.1
1993	60.1	59.6	59.6	59.1	58.4	58.3	57.9	57.2	57.1	56.7	56.3	56.3	58.0
1994	56.4	56.1	56.0	56.3	56.3	56.5	57.2	56.4	57.2	57.1	57.2	57.2	56.6
1995	57.7	58.2	58.3	57.7	57.5	57.9	57.7	57.3	58.3	58.6	51.8	58.8	57.4
1996	59.5	59.7	60.3	60.8	61.3	62.1	62.8	63.4	64.4	64.5	65.2	65.6	62.4
1997	65.8	66.3	67.1	67.8	68.6	69.4	69.8	70.6	71.2	71.7	72.7	73.2	69.5
1998	73.0	73.3	73.7	73.8	74.2	74.3	74.3	73.9	74.1	74.1	74.3	74.7	74.0
1999	75.1	75.2	75.5	74.5	74.3	74.0	73.8	72.7	72.6	72.5	72.3	72.6	73.8
2000	71.7	71.7	72.0	71.9	72.0	72.4	71.6	71.8	71.7	71.7	72.3	72.7	72.0
2001	71.4	71.7	72.4	72.5	72.2	72.7	72.8	72.6	72.4	71.3	70.8	69.9	71.9
2002	68.8	67.0	66.4	65.5	65.0	64.8	64.8	64.1	63.6	62.5	61.8	61.8	64.7
2003	59.4	60.4	59.6	58.4	58.2	55.3	57.2	56.8	57.1	57.0	56.9	56.9	57.8

Employment by Industry: Kansas—*Continued*

(Numbers in thousands. Not seasonally adjusted.)

Industry	January	February	March	April	May	June	July	August	September	October	November	December	Annual Average
WICHITA—*Continued*													
Service-providing													
1990	164.9	165.4	166.4	168.7	169.4	168.9	166.3	168.2	170.4	170.5	172.7	171.5	168.6
1991	166.4	167.2	168.6	169.3	170.1	168.8	168.1	168.4	170.7	171.6	172.0	172.1	169.4
1992	170.7	171.5	172.6	174.1	173.9	174.2	172.0	172.0	175.7	176.4	177.2	179.0	174.1
1993	174.4	176.3	177.3	181.1	180.2	181.1	176.0	175.8	178.6	178.7	178.9	180.3	178.2
1994	176.9	178.3	180.6	182.2	183.0	184.2	179.7	180.3	183.7	183.3	185.9	186.2	182.0
1995	181.0	183.0	184.2	184.8	185.6	185.9	181.2	182.0	185.3	184.9	186.9	188.9	184.4
1996	184.2	185.3	187.2	189.0	189.8	188.1	185.2	184.1	186.7	187.7	190.5	190.2	187.3
1997	184.7	186.3	187.7	190.7	192.3	192.6	188.5	187.7	191.6	193.5	194.9	196.3	190.6
1998	193.4	194.4	195.4	197.1	198.2	198.9	194.1	193.5	197.5	198.9	199.6	201.2	196.9
1999	193.0	194.0	194.7	198.0	197.1	197.3	193.2	192.0	196.5	198.2	199.1	200.2	196.1
2000	196.2	196.4	197.7	199.5	201.0	202.1	192.1	192.3	199.7	201.3	202.1	202.8	198.6
2001	199.9	200.1	202.4	203.6	205.0	204.2	194.4	194.8	203.0	204.5	204.7	205.3	201.8
2002	201.6	200.9	203.8	203.0	203.5	202.9	198.0	199.0	200.9	201.3	203.4	204.0	201.9
2003	200.5	200.9	202.5	203.3	203.8	202.7	196.3	196.9	201.5	202.2	202.8	202.8	201.4
Trade, transportation, and utilities													
1990	47.2	46.8	47.0	47.1	47.5	47.9	47.7	48.1	48.0	48.0	49.0	48.9	47.7
1991	45.0	44.4	44.8	44.9	44.9	45.2	45.0	45.0	44.9	44.8	45.4	45.9	45.0
1992	44.8	44.4	44.5	44.1	44.2	44.7	44.6	45.0	45.1	45.6	46.6	47.2	45.0
1993	45.0	44.9	44.9	46.3	45.1	45.0	44.4	44.6	44.6	44.9	45.7	46.3	45.1
1994	44.6	44.7	45.1	45.5	45.8	46.2	46.0	46.2	46.1	46.3	47.3	48.2	46.0
1995	46.1	45.9	45.9	45.9	46.2	46.4	46.4	46.8	46.5	46.9	48.1	48.8	46.6
1996	46.6	46.3	46.2	46.4	46.9	47.1	46.9	46.8	45.5	47.0	48.0	48.6	46.8
1997	47.0	46.6	46.8	46.9	47.4	47.3	47.5	47.8	47.9	48.3	49.0	49.7	47.7
1998	48.3	47.8	47.8	48.1	48.5	48.9	48.4	48.5	48.9	49.5	50.5	51.0	48.9
1999	48.5	48.1	48.4	48.7	48.6	49.0	48.8	48.5	48.6	49.1	50.0	50.6	48.9
2000	49.1	48.4	48.5	49.5	49.7	49.5	48.7	49.0	49.2	49.5	50.6	51.2	49.4
2001	49.2	48.6	48.6	48.8	49.1	49.1	48.9	49.5	49.6	49.7	50.2	50.5	49.3
2002	48.2	47.5	47.8	48.1	48.1	48.4	47.6	47.6	47.7	47.7	48.7	49.1	48.0
2003	48.1	47.7	47.8	47.7	47.1	46.5	46.6	46.7	47.0	47.1	47.4	47.7	47.3
Wholesale trade													
1990	11.5	11.6	11.6	11.6	11.6	11.8	11.7	11.7	11.6	11.4	11.4	11.5	11.5
1991	10.7	10.7	10.8	10.9	10.9	11.1	11.1	11.1	11.0	10.6	10.5	10.5	10.8
1992	10.5	10.5	10.5	10.5	10.5	10.7	10.7	10.7	10.6	10.6	10.6	10.6	10.5
1993	10.3	10.3	10.4	10.5	10.6	10.7	10.6	10.5	10.4	10.6	10.6	10.6	10.5
1994	10.6	10.6	10.7	10.7	10.8	10.9	10.9	10.8	10.8	10.8	10.9	10.9	10.7
1995	10.9	10.9	11.0	10.9	10.9	11.0	10.9	10.8	10.8	10.7	10.6	10.7	10.8
1996	10.6	10.7	10.6	10.7	10.8	10.9	11.0	10.9	11.0	10.8	10.9	10.9	10.8
1997	11.1	11.2	11.3	10.8	10.9	11.0	11.0	11.0	11.0	11.0	11.0	11.0	11.0
1998	11.0	11.0	11.0	11.3	11.4	11.5	11.2	11.2	11.2	11.3	11.3	11.4	11.2
1999	11.3	11.4	11.4	11.5	11.5	11.6	11.4	11.3	11.4	11.5	11.5	11.5	11.4
2000	11.7	11.5	11.5	11.8	11.8	11.8	11.6	11.6	11.6	11.5	11.6	11.6	11.6
2001	11.2	11.1	11.2	11.2	11.2	11.3	11.1	11.2	11.2	11.3	11.3	11.3	11.2
2002	11.1	11.1	11.0	11.3	11.2	11.2	11.3	11.3	11.3	11.0	11.0	11.2	11.2
2003	11.1	11.0	11.0	10.9	10.8	10.8	10.9	10.9	10.9	10.9	10.9	10.9	10.9
Retail trade													
1990	27.7	27.2	27.2	27.5	27.8	27.8	27.8	28.3	28.2	28.5	29.4	29.2	28.0
1991	25.5	25.0	25.2	25.8	25.8	25.8	25.6	25.6	25.6	25.7	26.4	26.8	25.7
1992	26.8	26.4	26.4	26.1	26.3	26.5	27.1	27.4	27.5	28.0	29.0	29.4	27.2
1993	27.8	27.7	27.6	28.8	27.5	27.2	26.8	27.0	27.1	27.2	28.0	28.5	27.6
1994	27.0	27.1	27.3	27.8	27.9	28.1	28.0	28.3	28.2	28.2	29.1	30.0	28.0
1995	28.2	27.9	27.8	27.8	28.1	28.2	28.2	28.8	28.5	28.8	30.0	30.5	28.5
1996	28.8	28.4	28.4	28.4	28.7	28.8	28.8	28.7	27.0	28.6	29.6	30.2	28.7
1997	28.6	28.1	28.2	28.4	28.8	28.9	29.3	29.5	29.3	29.8	30.4	31.3	29.2
1998	30.0	29.5	29.6	29.5	29.8	30.1	30.1	30.2	30.3	30.8	31.8	32.2	30.3
1999	30.0	29.6	29.9	30.0	29.9	30.3	30.4	30.3	30.0	30.2	31.2	31.8	30.3
2000	30.2	29.7	29.8	30.1	30.3	30.3	29.9	30.2	30.1	30.3	31.3	31.9	30.3
2001	30.2	29.7	29.5	29.7	30.0	30.1	30.2	30.7	30.5	30.4	31.1	31.5	30.3
2002	29.6	29.1	29.5	29.8	29.9	29.9	29.6	29.6	29.4	29.6	30.6	30.9	29.8
2003	29.5	29.2	29.3	29.6	29.8	29.9	30.0	30.0	30.0	30.1	30.5	30.8	29.9
Transportation and utilities													
1990	8.0	8.0	8.2	8.0	8.1	8.3	8.2	8.1	8.2	8.1	8.2	8.2	8.1
1991	8.8	8.7	8.8	8.2	8.2	8.3	8.3	8.3	8.3	8.5	8.5	8.6	8.4
1992	7.5	7.5	7.6	7.5	7.4	7.5	6.8	6.9	7.0	7.0	7.0	7.2	7.2
1993	6.9	6.9	6.9	7.0	7.0	7.1	7.0	7.1	7.1	7.1	7.1	7.2	7.0
1994	7.0	7.0	7.1	7.0	7.1	7.2	7.1	7.1	7.1	7.3	7.3	7.3	7.1
1995	7.0	7.1	7.1	7.2	7.2	7.2	7.3	7.2	7.2	7.4	7.5	7.6	7.2
1996	7.2	7.2	7.2	7.3	7.4	7.4	7.1	7.2	7.5	7.6	7.5	7.5	7.3
1997	7.3	7.3	7.3	7.7	7.7	7.4	7.2	7.3	7.6	7.5	7.6	7.4	7.4
1998	7.3	7.3	7.2	7.3	7.3	7.3	7.1	7.1	7.4	7.4	7.4	7.4	7.3
1999	7.2	7.1	7.1	7.2	7.2	7.1	7.0	6.9	7.2	7.4	7.3	7.3	7.2
2000	7.2	7.2	7.2	7.6	7.6	7.4	7.2	7.2	7.5	7.7	7.7	7.7	7.4
2001	7.8	7.8	7.9	7.9	7.9	7.7	7.6	7.6	7.9	8.0	7.8	7.7	7.8
2002	7.5	7.3	7.3	7.0	7.0	7.3	6.7	6.7	7.0	7.1	7.1	7.0	7.1
2003	7.5	7.5	7.5	7.2	6.5	5.8	5.7	5.8	6.1	6.1	6.0	6.0	6.5

Employment by Industry: Kansas—*Continued*

(Numbers in thousands. Not seasonally adjusted.)

Industry	January	February	March	April	May	June	July	August	September	October	November	December	Annual Average
WICHITA—*Continued*													
Information													
1990	5.4	5.4	5.5	5.4	5.3	5.3	5.4	5.3	5.2	5.3	5.2	5.2	5.3
1991	5.1	5.1	5.2	5.3	5.3	5.3	5.4	5.4	5.4	5.3	5.3	5.2	5.2
1992	5.0	4.9	5.0	4.9	4.9	4.9	4.9	4.9	4.9	4.7	4.7	4.7	4.8
1993	4.7	4.7	4.7	4.5	4.5	4.6	4.6	4.6	4.5	4.5	4.5	4.5	4.5
1994	4.9	5.0	5.0	4.9	5.0	5.0	4.9	4.9	4.9	4.9	5.1	5.2	4.9
1995	5.1	5.3	5.3	5.0	5.0	5.0	5.0	5.0	5.0	4.9	4.9	5.2	5.0
1996	5.1	5.2	5.2	5.2	5.4	5.2	5.3	5.2	5.2	5.0	5.0	5.1	5.1
1997	5.1	5.3	5.3	5.4	5.4	5.5	5.6	5.4	4.9	4.9	4.9	5.0	5.2
1998	5.5	5.5	5.5	5.6	5.3	5.2	5.2	5.2	5.1	5.2	5.3	5.5	5.3
1999	5.3	5.3	5.3	5.3	5.3	5.3	5.5	5.5	5.4	5.3	5.3	5.4	5.4
2000	5.4	5.8	5.8	5.6	5.6	5.7	5.9	5.9	5.9	5.8	5.8	5.8	5.8
2001	5.5	5.5	5.5	5.4	5.3	5.5	5.5	5.6	5.6	5.4	5.5	5.3	5.5
2002	5.0	5.2	5.1	5.4	5.6	5.6	5.6	5.6	5.4	5.3	5.6	5.7	5.4
2003	5.6	5.5	5.5	5.8	5.9	6.1	6.1	5.8	6.0	5.8	5.8	5.8	5.8
Financial activities													
1990	11.4	11.4	11.4	11.7	11.6	11.8	11.8	11.8	11.7	11.7	11.6	11.6	11.6
1991	11.2	11.4	11.3	11.4	11.6	11.6	11.7	11.7	11.7	11.6	11.6	11.6	11.5
1992	11.1	11.1	11.1	11.2	11.3	11.3	11.6	11.6	11.5	11.6	11.5	11.6	11.3
1993	10.9	11.0	11.1	10.9	10.9	11.2	11.2	11.1	11.0	11.0	11.0	11.1	11.0
1994	11.1	11.0	11.1	11.1	11.1	11.2	11.3	11.3	11.2	11.1	11.1	11.2	11.1
1995	10.9	10.9	10.9	11.1	11.1	11.3	11.4	11.4	11.3	11.3	11.2	11.3	11.1
1996	11.2	11.1	11.3	11.2	11.2	11.2	11.3	11.2	11.2	11.1	11.2	11.4	11.2
1997	11.4	11.5	11.5	11.0	11.0	11.1	11.4	11.2	11.2	11.2	11.2	11.6	11.3
1998	11.4	11.3	11.4	11.6	11.7	11.9	12.1	11.9	11.7	11.8	11.8	11.9	11.7
1999	11.4	11.4	11.3	11.7	11.6	12.0	12.1	12.0	11.9	11.8	11.7	11.8	11.7
2000	11.7	11.6	11.6	11.5	11.6	11.8	11.8	11.9	11.9	12.0	12.0	12.1	11.8
2001	12.6	12.5	12.6	12.4	12.4	12.4	12.4	12.3	12.2	12.3	12.3	12.5	12.4
2002	12.5	12.5	12.4	12.5	12.5	12.4	12.5	12.5	12.3	12.3	12.3	12.3	12.4
2003	12.1	12.2	12.3	12.5	12.5	12.5	12.4	12.4	12.3	12.2	12.3	12.2	12.3
Professional and business services													
1990	18.6	18.9	19.2	19.5	19.5	19.6	20.0	20.0	19.8	19.7	19.7	19.5	19.5
1991	19.0	19.3	19.8	20.2	20.4	20.5	21.2	21.1	21.0	21.3	21.2	21.0	20.5
1992	21.2	21.6	22.1	22.9	22.9	23.1	23.7	23.6	23.4	22.4	22.2	22.8	22.6
1993	23.2	23.9	24.0	24.3	24.5	24.7	24.4	24.3	24.2	24.0	24.0	24.5	24.1
1994	23.3	23.4	24.0	24.6	24.2	24.8	24.8	25.0	25.0	24.7	24.6	24.6	24.4
1995	24.4	25.1	25.5	24.8	24.6	24.7	24.9	25.6	25.3	25.5	25.6	25.8	25.1
1996	25.6	25.9	26.5	27.2	27.0	27.1	27.7	27.8	27.3	26.9	26.6	26.7	26.8
1997	25.9	26.7	26.9	27.8	27.9	28.4	28.5	28.5	28.2	28.7	29.1	29.4	28.0
1998	28.9	29.5	29.4	29.5	29.1	29.2	29.6	29.7	29.2	29.0	28.5	28.4	29.2
1999	27.8	27.6	27.6	28.5	28.3	28.3	28.9	28.6	28.9	28.4	28.5	28.8	28.4
2000	28.3	27.7	28.9	28.6	28.3	28.5	28.0	28.1	28.0	28.5	27.9	28.3	28.3
2001	27.0	27.4	28.0	29.3	29.4	29.5	28.6	28.5	28.6	28.3	27.8	27.8	28.4
2002	27.5	27.5	28.1	26.8	26.5	26.4	26.7	26.4	26.3	26.3	26.4	26.5	26.8
2003	26.0	26.1	26.3	26.3	26.3	26.4	26.3	26.3	26.1	26.1	26.1	26.2	26.2
Educational and health services													
1990	25.5	25.8	25.9	26.4	26.5	26.6	26.4	26.6	26.9	27.1	27.1	27.4	26.5
1991	27.4	27.4	27.2	27.6	27.6	27.7	27.7	27.9	28.1	28.3	28.3	28.4	27.8
1992	29.1	29.4	29.5	29.2	29.3	29.7	29.7	29.7	30.0	30.2	30.4	30.4	29.7
1993	30.1	30.3	30.4	30.7	30.8	30.8	30.7	30.7	30.6	30.6	30.5	30.4	30.5
1994	30.4	30.7	31.0	31.1	31.0	30.9	30.6	30.7	31.2	31.1	31.3	31.3	30.9
1995	31.1	31.5	31.7	31.7	31.9	32.0	32.0	32.1	32.5	32.4	32.5	32.6	32.0
1996	32.1	32.2	32.3	32.5	32.4	32.6	32.3	32.1	32.8	32.4	32.8	33.0	32.4
1997	31.6	32.0	32.1	32.7	33.1	33.2	32.9	33.2	33.5	33.7	33.9	34.0	33.0
1998	33.0	33.3	33.3	33.7	33.8	34.0	33.6	33.7	34.5	34.8	34.9	35.3	34.0
1999	35.0	35.4	35.4	35.1	34.9	35.0	35.0	34.7	35.1	34.9	35.1	34.8	35.0
2000	34.3	34.6	34.5	34.5	34.8	34.6	34.8	34.9	35.2	35.1	35.1	35.5	34.8
2001	34.9	35.4	35.6	35.5	35.6	35.3	34.9	35.2	35.8	35.7	36.1	36.3	35.5
2002	36.2	36.4	36.9	37.4	37.5	37.3	36.5	36.7	37.3	37.5	37.7	37.5	37.1
2003	37.0	37.2	37.2	37.2	37.3	36.5	36.4	36.2	36.9	37.0	37.2	37.0	36.9
Leisure and hospitality													
1990	19.6	19.7	20.2	20.7	21.0	21.5	21.0	21.1	20.6	20.7	20.8	20.7	20.6
1991	20.0	20.3	20.7	20.6	20.9	21.2	21.1	21.4	20.7	20.7	20.4	20.7	20.7
1992	20.4	20.5	20.7	21.1	21.6	21.4	21.5	21.5	21.1	21.0	21.1	21.1	21.0
1993	20.6	20.6	21.1	22.3	22.7	23.2	22.4	22.4	22.1	21.5	21.5	21.9	21.8
1994	21.1	21.3	22.0	22.8	23.5	23.8	23.2	23.6	23.2	22.3	22.4	22.8	22.6
1995	21.7	22.0	22.5	23.0	23.4	23.7	23.1	23.1	22.8	22.1	22.2	22.6	22.6
1996	22.2	22.3	22.7	23.0	23.2	23.5	23.1	23.2	23.4	22.5	22.5	22.6	22.8
1997	21.3	21.7	22.0	23.2	23.6	23.8	23.4	24.0	23.6	22.9	22.9	23.2	23.0
1998	22.7	23.1	23.7	23.8	24.7	25.3	25.1	25.3	24.7	24.3	24.1	24.4	24.3
1999	22.7	23.0	23.0	24.2	24.2	24.8	24.5	24.3	23.7	24.0	23.8	23.8	23.8
2000	22.9	23.2	23.2	24.1	24.4	25.1	24.7	24.6	24.4	24.2	24.0	23.7	24.0
2001	24.3	24.3	24.9	25.1	25.6	26.1	25.7	25.6	25.1	25.1	24.9	24.6	25.1
2002	24.0	24.1	24.7	24.7	24.8	24.9	24.6	24.6	23.9	23.9	23.8	23.4	24.3
2003	22.7	22.9	23.7	24.4	24.9	25.1	24.7	24.8	24.4	24.5	24.4	24.2	24.2

Employment by Industry: Kansas—*Continued*

(Numbers in thousands. Not seasonally adjusted.)

Industry	January	February	March	April	May	June	July	August	September	October	November	December	Annual Average
WICHITA—*Continued*													
Other services													
1990	8.5	8.1	8.0	8.3	8.3	8.5	8.6	8.7	9.1	8.2	8.1	8.3	8.3
1991	9.6	9.6	9.6	9.1	9.1	8.6	8.7	9.2	9.5	9.2	9.4	9.0	9.2
1992	8.9	8.7	8.9	8.8	8.6	8.6	8.5	8.7	8.5	9.0	8.7	8.9	8.7
1993	8.6	8.7	8.7	8.9	9.0	9.1	9.5	9.4	9.2	9.2	9.1	9.0	9.0
1994	9.2	9.3	9.4	9.3	9.3	9.2	8.9	9.1	9.3	9.1	8.9	8.8	9.1
1995	9.1	8.9	8.9	9.7	9.7	9.7	9.2	9.0	8.9	8.2	8.5	8.6	9.0
1996	8.5	8.7	9.0	9.5	9.6	9.1	8.7	8.7	8.9	9.3	8.9	8.9	8.9
1997	9.3	9.0	9.2	9.8	9.8	10.0	9.5	9.0	9.6	10.0	10.0	9.1	9.5
1998	10.2	10.1	10.3	10.3	10.3	10.5	10.4	10.2	10.2	10.4	10.3	10.4	10.3
1999	9.1	9.5	9.5	9.7	9.8	9.9	9.3	9.2	9.4	9.7	9.4	9.6	9.5
2000	10.1	10.2	9.5	10.0	10.1	10.6	10.6	10.0	10.6	10.3	10.4	10.0	10.2
2001	10.2	10.1	10.3	10.4	10.4	10.6	10.6	10.4	10.4	10.8	10.5	10.8	10.5
2002	11.2	11.3	11.4	10.8	10.8	11.3	11.1	11.1	11.3	10.9	11.0	11.3	11.1
2003	11.2	11.2	11.5	11.6	11.8	11.8	11.5	11.6	11.6	11.6	11.6	11.7	11.6
Government													
1990	28.7	29.3	29.2	29.6	29.7	27.7	25.4	26.6	29.1	29.8	31.2	29.9	28.8
1991	29.1	29.7	30.0	30.2	30.3	28.7	27.3	26.7	29.4	30.4	30.4	30.3	29.3
1992	30.2	30.9	30.8	31.9	31.1	30.5	27.5	27.0	31.2	31.9	32.0	32.3	30.6
1993	31.3	32.2	32.4	33.2	32.7	32.5	28.8	28.7	32.4	33.0	32.6	32.6	31.8
1994	32.3	32.9	33.0	32.9	33.1	33.1	30.0	29.5	32.8	33.8	35.2	34.1	32.7
1995	32.6	33.4	33.5	33.6	33.7	33.1	29.2	29.0	33.0	33.6	33.9	34.0	32.7
1996	32.9	33.6	34.0	34.0	34.1	32.3	29.9	29.1	32.4	33.5	35.5	33.9	32.9
1997	33.1	33.5	33.9	33.9	34.1	33.3	29.7	28.6	32.7	33.8	33.9	34.3	32.9
1998	33.4	33.8	34.0	34.5	34.8	33.9	29.7	29.0	33.2	33.9	34.2	34.3	33.2
1999	33.2	33.7	34.2	34.8	34.4	33.0	29.1	29.2	33.5	35.0	35.3	35.4	33.4
2000	34.4	34.9	35.7	35.7	36.5	36.3	27.6	27.9	34.5	35.9	36.3	36.2	34.3
2001	36.2	36.3	36.9	36.7	37.2	35.7	27.8	27.7	35.7	37.2	37.4	37.5	35.2
2002	37.0	36.4	37.4	37.3	37.7	36.6	33.4	34.5	36.7	37.4	37.9	38.2	36.7
2003	37.8	38.1	38.2	37.8	38.0	37.8	32.3	33.1	37.2	37.9	38.0	38.0	37.0

Average Weekly Hours by Industry: Kansas

(Not seasonally adjusted.)

Industry	January	February	March	April	May	June	July	August	September	October	November	December	Annual Average
STATEWIDE													
Manufacturing													
2001	40.8	40.8	40.6	39.8	40.4	40.9	40.0	40.8	41.4	41.0	40.7	40.8	40.7
2002	40.3	40.5	40.3	40.8	40.8	40.6	40.9	40.9	41.6	41.2	40.4	41.0	40.8
2003	40.4	39.7	40.0	40.3	39.7	40.2	39.8	40.2	40.8	40.8	41.2	41.3	40.4
WICHITA													
Manufacturing													
2001	42.1	41.7	41.1	40.2	40.8	41.6	40.8	41.2	41.6	40.9	39.9	39.7	41.0
2002	39.1	39.9	40.5	40.7	41.4	41.0	40.6	40.2	40.5	40.5	40.8	39.4	40.4
2003	38.6	39.5	39.9	39.9	39.5	40.0	39.8	40.0	38.5	39.6	39.9	40.2	39.6

Average Hourly Earnings by Industry: Kansas

(Dollars, not seasonally adjusted.)

Industry	January	February	March	April	May	June	July	August	September	October	November	December	Annual Average
STATEWIDE													
Manufacturing													
2001	15.48	15.37	15.29	15.27	15.33	15.37	15.51	15.53	15.57	15.67	15.62	15.71	15.48
2002	15.79	15.97	15.95	16.00	15.97	15.93	15.75	16.29	16.44	16.03	15.96	15.71	15.98
2003	15.84	15.82	15.70	15.59	15.57	15.62	15.71	15.87	15.87	16.11	16.14	16.13	15.83
WICHITA													
Manufacturing													
2001	19.33	18.77	18.61	18.52	18.60	18.51	18.66	18.66	18.72	18.98	18.88	18.97	18.77
2002	18.27	18.30	18.32	18.33	18.39	18.24	18.16	18.29	18.28	18.17	17.97	17.93	18.22
2003	18.37	18.36	18.40	18.11	18.09	18.23	18.56	18.81	18.32	19.15	18.87	19.08	18.53

Average Weekly Earnings by Industry: Kansas

(Dollars, not seasonally adjusted.)

Industry	January	February	March	April	May	June	July	August	September	October	November	December	Annual Average
STATEWIDE													
Manufacturing													
2001	631.58	627.10	620.77	607.75	619.33	628.63	620.40	633.62	644.60	642.47	635.73	640.97	630.04
2002	636.34	646.79	642.79	652.80	651.58	646.76	644.18	666.26	683.90	660.44	644.78	644.11	651.98
2003	639.94	628.05	628.00	628.28	618.13	627.92	625.26	637.97	647.50	657.29	664.97	666.17	639.53
WICHITA													
Manufacturing													
2001	813.79	782.71	764.87	744.50	758.88	770.02	761.33	768.79	778.75	776.28	753.31	753.11	769.57
2002	714.36	730.17	741.96	746.03	761.35	747.84	737.30	735.26	740.34	735.89	733.18	706.44	736.09
2003	709.08	725.22	734.16	722.59	714.56	729.20	738.69	752.40	705.32	758.34	752.91	767.02	733.79

KENTUCKY AT A GLANCE

(Population and total nonfarm employment numbers in thousands)

Population, Census 2000:	4,041.8
Total nonfarm employment, 2003:	1,782.9
Change in total nonfarm employment	
(Number)	
1990–2003:	312.4
1990–2001:	335.5
2001–2003:	-21.1
(Compound annual rate of change)	
1990–2003:	1.5%
1990–2001:	1.9%
2001–2003:	-0.6%
Unemployment rate	
1990:	6.1%
2001:	5.3%
2003:	6.2%

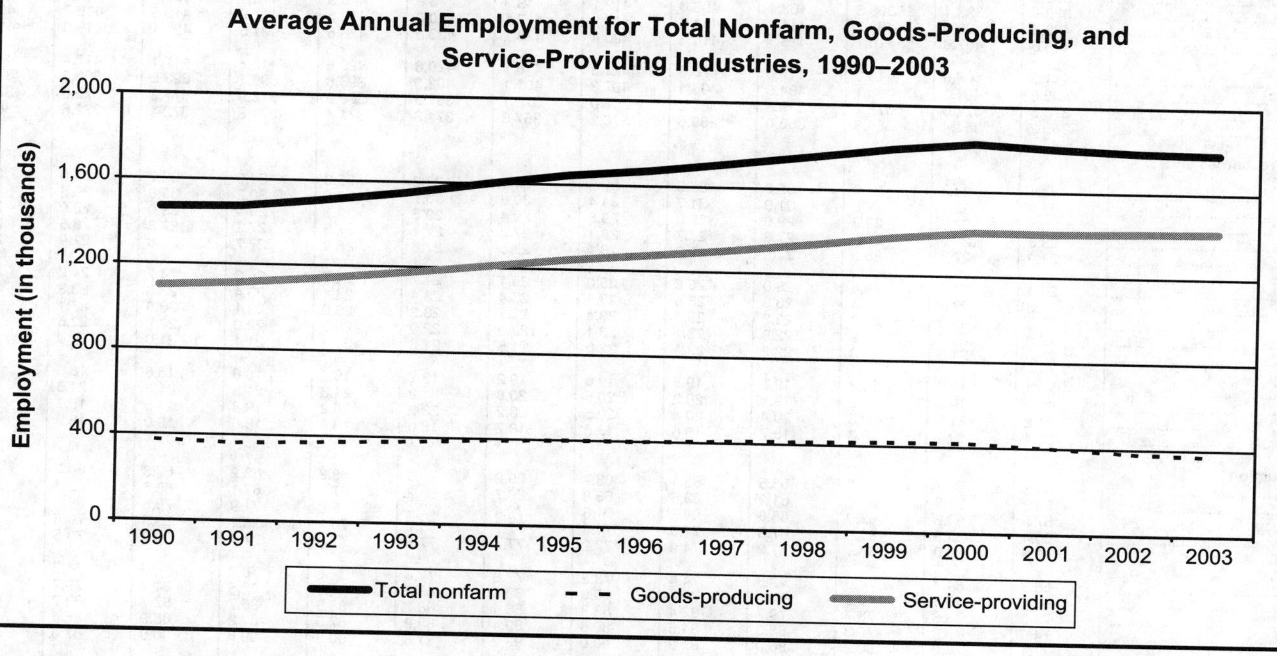

Following the 1990–1991 recession, when the growth of total nonfarm payroll employment was weak, the job picture in both the goods and services sectors strengthened until a downturn in both sectors occurred in 2001. Employment in the service-providing sector began to recover in 2002, however, employment in the goods-producing sector continued to decline, largely a reflection of a loss in manufacturing jobs.

Employment by Industry: Kentucky

(Numbers in thousands. Not seasonally adjusted.)

Industry	January	February	March	April	May	June	July	August	September	October	November	December	Annual Average
STATEWIDE													
Total nonfarm													
1990	1430.6	1435.9	1455.0	1461.2	1480.4	1479.3	1469.3	1480.5	1489.9	1487.4	1488.0	1489.1	1470.5
1991	1435.2	1438.6	1448.2	1468.7	1484.6	1482.0	1467.1	1479.9	1491.1	1493.0	1503.3	1505.4	1474.7
1992	1464.0	1470.3	1484.9	1503.4	1519.4	1520.6	1506.0	1510.0	1527.7	1528.4	1532.0	1536.4	1508.5
1993	1501.6	1508.3	1517.2	1537.9	1552.9	1556.6	1547.0	1550.2	1570.0	1571.5	1578.9	1582.0	1547.8
1994	1525.8	1542.0	1567.5	1588.3	1606.8	1610.1	1594.6	1604.8	1629.4	1622.0	1632.4	1642.6	1597.1
1995	1591.4	1600.7	1622.3	1637.3	1650.9	1659.9	1631.4	1651.4	1667.6	1661.2	1666.4	1673.3	1642.8
1996	1613.1	1628.7	1647.2	1660.5	1680.9	1680.6	1667.6	1682.3	1693.6	1695.5	1704.6	1705.8	1671.7
1997	1656.9	1668.5	1688.3	1707.9	1720.8	1724.7	1709.4	1715.7	1727.1	1732.7	1736.7	1745.8	1711.2
1998	1700.3	1705.6	1723.6	1748.2	1761.3	1764.2	1753.1	1764.8	1772.9	1773.2	1779.8	1786.2	1752.7
1999	1733.4	1749.8	1764.4	1794.3	1806.6	1809.4	1795.0	1803.9	1815.6	1819.3	1823.8	1830.1	1795.4
2000	1781.5	1793.4	1817.0	1827.7	1842.9	1840.2	1801.5	1820.2	1837.8	1842.7	1844.7	1845.0	1824.6
2001	1791.5	1796.6	1800.6	1813.4	1821.5	1824.7	1785.3	1805.0	1803.6	1801.4	1804.6	1799.8	1804.0
2002	1759.5	1762.0	1774.7	1787.6	1800.6	1801.8	1783.5	1790.8	1796.1	1799.6	1806.6	1803.0	1788.8
2003	1755.6	1753.3	1768.0	1781.4	1794.5	1794.0	1766.7	1782.8	1791.9	1798.0	1805.1	1802.9	1782.9
Total private													
1990	1171.6	1173.7	1187.8	1197.8	1211.7	1226.0	1224.3	1231.4	1229.0	1223.6	1223.0	1224.0	1210.3
1991	1174.5	1171.8	1180.4	1197.7	1211.0	1221.7	1214.0	1223.5	1220.9	1218.2	1226.3	1229.2	1207.4
1992	1190.8	1195.0	1209.2	1224.9	1240.2	1250.6	1248.6	1249.7	1251.5	1251.4	1253.9	1257.8	1235.3
1993	1226.8	1228.4	1237.2	1255.3	1269.5	1283.6	1287.6	1289.2	1291.6	1291.1	1296.3	1298.9	1271.2
1994	1249.3	1260.6	1283.9	1302.2	1320.2	1334.9	1331.5	1338.8	1344.3	1335.3	1344.4	1354.0	1316.6
1995	1312.6	1311.0	1330.3	1343.3	1355.9	1374.8	1362.9	1373.2	1377.9	1371.2	1375.7	1382.7	1355.9
1996	1331.9	1336.9	1353.8	1364.7	1384.2	1395.0	1392.9	1405.1	1404.2	1403.0	1410.7	1412.0	1382.8
1997	1373.1	1374.0	1392.6	1409.0	1422.2	1436.3	1432.8	1435.4	1437.4	1439.2	1441.4	1450.5	1420.3
1998	1410.6	1409.3	1425.6	1448.0	1461.9	1472.7	1472.3	1481.2	1476.7	1473.2	1479.5	1486.1	1458.0
1999	1440.2	1446.7	1460.6	1486.2	1495.7	1507.6	1512.8	1516.0	1514.5	1511.8	1516.3	1523.3	1494.3
2000	1484.1	1484.8	1503.6	1513.5	1525.5	1530.8	1526.2	1533.2	1532.3	1532.6	1533.1	1533.5	1519.4
2001	1482.9	1483.4	1486.5	1499.0	1505.4	1511.6	1498.9	1503.1	1489.9	1486.2	1488.4	1484.1	1493.3
2002	1447.2	1445.6	1456.5	1468.2	1480.9	1486.9	1480.8	1489.3	1480.3	1481.2	1486.9	1485.0	1474.1
2003	1442.9	1436.2	1450.2	1462.9	1474.2	1480.7	1471.2	1484.5	1481.8	1486.1	1492.7	1491.7	1471.3
Goods-producing													
1990	360.9	363.1	368.1	369.8	374.6	379.9	378.6	380.4	379.0	376.1	373.5	370.7	372.8
1991	352.7	350.8	351.9	356.5	360.1	363.9	363.4	367.0	366.7	366.5	366.7	364.7	360.9
1992	353.0	355.9	361.0	365.3	370.6	374.8	373.9	374.8	375.3	374.5	373.1	372.0	368.6
1993	363.0	363.8	364.7	371.0	375.6	381.3	383.9	383.6	385.3	384.6	383.5	382.8	376.9
1994	366.6	371.4	379.8	385.4	390.4	396.0	396.3	398.9	400.7	398.0	399.0	399.1	390.1
1995	389.9	387.6	393.3	394.9	397.4	403.7	400.0	402.6	403.5	401.2	400.7	400.4	397.9
1996	385.8	386.3	391.4	391.7	397.5	401.9	402.6	405.6	406.2	405.0	405.0	403.1	398.5
1997	393.9	393.4	399.5	403.1	406.0	412.1	413.3	416.9	415.8	413.1	409.4	412.3	407.4
1998	402.4	400.0	403.2	411.1	414.8	418.2	417.1	420.0	418.5	417.9	415.5	416.7	412.9
1999	406.5	407.6	410.7	415.1	416.5	420.4	423.7	423.8	423.6	421.5	421.1	419.6	417.5
2000	411.3	409.9	415.3	417.6	420.3	421.3	418.7	420.6	420.6	418.8	417.1	417.4	417.4
2001	400.6	401.1	400.1	404.0	405.4	407.3	401.1	402.0	398.8	395.1	393.5	390.2	399.9
2002	378.6	377.0	378.2	379.3	380.2	382.0	378.1	381.3	379.0	378.9	377.2	375.0	378.7
2003	365.2	361.4	364.3	366.0	368.6	370.2	367.8	371.3	371.4	371.8	372.4	372.6	368.6
Natural resources and mining													
1990	34.1	34.4	34.9	35.0	35.3	35.5	34.8	35.2	35.3	34.0	33.7	33.5	34.6
1991	32.6	32.3	32.5	31.9	31.7	31.4	30.8	30.7	30.5	30.2	30.0	29.8	31.2
1992	29.1	29.3	29.5	29.6	29.8	29.8	29.4	29.5	29.7	29.4	29.0	29.0	29.4
1993	28.8	28.6	27.9	27.6	27.7	28.1	27.3	27.1	27.5	27.2	27.3	28.5	27.8
1994	27.3	27.4	28.0	27.9	28.2	28.1	27.5	27.8	28.0	27.7	27.8	27.9	27.8
1995	27.1	26.5	26.6	26.0	25.8	25.6	25.1	24.7	24.7	24.3	24.2	24.2	25.4
1996	23.3	23.2	23.4	23.3	23.5	23.4	23.4	23.4	23.4	23.4	23.3	23.3	23.3
1997	23.1	23.3	23.2	23.2	23.3	23.4	23.7	23.2	23.0	23.1	23.0	23.1	23.2
1998	22.9	22.8	22.9	22.9	23.1	23.1	22.9	22.9	23.0	22.6	22.2	22.6	22.8
1999	22.0	21.8	21.9	22.2	22.1	22.0	21.5	21.6	21.6	21.1	21.0	21.0	21.6
2000	20.1	19.8	20.2	19.5	19.5	19.6	19.2	19.2	19.2	18.8	18.8	18.6	19.4
2001	18.7	19.0	19.2	19.8	20.2	20.6	20.8	21.2	21.3	21.5	21.8	21.8	20.5
2002	21.2	21.0	20.8	20.4	20.4	20.5	20.2	20.2	20.2	19.8	19.8	19.7	20.4
2003	19.4	19.3	19.3	18.7	18.6	18.8	18.7	18.9	18.9	18.8	19.0	18.9	18.9
Construction													
1990	58.7	58.7	61.2	63.8	66.1	68.7	69.2	70.0	68.8	68.2	67.8	64.7	65.4
1991	55.2	54.3	56.0	61.2	63.6	65.8	66.7	68.2	67.7	67.1	66.5	63.7	63.0
1992	57.9	59.3	62.9	65.6	69.2	71.3	72.4	72.4	72.0	71.9	70.6	68.0	67.7
1993	60.4	60.9	61.7	67.3	71.0	74.4	77.7	76.7	76.1	75.1	73.5	70.5	70.4
1994	60.3	63.0	68.1	71.9	74.9	77.2	77.4	77.6	77.9	77.1	76.2	73.5	72.9
1995	66.3	64.7	70.0	72.6	74.4	78.2	77.8	77.8	77.8	76.9	76.0	74.3	73.9
1996	65.4	66.6	70.8	74.1	78.1	80.9	82.6	83.2	82.8	82.5	81.7	79.7	77.3
1997	73.0	73.3	76.7	79.7	82.4	83.8	86.4	88.7	86.8	85.7	82.7	82.2	81.7
1998	74.9	73.9	76.3	82.3	84.5	86.8	89.4	88.9	87.5	87.2	85.9	85.4	83.5
1999	77.1	78.0	80.2	86.0	87.2	90.0	93.2	91.6	90.3	90.6	90.0	87.0	86.7
2000	81.8	81.8	86.1	87.3	88.9	89.9	90.1	89.2	89.3	89.8	88.8	88.6	87.6
2001	79.9	81.4	82.3	87.9	89.8	92.2	92.5	92.0	90.8	89.2	88.4	85.4	87.7
2002	77.9	78.2	79.7	82.0	83.4	85.1	85.7	86.7	86.2	86.1	85.3	83.3	83.3
2003	76.6	74.2	78.4	82.4	84.6	85.7	86.4	86.4	86.3	86.6	86.7	85.7	83.3

Employment by Industry: Kentucky—*Continued*

(Numbers in thousands. Not seasonally adjusted.)

Industry	January	February	March	April	May	June	July	August	September	October	November	December	Annual Average
STATEWIDE—*Continued*													
Manufacturing													
1990	268.1	270.0	272.0	271.0	273.2	275.7	274.6	275.2	274.9	273.9	272.0	272.5	272.7
1991	264.9	264.2	263.4	263.4	264.8	266.7	265.9	268.1	268.5	269.2	270.2	271.2	266.7
1992	266.0	267.3	268.6	270.1	271.6	273.7	272.1	272.9	273.6	273.2	273.5	275.0	271.4
1993	273.8	274.3	275.1	276.1	276.9	278.8	278.9	279.8	281.7	282.3	282.7	283.8	278.6
1994	279.0	281.0	283.7	285.6	287.3	290.7	291.4	293.5	294.8	293.2	295.0	297.7	289.4
1995	296.5	296.4	296.7	296.3	297.2	299.9	297.1	300.1	301.0	300.0	300.5	301.9	298.6
1996	297.1	296.5	297.2	294.3	295.9	297.6	296.6	299.0	300.0	299.1	300.0	300.1	297.7
1997	297.8	296.8	299.6	300.2	300.3	304.9	303.2	305.0	306.0	304.3	303.7	307.0	302.4
1998	304.6	303.3	304.0	305.9	307.2	308.3	304.8	308.2	308.0	308.1	307.4	308.7	306.5
1999	307.4	307.8	308.6	306.9	307.2	308.4	309.0	310.6	311.7	309.8	310.1	311.6	309.0
2000	309.4	308.3	309.0	310.8	311.9	311.8	309.4	312.2	312.1	310.2	309.5	310.2	310.4
2001	302.0	300.7	298.6	296.3	295.4	294.5	287.8	288.8	286.7	284.4	283.3	283.0	291.8
2002	279.5	277.8	277.7	276.9	276.4	276.4	272.2	274.4	272.6	273.0	272.1	272.0	275.1
2003	269.2	267.9	266.6	264.9	265.4	265.7	262.7	266.0	266.2	266.4	266.7	268.0	266.3
Service-providing													
1990	1069.7	1072.8	1086.9	1091.4	1105.8	1099.4	1090.7	1100.1	1110.9	1111.3	1114.5	1118.4	1097.6
1991	1082.5	1087.8	1096.3	1112.2	1124.5	1118.1	1103.7	1112.9	1124.4	1126.5	1136.6	1140.7	1113.8
1992	1111.0	1114.4	1123.9	1138.1	1148.8	1145.8	1132.1	1135.2	1152.4	1153.9	1158.9	1164.4	1139.9
1993	1138.6	1144.5	1152.5	1166.9	1177.3	1175.3	1163.1	1166.6	1184.7	1186.9	1195.4	1199.2	1170.9
1994	1159.2	1170.6	1187.7	1202.9	1216.4	1214.1	1198.3	1205.9	1228.7	1224.0	1233.4	1243.5	1207.0
1995	1201.5	1213.1	1229.0	1242.4	1253.5	1256.2	1231.4	1248.8	1264.1	1260.0	1265.7	1272.9	1244.8
1996	1227.3	1242.4	1255.8	1268.8	1283.4	1278.7	1265.0	1276.7	1287.4	1290.5	1299.6	1302.7	1273.1
1997	1263.0	1275.1	1288.8	1304.8	1314.8	1312.6	1296.1	1298.8	1311.3	1319.6	1327.3	1333.5	1303.8
1998	1297.9	1305.6	1320.4	1337.1	1346.5	1346.0	1336.0	1344.8	1354.4	1355.3	1364.3	1369.5	1339.8
1999	1326.9	1342.2	1353.7	1379.2	1390.1	1389.0	1371.3	1380.1	1392.0	1397.8	1402.7	1410.5	1377.9
2000	1370.2	1383.5	1401.7	1410.1	1422.6	1418.9	1382.8	1399.6	1417.2	1423.9	1427.6	1427.6	1407.1
2001	1390.9	1395.5	1400.5	1409.4	1416.1	1417.4	1384.2	1403.0	1404.8	1406.3	1411.1	1409.6	1404.1
2002	1380.9	1385.0	1396.5	1408.3	1420.4	1419.8	1405.4	1409.5	1417.1	1420.7	1429.4	1428.0	1410.1
2003	1390.4	1391.9	1403.7	1415.4	1425.9	1423.8	1398.9	1411.5	1420.5	1426.2	1432.7	1430.3	1414.3
Trade, transportation, and utilities													
1990	310.3	306.5	307.7	308.4	310.9	313.4	314.8	317.2	315.8	316.1	320.2	323.8	313.7
1991	309.7	304.3	305.6	305.4	309.5	312.0	308.9	311.6	310.9	311.2	319.0	323.6	310.9
1992	309.0	305.0	306.7	309.1	312.7	314.5	315.8	315.6	316.0	318.7	325.9	330.9	314.9
1993	316.4	312.5	313.3	317.2	321.0	324.1	325.9	326.8	325.8	329.8	336.7	340.7	324.1
1994	325.8	324.4	327.9	330.5	335.1	338.7	337.5	339.3	341.3	339.7	348.5	355.4	337.0
1995	339.4	335.4	338.5	341.7	344.4	348.3	346.5	348.9	351.2	353.4	360.2	365.3	347.7
1996	348.8	346.4	348.7	350.9	355.2	356.4	356.3	358.7	356.9	360.7	369.0	373.6	356.8
1997	360.2	355.2	357.5	360.1	362.0	363.9	363.5	358.6	363.3	368.2	374.5	380.1	363.9
1998	365.6	361.5	364.7	368.6	371.9	373.1	377.2	380.2	379.5	379.8	388.6	393.6	375.3
1999	377.2	374.5	377.1	382.4	385.8	388.5	389.0	390.4	388.8	392.0	398.7	404.2	387.3
2000	389.9	387.3	391.0	393.6	396.6	397.7	398.3	399.2	398.6	400.9	406.3	408.4	397.3
2001	383.0	379.4	378.9	379.5	379.8	380.0	377.9	378.2	375.8	378.2	383.2	384.3	379.9
2002	370.1	367.1	369.5	369.1	371.7	372.1	371.7	372.3	370.6	372.1	378.9	382.8	372.3
2003	366.0	362.9	365.2	367.1	369.9	370.6	370.3	372.8	371.6	373.3	378.2	380.6	370.7
Wholesale trade													
1990	60.6	59.7	59.5	59.4	59.6	60.0	60.2	60.4	60.2	60.2	61.7	62.4	60.3
1991	61.4	60.1	59.7	59.9	60.1	60.0	59.7	59.7	59.3	59.5	61.5	62.2	60.2
1992	61.2	59.7	59.9	59.4	59.9	60.2	60.5	60.1	60.0	59.4	61.1	62.0	60.2
1993	61.2	60.4	60.1	60.3	60.5	60.9	61.0	61.0	60.7	61.0	62.9	63.3	61.1
1994	61.4	61.2	61.5	61.5	62.1	62.6	62.8	62.8	62.8	62.7	64.7	65.5	62.6
1995	64.4	63.8	64.2	64.6	64.9	65.8	65.3	65.3	65.4	66.0	67.3	68.2	65.4
1996	67.1	66.5	66.4	65.7	66.3	66.9	67.2	67.3	67.2	67.1	68.7	69.4	67.1
1997	68.2	67.5	67.6	68.0	68.2	68.8	68.5	68.5	68.1	68.5	69.4	70.4	68.4
1998	68.7	68.3	68.4	68.5	68.5	69.0	69.3	69.4	69.5	69.6	70.9	71.7	69.3
1999	70.8	70.8	70.6	72.2	72.3	72.7	71.3	71.2	71.0	71.6	72.5	73.6	71.7
2000	72.7	72.6	73.1	73.3	73.5	73.5	73.0	73.1	73.1	74.5	75.3	75.1	73.6
2001	73.7	73.5	73.3	72.9	73.1	73.3	72.8	72.8	72.1	72.4	72.5	72.8	72.9
2002	72.2	72.1	71.5	71.8	72.3	72.2	71.9	72.1	71.8	72.3	72.8	73.2	72.2
2003	72.8	72.6	72.4	72.6	73.0	73.1	72.7	73.1	72.8	73.0	73.1	73.0	72.9
Retail trade													
1990	184.4	181.7	182.8	183.2	184.9	186.0	186.6	188.4	188.0	188.2	191.4	194.4	186.6
1991	182.7	179.5	180.9	179.1	182.3	184.1	181.8	183.7	183.8	183.5	188.6	191.8	183.4
1992	180.4	178.4	180.0	181.8	184.6	185.4	185.8	186.6	187.0	189.8	195.0	198.3	186.0
1993	187.4	185.1	185.8	188.4	191.3	193.1	193.9	194.8	193.8	196.4	201.1	204.3	192.9
1994	192.3	191.2	194.0	194.9	198.3	200.6	198.4	200.6	203.0	200.2	206.3	212.1	199.3
1995	198.5	195.7	198.2	199.8	202.2	204.9	202.0	204.6	206.9	206.8	212.9	216.8	204.1
1996	203.6	201.8	204.2	205.1	208.6	209.4	208.0	210.1	209.2	209.7	216.5	220.2	208.8
1997	209.4	206.0	208.5	208.8	210.5	211.8	211.3	213.1	211.6	213.8	219.5	224.2	212.3
1998	211.1	207.8	210.8	212.0	215.2	216.3	217.3	219.7	219.1	218.5	226.2	230.5	217.0
1999	215.4	213.7	216.3	218.6	221.5	223.7	223.2	224.7	223.5	222.7	228.5	232.6	222.0
2000	220.6	218.6	221.1	221.1	223.8	225.1	224.8	226.0	225.8	224.6	229.7	232.1	224.4
2001	217.0	214.1	214.6	214.8	216.4	216.6	213.5	214.1	213.0	214.0	219.3	220.6	215.7
2002	209.6	207.5	210.6	211.4	213.3	213.8	211.2	211.4	210.8	210.9	217.3	220.6	212.4
2003	207.3	204.3	206.4	207.7	210.1	210.7	210.4	211.9	211.7	213.3	217.7	220.2	211.0

Employment by Industry: Kentucky—*Continued*

(Numbers in thousands. Not seasonally adjusted.)

Industry	January	February	March	April	May	June	July	August	September	October	November	December	Annual Average
STATEWIDE—*Continued*													
Transportation and utilities													
1990	65.3	65.1	65.4	65.8	66.4	67.4	68.0	68.4	67.6	67.7	67.1	67.0	66.7
1991	65.6	64.7	65.0	66.4	67.1	67.9	67.4	68.2	67.8	68.2	68.9	69.6	67.2
1992	67.4	66.9	66.8	67.9	68.2	68.9	69.5	68.9	69.0	69.5	69.8	70.6	68.6
1993	67.8	67.0	67.4	68.5	69.2	70.1	71.0	71.0	71.3	72.4	72.7	73.1	70.1
1994	72.1	72.0	72.4	74.1	74.7	75.5	76.3	75.9	75.5	76.8	77.5	77.8	75.0
1995	76.5	75.9	76.1	77.3	77.3	77.6	79.2	79.0	78.9	80.6	80.0	80.3	78.2
1996	78.1	78.1	78.1	80.1	80.3	80.1	81.1	81.3	80.5	83.9	83.8	84.0	80.7
1997	82.6	81.7	81.4	83.3	83.3	83.3	83.7	77.0	83.6	85.9	85.6	85.5	83.0
1998	85.8	85.4	85.5	88.1	88.2	87.8	90.6	91.1	90.9	91.7	91.5	91.4	89.0
1999	91.0	90.0	90.2	91.6	92.0	92.1	94.5	94.5	94.3	97.7	97.7	98.0	93.6
2000	96.6	96.1	96.8	99.2	99.3	99.1	100.5	100.1	99.7	101.8	101.3	101.2	99.3
2001	92.3	91.8	91.0	91.8	90.3	90.1	91.6	91.3	90.7	91.8	91.4	90.9	91.3
2002	88.3	87.5	87.4	85.9	86.1	86.1	88.6	88.8	88.0	88.9	88.8	89.0	87.8
2003	85.9	86.0	86.4	86.8	86.8	86.8	87.2	87.8	87.1	87.0	87.4	87.4	86.9
Information													
1990	26.4	26.4	26.6	26.8	27.1	27.4	27.2	27.2	27.1	26.8	26.9	27.5	26.9
1991	26.8	26.7	26.8	26.7	26.6	26.8	26.8	26.7	26.4	26.2	26.2	26.5	26.6
1992	26.0	25.7	25.8	25.9	25.8	25.9	25.7	25.6	25.5	25.5	25.6	26.1	25.7
1993	26.2	25.8	26.1	26.0	26.1	26.1	26.2	26.3	26.2	26.3	26.6	27.1	26.2
1994	27.3	27.3	27.6	27.7	27.7	28.1	28.2	28.1	28.0	27.6	27.8	28.2	27.8
1995	26.9	27.0	27.4	27.3	27.7	28.2	27.9	27.8	28.0	27.5	27.8	28.1	27.6
1996	27.8	27.7	28.0	27.7	28.0	28.2	28.2	28.3	28.2	27.7	27.6	27.7	27.9
1997	27.8	28.0	28.6	28.8	29.0	29.4	29.2	29.4	29.1	29.3	29.4	29.7	28.9
1998	29.9	30.2	30.2	30.5	30.6	30.9	29.9	29.8	29.4	29.5	29.8	30.1	30.0
1999	30.1	30.3	30.5	30.7	30.9	31.2	30.6	30.8	30.6	31.4	31.3	31.9	30.8
2000	31.9	32.2	32.8	32.8	33.2	33.4	33.5	33.7	33.7	33.4	33.4	33.5	33.1
2001	33.3	33.4	33.6	33.3	33.4	33.4	33.0	32.7	32.2	31.9	31.8	31.9	32.8
2002	32.3	32.2	32.2	31.6	31.5	31.6	31.3	31.2	30.9	30.5	30.7	30.8	31.4
2003	30.5	30.6	30.8	30.3	30.6	30.3	30.1	30.2	29.8	30.3	30.4	30.3	30.4
Financial activities													
1990	65.3	65.4	65.8	66.5	67.0	67.7	67.9	68.0	67.1	67.0	66.9	67.2	66.8
1991	66.2	66.3	66.5	67.2	67.7	68.5	68.7	68.8	67.8	67.1	67.1	67.5	67.4
1992	66.5	66.5	66.8	67.3	67.8	68.6	68.0	67.9	67.4	66.7	66.6	67.0	67.2
1993	67.8	67.7	68.2	68.5	68.9	69.8	69.7	69.7	69.3	68.9	69.3	69.9	68.9
1994	68.5	68.8	69.6	70.2	70.9	72.1	72.6	72.8	72.5	70.4	70.8	71.6	70.9
1995	70.0	70.2	71.0	70.9	71.6	72.6	72.5	72.9	72.6	71.7	72.1	73.0	71.7
1996	71.9	72.1	72.5	72.9	74.0	74.5	75.1	75.2	74.7	77.0	77.1	77.6	74.5
1997	76.2	76.3	77.1	78.0	78.6	79.1	79.8	79.7	79.2	79.7	79.8	80.6	78.6
1998	79.3	79.2	79.4	79.8	80.4	81.1	81.2	81.2	79.8	79.8	79.7	80.4	80.1
1999	80.4	80.6	80.7	82.3	82.6	83.5	83.7	83.5	82.4	82.7	82.4	83.3	82.3
2000	84.7	84.8	84.4	84.2	84.7	85.7	83.0	83.1	82.6	82.8	83.0	82.9	83.8
2001	83.3	83.1	83.5	84.1	84.5	85.3	85.1	85.3	84.6	84.0	84.2	84.9	84.3
2002	83.6	83.9	84.1	84.5	85.1	85.6	85.3	85.4	84.9	84.8	85.0	85.4	84.8
2003	84.8	84.7	85.2	85.6	86.0	86.8	86.3	87.2	86.6	86.4	86.9	86.8	86.1
Professional and business services													
1990	97.1	97.8	100.5	101.8	102.7	104.6	104.6	105.2	105.6	103.7	103.2	102.7	102.4
1991	100.0	100.6	101.9	105.5	106.2	107.3	106.0	106.8	107.3	107.5	107.4	107.4	105.3
1992	104.4	106.8	108.9	110.8	112.0	113.0	112.7	112.6	113.0	112.3	111.5	111.7	110.8
1993	109.5	111.9	113.0	114.1	115.4	116.9	117.7	118.3	119.1	119.1	119.5	119.8	116.1
1994	114.9	118.9	122.3	124.7	127.7	128.6	128.0	129.0	129.1	130.0	129.3	130.3	126.0
1995	124.9	126.5	128.6	130.2	131.8	133.9	132.2	135.4	135.0	134.2	134.4	135.3	131.8
1996	129.2	131.5	134.1	135.1	137.4	138.8	139.2	142.6	143.5	141.6	141.3	139.6	137.8
1997	134.1	135.5	139.2	140.7	142.3	144.0	142.4	143.9	144.3	145.2	145.2	145.2	141.8
1998	139.9	142.0	144.9	145.3	146.1	148.3	149.8	152.8	152.8	152.3	153.4	153.3	148.4
1999	147.5	149.1	151.7	155.7	155.9	157.3	155.9	158.3	159.3	161.3	160.9	162.0	156.2
2000	157.5	157.9	161.7	160.7	161.5	162.3	163.9	166.0	166.9	167.9	168.1	166.9	163.4
2001	156.3	156.4	157.1	156.5	156.1	157.2	154.9	156.8	155.4	154.4	153.8	153.0	155.7
2002	149.2	149.2	151.1	152.7	154.6	156.3	155.8	159.5	158.1	158.0	158.7	157.5	155.1
2003	151.0	149.7	151.6	153.4	154.2	153.9	152.4	155.8	156.1	156.4	157.0	157.5	154.1
Educational and health services													
1990	144.6	145.9	146.9	147.5	148.1	148.0	148.1	149.2	150.8	153.6	154.3	154.6	149.3
1991	152.7	154.6	155.5	157.3	157.7	157.4	157.0	158.6	160.2	161.7	163.2	163.8	158.3
1992	162.2	164.2	165.3	165.6	165.8	165.1	164.2	165.7	168.0	169.8	170.1	170.4	166.3
1993	168.3	169.9	171.1	171.5	171.2	170.3	170.6	170.6	173.3	173.9	174.0	173.3	171.5
1994	169.3	171.0	172.1	173.1	172.9	172.3	170.3	171.4	174.5	175.1	176.0	176.7	172.8
1995	174.8	176.7	178.5	178.1	178.1	177.6	176.6	177.5	180.3	181.0	182.1	182.1	178.6
1996	178.4	180.7	181.7	182.3	182.7	182.1	180.4	182.3	184.2	185.6	187.6	187.4	182.9
1997	184.2	186.9	188.2	188.0	188.6	188.0	187.3	188.5	190.9	192.3	193.2	193.1	189.1
1998	191.1	192.9	193.9	195.4	195.1	193.7	192.7	193.6	196.0	197.3	197.7	197.8	194.7
1999	193.6	196.8	197.7	199.4	199.0	197.7	198.3	199.0	201.2	201.1	201.5	202.1	198.9
2000	199.7	201.8	202.7	203.0	203.4	203.1	202.8	204.4	204.9	205.4	205.6	205.4	203.5
2001	209.1	210.4	211.2	211.8	212.1	212.4	213.3	214.2	214.7	216.6	217.1	217.2	213.3
2002	217.3	218.2	218.7	221.5	222.0	222.2	222.3	223.4	224.6	226.1	227.3	227.5	222.6
2003	225.8	226.6	227.5	227.3	227.5	227.4	224.6	225.7	228.1	230.6	231.4	230.4	227.7

Employment by Industry: Kentucky—*Continued*

(Numbers in thousands. Not seasonally adjusted.)

Industry	January	February	March	April	May	June	July	August	September	October	November	December	Annual Average
STATEWIDE—*Continued*													
Leisure and hospitality													
1990	111.6	112.8	115.9	120.8	124.7	127.9	126.1	127.2	126.8	124.2	122.0	121.6	121.8
1991	111.9	113.7	117.1	123.1	127.0	128.9	126.3	127.1	125.2	121.5	120.1	118.8	121.7
1992	113.3	114.3	117.6	123.8	128.2	130.7	130.5	129.9	128.9	126.8	124.0	122.5	124.2
1993	118.5	119.7	123.2	129.0	133.0	135.9	135.4	135.9	134.9	131.1	129.3	128.1	129.5
1994	120.5	121.8	126.6	132.4	137.2	139.8	139.9	140.5	139.6	136.0	134.5	133.6	133.5
1995	128.4	129.2	133.6	140.9	145.3	149.6	146.7	147.5	146.8	142.1	138.4	138.1	140.5
1996	130.3	132.3	136.7	143.6	148.2	150.9	149.3	150.4	149.1	143.8	141.6	141.1	143.1
1997	135.5	137.1	140.1	147.5	152.1	154.9	152.2	152.8	149.6	146.3	144.6	143.4	146.3
1998	136.6	137.1	141.9	149.6	154.6	157.9	155.4	154.7	152.4	148.7	147.0	146.0	148.4
1999	137.5	139.8	143.4	151.1	155.3	158.0	161.8	160.8	159.5	153.4	152.0	151.4	152.0
2000	140.9	142.1	146.5	152.3	156.1	157.3	157.6	157.7	156.7	155.2	151.1	150.3	152.0
2001	143.2	145.2	147.4	155.0	159.0	160.0	159.0	159.3	154.6	152.3	151.1	148.3	152.9
2002	141.8	143.5	147.8	153.7	159.7	160.2	160.2	160.3	156.7	155.0	153.1	150.0	153.5
2003	144.1	144.7	149.4	156.6	160.3	163.6	162.4	163.5	160.4	159.1	158.3	155.5	156.5
Other services													
1990	55.4	55.8	56.3	56.2	56.6	57.1	57.0	57.0	56.8	56.1	56.0	55.9	56.3
1991	54.5	54.8	55.1	56.0	56.2	56.9	56.9	56.9	56.4	56.5	56.6	56.9	56.1
1992	56.4	56.6	57.1	57.1	57.3	58.0	57.8	57.6	57.4	57.1	57.1	57.2	57.2
1993	57.1	57.1	57.6	58.0	58.3	59.2	58.2	58.0	57.7	57.4	57.4	57.2	57.7
1994	56.4	57.0	58.0	58.2	58.3	59.3	58.7	58.8	58.6	58.5	58.5	59.1	58.2
1995	58.3	58.4	59.4	59.3	59.6	60.9	60.5	60.6	60.5	60.1	60.0	60.4	59.8
1996	59.7	59.9	60.7	60.5	61.2	62.2	61.8	62.0	61.4	61.6	61.5	61.9	61.2
1997	61.2	61.6	62.4	62.8	63.6	64.9	65.1	65.6	65.2	65.1	65.3	66.1	64.0
1998	65.8	66.4	67.4	67.7	68.4	69.5	69.0	68.9	68.3	67.9	67.8	68.2	67.9
1999	67.4	68.0	68.8	69.5	69.7	71.0	69.8	69.4	69.1	68.4	68.4	68.8	69.0
2000	68.2	68.8	69.2	69.3	69.7	70.0	68.4	68.5	68.3	68.2	68.5	68.7	68.8
2001	74.1	74.4	74.7	74.8	75.1	76.0	74.6	74.6	73.8	73.7	73.7	74.3	74.5
2002	74.3	74.5	74.9	75.8	76.1	76.9	76.1	75.9	75.5	75.8	76.0	76.0	75.7
2003	75.5	75.6	76.2	76.6	77.1	77.9	77.3	78.0	77.8	78.2	78.1	78.0	77.2
Government													
1990	259.0	262.2	267.2	263.4	268.7	253.3	245.0	249.1	260.9	263.8	265.0	265.1	260.2
1991	260.7	266.8	267.8	271.0	273.6	260.3	253.1	256.4	270.2	274.8	277.0	276.2	267.3
1992	273.2	275.3	275.7	278.5	279.2	270.0	257.4	260.3	276.2	277.0	278.1	278.6	273.2
1993	274.8	279.9	280.0	282.6	283.4	273.0	259.4	261.0	278.4	280.4	282.6	283.1	276.5
1994	276.5	281.4	283.6	286.1	286.6	275.2	263.1	266.0	285.1	286.7	288.0	288.6	280.5
1995	278.8	289.7	292.0	294.0	295.0	285.1	268.5	278.2	289.7	290.0	290.7	290.6	286.8
1996	281.2	291.8	293.4	295.8	296.7	285.6	274.7	277.2	289.4	292.5	293.9	293.8	288.8
1997	283.8	294.5	295.7	298.9	298.6	288.4	276.6	280.3	289.7	293.5	295.3	295.3	290.8
1998	289.7	296.3	298.0	300.2	299.4	291.5	280.8	283.6	296.2	300.0	300.3	300.1	294.6
1999	293.2	303.1	303.8	308.1	310.9	301.8	282.2	287.9	301.1	307.5	307.5	306.8	301.1
2000	297.4	308.6	313.4	314.2	317.4	309.4	275.3	287.0	305.5	310.1	311.6	311.5	305.1
2001	308.6	313.2	314.1	314.4	316.1	313.1	286.4	301.9	313.7	315.2	316.2	315.7	310.7
2002	312.3	316.4	318.2	319.4	319.7	314.9	302.7	301.5	315.8	318.4	319.7	318.0	314.8
2003	312.7	317.1	317.8	318.5	320.3	313.3	295.5	298.3	310.1	311.9	312.4	311.2	311.6
Federal government													
1990	46.2	46.6	50.7	47.1	51.9	47.0	46.3	45.1	43.8	44.0	44.0	44.0	46.3
1991	43.6	44.5	44.6	45.1	45.0	44.5	45.2	44.9	45.5	44.8	44.8	44.9	44.7
1992	44.9	44.7	44.5	45.0	45.0	45.3	44.4	44.3	44.2	43.6	43.5	43.9	44.4
1993	42.5	43.4	43.3	43.9	43.6	43.6	42.1	41.9	41.2	40.6	40.1	40.4	42.2
1994	41.3	42.5	42.7	43.1	42.4	42.4	41.4	41.4	41.1	40.5	39.7	39.8	41.5
1995	40.2	41.2	41.1	41.8	41.0	40.9	40.5	40.1	39.5	39.3	38.5	38.7	40.2
1996	39.1	40.4	40.4	41.5	40.3	40.0	38.9	38.3	38.1	37.9	37.9	38.0	39.2
1997	37.7	38.9	39.3	40.1	38.8	38.8	37.6	37.7	37.5	36.5	36.8	36.9	38.0
1998	37.0	38.4	38.5	38.8	39.0	37.8	36.8	36.6	36.1	35.3	35.4	35.7	37.1
1999	35.9	37.3	37.1	37.7	37.5	36.9	36.3	36.2	35.8	36.3	36.1	36.2	36.6
2000	36.8	39.4	41.2	40.0	45.4	42.2	40.8	39.8	36.1	35.7	36.0	36.4	39.2
2001	37.1	37.9	37.9	38.2	37.9	37.6	37.6	36.9	36.6	36.3	36.3	36.6	37.2
2002	37.2	37.4	38.1	38.2	37.8	38.0	38.1	37.7	37.7	37.8	38.2	38.3	37.9
2003	37.6	38.2	38.6	38.0	37.8	37.5	37.2	36.7	36.5	36.7	36.8	36.9	37.4
State government													
1990	82.3	84.1	84.4	84.9	85.2	78.2	78.1	80.2	86.0	87.1	86.8	86.7	83.6
1991	82.9	87.0	87.2	88.5	90.3	82.3	82.2	83.6	89.2	90.7	90.6	90.3	87.0
1992	87.8	89.3	89.5	90.4	90.3	81.2	80.9	82.5	89.4	89.1	89.1	88.9	87.3
1993	86.3	88.5	88.6	89.8	90.0	81.2	80.5	80.7	88.3	88.8	89.4	88.4	86.7
1994	85.5	88.2	88.2	90.0	90.2	80.5	80.3	81.3	89.7	90.3	90.6	90.1	87.0
1995	81.4	90.1	90.7	91.4	91.8	82.8	82.0	89.7	90.8	90.9	91.0	90.4	88.5
1996	82.9	90.1	90.5	91.3	92.1	82.8	83.7	84.0	88.6	90.6	91.1	90.2	88.1
1997	83.4	91.3	90.8	92.1	92.1	85.2	84.8	86.2	88.6	91.0	91.3	90.1	88.9
1998	87.1	91.3	91.8	92.0	89.6	85.0	85.1	86.2	91.4	93.5	92.6	91.4	89.7
1999	88.6	94.9	94.8	96.7	98.0	90.5	87.0	87.8	92.4	94.9	94.0	92.8	92.7
2000	89.0	95.6	97.3	98.4	94.9	90.2	89.9	91.1	96.8	99.2	99.3	98.6	95.0
2001	95.2	96.5	96.6	97.6	97.7	96.6	96.8	97.8	98.3	99.2	99.1	97.9	97.4
2002	97.8	99.7	100.0	101.4	100.6	98.9	97.5	97.7	99.1	100.8	100.8	99.4	99.5
2003	96.7	100.1	99.2	100.0	100.5	97.6	97.9	97.5	98.8	99.7	99.1	97.9	98.8

Employment by Industry: Kentucky—*Continued*

(Numbers in thousands. Not seasonally adjusted.)

Industry	January	February	March	April	May	June	July	August	September	October	November	December	Annual Average
STATEWIDE—*Continued*													
Local government													
1990	130.5	131.5	132.1	131.4	131.6	128.1	120.6	123.8	131.1	132.7	134.2	134.4	130.1
1991	134.2	135.3	136.0	137.4	138.3	133.5	125.7	127.9	135.5	139.3	141.6	141.0	135.4
1992	140.5	141.3	141.7	143.1	143.9	143.5	132.1	133.5	142.6	144.3	145.5	145.8	141.4
1993	146.0	148.0	148.1	148.9	149.8	148.2	136.8	138.4	148.9	151.0	153.1	154.3	147.6
1994	149.7	150.7	152.7	153.0	154.0	152.3	141.4	143.3	154.3	155.9	157.7	158.7	151.9
1995	157.2	158.4	160.2	160.8	162.2	161.4	146.0	148.4	159.4	159.8	161.2	161.5	158.0
1996	159.2	161.3	162.5	163.0	164.3	162.8	152.1	154.9	162.7	164.0	164.9	165.6	161.4
1997	162.7	164.3	165.6	166.7	167.7	164.4	154.2	156.4	163.6	166.0	167.2	168.3	163.9
1998	165.6	166.6	167.7	169.4	170.8	168.7	158.9	160.8	168.7	171.2	172.3	173.0	167.8
1999	168.7	170.9	171.9	173.7	175.4	174.4	158.9	163.9	172.9	176.3	177.4	177.8	171.8
2000	171.6	173.6	174.9	175.8	177.1	177.0	144.6	156.1	172.6	175.2	176.3	176.5	170.9
2001	176.3	178.8	179.6	178.6	180.5	178.9	152.0	167.2	178.8	179.7	180.8	181.2	176.0
2002	177.3	179.3	180.1	179.8	181.3	178.0	167.1	166.1	179.0	179.8	180.7	180.3	177.4
2003	178.4	178.8	180.0	180.5	182.0	178.2	160.4	164.1	174.8	175.5	176.5	176.4	175.5
LEXINGTON-FAYETTE													
Total nonfarm													
1990	215.5	219.2	221.3	223.4	223.3	221.7	218.5	221.2	224.7	226.4	226.4	226.4	222.3
1991	217.5	220.0	221.6	224.6	221.4	220.8	218.1	220.8	226.5	228.9	229.2	230.9	223.3
1992	223.1	225.9	227.3	230.7	227.5	226.4	224.9	223.8	230.6	235.8	236.1	237.4	229.1
1993	228.3	233.6	234.0	237.9	238.5	236.3	234.1	235.1	240.2	243.7	244.8	245.4	237.6
1994	231.2	237.6	241.3	244.1	241.4	242.3	238.0	240.2	249.6	248.9	250.4	251.3	243.0
1995	239.7	245.2	249.4	251.7	251.5	251.9	246.2	248.6	255.5	258.4	259.6	261.1	251.5
1996	248.0	255.1	257.3	261.0	262.3	258.8	255.3	258.1	262.8	265.6	267.1	266.8	259.8
1997	257.2	262.2	264.1	268.7	269.9	267.6	264.6	265.7	271.6	275.5	276.4	277.2	268.3
1998	267.9	270.6	272.9	277.0	275.3	275.9	272.9	274.8	280.4	284.9	286.2	285.8	277.0
1999	275.0	279.5	281.8	286.6	287.5	287.2	281.4	284.5	288.4	290.6	290.8	290.3	285.3
2000	284.1	286.6	289.7	290.5	289.1	289.2	284.9	287.0	290.4	294.4	294.6	293.5	289.5
2001	276.4	279.0	278.4	283.5	282.9	281.2	275.9	276.6	278.7	279.5	279.9	278.1	279.2
2002	271.6	273.1	274.6	277.5	277.6	275.2	273.0	274.2	278.2	278.9	280.2	279.0	276.1
2003	271.6	271.7	274.3	277.2	277.2	274.3	270.7	274.1	278.5	279.4	279.5	279.9	275.7
Total private													
1990	169.7	169.9	171.7	173.0	173.4	174.6	174.0	174.6	175.5	175.5	174.9	175.1	173.4
1991	169.3	168.7	170.1	172.6	172.8	173.4	171.7	173.1	175.1	175.4	175.0	176.4	172.8
1992	171.4	172.0	173.4	176.4	176.2	176.7	176.7	176.4	178.9	181.4	181.3	182.9	176.9
1993	178.3	179.0	179.6	183.4	184.3	185.8	184.5	185.3	187.2	189.2	189.3	190.2	184.6
1994	181.4	183.2	186.3	188.7	191.6	191.3	190.3	190.8	193.0	193.0	193.7	194.8	189.8
1995	189.0	189.4	192.7	194.6	195.8	199.1	197.0	198.8	200.9	202.4	202.9	204.7	197.2
1996	197.3	199.2	200.9	204.0	205.7	206.2	205.8	207.5	208.2	208.5	209.7	209.7	205.2
1997	204.6	205.5	207.6	211.0	213.2	214.9	214.9	215.0	216.4	218.6	219.2	220.3	213.4
1998	213.6	214.1	216.0	220.2	221.6	223.2	223.5	224.5	225.0	227.6	228.4	228.8	222.2
1999	221.6	222.5	224.6	229.2	229.5	230.7	231.2	232.2	232.3	233.6	233.3	233.5	229.5
2000	230.0	229.7	232.1	233.0	233.7	234.1	233.4	233.9	233.8	236.1	236.1	235.1	233.4
2001	223.3	223.0	222.2	226.9	226.3	225.9	223.9	223.8	222.6	223.2	223.4	222.0	223.9
2002	215.8	216.8	218.2	220.5	221.7	222.1	221.4	222.2	221.6	221.9	223.0	222.4	220.6
2003	215.8	214.9	217.3	220.4	220.8	221.5	220.0	221.4	222.0	222.5	222.4	223.0	220.2
Goods-producing													
1990	44.2	44.5	44.7	44.4	45.1	45.8	45.9	46.2	45.9	45.5	45.2	45.6	45.2
1991	44.1	44.0	44.3	44.6	44.9	45.3	45.1	45.4	45.8	45.7	45.7	45.5	45.0
1992	44.5	44.9	45.5	46.5	47.0	47.5	47.4	47.8	47.6	47.9	47.8	48.1	46.8
1993	47.1	47.2	47.3	48.1	48.7	49.4	49.5	50.2	50.4	50.7	50.2	50.5	49.1
1994	47.8	48.3	49.1	49.8	50.0	50.6	51.0	51.1	51.4	51.5	51.5	51.8	50.3
1995	51.1	51.1	52.3	52.1	52.5	53.9	54.3	54.5	55.1	54.8	55.1	55.5	53.5
1996	54.1	54.3	54.8	55.1	56.0	56.6	56.4	56.9	57.2	56.0	56.2	56.4	55.8
1997	55.5	55.7	56.6	57.3	58.4	59.2	59.9	60.0	59.9	59.8	59.7	59.9	58.4
1998	58.8	59.0	59.4	60.9	61.9	63.0	62.5	62.9	62.8	63.2	62.4	62.8	61.6
1999	61.4	61.8	62.3	62.2	62.7	63.6	63.7	64.2	64.0	63.5	63.4	63.3	63.0
2000	63.4	62.7	63.1	63.9	65.1	65.6	64.6	64.9	64.7	63.8	63.5	63.1	64.0
2001	60.2	59.9	58.6	60.4	60.3	60.6	59.9	59.6	58.7	57.9	57.5	57.3	59.2
2002	55.6	55.2	55.6	55.7	55.6	56.0	55.4	55.6	55.3	54.8	54.7	54.8	55.4
2003	53.2	52.6	53.2	54.2	54.5	55.1	54.9	55.1	55.0	54.9	54.8	54.4	54.3
Construction and mining													
1990	9.3	9.4	9.8	10.2	10.6	11.0	11.0	11.0	10.7	10.4	10.4	10.1	10.3
1991	9.1	9.0	9.5	10.2	10.5	10.8	10.9	11.0	10.8	10.6	10.6	10.2	10.2
1992	9.6	9.7	10.1	10.6	11.0	11.3	11.4	11.5	11.4	11.3	11.3	10.9	10.8
1993	10.1	10.2	10.2	11.0	11.6	12.4	12.4	12.8	12.5	12.0	11.6	11.1	11.4
1994	9.3	9.5	10.0	10.5	10.7	11.2	11.3	11.3	11.0	10.8	10.7	10.6	10.5
1995	9.7	9.5	10.4	10.7	11.0	11.7	11.9	11.7	11.8	11.5	11.4	11.4	11.0
1996	10.2	10.5	11.0	11.5	12.2	12.4	12.8	12.7	12.6	12.2	12.1	11.9	11.8
1997	11.3	11.5	11.9	12.0	12.6	12.7	13.0	13.0	12.8	12.8	12.7	12.4	12.3
1998	11.7	11.7	12.1	13.3	13.7	14.2	14.4	14.4	14.3	13.9	13.7	13.7	13.4
1999	12.6	12.9	13.1	13.9	14.2	14.8	15.1	14.8	14.7	14.3	14.2	14.1	14.0
2000	13.7	13.4	14.0	14.4	14.7	15.1	14.8	14.6	14.5	14.4	14.3	14.2	14.3
2001	13.9	13.9	14.1	15.0	15.2	15.5	15.7	15.4	15.0	14.6	14.6	14.3	14.8
2002	13.0	13.0	13.3	13.6	13.7	13.9	14.0	14.0	13.9	13.4	13.3	13.2	13.5
2003	12.3	11.8	12.4	13.4	13.7	14.1	14.5	14.4	14.4	14.5	14.5	14.1	13.7

Employment by Industry: Kentucky—*Continued*

(Numbers in thousands. Not seasonally adjusted.)

Industry	January	February	March	April	May	June	July	August	September	October	November	December	Annual Average
LEXINGTON-FAYETTE *—Continued*													
Manufacturing													
1990	34.9	35.1	34.9	34.2	34.5	34.8	34.9	35.2	35.2	35.1	34.8	35.5	34.9
1991	35.0	35.0	34.8	34.4	34.4	34.5	34.2	34.4	35.0	35.1	35.1	35.3	34.7
1992	34.9	35.2	35.4	35.9	36.0	36.2	36.0	36.3	36.2	36.6	36.5	37.2	36.0
1993	37.0	37.0	37.1	37.1	37.1	37.0	37.1	37.4	37.9	38.7	38.6	39.4	37.6
1994	38.5	38.8	39.1	39.3	39.3	39.4	39.7	39.8	40.4	40.7	40.8	41.2	39.7
1995	41.4	41.6	41.9	41.4	41.5	42.2	42.4	42.8	43.3	43.3	43.7	44.1	42.4
1996	43.9	43.8	43.8	43.6	43.8	44.2	43.6	44.2	44.6	43.8	44.1	44.5	43.9
1997	44.2	44.2	44.7	45.3	45.8	46.5	46.9	47.0	47.1	47.0	47.0	47.5	46.1
1998	47.1	47.3	47.3	47.6	48.2	48.8	48.1	48.5	48.5	49.3	48.7	49.1	48.2
1999	48.8	48.9	49.2	48.3	48.5	48.8	48.6	49.4	49.3	49.2	49.2	49.2	48.9
2000	49.7	49.3	49.1	49.5	50.4	50.5	49.8	50.3	50.2	49.4	49.2	48.9	49.6
2001	46.3	46.0	44.5	45.4	45.1	45.1	44.2	44.2	43.7	43.3	42.9	43.0	44.5
2002	42.6	42.2	42.3	42.1	41.9	42.1	41.4	41.6	41.4	41.4	41.4	41.6	41.8
2003	40.9	40.8	40.8	40.8	40.8	41.0	40.4	40.7	40.6	40.4	40.3	40.3	40.7
Service-providing													
1990	171.3	174.7	176.6	179.0	178.2	175.9	172.6	175.0	178.8	180.9	181.2	180.8	177.0
1991	173.4	176.0	177.3	180.0	176.5	175.5	173.0	175.4	180.7	183.2	183.5	185.4	178.3
1992	178.6	181.0	181.8	184.2	180.5	178.9	177.5	176.0	183.0	187.9	188.3	189.3	182.2
1993	181.2	186.4	186.7	189.8	189.8	186.9	184.6	184.9	189.8	193.0	194.6	194.9	188.5
1994	183.4	189.3	192.2	194.3	191.4	191.7	187.0	189.1	198.2	197.4	198.9	199.5	192.7
1995	188.6	194.1	197.1	199.6	199.0	198.0	191.9	194.1	200.4	203.6	204.5	205.6	198.0
1996	193.9	200.8	202.5	205.9	206.3	202.2	198.9	201.2	205.6	209.6	210.9	210.4	204.0
1997	201.7	206.5	207.5	211.4	211.5	208.4	204.7	205.7	211.7	215.7	216.7	217.3	209.9
1998	209.1	211.6	213.5	216.1	213.4	212.9	210.4	211.9	217.6	221.7	223.8	223.0	215.4
1999	213.6	217.7	219.5	224.4	224.8	223.6	217.7	220.3	224.4	227.1	227.4	227.0	222.2
2000	220.7	223.9	226.6	226.6	224.0	223.6	220.3	222.1	225.7	230.6	231.1	230.4	225.4
2001	216.2	219.1	219.8	223.1	222.6	220.6	216.0	217.0	220.0	221.6	222.4	220.8	219.9
2002	216.0	217.9	219.0	221.8	222.0	219.2	217.6	218.6	222.9	224.1	225.5	224.2	220.7
2003	218.4	219.1	221.1	223.0	222.7	219.2	215.8	219.0	223.5	224.5	224.7	225.5	221.4
Trade, transportation, and utilities													
1990	40.1	39.3	39.4	39.5	39.4	39.7	40.1	40.0	40.3	40.1	41.0	41.7	40.0
1991	39.5	38.4	38.6	38.2	38.8	38.9	38.6	39.5	39.9	39.6	40.6	42.0	39.3
1992	39.8	38.9	38.9	38.9	39.1	39.1	39.3	39.1	39.7	40.6	42.4	43.6	39.9
1993	41.1	40.4	40.2	41.0	41.6	41.9	41.8	42.1	42.6	43.9	45.3	46.3	42.3
1994	42.9	42.5	42.6	42.7	43.2	43.2	43.1	43.2	43.9	43.6	44.9	46.2	43.5
1995	43.3	42.7	42.9	42.8	43.5	44.4	44.1	44.7	45.4	46.0	47.3	48.3	44.6
1996	45.7	45.3	45.2	45.8	46.1	46.0	46.0	46.4	46.3	46.5	48.0	48.4	46.3
1997	46.4	45.8	46.0	45.9	46.1	46.4	46.8	46.9	47.8	49.2	50.2	51.3	47.4
1998	49.1	48.5	48.6	48.8	49.3	49.6	50.3	50.9	50.9	51.1	52.6	53.3	50.2
1999	50.9	50.5	50.6	50.9	51.3	51.6	52.0	52.2	51.7	52.1	53.2	54.1	51.7
2000	52.6	52.5	52.9	53.2	53.0	53.0	53.1	53.3	53.5	54.6	55.2	55.6	53.5
2001	50.8	50.3	50.2	50.1	50.0	49.9	49.6	49.8	49.7	49.9	50.7	50.9	50.2
2002	48.7	48.6	48.9	49.2	49.8	49.5	49.1	49.2	48.9	49.0	50.3	50.8	49.3
2003	48.3	47.7	48.1	48.4	48.8	48.9	49.2	49.2	49.5	49.7	50.1	51.0	49.1
Wholesale trade													
1990	7.1	6.9	6.8	6.7	6.7	6.7	6.9	6.8	6.9	6.9	7.1	7.2	6.8
1991	7.2	7.0	6.9	7.0	6.9	6.9	6.9	6.9	6.9	7.0	7.2	7.3	7.0
1992	7.2	6.9	6.9	7.1	6.9	6.9	7.0	6.9	7.0	7.0	7.3	7.4	7.0
1993	7.3	7.3	7.2	7.2	7.2	7.3	7.3	7.3	7.4	7.5	7.7	7.8	7.3
1994	7.6	7.6	7.6	7.4	7.4	7.4	7.6	7.5	7.6	7.7	7.9	8.0	7.6
1995	7.7	7.6	7.9	7.8	8.0	8.2	8.2	8.3	8.3	8.6	8.7	8.7	8.1
1996	8.6	8.5	8.5	8.3	8.3	8.4	8.5	8.5	8.6	8.6	8.8	8.8	8.5
1997	8.6	8.5	8.6	8.4	8.4	8.6	8.6	8.6	8.7	8.8	8.8	9.0	8.6
1998	8.9	8.9	9.0	8.9	8.9	8.9	8.9	8.9	9.1	9.2	9.3	9.2	9.0
1999	9.1	9.2	9.3	9.1	9.1	8.9	8.9	9.0	8.8	8.8	8.8	8.8	8.9
2000	9.0	9.0	9.1	9.2	9.2	9.2	9.4	9.3	9.4	9.5	9.4	9.4	9.2
2001	9.8	9.8	9.8	9.7	9.7	9.7	9.7	9.8	9.7	9.7	9.7	9.6	9.7
2002	9.6	9.7	9.7	9.7	10.0	9.8	9.7	9.9	9.9	9.9	10.1	10.1	9.8
2003	10.1	10.0	10.1	10.1	10.2	10.2	10.2	10.2	10.3	10.3	10.3	10.4	10.2
Retail trade													
1990	26.8	26.2	26.4	26.5	26.4	26.6	26.7	26.8	27.0	27.0	27.7	28.2	26.8
1991	26.0	25.3	25.6	25.1	25.7	25.8	25.4	26.3	26.6	26.3	27.1	28.0	26.1
1992	26.2	25.8	26.0	25.8	26.1	26.1	26.2	26.2	26.7	27.6	29.0	29.8	26.7
1993	27.5	27.2	27.2	27.8	28.4	28.5	28.4	28.8	29.1	29.9	31.1	31.7	28.8
1994	29.0	28.6	28.8	28.9	29.4	29.5	29.1	29.4	30.0	29.6	30.7	31.8	29.5
1995	29.3	28.9	29.0	28.9	29.3	29.9	29.2	29.7	30.3	30.5	31.6	32.4	29.9
1996	30.1	29.8	29.8	30.4	30.7	30.6	30.3	30.8	30.8	31.0	32.3	32.7	30.7
1997	31.1	30.8	31.0	30.8	30.9	31.0	31.3	31.9	32.0	32.9	33.9	34.7	31.8
1998	32.6	31.9	31.9	31.9	32.4	32.9	33.3	33.9	33.8	33.8	35.4	36.2	33.3
1999	33.8	33.5	33.5	33.6	34.0	34.4	34.4	34.6	34.3	34.4	35.6	36.4	34.3
2000	35.0	34.9	35.2	34.8	34.7	34.7	34.5	34.8	35.0	35.6	36.4	36.8	35.2
2001	33.0	32.4	32.3	32.2	32.2	32.0	31.6	31.8	31.8	31.8	32.7	33.0	32.2
2002	31.1	30.8	31.1	31.2	31.6	31.6	31.3	31.4	31.3	31.3	32.5	33.1	31.5
2003	30.7	30.3	30.6	30.9	31.1	31.3	31.4	31.5	31.7	32.0	32.3	33.0	31.4

Employment by Industry: Kentucky—*Continued*

(Numbers in thousands. Not seasonally adjusted.)

Industry	January	February	March	April	May	June	July	August	September	October	November	December	Annual Average
LEXINGTON-FAYETTE —*Continued*													
Transportation and utilities													
1990	6.2	6.2	6.2	6.3	6.3	6.4	6.5	6.4	6.4	6.2	6.2	6.3	6.3
1991	6.3	6.1	6.1	6.1	6.2	6.2	6.3	6.3	6.4	6.3	6.3	6.7	6.2
1992	6.4	6.2	6.0	6.0	6.1	6.1	6.1	6.0	6.0	6.0	6.1	6.4	6.1
1993	6.3	5.9	5.8	6.0	6.0	6.1	6.1	6.0	6.1	6.5	6.5	6.8	6.1
1994	6.3	6.3	6.2	6.4	6.4	6.3	6.4	6.3	6.3	6.3	6.3	6.4	6.3
1995	6.3	6.2	6.0	6.1	6.2	6.3	6.7	6.7	6.8	6.9	7.0	7.2	6.5
1996	7.0	7.0	6.9	7.1	7.1	7.0	7.2	7.1	6.9	6.9	6.9	6.9	7.0
1997	6.7	6.5	6.4	6.7	6.8	6.8	6.9	6.4	7.1	7.5	7.5	7.6	6.9
1998	7.6	7.7	7.7	8.0	8.0	7.8	8.1	8.1	8.0	8.1	7.9	7.9	7.9
1999	8.0	7.8	7.8	8.2	8.2	8.3	8.7	8.6	8.6	8.9	8.8	8.9	8.4
2000	8.6	8.6	8.6	9.2	9.1	9.1	9.2	9.2	9.1	9.5	9.4	9.4	9.0
2001	8.0	8.1	8.1	8.2	8.1	8.2	8.3	8.2	8.2	8.4	8.3	8.3	8.2
2002	8.0	8.1	8.1	8.3	8.2	8.1	8.1	7.9	7.7	7.8	7.7	7.6	8.0
2003	7.5	7.4	7.4	7.4	7.5	7.4	7.6	7.5	7.5	7.4	7.5	7.6	7.5
Information													
1990	4.6	4.7	4.7	4.7	4.7	4.8	4.7	4.7	4.7	4.6	4.7	4.7	4.6
1991	4.6	4.6	4.6	4.7	4.7	4.7	4.5	4.5	4.5	4.6	4.6	4.6	4.6
1992	4.5	4.6	4.6	4.5	4.4	4.4	4.5	4.4	4.4	4.4	4.3	4.4	4.4
1993	4.5	4.5	4.5	4.6	4.6	4.5	4.5	4.5	4.6	4.6	4.7	4.8	4.5
1994	4.7	4.8	4.8	4.8	4.8	5.0	5.0	4.9	4.9	4.8	4.9	5.0	4.8
1995	4.8	4.9	5.1	5.0	5.2	5.4	5.2	5.2	5.3	5.2	5.2	5.3	5.1
1996	5.1	5.2	5.4	5.1	5.1	5.1	5.1	5.2	5.2	4.9	5.0	5.0	5.1
1997	5.0	5.0	5.2	5.1	5.2	5.4	5.1	5.3	5.4	5.3	5.4	5.4	5.2
1998	5.3	5.4	5.4	5.3	5.3	5.4	5.4	5.3	5.3	5.3	5.4	5.4	5.3
1999	5.3	5.4	5.3	5.4	5.4	5.5	5.4	5.3	5.3	5.8	5.7	5.8	5.4
2000	5.7	5.8	5.9	6.0	6.0	6.1	6.0	6.0	5.9	6.1	6.1	6.4	6.0
2001	6.4	6.4	6.5	6.4	6.3	6.4	6.2	6.2	6.1	6.0	5.9	5.9	6.2
2002	5.9	6.1	6.1	6.1	6.1	6.1	6.1	6.1	6.0	6.0	6.0	6.0	6.1
2003	6.1	6.0	6.1	5.9	5.9	5.7	5.8	5.7	5.6	5.9	5.9	6.0	5.9
Financial activities													
1990	11.1	11.1	11.2	11.0	11.1	11.1	11.2	11.2	11.1	11.1	11.2	11.2	11.1
1991	11.1	10.9	11.0	10.9	10.9	10.9	11.0	10.9	10.8	10.8	10.8	10.9	10.9
1992	10.8	10.8	10.9	10.6	10.5	10.6	10.5	10.4	10.4	10.2	10.3	10.4	10.5
1993	10.5	10.4	10.6	10.6	10.6	10.6	10.4	10.3	10.3	10.3	10.6	10.7	10.4
1994	10.4	10.5	10.6	10.6	10.6	10.8	10.5	10.5	10.5	10.3	10.4	10.4	10.5
1995	10.3	10.4	10.4	10.4	10.4	10.5	10.3	10.4	10.4	10.4	10.5	10.6	10.4
1996	10.7	10.7	10.8	11.0	11.2	11.0	10.8	10.8	10.8	10.7	10.7	10.9	10.8
1997	10.6	10.6	10.7	10.7	10.7	10.8	10.8	10.7	10.8	11.0	11.1	11.3	10.8
1998	10.8	11.0	11.0	11.0	11.1	11.1	10.9	10.9	10.9	10.9	10.9	11.0	10.9
1999	11.1	11.1	11.2	11.2	11.2	11.3	11.5	11.5	11.4	11.3	11.3	11.5	11.3
2000	11.9	11.9	11.9	11.6	11.7	11.7	11.4	11.4	11.4	11.5	11.6	11.6	11.6
2001	11.2	11.2	11.2	11.3	11.2	11.3	11.2	11.2	11.1	11.3	11.4	11.5	11.3
2002	11.2	11.3	11.2	10.9	11.2	11.1	11.0	11.1	11.0	10.9	11.0	11.1	11.1
2003	11.0	11.0	11.0	11.0	11.1	11.2	11.0	11.2	11.0	11.0	11.0	10.9	11.0
Professional and business services													
1990	19.4	19.3	19.8	20.0	20.3	20.4	19.9	20.0	20.0	19.4	19.4	18.9	19.7
1991	19.0	19.4	19.6	19.7	19.5	19.6	19.2	19.3	19.2	18.8	19.0	19.3	19.3
1992	18.7	19.2	19.6	19.3	19.7	19.6	19.8	19.5	20.1	20.1	20.1	20.3	19.6
1993	20.2	21.0	20.7	20.8	21.5	21.8	21.2	21.1	21.2	20.9	20.8	20.8	21.0
1994	20.5	21.5	22.2	22.0	23.2	23.0	23.3	23.7	23.7	23.3	23.3	23.3	22.7
1995	22.6	22.9	23.7	23.9	24.2	24.7	23.9	24.6	24.3	24.5	24.5	24.9	24.0
1996	23.3	24.1	24.4	24.9	25.6	26.0	26.1	26.5	26.0	26.7	26.6	26.5	25.5
1997	25.8	26.4	26.9	27.6	28.2	28.7	28.4	28.2	28.0	27.6	27.9	28.3	27.6
1998	27.2	27.3	27.9	27.9	28.2	28.6	28.9	29.2	29.1	29.9	30.3	30.6	28.7
1999	29.1	28.9	29.8	31.2	31.3	31.5	31.2	31.8	31.8	31.7	31.4	31.2	30.9
2000	30.4	30.3	30.7	30.3	30.4	30.4	30.0	30.2	30.0	29.4	29.6	29.0	30.0
2001	28.3	28.3	28.3	28.1	28.0	28.0	27.5	27.4	27.1	26.8	27.0	27.2	27.7
2002	26.4	26.6	27.0	27.3	27.6	28.4	28.6	28.8	28.5	27.6	28.0	28.2	27.8
2003	26.9	26.7	27.0	27.1	27.1	27.3	26.9	27.5	27.8	27.7	27.7	28.0	27.3
Educational and health services													
1990	21.1	21.4	21.5	21.6	21.5	21.2	21.1	21.2	21.7	22.2	22.3	22.2	21.5
1991	22.2	22.5	22.5	22.8	22.8	22.7	22.4	22.6	23.2	23.3	23.5	23.6	22.8
1992	23.6	24.0	24.0	24.0	23.9	23.5	23.4	23.7	24.6	24.8	24.8	24.9	24.1
1993	24.5	24.8	25.0	25.1	24.9	24.7	25.1	25.1	25.8	25.9	25.9	25.7	25.2
1994	24.7	25.1	25.4	25.7	25.7	25.3	24.7	24.7	25.6	25.6	25.8	25.8	25.3
1995	25.3	25.7	25.9	25.9	25.8	25.8	25.3	25.5	26.0	26.2	26.3	26.4	25.8
1996	26.1	26.5	26.6	26.6	26.6	26.4	26.4	26.8	27.1	27.2	27.6	27.4	26.7
1997	27.1	27.6	27.7	27.5	27.7	27.4	27.4	27.6	28.2	28.6	28.9	28.8	27.8
1998	28.5	29.0	29.1	29.4	29.3	28.8	28.8	28.8	29.4	29.9	30.0	29.8	29.2
1999	28.8	29.4	29.5	30.1	30.0	29.5	29.4	29.5	29.8	30.2	30.2	29.9	29.6
2000	30.1	30.4	30.6	30.9	30.8	30.7	30.6	30.8	30.8	31.5	31.4	31.0	30.8
2001	31.4	31.8	32.1	32.0	32.1	31.9	32.0	32.2	32.5	32.8	32.9	32.6	32.2
2002	32.9	33.2	33.3	33.4	33.3	33.1	33.2	33.3	33.8	34.8	35.0	34.9	33.7
2003	34.7	34.9	35.1	35.0	35.2	34.9	34.3	34.5	34.7	34.8	34.9	34.6	34.8

Employment by Industry: Kentucky—*Continued*

(Numbers in thousands. Not seasonally adjusted.)

Industry	January	February	March	April	May	June	July	August	September	October	November	December	Annual Average
LEXINGTON-FAYETTE *—Continued*													
Leisure and hospitality													
1990	19.6	19.9	20.6	22.0	21.5	21.8	21.2	21.4	21.8	22.8	21.3	21.1	21.2
1991	19.5	19.6	20.1	22.2	21.7	21.7	21.4	21.3	22.0	23.0	21.2	20.9	21.2
1992	20.1	20.1	20.4	23.1	22.1	22.4	22.2	22.0	22.5	23.9	22.2	21.7	21.8
1993	21.0	21.3	21.9	23.7	22.9	23.2	22.6	22.6	22.9	23.6	22.5	22.0	22.5
1994	21.2	21.2	22.2	23.6	24.6	23.8	23.3	23.3	23.6	24.5	23.5	22.8	23.1
1995	22.2	22.3	22.9	24.9	24.6	24.7	24.2	24.4	24.8	25.8	24.5	24.2	24.1
1996	22.8	23.5	24.1	25.9	25.4	25.3	25.2	25.1	25.8	26.7	25.8	25.3	25.0
1997	24.5	24.7	24.7	27.1	27.0	27.0	26.5	26.4	26.4	27.2	26.1	25.5	26.0
1998	24.1	24.1	24.7	27.0	26.5	26.6	26.6	26.5	26.5	27.3	26.8	25.8	26.0
1999	24.9	25.2	25.6	27.9	27.2	27.2	27.5	27.2	27.8	28.7	27.8	27.4	27.0
2000	25.6	25.8	26.6	26.7	26.1	26.0	27.2	26.9	27.1	28.9	28.3	28.0	26.9
2001	25.2	25.3	25.4	28.5	28.3	27.6	27.6	27.4	27.5	28.5	28.0	26.6	27.2
2002	25.2	25.8	26.1	27.8	27.9	27.7	27.8	27.8	27.9	28.5	27.7	26.3	27.2
2003	25.3	25.8	26.4	28.4	27.7	28.0	27.3	27.6	27.8	27.9	27.4	27.5	27.3
Other services													
1990	9.6	9.7	9.8	9.8	9.8	9.8	9.9	9.9	10.0	9.8	9.8	9.7	9.8
1991	9.3	9.3	9.4	9.5	9.5	9.6	9.5	9.6	9.7	9.6	9.6	9.6	9.5
1992	9.4	9.5	9.5	9.5	9.5	9.6	9.6	9.5	9.6	9.5	9.4	9.5	9.5
1993	9.4	9.4	9.4	9.5	9.5	9.7	9.4	9.4	9.4	9.3	9.3	9.4	9.4
1994	9.2	9.3	9.4	9.5	9.5	9.6	9.4	9.4	9.4	9.4	9.4	9.5	9.4
1995	9.4	9.4	9.5	9.6	9.6	9.7	9.7	9.5	9.6	9.5	9.5	9.5	9.5
1996	9.5	9.6	9.6	9.6	9.7	9.8	9.8	9.8	9.8	9.8	9.8	9.8	9.7
1997	9.7	9.7	9.8	9.8	9.9	10.0	10.0	9.9	9.9	9.9	9.9	9.8	9.8
1998	9.8	9.8	9.9	9.9	10.0	10.1	10.1	10.0	10.1	10.0	10.0	10.1	9.9
1999	10.1	10.2	10.3	10.3	10.4	10.5	10.5	10.5	10.5	10.3	10.3	10.3	10.3
2000	10.3	10.3	10.4	10.4	10.6	10.6	10.5	10.4	10.4	10.3	10.4	10.4	10.4
2001	9.8	9.8	9.9	10.1	10.1	10.2	9.9	10.0	9.9	10.0	10.0	10.0	10.0
2002	9.9	10.0	10.0	10.1	10.2	10.2	10.2	10.3	10.2	10.3	10.3	10.3	10.2
2003	10.3	10.2	10.4	10.4	10.5	10.4	10.6	10.6	10.6	10.6	10.6	10.6	10.5
Government													
1990	45.8	49.3	49.6	50.4	49.9	47.1	44.5	46.6	49.2	50.9	51.5	51.3	48.8
1991	48.2	51.3	51.5	52.0	48.6	47.4	46.4	47.7	51.4	53.5	54.2	54.5	50.5
1992	51.7	53.9	53.9	54.3	51.3	49.7	48.2	47.4	51.7	54.4	54.8	54.5	52.1
1993	50.0	54.6	54.4	54.5	54.2	50.5	49.6	49.8	53.0	54.5	55.5	55.2	52.9
1994	49.8	54.4	55.0	55.4	49.8	51.0	47.7	49.4	56.6	55.9	56.7	56.5	53.1
1995	50.7	55.8	56.7	57.1	55.7	52.8	49.2	49.8	54.6	56.0	56.7	56.4	54.2
1996	50.7	55.9	56.4	57.0	56.6	52.6	49.5	50.6	54.6	57.1	57.4	57.1	54.6
1997	52.6	56.7	56.5	57.7	56.7	52.7	49.7	50.7	55.2	56.9	57.2	56.9	54.9
1998	54.3	56.5	56.9	56.8	53.7	52.7	49.4	50.3	55.4	57.3	57.8	57.0	54.8
1999	53.4	57.0	57.2	57.4	58.0	56.5	50.2	52.3	56.1	57.0	57.5	56.8	55.7
2000	54.1	56.9	57.6	57.5	55.4	55.1	51.5	53.1	56.6	58.3	58.5	58.4	56.0
2001	53.1	56.0	56.2	56.6	56.6	55.3	52.0	52.8	56.1	56.3	56.5	56.1	55.3
2002	55.8	56.3	56.4	57.0	55.9	53.1	51.6	52.0	56.6	57.0	57.2	56.6	55.5
2003	55.8	56.8	57.0	56.8	56.4	52.8	50.7	52.7	56.5	56.9	57.1	56.9	55.5
Federal government													
1992	6.6	6.6	6.6	6.5	6.5	6.5	6.6	6.6	6.6	6.6	6.6	6.7	6.5
1993	6.4	6.3	6.3	6.2	6.2	6.2	6.1	6.1	5.8	5.7	5.7	5.7	6.0
1994	5.7	5.7	5.6	5.7	5.7	5.7	5.7	5.7	5.7	5.6	5.6	5.7	5.6
1995	5.6	5.5	5.5	5.5	5.5	5.6	5.6	5.6	5.5	5.5	5.5	5.5	5.5
1996	5.4	5.4	5.4	5.4	5.4	5.4	5.4	5.4	5.4	5.4	5.4	5.4	5.4
1997	5.4	5.4	5.4	5.5	5.5	5.4	5.4	5.4	5.3	5.3	5.3	5.4	5.3
1998	5.3	5.2	5.3	5.3	5.3	5.3	5.3	5.3	5.3	5.3	5.4	5.4	5.3
1999	5.3	5.3	5.3	5.3	5.3	5.3	5.3	5.3	5.2	5.2	5.3	5.3	5.2
2000	5.3	5.4	5.3	5.4	6.0	5.9	5.5	5.7	5.3	5.2	5.3	5.4	5.4
2001	5.3	5.2	5.2	5.2	5.3	5.3	5.3	5.3	5.2	5.2	5.2	5.3	5.3
2002	5.2	5.2	5.2	5.2	5.2	5.2	5.2	5.2	5.1	5.2	5.2	5.2	5.2
2003	5.1	5.2	5.2	5.2	5.2	5.2	5.2	5.2	5.2	5.1	5.1	5.1	5.2
State government													
1992	29.3	31.4	31.4	31.5	28.2	26.9	28.4	27.4	30.4	31.7	31.8	31.7	30.0
1993	27.4	31.8	31.7	31.8	31.3	27.5	27.9	27.9	31.3	32.5	32.9	32.2	30.5
1994	27.6	32.2	32.7	32.9	27.1	28.3	28.6	28.6	35.3	33.2	33.5	33.2	31.1
1995	28.0	33.0	33.3	33.6	32.2	28.8	28.5	28.5	31.9	33.1	33.4	33.2	31.4
1996	27.8	32.7	33.1	33.5	32.8	28.8	28.9	28.9	32.1	33.8	34.0	33.6	31.6
1997	29.4	33.4	33.0	33.7	32.7	28.8	29.0	28.9	32.7	33.9	34.0	33.1	31.8
1998	31.2	33.3	33.5	33.4	30.0	29.1	29.0	28.8	33.1	33.7	33.9	33.1	31.8
1999	29.7	33.1	33.2	33.3	33.7	31.5	28.7	29.1	32.2	32.9	33.1	32.4	31.9
2000	29.5	31.9	32.6	32.8	29.9	29.3	29.1	29.9	32.9	33.4	33.4	33.2	31.4
2001	28.2	31.0	31.1	31.3	30.9	28.8	27.6	28.7	31.0	31.0	31.0	30.7	30.1
2002	30.8	30.8	30.9	31.3	30.1	27.7	27.8	28.2	31.2	31.4	31.6	31.2	30.3
2003	30.3	31.2	31.2	31.2	30.5	28.0	27.9	28.2	31.1	31.4	31.5	31.4	30.3

Employment by Industry: Kentucky—*Continued*

(Numbers in thousands. Not seasonally adjusted.)

Industry	January	February	March	April	May	June	July	August	September	October	November	December	Annual Average
LEXINGTON-FAYETTE *—Continued*													
Local government													
1992	15.8	15.9	15.9	16.3	16.6	16.3	13.2	13.4	14.7	16.1	16.4	16.1	15.5
1993	16.2	16.5	16.4	16.5	16.7	16.8	15.6	15.8	15.9	16.3	16.9	17.3	16.4
1994	16.5	16.5	16.7	16.8	17.0	17.0	13.4	15.1	15.6	17.1	17.6	17.6	16.4
1995	17.1	17.3	17.9	18.0	18.0	18.4	15.1	15.7	17.2	17.4	17.8	17.7	17.3
1996	17.5	17.8	17.9	18.1	18.4	18.4	15.2	16.3	17.1	17.9	18.0	18.1	17.5
1997	17.8	17.9	18.1	18.5	18.5	18.5	15.3	16.4	17.2	17.7	17.9	18.4	17.6
1998	17.8	18.0	18.1	18.1	18.4	18.3	15.1	16.2	17.0	18.3	18.5	18.5	17.6
1999	18.4	18.6	18.7	18.8	19.0	19.7	16.2	17.9	18.7	18.9	19.1	19.1	18.5
2000	19.3	19.6	19.7	19.3	19.5	19.9	16.9	17.5	18.4	19.7	19.8	19.8	19.1
2001	19.6	19.8	19.9	20.1	20.4	21.2	19.1	18.8	19.9	20.1	20.3	20.1	19.9
2002	19.8	20.3	20.3	20.5	20.6	20.2	18.6	18.6	20.3	20.4	20.4	20.2	20.0
2003	20.4	20.4	20.6	20.4	20.7	19.6	17.6	19.3	20.2	20.4	20.5	20.4	20.0
LOUISVILLE													
Total nonfarm													
1990	459.7	463.4	466.7	471.6	478.4	483.5	483.5	486.3	484.4	486.0	484.2	487.0	477.8
1991	464.6	466.3	468.5	474.2	479.2	482.1	478.4	482.0	481.1	479.9	484.5	484.7	477.1
1992	473.8	476.5	480.2	486.2	492.2	496.9	492.6	492.4	495.2	492.3	493.0	494.1	488.7
1993	482.3	484.8	488.7	495.9	499.9	504.3	502.9	503.3	506.0	505.3	508.9	509.3	499.3
1994	495.0	498.9	506.2	511.6	517.1	523.2	519.2	520.5	523.6	518.7	524.0	526.1	515.3
1995	511.5	514.5	521.2	522.8	528.4	533.2	529.8	532.6	535.8	531.4	534.5	535.8	527.6
1996	521.5	522.8	527.3	531.7	538.5	542.1	536.6	541.0	541.9	543.4	546.8	547.6	536.7
1997	533.2	534.4	541.3	547.8	551.7	556.5	551.9	548.1	553.8	556.6	558.5	562.0	549.6
1998	547.9	549.5	555.4	561.0	566.4	568.5	569.6	571.9	572.2	570.3	574.4	577.2	565.3
1999	561.7	564.9	568.8	576.0	579.0	583.6	584.5	584.1	584.1	587.0	588.0	592.6	579.5
2000	578.4	579.7	585.2	591.3	596.5	599.3	592.9	593.7	593.6	593.9	593.6	594.3	591.0
2001	577.8	578.6	580.7	585.0	587.2	586.4	583.8	582.8	580.7	576.6	576.7	574.0	580.9
2002	560.5	560.8	564.2	564.0	569.5	569.4	568.5	569.3	568.3	566.6	568.8	568.4	566.5
2003	552.5	552.4	557.0	561.4	565.8	568.2	559.8	562.5	562.6	563.7	564.9	565.7	561.4
Total private													
1990	396.8	400.1	402.8	406.6	412.3	418.2	421.5	423.1	420.0	421.1	419.1	421.5	413.5
1991	399.8	400.9	403.2	408.3	413.1	416.1	412.7	416.6	415.2	413.4	417.8	417.6	411.2
1992	407.1	409.8	413.4	419.0	424.9	428.5	427.3	426.9	428.3	425.4	425.5	426.5	421.8
1993	415.3	417.1	420.8	427.6	431.7	436.3	437.5	437.2	437.8	436.7	439.9	440.4	431.5
1994	426.7	430.6	437.6	443.1	448.7	454.7	452.9	454.4	456.2	451.0	456.0	458.0	447.4
1995	444.1	446.0	452.7	454.0	459.8	465.5	463.3	465.9	467.3	463.0	465.9	467.2	459.5
1996	453.6	454.3	458.4	462.9	469.0	473.1	470.9	475.3	474.8	475.4	478.8	479.2	468.8
1997	465.5	465.8	472.6	478.7	482.1	487.7	484.8	480.8	485.1	487.9	489.2	492.2	481.0
1998	478.6	479.2	484.6	490.8	495.0	498.2	501.2	503.5	501.1	499.1	502.5	505.0	494.9
1999	489.9	492.3	496.0	503.0	505.9	511.2	515.1	514.5	512.2	514.3	515.1	519.5	507.4
2000	506.0	505.6	510.3	515.4	519.6	521.5	521.5	522.2	520.5	520.5	520.4	520.7	517.0
2001	505.1	504.9	506.9	511.1	513.0	513.8	511.3	511.7	507.2	504.1	503.8	501.3	507.9
2002	489.5	488.7	491.9	491.9	496.9	497.7	499.7	500.2	497.0	494.3	496.2	495.9	495.0
2003	481.2	480.3	484.6	488.6	493.0	495.5	492.8	495.1	492.9	493.3	494.3	495.2	490.6
Goods-producing													
1990	101.4	102.3	102.7	103.5	104.5	106.1	107.6	107.3	106.2	105.8	104.7	105.0	104.7
1991	99.5	99.1	98.5	99.9	100.6	101.4	101.7	102.5	101.9	101.5	101.5	101.1	100.7
1992	99.0	99.6	100.4	101.6	102.8	103.8	104.8	104.7	104.9	104.5	103.5	103.4	102.7
1993	101.0	101.0	101.8	103.7	104.6	106.9	108.2	108.4	109.2	108.0	108.7	108.4	105.8
1994	104.9	105.4	107.7	109.1	110.2	111.8	113.0	113.2	113.4	111.7	112.2	112.6	110.4
1995	109.5	109.2	111.1	109.9	111.3	113.3	112.7	112.9	113.1	112.2	112.3	112.1	111.6
1996	108.5	108.3	109.4	109.4	109.9	111.2	112.7	112.8	113.6	114.8	115.1	113.8	111.6
1997	111.8	110.9	112.8	112.8	113.4	114.2	114.8	115.1	115.0	114.7	114.2	114.1	113.6
1998	113.9	112.8	113.8	115.3	115.3	115.8	118.1	118.2	117.8	117.8	117.4	117.9	116.1
1999	115.7	116.2	117.1	118.7	118.7	120.1	121.3	120.2	120.3	119.0	118.7	119.1	118.7
2000	117.1	116.7	118.1	119.0	119.4	119.5	120.3	119.8	119.5	119.3	118.8	118.4	118.8
2001	112.5	112.5	112.9	113.1	113.3	113.6	112.1	111.7	110.6	109.6	108.6	107.3	111.5
2002	104.4	104.0	104.1	104.2	104.1	104.9	105.8	106.0	105.7	104.6	104.0	103.8	104.6
2003	100.7	100.1	100.5	101.1	101.6	101.9	101.8	102.1	101.6	102.0	101.2	102.0	101.4
Construction and mining													
1990	20.4	20.8	21.5	22.2	23.1	23.9	24.8	24.9	24.2	23.8	23.1	22.8	22.9
1991	19.6	19.5	19.5	20.8	21.7	22.2	22.5	22.9	22.3	22.0	21.8	21.4	21.3
1992	20.0	20.4	20.9	21.6	22.2	23.1	23.9	23.8	23.6	23.7	22.9	22.8	22.4
1993	21.3	21.3	21.7	23.3	24.1	25.2	26.4	26.1	25.8	25.5	25.7	25.1	24.2
1994	22.1	22.5	24.0	25.0	25.3	26.2	26.7	26.6	26.7	26.2	25.9	25.6	25.2
1995	23.9	23.4	25.0	25.6	26.0	27.1	27.4	27.3	27.4	26.9	26.5	26.2	26.0
1996	23.7	24.2	25.2	26.0	26.8	27.6	28.5	28.6	28.4	28.3	28.3	27.9	26.9
1997	25.9	26.1	27.1	28.1	29.0	29.7	30.3	30.4	30.4	29.7	29.1	29.7	28.7
1998	27.6	26.9	27.7	28.7	29.3	29.9	31.0	30.9	30.7	30.4	30.0	30.2	29.4
1999	27.7	28.2	29.1	30.6	30.7	31.8	32.6	32.0	31.8	31.1	30.7	30.2	30.5
2000	28.7	28.7	30.1	30.9	31.4	31.9	32.1	31.9	31.7	31.0	30.6	30.2	30.7
2001	29.1	29.4	30.0	31.3	32.0	32.8	32.9	32.5	31.8	31.3	30.9	30.1	31.2
2002	28.0	28.2	28.6	28.9	29.5	30.3	30.7	31.0	31.1	30.4	30.2	30.0	29.7
2003	28.0	27.4	28.1	29.2	29.5	29.8	30.0	30.1	29.8	29.9	29.8	29.6	29.3

Employment by Industry: Kentucky—*Continued*

(Numbers in thousands. Not seasonally adjusted.)

Industry	January	February	March	April	May	June	July	August	September	October	November	December	Annual Average
LOUISVILLE—*Continued*													
Manufacturing													
1990	81.0	81.5	81.2	81.3	81.4	82.2	82.8	82.4	82.0	82.0	81.6	82.2	81.8
1991	79.9	79.6	79.0	79.1	78.9	79.2	79.2	79.6	79.6	79.5	79.7	79.7	79.4
1992	79.0	79.2	79.5	80.0	80.6	80.7	80.9	80.9	81.3	80.8	80.6	80.6	80.3
1993	79.7	79.7	80.1	80.4	80.5	81.7	81.8	82.3	83.4	82.5	83.0	83.3	81.5
1994	82.8	82.9	83.7	84.1	84.9	85.6	86.3	86.6	86.7	85.5	86.3	87.0	85.2
1995	85.6	85.8	86.1	84.3	85.3	86.2	85.3	85.6	85.7	85.3	85.8	85.9	85.5
1996	84.8	84.1	84.2	83.4	83.1	83.6	84.2	84.2	85.2	86.5	86.8	85.9	84.6
1997	85.9	84.8	85.7	84.7	84.4	84.5	84.5	84.7	84.6	85.0	85.1	84.4	84.8
1998	86.3	85.9	86.1	86.6	86.0	85.9	87.1	87.3	87.1	87.4	87.4	87.7	86.7
1999	88.0	88.0	88.0	88.1	88.0	88.3	88.7	88.2	88.5	87.9	88.0	88.9	88.2
2000	88.4	88.0	88.0	88.1	88.0	87.6	88.2	87.9	87.8	88.3	88.2	88.2	88.0
2001	83.4	83.1	82.9	81.8	81.3	80.8	79.2	79.2	78.8	78.3	77.7	77.2	80.3
2002	76.4	75.8	75.5	75.3	74.6	74.6	75.1	75.0	74.6	74.2	73.8	73.8	74.9
2003	72.7	72.7	72.4	71.9	72.1	72.1	71.8	72.0	71.8	72.1	71.4	72.4	72.1
Service-providing													
1990	358.3	361.1	364.0	368.1	373.9	377.4	375.9	379.0	378.2	380.2	379.5	382.0	373.1
1991	365.1	367.2	370.0	374.3	378.6	380.7	376.7	379.5	379.2	378.4	383.0	383.6	376.3
1992	374.8	376.9	379.8	384.6	389.4	393.1	387.8	387.7	390.3	387.8	389.5	390.7	386.0
1993	381.3	383.8	386.9	392.2	395.3	397.4	394.7	394.9	396.8	397.3	400.2	400.9	393.4
1994	390.1	393.5	398.5	402.5	406.9	411.4	406.2	407.3	410.2	407.0	411.8	413.5	404.9
1995	402.0	405.3	410.1	412.9	417.1	419.9	417.1	419.7	422.7	419.2	422.2	423.7	415.9
1996	413.0	414.5	417.9	422.3	428.6	430.9	423.9	428.2	428.3	428.6	431.7	433.8	425.1
1997	421.4	423.5	428.5	435.0	438.3	442.3	437.1	433.0	438.8	441.9	444.3	447.9	436.0
1998	434.0	436.7	441.6	445.7	451.1	452.7	451.5	453.7	454.4	452.5	457.0	459.3	449.1
1999	446.0	448.7	451.7	457.3	460.3	463.5	463.2	463.9	463.8	468.0	469.3	473.5	460.7
2000	461.3	463.0	467.1	472.3	477.1	479.8	472.6	473.9	474.1	474.6	474.8	475.9	472.2
2001	465.3	466.1	467.8	471.9	473.9	472.8	471.7	471.1	470.1	467.0	468.1	466.7	469.4
2002	456.1	456.8	460.1	459.8	465.4	464.5	462.7	463.3	462.6	462.0	464.8	464.6	461.9
2003	451.8	452.3	456.5	460.3	464.2	466.3	458.0	460.4	461.0	461.7	463.7	463.7	460.0
Trade, transportation, and utilities													
1990	109.1	108.6	109.0	108.8	109.6	110.9	112.3	113.0	112.1	113.8	113.6	115.2	111.3
1991	107.1	106.1	106.2	105.1	106.2	106.7	104.8	107.2	107.4	107.7	110.9	112.0	107.2
1992	107.1	106.3	106.8	108.6	109.8	110.6	110.9	110.6	111.1	111.6	113.6	115.0	110.1
1993	108.5	107.8	108.3	109.1	110.4	111.6	112.3	112.2	111.8	113.2	115.2	117.1	111.4
1994	113.9	113.7	114.8	116.0	117.5	119.2	118.4	118.9	119.6	119.3	122.1	123.6	118.0
1995	118.8	117.6	118.5	119.1	119.9	121.4	121.9	122.4	122.9	124.3	126.7	128.2	121.8
1996	123.4	122.4	122.9	123.7	124.9	124.8	125.4	125.5	124.5	128.6	131.3	132.9	125.8
1997	127.4	125.6	126.0	127.9	128.0	129.2	129.2	123.5	128.6	131.3	133.0	135.6	128.7
1998	129.0	128.0	129.0	130.2	131.4	131.3	134.0	135.6	134.2	134.1	136.4	138.0	132.6
1999	132.5	131.0	132.0	134.0	134.8	135.5	136.2	136.2	135.4	138.0	139.7	141.7	135.5
2000	138.2	136.5	137.0	138.9	139.7	139.5	138.6	138.9	138.0	138.5	140.1	141.3	138.7
2001	134.2	132.5	131.9	132.7	132.7	132.5	132.1	132.2	131.1	132.0	133.1	133.1	132.5
2002	128.4	127.2	127.6	125.0	125.4	125.6	127.9	127.3	126.5	126.0	128.4	129.3	127.1
2003	122.9	122.0	122.3	122.6	123.2	123.4	122.8	123.6	123.3	123.7	125.8	126.8	123.5
Wholesale trade													
1990	22.2	22.3	22.5	22.3	22.5	22.7	22.7	22.7	22.6	22.8	22.5	22.7	22.5
1991	21.7	21.8	21.8	21.9	22.0	22.0	21.6	21.7	21.5	21.4	21.5	21.5	21.7
1992	21.6	21.6	21.7	21.9	22.1	22.3	22.3	22.1	22.2	22.1	22.0	22.1	22.0
1993	22.1	22.2	22.2	22.4	22.4	22.5	22.4	22.4	22.4	22.5	22.6	22.8	22.4
1994	22.6	22.7	23.0	23.0	23.3	23.6	23.5	23.6	23.7	23.6	23.8	24.0	23.3
1995	24.0	24.2	24.4	24.3	24.5	24.9	24.8	24.8	25.1	25.1	25.2	25.4	24.7
1996	25.4	25.2	25.2	25.0	25.2	25.4	25.4	25.5	25.5	25.7	25.8	26.2	25.4
1997	26.0	26.1	26.2	26.5	26.5	26.7	26.8	26.8	26.8	26.7	26.6	27.0	26.5
1998	26.5	26.6	26.6	26.2	26.4	26.5	26.9	26.9	26.9	26.7	26.7	27.0	26.6
1999	27.4	27.3	27.4	27.9	27.7	27.8	27.4	27.3	27.3	27.7	27.7	28.1	27.5
2000	28.5	28.5	28.6	28.8	29.0	28.8	28.2	28.3	28.3	28.8	28.7	29.0	28.6
2001	29.7	29.6	29.6	29.5	29.5	29.4	29.3	29.2	29.1	29.1	28.6	28.4	29.3
2002	27.9	27.9	27.9	27.6	27.5	27.3	27.2	27.0	26.6	26.7	26.5	26.5	27.2
2003	26.4	26.5	26.5	26.5	26.5	26.5	26.4	26.3	26.4	26.5	26.6	26.7	26.5
Retail trade													
1990	59.6	59.0	59.1	58.9	59.2	59.9	60.8	61.5	61.1	62.0	62.8	64.5	60.7
1991	58.7	57.7	57.9	55.8	56.6	56.9	55.7	57.6	57.9	58.1	60.6	61.5	57.9
1992	57.7	56.7	57.2	57.4	58.3	58.5	58.8	58.9	59.1	59.8	61.6	62.7	58.8
1993	58.2	57.5	57.7	57.6	58.7	59.5	59.9	59.8	59.0	60.3	61.8	63.2	59.4
1994	59.5	59.2	59.9	59.9	61.1	62.4	61.5	62.4	63.1	62.2	64.5	66.1	61.8
1995	62.0	60.8	61.6	61.2	62.1	63.2	62.5	63.2	63.5	63.1	66.0	67.4	63.0
1996	63.4	62.5	63.1	62.9	64.2	64.4	63.9	64.1	63.9	64.6	67.7	69.5	64.5
1997	65.0	63.7	64.3	64.2	64.8	65.8	65.4	65.8	65.2	66.0	68.2	70.5	65.7
1998	65.6	64.7	65.7	65.5	66.7	67.2	67.5	68.7	67.5	67.4	70.4	72.0	67.4
1999	66.4	65.5	66.6	67.4	68.6	69.5	68.7	69.2	68.7	68.5	70.7	72.5	68.5
2000	68.3	67.1	67.6	67.6	68.5	69.1	67.4	67.9	67.5	66.4	68.7	70.0	68.0
2001	64.3	63.2	63.2	62.9	63.5	63.8	62.8	62.9	62.5	62.9	64.7	65.4	63.5
2002	62.3	61.5	62.3	61.7	62.3	63.0	62.4	62.1	61.8	61.4	64.1	65.2	62.5
2003	60.7	59.8	60.2	60.6	61.3	61.6	61.0	61.7	61.5	61.7	63.3	64.1	61.5

Employment by Industry: Kentucky—*Continued*

(Numbers in thousands. Not seasonally adjusted.)

Industry	January	February	March	April	May	June	July	August	September	October	November	December	Annual Average
LOUISVILLE—*Continued*													
Transportation and utilities													
1990	27.3	27.3	27.4	27.6	27.9	28.3	28.8	28.8	28.4	29.0	28.3	28.0	28.0
1991	26.7	26.6	26.5	27.4	27.6	27.8	27.5	27.9	28.0	28.2	28.8	29.0	27.6
1992	27.8	28.0	27.9	29.3	29.4	29.8	29.8	29.6	29.8	29.7	30.0	30.2	29.2
1993	28.2	28.1	28.4	29.1	29.3	29.6	30.0	30.0	30.4	30.4	30.8	31.1	29.6
1994	31.8	31.8	31.9	33.1	33.1	33.2	33.4	32.9	32.8	33.5	33.8	33.5	32.9
1995	32.8	32.6	32.5	33.6	33.3	33.3	34.6	34.4	34.3	36.1	35.5	35.4	34.0
1996	34.6	34.7	34.6	35.8	35.5	35.0	36.1	35.9	35.1	38.3	37.8	37.2	35.8
1997	36.4	35.8	35.5	37.2	36.7	36.7	37.0	30.9	36.6	38.6	38.2	38.1	36.4
1998	36.9	36.7	36.7	38.5	38.3	37.6	39.6	40.0	39.8	40.0	39.3	39.0	38.5
1999	38.7	38.2	38.0	38.7	38.5	38.2	40.1	39.7	39.4	41.8	41.3	41.1	39.4
2000	41.4	40.9	40.8	42.5	42.2	41.6	43.0	42.7	42.2	43.3	42.7	42.3	42.1
2001	40.2	39.7	39.1	40.3	39.7	39.3	40.0	40.1	39.5	40.0	39.8	39.3	39.8
2002	38.2	37.8	37.4	35.7	35.6	35.3	38.3	38.2	38.1	37.9	37.8	37.6	37.3
2003	35.8	35.7	35.6	35.5	35.4	35.3	35.4	35.6	35.4	35.5	35.9	36.0	35.6
Information													
1990	9.9	10.0	10.1	10.1	10.3	10.3	10.3	10.4	10.3	10.3	10.4	10.7	10.2
1991	10.5	10.5	10.5	10.3	10.2	10.3	10.5	10.5	10.4	10.3	10.3	10.3	10.3
1992	10.1	10.1	10.1	10.2	10.2	10.2	10.0	10.0	9.9	10.0	10.0	10.0	10.0
1993	10.0	9.9	10.0	9.9	9.9	10.0	10.1	10.1	10.0	10.2	10.3	10.4	10.0
1994	10.0	10.0	10.2	10.2	10.2	10.2	10.1	10.1	10.1	10.0	10.1	10.0	10.1
1995	10.2	10.2	10.2	10.2	10.2	10.3	10.3	10.3	10.2	10.1	10.1	10.2	10.2
1996	10.4	10.4	10.4	10.4	10.7	10.8	10.8	10.9	10.9	10.9	11.1	11.0	10.7
1997	11.3	11.5	11.6	12.0	11.8	11.8	12.0	11.9	11.7	12.0	12.0	12.1	11.8
1998	12.4	12.4	12.5	12.7	12.8	12.8	12.3	12.3	12.1	12.0	12.0	12.2	12.3
1999	12.3	12.4	12.5	12.2	12.3	12.5	12.0	12.1	11.9	12.4	12.4	12.6	12.3
2000	13.0	13.1	13.5	13.5	13.7	13.9	13.9	14.0	14.1	14.0	14.0	13.8	13.7
2001	13.2	13.2	13.3	13.2	13.1	12.9	12.9	12.7	12.5	12.3	12.1	12.1	12.8
2002	12.3	12.1	12.0	11.3	11.2	11.3	11.4	11.2	11.2	11.1	11.2	11.3	11.5
2003	11.1	11.1	11.2	10.9	11.0	11.1	11.1	11.1	11.0	11.1	11.1	10.9	11.1
Financial activities													
1990	28.0	28.2	28.1	28.1	28.2	28.7	29.0	28.8	28.4	28.4	28.2	28.4	28.3
1991	27.2	27.4	27.4	27.7	27.6	27.9	28.2	28.1	27.8	27.5	27.4	27.4	27.6
1992	27.4	27.6	27.7	28.0	28.2	28.6	28.3	28.2	28.0	27.8	27.6	27.8	27.9
1993	28.7	28.8	28.9	29.0	29.1	29.3	29.3	29.2	28.9	28.7	28.8	28.7	28.9
1994	28.5	28.4	28.6	29.0	29.4	29.8	30.1	30.1	29.9	29.7	29.7	29.6	29.4
1995	28.1	28.3	28.5	28.3	28.5	28.8	28.9	29.0	29.0	28.5	28.7	28.9	28.6
1996	28.5	28.5	28.5	28.7	29.1	29.5	29.8	29.9	29.8	29.6	29.6	29.7	29.2
1997	29.3	29.4	29.7	30.0	30.1	30.2	30.8	30.9	30.5	30.9	30.8	31.2	30.3
1998	30.4	30.4	30.4	30.4	30.8	30.8	30.9	30.8	30.6	30.3	30.3	30.6	30.5
1999	31.1	31.1	30.9	31.1	31.2	31.5	31.5	31.4	30.9	31.2	31.1	31.3	31.1
2000	35.9	35.8	35.5	36.4	36.6	37.3	37.1	37.0	36.6	36.5	36.3	36.4	36.4
2001	35.9	35.9	36.1	36.3	36.6	37.1	37.3	37.5	37.4	37.1	37.1	37.4	36.8
2002	36.9	37.1	37.1	37.1	37.2	37.2	37.1	37.1	37.0	36.9	36.9	37.0	37.1
2003	36.6	36.6	36.9	37.1	37.4	37.8	37.7	37.9	37.9	37.8	37.8	37.7	37.4
Professional and business services													
1990	41.9	42.7	43.8	45.5	46.1	47.2	47.9	48.3	48.4	47.7	47.3	47.5	46.1
1991	47.2	47.8	48.7	51.2	51.6	52.2	51.6	51.8	51.8	52.0	51.6	51.4	50.7
1992	50.3	51.5	52.3	52.9	53.6	54.1	53.3	53.4	54.0	53.1	52.3	52.6	52.7
1993	51.1	52.4	53.2	53.7	53.6	53.6	54.3	54.1	54.3	54.8	54.9	54.9	53.7
1994	50.9	53.0	54.0	55.5	55.9	56.6	55.6	55.4	56.1	55.4	56.1	56.4	55.0
1995	54.5	55.4	56.6	57.2	58.0	58.4	57.8	59.1	59.5	58.2	58.9	58.6	57.6
1996	56.6	57.4	58.4	59.0	60.1	60.7	59.2	61.7	62.5	57.9	58.1	57.9	59.1
1997	55.9	56.6	58.6	59.6	59.8	60.7	59.6	60.4	60.8	61.5	61.3	60.7	59.6
1998	58.2	59.3	60.4	60.2	60.5	61.7	62.3	63.2	63.3	62.7	63.4	63.4	61.5
1999	61.0	61.9	62.6	63.8	63.9	64.4	64.7	65.4	65.2	68.0	67.4	68.3	64.7
2000	66.1	66.5	67.9	67.9	68.4	68.7	69.4	70.0	70.4	70.8	70.5	70.0	68.8
2001	66.1	66.3	66.9	66.0	66.1	65.9	65.6	66.6	66.5	65.6	65.7	64.8	66.0
2002	62.8	62.8	63.7	63.5	64.9	64.6	63.9	65.0	64.3	63.9	64.3	63.6	63.9
2003	61.2	61.3	62.2	63.0	63.8	63.5	62.1	63.2	63.5	63.5	63.5	63.7	62.9
Educational and health services													
1990	48.2	48.9	49.1	49.3	49.5	49.8	50.0	50.5	50.6	51.6	51.6	51.9	50.0
1991	50.3	51.0	51.4	52.0	52.3	52.4	52.3	52.7	53.0	53.2	53.7	53.8	52.3
1992	53.7	54.6	54.8	54.7	54.6	54.4	53.7	54.5	55.1	55.0	55.1	55.2	54.6
1993	54.8	55.4	55.8	56.2	56.1	56.0	55.3	55.3	56.2	56.2	56.2	56.0	55.7
1994	55.6	56.3	56.7	56.3	56.1	56.2	55.6	56.1	57.3	57.0	57.4	57.5	56.5
1995	57.2	58.0	58.8	57.9	58.0	57.4	57.9	58.2	59.1	58.4	59.0	58.6	58.2
1996	58.6	59.4	59.6	59.7	59.8	59.7	58.8	59.3	59.7	60.9	61.6	61.5	59.8
1997	59.9	60.8	61.4	61.1	61.1	61.2	60.7	61.0	61.9	62.3	62.7	62.7	61.4
1998	61.4	62.0	62.3	63.1	63.0	62.5	62.5	62.7	63.4	63.4	63.3	63.3	62.7
1999	61.6	62.8	63.0	62.8	62.7	62.4	62.8	63.1	63.6	63.8	63.8	64.3	63.0
2000	58.6	59.3	59.1	59.1	59.3	59.0	59.2	59.8	60.1	59.6	59.3	59.3	59.3
2001	64.3	64.5	64.8	64.5	64.2	64.4	64.9	65.1	65.2	65.6	65.7	65.9	64.9
2002	66.4	66.5	66.7	68.3	68.1	68.4	68.9	69.1	69.2	69.2	69.6	69.6	68.3
2003	69.7	70.0	70.5	70.7	70.5	70.5	70.9	71.0	71.1	71.0	71.0	71.0	70.7

Employment by Industry: Kentucky—*Continued*

(Numbers in thousands. Not seasonally adjusted.)

Industry	January	February	March	April	May	June	July	August	September	October	November	December	Annual Average
LOUISVILLE—*Continued*													
Leisure and hospitality													
1990	39.0	39.8	40.2	41.3	44.0	44.7	44.1	44.5	43.9	43.4	43.3	42.8	42.5
1991	39.2	40.0	41.3	42.6	45.0	45.3	43.6	44.0	43.3	41.6	42.7	41.7	42.5
1992	39.5	40.0	41.0	42.8	45.4	46.1	45.6	45.0	44.9	43.0	42.9	41.9	43.1
1993	40.7	41.2	42.1	45.0	47.0	47.5	46.6	46.8	46.5	44.7	44.9	44.2	44.7
1994	42.4	42.8	44.2	45.8	48.1	49.1	48.7	49.2	48.4	46.5	46.9	46.5	46.5
1995	44.4	45.7	46.9	49.6	52.1	53.3	51.3	51.4	51.1	49.1	48.1	48.2	49.2
1996	45.7	46.0	47.0	50.0	52.2	53.6	51.7	52.6	51.5	49.9	49.2	49.4	49.9
1997	47.4	48.2	49.4	52.0	54.3	56.1	53.4	53.6	52.4	51.1	51.1	51.2	51.6
1998	49.0	49.8	51.1	53.8	55.8	57.3	55.1	54.9	54.3	53.5	54.4	54.1	53.5
1999	50.7	51.6	52.3	54.4	56.2	58.0	60.5	60.2	59.3	56.7	56.7	56.5	56.0
2000	51.4	51.7	53.1	54.5	56.4	57.1	57.6	57.4	56.6	56.4	56.2	56.1	55.3
2001	51.1	52.1	52.9	55.4	57.1	57.0	56.3	56.2	54.4	52.6	52.3	51.1	54.0
2002	49.0	49.6	51.1	52.6	56.0	55.2	54.5	54.4	53.2	52.5	51.7	51.0	52.6
2003	49.1	49.3	50.8	53.1	55.2	56.3	55.8	55.7	54.3	53.8	53.8	53.1	53.4
Other services													
1990	19.3	19.6	19.8	20.0	20.1	20.5	20.3	20.3	20.1	20.1	20.0	20.0	20.0
1991	18.8	19.0	19.2	19.5	19.6	19.9	20.0	19.8	19.6	19.6	19.7	19.9	19.5
1992	20.0	20.1	20.3	20.2	20.3	20.7	20.7	20.5	20.4	20.4	20.5	20.6	20.3
1993	20.5	20.6	20.7	21.0	21.0	21.4	21.4	21.1	20.9	20.9	20.9	20.7	20.9
1994	20.5	21.0	21.4	21.2	21.3	21.8	21.4	21.4	21.4	21.4	21.5	21.8	21.3
1995	21.4	21.6	22.1	21.8	21.8	22.6	22.5	22.6	22.4	22.2	22.1	22.4	22.1
1996	21.9	21.9	22.2	22.0	22.3	22.8	22.5	22.6	22.3	22.8	22.8	23.0	22.4
1997	22.5	22.8	23.1	23.3	23.6	24.3	24.3	24.4	24.2	24.1	24.1	24.6	23.7
1998	24.3	24.5	25.1	25.1	25.4	26.0	26.0	25.8	25.4	25.3	25.3	25.5	25.3
1999	25.0	25.3	25.6	26.0	26.1	26.8	26.1	25.9	25.6	25.2	25.3	25.7	25.7
2000	25.7	26.0	26.1	26.1	26.1	26.5	25.4	25.3	25.2	25.4	25.2	25.4	25.7
2001	27.8	27.9	28.1	29.9	29.9	30.4	30.1	29.7	29.5	29.3	29.2	29.6	29.3
2002	29.3	29.4	29.6	29.9	30.0	30.5	30.2	30.1	29.9	30.1	30.1	30.3	30.0
2003	29.9	29.9	30.2	30.1	30.3	31.0	30.6	30.5	30.2	30.4	30.1	30.0	30.3
Government													
1990	62.9	63.3	63.9	65.0	66.1	65.3	62.0	63.2	64.4	64.9	65.1	65.5	64.3
1991	64.8	65.4	65.3	65.9	66.1	66.0	65.7	65.4	65.9	66.5	66.7	67.1	65.9
1992	66.7	66.7	66.8	67.2	67.3	68.4	65.3	65.5	66.9	66.9	67.5	67.6	66.9
1993	67.0	67.7	67.9	68.3	68.2	68.0	65.4	66.1	68.2	68.6	69.0	68.9	67.7
1994	68.3	68.3	68.6	68.5	68.4	68.5	66.3	66.1	67.4	67.7	68.0	68.1	67.8
1995	67.4	68.5	68.5	68.8	68.6	67.7	66.5	66.7	68.5	68.4	68.6	68.6	68.0
1996	67.9	68.5	68.9	68.8	69.5	69.0	65.7	65.7	67.1	68.0	68.0	68.4	67.9
1997	67.7	68.6	68.7	69.1	69.6	68.8	67.1	67.3	68.7	68.7	69.3	69.8	68.6
1998	69.3	70.3	70.8	70.2	71.4	70.3	68.4	68.4	71.1	71.2	71.9	72.2	70.4
1999	71.8	72.6	72.8	73.0	73.1	72.4	69.4	69.6	71.9	72.7	72.9	73.1	72.1
2000	72.4	74.1	74.9	75.9	76.9	77.8	71.4	71.5	73.1	73.4	73.2	73.6	74.0
2001	72.7	73.7	73.8	73.9	74.2	72.6	72.5	71.1	73.5	72.5	72.9	72.7	73.0
2002	71.0	72.1	72.3	72.1	72.6	71.7	68.8	69.1	71.3	72.3	72.6	72.5	71.5
2003	71.3	72.1	72.4	72.8	72.8	72.7	67.0	67.4	69.7	70.4	70.6	70.5	70.8
Federal government													
1992	12.0	11.9	11.9	11.9	11.9	11.9	11.9	11.8	11.8	11.7	11.7	11.7	11.8
1993	11.6	11.7	11.7	11.5	11.6	11.7	11.8	11.8	11.7	11.7	11.7	11.7	11.6
1994	11.7	11.6	11.5	11.2	11.2	11.2	11.0	10.7	10.7	10.4	10.4	10.4	11.0
1995	10.2	10.3	10.2	10.3	10.2	10.2	10.3	10.3	10.2	10.1	10.1	10.2	10.2
1996	10.0	9.9	9.9	9.9	9.8	9.8	9.8	9.1	9.1	8.9	8.9	9.0	9.5
1997	9.0	9.1	9.1	9.2	9.2	9.2	9.3	9.3	9.2	9.0	9.3	9.7	9.2
1998	9.7	10.0	10.1	10.1	10.2	10.1	10.1	9.9	10.1	9.9	10.5	10.7	10.1
1999	10.9	10.8	10.8	10.6	10.5	10.5	10.2	10.1	10.3	10.5	10.6	10.8	10.5
2000	10.7	11.8	12.5	13.3	14.6	15.4	12.9	12.9	11.1	10.8	10.4	10.8	12.2
2001	10.4	10.5	10.5	10.6	10.6	10.6	10.6	10.5	10.2	9.5	9.6	9.6	10.3
2002	9.3	9.1	9.1	9.1	9.0	8.9	9.1	9.0	8.9	9.1	9.1	9.2	9.1
2003	9.3	9.4	9.4	9.3	9.1	9.1	9.1	9.0	8.9	9.0	8.9	9.0	9.1
State government													
1992	16.4	16.6	16.6	16.6	16.5	16.2	15.9	16.4	16.4	16.4	16.6	16.4	16.4
1993	16.1	16.4	16.5	16.7	16.6	15.8	15.9	16.5	16.7	16.5	16.7	16.4	16.4
1994	16.1	16.3	16.3	16.6	16.6	16.2	16.1	16.9	16.7	16.6	16.8	16.6	16.4
1995	16.2	16.6	16.7	16.8	16.5	16.2	16.1	16.9	16.8	16.7	16.9	16.7	16.5
1996	16.3	16.7	16.7	16.6	17.0	16.5	16.0	15.6	16.3	16.5	16.6	16.6	16.4
1997	16.4	16.8	16.8	16.9	17.0	16.6	16.3	15.9	16.6	16.8	16.8	16.8	16.6
1998	16.5	17.1	17.1	16.3	17.0	16.6	16.3	16.4	16.8	17.0	16.9	16.8	16.7
1999	16.6	17.0	17.0	17.1	16.9	16.7	15.5	15.9	16.7	17.0	16.9	16.9	16.6
2000	16.6	16.9	17.0	17.1	16.6	16.2	16.4	16.0	17.4	17.7	17.8	17.8	16.9
2001	17.5	17.9	17.9	18.1	18.0	17.2	17.0	16.8	17.8	18.2	18.4	17.9	17.7
2002	17.5	18.2	18.4	18.7	18.5	17.7	16.7	16.5	17.1	17.6	17.6	17.4	17.7
2003	17.1	17.4	17.4	17.5	17.3	17.1	16.8	16.9	17.6	17.9	18.0	17.9	17.4

Employment by Industry: Kentucky—*Continued*

(Numbers in thousands. Not seasonally adjusted.)

Industry	January	February	March	April	May	June	July	August	September	October	November	December	Annual Average
LOUISVILLE—*Continued*													
Local government													
1992	38.3	38.2	38.3	38.7	38.9	40.3	37.5	37.3	38.7	38.8	39.2	39.5	38.6
1993	39.3	39.6	39.7	40.1	40.0	40.5	37.7	37.8	39.8	40.4	40.6	40.8	39.6
1994	40.5	40.4	40.8	40.7	40.6	41.1	39.2	38.5	40.0	40.7	40.8	41.1	40.3
1995	41.0	41.6	41.6	41.7	41.9	41.3	40.1	39.5	41.5	41.6	41.6	41.7	41.2
1996	41.6	41.9	42.3	42.3	42.7	42.7	39.9	41.0	41.7	42.6	42.5	42.8	42.0
1997	42.3	42.7	42.8	43.0	43.4	43.0	41.5	42.1	42.9	42.9	43.2	43.3	42.7
1998	43.1	43.2	43.6	43.8	44.2	43.6	42.0	42.1	44.2	44.3	44.5	44.7	43.6
1999	44.3	44.8	45.0	45.3	45.7	45.2	43.7	43.6	44.9	45.2	45.4	45.4	44.8
2000	45.1	45.4	45.4	45.5	45.7	46.2	42.1	42.6	44.6	44.9	45.0	45.0	44.7
2001	44.8	45.3	45.4	45.2	45.6	44.8	44.9	43.8	45.5	44.8	44.9	45.2	45.0
2002	44.2	44.8	44.8	44.3	45.1	45.1	43.0	43.6	45.3	45.6	45.9	45.9	44.8
2003	44.9	45.3	45.6	46.0	46.4	46.5	41.1	41.5	43.2	43.5	43.7	43.6	44.3

Average Weekly Hours by Industry: Kentucky

(Not seasonally adjusted.)

Industry	January	February	March	April	May	June	July	August	September	October	November	December	Annual Average
STATEWIDE													
Natural resources and mining													
2001	51.3	50.5	50.6	49.9	49.8	49.2	49.4	49.6	49.8	49.2	48.6	50.1	49.8
2002	49.1	48.6	48.3	47.9	49.2	49.3	49.7	49.1	49.9	49.6	48.7	49.5	49.1
2003	48.3	47.1	49.0	48.8	49.3	48.4	48.4	48.3	48.3	48.8	49.4	48.2	48.5
Manufacturing													
2001	41.6	41.0	41.3	40.7	41.6	41.9	41.5	41.7	41.5	41.5	41.5	42.1	41.5
2002	41.9	41.8	42.0	41.9	41.8	42.5	42.2	42.4	42.6	42.3	42.3	42.9	42.2
2003	41.9	41.9	41.8	41.7	41.6	41.5	41.4	42.1	41.9	41.6	41.8	41.7	41.7
LEXINGTON-FAYETTE													
Manufacturing													
2001	40.8	38.7	38.6	38.1	38.9	38.6	38.7	38.8	38.7	38.9	38.9	38.7	38.9
2002	38.6	38.5	38.0	37.9	38.2	38.7	38.1	38.9	39.5	38.5	38.5	39.4	38.6
2003	38.6	38.8	38.2	39.2	38.6	39.2	38.9	39.9	39.3	38.5	38.1	38.8	38.8
LOUISVILLE													
Manufacturing													
2001	42.6	42.4	43.2	42.0	43.8	44.0	43.4	43.6	43.1	42.1	42.4	42.3	42.9
2002	41.9	41.6	41.6	41.6	42.3	41.7	41.4	42.3	42.4	42.5	42.6	43.3	42.1
2003	41.9	42.1	41.9	42.9	41.1	40.9	41.0	42.1	41.7	41.1	41.9	42.0	41.7

Average Hourly Earnings by Industry: Kentucky

(Dollars, not seasonally adjusted.)

Industry	January	February	March	April	May	June	July	August	September	October	November	December	Annual Average
STATEWIDE													
Natural resources and mining													
2001	14.67	14.65	14.64	14.51	14.67	14.85	14.79	14.79	14.87	14.74	14.81	14.70	14.73
2002	14.66	14.58	14.58	14.49	14.50	14.84	14.79	14.72	14.83	14.84	14.87	15.08	14.73
2003	15.33	15.47	15.69	15.41	15.34	15.19	15.28	15.45	15.40	15.54	15.87	16.58	15.55
Manufacturing													
2001	15.14	15.17	15.22	15.37	15.51	15.54	15.43	15.57	15.61	15.46	15.55	15.70	15.44
2002	15.54	15.61	15.59	15.76	15.72	15.80	15.39	15.76	15.87	15.95	15.80	15.96	15.73
2003	16.09	15.81	15.70	15.87	15.64	15.88	16.12	16.09	16.06	16.16	16.31	16.48	16.02
LEXINGTON-FAYETTE													
Manufacturing													
2001	13.38	13.28	13.23	13.67	13.48	13.46	13.36	13.62	13.61	13.58	13.66	13.69	13.50
2002	13.80	13.96	14.04	14.55	14.97	15.04	15.05	14.89	14.99	15.06	14.79	14.93	14.67
2003	14.77	15.12	15.04	15.14	14.77	14.86	15.15	15.06	15.17	15.30	15.31	15.50	15.10
LOUISVILLE													
Manufacturing													
2001	18.03	18.02	18.15	18.21	18.50	18.43	18.17	18.52	18.30	18.00	18.31	18.71	18.28
2002	18.28	18.39	18.40	18.69	18.91	18.83	17.64	18.83	19.04	19.18	19.31	19.62	18.75
2003	19.94	19.65	19.39	19.75	19.04	19.23	19.41	19.51	19.43	19.98	20.12	20.44	19.66

Average Weekly Earnings by Industry: Kentucky

(Dollars, not seasonally adjusted.)

Industry	January	February	March	April	May	June	July	August	September	October	November	December	Annual Average
STATEWIDE													
Natural resources and mining													
2001	752.57	739.83	740.78	724.05	730.57	730.62	730.63	733.58	740.53	725.21	719.77	736.47	733.55
2002	719.81	708.59	704.21	694.07	713.40	731.61	735.06	722.75	740.02	736.06	724.17	746.46	723.24
2003	740.44	728.64	768.81	752.01	756.26	735.20	739.55	746.24	743.82	758.35	783.98	799.16	754.18
Manufacturing													
2001	629.82	621.97	628.59	625.56	645.22	651.13	640.35	649.27	647.82	641.59	645.33	660.97	640.76
2002	651.13	652.50	654.78	660.34	657.10	671.50	649.46	668.22	676.06	674.69	668.34	684.68	663.81
2003	674.17	662.44	656.26	661.78	650.62	659.02	667.37	677.39	672.91	672.26	681.76	687.22	668.03
LEXINGTON-FAYETTE													
Manufacturing													
2001	545.90	513.94	510.68	520.83	524.37	519.56	517.03	528.46	526.71	528.26	531.37	529.80	525.15
2002	532.68	537.46	533.52	551.45	571.85	582.05	573.41	579.22	592.11	579.81	569.42	588.24	566.26
2003	570.12	586.66	574.53	593.49	570.12	582.51	589.34	600.89	596.18	589.05	583.31	601.40	585.88
LOUISVILLE													
Manufacturing													
2001	768.08	764.05	784.08	764.82	810.30	810.92	788.58	807.47	788.73	757.80	776.34	791.43	784.21
2002	765.93	765.02	765.44	777.50	799.89	785.21	730.30	796.51	807.30	815.15	822.61	849.55	789.38
2003	835.49	827.27	812.44	847.28	782.54	786.51	795.81	821.37	810.23	821.18	843.03	858.48	819.82

LOUISIANA AT A GLANCE

(Population and total nonfarm employment numbers in thousands)

Population, Census 2000:	4,469.0
Total nonfarm employment, 2003:	1,905.9
Change in total nonfarm employment	
(Number)	
1990–2003:	316.1
1990–2001:	327.7
2001–2003:	-11.6
(Compound annual rate of change)	
1990–2003:	1.4%
1990–2001:	1.7%
2001–2003:	-0.3%
Unemployment rate	
1990:	5.9%
2001:	5.4%
2003:	6.3%

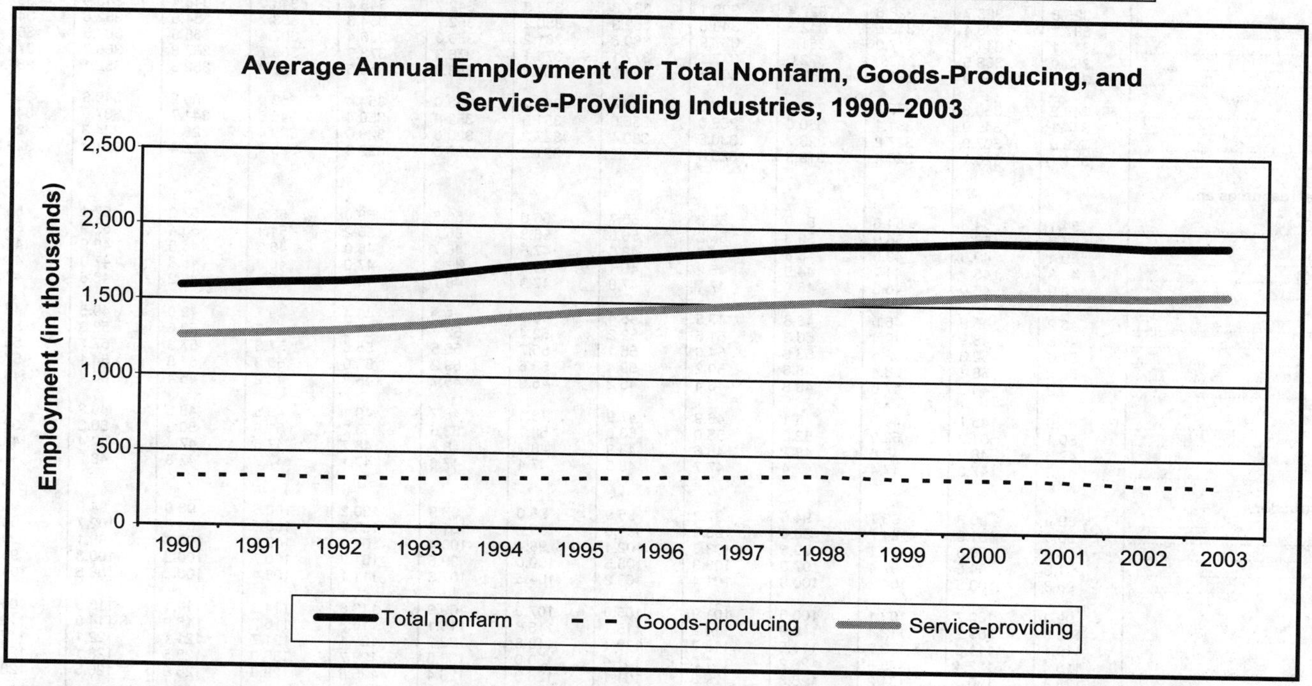

Total nonfarm payroll employment rose during the 1990–2000 period. The 2001 recession brought a decline in jobs, due in large part to weakness in the goods-producing sector, especially in the manufacturing industry. The growth in service-providing jobs, which had been steady during the 1990s, slowed significantly in 2001–2002, but strengthened in 2003. Employment in educational and health services, the fastest growing industry within the service sector, increased more than 9 percent from 2000 to 2003.

Employment by Industry: Louisiana

(Numbers in thousands. Not seasonally adjusted.)

Industry	January	February	March	April	May	June	July	August	September	October	November	December	Annual Average
STATEWIDE													
Total nonfarm													
1990	1543.6	1554.4	1568.0	1581.4	1600.3	1600.6	1589.2	1594.5	1605.9	1612.1	1614.8	1613.6	1589.8
1991	1578.4	1586.3	1597.2	1609.6	1624.4	1625.0	1608.7	1607.2	1623.3	1632.5	1632.3	1631.0	1612.9
1992	1593.4	1599.8	1608.7	1622.4	1633.6	1638.0	1624.2	1620.8	1634.4	1646.6	1649.2	1652.5	1626.9
1993	1615.4	1627.3	1636.6	1648.8	1658.7	1661.8	1650.6	1650.9	1673.0	1686.6	1692.3	1702.1	1658.6
1994	1667.2	1681.4	1702.1	1706.8	1716.4	1723.9	1719.1	1724.0	1747.6	1750.6	1759.6	1766.9	1722.1
1995	1727.4	1739.7	1753.1	1759.0	1774.3	1782.6	1770.4	1774.0	1798.1	1792.1	1797.5	1800.3	1772.3
1996	1764.2	1776.5	1789.7	1800.9	1816.3	1820.9	1803.5	1808.9	1829.3	1828.0	1837.3	1840.8	1809.6
1997	1799.8	1811.2	1827.3	1839.4	1848.3	1855.7	1847.3	1847.6	1870.4	1875.6	1884.0	1893.0	1849.9
1998	1845.6	1860.7	1873.1	1892.9	1903.8	1905.6	1889.0	1888.3	1905.3	1898.2	1902.1	1909.2	1889.4
1999	1868.4	1881.2	1890.4	1891.5	1893.5	1900.3	1885.5	1886.7	1906.0	1909.6	1918.6	1922.7	1896.2
2000	1890.0	1903.9	1918.7	1924.3	1940.5	1931.7	1906.6	1909.8	1924.6	1923.9	1928.0	1937.2	1919.9
2001	1899.5	1911.1	1925.3	1926.6	1933.0	1932.9	1902.8	1908.7	1920.7	1913.9	1918.0	1918.3	1917.5
2002	1874.4	1882.3	1893.1	1905.3	1909.3	1909.7	1886.1	1890.4	1902.0	1899.8	1910.9	1910.6	1897.8
2003	1886.0	1896.2	1902.4	1909.2	1916.9	1914.0	1889.5	1894.1	1905.8	1918.4	1921.2	1917.5	1905.9
Total private													
1990	1225.7	1230.9	1243.4	1250.5	1263.3	1272.8	1266.3	1277.4	1284.4	1281.7	1284.2	1283.9	1263.7
1991	1253.1	1255.6	1265.9	1272.7	1284.5	1290.6	1286.0	1290.2	1293.7	1293.1	1292.1	1290.7	1280.6
1992	1259.3	1259.9	1268.2	1279.8	1292.5	1297.6	1289.5	1290.8	1296.4	1301.6	1304.2	1309.8	1287.4
1993	1275.9	1284.4	1293.4	1302.8	1312.4	1318.4	1321.3	1325.2	1332.6	1336.2	1343.1	1354.6	1316.6
1994	1321.2	1333.5	1350.1	1351.2	1361.6	1372.6	1373.0	1382.9	1394.8	1393.4	1402.1	1411.3	1370.6
1995	1375.2	1383.3	1393.9	1396.2	1413.0	1424.6	1418.0	1426.8	1437.0	1428.7	1433.7	1438.1	1414.0
1996	1406.0	1412.4	1425.0	1432.9	1450.5	1458.9	1451.0	1458.9	1465.7	1463.2	1472.4	1477.6	1447.8
1997	1441.5	1447.4	1462.1	1471.7	1481.9	1490.2	1489.9	1495.6	1503.0	1506.2	1514.7	1525.6	1485.8
1998	1483.1	1492.1	1503.1	1521.9	1533.8	1538.6	1532.9	1535.7	1535.8	1524.4	1528.0	1537.2	1522.2
1999	1502.7	1507.8	1517.1	1518.2	1521.2	1531.2	1525.2	1527.9	1532.8	1534.6	1542.3	1549.5	1525.8
2000	1519.4	1527.3	1539.2	1545.1	1555.5	1557.8	1541.8	1550.1	1553.0	1550.1	1554.3	1564.2	1546.4
2001	1527.4	1533.0	1546.2	1549.2	1556.0	1558.4	1540.1	1548.0	1547.7	1537.9	1540.4	1541.3	1543.8
2002	1504.4	1506.8	1516.0	1527.8	1531.7	1533.3	1519.4	1525.9	1526.9	1521.1	1529.7	1531.7	1522.9
2003	1511.5	1514.5	1519.3	1526.1	1533.6	1533.3	1517.8	1525.8	1526.2	1534.9	1536.7	1536.0	1526.3
Goods-producing													
1990	314.1	316.4	320.9	323.3	327.9	330.0	329.5	334.8	336.8	337.9	336.6	332.3	328.3
1991	324.0	325.5	329.5	330.4	334.3	335.6	334.9	337.1	338.0	340.0	337.4	331.5	333.1
1992	319.4	318.4	321.5	324.5	330.6	330.5	323.8	325.1	324.9	328.4	326.3	324.7	324.8
1993	312.1	314.8	317.7	317.8	323.7	325.6	323.7	324.7	327.0	326.7	325.4	326.2	322.1
1994	316.1	319.9	325.8	324.2	327.2	331.3	332.8	337.6	341.8	339.0	339.0	339.6	331.1
1995	325.8	326.7	328.6	327.4	332.1	337.3	339.5	342.7	346.4	348.0	346.4	345.9	337.2
1996	337.1	338.4	342.5	342.5	349.6	352.3	350.2	352.7	354.8	353.7	354.5	352.6	348.4
1997	343.1	344.9	347.9	351.6	357.9	360.6	361.2	366.0	366.4	367.4	366.5	367.5	358.4
1998	359.0	363.5	367.8	372.0	377.1	377.1	374.1	376.3	373.9	369.7	367.6	366.3	370.3
1999	360.9	360.9	360.6	357.6	358.5	361.0	354.0	353.3	353.5	352.9	352.3	352.1	356.4
2000	349.2	350.3	353.5	355.2	359.5	360.4	353.7	356.0	354.4	353.0	350.2	349.8	353.7
2001	344.1	345.9	351.1	350.6	355.0	356.0	351.6	352.8	350.4	345.6	341.7	337.6	348.5
2002	328.8	327.0	327.8	328.7	330.6	330.4	327.2	329.0	328.0	329.4	326.4	324.3	328.1
2003	321.1	320.1	320.4	319.8	325.4	326.2	321.2	322.3	322.3	325.4	322.4	321.4	322.3
Natural resources and mining													
1990	54.1	54.3	54.8	54.9	55.0	55.7	56.0	56.5	56.0	56.8	57.2	57.1	55.7
1991	56.7	56.8	56.9	56.3	56.2	56.6	56.3	56.1	55.2	54.1	53.4	52.9	55.6
1992	50.4	49.6	49.0	48.3	48.3	48.5	47.5	46.7	45.0	46.3	46.6	46.9	47.7
1993	45.3	45.2	44.7	44.9	45.2	46.1	46.4	47.1	47.0	46.9	46.8	47.3	46.0
1994	45.9	46.0	46.3	46.9	47.1	47.6	47.9	48.7	48.9	48.0	48.2	48.6	47.5
1995	46.9	46.9	46.5	46.8	47.5	48.4	48.9	49.3	49.4	49.1	49.0	49.5	48.1
1996	48.5	48.9	49.4	50.3	51.5	52.2	52.4	52.7	52.6	52.2	52.6	53.3	51.3
1997	51.6	52.3	52.5	53.6	54.6	55.1	55.7	56.5	56.6	57.5	57.3	57.7	55.0
1998	57.7	58.1	58.4	58.6	59.2	59.4	59.6	59.2	58.0	55.3	54.8	54.1	57.7
1999	50.2	48.6	47.6	46.8	46.4	46.2	45.9	45.7	45.8	46.2	46.4	46.4	46.8
2000	45.0	45.1	44.9	46.1	46.9	47.9	48.1	48.7	49.1	48.5	48.5	49.2	47.3
2001	50.1	51.2	52.0	52.2	53.0	53.8	53.1	53.5	53.2	51.9	50.3	50.3	52.0
2002	49.6	48.9	48.6	48.2	48.6	48.9	48.7	48.8	48.7	47.5	47.4	47.4	48.4
2003	47.3	47.3	47.4	47.4	47.7	48.5	47.4	47.6	47.1	47.7	47.8	48.2	47.6
Construction													
1990	89.9	90.8	93.7	94.6	97.2	95.9	96.0	98.9	100.2	100.6	98.6	94.9	95.9
1991	90.9	91.9	94.7	96.9	98.9	98.6	99.7	101.4	103.4	105.1	104.0	102.7	99.0
1992	94.8	96.8	98.1	99.5	103.8	102.4	98.4	100.4	101.1	102.0	100.7	99.1	99.7
1993	91.8	94.5	97.4	97.8	103.3	103.5	100.0	99.6	101.2	100.7	100.2	100.8	99.2
1994	96.8	100.3	104.2	100.8	101.4	103.2	104.5	107.6	111.1	108.4	108.3	108.5	104.5
1995	99.8	100.7	102.1	100.0	101.9	105.0	107.9	109.9	113.6	114.9	114.1	113.9	106.9
1996	108.8	109.2	112.4	110.9	114.2	115.1	113.6	115.1	116.3	116.2	116.9	114.8	113.6
1997	110.1	111.6	113.7	114.5	116.7	118.1	118.8	122.2	122.1	121.7	121.1	122.1	117.7
1998	118.4	122.4	125.6	128.2	131.0	131.4	130.0	130.0	128.7	130.0	128.5	128.1	127.6
1999	128.8	130.4	131.2	128.8	129.3	131.1	126.3	126.4	125.8	126.9	126.6	126.5	128.1
2000	126.9	128.9	132.0	132.2	134.1	134.2	128.4	129.6	127.9	126.2	124.4	123.3	129.0
2001	119.0	120.6	124.6	124.7	127.4	127.3	126.5	127.7	126.6	125.4	124.5	121.8	124.6
2002	119.3	117.9	118.5	119.9	120.8	119.1	118.3	119.4	118.9	120.8	118.6	116.9	119.0
2003	117.2	117.3	117.0	118.1	121.0	120.4	119.4	119.5	119.6	120.9	118.8	118.3	119.0

Employment by Industry: Louisiana—*Continued*

(Numbers in thousands. Not seasonally adjusted.)

Industry	January	February	March	April	May	June	July	August	September	October	November	December	Annual Average
STATEWIDE—*Continued*													
Manufacturing													
1990	170.1	171.3	172.4	173.8	175.7	178.4	177.5	179.4	180.6	180.5	180.8	180.3	176.7
1991	176.4	176.8	177.9	177.2	179.2	180.4	178.9	179.6	179.4	180.8	180.0	175.9	178.5
1992	174.2	172.0	174.4	176.7	178.5	179.6	177.9	178.0	178.8	180.1	179.0	178.7	177.3
1993	175.0	175.1	175.6	175.1	175.2	176.0	177.3	178.0	178.8	179.1	178.4	178.1	176.8
1994	173.4	173.6	175.3	176.5	178.7	180.5	180.4	181.3	181.8	182.6	182.5	182.5	179.0
1995	179.1	179.1	180.0	180.6	182.7	183.9	182.7	183.5	183.4	184.0	183.3	182.5	182.0
1996	179.8	180.3	180.7	181.3	183.9	185.0	184.2	184.9	185.9	185.3	185.0	184.5	183.4
1997	181.4	181.0	181.7	183.5	186.6	187.4	186.7	187.3	187.7	188.2	188.1	187.7	185.6
1998	182.9	183.0	183.8	185.2	186.9	186.3	184.5	187.1	187.2	184.4	184.3	184.1	184.9
1999	181.9	181.9	181.8	182.0	182.8	183.7	181.8	181.2	181.9	179.8	179.3	179.2	181.4
2000	177.3	176.3	176.6	176.9	178.5	178.3	177.2	177.7	177.4	178.3	177.3	177.3	177.4
2001	175.0	174.1	174.5	173.7	174.6	174.9	172.0	171.6	170.6	168.3	166.9	165.5	171.8
2002	159.9	160.2	160.7	160.6	161.2	162.4	160.2	160.8	160.4	161.1	160.4	160.0	160.7
2003	156.6	155.5	156.0	154.3	156.7	157.3	154.4	155.2	155.6	156.8	155.8	154.9	155.8
Service-providing													
1990	1229.5	1238.0	1247.1	1258.1	1272.4	1270.6	1259.7	1259.7	1269.1	1274.2	1278.2	1281.3	1261.4
1991	1254.4	1260.8	1267.7	1279.2	1290.1	1289.4	1273.8	1270.1	1285.3	1292.5	1294.9	1299.5	1279.8
1992	1274.0	1281.4	1287.2	1297.9	1303.0	1307.5	1300.4	1295.7	1309.5	1318.2	1322.9	1327.8	1302.1
1993	1303.3	1312.5	1318.9	1331.0	1335.0	1336.2	1326.9	1326.2	1346.0	1359.9	1366.9	1375.9	1336.5
1994	1351.1	1361.5	1376.3	1382.6	1389.2	1392.6	1386.3	1386.4	1405.8	1411.6	1420.6	1427.3	1390.9
1995	1401.6	1413.0	1424.5	1431.6	1442.2	1445.3	1430.9	1431.3	1451.7	1444.1	1451.1	1454.4	1435.1
1996	1427.1	1438.1	1447.2	1458.4	1466.7	1468.6	1453.3	1456.2	1474.5	1474.3	1482.8	1488.2	1461.2
1997	1456.7	1466.3	1479.4	1487.8	1490.4	1495.1	1486.1	1481.6	1504.0	1508.2	1517.5	1525.5	1491.5
1998	1486.6	1497.2	1505.3	1520.9	1526.7	1528.5	1514.9	1512.0	1531.4	1528.5	1534.5	1542.9	1519.1
1999	1507.5	1520.3	1529.8	1533.9	1535.0	1539.3	1531.5	1533.4	1552.5	1556.7	1566.3	1570.6	1539.7
2000	1540.8	1553.6	1565.2	1569.1	1581.0	1571.3	1552.9	1553.8	1570.2	1570.9	1577.8	1587.4	1566.1
2001	1555.4	1565.2	1574.2	1576.0	1578.0	1576.9	1551.2	1555.9	1570.3	1568.3	1576.3	1580.7	1569.0
2002	1545.6	1555.3	1565.3	1576.6	1578.7	1579.3	1558.9	1561.4	1574.0	1570.4	1584.5	1586.3	1569.7
2003	1564.9	1576.1	1582.0	1589.4	1591.5	1587.8	1568.3	1571.8	1583.5	1593.0	1598.8	1596.1	1583.6
Trade, transportation, and utilities													
1990	351.0	349.5	351.2	352.6	355.1	357.9	355.3	356.8	357.5	356.3	360.0	363.1	355.5
1991	349.1	344.4	346.5	347.6	350.2	352.4	351.8	352.8	352.5	351.7	354.9	357.8	350.9
1992	342.9	341.2	342.0	345.4	347.5	349.3	346.8	347.0	348.0	348.9	353.7	359.8	347.7
1993	348.2	346.7	348.1	350.2	351.9	353.5	356.5	357.9	358.5	359.4	364.8	370.8	355.5
1994	358.2	357.3	360.8	360.4	362.1	364.4	364.3	365.4	366.7	367.2	373.1	378.5	364.8
1995	363.3	361.2	363.7	361.5	363.4	366.7	366.4	368.5	369.8	368.2	374.1	379.3	367.1
1996	365.8	362.9	364.3	366.9	370.6	373.8	371.9	373.0	373.1	373.1	378.6	383.7	371.4
1997	370.7	367.8	372.2	373.3	374.7	376.4	377.0	377.2	380.3	383.3	390.4	397.1	378.3
1998	378.6	376.5	379.3	382.6	385.1	387.4	387.6	389.1	390.2	387.9	392.3	398.4	386.2
1999	384.1	382.0	385.4	384.6	385.3	387.0	386.6	387.8	389.4	388.3	395.5	400.3	388.0
2000	384.7	385.9	388.9	387.8	390.6	392.4	388.3	391.4	392.2	390.9	397.1	403.1	391.1
2001	386.6	385.5	388.5	388.4	388.9	390.3	387.3	389.7	388.7	387.0	392.5	395.9	389.1
2002	380.5	379.0	382.2	383.6	384.8	386.6	383.8	384.3	383.8	381.8	388.2	393.0	384.3
2003	380.1	378.8	380.2	379.7	380.0	381.1	377.6	379.3	378.6	382.2	385.0	389.9	381.0
Wholesale trade													
1990	69.3	69.6	70.0	70.4	70.9	71.4	70.6	70.5	70.8	70.3	70.2	70.4	70.3
1991	68.2	68.1	68.7	70.0	70.5	70.9	70.2	70.1	69.7	69.3	68.9	68.7	69.4
1992	67.8	67.6	67.7	68.1	68.2	68.6	67.8	67.6	67.4	67.3	67.2	67.5	67.7
1993	67.5	67.5	67.8	68.7	68.8	69.0	69.1	69.0	69.1	68.6	68.7	69.1	68.5
1994	68.6	68.8	69.4	70.1	70.6	71.0	70.6	70.8	71.1	70.9	71.0	71.7	70.3
1995	70.7	71.0	71.9	72.1	72.8	73.4	73.4	73.6	73.8	72.4	72.5	72.9	72.5
1996	71.2	71.5	71.9	72.1	72.9	73.6	73.5	73.6	73.7	73.7	73.8	74.3	72.9
1997	73.9	74.3	74.8	75.4	75.6	76.3	76.5	76.9	77.0	76.6	76.7	77.1	75.9
1998	76.5	76.6	77.3	78.4	78.7	79.2	79.0	79.3	79.3	78.3	78.0	78.5	78.2
1999	77.0	77.2	77.6	77.7	77.8	78.1	78.3	78.1	78.0	77.2	76.9	77.3	77.6
2000	76.3	76.5	77.3	77.9	78.5	78.7	78.5	78.7	78.5	77.4	77.4	77.9	77.8
2001	76.8	77.1	77.6	78.1	78.2	79.0	77.8	78.1	78.1	77.7	77.7	78.0	77.8
2002	76.6	76.7	77.0	77.6	78.0	78.2	77.4	77.4	77.2	76.6	76.7	76.7	77.2
2003	76.2	76.1	76.3	75.7	75.8	76.3	75.3	75.4	75.4	75.6	75.1	74.9	75.7
Retail trade													
1990	199.4	197.1	198.0	199.2	200.7	202.0	200.5	201.4	201.1	200.9	204.8	207.8	201.0
1991	199.4	195.0	195.8	196.6	198.1	199.0	199.0	200.0	199.8	199.9	203.9	207.3	199.4
1992	196.7	194.7	195.4	198.7	200.9	202.0	200.6	201.2	201.8	202.0	207.3	212.3	201.1
1993	203.6	201.9	202.7	203.5	203.7	204.6	206.9	208.1	207.8	208.2	212.9	217.7	206.8
1994	207.4	205.6	207.7	206.9	208.1	210.0	210.8	212.6	213.9	214.0	220.2	225.1	211.8
1995	213.6	211.7	213.2	212.0	213.4	215.4	215.7	217.4	218.4	218.1	223.9	228.1	216.7
1996	217.6	214.0	215.2	217.5	219.5	221.5	220.8	221.8	221.4	221.3	226.9	231.0	220.7
1997	219.8	216.3	219.4	219.8	220.4	220.5	221.4	223.1	223.5	226.0	232.8	238.1	223.4
1998	224.2	221.8	223.4	225.0	226.9	227.9	226.7	228.0	228.7	228.5	233.6	238.6	227.7
1999	227.9	225.3	228.0	227.7	228.4	229.3	229.0	230.0	231.0	231.0	238.3	242.7	230.7
2000	229.6	229.8	232.1	230.6	232.4	233.3	229.4	231.2	231.9	231.8	238.0	242.8	232.7
2001	229.1	226.8	228.7	227.3	227.7	227.7	226.5	228.1	227.1	225.3	231.9	235.0	228.4
2002	223.5	222.1	224.8	225.0	225.1	226.5	224.0	224.2	223.7	221.8	227.9	232.4	225.1
2003	221.6	220.5	222.2	222.2	222.1	222.7	220.7	222.1	221.6	224.1	226.7	232.2	223.2

Employment by Industry: Louisiana—*Continued*

(Numbers in thousands. Not seasonally adjusted.)

Industry	January	February	March	April	May	June	July	August	September	October	November	December	Annual Average
STATEWIDE—*Continued*													
Transportation and utilities													
1990	82.3	82.8	83.2	83.0	83.5	84.5	84.2	84.9	85.6	85.1	85.0	84.9	84.0
1991	81.5	81.3	82.0	81.0	81.6	82.5	82.6	82.7	83.0	82.5	82.1	81.8	82.0
1992	78.4	78.9	78.9	78.6	78.4	78.7	78.4	78.2	78.8	79.6	79.2	80.0	78.8
1993	77.1	77.3	77.6	78.0	79.4	79.9	80.5	80.8	81.6	82.6	83.2	84.0	80.1
1994	82.2	82.9	83.7	83.4	83.4	83.4	82.9	82.0	81.7	82.3	81.9	81.7	82.6
1995	79.0	78.5	78.6	77.4	77.2	77.9	77.3	77.5	77.6	77.7	77.7	78.3	77.8
1996	77.0	77.4	77.2	77.3	78.2	78.7	77.6	77.6	78.0	78.1	77.9	78.4	77.7
1997	77.0	77.2	78.0	78.1	78.7	79.6	79.1	77.2	79.8	80.7	80.9	81.9	79.0
1998	77.9	78.1	78.6	79.2	79.5	80.3	81.9	81.8	82.2	81.1	80.7	81.3	80.2
1999	79.2	79.5	79.8	79.2	79.1	79.6	79.3	79.7	80.4	80.1	80.3	80.3	79.7
2000	78.8	79.6	79.5	79.3	79.7	80.4	80.4	81.5	81.8	81.7	81.7	82.4	80.5
2001	80.7	81.6	82.2	83.0	83.0	83.6	83.0	83.5	83.5	84.0	82.9	82.9	82.8
2002	80.4	80.2	80.4	81.0	81.7	81.9	82.4	82.7	82.9	83.4	83.6	83.9	82.0
2003	82.3	82.2	81.7	81.8	82.1	82.1	81.6	81.8	81.6	82.5	83.2	82.8	82.1
Information													
1990	26.6	26.6	26.7	26.6	26.7	26.9	27.3	27.1	27.4	26.4	26.4	26.5	26.7
1991	26.7	26.5	26.6	26.6	26.6	26.8	27.4	27.2	27.0	25.8	25.6	25.6	26.5
1992	25.7	25.3	25.3	25.5	25.5	26.0	24.0	23.9	23.8	23.7	23.7	23.9	24.6
1993	23.9	23.9	23.9	23.7	24.0	26.2	24.0	24.0	24.3	24.2	24.3	24.5	24.2
1994	23.8	23.9	24.0	24.0	24.1	24.5	24.5	24.4	24.3	24.2	24.3	24.7	24.2
1995	24.4	24.3	24.5	24.3	25.0	25.1	24.8	25.1	25.0	25.0	25.3	25.4	24.8
1996	25.3	25.3	25.3	26.1	26.6	26.7	26.3	26.7	26.5	26.4	26.7	26.8	26.2
1997	26.1	26.3	26.3	26.5	26.9	27.2	27.0	26.9	27.0	26.5	26.7	27.0	26.7
1998	26.4	26.5	26.5	26.6	27.0	27.2	27.4	27.3	27.2	27.9	27.9	28.1	27.1
1999	27.5	27.6	27.8	28.0	28.4	28.7	28.6	28.6	28.5	28.4	28.6	28.8	28.2
2000	28.9	28.5	28.8	29.1	29.2	29.9	30.7	30.9	30.5	30.3	30.5	31.0	29.8
2001	30.0	30.2	30.4	30.2	30.6	30.6	30.3	30.1	29.7	30.0	30.1	29.8	30.1
2002	29.3	29.3	29.5	29.0	28.9	29.3	29.0	29.0	28.9	28.5	28.8	28.9	29.0
2003	29.2	28.9	29.1	29.2	29.7	30.1	28.3	28.9	28.8	28.9	29.2	29.0	29.1
Financial activities													
1990	87.7	88.0	88.7	88.8	89.0	90.0	89.0	89.5	89.5	89.3	89.5	91.1	89.1
1991	85.5	85.6	85.7	86.5	86.7	87.0	86.4	86.2	85.6	84.6	84.6	85.9	85.8
1992	82.3	82.0	82.3	82.3	82.7	83.3	83.0	83.2	83.3	83.4	83.5	84.0	82.9
1993	83.4	83.6	83.8	84.4	84.4	84.9	85.5	85.7	85.8	85.6	85.7	86.6	84.9
1994	85.6	85.6	86.4	84.8	85.3	86.0	86.5	86.9	86.6	86.0	86.2	87.1	86.0
1995	86.8	86.7	87.3	87.5	88.0	88.7	88.8	88.9	88.8	88.2	88.5	89.2	88.1
1996	87.8	88.1	88.4	88.8	89.6	90.5	90.5	91.1	91.1	91.1	91.5	92.3	90.0
1997	91.2	91.6	92.3	92.5	92.8	93.7	94.3	94.7	94.6	94.4	94.6	95.3	93.5
1998	96.1	96.0	96.9	96.4	96.8	97.1	97.0	97.1	96.4	96.2	96.2	96.9	96.5
1999	95.1	95.3	95.7	95.5	95.7	96.1	96.9	97.0	96.5	97.1	97.1	98.0	96.3
2000	99.5	99.7	100.0	99.1	99.9	99.9	100.0	100.1	100.0	99.6	99.8	100.6	99.8
2001	98.9	99.5	99.3	99.4	99.3	99.9	100.0	100.1	99.4	99.1	99.1	99.2	99.4
2002	99.0	98.9	99.1	100.0	100.1	100.2	100.0	100.3	99.9	100.2	100.6	100.9	99.9
2003	100.8	101.0	100.8	101.1	101.3	101.7	101.6	102.0	101.7	100.6	99.8	100.7	101.1
Professional and business services													
1990	110.4	111.2	113.0	113.6	114.9	116.4	118.1	119.6	119.9	119.2	119.3	119.0	116.2
1991	123.1	125.1	126.6	125.6	126.2	127.5	127.4	128.0	128.4	127.8	127.4	127.4	126.7
1992	129.8	131.2	132.3	132.4	133.0	133.9	134.1	134.7	135.4	136.3	135.8	137.3	133.8
1993	135.2	136.8	137.8	139.5	139.5	139.3	140.2	140.7	141.5	141.5	141.8	143.5	139.7
1994	140.9	143.4	145.2	145.0	145.3	147.0	145.1	146.4	146.7	147.9	148.0	148.4	145.7
1995	148.4	151.0	152.4	151.9	153.6	155.3	152.6	153.5	155.2	152.5	152.5	153.5	152.7
1996	151.0	153.8	156.6	156.4	157.2	158.2	157.7	159.3	159.5	157.2	158.2	159.2	157.0
1997	157.3	159.2	161.3	163.7	163.7	165.6	165.6	166.1	166.9	167.1	166.9	168.8	164.3
1998	166.8	169.2	169.8	174.0	174.2	176.4	176.4	176.7	176.7	175.4	175.3	177.4	174.0
1999	173.3	174.9	176.2	177.4	176.2	178.8	182.7	183.7	183.2	183.7	183.6	184.1	179.8
2000	178.6	179.5	181.3	184.9	184.3	183.6	182.7	184.3	185.5	184.8	185.3	186.8	183.4
2001	183.9	183.7	183.8	183.6	183.3	184.3	181.3	182.4	183.0	182.2	182.5	184.1	183.1
2002	181.9	182.3	183.5	183.7	182.0	182.3	179.3	180.2	179.3	177.7	177.4	177.3	180.6
2003	177.8	178.8	179.7	180.9	179.3	178.9	178.5	179.2	178.5	178.8	178.4	178.1	178.9
Educational and health services													
1990	159.0	160.2	161.1	162.7	163.3	162.2	161.0	162.1	166.1	170.1	170.9	170.5	164.1
1991	168.3	170.7	171.8	172.9	173.0	171.5	170.8	172.0	176.4	178.8	178.9	179.0	173.6
1992	178.7	180.2	181.4	182.5	182.4	181.7	186.2	186.2	190.6	189.5	190.4	189.9	184.9
1993	188.1	191.0	192.4	194.7	193.5	191.9	195.0	195.4	198.9	202.0	202.9	202.7	195.7
1994	201.6	204.7	206.3	207.7	208.2	206.7	207.0	207.5	212.2	213.7	214.6	215.1	208.7
1995	211.8	215.1	216.0	217.8	217.4	216.4	212.6	212.2	216.2	216.9	217.6	217.3	215.6
1996	214.1	216.9	217.7	220.0	219.2	217.0	215.2	216.0	220.3	222.1	222.7	222.3	218.6
1997	218.6	221.3	222.2	223.3	222.7	221.1	220.1	220.0	223.9	225.3	225.6	225.2	222.4
1998	219.3	221.1	221.2	222.5	221.6	219.3	218.2	217.9	221.5	222.1	222.8	222.7	220.8
1999	218.8	221.8	222.3	224.6	223.5	221.5	219.2	219.4	224.0	225.2	225.7	225.4	222.6
2000	220.8	223.6	224.1	224.8	223.8	220.8	219.7	220.2	224.6	228.1	228.1	228.6	223.9
2001	226.1	228.0	228.5	229.8	229.4	226.9	223.3	225.7	231.2	232.2	234.4	234.6	229.1
2002	230.3	232.7	233.0	235.5	234.8	232.3	230.7	233.8	240.1	240.5	243.5	242.6	235.8
2003	242.2	243.2	242.7	244.7	244.9	240.7	239.4	241.7	246.5	249.1	252.2	249.4	244.7

Employment by Industry: Louisiana—*Continued*

(Numbers in thousands. Not seasonally adjusted.)

Industry	January	February	March	April	May	June	July	August	September	October	November	December	Annual Average
STATEWIDE—*Continued*													
Leisure and hospitality													
1990	121.4	123.3	125.7	126.3	129.7	132.3	128.9	130.4	130.0	125.6	124.7	124.6	126.9
1991	119.9	121.1	122.4	125.9	129.8	131.3	128.8	128.6	127.5	126.1	125.2	125.6	126.0
1992	123.3	124.5	125.9	129.4	132.9	134.5	133.3	132.7	132.3	133.4	133.0	132.2	130.6
1993	127.7	130.2	132.0	134.3	137.0	138.2	137.3	138.0	137.6	138.0	139.2	141.1	135.8
1994	136.6	140.1	142.4	145.7	149.8	152.6	152.3	154.5	156.3	155.6	157.1	157.8	150.0
1995	154.5	157.7	160.4	164.4	171.7	172.6	171.0	173.6	173.5	168.3	167.7	165.7	166.7
1996	163.2	165.0	167.8	169.6	174.4	176.5	175.8	176.9	177.1	176.1	176.7	177.1	173.0
1997	171.7	173.4	176.4	176.6	178.8	180.5	179.5	179.8	179.1	177.5	179.5	179.8	177.7
1998	172.2	174.5	176.4	181.1	184.8	186.2	184.6	184.1	182.8	179.1	179.9	181.1	180.5
1999	176.8	178.9	182.3	183.4	186.1	190.0	189.1	189.7	189.2	190.3	190.8	192.2	186.5
2000	189.4	191.1	193.4	195.2	198.8	201.2	197.6	197.5	196.1	194.3	194.6	195.5	195.3
2001	190.5	192.6	196.4	197.6	199.6	200.3	197.3	197.8	195.9	192.9	191.4	191.7	195.3
2002	186.9	189.5	192.2	196.2	198.9	200.3	198.4	198.2	195.7	192.1	193.6	193.1	194.6
2003	190.0	193.3	195.5	199.5	201.4	202.7	200.6	201.7	199.2	199.1	199.1	198.2	198.4
Other services													
1990	55.5	55.7	56.1	56.6	56.7	57.1	57.2	57.1	57.2	56.9	56.8	56.8	56.6
1991	56.5	56.7	56.8	57.2	57.7	58.5	58.5	58.3	58.3	58.3	58.1	57.9	57.7
1992	57.2	57.1	57.5	57.8	57.9	58.4	58.3	58.0	58.1	58.0	57.8	58.0	57.8
1993	57.3	57.4	57.7	58.2	58.4	58.8	59.1	58.8	59.0	58.8	59.0	59.2	58.4
1994	58.4	58.6	59.2	59.4	59.6	60.1	60.5	60.2	60.2	59.8	59.8	60.1	59.6
1995	60.2	60.6	61.0	61.4	61.8	62.5	62.3	62.3	62.1	61.6	61.6	61.8	61.6
1996	61.7	62.0	62.4	62.6	63.3	63.9	63.4	63.2	63.3	63.5	63.5	63.6	63.0
1997	62.8	62.9	63.5	64.2	64.4	65.1	65.2	64.9	64.8	64.7	64.5	64.9	64.3
1998	64.7	64.8	65.2	66.7	67.2	67.9	67.6	67.2	67.1	66.1	66.0	66.3	66.4
1999	66.2	66.4	66.8	67.1	67.5	68.1	68.1	68.4	68.5	68.7	68.7	68.6	67.7
2000	68.3	68.7	69.2	69.0	69.4	69.6	69.1	69.7	69.7	69.1	68.7	68.8	69.1
2001	67.3	67.6	68.2	69.6	69.9	70.1	69.0	69.4	69.4	68.9	68.7	68.4	68.8
2002	67.7	68.1	68.7	71.1	71.6	71.9	71.0	71.1	71.2	70.9	71.2	71.6	70.5
2003	70.3	70.4	70.9	71.2	71.6	71.9	70.6	70.7	70.6	70.8	70.6	69.3	70.7
Government													
1990	317.9	323.5	324.6	330.9	337.0	327.8	322.9	317.1	321.5	330.4	330.6	329.7	326.1
1991	325.3	330.7	331.3	336.9	339.9	334.4	322.7	317.0	329.6	339.4	340.2	340.3	332.3
1992	334.1	339.9	340.5	342.6	341.1	340.4	334.7	330.0	338.0	345.0	345.0	342.7	339.5
1993	339.5	342.9	343.2	346.0	346.3	343.4	329.3	325.7	340.4	350.4	349.2	347.5	341.9
1994	346.0	347.9	352.0	355.6	354.8	351.3	346.1	341.1	352.8	357.2	357.5	355.6	351.4
1995	352.2	356.4	359.2	362.8	361.3	358.0	352.4	347.2	361.1	363.4	363.8	362.2	358.3
1996	358.2	364.1	364.7	368.0	365.8	362.0	352.5	350.0	363.6	364.8	364.9	363.2	361.8
1997	358.3	363.8	365.2	367.7	366.4	365.5	357.4	352.0	367.4	369.4	369.3	367.4	364.1
1998	362.5	368.6	370.0	371.0	370.0	367.0	356.1	352.6	369.5	373.8	374.1	372.0	367.2
1999	365.7	373.4	373.3	373.3	372.3	369.1	360.3	358.8	373.2	375.0	376.3	373.2	370.3
2000	370.6	376.6	379.5	379.2	385.0	373.9	364.8	359.7	371.6	373.8	373.7	373.0	373.4
2001	372.1	378.1	379.1	377.4	377.0	374.5	362.7	360.7	373.0	376.0	377.6	377.0	373.7
2002	370.0	375.5	377.1	377.5	377.6	376.4	366.7	364.5	375.1	378.7	381.2	378.9	374.9
2003	374.5	381.7	383.1	383.1	383.3	380.7	371.7	368.3	379.6	383.5	384.5	381.5	379.6
Federal government													
1990	37.6	37.5	38.7	38.4	43.9	38.9	39.7	37.6	37.2	37.2	37.1	37.6	38.4
1991	36.6	36.5	36.5	37.1	37.3	37.8	37.6	37.9	37.6	37.9	38.0	38.3	37.4
1992	37.5	37.2	37.1	38.1	38.1	38.2	37.6	37.6	37.4	37.5	36.9	37.4	37.5
1993	36.9	36.7	36.8	37.1	37.3	37.2	37.5	37.3	37.2	36.9	36.6	36.7	37.0
1994	36.4	36.3	36.3	36.5	36.5	36.6	36.2	36.1	35.9	36.0	35.9	36.2	36.2
1995	35.4	35.3	35.4	35.6	35.9	35.9	36.1	36.1	36.0	35.7	35.7	36.1	35.7
1996	35.6	35.6	35.6	36.1	35.9	36.0	36.2	36.3	36.2	35.9	35.9	36.4	35.9
1997	35.7	35.6	35.5	35.5	35.4	35.5	35.6	35.6	35.5	35.3	35.4	35.8	35.5
1998	35.3	35.3	35.2	35.3	35.5	35.4	35.6	35.6	35.5	36.2	36.3	36.4	35.6
1999	35.4	37.0	35.7	35.6	35.3	35.6	35.5	35.5	35.4	35.6	35.4	36.1	35.6
2000	35.5	35.6	37.8	38.0	45.1	37.9	39.6	36.2	35.6	35.7	35.6	36.1	37.3
2001	35.5	35.3	35.3	35.4	35.4	35.7	35.9	35.7	35.7	35.6	35.5	35.5	35.5
2002	35.2	34.9	34.9	34.8	34.8	35.1	35.1	35.0	35.0	35.8	36.0	36.0	35.2
2003	35.6	35.5	35.5	35.4	35.3	35.4	34.8	34.6	35.0	35.0	34.8	34.9	35.2
State government													
1990	93.1	98.5	98.3	102.4	103.0	95.0	92.5	92.0	99.5	103.2	103.1	101.8	98.5
1991	97.3	102.1	102.5	105.4	105.7	97.5	95.9	93.9	103.2	108.1	108.4	107.9	102.3
1992	101.8	107.6	107.6	106.2	104.2	98.9	99.9	97.8	106.1	109.0	109.0	106.7	104.5
1993	104.7	107.8	107.9	108.4	107.9	102.6	102.5	101.8	109.3	111.2	110.4	108.7	106.9
1994	106.7	108.5	112.1	113.7	112.3	106.1	107.8	106.6	114.1	115.3	115.6	112.8	110.9
1995	110.2	113.8	115.7	118.0	115.8	109.2	110.8	108.4	115.9	118.0	117.7	116.9	114.2
1996	112.6	117.9	117.7	119.2	116.4	109.6	108.8	108.3	115.7	117.0	116.9	115.0	114.5
1997	110.2	115.4	115.8	116.6	114.4	107.9	108.3	107.4	115.7	118.1	117.8	115.8	113.6
1998	110.9	116.6	117.4	117.9	115.9	109.6	111.5	110.1	117.8	119.8	119.8	117.9	115.4
1999	112.8	118.5	119.1	119.8	118.2	110.5	112.1	111.1	119.0	120.7	120.7	118.7	116.7
2000	114.0	119.4	119.7	119.8	117.9	110.7	112.1	111.7	118.9	119.8	118.9	117.4	116.6
2001	112.1	117.8	117.8	117.2	116.2	109.8	108.7	109.3	116.6	116.4	117.7	117.2	114.7
2002	112.1	117.2	118.1	118.4	117.8	111.9	110.2	110.7	118.6	118.3	119.6	117.3	115.9
2003	112.5	119.3	120.2	120.3	119.9	113.1	111.8	112.4	121.0	122.6	122.3	119.2	117.9

Employment by Industry: Louisiana—*Continued*

(Numbers in thousands. Not seasonally adjusted.)

Industry	January	February	March	April	May	June	July	August	September	October	November	December	Annual Average
STATEWIDE—*Continued*													
Local government													
1990	187.2	187.5	187.6	190.1	190.1	193.9	190.7	187.5	184.8	190.0	190.4	190.3	189.1
1991	191.4	192.1	192.3	194.4	196.9	199.1	189.2	185.2	188.8	193.4	193.8	194.1	192.5
1992	194.8	195.1	195.8	198.3	198.8	203.3	197.2	194.6	194.5	198.5	199.1	198.6	197.3
1993	197.9	198.4	198.5	200.5	201.1	203.6	189.3	186.6	193.9	202.3	202.2	202.1	198.0
1994	202.9	203.1	203.6	205.4	206.0	208.6	202.1	198.4	202.8	205.9	206.0	206.6	204.2
1995	206.6	207.3	208.1	209.2	209.6	212.9	205.5	202.7	209.2	209.7	210.4	209.2	208.3
1996	210.0	210.6	211.4	212.7	213.5	216.4	207.5	205.4	211.7	211.9	212.1	211.8	211.2
1997	212.4	212.8	213.9	215.6	216.6	222.1	213.5	209.0	216.2	216.0	216.1	215.8	215.0
1998	216.3	216.7	217.4	217.8	218.6	222.0	209.0	206.9	216.2	217.8	218.0	217.7	216.2
1999	217.5	217.9	218.5	217.9	218.8	223.0	212.7	212.2	218.8	218.7	220.2	218.4	217.8
2000	221.1	221.6	222.0	221.4	222.0	225.3	213.1	211.8	217.1	218.3	219.2	219.5	219.3
2001	224.5	225.0	226.0	224.8	225.4	229.0	218.1	215.7	220.7	224.0	224.4	224.3	223.4
2002	222.7	223.4	224.1	224.3	225.0	229.4	221.4	218.8	221.5	224.6	225.6	225.6	223.9
2003	226.4	226.9	227.4	227.4	228.1	232.2	225.1	221.3	223.6	225.9	227.4	227.4	226.6
BATON ROUGE													
Total nonfarm													
1990	229.1	232.0	233.2	234.9	237.7	237.3	234.7	233.4	236.7	240.6	240.7	240.5	235.9
1991	234.3	237.9	239.2	240.4	241.9	243.7	243.0	240.3	245.3	245.8	246.0	246.2	242.0
1992	240.7	246.1	247.5	249.7	250.9	253.7	251.4	250.4	252.3	253.7	252.9	252.3	250.1
1993	246.7	251.4	252.1	254.3	255.4	256.8	254.2	250.7	254.7	255.8	256.9	257.4	253.8
1994	252.4	257.9	261.2	259.5	259.3	261.8	260.0	258.9	266.2	266.6	267.9	268.5	261.6
1995	262.4	265.9	266.4	266.1	267.0	269.7	269.4	267.2	272.5	274.2	274.6	273.0	269.0
1996	267.5	271.8	274.6	275.6	277.0	278.7	275.3	274.1	279.7	282.1	282.9	281.1	276.7
1997	273.0	277.6	280.6	280.1	279.5	281.7	279.4	277.3	283.1	285.9	287.6	289.5	281.2
1998	280.9	286.0	287.4	290.0	291.3	291.7	291.5	291.0	294.7	297.2	298.6	299.5	291.6
1999	291.1	295.1	295.7	298.3	298.2	300.7	300.2	300.6	304.2	305.5	307.9	308.0	300.5
2000	300.6	305.9	308.5	310.9	310.4	310.0	305.8	305.5	309.0	309.3	309.6	309.7	307.9
2001	301.9	304.1	306.0	306.1	307.7	307.2	301.7	302.1	307.5	306.1	306.9	306.0	305.2
2002	295.9	298.8	301.3	301.7	302.8	302.0	299.7	300.6	303.8	304.5	305.5	303.1	301.6
2003	300.1	304.3	304.9	305.2	306.5	305.3	302.0	303.3	307.1	309.6	311.1	308.6	305.7
Total private													
1990	177.9	177.8	178.5	179.2	181.3	182.2	181.1	182.7	183.3	184.0	184.4	185.1	181.4
1991	181.4	181.9	183.5	183.8	185.9	186.8	186.6	186.8	188.1	188.0	188.6	188.9	185.8
1992	186.1	188.1	189.5	191.5	194.6	196.6	193.6	195.1	195.4	196.0	195.7	196.5	193.2
1993	192.5	195.2	196.0	197.8	200.7	202.1	200.2	198.3	199.3	199.7	200.9	203.9	198.8
1994	198.2	201.2	204.3	202.3	204.0	205.8	203.7	205.7	209.1	208.7	210.4	212.4	205.4
1995	207.2	208.2	208.4	206.9	209.6	212.6	212.7	213.4	215.0	215.9	216.4	216.4	211.8
1996	212.1	213.6	216.7	217.0	220.1	221.6	219.9	220.8	222.0	223.2	224.0	223.5	219.5
1997	217.5	219.0	222.0	222.2	223.1	224.9	223.8	224.0	225.3	226.7	228.6	231.4	224.0
1998	224.6	226.8	228.9	231.6	233.4	234.5	234.3	235.0	235.2	236.7	238.1	240.2	233.2
1999	233.8	235.1	235.5	237.3	238.3	241.5	241.7	242.6	243.4	244.0	246.6	247.3	240.6
2000	243.7	245.6	248.3	249.2	249.1	250.2	246.6	247.8	247.9	247.3	247.9	249.2	247.7
2001	244.8	243.9	245.6	245.5	247.4	247.5	244.3	245.7	247.7	244.8	245.2	245.4	245.6
2002	237.6	238.6	240.5	241.3	242.3	242.6	241.1	242.5	242.6	242.4	242.6	242.9	241.4
2003	240.4	241.7	242.2	243.0	244.4	244.3	243.1	245.0	245.5	247.2	248.4	248.4	244.5
Goods-producing													
1990	48.8	49.3	48.9	47.9	49.3	48.7	48.1	49.5	49.3	50.4	50.5	49.9	49.2
1991	49.8	49.4	50.3	50.0	50.9	50.3	50.7	50.9	51.8	52.6	52.7	51.6	50.9
1992	49.0	50.9	51.5	51.5	53.8	54.0	51.1	51.9	51.5	52.4	51.7	51.2	51.7
1993	49.7	50.9	51.1	51.5	53.2	53.5	52.5	50.8	50.9	51.3	51.4	51.8	51.5
1994	50.8	52.7	54.7	52.0	52.3	52.5	52.1	53.5	55.4	54.9	55.0	55.4	53.4
1995	51.8	51.8	51.7	50.1	50.5	51.1	52.8	53.1	53.7	55.1	55.4	54.8	52.6
1996	53.7	54.4	56.4	55.6	56.8	57.4	56.2	56.6	57.3	58.0	58.1	57.3	56.4
1997	53.6	54.0	54.7	54.5	55.0	55.8	54.8	55.3	55.4	55.6	55.2	55.6	54.9
1998	54.0	55.9	56.8	56.3	57.3	57.4	57.2	58.0	57.6	58.9	59.5	59.2	57.3
1999	58.3	58.7	58.5	57.9	58.8	59.9	57.3	58.1	58.0	59.4	59.9	59.8	58.7
2000	60.4	60.9	62.2	62.8	62.8	61.9	59.3	60.1	58.9	58.5	58.1	57.7	60.3
2001	57.1	57.1	58.1	58.4	60.0	59.0	58.5	58.5	60.6	57.7	57.4	56.8	58.2
2002	53.7	53.8	54.6	54.5	54.9	54.3	53.5	54.3	55.0	55.6	54.2	53.5	54.3
2003	54.0	54.5	54.1	53.5	54.6	54.2	53.5	54.2	55.2	55.8	54.9	55.1	54.5
Natural resources and mining													
1990	0.6	0.6	0.6	0.7	0.7	0.7	0.8	0.8	0.8	0.7	0.8	0.8	0.7
1991	0.7	0.7	0.7	0.7	0.7	0.7	0.7	0.7	0.7	0.8	0.8	0.7	0.7
1992	0.7	0.7	0.7	0.7	0.7	0.7	0.7	0.7	0.7	0.7	0.7	0.7	0.7
1993	0.6	0.7	0.7	0.7	0.7	0.9	0.9	0.9	0.9	0.8	0.8	0.8	0.7
1994	0.9	0.8	0.8	0.8	0.8	0.8	0.8	0.8	0.8	0.8	0.8	0.8	0.8
1995	0.7	0.7	0.7	0.8	0.8	0.8	0.8	0.8	0.8	0.8	0.8	0.8	0.7
1996	0.8	0.8	0.8	1.0	1.0	1.0	0.9	0.9	0.9	1.0	1.0	1.0	0.9
1997	0.9	0.9	0.9	1.0	1.0	1.0	1.1	1.1	1.1	1.2	1.1	1.2	1.0
1998	1.1	1.1	1.1	1.2	1.2	1.3	1.1	1.1	1.1	1.1	1.1	1.1	1.1
1999	1.1	1.0	1.0	1.0	1.1	1.1	1.0	1.0	1.0	1.1	1.0	1.0	1.0
2000	1.1	1.0	1.1	1.1	1.0	1.1	1.1	1.1	1.1	1.0	1.0	1.0	1.1
2001	1.0	1.0	1.0	1.0	1.1	1.1	1.1	1.1	1.2	1.2	1.1	1.2	1.0
2002	1.2	1.2	1.2	1.1	1.2	1.2	1.2	1.2	1.2	1.3	1.3	1.3	1.2
2003	1.3	1.3	1.3	1.3	1.3	1.2	1.2	1.2	1.2	1.2	1.2	1.2	1.2

Employment by Industry: Louisiana—*Continued*

(Numbers in thousands. Not seasonally adjusted.)

Industry	January	February	March	April	May	June	July	August	September	October	November	December	Annual Average
BATON ROUGE—*Continued*													
Construction													
1990	27.3	27.7	27.2	26.0	27.3	26.5	25.5	26.9	26.8	27.9	27.9	27.3	27.0
1991	27.8	27.4	28.3	27.9	28.8	27.9	28.2	28.5	29.4	29.8	29.4	29.1	28.5
1992	27.7	29.6	30.2	30.0	32.2	32.1	29.3	30.2	29.9	30.6	30.1	29.6	30.1
1993	28.1	29.2	29.4	29.7	31.2	31.3	30.2	28.8	29.0	29.4	29.5	29.8	29.6
1994	28.9	31.0	32.9	29.6	29.8	29.6	29.4	30.8	32.8	32.0	32.1	32.4	30.9
1995	29.3	29.3	29.4	27.5	27.7	28.1	29.6	29.7	30.5	31.6	32.1	31.4	29.6
1996	30.2	30.8	32.8	31.7	32.5	33.0	32.0	32.6	33.2	33.7	33.9	33.1	32.4
1997	29.5	30.0	30.6	29.5	29.8	30.4	30.4	30.9	31.0	31.0	30.7	30.9	30.3
1998	30.1	31.9	32.8	31.7	32.4	32.1	32.4	33.2	32.9	34.4	34.8	34.4	32.7
1999	33.8	34.4	34.2	33.6	34.3	35.3	32.7	33.4	33.4	34.7	35.3	35.1	34.2
2000	35.9	36.5	37.7	38.3	38.3	37.1	34.7	35.4	34.3	33.3	32.9	32.3	35.6
2001	31.7	31.8	32.9	33.6	35.0	33.9	33.6	33.5	35.7	32.9	32.8	32.3	33.3
2002	29.9	30.5	31.3	31.5	31.8	31.0	30.3	31.0	31.7	32.2	30.9	30.3	31.0
2003	30.9	31.4	31.0	30.8	31.7	31.5	31.2	31.9	32.9	33.3	32.6	32.5	31.8
Manufacturing													
1990	20.9	21.0	21.1	21.2	21.3	21.5	21.8	21.8	21.7	21.8	21.8	21.8	21.4
1991	21.3	21.3	21.3	21.4	21.4	21.7	21.8	21.7	21.7	22.0	22.5	21.8	21.6
1992	20.6	20.6	20.6	20.8	20.9	21.2	21.1	21.0	20.9	21.1	20.9	20.9	20.8
1993	21.0	21.0	21.0	21.1	21.3	21.3	21.4	21.1	21.0	21.1	21.1	21.2	21.1
1994	21.0	20.9	21.0	21.6	21.7	22.1	21.9	21.9	21.8	22.1	22.1	22.2	21.6
1995	21.8	21.8	21.6	21.8	22.0	22.2	22.4	22.6	22.4	22.7	22.5	22.6	22.2
1996	22.7	22.8	22.8	22.9	23.3	23.4	23.3	23.1	23.2	23.3	23.2	23.2	23.1
1997	23.2	23.1	23.2	24.0	24.2	24.4	23.3	23.3	23.3	23.4	23.4	23.5	23.5
1998	22.8	22.9	22.9	23.4	23.7	24.0	23.7	23.7	23.6	23.4	23.6	23.7	23.4
1999	23.4	23.3	23.3	23.3	23.4	23.5	23.6	23.7	23.6	23.6	23.6	23.7	23.5
2000	23.4	23.4	23.4	23.4	23.5	23.7	23.5	23.6	23.5	24.2	24.2	24.4	23.7
2001	24.4	24.3	24.2	23.8	23.9	24.0	23.8	23.9	23.7	23.6	23.5	23.3	23.8
2002	22.6	22.1	22.1	21.9	21.9	22.1	22.0	22.1	22.1	22.1	22.0	21.9	22.1
2003	21.8	21.8	21.8	21.4	21.6	21.5	21.1	21.1	21.1	21.3	21.1	21.4	21.4
Service-providing													
1990	180.3	182.7	184.3	187.0	188.4	188.6	186.6	183.9	187.4	190.2	190.2	190.6	186.6
1991	184.5	188.5	188.9	190.4	191.0	193.4	192.3	189.4	193.5	193.2	193.3	194.6	191.0
1992	191.7	195.2	196.0	198.2	197.1	199.7	200.3	198.5	200.8	201.3	201.2	201.1	198.4
1993	197.0	200.5	201.0	202.8	202.2	203.3	201.7	199.9	203.8	204.5	205.5	205.6	202.3
1994	201.6	205.2	206.5	207.5	207.0	209.3	207.9	205.4	210.8	211.7	212.9	213.1	208.2
1995	210.6	214.1	214.7	216.0	216.5	218.6	216.6	214.1	218.8	219.1	219.2	218.2	216.3
1996	213.8	217.4	218.2	220.0	220.2	221.3	219.1	217.5	222.4	224.1	224.8	223.8	220.2
1997	219.4	223.6	225.9	225.6	224.5	225.9	224.6	222.0	227.7	230.3	232.4	233.9	226.3
1998	226.9	230.1	230.6	233.7	234.0	234.3	234.3	233.0	237.1	238.3	239.1	240.3	234.3
1999	232.8	236.4	237.2	240.4	239.4	240.8	242.9	242.5	246.2	246.1	248.0	248.2	241.7
2000	240.2	245.0	246.3	248.1	247.6	248.1	246.5	245.4	250.1	250.8	251.5	252.0	247.6
2001	244.8	247.0	247.9	247.7	247.7	248.2	243.2	243.6	246.9	248.4	249.5	249.2	247.0
2002	242.2	245.0	246.7	247.2	247.9	247.7	246.2	246.3	248.8	248.9	251.3	249.6	247.3
2003	246.1	249.8	250.8	251.7	251.9	251.1	248.5	249.1	251.9	253.8	256.2	253.5	251.2
Trade, transportation, and utilities													
1990	44.5	44.1	44.3	44.7	45.0	45.4	44.9	44.9	44.9	44.6	44.9	45.9	44.8
1991	44.9	44.4	44.7	44.8	45.1	45.6	45.7	45.6	45.5	45.2	46.0	46.9	45.3
1992	45.9	45.3	45.5	46.0	46.2	46.9	46.7	46.9	46.9	46.6	47.4	48.2	46.5
1993	46.5	46.5	46.5	46.5	46.9	47.4	47.4	47.3	47.4	47.4	48.3	49.6	47.3
1994	47.2	47.3	47.3	47.4	47.9	48.5	48.3	48.7	49.1	49.0	49.9	50.8	48.4
1995	49.5	49.2	49.3	48.9	49.7	50.6	50.1	50.3	50.1	50.4	50.9	51.7	50.0
1996	49.7	49.5	49.6	49.7	50.6	51.0	51.3	51.5	51.2	51.4	52.3	52.9	50.8
1997	51.7	51.3	52.4	52.1	52.1	52.3	52.7	52.7	53.0	54.5	56.1	57.6	53.2
1998	54.6	54.3	54.6	55.5	55.8	56.3	56.2	56.5	56.9	56.6	57.5	58.7	56.1
1999	56.5	56.2	56.5	56.9	56.9	57.5	58.7	58.8	59.3	58.7	60.0	61.1	58.1
2000	58.4	58.3	59.0	58.6	58.8	59.6	59.9	60.5	60.9	60.8	62.0	63.0	60.0
2001	61.4	60.4	60.6	60.2	60.1	60.4	59.6	60.3	60.1	60.4	61.5	62.1	60.5
2002	59.7	59.8	59.9	59.9	59.8	59.8	59.3	59.4	59.2	58.7	60.0	60.5	59.7
2003	57.9	57.8	58.1	58.3	58.4	58.5	57.8	58.0	57.9	58.5	59.8	60.1	58.4
Wholesale trade													
1990	10.4	10.4	10.4	10.5	10.5	10.5	10.6	10.6	10.5	10.3	10.3	10.4	10.4
1991	10.1	10.2	10.3	10.6	10.6	10.8	10.8	10.7	10.7	10.7	10.7	10.7	10.5
1992	10.8	10.7	10.7	10.8	10.8	10.9	10.9	11.0	10.9	10.9	10.8	10.9	10.8
1993	10.9	10.9	10.9	10.9	10.9	11.0	10.9	10.8	10.8	10.7	10.7	10.9	10.8
1994	10.7	10.7	10.7	10.8	10.9	11.1	11.0	11.0	11.1	11.1	11.1	11.2	10.9
1995	11.2	11.2	11.2	11.2	11.4	11.6	11.5	11.6	11.6	11.7	11.6	11.7	11.4
1996	11.5	11.6	11.5	11.6	11.8	12.0	12.0	12.1	12.0	12.0	12.1	12.1	11.8
1997	12.3	12.2	12.3	12.2	12.3	12.4	12.5	12.5	12.5	12.3	12.4	12.5	12.3
1998	12.4	12.4	12.5	12.7	12.7	12.9	12.9	12.9	12.9	12.7	12.7	12.8	12.7
1999	12.7	12.8	12.9	13.1	13.1	13.2	13.3	13.3	13.2	13.0	13.0	13.1	13.1
2000	13.2	13.1	13.4	13.4	13.5	13.7	13.6	13.6	13.5	13.5	13.4	13.6	13.5
2001	13.7	13.7	13.9	13.9	13.7	13.9	13.6	13.5	13.6	13.4	13.5	13.4	13.6
2002	13.1	13.2	13.2	13.1	13.1	13.2	13.0	13.0	13.0	12.8	12.8	12.8	13.0
2003	13.0	13.0	13.0	12.8	12.9	13.0	12.8	12.8	12.8	13.0	12.9	12.8	12.9

Employment by Industry: Louisiana—*Continued*

(Numbers in thousands. Not seasonally adjusted.)

Industry	January	February	March	April	May	June	July	August	September	October	November	December	Annual Average
BATON ROUGE—*Continued*													
Retail trade													
1990	27.5	27.0	27.2	27.5	27.8	28.1	27.5	27.5	27.5	27.4	27.8	28.6	27.6
1991	28.1	27.4	27.5	27.4	27.6	27.9	27.9	27.9	27.9	27.6	28.4	29.3	27.9
1992	27.8	27.3	27.4	27.8	28.0	28.4	28.1	28.2	28.3	28.3	29.2	29.9	28.2
1993	28.2	28.2	28.2	28.0	28.2	28.5	28.6	28.7	28.8	28.7	29.6	30.5	28.6
1994	28.5	28.5	28.4	28.5	28.9	29.2	29.1	29.6	30.0	29.8	30.8	31.5	29.4
1995	30.2	29.9	30.0	29.5	30.2	30.7	30.4	30.5	30.5	30.8	31.5	32.3	30.5
1996	30.5	30.1	30.4	30.4	31.0	31.3	31.4	31.5	31.3	31.6	32.4	33.0	31.2
1997	31.6	31.2	32.0	31.8	31.7	31.6	31.9	32.2	32.3	34.1	35.5	36.8	32.7
1998	34.0	33.7	33.9	34.4	34.6	34.8	34.7	35.0	35.4	35.5	36.4	37.4	34.9
1999	35.0	34.6	34.7	34.8	34.9	35.2	36.3	36.3	36.8	36.3	37.6	38.4	35.9
2000	36.1	36.0	36.6	36.1	36.2	36.6	36.7	36.8	37.3	37.0	38.3	39.1	36.9
2001	37.1	36.2	36.2	35.8	35.9	35.9	35.6	36.3	36.0	36.3	37.4	38.0	36.3
2002	36.2	35.9	35.8	35.7	35.5	35.4	35.0	35.0	34.9	34.6	35.9	36.5	35.5
2003	34.2	34.0	34.2	34.5	34.4	34.5	34.1	34.2	34.1	34.5	35.8	36.3	34.6
Transportation and utilities													
1990	6.6	6.7	6.7	6.7	6.7	6.8	6.8	6.8	6.9	6.9	6.8	6.9	6.7
1991	6.7	6.8	6.9	6.8	6.9	6.9	7.0	7.0	6.9	6.9	6.9	6.9	6.8
1992	7.3	7.3	7.4	7.4	7.4	7.6	7.7	7.7	7.7	7.4	7.4	7.4	7.4
1993	7.4	7.4	7.4	7.6	7.8	7.9	7.9	7.8	7.8	8.0	8.0	8.2	7.7
1994	8.0	8.1	8.2	8.1	8.1	8.2	8.2	8.1	8.0	8.1	8.0	8.1	8.1
1995	8.1	8.1	8.1	8.2	8.1	8.3	8.2	8.2	8.0	7.9	7.8	7.7	8.0
1996	7.7	7.8	7.7	7.7	7.8	7.7	7.9	7.9	7.9	7.8	7.8	7.8	7.7
1997	7.8	7.9	8.1	8.1	8.1	8.3	8.3	8.0	8.2	8.1	8.2	8.3	8.1
1998	8.2	8.2	8.2	8.4	8.5	8.6	8.6	8.6	8.6	8.4	8.4	8.5	8.4
1999	8.8	8.8	8.9	9.0	8.9	9.1	9.1	9.2	9.3	9.4	9.4	9.6	9.1
2000	9.1	9.2	9.0	9.1	9.1	9.3	9.6	10.1	10.1	10.3	10.3	10.3	9.6
2001	10.6	10.5	10.5	10.5	10.5	10.6	10.4	10.5	10.5	10.7	10.6	10.7	10.5
2002	10.4	10.7	10.9	11.1	11.2	11.2	11.3	11.4	11.3	11.3	11.3	11.2	11.1
2003	10.7	10.8	10.9	11.0	11.1	11.0	10.9	11.0	11.0	11.0	11.1	11.0	11.0
Information													
1990	4.0	4.0	3.9	3.8	3.9	3.9	3.9	3.9	3.9	3.8	3.8	3.8	3.8
1991	3.8	3.8	3.8	3.7	3.7	3.7	3.7	3.7	3.7	3.5	3.4	3.5	3.6
1992	3.5	3.4	3.4	3.5	3.5	3.5	3.6	3.6	3.5	3.5	3.5	3.5	3.5
1993	3.6	3.6	3.5	3.6	3.8	3.9	3.6	3.6	3.8	3.8	3.9	3.9	3.7
1994	3.7	3.7	3.7	3.7	3.7	3.7	3.7	3.6	3.6	3.7	3.7	3.7	3.6
1995	3.8	3.8	3.9	3.8	3.9	4.0	4.0	4.0	4.0	4.0	4.0	3.9	3.9
1996	3.9	3.9	3.9	4.1	4.1	4.1	4.0	4.1	4.1	4.3	4.4	4.3	4.1
1997	4.2	4.2	4.2	4.1	4.1	4.1	4.3	4.1	4.2	4.0	4.1	4.1	4.1
1998	4.3	4.3	4.3	4.3	4.4	4.4	4.4	4.4	4.3	4.5	4.4	4.4	4.3
1999	4.5	4.5	4.6	4.5	4.5	4.6	4.7	4.7	4.7	4.6	4.6	4.7	4.6
2000	4.6	4.6	4.8	5.0	4.9	5.0	5.3	5.3	5.3	5.3	5.3	5.4	5.1
2001	5.1	5.1	5.2	5.5	5.5	5.5	5.3	5.2	5.2	5.3	5.2	5.1	5.2
2002	5.0	5.0	5.0	4.9	5.0	5.1	5.0	5.0	5.1	5.0	5.0	5.0	5.0
2003	5.0	5.0	5.1	5.1	5.1	5.2	5.2	5.5	5.4	5.5	5.5	5.6	5.3
Financial activities													
1990	13.1	12.9	13.0	13.3	13.2	13.4	13.2	13.1	13.1	13.1	13.1	13.0	13.1
1991	13.0	13.0	13.0	13.0	13.1	13.1	13.0	13.1	13.1	13.0	13.1	13.1	13.0
1992	12.7	12.6	12.8	12.8	12.8	13.0	12.9	13.0	13.0	13.1	13.1	13.1	12.9
1993	13.1	13.1	13.2	13.1	13.3	13.5	13.4	13.4	13.5	13.5	13.4	13.7	13.3
1994	13.5	13.4	13.5	12.6	12.7	12.8	12.8	12.9	12.8	12.8	12.8	13.0	12.9
1995	12.9	12.9	13.0	13.2	13.3	13.4	13.6	13.7	13.7	13.9	13.9	13.9	13.4
1996	14.0	14.1	14.2	14.5	14.7	14.8	14.6	14.7	14.7	14.8	14.8	14.8	14.5
1997	15.1	15.3	15.4	15.4	15.6	15.7	15.5	15.6	15.5	15.8	15.8	15.9	15.5
1998	15.7	15.7	15.8	16.1	16.1	16.1	16.0	16.0	15.8	16.2	16.1	16.3	15.9
1999	15.7	15.7	15.7	15.8	15.8	15.8	16.0	15.9	15.8	16.0	16.1	16.3	15.9
2000	17.0	17.0	17.1	16.7	16.7	16.9	16.6	16.6	16.6	16.5	16.5	16.7	16.7
2001	15.9	15.9	15.9	15.9	15.8	16.0	15.7	15.8	15.7	15.7	15.8	15.8	15.8
2002	16.1	16.1	16.0	16.4	16.3	16.2	16.2	16.3	16.1	16.2	16.1	16.3	16.2
2003	16.5	16.6	16.6	16.5	16.5	16.6	16.7	16.8	16.8	16.8	16.9	17.1	16.7
Professional and business services													
1990	22.7	22.7	23.1	23.2	23.4	23.6	24.1	24.3	24.2	24.0	24.1	24.3	23.6
1991	24.9	25.4	25.5	25.7	26.1	26.5	26.2	26.5	26.5	26.2	25.8	26.1	25.9
1992	27.5	27.8	28.0	28.1	28.2	28.5	28.7	29.0	29.1	29.0	28.7	29.1	28.4
1993	28.7	28.9	29.0	28.7	28.9	29.2	29.0	28.9	28.8	28.6	28.5	29.0	28.8
1994	28.1	28.5	28.9	29.4	29.4	30.0	29.5	29.6	29.8	29.3	29.5	29.6	29.3
1995	29.4	29.7	29.8	29.4	29.8	30.3	29.8	29.8	30.1	29.6	29.5	29.3	29.7
1996	28.9	29.0	29.2	29.1	29.1	29.2	29.6	29.7	29.8	29.5	29.5	29.4	29.3
1997	29.0	29.2	29.7	30.0	29.9	30.1	30.1	30.2	30.6	30.6	30.7	31.3	30.1
1998	31.2	31.3	31.7	33.0	33.1	33.5	33.7	33.6	33.6	34.1	34.3	34.9	33.1
1999	34.0	34.4	34.2	35.9	35.8	36.6	37.4	37.7	37.6	37.1	37.7	37.5	36.3
2000	36.5	37.0	37.1	37.1	37.2	37.7	37.3	37.3	37.5	38.0	37.9	38.0	37.4
2001	38.4	37.7	37.5	37.0	36.9	37.4	37.3	37.6	37.5	37.6	37.5	38.0	37.5
2002	36.9	37.0	37.2	36.9	36.8	36.8	36.6	36.5	36.1	36.2	36.1	36.2	36.6
2003	36.0	35.8	36.1	36.4	36.1	36.1	35.8	35.9	35.4	35.5	35.9	35.8	35.9

Employment by Industry: Louisiana—*Continued*

(Numbers in thousands. Not seasonally adjusted.)

Industry	January	February	March	April	May	June	July	August	September	October	November	December	Annual Average
BATON ROUGE—*Continued*													
Educational and health services													
1990	20.2	20.2	20.4	21.0	21.0	20.8	20.8	20.9	21.9	22.6	22.7	22.8	21.2
1991	21.1	21.6	21.9	21.8	21.7	21.6	21.5	21.5	22.2	22.6	22.7	22.6	21.9
1992	22.4	22.8	22.9	23.2	23.1	23.1	22.9	23.1	23.9	24.2	24.3	24.4	23.3
1993	24.6	25.2	25.3	26.2	26.0	25.8	25.7	25.8	26.5	27.3	27.5	27.8	26.1
1994	27.2	27.6	27.7	28.3	28.5	28.3	27.9	28.0	28.6	28.9	29.1	29.2	28.2
1995	28.4	28.8	28.6	28.9	28.9	28.9	28.5	28.4	28.9	29.4	29.3	29.2	28.8
1996	28.5	28.9	29.1	29.2	29.2	29.0	28.7	28.8	29.4	29.8	29.8	29.6	29.1
1997	29.3	29.8	30.0	30.4	30.3	30.2	29.8	29.7	30.1	30.2	30.3	30.3	30.0
1998	29.1	29.2	29.3	29.8	29.6	29.4	29.2	29.1	29.8	29.9	29.9	29.9	29.5
1999	29.4	29.9	29.7	29.9	29.6	29.5	29.5	29.7	30.3	30.7	30.8	30.7	30.0
2000	30.3	30.7	30.8	31.0	30.6	30.4	29.9	29.9	30.8	31.2	31.1	31.1	30.7
2001	30.2	30.4	30.6	30.5	30.4	30.3	29.7	29.8	30.1	30.2	30.2	30.2	30.2
2002	30.0	30.1	30.3	30.3	30.5	30.9	30.9	31.4	31.9	32.0	32.3	32.6	31.1
2003	32.8	33.0	33.0	33.1	33.3	33.3	34.0	34.4	34.5	34.8	35.0	34.7	33.8
Leisure and hospitality													
1990	15.5	15.5	15.7	16.1	16.3	17.0	16.8	16.9	16.7	16.2	16.1	16.2	16.2
1991	14.7	15.0	15.0	15.4	15.9	16.3	16.1	15.9	15.8	15.3	15.4	15.6	15.5
1992	15.6	15.8	15.9	16.7	17.3	17.6	17.7	17.6	17.6	17.4	17.2	17.2	16.9
1993	16.6	17.2	17.5	18.2	18.5	18.5	18.2	18.3	18.2	17.7	17.7	17.8	17.8
1994	17.5	17.8	18.2	18.5	19.1	19.4	18.8	18.9	19.3	19.7	20.0	20.3	18.9
1995	20.9	21.4	21.6	22.0	22.8	23.3	22.9	23.2	23.7	22.7	22.6	22.8	22.4
1996	22.6	22.9	23.3	23.7	24.3	24.6	24.2	24.2	24.4	24.2	24.0	24.1	23.8
1997	23.6	24.1	24.4	24.5	24.7	25.1	24.9	24.8	25.0	24.4	24.8	24.9	24.6
1998	23.8	24.2	24.4	24.5	24.9	25.1	25.3	25.1	25.0	24.4	24.4	24.8	24.6
1999	23.5	23.7	24.3	24.5	25.0	25.7	26.2	25.8	25.8	25.9	25.9	25.8	25.2
2000	25.1	25.6	25.9	26.6	26.7	27.4	27.0	26.9	26.8	26.1	26.3	26.7	26.4
2001	26.0	26.5	26.9	27.0	27.7	27.7	27.3	27.5	27.4	26.9	26.7	26.5	27.0
2002	25.4	25.9	26.5	27.0	27.6	27.9	28.0	28.2	27.8	27.1	27.4	27.3	27.2
2003	26.9	27.7	27.8	28.5	28.7	28.7	28.6	28.7	28.9	28.9	29.0	28.8	28.4
Other services													
1990	9.1	9.1	9.2	9.2	9.2	9.4	9.3	9.2	9.3	9.3	9.2	9.2	9.2
1991	9.2	9.3	9.3	9.4	9.4	9.7	9.7	9.6	9.5	9.6	9.5	9.5	9.4
1992	9.5	9.5	9.5	9.7	9.7	10.0	10.0	10.0	9.9	9.8	9.8	9.8	9.7
1993	9.7	9.8	9.9	10.0	10.1	10.3	10.4	10.2	10.2	10.1	10.2	10.3	10.1
1994	10.2	10.2	10.3	10.4	10.4	10.6	10.6	10.5	10.5	10.4	10.4	10.4	10.4
1995	10.5	10.6	10.5	10.6	10.7	11.0	11.0	10.9	10.8	10.8	10.8	10.8	10.7
1996	10.8	10.9	11.0	11.1	11.3	11.5	11.3	11.2	11.1	11.2	11.1	11.1	11.1
1997	11.0	11.1	11.2	11.2	11.4	11.6	11.7	11.6	11.5	11.6	11.6	11.7	11.4
1998	11.9	11.9	12.0	12.1	12.2	12.3	12.3	12.3	12.2	12.1	12.0	12.0	12.1
1999	11.9	12.0	12.0	11.9	11.9	11.9	11.9	11.9	11.9	11.6	11.6	11.4	11.8
2000	11.4	11.5	11.4	11.4	11.4	11.3	11.3	11.2	11.1	10.9	10.7	10.6	11.2
2001	10.7	10.8	10.8	11.0	11.0	11.2	10.9	11.0	11.1	11.0	10.9	10.9	10.9
2002	10.8	10.9	11.0	11.4	11.4	11.6	11.6	11.4	11.4	11.6	11.5	11.5	11.3
2003	11.3	11.3	11.4	11.6	11.7	11.7	11.5	11.5	11.4	11.4	11.4	11.2	11.5
Government													
1990	51.2	54.2	54.7	55.7	56.4	55.1	53.6	50.7	53.4	56.6	56.3	55.4	54.4
1991	52.9	56.0	55.7	56.6	56.0	56.9	56.4	53.5	57.2	57.8	57.4	57.3	56.1
1992	54.6	58.0	58.0	58.2	56.3	57.1	57.8	55.3	56.9	57.7	57.2	55.8	56.9
1993	54.2	56.2	56.1	56.5	54.7	54.7	54.0	52.4	55.4	56.1	56.0	53.5	54.9
1994	54.2	56.7	56.9	57.2	55.3	56.0	56.3	53.2	57.1	57.9	57.5	56.1	56.2
1995	55.2	57.7	58.0	59.2	57.4	57.1	56.7	53.8	57.5	58.3	58.2	56.6	57.1
1996	55.4	58.2	57.9	58.6	56.9	57.1	55.4	53.3	57.7	58.9	58.9	57.6	57.1
1997	55.5	58.6	58.6	57.9	56.4	56.8	55.6	53.3	57.8	59.2	59.0	58.1	57.2
1998	56.3	59.2	58.5	58.4	57.9	57.2	57.2	56.0	59.5	60.5	60.5	59.3	58.3
1999	57.3	60.0	60.2	61.0	59.9	59.2	58.5	58.0	60.8	61.5	61.3	60.7	59.9
2000	56.9	60.3	60.2	61.7	61.3	59.8	59.2	57.7	61.1	62.0	61.7	60.5	60.2
2001	57.1	60.2	60.4	60.6	60.3	59.7	57.4	56.4	59.8	61.3	61.7	60.6	59.6
2002	58.3	60.2	60.8	60.4	60.5	59.4	58.6	58.1	61.2	62.1	62.9	60.2	60.2
2003	59.7	62.6	62.7	62.2	62.1	61.0	58.9	58.3	61.6	62.4	62.7	60.2	61.2
Federal government													
1990	2.4	2.5	2.7	2.8	3.5	3.0	3.0	2.6	2.6	2.6	2.6	2.7	2.7
1991	2.6	2.6	2.6	2.6	2.6	2.7	2.7	2.7	2.7	2.7	2.7	2.7	2.6
1992	2.7	2.7	2.7	2.7	2.7	2.7	2.6	2.5	2.5	2.5	2.4	2.5	2.6
1993	2.4	2.3	2.3	2.3	2.3	2.3	2.3	2.3	2.3	2.3	2.3	2.3	2.3
1994	2.3	2.3	2.3	2.3	2.3	2.3	2.3	2.3	2.3	2.3	2.3	2.3	2.3
1995	2.3	2.3	2.3	2.3	2.4	2.4	2.4	2.4	2.4	2.3	2.3	2.4	2.3
1996	2.3	2.3	2.3	2.6	2.6	2.6	2.6	2.7	2.6	2.6	2.7	2.7	2.5
1997	2.6	2.6	2.7	2.6	2.6	2.6	2.7	2.7	2.7	2.7	2.7	2.7	2.6
1998	2.7	2.7	2.7	2.6	2.6	2.6	2.6	2.6	2.6	2.7	2.8	2.8	2.6
1999	2.7	2.6	2.6	2.7	2.7	2.7	2.7	2.6	2.6	2.7	2.7	2.7	2.7
2000	2.7	2.7	2.8	3.0	3.9	3.2	3.1	2.8	2.7	2.7	2.7	2.7	2.9
2001	2.6	2.6	2.6	2.6	2.6	2.6	2.6	2.6	2.6	2.5	2.6	2.5	2.5
2002	2.5	2.5	2.5	2.5	2.5	2.5	2.5	2.5	2.5	2.7	2.6	2.6	2.5
2003	2.6	2.6	2.5	2.5	2.5	2.5	2.5	2.5	2.5	2.5	2.5	2.5	2.5

Employment by Industry: Louisiana—*Continued*

(Numbers in thousands. Not seasonally adjusted.)

Industry	January	February	March	April	May	June	July	August	September	October	November	December	Annual Average
BATON ROUGE—*Continued*													
State government													
1990	26.4	29.4	29.7	29.9	29.9	27.5	26.7	25.9	28.7	30.7	30.5	29.5	28.7
1991	27.3	30.5	30.2	30.5	29.9	28.9	28.7	27.5	31.0	31.5	31.2	31.1	29.8
1992	28.3	31.7	31.6	31.8	29.9	29.5	29.4	28.6	30.6	31.3	31.0	29.5	30.2
1993	28.1	30.2	30.2	30.3	28.4	27.2	27.6	27.1	29.9	30.4	30.3	27.9	28.9
1994	28.0	30.6	30.7	30.4	28.5	27.8	28.7	27.4	30.5	31.3	31.0	29.8	29.5
1995	28.5	30.9	31.2	31.9	30.0	29.0	29.7	28.4	31.0	31.9	31.6	30.8	30.4
1996	28.7	31.3	30.9	31.8	30.0	29.3	29.4	28.5	31.7	32.1	31.9	30.6	30.5
1997	28.5	31.5	31.4	31.4	29.6	28.8	28.5	27.8	30.8	31.7	31.3	30.5	30.1
1998	28.6	31.6	31.5	31.4	30.6	29.5	30.3	29.6	32.5	33.0	32.9	31.9	31.1
1999	29.7	32.3	32.5	33.5	32.2	30.5	30.9	30.2	33.1	33.6	33.4	32.8	32.1
2000	29.1	32.3	32.0	33.3	31.9	30.6	31.2	30.5	33.4	34.0	33.5	32.4	32.0
2001	29.3	32.3	32.2	32.6	31.9	31.1	30.3	29.9	32.4	33.1	33.5	32.8	31.7
2002	30.9	32.5	33.0	33.2	33.0	31.7	31.4	31.2	33.6	33.9	34.5	32.3	32.6
2003	31.1	33.7	33.8	34.4	33.9	32.6	32.3	31.9	34.4	34.9	35.0	32.9	33.4
Local government													
1990	22.4	22.3	22.3	23.0	23.0	24.6	23.9	22.2	22.1	23.3	23.2	23.2	22.9
1991	23.0	22.9	22.9	23.5	23.5	25.3	25.0	23.3	23.5	23.6	23.5	23.5	23.6
1992	23.6	23.6	23.7	23.7	23.7	24.9	25.8	24.2	23.8	23.9	23.8	23.8	24.0
1993	23.7	23.7	23.6	23.9	24.0	25.2	24.1	23.0	23.2	23.4	23.4	23.3	23.7
1994	23.9	23.8	23.9	24.5	24.5	25.9	25.3	23.5	24.3	24.3	24.2	24.0	24.3
1995	24.4	24.5	24.5	25.0	25.0	25.7	24.6	23.0	24.1	24.1	24.3	23.4	24.3
1996	24.4	24.6	24.7	24.2	24.3	25.2	23.4	22.1	23.4	24.2	24.3	24.3	24.0
1997	24.4	24.5	24.5	23.9	24.2	25.4	24.4	22.8	24.3	24.8	25.0	24.9	24.4
1998	25.0	24.9	24.3	24.4	24.7	25.1	24.3	23.8	24.4	24.8	24.8	24.6	24.5
1999	24.9	25.1	25.1	24.8	25.0	26.0	24.9	25.2	25.1	25.2	25.2	25.2	25.1
2000	25.1	25.3	25.4	25.4	25.5	26.0	24.9	24.4	25.0	25.3	25.5	25.4	25.3
2001	25.2	25.3	25.6	25.4	25.8	26.0	24.5	23.9	24.8	25.7	25.6	25.3	25.2
2002	24.9	25.2	25.3	24.7	25.0	25.2	24.7	24.4	25.1	25.5	25.8	25.3	25.1
2003	26.0	26.3	26.4	25.3	25.7	25.9	24.1	23.9	24.7	25.0	25.2	24.8	25.3
LAFAYETTE													
Total nonfarm													
1990	120.8	122.7	124.4	126.2	128.2	128.1	127.8	131.3	129.8	130.3	131.0	131.2	127.6
1991	129.0	129.2	131.0	132.7	134.3	133.4	132.8	132.6	133.5	133.1	132.9	133.2	132.3
1992	128.7	129.0	129.6	131.1	131.9	131.7	130.4	131.3	131.3	132.0	132.7	133.6	131.1
1993	130.7	132.0	133.3	135.1	135.5	135.7	135.9	137.4	137.9	138.1	138.6	139.5	135.8
1994	136.2	137.7	139.9	141.7	142.7	142.5	143.0	143.8	144.7	143.6	144.3	145.2	142.1
1995	141.6	142.8	144.7	146.1	146.5	147.0	146.7	148.0	149.5	148.4	149.9	151.4	146.8
1996	147.3	148.5	149.6	151.2	152.8	153.0	152.4	154.4	154.7	155.7	156.7	157.7	152.8
1997	154.6	155.5	157.4	159.4	161.2	161.4	161.5	162.4	162.6	163.9	163.9	165.5	160.7
1998	161.5	162.8	164.4	166.7	168.0	167.7	167.6	168.6	167.3	165.5	165.9	165.6	165.9
1999	159.8	160.6	161.6	162.4	163.0	162.7	160.7	161.2	161.8	161.9	162.3	162.9	161.7
2000	158.6	160.6	161.8	163.8	165.6	165.4	164.2	165.5	165.9	166.4	167.0	169.0	164.5
2001	167.0	167.9	170.0	169.0	170.1	170.2	168.1	170.6	170.6	169.9	170.0	170.7	169.5
2002	165.9	166.4	167.2	170.0	171.1	169.6	167.2	168.9	168.7	168.1	169.4	169.9	168.5
2003	168.3	169.0	170.1	170.5	171.2	170.5	168.0	169.3	170.0	169.9	170.3	170.0	169.8
Total private													
1990	100.4	101.6	103.2	104.7	106.3	107.1	106.4	109.1	108.6	108.9	109.5	109.8	106.3
1991	108.3	108.2	109.7	110.9	112.5	112.2	111.3	111.7	112.3	111.7	111.3	111.7	110.9
1992	107.9	107.4	108.0	109.3	110.2	110.4	108.8	109.4	109.6	110.0	110.5	111.4	109.4
1993	109.3	110.1	111.3	112.8	113.5	114.2	114.2	115.8	115.8	115.5	116.0	116.9	113.7
1994	114.6	115.5	117.5	119.3	120.3	120.4	120.9	121.7	122.0	120.8	121.5	122.4	119.7
1995	119.5	120.1	121.8	123.1	123.5	124.5	124.0	125.4	126.4	125.1	126.4	127.8	123.9
1996	124.5	125.0	126.2	127.7	129.4	130.1	130.5	132.1	131.8	132.4	133.5	134.5	129.8
1997	131.9	132.4	134.2	136.0	137.9	138.0	138.4	140.1	139.5	140.4	140.4	141.9	137.5
1998	138.6	139.5	140.7	143.0	144.2	144.5	144.3	145.7	143.8	141.5	141.9	141.6	142.4
1999	136.5	136.6	137.4	138.3	138.8	139.0	136.9	137.8	137.8	137.5	138.0	138.4	137.7
2000	135.1	136.4	137.2	139.2	140.5	141.8	140.6	142.0	142.1	142.3	142.9	144.7	140.4
2001	143.9	144.0	145.9	145.1	146.2	146.8	145.5	147.7	147.0	146.0	145.9	146.5	145.8
2002	142.7	142.6	143.2	145.8	146.9	146.3	144.5	146.0	145.3	144.2	145.4	145.8	144.9
2003	144.6	144.7	145.4	145.8	146.4	146.8	145.0	145.7	145.3	145.5	145.7	145.5	145.5
Goods-producing													
1990	30.5	31.1	31.8	32.7	33.4	33.9	34.3	35.1	35.1	35.3	35.4	35.3	33.6
1991	34.3	34.1	34.6	34.7	35.3	35.2	34.5	34.8	34.8	34.3	33.7	33.6	34.4
1992	32.0	31.6	31.8	32.1	32.6	32.8	31.9	32.1	31.9	32.0	32.3	32.4	32.1
1993	31.9	32.2	32.4	32.6	33.1	33.4	33.3	33.9	34.0	33.6	33.5	33.6	33.1
1994	32.8	32.9	33.6	34.6	35.1	35.7	35.7	36.1	36.0	35.5	35.6	35.7	34.9
1995	34.5	34.7	35.2	36.1	36.1	36.8	36.4	37.1	37.4	37.0	37.1	37.5	36.3
1996	35.9	36.2	36.7	37.1	37.7	38.1	38.6	39.0	38.9	38.9	39.0	39.4	37.9
1997	38.3	38.5	39.0	39.6	40.6	40.9	41.0	41.5	41.3	41.8	41.0	41.2	40.3
1998	40.9	41.4	41.9	41.8	42.2	42.6	42.6	42.7	41.8	40.5	40.1	39.7	41.5
1999	36.7	36.5	36.2	36.1	36.4	36.3	35.3	35.2	35.4	34.9	34.8	35.0	35.7
2000	35.0	35.3	35.5	36.0	36.9	37.7	37.5	37.8	37.7	37.7	38.0	38.7	37.0
2001	39.3	39.7	40.6	40.2	40.7	41.5	40.3	40.7	40.6	40.1	39.4	39.3	40.2
2002	37.9	37.6	37.6	38.1	38.1	38.3	37.3	37.6	37.1	36.2	36.4	36.6	37.4
2003	36.8	36.6	36.7	36.8	37.1	37.4	36.2	36.4	36.3	36.4	36.0	35.7	36.5

Employment by Industry: Louisiana—*Continued*

(Numbers in thousands. Not seasonally adjusted.)

Industry	January	February	March	April	May	June	July	August	September	October	November	December	Annual Average
LAFAYETTE—*Continued*													
Natural resources and mining													
1990	11.7	11.8	11.9	12.7	12.7	12.8	13.1	13.4	13.4	13.7	14.0	14.2	12.9
1991	14.1	13.9	14.0	13.8	14.0	14.0	13.3	13.3	13.1	12.6	12.4	12.3	13.4
1992	11.5	11.1	11.0	10.5	10.5	10.6	10.6	10.5	10.3	10.4	10.5	10.7	10.6
1993	10.3	10.3	10.2	10.3	10.4	10.6	10.7	11.1	11.1	11.1	11.1	11.2	10.7
1994	10.9	10.9	11.0	11.4	11.4	11.4	11.5	11.7	11.6	11.2	11.4	11.4	11.3
1995	11.3	11.4	11.6	12.1	12.1	12.3	12.5	12.7	12.8	12.8	13.0	13.3	12.3
1996	13.3	13.5	13.6	13.8	14.0	14.2	14.1	14.2	14.1	14.0	14.2	14.7	13.9
1997	13.7	13.9	14.0	14.7	15.1	15.3	15.4	15.7	15.7	16.3	16.2	16.3	15.1
1998	16.9	17.2	17.3	16.4	16.6	16.7	16.7	16.7	16.4	14.9	14.6	14.5	16.2
1999	12.8	12.4	11.9	11.5	11.6	11.4	11.3	11.5	11.6	11.5	11.6	11.9	11.7
2000	11.9	11.9	11.8	12.5	12.8	13.3	13.5	14.0	14.3	14.5	14.8	15.3	13.4
2001	15.8	16.1	16.5	16.7	17.1	17.7	17.5	17.6	17.8	17.7	17.1	17.3	17.0
2002	16.4	16.3	16.1	16.4	16.3	16.5	16.3	16.6	16.3	15.6	15.6	15.7	16.2
2003	16.1	16.2	16.1	16.0	16.1	16.5	16.1	16.2	16.1	16.0	15.8	15.7	16.1
Construction													
1990	6.8	6.8	7.0	7.1	7.4	7.6	8.0	8.2	8.2	7.9	7.7	7.5	7.5
1991	6.8	6.8	7.0	7.5	7.7	7.7	7.9	8.1	8.2	8.2	7.9	7.9	7.6
1992	6.8	6.7	6.9	7.2	7.5	7.8	7.5	7.7	7.7	7.4	7.4	7.2	7.3
1993	6.8	7.0	7.1	7.0	7.3	7.4	7.4	7.6	7.8	7.4	7.3	7.3	7.2
1994	6.9	7.0	7.3	7.3	7.6	8.2	8.7	8.9	9.0	8.8	8.7	8.6	8.0
1995	7.6	7.7	7.8	7.7	7.8	8.3	8.3	8.7	9.0	8.5	8.4	8.5	8.1
1996	7.7	7.8	8.0	8.0	8.3	8.6	9.0	9.3	9.3	9.3	9.2	9.0	8.6
1997	8.6	8.8	9.0	9.2	9.7	9.7	10.0	10.5	10.5	10.5	10.4	10.4	9.7
1998	9.6	9.6	9.9	10.4	10.6	11.0	10.9	11.0	10.6	11.0	10.9	10.8	10.5
1999	9.8	9.7	9.8	9.9	10.0	10.2	10.0	9.8	9.9	9.7	9.5	9.3	9.8
2000	9.2	9.5	9.7	9.9	10.3	10.8	10.4	10.3	9.7	9.9	9.8	10.0	10.0
2001	10.0	10.1	10.6	10.0	10.1	10.3	10.0	10.2	10.2	9.9	9.9	9.7	10.0
2002	9.2	9.2	9.2	9.4	9.5	9.6	9.3	9.3	9.1	8.9	9.1	9.2	9.3
2003	9.2	9.0	9.1	9.2	9.5	9.6	9.2	9.3	9.3	9.4	9.3	9.2	9.3
Manufacturing													
1990	12.0	12.5	12.9	12.9	13.3	13.5	13.2	13.5	13.5	13.7	13.7	13.6	13.1
1991	13.4	13.4	13.6	13.4	13.6	13.5	13.3	13.4	13.5	13.5	13.4	13.4	13.4
1992	13.7	13.8	13.9	14.4	14.6	14.4	13.8	13.9	13.9	14.2	14.4	14.5	14.1
1993	14.8	14.9	15.1	15.3	15.4	15.4	15.2	15.2	15.1	15.1	15.1	15.1	15.1
1994	15.0	15.0	15.3	15.9	16.1	16.1	15.5	15.5	15.4	15.5	15.5	15.7	15.5
1995	15.6	15.6	15.8	16.3	16.2	16.2	15.6	15.7	15.6	15.7	15.7	15.7	15.8
1996	14.9	14.9	15.1	15.3	15.4	15.3	15.5	15.5	15.5	15.6	15.6	15.7	15.3
1997	16.0	15.8	16.0	15.7	15.8	15.9	15.6	15.3	15.1	15.0	14.4	14.5	15.4
1998	14.4	14.6	14.7	15.0	15.0	14.9	15.0	15.0	14.8	14.6	14.6	14.4	14.7
1999	14.1	14.4	14.5	14.7	14.8	14.7	14.0	13.9	13.9	13.7	13.7	13.8	14.1
2000	13.9	13.9	14.0	13.6	13.8	13.6	13.6	13.5	13.7	13.3	13.4	13.4	13.6
2001	13.5	13.5	13.5	13.5	13.5	13.5	12.8	12.9	12.6	12.5	12.4	12.3	13.0
2002	12.3	12.1	12.3	12.3	12.3	12.2	11.7	11.7	11.7	11.7	11.7	11.7	12.0
2003	11.5	11.4	11.5	11.6	11.5	11.3	10.9	10.9	10.9	11.0	10.9	10.8	11.2
Service-providing													
1990	90.3	91.6	92.6	93.5	94.8	94.2	93.5	96.2	94.7	95.0	95.6	95.9	93.9
1991	94.7	95.1	96.4	98.0	99.0	98.2	98.3	97.8	98.7	98.8	99.2	99.6	97.8
1992	96.7	97.4	97.8	99.0	99.3	98.9	98.5	99.2	99.4	100.0	100.4	101.2	98.9
1993	98.8	99.8	100.9	102.5	102.4	102.3	102.6	103.5	103.9	104.5	105.1	105.9	102.6
1994	103.4	104.8	106.3	107.1	107.6	106.8	107.3	107.7	108.7	108.1	108.7	109.5	107.1
1995	107.1	108.1	109.5	110.0	110.4	110.2	110.3	110.9	112.1	111.4	112.8	113.9	110.5
1996	111.4	112.3	112.9	114.1	115.1	114.9	113.8	115.4	115.8	116.8	117.7	118.3	114.8
1997	116.3	117.0	118.4	119.8	120.6	120.5	120.5	120.9	121.3	122.1	122.9	124.3	120.3
1998	120.6	121.4	122.5	124.9	125.8	125.1	125.0	125.9	125.5	125.0	125.8	125.9	124.4
1999	123.1	124.1	125.4	126.3	126.6	126.4	125.4	126.0	126.4	127.0	127.5	127.9	126.0
2000	123.6	125.3	126.3	127.8	128.7	127.7	126.7	127.7	128.2	128.7	129.0	130.3	127.5
2001	127.7	128.2	129.4	128.8	129.4	128.7	127.8	129.9	130.0	129.8	130.6	131.4	129.3
2002	128.0	128.8	129.6	131.9	133.0	131.3	129.9	131.3	131.6	131.9	133.0	133.3	131.1
2003	131.5	132.4	133.4	133.7	134.1	133.1	131.8	132.9	133.7	133.5	134.3	134.3	133.2
Trade, transportation, and utilities													
1990	27.8	27.8	28.1	27.9	28.3	28.1	28.1	28.7	28.6	28.7	28.9	29.2	28.3
1991	28.2	27.9	28.5	27.7	28.0	28.0	28.5	28.6	28.7	28.8	29.2	29.4	28.4
1992	27.9	27.8	27.8	28.3	28.5	28.3	27.9	28.1	28.1	28.4	28.7	29.1	28.2
1993	28.8	28.5	28.8	29.5	29.6	29.7	29.7	29.9	29.8	29.8	30.4	30.6	29.5
1994	30.0	30.0	30.3	30.8	30.9	30.8	31.0	31.5	31.4	31.1	31.5	32.1	30.9
1995	30.7	30.5	31.0	31.0	31.0	30.9	31.3	31.6	31.7	31.7	32.3	32.7	31.3
1996	32.0	31.7	32.0	32.4	32.8	33.4	33.4	33.7	33.6	33.6	34.3	34.6	33.1
1997	33.5	33.2	33.8	34.3	34.3	34.2	34.7	34.8	35.0	35.0	35.6	36.2	34.5
1998	34.9	34.6	34.9	35.4	35.6	35.5	35.3	36.1	35.7	35.7	36.1	36.4	35.5
1999	34.9	34.7	35.2	35.6	35.6	35.7	35.0	35.5	35.3	35.1	35.6	35.8	35.3
2000	33.9	34.1	34.4	34.7	34.9	35.0	34.8	35.4	35.8	35.6	36.0	36.2	35.1
2001	35.7	35.6	35.9	35.7	35.9	36.0	36.0	36.3	36.2	35.7	36.3	36.8	36.0
2002	35.7	35.6	36.1	36.5	36.9	36.7	36.1	36.0	36.3	36.2	36.9	37.3	36.4
2003	36.0	35.9	36.1	36.2	36.2	36.1	35.9	36.1	35.9	35.7	35.9	36.4	36.0

Employment by Industry: Louisiana—*Continued*

(Numbers in thousands. Not seasonally adjusted.)

Industry	January	February	March	April	May	June	July	August	September	October	November	December	Annual Average
LAFAYETTE—*Continued*													
Wholesale trade													
1990	5.9	6.0	6.1	6.1	6.2	6.2	6.2	6.2	6.2	6.2	6.2	6.2	6.1
1991	6.1	6.1	6.3	6.5	6.6	6.5	6.3	6.2	6.2	6.2	6.2	6.1	6.2
1992	6.1	6.1	6.2	6.2	6.2	6.1	6.0	5.9	5.9	5.8	5.8	5.9	6.0
1993	6.0	5.9	6.0	6.3	6.2	6.2	5.9	5.9	6.0	5.9	6.0	6.0	6.0
1994	6.0	6.1	6.2	6.5	6.5	6.4	6.2	6.3	6.3	6.3	6.3	6.4	6.2
1995	6.3	6.4	6.5	6.7	6.6	6.7	6.8	6.8	6.8	6.6	6.6	6.7	6.6
1996	6.7	6.7	6.8	6.9	7.0	7.0	7.1	7.1	7.2	7.1	7.1	7.2	6.9
1997	7.2	7.2	7.3	7.5	7.5	7.5	7.4	7.4	7.5	7.6	7.6	7.6	7.4
1998	7.7	7.7	7.8	8.0	8.0	7.9	7.8	7.9	7.8	7.7	7.6	7.6	7.7
1999	7.4	7.5	7.6	7.5	7.5	7.5	7.4	7.5	7.5	7.5	7.4	7.4	7.4
2000	7.3	7.4	7.5	7.7	7.8	7.8	7.9	7.9	7.8	7.6	7.6	7.6	7.7
2001	7.6	7.7	7.7	7.8	7.9	8.0	7.8	8.0	8.0	7.7	7.7	7.8	7.8
2002	7.8	7.8	7.9	8.0	8.1	8.0	7.9	7.9	7.9	7.9	7.9	7.9	7.9
2003	7.7	7.7	7.8	7.7	7.8	7.7	7.7	7.6	7.6	7.6	7.5	7.6	7.7
Retail trade													
1990	16.7	16.6	16.7	16.7	16.9	16.7	16.6	17.0	16.9	17.1	17.3	17.6	16.9
1991	17.0	16.7	17.0	17.0	17.2	17.3	17.1	17.3	17.5	17.5	18.0	18.3	17.3
1992	17.2	17.1	17.0	17.5	17.7	17.6	17.3	17.5	17.6	17.9	18.3	18.6	17.6
1993	17.9	17.7	17.9	18.1	18.2	18.2	18.3	18.5	18.3	18.3	18.8	19.0	18.2
1994	18.3	18.2	18.4	18.4	18.5	18.5	19.0	19.4	19.4	19.2	19.7	20.1	18.9
1995	19.0	18.7	19.1	19.1	19.2	19.0	19.2	19.6	19.7	19.9	20.6	20.9	19.5
1996	20.2	19.9	20.1	20.2	20.4	21.0	20.9	21.2	21.0	21.1	21.7	21.9	20.8
1997	20.8	20.5	20.9	21.3	21.2	21.0	21.5	21.7	21.7	21.6	22.2	22.7	21.4
1998	21.4	21.1	21.2	21.7	21.8	21.7	21.6	22.2	22.0	22.2	22.7	22.9	21.8
1999	22.0	21.7	22.0	22.1	22.1	22.1	21.7	22.0	21.8	21.9	22.5	22.7	22.0
2000	21.6	21.7	21.9	21.9	21.9	22.0	21.8	22.3	22.7	22.5	23.0	23.2	22.2
2001	22.2	21.9	22.2	22.1	22.2	22.2	22.5	22.6	22.6	22.3	23.1	23.5	22.4
2002	22.6	22.5	22.9	23.3	23.6	23.4	22.9	22.8	23.0	23.1	23.7	24.1	23.2
2003	23.0	22.9	23.0	23.2	23.1	23.1	22.8	23.0	22.9	22.7	23.0	23.4	23.0
Transportation and utilities													
1990	5.2	5.2	5.3	5.1	5.2	5.2	5.3	5.5	5.5	5.4	5.4	5.4	5.3
1991	5.1	5.1	5.2	4.2	4.2	4.2	5.1	5.1	5.0	5.1	5.0	5.0	4.8
1992	4.6	4.6	4.6	4.6	4.6	4.6	4.6	4.7	4.6	4.7	4.6	4.6	4.6
1993	4.9	4.9	4.9	5.1	5.2	5.3	5.5	5.5	5.5	5.6	5.6	5.6	5.3
1994	5.7	5.7	5.7	5.9	5.9	5.9	5.8	5.8	5.7	5.6	5.5	5.6	5.7
1995	5.4	5.4	5.4	5.2	5.2	5.2	5.3	5.2	5.2	5.2	5.1	5.1	5.2
1996	5.1	5.1	5.1	5.3	5.4	5.4	5.4	5.4	5.4	5.4	5.5	5.5	5.3
1997	5.5	5.5	5.6	5.5	5.6	5.7	5.8	5.7	5.8	5.8	5.8	5.9	5.6
1998	5.8	5.8	5.9	5.7	5.8	5.9	5.9	6.0	5.9	5.8	5.8	5.9	5.8
1999	5.5	5.5	5.6	6.0	6.0	6.1	5.9	6.0	6.0	5.7	5.7	5.7	5.8
2000	5.0	5.0	5.0	5.1	5.2	5.2	5.1	5.2	5.3	5.5	5.4	5.4	5.2
2001	5.9	6.0	6.0	5.8	5.8	5.8	5.7	5.7	5.6	5.7	5.5	5.5	5.7
2002	5.3	5.3	5.3	5.2	5.2	5.3	5.3	5.3	5.4	5.2	5.3	5.3	5.3
2003	5.3	5.3	5.3	5.3	5.3	5.3	5.4	5.5	5.4	5.4	5.4	5.4	5.4
Information													
1990	1.8	1.8	1.8	1.8	1.8	1.8	1.8	1.8	1.8	1.8	1.8	1.8	1.8
1991	2.0	2.0	2.0	2.0	2.0	2.0	2.0	2.0	2.0	2.0	2.0	2.0	2.0
1992	2.0	2.0	2.0	2.0	2.0	2.0	2.0	2.0	2.0	2.0	2.0	2.0	2.0
1993	2.0	2.0	2.0	2.0	2.0	2.0	2.1	2.1	2.1	2.0	2.0	2.0	2.0
1994	2.1	2.0	2.1	2.1	2.1	2.1	2.1	2.1	2.1	2.1	2.1	2.1	2.0
1995	2.1	2.1	2.2	2.1	2.2	2.2	2.2	2.2	2.2	2.2	2.3	2.3	2.1
1996	2.3	2.3	2.4	2.3	2.3	2.3	2.4	2.4	2.3	2.4	2.4	2.4	2.3
1997	2.4	2.4	2.4	2.4	2.4	2.4	2.4	2.5	2.4	2.5	2.5	2.5	2.4
1998	2.4	2.4	2.4	2.5	2.5	2.5	2.5	2.6	2.5	2.5	2.5	2.6	2.4
1999	2.5	2.5	2.5	2.6	2.7	2.7	2.6	2.7	2.6	2.5	2.5	2.5	2.5
2000	2.4	2.4	2.4	2.5	2.5	2.5	2.5	2.5	2.5	2.5	2.5	2.6	2.5
2001	2.6	2.6	2.6	2.5	2.5	2.6	2.6	2.7	2.6	2.5	2.6	2.5	2.5
2002	2.6	2.6	2.6	2.8	2.8	2.8	2.7	2.7	2.7	2.9	3.0	3.0	2.8
2003	3.0	3.0	2.9	2.9	2.9	2.9	2.9	3.0	3.1	3.1	3.1	3.1	3.0
Financial activities													
1990	6.5	6.6	6.6	6.8	6.8	6.8	6.8	7.0	6.9	6.9	7.0	7.0	6.8
1991	6.9	6.9	6.9	7.1	7.1	7.1	7.1	7.0	7.1	7.0	6.9	7.0	7.0
1992	6.9	6.9	6.9	6.7	6.7	6.7	6.6	6.7	6.7	6.8	6.8	6.9	6.7
1993	6.8	6.9	6.9	6.9	6.8	6.9	7.0	7.1	7.1	7.0	7.1	7.1	6.9
1994	7.1	7.2	7.2	7.1	7.2	7.2	7.3	7.4	7.4	7.3	7.4	7.4	7.2
1995	7.4	7.4	7.5	7.6	7.6	7.8	7.8	7.8	7.8	7.7	7.7	7.8	7.6
1996	7.8	7.8	7.8	7.8	7.9	7.9	7.9	8.0	8.0	8.1	8.1	8.2	7.9
1997	8.2	8.2	8.3	8.4	8.6	8.7	8.7	8.9	8.9	8.8	8.9	9.0	8.6
1998	8.8	8.9	8.9	8.9	9.0	9.0	9.1	9.0	9.1	8.9	8.9	8.9	8.9
1999	8.7	8.7	8.7	8.5	8.6	8.7	8.8	8.9	8.9	8.7	8.7	8.8	8.7
2000	8.7	8.8	8.8	9.0	9.0	9.1	9.0	9.0	8.9	8.9	8.9	9.0	8.9
2001	9.4	9.5	9.6	9.2	9.3	9.4	9.5	9.6	9.5	9.6	9.6	9.7	9.4
2002	9.4	9.4	9.4	10.1	10.1	10.0	10.1	10.0	10.0	10.0	10.3	10.1	9.9
2003	9.9	9.9	9.9	9.8	9.8	9.8	9.8	9.7	9.8	9.6	9.6	9.6	9.8

Employment by Industry: Louisiana—*Continued*

(Numbers in thousands. Not seasonally adjusted.)

Industry	January	February	March	April	May	June	July	August	September	October	November	December	Annual Average
LAFAYETTE—*Continued*													
Professional and business services													
1990	8.6	8.7	8.9	8.8	9.0	9.1	8.9	9.1	9.1	9.2	9.2	9.2	8.9
1991	9.5	9.5	9.6	10.1	10.2	10.3	10.1	10.0	10.2	10.0	9.9	10.0	9.9
1992	10.0	10.0	10.1	10.4	10.3	10.3	10.3	10.2	10.4	10.2	10.1	10.3	10.2
1993	10.1	10.3	10.5	10.5	10.5	10.6	10.6	10.7	10.7	10.9	10.9	11.1	10.6
1994	11.1	11.4	11.7	11.1	11.2	11.3	11.2	11.2	11.3	11.5	11.5	11.6	11.3
1995	11.9	11.8	11.9	11.8	11.8	11.9	11.8	12.0	12.2	12.0	12.0	12.2	11.9
1996	12.0	12.1	12.2	12.6	12.8	13.0	12.7	12.9	12.7	12.7	12.9	13.0	12.6
1997	13.1	13.3	13.6	13.9	14.1	14.2	14.3	14.5	14.4	14.5	14.4	14.7	14.0
1998	14.2	14.3	14.5	15.4	15.4	15.3	15.6	15.6	15.5	15.1	15.2	15.0	15.0
1999	14.7	14.8	14.9	15.2	15.2	15.4	15.6	15.7	15.6	15.8	16.0	16.0	15.4
2000	15.1	15.2	15.3	15.5	15.6	15.5	15.3	15.6	15.5	15.8	15.8	16.1	15.5
2001	15.7	15.6	15.8	16.0	16.2	16.4	16.6	16.7	16.6	16.7	16.6	16.5	16.2
2002	16.3	16.3	16.2	16.2	16.4	16.6	16.7	16.7	16.6	16.2	16.0	16.0	16.4
2003	16.2	16.3	16.3	16.0	15.9	16.0	16.0	16.2	16.2	15.9	16.0	15.9	16.1
Educational and health services													
1990	11.8	11.8	11.9	11.9	12.0	11.8	11.7	12.1	12.2	12.5	12.6	12.7	12.0
1991	12.7	12.8	13.0	13.3	13.4	13.2	13.2	13.4	13.7	14.0	14.0	14.1	13.4
1992	13.9	14.0	14.1	14.3	14.3	14.1	14.2	14.3	14.7	14.7	14.9	15.0	14.3
1993	14.8	15.0	15.2	15.4	15.2	15.2	15.3	15.5	15.7	16.0	15.9	16.0	15.4
1994	16.1	16.3	16.5	16.7	16.7	16.4	16.4	16.4	16.7	16.6	16.7	16.7	16.5
1995	16.6	16.9	17.0	16.9	16.9	16.9	16.8	16.8	17.1	17.1	17.3	17.4	16.9
1996	17.2	17.4	17.5	17.7	17.9	17.6	17.6	17.8	18.1	18.4	18.4	18.3	17.8
1997	18.0	18.2	18.3	18.3	18.4	18.4	18.3	18.5	18.7	18.9	19.0	19.0	18.5
1998	18.7	19.0	19.0	18.9	18.9	18.9	18.9	19.1	19.3	19.4	19.5	19.5	19.0
1999	19.5	19.6	19.8	20.0	19.9	19.8	19.7	19.8	20.2	20.5	20.5	20.6	19.9
2000	20.3	20.5	20.6	20.8	20.6	20.8	20.8	21.0	21.1	21.4	21.4	21.7	20.9
2001	21.1	21.3	21.4	21.1	21.1	20.6	20.3	21.2	21.2	21.3	21.3	21.6	21.1
2002	21.3	21.4	21.4	21.8	22.0	21.4	21.6	22.7	22.7	22.5	22.6	22.7	22.0
2003	22.8	22.9	23.0	23.0	23.1	23.2	23.1	23.1	23.2	23.6	23.7	23.5	23.2
Leisure and hospitality													
1990	9.3	9.6	9.9	10.7	10.9	11.6	10.8	11.1	10.8	10.4	10.5	10.5	10.5
1991	10.6	10.9	11.0	11.8	12.2	12.2	11.8	11.7	11.5	11.3	11.3	11.3	11.4
1992	11.1	11.0	11.1	11.3	11.6	12.0	11.8	11.8	11.6	11.7	11.5	11.5	11.5
1993	10.7	11.0	11.3	11.6	12.0	12.1	12.0	12.3	12.1	11.9	11.9	12.1	11.7
1994	11.0	11.3	11.7	12.4	12.6	12.5	12.7	12.5	12.5	12.1	12.2	12.3	12.1
1995	11.8	12.2	12.4	13.0	13.3	13.4	13.2	13.3	13.4	12.8	13.1	13.2	12.9
1996	12.7	12.9	13.0	13.2	13.3	13.2	13.2	13.6	13.5	13.4	13.4	13.6	13.2
1997	13.4	13.6	13.7	14.0	14.4	14.2	14.1	14.4	13.8	13.9	14.0	14.3	13.9
1998	13.8	14.0	14.2	15.1	15.6	15.6	15.2	15.6	14.9	14.4	14.6	14.5	14.7
1999	14.4	14.7	15.0	15.3	15.4	15.4	14.9	14.9	14.7	14.9	14.8	14.6	14.9
2000	14.6	14.9	15.0	15.4	15.7	15.9	15.5	15.4	15.2	15.0	15.0	15.1	15.2
2001	14.9	14.4	14.7	15.0	15.1	14.9	14.9	15.1	14.9	14.8	14.8	14.8	14.8
2002	14.2	14.4	14.6	14.9	15.2	15.1	14.8	14.9	14.5	14.8	14.8	14.7	14.7
2003	14.5	14.7	15.0	15.6	15.8	15.8	15.7	15.7	15.3	15.7	15.9	15.8	15.5
Other services													
1990	4.1	4.2	4.2	4.1	4.1	4.0	4.0	4.2	4.1	4.1	4.1	4.1	4.1
1991	4.1	4.1	4.1	4.2	4.3	4.2	4.1	4.2	4.3	4.3	4.3	4.3	4.2
1992	4.1	4.1	4.2	4.2	4.2	4.2	4.1	4.2	4.2	4.2	4.2	4.2	4.1
1993	4.2	4.2	4.2	4.3	4.3	4.3	4.2	4.3	4.3	4.3	4.3	4.4	4.2
1994	4.4	4.4	4.4	4.5	4.5	4.4	4.5	4.5	4.6	4.6	4.5	4.5	4.4
1995	4.5	4.5	4.6	4.6	4.6	4.6	4.5	4.6	4.6	4.6	4.6	4.7	4.5
1996	4.6	4.6	4.6	4.6	4.7	4.6	4.7	4.7	4.7	4.9	5.0	5.0	4.7
1997	5.0	5.0	5.1	5.1	5.1	5.0	4.9	5.0	5.0	5.0	5.0	5.0	5.0
1998	4.9	4.9	4.9	5.0	5.0	5.1	5.1	5.0	5.0	5.0	5.0	5.0	4.9
1999	5.1	5.1	5.1	5.0	5.0	5.0	5.0	5.1	5.1	5.1	5.1	5.1	5.0
2000	5.1	5.2	5.2	5.3	5.3	5.3	5.2	5.3	5.4	5.4	5.3	5.3	5.3
2001	5.2	5.3	5.3	5.4	5.4	5.4	5.3	5.4	5.4	5.3	5.3	5.3	5.3
2002	5.3	5.3	5.3	5.4	5.4	5.4	5.2	5.4	5.4	5.4	5.4	5.4	5.4
2003	5.4	5.4	5.5	5.5	5.6	5.6	5.4	5.5	5.5	5.5	5.5	5.5	5.5
Government													
1990	20.4	21.1	21.2	21.5	21.9	21.0	21.4	22.2	21.2	21.4	21.5	21.4	21.3
1991	20.7	21.0	21.3	21.8	21.8	21.2	21.5	20.9	21.2	21.4	21.6	21.5	21.3
1992	20.8	21.6	21.6	21.8	21.7	21.3	21.6	21.9	21.7	22.0	22.2	22.2	21.7
1993	21.4	21.9	22.0	22.3	22.0	21.5	21.7	21.6	22.1	22.6	22.6	22.6	22.0
1994	21.6	22.2	22.4	22.4	22.4	22.1	22.1	22.1	22.7	22.8	22.8	22.8	22.3
1995	22.1	22.7	22.9	23.0	23.0	22.5	22.7	22.6	23.1	23.3	23.5	23.6	22.9
1996	22.8	23.5	23.4	23.5	23.4	22.9	21.9	22.3	22.9	23.3	23.2	23.2	23.0
1997	22.7	23.1	23.2	23.4	23.3	23.4	23.1	22.3	23.1	23.5	23.5	23.6	23.1
1998	22.9	23.3	23.7	23.7	23.8	23.2	23.3	22.9	23.5	24.0	24.0	24.0	23.5
1999	23.3	24.0	24.2	24.1	24.2	23.7	23.8	23.4	24.0	24.4	24.3	24.5	23.9
2000	23.5	24.2	24.6	24.6	25.1	23.6	23.6	23.5	23.8	24.1	24.1	24.3	24.1
2001	23.1	23.9	24.1	23.9	23.9	23.4	22.6	22.9	23.6	23.9	24.1	24.2	23.6
2002	23.2	23.8	24.0	24.2	24.2	23.3	22.7	22.9	23.4	23.9	24.0	24.1	23.6
2003	23.7	24.3	24.7	24.7	24.8	23.7	23.0	23.6	24.7	24.4	24.6	24.5	24.2

Employment by Industry: Louisiana—*Continued*

(Numbers in thousands. Not seasonally adjusted.)

Industry	January	February	March	April	May	June	July	August	September	October	November	December	Annual Average
LAFAYETTE—*Continued*													
Federal government													
1990	1.3	1.3	1.4	1.5	1.9	1.5	1.5	1.3	1.2	1.2	1.2	1.3	1.3
1991	1.3	1.2	1.3	1.2	1.2	1.2	1.2	1.2	1.2	1.2	1.2	1.2	1.2
1992	1.3	1.3	1.3	1.3	1.3	1.3	1.3	1.3	1.3	1.3	1.3	1.4	1.3
1993	1.3	1.3	1.3	1.3	1.3	1.3	1.3	1.3	1.4	1.4	1.4	1.4	1.3
1994	1.4	1.4	1.4	1.4	1.4	1.4	1.4	1.4	1.4	1.4	1.4	1.4	1.4
1995	1.4	1.4	1.4	1.4	1.4	1.4	1.4	1.4	1.4	1.4	1.4	1.4	1.4
1996	1.4	1.4	1.4	1.4	1.4	1.4	1.4	1.4	1.4	1.4	1.4	1.4	1.4
1997	1.4	1.4	1.4	1.4	1.4	1.3	1.4	1.4	1.4	1.4	1.4	1.4	1.3
1998	1.4	1.4	1.4	1.4	1.4	1.4	1.4	1.4	1.4	1.4	1.4	1.4	1.4
1999	1.4	1.4	1.4	1.4	1.4	1.4	1.4	1.4	1.4	1.5	1.4	1.5	1.4
2000	1.5	1.5	1.7	1.7	2.2	1.6	1.8	1.5	1.5	1.4	1.4	1.4	1.6
2001	1.4	1.4	1.4	1.4	1.4	1.5	1.4	1.4	1.4	1.4	1.4	1.4	1.4
2002	1.4	1.4	1.4	1.4	1.4	1.4	1.4	1.4	1.4	1.4	1.4	1.5	1.4
2003	1.4	1.4	1.5	1.4	1.4	1.4	1.4	1.4	1.5	1.4	1.4	1.4	1.4
State government													
1990	5.3	6.0	6.0	5.9	6.0	5.1	5.3	5.5	6.1	6.2	6.3	6.2	5.8
1991	5.3	5.7	5.8	6.2	6.2	5.4	5.5	5.3	5.9	6.0	6.1	5.9	5.7
1992	5.4	6.1	6.1	6.1	6.0	5.3	5.4	5.6	6.0	6.3	6.3	6.3	5.9
1993	5.7	6.2	6.3	6.5	6.3	5.7	5.8	5.8	6.3	6.5	6.5	6.5	6.1
1994	5.7	6.3	6.4	6.4	6.3	5.9	5.9	5.9	6.5	6.5	6.5	6.5	6.2
1995	5.8	6.5	6.5	6.6	6.6	5.9	6.0	5.9	6.5	6.6	6.7	6.7	6.3
1996	5.9	6.6	6.6	6.6	6.5	5.8	5.5	6.0	6.1	6.4	6.4	6.4	6.2
1997	5.8	6.3	6.4	6.5	6.4	5.4	5.6	5.9	6.2	6.5	6.5	6.5	6.1
1998	5.7	6.1	6.4	6.5	6.5	5.4	5.7	6.0	6.3	6.6	6.6	6.5	6.1
1999	5.8	6.4	6.6	6.6	6.6	5.5	5.5	5.9	6.3	6.6	6.6	6.7	6.2
2000	5.7	6.4	6.6	6.6	6.6	5.3	5.4	5.8	6.3	6.5	6.5	6.6	6.2
2001	5.6	6.3	6.4	6.3	6.3	5.4	5.3	5.8	6.1	6.4	6.5	6.5	6.0
2002	5.5	6.1	6.2	6.3	6.2	5.1	5.1	5.6	5.8	6.0	6.1	6.1	5.8
2003	5.6	6.2	6.5	6.5	6.5	5.2	5.1	5.8	6.3	6.6	6.6	6.6	6.1
Local government													
1990	13.8	13.8	13.8	14.1	14.0	14.4	14.6	15.4	13.9	14.0	14.0	13.9	14.1
1991	14.1	14.1	14.2	14.4	14.4	14.6	14.8	14.4	14.1	14.2	14.3	14.4	14.3
1992	14.1	14.2	14.2	14.4	14.4	14.7	14.9	15.0	14.4	14.4	14.6	14.5	14.4
1993	14.4	14.4	14.4	14.5	14.4	14.5	14.6	14.5	14.4	14.7	14.7	14.7	14.5
1994	14.5	14.5	14.6	14.6	14.7	14.8	14.8	14.8	14.8	14.9	14.9	14.9	14.7
1995	14.9	14.8	15.0	15.0	15.0	15.2	15.3	15.3	15.2	15.3	15.4	15.5	15.1
1996	15.5	15.5	15.4	15.5	15.5	15.7	15.0	14.9	15.4	15.5	15.4	15.4	15.3
1997	15.5	15.4	15.4	15.5	15.5	16.7	16.1	15.0	15.5	15.6	15.6	15.7	15.6
1998	15.8	15.8	15.9	15.8	15.9	16.4	16.2	15.5	15.8	16.0	16.0	16.1	15.9
1999	16.1	16.2	16.2	16.1	16.2	16.8	16.9	16.1	16.3	16.3	16.3	16.3	16.3
2000	16.3	16.3	16.3	16.3	16.3	16.7	16.4	16.2	16.0	16.2	16.2	16.3	16.3
2001	16.1	16.2	16.3	16.2	16.2	16.5	15.9	15.7	16.1	16.1	16.2	16.3	16.1
2002	16.3	16.3	16.4	16.5	16.6	16.8	16.2	15.9	16.2	16.5	16.5	16.5	16.4
2003	16.7	16.7	16.7	16.8	16.9	17.1	16.5	16.4	16.9	16.4	16.6	16.5	16.7
NEW ORLEANS													
Total nonfarm													
1990	547.6	549.7	552.8	552.8	557.4	555.6	558.0	560.8	559.4	560.3	562.2	561.3	556.5
1991	554.2	555.9	560.4	560.6	563.1	562.4	560.9	559.4	561.5	562.1	563.1	565.8	560.8
1992	556.4	558.0	559.0	559.3	561.9	560.3	558.2	555.3	559.6	566.3	568.3	571.1	561.1
1993	558.2	561.5	561.7	566.3	568.5	569.6	569.1	569.1	574.4	575.7	579.4	584.3	569.8
1994	573.6	577.6	580.8	579.5	581.3	581.1	582.0	583.4	590.5	593.0	596.7	600.5	585.0
1995	589.3	591.4	594.7	595.6	603.1	602.1	597.8	597.4	603.7	601.0	604.4	605.5	598.8
1996	592.7	594.1	598.7	601.5	605.7	605.7	602.1	603.4	610.1	606.0	611.0	615.0	603.8
1997	604.2	604.2	609.0	612.4	616.6	617.6	611.0	608.0	621.5	616.6	620.9	625.6	614.0
1998	611.2	613.4	615.1	621.5	625.4	627.3	619.2	616.3	625.7	622.8	623.6	628.5	620.8
1999	617.3	618.8	622.9	619.8	620.5	620.3	615.2	613.5	623.4	625.0	629.3	633.5	621.6
2000	621.5	624.0	626.9	627.3	633.3	628.1	618.9	619.1	624.2	624.5	626.5	631.9	625.5
2001	623.3	628.0	632.2	629.5	630.4	629.5	617.7	615.7	623.5	620.0	622.5	623.5	624.6
2002	608.5	610.7	613.9	618.8	616.6	619.7	609.2	608.4	613.0	612.1	618.8	619.3	614.1
2003	610.6	613.2	614.8	622.3	620.5	622.6	611.8	609.0	614.1	615.3	617.2	615.1	615.5
Total private													
1990	454.1	456.3	459.4	458.8	461.0	462.2	461.1	463.4	466.1	466.1	467.6	467.1	461.9
1991	459.3	461.1	465.2	464.7	466.6	466.3	461.7	461.3	465.9	465.1	466.0	468.6	464.3
1992	459.8	461.4	461.9	460.1	462.4	461.2	461.0	458.3	461.3	466.2	467.7	470.5	462.7
1993	458.8	461.7	461.8	464.8	467.0	468.6	467.1	467.2	470.7	473.2	476.5	480.6	468.2
1994	470.4	474.2	477.6	477.5	479.0	480.0	481.1	483.0	487.0	489.4	493.0	496.3	482.4
1995	485.8	488.2	491.4	492.3	499.0	499.1	494.1	495.2	499.7	497.6	501.4	502.3	495.5
1996	489.2	490.8	495.0	496.5	500.7	502.4	499.3	500.4	503.8	502.2	507.2	511.2	499.9
1997	500.6	500.2	504.7	506.9	510.6	512.1	510.1	507.8	513.4	511.8	516.1	520.9	509.6
1998	506.0	508.8	509.8	515.6	519.6	522.0	518.6	516.2	519.7	517.4	519.4	523.6	516.4
1999	512.7	514.3	518.0	515.3	516.1	516.5	514.9	513.3	517.4	519.9	524.6	528.0	517.6
2000	516.0	518.1	520.5	520.4	524.5	521.7	517.1	517.8	519.7	520.1	522.2	526.5	520.4
2001	518.2	522.3	526.5	523.2	524.5	523.7	517.0	516.2	519.0	515.7	518.5	518.8	520.3
2002	504.1	505.2	508.3	513.4	511.6	513.2	506.1	506.1	508.8	507.4	513.1	513.3	509.2
2003	507.2	509.0	510.3	517.4	515.9	517.3	508.1	508.5	509.8	510.5	512.1	509.9	511.3

Employment by Industry: Louisiana—*Continued*

(Numbers in thousands. Not seasonally adjusted.)

Industry	January	February	March	April	May	June	July	August	September	October	November	December	Annual Average
NEW ORLEANS—*Continued*													
Goods-producing													
1990	88.6	89.2	90.7	91.4	91.8	92.0	92.6	93.3	92.3	93.5	92.6	91.8	91.7
1991	90.6	91.2	92.5	93.3	93.3	93.5	93.0	93.0	93.2	93.3	92.5	92.4	92.7
1992	90.0	89.6	89.0	88.2	88.8	88.6	87.1	86.6	85.8	88.0	86.9	86.9	88.0
1993	83.9	84.0	84.1	83.6	84.5	85.6	83.9	84.4	84.4	84.5	84.9	85.4	84.4
1994	82.7	83.4	84.5	84.7	85.0	86.2	86.9	87.8	88.4	88.1	88.0	87.9	86.1
1995	85.1	85.2	85.4	84.8	85.9	87.0	87.7	88.3	88.7	89.1	89.3	89.3	87.2
1996	87.4	87.3	88.6	87.9	89.4	90.1	90.2	90.6	90.2	89.6	90.2	90.1	89.3
1997	90.6	90.3	91.7	91.7	93.3	94.1	94.1	95.3	95.5	95.3	96.6	97.8	93.9
1998	94.9	95.8	96.4	99.0	100.4	100.8	99.8	99.6	98.8	96.9	96.5	96.4	97.9
1999	95.9	96.1	96.4	95.2	95.4	95.1	93.3	92.6	92.2	91.6	91.5	91.5	93.9
2000	89.7	89.4	89.9	89.1	90.2	90.6	90.0	90.5	89.1	88.4	87.4	87.2	89.3
2001	86.7	87.8	89.7	87.2	87.8	88.1	87.4	86.8	86.2	85.1	84.0	83.2	86.6
2002	81.6	81.0	81.7	81.7	82.2	82.5	81.5	82.1	81.8	82.9	82.8	82.6	82.0
2003	81.4	81.5	81.4	83.1	83.5	84.1	82.7	82.2	81.6	82.0	81.4	80.9	82.2
Natural resources and mining													
1990	16.1	16.2	16.2	16.9	16.9	17.1	17.2	17.1	16.4	17.1	17.0	17.0	16.8
1991	18.1	18.1	18.2	17.8	17.8	18.1	18.1	18.0	17.8	17.5	17.2	17.1	17.8
1992	16.4	16.2	16.2	15.3	15.2	15.1	14.3	13.8	13.0	13.6	13.5	13.7	14.7
1993	13.1	13.0	12.9	13.0	13.0	13.2	12.8	13.0	12.9	12.5	12.4	12.6	12.9
1994	12.3	12.3	12.3	12.8	12.9	13.0	13.3	13.5	13.5	13.3	13.3	13.5	13.0
1995	12.9	12.9	12.6	12.6	12.7	12.9	13.2	13.2	13.2	13.1	13.1	13.2	13.0
1996	12.5	12.7	13.0	13.7	14.0	14.3	14.5	14.5	14.4	14.1	14.2	14.3	13.9
1997	14.4	14.5	14.7	14.4	14.5	14.5	14.7	14.8	14.7	14.8	14.7	15.0	14.6
1998	14.6	14.7	14.8	14.8	15.1	15.3	15.5	15.4	15.1	15.0	14.9	14.7	15.0
1999	13.8	13.6	13.6	13.2	13.0	12.8	11.7	11.5	11.4	11.8	12.0	11.7	12.5
2000	11.3	11.2	11.3	11.2	11.4	11.3	11.4	11.4	11.4	11.0	10.9	11.0	11.2
2001	10.8	11.3	11.5	11.4	11.2	11.2	10.9	10.8	10.5	9.9	9.6	9.6	10.7
2002	9.5	9.6	9.6	9.4	9.4	9.4	9.3	9.2	9.1	9.1	9.1	9.1	9.3
2003	9.2	9.2	9.1	9.3	9.4	9.5	9.3	9.1	9.0	9.2	9.0	9.0	9.2
Construction													
1990	24.8	25.3	26.9	27.1	27.2	26.2	26.7	27.3	26.9	27.4	26.6	25.6	26.5
1991	23.7	23.9	24.9	25.9	25.5	25.1	25.0	25.3	26.0	26.4	26.1	26.2	25.3
1992	24.7	24.8	24.3	24.5	25.1	24.9	24.7	24.9	25.4	26.4	25.8	25.4	25.1
1993	24.3	24.6	25.0	24.9	25.8	26.2	25.3	25.5	25.6	25.7	26.0	26.2	25.4
1994	24.6	25.3	26.1	25.5	25.4	25.9	26.0	27.1	28.0	27.7	27.7	27.4	26.4
1995	25.9	26.1	26.5	26.0	26.7	27.3	27.9	28.7	29.5	30.1	30.1	29.9	27.9
1996	28.5	28.1	29.0	27.8	28.5	28.4	28.0	28.5	28.4	28.2	28.5	28.2	28.3
1997	28.9	28.6	29.8	30.1	30.4	31.2	31.0	32.0	32.3	32.3	32.8	33.6	31.1
1998	32.3	33.4	33.9	36.4	36.8	36.5	35.3	35.3	34.8	33.9	33.4	33.3	34.6
1999	33.7	33.8	34.3	33.4	33.4	33.0	32.7	32.7	32.4	32.2	32.0	32.4	33.0
2000	31.4	31.7	32.1	32.2	32.5	32.9	32.2	32.7	32.0	32.0	31.3	31.1	32.0
2001	30.6	31.3	32.9	31.1	31.6	31.6	32.0	31.9	31.6	31.8	31.1	30.4	31.4
2002	29.8	29.2	30.0	30.0	30.4	30.4	30.1	30.6	31.1	31.1	30.9	30.7	30.4
2003	30.4	30.6	30.7	32.3	32.5	32.8	31.8	31.5	31.3	31.4	31.2	31.1	31.5
Manufacturing													
1990	47.7	47.7	47.6	47.4	47.7	48.7	48.7	48.9	49.0	49.0	49.0	49.2	48.4
1991	48.8	49.2	49.4	49.6	50.0	50.3	49.9	49.7	49.4	49.4	49.2	49.1	49.5
1992	48.9	48.6	48.5	48.4	48.5	48.6	48.1	47.9	47.4	48.0	47.6	47.8	48.2
1993	46.5	46.4	46.2	45.7	45.7	46.2	45.8	45.9	45.9	46.3	46.5	46.6	46.1
1994	45.8	45.8	46.1	46.4	46.7	47.3	47.6	47.2	46.9	47.1	47.0	47.0	46.7
1995	46.3	46.2	46.3	46.2	46.5	46.8	46.6	46.4	46.0	45.9	46.1	46.2	46.3
1996	46.4	46.5	46.6	46.4	46.9	47.4	47.7	47.6	47.4	47.3	47.5	47.6	47.1
1997	47.3	47.2	47.2	47.2	48.4	48.4	48.4	48.5	48.5	48.2	49.1	49.2	48.1
1998	48.0	47.7	47.7	47.8	48.5	49.0	49.0	48.9	48.9	48.0	48.2	48.4	48.3
1999	48.4	48.7	48.5	48.6	49.0	49.3	48.9	48.4	48.4	47.6	47.5	47.4	48.4
2000	47.0	46.5	46.5	45.7	46.3	46.4	46.4	46.4	45.7	45.4	45.2	45.1	46.1
2001	45.3	45.2	45.3	44.7	45.0	45.3	44.5	44.1	44.1	43.4	43.3	43.2	44.4
2002	42.3	42.2	42.1	42.3	42.4	42.7	42.1	42.3	41.6	42.7	42.8	42.8	42.4
2003	41.8	41.7	41.6	41.5	41.6	41.8	41.6	41.6	41.3	41.4	41.2	40.8	41.5
Service-providing													
1990	459.0	460.5	462.1	461.4	465.6	463.6	465.4	467.5	467.1	466.8	469.6	469.5	464.8
1991	463.6	464.7	467.9	467.3	469.8	468.9	467.9	466.4	468.3	468.8	470.6	473.4	468.1
1992	466.4	468.4	470.0	471.1	473.1	471.7	471.1	468.7	473.8	478.3	481.4	484.2	473.2
1993	474.3	477.5	477.6	482.7	484.0	484.0	485.2	484.7	490.0	491.2	494.5	498.9	485.4
1994	490.9	494.2	496.3	494.8	496.3	494.9	495.1	495.6	502.1	504.9	508.7	512.6	498.9
1995	504.2	506.2	509.3	510.8	517.2	515.1	510.1	509.1	515.0	511.9	515.1	516.2	511.7
1996	505.3	506.8	510.1	513.6	516.3	515.6	511.9	512.8	519.9	516.4	520.8	524.9	514.5
1997	513.6	513.9	517.3	520.7	523.3	523.5	516.9	512.7	526.0	521.3	524.3	527.8	520.1
1998	516.3	517.6	518.7	522.5	525.0	526.5	519.4	516.7	526.9	525.9	527.1	532.1	522.9
1999	521.4	522.7	526.5	524.6	525.1	525.2	521.9	520.9	531.2	533.4	537.8	542.0	527.7
2000	531.8	534.6	537.0	538.2	543.1	537.5	528.9	528.6	535.1	536.1	539.1	544.7	536.2
2001	536.6	540.2	542.5	542.3	542.6	541.4	530.3	528.9	537.3	534.9	538.5	540.3	537.9
2002	526.9	529.7	532.2	537.1	534.4	537.2	527.7	526.3	531.2	529.2	536.0	536.7	532.1
2003	529.2	531.7	533.4	539.2	537.0	538.5	529.1	526.8	532.5	533.3	535.8	534.2	533.4

Employment by Industry: Louisiana—*Continued*

(Numbers in thousands. Not seasonally adjusted.)

Industry	January	February	March	April	May	June	July	August	September	October	November	December	Annual Average
NEW ORLEANS—*Continued*													
Trade, transportation, and utilities													
1990	134.5	133.7	133.4	134.6	134.9	136.4	135.5	135.8	135.4	135.6	137.3	138.0	135.4
1991	133.6	132.0	132.6	131.5	132.6	133.5	131.9	132.1	132.4	132.2	133.6	134.9	132.7
1992	129.8	129.4	129.4	128.7	129.4	130.1	129.5	129.0	128.9	130.4	132.5	135.3	130.2
1993	130.2	129.5	129.6	130.1	130.5	131.4	131.8	132.1	131.2	132.0	133.4	136.0	131.5
1994	132.2	130.9	132.0	130.9	130.6	131.8	131.9	131.3	130.7	131.6	134.0	136.6	132.0
1995	131.5	130.1	130.3	129.5	129.1	130.9	131.4	131.6	131.3	130.7	133.2	135.5	131.3
1996	129.5	128.1	128.9	129.1	129.9	131.4	129.6	129.3	129.0	129.5	131.5	134.2	130.0
1997	129.2	127.6	128.4	129.1	130.1	131.0	130.4	129.4	130.4	130.2	132.6	134.8	130.3
1998	127.6	126.4	126.9	126.7	127.5	129.5	130.1	130.0	130.2	129.8	131.5	133.8	129.2
1999	129.6	128.0	129.0	128.5	128.6	130.0	129.6	129.3	129.6	129.3	132.4	134.4	129.9
2000	128.7	129.0	129.5	128.6	129.6	130.5	128.2	128.4	127.9	127.9	129.9	132.8	129.3
2001	128.4	128.4	129.0	128.5	128.4	128.8	127.1	127.6	127.3	126.4	127.9	129.4	128.1
2002	123.7	122.9	124.4	124.4	124.3	126.0	123.8	123.7	123.3	122.7	124.2	126.5	124.2
2003	122.1	121.6	122.0	121.9	121.6	122.1	122.2	122.7	122.0	123.1	123.4	123.8	122.4
Wholesale trade													
1990	27.5	27.5	27.5	28.3	28.5	28.8	28.4	28.3	28.3	28.3	28.3	28.3	28.2
1991	27.7	27.6	27.9	28.0	28.3	28.3	28.1	28.0	27.9	27.6	27.6	27.4	27.9
1992	27.1	27.1	27.1	26.8	26.9	27.1	26.9	26.6	26.4	26.6	26.7	26.8	26.8
1993	26.8	26.8	26.7	27.1	27.1	27.2	27.3	27.3	27.3	27.1	27.2	27.2	27.1
1994	27.1	27.1	27.2	27.3	27.5	27.7	27.8	27.8	27.7	27.7	27.8	28.2	27.6
1995	27.9	28.0	28.2	28.1	28.3	28.5	28.8	28.8	28.7	27.8	27.8	28.0	28.2
1996	27.0	27.2	27.4	27.1	27.3	27.6	27.6	27.6	27.7	27.8	27.8	28.1	27.5
1997	27.7	28.0	28.2	28.4	28.3	28.5	28.6	28.7	28.7	28.7	28.7	28.9	28.5
1998	28.3	28.4	28.5	29.0	29.2	29.6	29.4	29.6	29.5	29.4	29.4	29.6	29.2
1999	28.8	28.7	29.0	29.1	29.0	29.3	29.3	29.1	29.0	29.0	28.9	29.0	29.0
2000	28.2	28.4	28.7	28.8	29.0	29.1	29.0	28.9	28.8	28.4	28.4	28.7	28.7
2001	28.6	28.7	28.8	28.7	28.8	29.0	28.4	28.4	28.3	28.2	28.0	28.0	28.5
2002	27.2	27.2	27.4	27.5	27.6	27.7	27.2	27.3	27.1	27.0	26.9	26.9	27.3
2003	27.0	27.0	27.1	26.7	26.6	26.7	26.7	26.7	26.4	26.7	26.7	26.5	26.7
Retail trade													
1990	70.2	69.2	68.9	69.4	69.6	70.3	70.0	70.1	69.4	69.8	71.4	72.2	70.0
1991	69.3	67.6	67.7	67.2	67.4	67.8	67.5	67.6	67.7	68.2	69.7	71.1	68.2
1992	67.5	66.9	66.8	67.1	67.8	68.2	67.9	67.8	67.9	68.4	70.4	72.6	68.3
1993	69.7	69.0	69.1	69.4	69.2	70.0	70.2	70.4	69.5	70.0	71.1	73.1	70.1
1994	70.3	68.8	69.6	68.8	68.4	69.3	69.2	69.3	68.8	69.7	72.3	74.3	69.9
1995	70.5	69.3	69.4	68.8	68.4	69.7	70.4	70.6	70.4	70.7	73.0	74.6	70.5
1996	70.6	69.2	69.6	70.5	70.8	71.5	71.4	71.2	70.8	70.9	73.1	75.1	71.2
1997	71.0	69.2	69.5	70.1	70.6	70.9	70.9	71.4	71.1	70.8	73.1	74.9	71.1
1998	70.2	69.2	69.4	69.0	69.5	70.4	70.2	70.0	69.9	70.0	71.8	73.7	70.3
1999	71.2	69.6	70.1	69.4	69.8	70.6	70.4	70.4	70.5	71.1	74.2	76.0	71.1
2000	71.2	70.9	71.1	70.6	71.3	71.8	70.1	70.5	70.0	70.0	72.2	74.3	71.2
2001	70.1	69.5	69.9	69.3	69.3	69.5	69.0	69.4	69.3	68.8	71.0	72.2	69.7
2002	68.2	67.5	68.8	68.1	68.0	69.3	67.7	67.5	67.2	66.4	68.2	70.1	68.1
2003	66.5	66.3	66.8	66.9	66.9	67.3	67.0	67.5	67.2	67.8	68.0	68.7	67.2
Transportation and utilities													
1990	36.8	37.0	37.0	36.9	36.8	37.3	37.1	37.4	37.7	37.5	37.6	37.5	37.2
1991	36.6	36.8	37.0	36.3	36.9	37.4	36.3	36.5	36.8	36.4	36.3	36.4	36.6
1992	35.2	35.4	35.5	34.8	34.7	34.8	34.7	34.6	34.6	35.4	35.4	35.9	35.1
1993	33.7	33.7	33.8	33.6	34.2	34.2	34.3	34.4	34.4	34.9	35.1	35.7	34.3
1994	34.8	35.0	35.2	34.8	34.7	34.8	34.9	34.2	34.2	34.2	33.9	34.1	34.6
1995	33.1	32.8	32.7	32.6	32.4	32.7	32.2	32.2	32.2	32.2	32.4	32.9	32.5
1996	31.9	31.7	31.9	31.5	31.8	32.3	30.6	30.5	30.5	30.8	30.6	31.0	31.3
1997	30.5	30.4	30.7	30.6	31.2	31.6	30.9	29.3	30.6	30.7	30.8	31.0	30.7
1998	29.1	28.8	29.0	28.7	28.8	29.5	30.5	30.4	30.8	30.4	30.3	30.5	29.7
1999	29.6	29.7	29.9	30.0	29.8	30.1	29.9	29.8	30.1	29.2	29.3	29.4	29.7
2000	29.3	29.7	29.7	29.2	29.3	29.6	29.1	29.0	29.1	29.5	29.3	29.8	29.4
2001	29.7	30.2	30.3	30.5	30.3	30.3	29.7	29.8	29.7	29.4	28.9	29.2	29.8
2002	28.3	28.2	28.2	28.8	28.7	29.0	28.9	28.9	29.0	29.3	29.1	29.5	28.8
2003	28.6	28.3	28.1	28.3	28.1	28.1	28.5	28.5	28.4	28.6	28.7	28.6	28.4
Information													
1990	10.0	10.0	10.0	10.0	10.0	10.1	10.4	10.4	10.7	9.8	9.8	9.8	10.1
1991	10.3	10.3	10.3	10.4	10.4	10.5	10.9	10.8	10.9	10.1	10.0	10.0	10.4
1992	10.0	9.8	9.9	9.8	9.8	10.1	8.1	8.1	8.1	8.2	8.2	8.3	9.0
1993	8.3	8.3	8.3	8.1	8.2	10.3	8.3	8.3	8.5	8.4	8.5	8.7	8.5
1994	8.3	8.4	8.4	8.6	8.6	8.7	8.7	8.8	8.7	8.6	8.6	8.8	8.6
1995	8.6	8.4	8.6	8.6	9.0	9.0	8.8	8.9	8.9	8.9	9.0	9.1	8.8
1996	9.1	9.1	9.1	9.6	10.0	10.0	9.6	9.8	9.8	9.4	9.6	9.7	9.6
1997	9.4	9.5	9.6	9.8	10.1	10.4	10.2	10.3	10.3	9.9	10.0	10.1	10.0
1998	9.5	9.5	9.5	9.4	9.4	9.7	9.5	9.3	9.4	10.0	10.0	10.1	9.6
1999	9.8	9.8	9.8	9.7	9.9	10.0	10.1	10.1	10.1	10.1	10.2	10.2	10.0
2000	10.3	10.3	10.4	10.4	10.5	10.8	11.3	11.3	11.0	10.8	10.9	11.2	10.8
2001	11.0	11.1	11.2	10.7	10.8	10.8	10.6	10.5	10.3	10.3	10.4	10.2	10.6
2002	10.0	10.0	10.0	9.6	9.5	9.7	9.6	9.6	9.5	9.3	9.3	9.4	9.6
2003	9.8	9.7	9.9	10.3	10.6	11.0	9.2	9.5	9.4	9.4	9.6	9.5	9.8

Employment by Industry: Louisiana—*Continued*

(Numbers in thousands. Not seasonally adjusted.)

Industry	January	February	March	April	May	June	July	August	September	October	November	December	Annual Average
NEW ORLEANS—*Continued*													
Financial activities													
1990	33.7	34.0	34.5	34.1	34.0	34.5	34.0	34.2	34.2	34.0	34.2	35.3	34.2
1991	32.4	32.5	32.6	32.7	32.7	32.8	32.3	32.1	31.9	31.4	31.4	32.6	32.3
1992	30.4	30.5	30.5	30.7	30.9	30.9	30.9	30.9	30.9	30.8	30.9	31.0	30.8
1993	31.0	31.1	31.0	31.2	31.3	31.5	31.5	31.5	31.4	31.1	31.2	31.4	31.3
1994	31.0	31.0	31.1	31.3	31.3	31.7	31.8	31.8	31.6	31.4	31.4	31.7	31.4
1995	31.7	31.7	31.8	32.1	32.2	32.5	32.4	32.5	32.3	32.1	32.2	32.5	32.2
1996	31.6	31.7	31.8	32.1	32.2	32.6	33.0	33.1	33.0	32.8	33.0	33.2	32.5
1997	32.6	32.7	32.8	32.8	32.9	33.2	33.4	33.3	33.2	33.0	33.0	33.1	33.0
1998	34.2	34.3	34.5	33.8	33.8	34.2	34.1	34.0	33.7	33.4	33.5	33.7	33.9
1999	33.4	33.6	33.8	34.0	34.0	34.3	34.5	34.2	34.0	34.0	34.1	34.3	34.0
2000	34.9	35.1	35.2	34.6	35.1	34.9	35.4	35.4	35.1	34.8	34.8	35.0	35.0
2001	35.1	35.2	35.0	35.1	35.1	35.1	35.3	35.2	34.9	35.0	35.0	34.9	35.0
2002	34.4	34.6	34.7	35.1	35.1	35.3	35.1	35.5	35.3	35.7	35.9	35.9	35.2
2003	36.1	36.1	35.9	35.9	35.9	36.0	36.0	36.2	36.0	35.8	35.8	35.6	35.9
Professional and business services													
1990	49.7	50.1	50.6	50.7	51.2	52.1	53.2	53.9	53.7	53.6	53.7	53.1	52.1
1991	54.9	56.1	57.3	55.7	55.6	56.1	56.1	56.0	56.3	56.2	56.7	56.7	56.1
1992	57.5	58.6	58.8	57.9	57.9	58.4	59.3	59.3	59.2	60.2	60.4	61.2	59.1
1993	60.2	61.0	60.9	61.7	61.8	61.8	62.0	62.2	62.9	62.7	63.0	63.9	62.0
1994	62.9	64.0	64.7	63.8	64.2	64.7	63.2	63.8	63.4	65.0	65.4	65.3	64.2
1995	65.0	66.4	67.2	66.7	67.7	68.4	66.5	66.8	66.7	66.4	66.5	67.1	66.8
1996	65.1	66.4	67.5	67.7	68.2	68.8	68.7	69.6	69.2	68.0	68.8	69.6	68.1
1997	68.7	69.4	70.3	71.2	71.0	72.3	71.1	70.1	70.3	70.3	70.2	71.3	70.5
1998	70.4	71.7	71.3	72.7	72.7	74.6	73.6	73.6	73.5	73.5	73.3	74.4	72.9
1999	71.3	72.2	72.9	71.4	70.8	72.1	73.4	73.8	73.4	74.0	74.3	74.8	72.9
2000	72.4	72.3	72.9	74.5	74.4	73.8	73.5	74.1	74.7	74.0	75.0	75.2	73.9
2001	75.3	75.9	76.3	74.7	75.6	75.4	74.2	74.3	74.6	74.3	74.5	75.2	75.0
2002	73.3	73.4	73.7	74.0	72.6	72.7	72.0	72.5	71.9	71.0	71.0	71.4	72.5
2003	71.1	71.6	72.8	74.1	72.2	72.6	71.9	71.8	71.4	71.5	71.1	71.2	71.9
Educational and health services													
1990	60.3	60.7	61.0	60.5	60.9	58.0	57.8	57.9	61.6	62.8	63.1	62.7	60.6
1991	62.3	63.2	63.7	64.1	63.9	60.9	60.0	60.1	64.3	64.8	64.7	64.9	63.1
1992	65.6	65.9	66.2	66.4	66.2	63.5	67.1	66.0	69.8	68.7	69.1	68.3	66.9
1993	67.3	68.5	68.7	70.3	70.1	66.8	68.5	67.7	71.5	72.4	72.7	71.8	69.7
1994	71.4	72.6	73.0	73.6	73.9	70.6	72.6	72.5	76.5	76.7	76.7	77.1	73.9
1995	76.2	77.0	77.5	79.1	79.0	76.1	72.6	71.9	77.3	77.7	78.2	78.4	76.8
1996	76.7	77.7	78.1	78.4	77.5	74.7	73.0	72.5	77.9	77.8	78.0	77.9	76.7
1997	76.6	77.3	77.4	78.4	78.2	75.1	74.9	74.1	78.6	79.0	79.1	79.0	77.3
1998	76.9	77.5	77.5	78.3	78.3	74.9	74.3	73.8	77.9	78.8	79.0	78.9	77.2
1999	78.0	79.1	79.3	79.4	79.3	75.1	73.8	73.3	78.4	78.7	79.1	78.9	77.7
2000	77.2	78.1	78.2	78.4	78.0	73.8	73.3	73.2	78.7	79.8	79.7	79.8	77.4
2001	79.1	79.6	79.5	81.4	80.6	78.6	77.1	76.6	81.6	81.8	84.0	83.2	80.2
2002	80.2	81.5	81.1	83.2	81.5	80.1	78.5	78.2	83.5	83.9	85.9	84.0	81.8
2003	83.1	83.5	82.6	84.6	84.2	82.1	81.0	80.7	85.1	84.9	86.9	85.4	83.7
Leisure and hospitality													
1990	57.3	58.6	59.1	57.1	57.8	58.5	56.9	57.5	57.7	56.5	56.6	56.1	57.5
1991	54.6	55.1	55.5	56.3	57.4	57.9	56.4	56.3	56.0	56.3	56.5	56.5	56.2
1992	56.0	57.1	57.5	57.9	58.9	58.9	58.2	57.9	58.3	59.5	59.4	59.1	58.2
1993	57.3	58.6	58.5	58.9	59.6	59.9	59.8	59.9	59.7	61.3	62.0	62.6	59.8
1994	61.3	63.1	63.0	63.6	64.3	65.1	64.7	65.7	66.6	67.1	67.9	67.8	65.0
1995	66.5	68.0	69.1	69.8	74.3	73.1	72.7	73.1	72.8	71.2	71.5	69.0	70.9
1996	68.2	68.9	69.3	69.8	71.5	72.4	72.9	73.4	72.8	73.1	74.1	74.4	71.7
1997	71.8	71.7	72.6	71.7	72.6	73.4	73.3	72.8	72.8	71.8	72.5	72.5	72.5
1998	70.4	71.5	71.5	72.9	74.5	75.1	74.2	73.1	73.5	72.5	73.0	73.6	73.0
1999	72.0	72.8	73.9	74.0	74.8	76.2	76.4	76.2	76.0	78.1	79.2	80.1	75.8
2000	79.3	80.2	80.5	81.1	83.0	83.3	81.5	81.0	79.6	80.8	81.1	81.9	81.1
2001	80.3	81.9	83.2	83.1	83.5	84.0	82.7	82.6	81.5	80.1	80.0	80.0	81.9
2002	78.8	79.6	80.3	82.1	82.9	83.3	82.0	81.0	80.1	79.0	80.2	79.5	80.7
2003	79.9	81.3	81.9	83.6	83.9	86.1	82.3	82.6	81.6	81.1	81.1	80.8	82.2
Other services													
1990	20.0	20.0	20.1	20.4	20.4	20.6	20.7	20.4	20.5	20.3	20.3	20.3	20.3
1991	20.6	20.7	20.7	20.7	20.7	21.1	21.1	20.9	20.9	20.8	20.6	20.6	20.8
1992	20.5	20.5	20.6	20.5	20.5	20.7	20.8	20.5	20.3	20.4	20.3	20.4	20.5
1993	20.6	20.7	20.7	20.9	21.0	21.3	21.3	21.1	21.1	20.8	20.8	20.8	20.9
1994	20.6	20.8	20.9	21.0	21.1	21.2	21.3	21.3	21.1	20.9	21.0	21.1	21.0
1995	21.2	21.4	21.5	21.7	21.8	22.1	22.0	22.1	21.7	21.5	21.5	21.4	21.7
1996	21.6	21.6	21.7	21.9	22.0	22.4	22.3	22.1	21.9	22.0	22.0	22.1	22.0
1997	21.7	21.7	21.9	22.2	22.4	22.6	22.7	22.5	22.3	22.3	22.1	22.3	22.2
1998	22.1	22.1	22.2	22.8	23.0	23.2	23.0	22.8	22.7	22.5	22.6	22.7	22.6
1999	22.7	22.7	22.9	23.1	23.3	23.7	23.8	23.8	23.7	24.1	23.8	23.8	23.5
2000	23.5	23.7	23.9	23.7	23.7	24.0	23.9	23.9	23.6	23.6	23.4	23.4	23.7
2001	22.3	22.4	22.6	22.5	22.7	22.9	22.6	22.6	22.6	22.7	22.7	22.7	22.6
2002	22.1	22.2	22.4	23.3	23.5	23.6	23.6	23.5	23.4	22.9	23.8	24.0	23.2
2003	23.7	23.7	23.8	23.9	24.0	23.3	22.8	22.8	22.7	22.7	22.8	22.7	23.2

Employment by Industry: Louisiana—*Continued*

(Numbers in thousands. Not seasonally adjusted.)

Industry	January	February	March	April	May	June	July	August	September	October	November	December	Annual Average
NEW ORLEANS—*Continued*													
Government													
1990	93.5	93.4	93.4	94.0	96.4	93.4	96.9	97.4	93.3	94.2	94.6	94.2	94.6
1991	94.9	94.8	95.2	95.9	96.5	96.1	99.2	98.1	95.6	97.0	97.1	97.2	96.5
1992	96.6	96.6	97.1	99.2	99.5	99.1	97.2	97.0	98.3	100.1	100.6	100.6	98.5
1993	99.4	99.8	99.9	101.5	101.5	101.0	102.0	101.9	103.7	102.5	102.9	103.7	101.7
1994	103.2	103.4	103.2	102.0	102.3	101.1	100.9	100.4	103.5	103.6	103.7	104.2	102.6
1995	103.5	103.2	103.3	103.3	104.1	103.0	103.7	102.2	104.0	103.4	103.0	103.2	103.3
1996	103.5	103.3	103.7	105.0	105.0	103.3	102.8	103.0	106.3	103.8	103.8	103.8	103.9
1997	103.6	104.0	104.3	105.5	106.0	105.5	100.9	100.2	108.1	104.8	104.8	104.7	104.4
1998	105.2	104.6	105.3	105.9	105.8	105.3	100.6	100.1	106.0	105.4	104.2	104.9	104.4
1999	104.6	104.5	104.9	104.5	104.4	103.8	100.3	100.2	106.0	105.1	104.7	105.5	104.0
2000	105.5	105.9	106.4	106.9	108.8	106.4	101.8	101.3	104.5	104.4	104.3	105.4	105.1
2001	105.1	105.7	105.7	106.3	105.9	105.8	100.7	99.5	104.5	104.3	104.0	104.7	104.3
2002	104.4	105.5	105.6	105.4	105.0	106.5	103.1	102.3	104.2	104.7	105.7	106.0	104.9
2003	103.4	104.2	104.5	104.9	104.6	105.3	103.7	100.5	104.3	104.8	105.1	105.2	104.2
Federal government													
1990	17.1	17.0	17.0	17.1	19.0	17.5	17.7	16.9	16.8	16.7	16.8	16.8	17.2
1991	16.7	16.6	16.6	17.0	17.1	17.2	17.2	17.4	17.2	17.2	17.3	17.4	17.1
1992	17.2	17.2	17.2	17.6	17.6	17.7	17.2	17.1	17.1	17.3	17.2	17.3	17.3
1993	17.0	17.1	17.0	17.4	17.5	17.6	17.4	17.4	17.2	17.1	17.1	17.3	17.3
1994	17.2	17.2	16.9	16.9	16.9	16.9	16.7	16.7	16.6	16.7	16.4	16.7	16.8
1995	16.4	16.4	16.4	16.4	16.4	16.6	16.6	16.5	16.5	16.5	16.3	16.7	16.5
1996	16.4	16.4	16.4	16.5	16.5	16.5	16.6	16.7	16.6	16.5	16.5	17.0	16.6
1997	16.6	16.6	16.4	16.3	16.3	16.4	16.3	16.4	16.3	16.2	16.3	16.7	16.4
1998	16.3	16.3	16.2	16.4	16.5	16.4	16.5	16.5	16.4	16.3	16.3	16.8	16.4
1999	16.4	16.4	16.4	16.5	16.4	16.4	16.5	16.4	16.4	16.3	16.3	16.6	16.4
2000	16.3	16.3	16.5	17.1	19.3	17.2	17.6	16.5	16.4	16.3	16.3	16.7	16.9
2001	16.3	16.2	16.2	16.3	16.2	16.3	16.4	16.3	16.3	16.2	16.1	16.2	16.2
2002	16.0	16.0	16.1	16.0	15.9	16.0	16.0	16.0	16.0	16.3	16.4	16.5	16.1
2003	16.4	16.3	16.3	16.3	16.2	16.3	16.2	16.1	16.5	16.5	16.4	16.4	16.3
State government													
1990	20.5	20.6	20.4	20.5	21.0	19.2	20.1	20.5	21.4	21.2	21.3	21.0	20.6
1991	21.0	21.0	21.2	21.2	21.5	20.0	20.8	20.7	21.8	22.0	21.9	22.0	21.3
1992	21.2	21.4	21.4	22.6	22.9	21.3	22.2	21.9	23.0	22.9	23.2	23.2	22.3
1993	23.2	23.4	23.5	23.9	23.8	22.9	23.0	23.1	24.4	24.5	25.0	24.8	23.8
1994	25.3	25.3	25.3	25.2	25.4	24.2	25.1	24.7	25.8	25.4	25.8	25.4	25.2
1995	25.8	25.6	25.4	25.6	26.2	24.7	26.5	25.4	26.2	25.8	26.1	25.8	25.8
1996	26.5	26.4	26.5	26.7	26.5	24.5	25.3	24.9	25.7	25.7	25.8	25.3	25.8
1997	25.2	25.5	25.4	25.9	25.9	24.1	25.3	24.6	26.1	25.8	25.7	25.2	25.4
1998	25.2	25.3	25.6	25.8	25.8	24.2	25.2	24.8	25.7	24.9	24.7	24.6	25.2
1999	24.6	24.9	25.1	25.3	25.3	24.0	25.0	24.8	25.7	25.0	24.9	25.2	25.0
2000	24.6	25.1	25.2	25.1	25.0	24.0	24.3	24.5	25.4	24.9	24.7	25.1	24.8
2001	25.1	25.8	25.7	25.8	25.4	23.7	24.1	24.6	25.3	24.5	24.6	25.0	24.9
2002	25.0	25.8	25.8	25.6	25.2	24.4	24.5	24.7	25.8	24.9	25.2	25.4	25.2
2003	23.6	24.5	24.7	24.5	24.2	23.4	23.1	23.1	24.7	24.7	24.7	24.7	24.2
Local government													
1990	55.9	55.8	56.0	56.4	56.4	56.7	59.1	60.0	55.1	56.3	56.5	56.4	56.7
1991	57.2	57.2	57.4	57.7	57.9	58.9	61.2	60.0	56.6	57.8	57.9	57.8	58.1
1992	58.2	58.0	58.5	59.0	59.0	60.1	57.8	58.0	58.2	59.9	60.2	60.1	58.9
1993	59.2	59.3	59.4	60.2	60.2	60.5	61.6	61.4	62.1	60.9	60.8	61.6	60.6
1994	60.7	60.9	61.0	59.9	60.0	60.0	59.1	59.0	61.1	61.5	61.5	62.1	60.6
1995	61.3	61.2	61.5	61.3	61.5	61.7	60.6	60.3	61.3	61.1	60.6	60.7	61.1
1996	60.6	60.5	60.8	61.8	62.0	62.3	60.9	61.4	64.0	61.6	61.5	61.5	61.6
1997	61.8	61.9	62.5	63.3	63.8	65.0	59.3	59.2	65.7	62.8	62.8	62.8	62.6
1998	63.7	63.0	63.5	63.7	63.5	64.7	58.9	58.8	63.9	64.2	63.2	63.5	62.9
1999	63.6	63.2	63.4	62.7	62.7	63.4	58.8	59.0	63.9	63.8	63.5	63.7	62.6
2000	64.6	64.5	64.7	64.7	64.5	65.2	59.9	60.3	62.7	63.2	63.3	63.6	63.4
2001	63.7	63.7	63.8	64.2	64.3	65.8	60.2	58.6	62.9	63.6	63.3	63.5	63.1
2002	63.4	63.7	63.7	63.8	63.9	66.1	62.6	61.6	62.4	63.5	64.1	64.1	63.6
2003	63.4	63.4	63.5	64.1	64.2	65.6	64.4	61.3	63.1	63.6	64.0	64.1	63.7
SHREVEPORT													
Total nonfarm													
1990	139.5	142.0	143.2	144.7	147.0	146.9	145.3	145.3	147.7	147.1	146.9	146.4	145.2
1991	145.6	144.0	143.4	145.6	147.4	148.6	145.4	146.3	148.2	148.5	146.7	146.9	146.4
1992	145.7	143.7	147.1	148.2	150.3	151.1	147.6	148.5	151.4	151.7	152.4	152.7	149.2
1993	150.1	151.2	151.7	152.1	153.6	154.6	153.4	154.0	154.8	154.2	154.2	154.8	153.2
1994	151.7	153.1	154.9	157.2	159.1	161.2	159.6	160.2	162.3	161.4	161.5	162.0	158.7
1995	158.4	159.5	160.6	162.3	163.5	165.5	163.0	163.5	165.1	165.0	164.8	165.0	163.0
1996	162.8	163.4	163.0	166.4	167.9	169.2	167.1	167.0	168.9	169.1	169.4	169.8	167.0
1997	166.2	167.0	167.9	168.7	168.1	172.1	170.9	170.0	171.1	171.5	172.3	172.8	169.9
1998	169.0	169.7	171.2	173.3	173.8	173.7	172.1	174.1	174.3	173.1	173.4	173.1	172.6
1999	170.8	171.1	172.8	173.9	174.2	176.4	175.2	174.8	175.2	175.3	175.4	175.6	174.2
2000	173.5	173.8	175.8	174.4	175.7	175.9	175.2	175.2	176.0	176.8	176.5	176.5	175.4
2001	175.9	176.0	177.1	176.9	176.8	178.0	174.7	175.1	174.5	172.8	173.2	172.1	175.2
2002	168.0	169.7	170.7	172.1	173.4	173.6	171.5	171.9	172.4	171.2	171.6	171.6	171.5
2003	170.0	169.9	170.8	169.7	172.1	173.1	171.2	172.3	172.5	173.8	173.4	173.2	171.8

Employment by Industry: Louisiana—*Continued*

(Numbers in thousands. Not seasonally adjusted.)

Industry	January	February	March	April	May	June	July	August	September	October	November	December	Annual Average
SHREVEPORT—*Continued*													
Total private													
1990	111.0	113.4	114.5	115.5	117.6	118.9	118.8	119.0	119.3	118.2	118.3	117.8	116.9
1991	116.6	114.6	114.0	116.0	117.7	118.9	118.2	119.0	119.0	118.9	117.0	117.0	117.2
1992	116.0	113.8	117.2	118.2	120.0	121.1	120.2	121.2	121.5	121.1	121.7	121.9	119.5
1993	119.2	120.2	120.8	121.0	122.6	123.7	122.8	123.7	123.7	122.9	123.0	123.6	122.3
1994	120.8	122.1	123.9	126.1	128.0	130.0	129.9	130.8	131.3	129.8	129.9	130.3	127.7
1995	126.6	127.5	128.6	129.9	131.6	133.7	132.2	133.2	133.2	132.8	132.6	132.8	131.2
1996	130.5	131.0	130.4	133.6	135.2	136.7	136.0	136.2	136.6	136.3	136.6	137.1	134.7
1997	133.6	134.4	135.1	135.9	135.5	138.7	138.9	139.2	139.3	138.8	139.2	140.1	137.4
1998	136.2	136.7	138.0	140.0	140.6	139.9	139.3	142.0	141.8	140.1	140.2	140.2	139.6
1999	138.0	138.1	139.6	140.9	141.2	142.7	142.0	142.9	142.5	142.7	142.9	143.2	141.4
2000	141.2	141.2	143.1	141.7	142.4	143.5	143.7	144.3	144.1	144.3	144.1	144.4	143.2
2001	143.9	143.7	144.8	144.9	144.7	145.7	143.8	144.2	142.7	140.6	140.9	140.3	143.3
2002	136.3	137.8	138.6	139.5	140.8	140.8	139.3	139.9	139.6	138.1	138.5	138.3	139.0
2003	137.0	136.5	137.3	136.7	139.1	139.6	138.3	139.3	139.5	140.2	139.6	139.6	138.6
Goods-producing													
1990	29.5	30.2	30.4	30.4	30.8	31.4	31.0	31.3	31.3	31.1	31.3	30.9	30.8
1991	30.4	30.3	30.2	30.0	30.2	30.6	30.3	30.7	30.7	30.6	30.4	29.1	30.3
1992	29.7	27.7	29.7	30.0	30.4	30.6	30.9	31.2	31.3	30.7	31.0	30.9	30.3
1993	29.8	30.0	30.3	29.7	30.4	30.6	30.8	31.4	31.2	30.1	29.8	29.7	30.3
1994	29.0	29.2	29.5	30.0	30.1	30.5	30.2	30.5	30.6	29.8	29.5	29.7	29.9
1995	29.1	29.2	29.3	29.3	29.7	30.6	30.5	30.8	30.7	30.7	30.3	30.3	30.0
1996	29.7	29.7	29.4	30.5	31.0	31.3	31.2	31.4	31.3	31.5	31.7	31.3	30.8
1997	30.6	30.5	30.3	30.2	30.3	31.4	31.2	31.2	31.4	31.1	30.8	31.0	30.8
1998	30.3	30.2	30.4	30.9	31.3	30.1	29.6	31.7	31.6	31.2	30.6	30.4	30.7
1999	29.8	29.7	29.8	29.4	29.4	30.1	30.3	30.1	30.1	29.8	29.8	29.6	29.8
2000	29.6	29.5	29.7	29.8	30.2	30.9	30.5	30.5	30.5	30.7	30.4	30.4	30.2
2001	30.3	29.9	30.2	30.3	30.4	30.7	30.5	30.2	29.3	28.0	28.3	27.8	29.6
2002	25.1	26.4	26.8	26.4	26.9	27.3	27.0	27.0	26.9	26.5	26.8	26.6	26.6
2003	25.6	25.5	25.8	24.7	26.7	27.2	26.7	27.3	27.5	27.5	26.5	26.3	26.4
Natural resources and mining													
1990	3.4	3.5	3.5	3.3	3.4	3.5	3.3	3.4	3.4	3.4	3.5	3.4	3.4
1991	3.3	3.3	3.3	3.2	3.2	3.2	3.3	3.2	3.1	3.1	3.0	3.0	3.2
1992	3.0	2.9	2.8	2.9	2.9	2.9	2.9	2.9	2.9	3.0	3.0	3.1	2.9
1993	3.0	2.9	2.9	2.8	2.8	2.9	3.0	2.9	3.0	2.9	2.9	2.9	2.9
1994	2.7	2.7	2.6	2.8	2.9	2.9	2.7	2.7	2.7	2.7	2.6	2.6	2.7
1995	2.5	2.5	2.5	2.4	2.4	2.5	2.5	2.5	2.5	2.5	2.5	2.5	2.5
1996	2.4	2.4	2.4	2.5	2.6	2.5	2.6	2.6	2.7	2.7	2.6	2.6	2.6
1997	2.6	2.6	2.6	2.7	2.7	2.8	2.9	2.9	2.9	3.0	2.9	3.0	2.8
1998	2.9	2.9	2.9	2.9	3.0	3.0	3.1	3.0	3.0	2.7	2.6	2.6	2.9
1999	2.3	2.2	2.2	2.2	2.2	2.3	2.5	2.4	2.5	2.7	2.7	2.7	2.4
2000	2.7	2.7	2.7	2.4	2.5	2.6	2.7	2.7	2.8	3.0	3.0	3.0	2.7
2001	3.3	3.3	3.3	3.3	3.4	3.5	3.4	3.5	3.4	3.3	3.3	3.3	3.3
2002	3.0	3.1	3.2	2.9	3.1	3.2	3.0	3.1	3.2	3.0	3.1	3.2	3.1
2003	2.9	3.0	3.1	3.0	3.2	3.4	3.1	3.3	3.3	3.3	3.3	3.3	3.2
Construction													
1990	6.1	6.2	6.3	6.6	6.8	6.9	7.1	7.4	7.3	7.1	7.0	6.8	6.8
1991	6.1	6.2	6.2	6.7	7.0	7.2	7.2	7.4	7.5	7.4	7.4	7.4	7.0
1992	6.3	6.3	6.5	6.6	7.0	7.2	7.8	8.0	8.2	7.7	7.8	7.6	7.3
1993	6.8	7.2	7.6	8.5	9.2	9.0	8.0	8.2	8.0	7.7	7.6	7.6	8.0
1994	7.3	7.3	7.5	7.9	7.8	8.1	8.3	8.3	8.3	7.4	7.4	7.4	7.8
1995	7.0	7.0	7.0	7.1	7.5	7.9	7.9	8.1	8.0	8.0	7.7	7.7	7.6
1996	7.5	7.4	7.5	8.1	8.6	8.7	9.1	9.0	9.0	9.3	9.6	9.3	8.6
1997	8.8	8.5	8.3	8.4	8.6	9.2	9.3	9.3	9.3	8.9	8.8	8.9	8.9
1998	8.4	8.5	8.6	8.9	9.1	9.5	9.7	9.7	9.6	9.6	9.2	9.2	9.2
1999	8.6	8.6	8.7	8.5	8.5	8.9	9.0	9.0	8.8	8.6	8.6	8.4	8.7
2000	8.4	8.4	8.6	8.7	8.9	9.2	9.0	9.0	8.9	9.0	8.9	8.9	8.8
2001	8.6	8.6	8.8	8.9	9.0	9.3	9.6	9.5	9.2	8.9	8.9	8.7	8.9
2002	8.3	8.3	8.4	8.4	8.6	8.5	8.6	8.5	8.4	8.2	8.2	8.0	8.4
2003	7.9	7.8	7.9	8.2	8.5	8.5	8.6	8.5	8.5	8.4	7.7	7.6	8.2
Manufacturing													
1990	20.0	20.5	20.6	20.5	20.6	21.0	20.6	20.5	20.6	20.6	20.8	20.7	20.6
1991	21.0	20.8	20.7	20.1	20.0	20.2	19.8	20.1	20.1	20.1	20.0	18.7	20.1
1992	20.4	18.5	20.4	20.5	20.5	20.5	20.2	20.3	20.2	20.0	20.2	20.2	20.2
1993	20.0	19.9	19.8	18.4	18.4	18.7	19.8	20.3	20.2	19.5	19.3	19.2	19.5
1994	19.0	19.2	19.4	19.3	19.4	19.5	19.2	19.5	19.6	19.7	19.5	19.7	19.4
1995	19.6	19.7	19.8	19.8	19.8	20.2	20.1	20.2	20.2	20.2	20.1	20.1	20.0
1996	19.8	19.9	19.5	19.9	19.8	20.1	19.5	19.8	19.6	19.5	19.5	19.4	19.7
1997	19.2	19.4	19.4	19.1	19.0	19.4	19.0	19.0	19.2	19.2	19.1	19.1	19.2
1998	19.0	18.8	18.9	19.1	19.2	17.6	16.8	19.0	19.0	18.9	18.8	18.6	18.6
1999	18.9	18.9	18.9	18.7	18.7	18.9	18.8	18.7	18.8	18.5	18.5	18.5	18.7
2000	18.5	18.4	18.4	18.7	18.8	19.1	18.8	18.8	18.8	18.7	18.5	18.5	18.7
2001	18.4	18.0	18.1	18.1	18.0	17.9	17.5	17.2	16.7	15.8	16.1	15.8	17.3
2002	13.8	15.0	15.2	15.1	15.2	15.6	15.4	15.4	15.3	15.3	15.5	15.4	15.2
2003	14.8	14.7	14.8	13.5	15.0	15.3	15.0	15.5	15.7	15.8	15.5	15.4	15.1

Employment by Industry: Louisiana—*Continued*

(Numbers in thousands. Not seasonally adjusted.)

Industry	January	February	March	April	May	June	July	August	September	October	November	December	Annual Average
SHREVEPORT—*Continued*													
Service-providing													
1990	110.0	111.8	112.8	114.3	116.2	115.5	114.3	114.0	116.4	116.0	115.6	115.5	114.4
1991	115.2	113.7	113.2	115.6	117.2	118.0	115.1	115.6	117.5	117.9	116.3	117.8	116.1
1992	116.0	116.0	117.4	118.2	119.9	120.5	116.7	117.3	120.1	121.0	121.4	121.8	118.9
1993	120.3	121.2	121.4	122.4	123.2	124.0	122.6	122.6	123.6	124.1	124.4	125.1	122.9
1994	122.7	123.9	125.4	127.2	129.0	130.7	129.4	129.7	131.7	131.6	132.0	132.3	128.8
1995	129.3	130.3	131.3	133.0	133.8	134.9	132.5	132.7	134.4	134.3	134.5	134.7	133.0
1996	133.1	133.7	133.6	135.9	136.9	137.9	135.9	135.6	137.6	137.6	137.7	138.5	136.2
1997	135.6	136.5	137.6	138.5	137.8	140.7	139.7	138.8	139.7	140.4	141.5	141.8	139.1
1998	138.7	139.5	140.8	142.4	142.5	143.6	142.5	142.4	142.7	141.9	142.8	142.7	141.9
1999	141.0	141.4	143.0	144.5	144.8	146.3	144.9	144.7	145.1	145.5	145.6	146.0	144.4
2000	143.9	144.3	146.1	144.6	145.5	145.0	144.7	144.7	145.5	146.1	146.1	146.1	145.2
2001	145.6	146.1	146.9	146.6	146.4	147.3	144.2	144.9	145.2	144.8	144.9	144.3	145.6
2002	142.9	143.3	143.9	145.7	146.5	146.3	144.5	144.9	145.5	144.7	144.8	145.0	144.8
2003	144.4	144.4	145.0	145.0	145.4	145.9	145.5	145.0	145.0	146.3	146.9	146.9	145.5
Trade, transportation, and utilities													
1990	31.0	31.4	31.8	31.9	32.0	32.3	32.2	32.3	32.4	32.1	32.7	32.8	32.1
1991	31.6	30.1	29.8	30.9	30.9	31.4	31.1	31.5	31.3	31.1	31.1	31.5	31.0
1992	29.9	29.5	29.9	30.3	30.6	30.8	30.5	30.8	30.7	30.8	31.4	31.9	30.6
1993	31.2	31.1	31.1	30.8	31.0	31.3	30.9	31.2	31.0	31.1	31.5	32.3	31.2
1994	31.4	31.3	31.6	31.8	31.9	32.1	32.3	32.2	32.4	32.4	33.0	33.6	32.2
1995	31.8	31.7	32.0	31.8	32.1	32.2	32.0	32.4	32.3	32.3	32.9	33.2	32.2
1996	32.3	31.8	31.3	32.1	32.4	33.0	32.5	32.4	32.4	32.0	32.6	33.1	32.3
1997	31.9	31.5	31.9	31.6	31.5	32.3	32.1	32.3	32.5	32.9	33.4	34.0	32.3
1998	32.4	32.3	32.4	32.6	32.7	32.8	32.5	32.8	32.8	32.5	32.9	33.1	32.7
1999	32.1	31.9	32.4	32.4	32.2	32.3	32.0	32.2	32.2	32.4	33.2	33.4	32.4
2000	32.5	32.6	33.0	32.4	32.7	32.9	32.4	32.5	32.3	32.6	33.2	33.8	32.7
2001	33.4	33.1	33.4	33.3	33.1	33.3	33.4	33.7	33.4	33.0	33.5	33.8	33.3
2002	32.6	32.6	32.7	33.4	33.5	33.9	33.0	33.0	32.7	32.2	32.8	32.9	32.9
2003	32.7	32.6	32.9	32.7	32.5	32.8	32.5	32.6	32.7	32.8	33.4	34.1	32.9
Wholesale trade													
1990	6.0	6.1	6.2	6.5	6.5	6.6	6.6	6.6	6.5	6.5	6.5	6.5	6.4
1991	6.6	6.4	6.4	6.5	6.5	6.7	6.6	6.6	6.5	6.6	6.5	6.6	6.5
1992	6.6	6.6	6.6	6.6	6.6	6.7	6.6	6.6	6.6	6.6	6.6	6.6	6.6
1993	6.7	6.7	6.7	6.7	6.8	6.9	6.8	6.9	6.8	6.7	6.6	6.7	6.8
1994	6.8	6.8	6.8	6.9	6.9	7.0	7.0	6.9	7.0	7.0	7.0	7.0	6.9
1995	6.8	6.8	6.9	6.8	6.9	6.9	6.9	7.0	7.0	6.9	6.9	6.8	6.9
1996	6.9	6.9	6.8	7.1	7.1	7.3	7.2	7.1	7.0	6.9	6.9	7.0	7.0
1997	7.0	7.0	7.0	7.0	6.9	7.1	7.0	7.0	7.0	7.0	7.0	7.0	7.0
1998	7.1	7.1	7.1	7.1	7.1	7.0	7.1	7.1	7.1	7.0	7.0	7.0	7.1
1999	6.9	6.9	6.9	7.0	7.0	7.0	7.0	7.0	7.0	6.9	6.9	6.9	7.0
2000	6.9	6.9	7.0	6.9	6.9	6.9	7.0	7.0	6.9	7.1	7.1	7.1	7.0
2001	7.2	7.2	7.2	7.1	7.1	7.1	7.1	7.1	7.1	7.1	7.1	7.1	7.1
2002	7.2	7.2	7.2	7.3	7.2	7.2	7.3	7.2	7.1	7.1	7.1	7.1	7.2
2003	7.1	7.0	7.0	7.0	7.0	7.1	6.9	6.9	6.9	6.8	6.9	7.0	7.0
Retail trade													
1990	18.6	18.7	18.9	18.7	18.7	18.8	18.7	18.8	19.0	18.9	19.5	19.7	18.9
1991	19.0	18.2	18.0	18.6	18.7	18.9	18.6	18.9	18.9	18.7	18.8	19.3	18.7
1992	18.0	17.7	17.9	18.3	18.5	18.6	18.6	18.9	18.8	18.9	19.5	20.0	18.6
1993	19.0	18.9	18.9	18.6	18.7	18.8	18.8	19.0	18.8	18.8	19.3	19.9	19.0
1994	18.9	18.8	19.0	19.0	19.1	19.2	19.4	19.4	19.5	19.6	20.2	20.8	19.4
1995	19.3	19.1	19.3	19.4	19.6	19.7	19.6	19.9	19.9	19.8	20.5	20.9	19.8
1996	20.1	19.5	19.3	19.7	19.9	20.3	20.0	20.0	20.0	19.8	20.4	20.8	20.0
1997	19.9	19.4	19.7	19.4	19.3	19.8	19.8	20.2	20.2	20.6	21.0	21.6	20.1
1998	20.1	19.9	20.0	20.3	20.3	20.5	20.2	20.4	20.5	20.5	20.9	21.2	20.4
1999	20.1	19.9	20.4	20.3	20.1	20.2	19.9	20.1	20.1	20.2	21.0	21.2	20.3
2000	20.4	20.5	20.8	20.2	20.4	20.6	20.0	20.1	20.1	20.2	20.8	21.4	20.5
2001	20.4	20.1	20.4	20.3	20.2	20.3	20.5	20.7	20.4	20.0	20.7	21.1	20.4
2002	20.0	19.9	20.0	19.9	19.9	20.3	20.1	20.1	20.0	20.0	20.6	20.9	20.1
2003	20.0	19.9	20.0	19.9	19.7	19.9	19.8	19.9	20.0	20.1	20.6	21.3	20.1
Transportation and utilities													
1990	6.4	6.6	6.7	6.7	6.8	6.9	6.9	6.9	6.9	6.7	6.7	6.6	6.7
1991	6.0	5.5	5.4	5.8	5.7	5.8	5.9	6.0	5.9	5.8	5.8	5.6	5.8
1992	5.3	5.2	5.4	5.4	5.5	5.5	5.3	5.3	5.3	5.3	5.3	5.3	5.3
1993	5.5	5.5	5.5	5.5	5.5	5.6	5.3	5.3	5.4	5.6	5.6	5.7	5.5
1994	5.7	5.7	5.8	5.9	5.9	5.9	5.9	5.9	5.9	5.8	5.8	5.8	5.8
1995	5.7	5.8	5.8	5.6	5.6	5.6	5.5	5.5	5.4	5.6	5.5	5.5	5.6
1996	5.3	5.4	5.2	5.3	5.4	5.4	5.3	5.3	5.4	5.3	5.3	5.3	5.3
1997	5.0	5.1	5.2	5.2	5.3	5.4	5.3	5.1	5.3	5.3	5.4	5.4	5.3
1998	5.2	5.3	5.3	5.2	5.3	5.3	5.2	5.3	5.2	5.0	5.0	4.9	5.2
1999	5.1	5.1	5.1	5.1	5.1	5.1	5.1	5.1	5.1	5.3	5.3	5.3	5.2
2000	5.2	5.2	5.2	5.3	5.4	5.4	5.4	5.4	5.3	5.3	5.3	5.3	5.3
2001	5.8	5.8	5.8	5.9	5.8	5.9	5.8	5.9	5.9	5.9	5.7	5.6	5.8
2002	5.4	5.5	5.5	6.2	6.4	6.4	5.6	5.7	5.6	5.1	5.1	4.9	5.6
2003	5.6	5.7	5.9	5.8	5.8	5.8	5.8	5.8	5.8	5.9	5.9	5.8	5.8

Employment by Industry: Louisiana—*Continued*

(Numbers in thousands. Not seasonally adjusted.)

Industry	January	February	March	April	May	June	July	August	September	October	November	December	Annual Average
SHREVEPORT—*Continued*													
Information													
1990	3.5	3.5	3.5	3.4	3.4	3.5	3.5	3.5	3.5	3.4	3.4	3.4	3.5
1991	3.2	3.2	3.1	3.2	3.1	3.2	3.2	3.2	3.1	3.0	3.0	3.1	3.1
1992	3.2	3.1	3.1	3.1	3.1	3.1	3.1	3.1	3.0	3.0	3.0	3.1	3.1
1993	3.1	3.1	3.0	3.0	3.0	3.0	3.0	3.0	3.0	3.0	2.9	2.9	3.0
1994	2.9	2.8	2.8	2.8	2.8	2.8	2.9	2.9	2.8	2.8	2.8	2.8	2.8
1995	2.7	2.7	2.7	2.7	2.7	2.8	2.8	2.8	2.7	2.7	2.8	2.8	2.7
1996	2.8	2.7	2.7	2.8	2.9	2.9	3.0	3.0	2.9	2.9	2.9	2.9	2.9
1997	2.9	2.9	2.8	2.9	2.9	3.0	3.0	2.9	2.9	2.9	2.9	2.9	2.9
1998	2.9	2.9	2.9	2.9	2.9	2.9	3.0	3.0	3.0	3.1	3.1	3.1	3.0
1999	2.9	2.9	2.9	3.1	3.2	3.2	3.2	3.2	3.1	3.1	3.1	3.1	3.1
2000	3.1	3.0	3.1	2.9	2.9	3.0	3.1	3.1	2.9	2.9	2.9	2.9	3.0
2001	2.9	2.9	2.9	2.8	2.8	2.8	3.1	3.1	3.1	3.1	3.1	3.1	2.9
2002	3.1	3.1	3.1	3.1	3.2	3.1	3.2	3.2	3.2	3.1	3.1	3.1	3.1
2003	3.1	3.0	3.0	3.0	3.0	3.0	3.0	3.0	3.0	3.0	3.0	2.9	3.0
Financial activities													
1990	7.6	7.8	7.8	7.8	7.8	8.0	8.0	7.9	7.9	7.8	7.8	7.8	7.8
1991	7.6	7.5	7.4	7.5	7.6	7.6	7.5	7.5	7.5	7.4	7.3	7.5	7.5
1992	7.4	7.4	7.4	7.3	7.3	7.4	7.3	7.4	7.3	7.3	7.3	7.4	7.4
1993	7.2	7.3	7.3	7.2	7.2	7.3	7.3	7.3	7.3	7.2	7.2	7.3	7.3
1994	7.3	7.3	7.4	7.1	7.1	7.1	7.3	7.2	7.1	6.9	6.9	7.0	7.1
1995	7.0	7.0	7.0	7.0	7.0	7.1	6.9	7.0	7.0	7.0	7.0	7.0	7.0
1996	7.1	7.2	7.2	7.2	7.2	7.4	7.4	7.4	7.3	7.2	7.2	7.3	7.3
1997	7.1	7.1	7.1	7.1	7.0	7.2	7.3	7.3	7.3	7.2	7.2	7.3	7.2
1998	7.0	7.0	7.0	7.0	7.1	7.1	7.1	7.1	7.1	7.1	7.1	7.2	7.1
1999	7.2	7.2	7.3	7.3	7.3	7.4	7.5	7.5	7.4	7.6	7.6	7.6	7.4
2000	7.4	7.4	7.4	7.5	7.6	7.6	7.7	7.8	7.7	7.9	8.0	8.0	7.7
2001	7.5	7.6	7.6	7.6	7.6	7.7	7.7	7.7	7.7	7.6	7.5	7.5	7.6
2002	7.7	7.7	7.7	7.8	7.8	7.7	7.7	7.7	7.7	7.8	7.7	7.7	7.7
2003	7.9	7.9	7.9	7.7	7.7	7.8	7.9	7.9	7.9	7.9	7.9	7.7	7.8
Professional and business services													
1990	7.0	7.2	7.2	7.7	7.7	7.7	8.1	8.2	8.2	7.9	7.9	7.8	7.7
1991	8.5	8.4	8.3	8.6	8.8	9.0	9.1	9.1	9.1	9.1	8.9	9.1	8.8
1992	9.4	9.5	9.7	9.8	10.1	10.3	9.6	9.9	9.9	9.9	9.8	9.8	9.8
1993	10.0	10.2	10.3	10.5	10.6	10.6	10.7	10.7	10.7	11.1	11.0	11.1	10.6
1994	10.4	10.9	11.1	11.4	11.2	11.5	11.4	11.7	11.7	11.7	11.4	11.4	11.3
1995	11.4	11.7	11.7	12.2	12.3	12.5	12.3	12.4	12.6	12.2	12.1	12.2	12.1
1996	12.2	12.6	12.5	12.4	12.3	12.5	12.6	12.6	12.6	12.7	12.5	12.7	12.5
1997	12.5	12.7	12.8	13.0	13.0	13.2	13.8	13.9	13.6	13.4	13.3	13.2	13.2
1998	13.4	13.7	13.9	13.8	13.7	13.8	14.1	14.4	14.3	13.6	13.5	13.5	13.8
1999	14.5	14.6	14.6	14.7	14.5	14.8	14.9	15.2	15.0	15.5	14.8	14.7	14.8
2000	15.3	15.2	15.6	15.5	15.2	15.2	15.6	15.6	15.5	15.4	14.9	15.0	15.3
2001	15.4	15.4	15.3	15.3	14.7	15.0	14.4	14.4	14.3	14.1	14.2	14.2	14.7
2002	14.3	14.4	14.2	14.5	14.5	13.7	13.0	13.3	13.4	13.5	13.0	12.9	13.7
2003	13.3	13.3	13.3	13.7	13.6	13.4	12.8	13.0	13.2	13.4	13.4	13.4	13.3
Educational and health services													
1990	16.5	16.9	17.0	17.1	17.1	16.9	16.8	16.7	17.1	18.0	18.3	18.0	17.2
1991	18.4	18.4	18.2	18.3	18.4	18.0	18.1	18.3	18.8	19.1	18.8	19.0	18.5
1992	19.0	19.2	19.5	19.6	19.4	19.3	19.4	19.6	20.2	20.3	20.3	20.4	19.7
1993	20.0	20.3	20.4	20.7	20.5	20.5	20.1	20.2	20.8	21.1	21.1	21.2	20.6
1994	21.6	21.9	22.2	22.0	22.1	22.0	21.6	21.6	22.1	22.4	22.4	22.4	22.0
1995	21.6	22.1	22.2	22.0	22.0	22.0	21.5	21.5	22.1	22.3	22.5	22.2	22.0
1996	22.1	22.4	22.3	22.8	22.7	22.6	22.5	22.7	22.9	23.2	23.3	23.4	22.7
1997	23.0	23.4	23.4	23.8	23.5	23.6	23.2	23.4	23.7	23.7	23.7	23.8	23.5
1998	23.3	23.5	23.6	23.7	23.5	23.3	23.4	23.4	23.7	23.5	23.6	23.6	23.5
1999	22.9	23.2	23.4	24.1	24.0	23.9	23.4	23.6	24.0	24.0	24.1	24.1	23.7
2000	23.5	23.6	23.8	23.3	23.0	22.8	23.1	23.1	23.6	23.7	23.7	23.5	23.4
2001	22.2	22.4	22.6	22.8	22.9	23.0	22.7	22.8	22.9	23.1	23.1	23.2	22.8
2002	23.2	23.2	23.4	23.4	23.5	23.4	23.4	23.5	23.5	23.7	23.8	23.8	23.5
2003	23.8	23.8	23.6	23.7	23.8	23.5	23.3	23.5	23.7	24.0	23.9	23.7	23.7
Leisure and hospitality													
1990	10.4	10.7	11.0	11.2	12.7	13.0	13.0	12.9	12.7	11.8	10.8	11.0	11.8
1991	10.7	10.6	10.9	11.4	12.5	12.8	12.5	12.4	12.1	12.1	11.0	11.2	11.7
1992	11.1	11.1	11.6	11.7	12.6	13.0	12.8	12.7	12.4	12.5	12.3	11.7	12.1
1993	11.3	11.4	11.6	12.3	13.1	13.5	13.1	13.1	12.8	12.3	12.4	12.1	12.4
1994	11.6	12.0	12.6	14.3	16.1	17.0	17.2	17.9	17.7	17.0	17.1	16.6	15.6
1995	16.0	16.1	16.6	17.8	18.7	19.2	18.8	19.0	18.5	18.3	17.7	17.8	17.9
1996	17.1	17.3	17.8	18.6	19.4	19.6	19.6	19.5	19.8	19.5	19.1	19.1	18.9
1997	18.4	19.0	19.4	19.8	19.9	20.4	20.8	20.7	20.4	20.3	20.5	20.4	20.0
1998	19.5	19.7	20.4	21.5	21.7	22.0	21.9	21.9	21.6	21.4	21.8	21.6	21.3
1999	20.9	20.8	21.3	21.9	22.6	22.9	22.8	23.1	22.7	22.2	22.0	22.3	22.1
2000	21.6	21.7	22.2	22.1	22.5	22.9	23.1	23.2	23.1	22.7	22.7	22.5	22.5
2001	23.6	23.8	24.2	24.1	24.5	24.6	23.6	23.8	23.5	23.3	22.8	22.4	23.6
2002	22.0	22.1	22.4	22.5	23.0	23.2	23.6	23.8	23.8	23.1	23.1	23.1	23.0
2003	22.6	22.5	22.8	23.2	23.7	23.8	24.1	24.0	23.5	23.6	23.6	23.7	23.4

Employment by Industry: Louisiana—*Continued*

(Numbers in thousands. Not seasonally adjusted.)

Industry	January	February	March	April	May	June	July	August	September	October	November	December	Annual Average
SHREVEPORT—*Continued*													
Other services													
1990	5.5	5.7	5.8	6.0	6.1	6.1	6.2	6.2	6.2	6.1	6.1	6.1	6.0
1991	6.2	6.1	6.1	6.1	6.2	6.3	6.4	6.3	6.4	6.5	6.5	6.5	6.3
1992	6.3	6.3	6.3	6.4	6.5	6.6	6.6	6.5	6.7	6.6	6.6	6.7	6.5
1993	6.6	6.8	6.8	6.8	6.8	6.9	6.9	6.8	6.9	7.0	7.1	7.0	6.9
1994	6.6	6.7	6.7	6.7	6.7	7.0	7.0	6.8	6.9	6.8	6.8	6.8	6.8
1995	7.0	7.0	7.1	7.1	7.1	7.3	7.4	7.3	7.3	7.3	7.3	7.3	7.2
1996	7.2	7.3	7.2	7.2	7.3	7.4	7.2	7.2	7.4	7.3	7.3	7.3	7.3
1997	7.2	7.3	7.4	7.5	7.4	7.6	7.5	7.5	7.5	7.3	7.4	7.5	7.4
1998	7.4	7.4	7.4	7.6	7.7	7.9	7.7	7.7	7.7	7.7	7.6	7.7	7.6
1999	7.7	7.8	7.9	8.0	8.0	8.1	7.9	8.0	8.0	8.1	8.3	8.4	8.0
2000	8.2	8.2	8.3	8.2	8.3	8.2	8.2	8.5	8.5	8.4	8.3	8.3	8.3
2001	8.6	8.6	8.6	8.7	8.7	8.6	8.4	8.5	8.5	8.4	8.4	8.3	8.5
2002	8.3	8.3	8.3	8.4	8.4	8.5	8.4	8.4	8.4	8.2	8.2	8.2	8.3
2003	8.0	7.9	8.0	8.0	8.1	8.1	8.0	8.0	8.0	8.0	7.9	7.8	8.0
Government													
1990	28.5	28.6	28.7	29.2	29.4	28.0	26.5	26.3	28.4	28.9	28.6	28.6	28.3
1991	29.0	29.4	29.4	29.6	29.7	29.7	27.2	27.3	29.2	29.6	29.7	29.9	29.1
1992	29.7	29.9	29.9	30.0	30.3	30.0	27.4	27.3	29.9	30.6	30.7	30.8	29.7
1993	30.9	31.0	30.9	31.1	31.0	30.9	30.6	30.3	31.1	31.3	31.2	31.2	31.0
1994	30.9	31.0	31.0	31.1	31.1	31.2	29.7	29.4	31.0	31.6	31.6	31.7	30.9
1995	31.8	32.0	32.0	32.4	31.9	31.8	30.8	30.3	31.9	32.2	32.2	32.2	31.8
1996	32.3	32.4	32.6	32.8	32.7	32.5	31.1	30.8	32.3	32.8	32.8	32.7	32.3
1997	32.6	32.6	32.8	32.8	32.6	33.4	32.0	30.8	31.8	32.7	33.1	32.7	32.5
1998	32.8	33.0	33.2	33.3	33.2	33.8	32.8	32.1	32.5	33.0	33.2	32.9	33.0
1999	32.8	33.0	33.2	33.0	33.0	33.7	33.2	31.9	32.7	32.6	32.5	32.4	32.8
2000	32.3	32.6	32.7	32.7	33.3	32.4	31.5	30.9	31.9	32.5	32.4	32.1	32.3
2001	32.0	32.3	32.3	32.0	32.1	32.3	30.9	30.9	31.8	32.2	32.3	31.8	31.9
2002	31.7	31.9	32.1	32.6	32.6	32.8	32.2	32.0	32.8	33.1	33.1	33.3	32.5
2003	33.0	33.4	33.5	33.0	33.0	33.5	32.9	33.0	33.0	33.6	33.8	33.6	33.3
Federal government													
1990	5.1	5.0	5.1	5.3	5.7	5.3	5.4	5.2	5.2	5.2	5.0	5.1	5.2
1991	5.1	5.0	5.1	5.1	5.2	5.3	5.2	5.3	5.3	5.0	5.0	5.1	5.1
1992	5.0	5.0	5.0	5.0	5.0	5.0	5.0	5.0	5.0	5.0	5.1	5.1	5.0
1993	5.1	5.1	5.0	5.1	5.0	5.1	5.2	5.2	5.1	5.1	5.0	4.9	5.1
1994	4.8	4.8	4.8	4.8	4.7	4.8	4.8	4.7	4.7	4.7	4.7	4.8	4.8
1995	4.7	4.7	4.6	4.7	4.7	4.7	4.8	4.8	4.8	4.8	4.7	4.8	4.7
1996	4.9	4.9	4.9	4.9	4.8	4.9	4.9	4.9	4.9	4.9	4.9	4.9	4.9
1997	4.9	4.8	4.8	4.8	4.8	4.8	4.8	4.8	4.7	4.7	4.8	4.8	4.8
1998	4.7	4.7	4.8	4.8	4.8	4.8	4.8	4.8	4.8	4.8	4.8	4.8	4.8
1999	4.8	4.8	4.8	4.7	4.7	4.8	4.8	4.8	4.7	4.8	4.7	4.8	4.8
2000	4.8	4.8	4.9	4.9	5.6	4.9	5.2	4.9	4.8	4.9	4.8	4.8	4.9
2001	4.7	4.7	4.7	4.7	4.7	4.8	4.9	4.8	4.7	4.8	4.7	4.7	4.7
2002	4.7	4.6	4.5	4.5	4.5	4.6	4.6	4.6	4.6	4.8	4.8	4.8	4.6
2003	4.8	4.8	4.8	4.7	4.7	4.8	4.8	4.8	4.7	4.7	4.6	4.7	4.7
State government													
1990	7.0	7.0	7.0	7.1	6.9	6.8	6.7	6.7	7.0	7.3	7.2	7.1	7.0
1991	7.2	7.3	7.4	7.4	7.2	7.1	7.3	7.2	7.4	7.6	7.6	7.6	7.4
1992	7.6	7.6	7.6	7.7	7.8	7.5	7.7	7.4	7.8	8.3	8.2	8.2	7.8
1993	8.4	8.4	8.4	8.5	8.5	8.4	8.3	8.2	8.5	8.5	8.5	8.5	8.4
1994	8.4	8.4	8.5	8.3	8.4	8.3	8.2	8.1	8.6	8.7	8.7	8.7	8.4
1995	8.7	8.8	8.8	9.0	8.5	8.3	8.3	8.2	8.4	8.4	8.3	8.3	8.5
1996	8.3	8.3	8.4	8.6	8.5	8.2	8.4	8.4	8.5	8.4	8.4	8.3	8.4
1997	8.3	8.3	8.4	8.4	8.3	8.2	8.7	8.6	8.8	9.1	9.2	9.0	8.6
1998	9.0	9.1	9.1	9.3	9.1	8.9	9.2	9.0	9.2	9.1	9.2	8.9	9.1
1999	8.8	9.0	9.1	9.1	9.0	8.8	9.3	9.0	9.2	9.2	9.2	9.0	9.1
2000	8.8	9.1	9.0	9.0	8.9	8.7	8.9	8.7	8.9	9.0	9.0	8.8	8.9
2001	8.7	8.9	8.8	8.7	8.7	8.6	8.5	8.5	8.8	8.8	8.9	8.8	8.7
2002	8.6	8.8	9.0	9.5	9.3	9.4	9.3	9.6	10.0	9.9	9.8	9.7	9.4
2003	9.6	10.0	10.0	9.7	9.6	9.8	9.7	9.9	10.3	10.3	10.4	9.7	9.9
Local government													
1990	16.4	16.6	16.6	16.8	16.8	15.9	14.4	14.4	16.2	16.4	16.4	16.4	16.1
1991	16.7	17.1	16.9	17.1	17.3	17.3	14.7	14.8	16.5	17.0	17.1	17.2	16.6
1992	17.1	17.3	17.3	17.3	17.5	17.5	14.7	14.9	17.1	17.3	17.4	17.5	16.9
1993	17.4	17.5	17.5	17.5	17.5	17.4	17.1	16.9	17.5	17.7	17.7	17.8	17.5
1994	17.7	17.8	17.7	18.0	18.0	18.1	16.7	16.6	17.7	18.2	18.2	18.2	17.7
1995	18.4	18.5	18.6	18.7	18.7	18.8	17.7	17.3	18.7	19.0	19.2	19.1	18.6
1996	19.1	19.2	19.3	19.3	19.4	19.4	17.8	17.5	18.9	19.5	19.5	19.5	19.0
1997	19.4	19.5	19.6	19.6	19.5	20.4	18.5	17.4	18.3	18.9	19.1	18.9	19.1
1998	19.1	19.2	19.3	19.2	19.3	20.1	18.8	18.3	18.5	19.1	19.2	19.2	19.1
1999	19.2	19.2	19.3	19.2	19.3	20.1	19.1	18.1	18.8	18.6	18.6	18.6	19.0
2000	18.7	18.7	18.8	18.8	18.8	18.8	17.4	17.3	18.2	18.6	18.6	18.5	18.4
2001	18.6	18.7	18.8	18.6	18.7	18.9	17.5	17.6	18.3	18.6	18.7	18.3	18.4
2002	18.4	18.5	18.6	18.6	18.8	18.8	18.3	17.8	18.2	18.4	18.5	18.8	18.5
2003	18.6	18.6	18.7	18.6	18.7	18.9	18.4	18.3	18.0	18.6	18.8	19.2	18.6

Average Weekly Hours by Industry: Louisiana

(Not seasonally adjusted.)

Industry	January	February	March	April	May	June	July	August	September	October	November	December	Annual Average
STATEWIDE													
Natural resources and mining													
2001	50.1	49.8	42.5	43.4	43.3	41.9	44.9	47.0	47.4	45.1	46.5	44.4	45.5
2002	48.0	49.4	42.8	43.7	47.5	51.9	52.0	47.0	51.0	45.1	40.9	43.1	46.9
2003	40.3	47.3	51.5	47.8	48.7	48.2	49.9	52.7	50.7	53.5	46.1	49.0	48.8
Manufacturing													
2001	40.9	42.5	42.5	41.4	43.4	43.9	43.3	43.6	43.4	43.8	44.1	44.0	43.1
2002	42.2	40.7	43.9	43.2	43.7	45.1	44.4	44.6	45.3	43.7	44.9	44.5	43.9
2003	43.0	42.8	42.3	43.7	44.7	44.5	43.6	44.2	45.4	45.2	45.0	44.5	44.1
Financial activities													
2001	40.2	41.6	40.5	39.3	38.7	40.1	39.0	39.0	40.8	40.0	39.7	41.9	40.1
2002	40.4	41.9	42.0	40.3	40.2	43.7	40.6	40.6	42.8	39.5	38.7	42.0	41.0
2003	39.5	40.1	41.1	38.4	38.8	41.2	38.3	37.1	38.6	38.2	37.7	37.3	38.9
BATON ROUGE													
Manufacturing													
2001	45.5	44.7	43.6	43.7	42.5	44.0	43.0	43.0	43.0	44.8	44.8	45.9	44.1
2002	43.8	42.1	43.4	43.1	43.0	45.5	43.2	44.5	43.1	45.2	44.7	43.0	43.7
2003	42.7	42.8	44.4	42.5	44.2	42.9	42.3	41.5	41.7	46.4	43.6	44.7	43.3
NEW ORLEANS													
Manufacturing													
2001	45.1	45.7	46.4	45.6	46.2	45.8	45.8	45.5	46.2	45.8	46.0	45.4	45.8
2002	45.5	45.4	45.3	45.7	45.5	45.6	45.8	45.9	46.0	46.3	46.5	46.7	45.9
2003	45.2	46.0	46.3	45.8	45.7	45.9	43.7	43.5	44.3	44.4	44.0	44.4	44.9

Average Hourly Earnings by Industry: Louisiana

(Dollars, not seasonally adjusted.)

Industry	January	February	March	April	May	June	July	August	September	October	November	December	Annual Average
STATEWIDE													
Natural resources and mining													
2001	16.17	16.23	16.42	16.34	16.00	16.04	16.18	14.66	14.62	14.71	14.78	15.93	15.66
2002	14.93	15.71	15.35	15.01	14.90	14.78	15.82	15.23	15.81	15.51	16.70	16.58	15.50
2003	17.05	16.51	16.00	16.55	15.98	16.60	16.50	17.05	16.52	16.95	16.35	17.77	16.66
Manufacturing													
2001	15.84	15.82	15.84	16.21	16.16	16.11	16.19	16.05	16.31	16.27	16.51	16.81	16.18
2002	16.53	16.95	16.94	17.16	17.09	17.15	17.03	16.93	16.90	16.93	17.20	17.56	17.03
2003	17.10	17.58	17.21	17.03	17.07	17.21	16.78	16.55	16.68	16.35	16.08	16.78	16.86
Financial activities													
2001	12.01	12.12	12.83	12.49	12.20	12.22	12.83	12.73	12.94	12.49	12.48	12.51	12.49
2002	12.52	12.21	12.60	12.61	12.65	12.57	12.84	13.05	12.89	13.15	13.36	12.99	12.78
2003	13.48	13.84	13.29	13.95	13.73	14.04	14.02	13.83	13.62	13.62	13.82	13.52	13.73
BATON ROUGE													
Manufacturing													
2001	16.77	17.62	17.35	18.00	17.76	17.83	18.56	17.79	19.35	18.24	18.09	18.57	17.99
2002	19.22	20.20	19.04	20.07	18.89	18.99	17.97	18.15	18.45	17.72	17.31	17.86	18.63
2003	17.87	17.51	17.02	18.05	17.67	17.52	17.09	17.06	18.26	17.63	17.76	17.49	17.57
NEW ORLEANS													
Manufacturing													
2001	17.21	16.92	16.88	16.99	17.09	16.69	16.86	16.80	17.03	16.98	17.11	17.05	16.97
2002	17.05	17.00	16.78	17.31	17.05	17.01	17.23	17.13	17.36	18.13	17.74	17.76	17.30
2003	17.40	17.85	17.99	16.96	17.10	16.86	16.78	16.14	16.63	16.50	16.14	16.40	16.91

Average Weekly Earnings by Industry: Louisiana

(Dollars, not seasonally adjusted.)

Industry	January	February	March	April	May	June	July	August	September	October	November	December	Annual Average
STATEWIDE													
Natural resources and mining													
2001	810.12	808.25	697.85	709.16	692.80	672.08	726.48	689.02	692.99	663.42	687.27	707.29	712.53
2002	716.64	776.07	656.98	655.94	707.75	767.08	822.64	715.81	806.31	699.50	683.03	714.60	726.95
2003	687.12	780.92	824.00	791.09	778.23	800.12	823.35	898.54	837.56	906.83	753.74	870.73	813.01
Manufacturing													
2001	647.86	672.35	673.20	671.09	701.34	707.23	701.03	699.78	707.85	712.63	728.09	739.64	697.36
2002	697.57	689.87	743.67	741.31	746.83	773.47	756.13	755.08	765.57	739.84	772.28	781.42	747.62
2003	735.30	752.42	727.98	744.21	763.03	765.85	731.61	731.51	757.27	739.02	723.60	746.71	743.53
Financial activities													
2001	482.80	504.19	519.62	490.86	472.14	490.02	500.37	496.47	527.95	499.60	495.46	524.17	500.85
2002	505.81	511.60	529.20	508.18	508.53	549.31	521.30	529.83	551.69	519.43	517.03	545.58	523.98
2003	532.46	554.98	546.22	535.68	532.72	578.45	536.97	513.09	525.73	520.28	521.01	504.30	534.10
BATON ROUGE													
Manufacturing													
2001	763.04	787.61	756.46	786.60	754.80	784.52	798.08	764.97	832.05	817.15	810.43	852.36	793.36
2002	841.84	850.42	826.34	865.02	812.27	864.05	776.30	807.68	795.20	800.94	773.76	767.98	814.13
2003	763.05	749.43	755.69	767.13	781.01	751.61	722.91	707.99	761.44	818.03	774.34	781.80	760.78
NEW ORLEANS													
Manufacturing													
2001	776.17	773.24	783.23	774.74	789.56	764.40	772.19	764.40	786.79	777.68	787.06	774.07	777.23
2002	775.78	771.80	760.13	791.07	775.78	775.66	789.13	786.27	798.56	839.42	824.91	829.39	794.07
2003	786.48	821.10	832.94	776.77	781.47	773.87	733.29	702.09	736.71	732.60	710.16	728.16	759.26

MAINE AT A GLANCE

(Population and total nonfarm employment numbers in thousands)

Population, Census 2000:	1,274.9
Total nonfarm employment, 2003:	606.1
Change in total nonfarm employment	
(Number)	
1990–2003:	71.1
1990–2001:	73.1
2001–2003:	-2.0
(Compound annual rate of change)	
1990–2003:	1.0%
1990–2001:	1.2%
2001–2003:	-0.2%
Unemployment rate	
1990:	5.3%
2001:	3.9%
2003:	5.0%

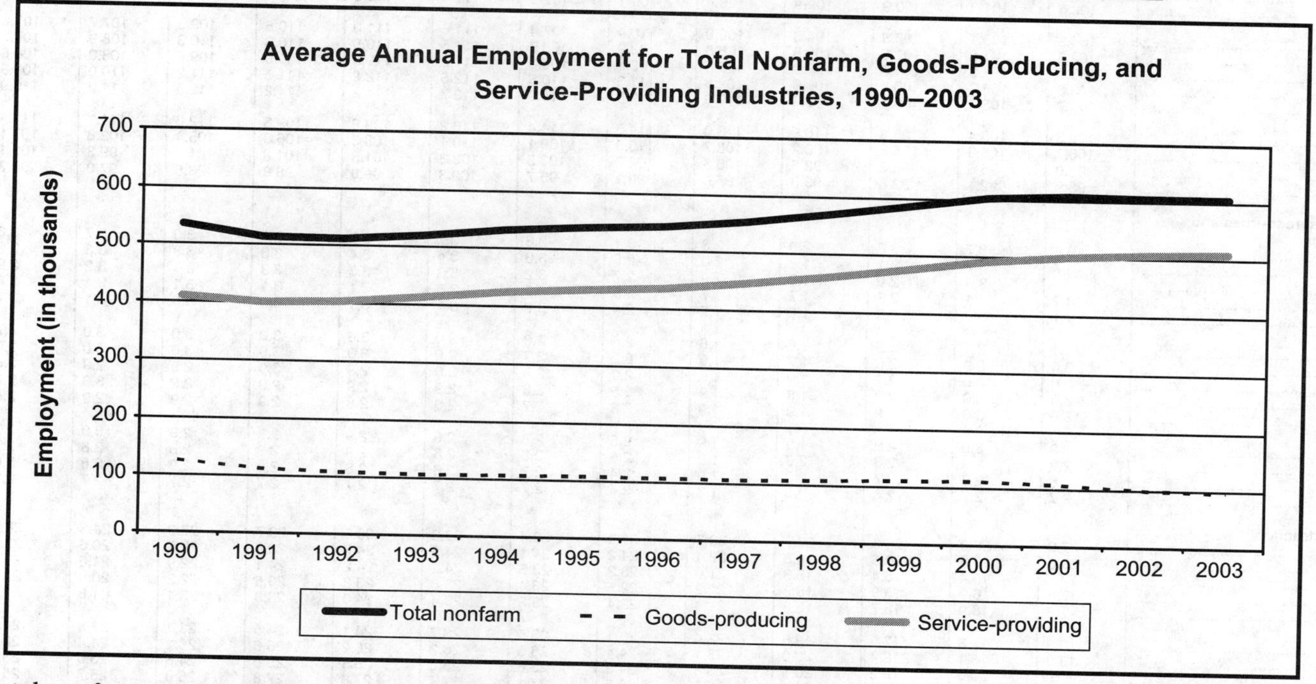

Total nonfarm payroll employment declined during the 1990–1991 recession, but recovered throughout the decade. Employment in the goods-producing sector declined sharply in the 1990–1991 period, remained sluggish throughout the rest of the decade, and then fell again following the 2001 recession. In 2003, goods-producing industries employed 28,400 fewer people than they had in 1990. Much of this decline can be attributed to a 31 percent drop in manufacturing employment from 1990 to 2003. Similarly, the service-producing sector weakened during the 1990 to 1991 contraction and slowed considerably during the 2001 recession. However, employment in the service-producing industries increased nearly 100,000 from 1990 to 2003.

Employment by Industry: Maine

(Numbers in thousands. Not seasonally adjusted.)

Industry	January	February	March	April	May	June	July	August	September	October	November	December	Annual Average
STATEWIDE													
Total nonfarm													
1990	526.0	522.8	525.1	530.2	541.1	554.4	542.1	540.7	541.4	539.7	530.9	525.6	535.0
1991	506.6	500.3	498.5	503.5	513.5	525.2	517.6	522.6	524.0	521.8	516.9	511.3	513.4
1992	490.3	490.2	490.7	498.9	510.5	523.2	520.5	523.9	526.7	527.2	522.6	518.0	511.8
1993	493.5	495.0	498.1	506.5	519.7	530.8	525.7	530.2	533.9	537.1	532.7	529.1	519.3
1994	506.5	508.3	510.9	518.4	531.5	542.9	536.7	541.1	547.1	547.0	545.4	543.0	531.5
1995	516.8	520.8	522.3	528.7	542.8	553.2	540.6	547.3	550.5	548.9	545.0	540.7	538.1
1996	519.5	521.0	522.7	529.3	541.0	554.3	549.2	553.9	555.5	554.5	555.5	552.8	542.4
1997	527.2	528.9	532.2	539.5	553.3	565.9	560.9	565.8	568.8	567.6	567.5	567.3	553.7
1998	537.4	545.9	547.6	557.2	569.5	582.4	575.9	578.9	584.6	584.4	583.0	582.9	569.1
1999	556.0	562.1	565.6	574.5	584.5	599.2	595.1	597.1	601.1	605.3	597.9	597.3	586.3
2000	576.1	580.2	586.0	593.8	606.9	617.8	615.8	614.4	614.7	611.5	612.8	611.7	603.4
2001	588.5	590.3	592.6	601.5	613.1	625.2	618.0	618.4	618.0	614.6	610.4	607.1	608.1
2002	583.7	585.5	588.9	598.3	610.4	622.3	618.5	618.2	617.1	614.2	610.5	609.9	606.5
2003	584.0	585.1	587.8	594.9	608.1	618.2	617.1	618.9	617.8	615.9	613.2	612.6	606.1
Total private													
1990	429.4	425.4	426.9	431.0	441.8	456.9	456.8	456.9	446.5	441.6	430.9	426.5	439.2
1991	409.5	401.2	399.5	404.5	414.8	428.5	433.6	439.4	428.8	423.2	416.4	412.0	417.6
1992	394.4	391.8	391.7	399.8	411.8	425.5	436.5	441.1	431.4	428.2	422.3	419.8	416.1
1993	397.7	396.2	398.6	408.0	421.9	435.0	441.9	447.7	439.8	438.3	432.7	430.2	424.0
1994	412.6	410.8	412.9	421.0	433.8	447.2	454.0	460.0	454.4	450.5	446.5	445.5	437.4
1995	423.8	424.0	425.6	431.8	445.9	459.1	459.5	466.6	458.7	452.9	447.1	444.1	444.9
1996	427.0	425.1	426.1	433.4	446.2	459.7	467.8	472.9	463.7	459.2	457.8	456.5	449.6
1997	434.9	433.3	435.8	443.0	457.9	471.9	480.4	484.9	476.8	471.2	469.4	469.7	460.7
1998	445.4	447.9	450.0	459.7	473.1	486.2	493.1	496.8	490.6	485.5	483.1	482.6	474.5
1999	460.6	463.1	465.9	475.2	486.4	502.1	510.3	513.2	503.0	504.6	496.0	495.0	489.6
2000	478.7	479.0	482.2	491.5	502.7	517.0	528.3	528.4	515.0	508.7	508.4	507.0	503.9
2001	488.0	486.4	488.3	496.8	508.0	522.1	528.1	528.7	515.5	508.4	503.5	499.4	506.1
2002	481.8	480.3	482.7	492.8	504.1	517.6	526.8	527.6	514.5	508.1	502.7	501.9	503.4
2003	481.1	478.6	480.8	488.2	501.4	513.7	525.6	528.0	515.1	509.7	505.1	504.2	502.6
Goods-producing													
1990	124.0	122.3	122.3	123.0	126.9	130.6	128.0	131.6	128.0	125.5	121.2	118.0	125.1
1991	112.4	109.2	108.0	108.7	111.9	115.8	113.9	117.2	116.0	114.9	113.8	111.0	112.7
1992	104.0	102.5	101.8	103.6	107.7	110.6	110.3	114.0	113.1	111.8	110.2	108.2	108.1
1993	101.6	100.4	100.3	101.7	105.4	108.3	108.1	111.6	109.8	110.4	109.1	107.5	106.1
1994	102.8	101.3	100.9	102.9	106.4	109.1	107.5	111.5	112.0	111.1	111.4	109.7	107.2
1995	104.9	103.1	102.8	104.3	108.0	110.4	107.4	111.6	111.0	110.6	109.5	107.7	107.6
1996	102.9	101.2	101.3	102.8	106.5	108.9	108.7	111.5	110.9	110.3	110.3	108.9	107.0
1997	103.0	101.3	101.3	102.2	106.5	109.1	108.3	111.2	110.3	109.0	109.5	108.0	106.6
1998	103.8	103.7	103.8	106.0	109.6	111.3	110.5	112.5	112.2	111.5	111.2	110.0	108.8
1999	105.7	105.2	106.1	108.3	110.6	113.8	114.0	115.7	114.2	114.2	112.9	111.2	110.9
2000	108.3	108.4	108.8	110.9	113.0	114.5	114.4	116.2	109.9	109.3	112.6	111.1	111.4
2001	106.7	105.3	105.8	106.2	108.7	110.9	109.1	110.1	108.3	106.0	105.4	102.8	107.1
2002	98.0	96.5	96.3	98.5	100.5	102.7	101.5	103.3	101.8	101.3	101.2	99.3	100.1
2003	93.9	92.1	92.6	93.8	97.0	99.1	98.7	100.3	99.0	98.8	98.5	97.0	96.7
Natural resources and mining													
1990	3.8	3.7	3.3	2.0	2.3	3.1	3.6	3.7	3.7	3.6	3.6	3.7	3.3
1991	3.7	3.7	3.1	1.8	2.0	2.8	3.3	3.4	3.4	3.3	3.3	3.3	3.0
1992	3.5	3.5	2.9	1.9	1.9	2.7	3.2	3.3	3.3	3.3	3.1	3.2	2.9
1993	3.2	3.1	2.7	1.7	1.7	2.5	2.9	3.0	3.1	3.1	3.1	3.1	2.7
1994	3.1	3.0	2.8	1.8	1.6	2.4	2.9	3.1	3.1	3.0	3.0	3.1	2.7
1995	3.1	3.1	2.9	1.8	1.8	2.5	2.8	3.0	3.0	3.0	3.0	3.0	2.7
1996	3.0	2.9	2.6	1.7	1.6	2.2	2.7	2.9	3.0	3.0	3.0	3.0	2.6
1997	3.0	3.0	2.7	1.9	1.6	2.2	2.8	3.0	2.9	3.0	2.9	2.9	2.6
1998	3.0	3.0	2.6	1.8	1.9	2.5	2.8	2.9	2.9	2.9	2.9	3.0	2.6
1999	3.0	3.0	2.9	1.9	1.9	2.3	2.7	2.8	2.8	2.9	2.9	2.9	2.6
2000	2.9	3.0	2.8	1.9	1.9	2.5	2.8	2.9	2.9	2.9	2.9	3.0	2.7
2001	2.9	2.9	2.8	2.0	1.9	2.5	2.8	2.8	2.9	2.8	2.8	2.8	2.7
2002	2.8	2.8	2.7	2.0	1.9	2.4	2.7	2.8	2.8	2.8	2.8	2.8	2.6
2003	2.7	2.7	2.6	2.0	1.8	2.4	2.7	2.7	2.7	2.7	2.7	2.7	2.5
Construction													
1990	27.0	26.0	26.3	27.7	30.7	31.8	32.4	32.2	30.6	29.7	27.0	24.3	28.8
1991	20.6	18.8	18.5	19.8	22.4	24.2	24.1	24.5	24.7	23.8	22.6	20.5	22.0
1992	17.2	16.4	16.4	18.3	21.6	23.2	23.5	24.2	24.2	24.1	22.9	21.6	21.1
1993	17.8	16.9	16.9	18.3	21.2	22.5	23.4	23.8	23.3	23.6	22.2	20.9	20.9
1994	17.7	16.9	16.7	18.6	21.4	22.4	23.2	23.4	24.0	23.8	23.1	21.8	21.0
1995	18.3	17.8	17.9	19.6	22.4	23.1	23.5	23.7	24.1	24.5	23.1	21.8	21.6
1996	18.9	18.1	18.4	20.0	23.1	24.4	25.5	26.2	26.2	26.6	26.1	24.4	23.1
1997	20.9	20.0	19.9	20.8	23.8	24.9	25.6	25.8	25.5	25.0	24.5	23.0	23.3
1998	20.8	20.4	20.8	23.1	26.0	26.5	27.1	27.4	27.8	27.8	26.8	25.7	25.0
1999	23.2	22.7	23.2	26.0	28.0	30.1	31.7	31.6	30.5	30.2	28.6	27.4	27.7
2000	25.7	25.4	25.8	28.4	30.2	30.8	31.7	31.7	31.2	31.0	29.9	28.8	29.2
2001	26.6	26.1	26.7	28.3	30.8	32.0	32.5	32.2	31.7	31.3	30.6	29.0	29.8
2002	26.4	25.5	25.6	28.0	30.1	31.2	31.7	31.8	31.3	31.4	30.8	29.5	29.4
2003	27.0	26.0	26.5	28.5	31.3	32.6	33.1	33.1	32.5	32.4	31.8	30.5	30.4

Employment by Industry: Maine—*Continued*

(Numbers in thousands. Not seasonally adjusted.)

Industry	January	February	March	April	May	June	July	August	September	October	November	December	Annual Average
STATEWIDE—*Continued*													
Manufacturing													
1990	93.2	92.6	92.7	93.3	93.9	95.7	92.0	95.7	93.7	92.2	90.6	90.0	92.9
1991	88.1	86.7	86.4	87.1	87.5	88.8	86.5	89.3	87.9	87.8	87.9	87.2	87.6
1992	83.3	82.6	82.5	83.4	84.2	84.7	83.6	86.5	85.6	84.4	84.2	83.4	84.0
1993	80.6	80.4	80.7	81.7	82.5	83.3	81.8	84.8	83.4	83.7	83.8	83.5	82.5
1994	82.0	81.4	81.4	82.5	83.4	84.3	81.4	85.0	84.9	84.3	85.3	84.8	83.3
1995	83.5	82.2	82.0	82.9	83.8	84.8	81.1	84.9	83.9	83.1	83.4	82.9	83.2
1996	81.0	80.2	80.3	81.1	81.8	82.3	80.5	82.4	81.7	80.7	81.2	81.5	81.2
1997	79.1	78.3	78.7	79.5	81.1	82.0	79.9	82.4	81.9	81.0	82.1	82.1	80.6
1998	80.0	80.3	80.4	81.1	81.7	82.3	80.6	82.2	81.5	80.8	81.5	81.3	81.1
1999	79.5	79.5	80.0	80.4	80.7	81.4	79.6	81.3	80.9	81.1	81.4	80.9	80.5
2000	79.7	80.0	80.2	80.6	80.9	81.2	79.9	81.6	75.8	75.4	79.8	79.3	79.5
2001	77.2	76.3	76.3	75.9	76.0	76.4	73.8	75.1	73.7	71.9	72.0	71.0	74.6
2002	68.8	68.2	68.0	68.5	68.5	69.1	67.1	68.7	67.7	67.1	67.6	67.0	68.0
2003	64.2	63.4	63.5	63.3	63.9	64.1	62.9	64.5	63.8	63.7	64.0	63.8	63.8
Service-providing													
1990	402.0	400.5	402.8	407.2	414.2	423.8	414.1	409.1	413.4	414.2	409.7	407.6	409.8
1991	394.2	391.1	390.5	394.8	401.6	409.4	403.7	405.4	408.0	406.9	403.1	400.3	400.7
1992	386.3	387.7	388.9	395.3	402.8	412.6	410.2	409.9	413.6	415.4	412.4	409.8	403.7
1993	391.9	394.6	397.8	404.8	414.3	422.5	417.6	418.6	424.1	426.7	423.6	421.6	413.1
1994	403.7	407.0	410.0	415.5	425.1	433.8	429.2	429.6	435.1	435.9	434.0	433.3	424.3
1995	411.9	417.7	419.5	424.4	434.8	442.8	433.2	435.7	439.5	438.3	435.5	433.0	430.5
1996	416.6	419.8	421.4	426.5	434.5	445.4	440.5	442.4	444.6	444.2	445.2	443.9	435.4
1997	424.2	427.6	430.9	437.3	446.8	456.8	452.6	454.6	458.5	458.6	458.0	459.3	447.1
1998	433.6	442.2	443.8	451.2	459.9	471.1	465.4	466.4	472.4	472.9	471.8	472.9	460.3
1999	450.3	456.9	459.5	466.2	473.9	485.4	481.1	481.4	486.9	491.1	485.0	486.1	475.3
2000	467.8	471.8	477.2	482.9	493.9	503.3	501.4	498.2	504.8	502.2	500.2	500.6	492.0
2001	481.8	485.0	486.8	495.3	504.4	514.3	508.9	508.3	509.7	508.6	505.0	504.3	501.0
2002	485.7	489.0	492.6	499.8	509.9	519.6	517.0	514.9	515.3	512.9	509.3	510.6	506.4
2003	490.1	493.0	495.2	501.1	511.1	519.1	518.4	518.6	518.8	517.1	514.7	515.6	509.4
Trade, transportation, and utilities													
1990	112.4	109.6	109.3	108.7	110.9	113.6	113.6	114.0	112.3	113.5	114.5	115.3	112.3
1991	106.4	102.9	102.2	101.9	103.8	106.8	107.5	109.0	106.8	106.6	107.4	108.3	105.8
1992	102.5	100.3	99.9	100.9	103.1	106.8	108.1	108.6	107.2	108.0	109.8	111.1	105.5
1993	103.7	102.3	102.2	103.8	106.4	109.1	110.7	111.8	110.9	112.9	114.3	114.2	108.5
1994	107.4	105.5	105.0	105.9	108.1	111.6	113.1	113.7	113.3	114.9	116.1	117.1	110.9
1995	109.9	108.2	107.6	108.8	111.0	114.4	113.7	114.7	114.2	115.0	116.0	116.1	112.4
1996	109.6	106.9	106.1	107.4	110.0	113.0	114.7	115.5	114.1	115.5	118.9	119.2	112.5
1997	110.6	108.3	108.5	109.9	112.3	115.6	116.8	117.6	116.5	118.3	120.7	121.7	114.7
1998	111.5	109.5	109.8	110.6	112.8	116.7	117.3	118.2	118.5	119.7	122.8	123.7	115.9
1999	114.1	113.1	113.3	114.1	116.4	120.6	122.0	122.6	120.9	124.0	125.7	127.0	119.4
2000	118.4	116.1	116.3	117.4	119.4	123.8	126.1	126.1	125.2	126.1	128.8	128.7	122.7
2001	120.9	118.2	117.7	119.3	121.8	125.4	126.7	126.6	124.7	126.0	127.9	128.1	123.6
2002	120.3	118.1	118.1	119.6	121.7	125.2	127.1	127.0	124.5	124.0	125.7	127.4	123.2
2003	119.5	116.9	116.8	118.0	121.0	124.2	126.2	127.1	124.6	125.2	127.4	128.8	123.0
Wholesale trade													
1990	18.3	18.2	18.2	18.1	18.3	18.5	18.4	18.6	18.2	18.1	18.0	17.9	18.2
1991	17.2	17.0	17.0	16.8	16.9	17.2	17.1	17.1	16.8	16.5	16.5	16.4	16.8
1992	16.1	16.1	16.1	16.0	16.2	16.5	16.8	16.9	16.8	16.5	16.7	16.7	16.4
1993	16.5	16.5	16.6	16.6	16.8	17.1	17.2	17.3	17.3	17.4	17.4	17.4	17.0
1994	17.0	17.0	17.0	17.1	17.1	17.4	17.6	17.7	17.6	17.7	17.8	17.9	17.4
1995	17.5	17.6	17.6	17.8	17.8	18.0	17.8	17.9	17.9	17.9	17.8	18.1	17.8
1996	17.8	17.8	17.9	17.9	18.1	18.4	18.4	18.7	18.7	18.5	18.7	19.0	18.3
1997	18.3	18.3	18.4	18.4	18.5	18.3	18.3	18.3	18.3	18.3	18.2	18.3	18.3
1998	18.0	18.0	18.1	18.3	18.6	19.2	19.1	19.1	19.1	19.1	19.2	19.1	18.7
1999	18.6	18.7	18.8	19.0	19.2	19.5	19.7	19.9	19.6	20.0	19.7	19.5	19.3
2000	18.9	18.8	18.9	19.2	19.3	19.6	19.9	20.0	19.9	20.0	19.9	20.0	19.5
2001	20.0	19.8	19.8	20.1	20.1	20.5	20.7	20.6	20.3	20.4	20.2	20.3	20.2
2002	19.8	19.7	19.7	20.0	20.1	20.4	20.9	20.9	20.8	20.8	20.8	20.8	20.4
2003	20.4	20.2	20.3	20.5	20.8	21.1	21.3	21.4	21.1	21.1	21.2	21.1	20.9
Retail trade													
1990	77.0	74.2	73.8	73.6	75.1	77.1	76.8	77.0	76.0	77.3	78.6	79.5	76.3
1991	71.0	68.1	67.5	67.5	69.1	71.3	72.3	73.5	71.8	72.1	73.1	73.9	70.9
1992	68.8	66.5	66.2	67.2	68.9	71.6	73.3	73.8	72.5	73.4	74.9	76.2	71.1
1993	69.7	68.3	68.0	69.7	71.6	73.3	75.1	76.0	74.8	76.3	78.0	78.4	73.2
1994	72.5	70.7	70.3	71.4	73.1	75.8	76.8	77.8	77.1	78.2	79.8	80.7	75.3
1995	74.7	72.5	72.0	73.2	75.1	77.7	77.5	78.3	78.0	78.1	79.4	79.7	76.3
1996	73.9	71.3	70.5	72.0	74.1	76.5	77.7	78.2	76.9	78.3	81.0	81.7	76.0
1997	75.1	72.4	72.3	74.3	76.5	79.6	80.7	81.3	80.2	81.8	84.6	85.3	78.6
1998	76.6	74.7	75.0	75.3	77.5	80.5	81.4	82.2	81.8	82.8	86.1	87.2	80.0
1999	78.9	77.7	77.8	78.6	80.3	83.2	84.4	85.0	83.8	86.1	88.5	89.7	82.8
2000	82.2	80.3	80.4	81.3	82.9	86.1	87.8	88.3	87.5	88.3	90.7	91.1	85.5
2001	83.9	81.6	81.1	82.5	84.9	87.4	88.5	88.5	87.0	88.1	90.4	90.4	86.2
2002	83.8	81.8	81.9	83.0	84.7	87.5	88.8	88.8	86.4	85.9	88.0	89.6	85.9
2003	82.7	80.5	80.4	81.6	83.9	86.4	88.0	88.8	86.6	87.2	89.4	90.9	85.5

Employment by Industry: Maine—*Continued*

(Numbers in thousands. Not seasonally adjusted.)

Industry	January	February	March	April	May	June	July	August	September	October	November	December	Annual Average
STATEWIDE—*Continued*													
Transportation and utilities													
1990	17.1	17.2	17.3	17.0	17.5	18.0	18.4	18.4	18.1	18.1	17.9	17.9	17.7
1991	18.2	17.8	17.7	17.6	17.8	18.3	18.1	18.4	18.2	18.0	17.8	18.0	17.9
1992	17.6	17.7	17.6	17.7	18.0	18.7	18.0	17.9	17.9	18.1	18.2	18.2	17.9
1993	17.5	17.5	17.6	17.5	18.0	18.7	18.4	18.5	18.8	19.2	18.9	18.4	18.2
1994	17.9	17.8	17.7	17.4	17.9	18.4	18.7	18.2	18.6	19.0	18.5	18.5	18.2
1995	17.7	18.1	18.0	17.8	18.1	18.7	18.4	18.5	18.3	19.0	18.8	18.3	18.3
1996	17.9	17.8	17.7	17.5	17.8	18.1	18.6	18.6	18.5	18.7	19.2	18.5	18.2
1997	17.2	17.6	17.8	17.2	17.3	17.7	17.8	18.0	18.0	18.2	17.9	18.1	17.7
1998	16.9	16.8	16.7	17.0	16.7	17.0	16.8	16.9	17.6	17.8	17.5	17.4	17.0
1999	16.6	16.7	16.7	16.5	16.9	17.9	17.9	17.7	17.5	17.9	17.5	17.8	17.3
2000	17.3	17.0	17.0	16.9	17.2	18.1	18.4	17.8	17.8	17.8	18.2	17.6	17.5
2001	17.0	16.8	16.8	16.7	16.8	17.5	17.5	17.5	17.4	17.5	17.3	17.4	17.2
2002	16.7	16.6	16.5	16.6	16.9	17.3	17.4	17.3	17.3	17.3	16.9	17.0	17.0
2003	16.4	16.2	16.1	15.9	16.3	16.7	16.9	16.9	16.9	16.9	16.8	16.8	16.6
Information													
1990	10.5	10.4	10.4	10.4	10.3	10.4	10.3	10.2	10.1	10.0	9.9	9.9	10.2
1991	10.0	10.0	9.9	9.8	9.8	9.9	9.8	9.7	9.7	9.6	9.4	9.6	9.7
1992	9.4	9.5	9.5	9.4	9.5	9.5	9.9	9.9	9.8	10.0	9.8	9.8	9.6
1993	9.6	9.5	9.6	9.7	9.8	9.8	9.8	9.8	9.8	9.9	10.0	10.0	9.7
1994	9.8	9.9	9.9	10.0	10.1	10.2	10.2	10.3	10.2	10.2	10.2	10.2	10.1
1995	10.0	10.0	10.1	10.2	10.3	10.5	10.5	10.5	10.4	10.4	10.5	10.5	10.3
1996	10.2	10.3	10.2	10.2	10.2	10.3	10.3	10.3	10.3	10.2	10.2	10.3	10.2
1997	10.3	10.3	10.4	10.4	10.6	10.8	10.8	10.8	10.8	10.7	10.8	11.0	10.6
1998	10.8	10.9	10.9	10.9	11.2	11.1	11.0	11.1	11.0	11.2	11.3	11.4	11.0
1999	11.5	11.5	11.6	11.4	11.5	11.7	11.8	11.8	11.8	11.9	11.9	12.0	11.7
2000	12.1	12.1	12.2	12.3	12.3	12.2	12.3	11.0	12.2	12.2	12.3	12.3	12.1
2001	12.3	12.4	12.3	12.3	12.3	12.3	12.2	12.1	12.0	11.8	11.9	11.9	12.2
2002	11.8	11.7	11.6	11.6	11.7	11.7	11.6	11.5	11.4	11.3	11.5	11.6	11.6
2003	11.3	11.4	11.3	11.3	11.2	11.2	11.2	11.2	11.1	10.9	11.2	11.2	11.2
Financial activities													
1990	26.4	26.3	26.4	26.4	26.6	27.1	27.0	26.8	26.6	26.5	26.3	26.1	26.5
1991	26.0	25.8	25.8	25.7	25.9	26.4	26.3	26.2	25.8	25.5	25.4	25.4	25.8
1992	25.0	25.0	25.0	25.2	25.4	25.8	26.1	26.0	25.9	26.0	25.9	26.0	25.6
1993	25.6	25.6	25.8	26.2	26.5	26.9	27.0	27.1	27.0	26.9	26.9	26.9	26.5
1994	26.4	26.2	26.5	26.6	26.9	27.3	27.1	27.1	26.8	26.4	26.4	26.6	26.6
1995	26.5	26.7	27.4	27.2	27.5	28.2	28.0	28.3	27.9	27.4	27.3	27.4	27.4
1996	27.3	27.5	27.9	28.0	28.4	29.0	29.2	29.6	29.1	28.9	28.8	29.0	28.5
1997	28.7	29.1	29.4	29.0	29.4	30.1	30.6	30.5	30.4	29.3	29.6	29.8	29.6
1998	30.2	30.4	30.6	30.8	31.2	31.8	31.7	31.8	31.4	31.4	31.3	31.6	31.1
1999	31.8	32.0	32.2	32.3	32.6	33.2	33.3	33.3	32.8	33.2	33.2	33.4	32.7
2000	33.4	33.3	33.5	33.7	33.8	34.3	34.9	34.9	34.4	34.2	34.1	34.6	34.0
2001	34.2	34.5	34.7	35.0	35.0	35.4	35.9	35.9	35.2	35.1	35.1	35.4	35.1
2002	34.6	34.6	34.8	34.7	34.9	35.5	35.7	35.6	35.2	35.2	35.2	35.4	35.1
2003	34.8	34.8	34.9	35.0	35.0	35.2	35.5	35.4	34.8	34.8	34.8	35.0	35.0
Professional and business services													
1990	33.1	32.9	33.2	34.2	34.6	35.4	34.4	34.3	33.3	33.1	32.6	32.5	33.6
1991	32.3	31.8	31.6	32.0	32.5	33.3	33.2	33.1	32.8	32.6	32.4	31.8	32.4
1992	31.4	31.4	31.7	32.4	32.9	33.8	34.8	34.9	34.4	34.2	34.0	33.8	33.3
1993	31.9	32.1	33.1	34.2	35.6	36.0	35.9	36.1	36.2	36.2	35.8	35.4	34.8
1994	35.2	35.4	36.1	37.2	38.1	39.3	40.4	41.2	41.0	40.5	40.8	40.4	38.8
1995	37.6	38.7	38.8	39.1	40.4	41.0	39.8	40.7	40.1	39.6	40.1	39.6	39.6
1996	38.7	38.3	38.5	39.1	40.0	41.0	41.5	42.0	41.6	41.6	41.9	41.9	40.5
1997	41.0	41.0	41.3	42.6	44.2	44.6	45.2	46.0	45.3	45.5	45.8	45.9	44.0
1998	42.9	43.4	43.9	45.5	46.7	47.7	48.4	48.8	48.5	47.9	47.8	47.5	46.5
1999	45.1	45.7	46.0	47.8	48.7	49.7	49.5	49.6	48.7	49.7	49.4	49.3	48.2
2000	49.0	49.1	49.8	51.2	52.0	53.3	53.7	53.7	53.1	52.4	52.0	52.6	51.8
2001	50.8	51.0	51.4	52.7	53.2	53.8	52.8	52.5	51.4	51.1	50.6	50.4	51.8
2002	49.4	49.4	50.0	51.4	52.0	53.1	52.9	52.8	51.7	51.7	51.3	50.8	51.4
2003	49.2	49.1	49.3	50.1	50.6	51.2	51.5	51.9	51.4	51.3	51.2	50.9	50.6
Educational and health services													
1990	64.7	66.0	66.2	67.1	66.6	66.9	65.5	65.1	66.8	67.3	67.1	67.1	66.3
1991	68.0	68.1	68.1	68.6	68.5	67.5	68.0	68.5	69.4	69.8	70.1	69.7	68.6
1992	68.8	69.7	69.6	70.3	70.1	69.6	70.9	70.3	70.8	72.8	72.7	72.2	70.6
1993	71.5	72.4	73.2	73.3	73.2	73.4	73.7	73.5	74.5	75.7	75.8	75.6	73.8
1994	74.9	76.5	77.5	77.7	77.6	77.0	76.7	76.4	77.9	79.7	79.9	80.1	77.6
1995	77.4	79.2	79.9	79.9	80.1	79.3	79.3	79.1	80.4	81.4	81.6	81.4	79.9
1996	79.7	81.7	82.1	82.4	81.5	81.1	81.2	81.2	82.4	84.0	84.6	84.8	82.2
1997	82.9	84.8	85.6	85.5	85.0	85.2	85.8	85.9	87.3	88.3	88.6	88.9	86.1
1998	86.1	89.0	89.1	90.0	88.9	88.8	89.5	89.2	90.3	92.7	93.1	93.3	90.0
1999	91.1	93.6	93.9	94.1	93.2	92.7	93.3	93.4	95.2	96.6	96.3	96.4	94.1
2000	94.2	96.5	96.9	97.2	97.2	95.8	96.8	96.7	98.8	99.5	100.0	100.0	97.4
2001	97.7	100.1	100.5	100.5	100.5	99.7	99.7	99.9	101.3	102.8	102.9	103.2	100.7
2002	101.9	104.2	104.8	105.5	105.3	104.0	104.4	104.0	105.2	106.4	106.8	106.6	104.9
2003	104.3	106.3	107.0	107.2	106.7	105.6	106.4	105.9	107.3	108.2	108.5	108.1	106.8

Employment by Industry: Maine—*Continued*

(Numbers in thousands. Not seasonally adjusted.)

Industry	January	February	March	April	May	June	July	August	September	October	November	December	Annual Average
STATEWIDE—*Continued*													
Leisure and hospitality													
1990	40.8	40.6	41.8	43.9	48.4	55.4	60.3	57.5	52.3	48.6	42.5	40.9	47.7
1991	38.2	37.6	38.0	41.5	46.2	52.4	58.1	59.0	52.0	47.9	41.7	39.9	46.0
1992	37.5	37.6	38.4	41.7	46.6	52.8	59.1	60.3	53.7	49.0	43.5	42.4	46.8
1993	38.1	38.3	38.6	42.9	48.6	54.8	59.6	60.7	54.6	49.2	43.7	43.4	47.7
1994	39.7	39.6	40.5	44.2	49.7	55.8	61.4	62.1	55.8	50.3	44.5	44.0	48.9
1995	40.6	41.3	42.1	45.3	51.2	57.8	63.0	63.8	57.2	50.7	44.7	43.8	50.1
1996	41.7	42.3	43.0	46.3	52.2	58.7	64.2	64.9	57.6	51.8	46.2	45.6	51.2
1997	42.1	42.3	43.0	46.7	52.9	59.2	65.2	65.3	58.6	52.6	47.1	46.9	51.8
1998	43.0	43.9	44.6	48.4	54.9	61.0	66.4	67.0	60.6	53.4	48.0	47.5	53.2
1999	43.9	44.5	45.1	49.3	55.4	62.1	68.0	68.4	61.3	57.0	48.7	47.7	54.2
2000	45.5	45.7	46.8	50.6	56.6	64.4	71.1	70.9	62.9	56.7	50.4	49.4	55.9
2001	46.7	46.2	47.0	51.9	57.4	65.2	71.9	72.1	63.5	56.6	50.7	48.7	56.5
2002	46.7	46.7	47.9	51.9	58.2	65.4	73.0	72.8	64.6	58.5	51.3	51.1	57.3
2003	48.0	47.9	48.7	52.5	59.4	66.3	74.1	74.2	65.3	59.1	52.2	51.9	58.3
Other services													
1990	17.5	17.3	17.3	17.3	17.5	17.5	17.7	17.4	17.1	17.1	16.8	16.7	17.2
1991	16.2	15.8	15.9	16.3	16.2	16.4	16.8	16.7	16.3	16.3	16.2	16.3	16.2
1992	15.8	15.8	15.8	16.3	16.5	16.6	17.3	17.1	16.5	16.4	16.4	16.3	16.4
1993	15.7	15.6	15.8	16.2	16.4	16.7	17.1	17.1	17.0	17.1	17.1	17.2	16.5
1994	16.4	16.4	16.5	16.5	16.9	16.9	17.6	17.7	17.4	17.4	17.2	17.4	17.0
1995	16.9	16.8	16.9	17.0	17.4	17.5	17.8	17.9	17.5	17.8	17.4	17.6	17.3
1996	16.9	16.9	17.0	17.2	17.4	17.7	18.0	17.9	17.7	16.9	16.9	16.8	17.2
1997	16.3	16.2	16.3	16.7	17.0	17.3	17.7	17.6	17.6	17.5	17.3	17.5	17.0
1998	17.1	17.1	17.3	17.5	17.8	17.8	18.3	18.2	18.1	17.7	17.6	17.6	17.6
1999	17.4	17.5	17.7	17.9	18.0	18.3	18.4	18.4	18.1	18.0	17.9	18.0	17.9
2000	17.8	17.8	17.9	18.2	18.4	18.7	19.0	18.9	18.5	18.3	18.2	18.3	18.3
2001	18.7	18.7	18.9	18.9	19.1	19.4	19.8	19.5	19.1	19.0	19.0	18.9	19.1
2002	19.1	19.1	19.2	19.6	19.8	20.0	20.6	20.6	20.1	19.7	19.7	19.7	19.8
2003	20.1	20.1	20.2	20.3	20.5	20.9	22.0	22.0	21.6	21.4	21.3	21.3	21.0
Government													
1990	96.6	97.4	98.2	99.2	99.3	97.5	85.3	83.8	94.9	98.1	100.0	99.1	95.7
1991	97.1	99.1	99.0	99.0	98.7	96.7	84.0	83.2	95.2	98.6	100.5	99.3	95.8
1992	95.9	98.4	99.0	99.1	98.7	97.7	84.0	82.8	95.3	99.0	100.3	98.2	95.7
1993	95.8	98.8	99.5	98.5	97.8	95.8	83.8	82.5	94.1	98.8	100.0	98.9	95.3
1994	93.9	97.5	98.0	97.4	97.7	95.7	82.7	81.1	92.7	96.5	98.9	97.5	94.1
1995	93.0	96.8	96.7	96.9	96.9	94.1	81.1	80.7	91.8	96.0	97.9	96.6	93.2
1996	92.5	95.9	96.6	95.9	94.8	94.6	81.4	81.0	91.8	95.3	97.7	96.3	92.8
1997	92.3	95.6	96.4	96.5	95.4	94.0	80.5	80.9	92.0	96.4	98.1	97.6	92.9
1998	92.0	98.0	97.6	97.5	96.4	96.2	82.8	82.1	94.0	98.9	99.9	100.3	94.6
1999	95.4	99.0	99.7	99.3	98.1	97.1	84.8	83.9	98.1	100.7	101.9	102.3	96.6
2000	97.4	101.2	103.8	102.3	104.2	100.8	87.5	86.0	99.7	102.8	104.4	104.7	99.5
2001	100.5	103.9	104.3	104.7	105.1	103.1	89.9	89.7	102.5	106.2	106.9	107.7	102.0
2002	101.9	105.2	106.2	105.5	106.3	104.7	91.7	90.6	102.6	106.1	107.8	108.0	103.1
2003	102.9	106.5	107.0	106.7	106.7	104.5	91.5	90.9	102.7	106.2	108.1	108.4	103.5
Federal government													
1990	19.3	18.8	19.1	20.3	20.3	20.0	19.8	19.1	18.6	18.4	18.3	18.3	19.1
1991	18.2	18.2	18.5	17.9	17.9	18.0	18.1	18.1	18.0	17.9	17.9	18.0	18.0
1992	17.8	17.8	17.7	17.7	17.6	17.1	17.2	17.2	17.0	17.0	16.6	16.7	17.2
1993	16.6	16.5	16.5	16.4	15.9	16.0	16.1	16.1	15.9	15.9	15.7	15.5	16.0
1994	15.3	15.1	15.0	14.8	14.8	14.7	14.4	13.9	13.9	13.8	13.7	13.8	14.4
1995	13.8	13.8	13.7	13.7	13.7	13.7	13.7	13.8	13.7	13.5	13.4	12.9	13.6
1996	13.3	13.2	13.1	13.2	13.2	13.2	13.1	13.1	13.0	12.5	12.6	12.8	13.0
1997	13.2	13.1	13.1	13.1	13.1	13.1	13.1	13.1	13.0	12.9	13.0	13.3	13.0
1998	13.2	13.2	13.1	13.0	13.1	13.2	13.2	13.5	13.4	13.2	13.3	13.7	13.2
1999	13.2	13.2	13.2	13.3	13.5	13.5	13.4	13.5	13.4	13.4	13.5	13.7	13.4
2000	13.5	13.6	15.6	14.7	16.0	14.7	14.7	14.0	13.7	13.6	13.7	14.0	14.3
2001	13.8	13.7	13.7	13.8	13.8	14.0	14.2	14.2	14.1	14.0	13.8	13.9	13.9
2002	13.8	13.8	13.8	13.8	13.8	14.0	14.1	14.0	13.9	14.0	14.0	14.3	13.9
2003	13.9	14.1	14.1	14.1	14.1	14.2	14.3	14.3	14.3	14.2	14.1	14.6	14.2
State government													
1990	26.4	27.1	26.9	26.9	26.6	24.2	24.3	23.8	25.9	27.2	27.2	27.1	26.1
1991	25.8	26.9	26.4	27.1	26.1	24.1	24.3	24.0	26.4	27.4	27.8	27.5	26.1
1992	25.8	27.2	27.1	27.6	26.7	24.7	24.5	24.3	27.0	28.1	28.2	26.8	26.5
1993	26.2	28.0	28.1	27.5	26.5	24.3	24.0	23.7	25.7	27.9	28.2	27.7	26.4
1994	24.9	27.4	27.6	27.4	26.9	24.1	24.2	23.9	25.7	27.6	27.7	27.3	26.2
1995	25.0	27.4	27.5	27.3	26.8	24.2	24.0	23.7	25.5	27.2	27.3	26.9	26.0
1996	24.3	26.5	26.5	26.3	24.2	22.9	23.2	23.2	24.9	26.4	26.6	26.2	25.1
1997	23.7	26.1	26.2	26.1	24.3	23.0	23.0	22.9	24.7	26.8	26.7	26.3	24.9
1998	23.2	26.6	26.3	26.4	24.6	23.2	23.1	23.0	24.3	27.5	27.4	27.2	25.2
1999	24.4	27.2	27.3	27.2	25.3	24.0	24.2	24.1	27.1	27.9	27.9	27.8	26.2
2000	24.5	27.7	27.8	27.5	27.0	24.4	24.6	24.5	27.5	28.5	28.5	28.4	26.7
2001	25.4	28.3	28.6	28.5	27.9	25.2	25.3	25.2	28.1	29.3	29.4	29.2	27.5
2002	26.0	29.1	29.4	28.8	28.4	25.7	25.9	25.3	28.1	29.2	29.3	29.4	27.9
2003	26.0	28.8	28.9	28.8	28.1	25.5	25.5	25.3	27.9	29.2	29.5	29.6	27.8

Employment by Industry: Maine—*Continued*

(Numbers in thousands. Not seasonally adjusted.)

Industry	January	February	March	April	May	June	July	August	September	October	November	December	Annual Average
STATEWIDE—*Continued*													
Local government													
1990	50.9	51.5	52.2	52.0	52.4	53.3	41.2	40.9	50.4	52.5	54.5	53.7	50.4
1991	53.1	54.0	54.1	54.0	54.7	54.6	41.6	41.1	50.8	53.3	54.8	53.8	51.6
1992	52.3	53.4	54.2	53.8	54.4	55.9	42.3	41.3	51.3	53.9	55.5	54.7	51.9
1993	53.0	54.3	54.9	54.6	55.4	55.5	43.7	42.7	52.5	55.0	56.1	55.7	52.7
1994	53.7	55.0	55.4	55.2	56.0	56.9	44.1	43.3	53.1	55.1	57.5	56.4	53.4
1995	54.2	55.6	55.5	55.9	56.4	56.2	43.4	43.2	52.6	55.3	57.2	56.8	53.5
1996	54.9	56.2	57.0	56.4	57.4	58.5	45.1	44.7	53.9	56.4	58.5	57.3	54.6
1997	55.4	56.4	57.1	57.3	58.0	57.9	44.4	44.9	54.3	56.7	58.4	58.0	54.9
1998	55.6	58.2	58.2	58.1	58.7	59.8	46.5	45.6	56.3	58.2	59.2	59.4	56.1
1999	57.8	58.6	59.2	58.8	59.3	59.6	47.2	46.3	57.6	59.4	60.5	60.8	57.0
2000	59.4	59.9	60.4	60.1	61.2	61.7	48.2	47.5	58.5	60.7	62.2	62.3	58.5
2001	61.3	61.9	62.0	62.4	63.4	63.9	50.4	50.3	60.3	62.9	63.7	64.6	60.6
2002	62.1	62.3	63.0	62.9	64.1	65.0	51.7	51.3	60.6	62.9	64.5	64.3	61.2
2003	63.0	63.6	64.0	63.8	64.5	64.8	51.7	51.3	60.5	62.8	64.5	64.2	61.6
LEWISTON-AUBURN													
Total nonfarm													
1990	39.6	39.4	39.6	39.8	40.4	40.2	38.5	38.7	39.3	40.3	39.8	39.4	39.6
1991	38.1	37.5	36.9	37.5	38.1	37.9	36.3	37.3	38.0	38.3	38.1	38.0	37.7
1992	37.3	37.1	37.2	37.3	38.0	38.2	37.4	37.7	38.3	39.7	40.0	39.9	38.2
1993	38.2	38.1	38.0	39.0	39.7	39.5	38.7	39.6	40.1	41.2	41.7	41.2	39.6
1994	39.2	39.5	39.5	39.9	40.7	40.9	40.0	40.4	41.7	42.4	42.7	42.5	40.8
1995	40.5	40.4	40.5	40.5	41.6	41.5	40.5	41.0	41.7	42.0	42.1	42.1	41.2
1996	40.8	40.0	40.0	40.1	40.4	40.3	39.6	40.0	41.3	41.8	42.5	42.6	40.8
1997	40.6	39.9	40.2	40.5	40.6	41.7	40.1	40.9	42.2	42.4	43.2	43.0	41.3
1998	41.4	41.6	41.3	41.9	42.4	43.3	42.1	42.3	43.8	44.6	44.9	45.1	42.9
1999	43.0	43.6	43.5	43.7	44.5	45.3	43.5	43.9	44.8	46.4	46.2	46.0	44.5
2000	45.7	45.4	45.8	46.5	46.5	47.3	45.5	45.5	46.6	46.8	46.6	47.0	46.3
2001	46.2	45.5	45.4	45.6	46.1	46.5	45.5	45.4	46.0	46.5	46.7	46.4	46.0
2002	45.9	45.5	45.5	46.2	46.5	46.9	46.0	45.8	46.6	47.2	47.4	47.2	46.4
2003	46.1	45.9	46.2	46.2	46.4	46.9	45.9	46.0	46.5	47.5	47.7	47.4	46.6
Total private													
1990	35.3	35.0	35.2	35.3	36.0	35.8	34.6	34.8	35.1	35.9	35.4	34.9	35.3
1991	33.7	33.2	32.5	33.2	33.8	33.6	32.7	33.7	33.6	34.0	33.7	33.6	33.4
1992	32.7	32.4	32.5	32.6	33.3	33.5	33.6	34.0	33.8	34.9	35.2	35.0	33.6
1993	33.4	33.2	33.2	34.4	35.0	35.0	34.9	35.8	35.6	36.4	36.8	36.4	35.0
1994	34.5	34.7	34.7	35.1	35.8	36.3	36.3	36.8	37.1	37.6	37.7	37.7	36.2
1995	35.7	35.5	35.6	35.7	36.7	36.8	36.7	37.3	37.1	37.1	37.2	37.2	36.6
1996	36.0	35.2	35.1	35.2	35.5	35.6	35.7	36.3	36.7	37.0	37.6	37.6	36.1
1997	35.8	35.0	35.3	35.5	35.8	36.9	36.4	36.8	37.4	37.5	38.1	38.0	36.5
1998	36.7	36.6	36.4	36.9	37.4	38.4	38.2	38.4	38.9	39.6	39.9	40.1	38.1
1999	38.1	38.4	38.4	38.7	39.5	40.2	39.4	39.9	39.7	41.3	41.0	40.8	39.6
2000	40.6	40.1	40.5	41.2	41.1	41.8	41.0	41.2	41.5	41.5	41.1	41.5	41.1
2001	40.8	40.0	40.0	40.2	40.6	41.0	41.3	41.1	40.7	41.0	41.2	40.9	40.7
2002	40.4	40.0	40.0	40.7	40.9	41.2	41.5	41.2	41.1	41.6	41.8	41.6	41.0
2003	40.6	40.3	40.6	40.6	40.7	41.3	41.4	41.4	41.1	41.8	42.0	41.8	41.1
Goods-producing													
1990	10.9	10.7	10.8	10.9	11.2	11.0	10.1	10.5	10.7	10.7	10.4	10.0	10.7
1991	9.5	9.2	8.9	9.3	9.6	9.7	9.0	9.6	9.6	9.6	9.3	9.1	9.4
1992	8.9	8.9	9.0	9.1	9.4	9.5	9.1	9.4	9.2	9.8	9.6	9.3	9.3
1993	9.1	9.1	9.2	9.4	9.6	9.7	9.6	9.8	9.8	9.8	9.8	9.6	9.5
1994	9.3	9.3	9.4	9.7	10.0	10.3	10.3	10.5	10.6	10.7	10.5	10.4	10.1
1995	10.0	9.8	10.0	10.0	10.2	10.3	10.1	10.3	10.1	10.1	10.0	9.9	10.1
1996	9.4	9.3	9.2	9.2	9.2	9.3	9.0	9.2	9.3	9.3	9.3	9.2	9.2
1997	8.9	8.8	8.8	9.0	9.2	9.5	9.1	9.3	9.4	9.2	9.2	9.1	9.1
1998	8.8	8.9	9.0	9.1	9.2	9.4	9.1	9.1	9.3	9.2	9.2	9.3	9.1
1999	9.0	9.1	9.2	9.2	9.4	9.6	9.1	9.4	9.3	9.6	9.5	9.3	9.3
2000	9.4	9.3	9.4	9.7	9.7	9.8	9.5	9.7	9.5	9.6	9.3	9.5	9.5
2001	9.4	9.3	9.2	9.2	9.2	9.3	9.2	9.2	9.1	9.0	8.9	8.9	9.2
2002	8.7	8.7	8.6	8.8	8.8	8.9	8.8	8.9	8.9	8.9	8.8	8.7	8.8
2003	8.7	8.6	8.7	8.7	8.8	9.0	8.9	9.0	9.0	9.0	8.8	8.6	8.8
Construction and mining													
1990	2.0	1.9	2.0	2.0	2.1	2.1	2.1	2.0	2.0	2.0	2.0	1.8	2.0
1991	1.6	1.5	1.5	1.6	1.7	1.9	1.9	1.9	1.9	1.8	1.7	1.5	1.7
1992	1.3	1.3	1.3	1.4	1.5	1.6	1.7	1.7	1.7	1.8	1.7	1.6	1.6
1993	1.4	1.3	1.4	1.4	1.5	1.6	1.6	1.6	1.6	1.6	1.6	1.6	1.5
1994	1.3	1.3	1.3	1.4	1.5	1.7	1.7	1.7	1.7	1.7	1.7	1.7	1.6
1995	1.5	1.4	1.4	1.5	1.7	1.8	1.8	1.8	1.7	1.7	1.7	1.7	1.6
1996	1.5	1.5	1.5	1.5	1.7	1.7	1.8	1.9	2.0	1.9	1.9	1.8	1.7
1997	1.6	1.5	1.5	1.5	1.7	1.8	1.7	1.7	1.7	1.7	1.7	1.6	1.6
1998	1.5	1.5	1.5	1.6	1.7	1.8	1.8	1.7	1.7	1.7	1.7	1.7	1.7
1999	1.6	1.6	1.6	1.7	1.8	1.9	1.9	1.9	1.8	2.0	1.9	1.8	1.8
2000	1.8	1.8	1.8	2.0	2.1	2.2	2.2	2.2	2.2	2.3	2.1	2.2	2.1
2001	2.1	2.1	2.1	2.2	2.3	2.4	2.5	2.5	2.4	2.4	2.3	2.2	2.3
2002	2.1	2.1	2.0	2.2	2.2	2.3	2.4	2.4	2.4	2.4	2.3	2.2	2.3
2003	2.2	2.2	2.3	2.3	2.5	2.7	2.7	2.7	2.7	2.7	2.6	2.4	2.5

Employment by Industry: Maine—*Continued*

(Numbers in thousands. Not seasonally adjusted.)

Industry	January	February	March	April	May	June	July	August	September	October	November	December	Annual Average
LEWISTON-AUBURN *—Continued*													
Manufacturing													
1990	8.9	8.8	8.8	8.9	9.1	8.9	8.0	8.5	8.7	8.7	8.4	8.2	8.7
1991	7.9	7.7	7.4	7.7	7.9	7.8	7.1	7.7	7.7	7.8	7.6	7.6	7.7
1992	7.6	7.6	7.7	7.7	7.9	7.9	7.4	7.7	7.5	8.0	7.9	7.7	7.7
1993	7.7	7.8	7.8	8.0	8.1	8.1	8.0	8.2	8.2	8.2	8.2	8.0	8.0
1994	8.0	8.0	8.1	8.3	8.5	8.6	8.6	8.8	8.9	9.0	8.8	8.7	8.5
1995	8.5	8.4	8.6	8.5	8.5	8.5	8.3	8.5	8.4	8.4	8.3	8.2	8.4
1996	7.9	7.8	7.7	7.7	7.5	7.6	7.2	7.3	7.3	7.4	7.4	7.4	7.5
1997	7.3	7.3	7.3	7.5	7.5	7.7	7.4	7.6	7.7	7.5	7.5	7.5	7.5
1998	7.3	7.4	7.5	7.5	7.5	7.6	7.3	7.4	7.6	7.5	7.5	7.6	7.5
1999	7.4	7.5	7.6	7.5	7.6	7.7	7.2	7.5	7.5	7.6	7.6	7.5	7.5
2000	7.6	7.5	7.6	7.7	7.6	7.6	7.3	7.5	7.3	7.3	7.2	7.3	7.5
2001	7.3	7.2	7.1	7.0	6.9	6.9	6.7	6.7	6.7	6.6	6.6	6.7	6.9
2002	6.6	6.6	6.6	6.6	6.6	6.6	6.4	6.5	6.5	6.5	6.5	6.5	6.5
2003	6.5	6.4	6.4	6.4	6.3	6.3	6.2	6.3	6.3	6.3	6.2	6.2	6.3
Service-providing													
1990	28.7	28.7	28.8	28.9	29.2	29.2	28.4	28.2	28.6	29.6	29.4	29.4	28.9
1991	28.6	28.3	28.0	28.2	28.5	28.2	27.3	27.7	28.4	28.7	28.8	28.9	28.3
1992	28.4	28.2	28.2	28.2	28.6	28.7	28.3	28.3	29.1	29.9	30.4	30.6	28.9
1993	29.1	29.0	28.8	29.6	30.1	29.8	29.1	29.8	30.3	31.4	31.9	31.6	30.0
1994	29.9	30.2	30.1	30.2	30.7	30.6	29.7	29.9	31.1	31.7	32.2	32.1	30.7
1995	30.5	30.6	30.5	30.5	31.4	31.2	30.4	30.7	31.6	31.9	32.1	32.2	31.1
1996	31.4	30.7	30.8	30.9	31.2	31.0	30.6	30.8	32.0	32.5	33.2	33.4	31.5
1997	31.7	31.1	31.4	31.5	31.4	32.2	31.0	31.6	32.8	33.2	34.0	33.9	32.2
1998	32.6	32.7	32.3	32.8	33.2	33.9	33.0	33.2	34.5	35.4	35.7	35.8	33.8
1999	34.0	34.5	34.3	34.5	35.1	35.7	34.4	34.5	35.5	36.8	36.7	36.7	35.2
2000	36.3	36.1	36.4	36.8	36.8	37.5	36.0	35.8	37.1	37.2	37.3	37.5	36.7
2001	36.8	36.2	36.2	36.4	36.9	37.2	36.3	36.2	36.9	37.5	37.8	37.5	36.8
2002	37.2	36.8	36.9	37.4	37.7	38.0	37.2	36.9	37.7	38.3	38.6	38.5	37.6
2003	37.4	37.3	37.5	37.5	37.6	37.9	37.0	37.0	37.5	38.5	38.9	38.8	37.7
Trade, transportation, and utilities													
1990	7.7	7.6	7.7	7.7	7.8	7.8	7.7	7.8	7.8	8.1	8.2	8.2	7.8
1991	7.9	7.6	7.4	7.5	7.6	7.6	7.5	7.6	7.6	7.9	8.2	8.3	7.7
1992	7.5	7.2	7.1	7.3	7.4	7.4	7.5	7.6	7.7	7.8	8.1	8.2	7.6
1993	7.7	7.5	7.4	7.7	7.8	7.7	7.8	8.0	8.2	8.8	9.2	9.2	8.1
1994	7.9	8.0	7.8	7.7	7.9	8.0	7.9	8.0	8.3	8.6	9.0	9.0	8.2
1995	8.2	7.9	7.8	7.9	8.2	8.2	8.0	8.2	8.5	8.7	8.9	9.0	8.3
1996	8.3	7.9	7.8	7.9	8.0	8.2	8.0	8.2	8.6	8.9	9.3	9.4	8.4
1997	8.5	8.0	8.0	8.2	8.1	8.6	8.4	8.3	8.9	9.2	9.6	9.6	8.6
1998	8.6	8.2	8.2	8.3	8.4	8.8	8.7	8.8	9.1	9.6	9.8	9.8	8.9
1999	8.9	8.8	8.8	8.8	9.1	9.3	9.0	9.0	9.0	9.7	9.9	9.9	9.2
2000	9.4	9.0	9.0	9.3	9.4	9.6	9.5	9.4	9.7	10.1	10.3	10.3	9.6
2001	9.9	9.5	9.5	9.5	9.7	9.8	9.8	9.8	9.9	10.3	10.6	10.5	9.9
2002	9.8	9.5	9.5	9.6	9.6	9.6	9.8	9.7	9.6	9.8	10.3	10.2	9.8
2003	9.5	9.2	9.3	9.3	9.2	9.5	9.5	9.4	9.3	9.6	10.2	10.2	9.5
Wholesale trade													
1990	1.3	1.3	1.3	1.3	1.3	1.3	1.3	1.3	1.3	1.3	1.3	1.3	1.3
1991	1.2	1.2	1.2	1.2	1.2	1.2	1.3	1.3	1.3	1.2	1.2	1.2	1.2
1992	1.1	1.1	1.1	1.1	1.1	1.1	1.2	1.2	1.2	1.2	1.2	1.2	1.2
1993	1.1	1.1	1.1	1.2	1.2	1.2	1.2	1.2	1.2	1.2	1.2	1.2	1.2
1994	1.1	1.2	1.2	1.2	1.2	1.2	1.2	1.2	1.2	1.2	1.2	1.2	1.2
1995	1.2	1.2	1.2	1.2	1.3	1.3	1.3	1.3	1.3	1.3	1.3	1.3	1.3
1996	1.2	1.2	1.2	1.2	1.2	1.2	1.2	1.2	1.3	1.2	1.2	1.2	1.2
1997	1.1	1.1	1.1	1.1	1.1	1.2	1.1	1.1	1.1	1.1	1.1	1.1	1.1
1998	1.1	1.1	1.1	1.1	1.1	1.2	1.2	1.2	1.1	1.2	1.2	1.2	1.2
1999	1.1	1.1	1.2	1.1	1.2	1.2	1.2	1.1	1.1	1.2	1.1	1.1	1.1
2000	1.1	1.1	1.1	1.2	1.2	1.2	1.2	1.2	1.2	1.2	1.2	1.2	1.2
2001	1.3	1.3	1.3	1.3	1.3	1.3	1.3	1.3	1.3	1.3	1.3	1.3	1.3
2002	1.3	1.2	1.2	1.3	1.3	1.3	1.3	1.3	1.3	1.4	1.4	1.4	1.3
2003	1.4	1.4	1.4	1.4	1.3	1.4	1.4	1.3	1.3	1.3	1.3	1.3	1.4
Retail trade													
1990	5.4	5.3	5.3	5.4	5.4	5.4	5.4	5.5	5.5	5.7	5.8	5.8	5.5
1991	5.7	5.5	5.3	5.4	5.5	5.5	5.3	5.4	5.4	5.7	6.0	6.1	5.6
1992	5.5	5.2	5.1	5.3	5.4	5.4	5.4	5.5	5.5	5.6	5.8	5.9	5.5
1993	5.7	5.5	5.4	5.5	5.6	5.5	5.6	5.8	5.9	6.5	6.8	6.8	5.9
1994	5.8	5.8	5.6	5.5	5.6	5.7	5.7	5.8	6.0	6.2	6.6	6.6	5.9
1995	6.0	5.6	5.5	5.6	5.7	5.8	5.6	5.7	6.0	6.1	6.3	6.4	5.9
1996	5.9	5.5	5.4	5.4	5.5	5.6	5.5	5.6	5.9	6.2	6.7	6.7	5.8
1997	6.2	5.7	5.7	5.8	5.8	6.1	6.0	6.0	6.4	6.7	7.1	7.1	6.2
1998	6.3	5.9	5.9	5.9	6.0	6.3	6.2	6.3	6.6	7.0	7.2	7.2	6.4
1999	6.4	6.3	6.2	6.3	6.4	6.6	6.4	6.5	6.5	6.9	7.3	7.3	6.6
2000	6.8	6.4	6.4	6.6	6.6	6.8	6.7	6.6	6.9	7.2	7.5	7.5	6.8
2001	7.0	6.7	6.7	6.7	6.8	6.9	6.9	6.9	7.1	7.4	7.7	7.6	7.0
2002	7.0	6.8	6.8	6.8	6.8	6.8	6.9	6.9	6.8	6.9	7.4	7.4	6.9
2003	6.8	6.5	6.5	6.6	6.6	6.7	6.8	6.8	6.7	6.9	7.5	7.5	6.8

Employment by Industry: Maine—*Continued*

(Numbers in thousands. Not seasonally adjusted.)

Industry	January	February	March	April	May	June	July	August	September	October	November	December	Annual Average
LEWISTON-AUBURN *—Continued*													
Transportation and utilities													
1990	1.0	1.0	1.1	1.0	1.1	1.1	1.0	1.0	1.0	1.1	1.1	1.1	1.1
1991	1.0	0.9	0.9	0.9	0.9	0.9	0.9	0.9	0.9	1.0	1.0	1.0	0.9
1992	0.9	0.9	0.9	0.9	0.9	0.9	0.9	0.9	1.0	1.0	1.1	1.1	1.0
1993	0.9	0.9	0.9	1.0	1.0	1.0	1.0	1.0	1.1	1.1	1.2	1.2	1.0
1994	1.0	1.0	1.0	1.0	1.1	1.1	1.0	1.0	1.1	1.2	1.2	1.2	1.1
1995	1.0	1.1	1.1	1.1	1.2	1.1	1.1	1.2	1.2	1.3	1.3	1.3	1.2
1996	1.2	1.2	1.2	1.3	1.3	1.4	1.3	1.4	1.4	1.5	1.4	1.5	1.3
1997	1.2	1.2	1.2	1.3	1.2	1.3	1.3	1.2	1.4	1.4	1.4	1.4	1.3
1998	1.2	1.2	1.2	1.3	1.3	1.3	1.3	1.3	1.4	1.4	1.4	1.4	1.3
1999	1.4	1.4	1.4	1.4	1.5	1.5	1.4	1.4	1.4	1.6	1.5	1.5	1.5
2000	1.5	1.5	1.5	1.5	1.6	1.6	1.6	1.6	1.6	1.7	1.6	1.6	1.6
2001	1.6	1.5	1.5	1.5	1.6	1.6	1.6	1.6	1.5	1.6	1.6	1.6	1.6
2002	1.5	1.5	1.5	1.5	1.5	1.5	1.6	1.5	1.5	1.5	1.5	1.4	1.5
2003	1.3	1.3	1.4	1.3	1.3	1.4	1.3	1.3	1.3	1.4	1.4	1.4	1.3
Information													
1990	0.8	0.8	0.8	0.8	0.8	0.8	0.8	0.8	0.8	0.8	0.8	0.8	0.8
1991	0.8	0.8	0.8	0.8	0.8	0.7	0.7	0.7	0.7	0.7	0.7	0.7	0.7
1992	0.8	0.7	0.8	0.8	0.8	0.8	0.8	0.8	0.8	0.8	0.9	0.9	0.8
1993	0.9	0.9	0.8	0.9	0.9	0.9	0.8	0.9	0.9	0.9	0.9	0.9	0.9
1994	0.9	0.9	0.9	0.9	0.9	0.9	0.9	0.9	0.9	0.9	0.9	0.9	0.9
1995	0.8	0.8	0.8	0.8	0.8	0.8	0.9	0.8	0.8	0.8	0.8	0.8	0.8
1996	0.8	0.7	0.8	0.7	0.7	0.7	0.8	0.8	0.8	0.8	0.8	0.8	0.8
1997	0.8	0.8	0.8	0.8	0.8	0.8	0.8	0.8	0.8	0.8	0.7	0.8	0.8
1998	0.7	0.7	0.7	0.7	0.7	0.7	0.7	0.7	0.7	0.8	0.8	0.8	0.7
1999	0.8	0.8	0.8	0.8	0.8	0.8	0.8	0.8	0.8	0.9	0.9	0.9	0.8
2000	0.8	0.8	0.9	0.8	0.8	0.8	0.7	0.7	0.8	0.8	0.7	0.8	0.8
2001	0.7	0.7	0.7	0.7	0.7	0.7	0.7	0.7	0.7	0.7	0.7	0.7	0.7
2002	0.7	0.7	0.7	0.7	0.7	0.7	0.7	0.7	0.6	0.7	0.7	0.7	0.7
2003	0.6	0.7	0.7	0.7	0.7	0.7	0.7	0.7	0.7	0.7	0.7	0.7	0.7
Financial activities													
1990	2.3	2.3	2.3	2.3	2.3	2.3	2.3	2.2	2.2	2.3	2.3	2.3	2.3
1991	2.2	2.2	2.2	2.2	2.2	2.2	2.1	2.1	2.1	2.1	2.1	2.1	2.2
1992	2.0	2.1	2.1	2.0	2.1	2.1	2.1	2.1	2.1	2.1	2.2	2.2	2.1
1993	2.0	2.0	2.0	2.1	2.1	2.1	2.0	2.1	2.0	2.1	2.1	2.1	2.1
1994	2.1	2.0	2.1	2.1	2.1	2.1	2.1	2.1	2.1	2.1	2.1	2.1	2.1
1995	2.1	2.1	2.2	2.1	2.2	2.2	2.2	2.2	2.2	2.2	2.2	2.2	2.2
1996	2.2	2.2	2.2	2.2	2.2	2.2	2.3	2.3	2.3	2.3	2.4	2.4	2.3
1997	2.4	2.3	2.4	2.4	2.3	2.4	2.4	2.4	2.4	2.4	2.4	2.4	2.4
1998	2.6	2.6	2.6	2.6	2.6	2.7	2.7	2.7	2.7	2.7	2.7	2.8	2.7
1999	2.7	2.7	2.7	2.7	2.7	2.7	2.8	2.8	2.8	2.8	2.8	2.8	2.8
2000	2.7	2.7	2.8	2.7	2.7	2.8	2.7	2.8	2.8	2.7	2.8	2.8	2.8
2001	2.7	2.7	2.7	2.7	2.7	2.8	2.7	2.8	2.8	2.7	2.8	2.8	2.7
2002	2.8	2.8	2.8	2.9	2.9	2.9	3.0	3.0	3.0	2.9	3.0	3.0	2.9
2003	3.0	3.0	3.0	3.0	3.0	3.0	3.0	3.0	3.0	3.0	3.0	3.0	3.0
Professional and business services													
1990	2.6	2.5	2.5	2.5	2.6	2.6	2.5	2.5	2.6	2.6	2.6	2.5	2.6
1991	2.7	2.7	2.7	2.6	2.6	2.6	2.5	2.5	2.5	2.6	2.5	2.5	2.6
1992	2.6	2.5	2.5	2.5	2.5	2.6	2.8	2.8	2.9	3.0	3.0	3.0	2.7
1993	2.7	2.7	2.8	2.9	3.0	3.0	2.9	3.0	3.0	3.1	3.1	3.0	2.9
1994	2.9	3.0	2.9	3.1	3.2	3.3	3.3	3.3	3.4	3.4	3.3	3.3	3.2
1995	3.3	3.3	3.4	3.4	3.6	3.6	3.7	3.8	3.7	3.6	3.8	3.7	3.6
1996	3.7	3.5	3.5	3.5	3.6	3.6	3.7	3.8	3.8	3.8	4.0	4.0	3.7
1997	3.6	3.5	3.6	3.4	3.5	3.6	3.8	4.0	4.0	3.8	3.9	3.9	3.7
1998	3.8	3.8	3.8	3.7	3.9	3.9	4.2	4.2	4.1	4.4	4.4	4.5	4.1
1999	4.0	4.1	4.2	4.4	4.6	4.7	4.6	4.7	4.7	4.8	4.9	4.9	4.6
2000	5.2	5.2	5.2	5.3	5.1	5.2	5.2	5.2	5.2	5.1	5.0	5.1	5.2
2001	5.1	5.0	5.0	5.0	5.1	5.1	5.2	5.2	5.1	5.3	5.3	5.4	5.2
2002	5.5	5.4	5.5	5.6	5.7	5.9	5.9	5.7	5.6	5.8	5.8	5.8	5.7
2003	5.6	5.6	5.6	5.7	5.7	5.7	5.6	5.6	5.5	5.6	5.6	5.7	5.6
Educational and health services													
1990	6.6	6.7	6.7	6.7	6.8	6.8	6.7	6.7	6.8	7.0	6.9	6.9	6.8
1991	6.6	6.7	6.6	6.7	6.8	6.6	6.6	6.8	6.9	6.9	6.8	6.8	6.7
1992	6.8	6.9	6.8	6.9	6.9	6.8	6.9	6.8	6.9	7.1	7.2	7.2	6.9
1993	6.9	7.0	7.0	7.2	7.2	7.1	7.2	7.3	7.3	7.5	7.5	7.4	7.2
1994	7.3	7.4	7.4	7.5	7.4	7.4	7.5	7.4	7.5	7.6	7.6	7.7	7.5
1995	7.2	7.3	7.2	7.3	7.3	7.3	7.4	7.3	7.3	7.3	7.3	7.4	7.3
1996	7.3	7.3	7.4	7.4	7.4	7.1	7.4	7.4	7.5	7.6	7.6	7.6	7.4
1997	7.5	7.5	7.6	7.6	7.6	7.7	7.6	7.6	7.6	7.9	8.0	8.0	7.7
1998	8.1	8.2	8.0	8.2	8.0	8.4	8.3	8.2	8.4	8.5	8.6	8.5	8.3
1999	8.5	8.6	8.5	8.5	8.5	8.7	8.6	8.7	8.7	8.9	8.8	8.8	8.7
2000	8.8	8.8	8.9	8.8	8.8	8.9	8.7	8.7	8.9	8.7	8.7	8.7	8.8
2001	8.6	8.5	8.5	8.5	8.5	8.6	8.8	8.6	8.6	8.4	8.5	8.4	8.5
2002	8.5	8.5	8.6	8.6	8.5	8.5	8.4	8.4	8.7	8.8	8.8	8.8	8.6
2003	8.8	8.7	8.8	8.7	8.7	8.7	8.6	8.6	8.8	9.1	9.1	9.0	8.8

Employment by Industry: Maine—*Continued*

(Numbers in thousands. Not seasonally adjusted.)

Industry	January	February	March	April	May	June	July	August	September	October	November	December	Annual Average
LEWISTON-AUBURN *—Continued*													
Leisure and hospitality													
1990	3.0	3.0	3.0	3.0	3.1	3.1	3.1	3.0	2.9	3.0	2.8	2.8	3.0
1991	2.7	2.7	2.6	2.8	2.9	2.9	3.0	3.1	2.9	2.9	2.8	2.8	2.8
1992	2.8	2.8	2.9	2.7	2.9	3.0	3.1	3.2	2.9	3.0	2.9	2.9	2.9
1993	2.8	2.7	2.7	2.8	3.0	3.1	3.2	3.3	3.0	2.8	2.8	2.8	2.9
1994	2.8	2.8	2.8	2.7	2.9	2.9	2.9	3.1	2.8	2.8	2.8	2.8	2.8
1995	2.7	2.9	2.8	2.8	3.0	3.0	3.0	3.2	3.0	3.0	2.8	2.8	2.9
1996	2.9	2.9	2.8	2.9	3.0	3.1	3.1	3.2	3.0	2.9	2.8	2.8	3.0
1997	2.7	2.7	2.7	2.7	2.9	2.9	2.9	3.0	2.8	2.8	2.9	2.8	2.8
1998	2.7	2.8	2.7	2.8	3.1	3.0	3.0	3.2	3.1	2.9	2.9	2.9	2.9
1999	2.7	2.8	2.7	2.8	2.9	2.9	3.0	3.0	2.9	3.1	2.7	2.7	2.9
2000	2.8	2.8	2.8	3.0	3.1	3.2	3.2	3.2	3.1	3.0	2.8	2.8	3.0
2001	3.0	2.9	3.0	3.2	3.3	3.4	3.5	3.4	3.3	3.2	3.0	2.9	3.2
2002	3.0	3.0	2.9	3.1	3.3	3.3	3.5	3.4	3.3	3.3	3.1	3.1	3.2
2003	3.0	3.1	3.1	3.2	3.3	3.4	3.7	3.7	3.4	3.4	3.2	3.2	3.3
Other services													
1990	1.4	1.4	1.4	1.4	1.4	1.4	1.4	1.3	1.3	1.4	1.4	1.4	1.4
1991	1.3	1.3	1.3	1.3	1.3	1.3	1.3	1.3	1.3	1.3	1.3	1.3	1.3
1992	1.3	1.3	1.3	1.3	1.3	1.3	1.3	1.3	1.3	1.3	1.3	1.3	1.3
1993	1.3	1.3	1.3	1.4	1.4	1.4	1.4	1.4	1.4	1.4	1.4	1.4	1.4
1994	1.3	1.3	1.4	1.4	1.4	1.4	1.4	1.5	1.5	1.5	1.5	1.5	1.4
1995	1.4	1.4	1.4	1.4	1.4	1.4	1.4	1.5	1.5	1.4	1.4	1.4	1.4
1996	1.4	1.4	1.4	1.4	1.4	1.4	1.4	1.4	1.4	1.4	1.4	1.4	1.4
1997	1.4	1.4	1.4	1.4	1.4	1.4	1.4	1.4	1.5	1.4	1.4	1.4	1.4
1998	1.4	1.4	1.4	1.5	1.5	1.5	1.5	1.5	1.5	1.5	1.5	1.5	1.5
1999	1.5	1.5	1.5	1.5	1.5	1.5	1.5	1.5	1.5	1.5	1.5	1.5	1.5
2000	1.5	1.5	1.5	1.6	1.5	1.5	1.5	1.5	1.5	1.5	1.5	1.5	1.5
2001	1.4	1.4	1.4	1.4	1.4	1.3	1.4	1.4	1.2	1.4	1.4	1.3	1.4
2002	1.4	1.4	1.4	1.4	1.4	1.4	1.4	1.4	1.4	1.4	1.3	1.3	1.4
2003	1.4	1.4	1.4	1.3	1.3	1.3	1.4	1.4	1.4	1.4	1.4	1.4	1.4
Government													
1990	4.3	4.4	4.4	4.5	4.4	4.4	3.9	3.9	4.2	4.4	4.4	4.5	4.3
1991	4.4	4.3	4.4	4.3	4.3	4.3	3.6	3.6	4.4	4.3	4.4	4.4	4.2
1992	4.6	4.7	4.7	4.7	4.7	4.7	3.8	3.7	4.5	4.8	4.8	4.9	4.6
1993	4.8	4.9	4.8	4.6	4.7	4.5	3.8	3.8	4.5	4.8	4.9	4.8	4.6
1994	4.7	4.8	4.8	4.8	4.9	4.6	3.7	3.6	4.6	4.8	5.0	4.8	4.6
1995	4.8	4.9	4.9	4.8	4.9	4.7	3.8	3.7	4.6	4.9	4.9	4.9	4.7
1996	4.8	4.8	4.9	4.9	4.9	4.7	3.9	3.7	4.6	4.8	4.9	5.0	4.7
1997	4.8	4.9	4.9	5.0	4.8	4.8	3.7	4.1	4.8	4.9	5.1	5.0	4.7
1998	4.7	5.0	4.9	5.0	5.0	4.9	3.9	3.9	4.9	5.0	5.0	5.0	4.8
1999	4.9	5.2	5.1	5.0	5.0	5.1	4.1	4.0	5.1	5.1	5.2	5.2	4.9
2000	5.1	5.3	5.3	5.3	5.4	5.5	4.5	4.3	5.1	5.3	5.5	5.5	5.2
2001	5.4	5.5	5.4	5.4	5.5	5.5	4.2	4.3	5.3	5.5	5.5	5.5	5.3
2002	5.5	5.5	5.5	5.5	5.6	5.7	4.5	4.6	5.5	5.6	5.6	5.6	5.4
2003	5.5	5.6	5.6	5.6	5.7	5.6	4.5	4.6	5.4	5.7	5.7	5.6	5.4
Federal government													
1997	0.3	0.3	0.3	0.3	0.3	0.3	0.3	0.3	0.3	0.3	0.3	0.3	0.3
1998	0.3	0.3	0.3	0.3	0.3	0.3	0.3	0.3	0.3	0.3	0.3	0.3	0.3
1999	0.3	0.3	0.3	0.3	0.3	0.3	0.3	0.3	0.3	0.3	0.3	0.3	0.3
2000	0.3	0.3	0.4	0.4	0.4	0.4	0.4	0.3	0.3	0.3	0.3	0.3	0.3
2001	0.3	0.3	0.3	0.3	0.3	0.3	0.3	0.3	0.3	0.3	0.3	0.3	0.3
2002	0.3	0.3	0.3	0.3	0.3	0.3	0.3	0.3	0.3	0.3	0.3	0.3	0.3
2003	0.3	0.3	0.3	0.3	0.3	0.3	0.3	0.3	0.3	0.3	0.3	0.3	0.3
State government													
1997	0.7	0.7	0.7	0.7	0.6	0.6	0.6	0.6	0.7	0.7	0.7	0.7	0.7
1998	0.7	0.7	0.7	0.7	0.7	0.6	0.6	0.6	0.7	0.7	0.7	0.7	0.7
1999	0.7	0.8	0.8	0.8	0.7	0.7	0.7	0.7	0.8	0.8	0.8	0.8	0.8
2000	0.7	0.8	0.8	0.8	0.8	0.8	0.8	0.7	0.9	0.8	0.8	0.9	0.8
2001	0.9	0.9	0.9	0.9	0.9	0.9	0.7	0.7	0.9	0.9	0.9	0.9	0.9
2002	0.9	0.9	0.9	0.9	0.9	0.9	0.8	0.8	0.9	0.9	0.9	0.9	0.9
2003	0.9	0.9	0.9	0.9	0.9	0.9	0.8	0.8	0.9	1.0	1.0	0.9	0.9
Local government													
1997	3.8	3.9	3.9	4.0	3.9	3.9	2.8	3.2	3.8	3.9	4.1	4.0	3.8
1998	3.7	4.0	3.9	4.0	4.0	4.0	3.0	3.0	3.9	4.0	4.0	4.0	3.8
1999	3.9	4.1	4.0	3.9	4.0	4.1	3.1	3.0	4.0	4.0	4.1	4.1	3.9
2000	4.1	4.2	4.1	4.1	4.2	4.3	3.3	3.3	3.9	4.2	4.4	4.3	4.0
2001	4.2	4.3	4.2	4.2	4.3	4.3	3.2	3.3	4.1	4.3	4.3	4.3	4.1
2002	4.3	4.3	4.3	4.3	4.4	4.5	3.4	3.5	4.3	4.4	4.4	4.4	4.2
2003	4.3	4.4	4.4	4.4	4.5	4.4	3.4	3.5	4.2	4.4	4.4	4.4	4.2

Employment by Industry: Maine—*Continued*

(Numbers in thousands. Not seasonally adjusted.)

Industry	January	February	March	April	May	June	July	August	September	October	November	December	Annual Average
PORTLAND													
Total nonfarm													
1990	129.1	128.2	128.4	129.3	130.8	133.0	131.6	129.3	129.8	131.5	130.6	130.0	130.1
1991	123.3	121.8	121.4	120.2	121.1	123.1	123.4	123.9	124.7	124.5	125.1	122.9	122.9
1992	120.6	120.1	120.0	121.8	122.6	125.2	126.0	126.4	125.8	126.7	127.0	127.6	124.1
1993	119.9	119.6	120.7	122.8	124.8	126.3	125.3	125.2	127.4	128.7	129.6	129.0	124.9
1994	123.9	123.6	124.4	126.5	128.7	130.5	131.3	131.1	132.3	133.8	135.3	135.3	129.7
1995	128.0	128.8	128.7	129.6	132.1	133.5	133.6	133.9	134.5	137.7	137.1	136.9	132.8
1996	130.8	131.1	131.0	133.2	135.0	137.3	137.4	138.1	137.4	139.1	141.6	140.9	136.0
1997	136.6	136.0	136.7	137.6	140.1	142.7	143.8	144.4	144.8	145.8	148.4	149.3	142.1
1998	140.3	139.7	140.5	142.5	144.6	147.3	147.4	146.9	148.3	148.3	150.8	151.3	145.6
1999	141.8	142.3	143.2	143.9	145.7	150.4	150.1	149.3	148.5	151.4	151.2	151.9	147.4
2000	146.7	146.3	147.1	149.3	151.5	154.5	155.1	154.0	154.2	154.7	156.1	156.4	152.1
2001	152.4	151.6	151.8	154.4	156.0	158.7	159.3	158.1	157.8	158.3	158.1	158.2	156.2
2002	151.4	151.3	152.0	154.1	155.6	158.6	159.5	159.3	158.3	158.3	158.6	159.4	156.4
2003	153.5	152.9	153.0	154.5	156.4	159.2	160.4	159.9	158.6	160.0	161.6	161.3	157.6
Total private													
1990	113.3	112.2	112.0	112.4	113.8	117.2	117.7	115.9	114.4	115.2	114.1	113.5	114.3
1991	107.6	105.5	105.2	104.3	105.2	107.9	109.8	110.5	109.3	108.1	108.6	106.8	107.4
1992	104.9	103.7	103.5	105.6	106.4	109.6	111.6	112.4	109.9	110.0	110.3	110.8	108.2
1993	104.4	103.1	103.9	106.3	108.2	110.1	110.8	111.1	111.1	111.4	112.2	111.8	108.7
1994	107.4	106.1	106.9	109.0	111.2	113.8	116.2	116.3	115.8	116.2	117.2	117.7	112.8
1995	111.2	111.2	111.2	111.9	114.4	116.5	118.2	118.7	117.6	119.9	118.8	118.9	115.7
1996	113.7	113.2	112.7	115.1	117.0	119.7	121.5	122.6	119.9	120.8	122.8	122.6	118.4
1997	118.9	117.7	118.3	119.3	121.8	125.0	127.9	128.4	127.4	127.1	129.2	130.1	124.2
1998	122.4	121.0	121.6	123.6	125.8	128.8	130.4	130.6	130.2	129.9	131.5	131.8	127.3
1999	123.2	123.2	123.8	124.6	127.0	131.5	132.8	132.5	129.8	131.9	131.3	131.8	128.6
2000	128.1	127.0	127.5	129.9	131.6	135.3	137.9	137.1	135.5	135.3	136.5	136.3	133.1
2001	133.2	132.0	132.1	134.6	136.4	139.4	141.7	141.1	138.7	138.3	138.0	137.8	136.9
2002	131.6	131.0	131.4	133.6	135.2	138.3	141.0	141.4	138.3	137.4	137.5	138.2	136.2
2003	133.2	132.2	132.1	133.5	135.7	138.8	141.9	141.6	138.7	138.6	139.7	139.4	137.1
Goods-producing													
1990	20.5	20.3	20.0	20.0	20.4	20.8	20.8	20.4	20.2	20.2	19.9	19.3	20.2
1991	18.1	17.7	17.6	17.5	17.5	18.1	17.8	17.9	18.0	17.6	17.3	16.7	17.6
1992	16.4	16.0	16.0	16.5	16.7	17.2	17.3	17.8	17.5	17.4	17.4	17.2	16.9
1993	15.8	15.4	15.6	15.8	16.1	16.5	16.3	16.5	16.6	16.6	16.5	16.3	16.1
1994	15.6	15.4	15.6	16.1	16.6	16.7	16.8	17.0	17.3	17.1	17.1	17.0	16.5
1995	16.3	16.3	16.4	16.9	17.5	17.7	17.7	17.9	18.0	18.6	17.9	17.9	17.4
1996	17.3	17.1	17.3	17.8	18.3	18.4	18.4	18.6	18.4	18.6	18.7	18.7	18.1
1997	17.9	17.8	17.8	17.6	18.2	19.0	19.4	19.5	19.4	19.4	19.4	19.3	18.7
1998	18.8	18.5	18.7	19.3	19.5	19.6	19.7	19.8	19.9	19.8	19.7	19.6	19.4
1999	19.2	19.3	19.5	19.3	19.7	20.1	19.7	19.8	19.6	19.8	19.6	19.6	19.6
2000	19.4	19.3	19.5	19.9	20.2	20.7	20.7	21.0	20.8	20.3	20.3	20.3	20.2
2001	20.3	20.0	20.0	20.2	20.5	20.7	20.9	20.6	20.4	19.8	19.5	19.4	20.2
2002	18.5	18.3	18.4	18.8	18.9	19.2	19.4	20.3	20.0	19.8	19.5	19.5	19.2
2003	18.9	18.6	18.6	18.3	18.7	19.0	19.4	19.5	19.3	19.3	19.4	19.3	19.0
Construction and mining													
1990	6.8	6.6	6.3	6.4	6.8	6.8	7.1	6.7	6.7	6.7	6.6	5.9	6.6
1991	5.3	5.0	4.9	5.0	5.2	5.6	5.5	5.5	5.8	5.5	5.2	4.7	5.2
1992	4.2	4.0	3.9	4.4	4.8	5.2	5.4	5.9	5.6	5.5	5.4	5.3	4.9
1993	4.6	4.4	4.5	4.6	5.0	5.2	5.3	5.3	5.3	5.3	5.2	5.0	4.9
1994	4.6	4.5	4.6	5.0	5.5	5.5	5.8	5.8	6.0	6.0	5.8	5.7	5.4
1995	5.0	5.0	5.0	5.4	5.9	6.0	6.0	6.1	6.1	6.4	5.8	5.7	5.7
1996	5.2	5.0	5.2	5.5	6.0	6.1	6.2	6.4	6.3	6.5	6.5	6.5	5.9
1997	5.7	5.6	5.5	5.4	5.9	6.4	6.7	6.7	6.5	6.4	6.3	6.1	6.1
1998	5.6	5.4	5.6	6.1	6.4	6.6	6.7	6.8	6.7	6.7	6.5	6.4	6.2
1999	6.1	6.1	6.3	6.5	6.8	7.1	7.1	7.1	6.9	7.0	6.9	6.8	6.7
2000	6.5	6.4	6.6	7.0	7.3	7.6	7.7	7.8	7.6	7.4	7.4	7.3	7.2
2001	7.0	6.9	7.0	7.3	7.8	8.0	8.2	8.1	8.0	7.9	7.7	7.6	7.6
2002	7.0	6.8	6.9	7.4	7.6	7.8	8.0	8.7	8.5	8.4	8.2	8.1	7.8
2003	7.8	7.6	7.6	7.4	7.9	8.1	8.8	8.7	8.6	8.5	8.6	8.5	8.2
Manufacturing													
1990	13.7	13.7	13.7	13.6	13.6	14.0	13.7	13.7	13.5	13.5	13.3	13.4	13.6
1991	12.8	12.7	12.7	12.5	12.3	12.5	12.3	12.4	12.2	12.1	12.1	12.0	12.3
1992	12.2	12.0	12.1	12.1	11.9	12.0	11.9	11.9	11.9	11.9	12.0	11.9	11.9
1993	11.2	11.0	11.1	11.2	11.1	11.3	11.0	11.2	11.3	11.3	11.3	11.3	11.1
1994	11.0	10.9	11.0	11.1	11.1	11.2	11.0	11.2	11.3	11.1	11.3	11.3	11.1
1995	11.3	11.3	11.4	11.5	11.6	11.7	11.7	11.8	11.9	12.2	12.1	12.2	11.7
1996	12.1	12.1	12.1	12.3	12.3	12.3	12.2	12.2	12.1	12.1	12.2	12.2	12.1
1997	12.2	12.2	12.3	12.2	12.3	12.6	12.7	12.8	12.9	13.0	13.1	13.2	12.6
1998	13.2	13.1	13.1	13.2	13.1	13.0	13.0	13.0	13.2	13.1	13.2	13.2	13.1
1999	13.1	13.2	13.2	12.8	12.9	13.0	12.6	12.7	12.7	12.8	12.7	12.8	12.8
2000	12.9	12.9	12.9	12.9	12.9	13.1	13.0	13.2	13.2	12.9	12.9	13.0	12.9
2001	13.3	13.1	13.0	12.9	12.7	12.7	12.7	12.5	12.4	11.9	11.8	11.8	12.6
2002	11.5	11.5	11.5	11.4	11.3	11.4	11.4	11.6	11.5	11.4	11.3	11.4	11.4
2003	11.1	11.0	11.0	10.9	10.8	10.9	10.6	10.8	10.7	10.8	10.8	10.8	10.9

Employment by Industry: Maine—*Continued*

(Numbers in thousands. Not seasonally adjusted.)

Industry	January	February	March	April	May	June	July	August	September	October	November	December	Annual Average
PORTLAND—*Continued*													
Service-providing													
1990	108.6	107.9	108.4	109.3	110.4	112.2	110.8	108.9	109.6	111.3	110.7	110.7	109.9
1991	105.2	104.1	103.8	102.7	103.6	105.0	105.6	106.0	106.7	106.9	107.8	106.2	105.3
1992	104.2	104.1	104.0	105.3	105.9	108.0	108.7	108.6	108.3	109.3	109.6	110.4	107.2
1993	104.1	104.2	105.1	107.0	108.7	109.8	109.0	108.7	110.8	112.1	113.1	112.7	108.7
1994	108.3	108.2	108.8	110.4	112.1	113.8	114.5	114.1	115.0	116.7	118.2	118.3	113.2
1995	111.7	112.5	112.3	112.7	114.6	115.8	115.9	116.0	116.5	119.1	119.2	119.0	115.4
1996	113.5	114.0	113.7	115.4	116.7	118.9	119.0	119.5	119.0	120.5	122.9	122.2	117.9
1997	118.7	118.2	118.9	120.0	121.9	123.7	124.4	124.9	125.4	126.4	129.0	130.0	123.4
1998	121.5	121.2	121.8	123.2	125.1	127.7	127.7	127.1	128.4	128.5	131.1	131.7	126.2
1999	122.6	123.0	123.7	124.6	126.0	130.3	130.4	129.5	128.9	131.6	131.6	132.3	127.8
2000	127.3	127.0	127.6	129.4	131.3	133.8	134.4	133.0	133.4	134.4	135.8	136.1	131.9
2001	132.1	131.6	131.8	134.2	135.5	138.0	138.4	137.5	137.4	138.5	138.6	138.8	136.0
2002	132.9	133.0	133.6	135.3	136.7	139.4	140.1	139.0	138.3	138.5	139.1	139.9	137.2
2003	134.6	134.3	134.4	136.2	137.7	140.2	141.0	140.4	139.3	140.7	142.2	142.0	138.6
Trade, transportation, and utilities													
1990	33.3	32.1	31.6	31.2	31.5	32.9	32.4	32.5	32.4	33.0	33.7	34.1	32.5
1991	30.8	29.5	29.1	28.1	28.2	28.8	29.4	30.0	29.9	29.8	30.7	30.9	29.6
1992	30.4	29.6	29.1	29.3	29.4	30.5	30.3	30.5	30.2	31.0	32.2	33.0	30.4
1993	30.0	29.2	28.8	29.0	29.4	29.7	30.2	30.4	30.8	31.8	32.9	32.6	30.4
1994	30.6	29.7	29.3	29.3	29.8	30.6	31.1	30.8	31.2	32.6	33.6	34.4	31.0
1995	31.8	31.0	30.3	30.3	30.6	31.2	31.5	31.8	32.0	34.0	34.7	34.7	31.9
1996	32.0	31.1	30.3	30.4	30.7	31.4	32.0	32.5	32.2	33.8	36.3	36.2	32.4
1997	32.8	31.5	31.4	31.3	31.7	32.3	32.7	33.2	33.1	34.2	36.2	36.7	33.0
1998	32.4	31.1	30.8	30.8	31.1	32.0	32.7	32.8	33.4	34.3	36.6	36.8	32.9
1999	32.1	31.5	31.3	31.1	31.5	33.3	34.0	34.3	33.7	35.1	36.1	37.0	33.4
2000	33.5	32.4	32.2	32.3	32.5	33.9	34.5	34.2	34.5	35.4	37.2	36.9	34.1
2001	35.1	33.8	33.4	33.6	33.9	34.8	35.6	35.6	35.3	36.5	37.6	37.8	35.3
2002	34.5	33.6	33.3	33.4	33.4	34.2	34.7	34.8	34.4	34.6	35.6	36.6	34.4
2003	33.8	32.9	32.4	32.5	33.1	34.2	34.6	34.8	34.5	34.9	36.7	37.2	34.3
Wholesale trade													
1990	7.1	7.2	7.2	7.0	7.0	7.1	7.0	7.0	6.9	6.9	6.8	6.9	7.0
1991	6.9	6.8	6.8	6.4	6.4	6.4	6.5	6.5	6.4	6.2	6.2	6.1	6.4
1992	6.1	6.1	6.1	6.1	6.1	6.2	6.3	6.3	6.3	6.1	6.1	6.1	6.1
1993	6.2	6.2	6.2	6.2	6.2	6.3	6.3	6.3	6.4	6.4	6.4	6.4	6.2
1994	6.4	6.4	6.4	6.3	6.3	6.4	6.4	6.4	6.3	6.3	6.3	6.4	6.3
1995	6.3	6.4	6.3	6.4	6.4	6.5	6.5	6.6	6.6	6.8	6.7	6.9	6.5
1996	7.1	7.2	7.2	7.2	7.2	7.3	7.2	7.4	7.4	7.4	7.6	7.8	7.3
1997	7.7	7.8	7.7	7.7	7.6	7.1	6.8	6.9	6.9	6.9	6.9	6.9	7.2
1998	6.8	6.9	6.8	6.9	7.0	7.0	7.1	6.9	6.9	6.9	7.0	7.0	6.9
1999	6.6	6.7	6.7	6.7	6.7	6.8	6.8	6.9	6.8	7.0	6.8	6.8	6.7
2000	6.8	6.9	6.9	7.2	7.1	7.2	7.2	7.2	7.2	7.3	7.3	7.4	7.1
2001	7.7	7.6	7.6	7.7	7.6	7.6	7.7	7.7	7.6	7.6	7.6	7.7	7.6
2002	7.3	7.3	7.3	7.3	7.2	7.2	7.2	7.1	7.1	7.1	7.1	7.0	7.2
2003	7.2	7.2	7.2	7.2	7.4	7.5	7.5	7.5	7.4	7.4	7.4	7.3	7.4
Retail trade													
1990	21.7	20.3	19.8	19.6	19.8	21.0	20.5	20.5	20.6	21.1	22.0	22.3	20.7
1991	19.0	17.8	17.4	16.8	16.9	17.4	17.8	18.4	18.4	18.6	19.5	19.9	18.1
1992	18.5	17.5	17.2	17.2	17.3	18.1	18.6	18.9	18.6	19.7	20.9	21.7	18.6
1993	18.4	17.6	17.1	17.4	17.6	17.8	18.4	18.6	18.6	19.4	20.5	20.8	18.5
1994	18.5	17.6	17.4	17.5	17.8	18.5	18.7	18.9	19.3	20.3	21.8	22.4	19.0
1995	20.1	18.9	18.4	18.3	18.6	19.0	19.3	19.5	20.0	21.2	22.0	22.3	19.8
1996	19.3	18.2	17.5	17.9	18.1	18.7	19.0	19.3	19.3	20.5	22.2	22.5	19.3
1997	20.2	18.3	18.2	18.4	18.9	20.0	20.6	20.9	20.9	21.8	23.7	24.1	20.5
1998	20.5	19.3	19.2	18.8	19.1	19.9	20.5	20.8	20.9	21.7	23.9	24.3	20.7
1999	20.4	19.7	19.5	19.3	19.6	20.6	21.3	21.7	21.5	22.6	23.9	24.4	21.2
2000	21.0	20.1	20.0	19.8	20.1	20.9	21.4	21.6	21.9	22.7	24.0	24.1	21.4
2001	22.1	21.0	20.7	20.8	21.2	21.9	22.6	22.7	22.5	23.6	24.7	24.8	22.4
2002	22.0	21.2	21.0	21.1	21.2	21.9	22.3	22.6	22.2	22.4	23.5	24.5	22.2
2003	21.6	20.6	20.3	20.5	20.8	21.7	22.2	22.4	22.0	22.3	24.0	24.5	21.9
Transportation and utilities													
1990	4.5	4.6	4.6	4.6	4.7	4.8	4.9	5.0	4.9	5.0	4.9	4.9	4.7
1991	4.9	4.9	4.9	4.9	4.9	5.0	5.1	5.1	5.1	5.0	5.0	4.9	4.9
1992	5.8	6.0	5.8	6.0	6.0	6.2	5.4	5.3	5.3	5.2	5.2	5.2	5.6
1993	5.4	5.4	5.5	5.4	5.6	5.6	5.5	5.5	5.8	6.0	6.0	5.4	5.5
1994	5.7	5.7	5.5	5.5	5.7	5.7	6.0	5.5	5.6	6.0	5.5	5.6	5.6
1995	5.4	5.7	5.6	5.6	5.6	5.7	5.7	5.7	5.4	6.0	6.0	5.5	5.6
1996	5.6	5.7	5.6	5.3	5.4	5.4	5.8	5.8	5.5	5.9	6.5	5.9	5.7
1997	4.9	5.4	5.5	5.2	5.2	5.2	5.3	5.4	5.3	5.5	5.6	5.7	5.3
1998	5.1	4.9	4.8	5.1	5.0	5.1	5.1	5.1	5.6	5.7	5.7	5.5	5.2
1999	5.1	5.1	5.1	5.1	5.2	5.9	5.9	5.7	5.4	5.5	5.4	5.8	5.4
2000	5.7	5.4	5.3	5.3	5.3	5.8	5.9	5.4	5.4	5.4	5.9	5.4	5.5
2001	5.3	5.2	5.1	5.1	5.1	5.3	5.3	5.2	5.2	5.3	5.3	5.3	5.2
2002	5.2	5.1	5.0	5.0	5.0	5.1	5.2	5.1	5.1	5.1	5.0	5.1	5.1
2003	5.0	5.1	4.9	4.8	4.9	5.0	4.9	4.9	5.1	5.2	5.3	5.4	5.0

Employment by Industry: Maine—*Continued*

(Numbers in thousands. Not seasonally adjusted.)

Industry	January	February	March	April	May	June	July	August	September	October	November	December	Annual Average
PORTLAND—*Continued*													
Information													
1990	3.7	3.6	3.6	3.7	3.7	3.7	3.7	3.7	3.6	3.6	3.6	3.6	3.6
1991	3.5	3.4	3.4	3.4	3.4	3.4	3.4	3.4	3.4	3.3	3.3	3.2	3.3
1992	3.2	3.2	3.2	3.2	3.2	3.3	3.4	3.4	3.4	3.4	3.3	3.3	3.2
1993	3.3	3.3	3.4	3.4	3.4	3.5	3.5	3.4	3.4	3.4	3.4	3.5	3.4
1994	3.5	3.5	3.6	3.6	3.6	3.6	3.6	3.7	3.7	3.7	3.7	3.7	3.6
1995	3.6	3.6	3.7	3.7	3.7	3.8	3.8	3.8	3.8	4.0	4.0	4.0	3.7
1996	3.7	3.7	3.6	3.6	3.7	3.7	3.7	3.7	3.6	3.5	3.5	3.6	3.6
1997	3.7	3.7	3.7	3.7	3.7	3.8	3.9	3.9	4.0	3.9	4.0	4.0	3.8
1998	4.0	4.0	4.0	4.0	4.1	4.1	4.0	4.0	4.0	4.0	4.0	4.1	4.0
1999	3.9	3.8	3.8	3.8	3.9	3.9	4.0	4.0	4.0	4.0	4.1	4.1	3.9
2000	4.2	4.2	4.2	4.2	4.3	4.2	4.3	3.7	4.3	4.3	4.4	4.3	4.2
2001	4.6	4.6	4.6	4.6	4.6	4.6	4.6	4.6	4.6	4.5	4.5	4.5	4.6
2002	4.4	4.3	4.3	4.3	4.3	4.3	4.3	4.3	4.2	4.2	4.3	4.2	4.3
2003	4.2	4.2	4.2	4.2	4.2	4.2	4.2	4.2	4.2	4.1	4.1	4.1	4.2
Financial activities													
1990	12.1	12.2	12.2	12.2	12.2	12.4	12.4	12.3	12.3	12.5	12.3	12.2	12.2
1991	12.2	12.3	12.2	12.0	12.0	12.2	12.2	12.1	12.2	11.9	12.0	11.8	12.0
1992	11.9	11.8	11.8	11.8	11.8	12.0	12.1	12.1	12.0	12.0	11.9	12.0	11.9
1993	12.2	12.2	12.2	12.3	12.4	12.5	12.6	12.6	12.6	12.5	12.6	12.6	12.4
1994	12.4	12.4	12.5	12.7	12.7	12.8	12.6	12.6	12.5	12.4	12.5	12.5	12.5
1995	12.0	12.1	12.3	12.1	12.2	12.4	12.5	12.5	12.4	12.3	12.1	12.2	12.2
1996	12.1	12.2	12.3	12.5	12.6	12.9	12.9	13.0	12.7	12.7	12.6	12.6	12.5
1997	12.8	12.9	13.1	12.6	12.7	13.0	13.3	13.2	13.2	12.9	13.0	13.0	12.9
1998	13.1	13.1	13.3	13.6	13.7	14.0	14.0	14.1	13.9	13.9	13.9	14.0	13.7
1999	14.0	14.1	14.1	14.1	14.2	14.5	14.4	14.2	13.9	14.1	13.9	13.9	14.1
2000	14.0	13.9	13.9	14.0	13.9	14.1	14.1	14.2	14.0	14.1	14.1	14.2	14.0
2001	14.1	14.3	14.3	14.4	14.4	14.6	14.6	14.6	14.5	14.5	14.5	14.6	14.5
2002	14.3	14.3	14.3	14.2	14.4	14.6	14.6	14.6	14.3	14.5	14.5	14.5	14.4
2003	14.3	14.3	14.3	14.3	14.3	14.4	14.6	14.6	14.3	14.4	14.4	14.4	14.4
Professional and business services													
1990	12.8	12.8	12.9	12.9	12.9	13.2	13.0	12.9	12.8	12.9	12.7	12.8	12.8
1991	12.5	12.4	12.4	12.3	12.4	12.7	12.8	12.9	12.8	12.8	12.9	12.7	12.6
1992	12.4	12.4	12.5	12.9	12.9	13.2	13.7	13.7	13.4	13.2	13.3	13.3	13.0
1993	12.4	12.4	12.6	13.0	13.4	13.3	13.2	13.2	13.4	13.4	13.4	13.4	13.0
1994	13.4	13.4	13.7	14.0	14.1	14.8	15.3	15.5	15.5	15.4	16.0	15.9	14.7
1995	14.8	15.3	15.3	14.7	15.4	15.6	15.2	15.3	15.3	15.6	15.6	15.5	15.3
1996	15.1	15.1	15.0	15.1	15.2	15.5	15.6	15.7	15.5	15.9	15.7	15.7	15.4
1997	16.3	16.2	16.3	16.6	16.8	17.1	17.5	17.9	17.7	18.2	18.6	18.9	17.3
1998	17.2	17.3	17.4	18.0	18.2	18.6	18.8	18.8	18.9	18.8	18.8	19.0	18.3
1999	17.5	17.7	17.7	18.0	18.1	18.5	18.3	18.0	17.7	18.1	18.0	18.0	17.9
2000	17.8	17.7	17.9	18.3	18.4	18.7	19.1	19.2	19.0	19.0	18.8	19.2	18.5
2001	18.8	18.8	18.9	19.2	19.4	19.7	19.7	19.7	19.5	19.5	19.3	19.3	19.3
2002	18.8	18.9	19.0	19.1	19.2	19.5	19.7	19.4	19.1	19.0	19.1	18.9	19.1
2003	18.8	18.6	18.8	18.9	19.0	19.3	19.0	19.1	18.7	18.7	18.8	18.6	18.9
Educational and health services													
1990	15.5	15.8	15.9	15.9	15.9	15.9	15.5	15.3	15.6	16.1	16.0	16.0	15.7
1991	16.0	16.1	16.1	16.1	16.1	15.9	15.7	15.8	16.2	16.6	16.9	16.5	16.1
1992	16.3	16.5	16.5	16.5	16.4	16.3	16.2	16.1	16.2	16.8	16.7	16.7	16.4
1993	16.7	16.9	17.2	17.2	17.2	17.2	16.7	16.6	17.1	17.4	17.5	17.5	17.1
1994	17.2	17.3	17.6	17.6	17.7	17.4	17.1	17.2	17.6	17.9	18.0	18.0	17.5
1995	17.7	17.8	17.9	17.9	17.9	17.7	17.8	17.7	18.1	18.4	18.3	18.6	17.9
1996	18.4	18.8	18.9	18.9	18.8	18.8	18.6	19.0	19.3	19.6	19.7	19.8	19.0
1997	20.1	20.3	20.5	20.3	20.4	20.4	20.5	20.5	21.0	21.0	21.2	21.4	20.6
1998	21.1	21.3	21.3	20.8	20.8	20.8	20.5	20.5	20.9	21.3	21.5	21.5	21.0
1999	21.0	21.3	21.5	21.3	21.3	21.4	21.2	21.3	21.7	22.3	22.3	22.3	21.5
2000	23.0	23.3	23.3	23.2	23.3	23.1	23.2	23.1	23.4	23.7	23.8	23.8	23.3
2001	23.0	23.2	23.3	23.4	23.3	23.4	23.2	23.3	23.6	24.1	23.8	23.9	23.5
2002	23.9	24.2	24.2	24.6	24.6	24.6	24.7	24.6	24.7	25.0	24.9	25.0	24.6
2003	25.0	25.2	25.2	25.5	25.2	25.3	25.6	25.2	25.4	26.0	26.1	25.8	25.5
Leisure and hospitality													
1990	9.9	9.9	10.3	11.0	11.7	13.0	14.4	13.4	12.3	11.7	10.8	10.4	11.5
1991	9.6	9.3	9.6	10.2	10.9	12.1	13.5	13.5	12.1	11.3	10.7	10.2	11.0
1992	9.8	9.7	10.0	10.8	11.4	12.5	13.8	14.0	12.5	11.5	10.8	10.6	11.4
1993	9.5	9.3	9.6	11.0	11.7	12.7	13.5	13.6	12.5	11.5	11.1	11.1	11.4
1994	10.1	10.1	10.3	11.3	12.3	13.4	14.7	14.5	13.2	12.3	11.5	11.3	12.0
1995	10.2	10.3	10.5	11.6	12.4	13.3	14.7	14.7	13.2	12.2	11.4	11.2	12.1
1996	10.4	10.5	10.6	12.0	12.9	14.1	15.1	15.1	13.4	12.2	11.8	11.5	12.4
1997	10.9	10.8	11.0	12.8	13.8	14.9	15.7	15.5	14.3	13.0	12.2	12.1	13.0
1998	11.2	11.2	11.5	12.5	13.7	14.9	15.6	15.6	14.2	13.1	12.3	12.1	13.1
1999	10.9	10.9	11.2	12.2	13.5	14.8	16.4	16.2	14.6	13.9	12.7	12.3	13.3
2000	11.7	11.7	11.9	13.4	14.4	15.9	17.1	16.8	14.8	13.9	13.3	13.0	13.9
2001	12.5	12.4	12.6	14.1	15.2	16.6	17.9	17.7	15.7	14.2	13.6	13.3	14.7
2002	12.2	12.2	12.6	13.9	15.1	16.6	18.1	17.9	16.1	14.7	14.1	14.0	14.8
2003	12.9	12.8	13.1	14.2	15.6	16.9	18.5	18.4	16.4	15.3	14.2	14.0	15.2

Employment by Industry: Maine—*Continued*

(Numbers in thousands. Not seasonally adjusted.)

Industry	January	February	March	April	May	June	July	August	September	October	November	December	Annual Average
PORTLAND—*Continued*													
Other services													
1990	5.5	5.5	5.5	5.5	5.5	5.3	5.5	5.4	5.2	5.2	5.1	5.1	5.3
1991	4.9	4.8	4.8	4.7	4.7	4.7	5.0	4.9	4.7	4.8	4.8	4.8	4.8
1992	4.5	4.5	4.4	4.6	4.6	4.6	4.8	4.8	4.7	4.7	4.7	4.7	4.6
1993	4.5	4.4	4.5	4.6	4.6	4.7	4.8	4.8	4.7	4.8	4.8	4.8	4.6
1994	4.6	4.3	4.3	4.4	4.4	4.5	5.0	5.0	4.8	4.8	4.8	4.9	4.6
1995	4.8	4.8	4.8	4.7	4.7	4.8	5.0	5.0	4.8	4.8	4.8	4.8	4.8
1996	4.7	4.7	4.7	4.8	4.8	4.9	5.2	5.0	4.8	4.5	4.5	4.5	4.7
1997	4.4	4.5	4.5	4.4	4.5	4.5	4.9	4.7	4.7	4.5	4.6	4.7	4.5
1998	4.6	4.5	4.6	4.6	4.7	4.8	5.1	5.0	5.0	4.7	4.7	4.7	4.7
1999	4.6	4.6	4.7	4.8	4.8	5.0	4.8	4.7	4.6	4.6	4.6	4.6	4.7
2000	4.5	4.5	4.6	4.6	4.6	4.7	4.9	4.9	4.7	4.6	4.6	4.6	4.6
2001	4.8	4.9	5.0	5.1	5.1	5.0	5.2	5.0	5.1	5.2	5.2	5.0	5.1
2002	5.0	5.2	5.3	5.3	5.3	5.3	5.5	5.5	5.5	5.6	5.5	5.5	5.4
2003	5.3	5.6	5.5	5.6	5.6	5.5	6.0	5.8	5.9	5.9	6.0	6.0	5.7
Government													
1990	15.8	16.0	16.4	16.9	17.0	15.8	13.9	13.4	15.4	16.3	16.5	16.5	15.8
1991	15.7	16.3	16.2	15.9	15.9	15.2	13.6	13.4	15.4	16.4	16.5	16.1	15.5
1992	15.7	16.4	16.5	16.2	16.2	15.6	14.4	14.0	15.9	16.7	16.7	16.8	15.9
1993	15.5	16.5	16.8	16.5	16.6	16.2	14.5	14.1	16.3	17.3	17.4	17.2	16.2
1994	16.5	17.5	17.5	17.5	17.5	16.7	15.1	14.8	16.5	17.6	18.1	17.6	16.9
1995	16.8	17.6	17.5	17.7	17.7	17.0	15.4	15.2	16.9	17.8	18.3	18.0	17.1
1996	17.1	17.9	18.3	18.1	18.0	17.6	15.9	15.5	17.5	18.3	18.8	18.3	17.6
1997	17.7	18.3	18.4	18.3	18.3	17.7	15.9	16.0	17.4	18.7	19.2	19.2	17.9
1998	17.9	18.7	18.9	18.9	18.8	18.5	17.0	16.3	18.1	18.4	19.3	19.5	18.3
1999	18.6	19.1	19.4	19.3	18.7	18.9	17.3	16.8	18.7	19.5	19.9	20.1	18.8
2000	18.6	19.3	19.6	19.4	19.9	19.2	17.2	16.9	18.7	19.4	19.6	20.1	18.9
2001	19.2	19.6	19.7	19.8	19.6	19.3	17.6	17.0	19.1	20.0	20.1	20.4	19.3
2002	19.8	20.3	20.6	20.5	20.4	20.3	18.5	17.9	20.0	20.9	21.1	21.2	20.1
2003	20.3	20.7	20.9	21.0	20.7	20.4	18.5	18.3	19.9	21.4	21.9	21.9	20.5
Federal government													
1990	2.0	2.0	2.1	2.8	2.9	2.3	2.3	2.1	2.0	2.0	2.0	2.1	2.2
1991	2.0	2.1	2.1	1.9	1.9	2.0	2.0	2.0	2.0	2.0	2.0	2.0	2.0
1992	2.0	2.1	2.1	2.0	2.0	2.0	2.1	2.1	2.1	2.0	1.9	2.0	2.0
1993	1.9	1.9	1.9	1.9	1.9	2.0	2.0	2.0	2.0	2.0	2.0	2.0	1.9
1994	2.1	2.1	2.0	2.1	2.1	2.1	2.1	2.1	2.1	2.1	2.1	2.2	2.1
1995	2.1	2.1	2.1	2.1	2.2	2.2	2.1	2.2	2.1	2.2	2.2	2.2	2.1
1996	2.2	2.1	2.2	2.2	2.2	2.2	2.2	2.1	2.2	2.3	2.4	2.3	2.2
1997	2.3	2.3	2.3	2.2	2.2	2.2	2.2	2.4	2.2	2.2	2.3	2.5	2.2
1998	2.4	2.4	2.4	2.4	2.4	2.4	2.4	2.4	2.4	2.4	2.5	2.7	2.4
1999	2.4	2.4	2.4	2.4	2.4	2.4	2.4	2.5	2.4	2.5	2.5	2.7	2.4
2000	2.5	2.5	2.7	2.6	2.9	2.7	2.6	2.5	2.4	2.4	2.5	2.7	2.5
2001	2.5	2.4	2.4	2.4	2.4	2.4	2.4	2.4	2.4	2.4	2.4	2.4	2.4
2002	2.3	2.3	2.3	2.3	2.3	2.3	2.3	2.3	2.3	2.4	2.4	2.5	2.3
2003	2.3	2.3	2.3	2.3	2.3	2.3	2.1	2.1	2.3	2.2	2.2	2.3	2.3
State government													
1990	4.2	4.4	4.5	4.5	4.4	3.7	3.7	3.7	4.2	4.6	4.6	4.6	4.2
1991	4.3	4.5	4.6	4.4	4.4	3.6	3.6	3.6	4.3	4.6	4.6	4.6	4.2
1992	4.2	4.5	4.6	4.5	4.4	3.7	3.8	3.7	4.4	4.8	4.8	4.8	4.3
1993	4.0	4.7	4.8	4.6	4.5	3.8	3.8	3.8	4.3	5.0	5.0	5.0	4.4
1994	4.2	5.0	5.1	5.0	4.9	3.9	3.9	3.9	4.2	4.8	5.0	4.9	4.5
1995	4.1	4.8	4.8	4.7	4.6	3.9	3.8	3.9	4.3	4.8	4.8	4.8	4.4
1996	4.1	4.8	4.8	4.7	4.6	3.9	3.8	3.8	4.7	4.8	4.8	4.8	4.4
1997	4.3	4.8	4.9	4.7	4.7	4.0	4.0	4.0	4.5	5.0	5.0	5.0	4.5
1998	4.3	4.7	4.9	4.8	4.8	4.1	4.1	4.1	4.3	4.5	5.2	5.2	4.5
1999	4.5	5.1	5.2	5.2	4.8	4.4	4.4	4.3	4.9	5.1	5.3	5.3	4.8
2000	4.3	4.9	4.9	4.9	4.8	4.1	4.1	4.1	4.6	4.9	5.0	5.0	4.6
2001	4.4	4.9	5.0	5.0	4.7	4.2	4.1	4.0	4.6	5.0	5.0	5.1	4.7
2002	5.0	5.5	5.6	5.6	5.3	4.8	4.9	4.8	5.4	5.7	5.7	5.8	5.3
2003	5.2	5.5	5.7	5.7	5.4	4.9	4.8	4.7	5.3	5.4	5.6	5.9	5.3
Local government													
1990	9.6	9.6	9.8	9.6	9.7	9.8	7.9	7.6	9.2	9.7	9.9	9.8	9.3
1991	9.4	9.7	9.5	9.6	9.6	9.6	8.0	7.8	9.1	9.8	9.9	9.5	9.2
1992	9.5	9.8	9.8	9.7	9.8	9.9	8.5	8.2	9.4	9.9	10.0	10.0	9.5
1993	9.6	9.9	10.1	10.0	10.2	10.4	8.7	8.3	10.0	10.3	10.4	10.2	9.8
1994	10.2	10.4	10.4	10.4	10.5	10.7	9.1	8.8	10.2	10.7	11.0	10.5	10.2
1995	10.6	10.7	10.6	10.9	10.9	10.9	9.5	9.1	10.5	10.8	11.3	11.0	10.5
1996	10.8	11.0	11.3	11.2	11.2	11.5	9.9	9.6	10.6	11.2	11.6	11.2	10.9
1997	11.1	11.2	11.2	11.4	11.4	11.5	9.7	9.6	10.7	11.5	11.9	11.7	11.0
1998	11.2	11.6	11.6	11.7	11.6	12.0	10.5	9.8	11.4	11.5	11.6	11.6	11.3
1999	11.7	11.6	11.8	11.7	11.5	12.1	10.5	10.0	11.4	11.9	12.1	12.1	11.5
2000	11.8	11.9	12.0	11.9	12.2	12.4	10.5	10.3	11.7	12.1	12.1	12.4	11.7
2001	12.3	12.3	12.3	12.4	12.5	12.7	11.1	10.6	12.1	12.6	12.7	12.9	12.2
2002	12.5	12.5	12.7	12.6	12.8	13.2	11.3	10.8	12.3	12.8	13.0	12.9	12.5
2003	12.8	12.9	12.9	13.0	13.0	13.2	11.6	11.5	12.3	13.8	14.1	13.7	12.9

Employment by Industry: Maine—*Continued*

(Numbers in thousands. Not seasonally adjusted.)

Industry	January	February	March	April	May	June	July	August	September	October	November	December	Annual Average
PORTLAND—*Continued*													
Local government													
1990	9.6	9.6	9.8	9.6	9.7	9.8	7.9	7.6	9.2	9.7	9.9	9.8	9.3
1991	9.4	9.7	9.5	9.6	9.6	9.6	8.0	7.8	9.1	9.8	9.9	9.5	9.2
1992	9.5	9.8	9.8	9.7	9.8	9.9	8.5	8.2	9.4	9.9	10.0	10.0	9.5
1993	9.6	9.9	10.1	10.0	10.2	10.4	8.7	8.3	10.0	10.3	10.4	10.2	9.8
1994	10.2	10.4	10.4	10.4	10.5	10.7	9.1	8.8	10.2	10.7	11.0	10.5	10.2
1995	10.6	10.7	10.6	10.9	10.9	10.9	9.5	9.1	10.5	10.8	11.3	11.0	10.5
1996	10.8	11.0	11.3	11.2	11.2	11.5	9.9	9.6	10.6	11.2	11.6	11.2	10.9
1997	11.1	11.2	11.2	11.4	11.4	11.5	9.7	9.6	10.7	11.5	11.9	11.7	11.0
1998	11.2	11.6	11.6	11.7	11.6	12.0	10.5	9.8	11.4	11.5	11.6	11.6	11.3
1999	11.7	11.6	11.8	11.7	11.5	12.1	10.5	10.0	11.4	11.9	12.1	12.1	11.5
2000	11.8	11.9	12.0	11.9	12.2	12.4	10.5	10.3	11.7	12.1	12.1	12.4	11.7
2001	12.3	12.3	12.3	12.4	12.5	12.7	11.1	10.6	12.1	12.6	12.7	12.9	12.2
2002	12.5	12.5	12.7	12.6	12.8	13.2	11.3	10.8	12.3	12.8	13.0	12.9	12.5
2003	12.8	12.9	12.9	13.0	13.0	13.2	11.6	11.5	12.3	13.8	14.1	13.7	12.9

Average Weekly Hours by Industry: Maine

(Not seasonally adjusted.)

Industry	January	February	March	April	May	June	July	August	September	October	November	December	Annual Average
STATEWIDE													
Manufacturing													
2001	40.1	39.9	39.6	39.5	39.8	39.4	40.0	39.1	39.3	39.9	40.2	40.4	39.8
2002	39.5	39.5	40.0	39.8	39.6	39.9	39.3	39.0	40.5	40.3	40.3	40.8	39.9
2003	40.0	39.4	40.0	40.3	39.8	39.7	40.0	39.8	40.6	40.2	40.1	40.7	40.0
PORTLAND													
Manufacturing													
2001	42.2	40.8	40.5	42.2	41.6	42.6	39.5	41.0	43.4	43.3	43.2	42.4	41.9
2002	40.5	40.2	41.2	40.5	41.4	41.7	40.2	40.5	41.5	41.8	41.5	41.8	41.1
2003	41.7	41.7	41.4	41.9	42.1	41.5	42.8	41.4	43.0	44.0	42.8	44.4	42.4

Average Hourly Earnings by Industry: Maine

(Dollars, not seasonally adjusted.)

Industry	January	February	March	April	May	June	July	August	September	October	November	December	Annual Average
STATEWIDE													
Manufacturing													
2001	14.26	14.39	14.47	14.56	14.55	14.66	15.05	14.77	14.88	14.93	14.99	15.09	14.71
2002	15.21	15.33	15.02	15.23	15.33	15.36	15.93	15.65	15.71	15.82	15.85	16.13	15.55
2003	16.11	16.16	16.05	16.03	16.23	16.16	16.21	16.29	16.41	16.54	16.59	16.53	16.28
PORTLAND													
Manufacturing													
2001	12.22	12.41	12.39	12.31	12.34	12.54	12.89	12.24	12.36	12.58	13.37	12.74	12.52
2002	12.70	12.81	12.67	12.71	12.82	12.70	12.83	12.98	13.17	13.00	13.50	13.16	12.92
2003	13.02	12.93	12.88	13.15	13.04	12.98	13.17	13.18	13.07	12.90	13.58	12.86	13.06

Average Weekly Earnings by Industry: Maine

(Dollars, not seasonally adjusted.)

Industry	January	February	March	April	May	June	July	August	September	October	November	December	Annual Average
STATEWIDE													
Manufacturing													
2001	571.83	574.16	573.01	575.12	579.09	577.60	602.00	577.51	584.78	595.71	602.60	609.64	585.46
2002	600.80	605.54	600.80	606.15	607.07	612.86	626.05	610.35	636.26	637.55	638.76	658.10	620.45
2003	644.40	636.70	642.00	646.01	645.95	641.55	648.40	648.34	666.25	664.91	665.26	672.77	651.20
PORTLAND													
Manufacturing													
2001	515.68	506.33	501.80	519.48	513.34	534.20	509.16	501.84	536.42	544.71	577.58	540.18	524.59
2002	514.35	514.96	522.00	514.76	530.75	529.59	515.77	525.69	546.56	543.40	560.25	550.09	531.01
2003	542.93	539.18	533.23	550.99	548.98	538.67	563.68	545.65	562.01	567.60	581.22	570.98	553.74

MARYLAND AT A GLANCE

(Population and total nonfarm employment numbers in thousands)

Population, Census 2000:	5,296.5
Total nonfarm employment, 2003:	2,482.5
Change in total nonfarm employment	
(Number)	
1990–2003:	311.3
1990–2001:	296.1
2001–2003:	15.2
(Compound annual rate of change)	
1990–2003:	1.0%
1990–2001:	1.2%
2001–2003:	0.3%
Unemployment rate	
1990:	4.6%
2001:	4.0%
2003:	4.5%

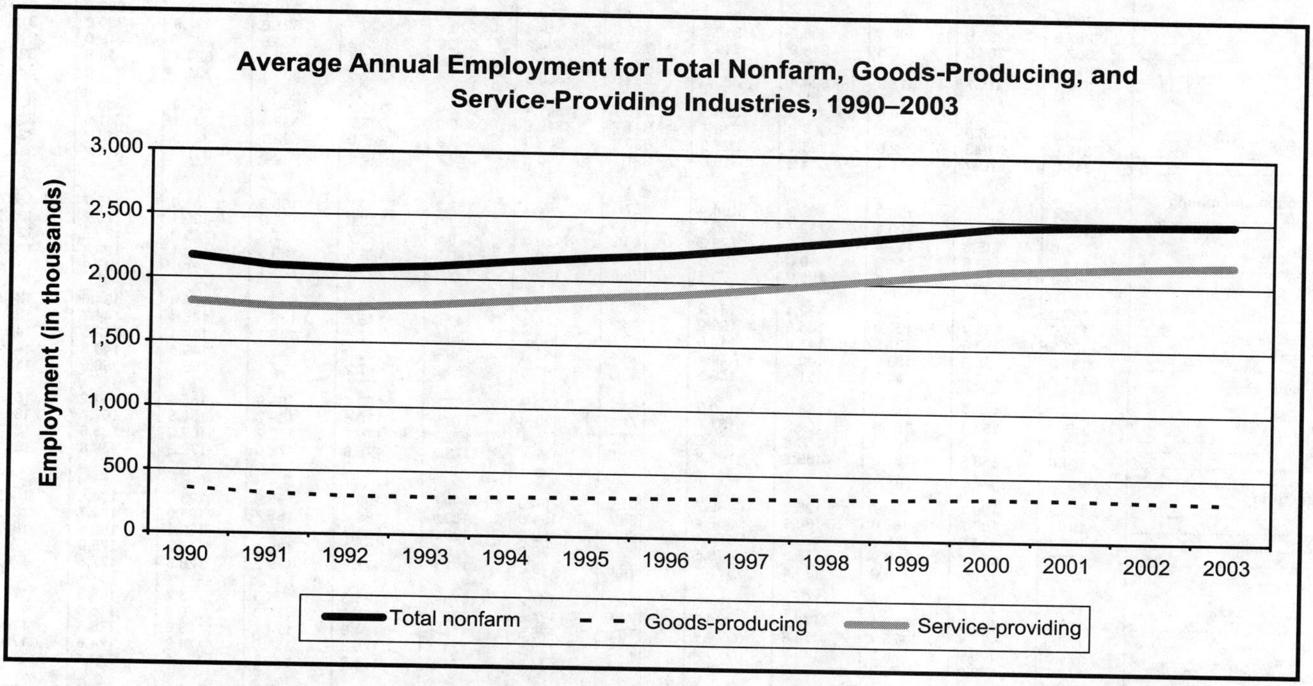

The total number of nonfarm payroll jobs declined during the 1990–1991 recession as employment in the goods-producing sector fell sharply. Although employment fell in the service-providing sector as well, it did so at a slower rate. After stable growth in the mid 1990s, total nonfarm employment was relatively flat from 2000 to 2003, increasing only 1.3 percent. During this period, goods-producing employment decreased while the service-providing sector experienced modest gains. However, employment in the information industry fell 14.2 percent from 2000 to 2003.

Employment by Industry: Maryland

(Numbers in thousands. Not seasonally adjusted.)

Industry	January	February	March	April	May	June	July	August	September	October	November	December	Annual Average
STATEWIDE													
Total nonfarm													
1990	2116.1	2135.5	2161.0	2172.1	2186.6	2214.4	2180.5	2183.5	2191.3	2170.2	2172.8	2170.7	2171.2
1991	2071.4	2076.3	2089.8	2095.0	2113.6	2130.2	2099.1	2097.6	2107.5	2100.4	2110.9	2106.1	2099.8
1992	2034.4	2037.3	2053.4	2075.4	2096.1	2107.8	2092.2	2084.4	2090.1	2098.1	2100.7	2105.8	2081.3
1993	2041.9	2051.7	2059.0	2088.9	2114.0	2127.1	2114.8	2104.6	2120.7	2126.3	2134.7	2145.0	2102.3
1994	2068.4	2071.2	2105.5	2135.6	2158.2	2177.7	2161.7	2152.1	2172.2	2171.9	2183.9	2192.3	2145.8
1995	2121.5	2129.5	2154.4	2176.0	2193.4	2219.3	2188.6	2186.7	2199.0	2198.0	2208.5	2217.3	2182.6
1996	2108.5	2145.4	2175.1	2194.7	2221.0	2247.7	2225.0	2222.8	2236.9	2244.2	2253.9	2258.7	2211.1
1997	2186.5	2198.6	2231.1	2248.5	2275.3	2296.5	2281.2	2267.8	2288.7	2298.9	2310.0	2323.6	2267.2
1998	2250.0	2263.1	2288.6	2299.8	2323.8	2352.5	2332.3	2334.7	2344.4	2356.4	2366.6	2379.7	2324.3
1999	2305.7	2324.4	2346.2	2372.8	2392.3	2414.4	2383.8	2371.1	2405.9	2427.4	2441.1	2453.2	2386.5
2000	2369.5	2377.8	2419.0	2441.7	2464.3	2489.0	2441.9	2431.1	2477.2	2483.8	2495.9	2509.8	2450.0
2001	2415.0	2429.3	2450.9	2462.7	2482.8	2506.6	2451.1	2460.3	2472.8	2481.9	2493.2	2500.7	2467.3
2002	2421.1	2436.6	2462.2	2472.8	2494.5	2512.8	2461.3	2479.1	2488.9	2490.0	2499.6	2501.6	2476.7
2003	2429.3	2426.9	2452.7	2477.4	2501.8	2518.3	2471.9	2484.8	2493.5	2507.4	2513.1	2513.0	2482.5
Total private													
1990	1704.7	1715.5	1737.6	1746.7	1759.2	1788.6	1777.1	1781.5	1773.1	1745.3	1747.2	1746.1	1751.8
1991	1661.8	1655.7	1668.1	1673.5	1688.9	1710.2	1698.0	1704.4	1697.4	1677.7	1685.2	1681.4	1683.5
1992	1624.6	1619.1	1632.4	1654.7	1674.4	1693.4	1690.1	1687.5	1682.8	1677.5	1678.1	1683.8	1666.5
1993	1630.8	1631.1	1636.1	1665.5	1689.4	1709.5	1714.4	1709.4	1704.0	1702.8	1708.8	1718.6	1685.0
1994	1652.9	1650.0	1679.4	1709.4	1732.4	1758.5	1757.4	1755.2	1754.3	1744.5	1753.3	1762.0	1725.7
1995	1703.4	1705.4	1727.4	1748.0	1766.2	1791.9	1782.7	1784.2	1781.9	1771.3	1780.3	1788.5	1760.9
1996	1690.9	1718.3	1747.4	1767.5	1792.8	1821.3	1818.2	1824.9	1818.4	1819.9	1830.4	1836.3	1790.5
1997	1775.8	1780.1	1807.3	1825.6	1850.2	1872.7	1873.6	1871.5	1866.8	1868.3	1875.6	1890.2	1846.4
1998	1823.0	1830.1	1852.6	1865.4	1886.0	1917.6	1918.5	1920.9	1913.9	1918.3	1926.1	1937.7	1892.5
1999	1867.6	1878.1	1896.4	1923.6	1942.7	1971.7	1983.5	1978.1	1966.3	1977.1	1986.9	1998.7	1947.5
2000	1927.6	1931.0	1962.5	1984.5	2001.5	2034.9	2035.8	2036.5	2033.5	2027.0	2036.6	2050.2	2005.1
2001	1966.8	1971.7	1990.1	2000.9	2021.6	2052.1	2041.4	2042.4	2020.2	2017.1	2024.2	2031.7	2015.0
2002	1963.7	1969.2	1990.3	2004.4	2025.2	2049.6	2043.3	2043.2	2027.4	2017.5	2025.6	2028.9	2015.7
2003	1970.1	1958.5	1981.3	2005.6	2029.2	2054.3	2042.1	2045.2	2033.2	2034.9	2039.9	2040.5	2019.6
Goods-producing													
1990	348.7	353.3	359.6	361.8	363.7	368.1	363.1	362.6	360.0	351.1	346.9	340.5	356.6
1991	320.5	315.9	317.8	319.6	322.7	326.8	323.8	327.4	324.8	318.6	315.1	309.9	320.2
1992	297.1	294.4	296.9	301.0	304.6	308.9	309.6	309.9	308.8	307.8	305.8	303.6	304.0
1993	291.5	290.6	291.2	295.3	300.1	304.3	307.0	307.3	306.1	305.4	304.8	302.8	300.5
1994	287.9	285.2	292.4	302.3	308.2	313.4	317.0	317.1	316.7	316.3	315.4	313.4	307.1
1995	303.1	299.7	304.9	309.3	312.1	316.7	315.4	317.1	316.9	313.7	312.1	309.8	310.9
1996	287.8	295.6	302.5	308.8	313.5	318.8	319.7	322.4	320.7	321.6	321.9	320.2	312.7
1997	307.6	308.0	312.6	315.9	319.4	323.3	324.2	325.0	322.2	320.8	320.7	319.0	318.2
1998	311.4	312.2	315.1	317.8	320.3	326.7	324.3	325.6	325.8	326.2	324.4	324.6	321.2
1999	314.1	315.7	317.8	324.4	326.0	332.0	335.3	333.8	332.0	331.1	331.0	331.0	327.0
2000	322.4	320.4	328.6	331.6	334.3	340.1	341.4	342.4	341.8	340.3	338.9	338.1	335.0
2001	326.0	328.0	332.4	334.8	336.7	341.7	340.6	340.9	337.7	335.1	333.1	331.6	334.9
2002	318.5	319.3	322.8	325.1	327.0	330.5	328.3	328.8	326.0	322.1	321.5	318.7	324.1
2003	311.0	307.7	311.4	314.2	318.0	321.1	318.5	320.2	318.4	318.5	317.7	314.7	316.0
Construction and mining													
1990	152.4	154.2	159.9	163.3	164.4	167.1	163.1	163.2	160.7	155.3	151.0	145.7	158.3
1991	128.7	126.2	128.0	132.7	135.3	138.4	139.0	139.3	136.6	132.9	130.1	126.2	132.7
1992	117.0	115.6	117.4	122.0	125.2	128.2	129.3	129.0	127.7	127.4	125.7	123.5	124.0
1993	114.3	113.9	114.3	119.0	123.6	126.9	130.1	130.5	129.5	129.6	129.1	127.8	124.0
1994	114.4	112.5	118.4	125.9	130.8	134.6	138.4	139.5	139.2	138.1	137.1	135.8	130.3
1995	127.2	124.2	128.9	132.4	134.2	138.0	138.2	139.1	138.6	137.4	136.4	134.5	134.0
1996	117.0	123.4	130.0	135.6	139.9	143.9	145.4	147.0	145.5	146.6	146.4	144.7	138.7
1997	133.9	133.6	137.5	141.6	144.5	147.5	148.7	148.6	147.4	146.1	144.1	142.5	143.0
1998	137.2	136.3	138.6	142.1	144.4	149.4	151.3	150.9	150.0	151.2	149.5	149.8	145.8
1999	141.5	142.8	144.9	151.6	153.5	158.3	160.6	159.3	157.2	157.1	156.9	156.6	153.3
2000	150.3	148.2	155.1	158.0	160.3	164.2	166.3	167.8	167.1	165.9	165.4	164.2	161.0
2001	155.7	157.4	161.9	164.9	167.8	171.8	171.8	172.9	170.6	169.7	168.8	167.4	166.7
2002	159.4	160.4	164.0	166.4	168.5	171.6	172.1	172.7	170.7	169.2	169.0	166.6	167.6
2003	161.0	158.5	161.9	165.2	168.8	171.6	172.4	173.7	172.6	173.0	172.2	169.8	168.4
Manufacturing													
1990	196.3	199.1	199.7	198.5	199.3	201.0	200.0	199.4	199.3	195.8	195.9	194.8	198.2
1991	191.8	189.7	189.8	186.9	187.4	188.4	184.8	188.1	188.2	185.7	185.0	183.7	187.4
1992	180.1	178.8	179.5	179.0	179.4	180.7	180.3	180.9	181.1	180.4	180.1	180.1	180.0
1993	177.2	176.7	176.9	176.3	176.5	177.4	176.9	176.8	176.6	175.8	175.7	175.0	176.4
1994	173.5	172.7	174.0	176.4	177.4	178.8	178.6	177.6	177.5	178.2	178.3	177.6	176.7
1995	175.9	175.5	176.0	176.9	177.9	178.7	177.2	178.0	178.3	176.3	175.7	175.3	176.8
1996	170.8	172.2	172.5	173.2	173.6	174.9	174.3	175.4	175.2	175.0	175.5	175.5	174.0
1997	173.7	174.4	175.1	174.3	174.9	175.8	175.5	176.4	174.8	174.7	176.6	176.5	175.2
1998	174.2	175.9	176.5	175.7	175.9	177.3	173.0	174.7	175.8	175.0	174.9	174.8	175.3
1999	172.6	172.9	172.9	172.8	172.5	173.7	174.7	174.5	174.8	174.0	174.1	174.4	173.6
2000	172.1	172.2	173.5	173.6	174.0	175.9	175.1	174.6	174.7	174.4	173.5	173.9	173.9
2001	170.3	170.6	170.5	169.9	168.9	169.9	168.8	168.0	167.1	165.4	164.3	164.2	168.2
2002	159.1	158.9	158.8	158.7	158.5	158.9	156.2	156.1	155.3	152.9	152.5	152.1	156.5
2003	150.0	149.2	149.5	149.0	149.2	149.5	146.1	146.5	145.8	145.5	145.5	144.9	147.6

Employment by Industry: Maryland—*Continued*

(Numbers in thousands. Not seasonally adjusted.)

Industry	January	February	March	April	May	June	July	August	September	October	November	December	Annual Average
STATEWIDE—*Continued*													
Service-providing													
1990	1767.4	1782.2	1801.4	1810.3	1822.9	1846.3	1817.4	1820.9	1831.3	1819.1	1825.9	1830.2	1814.6
1991	1750.9	1760.4	1772.0	1775.4	1790.9	1803.4	1775.3	1770.2	1782.7	1781.8	1795.8	1796.2	1779.5
1992	1737.3	1742.9	1756.5	1774.4	1791.5	1798.9	1782.6	1774.5	1781.3	1790.3	1794.9	1802.2	1777.2
1993	1750.4	1761.1	1767.8	1793.6	1813.9	1822.8	1807.8	1797.3	1814.6	1820.9	1829.9	1842.2	1801.8
1994	1780.5	1786.0	1813.1	1833.3	1850.0	1864.3	1844.7	1835.0	1855.5	1855.6	1868.5	1878.9	1838.7
1995	1818.4	1829.8	1849.5	1866.7	1881.3	1902.6	1873.2	1869.6	1882.1	1884.3	1896.4	1907.5	1871.7
1996	1820.7	1849.8	1872.6	1885.9	1907.5	1928.9	1905.3	1900.4	1916.2	1922.6	1932.0	1938.5	1898.3
1997	1878.9	1890.6	1918.5	1932.6	1955.9	1973.2	1957.0	1942.8	1966.5	1978.1	1989.3	2004.6	1949.0
1998	1938.6	1950.9	1973.5	1982.0	2003.5	2025.8	2008.0	2009.1	2018.6	2030.2	2042.2	2055.1	2003.1
1999	1991.6	2008.7	2028.4	2048.4	2066.3	2082.4	2048.5	2037.3	2073.9	2096.3	2110.1	2122.2	2059.5
2000	2047.1	2057.4	2090.4	2110.1	2130.0	2148.9	2100.5	2088.7	2135.4	2143.5	2157.0	2171.7	2115.0
2001	2089.0	2101.3	2118.5	2127.9	2146.1	2164.9	2110.5	2119.4	2135.1	2146.8	2160.1	2169.1	2132.4
2002	2102.6	2117.3	2139.4	2147.7	2167.5	2182.3	2133.0	2150.3	2162.9	2167.9	2178.1	2182.9	2152.7
2003	2118.3	2119.2	2141.3	2163.2	2183.8	2197.2	2153.4	2164.6	2175.1	2188.9	2195.4	2198.3	2166.6
Trade, transportation, and utilities													
1990	450.3	444.9	447.9	445.7	447.1	451.8	446.8	448.5	449.4	447.3	454.4	460.6	449.5
1991	425.6	418.2	419.3	419.9	423.1	425.9	423.2	424.7	426.4	423.2	433.5	438.9	425.1
1992	419.5	412.1	412.5	415.0	419.1	421.1	417.7	416.8	417.4	420.5	428.1	436.1	419.6
1993	415.9	410.0	409.1	411.6	416.5	418.8	419.5	418.8	418.9	423.3	431.5	441.1	419.5
1994	421.3	414.9	419.7	423.8	428.8	433.2	428.6	429.3	433.3	436.3	446.2	455.5	430.9
1995	428.2	425.0	428.1	431.5	434.4	437.2	432.6	434.0	435.9	438.2	446.2	454.7	435.5
1996	426.8	424.5	427.7	428.7	433.8	439.6	436.9	436.9	441.2	442.9	452.8	460.3	437.6
1997	442.1	435.8	439.8	439.1	442.9	446.4	443.7	444.8	445.2	449.2	459.0	468.0	446.3
1998	443.1	439.9	442.1	442.8	446.7	450.8	448.5	450.0	452.5	458.8	469.1	477.1	451.7
1999	450.6	446.0	451.3	454.2	458.7	462.7	462.9	462.9	462.4	470.2	480.5	487.7	462.5
2000	460.6	457.2	460.8	464.1	467.0	472.7	470.1	472.5	473.4	477.8	489.0	499.3	472.0
2001	469.7	462.9	464.0	462.7	466.3	470.1	465.4	466.1	466.5	468.4	477.2	484.2	468.6
2002	461.4	455.8	460.1	461.3	464.8	469.5	464.5	463.9	464.2	466.0	473.4	480.7	465.5
2003	456.0	450.1	453.3	455.5	460.0	464.5	460.3	462.7	462.9	465.7	473.9	479.2	462.0
Wholesale trade													
1990	91.5	91.6	92.2	92.2	92.0	92.7	92.3	92.3	92.3	90.7	90.7	90.6	91.7
1991	87.9	87.3	87.7	87.5	87.2	87.4	87.1	87.0	86.8	85.8	85.8	85.2	86.8
1992	83.6	83.4	83.7	84.1	84.5	84.5	83.8	83.5	83.4	83.8	83.6	83.5	83.7
1993	81.7	81.6	81.9	82.3	82.8	83.2	83.3	83.5	83.5	83.5	83.3	84.0	82.8
1994	82.4	82.4	82.9	83.2	83.9	85.0	85.2	85.3	85.2	83.7	84.0	84.3	83.9
1995	82.7	83.2	84.1	84.7	85.5	86.4	85.8	86.0	85.8	86.0	85.8	86.2	85.1
1996	83.4	84.4	85.1	85.6	86.3	86.9	87.2	87.6	87.1	87.6	87.9	88.1	86.4
1997	86.6	87.3	88.1	87.7	88.5	88.9	89.3	89.5	89.5	89.2	89.5	89.9	88.6
1998	88.2	88.9	89.6	89.1	89.5	89.9	89.9	89.8	89.5	90.0	90.1	90.5	89.5
1999	88.3	88.8	89.2	90.1	90.8	91.1	91.3	91.4	90.9	91.2	91.5	92.4	90.5
2000	89.8	90.6	91.8	92.0	92.3	93.4	93.6	94.1	93.7	94.2	94.4	94.9	92.9
2001	93.4	93.8	94.5	94.9	95.0	95.1	94.6	94.6	94.4	94.2	94.2	94.3	94.4
2002	93.4	93.3	93.6	93.1	93.3	93.6	93.2	93.3	92.8	93.0	93.0	93.0	93.2
2003	91.2	90.8	91.4	91.0	91.4	91.7	90.8	90.7	90.5	90.7	90.9	91.2	91.0
Retail trade													
1990	288.6	283.3	284.6	281.7	283.3	286.2	284.2	286.0	285.0	284.5	291.9	298.2	286.4
1991	274.1	267.1	267.6	268.3	271.5	273.4	272.3	274.1	273.8	272.5	282.1	287.2	273.6
1992	268.3	261.2	261.4	262.5	265.5	266.8	266.0	265.7	265.2	267.6	275.6	282.8	267.3
1993	263.6	258.5	257.5	259.0	263.0	265.0	266.3	265.4	264.0	267.8	275.9	284.6	265.8
1994	267.1	260.5	263.8	267.2	269.8	272.0	267.8	268.4	270.6	274.3	283.3	291.6	271.3
1995	272.2	267.5	269.5	271.9	273.9	275.7	273.2	274.7	275.5	275.4	283.8	291.8	275.4
1996	270.1	266.4	268.2	269.0	272.4	277.2	276.2	278.9	278.7	278.9	289.2	296.6	276.8
1997	281.5	274.8	277.7	276.6	279.1	282.1	280.9	281.5	281.1	283.5	292.9	301.3	282.7
1998	281.2	277.4	278.6	278.3	281.6	285.0	284.2	285.5	286.8	291.4	301.9	308.8	286.7
1999	287.1	283.6	285.9	286.6	289.9	292.7	292.3	292.6	291.2	296.4	306.9	313.7	293.2
2000	292.3	288.5	290.5	293.2	295.8	299.8	298.3	299.5	299.2	301.2	312.6	321.8	299.3
2001	298.4	291.7	292.3	290.0	293.0	296.5	294.5	295.2	294.6	295.5	304.8	311.7	296.5
2002	292.7	287.6	291.3	290.9	293.3	297.8	295.6	294.8	294.6	295.0	302.9	310.1	295.6
2003	290.3	285.1	286.8	289.9	293.1	297.2	295.9	298.1	297.2	298.5	306.4	310.5	295.8
Transportation and utilities													
1990	70.2	70.0	71.1	71.8	71.8	72.9	70.3	70.2	72.1	72.1	71.8	71.8	71.3
1991	63.6	63.8	64.0	64.1	64.4	65.1	63.8	63.6	65.8	64.9	65.6	66.5	64.6
1992	67.6	67.5	67.4	68.4	69.1	69.8	67.9	67.6	68.8	69.1	68.9	69.8	68.4
1993	70.6	69.9	69.7	70.3	70.7	70.6	69.9	69.9	71.4	72.0	72.3	72.5	70.8
1994	71.8	72.0	73.0	73.4	75.1	76.2	75.6	75.6	77.5	78.3	78.9	79.6	75.5
1995	73.3	74.3	74.5	74.9	75.0	75.1	73.6	73.3	74.6	76.8	76.6	76.7	74.8
1996	73.3	73.7	74.4	74.1	75.1	75.5	73.5	70.4	75.4	76.4	75.7	75.6	74.4
1997	74.0	73.7	74.0	74.8	75.3	75.4	73.5	73.8	74.6	76.5	76.6	76.8	74.9
1998	73.7	73.6	73.9	75.4	75.6	75.9	74.4	74.7	76.2	77.4	77.1	77.8	75.4
1999	75.2	73.6	76.2	77.5	78.0	78.9	79.3	78.9	80.3	82.6	82.1	81.6	78.6
2000	78.5	78.1	78.5	78.9	78.9	79.5	78.2	78.9	80.5	82.4	82.0	82.6	79.7
2001	77.9	77.4	77.2	77.8	78.3	78.5	76.3	76.3	77.5	78.7	78.2	78.2	77.7
2002	75.3	74.9	75.2	77.3	78.2	78.1	75.7	75.8	76.8	78.0	77.5	77.6	76.7
2003	74.5	74.2	75.1	74.6	75.5	75.6	73.6	73.9	75.2	76.5	76.6	77.5	75.2

Employment by Industry: Maryland—*Continued*

(Numbers in thousands. Not seasonally adjusted.)

Industry	January	February	March	April	May	June	July	August	September	October	November	December	Annual Average
STATEWIDE—*Continued*													
Information													
1990	52.4	53.0	53.3	53.0	52.8	52.9	53.6	53.5	52.7	53.3	53.3	53.1	53.0
1991	52.1	52.1	52.0	51.7	51.6	51.3	45.4	45.2	45.2	45.5	45.7	44.9	48.5
1992	44.5	44.4	44.2	44.3	44.5	44.6	44.5	44.4	44.2	44.3	44.4	44.4	44.3
1993	43.3	43.2	43.4	43.4	43.7	44.5	44.7	44.7	44.2	43.9	44.3	44.6	43.9
1994	44.5	44.7	45.3	45.3	45.3	45.5	45.1	45.5	45.1	45.2	45.6	45.8	45.2
1995	44.4	44.9	45.1	46.3	46.5	46.6	46.4	47.1	46.9	46.4	46.7	47.2	46.2
1996	46.6	47.6	48.1	47.8	48.6	48.8	49.5	49.4	48.9	48.6	49.4	49.7	48.5
1997	49.6	49.8	50.2	49.6	50.0	50.3	50.7	50.8	49.8	50.4	50.5	51.6	50.2
1998	51.1	51.5	51.8	51.8	51.9	52.5	52.6	52.8	52.4	52.5	52.5	53.0	52.2
1999	52.7	53.1	53.0	52.7	53.1	53.4	54.3	54.4	54.5	56.2	57.0	56.3	54.2
2000	56.3	56.6	57.3	57.7	58.2	59.1	59.4	54.2	60.0	60.3	60.8	62.1	58.5
2001	59.7	60.1	60.1	59.3	59.4	59.5	58.4	58.1	57.0	56.8	56.7	56.6	58.5
2002	55.2	54.9	54.8	54.4	54.4	54.0	53.3	53.0	52.2	50.7	51.4	51.1	53.3
2003	50.4	50.5	50.6	50.9	51.3	51.0	50.1	49.7	49.5	49.2	49.7	49.6	50.2
Financial activities													
1990	140.1	140.8	141.4	141.9	142.4	144.5	141.8	142.8	141.9	142.7	143.2	143.5	142.2
1991	136.7	136.6	136.7	135.7	136.0	137.0	135.6	136.1	135.1	133.7	134.0	134.3	135.6
1992	132.4	132.3	132.8	133.5	134.3	135.5	134.3	134.0	133.2	132.3	132.6	133.4	133.3
1993	132.1	131.9	132.4	133.0	133.7	135.3	136.2	136.5	135.9	136.5	137.1	138.2	134.9
1994	136.0	137.0	138.1	138.7	139.4	140.1	139.8	139.6	138.5	137.1	137.5	137.9	138.3
1995	134.4	134.9	135.1	135.0	135.0	136.5	135.7	136.3	135.5	134.3	134.9	135.8	135.2
1996	132.9	133.7	134.9	134.5	135.3	136.7	137.6	138.9	138.2	137.7	138.6	139.8	136.5
1997	137.8	138.3	139.7	138.6	140.9	142.2	142.7	142.8	142.6	142.1	142.4	144.0	141.1
1998	141.7	141.9	143.2	142.7	144.0	145.9	146.1	146.5	145.2	145.3	145.3	146.9	144.5
1999	145.3	146.1	146.6	146.9	147.3	148.8	149.5	149.2	147.8	147.0	146.6	147.7	147.4
2000	144.1	144.3	145.3	145.5	146.2	148.5	148.8	148.8	147.9	147.2	148.0	149.3	146.9
2001	145.2	146.1	147.1	147.3	148.1	150.1	150.4	150.6	149.3	149.1	149.8	150.6	148.6
2002	148.8	149.3	149.4	149.9	150.7	152.3	152.6	152.9	152.2	152.1	152.7	153.8	151.4
2003	153.2	153.3	154.3	154.9	156.2	157.8	157.7	157.8	156.4	156.2	156.5	156.9	155.9
Professional and business services													
1990	238.2	241.3	245.5	248.6	249.5	253.6	253.7	254.4	254.4	246.9	246.7	246.0	248.2
1991	242.8	243.0	246.5	246.2	246.0	248.7	247.8	248.1	247.7	250.0	250.1	249.5	247.2
1992	243.9	244.7	248.3	251.9	251.6	253.6	256.5	255.9	256.0	257.1	254.8	255.2	252.4
1993	250.2	250.3	252.8	261.3	263.4	265.2	266.3	264.4	264.2	264.4	264.0	264.9	260.9
1994	254.9	257.4	261.9	263.7	265.5	269.7	269.1	268.5	270.3	266.7	267.4	267.5	265.2
1995	264.3	265.9	270.8	273.6	275.3	278.0	278.3	278.7	278.4	278.4	279.1	280.9	275.1
1996	263.2	272.5	280.0	286.1	289.1	292.6	293.6	296.8	294.6	297.6	297.8	297.4	288.4
1997	287.1	289.9	297.5	305.2	308.7	313.6	315.7	316.0	316.7	319.0	319.2	321.3	309.1
1998	305.3	307.9	315.2	318.1	321.9	328.3	332.0	333.8	332.3	334.4	335.4	336.9	325.1
1999	323.9	330.0	334.7	340.8	343.5	349.4	352.9	352.9	353.3	355.9	356.5	358.7	346.0
2000	345.7	350.2	358.2	360.4	362.4	367.4	366.7	370.7	368.2	365.7	365.8	365.9	362.2
2001	355.9	358.2	361.9	364.9	367.5	369.8	369.8	370.8	364.8	363.7	364.8	364.9	364.8
2002	350.5	353.4	357.6	360.5	363.3	365.7	365.2	367.7	364.3	362.8	363.3	363.2	361.5
2003	351.8	350.0	355.1	361.5	364.0	367.1	363.6	365.7	363.9	365.1	365.1	363.8	361.4
Educational and health services													
1990	215.2	219.8	222.0	221.4	221.8	221.6	223.0	224.3	227.6	229.8	231.9	232.5	224.2
1991	229.3	233.0	234.9	234.5	236.2	235.1	235.5	235.5	239.5	242.0	243.5	243.5	236.8
1992	237.3	240.4	242.5	244.9	245.3	245.0	244.1	243.3	247.1	251.4	252.4	253.2	245.5
1993	246.5	252.1	253.1	253.9	254.4	253.8	252.5	251.7	255.6	257.9	259.1	259.8	254.2
1994	253.0	255.2	258.1	260.8	260.5	260.7	258.2	257.8	261.5	264.5	264.6	265.5	260.0
1995	262.4	266.3	268.1	268.6	269.4	269.2	267.6	267.0	272.8	273.0	275.3	275.8	269.6
1996	268.3	273.8	276.0	275.5	275.8	276.2	273.7	273.2	276.9	279.8	281.4	281.6	276.0
1997	277.1	281.0	283.0	283.2	283.7	283.2	281.9	280.1	284.6	286.0	286.9	288.7	283.2
1998	286.7	289.9	292.1	292.4	292.4	292.8	291.8	290.2	292.8	296.0	297.6	297.8	292.7
1999	292.1	295.1	296.2	298.0	298.1	298.6	299.2	298.0	299.8	303.3	305.1	307.7	299.2
2000	299.3	302.2	304.1	308.7	308.4	308.4	308.9	308.2	312.1	314.1	316.0	317.8	309.0
2001	311.0	314.6	316.6	318.2	319.3	321.4	317.7	316.9	319.6	323.8	326.5	328.5	319.5
2002	324.3	329.2	330.2	329.1	330.2	329.7	328.1	327.0	329.8	334.4	337.2	337.8	330.6
2003	333.6	335.2	337.5	339.0	339.9	339.7	336.4	335.1	338.4	342.8	343.8	344.3	338.8
Leisure and hospitality													
1990	166.8	168.8	173.0	179.8	186.3	198.5	198.8	198.4	190.5	179.6	176.2	175.0	182.6
1991	164.2	165.4	168.6	174.0	180.7	191.5	192.0	193.2	185.5	174.1	172.2	169.0	177.5
1992	161.0	161.6	165.4	173.6	183.5	191.6	190.2	190.7	184.1	172.6	168.6	166.1	175.7
1993	161.3	162.7	163.3	175.1	184.8	193.0	193.5	192.1	185.6	178.7	175.4	174.0	178.2
1994	164.6	164.2	170.6	180.5	189.6	198.8	201.1	199.3	191.5	181.6	179.5	178.7	183.3
1995	171.2	172.5	177.7	185.3	194.1	205.8	204.6	202.7	195.0	188.0	186.2	183.9	188.9
1996	169.7	172.8	178.5	186.4	195.7	205.7	204.3	204.2	196.2	189.7	186.0	184.5	189.4
1997	174.9	177.1	182.8	191.6	201.4	209.4	210.0	207.5	201.5	196.1	192.3	192.1	194.7
1998	179.6	182.4	187.9	193.7	202.4	213.3	215.3	214.6	206.4	198.0	194.4	193.2	198.4
1999	183.1	185.4	189.4	198.3	207.1	216.8	219.4	217.3	207.2	202.7	199.1	197.8	201.9
2000	188.7	188.7	195.0	202.4	210.0	221.8	224.6	223.9	214.5	206.7	203.1	202.1	206.7
2001	190.2	191.6	196.9	203.2	212.2	225.2	225.7	226.0	214.5	209.3	205.2	203.6	208.6
2002	194.9	196.0	202.6	210.5	220.3	231.5	233.6	233.6	224.1	215.3	211.7	208.6	215.2
2003	201.0	198.2	203.8	214.2	223.7	234.5	235.4	235.8	227.0	220.9	216.7	215.7	218.9

Employment by Industry: Maryland—*Continued*

(Numbers in thousands. Not seasonally adjusted.)

Industry	January	February	March	April	May	June	July	August	September	October	November	December	Annual Average
STATEWIDE—*Continued*													
Other services													
1990	93.0	93.6	94.9	94.5	95.6	97.6	96.3	97.0	96.6	94.6	94.6	94.9	95.2
1991	90.6	91.5	92.3	91.9	92.6	93.9	94.7	94.2	93.2	90.6	91.1	91.4	92.3
1992	88.9	89.2	89.8	90.5	91.5	93.1	93.2	92.5	92.0	91.5	91.4	91.8	91.2
1993	90.0	90.3	90.8	91.9	92.8	94.6	94.7	93.9	93.5	92.7	92.6	93.2	92.5
1994	90.7	91.4	93.3	94.3	95.1	97.1	98.5	98.1	97.4	96.8	97.1	97.7	95.6
1995	95.4	96.2	97.6	98.4	99.4	101.9	102.1	101.3	100.5	99.3	99.8	100.4	99.3
1996	95.6	97.8	99.7	99.7	101.0	102.9	102.9	103.1	101.7	102.0	102.5	102.8	100.9
1997	99.6	100.2	101.7	102.4	103.2	104.3	104.7	104.5	104.2	104.7	104.6	105.5	103.3
1998	104.1	104.4	105.2	106.1	106.4	107.3	107.9	107.4	106.5	107.1	107.4	108.2	106.5
1999	105.8	106.7	107.4	108.3	108.9	110.0	110.0	109.6	109.3	110.7	111.1	111.8	109.1
2000	110.5	111.4	113.2	114.1	115.0	116.9	115.9	115.8	115.6	114.9	115.0	115.6	114.4
2001	109.1	110.2	111.1	110.5	112.1	114.3	113.4	113.0	110.8	110.9	110.9	111.7	111.5
2002	110.1	111.3	112.8	113.6	114.5	116.4	117.7	116.3	114.6	114.1	114.4	115.0	114.2
2003	113.1	113.5	115.3	115.4	116.1	118.6	120.1	118.2	116.7	116.5	116.5	116.3	116.4
Government													
1990	411.4	420.0	423.4	425.4	427.4	425.8	403.4	402.0	418.2	424.9	425.6	424.6	419.3
1991	409.6	420.6	421.7	421.5	424.7	420.0	401.1	393.2	410.1	422.7	425.7	424.7	416.3
1992	409.8	418.2	421.0	420.7	421.7	414.4	402.1	396.9	407.3	420.6	422.6	422.0	414.7
1993	411.1	420.6	422.9	423.4	424.6	417.6	400.4	395.2	416.7	423.5	425.9	426.4	417.3
1994	415.5	421.2	426.1	426.2	425.8	419.2	404.3	396.9	417.9	427.4	430.6	430.3	420.1
1995	418.1	424.1	427.0	428.0	427.2	427.4	405.9	402.5	417.1	426.7	428.2	428.8	421.7
1996	417.6	427.1	427.7	427.2	428.2	426.4	406.8	397.9	418.5	424.3	423.5	422.4	420.6
1997	410.7	418.5	423.8	422.9	425.1	423.8	407.6	396.3	421.9	430.6	434.4	433.4	420.7
1998	427.0	433.0	436.0	434.4	437.8	434.9	413.8	413.8	430.5	438.1	440.5	442.0	431.8
1999	438.1	446.3	449.8	449.2	449.6	442.7	400.3	393.0	439.6	450.3	454.2	454.5	438.9
2000	441.9	446.8	456.5	457.2	462.8	454.1	406.1	394.6	443.7	456.8	459.3	459.6	444.9
2001	448.2	457.6	460.8	461.8	461.2	454.5	409.7	417.9	452.6	464.8	469.0	469.0	452.3
2002	457.4	467.4	471.9	468.4	469.3	463.2	418.0	435.9	461.5	472.5	474.0	472.7	461.0
2003	459.2	468.4	471.4	471.8	472.6	464.0	429.8	439.6	460.3	472.5	473.2	472.5	462.9
Federal government													
1990	133.1	132.9	133.2	138.0	139.0	142.4	142.2	138.6	137.7	135.5	135.1	136.1	136.9
1991	135.3	134.5	134.7	135.0	135.8	138.5	137.1	136.9	135.9	135.5	135.7	136.7	135.9
1992	135.3	134.8	135.0	135.2	135.4	136.4	136.8	136.2	135.2	135.0	134.7	135.2	135.4
1993	135.1	134.9	135.0	134.5	134.9	135.6	135.5	135.6	135.1	134.2	134.0	134.5	134.9
1994	133.0	132.7	132.3	131.9	131.8	132.2	132.7	132.8	132.1	131.6	131.7	132.2	132.2
1995	131.4	131.1	130.7	130.4	130.1	130.9	131.0	130.7	129.6	129.3	129.2	130.1	130.3
1996	128.3	128.3	128.4	128.2	128.0	128.8	129.0	129.4	128.8	124.4	124.9	125.4	127.6
1997	123.3	123.2	124.5	124.5	124.4	125.1	127.0	127.0	127.0	126.8	127.1	127.7	125.6
1998	126.2	125.9	125.9	125.6	126.1	127.0	127.8	128.1	126.9	126.7	126.5	127.5	126.6
1999	126.2	126.0	126.0	126.4	126.4	127.3	127.7	128.1	127.1	127.1	127.1	128.3	126.9
2000	126.9	127.2	128.5	128.4	134.6	132.0	130.0	128.0	125.7	125.2	125.2	126.1	128.1
2001	126.4	125.6	125.1	125.5	125.6	126.8	127.7	127.7	127.5	127.6	127.5	128.2	126.8
2002	127.7	127.1	127.3	126.0	126.4	128.5	129.7	130.0	129.1	128.8	128.8	130.1	128.3
2003	129.0	128.5	128.6	127.6	127.8	128.8	130.7	130.1	129.2	128.8	128.3	129.0	128.9
State government													
1990	95.3	98.6	99.4	98.5	97.7	95.6	93.1	94.4	97.1	98.3	97.9	96.3	96.8
1991	90.3	95.3	95.6	95.5	95.4	91.7	87.9	90.1	92.2	95.1	95.8	94.7	93.3
1992	90.5	94.7	95.4	95.7	95.7	91.2	88.6	90.3	90.7	95.0	95.4	95.2	93.2
1993	91.4	95.3	96.2	96.7	97.3	93.7	91.9	91.2	92.6	96.9	97.1	97.4	94.8
1994	93.2	95.2	97.2	97.8	98.4	96.0	95.2	94.5	94.5	97.7	98.3	98.5	96.3
1995	94.0	96.3	98.1	98.7	98.0	96.7	95.0	94.9	94.5	97.5	97.8	97.5	96.5
1996	93.4	95.8	97.9	98.3	97.4	96.8	95.0	95.1	95.6	98.9	95.2	94.5	96.1
1997	91.4	93.5	95.4	95.3	95.4	95.4	93.7	94.1	95.0	96.9	98.8	97.9	95.2
1998	96.1	96.5	97.7	96.7	96.9	96.0	93.8	94.8	96.5	98.3	98.7	99.1	96.7
1999	102.2	103.7	105.9	105.2	104.1	100.1	96.8	96.2	102.0	106.3	106.7	105.4	102.8
2000	100.3	102.0	106.5	106.9	105.6	101.8	97.5	98.1	103.5	108.4	108.7	108.5	103.9
2001	103.5	107.5	109.8	109.8	108.9	103.1	100.7	102.4	105.5	109.9	111.5	110.9	107.0
2002	103.8	109.7	112.4	111.9	111.3	106.2	102.7	103.8	108.3	112.3	112.3	111.7	108.9
2003	103.3	109.5	112.6	111.7	111.7	104.7	101.7	102.5	105.6	109.8	109.0	109.5	107.6
Local government													
1990	183.0	188.5	190.8	188.9	190.7	187.8	168.1	169.0	183.4	191.1	192.6	192.2	185.5
1991	184.0	190.8	191.4	191.0	193.5	189.8	176.1	166.2	182.0	192.1	194.2	193.3	187.0
1992	184.0	188.7	190.6	189.8	190.6	186.8	176.7	170.4	181.4	190.6	192.5	191.6	186.1
1993	184.6	190.4	191.7	192.2	192.4	188.3	173.0	168.4	189.0	192.4	194.8	194.5	187.6
1994	189.3	193.3	196.6	196.5	195.6	191.0	176.4	169.6	191.3	198.1	200.6	199.6	191.4
1995	192.7	196.7	198.2	198.9	199.1	199.8	179.9	176.9	193.0	199.9	201.2	201.2	194.7
1996	195.9	203.0	201.4	200.7	202.8	200.8	182.8	173.4	194.1	201.0	203.4	202.5	196.8
1997	196.0	201.8	203.9	203.1	205.3	203.3	186.9	175.3	199.9	206.9	208.5	207.8	199.8
1998	204.7	210.6	212.4	212.1	214.8	211.9	192.2	190.9	207.1	213.1	215.3	215.4	208.3
1999	209.7	216.6	217.9	217.6	219.1	215.3	175.8	168.7	210.5	216.9	220.4	220.8	209.1
2000	214.7	217.6	221.5	221.9	222.6	220.3	178.6	168.5	214.5	223.2	225.4	225.0	212.8
2001	218.3	224.5	225.9	226.5	226.7	224.6	181.3	187.8	219.6	227.3	230.0	229.9	218.5
2002	225.9	230.6	232.2	230.5	231.6	228.5	185.6	202.1	224.1	231.4	232.9	230.9	223.9
2003	226.9	230.4	230.2	232.5	233.1	230.5	197.4	207.0	225.5	233.9	235.9	234.0	226.4

Employment by Industry: Maryland—*Continued*

(Numbers in thousands. Not seasonally adjusted.)

Industry	January	February	March	April	May	June	July	August	September	October	November	December	Annual Average
BALTIMORE MSA													
Total nonfarm													
1990	1127.7	1139.2	1153.3	1154.4	1161.9	1168.1	1153.5	1155.1	1156.2	1148.6	1151.5	1149.5	1151.5
1991	1095.2	1096.5	1102.8	1106.8	1113.0	1118.9	1104.1	1102.6	1107.4	1109.3	1116.1	1114.2	1107.2
1992	1069.0	1070.1	1078.4	1090.8	1098.0	1101.1	1101.5	1096.7	1093.6	1102.3	1104.3	1107.7	1092.7
1993	1070.9	1074.0	1078.0	1090.3	1101.5	1104.5	1108.2	1102.6	1105.9	1109.5	1115.9	1121.3	1098.5
1994	1077.1	1077.1	1093.9	1108.9	1118.5	1125.4	1123.2	1119.7	1129.3	1131.5	1139.1	1142.3	1115.5
1995	1104.7	1109.2	1120.4	1130.5	1136.2	1141.5	1125.4	1125.5	1133.7	1134.2	1142.8	1146.7	1129.2
1996	1089.9	1110.4	1124.8	1135.1	1145.5	1151.7	1139.9	1138.3	1150.0	1157.7	1161.3	1161.5	1138.8
1997	1129.4	1136.4	1149.5	1160.7	1172.2	1180.5	1172.1	1165.2	1176.1	1184.8	1192.3	1199.0	1168.1
1998	1156.0	1163.1	1174.1	1178.3	1187.3	1199.0	1184.7	1189.1	1195.7	1203.8	1210.1	1216.2	1188.1
1999	1175.9	1185.8	1196.7	1212.2	1222.2	1228.3	1216.4	1211.4	1227.3	1241.8	1248.4	1253.8	1218.3
2000	1209.6	1212.9	1230.9	1243.3	1254.6	1264.6	1241.2	1239.6	1259.4	1266.8	1275.4	1284.1	1248.5
2001	1231.6	1238.3	1249.6	1255.3	1262.8	1271.8	1251.9	1257.1	1257.6	1260.1	1268.0	1271.2	1256.3
2002	1227.4	1234.2	1246.4	1248.7	1259.1	1265.1	1245.0	1250.4	1251.9	1254.3	1260.2	1261.2	1250.3
2003	1225.9	1223.0	1235.3	1249.1	1259.1	1261.5	1237.2	1244.2	1250.1	1255.7	1258.2	1258.0	1246.4
Total private													
1990	914.1	921.3	933.2	932.5	938.8	947.9	943.3	946.9	946.5	935.4	938.3	937.3	936.2
1991	888.1	885.3	891.4	893.9	899.6	906.9	897.6	902.1	903.5	897.5	903.4	902.6	897.6
1992	863.7	862.3	868.9	880.8	889.0	895.0	892.5	891.4	892.8	893.3	893.9	897.6	885.1
1993	865.9	866.3	868.7	882.0	891.9	897.6	900.5	898.9	900.0	901.0	905.8	910.7	890.7
1994	872.8	871.7	886.1	901.0	910.0	919.3	917.2	917.5	920.6	918.3	924.2	928.0	907.2
1995	897.1	899.1	908.7	917.9	925.1	932.5	924.5	925.3	928.2	924.8	932.5	936.0	920.9
1996	883.1	899.8	912.3	922.9	933.6	941.7	937.5	941.9	943.4	946.3	952.5	954.4	930.7
1997	922.1	925.6	937.3	948.4	959.7	968.5	965.3	966.0	966.6	971.3	976.6	983.6	957.5
1998	942.5	946.7	956.6	963.5	971.6	985.3	980.7	984.7	985.2	990.2	995.3	1000.6	975.2
1999	960.9	966.9	976.1	992.7	1002.5	1012.6	1017.7	1016.0	1014.0	1023.1	1028.2	1033.2	1003.6
2000	993.7	994.7	1008.8	1021.8	1030.2	1043.8	1040.8	1042.9	1045.2	1044.7	1053.4	1061.7	1031.8
2001	1014.3	1016.9	1026.7	1032.3	1040.9	1053.1	1047.2	1046.8	1040.2	1038.1	1044.2	1047.8	1037.4
2002	1006.9	1010.0	1020.1	1025.4	1035.3	1044.6	1037.9	1038.4	1031.9	1029.7	1035.1	1037.6	1029.4
2003	1007.5	1000.8	1011.2	1024.6	1034.6	1042.9	1031.2	1035.0	1032.4	1034.7	1037.3	1037.9	1027.5
Goods-producing													
1990	193.9	197.3	200.9	199.7	200.8	202.6	200.3	200.7	199.3	194.3	192.9	190.1	197.7
1991	179.4	176.3	177.3	178.1	179.9	182.3	178.7	181.6	180.6	177.5	176.3	173.9	178.4
1992	165.5	164.4	165.5	168.1	169.8	171.9	172.0	172.3	171.5	170.4	169.7	168.8	169.1
1993	162.5	161.6	161.7	162.8	164.6	166.8	169.0	169.6	168.8	167.9	168.2	167.8	165.9
1994	159.4	157.5	160.6	163.8	166.4	168.7	169.8	170.7	170.0	172.6	169.2	168.1	166.4
1995	161.3	159.2	162.1	164.8	165.9	168.0	167.4	168.0	167.8	165.6	165.2	164.2	164.9
1996	153.3	157.0	159.9	162.8	164.8	166.6	166.7	167.8	167.4	168.1	168.3	167.5	164.1
1997	161.6	162.1	163.8	164.5	166.2	167.6	168.2	169.2	167.3	166.6	167.2	166.7	165.9
1998	162.6	163.4	164.7	164.3	165.3	168.1	166.2	167.6	168.6	168.3	168.3	168.7	166.3
1999	162.7	163.6	164.5	166.3	167.5	170.6	173.2	171.9	170.8	170.2	170.0	169.6	168.4
2000	164.6	163.2	167.0	168.0	169.5	171.9	171.5	172.4	172.7	171.5	171.7	171.5	169.6
2001	163.0	164.3	166.3	166.9	166.8	169.6	169.3	169.5	168.2	166.4	165.6	165.2	166.8
2002	156.7	157.7	158.9	160.3	161.1	162.8	161.0	161.5	160.0	158.5	158.2	157.1	159.5
2003	153.3	151.3	152.3	153.6	154.9	156.4	154.7	155.9	155.2	153.7	153.4	152.3	153.9
Construction and mining													
1990	68.5	68.8	71.7	72.4	73.2	74.3	72.5	72.8	71.7	69.5	67.7	65.4	70.7
1991	57.6	56.5	57.4	60.5	61.9	63.8	63.9	64.0	62.7	60.8	59.7	57.9	60.5
1992	52.9	52.4	53.1	55.5	56.9	58.5	59.4	59.4	58.5	58.2	57.4	56.4	56.5
1993	52.8	52.4	52.5	54.3	56.4	58.2	60.3	60.5	60.1	59.9	60.0	59.4	57.2
1994	52.9	51.6	54.3	58.4	60.6	62.4	63.4	64.0	63.9	62.9	62.7	62.0	59.9
1995	57.5	55.9	58.1	59.8	60.6	62.6	63.0	63.3	63.0	62.2	62.2	61.2	60.7
1996	53.1	55.8	58.6	61.3	63.0	64.6	65.3	65.8	65.3	66.0	65.9	65.0	62.4
1997	61.0	61.1	62.5	63.9	65.2	66.6	67.2	67.3	67.0	66.6	65.4	65.1	64.9
1998	63.5	62.7	63.7	63.8	64.8	67.1	68.6	68.2	68.0	68.3	68.1	68.4	66.2
1999	64.2	65.0	66.0	68.7	70.0	72.8	74.8	73.3	72.1	72.3	72.0	71.9	70.2
2000	68.8	67.5	70.9	72.3	73.7	75.2	75.8	76.6	76.5	75.5	75.5	74.9	73.6
2001	70.4	71.2	73.4	74.3	75.2	77.0	76.6	77.1	76.1	75.1	74.7	74.2	74.6
2002	69.7	70.2	71.8	73.2	74.2	75.6	76.1	76.5	75.6	75.3	75.1	74.2	74.0
2003	71.3	69.6	70.6	72.0	73.5	74.8	75.5	76.0	75.6	75.4	75.2	74.6	73.7
Manufacturing													
1990	125.4	128.5	129.2	127.3	127.6	128.3	127.8	127.9	127.6	124.8	125.2	124.7	127.0
1991	121.8	119.8	119.9	117.6	118.0	118.5	114.8	117.6	117.9	116.7	116.6	116.0	117.9
1992	112.6	112.0	112.4	112.6	112.9	113.4	112.6	112.9	113.0	112.2	112.3	112.4	112.6
1993	109.7	109.2	109.2	108.5	108.2	108.6	108.7	109.1	108.7	108.0	108.2	108.4	108.7
1994	106.5	105.9	106.3	105.4	105.8	106.3	106.4	106.7	106.1	109.7	106.5	106.1	106.4
1995	103.8	103.3	104.0	105.0	105.3	105.4	104.4	104.7	104.8	103.4	103.0	103.0	104.1
1996	100.2	101.2	101.3	101.5	101.8	102.0	101.4	102.0	102.1	102.1	102.4	102.5	101.7
1997	100.6	101.0	101.3	100.6	101.0	101.0	101.0	101.9	100.3	100.0	101.8	101.6	101.0
1998	99.1	100.7	101.0	100.5	100.5	101.0	97.6	99.4	100.6	100.0	100.2	100.3	100.0
1999	98.5	98.6	98.5	97.6	97.5	97.8	98.4	98.6	98.7	97.9	98.0	97.7	98.1
2000	95.8	95.7	96.1	95.7	95.8	96.7	95.7	95.8	96.2	96.0	96.2	96.6	96.0
2001	92.6	93.1	92.9	92.6	91.6	92.6	92.7	92.4	92.1	91.3	90.9	91.0	92.2
2002	87.0	87.5	87.1	87.1	86.9	87.2	84.9	85.0	84.4	83.2	83.1	82.9	85.5
2003	82.0	81.7	81.7	81.6	81.4	81.6	79.2	79.9	79.6	78.3	78.2	77.7	80.2

Employment by Industry: Maryland—*Continued*

(Numbers in thousands. Not seasonally adjusted.)

Industry	January	February	March	April	May	June	July	August	September	October	November	December	Annual Average
BALTIMORE MSA *—Continued*													
Service-providing													
1990	933.8	941.9	952.4	954.7	961.1	965.5	953.2	954.4	956.9	954.3	958.6	959.4	953.8
1991	915.8	920.2	925.5	928.7	933.1	936.6	925.4	921.0	926.8	931.8	939.8	940.3	928.7
1992	903.5	905.7	912.9	922.7	928.2	929.2	929.5	924.4	922.1	931.9	934.6	938.9	923.6
1993	908.4	912.4	916.3	927.5	936.9	937.7	939.2	933.0	937.1	941.6	947.7	953.5	932.6
1994	917.7	919.6	933.3	945.1	952.1	956.7	953.4	949.0	959.3	958.9	969.9	974.2	949.1
1995	943.4	950.0	958.3	965.7	970.3	973.5	958.0	957.5	965.9	968.6	977.6	982.5	964.2
1996	936.6	953.4	964.9	972.3	980.7	985.1	973.2	970.5	982.6	989.6	993.0	994.0	974.6
1997	967.8	974.3	985.7	996.2	1006.0	1012.9	1003.9	996.0	1008.8	1018.2	1025.1	1032.3	1002.2
1998	993.4	999.7	1009.4	1014.0	1022.0	1030.9	1018.5	1021.5	1027.1	1035.5	1041.8	1047.5	1021.7
1999	1013.2	1022.2	1032.2	1045.9	1054.7	1057.7	1043.2	1039.5	1056.5	1071.6	1078.4	1084.2	1049.9
2000	1045.0	1049.7	1063.9	1075.3	1085.1	1092.7	1069.7	1067.2	1086.7	1095.3	1103.7	1112.6	1078.9
2001	1068.6	1074.0	1083.3	1088.4	1096.0	1102.2	1082.6	1087.6	1089.4	1093.7	1102.4	1106.0	1089.5
2002	1070.7	1076.5	1087.5	1088.4	1098.0	1102.3	1084.0	1088.9	1091.9	1095.8	1102.0	1104.1	1090.8
2003	1072.6	1071.7	1083.0	1095.5	1104.2	1105.1	1082.5	1088.3	1094.9	1102.0	1104.8	1105.7	1092.5
Trade, transportation, and utilities													
1990	235.2	232.2	233.9	231.2	231.5	232.7	231.2	232.8	233.3	233.1	236.7	239.1	233.5
1991	224.4	220.9	220.9	221.2	222.9	223.8	222.4	223.3	225.2	224.2	229.7	232.3	224.2
1992	218.3	215.0	215.0	216.9	219.1	219.7	217.4	217.2	218.1	220.1	224.0	228.1	219.0
1993	215.2	212.7	212.1	212.2	214.5	215.0	215.4	215.4	216.0	218.2	222.6	227.5	216.4
1994	219.9	216.8	219.0	220.3	222.4	224.3	220.5	220.5	223.2	225.3	231.3	235.7	223.2
1995	222.2	221.5	222.5	224.2	225.6	225.9	223.9	223.7	224.8	225.3	229.9	234.4	225.3
1996	218.9	218.6	220.0	220.2	222.8	224.9	222.0	223.4	225.0	226.0	230.9	234.7	223.9
1997	225.9	222.9	224.3	225.7	227.7	229.5	227.1	228.1	227.8	230.9	235.6	239.9	228.7
1998	226.5	225.3	226.1	227.1	228.9	230.5	228.6	228.9	230.6	235.2	240.4	244.3	231.0
1999	230.0	229.0	230.5	232.1	234.6	235.8	236.0	236.8	237.3	241.8	247.2	250.5	236.8
2000	237.2	235.4	236.7	238.8	240.9	242.8	241.7	243.9	244.5	247.6	253.5	258.7	243.4
2001	245.0	241.6	242.5	242.0	243.6	244.9	241.2	241.4	242.1	243.0	247.2	250.8	243.8
2002	237.8	234.7	236.7	237.1	239.0	240.8	237.1	237.0	238.0	238.5	242.1	246.4	238.8
2003	234.5	231.5	233.3	234.4	236.7	238.6	235.1	237.0	238.0	238.8	241.6	244.3	237.0
Wholesale trade													
1990	52.4	52.6	53.0	52.6	52.3	52.6	52.8	52.9	52.7	52.0	52.0	51.8	52.4
1991	50.0	49.6	49.7	49.5	49.3	49.3	49.2	49.3	49.4	48.9	48.9	48.7	49.3
1992	47.9	47.8	47.9	48.6	48.8	48.8	48.3	48.3	48.3	48.1	48.1	48.2	48.2
1993	46.3	46.4	46.5	46.0	46.2	46.3	46.6	46.7	46.8	46.7	46.6	47.0	46.5
1994	45.8	45.7	45.9	45.8	45.9	46.5	46.9	47.0	47.0	46.5	46.9	47.0	46.4
1995	45.8	46.1	46.5	47.1	47.4	47.8	47.7	47.7	47.6	47.7	47.5	47.7	47.2
1996	46.0	46.6	46.8	47.5	47.9	48.1	48.3	48.4	48.3	48.5	48.7	48.9	47.8
1997	48.1	48.4	48.5	48.8	49.2	49.5	50.0	50.3	50.3	50.3	50.6	50.9	49.5
1998	49.6	50.3	50.5	49.5	49.7	50.0	49.7	49.7	49.6	49.9	50.0	50.3	49.9
1999	49.1	49.4	49.4	50.2	50.5	50.6	50.7	50.8	50.6	50.2	50.5	50.9	50.2
2000	49.5	49.8	50.4	50.8	51.1	51.8	52.2	52.6	52.5	52.5	52.8	53.2	51.6
2001	55.4	55.6	56.1	56.4	56.5	56.5	56.2	56.1	56.0	55.7	55.5	55.7	56.0
2002	54.6	54.6	54.6	54.3	54.4	54.5	54.4	54.6	54.5	54.3	54.2	54.4	54.5
2003	53.3	52.9	53.3	53.2	53.3	53.5	52.6	52.6	52.7	52.5	52.6	52.8	52.9
Retail trade													
1990	142.5	139.8	140.3	137.3	138.0	138.3	138.0	139.4	139.3	139.7	143.9	146.8	140.2
1991	138.1	134.9	134.8	134.9	136.5	137.0	137.0	137.9	138.2	138.2	143.4	146.0	138.0
1992	133.2	130.0	129.9	131.1	132.5	132.5	132.3	132.3	132.2	134.2	138.3	141.9	133.3
1993	132.0	129.7	129.1	129.7	131.2	131.7	132.9	132.6	132.1	134.2	138.4	142.7	133.0
1994	134.8	131.4	132.9	134.4	135.6	136.1	132.8	133.1	134.3	136.7	141.9	145.9	135.8
1995	134.8	132.9	133.7	134.7	135.7	135.7	134.4	134.7	134.9	135.2	140.2	144.3	135.9
1996	132.2	130.9	131.8	131.5	133.1	134.7	133.2	134.0	134.9	135.4	140.5	143.9	134.6
1997	136.8	133.5	134.6	134.9	136.2	137.8	136.5	136.9	136.5	138.2	142.4	146.2	137.5
1998	137.2	135.2	135.4	136.3	137.9	139.0	138.5	138.7	139.2	143.1	148.5	152.0	140.0
1999	140.5	138.7	139.8	140.1	141.7	142.3	142.1	142.5	142.0	146.1	151.3	154.5	143.4
2000	144.1	142.1	142.7	143.7	145.3	146.3	145.6	146.6	146.0	148.5	154.2	158.4	146.9
2001	145.0	141.6	142.0	140.9	142.2	143.4	142.1	142.5	142.1	143.0	147.8	151.0	143.6
2002	141.1	138.3	140.2	139.9	141.0	142.8	141.5	141.1	141.2	141.5	145.6	149.2	142.0
2003	140.1	137.7	138.4	139.9	141.4	143.2	142.4	144.1	143.9	145.0	147.7	149.9	142.8
Transportation and utilities													
1990	40.3	39.8	40.6	41.3	41.2	41.8	40.4	40.5	41.3	41.4	40.8	40.5	40.8
1991	36.3	36.4	36.4	36.8	37.1	37.5	36.2	36.1	37.6	37.1	37.4	37.6	36.8
1992	37.2	37.2	37.2	37.2	37.8	38.4	36.8	36.6	37.6	37.8	37.6	38.0	37.4
1993	36.9	36.6	36.5	36.5	37.1	37.0	35.9	36.1	37.1	37.3	37.6	37.8	36.8
1994	39.3	39.7	40.2	40.1	40.9	41.7	40.8	40.4	41.9	42.1	42.5	42.8	41.0
1995	41.6	42.5	42.3	42.4	42.5	42.4	41.8	41.3	42.3	42.4	42.2	42.4	42.1
1996	40.7	41.1	41.4	41.2	41.8	42.1	40.5	41.0	41.8	42.1	41.7	41.9	41.4
1997	41.0	41.0	41.2	42.0	42.3	42.2	40.6	40.9	41.0	42.4	42.6	42.8	41.6
1998	39.7	39.8	40.2	41.3	41.3	41.5	40.4	40.5	41.8	42.2	41.9	42.0	41.0
1999	40.4	40.9	41.3	41.8	42.4	42.9	43.2	43.5	44.7	45.5	45.4	45.1	43.0
2000	43.6	43.5	43.6	44.3	44.5	44.7	43.9	44.7	46.0	46.6	46.5	47.1	44.9
2001	44.6	44.4	44.4	44.7	44.9	45.0	42.9	42.8	44.0	44.3	43.9	44.1	44.2
2002	42.1	41.8	41.9	42.9	43.6	43.5	41.2	41.3	42.3	42.7	42.3	42.8	42.4
2003	41.1	40.9	41.6	41.3	42.0	41.9	40.1	40.3	41.4	41.3	41.3	41.6	41.2

Employment by Industry: Maryland—*Continued*

(Numbers in thousands. Not seasonally adjusted.)

Industry	January	February	March	April	May	June	July	August	September	October	November	December	Annual Average
BALTIMORE MSA *—Continued*													
Information													
1990	20.5	21.0	21.1	20.6	20.6	20.7	20.8	20.7	20.6	20.7	20.7	20.6	20.7
1991	20.1	20.0	20.0	19.6	19.6	19.6	19.5	19.4	19.3	20.0	20.1	20.0	19.7
1992	19.4	19.2	19.2	19.1	19.4	19.5	19.4	19.5	19.3	19.3	19.3	19.4	19.3
1993	18.9	18.9	18.9	18.6	18.7	18.8	19.2	19.2	19.0	18.6	18.7	19.0	18.8
1994	19.0	19.1	19.2	18.9	19.0	19.2	19.1	19.4	19.3	19.1	19.3	19.4	19.1
1995	19.2	19.3	19.3	19.5	19.6	19.8	19.3	19.9	19.9	19.8	20.0	20.3	19.6
1996	20.1	20.7	20.9	20.7	20.9	21.3	21.7	21.6	21.4	21.6	22.1	22.2	21.2
1997	22.1	22.3	22.4	22.1	22.3	22.5	22.7	22.8	22.6	22.7	22.8	23.2	22.5
1998	22.7	22.9	22.9	22.7	22.7	23.1	23.0	23.1	22.8	22.9	23.1	23.4	22.9
1999	23.3	23.5	23.5	23.2	23.5	23.7	24.0	24.1	24.2	24.4	24.8	24.7	23.9
2000	24.6	24.4	24.6	24.2	24.5	25.1	25.1	22.6	25.4	25.4	25.9	26.6	24.8
2001	25.8	26.1	26.0	25.1	25.2	25.2	24.3	24.3	23.7	23.5	23.6	23.4	24.7
2002	22.5	22.5	22.4	22.3	22.3	22.2	21.7	21.8	21.2	20.6	21.1	20.8	21.8
2003	20.8	20.8	20.8	21.1	21.3	21.0	20.6	20.5	20.3	19.8	20.1	19.9	20.6
Financial activities													
1990	79.6	79.8	79.9	79.8	80.4	81.1	78.2	78.7	78.6	80.3	80.7	80.7	79.8
1991	76.3	76.1	76.3	75.7	75.6	76.0	74.0	74.5	74.1	74.3	74.5	74.9	75.1
1992	74.0	74.1	74.4	74.2	74.7	75.1	75.3	75.3	75.1	74.1	74.2	74.7	74.6
1993	73.5	73.4	73.7	73.7	73.8	74.4	75.0	75.3	75.2	75.4	75.9	76.2	74.6
1994	74.7	75.1	75.5	75.6	75.9	76.1	76.3	76.3	76.2	75.2	75.5	75.7	75.6
1995	74.2	74.3	74.2	73.9	73.5	74.0	73.8	74.2	73.7	73.5	74.0	74.2	73.9
1996	73.1	73.4	73.9	74.0	74.3	74.6	74.6	74.9	74.9	74.8	75.1	75.6	74.4
1997	73.8	74.3	74.9	75.5	76.0	76.7	76.9	76.8	76.8	76.8	77.1	78.1	76.1
1998	75.5	75.5	76.2	76.0	76.5	77.6	78.0	78.0	77.5	77.6	77.6	78.6	77.0
1999	77.1	77.5	77.8	78.3	78.5	79.1	79.5	79.5	79.0	78.8	78.7	79.0	78.5
2000	77.0	77.4	77.9	77.3	77.8	79.0	79.3	79.4	79.0	79.0	79.5	80.2	78.5
2001	77.4	77.9	78.5	78.5	78.9	80.0	80.3	80.4	80.1	80.0	80.8	81.1	79.5
2002	79.0	79.2	79.3	79.6	79.9	80.7	80.7	80.8	80.9	80.6	81.1	81.4	80.3
2003	81.0	81.0	81.5	81.7	82.2	83.0	82.2	82.3	81.6	81.4	81.7	81.4	81.8
Professional and business services													
1990	115.3	116.6	118.7	121.5	122.1	123.7	124.5	124.8	125.4	120.1	119.9	119.4	121.0
1991	116.2	116.0	117.1	118.4	118.4	120.1	119.3	119.1	119.4	117.5	117.3	117.2	118.0
1992	112.7	113.2	114.4	115.3	115.1	115.8	116.4	116.4	117.0	117.6	115.8	115.3	115.4
1993	111.7	112.2	113.4	119.1	120.2	121.0	121.8	121.1	122.0	121.7	121.5	121.2	118.9
1994	114.5	116.0	119.1	121.7	122.9	124.5	124.4	124.5	125.8	123.2	123.9	124.1	122.0
1995	123.4	124.5	125.6	125.9	126.7	127.5	126.0	126.7	126.9	127.5	127.7	128.0	126.3
1996	119.3	124.7	127.7	131.5	132.8	134.2	134.3	135.9	135.7	136.3	136.7	135.4	132.0
1997	131.3	133.0	136.4	141.1	143.0	145.6	146.0	146.5	146.8	149.5	149.6	149.7	143.2
1998	138.7	139.8	141.9	144.9	146.4	149.9	151.4	152.6	152.5	153.7	153.9	154.2	148.3
1999	146.5	149.0	152.2	159.9	161.5	164.6	164.2	163.9	164.4	168.5	167.9	168.9	160.9
2000	161.6	162.7	166.6	173.0	174.0	176.8	175.9	177.4	175.8	176.4	176.1	176.0	172.6
2001	173.2	173.8	175.6	177.6	179.5	179.7	181.9	182.0	179.0	177.4	178.8	177.9	178.0
2002	170.8	171.6	173.7	174.2	176.3	177.3	177.0	178.5	176.0	175.0	175.1	174.8	175.0
2003	168.3	166.3	168.9	173.2	174.5	175.5	172.0	173.9	173.0	172.7	172.8	172.5	172.0
Educational and health services													
1990	137.6	141.3	142.9	141.1	141.2	139.9	141.5	142.4	145.1	147.8	149.1	149.1	143.2
1991	145.4	148.6	150.2	150.0	149.4	147.5	147.7	147.2	150.4	153.8	155.0	154.9	150.0
1992	150.5	153.3	154.7	155.8	155.6	154.6	154.1	153.6	156.3	159.5	160.1	160.9	155.7
1993	157.3	159.7	160.6	160.8	160.7	159.3	159.0	158.2	161.1	162.6	163.5	163.5	160.5
1994	157.7	159.5	160.9	163.3	162.1	161.7	161.2	161.0	163.5	164.9	166.7	167.0	162.4
1995	163.5	166.3	167.4	167.3	167.4	166.2	166.1	165.7	170.2	170.4	172.3	172.0	167.9
1996	166.5	170.6	171.7	172.1	171.8	170.7	170.1	169.6	172.4	174.3	175.3	175.0	171.6
1997	171.7	174.5	175.2	175.1	174.9	174.7	173.6	172.9	176.2	176.6	177.3	178.2	175.0
1998	175.4	177.3	178.9	179.2	178.9	178.7	176.8	179.1	180.3	182.1	182.4	181.1	179.1
1999	177.5	179.9	181.0	180.9	180.6	180.3	181.7	181.3	182.9	185.0	186.1	187.8	182.0
2000	181.5	183.8	184.6	186.9	186.4	186.0	186.3	186.3	189.3	190.0	191.4	192.9	187.1
2001	183.6	186.2	187.2	188.3	189.0	189.9	187.8	187.1	188.4	191.1	192.9	193.9	188.8
2002	190.1	193.7	194.5	193.5	193.8	193.2	192.4	191.4	193.2	196.3	198.4	198.5	194.1
2003	196.0	197.7	198.8	199.4	199.7	198.5	197.0	195.8	198.6	203.4	204.4	204.9	199.5
Leisure and hospitality													
1990	88.6	89.6	91.5	94.4	97.4	101.8	100.9	100.5	98.3	94.6	93.9	93.6	95.4
1991	84.0	84.6	86.2	87.5	90.3	93.4	91.8	92.9	90.7	87.5	87.7	86.5	88.5
1992	81.7	81.4	83.5	88.8	92.5	95.0	93.7	93.5	91.9	89.0	87.6	87.1	88.8
1993	84.6	85.3	85.6	91.4	95.7	97.8	96.6	96.0	94.2	93.1	92.0	91.9	92.0
1994	85.9	85.6	88.7	93.9	97.5	100.1	100.5	99.8	97.8	93.3	93.5	93.0	94.1
1995	89.2	89.9	92.7	97.2	100.6	104.4	101.3	100.5	98.8	97.2	97.4	96.6	97.1
1996	88.2	90.0	92.5	95.7	99.7	102.1	100.5	101.1	99.4	98.0	96.6	96.3	96.6
1997	90.6	91.4	94.2	97.6	102.4	104.1	103.0	101.9	100.8	99.9	98.7	99.1	98.6
1998	92.9	94.0	96.9	100.6	103.9	107.7	107.1	106.3	104.2	101.2	100.2	100.7	101.3
1999	95.5	95.6	97.6	102.4	106.2	108.0	108.8	108.3	105.2	103.7	102.7	101.8	102.9
2000	97.1	97.3	100.3	102.4	105.3	109.5	108.6	108.4	105.9	102.9	103.3	103.6	103.7
2001	94.3	94.4	97.3	101.0	104.2	109.1	107.8	107.6	105.2	103.1	101.6	101.5	102.3
2002	97.1	97.3	100.6	103.9	107.9	112.0	112.1	112.3	107.7	105.4	104.1	103.5	105.3
2003	99.7	98.2	100.7	106.0	109.7	113.6	112.3	113.1	109.7	108.8	107.3	106.6	107.1

Employment by Industry: Maryland—*Continued*

(Numbers in thousands. Not seasonally adjusted.)

Industry	January	February	March	April	May	June	July	August	September	October	November	December	Annual Average
BALTIMORE MSA *—Continued*													
Other services													
1990	43.4	43.5	44.3	44.2	44.8	45.4	45.9	46.3	45.9	44.5	44.4	44.7	44.7
1991	42.3	42.8	43.4	43.4	43.5	44.2	44.2	44.1	43.8	42.7	42.8	42.9	43.3
1992	41.6	41.7	42.2	42.6	42.8	43.4	44.2	43.6	43.6	43.3	43.2	43.3	42.9
1993	42.2	42.5	42.7	43.4	43.7	44.5	44.5	44.1	43.7	43.5	43.4	43.6	43.4
1994	41.7	42.1	43.1	43.5	43.8	44.7	45.4	45.3	44.8	44.7	44.8	45.0	44.0
1995	44.1	44.1	44.9	45.1	45.8	46.7	46.7	46.6	46.1	45.5	46.0	46.3	45.6
1996	43.7	44.8	45.7	45.9	46.5	47.3	47.6	47.6	47.2	47.2	47.5	47.7	46.5
1997	45.1	45.1	46.1	46.8	47.2	47.8	47.8	47.8	48.3	48.3	48.3	48.7	47.2
1998	48.2	48.5	49.0	48.7	49.0	49.7	49.6	49.1	48.7	49.2	49.4	49.6	49.0
1999	48.3	48.8	49.0	49.6	50.1	50.5	50.3	50.2	50.2	50.7	50.8	50.9	49.9
2000	50.1	50.5	51.1	51.2	51.8	52.7	52.4	52.5	52.6	51.9	52.0	52.2	51.7
2001	52.0	52.6	53.3	52.9	53.7	54.7	54.6	54.5	53.5	53.6	53.7	54.0	53.6
2002	52.9	53.3	54.0	54.5	55.0	55.6	55.9	55.1	54.9	54.8	55.0	55.1	54.7
2003	53.9	54.0	54.9	55.2	55.6	56.3	57.3	56.5	56.0	56.1	56.0	56.0	55.7
Government													
1990	213.6	217.9	220.1	221.9	223.1	220.2	210.2	208.2	209.7	213.2	213.2	212.2	215.2
1991	207.1	211.2	211.4	212.9	213.4	212.0	206.5	200.5	203.9	211.8	212.7	211.6	209.5
1992	205.3	207.8	209.5	210.0	209.0	206.1	209.0	205.3	200.8	209.0	210.4	210.1	207.6
1993	205.0	207.7	209.3	208.3	209.6	206.9	207.7	203.7	205.9	208.5	210.1	210.6	207.7
1994	204.3	205.4	207.8	207.9	208.5	206.1	206.0	202.2	208.7	213.2	214.9	214.3	208.2
1995	207.6	210.1	211.7	212.6	211.1	209.0	200.9	200.2	205.5	209.4	210.3	210.7	208.2
1996	206.8	210.6	212.5	212.2	211.9	210.0	202.4	196.4	206.6	211.4	208.8	207.1	208.0
1997	207.3	210.8	212.2	212.3	212.5	212.0	206.8	199.2	209.5	213.5	215.7	215.4	210.6
1998	213.5	216.4	217.5	214.8	215.7	213.7	204.0	204.4	210.5	213.6	214.8	215.6	212.8
1999	215.0	218.9	220.6	219.5	219.7	215.7	198.7	195.4	213.3	218.7	220.2	220.6	214.6
2000	215.9	218.2	222.1	221.5	224.4	220.8	200.4	196.7	214.2	222.1	222.0	222.4	216.7
2001	217.3	221.4	222.9	223.0	221.9	218.7	204.7	210.3	217.4	222.0	223.8	223.4	218.9
2002	220.5	224.2	226.3	223.3	223.8	220.5	207.1	212.0	220.0	224.6	225.1	223.6	220.9
2003	218.4	222.2	224.1	224.5	224.5	218.6	206.0	209.2	217.7	221.0	220.9	220.1	218.9
Federal government													
1990	52.0	52.0	52.0	54.3	55.7	55.6	55.8	54.1	53.8	51.8	51.6	51.7	53.3
1991	52.3	51.8	51.8	51.9	51.9	52.1	51.1	51.3	51.1	50.6	50.7	51.0	51.4
1992	50.0	49.7	49.7	49.8	49.8	49.9	49.8	49.7	49.4	50.2	50.2	50.4	49.8
1993	49.5	49.2	49.4	48.8	48.8	48.9	49.1	49.3	49.2	48.6	48.5	48.8	49.0
1994	48.3	48.0	48.0	47.8	47.8	47.8	48.4	48.7	49.0	48.5	48.7	48.9	48.3
1995	48.4	48.2	48.2	48.1	47.9	48.0	47.8	47.9	47.7	47.0	47.1	47.3	47.8
1996	46.6	46.5	46.8	46.4	46.0	45.8	45.6	45.3	44.9	44.4	44.3	43.6	45.5
1997	46.9	46.9	47.1	47.4	47.3	47.4	48.1	47.5	47.3	47.1	47.3	47.7	47.3
1998	47.1	46.9	47.0	46.0	46.0	46.3	46.2	46.4	46.2	46.1	46.1	46.7	46.4
1999	45.4	45.4	45.4	45.1	45.0	45.0	45.2	45.2	45.0	44.9	44.8	45.4	45.1
2000	44.6	44.7	45.1	45.6	48.6	47.0	44.5	44.0	43.4	43.4	43.3	43.8	44.8
2001	42.4	42.2	42.4	42.2	42.3	42.5	42.6	42.7	42.9	42.4	42.2	42.6	42.5
2002	42.0	41.8	42.1	41.3	41.5	42.3	42.5	42.6	42.5	42.4	42.4	42.9	42.2
2003	42.3	42.1	42.3	41.9	42.0	42.3	42.0	41.8	41.9	41.5	41.3	41.7	41.9
State government													
1990	70.8	72.2	73.1	72.5	72.0	71.3	70.6	70.1	69.9	70.1	69.2	67.9	70.8
1991	65.4	67.3	67.5	67.7	67.9	66.4	65.6	66.4	67.0	68.0	67.9	67.1	67.0
1992	65.4	66.6	67.4	67.4	67.4	65.6	65.1	65.6	65.4	67.1	67.0	67.2	66.4
1993	66.2	66.8	67.7	67.8	68.6	67.6	68.1	66.4	65.9	67.9	68.0	68.4	67.4
1994	67.0	67.2	68.2	68.5	69.1	68.3	68.1	67.6	66.7	68.2	68.7	68.9	68.0
1995	67.5	68.4	69.1	70.0	69.2	68.9	68.1	68.1	67.5	68.4	67.4	67.2	68.3
1996	66.4	68.3	69.4	69.1	68.9	68.9	67.7	68.0	68.8	70.8	66.7	66.5	68.2
1997	65.9	66.9	67.4	67.3	67.3	67.6	65.9	66.2	66.6	67.4	68.5	67.7	67.0
1998	67.1	67.6	67.6	65.6	65.5	65.1	64.5	64.8	65.2	65.4	65.5	65.6	65.7
1999	68.3	69.5	70.7	69.8	69.5	68.0	67.5	67.3	69.3	70.5	70.1	69.7	69.1
2000	68.7	69.7	71.4	70.0	69.4	68.4	67.8	68.3	70.4	71.6	71.1	71.2	69.8
2001	70.5	72.3	73.1	73.0	71.9	70.0	69.5	70.6	71.1	72.1	72.8	72.3	71.6
2002	71.1	73.5	74.4	74.0	73.6	71.4	70.5	71.1	72.8	73.4	73.4	72.4	72.6
2003	70.1	72.7	73.8	73.8	73.9	69.2	69.8	70.2	71.0	71.7	71.3	71.0	71.5
Local government													
1990	90.8	93.7	95.0	95.1	95.4	93.3	83.8	84.0	86.0	91.3	92.4	92.6	91.1
1991	89.4	92.1	92.1	93.3	93.6	93.5	89.8	82.8	85.8	93.2	94.1	93.5	91.1
1992	89.9	91.5	92.4	92.8	91.8	90.6	94.1	90.0	86.0	91.7	93.2	92.5	91.3
1993	89.3	91.7	92.2	91.7	92.2	90.4	90.5	88.0	90.8	92.0	93.6	93.4	91.3
1994	89.0	90.2	91.6	91.6	91.6	90.0	89.5	85.9	93.0	96.5	97.5	96.5	91.9
1995	91.7	93.5	94.4	94.5	94.0	92.1	85.0	84.2	90.3	94.0	95.8	96.2	92.1
1996	93.8	95.8	96.3	96.7	97.0	95.3	89.1	83.1	92.9	96.2	97.8	97.0	94.2
1997	94.5	97.0	97.7	97.6	97.9	97.0	92.7	85.4	95.6	99.0	99.9	100.0	96.1
1998	99.3	101.9	102.9	103.2	104.2	102.3	93.3	93.2	99.1	102.1	103.2	103.3	100.6
1999	101.3	104.0	104.5	104.6	105.2	102.7	86.0	82.9	99.0	103.3	105.3	105.5	100.3
2000	102.6	103.8	105.6	105.9	106.4	105.4	88.1	84.4	100.4	107.1	107.6	107.4	102.0
2001	104.4	106.9	107.4	107.8	107.7	106.2	92.6	97.0	103.4	107.5	108.8	108.5	104.9
2002	107.4	108.9	109.8	108.0	108.7	106.8	94.1	98.3	104.7	108.8	109.3	108.3	106.1
2003	106.0	107.4	108.0	108.8	108.6	107.1	94.2	97.2	104.8	107.8	108.3	107.4	105.5

Employment by Industry: Maryland—*Continued*

(Numbers in thousands. Not seasonally adjusted.)

Industry	January	February	March	April	May	June	July	August	September	October	November	December	Annual Average
BALTIMORE CITY													
Total nonfarm													
1990	459.1	466.3	470.8	468.0	467.5	466.9	462.2	461.7	459.5	454.4	453.1	448.3	461.4
1991	431.8	432.3	433.4	433.2	433.7	432.8	429.6	428.5	429.8	428.8	429.0	427.6	430.8
1992	415.9	416.6	419.4	422.1	421.7	421.0	427.1	423.8	419.2	420.2	419.3	419.1	420.4
1993	407.5	409.8	410.9	414.0	416.1	415.7	418.4	415.1	413.1	415.0	415.4	415.8	413.9
1994	401.8	403.5	409.8	411.5	413.7	413.2	413.7	410.2	408.9	410.0	410.8	410.5	409.8
1995	400.0	402.6	405.2	408.1	409.7	409.0	405.7	406.0	407.7	404.2	408.1	408.3	406.2
1996	386.9	396.8	401.4	403.3	405.1	405.1	401.9	403.7	404.5	407.3	405.8	405.8	402.3
1997	393.0	396.9	400.7	402.8	405.9	406.5	406.2	403.9	401.7	404.9	407.2	407.8	403.1
1998	392.8	395.6	397.9	399.3	399.3	401.7	398.7	401.9	401.7	402.5	403.6	404.2	399.9
1999	391.3	394.2	396.5	404.0	406.3	407.3	412.0	409.9	409.7	412.2	411.3	412.3	405.5
2000	401.2	402.1	406.6	407.7	408.9	410.3	412.5	408.5	411.6	409.2	409.1	413.2	408.4
2001	393.7	396.0	398.1	398.1	398.8	401.3	397.1	396.3	392.4	390.8	389.8	391.3	395.3
2002	380.8	384.5	387.8	386.8	388.0	389.9	387.4	389.0	388.8	387.5	389.7	391.7	387.7
2003	381.2	381.8	381.5	384.3	386.1	386.4	382.0	383.4	384.0	387.3	389.3	391.0	384.9
Total private													
1990	368.1	374.2	378.2	375.8	374.7	374.8	369.5	368.8	369.1	363.3	361.9	357.1	369.6
1991	341.7	342.1	343.2	342.6	343.1	342.6	336.0	338.6	339.1	337.9	337.8	336.5	340.1
1992	325.7	325.9	328.5	331.3	331.3	331.8	331.0	329.6	330.0	330.5	329.9	329.5	329.5
1993	318.3	320.4	321.4	323.9	325.4	325.2	325.2	323.3	323.6	325.0	325.1	324.3	323.4
1994	311.6	312.8	318.3	320.0	321.8	321.9	320.4	319.7	319.7	319.4	320.0	319.1	318.7
1995	310.0	311.9	313.8	317.8	319.7	319.7	318.4	319.1	320.0	316.3	319.8	319.4	317.1
1996	299.8	309.0	313.0	314.8	316.6	317.2	314.8	316.7	316.7	318.6	318.8	318.4	314.5
1997	306.5	309.9	313.3	314.5	317.6	318.3	314.6	314.5	313.4	316.2	317.7	318.0	314.5
1998	304.8	307.4	309.8	311.8	312.1	315.1	312.3	314.4	314.1	315.7	316.6	316.4	312.5
1999	305.0	307.5	309.7	317.6	319.9	321.2	324.9	323.8	323.4	326.1	325.0	325.5	319.1
2000	315.5	316.2	319.6	323.1	323.6	325.0	324.6	323.5	326.0	324.3	324.3	327.7	322.7
2001	310.6	313.0	315.3	315.6	316.6	318.2	314.6	312.6	309.8	308.6	308.6	307.9	312.6
2002	297.6	301.6	304.6	304.5	306.3	307.4	305.7	306.1	305.2	305.3	307.1	306.9	304.9
2003	296.4	297.4	299.6	303.0	305.0	305.6	301.0	301.6	302.3	305.8	307.4	306.7	302.7
Goods-producing													
1990	57.4	60.5	61.2	60.4	60.5	60.9	59.9	59.5	59.0	57.1	56.5	55.1	59.0
1991	54.2	53.3	53.4	52.6	52.2	52.7	49.5	52.5	52.5	51.3	51.0	50.3	52.1
1992	48.9	48.5	48.8	49.5	49.5	50.3	50.3	50.4	50.1	49.5	49.5	49.3	49.5
1993	47.4	47.4	47.6	47.4	47.5	48.1	48.4	48.5	48.3	48.2	48.2	48.0	47.9
1994	46.3	45.8	46.9	44.5	45.4	45.5	45.4	45.5	45.5	45.3	45.3	44.9	45.5
1995	43.2	42.8	43.3	44.3	44.6	45.1	44.6	44.9	45.2	43.9	44.2	44.1	44.1
1996	41.4	42.9	43.4	44.1	44.5	44.9	44.3	44.8	44.7	44.9	45.0	44.9	44.1
1997	43.1	43.5	43.8	43.0	43.3	43.4	43.3	43.6	41.4	41.0	42.9	42.5	42.9
1998	40.1	41.1	41.3	41.2	41.4	41.8	39.1	40.6	41.7	41.0	41.2	41.3	40.9
1999	40.9	41.2	41.3	41.5	41.5	42.5	43.8	42.7	42.2	41.6	41.4	41.2	41.8
2000	40.3	39.9	40.5	39.9	40.2	40.4	40.0	39.8	39.9	39.6	39.3	39.4	39.9
2001	36.8	37.2	37.7	37.5	36.7	37.7	37.5	37.1	36.8	36.3	36.3	35.9	37.0
2002	33.5	34.7	34.9	35.1	35.3	35.4	35.4	35.1	35.0	34.6	34.5	34.4	34.8
2003	32.4	32.5	32.7	32.9	33.0	33.1	32.4	32.4	32.2	31.7	31.5	31.8	32.4
Construction and mining													
1990	17.6	17.7	18.3	18.0	18.1	18.2	17.9	17.7	17.4	17.1	16.5	16.0	17.5
1991	14.7	14.3	14.4	14.2	14.0	14.4	14.5	14.4	14.2	13.9	13.7	13.2	14.1
1992	12.2	12.0	12.2	12.8	12.7	13.2	13.6	13.6	13.2	13.1	12.9	12.5	12.8
1993	11.6	11.5	11.7	11.6	11.9	12.3	12.8	12.9	12.7	13.1	13.0	12.9	12.3
1994	11.4	11.0	11.7	11.3	11.8	12.0	12.3	12.2	12.2	12.2	12.1	12.1	11.8
1995	11.3	10.8	11.0	11.4	11.5	11.8	12.1	12.1	12.0	11.9	12.1	11.9	11.6
1996	10.5	11.3	11.7	12.3	12.5	12.6	12.8	12.8	12.6	12.9	12.9	12.7	12.3
1997	11.9	11.8	12.0	11.7	12.0	12.3	12.5	12.5	12.5	12.5	12.3	12.1	12.1
1998	11.5	11.4	11.4	11.7	11.9	12.2	12.4	12.5	12.4	12.5	12.4	12.4	12.0
1999	12.2	12.5	12.7	13.3	13.4	14.4	15.6	14.6	14.1	14.1	14.1	14.0	13.7
2000	13.5	13.3	13.9	12.5	12.7	12.8	12.9	13.1	13.0	12.9	12.8	12.7	13.0
2001	11.9	12.0	12.6	12.5	12.5	12.7	12.8	12.7	12.4	12.3	12.2	11.9	12.4
2002	11.2	11.3	11.5	11.8	12.0	12.0	12.4	12.4	12.4	12.1	12.0	11.9	11.9
2003	11.4	11.1	11.3	11.6	11.7	11.9	12.0	12.0	11.9	11.6	11.5	11.9	11.7
Manufacturing													
1990	39.8	42.8	42.9	42.4	42.4	42.7	42.0	41.8	41.6	40.0	40.0	39.1	41.4
1991	39.5	39.0	39.0	38.4	38.2	38.3	35.0	38.1	38.3	37.4	37.3	37.1	37.9
1992	36.7	36.5	36.6	36.7	36.8	37.1	36.7	36.8	36.9	36.4	36.6	36.8	36.7
1993	35.8	35.9	35.9	35.8	35.6	35.8	35.6	35.6	35.6	35.1	35.2	35.1	35.5
1994	34.9	34.8	35.2	33.2	33.6	33.5	33.1	33.3	33.3	33.1	33.2	32.8	33.6
1995	31.9	32.0	32.3	32.9	33.1	33.3	32.5	32.8	33.2	32.0	32.1	32.2	32.5
1996	30.9	31.6	31.7	31.8	32.0	32.3	31.5	32.0	32.1	32.0	32.1	32.2	31.8
1997	31.2	31.7	31.8	31.3	31.3	31.1	30.8	31.1	28.9	28.5	30.6	30.4	30.7
1998	28.6	29.7	29.9	29.5	29.5	29.6	26.7	28.1	29.3	28.5	28.8	28.9	28.9
1999	28.7	28.7	28.6	28.2	28.1	28.1	28.2	28.1	28.1	27.5	27.3	27.2	28.0
2000	26.8	26.6	26.6	27.4	27.5	27.6	27.1	26.7	26.9	26.7	26.5	26.7	26.9
2001	24.9	25.2	25.1	25.0	24.2	25.0	24.7	24.4	24.4	24.0	24.1	24.0	24.6
2002	22.3	23.4	23.4	23.3	23.3	23.4	23.0	22.7	22.6	22.5	22.5	22.5	22.9
2003	21.0	21.4	21.4	21.3	21.3	21.2	20.4	20.4	20.3	20.1	20.0	19.9	20.7

Employment by Industry: Maryland—*Continued*

(Numbers in thousands. Not seasonally adjusted.)

Industry	January	February	March	April	May	June	July	August	September	October	November	December	Annual Average
BALTIMORE CITY *—Continued*													
Service-providing													
1990	401.7	405.8	409.6	407.6	407.0	406.0	402.3	402.2	400.5	397.3	396.6	393.2	402.4
1991	377.6	379.0	380.0	380.6	381.5	380.1	380.1	376.0	377.3	377.5	378.0	377.3	378.7
1992	367.0	368.1	370.6	372.6	372.2	370.7	376.8	373.4	369.1	370.7	369.8	369.8	370.9
1993	360.1	362.4	363.3	366.6	368.6	367.6	370.0	366.6	364.8	366.8	367.2	367.8	365.9
1994	355.5	357.7	362.9	367.0	368.3	367.7	368.3	364.7	363.4	364.7	365.5	365.6	364.2
1995	356.8	359.8	361.9	363.8	365.1	363.9	361.1	361.1	362.5	360.3	363.9	364.2	362.0
1996	345.5	353.9	358.0	359.2	360.6	360.2	357.6	358.9	359.8	362.4	360.8	360.9	358.1
1997	349.9	353.4	356.9	359.8	362.6	363.1	362.9	360.3	360.3	363.9	364.3	365.3	360.2
1998	352.7	354.5	356.6	358.1	357.9	359.9	359.6	361.3	360.0	361.5	362.4	362.9	358.9
1999	350.4	353.0	355.2	362.5	364.8	364.8	368.2	367.2	367.5	370.6	369.9	371.1	363.7
2000	360.9	362.2	366.1	367.8	368.7	369.9	372.5	368.7	371.7	369.6	369.8	373.8	368.4
2001	356.9	358.8	360.4	360.6	362.1	363.6	359.6	359.2	355.6	354.5	353.5	355.4	358.4
2002	347.3	349.8	352.9	351.7	352.7	354.5	352.0	353.9	353.8	352.9	355.2	357.3	352.8
2003	348.8	349.3	348.8	351.4	353.1	353.3	349.6	351.0	351.8	355.6	357.8	359.2	352.5
Trade, transportation, and utilities													
1990	82.9	82.4	82.7	82.0	81.4	81.3	80.8	80.5	80.6	79.4	79.4	78.8	81.0
1991	71.9	71.2	70.9	71.5	71.8	72.0	71.6	71.5	71.7	71.0	71.2	71.5	71.4
1992	69.0	67.9	67.8	66.1	66.6	66.8	65.9	65.9	65.5	65.4	65.6	65.9	66.5
1993	62.7	62.4	62.1	62.4	62.8	63.2	63.3	63.2	62.9	62.6	62.9	63.6	62.8
1994	61.0	60.9	61.4	61.5	62.2	62.5	62.2	62.2	62.0	62.4	62.6	62.9	61.9
1995	60.7	60.9	60.8	61.4	61.7	62.1	62.3	62.2	61.3	60.4	60.8	61.4	61.3
1996	57.5	58.5	58.9	58.4	58.7	59.2	58.3	58.4	58.3	58.7	58.8	59.3	58.5
1997	56.8	56.7	57.0	58.1	58.4	59.0	57.0	57.0	56.9	58.2	58.2	58.8	57.6
1998	56.1	56.1	56.3	56.0	56.1	56.3	55.9	56.1	55.9	56.7	55.4	55.6	56.0
1999	53.3	53.4	53.2	54.4	55.0	55.1	55.7	56.1	55.9	56.1	56.0	56.3	55.0
2000	54.4	54.2	54.8	52.4	52.4	53.5	52.2	52.8	52.6	52.5	52.6	53.2	53.1
2001	52.0	51.5	51.7	51.4	51.4	51.1	49.8	49.4	49.2	48.9	48.5	48.9	50.3
2002	46.7	46.6	47.1	46.7	47.2	47.4	46.9	47.0	47.2	47.1	48.0	48.3	47.2
2003	45.5	45.2	45.6	46.0	46.6	46.5	45.8	46.4	46.6	45.5	46.1	46.5	46.0
Wholesale trade													
1990	21.9	22.0	22.1	21.8	21.7	21.8	22.0	21.8	21.6	21.0	21.0	20.7	21.6
1991	20.4	20.3	20.2	20.9	20.8	20.9	20.9	20.8	20.8	20.6	20.5	20.4	20.6
1992	20.1	20.0	20.0	19.3	19.3	19.4	19.1	19.1	19.0	18.9	18.9	18.8	19.3
1993	17.6	17.7	17.7	17.5	17.6	17.6	17.7	17.6	17.4	17.3	17.1	17.2	17.5
1994	16.9	16.9	16.9	16.8	16.8	16.8	16.9	16.9	16.9	16.8	16.8	16.7	16.8
1995	16.0	16.2	16.2	16.2	16.3	16.5	16.5	16.5	16.5	16.5	16.6	16.7	16.3
1996	15.8	16.1	16.1	15.9	16.0	16.1	16.1	16.1	16.0	16.0	16.1	16.1	16.0
1997	15.7	15.8	15.7	15.3	15.4	15.4	15.6	15.8	15.7	15.7	15.8	15.8	15.6
1998	15.1	15.4	15.4	14.5	14.6	14.7	14.5	14.5	14.4	14.4	14.5	14.5	14.7
1999	14.0	14.0	14.0	14.4	14.5	14.5	14.6	14.6	14.5	13.9	13.8	14.0	14.2
2000	13.9	14.0	14.2	13.0	13.1	13.1	13.3	13.2	13.2	12.9	12.9	13.0	13.3
2001	14.3	14.2	14.4	14.4	14.4	14.4	14.3	14.2	14.1	13.8	13.7	13.7	14.2
2002	13.1	13.1	13.3	13.1	13.1	13.1	13.0	13.2	13.2	13.0	13.0	13.1	13.1
2003	12.5	12.3	12.4	12.5	12.4	12.4	12.2	12.2	12.2	12.2	12.3	12.3	12.3
Retail trade													
1990	39.7	39.3	39.3	38.8	38.6	38.5	37.9	38.0	38.0	37.6	37.9	38.0	38.4
1991	34.5	33.8	33.5	33.3	33.6	33.7	33.5	33.5	33.5	33.1	33.4	33.8	33.6
1992	31.8	30.9	30.9	30.1	30.5	30.4	30.3	30.3	30.0	30.1	30.3	30.6	30.5
1993	29.3	29.0	28.8	29.6	29.8	30.0	30.4	30.3	30.1	30.1	30.7	31.2	29.9
1994	29.9	29.5	29.7	30.1	30.5	30.6	30.4	30.5	30.4	30.6	30.9	31.3	30.3
1995	29.7	29.6	29.5	29.5	29.7	29.9	30.0	29.9	29.4	29.2	29.8	30.2	29.7
1996	27.8	28.3	28.7	28.2	28.4	28.7	28.0	28.0	28.0	28.3	28.7	29.1	28.3
1997	27.8	27.6	27.8	27.9	28.1	28.5	28.2	28.3	28.1	28.2	28.3	28.8	28.1
1998	28.0	27.5	27.6	27.7	27.9	28.0	27.9	28.1	28.0	28.2	26.8	27.2	27.7
1999	26.5	26.4	26.3	26.5	26.9	26.9	26.7	27.0	27.1	27.8	28.1	28.3	27.0
2000	26.8	26.5	26.7	25.0	25.1	26.3	24.8	25.1	25.1	24.7	25.2	25.5	25.5
2001	23.6	23.4	23.5	23.0	22.9	22.6	21.8	21.5	21.3	21.0	21.1	21.3	22.3
2002	20.3	20.1	20.5	20.2	20.4	20.6	20.3	20.3	20.4	20.3	20.9	21.2	20.5
2003	19.7	19.5	19.6	19.8	20.0	20.1	20.2	20.7	20.7	20.4	21.2	21.5	20.3
Transportation and utilities													
1990	21.3	21.1	21.3	21.4	21.1	21.0	20.9	20.7	21.0	20.8	20.5	20.1	20.9
1991	17.0	17.1	17.2	17.3	17.4	17.4	17.2	17.2	17.4	17.3	17.3	17.3	17.2
1992	17.1	17.0	16.9	16.7	16.8	17.0	16.5	16.5	16.5	16.4	16.4	16.5	16.6
1993	15.8	15.7	15.6	15.3	15.4	15.6	15.2	15.3	15.4	15.2	15.1	15.2	15.4
1994	14.2	14.5	14.8	14.6	14.9	15.1	14.9	14.8	14.7	15.0	14.9	14.9	14.7
1995	15.0	15.1	15.1	15.7	15.7	15.7	15.8	15.8	15.4	14.7	14.4	14.5	15.2
1996	13.9	14.1	14.1	14.3	14.3	14.4	14.2	14.3	14.3	14.4	14.0	14.1	14.2
1997	13.3	13.3	13.5	14.9	14.9	15.1	13.2	12.9	13.1	14.3	14.1	14.2	13.9
1998	13.0	13.2	13.3	13.8	13.6	13.6	13.5	13.5	13.5	14.1	14.1	13.9	13.5
1999	12.8	13.0	12.9	13.5	13.6	13.7	14.4	14.5	14.3	14.4	14.1	14.0	13.7
2000	13.7	13.7	13.9	14.4	14.2	14.1	14.1	14.5	14.3	14.9	14.5	14.7	14.2
2001	14.1	13.9	13.8	14.0	14.1	14.1	13.7	13.7	13.8	14.1	13.7	13.9	13.9
2002	13.3	13.4	13.3	13.4	13.7	13.7	13.6	13.5	13.6	13.8	14.1	14.0	13.6
2003	13.3	13.4	13.6	13.7	14.2	14.0	13.4	13.5	13.7	12.9	12.6	12.7	13.4

Employment by Industry: Maryland—*Continued*

(Numbers in thousands. Not seasonally adjusted.)

Industry	January	February	March	April	May	June	July	August	September	October	November	December	Annual Average
BALTIMORE CITY *—Continued*													
Information													
1990	10.4	10.4	10.5	10.4	10.4	10.3	10.2	10.1	9.9	9.8	9.8	9.6	10.1
1991	9.9	9.9	9.8	9.6	9.7	9.7	9.7	9.6	9.4	9.2	9.2	9.1	9.5
1992	9.0	8.8	8.8	8.6	8.7	8.8	8.7	8.6	8.5	8.4	8.4	8.4	8.6
1993	8.3	8.2	8.2	8.1	8.2	8.2	8.4	8.2	8.1	8.2	8.2	8.1	8.2
1994	8.1	8.1	8.1	7.6	7.6	7.7	7.5	7.6	7.4	7.3	7.3	7.3	7.6
1995	7.4	7.3	7.2	7.6	7.6	7.6	7.6	8.0	8.0	7.9	8.1	8.2	7.7
1996	7.8	8.2	8.3	8.0	8.2	8.3	8.6	8.5	8.4	8.4	8.7	8.6	8.3
1997	8.6	8.7	8.7	8.6	8.7	8.8	8.8	8.9	8.7	8.9	8.9	9.0	8.7
1998	8.8	9.0	8.8	8.9	8.9	9.0	9.1	9.2	9.0	9.0	9.1	9.1	8.9
1999	8.7	8.7	8.7	8.9	9.0	9.1	9.3	9.4	9.3	9.2	9.3	9.1	9.0
2000	9.4	9.2	9.2	9.3	9.5	9.5	9.6	8.6	9.6	9.6	9.8	9.9	9.4
2001	10.2	10.5	10.3	9.6	9.6	9.3	8.9	8.9	8.4	8.2	8.1	7.8	9.2
2002	7.7	7.9	7.8	7.6	7.6	7.5	7.3	7.4	7.1	6.9	7.0	6.9	7.4
2003	6.8	6.9	6.9	7.1	7.3	7.0	7.1	6.9	6.7	6.8	6.8	6.7	6.9
Financial activities													
1990	46.4	46.5	46.7	47.0	47.0	47.1	43.6	43.6	43.5	45.1	45.2	44.7	45.5
1991	39.5	39.1	39.3	37.7	38.0	38.0	36.0	36.1	35.9	36.3	36.2	36.4	37.3
1992	35.9	35.8	36.0	36.1	36.2	36.4	36.4	36.2	36.0	35.5	35.4	35.5	35.9
1993	34.9	34.9	35.0	35.2	35.1	35.3	35.6	35.7	35.3	35.5	35.6	35.8	35.3
1994	35.5	35.6	36.0	36.0	36.2	36.2	36.0	35.9	35.6	35.5	35.4	35.4	35.7
1995	34.0	34.1	34.1	33.7	33.7	33.8	33.6	33.5	32.9	32.6	33.0	33.0	33.5
1996	31.7	32.1	32.2	32.2	32.1	32.2	32.1	32.1	32.1	32.2	32.3	32.6	32.1
1997	31.4	31.6	31.8	32.5	32.7	32.9	32.8	32.8	32.8	32.4	32.4	32.8	32.4
1998	31.1	30.9	31.3	31.2	31.3	31.7	31.8	31.9	31.6	32.0	31.9	32.1	31.5
1999	31.8	31.8	32.1	31.8	31.8	31.9	32.5	32.5	32.4	32.2	32.0	31.9	32.0
2000	31.3	31.4	31.5	31.1	31.2	31.3	31.8	31.7	31.6	31.4	31.5	31.9	31.4
2001	30.8	30.9	31.2	30.7	30.6	30.8	30.4	30.1	29.9	29.4	29.4	29.2	30.3
2002	29.3	29.1	29.1	28.9	28.9	29.1	28.9	28.8	28.8	28.6	28.6	28.6	28.9
2003	27.3	27.4	27.5	27.4	27.3	27.5	27.0	27.0	26.9	26.7	26.9	26.7	27.1
Professional and business services													
1990	46.3	46.7	47.4	46.6	46.0	46.5	46.2	46.1	46.5	43.3	43.0	42.5	45.5
1991	43.7	43.3	43.2	44.0	44.3	45.3	44.7	44.7	44.6	43.5	43.2	43.2	43.9
1992	41.9	41.9	42.2	41.4	41.0	41.2	41.6	41.4	41.5	42.4	42.2	41.9	41.7
1993	40.9	41.1	41.4	42.7	42.9	43.1	43.4	43.0	43.3	43.0	43.0	42.7	42.5
1994	39.9	40.4	41.7	42.4	42.9	43.1	42.9	43.0	43.5	43.0	43.4	43.3	42.4
1995	43.4	44.0	43.9	43.9	43.8	43.5	43.2	43.6	43.6	43.2	43.7	43.9	43.6
1996	40.0	42.1	43.1	43.5	44.2	44.7	44.3	45.3	45.3	45.6	45.9	45.1	44.0
1997	43.0	43.7	44.7	44.0	44.9	46.1	45.8	46.1	45.8	47.0	46.7	46.6	45.3
1998	43.1	43.5	43.4	43.2	43.7	44.8	46.0	46.3	46.1	46.1	46.7	46.7	44.9
1999	43.7	44.5	45.2	48.7	49.4	50.4	51.2	50.7	51.3	53.4	52.4	52.8	49.4
2000	49.9	49.9	50.5	51.9	52.1	52.8	53.3	53.2	52.7	53.4	53.0	53.5	52.1
2001	52.6	52.8	52.7	52.8	53.9	53.8	54.9	54.5	53.4	52.9	52.9	52.7	53.3
2002	48.5	49.0	49.5	49.6	50.3	50.7	50.7	51.9	51.2	50.9	51.2	51.4	50.4
2003	50.1	49.5	49.8	51.5	52.3	53.0	51.4	51.9	51.4	51.3	51.3	50.6	51.2
Educational and health services													
1990	80.7	83.5	84.5	83.2	82.5	80.5	81.3	81.3	82.7	83.7	83.8	82.9	82.5
1991	81.2	83.6	84.2	84.5	83.8	81.3	82.3	81.6	82.7	85.6	86.1	85.8	83.5
1992	83.1	85.0	85.9	86.9	86.1	84.7	84.9	84.4	85.6	87.7	88.0	88.2	85.8
1993	85.7	87.5	88.0	88.1	87.6	86.2	85.5	84.9	86.1	87.0	87.3	86.6	86.7
1994	84.0	85.2	86.0	86.7	85.2	84.5	84.6	84.0	84.7	86.3	86.6	86.4	85.3
1995	84.3	85.5	86.0	85.8	85.3	84.2	85.8	85.5	87.9	87.4	88.9	88.3	86.2
1996	85.6	88.3	88.7	88.8	88.0	87.0	86.5	86.5	87.2	88.2	88.2	88.1	87.5
1997	85.9	87.6	87.8	88.2	87.6	87.4	86.5	86.3	87.7	87.8	88.0	87.9	87.3
1998	86.6	87.3	87.8	88.8	87.8	87.5	87.6	87.9	88.0	89.3	90.7	89.9	88.2
1999	86.7	87.7	88.2	88.4	87.8	87.7	88.1	88.1	88.4	89.6	90.4	91.5	88.5
2000	89.4	90.6	90.8	94.6	93.4	92.5	93.3	93.1	95.0	94.4	94.7	96.1	93.1
2001	87.6	89.2	89.8	90.4	90.4	91.1	89.8	89.6	89.3	91.0	91.8	92.1	90.2
2002	90.8	93.0	93.3	92.3	91.7	91.7	91.1	90.8	91.4	93.5	94.1	94.4	92.3
2003	93.0	94.5	95.1	94.5	94.2	93.4	92.8	92.5	94.2	99.6	100.7	100.7	95.4
Leisure and hospitality													
1990	27.7	27.8	28.6	29.6	30.2	31.4	30.7	30.8	30.4	28.9	28.4	27.6	29.3
1991	25.7	25.9	26.5	27.1	27.6	27.8	26.3	26.9	26.7	25.7	25.6	25.0	26.4
1992	23.2	23.2	24.0	27.3	27.9	28.2	27.6	27.4	27.7	26.6	25.8	25.3	26.1
1993	23.7	24.1	24.3	25.2	26.4	26.1	25.6	25.1	25.1	25.9	25.5	25.2	25.1
1994	22.8	22.8	23.9	26.7	27.7	27.6	26.8	26.5	26.4	24.9	24.8	24.3	25.4
1995	22.8	23.1	24.1	26.2	27.6	27.7	25.5	25.7	25.7	25.9	26.0	25.3	25.4
1996	21.9	22.6	23.7	25.0	26.0	25.7	25.5	25.9	25.6	25.6	24.9	24.7	24.7
1997	23.2	23.7	24.8	25.7	27.5	26.1	25.7	25.2	25.3	25.9	25.5	25.3	25.3
1998	24.1	24.7	25.8	27.4	27.7	28.9	27.8	27.5	27.1	26.6	26.5	26.7	26.7
1999	25.4	25.5	26.3	28.2	29.7	28.9	28.8	28.7	28.4	28.4	27.8	27.1	27.7
2000	25.5	25.6	26.7	27.8	28.6	28.8	28.1	28.0	28.1	27.2	27.0	27.2	27.3
2001	24.4	24.4	25.3	26.8	27.3	27.5	26.5	26.3	26.3	25.3	24.9	24.5	25.8
2002	24.7	24.9	26.4	27.6	28.3	28.8	28.5	28.6	28.1	27.1	27.0	26.2	27.2
2003	25.0	25.1	25.6	27.3	27.9	28.7	28.0	28.2	28.0	27.6	27.5	27.1	27.2

Employment by Industry: Maryland—*Continued*

(Numbers in thousands. Not seasonally adjusted.)

Industry	January	February	March	April	May	June	July	August	September	October	November	December	Annual Average
BALTIMORE CITY *—Continued*													
Other services													
1990	16.3	16.4	16.6	16.6	16.7	16.8	16.8	16.9	16.5	16.0	15.8	15.9	16.4
1991	15.6	15.8	15.9	15.6	15.7	15.8	15.9	15.7	15.6	15.3	15.3	15.2	15.6
1992	14.7	14.8	15.0	15.4	15.3	15.4	15.6	15.3	15.1	15.0	15.0	15.0	15.1
1993	14.7	14.8	14.8	14.8	14.9	15.0	15.0	14.7	14.5	14.6	14.4	14.3	14.7
1994	14.0	14.0	14.3	14.6	14.6	14.8	15.0	15.0	14.6	14.7	14.6	14.6	14.5
1995	14.2	14.2	14.4	14.9	15.4	15.7	15.8	15.7	15.4	15.0	15.1	15.2	15.0
1996	13.9	14.3	14.7	14.8	14.9	15.2	15.2	15.2	15.1	15.0	15.0	15.1	14.8
1997	14.5	14.4	14.7	14.4	14.5	14.6	14.7	14.6	14.8	15.0	15.1	15.1	14.7
1998	14.9	14.8	15.1	15.1	15.2	15.1	15.0	14.9	14.7	15.0	15.1	15.0	14.9
1999	14.5	14.7	14.7	15.7	15.7	15.6	15.5	15.6	15.5	15.6	15.7	15.6	15.3
2000	15.3	15.4	15.6	16.1	16.2	16.2	16.3	16.3	16.5	16.2	16.4	16.5	16.0
2001	16.2	16.5	16.6	16.4	16.7	16.9	16.8	16.7	16.5	16.6	16.7	16.8	16.6
2002	16.4	16.4	16.5	16.7	17.0	16.8	16.9	16.5	16.4	16.6	16.7	16.7	16.6
2003	16.3	16.3	16.4	16.3	16.4	16.4	16.5	16.3	16.3	16.6	16.6	16.6	16.4
Government													
1990	91.0	92.1	92.6	92.2	92.8	92.1	92.7	92.9	90.4	91.1	91.2	91.2	91.8
1991	90.1	90.2	90.2	90.6	90.6	90.2	93.6	89.9	90.7	90.9	91.2	91.1	90.7
1992	90.2	90.7	90.9	90.8	90.4	89.2	96.1	94.2	89.2	89.7	89.4	89.6	90.8
1993	89.2	89.4	89.5	90.1	90.7	90.5	93.2	91.8	89.5	90.0	90.3	91.5	90.4
1994	90.2	90.7	91.5	91.5	91.9	91.3	93.3	90.5	89.2	90.6	90.8	91.4	91.0
1995	90.0	90.7	91.4	90.3	90.0	89.3	87.3	86.9	87.7	87.9	88.3	88.9	89.0
1996	87.1	87.8	88.4	88.5	88.5	87.9	87.1	87.0	87.8	88.7	87.0	87.4	87.7
1997	86.5	87.0	87.4	88.3	88.3	88.2	91.6	89.4	88.3	88.7	89.5	89.8	88.5
1998	88.0	88.2	88.1	87.5	87.2	86.6	86.4	87.5	87.6	86.8	87.0	87.8	87.3
1999	86.3	86.7	86.8	86.4	86.4	86.1	87.1	86.1	86.3	86.1	86.3	86.8	86.4
2000	85.7	85.9	87.0	84.6	85.3	85.3	87.9	85.0	85.6	84.9	84.8	85.5	85.6
2001	83.1	83.0	82.8	82.5	82.2	83.1	82.5	83.7	82.6	82.2	81.2	83.4	82.7
2002	83.2	82.9	83.2	82.3	81.7	82.5	81.7	82.9	83.6	82.2	82.6	84.8	82.8
2003	84.8	84.4	81.9	81.3	81.1	80.8	81.0	81.8	81.7	81.5	81.9	84.3	82.2
Federal government													
1990	15.2	15.3	15.3	17.1	17.8	17.8	17.9	17.1	17.1	17.1	17.0	17.1	16.8
1991	17.0	16.5	16.3	16.3	16.3	16.4	16.4	16.5	16.4	16.2	16.2	16.3	16.4
1992	16.2	16.0	16.0	16.0	15.9	15.9	15.7	15.5	15.4	15.5	15.3	15.4	15.7
1993	15.8	15.7	15.7	15.6	15.6	15.6	15.6	15.6	15.8	15.4	15.4	15.8	15.6
1994	15.3	15.3	15.3	15.5	15.5	15.5	15.6	15.6	15.9	15.6	15.7	16.1	15.5
1995	15.6	15.5	15.6	15.4	15.4	15.3	15.3	15.2	15.1	14.9	14.8	15.2	15.2
1996	14.8	14.7	14.7	14.8	14.7	14.8	14.7	14.8	14.9	14.8	15.0	15.4	14.8
1997	14.7	14.8	14.9	15.3	15.3	15.3	15.2	15.2	15.1	15.1	15.4	15.7	15.1
1998	13.7	13.7	13.7	12.7	12.6	12.7	13.0	13.1	13.0	13.2	13.2	13.9	13.2
1999	12.5	12.5	12.5	12.5	12.4	12.4	12.4	12.4	12.3	12.4	12.4	12.9	12.4
2000	12.5	12.6	12.7	12.8	14.3	13.3	12.2	11.6	11.2	11.0	10.8	11.1	12.1
2001	10.6	10.6	10.6	10.6	10.6	10.7	10.7	10.7	10.7	10.6	10.6	10.9	10.7
2002	10.4	10.4	10.5	10.4	10.3	10.4	10.4	10.4	10.4	10.3	10.3	10.6	10.4
2003	10.3	10.2	10.5	10.4	10.4	10.5	10.5	10.4	10.4	10.4	10.3	10.7	10.4
State government													
1990	39.1	39.3	39.6	38.4	38.5	38.6	39.5	39.5	39.2	39.7	39.7	39.4	39.2
1991	38.5	38.9	39.2	39.5	39.5	39.4	39.8	39.5	40.5	40.8	41.0	40.9	39.7
1992	40.2	40.9	41.1	41.0	40.7	40.3	40.4	40.6	40.6	40.6	40.4	40.5	40.6
1993	40.1	40.2	40.4	40.4	40.6	40.5	41.8	40.4	40.3	40.6	40.6	40.7	40.5
1994	40.4	40.4	40.8	40.8	41.0	41.0	41.6	41.1	40.5	41.0	41.1	41.4	40.9
1995	40.9	41.2	41.6	41.6	41.8	41.9	41.4	41.3	41.5	41.9	42.3	42.5	41.6
1996	41.5	42.2	42.6	42.4	42.3	41.8	41.1	41.2	41.9	43.0	40.7	40.6	41.7
1997	40.5	40.7	41.0	41.0	41.0	40.9	40.3	40.6	40.8	41.5	41.7	41.7	40.9
1998	41.7	41.8	41.7	41.6	41.4	40.6	40.4	40.5	40.8	41.0	41.0	41.1	41.1
1999	40.9	41.3	41.4	40.9	40.7	40.4	39.7	39.9	40.8	40.9	41.0	41.0	40.7
2000	40.7	40.6	41.5	39.6	38.6	39.5	40.1	40.3	41.6	41.6	41.5	41.8	40.6
2001	40.4	40.2	40.2	40.0	39.7	40.5	40.6	41.1	40.1	39.7	38.6	40.4	40.1
2002	41.0	40.7	41.0	40.7	40.0	40.8	40.2	41.0	41.0	40.7	41.1	43.0	40.9
2003	43.6	43.4	40.6	40.2	39.9	39.5	39.8	40.0	40.0	39.5	39.9	41.9	40.7
Local government													
1990	36.7	37.5	37.7	36.7	36.5	35.7	35.3	36.3	34.1	34.3	34.5	34.7	35.8
1991	34.6	34.8	34.7	34.8	34.8	34.4	37.4	33.9	33.8	33.9	34.0	33.9	34.5
1992	33.8	33.8	33.8	33.8	33.8	33.0	40.0	38.1	33.2	33.6	33.7	33.7	34.5
1993	33.3	33.5	33.4	34.1	34.5	34.4	35.8	35.8	33.4	34.0	34.3	35.0	34.2
1994	34.5	35.0	35.4	35.2	35.4	34.8	36.1	33.8	32.8	34.0	34.0	33.9	34.5
1995	33.5	34.0	34.2	33.3	32.8	32.1	30.6	30.4	31.1	31.1	31.2	31.2	32.1
1996	30.8	30.9	31.1	31.3	31.5	31.3	31.3	31.0	31.0	30.9	31.3	31.4	31.1
1997	31.3	31.5	31.5	32.0	32.0	32.0	36.1	33.6	32.4	32.1	32.4	32.4	32.4
1998	32.6	32.7	32.7	33.2	33.2	33.3	33.0	33.9	33.8	32.6	32.8	32.8	33.0
1999	32.9	32.9	32.9	33.0	33.3	33.3	35.0	33.8	33.2	32.8	32.9	32.9	33.2
2000	32.5	32.7	32.8	32.2	32.4	32.5	35.6	33.1	32.8	32.3	32.5	32.6	32.8
2001	32.1	32.2	32.0	31.9	31.9	31.9	31.2	31.9	31.8	31.9	32.0	32.1	31.9
2002	31.8	31.8	31.7	31.2	31.4	31.3	31.1	31.5	32.2	31.2	31.2	31.2	31.5
2003	30.9	30.8	30.8	30.7	30.8	30.8	30.7	31.4	31.3	31.6	31.7	31.7	31.1

Employment by Industry: Maryland—*Continued*

(Numbers in thousands. Not seasonally adjusted.)

Industry	January	February	March	April	May	June	July	August	September	October	November	December	Annual Average
SUBURBAN MARYLAND-DC													
Total nonfarm													
1990	762.0	765.9	773.0	774.3	781.1	793.4	781.4	783.0	787.4	778.6	779.6	781.8	778.4
1991	748.1	750.0	754.2	753.4	759.6	765.8	752.7	753.1	760.4	757.3	762.1	763.0	756.6
1992	739.5	740.0	745.8	750.2	758.0	760.9	749.3	748.2	756.5	759.8	762.2	767.9	753.1
1993	745.6	750.1	752.5	760.8	770.0	775.2	764.1	762.0	772.7	777.4	782.1	788.0	766.7
1994	762.1	764.1	774.5	783.0	790.3	796.0	785.6	783.6	795.2	796.3	801.4	807.7	786.6
1995	781.3	785.8	795.0	799.4	805.7	812.7	799.0	798.3	807.9	809.0	812.3	817.4	801.9
1996	781.2	792.1	803.1	808.5	816.5	825.9	815.2	815.2	821.1	824.7	830.9	836.9	814.2
1997	805.4	808.9	820.7	824.0	831.0	840.4	832.8	828.1	839.8	842.3	847.5	855.4	831.3
1998	831.0	834.1	845.0	847.1	855.6	867.3	863.6	864.6	869.1	876.5	882.6	890.6	860.5
1999	860.6	866.9	875.7	883.5	889.0	897.0	883.8	879.0	894.4	904.4	910.5	918.8	888.6
2000	890.2	894.1	909.5	913.2	920.7	929.9	913.4	906.9	929.9	932.5	936.9	944.4	918.4
2001	906.2	910.9	917.8	920.7	927.6	935.5	908.9	913.0	923.4	930.7	934.7	941.0	922.5
2002	913.5	918.8	927.4	927.1	933.0	937.3	914.9	927.2	932.2	935.1	939.9	942.0	929.0
2003	918.1	917.2	927.4	930.9	938.7	946.5	931.6	938.2	939.5	948.5	951.2	954.2	936.8
Total private													
1990	603.9	606.3	612.9	614.8	619.1	629.4	627.1	628.5	623.1	613.3	613.7	615.3	617.2
1991	585.1	583.7	586.8	587.0	591.2	598.3	597.3	598.1	595.2	588.9	592.5	593.6	591.4
1992	575.8	572.6	577.6	582.8	589.2	594.9	593.6	592.6	591.0	590.8	592.5	597.7	587.5
1993	580.4	579.9	581.4	590.3	598.5	606.0	606.7	604.9	602.8	604.5	608.7	614.3	598.2
1994	594.3	592.6	601.9	610.7	617.8	626.0	625.7	624.7	623.9	621.9	626.1	631.7	616.4
1995	610.9	611.6	620.2	625.4	631.3	639.8	636.6	637.0	637.3	636.0	639.2	644.7	630.8
1996	610.3	619.5	630.0	635.4	643.1	653.6	653.2	655.4	653.1	652.9	658.1	663.9	644.0
1997	643.6	644.3	653.7	658.0	665.2	674.8	676.3	674.4	674.7	674.5	678.1	686.4	667.0
1998	665.5	667.1	676.3	679.2	685.8	697.9	701.7	702.0	698.7	702.7	707.4	714.6	691.5
1999	687.8	690.6	697.6	704.5	709.7	720.4	725.7	723.4	717.9	724.6	729.1	736.8	714.0
2000	712.9	715.7	727.6	730.4	736.4	749.2	751.4	751.9	750.5	750.0	752.7	759.4	740.6
2001	725.9	727.5	733.3	735.5	742.1	753.1	749.2	750.1	740.3	743.8	746.6	751.7	741.6
2002	727.4	728.9	735.6	737.0	742.6	750.1	749.9	749.1	744.1	742.7	746.7	748.2	741.9
2003	729.4	725.6	735.0	739.3	746.4	756.2	755.3	754.7	750.0	752.7	754.8	757.3	746.4
Goods-producing													
1990	102.0	102.5	104.4	105.2	105.9	106.8	105.9	105.4	104.2	101.1	99.4	97.2	103.3
1991	89.1	87.8	88.1	88.9	89.8	90.8	91.8	92.0	91.0	89.0	88.0	86.9	89.4
1992	83.1	82.1	83.4	84.7	86.1	87.3	86.6	86.4	86.4	86.7	86.1	85.6	85.3
1993	82.1	82.4	82.9	84.5	86.1	87.4	87.7	87.9	87.8	87.8	87.5	87.1	85.9
1994	83.3	82.5	84.8	89.6	91.5	93.3	96.3	95.5	95.5	96.1	96.4	96.5	91.7
1995	93.5	92.9	94.4	95.4	96.2	97.5	96.7	97.2	97.6	97.4	96.8	96.6	96.0
1996	89.2	92.3	94.5	96.7	98.7	100.7	101.6	102.4	102.6	102.3	102.4	102.3	98.8
1997	97.6	97.4	99.0	98.7	100.0	101.4	104.1	104.2	104.0	103.1	102.6	102.2	101.1
1998	99.9	100.0	101.5	103.7	104.4	106.4	107.0	107.4	107.3	108.4	107.3	107.6	105.0
1999	103.6	104.1	105.2	108.2	108.7	110.4	111.2	111.3	110.8	110.9	111.0	111.8	108.9
2000	109.2	109.4	112.0	112.4	113.7	116.2	117.6	117.7	117.8	117.4	116.4	116.0	114.6
2001	111.8	112.3	114.2	115.1	116.5	118.2	118.4	118.9	117.8	117.3	116.5	115.6	116.1
2002	112.3	112.5	113.9	114.2	114.9	115.7	115.5	115.2	114.0	112.6	112.3	111.0	113.7
2003	108.7	108.2	110.4	110.9	112.4	113.3	113.2	113.8	112.8	113.0	112.7	112.0	111.8
Construction and mining													
1990	64.4	64.9	66.7	67.6	68.2	69.0	68.1	68.1	67.0	64.5	62.7	60.6	65.9
1991	53.7	52.5	52.7	54.8	55.6	56.6	57.5	57.8	56.7	55.1	54.0	53.1	55.0
1992	49.5	49.0	49.8	51.0	52.3	53.3	53.2	53.0	52.9	52.7	52.0	51.5	51.6
1993	47.6	47.9	48.2	49.8	51.4	52.4	53.3	53.5	53.0	52.8	52.4	52.3	51.2
1994	48.1	47.3	49.3	51.8	53.7	55.3	58.0	58.7	58.2	57.9	58.0	57.9	54.5
1995	55.0	54.2	55.7	57.0	57.5	58.5	58.1	58.4	58.5	58.4	57.7	57.4	57.2
1996	50.7	53.5	55.8	57.9	59.6	61.3	62.1	63.0	62.9	62.8	62.6	62.5	59.5
1997	56.9	56.7	58.1	59.9	61.0	61.9	62.9	63.1	62.8	61.9	61.2	60.7	60.5
1998	58.1	58.1	59.3	61.9	62.5	64.1	65.5	65.9	65.7	66.8	65.4	65.8	63.2
1999	62.3	62.8	63.7	66.7	67.2	68.6	69.1	69.3	68.8	68.5	68.5	68.8	67.0
2000	66.1	65.9	68.2	69.3	70.2	72.1	73.3	73.4	73.4	73.1	73.0	72.6	70.8
2001	69.6	70.3	72.2	73.4	74.7	76.4	77.0	77.6	76.8	77.0	76.5	75.7	74.8
2002	73.0	73.6	74.9	75.4	76.2	77.2	77.2	77.3	76.4	75.4	75.4	74.1	75.5
2003	72.4	72.1	74.0	75.0	76.4	77.3	77.5	78.2	77.6	77.7	77.6	76.7	76.0
Manufacturing													
1990	37.6	37.6	37.7	37.6	37.7	37.8	37.8	37.3	37.2	36.6	36.7	36.6	37.3
1991	35.4	35.3	35.4	34.1	34.2	34.2	34.3	34.2	34.3	33.9	34.0	33.8	34.4
1992	33.6	33.1	33.6	33.7	33.8	34.0	33.4	33.4	33.5	34.0	34.1	34.1	33.6
1993	34.5	34.5	34.7	34.7	34.7	35.0	34.4	34.4	34.8	35.0	35.1	34.8	34.7
1994	35.2	35.2	35.5	37.8	37.8	38.0	38.3	36.8	37.3	38.2	38.4	38.6	37.2
1995	38.5	38.7	38.7	38.4	38.7	39.0	38.6	38.8	39.1	39.0	39.1	39.2	38.8
1996	38.5	38.8	38.7	38.8	39.1	39.4	39.5	39.4	39.7	39.5	39.8	39.8	39.2
1997	40.7	40.7	40.9	38.8	39.0	39.5	41.2	41.1	41.2	41.2	41.4	41.5	40.6
1998	41.8	41.9	42.2	41.8	41.9	42.3	41.5	41.5	41.6	41.6	41.9	41.8	41.8
1999	41.3	41.3	41.5	41.5	41.5	41.8	42.1	42.0	42.0	42.4	42.5	43.0	41.9
2000	43.1	43.5	43.8	43.1	43.5	44.1	44.3	44.3	44.4	44.3	43.4	43.4	43.7
2001	42.2	42.0	42.0	41.7	41.8	41.8	41.4	41.3	41.0	40.3	40.0	39.9	41.3
2002	39.3	38.9	39.0	38.8	38.7	38.5	38.3	37.9	37.6	37.2	36.9	36.9	38.2
2003	36.3	36.1	36.4	35.9	36.0	36.0	35.7	35.6	35.2	35.3	35.1	35.3	35.7

Employment by Industry: Maryland—*Continued*

(Numbers in thousands. Not seasonally adjusted.)

Industry	January	February	March	April	May	June	July	August	September	October	November	December	Annual Average
SUBURBAN MARYLAND-DC *—Continued*													
Service-providing													
1990	660.0	663.4	668.6	669.1	675.2	686.6	675.5	677.6	683.2	677.5	680.2	684.6	675.1
1991	659.0	662.2	666.1	664.5	669.8	675.0	660.9	661.1	669.4	668.3	674.1	676.1	667.2
1992	656.4	657.9	662.4	665.5	671.9	673.6	662.7	661.8	670.1	673.1	676.1	682.3	667.8
1993	663.5	667.7	669.6	676.3	683.9	687.8	676.4	674.1	684.9	689.6	694.6	700.9	680.7
1994	678.8	681.6	689.7	693.4	698.8	702.7	689.3	688.1	699.7	700.2	705.0	711.2	694.8
1995	687.8	692.9	700.6	704.0	709.5	715.2	702.3	701.1	710.3	711.6	715.5	720.8	705.9
1996	692.0	699.8	708.6	711.8	717.8	725.2	713.6	712.8	718.5	722.4	728.5	734.6	715.4
1997	707.8	711.5	721.7	725.3	731.0	739.0	728.7	723.9	735.8	739.2	744.9	753.2	730.1
1998	731.1	734.1	743.5	743.4	751.2	760.9	756.6	757.2	761.8	768.1	775.3	783.0	755.5
1999	757.0	762.8	770.5	775.3	780.3	786.6	772.6	767.7	783.6	793.5	799.5	807.0	779.7
2000	781.0	784.7	797.5	800.8	807.0	813.7	795.8	789.2	812.1	815.1	820.5	828.4	803.8
2001	794.4	798.6	803.6	805.6	811.1	817.3	790.5	794.1	805.6	813.4	818.2	825.4	806.5
2002	801.2	806.3	813.5	812.9	818.1	821.6	799.4	812.0	818.2	822.5	827.6	831.0	815.4
2003	809.4	809.0	817.0	820.0	826.3	833.2	818.4	824.4	826.7	835.5	838.5	842.2	825.1
Trade, transportation, and utilities													
1990	158.1	156.3	156.9	157.1	157.8	159.4	157.3	157.7	158.0	157.2	160.0	163.9	158.3
1991	149.2	146.5	147.2	146.7	147.4	148.3	149.6	150.4	150.7	149.0	153.1	156.4	149.5
1992	148.8	145.5	145.7	144.7	145.5	146.0	145.5	145.1	145.3	147.2	150.3	154.3	146.9
1993	146.1	143.7	142.8	144.2	146.0	146.8	148.0	147.5	147.1	149.6	153.4	157.8	147.7
1994	147.5	144.6	146.2	148.0	149.1	150.2	149.8	150.1	151.2	152.6	156.9	161.1	150.6
1995	153.1	151.0	152.2	152.9	153.6	154.5	152.1	153.2	154.4	156.2	159.5	162.9	154.6
1996	153.3	151.9	152.3	152.5	153.9	156.3	156.4	157.7	157.9	158.5	163.0	166.8	156.7
1997	159.5	156.7	158.0	157.0	158.0	159.6	159.0	159.2	159.8	161.3	165.9	170.3	160.3
1998	161.2	159.1	160.2	158.4	159.5	161.6	162.3	162.8	163.5	166.3	171.6	175.8	163.5
1999	163.4	161.5	163.2	162.2	163.5	164.9	166.3	165.7	165.1	168.3	172.5	176.3	166.0
2000	165.0	163.9	165.0	164.4	165.3	167.7	167.0	167.1	167.5	169.8	174.6	179.3	168.0
2001	166.6	163.8	163.7	162.8	163.9	165.5	164.9	165.0	164.9	166.1	169.8	173.1	165.8
2002	164.9	162.7	163.8	164.4	165.4	167.4	166.1	165.8	165.5	167.4	170.5	173.3	166.4
2003	164.1	161.6	162.8	161.6	162.7	164.5	164.9	165.3	165.1	166.8	169.3	172.4	165.1
Wholesale trade													
1990	26.0	26.0	26.0	26.1	26.2	26.3	26.2	26.2	26.2	25.6	25.5	25.6	25.9
1991	24.4	24.3	24.6	24.7	24.7	24.9	24.7	24.7	24.6	24.1	24.1	24.1	24.4
1992	23.6	23.5	23.7	23.4	23.4	23.4	23.4	23.3	23.2	23.6	23.4	23.4	23.4
1993	23.4	23.4	23.5	24.1	24.2	24.5	24.5	24.5	24.6	24.5	24.5	24.7	24.2
1994	24.5	24.5	24.7	24.8	25.0	25.3	25.4	25.4	25.3	25.3	25.4	25.4	25.0
1995	25.0	25.2	25.5	25.5	25.6	25.9	25.7	25.8	25.8	25.8	25.8	25.8	25.6
1996	25.0	25.3	25.5	25.3	25.3	25.6	25.7	25.7	25.6	25.8	25.8	25.8	25.5
1997	25.5	25.8	26.1	25.8	26.0	26.1	26.2	26.2	26.2	26.0	25.9	26.0	25.9
1998	25.4	25.5	25.7	25.8	25.7	25.8	26.7	26.7	26.4	26.7	26.9	27.1	26.2
1999	26.3	26.3	26.5	27.0	27.2	27.3	27.7	27.6	27.4	27.8	27.9	28.2	27.2
2000	27.3	27.6	27.8	27.2	27.3	27.6	27.8	27.7	27.6	27.8	27.9	28.0	27.6
2001	29.3	29.4	29.5	29.5	29.5	29.5	29.5	29.4	29.3	29.4	29.6	29.6	29.5
2002	29.9	29.7	29.8	29.8	29.8	29.9	29.4	29.4	29.2	29.5	29.6	29.6	29.6
2003	29.4	29.4	29.5	29.0	29.2	29.2	29.1	29.0	28.8	29.1	29.1	29.2	29.2
Retail trade													
1990	111.1	109.2	109.6	109.4	110.0	111.0	109.6	110.1	109.8	109.6	112.1	115.4	110.5
1991	103.0	100.2	100.4	99.9	100.5	100.9	101.7	102.6	102.6	102.0	105.6	108.1	102.2
1992	103.4	100.3	100.5	99.2	100.0	100.3	100.0	99.7	100.0	101.3	104.5	107.9	101.4
1993	101.0	98.8	98.0	98.3	99.9	100.6	101.0	100.7	100.2	102.3	106.2	110.4	101.4
1994	102.5	99.8	101.0	102.4	103.0	103.8	102.9	103.2	104.5	105.5	109.6	113.6	104.3
1995	106.4	104.1	104.7	105.3	105.9	106.4	105.1	106.1	107.2	107.2	110.4	113.9	106.8
1996	106.7	104.9	105.0	105.7	106.8	108.8	108.9	110.1	110.1	110.0	114.7	118.6	109.1
1997	112.3	109.5	110.6	109.5	109.9	111.1	110.7	110.9	111.4	112.4	117.3	121.6	112.2
1998	113.1	111.3	112.2	109.7	110.8	112.5	112.1	112.8	113.9	115.6	120.7	124.2	114.0
1999	113.9	112.3	113.5	111.6	112.8	113.9	114.2	114.1	113.8	115.1	119.6	123.1	114.8
2000	114.0	112.8	113.6	113.8	114.7	116.6	115.9	116.2	116.8	117.8	122.7	127.2	116.8
2001	115.0	112.2	112.2	111.0	112.0	113.5	112.7	112.9	113.1	113.5	117.2	120.6	113.8
2002	112.8	111.0	111.9	111.6	112.4	114.1	113.1	112.8	112.8	113.5	116.6	119.6	113.5
2003	111.5	109.2	110.0	110.7	111.5	113.1	112.7	113.1	112.9	113.4	115.7	117.7	112.6
Transportation and utilities													
1990	21.0	21.1	21.3	21.6	21.6	22.1	21.5	21.4	22.0	22.0	22.4	22.9	21.7
1991	21.8	22.0	22.2	22.1	22.2	22.5	23.2	23.1	23.5	22.9	23.4	24.2	22.7
1992	21.8	21.7	21.5	22.1	22.1	22.3	22.1	22.1	22.1	22.3	22.4	23.0	22.1
1993	21.7	21.5	21.3	21.8	21.9	21.7	22.5	22.3	22.3	22.8	22.7	22.7	22.1
1994	20.5	20.3	20.5	20.8	21.1	21.1	21.5	21.5	21.4	21.8	21.9	22.1	21.2
1995	21.7	21.7	22.0	22.1	22.1	22.2	21.3	21.3	21.4	23.2	23.3	23.2	22.1
1996	21.6	21.7	21.8	21.5	21.8	21.9	21.8	21.9	22.2	22.7	22.5	22.4	21.9
1997	21.7	21.4	21.3	21.7	22.1	22.4	22.1	22.1	22.2	22.9	22.7	22.7	22.1
1998	22.7	22.3	22.3	22.9	23.0	23.3	23.5	23.3	23.2	24.0	24.0	24.5	23.2
1999	23.2	22.9	23.2	23.6	23.5	23.7	24.4	24.0	23.9	25.4	25.0	25.0	23.9
2000	23.7	23.5	23.6	23.4	23.3	23.5	23.3	23.2	23.1	24.2	24.0	24.1	23.5
2001	22.3	22.2	22.0	22.3	22.4	22.5	22.7	22.7	22.5	23.2	23.0	22.9	22.6
2002	22.2	22.0	22.1	23.0	23.2	23.4	23.6	23.6	23.5	24.4	24.3	24.1	23.3
2003	23.2	23.0	23.3	21.9	22.0	22.2	23.1	23.2	23.4	24.3	24.5	25.5	23.3

Employment by Industry: Maryland—*Continued*

(Numbers in thousands. Not seasonally adjusted.)

Industry	January	February	March	April	May	June	July	August	September	October	November	December	Annual Average
SUBURBAN MARYLAND-DC —*Continued*													
Information													
1990	28.4	28.5	28.6	28.7	28.5	28.5	29.1	29.1	28.5	29.1	29.0	28.9	28.7
1991	28.2	28.4	28.3	28.7	28.6	28.4	22.3	22.2	22.3	22.1	22.1	21.6	25.2
1992	21.7	21.7	21.6	21.7	21.6	21.6	21.6	21.4	21.3	21.6	21.6	21.6	21.5
1993	21.1	21.1	21.2	21.3	21.3	22.1	22.1	22.1	21.8	22.0	22.1	22.2	21.7
1994	22.1	22.3	22.8	23.0	22.9	22.9	22.6	22.6	22.3	22.4	22.7	22.8	22.6
1995	21.4	21.8	22.0	22.7	22.8	23.0	23.1	23.2	23.1	22.8	22.8	23.1	22.6
1996	22.7	23.0	23.2	23.3	23.6	23.7	23.8	23.7	23.5	23.1	23.4	23.6	23.3
1997	23.8	23.7	23.9	24.0	24.1	24.3	23.8	23.7	23.6	23.9	23.9	24.5	23.9
1998	24.7	24.9	25.3	24.8	25.1	25.3	25.6	25.7	25.5	25.0	24.7	25.0	25.1
1999	25.1	25.2	25.2	26.0	26.1	26.3	26.9	26.7	26.7	27.4	27.6	27.7	26.4
2000	28.0	28.4	28.7	29.4	29.8	30.1	30.2	30.4	30.7	31.1	31.0	31.5	29.9
2001	29.9	30.1	30.1	30.4	30.4	30.5	30.3	30.2	29.8	29.8	29.6	29.8	30.1
2002	28.9	28.7	28.6	28.4	28.3	28.2	27.8	27.5	27.2	26.3	26.4	26.3	27.7
2003	26.1	26.2	26.3	26.3	26.4	26.4	25.9	25.7	25.7	25.9	26.1	26.1	26.1
Financial activities													
1990	51.0	51.2	51.5	51.4	51.5	52.5	53.0	53.5	52.7	52.0	52.0	52.3	52.0
1991	49.1	49.3	49.1	49.7	50.0	50.5	51.2	51.2	50.9	49.6	49.4	49.6	49.9
1992	48.0	47.9	48.1	48.7	49.1	49.4	49.2	49.0	48.7	49.0	49.0	49.5	48.8
1993	47.8	47.9	48.0	48.3	48.8	49.5	50.0	50.1	49.7	50.1	50.3	50.8	49.2
1994	50.5	50.9	51.3	52.1	52.3	52.6	52.0	52.0	51.2	50.4	50.7	50.8	51.4
1995	49.2	49.6	49.7	49.4	49.7	50.4	49.9	50.2	50.1	49.2	49.2	49.8	49.7
1996	48.1	48.5	49.2	48.9	49.2	49.6	50.4	50.9	50.6	50.2	50.7	51.2	49.7
1997	50.8	50.9	51.5	50.4	52.1	52.6	52.7	52.8	52.7	52.1	52.1	52.7	51.9
1998	52.5	52.7	53.3	53.2	53.6	54.5	54.4	54.5	54.0	54.2	54.3	55.0	53.8
1999	54.3	54.7	55.0	55.5	55.5	56.2	56.2	56.0	55.4	55.1	55.0	55.6	55.3
2000	54.2	54.2	54.5	55.0	55.2	55.9	55.7	55.6	55.3	54.8	55.3	55.7	55.1
2001	54.2	54.5	54.7	55.0	55.4	56.0	56.1	56.1	55.4	55.6	55.7	56.2	55.4
2002	55.7	56.1	56.0	56.1	56.3	56.9	57.1	57.0	56.7	56.8	57.0	57.5	56.6
2003	57.4	57.5	57.8	58.2	58.7	59.4	59.8	60.0	59.5	59.4	59.5	59.9	58.9
Professional and business services													
1990	106.1	107.6	109.3	108.8	109.5	111.6	111.7	112.0	110.8	108.8	108.5	108.1	109.4
1991	107.2	107.7	109.3	108.2	108.1	109.0	109.2	109.3	108.6	113.1	113.2	112.6	109.6
1992	112.0	112.1	113.9	115.9	115.5	116.9	118.5	117.8	117.6	117.6	116.9	117.8	116.0
1993	118.0	118.0	119.2	121.3	122.2	122.9	122.3	121.4	121.0	121.2	121.3	121.9	120.8
1994	120.4	121.0	121.8	120.3	120.9	122.4	121.3	121.5	121.8	120.1	120.2	119.9	120.9
1995	116.8	117.3	120.6	122.2	122.9	124.1	124.8	124.7	124.4	123.5	123.6	124.8	122.4
1996	117.9	120.9	124.5	126.3	127.1	128.4	128.5	129.7	128.5	129.5	128.9	129.7	126.6
1997	125.5	126.7	129.8	132.9	133.6	135.9	136.0	135.7	135.6	135.8	135.4	136.8	133.3
1998	133.3	134.2	137.8	136.1	137.2	140.0	141.1	141.3	139.8	141.0	141.5	142.8	138.8
1999	141.2	143.1	145.2	147.8	147.8	150.3	151.5	152.1	151.4	151.8	151.9	153.3	148.9
2000	149.6	151.9	156.7	154.7	154.7	157.5	157.2	158.1	158.5	156.6	156.2	157.2	155.7
2001	158.5	160.1	161.8	162.5	162.8	164.5	162.3	163.3	160.7	161.5	161.2	162.6	161.8
2002	155.6	157.3	159.0	156.9	157.0	157.5	158.6	159.3	158.7	158.3	158.7	158.8	158.0
2003	155.6	155.6	157.8	160.0	160.8	162.4	161.4	161.3	160.8	161.5	161.9	161.9	160.1
Educational and health services													
1990	62.8	63.6	64.1	64.4	64.8	65.0	65.1	65.5	66.0	66.2	66.9	67.0	65.1
1991	66.7	67.7	67.7	67.3	67.9	68.2	68.2	68.3	69.5	68.9	69.3	69.4	68.2
1992	68.3	68.8	69.4	70.3	70.8	70.8	70.6	70.4	71.3	72.8	73.0	73.4	70.8
1993	72.5	73.2	73.5	73.6	73.9	74.3	73.5	73.5	74.9	75.4	76.1	76.3	74.2
1994	75.1	75.7	76.7	76.9	77.4	77.8	76.2	76.0	77.4	78.5	77.3	77.9	76.9
1995	77.8	78.9	79.6	80.1	80.5	80.9	79.8	79.4	80.8	81.6	82.1	82.5	80.3
1996	80.2	81.8	82.7	81.5	81.8	82.3	81.0	80.0	81.3	82.4	82.9	83.3	81.7
1997	82.5	83.5	84.5	83.3	83.7	83.9	83.6	82.4	83.9	84.7	85.0	85.8	83.9
1998	86.4	87.4	88.1	88.8	89.1	89.5	89.6	88.6	89.4	89.9	90.6	90.8	89.0
1999	89.0	89.4	89.8	89.7	90.1	90.3	90.8	89.8	89.9	92.5	92.9	92.9	90.5
2000	91.1	92.0	92.2	93.6	94.0	94.0	94.3	93.6	94.4	95.8	96.5	96.6	94.0
2001	91.1	92.1	92.6	93.3	93.5	94.4	93.2	92.7	93.8	95.3	95.9	96.6	93.7
2002	96.0	96.8	97.2	97.1	97.5	97.7	97.3	96.7	97.2	98.8	99.3	99.7	97.6
2003	98.3	98.3	99.2	99.6	99.9	100.6	99.4	99.1	99.6	100.4	100.3	100.5	99.6
Leisure and hospitality													
1990	58.9	59.7	61.1	63.0	64.4	67.9	68.3	68.3	65.9	62.4	61.3	61.2	63.5
1991	60.3	60.8	61.5	62.1	63.5	66.9	67.9	67.9	65.9	62.1	62.0	61.5	63.5
1992	59.2	59.6	60.5	61.8	65.0	66.6	65.5	66.5	64.8	60.2	59.9	59.5	62.4
1993	57.4	58.0	58.1	60.9	63.6	65.6	65.7	65.2	63.4	61.6	61.2	61.2	61.8
1994	58.8	58.8	60.8	63.0	65.5	67.8	68.0	67.7	65.4	63.3	63.1	63.8	63.8
1995	61.3	61.9	63.1	63.6	66.0	68.8	69.4	68.8	66.7	65.5	65.2	64.8	65.4
1996	60.4	61.8	63.6	66.3	68.5	71.6	70.6	70.0	68.4	66.4	66.0	66.0	66.6
1997	63.6	64.7	66.0	69.7	71.3	74.4	73.9	73.3	72.5	71.1	70.7	71.1	70.1
1998	65.4	66.8	68.1	70.3	73.1	76.6	77.2	77.4	75.2	73.5	73.0	72.5	72.4
1999	67.8	69.1	70.1	71.2	74.0	77.4	77.8	77.0	74.2	73.7	73.1	73.6	73.2
2000	70.7	70.5	72.2	74.3	76.7	80.0	81.1	81.3	78.5	76.4	74.5	74.6	75.9
2001	69.4	69.8	71.2	71.6	74.2	77.8	78.2	78.6	73.6	73.8	73.6	73.2	73.8
2002	70.0	70.2	71.9	74.3	77.3	79.9	80.2	80.7	78.9	76.9	76.8	75.6	76.1
2003	73.6	72.4	74.2	76.6	79.2	82.5	82.8	82.5	80.1	79.1	78.5	78.1	78.3

Employment by Industry: Maryland—*Continued*

(Numbers in thousands. Not seasonally adjusted.)

Industry	January	February	March	April	May	June	July	August	September	October	November	December	Annual Average
SUBURBAN MARYLAND-DC *—Continued*													
Other services													
1990	36.6	36.9	37.0	36.2	36.7	37.7	36.7	37.0	37.0	36.5	36.6	36.7	36.8
1991	35.3	35.5	35.6	35.4	35.9	36.2	37.1	36.8	36.3	35.1	35.4	35.6	35.8
1992	34.7	34.9	35.0	35.0	35.6	36.3	36.1	36.0	35.6	35.7	35.7	36.0	35.5
1993	35.4	35.6	35.7	36.2	36.6	37.4	37.4	37.2	37.1	36.8	36.8	37.0	36.6
1994	36.6	36.8	37.5	37.8	38.2	39.0	39.5	39.3	39.1	38.5	38.8	38.9	38.3
1995	37.8	38.2	38.6	39.1	39.6	40.6	40.8	40.3	40.2	39.8	40.0	40.2	39.6
1996	38.5	39.3	40.0	39.9	40.3	41.0	40.9	41.0	40.3	40.5	40.8	41.0	40.2
1997	40.3	40.7	41.0	42.0	42.4	42.7	43.2	43.1	42.6	42.5	42.5	43.0	42.1
1998	42.1	42.0	42.0	43.9	43.8	44.0	44.5	44.3	44.0	44.4	44.4	45.1	43.7
1999	43.4	43.5	43.9	43.9	44.0	44.6	45.0	44.8	44.4	44.9	45.1	45.6	44.4
2000	45.1	45.4	46.3	46.6	47.0	47.8	48.3	48.1	47.8	48.1	48.2	48.5	47.2
2001	44.4	44.8	45.0	44.8	45.4	46.2	45.8	45.3	44.3	44.4	44.3	44.6	44.9
2002	44.0	44.6	45.2	45.6	45.9	46.8	47.3	46.9	45.9	45.6	45.7	46.0	45.8
2003	45.6	45.8	46.5	46.1	46.3	47.1	47.9	47.0	46.4	46.6	46.5	46.4	46.5
Government													
1990	158.1	159.6	160.1	159.5	162.0	164.0	154.3	154.5	164.3	165.3	165.9	166.5	161.1
1991	163.0	166.3	167.4	166.4	168.4	167.5	155.4	155.0	165.2	168.4	169.6	169.4	165.1
1992	163.7	167.4	168.2	167.4	168.8	166.0	155.7	155.6	165.5	169.0	169.7	170.2	165.6
1993	165.2	170.2	171.1	170.5	171.5	169.2	157.4	157.1	169.9	172.9	173.4	173.7	168.5
1994	167.8	171.5	172.6	172.3	172.5	170.0	159.9	158.9	171.3	174.4	175.3	176.0	170.2
1995	170.4	174.2	174.8	174.0	174.4	172.9	162.4	161.3	170.6	173.0	173.1	172.7	171.1
1996	170.9	172.6	173.1	173.1	173.4	172.3	162.0	159.8	168.0	171.8	172.8	173.0	170.2
1997	161.8	164.6	167.0	166.0	165.8	165.6	156.5	153.7	165.1	167.8	169.4	169.0	164.3
1998	165.5	167.0	168.7	167.9	169.8	169.4	161.9	162.6	170.4	173.8	175.2	176.0	169.0
1999	172.8	176.3	178.1	179.0	179.3	176.6	158.1	155.6	176.5	179.8	181.4	182.0	174.6
2000	177.3	178.4	181.9	182.8	184.3	180.7	162.0	155.0	179.4	182.5	184.2	185.0	177.7
2001	180.3	183.4	184.5	185.2	185.5	182.4	159.7	162.9	183.1	186.9	188.1	189.3	180.9
2002	186.1	189.9	191.8	190.1	190.4	187.2	165.0	178.1	188.1	192.4	193.2	193.8	187.2
2003	188.7	191.6	192.4	191.6	192.3	190.3	176.3	183.5	189.5	195.8	196.4	196.9	190.4
Federal government													
1990	73.1	72.8	73.0	72.7	74.4	76.6	76.9	75.3	75.4	73.3	73.2	74.0	74.2
1991	74.0	74.0	74.1	74.4	75.1	76.9	77.0	76.7	76.0	76.1	76.1	76.7	75.5
1992	76.4	76.2	76.3	76.5	76.8	77.6	78.0	77.8	77.1	76.1	76.0	76.7	76.7
1993	76.5	76.5	76.8	76.7	77.0	77.5	77.8	77.6	77.5	77.1	76.9	77.4	77.1
1994	76.6	76.3	76.0	75.7	75.6	76.0	75.9	75.7	74.7	74.5	74.3	74.5	75.4
1995	74.0	73.9	73.7	73.3	73.3	73.8	74.2	73.9	72.8	73.1	73.0	73.1	73.5
1996	72.1	72.2	72.1	72.3	72.3	73.3	73.4	73.4	72.9	73.5	73.7	73.9	72.9
1997	67.0	66.8	67.9	67.5	67.5	68.1	69.1	69.4	68.5	68.1	68.3	68.5	68.0
1998	67.7	67.4	67.5	67.5	67.9	68.5	69.8	69.9	68.9	69.0	69.2	69.5	68.5
1999	69.5	69.3	69.3	69.9	70.1	70.8	71.0	71.5	70.7	70.9	71.0	71.6	70.4
2000	71.2	71.3	71.6	71.5	73.4	73.1	73.5	72.4	71.0	70.6	70.6	71.0	71.7
2001	71.6	71.0	70.4	71.0	70.9	71.7	72.8	72.7	72.1	72.3	72.4	72.8	71.8
2002	72.8	72.4	72.3	71.8	72.1	73.0	74.0	74.2	73.4	73.4	73.4	74.1	73.1
2003	73.7	73.4	73.4	72.9	73.0	73.6	75.6	75.2	74.4	74.7	74.4	74.5	74.1
State government													
1990	16.1	16.9	16.6	17.0	16.3	16.7	15.7	17.0	17.7	18.1	18.0	17.7	16.9
1991	17.3	17.9	18.1	18.1	17.9	16.9	14.5	16.0	17.0	17.9	17.9	17.5	17.2
1992	15.8	17.5	17.4	17.7	17.5	16.2	14.3	15.8	15.7	18.1	18.4	18.3	16.8
1993	16.5	18.3	18.3	18.4	18.2	18.1	15.7	17.1	17.8	19.7	19.6	19.5	18.1
1994	17.6	18.9	19.2	19.3	19.2	19.0	17.2	17.9	18.6	19.4	19.6	19.7	18.8
1995	17.6	19.0	19.1	19.1	19.1	18.5	17.3	18.1	18.8	19.4	19.6	19.5	18.7
1996	17.6	17.8	17.9	18.6	18.7	18.3	17.1	17.8	18.3	18.8	18.8	18.7	18.2
1997	17.0	17.1	17.5	17.0	16.8	16.7	16.6	16.9	17.3	18.0	18.7	18.7	17.3
1998	17.9	17.1	18.3	17.8	18.0	18.1	17.0	17.7	19.1	20.3	20.6	21.1	18.5
1999	21.0	21.2	22.6	23.4	22.8	20.8	17.9	18.2	21.0	23.1	23.4	23.3	21.5
2000	20.9	20.5	22.5	23.4	22.8	20.9	18.7	19.0	21.4	23.8	24.1	24.6	21.8
2001	21.9	22.8	23.9	24.0	24.1	21.0	19.5	20.2	22.0	23.2	23.3	23.8	22.5
2002	22.7	24.5	25.9	24.8	24.6	21.8	20.6	21.2	23.1	25.4	25.4	26.2	23.9
2003	22.4	24.3	25.7	24.8	24.7	23.2	20.4	21.0	22.6	24.8	24.6	25.6	23.7
Local government													
1990	68.9	69.9	70.5	69.8	71.3	70.7	61.7	62.2	71.2	73.9	74.7	74.8	69.9
1991	71.7	74.4	75.2	73.9	75.4	73.7	63.9	62.3	72.2	74.4	75.6	75.2	72.3
1992	71.5	73.7	74.5	73.2	74.5	72.2	63.4	62.0	72.7	74.8	75.3	75.2	71.9
1993	72.2	75.4	76.0	75.4	76.3	73.6	63.9	62.4	74.6	76.1	76.9	76.8	73.3
1994	73.6	76.3	77.4	77.3	77.7	75.0	66.8	65.3	78.0	80.5	81.4	81.8	75.9
1995	78.8	81.3	82.0	81.6	82.0	80.6	70.9	69.3	79.0	80.5	80.5	80.1	78.8
1996	81.2	82.6	83.1	82.2	82.4	80.7	71.5	68.6	76.8	79.5	80.3	80.4	79.1
1997	77.8	80.7	81.6	81.5	81.5	80.8	70.7	67.3	79.3	81.7	82.4	81.8	78.9
1998	79.9	82.5	82.9	82.6	83.9	82.8	75.1	75.0	82.4	84.5	85.4	85.4	81.8
1999	82.3	85.8	86.2	85.7	86.4	85.0	69.2	65.9	84.8	85.8	87.0	87.1	82.6
2000	85.2	86.6	87.8	87.9	88.1	86.7	69.8	63.6	87.0	88.1	89.5	89.4	84.1
2001	86.8	89.6	90.2	90.2	90.5	89.7	67.4	70.0	89.0	91.4	92.4	92.7	86.7
2002	90.6	93.0	93.6	93.5	93.7	92.4	70.4	82.7	91.6	93.6	94.4	93.5	90.3
2003	92.6	93.9	93.3	93.9	94.6	93.5	80.3	87.3	92.5	96.3	97.4	96.8	92.7

Average Weekly Hours by Industry: Maryland

(Not seasonally adjusted.)

Industry	January	February	March	April	May	June	July	August	September	October	November	December	Annual Average
STATEWIDE													
Manufacturing													
2001	39.5	37.9	37.9	39.2	40.6	39.0	38.0	38.4	39.6	38.7	39.5	39.8	39.0
2002	39.4	39.2	39.9	39.9	39.4	40.1	40.6	40.2	40.4	40.8	40.3	40.2	40.0
2003	39.0	38.0	39.2	39.5	40.1	40.1	39.4	39.3	39.3	39.9	40.3	40.5	39.5

Average Hourly Earnings by Industry: Maryland

(Dollars, not seasonally adjusted.)

Industry	January	February	March	April	May	June	July	August	September	October	November	December	Annual Average
STATEWIDE													
Manufacturing													
2001	14.55	14.28	14.26	14.22	14.24	14.52	14.61	14.49	14.92	14.65	14.90	15.14	14.56
2002	14.83	14.92	15.24	15.13	15.11	15.25	15.10	15.27	15.30	15.41	15.40	15.51	15.21
2003	15.43	15.43	15.16	15.62	15.79	15.67	16.05	15.96	15.85	15.81	16.01	16.22	15.75

Average Weekly Earnings by Industry: Maryland

(Dollars, not seasonally adjusted.)

Industry	January	February	March	April	May	June	July	August	September	October	November	December	Annual Average
STATEWIDE													
Manufacturing													
2001	574.73	541.21	540.45	557.42	578.14	566.28	555.18	556.42	590.83	566.96	588.55	602.57	567.84
2002	584.30	584.86	608.08	603.69	595.33	611.53	613.06	613.85	618.12	628.73	620.62	623.50	608.40
2003	601.77	586.34	594.27	616.99	633.18	628.37	632.37	627.23	622.91	630.82	645.20	656.91	622.13

MASSACHUSETTS AT A GLANCE

(Population and total nonfarm employment numbers in thousands)

Population, Census 2000:	6,349.1
Total nonfarm employment, 2003:	3,186.3
Change in total nonfarm employment	
(Number)	
1990–2003:	201.5
1990–2001:	344.3
2001–2003:	-142.8
(Compound annual rate of change)	
1990–2003:	0.5%
1990–2001:	1.0%
2001–2003:	-2.2%
Unemployment rate	
1990:	6.3%
2001:	3.7%
2003:	5.8%

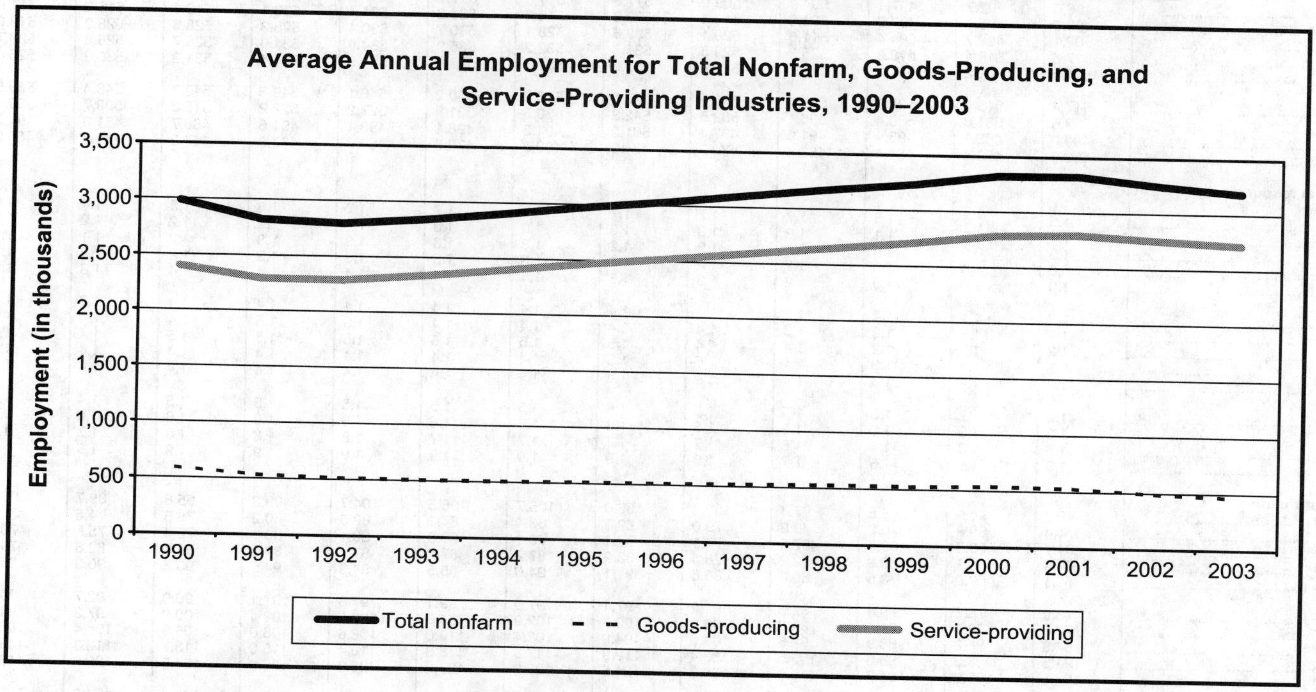

Following a recovery from the recession in the early 1990s, total employment grew steadily. It peaked in 2001 before falling in both 2002 and 2003. Employment in the goods-producing sector dropped during both recessions and was relatively stagnant between these contractionary periods, while jobs in the service-providing sector expanded moderately over the 1990s.

Employment by Industry: Massachusetts

(Numbers in thousands. Not seasonally adjusted.)

Industry	January	February	March	April	May	June	July	August	September	October	November	December	Annual Average
STATEWIDE													
Total nonfarm													
1990	2984.2	2984.1	2995.4	2993.8	3019.8	3042.2	2977.9	2971.9	2982.6	2961.4	2955.5	2949.9	2984.8
1991	2817.3	2804.1	2811.5	2816.9	2837.7	2865.1	2804.5	2806.0	2820.4	2821.4	2822.3	2826.0	2821.1
1992	2737.9	2742.8	2755.4	2774.6	2805.3	2829.6	2790.1	2788.7	2815.9	2831.4	2833.6	2836.3	2795.1
1993	2758.0	2765.3	2771.2	2817.3	2847.5	2876.5	2844.2	2845.3	2870.2	2885.2	2894.5	2906.0	2840.1
1994	2810.6	2819.8	2838.8	2877.1	2903.6	2939.6	2900.7	2909.5	2940.7	2951.6	2968.1	2983.8	2903.6
1995	2891.5	2903.0	2925.2	2954.8	2975.8	3008.8	2969.0	2979.4	3008.2	3023.3	3033.9	3046.8	2976.6
1996	2934.4	2956.8	2976.5	3006.1	3041.3	3073.6	3031.3	3040.7	3068.3	3082.3	3101.3	3111.9	3035.3
1997	3022.7	3033.9	3059.1	3084.7	3118.9	3149.6	3099.0	3104.2	3132.9	3153.3	3162.4	3189.8	3109.2
1998	3089.7	3106.8	3126.4	3159.5	3185.4	3214.3	3180.9	3180.6	3205.3	3219.7	3227.6	3248.0	3178.6
1999	3139.6	3156.7	3175.9	3222.3	3238.7	3275.3	3243.5	3238.4	3263.7	3283.5	3291.3	3313.0	3236.8
2000	3217.1	3232.1	3255.0	3299.6	3323.9	3361.5	3333.3	3324.0	3358.2	3377.0	3390.1	3407.0	3323.2
2001	3308.5	3313.7	3322.7	3343.5	3361.3	3384.3	3325.0	3317.0	3324.5	3319.4	3313.5	3315.2	3329.1
2002	3209.7	3204.0	3223.4	3249.4	3272.1	3292.9	3253.3	3244.5	3261.7	3260.8	3262.5	3261.7	3249.7
2003	3151.6	3137.0	3149.7	3184.6	3210.6	3228.9	3188.6	3176.6	3196.7	3205.6	3203.5	3201.7	3186.3
Total private													
1990	2578.8	2574.2	2585.2	2583.1	2602.0	2627.7	2592.3	2594.9	2590.2	2562.9	2554.0	2547.5	2582.7
1991	2421.7	2403.7	2410.8	2419.5	2439.1	2465.7	2433.5	2438.0	2439.5	2434.4	2433.0	2435.3	2431.1
1992	2354.6	2354.8	2365.5	2385.8	2415.0	2440.4	2428.2	2429.6	2438.5	2446.1	2445.7	2446.6	2412.5
1993	2375.3	2377.0	2381.5	2423.5	2451.6	2480.6	2472.8	2479.0	2486.2	2493.1	2500.6	2510.2	2452.6
1994	2420.7	2425.3	2444.4	2482.1	2507.1	2541.3	2530.3	2543.3	2555.2	2557.9	2571.5	2585.0	2513.6
1995	2500.6	2505.9	2527.0	2554.3	2574.2	2607.0	2593.5	2608.5	2617.2	2621.3	2629.4	2640.1	2581.5
1996	2536.2	2552.7	2570.0	2600.1	2634.3	2666.0	2654.0	2666.7	2671.9	2677.3	2693.1	2702.7	2635.4
1997	2621.9	2628.8	2651.8	2674.7	2707.0	2736.8	2716.2	2725.4	2731.0	2741.5	2748.6	2772.0	2704.6
1998	2683.0	2694.7	2712.6	2742.8	2766.4	2794.9	2792.2	2794.7	2794.2	2800.3	2805.8	2823.7	2767.1
1999	2724.3	2735.8	2753.5	2799.1	2814.1	2849.7	2851.8	2850.5	2847.3	2858.1	2864.6	2884.0	2819.4
2000	2794.7	2804.7	2827.8	2868.1	2884.4	2928.8	2932.4	2930.7	2933.9	2947.4	2957.4	2974.1	2898.7
2001	2877.9	2878.5	2886.9	2906.5	2922.3	2949.1	2921.4	2917.8	2893.2	2883.0	2875.7	2875.3	2899.0
2002	2776.2	2767.3	2785.9	2814.2	2836.3	2860.5	2851.1	2847.4	2834.7	2835.9	2834.4	2834.2	2823.2
2003	2729.1	2712.0	2724.6	2759.4	2785.0	2805.4	2796.0	2789.5	2780.2	2787.8	2784.7	2782.3	2769.7
Goods-producing													
1990	595.7	589.4	589.0	588.9	594.2	600.2	589.9	593.7	589.8	577.7	572.3	564.0	587.0
1991	536.9	527.8	527.0	528.9	533.9	541.5	530.1	537.1	535.1	528.9	525.8	520.4	531.1
1992	503.8	499.8	500.6	506.6	514.3	521.1	515.0	517.8	518.1	515.9	513.4	508.9	511.2
1993	494.9	492.3	490.6	502.6	508.3	515.4	509.9	513.3	511.6	510.6	508.6	505.3	505.2
1994	487.7	485.0	487.7	498.1	505.8	515.0	511.2	516.7	517.2	514.8	515.2	512.4	505.5
1995	496.0	492.7	497.1	504.9	509.9	517.8	511.8	517.7	517.4	517.7	517.7	515.0	509.6
1996	495.0	495.0	497.9	505.0	514.4	522.3	515.2	521.2	521.4	520.1	519.1	516.2	511.9
1997	502.1	499.7	504.4	511.6	520.1	528.6	523.1	530.7	530.4	528.3	528.3	528.2	519.6
1998	517.6	516.4	518.8	525.8	529.8	536.5	532.2	535.9	534.0	531.0	528.7	526.6	527.7
1999	511.5	509.2	511.1	523.3	526.9	533.5	531.1	532.8	531.9	531.4	531.2	530.9	525.4
2000	517.4	515.4	522.2	532.4	537.3	547.9	545.8	550.2	546.1	549.6	549.7	548.4	538.5
2001	533.6	531.0	530.4	536.1	539.5	542.3	530.5	531.8	527.2	522.2	515.3	509.7	529.1
2002	490.0	483.7	485.9	491.6	497.4	501.2	494.2	496.1	493.4	491.5	488.7	481.3	491.3
2003	462.9	453.4	454.4	463.8	470.2	474.0	469.0	470.5	467.0	467.5	467.2	462.5	465.2
Natural resources and mining													
1990	1.5	1.5	1.5	1.7	1.7	1.7	1.7	1.7	1.7	1.6	1.5	1.4	1.6
1991	1.1	1.0	1.1	1.2	1.3	1.3	1.3	1.3	1.2	1.2	1.2	1.2	1.2
1992	1.0	0.9	1.0	1.1	1.2	1.2	1.3	1.3	1.3	1.3	1.2	1.1	1.1
1993	1.0	1.0	1.0	1.2	1.2	1.3	1.3	1.3	1.3	1.2	1.2	1.2	1.1
1994	1.0	1.0	1.0	1.2	1.3	1.3	1.4	1.4	1.4	1.4	1.4	1.3	1.2
1995	1.2	1.1	1.2	1.3	1.4	1.4	1.4	1.4	1.4	1.4	1.4	1.3	1.3
1996	1.1	1.1	1.2	1.3	1.4	1.4	1.4	1.4	1.5	1.5	1.4	1.4	1.3
1997	1.2	1.2	1.2	1.4	1.4	1.5	1.5	1.5	1.5	1.5	1.5	1.4	1.4
1998	1.3	1.3	1.3	1.4	1.5	1.5	1.4	1.4	1.4	1.4	1.4	1.4	1.3
1999	1.2	1.2	1.3	1.4	1.4	1.5	1.4	1.4	1.4	1.4	1.4	1.4	1.3
2000	1.2	1.2	1.3	1.5	1.5	1.5	1.5	1.5	1.5	1.5	1.5	1.4	1.4
2001	1.3	1.3	1.3	1.5	1.6	1.6	1.6	1.6	1.6	1.6	1.6	1.6	1.5
2002	1.3	1.3	1.4	1.6	1.7	1.7	1.7	1.7	1.8	1.8	1.8	1.7	1.6
2003	1.5	1.5	1.5	1.7	1.8	1.9	1.9	1.9	1.9	1.9	1.9	1.8	1.8
Construction													
1990	98.7	94.9	95.5	97.4	102.3	106.0	105.7	106.5	104.7	99.3	95.8	89.7	99.7
1991	74.4	69.8	70.2	73.9	79.0	82.5	83.4	84.1	82.5	80.2	78.5	74.6	77.7
1992	64.7	62.5	63.5	67.5	73.1	77.1	79.1	80.3	80.1	80.1	78.4	75.5	73.4
1993	67.4	66.1	65.9	72.2	78.4	83.2	87.2	87.7	87.1	87.3	85.5	82.6	79.2
1994	71.1	69.0	70.5	80.0	85.6	91.1	94.0	95.5	94.9	94.5	93.3	90.3	85.8
1995	78.9	76.6	79.4	87.3	91.9	97.1	97.9	99.1	97.6	97.1	96.0	92.7	90.9
1996	78.8	78.9	81.5	89.0	96.2	100.7	102.9	104.0	102.5	102.4	100.9	97.3	94.5
1997	87.9	86.2	88.9	94.6	101.0	104.9	108.4	110.0	108.6	108.0	106.5	104.4	100.7
1998	94.5	93.3	95.3	103.5	108.4	112.9	117.8	118.3	116.4	115.0	113.7	112.3	108.4
1999	103.5	102.3	104.7	116.0	120.3	124.5	127.3	127.2	126.3	126.0	124.5	122.8	118.7
2000	112.5	110.1	115.6	124.5	129.0	134.6	138.3	139.4	137.7	137.6	136.9	134.0	129.1
2001	124.5	123.3	125.4	135.6	142.1	146.4	147.9	148.4	146.1	145.5	143.5	139.9	139.1
2002	128.4	125.8	128.8	137.8	144.3	147.0	148.6	149.4	146.6	147.5	145.9	139.3	140.8
2003	126.9	120.6	122.7	133.2	140.4	143.5	146.4	146.0	143.1	143.6	142.2	138.0	137.2

Employment by Industry: Massachusetts—*Continued*

(Numbers in thousands. Not seasonally adjusted.)

Industry	January	February	March	April	May	June	July	August	September	October	November	December	Annual Average
STATEWIDE—*Continued*													
Manufacturing													
1990	495.5	493.0	492.0	489.8	490.2	492.5	482.5	485.5	483.4	476.8	475.0	472.9	485.7
1991	461.4	457.0	455.7	453.8	453.6	457.7	445.4	451.7	451.4	447.5	446.1	444.6	452.1
1992	438.1	436.4	436.1	438.0	440.0	442.8	434.6	436.2	436.7	434.5	433.8	432.3	436.6
1993	426.5	425.2	423.7	429.2	428.7	430.9	421.4	424.3	423.2	422.1	421.9	421.5	424.8
1994	415.6	415.0	416.2	416.9	418.9	422.6	415.8	419.8	420.9	418.9	420.5	420.8	418.4
1995	415.9	415.0	416.5	416.3	416.6	419.3	412.5	417.2	418.4	419.2	420.3	421.0	417.3
1996	415.1	415.0	415.2	414.7	416.8	420.2	410.9	415.8	417.4	416.2	416.8	417.5	415.9
1997	413.0	412.3	414.3	415.6	417.7	422.2	413.2	419.2	420.3	418.8	420.3	422.4	417.4
1998	421.8	421.8	422.2	420.9	419.9	422.1	413.0	416.2	416.2	414.6	413.6	412.9	417.9
1999	406.8	405.7	405.1	405.9	405.2	407.5	402.4	404.2	404.2	404.0	405.3	406.7	405.2
2000	403.7	404.1	405.3	406.4	406.8	411.8	406.0	409.3	406.9	410.5	411.3	413.0	407.9
2001	407.8	406.4	403.7	399.0	395.8	394.3	381.0	381.8	379.5	375.1	370.2	368.2	388.6
2002	360.3	356.6	355.7	352.2	351.4	352.5	343.9	345.0	345.0	342.2	341.0	340.3	348.8
2003	334.5	331.3	330.2	328.9	328.0	328.6	320.7	322.6	322.0	322.0	323.1	322.7	326.2
Service-providing													
1990	2388.5	2394.7	2406.4	2404.9	2425.6	2442.0	2388.0	2378.2	2392.8	2383.7	2383.2	2385.9	2397.8
1991	2280.4	2276.3	2284.5	2288.0	2303.8	2323.6	2274.4	2268.9	2285.3	2292.5	2296.5	2305.6	2289.9
1992	2234.1	2243.0	2254.8	2268.0	2291.0	2308.5	2275.1	2270.9	2297.8	2315.5	2320.2	2327.4	2283.8
1993	2263.1	2273.0	2280.6	2314.7	2339.2	2361.1	2334.3	2332.0	2358.6	2374.6	2385.9	2400.7	2334.8
1994	2322.9	2334.8	2351.1	2379.0	2397.8	2424.6	2389.5	2392.8	2423.5	2436.8	2452.9	2471.4	2398.0
1995	2395.5	2410.3	2428.1	2449.9	2465.9	2491.0	2457.2	2461.7	2490.8	2505.6	2516.2	2531.8	2467.0
1996	2439.4	2461.8	2478.6	2501.1	2526.9	2551.3	2516.1	2519.5	2546.9	2562.2	2582.2	2595.7	2523.4
1997	2520.6	2534.2	2554.7	2573.1	2598.8	2621.0	2575.9	2573.5	2602.5	2625.0	2634.1	2661.6	2589.5
1998	2572.1	2590.4	2607.6	2633.7	2655.6	2677.8	2648.7	2644.7	2671.3	2688.7	2698.9	2721.4	2650.9
1999	2628.1	2647.5	2664.8	2699.0	2711.8	2741.8	2712.4	2705.6	2731.8	2752.1	2760.1	2782.1	2711.4
2000	2699.7	2716.7	2732.8	2767.2	2786.6	2813.6	2787.5	2773.8	2812.1	2827.4	2840.4	2858.6	2784.7
2001	2774.9	2782.7	2792.3	2807.4	2821.8	2842.0	2794.5	2785.2	2797.3	2797.2	2798.2	2805.5	2799.9
2002	2719.7	2720.3	2737.5	2757.8	2774.7	2791.7	2759.1	2748.4	2768.3	2769.3	2773.8	2780.4	2758.4
2003	2688.7	2683.6	2695.3	2720.8	2740.4	2754.9	2719.6	2706.1	2729.7	2738.1	2736.3	2739.2	2721.1
Trade, transportation, and utilities													
1990	586.7	572.9	573.7	567.3	571.7	581.7	565.4	565.5	567.8	561.0	567.1	573.2	571.1
1991	538.9	524.3	522.7	520.4	525.7	533.1	521.2	521.5	523.7	521.9	529.4	536.9	526.6
1992	512.7	505.9	506.6	506.8	512.2	518.9	510.9	510.4	514.2	519.8	527.1	535.7	515.1
1993	510.3	503.0	501.0	507.7	514.4	522.7	516.6	518.5	521.6	525.3	534.6	543.7	518.2
1994	519.6	512.1	512.9	516.1	522.2	531.2	525.0	527.6	531.8	540.0	552.7	563.7	529.5
1995	535.7	527.1	528.7	530.6	535.7	543.0	535.4	538.6	542.7	546.7	557.5	567.5	540.7
1996	544.1	536.7	536.8	539.4	546.7	554.9	546.5	548.1	552.2	555.5	569.8	580.6	550.9
1997	558.6	551.0	554.6	552.7	559.0	567.7	558.6	558.5	566.7	571.2	581.8	596.2	564.7
1998	566.2	559.6	560.0	562.9	569.9	577.1	572.9	573.4	578.3	583.4	595.6	609.1	575.7
1999	578.6	572.1	574.4	577.9	581.9	590.8	586.7	587.7	589.4	592.1	604.3	619.7	587.9
2000	591.3	584.4	585.5	587.1	590.5	599.2	592.1	592.1	595.6	602.0	613.9	627.6	596.7
2001	595.1	584.9	585.4	587.4	591.1	600.3	589.7	588.3	588.2	589.7	599.9	607.0	592.3
2002	577.4	567.4	569.5	572.3	577.4	586.5	580.5	578.1	579.6	581.0	589.3	598.8	579.8
2003	568.8	560.2	562.2	566.4	572.1	580.2	570.5	568.1	572.5	576.2	582.2	590.1	572.5
Wholesale trade													
1990	146.0	145.8	146.2	144.8	144.9	146.4	144.5	144.3	143.2	142.3	141.3	141.1	144.2
1991	134.6	133.3	133.2	132.6	132.5	133.7	132.5	132.3	131.8	131.1	131.2	130.8	132.4
1992	128.2	127.9	128.5	127.6	128.7	129.7	128.6	128.1	127.6	127.9	128.3	128.5	128.3
1993	124.6	124.5	124.6	126.1	127.0	128.4	127.6	127.8	127.7	127.4	128.1	128.3	126.8
1994	125.5	125.3	125.9	126.8	127.3	128.7	128.3	128.5	128.3	127.3	128.3	129.6	127.4
1995	125.9	125.8	126.4	126.8	127.1	128.4	128.0	129.0	129.5	129.9	131.1	132.0	128.3
1996	129.3	129.4	129.9	130.0	131.1	132.6	131.2	131.7	131.5	132.1	133.3	134.2	131.3
1997	132.0	132.2	133.4	133.2	134.3	135.9	133.7	134.9	135.0	134.2	135.6	136.8	134.2
1998	135.2	135.2	135.7	137.0	137.7	138.7	137.5	137.2	137.4	139.2	140.3	141.2	137.6
1999	137.1	137.0	138.0	137.2	137.1	138.0	139.2	139.7	139.5	139.0	139.9	141.1	138.5
2000	137.1	137.1	137.9	138.4	138.9	140.7	139.6	139.6	139.7	140.7	141.3	143.0	139.5
2001	141.5	141.6	142.0	142.5	142.3	143.3	142.4	142.0	140.8	140.1	139.8	139.9	141.5
2002	136.4	135.7	136.2	136.0	136.5	137.7	136.9	136.6	135.8	135.4	135.5	136.3	136.3
2003	135.0	134.5	134.6	134.6	135.0	135.7	135.3	135.0	134.1	134.0	134.1	134.5	134.7
Retail trade													
1990	360.9	347.0	346.6	343.1	346.1	353.7	343.2	342.8	342.1	338.3	345.7	351.8	346.7
1991	326.5	314.0	312.7	311.4	315.3	320.1	314.3	314.8	313.7	313.3	321.3	329.0	317.2
1992	309.9	303.5	303.1	303.6	306.9	311.2	307.5	308.2	308.5	312.9	321.2	328.7	310.4
1993	309.7	304.0	301.5	305.1	310.0	314.7	312.4	314.6	314.1	316.6	325.6	334.7	313.5
1994	316.8	309.4	309.2	310.3	314.6	320.8	318.0	320.1	321.3	328.4	340.6	350.5	321.6
1995	329.3	321.8	322.5	323.1	325.8	330.8	327.9	330.2	330.0	332.0	342.1	350.5	330.5
1996	333.5	325.7	324.8	327.5	332.4	337.8	335.2	336.5	336.7	338.6	351.5	361.4	336.8
1997	342.8	335.5	337.2	334.9	338.7	344.6	341.9	343.8	344.3	348.7	358.4	371.2	345.1
1998	344.9	338.2	337.8	338.2	343.4	348.7	349.5	350.4	350.5	353.5	365.0	377.1	349.7
1999	353.2	346.6	347.4	349.6	352.8	359.8	358.4	359.4	357.5	359.3	371.0	384.2	358.2
2000	361.8	354.9	355.4	354.0	356.4	362.3	360.0	360.2	359.7	364.2	376.4	387.9	362.7
2001	360.9	350.7	351.0	351.7	354.9	361.9	357.2	357.2	354.1	357.2	369.7	378.0	358.7
2002	354.8	346.0	347.8	349.5	353.2	360.1	359.3	358.0	355.5	356.6	365.9	375.4	356.8
2003	348.4	341.1	342.7	346.7	351.0	357.8	353.2	352.1	352.7	355.9	362.6	370.0	352.9

Employment by Industry: Massachusetts—*Continued*

(Numbers in thousands. Not seasonally adjusted.)

Industry	January	February	March	April	May	June	July	August	September	October	November	December	Annual Average
STATEWIDE—*Continued*													
Transportation and utilities													
1990	79.8	80.1	80.9	79.4	80.7	81.6	77.7	78.4	82.5	80.4	80.1	80.3	80.1
1991	77.8	77.0	76.8	76.4	77.9	79.3	74.4	74.4	78.2	77.5	76.9	77.1	76.9
1992	74.6	74.5	75.0	75.6	76.6	78.0	74.8	74.1	78.1	79.0	77.6	78.5	76.3
1993	76.0	74.5	74.9	76.5	77.4	79.6	76.6	76.1	79.8	81.3	80.9	80.7	77.8
1994	77.3	77.4	77.8	79.0	80.3	81.7	78.7	79.0	82.2	84.3	83.8	83.6	80.4
1995	80.5	79.5	79.8	80.7	82.8	83.8	79.5	79.4	83.2	84.8	84.3	85.0	81.9
1996	81.3	81.6	82.1	81.9	83.2	84.5	80.1	79.9	84.0	84.8	85.0	85.0	82.7
1997	83.8	83.3	84.0	84.6	86.0	87.2	83.0	79.8	87.4	88.3	87.8	88.2	85.2
1998	86.1	86.2	86.5	87.7	88.8	89.7	85.9	85.8	90.4	90.7	90.3	90.8	88.2
1999	88.3	88.5	89.0	91.1	92.0	93.0	89.1	88.6	92.4	93.8	93.4	94.4	91.1
2000	92.4	92.4	92.2	94.7	95.2	96.2	92.5	92.3	96.2	97.1	96.2	96.7	94.5
2001	92.7	92.6	92.4	93.2	93.9	95.1	90.1	89.1	93.3	92.4	90.4	89.1	92.0
2002	86.2	85.7	85.5	86.8	87.7	88.7	84.3	83.5	88.3	89.0	87.9	87.1	86.7
2003	85.4	84.6	84.9	85.1	86.1	86.7	82.0	81.0	85.7	86.3	85.5	85.6	84.9
Information													
1990	85.3	84.7	84.7	85.2	86.8	89.0	90.2	90.3	89.8	88.4	88.4	88.2	87.5
1991	86.8	86.7	86.7	85.1	85.0	85.6	84.9	84.4	83.0	83.5	83.9	84.4	85.0
1992	81.1	78.3	76.7	77.4	77.9	78.6	78.6	78.5	78.5	78.6	79.1	79.6	78.5
1993	78.4	78.5	78.6	78.1	78.6	81.6	84.1	84.4	83.6	84.4	84.7	85.3	81.6
1994	83.7	84.2	84.7	85.1	85.4	86.4	86.6	86.7	86.5	85.7	86.6	87.7	85.7
1995	87.2	87.2	87.9	87.8	88.4	89.6	90.1	90.8	90.3	90.6	90.5	90.3	89.2
1996	89.0	90.3	90.4	90.1	90.6	92.0	92.9	93.7	93.3	94.0	95.2	95.2	92.2
1997	94.2	94.8	94.3	93.9	95.3	96.1	96.3	95.7	94.9	95.4	95.9	96.6	95.2
1998	96.3	96.8	97.0	96.5	96.9	97.8	98.9	98.8	98.1	98.0	98.7	99.5	97.7
1999	96.8	97.1	97.3	98.4	99.0	100.4	101.8	102.0	101.5	101.9	102.9	104.3	100.2
2000	104.1	105.2	106.8	108.6	110.4	112.7	115.4	107.3	115.1	115.0	115.9	116.7	111.1
2001	116.4	116.2	115.8	115.0	113.8	113.4	111.6	110.5	108.0	106.1	105.4	104.7	111.4
2002	103.5	102.7	102.5	100.4	100.0	99.9	99.5	98.8	96.9	96.9	96.7	96.9	99.6
2003	93.7	93.1	93.0	92.0	91.8	92.6	91.2	91.1	89.9	90.1	89.7	89.6	91.5
Financial activities													
1990	206.5	206.9	207.4	203.8	201.9	202.4	200.7	200.1	197.6	196.0	194.7	194.7	201.0
1991	191.3	190.4	190.2	189.5	190.3	192.6	189.8	189.0	187.0	185.6	185.7	186.3	188.9
1992	183.3	183.9	184.7	185.4	187.1	189.4	188.7	188.5	186.2	186.1	186.4	187.0	186.3
1993	186.0	186.4	186.5	188.2	190.0	192.3	190.9	189.9	188.4	192.0	193.3	194.7	189.8
1994	193.9	194.2	195.4	195.9	197.0	199.4	199.1	199.2	197.8	195.3	195.3	197.5	196.6
1995	194.0	194.7	195.6	195.4	196.3	199.1	199.7	199.7	199.0	198.1	198.4	200.8	197.5
1996	194.8	196.0	197.3	199.1	200.5	204.6	205.7	207.6	206.8	207.2	208.6	210.4	203.2
1997	208.3	208.2	209.1	208.6	210.1	213.4	215.2	217.7	216.0	214.9	216.2	218.6	213.0
1998	216.6	217.0	218.3	219.3	219.6	223.0	224.2	224.9	222.1	224.2	224.6	225.7	221.6
1999	223.5	224.1	224.9	224.6	224.5	228.4	231.3	230.6	227.7	227.0	226.8	228.6	226.8
2000	224.7	224.0	224.6	225.7	226.0	230.0	230.3	230.6	229.0	229.5	230.0	232.4	228.0
2001	228.4	228.7	229.9	229.7	229.7	233.1	234.1	233.7	230.5	229.4	229.7	230.6	230.6
2002	230.2	228.9	228.3	226.8	227.2	229.7	230.8	230.3	226.9	226.4	225.6	226.4	228.1
2003	224.7	223.2	223.5	223.5	224.0	226.1	226.0	225.9	222.3	222.1	221.3	222.0	223.7
Professional and business services													
1990	339.7	342.4	345.2	344.3	345.2	349.2	345.8	347.1	343.4	337.4	335.7	333.7	342.4
1991	320.2	318.5	320.1	323.0	325.2	330.0	326.0	326.8	327.3	326.1	326.2	325.8	324.6
1992	317.3	319.4	322.3	327.4	331.3	336.5	335.7	337.0	336.9	335.1	335.8	335.3	330.8
1993	326.8	329.1	330.9	335.8	339.8	343.6	343.8	344.7	346.6	347.1	348.7	349.3	340.5
1994	340.8	343.3	347.0	353.4	355.6	362.4	360.1	364.2	364.4	363.7	366.6	367.8	357.4
1995	360.4	363.8	369.2	375.3	377.5	383.2	382.2	386.7	385.9	384.3	387.0	387.7	378.6
1996	374.3	379.0	384.2	392.7	397.1	402.8	404.9	408.9	408.0	407.3	411.1	411.7	398.5
1997	400.6	402.7	408.9	418.0	422.9	429.4	428.6	428.0	426.1	428.2	429.0	434.4	421.4
1998	420.8	422.9	428.7	438.4	440.1	447.5	450.4	451.3	449.2	448.7	448.8	452.0	441.5
1999	439.2	442.7	448.7	457.7	459.9	469.6	469.6	469.8	468.3	471.9	473.2	476.1	462.2
2000	464.8	468.5	475.2	485.3	487.0	499.4	504.1	508.0	505.5	504.3	506.0	507.8	492.9
2001	494.3	492.1	493.3	493.1	493.4	496.5	487.0	485.9	479.5	472.3	468.0	466.6	485.2
2002	448.6	445.3	448.4	455.8	456.9	460.7	458.9	458.5	455.0	453.5	452.2	449.8	453.6
2003	433.5	428.3	429.5	438.5	440.1	443.6	443.2	442.3	439.0	437.0	435.2	435.1	437.1
Educational and health services													
1990	448.0	459.7	461.6	464.6	460.9	450.7	445.7	443.8	457.5	470.2	473.1	474.2	459.1
1991	454.2	464.4	468.9	468.8	462.7	452.7	450.5	448.9	462.5	473.5	476.6	477.7	463.4
1992	466.4	476.1	479.4	479.7	475.2	465.3	464.1	462.8	478.5	490.5	492.8	492.1	476.9
1993	485.3	492.6	495.4	498.3	493.3	482.5	480.0	478.8	493.8	502.3	506.6	508.0	493.0
1994	489.1	499.6	503.6	507.7	502.4	491.5	486.1	484.9	505.4	514.5	518.0	520.7	501.9
1995	509.8	522.0	524.9	525.9	518.2	508.6	504.7	503.0	522.3	535.5	539.3	540.9	521.2
1996	521.1	534.1	536.5	536.1	529.5	516.7	513.4	510.6	525.7	537.1	541.5	542.9	528.7
1997	529.3	541.1	543.8	542.8	535.8	522.4	513.1	511.7	526.7	540.3	543.8	544.2	532.9
1998	530.7	542.2	546.4	544.0	538.4	526.6	520.6	517.3	531.6	543.8	547.4	548.3	536.4
1999	528.5	540.8	543.1	545.0	536.7	525.0	524.9	522.6	537.0	549.2	552.7	552.9	538.2
2000	537.9	549.8	551.0	552.4	544.5	532.1	530.0	529.6	543.4	555.2	560.0	560.8	545.5
2001	543.4	556.3	557.2	560.0	553.5	541.5	541.6	541.5	553.0	566.9	571.1	572.5	554.9
2002	558.0	569.3	573.1	575.3	568.5	555.9	553.2	551.6	566.6	578.5	584.9	585.7	568.4
2003	568.3	578.1	581.5	583.3	574.9	561.1	560.6	557.7	573.0	584.4	588.8	586.1	574.8

Employment by Industry: Massachusetts—*Continued*

(Numbers in thousands. Not seasonally adjusted.)

Industry	January	February	March	April	May	June	July	August	September	October	November	December	Annual Average
STATEWIDE—*Continued*													
Leisure and hospitality													
1990	219.8	220.9	225.2	231.4	243.0	255.2	256.5	256.5	248.2	236.2	227.3	223.9	237.0
1991	202.6	201.4	204.8	213.8	225.9	238.7	239.5	239.5	231.6	225.8	216.5	214.0	221.1
1992	202.2	203.7	207.1	215.2	228.5	240.6	244.4	244.0	237.4	230.9	221.7	217.8	224.4
1993	205.2	206.6	209.9	222.1	235.5	249.2	253.6	255.6	248.4	239.2	230.8	229.3	232.1
1994	214.4	215.2	220.1	232.0	244.1	259.1	264.8	266.5	256.0	247.7	240.0	237.3	241.4
1995	223.3	224.1	228.3	239.1	252.1	268.0	270.9	272.4	262.1	250.5	242.3	240.1	247.7
1996	223.6	226.5	230.9	240.8	257.0	272.4	275.3	276.8	266.9	258.0	249.1	246.8	252.0
1997	232.1	234.4	238.5	248.0	263.7	277.6	278.8	280.5	269.6	262.5	252.9	252.0	257.5
1998	235.1	239.4	242.3	253.7	268.4	281.9	287.2	287.6	277.1	267.2	257.6	256.6	262.8
1999	242.1	244.8	248.1	265.1	277.4	292.4	295.4	294.6	283.0	276.1	264.9	262.0	270.4
2000	246.9	249.0	253.4	266.8	277.8	294.8	301.1	299.6	287.6	280.1	270.1	267.8	274.5
2001	254.3	256.3	260.9	271.0	285.8	303.4	306.3	305.7	291.0	280.6	270.4	267.7	279.5
2002	254.1	255.4	262.0	275.6	291.3	306.8	312.4	312.7	299.5	291.1	279.9	278.0	284.9
2003	262.2	260.9	264.5	275.6	294.3	308.2	314.3	314.1	300.2	293.8	283.2	279.6	287.6
Other services													
1990	97.1	97.3	98.4	97.6	98.3	99.3	98.1	97.9	96.1	96.0	95.4	95.6	97.2
1991	90.8	90.2	90.4	90.0	90.4	91.5	91.5	90.8	89.3	89.1	88.9	89.8	90.2
1992	87.8	87.7	88.1	87.3	88.5	90.0	90.8	90.6	88.7	89.2	89.4	90.2	89.0
1993	88.4	88.5	88.6	90.7	91.7	93.3	93.9	93.8	92.2	92.2	93.3	94.6	91.7
1994	91.5	91.7	93.0	93.8	94.6	96.3	97.4	97.5	96.1	96.2	97.1	97.9	95.2
1995	94.2	94.3	95.3	95.3	96.1	97.7	98.7	99.6	97.5	97.9	96.7	97.8	96.7
1996	94.3	95.1	96.0	96.9	98.5	100.3	100.1	99.8	97.6	98.1	98.7	98.9	97.8
1997	96.7	96.9	98.2	99.1	100.1	101.6	102.5	102.6	100.6	100.7	100.7	101.8	100.1
1998	99.7	100.4	101.1	102.2	103.3	104.5	105.8	105.5	103.8	104.0	104.4	105.9	103.3
1999	104.1	105.0	105.9	107.1	107.8	109.6	111.0	110.4	108.5	108.5	108.6	109.5	108.0
2000	107.6	108.4	109.1	109.8	110.9	112.7	113.6	113.3	111.6	111.7	111.8	112.6	111.0
2001	112.4	113.0	114.0	114.2	115.5	118.6	120.6	120.4	115.8	115.8	115.9	116.5	116.1
2002	114.4	114.6	116.2	116.4	117.6	119.8	121.6	121.3	116.8	117.0	117.1	117.3	117.5
2003	115.0	114.8	116.0	116.3	117.6	119.6	121.2	119.8	116.3	116.7	117.1	117.3	117.3
Government													
1990	405.4	409.9	410.2	410.7	417.8	414.5	385.6	377.0	392.4	398.5	401.5	402.4	402.1
1991	395.6	400.4	400.7	397.4	398.6	399.4	371.0	368.0	380.9	387.0	389.3	390.7	389.9
1992	383.3	388.0	389.9	388.8	390.3	389.2	361.9	359.1	377.4	385.3	387.9	389.7	382.5
1993	382.7	388.3	389.7	393.8	395.9	395.9	371.4	366.3	384.0	392.1	393.9	395.8	387.4
1994	389.9	394.5	394.4	395.0	396.5	398.3	370.4	366.2	385.5	393.7	396.6	398.8	389.9
1995	390.9	397.1	398.2	400.5	401.6	401.8	375.5	370.9	391.0	402.0	404.5	406.7	395.0
1996	398.2	404.1	406.5	406.0	407.0	407.6	377.3	374.0	396.4	405.0	408.2	409.2	399.9
1997	400.8	405.1	407.3	410.0	411.9	412.8	382.8	378.8	401.9	411.8	413.8	417.8	404.5
1998	406.7	412.1	413.8	416.7	419.0	419.4	388.7	385.9	411.1	419.4	421.8	424.3	411.5
1999	415.3	420.9	422.4	423.2	424.6	425.6	391.7	387.9	416.4	425.4	426.7	429.0	417.4
2000	422.4	427.4	427.2	431.5	439.5	432.7	400.9	393.3	424.3	429.6	432.7	432.9	424.5
2001	430.6	435.2	435.8	437.0	439.0	435.2	403.6	399.2	431.3	436.4	437.8	439.9	430.1
2002	433.5	436.7	437.5	435.2	435.8	432.4	402.2	397.1	427.0	424.9	428.1	427.5	426.5
2003	422.5	425.0	425.1	425.2	425.6	423.5	392.6	387.1	416.5	417.8	418.8	419.4	416.6
Federal government													
1990	61.8	62.2	62.9	65.3	70.1	69.5	65.7	62.6	60.9	60.2	60.2	61.5	63.5
1991	61.1	61.4	61.3	61.4	60.9	61.4	61.2	61.2	60.3	59.7	59.8	61.0	60.8
1992	60.6	60.9	60.8	61.0	60.4	60.5	60.2	59.9	59.4	59.1	58.3	59.7	60.0
1993	59.1	59.7	59.8	60.9	60.5	60.5	60.4	60.0	59.7	59.1	59.0	60.7	59.9
1994	60.0	60.7	60.4	60.5	60.3	60.3	60.2	59.8	59.3	57.2	56.9	58.2	59.4
1995	58.0	58.9	58.7	58.9	58.2	58.8	58.5	58.3	57.5	57.1	56.6	57.8	58.1
1996	56.4	57.0	57.0	56.9	55.8	55.9	55.1	54.7	54.1	54.0	54.3	55.6	55.5
1997	54.9	55.4	55.7	56.2	55.4	55.6	54.7	55.0	54.3	53.4	53.8	55.7	55.0
1998	54.0	54.9	55.0	55.4	55.5	54.9	54.9	54.6	54.0	53.4	53.9	55.4	54.6
1999	54.2	55.0	55.1	56.0	55.2	55.5	55.3	55.2	54.2	54.5	54.6	55.9	55.0
2000	55.2	56.2	57.4	58.5	64.9	61.0	59.9	55.9	54.1	53.5	53.6	54.2	57.0
2001	53.6	54.2	54.3	54.5	54.0	54.7	55.2	54.6	53.6	53.0	52.8	53.2	54.0
2002	52.6	52.3	52.6	52.5	52.1	52.6	52.8	52.5	51.8	52.4	52.6	53.6	52.5
2003	53.1	53.3	53.1	53.0	52.5	52.5	52.2	51.8	50.6	51.0	50.5	51.2	52.1
State government													
1990	101.7	104.8	104.5	104.4	104.3	101.0	101.7	101.1	103.1	104.1	103.4	103.3	103.1
1991	98.1	101.4	101.9	101.7	101.4	100.3	100.5	99.5	99.7	99.7	99.7	99.0	100.2
1992	96.2	98.7	98.4	98.6	98.9	96.5	95.8	94.8	95.0	97.3	96.9	97.1	97.0
1993	94.7	97.9	98.2	98.4	98.8	96.5	97.1	96.3	95.4	97.5	97.1	96.8	97.0
1994	93.9	97.0	97.1	96.6	96.7	94.5	94.6	94.7	94.2	96.9	96.9	96.9	95.8
1995	93.7	96.9	97.3	98.1	98.7	95.0	95.8	95.6	97.0	98.7	98.7	98.6	97.0
1996	95.8	98.9	99.2	99.5	99.7	96.9	98.4	98.7	97.7	99.5	99.5	99.3	98.5
1997	96.0	99.3	100.0	100.9	102.1	99.6	99.8	99.0	98.1	102.8	102.8	102.8	100.2
1998	98.4	101.6	102.3	104.0	104.7	102.4	103.5	104.4	104.4	107.3	106.3	106.4	103.8
1999	102.2	105.3	106.0	105.2	105.8	103.2	101.2	101.1	101.5	105.9	105.3	104.8	103.9
2000	101.3	104.7	101.3	104.9	105.1	101.6	103.6	103.5	103.6	106.4	106.3	106.0	104.0
2001	105.6	109.1	109.3	109.3	109.6	105.5	106.0	105.9	107.5	109.6	109.2	108.9	108.0
2002	104.3	107.3	107.3	104.8	104.7	101.5	103.7	103.7	103.0	102.0	101.9	101.6	103.8
2003	100.7	103.3	103.3	102.1	102.3	99.5	103.8	104.0	103.4	103.1	102.9	102.8	102.6

Employment by Industry: Massachusetts—*Continued*

(Numbers in thousands. Not seasonally adjusted.)

Industry	January	February	March	April	May	June	July	August	September	October	November	December	Annual Average
STATEWIDE—*Continued*													
Local government													
1990	241.9	242.9	242.8	241.0	243.4	244.0	218.2	213.3	228.4	234.2	237.9	237.6	235.4
1991	236.4	237.6	237.5	234.3	236.3	237.7	209.3	207.3	220.9	227.6	229.8	230.7	228.7
1992	226.5	228.4	230.7	229.2	231.0	232.2	205.9	204.4	223.0	228.9	232.7	232.9	225.4
1993	228.9	230.7	231.7	234.5	236.6	238.9	213.9	210.0	228.9	235.5	237.8	238.3	230.4
1994	236.0	236.8	236.9	237.9	239.5	243.5	215.6	211.7	232.0	239.6	242.8	243.7	234.6
1995	239.2	241.3	242.2	243.5	244.7	248.0	221.2	217.0	236.5	246.2	249.2	250.3	239.9
1996	246.0	248.2	250.3	249.6	251.5	254.8	223.8	220.6	244.6	251.5	254.4	254.3	245.8
1997	249.9	250.4	251.6	252.9	254.4	257.6	228.3	224.8	249.5	255.6	257.2	259.3	249.2
1998	254.3	255.6	256.5	257.3	258.8	262.1	230.3	226.9	252.7	258.7	261.6	262.5	253.1
1999	258.9	260.6	261.3	262.0	263.6	266.9	235.2	231.6	260.7	265.0	266.8	268.3	258.4
2000	265.9	266.5	268.5	268.1	269.5	270.1	237.4	233.9	266.6	269.7	272.8	272.7	263.4
2001	271.4	271.9	272.2	273.2	275.4	275.0	242.4	238.7	270.2	273.8	275.8	277.8	268.2
2002	276.6	277.1	277.6	277.9	279.0	278.3	245.7	240.9	272.2	270.5	273.6	272.3	270.1
2003	268.7	268.4	268.7	270.1	270.8	271.5	236.6	231.3	262.5	263.7	265.4	265.4	261.9
BARNSTABLE-YARMOUTH													
Total nonfarm													
1995	46.6	46.8	47.5	50.6	53.8	59.6	62.9	62.7	57.8	54.8	52.3	51.4	53.9
1996	48.1	48.4	49.2	51.9	55.8	61.8	65.0	64.2	58.9	56.3	53.7	52.6	55.4
1997	49.7	49.4	50.5	53.4	57.2	62.1	65.3	64.4	59.9	58.0	54.9	54.2	56.5
1998	51.2	51.0	52.0	54.9	58.9	63.9	67.4	66.5	62.3	59.4	57.2	57.0	58.4
1999	53.5	53.4	54.1	58.4	61.6	66.5	71.1	70.5	64.9	62.2	59.4	58.9	61.2
2000	55.8	56.1	57.4	60.1	63.5	69.2	72.2	71.4	66.3	64.0	61.9	60.9	63.2
2001	58.2	58.4	58.7	60.9	64.7	71.0	74.4	73.4	67.7	64.7	62.1	61.4	64.6
2002	58.2	57.7	59.0	61.6	65.5	71.8	75.7	75.0	69.3	66.5	64.0	63.1	65.6
2003	59.0	58.6	59.2	62.6	67.0	73.1	76.1	76.1	70.6	68.2	65.2	64.1	66.7
Total private													
1995	39.5	39.6	40.3	43.3	46.4	51.8	55.6	55.6	50.5	47.6	45.2	44.2	46.6
1996	40.8	41.0	41.8	44.5	48.3	53.8	57.5	56.9	51.6	49.0	46.3	45.3	48.0
1997	42.6	42.1	43.2	46.0	49.7	54.3	57.8	57.2	52.4	50.5	47.4	46.7	49.1
1998	43.8	43.6	44.5	47.4	51.3	55.9	59.7	58.8	54.6	51.6	49.3	49.2	50.8
1999	45.8	45.7	46.4	50.5	53.6	58.2	62.6	62.1	57.0	54.1	51.3	50.9	53.1
2000	47.8	47.8	48.8	51.5	54.6	60.1	63.6	63.0	58.1	55.6	53.5	52.6	54.7
2001	49.9	49.6	50.3	52.5	56.0	61.8	65.4	64.6	58.9	56.0	53.5	52.7	55.9
2002	49.6	49.0	50.3	52.9	56.7	62.4	66.6	66.1	60.4	57.7	55.1	54.3	56.8
2003	50.4	50.0	50.6	53.7	58.0	63.6	66.9	67.0	61.8	59.1	56.2	55.3	57.7
Goods-producing													
1995	3.9	4.0	4.1	4.4	4.7	5.0	4.8	4.9	4.7	4.6	4.4	4.4	4.4
1996	4.0	4.0	4.1	4.2	4.4	4.7	4.7	4.7	4.4	4.3	4.3	4.2	4.3
1997	4.0	3.9	4.0	4.4	4.6	4.8	4.9	4.8	4.6	4.5	4.4	4.4	4.4
1998	4.2	4.1	4.1	4.5	4.9	5.1	5.2	5.0	4.9	4.8	4.9	4.7	4.7
1999	4.7	4.7	4.8	5.0	5.3	5.5	5.7	5.6	5.3	5.2	5.1	5.2	5.1
2000	5.0	5.0	5.2	5.5	5.7	6.1	6.1	6.1	5.9	5.8	5.8	5.7	5.6
2001	5.7	5.7	5.7	5.9	6.0	6.3	6.3	6.3	6.0	5.9	5.8	5.8	6.0
2002	5.4	5.4	5.5	5.7	5.9	6.2	6.4	6.3	6.0	6.0	5.9	5.9	5.9
2003	5.5	5.4	5.5	5.7	6.0	6.2	6.3	6.3	6.0	6.0	6.0	5.9	5.9
Construction and mining													
1995	2.2	2.2	2.3	2.5	2.7	2.8	2.7	2.7	2.6	2.6	2.4	2.4	2.5
1996	2.2	2.2	2.3	2.5	2.7	2.9	2.9	2.9	2.8	2.7	2.7	2.6	2.6
1997	2.5	2.4	2.5	2.8	2.9	3.0	3.1	3.0	2.9	2.9	2.8	2.8	2.8
1998	2.6	2.6	2.6	2.8	3.0	3.1	3.1	3.0	2.9	2.9	2.9	2.8	2.8
1999	2.8	2.8	2.8	3.1	3.3	3.5	3.6	3.5	3.3	3.3	3.2	3.2	3.2
2000	3.2	3.1	3.3	3.6	3.8	4.0	4.0	4.0	3.9	3.8	3.8	3.7	3.6
2001	3.7	3.7	3.7	3.8	3.9	4.1	4.1	4.1	3.9	3.9	3.9	3.9	3.9
2002	3.6	3.6	3.7	3.9	4.1	4.3	4.4	4.3	4.1	4.1	4.0	4.0	4.0
2003	3.8	3.7	3.8	4.0	4.3	4.4	4.5	4.5	4.3	4.3	4.3	4.2	4.2
Manufacturing													
1995	1.7	1.8	1.8	1.9	2.0	2.2	2.1	2.2	2.1	2.0	2.0	2.0	1.9
1996	1.8	1.8	1.8	1.7	1.7	1.8	1.8	1.8	1.6	1.6	1.6	1.6	1.7
1997	1.5	1.5	1.5	1.6	1.7	1.8	1.8	1.8	1.7	1.6	1.6	1.6	1.6
1998	1.6	1.5	1.5	1.7	1.9	2.0	2.1	2.0	2.0	1.9	2.0	1.9	1.8
1999	1.9	1.9	2.0	1.9	2.0	2.0	2.1	2.1	2.0	1.9	1.9	2.0	1.9
2000	1.8	1.9	1.9	1.9	1.9	2.1	2.1	2.1	2.0	2.0	2.0	2.0	1.9
2001	2.0	2.0	2.0	2.1	2.1	2.2	2.2	2.2	2.1	2.0	1.9	1.9	2.1
2002	1.8	1.8	1.8	1.8	1.8	1.9	2.0	2.0	1.9	1.9	1.9	1.9	1.9
2003	1.7	1.7	1.7	1.7	1.7	1.8	1.8	1.8	1.7	1.7	1.7	1.7	1.7
Service-providing													
1995	42.7	42.8	43.4	46.2	49.1	54.6	58.1	57.8	53.1	50.2	47.9	47.0	49.4
1996	44.1	44.4	45.1	47.7	51.4	57.1	60.3	59.5	54.5	52.0	49.4	48.4	51.1
1997	45.7	45.5	46.5	49.0	52.6	57.3	60.4	59.6	55.3	53.5	50.5	49.8	52.1
1998	47.0	46.9	47.9	50.4	54.0	58.8	62.2	61.5	57.4	54.6	52.3	52.3	53.7
1999	48.8	48.7	49.3	53.4	56.3	61.0	65.4	64.9	59.6	57.0	54.3	53.7	56.0
2000	50.8	51.1	52.2	54.6	57.8	63.1	66.1	65.3	60.4	58.2	56.1	55.2	57.5
2001	52.5	52.7	53.0	55.0	58.7	64.7	68.1	67.1	61.7	58.8	56.3	55.6	58.7
2002	52.8	52.3	53.5	55.9	59.6	65.6	69.3	68.7	63.3	60.5	58.1	57.2	59.7
2003	53.5	53.2	53.7	56.9	61.0	66.9	69.8	69.8	64.6	62.2	59.2	58.2	60.8

Employment by Industry: Massachusetts—*Continued*

(Numbers in thousands. Not seasonally adjusted.)

Industry	January	February	March	April	May	June	July	August	September	October	November	December	Annual Average
BARNSTABLE-YARMOUTH *—Continued*													
Trade, transportation, and utilities													
1995	11.0	10.8	10.9	11.4	12.0	13.0	14.1	14.1	13.1	12.5	12.5	12.7	12.3
1996	11.7	11.4	11.4	12.0	12.7	14.0	15.3	14.9	13.6	13.1	13.0	13.2	13.0
1997	12.3	11.8	12.1	12.5	13.2	14.3	15.2	15.2	13.9	13.6	13.4	13.5	13.4
1998	12.6	12.1	12.2	12.6	13.4	14.5	15.3	15.2	14.3	13.7	13.7	14.1	13.6
1999	12.7	12.4	12.7	13.4	14.1	15.3	16.3	16.2	14.9	14.2	14.3	14.8	14.2
2000	13.7	13.4	13.4	13.7	14.3	15.7	16.7	16.5	15.6	15.2	15.1	15.4	14.8
2001	14.4	13.9	14.1	14.2	15.1	16.6	17.5	17.2	16.0	15.4	15.4	15.5	15.4
2002	14.3	13.8	14.0	14.1	15.1	16.5	17.4	17.2	16.1	15.8	15.8	15.9	15.5
2003	14.2	14.0	14.0	14.5	15.5	16.9	17.4	17.3	16.2	15.9	15.6	15.8	15.6
Wholesale trade													
1995	0.7	0.7	0.7	0.7	0.7	0.7	0.8	0.8	0.7	0.7	0.7	0.7	0.7
1996	0.6	0.6	0.6	0.7	0.7	0.8	0.8	0.8	0.7	0.7	0.7	0.7	0.7
1997	0.7	0.7	0.7	0.7	0.7	0.8	0.8	0.8	0.8	0.8	0.7	0.7	0.7
1998	0.7	0.7	0.7	0.7	0.8	0.8	0.8	0.8	0.8	0.8	0.7	0.8	0.7
1999	0.7	0.7	0.8	0.8	0.8	0.8	0.9	0.9	0.8	0.8	0.8	0.8	0.8
2000	0.8	0.8	0.8	0.8	0.8	0.9	0.9	0.9	0.9	0.9	0.9	0.9	0.8
2001	0.9	0.9	0.9	1.0	1.0	1.1	1.1	1.0	1.0	1.0	1.0	0.9	1.0
2002	1.0	1.0	1.0	0.9	1.0	1.0	1.0	1.0	1.0	1.0	1.0	0.9	1.0
2003	1.0	1.0	1.0	1.0	1.1	1.1	1.1	1.1	1.0	1.0	1.0	1.0	1.0
Retail trade													
1995	9.0	8.8	8.9	9.3	9.8	10.6	11.6	11.6	10.6	10.1	10.2	10.4	10.0
1996	9.6	9.3	9.3	9.7	10.2	11.3	12.6	12.2	11.0	10.6	10.6	10.8	10.6
1997	10.0	9.6	9.8	10.2	10.7	11.6	12.6	12.6	11.3	11.0	11.0	11.2	10.9
1998	10.3	9.8	9.9	10.3	10.8	11.7	12.5	12.4	11.5	11.1	11.3	11.6	11.1
1999	10.3	10.0	10.2	10.8	11.3	12.4	13.4	13.2	12.1	11.5	11.7	12.1	11.5
2000	11.1	10.8	10.8	11.1	11.6	12.7	13.7	13.5	12.6	12.3	12.4	12.7	12.1
2001	11.7	11.2	11.4	11.5	12.2	13.4	14.3	14.1	13.0	12.5	12.7	12.9	12.6
2002	11.7	11.2	11.4	11.5	12.2	13.4	14.4	14.2	13.2	12.9	13.1	13.3	12.7
2003	11.6	11.4	11.4	11.8	12.6	13.9	14.4	14.3	13.4	13.1	12.9	13.1	12.8
Transportation and utilities													
1995	1.3	1.3	1.3	1.4	1.5	1.7	1.7	1.7	1.8	1.7	1.6	1.6	1.5
1996	1.5	1.5	1.5	1.6	1.8	1.9	1.9	1.9	1.9	1.8	1.7	1.7	1.7
1997	1.6	1.5	1.6	1.6	1.8	1.9	1.8	1.8	1.8	1.8	1.7	1.6	1.7
1998	1.6	1.6	1.6	1.6	1.8	2.0	2.0	2.0	2.0	1.8	1.7	1.7	1.7
1999	1.7	1.7	1.7	1.8	2.0	2.1	2.0	2.1	2.0	1.9	1.8	1.9	1.8
2000	1.8	1.8	1.8	1.8	1.9	2.1	2.1	2.1	2.1	2.0	1.8	1.8	1.9
2001	1.8	1.8	1.8	1.7	1.9	2.1	2.1	2.1	2.0	1.9	1.7	1.7	1.9
2002	1.6	1.6	1.6	1.7	1.9	2.1	2.0	2.0	1.9	1.9	1.7	1.7	1.8
2003	1.6	1.6	1.6	1.7	1.8	1.9	1.9	1.9	1.8	1.8	1.7	1.7	1.8
Information													
1995	1.7	1.7	1.7	1.7	1.8	1.7	1.8	1.8	1.8	1.7	1.7	1.7	1.7
1996	1.7	1.7	1.7	1.7	1.7	1.8	1.9	1.9	1.8	1.8	1.8	1.8	1.7
1997	1.8	1.8	1.8	1.9	1.9	1.9	2.0	1.9	1.9	1.9	1.8	1.8	1.8
1998	1.8	1.8	1.8	1.8	1.8	1.8	1.9	1.8	1.8	1.8	1.8	1.9	1.8
1999	1.8	1.8	1.7	1.7	1.7	1.8	1.8	1.8	1.7	1.7	1.7	1.7	1.7
2000	1.6	1.6	1.6	1.6	1.6	1.7	1.7	1.5	1.6	1.6	1.6	1.6	1.6
2001	1.6	1.6	1.6	1.5	1.6	1.6	1.7	1.6	1.5	1.5	1.5	1.5	1.6
2002	1.6	1.5	1.5	1.5	1.6	1.6	1.6	1.6	1.5	1.5	1.5	1.5	1.5
2003	1.5	1.5	1.5	1.5	1.5	1.6	1.5	1.5	1.5	1.5	1.5	1.5	1.5
Financial activities													
1995	2.6	2.6	2.6	2.7	2.7	2.8	2.9	2.9	2.8	2.8	2.7	2.7	2.7
1996	2.8	2.8	2.9	3.0	3.1	3.2	3.3	3.3	3.2	3.2	3.1	3.1	3.0
1997	3.1	3.0	3.1	3.1	3.2	3.3	3.5	3.4	3.3	3.2	3.2	3.2	3.2
1998	3.1	3.1	3.2	3.2	3.3	3.4	3.5	3.5	3.3	3.3	3.2	3.3	3.2
1999	3.2	3.2	3.2	3.4	3.4	3.5	3.7	3.6	3.5	3.5	3.3	3.4	3.4
2000	3.3	3.3	3.3	3.4	3.5	3.6	3.6	3.6	3.5	3.5	3.4	3.4	3.4
2001	3.4	3.4	3.4	3.5	3.6	3.7	3.8	3.8	3.6	3.5	3.4	3.4	3.5
2002	3.4	3.4	3.4	3.5	3.6	3.8	3.9	3.9	3.7	3.6	3.5	3.5	3.6
2003	3.5	3.5	3.5	3.6	3.7	3.8	3.9	3.9	3.8	3.7	3.6	3.6	3.7
Professional and business services													
1995	3.0	3.0	3.1	3.5	3.7	3.9	3.9	3.9	3.6	3.7	3.6	3.5	3.5
1996	3.1	3.1	3.2	3.5	3.8	4.0	3.9	4.0	3.8	3.8	3.8	3.7	3.6
1997	3.2	3.2	3.4	3.7	4.0	4.1	4.2	4.2	4.1	4.1	3.9	3.9	3.8
1998	3.4	3.4	3.6	4.3	4.7	4.9	5.0	4.8	4.8	4.7	4.6	4.6	4.4
1999	4.3	4.3	4.4	5.1	5.3	5.5	5.7	5.7	5.5	5.3	5.1	5.0	5.1
2000	4.6	4.6	4.9	5.3	5.6	5.9	6.0	5.9	5.7	5.5	5.5	5.4	5.4
2001	5.0	5.0	5.2	5.6	5.8	6.0	6.2	6.1	5.8	5.6	5.5	5.3	5.6
2002	4.9	4.8	5.2	5.6	5.8	6.1	6.3	6.1	5.8	5.8	5.7	5.6	5.6
2003	5.0	4.8	5.0	5.8	6.0	6.2	6.3	6.4	6.1	6.0	5.9	5.8	5.8

Employment by Industry: Massachusetts—*Continued*

(Numbers in thousands. Not seasonally adjusted.)

Industry	January	February	March	April	May	June	July	August	September	October	November	December	Annual Average
BARNSTABLE-YARMOUTH *—Continued*													
Educational and health services													
1995	8.6	8.8	8.8	8.8	8.9	9.0	9.0	9.0	9.0	9.1	9.2	9.2	8.9
1996	9.0	9.2	9.3	9.1	9.2	9.2	9.1	9.0	9.2	9.3	9.3	9.3	9.1
1997	9.3	9.3	9.3	9.4	9.3	9.3	9.0	8.9	9.2	9.4	9.5	9.4	9.2
1998	9.4	9.5	9.6	9.4	9.3	9.3	9.1	9.0	9.3	9.6	9.6	9.7	9.4
1999	9.6	9.6	9.7	9.8	9.8	9.7	9.6	9.5	9.7	9.7	9.7	9.7	9.6
2000	9.7	9.8	9.9	9.7	9.8	9.8	9.7	9.8	9.8	9.8	9.9	10.0	9.8
2001	9.7	9.8	9.8	9.8	9.9	10.0	9.8	9.8	9.8	9.8	9.9	10.0	9.8
2002	9.9	9.9	9.9	10.0	10.1	10.2	10.1	10.1	10.1	10.1	10.2	10.3	10.1
2003	10.3	10.3	10.3	10.4	10.5	10.5	10.5	10.7	10.8	10.7	10.9	10.9	10.6
Leisure and hospitality													
1995	6.5	6.5	6.9	8.5	10.3	13.9	16.5	16.4	13.1	10.8	8.8	7.7	10.4
1996	6.3	6.6	7.0	8.7	11.0	14.4	16.6	16.5	13.1	11.1	8.8	7.8	10.6
1997	6.7	6.9	7.3	8.8	11.2	14.2	16.4	16.2	12.9	11.4	8.9	8.2	10.7
1998	7.1	7.4	7.7	9.3	11.5	14.4	17.0	16.8	13.7	11.3	9.2	8.6	11.1
1999	7.2	7.4	7.6	9.8	11.6	14.4	17.1	17.0	13.9	12.1	9.8	8.8	11.3
2000	7.6	7.7	8.1	9.8	11.6	14.7	17.1	16.9	13.4	11.7	9.7	8.6	11.4
2001	7.8	7.8	8.1	9.6	11.5	15.0	17.3	17.0	13.6	11.7	9.5	8.7	11.5
2002	7.6	7.8	8.3	10.0	12.0	15.3	18.1	18.0	14.5	12.3	9.9	9.1	11.9
2003	7.9	8.0	8.3	9.7	12.2	15.6	18.1	18.0	14.5	12.5	9.9	9.2	12.0
Other services													
1995	2.2	2.2	2.2	2.3	2.3	2.5	2.6	2.6	2.4	2.4	2.3	2.3	2.3
1996	2.2	2.2	2.2	2.3	2.4	2.5	2.7	2.6	2.5	2.4	2.2	2.2	2.3
1997	2.2	2.2	2.2	2.2	2.3	2.4	2.6	2.6	2.5	2.4	2.3	2.3	2.3
1998	2.2	2.2	2.3	2.3	2.4	2.5	2.7	2.7	2.5	2.4	2.3	2.3	2.4
1999	2.3	2.3	2.3	2.3	2.4	2.5	2.7	2.7	2.5	2.4	2.3	2.3	2.4
2000	2.3	2.4	2.4	2.5	2.5	2.6	2.7	2.7	2.6	2.5	2.5	2.5	2.5
2001	2.3	2.4	2.4	2.4	2.5	2.6	2.8	2.8	2.6	2.6	2.5	2.5	2.5
2002	2.5	2.4	2.5	2.5	2.6	2.7	2.8	2.9	2.7	2.6	2.6	2.5	2.6
2003	2.5	2.5	2.5	2.5	2.6	2.8	2.9	2.9	2.9	2.8	2.8	2.6	2.7
Government													
1995	7.1	7.2	7.2	7.3	7.4	7.8	7.3	7.1	7.3	7.2	7.1	7.2	7.2
1996	7.3	7.4	7.4	7.4	7.5	8.0	7.5	7.3	7.3	7.3	7.4	7.3	7.4
1997	7.1	7.3	7.3	7.4	7.5	7.8	7.5	7.2	7.5	7.5	7.5	7.5	7.4
1998	7.4	7.4	7.5	7.5	7.6	8.0	7.7	7.7	7.7	7.8	7.9	7.8	7.6
1999	7.7	7.7	7.7	7.9	8.0	8.3	8.5	8.4	7.9	8.1	8.1	8.0	8.0
2000	8.0	8.3	8.6	8.6	8.9	9.1	8.6	8.4	8.2	8.4	8.4	8.3	8.4
2001	8.3	8.8	8.4	8.4	8.7	9.2	9.0	8.8	8.8	8.7	8.6	8.7	8.7
2002	8.6	8.7	8.7	8.7	8.8	9.4	9.1	8.9	8.9	8.8	8.9	8.8	8.9
2003	8.6	8.6	8.6	8.9	9.0	9.5	9.2	9.1	8.8	9.1	9.0	8.8	8.9
Federal government													
2001	0.4	0.4	0.4	0.4	0.4	0.4	0.4	0.4	0.4	0.4	0.4	0.4	0.4
2002	0.4	0.4	0.4	0.4	0.4	0.4	0.4	0.4	0.4	0.4	0.5	0.5	0.4
2003	0.4	0.4	0.4	0.5	0.5	0.4	0.4	0.4	0.4	0.4	0.4	0.4	0.4
State government													
1995	0.9	0.9	0.9	0.9	0.9	0.9	0.9	0.9	0.9	0.9	0.9	0.9	0.9
1996	0.9	0.9	0.9	0.9	0.9	0.9	0.9	0.8	0.8	0.8	0.8	0.8	0.8
1997	0.7	0.8	0.8	0.8	0.8	0.7	0.7	0.7	0.7	0.7	0.8	0.8	0.7
1998	0.8	0.8	0.8	0.8	0.8	0.8	0.7	0.8	0.8	0.8	0.8	0.8	0.7
1999	0.8	0.8	0.8	0.8	0.8	0.8	0.8	0.8	0.8	0.8	0.8	0.8	0.8
2000	0.9	1.1	1.0	0.9	0.9	0.9	0.8	0.8	0.9	0.9	0.9	0.9	0.9
2001	1.0	1.2	1.0	0.9	0.9	0.9	0.9	0.9	1.0	1.0	1.0	1.0	1.0
2002	1.0	1.0	1.0	0.9	0.9	0.9	0.9	0.9	0.9	0.9	0.9	0.9	0.9
2003	0.9	0.9	0.9	0.9	0.9	0.9	0.9	0.9	0.9	0.9	0.9	0.9	0.9
Local government													
1995	5.8	5.9	5.9	6.0	6.1	6.5	6.0	5.8	6.0	5.9	5.8	5.9	5.9
1996	6.0	6.1	6.1	6.1	6.2	6.7	6.2	6.1	6.1	6.1	6.2	6.1	6.1
1997	6.0	6.1	6.1	6.2	6.3	6.7	6.4	6.1	6.4	6.4	6.3	6.3	6.2
1998	6.2	6.2	6.3	6.3	6.4	6.8	6.6	6.5	6.5	6.6	6.7	6.6	6.4
1999	6.5	6.5	6.5	6.7	6.8	7.1	7.3	7.2	6.7	6.9	6.9	6.8	6.8
2000	6.7	6.8	6.8	6.8	7.0	7.5	7.3	7.2	6.9	7.1	7.1	7.0	7.0
2001	6.9	7.2	7.0	7.1	7.4	7.9	7.7	7.5	7.4	7.3	7.2	7.3	7.3
2002	7.2	7.3	7.3	7.4	7.5	8.1	7.8	7.6	7.6	7.5	7.5	7.4	7.5
2003	7.3	7.3	7.3	7.5	7.6	8.2	7.9	7.8	7.5	7.8	7.7	7.5	7.6

Employment by Industry: Massachusetts—*Continued*

(Numbers in thousands. Not seasonally adjusted.)

Industry	January	February	March	April	May	June	July	August	September	October	November	December	Annual Average
BOSTON													
Total nonfarm													
1990	1833.1	1826.7	1842.1	1829.8	1840.8	1862.0	1818.9	1810.0	1812.8	1806.2	1806.9	1805.7	1824.6
1991	1725.5	1714.4	1720.9	1719.4	1726.7	1738.6	1704.4	1698.7	1706.4	1718.6	1725.3	1729.2	1719.0
1992	1678.9	1680.2	1689.8	1695.5	1707.3	1719.4	1701.0	1695.3	1710.7	1726.6	1730.8	1736.9	1706.0
1993	1686.3	1687.2	1690.1	1713.7	1727.7	1744.3	1726.4	1725.1	1738.6	1751.8	1761.8	1771.7	1727.1
1994	1727.7	1732.8	1745.7	1764.6	1777.5	1798.7	1775.7	1777.8	1789.2	1797.7	1811.9	1824.3	1777.0
1995	1777.5	1779.8	1792.6	1808.1	1819.0	1840.5	1816.9	1821.0	1831.9	1840.5	1853.7	1863.0	1820.4
1996	1804.6	1815.6	1827.3	1841.7	1860.7	1880.6	1859.0	1865.8	1877.0	1883.1	1900.8	1911.5	1860.6
1997	1864.2	1867.5	1881.4	1891.5	1910.0	1927.1	1898.9	1901.1	1913.5	1924.3	1933.8	1953.1	1905.5
1998	1900.1	1906.6	1915.9	1933.9	1945.5	1964.2	1949.2	1949.0	1958.4	1969.1	1977.6	1991.0	1946.7
1999	1931.8	1938.1	1949.2	1970.0	1979.0	2003.5	1985.0	1983.5	1996.2	2009.7	2018.9	2034.3	1983.3
2000	1983.5	1988.6	2002.6	2020.0	2032.2	2058.7	2046.2	2041.8	2058.0	2073.6	2087.4	2098.7	2040.9
2001	2041.7	2041.1	2044.4	2051.8	2057.2	2070.8	2038.3	2032.6	2028.3	2025.1	2025.3	2028.3	2040.4
2002	1970.8	1962.6	1972.3	1980.1	1989.4	2000.9	1980.0	1974.0	1977.7	1979.4	1985.1	1986.5	1979.9
2003	1924.3	1911.2	1917.0	1933.1	1942.7	1954.6	1931.4	1921.0	1927.3	1935.1	1935.8	1934.0	1930.6
Total private													
1990	1605.4	1598.5	1613.6	1600.3	1606.9	1626.7	1598.0	1597.5	1593.7	1584.1	1582.9	1581.7	1599.1
1991	1504.5	1492.5	1498.8	1498.5	1506.0	1515.8	1493.3	1492.5	1491.9	1502.0	1507.7	1510.6	1501.2
1992	1464.5	1465.3	1474.5	1480.8	1492.1	1503.1	1496.5	1495.2	1499.9	1513.4	1516.1	1521.6	1493.6
1993	1474.5	1474.3	1476.8	1496.5	1510.0	1525.0	1517.8	1520.0	1525.3	1536.1	1545.1	1553.8	1512.9
1994	1503.2	1507.8	1520.7	1539.2	1551.4	1570.2	1559.8	1564.2	1567.5	1572.6	1585.9	1596.9	1553.3
1995	1552.7	1553.7	1565.8	1580.6	1591.1	1609.8	1595.9	1602.9	1605.6	1611.2	1623.6	1631.9	1593.7
1996	1576.8	1586.5	1597.4	1612.4	1631.2	1649.5	1641.8	1650.5	1652.0	1655.2	1672.0	1681.5	1633.9
1997	1637.0	1640.0	1653.2	1662.2	1679.6	1695.5	1680.6	1685.1	1686.6	1693.0	1701.4	1719.0	1677.8
1998	1670.3	1676.1	1684.9	1701.7	1712.4	1729.0	1728.2	1729.2	1725.4	1734.0	1741.4	1753.5	1715.5
1999	1697.5	1702.0	1712.5	1732.9	1740.8	1763.8	1760.5	1760.6	1759.7	1768.4	1777.0	1791.7	1747.3
2000	1743.0	1747.7	1760.2	1777.7	1786.2	1815.4	1816.3	1815.7	1817.6	1831.9	1844.5	1855.7	1801.0
2001	1798.8	1797.6	1801.1	1807.7	1812.5	1827.5	1808.6	1804.6	1785.3	1782.5	1781.9	1783.8	1799.3
2002	1728.3	1719.9	1729.3	1739.3	1748.6	1761.5	1752.1	1748.3	1739.0	1743.7	1748.0	1750.0	1742.3
2003	1689.7	1676.7	1682.7	1699.0	1708.7	1720.6	1709.2	1704.5	1698.9	1704.3	1705.2	1703.4	1700.2
Goods-producing													
1990	313.4	309.5	311.2	310.2	311.8	315.4	309.1	310.2	307.6	301.6	298.9	294.8	307.8
1991	280.3	275.6	275.8	273.2	275.3	278.3	274.0	276.3	275.2	272.4	270.5	267.9	274.6
1992	259.0	257.0	257.8	260.4	262.9	264.1	262.4	263.3	262.8	262.6	261.4	259.8	261.1
1993	251.6	249.9	249.3	253.2	256.1	260.3	259.5	260.4	259.0	258.6	257.3	256.1	255.9
1994	247.6	246.5	248.1	252.6	256.5	260.5	258.8	260.7	260.8	259.8	260.5	259.5	256.0
1995	251.4	249.5	251.5	256.3	259.0	263.1	258.8	261.7	261.7	261.2	262.0	260.6	258.1
1996	250.4	251.0	252.6	255.4	260.0	264.3	261.8	264.8	264.3	262.9	262.6	260.8	259.2
1997	254.1	252.8	255.3	260.0	265.0	269.1	267.2	270.1	270.2	269.0	268.9	268.8	264.2
1998	262.7	262.8	263.9	266.2	266.5	270.0	269.3	270.8	269.4	266.1	265.8	263.6	266.4
1999	255.9	255.6	255.2	260.7	262.9	266.3	266.5	267.9	267.6	267.2	266.7	267.1	263.3
2000	260.5	259.7	263.0	267.9	270.6	276.3	273.4	275.8	274.1	278.2	278.6	277.7	271.3
2001	271.8	270.5	270.8	275.0	276.5	278.1	273.7	273.4	270.2	267.9	264.5	260.9	271.1
2002	251.8	248.3	249.1	252.2	255.1	257.0	255.9	256.5	254.5	254.5	253.0	248.8	253.1
2003	238.5	232.8	233.1	238.1	241.2	242.9	242.1	241.6	239.9	240.1	240.6	238.0	239.1
Natural resources and mining													
1990	0.8	0.8	0.8	0.8	0.8	0.8	0.8	0.7	0.7	0.7	0.7	0.7	0.8
1991	0.5	0.4	0.4	0.5	0.5	0.5	0.5	0.5	0.5	0.5	0.5	0.5	0.5
1992	0.4	0.4	0.4	0.5	0.5	0.5	0.5	0.5	0.5	0.5	0.5	0.5	0.5
1993	0.4	0.4	0.4	0.4	0.4	0.5	0.5	0.5	0.5	0.5	0.5	0.4	0.5
1994	0.4	0.4	0.4	0.4	0.5	0.5	0.5	0.5	0.5	0.5	0.5	0.5	0.5
1995	0.4	0.4	0.5	0.5	0.5	0.5	0.5	0.5	0.5	0.5	0.5	0.5	0.5
1996	0.4	0.4	0.4	0.5	0.5	0.5	0.5	0.5	0.5	0.5	0.5	0.5	0.5
1997	0.4	0.4	0.5	0.5	0.6	0.6	0.6	0.6	0.6	0.6	0.6	0.6	0.6
1998	0.5	0.5	0.5	0.6	0.6	0.6	0.6	0.6	0.6	0.6	0.6	0.6	0.6
1999	0.5	0.5	0.5	0.5	0.5	0.5	0.5	0.5	0.5	0.6	0.6	0.6	0.5
2000	0.5	0.4	0.5	0.7	0.7	0.8	0.6	0.7	0.7	0.7	0.7	0.6	0.6
2001	0.5	0.5	0.5	0.6	0.7	0.7	0.7	0.7	0.7	0.7	0.7	0.7	0.6
2002	0.6	0.6	0.6	0.7	0.8	0.8	0.8	0.8	0.9	0.9	0.9	0.9	0.8
2003	0.7	0.7	0.6	0.7	0.9	0.9	0.9	0.9	0.9	0.9	0.9	0.8	0.8
Construction													
1990	58.4	56.0	56.5	57.1	59.4	61.5	60.7	61.5	60.5	57.5	56.0	53.2	58.2
1991	44.6	42.3	42.6	43.6	46.1	48.1	48.2	48.8	48.1	46.2	45.1	43.3	45.6
1992	38.2	37.3	37.9	39.4	41.9	44.0	45.3	46.1	45.6	45.9	45.2	43.7	42.5
1993	39.6	39.0	39.2	41.8	44.8	47.8	50.2	50.6	50.3	50.1	49.0	47.8	45.9
1994	42.2	41.3	42.1	46.6	49.4	52.1	53.6	54.4	54.0	53.9	53.5	52.0	49.6
1995	45.9	44.6	46.0	49.8	52.3	55.5	56.1	56.9	56.0	55.4	55.3	53.4	52.3
1996	46.2	46.3	47.7	51.3	54.8	57.6	58.6	59.5	58.7	58.6	57.8	55.8	54.4
1997	51.2	50.0	51.6	55.0	58.8	60.8	62.3	63.0	62.5	62.1	61.3	60.4	58.3
1998	55.3	54.9	55.9	60.2	62.8	65.2	68.7	69.0	67.9	67.0	66.8	66.1	63.3
1999	61.7	61.6	62.3	68.1	70.4	72.9	74.5	74.8	74.4	73.9	73.0	72.7	70.0
2000	67.1	66.1	68.9	73.9	76.4	79.5	82.3	83.0	82.0	82.5	82.0	80.4	77.0
2001	74.7	73.9	75.1	81.0	84.2	86.3	87.3	87.2	85.5	86.0	84.8	82.6	82.4
2002	76.7	75.2	76.7	81.4	84.8	85.8	86.7	86.8	85.8	86.7	86.0	82.2	82.9
2003	75.4	71.5	72.4	77.6	80.6	82.0	82.8	82.5	81.2	81.6	80.9	78.7	78.9

Employment by Industry: Massachusetts—*Continued*

(Numbers in thousands. Not seasonally adjusted.)

Industry	January	February	March	April	May	June	July	August	September	October	November	December	Annual Average
BOSTON—*Continued*													
Manufacturing													
1990	254.2	252.7	253.9	252.3	251.6	253.1	247.6	248.0	246.4	243.4	242.2	240.9	248.9
1991	235.2	232.9	232.8	229.1	228.7	229.7	225.3	227.0	226.6	225.7	224.9	224.1	228.5
1992	220.4	219.3	219.5	220.5	220.5	219.6	216.6	216.7	216.7	216.2	215.7	215.6	218.1
1993	211.6	210.5	209.7	211.0	210.9	212.0	208.8	209.3	208.2	208.0	207.8	207.9	209.6
1994	205.0	204.8	205.6	205.6	206.6	207.9	204.7	205.8	206.3	205.4	206.5	207.0	205.9
1995	205.1	204.5	205.0	206.0	206.2	207.1	202.2	204.3	205.2	205.3	206.2	206.7	205.3
1996	203.8	204.3	204.5	203.6	204.7	206.2	202.7	204.8	205.1	203.8	204.3	204.5	204.4
1997	202.5	202.4	203.2	204.5	205.6	207.7	204.3	206.5	207.1	206.3	207.0	207.8	205.4
1998	206.9	207.4	207.5	205.4	203.1	204.2	200.0	201.2	200.9	198.5	198.4	196.9	202.5
1999	193.7	193.5	192.4	192.1	192.0	192.9	191.5	192.6	192.7	192.7	193.1	193.8	192.8
2000	192.9	193.2	193.6	193.3	193.5	196.0	190.5	192.1	191.4	195.0	195.9	196.7	193.7
2001	196.6	196.1	195.2	193.4	191.6	191.1	185.7	185.5	184.0	181.2	179.0	177.6	188.1
2002	174.5	172.5	171.8	170.1	169.5	170.4	168.4	168.9	167.8	166.9	166.1	165.7	169.4
2003	162.4	160.6	160.1	159.8	159.7	160.0	158.4	158.2	157.8	157.6	158.8	158.5	159.3
Service-providing													
1990	1519.7	1517.2	1530.9	1519.6	1529.0	1546.6	1509.8	1499.8	1505.2	1504.6	1508.0	1510.9	1516.8
1991	1445.2	1438.8	1445.1	1446.2	1451.4	1460.3	1430.4	1422.4	1431.2	1446.2	1454.8	1461.3	1444.4
1992	1419.9	1423.2	1432.0	1435.1	1444.4	1455.3	1438.6	1432.0	1447.9	1464.0	1469.4	1477.1	1444.9
1993	1434.7	1437.3	1440.8	1460.5	1471.6	1484.0	1466.9	1464.7	1479.6	1493.2	1504.5	1515.6	1471.1
1994	1480.1	1486.3	1497.6	1512.0	1521.0	1538.2	1516.9	1517.1	1528.4	1537.9	1551.4	1564.8	1521.0
1995	1526.1	1530.3	1541.1	1551.8	1560.0	1577.4	1558.1	1559.3	1570.2	1579.3	1591.7	1602.4	1562.3
1996	1554.2	1564.6	1574.7	1586.3	1600.7	1616.3	1597.2	1601.0	1612.7	1620.2	1638.2	1650.7	1601.4
1997	1610.1	1614.7	1626.1	1631.5	1645.0	1658.0	1631.7	1631.0	1643.3	1655.3	1664.9	1684.3	1641.3
1998	1637.4	1643.8	1652.0	1667.7	1679.0	1694.2	1679.9	1678.2	1689.0	1703.0	1711.8	1727.4	1680.3
1999	1675.9	1682.5	1694.0	1709.3	1716.1	1737.2	1718.5	1715.6	1728.6	1742.5	1752.2	1767.2	1720.0
2000	1723.0	1728.9	1739.6	1752.1	1761.6	1782.4	1772.8	1766.0	1783.9	1795.4	1808.8	1821.0	1769.6
2001	1769.9	1770.6	1773.6	1776.8	1780.7	1792.7	1764.6	1759.2	1758.1	1757.2	1760.8	1767.4	1769.3
2002	1719.0	1714.3	1723.2	1727.9	1734.3	1743.9	1724.1	1717.5	1723.2	1724.9	1732.1	1737.7	1726.8
2003	1685.8	1678.4	1683.9	1695.0	1701.5	1711.7	1689.3	1679.4	1687.4	1695.0	1695.2	1696.0	1691.6
Trade, transportation, and utilities													
1990	351.0	341.7	343.7	337.0	338.5	345.4	333.0	332.5	334.4	331.8	335.9	340.7	338.8
1991	320.0	311.1	310.1	308.8	310.8	313.3	305.9	305.1	306.5	308.5	313.6	318.7	311.0
1992	303.7	299.6	300.2	298.9	300.9	303.1	298.3	297.6	299.4	304.5	309.1	315.2	302.5
1993	300.7	296.1	294.8	297.7	300.4	304.5	300.0	300.1	303.3	306.2	312.2	318.6	302.9
1994	305.1	301.2	301.5	303.1	305.7	309.7	303.9	304.8	307.7	312.3	320.1	327.5	308.6
1995	311.6	307.0	307.9	308.5	310.0	313.1	306.7	308.4	310.9	313.8	321.0	327.1	312.2
1996	315.6	312.1	311.8	311.3	315.1	318.9	313.3	314.9	318.2	320.5	330.4	338.1	318.4
1997	328.0	323.5	325.3	321.5	324.5	328.3	320.3	320.8	325.5	330.5	336.8	345.9	327.6
1998	330.6	326.3	326.1	325.7	328.1	331.5	328.4	328.2	331.1	335.7	344.8	352.7	332.4
1999	336.3	333.6	333.1	334.2	336.3	340.6	337.6	337.5	339.2	341.7	349.0	358.9	339.8
2000	343.7	339.7	339.8	341.0	342.4	346.8	342.0	342.1	344.9	349.5	357.7	366.2	346.3
2001	347.0	341.1	340.9	340.8	341.7	346.0	339.7	338.8	338.0	339.7	346.3	351.2	342.6
2002	334.3	328.4	329.1	329.4	331.5	336.0	331.4	329.8	330.8	331.9	337.8	344.2	332.9
2003	326.5	321.5	321.7	322.8	324.6	328.1	321.4	321.0	322.4	324.5	327.4	331.3	324.4
Wholesale trade													
1990	96.8	96.4	96.9	94.6	94.4	95.7	93.8	93.3	92.6	92.5	92.1	92.1	94.3
1991	87.8	87.0	86.8	86.8	86.4	86.8	86.1	85.6	85.1	85.0	85.3	85.2	86.2
1992	83.6	83.4	83.7	82.6	83.1	83.5	83.1	82.6	82.3	82.5	82.5	83.0	83.0
1993	79.8	79.9	79.9	80.4	80.7	81.4	80.9	80.6	80.8	80.1	80.6	80.8	80.5
1994	79.5	79.4	79.9	79.6	79.7	80.4	80.0	79.7	79.3	78.6	79.2	80.1	79.6
1995	77.1	77.0	77.2	78.5	78.5	79.1	78.8	79.3	79.4	79.7	80.5	81.0	78.8
1996	80.5	80.5	80.7	80.4	81.1	81.8	81.1	81.5	81.6	81.7	82.6	83.3	81.4
1997	81.8	82.0	82.6	82.7	83.2	83.8	82.7	83.4	83.6	83.4	84.0	84.5	83.1
1998	85.2	85.1	85.2	84.2	84.4	84.8	83.8	83.4	83.7	85.5	86.4	86.5	84.9
1999	84.6	85.0	85.1	84.9	84.8	85.3	86.2	86.2	86.3	87.3	87.7	88.4	86.0
2000	85.8	85.8	86.1	86.1	86.5	87.7	86.6	86.5	86.7	87.4	87.8	88.9	86.8
2001	87.5	87.5	87.6	87.9	87.6	88.0	87.7	87.2	86.4	86.4	86.1	86.3	87.2
2002	84.0	83.5	83.8	83.2	83.3	83.7	83.0	82.6	82.2	81.9	81.9	82.3	83.0
2003	81.8	81.5	81.4	81.1	81.1	81.4	80.7	80.5	79.8	80.1	80.0	80.3	80.8
Retail trade													
1990	206.7	197.7	198.4	194.5	195.4	200.5	191.4	191.2	192.3	191.5	196.0	200.5	196.3
1991	186.2	178.3	177.4	175.7	177.2	178.7	173.9	173.6	174.2	176.4	181.3	186.4	178.3
1992	174.2	170.3	170.1	169.6	170.7	172.1	169.2	169.5	170.7	175.5	180.5	186.0	173.2
1993	173.9	170.4	168.9	170.5	172.3	174.0	172.0	172.8	173.9	177.1	182.9	189.0	174.8
1994	178.7	174.6	174.1	175.3	177.1	179.7	176.3	177.2	178.6	183.0	190.3	196.8	180.1
1995	185.3	180.7	181.0	180.7	181.3	183.1	179.7	181.0	181.7	183.9	190.2	195.5	183.7
1996	186.6	182.6	181.7	181.8	184.2	186.4	183.4	184.6	185.9	188.5	197.1	204.0	187.2
1997	195.4	190.8	191.3	187.7	189.3	191.5	188.6	189.2	191.0	194.4	200.3	208.7	193.2
1998	193.6	189.3	188.7	188.5	190.0	192.6	192.1	192.4	193.1	195.8	203.9	211.6	194.3
1999	198.2	194.6	193.8	194.3	195.8	198.9	196.7	196.7	196.8	198.0	205.0	214.0	198.6
2000	202.2	198.0	198.0	198.3	198.9	201.1	199.0	199.1	200.1	204.1	212.3	219.9	202.6
2001	203.9	197.7	197.6	196.9	197.8	201.0	197.3	197.2	196.0	198.8	207.0	212.7	200.3
2002	199.5	194.2	194.8	195.1	196.5	199.8	197.8	196.9	196.5	198.1	204.3	210.9	198.7
2003	194.8	190.5	190.7	191.7	193.0	196.1	192.2	192.7	192.8	194.6	198.3	202.2	194.1

Employment by Industry: Massachusetts—*Continued*

(Numbers in thousands. Not seasonally adjusted.)

Industry	January	February	March	April	May	June	July	August	September	October	November	December	Annual Average
BOSTON—*Continued*													
Transportation and utilities													
1990	47.5	47.6	48.4	47.9	48.7	49.2	47.8	48.0	49.5	47.8	47.8	48.1	48.2
1991	46.0	45.8	45.9	46.3	47.2	47.8	45.9	45.9	47.2	47.1	47.0	47.1	46.6
1992	45.9	45.9	46.4	46.7	47.1	47.5	46.0	45.5	46.4	46.5	46.1	46.2	46.4
1993	47.0	45.8	46.0	46.8	47.4	49.1	47.1	46.7	48.6	49.0	48.7	48.8	47.6
1994	46.9	47.2	47.5	48.2	48.9	49.6	47.6	47.9	49.8	50.7	50.6	50.6	48.8
1995	49.2	49.3	49.7	49.3	50.2	50.9	48.2	48.1	49.8	50.2	50.3	50.6	49.7
1996	48.5	49.0	49.4	49.1	49.8	50.7	48.8	48.8	50.7	50.3	50.7	50.8	49.7
1997	50.8	50.7	51.4	51.1	52.0	53.0	49.0	48.2	50.9	52.7	52.5	52.7	51.3
1998	51.8	51.9	52.2	53.0	53.7	54.1	52.5	52.4	54.3	54.4	54.5	54.6	53.3
1999	53.5	54.0	54.2	55.0	55.7	56.4	54.7	54.6	56.1	56.4	56.3	56.5	55.3
2000	55.7	55.9	55.7	56.6	57.0	58.0	56.4	56.5	58.1	58.0	57.6	57.4	56.9
2001	55.6	55.9	55.7	56.0	56.3	57.0	54.7	54.4	55.6	54.5	53.2	52.2	55.1
2002	50.8	50.7	50.5	51.1	51.7	52.5	50.6	50.3	52.1	51.9	51.6	51.0	51.2
2003	49.9	49.5	49.6	50.0	50.5	50.6	48.5	47.8	49.8	49.8	49.1	48.8	49.5
Information													
1990	53.2	53.6	53.9	55.7	55.4	55.9	59.5	59.6	59.2	58.4	58.4	58.3	56.8
1991	57.1	56.8	56.9	55.8	55.9	56.0	55.5	55.1	54.5	55.9	56.4	56.8	56.1
1992	54.7	53.9	54.0	54.7	55.2	55.4	55.7	55.7	55.8	56.3	56.5	57.1	55.4
1993	55.7	56.0	56.0	57.4	58.1	58.7	59.2	61.1	60.7	61.9	62.2	62.5	59.1
1994	61.1	61.4	62.0	62.5	62.6	63.5	63.5	63.7	63.5	63.3	64.0	64.9	63.0
1995	64.6	64.4	64.9	64.6	65.0	65.5	66.1	66.5	66.3	65.3	65.7	65.8	65.4
1996	65.1	66.3	66.5	66.2	66.7	67.6	68.0	68.8	68.6	68.9	69.6	69.6	67.7
1997	69.2	69.7	70.3	68.3	69.1	69.7	69.5	69.3	68.9	68.8	69.1	69.5	69.3
1998	69.1	69.6	69.6	69.2	69.3	69.9	70.7	70.5	69.8	69.9	70.6	70.7	69.9
1999	69.2	69.7	69.7	70.3	70.7	71.6	72.5	72.7	72.6	73.2	74.0	75.0	71.8
2000	74.2	74.8	76.0	77.4	78.6	80.6	82.6	78.6	82.9	82.9	83.5	84.2	79.7
2001	83.7	83.7	83.3	82.8	81.6	81.3	80.1	79.2	77.5	75.7	75.2	74.7	79.9
2002	73.4	72.9	72.8	70.8	70.2	70.0	69.5	69.0	67.9	67.5	67.2	67.4	69.9
2003	65.6	65.4	65.3	64.5	64.2	64.8	63.9	63.8	63.0	63.2	62.9	62.8	64.1
Financial activities													
1990	151.7	151.4	152.4	145.8	145.9	146.3	144.7	144.3	142.9	142.3	141.6	141.8	145.9
1991	139.4	138.7	138.7	138.9	139.2	140.3	137.9	137.4	135.9	135.1	135.7	136.3	137.8
1992	134.0	134.9	135.7	135.8	136.9	138.0	138.3	138.2	136.6	137.9	138.0	138.9	136.9
1993	136.7	137.0	137.3	138.9	139.3	140.7	138.5	138.6	137.9	141.3	142.4	143.3	139.3
1994	142.8	143.1	144.2	145.0	145.5	147.2	147.5	147.4	146.4	145.4	145.5	147.1	145.6
1995	144.9	145.3	146.1	146.1	146.8	148.5	148.9	148.8	148.5	148.1	148.2	149.8	147.5
1996	145.7	146.9	148.0	149.7	150.6	153.9	154.1	155.1	155.0	154.0	155.4	157.0	152.1
1997	152.8	152.6	153.3	153.1	154.0	156.3	159.4	162.4	161.6	160.8	162.1	164.2	157.7
1998	162.9	163.4	164.2	165.5	165.4	167.8	168.4	169.2	166.8	169.1	170.4	170.5	167.0
1999	168.9	170.2	170.1	169.3	169.2	170.8	174.6	173.9	172.3	171.7	171.7	173.1	171.3
2000	170.7	170.1	170.5	171.1	171.1	174.4	174.7	175.4	174.2	175.1	175.5	177.3	173.3
2001	173.8	174.1	174.9	174.1	173.7	175.8	176.6	176.3	174.0	172.9	173.1	173.9	174.4
2002	173.7	172.7	172.0	169.9	170.0	171.6	172.3	171.7	169.1	169.1	168.3	168.9	170.8
2003	167.6	166.3	166.2	165.9	166.0	167.1	167.2	166.7	164.1	164.0	163.4	163.5	165.7
Professional and business services													
1990	249.5	250.1	253.2	250.1	250.1	253.5	250.7	251.6	248.5	245.4	244.4	243.4	249.2
1991	232.8	231.8	232.9	233.7	235.1	237.3	233.9	233.8	233.9	236.3	237.0	237.1	234.6
1992	233.7	234.9	237.5	239.2	241.3	244.0	244.2	245.5	246.0	246.0	246.4	246.9	242.1
1993	239.8	241.3	242.7	242.6	245.5	247.4	248.8	248.8	250.1	252.0	253.2	254.5	247.2
1994	248.0	249.6	252.3	256.9	258.3	262.3	260.5	263.1	262.9	262.6	265.1	266.4	259.0
1995	260.9	263.0	266.3	270.9	272.6	276.3	275.6	277.9	277.2	277.8	280.5	281.5	273.4
1996	272.0	273.1	276.1	281.9	284.6	288.4	290.8	293.3	292.5	292.7	296.6	298.1	286.7
1997	289.8	291.9	295.4	300.9	303.7	308.1	304.6	304.4	303.1	304.3	305.3	309.0	301.7
1998	300.5	302.3	305.4	313.0	314.1	319.1	323.0	323.6	322.1	323.2	324.8	325.9	316.4
1999	320.3	324.0	326.5	332.9	333.7	340.9	341.0	340.7	339.7	342.9	344.2	345.8	336.1
2000	337.7	340.6	344.9	350.2	351.5	360.7	365.3	366.7	366.1	365.8	367.7	369.0	357.2
2001	359.4	357.6	357.7	355.4	354.6	356.0	349.4	347.8	342.3	339.5	336.6	336.0	349.4
2002	323.8	321.0	322.0	324.7	325.0	327.4	325.3	324.3	321.6	322.4	321.8	321.0	323.4
2003	310.9	307.2	307.5	312.6	312.7	314.9	314.3	313.3	311.2	310.6	310.8	310.4	311.4
Educational and health services													
1990	297.7	302.9	306.0	306.0	304.4	303.8	298.4	297.5	301.4	308.8	311.1	311.3	304.1
1991	300.0	305.7	309.3	308.2	304.8	301.5	300.1	299.4	302.5	309.6	312.6	312.7	305.5
1992	307.4	312.3	314.6	314.2	311.1	309.7	308.6	307.0	312.9	319.0	320.6	320.5	313.2
1993	316.2	319.9	322.5	322.0	319.9	316.9	315.8	315.0	319.2	323.0	325.9	326.3	320.2
1994	317.8	324.0	327.0	327.7	325.5	323.3	320.9	319.2	325.4	328.6	330.8	332.6	325.2
1995	331.4	336.3	338.1	336.6	334.4	333.0	330.3	328.4	334.0	342.3	345.1	346.1	336.3
1996	338.7	345.7	347.6	348.2	347.1	342.1	340.0	339.0	342.8	346.8	349.1	350.3	344.8
1997	346.5	351.7	352.9	351.6	349.2	343.0	340.8	339.3	342.9	347.1	349.0	351.0	347.1
1998	344.2	348.9	351.0	350.4	351.1	346.8	343.7	341.5	345.1	351.3	347.6	353.0	347.9
1999	340.9	340.4	348.0	346.4	343.4	341.5	337.6	338.2	342.8	347.2	349.7	350.6	343.9
2000	345.7	350.4	351.2	349.1	346.3	343.4	342.7	342.5	345.7	350.6	353.8	354.5	348.0
2001	346.2	351.8	352.0	352.6	350.4	348.4	348.3	348.1	350.2	356.9	358.9	360.2	352.0
2002	355.2	359.8	362.6	362.9	360.1	356.6	355.0	354.0	358.6	362.8	367.1	367.2	360.2
2003	359.8	363.4	366.0	366.5	363.3	360.2	358.6	356.0	362.2	366.5	368.6	367.3	363.2

Employment by Industry: Massachusetts—*Continued*

(Numbers in thousands. Not seasonally adjusted.)

Industry	January	February	March	April	May	June	July	August	September	October	November	December	Annual Average
BOSTON—*Continued*													
Leisure and hospitality													
1990	133.1	133.4	136.3	139.5	144.5	149.1	147.0	146.4	144.6	140.7	137.7	136.4	140.7
1991	122.7	120.9	123.1	128.0	132.7	136.5	133.8	133.5	132.1	132.9	130.5	129.2	129.7
1992	121.5	122.2	123.9	127.3	133.0	137.2	137.0	136.0	135.2	135.3	132.3	130.8	131.0
1993	122.5	122.7	122.7	131.8	137.4	142.4	141.7	141.9	141.3	139.4	137.2	137.0	134.8
1994	128.2	129.1	131.6	137.8	143.0	148.2	148.2	148.7	145.3	144.8	143.6	142.3	140.9
1995	133.8	134.1	136.2	142.6	147.6	153.3	151.9	153.0	150.3	145.7	144.2	143.3	144.7
1996	133.6	135.7	138.2	142.6	149.0	154.9	154.2	155.3	152.4	150.6	148.8	148.4	147.0
1997	139.3	140.4	142.4	148.0	154.2	160.0	157.5	157.6	154.5	152.6	150.2	150.3	150.6
1998	140.8	142.7	144.4	150.7	156.1	161.0	161.4	161.9	158.9	156.4	154.6	154.1	153.6
1999	145.0	146.9	148.0	156.6	161.8	167.8	165.8	165.0	161.8	160.8	157.8	156.9	157.9
2000	146.9	148.3	150.4	156.4	160.7	166.8	168.3	167.5	164.3	163.2	160.7	159.6	159.4
2001	151.6	153.0	155.1	160.5	166.9	173.7	172.5	172.6	166.5	162.8	160.1	159.5	162.9
2002	150.4	151.0	155.0	162.5	169.0	174.4	174.0	174.2	169.4	167.8	165.0	164.5	164.8
2003	154.5	153.9	156.0	161.8	169.5	174.6	174.3	174.3	169.4	168.3	164.4	162.6	165.3
Other services													
1990	55.8	55.9	56.9	56.0	56.3	57.3	55.6	55.4	55.1	55.1	54.9	55.0	55.8
1991	52.2	51.9	52.0	51.9	52.2	52.6	52.2	51.9	51.3	51.3	51.4	51.9	51.9
1992	50.5	50.5	50.8	50.3	50.8	51.6	52.0	51.9	51.2	51.8	51.8	52.4	51.3
1993	51.3	51.4	51.5	52.9	53.3	54.1	54.3	54.1	53.8	53.7	54.7	55.5	53.4
1994	52.6	52.9	54.0	53.6	54.3	55.5	56.5	56.6	55.5	55.8	56.3	56.6	55.0
1995	54.1	54.1	54.8	55.0	55.7	57.0	57.6	58.2	56.7	57.0	56.9	57.7	56.2
1996	55.7	55.7	56.6	57.1	58.1	59.4	59.6	59.3	58.2	58.8	59.5	59.2	58.1
1997	57.3	57.4	58.3	58.8	59.9	61.0	61.3	61.2	59.9	59.9	60.0	60.3	59.6
1998	59.5	60.1	60.3	61.0	61.8	62.9	63.3	63.5	62.2	62.3	62.8	63.0	61.9
1999	61.0	61.6	61.9	62.5	62.8	64.3	64.9	64.7	63.7	63.7	63.9	64.3	63.3
2000	63.6	64.1	64.4	64.6	65.0	66.4	67.3	67.1	65.4	66.6	67.0	67.2	65.7
2001	65.3	65.8	66.4	66.5	67.1	68.2	68.3	68.4	66.6	67.1	67.2	67.4	67.0
2002	65.7	65.8	66.7	66.9	67.7	68.5	68.7	68.8	67.1	67.7	67.8	68.0	67.5
2003	66.3	66.2	66.9	66.8	67.2	68.0	67.4	67.8	66.7	67.1	67.1	67.5	67.1
Government													
1990	227.7	228.2	228.5	229.5	233.9	235.3	220.9	212.5	219.1	222.1	224.0	224.0	225.5
1991	221.0	221.9	222.1	220.9	220.7	222.8	211.1	206.2	214.5	216.6	217.6	218.6	217.8
1992	214.4	214.9	215.3	214.7	215.2	216.3	204.5	200.1	210.8	213.2	214.7	215.3	212.5
1993	211.8	212.9	213.3	217.2	217.7	219.3	208.6	205.1	213.3	215.7	216.7	217.9	214.1
1994	224.5	225.0	225.0	225.4	226.1	228.5	215.9	213.6	221.7	225.1	226.0	227.4	223.7
1995	224.8	226.1	226.8	227.5	227.9	230.7	221.0	218.1	226.3	229.3	230.1	231.1	226.6
1996	227.8	229.1	229.9	229.3	229.5	231.1	217.2	215.3	225.0	227.9	228.8	230.0	226.7
1997	227.2	227.5	228.2	229.3	230.4	231.6	218.3	216.0	226.9	231.3	232.4	234.1	227.8
1998	229.8	230.5	231.0	232.2	233.1	235.2	221.0	219.8	233.0	235.1	236.2	237.5	231.2
1999	234.3	236.1	236.7	237.1	238.2	239.7	224.5	222.9	236.5	241.3	241.9	242.6	236.0
2000	240.5	240.9	242.4	242.3	246.0	243.3	229.9	226.1	240.4	241.7	242.9	243.0	240.0
2001	242.9	243.5	243.3	244.1	244.7	243.3	229.7	228.0	243.0	242.6	243.4	244.5	241.1
2002	242.5	242.7	243.0	240.8	240.8	239.4	227.9	225.7	238.7	235.7	237.1	236.5	237.6
2003	234.6	234.5	234.3	234.1	234.0	234.0	222.2	216.5	228.4	230.8	230.6	230.6	230.4
Federal government													
1990	38.7	38.6	39.3	41.5	44.9	44.3	42.7	39.6	38.3	38.2	38.2	39.0	40.3
1991	38.6	38.4	38.4	38.1	38.1	38.6	38.5	38.3	37.9	37.4	37.4	38.4	38.2
1992	37.9	37.5	37.4	37.3	37.2	37.5	37.5	37.4	37.0	37.0	36.6	37.4	37.3
1993	37.3	37.2	37.1	38.4	38.4	38.6	38.6	38.5	38.3	38.0	38.0	39.1	38.1
1994	38.3	38.2	38.0	37.7	37.7	37.7	37.7	37.4	37.1	36.4	36.2	37.0	37.5
1995	36.7	36.9	36.8	36.7	36.7	37.2	37.3	37.2	36.6	36.4	36.0	36.8	36.8
1996	35.6	35.5	35.5	35.2	34.9	35.0	35.0	34.9	34.5	34.5	34.6	35.8	35.1
1997	34.6	34.4	34.3	34.5	34.4	34.7	34.5	34.6	34.1	33.6	33.6	35.1	34.4
1998	33.8	33.5	33.4	33.5	33.5	33.6	33.9	33.9	33.5	33.2	33.4	34.6	33.7
1999	33.7	34.0	34.1	33.6	33.5	33.7	34.0	34.0	33.4	34.1	34.1	34.9	33.9
2000	34.1	34.2	34.6	35.3	38.4	36.7	37.1	34.7	33.6	33.5	33.5	33.9	35.0
2001	33.2	33.0	32.9	33.0	32.9	33.4	33.8	33.6	33.1	32.8	32.8	33.3	33.2
2002	32.7	32.4	32.6	32.3	32.3	32.7	33.0	33.1	32.8	33.1	33.3	33.9	32.9
2003	33.0	32.8	32.8	32.8	32.7	32.8	33.0	32.6	32.1	32.0	31.7	31.8	32.5
State government													
1990	56.8	56.7	56.4	56.3	56.4	56.9	57.5	57.1	57.0	56.5	55.9	55.8	56.6
1991	54.6	54.7	54.8	54.1	53.8	53.9	54.6	53.9	53.4	52.8	52.8	52.3	53.8
1992	52.2	52.2	52.1	52.1	52.3	53.0	52.3	51.6	51.5	51.2	51.2	51.3	51.9
1993	51.2	51.4	51.6	51.7	52.0	52.5	52.3	51.9	51.2	50.9	50.7	50.5	51.5
1994	59.1	59.5	59.5	59.7	59.8	60.7	60.5	60.7	59.8	59.9	60.0	60.0	59.9
1995	59.9	59.9	59.9	60.6	61.0	61.9	63.0	62.9	62.1	61.3	61.3	61.1	61.2
1996	60.9	61.1	61.2	61.4	61.4	61.8	62.2	61.9	61.1	60.6	60.3	60.2	61.2
1997	60.3	60.5	61.0	61.5	62.0	62.8	62.5	62.0	61.3	62.8	62.8	62.4	61.8
1998	61.1	61.4	61.9	63.2	63.4	64.4	64.0	64.4	64.6	64.4	64.0	63.8	63.4
1999	62.6	63.0	63.5	64.6	64.9	65.5	64.9	64.8	64.6	66.0	65.6	65.0	64.6
2000	64.6	64.8	65.1	64.9	65.0	65.7	65.5	65.4	65.4	65.6	65.6	65.6	65.3
2001	66.7	67.3	67.2	67.4	67.4	67.4	67.2	67.1	67.1	66.2	66.1	66.0	66.9
2002	64.3	64.5	64.5	62.7	62.7	63.0	64.7	64.5	63.7	61.2	61.2	61.1	63.2
2003	61.8	61.9	61.9	61.0	61.1	61.5	63.8	63.7	63.2	61.6	61.4	61.5	62.0

Employment by Industry: Massachusetts—*Continued*

(Numbers in thousands. Not seasonally adjusted.)

Industry	January	February	March	April	May	June	July	August	September	October	November	December	Annual Average
BOSTON—*Continued*													
Local government													
1990	132.2	132.9	132.8	131.7	132.6	134.1	120.7	115.8	123.8	127.4	129.9	129.2	128.6
1991	127.8	128.8	128.9	128.7	128.8	130.3	118.0	114.0	123.2	126.4	127.4	127.9	125.9
1992	124.3	125.2	125.8	125.3	125.7	125.8	114.7	111.1	122.3	125.0	126.9	126.6	123.2
1993	123.3	124.3	124.6	127.1	127.3	128.2	117.7	114.7	123.8	126.8	128.0	128.3	124.5
1994	127.1	127.3	127.5	128.0	128.6	130.1	117.7	115.5	124.8	128.8	129.8	130.4	126.3
1995	128.2	129.3	130.1	130.2	130.2	131.6	120.7	118.0	127.6	131.6	132.8	133.2	128.6
1996	131.3	132.5	133.2	132.7	133.2	134.3	120.0	118.5	129.4	132.8	133.9	134.0	130.5
1997	132.3	132.6	132.9	133.3	134.0	134.1	121.3	119.4	131.5	134.9	136.0	136.6	131.6
1998	134.9	135.6	135.7	135.5	136.2	137.2	123.1	121.5	134.9	137.5	138.8	139.1	134.2
1999	138.0	139.1	139.1	138.9	139.8	140.5	125.6	124.1	138.5	141.2	142.2	142.7	137.5
2000	141.8	141.9	142.7	142.1	142.6	140.9	127.3	126.0	141.4	142.6	143.8	143.5	139.7
2001	143.0	143.2	143.2	143.7	144.4	142.5	128.7	127.3	142.8	143.6	144.5	145.2	141.0
2002	145.5	145.8	145.9	145.8	145.8	143.7	130.2	128.1	142.2	141.4	142.6	141.5	141.5
2003	139.8	139.8	139.6	140.3	140.2	139.7	125.4	120.2	133.1	137.2	137.5	137.3	135.8
LAWRENCE-HAVERHILL													
Total nonfarm													
1990	134.1	133.5	134.0	134.3	134.3	134.6	130.5	131.3	131.2	130.6	130.8	130.9	132.5
1991	129.4	128.1	128.0	128.1	128.3	129.0	125.2	126.4	126.9	126.7	127.8	127.3	127.6
1992	127.8	127.6	128.1	128.6	129.8	130.3	128.4	128.5	129.8	130.8	131.3	132.0	129.4
1993	129.6	129.9	130.0	132.3	133.5	135.1	132.1	132.1	133.3	133.2	133.6	134.8	132.5
1994	132.2	132.8	133.2	135.5	137.0	138.4	135.9	136.6	138.9	138.4	139.6	141.0	136.6
1995	137.0	137.4	138.3	141.0	141.5	143.3	139.8	140.7	142.0	146.1	146.7	148.0	141.8
1996	144.5	144.9	145.4	146.7	147.8	149.0	145.6	145.9	147.6	148.2	148.3	148.8	146.9
1997	146.5	146.4	148.2	150.2	152.0	153.6	149.9	150.2	152.3	153.1	153.1	154.5	150.8
1998	150.7	151.7	152.7	153.9	155.8	156.7	154.9	154.7	155.7	155.7	156.9	157.8	154.8
1999	155.7	155.7	157.1	160.4	160.9	162.6	160.9	160.5	162.6	163.0	163.6	164.6	160.6
2000	159.5	160.8	161.7	164.3	166.3	168.8	165.2	164.4	165.7	166.2	167.3	168.7	164.9
2001	164.3	163.8	164.2	164.8	166.0	167.3	163.2	162.4	162.8	161.8	161.3	161.6	163.6
2002	156.4	156.0	157.1	158.3	159.6	160.7	157.1	157.1	158.5	157.2	157.8	157.4	157.8
2003	153.1	152.0	152.7	153.9	155.7	156.8	153.3	152.1	154.0	154.1	154.4	154.2	153.9
Total private													
1990	116.8	115.9	116.4	116.4	116.9	118.3	115.0	115.5	115.3	113.9	113.9	113.9	115.7
1991	111.9	110.0	110.4	110.4	111.0	112.1	110.0	110.9	110.4	110.2	111.1	110.8	110.8
1992	111.2	110.3	110.8	111.2	112.7	113.6	113.5	113.8	113.8	114.3	114.7	115.3	112.9
1993	113.0	112.6	112.7	114.4	116.1	117.7	116.5	116.7	117.0	116.7	116.9	118.1	115.7
1994	115.4	115.2	115.7	117.2	118.9	120.5	119.7	120.5	121.5	121.5	122.3	123.8	119.4
1995	119.7	119.4	120.2	122.5	123.5	125.7	124.1	125.0	125.4	128.5	128.9	130.2	124.4
1996	126.8	126.6	126.8	127.9	129.4	131.1	130.0	130.4	130.6	130.7	130.5	131.0	129.3
1997	128.6	127.9	129.2	130.9	133.2	135.3	133.6	134.0	134.5	135.0	134.7	136.2	132.8
1998	132.3	132.3	133.2	134.2	136.0	137.7	137.9	137.8	137.5	137.2	137.9	138.9	136.1
1999	136.8	136.3	137.4	139.9	140.9	142.8	143.2	142.8	143.5	143.8	144.1	145.0	141.4
2000	140.3	140.8	141.3	143.7	145.5	148.4	147.3	146.6	146.3	146.9	147.7	149.0	145.3
2001	144.3	143.2	143.5	143.7	145.4	146.8	144.3	143.7	143.1	141.9	141.2	141.4	143.5
2002	135.9	135.2	136.0	137.1	138.8	140.0	139.0	139.2	138.5	137.3	137.6	137.2	137.7
2003	132.6	131.1	131.6	132.2	134.3	135.7	135.3	134.5	133.6	132.9	133.0	133.0	133.3
Goods-producing													
1990	43.7	43.4	43.5	43.8	43.9	44.3	42.5	42.9	42.7	42.6	42.3	42.1	43.1
1991	41.2	40.7	40.7	40.1	40.1	40.4	39.3	39.8	39.4	39.3	39.6	39.1	40.0
1992	38.7	38.4	38.5	38.2	38.5	38.4	38.9	38.8	39.1	39.0	39.1	39.0	38.7
1993	38.2	38.0	38.2	38.3	38.4	38.8	38.2	38.2	38.2	38.0	37.7	37.8	38.2
1994	37.2	37.1	37.2	37.7	38.3	38.6	38.2	38.7	38.8	38.8	39.0	38.9	38.2
1995	38.3	38.1	38.2	39.5	39.7	40.1	39.4	39.9	40.2	42.7	42.5	42.9	40.1
1996	41.9	41.9	41.9	41.9	42.2	42.4	42.1	42.2	42.3	42.5	41.8	41.6	42.1
1997	42.2	42.2	42.6	43.1	43.7	44.2	43.8	44.3	44.4	44.8	44.8	44.8	43.7
1998	44.2	44.1	44.1	44.3	44.4	44.8	44.5	44.3	44.3	44.4	44.3	44.2	44.3
1999	43.8	43.7	44.1	45.5	45.4	45.7	46.0	45.9	45.7	45.6	45.5	45.5	45.2
2000	44.4	44.5	44.6	44.9	45.2	45.9	45.8	46.0	44.9	45.5	45.5	45.7	45.2
2001	44.6	44.5	44.6	44.3	44.6	44.2	42.9	42.6	42.3	42.2	41.1	40.9	43.2
2002	38.3	38.0	38.2	37.9	38.3	38.0	37.7	37.5	37.5	36.9	36.7	36.3	37.6
2003	35.3	34.7	34.6	34.4	35.0	35.2	35.2	34.8	34.3	34.1	33.8	33.7	34.6
Construction and mining													
1990	4.6	4.4	4.5	4.6	4.8	4.9	4.9	4.9	4.8	4.7	4.5	4.2	4.7
1991	3.6	3.3	3.3	3.6	3.9	3.9	3.8	3.9	3.9	3.8	3.9	3.7	3.7
1992	3.0	2.8	2.9	3.3	3.6	3.7	4.0	4.1	4.1	4.2	4.1	4.0	3.7
1993	3.4	3.3	3.4	3.6	3.8	4.0	4.3	4.4	4.4	4.3	4.3	4.2	4.0
1994	3.6	3.5	3.6	4.1	4.4	4.7	4.8	4.8	4.9	4.8	4.7	4.6	4.4
1995	4.1	3.9	4.1	4.8	5.1	5.3	5.3	5.4	5.6	5.8	5.6	5.6	5.1
1996	4.6	4.7	4.8	5.0	5.4	5.6	5.6	5.5	5.5	5.6	5.4	5.2	5.2
1997	4.9	4.8	4.9	5.2	5.4	5.6	5.7	5.7	5.7	5.7	5.6	5.5	5.4
1998	5.0	4.9	5.0	5.4	5.5	5.8	5.9	5.9	5.9	6.0	5.9	6.0	5.6
1999	5.5	5.4	5.5	5.9	6.1	6.3	6.5	6.5	6.5	6.5	6.3	6.3	6.1
2000	5.7	5.6	5.7	6.1	6.3	6.5	6.7	6.8	6.8	6.7	6.7	6.6	6.4
2001	6.2	6.1	6.1	6.6	6.9	7.1	7.0	7.1	7.0	7.0	6.9	6.8	6.7
2002	6.2	6.1	6.2	6.8	7.2	7.2	7.4	7.4	7.3	7.4	7.2	6.9	6.9
2003	6.3	6.1	6.1	6.4	7.0	7.0	7.3	7.2	7.1	7.2	6.9	6.7	6.8

Employment by Industry: Massachusetts—*Continued*

(Numbers in thousands. Not seasonally adjusted.)

Industry	January	February	March	April	May	June	July	August	September	October	November	December	Annual Average
LAWRENCE-HAVERHILL *—Continued*													
Manufacturing													
1990	39.1	39.0	39.0	39.2	39.1	39.4	37.6	38.0	37.9	37.9	37.8	37.9	38.5
1991	37.6	37.4	37.4	36.5	36.2	36.5	35.5	35.9	35.5	35.5	35.7	35.4	36.3
1992	35.7	35.6	35.6	34.9	34.9	34.7	34.9	34.7	35.0	34.8	35.0	35.0	35.1
1993	34.8	34.7	34.8	34.7	34.6	34.8	33.9	33.8	33.8	33.7	33.4	33.6	34.2
1994	33.6	33.6	33.6	33.6	33.9	33.9	33.4	33.9	33.9	34.0	34.3	34.3	33.8
1995	34.2	34.2	34.1	34.7	34.6	34.8	34.1	34.5	34.6	36.9	36.9	37.3	35.1
1996	37.3	37.2	37.1	36.9	36.8	36.8	36.5	36.7	36.8	36.9	36.4	36.4	36.8
1997	37.3	37.4	37.7	37.9	38.3	38.6	38.1	38.6	38.7	39.1	39.2	39.3	38.4
1998	39.2	39.2	39.1	38.9	38.9	39.0	38.6	38.4	38.4	38.4	38.4	38.2	38.7
1999	38.3	38.3	38.6	39.6	39.3	39.4	39.5	39.4	39.2	39.1	39.2	39.2	39.1
2000	38.7	38.9	38.9	38.8	38.9	39.4	39.1	39.2	38.1	38.8	38.8	39.1	38.9
2001	38.4	38.4	38.5	37.7	37.7	37.1	35.9	35.5	35.3	35.2	34.2	34.1	36.5
2002	32.1	31.9	32.0	31.1	31.1	30.8	30.3	30.1	30.2	29.5	29.5	29.4	30.7
2003	29.0	28.6	28.5	28.0	28.0	28.2	27.9	27.6	27.2	26.9	26.9	27.0	27.8
Service-providing													
1990	90.4	90.1	90.5	90.5	90.4	90.3	88.0	88.4	88.5	88.0	88.5	88.8	89.4
1991	88.2	87.4	87.3	88.0	88.2	88.6	85.9	86.6	87.5	87.4	88.2	88.2	87.6
1992	89.1	89.2	89.6	90.4	91.3	91.9	89.5	89.7	90.7	91.8	92.2	93.0	90.7
1993	91.4	91.9	91.8	94.0	95.1	96.3	93.9	93.9	95.1	95.2	95.9	97.0	94.3
1994	95.0	95.7	96.0	97.8	98.7	99.8	97.7	97.9	100.1	99.6	100.6	102.1	98.4
1995	98.7	99.3	100.1	101.5	101.8	103.2	100.4	100.8	101.8	103.4	104.2	105.1	101.7
1996	102.6	103.0	103.5	104.8	105.6	106.6	103.5	103.7	105.3	105.7	106.5	107.2	104.8
1997	104.3	104.2	105.6	107.1	108.3	109.4	106.1	105.9	107.9	108.3	108.3	109.7	107.1
1998	106.5	107.6	108.6	109.6	111.4	111.9	110.4	110.4	111.4	111.3	112.6	113.6	110.4
1999	111.9	112.0	113.0	114.9	115.5	116.9	114.9	114.6	116.9	117.4	118.1	119.1	115.4
2000	115.1	116.3	117.1	119.4	121.1	122.9	119.4	118.4	120.8	120.7	121.8	123.0	119.7
2001	119.7	119.3	119.6	120.5	121.4	123.1	120.3	119.8	120.5	119.6	120.2	120.7	120.4
2002	118.1	118.0	118.9	120.4	121.3	122.7	119.4	119.6	121.0	120.3	121.1	121.1	120.2
2003	117.8	117.3	118.1	119.5	120.7	121.6	118.1	117.3	119.7	120.0	120.6	120.5	119.3
Trade, transportation, and utilities													
1990	25.8	25.1	25.2	24.8	24.9	25.0	24.3	24.4	24.6	24.0	24.4	24.9	24.8
1991	23.7	22.8	22.7	22.9	23.0	23.0	22.5	22.7	22.8	23.1	23.6	24.0	23.1
1992	26.0	25.6	25.5	25.3	25.5	25.9	25.6	25.8	26.1	26.3	26.8	27.6	26.0
1993	27.1	26.8	26.8	27.0	27.7	27.9	27.4	27.5	27.6	27.8	28.4	29.1	27.6
1994	27.6	27.2	27.1	26.9	27.4	27.7	26.8	27.0	27.4	27.9	28.4	29.3	27.6
1995	28.0	27.6	27.7	27.9	28.2	28.5	27.8	27.9	28.2	29.2	30.0	30.5	28.5
1996	29.4	28.7	28.3	28.6	29.0	29.3	28.7	28.9	28.9	28.9	29.6	30.1	29.0
1997	27.9	27.3	27.2	28.0	28.5	28.9	28.1	27.8	28.6	28.9	29.5	30.2	28.4
1998	28.7	28.1	28.3	28.1	28.6	28.9	28.5	28.8	29.0	29.4	30.3	31.1	29.0
1999	30.1	29.5	29.8	29.5	29.8	30.2	29.5	29.8	30.6	30.9	31.6	32.4	30.3
2000	30.2	30.0	29.9	29.9	30.4	30.8	30.1	30.1	30.3	30.9	31.9	32.6	30.6
2001	31.1	30.3	30.3	30.0	30.4	30.8	30.1	30.1	30.3	30.5	31.4	31.9	30.6
2002	30.4	29.8	29.9	30.4	30.8	30.9	30.3	30.6	30.8	30.8	31.5	32.0	30.7
2003	30.2	29.6	29.9	29.7	30.0	30.3	29.6	29.9	29.9	29.8	30.3	30.9	30.0
Wholesale trade													
1990	5.4	5.3	5.4	5.3	5.3	5.4	5.4	5.5	5.4	5.3	5.2	5.3	5.4
1991	5.1	5.0	5.0	5.1	5.1	5.1	5.1	5.1	5.1	5.1	5.0	5.0	5.1
1992	5.1	5.1	5.0	5.2	5.2	5.3	5.1	5.1	5.1	5.2	5.2	5.2	5.2
1993	5.2	5.2	5.3	5.3	5.4	5.5	5.3	5.4	5.3	5.3	5.3	5.4	5.3
1994	5.0	5.1	5.0	5.1	5.1	5.2	5.2	5.2	5.2	5.3	5.3	5.3	5.2
1995	5.3	5.2	5.2	5.4	5.5	5.5	5.5	5.5	5.6	5.6	5.6	5.7	5.5
1996	5.4	5.4	5.5	5.6	5.7	5.8	5.7	5.7	5.7	5.7	5.7	5.7	5.6
1997	5.7	5.7	5.7	5.7	5.8	5.9	5.8	5.8	5.9	5.9	5.9	5.9	5.8
1998	5.9	5.9	5.9	6.0	6.0	6.1	6.0	6.1	6.0	6.1	6.1	6.1	6.0
1999	6.1	6.0	6.1	5.8	5.8	5.9	5.8	5.7	5.7	5.7	5.7	5.8	5.8
2000	5.6	5.7	5.7	5.6	5.7	5.9	5.9	5.9	6.0	6.0	6.0	6.1	5.8
2001	6.1	6.0	6.1	5.9	5.9	6.0	6.1	6.1	6.1	5.9	5.8	5.8	6.0
2002	5.8	5.8	5.8	5.9	5.9	6.0	6.0	6.0	5.9	5.9	6.0	5.9	5.9
2003	5.9	5.8	5.7	5.6	5.6	5.6	5.6	5.6	5.5	5.5	5.5	5.5	5.6
Retail trade													
1990	17.3	16.6	16.6	16.8	16.9	16.9	16.2	16.2	16.2	16.0	16.4	16.7	16.6
1991	15.6	14.9	14.9	14.9	15.0	15.0	14.9	15.0	15.0	15.3	15.9	16.2	15.2
1992	18.2	17.8	17.8	17.4	17.6	17.8	18.0	18.2	18.3	18.4	18.9	19.6	18.2
1993	19.2	18.9	18.9	19.1	19.6	19.7	19.5	19.6	19.5	19.7	20.2	20.9	19.6
1994	19.9	19.5	19.3	19.0	19.5	19.6	19.0	19.2	19.3	19.8	20.4	21.1	19.6
1995	20.1	19.7	19.8	19.9	20.1	20.3	19.9	20.0	20.0	20.7	21.5	21.9	20.3
1996	21.3	20.5	20.1	20.1	20.4	20.7	20.6	20.8	20.5	20.5	21.2	21.7	20.7
1997	19.5	18.9	18.8	18.7	18.9	19.2	18.9	18.6	19.0	19.3	19.9	20.5	19.2
1998	19.2	18.7	18.8	18.5	18.9	19.1	19.1	19.3	19.2	19.5	20.4	21.2	19.3
1999	20.2	19.6	19.8	19.6	19.8	20.2	19.8	20.2	20.5	20.9	21.6	22.3	20.4
2000	20.3	20.0	20.0	20.0	20.3	20.6	20.3	20.3	20.2	20.6	21.5	22.2	20.5
2001	21.0	20.2	20.3	20.2	20.6	20.9	20.4	20.4	20.4	20.8	21.7	22.3	20.8
2002	20.7	20.1	20.2	20.7	20.9	21.0	20.8	21.0	20.9	20.9	21.5	22.1	20.9
2003	20.4	19.9	20.3	20.2	20.5	20.8	20.4	20.7	20.9	21.4	21.7	22.2	20.8

Employment by Industry: Massachusetts—*Continued*

(Numbers in thousands. Not seasonally adjusted.)

Industry	January	February	March	April	May	June	July	August	September	October	November	December	Annual Average
LAWRENCE-HAVERHILL —*Continued*													
Information													
1990	3.0	3.0	3.0	2.6	2.6	2.7	2.6	2.6	2.6	2.5	2.5	2.5	2.7
1991	2.9	2.9	2.9	2.9	2.9	2.9	2.8	2.8	2.8	2.8	2.8	2.8	2.9
1992	2.4	2.4	2.5	2.4	2.4	2.4	2.5	2.5	2.5	2.5	2.6	2.6	2.5
1993	2.5	2.5	2.5	2.4	2.4	2.5	2.7	2.7	2.7	2.8	2.8	2.9	2.6
1994	2.9	2.9	2.9	2.9	2.9	3.0	3.0	3.0	3.0	2.9	2.9	3.0	2.9
1995	3.1	3.1	3.2	3.1	3.1	3.3	3.3	3.4	3.4	3.6	3.6	3.7	3.3
1996	3.6	3.6	3.6	3.5	3.4	3.5	3.5	3.5	3.5	3.5	3.5	3.5	3.5
1997	3.6	3.6	3.6	3.7	3.7	3.8	3.8	3.8	3.8	3.8	3.7	3.7	3.7
1998	3.8	3.8	3.8	4.0	4.0	4.1	4.2	4.2	4.2	4.2	4.3	4.4	4.1
1999	4.4	4.4	4.4	4.4	4.4	4.5	4.6	4.7	4.7	4.7	4.8	5.0	4.6
2000	5.0	5.1	5.2	5.4	5.5	5.6	5.8	4.9	5.8	5.7	5.6	5.6	5.4
2001	5.6	5.5	5.4	5.2	5.2	5.1	5.1	4.9	4.8	4.8	4.5	4.5	5.1
2002	4.5	4.5	4.5	4.2	4.1	4.1	4.0	4.0	3.9	3.9	3.9	3.8	4.1
2003	3.8	3.7	3.7	3.6	3.6	3.6	3.7	3.5	3.5	3.5	3.6	3.6	3.6
Financial activities													
1990	6.0	6.0	6.0	5.9	5.9	5.9	5.8	5.8	5.7	5.6	5.6	5.5	5.8
1991	5.5	5.4	5.4	5.3	5.3	5.3	5.3	5.3	5.2	5.3	5.4	5.4	5.3
1992	5.1	5.1	5.1	5.1	5.2	5.2	5.2	5.2	5.1	5.2	5.1	5.2	5.2
1993	5.1	5.1	5.1	5.2	5.2	5.3	5.2	5.3	5.2	5.1	5.2	5.2	5.2
1994	5.2	5.2	5.2	5.3	5.3	5.4	5.4	5.4	5.4	5.4	5.3	5.4	5.3
1995	5.4	5.3	5.3	5.3	5.3	5.4	5.4	5.4	5.3	5.3	5.3	5.4	5.3
1996	5.2	5.2	5.2	5.2	5.2	5.4	5.5	5.5	5.4	5.4	5.5	5.5	5.4
1997	5.5	5.5	5.6	5.5	5.5	5.6	5.7	5.7	5.6	5.6	5.5	5.6	5.6
1998	5.5	5.6	5.6	5.6	5.7	5.8	5.8	5.9	5.8	5.9	5.9	6.0	5.8
1999	5.9	5.9	5.9	5.9	5.9	6.0	6.0	6.0	5.9	5.9	5.9	5.9	5.9
2000	5.8	5.8	5.8	5.8	5.8	5.9	5.8	5.7	5.6	5.8	5.8	5.8	5.8
2001	5.6	5.6	5.6	5.6	5.6	5.7	5.8	5.7	5.6	5.6	5.6	5.7	5.6
2002	5.8	5.7	5.8	5.7	5.8	5.9	6.0	6.1	6.0	5.9	6.0	6.0	5.9
2003	6.1	6.1	6.1	6.2	6.3	6.3	6.3	6.3	6.0	5.8	5.9	5.9	6.1
Professional and business services													
1990	9.0	9.1	9.1	9.7	9.6	9.8	9.6	9.5	9.5	9.2	9.2	9.1	9.4
1991	9.2	8.9	9.1	9.4	9.5	9.7	9.7	9.8	9.7	9.5	9.6	9.4	9.5
1992	9.6	9.6	9.7	9.9	9.9	10.0	10.2	10.3	10.2	10.3	10.3	10.2	10.0
1993	9.9	10.0	10.0	10.6	10.9	11.0	11.0	11.2	11.2	11.3	11.2	11.3	10.8
1994	11.4	11.6	11.8	12.4	12.4	12.4	12.8	13.0	13.1	12.9	12.9	13.1	12.5
1995	12.5	12.8	12.9	13.4	13.3	13.5	14.3	14.6	14.7	13.5	13.8	13.8	13.6
1996	13.6	13.8	14.0	15.0	15.3	15.5	15.4	15.7	16.1	16.3	16.1	16.2	15.3
1997	15.3	15.3	15.5	15.6	16.1	16.2	16.0	16.4	16.1	15.9	16.0	16.2	15.9
1998	16.1	16.2	16.4	16.4	16.8	16.9	17.4	17.4	17.3	16.9	16.9	17.0	16.8
1999	16.8	17.0	17.2	17.9	18.1	18.4	18.6	18.6	18.7	19.0	19.0	19.3	18.2
2000	19.6	19.7	19.9	20.8	21.1	21.6	21.5	21.9	22.0	21.8	21.8	22.0	21.1
2001	21.3	21.2	21.1	21.3	21.4	21.7	21.3	21.4	21.4	20.4	20.4	20.1	21.1
2002	19.0	18.8	18.9	19.9	20.0	20.1	20.3	20.4	20.2	20.5	20.4	20.1	19.9
2003	18.8	18.7	18.8	19.3	19.5	19.4	19.8	19.6	19.7	19.7	19.5	19.3	19.3
Educational and health services													
1990	15.9	16.0	16.1	15.9	15.8	15.8	15.3	15.1	15.7	16.1	16.1	16.2	15.8
1991	16.7	16.7	16.7	16.5	16.5	16.5	16.0	15.9	16.5	16.6	16.8	16.8	16.5
1992	16.7	16.7	16.9	16.8	17.0	16.8	16.5	16.3	16.6	17.2	17.3	17.3	16.8
1993	17.4	17.5	17.5	17.6	17.6	17.7	17.2	16.9	17.8	17.8	17.9	18.1	17.6
1994	18.2	18.3	18.4	18.4	18.6	18.6	18.4	18.2	19.2	19.4	19.4	19.6	18.7
1995	19.2	19.4	19.5	19.6	19.7	19.7	18.8	18.6	19.4	20.1	19.9	20.0	19.5
1996	19.8	20.0	20.0	19.7	19.7	19.6	19.3	19.0	19.6	19.9	19.9	20.2	19.7
1997	20.0	20.1	20.3	20.5	20.4	20.3	19.9	19.5	20.2	20.4	20.3	20.6	20.2
1998	20.0	20.3	20.4	20.5	20.3	20.3	20.2	19.9	20.3	20.6	20.8	20.9	20.4
1999	20.4	20.5	20.6	20.6	20.6	20.6	20.8	20.2	20.9	21.2	21.2	21.2	20.7
2000	20.3	20.6	20.6	20.9	21.0	21.0	20.6	20.3	20.8	20.8	21.0	21.3	20.8
2001	20.9	21.1	21.2	21.4	21.5	21.5	21.2	21.2	22.0	22.0	22.2	22.4	21.6
2002	22.4	22.6	22.7	22.6	22.7	22.8	22.3	22.2	22.7	22.7	22.8	22.8	22.6
2003	22.6	22.6	22.7	22.6	22.6	22.7	22.4	22.3	23.1	23.2	23.3	23.4	22.8
Leisure and hospitality													
1990	9.5	9.4	9.6	9.9	10.4	11.0	10.8	11.1	10.6	10.0	9.9	9.7	10.2
1991	8.8	8.7	9.0	9.3	9.7	10.3	10.3	10.5	10.1	9.6	9.4	9.4	9.6
1992	8.8	8.6	8.7	9.6	10.3	10.8	10.6	10.9	10.4	9.9	9.6	9.4	9.8
1993	8.9	8.8	8.7	9.4	9.9	10.5	10.6	10.7	10.3	9.8	9.6	9.6	9.7
1994	8.9	8.9	9.1	9.5	9.9	10.6	10.8	10.9	10.5	10.0	10.2	10.3	10.0
1995	9.0	8.9	9.2	9.6	10.1	11.0	10.8	10.9	10.1	10.0	9.6	9.7	9.9
1996	9.1	9.2	9.5	9.7	10.3	11.1	11.1	11.2	10.6	10.0	9.9	9.7	10.1
1997	9.8	9.7	10.1	10.2	11.0	11.9	12.0	12.1	11.5	11.3	10.7	10.8	10.9
1998	9.8	10.0	10.3	11.0	11.8	12.4	12.8	12.8	12.2	11.3	10.9	10.8	11.3
1999	11.0	10.9	10.9	11.5	12.1	12.7	13.0	13.0	12.4	12.0	11.5	11.1	11.8
2000	10.6	10.6	10.8	11.4	11.9	12.9	13.1	13.1	12.4	11.9	11.6	11.4	11.8
2001	10.6	10.5	10.7	11.2	12.0	13.0	13.1	13.0	12.1	11.7	11.3	11.1	11.7
2002	10.9	11.1	11.3	11.8	12.5	13.5	13.6	13.6	12.8	12.0	11.7	11.6	12.2
2003	11.3	11.3	11.3	11.9	12.8	13.6	13.7	13.7	12.8	12.4	12.2	11.9	12.4

Employment by Industry: Massachusetts—*Continued*

(Numbers in thousands. Not seasonally adjusted.)

Industry	January	February	March	April	May	June	July	August	September	October	November	December	Annual Average
LAWRENCE-HAVERHILL *—Continued*													
Other services													
1990	3.9	3.9	3.9	3.8	3.8	3.8	4.1	4.1	3.9	3.9	3.9	3.9	3.9
1991	3.9	3.9	3.9	4.0	4.0	4.0	4.1	4.1	3.9	4.0	3.9	3.9	4.0
1992	3.9	3.9	3.9	3.9	3.9	4.1	4.0	4.0	3.8	3.9	3.9	4.0	3.9
1993	3.9	3.9	3.9	3.9	4.0	4.0	4.2	4.2	4.0	4.1	4.1	4.1	4.0
1994	4.0	4.0	4.0	4.1	4.1	4.2	4.3	4.3	4.1	4.2	4.2	4.2	4.1
1995	4.2	4.2	4.2	4.1	4.1	4.2	4.3	4.3	4.1	4.1	4.2	4.2	4.2
1996	4.2	4.2	4.3	4.3	4.3	4.3	4.4	4.4	4.2	4.2	4.2	4.2	4.3
1997	4.3	4.2	4.3	4.3	4.3	4.4	4.3	4.4	4.3	4.3	4.2	4.3	4.3
1998	4.2	4.2	4.3	4.3	4.4	4.5	4.5	4.5	4.4	4.5	4.5	4.5	4.4
1999	4.4	4.4	4.5	4.6	4.6	4.7	4.7	4.6	4.6	4.5	4.6	4.6	4.6
2000	4.4	4.5	4.5	4.6	4.6	4.7	4.6	4.6	4.5	4.5	4.5	4.6	4.6
2001	4.6	4.5	4.6	4.7	4.7	4.8	4.8	4.8	4.6	4.7	4.7	4.8	4.7
2002	4.6	4.7	4.7	4.6	4.6	4.7	4.8	4.8	4.6	4.6	4.6	4.6	4.7
2003	4.5	4.4	4.5	4.5	4.5	4.6	4.6	4.4	4.3	4.4	4.4	4.3	4.5
Government													
1990	17.3	17.6	17.6	17.9	17.4	16.3	15.5	15.8	15.9	16.7	16.9	17.0	16.8
1991	17.5	18.1	17.6	17.7	17.3	16.9	15.2	15.5	16.5	16.5	16.7	16.5	16.8
1992	16.6	17.3	17.3	17.4	17.1	16.7	14.9	14.7	16.0	16.5	16.6	16.7	16.5
1993	16.6	17.3	17.3	17.9	17.4	17.4	15.6	15.4	16.3	16.5	16.7	16.7	16.8
1994	16.8	17.6	17.5	18.3	18.1	17.9	16.2	16.1	17.4	16.9	17.3	17.2	17.3
1995	17.3	18.0	18.1	18.5	18.0	17.6	15.7	15.7	16.6	17.6	17.8	17.8	17.4
1996	17.7	18.3	18.6	18.8	18.4	17.9	15.6	15.5	17.0	17.5	17.8	17.8	17.6
1997	17.9	18.5	19.0	19.3	18.8	18.3	16.3	16.2	17.8	18.1	18.4	18.3	18.1
1998	18.4	19.4	19.5	19.7	19.8	19.0	17.0	16.9	18.2	18.5	19.0	18.9	18.7
1999	18.9	19.4	19.7	20.5	20.0	19.8	17.7	17.7	19.1	19.2	19.5	19.6	19.3
2000	19.2	20.0	20.4	20.6	20.8	20.4	17.9	17.8	19.4	19.3	19.6	19.7	19.6
2001	20.0	20.6	20.7	21.1	20.6	20.5	18.9	18.7	19.7	19.9	20.1	20.2	20.1
2002	20.5	20.8	21.1	21.2	20.8	20.7	18.1	17.9	20.0	19.9	20.2	20.2	20.1
2003	20.5	20.9	21.1	21.7	21.4	21.1	18.0	17.6	20.4	21.2	21.4	21.2	20.5
Federal government													
1990	3.6	4.2	4.1	4.4	3.8	3.6	3.5	3.7	3.5	3.4	3.4	3.5	3.7
1991	3.6	4.2	4.1	4.3	3.8	3.6	3.5	3.7	3.5	3.5	3.5	3.3	3.7
1992	3.5	4.2	4.2	4.4	4.0	3.7	3.5	3.4	3.4	3.3	3.1	3.1	3.7
1993	3.4	3.9	4.0	4.3	3.9	3.7	3.4	3.2	3.3	3.0	2.8	2.8	3.5
1994	3.3	3.9	3.8	4.5	4.3	4.1	3.9	3.9	3.9	3.0	2.9	2.9	3.7
1995	3.2	3.8	3.9	4.2	3.6	3.5	3.2	3.1	3.3	3.0	2.9	2.9	3.4
1996	3.2	3.7	3.8	4.2	3.6	3.4	2.7	2.6	2.5	2.5	2.4	2.4	3.1
1997	2.8	3.4	3.6	3.9	3.4	3.2	2.8	2.7	2.7	2.5	2.5	2.4	3.0
1998	2.8	3.7	3.7	4.0	4.0	3.3	2.9	2.7	2.7	2.6	2.6	2.5	3.1
1999	2.7	3.1	3.2	4.0	3.4	3.4	3.0	3.0	2.9	2.6	2.6	2.6	3.0
2000	2.8	3.6	3.7	4.1	4.3	3.7	3.2	3.0	2.8	2.6	2.6	2.6	3.3
2001	2.9	3.5	3.7	4.0	3.5	3.4	3.4	3.2	3.0	2.8	2.8	2.7	3.2
2002	3.3	3.5	3.7	3.9	3.4	3.2	2.8	2.5	2.3	2.3	2.3	2.2	3.0
2003	2.7	3.2	3.3	3.5	3.1	2.9	2.5	2.4	2.1	2.3	2.3	2.2	2.7
State government													
1990	0.7	0.7	0.7	0.7	0.7	0.7	0.7	0.7	0.7	0.7	0.7	0.7	0.7
1991	0.7	0.7	0.7	0.7	0.7	0.7	0.7	0.7	0.7	0.7	0.7	0.7	0.7
1992	0.7	0.7	0.7	0.7	0.8	0.8	0.7	0.7	0.7	0.7	0.7	0.7	0.7
1993	0.7	0.8	0.8	0.8	0.8	0.8	0.8	0.7	0.7	0.7	0.7	0.7	0.8
1994	0.7	0.7	0.7	0.7	0.7	0.8	0.8	0.8	0.8	0.8	0.8	0.8	0.8
1995	0.9	0.8	0.8	0.8	0.9	0.9	0.9	0.9	0.9	0.9	0.9	0.9	0.9
1996	0.9	0.8	0.8	0.8	0.9	0.9	0.9	1.0	1.0	1.0	1.0	1.0	0.9
1997	1.1	1.1	1.2	1.2	1.2	1.2	1.2	1.2	1.2	1.3	1.3	1.2	1.2
1998	1.2	1.2	1.2	1.2	1.2	1.2	1.2	1.3	1.3	1.2	1.2	1.3	1.2
1999	1.2	1.2	1.3	1.3	1.3	1.3	1.4	1.3	1.3	1.3	1.3	1.3	1.3
2000	1.3	1.2	1.3	1.3	1.2	1.3	1.3	1.3	1.3	1.3	1.3	1.3	1.3
2001	1.3	1.3	1.3	1.3	1.3	1.3	1.8	1.8	1.7	1.8	1.7	1.7	1.5
2002	1.8	1.7	1.7	1.7	1.7	1.7	1.8	1.8	1.8	1.7	1.6	1.7	1.7
2003	1.7	1.6	1.6	1.6	1.6	1.6	1.8	1.8	1.8	1.8	1.8	1.8	1.7
Local government													
1990	13.0	12.7	12.8	12.8	12.9	12.0	11.3	11.4	11.7	12.6	12.8	12.8	12.4
1991	13.2	13.2	12.8	12.7	12.8	12.6	11.0	11.1	12.3	12.3	12.5	12.5	12.4
1992	12.4	12.4	12.4	12.3	12.3	12.2	10.7	10.6	11.9	12.5	12.8	12.9	12.1
1993	12.5	12.6	12.5	12.8	12.7	12.9	11.4	11.5	12.3	12.8	13.2	13.2	12.5
1994	12.8	13.0	13.0	13.1	13.1	13.0	11.5	11.4	12.7	13.1	13.6	13.5	12.8
1995	13.2	13.4	13.4	13.5	13.5	13.2	11.6	11.7	12.4	13.7	14.0	14.0	13.1
1996	13.6	13.8	14.0	13.8	13.9	13.6	12.0	11.9	13.5	14.0	14.4	14.4	13.6
1997	14.0	14.0	14.2	14.2	14.2	13.9	12.3	12.3	13.9	14.3	14.6	14.7	13.9
1998	14.4	14.5	14.6	14.5	14.6	14.5	12.9	12.9	14.2	14.7	15.2	15.1	14.3
1999	15.0	15.1	15.2	15.2	15.3	15.1	13.3	13.4	14.9	15.3	15.6	15.7	14.9
2000	15.1	15.2	15.4	15.2	15.3	15.4	13.4	13.5	15.3	15.4	15.7	15.8	15.1
2001	15.8	15.8	15.7	15.8	15.8	15.8	13.7	13.7	15.0	15.3	15.6	15.8	15.3
2002	15.4	15.6	15.7	15.6	15.7	15.8	13.5	13.6	15.9	15.9	16.3	16.3	15.4
2003	16.1	16.1	16.2	16.6	16.7	16.6	13.7	13.4	16.5	17.1	17.3	17.2	16.1

Employment by Industry: Massachusetts—*Continued*

(Numbers in thousands. Not seasonally adjusted.)

Industry	January	February	March	April	May	June	July	August	September	October	November	December	Annual Average
LOWELL													
Total nonfarm													
1990	109.5	108.1	108.4	108.2	108.9	109.1	106.5	106.3	109.7	107.6	107.6	107.7	108.1
1991	104.7	103.8	103.5	103.1	103.6	103.7	100.1	100.2	100.4	101.2	101.2	101.4	102.2
1992	101.8	101.6	101.7	100.9	102.3	102.0	100.0	99.5	100.8	102.2	101.5	101.5	101.3
1993	98.9	98.7	99.0	101.7	102.8	103.2	100.6	100.4	102.2	104.1	103.8	103.6	101.6
1994	101.2	101.1	101.5	102.6	103.1	104.2	101.9	102.5	104.0	105.1	104.9	105.2	103.1
1995	102.5	102.5	103.1	105.2	106.0	107.6	106.0	107.3	108.4	108.3	108.4	109.3	106.2
1996	106.0	106.9	108.0	109.5	111.0	112.3	109.2	109.3	111.7	112.8	113.4	113.3	110.3
1997	111.8	111.6	112.7	114.1	115.7	116.7	114.4	113.6	116.4	117.3	117.7	118.8	115.1
1998	114.9	115.6	116.5	118.6	120.0	120.3	117.3	117.9	119.6	121.5	121.7	122.4	118.9
1999	120.2	120.5	120.8	123.4	124.0	125.2	123.2	123.4	124.7	125.6	126.5	127.5	123.8
2000	125.2	125.7	127.0	129.1	131.0	132.0	130.6	130.7	131.2	131.8	132.8	132.4	130.0
2001	130.8	131.0	131.5	131.4	132.8	133.4	128.9	128.8	129.9	129.9	128.9	128.6	130.5
2002	126.4	125.9	125.7	128.0	128.7	129.1	123.9	123.4	125.5	125.9	125.1	125.2	126.1
2003	120.2	119.7	120.1	121.3	121.4	122.6	118.6	119.3	122.7	123.8	124.5	123.9	121.5
Total private													
1990	95.9	93.7	94.3	94.2	94.9	95.5	94.7	94.7	95.2	93.8	93.7	93.7	94.5
1991	91.2	90.1	90.0	89.7	90.0	90.2	88.3	88.5	88.1	88.1	87.9	88.2	89.2
1992	88.2	87.8	87.8	87.2	88.4	88.2	87.8	87.3	87.8	88.4	87.7	87.7	87.9
1993	85.2	84.9	85.3	88.0	89.2	89.9	88.6	88.5	89.3	90.6	90.3	90.2	88.3
1994	87.8	87.6	87.8	88.8	89.4	90.7	89.8	90.4	91.1	91.5	91.1	91.4	89.8
1995	89.0	88.4	89.0	90.8	91.4	93.5	93.1	94.5	94.9	93.8	93.9	94.9	92.3
1996	92.0	92.5	93.5	95.1	96.6	97.9	96.6	96.7	97.5	98.0	98.4	98.3	96.1
1997	96.9	96.6	97.5	98.6	100.2	101.5	101.1	100.3	101.4	101.6	102.2	103.2	100.1
1998	99.7	100.0	100.7	102.6	103.9	104.7	103.6	104.0	104.5	105.4	105.5	106.3	103.4
1999	104.8	104.7	104.7	107.1	107.7	108.9	108.7	108.8	108.9	109.1	109.9	110.9	107.9
2000	109.0	109.3	110.4	112.2	113.5	115.1	115.4	115.9	115.2	115.1	115.7	115.6	113.5
2001	114.2	113.9	114.3	114.4	115.6	116.8	114.1	114.1	113.2	112.4	111.2	110.9	113.8
2002	109.1	108.2	108.1	110.1	110.6	111.5	108.8	108.3	107.7	107.9	107.2	107.1	108.7
2003	102.8	101.7	102.4	103.6	104.3	105.3	104.0	104.9	105.3	106.2	106.7	106.1	104.4
Goods-producing													
1990	31.3	30.3	30.2	30.8	31.2	31.4	31.2	31.4	31.4	31.0	30.7	30.8	31.0
1991	29.9	29.3	29.1	30.3	30.2	30.3	30.0	30.3	30.3	30.2	30.1	29.9	30.0
1992	30.3	30.8	31.6	32.4	32.6	32.5	31.8	31.3	31.1	31.3	31.5	31.9	31.6
1993	32.0	31.7	31.8	32.9	33.3	33.3	32.6	32.6	32.7	32.7	32.7	32.5	32.6
1994	31.7	31.5	31.3	32.0	32.5	32.8	32.3	32.4	32.3	32.1	32.1	31.9	32.1
1995	31.1	30.6	30.7	31.2	31.2	32.0	32.1	32.7	32.8	31.3	31.3	31.5	31.5
1996	29.3	29.4	29.8	30.5	31.3	31.9	31.9	32.0	32.1	31.8	31.7	31.5	31.1
1997	30.8	30.6	30.7	31.2	31.7	32.2	32.1	32.3	32.4	32.5	32.8	33.1	31.9
1998	31.6	31.6	31.8	32.1	32.5	32.7	32.6	32.7	32.7	33.0	32.7	32.7	32.4
1999	32.9	32.8	32.6	32.7	32.9	33.2	33.5	33.5	33.2	33.7	33.9	34.2	33.3
2000	33.6	33.7	34.3	35.1	35.5	36.2	36.2	36.6	35.8	35.3	35.5	35.4	35.3
2001	34.9	34.7	34.5	34.7	34.7	35.0	34.2	34.1	33.5	32.9	32.1	31.9	33.9
2002	31.6	31.0	30.7	31.0	31.2	31.3	29.3	29.1	29.1	28.6	28.3	27.9	29.9
2003	27.4	26.9	27.0	27.6	27.7	27.9	27.8	28.0	28.0	28.3	28.5	28.0	27.8
Construction and mining													
1990	3.9	3.7	3.6	3.9	4.1	4.2	4.2	4.2	4.2	4.1	3.9	3.7	4.0
1991	3.0	2.8	2.8	3.4	3.5	3.7	4.0	4.1	4.0	3.9	3.9	3.8	3.6
1992	3.2	3.1	3.0	3.2	3.5	3.7	4.0	3.9	4.0	4.1	3.9	3.7	3.6
1993	3.1	3.0	3.0	3.4	3.8	4.0	4.1	4.1	4.1	4.1	4.1	4.0	3.7
1994	3.2	3.1	3.1	3.7	4.1	4.4	4.6	4.6	4.6	4.6	4.6	4.4	4.1
1995	3.6	3.5	3.6	4.2	4.4	4.7	4.7	4.8	4.8	4.9	4.8	4.7	4.4
1996	3.7	3.8	4.0	4.4	5.0	5.3	5.4	5.4	5.3	5.3	5.2	5.0	4.8
1997	4.3	4.3	4.4	4.4	4.8	5.0	5.3	5.4	5.4	5.3	5.3	5.2	4.9
1998	4.6	4.5	4.7	4.9	5.1	5.3	5.4	5.5	5.5	5.4	5.2	5.1	5.1
1999	4.8	4.7	4.7	5.3	5.5	5.6	5.9	5.9	5.8	5.9	5.8	5.7	5.5
2000	5.1	5.1	5.4	5.8	6.1	6.3	6.3	6.4	6.4	6.5	6.5	6.3	6.0
2001	5.9	5.8	5.8	6.2	6.6	7.0	7.0	7.0	6.6	6.7	6.5	6.4	6.5
2002	5.8	5.6	5.7	6.2	6.6	6.8	7.0	7.0	7.0	7.0	7.0	6.7	6.5
2003	6.1	5.9	6.0	6.6	7.0	7.2	7.3	7.3	7.3	7.3	7.2	7.0	6.9
Manufacturing													
1990	27.4	26.6	26.6	26.9	27.1	27.2	27.0	27.2	27.2	26.9	26.8	27.1	27.0
1991	26.9	26.5	26.3	26.9	26.7	26.6	26.0	26.2	26.3	26.3	26.2	26.1	26.4
1992	27.1	27.7	28.6	29.2	29.1	28.8	27.8	27.4	27.1	27.2	27.6	28.2	28.0
1993	28.9	28.7	28.8	29.5	29.5	29.3	28.5	28.5	28.6	28.6	28.6	28.5	28.8
1994	28.5	28.4	28.2	28.3	28.4	28.4	27.7	27.8	27.7	27.5	27.5	27.5	28.0
1995	27.5	27.1	27.1	27.0	26.8	27.3	27.4	27.9	28.0	26.4	26.5	26.8	27.2
1996	25.6	25.6	25.8	26.1	26.3	26.6	26.5	26.6	26.8	26.5	26.5	26.5	26.3
1997	26.5	26.3	26.3	26.8	26.9	27.2	26.8	26.9	27.0	27.2	27.5	27.9	26.9
1998	27.0	27.1	27.1	27.2	27.4	27.4	27.2	27.2	27.2	27.6	27.5	27.6	27.3
1999	28.1	28.1	27.9	27.4	27.4	27.6	27.6	27.6	27.4	27.8	28.1	28.5	27.8
2000	28.5	28.6	28.9	29.3	29.4	29.9	29.9	30.2	29.4	28.8	29.0	29.1	29.3
2001	29.0	28.9	28.7	28.5	28.1	28.0	27.2	27.1	26.9	26.2	25.6	25.5	27.5
2002	25.8	25.4	25.0	24.8	24.6	24.5	22.3	22.1	22.1	21.6	21.3	21.2	23.4
2003	21.3	21.0	21.0	21.0	20.7	20.7	20.5	20.7	20.7	21.0	21.3	21.0	20.9

Employment by Industry: Massachusetts—*Continued*

(Numbers in thousands. Not seasonally adjusted.)

Industry	January	February	March	April	May	June	July	August	September	October	November	December	Annual Average
LOWELL—*Continued*													
Service-providing													
1990	78.2	77.8	78.2	77.4	77.7	77.7	75.3	74.9	78.3	76.6	76.9	76.9	77.2
1991	74.8	74.5	74.4	72.8	73.4	73.4	70.1	69.9	70.1	71.0	71.1	71.5	72.3
1992	71.5	70.8	70.1	68.5	69.7	69.5	68.2	68.2	69.7	70.9	70.0	69.6	69.7
1993	66.9	67.0	67.2	68.8	69.5	69.9	68.0	67.8	69.5	71.4	71.1	71.1	69.0
1994	69.5	69.6	70.2	70.6	70.6	71.4	69.6	70.1	71.7	73.0	72.8	73.3	71.0
1995	71.4	71.9	72.4	74.0	74.8	75.6	73.9	74.6	75.6	77.0	77.1	77.8	74.7
1996	76.7	77.5	78.2	79.0	79.7	80.4	77.3	77.3	79.6	81.0	81.7	81.8	79.2
1997	81.0	81.0	82.0	82.9	84.0	84.5	82.3	81.3	84.0	84.8	84.9	85.7	83.2
1998	83.3	84.0	84.7	86.5	87.5	87.6	84.7	85.2	86.9	88.5	89.0	89.7	86.5
1999	87.3	87.7	88.2	90.7	91.1	92.0	89.7	89.9	91.5	91.9	92.6	93.3	90.5
2000	91.6	92.0	92.7	94.0	95.5	95.8	94.4	94.1	95.4	96.5	97.3	97.0	94.7
2001	95.9	96.3	97.0	96.7	98.1	98.4	94.7	94.7	96.4	97.0	96.8	96.7	96.6
2002	94.8	94.9	95.0	97.0	97.5	97.8	94.6	94.3	96.4	97.3	96.8	97.3	96.1
2003	92.8	92.8	93.1	93.7	93.7	94.7	90.8	91.3	94.7	95.5	96.0	95.9	93.8
Trade, transportation, and utilities													
1990	21.8	21.2	21.2	21.0	21.1	21.3	20.7	20.7	21.3	21.4	21.7	21.6	21.3
1991	21.1	20.5	20.1	19.7	19.8	19.8	19.3	19.2	19.4	19.5	19.8	19.9	19.8
1992	19.3	18.8	18.4	17.3	17.4	17.5	17.5	17.4	18.3	18.8	18.5	18.8	18.2
1993	16.9	16.7	16.9	17.5	17.5	17.6	17.8	17.8	18.1	18.6	18.7	18.9	17.8
1994	18.5	18.4	18.4	18.5	18.5	18.7	18.7	18.9	19.1	19.6	19.7	19.8	18.9
1995	19.0	18.5	18.5	19.2	19.3	19.4	19.3	19.5	19.7	20.2	20.5	20.7	19.5
1996	20.2	20.2	20.3	20.4	20.5	20.6	20.2	20.2	20.3	21.0	21.2	21.3	20.5
1997	20.9	20.9	21.0	21.4	21.5	21.5	21.1	20.1	21.3	21.9	21.8	22.0	21.3
1998	21.1	21.1	21.2	21.7	21.7	21.7	21.6	21.8	22.3	22.6	22.8	23.1	21.9
1999	22.4	22.1	22.1	22.8	22.9	23.1	22.7	22.7	23.0	23.2	23.6	23.8	22.9
2000	22.9	22.8	22.8	23.1	23.1	23.1	23.1	23.1	23.2	23.9	23.9	24.0	23.3
2001	23.6	23.4	23.4	23.6	23.8	24.1	23.4	23.4	23.4	23.6	23.6	23.5	23.6
2002	23.1	22.8	22.7	23.0	22.9	23.0	22.8	22.6	22.5	23.1	23.0	23.2	22.9
2003	22.6	22.5	23.0	23.0	23.1	23.5	22.7	23.1	23.6	23.9	24.2	24.3	23.3
Wholesale trade													
1990	4.8	4.8	4.7	4.6	4.6	4.7	4.6	4.6	4.6	4.5	4.5	4.5	4.6
1991	4.3	4.3	4.3	4.2	4.2	4.2	4.2	4.2	4.2	4.3	4.3	4.3	4.3
1992	4.4	4.3	4.3	4.1	4.1	4.1	4.0	4.1	4.0	4.0	3.8	3.8	4.1
1993	3.8	3.9	4.0	4.3	4.3	4.3	4.5	4.6	4.6	4.5	4.5	4.5	4.3
1994	4.5	4.5	4.5	4.5	4.5	4.6	4.7	4.8	4.9	4.9	4.9	4.9	4.7
1995	4.9	4.9	5.0	5.3	5.3	5.4	5.4	5.5	5.6	5.6	5.6	5.7	5.4
1996	5.6	5.7	5.7	5.7	5.8	5.9	6.0	6.0	5.9	6.1	6.2	6.1	5.9
1997	6.4	6.7	6.8	6.9	6.9	6.7	6.4	6.4	6.3	6.0	5.7	5.8	6.4
1998	5.9	6.0	6.2	6.3	6.3	6.4	6.5	6.6	6.6	6.6	6.6	6.7	6.4
1999	6.7	6.7	6.7	6.9	6.9	7.0	6.9	7.0	7.0	6.9	7.0	7.1	6.9
2000	6.8	6.8	6.8	6.9	7.0	7.1	7.2	7.3	7.3	7.4	7.4	7.5	7.1
2001	7.4	7.5	7.5	7.6	7.6	7.6	7.5	7.5	7.3	7.2	7.1	7.0	7.4
2002	7.0	6.8	6.8	6.6	6.6	6.7	6.8	6.7	6.6	6.6	6.6	6.7	6.7
2003	6.8	6.7	6.9	6.9	6.8	6.9	6.9	7.1	7.0	7.0	7.0	7.0	6.9
Retail trade													
1990	12.4	11.9	11.9	11.9	12.0	12.1	12.0	11.9	12.2	11.9	12.3	12.4	12.1
1991	11.9	11.6	11.5	11.4	11.5	11.5	11.3	11.2	11.1	11.0	11.2	11.3	11.4
1992	11.2	10.8	10.5	9.7	9.8	9.8	9.7	9.7	9.7	10.0	10.0	9.9	10.1
1993	9.4	9.2	9.2	9.2	9.2	9.3	9.3	9.2	9.3	9.5	9.6	9.8	9.4
1994	9.7	9.6	9.6	9.5	9.5	9.6	9.3	9.5	9.7	9.9	10.1	10.3	9.7
1995	9.5	9.2	9.2	9.2	9.3	9.4	9.3	9.4	9.4	9.5	9.9	10.0	9.4
1996	9.6	9.5	9.6	9.7	9.8	9.8	9.6	9.7	9.8	9.8	10.0	10.2	9.8
1997	9.7	9.6	9.7	9.8	10.0	10.2	10.3	10.1	10.4	10.6	10.9	11.1	10.2
1998	10.3	10.3	10.3	10.5	10.6	10.6	10.7	10.8	10.9	10.9	11.2	11.5	10.7
1999	10.7	10.6	10.7	10.9	11.1	11.2	11.0	11.0	11.1	11.1	11.4	11.6	11.0
2000	10.8	10.8	10.9	10.8	10.9	11.0	10.8	10.8	10.8	10.9	11.0	11.1	10.9
2001	10.7	10.5	10.7	10.7	10.9	11.1	10.9	10.9	10.9	10.8	11.0	11.1	10.9
2002	10.9	10.9	10.9	11.2	11.2	11.2	11.0	11.0	10.8	10.9	10.9	11.1	11.0
2003	10.3	10.2	10.4	10.7	10.8	10.9	10.6	10.8	10.9	11.2	11.5	11.5	10.8
Transportation and utilities													
1990	4.6	4.5	4.6	4.5	4.5	4.5	4.1	4.2	4.5	5.0	4.9	4.7	4.6
1991	4.9	4.6	4.3	4.1	4.1	4.1	3.8	3.8	4.1	4.2	4.3	4.3	4.2
1992	3.7	3.7	3.6	3.5	3.5	3.6	3.8	3.6	4.6	4.8	4.7	5.1	4.0
1993	3.7	3.6	3.7	4.0	4.0	4.0	4.0	4.0	4.2	4.6	4.6	4.6	4.1
1994	4.3	4.3	4.3	4.5	4.5	4.5	4.7	4.6	4.5	4.8	4.7	4.6	4.5
1995	4.6	4.4	4.3	4.7	4.7	4.6	4.6	4.6	4.7	5.1	5.0	5.0	4.7
1996	5.0	5.0	5.0	5.0	4.9	4.9	4.6	4.5	4.6	5.1	5.0	5.0	4.9
1997	4.8	4.6	4.5	4.7	4.6	4.6	4.4	3.6	4.6	5.3	5.2	5.1	4.7
1998	4.9	4.8	4.7	4.9	4.8	4.7	4.4	4.4	4.8	5.1	5.0	4.9	4.8
1999	5.0	4.8	4.7	5.0	4.9	4.9	4.8	4.7	4.9	5.2	5.2	5.1	4.9
2000	5.3	5.2	5.1	5.4	5.2	5.0	5.1	5.0	5.1	5.6	5.5	5.4	5.2
2001	5.5	5.4	5.2	5.3	5.3	5.4	5.0	5.0	5.2	5.6	5.5	5.4	5.3
2002	5.2	5.1	5.0	5.2	5.1	5.1	5.0	4.9	5.1	5.6	5.5	5.4	5.2
2003	5.5	5.6	5.7	5.4	5.5	5.7	5.2	5.2	5.7	5.7	5.7	5.8	5.6

Employment by Industry: Massachusetts—*Continued*

(Numbers in thousands. Not seasonally adjusted.)

Industry	January	February	March	April	May	June	July	August	September	October	November	December	Annual Average
LOWELL—*Continued*													
Information													
1990	5.9	5.8	5.8	5.8	5.6	5.6	5.7	5.8	5.8	5.4	5.6	5.6	5.7
1991	5.5	5.6	5.6	5.0	4.9	4.8	4.5	4.5	3.7	3.7	3.6	3.6	4.6
1992	4.1	4.0	3.9	3.6	3.6	3.6	3.7	3.7	3.7	3.7	3.7	3.6	3.7
1993	3.6	3.6	3.6	3.0	3.0	3.1	3.5	3.5	3.5	3.7	3.6	3.6	3.4
1994	3.6	3.6	3.6	3.5	3.4	3.4	3.4	3.4	3.4	3.4	3.4	3.4	3.5
1995	3.4	3.4	3.4	3.8	3.8	4.0	4.0	4.1	4.1	4.1	4.1	4.2	3.9
1996	4.3	4.3	4.3	4.2	4.2	4.3	4.5	4.5	4.6	4.7	4.9	5.0	4.5
1997	5.3	5.3	5.4	5.1	5.3	5.4	5.7	5.7	5.6	5.1	5.2	5.4	5.4
1998	6.2	6.2	6.2	6.4	6.5	6.5	6.5	6.6	6.7	6.6	6.7	6.9	6.5
1999	6.0	6.0	5.9	6.2	6.2	6.2	6.3	6.3	6.3	6.3	6.3	6.4	6.2
2000	6.4	6.5	6.6	6.5	6.6	6.7	6.9	6.4	6.8	6.8	6.8	6.8	6.7
2001	6.8	6.9	6.9	6.9	6.9	6.9	6.7	6.7	6.6	6.6	6.5	6.4	6.7
2002	6.8	6.8	6.7	7.2	7.1	7.1	7.2	7.1	6.9	6.9	6.9	6.9	7.0
2003	6.5	6.4	6.4	6.3	6.3	6.3	6.1	6.1	6.1	6.1	6.0	5.8	6.2
Financial activities													
1990	4.1	4.1	4.1	3.9	3.9	3.9	3.8	3.8	3.8	3.7	3.7	3.7	3.9
1991	3.7	3.7	3.7	3.5	3.5	3.5	3.4	3.4	3.4	3.4	3.3	3.3	3.5
1992	3.2	3.1	3.2	3.3	3.3	3.4	3.4	3.4	3.3	3.2	3.2	3.1	3.3
1993	3.2	3.2	3.2	3.4	3.4	3.5	3.5	3.5	3.5	3.5	3.5	3.6	3.4
1994	3.4	3.4	3.4	3.6	3.6	3.6	3.7	3.7	3.7	3.9	3.8	3.9	3.6
1995	3.8	3.8	3.8	3.8	3.8	3.9	3.9	3.9	3.9	4.0	4.0	4.1	3.9
1996	3.9	3.9	4.0	3.9	3.9	4.0	4.0	4.0	4.0	4.0	4.1	4.1	4.0
1997	3.9	3.9	3.9	3.9	3.9	4.0	3.9	3.8	3.8	3.8	3.9	3.9	3.9
1998	3.5	3.4	3.4	3.5	3.7	3.7	3.6	3.6	3.6	3.6	3.6	3.6	3.6
1999	3.6	3.6	3.6	3.7	3.7	3.8	3.7	3.7	3.7	3.8	3.8	3.9	3.7
2000	3.8	3.8	3.8	3.8	3.8	3.9	4.1	4.1	4.1	4.2	4.2	4.3	4.0
2001	4.2	4.2	4.2	4.3	4.4	4.4	4.4	4.4	4.4	4.4	4.4	4.4	4.3
2002	4.4	4.3	4.3	4.3	4.4	4.3	4.3	4.3	4.3	4.3	4.3	4.2	4.3
2003	4.3	4.3	4.2	4.2	4.3	4.3	4.3	4.3	4.3	4.3	4.3	4.2	4.3
Professional and business services													
1990	9.8	9.5	9.5	9.8	9.8	9.9	9.8	9.7	9.6	9.1	9.0	8.8	9.5
1991	8.4	8.4	8.5	8.6	8.7	8.7	8.7	8.7	8.7	8.8	8.9	8.8	8.7
1992	8.3	8.3	8.0	8.5	8.7	8.7	8.7	8.8	8.8	8.6	8.5	8.4	8.5
1993	8.0	8.1	8.2	9.1	9.5	9.6	8.7	8.8	8.8	9.3	9.2	8.7	8.8
1994	8.0	8.1	8.2	8.2	8.3	8.6	8.5	8.6	8.7	8.7	8.6	8.7	8.4
1995	8.5	8.8	9.1	9.8	10.0	10.2	10.2	10.4	10.5	10.5	10.4	10.4	9.9
1996	11.1	11.5	11.6	12.5	12.6	12.8	12.3	12.4	12.7	12.6	12.7	12.6	12.3
1997	12.4	12.2	12.6	13.1	13.5	13.7	13.9	14.1	14.1	14.0	14.2	14.2	13.5
1998	13.5	13.6	13.9	14.5	14.8	15.0	14.8	14.9	15.0	15.1	15.3	15.4	14.7
1999	15.4	15.6	15.7	16.4	16.4	16.8	16.8	16.9	17.0	16.4	16.7	16.8	16.4
2000	16.6	16.7	17.0	18.0	18.3	18.8	18.7	19.3	19.2	19.0	19.4	19.2	18.4
2001	19.2	19.1	19.3	18.9	19.2	19.4	18.7	18.8	18.9	18.6	18.5	18.4	18.9
2002	17.6	17.5	17.6	18.1	18.4	18.6	18.3	18.3	18.2	18.3	18.2	18.3	18.1
2003	16.1	15.9	16.0	16.3	16.4	16.4	16.5	16.6	16.4	16.6	16.6	16.6	16.4
Educational and health services													
1990	10.6	10.5	10.9	10.7	11.0	10.8	11.1	10.9	11.0	11.1	11.1	11.2	10.9
1991	11.0	10.9	11.2	10.9	11.1	11.1	10.7	10.7	10.9	11.0	10.9	11.2	11.0
1992	11.4	11.3	11.3	10.9	11.2	10.8	11.1	11.1	11.0	11.2	11.0	10.8	11.1
1993	10.8	10.8	10.8	10.8	10.9	10.9	10.7	10.5	10.8	11.0	11.0	11.1	10.8
1994	11.1	11.0	11.1	11.2	11.2	11.3	10.9	10.9	11.2	11.4	11.3	11.4	11.2
1995	11.4	11.4	11.5	11.3	11.3	11.5	11.3	11.3	11.5	11.5	11.6	11.7	11.4
1996	11.3	11.3	11.4	11.4	11.5	11.4	11.2	11.0	11.2	11.4	11.4	11.4	11.3
1997	11.5	11.5	11.5	11.6	11.7	11.7	11.6	11.5	11.5	11.5	11.6	11.7	11.6
1998	11.6	11.7	11.7	11.6	11.7	11.8	11.4	11.4	11.5	11.5	11.5	11.7	11.6
1999	11.7	11.6	11.6	11.7	11.8	11.8	11.7	11.7	11.7	11.8	11.9	11.9	11.7
2000	12.2	12.2	12.2	11.9	11.9	11.9	12.1	12.1	12.1	12.2	12.3	12.2	12.1
2001	12.4	12.4	12.4	12.4	12.6	12.7	12.6	12.6	12.7	12.8	12.9	13.0	12.6
2002	12.9	12.9	13.0	13.0	12.9	13.1	12.8	12.8	12.9	13.0	13.1	13.2	13.0
2003	12.8	12.7	12.7	12.8	12.8	12.8	12.5	12.8	13.0	13.1	13.2	13.4	12.9
Leisure and hospitality													
1990	7.8	7.8	8.0	7.6	7.8	8.0	7.9	7.9	7.9	7.7	7.5	7.6	7.8
1991	7.2	7.3	7.3	7.4	7.6	7.8	7.4	7.4	7.5	7.4	7.2	7.3	7.4
1992	7.3	7.3	7.2	7.2	7.5	7.6	7.5	7.5	7.5	7.5	7.3	7.1	7.4
1993	6.8	6.9	6.9	7.2	7.4	7.7	7.5	7.6	7.7	7.6	7.3	7.5	7.3
1994	7.3	7.4	7.5	7.5	7.7	8.0	8.0	8.3	8.4	8.1	7.9	7.9	7.8
1995	7.8	7.8	7.9	7.6	7.9	8.4	8.2	8.4	8.3	8.1	8.0	8.2	8.1
1996	7.9	7.9	8.0	8.2	8.5	8.8	8.4	8.5	8.6	8.5	8.3	8.3	8.3
1997	8.0	8.2	8.3	8.3	8.5	8.8	8.6	8.6	8.5	8.7	8.6	8.7	8.5
1998	8.1	8.3	8.4	8.6	8.8	9.1	8.9	8.7	8.5	8.8	8.6	8.6	8.6
1999	8.6	8.7	8.9	9.2	9.4	9.6	9.6	9.6	9.6	9.4	9.2	9.3	9.3
2000	9.2	9.2	9.4	9.5	9.8	10.0	10.1	10.1	9.8	9.6	9.5	9.5	9.6
2001	9.2	9.3	9.6	9.6	10.0	10.3	10.1	10.1	9.7	9.5	9.2	9.3	9.7
2002	8.9	9.0	9.2	9.6	9.8	10.1	10.1	10.1	9.8	9.7	9.4	9.4	9.6
2003	9.3	9.1	9.2	9.5	9.8	10.1	10.1	10.1	9.9	9.9	9.8	9.7	9.7

Employment by Industry: Massachusetts—*Continued*

(Numbers in thousands. Not seasonally adjusted.)

Industry	January	February	March	April	May	June	July	August	September	October	November	December	Annual Average
LOWELL—*Continued*													
Other services													
1990	4.6	4.5	4.6	4.6	4.5	4.6	4.5	4.5	4.4	4.4	4.4	4.4	4.5
1991	4.4	4.4	4.5	4.3	4.2	4.2	4.3	4.3	4.2	4.1	4.1	4.2	4.3
1992	4.3	4.2	4.2	4.0	4.1	4.1	4.1	4.1	4.1	4.1	4.0	4.0	4.1
1993	3.9	3.9	3.9	4.1	4.2	4.2	4.3	4.2	4.2	4.2	4.3	4.3	4.1
1994	4.2	4.2	4.3	4.3	4.2	4.3	4.3	4.2	4.3	4.3	4.3	4.4	4.3
1995	4.0	4.1	4.1	4.1	4.1	4.1	4.1	4.2	4.1	4.1	4.0	4.1	4.1
1996	4.0	4.0	4.1	4.0	4.1	4.1	4.1	4.1	4.0	4.0	4.1	4.1	4.1
1997	4.1	4.0	4.1	4.0	4.1	4.2	4.2	4.2	4.2	4.1	4.1	4.2	4.1
1998	4.1	4.1	4.1	4.2	4.2	4.2	4.2	4.3	4.2	4.2	4.3	4.3	4.2
1999	4.2	4.3	4.3	4.4	4.4	4.4	4.4	4.4	4.4	4.5	4.5	4.6	4.4
2000	4.3	4.4	4.3	4.3	4.5	4.5	4.2	4.2	4.2	4.1	4.1	4.2	4.3
2001	3.9	3.9	4.0	4.0	4.0	4.0	4.0	4.0	4.0	4.0	4.0	4.0	4.0
2002	3.8	3.9	3.9	3.9	3.9	4.0	4.0	4.0	4.0	4.0	4.0	4.0	4.0
2003	3.8	3.9	3.9	3.9	3.9	4.0	4.0	3.9	4.0	4.0	4.1	4.1	4.0
Government													
1990	13.6	14.4	14.1	14.0	14.0	13.6	11.8	11.6	14.5	13.8	13.9	14.0	13.6
1991	13.5	13.7	13.5	13.4	13.6	13.5	11.8	11.7	12.3	13.1	13.3	13.2	13.1
1992	13.6	13.8	13.9	13.7	13.9	13.8	12.2	12.2	13.0	13.8	13.8	13.8	13.5
1993	13.7	13.8	13.7	13.7	13.6	13.3	12.0	11.9	12.9	13.5	13.5	13.4	13.3
1994	13.4	13.5	13.7	13.8	13.7	13.5	12.1	12.1	12.9	13.6	13.8	13.8	13.3
1995	13.5	14.1	14.1	14.4	14.6	14.1	12.9	12.8	13.5	14.5	14.5	14.4	14.0
1996	14.0	14.4	14.5	14.4	14.4	14.4	12.6	12.6	14.2	14.8	15.0	15.0	14.2
1997	14.9	15.0	15.2	15.5	15.5	15.2	13.3	13.3	15.0	15.7	15.5	15.6	15.0
1998	15.2	15.6	15.8	16.0	16.1	15.6	13.7	13.9	15.1	16.1	16.2	16.1	15.5
1999	15.4	15.8	16.1	16.3	16.3	16.3	14.5	14.6	15.8	16.5	16.6	16.6	15.9
2000	16.2	16.4	16.6	16.9	17.5	16.9	15.2	14.8	16.0	16.7	17.1	16.8	16.4
2001	16.6	17.1	17.2	17.0	17.2	16.6	14.8	14.7	16.7	17.5	17.7	17.7	16.7
2002	17.3	17.7	17.6	17.9	18.1	17.6	15.1	15.1	17.8	18.0	17.9	18.1	17.4
2003	17.4	18.0	17.7	17.7	17.1	17.3	14.6	14.4	17.4	17.6	17.8	17.8	17.1
Federal government													
2001	1.2	1.2	1.2	1.2	1.2	1.2	1.2	1.2	1.2	1.2	1.2	1.2	1.2
2002	1.2	1.1	1.1	1.2	1.3	1.4	1.4	1.4	1.3	1.4	1.3	1.4	1.3
2003	1.4	1.4	1.4	1.4	1.4	1.4	1.4	1.4	1.3	1.4	1.4	1.3	1.4
State government													
1990	3.1	3.1	3.1	3.1	3.0	2.9	2.8	2.7	2.8	3.0	3.0	3.0	3.0
1991	3.0	3.0	3.0	3.0	3.0	2.9	2.8	2.7	2.8	3.0	3.0	3.0	2.9
1992	3.1	3.1	3.1	3.1	3.1	3.0	2.9	2.9	3.0	3.2	3.2	3.1	3.1
1993	3.1	3.2	3.2	3.2	3.0	2.8	2.7	2.7	2.6	2.8	2.8	2.7	2.9
1994	2.7	2.8	3.0	3.0	2.8	2.6	2.5	2.6	2.5	2.7	2.9	2.9	2.8
1995	2.5	2.9	2.9	2.9	2.9	2.7	2.6	2.6	2.5	2.8	2.8	2.8	2.7
1996	2.5	2.8	2.8	2.8	2.8	2.8	2.5	2.4	2.5	2.8	2.8	2.8	2.7
1997	2.5	2.6	2.8	2.9	2.9	2.5	2.2	2.3	2.4	2.9	3.6	3.6	2.8
1998	3.2	3.3	3.5	3.5	3.6	3.0	2.9	3.0	3.0	3.5	3.5	3.5	3.3
1999	3.1	3.3	3.5	3.5	3.5	3.4	3.0	3.1	3.1	3.5	3.6	3.6	3.4
2000	3.1	3.3	3.5	3.5	3.5	3.1	3.1	3.1	3.1	3.6	3.7	3.7	3.4
2001	3.3	3.7	3.9	3.7	3.7	3.2	3.5	3.6	3.5	4.1	4.1	4.1	3.7
2002	3.6	4.1	3.9	4.0	4.1	3.5	3.8	3.9	4.0	4.2	4.2	4.2	4.0
2003	3.6	4.2	3.9	3.8	3.3	3.4	3.6	3.6	3.8	3.7	3.7	3.7	3.7
Local government													
1990	9.6	10.4	10.1	10.0	10.0	9.7	8.1	8.0	10.8	9.9	10.0	10.1	9.7
1991	9.6	9.8	9.6	9.5	9.7	9.7	8.1	8.1	8.6	9.2	9.4	9.3	9.2
1992	9.6	9.8	9.9	9.7	9.9	9.9	8.4	8.4	9.2	9.8	9.8	9.8	9.5
1993	9.7	9.8	9.7	9.7	9.8	9.8	8.4	8.4	9.5	9.9	9.9	9.9	9.5
1994	9.9	9.9	9.9	10.0	10.1	10.1	8.8	8.7	9.6	10.1	10.2	10.2	9.8
1995	10.3	10.4	10.4	10.8	10.9	10.6	9.5	9.4	10.2	10.9	11.0	10.9	10.4
1996	10.8	10.9	11.0	10.9	10.9	10.8	9.3	9.4	10.9	11.3	11.5	11.5	10.8
1997	11.3	11.3	11.3	11.5	11.5	11.6	10.0	9.9	11.4	11.7	10.9	11.0	11.1
1998	11.0	11.1	11.1	11.3	11.3	11.4	9.6	9.7	10.9	11.4	11.5	11.4	11.0
1999	11.1	11.2	11.3	11.5	11.5	11.6	10.2	10.2	11.5	11.8	11.8	11.8	11.3
2000	11.9	11.9	11.9	12.0	12.1	12.2	10.6	10.5	11.7	11.9	12.2	12.0	11.7
2001	12.1	12.2	12.1	12.1	12.3	12.2	10.1	9.9	12.0	12.2	12.4	12.4	11.8
2002	12.5	12.5	12.6	12.7	12.7	12.7	9.9	9.8	12.5	12.4	12.4	12.5	12.1
2003	12.4	12.4	12.4	12.5	12.4	12.5	9.6	9.4	12.3	12.5	12.7	12.8	12.0
NEW BEDFORD													
Total nonfarm													
1990	64.0	63.8	63.7	63.6	64.8	65.8	64.5	64.9	64.2	63.5	63.5	63.1	64.1
1991	60.6	59.8	59.7	59.5	60.2	61.3	59.1	60.3	60.6	59.9	59.9	60.5	60.1
1992	58.4	58.5	58.6	59.0	59.7	60.2	56.9	56.8	60.0	60.1	60.0	60.1	59.0
1993	58.5	58.6	58.8	60.0	61.1	61.6	60.3	60.8	61.6	61.4	62.0	62.0	60.5
1994	60.5	60.4	60.8	61.4	61.9	62.6	60.9	61.4	62.3	62.4	62.5	63.3	61.7
1995	60.8	60.6	60.8	61.3	61.8	63.2	61.7	62.5	63.0	62.9	62.9	63.4	62.0
1996	60.5	60.8	60.5	61.1	62.2	62.7	61.4	61.9	62.1	62.6	62.7	63.1	61.8
1997	62.1	61.6	62.5	62.9	63.4	64.4	62.3	63.0	64.1	64.2	64.5	64.8	63.3
1998	63.2	62.9	63.2	64.5	65.3	65.9	64.4	64.0	64.7	64.5	64.8	64.9	64.3
1999	63.0	63.2	63.8	64.6	65.2	66.2	65.0	65.4	66.0	66.2	66.4	66.7	65.1
2000	64.6	64.2	65.2	66.3	67.4	68.1	66.4	66.2	66.7	67.0	66.9	66.7	66.3
2001	65.1	65.0	65.0	66.3	66.8	67.7	65.2	65.1	65.9	65.8	66.0	65.8	65.8
2002	64.1	64.0	64.4	65.4	66.6	67.2	65.8	64.9	66.0	65.7	65.6	65.4	65.4
2003	63.6	63.0	63.2	64.3	65.0	65.6	64.7	64.9	65.6	65.0	65.2	65.0	64.6

Employment by Industry: Massachusetts—*Continued*

(Numbers in thousands. Not seasonally adjusted.)

Industry	January	February	March	April	May	June	July	August	September	October	November	December	Annual Average
NEW BEDFORD—*Continued*													
Total private													
1990	54.3	54.1	53.9	53.7	54.8	55.8	55.1	55.7	54.8	53.9	53.7	53.3	54.4
1991	51.0	50.1	49.9	49.7	50.3	51.4	49.8	50.9	51.1	50.4	50.4	50.9	50.4
1992	49.2	49.2	49.2	49.7	50.3	50.8	50.4	50.6	50.9	50.8	50.6	50.5	50.1
1993	49.3	49.3	49.4	50.6	51.5	52.2	51.4	52.1	52.3	51.9	52.5	52.4	51.2
1994	50.8	50.6	51.0	51.5	51.9	52.8	51.8	52.4	52.8	52.7	52.7	53.5	52.0
1995	51.2	50.9	51.1	51.5	52.1	53.4	52.7	53.6	53.5	53.1	53.0	53.5	52.4
1996	50.7	50.9	50.5	51.2	52.2	52.9	52.3	53.0	52.6	52.7	52.8	53.1	52.0
1997	52.2	51.8	52.6	52.9	53.5	54.4	53.0	53.9	54.4	54.3	54.5	54.8	53.5
1998	53.3	53.0	53.3	54.6	55.3	55.9	55.0	54.8	54.9	54.5	54.7	54.7	54.5
1999	53.0	53.1	53.7	54.5	55.1	56.0	55.4	56.1	56.0	56.1	56.2	56.4	55.1
2000	54.4	53.8	54.7	55.8	56.2	57.2	56.5	56.6	56.5	56.5	56.3	56.1	55.8
2001	54.5	54.4	54.4	55.5	56.0	56.7	55.4	55.4	55.3	55.0	55.2	55.0	55.2
2002	53.3	53.1	53.6	54.5	55.7	56.3	55.9	55.0	55.5	55.6	55.4	55.3	54.9
2003	53.6	53.0	53.3	54.3	55.2	55.7	55.1	55.3	55.3	54.9	55.0	54.9	54.6
Goods-producing													
1990	17.3	17.2	17.1	16.7	17.0	17.2	17.1	17.5	17.2	16.8	16.8	16.5	17.0
1991	16.4	16.1	15.8	16.1	16.5	16.8	16.1	16.6	16.9	16.7	16.8	16.7	16.4
1992	15.9	16.1	16.2	16.2	16.4	16.7	16.3	16.5	16.6	16.6	16.5	16.4	16.3
1993	15.9	16.1	16.1	16.6	16.8	17.1	16.6	17.0	17.1	17.2	17.2	17.1	16.7
1994	16.4	16.3	16.4	16.6	16.8	17.0	16.7	17.0	17.1	16.9	16.7	16.5	16.7
1995	15.6	15.5	15.6	15.6	15.7	16.3	15.6	15.9	16.1	16.1	16.1	16.0	15.8
1996	15.3	15.3	14.9	15.2	15.5	15.6	15.0	15.6	15.6	15.6	15.7	15.7	15.4
1997	15.2	15.1	15.4	15.3	15.5	15.7	15.0	15.1	15.2	15.5	15.9	16.0	15.4
1998	15.4	15.2	15.2	15.8	16.0	16.0	16.1	16.1	16.2	15.9	16.0	15.9	15.8
1999	15.6	15.4	15.4	15.9	16.0	16.2	16.1	16.3	16.3	16.3	16.3	16.2	16.0
2000	15.5	15.2	15.5	16.1	16.0	16.3	15.9	15.9	15.7	15.7	15.6	15.3	15.7
2001	15.5	15.5	15.2	15.6	15.6	15.7	15.0	15.2	15.1	15.0	14.8	14.5	15.2
2002	14.0	14.0	14.1	14.3	14.8	15.0	14.6	14.2	14.6	14.5	14.5	14.3	14.4
2003	13.8	13.6	13.7	13.9	14.2	14.3	14.0	14.2	14.2	14.3	14.3	14.2	14.1
Construction and mining													
1990	2.1	2.1	2.2	2.3	2.5	2.6	2.6	2.5	2.4	2.2	2.1	1.9	2.2
1991	1.5	1.5	1.5	1.7	1.9	2.0	2.0	1.9	2.0	2.1	2.0	1.8	1.8
1992	1.5	1.4	1.5	1.7	1.9	2.0	2.0	2.0	2.0	2.0	1.9	1.9	1.8
1993	1.4	1.4	1.4	1.6	1.8	2.0	2.1	2.2	2.2	2.3	2.3	2.1	1.9
1994	1.6	1.5	1.6	1.9	2.1	2.1	2.3	2.3	2.3	2.2	2.1	2.0	2.0
1995	1.6	1.5	1.6	2.0	2.1	2.3	2.3	2.3	2.3	2.3	2.2	2.1	2.0
1996	1.5	1.6	1.6	2.0	2.2	2.2	2.3	2.4	2.3	2.4	2.3	2.2	2.0
1997	1.9	1.9	2.0	2.0	2.2	2.2	2.4	2.5	2.4	2.4	2.3	2.3	2.2
1998	2.2	2.1	2.2	2.4	2.6	2.6	2.7	2.7	2.7	2.6	2.6	2.5	2.4
1999	2.2	2.2	2.3	2.6	2.7	2.8	2.8	2.9	2.9	2.9	2.9	2.8	2.6
2000	2.5	2.4	2.5	2.9	3.0	3.1	3.1	3.1	3.1	3.1	3.1	2.9	2.9
2001	2.6	2.5	2.5	2.8	2.9	3.0	3.0	3.1	3.1	3.1	3.1	2.9	2.9
2002	2.6	2.6	2.8	3.0	3.3	3.4	3.5	3.5	3.5	3.4	3.4	3.2	3.2
2003	2.8	2.7	2.7	3.1	3.4	3.5	3.4	3.5	3.5	3.5	3.4	3.3	3.2
Manufacturing													
1990	15.2	15.1	14.9	14.4	14.5	14.6	14.5	15.0	14.8	14.6	14.7	14.6	14.7
1991	14.9	14.6	14.3	14.4	14.6	14.8	14.1	14.7	14.9	14.6	14.8	14.9	14.6
1992	14.4	14.7	14.7	14.5	14.5	14.7	14.3	14.5	14.6	14.6	14.6	14.5	14.5
1993	14.5	14.7	14.7	15.0	15.0	15.1	14.5	14.8	14.9	14.9	14.9	15.0	14.8
1994	14.8	14.8	14.8	14.7	14.7	14.9	14.4	14.7	14.8	14.7	14.6	14.5	14.7
1995	14.0	14.0	14.0	13.6	13.6	14.0	13.3	13.6	13.8	13.8	13.9	13.9	13.7
1996	13.8	13.7	13.3	13.2	13.3	13.4	12.7	13.2	13.3	13.2	13.4	13.5	13.3
1997	13.3	13.2	13.4	13.3	13.3	13.5	12.6	12.6	12.8	13.1	13.6	13.7	13.2
1998	13.2	13.1	13.0	13.4	13.4	13.4	13.4	13.4	13.5	13.3	13.4	13.4	13.3
1999	13.4	13.2	13.1	13.3	13.3	13.4	13.3	13.4	13.4	13.4	13.4	13.4	13.3
2000	13.0	12.8	13.0	13.2	13.0	13.2	12.8	12.8	12.6	12.6	12.5	12.4	12.8
2001	12.9	13.0	12.7	12.8	12.7	12.7	12.0	12.1	12.0	11.9	11.7	11.6	12.3
2002	11.4	11.4	11.3	11.3	11.5	11.6	11.1	10.7	11.1	11.1	11.1	11.1	11.2
2003	11.0	10.9	11.0	10.8	10.8	10.8	10.6	10.7	10.7	10.8	10.9	10.9	10.8
Service-providing													
1990	46.7	46.6	46.6	46.9	47.8	48.6	47.4	47.4	47.0	46.7	46.7	46.6	47.0
1991	44.2	43.7	43.9	43.4	43.7	44.5	43.0	43.7	43.7	43.2	43.1	43.8	43.6
1992	42.5	42.4	42.4	42.8	43.3	43.5	40.6	40.3	43.4	43.5	43.5	43.7	42.6
1993	42.6	42.5	42.7	43.4	44.3	44.5	43.7	43.8	44.5	44.2	44.8	44.9	43.8
1994	44.1	44.1	44.4	44.8	45.1	45.6	44.2	44.4	45.2	45.5	45.8	46.8	45.0
1995	45.2	45.1	45.2	45.7	46.1	46.9	46.1	46.6	46.9	46.8	46.8	47.4	46.2
1996	45.2	45.5	45.6	45.9	46.7	47.1	46.4	46.3	46.5	47.0	47.0	47.4	46.3
1997	46.9	46.5	47.1	47.6	47.9	48.7	47.3	47.9	48.9	48.7	48.6	48.8	47.9
1998	47.8	47.7	48.0	48.7	49.3	49.9	48.3	47.9	48.5	48.6	48.8	49.0	48.5
1999	47.4	47.8	48.4	48.7	49.2	50.0	48.9	49.1	49.7	49.9	50.1	50.5	49.1
2000	49.1	49.0	49.7	50.2	51.4	51.8	50.5	50.3	51.0	51.3	51.3	51.4	50.5
2001	49.6	49.5	49.8	50.7	51.2	52.0	50.2	49.9	50.8	50.8	51.2	51.3	50.6
2002	50.1	50.0	50.3	51.1	51.8	52.2	51.2	50.7	51.4	51.2	51.1	51.1	51.0
2003	49.8	49.4	49.5	50.4	50.8	51.3	50.7	50.7	51.4	50.7	50.9	50.8	50.5

Employment by Industry: Massachusetts—*Continued*

(Numbers in thousands. Not seasonally adjusted.)

Industry	January	February	March	April	May	June	July	August	September	October	November	December	Annual Average
NEW BEDFORD—*Continued*													
Trade, transportation, and utilities													
1990	13.2	13.1	13.0	12.9	13.2	13.7	13.5	13.7	13.5	13.2	13.3	13.4	13.3
1991	12.4	12.1	12.1	11.9	11.9	12.2	11.8	12.1	12.2	12.0	12.0	12.4	12.0
1992	11.6	11.4	11.4	11.5	11.6	11.6	11.5	11.6	11.8	11.9	12.0	12.1	11.6
1993	11.2	11.1	11.1	11.0	11.4	11.5	11.1	11.2	11.3	11.2	11.5	11.6	11.2
1994	10.9	10.8	10.8	11.1	11.0	11.2	10.9	11.2	11.3	11.3	11.6	11.9	11.1
1995	11.2	11.0	11.0	10.9	11.0	11.4	11.4	11.7	11.6	11.8	12.0	12.4	11.4
1996	11.6	11.4	11.5	11.7	11.8	12.2	12.1	12.2	12.1	12.3	12.4	12.6	11.9
1997	12.1	11.9	12.0	12.3	12.5	12.6	12.4	12.6	12.8	12.7	12.7	12.9	12.4
1998	12.5	12.3	12.3	12.2	12.4	12.6	12.3	12.3	12.4	12.5	12.6	12.7	12.4
1999	12.1	12.2	12.4	12.3	12.4	12.5	12.3	12.7	12.8	12.8	13.1	13.5	12.5
2000	12.4	12.0	12.2	12.6	12.9	13.0	12.6	12.8	13.1	13.4	13.6	13.8	12.8
2001	13.0	12.7	12.9	13.3	13.2	13.3	13.1	13.0	13.1	13.2	13.5	13.5	13.2
2002	13.0	12.7	12.7	12.9	13.0	13.2	13.1	12.8	12.9	13.1	13.2	13.3	13.0
2003	12.5	12.3	12.3	12.5	12.7	12.8	12.6	12.5	12.6	12.5	12.7	13.0	12.6
Wholesale trade													
1990	3.0	3.0	3.0	3.0	3.1	3.1	3.1	3.1	3.0	3.0	3.0	3.0	3.0
1991	2.8	2.8	2.8	2.7	2.7	2.8	2.7	2.8	2.8	2.7	2.7	2.7	2.7
1992	2.5	2.5	2.5	2.5	2.6	2.6	2.6	2.6	2.6	2.6	2.6	2.5	2.5
1993	2.4	2.4	2.5	2.4	2.5	2.5	2.5	2.6	2.5	2.5	2.5	2.5	2.4
1994	2.3	2.3	2.3	2.4	2.4	2.5	2.4	2.5	2.4	2.3	2.3	2.4	2.3
1995	2.3	2.3	2.3	2.4	2.4	2.5	2.6	2.7	2.7	2.7	2.7	2.7	2.5
1996	2.6	2.6	2.6	2.6	2.6	2.7	2.7	2.7	2.6	2.6	2.6	2.6	2.6
1997	2.6	2.6	2.6	2.7	2.7	2.8	2.8	2.8	2.8	2.8	2.7	2.7	2.7
1998	2.6	2.6	2.6	2.6	2.6	2.7	2.6	2.6	2.6	2.6	2.6	2.6	2.6
1999	2.6	2.7	2.8	2.7	2.8	2.8	2.8	2.8	2.8	2.8	2.7	2.8	2.7
2000	2.6	2.5	2.6	2.8	2.9	2.9	2.9	2.9	3.0	3.0	3.0	3.0	2.8
2001	2.9	2.9	2.9	3.1	3.0	3.1	3.1	3.0	3.0	3.1	3.1	3.0	3.0
2002	2.8	2.8	2.8	2.8	2.9	3.0	3.0	2.9	2.9	2.9	2.9	2.9	2.9
2003	2.7	2.7	2.7	2.7	2.7	2.8	2.8	2.7	2.7	2.7	2.7	2.7	2.7
Retail trade													
1990	8.3	8.2	8.1	8.1	8.3	8.7	8.6	8.7	8.5	8.4	8.5	8.6	8.4
1991	7.9	7.6	7.6	7.6	7.6	7.7	7.6	7.7	7.7	7.7	7.7	8.0	7.7
1992	7.4	7.3	7.3	7.5	7.5	7.5	7.4	7.6	7.7	7.8	7.9	8.0	7.5
1993	7.5	7.4	7.3	7.3	7.5	7.6	7.3	7.3	7.4	7.3	7.5	7.6	7.4
1994	7.2	7.1	7.1	7.2	7.1	7.2	7.2	7.4	7.5	7.5	7.8	8.0	7.3
1995	7.6	7.4	7.4	7.1	7.2	7.4	7.5	7.6	7.5	7.5	7.8	8.1	7.5
1996	7.6	7.5	7.5	7.8	7.9	8.1	8.1	8.2	8.1	8.2	8.4	8.6	8.0
1997	8.1	7.9	8.0	8.1	8.3	8.3	8.3	8.5	8.5	8.4	8.6	8.8	8.3
1998	8.5	8.3	8.3	8.2	8.3	8.4	8.4	8.4	8.4	8.5	8.7	8.8	8.4
1999	8.2	8.2	8.3	8.3	8.3	8.4	8.3	8.6	8.6	8.6	9.1	9.3	8.5
2000	8.6	8.3	8.4	8.6	8.7	8.8	8.5	8.6	8.8	9.1	9.3	9.5	8.7
2001	8.9	8.6	8.8	9.0	9.0	9.0	8.9	8.9	8.9	9.0	9.3	9.4	9.0
2002	8.9	8.7	8.7	8.8	8.8	8.9	8.9	8.8	8.8	8.9	9.1	9.2	8.9
2003	8.6	8.4	8.4	8.5	8.7	8.7	8.6	8.6	8.6	8.6	8.8	9.1	8.6
Transportation and utilities													
1990	1.9	1.9	1.9	1.8	1.8	1.9	1.8	1.9	2.0	1.8	1.8	1.8	1.8
1991	1.7	1.7	1.7	1.6	1.6	1.7	1.5	1.6	1.7	1.6	1.6	1.7	1.6
1992	1.7	1.6	1.6	1.5	1.5	1.5	1.5	1.4	1.5	1.5	1.5	1.6	1.5
1993	1.3	1.3	1.3	1.3	1.4	1.4	1.3	1.3	1.4	1.4	1.5	1.5	1.3
1994	1.4	1.4	1.4	1.5	1.5	1.5	1.3	1.3	1.4	1.5	1.5	1.5	1.4
1995	1.3	1.3	1.3	1.4	1.4	1.5	1.3	1.4	1.4	1.6	1.5	1.6	1.4
1996	1.4	1.3	1.4	1.3	1.3	1.4	1.3	1.3	1.4	1.5	1.4	1.4	1.3
1997	1.4	1.4	1.4	1.5	1.5	1.5	1.3	1.3	1.5	1.5	1.4	1.4	1.4
1998	1.4	1.4	1.4	1.4	1.5	1.5	1.3	1.3	1.4	1.4	1.3	1.3	1.3
1999	1.3	1.3	1.3	1.3	1.3	1.3	1.2	1.3	1.4	1.4	1.3	1.4	1.3
2000	1.2	1.2	1.2	1.2	1.3	1.3	1.2	1.3	1.3	1.3	1.3	1.3	1.2
2001	1.2	1.2	1.2	1.2	1.2	1.2	1.1	1.1	1.2	1.1	1.1	1.1	1.2
2002	1.3	1.2	1.2	1.3	1.3	1.3	1.2	1.1	1.2	1.3	1.2	1.2	1.2
2003	1.2	1.2	1.2	1.3	1.3	1.3	1.2	1.2	1.3	1.2	1.2	1.2	1.2
Information													
1990	2.2	2.2	2.2	2.1	2.2	2.2	2.1	2.1	2.1	2.1	2.1	2.1	2.1
1991	2.0	2.0	2.0	1.9	1.9	1.9	1.8	1.8	1.8	1.8	1.8	1.8	1.8
1992	1.6	1.6	1.6	1.7	1.7	1.6	1.6	1.6	1.6	1.6	1.7	1.6	1.6
1993	1.6	1.6	1.6	1.6	1.6	1.6	1.7	1.7	1.7	1.7	1.7	1.6	1.6
1994	1.7	1.7	1.7	1.6	1.6	1.7	1.6	1.6	1.6	1.6	1.6	1.6	1.6
1995	1.6	1.6	1.6	1.7	1.7	1.7	1.7	1.7	1.7	1.7	1.6	1.6	1.6
1996	1.6	1.6	1.6	1.5	1.5	1.5	1.5	1.5	1.5	1.5	1.5	1.5	1.5
1997	1.5	1.5	1.5	1.5	1.5	1.5	1.5	1.5	1.6	1.6	1.7	1.7	1.5
1998	1.8	1.8	1.8	1.7	1.7	1.7	1.7	1.7	1.6	1.6	1.6	1.6	1.6
1999	1.7	1.7	1.7	1.6	1.6	1.7	1.7	1.8	1.8	1.7	1.7	1.6	1.6
2000	1.6	1.6	1.6	1.5	1.5	1.5	1.5	1.4	1.5	1.5	1.5	1.5	1.5
2001	1.4	1.4	1.4	1.4	1.4	1.4	1.3	1.3	1.3	1.3	1.3	1.3	1.4
2002	1.3	1.3	1.2	1.2	1.3	1.2	1.2	1.2	1.2	1.2	1.2	1.2	1.2
2003	1.2	1.2	1.2	1.2	1.2	1.2	1.1	1.2	1.1	1.1	1.1	1.1	1.2

Employment by Industry: Massachusetts—*Continued*

(Numbers in thousands. Not seasonally adjusted.)

Industry	January	February	March	April	May	June	July	August	September	October	November	December	Annual Average
NEW BEDFORD—*Continued*													
Financial activities													
1990	3.0	3.0	3.0	2.8	2.9	2.8	2.9	2.8	2.7	2.7	2.6	2.5	2.8
1991	2.6	2.4	2.4	2.1	2.1	2.2	2.1	2.2	2.2	2.1	2.1	2.1	2.2
1992	2.0	2.0	2.0	2.0	2.0	2.0	1.9	1.9	1.9	1.9	1.9	1.9	1.9
1993	1.9	1.9	1.9	1.9	1.9	1.9	1.9	1.9	1.9	1.9	1.9	1.9	1.9
1994	1.9	1.9	1.9	1.8	1.8	1.9	1.8	1.8	1.8	1.8	1.8	1.8	1.8
1995	1.9	1.9	1.9	1.9	1.9	1.9	1.9	1.9	1.9	1.8	1.8	1.9	1.8
1996	1.8	1.8	1.8	1.9	1.9	1.9	1.9	2.0	1.9	1.8	1.8	1.8	1.8
1997	1.8	1.8	1.8	1.8	1.8	1.8	1.8	1.8	1.8	1.7	1.7	1.7	1.7
1998	1.8	1.7	1.7	1.8	1.9	1.9	1.9	1.9	1.9	1.9	1.9	1.9	1.8
1999	1.9	1.9	1.9	1.9	1.9	2.0	2.0	2.0	1.9	1.9	1.9	2.0	1.9
2000	1.9	1.9	1.9	1.9	1.9	2.0	1.9	1.9	1.8	1.8	1.8	1.8	1.8
2001	1.8	1.8	1.8	1.8	1.9	1.9	1.9	1.9	1.9	1.9	1.9	1.9	1.9
2002	1.8	1.8	1.9	1.9	1.9	2.0	2.0	2.0	1.9	1.9	1.9	2.0	1.9
2003	2.0	2.0	2.0	2.0	2.0	2.1	2.1	2.1	2.0	2.0	2.0	2.0	2.0
Professional and business services													
1990	3.0	3.0	3.0	3.2	3.2	3.3	3.1	3.0	3.0	2.9	2.9	2.7	3.0
1991	2.5	2.4	2.4	2.6	2.5	2.6	2.5	2.6	2.6	2.6	2.5	2.6	2.5
1992	2.5	2.5	2.5	2.7	2.7	2.7	2.7	2.7	2.7	2.7	2.5	2.5	2.6
1993	2.8	2.9	2.9	3.0	3.0	3.0	2.8	2.9	3.0	3.1	3.1	3.1	2.9
1994	3.1	3.1	3.2	3.1	3.3	3.2	3.0	2.9	3.1	3.1	3.1	3.2	3.1
1995	3.1	3.2	3.2	3.2	3.2	3.3	3.1	3.1	3.1	3.1	3.0	3.0	3.1
1996	2.8	2.9	2.9	2.8	2.9	3.0	3.0	3.1	3.0	3.2	3.2	3.2	3.0
1997	3.3	3.2	3.3	3.3	3.4	3.5	3.4	3.5	3.5	3.5	3.3	3.3	3.3
1998	3.0	3.0	3.0	3.3	3.2	3.3	3.2	3.2	3.3	3.4	3.4	3.4	3.2
1999	3.4	3.5	3.6	3.6	3.7	3.8	3.6	3.6	3.6	3.7	3.7	3.7	3.6
2000	3.5	3.5	3.7	3.8	3.8	3.9	3.8	3.8	3.9	3.9	3.8	3.9	3.7
2001	3.7	3.6	3.6	3.7	3.7	3.7	3.5	3.5	3.6	3.5	3.5	3.4	3.6
2002	3.2	3.2	3.3	3.6	3.6	3.7	3.6	3.6	3.7	3.8	3.7	3.7	3.6
2003	3.4	3.4	3.5	3.8	3.9	3.9	3.7	3.7	3.9	3.9	3.9	3.8	3.7
Educational and health services													
1990	8.2	8.3	8.2	8.2	8.2	8.2	8.2	8.3	8.3	8.4	8.4	8.4	8.2
1991	8.0	8.0	8.1	7.9	7.9	7.9	7.9	7.9	8.0	7.9	8.0	8.2	7.9
1992	8.7	8.7	8.5	8.4	8.4	8.5	8.6	8.5	8.6	8.6	8.7	8.7	8.5
1993	8.9	8.7	8.8	9.2	9.2	9.2	9.4	9.4	9.4	9.2	9.3	9.3	9.1
1994	9.5	9.5	9.6	9.7	9.6	9.7	9.5	9.6	9.7	10.1	10.1	10.3	9.7
1995	10.1	10.2	10.3	10.5	10.6	10.5	10.5	10.5	10.5	10.4	10.5	10.6	10.4
1996	10.5	10.7	10.6	10.6	10.7	10.6	10.7	10.5	10.6	10.8	10.9	11.0	10.6
1997	11.0	11.0	11.2	11.1	11.0	11.2	10.8	11.0	11.3	11.4	11.4	11.4	11.1
1998	11.4	11.4	11.6	11.9	11.9	12.0	11.3	11.2	11.2	11.1	11.2	11.2	11.4
1999	10.8	10.9	10.9	11.1	11.1	11.0	10.8	10.8	10.9	11.1	11.1	11.1	10.9
2000	11.5	11.6	11.7	11.4	11.3	11.4	11.2	11.4	11.4	11.5	11.5	11.2	11.4
2001	10.9	11.0	11.0	11.0	11.2	11.4	11.4	11.3	11.4	11.5	11.7	11.8	11.3
2002	11.7	11.8	11.9	11.9	12.0	12.0	12.0	11.8	11.9	12.1	12.1	12.1	11.9
2003	12.1	12.0	12.0	12.0	12.0	12.0	12.1	11.9	12.0	12.0	12.1	12.0	12.0
Leisure and hospitality													
1990	4.7	4.6	4.7	5.1	5.3	5.6	5.4	5.5	5.3	5.1	5.0	5.0	5.1
1991	4.7	4.7	4.7	4.8	5.1	5.3	5.2	5.3	5.1	4.9	4.8	4.7	4.9
1992	4.5	4.5	4.6	4.8	5.1	5.3	5.2	5.2	5.2	5.1	4.9	4.9	4.9
1993	4.6	4.6	4.6	4.9	5.1	5.4	5.4	5.5	5.4	5.2	5.3	5.3	5.1
1994	4.9	4.9	5.0	5.2	5.4	5.6	5.8	5.8	5.7	5.5	5.4	5.7	5.4
1995	5.4	5.3	5.3	5.5	5.7	6.0	6.1	6.4	6.3	5.9	5.8	5.8	5.7
1996	4.9	5.0	5.0	5.3	5.6	5.8	5.8	5.8	5.7	5.5	5.3	5.3	5.4
1997	5.2	5.2	5.3	5.5	5.7	5.9	5.9	6.1	6.0	5.8	5.7	5.6	5.6
1998	5.3	5.4	5.5	5.7	6.0	6.1	6.2	6.1	6.1	5.9	5.8	5.8	5.8
1999	5.3	5.3	5.5	5.8	6.1	6.4	6.5	6.5	6.3	6.2	6.0	5.9	5.9
2000	5.6	5.6	5.7	6.0	6.3	6.6	6.9	6.8	6.6	6.2	6.0	6.1	6.2
2001	5.8	6.0	6.1	6.3	6.6	6.8	6.7	6.7	6.5	6.2	6.1	6.2	6.3
2002	5.9	5.9	6.1	6.3	6.7	6.8	6.9	6.9	6.8	6.6	6.4	6.3	6.5
2003	6.2	6.1	6.2	6.4	6.7	6.8	7.0	7.1	6.9	6.6	6.4	6.2	6.6
Other services													
1990	2.7	2.7	2.7	2.7	2.8	2.8	2.8	2.8	2.7	2.7	2.6	2.7	2.7
1991	2.4	2.4	2.4	2.4	2.4	2.5	2.4	2.4	2.3	2.4	2.4	2.4	2.4
1992	2.4	2.4	2.4	2.4	2.4	2.4	2.6	2.6	2.5	2.4	2.4	2.4	2.4
1993	2.4	2.4	2.4	2.4	2.5	2.5	2.5	2.5	2.5	2.4	2.5	2.5	2.4
1994	2.4	2.4	2.4	2.4	2.4	2.5	2.5	2.5	2.5	2.4	2.4	2.5	2.4
1995	2.3	2.2	2.2	2.2	2.3	2.3	2.4	2.4	2.3	2.3	2.2	2.2	2.2
1996	2.2	2.2	2.2	2.2	2.3	2.3	2.3	2.3	2.2	2.0	2.0	2.0	2.1
1997	2.1	2.1	2.1	2.1	2.1	2.2	2.2	2.3	2.2	2.1	2.1	2.2	2.1
1998	2.1	2.2	2.2	2.2	2.2	2.3	2.3	2.3	2.2	2.2	2.2	2.2	2.2
1999	2.2	2.2	2.3	2.3	2.3	2.4	2.4	2.4	2.4	2.4	2.4	2.4	2.3
2000	2.4	2.4	2.4	2.5	2.5	2.5	2.7	2.6	2.5	2.5	2.5	2.5	2.5
2001	2.4	2.4	2.4	2.4	2.4	2.5	2.5	2.5	2.4	2.4	2.4	2.4	2.4
2002	2.4	2.4	2.4	2.4	2.4	2.4	2.5	2.5	2.5	2.4	2.4	2.4	2.4
2003	2.4	2.4	2.4	2.5	2.5	2.6	2.5	2.6	2.6	2.5	2.5	2.6	2.5

Employment by Industry: Massachusetts—*Continued*

(Numbers in thousands. Not seasonally adjusted.)

Industry	January	February	March	April	May	June	July	August	September	October	November	December	Annual Average
NEW BEDFORD—*Continued*													
Government													
1990	9.7	9.7	9.8	9.9	10.0	10.0	9.4	9.2	9.4	9.6	9.8	9.8	9.6
1991	9.6	9.7	9.8	9.8	9.9	9.9	9.3	9.4	9.5	9.5	9.5	9.6	9.6
1992	9.2	9.3	9.4	9.3	9.4	9.4	6.5	6.2	9.1	9.3	9.4	9.6	8.8
1993	9.2	9.3	9.4	9.4	9.6	9.4	8.9	8.7	9.3	9.5	9.5	9.6	9.3
1994	9.7	9.8	9.8	9.9	10.0	9.8	9.1	9.0	9.5	9.7	9.8	9.8	9.6
1995	9.6	9.7	9.7	9.8	9.7	9.8	9.0	8.9	9.5	9.8	9.9	9.9	9.6
1996	9.8	9.9	10.0	9.9	10.0	9.8	9.1	8.9	9.5	9.9	9.9	10.0	9.7
1997	9.9	9.8	9.9	10.0	9.9	10.0	9.3	9.1	9.7	9.9	10.0	10.0	9.7
1998	9.9	9.9	9.9	9.9	10.0	10.0	9.4	9.2	9.8	10.0	10.1	10.2	9.8
1999	10.0	10.1	10.1	10.1	10.1	10.2	9.6	9.3	10.0	10.1	10.2	10.3	10.0
2000	10.2	10.4	10.5	10.5	11.2	10.9	9.9	9.6	10.2	10.5	10.6	10.6	10.4
2001	10.6	10.6	10.6	10.8	10.8	11.0	9.8	9.7	10.6	10.8	10.8	10.8	10.6
2002	10.8	10.9	10.8	10.9	10.9	10.9	9.9	9.9	10.5	10.1	10.2	10.1	10.5
2003	10.0	10.0	9.9	10.0	9.8	9.9	9.6	9.6	10.3	10.1	10.2	10.1	10.0
Federal government													
2001	0.4	0.4	0.4	0.4	0.4	0.4	0.4	0.4	0.4	0.4	0.4	0.4	0.4
2002	0.4	0.4	0.4	0.4	0.4	0.4	0.4	0.4	0.4	0.4	0.4	0.4	0.4
2003	0.4	0.4	0.4	0.4	0.4	0.4	0.4	0.4	0.4	0.4	0.4	0.4	0.4
State government													
1990	1.7	1.7	1.7	1.7	1.7	1.7	1.7	1.7	1.7	1.7	1.7	1.7	1.7
1991	1.7	1.7	1.7	1.8	1.8	1.8	1.7	1.7	1.7	1.7	1.7	1.7	1.7
1992	1.8	1.9	1.9	1.9	1.9	1.8	1.7	1.7	1.8	1.9	1.9	1.9	1.8
1993	1.9	2.0	2.0	2.0	2.0	1.9	1.8	1.7	1.8	1.9	1.9	1.9	1.9
1994	1.8	1.9	1.9	1.9	1.9	1.8	1.6	1.6	1.8	1.9	1.9	1.9	1.8
1995	1.8	1.9	1.9	1.9	1.9	1.8	1.6	1.6	1.8	1.9	1.9	1.9	1.8
1996	1.8	1.9	1.9	1.9	1.9	1.7	1.6	1.6	1.7	1.9	1.9	1.9	1.8
1997	1.8	1.8	1.8	1.8	1.8	1.8	1.8	1.6	1.7	1.8	1.8	1.8	1.7
1998	1.8	1.8	1.8	1.8	1.8	1.8	1.8	1.7	1.7	1.8	1.8	1.8	1.7
1999	1.8	1.8	1.8	1.8	1.8	1.8	1.8	1.8	1.8	1.8	1.8	1.8	1.8
2000	1.8	1.8	1.8	1.8	1.8	1.8	1.8	1.8	1.8	1.9	1.9	1.9	1.8
2001	1.9	1.9	1.9	2.0	1.9	2.0	1.8	1.8	1.9	1.9	1.9	1.9	1.9
2002	1.9	1.9	1.9	1.9	1.9	1.8	1.8	1.8	1.8	1.7	1.7	1.7	1.8
2003	1.7	1.7	1.7	1.7	1.7	1.7	1.8	1.8	1.8	1.8	1.8	1.8	1.8
Local government													
1990	6.9	6.9	7.0	7.0	7.1	7.1	6.5	6.4	6.6	6.7	7.0	7.0	6.8
1991	6.8	6.9	7.0	7.0	7.1	7.1	6.5	6.6	6.7	6.7	6.8	6.8	6.8
1992	6.8	6.8	6.8	6.8	6.8	6.9	4.2	3.9	6.7	6.8	6.9	7.0	6.3
1993	6.9	6.9	7.0	7.0	7.1	7.0	6.6	6.5	6.9	7.1	7.1	7.3	6.9
1994	7.4	7.4	7.4	7.5	7.6	7.5	7.0	6.9	7.2	7.3	7.4	7.4	7.3
1995	7.3	7.3	7.3	7.4	7.3	7.5	6.9	6.8	7.2	7.4	7.5	7.5	7.2
1996	7.5	7.5	7.6	7.5	7.6	7.6	7.0	6.8	7.3	7.5	7.5	7.6	7.4
1997	7.6	7.5	7.6	7.7	7.6	7.7	7.0	7.0	7.5	7.6	7.7	7.7	7.5
1998	7.6	7.6	7.6	7.7	7.8	7.8	7.2	7.1	7.7	7.8	7.9	8.0	7.6
1999	7.8	7.9	7.9	7.9	7.9	8.0	7.3	7.1	7.8	7.9	8.0	8.1	7.8
2000	8.0	8.1	8.1	8.1	8.2	8.3	7.4	7.3	8.0	8.2	8.3	8.3	8.0
2001	8.3	8.3	8.3	8.4	8.5	8.6	7.6	7.5	8.3	8.5	8.5	8.5	8.3
2002	8.5	8.6	8.5	8.6	8.6	8.7	7.7	7.7	8.3	8.0	8.1	8.0	8.3
2003	7.9	7.9	7.8	7.9	7.7	7.8	7.4	7.4	8.1	7.9	8.0	7.9	7.8
SPRINGFIELD													
Total nonfarm													
1990	253.7	254.7	255.9	256.0	257.1	256.4	248.5	248.6	253.0	251.6	251.6	250.1	253.1
1991	236.4	237.1	238.2	239.5	241.3	240.2	232.5	232.4	237.9	238.7	239.4	238.6	237.6
1992	231.8	234.3	235.5	237.7	239.6	239.2	232.7	231.5	237.8	240.4	241.0	240.7	236.8
1993	230.2	232.5	232.5	237.1	239.6	238.7	233.4	233.5	240.0	241.1	241.4	241.2	236.7
1994	231.5	233.5	235.2	237.5	240.5	240.8	235.2	236.3	242.7	243.2	244.9	243.7	238.7
1995	235.5	237.7	239.2	242.3	244.5	244.4	239.3	239.1	246.1	246.0	246.8	247.0	242.3
1996	236.2	239.2	240.9	245.2	248.0	247.8	241.0	242.1	248.6	250.7	252.6	251.7	245.3
1997	243.7	246.3	248.2	250.9	253.3	253.7	246.0	246.5	253.0	255.0	257.2	257.2	250.9
1998	246.6	249.1	250.9	253.0	255.2	255.7	249.0	249.4	255.7	259.2	259.9	261.3	253.7
1999	247.8	251.7	253.3	257.6	259.6	259.9	252.4	251.4	258.5	261.4	262.1	263.1	256.5
2000	253.9	256.2	256.4	262.5	264.6	265.4	257.2	256.1	263.7	266.3	267.6	268.4	261.5
2001	259.7	260.9	262.2	264.0	266.0	266.1	257.8	257.8	263.5	264.6	264.5	263.8	262.6
2002	253.7	255.1	257.1	259.4	262.8	262.0	254.2	254.0	260.9	260.5	260.9	259.9	258.4
2003	249.7	250.2	251.9	255.5	258.5	257.8	249.4	249.0	255.8	257.4	258.6	257.2	254.3
Total private													
1990	208.3	208.3	209.3	210.0	210.9	210.9	206.2	206.7	208.9	206.8	206.7	205.5	208.2
1991	194.4	194.1	195.2	196.4	197.9	197.2	193.2	193.6	196.8	196.2	196.8	196.1	195.6
1992	190.0	191.1	192.1	194.4	196.1	196.1	193.2	192.5	196.1	197.4	198.2	197.9	194.5
1993	187.8	188.8	188.6	193.2	195.3	195.1	193.2	194.2	197.5	197.2	197.3	197.1	193.7
1994	188.6	189.6	191.3	193.5	196.4	197.1	195.5	197.0	200.1	199.0	200.2	199.2	195.6
1995	192.4	193.3	194.7	197.6	199.6	200.2	198.6	199.0	203.0	200.9	201.2	201.5	198.5
1996	192.5	194.1	195.6	199.5	201.9	202.3	199.8	201.2	204.3	204.7	205.9	205.9	200.6
1997	199.1	200.6	202.3	204.8	207.0	208.0	204.4	205.3	208.1	209.2	210.5	211.0	205.8
1998	201.9	203.1	204.7	206.9	208.7	209.6	207.3	207.9	210.4	212.7	212.9	214.4	208.3
1999	202.3	205.0	206.4	210.4	212.3	212.9	211.0	210.3	211.9	214.0	214.3	215.3	210.5
2000	207.2	208.4	209.9	214.3	215.7	217.2	214.6	214.1	216.2	218.1	218.8	220.0	214.5
2001	211.3	211.7	212.7	214.4	216.4	216.9	213.4	213.7	214.6	214.2	213.9	213.3	213.9
2002	204.9	205.3	207.2	209.9	213.2	213.2	210.6	210.5	212.6	211.7	211.8	210.9	210.2
2003	202.0	201.4	203.1	207.1	210.1	209.7	206.5	206.1	208.3	209.4	210.3	208.7	206.9

Employment by Industry: Massachusetts—*Continued*

(Numbers in thousands. Not seasonally adjusted.)

Industry	January	February	March	April	May	June	July	August	September	October	November	December	Annual Average
SPRINGFIELD—*Continued*													
Goods-producing													
1990	52.7	52.2	52.2	52.8	53.2	53.9	52.7	52.7	52.7	51.9	51.6	50.7	52.4
1991	48.3	47.7	47.8	48.1	48.5	48.8	48.0	48.0	48.5	48.4	48.3	47.3	48.1
1992	45.8	45.6	45.7	45.6	46.2	46.7	45.9	46.0	46.6	46.3	46.0	45.7	46.0
1993	43.7	43.6	43.6	44.0	44.5	45.1	44.7	45.1	45.4	44.8	44.5	43.9	44.4
1994	42.4	42.2	42.6	43.4	44.3	45.2	44.9	45.2	45.8	45.3	45.3	44.7	44.2
1995	43.5	43.2	43.7	44.6	45.1	45.7	45.1	45.2	45.2	45.2	44.9	44.4	44.6
1996	42.7	42.6	43.0	44.0	44.6	45.1	44.4	45.0	45.1	45.2	45.4	45.0	44.3
1997	43.1	43.1	43.4	44.1	44.9	45.2	44.3	44.7	44.4	43.7	43.9	43.5	44.0
1998	42.6	42.7	43.2	44.1	44.6	45.1	44.5	45.0	45.0	45.6	45.5	45.3	44.4
1999	42.2	42.3	42.8	44.1	44.8	45.2	44.8	44.4	44.9	44.8	44.8	44.4	44.1
2000	42.6	42.4	43.4	44.4	44.8	45.1	45.0	45.3	45.1	45.6	45.4	45.0	44.5
2001	43.0	42.8	42.9	43.0	43.3	43.8	42.6	43.1	42.8	42.4	42.0	41.5	42.8
2002	39.9	39.1	39.5	40.1	40.7	41.1	40.5	40.9	40.7	40.3	40.0	39.3	40.2
2003	37.2	36.7	36.9	37.9	38.5	38.8	38.0	38.6	38.0	38.0	37.5	36.7	37.7
Construction and mining													
1990	7.9	7.4	7.5	8.2	8.6	9.0	9.1	9.0	9.0	8.6	8.2	7.6	8.3
1991	6.2	5.8	5.9	6.4	7.0	7.3	7.4	7.5	7.4	7.3	7.0	6.3	6.7
1992	5.3	5.0	5.1	5.7	6.3	6.5	6.6	6.8	6.8	6.9	6.7	6.3	6.1
1993	5.4	5.2	5.2	5.8	6.4	6.8	7.2	7.3	7.4	7.4	7.2	6.7	6.5
1994	5.5	5.2	5.3	6.2	6.8	7.4	7.7	7.8	7.8	7.5	7.4	6.9	6.7
1995	6.0	5.8	6.0	6.9	7.3	7.8	7.9	8.0	7.7	7.7	7.5	7.0	7.1
1996	5.9	5.9	6.2	7.1	7.6	8.1	8.3	8.4	8.1	8.2	8.1	7.6	7.4
1997	6.3	6.1	6.3	7.2	7.8	8.1	8.2	8.4	8.2	8.2	8.1	7.8	7.5
1998	6.6	6.6	6.8	7.8	8.2	8.5	8.8	8.9	8.5	8.5	8.4	8.1	7.9
1999	6.8	6.8	7.1	8.3	8.8	9.1	9.4	9.2	9.2	9.1	8.9	8.5	8.4
2000	7.5	7.1	7.8	8.6	9.0	9.3	9.6	9.7	9.4	9.3	9.2	8.7	8.7
2001	7.6	7.6	7.9	8.7	9.4	9.9	9.9	10.1	9.8	9.8	9.8	9.4	9.2
2002	8.3	7.9	8.2	9.2	9.7	10.1	10.1	10.1	9.8	9.7	9.5	8.9	9.3
2003	7.8	7.5	7.7	8.7	9.4	9.7	9.9	9.9	9.5	9.7	9.3	8.6	9.0
Manufacturing													
1990	44.8	44.8	44.7	44.6	44.6	44.9	43.6	43.7	43.7	43.3	43.4	43.1	44.1
1991	42.1	41.9	41.9	41.7	41.5	41.5	40.6	40.5	41.1	41.1	41.3	41.0	41.3
1992	40.5	40.6	40.6	39.9	39.9	40.2	39.3	39.2	39.8	39.4	39.3	39.4	39.8
1993	38.3	38.4	38.4	38.2	38.1	38.3	37.5	37.8	38.0	37.4	37.3	37.2	37.9
1994	36.9	37.0	37.3	37.2	37.5	37.8	37.2	37.4	38.0	37.8	37.9	37.8	37.4
1995	37.5	37.4	37.7	37.7	37.8	37.9	37.2	37.2	37.5	37.5	37.4	37.4	37.5
1996	36.8	36.7	36.8	36.9	37.0	37.0	36.1	36.6	37.0	37.0	37.3	37.4	36.8
1997	36.8	37.0	37.1	36.9	37.1	37.1	36.1	36.3	36.2	35.5	35.8	35.7	36.4
1998	36.0	36.1	36.4	36.3	36.4	36.6	35.7	36.1	36.5	37.1	37.1	37.2	36.4
1999	35.4	35.5	35.7	35.8	36.0	36.1	35.4	35.2	35.7	35.7	35.9	35.9	35.6
2000	35.1	35.3	35.6	35.8	35.8	35.8	35.4	35.6	35.7	36.3	36.2	36.3	35.7
2001	35.4	35.2	35.0	34.3	33.9	33.9	32.7	33.0	33.0	32.6	32.2	32.1	33.6
2002	31.6	31.2	31.3	30.9	31.0	31.0	30.4	30.8	30.9	30.6	30.5	30.4	30.9
2003	29.4	29.2	29.2	29.2	29.1	29.1	28.1	28.7	28.5	28.3	28.2	28.1	28.8
Service-providing													
1990	201.0	202.5	203.7	203.2	203.9	202.5	195.8	195.9	200.3	199.7	200.0	199.4	200.6
1991	188.1	189.4	190.4	191.4	192.8	191.4	184.5	184.4	189.4	190.3	191.1	191.3	189.5
1992	186.0	188.7	189.8	192.1	193.4	192.5	186.8	185.5	191.2	194.1	195.0	195.0	190.8
1993	186.5	188.9	188.9	193.1	195.1	193.6	188.7	188.4	194.6	196.3	196.9	197.3	192.3
1994	189.1	191.3	192.6	194.1	196.2	195.6	190.3	191.1	196.9	197.9	199.6	199.0	194.4
1995	192.0	194.5	195.5	197.7	199.4	198.7	194.2	193.9	200.9	200.8	201.9	202.6	197.6
1996	193.5	196.6	197.9	201.2	203.4	202.7	196.6	197.1	203.5	205.5	207.2	206.7	200.9
1997	200.6	203.2	204.8	206.8	208.4	208.5	201.7	201.8	208.6	211.3	213.3	213.7	206.8
1998	204.0	206.4	207.7	208.9	210.6	210.6	204.5	204.4	210.7	213.6	214.4	216.0	209.3
1999	205.6	209.4	210.5	213.5	214.8	214.7	207.6	207.0	213.6	216.6	217.3	218.7	212.4
2000	211.3	213.8	213.0	218.1	219.8	220.3	212.2	210.8	218.6	220.7	222.2	223.4	217.0
2001	216.7	218.1	219.3	221.0	222.7	222.3	215.2	214.7	220.7	222.2	222.5	222.3	219.8
2002	213.8	216.0	217.6	219.3	222.1	220.9	213.7	213.1	220.2	220.2	220.9	220.6	218.2
2003	212.5	213.5	215.0	217.6	220.0	219.0	211.4	210.4	217.8	219.4	221.1	220.5	216.5
Trade, transportation, and utilities													
1990	50.1	49.4	49.5	48.9	48.9	48.7	47.3	47.3	48.4	47.6	48.2	48.5	48.5
1991	45.0	44.2	44.3	44.0	44.5	44.3	42.7	43.0	44.2	44.0	44.7	45.2	44.1
1992	43.0	42.7	42.7	43.4	43.6	43.5	42.4	42.2	43.2	43.8	44.7	45.1	43.3
1993	42.2	41.8	41.6	42.3	42.8	42.7	41.8	41.9	43.3	43.6	44.2	44.7	42.7
1994	42.3	41.8	42.3	42.2	42.6	42.6	42.2	42.8	43.8	44.4	45.6	46.0	43.2
1995	43.9	43.4	43.4	44.0	44.4	44.6	44.3	44.7	45.7	45.6	46.4	47.1	44.7
1996	44.9	44.4	44.5	45.4	45.9	46.0	45.0	45.4	46.4	47.1	48.2	48.9	46.0
1997	46.6	46.3	46.7	46.8	47.0	47.3	46.4	46.4	47.7	48.7	49.7	51.1	47.5
1998	48.0	47.8	47.9	47.7	48.2	48.4	47.9	48.0	49.3	50.4	51.2	52.3	48.9
1999	49.0	49.1	49.1	49.3	49.9	50.2	49.6	49.8	50.6	51.5	52.8	53.9	50.4
2000	51.3	51.0	50.1	49.9	50.0	50.3	49.3	49.5	50.5	51.3	52.7	54.1	50.8
2001	50.4	49.6	49.5	49.5	49.8	49.7	48.1	48.2	48.9	49.3	50.2	50.6	49.5
2002	48.1	47.4	47.5	47.8	48.2	48.7	47.5	47.7	48.5	48.3	48.8	49.3	48.2
2003	46.9	46.2	46.5	47.3	47.7	47.9	46.2	46.0	47.2	47.9	49.0	49.1	47.3

Employment by Industry: Massachusetts—*Continued*

(Numbers in thousands. Not seasonally adjusted.)

Industry	January	February	March	April	May	June	July	August	September	October	November	December	Annual Average
SPRINGFIELD—*Continued*													
Wholesale trade													
1990	8.3	8.3	8.4	8.4	8.4	8.4	8.3	8.3	8.4	8.2	8.1	8.1	8.3
1991	7.7	7.6	7.6	7.7	7.7	7.7	7.5	7.5	7.6	7.5	7.4	7.3	7.5
1992	7.2	7.2	7.2	7.2	7.2	7.3	7.4	7.4	7.4	7.5	7.5	7.5	7.3
1993	7.2	7.2	7.1	7.3	7.4	7.4	7.3	7.3	7.4	7.4	7.4	7.3	7.3
1994	7.0	7.0	7.0	7.5	7.5	7.5	7.4	7.4	7.5	7.4	7.4	7.4	7.3
1995	7.6	7.6	7.6	7.4	7.5	7.6	7.7	7.8	7.9	7.9	7.8	7.9	7.6
1996	7.5	7.5	7.6	7.7	7.8	7.9	7.7	7.6	7.6	7.9	7.9	8.0	7.7
1997	7.8	7.8	7.9	7.9	7.9	8.1	8.0	8.0	8.1	8.1	8.1	8.1	7.9
1998	7.9	7.8	7.9	8.1	8.0	8.1	8.2	8.2	8.2	8.3	8.3	8.3	8.1
1999	8.1	8.2	8.2	8.3	8.3	8.3	8.3	8.3	8.4	8.1	8.3	8.3	8.2
2000	8.2	8.2	8.3	8.4	8.3	8.5	8.5	8.5	8.5	8.5	8.6	8.7	8.4
2001	8.7	8.6	8.6	8.4	8.3	8.4	8.2	8.3	8.4	8.4	8.4	8.4	8.4
2002	8.2	8.2	8.2	8.3	8.3	8.4	8.3	8.3	8.3	8.1	8.1	8.2	8.2
2003	7.8	7.8	7.9	7.8	7.9	8.0	7.9	7.8	7.9	8.0	8.2	7.9	7.9
Retail trade													
1990	34.6	33.8	33.7	33.6	33.5	33.3	32.7	32.6	33.0	32.2	33.0	33.3	33.2
1991	30.6	29.9	30.0	29.9	30.2	30.1	29.3	29.6	30.0	30.0	30.8	31.5	30.1
1992	29.7	29.4	29.4	30.0	30.1	30.0	29.4	29.2	29.6	30.1	31.0	31.5	29.9
1993	29.2	28.9	28.8	29.2	29.5	29.4	29.1	29.2	29.8	29.9	30.5	31.2	29.5
1994	29.5	29.0	29.3	28.8	29.1	29.1	29.0	29.4	29.9	30.4	31.6	32.0	29.7
1995	29.9	29.3	29.3	30.0	30.3	30.3	30.3	30.6	31.0	30.8	31.8	32.5	30.5
1996	30.9	30.4	30.4	31.1	31.4	31.4	31.0	31.5	32.0	32.3	33.3	33.8	31.6
1997	31.9	31.7	31.9	32.0	32.1	32.1	32.1	32.3	32.7	33.3	34.2	35.3	32.6
1998	32.8	32.6	32.6	32.2	32.8	32.9	32.8	33.0	33.4	34.2	35.0	35.6	33.3
1999	33.3	33.1	33.1	33.2	33.7	34.0	34.0	34.2	34.3	35.1	36.1	36.9	34.2
2000	34.6	34.3	33.3	32.5	32.7	32.8	32.5	32.8	33.1	33.6	34.8	35.7	33.5
2001	33.1	32.5	32.4	32.6	32.9	32.8	32.1	32.2	32.2	32.5	33.4	34.0	32.7
2002	31.8	31.2	31.3	31.5	31.8	32.2	31.8	32.0	32.2	32.1	32.8	33.4	32.0
2003	31.4	30.8	31.0	31.9	32.2	32.3	31.4	31.5	31.9	32.6	33.5	33.8	32.0
Transportation and utilities													
1990	7.2	7.3	7.4	6.9	7.0	7.0	6.3	6.4	7.0	7.2	7.1	7.1	6.9
1991	6.7	6.7	6.7	6.4	6.6	6.5	5.9	5.9	6.6	6.5	6.5	6.4	6.4
1992	6.1	6.1	6.1	6.2	6.3	6.2	5.6	5.6	6.2	6.2	6.2	6.1	6.0
1993	5.8	5.7	5.7	5.8	5.9	5.9	5.4	5.4	6.1	6.3	6.3	6.2	5.8
1994	5.8	5.8	6.0	5.9	6.0	6.0	5.8	6.0	6.4	6.6	6.6	6.6	6.1
1995	6.4	6.5	6.5	6.6	6.6	6.7	6.3	6.3	6.8	6.9	6.8	6.7	6.5
1996	6.5	6.5	6.5	6.6	6.7	6.7	6.3	6.3	6.8	6.9	7.0	7.1	6.6
1997	6.9	6.8	6.9	6.9	7.0	7.1	6.3	6.1	6.9	7.3	7.4	7.7	6.9
1998	7.3	7.4	7.4	7.4	7.4	7.4	6.9	6.8	7.7	7.9	7.9	8.4	7.4
1999	7.6	7.8	7.8	7.8	7.9	7.9	7.3	7.3	7.9	8.3	8.4	8.7	7.8
2000	8.5	8.5	8.5	9.0	9.0	9.0	8.3	8.2	8.9	9.2	9.3	9.7	8.8
2001	8.6	8.5	8.5	8.5	8.6	8.5	7.8	7.7	8.3	8.4	8.4	8.2	8.3
2002	8.1	8.0	8.0	8.0	8.1	8.1	7.4	7.4	8.0	8.1	7.9	7.7	7.9
2003	7.7	7.6	7.6	7.6	7.6	7.6	6.9	6.7	7.4	7.3	7.3	7.4	7.4
Information													
1990	5.7	5.7	5.7	5.7	5.7	5.7	5.6	5.6	5.6	5.7	5.7	5.7	5.6
1991	5.4	5.4	5.5	5.5	5.5	5.5	5.4	5.4	5.4	5.3	5.4	5.4	5.4
1992	5.2	5.1	5.1	5.2	5.2	5.2	5.2	5.1	5.2	5.2	5.2	5.3	5.1
1993	5.1	5.1	5.0	4.9	4.8	4.8	5.0	4.9	5.0	4.9	4.9	5.0	4.9
1994	4.9	4.9	4.9	4.9	5.0	5.0	5.0	5.0	5.0	5.1	5.1	5.1	4.9
1995	4.9	5.0	4.9	5.0	5.0	5.0	5.0	5.1	5.0	5.0	5.0	5.1	5.0
1996	4.9	5.0	5.0	5.0	5.0	5.0	5.2	5.3	5.3	5.3	5.3	5.4	5.1
1997	4.9	4.6	4.6	4.5	4.6	4.6	4.5	4.5	4.4	4.4	4.4	4.4	4.5
1998	4.4	4.4	4.4	4.3	4.3	4.4	4.4	4.4	4.4	4.4	4.5	4.5	4.4
1999	4.3	4.2	4.3	4.4	4.5	4.5	4.5	4.5	4.5	4.5	4.5	4.9	4.4
2000	5.1	5.1	5.1	5.3	5.3	5.3	5.4	4.8	5.4	5.4	5.5	5.6	5.2
2001	5.6	5.5	5.5	5.6	5.5	5.5	5.4	5.3	5.2	5.3	5.3	5.3	5.4
2002	5.2	5.2	5.2	5.0	5.1	5.0	5.0	5.0	4.9	4.9	5.0	5.0	5.0
2003	4.9	4.8	4.8	4.8	4.8	4.7	4.6	4.7	4.6	4.6	4.7	4.8	4.7
Financial activities													
1990	14.5	14.5	14.6	14.6	14.6	14.5	14.4	14.4	14.3	14.3	14.3	14.3	14.4
1991	13.8	13.8	13.8	13.6	13.6	13.6	13.5	13.5	13.5	13.5	13.6	13.6	13.6
1992	13.4	13.4	13.4	13.2	13.3	13.3	13.4	13.3	13.2	13.2	13.2	13.3	13.3
1993	12.6	12.7	12.7	12.8	12.8	12.8	12.6	12.7	12.7	13.1	13.1	13.1	12.8
1994	13.1	13.1	13.1	12.8	12.8	12.9	12.8	12.8	12.7	12.6	12.6	12.6	12.8
1995	12.4	12.5	12.5	12.4	12.4	12.4	12.4	12.4	12.4	12.2	12.3	12.4	12.3
1996	12.2	12.2	12.2	12.4	12.4	12.4	12.5	12.6	12.6	12.6	12.7	12.8	12.4
1997	12.7	12.8	12.8	12.8	12.8	13.0	13.5	13.6	13.5	13.6	13.6	13.7	13.2
1998	13.5	13.6	13.7	13.9	13.9	13.9	14.1	14.1	14.0	13.9	13.9	13.9	13.8
1999	13.4	13.4	13.4	13.6	13.6	13.6	13.7	13.7	13.5	13.6	13.6	13.7	13.5
2000	13.7	13.7	13.8	14.0	13.9	14.1	14.1	14.1	14.1	14.2	14.3	14.5	14.0
2001	14.3	14.3	14.4	14.4	14.5	14.8	14.6	14.6	14.5	14.5	14.6	14.5	14.5
2002	14.4	14.3	14.3	14.3	14.4	14.5	14.5	14.5	14.4	14.2	14.3	14.4	14.4
2003	14.3	14.2	14.3	14.3	14.4	14.5	14.3	14.3	14.1	14.0	13.9	14.0	14.2

Employment by Industry: Massachusetts—*Continued*

(Numbers in thousands. Not seasonally adjusted.)

Industry	January	February	March	April	May	June	July	August	September	October	November	December	Annual Average
SPRINGFIELD—*Continued*													
Professional and business services													
1990	17.1	17.5	17.7	17.7	17.5	17.7	17.5	18.0	17.9	17.1	17.2	17.0	17.4
1991	16.1	16.1	16.1	16.6	16.4	16.7	16.3	16.6	16.9	16.3	16.2	16.1	16.3
1992	15.8	16.3	16.4	16.8	17.1	17.5	17.2	17.1	17.4	17.8	17.7	17.5	17.0
1993	16.4	16.7	16.9	17.7	18.0	17.9	17.5	17.6	17.9	17.5	17.6	17.4	17.4
1994	16.6	16.9	17.0	17.6	17.9	18.2	18.2	18.7	18.9	18.3	18.4	18.1	17.9
1995	17.4	17.8	18.2	18.7	18.9	19.0	19.1	19.7	20.2	19.6	19.7	19.5	18.9
1996	18.4	18.7	18.9	19.6	20.1	20.3	20.4	21.2	21.0	20.3	20.2	20.0	19.9
1997	20.6	20.8	21.2	21.7	21.9	22.5	21.8	22.1	22.3	22.3	22.3	21.9	21.7
1998	20.1	19.5	19.9	20.3	20.4	20.5	19.9	20.2	20.3	20.4	20.4	21.0	20.2
1999	20.0	20.5	20.8	21.0	21.1	21.3	21.0	20.9	21.1	21.7	21.7	21.7	21.0
2000	20.2	20.5	20.9	21.7	21.6	21.7	21.6	21.8	21.9	21.7	21.5	21.4	21.3
2001	20.4	20.5	20.7	21.0	21.1	21.3	21.3	21.2	21.0	20.4	20.2	19.9	20.8
2002	18.8	19.3	19.7	20.4	20.4	20.3	20.1	20.0	20.1	19.6	19.5	19.3	19.8
2003	18.3	18.0	18.3	19.3	19.4	19.6	19.3	19.4	19.2	18.9	19.3	19.5	19.0
Educational and health services													
1990	40.6	41.2	41.3	41.5	41.5	40.8	40.1	40.2	41.2	41.7	41.9	41.7	41.1
1991	40.6	41.3	41.8	41.8	41.7	40.8	40.1	40.0	40.9	42.0	42.2	42.2	41.2
1992	41.5	42.1	42.4	42.9	42.6	42.0	41.4	41.3	42.6	43.5	43.8	43.5	42.4
1993	42.2	42.9	42.8	43.7	43.6	42.8	42.3	42.4	43.7	44.7	44.8	44.9	43.4
1994	43.2	44.2	44.5	44.4	44.5	43.8	42.9	42.7	44.2	44.7	45.1	45.0	44.1
1995	44.2	45.0	45.2	44.9	44.8	44.3	43.9	43.2	45.5	44.9	45.3	45.5	44.7
1996	43.3	44.6	45.0	45.0	44.8	44.3	43.3	43.1	44.5	45.4	45.8	45.7	44.5
1997	44.6	45.8	46.1	46.4	46.2	45.7	44.3	44.4	45.5	47.0	47.4	47.7	45.9
1998	46.3	47.2	47.5	47.5	47.2	46.8	46.2	45.9	47.1	48.1	48.2	48.3	47.1
1999	46.2	47.4	47.6	47.2	46.9	46.4	45.9	45.5	46.2	47.1	47.2	47.1	46.7
2000	46.3	47.2	47.4	48.0	48.2	48.2	47.1	46.8	47.5	48.4	48.8	49.0	47.7
2001	48.2	49.2	49.3	49.5	49.6	48.9	48.4	48.4	49.5	50.2	50.4	50.3	49.3
2002	49.2	50.4	50.6	51.0	51.5	50.5	49.7	49.4	50.9	51.9	52.7	52.4	50.9
2003	50.9	51.8	52.0	52.0	52.3	50.9	50.5	49.8	52.2	53.6	54.6	53.6	52.0
Leisure and hospitality													
1990	18.1	18.3	18.8	19.3	19.9	20.0	19.1	19.0	19.6	19.2	18.7	18.4	19.0
1991	16.6	17.0	17.2	18.2	19.1	19.0	18.8	18.8	19.3	18.4	18.0	17.9	18.1
1992	16.9	17.5	18.0	18.8	19.5	19.3	19.1	19.1	19.6	19.2	19.1	19.0	18.7
1993	17.3	17.7	17.6	19.1	20.2	20.3	20.6	20.8	20.9	19.9	19.5	19.3	19.4
1994	17.6	17.9	18.1	19.3	20.4	20.4	20.5	20.8	20.7	19.7	19.1	18.6	19.4
1995	17.3	17.6	17.8	19.1	20.2	20.3	19.8	19.7	20.2	19.7	19.0	18.7	19.1
1996	17.8	18.1	18.4	19.4	20.3	20.5	20.2	19.9	20.8	20.3	19.8	19.5	19.5
1997	18.3	18.8	19.0	19.7	20.8	20.9	20.8	20.9	21.7	20.7	20.4	19.7	20.1
1998	18.3	19.1	19.2	20.2	21.2	21.5	21.2	21.4	21.5	20.7	20.0	19.8	20.3
1999	18.3	19.0	19.3	21.6	22.2	22.4	22.1	22.2	22.0	21.6	20.6	20.3	20.9
2000	19.1	19.5	20.0	21.8	22.5	23.1	22.6	22.4	22.5	22.1	21.2	20.9	21.4
2001	20.2	20.5	21.1	22.1	23.1	23.4	23.2	23.2	23.4	22.7	21.8	21.6	22.2
2002	20.0	20.3	21.0	22.0	23.3	23.6	23.6	23.4	23.9	23.2	22.1	21.7	22.3
2003	20.3	20.5	21.0	22.1	23.5	23.9	24.0	23.8	23.8	23.1	22.0	21.6	22.5
Other services													
1990	9.5	9.5	9.5	9.5	9.6	9.6	9.5	9.5	9.2	9.3	9.1	9.2	9.4
1991	8.6	8.6	8.7	8.6	8.6	8.5	8.4	8.3	8.1	8.3	8.4	8.4	8.4
1992	8.4	8.4	8.4	8.5	8.6	8.6	8.6	8.4	8.3	8.4	8.5	8.5	8.4
1993	8.3	8.3	8.4	8.7	8.6	8.7	8.7	8.8	8.6	8.7	8.7	8.8	8.6
1994	8.5	8.6	8.8	8.9	8.9	9.0	9.0	9.0	9.0	8.9	9.0	9.1	8.8
1995	8.8	8.8	9.0	8.9	8.8	8.9	9.0	9.0	8.8	8.7	8.6	8.8	8.8
1996	8.3	8.5	8.6	8.7	8.8	8.7	8.8	8.7	8.6	8.5	8.5	8.6	8.6
1997	8.3	8.4	8.5	8.8	8.8	8.8	8.8	8.7	8.6	8.8	8.8	9.0	8.6
1998	8.7	8.8	8.9	8.9	8.9	9.0	9.1	8.9	8.8	9.2	9.2	9.3	8.9
1999	8.9	9.1	9.1	9.2	9.3	9.3	9.4	9.3	9.1	9.2	9.1	9.3	9.1
2000	8.9	9.0	9.2	9.2	9.4	9.4	9.5	9.4	9.2	9.4	9.4	9.5	9.2
2001	9.2	9.3	9.3	9.3	9.5	9.5	9.8	9.7	9.3	9.4	9.4	9.6	9.4
2002	9.3	9.3	9.4	9.3	9.6	9.5	9.7	9.6	9.2	9.3	9.4	9.5	9.4
2003	9.2	9.2	9.3	9.4	9.5	9.4	9.6	9.5	9.2	9.3	9.3	9.4	9.4
Government													
1990	45.4	46.4	46.6	46.0	46.2	45.5	42.3	41.9	44.1	44.8	44.9	44.6	44.8
1991	42.0	43.0	43.0	43.1	43.4	43.0	39.3	38.8	41.1	42.5	42.6	42.5	42.0
1992	41.8	43.2	43.4	43.3	43.5	43.1	39.5	39.0	41.7	43.0	42.8	42.8	42.2
1993	42.4	43.7	43.9	43.9	44.3	43.6	40.2	39.3	42.5	43.9	44.1	44.1	42.9
1994	42.9	43.9	43.9	44.0	44.1	43.7	39.7	39.3	42.6	44.2	44.7	44.5	43.1
1995	43.1	44.4	44.5	44.7	44.9	44.2	40.7	40.1	43.1	45.1	45.6	45.5	43.8
1996	43.7	45.1	45.3	45.7	46.1	45.5	41.2	40.9	44.3	46.0	46.7	45.8	44.6
1997	44.6	45.7	45.9	46.1	46.3	45.7	41.6	41.2	44.9	45.8	46.7	46.2	45.0
1998	44.7	46.0	46.2	46.1	46.5	46.1	41.7	41.5	45.3	46.5	47.0	46.9	45.3
1999	45.5	46.7	46.9	47.2	47.3	47.0	41.4	41.1	46.6	47.4	47.8	47.8	46.0
2000	46.7	47.8	46.5	48.2	48.9	48.2	42.6	42.0	47.5	48.2	48.8	48.4	46.9
2001	48.4	49.2	49.5	49.6	49.6	49.2	44.4	44.1	48.9	50.4	50.6	50.5	48.7
2002	48.8	49.8	49.9	49.5	49.6	48.8	43.6	43.5	48.3	48.8	49.1	49.0	48.2
2003	47.7	48.8	48.8	48.4	48.4	48.1	42.9	42.9	47.5	48.0	48.3	48.5	47.4

Employment by Industry: Massachusetts—*Continued*

(Numbers in thousands. Not seasonally adjusted.)

Industry	January	February	March	April	May	June	July	August	September	October	November	December	Annual Average
SPRINGFIELD—*Continued*													
Federal government													
1990	6.7	6.6	6.6	6.7	6.7	6.8	6.9	6.9	6.7	6.7	6.7	6.9	6.7
1991	6.7	6.7	6.7	6.7	6.7	6.9	7.0	6.9	6.9	6.8	6.9	7.1	6.8
1992	7.0	7.0	7.0	7.1	7.0	7.2	7.2	7.2	7.1	7.1	7.1	7.3	7.1
1993	6.5	6.6	6.6	6.6	6.6	6.6	6.6	6.6	6.7	6.7	6.7	7.0	6.6
1994	7.0	7.0	6.9	6.8	6.9	6.9	6.9	6.8	6.8	6.8	6.9	7.1	6.9
1995	6.9	6.9	6.8	6.8	6.8	6.9	7.0	6.9	6.8	6.8	6.9	7.0	6.8
1996	6.8	6.8	6.7	6.7	6.7	6.8	6.7	6.7	6.7	6.6	6.8	6.9	6.7
1997	6.7	6.6	6.6	6.6	6.6	6.5	6.5	6.7	6.6	6.4	6.8	6.9	6.6
1998	6.6	6.6	6.6	6.6	6.6	6.7	6.7	6.7	6.6	6.6	6.7	6.9	6.6
1999	6.6	6.6	6.6	6.9	6.8	6.8	6.8	6.9	6.8	6.8	6.9	7.1	6.8
2000	6.8	6.8	6.8	7.0	7.5	7.2	7.1	6.7	6.6	6.5	6.6	6.7	6.8
2001	6.9	6.8	6.8	6.7	6.7	6.7	6.8	6.8	6.6	6.7	6.7	6.7	6.7
2002	6.2	6.2	6.1	6.1	6.1	6.1	6.1	6.2	6.1	6.5	6.5	6.7	6.2
2003	6.4	6.4	6.1	5.8	5.7	5.7	5.8	5.8	5.7	5.8	5.8	6.1	5.9
State government													
1990	12.5	13.4	13.4	13.4	13.4	12.4	11.7	11.6	12.8	13.2	13.1	12.5	12.7
1991	12.0	12.9	12.9	12.9	12.9	11.8	11.3	11.3	12.2	12.5	12.5	12.0	12.2
1992	11.3	12.3	12.3	12.3	12.3	11.1	10.3	10.2	11.3	11.8	11.4	10.9	11.4
1993	11.0	12.0	12.0	12.0	11.9	11.0	10.5	10.2	11.1	11.5	11.4	10.9	11.2
1994	10.4	11.3	11.3	11.3	11.3	10.2	9.6	9.6	10.7	11.2	11.3	10.8	10.7
1995	10.3	11.3	11.5	11.5	11.5	10.4	9.8	9.7	10.8	11.3	11.3	10.8	10.8
1996	10.2	11.3	11.3	11.3	11.4	10.3	9.7	9.8	10.8	11.4	11.4	11.0	10.8
1997	10.4	11.5	11.5	11.6	11.7	10.8	10.3	10.2	11.1	11.7	11.9	11.0	11.1
1998	10.5	11.5	11.5	11.6	11.7	11.0	11.2	11.2	12.1	12.6	12.6	12.0	11.6
1999	11.7	12.7	12.8	12.9	13.0	12.2	11.5	11.4	12.7	13.1	13.2	12.7	12.4
2000	12.1	13.1	11.6	13.2	13.3	12.5	12.0	12.0	13.0	13.4	13.4	12.8	12.7
2001	13.0	14.0	14.1	14.1	14.1	13.2	13.2	13.2	14.3	14.8	14.8	14.3	13.9
2002	13.6	14.6	14.6	14.3	14.3	13.0	12.6	12.6	13.7	13.9	13.9	13.3	13.7
2003	13.1	14.2	14.2	14.3	14.3	13.4	13.2	13.2	14.2	14.1	14.2	14.1	13.9
Local government													
1990	26.2	26.4	26.6	25.9	26.1	26.3	23.7	23.4	24.6	24.9	25.1	25.2	25.3
1991	23.3	23.4	23.4	23.5	23.8	24.3	21.0	20.6	22.0	23.2	23.2	23.4	22.9
1992	23.5	23.9	24.1	23.9	24.2	24.8	22.0	21.6	23.3	24.1	24.3	24.6	23.6
1993	24.9	25.1	25.3	25.3	25.8	26.0	23.1	22.5	24.7	25.7	26.0	26.2	25.0
1994	25.5	25.6	25.7	25.9	25.9	26.6	23.2	22.9	25.1	26.2	26.5	26.6	25.4
1995	25.9	26.2	26.2	26.4	26.6	26.9	23.9	23.5	25.5	27.0	27.4	27.7	26.1
1996	26.7	27.0	27.3	27.7	28.0	28.4	24.8	24.4	26.8	28.0	28.5	27.9	27.1
1997	27.5	27.6	27.8	27.9	28.0	28.4	24.8	24.3	27.2	27.7	28.0	28.3	27.2
1998	27.6	27.9	28.1	27.9	28.2	28.4	23.8	23.6	26.6	27.3	27.7	28.0	27.0
1999	27.2	27.4	27.5	27.4	27.5	28.0	23.1	22.8	27.1	27.5	27.7	28.0	26.7
2000	27.8	27.9	28.1	28.0	28.1	28.5	23.5	23.3	27.9	28.3	28.8	28.9	27.4
2001	28.5	28.4	28.6	28.8	28.8	29.3	24.4	24.1	28.0	28.9	29.1	29.5	28.0
2002	29.0	29.0	29.2	29.1	29.2	29.7	24.9	24.7	28.5	28.4	28.7	29.0	28.3
2003	28.2	28.2	28.5	28.3	28.4	29.0	23.9	23.9	27.6	28.1	28.3	28.3	27.6
WORCESTER													
Total nonfarm													
1990	215.1	214.0	214.0	213.3	214.1	214.3	206.9	206.6	210.7	210.5	210.4	210.4	211.6
1991	201.4	200.4	201.1	200.1	200.9	201.2	193.8	194.0	198.0	199.7	200.7	200.9	199.3
1992	197.0	197.9	198.6	199.2	201.3	202.0	195.8	196.3	200.7	204.3	204.8	204.7	200.2
1993	202.2	202.7	202.7	205.6	206.8	208.0	203.0	202.7	207.5	209.3	210.2	211.5	206.0
1994	206.4	207.0	207.4	210.2	212.2	215.0	208.7	208.8	212.7	214.8	217.3	218.3	211.5
1995	209.5	209.8	211.3	211.3	213.2	214.1	210.8	212.2	215.1	215.8	217.2	218.7	213.2
1996	211.7	212.6	213.7	214.7	217.3	219.0	213.0	214.3	219.0	220.1	222.6	223.1	216.7
1997	217.6	217.8	219.6	221.2	223.6	225.1	218.8	219.4	224.1	227.3	229.0	231.8	222.9
1998	224.1	225.0	226.2	230.1	230.8	231.8	225.6	225.4	229.5	231.2	232.2	234.6	228.8
1999	226.8	227.8	228.4	231.4	231.7	233.3	227.8	227.3	231.0	233.5	234.0	235.1	230.6
2000	229.3	229.9	231.3	234.9	236.6	237.8	231.4	231.6	235.3	236.9	237.4	240.0	234.3
2001	234.4	234.0	235.0	237.7	239.3	240.4	233.5	233.1	235.4	238.2	238.6	239.2	236.6
2002	230.6	229.5	230.5	232.5	234.1	234.5	231.2	231.3	234.5	233.0	233.6	234.2	232.5
2003	228.6	227.0	227.8	230.7	232.9	233.0	228.3	227.6	231.2	232.0	232.8	233.1	230.4
Total private													
1990	184.2	183.4	183.4	182.6	183.1	183.4	178.6	178.5	181.0	179.8	179.7	179.4	181.4
1991	170.5	169.4	170.1	169.2	169.8	170.0	165.0	165.6	168.8	169.8	170.6	170.8	169.1
1992	167.0	167.7	168.1	168.5	170.2	170.7	167.1	167.8	170.2	173.2	173.3	173.2	169.7
1993	170.8	171.2	171.2	173.8	174.8	175.9	172.9	173.1	176.2	177.1	178.0	179.0	174.5
1994	174.6	175.1	175.6	178.4	180.2	182.7	178.3	178.9	181.3	183.0	185.0	186.0	179.9
1995	178.1	178.6	180.3	180.0	181.6	182.3	180.3	182.2	184.0	184.2	185.4	186.6	181.9
1996	179.9	180.8	181.8	182.4	184.5	185.9	181.8	183.4	186.1	186.9	189.1	189.3	184.3
1997	184.3	184.3	185.9	187.2	189.0	190.0	186.1	187.2	190.0	192.2	193.4	195.6	188.7
1998	189.3	190.1	190.9	194.1	194.7	195.3	191.2	191.3	194.5	195.0	196.1	198.0	193.3
1999	190.9	192.0	192.4	196.8	197.0	198.2	196.7	196.6	199.0	200.7	201.4	202.1	196.9
2000	197.0	197.5	198.6	201.6	202.6	203.8	200.0	200.9	202.8	203.8	204.2	206.4	201.6
2001	201.2	201.0	201.6	204.2	205.1	205.8	201.4	201.5	201.6	203.7	203.8	204.1	202.9
2002	196.1	194.9	195.9	198.0	199.2	199.5	199.0	199.6	200.1	199.1	199.4	200.0	198.4
2003	194.7	193.3	193.9	196.6	198.6	198.4	196.0	195.6	197.2	197.5	198.1	198.2	196.5

Employment by Industry: Massachusetts—*Continued*

(Numbers in thousands. Not seasonally adjusted.)

Industry	January	February	March	April	May	June	July	August	September	October	November	December	Annual Average
WORCESTER—*Continued*													
Goods-producing													
1990	50.4	49.7	49.5	49.4	49.7	50.2	49.2	49.3	49.2	48.7	48.5	48.0	49.3
1991	45.5	44.7	44.7	44.9	45.2	45.7	44.3	44.9	45.2	45.3	45.4	45.1	45.0
1992	42.5	42.1	42.8	43.7	44.5	44.9	43.7	44.2	44.6	44.9	44.6	44.4	43.9
1993	43.2	42.8	42.8	43.1	43.5	44.2	43.3	43.4	43.7	43.7	43.8	43.8	43.4
1994	42.5	42.3	42.5	43.4	43.9	44.9	44.4	44.8	44.9	44.8	44.8	44.8	44.0
1995	44.0	44.0	44.4	44.9	45.3	45.9	45.3	46.0	45.9	45.7	45.8	45.6	45.2
1996	45.0	45.2	45.3	45.6	46.3	47.0	45.0	45.5	45.7	46.2	46.5	46.2	45.7
1997	45.5	45.1	45.4	45.4	46.2	47.0	46.5	46.9	47.1	47.2	47.2	47.4	46.4
1998	46.1	45.9	46.1	47.0	47.3	47.7	46.5	46.7	46.8	46.4	46.3	46.3	46.5
1999	45.0	44.9	44.9	45.7	45.9	46.6	45.5	45.6	45.6	45.4	45.3	45.3	45.4
2000	44.6	44.2	44.5	45.4	46.0	46.7	46.0	46.4	46.5	46.9	46.8	47.0	45.9
2001	45.6	45.2	45.0	45.4	45.3	45.4	44.3	44.1	43.9	43.8	43.4	43.3	44.6
2002	40.7	39.9	40.0	40.6	40.9	41.0	40.7	41.1	40.9	39.7	39.5	39.3	40.4
2003	38.4	37.4	37.3	38.1	38.4	38.7	38.0	37.8	37.9	37.7	38.0	37.5	37.9
Construction and mining													
1990	6.9	6.5	6.5	6.6	6.9	7.2	7.3	7.4	7.3	6.9	6.7	6.4	6.8
1991	5.1	4.8	4.7	5.0	5.2	5.5	5.7	5.8	5.7	5.7	5.6	5.3	5.3
1992	4.5	4.3	4.3	4.8	5.4	5.6	5.8	5.9	6.0	5.9	5.7	5.6	5.3
1993	5.1	5.0	5.0	5.2	5.6	5.9	6.0	5.9	6.0	6.0	6.0	5.8	5.6
1994	5.2	4.9	5.0	5.6	5.9	6.3	6.5	6.6	6.5	6.6	6.5	6.3	5.9
1995	5.6	5.4	5.5	6.0	6.3	6.6	6.6	6.7	6.6	6.6	6.5	6.3	6.2
1996	5.5	5.4	5.5	6.0	6.5	6.8	6.9	7.1	7.0	7.2	7.1	6.8	6.4
1997	6.3	6.0	6.2	6.5	6.9	7.3	7.6	7.8	7.7	7.6	7.5	7.3	7.0
1998	6.5	6.3	6.5	7.1	7.4	7.7	7.7	7.8	7.7	7.7	7.6	7.5	7.2
1999	7.0	6.9	6.9	7.6	7.9	8.2	8.4	8.4	8.4	8.4	8.3	8.2	7.8
2000	7.7	7.4	7.6	8.4	8.7	9.2	9.5	9.5	9.5	9.3	9.3	9.1	8.7
2001	8.5	8.4	8.4	9.3	9.7	9.9	10.2	10.4	10.3	9.8	9.7	9.5	9.5
2002	8.5	8.2	8.3	9.1	9.5	9.7	9.8	9.9	9.7	9.5	9.5	9.2	9.2
2003	8.3	7.7	7.8	8.7	9.3	9.6	9.7	9.8	9.7	9.8	10.0	9.5	9.2
Manufacturing													
1990	43.5	43.2	43.0	42.8	42.8	43.0	41.9	41.9	41.9	41.8	41.8	41.6	42.4
1991	40.4	39.9	40.0	39.9	40.0	40.2	38.6	39.1	39.5	39.6	39.8	39.8	39.7
1992	38.0	37.8	38.5	38.9	39.1	39.3	37.9	38.3	38.6	39.0	38.9	38.8	38.5
1993	38.1	37.8	37.8	37.9	37.9	38.3	37.3	37.5	37.7	37.7	37.8	38.0	37.8
1994	37.3	37.4	37.5	37.8	38.0	38.6	37.9	38.2	38.4	38.2	38.3	38.5	38.0
1995	38.4	38.6	38.9	38.9	39.0	39.3	38.7	39.3	39.3	39.1	39.3	39.3	39.0
1996	39.5	39.8	39.8	39.6	39.8	40.2	38.1	38.4	38.7	39.0	39.4	39.4	39.3
1997	39.2	39.1	39.2	38.9	39.3	39.7	38.9	39.1	39.4	39.6	39.7	40.1	39.3
1998	39.6	39.6	39.6	39.9	39.9	40.0	38.8	38.9	39.1	38.7	38.7	38.8	39.3
1999	38.0	38.0	38.0	38.1	38.0	38.4	37.1	37.2	37.2	37.0	37.0	37.1	37.5
2000	36.9	36.8	36.9	37.0	37.3	37.5	36.5	36.9	37.0	37.6	37.5	37.9	37.1
2001	37.1	36.8	36.6	36.1	35.6	35.5	34.1	33.7	33.6	34.0	33.7	33.8	35.1
2002	32.2	31.7	31.7	31.5	31.4	31.3	30.9	31.2	31.2	30.2	30.0	30.1	31.1
2003	30.1	29.7	29.5	29.4	29.1	29.1	28.3	28.0	28.2	27.9	28.0	28.0	28.8
Service-providing													
1990	164.7	164.3	164.5	163.9	164.4	164.1	157.7	157.3	161.5	161.8	161.9	162.4	162.3
1991	155.9	155.7	156.4	155.2	155.7	155.5	149.5	149.1	152.8	154.4	155.3	155.8	154.2
1992	154.5	155.8	155.5	155.5	156.8	157.1	152.1	152.1	156.1	159.4	160.2	160.3	156.3
1993	159.0	159.9	159.9	162.5	163.3	163.8	159.7	159.3	163.8	165.6	166.4	167.7	162.5
1994	163.9	164.7	164.9	166.8	168.3	170.1	164.3	164.0	167.8	170.0	172.5	173.5	167.5
1995	165.5	165.8	166.9	166.4	167.9	168.2	165.5	166.2	169.2	170.1	171.4	173.1	168.0
1996	166.7	167.4	168.4	169.1	171.0	172.0	168.0	168.8	173.3	173.9	176.1	176.9	170.9
1997	172.1	172.7	174.2	175.8	177.4	178.1	172.3	172.5	177.0	180.1	181.8	184.4	176.5
1998	178.0	179.1	180.1	183.1	183.5	184.1	179.1	178.7	182.7	184.8	185.9	188.3	182.2
1999	181.8	182.9	183.5	185.7	185.8	186.7	182.3	181.7	185.4	188.1	188.7	189.8	185.2
2000	184.7	185.7	186.8	189.5	190.6	191.1	185.4	185.2	188.8	190.0	190.6	193.0	188.4
2001	188.8	188.8	190.0	192.3	194.0	195.0	189.2	189.0	191.5	194.4	195.2	195.9	192.0
2002	189.9	189.6	190.5	191.9	193.2	193.5	190.5	190.2	193.6	193.3	194.1	194.9	192.1
2003	190.2	189.6	190.5	192.6	194.5	194.3	190.3	189.8	193.3	194.3	194.8	195.6	192.5
Trade, transportation, and utilities													
1990	42.3	41.2	41.3	41.2	40.9	41.2	39.6	39.7	40.5	40.3	40.8	40.9	40.8
1991	38.6	37.7	37.7	37.0	37.4	37.5	35.8	35.8	36.9	37.1	38.2	38.5	37.3
1992	37.5	37.2	37.2	37.3	37.5	37.5	36.1	36.1	36.8	38.0	38.6	39.1	37.4
1993	37.6	37.0	37.0	37.5	37.6	38.1	37.5	37.6	38.3	38.5	39.4	39.9	38.0
1994	38.3	37.7	37.7	38.4	38.6	39.4	38.6	38.4	39.3	40.0	41.2	41.8	39.1
1995	39.0	38.4	38.7	37.9	38.2	38.4	38.0	38.4	39.2	39.6	40.3	40.8	38.9
1996	38.9	38.4	38.4	38.3	38.5	38.9	37.8	38.2	38.8	39.8	41.0	41.4	39.0
1997	39.8	39.4	39.9	40.4	40.7	41.5	40.0	39.4	40.4	41.7	42.9	43.9	40.8
1998	41.5	41.4	41.4	41.5	42.1	42.5	41.5	41.4	42.5	43.2	44.5	45.2	42.3
1999	42.7	42.5	42.8	43.6	43.8	44.2	43.0	42.9	43.6	44.4	45.5	46.3	43.7
2000	44.7	43.9	44.1	44.4	44.4	44.4	43.0	43.2	43.5	44.0	44.9	45.8	44.1
2001	43.9	43.1	43.2	43.6	43.7	44.2	43.2	43.3	43.4	44.2	45.1	45.6	43.9
2002	43.4	42.8	43.2	43.4	43.3	43.7	43.2	43.0	43.5	43.8	44.5	44.9	43.6
2003	43.3	42.5	42.7	43.4	43.7	44.0	43.4	43.7	44.2	44.4	44.9	44.8	43.8

Employment by Industry: Massachusetts—*Continued*

(Numbers in thousands. Not seasonally adjusted.)

Industry	January	February	March	April	May	June	July	August	September	October	November	December	Annual Average
WORCESTER—*Continued*													
Wholesale trade													
1990	11.3	11.3	11.3	11.6	11.4	11.5	11.3	11.4	11.4	11.3	11.0	11.0	11.3
1991	10.3	10.1	10.1	9.8	9.9	10.0	9.8	9.8	9.9	9.8	9.9	9.8	9.9
1992	9.7	9.7	9.8	10.0	10.1	10.1	9.9	9.8	9.9	10.1	10.2	10.2	9.9
1993	10.1	10.0	10.1	10.1	10.1	10.4	10.2	10.2	10.2	10.3	10.5	10.5	10.2
1994	10.3	10.3	10.3	10.8	10.8	10.9	10.8	10.9	11.0	11.2	11.4	11.5	10.8
1995	10.6	10.6	10.7	10.4	10.4	10.5	10.3	10.5	10.7	10.9	11.0	11.1	10.6
1996	10.5	10.5	10.5	10.3	10.2	10.2	9.9	10.1	10.0	10.2	10.3	10.4	10.2
1997	10.0	10.0	10.2	10.1	10.3	10.4	10.2	10.3	10.3	10.4	10.7	11.0	10.3
1998	10.2	10.2	10.3	10.1	10.2	10.3	10.0	10.0	10.2	10.1	10.5	10.7	10.2
1999	10.1	10.1	10.1	10.4	10.5	10.5	10.1	10.1	10.2	10.2	10.3	10.3	10.2
2000	10.0	10.0	10.0	10.4	10.2	9.9	9.7	9.8	9.8	9.8	9.8	9.9	9.9
2001	9.7	9.7	9.7	9.8	9.8	9.9	9.7	9.9	9.7	9.9	9.9	9.8	9.8
2002	9.5	9.4	9.5	9.6	9.5	9.7	9.6	9.6	9.6	9.8	9.8	9.8	9.6
2003	9.8	9.7	9.7	9.9	9.9	10.0	10.0	10.1	10.0	10.1	10.1	10.1	10.0
Retail trade													
1990	25.6	24.5	24.5	24.3	24.2	24.4	23.3	23.1	23.3	23.4	24.2	24.3	24.0
1991	22.9	22.2	22.2	21.9	22.2	22.1	21.3	21.3	21.8	22.0	23.0	23.4	22.1
1992	22.4	22.1	21.9	22.1	22.2	22.1	21.3	21.4	21.6	22.5	23.0	23.4	22.1
1993	22.2	21.7	21.6	21.9	22.1	22.3	21.9	22.0	22.3	22.3	23.0	23.5	22.2
1994	22.4	21.8	21.7	21.9	22.1	22.7	22.3	22.0	22.5	22.7	23.7	24.3	22.5
1995	22.7	22.2	22.4	22.0	22.2	22.4	22.4	22.7	23.0	23.0	23.7	24.1	22.7
1996	22.9	22.4	22.5	22.9	23.1	23.4	23.0	23.1	23.5	23.7	24.7	25.1	23.3
1997	24.1	23.7	24.0	24.5	24.6	25.3	24.3	24.3	24.3	25.2	26.2	26.7	24.7
1998	25.1	25.1	24.9	25.1	25.6	25.9	25.5	25.5	25.8	26.7	27.5	28.1	25.9
1999	26.3	26.1	26.3	26.4	26.5	26.9	26.5	26.6	26.7	27.1	28.1	29.0	26.8
2000	27.8	27.1	27.2	26.9	27.0	27.5	26.7	26.9	26.8	27.0	28.0	28.9	27.3
2001	27.2	26.5	26.5	26.7	26.8	27.1	26.6	26.6	26.4	27.0	27.9	28.5	27.0
2002	26.8	26.3	26.6	26.5	26.6	26.8	26.8	26.7	26.7	26.6	27.3	27.7	26.8
2003	26.3	25.7	25.9	26.2	26.5	26.8	26.5	26.8	27.0	27.1	27.6	27.7	26.7
Transportation and utilities													
1990	5.4	5.4	5.5	5.3	5.3	5.3	5.0	5.2	5.8	5.6	5.6	5.6	5.4
1991	5.4	5.4	5.4	5.3	5.3	5.4	4.7	4.7	5.2	5.3	5.3	5.3	5.2
1992	5.4	5.4	5.5	5.2	5.2	5.3	4.9	4.9	5.3	5.4	5.4	5.5	5.2
1993	5.3	5.3	5.3	5.5	5.4	5.4	5.4	5.4	5.8	5.9	5.9	5.9	5.5
1994	5.6	5.6	5.7	5.7	5.7	5.8	5.5	5.5	5.8	6.1	6.1	6.0	5.7
1995	5.7	5.6	5.6	5.5	5.6	5.5	5.3	5.2	5.5	5.7	5.6	5.6	5.5
1996	5.5	5.5	5.4	5.1	5.2	5.3	4.9	5.0	5.3	5.9	6.0	5.9	5.4
1997	5.7	5.7	5.7	5.8	5.8	5.8	5.5	4.8	5.8	6.1	6.0	6.2	5.7
1998	6.2	6.1	6.2	6.3	6.3	6.3	6.0	5.9	6.5	6.4	6.5	6.4	6.2
1999	6.3	6.3	6.4	6.8	6.8	6.8	6.4	6.2	6.7	7.1	7.1	7.0	6.6
2000	6.9	6.8	6.9	7.1	7.2	7.0	6.6	6.5	6.9	7.2	7.1	7.0	6.9
2001	7.0	6.9	7.0	7.1	7.1	7.2	6.9	6.8	7.3	7.3	7.3	7.3	7.1
2002	7.1	7.1	7.1	7.3	7.2	7.2	6.8	6.7	7.2	7.4	7.4	7.4	7.2
2003	7.2	7.1	7.1	7.3	7.3	7.2	6.9	6.8	7.2	7.2	7.2	7.0	7.1
Information													
1990	3.8	3.8	3.8	3.9	3.9	3.9	3.7	3.7	3.7	3.7	3.7	3.7	3.7
1991	3.6	3.6	3.6	3.6	3.6	3.6	3.6	3.6	3.6	3.5	3.6	3.6	3.5
1992	3.5	3.5	3.3	3.2	3.2	3.2	3.3	3.2	3.2	3.2	3.2	3.2	3.2
1993	3.2	3.2	3.0	2.8	2.8	2.9	3.0	3.0	3.0	3.0	3.0	3.0	2.9
1994	3.0	3.0	2.9	2.9	2.9	2.9	2.9	2.9	2.8	2.7	2.7	2.8	2.8
1995	2.7	2.7	2.7	2.7	2.7	2.8	2.7	2.7	2.7	2.7	2.7	2.7	2.7
1996	2.7	2.6	2.6	2.6	2.6	2.6	2.7	2.7	2.8	2.8	2.9	2.9	2.7
1997	2.8	2.8	2.8	3.0	3.0	3.0	3.0	3.0	3.1	2.9	3.0	3.0	2.9
1998	2.9	2.9	3.0	3.0	3.0	3.0	2.9	2.9	2.8	2.9	2.9	3.0	2.9
1999	3.0	3.0	3.0	3.1	3.2	3.2	3.2	3.2	3.2	3.2	3.3	3.3	3.1
2000	3.4	3.5	3.5	3.7	3.8	3.9	3.9	3.6	4.1	4.1	4.3	4.3	3.8
2001	4.4	4.4	4.4	4.4	4.5	4.5	4.4	4.4	4.3	4.4	4.4	4.3	4.4
2002	4.4	4.3	4.3	4.3	4.3	4.3	4.3	4.3	4.2	4.1	4.1	4.1	4.3
2003	4.1	4.0	4.0	3.9	3.9	4.0	3.9	3.9	3.8	3.9	3.9	3.9	3.9
Financial activities													
1990	14.6	14.6	14.6	14.7	14.8	14.9	14.6	14.6	14.5	14.2	14.2	14.2	14.5
1991	14.2	14.1	14.2	14.1	14.1	14.1	13.8	13.7	13.7	13.8	13.7	13.7	13.9
1992	14.3	14.3	14.3	14.3	14.3	14.4	13.7	13.8	13.8	14.0	14.0	14.0	14.1
1993	14.8	15.5	15.5	15.6	15.6	15.8	15.2	15.2	15.3	15.6	15.6	15.7	15.4
1994	15.6	15.7	15.8	15.9	16.1	16.3	15.7	15.6	15.7	15.1	15.2	15.3	15.6
1995	14.4	14.5	14.5	14.4	14.5	14.6	14.8	14.8	14.8	14.6	14.8	15.0	14.6
1996	14.4	14.5	14.6	14.0	14.1	14.3	14.3	14.4	14.4	14.2	14.2	14.3	14.3
1997	14.2	14.2	14.3	14.4	14.4	14.5	14.1	14.2	14.2	13.9	14.0	13.9	14.1
1998	14.2	14.4	14.4	14.1	14.0	14.0	14.2	14.2	14.2	14.4	14.4	14.5	14.2
1999	14.5	14.7	14.7	14.8	14.7	14.9	15.0	14.9	14.7	14.6	14.6	14.6	14.7
2000	13.7	13.6	13.6	13.6	13.6	13.6	13.2	13.2	13.1	13.1	13.2	13.3	13.4
2001	13.4	13.3	13.4	13.7	13.7	13.9	13.9	13.9	13.8	14.0	14.0	14.0	13.8
2002	13.9	13.8	13.8	13.9	13.9	14.0	14.1	14.1	13.9	14.1	14.0	14.0	14.0
2003	13.6	13.7	13.7	13.8	13.8	13.9	13.9	14.0	13.9	13.8	13.6	13.6	13.8

Employment by Industry: Massachusetts—*Continued*

(Numbers in thousands. Not seasonally adjusted.)

Industry	January	February	March	April	May	June	July	August	September	October	November	December	Annual Average
WORCESTER—*Continued*													
Professional and business services													
1990	21.0	21.2	21.1	21.2	21.1	21.1	21.0	21.1	21.2	20.5	20.5	20.5	20.9
1991	19.4	19.4	19.6	19.4	19.2	19.4	19.0	19.2	19.5	19.1	18.8	18.8	19.2
1992	18.9	19.3	19.4	19.7	19.9	20.3	20.0	20.0	19.9	20.0	19.9	19.9	19.7
1993	19.6	19.8	20.0	20.5	20.6	20.6	20.7	20.7	21.0	21.2	21.1	21.2	20.5
1994	21.4	21.8	21.8	21.5	21.6	22.0	21.6	21.9	22.1	22.8	23.2	22.9	22.0
1995	22.1	22.2	22.6	22.1	22.1	22.3	21.8	22.3	22.3	22.1	22.2	22.1	22.1
1996	21.1	21.6	21.8	22.1	22.4	22.8	23.2	23.5	23.9	23.6	23.9	23.8	22.8
1997	22.8	22.8	23.0	24.0	24.1	24.5	24.0	24.7	24.9	25.4	25.4	25.7	24.2
1998	24.6	24.7	25.2	26.7	26.0	26.2	25.8	25.8	25.9	25.5	25.4	25.8	25.6
1999	24.8	25.3	25.7	26.0	25.5	25.9	25.9	26.1	26.4	27.4	27.5	27.6	26.1
2000	26.8	27.3	27.5	28.3	28.0	28.2	28.0	28.4	28.5	27.8	27.9	28.1	27.9
2001	27.8	27.9	28.1	28.5	28.5	28.8	27.9	28.3	28.0	27.4	27.2	27.4	28.0
2002	26.2	26.3	26.4	26.8	26.8	26.8	27.6	27.9	28.0	26.8	27.0	26.7	26.9
2003	26.0	26.0	26.0	26.6	26.6	26.7	26.8	26.8	26.8	26.7	27.0	27.2	26.6
Educational and health services													
1990	29.2	29.8	30.0	29.1	29.2	28.6	27.4	27.3	28.9	29.8	29.8	30.0	29.0
1991	28.6	29.2	29.5	29.6	29.5	28.9	27.8	27.7	29.0	30.0	30.1	30.1	29.1
1992	29.9	30.4	30.4	29.9	29.9	29.3	29.9	29.9	31.3	31.7	31.9	31.8	30.5
1993	31.9	32.1	32.2	32.9	32.6	31.9	30.8	30.8	32.2	32.8	32.9	33.1	32.1
1994	32.3	32.9	33.0	33.7	33.9	33.3	31.8	31.8	33.3	34.3	34.7	34.9	33.3
1995	33.3	34.1	34.4	34.6	34.6	34.0	33.6	33.8	34.9	35.6	35.9	36.0	34.5
1996	34.5	35.4	35.5	35.6	35.5	35.1	34.0	34.2	35.4	35.8	36.3	36.3	35.3
1997	35.6	36.4	36.7	36.2	36.0	35.0	34.4	34.5	35.8	36.6	36.7	37.0	35.9
1998	36.6	37.0	37.0	37.2	37.2	36.7	35.5	35.6	37.4	38.0	38.2	38.5	37.0
1999	36.6	36.8	36.5	38.2	38.0	37.0	38.4	38.1	39.8	40.1	40.2	40.0	38.3
2000	39.4	40.3	40.3	40.6	40.7	40.4	39.9	39.9	41.0	41.5	41.4	41.6	40.5
2001	40.7	41.7	41.8	42.5	42.6	41.3	40.3	40.4	41.4	42.7	42.8	42.8	41.8
2002	41.2	41.7	41.9	42.1	42.2	41.4	40.7	40.5	41.2	42.7	42.6	42.9	41.8
2003	42.3	42.9	43.1	43.5	43.3	42.2	41.1	40.8	42.3	42.9	43.3	43.5	42.6
Leisure and hospitality													
1990	14.8	15.0	15.0	15.0	15.4	15.4	15.2	15.0	15.3	14.8	14.5	14.4	14.9
1991	13.3	13.5	13.6	13.6	13.8	13.9	13.8	13.9	14.2	14.2	14.0	14.1	13.8
1992	13.5	13.8	13.8	13.8	14.2	14.4	13.9	14.1	14.2	14.8	14.5	14.2	14.1
1993	14.0	14.3	14.1	14.5	15.1	15.3	15.1	15.2	15.6	15.2	15.0	15.1	14.8
1994	14.5	14.5	14.6	15.2	15.7	16.3	15.7	15.9	15.7	15.7	15.5	15.7	15.4
1995	15.2	15.3	15.5	15.9	16.6	16.7	16.4	16.4	16.5	16.2	15.9	16.4	16.0
1996	15.8	15.5	15.9	16.2	17.0	17.3	17.1	17.2	17.5	17.1	16.9	17.0	16.7
1997	16.3	16.3	16.5	16.5	17.3	17.2	16.7	17.1	17.2	17.1	16.8	17.2	16.8
1998	16.1	16.5	16.4	17.1	17.6	17.6	17.1	17.1	17.4	17.1	16.8	17.0	16.9
1999	16.5	16.9	16.9	17.5	17.9	18.3	17.7	17.8	17.9	17.7	17.1	17.0	17.4
2000	16.7	16.9	17.3	17.7	18.2	18.5	18.0	18.1	18.1	18.3	17.6	18.1	17.7
2001	17.5	17.5	17.8	18.1	18.7	19.4	19.0	18.8	18.7	19.0	18.6	18.4	18.5
2002	18.1	18.0	18.1	18.7	19.6	20.0	20.0	20.4	20.3	20.0	19.7	20.1	19.4
2003	19.1	18.9	19.1	19.3	20.8	20.7	20.6	20.5	20.4	20.0	19.6	19.6	19.9
Other services													
1990	8.1	8.1	8.1	8.1	8.1	8.1	7.9	7.8	7.7	7.8	7.7	7.7	7.9
1991	7.3	7.2	7.2	7.0	7.0	6.9	6.9	6.8	6.7	6.8	6.8	6.9	6.9
1992	6.9	7.1	6.9	6.6	6.7	6.7	6.5	6.5	6.4	6.6	6.6	6.6	6.6
1993	6.5	6.5	6.6	6.9	7.0	7.1	7.3	7.2	7.1	7.1	7.2	7.2	6.9
1994	7.0	7.2	7.3	7.4	7.5	7.6	7.6	7.6	7.5	7.6	7.7	7.8	7.4
1995	7.4	7.4	7.5	7.5	7.6	7.6	7.7	7.8	7.7	7.7	7.8	8.0	7.6
1996	7.5	7.6	7.7	8.0	8.1	7.9	7.7	7.7	7.6	7.4	7.4	7.4	7.6
1997	7.3	7.3	7.3	7.3	7.3	7.3	7.4	7.4	7.3	7.4	7.4	7.5	7.3
1998	7.3	7.3	7.4	7.5	7.5	7.6	7.7	7.6	7.5	7.5	7.6	7.7	7.5
1999	7.8	7.9	7.9	7.9	8.0	8.1	8.0	8.0	7.8	7.9	7.9	8.0	7.9
2000	7.7	7.8	7.8	7.9	7.9	8.1	8.0	8.1	8.0	8.1	8.1	8.2	7.9
2001	7.9	7.9	7.9	8.0	8.1	8.3	8.4	8.3	8.1	8.2	8.3	8.3	8.1
2002	8.2	8.1	8.2	8.2	8.2	8.3	8.4	8.3	8.1	7.9	8.0	8.0	8.2
2003	7.9	7.9	8.0	8.0	8.1	8.2	8.3	8.1	7.9	8.1	7.8	8.1	8.0
Government													
1990	30.9	30.6	30.6	30.7	31.0	30.9	28.3	28.1	29.7	30.7	30.7	31.0	30.2
1991	30.9	31.0	31.0	30.9	31.1	31.2	28.8	28.4	29.2	29.9	30.1	30.1	30.2
1992	30.0	30.2	30.5	30.7	31.1	31.3	28.7	28.5	30.5	31.1	31.5	31.5	30.4
1993	31.4	31.5	31.5	31.8	32.0	32.1	30.1	29.6	31.3	32.2	32.2	32.5	31.5
1994	31.8	31.9	31.8	31.8	32.0	32.3	30.4	29.9	31.4	31.8	32.3	32.3	31.6
1995	31.4	31.2	31.0	31.3	31.6	31.8	30.5	30.0	31.1	31.6	31.8	32.1	31.2
1996	31.8	31.8	31.9	32.3	32.8	33.1	31.2	30.9	32.9	33.2	33.5	33.8	32.4
1997	33.3	33.5	33.7	34.0	34.6	35.1	32.7	32.2	34.1	35.1	35.6	36.2	34.1
1998	34.8	34.9	35.3	36.0	36.1	36.5	34.4	34.1	35.0	36.2	36.1	36.6	35.5
1999	35.9	35.8	36.0	34.6	34.7	35.1	31.1	30.7	32.0	32.8	32.6	33.0	33.6
2000	32.3	32.4	32.7	33.3	34.0	34.0	31.4	30.7	32.5	33.1	33.2	33.6	32.7
2001	33.2	33.0	33.4	33.5	34.2	34.6	32.1	31.6	33.8	34.5	34.8	35.1	33.7
2002	34.5	34.6	34.6	34.5	34.9	35.0	32.2	31.7	34.4	33.9	34.2	34.2	34.1
2003	33.9	33.7	33.9	34.1	34.3	34.6	32.3	32.0	34.0	34.5	34.7	34.9	33.9

Employment by Industry: Massachusetts—*Continued*

(Numbers in thousands. Not seasonally adjusted.)

Industry	January	February	March	April	May	June	July	August	September	October	November	December	Annual Average
WORCESTER—*Continued*													
Federal government													
1990	2.0	2.0	2.0	2.0	2.0	2.0	2.0	2.0	2.0	2.0	2.0	2.0	2.0
1991	2.0	2.0	2.0	2.0	2.0	2.1	2.2	2.2	2.2	2.2	2.3	2.3	2.1
1992	2.3	2.3	2.3	2.3	2.3	2.3	2.3	2.3	2.3	2.3	2.3	2.4	2.3
1993	2.6	2.7	2.7	2.8	2.8	2.8	2.9	2.9	2.9	2.9	2.8	3.0	2.8
1994	2.8	2.8	2.8	2.8	2.8	2.8	2.8	2.8	2.8	2.6	2.6	2.7	2.7
1995	2.6	2.4	2.3	2.3	2.3	2.3	2.3	2.3	2.3	2.3	2.3	2.4	2.3
1996	2.3	2.3	2.2	2.3	2.3	2.3	2.3	2.3	2.2	2.2	2.3	2.4	2.2
1997	2.3	2.3	2.3	2.3	2.3	2.3	2.3	2.3	2.4	2.3	2.4	2.7	2.3
1998	2.4	2.4	2.4	2.4	2.4	2.4	2.4	2.4	2.4	2.4	2.5	2.6	2.4
1999	2.4	2.4	2.4	2.4	2.4	2.4	2.4	2.4	2.4	2.4	2.4	2.6	2.4
2000	2.4	2.4	2.4	2.6	3.2	3.0	2.7	2.4	2.3	2.3	2.3	2.5	2.5
2001	2.4	2.3	2.4	2.4	2.4	2.5	2.4	2.4	2.4	2.4	2.4	2.5	2.4
2002	2.3	2.3	2.3	2.2	2.3	2.4	2.4	2.4	2.3	2.3	2.4	2.5	2.3
2003	2.3	2.3	2.2	2.3	2.3	2.3	2.3	2.3	2.3	2.3	2.3	2.3	2.3
State government													
1990	10.7	10.6	10.6	10.6	10.5	10.6	10.3	10.3	10.5	10.5	10.6	10.6	10.5
1991	10.6	10.5	10.6	10.5	10.6	10.6	10.3	10.2	10.5	10.4	10.4	10.4	10.4
1992	10.7	10.8	10.8	10.8	10.8	10.8	10.4	10.4	10.7	10.8	10.8	10.9	10.7
1993	10.8	10.8	10.8	10.8	10.9	10.8	10.7	10.6	10.8	10.9	10.9	10.8	10.8
1994	10.8	10.8	10.8	11.0	11.1	11.1	10.9	10.8	10.8	10.9	10.9	10.9	10.9
1995	10.7	10.7	10.7	10.7	10.7	10.7	10.7	10.6	10.7	10.7	10.7	10.8	10.7
1996	10.8	10.8	10.7	11.0	11.2	11.4	11.5	11.5	11.5	11.6	11.7	11.8	11.2
1997	11.9	12.1	12.2	12.4	12.7	12.8	12.6	12.6	12.5	12.7	12.8	12.8	12.5
1998	12.5	12.6	12.7	12.9	13.0	13.0	13.6	13.7	13.6	13.8	13.5	13.7	13.2
1999	13.5	13.5	13.6	12.0	12.1	12.0	9.8	9.8	9.7	10.0	9.9	9.9	11.3
2000	9.5	9.5	9.6	9.5	9.5	9.5	9.7	9.6	9.6	9.6	9.6	9.6	9.5
2001	9.8	9.8	9.8	9.9	10.0	10.1	10.1	10.1	10.1	10.1	10.1	10.1	10.0
2002	10.2	10.2	10.2	10.1	10.1	9.9	9.9	9.9	10.0	9.7	9.7	9.7	10.0
2003	9.9	9.9	9.9	9.9	9.9	9.9	10.5	10.5	10.4	10.4	10.4	10.3	10.2
Local government													
1990	18.2	18.0	18.0	18.1	18.5	18.3	16.0	15.8	17.2	18.2	18.1	18.4	17.7
1991	18.3	18.5	18.4	18.4	18.5	18.5	16.3	16.0	16.5	17.3	17.4	17.4	17.6
1992	17.0	17.1	17.4	17.6	18.0	18.2	16.0	15.8	17.5	18.0	18.4	18.2	17.4
1993	18.0	18.0	18.0	18.2	18.3	18.5	16.5	16.1	17.6	18.4	18.5	18.7	17.9
1994	18.2	18.3	18.2	18.0	18.1	18.4	16.7	16.3	17.8	18.3	18.8	18.7	17.9
1995	18.1	18.1	18.0	18.3	18.6	18.8	17.5	17.1	18.1	18.6	18.8	18.9	18.2
1996	18.7	18.7	19.0	19.0	19.3	19.4	17.4	17.1	19.2	19.4	19.5	19.6	18.8
1997	19.1	19.1	19.2	19.3	19.6	20.0	17.8	17.3	19.2	20.1	20.4	20.7	19.3
1998	19.9	19.9	20.2	20.7	20.7	21.1	18.4	18.0	19.0	20.0	20.1	20.3	19.8
1999	20.0	19.9	20.0	20.2	20.2	20.7	18.9	18.5	19.9	20.4	20.3	20.5	19.9
2000	20.4	20.5	20.7	21.2	21.3	21.5	19.0	18.7	20.6	21.2	21.3	21.5	20.6
2001	21.0	20.9	21.2	21.2	21.8	22.0	19.6	19.1	21.3	22.0	22.3	22.5	21.2
2002	22.0	22.1	22.1	22.2	22.5	22.7	19.9	19.4	22.1	21.9	22.1	22.0	21.8
2003	21.7	21.5	21.8	21.9	22.1	22.4	19.5	19.2	21.3	21.8	22.0	22.3	21.5

Average Weekly Hours by Industry: Massachusetts

(Not seasonally adjusted.)

Industry	January	February	March	April	May	June	July	August	September	October	November	December	Annual Average
STATEWIDE													
Manufacturing													
2001	40.7	40.4	40.9	39.6	40.4	40.7	39.3	39.8	40.4	39.8	40.3	41.3	40.3
2002	40.2	40.5	40.9	40.8	41.0	41.6	39.5	40.9	41.1	40.4	40.5	41.6	40.8
2003	40.3	40.5	41.0	40.3	40.4	40.7	39.8	40.3	40.8	40.2	40.9	41.4	40.6
BOSTON													
Manufacturing													
2001	40.5	40.7	40.9	40.2	40.7	40.9	38.9	39.9	40.3	39.6	40.3	41.3	40.4
2002	40.7	40.7	41.2	40.9	40.9	41.9	40.6	40.8	41.6	40.6	40.9	41.3	41.0
2003	39.5	39.0	39.3	38.6	38.9	39.4	39.8	40.1	41.0	39.8	41.4	42.0	39.9
LAWRENCE-HAVERHILL													
Manufacturing													
2001	38.9	37.9	36.7	36.1	36.7	36.4	36.3	37.4	37.1	38.8	38.7	40.5	37.6
2002	39.1	39.4	40.4	40.6	40.3	41.0	40.7	40.7	40.4	39.8	41.0	40.2	40.3
2003	38.5	39.1	40.0	39.8	40.0	40.4	39.5	39.4	40.8	40.7	41.1	41.3	40.0
LOWELL													
Manufacturing													
2001	40.8	37.8	42.6	40.1	41.7	41.6	38.4	41.2	41.6	41.5	42.0	41.5	40.9
2002	40.4	40.4	40.7	40.5	41.2	40.8	39.0	37.7	38.3	37.7	38.7	37.6	39.5
2003	39.2	39.4	39.8	39.2	39.3	40.1	38.1	39.5	39.9	39.7	40.2	39.7	39.5
SPRINGFIELD													
Manufacturing													
2001	39.5	39.6	40.4	38.2	39.8	40.3	39.6	39.2	40.4	39.7	40.6	41.4	39.9
2002	39.7	39.4	39.9	40.0	40.2	40.7	40.5	40.7	40.8	40.7	41.0	40.8	40.4
2003	40.7	40.6	40.9	40.8	40.8	40.4	38.5	40.1	40.5	40.0	41.0	40.3	40.4
WORCESTER													
Manufacturing													
2001	40.9	40.3	40.6	39.6	39.8	39.9	39.4	39.0	39.8	39.2	40.1	41.6	40.0
2002	39.7	41.2	41.3	40.9	40.9	41.0	40.9	41.0	40.6	40.8	40.9	40.8	40.8
2003	40.7	40.7	41.0	40.7	40.4	41.0	39.3	40.4	40.4	39.4	39.9	40.2	40.4

Average Hourly Earnings by Industry: Massachusetts

(Dollars, not seasonally adjusted.)

Industry	January	February	March	April	May	June	July	August	September	October	November	December	Annual Average
STATEWIDE													
Manufacturing													
2001	15.34	15.42	15.49	15.56	15.52	15.75	16.01	15.88	15.91	16.04	16.06	16.17	15.75
2002	16.00	15.96	16.04	16.06	16.09	16.19	16.49	16.47	16.43	16.26	16.38	16.67	16.25
2003	16.48	16.37	16.44	16.54	16.49	16.55	16.49	16.50	16.53	16.59	16.69	16.71	16.53
BOSTON													
Manufacturing													
2001	17.36	17.41	17.57	17.49	17.56	17.62	17.87	17.74	18.01	18.20	17.81	18.07	17.72
2002	17.78	17.74	17.79	17.89	17.70	17.96	17.88	17.89	17.95	17.92	17.99	18.04	17.88
2003	17.94	17.96	18.01	18.04	18.02	18.04	18.13	18.07	18.13	18.03	18.13	18.08	18.05
LAWRENCE-HAVERHILL													
Manufacturing													
2001	14.20	14.41	14.91	14.78	14.60	14.73	15.36	14.94	15.99	15.87	15.86	16.46	15.16
2002	16.09	16.29	16.00	16.20	16.44	15.52	15.33	15.20	15.07	15.13	15.08	15.20	15.64
2003	14.68	14.86	14.98	15.03	15.03	15.18	15.29	15.37	15.36	15.26	15.60	15.68	15.18
LOWELL													
Manufacturing													
2001	16.17	16.65	16.45	16.53	16.60	16.14	16.91	17.01	17.02	17.45	17.08	17.03	16.74
2002	17.33	17.13	16.99	17.40	17.21	17.23	17.46	18.18	18.02	17.72	17.72	17.92	17.50
2003	17.58	17.16	17.25	16.95	17.25	16.81	16.76	16.88	16.98	17.01	16.90	16.88	17.04
SPRINGFIELD													
Manufacturing													
2001	14.58	14.54	14.52	14.85	14.83	15.02	15.33	15.24	15.21	15.45	15.40	15.19	15.01
2002	15.30	15.36	15.54	15.42	15.70	15.68	15.70	15.71	15.72	15.77	15.79	15.81	15.63
2003	15.78	15.77	15.78	15.76	15.73	15.92	16.05	15.89	15.90	16.13	16.12	16.28	15.92
WORCESTER													
Manufacturing													
2001	14.39	14.51	14.32	14.54	14.51	14.60	14.78	14.63	14.72	14.80	14.83	15.20	14.64
2002	14.92	14.83	14.97	15.03	15.15	15.30	15.36	15.37	15.38	15.42	15.43	15.43	15.21
2003	15.41	15.41	15.41	15.35	15.32	15.45	15.50	15.60	15.78	15.53	15.70	15.67	15.50

Average Weekly Earnings by Industry: Massachusetts

(Dollars, not seasonally adjusted.)

Industry	January	February	March	April	May	June	July	August	September	October	November	December	Annual Average
STATEWIDE													
Manufacturing													
2001	624.34	622.97	633.54	616.18	627.01	641.03	629.19	632.02	642.76	638.39	647.22	667.82	634.73
2002	643.20	646.38	656.04	655.25	659.69	673.50	651.36	673.62	675.27	656.90	663.39	693.47	663.00
2003	664.14	662.99	674.04	666.56	666.20	673.59	656.30	664.95	674.42	666.92	682.62	691.79	671.12
BOSTON													
Manufacturing													
2001	703.08	708.59	718.61	703.10	714.69	720.66	695.14	707.83	725.80	720.72	717.74	746.29	715.89
2002	723.65	722.02	732.95	731.70	723.93	752.52	725.93	729.91	746.72	727.55	735.79	745.05	733.08
2003	708.63	700.44	707.79	696.34	700.98	710.78	721.57	724.61	743.33	717.59	750.58	759.36	720.20
LAWRENCE-HAVERHILL													
Manufacturing													
2001	552.38	546.14	547.20	533.56	535.82	536.17	557.57	558.76	593.23	615.76	613.78	666.63	570.02
2002	629.12	641.83	646.40	657.72	662.53	636.32	623.93	618.64	608.83	602.17	618.28	611.04	630.29
2003	565.18	581.03	599.20	598.19	601.20	613.27	603.96	605.58	626.69	621.08	641.16	647.58	607.20
LOWELL													
Manufacturing													
2001	659.74	629.37	700.77	662.85	692.22	671.42	649.34	700.81	708.03	724.18	717.36	706.75	684.67
2002	700.13	692.05	691.49	704.70	709.05	702.98	680.94	685.39	690.17	668.04	685.76	673.79	691.25
2003	689.14	676.10	686.55	664.44	677.93	674.08	638.56	666.76	677.50	675.30	679.38	670.14	673.08
SPRINGFIELD													
Manufacturing													
2001	575.91	575.78	586.61	567.27	590.23	605.31	607.07	597.41	614.48	613.37	625.24	628.87	598.90
2002	607.41	605.18	620.05	616.80	631.14	638.18	635.85	639.40	641.38	641.84	647.39	645.05	631.45
2003	642.25	640.26	645.40	643.01	641.78	643.17	617.93	637.19	643.95	645.20	660.92	656.08	643.17
WORCESTER													
Manufacturing													
2001	588.55	584.75	581.39	575.78	577.50	582.54	582.33	570.57	585.86	580.16	594.68	632.32	585.60
2002	592.32	611.00	618.26	614.73	619.64	627.30	628.22	630.17	624.43	629.14	631.09	629.54	620.57
2003	627.19	627.19	631.81	624.75	618.93	633.45	609.15	630.24	637.51	611.88	626.43	629.93	626.20

MICHIGAN AT A GLANCE

(Population and total nonfarm employment numbers in thousands)

Population, Census 2000:	9,938.4
Total nonfarm employment, 2003:	4,411.8
Change in total nonfarm employment	
(Number)	
1990–2003:	442.1
1990–2001:	586.2
2001–2003:	-144.1
(Compound annual rate of change)	
1990–2003:	0.8%
1990–2001:	1.3%
2001–2003:	-1.6%
Unemployment rate	
1990:	7.7%
2001:	5.2%
2003:	7.1%

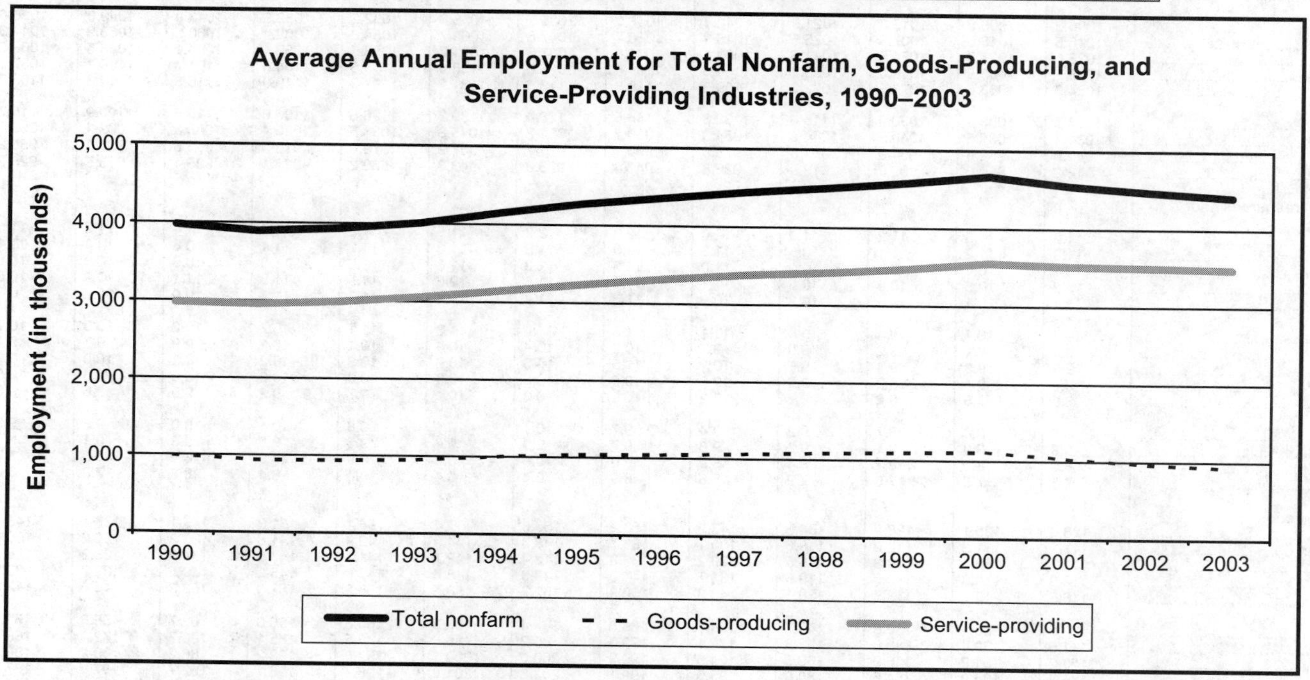

After the 1990–1991 recession, nonfarm payroll employment rose steadily in Michigan until it was hard-hit by the 2001 recession, losing nearly 200,000 jobs from 2000 to 2002. Employment in goods-producing industries, after recovering from the earlier recession, fell sharply during the 2001–2002 period. In manufacturing alone, employment declined 18 percent from 2000 to 2002. These declines were accompanied by losses in service industries as well. After growing steadily from 1992 to 2000, the service-providing industry began to decline in 2001. Improvement was not yet evident in 2003.

Employment by Industry: Michigan

(Numbers in thousands. Not seasonally adjusted.)

Industry	January	February	March	April	May	June	July	August	September	October	November	December	Annual Average
STATEWIDE													
Total nonfarm													
1990	3842.1	3896.8	3928.0	3954.9	4012.2	4031.9	3976.0	3989.5	4016.5	4015.1	3986.6	3986.5	3969.7
1991	3829.9	3822.4	3826.0	3847.7	3907.5	3916.1	3870.4	3883.2	3934.1	3954.9	3952.9	3948.9	3891.2
1992	3814.0	3838.6	3859.1	3892.3	3947.1	3964.1	3916.2	3929.3	3970.4	3998.6	3997.6	4002.7	3927.5
1993	3899.9	3912.5	3927.5	3962.8	4016.8	4028.1	3983.9	3983.5	4053.2	4091.8	4097.0	4113.1	4005.8
1994	4007.3	4024.8	4060.5	4091.9	4149.6	4169.5	4123.6	4160.5	4225.0	4230.4	4254.5	4264.7	4146.9
1995	4142.3	4174.4	4209.4	4233.9	4293.3	4311.9	4233.3	4273.2	4338.4	4346.7	4349.0	4381.2	4273.9
1996	4244.2	4272.5	4281.5	4308.0	4380.5	4401.2	4314.0	4364.8	4414.6	4437.9	4451.7	4459.1	4360.8
1997	4332.4	4354.6	4393.5	4415.6	4483.2	4478.6	4409.3	4441.6	4500.6	4516.7	4517.9	4532.9	4448.1
1998	4419.2	4440.3	4456.9	4501.0	4557.9	4558.0	4401.8	4492.1	4544.1	4574.2	4583.6	4592.9	4510.2
1999	4444.3	4478.9	4507.4	4556.1	4614.2	4623.4	4551.8	4578.5	4627.7	4652.1	4665.1	4683.8	4581.9
2000	4561.4	4584.4	4620.9	4671.9	4728.0	4742.9	4637.8	4664.7	4706.7	4724.8	4725.0	4718.1	4673.9
2001	4502.0	4525.1	4547.3	4575.8	4621.3	4633.6	4512.4	4540.9	4565.1	4554.5	4548.6	4543.6	4555.9
2002	4381.7	4401.3	4427.5	4460.4	4522.8	4539.7	4441.5	4479.2	4517.8	4523.7	4524.7	4513.3	4477.8
2003	4354.0	4357.4	4368.3	4395.4	4468.7	4475.9	4362.0	4374.4	4437.2	4461.1	4458.6	4428.9	4411.8
Total private													
1990	3214.9	3249.3	3276.6	3305.1	3361.6	3408.4	3386.3	3403.8	3397.9	3363.8	3328.4	3333.6	3335.8
1991	3196.0	3166.7	3167.9	3196.7	3260.7	3293.2	3288.1	3307.8	3311.5	3296.4	3289.6	3289.3	3255.3
1992	3171.9	3179.2	3195.4	3236.4	3297.0	3333.9	3333.4	3350.2	3344.9	3342.1	3333.1	3344.9	3288.5
1993	3255.2	3252.1	3263.7	3303.7	3363.0	3398.6	3402.9	3412.1	3421.7	3433.5	3435.1	3456.1	3366.5
1994	3367.3	3369.3	3398.0	3435.5	3500.5	3545.7	3544.6	3581.0	3589.5	3573.4	3586.2	3603.8	3507.9
1995	3509.1	3516.2	3545.5	3575.6	3640.8	3685.2	3651.5	3697.0	3692.1	3686.0	3683.5	3713.9	3633.0
1996	3605.1	3610.8	3614.8	3649.2	3726.6	3767.9	3733.8	3786.5	3771.6	3771.2	3778.6	3788.3	3717.0
1997	3683.2	3686.3	3720.3	3751.2	3821.8	3848.2	3831.9	3864.7	3850.6	3846.7	3843.9	3859.4	3800.7
1998	3763.7	3767.8	3781.4	3829.1	3889.9	3908.8	3811.3	3906.8	3888.0	3895.3	3897.0	3910.5	3854.1
1999	3787.2	3796.9	3820.9	3871.1	3933.1	3965.4	3945.5	3977.7	3959.5	3960.6	3965.9	3988.0	3914.3
2000	3888.8	3888.8	3915.9	3971.5	4027.7	4069.9	4018.8	4052.5	4025.6	4021.2	4014.8	4012.2	3992.3
2001	3819.1	3823.2	3838.8	3870.8	3920.4	3951.5	3888.3	3918.9	3883.8	3848.1	3837.0	3835.1	3869.6
2002	3692.9	3695.5	3718.3	3763.3	3828.2	3864.9	3822.7	3859.5	3832.9	3808.9	3806.8	3800.6	3791.2
2003	3663.9	3648.2	3660.1	3691.3	3767.9	3802.5	3759.4	3777.5	3756.9	3755.3	3751.0	3731.4	3730.5
Goods-producing													
1990	942.3	972.2	979.7	992.8	1008.1	1023.2	1008.5	1017.1	1020.0	1009.0	974.9	958.6	992.2
1991	908.0	907.7	894.8	906.5	935.0	945.0	945.7	955.9	963.1	959.9	949.9	937.4	934.1
1992	890.8	900.6	903.6	922.8	942.6	953.3	947.2	959.9	959.5	954.3	948.2	943.5	935.5
1993	922.5	918.5	916.9	927.4	946.0	956.5	961.0	958.1	968.1	971.9	969.5	971.8	949.0
1994	951.8	950.1	960.3	975.0	995.2	1014.2	1004.3	1026.8	1033.1	1032.8	1035.3	1036.3	1001.3
1995	1006.6	1006.8	1015.3	1021.9	1042.1	1056.9	1035.7	1055.6	1052.2	1052.8	1043.9	1049.3	1036.6
1996	1018.5	1015.0	1007.3	1025.5	1045.9	1060.4	1047.5	1069.7	1064.6	1062.4	1060.5	1053.9	1044.3
1997	1023.1	1025.3	1034.5	1041.5	1063.1	1073.8	1067.8	1091.7	1088.5	1086.4	1084.1	1083.5	1063.6
1998	1068.1	1068.5	1069.0	1085.7	1104.6	1104.5	1026.8	1108.0	1105.5	1104.6	1101.7	1100.1	1087.3
1999	1064.3	1063.6	1073.5	1092.2	1109.3	1118.6	1113.5	1131.2	1127.9	1119.0	1116.8	1114.2	1103.7
2000	1083.7	1083.9	1090.9	1116.0	1132.8	1146.5	1123.4	1139.3	1126.8	1126.0	1115.5	1103.9	1115.7
2001	1034.1	1039.5	1040.2	1044.2	1054.0	1060.2	1032.2	1045.8	1038.5	1020.4	1008.3	1002.4	1035.0
2002	945.9	952.6	954.9	961.8	978.5	990.1	971.7	987.9	979.4	973.3	966.6	955.4	968.2
2003	916.2	910.0	909.9	912.8	936.8	947.4	925.8	943.3	932.2	925.1	925.4	918.5	925.3
Natural resources and mining													
1990	11.2	11.3	11.2	11.0	12.0	12.3	12.3	11.5	11.2	11.2	11.4	11.2	11.5
1991	11.3	11.2	11.1	10.6	11.3	11.5	11.2	11.3	11.2	11.1	10.8	10.4	11.1
1992	10.1	10.1	10.1	10.0	11.0	11.3	11.3	11.3	11.3	11.3	10.9	10.8	10.8
1993	10.3	10.3	10.3	10.5	11.1	11.4	11.5	9.6	11.5	11.3	11.1	10.9	10.8
1994	10.1	10.1	10.4	10.2	10.9	11.3	11.4	11.4	11.2	11.1	10.9	10.7	10.8
1995	10.1	10.1	10.4	10.4	11.1	11.3	11.4	11.3	11.1	10.7	10.2	10.0	10.7
1996	9.1	9.1	9.2	9.0	9.7	10.2	10.4	10.4	10.1	10.1	9.9	9.7	9.7
1997	9.2	9.3	9.4	9.5	10.1	10.5	10.3	10.2	10.3	10.2	10.2	10.0	9.9
1998	9.6	9.4	9.2	9.6	10.3	10.5	10.5	10.5	10.3	10.2	10.0	9.6	10.0
1999	8.9	8.8	8.8	9.7	10.2	10.5	10.2	10.1	9.7	9.5	9.6	9.5	9.6
2000	8.8	8.6	8.7	9.2	9.4	9.7	10.1	10.1	9.8	10.1	10.0	9.6	9.5
2001	8.8	8.9	9.1	9.2	9.6	9.7	9.6	9.6	9.5	9.5	9.3	9.1	9.3
2002	8.0	8.0	8.1	8.4	8.9	9.0	9.0	8.8	8.9	8.9	8.8	8.5	8.6
2003	7.6	7.6	7.6	7.9	8.6	8.9	8.4	8.4	8.4	8.4	8.3	7.8	8.2
Construction													
1990	128.6	125.1	126.2	134.5	147.2	153.2	156.6	157.4	156.1	151.3	145.1	136.1	143.1
1991	117.1	111.3	112.0	118.6	130.1	136.7	143.3	144.9	142.2	141.8	135.2	126.2	130.0
1992	111.1	108.1	109.3	116.5	129.2	136.3	142.4	142.7	141.7	141.5	134.8	128.2	128.5
1993	113.3	110.8	110.7	119.6	133.7	141.0	148.0	148.6	147.0	145.2	139.5	132.7	132.5
1994	116.5	113.7	118.5	130.1	143.0	150.9	157.7	158.5	158.2	157.3	153.3	146.6	142.0
1995	130.9	126.3	130.8	140.7	154.1	163.3	167.4	168.3	166.8	166.6	162.7	156.8	152.9
1996	141.5	139.4	143.8	153.8	171.1	179.3	185.2	186.6	183.5	185.1	180.7	172.4	168.5
1997	153.2	151.9	156.9	169.5	184.5	190.9	200.0	200.1	197.6	192.2	186.2	180.2	180.3
1998	165.5	164.0	164.6	180.0	193.3	199.1	203.8	201.6	198.7	198.1	192.7	187.4	187.4
1999	164.9	164.4	167.9	190.8	200.9	206.7	211.2	210.3	208.5	212.7	209.0	203.6	195.9
2000	182.3	180.4	188.3	205.6	216.6	224.8	227.7	227.1	224.2	220.6	213.9	203.2	209.6
2001	182.5	180.8	185.6	198.3	211.8	218.7	222.6	223.1	219.2	215.7	210.7	203.9	206.1
2002	182.3	177.8	180.4	192.3	206.9	213.0	216.0	215.8	210.7	207.6	201.5	190.6	199.6
2003	168.8	163.0	164.5	178.6	196.2	204.2	207.8	207.0	202.9	201.8	196.4	188.3	190.0

Employment by Industry: Michigan—*Continued*

(Numbers in thousands. Not seasonally adjusted.)

Industry	January	February	March	April	May	June	July	August	September	October	November	December	Annual Average
STATEWIDE—*Continued*													
Manufacturing													
1990	802.5	835.8	842.3	847.3	848.9	857.7	839.6	848.2	852.7	846.5	818.4	811.3	837.6
1991	779.6	785.2	771.7	777.3	793.6	796.8	791.2	799.7	809.7	807.0	803.9	800.8	793.0
1992	769.6	782.4	784.2	796.3	802.4	805.7	793.5	805.9	806.5	801.5	802.5	804.5	796.3
1993	798.9	797.4	795.9	797.3	801.2	804.1	801.5	799.9	809.6	815.4	818.9	828.2	805.7
1994	825.2	826.3	831.4	834.7	841.3	852.0	835.2	856.9	863.7	864.4	871.1	879.0	848.4
1995	865.6	870.4	874.1	870.8	876.9	882.3	856.9	876.0	874.3	875.5	871.0	882.5	873.0
1996	867.9	866.5	854.3	862.7	865.1	870.9	851.9	872.7	871.0	867.2	869.9	871.8	866.0
1997	860.7	864.1	868.2	862.5	868.5	872.4	857.5	881.4	880.6	884.0	887.7	893.3	873.4
1998	893.0	895.1	895.2	896.1	901.0	894.9	812.5	895.9	896.5	896.3	899.0	903.1	889.9
1999	890.5	890.4	896.8	891.7	898.2	901.4	892.1	910.8	909.7	896.8	898.2	901.1	898.1
2000	892.6	894.9	893.9	901.2	906.8	912.0	885.6	902.1	892.8	895.3	891.6	891.1	896.7
2001	842.8	849.8	845.5	836.7	832.6	831.8	800.0	813.1	809.8	795.2	788.3	789.4	819.6
2002	755.6	766.8	766.4	761.1	762.7	768.1	746.7	763.3	759.8	756.8	756.3	756.3	760.0
2003	739.8	739.4	737.8	726.3	732.0	734.3	709.6	727.9	720.9	714.9	720.7	722.4	727.2
Service-providing													
1990	2899.8	2924.6	2948.3	2962.1	3004.1	3008.7	2967.5	2972.4	2996.5	3006.1	3011.7	3027.9	2977.5
1991	2921.9	2914.7	2931.2	2941.2	2972.5	2971.1	2924.7	2927.3	2971.0	2995.0	3003.0	3011.5	2957.1
1992	2923.2	2938.0	2955.5	2969.5	3004.5	3010.8	2969.0	2969.4	3010.9	3044.3	3049.4	3059.2	2992.0
1993	2977.4	2994.0	3010.6	3035.4	3070.8	3071.6	3022.9	3025.4	3085.1	3119.9	3127.5	3141.3	3056.8
1994	3055.5	3074.7	3100.2	3116.9	3154.4	3155.3	3119.3	3133.7	3191.9	3197.6	3219.2	3228.4	3145.6
1995	3135.7	3167.6	3194.1	3212.0	3251.2	3255.0	3197.6	3217.6	3286.2	3293.9	3305.1	3331.9	3237.3
1996	3225.7	3257.5	3274.2	3282.5	3334.6	3340.8	3266.5	3295.1	3350.0	3375.5	3391.2	3405.2	3316.6
1997	3309.3	3329.3	3359.0	3374.1	3420.1	3404.8	3341.5	3349.9	3412.1	3430.3	3433.8	3449.4	3384.5
1998	3351.1	3371.8	3387.9	3415.3	3453.3	3453.5	3375.0	3384.1	3438.6	3469.6	3481.9	3492.8	3422.9
1999	3380.0	3415.3	3433.9	3463.9	3504.9	3504.8	3438.3	3447.3	3499.8	3533.1	3548.3	3569.6	3478.3
2000	3477.7	3500.5	3530.0	3555.9	3595.2	3596.4	3514.4	3525.4	3579.9	3598.8	3609.5	3614.2	3558.2
2001	3467.9	3485.6	3507.1	3531.6	3567.3	3573.4	3480.2	3495.1	3526.6	3534.1	3540.3	3541.2	3520.9
2002	3435.8	3448.7	3472.6	3498.6	3544.3	3549.6	3469.8	3491.3	3538.4	3550.4	3558.1	3557.9	3509.6
2003	3437.8	3447.4	3458.4	3482.6	3531.9	3528.5	3436.2	3431.1	3505.0	3536.0	3533.2	3510.4	3486.5
Trade, transportation, and utilities													
1990	771.2	764.7	767.5	769.2	781.2	789.1	788.5	790.6	780.5	783.4	792.3	809.8	782.3
1991	767.3	745.4	747.0	742.1	752.7	758.1	759.4	757.1	756.9	753.1	764.7	776.1	756.7
1992	740.5	730.4	730.5	735.0	746.3	757.2	757.2	759.5	757.4	761.1	771.5	785.5	752.7
1993	749.5	740.1	739.5	745.9	756.8	764.2	769.0	772.7	771.2	781.0	794.1	806.7	765.9
1994	770.8	762.8	766.8	770.8	786.0	794.4	798.6	800.2	803.3	803.3	818.2	832.4	792.3
1995	789.6	781.4	786.0	793.6	807.0	814.3	809.2	818.3	819.0	823.6	836.9	855.2	811.2
1996	814.2	805.5	806.6	803.1	818.9	826.7	820.5	830.2	826.7	834.7	852.3	866.1	825.5
1997	824.5	814.7	818.9	822.9	836.5	841.0	845.0	844.0	846.6	856.1	869.3	879.9	841.6
1998	838.0	831.6	831.0	839.4	853.5	859.4	854.5	855.4	852.4	859.2	876.5	890.6	853.5
1999	853.5	846.2	850.3	854.2	865.3	872.5	871.1	873.1	867.6	872.8	888.3	904.2	868.3
2000	866.5	858.9	864.7	869.5	881.2	886.7	874.0	879.9	878.4	889.3	905.2	919.7	881.2
2001	865.3	854.8	855.5	859.5	867.4	870.6	857.1	860.2	853.7	853.6	865.3	871.7	861.2
2002	826.1	814.9	820.4	825.6	838.6	843.5	834.7	838.3	836.8	832.8	845.8	854.0	834.3
2003	807.5	798.5	800.3	803.5	816.6	822.6	816.7	819.0	816.0	822.7	830.2	830.1	815.3
Wholesale trade													
1990	157.0	157.5	158.3	158.7	159.9	161.0	160.8	161.8	161.5	159.3	158.7	159.8	159.5
1991	153.0	151.0	151.3	150.1	150.9	151.9	152.5	152.4	151.0	151.0	150.6	150.8	151.4
1992	148.0	147.8	148.3	149.0	150.3	151.3	153.0	152.0	151.4	151.5	150.6	151.3	150.4
1993	149.5	149.5	150.0	151.7	153.2	154.1	153.9	154.1	153.7	153.9	154.2	154.8	152.7
1994	152.6	152.9	153.9	154.6	156.1	157.6	158.4	158.3	158.0	157.4	158.2	159.2	156.4
1995	154.1	154.9	156.2	157.2	159.4	161.1	161.4	162.1	161.8	161.3	161.0	162.4	159.4
1996	159.3	159.5	160.1	161.3	163.5	165.2	164.5	165.1	164.3	165.4	165.8	166.9	163.4
1997	164.5	165.6	166.5	167.3	169.5	170.7	176.1	176.1	175.9	176.8	176.7	177.6	171.9
1998	176.2	176.3	177.5	179.9	181.3	182.6	181.6	181.3	180.1	179.9	180.4	180.8	179.8
1999	178.5	180.3	181.2	180.9	182.6	183.7	186.1	185.7	184.1	186.4	186.4	187.2	183.6
2000	184.0	184.8	185.8	185.8	187.1	188.0	187.0	186.7	185.2	185.8	185.3	186.4	186.0
2001	180.3	180.8	181.2	183.2	183.4	183.0	181.1	180.7	178.9	177.9	176.9	177.1	180.4
2002	173.0	173.0	173.6	175.0	177.1	177.8	176.5	176.7	175.4	175.3	175.5	175.9	175.4
2003	171.7	171.7	172.2	172.8	173.7	174.6	173.9	174.6	172.7	175.1	175.7	174.8	173.6
Retail trade													
1990	500.7	492.7	493.8	494.7	503.1	507.5	509.1	509.6	499.7	507.1	517.1	531.5	505.6
1991	498.7	480.0	480.7	478.6	486.4	489.3	490.6	487.7	489.0	486.5	498.5	509.2	489.6
1992	480.1	469.7	469.1	470.9	478.4	487.3	486.5	490.2	488.4	492.2	503.3	516.1	486.0
1993	485.0	475.6	474.4	478.9	486.2	490.5	494.2	497.7	495.6	502.8	515.5	526.3	493.6
1994	494.5	485.6	487.4	490.1	501.7	507.8	511.7	513.5	517.1	518.0	533.0	546.2	508.9
1995	510.0	501.5	504.6	509.7	520.1	524.5	519.4	527.4	528.7	531.5	546.0	562.2	523.8
1996	527.9	519.1	519.5	517.3	528.7	533.4	528.7	537.1	534.3	539.9	557.4	569.9	534.4
1997	532.9	521.9	524.6	526.0	535.7	538.4	539.7	542.5	540.6	546.8	558.6	572.9	540.1
1998	533.7	527.0	525.2	529.7	540.1	544.5	541.9	541.8	539.2	546.1	563.3	577.3	542.5
1999	543.1	536.6	540.2	538.4	546.4	551.1	550.5	552.0	548.3	551.0	566.9	582.5	550.6
2000	550.0	541.8	546.3	549.1	558.5	562.1	552.8	557.5	557.9	564.6	581.7	595.5	559.8
2001	553.8	544.2	544.9	544.2	550.8	553.0	543.8	546.0	542.5	542.4	556.8	563.5	548.8
2002	526.7	515.8	519.5	522.8	531.8	534.9	530.1	532.2	532.6	528.2	542.1	551.1	530.7
2003	511.0	503.1	503.9	505.7	516.3	520.8	517.0	518.6	517.3	523.0	530.4	531.7	516.6

Employment by Industry: Michigan—*Continued*

(Numbers in thousands. Not seasonally adjusted.)

Industry	January	February	March	April	May	June	July	August	September	October	November	December	Annual Average
STATEWIDE—*Continued*													
Transportation and utilities													
1990	113.5	114.5	115.4	115.8	118.2	120.6	118.6	119.2	119.3	117.0	116.5	118.5	117.3
1991	115.6	114.4	115.0	113.4	115.4	116.9	116.3	117.0	116.9	115.6	115.6	116.1	115.7
1992	112.4	112.9	113.1	115.1	117.6	118.6	117.7	117.3	117.6	117.4	117.6	118.1	116.3
1993	115.0	115.0	115.1	115.3	117.4	119.6	120.9	120.9	121.9	124.3	124.4	125.6	119.6
1994	123.7	124.3	125.5	126.1	128.2	129.0	128.5	128.4	128.2	127.9	127.0	127.0	127.0
1995	125.5	125.0	125.2	126.7	127.5	128.7	128.4	128.8	128.5	130.8	129.9	130.6	128.0
1996	127.0	126.9	127.0	124.5	126.7	128.1	127.3	128.0	128.1	129.4	129.1	129.3	127.6
1997	127.1	127.2	127.8	129.6	131.3	131.9	129.2	125.4	130.1	132.5	134.0	129.4	129.6
1998	128.1	128.3	128.3	129.8	132.1	132.3	131.0	132.3	133.1	133.2	132.8	132.5	131.2
1999	131.9	129.3	128.9	134.9	136.3	137.7	134.5	135.4	135.2	135.4	135.0	134.5	134.1
2000	132.5	132.3	132.6	134.6	135.6	136.6	134.2	135.7	135.3	138.9	138.2	137.8	135.4
2001	131.2	129.8	129.4	132.1	133.2	134.6	132.2	133.5	132.3	133.3	131.6	131.1	132.0
2002	126.4	126.1	127.3	127.8	129.7	130.8	128.1	129.4	128.8	129.3	128.2	127.0	128.2
2003	124.8	123.7	124.2	125.0	126.6	127.2	125.8	125.8	126.0	124.6	124.1	123.6	125.1
Information													
1990	70.6	70.4	70.9	70.1	70.7	71.5	71.1	71.2	71.0	70.9	70.2	71.3	70.8
1991	70.3	69.8	69.8	68.4	68.8	69.0	69.1	69.3	69.0	68.8	69.1	69.3	69.2
1992	68.7	68.0	68.4	67.5	68.1	67.7	68.4	67.9	67.2	67.3	67.5	68.0	67.9
1993	67.2	67.4	67.4	66.9	67.4	68.1	68.5	68.8	68.0	67.5	67.8	68.2	67.8
1994	66.9	66.8	66.9	66.3	67.0	67.6	67.1	67.2	66.8	66.5	67.2	67.6	67.0
1995	66.7	67.3	67.5	67.0	67.9	68.8	68.2	67.6	68.3	67.8	68.7	69.2	67.9
1996	69.3	69.5	70.3	68.9	69.8	70.3	70.4	70.7	70.2	70.5	71.0	71.7	70.2
1997	70.4	71.1	71.4	70.6	71.0	71.4	72.9	72.7	72.0	72.2	72.4	72.9	71.8
1998	73.4	73.5	73.6	72.4	73.3	73.7	75.0	75.2	74.4	74.1	74.8	75.5	74.1
1999	71.9	72.1	72.3	72.7	73.7	74.4	74.7	75.2	74.4	74.9	75.3	75.5	73.9
2000	76.1	75.8	76.7	76.0	76.7	77.2	77.0	77.1	77.7	75.8	76.5	77.2	76.7
2001	74.4	74.4	74.6	76.3	76.8	77.3	77.2	75.8	74.8	75.4	76.5	76.3	75.8
2002	76.1	75.9	75.8	74.4	74.7	74.7	73.1	72.7	71.7	71.7	72.3	72.6	73.8
2003	71.0	70.8	71.1	70.8	71.0	71.1	70.6	70.3	70.1	70.4	70.0	70.0	70.6
Financial activities													
1990	193.8	194.6	196.2	192.3	194.7	197.2	197.6	197.9	197.0	193.0	194.1	196.5	195.4
1991	189.2	187.7	188.6	188.1	190.3	192.7	191.8	192.6	190.7	187.8	188.6	190.2	189.9
1992	185.4	185.0	185.7	186.2	188.8	190.7	191.0	190.8	189.4	189.2	189.4	190.6	188.5
1993	187.8	187.8	188.8	188.2	190.0	192.3	192.2	193.0	191.7	191.8	192.4	193.5	190.8
1994	191.6	191.7	192.1	192.4	194.1	196.0	197.4	197.3	195.9	192.9	192.4	193.5	193.9
1995	195.1	195.7	196.4	193.7	195.4	197.3	197.5	198.2	196.9	195.3	195.5	197.6	196.2
1996	195.2	195.9	197.3	199.4	201.7	203.6	204.3	205.3	203.0	201.8	202.0	203.4	201.1
1997	200.4	201.0	202.2	201.9	204.9	206.5	207.8	208.4	207.3	203.8	203.8	205.7	204.5
1998	206.5	205.8	206.8	206.9	208.8	209.6	208.9	209.7	206.5	207.1	207.4	208.8	207.7
1999	205.3	205.6	204.0	206.2	207.2	209.5	209.7	210.2	206.6	206.3	205.2	206.5	206.9
2000	206.7	206.4	206.4	208.7	209.9	212.3	212.2	211.4	209.3	209.3	209.3	210.9	209.4
2001	205.1	206.1	207.3	208.8	212.1	214.3	213.1	213.4	210.5	210.4	210.7	212.4	210.4
2002	212.0	212.2	212.2	213.7	215.6	216.6	216.8	217.6	215.2	214.8	215.3	216.5	214.9
2003	214.7	214.7	215.0	218.1	220.5	222.5	223.3	224.0	219.7	218.0	218.4	217.7	218.9
Professional and business services													
1990	382.4	385.1	390.5	406.6	413.4	420.2	419.0	421.2	423.3	415.4	410.9	409.5	408.1
1991	387.8	384.6	386.4	408.8	412.4	417.9	419.2	423.4	424.5	424.3	422.6	421.6	411.1
1992	405.7	410.2	415.7	427.1	433.7	439.2	445.1	445.5	446.9	445.6	442.8	443.9	433.5
1993	432.2	435.8	441.0	450.1	458.9	462.4	459.9	464.3	468.6	473.8	473.5	476.7	458.1
1994	465.2	469.5	475.4	485.2	491.4	497.2	502.5	509.3	511.4	509.4	511.0	511.8	494.9
1995	503.9	508.8	514.8	518.5	526.1	532.7	530.1	541.7	541.1	538.3	538.1	538.7	527.7
1996	523.0	529.1	531.9	543.6	556.4	564.2	558.1	571.1	571.1	571.3	569.4	568.7	554.8
1997	565.2	568.2	577.4	584.4	593.6	597.3	584.6	590.0	589.6	590.9	589.0	590.1	585.0
1998	570.4	577.0	583.8	595.5	602.2	608.9	600.3	613.6	611.2	615.4	614.1	613.2	600.5
1999	591.9	595.4	600.9	608.4	615.8	624.2	612.5	624.0	626.9	630.4	632.0	634.6	616.4
2000	625.4	623.3	629.7	638.0	645.3	651.8	642.0	652.7	648.1	640.4	636.1	632.2	638.8
2001	599.3	599.6	601.7	608.2	612.0	617.5	605.0	615.8	609.8	599.3	594.3	591.6	604.5
2002	574.5	575.4	578.8	590.3	599.5	604.7	596.8	609.2	604.5	601.8	600.3	597.3	594.4
2003	576.8	575.2	577.4	587.1	595.2	597.9	592.7	593.3	595.1	589.1	586.2	578.3	587.0
Educational and health services													
1990	404.7	408.5	411.5	408.4	408.4	410.0	406.6	408.7	415.9	417.2	418.9	421.9	411.7
1991	419.0	419.9	423.0	422.1	421.3	421.1	414.4	416.9	423.1	429.5	431.8	431.4	422.8
1992	429.4	432.7	433.7	433.2	433.6	432.4	428.9	429.7	435.9	440.7	442.0	442.4	434.6
1993	437.9	441.8	443.7	447.7	447.3	447.4	441.1	441.4	447.5	452.6	454.2	453.2	446.3
1994	447.7	452.9	454.1	453.3	453.8	453.7	450.6	451.4	458.4	460.5	463.4	462.6	455.2
1995	460.5	464.8	466.2	468.6	468.3	468.3	464.4	466.2	472.1	479.1	481.7	481.9	470.2
1996	478.3	484.4	484.4	487.1	488.1	487.7	477.5	478.9	484.7	490.5	493.3	492.5	485.6
1997	484.0	488.4	490.3	494.5	494.5	492.2	483.5	483.6	488.5	490.0	490.9	491.6	489.3
1998	484.4	487.3	487.9	486.2	485.7	483.4	477.1	476.0	481.3	489.2	490.0	489.4	484.8
1999	486.6	494.4	494.5	492.0	491.9	490.2	486.6	485.4	489.1	495.0	497.7	496.9	491.7
2000	492.6	499.1	500.0	501.5	501.5	502.1	498.0	499.1	504.1	507.0	511.0	509.3	502.1
2001	500.4	505.2	508.2	511.8	513.7	515.8	510.7	512.1	515.3	519.6	523.7	523.7	513.4
2002	520.2	524.7	527.3	533.0	534.6	537.1	532.3	533.5	536.3	538.8	542.6	541.7	533.5
2003	538.6	540.8	541.2	541.0	543.4	544.4	533.8	532.4	542.8	556.8	558.6	556.4	544.2

Employment by Industry: Michigan—*Continued*

(Numbers in thousands. Not seasonally adjusted.)

Industry	January	February	March	April	May	June	July	August	September	October	November	December	Annual Average
STATEWIDE—*Continued*													
Leisure and hospitality													
1990	309.9	311.8	316.5	323.2	340.5	351.4	351.2	352.6	346.3	330.8	323.5	321.2	331.6
1991	312.3	309.3	314.6	319.1	337.5	345.8	346.6	350.3	342.6	328.6	319.9	319.7	328.9
1992	309.6	309.6	314.2	320.7	338.9	347.1	348.9	351.1	343.2	336.8	326.3	324.9	330.9
1993	314.0	315.2	319.4	330.3	347.7	357.4	361.0	364.0	357.6	344.7	333.0	334.1	339.9
1994	324.0	324.8	329.9	338.5	357.5	366.0	367.9	371.7	364.1	350.2	341.7	341.7	348.2
1995	332.5	335.9	341.6	354.6	374.6	385.4	386.7	388.7	382.6	367.8	358.3	359.4	364.0
1996	345.8	348.8	353.6	358.0	380.3	388.3	391.4	395.5	387.4	374.9	364.9	367.3	371.4
1997	351.6	352.6	359.1	369.4	391.0	398.2	402.3	405.4	390.6	381.1	369.5	369.6	378.4
1998	357.8	358.2	362.4	374.9	393.0	399.9	400.6	400.4	389.8	378.8	366.5	366.0	379.0
1999	350.7	354.0	358.9	377.7	397.1	405.9	408.8	409.6	399.7	394.9	384.1	388.7	385.8
2000	373.8	375.6	380.1	393.4	411.4	423.0	422.4	422.9	412.9	405.5	393.4	390.7	400.4
2001	368.0	369.5	375.5	386.2	407.1	417.0	416.9	419.3	407.6	396.5	384.7	382.8	394.3
2002	367.2	367.8	375.6	390.1	411.0	421.1	421.3	424.0	414.3	402.1	391.1	389.3	397.9
2003	369.0	368.0	373.5	387.1	412.2	423.4	424.8	424.0	410.5	401.6	391.5	390.5	398.0
Other services													
1990	140.0	142.0	143.8	142.5	144.6	145.8	143.8	144.5	143.9	144.1	143.6	144.8	143.6
1991	142.1	142.3	143.7	141.6	142.7	143.6	141.9	142.3	141.6	144.4	143.0	143.6	142.7
1992	141.8	142.7	143.6	143.9	145.0	146.3	146.7	145.8	145.4	147.1	145.4	146.1	145.0
1993	144.1	145.5	147.0	147.2	148.9	150.3	150.2	149.8	149.0	150.2	150.6	151.9	148.7
1994	149.3	150.7	152.5	154.0	155.5	156.6	156.2	157.1	156.5	157.8	157.0	157.9	155.1
1995	154.2	155.5	157.7	157.7	159.4	161.5	159.7	160.7	159.9	161.3	160.4	162.6	159.2
1996	160.8	162.6	163.4	163.6	165.5	166.7	164.1	165.1	163.9	165.1	165.2	164.7	164.2
1997	164.0	165.0	166.5	166.0	167.2	167.8	168.0	168.9	167.5	166.2	164.9	166.1	166.5
1998	165.1	165.9	166.9	168.1	168.8	169.4	168.1	168.5	166.9	166.9	166.0	166.9	167.3
1999	163.0	165.6	166.5	167.7	172.8	170.1	168.6	169.0	167.3	167.3	166.5	167.4	167.7
2000	164.0	165.8	167.4	168.4	168.9	170.3	169.8	170.1	168.3	167.9	167.8	168.3	168.1
2001	172.5	174.1	175.8	175.8	177.3	178.8	176.1	176.5	173.6	172.9	173.5	174.2	175.1
2002	170.9	172.0	173.3	174.4	175.7	177.1	176.0	176.3	174.7	173.6	172.8	173.8	174.2
2003	170.1	170.2	171.7	170.9	172.2	173.2	171.7	171.2	170.5	171.6	170.7	169.9	171.2
Government													
1990	627.2	647.5	651.4	649.8	650.6	623.5	589.7	585.7	618.6	651.3	658.2	652.9	633.9
1991	633.9	655.7	658.1	651.0	646.8	622.9	582.3	575.4	622.6	658.5	663.3	659.6	635.8
1992	642.1	659.4	663.7	655.9	650.1	630.2	582.8	579.1	625.5	656.5	664.5	657.8	639.0
1993	644.7	660.4	663.8	659.1	653.8	629.5	581.0	571.4	631.5	658.3	661.9	657.0	639.4
1994	640.0	655.5	662.5	656.4	649.1	623.8	579.0	579.5	635.5	657.0	668.3	660.9	639.0
1995	633.2	658.2	663.9	658.3	652.5	626.7	581.8	576.2	646.3	660.7	665.5	667.3	640.9
1996	639.1	661.7	666.7	658.8	653.9	633.3	580.2	578.3	643.0	666.7	673.1	670.8	643.8
1997	649.2	668.3	673.2	664.4	661.4	630.4	577.4	576.9	650.0	670.0	674.0	673.5	647.4
1998	655.5	672.5	675.5	671.9	668.0	649.2	590.5	585.3	656.1	678.9	686.6	682.4	656.0
1999	657.1	682.0	686.5	685.0	681.1	658.0	606.3	600.8	668.2	691.5	699.2	695.8	667.6
2000	672.6	695.6	705.0	700.4	700.3	673.0	619.0	612.2	681.1	703.6	710.2	705.9	681.6
2001	682.9	701.9	708.5	705.0	700.9	682.1	624.1	622.0	681.3	706.4	711.6	708.5	686.3
2002	688.8	705.8	709.2	697.1	694.6	674.8	618.8	619.7	684.9	714.8	717.9	712.7	686.6
2003	690.1	709.2	708.2	704.1	700.8	673.4	602.6	596.9	680.3	705.8	707.6	697.5	681.4
Federal government													
1990	60.0	59.8	60.7	64.7	69.3	64.0	64.0	59.5	58.4	57.9	57.8	58.7	61.2
1991	57.9	58.0	57.9	58.1	58.2	58.7	58.8	58.4	58.2	58.1	58.2	59.3	58.3
1992	59.0	58.3	58.1	58.3	58.3	58.3	58.8	58.2	57.7	57.7	57.3	58.2	58.2
1993	57.5	57.0	56.9	56.5	56.7	56.6	56.7	56.5	56.4	56.4	56.5	58.6	56.9
1994	56.4	56.2	56.3	56.6	56.6	56.9	56.9	57.1	57.1	56.9	56.7	59.7	57.0
1995	57.0	57.0	57.1	57.3	57.4	57.8	56.9	57.0	56.8	56.6	56.5	59.2	57.2
1996	56.0	56.1	56.0	56.6	56.4	56.4	56.5	56.6	56.4	56.1	56.5	58.4	56.5
1997	55.9	55.6	55.6	55.6	55.7	55.8	55.9	56.3	56.5	55.7	56.6	59.0	56.2
1998	56.2	56.0	55.9	56.7	57.2	57.0	56.0	56.0	56.1	56.0	56.9	58.6	56.6
1999	56.9	56.7	58.6	57.9	56.9	57.1	56.9	57.0	56.8	56.6	57.1	59.2	57.3
2000	57.5	57.7	60.0	61.8	72.5	64.0	63.5	58.7	56.7	56.3	56.9	58.6	60.4
2001	56.4	56.3	56.3	56.2	56.4	56.6	56.6	56.6	56.1	55.3	55.3	56.8	56.2
2002	55.3	54.8	55.1	55.1	55.4	56.3	55.7	55.6	55.7	56.3	56.3	57.5	55.8
2003	56.1	55.8	56.0	56.1	56.1	56.3	56.4	56.2	55.8	55.5	54.9	56.2	56.0
State government													
1990	167.4	174.1	173.5	173.5	161.7	155.4	149.0	149.6	163.6	176.2	176.8	173.7	166.2
1991	168.3	175.5	174.0	174.8	162.6	155.1	150.7	148.4	159.0	173.6	174.6	172.2	165.7
1992	168.1	172.4	169.7	170.7	158.4	155.4	148.4	147.5	159.6	168.3	172.6	169.7	163.4
1993	167.4	170.8	169.9	172.3	159.3	147.9	149.1	145.9	163.7	173.9	173.1	171.9	163.8
1994	165.2	172.0	171.0	171.7	157.8	148.8	148.8	147.5	165.1	172.5	174.3	172.4	163.9
1995	160.9	172.6	173.3	173.7	159.7	151.1	151.0	150.4	168.8	173.9	175.0	174.0	165.4
1996	165.8	175.3	175.4	174.7	162.8	157.6	153.4	151.6	170.8	175.4	175.8	173.1	167.6
1997	167.6	174.4	173.7	173.5	161.0	147.8	149.6	148.1	168.0	173.5	174.2	172.6	165.3
1998	169.2	173.3	172.8	173.3	160.3	155.3	155.2	153.0	169.0	175.4	176.8	175.1	167.4
1999	164.7	176.3	173.7	177.1	166.1	157.1	158.3	154.8	167.3	176.9	179.3	176.5	169.0
2000	164.3	175.9	177.2	177.4	163.2	157.9	157.9	155.2	170.8	179.6	181.0	178.6	169.9
2001	171.0	178.6	179.9	179.8	169.0	164.5	162.3	160.2	174.3	182.6	184.5	180.2	173.9
2002	176.0	183.0	181.1	179.1	167.7	163.0	162.3	161.3	175.0	182.0	181.0	177.2	174.1
2003	171.3	178.3	175.6	175.7	164.3	152.0	152.2	150.9	165.8	172.8	172.4	167.0	166.5

Employment by Industry: Michigan—*Continued*

(Numbers in thousands. Not seasonally adjusted.)

Industry	January	February	March	April	May	June	July	August	September	October	November	December	Annual Average
STATEWIDE—*Continued*													
Local government													
1990	399.8	413.6	417.2	411.6	419.6	404.1	376.7	376.6	396.6	417.2	423.5	420.5	406.4
1991	407.7	422.2	426.2	418.1	426.1	409.2	372.8	368.5	405.4	426.8	430.6	428.0	411.8
1992	414.9	428.8	435.8	426.9	433.4	416.4	375.6	373.5	408.2	430.5	434.6	429.9	417.4
1993	419.7	432.6	437.0	430.3	437.8	424.9	375.2	369.0	411.4	428.0	432.3	426.6	418.7
1994	418.3	427.2	435.2	428.1	434.7	418.1	373.3	374.9	413.3	427.6	437.3	428.8	418.1
1995	415.3	428.6	433.6	427.3	435.3	417.9	373.9	368.8	420.7	430.3	434.0	434.2	418.3
1996	417.3	430.4	435.3	427.5	434.7	419.2	370.3	370.1	415.8	435.2	440.7	439.3	419.7
1997	425.7	438.3	443.9	435.3	444.7	426.8	371.9	372.5	425.5	440.8	443.2	441.9	425.9
1998	430.1	443.2	446.8	441.9	450.5	436.9	379.3	376.3	431.0	447.5	452.9	448.7	432.1
1999	435.5	449.0	454.2	450.0	458.1	443.8	391.1	389.0	444.1	458.0	462.8	460.1	441.3
2000	450.8	462.0	467.8	461.2	464.6	451.1	397.6	398.3	453.6	467.7	472.3	468.7	451.3
2001	455.5	467.0	472.3	469.0	475.5	461.0	405.2	405.2	450.9	468.5	471.8	471.5	456.1
2002	457.5	468.0	473.0	462.9	471.5	455.5	400.8	402.8	454.2	476.5	480.6	478.0	456.8
2003	462.7	475.1	476.6	472.3	480.4	465.1	394.0	389.8	458.7	477.5	480.3	474.3	458.9
ANN ARBOR													
Total nonfarm													
1990	236.0	242.5	245.5	243.8	243.4	242.9	233.0	233.0	245.3	244.6	248.0	250.0	242.3
1991	237.9	241.2	242.5	239.8	240.0	236.7	230.5	230.6	240.6	245.9	247.0	245.4	239.8
1992	239.0	242.5	242.9	244.0	242.9	242.0	237.8	235.5	241.0	245.1	250.1	249.9	242.7
1993	241.3	243.9	242.1	245.6	242.4	242.1	237.3	235.3	243.0	249.7	250.7	251.1	243.7
1994	243.1	246.9	247.7	249.3	247.8	248.2	244.2	243.8	250.8	254.4	256.7	258.1	249.3
1995	248.2	253.2	255.7	256.5	253.4	254.9	250.9	250.3	259.4	260.3	260.4	263.4	255.6
1996	251.9	258.9	261.9	261.4	261.0	264.4	257.4	258.5	264.5	266.7	268.3	269.0	262.0
1997	260.6	263.3	265.2	265.5	265.6	265.0	259.5	260.5	269.1	271.6	273.5	275.0	266.2
1998	267.2	270.4	272.2	275.4	276.0	275.1	266.8	270.2	276.2	280.1	282.9	283.9	274.7
1999	273.7	278.6	280.2	283.9	282.9	283.7	279.1	277.5	283.1	286.2	288.1	288.8	282.2
2000	280.4	283.9	285.9	289.4	287.6	288.3	281.0	282.2	286.3	291.2	293.5	293.1	286.9
2001	293.7	296.6	298.3	296.8	298.4	299.5	289.0	290.7	293.5	297.2	299.0	298.0	295.9
2002	286.1	289.6	290.4	290.0	291.7	292.3	284.1	285.0	289.8	294.2	296.8	295.4	290.5
2003	285.1	287.6	286.7	288.1	290.1	289.2	281.7	282.5	291.1	296.5	296.6	294.7	289.2
Total private													
1990	173.5	176.3	177.9	177.2	180.2	182.4	176.8	177.6	183.2	176.6	177.9	181.7	178.4
1991	173.9	172.7	173.4	169.9	174.7	176.0	172.6	173.6	178.3	177.7	177.4	175.3	174.6
1992	172.2	172.1	173.0	173.7	175.9	176.9	177.7	175.7	178.0	178.5	178.5	179.7	176.0
1993	173.9	173.7	171.5	174.1	176.5	178.5	176.7	176.7	177.8	178.1	178.7	180.1	176.4
1994	175.1	175.8	176.7	178.8	181.7	183.6	182.9	183.0	185.6	184.2	185.2	187.2	181.7
1995	180.8	181.7	183.3	184.1	187.1	189.1	188.4	189.1	189.8	189.3	188.9	191.9	187.0
1996	186.2	187.7	188.6	189.4	192.4	194.6	193.9	195.6	195.3	195.0	195.7	196.9	192.6
1997	191.4	191.6	193.0	193.6	197.2	199.2	197.5	199.0	199.6	198.9	200.4	201.9	196.9
1998	196.6	197.5	198.7	202.3	204.8	206.5	201.6	206.2	205.8	206.3	207.3	208.2	203.5
1999	201.4	203.4	204.8	208.3	210.7	213.1	212.3	213.1	211.7	210.8	211.3	212.4	209.4
2000	207.5	208.0	209.3	213.3	215.4	217.6	215.1	216.3	215.4	215.3	215.6	216.0	213.7
2001	217.0	216.7	217.7	218.5	221.2	222.6	217.3	220.3	218.0	216.1	216.0	215.5	218.1
2002	207.8	208.0	208.9	210.6	214.3	215.4	211.4	212.7	211.4	211.4	211.6	211.4	211.2
2003	205.9	205.0	205.3	207.0	211.2	213.4	210.8	212.7	213.4	213.7	213.9	212.7	210.4
Goods-producing													
1990	53.3	54.2	54.1	56.0	57.0	57.5	55.9	54.5	58.2	54.6	54.7	55.3	55.4
1991	55.4	55.3	55.2	53.1	55.2	56.1	54.6	54.3	57.7	58.3	58.0	56.0	55.8
1992	56.0	55.4	56.2	56.9	57.1	57.3	56.2	54.7	56.9	57.1	57.1	56.8	56.5
1993	55.2	55.4	54.3	54.7	55.5	56.3	53.6	53.4	54.2	54.4	54.7	54.7	54.7
1994	53.7	53.6	53.9	55.8	56.7	57.6	57.6	57.9	58.9	58.5	58.6	58.9	56.8
1995	57.8	57.0	57.3	57.6	58.5	59.4	58.6	58.7	58.9	58.9	59.3	59.2	58.4
1996	57.4	57.5	58.0	57.9	58.6	59.5	59.2	60.0	59.7	59.5	59.2	59.4	58.8
1997	57.4	57.5	57.8	57.5	58.9	59.5	59.6	59.9	59.8	59.0	59.4	59.7	58.8
1998	58.4	58.6	58.6	60.3	61.1	61.7	59.7	61.1	61.6	61.3	61.4	61.7	60.5
1999	58.9	59.4	59.9	60.7	61.1	61.8	61.7	62.3	61.9	60.7	60.4	60.6	60.8
2000	60.2	60.1	60.2	60.9	61.9	63.0	61.8	62.3	61.0	61.2	61.0	60.9	61.2
2001	59.3	58.7	58.6	57.8	58.7	59.0	57.6	59.2	58.3	57.1	57.1	56.7	58.2
2002	54.5	54.6	54.5	54.4	55.7	56.1	55.6	56.2	55.3	55.9	55.7	55.4	55.3
2003	53.0	52.5	52.5	52.4	53.9	54.3	53.2	54.1	53.6	53.7	53.7	53.3	53.4
Construction and mining													
1990	6.7	6.7	6.7	7.3	7.9	8.1	8.2	8.4	8.4	7.8	7.6	7.5	7.6
1991	6.2	5.7	5.9	6.0	6.4	6.8	7.1	7.3	7.0	7.0	6.8	6.3	6.5
1992	5.7	5.6	5.6	5.8	6.2	6.6	6.9	6.9	6.8	6.8	6.6	6.3	6.3
1993	5.6	5.5	5.5	5.9	6.6	7.0	7.3	7.3	7.1	7.2	7.1	6.9	6.6
1994	6.3	6.2	6.4	7.1	7.7	7.9	8.4	8.4	8.5	8.5	8.3	8.1	7.7
1995	7.3	7.2	7.4	7.9	8.6	9.3	9.5	9.5	9.4	9.2	9.0	9.0	8.6
1996	8.1	7.9	8.2	8.9	9.7	10.1	10.4	10.5	10.3	10.3	10.2	10.0	9.6
1997	9.0	9.0	9.2	9.7	10.5	10.8	11.4	11.5	11.1	10.4	10.2	10.1	10.2
1998	9.4	9.5	9.5	10.3	10.9	11.2	11.3	11.6	11.4	11.2	11.0	10.9	10.7
1999	9.6	9.8	9.9	10.8	11.1	11.5	12.1	12.2	12.0	11.9	11.7	11.4	11.2
2000	10.5	10.2	10.5	11.6	12.2	12.6	12.6	12.8	12.5	12.3	12.1	11.6	11.8
2001	10.8	10.8	11.1	11.7	12.5	12.9	13.1	13.3	12.9	12.6	12.3	11.9	12.2
2002	11.0	10.7	10.8	11.5	12.2	12.6	12.8	12.7	12.3	12.3	12.0	11.6	11.9
2003	10.2	9.9	10.0	10.8	11.8	12.1	12.4	12.6	12.5	12.4	12.0	11.7	11.5

Employment by Industry: Michigan—*Continued*

(Numbers in thousands. Not seasonally adjusted.)

Industry	January	February	March	April	May	June	July	August	September	October	November	December	Annual Average
ANN ARBOR—*Continued*													
Manufacturing													
1990	46.6	47.5	47.4	48.7	49.1	49.4	47.7	46.1	49.8	46.8	47.1	47.8	47.8
1991	49.2	49.6	49.3	47.1	48.8	49.3	47.5	47.0	50.7	51.3	51.2	49.7	49.2
1992	50.3	49.8	50.6	51.1	50.9	50.7	49.3	47.8	50.1	50.3	50.5	50.5	50.2
1993	49.6	49.9	48.8	48.8	48.9	49.3	46.3	46.1	47.1	47.2	47.6	47.8	48.1
1994	47.4	47.4	47.5	48.7	49.0	49.7	49.2	49.5	50.4	50.0	50.3	50.8	49.2
1995	50.5	49.8	49.9	49.7	49.9	50.1	49.1	49.2	49.5	49.7	50.3	50.2	49.8
1996	49.3	49.6	49.8	49.0	48.9	49.4	48.8	49.5	49.4	49.2	49.0	49.4	49.3
1997	48.4	48.5	48.6	47.8	48.4	48.7	48.2	48.4	48.7	48.6	49.2	49.6	48.6
1998	49.0	49.1	49.1	50.0	50.2	50.5	48.4	49.5	50.2	50.1	50.4	50.8	49.8
1999	49.3	49.6	50.0	49.9	50.0	50.3	49.6	50.1	49.9	48.8	48.7	49.2	49.6
2000	49.7	49.9	49.7	49.3	49.7	50.4	49.2	49.5	48.5	48.9	48.9	49.3	49.4
2001	48.5	47.9	47.5	46.1	46.2	46.1	44.5	45.9	45.4	44.5	44.8	44.8	46.0
2002	43.5	43.9	43.7	42.9	43.5	43.5	42.8	43.5	43.0	43.6	43.7	43.8	43.5
2003	42.8	42.6	42.5	41.6	42.1	42.2	40.8	41.5	41.1	41.3	41.7	41.6	41.8
Service-providing													
1990	182.7	188.3	191.4	187.8	186.4	185.4	177.1	178.5	187.1	190.0	193.3	194.7	186.9
1991	182.5	185.9	187.3	186.7	184.8	180.6	175.9	176.3	182.9	187.6	189.0	189.4	184.1
1992	183.0	187.1	186.7	187.1	185.8	184.7	181.6	180.8	184.1	188.0	193.0	193.1	186.3
1993	186.1	188.5	187.8	190.9	186.9	185.8	183.7	181.9	188.8	195.3	196.0	196.4	189.0
1994	189.4	193.3	193.8	193.5	191.1	190.6	186.6	185.9	191.9	195.9	198.1	199.2	192.4
1995	190.4	196.2	198.4	198.9	194.9	195.5	192.3	191.6	200.5	201.4	201.1	204.2	197.1
1996	194.5	201.4	203.9	203.5	202.4	204.9	198.2	198.5	204.8	207.2	209.1	209.6	203.2
1997	203.2	205.8	207.4	208.0	206.7	205.5	199.9	200.6	209.3	212.6	214.1	215.3	207.4
1998	208.8	211.8	213.6	215.1	214.9	213.4	207.1	209.1	214.6	218.8	221.5	222.2	214.2
1999	214.8	219.2	220.3	223.2	221.8	221.9	217.4	215.2	221.2	225.5	227.7	228.2	221.4
2000	220.2	223.8	225.7	228.5	225.7	225.3	219.2	219.9	225.3	230.0	232.5	232.2	225.7
2001	234.4	237.9	239.7	239.0	239.7	240.5	231.4	231.5	235.2	240.1	241.9	241.3	237.7
2002	231.6	235.0	235.9	235.6	236.0	236.2	228.5	228.8	234.5	238.3	241.1	240.0	235.1
2003	232.1	235.1	234.2	235.7	236.2	234.9	228.5	228.4	237.5	242.8	242.9	241.4	235.8
Trade, transportation, and utilities													
1990	34.5	34.5	34.4	34.7	35.1	35.4	34.3	34.9	35.5	34.4	35.4	36.7	35.0
1991	34.1	33.1	33.6	32.5	32.9	33.0	32.6	33.1	33.5	33.1	33.4	33.8	33.2
1992	32.1	31.4	31.1	31.3	30.9	31.5	32.6	32.3	32.7	32.5	33.0	34.0	32.1
1993	33.3	32.5	32.1	32.2	32.8	33.2	33.5	33.7	34.0	34.1	34.9	35.9	33.5
1994	34.0	33.7	34.1	34.2	35.1	35.4	34.8	34.9	35.7	35.6	36.4	37.7	35.1
1995	35.2	35.0	35.5	35.1	35.8	35.9	35.4	36.0	36.3	36.5	36.9	38.3	36.0
1996	36.7	36.5	36.2	36.6	37.0	37.3	37.3	37.3	37.5	37.7	38.7	39.8	37.4
1997	38.4	37.8	38.0	37.9	38.4	39.2	38.9	39.4	39.9	40.1	41.1	41.8	39.2
1998	40.0	39.7	39.7	39.4	39.8	40.3	39.2	40.2	40.2	40.9	41.8	42.4	40.3
1999	40.7	40.3	40.6	40.2	40.6	40.9	41.6	42.0	41.8	42.0	43.0	44.1	41.5
2000	41.8	41.4	41.9	42.4	42.8	42.9	41.9	42.2	42.7	43.0	43.9	44.9	42.7
2001	45.8	45.3	45.4	45.5	45.8	45.9	44.7	45.0	44.9	45.0	45.6	45.9	45.4
2002	43.7	43.0	43.1	43.0	43.7	43.8	43.3	43.3	43.6	43.2	44.0	44.7	43.5
2003	42.4	41.8	41.6	41.9	42.5	42.9	42.6	43.0	43.0	43.7	44.3	44.0	42.8
Wholesale trade													
1990	4.4	4.5	4.5	4.6	4.6	4.6	4.5	4.6	4.6	4.5	4.5	4.6	4.5
1991	4.5	4.5	4.6	4.4	4.4	4.4	4.4	4.5	4.5	4.5	4.4	4.5	4.5
1992	4.4	4.4	4.4	4.5	4.4	4.4	4.6	4.5	4.5	4.4	4.4	4.5	4.5
1993	4.5	4.5	4.5	4.7	4.7	4.7	4.7	4.7	4.7	4.7	4.7	4.7	4.7
1994	4.6	4.6	4.7	4.7	4.8	4.8	4.8	4.8	4.8	4.8	4.8	4.8	4.8
1995	4.5	4.5	4.6	4.3	4.3	4.4	4.4	4.4	4.4	4.5	4.4	4.5	4.4
1996	4.6	4.6	4.6	4.7	4.7	4.8	4.8	4.8	4.8	5.1	5.2	5.3	4.8
1997	5.2	5.2	5.3	5.4	5.5	5.6	5.5	5.6	5.6	5.6	5.7	5.7	5.5
1998	5.8	5.8	5.8	5.8	5.8	5.9	5.5	5.6	5.5	5.7	5.7	5.7	5.7
1999	5.6	5.7	5.7	5.8	5.9	5.9	5.9	5.9	5.9	6.1	6.1	6.2	5.9
2000	6.1	6.1	6.2	6.2	6.3	6.3	6.2	6.2	6.1	6.2	6.3	6.3	6.2
2001	7.2	7.3	7.3	7.4	7.4	7.4	7.5	7.6	7.5	7.5	7.5	7.5	7.4
2002	7.3	7.4	7.4	7.2	7.4	7.4	7.3	7.4	7.4	7.4	7.5	7.6	7.4
2003	7.5	7.5	7.5	7.5	7.5	7.5	7.5	7.6	7.5	7.6	7.6	7.6	7.5
Retail trade													
1990	25.3	25.1	25.0	25.3	25.6	25.8	25.0	25.4	25.9	25.2	26.0	27.2	25.6
1991	24.5	23.5	23.8	23.4	23.7	23.8	23.5	23.8	24.3	24.0	24.4	24.9	24.0
1992	24.0	23.3	23.1	23.5	23.1	23.6	24.5	24.4	24.8	24.7	25.1	25.9	24.2
1993	25.2	24.4	24.0	24.0	24.5	24.7	24.9	25.0	25.2	25.2	25.9	26.4	25.0
1994	25.2	24.8	24.7	25.2	26.0	26.3	26.1	26.2	27.0	26.8	27.6	28.7	26.2
1995	26.6	26.2	26.5	26.4	27.0	27.2	26.6	27.2	27.6	27.5	28.0	29.2	27.2
1996	27.2	27.1	26.9	27.3	27.6	27.9	27.8	27.9	28.2	28.1	28.9	29.9	27.9
1997	28.6	27.8	27.9	27.6	27.8	28.5	28.3	28.8	28.9	28.9	29.3	30.0	28.5
1998	28.3	28.0	28.0	27.7	27.9	28.3	27.8	28.5	28.5	29.1	30.1	30.9	28.6
1999	29.7	29.2	29.5	29.8	30.0	30.3	30.9	31.4	31.2	31.1	32.0	33.1	30.7
2000	31.1	30.7	31.1	31.5	31.7	31.8	30.9	31.2	31.8	31.8	32.6	33.6	31.7
2001	33.8	33.2	33.4	33.2	33.5	33.5	32.2	32.4	32.5	32.4	33.0	33.4	33.0
2002	31.7	30.9	31.0	31.1	31.6	31.6	31.3	31.2	31.5	30.9	31.6	32.3	31.4
2003	30.3	29.7	29.6	29.7	30.2	30.5	30.4	30.6	30.8	31.3	31.9	31.7	30.6

Employment by Industry: Michigan—*Continued*

(Numbers in thousands. Not seasonally adjusted.)

Industry	January	February	March	April	May	June	July	August	September	October	November	December	Annual Average
ANN ARBOR—*Continued*													
Transportation and utilities													
1990	4.8	4.9	4.9	4.8	4.9	5.0	4.8	4.9	5.0	4.7	4.9	4.9	4.9
1991	5.1	5.1	5.2	4.7	4.8	4.8	4.7	4.8	4.7	4.6	4.6	4.4	4.8
1992	3.7	3.7	3.6	3.3	3.4	3.5	3.5	3.4	3.4	3.4	3.5	3.6	3.5
1993	3.6	3.6	3.6	3.5	3.6	3.8	3.9	4.0	4.1	4.2	4.3	4.8	3.9
1994	4.2	4.3	4.7	4.3	4.3	4.3	3.9	3.9	3.9	4.0	4.0	4.2	4.2
1995	4.1	4.3	4.4	4.4	4.5	4.3	4.4	4.4	4.3	4.5	4.5	4.6	4.4
1996	4.9	4.8	4.7	4.6	4.7	4.6	4.7	4.6	4.5	4.5	4.6	4.6	4.7
1997	4.6	4.8	4.8	4.9	5.1	5.1	5.1	5.0	5.4	5.6	6.1	6.1	5.2
1998	5.9	5.9	5.9	5.9	6.1	6.1	5.9	6.1	6.2	6.1	6.0	5.8	6.0
1999	5.4	5.4	5.4	4.6	4.7	4.7	4.8	4.7	4.7	4.8	4.9	4.8	4.9
2000	4.6	4.6	4.6	4.7	4.8	4.8	4.8	4.8	4.8	5.0	5.0	5.0	4.8
2001	4.8	4.8	4.7	4.9	4.9	5.0	5.0	5.0	4.9	5.1	5.1	5.0	4.9
2002	4.7	4.7	4.7	4.7	4.7	4.8	4.7	4.7	4.7	4.9	4.9	4.8	4.8
2003	4.6	4.6	4.5	4.7	4.8	4.9	4.7	4.8	4.7	4.8	4.8	4.7	4.7
Information													
1990	3.8	4.0	4.0	3.4	3.4	3.5	3.5	3.6	3.5	3.5	3.5	3.6	3.6
1991	3.5	3.5	3.5	3.5	3.6	3.6	3.6	3.6	3.6	3.6	3.6	3.6	3.6
1992	3.4	3.5	3.5	3.5	3.5	3.5	3.6	3.5	3.5	3.5	3.5	3.6	3.5
1993	3.0	3.0	3.2	3.7	3.7	3.8	3.8	3.8	3.8	3.7	3.7	3.8	3.6
1994	3.9	4.0	4.0	3.9	3.9	3.9	3.8	3.8	3.8	3.8	3.8	3.9	3.9
1995	4.1	4.2	4.2	4.7	4.7	4.7	4.6	4.6	4.7	4.6	4.6	4.7	4.5
1996	4.7	4.8	4.8	5.1	5.2	5.2	5.1	5.2	5.1	5.2	5.3	5.3	5.1
1997	5.2	5.2	5.3	4.9	5.0	5.0	4.9	4.9	4.8	4.5	4.5	4.5	4.9
1998	5.1	5.1	5.1	5.2	5.2	5.2	5.1	5.3	5.2	5.2	5.3	5.3	5.2
1999	5.2	5.3	5.3	5.4	5.5	5.6	5.3	5.3	5.3	5.2	5.2	5.2	5.3
2000	5.3	5.3	5.4	5.5	5.5	5.6	5.5	5.4	5.5	5.6	5.6	5.6	5.5
2001	6.0	6.1	6.1	6.3	6.3	6.4	6.3	6.2	6.2	6.3	6.3	6.3	6.2
2002	5.9	5.9	5.8	5.9	5.9	5.9	5.5	5.5	5.5	5.5	5.5	5.4	5.7
2003	5.3	5.4	5.4	5.3	5.2	5.3	5.3	5.2	5.2	5.2	5.2	5.2	5.3
Financial activities													
1990	10.2	10.4	10.5	10.0	10.1	10.2	9.7	9.8	9.8	9.6	9.6	9.8	10.0
1991	9.4	9.3	9.3	9.6	9.9	9.9	10.0	10.1	10.1	9.8	9.8	9.8	9.8
1992	9.2	9.2	9.2	9.3	9.4	9.5	9.5	9.7	9.5	9.6	9.6	9.8	9.5
1993	9.5	9.5	9.3	9.4	9.6	9.8	9.8	9.9	9.8	9.6	9.7	9.8	9.6
1994	9.8	9.8	9.9	9.6	9.8	10.1	10.0	9.9	9.9	9.8	9.6	9.8	9.8
1995	9.1	9.2	9.2	9.2	9.3	9.5	9.5	9.5	9.5	9.3	9.2	9.4	9.3
1996	9.3	9.4	9.5	9.7	9.8	9.9	9.9	9.9	9.8	9.6	9.7	9.6	9.7
1997	9.5	9.5	9.5	9.9	10.0	10.1	10.2	10.3	10.1	9.8	9.9	9.9	9.9
1998	10.0	9.8	10.0	9.9	10.1	10.2	10.5	10.8	10.5	10.6	10.7	10.8	10.3
1999	10.5	10.8	10.8	11.0	11.2	11.3	11.2	11.2	10.9	10.6	10.6	10.6	10.9
2000	10.6	10.7	10.6	10.8	10.9	11.1	11.1	11.1	10.9	10.6	10.7	10.7	10.8
2001	11.0	11.2	11.3	11.5	11.7	11.8	11.5	11.6	11.3	11.2	11.3	11.3	11.4
2002	11.1	11.2	11.2	11.3	11.4	11.6	11.4	11.4	11.2	11.3	11.3	11.4	11.3
2003	11.2	11.2	11.2	11.1	11.4	11.6	11.6	11.8	11.4	11.5	11.1	11.1	11.4
Professional and business services													
1990	23.7	23.9	24.1	24.3	24.8	25.4	24.8	25.2	25.6	24.4	24.3	24.8	24.6
1991	23.4	23.2	23.1	23.6	24.2	24.4	24.4	24.6	24.6	24.3	24.0	23.8	24.0
1992	24.1	24.8	25.1	25.1	27.0	27.3	27.3	27.2	26.9	26.7	26.5	26.5	26.2
1993	25.4	25.5	25.4	26.0	26.5	26.7	27.0	27.0	26.7	26.7	26.7	27.0	26.4
1994	25.9	26.3	26.6	26.7	26.4	26.4	26.1	26.1	26.0	26.2	26.3	26.4	26.3
1995	26.3	26.5	26.9	27.7	28.2	28.7	29.2	29.5	29.3	29.8	29.2	29.7	28.4
1996	28.3	28.6	28.7	28.1	28.8	29.3	29.9	30.4	30.0	29.8	29.6	29.5	29.3
1997	29.2	29.5	30.0	30.6	31.3	31.7	31.2	31.6	31.4	30.6	30.8	31.4	30.8
1998	31.9	32.4	32.7	33.3	33.4	33.8	33.1	34.3	34.1	34.4	34.7	34.7	33.6
1999	34.0	34.7	34.9	36.3	37.0	37.9	37.7	38.1	37.9	37.4	37.4	37.2	36.7
2000	35.6	35.7	35.9	36.8	36.9	37.2	37.5	38.2	38.0	37.3	37.0	37.0	36.9
2001	38.5	38.6	38.7	39.5	39.7	40.0	38.2	39.2	38.7	37.8	37.2	37.0	38.6
2002	35.3	35.2	35.4	36.0	36.8	36.9	36.3	36.7	36.5	36.6	36.6	36.3	36.2
2003	36.9	36.8	36.9	37.1	37.9	38.1	37.4	37.8	37.7	37.7	38.2	37.9	37.5
Educational and health services													
1990	23.2	23.8	24.8	23.5	23.4	23.8	22.8	23.2	24.2	24.4	24.5	25.2	23.9
1991	23.9	24.1	24.2	23.3	23.3	23.1	21.8	22.0	22.5	22.7	22.7	22.6	23.0
1992	22.4	22.7	22.8	22.6	22.4	22.2	22.1	22.0	22.5	22.9	22.9	23.0	22.5
1993	22.5	22.7	22.5	22.9	22.7	22.6	22.4	22.4	22.9	23.5	23.2	23.0	22.8
1994	22.5	23.0	23.1	22.7	22.9	22.8	23.3	23.1	23.9	23.6	24.1	24.2	23.3
1995	23.2	23.8	23.9	23.2	23.1	23.0	23.2	23.2	23.7	23.5	23.7	24.2	23.5
1996	23.9	24.3	24.4	24.7	24.6	24.5	23.7	23.9	24.4	24.9	25.1	25.2	24.5
1997	24.2	24.4	24.5	24.3	24.1	24.1	23.2	23.5	24.0	24.1	24.3	24.2	24.1
1998	23.2	23.5	23.6	24.2	24.2	24.1	23.6	24.1	24.3	24.6	24.8	24.6	24.1
1999	24.8	25.1	25.2	25.3	25.4	25.1	25.0	24.7	24.8	25.7	25.9	25.9	25.2
2000	26.1	26.5	26.6	26.9	26.8	26.8	26.7	26.7	27.2	27.4	27.7	27.4	26.9
2001	27.5	27.8	28.0	28.1	28.1	28.0	27.9	28.0	28.2	28.7	28.8	28.8	28.2
2002	28.5	29.2	29.4	30.0	30.1	30.0	28.2	28.4	28.6	28.7	29.0	28.9	29.1
2003	28.8	29.0	28.9	29.7	29.6	29.7	28.9	29.3	30.8	30.9	31.1	30.9	29.8

Employment by Industry: Michigan—*Continued*

(Numbers in thousands. Not seasonally adjusted.)

Industry	January	February	March	April	May	June	July	August	September	October	November	December	Annual Average
ANN ARBOR—*Continued*													
Leisure and hospitality													
1990	17.8	18.3	18.7	18.1	19.0	19.2	18.7	19.1	19.1	18.4	18.7	19.0	18.7
1991	17.3	17.3	17.5	17.4	18.5	18.8	18.6	18.8	19.2	18.6	18.7	18.5	18.3
1992	17.7	17.8	17.8	17.7	18.2	18.3	18.9	19.0	18.8	18.8	18.6	18.6	18.4
1993	17.7	17.8	17.4	17.9	18.4	18.7	19.0	18.9	18.8	18.6	18.3	18.3	18.3
1994	18.0	18.1	17.7	18.4	19.3	19.7	19.7	19.7	19.8	19.0	18.7	18.5	18.9
1995	17.5	18.3	18.4	18.9	19.8	20.1	20.2	19.8	19.7	19.0	18.4	18.6	19.1
1996	18.0	18.7	18.9	19.2	20.2	20.6	20.6	20.6	20.6	20.0	19.8	19.9	19.8
1997	19.2	19.4	19.5	20.5	21.4	21.5	21.4	21.2	21.4	22.6	22.3	22.2	21.1
1998	20.2	20.5	21.0	22.0	22.9	23.1	22.6	22.4	22.0	21.4	20.8	20.8	21.6
1999	19.4	19.8	20.0	21.3	21.8	22.3	21.8	21.5	21.1	21.0	20.7	20.7	21.0
2000	19.9	20.2	20.6	21.7	22.4	22.8	22.6	22.4	22.1	22.1	21.5	21.3	21.6
2001	20.7	20.7	21.3	21.5	22.6	23.2	22.9	22.9	22.4	21.9	21.6	21.3	21.9
2002	20.7	20.7	21.2	21.7	22.5	22.8	22.7	22.8	22.4	21.8	21.2	20.8	21.8
2003	19.8	19.8	20.2	20.9	22.1	22.9	23.2	22.9	23.1	22.4	21.7	21.8	21.7
Other services													
1990	7.0	7.2	7.3	7.2	7.4	7.4	7.1	7.3	7.3	7.3	7.2	7.3	7.3
1991	6.9	6.9	7.0	6.9	7.1	7.1	7.0	7.1	7.1	7.3	7.2	7.2	7.1
1992	7.3	7.3	7.3	7.3	7.4	7.3	7.5	7.3	7.2	7.4	7.3	7.4	7.3
1993	7.3	7.3	7.3	7.3	7.3	7.4	7.6	7.6	7.6	7.5	7.5	7.6	7.4
1994	7.3	7.3	7.4	7.5	7.6	7.7	7.6	7.6	7.6	7.7	7.7	7.8	7.6
1995	7.6	7.7	7.9	7.7	7.7	7.8	7.7	7.8	7.7	7.7	7.6	7.8	7.7
1996	7.9	7.9	8.1	8.1	8.2	8.3	8.2	8.3	8.2	8.3	8.3	8.2	8.2
1997	8.3	8.3	8.4	8.0	8.1	8.1	8.1	8.2	8.2	8.2	8.1	8.2	8.2
1998	7.8	7.9	8.0	8.0	8.1	8.1	7.8	8.0	7.9	7.9	7.8	7.9	7.9
1999	7.9	8.0	8.1	8.1	8.1	8.2	8.0	8.0	8.0	8.2	8.1	8.1	8.1
2000	8.0	8.1	8.1	8.3	8.2	8.2	8.0	8.0	8.0	8.1	8.2	8.2	8.1
2001	8.2	8.3	8.3	8.3	8.3	8.3	8.2	8.2	8.0	8.1	8.1	8.2	8.2
2002	8.1	8.2	8.3	8.3	8.2	8.3	8.4	8.4	8.3	8.4	8.3	8.5	8.3
2003	8.5	8.5	8.6	8.6	8.6	8.6	8.6	8.6	8.6	8.6	8.6	8.5	8.6
Government													
1990	62.5	66.2	67.6	66.6	63.2	60.5	56.2	55.4	62.1	68.0	70.1	68.3	63.9
1991	64.0	68.5	69.1	69.9	65.3	60.7	57.9	57.0	62.3	68.2	69.6	70.1	65.2
1992	66.8	70.4	69.9	70.3	67.0	65.1	60.1	59.8	63.0	66.6	71.6	70.2	66.7
1993	67.4	70.2	70.6	71.5	65.9	63.6	60.6	58.6	65.2	71.6	72.0	71.0	67.4
1994	68.0	71.1	71.0	70.5	66.1	64.6	61.3	60.8	65.2	70.2	71.5	70.9	67.6
1995	67.4	71.5	72.4	72.4	66.3	65.8	62.5	61.2	69.6	71.0	71.5	71.5	68.6
1996	65.7	71.2	73.3	72.0	68.6	69.8	63.5	62.9	69.2	71.7	72.6	72.1	69.4
1997	69.2	71.7	72.2	71.9	68.4	65.8	62.0	61.5	69.5	72.7	73.1	73.1	69.3
1998	70.6	72.9	73.5	73.1	71.2	68.6	65.2	64.0	70.4	73.8	75.6	75.7	71.2
1999	72.3	75.2	75.4	75.6	72.2	70.6	66.8	64.4	71.4	75.4	76.8	76.4	72.7
2000	72.9	75.9	76.6	76.1	72.2	70.7	65.9	65.9	70.9	75.9	77.9	77.1	73.2
2001	76.7	79.9	80.6	78.3	77.2	76.9	71.7	70.4	75.5	81.1	83.0	82.5	77.8
2002	78.3	81.6	81.5	79.4	77.4	76.9	72.7	72.3	78.4	82.8	85.2	84.0	79.2
2003	79.2	82.6	81.4	81.1	78.9	75.8	70.9	69.8	77.7	82.8	82.7	82.0	78.7
Federal government													
1990	3.2	3.2	3.4	3.6	3.7	3.5	3.4	3.2	3.2	3.2	3.2	3.3	3.3
1991	3.2	3.2	3.2	3.2	3.2	3.2	3.2	3.2	3.2	3.3	3.3	3.3	3.2
1992	3.3	3.3	3.3	3.4	3.4	3.4	3.4	3.4	3.4	3.4	3.4	3.4	3.4
1993	3.4	3.4	3.4	3.4	3.4	3.4	3.4	3.4	3.5	3.5	3.5	3.5	3.4
1994	3.5	3.5	3.5	3.5	3.5	3.5	3.5	3.5	3.5	3.5	3.4	3.5	3.5
1995	3.4	3.5	3.4	3.4	3.4	3.4	3.5	3.5	3.5	3.5	3.4	3.4	3.4
1996	3.4	3.4	3.4	3.4	3.4	3.4	3.4	3.5	3.5	3.4	3.4	3.4	3.4
1997	3.4	3.4	3.4	3.4	3.4	3.4	3.4	3.4	3.4	3.4	3.4	3.4	3.4
1998	3.3	3.3	3.3	3.4	3.4	3.4	3.4	3.4	3.4	3.4	3.4	3.4	3.4
1999	3.5	3.4	3.5	3.5	3.5	3.5	3.5	3.5	3.5	3.5	3.5	3.5	3.5
2000	3.5	3.6	3.6	3.8	4.3	4.0	3.8	3.6	3.5	3.4	3.5	3.5	3.7
2001	3.4	3.3	3.3	3.3	3.3	3.3	3.3	3.3	3.3	3.2	3.3	3.3	3.3
2002	3.2	3.2	3.3	3.2	3.2	3.2	3.2	3.2	3.2	3.2	3.2	3.2	3.2
2003	3.2	3.2	3.2	3.2	3.2	3.2	3.2	3.3	3.2	3.2	3.2	3.2	3.2
State government													
1990	40.6	42.6	42.9	42.7	39.3	38.0	36.3	36.0	40.4	44.4	45.6	44.3	41.1
1991	41.5	44.5	44.7	45.2	41.3	37.4	37.0	36.2	39.7	43.6	44.9	45.3	41.8
1992	42.9	44.8	44.0	44.3	41.2	39.9	38.2	37.8	38.5	40.7	44.7	44.2	41.8
1993	42.3	44.1	44.2	45.6	39.9	38.4	38.6	37.0	41.0	46.0	46.0	45.8	42.4
1994	43.4	45.6	44.9	45.3	40.1	39.3	39.1	38.6	41.5	45.1	45.9	46.2	42.9
1995	44.2	46.7	47.3	47.3	41.3	41.3	40.8	39.8	45.8	45.7	46.0	46.2	44.4
1996	42.0	45.9	47.7	46.8	43.1	44.8	41.6	41.2	45.2	46.1	46.5	46.6	44.8
1997	45.2	46.2	46.5	46.3	42.4	39.8	39.6	39.5	45.0	46.7	47.3	47.3	44.3
1998	46.2	47.0	47.3	47.2	44.8	42.4	42.8	41.7	45.6	47.6	48.8	49.1	45.9
1999	47.2	49.0	48.8	49.4	45.2	44.3	43.9	41.9	46.1	48.7	49.8	49.4	47.0
2000	47.1	48.9	49.3	49.1	44.3	43.6	41.8	41.8	44.7	48.6	49.9	49.6	46.6
2001	49.2	51.3	51.9	50.6	48.9	49.2	46.6	45.7	48.1	52.6	54.1	53.4	50.1
2002	50.8	53.3	53.0	51.1	49.1	49.2	48.0	47.7	50.6	53.5	55.7	54.8	51.4
2003	51.6	53.7	52.6	52.3	49.9	47.0	46.6	46.1	50.2	53.5	53.2	52.8	50.8

Employment by Industry: Michigan—*Continued*

(Numbers in thousands. Not seasonally adjusted.)

Industry	January	February	March	April	May	June	July	August	September	October	November	December	Annual Average
ANN ARBOR—*Continued*													
Local government													
1990	18.8	20.4	21.3	20.3	20.3	19.0	16.5	16.2	18.5	20.4	21.2	20.7	19.5
1991	19.3	20.8	21.3	21.5	20.8	20.1	17.6	17.6	19.4	21.4	21.4	21.5	20.2
1992	20.7	22.3	22.6	22.7	22.3	21.8	18.5	18.6	21.1	22.5	23.5	22.6	21.6
1993	21.7	22.7	23.0	22.6	22.5	21.9	18.5	18.2	20.6	22.1	22.5	21.7	21.5
1994	21.1	22.0	22.6	21.7	22.5	21.7	18.7	18.8	20.2	21.7	22.2	21.3	21.2
1995	19.8	21.4	21.6	21.7	21.6	21.0	18.2	17.9	20.3	21.8	22.1	21.9	20.8
1996	20.3	21.8	22.1	21.7	22.1	21.6	18.4	18.2	20.5	22.2	22.7	22.0	21.1
1997	20.6	22.1	22.3	22.2	22.6	22.6	19.0	18.6	21.1	22.6	22.4	22.4	21.5
1998	21.1	22.6	22.9	22.5	23.0	22.8	19.0	18.9	21.4	22.8	23.4	23.2	22.0
1999	21.6	22.8	23.1	22.7	23.5	22.8	19.4	19.0	21.8	23.2	23.5	23.5	22.2
2000	22.3	23.4	23.7	23.2	23.6	23.1	20.3	20.5	22.7	23.9	24.5	24.0	22.9
2001	24.1	25.3	25.4	24.4	25.0	24.4	21.8	21.4	24.1	25.3	25.6	25.8	24.4
2002	24.3	25.1	25.2	25.1	25.1	24.5	21.5	21.4	24.6	26.1	26.3	26.0	24.6
2003	24.4	25.7	25.6	25.6	25.8	25.6	21.1	20.4	24.3	26.1	26.3	26.0	24.7
DETROIT													
Total nonfarm													
1990	1857.2	1875.1	1886.3	1891.8	1918.1	1926.8	1907.0	1918.9	1914.7	1913.1	1903.5	1909.3	1901.8
1991	1822.2	1814.9	1821.0	1832.1	1859.3	1864.8	1842.4	1846.5	1861.8	1863.5	1871.2	1875.6	1847.9
1992	1798.1	1813.6	1825.7	1841.9	1863.7	1870.3	1844.1	1857.0	1869.6	1877.5	1879.9	1888.3	1852.5
1993	1838.5	1848.0	1855.9	1870.4	1893.5	1899.2	1882.9	1884.3	1902.9	1921.1	1931.9	1945.7	1889.5
1994	1894.4	1901.8	1918.8	1926.8	1949.0	1960.2	1936.2	1958.6	1976.5	1975.9	1992.9	2002.8	1949.5
1995	1947.0	1958.5	1975.7	1988.7	2014.5	2027.9	1982.3	2006.4	2028.5	2033.8	2043.4	2068.0	2006.2
1996	1999.8	2013.4	2013.8	2030.1	2059.9	2074.0	2026.1	2054.3	2063.7	2078.3	2087.8	2098.0	2049.9
1997	2037.9	2046.2	2064.0	2060.9	2085.8	2088.5	2050.8	2070.0	2089.1	2099.9	2107.2	2119.7	2076.7
1998	2069.0	2082.5	2094.4	2121.4	2148.9	2151.7	2071.0	2104.9	2122.2	2136.0	2148.2	2157.3	2117.3
1999	2093.9	2102.6	2119.1	2148.1	2173.3	2182.5	2138.5	2162.5	2181.5	2193.8	2207.9	2222.7	2160.5
2000	2169.2	2173.3	2187.4	2202.3	2226.2	2236.7	2176.9	2195.9	2204.1	2218.2	2227.4	2228.1	2203.8
2001	2122.6	2140.1	2148.0	2160.2	2176.9	2184.9	2120.8	2134.3	2136.1	2135.0	2139.3	2144.7	2145.2
2002	2059.6	2067.1	2079.3	2085.8	2108.1	2118.1	2071.9	2091.1	2098.2	2108.3	2115.5	2118.1	2093.4
2003	2044.7	2045.9	2052.0	2060.2	2087.7	2097.0	2039.1	2046.4	2059.9	2064.5	2066.8	2057.1	2060.1
Total private													
1990	1627.5	1641.1	1651.3	1656.7	1678.8	1695.9	1680.3	1693.1	1691.0	1679.8	1667.1	1674.2	1669.7
1991	1592.7	1579.4	1584.8	1598.6	1623.2	1633.3	1626.8	1635.3	1635.5	1629.0	1633.7	1639.6	1617.7
1992	1568.8	1578.6	1588.2	1607.4	1628.6	1638.5	1628.3	1644.1	1644.3	1641.9	1642.9	1652.9	1622.0
1993	1605.4	1610.3	1617.0	1632.8	1655.4	1663.6	1666.5	1673.2	1674.6	1685.4	1693.8	1709.4	1657.3
1994	1667.5	1670.7	1685.4	1695.7	1718.8	1734.5	1725.3	1748.4	1752.0	1745.8	1758.6	1770.3	1722.8
1995	1722.4	1728.5	1743.9	1758.7	1784.1	1800.9	1772.9	1798.4	1799.4	1802.9	1810.2	1832.1	1779.5
1996	1773.8	1781.3	1783.3	1801.0	1830.5	1845.2	1817.7	1846.9	1842.6	1846.7	1853.3	1862.5	1823.7
1997	1808.9	1813.3	1829.3	1828.8	1852.3	1858.5	1847.2	1864.3	1860.7	1865.9	1870.9	1883.0	1848.6
1998	1838.2	1846.6	1857.5	1885.2	1911.2	1917.4	1864.8	1902.4	1893.3	1900.4	1909.1	1920.5	1887.2
1999	1863.3	1867.6	1880.6	1910.3	1935.6	1948.1	1925.0	1951.5	1947.8	1955.2	1966.1	1982.4	1927.8
2000	1932.0	1932.5	1943.6	1960.4	1981.6	1995.6	1959.0	1981.5	1967.6	1977.3	1984.0	1985.4	1966.7
2001	1881.2	1894.2	1900.8	1913.5	1930.6	1940.3	1898.4	1914.8	1903.7	1891.2	1893.3	1899.2	1905.1
2002	1817.8	1821.6	1833.0	1843.2	1864.5	1876.6	1855.9	1876.8	1867.1	1862.4	1869.4	1872.5	1855.1
2003	1806.0	1801.6	1807.8	1815.5	1842.8	1854.1	1825.2	1837.0	1824.9	1821.0	1821.7	1816.0	1822.8
Goods-producing													
1990	414.6	426.1	427.3	434.0	441.0	446.2	436.6	444.4	444.1	445.7	428.0	429.4	434.8
1991	394.3	389.9	383.9	392.1	404.1	406.6	407.2	412.7	412.3	408.5	405.7	401.3	401.6
1992	370.0	380.7	383.0	397.6	404.4	406.3	396.2	410.7	410.7	405.3	401.9	400.5	397.3
1993	387.8	392.8	392.5	394.6	400.1	401.7	409.3	411.3	410.9	413.8	414.3	417.5	403.9
1994	409.0	410.6	415.0	417.8	423.9	430.3	421.2	436.6	440.1	440.4	443.1	444.7	427.7
1995	427.2	429.9	434.9	436.6	443.9	450.7	433.1	448.1	447.5	449.3	449.0	452.5	441.9
1996	434.3	434.7	431.5	441.9	448.2	452.7	442.1	456.0	455.9	458.9	457.8	456.5	447.5
1997	438.2	441.6	446.0	447.9	454.8	457.8	457.6	474.8	477.3	474.9	475.8	475.7	460.2
1998	466.3	470.7	471.2	477.2	486.5	484.4	465.3	483.4	484.3	483.4	483.7	483.6	478.3
1999	467.7	469.3	474.9	483.1	491.0	495.0	489.1	504.6	506.1	502.2	503.6	503.3	490.8
2000	490.5	492.9	496.4	504.8	511.3	514.2	497.9	509.8	503.4	504.9	503.1	498.0	502.3
2001	448.0	460.4	460.7	461.9	464.7	466.0	447.8	456.3	455.9	449.3	445.4	445.7	455.2
2002	413.6	420.0	421.2	421.5	425.8	430.0	420.6	430.5	426.7	424.8	423.4	420.0	423.2
2003	401.5	400.6	400.8	400.9	409.4	412.9	398.6	408.5	405.0	403.4	406.0	403.8	404.3
Construction and mining													
1990	59.7	57.7	57.8	59.5	65.6	68.3	69.9	70.2	68.9	67.4	65.5	60.8	64.3
1991	53.4	51.7	52.3	54.6	59.0	60.3	62.5	62.9	62.0	62.0	59.8	56.1	58.1
1992	48.6	47.6	48.0	51.4	56.6	59.5	62.1	62.4	62.3	62.0	59.2	56.7	56.4
1993	49.9	49.2	48.8	52.1	57.7	60.5	64.2	64.0	63.7	63.1	61.2	59.1	57.8
1994	51.8	51.2	53.1	56.7	61.5	64.7	68.1	68.3	68.1	67.9	66.6	64.5	61.9
1995	57.8	56.3	59.0	62.4	68.0	71.2	73.6	74.1	73.6	74.0	73.4	71.7	67.9
1996	63.7	63.2	65.0	69.1	75.9	78.5	81.5	81.9	80.4	81.5	80.4	77.5	74.9
1997	69.3	69.2	71.3	76.5	82.1	84.4	89.2	89.2	88.5	86.2	84.8	82.6	81.1
1998	75.6	75.7	76.1	82.8	88.5	90.8	91.7	90.7	89.9	89.7	87.6	85.7	85.4
1999	74.9	76.5	78.0	86.8	91.2	94.4	96.6	95.8	94.9	97.3	96.0	95.2	89.8
2000	86.0	86.0	89.5	95.3	99.0	101.3	103.2	101.8	100.7	100.0	98.3	94.1	96.3
2001	83.6	83.0	85.4	89.9	95.0	97.3	99.1	99.2	97.9	96.5	95.4	93.2	93.0
2002	83.7	82.2	83.1	86.4	91.5	94.0	95.5	95.2	92.7	91.4	88.9	85.2	89.2
2003	75.4	73.3	74.1	79.0	86.9	90.5	90.0	89.1	88.3	88.0	87.0	83.6	83.8

Employment by Industry: Michigan—*Continued*

(Numbers in thousands. Not seasonally adjusted.)

Industry	January	February	March	April	May	June	July	August	September	October	November	December	Annual Average
DETROIT—*Continued*													
Manufacturing													
1990	354.9	368.4	369.5	374.5	375.4	377.9	366.7	374.2	375.2	378.3	362.5	368.6	370.5
1991	340.9	338.2	331.6	337.5	345.1	346.3	344.7	349.8	350.3	346.5	345.9	345.2	343.5
1992	321.4	333.1	335.0	346.2	347.8	346.8	334.1	348.3	348.4	343.3	342.7	343.8	340.9
1993	337.9	343.6	343.7	342.5	342.4	341.2	345.1	347.3	347.2	350.7	353.1	358.4	346.1
1994	357.2	359.4	361.9	361.1	362.4	365.6	353.1	368.3	372.0	372.5	376.5	380.2	365.9
1995	369.4	373.6	375.9	374.2	375.9	379.5	359.5	374.0	373.9	375.3	375.6	380.8	374.0
1996	370.6	371.5	366.5	372.8	372.3	374.2	360.6	374.1	375.5	377.4	377.4	379.0	372.7
1997	368.9	372.4	374.7	371.4	372.7	373.4	368.4	385.6	388.8	388.7	391.0	393.1	379.1
1998	390.7	395.0	395.1	394.4	398.0	393.6	373.6	392.7	394.4	393.7	396.1	397.9	392.9
1999	392.8	392.8	396.9	396.3	399.8	400.6	392.5	408.8	411.2	404.9	407.6	408.1	401.0
2000	404.5	406.9	406.9	409.5	412.3	412.9	394.7	408.0	402.7	404.9	404.8	403.9	406.0
2001	364.4	377.4	375.3	372.0	369.7	368.7	348.7	357.1	358.0	352.8	350.0	352.5	362.2
2002	329.9	337.8	338.1	335.1	334.3	336.0	325.1	335.3	334.0	333.4	334.5	334.8	334.0
2003	326.1	327.3	326.7	321.9	322.5	322.4	308.6	319.4	316.7	315.4	319.0	320.2	320.5
Service-providing													
1990	1442.6	1449.0	1459.0	1457.8	1477.1	1480.6	1470.4	1474.5	1470.6	1467.4	1475.5	1479.9	1467.0
1991	1427.9	1425.0	1437.1	1440.0	1455.2	1458.2	1435.2	1433.8	1449.5	1455.0	1465.5	1474.3	1446.4
1992	1428.1	1432.9	1442.7	1444.3	1459.3	1464.0	1447.9	1446.3	1458.9	1472.2	1478.0	1487.8	1455.2
1993	1450.7	1455.2	1463.4	1475.8	1493.4	1497.5	1473.6	1473.0	1492.0	1507.3	1517.6	1528.2	1485.6
1994	1485.4	1491.2	1503.8	1509.0	1525.1	1529.9	1515.0	1522.0	1536.4	1535.5	1549.8	1558.1	1521.8
1995	1519.8	1528.6	1540.8	1552.1	1570.6	1577.2	1549.2	1558.3	1581.0	1584.5	1594.4	1615.5	1564.3
1996	1565.5	1578.7	1582.3	1588.2	1611.7	1621.3	1584.0	1598.3	1607.8	1619.4	1630.0	1641.5	1602.4
1997	1599.7	1604.6	1618.0	1613.0	1631.0	1630.7	1593.2	1595.2	1611.8	1625.0	1631.4	1644.0	1616.5
1998	1602.7	1611.8	1623.2	1644.2	1662.4	1667.3	1605.7	1621.5	1637.9	1652.6	1664.5	1673.7	1639.0
1999	1626.2	1633.3	1644.2	1665.0	1682.3	1687.5	1649.4	1657.9	1675.4	1691.6	1704.3	1719.4	1669.7
2000	1678.7	1680.4	1691.0	1697.5	1714.9	1722.5	1679.0	1686.1	1700.7	1713.3	1724.3	1730.1	1701.5
2001	1674.6	1679.7	1687.3	1698.3	1712.2	1718.9	1673.0	1678.0	1680.2	1685.7	1693.9	1699.0	1690.1
2002	1646.0	1647.1	1658.1	1664.3	1682.3	1688.1	1651.3	1660.6	1671.5	1683.5	1692.1	1698.1	1670.3
2003	1643.2	1645.3	1651.2	1659.3	1678.3	1684.1	1640.5	1637.9	1654.9	1661.1	1660.8	1653.3	1655.8
Trade, transportation, and utilities													
1990	387.6	384.2	385.6	381.4	385.4	387.4	384.5	386.9	385.3	384.4	390.1	398.2	386.8
1991	380.6	371.7	373.8	367.9	371.5	373.6	371.2	371.3	371.8	369.9	377.9	385.4	373.9
1992	368.7	363.8	364.0	363.8	366.2	370.4	370.6	370.1	370.7	373.0	379.7	388.7	370.8
1993	369.9	364.9	364.7	367.5	370.8	372.7	373.5	375.2	375.1	382.0	389.7	397.5	375.3
1994	381.1	377.1	378.5	377.5	382.9	386.5	386.3	388.5	390.1	389.7	399.1	406.8	387.0
1995	380.7	377.3	379.1	385.6	390.1	392.6	389.0	393.0	394.7	397.2	405.6	417.1	391.8
1996	395.4	391.2	391.7	387.0	393.3	396.6	389.7	394.5	394.2	398.3	408.1	416.1	396.3
1997	393.4	388.6	390.7	390.0	394.8	396.1	397.5	396.2	396.8	402.0	409.9	419.0	397.9
1998	403.6	401.8	405.1	399.4	404.8	407.8	396.8	401.5	400.3	404.8	416.4	424.7	405.6
1999	408.9	405.6	409.5	409.7	412.3	416.7	411.1	415.0	413.7	413.4	423.7	433.3	414.4
2000	412.0	407.7	409.1	407.0	410.1	414.0	406.8	410.3	409.4	418.6	428.7	437.6	414.3
2001	421.1	415.5	415.9	416.0	418.1	419.2	411.9	413.5	411.1	411.4	418.5	424.2	416.4
2002	400.2	394.7	397.2	396.3	400.9	402.3	397.5	398.6	398.7	398.9	406.9	412.5	400.4
2003	390.3	387.1	387.6	385.8	389.6	391.3	387.2	387.9	388.2	391.2	396.5	397.0	390.0
Wholesale trade													
1990	83.8	83.9	84.4	83.4	83.9	84.4	84.8	84.6	84.5	83.5	83.4	83.6	84.0
1991	82.3	81.7	81.8	81.4	81.5	81.7	81.9	81.6	81.1	81.1	81.2	81.4	81.6
1992	80.5	80.3	80.6	81.6	81.9	82.4	83.3	82.9	82.6	82.7	82.3	82.9	82.0
1993	81.7	81.6	81.9	82.9	83.4	83.7	83.9	84.0	83.9	83.8	84.1	84.7	83.3
1994	83.8	83.8	84.3	84.5	85.0	85.5	86.1	86.1	85.9	85.4	86.2	86.1	85.2
1995	82.6	83.2	83.7	85.2	86.1	86.7	87.2	87.3	87.2	86.4	86.4	87.5	85.8
1996	85.7	85.8	86.0	86.4	87.5	88.5	87.5	88.0	87.6	88.8	88.9	89.7	87.5
1997	88.3	89.2	90.2	89.6	90.5	91.0	93.6	92.9	93.2	93.5	93.6	94.3	91.7
1998	92.1	92.3	93.2	95.5	96.1	96.9	94.4	95.2	94.4	94.4	95.1	95.1	94.6
1999	94.6	95.4	95.8	96.7	97.3	98.2	99.6	99.9	99.4	99.4	99.7	100.0	98.0
2000	98.8	98.8	99.0	98.9	99.4	100.1	99.5	99.4	98.5	99.4	99.0	99.6	99.2
2001	103.4	103.9	103.9	104.7	104.7	104.2	103.1	102.8	101.8	101.2	100.7	101.1	103.0
2002	98.6	99.0	99.0	99.1	99.8	100.1	99.0	98.8	98.3	97.8	98.1	98.6	98.9
2003	96.8	97.1	97.2	96.8	96.5	97.1	96.6	97.7	95.9	96.4	97.4	96.3	96.8
Retail trade													
1990	239.9	235.6	235.7	232.4	234.6	235.2	233.7	235.8	234.1	235.6	242.0	249.2	237.0
1991	234.4	226.3	227.6	223.4	226.2	227.6	225.2	225.5	226.2	225.1	232.7	239.5	228.3
1992	223.6	218.5	218.3	216.8	217.8	221.6	221.7	221.9	222.3	224.6	231.2	239.5	223.2
1993	223.3	218.2	217.9	219.9	221.8	222.8	222.8	224.6	224.0	229.7	236.8	243.5	225.4
1994	228.4	223.9	224.3	222.4	226.3	229.0	228.2	230.5	232.3	232.6	241.2	249.1	230.7
1995	228.1	224.2	225.5	229.1	232.7	234.0	230.2	233.9	235.4	237.5	246.0	255.8	234.4
1996	238.1	233.7	233.7	231.2	235.6	237.7	233.2	236.9	236.7	239.2	249.1	256.4	238.5
1997	235.9	230.6	231.7	230.3	233.5	234.2	234.1	235.2	235.7	239.7	247.3	255.4	237.0
1998	242.4	239.9	242.0	233.7	237.3	239.5	232.9	235.4	234.4	239.2	249.7	258.1	240.4
1999	243.6	239.9	240.7	237.6	239.3	242.2	239.1	241.9	241.0	241.6	251.5	260.8	243.3
2000	241.5	237.4	238.4	235.8	238.6	241.4	237.3	239.7	240.0	245.9	256.5	265.0	243.1
2001	245.7	240.5	241.2	238.7	240.7	241.7	237.1	238.2	237.2	238.3	246.6	251.7	241.5
2002	232.1	226.5	228.1	227.1	230.4	231.1	229.1	229.4	229.9	230.3	238.3	244.2	231.4
2003	224.9	221.6	222.0	220.8	224.7	225.8	223.6	223.5	224.2	227.6	231.8	233.6	225.3

Employment by Industry: Michigan—*Continued*

(Numbers in thousands. Not seasonally adjusted.)

Industry	January	February	March	April	May	June	July	August	September	October	November	December	Annual Average
DETROIT—*Continued*													
Transportation and utilities													
1990	63.9	64.7	65.5	65.6	66.9	67.8	66.0	66.5	66.7	65.3	64.7	65.4	65.8
1991	63.9	63.7	64.4	63.1	63.8	64.3	64.1	64.2	64.5	63.7	64.0	64.5	64.0
1992	64.6	65.0	65.1	65.4	66.5	66.4	65.6	65.3	65.8	65.7	66.2	66.3	65.7
1993	64.9	65.1	64.9	64.7	65.6	66.2	66.8	66.6	67.2	68.5	68.8	69.3	66.6
1994	68.9	69.4	69.9	70.6	71.6	72.0	72.0	71.9	71.9	71.7	71.7	71.6	71.1
1995	70.0	69.9	69.9	71.3	71.3	71.9	71.6	71.8	72.1	73.3	73.2	73.8	71.7
1996	71.6	71.7	72.0	69.4	70.2	70.4	69.0	69.6	69.9	70.3	70.1	70.0	70.4
1997	69.2	68.8	68.8	70.1	70.8	70.9	69.8	68.1	67.9	68.8	69.0	69.3	69.3
1998	69.1	69.6	69.9	70.2	71.4	71.4	69.5	70.9	71.5	71.2	71.6	71.5	70.7
1999	70.7	70.3	73.0	75.4	75.7	76.3	72.4	73.2	73.3	72.4	72.5	72.5	73.1
2000	71.7	71.5	71.7	72.3	72.1	72.5	70.0	71.2	70.9	73.3	73.2	73.0	72.0
2001	72.0	71.1	70.8	72.6	72.7	73.3	71.7	72.5	72.1	71.9	71.2	71.4	71.9
2002	69.5	69.2	70.1	70.1	70.7	71.1	69.4	70.4	70.5	70.8	70.5	69.7	70.2
2003	68.6	68.4	68.4	68.2	68.4	68.4	67.0	66.7	68.1	67.2	67.3	67.1	67.8
Information													
1990	38.4	38.3	38.6	38.2	38.3	38.7	38.2	38.2	38.0	38.2	38.2	38.3	38.3
1991	38.3	38.2	38.3	37.1	37.6	37.5	37.5	37.5	37.5	37.0	37.2	37.3	37.6
1992	37.8	37.4	37.7	37.7	38.1	37.5	37.9	37.5	37.0	37.0	37.3	37.4	37.5
1993	37.7	37.9	37.8	37.1	37.4	37.7	37.8	37.9	37.5	37.1	37.3	37.6	37.6
1994	36.7	36.6	36.7	36.3	36.8	37.2	36.7	36.9	36.4	36.5	37.0	37.0	36.7
1995	35.8	36.1	36.3	35.7	36.3	36.6	36.7	36.0	36.4	36.1	36.8	37.0	36.3
1996	36.4	36.6	37.0	36.1	36.7	36.9	37.2	37.4	37.0	37.4	37.7	38.1	37.0
1997	37.6	37.9	38.0	38.0	38.1	38.2	39.7	39.5	39.1	39.3	39.6	39.6	38.7
1998	39.4	39.4	39.5	38.6	39.0	39.3	39.5	40.0	39.2	39.2	39.6	40.0	39.4
1999	38.4	38.3	38.4	39.1	39.5	39.9	40.0	40.4	40.2	40.0	40.2	40.1	39.5
2000	40.1	40.1	40.6	40.0	40.4	40.7	40.4	40.5	41.2	39.8	40.3	40.6	40.4
2001	40.0	40.2	40.2	41.7	42.1	42.3	42.3	41.4	40.7	41.0	41.5	41.0	41.2
2002	40.6	40.5	40.4	39.1	39.2	39.0	38.4	38.1	37.6	37.6	37.7	37.9	38.8
2003	37.7	37.7	37.8	37.3	37.5	37.7	37.5	37.1	37.0	37.1	36.7	37.0	37.3
Financial activities													
1990	112.7	113.5	114.1	111.0	112.4	114.0	115.2	115.5	115.5	113.1	114.7	115.3	113.9
1991	114.5	114.3	115.1	110.1	111.6	113.0	112.6	112.7	111.5	110.0	110.8	112.2	112.4
1992	109.1	109.0	109.4	109.0	110.5	111.5	111.5	111.2	110.2	110.1	110.5	111.2	110.3
1993	109.8	109.8	110.6	109.8	110.6	111.8	111.3	111.6	110.7	111.4	111.9	112.4	111.0
1994	108.0	108.2	108.4	108.3	108.9	110.2	110.9	110.6	109.6	107.3	107.1	107.6	108.8
1995	111.5	110.9	111.3	106.8	107.6	108.3	108.8	109.4	108.7	107.7	107.8	109.0	109.0
1996	107.9	108.7	109.3	111.1	112.4	113.3	113.5	114.1	112.8	112.1	112.2	112.8	111.7
1997	110.6	111.0	111.6	112.2	113.6	114.5	113.9	113.8	113.8	112.5	112.7	114.0	112.9
1998	114.4	114.7	115.4	114.2	115.5	115.0	114.9	116.6	114.6	114.4	114.8	115.2	115.0
1999	114.3	114.3	113.3	113.4	113.5	114.5	112.8	113.1	111.1	110.5	109.7	110.4	112.6
2000	110.0	109.6	110.0	114.0	114.5	116.3	116.2	115.4	114.1	111.4	111.2	112.1	112.9
2001	109.8	111.1	111.6	112.9	114.9	116.0	115.0	115.0	113.5	113.0	113.3	114.4	113.4
2002	114.6	114.5	114.3	115.7	116.4	116.7	117.2	117.7	116.3	115.4	116.0	116.6	116.0
2003	115.6	115.6	115.7	117.5	118.8	119.9	120.1	120.7	118.5	117.5	117.4	117.4	117.9
Professional and business services													
1990	250.9	252.7	254.8	267.2	269.9	273.7	272.8	273.5	273.2	270.1	267.8	266.0	266.1
1991	242.2	241.6	243.4	262.9	264.3	266.9	266.7	268.3	268.6	268.1	268.0	268.0	260.8
1992	256.0	258.3	261.0	264.5	268.2	270.4	273.3	273.5	275.0	273.6	272.9	273.5	268.4
1993	269.0	271.3	273.7	279.5	284.7	286.1	284.8	286.4	289.0	289.4	290.9	293.0	283.2
1994	289.0	291.5	295.1	302.6	305.4	308.5	313.0	316.4	316.5	315.1	316.2	317.1	307.2
1995	316.9	320.3	323.7	325.9	330.4	334.0	332.7	337.8	336.6	337.8	337.8	339.3	331.1
1996	330.6	335.5	336.3	346.1	352.9	357.7	353.1	359.9	358.4	357.4	355.9	356.2	350.0
1997	355.8	357.9	362.4	354.2	357.7	358.8	346.1	346.5	347.0	349.9	348.9	349.3	352.9
1998	339.6	342.6	345.0	367.3	370.5	374.5	364.5	373.5	369.6	371.8	371.1	372.1	363.5
1999	360.4	360.7	361.9	373.4	376.8	381.7	372.7	379.4	379.4	386.9	388.7	389.9	376.0
2000	382.9	380.9	382.8	385.9	391.0	393.2	385.7	392.9	389.5	388.4	386.6	384.2	387.0
2001	379.4	381.0	381.5	383.3	384.2	386.6	379.3	385.5	382.3	376.6	374.5	373.8	380.7
2002	360.3	361.0	362.1	365.5	369.9	372.1	368.0	376.3	374.9	374.2	374.4	374.0	369.4
2003	360.7	359.6	360.9	366.2	370.3	371.4	366.4	368.1	366.7	361.2	358.3	352.6	363.5
Educational and health services													
1990	206.8	208.3	209.5	203.7	204.8	205.3	205.5	206.1	208.6	207.6	208.2	208.2	206.9
1991	209.7	210.8	213.4	211.2	211.1	211.4	209.9	210.5	214.3	218.1	219.0	219.5	213.2
1992	216.6	217.7	218.4	218.7	219.2	218.5	216.1	217.2	219.4	221.4	221.7	222.5	219.0
1993	219.0	220.7	222.1	223.2	223.7	222.8	220.3	220.6	223.0	226.1	226.8	226.7	222.9
1994	223.7	225.9	227.0	225.0	225.7	225.3	223.8	224.3	227.2	228.0	228.7	228.5	226.1
1995	226.5	228.5	229.1	232.0	232.3	232.0	228.3	228.7	231.4	234.9	235.0	236.2	231.2
1996	236.4	239.4	239.7	240.3	240.8	239.9	235.0	236.1	238.5	240.1	240.8	241.2	239.0
1997	238.4	240.4	241.1	243.4	243.1	241.7	240.1	239.6	241.8	242.1	242.1	242.5	241.4
1998	239.6	242.0	242.6	241.2	241.1	240.5	235.2	236.6	239.2	243.7	243.6	243.4	240.7
1999	242.2	245.5	245.4	242.2	242.0	241.2	240.9	240.5	242.4	244.7	244.9	244.6	243.0
2000	244.4	247.5	247.5	246.9	247.1	246.7	245.9	246.1	247.9	249.8	251.3	250.6	247.6
2001	234.0	236.0	236.8	239.6	241.2	242.0	238.7	239.6	240.8	242.6	245.0	244.5	240.1
2002	242.5	244.2	245.3	247.4	247.9	249.4	249.5	249.6	250.3	251.2	252.7	252.6	248.6
2003	250.8	251.6	251.8	249.7	250.7	251.2	249.7	249.0	249.3	251.4	251.0	251.3	250.6

Employment by Industry: Michigan—*Continued*

(Numbers in thousands. Not seasonally adjusted.)

Industry	January	February	March	April	May	June	July	August	September	October	November	December	Annual Average
DETROIT—*Continued*													
Leisure and hospitality													
1990	145.6	146.3	148.6	150.2	155.1	158.6	156.8	157.2	155.3	149.8	148.9	147.7	151.7
1991	142.2	141.9	144.9	147.4	152.8	153.6	151.9	152.3	149.6	146.3	145.0	145.2	147.8
1992	141.4	142.4	144.8	146.0	151.6	152.7	151.5	152.9	150.6	150.3	148.0	147.6	148.3
1993	141.7	142.0	144.0	149.4	155.6	157.6	156.4	157.0	155.5	152.6	149.7	150.9	151.0
1994	147.3	147.8	150.6	152.9	159.5	160.5	157.7	159.3	156.2	152.5	151.5	152.2	154.0
1995	149.8	151.0	154.0	160.1	166.7	168.8	167.5	168.0	167.1	162.2	160.8	162.1	161.5
1996	155.4	157.0	159.4	160.0	167.1	168.3	169.0	170.2	168.0	164.3	162.4	163.3	163.7
1997	156.9	157.4	160.4	163.6	170.2	171.0	172.2	173.3	165.0	165.3	162.3	162.9	165.0
1998	155.8	155.8	158.4	166.3	172.6	174.2	168.8	169.9	166.2	163.9	160.7	162.0	164.6
1999	153.9	155.5	158.3	168.9	175.7	177.8	176.9	176.6	173.8	177.0	175.0	180.1	170.8
2000	173.5	174.4	176.7	180.8	186.2	188.8	184.7	184.8	181.1	183.6	181.5	180.9	181.4
2001	169.8	170.1	173.4	177.4	183.9	186.5	183.2	182.9	180.1	178.4	175.9	176.0	178.1
2002	168.3	168.6	173.5	178.8	184.9	187.1	184.6	185.8	182.8	181.9	180.3	180.2	179.7
2003	172.1	172.2	175.3	181.1	189.0	192.1	188.4	188.2	185.1	182.4	180.2	181.4	182.3
Other services													
1990	70.9	71.7	72.8	71.0	71.9	72.0	70.7	71.3	71.0	70.9	71.2	71.1	71.4
1991	70.9	71.0	72.0	69.9	70.2	70.7	69.8	70.0	69.9	71.1	70.1	70.7	70.5
1992	69.2	69.3	69.9	70.1	70.4	71.2	71.2	71.0	70.7	71.2	70.9	71.5	70.6
1993	70.5	70.9	71.6	71.7	72.5	73.2	73.1	73.2	72.9	73.0	73.2	73.8	72.5
1994	72.7	73.0	74.1	75.3	75.7	76.0	75.7	75.8	75.9	76.3	75.9	76.4	75.2
1995	74.0	74.5	75.5	76.0	76.8	77.9	76.8	77.4	77.0	77.7	77.4	78.9	76.7
1996	77.4	78.2	78.4	78.5	79.1	79.8	78.1	78.7	77.8	78.2	78.4	78.3	78.4
1997	78.0	78.5	79.1	79.5	80.0	80.4	80.1	80.6	79.9	79.9	79.6	80.0	79.6
1998	79.5	79.6	80.3	81.0	81.2	81.7	79.8	80.9	79.9	79.2	79.2	79.5	80.2
1999	77.5	78.4	78.9	80.5	84.8	81.3	81.5	81.9	81.1	80.5	80.3	80.7	80.6
2000	78.6	79.4	80.5	81.0	81.0	81.7	81.4	81.7	81.0	80.8	81.3	81.4	80.8
2001	79.1	79.9	80.7	80.7	81.5	81.7	80.2	80.6	79.3	78.9	79.2	79.6	80.1
2002	77.7	78.1	79.0	78.9	79.5	80.0	80.1	80.2	79.8	78.4	78.0	78.7	79.0
2003	77.3	77.2	77.9	77.0	77.5	77.6	77.3	77.5	75.1	76.8	75.6	75.5	76.9
Government													
1990	229.7	234.0	235.0	235.1	239.3	230.9	226.7	225.8	223.7	233.3	236.4	235.1	232.1
1991	229.5	235.5	236.2	233.5	236.1	231.5	215.6	211.2	226.3	234.5	237.5	236.0	230.3
1992	229.3	235.0	237.5	234.5	235.1	231.8	215.8	212.9	225.3	235.6	237.0	235.4	230.4
1993	233.1	237.7	238.9	237.6	238.1	235.6	216.4	211.1	228.3	235.7	238.1	236.3	232.2
1994	226.9	231.1	233.4	231.1	230.2	225.7	210.9	210.2	224.5	230.1	234.3	232.5	226.7
1995	224.6	230.0	231.8	230.0	230.4	227.0	209.4	208.0	229.1	230.9	233.2	235.9	226.7
1996	226.0	232.1	230.5	229.1	229.4	228.8	208.4	207.4	221.1	231.6	234.5	235.5	226.2
1997	229.0	232.9	234.7	232.1	233.5	230.0	203.6	205.7	228.4	234.0	236.3	236.7	228.1
1998	230.8	235.9	236.9	236.2	237.7	234.3	206.2	202.5	228.9	235.6	239.1	236.8	230.1
1999	230.6	235.0	238.5	237.8	237.7	234.4	213.5	211.0	233.7	238.6	241.8	240.3	232.7
2000	237.2	240.8	243.8	241.9	244.6	241.1	217.9	214.4	236.5	240.9	243.4	242.7	237.1
2001	241.4	245.9	247.2	246.7	246.3	244.6	222.4	219.5	232.4	243.8	246.0	245.5	240.1
2002	241.8	245.5	246.3	242.6	243.6	241.5	216.0	214.3	231.1	245.9	246.1	245.6	238.4
2003	238.7	244.3	244.2	244.7	244.9	242.9	213.9	209.4	235.0	243.5	245.1	241.1	237.3
Federal government													
1990	31.8	31.6	31.7	32.3	35.4	32.5	32.4	31.1	30.5	30.3	30.6	31.1	31.8
1991	30.7	30.9	30.8	30.7	30.7	30.7	30.9	30.6	30.5	30.4	30.4	31.2	30.7
1992	30.9	30.4	30.4	30.4	30.3	30.4	30.7	30.3	30.0	30.3	30.2	30.6	30.4
1993	30.4	30.0	30.0	29.6	29.7	29.6	29.6	29.5	29.5	29.6	29.7	31.2	29.9
1994	29.7	29.6	29.6	29.7	29.6	29.8	29.7	29.9	30.0	30.1	30.0	32.2	30.0
1995	30.4	30.4	30.5	30.7	30.7	30.9	30.2	30.2	30.1	30.1	30.2	32.2	30.6
1996	29.9	30.0	30.0	30.4	30.2	30.1	30.1	30.1	30.0	29.9	30.4	31.6	30.2
1997	30.2	30.0	29.9	29.7	29.7	29.7	29.6	30.0	30.2	29.7	30.5	32.2	30.1
1998	31.0	30.9	30.8	30.9	31.1	30.9	29.9	29.9	30.0	30.0	30.7	32.0	30.7
1999	30.5	30.4	31.5	30.8	30.5	30.4	30.2	30.1	30.0	30.0	30.4	31.8	30.6
2000	30.5	30.3	30.7	31.8	36.4	33.3	32.4	30.5	29.8	29.8	30.3	31.5	31.4
2001	30.0	30.0	29.9	29.9	29.9	29.9	29.9	29.9	29.7	29.1	29.2	30.2	29.8
2002	29.4	29.1	29.2	29.2	29.2	29.4	29.3	29.3	29.5	30.2	30.2	31.1	29.6
2003	30.1	29.9	30.0	30.1	29.9	30.0	30.0	29.9	29.7	29.6	29.5	30.2	29.9
State government													
1990	29.3	29.9	30.1	30.2	28.7	28.1	28.2	29.1	29.0	29.8	30.2	30.2	29.4
1991	29.6	30.1	29.8	30.0	29.6	28.9	28.9	28.3	29.2	29.7	29.9	29.7	29.5
1992	29.1	29.7	29.6	29.4	28.1	28.5	28.4	28.6	29.5	30.0	30.3	30.4	29.3
1993	29.9	30.1	30.1	30.0	27.7	27.9	28.0	27.3	28.5	29.3	29.3	29.6	29.0
1994	28.7	29.2	29.3	29.2	26.7	27.2	27.0	27.1	28.6	29.3	29.5	29.4	28.4
1995	28.7	29.2	29.2	29.3	27.0	27.3	27.1	28.6	28.5	29.4	29.6	29.4	28.6
1996	28.8	30.4	29.4	28.8	27.4	28.0	26.8	26.6	27.9	28.4	28.6	28.3	28.3
1997	27.5	28.2	28.2	28.1	26.4	25.8	26.0	24.9	26.6	27.2	27.3	27.1	26.9
1998	26.3	27.2	27.4	27.5	26.5	26.2	25.2	25.1	25.7	26.9	26.9	26.5	26.5
1999	26.1	26.7	26.8	26.9	24.3	24.7	24.8	24.7	25.7	26.9	27.0	26.8	26.0
2000	25.7	26.7	26.8	26.8	24.9	25.3	25.3	24.6	25.8	26.7	27.0	26.8	26.0
2001	28.0	28.9	28.8	28.9	27.6	27.7	27.1	26.5	27.3	28.4	28.8	28.7	28.1
2002	28.3	29.1	28.3	27.2	25.4	25.5	26.2	25.9	27.1	27.8	26.5	26.4	27.0
2003	25.8	26.6	26.5	26.5	25.1	24.6	24.6	24.3	24.7	25.8	25.6	25.5	25.5

Employment by Industry: Michigan—*Continued*

(Numbers in thousands. Not seasonally adjusted.)

Industry	January	February	March	April	May	June	July	August	September	October	November	December	Annual Average
DETROIT—*Continued*													
Local government													
1990	168.7	172.5	173.2	172.6	175.2	170.3	166.1	165.5	164.2	173.1	175.7	173.8	170.9
1991	169.2	174.6	175.6	172.8	175.7	171.9	155.8	152.4	166.6	174.4	177.1	175.0	170.1
1992	169.4	175.0	177.5	174.7	176.8	173.0	156.8	154.1	165.8	175.3	176.5	174.4	170.8
1993	172.9	177.6	178.8	178.0	180.8	178.1	158.7	154.4	170.3	176.9	179.1	175.5	173.4
1994	168.5	172.3	174.5	172.1	173.8	168.8	154.2	153.3	165.8	170.7	174.8	170.9	168.3
1995	165.5	170.4	172.1	170.0	172.8	168.8	152.1	149.2	170.5	171.5	173.4	174.2	167.5
1996	167.3	171.7	171.1	170.0	171.9	170.7	151.4	150.6	163.2	173.2	175.5	175.6	167.7
1997	171.3	174.7	176.6	174.3	177.4	174.5	148.0	150.8	171.6	177.1	178.5	177.4	171.0
1998	173.5	177.8	178.7	177.8	180.1	177.2	151.1	147.5	173.2	178.7	181.5	178.3	173.0
1999	174.0	177.9	180.2	180.1	182.9	179.3	158.5	156.2	178.0	181.7	184.4	181.7	176.2
2000	181.0	183.8	186.3	183.3	183.3	182.5	160.2	159.3	180.9	184.4	186.1	184.4	179.6
2001	183.4	187.0	188.5	187.9	188.8	187.0	165.4	163.1	175.4	186.3	188.0	186.6	182.3
2002	184.1	187.3	188.8	186.2	189.0	186.6	160.5	159.1	174.5	187.9	189.4	188.1	181.8
2003	182.8	187.8	187.7	188.1	189.9	188.3	159.3	155.2	180.6	188.1	190.0	185.4	181.9
FLINT													
Total nonfarm													
1990	158.5	169.5	171.2	171.3	174.8	174.9	170.6	170.4	174.0	170.4	165.9	170.7	170.2
1991	168.7	163.7	160.4	163.2	168.6	168.6	163.8	163.0	165.7	167.7	167.5	168.2	165.8
1992	161.5	163.5	163.7	164.0	165.8	164.3	161.8	163.1	163.4	167.4	168.5	169.3	164.7
1993	165.3	165.3	163.4	164.4	166.7	166.0	163.0	162.8	166.4	168.0	169.1	171.1	166.0
1994	168.1	169.4	171.9	173.6	176.7	176.0	172.9	174.9	177.7	178.2	179.8	181.0	175.0
1995	176.6	177.9	178.8	178.5	180.7	180.3	179.4	180.5	182.9	184.8	182.4	186.9	180.8
1996	180.6	180.6	179.7	181.0	183.9	185.4	179.8	181.1	182.7	183.5	184.1	184.0	182.2
1997	178.4	178.5	179.1	183.2	185.8	186.5	178.7	180.8	183.8	183.6	184.8	185.1	182.4
1998	175.4	175.6	176.3	179.1	181.4	176.1	154.3	175.1	177.5	179.1	180.8	180.1	175.9
1999	174.2	173.9	175.0	174.3	176.1	175.6	169.7	170.3	172.2	171.7	171.8	172.6	173.1
2000	167.6	167.7	168.8	170.0	170.6	170.8	167.8	166.9	169.8	170.5	170.5	170.3	169.3
2001	167.6	167.2	167.8	168.9	170.3	170.1	164.7	166.2	168.6	167.4	168.6	168.9	168.0
2002	161.4	164.6	165.5	166.0	168.4	167.3	159.4	162.2	165.2	166.0	167.2	166.8	165.0
2003	158.9	159.3	160.7	160.2	163.1	162.9	156.5	158.0	161.1	162.8	162.9	161.4	160.7
Total private													
1990	135.4	145.8	147.3	146.9	149.5	151.3	149.5	149.3	150.4	146.1	141.1	145.7	146.5
1991	144.5	139.0	135.4	138.6	143.6	145.5	142.8	142.1	142.0	142.4	142.5	143.2	141.8
1992	137.1	138.4	138.4	139.0	140.7	141.2	141.0	142.1	140.0	143.0	143.7	144.6	140.8
1993	141.0	140.4	138.2	139.8	141.6	142.7	142.3	142.5	142.9	143.7	144.6	146.3	142.2
1994	143.8	144.7	146.7	148.9	151.7	153.2	152.3	154.0	154.1	153.9	154.9	156.0	151.2
1995	152.2	152.9	153.5	153.5	155.4	157.2	158.3	159.6	159.2	159.6	157.1	161.4	156.7
1996	155.9	155.3	154.0	155.8	158.6	160.1	158.6	159.3	158.4	158.3	158.8	158.8	157.7
1997	153.7	153.1	153.6	158.6	160.8	162.6	159.0	161.5	160.1	159.1	159.9	160.4	158.5
1998	150.5	150.2	150.8	153.5	155.4	151.3	133.0	154.0	152.7	153.6	154.9	154.2	151.2
1999	149.1	148.1	148.9	148.6	150.2	150.8	148.1	148.4	146.9	145.7	145.7	146.4	148.1
2000	141.8	141.5	142.4	143.5	143.8	146.1	145.7	144.4	144.4	144.1	143.9	143.8	143.8
2001	141.9	141.2	141.5	142.6	143.6	144.7	142.8	143.6	142.5	140.4	141.3	141.6	142.3
2002	135.6	138.3	139.2	140.0	141.9	142.7	138.7	141.0	139.9	139.8	140.8	140.3	139.9
2003	133.6	133.6	134.8	134.5	137.0	138.0	135.7	137.6	136.4	136.8	136.8	135.7	135.9
Goods-producing													
1990	52.0	56.8	57.5	59.2	60.2	60.8	60.3	59.3	59.9	56.7	51.5	55.5	57.5
1991	45.6	44.1	44.6	48.8	53.2	54.1	52.9	52.2	52.2	52.1	52.1	52.3	50.4
1992	49.7	51.3	50.9	51.4	52.1	52.0	52.3	53.0	51.0	53.5	54.1	54.4	52.1
1993	53.0	52.0	49.0	48.9	50.1	50.4	50.2	50.1	50.6	50.4	50.5	51.2	50.5
1994	50.7	50.5	51.5	52.7	53.6	54.5	53.9	54.7	54.8	54.2	54.5	54.7	53.4
1995	53.2	53.3	53.3	53.5	54.4	55.0	55.5	54.8	54.4	54.6	51.4	54.1	54.0
1996	52.2	51.3	49.7	51.5	52.3	53.1	53.3	52.9	52.5	51.1	50.9	50.8	51.8
1997	49.4	48.9	48.7	50.2	51.3	52.1	48.0	49.0	48.7	47.9	48.1	47.6	49.2
1998	45.8	45.3	45.3	46.0	46.5	42.7	27.1	45.5	45.0	44.9	45.0	44.3	43.6
1999	44.4	42.3	43.6	43.6	43.9	44.0	44.1	43.8	43.2	40.5	39.7	39.8	42.7
2000	38.6	38.0	38.2	38.5	38.9	39.8	40.8	38.5	39.0	38.6	37.9	37.8	38.7
2001	36.0	35.5	35.6	35.9	36.2	37.0	37.6	37.3	37.1	36.3	36.3	36.4	36.4
2002	31.0	33.6	33.7	34.2	34.8	35.4	34.2	34.8	34.2	33.7	33.6	33.0	33.9
2003	30.6	30.9	30.9	30.2	31.4	32.0	32.0	33.0	32.4	32.3	31.8	31.3	31.6
Construction and mining													
1990	4.2	4.4	4.5	4.7	5.3	5.7	6.1	6.1	6.2	5.8	5.8	5.3	5.3
1991	4.8	4.4	4.3	4.5	4.9	5.3	5.6	5.5	5.3	5.4	5.3	5.0	5.0
1992	4.3	4.1	4.1	4.5	5.1	5.4	5.6	5.8	5.5	5.5	5.0	4.9	5.0
1993	4.3	4.0	4.1	4.3	4.8	5.1	5.7	6.1	5.6	5.4	5.1	4.8	4.9
1994	4.3	4.1	4.3	4.8	5.3	5.6	6.3	6.1	6.0	5.9	5.7	5.5	5.3
1995	4.8	4.8	4.9	5.2	5.6	5.9	6.3	6.3	6.3	6.4	6.2	6.0	5.7
1996	5.5	5.3	5.5	5.9	6.5	6.9	7.3	7.3	7.2	7.3	7.1	6.9	6.6
1997	6.2	6.1	6.1	6.6	7.1	7.4	7.6	7.7	7.7	7.5	7.2	7.0	7.0
1998	6.5	6.3	6.3	6.8	7.3	7.4	7.6	7.5	7.3	7.3	7.2	7.0	7.0
1999	6.1	6.1	6.2	6.7	7.2	7.5	8.0	7.9	7.8	7.9	7.9	7.8	7.3
2000	6.8	6.6	6.9	7.7	8.0	8.5	8.8	8.6	8.5	8.4	8.1	7.8	7.9
2001	6.8	6.8	6.9	7.4	7.9	8.3	8.8	8.9	8.6	8.3	8.2	8.1	7.9
2002	7.0	6.7	6.8	7.3	7.8	8.1	8.1	8.0	7.7	7.5	7.2	6.7	7.4
2003	5.9	5.8	5.7	6.4	7.0	7.4	8.3	8.0	7.6	7.5	7.3	7.1	7.0

Employment by Industry: Michigan—*Continued*

(Numbers in thousands. Not seasonally adjusted.)

Industry	January	February	March	April	May	June	July	August	September	October	November	December	Annual Average
FLINT—*Continued*													
Manufacturing													
1990	47.8	52.4	53.0	54.5	54.9	55.1	54.2	53.2	53.7	50.9	45.7	50.2	52.1
1991	40.8	39.7	40.3	44.3	48.3	48.8	47.3	46.7	46.9	46.7	46.8	47.3	45.3
1992	45.4	47.2	46.8	46.9	47.0	46.6	46.7	47.2	45.5	48.0	49.1	49.5	47.2
1993	48.7	48.0	44.9	44.6	45.3	45.3	44.5	44.0	45.0	45.0	45.4	46.4	45.6
1994	46.4	46.4	47.2	47.9	48.3	48.9	47.6	48.6	48.8	48.3	48.8	49.2	48.0
1995	48.4	48.5	48.4	48.3	48.8	49.1	49.2	48.5	48.1	48.2	45.2	48.1	48.2
1996	46.7	46.0	44.2	45.6	45.8	46.2	46.0	45.6	45.3	43.8	43.8	43.9	45.2
1997	43.2	42.8	42.6	43.6	44.2	44.7	40.4	41.3	41.0	40.4	40.9	40.6	42.1
1998	39.3	39.0	39.0	39.2	39.2	35.3	19.5	38.0	37.7	37.6	37.8	37.3	36.6
1999	38.3	36.2	37.4	36.9	36.7	36.5	36.1	35.9	35.4	32.6	31.8	32.0	35.5
2000	31.8	31.4	31.3	30.8	30.9	31.3	32.0	29.9	30.5	30.2	29.8	30.0	30.8
2001	29.2	28.7	28.7	28.5	28.3	28.7	28.8	28.4	28.5	28.0	28.1	28.3	28.5
2002	24.0	26.9	26.9	26.9	27.0	27.3	26.1	26.8	26.5	26.2	26.4	26.3	26.4
2003	24.7	25.1	25.2	23.8	24.4	24.6	23.7	25.0	24.8	24.8	24.5	24.2	24.6
Service-providing													
1990	106.5	112.7	113.7	112.1	114.6	114.1	110.3	111.1	114.1	113.7	114.4	115.2	112.7
1991	123.1	119.6	115.8	114.4	115.4	114.5	110.9	110.8	113.5	115.6	115.4	115.9	115.4
1992	111.8	112.2	112.8	112.6	113.7	112.3	109.5	110.1	112.4	113.9	114.4	114.9	112.6
1993	112.3	113.3	114.4	115.5	116.6	115.6	112.8	112.7	115.8	117.6	118.6	119.9	115.4
1994	117.4	118.9	120.4	120.9	123.1	121.5	119.0	120.2	122.9	124.0	125.3	126.3	121.7
1995	123.4	124.6	125.5	125.0	126.3	125.3	123.9	125.7	128.5	130.2	131.0	132.8	126.9
1996	128.4	129.3	130.0	129.5	131.6	132.3	126.5	128.2	130.2	132.4	133.2	133.2	130.4
1997	129.0	129.6	130.4	133.0	134.5	134.4	130.7	131.8	135.1	135.7	136.7	137.5	133.2
1998	129.6	130.3	131.0	133.1	134.9	133.4	127.2	129.6	132.5	134.2	135.8	135.8	132.3
1999	129.8	131.6	131.4	130.7	132.2	131.6	125.6	126.5	129.0	131.2	132.1	132.8	130.4
2000	129.0	129.7	130.6	131.5	131.7	131.0	127.0	128.4	130.8	131.9	132.6	132.5	130.6
2001	131.6	131.7	132.2	133.0	134.1	133.1	127.1	128.9	131.5	131.1	132.3	132.5	131.6
2002	130.4	131.0	131.8	131.8	133.6	131.9	125.2	127.4	131.0	132.3	133.6	133.8	131.2
2003	128.3	128.4	129.8	130.0	131.7	130.9	124.5	125.0	128.7	130.5	131.1	130.1	129.1
Trade, transportation, and utilities													
1990	33.1	34.8	34.9	33.6	34.2	34.5	34.2	34.7	34.2	33.7	34.2	34.4	34.2
1991	35.9	33.6	31.9	31.5	31.5	31.6	31.6	31.1	31.4	31.4	32.0	32.6	32.2
1992	31.0	30.2	30.2	30.2	30.7	31.1	30.8	30.8	30.8	31.0	31.6	32.3	30.9
1993	30.9	30.5	30.5	31.0	31.2	31.7	32.0	32.1	31.8	32.2	33.1	33.8	31.7
1994	32.1	31.9	32.2	32.3	33.5	33.5	33.2	33.5	33.3	33.3	34.0	34.8	33.1
1995	32.6	32.1	32.4	32.9	33.3	34.1	34.1	34.4	34.4	34.7	35.4	36.5	33.9
1996	34.4	33.5	33.4	32.6	33.1	33.5	33.3	33.4	33.1	33.5	34.5	35.1	33.6
1997	33.9	33.1	33.1	33.7	33.8	34.3	34.4	34.9	34.6	34.7	35.2	36.0	34.3
1998	33.1	32.6	32.8	33.6	33.9	33.9	33.6	33.8	33.4	34.1	35.2	35.4	33.8
1999	34.0	33.6	33.4	32.1	32.7	32.9	32.4	32.3	32.1	32.1	32.8	33.5	32.8
2000	31.6	31.5	31.6	32.4	32.5	32.9	31.9	32.1	32.1	32.5	33.4	33.9	32.4
2001	34.4	34.0	33.8	34.1	34.4	34.5	33.8	33.8	33.7	33.3	34.3	34.6	34.1
2002	33.0	32.4	32.5	32.5	32.9	32.9	32.2	32.3	32.1	32.0	32.7	33.1	32.6
2003	31.2	30.7	31.1	31.2	31.6	31.8	31.2	31.4	31.0	31.2	31.4	31.4	31.3
Wholesale trade													
1990	5.2	5.5	5.6	5.6	5.7	5.7	5.8	6.0	5.7	5.6	5.6	5.6	5.6
1991	6.0	5.7	5.5	5.4	5.3	5.4	5.4	5.3	5.3	5.3	5.3	5.3	5.4
1992	5.2	5.2	5.3	5.2	5.3	5.3	5.2	5.2	5.2	5.1	5.1	5.2	5.2
1993	5.1	5.1	5.1	5.2	5.2	5.3	5.1	5.1	5.1	5.1	5.2	5.2	5.2
1994	5.3	5.3	5.3	5.4	5.5	5.5	5.4	5.5	5.5	5.5	5.5	5.5	5.4
1995	5.3	5.3	5.4	5.5	5.5	5.7	5.7	5.7	5.7	5.7	5.6	5.6	5.6
1996	5.7	5.7	5.7	5.5	5.6	5.8	5.8	5.8	5.8	5.8	5.8	5.8	5.7
1997	5.8	5.7	5.7	5.8	5.7	5.8	6.1	6.2	6.1	6.1	6.0	6.1	5.9
1998	5.8	5.8	5.9	6.0	6.1	6.1	6.2	6.1	6.0	6.0	6.0	6.0	6.0
1999	6.1	6.1	6.0	6.1	6.3	6.4	6.4	6.3	6.1	5.9	5.9	5.9	6.1
2000	5.8	5.9	5.9	5.8	5.8	6.0	6.0	6.0	5.8	5.8	5.7	5.7	5.9
2001	6.7	6.7	6.7	6.8	6.9	6.9	6.8	6.7	6.7	6.6	6.6	6.6	6.7
2002	6.6	6.5	6.6	6.5	6.6	6.6	6.5	6.5	6.4	6.5	6.5	6.5	6.5
2003	6.4	6.5	6.5	6.4	6.5	6.6	6.5	6.6	6.5	6.6	6.6	6.6	6.5
Retail trade													
1990	24.5	25.7	25.6	25.0	25.4	25.5	25.2	25.8	25.4	25.1	25.6	25.8	25.4
1991	26.5	24.7	23.4	23.2	23.4	23.1	23.2	22.7	23.1	23.3	23.9	24.4	23.7
1992	23.0	22.3	22.1	22.3	22.6	22.9	22.9	23.0	23.0	23.2	23.8	24.3	23.0
1993	23.3	22.9	22.8	23.1	23.3	23.6	24.1	24.3	23.9	24.1	24.9	25.6	23.8
1994	23.9	23.6	23.8	23.9	24.8	24.9	24.8	24.9	24.8	24.9	25.7	26.5	24.7
1995	24.5	24.0	24.1	24.6	25.0	25.4	25.4	25.6	25.7	26.0	26.8	27.8	25.4
1996	26.0	25.2	25.1	24.5	24.9	24.9	24.6	24.7	24.5	24.8	25.9	26.5	25.1
1997	25.4	24.7	24.6	25.0	25.4	25.6	25.5	25.9	25.6	25.6	26.2	26.9	25.5
1998	24.5	24.0	24.1	24.7	24.9	24.9	24.6	24.7	24.4	25.0	26.1	26.3	24.9
1999	24.9	24.5	24.4	22.7	23.1	23.2	22.9	22.9	22.8	23.0	23.8	24.4	23.6
2000	22.7	22.5	22.6	23.4	23.5	23.6	22.6	22.7	22.7	22.9	23.9	24.3	23.1
2001	23.7	23.2	23.1	23.0	23.2	23.2	22.9	23.0	22.9	22.7	23.7	24.0	23.2
2002	22.6	22.1	22.2	22.2	22.4	22.4	22.2	22.2	22.2	22.0	22.7	23.1	22.4
2003	21.3	21.0	21.1	21.3	21.6	21.7	21.3	21.4	21.1	21.3	21.5	21.5	21.3

Employment by Industry: Michigan—*Continued*

(Numbers in thousands. Not seasonally adjusted.)

Industry	January	February	March	April	May	June	July	August	September	October	November	December	Annual Average
FLINT—*Continued*													
Transportation and utilities													
1990	3.4	3.6	3.7	3.0	3.1	3.3	3.2	2.9	3.1	3.0	3.0	3.0	3.2
1991	3.4	3.2	3.0	2.9	2.8	3.1	3.0	3.1	3.0	2.8	2.8	2.9	3.0
1992	2.8	2.7	2.8	2.7	2.8	2.9	2.7	2.6	2.6	2.7	2.7	2.8	2.7
1993	2.5	2.5	2.6	2.7	2.7	2.8	2.8	2.7	2.8	3.0	3.0	3.0	2.8
1994	2.9	3.0	3.1	3.0	3.2	3.1	3.0	3.1	3.0	2.9	2.8	2.8	3.0
1995	2.8	2.8	2.9	2.8	2.8	3.0	3.0	3.1	3.0	3.0	3.0	3.1	2.9
1996	2.7	2.6	2.6	2.6	2.6	2.8	2.9	2.9	2.8	2.9	2.8	2.8	2.8
1997	2.7	2.7	2.8	2.9	2.7	2.9	2.8	2.8	2.9	3.0	3.0	3.0	2.9
1998	2.8	2.8	2.8	2.9	2.9	2.9	2.8	3.0	3.0	3.1	3.1	3.1	2.9
1999	3.0	3.0	3.0	3.3	3.3	3.3	3.1	3.1	3.2	3.2	3.1	3.2	3.2
2000	3.1	3.1	3.1	3.2	3.2	3.3	3.3	3.4	3.6	3.8	3.8	3.9	3.4
2001	4.0	4.1	4.0	4.3	4.3	4.4	4.1	4.1	4.1	4.0	4.0	4.0	4.1
2002	3.8	3.8	3.7	3.8	3.9	3.9	3.5	3.6	3.5	3.5	3.5	3.5	3.7
2003	3.5	3.2	3.5	3.5	3.5	3.5	3.4	3.4	3.4	3.3	3.3	3.3	3.4
Information													
1990	1.9	2.0	2.0	2.0	2.0	2.0	2.0	2.0	2.1	2.0	1.9	1.9	2.0
1991	2.2	2.1	2.0	2.0	2.0	2.0	2.0	2.0	2.0	2.0	2.0	2.0	2.0
1992	1.9	1.9	1.9	1.8	1.9	1.9	1.9	1.9	1.9	1.8	1.8	1.8	1.9
1993	1.9	1.9	1.9	1.9	1.9	1.9	1.9	1.9	1.9	1.9	1.9	1.9	1.9
1994	1.9	2.0	2.0	2.0	2.0	2.0	2.0	2.1	2.1	2.0	2.0	2.0	2.0
1995	1.9	1.9	1.9	1.8	1.8	1.8	1.8	1.8	1.8	1.8	1.8	1.8	1.8
1996	1.8	1.8	1.8	1.8	1.8	1.8	1.9	1.9	1.9	1.9	1.9	1.9	1.9
1997	1.9	1.9	2.0	2.0	2.0	2.0	2.0	2.0	2.0	2.2	2.2	2.2	2.0
1998	2.2	2.3	2.3	2.2	2.4	2.3	2.4	2.4	2.4	2.4	2.4	2.5	2.4
1999	2.4	2.4	2.4	2.5	2.5	2.6	2.5	2.6	2.6	2.9	2.9	2.9	2.6
2000	2.9	2.8	2.9	2.6	2.6	2.6	2.7	2.7	2.7	2.4	2.4	2.5	2.7
2001	2.6	2.6	2.6	2.6	2.6	2.6	2.7	2.6	2.6	2.6	2.6	2.6	2.6
2002	2.5	2.5	2.5	2.5	2.5	2.4	2.4	2.3	2.3	2.3	2.3	2.3	2.4
2003	2.2	2.2	2.2	2.2	2.2	2.2	2.2	2.2	2.2	2.2	2.2	2.2	2.2
Financial activities													
1990	5.2	5.5	5.6	5.4	5.4	5.5	5.4	5.4	5.6	5.4	5.4	5.6	5.5
1991	5.9	5.6	5.4	5.3	5.4	5.6	5.5	5.5	5.5	5.5	5.5	5.4	5.5
1992	5.4	5.3	5.3	5.3	5.4	5.5	5.5	5.6	5.5	5.4	5.4	5.4	5.4
1993	5.4	5.4	5.4	5.4	5.5	5.5	5.6	5.6	5.6	5.4	5.4	5.4	5.5
1994	6.2	6.2	6.3	6.3	6.3	6.3	6.3	6.3	6.3	6.2	6.2	6.2	6.3
1995	6.5	6.5	6.5	6.3	6.3	6.4	6.5	6.5	6.5	6.3	6.3	6.4	6.4
1996	6.4	6.4	6.4	6.4	6.6	6.6	6.6	6.6	6.5	6.5	6.5	6.4	6.5
1997	6.5	6.5	6.4	6.6	6.7	6.8	6.7	6.8	6.8	6.6	6.5	6.6	6.6
1998	6.3	6.3	6.4	6.4	6.5	6.6	6.6	6.7	6.6	6.7	6.7	6.7	6.5
1999	6.6	6.6	6.5	6.9	6.9	6.9	6.8	6.9	6.8	6.7	6.7	6.7	6.8
2000	6.5	6.6	6.5	6.4	6.5	6.5	6.5	6.6	6.5	6.4	6.4	6.4	6.5
2001	5.6	5.6	5.6	5.7	5.7	5.8	5.7	5.7	5.6	5.6	5.6	5.6	5.7
2002	5.8	5.8	6.0	5.9	6.0	6.0	5.8	5.8	5.8	5.9	5.9	5.9	5.9
2003	6.2	6.2	6.2	6.4	6.5	6.6	6.8	6.9	6.7	7.0	7.0	7.0	6.6
Professional and business services													
1990	8.9	9.5	9.8	9.8	10.1	10.2	10.0	10.0	10.0	9.8	9.9	9.9	9.8
1991	13.7	13.2	12.6	12.6	12.5	12.8	12.7	12.8	12.6	12.8	12.7	12.8	12.8
1992	11.6	11.8	11.7	11.8	11.7	11.7	11.8	12.0	11.9	12.2	12.0	12.1	11.9
1993	11.9	12.2	12.6	13.0	13.1	13.0	12.9	13.3	13.3	13.5	13.6	14.0	13.0
1994	13.8	14.4	14.7	15.1	15.5	15.9	15.9	16.3	16.5	16.6	16.6	16.9	15.7
1995	16.4	17.0	17.0	16.3	16.7	17.1	17.1	18.3	18.3	18.1	18.2	18.3	17.4
1996	18.0	18.6	18.8	19.5	19.9	20.2	19.6	20.4	20.1	20.1	20.1	20.0	19.6
1997	20.2	20.7	21.2	21.4	21.6	21.8	22.7	23.4	23.4	23.4	23.7	23.8	22.3
1998	21.8	22.1	22.4	22.6	22.7	22.8	20.4	22.8	23.0	22.9	22.7	22.4	22.4
1999	19.2	19.8	19.9	20.3	20.3	20.5	19.7	20.1	20.1	20.8	20.7	20.7	20.2
2000	20.8	20.7	20.9	21.4	21.3	21.7	20.1	20.7	20.4	19.9	19.8	19.7	20.6
2001	20.1	19.9	20.0	20.2	20.0	20.2	18.7	19.4	18.9	18.4	18.0	18.1	19.3
2002	19.6	19.7	19.8	19.9	20.0	19.9	18.8	19.9	19.6	19.5	19.7	19.6	19.7
2003	18.9	18.6	19.2	19.0	19.0	19.0	18.7	18.9	18.9	18.1	18.2	18.0	18.7
Educational and health services													
1990	17.2	18.6	18.7	18.6	18.7	18.9	18.7	19.0	19.4	19.4	19.5	19.7	18.9
1991	21.5	21.0	20.3	19.9	20.0	20.1	19.8	19.9	20.1	20.5	20.4	20.4	20.3
1992	20.1	20.3	20.4	20.0	20.1	20.2	20.0	20.0	20.2	20.5	20.4	20.5	20.2
1993	20.2	20.4	20.7	20.7	20.7	20.8	20.4	20.2	20.4	20.6	20.6	20.5	20.5
1994	20.3	20.6	20.6	20.7	20.7	20.7	20.8	20.8	21.0	21.3	21.3	21.3	20.8
1995	21.5	21.7	21.8	21.6	21.5	21.2	21.7	21.9	22.0	22.5	22.5	22.6	21.9
1996	22.0	22.3	22.3	22.2	22.4	22.2	21.8	21.9	22.1	22.6	22.5	22.3	22.2
1997	20.3	20.3	20.2	22.3	22.3	22.2	21.9	22.1	21.9	21.6	21.5	21.5	21.5
1998	20.2	20.1	20.1	20.5	20.6	20.3	20.8	20.6	20.5	21.1	21.3	21.4	20.6
1999	21.3	21.7	21.4	21.8	22.0	21.8	21.1	21.1	20.9	21.7	21.8	21.9	21.5
2000	21.2	21.6	21.7	21.2	21.1	21.1	22.1	22.1	22.0	22.3	22.3	22.2	21.7
2001	21.9	22.1	22.2	22.3	22.5	22.2	22.1	22.3	22.3	22.3	22.5	22.5	22.3
2002	22.2	22.8	22.9	23.1	23.2	23.5	23.1	23.4	23.6	24.2	24.3	24.4	23.4
2003	23.5	24.1	24.2	24.0	24.2	24.3	23.1	23.5	23.5	24.0	24.3	24.2	23.9

Employment by Industry: Michigan—*Continued*

(Numbers in thousands. Not seasonally adjusted.)

Industry	January	February	March	April	May	June	July	August	September	October	November	December	Annual Average
FLINT—*Continued*													
Leisure and hospitality													
1990	11.5	12.4	12.7	12.4	12.9	13.3	12.8	12.8	13.0	13.1	12.7	12.7	12.7
1991	13.4	13.2	12.7	12.8	13.3	13.5	12.8	13.0	12.7	12.4	12.2	12.2	12.9
1992	12.1	12.2	12.4	12.9	13.3	13.3	13.1	13.2	13.1	13.0	12.9	12.6	12.8
1993	12.3	12.5	12.5	13.2	13.4	13.7	13.5	13.6	13.7	13.8	13.6	13.6	13.3
1994	13.0	13.2	13.4	13.9	14.2	14.4	14.2	14.3	14.1	14.2	14.2	14.0	13.9
1995	14.2	14.3	14.5	15.0	15.3	15.4	15.4	15.8	15.6	15.4	15.4	15.6	15.2
1996	15.1	15.3	15.5	15.5	16.1	16.3	15.9	16.0	16.0	16.3	16.0	16.0	15.8
1997	15.4	15.5	15.7	16.1	16.8	17.1	17.0	16.9	16.2	16.0	16.0	15.9	16.2
1998	15.1	15.3	15.3	15.8	16.4	16.3	15.9	16.0	15.7	15.3	15.4	15.3	15.7
1999	15.0	15.3	15.3	15.0	15.4	15.5	15.2	15.3	15.0	14.8	14.8	14.7	15.1
2000	14.1	14.1	14.4	14.8	14.8	15.2	15.4	15.4	15.5	15.7	15.6	15.2	15.0
2001	14.8	14.9	15.1	15.2	15.6	15.7	15.5	15.8	15.7	15.3	15.3	15.2	15.3
2002	14.8	14.8	15.1	15.2	15.9	15.9	15.6	15.9	15.8	15.5	15.7	15.4	15.5
2003	14.5	14.4	14.5	15.1	15.6	15.5	15.2	15.3	15.3	15.5	15.4	15.3	15.1
Other services													
1990	5.6	6.2	6.1	5.9	6.0	6.1	6.1	6.1	6.2	6.0	6.0	6.0	6.0
1991	6.3	6.2	5.9	5.7	5.7	5.8	5.5	5.6	5.5	5.7	5.6	5.5	5.8
1992	5.3	5.4	5.6	5.6	5.5	5.5	5.6	5.6	5.6	5.6	5.5	5.5	5.5
1993	5.4	5.5	5.6	5.7	5.7	5.7	5.8	5.7	5.6	5.9	5.9	5.9	5.7
1994	5.8	5.9	6.0	5.9	5.9	5.9	6.0	6.0	6.0	6.1	6.1	6.1	6.0
1995	5.9	6.1	6.1	6.1	6.1	6.2	6.2	6.1	6.2	6.2	6.1	6.1	6.1
1996	6.0	6.1	6.1	6.3	6.4	6.4	6.2	6.2	6.2	6.3	6.4	6.3	6.2
1997	6.1	6.2	6.3	6.3	6.3	6.3	6.3	6.4	6.5	6.7	6.7	6.8	6.4
1998	6.0	6.2	6.2	6.4	6.4	6.4	6.2	6.2	6.1	6.2	6.2	6.2	6.2
1999	6.2	6.4	6.4	6.4	6.5	6.6	6.3	6.3	6.2	6.2	6.3	6.2	6.3
2000	6.1	6.2	6.2	6.2	6.1	6.3	6.2	6.3	6.2	6.3	6.1	6.1	6.2
2001	6.5	6.6	6.6	6.6	6.6	6.7	6.7	6.7	6.6	6.6	6.7	6.6	6.6
2002	6.7	6.7	6.7	6.7	6.6	6.7	6.6	6.6	6.5	6.7	6.6	6.6	6.6
2003	6.5	6.5	6.5	6.4	6.5	6.6	6.5	6.4	6.4	6.5	6.5	6.3	6.5
Government													
1990	23.1	23.7	23.9	24.4	25.3	23.6	21.1	21.1	23.6	24.3	24.8	25.0	23.7
1991	24.2	24.7	25.0	24.6	25.0	23.1	21.0	20.9	23.7	25.3	25.0	25.0	24.0
1992	24.4	25.1	25.3	25.0	25.1	23.1	20.8	21.0	23.4	24.4	24.8	24.7	23.9
1993	24.3	24.9	25.2	24.6	25.1	23.3	20.7	20.3	23.5	24.3	24.5	24.8	23.8
1994	24.3	24.7	25.2	24.7	25.0	22.8	20.6	20.9	23.6	24.3	24.9	25.0	23.8
1995	24.4	25.0	25.3	25.0	25.3	23.1	21.1	20.9	23.7	25.2	25.3	25.5	24.2
1996	24.7	25.3	25.7	25.2	25.3	25.3	21.2	21.8	24.3	25.2	25.3	25.2	24.5
1997	24.7	25.4	25.5	24.6	25.0	23.9	19.7	19.3	23.7	24.5	24.9	24.7	23.8
1998	24.9	25.4	25.5	25.6	26.0	24.8	21.3	21.1	24.8	25.5	25.9	25.9	24.7
1999	25.1	25.8	26.1	25.7	25.9	24.8	21.6	21.9	25.3	26.0	26.1	26.2	25.0
2000	25.8	26.2	26.4	26.5	26.8	24.7	22.1	22.5	25.4	26.4	26.6	26.5	25.5
2001	25.7	26.0	26.3	26.3	26.7	25.4	21.9	22.6	26.1	27.0	27.3	27.3	25.7
2002	25.8	26.3	26.3	26.0	26.5	24.6	20.7	21.2	25.3	26.2	26.4	26.5	25.2
2003	25.3	25.7	25.9	25.7	26.1	24.9	20.8	20.4	24.7	26.0	26.1	25.7	24.8
Federal government													
1990	1.5	1.5	1.5	1.6	1.9	1.7	1.5	1.4	1.4	1.4	1.4	1.4	1.5
1991	1.4	1.4	1.4	1.4	1.4	1.4	1.4	1.4	1.4	1.4	1.4	1.4	1.4
1992	1.4	1.4	1.4	1.4	1.4	1.4	1.4	1.4	1.4	1.3	1.3	1.4	1.4
1993	1.3	1.3	1.3	1.3	1.3	1.4	1.4	1.4	1.3	1.3	1.3	1.5	1.3
1994	1.4	1.4	1.4	1.4	1.4	1.4	1.4	1.4	1.4	1.4	1.4	1.5	1.4
1995	1.4	1.4	1.4	1.4	1.5	1.5	1.4	1.5	1.4	1.4	1.4	1.5	1.4
1996	1.4	1.4	1.4	1.4	1.4	1.4	1.4	1.4	1.4	1.4	1.4	1.5	1.4
1997	1.4	1.4	1.4	1.4	1.4	1.4	1.4	1.4	1.4	1.4	1.4	1.4	1.4
1998	1.4	1.4	1.4	1.4	1.4	1.4	1.4	1.4	1.4	1.4	1.5	1.5	1.4
1999	1.4	1.5	1.6	1.5	1.5	1.5	1.5	1.5	1.5	1.5	1.5	1.6	1.5
2000	1.6	1.6	1.6	1.7	2.1	1.8	1.7	1.6	1.6	1.6	1.6	1.7	1.7
2001	1.5	1.5	1.5	1.5	1.5	1.5	1.5	1.5	1.5	1.5	1.5	1.5	1.5
2002	1.5	1.5	1.5	1.5	1.5	1.5	1.5	1.5	1.5	1.5	1.5	1.6	1.5
2003	1.5	1.5	1.5	1.5	1.5	1.5	1.5	1.5	1.5	1.5	1.5	1.5	1.5
State government													
1990	2.2	2.3	2.3	2.4	2.3	2.3	2.3	2.3	2.5	2.4	2.5	2.5	2.4
1991	2.3	2.4	2.4	2.4	2.2	2.2	2.2	2.1	2.2	2.3	2.4	2.4	2.3
1992	2.3	2.4	2.4	2.4	2.2	2.1	2.0	2.0	2.2	2.3	2.4	2.4	2.3
1993	2.3	2.3	2.3	2.3	2.1	2.1	2.0	2.0	2.2	2.3	2.3	2.3	2.2
1994	2.2	2.3	2.3	2.4	2.2	2.2	2.1	2.1	2.2	2.3	2.3	2.3	2.2
1995	2.2	2.3	2.3	2.4	2.2	2.2	2.1	2.1	2.3	2.6	2.7	2.6	2.3
1996	2.5	2.6	2.7	2.7	2.4	2.6	2.5	2.5	2.5	2.7	2.7	2.7	2.6
1997	2.6	2.7	2.7	2.7	2.5	2.3	2.3	2.3	2.5	2.6	2.7	2.7	2.6
1998	2.7	2.7	2.7	2.7	2.6	2.5	2.5	2.4	2.5	2.7	2.7	2.7	2.6
1999	2.6	2.7	2.7	2.7	2.5	2.4	2.3	2.2	2.4	2.6	2.6	2.7	2.5
2000	2.5	2.7	2.6	2.6	2.4	2.4	2.4	2.4	2.5	2.7	2.7	2.7	2.6
2001	2.8	2.9	2.9	2.9	2.9	2.8	2.7	2.7	2.7	2.9	3.0	2.9	2.8
2002	2.8	2.9	2.9	2.9	2.8	2.7	2.5	2.4	2.7	2.8	2.8	2.8	2.8
2003	2.6	2.7	2.7	2.7	2.7	2.5	2.5	2.5	2.5	2.7	2.7	2.7	2.6

Employment by Industry: Michigan—*Continued*

(Numbers in thousands. Not seasonally adjusted.)

Industry	January	February	March	April	May	June	July	August	September	October	November	December	Annual Average
FLINT—*Continued*													
Local government													
1990	19.4	19.9	20.1	20.4	21.1	19.7	17.3	17.4	19.6	20.5	20.9	21.2	19.8
1991	20.5	20.9	21.2	20.8	21.4	19.5	17.5	17.3	20.0	21.6	21.2	21.1	20.3
1992	20.7	21.3	21.5	21.2	21.5	19.6	17.4	17.6	19.9	20.7	21.1	20.9	20.3
1993	20.8	21.3	21.5	21.0	21.6	19.8	17.3	16.9	20.0	20.6	20.8	21.0	20.2
1994	20.7	21.0	21.5	21.0	21.4	19.3	17.1	17.4	20.0	20.6	21.1	21.1	20.2
1995	20.7	21.3	21.6	21.2	21.6	19.4	17.5	17.3	20.0	21.1	21.2	21.4	20.4
1996	20.7	21.3	21.6	21.1	21.4	21.3	17.3	17.8	20.3	21.1	21.1	21.0	20.5
1997	20.7	21.3	21.4	20.5	21.1	20.2	16.0	15.6	19.8	20.5	20.8	20.6	19.9
1998	20.8	21.3	21.4	21.5	22.0	20.9	17.4	17.3	20.9	21.4	21.7	21.7	20.7
1999	21.1	21.6	21.8	21.5	21.9	20.9	17.8	18.2	21.4	21.9	22.0	21.9	21.0
2000	21.7	21.9	22.2	22.2	22.3	20.5	18.0	18.5	21.3	22.1	22.3	22.1	21.3
2001	21.4	21.6	21.9	21.9	22.3	21.1	17.7	18.4	21.9	22.6	22.8	22.9	21.4
2002	21.5	21.9	21.9	21.6	22.2	20.4	16.7	17.3	21.1	21.9	22.1	22.1	20.9
2003	21.2	21.5	21.7	21.5	21.9	20.9	16.8	16.4	20.7	21.8	21.9	21.5	20.7
GRAND RAPIDS													
Total nonfarm													
1990	432.9	437.3	440.6	443.9	448.6	450.4	443.2	444.8	455.0	456.1	455.0	453.8	446.8
1991	437.3	436.7	437.2	440.5	444.4	442.9	437.2	440.0	451.6	453.8	455.1	453.4	444.2
1992	440.6	442.3	444.5	447.8	454.2	456.9	452.2	452.1	460.4	464.2	464.8	464.3	453.7
1993	454.6	455.7	458.1	466.1	472.8	474.2	466.9	469.4	479.9	486.4	486.5	488.1	471.6
1994	477.5	477.8	482.4	489.4	495.3	499.6	494.4	499.1	509.2	511.0	513.7	514.2	497.0
1995	502.8	506.1	510.0	515.4	522.1	522.9	515.5	518.9	527.5	528.4	529.8	531.6	519.3
1996	519.3	519.8	522.8	525.3	531.2	531.8	525.2	530.8	541.1	545.7	546.7	549.7	532.5
1997	535.5	537.1	542.7	544.7	553.6	553.2	547.5	550.3	558.6	559.6	560.5	564.3	550.6
1998	549.2	552.9	555.4	562.6	569.7	571.0	556.1	562.8	568.9	572.4	574.0	577.7	564.4
1999	559.3	563.1	566.9	576.6	582.9	583.1	575.4	578.4	586.0	589.1	591.6	595.6	579.0
2000	580.0	583.2	586.9	589.6	596.4	597.4	586.7	589.8	596.2	598.4	597.9	598.2	591.7
2001	581.1	579.7	581.2	588.6	593.5	593.2	580.2	582.6	586.1	585.3	581.9	581.0	584.5
2002	563.0	562.9	566.0	572.0	579.7	580.3	570.0	574.6	579.8	579.1	579.8	578.1	573.8
2003	556.3	556.2	556.1	553.5	565.7	565.6	557.9	556.8	564.2	566.8	565.4	565.6	560.8
Total private													
1990	386.0	389.0	391.9	395.2	399.9	405.1	402.3	404.4	407.1	406.4	404.8	403.7	399.7
1991	388.9	386.3	386.4	390.9	395.2	396.9	395.4	398.1	401.4	402.1	403.2	401.8	395.6
1992	389.4	390.4	391.9	396.8	403.0	408.1	408.1	408.1	410.6	412.1	412.1	412.0	403.6
1993	403.3	403.4	405.6	414.2	421.0	424.1	422.4	425.7	429.2	433.8	433.8	435.7	421.0
1994	426.2	425.6	429.0	437.2	443.3	449.4	449.8	454.1	457.5	457.8	459.5	461.4	445.9
1995	450.9	453.0	456.7	462.6	469.2	472.4	470.6	474.4	475.5	474.4	475.9	477.7	467.8
1996	467.0	466.4	468.3	471.5	478.1	481.9	480.3	486.2	488.0	490.8	491.3	494.9	480.4
1997	481.8	482.1	487.4	490.5	499.3	501.7	500.3	503.5	505.2	504.0	505.2	509.0	497.5
1998	494.4	496.9	499.1	507.0	513.9	517.2	508.2	514.7	514.4	515.6	517.0	520.7	509.9
1999	503.7	506.1	509.4	519.1	525.2	528.2	527.1	530.2	529.6	530.0	532.5	537.0	523.2
2000	523.3	524.6	528.0	531.1	536.5	541.5	537.5	541.1	538.8	538.8	538.0	539.2	534.9
2001	522.5	519.8	520.8	529.3	533.4	536.8	528.6	532.5	527.6	525.1	521.8	520.7	526.6
2002	504.3	503.1	505.7	512.8	519.8	524.4	520.0	524.4	521.4	517.7	517.9	516.2	515.6
2003	497.2	494.7	494.1	494.0	504.9	508.7	508.0	506.9	506.0	507.1	505.3	505.5	502.7
Goods-producing													
1990	147.7	148.5	149.6	153.4	153.3	155.2	154.7	155.7	156.4	157.3	155.5	154.0	153.4
1991	148.2	147.0	146.3	147.4	148.4	149.5	147.9	149.4	151.6	152.9	152.3	150.6	149.3
1992	146.6	146.9	147.1	146.8	149.2	151.4	152.0	151.8	153.3	153.3	152.9	152.3	150.3
1993	148.5	148.2	148.9	151.5	153.8	155.5	153.8	155.4	156.6	158.6	158.4	158.8	154.0
1994	156.6	156.0	157.8	161.4	164.1	167.2	165.9	168.0	168.8	169.8	170.7	171.6	164.8
1995	170.6	171.5	172.7	174.3	177.1	178.1	176.7	178.5	178.2	178.2	178.4	178.2	176.0
1996	176.0	175.0	175.6	177.3	179.4	181.4	179.2	181.9	182.1	182.0	182.2	182.4	179.5
1997	179.5	180.6	182.1	182.2	184.9	187.1	185.5	186.5	186.4	186.1	186.3	187.5	184.6
1998	185.6	186.2	188.2	193.3	195.8	197.3	194.0	196.4	196.2	196.7	197.0	198.3	193.8
1999	191.3	192.0	192.7	194.6	196.4	197.3	197.0	197.4	196.7	196.3	196.8	196.9	195.5
2000	192.3	192.7	193.7	195.1	195.9	198.4	196.0	197.8	197.2	197.6	196.4	195.8	195.7
2001	181.6	179.7	178.8	180.5	181.1	181.6	178.7	180.3	178.7	175.2	172.6	171.4	178.4
2002	165.9	164.7	164.9	165.5	167.4	168.6	166.4	168.1	166.7	165.7	164.4	163.3	166.0
2003	158.6	156.6	156.2	154.3	158.2	158.7	156.4	157.7	156.2	155.6	153.4	153.7	156.3
Natural resources and mining													
1990	0.4	0.4	0.4	0.5	0.5	0.5	0.5	0.5	0.5	0.5	0.5	0.4	0.5
1991	0.4	0.4	0.4	0.4	0.4	0.4	0.4	0.4	0.4	0.4	0.4	0.4	0.4
1992	0.3	0.3	0.3	0.4	0.4	0.4	0.4	0.4	0.4	0.4	0.4	0.4	0.4
1993	0.4	0.4	0.4	0.4	0.4	0.4	0.4	0.4	0.5	0.5	0.4	0.4	0.4
1994	0.4	0.4	0.4	0.4	0.5	0.5	0.5	0.5	0.5	0.5	0.5	0.4	0.5
1995	0.4	0.4	0.4	0.5	0.5	0.5	0.5	0.5	0.4	0.4	0.4	0.4	0.4
1996	0.3	0.3	0.4	0.4	0.4	0.4	0.4	0.5	0.5	0.5	0.5	0.4	0.4
1997	0.4	0.4	0.4	0.5	0.5	0.5	0.5	0.5	0.5	0.5	0.5	0.5	0.5
1998	0.4	0.4	0.4	0.5	0.5	0.5	0.5	0.5	0.5	0.5	0.5	0.4	0.5
1999	0.3	0.4	0.4	0.5	0.5	0.5	0.5	0.4	0.4	0.4	0.4	0.4	0.4
2000	0.3	0.3	0.4	0.4	0.4	0.5	0.5	0.5	0.5	0.6	0.6	0.6	0.5
2001	0.4	0.4	0.5	0.5	0.5	0.5	0.6	0.6	0.6	0.5	0.5	0.5	0.5
2002	0.4	0.4	0.4	0.5	0.6	0.6	0.6	0.6	0.5	0.5	0.5	0.5	0.5
2003	0.4	0.4	0.4	0.5	0.5	0.5	0.5	0.5	0.5	0.5	0.5	0.5	0.5

Employment by Industry: Michigan—*Continued*

(Numbers in thousands. Not seasonally adjusted.)

Industry	January	February	March	April	May	June	July	August	September	October	November	December	Annual Average
GRAND RAPIDS—*Continued*													
Construction													
1990	18.3	18.2	18.7	20.2	21.0	21.6	21.6	21.7	21.9	21.3	20.4	19.6	20.4
1991	17.0	16.4	16.4	16.9	17.8	18.4	18.8	19.1	19.0	19.1	18.4	17.6	17.9
1992	15.9	15.6	15.8	17.0	18.2	18.8	19.6	19.7	19.7	19.7	19.1	18.6	18.1
1993	16.9	16.7	16.9	18.4	19.7	20.3	20.5	20.5	20.1	20.2	19.8	19.1	19.1
1994	17.4	17.1	17.8	19.6	20.8	21.8	22.5	22.7	22.4	22.1	21.7	21.1	20.6
1995	19.0	18.9	19.6	21.1	22.4	23.3	23.5	23.5	23.2	23.2	22.5	21.9	21.8
1996	20.4	20.3	20.9	22.4	24.1	25.1	25.9	26.1	25.6	25.5	25.1	24.4	23.8
1997	22.0	22.1	22.7	24.7	26.1	27.0	27.8	27.8	27.4	26.4	25.6	25.1	25.4
1998	23.3	23.1	23.4	26.0	27.1	27.9	28.3	28.4	28.1	27.6	27.2	26.9	26.4
1999	23.4	23.5	24.0	27.3	28.5	29.2	29.0	28.9	28.3	28.5	28.4	27.7	27.2
2000	25.3	25.1	26.2	28.5	29.4	30.3	30.1	30.3	29.8	29.6	28.9	28.0	28.5
2001	25.6	25.3	25.8	27.9	29.1	29.8	30.3	30.4	29.9	29.3	28.6	27.8	28.3
2002	25.6	25.2	25.8	27.4	28.9	29.4	29.7	29.7	29.1	28.7	28.0	27.0	27.9
2003	24.7	24.1	24.2	26.0	27.2	28.1	28.8	29.4	28.3	28.2	26.7	26.7	26.9
Manufacturing													
1990	129.0	129.9	130.5	132.7	131.8	133.1	132.6	133.5	134.0	135.5	134.6	134.0	132.6
1991	130.8	130.2	129.5	130.1	130.2	130.7	128.7	129.9	132.2	133.4	133.5	132.6	131.0
1992	130.4	131.0	131.0	129.4	130.6	132.2	132.0	131.7	133.2	133.2	133.4	133.3	131.8
1993	131.2	131.1	131.6	132.7	133.7	134.8	132.9	134.5	136.0	137.9	138.2	139.3	134.5
1994	138.8	138.5	139.6	141.4	142.8	144.9	142.9	144.8	145.9	147.2	148.5	150.1	143.8
1995	151.2	152.2	152.7	152.7	154.2	154.3	152.7	154.5	154.6	154.6	155.5	155.9	153.8
1996	155.3	154.4	154.3	154.5	154.9	155.9	152.9	155.3	156.0	156.0	156.6	157.6	155.3
1997	157.1	158.1	159.0	157.0	158.3	159.6	157.2	158.2	158.5	159.2	160.2	161.9	158.7
1998	161.9	162.7	164.4	166.8	168.2	168.9	165.2	167.5	167.6	168.6	169.3	171.0	166.8
1999	167.6	168.1	168.3	166.8	167.4	167.6	167.5	168.1	168.0	167.4	168.0	168.8	167.8
2000	166.7	167.3	167.1	166.2	166.1	167.6	165.4	167.0	166.9	167.4	166.9	167.2	166.8
2001	155.6	154.0	152.5	152.1	151.5	151.3	147.8	149.3	148.2	145.4	143.5	143.1	149.5
2002	139.9	139.1	138.7	137.6	137.9	138.6	136.1	137.8	137.1	136.5	135.9	135.8	137.6
2003	133.5	132.1	131.6	127.8	130.5	130.1	127.1	127.8	127.4	126.9	126.2	126.5	129.0
Service-providing													
1990	285.2	288.8	291.0	290.5	295.3	295.2	288.5	289.1	298.6	298.8	299.5	299.8	293.4
1991	289.1	289.7	290.9	293.1	296.0	293.4	289.3	290.6	300.0	300.9	302.8	302.8	294.9
1992	294.0	295.4	297.4	301.0	305.0	305.5	300.2	300.3	307.1	310.9	311.9	312.0	303.4
1993	306.1	307.5	309.2	314.6	319.0	318.7	313.1	314.0	323.3	327.8	328.1	329.3	317.6
1994	320.9	321.8	324.6	328.0	331.2	332.4	328.5	331.1	340.4	341.2	343.0	342.6	332.1
1995	332.2	334.6	337.3	341.1	345.0	344.8	338.8	340.4	349.3	350.2	351.4	353.4	343.2
1996	343.3	344.8	347.2	348.0	351.8	350.4	346.0	348.9	359.0	363.7	364.5	367.3	352.9
1997	356.0	356.5	360.6	362.5	368.7	366.1	362.0	363.8	372.2	373.5	374.2	376.8	366.1
1998	363.6	366.7	367.2	369.3	373.9	373.7	362.1	366.4	372.7	375.7	377.0	379.4	370.6
1999	368.0	371.1	374.2	382.0	386.5	385.8	378.4	381.0	389.3	392.8	394.8	398.7	383.6
2000	387.7	390.5	393.2	394.5	400.5	399.0	390.7	392.0	399.0	400.8	401.5	402.4	396.0
2001	399.5	400.0	402.4	408.1	412.4	411.6	401.5	402.3	407.4	410.1	409.3	409.6	406.2
2002	397.1	398.2	401.1	406.5	412.3	411.7	403.6	406.5	413.1	413.4	415.4	414.8	407.8
2003	397.7	399.6	399.9	399.2	407.5	406.9	401.5	399.1	408.0	411.2	412.0	411.9	404.5
Trade, transportation, and utilities													
1990	92.9	93.1	93.4	93.4	95.0	95.3	94.2	95.4	96.1	96.0	97.2	97.8	95.0
1991	90.9	89.3	89.5	90.2	91.1	90.2	89.6	90.0	90.7	91.1	92.7	93.2	90.7
1992	89.7	89.5	89.5	89.9	91.3	92.0	90.9	91.3	91.8	93.6	94.8	95.2	91.6
1993	92.8	92.1	92.3	93.6	94.8	94.9	95.1	96.0	97.1	99.7	100.8	101.4	95.9
1994	97.7	96.9	97.7	99.3	100.4	101.0	101.6	102.4	103.6	104.9	106.0	107.1	101.6
1995	103.7	103.5	104.1	104.7	106.2	106.1	105.6	106.3	107.3	108.6	110.1	111.6	106.5
1996	108.3	107.8	108.2	108.4	109.5	109.0	108.6	109.5	110.5	112.7	114.3	115.6	110.2
1997	110.4	109.7	110.4	110.6	112.3	111.9	111.1	111.1	112.7	113.8	115.4	116.3	112.1
1998	111.2	111.2	111.2	113.6	115.3	115.1	113.5	115.0	116.2	117.0	118.9	120.7	114.9
1999	115.7	115.8	116.3	115.6	117.1	116.3	115.8	115.6	115.9	116.2	117.8	119.6	116.5
2000	116.5	116.1	117.3	116.8	118.0	117.4	115.4	116.1	116.7	118.1	119.9	121.3	117.5
2001	115.4	114.1	113.9	114.9	115.3	115.0	112.4	112.4	111.7	112.5	113.5	113.7	113.7
2002	109.2	108.0	108.3	109.6	110.8	111.2	111.1	112.1	111.6	111.4	112.7	113.5	110.8
2003	108.1	106.4	106.5	107.2	109.1	109.8	109.7	109.9	109.4	109.4	110.1	110.3	108.8
Wholesale trade													
1990	24.0	24.1	24.2	24.1	24.5	24.4	24.3	24.4	24.6	24.4	24.3	24.3	24.3
1991	23.2	23.2	23.2	23.3	23.3	23.3	23.3	23.3	23.3	23.4	23.5	23.5	23.3
1992	23.3	23.4	23.5	23.5	23.7	23.9	23.9	23.8	23.7	24.0	24.0	24.0	23.7
1993	24.4	24.5	24.5	25.1	25.2	25.2	25.3	25.3	25.4	25.9	25.9	26.0	25.2
1994	25.6	25.8	25.9	26.3	26.5	27.0	27.1	27.1	27.0	27.3	27.3	27.5	26.7
1995	27.5	27.6	27.9	28.0	28.4	28.7	28.9	28.9	29.0	29.2	29.3	29.3	28.6
1996	28.9	29.1	29.2	29.6	29.8	30.0	29.9	30.1	30.3	30.5	30.6	30.6	29.9
1997	30.4	30.8	31.0	30.8	31.5	31.6	31.7	31.8	32.0	32.6	32.8	32.6	31.6
1998	31.9	32.2	32.3	32.2	32.8	32.9	33.3	33.6	33.8	33.7	33.7	33.7	33.0
1999	33.4	33.5	33.7	32.8	33.3	33.0	33.3	33.0	32.9	33.3	33.4	33.3	33.2
2000	33.0	33.3	33.3	32.8	32.8	32.9	32.6	32.4	32.5	32.6	32.6	32.8	32.8
2001	31.0	30.6	30.9	31.3	30.9	30.8	30.2	30.0	29.8	29.9	29.8	29.6	30.4
2002	29.0	28.7	28.7	29.5	29.7	29.9	30.1	30.1	29.7	30.0	30.0	29.9	29.6
2003	29.2	29.0	29.1	29.3	29.7	29.8	29.7	29.7	30.1	29.9	29.8	30.0	29.6

Employment by Industry: Michigan—*Continued*

(Numbers in thousands. Not seasonally adjusted.)

Industry	January	February	March	April	May	June	July	August	September	October	November	December	Annual Average
GRAND RAPIDS—*Continued*													
Retail trade													
1990	58.8	58.7	59.0	58.9	60.0	60.0	59.3	60.2	60.7	60.8	62.0	62.5	60.1
1991	56.6	55.1	55.2	55.8	56.4	55.4	54.9	55.0	55.7	55.9	57.3	57.8	55.9
1992	55.0	54.6	54.5	54.5	55.5	55.8	54.7	55.1	55.7	57.0	58.2	58.7	55.8
1993	56.5	55.7	55.7	56.3	57.2	57.1	57.1	57.9	58.7	60.1	61.2	61.6	57.9
1994	58.7	57.6	58.2	59.2	60.1	60.2	60.5	61.5	62.7	63.8	65.1	66.0	61.1
1995	62.5	62.1	62.3	62.9	63.9	63.6	62.9	63.5	64.5	65.3	66.9	68.4	64.1
1996	65.7	65.0	65.2	65.0	65.8	65.2	64.9	65.5	66.2	68.2	69.9	71.2	66.5
1997	66.9	65.8	66.3	66.5	67.6	67.1	66.2	67.0	67.5	67.9	69.3	70.4	67.4
1998	66.1	65.7	65.7	67.4	68.4	68.2	66.4	67.4	68.2	68.9	70.8	72.6	68.0
1999	68.3	68.4	68.9	68.7	69.7	69.1	68.3	68.5	68.9	68.7	70.3	72.1	69.2
2000	69.6	68.9	70.1	69.8	71.0	70.3	68.5	69.2	69.7	70.6	72.5	73.6	70.3
2001	69.9	69.1	68.6	69.0	69.7	69.4	67.4	67.5	67.1	67.7	69.2	69.7	68.7
2002	66.2	65.3	65.4	66.0	66.9	67.1	67.1	67.8	67.8	67.2	68.7	69.6	67.1
2003	65.0	63.7	63.7	63.8	65.2	65.7	65.8	65.7	65.1	65.3	65.9	66.0	65.1
Transportation and utilities													
1990	10.1	10.3	10.2	10.4	10.5	10.9	10.6	10.8	10.8	10.8	10.9	11.0	10.6
1991	11.1	11.0	11.1	11.1	11.4	11.5	11.4	11.7	11.7	11.8	11.9	11.9	11.5
1992	11.4	11.5	11.5	11.9	12.1	12.3	12.3	12.4	12.4	12.6	12.6	12.5	12.1
1993	11.9	11.9	12.1	12.2	12.4	12.6	12.7	12.8	13.0	13.7	13.7	13.8	12.7
1994	13.4	13.5	13.6	13.8	13.8	13.8	14.0	13.8	13.9	13.8	13.6	13.6	13.7
1995	13.7	13.8	13.9	13.8	13.9	13.8	13.8	13.9	13.8	14.1	13.9	13.9	13.9
1996	13.7	13.7	13.8	13.8	13.9	13.8	13.8	13.9	14.0	14.0	13.8	13.8	13.8
1997	13.1	13.1	13.1	13.3	13.2	13.2	13.2	12.3	13.2	13.3	13.3	13.3	13.1
1998	13.2	13.3	13.2	14.0	14.1	14.0	13.8	14.0	14.2	14.4	14.4	14.4	13.9
1999	14.0	13.9	13.7	14.1	14.1	14.2	14.2	14.1	14.1	14.2	14.1	14.2	14.1
2000	13.9	13.9	13.9	14.2	14.2	14.2	14.3	14.5	14.5	14.9	14.8	14.9	14.4
2001	14.5	14.4	14.4	14.6	14.7	14.8	14.8	14.9	14.8	14.9	14.5	14.4	14.6
2002	14.0	14.0	14.2	14.1	14.2	14.2	13.9	14.2	14.1	14.2	14.0	14.0	14.1
2003	13.9	13.7	13.7	14.1	14.2	14.3	14.2	14.5	14.2	14.2	14.4	14.3	14.1
Information													
1990	8.2	8.2	8.2	8.2	8.3	8.4	8.3	8.3	8.3	8.4	8.4	8.6	8.3
1991	8.1	8.2	8.2	8.2	8.1	8.1	8.1	8.1	8.1	8.5	8.6	8.6	8.2
1992	7.4	7.3	7.5	7.2	7.2	7.2	7.2	7.2	7.2	7.1	7.1	7.1	7.2
1993	7.0	7.0	7.0	6.4	6.4	6.4	6.6	6.6	6.6	6.7	6.8	6.8	6.7
1994	6.6	6.6	6.6	6.5	6.5	6.6	6.6	6.6	6.8	6.6	6.7	6.7	6.6
1995	6.8	6.9	6.9	6.7	6.7	6.9	6.9	6.9	6.9	6.8	6.8	6.9	6.8
1996	7.0	6.8	7.0	7.0	7.0	7.0	7.3	7.3	7.4	7.5	7.6	7.6	7.2
1997	7.2	7.3	7.4	7.3	7.4	7.5	7.6	7.7	7.7	7.8	7.7	7.8	7.5
1998	7.8	7.9	7.9	7.9	8.0	8.0	7.8	7.8	7.9	7.9	8.0	8.2	7.9
1999	7.5	7.5	7.6	8.0	8.0	8.1	8.2	8.2	8.1	8.0	8.0	8.0	7.9
2000	7.9	7.8	7.9	8.5	8.6	8.7	8.6	8.7	8.6	8.3	8.3	8.4	8.4
2001	8.1	8.2	8.2	8.4	8.5	8.7	8.4	8.3	8.3	8.6	8.9	8.9	8.5
2002	9.0	9.0	9.1	8.5	8.5	8.5	8.4	8.4	8.2	8.5	8.5	8.6	8.6
2003	7.9	7.9	7.8	8.2	8.1	8.1	7.8	7.9	8.1	8.3	8.2	8.3	8.1
Financial activities													
1990	18.0	18.2	18.4	18.0	18.2	18.4	17.8	17.9	18.2	18.0	18.0	18.2	18.1
1991	17.2	17.3	17.4	17.4	17.5	17.7	17.5	17.6	17.7	17.2	17.6	17.7	17.5
1992	16.8	16.8	16.7	17.9	18.0	18.1	18.2	18.1	18.3	18.3	18.4	18.4	17.8
1993	18.0	18.1	18.2	18.1	18.2	18.4	18.3	18.4	18.5	18.7	18.9	19.0	18.4
1994	19.8	19.8	19.8	19.9	20.1	20.2	20.3	20.3	20.3	20.3	20.3	20.5	20.1
1995	21.0	21.1	21.3	21.1	21.3	21.4	21.1	21.1	21.2	21.0	21.0	21.2	21.2
1996	21.2	21.2	21.4	20.3	20.4	20.6	20.9	21.0	21.0	20.8	20.8	21.1	20.9
1997	21.0	21.1	21.2	21.2	22.0	22.1	23.0	23.1	23.1	23.0	23.1	23.4	22.3
1998	23.6	23.8	23.8	23.8	23.9	24.0	23.8	24.0	23.8	24.1	24.1	24.2	23.9
1999	23.8	23.7	23.6	24.2	23.8	24.2	23.9	25.6	26.0	25.7	25.5	25.8	24.7
2000	25.4	25.5	25.4	24.7	24.7	24.8	24.5	24.6	24.6	25.1	25.1	25.4	25.0
2001	24.2	24.1	24.3	24.3	24.6	24.6	24.2	24.3	24.0	24.9	24.6	24.8	24.4
2002	24.4	24.6	24.7	24.4	24.4	24.2	24.1	24.2	23.9	24.3	24.1	24.2	24.3
2003	24.3	24.3	24.2	24.5	24.4	24.5	25.1	24.3	23.7	22.9	23.1	22.7	24.0
Professional and business services													
1990	29.5	29.7	30.0	30.2	30.9	32.4	32.0	32.2	32.9	32.3	32.0	31.4	31.3
1991	31.7	31.3	31.2	32.6	33.1	33.8	34.6	35.1	35.5	35.4	35.6	35.2	33.8
1992	34.6	34.9	35.6	37.7	38.2	39.5	39.2	39.3	39.4	39.7	39.6	39.8	38.1
1993	38.5	38.6	38.8	42.3	42.8	43.3	43.3	44.1	44.9	47.0	46.6	46.9	43.1
1994	45.3	45.2	45.4	46.8	46.9	48.1	48.8	49.7	50.7	49.9	50.4	50.2	48.1
1995	47.3	47.4	47.7	49.6	49.7	50.4	50.7	51.7	52.1	50.4	50.7	50.4	49.8
1996	47.4	47.5	47.3	47.7	49.0	49.9	49.9	51.3	52.2	53.3	52.9	53.4	50.2
1997	52.2	51.3	52.5	54.5	55.5	55.3	56.2	57.4	57.9	57.3	57.0	57.7	55.4
1998	53.9	53.9	53.5	53.5	54.2	55.4	53.2	55.2	55.1	55.4	55.3	55.4	54.5
1999	53.0	53.2	54.2	57.6	58.4	60.0	60.2	61.5	61.6	63.0	64.4	65.7	59.4
2000	64.6	64.7	65.0	66.5	67.4	69.2	69.7	70.2	69.2	68.2	67.7	67.6	67.5
2001	62.6	61.7	61.7	64.7	66.2	67.3	66.5	68.1	67.3	65.2	64.7	64.1	65.0
2002	61.9	61.8	62.3	65.5	67.1	68.2	68.5	69.3	68.4	66.8	66.8	66.1	66.1
2003	61.1	60.7	60.3	61.7	63.4	63.9	65.3	64.2	62.5	63.0	63.3	64.0	62.8

Employment by Industry: Michigan—*Continued*

(Numbers in thousands. Not seasonally adjusted.)

Industry	January	February	March	April	May	June	July	August	September	October	November	December	Annual Average
GRAND RAPIDS—*Continued*													
Educational and health services													
1990	40.2	40.9	41.1	40.6	40.8	40.8	41.3	41.0	41.5	41.9	41.9	42.0	41.2
1991	42.3	42.4	42.6	42.6	42.6	42.5	42.8	43.0	43.2	43.6	43.8	44.2	43.0
1992	43.6	43.8	43.9	43.8	44.0	43.9	44.0	44.0	44.6	44.5	44.7	44.9	44.1
1993	45.4	45.7	45.9	45.8	46.0	45.7	45.2	45.2	45.9	44.8	44.9	45.3	45.5
1994	44.1	44.3	44.4	44.6	44.7	44.7	44.5	44.8	45.3	45.3	45.5	45.2	44.8
1995	44.8	45.1	45.3	45.9	45.9	46.0	46.1	46.2	46.7	47.1	47.4	47.5	46.2
1996	46.8	47.2	47.3	48.1	47.9	47.9	47.7	47.9	48.5	49.3	49.3	49.6	48.1
1997	48.9	49.2	49.6	49.6	49.9	49.8	48.6	48.9	49.6	49.6	49.5	49.8	49.4
1998	49.6	50.2	50.3	48.5	48.7	48.7	47.3	47.7	48.0	48.1	48.2	48.3	48.6
1999	49.8	50.3	50.4	51.7	51.8	51.6	51.6	51.5	52.0	51.9	51.8	52.1	51.4
2000	50.9	51.2	51.4	51.3	51.4	51.3	51.2	51.5	52.0	52.5	52.5	52.7	51.7
2001	64.3	65.1	66.2	66.5	65.4	66.7	65.5	65.4	66.3	67.8	68.4	68.7	66.4
2002	68.0	68.8	69.7	70.3	70.1	70.5	68.0	68.1	69.0	69.9	71.1	70.3	69.5
2003	70.1	71.9	71.8	69.4	70.2	70.6	70.5	70.2	73.4	76.1	76.5	75.9	72.2
Leisure and hospitality													
1990	34.2	34.8	35.4	35.8	37.6	38.7	38.4	38.1	38.0	36.7	36.1	35.9	36.6
1991	35.0	35.1	35.4	36.7	38.4	39.2	39.2	39.2	38.9	37.3	36.7	36.3	37.3
1992	34.9	35.1	35.5	37.4	38.8	39.6	40.0	39.9	39.5	38.8	38.0	37.7	37.9
1993	36.5	36.8	37.4	39.4	41.4	42.3	42.6	42.6	42.1	40.6	39.6	39.5	40.1
1994	38.4	38.7	39.1	40.5	42.0	42.8	43.1	43.2	43.0	41.9	40.8	41.0	41.2
1995	38.2	38.7	39.5	41.1	42.8	43.9	43.9	43.9	43.5	42.2	41.5	41.7	41.7
1996	40.2	40.6	41.1	42.4	44.5	45.5	46.3	46.6	45.7	44.3	43.5	44.6	43.8
1997	42.3	42.6	43.7	44.8	46.8	47.4	47.5	48.0	47.2	45.5	45.3	45.5	45.6
1998	42.9	43.5	43.9	45.8	47.4	48.1	48.2	48.1	46.7	45.8	44.9	44.8	45.8
1999	42.6	43.3	44.1	46.2	48.4	49.1	48.8	48.9	48.1	47.6	47.0	47.4	46.8
2000	44.5	45.2	45.7	46.5	48.8	49.8	50.0	50.1	48.8	47.2	46.4	46.1	47.4
2001	43.3	43.7	44.3	46.2	48.5	48.8	49.1	49.8	47.9	47.4	45.6	45.5	46.7
2002	42.9	43.1	43.5	45.6	47.9	49.3	49.4	50.2	49.7	47.3	46.6	46.4	46.8
2003	43.7	43.6	43.9	45.3	48.0	49.5	49.6	49.8	49.6	48.5	47.0	47.3	47.2
Other services													
1990	15.3	15.6	15.8	15.6	15.8	15.9	15.6	15.8	15.7	15.8	15.7	15.8	15.7
1991	15.5	15.7	15.8	15.8	16.0	15.9	15.7	15.7	15.7	16.1	15.9	16.0	15.8
1992	15.8	16.1	16.1	16.1	16.3	16.4	16.6	16.5	16.5	16.8	16.6	16.6	16.4
1993	16.6	16.9	17.1	17.1	17.6	17.6	17.5	17.4	17.5	17.7	17.8	18.0	17.4
1994	17.7	18.1	18.2	18.2	18.6	18.8	19.0	19.1	19.0	19.1	19.1	19.1	18.7
1995	18.5	18.8	19.2	19.2	19.5	19.6	19.6	19.8	19.6	20.1	20.0	20.2	19.5
1996	20.1	20.3	20.4	20.3	20.4	20.6	20.4	20.7	20.6	20.9	20.7	20.6	20.5
1997	20.3	20.3	20.5	20.3	20.5	20.6	20.8	20.8	20.6	20.9	20.9	21.0	20.6
1998	19.8	20.2	20.3	20.6	20.6	20.6	20.4	20.5	20.5	20.6	20.6	20.8	20.5
1999	20.0	20.3	20.5	21.2	21.3	21.6	21.6	21.5	21.2	21.3	21.2	21.5	21.1
2000	21.2	21.4	21.6	21.7	21.7	21.9	22.1	22.1	21.7	21.8	21.7	21.9	21.7
2001	23.0	23.2	23.4	23.8	23.8	24.1	23.8	23.9	23.4	23.5	23.5	23.6	23.6
2002	23.0	23.1	23.2	23.4	23.6	23.9	24.1	24.0	23.9	23.8	23.7	23.8	23.6
2003	23.4	23.3	23.4	23.4	23.5	23.6	23.6	22.9	23.1	23.3	23.7	23.3	23.4
Government													
1990	46.9	48.3	48.7	48.7	48.7	45.3	40.9	40.4	47.9	49.7	50.2	50.1	47.2
1991	48.4	50.4	50.8	49.6	49.2	46.0	41.8	41.9	50.2	51.7	51.9	51.6	48.6
1992	51.2	51.9	52.6	51.0	51.2	48.8	44.1	44.0	49.8	52.1	52.7	52.3	50.1
1993	51.3	52.3	52.5	51.9	51.8	50.1	44.5	43.7	50.7	52.6	52.7	52.4	50.5
1994	51.3	52.2	53.4	52.2	52.0	50.2	44.6	45.0	51.7	53.2	54.2	52.8	51.1
1995	51.9	53.1	53.3	52.8	52.9	50.5	44.9	44.5	52.0	54.0	53.9	53.9	51.5
1996	52.3	53.4	54.5	53.8	53.1	49.9	44.9	44.6	53.1	54.9	55.4	54.8	52.1
1997	53.7	55.0	55.3	54.2	54.3	51.5	47.2	46.8	53.4	55.6	55.3	55.3	53.1
1998	54.8	56.0	56.3	55.6	55.8	53.8	47.9	48.1	54.5	56.8	57.0	57.0	54.5
1999	55.6	57.0	57.5	57.5	57.7	54.9	48.3	48.2	56.4	59.1	59.1	58.6	55.8
2000	56.7	58.6	58.9	58.5	59.9	55.9	49.2	48.7	57.4	59.6	59.9	59.0	56.9
2001	58.6	59.9	60.4	59.3	60.1	56.4	51.6	50.1	58.5	60.2	60.1	60.3	58.0
2002	58.7	59.8	60.3	59.2	59.9	55.9	50.0	50.2	58.4	61.4	61.9	61.9	58.1
2003	59.1	61.5	62.0	59.5	60.8	56.9	49.9	49.9	58.2	59.7	60.1	60.1	58.1
Federal government													
1990	3.5	3.5	3.5	3.8	4.3	3.8	3.8	3.6	3.5	3.5	3.5	3.5	3.7
1991	3.5	3.5	3.5	3.4	3.5	3.5	3.5	3.5	3.5	3.5	3.6	3.7	3.5
1992	3.7	3.7	3.7	3.6	3.6	3.6	3.6	3.6	3.6	3.6	3.5	3.6	3.6
1993	3.6	3.6	3.6	3.6	3.6	3.6	3.6	3.6	3.6	3.6	3.6	3.7	3.6
1994	3.6	3.6	3.7	3.7	3.7	3.7	3.7	3.7	3.7	3.7	3.7	4.0	3.7
1995	3.8	3.8	3.8	3.8	3.8	3.9	3.8	3.8	3.8	3.8	3.9	4.0	3.8
1996	3.8	3.8	3.7	3.8	3.8	3.9	3.9	3.9	3.9	3.8	3.9	4.1	3.9
1997	4.0	4.0	4.0	4.0	4.0	4.0	4.0	4.0	4.0	4.0	4.0	4.4	4.0
1998	4.2	4.2	4.2	4.1	4.1	4.1	4.1	4.1	4.1	4.1	4.1	4.3	4.1
1999	4.2	4.2	4.2	4.4	4.2	4.3	4.3	4.3	4.3	4.2	4.3	4.5	4.3
2000	4.3	4.4	4.4	4.7	5.6	4.9	4.8	4.4	4.2	4.2	4.2	4.3	4.5
2001	4.2	4.2	4.2	4.1	4.1	4.2	4.2	4.2	4.2	4.1	4.1	4.2	4.2
2002	4.1	4.1	4.1	4.1	4.1	4.2	4.1	4.1	4.2	4.3	4.2	4.3	4.2
2003	4.2	4.2	4.2	4.2	4.2	4.2	4.3	4.2	4.2	4.1	4.1	4.2	4.2

Employment by Industry: Michigan—*Continued*

(Numbers in thousands. Not seasonally adjusted.)

Industry	January	February	March	April	May	June	July	August	September	October	November	December	Annual Average
GRAND RAPIDS—*Continued*													
State government													
1990	6.2	6.3	6.1	6.4	4.7	4.7	4.8	4.7	6.4	6.4	6.1	6.4	5.8
1991	5.9	6.3	6.6	6.5	4.7	4.8	4.8	4.7	6.3	6.3	6.2	5.8	5.7
1992	6.2	6.2	6.1	6.1	5.1	5.2	5.3	5.1	6.3	6.2	6.2	6.2	5.9
1993	6.2	6.1	6.1	6.2	5.0	5.0	5.2	5.1	6.3	6.4	6.4	5.8	5.8
1994	6.1	6.3	6.2	6.3	5.2	5.3	5.3	5.3	6.5	6.6	6.5	6.1	6.0
1995	6.3	6.5	6.4	6.5	5.3	5.4	5.5	5.4	6.6	6.9	6.8	6.8	6.2
1996	6.5	6.7	6.7	6.7	5.4	5.5	5.6	5.5	7.0	6.9	6.9	6.5	6.3
1997	6.6	6.8	6.7	6.8	5.5	5.4	5.5	5.5	6.8	7.1	6.9	6.4	6.3
1998	6.9	7.1	7.0	7.0	5.6	5.7	5.7	5.7	7.0	7.3	7.3	7.2	6.6
1999	6.9	7.2	7.2	7.3	6.5	5.8	5.9	5.9	7.2	7.6	7.5	6.9	6.8
2000	6.7	7.3	7.2	7.3	6.6	6.0	6.0	5.7	7.2	7.6	7.6	7.0	6.9
2001	7.3	7.7	7.7	7.8	7.0	6.3	6.4	6.3	7.6	8.2	8.2	8.2	7.4
2002	7.2	7.9	7.8	7.8	7.1	6.3	6.3	6.2	6.8	8.0	8.0	8.1	7.3
2003	6.2	8.0	8.0	7.1	6.5	5.0	5.3	5.3	6.5	7.0	7.0	7.0	6.6
Local government													
1990	37.2	38.4	39.1	38.6	39.7	36.8	32.3	32.1	38.0	39.8	40.6	40.2	37.7
1991	38.9	40.6	40.8	39.6	41.0	37.7	33.5	33.7	40.4	41.9	42.1	42.1	39.4
1992	41.3	42.1	42.9	41.2	42.5	40.1	35.2	35.3	39.9	42.3	43.0	42.5	40.7
1993	41.5	42.6	42.9	42.1	43.2	41.5	35.7	35.0	40.8	42.6	42.7	42.8	41.1
1994	41.6	42.3	43.5	42.2	43.1	41.2	35.6	36.1	41.4	42.9	43.9	42.8	41.4
1995	41.8	42.9	43.2	42.5	43.7	41.3	35.5	35.3	41.6	43.3	43.3	43.0	41.5
1996	42.0	43.0	44.1	43.2	43.9	40.6	35.4	35.2	42.2	44.1	44.6	44.3	41.9
1997	43.1	44.2	44.6	43.4	44.8	42.1	37.7	37.3	42.6	44.5	44.4	44.5	42.8
1998	43.7	44.7	45.1	44.5	46.1	44.0	38.1	38.3	43.4	45.4	45.6	45.5	43.7
1999	44.5	45.6	46.1	45.8	47.0	44.8	38.1	38.0	44.9	47.3	47.3	47.2	44.7
2000	45.7	46.9	47.3	46.5	47.7	45.0	38.4	38.6	46.0	47.8	48.1	47.7	45.5
2001	47.1	48.0	48.5	47.4	49.0	45.9	41.0	39.6	46.7	47.9	47.8	47.9	46.4
2002	47.4	47.8	48.4	47.3	48.7	45.4	39.6	39.9	47.4	49.1	49.7	49.5	46.7
2003	48.7	49.3	49.8	48.2	50.1	47.7	40.3	40.4	47.5	48.6	49.0	48.9	47.4
KALAMAZOO													
Total nonfarm													
1990	189.9	191.9	194.1	193.1	192.8	194.0	192.7	192.8	197.1	196.7	196.5	196.0	194.0
1991	187.0	187.4	187.5	188.4	188.9	189.0	184.8	187.0	192.8	193.8	194.7	195.4	189.7
1992	189.1	190.2	191.0	192.0	192.5	193.5	190.8	191.4	194.8	197.5	197.3	196.6	193.1
1993	191.9	193.2	194.1	196.2	195.2	195.9	192.6	193.9	198.7	200.8	201.0	201.2	196.2
1994	196.0	197.3	199.3	200.6	200.5	201.0	199.1	200.0	205.3	206.4	207.1	207.8	201.7
1995	201.3	202.3	204.0	205.1	205.5	205.5	201.6	203.3	208.0	209.1	209.6	209.9	205.4
1996	204.0	204.8	206.4	207.3	208.1	207.2	202.7	205.3	209.9	211.5	211.7	212.0	207.6
1997	204.4	206.2	207.6	208.5	208.8	208.6	206.0	207.2	210.8	212.5	212.8	213.0	208.9
1998	206.4	208.3	209.9	212.9	213.6	214.8	208.2	210.8	214.8	217.4	218.1	217.0	212.7
1999	210.0	212.1	213.4	216.3	216.3	216.8	213.4	213.8	217.2	218.4	219.0	219.3	215.5
2000	212.1	212.8	214.7	216.6	217.0	216.7	211.2	212.7	217.2	218.6	219.0	218.3	215.6
2001	209.2	210.0	211.1	211.8	212.2	210.4	204.3	208.1	212.6	212.5	212.8	209.7	210.4
2002	207.1	208.1	209.5	210.8	212.6	211.9	209.5	211.9	215.1	215.1	215.1	212.7	211.6
2003	208.1	207.8	208.8	210.9	211.1	210.9	206.1	205.4	210.8	214.7	213.8	210.0	209.9
Total private													
1990	156.8	156.9	158.5	157.7	159.3	160.7	161.0	161.8	162.4	161.2	160.9	160.6	159.8
1991	153.3	151.7	151.8	153.6	155.9	156.7	154.8	157.5	157.9	158.2	158.7	158.9	155.8
1992	154.6	154.3	155.0	157.2	159.7	161.5	161.5	162.1	162.3	161.9	161.3	161.8	159.4
1993	157.4	157.8	158.7	161.0	162.0	163.7	163.3	164.8	165.1	165.4	165.4	165.7	162.5
1994	162.0	162.1	163.6	165.5	167.9	169.0	169.9	170.8	171.5	171.1	171.6	172.5	168.1
1995	167.0	166.9	168.4	169.9	172.2	173.3	172.2	174.3	173.8	173.8	174.1	174.3	171.7
1996	170.1	169.4	170.7	171.9	174.9	175.2	173.5	176.1	175.6	175.8	175.7	176.3	173.8
1997	170.4	170.5	171.6	172.9	175.5	176.7	175.6	176.9	175.9	176.9	176.9	177.1	174.7
1998	171.7	172.2	173.5	177.2	180.0	181.1	177.8	180.2	179.3	180.7	181.1	180.8	178.0
1999	174.7	175.3	176.5	179.8	181.9	183.0	182.3	182.6	182.6	182.4	182.6	183.1	180.6
2000	177.1	176.4	178.3	180.4	182.5	183.4	180.8	182.5	182.5	181.8	181.7	181.1	180.7
2001	171.7	171.2	172.1	174.6	176.7	176.5	174.1	176.2	175.5	174.5	174.6	173.9	174.3
2002	170.1	170.0	171.6	174.4	177.8	178.9	178.0	179.9	178.4	177.1	177.0	175.7	175.7
2003	171.4	170.3	171.4	174.1	176.3	178.0	176.1	174.6	174.0	176.3	175.2	172.5	174.2
Goods-producing													
1990	56.4	56.3	56.7	56.6	57.1	57.9	58.7	58.6	58.3	57.7	57.0	56.9	57.4
1991	51.8	51.3	50.5	51.7	52.9	53.7	52.6	53.7	53.6	53.4	53.5	53.6	52.7
1992	52.5	52.3	52.5	53.2	54.2	55.1	55.1	54.7	55.1	54.6	54.3	54.3	54.0
1993	52.8	52.8	52.7	53.6	54.0	54.5	54.2	54.4	54.4	54.0	54.1	53.8	53.8
1994	53.0	53.0	53.3	53.7	54.9	55.5	55.2	55.7	55.8	55.8	55.8	56.1	54.8
1995	54.6	54.2	54.4	55.1	56.1	56.3	55.7	56.4	55.9	56.5	56.1	55.7	55.6
1996	56.0	55.3	55.2	55.0	55.8	56.0	56.0	56.4	56.1	55.3	55.0	54.9	55.6
1997	53.8	53.5	53.7	54.0	55.1	55.6	55.2	55.8	55.3	56.1	55.8	55.7	55.0
1998	54.3	54.1	54.4	56.2	57.3	57.5	55.7	57.3	56.9	56.8	57.0	56.7	56.2
1999	54.9	54.8	55.1	58.0	58.8	59.7	59.8	59.7	59.9	59.5	59.7	59.6	58.3
2000	57.2	56.8	57.2	58.7	59.5	59.9	58.3	59.3	58.8	59.1	58.8	58.5	58.5
2001	53.2	52.9	52.9	53.0	53.4	53.6	52.6	53.9	53.1	52.5	52.0	51.7	52.9
2002	50.2	49.7	50.0	50.4	51.6	52.2	51.3	52.0	51.7	50.9	50.7	49.8	50.9
2003	49.1	48.7	48.9	49.5	50.1	51.2	51.2	50.6	50.3	50.7	50.4	50.2	50.1

Employment by Industry: Michigan—*Continued*

(Numbers in thousands. Not seasonally adjusted.)

Industry	January	February	March	April	May	June	July	August	September	October	November	December	Annual Average
KALAMAZOO—*Continued*													
Construction and mining													
1990	6.3	6.1	6.1	6.2	6.7	6.8	7.2	7.2	7.1	7.0	6.9	6.5	6.7
1991	5.2	5.0	5.2	5.6	6.2	6.5	6.7	7.0	6.7	6.8	6.8	6.5	6.2
1992	6.1	5.9	5.9	6.0	6.4	6.8	6.9	6.8	6.7	6.7	6.5	6.2	6.4
1993	5.6	5.5	5.5	6.1	6.6	6.8	7.0	7.0	6.9	7.0	6.8	6.4	6.4
1994	5.7	5.5	5.8	6.4	7.0	7.3	7.6	7.7	7.6	7.5	7.3	7.1	6.9
1995	6.3	6.1	6.3	6.8	7.4	7.7	7.9	7.9	7.7	7.6	7.4	7.0	7.2
1996	6.6	6.4	6.7	7.3	7.9	8.3	8.3	8.3	8.2	8.4	8.2	7.9	7.7
1997	7.1	6.9	7.2	7.8	8.6	8.9	9.1	9.0	8.9	9.0	8.7	8.4	8.3
1998	7.4	7.2	7.4	8.2	9.1	9.3	9.6	9.3	9.1	9.0	8.9	8.6	8.6
1999	7.7	7.6	7.8	8.9	9.3	10.0	9.9	9.9	9.7	9.9	9.9	9.4	9.2
2000	8.3	8.0	8.5	9.5	10.0	10.2	10.3	10.4	10.2	9.9	9.6	9.3	9.5
2001	8.4	8.2	8.4	9.0	9.5	9.9	10.3	10.3	10.0	10.1	9.9	9.6	9.5
2002	8.7	8.3	8.6	9.2	10.0	10.2	10.6	10.6	10.4	10.4	10.3	9.6	9.7
2003	9.0	8.6	8.7	9.4	10.1	10.4	10.7	10.3	10.3	10.8	10.3	10.1	9.9
Manufacturing													
1990	50.1	50.2	50.6	50.4	50.4	51.1	51.5	51.4	51.2	50.7	50.1	50.4	50.7
1991	46.6	46.3	45.3	46.1	46.7	47.2	45.9	46.7	46.9	46.6	46.7	47.1	46.5
1992	46.4	46.4	46.6	47.2	47.8	48.3	48.2	47.9	48.4	47.9	47.8	48.1	47.6
1993	47.2	47.3	47.2	47.5	47.4	47.7	47.2	47.4	47.5	47.0	47.3	47.4	47.3
1994	47.3	47.5	47.5	47.3	47.9	48.2	47.6	48.0	48.2	48.3	48.5	49.0	47.9
1995	48.3	48.1	48.1	48.3	48.7	48.6	47.8	48.5	48.2	48.9	48.7	48.7	48.4
1996	49.4	48.9	48.5	47.7	47.9	47.7	47.7	48.1	47.9	46.9	46.8	47.0	47.9
1997	46.7	46.6	46.5	46.2	46.5	46.7	46.1	46.8	46.4	47.1	47.1	47.3	46.7
1998	46.9	46.9	47.0	48.0	48.2	48.2	46.1	48.0	47.8	47.8	48.1	48.1	47.6
1999	47.2	47.2	47.3	49.1	49.5	49.7	49.9	49.8	50.2	49.6	49.8	50.2	49.1
2000	48.9	48.8	48.7	49.2	49.5	49.7	48.0	48.9	48.6	49.2	49.2	49.2	49.0
2001	44.8	44.7	44.5	44.0	43.9	43.7	42.3	43.6	43.1	42.4	42.1	42.1	43.4
2002	41.5	41.4	41.4	41.2	41.6	42.0	40.7	41.4	41.3	40.5	40.4	40.2	41.1
2003	40.1	40.1	40.2	40.1	40.0	40.8	40.5	40.3	40.0	39.9	40.1	40.1	40.2
Service-providing													
1990	133.5	135.6	137.4	136.5	135.7	136.1	134.0	134.2	138.8	139.0	139.5	139.1	136.6
1991	135.2	136.1	137.0	136.7	136.0	135.3	132.2	133.3	139.2	140.4	141.2	141.8	137.0
1992	136.6	137.9	138.5	138.8	138.3	138.4	135.7	136.7	139.7	142.9	143.0	142.3	139.1
1993	139.1	140.4	141.4	142.6	141.2	141.4	138.4	139.5	144.3	146.8	146.9	147.4	142.5
1994	143.0	144.3	146.0	146.9	145.6	145.5	143.9	144.3	149.5	150.6	151.3	151.7	146.9
1995	146.7	148.1	149.6	150.0	149.4	149.2	145.9	146.9	152.1	152.6	153.5	154.2	149.9
1996	148.0	149.5	151.2	152.3	152.3	151.2	146.7	148.9	153.8	156.2	156.7	157.1	152.0
1997	150.6	152.7	153.9	154.5	153.7	153.0	150.8	151.4	155.5	156.4	157.0	157.3	153.9
1998	152.1	154.2	155.5	156.7	156.3	157.3	152.5	153.5	157.9	160.6	161.1	160.3	156.5
1999	155.1	157.3	158.3	158.3	157.5	157.1	153.6	154.1	157.3	158.9	159.3	159.7	157.2
2000	154.9	156.0	157.5	157.9	157.5	156.8	152.9	153.4	158.4	159.5	160.2	159.8	157.1
2001	156.0	157.1	158.2	158.8	158.8	156.8	151.7	154.2	159.5	160.0	160.8	158.0	157.5
2002	156.9	158.4	159.5	160.4	161.0	159.7	158.2	159.9	163.4	164.2	164.4	162.9	160.7
2003	159.0	159.1	159.9	161.4	161.0	159.7	154.9	154.8	160.5	164.0	163.4	159.8	159.8
Trade, transportation, and utilities													
1990	30.9	30.4	30.4	29.7	29.8	29.9	30.1	30.4	30.4	30.2	30.8	31.4	30.4
1991	30.2	29.4	29.3	29.1	29.5	29.5	29.0	29.4	29.4	29.3	29.9	30.6	29.6
1992	29.8	29.4	29.4	30.0	30.4	30.7	29.9	30.2	30.3	30.7	31.0	31.6	30.3
1993	30.0	29.7	29.8	30.3	30.4	31.1	31.1	31.5	31.4	31.5	32.0	32.5	30.9
1994	31.0	30.7	30.9	31.1	31.4	31.7	31.6	31.9	31.9	32.3	33.0	33.3	31.7
1995	32.0	31.5	31.7	32.0	32.2	32.5	32.3	32.6	32.6	33.1	33.6	34.1	32.5
1996	33.1	32.6	32.8	32.7	33.0	33.3	33.4	33.9	33.7	34.0	34.8	35.3	33.6
1997	33.1	32.8	32.9	33.1	33.4	33.8	33.6	33.5	33.5	34.0	34.5	35.3	33.6
1998	32.8	32.9	32.9	34.4	35.0	35.4	34.9	35.1	34.9	35.4	36.2	36.7	34.7
1999	33.6	33.3	33.6	36.4	36.9	37.0	37.0	37.0	36.9	37.2	38.0	38.5	36.3
2000	36.7	36.4	36.8	36.6	36.9	36.8	36.5	36.7	36.6	36.8	37.8	38.3	36.9
2001	36.0	35.6	35.8	37.4	37.7	37.2	36.2	36.4	36.1	36.7	37.5	37.9	36.7
2002	35.9	36.0	36.6	37.2	37.7	37.8	37.3	37.7	37.7	37.1	37.9	38.3	37.3
2003	35.9	35.7	35.9	36.2	36.5	36.5	36.3	36.1	36.5	37.0	37.2	36.8	36.4
Wholesale trade													
1990	4.7	4.7	4.8	4.8	4.8	4.8	4.9	5.0	4.9	4.8	4.7	4.8	4.8
1991	4.6	4.6	4.6	4.5	4.6	4.5	4.5	4.5	4.5	4.5	4.5	4.5	4.5
1992	4.4	4.4	4.4	4.5	4.5	4.5	4.5	4.6	4.6	4.6	4.5	4.6	4.5
1993	4.6	4.6	4.7	4.7	4.8	4.8	4.8	4.9	4.8	4.8	4.7	4.8	4.8
1994	4.7	4.7	4.8	4.9	4.9	5.0	5.1	5.1	5.0	4.9	4.9	4.9	4.9
1995	4.7	4.7	4.8	4.8	4.8	4.9	5.0	5.0	4.9	5.0	5.0	5.1	4.9
1996	5.0	5.0	5.1	5.1	5.1	5.1	5.0	5.1	5.0	4.9	4.8	4.9	5.0
1997	4.8	4.8	4.8	4.9	5.0	5.1	5.0	5.1	5.0	4.9	4.9	5.0	4.9
1998	4.8	4.9	4.9	5.1	5.1	5.2	5.3	5.3	5.2	5.1	5.1	5.2	5.1
1999	5.0	5.0	5.0	5.3	5.3	5.4	5.4	5.4	5.3	5.4	5.4	5.4	5.3
2000	5.3	5.3	5.3	5.4	5.4	5.4	5.5	5.5	5.4	5.3	5.3	5.4	5.4
2001	5.4	5.5	5.5	5.7	5.7	5.7	5.6	5.7	5.6	5.5	5.6	5.7	5.6
2002	5.6	5.6	5.7	5.8	5.8	5.8	5.6	5.7	5.7	5.7	5.8	5.8	5.7
2003	5.6	5.6	5.6	5.7	5.7	5.6	5.5	5.5	5.9	6.0	6.3	6.0	5.8

Employment by Industry: Michigan—*Continued*

(Numbers in thousands. Not seasonally adjusted.)

Industry	January	February	March	April	May	June	July	August	September	October	November	December	Annual Average
KALAMAZOO—*Continued*													
Retail trade													
1990	22.5	22.0	21.9	21.3	21.4	21.4	21.3	21.4	21.6	21.6	22.2	22.8	21.8
1991	22.1	21.3	21.2	21.0	21.3	21.3	20.8	21.1	21.2	21.2	21.8	22.4	21.4
1992	21.7	21.2	21.2	21.6	22.0	22.3	21.5	21.7	21.9	22.2	22.6	23.1	21.9
1993	21.7	21.4	21.3	21.7	21.7	22.2	22.3	22.5	22.5	22.6	23.2	23.6	22.2
1994	22.2	21.9	21.9	22.1	22.3	22.5	22.3	22.7	22.8	23.2	23.9	24.3	22.7
1995	23.1	22.6	22.7	22.7	22.9	23.1	22.9	23.2	23.3	23.7	24.2	24.6	23.3
1996	23.8	23.3	23.4	23.3	23.6	23.9	24.1	24.5	24.5	24.8	25.6	26.0	24.2
1997	24.2	23.9	24.0	24.0	24.2	24.4	24.3	24.3	24.2	24.8	25.2	25.9	24.5
1998	23.7	23.7	23.7	24.8	25.3	25.6	25.3	25.5	25.4	25.7	26.5	27.0	25.2
1999	24.1	23.9	24.2	26.4	26.9	26.8	26.7	26.7	26.7	26.9	27.7	28.2	26.3
2000	26.6	26.3	26.7	26.3	26.6	26.4	26.0	26.2	26.3	26.5	27.4	27.8	26.6
2001	25.5	25.1	25.3	26.6	26.9	26.4	25.9	26.0	25.8	26.0	26.7	27.0	26.1
2002	25.3	25.3	25.8	26.2	26.7	26.7	26.5	26.9	26.9	26.3	27.0	27.4	26.4
2003	25.4	25.2	25.4	25.6	25.9	26.0	25.9	25.7	25.7	26.2	26.1	26.0	25.8
Transportation and utilities													
1990	3.7	3.7	3.7	3.6	3.6	3.7	3.9	4.0	3.9	3.8	3.9	3.8	3.8
1991	3.5	3.5	3.5	3.6	3.6	3.7	3.7	3.8	3.7	3.6	3.6	3.7	3.6
1992	3.7	3.8	3.8	3.9	3.9	3.9	3.9	3.9	3.8	3.9	3.9	3.9	3.9
1993	3.7	3.7	3.8	3.9	3.9	4.1	4.0	4.1	4.1	4.1	4.1	4.1	4.0
1994	4.1	4.1	4.2	4.1	4.2	4.2	4.2	4.1	4.1	4.2	4.2	4.1	4.2
1995	4.2	4.2	4.2	4.5	4.5	4.5	4.4	4.4	4.4	4.4	4.4	4.4	4.4
1996	4.3	4.3	4.3	4.3	4.3	4.3	4.3	4.3	4.2	4.3	4.4	4.4	4.3
1997	4.1	4.1	4.1	4.2	4.2	4.3	4.3	4.1	4.3	4.3	4.4	4.4	4.2
1998	4.3	4.3	4.3	4.5	4.6	4.6	4.3	4.3	4.3	4.6	4.6	4.5	4.4
1999	4.5	4.4	4.4	4.7	4.7	4.8	4.9	4.9	4.9	4.9	4.9	4.9	4.7
2000	4.8	4.8	4.8	4.9	4.9	5.0	5.0	5.0	4.9	5.0	5.1	5.1	4.9
2001	5.1	5.0	5.0	5.1	5.1	5.1	4.7	4.7	4.7	5.2	5.2	5.2	5.0
2002	5.0	5.1	5.1	5.2	5.2	5.3	5.2	5.1	5.1	5.1	5.1	5.1	5.1
2003	4.9	4.9	4.9	4.9	4.9	4.9	4.9	4.9	4.9	4.8	4.8	4.8	4.9
Information													
1990	2.1	2.1	2.1	2.0	2.0	2.1	2.1	2.1	2.1	2.1	2.1	2.1	2.1
1991	2.2	2.1	2.1	2.2	2.2	2.2	2.2	2.2	2.1	2.1	2.2	2.2	2.2
1992	2.2	2.2	2.2	2.2	2.2	2.2	2.2	2.2	2.2	2.3	2.3	2.3	2.2
1993	2.2	2.2	2.2	2.2	2.2	2.2	2.2	2.2	2.2	2.2	2.2	2.2	2.2
1994	2.2	2.2	2.2	2.2	2.3	2.3	2.3	2.3	2.3	2.2	2.3	2.3	2.3
1995	2.3	2.3	2.3	2.4	2.4	2.5	2.4	2.4	2.4	2.4	2.5	2.5	2.4
1996	2.6	2.6	2.6	2.6	2.6	2.6	2.6	2.6	2.5	2.5	2.5	2.6	2.6
1997	2.5	2.5	2.5	2.5	2.5	2.6	2.6	2.6	2.5	2.5	2.6	2.6	2.5
1998	2.6	2.6	2.7	2.6	2.6	2.7	2.9	2.9	2.8	2.7	2.8	2.8	2.7
1999	2.4	2.4	2.4	2.6	2.6	2.6	2.6	2.6	2.6	2.6	2.6	2.6	2.6
2000	2.4	2.4	2.4	2.3	2.3	2.3	2.4	2.4	2.4	2.5	2.4	2.5	2.4
2001	2.5	2.4	2.5	2.5	2.5	2.5	2.5	2.4	2.4	2.3	2.4	2.4	2.4
2002	2.4	2.3	2.3	2.4	2.4	2.4	2.4	2.4	2.3	2.3	2.3	2.3	2.4
2003	2.2	2.2	2.3	2.2	2.2	2.1	2.1	2.1	2.1	2.1	2.1	2.1	2.2
Financial activities													
1990	7.1	7.2	7.2	7.1	7.2	7.2	7.3	7.2	7.2	7.3	7.3	7.3	7.2
1991	6.9	6.9	6.9	7.1	7.1	7.0	6.8	6.7	6.7	6.8	6.8	6.8	6.9
1992	7.1	7.1	7.1	7.2	7.3	7.3	7.0	7.2	7.1	7.2	7.2	7.2	7.2
1993	7.0	7.0	7.1	7.2	7.2	7.3	7.3	7.2	7.2	7.3	7.3	7.4	7.2
1994	7.3	7.3	7.4	7.5	7.5	7.5	7.6	7.5	7.5	7.4	7.5	7.5	7.5
1995	7.3	7.3	7.4	7.3	7.4	7.3	7.3	7.5	7.3	7.5	7.6	7.6	7.4
1996	7.4	7.5	7.6	7.7	7.7	7.6	7.5	7.7	7.5	7.6	7.6	7.6	7.6
1997	7.6	7.6	7.6	7.5	7.6	7.5	7.5	7.6	7.4	7.5	7.5	7.5	7.5
1998	7.4	7.4	7.4	7.5	7.5	7.5	7.8	7.6	7.5	7.6	7.7	7.7	7.6
1999	7.7	7.7	7.6	7.8	7.7	7.7	7.7	7.7	7.6	7.4	7.5	7.5	7.6
2000	7.3	7.3	7.3	7.3	7.2	7.2	7.2	7.1	7.2	7.2	7.1	7.2	7.2
2001	9.0	8.9	9.0	9.1	9.0	9.1	9.2	9.2	9.2	9.2	9.2	9.3	9.1
2002	9.3	9.3	9.3	9.3	9.3	9.2	9.0	9.1	9.2	9.2	9.3	9.2	9.2
2003	9.1	9.1	9.1	9.3	9.3	9.3	9.2	9.2	9.2	8.9	9.1	9.7	9.2
Professional and business services													
1990	13.8	14.2	15.1	15.1	15.5	15.8	15.9	16.4	16.8	16.5	16.2	15.8	15.6
1991	15.9	15.9	16.4	16.4	16.7	17.0	16.9	17.4	17.6	18.1	17.9	17.5	17.0
1992	16.9	17.0	17.2	17.7	18.1	18.4	20.1	20.6	20.3	19.3	19.0	19.3	18.7
1993	18.8	18.9	19.1	19.0	19.4	19.6	20.0	20.4	20.5	20.8	20.6	20.6	19.8
1994	20.3	20.3	20.5	21.2	21.4	21.6	22.4	22.5	22.4	22.4	22.4	22.6	21.7
1995	21.4	21.7	22.1	22.0	22.4	22.7	22.5	23.1	23.2	22.2	22.1	22.2	22.3
1996	21.3	21.5	21.9	22.6	23.1	23.4	22.9	23.8	24.1	24.1	23.8	23.5	23.0
1997	22.8	23.0	23.1	24.0	24.3	24.5	23.8	24.3	24.2	23.4	23.7	23.6	23.7
1998	23.9	24.3	24.8	23.7	23.9	24.4	23.5	24.4	24.4	25.2	24.8	24.4	24.3
1999	22.8	23.1	23.5	20.4	20.5	20.6	19.8	20.1	20.2	20.0	19.9	19.8	20.9
2000	20.0	20.0	20.4	20.6	20.6	20.9	20.2	20.5	20.7	20.1	20.0	19.4	20.3
2001	19.2	18.8	19.0	19.1	19.6	19.9	19.6	19.8	19.7	19.2	19.2	18.9	19.3
2002	18.7	18.8	19.0	19.6	19.9	20.2	20.0	20.3	20.1	20.7	20.2	20.0	19.8
2003	19.3	19.5	19.6	20.1	20.2	20.4	19.9	20.4	20.2	20.5	19.9	19.2	19.9

Employment by Industry: Michigan—*Continued*

(Numbers in thousands. Not seasonally adjusted.)

Industry	January	February	March	April	May	June	July	August	September	October	November	December	Annual Average
KALAMAZOO—*Continued*													
Educational and health services													
1990	23.7	23.7	23.8	23.5	23.2	23.1	21.7	21.8	22.4	22.8	23.0	22.9	23.0
1991	21.6	21.7	21.6	21.9	21.6	21.4	20.8	21.2	21.5	21.6	21.8	21.7	21.5
1992	21.7	21.9	21.9	21.4	21.5	21.5	21.1	21.2	21.6	21.9	22.0	21.9	21.6
1993	22.0	22.1	22.2	22.3	22.2	22.2	21.7	21.9	22.2	22.7	22.8	22.8	22.3
1994	22.8	23.0	23.1	23.1	23.0	22.9	22.9	22.9	23.3	23.2	23.2	23.4	23.1
1995	23.0	23.0	23.1	23.0	23.0	22.8	22.7	22.8	23.0	23.3	23.5	23.2	23.0
1996	23.6	23.7	23.7	23.8	24.0	23.7	23.1	23.2	23.5	24.0	24.1	24.1	23.7
1997	23.7	23.9	24.0	23.8	23.9	23.8	23.5	23.7	24.0	24.3	24.2	24.2	23.9
1998	23.4	23.5	23.5	24.4	24.6	24.5	23.6	23.6	23.6	24.0	24.0	24.0	23.9
1999	23.8	24.2	24.2	25.2	25.3	25.1	25.7	25.6	26.0	26.4	26.4	26.5	25.4
2000	26.1	26.2	26.4	26.1	26.2	26.2	26.2	26.4	26.7	26.6	26.7	26.7	26.4
2001	24.5	24.7	24.6	24.8	24.9	24.4	24.4	24.5	25.4	25.9	26.1	25.9	25.0
2002	25.7	25.7	25.8	26.2	26.3	26.3	26.8	27.0	27.2	27.5	27.8	27.5	26.7
2003	28.0	27.9	28.0	28.4	28.4	28.4	26.8	26.7	26.4	27.6	27.6	26.8	27.6
Leisure and hospitality													
1990	15.7	15.9	16.0	16.6	17.4	17.5	17.9	18.0	18.0	17.3	17.1	16.8	17.0
1991	17.7	17.4	18.0	18.2	18.8	18.9	19.4	19.7	19.9	19.7	19.4	19.2	18.9
1992	17.2	17.1	17.4	17.9	18.4	18.6	18.5	18.4	18.2	18.4	18.0	17.7	18.0
1993	17.2	17.6	17.9	18.6	18.9	19.0	19.0	19.2	19.3	19.0	18.5	18.4	18.6
1994	17.5	17.6	18.1	18.5	19.1	19.3	19.6	19.6	19.9	19.4	19.0	18.9	18.9
1995	18.3	18.6	19.0	19.9	20.5	20.9	21.0	21.2	21.1	20.5	20.4	20.6	20.2
1996	17.7	17.7	18.3	18.9	20.0	20.0	19.6	20.0	19.7	19.7	19.4	19.7	19.2
1997	18.4	18.7	19.2	19.5	20.3	20.6	21.0	21.0	20.7	20.4	20.0	19.6	20.0
1998	18.9	18.9	19.3	19.8	20.4	20.4	20.6	20.5	20.5	20.2	19.7	19.6	19.9
1999	20.7	20.9	21.1	20.4	21.1	21.3	21.0	21.2	20.7	20.7	19.9	19.9	20.7
2000	18.8	18.6	19.0	20.0	21.1	21.3	21.3	21.4	21.3	20.8	20.2	19.7	20.3
2001	18.5	18.9	19.2	19.7	20.6	20.8	20.7	21.1	20.7	19.9	19.3	18.9	19.9
2002	19.1	19.4	19.7	20.4	21.6	21.8	21.8	22.0	20.9	20.0	19.4	19.1	20.4
2003	18.5	18.1	18.3	19.1	20.3	20.6	21.2	20.2	20.0	20.2	19.6	18.5	19.6
Other services													
1990	7.1	7.1	7.2	7.1	7.1	7.2	7.3	7.3	7.2	7.3	7.4	7.4	7.2
1991	7.0	7.0	7.0	7.0	7.1	7.0	7.1	7.2	7.1	7.2	7.2	7.3	7.1
1992	7.2	7.3	7.3	7.6	7.6	7.7	7.6	7.6	7.5	7.5	7.5	7.5	7.5
1993	7.4	7.5	7.7	7.8	7.7	7.8	7.8	8.0	7.9	7.9	7.9	8.0	7.8
1994	7.9	8.0	8.1	8.2	8.3	8.2	8.3	8.4	8.4	8.4	8.4	8.4	8.3
1995	8.1	8.3	8.4	8.2	8.2	8.3	8.3	8.3	8.3	8.3	8.3	8.4	8.3
1996	8.4	8.5	8.6	8.6	8.7	8.6	8.4	8.5	8.5	8.6	8.5	8.6	8.5
1997	8.5	8.5	8.6	8.5	8.4	8.4	8.4	8.4	8.3	8.7	8.6	8.6	8.5
1998	8.4	8.5	8.5	8.6	8.7	8.7	8.8	8.8	8.7	8.8	8.9	8.9	8.7
1999	8.8	8.9	9.0	9.0	9.0	9.0	8.7	8.7	8.7	8.6	8.6	8.7	8.8
2000	8.6	8.7	8.8	8.8	8.7	8.8	8.7	8.7	8.8	8.7	8.7	8.8	8.7
2001	8.8	9.0	9.1	9.0	9.0	9.0	8.9	8.9	8.9	8.8	8.9	8.9	8.9
2002	8.8	8.8	8.9	8.9	9.0	9.0	9.4	9.4	9.3	9.4	9.4	9.5	9.2
2003	9.3	9.1	9.3	9.3	9.3	9.5	9.4	9.3	9.3	9.3	9.3	9.2	9.3
Government													
1990	33.1	35.0	35.6	35.4	33.5	33.3	31.7	31.0	34.7	35.5	35.6	35.4	34.2
1991	33.7	35.7	35.7	34.8	33.0	32.3	30.0	29.5	34.9	35.6	36.0	36.5	34.0
1992	34.5	35.9	36.0	34.8	32.8	32.0	29.3	29.3	32.5	35.6	36.0	34.8	33.6
1993	34.5	35.4	35.4	35.2	33.2	32.2	29.3	29.1	33.6	35.4	35.6	35.5	33.7
1994	34.0	35.2	35.7	35.1	32.6	32.0	29.2	29.2	33.8	35.3	35.5	35.3	33.6
1995	34.3	35.4	35.6	35.2	33.3	32.2	29.4	29.0	34.2	35.3	35.5	35.6	33.8
1996	33.9	35.4	35.7	35.4	33.2	32.0	29.2	29.2	34.3	35.7	36.0	35.7	33.8
1997	34.0	35.7	36.0	35.6	33.3	31.9	30.4	30.3	34.9	35.6	35.9	35.9	34.1
1998	34.7	36.1	36.4	35.7	33.6	33.7	30.4	30.6	35.5	36.7	37.0	36.2	34.7
1999	35.3	36.8	36.9	36.5	34.4	33.8	31.1	31.2	34.6	36.0	36.4	36.2	34.9
2000	35.0	36.4	36.4	36.2	34.5	33.3	30.4	30.2	34.7	36.8	37.3	37.2	34.9
2001	37.5	38.8	39.0	37.2	35.5	33.9	30.2	31.9	37.1	38.0	38.2	35.8	36.1
2002	37.0	38.1	37.9	36.4	34.8	33.0	31.5	32.0	36.7	38.0	38.1	37.0	35.9
2003	36.7	37.5	37.4	36.8	34.8	32.9	30.0	30.8	36.8	38.4	38.6	37.5	35.7
Federal government													
1990	5.6	5.7	6.1	6.7	7.0	6.8	6.8	5.9	5.7	5.6	5.6	5.7	6.1
1991	5.6	5.5	5.5	5.5	5.5	5.5	5.6	5.6	5.5	5.5	5.5	5.8	5.6
1992	5.7	5.6	5.6	5.6	5.6	5.6	5.6	5.6	5.6	5.6	5.6	5.6	5.6
1993	5.2	5.2	5.2	5.2	5.2	5.2	5.2	5.3	5.3	5.3	5.3	5.4	5.3
1994	5.3	5.3	5.3	5.3	5.2	5.3	5.3	5.3	5.3	5.2	5.2	5.2	5.3
1995	5.2	5.2	5.2	5.2	5.2	5.2	5.2	5.2	5.2	5.1	5.1	5.2	5.2
1996	5.2	5.1	5.1	5.2	5.2	5.2	5.1	5.2	5.2	5.2	5.2	5.3	5.2
1997	5.0	5.0	5.1	5.0	4.9	4.9	4.9	5.0	5.0	4.9	4.9	5.0	5.0
1998	4.9	4.9	4.9	4.9	4.9	4.9	4.9	4.9	4.9	5.0	5.0	5.0	4.9
1999	5.0	4.9	5.0	4.9	4.8	4.7	4.9	4.9	4.9	4.9	4.9	4.9	4.9
2000	5.0	5.0	5.0	5.3	5.7	5.3	5.2	5.0	4.8	4.8	4.8	4.9	5.1
2001	4.8	4.8	4.8	4.8	4.8	4.8	4.8	4.8	4.8	4.8	4.8	4.8	4.8
2002	4.8	4.8	4.8	4.8	4.8	4.9	4.8	4.9	4.8	4.8	4.8	4.8	4.8
2003	4.8	4.8	4.7	4.7	4.6	4.7	4.8	4.7	4.7	4.7	4.6	4.7	4.7

Employment by Industry: Michigan—*Continued*

(Numbers in thousands. Not seasonally adjusted.)

Industry	January	February	March	April	May	June	July	August	September	October	November	December	Annual Average
KALAMAZOO—*Continued*													
State government													
1990	9.0	9.6	9.4	9.6	6.8	6.8	6.4	6.4	9.7	9.7	9.7	9.5	8.6
1991	9.1	9.7	9.6	9.5	6.7	6.6	6.3	6.0	9.2	9.4	9.3	9.4	8.4
1992	8.9	9.5	9.3	9.4	6.7	6.6	6.3	6.2	7.2	9.4	9.5	8.6	8.1
1993	9.4	9.5	9.2	9.4	6.9	6.8	6.6	6.4	8.5	9.5	9.5	9.7	8.5
1994	8.9	9.4	9.4	9.3	6.8	6.7	6.5	6.3	8.4	9.4	9.4	9.3	8.3
1995	8.9	9.3	9.2	9.3	6.7	6.6	6.4	6.2	8.8	9.3	9.3	9.4	8.3
1996	9.1	9.2	9.1	9.1	6.6	6.5	6.3	6.2	8.4	9.3	9.3	9.0	8.2
1997	8.8	9.3	9.2	9.3	6.6	6.5	6.8	6.9	9.1	9.3	9.4	9.3	8.4
1998	9.2	9.4	9.4	9.3	7.0	7.5	6.7	7.1	9.2	9.7	9.8	9.1	8.6
1999	9.3	9.8	9.7	9.8	7.6	7.8	7.6	7.5	8.3	8.8	8.9	8.9	8.7
2000	8.6	8.8	8.8	8.8	6.8	6.7	6.7	6.4	8.3	9.3	9.6	9.6	8.2
2001	10.1	10.8	10.9	9.6	7.5	7.3	6.2	7.4	9.4	9.8	9.9	7.5	8.9
2002	9.5	9.8	9.7	8.7	6.6	6.4	7.5	7.7	9.2	9.8	9.7	8.7	8.6
2003	9.3	9.6	9.5	9.5	7.3	7.0	6.8	7.2	9.2	9.6	9.8	8.8	8.6
Local government													
1990	18.5	19.7	20.2	19.2	19.7	19.7	18.6	18.7	19.3	20.1	20.3	20.2	19.5
1991	19.0	20.4	20.5	19.8	20.8	20.1	18.2	17.9	20.2	20.7	21.1	21.3	20.0
1992	19.9	20.7	21.2	19.9	20.5	19.8	17.4	17.5	19.7	20.6	20.9	20.6	19.9
1993	20.0	20.8	21.0	20.7	21.1	20.2	17.5	17.4	19.9	20.6	20.8	20.5	20.0
1994	19.9	20.5	21.1	20.5	20.5	20.0	17.5	17.7	20.1	20.7	21.0	20.8	20.0
1995	20.2	20.9	21.2	20.8	21.4	20.4	17.8	17.7	20.1	20.9	21.0	21.0	20.3
1996	19.7	21.1	21.5	21.2	21.4	20.4	17.8	17.9	20.6	21.2	21.6	21.4	20.5
1997	20.2	21.4	21.7	21.3	21.8	20.5	18.7	18.4	20.8	21.4	21.6	21.6	20.8
1998	20.6	21.8	22.1	21.5	21.7	21.3	18.8	18.6	21.4	22.0	22.2	22.1	21.2
1999	21.0	22.1	22.2	21.8	22.0	21.3	18.6	18.8	21.4	22.3	22.6	22.4	21.4
2000	21.4	22.6	22.6	22.1	22.0	21.3	18.5	18.8	21.6	22.7	22.9	22.7	21.6
2001	22.6	23.2	23.3	22.8	23.2	21.8	19.2	19.7	22.9	23.4	23.5	23.5	22.4
2002	22.7	23.5	23.4	22.9	23.4	21.7	19.2	19.4	22.7	23.4	23.6	23.5	22.5
2003	22.6	23.1	23.2	22.6	22.9	21.2	18.4	18.9	22.9	24.1	24.2	24.0	22.3
LANSING-EAST LANSING													
Total nonfarm													
1990	209.7	213.5	218.3	217.4	222.0	220.6	211.2	210.7	214.0	221.6	221.6	217.2	216.5
1991	209.0	214.9	214.7	214.9	214.6	210.6	203.6	206.4	210.0	220.2	220.5	218.5	213.2
1992	213.4	214.2	215.2	215.4	218.6	218.1	209.0	208.5	216.2	217.9	219.5	218.6	215.4
1993	213.9	209.3	214.7	215.8	218.5	212.9	207.6	201.7	215.7	219.4	219.8	220.3	214.1
1994	215.1	217.1	218.4	219.7	222.0	217.7	213.4	214.4	223.2	225.3	228.2	228.4	220.2
1995	215.9	223.9	224.6	226.7	229.0	222.6	219.6	220.6	227.8	230.8	232.8	233.7	225.7
1996	224.8	228.7	222.0	230.4	234.2	228.9	223.6	223.5	231.6	235.4	236.7	236.1	229.7
1997	227.8	231.3	232.5	233.3	235.2	228.6	224.8	229.6	233.2	235.8	236.6	236.8	232.1
1998	231.5	231.9	232.4	235.4	233.5	231.7	217.2	227.2	235.2	239.3	240.6	240.0	233.0
1999	226.1	234.4	232.8	237.1	235.1	231.4	229.7	229.9	234.8	240.3	241.6	241.2	234.5
2000	229.1	236.0	237.8	240.7	239.9	236.1	232.8	232.4	240.8	243.5	244.0	242.8	238.0
2001	237.6	240.5	242.3	244.5	244.3	240.9	237.9	237.4	244.0	245.1	246.4	246.2	242.3
2002	238.3	240.2	241.8	244.0	245.2	241.3	237.6	238.9	246.4	245.9	244.9	244.3	242.4
2003	236.4	238.4	238.7	240.4	241.8	238.7	234.8	235.5	243.7	242.2	244.8	241.3	239.7
Total private													
1990	142.3	141.8	146.5	147.5	150.1	151.1	149.3	148.8	149.4	150.0	149.9	146.8	147.8
1991	140.1	143.0	142.9	144.1	143.0	141.2	140.9	144.2	148.0	148.2	147.9	147.4	144.2
1992	143.9	143.3	144.2	145.4	147.6	148.7	147.5	147.4	148.6	147.2	148.1	148.7	146.7
1993	147.0	140.6	145.9	148.1	149.3	150.4	148.6	143.4	150.1	150.5	151.0	151.5	148.0
1994	149.0	148.8	149.8	151.6	154.2	155.6	154.7	155.9	157.5	157.2	158.7	159.2	154.4
1995	155.3	155.9	156.0	158.3	160.4	161.5	160.0	161.7	162.9	162.9	163.7	164.5	160.3
1996	158.9	159.7	153.3	161.6	164.6	165.5	163.5	164.9	164.9	166.1	167.1	166.9	163.1
1997	161.6	162.7	163.6	165.2	166.7	167.6	166.3	167.3	167.8	167.8	168.4	168.6	166.1
1998	163.9	164.2	165.3	168.1	169.8	170.6	159.0	169.9	170.1	171.4	172.5	172.2	168.1
1999	166.3	166.5	166.9	169.1	169.7	170.5	170.4	171.2	170.7	171.9	171.9	171.9	169.8
2000	167.4	167.4	169.0	171.9	172.5	173.6	171.9	173.2	173.7	174.0	174.0	173.5	171.8
2001	166.8	166.3	167.4	168.2	169.3	170.4	168.8	169.5	169.3	168.3	169.3	169.2	168.6
2002	164.2	164.0	165.5	167.1	169.4	171.1	169.0	170.7	171.2	169.6	169.8	169.4	168.4
2003	164.0	163.5	163.8	165.5	168.2	169.8	169.4	172.0	170.8	167.5	169.8	168.9	167.8
Goods-producing													
1990	35.2	36.5	39.2	39.3	39.9	40.8	40.4	39.9	39.8	40.0	39.6	36.5	38.9
1991	32.8	35.9	35.5	36.5	34.2	31.6	32.9	34.9	38.3	38.5	38.1	37.6	35.6
1992	35.5	35.2	35.3	37.1	37.4	37.7	37.8	38.0	37.4	36.0	36.8	37.0	36.8
1993	37.6	31.7	35.9	35.5	36.0	36.5	35.9	29.9	35.9	35.7	35.8	36.2	35.2
1994	35.8	35.5	35.7	36.0	37.0	37.6	37.3	38.0	38.1	37.9	38.0	37.9	37.1
1995	36.9	36.5	36.6	37.8	38.6	39.4	38.7	39.2	38.7	37.9	37.5	38.0	38.0
1996	37.7	38.0	33.5	38.6	39.5	39.8	39.5	40.7	39.6	39.8	39.8	38.9	38.8
1997	38.0	38.2	38.3	39.3	39.9	40.3	40.1	40.8	39.6	39.2	39.2	38.9	39.3
1998	38.1	38.1	38.7	39.6	40.2	40.7	30.2	41.0	40.5	40.1	40.2	39.9	38.9
1999	38.1	38.0	37.9	38.4	38.8	39.4	39.1	39.4	39.1	38.8	38.0	37.6	38.6
2000	37.3	37.2	37.7	38.9	39.3	40.2	40.0	40.5	40.2	39.8	39.0	38.5	39.1
2001	36.2	35.9	36.1	36.1	36.4	36.6	36.5	36.0	36.1	35.1	34.6	34.3	35.8
2002	32.9	33.0	32.9	33.4	34.1	35.0	34.6	35.1	34.9	34.3	34.0	33.5	34.0
2003	32.3	32.0	31.9	32.2	33.7	34.5	34.3	35.2	34.2	30.2	33.9	33.6	33.2

Employment by Industry: Michigan—*Continued*

(Numbers in thousands. Not seasonally adjusted.)

Industry	January	February	March	April	May	June	July	August	September	October	November	December	Annual Average
LANSING-EAST LANSING *—Continued*													
Construction and mining													
1990	6.0	5.6	5.8	6.2	6.8	7.2	7.3	7.3	7.1	7.0	6.7	6.3	6.6
1991	5.3	5.1	5.1	5.7	6.2	6.6	6.7	6.8	6.8	6.7	6.4	5.8	6.1
1992	5.5	5.3	5.3	5.5	6.0	6.4	6.6	6.7	6.5	6.5	6.2	6.0	6.0
1993	5.6	5.4	5.5	6.0	6.5	6.7	6.9	6.9	6.7	6.5	6.2	5.9	6.2
1994	5.3	5.2	5.4	5.8	6.5	6.8	7.2	7.1	7.2	7.1	7.0	6.6	6.4
1995	5.9	5.7	5.8	6.3	6.7	7.2	7.4	7.5	7.5	7.6	7.5	7.2	6.9
1996	6.7	6.7	6.7	7.3	8.1	8.4	8.8	8.8	8.6	8.8	8.6	8.1	8.0
1997	7.3	7.5	7.5	8.0	8.7	8.9	9.2	9.2	8.8	8.5	8.3	8.0	8.3
1998	7.6	7.5	7.6	8.3	9.0	9.4	9.7	9.8	9.4	9.4	9.2	8.8	8.8
1999	7.5	7.6	7.7	8.8	9.2	9.7	9.9	10.1	9.8	9.9	9.7	9.2	9.1
2000	8.5	8.4	8.8	9.7	10.3	10.7	10.9	11.1	10.9	10.8	10.3	9.9	10.0
2001	9.1	9.0	9.3	9.8	10.2	10.5	10.9	10.8	10.7	10.3	9.9	9.6	10.0
2002	8.8	8.7	8.7	9.4	10.1	10.4	10.4	10.5	10.3	10.0	9.5	8.9	9.6
2003	8.2	7.8	7.8	8.4	9.3	9.8	10.3	10.4	10.2	10.2	10.2	10.0	9.4
Manufacturing													
1990	29.2	30.9	33.4	33.1	33.1	33.6	33.1	32.6	32.7	33.0	32.9	30.2	32.3
1991	27.5	30.8	30.4	30.8	28.0	25.0	26.2	28.1	31.5	31.8	31.7	31.8	29.5
1992	30.0	29.9	30.0	31.6	31.4	31.3	31.2	31.3	30.9	29.5	30.6	31.0	30.7
1993	32.0	26.3	30.4	29.5	29.5	29.8	29.0	23.0	29.2	29.2	29.6	30.3	29.0
1994	30.5	30.3	30.3	30.2	30.5	30.8	30.1	30.9	30.9	30.8	31.0	31.3	30.6
1995	31.0	30.8	30.8	31.5	31.9	32.2	31.3	31.7	31.2	30.3	30.0	30.8	31.1
1996	31.0	31.3	26.8	31.3	31.4	31.4	30.7	31.9	31.0	31.0	31.2	30.8	30.8
1997	30.7	30.7	30.8	31.3	31.2	31.4	30.9	31.6	30.8	30.7	30.9	30.9	31.0
1998	30.5	30.6	31.1	31.3	31.2	31.3	20.5	31.2	31.1	30.7	31.0	31.1	30.1
1999	30.6	30.4	30.2	29.6	29.6	29.7	29.2	29.3	29.3	28.9	28.3	28.4	29.5
2000	28.8	28.8	28.9	29.2	29.0	29.5	29.1	29.4	29.3	29.0	28.7	28.6	29.0
2001	27.1	26.9	26.8	26.3	26.2	26.1	25.6	25.2	25.4	24.8	24.7	24.7	25.8
2002	24.1	24.3	24.2	24.0	24.0	24.6	24.2	24.6	24.6	24.3	24.5	24.6	24.3
2003	24.1	24.2	24.1	23.8	24.4	24.7	24.0	24.8	24.0	20.0	23.7	23.6	23.8
Service-providing													
1990	174.5	177.0	179.1	178.1	182.1	179.8	170.8	170.8	174.2	181.6	182.0	180.7	177.6
1991	176.2	179.0	179.2	178.4	180.4	179.0	170.7	171.5	171.7	181.7	182.4	180.9	177.6
1992	177.9	179.0	179.9	178.3	181.2	180.4	171.2	170.5	178.8	181.9	182.7	181.6	178.6
1993	176.3	177.6	178.8	180.3	182.5	176.4	171.7	171.8	179.8	183.7	184.0	184.1	178.9
1994	179.3	181.6	182.7	183.7	185.0	180.1	176.1	176.4	185.1	187.4	190.2	190.5	183.2
1995	179.0	187.4	188.0	188.9	190.4	183.2	180.9	181.4	189.1	192.9	195.3	195.7	187.7
1996	187.1	190.7	188.5	191.8	194.7	189.1	184.1	182.8	192.0	195.6	196.9	197.2	190.9
1997	189.8	193.1	194.2	194.0	195.3	188.3	184.7	188.8	193.6	196.6	197.4	197.9	192.8
1998	193.4	193.8	193.7	195.8	193.3	191.0	187.0	186.2	194.7	199.2	200.4	200.1	194.1
1999	188.0	196.4	194.9	198.7	196.3	192.0	190.6	190.5	195.7	201.5	203.6	203.6	196.0
2000	191.8	198.8	200.1	201.8	200.6	195.9	192.8	191.9	200.6	203.7	205.0	204.3	198.9
2001	201.4	204.6	206.2	208.4	207.9	204.3	201.4	201.4	207.9	210.0	211.8	211.9	206.4
2002	205.4	207.2	208.9	210.6	211.1	206.3	203.0	203.8	211.5	211.6	210.9	210.8	208.4
2003	204.1	206.4	206.8	208.2	208.1	204.2	200.5	200.3	209.5	212.0	210.9	207.7	206.6
Trade, transportation, and utilities													
1990	36.3	35.2	35.5	35.7	35.8	36.5	36.1	36.0	36.0	36.9	37.7	38.2	36.3
1991	35.1	34.3	34.2	34.2	34.5	34.7	33.7	33.9	34.0	34.6	35.3	35.7	34.5
1992	35.0	34.3	34.3	33.6	34.0	34.3	33.9	33.8	34.5	34.1	34.9	35.5	34.4
1993	34.4	33.8	33.8	34.7	34.9	34.9	34.1	33.9	34.1	34.5	35.4	35.9	34.5
1994	34.9	34.3	34.4	34.8	35.4	35.9	35.5	35.8	36.2	36.5	37.4	38.0	35.8
1995	36.1	35.7	35.5	35.6	35.8	36.0	36.3	36.5	36.9	37.2	38.2	38.7	36.5
1996	36.5	36.0	35.3	35.8	36.4	36.6	36.9	36.4	36.6	37.4	38.5	39.1	36.8
1997	37.2	36.7	36.8	36.2	36.2	36.4	36.3	35.9	36.7	37.4	38.3	39.1	36.9
1998	37.6	37.1	37.0	37.3	37.6	37.6	37.7	37.6	37.7	38.1	39.4	39.9	37.9
1999	38.1	37.7	37.3	37.2	37.1	37.2	37.4	37.5	37.4	37.8	38.7	39.5	37.7
2000	37.9	37.6	37.8	38.4	38.5	38.5	38.3	38.7	39.0	40.0	41.0	41.6	38.9
2001	40.2	39.6	39.4	39.3	39.3	39.6	39.0	39.3	39.2	39.6	40.7	40.7	39.7
2002	38.7	38.0	38.6	38.4	38.6	39.0	38.3	38.5	38.9	38.7	39.5	39.9	38.8
2003	38.0	37.5	37.3	37.4	37.9	38.2	38.5	38.6	38.6	39.2	39.5	39.7	38.4
Wholesale trade													
1990	5.2	5.2	5.2	5.3	5.3	5.4	5.4	5.3	5.3	5.4	5.5	5.4	5.3
1991	5.4	5.4	5.5	5.2	5.3	5.3	5.2	5.2	5.2	5.4	5.4	5.3	5.3
1992	5.5	5.4	5.5	5.5	5.5	5.6	5.6	5.5	5.6	5.5	5.4	5.4	5.5
1993	4.9	4.9	4.9	5.2	5.2	5.2	5.0	5.0	5.0	5.1	5.1	5.1	5.1
1994	5.1	5.1	5.2	5.1	5.2	5.3	5.3	5.3	5.3	5.4	5.3	5.3	5.2
1995	5.1	5.2	5.2	5.2	5.2	5.3	5.4	5.3	5.3	5.3	5.4	5.5	5.3
1996	5.5	5.4	5.4	5.4	5.6	5.7	6.0	5.6	5.5	5.5	5.6	5.6	5.6
1997	5.2	5.1	5.2	5.1	5.1	5.2	5.3	5.2	5.2	5.6	5.6	5.7	5.3
1998	5.3	5.3	5.3	5.4	5.5	5.6	5.5	5.4	5.4	5.4	5.5	5.5	5.4
1999	5.4	5.4	5.3	5.6	5.6	5.7	5.7	5.6	5.6	5.6	5.6	5.7	5.6
2000	5.5	5.6	5.7	5.8	5.9	5.8	5.9	5.8	5.8	5.7	5.7	5.8	5.8
2001	6.0	6.0	6.0	6.1	6.2	6.2	6.2	6.1	6.1	6.0	6.0	6.0	6.1
2002	5.8	5.8	5.8	5.9	5.9	6.0	5.9	5.9	5.8	5.8	5.8	5.8	5.9
2003	5.6	5.6	5.6	5.8	5.9	5.9	6.1	6.1	6.0	6.3	6.2	6.1	5.9

Employment by Industry: Michigan—*Continued*

(Numbers in thousands. Not seasonally adjusted.)

Industry	January	February	March	April	May	June	July	August	September	October	November	December	Annual Average
LANSING-EAST LANSING *—Continued*													
Retail trade													
1990	25.3	24.3	24.6	24.7	24.8	25.2	24.8	24.8	24.9	25.6	26.2	26.8	25.2
1991	24.0	23.3	23.1	23.3	23.5	23.6	23.0	23.2	23.2	23.4	24.1	24.5	23.5
1992	23.5	23.0	22.9	22.4	22.7	22.8	22.4	22.5	23.0	22.9	23.8	24.3	23.0
1993	23.8	23.3	23.3	23.7	23.9	23.8	23.4	23.2	23.3	23.8	24.6	25.0	23.8
1994	24.1	23.5	23.5	23.9	24.3	24.7	24.5	24.8	25.2	25.4	26.4	27.1	24.8
1995	25.5	25.0	24.9	24.9	25.1	25.2	25.3	25.7	26.2	26.3	27.2	27.7	25.8
1996	25.6	25.2	24.7	25.0	25.3	25.4	25.3	25.4	25.7	26.5	27.4	28.1	25.8
1997	26.7	26.4	26.4	25.8	25.8	25.9	25.8	26.0	26.3	26.5	27.4	28.1	26.4
1998	26.9	26.5	26.4	26.6	26.7	26.6	26.6	26.6	26.7	26.9	28.0	28.5	26.9
1999	27.1	26.7	26.5	26.1	26.0	25.9	25.9	26.1	26.1	26.4	27.2	27.9	26.5
2000	26.6	26.2	26.3	26.8	26.8	26.8	26.3	26.6	26.9	27.8	28.8	29.3	27.1
2001	28.1	27.6	27.4	27.0	26.8	26.9	26.4	26.7	26.6	26.9	28.0	28.1	27.2
2002	26.5	25.9	26.5	26.2	26.3	26.5	25.8	26.0	26.6	26.4	27.2	27.6	26.5
2003	26.1	25.6	25.4	25.3	25.7	26.0	26.1	26.3	26.4	26.6	27.1	27.4	26.2
Transportation and utilities													
1990	5.8	5.7	5.7	5.7	5.7	5.9	5.9	5.9	5.8	5.9	6.0	6.0	5.8
1991	5.7	5.6	5.6	5.7	5.7	5.8	5.5	5.5	5.6	5.8	5.8	5.9	5.7
1992	6.0	5.9	5.9	5.7	5.8	5.9	5.9	5.8	5.9	5.7	5.7	5.8	5.8
1993	5.7	5.6	5.6	5.8	5.8	5.9	5.7	5.7	5.8	5.6	5.7	5.8	5.7
1994	5.7	5.7	5.7	5.8	5.9	5.9	5.7	5.7	5.7	5.7	5.7	5.6	5.7
1995	5.5	5.5	5.4	5.5	5.5	5.5	5.6	5.5	5.4	5.6	5.6	5.5	5.5
1996	5.4	5.4	5.2	5.4	5.5	5.5	5.6	5.4	5.4	5.4	5.5	5.4	5.4
1997	5.3	5.2	5.2	5.3	5.3	5.3	5.2	4.7	5.2	5.3	5.3	5.3	5.2
1998	5.4	5.3	5.3	5.3	5.4	5.4	5.6	5.6	5.6	5.8	5.9	5.9	5.5
1999	5.6	5.6	5.5	5.5	5.5	5.6	5.8	5.8	5.7	5.8	5.9	5.9	5.7
2000	5.8	5.8	5.8	5.8	5.8	5.9	6.1	6.3	6.3	6.5	6.5	6.5	6.1
2001	6.1	6.0	6.0	6.2	6.3	6.5	6.4	6.5	6.5	6.7	6.7	6.6	6.4
2002	6.4	6.3	6.3	6.3	6.4	6.5	6.6	6.6	6.5	6.5	6.5	6.5	6.5
2003	6.3	6.3	6.3	6.3	6.3	6.3	6.3	6.2	6.2	6.3	6.2	6.2	6.3
Information													
1990	3.5	3.4	3.4	3.5	3.5	3.5	3.6	3.5	3.5	3.5	3.5	3.5	3.5
1991	3.3	3.3	3.3	3.3	3.3	3.3	3.4	3.5	3.4	3.4	3.4	3.4	3.4
1992	3.5	3.4	3.4	3.4	3.4	3.4	3.4	3.4	3.3	3.3	3.3	3.4	3.4
1993	3.4	3.3	3.2	3.4	3.4	3.5	3.5	3.5	3.4	3.3	3.4	3.4	3.4
1994	3.4	3.4	3.4	3.4	3.4	3.4	3.4	3.4	3.3	3.3	3.4	3.5	3.4
1995	3.5	3.5	3.5	3.5	3.5	3.6	3.6	3.6	3.6	3.6	3.6	3.7	3.6
1996	3.8	3.8	3.7	3.6	3.7	3.8	3.9	3.8	3.7	3.6	3.7	3.8	3.7
1997	3.7	3.7	3.7	3.7	3.8	3.7	3.9	3.9	3.9	3.7	3.7	3.8	3.8
1998	4.0	3.9	4.0	3.9	3.9	3.9	4.2	4.1	4.2	4.1	4.1	4.1	4.0
1999	3.9	3.9	3.8	3.6	3.7	3.6	3.8	3.8	3.7	3.7	3.8	3.8	3.8
2000	3.9	3.9	3.9	3.9	3.9	3.9	4.0	3.9	3.8	3.7	3.7	3.8	3.9
2001	3.8	3.5	3.5	3.6	3.5	3.6	3.6	3.5	3.5	3.5	3.6	3.7	3.6
2002	3.5	3.5	3.5	3.6	3.7	3.8	3.7	3.8	3.8	3.7	3.8	3.9	3.7
2003	3.8	3.8	3.9	3.5	3.5	3.5	3.5	3.5	3.5	3.5	3.5	3.5	3.6
Financial activities													
1990	12.0	11.7	11.9	11.3	11.3	11.5	11.7	11.5	11.6	11.4	11.4	11.4	11.6
1991	11.0	11.0	11.0	11.4	11.6	11.7	11.5	11.7	11.6	11.0	11.0	10.9	11.3
1992	11.3	11.2	11.3	10.8	10.9	11.1	11.0	11.0	10.9	10.8	10.8	10.9	11.0
1993	10.1	9.9	9.9	10.1	10.1	10.3	10.4	10.4	10.5	10.3	10.4	10.5	10.2
1994	10.6	10.6	10.6	10.7	10.7	10.8	11.0	11.0	10.9	10.7	10.7	10.8	10.8
1995	10.9	10.9	10.9	11.0	11.0	11.2	11.3	11.3	11.3	11.0	11.1	11.3	11.1
1996	11.0	11.0	10.8	11.0	11.1	11.3	11.5	11.4	11.3	11.4	11.4	11.6	11.2
1997	11.4	11.5	11.5	11.3	11.4	11.6	11.7	11.7	11.5	11.8	11.8	11.9	11.6
1998	12.4	12.4	12.5	12.1	12.2	12.3	12.2	12.3	12.1	12.2	12.3	12.4	12.3
1999	12.4	12.4	13.0	12.9	12.9	12.9	13.2	13.2	13.0	13.5	13.6	13.6	13.1
2000	13.7	13.6	13.6	13.7	13.7	13.9	14.1	14.0	13.9	14.0	14.1	14.1	13.9
2001	13.8	13.9	13.9	14.1	14.3	14.4	14.4	14.5	14.2	14.3	14.5	14.5	14.2
2002	14.3	14.2	14.2	14.4	14.7	14.9	15.2	15.3	15.1	15.2	15.3	15.4	14.9
2003	15.3	15.3	15.3	15.6	15.8	16.0	16.5	17.2	17.0	17.0	17.0	16.9	16.2
Professional and business services													
1990	12.7	12.6	13.2	13.6	14.6	13.4	13.4	13.6	13.7	12.4	11.9	11.4	13.0
1991	13.8	13.8	13.7	13.8	13.9	14.4	15.4	15.6	15.6	15.7	15.2	14.9	14.7
1992	14.6	14.9	15.4	16.1	16.6	17.0	16.8	16.7	17.0	17.6	17.1	17.1	16.4
1993	17.1	17.4	18.1	18.3	18.4	18.6	18.5	19.5	19.6	20.1	19.5	19.2	18.7
1994	18.7	18.9	19.3	19.8	19.9	20.0	20.1	20.4	20.6	20.9	21.0	21.0	20.1
1995	20.6	21.1	21.3	21.3	21.5	21.6	21.2	22.3	22.6	23.1	23.1	22.8	21.9
1996	21.6	21.6	21.6	22.7	23.1	23.6	21.7	22.7	22.9	22.8	22.6	22.5	22.5
1997	21.8	22.6	22.9	23.2	23.3	23.8	23.6	24.3	24.5	24.3	24.2	24.2	23.6
1998	21.0	21.2	21.5	22.1	22.2	22.5	22.6	23.1	23.4	24.1	24.1	23.7	22.6
1999	23.2	23.2	23.4	25.2	25.3	25.8	25.4	25.8	25.6	25.8	25.5	25.4	25.0
2000	23.1	23.0	23.5	23.6	23.5	23.8	23.3	23.6	23.6	23.2	23.0	22.8	23.3
2001	22.7	22.8	23.3	22.9	22.9	23.2	22.8	23.3	23.2	22.8	22.6	22.4	22.9
2002	22.1	22.2	22.7	22.9	22.9	23.2	22.3	22.8	22.6	22.7	22.5	22.5	22.6
2003	21.5	21.6	21.9	22.1	21.7	22.1	21.2	21.4	21.4	21.3	21.1	21.0	21.5

Employment by Industry: Michigan—*Continued*

(Numbers in thousands. Not seasonally adjusted.)

Industry	January	February	March	April	May	June	July	August	September	October	November	December	Annual Average
LANSING-EAST LANSING —*Continued*													
Educational and health services													
1990	18.6	18.5	18.8	19.0	19.0	19.1	18.8	19.2	19.6	19.9	20.0	20.1	19.2
1991	19.6	19.9	20.1	19.5	19.4	19.3	18.8	19.2	19.5	19.8	19.8	19.7	19.6
1992	19.7	19.7	19.7	19.6	19.6	19.3	19.5	19.5	20.0	20.1	20.1	20.2	19.8
1993	20.1	20.1	20.2	20.8	20.8	20.8	20.6	20.6	21.0	21.1	21.2	21.2	20.7
1994	21.2	21.3	21.4	21.2	21.2	21.1	20.9	20.8	21.2	21.4	21.6	21.6	21.2
1995	21.5	21.6	21.7	21.9	22.1	22.2	21.8	21.8	22.4	22.6	22.8	22.8	22.1
1996	22.0	22.3	21.8	22.4	22.5	22.3	22.2	22.1	22.6	23.0	23.1	23.1	22.5
1997	22.5	22.7	22.8	23.0	22.8	22.5	22.3	22.4	22.9	23.2	23.2	23.3	22.8
1998	22.9	23.0	23.0	23.8	23.8	23.4	22.7	22.6	22.9	23.5	23.6	23.5	23.2
1999	23.4	23.6	23.6	23.3	23.2	23.0	23.0	23.1	23.5	23.6	23.8	23.7	23.4
2000	23.9	24.1	24.3	24.2	24.1	23.9	23.0	23.1	23.5	23.9	24.0	23.9	23.8
2001	22.1	22.3	22.6	22.7	22.9	22.8	22.7	22.9	23.0	23.2	23.2	23.4	22.8
2002	23.4	23.4	23.5	23.7	24.0	24.0	23.8	24.0	24.1	23.8	23.9	23.9	23.8
2003	24.3	24.1	24.1	24.6	24.7	24.5	24.6	24.9	25.0	25.4	25.2	25.0	24.7
Leisure and hospitality													
1990	15.5	15.4	15.7	16.3	17.2	17.4	16.4	16.4	16.4	16.5	16.4	16.5	16.3
1991	15.9	16.0	16.3	16.5	17.2	17.3	16.7	16.9	17.2	16.4	16.4	16.5	16.6
1992	15.4	15.5	15.7	15.7	16.6	16.8	16.1	16.1	16.4	16.2	16.2	15.9	16.1
1993	15.5	15.6	15.9	16.3	16.7	16.7	16.8	16.9	17.0	16.7	16.5	16.3	16.4
1994	15.7	15.9	16.1	16.7	17.5	17.5	17.4	17.4	18.0	17.3	17.5	17.3	17.0
1995	16.9	17.6	17.4	18.2	18.7	18.2	17.9	17.9	18.3	18.2	18.2	17.9	18.0
1996	17.1	17.6	17.3	18.0	18.6	18.3	18.2	18.3	18.8	18.4	18.1	18.1	18.1
1997	17.3	17.6	17.8	18.7	19.6	19.4	18.4	18.3	18.9	18.0	17.7	17.3	18.3
1998	18.0	18.5	18.5	19.2	19.8	19.9	19.1	19.1	19.3	19.1	18.7	18.6	19.0
1999	17.3	17.6	17.8	18.4	18.6	18.4	18.5	18.4	18.5	18.8	18.7	18.5	18.3
2000	17.8	18.0	18.2	19.1	19.3	19.0	18.8	19.0	19.4	19.2	19.0	18.7	18.8
2001	17.2	17.4	17.6	18.4	18.8	18.8	18.7	19.0	19.2	18.9	19.1	19.2	18.5
2002	18.4	18.6	19.0	19.5	20.1	19.9	19.7	19.9	20.6	19.9	19.7	19.2	19.5
2003	18.0	18.3	18.4	19.2	19.9	19.9	19.8	20.3	20.3	20.0	18.7	18.5	19.3
Other services													
1990	8.5	8.5	8.8	8.8	8.8	8.9	8.9	8.7	8.8	9.4	9.4	9.2	8.9
1991	8.6	8.8	8.8	8.9	8.9	8.9	8.5	8.5	8.4	8.8	8.7	8.7	8.7
1992	8.9	9.1	9.1	9.1	9.1	9.1	9.0	8.9	9.1	9.1	8.9	8.7	9.0
1993	8.8	8.8	8.9	9.0	9.0	9.1	8.8	8.7	8.6	8.8	8.8	8.8	8.8
1994	8.7	8.9	8.9	9.0	9.1	9.3	9.1	9.1	9.2	9.2	9.1	9.1	9.1
1995	8.9	9.0	9.1	9.0	9.2	9.3	9.2	9.1	9.1	9.3	9.2	9.3	9.1
1996	9.2	9.4	9.3	9.5	9.7	9.8	9.6	9.5	9.4	9.7	9.9	9.8	9.6
1997	9.7	9.7	9.8	9.8	9.7	9.9	10.0	10.0	9.8	10.2	10.3	10.1	9.9
1998	9.9	10.0	10.1	10.1	10.1	10.3	10.3	10.1	10.0	10.2	10.1	10.1	10.1
1999	9.9	10.1	10.1	10.1	10.1	10.2	10.0	10.0	9.9	9.9	9.8	9.8	10.0
2000	9.8	10.0	10.0	10.1	10.2	10.4	10.4	10.4	10.3	10.2	10.2	10.1	10.2
2001	10.8	10.9	11.0	11.1	11.2	11.4	11.1	11.0	10.9	10.9	11.0	11.0	11.0
2002	10.9	11.1	11.1	11.2	11.3	11.3	11.4	11.3	11.2	11.3	11.1	11.1	11.2
2003	10.8	10.9	11.0	10.9	11.0	11.1	11.0	10.9	10.8	10.9	10.9	10.7	10.9
Government													
1990	67.4	71.7	71.8	69.9	71.9	69.5	61.9	61.9	64.6	71.6	71.7	70.4	68.7
1991	68.9	71.9	71.8	70.8	71.6	69.4	62.7	62.2	62.0	72.0	72.6	71.1	68.9
1992	69.5	70.9	71.0	70.0	71.0	69.4	61.5	61.1	67.6	70.7	71.4	69.9	68.7
1993	66.9	68.7	68.8	67.7	69.2	62.5	59.0	58.3	65.6	68.9	68.8	68.8	66.1
1994	66.1	68.3	68.6	68.1	67.8	62.1	58.7	58.5	65.7	68.1	69.5	69.2	65.9
1995	60.6	68.0	68.6	68.4	68.6	61.1	59.6	58.9	64.9	67.9	69.1	69.2	65.4
1996	65.9	69.0	68.7	68.8	69.6	63.4	60.1	58.6	66.7	69.3	69.6	69.2	66.6
1997	66.2	68.6	68.9	68.1	68.5	61.0	58.5	62.3	65.4	68.0	68.2	68.2	66.0
1998	67.6	67.7	67.1	67.3	63.7	61.1	58.2	57.3	65.1	67.9	68.1	67.8	64.9
1999	59.8	67.9	65.9	68.0	65.4	60.9	59.3	58.7	64.1	68.4	69.7	69.3	64.8
2000	61.7	68.6	68.8	68.8	67.4	62.5	60.9	59.2	67.1	69.5	70.0	69.3	66.2
2001	70.8	74.2	74.9	76.3	75.0	70.5	69.1	67.9	74.7	76.8	77.1	77.0	73.7
2002	74.1	76.2	76.3	76.9	75.8	70.2	68.6	68.2	75.2	76.3	75.1	74.9	74.0
2003	72.4	74.9	74.9	74.9	73.6	68.9	65.4	63.5	72.9	74.7	75.0	72.4	72.0
Federal government													
1990	3.2	3.2	3.2	3.4	3.7	3.5	3.5	3.3	3.2	3.2	3.1	3.2	3.3
1991	3.1	3.1	3.1	3.1	3.1	3.2	3.2	3.2	3.2	3.2	3.2	3.3	3.2
1992	3.2	3.2	3.2	3.2	3.2	3.2	3.2	3.1	3.1	3.1	3.1	3.2	3.2
1993	3.1	3.0	3.0	3.1	3.1	3.1	3.1	3.1	3.0	3.1	3.1	3.2	3.1
1994	3.1	3.1	3.1	3.1	3.1	3.2	3.1	3.1	3.1	3.1	3.1	3.4	3.1
1995	3.2	3.2	3.2	3.2	3.2	3.3	3.2	3.2	3.2	3.2	3.2	3.4	3.2
1996	3.2	3.2	3.2	3.2	3.2	3.2	3.2	3.2	3.2	3.2	3.2	3.4	3.2
1997	2.9	2.9	2.8	2.9	2.8	2.8	2.8	2.8	2.8	2.8	2.8	2.9	2.8
1998	2.9	2.9	2.9	2.9	2.9	2.9	2.8	2.8	2.8	2.8	2.9	3.0	2.9
1999	3.0	2.9	3.0	3.0	2.9	2.9	2.9	3.0	2.9	2.9	2.9	3.0	2.9
2000	3.1	3.0	3.0	3.1	3.5	3.2	3.1	3.0	2.9	2.8	2.9	2.9	3.0
2001	2.9	2.9	2.9	2.9	2.9	2.9	2.9	2.9	2.9	2.9	2.8	2.9	2.9
2002	2.8	2.8	2.8	2.8	2.8	2.9	2.8	2.8	2.8	2.8	2.8	2.8	2.8
2003	2.8	2.8	2.8	2.8	2.8	2.8	2.8	2.8	2.8	2.8	2.8	2.8	2.8

Employment by Industry: Michigan—*Continued*

(Numbers in thousands. Not seasonally adjusted.)

Industry	January	February	March	April	May	June	July	August	September	October	November	December	Annual Average
LANSING-EAST LANSING *—Continued*													
State government													
1990	43.1	45.2	45.1	44.2	44.7	43.0	38.3	38.7	40.1	44.9	45.0	43.3	43.0
1991	43.0	44.8	44.6	44.1	44.3	43.3	39.0	38.7	37.1	44.6	44.9	43.5	42.7
1992	42.9	43.4	43.2	42.8	43.2	43.0	38.0	37.8	42.3	43.3	43.6	43.2	42.2
1993	42.4	43.0	43.0	42.9	43.1	36.9	37.4	37.1	42.4	43.9	43.4	43.4	41.6
1994	42.2	43.2	43.2	43.0	42.1	37.1	37.7	37.2	42.5	43.2	44.1	43.8	41.6
1995	36.0	42.6	43.0	43.0	42.8	36.9	37.3	36.8	40.7	42.7	43.8	43.5	40.8
1996	42.0	43.5	43.1	43.5	43.6	38.0	38.3	37.6	42.5	44.0	44.1	43.6	42.0
1997	42.1	43.7	43.7	43.3	43.1	36.2	37.0	37.2	41.4	43.2	43.4	43.2	41.5
1998	43.3	43.1	42.2	42.9	38.6	36.8	37.3	36.4	42.0	43.2	43.4	42.9	41.0
1999	36.7	42.9	40.8	43.3	41.0	36.9	37.9	37.2	40.6	43.6	44.7	44.0	40.8
2000	37.6	43.3	43.3	43.5	41.3	37.7	39.0	37.7	42.8	44.3	44.5	43.9	41.6
2001	46.7	48.4	48.9	50.8	49.0	45.1	46.5	45.1	49.8	51.0	51.1	51.0	48.6
2002	49.8	50.4	50.1	50.9	49.0	45.4	46.4	46.0	49.7	50.3	48.8	48.5	48.8
2003	47.8	48.6	48.4	48.8	47.0	43.0	43.8	42.9	48.4	49.6	49.7	47.2	47.1
Local government													
1990	21.1	23.3	23.5	22.3	23.4	23.0	20.2	20.0	21.4	23.6	23.6	23.9	22.4
1991	22.8	24.0	24.1	23.6	24.1	22.9	20.5	20.3	21.7	24.2	24.4	24.3	23.1
1992	23.4	24.3	24.6	24.0	24.6	23.3	20.4	20.2	22.2	24.4	24.7	23.4	23.3
1993	21.4	22.6	22.7	21.7	23.0	22.5	18.5	18.1	20.2	21.9	22.3	22.2	21.4
1994	20.7	22.0	22.3	22.0	22.6	21.9	17.9	18.1	20.1	21.8	22.3	22.0	21.1
1995	21.5	22.3	22.4	22.2	22.6	20.9	19.1	18.9	21.1	21.9	22.1	22.3	21.4
1996	20.7	22.2	22.5	22.0	22.8	22.2	18.6	17.8	21.0	22.1	22.3	22.2	21.4
1997	21.2	22.0	22.4	21.9	22.6	22.0	18.7	22.3	21.2	22.0	22.0	22.1	21.7
1998	21.4	21.7	22.0	21.5	22.2	21.4	18.1	18.1	20.3	21.9	21.8	21.9	21.0
1999	20.1	22.1	22.1	21.7	21.5	21.1	18.5	18.5	20.6	21.9	22.1	22.3	21.0
2000	21.0	22.3	22.5	22.2	22.6	21.6	18.8	18.5	21.4	22.4	22.6	22.5	21.5
2001	21.2	22.9	23.1	22.6	23.1	22.5	19.7	19.9	22.0	22.9	23.2	23.1	22.2
2002	21.5	23.0	23.4	23.2	24.0	21.9	19.4	19.4	22.7	23.2	23.5	23.6	22.4
2003	21.8	23.5	23.7	23.3	23.8	23.1	18.8	17.8	21.7	22.3	22.5	22.4	22.1

Average Weekly Hours by Industry: Michigan

(Not seasonally adjusted.)

Industry	January	February	March	April	May	June	July	August	September	October	November	December	Annual Average
STATEWIDE													
Construction													
2001	37.7	37.0	38.0	37.9	40.4	41.5	41.5	40.7	40.9	39.0	38.0	38.8	39.4
2002	38.3	38.2	38.8	38.6	39.6	41.2	42.0	41.2	41.8	41.5	38.0	39.2	40.0
2003	37.9	37.0	37.5	37.8	38.6	39.2	38.3	39.0	40.2	39.7	37.7	37.1	38.4
Manufacturing													
2001	41.4	41.9	42.3	41.1	42.7	42.3	40.4	42.7	42.4	41.8	41.3	42.6	41.9
2002	42.2	41.9	42.5	43.0	42.9	42.9	40.1	43.3	43.6	43.3	42.3	44.0	42.7
2003	43.1	41.8	41.8	42.0	42.2	42.4	40.2	39.1	42.9	42.6	43.1	44.1	42.1
Wholesale trade													
2001	39.7	37.7	37.7	37.4	37.3	38.3	38.9	38.1	38.4	37.3	37.9	38.5	38.1
2002	37.4	37.9	37.5	37.6	38.2	39.0	37.6	37.9	37.2	36.2	36.8	36.7	37.5
2003	35.8	35.9	35.4	35.1	36.4	35.9	36.2	35.1	36.2	36.4	37.3	36.5	36.0
Retail trade													
2001	28.3	28.6	28.7	28.9	29.2	29.3	29.8	29.6	28.9	28.6	28.9	29.4	29.0
2002	28.0	28.4	28.6	28.6	29.0	29.6	30.0	29.4	29.1	29.2	28.9	30.3	29.1
2003	28.1	28.6	28.7	28.6	29.0	29.6	29.9	29.2	29.3	29.0	28.9	29.7	29.1
Information													
2001	34.9	33.9	34.3	33.2	33.3	34.7	34.2	34.0	33.7	33.6	33.9	33.5	33.9
2002	32.8	33.6	33.5	33.1	32.8	32.7	31.7	31.9	33.2	32.3	31.7	32.7	32.7
2003	31.8	32.2	31.8	32.0	31.5	31.7	33.0	31.7	31.5	31.7	32.9	32.5	32.0
Financial activities													
2001	35.8	35.2	35.2	35.2	35.3	35.7	36.0	35.4	35.9	35.5	36.0	36.2	35.6
2002	35.3	35.6	35.8	35.6	35.6	36.8	36.3	35.9	36.6	35.8	36.1	36.6	36.0
2003	37.2	37.1	37.2	36.6	36.3	36.7	36.0	36.0	35.8	35.1	35.2	34.3	36.1
Professional and business services													
2001	35.2	35.2	35.4	34.9	35.7	35.9	35.1	35.3	36.2	36.5	35.9	35.7	35.6
2002	33.8	34.4	34.3	34.6	35.5	35.5	35.2	36.2	35.4	35.0	34.7	34.1	34.9
2003	33.2	33.7	33.4	32.9	34.8	35.1	33.9	33.9	34.2	34.5	34.8	34.0	34.0
ANN ARBOR													
Manufacturing													
2001	42.2	43.1	42.8	42.1	42.9	42.5	40.6	42.9	42.5	42.1	42.1	42.2	42.3
2002	42.6	42.5	43.2	44.7	45.0	44.8	38.1	43.5	43.8	43.4	42.5	44.2	43.2
2003	43.6	42.2	41.3	43.6	42.8	43.7	39.8	38.0	43.0	41.8	43.7	44.9	42.4
DETROIT													
Manufacturing													
2001	42.2	43.0	44.3	43.1	44.2	43.2	41.2	43.8	44.1	43.0	42.6	44.6	43.3
2002	43.8	43.4	44.0	44.5	44.9	44.6	41.3	45.2	45.1	44.9	44.5	45.7	44.4
2003	44.8	43.4	43.3	42.6	43.2	43.4	40.6	37.6	43.3	43.0	43.8	44.8	42.8
Wholesale trade													
2001	39.7	37.8	37.9	37.1	37.5	36.9	37.6	37.7	37.5	36.4	37.5	37.8	37.6
2002	36.1	37.0	37.0	37.0	38.4	39.1	38.1	38.3	37.0	36.3	37.0	36.2	37.3
2003	35.1	35.2	34.4	33.5	35.8	34.5	35.2	33.3	35.0	36.6	36.9	36.4	35.2
Retail trade													
2001	28.0	28.3	28.5	28.9	29.2	29.3	29.4	29.4	28.6	28.4	29.1	29.6	28.9
2002	27.9	28.5	28.7	28.7	28.8	29.2	29.0	29.0	28.6	29.0	28.3	30.3	28.8
2003	27.5	28.2	28.2	28.1	28.9	29.5	29.4	28.1	29.4	28.9	28.8	30.0	28.8
Information													
2001	31.5	31.5	30.2	30.6	31.0	31.2	30.8	30.4	30.7	32.3	32.0	30.5	31.0
2002	29.9	30.4	31.0	30.5	31.3	31.1	30.6	32.1	32.6	34.0	30.7	33.2	31.4
2003	32.5	33.9	32.7	34.3	32.4	34.8	35.0	33.6	33.1	34.3	35.2	35.2	33.9
Professional and business services													
2001	36.5	36.5	36.6	36.1	37.4	37.1	36.0	36.3	36.4	37.0	36.7	36.4	36.6
2002	35.3	35.9	35.7	35.2	35.9	35.8	36.2	37.1	35.8	35.7	35.0	34.8	35.7
2003	34.6	35.3	34.7	34.6	37.7	37.4	36.5	36.2	37.6	38.0	38.2	37.5	36.6
FLINT													
Manufacturing													
2001	40.0	42.7	42.2	43.0	44.2	44.3	40.5	45.3	41.9	42.3	42.9	43.5	42.7
2002	41.8	42.7	43.0	43.9	44.7	44.6	40.0	44.9	45.7	45.4	44.4	46.9	44.0
2003	44.6	43.2	42.9	43.9	44.3	44.5	40.7	41.1	46.2	46.2	46.2	47.7	44.3
GRAND RAPIDS													
Manufacturing													
2001	40.6	40.8	40.9	39.7	40.2	40.7	39.7	40.5	40.5	40.4	39.7	40.7	40.4
2002	40.1	39.5	40.3	40.0	39.9	39.7	38.3	39.9	40.0	39.9	39.4	41.1	39.8
2003	40.5	39.6	40.1	39.1	39.7	39.8	38.5	39.9	40.4	39.9	40.0	40.1	39.8
Trade, transportation, and utilities													
2001	32.8	32.7	33.3	32.8	31.6	31.5	32.5	32.5	32.1	31.6	31.6	32.3	32.3
2002	32.0	32.6	32.4	32.1	32.1	32.9	32.7	32.1	32.8	32.2	31.8	32.2	32.3
2003	31.6	32.0	32.1	32.5	32.0	31.7	32.3	32.0	31.5	31.2	31.9	31.3	31.8
KALAMAZOO													
Manufacturing													
2001	39.5	38.8	39.8	37.5	39.5	40.3	40.0	40.3	41.4	40.7	39.9	40.8	39.9
2002	41.2	41.4	41.7	40.1	40.3	41.6	41.0	40.7	40.9	41.1	38.8	41.0	40.8
2003	39.6	38.7	39.3	38.2	39.4	39.1	39.6	39.0	39.7	40.0	40.5	42.7	39.6

Average Hourly Earnings by Industry: Michigan

(Dollars, not seasonally adjusted.)

Industry	January	February	March	April	May	June	July	August	September	October	November	December	Annual Average
STATEWIDE													
Construction													
2001	21.35	20.87	20.82	20.64	20.61	20.78	21.00	20.84	21.00	20.98	21.01	21.46	20.94
2002	21.36	21.33	21.43	21.33	21.23	21.63	21.91	21.58	22.08	21.80	21.60	21.99	21.62
2003	22.13	22.18	22.04	22.13	21.41	21.56	21.77	21.37	21.94	21.66	21.96	21.84	21.81
Manufacturing													
2001	19.06	19.13	19.29	19.28	19.40	19.40	19.03	19.49	19.69	19.61	19.92	20.13	19.45
2002	19.96	20.14	20.21	20.37	20.26	20.43	19.64	20.48	20.69	21.06	21.49	21.33	20.51
2003	21.02	20.99	20.89	21.05	21.09	21.20	20.61	21.28	21.71	21.54	21.79	22.15	21.28
Wholesale trade													
2001	18.86	18.69	18.64	18.66	18.32	18.64	18.74	19.11	18.46	18.20	18.68	18.65	18.64
2002	18.58	18.99	18.49	18.53	18.04	18.37	18.44	18.77	19.24	18.84	19.08	18.85	18.68
2003	18.77	18.62	18.61	17.99	17.76	18.43	18.14	18.52	18.50	18.22	18.48	18.04	18.34
Retail trade													
2001	11.10	11.13	11.45	11.14	11.31	11.30	11.04	11.04	11.15	11.21	11.18	11.17	11.18
2002	11.20	11.40	11.45	11.17	11.26	11.04	11.10	11.12	11.23	11.18	11.00	11.07	11.18
2003	10.94	11.08	11.02	10.98	11.04	11.07	11.01	10.97	10.99	11.07	11.13	11.03	11.03
Information													
2001	15.38	14.99	15.18	15.75	15.25	15.31	15.33	15.32	15.26	15.15	15.29	15.60	15.32
2002	15.28	15.62	15.15	15.04	15.00	15.20	15.43	15.48	15.76	15.64	15.75	15.67	15.41
2003	15.96	15.43	15.69	16.63	15.98	16.34	16.35	15.95	16.38	16.48	16.51	16.26	16.16
Financial activities													
2001	14.67	14.48	14.48	14.69	14.56	14.83	14.88	14.83	14.93	14.93	14.84	15.46	14.80
2002	15.29	15.18	14.94	14.87	14.46	14.86	14.90	14.96	15.13	15.22	15.24	15.60	15.05
2003	14.93	15.51	15.62	15.67	15.64	15.65	15.49	16.03	15.94	15.86	15.82	15.89	15.67
Professional and business services													
2001	15.99	16.04	16.04	16.16	15.95	15.81	15.84	16.00	16.30	16.16	16.15	16.46	16.07
2002	16.13	16.20	16.21	16.01	15.98	15.92	15.65	15.77	16.16	16.46	16.16	16.53	16.09
2003	16.73	16.73	16.60	16.89	16.47	16.38	16.14	15.76	15.92	16.06	16.31	16.45	16.36
ANN ARBOR													
Manufacturing													
2001	21.32	21.14	21.57	21.45	21.36	21.54	20.66	22.24	22.03	22.12	22.18	22.24	21.65
2002	22.22	23.17	22.66	22.83	22.94	23.31	20.42	22.54	22.85	23.30	23.84	23.55	22.83
2003	23.68	23.59	23.41	23.49	23.47	23.69	22.57	23.72	24.21	23.86	24.11	24.80	23.73
DETROIT													
Manufacturing													
2001	21.81	21.96	21.93	22.17	22.25	22.20	21.91	22.70	24.20	24.05	23.35	23.74	22.68
2002	23.37	23.53	23.57	23.62	23.40	23.74	23.00	23.50	23.88	24.39	24.96	24.57	23.81
2003	24.17	24.13	23.98	23.80	23.85	24.25	23.79	24.32	24.61	24.58	24.84	24.99	24.28
Wholesale trade													
2001	20.48	20.16	20.49	20.62	20.35	20.50	20.60	20.78	20.93	20.56	21.07	21.02	20.63
2002	20.64	20.77	20.01	20.17	19.95	20.14	20.14	20.20	20.62	20.28	20.36	20.26	20.29
2003	20.01	20.19	20.32	20.22	19.69	20.62	20.23	20.60	20.38	20.08	20.77	19.93	20.25
Retail trade													
2001	12.14	12.03	12.59	12.04	12.33	12.25	11.88	11.78	11.78	11.65	11.83	12.27	12.05
2002	12.34	12.53	12.58	12.21	12.48	12.05	12.21	12.04	12.18	12.21	11.67	11.68	12.17
2003	11.64	11.74	11.82	11.79	11.93	11.91	11.97	11.92	11.76	11.86	11.86	11.70	11.83
Information													
2001	14.71	14.71	14.69	15.00	14.92	14.91	15.00	14.94	14.82	15.10	15.06	14.97	14.91
2002	14.69	14.90	15.48	15.58	14.75	14.41	14.55	14.07	14.98	14.40	14.08	14.27	14.68
2003	14.53	14.67	14.59	15.28	14.18	14.49	14.42	14.31	14.54	14.26	13.66	13.33	14.36
Professional and business services													
2001	17.76	18.11	18.12	17.98	17.75	17.56	17.87	17.89	18.12	17.99	18.04	18.55	17.97
2002	18.38	18.56	18.32	18.15	18.04	18.30	17.94	17.79	17.82	17.97	17.92	18.07	18.10
2003	18.37	18.25	18.44	18.17	17.51	17.83	17.97	17.71	18.01	18.13	18.33	18.41	18.09
FLINT													
Manufacturing													
2001	27.12	26.88	26.95	27.00	27.00	27.56	26.06	26.83	27.46	27.47	27.93	28.05	27.20
2002	27.82	27.74	27.85	28.03	28.00	28.12	26.12	28.71	28.96	29.65	30.81	30.65	28.60
2003	30.12	29.78	29.71	29.96	29.65	29.84	28.45	30.29	30.57	30.57	30.57	31.56	30.12
GRAND RAPIDS													
Manufacturing													
2001	15.41	15.23	15.40	15.59	15.49	15.61	15.82	15.58	15.89	15.74	16.01	16.08	15.65
2002	15.85	15.98	16.05	16.12	16.13	16.06	15.70	16.00	16.20	16.38	16.55	16.64	16.14
2003	16.39	16.43	16.40	16.51	16.42	16.37	16.37	16.59	16.63	16.54	16.24	16.78	16.47
Trade, transportation, and utilities													
2001	12.99	13.30	13.27	13.35	13.21	13.17	13.04	13.34	13.24	13.72	13.18	13.31	13.26
2002	13.26	13.63	13.30	13.44	13.32	13.53	13.46	13.61	13.20	13.32	13.28	13.21	13.38
2003	13.11	13.23	13.38	12.98	13.15	13.15	12.97	12.62	12.85	12.79	13.07	13.23	13.04
KALAMAZOO													
Manufacturing													
2001	15.64	15.87	16.06	16.26	15.91	16.14	16.01	16.22	16.40	16.09	16.05	16.55	16.10
2002	16.10	16.31	16.25	16.09	16.08	15.98	15.81	15.59	15.62	15.45	15.49	15.75	15.89
2003	15.56	15.57	15.15	15.31	15.80	15.66	15.27	15.25	15.10	15.62	15.49	15.76	15.46

Average Weekly Earnings by Industry: Michigan

(Dollars, not seasonally adjusted.)

Industry	January	February	March	April	May	June	July	August	September	October	November	December	Annual Average
STATEWIDE													
Construction													
2001	804.90	772.19	791.16	782.26	832.64	862.37	871.50	848.19	858.90	818.22	798.38	832.65	825.04
2002	818.09	814.81	831.48	823.34	840.71	891.16	920.22	889.10	922.94	904.70	820.80	862.01	864.80
2003	838.73	820.66	826.50	836.51	826.43	845.15	833.79	833.43	881.99	859.90	827.89	810.26	837.50
Manufacturing													
2001	789.08	801.55	815.97	792.41	828.38	820.62	768.81	832.22	834.86	819.70	822.70	857.54	814.96
2002	842.31	843.87	858.93	875.91	869.15	876.45	787.56	886.78	902.08	911.90	909.03	938.52	875.78
2003	905.96	877.38	873.20	884.10	890.00	898.88	828.52	832.05	931.36	917.60	939.15	976.82	895.89
Wholesale trade													
2001	748.74	704.61	702.73	697.88	683.34	713.91	728.99	728.09	708.86	678.86	707.97	718.03	710.18
2002	694.89	719.72	693.38	696.73	689.13	716.43	693.34	711.38	715.73	682.01	702.14	691.80	700.50
2003	671.97	668.46	658.79	631.45	646.46	661.64	656.67	650.05	669.70	663.21	689.30	658.46	660.24
Retail trade													
2001	314.13	318.32	328.62	321.95	330.25	331.09	328.99	326.78	322.24	320.61	323.10	328.40	324.22
2002	313.60	323.76	327.47	319.46	326.54	326.78	333.00	326.93	326.79	326.46	317.90	335.42	325.34
2003	307.41	316.89	316.27	314.03	320.16	327.67	329.20	320.32	322.01	321.03	321.66	327.59	320.97
Information													
2001	536.76	508.16	520.67	522.90	507.83	531.26	524.29	520.88	514.26	509.04	518.33	522.60	519.35
2002	501.18	524.83	507.53	497.82	492.00	497.04	489.13	493.81	523.23	505.17	499.28	512.41	503.91
2003	507.53	496.85	498.94	532.16	503.37	517.98	539.55	505.62	515.97	522.42	543.18	528.45	517.12
Financial activities													
2001	525.19	509.70	509.70	517.09	513.97	529.43	535.68	524.98	535.99	530.02	534.24	559.65	526.88
2002	539.74	540.41	534.85	529.37	514.78	546.85	540.87	537.06	553.76	544.88	550.16	570.96	541.80
2003	555.40	575.42	581.06	573.52	567.73	574.36	557.64	577.08	570.65	556.69	556.86	545.03	565.69
Professional and business services													
2001	562.85	564.61	567.82	563.98	569.42	567.58	555.98	564.80	590.06	589.84	579.79	587.62	572.09
2002	545.19	557.28	556.00	553.95	567.29	565.16	550.88	570.87	572.06	576.10	560.75	563.67	561.54
2003	555.44	563.80	554.44	555.68	573.16	574.94	547.15	534.26	544.46	554.07	567.59	559.30	556.24
ANN ARBOR													
Manufacturing													
2001	899.70	911.13	923.20	903.05	916.34	915.45	838.80	954.10	936.28	931.25	933.78	938.53	915.80
2002	946.57	984.73	978.91	1020.50	1032.30	1044.29	778.00	980.49	1000.83	1011.22	1013.20	1040.91	986.26
2003	1032.45	995.50	966.83	1024.16	1004.52	1035.25	898.29	901.36	1041.03	997.35	1053.61	1113.52	1006.15
DETROIT													
Manufacturing													
2001	920.38	944.28	971.50	955.53	983.45	959.04	902.69	994.26	1067.22	1034.15	994.71	1058.80	982.04
2002	1023.61	1021.20	1037.08	1051.09	1050.66	1058.80	949.90	1062.20	1076.99	1095.11	1110.72	1122.85	1057.16
2003	1082.82	1047.24	1038.33	1013.88	1030.32	1052.45	965.87	914.43	1065.61	1056.94	1087.99	1119.55	1039.18
Wholesale trade													
2001	813.06	762.05	776.57	765.00	763.13	756.45	774.56	783.41	784.88	748.38	790.13	794.56	775.69
2002	745.10	768.49	740.37	746.29	766.08	787.47	767.33	773.66	762.94	736.16	753.32	733.41	756.82
2003	702.35	710.69	699.01	677.37	704.90	711.39	712.10	685.98	713.30	734.93	766.41	725.45	712.80
Retail trade													
2001	339.92	340.45	358.82	347.96	360.04	358.93	349.27	346.33	336.91	330.86	344.25	363.19	348.25
2002	344.29	357.11	361.05	350.43	359.42	351.86	354.09	349.16	348.35	354.09	330.26	353.90	350.50
2003	320.10	331.07	333.32	331.30	344.78	351.35	351.92	334.95	345.74	342.75	341.57	351.00	340.70
Information													
2001	463.37	463.37	443.64	459.00	462.52	465.19	462.00	454.18	454.97	487.73	481.92	456.59	462.21
2002	439.23	452.96	479.88	475.19	461.68	448.15	445.23	451.65	488.35	489.60	432.26	473.76	460.95
2003	472.23	497.31	477.09	524.10	459.43	504.25	504.70	480.82	481.27	489.12	480.83	469.22	486.80
Professional and business services													
2001	648.24	661.02	663.19	649.08	663.85	651.48	643.32	649.41	659.57	665.63	662.07	675.22	657.70
2002	648.81	666.30	654.02	638.88	647.64	655.14	649.43	660.01	637.96	641.53	627.20	628.84	646.17
2003	635.60	644.23	639.87	628.68	660.13	666.84	655.91	641.10	677.18	688.94	700.21	690.38	662.09
FLINT													
Manufacturing													
2001	1084.80	1147.78	1137.29	1161.00	1193.40	1220.91	1055.43	1215.40	1150.57	1161.98	1198.20	1220.18	1161.44
2002	1162.88	1184.50	1197.55	1230.52	1251.60	1254.15	1044.80	1289.08	1323.47	1346.11	1367.96	1437.49	1258.40
2003	1343.35	1286.50	1274.56	1315.24	1313.50	1327.88	1157.92	1244.92	1412.33	1412.33	1412.33	1505.41	1334.32
GRAND RAPIDS													
Manufacturing													
2001	625.65	621.38	629.86	618.92	622.70	635.33	628.05	630.99	643.55	635.90	635.60	654.46	632.26
2002	635.59	631.21	646.82	644.80	643.59	637.58	601.31	638.40	648.00	653.56	652.07	683.90	642.37
2003	663.80	650.63	657.64	645.54	651.87	651.53	630.25	661.94	671.85	659.95	649.60	672.88	655.51
Trade, transportation, and utilities													
2001	426.07	434.91	441.89	437.88	417.44	414.86	423.80	433.55	425.00	433.55	416.49	429.91	428.30
2002	424.32	444.34	430.92	431.42	427.57	445.14	440.14	436.88	432.96	428.90	422.30	425.36	432.17
2003	414.28	423.36	429.50	421.85	420.80	416.86	418.93	403.84	404.78	399.05	416.93	414.10	414.67
KALAMAZOO													
Manufacturing													
2001	617.78	615.76	639.19	609.75	628.45	650.44	640.40	653.67	678.96	654.86	640.40	675.24	642.39
2002	663.32	675.23	677.63	645.21	648.02	664.77	648.21	634.51	638.86	635.00	601.01	645.75	648.31
2003	616.18	602.56	595.40	584.84	622.52	612.31	604.69	594.75	599.47	624.80	627.35	672.95	612.22

MINNESOTA AT A GLANCE

(Population and total nonfarm employment numbers in thousands)

Population, Census 2000:	4,919.5
Total nonfarm employment, 2003:	2,651.3
Change in total nonfarm employment	
(Number)	
1990–2003:	524.6
1990–2001:	553.6
2001–2003:	-29.0
(Compound annual rate of change)	
1990–2003:	1.7%
1990–2001:	2.1%
2001–2003:	-0.5%
Unemployment rate	
1990:	4.8%
2001:	3.9%
2003:	4.9%

Average Annual Employment for Total Nonfarm, Goods-Producing, and Service-Providing Industries, 1990–2003

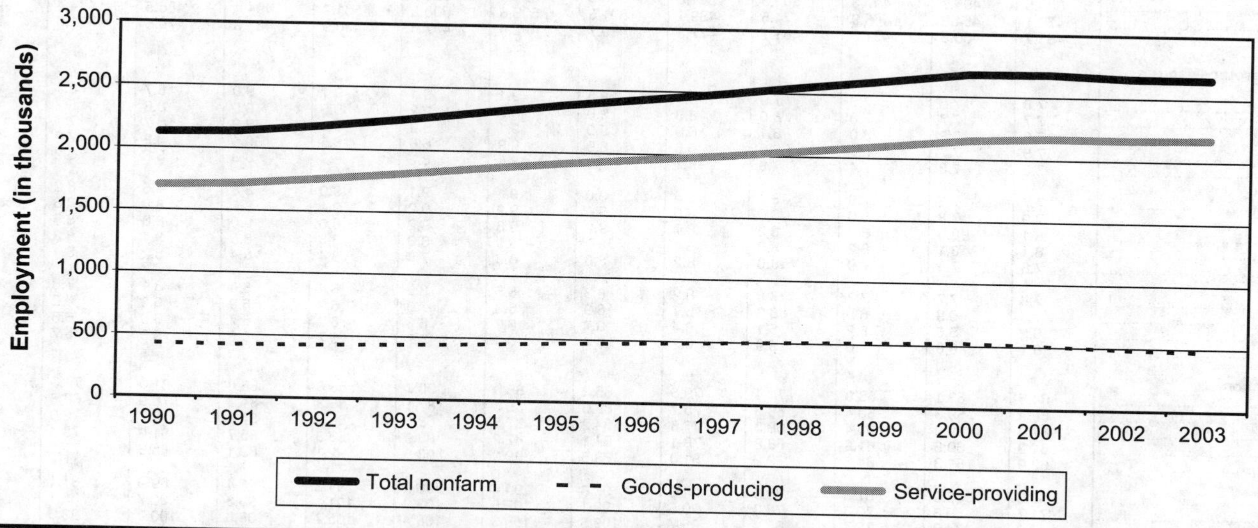

Nonfarm payroll employment rose steadily during the 1990–2000 period, but turned down following the 2001 recession, mainly due to decreases in the goods-producing sector. Construction employment remained relatively flat and employment declined in both natural resources and mining and manufacturing. In the service-providing sector, employment increased at a steady pace from 1990 to 2001 before declining in 2002. It showed some signs of recovery in 2003 as employment edged up.

Employment by Industry: Minnesota

(Numbers in thousands. Not seasonally adjusted.)

Industry	January	February	March	April	May	June	July	August	September	October	November	December	Annual Average
STATEWIDE													
Total nonfarm													
1990	2069.9	2077.4	2086.2	2109.5	2141.1	2157.3	2129.5	2135.5	2148.3	2157.7	2158.3	2150.0	2126.7
1991	2089.5	2085.9	2094.7	2116.7	2150.6	2166.4	2135.3	2143.4	2155.7	2172.4	2164.7	2166.7	2136.8
1992	2112.6	2116.8	2131.7	2165.4	2199.3	2212.2	2186.6	2190.5	2209.8	2232.6	2230.8	2231.4	2184.9
1993	2172.3	2178.7	2193.8	2223.9	2253.2	2267.9	2240.5	2242.9	2258.5	2290.4	2293.2	2297.1	2242.7
1994	2230.5	2239.3	2257.1	2289.2	2323.3	2346.0	2310.0	2314.7	2338.6	2350.9	2362.8	2362.7	2310.4
1995	2304.4	2314.4	2332.6	2351.1	2387.9	2414.1	2380.0	2385.3	2398.7	2419.8	2428.1	2426.5	2378.5
1996	2364.0	2369.5	2387.8	2405.5	2447.1	2468.3	2435.0	2440.8	2454.3	2470.3	2480.7	2476.2	2433.2
1997	2404.7	2415.1	2431.5	2451.7	2499.7	2524.0	2498.5	2504.1	2523.2	2541.8	2545.7	2549.6	2490.8
1998	2479.2	2487.8	2503.5	2538.6	2578.8	2600.4	2555.5	2564.8	2563.8	2591.2	2595.3	2602.1	2555.0
1999	2526.5	2534.0	2550.2	2594.9	2624.7	2649.9	2625.3	2628.0	2633.1	2659.8	2662.6	2667.7	2613.0
2000	2590.9	2604.0	2624.2	2656.6	2691.1	2718.6	2681.6	2689.7	2703.8	2714.3	2718.2	2715.8	2675.7
2001	2639.6	2645.0	2655.7	2672.4	2706.8	2726.5	2680.8	2679.4	2690.1	2694.8	2691.6	2680.3	2680.3
2002	2603.0	2601.0	2607.9	2632.3	2672.4	2697.0	2663.0	2662.5	2679.2	2679.4	2682.7	2673.2	2654.5
2003	2594.7	2596.6	2602.6	2633.9	2673.2	2689.8	2661.7	2662.5	2664.6	2683.2	2681.8	2670.7	2651.3
Total private													
1990	1733.1	1733.9	1744.5	1762.4	1790.0	1814.9	1815.2	1829.7	1822.8	1812.5	1806.8	1802.0	1788.9
1991	1745.8	1735.8	1746.6	1766.2	1796.1	1819.2	1818.2	1832.3	1828.5	1824.3	1813.0	1814.1	1795.0
1992	1765.1	1763.6	1778.3	1807.4	1840.8	1861.2	1866.2	1877.4	1879.4	1879.9	1872.1	1875.1	1838.8
1993	1818.2	1818.8	1833.5	1862.6	1888.6	1910.7	1915.1	1923.7	1923.5	1931.6	1929.1	1932.3	1890.6
1994	1872.8	1876.9	1894.5	1922.5	1953.1	1978.9	1976.7	1987.9	1990.6	1982.8	1985.6	1988.7	1950.9
1995	1920.6	1925.5	1943.2	1963.0	1996.5	2026.8	2027.4	2042.7	2041.0	2039.0	2041.2	2041.7	2000.7
1996	1983.0	1984.2	2002.6	2019.5	2056.6	2084.3	2080.7	2093.7	2086.8	2082.8	2085.5	2085.6	2053.7
1997	2023.0	2028.0	2044.3	2064.6	2109.4	2137.5	2144.6	2156.7	2156.6	2156.0	2154.8	2158.7	2111.1
1998	2094.9	2098.7	2113.8	2147.9	2185.0	2213.0	2206.1	2219.2	2194.7	2201.7	2201.7	2208.8	2173.7
1999	2137.9	2140.5	2155.0	2197.3	2227.0	2260.5	2264.7	2274.6	2255.9	2263.2	2262.5	2268.7	2225.6
2000	2198.8	2201.6	2218.7	2246.8	2276.2	2312.7	2311.0	2322.7	2312.5	2311.1	2308.3	2307.3	2277.3
2001	2243.9	2237.8	2247.7	2263.6	2295.9	2318.8	2308.5	2314.8	2295.1	2286.9	2280.4	2268.2	2280.1
2002	2197.9	2189.8	2197.1	2223.3	2261.5	2285.3	2280.8	2291.9	2278.0	2268.7	2264.5	2257.4	2249.7
2003	2191.1	2184.2	2190.4	2220.3	2260.1	2280.8	2284.3	2288.2	2275.7	2276.8	2273.3	2261.9	2248.9
Goods-producing													
1990	408.8	407.2	409.5	415.8	426.5	440.0	444.4	450.1	445.1	438.5	429.9	418.0	427.8
1991	403.0	399.3	399.7	410.7	421.4	434.6	438.6	444.6	439.7	436.1	423.9	416.5	422.3
1992	401.8	400.0	403.7	413.2	425.1	438.7	443.9	446.7	445.7	442.8	433.5	425.4	426.7
1993	410.0	409.9	414.2	424.5	435.5	446.2	453.4	456.6	452.5	449.1	443.7	434.4	435.8
1994	419.1	418.4	424.3	434.2	446.2	460.8	466.4	471.9	470.3	465.1	462.1	454.6	449.4
1995	438.1	437.8	442.9	452.1	464.6	479.3	483.9	490.4	486.5	479.1	475.2	466.6	466.3
1996	451.0	448.9	454.3	461.9	476.7	491.9	497.3	502.9	498.5	492.5	486.3	478.0	478.3
1997	462.3	463.4	468.7	477.4	494.0	508.5	510.7	516.4	512.0	510.9	504.0	496.4	493.7
1998	481.9	479.7	485.1	497.9	510.3	524.6	526.1	528.5	522.2	517.4	510.9	505.9	507.5
1999	488.6	487.3	491.7	504.3	514.9	530.2	533.1	537.5	531.2	525.7	520.6	513.2	514.8
2000	496.0	495.2	501.1	513.6	525.5	540.1	542.8	547.2	540.4	534.5	526.9	519.2	523.5
2001	500.5	496.7	497.3	501.3	511.8	520.9	523.2	524.8	519.5	511.1	502.3	490.7	508.3
2002	470.1	464.8	466.9	474.5	489.1	501.5	503.6	508.2	501.7	494.4	486.5	474.4	486.3
2003	455.7	450.3	451.6	461.7	477.3	489.7	492.9	497.6	490.9	487.3	479.5	471.0	475.5
Natural resources and mining													
1990	7.6	7.5	7.8	7.9	8.4	8.8	9.1	9.1	9.1	9.0	8.7	8.1	8.4
1991	7.7	7.7	7.8	8.0	8.6	9.0	8.9	9.2	9.0	9.0	8.6	8.2	8.4
1992	7.9	7.8	8.0	8.1	8.6	9.0	9.1	8.3	9.1	8.9	8.7	7.9	8.4
1993	7.5	7.7	8.0	8.0	8.5	8.9	8.9	8.6	8.5	8.4	8.2	7.7	8.2
1994	7.3	7.3	7.4	7.8	8.1	8.5	8.5	8.9	8.8	8.8	8.6	8.2	8.1
1995	7.7	7.7	7.9	8.0	8.5	9.0	9.1	9.1	9.0	8.8	8.6	8.2	8.4
1996	7.9	7.8	8.0	8.0	8.5	9.0	9.2	9.2	9.1	8.9	8.8	8.6	8.5
1997	8.1	8.0	8.2	8.2	8.7	9.2	9.3	9.2	9.0	9.0	8.8	8.5	8.6
1998	8.1	8.1	8.2	8.0	8.4	8.8	8.9	8.8	8.6	8.5	8.4	8.2	8.4
1999	7.8	7.9	7.9	8.0	8.2	8.6	8.5	7.8	8.4	8.4	8.2	8.1	8.1
2000	7.8	7.7	7.7	7.8	8.2	8.3	8.5	8.5	8.4	8.4	8.1	7.8	8.1
2001	7.5	6.9	6.6	6.3	6.7	6.9	6.3	7.0	6.9	6.9	6.3	6.2	6.7
2002	6.2	5.6	6.2	6.1	6.4	6.7	6.7	6.8	6.7	6.7	6.6	6.3	6.4
2003	6.1	6.0	6.0	5.9	6.2	6.4	6.4	5.9	5.7	5.6	5.5	5.7	6.0
Construction													
1990	64.5	63.1	63.9	71.4	79.6	86.2	88.9	90.7	88.6	86.0	81.0	71.3	77.9
1991	60.9	59.3	60.4	68.3	75.7	82.6	85.2	87.1	85.3	84.2	76.9	69.6	74.6
1992	61.0	59.3	60.4	68.2	77.6	84.2	87.5	88.0	86.3	84.8	78.7	72.0	75.6
1993	61.9	60.6	61.9	68.8	78.1	84.1	87.9	88.9	86.8	85.7	81.0	73.0	76.5
1994	62.9	61.3	64.3	72.2	81.0	88.5	92.0	93.5	92.1	89.1	85.6	77.6	80.0
1995	66.5	65.0	67.3	73.9	84.0	92.8	94.4	96.3	94.2	93.4	89.0	81.1	83.1
1996	71.7	69.8	72.3	78.3	90.5	99.1	102.5	103.9	101.1	98.3	93.7	85.1	88.8
1997	74.6	74.0	75.7	82.9	95.7	103.5	106.3	108.4	105.7	106.0	100.2	93.3	93.8
1998	82.5	81.6	83.0	94.1	104.4	112.3	116.3	115.9	113.4	112.5	107.8	102.7	102.2
1999	89.0	88.8	92.0	103.4	112.9	121.7	126.0	127.3	125.2	121.9	117.0	110.3	111.2
2000	97.3	97.0	101.2	112.4	122.6	130.7	132.7	134.2	131.1	129.0	122.9	115.1	118.8
2001	104.0	102.6	104.9	112.5	123.9	134.0	138.1	139.3	135.0	133.6	129.2	120.0	123.1
2002	106.1	103.2	104.1	113.0	126.5	134.5	139.6	141.2	138.1	134.5	128.6	119.3	124.1
2003	106.0	102.6	103.6	113.4	127.3	136.0	140.1	142.7	139.4	138.2	131.3	121.8	125.2

Employment by Industry: Minnesota—*Continued*

(Numbers in thousands. Not seasonally adjusted.)

Industry	January	February	March	April	May	June	July	August	September	October	November	December	Annual Average
STATEWIDE—*Continued*													
Manufacturing													
1990	336.7	336.6	337.8	336.5	338.5	345.0	346.4	350.3	347.4	343.5	340.2	338.6	341.4
1991	334.4	332.3	331.5	334.4	337.1	343.0	344.5	348.3	345.4	342.9	338.4	338.7	339.2
1992	332.9	332.9	335.3	336.9	338.9	345.5	347.3	350.4	350.3	349.1	346.1	345.5	342.5
1993	340.6	341.6	344.3	347.7	348.9	353.2	356.6	359.1	357.2	355.0	354.5	353.7	351.0
1994	348.9	349.8	352.6	354.2	357.1	363.8	365.9	369.5	369.4	367.2	367.9	368.8	361.2
1995	363.9	365.1	367.7	370.2	372.1	377.5	380.4	385.0	383.3	376.9	377.6	377.3	374.7
1996	371.4	371.3	374.0	375.6	377.7	383.8	385.6	389.8	388.3	385.3	383.8	384.3	380.9
1997	379.6	381.4	384.8	386.3	389.6	395.8	395.1	398.8	397.3	395.9	395.0	394.6	391.1
1998	391.3	390.0	393.9	395.8	397.5	403.5	400.9	403.8	400.2	396.4	394.7	395.0	396.9
1999	391.8	390.6	391.8	392.9	393.8	399.9	398.6	402.4	397.6	395.4	395.4	394.8	395.4
2000	390.9	390.5	392.2	393.4	394.7	401.1	401.6	404.5	400.9	397.1	395.9	396.3	396.5
2001	389.0	387.2	385.8	382.5	381.2	380.0	378.8	378.5	377.6	370.6	366.8	364.5	378.5
2002	357.8	356.0	356.6	355.4	356.2	360.3	357.3	360.2	356.9	353.2	351.3	348.8	355.8
2003	343.6	341.7	342.0	342.4	343.8	347.3	346.4	349.0	345.8	343.5	342.7	343.5	344.3
Service-providing													
1990	1661.1	1670.2	1676.7	1693.7	1714.6	1717.3	1685.1	1685.4	1703.2	1719.2	1728.4	1732.0	1698.9
1991	1686.5	1686.6	1695.0	1706.0	1729.2	1731.8	1696.7	1698.8	1716.0	1736.3	1740.8	1750.2	1714.4
1992	1710.8	1716.8	1728.0	1752.2	1774.2	1773.5	1742.7	1743.8	1764.1	1789.8	1797.3	1806.0	1758.2
1993	1762.3	1768.8	1779.6	1799.4	1817.7	1821.7	1787.1	1786.3	1806.0	1841.3	1849.5	1862.7	1806.8
1994	1811.4	1820.9	1832.8	1855.0	1877.1	1885.2	1843.6	1842.8	1868.3	1885.8	1900.7	1908.1	1860.9
1995	1866.3	1876.6	1889.7	1899.0	1923.3	1934.8	1896.1	1894.9	1912.2	1940.7	1952.9	1959.9	1912.2
1996	1913.0	1920.6	1933.5	1943.6	1970.4	1976.4	1937.7	1937.9	1955.8	1977.8	1994.4	1998.2	1954.9
1997	1942.4	1951.7	1962.8	1974.3	2005.7	2015.5	1987.8	1987.7	2011.2	2030.9	2041.7	2053.2	1997.0
1998	1997.3	2008.1	2018.4	2040.7	2068.5	2075.8	2029.4	2036.3	2041.6	2073.8	2084.4	2096.2	2047.5
1999	2037.9	2046.7	2058.5	2090.6	2109.8	2119.7	2092.2	2090.5	2101.9	2134.1	2142.0	2154.5	2098.2
2000	2094.9	2108.8	2123.1	2143.0	2165.6	2178.5	2138.8	2142.5	2163.4	2179.8	2191.3	2196.6	2152.1
2001	2139.1	2148.3	2158.4	2171.1	2195.0	2205.6	2157.6	2154.6	2170.6	2183.7	2189.3	2189.6	2171.9
2002	2132.9	2136.2	2141.0	2157.8	2183.3	2195.5	2159.4	2154.3	2177.5	2185.0	2196.2	2198.8	2168.2
2003	2139.0	2146.3	2151.0	2172.2	2195.9	2200.1	2168.8	2164.9	2173.7	2195.9	2202.3	2199.7	2175.8
Trade, transportation, and utilities													
1990	441.7	436.7	437.9	441.9	447.2	451.4	447.2	451.1	450.5	450.4	458.1	461.7	447.9
1991	442.4	434.3	436.0	438.8	444.0	446.9	443.7	445.3	446.2	449.5	455.6	460.3	445.2
1992	441.5	436.3	438.1	442.4	447.9	448.5	447.5	451.0	451.3	457.3	464.8	469.9	449.7
1993	450.4	445.0	446.3	452.2	457.2	460.7	458.8	459.5	462.0	469.7	477.1	482.5	460.1
1994	463.3	460.3	462.3	465.8	471.9	475.4	476.2	476.8	480.1	485.6	493.8	499.0	475.8
1995	479.3	474.5	475.2	478.1	484.1	488.6	485.3	486.7	488.3	498.5	506.4	510.5	487.9
1996	491.6	485.4	487.6	490.3	496.4	498.5	493.9	495.2	495.7	501.9	512.0	516.7	497.1
1997	495.3	489.8	492.0	496.3	505.1	508.3	506.9	505.7	511.9	518.2	527.0	534.8	507.6
1998	511.5	507.7	508.9	516.4	523.4	526.0	521.0	522.3	510.3	528.0	536.4	543.3	521.2
1999	517.6	513.4	515.0	524.1	529.6	533.0	530.8	531.2	529.0	535.9	545.1	553.4	529.8
2000	532.2	527.9	529.0	531.8	536.8	541.1	538.3	540.0	539.1	544.9	553.9	559.9	539.5
2001	540.6	533.4	534.3	536.0	542.4	544.2	540.1	539.3	534.9	538.4	544.9	547.1	539.6
2002	525.2	516.0	516.8	521.8	527.7	529.1	523.4	523.1	521.7	524.5	534.3	538.9	525.2
2003	518.6	511.2	511.4	516.9	523.4	524.6	521.3	520.9	519.6	521.7	533.0	536.7	521.6
Wholesale trade													
1990	103.3	103.8	104.1	106.3	106.9	108.3	108.7	109.9	108.0	107.1	106.8	107.0	106.6
1991	104.0	103.6	104.3	105.6	106.5	107.2	106.7	107.4	106.4	106.2	105.6	105.9	105.7
1992	104.4	103.8	105.0	105.5	106.7	107.1	108.9	108.9	108.1	107.8	107.8	107.9	106.8
1993	106.0	106.2	106.9	108.5	109.7	110.5	111.7	111.5	110.4	109.7	109.4	109.9	109.2
1994	108.1	108.2	109.2	110.9	112.0	113.1	113.4	113.5	113.2	113.0	113.4	114.0	111.8
1995	112.1	112.6	113.4	114.6	116.2	117.3	116.0	116.1	115.3	118.0	118.1	118.4	115.6
1996	117.2	117.1	118.0	119.6	121.2	122.9	122.5	122.7	121.5	121.3	121.8	122.0	120.6
1997	120.1	120.4	121.3	122.2	123.9	124.9	125.9	125.9	125.1	125.6	125.7	126.2	123.9
1998	124.2	124.7	125.3	126.8	127.9	128.3	127.8	127.9	126.5	126.8	127.0	126.7	126.6
1999	123.5	123.7	124.2	126.7	127.4	128.1	128.5	128.6	126.4	127.7	127.8	128.7	126.7
2000	126.6	126.5	127.3	128.2	129.0	131.2	130.0	130.5	129.0	129.6	130.0	130.4	129.0
2001	130.3	129.8	130.3	131.1	131.9	132.1	132.0	131.2	129.6	129.3	129.0	128.6	130.4
2002	126.6	126.4	126.2	127.4	128.1	128.6	128.7	128.1	126.5	127.0	126.6	126.3	127.2
2003	126.6	126.7	126.7	127.3	128.1	129.3	130.2	129.6	127.5	126.5	127.5	127.8	127.8
Retail trade													
1990	255.0	249.4	249.5	250.4	253.6	256.1	253.8	255.6	254.2	256.0	263.8	267.5	255.4
1991	253.3	246.1	246.5	248.1	251.0	253.2	252.3	252.9	252.2	255.2	261.7	265.5	253.1
1992	251.5	246.7	246.8	249.9	253.4	255.1	253.2	257.3	255.7	261.1	269.0	273.8	256.1
1993	258.2	253.1	253.5	256.6	259.4	262.1	259.8	261.0	260.7	266.2	273.5	278.3	261.8
1994	262.5	258.5	259.2	262.2	265.9	268.7	270.1	272.3	272.0	275.4	284.6	289.5	270.0
1995	274.0	269.0	269.4	270.8	274.6	278.2	277.8	279.5	278.4	284.3	292.1	296.4	278.7
1996	281.5	275.1	276.2	277.9	282.2	283.9	281.5	282.9	281.8	287.1	297.1	302.2	284.1
1997	284.8	279.5	281.4	283.7	289.0	291.6	289.8	290.9	291.0	295.1	303.7	311.1	290.9
1998	290.8	286.2	286.1	291.3	296.1	299.3	296.7	297.7	296.1	299.4	307.7	315.3	296.8
1999	295.6	291.1	292.1	296.4	300.7	303.6	302.6	302.8	300.0	304.1	313.5	321.2	301.9
2000	303.8	299.5	299.4	300.7	304.2	306.9	306.0	307.2	305.3	309.7	318.8	324.5	307.1
2001	307.6	301.6	301.6	301.7	306.5	309.0	306.8	307.7	303.2	307.4	316.2	319.9	307.4
2002	302.5	294.6	295.8	298.4	302.6	304.8	302.7	303.4	300.7	301.4	311.7	317.5	303.0
2003	299.0	292.2	292.5	297.1	302.5	304.1	300.9	301.5	300.4	302.4	312.4	315.3	301.7

Employment by Industry: Minnesota—*Continued*

(Numbers in thousands. Not seasonally adjusted.)

Industry	January	February	March	April	May	June	July	August	September	October	November	December	Annual Average
STATEWIDE—*Continued*													
Transportation and utilities													
1990	83.4	83.5	84.3	85.2	86.7	87.0	84.7	85.6	88.3	87.3	87.5	87.2	85.8
1991	85.1	84.6	85.2	85.1	86.5	86.5	84.7	85.0	87.6	88.1	88.3	88.9	86.3
1992	85.6	85.8	86.3	87.0	87.8	86.3	85.4	84.8	87.5	88.4	88.0	88.2	86.7
1993	86.2	85.7	85.9	87.1	88.1	88.1	87.3	87.0	90.9	93.8	94.2	94.3	89.0
1994	92.7	93.6	93.9	92.7	94.0	93.6	92.7	91.0	94.9	97.2	95.8	95.5	93.9
1995	93.2	92.9	92.4	92.7	93.3	93.1	91.5	91.1	94.6	96.2	96.2	95.7	93.5
1996	92.9	93.2	93.4	92.8	93.0	91.7	89.9	89.6	92.4	93.5	93.1	92.5	92.3
1997	90.4	89.9	89.3	90.4	92.2	91.8	91.2	88.9	95.8	97.5	97.6	97.5	92.7
1998	96.5	96.8	97.5	98.3	99.4	98.4	96.5	96.7	87.7	101.8	101.7	101.3	97.7
1999	98.5	98.6	98.7	101.0	101.5	101.3	99.7	99.8	102.6	104.1	103.8	103.5	101.0
2000	101.8	101.9	102.3	102.9	103.6	103.0	102.3	102.3	104.8	105.6	105.1	105.0	103.3
2001	102.7	102.0	102.4	103.2	104.0	103.1	101.3	100.4	102.1	101.7	99.7	98.6	101.8
2002	96.1	95.0	94.8	96.0	97.0	95.7	92.0	91.6	94.5	96.1	96.0	95.1	95.0
2003	93.0	92.3	92.2	92.5	92.8	91.2	90.2	89.8	91.7	92.8	93.1	93.6	92.1
Information													
1990	52.9	53.1	53.6	54.0	54.4	55.0	55.2	55.4	55.0	54.3	54.6	54.8	54.3
1991	54.0	54.0	54.4	54.0	54.1	54.4	54.0	54.1	53.8	53.6	53.3	53.6	53.9
1992	52.5	52.6	53.2	54.4	53.7	54.3	54.1	54.0	53.9	53.3	53.5	53.8	53.6
1993	53.4	53.6	55.0	54.6	54.5	55.6	55.2	55.4	55.5	55.7	56.3	56.3	55.0
1994	55.7	55.8	56.2	56.6	56.7	57.4	57.5	57.6	57.0	57.0	57.5	58.0	56.9
1995	57.4	57.8	58.7	59.5	60.2	61.2	60.6	60.9	60.8	59.6	59.9	60.3	59.7
1996	60.2	61.0	61.3	61.5	62.1	64.6	62.2	62.8	62.3	62.1	62.3	62.7	62.0
1997	60.5	60.8	61.5	61.3	61.7	62.6	63.3	63.7	63.0	62.4	62.8	63.6	62.2
1998	62.6	62.6	62.8	63.1	63.2	63.7	64.4	65.2	65.0	63.4	64.1	64.6	63.7
1999	64.0	64.2	64.5	65.5	66.0	66.8	67.7	68.5	66.6	66.4	66.8	67.3	66.1
2000	66.7	67.3	67.5	68.2	68.7	70.3	70.7	70.8	69.8	70.0	70.5	70.6	69.2
2001	70.6	70.6	70.6	69.8	70.6	71.5	70.3	69.7	68.5	68.9	69.1	69.0	69.9
2002	67.5	67.2	67.2	67.4	67.3	67.7	67.2	66.1	64.9	64.4	64.5	64.3	66.3
2003	62.5	62.3	62.3	63.0	63.0	62.7	64.0	62.4	61.5	62.7	63.1	62.2	62.6
Financial activities													
1990	127.1	127.5	128.2	127.9	128.2	129.5	131.7	131.9	130.7	130.1	129.2	129.8	129.3
1991	129.3	128.5	129.6	128.6	129.9	131.2	131.7	133.0	131.5	130.0	130.0	131.2	130.3
1992	132.0	132.2	133.2	133.1	133.9	136.0	137.6	139.0	137.9	136.7	136.5	138.0	135.5
1993	136.9	136.9	138.2	138.9	139.8	142.0	142.1	142.6	142.2	141.8	142.2	144.0	140.6
1994	142.8	142.9	143.3	144.5	144.8	145.4	145.3	145.7	144.3	143.0	142.3	143.6	143.9
1995	141.5	141.2	142.0	141.9	142.4	144.1	145.7	146.3	146.0	145.4	145.8	146.9	144.1
1996	145.3	145.8	146.7	147.4	148.1	150.3	150.7	151.3	150.7	150.5	150.8	152.1	149.1
1997	149.8	149.9	150.6	151.4	151.5	152.7	156.2	156.2	155.1	154.1	154.0	155.2	153.0
1998	152.8	153.6	154.6	157.7	158.2	160.5	162.7	163.2	160.9	163.1	163.5	165.0	159.6
1999	161.5	161.5	161.9	163.3	163.6	165.1	165.8	165.8	164.2	164.4	164.0	165.4	163.8
2000	162.0	161.9	162.5	163.1	163.6	166.0	166.4	166.7	165.6	166.3	166.3	167.7	164.8
2001	166.2	166.9	167.6	168.0	168.7	170.7	170.6	170.7	168.8	168.2	168.7	169.4	168.7
2002	168.3	168.6	168.6	169.6	170.4	171.5	173.3	173.9	173.1	173.0	173.8	174.8	171.6
2003	172.0	172.6	173.2	174.6	175.6	177.2	179.1	177.5	176.5	177.3	177.8	178.1	176.0
Professional and business services													
1990	208.9	210.3	211.6	211.6	214.3	216.8	215.4	217.7	216.6	218.0	217.0	215.9	214.5
1991	207.2	206.3	207.9	210.7	212.6	216.0	216.8	218.9	219.0	218.2	217.5	217.2	214.0
1992	213.0	213.7	216.6	220.8	222.6	225.8	228.0	230.8	231.0	231.2	229.2	230.1	224.4
1993	223.7	224.1	225.6	229.0	230.6	234.3	235.6	236.7	237.1	240.4	240.2	241.9	233.2
1994	233.9	235.8	239.0	243.1	245.6	250.4	248.8	251.7	252.0	249.9	251.0	251.9	246.0
1995	245.4	247.7	251.5	252.6	255.1	259.4	261.9	265.0	264.6	265.1	265.3	267.3	258.4
1996	257.7	260.8	263.2	265.7	268.9	272.3	272.0	273.7	273.4	275.6	276.6	276.5	269.7
1997	269.6	272.0	274.5	276.5	281.6	286.2	290.8	294.3	293.1	292.9	295.1	295.8	285.2
1998	289.8	290.4	292.1	294.8	298.4	303.5	302.7	304.5	302.2	302.6	303.3	303.9	299.0
1999	296.6	297.6	300.1	306.2	308.2	312.7	315.3	317.4	313.3	319.3	318.1	318.8	310.3
2000	308.6	307.9	311.6	316.3	317.8	325.0	323.6	325.5	323.7	325.0	324.0	322.1	319.2
2001	312.2	309.5	310.4	314.0	314.4	317.5	313.2	312.6	309.6	307.9	305.0	302.6	310.7
2002	290.1	289.8	290.4	292.7	295.5	299.7	301.3	304.4	302.2	302.9	300.3	297.7	297.3
2003	287.8	288.1	288.9	291.7	293.8	296.8	296.8	297.6	297.4	300.7	299.4	295.8	294.6
Educational and health services													
1990	237.0	240.8	242.0	242.3	243.3	236.9	235.1	236.0	242.1	247.7	248.6	250.2	241.8
1991	246.7	250.0	252.2	252.0	253.3	246.5	244.8	244.5	251.0	257.5	258.0	258.8	251.2
1992	255.5	259.7	260.5	261.4	262.5	255.0	253.7	252.7	259.8	265.5	266.4	268.3	260.0
1993	262.1	266.0	267.9	269.8	270.2	263.4	261.1	260.4	266.9	272.9	273.7	275.0	267.4
1994	267.0	271.3	273.4	274.1	274.6	267.4	264.2	263.6	271.6	275.0	276.1	277.3	271.3
1995	271.6	276.5	279.0	279.8	280.8	274.4	272.6	273.0	280.2	285.1	286.6	286.8	278.8
1996	281.8	285.8	288.7	287.9	288.3	282.0	279.0	279.1	285.3	289.7	290.8	292.1	285.8
1997	290.0	294.1	296.1	295.1	296.1	290.3	286.9	287.0	293.2	299.3	300.3	299.6	294.0
1998	292.5	298.4	300.9	301.9	303.8	298.4	293.7	295.1	300.6	306.1	308.1	308.8	300.6
1999	301.5	306.0	308.0	311.6	311.8	309.6	310.1	307.3	312.8	320.5	322.5	323.6	312.1
2000	315.7	321.3	323.5	324.6	324.7	320.4	318.5	317.4	325.8	332.3	334.5	335.6	324.5
2001	328.1	332.9	335.8	337.5	339.4	334.3	332.0	332.7	339.5	348.1	350.4	350.6	338.4
2002	346.3	353.1	355.2	357.1	359.4	352.9	348.3	349.4	355.1	361.6	363.9	364.3	355.6
2003	360.2	366.7	368.2	368.6	370.3	364.6	362.2	362.0	365.3	372.2	371.2	369.8	366.8

Employment by Industry: Minnesota—*Continued*

(Numbers in thousands. Not seasonally adjusted.)

Industry	January	February	March	April	May	June	July	August	September	October	November	December	Annual Average
STATEWIDE—*Continued*													
Leisure and hospitality													
1990	167.0	168.1	171.3	177.2	184.1	191.5	193.1	194.4	190.2	180.8	176.4	177.9	181.0
1991	170.3	171.0	173.6	179.1	187.8	194.8	194.2	197.4	193.6	185.1	180.5	181.0	184.0
1992	175.7	175.7	178.7	187.7	200.0	206.1	205.1	206.8	203.4	196.7	191.7	192.3	193.3
1993	185.6	186.3	188.7	195.1	202.1	208.6	209.9	213.8	208.9	202.7	196.6	198.1	199.7
1994	192.4	193.2	195.8	204.3	212.9	220.4	216.9	219.0	213.5	205.9	201.4	202.3	206.5
1995	188.6	190.5	193.4	198.6	208.3	217.6	215.8	218.8	212.7	204.8	200.4	200.7	204.1
1996	193.4	193.9	196.8	200.5	211.3	219.1	219.6	222.9	214.9	205.3	201.2	200.7	206.6
1997	191.6	193.3	195.1	200.5	212.6	221.7	223.2	226.3	220.6	210.2	203.6	204.5	208.6
1998	196.5	198.3	200.8	206.9	218.4	226.3	226.3	231.0	223.9	211.1	205.5	206.2	212.6
1999	199.1	201.2	203.4	211.5	221.7	230.7	230.1	234.9	227.0	217.7	211.7	212.2	216.7
2000	204.8	206.4	208.8	215.1	225.1	235.0	236.6	240.4	234.0	222.1	216.3	215.3	221.6
2001	209.7	211.5	214.2	219.2	230.4	241.0	242.4	248.0	237.9	226.5	220.5	220.0	226.8
2002	213.8	213.6	215.0	222.3	233.9	243.6	244.2	246.9	240.1	228.7	221.7	222.8	228.9
2003	216.6	215.1	216.4	225.5	237.9	245.5	248.2	250.4	244.8	235.7	230.1	230.0	233.0
Other services													
1990	89.7	90.2	90.4	91.7	92.0	93.8	93.1	93.1	92.6	92.7	93.0	93.7	92.1
1991	92.9	92.4	93.2	92.3	93.0	94.8	94.4	94.5	93.7	94.3	94.2	95.5	93.7
1992	93.1	93.4	94.3	94.4	95.1	96.8	96.3	96.4	96.4	96.4	96.5	97.3	95.5
1993	96.1	97.0	97.6	98.5	98.7	99.9	99.0	98.7	98.4	99.3	99.3	100.1	98.5
1994	98.6	99.2	100.2	99.9	100.4	101.7	101.4	101.6	101.8	101.3	101.4	102.0	100.7
1995	98.7	99.5	100.5	100.4	101.0	102.2	101.6	101.6	101.9	101.4	101.6	102.6	101.0
1996	102.0	102.6	104.0	104.3	104.8	105.6	106.0	105.8	106.0	105.2	105.5	106.8	104.8
1997	103.9	104.7	105.8	106.1	106.8	107.2	106.6	107.1	107.7	108.0	108.0	108.8	106.7
1998	107.3	108.0	108.6	109.2	109.3	110.0	109.2	109.4	109.6	110.0	109.9	111.1	109.3
1999	109.0	109.3	110.4	110.8	111.2	112.4	111.8	112.0	111.8	113.3	113.7	114.8	111.7
2000	112.8	113.7	114.7	114.1	114.0	114.8	114.1	114.7	114.1	116.0	115.9	116.9	114.6
2001	116.0	116.3	117.5	117.8	118.2	118.7	116.7	117.0	116.4	117.8	119.5	118.8	117.6
2002	116.6	116.7	117.0	117.9	118.2	119.3	119.5	119.9	119.2	119.2	119.5	120.2	118.6
2003	117.7	117.9	118.4	118.3	118.8	119.7	119.8	119.8	119.7	119.2	119.2	118.3	118.9
Government													
1990	336.8	343.5	341.7	347.1	351.1	342.4	314.3	305.8	325.5	345.2	351.5	348.0	337.7
1991	343.7	350.1	348.1	350.5	354.5	347.2	317.1	311.1	327.2	348.1	351.7	352.6	341.8
1992	347.5	353.2	353.4	358.0	358.5	351.0	320.4	313.1	330.4	352.7	358.7	356.3	346.1
1993	354.1	359.9	360.3	361.3	364.6	357.2	325.4	319.2	335.0	358.8	364.1	364.8	352.0
1994	357.7	362.4	362.6	366.7	370.2	367.1	333.3	326.8	348.0	368.1	377.2	374.0	359.5
1995	383.8	388.9	389.4	388.1	391.4	387.3	352.6	342.6	357.7	380.8	386.9	384.8	377.8
1996	381.0	385.3	385.2	386.0	390.5	384.0	354.3	347.1	367.5	387.5	395.2	390.6	379.5
1997	381.7	387.1	387.2	387.1	390.3	386.5	353.9	347.4	366.6	385.8	390.9	390.9	379.6
1998	384.3	389.1	389.7	390.7	393.8	387.4	349.4	345.6	369.1	389.5	393.6	393.3	381.2
1999	388.6	393.5	395.2	397.6	397.7	389.4	360.6	353.4	377.2	396.6	400.1	399.0	387.4
2000	392.1	402.4	405.5	409.8	414.9	405.9	370.6	367.0	391.3	403.2	409.9	408.5	398.4
2001	395.7	407.2	408.0	408.8	410.9	407.7	372.3	364.6	395.0	407.9	411.2	412.1	400.1
2002	405.1	411.2	410.8	409.0	410.9	411.7	382.2	370.6	401.2	410.7	418.2	415.8	404.8
2003	403.6	412.4	412.2	413.6	413.1	409.0	377.4	374.3	388.9	406.4	408.5	408.8	402.4
Federal government													
1990	34.1	34.0	35.1	37.0	38.2	35.8	36.6	34.8	34.2	33.7	33.7	34.2	35.1
1991	33.8	33.6	33.7	34.0	34.1	34.7	34.8	34.6	34.5	34.2	34.3	34.8	34.2
1992	34.7	34.4	34.4	34.6	34.5	34.6	34.4	34.3	34.2	34.1	33.4	34.2	34.3
1993	33.5	33.6	33.5	33.5	33.7	33.9	34.1	34.2	34.3	34.0	34.1	34.9	33.9
1994	33.8	33.7	34.0	34.1	34.0	34.1	33.9	34.1	33.9	33.9	33.9	34.6	34.0
1995	34.1	33.8	34.0	33.7	33.7	34.4	34.1	34.1	34.0	33.8	33.8	34.7	34.0
1996	33.6	33.9	33.9	34.0	34.1	34.3	34.5	34.6	34.0	33.8	33.7	35.0	34.1
1997	34.0	33.7	33.7	34.0	34.1	34.2	34.2	34.1	34.1	33.8	33.9	35.0	34.0
1998	33.2	33.0	32.7	33.2	33.4	33.4	33.5	33.6	33.5	33.3	33.6	34.5	33.4
1999	33.2	33.0	32.8	33.8	33.7	33.3	33.2	33.1	33.2	32.7	33.1	34.0	33.2
2000	32.9	33.1	35.0	35.9	41.7	40.7	38.2	38.7	34.1	33.9	34.3	35.2	36.1
2001	33.8	33.5	33.4	33.6	33.7	34.1	34.0	33.8	33.7	33.4	33.3	33.8	33.7
2002	33.0	32.7	32.7	32.5	32.5	33.3	33.0	32.8	33.1	33.2	33.5	33.9	33.0
2003	34.2	34.1	34.4	34.2	34.3	34.4	34.5	34.5	34.2	34.1	33.8	34.2	34.2
State government													
1990	84.8	87.0	84.5	87.2	87.3	78.7	72.9	72.8	78.4	87.0	87.3	85.8	82.8
1991	85.3	87.7	85.3	87.7	87.3	79.4	73.3	73.1	77.8	85.8	85.6	84.3	82.7
1992	84.0	86.3	85.2	86.2	86.9	79.6	73.1	72.0	75.6	86.1	86.9	83.9	82.1
1993	85.9	87.4	85.9	87.0	87.7	80.4	73.5	72.7	78.3	86.4	87.3	85.9	83.2
1994	85.3	87.6	86.0	87.7	88.4	82.1	74.5	73.8	78.8	88.1	88.8	87.3	84.0
1995	89.0	90.2	89.2	90.6	91.3	84.4	77.7	76.2	80.6	91.7	92.7	89.1	86.8
1996	91.7	93.4	91.1	92.5	93.4	85.1	79.8	79.2	82.0	93.0	92.9	90.4	88.7
1997	88.1	89.6	88.2	89.0	88.5	82.9	77.3	76.8	79.8	88.2	89.6	87.2	85.4
1998	87.7	88.3	89.1	89.4	89.1	82.5	78.0	76.5	79.1	87.6	87.6	86.9	85.1
1999	86.3	88.7	89.9	91.1	89.4	83.8	79.7	78.6	85.3	92.9	92.8	89.2	87.3
2000	86.7	93.0	94.0	94.7	91.3	84.7	80.7	80.0	89.2	91.2	91.6	89.8	88.9
2001	82.4	90.5	90.4	91.8	89.2	82.8	81.3	80.1	91.3	91.3	91.3	90.6	87.8
2002	88.2	91.8	91.1	91.7	87.4	83.1	82.8	80.5	93.5	92.4	92.9	92.4	89.0
2003	86.0	91.1	90.5	93.1	89.9	83.0	83.0	82.1	91.5	92.8	93.0	92.7	89.1

Employment by Industry: Minnesota—*Continued*

(Numbers in thousands. Not seasonally adjusted.)

Industry	January	February	March	April	May	June	July	August	September	October	November	December	Annual Average
STATEWIDE—*Continued*													
Local government													
1990	217.9	222.5	222.1	222.9	225.6	227.9	204.8	198.2	212.9	224.5	230.5	228.0	219.8
1991	224.6	228.8	229.1	228.8	233.1	233.1	209.0	203.4	214.9	228.1	231.8	233.5	224.8
1992	228.8	232.5	233.8	237.2	237.1	236.8	212.9	206.8	220.6	232.5	238.4	238.2	229.6
1993	234.7	238.9	240.9	240.8	243.2	242.9	217.8	212.3	222.4	238.4	242.7	244.0	234.9
1994	238.6	241.1	242.6	244.9	247.8	250.9	224.9	218.9	235.3	246.1	254.5	252.1	241.4
1995	260.7	264.9	266.2	263.8	266.4	268.5	240.8	232.3	243.1	255.3	260.4	261.0	256.9
1996	255.7	258.0	260.2	259.5	263.0	264.6	240.0	233.3	251.5	260.7	268.6	265.2	256.6
1997	259.6	263.8	265.3	264.1	267.7	269.4	242.4	236.5	252.7	263.8	267.4	268.7	260.1
1998	263.4	267.8	267.9	268.1	271.3	271.5	237.9	235.5	256.5	268.6	272.4	271.9	262.7
1999	269.1	271.8	272.5	272.7	274.6	272.3	247.7	241.7	258.7	271.0	274.2	275.8	266.8
2000	272.5	276.3	276.5	279.2	281.9	280.5	251.7	248.3	268.0	278.1	284.0	283.5	273.3
2001	279.5	283.2	284.2	283.4	288.0	290.8	257.0	250.7	270.0	283.2	286.6	287.7	278.7
2002	283.9	286.7	287.0	284.8	291.0	295.3	266.4	257.3	274.6	285.1	291.8	289.5	282.8
2003	283.4	287.2	287.3	286.3	288.9	291.6	259.9	257.7	263.2	279.5	281.7	281.9	279.1
DULUTH													
Total nonfarm													
1990	94.8	94.2	94.8	96.2	98.0	98.7	98.3	99.4	99.7	99.2	99.5	98.2	97.5
1991	96.0	95.6	96.1	97.2	99.9	100.4	100.3	100.9	101.9	101.2	100.6	100.7	99.2
1992	98.5	97.7	97.7	99.5	101.5	102.7	102.6	100.7	102.1	101.5	100.7	100.2	100.4
1993	98.2	97.8	98.4	99.8	101.1	102.7	102.1	101.5	102.3	102.7	102.8	102.0	100.9
1994	99.6	100.0	100.2	102.0	104.1	105.0	105.0	104.4	104.8	105.0	104.9	104.3	103.2
1995	102.5	102.8	103.1	104.0	106.1	108.3	108.4	107.2	108.7	108.8	109.2	108.2	106.4
1996	104.7	105.2	105.4	106.7	108.8	109.9	109.5	109.2	109.8	110.6	111.1	110.4	108.4
1997	106.7	107.1	107.4	107.6	110.6	112.3	112.2	111.9	112.3	114.6	113.7	113.0	110.7
1998	109.4	109.7	109.5	111.5	114.7	116.2	114.9	114.0	113.2	114.4	114.6	114.2	113.0
1999	109.9	110.0	110.8	112.8	114.5	116.1	116.0	114.8	115.3	116.9	116.9	117.2	114.2
2000	112.8	114.1	114.8	115.8	117.5	119.1	118.5	118.3	118.7	119.0	119.4	118.7	117.2
2001	114.2	115.1	114.9	115.2	116.9	118.6	116.3	116.3	117.1	118.2	118.6	117.1	116.5
2002	112.9	112.7	113.6	114.5	116.1	117.2	116.7	116.2	117.6	117.9	118.3	117.4	115.9
2003	113.3	114.7	114.5	115.5	117.8	117.1	116.1	115.3	116.1	116.8	117.0	117.0	115.9
Total private													
1990	72.8	72.0	72.8	73.9	75.6	77.7	77.7	78.5	78.0	77.6	77.4	76.6	75.8
1991	74.2	73.8	74.4	75.6	78.1	79.4	79.6	80.7	80.8	79.8	79.0	79.0	77.8
1992	76.8	75.9	76.1	77.3	79.9	81.3	81.6	80.7	81.2	80.2	79.0	78.9	79.0
1993	76.7	76.2	76.7	77.9	79.2	81.1	81.3	81.3	81.7	81.7	81.3	80.5	79.6
1994	78.0	78.0	78.4	80.3	82.2	83.5	84.0	83.7	83.9	83.2	82.8	82.6	81.7
1995	80.1	79.9	80.3	81.4	83.5	85.7	86.5	86.4	86.7	86.2	86.1	85.3	84.0
1996	81.8	81.3	81.8	82.9	85.1	87.1	87.3	87.8	87.4	87.2	87.0	86.8	85.2
1997	83.2	82.9	83.3	83.4	86.5	88.8	89.7	90.2	89.8	90.6	89.2	88.9	87.2
1998	85.7	85.4	85.2	88.2	91.4	93.2	92.3	92.2	91.1	90.6	90.5	90.4	89.6
1999	86.7	86.6	87.3	89.4	91.2	93.4	94.2	93.3	92.9	93.4	93.2	93.8	91.2
2000	89.7	90.3	90.8	91.7	93.3	95.2	95.4	95.9	95.3	95.1	94.7	94.3	93.4
2001	91.3	90.6	90.7	90.9	93.0	94.9	94.5	95.0	93.8	93.4	93.3	92.6	92.8
2002	89.6	88.3	89.3	90.3	92.3	94.5	94.9	95.2	94.2	93.7	93.5	93.0	92.4
2003	90.7	90.4	90.4	91.2	94.0	95.0	95.3	94.8	93.6	93.2	93.1	93.3	92.9
Goods-producing													
1990	14.7	14.4	14.7	15.1	15.5	16.6	16.3	16.6	16.3	16.6	16.3	15.5	15.7
1991	14.6	14.4	14.6	15.6	16.3	16.9	16.9	17.3	17.5	17.3	16.7	16.2	16.1
1992	15.4	15.1	15.2	15.3	15.9	16.6	16.9	16.2	17.0	16.6	16.2	15.2	15.9
1993	14.5	14.3	14.7	15.0	15.5	16.2	16.2	16.2	16.3	16.5	16.2	15.5	15.5
1994	14.6	14.5	14.7	15.6	16.3	16.8	16.7	16.8	16.9	16.7	16.4	16.2	16.0
1995	15.4	15.2	15.3	15.6	16.3	17.0	17.3	17.1	17.1	17.1	16.8	16.2	16.3
1996	15.0	14.8	15.1	15.4	16.1	16.9	17.2	17.4	17.4	17.2	17.1	16.7	16.3
1997	15.6	15.6	15.6	15.5	16.5	17.2	17.6	17.7	17.7	17.6	17.2	16.7	16.7
1998	16.0	15.8	15.8	16.5	17.2	17.5	17.4	17.4	17.2	17.4	17.2	16.6	16.8
1999	15.6	15.6	15.8	16.3	17.0	17.9	18.2	17.6	18.1	18.2	17.7	17.4	17.1
2000	16.4	16.5	16.4	16.5	17.3	17.9	18.4	18.4	18.3	17.9	17.5	16.9	17.3
2001	15.9	15.3	14.9	14.6	15.2	15.8	15.5	16.0	15.7	15.7	15.3	14.7	15.4
2002	13.7	12.8	13.6	13.7	14.4	15.1	15.5	15.6	15.4	15.3	15.0	14.3	14.5
2003	13.5	13.4	13.5	13.5	14.9	14.9	15.2	14.8	14.5	14.4	14.0	13.8	14.2
Natural resources and mining													
1990	5.3	5.2	5.3	5.3	5.2	5.5	5.5	5.5	5.5	5.5	5.4	5.3	5.3
1991	5.4	5.4	5.3	5.4	5.5	5.6	5.5	5.6	5.5	5.5	5.5	5.5	5.4
1992	5.5	5.4	5.4	5.4	5.4	5.5	5.6	4.8	5.6	5.5	5.4	4.9	5.3
1993	4.9	5.0	5.2	5.1	5.2	5.3	5.4	5.3	5.3	5.2	5.2	5.2	5.1
1994	5.1	5.1	5.1	5.2	5.3	5.4	5.3	5.4	5.3	5.3	5.2	5.3	5.2
1995	5.3	5.2	5.2	5.2	5.3	5.5	5.6	5.5	5.5	5.4	5.4	5.3	5.3
1996	5.3	5.2	5.2	5.2	5.3	5.5	5.6	5.5	5.5	5.4	5.4	5.5	5.3
1997	5.3	5.3	5.3	5.2	5.3	5.5	5.6	5.5	5.4	5.3	5.2	5.3	5.3
1998	5.2	5.1	5.1	5.1	5.2	5.4	5.3	5.3	5.2	5.2	5.2	5.1	5.2
1999	5.1	5.1	5.1	5.1	5.0	5.2	5.1	4.4	5.0	5.0	5.0	5.0	5.0
2000	5.0	4.9	4.8	4.9	4.9	4.9	5.0	5.0	4.9	4.9	4.8	4.8	4.9
2001	4.6	4.1	3.7	3.5	3.5	3.5	2.8	3.5	3.5	3.5	3.4	3.4	3.6
2002	3.3	2.7	3.3	3.2	3.2	3.3	3.3	3.3	3.3	3.3	3.3	3.2	3.2
2003	3.3	3.3	3.2	3.1	3.1	3.1	3.1	2.7	2.6	2.5	2.4	2.8	2.9

Employment by Industry: Minnesota—*Continued*

(Numbers in thousands. Not seasonally adjusted.)

Industry	January	February	March	April	May	June	July	August	September	October	November	December	Annual Average
DULUTH—*Continued*													
Construction													
1990	2.9	2.7	2.8	3.1	3.5	4.1	4.1	4.3	4.1	4.1	4.0	3.5	3.6
1991	2.7	2.6	2.7	3.2	3.7	4.1	4.2	4.4	4.7	4.5	4.0	3.6	3.7
1992	3.0	2.9	2.9	3.0	3.5	4.0	4.0	4.1	4.1	4.0	3.7	3.3	3.5
1993	2.9	2.7	2.7	3.0	3.4	3.8	4.0	4.1	4.2	4.1	3.8	3.2	3.4
1994	2.7	2.6	2.7	3.3	3.9	4.1	4.2	4.2	4.3	4.2	4.0	3.7	3.6
1995	3.0	2.9	2.9	3.2	3.7	4.2	4.3	4.3	4.3	4.3	4.1	3.5	3.7
1996	2.9	2.8	2.9	3.1	3.6	4.1	4.3	4.5	4.5	4.5	4.3	3.8	3.7
1997	3.2	3.0	3.0	3.1	3.9	4.3	4.6	4.8	4.9	4.8	4.4	3.9	3.9
1998	3.4	3.3	3.3	3.9	4.4	4.4	4.6	4.6	4.7	4.6	4.4	4.1	4.1
1999	3.3	3.3	3.4	4.0	4.7	5.2	5.4	5.5	5.5	5.5	5.0	4.7	4.6
2000	3.8	3.8	3.8	3.9	4.6	5.0	5.2	5.4	5.5	5.2	4.9	4.5	4.6
2001	3.7	3.6	3.6	3.8	4.4	5.0	5.5	5.3	5.1	5.1	4.9	4.4	4.5
2002	3.6	3.3	3.3	3.6	4.2	4.8	5.0	5.2	5.1	5.1	4.8	4.3	4.4
2003	3.6	3.5	3.7	3.9	5.1	5.0	5.2	5.2	5.1	5.1	4.8	4.3	4.5
Manufacturing													
1990	6.5	6.5	6.6	6.7	6.8	7.0	6.7	6.8	6.7	7.0	6.9	6.7	6.7
1991	6.5	6.4	6.6	7.0	7.1	7.2	7.2	7.3	7.3	7.3	7.2	7.1	7.0
1992	6.9	6.8	6.9	6.9	7.0	7.1	7.3	7.3	7.3	7.1	7.1	7.0	7.0
1993	6.7	6.6	6.8	6.9	6.9	7.1	6.8	6.8	6.8	7.2	7.2	7.1	6.9
1994	6.8	6.8	6.9	7.1	7.1	7.3	7.2	7.2	7.3	7.2	7.2	7.2	7.1
1995	7.1	7.1	7.2	7.2	7.3	7.3	7.4	7.3	7.3	7.4	7.3	7.4	7.2
1996	6.8	6.8	7.0	7.1	7.2	7.3	7.3	7.4	7.4	7.3	7.4	7.4	7.2
1997	7.1	7.3	7.3	7.2	7.3	7.4	7.4	7.4	7.4	7.5	7.6	7.5	7.3
1998	7.4	7.4	7.4	7.5	7.6	7.7	7.5	7.5	7.3	7.6	7.6	7.4	7.4
1999	7.2	7.2	7.3	7.2	7.3	7.5	7.7	7.7	7.6	7.7	7.7	7.7	7.4
2000	7.6	7.8	7.8	7.7	7.8	8.0	8.2	8.0	7.9	7.8	7.8	7.6	7.8
2001	7.6	7.6	7.6	7.3	7.3	7.3	7.2	7.2	7.1	7.1	7.0	6.9	7.3
2002	6.8	6.8	7.0	6.9	7.0	7.0	7.2	7.1	7.0	6.9	6.9	6.8	7.0
2003	6.6	6.6	6.6	6.5	6.7	6.8	6.9	6.9	6.8	6.8	6.8	6.7	6.7
Service-providing													
1990	80.1	79.8	80.1	81.1	82.5	82.1	82.0	82.8	83.4	82.6	83.2	82.7	81.8
1991	81.4	81.2	81.5	81.6	83.6	83.5	83.4	83.6	84.4	83.9	83.9	84.5	83.0
1992	83.1	82.6	82.5	84.2	85.6	86.1	85.7	84.5	85.1	84.9	84.5	85.0	84.4
1993	83.7	83.5	83.7	84.8	85.6	86.5	85.9	85.3	86.0	86.2	86.6	86.5	85.3
1994	85.0	85.5	85.5	86.4	87.8	88.2	88.3	87.6	87.9	88.3	88.5	88.1	87.2
1995	87.1	87.6	87.8	88.4	89.8	91.3	91.1	90.1	91.6	91.7	92.4	92.0	90.0
1996	89.7	90.4	90.3	91.3	92.7	93.0	92.3	91.8	92.4	93.4	94.0	93.7	92.0
1997	91.1	91.5	91.8	92.1	94.1	95.1	94.6	94.2	94.6	97.0	96.5	96.3	94.0
1998	93.4	93.9	93.7	95.0	97.5	98.7	97.5	96.6	96.0	97.0	97.4	97.6	96.1
1999	94.3	94.4	95.0	96.5	97.5	98.2	97.8	97.2	97.2	98.7	99.2	99.8	97.1
2000	96.4	97.6	98.4	99.3	100.2	101.2	100.1	99.9	100.4	101.1	101.9	101.8	99.8
2001	98.3	99.8	100.0	100.6	101.7	102.8	100.8	100.3	101.4	102.5	103.3	102.4	101.2
2002	99.2	99.9	100.0	100.8	101.7	102.1	101.2	100.6	102.2	102.6	103.3	103.1	101.4
2003	99.8	101.3	101.0	102.0	102.9	102.2	100.9	100.5	101.6	102.4	103.0	103.2	101.7
Trade, transportation, and utilities													
1990	20.4	19.9	19.9	20.2	20.9	21.2	21.1	21.3	21.1	21.1	21.4	21.6	20.8
1991	20.6	20.3	20.4	20.6	21.2	21.5	21.4	21.7	21.7	21.9	22.1	22.2	21.3
1992	21.5	20.8	20.7	21.1	21.6	21.9	22.2	22.5	22.2	22.1	22.1	22.4	21.7
1993	21.7	21.2	21.1	21.9	21.9	22.5	22.7	22.6	22.6	22.9	23.2	23.1	22.2
1994	22.1	22.1	22.2	22.7	23.0	23.2	23.6	23.6	23.6	23.5	23.6	23.3	23.0
1995	22.7	22.3	22.2	22.7	23.1	23.6	24.1	24.0	24.0	23.9	24.2	24.1	23.4
1996	23.3	22.9	22.9	23.0	23.5	24.0	23.9	24.0	24.0	24.3	24.6	24.7	23.7
1997	23.2	22.8	22.9	22.9	23.5	23.8	24.0	24.1	23.9	24.2	24.6	24.9	23.7
1998	23.1	22.7	22.6	23.4	24.2	24.6	24.0	24.0	23.7	23.7	24.1	24.2	23.6
1999	22.8	22.6	22.9	23.6	24.0	24.3	24.3	24.2	24.1	24.3	24.8	25.1	23.9
2000	23.5	23.5	23.6	24.0	24.4	24.7	24.5	24.7	24.6	24.5	24.9	25.1	24.3
2001	24.7	24.7	25.0	24.9	25.4	25.7	25.5	25.4	25.1	25.0	25.6	25.5	25.2
2002	24.6	24.0	24.0	24.2	24.5	24.7	24.4	24.5	24.1	24.3	24.5	24.5	24.4
2003	23.7	23.5	23.2	23.7	23.9	24.2	24.1	24.1	23.8	23.9	24.2	24.4	23.9
Wholesale trade													
1990	3.3	3.3	3.3	3.3	3.3	3.4	3.4	3.5	3.4	3.4	3.4	3.4	3.3
1991	3.4	3.4	3.4	3.3	3.4	3.4	3.5	3.5	3.5	3.5	3.4	3.5	3.4
1992	3.5	3.4	3.4	3.5	3.5	3.6	3.6	3.6	3.6	3.5	3.4	3.4	3.5
1993	3.3	3.3	3.3	3.4	3.4	3.5	3.6	3.5	3.5	3.5	3.5	3.4	3.4
1994	3.4	3.4	3.4	3.5	3.6	3.7	3.7	3.6	3.6	3.6	3.6	3.6	3.5
1995	3.5	3.5	3.5	3.6	3.6	3.7	3.8	3.8	3.7	3.7	3.7	3.6	3.6
1996	3.6	3.6	3.6	3.6	3.6	3.7	3.7	3.7	3.7	3.6	3.6	3.6	3.6
1997	3.4	3.4	3.5	3.5	3.5	3.6	3.6	3.6	3.6	3.7	3.7	3.6	3.5
1998	3.5	3.5	3.5	3.5	3.6	3.7	3.6	3.6	3.5	3.6	3.5	3.5	3.5
1999	3.3	3.3	3.3	3.3	3.3	3.4	3.5	3.4	3.4	3.3	3.4	3.5	3.3
2000	3.4	3.4	3.4	3.4	3.5	3.6	3.6	3.6	3.7	3.6	3.6	3.6	3.5
2001	3.4	3.3	3.4	3.6	3.6	3.7	3.7	3.7	3.6	3.6	3.6	3.5	3.6
2002	3.5	3.5	3.5	3.5	3.5	3.6	3.6	3.5	3.5	3.6	3.5	3.5	3.5
2003	3.4	3.4	3.4	3.4	3.4	3.5	3.6	3.5	3.5	3.5	3.5	3.5	3.5

Employment by Industry: Minnesota—*Continued*

(Numbers in thousands. Not seasonally adjusted.)

Industry	January	February	March	April	May	June	July	August	September	October	November	December	Annual Average
DULUTH—*Continued*													
Retail trade													
1990	13.1	12.8	12.8	13.0	13.3	13.5	13.4	13.5	13.5	13.4	13.8	14.0	13.3
1991	13.3	13.1	13.1	13.3	13.6	13.8	13.7	13.8	13.9	14.0	14.3	14.4	13.6
1992	14.0	13.7	13.6	13.7	14.0	14.1	14.1	14.3	14.1	14.4	14.6	14.8	14.1
1993	14.3	14.0	14.0	14.2	14.1	14.4	14.6	14.5	14.5	14.8	15.1	15.1	14.4
1994	14.4	14.3	14.5	14.8	14.9	15.0	15.4	15.5	15.5	15.5	15.7	15.3	15.0
1995	15.1	14.8	14.9	15.0	15.3	15.6	15.9	15.9	15.9	15.9	16.3	16.3	15.5
1996	15.7	15.4	15.3	15.4	15.7	15.9	15.8	15.8	15.8	16.2	16.6	16.8	15.8
1997	15.7	15.4	15.3	15.2	15.6	15.7	15.8	15.8	15.6	15.7	16.1	16.4	15.6
1998	15.2	15.0	14.9	15.3	15.7	15.9	15.5	15.5	15.3	15.1	15.6	15.7	15.3
1999	15.0	14.8	14.9	15.1	15.4	15.5	15.5	15.5	15.4	15.6	16.0	16.2	15.4
2000	15.3	15.2	15.1	15.3	15.5	15.7	15.4	15.5	15.3	15.4	15.8	16.0	15.4
2001	14.9	15.0	15.0	14.8	15.1	15.3	15.1	15.1	14.9	15.0	15.4	15.4	15.1
2002	14.7	14.4	14.4	14.6	14.5	14.6	14.6	14.7	14.5	14.4	14.7	14.9	14.6
2003	14.3	14.1	14.0	14.3	14.5	14.7	14.6	14.7	14.4	14.5	14.8	15.0	14.5
Transportation and utilities													
1990	4.0	3.8	3.8	3.9	4.3	4.3	4.3	4.3	4.2	4.3	4.2	4.2	4.1
1991	3.9	3.8	3.9	4.0	4.2	4.3	4.2	4.4	4.3	4.4	4.4	4.3	4.1
1992	4.0	3.7	3.7	3.9	4.1	4.2	4.5	4.6	4.5	4.2	4.1	4.2	4.1
1993	4.1	3.9	3.8	4.3	4.4	4.6	4.5	4.6	4.6	4.6	4.6	4.6	4.3
1994	4.3	4.4	4.3	4.4	4.5	4.5	4.5	4.5	4.5	4.4	4.3	4.4	4.4
1995	4.1	4.0	3.8	4.1	4.2	4.3	4.4	4.3	4.4	4.3	4.2	4.2	4.1
1996	4.0	3.9	4.0	4.0	4.2	4.4	4.4	4.5	4.5	4.5	4.4	4.3	4.2
1997	4.1	4.0	4.1	4.2	4.4	4.5	4.6	4.7	4.7	4.8	4.8	4.9	4.4
1998	4.4	4.2	4.2	4.6	4.9	5.0	4.9	4.9	4.9	5.0	5.0	5.0	4.7
1999	4.5	4.5	4.7	5.2	5.3	5.4	5.3	5.3	5.3	5.4	5.4	5.4	5.1
2000	4.8	4.9	5.1	5.3	5.4	5.4	5.5	5.6	5.6	5.5	5.5	5.5	5.3
2001	6.4	6.4	6.6	6.5	6.7	6.7	6.7	6.6	6.6	6.4	6.6	6.6	6.6
2002	6.4	6.1	6.1	6.1	6.5	6.5	6.2	6.3	6.1	6.3	6.3	6.1	6.3
2003	6.0	6.0	5.8	6.0	6.0	6.0	5.9	5.9	5.9	5.9	5.9	5.9	5.9
Information													
1990	2.8	2.8	2.8	2.8	2.8	2.8	2.8	2.8	2.8	2.7	2.7	2.7	2.7
1991	2.5	2.5	2.5	2.5	2.5	2.5	2.5	2.5	2.4	2.4	2.4	2.4	2.4
1992	2.4	2.4	2.4	2.3	2.3	2.3	2.3	2.3	2.3	2.3	2.3	2.3	2.3
1993	2.2	2.3	2.2	2.2	2.2	2.2	2.2	2.2	2.2	2.2	2.2	2.2	2.2
1994	2.2	2.2	2.2	2.3	2.3	2.3	2.3	2.3	2.3	2.3	2.3	2.3	2.2
1995	2.3	2.3	2.3	2.2	2.2	2.3	2.3	2.3	2.5	2.5	2.6	2.6	2.3
1996	2.2	2.2	2.2	2.3	2.3	2.3	2.2	2.2	2.2	2.2	2.2	2.2	2.2
1997	2.2	2.2	2.2	2.2	2.2	2.3	2.3	2.3	2.3	2.3	2.3	2.4	2.2
1998	2.3	2.4	2.3	2.4	2.4	2.5	2.5	2.5	2.5	2.5	2.6	2.6	2.4
1999	2.5	2.5	2.5	2.5	2.5	2.6	2.6	2.6	2.6	2.6	2.6	2.7	2.5
2000	2.7	2.7	2.7	2.7	2.6	2.7	2.7	2.7	2.7	2.7	2.6	2.7	2.6
2001	2.7	2.7	2.6	2.6	2.7	2.7	2.7	2.7	2.7	2.6	2.7	2.7	2.7
2002	2.7	2.7	2.7	2.7	2.7	2.7	2.7	2.7	2.7	2.8	2.8	2.8	2.7
2003	2.7	2.7	2.7	2.7	2.7	2.7	2.7	2.7	2.7	2.7	2.7	2.7	2.7
Financial activities													
1990	3.6	3.5	3.6	3.6	3.5	3.6	3.6	3.6	3.6	3.6	3.6	3.6	3.5
1991	3.6	3.6	3.6	3.6	3.7	3.7	3.8	3.8	3.7	3.6	3.6	3.7	3.6
1992	3.7	3.7	3.7	3.7	3.8	3.9	3.8	3.8	3.8	3.7	3.6	3.7	3.7
1993	3.6	3.6	3.5	3.6	3.6	3.7	3.8	3.8	3.8	3.7	3.6	3.7	3.6
1994	3.6	3.6	3.6	3.6	3.7	3.7	3.7	3.7	3.7	3.6	3.6	3.6	3.6
1995	3.6	3.6	3.6	3.6	3.6	3.7	3.7	3.7	3.7	3.7	3.7	3.8	3.6
1996	4.2	4.2	4.2	4.0	4.1	4.2	4.3	4.3	4.2	4.2	4.3	4.3	4.2
1997	4.2	4.2	4.2	4.2	4.2	4.3	4.3	4.3	4.3	4.2	4.1	4.1	4.2
1998	4.1	4.1	4.1	4.3	4.4	4.5	4.4	4.4	4.4	4.3	4.2	4.2	4.2
1999	4.3	4.2	4.3	4.3	4.3	4.4	4.4	4.4	4.4	4.3	4.3	4.3	4.3
2000	4.2	4.3	4.3	4.2	4.3	4.4	4.4	4.4	4.4	4.6	4.6	4.6	4.3
2001	4.6	4.6	4.6	4.6	4.7	4.9	4.8	4.8	4.7	4.7	4.7	4.7	4.7
2002	4.7	4.7	4.7	4.7	4.7	4.9	4.9	4.9	4.9	4.8	4.8	4.9	4.8
2003	4.9	4.8	4.9	4.9	5.0	5.0	5.1	5.0	5.1	5.1	5.1	5.1	5.0
Professional and business services													
1990	4.2	4.2	4.3	4.5	4.5	4.6	5.0	5.0	5.1	4.8	4.7	4.6	4.6
1991	4.3	4.3	4.3	4.6	4.8	4.8	4.9	4.9	4.9	4.9	4.7	4.7	4.6
1992	4.6	4.6	4.6	4.7	4.8	5.0	4.9	4.8	4.9	4.7	4.5	4.6	4.7
1993	4.6	4.7	4.7	4.6	4.7	4.8	4.8	4.9	5.0	5.1	5.0	4.9	4.8
1994	4.8	4.9	4.9	5.0	5.1	5.1	5.2	5.1	5.1	4.9	4.9	4.8	4.9
1995	5.0	5.0	5.1	5.1	5.3	5.3	5.5	5.6	5.7	5.6	5.5	5.5	5.3
1996	5.5	5.6	5.7	5.8	5.9	6.1	6.1	6.1	6.1	6.2	6.2	6.1	5.9
1997	6.1	6.1	6.1	6.3	6.6	6.8	7.1	7.2	7.1	8.3	7.2	7.2	6.8
1998	6.9	7.0	7.0	7.5	8.0	8.2	8.2	7.9	7.8	7.5	7.5	7.6	7.5
1999	7.2	7.3	7.4	7.6	7.7	7.9	7.9	7.7	7.3	7.7	7.7	7.8	7.6
2000	7.5	7.6	7.9	8.1	7.8	8.0	8.1	8.2	8.2	8.3	8.4	8.3	8.0
2001	7.1	6.9	6.9	6.9	6.9	7.0	6.8	6.7	6.7	6.7	6.7	6.5	6.8
2002	6.4	6.5	6.4	6.6	6.6	7.0	7.2	7.4	7.3	6.9	6.9	6.9	6.8
2003	7.1	7.0	7.0	7.1	7.2	7.3	7.2	7.2	7.0	7.0	7.2	7.1	7.1

Employment by Industry: Minnesota—*Continued*

(Numbers in thousands. Not seasonally adjusted.)

Industry	January	February	March	April	May	June	July	August	September	October	November	December	Annual Average
DULUTH—*Continued*													
Educational and health services													
1990	13.3	13.3	13.4	13.3	13.4	13.2	13.4	13.5	13.8	14.0	14.2	14.3	13.5
1991	14.5	14.5	14.6	14.4	14.5	14.1	14.1	14.3	14.5	14.7	15.0	15.1	14.5
1992	14.9	15.0	14.9	15.0	15.2	14.8	14.7	14.7	15.0	15.3	15.3	15.4	15.0
1993	15.2	15.1	15.3	15.4	15.4	15.1	15.2	15.0	15.5	15.6	15.7	15.7	15.3
1994	15.7	15.7	15.7	15.6	15.6	15.4	15.2	15.1	15.6	16.0	16.2	16.3	15.6
1995	16.0	16.2	16.3	16.4	16.4	16.1	16.2	16.4	16.7	16.9	17.2	17.1	16.4
1996	16.5	16.5	16.5	16.9	16.9	16.5	16.4	16.4	16.9	17.0	17.1	17.2	16.7
1997	16.9	17.0	17.2	17.0	17.1	17.1	16.8	16.9	17.4	17.4	17.7	17.6	17.1
1998	17.6	17.7	17.7	18.4	18.6	18.3	17.9	18.0	18.3	18.6	18.8	18.9	18.2
1999	18.6	18.6	18.6	18.7	18.7	18.5	18.6	18.6	18.9	19.5	19.7	19.9	18.9
2000	19.6	19.6	19.8	19.8	19.8	19.5	19.5	19.4	19.7	19.9	20.0	19.9	19.7
2001	19.7	19.8	19.8	20.2	20.5	20.1	20.4	20.5	20.9	21.2	21.3	21.5	20.5
2002	21.4	21.5	21.5	21.6	21.7	21.5	21.1	21.3	21.7	22.1	22.3	22.4	21.7
2003	22.1	22.4	22.4	22.3	22.4	22.1	22.1	22.1	22.4	22.5	22.6	22.8	22.4
Leisure and hospitality													
1990	9.2	9.3	9.5	9.8	10.4	11.0	10.9	11.1	10.7	10.2	9.9	9.7	10.1
1991	9.6	9.7	9.8	9.7	10.3	11.1	11.2	11.4	11.3	10.3	9.8	10.0	10.3
1992	9.6	9.6	9.8	10.4	11.3	11.8	11.9	11.5	11.1	10.5	10.1	10.3	10.6
1993	10.0	10.1	10.2	10.3	10.9	11.5	11.5	11.7	11.4	10.7	10.4	10.4	10.7
1994	10.2	10.2	10.2	10.7	11.3	12.0	12.2	12.0	11.6	11.2	10.8	11.0	11.1
1995	10.2	10.4	10.5	10.9	11.6	12.5	12.3	12.2	11.9	11.5	11.2	11.1	11.3
1996	10.3	10.3	10.3	10.6	11.3	12.0	12.2	12.3	11.6	11.1	10.6	10.6	11.1
1997	10.2	10.2	10.2	10.4	11.4	12.0	12.4	12.5	11.9	11.4	11.0	10.9	11.2
1998	10.7	10.7	10.7	11.0	11.8	12.6	13.0	13.1	12.4	11.9	11.4	11.5	11.7
1999	11.0	11.1	11.1	11.5	12.2	12.7	13.1	13.1	12.5	11.8	11.4	11.5	11.9
2000	10.9	11.1	11.1	11.4	12.0	12.7	12.6	12.8	12.4	12.1	11.7	11.7	11.8
2001	11.4	11.5	11.7	11.9	12.4	13.2	13.5	13.6	12.9	12.3	11.9	11.8	12.3
2002	11.1	11.0	11.2	11.6	12.4	13.1	13.6	13.4	12.8	12.2	11.9	11.8	12.2
2003	11.4	11.3	11.4	11.7	12.6	13.1	13.3	13.3	12.7	12.2	11.9	11.9	12.2
Other services													
1990	4.6	4.6	4.6	4.6	4.6	4.7	4.6	4.6	4.6	4.6	4.6	4.6	4.6
1991	4.5	4.5	4.6	4.6	4.8	4.8	4.8	4.8	4.8	4.7	4.7	4.7	4.6
1992	4.7	4.7	4.8	4.8	5.0	5.0	4.9	4.9	4.9	5.0	4.9	5.0	4.8
1993	4.9	4.9	5.0	4.9	5.0	5.1	4.9	4.9	4.9	5.0	5.0	5.0	4.9
1994	4.8	4.8	4.9	4.8	4.9	5.0	5.1	5.1	5.1	5.0	5.0	5.1	4.9
1995	4.9	4.9	5.0	4.9	5.0	5.2	5.1	5.1	5.1	5.0	4.9	4.9	5.0
1996	4.8	4.8	4.9	4.9	5.0	5.1	5.0	5.1	5.0	5.0	4.9	5.0	4.9
1997	4.8	4.8	4.9	4.9	5.0	5.3	5.2	5.2	5.2	5.2	5.1	5.1	5.0
1998	5.0	5.0	5.0	4.7	4.8	5.0	4.9	4.9	4.8	4.7	4.7	4.8	4.8
1999	4.7	4.7	4.7	4.9	4.8	5.1	5.1	5.1	5.0	5.0	5.0	5.1	4.9
2000	4.9	5.0	5.0	5.0	5.1	5.3	5.2	5.3	5.0	5.1	5.0	5.1	5.0
2001	5.2	5.1	5.2	5.2	5.2	5.5	5.3	5.3	5.1	5.2	5.1	5.2	5.2
2002	5.0	5.1	5.2	5.2	5.3	5.5	5.5	5.4	5.3	5.3	5.3	5.4	5.3
2003	5.3	5.3	5.3	5.3	5.3	5.7	5.6	5.6	5.4	5.4	5.4	5.5	5.4
Government													
1990	22.0	22.2	22.0	22.3	22.4	21.0	20.6	20.9	21.7	21.6	22.1	21.6	21.7
1991	21.8	21.8	21.7	21.6	21.8	21.0	20.7	20.2	21.1	21.4	21.6	21.7	21.3
1992	21.7	21.8	21.6	22.2	21.6	21.4	21.0	20.0	20.9	21.3	21.7	21.3	21.3
1993	21.5	21.6	21.7	21.9	21.9	21.6	20.8	20.2	20.6	21.0	21.5	21.5	21.3
1994	21.6	22.0	21.8	21.7	21.9	21.5	21.0	20.7	20.9	21.8	22.1	21.7	21.5
1995	22.4	22.9	22.8	22.6	22.6	22.6	21.9	20.8	22.0	22.6	23.1	22.9	22.4
1996	22.9	23.9	23.6	23.8	23.7	22.8	22.2	21.4	22.4	23.4	24.1	23.6	23.1
1997	23.5	24.2	24.1	24.2	24.1	23.5	22.5	21.7	22.5	24.0	24.5	24.1	23.5
1998	23.7	24.3	24.3	23.3	23.3	23.0	22.6	21.8	22.1	23.8	24.1	23.8	23.3
1999	23.2	23.4	23.5	23.4	23.3	22.7	21.8	21.5	22.4	23.5	23.7	23.4	22.9
2000	23.1	23.8	24.0	24.1	24.2	23.9	23.1	22.4	23.4	23.9	24.7	24.4	23.7
2001	22.9	24.5	24.2	24.3	23.9	23.7	21.8	21.3	23.3	24.8	25.3	24.5	23.7
2002	23.3	24.4	24.3	24.2	23.8	22.7	21.8	21.0	23.4	24.2	24.8	24.4	23.5
2003	22.6	24.3	24.1	24.3	23.8	22.1	20.8	20.5	22.5	23.6	23.9	23.7	23.0
Federal government													
1990	1.8	1.8	1.8	2.1	2.1	1.9	2.0	1.9	1.8	1.8	1.8	1.8	1.8
1991	1.8	1.8	1.7	1.8	1.8	1.8	1.9	1.8	1.8	1.8	1.8	1.8	1.8
1992	1.8	1.8	1.8	1.8	1.8	1.8	1.9	1.9	1.8	1.8	1.7	1.8	1.8
1993	1.7	1.7	1.7	1.7	1.7	1.8	1.8	1.8	1.8	1.8	1.8	1.8	1.7
1994	1.7	1.7	1.7	1.7	1.8	1.7	1.7	1.7	1.7	1.7	1.7	1.7	1.7
1995	1.7	1.7	1.7	1.7	1.7	1.8	2.1	2.0	2.0	2.0	2.1	2.1	1.8
1996	2.1	2.6	2.5	2.5	2.4	2.4	2.4	2.5	2.4	2.4	2.4	2.4	2.4
1997	2.3	2.3	2.3	2.3	2.3	2.3	2.3	2.3	2.3	2.3	2.3	2.5	2.3
1998	2.2	2.2	2.2	2.2	2.2	2.3	2.2	2.3	2.2	2.2	2.2	2.4	2.2
1999	2.2	2.1	2.1	2.1	2.1	2.1	2.1	2.1	2.2	2.1	2.2	2.2	2.1
2000	2.2	2.2	2.4	2.4	2.8	2.6	2.5	2.5	2.2	2.2	2.2	2.3	2.3
2001	2.1	2.1	2.1	2.1	2.2	2.2	2.2	2.2	2.2	2.1	2.2	2.2	2.2
2002	2.1	2.1	2.1	2.1	2.1	2.2	2.2	2.2	2.1	2.2	2.3	2.3	2.2
2003	2.2	2.1	2.2	2.2	2.2	2.2	2.2	2.2	2.2	2.2	2.2	2.2	2.2

Employment by Industry: Minnesota—*Continued*

(Numbers in thousands. Not seasonally adjusted.)

Industry	January	February	March	April	May	June	July	August	September	October	November	December	Annual Average
DULUTH—*Continued*													
State government													
1990	4.5	4.5	4.5	4.5	4.6	3.9	3.9	3.9	4.2	4.5	4.5	4.5	4.3
1991	4.5	4.5	4.5	4.5	4.6	4.0	3.9	3.8	4.4	4.5	4.5	4.5	4.3
1992	4.5	4.6	4.5	4.5	4.6	4.2	4.0	3.8	4.1	4.6	4.6	4.5	4.3
1993	4.6	4.6	4.6	4.6	4.7	4.1	3.6	3.5	3.7	4.3	4.3	4.3	4.2
1994	4.5	4.7	4.6	4.6	4.7	4.2	4.0	4.0	4.2	4.8	4.8	4.6	4.4
1995	4.5	4.8	4.7	4.7	4.8	4.3	4.2	4.3	4.8	5.4	5.4	5.2	4.7
1996	5.1	5.4	5.4	5.3	5.3	4.5	4.3	4.2	4.5	5.2	5.3	5.2	4.9
1997	5.0	5.5	5.5	5.5	5.5	4.7	4.4	4.4	4.8	5.5	5.7	5.4	5.1
1998	5.3	5.5	5.6	5.6	5.6	4.8	4.9	4.8	5.1	5.7	5.8	5.6	5.3
1999	5.5	5.7	5.8	6.0	5.8	5.1	4.9	4.8	5.6	6.1	6.1	5.9	5.6
2000	5.5	6.0	6.1	6.2	5.9	5.4	5.3	5.1	6.3	6.6	6.7	6.6	5.9
2001	5.3	6.7	6.5	6.6	6.3	5.6	5.4	5.2	6.3	6.9	6.9	6.9	6.2
2002	5.8	6.9	6.7	6.9	6.3	5.5	5.3	5.1	6.6	6.9	7.1	6.9	6.3
2003	5.5	7.0	6.9	7.1	6.7	5.5	5.5	5.4	6.5	6.8	6.8	6.7	6.4
Local government													
1990	15.7	15.9	15.7	15.7	15.7	15.2	14.7	15.1	15.7	15.3	15.8	15.3	15.4
1991	15.5	15.5	15.5	15.3	15.4	15.2	14.9	14.6	14.9	15.1	15.3	15.4	15.2
1992	15.4	15.4	15.3	15.9	15.2	15.4	15.1	14.3	15.0	14.9	15.4	15.0	15.1
1993	15.2	15.3	15.4	15.6	15.5	15.7	15.4	14.9	15.1	14.9	15.4	15.4	15.3
1994	15.4	15.6	15.5	15.4	15.4	15.6	15.3	15.0	15.0	15.3	15.6	15.4	15.3
1995	16.2	16.4	16.4	16.2	16.1	16.5	15.6	14.5	15.2	15.2	15.6	15.6	15.7
1996	15.7	15.9	15.7	16.0	16.0	15.9	15.5	14.7	15.5	15.8	16.4	16.0	15.7
1997	16.2	16.4	16.3	16.4	16.3	16.5	15.8	15.0	15.4	16.2	16.5	16.2	16.1
1998	16.2	16.6	16.5	15.5	15.5	15.9	15.5	14.8	14.8	15.9	16.1	15.8	15.7
1999	15.5	15.6	15.6	15.3	15.4	15.5	14.8	14.6	14.6	15.3	15.4	15.3	15.2
2000	15.4	15.6	15.5	15.5	15.5	15.9	15.3	14.8	14.9	15.1	15.8	15.5	15.4
2001	15.5	15.7	15.6	15.6	15.4	15.9	14.2	13.9	14.8	15.8	16.2	15.4	15.3
2002	15.4	15.4	15.5	15.2	15.4	15.0	14.3	13.7	14.7	15.1	15.4	15.2	15.0
2003	14.9	15.2	15.0	15.0	14.9	14.4	13.1	12.9	13.8	14.6	14.9	14.8	14.5
MINNEAPOLIS-ST. PAUL													
Total nonfarm													
1990	1359.5	1364.7	1370.9	1381.8	1396.5	1405.9	1390.9	1395.4	1398.5	1406.4	1410.7	1408.1	1390.7
1991	1362.1	1358.5	1365.4	1374.9	1390.4	1401.6	1383.6	1386.7	1390.8	1402.4	1403.6	1407.4	1385.6
1992	1371.5	1374.7	1384.3	1401.8	1419.1	1425.7	1414.7	1417.4	1425.7	1439.0	1443.5	1447.5	1413.7
1993	1407.5	1412.9	1420.6	1438.6	1452.3	1461.8	1449.0	1452.4	1457.9	1479.3	1484.2	1492.0	1450.7
1994	1452.6	1460.1	1471.4	1485.3	1503.7	1515.2	1498.8	1501.5	1512.0	1519.4	1534.7	1536.9	1499.3
1995	1501.8	1509.6	1520.0	1528.5	1547.5	1562.2	1543.9	1551.0	1556.2	1572.3	1582.2	1588.0	1546.9
1996	1540.1	1545.6	1556.5	1564.4	1587.1	1599.0	1577.8	1584.2	1592.7	1603.5	1619.4	1620.3	1582.5
1997	1563.1	1572.0	1582.6	1593.9	1617.6	1629.6	1618.8	1624.3	1634.3	1646.4	1655.3	1661.4	1616.6
1998	1610.7	1614.1	1626.6	1647.6	1668.3	1676.6	1656.5	1662.4	1657.9	1684.4	1692.8	1700.2	1658.1
1999	1648.9	1655.7	1664.9	1690.1	1706.0	1716.7	1700.9	1708.6	1710.0	1733.0	1739.6	1746.3	1701.7
2000	1698.7	1705.0	1717.6	1736.3	1753.7	1769.7	1747.1	1754.6	1763.1	1771.3	1778.1	1779.4	1747.8
2001	1729.3	1732.1	1737.7	1745.2	1762.5	1770.8	1746.7	1748.2	1752.9	1754.0	1755.3	1750.4	1748.8
2002	1695.8	1694.4	1697.1	1708.1	1728.9	1737.8	1720.8	1719.6	1733.2	1736.1	1742.8	1737.1	1721.0
2003	1691.1	1693.7	1696.2	1714.5	1734.9	1741.2	1719.5	1716.9	1723.5	1740.2	1748.8	1744.9	1722.1
Total private													
1990	1170.2	1171.6	1178.6	1187.4	1199.2	1212.3	1209.8	1218.9	1214.9	1211.2	1212.4	1211.3	1199.8
1991	1168.3	1160.6	1167.9	1176.5	1190.0	1203.5	1200.2	1207.0	1205.0	1205.5	1204.7	1208.3	1191.4
1992	1176.0	1174.9	1184.0	1199.6	1216.0	1225.8	1228.6	1235.4	1236.9	1239.2	1240.7	1245.2	1216.8
1993	1207.1	1208.5	1215.8	1233.2	1244.9	1257.9	1259.0	1266.1	1265.3	1275.0	1277.1	1284.2	1249.5
1994	1249.2	1252.5	1263.8	1275.4	1291.4	1304.3	1302.2	1308.5	1310.6	1307.7	1316.7	1322.2	1292.0
1995	1285.5	1290.4	1299.9	1309.5	1326.8	1342.6	1342.7	1351.9	1350.5	1353.8	1359.6	1366.9	1331.6
1996	1322.6	1324.9	1335.4	1344.0	1363.3	1379.2	1376.4	1384.4	1383.2	1382.3	1392.6	1396.6	1365.4
1997	1345.0	1349.7	1359.7	1370.8	1391.7	1406.7	1414.4	1421.4	1423.7	1423.7	1428.3	1435.7	1397.5
1998	1388.2	1389.5	1399.9	1419.8	1438.0	1453.4	1451.3	1459.3	1442.7	1455.9	1462.1	1470.2	1435.8
1999	1420.2	1423.5	1432.5	1455.3	1470.5	1486.5	1488.5	1498.0	1487.0	1498.4	1502.4	1510.6	1472.7
2000	1465.2	1467.7	1478.3	1495.2	1509.9	1531.4	1530.4	1538.5	1533.3	1536.7	1540.3	1542.4	1514.1
2001	1498.3	1494.4	1499.4	1506.5	1520.8	1533.5	1526.9	1529.6	1519.2	1514.6	1513.9	1509.1	1513.9
2002	1459.0	1452.5	1454.7	1465.7	1484.4	1498.7	1497.5	1504.2	1495.4	1494.1	1496.0	1492.7	1482.9
2003	1453.4	1449.5	1452.2	1467.5	1487.4	1499.5	1493.6	1495.6	1494.0	1505.2	1511.7	1508.0	1484.8
Goods-producing													
1990	258.4	257.6	258.9	262.7	266.7	271.5	273.0	275.1	272.2	269.4	266.7	261.0	266.1
1991	251.6	249.0	249.8	256.1	259.9	265.2	266.4	268.1	265.4	264.2	260.2	257.6	259.4
1992	249.8	248.4	250.2	255.0	261.4	266.7	269.8	269.5	268.4	267.5	264.6	260.9	261.0
1993	252.3	252.2	253.9	259.1	263.9	268.9	272.1	274.0	270.7	270.7	268.3	264.8	264.2
1994	257.3	256.7	259.8	263.4	269.6	275.7	279.8	282.0	280.5	280.1	279.2	276.0	271.6
1995	268.2	268.1	270.7	276.2	282.4	288.8	291.3	293.7	291.7	289.3	287.7	284.6	282.7
1996	275.2	273.6	276.7	280.8	288.4	296.8	298.6	300.1	298.3	296.6	295.3	291.4	289.3
1997	279.5	280.0	282.9	287.6	295.1	301.2	301.8	304.2	302.1	302.6	300.1	296.1	294.4
1998	287.7	285.0	288.9	297.3	303.2	309.4	310.6	312.2	309.7	309.1	306.3	304.2	301.9
1999	294.9	294.8	296.6	303.6	308.3	314.9	315.8	318.6	314.9	313.0	311.4	308.2	307.9
2000	299.9	299.8	303.3	309.9	315.2	321.8	323.3	325.9	321.3	321.6	319.2	315.0	314.6
2001	305.1	303.4	303.7	305.7	310.2	314.0	315.2	315.3	313.8	308.7	304.4	298.8	308.2
2002	286.1	283.6	283.7	287.3	293.7	299.3	300.9	303.5	299.4	296.9	293.5	286.8	292.9
2003	277.5	274.2	274.4	279.3	286.4	292.9	293.3	294.8	291.5	292.3	289.7	287.1	286.1

Employment by Industry: Minnesota—*Continued*

(Numbers in thousands. Not seasonally adjusted.)

Industry	January	February	March	April	May	June	July	August	September	October	November	December	Annual Average
MINNEAPOLIS-ST. PAUL —*Continued*													
Natural resources and mining													
1990	0.4	0.4	0.4	0.6	0.6	0.6	0.6	0.6	0.5	0.5	0.5	0.4	0.5
1991	0.2	0.3	0.3	0.4	0.5	0.5	0.5	0.5	0.5	0.5	0.4	0.3	0.4
1992	0.2	0.2	0.3	0.4	0.5	0.5	0.5	0.5	0.5	0.5	0.5	0.4	0.4
1993	0.3	0.4	0.4	0.5	0.5	0.6	0.6	0.6	0.6	0.6	0.5	0.4	0.5
1994	0.3	0.3	0.4	0.5	0.6	0.6	0.6	0.6	0.6	0.6	0.6	0.4	0.5
1995	0.3	0.4	0.4	0.5	0.6	0.6	0.6	0.6	0.6	0.6	0.6	0.5	0.5
1996	0.4	0.4	0.4	0.5	0.6	0.6	0.6	0.6	0.6	0.7	0.6	0.6	0.5
1997	0.4	0.4	0.5	0.6	0.7	0.7	0.7	0.7	0.7	0.7	0.7	0.6	0.6
1998	0.4	0.5	0.5	0.6	0.6	0.7	0.6	0.6	0.6	0.6	0.6	0.6	0.5
1999	0.4	0.5	0.5	0.6	0.6	0.6	0.6	0.6	0.6	0.6	0.6	0.5	0.5
2000	0.5	0.5	0.5	0.5	0.6	0.6	0.6	0.6	0.6	0.6	0.6	0.5	0.5
2001	0.4	0.4	0.5	0.6	0.6	0.6	0.7	0.7	0.7	0.7	0.7	0.6	0.6
2002	0.5	0.5	0.5	0.6	0.7	0.7	0.7	0.7	0.7	0.7	0.7	0.6	0.6
2003	0.5	0.5	0.6	0.7	0.7	0.7	0.7	0.7	0.6	0.6	0.6	0.6	0.6
Construction													
1990	42.7	41.7	42.1	47.2	51.0	54.1	55.5	56.4	55.2	54.1	51.6	46.4	49.8
1991	40.4	39.3	40.2	45.4	48.1	51.5	53.0	53.7	52.6	51.5	48.1	44.9	47.3
1992	40.0	38.9	39.3	43.9	48.8	52.2	54.4	54.5	53.1	52.9	49.9	46.4	47.8
1993	40.6	39.9	40.5	44.2	48.8	51.8	54.1	54.6	53.4	52.6	50.6	46.7	48.1
1994	41.5	40.7	42.3	46.0	50.5	54.0	56.7	57.6	56.7	55.5	53.9	49.8	50.4
1995	44.1	43.0	44.3	48.3	53.3	57.5	58.5	59.4	58.2	58.2	56.3	52.4	52.7
1996	47.6	46.4	47.8	51.1	57.5	61.8	63.8	64.2	62.9	61.5	59.5	55.5	56.6
1997	48.8	48.6	49.7	53.9	60.0	63.9	65.7	66.7	65.3	65.7	62.9	59.4	59.2
1998	53.5	53.1	53.9	60.5	65.5	69.6	72.0	71.9	70.9	70.9	68.7	66.4	64.7
1999	59.1	59.1	61.0	67.5	72.0	76.5	78.8	79.6	78.3	76.3	74.6	71.8	71.2
2000	65.8	65.6	68.1	73.9	78.8	83.3	84.8	85.7	84.0	83.2	80.4	76.7	77.5
2001	71.1	70.3	71.6	75.8	81.5	87.2	89.4	90.6	88.3	87.2	84.8	80.1	81.5
2002	71.8	70.4	70.5	75.2	81.9	85.9	88.9	90.0	88.1	86.6	83.9	78.7	81.0
2003	71.0	69.0	69.3	74.7	81.4	86.2	88.3	89.4	87.2	88.1	84.8	80.5	80.8
Manufacturing													
1990	215.3	215.5	216.4	214.9	215.1	216.8	216.9	218.1	216.5	214.8	214.6	214.2	215.7
1991	211.0	209.4	209.3	210.3	211.3	213.2	212.9	213.9	212.3	212.2	211.7	212.4	211.6
1992	209.6	209.3	210.6	210.7	212.1	214.0	214.9	214.5	214.8	214.1	214.2	214.1	212.7
1993	211.4	211.9	213.0	214.4	214.6	216.5	217.4	218.8	216.7	217.5	217.2	217.7	215.5
1994	215.5	215.7	217.1	216.9	218.5	221.1	222.5	223.8	223.2	224.0	224.7	225.8	220.7
1995	223.8	224.7	226.0	227.4	228.5	230.7	232.2	233.7	232.9	230.5	230.8	231.7	229.4
1996	227.2	226.8	228.5	229.2	230.3	234.4	234.2	235.3	234.8	234.4	235.2	235.3	232.1
1997	230.3	231.0	232.7	233.1	234.4	236.6	235.4	236.8	236.1	236.2	236.5	236.1	234.6
1998	233.8	231.4	234.5	236.2	237.1	239.1	238.0	239.7	238.2	237.6	237.0	237.2	236.6
1999	235.4	235.2	235.1	235.5	235.7	237.8	236.4	238.4	236.0	236.1	236.2	235.9	236.1
2000	233.6	233.7	234.7	235.5	235.8	237.9	237.9	239.6	236.7	237.8	238.2	237.8	236.6
2001	233.6	232.7	231.6	229.3	228.1	226.2	225.1	224.0	224.8	220.8	218.9	218.1	226.1
2002	213.8	212.7	212.7	211.5	211.1	212.7	211.3	212.8	210.6	209.6	208.9	207.5	211.3
2003	206.0	204.7	204.5	203.9	204.3	206.0	204.3	204.7	203.7	203.6	204.3	206.0	204.7
Service-providing													
1990	1101.1	1107.1	1112.0	1119.1	1129.8	1134.4	1117.9	1120.3	1126.3	1137.0	1144.0	1147.1	1124.6
1991	1110.5	1109.5	1115.6	1118.8	1130.5	1136.4	1117.2	1118.6	1125.4	1138.2	1143.4	1149.8	1126.1
1992	1121.7	1126.3	1134.1	1146.8	1157.7	1159.0	1144.9	1147.9	1157.3	1171.5	1178.9	1186.6	1152.7
1993	1155.2	1160.7	1166.7	1179.5	1188.4	1192.9	1176.9	1178.4	1187.2	1208.6	1215.9	1227.2	1186.4
1994	1195.3	1203.4	1211.6	1221.9	1234.1	1239.5	1219.0	1219.5	1231.5	1239.3	1255.5	1260.9	1227.6
1995	1233.6	1241.5	1249.3	1252.3	1265.1	1273.4	1252.6	1257.3	1264.5	1283.0	1294.5	1303.4	1264.2
1996	1264.9	1272.0	1279.8	1283.6	1298.7	1302.2	1279.2	1284.1	1294.4	1306.9	1324.1	1328.9	1293.2
1997	1283.6	1292.0	1299.7	1306.3	1322.5	1328.4	1317.0	1320.1	1332.2	1343.8	1355.2	1365.3	1322.1
1998	1323.0	1329.1	1337.7	1350.3	1365.1	1367.2	1345.9	1350.2	1348.2	1375.3	1386.5	1396.0	1356.2
1999	1354.0	1360.9	1368.3	1386.5	1397.7	1401.8	1385.1	1390.0	1395.1	1420.0	1428.2	1438.1	1393.8
2000	1398.8	1405.2	1414.3	1426.4	1438.5	1447.9	1423.8	1428.7	1441.8	1449.7	1458.9	1464.4	1433.2
2001	1424.2	1428.7	1434.0	1439.5	1452.3	1456.8	1431.5	1432.9	1439.1	1445.3	1450.9	1451.6	1440.6
2002	1409.7	1410.8	1413.4	1420.8	1435.2	1438.5	1419.9	1416.1	1433.8	1439.2	1449.3	1450.3	1428.1
2003	1413.6	1419.5	1421.8	1435.2	1448.5	1448.3	1426.2	1422.1	1432.0	1447.9	1459.1	1457.8	1436.0
Trade, transportation, and utilities													
1990	291.2	287.9	289.2	289.6	291.8	294.2	290.5	293.1	292.5	292.7	299.3	302.2	292.8
1991	287.3	281.8	282.4	282.9	285.0	287.4	284.1	284.7	284.9	287.7	292.8	296.3	286.4
1992	282.8	279.8	280.5	282.6	285.4	285.8	284.8	287.9	287.8	292.2	298.6	302.5	287.5
1993	288.0	285.0	285.4	288.1	289.9	292.8	292.4	293.2	294.4	300.1	306.4	310.7	293.8
1994	299.0	297.2	297.9	297.3	300.6	303.0	304.6	304.7	307.2	311.5	318.7	323.3	305.4
1995	310.6	308.2	307.3	307.4	310.2	312.9	311.1	312.3	312.6	320.7	327.1	331.4	314.3
1996	317.7	313.7	314.7	315.1	317.9	320.7	317.1	318.1	318.4	323.3	332.5	337.3	320.5
1997	320.5	317.6	318.3	318.4	322.1	325.0	325.1	323.4	328.1	331.6	338.8	345.8	326.2
1998	328.9	326.0	326.3	329.7	333.4	334.6	333.5	334.7	322.3	338.6	345.9	351.6	333.7
1999	333.9	332.3	333.0	336.2	338.8	341.1	341.1	342.1	339.1	344.4	351.3	358.3	340.9
2000	344.6	341.2	340.9	341.2	343.3	346.8	346.0	347.2	346.8	351.3	358.5	363.6	347.6
2001	352.3	347.1	346.8	346.8	349.1	351.1	349.0	348.0	344.4	347.3	352.1	354.0	349.0
2002	339.5	332.6	332.6	333.9	336.8	338.4	335.1	335.3	333.7	336.5	343.6	347.5	337.1
2003	335.0	330.3	330.2	331.3	334.4	335.2	332.1	332.9	332.0	336.0	343.8	345.1	334.9

Employment by Industry: Minnesota—*Continued*

(Numbers in thousands. Not seasonally adjusted.)

Industry	January	February	March	April	May	June	July	August	September	October	November	December	Annual Average
MINNEAPOLIS-ST. PAUL *—Continued*													
Wholesale trade													
1990	69.6	69.8	70.4	70.3	70.5	71.5	71.0	71.7	70.4	69.8	69.9	70.1	70.4
1991	67.6	67.3	67.6	68.4	68.8	69.5	69.0	69.5	68.7	68.3	68.3	68.5	68.4
1992	67.7	67.3	67.8	68.1	68.6	69.1	70.1	69.9	69.4	69.6	69.9	70.0	68.9
1993	68.7	68.9	69.2	69.9	70.3	71.1	72.2	72.1	71.5	71.0	71.1	71.6	70.6
1994	70.7	70.9	71.5	71.7	72.2	73.2	73.7	73.9	73.8	73.8	74.1	74.9	72.8
1995	73.5	74.1	74.4	75.3	76.0	76.8	76.0	76.1	75.8	77.5	77.7	78.5	75.9
1996	78.3	78.3	78.8	79.6	80.1	82.0	81.8	82.1	81.2	80.8	81.4	81.9	80.5
1997	79.7	80.2	80.4	79.9	80.2	81.3	82.5	82.6	82.2	81.3	81.6	82.9	81.2
1998	81.4	81.5	81.7	82.5	83.1	83.4	83.8	83.8	82.9	83.0	83.3	83.2	82.8
1999	81.3	81.7	81.9	83.4	83.7	84.3	86.5	86.6	84.9	84.2	84.3	85.2	84.0
2000	83.8	83.8	84.2	84.4	85.0	86.8	85.7	85.8	85.0	85.3	85.5	85.9	85.1
2001	86.9	86.8	86.8	86.5	86.4	86.9	86.8	86.3	85.3	85.2	85.3	85.1	86.2
2002	83.8	83.8	83.6	83.6	83.7	84.2	84.4	84.3	83.3	83.6	83.4	83.4	83.8
2003	83.7	83.7	83.7	83.0	83.4	84.0	84.7	84.7	83.6	83.8	84.1	84.9	83.9
Retail trade													
1990	160.5	156.5	156.5	156.3	157.4	158.1	156.7	157.6	157.1	159.3	165.2	168.1	159.1
1991	157.2	152.3	152.0	151.8	152.6	153.7	152.3	152.2	152.0	154.7	159.5	162.1	154.3
1992	152.2	149.2	149.0	150.6	152.2	153.0	151.8	155.5	154.6	158.4	164.5	168.3	154.9
1993	156.6	153.4	153.4	154.4	155.5	157.5	155.8	157.2	156.8	161.4	167.1	170.9	158.3
1994	160.8	158.3	158.2	158.3	160.0	161.4	162.5	163.9	163.8	166.6	174.0	178.2	163.8
1995	168.0	165.0	164.1	163.6	165.5	167.2	167.3	168.7	167.3	172.5	178.7	182.4	169.1
1996	171.4	167.2	167.5	168.2	170.5	171.9	169.8	170.9	170.4	175.1	183.2	187.7	172.8
1997	174.4	171.2	172.2	172.5	174.6	176.3	175.4	176.0	176.0	179.6	186.3	192.3	177.2
1998	177.4	174.1	173.9	175.9	178.2	179.7	179.2	180.0	179.1	181.9	188.8	194.7	180.2
1999	180.8	178.6	179.2	180.0	182.1	183.5	182.3	182.8	180.3	185.1	191.9	198.0	183.7
2000	186.5	183.1	182.5	181.9	183.3	185.2	185.7	186.7	186.0	189.7	196.7	201.5	187.4
2001	190.8	186.3	185.9	185.7	187.9	189.7	188.6	189.2	185.8	189.7	196.0	199.1	189.6
2002	187.5	181.7	181.9	182.6	185.0	186.7	185.5	185.9	183.7	185.6	193.0	197.3	186.4
2003	185.4	181.0	181.0	182.9	185.6	186.6	183.8	184.2	183.0	185.8	192.7	193.9	185.5
Transportation and utilities													
1990	61.1	61.6	62.3	63.0	63.9	64.6	62.8	63.8	65.0	63.6	64.2	64.0	63.3
1991	62.5	62.2	62.8	62.7	63.6	64.2	62.8	63.0	64.2	64.7	65.0	65.7	63.6
1992	62.9	63.3	63.7	63.9	64.6	63.7	62.9	62.5	63.8	64.2	64.2	64.2	63.6
1993	62.7	62.7	62.8	63.8	64.1	64.2	64.4	63.9	66.1	67.7	68.2	68.2	64.9
1994	67.5	68.0	68.2	67.3	68.4	68.4	68.4	66.9	69.6	71.1	70.6	70.2	68.7
1995	69.1	69.1	68.8	68.5	68.7	68.9	67.8	67.5	69.5	70.7	70.7	70.5	69.1
1996	68.0	68.2	68.4	67.3	67.3	66.8	65.5	65.1	66.8	67.4	67.9	67.7	67.2
1997	66.4	66.2	65.7	66.0	67.3	67.4	67.2	64.8	69.9	70.7	70.9	70.6	67.7
1998	70.1	70.4	70.7	71.3	72.1	71.5	70.5	70.9	60.3	73.7	73.8	73.7	70.7
1999	71.8	72.0	71.9	72.8	73.0	73.3	72.3	72.7	73.9	75.1	75.1	75.1	73.2
2000	74.3	74.3	74.2	74.9	75.0	74.8	74.6	74.7	75.8	76.3	76.3	76.2	75.1
2001	74.6	74.0	74.1	74.6	74.8	74.5	73.6	72.5	73.3	72.4	70.8	69.8	73.3
2002	68.2	67.1	67.1	67.7	68.1	67.5	65.2	65.1	66.7	67.3	67.2	66.8	67.0
2003	65.9	65.6	65.5	65.4	65.4	64.6	63.6	64.0	65.4	66.4	67.0	66.3	65.4
Information													
1990	38.0	38.2	38.5	38.8	39.0	39.6	39.8	40.0	39.7	38.9	39.1	39.3	39.0
1991	39.0	39.1	39.4	38.7	38.8	39.1	38.8	38.8	38.7	38.5	38.5	38.7	38.8
1992	38.0	38.1	38.4	39.6	39.2	39.7	39.1	38.9	38.8	38.3	38.5	38.7	38.7
1993	38.4	38.5	38.7	39.5	39.5	39.9	40.2	40.3	40.2	40.3	40.5	40.9	39.7
1994	40.8	40.9	41.2	41.5	41.6	42.1	42.0	42.0	41.7	41.6	42.1	42.4	41.6
1995	42.3	42.6	43.3	44.1	44.5	45.2	44.5	44.7	44.6	43.5	43.8	44.3	43.9
1996	44.7	45.5	45.7	45.7	46.1	46.6	46.7	47.3	46.9	46.7	46.9	47.3	46.3
1997	44.9	45.2	45.8	45.7	45.8	46.3	46.9	47.1	46.6	46.1	46.2	46.9	46.1
1998	46.1	46.2	46.5	46.6	46.6	47.0	47.6	48.1	47.8	46.8	47.4	47.7	47.0
1999	47.4	47.5	47.9	48.8	49.1	49.7	50.1	50.6	49.6	49.6	49.9	50.3	49.2
2000	49.8	50.2	50.4	51.1	51.3	52.6	53.0	53.0	52.3	52.6	52.8	53.0	51.8
2001	52.8	52.7	53.0	52.3	52.3	53.0	52.7	51.9	51.3	51.6	51.7	51.5	52.2
2002	50.1	49.9	49.8	50.2	49.9	50.2	49.6	48.4	47.4	47.1	47.1	47.0	48.9
2003	45.6	45.4	45.3	46.1	45.9	45.6	45.2	45.4	44.6	45.0	45.4	44.8	45.4
Financial activities													
1990	99.9	100.4	100.8	100.8	100.9	102.1	103.5	103.6	103.3	102.7	101.9	102.3	101.8
1991	101.6	101.1	102.3	101.9	102.9	103.9	103.9	104.3	103.8	102.8	102.9	103.6	102.9
1992	104.7	104.9	105.7	105.6	106.1	107.7	109.2	109.8	109.8	108.7	108.7	109.7	107.5
1993	108.9	109.1	110.3	110.6	111.2	112.9	112.8	113.0	112.9	112.3	112.9	114.0	111.7
1994	114.1	114.2	114.7	115.4	115.4	115.5	115.3	115.3	114.5	113.4	113.1	114.2	114.5
1995	112.7	112.7	113.1	113.2	113.6	114.9	115.8	116.2	116.0	115.7	116.1	117.0	114.7
1996	114.3	114.7	115.3	116.4	117.0	118.8	118.9	119.7	119.3	118.8	119.1	120.2	117.7
1997	117.5	117.6	118.3	119.1	118.8	119.6	122.7	123.1	122.4	121.3	121.2	122.1	120.3
1998	119.6	120.5	121.3	123.8	124.2	125.9	128.2	128.8	126.8	129.1	129.6	131.1	125.7
1999	127.0	127.1	127.4	128.6	128.9	129.8	130.6	130.5	129.3	129.9	129.9	130.9	129.1
2000	127.6	127.6	128.0	128.8	129.4	131.2	131.6	131.8	131.1	131.3	131.2	132.4	130.1
2001	130.8	131.5	132.0	132.6	132.9	134.3	134.7	134.7	133.2	132.8	133.2	133.7	133.0
2002	132.8	133.1	133.1	133.5	134.0	134.7	136.5	137.1	136.5	136.5	137.4	138.1	135.3
2003	136.0	136.4	137.0	138.4	139.2	140.3	140.2	138.9	138.5	139.1	139.7	140.0	138.6

Employment by Industry: Minnesota—*Continued*

(Numbers in thousands. Not seasonally adjusted.)

Industry	January	February	March	April	May	June	July	August	September	October	November	December	Annual Average
MINNEAPOLIS-ST. PAUL *—Continued*													
Professional and business services													
1990	178.1	179.6	180.4	179.7	182.0	184.1	182.5	184.6	183.4	185.5	184.7	183.5	182.3
1991	176.2	175.5	176.9	178.5	180.3	182.9	184.1	185.8	185.8	185.6	185.4	185.2	181.8
1992	179.8	180.7	182.8	186.4	187.8	190.0	192.0	193.6	194.1	195.2	194.1	194.8	189.2
1993	188.8	189.3	190.6	193.9	195.3	198.0	198.3	199.8	199.9	203.0	202.9	204.5	197.0
1994	198.8	200.4	203.2	205.8	207.7	211.2	209.4	212.1	212.1	210.2	212.1	213.0	208.0
1995	208.0	210.4	213.2	213.4	215.5	218.6	220.7	222.8	222.4	224.2	224.3	226.4	218.3
1996	216.5	218.8	220.3	222.1	224.2	226.1	226.4	228.0	227.7	229.3	229.7	230.1	224.9
1997	223.5	225.4	227.3	228.2	232.0	235.7	240.2	243.6	242.5	241.9	243.8	244.3	235.7
1998	238.2	238.8	239.9	241.6	243.9	247.7	247.7	249.6	247.7	249.0	249.5	250.2	245.3
1999	244.8	245.1	246.9	250.7	252.4	255.6	257.7	259.8	257.3	263.1	261.9	262.8	254.8
2000	255.4	254.7	257.9	262.5	264.2	270.0	268.8	270.5	268.8	269.6	268.5	266.8	264.8
2001	260.5	258.3	258.4	261.8	261.7	263.5	260.6	260.5	257.6	255.8	253.2	251.8	258.6
2002	241.8	241.0	241.0	242.2	244.2	247.3	247.8	249.2	247.5	248.4	246.7	244.6	245.1
2003	237.2	237.5	237.7	239.4	240.5	242.4	240.8	240.2	239.6	242.9	243.3	241.4	240.2
Educational and health services													
1990	136.8	139.1	139.9	140.3	140.9	138.0	137.6	138.6	141.8	144.6	144.8	145.6	140.6
1991	141.7	143.2	144.6	144.5	145.1	142.3	141.6	141.8	144.8	148.1	148.1	149.0	144.5
1992	147.5	149.7	151.0	151.4	152.1	148.6	148.3	148.1	151.5	154.1	154.6	155.8	151.0
1993	151.4	153.7	154.7	156.0	156.3	153.4	152.7	152.5	155.5	158.4	158.7	159.5	155.2
1994	154.4	157.0	158.5	159.0	159.5	155.8	153.9	154.0	158.2	158.7	159.8	160.6	157.4
1995	157.3	160.3	161.9	162.7	163.2	159.7	159.5	160.0	163.7	165.4	166.1	166.9	162.2
1996	163.1	166.3	168.0	167.3	168.1	164.9	162.7	163.1	166.8	167.8	169.2	169.7	166.4
1997	167.3	170.4	171.9	173.2	173.7	170.0	168.8	168.8	172.5	175.4	175.7	176.2	171.9
1998	170.7	174.1	175.9	176.2	177.1	174.6	170.5	170.7	174.8	177.0	178.5	178.8	174.9
1999	172.0	174.4	176.3	178.1	178.5	175.9	175.4	175.9	179.8	184.1	185.2	185.7	178.4
2000	180.2	184.3	185.7	186.3	186.8	183.8	182.3	182.7	187.5	190.3	191.7	192.9	186.2
2001	185.9	189.0	190.9	191.0	192.3	189.2	187.9	188.5	193.2	197.0	198.7	199.1	191.9
2002	194.5	197.8	198.9	199.6	201.1	198.2	198.7	199.3	203.1	206.3	207.9	208.1	201.1
2003	205.7	210.0	210.9	211.1	212.2	210.3	208.3	208.4	213.8	218.2	218.8	219.0	212.2
Leisure and hospitality													
1990	109.4	110.0	112.0	115.6	117.9	121.7	122.4	123.2	121.8	117.2	115.5	116.7	116.9
1991	110.1	110.6	111.8	114.4	118.2	121.6	120.7	122.6	121.6	117.8	116.1	116.3	116.8
1992	113.4	113.2	114.6	118.3	122.9	125.1	123.4	125.4	124.5	121.4	119.5	120.2	120.1
1993	117.7	118.3	119.5	122.7	125.5	127.8	127.1	129.8	128.6	126.3	123.5	125.3	124.3
1994	121.5	122.4	124.2	129.1	132.8	135.9	132.8	133.5	131.5	127.7	126.7	127.6	128.8
1995	122.4	123.5	125.2	127.7	132.2	136.6	134.2	136.3	133.8	129.6	128.8	129.8	130.0
1996	124.6	125.2	126.7	128.3	132.9	136.5	136.6	138.4	135.9	130.5	130.2	130.0	131.3
1997	123.8	125.0	125.9	129.4	134.6	139.0	139.2	141.0	139.1	134.1	131.8	133.2	133.0
1998	127.0	128.3	130.1	133.1	138.3	142.3	141.3	143.2	141.7	134.2	132.8	133.9	135.5
1999	128.8	130.5	131.9	136.4	141.2	145.3	144.1	146.6	143.6	139.6	137.9	138.8	138.7
2000	133.5	134.8	136.4	140.1	144.6	149.5	149.8	151.5	150.2	143.5	141.8	141.7	143.1
2001	138.2	139.5	141.0	143.2	148.7	154.4	153.6	157.3	153.0	147.3	145.0	145.5	147.2
2002	141.3	141.5	142.5	145.3	150.8	156.0	153.9	156.1	153.5	148.0	145.1	145.8	148.3
2003	143.1	142.3	142.8	148.1	154.4	157.5	157.7	160.2	157.7	153.9	152.4	152.9	151.9
Other services													
1990	58.4	58.8	58.9	59.9	60.0	61.1	60.5	60.7	60.2	60.2	60.4	60.7	59.9
1991	60.8	60.3	60.7	59.5	59.8	61.1	60.6	60.9	60.0	60.8	60.7	61.6	60.5
1992	60.0	60.1	60.8	60.7	61.1	62.2	62.0	62.2	62.0	61.8	62.1	62.6	61.4
1993	61.6	62.4	62.7	63.3	63.3	64.2	63.4	63.5	63.1	63.9	63.9	64.5	63.3
1994	63.3	63.7	64.3	63.9	64.2	65.1	64.4	64.9	64.9	64.5	65.0	65.1	64.4
1995	64.0	64.6	65.2	64.8	65.2	65.9	65.6	65.9	65.7	65.4	65.7	66.5	65.3
1996	66.5	67.1	68.0	68.3	68.7	68.8	69.4	69.7	69.9	69.3	69.7	70.6	68.8
1997	68.0	68.5	69.3	69.2	69.6	69.9	69.7	70.2	70.4	70.7	70.7	71.1	69.7
1998	70.0	70.6	71.0	71.5	71.3	71.9	71.9	72.0	71.9	72.1	72.1	72.7	71.5
1999	71.4	71.8	72.5	72.9	73.3	74.2	73.7	73.9	73.4	74.7	74.9	75.6	73.5
2000	74.2	75.1	75.7	75.3	75.1	75.7	75.6	75.9	75.3	76.5	76.6	77.0	75.6
2001	72.7	72.9	73.6	73.1	73.6	74.0	73.2	73.4	72.7	74.1	75.6	74.7	73.6
2002	72.9	73.0	73.1	73.7	73.9	74.6	75.0	75.3	74.3	74.4	74.7	74.8	74.1
2003	73.3	73.4	73.9	73.8	74.4	75.3	76.0	74.8	76.3	77.8	78.6	77.7	75.4
Government													
1990	189.3	193.1	192.3	194.4	197.3	193.6	181.1	176.5	183.6	195.2	198.3	196.8	190.9
1991	193.8	197.9	197.5	198.4	200.4	198.1	183.4	179.7	185.8	196.9	198.9	199.1	194.1
1992	195.5	199.8	200.3	202.2	203.1	199.9	186.1	182.0	188.8	199.8	202.8	202.3	196.8
1993	200.4	204.4	204.8	205.4	207.4	203.9	190.0	186.3	192.6	204.3	207.1	207.8	201.2
1994	203.4	207.6	207.6	209.9	212.3	210.9	196.6	193.0	201.4	211.7	218.0	214.7	207.2
1995	216.3	219.2	220.1	219.0	220.7	219.6	201.2	199.1	205.7	218.5	222.6	221.1	215.2
1996	217.5	220.7	221.1	220.4	223.8	219.8	201.4	199.8	209.5	221.2	226.8	223.7	217.1
1997	218.1	222.3	222.9	223.1	225.9	222.9	204.4	202.9	210.6	222.7	227.0	225.7	219.0
1998	222.5	224.6	226.7	227.8	230.3	223.2	205.2	203.1	215.2	228.5	230.7	230.0	222.3
1999	228.7	232.2	232.4	234.8	235.5	230.2	212.4	210.6	223.0	234.6	237.2	235.7	228.9
2000	233.5	237.3	239.3	241.1	243.8	238.3	216.7	216.1	229.8	234.6	237.8	237.0	233.7
2001	231.0	237.7	238.3	238.7	241.7	237.3	219.8	218.6	233.7	239.4	241.4	241.3	234.9
2002	236.8	241.9	242.4	242.4	244.5	239.1	223.3	215.4	237.8	242.0	246.8	244.4	238.1
2003	237.7	244.2	244.0	247.0	247.5	241.7	225.9	221.3	229.5	235.0	237.1	236.9	237.3

Employment by Industry: Minnesota—*Continued*

(Numbers in thousands. Not seasonally adjusted.)

Industry	January	February	March	April	May	June	July	August	September	October	November	December	Annual Average
MINNEAPOLIS-ST. PAUL *—Continued*													
Federal government													
1990	21.6	21.6	21.7	22.2	23.6	22.4	22.7	21.8	21.4	21.4	21.3	21.7	21.9
1991	21.5	21.4	21.4	21.4	21.5	21.7	21.9	21.8	21.8	21.8	21.8	22.3	21.6
1992	22.3	22.2	22.2	22.3	22.2	22.1	22.0	21.8	21.7	21.8	21.4	22.0	22.0
1993	21.5	21.6	21.5	21.4	21.5	21.6	21.6	21.8	21.8	21.6	21.7	22.3	21.6
1994	21.7	21.6	21.8	21.8	21.8	21.7	21.7	21.9	21.8	21.8	22.0	22.5	21.8
1995	22.4	22.1	22.3	21.8	21.9	22.2	21.8	21.8	21.7	21.7	21.7	22.6	22.0
1996	21.5	21.4	21.5	21.5	21.7	21.9	22.1	22.2	21.8	21.9	21.9	23.0	21.8
1997	22.4	22.1	22.1	22.4	22.4	22.4	22.3	22.3	22.4	22.2	22.3	23.2	22.3
1998	21.9	21.6	21.7	22.2	22.3	22.2	22.3	22.3	22.3	22.3	22.5	23.2	22.2
1999	22.2	22.0	21.8	22.8	22.6	22.1	21.8	21.8	21.9	21.6	22.0	22.8	22.1
2000	21.8	21.9	22.3	23.1	26.0	26.8	24.1	25.0	22.0	21.9	22.2	22.9	23.3
2001	21.9	21.8	21.7	21.8	21.9	21.9	21.8	21.7	21.6	21.4	21.4	21.6	21.7
2002	21.1	21.0	20.9	20.7	20.7	20.9	20.7	20.7	21.1	21.4	21.6	21.8	21.1
2003	22.4	22.3	22.5	22.3	22.3	22.2	22.3	22.2	22.1	22.1	21.9	22.2	22.2
State government													
1990	54.4	55.7	55.0	56.0	56.0	53.6	48.7	48.6	49.3	55.5	56.1	55.4	53.6
1991	54.9	56.6	55.9	56.4	55.9	54.3	48.6	48.6	49.1	55.0	55.3	54.7	53.7
1992	55.5	57.4	57.1	57.4	57.6	54.7	49.6	49.2	50.1	56.6	57.2	56.4	54.9
1993	56.5	57.5	57.3	57.8	57.8	55.9	50.7	50.2	51.1	57.3	58.2	57.8	55.6
1994	57.3	59.5	59.1	59.7	60.0	57.7	52.6	52.5	52.3	60.0	61.3	59.1	57.5
1995	60.2	61.0	60.9	62.0	62.1	58.6	55.1	54.6	55.9	63.6	64.8	61.7	60.0
1996	63.1	64.5	63.3	64.5	64.8	60.2	56.2	56.0	56.1	63.3	64.5	62.4	61.5
1997	60.4	62.0	61.8	62.1	62.1	58.8	53.9	53.5	53.3	60.9	63.2	60.6	59.3
1998	61.7	61.5	63.1	62.9	63.0	59.7	55.4	54.3	54.3	62.6	63.1	62.1	60.3
1999	63.0	64.9	64.8	65.1	65.2	61.0	57.2	56.4	60.9	67.6	68.1	65.5	63.3
2000	65.5	66.6	68.0	67.8	65.8	60.3	56.5	56.2	62.5	62.8	63.1	62.6	63.1
2001	58.6	63.2	63.3	63.8	63.9	59.5	58.8	58.5	65.4	65.1	65.3	64.9	62.5
2002	62.2	65.7	66.1	67.5	65.6	60.6	60.4	59.0	67.8	66.5	67.0	66.7	64.6
2003	62.8	67.2	66.8	70.3	69.3	63.7	64.5	63.0	68.5	69.7	69.9	69.8	67.1
Local government													
1990	108.3	110.6	110.4	110.8	112.3	113.1	105.5	101.9	107.7	112.7	115.2	114.0	110.2
1991	111.9	114.4	114.6	114.9	117.2	117.3	108.5	105.0	109.7	114.5	116.0	116.5	113.3
1992	117.7	120.2	121.0	122.5	123.3	123.1	114.5	111.0	117.0	121.4	124.2	123.9	119.9
1993	122.4	125.3	126.0	126.2	128.1	126.4	117.7	114.3	119.7	125.4	127.2	127.7	123.8
1994	124.4	126.5	126.7	128.4	130.5	131.5	122.3	118.6	127.3	129.9	134.7	133.1	127.8
1995	133.7	136.1	136.9	135.2	136.7	138.8	124.3	122.7	128.1	133.2	136.1	136.8	133.2
1996	132.9	134.8	136.3	134.4	137.3	137.7	123.1	121.6	131.6	136.0	140.4	138.3	133.7
1997	135.3	138.2	139.0	138.6	141.4	141.7	128.2	127.1	134.9	139.6	141.5	141.9	137.2
1998	138.9	141.5	141.9	142.7	145.0	141.3	127.5	126.5	138.6	143.6	145.1	144.7	139.7
1999	143.5	145.3	145.8	146.9	147.7	147.1	133.4	132.4	140.2	145.4	147.1	147.4	143.5
2000	146.2	148.8	149.0	150.2	152.0	151.2	136.1	134.9	145.3	149.9	152.5	151.5	147.3
2001	150.5	152.7	153.3	153.1	155.9	155.9	139.2	138.4	146.7	152.9	154.7	154.8	150.7
2002	153.5	155.2	155.4	154.2	158.2	157.6	142.2	135.7	148.9	154.1	158.2	155.9	152.4
2003	152.5	154.7	154.7	154.4	155.9	155.8	139.1	136.1	138.9	143.2	145.3	144.9	148.0
ROCHESTER													
Total nonfarm													
1990	63.4	63.3	63.8	64.9	65.9	67.0	66.6	66.9	67.1	66.5	66.9	66.6	65.7
1991	65.8	65.6	66.1	66.4	66.9	67.9	67.9	68.2	68.3	67.5	67.8	67.4	67.1
1992	66.1	65.9	66.1	67.0	67.7	68.8	68.3	68.4	68.6	68.7	68.7	69.2	67.7
1993	67.4	67.4	67.9	69.2	69.5	70.6	70.2	69.8	70.0	69.4	69.4	69.3	69.1
1994	67.1	67.3	67.6	67.6	68.1	69.1	68.4	68.5	68.9	68.2	68.3	68.5	68.1
1995	66.9	66.7	67.4	67.5	68.1	69.6	69.5	69.6	70.0	69.5	69.9	70.0	68.7
1996	68.5	68.3	68.9	69.2	70.3	71.1	70.7	71.3	70.7	71.1	71.6	71.6	70.2
1997	70.8	70.7	71.3	72.0	73.0	74.7	74.6	74.8	74.7	75.6	76.0	76.3	73.7
1998	75.9	75.8	76.4	77.5	78.1	79.8	79.1	79.4	79.4	78.9	79.0	79.7	78.2
1999	78.9	78.5	79.0	79.9	80.7	82.5	83.0	83.2	82.9	83.2	83.6	83.6	81.5
2000	82.9	83.2	83.9	83.6	84.5	86.1	85.6	85.6	85.8	86.0	86.6	86.7	85.0
2001	85.9	85.6	86.0	86.6	87.4	88.9	88.5	88.3	87.6	88.1	87.8	88.0	87.4
2002	86.4	85.6	86.2	86.5	87.5	89.0	88.8	88.9	88.4	88.9	89.5	89.9	88.0
2003	87.8	87.3	87.7	88.4	89.3	90.2	89.8	89.9	88.9	89.4	89.5	90.0	89.0
Total private													
1990	56.9	56.6	56.9	57.9	58.7	60.1	60.4	60.8	60.4	59.7	60.0	59.7	59.0
1991	59.0	58.7	59.1	59.5	59.9	61.3	62.1	62.4	61.5	60.5	60.6	60.3	60.4
1992	59.1	58.9	58.9	59.8	60.6	61.8	62.1	62.5	61.9	61.7	61.4	62.0	60.8
1993	60.4	60.3	60.6	62.0	62.3	63.4	63.9	63.6	63.2	62.2	62.0	62.0	62.1
1994	59.9	59.8	60.1	60.2	60.6	61.9	61.9	62.1	61.6	60.8	60.9	61.0	60.9
1995	59.6	59.4	59.9	60.1	60.8	62.3	63.2	63.4	62.9	62.6	62.8	62.7	61.6
1996	61.5	61.4	61.8	62.1	63.1	63.9	64.4	64.9	63.8	64.1	64.4	64.4	63.3
1997	63.6	63.4	64.0	64.8	65.7	67.3	67.9	68.2	67.4	68.5	68.8	69.0	66.5
1998	68.7	68.5	69.1	70.2	70.8	72.5	72.5	72.8	72.1	71.6	71.7	72.3	71.0
1999	71.5	71.0	71.4	72.6	73.2	75.0	76.2	76.5	75.4	75.8	76.1	76.1	74.2
2000	75.4	75.4	76.1	75.8	76.4	78.1	78.3	78.5	78.1	78.2	78.7	78.7	77.3
2001	78.2	77.6	77.9	78.6	79.3	80.9	81.0	80.8	79.8	80.1	79.8	79.9	79.5
2002	78.3	77.6	78.3	78.8	79.7	81.1	81.5	81.5	80.8	81.1	81.2	81.9	80.2
2003	79.9	79.3	79.8	80.7	81.6	82.4	82.5	82.5	81.5	81.8	81.9	82.3	81.4

Employment by Industry: Minnesota—*Continued*

(Numbers in thousands. Not seasonally adjusted.)

Industry	January	February	March	April	May	June	July	August	September	October	November	December	Annual Average
ROCHESTER—*Continued*													
Goods-producing													
1990	13.3	13.2	13.3	13.6	13.9	14.5	14.7	14.8	14.5	14.5	14.3	13.7	14.0
1991	13.4	13.4	13.4	13.7	14.0	14.4	14.7	14.7	14.2	14.0	13.7	13.2	13.9
1992	12.9	13.0	13.0	13.4	13.8	14.2	14.4	14.8	14.6	14.8	14.5	14.3	13.9
1993	14.0	14.0	14.1	14.2	14.5	14.8	15.1	15.0	14.4	13.6	13.2	12.5	14.1
1994	12.2	12.2	12.3	12.1	12.3	12.9	13.1	13.3	13.0	12.6	12.5	12.1	12.5
1995	11.9	12.0	12.1	12.3	12.7	13.1	13.2	13.6	13.2	12.9	12.9	12.7	12.7
1996	12.1	12.0	12.0	12.2	12.7	12.8	13.3	13.8	13.5	13.0	13.0	12.8	12.7
1997	13.1	13.3	13.5	13.4	13.9	14.5	15.0	15.4	15.1	15.3	15.3	15.0	14.4
1998	15.3	15.3	15.6	15.8	16.1	16.6	16.4	16.4	16.1	15.9	15.7	15.5	15.8
1999	15.3	15.1	15.3	15.2	15.5	16.1	16.7	16.9	16.5	16.3	16.1	15.8	15.9
2000	15.5	15.4	15.5	15.2	15.5	16.0	16.2	16.3	16.3	16.0	15.9	15.6	15.7
2001	15.6	15.4	15.4	15.8	16.1	16.4	16.6	16.6	16.1	15.8	15.5	15.4	15.9
2002	15.0	14.8	15.1	14.9	15.3	15.6	15.7	15.8	15.4	15.1	15.0	14.7	15.2
2003	14.1	13.8	14.1	14.3	14.5	14.6	14.6	14.6	14.5	14.3	14.2	13.8	14.3
Construction and mining													
1990	1.9	1.8	1.8	1.9	2.2	2.4	2.5	2.5	2.5	2.5	2.4	2.1	2.2
1991	1.9	1.8	1.8	1.9	2.2	2.4	2.4	2.5	2.5	2.4	2.1	2.0	2.1
1992	1.9	1.9	2.0	2.2	2.5	2.6	2.7	2.7	2.6	2.6	2.4	2.2	2.3
1993	1.9	1.9	2.0	2.1	2.4	2.6	2.6	2.6	2.5	2.5	2.4	2.2	2.3
1994	1.8	1.7	1.8	2.0	2.2	2.5	2.5	2.5	2.5	2.5	2.4	2.2	2.2
1995	2.0	2.0	2.0	2.2	2.5	2.7	2.7	2.7	2.6	2.6	2.5	2.4	2.4
1996	2.1	2.0	2.0	2.2	2.6	2.7	2.8	2.9	2.8	2.8	2.7	2.5	2.5
1997	2.2	2.3	2.3	2.6	3.0	3.1	3.2	3.2	3.2	3.2	3.1	2.9	2.8
1998	2.7	2.6	2.7	2.7	2.9	3.1	3.1	3.1	3.1	3.1	2.9	2.8	2.9
1999	2.5	2.6	2.6	2.8	3.1	3.3	3.6	3.6	3.6	3.6	3.5	3.3	3.1
2000	2.9	2.9	3.0	3.3	3.6	3.7	3.8	3.7	3.7	3.7	3.6	3.4	3.4
2001	3.1	3.0	3.1	3.5	3.8	4.0	4.1	4.1	3.9	3.9	3.8	3.7	3.7
2002	3.4	3.3	3.3	3.6	3.9	4.1	4.2	4.2	4.1	4.0	4.0	3.8	3.8
2003	3.5	3.2	3.3	3.6	3.9	4.1	4.2	4.2	4.1	4.1	4.0	3.8	3.8
Manufacturing													
1990	11.4	11.4	11.5	11.7	11.7	12.1	12.2	12.3	12.0	12.0	11.9	11.6	11.8
1991	11.5	11.6	11.6	11.8	11.8	12.0	12.3	12.2	11.7	11.6	11.6	11.2	11.7
1992	11.0	11.1	11.0	11.2	11.3	11.6	11.7	12.1	12.0	12.2	12.1	12.1	11.6
1993	12.1	12.1	12.1	12.1	12.1	12.2	12.5	12.4	11.9	11.1	10.8	10.3	11.8
1994	10.4	10.5	10.5	10.1	10.1	10.4	10.6	10.8	10.5	10.1	10.1	9.9	10.3
1995	9.9	10.0	10.1	10.1	10.2	10.4	10.5	10.9	10.6	10.3	10.4	10.3	10.3
1996	10.0	10.0	10.0	10.0	10.1	10.1	10.5	10.9	10.7	10.2	10.3	10.3	10.2
1997	10.9	11.0	11.2	10.8	10.9	11.4	11.8	12.2	11.9	12.1	12.2	12.1	11.5
1998	12.6	12.7	12.9	13.1	13.2	13.5	13.3	13.3	13.0	12.8	12.8	12.7	12.9
1999	12.8	12.5	12.7	12.4	12.4	12.8	13.1	13.3	12.9	12.7	12.6	12.5	12.7
2000	12.6	12.5	12.5	11.9	11.9	12.3	12.4	12.6	12.6	12.3	12.3	12.2	12.3
2001	12.5	12.4	12.3	12.3	12.3	12.4	12.5	12.5	12.2	11.9	11.7	11.7	12.2
2002	11.6	11.5	11.8	11.3	11.4	11.5	11.5	11.6	11.3	11.1	11.0	10.9	11.4
2003	10.6	10.6	10.8	10.7	10.6	10.5	10.4	10.4	10.4	10.2	10.2	10.0	10.5
Service-providing													
1990	50.1	50.1	50.5	51.3	52.0	52.5	51.9	52.1	52.6	52.0	52.6	52.9	51.7
1991	52.4	52.2	52.7	52.7	52.9	53.5	53.2	53.5	54.1	53.5	54.1	54.2	53.2
1992	53.2	52.9	53.1	53.6	53.9	54.6	53.9	53.6	54.0	53.9	54.2	54.9	53.8
1993	53.4	53.4	53.8	55.0	55.0	55.8	55.1	54.8	55.6	55.8	56.2	56.8	55.0
1994	54.9	55.1	55.3	55.5	55.8	56.2	55.3	55.2	55.9	55.6	55.8	56.4	55.5
1995	55.0	54.7	55.3	55.2	55.4	56.5	56.3	56.0	56.8	56.6	57.0	57.3	56.0
1996	56.4	56.3	56.9	57.0	57.6	58.3	57.4	57.5	57.2	58.1	58.6	58.8	57.5
1997	57.7	57.4	57.8	58.6	59.1	60.2	59.6	59.4	59.6	60.3	60.7	61.3	59.3
1998	60.6	60.5	60.8	61.7	62.0	63.2	62.7	63.0	63.3	63.0	63.3	64.2	62.3
1999	63.6	63.4	63.7	64.7	65.2	66.4	66.3	66.3	66.4	66.9	67.5	67.8	65.6
2000	67.4	67.8	68.4	68.4	69.0	70.1	69.4	69.3	69.5	70.0	70.7	71.1	69.2
2001	70.3	70.2	70.6	70.8	71.3	72.5	71.9	71.7	71.5	72.3	72.3	72.6	71.5
2002	71.4	70.8	71.1	71.6	72.2	73.4	73.1	73.1	73.0	73.8	74.5	75.2	72.8
2003	73.7	73.5	73.6	74.1	74.8	75.6	75.2	75.3	74.4	75.1	75.3	76.2	74.7
Trade, transportation, and utilities													
1990	10.0	9.9	9.9	10.0	10.1	10.3	10.1	10.1	10.1	10.2	10.6	10.8	10.1
1991	10.5	10.1	10.1	10.1	10.1	10.4	10.3	10.3	10.2	10.3	10.6	10.8	10.3
1992	10.3	10.1	10.2	10.4	10.4	10.5	10.0	9.9	9.8	10.2	10.4	10.8	10.2
1993	10.3	10.1	10.1	10.5	10.6	10.6	10.6	10.5	10.7	10.8	11.3	11.7	10.6
1994	10.8	10.7	10.7	10.8	10.9	11.0	10.8	10.8	10.8	10.9	11.1	11.4	10.8
1995	10.7	10.5	10.6	10.4	10.7	10.8	11.0	11.0	11.0	11.1	11.5	11.7	10.9
1996	11.3	11.1	11.2	11.0	11.2	11.2	11.0	11.0	10.9	11.3	11.6	11.8	11.2
1997	11.0	10.8	11.1	11.0	11.3	11.4	11.3	11.4	11.4	11.8	12.1	12.4	11.4
1998	12.0	11.8	11.8	12.1	12.2	12.7	12.6	12.6	12.6	12.7	13.0	13.3	12.4
1999	12.4	12.1	12.1	12.4	12.5	12.5	12.7	12.6	12.6	12.6	13.1	13.3	12.5
2000	12.8	13.0	13.1	13.4	13.6	13.5	13.5	13.4	13.4	13.6	14.1	14.2	13.4
2001	13.6	13.3	13.1	13.2	13.5	13.4	13.2	13.3	13.1	13.5	13.8	14.0	13.4
2002	13.4	13.0	13.2	13.1	13.3	13.4	13.3	13.2	13.1	13.4	14.0	14.3	13.4
2003	13.2	12.9	12.9	13.2	13.5	13.5	13.4	13.4	13.2	13.4	13.8	14.0	13.4

Employment by Industry: Minnesota—*Continued*

(Numbers in thousands. Not seasonally adjusted.)

Industry	January	February	March	April	May	June	July	August	September	October	November	December	Annual Average
ROCHESTER—*Continued*													
Wholesale trade													
1990	1.4	1.4	1.4	1.4	1.4	1.4	1.4	1.4	1.4	1.4	1.4	1.4	1.4
1991	1.5	1.5	1.5	1.5	1.5	1.5	1.6	1.6	1.6	1.6	1.6	1.6	1.5
1992	1.5	1.5	1.5	1.5	1.5	1.5	1.2	1.2	1.2	1.2	1.2	1.2	1.3
1993	1.2	1.2	1.2	1.2	1.2	1.2	1.4	1.3	1.3	1.3	1.3	1.3	1.2
1994	1.3	1.3	1.3	1.3	1.3	1.3	1.3	1.3	1.3	1.3	1.3	1.3	1.3
1995	1.2	1.2	1.3	1.3	1.3	1.3	1.4	1.4	1.4	1.4	1.4	1.4	1.3
1996	1.4	1.4	1.4	1.5	1.5	1.5	1.5	1.4	1.4	1.4	1.4	1.4	1.4
1997	1.4	1.4	1.4	1.4	1.4	1.5	1.4	1.4	1.4	1.3	1.3	1.3	1.3
1998	1.4	1.4	1.4	1.5	1.5	1.5	1.6	1.6	1.6	1.6	1.5	1.6	1.5
1999	1.5	1.5	1.5	1.5	1.5	1.5	1.5	1.5	1.5	1.5	1.5	1.5	1.5
2000	1.5	1.4	1.5	1.5	1.5	1.5	1.5	1.5	1.5	1.5	1.5	1.5	1.4
2001	1.4	1.4	1.4	1.4	1.5	1.4	1.4	1.4	1.4	1.4	1.4	1.4	1.4
2002	1.4	1.4	1.4	1.4	1.4	1.4	1.5	1.5	1.5	1.5	1.5	1.5	1.5
2003	1.4	1.4	1.4	1.5	1.5	1.5	1.5	1.5	1.5	1.5	1.5	1.5	1.5
Retail trade													
1990	7.1	7.0	7.0	7.1	7.2	7.4	7.3	7.3	7.3	7.3	7.7	7.9	7.3
1991	7.5	7.1	7.1	7.1	7.1	7.3	7.2	7.2	7.1	7.2	7.5	7.7	7.2
1992	7.3	7.1	7.2	7.4	7.4	7.5	7.4	7.3	7.2	7.6	7.8	8.2	7.4
1993	7.7	7.5	7.5	7.9	8.0	8.0	7.8	7.8	7.9	8.0	8.5	8.8	7.9
1994	7.9	7.7	7.7	7.8	7.9	8.0	7.9	7.9	7.9	8.0	8.3	8.5	7.9
1995	8.0	7.8	7.8	7.7	7.9	8.0	8.1	8.1	8.1	8.2	8.6	8.8	8.0
1996	8.4	8.2	8.3	7.9	8.1	8.1	8.0	8.1	8.0	8.3	8.6	8.8	8.2
1997	8.2	8.0	8.3	8.2	8.4	8.4	8.4	8.5	8.4	8.8	9.1	9.4	8.5
1998	8.7	8.5	8.5	8.7	8.8	9.3	9.2	9.2	9.1	9.2	9.5	9.8	9.0
1999	9.1	8.7	8.7	8.9	9.0	9.0	9.3	9.2	9.1	9.1	9.6	9.8	9.1
2000	9.3	9.6	9.6	9.9	10.1	10.0	10.0	10.0	9.9	10.0	10.4	10.5	9.9
2001	10.2	9.9	9.7	9.7	9.9	9.9	9.8	10.0	9.8	10.1	10.5	10.6	10.0
2002	10.1	9.7	9.9	9.8	10.0	10.1	9.9	9.9	9.7	9.9	10.5	10.8	10.0
2003	10.0	9.7	9.6	9.8	10.1	10.1	10.0	10.0	9.8	9.9	10.4	10.5	10.0
Transportation and utilities													
1990	1.5	1.5	1.5	1.5	1.5	1.5	1.4	1.4	1.4	1.5	1.5	1.5	1.4
1991	1.5	1.5	1.5	1.5	1.5	1.6	1.5	1.5	1.5	1.5	1.5	1.5	1.5
1992	1.5	1.5	1.5	1.5	1.5	1.5	1.4	1.4	1.4	1.4	1.4	1.4	1.4
1993	1.4	1.4	1.4	1.4	1.4	1.4	1.4	1.4	1.5	1.5	1.5	1.6	1.4
1994	1.6	1.7	1.7	1.7	1.7	1.7	1.6	1.6	1.6	1.6	1.5	1.6	1.6
1995	1.5	1.5	1.5	1.4	1.5	1.5	1.5	1.5	1.5	1.5	1.5	1.5	1.4
1996	1.5	1.5	1.5	1.6	1.6	1.6	1.5	1.5	1.5	1.6	1.6	1.6	1.5
1997	1.4	1.4	1.4	1.4	1.5	1.5	1.5	1.5	1.6	1.7	1.7	1.7	1.5
1998	1.9	1.9	1.9	1.9	1.9	1.9	1.8	1.8	1.9	1.9	2.0	1.9	1.8
1999	1.8	1.9	1.9	2.0	2.0	2.0	1.9	1.9	2.0	2.0	2.0	2.0	1.9
2000	2.0	2.0	2.0	2.0	2.0	2.0	2.0	1.9	2.0	2.1	2.2	2.2	2.0
2001	2.0	2.0	2.0	2.1	2.1	2.1	2.0	1.9	1.9	2.0	1.9	2.0	2.0
2002	1.9	1.9	1.9	1.9	1.9	1.9	1.9	1.8	1.9	2.0	2.0	2.0	1.9
2003	1.8	1.8	1.9	1.9	1.9	1.9	1.9	1.9	1.9	2.0	1.9	2.0	1.9
Information													
1990	1.0	1.0	1.0	1.0	1.0	1.0	1.0	1.0	0.9	1.1	1.1	1.0	1.0
1991	1.1	1.1	1.1	1.1	1.1	1.1	1.1	1.1	1.1	1.0	1.0	1.1	1.0
1992	1.0	1.0	1.0	1.0	1.0	1.1	1.1	1.1	1.1	1.1	1.1	1.1	1.0
1993	1.1	1.1	1.1	1.1	1.1	1.1	1.1	1.1	1.1	1.1	1.1	1.1	1.1
1994	1.1	1.1	1.1	1.1	1.1	1.1	1.1	1.1	1.1	1.0	1.0	1.0	1.0
1995	1.1	1.1	1.1	1.0	0.9	1.0	1.0	0.9	0.9	0.9	0.9	0.9	0.9
1996	0.9	0.9	0.9	0.9	0.9	0.9	0.9	0.9	0.8	0.8	0.8	0.8	0.8
1997	0.9	0.8	0.8	0.8	0.8	0.9	0.9	0.9	0.9	0.9	0.8	0.9	0.8
1998	0.9	0.8	0.8	0.8	0.8	0.8	0.8	0.8	0.8	0.8	0.8	0.8	0.8
1999	0.8	0.8	0.8	0.8	0.8	0.9	0.9	0.9	0.9	0.9	0.9	0.9	0.8
2000	0.9	0.9	1.0	0.9	0.9	0.9	1.0	1.0	1.0	0.9	0.9	0.9	0.9
2001	0.9	0.9	0.9	0.9	0.9	1.0	0.9	0.9	0.9	0.9	0.8	0.9	0.9
2002	0.9	1.0	1.0	1.0	1.0	1.0	1.0	1.0	1.0	1.0	1.0	1.0	1.0
2003	1.2	1.2	1.2	1.2	1.2	1.2	1.2	1.2	1.2	1.2	1.2	1.2	1.2
Financial activities													
1990	2.0	2.0	2.0	2.1	2.1	2.1	2.1	2.1	2.1	2.0	2.0	2.1	2.0
1991	2.1	2.1	2.0	2.1	2.1	2.2	2.1	2.2	2.1	2.1	2.1	2.1	2.1
1992	2.1	2.1	2.2	2.2	2.2	2.3	2.3	2.2	2.2	2.1	2.1	2.2	2.1
1993	2.2	2.1	2.2	2.3	2.3	2.3	2.3	2.3	2.3	2.3	2.3	2.4	2.2
1994	2.3	2.3	2.3	2.4	2.4	2.5	2.4	2.4	2.4	2.3	2.3	2.4	2.3
1995	2.3	2.2	2.2	2.3	2.3	2.3	2.4	2.3	2.3	2.4	2.4	2.4	2.3
1996	2.5	2.6	2.6	2.4	2.5	2.5	2.5	2.5	2.4	2.4	2.4	2.3	2.4
1997	2.3	2.2	2.2	2.3	2.3	2.3	2.3	2.1	2.0	2.0	2.0	2.0	2.1
1998	2.1	2.1	2.1	2.2	2.2	2.3	2.2	2.2	2.2	2.1	2.1	2.1	2.1
1999	2.2	2.2	2.2	2.3	2.3	2.3	2.3	2.3	2.3	2.3	2.3	2.3	2.2
2000	2.3	2.3	2.3	2.4	2.4	2.5	2.4	2.4	2.4	2.3	2.3	2.3	2.3
2001	2.3	2.3	2.3	2.4	2.4	2.4	2.4	2.4	2.3	2.4	2.4	2.4	2.4
2002	2.2	2.2	2.2	2.3	2.3	2.3	2.3	2.3	2.3	2.4	2.3	2.4	2.3
2003	2.3	2.3	2.3	2.4	2.4	2.4	2.4	2.4	2.4	2.4	2.4	2.4	2.4

Employment by Industry: Minnesota—*Continued*

(Numbers in thousands. Not seasonally adjusted.)

Industry	January	February	March	April	May	June	July	August	September	October	November	December	Annual Average
ROCHESTER—*Continued*													
Professional and business services													
1990	2.2	2.2	2.3	2.3	2.4	2.4	2.4	2.5	2.7	2.4	2.5	2.5	2.4
1991	2.4	2.3	2.4	2.5	2.5	2.6	2.7	2.7	2.9	2.8	2.7	2.7	2.6
1992	2.5	2.4	2.4	2.7	2.8	2.9	3.0	3.1	3.1	3.0	2.9	2.9	2.8
1993	2.9	3.0	2.9	2.9	2.9	3.2	3.0	2.9	3.0	3.0	3.0	3.1	2.9
1994	2.9	2.8	2.9	2.9	3.0	3.1	3.2	3.1	3.3	3.3	3.3	3.3	3.0
1995	3.1	3.0	3.1	3.3	3.3	3.4	3.7	3.7	3.8	3.7	3.6	3.6	3.4
1996	3.5	3.5	3.6	3.6	3.7	3.7	3.8	3.7	3.8	3.9	3.9	4.0	3.7
1997	3.8	3.9	3.9	4.2	4.2	4.3	4.5	4.4	4.5	4.5	4.5	4.5	4.2
1998	4.4	4.4	4.5	4.7	4.7	4.7	4.8	4.8	4.8	4.8	4.8	5.0	4.7
1999	5.1	5.1	5.2	5.5	5.5	5.6	5.6	5.5	5.4	5.8	5.7	5.6	5.4
2000	5.7	5.7	5.6	5.1	5.1	5.2	5.1	5.1	5.1	5.4	5.5	5.6	5.3
2001	5.5	5.4	5.5	5.4	5.4	5.4	5.2	5.1	5.2	5.3	5.1	5.0	5.3
2002	4.7	4.4	4.4	4.7	4.7	4.8	4.8	4.9	5.0	5.0	4.9	5.0	4.8
2003	4.7	4.7	4.8	4.8	4.9	5.0	5.0	5.0	5.0	5.2	5.2	5.7	5.0
Educational and health services													
1990	20.4	20.3	20.3	20.6	20.7	21.1	21.3	21.4	21.3	21.1	21.1	21.1	20.8
1991	21.1	21.2	21.4	21.4	21.5	21.7	22.4	22.4	22.2	21.7	21.8	21.7	21.7
1992	21.8	21.8	21.6	21.6	21.6	21.8	22.2	22.3	22.3	21.8	21.8	22.0	21.8
1993	21.5	21.6	21.7	22.2	22.1	22.3	22.7	22.7	22.7	22.5	22.3	22.4	22.2
1994	21.8	21.9	21.9	21.9	21.8	21.9	22.1	22.0	21.8	21.8	21.8	21.9	21.8
1995	22.0	22.1	22.1	22.1	22.1	22.4	22.7	22.6	22.6	22.7	22.7	22.7	22.4
1996	22.8	22.9	22.9	23.3	23.4	23.8	23.9	23.9	23.5	23.8	23.9	23.9	23.5
1997	24.0	24.0	24.0	24.3	24.2	24.7	24.8	24.8	24.6	25.1	25.2	25.2	24.5
1998	25.1	25.1	25.2	25.3	25.3	25.7	26.1	26.4	26.1	26.1	26.2	26.3	25.7
1999	26.5	26.5	26.5	27.1	27.2	27.9	28.5	28.6	28.2	28.5	28.6	28.7	27.7
2000	28.9	28.8	29.0	29.2	29.2	29.9	30.1	30.2	30.1	30.1	30.1	30.1	29.6
2001	30.5	30.6	30.7	31.0	31.0	31.9	32.2	32.0	32.0	32.1	32.2	32.3	31.5
2002	32.5	32.6	32.7	32.7	32.8	33.6	34.0	33.9	33.8	34.0	34.0	34.2	33.4
2003	34.3	34.3	34.4	34.5	34.6	35.1	35.3	35.3	34.9	35.0	35.0	35.0	34.8
Leisure and hospitality													
1990	5.6	5.6	5.7	5.9	6.1	6.2	6.2	6.3	6.3	5.9	5.9	6.0	5.9
1991	5.9	6.0	6.1	6.1	6.1	6.3	6.1	6.3	6.2	6.0	6.1	6.1	6.1
1992	5.8	5.8	5.8	5.9	6.1	6.2	6.2	6.3	6.0	5.9	5.8	5.9	5.9
1993	5.6	5.6	5.7	6.0	6.0	6.2	6.2	6.3	6.2	6.2	6.1	6.1	6.0
1994	6.1	6.1	6.1	6.2	6.3	6.5	6.4	6.6	6.4	6.1	6.1	6.1	6.2
1995	5.8	5.8	5.9	6.0	6.1	6.4	6.4	6.4	6.3	6.1	6.0	5.9	6.0
1996	5.7	5.7	5.9	5.9	5.9	6.1	6.1	6.2	6.1	6.1	6.0	6.0	5.9
1997	5.8	5.7	5.8	6.0	6.2	6.3	6.3	6.4	6.1	6.2	6.2	6.2	6.1
1998	6.0	6.1	6.2	6.4	6.6	6.7	6.7	6.8	6.5	6.4	6.3	6.4	6.4
1999	6.3	6.3	6.4	6.4	6.5	6.7	6.5	6.7	6.5	6.4	6.4	6.4	6.4
2000	6.3	6.3	6.5	6.6	6.7	7.0	7.0	7.1	6.8	6.8	6.8	6.9	6.7
2001	6.9	6.8	7.0	6.9	7.0	7.5	7.6	7.6	7.3	7.2	7.0	7.0	7.2
2002	6.7	6.7	6.8	7.1	7.3	7.4	7.4	7.5	7.2	7.2	7.0	7.3	7.1
2003	7.1	7.1	7.1	7.2	7.4	7.6	7.6	7.6	7.3	7.3	7.1	7.2	7.3
Other services													
1990	2.4	2.4	2.4	2.4	2.4	2.5	2.6	2.6	2.5	2.5	2.5	2.5	2.4
1991	2.5	2.5	2.6	2.5	2.5	2.6	2.7	2.7	2.6	2.6	2.6	2.6	2.5
1992	2.7	2.7	2.7	2.6	2.7	2.8	2.9	2.8	2.8	2.8	2.8	2.8	2.7
1993	2.8	2.8	2.8	2.8	2.8	2.9	2.9	2.8	2.8	2.7	2.7	2.7	2.7
1994	2.7	2.7	2.8	2.8	2.8	2.9	2.8	2.8	2.8	2.8	2.8	2.8	2.7
1995	2.7	2.7	2.8	2.7	2.7	2.9	2.8	2.9	2.8	2.8	2.8	2.8	2.7
1996	2.7	2.7	2.7	2.8	2.8	2.9	2.9	2.9	2.8	2.8	2.8	2.8	2.8
1997	2.7	2.7	2.7	2.8	2.8	2.9	2.8	2.8	2.8	2.7	2.7	2.8	2.7
1998	2.9	2.9	2.9	2.9	2.9	3.0	2.9	2.8	3.0	2.8	2.8	2.9	2.8
1999	2.9	2.9	2.9	2.9	2.9	3.0	3.0	3.0	3.0	3.0	3.0	3.1	2.9
2000	3.0	3.0	3.1	3.0	3.0	3.1	3.0	3.0	3.0	3.1	3.1	3.1	3.0
2001	2.9	2.9	3.0	3.0	3.0	2.9	2.9	2.9	2.9	2.9	3.0	2.9	2.9
2002	2.9	2.9	2.9	3.0	3.0	3.0	3.0	2.9	3.0	3.0	3.0	3.0	3.0
2003	3.0	3.0	3.0	3.1	3.1	3.0	3.0	3.0	3.0	3.0	3.0	3.0	3.0
Government													
1990	6.5	6.7	6.9	7.0	7.2	6.9	6.2	6.1	6.7	6.8	6.9	6.9	6.7
1991	6.8	6.9	7.0	6.9	7.0	6.6	5.8	5.8	6.8	7.0	7.2	7.1	6.7
1992	7.0	7.0	7.2	7.2	7.1	7.0	6.2	5.9	6.7	7.0	7.3	7.2	6.9
1993	7.0	7.1	7.3	7.2	7.2	7.2	6.3	6.2	6.8	7.2	7.4	7.3	7.0
1994	7.2	7.5	7.5	7.4	7.5	7.2	6.5	6.4	7.3	7.4	7.4	7.5	7.2
1995	7.3	7.3	7.5	7.4	7.3	7.3	6.3	6.2	7.1	6.9	7.1	7.3	7.0
1996	7.0	6.9	7.1	7.1	7.2	7.2	6.3	6.4	6.9	7.0	7.2	7.2	6.9
1997	7.2	7.3	7.3	7.2	7.3	7.4	6.7	6.6	7.3	7.1	7.2	7.3	7.1
1998	7.2	7.3	7.3	7.3	7.3	7.3	6.6	6.6	7.3	7.3	7.3	7.4	7.1
1999	7.4	7.5	7.6	7.3	7.5	7.5	6.8	6.7	7.5	7.4	7.5	7.5	7.3
2000	7.5	7.8	7.8	7.8	8.1	8.0	7.3	7.1	7.7	7.8	7.9	8.0	7.7
2001	7.7	8.0	8.1	8.0	8.1	8.0	7.5	7.5	7.8	8.0	8.0	8.1	7.9
2002	8.1	8.0	7.9	7.7	7.8	7.9	7.3	7.4	7.6	7.8	8.3	8.0	7.8
2003	7.9	8.0	7.9	7.7	7.7	7.8	7.3	7.4	7.4	7.6	7.6	7.7	7.7

Employment by Industry: Minnesota—*Continued*

(Numbers in thousands. Not seasonally adjusted.)

Industry	January	February	March	April	May	June	July	August	September	October	November	December	Annual Average
ROCHESTER—*Continued*													
Federal government													
1990	0.9	0.9	1.0	1.0	1.0	1.0	0.9	0.9	0.9	0.9	0.9	0.9	0.9
1991	0.9	0.9	0.9	0.9	0.9	0.9	0.9	0.9	0.9	0.9	0.9	0.9	0.9
1992	0.9	0.9	0.9	0.9	0.9	0.9	1.0	1.0	0.9	0.9	0.9	0.9	0.9
1993	0.9	0.9	0.9	0.9	0.9	0.9	0.9	0.9	0.9	0.9	0.9	0.9	0.9
1994	0.9	0.9	0.9	1.0	1.0	1.0	0.9	0.9	0.9	1.0	0.9	0.9	0.9
1995	0.9	0.9	0.9	0.9	0.9	0.9	0.9	0.9	0.9	0.9	0.9	0.9	0.9
1996	0.9	0.9	0.9	0.9	0.9	0.9	0.9	0.9	0.9	0.9	0.9	0.9	0.9
1997	0.9	0.9	0.9	0.9	0.9	0.9	0.9	0.9	0.9	0.9	0.9	0.9	0.9
1998	0.9	0.9	0.9	0.9	0.9	0.9	0.9	0.9	0.9	0.9	0.9	0.9	0.9
1999	0.9	0.9	0.9	0.9	0.9	0.9	0.9	0.9	0.9	0.9	0.9	0.9	0.9
2000	1.0	1.0	1.0	1.0	1.1	1.2	1.1	1.1	0.9	0.9	0.9	0.9	1.0
2001	0.9	0.9	0.9	0.9	0.9	0.9	0.9	0.9	0.9	0.9	0.9	0.9	0.9
2002	0.9	0.9	0.9	0.9	0.9	0.9	0.9	0.9	0.9	0.9	0.9	1.0	0.9
2003	0.9	0.9	0.9	0.9	0.9	0.9	0.9	0.9	0.9	0.9	0.9	0.9	0.9
State government													
1990	1.0	1.0	1.1	1.1	1.1	0.9	0.8	0.8	1.0	1.1	1.1	1.1	1.0
1991	1.1	1.1	1.1	1.1	1.1	0.9	0.8	0.8	1.0	1.1	1.1	1.1	1.0
1992	1.1	1.1	1.1	1.1	1.1	0.9	0.8	0.8	1.0	1.1	1.1	1.1	1.0
1993	1.1	1.1	1.1	1.1	1.1	0.9	0.8	0.8	1.0	1.1	1.1	1.1	1.0
1994	1.1	1.1	1.1	1.1	1.1	0.9	0.8	0.8	1.1	1.1	1.1	1.1	1.0
1995	1.1	1.1	1.1	1.1	1.1	1.0	0.9	0.9	1.1	1.1	1.2	1.3	1.0
1996	1.2	1.1	1.1	1.1	1.1	0.9	1.0	1.1	1.1	1.1	1.1	1.1	1.0
1997	1.2	1.2	1.2	1.2	1.2	1.2	1.3	1.3	1.4	1.2	1.2	1.2	1.2
1998	1.2	1.2	1.2	1.2	1.2	1.0	1.0	1.0	1.1	1.1	1.1	1.1	1.1
1999	1.1	1.2	1.2	1.2	1.2	1.1	1.1	1.1	1.2	1.2	1.2	1.2	1.1
2000	1.1	1.3	1.3	1.3	1.4	1.2	1.2	1.2	1.4	1.4	1.4	1.4	1.3
2001	1.3	1.5	1.5	1.5	1.5	1.3	1.3	1.3	1.5	1.5	1.5	1.5	1.4
2002	1.5	1.4	1.4	1.1	1.1	1.1	1.1	1.1	1.2	1.2	1.2	1.2	1.2
2003	1.2	1.2	1.2	1.1	1.0	1.1	1.0	1.1	1.1	1.1	1.1	1.1	1.1
Local government													
1990	4.6	4.8	4.8	4.9	5.1	5.0	4.5	4.4	4.8	4.8	4.9	4.9	4.7
1991	4.8	4.9	5.0	4.9	5.0	4.8	4.1	4.1	4.9	5.0	5.2	5.1	4.8
1992	5.0	5.0	5.2	5.2	5.1	5.2	4.4	4.1	4.8	5.0	5.3	5.2	4.9
1993	5.0	5.1	5.3	5.2	5.2	5.4	4.6	4.5	4.9	5.2	5.4	5.3	5.0
1994	5.2	5.5	5.5	5.3	5.4	5.3	4.8	4.7	5.3	5.3	5.4	5.5	5.2
1995	5.3	5.3	5.5	5.4	5.3	5.4	4.5	4.4	5.1	4.9	5.0	5.1	5.1
1996	4.9	4.9	5.1	5.1	5.2	5.4	4.4	4.4	4.9	5.0	5.2	5.2	4.9
1997	5.1	5.2	5.2	5.1	5.2	5.3	4.5	4.4	5.0	5.0	5.1	5.2	5.0
1998	5.1	5.2	5.2	5.2	5.2	5.4	4.7	4.7	5.3	5.3	5.3	5.4	5.1
1999	5.4	5.4	5.5	5.2	5.4	5.5	4.8	4.7	5.4	5.3	5.4	5.4	5.2
2000	5.4	5.5	5.5	5.5	5.6	5.6	5.0	4.8	5.4	5.5	5.6	5.7	5.4
2001	5.5	5.6	5.7	5.6	5.7	5.8	5.3	5.3	5.4	5.6	5.6	5.7	5.6
2002	5.7	5.7	5.6	5.7	5.8	5.9	5.3	5.4	5.5	5.7	6.2	5.8	5.7
2003	5.8	5.9	5.8	5.7	5.8	5.8	5.4	5.4	5.4	5.6	5.6	5.7	5.7
ST. CLOUD													
Total nonfarm													
1990	67.6	68.2	67.2	68.4	70.1	68.4	67.4	67.9	71.0	72.8	73.4	72.9	69.6
1991	70.4	70.7	69.7	71.7	73.2	71.0	69.9	70.4	73.4	74.5	74.6	74.6	72.0
1992	72.3	72.1	72.9	73.1	74.8	73.6	72.3	72.8	75.6	76.7	77.6	77.1	74.2
1993	75.0	75.2	75.4	77.0	78.1	75.5	74.6	74.2	77.5	78.7	79.0	79.3	76.6
1994	76.4	77.0	77.5	79.3	80.6	78.6	77.4	77.5	80.5	81.6	82.5	82.9	79.3
1995	80.6	80.8	82.0	82.4	83.4	81.3	80.4	80.1	83.4	85.0	85.1	85.4	82.4
1996	82.9	82.9	83.8	84.7	86.0	83.3	81.6	81.3	84.5	85.2	85.9	85.5	83.9
1997	82.0	82.8	83.4	84.6	86.1	83.7	83.0	82.6	85.7	87.2	87.3	87.8	84.6
1998	84.7	85.9	85.9	87.7	89.0	87.6	85.2	85.8	88.5	90.1	90.4	90.8	87.6
1999	88.1	89.3	89.7	92.2	92.2	91.5	90.7	90.2	91.8	95.1	95.5	95.7	91.8
2000	91.7	93.3	94.2	95.2	95.7	94.0	93.7	93.0	94.8	96.8	95.9	97.5	94.6
2001	92.9	93.9	94.8	95.5	96.5	94.7	92.9	93.3	95.8	97.2	97.9	97.5	95.2
2002	93.1	94.3	94.7	95.3	96.5	93.6	92.8	93.5	95.7	95.7	96.1	96.0	94.8
2003	92.9	92.7	92.9	94.5	95.5	94.1	93.2	93.1	95.1	96.3	96.2	96.2	94.4
Total private													
1990	55.8	56.0	55.9	56.5	57.9	57.8	58.3	58.2	59.8	60.6	61.1	60.8	58.2
1991	58.2	58.1	57.9	59.4	60.6	60.1	60.1	60.7	61.9	62.3	62.4	62.3	60.3
1992	60.0	59.8	60.5	60.8	62.5	62.4	61.8	62.5	63.5	64.2	64.6	64.4	62.2
1993	62.3	62.4	62.7	64.1	65.0	64.0	64.3	64.1	65.2	65.8	66.0	66.1	64.3
1994	63.6	64.0	64.4	65.9	67.2	66.8	66.5	66.9	68.3	68.8	69.3	69.6	66.7
1995	67.4	67.5	68.8	69.1	69.9	69.2	69.6	69.6	70.7	71.9	71.9	72.1	69.8
1996	69.8	69.6	70.6	71.5	72.7	71.2	70.6	70.8	71.7	71.9	72.2	72.0	71.2
1997	68.8	69.5	70.2	71.3	72.7	71.7	71.9	72.0	73.2	74.1	74.1	74.5	72.0
1998	71.8	72.7	72.9	74.5	75.7	75.1	74.0	74.8	75.9	76.7	76.8	77.1	74.8
1999	74.8	75.6	76.1	78.5	79.4	78.9	79.0	79.2	79.6	81.6	81.8	81.9	78.8
2000	79.0	79.6	80.3	81.4	82.2	81.0	81.8	81.7	82.4	83.0	81.7	83.2	81.4
2001	79.9	79.8	80.7	81.4	82.8	81.7	81.1	81.8	82.5	83.1	83.5	83.2	81.8
2002	79.6	80.1	80.5	81.3	82.9	80.8	81.1	81.6	82.4	81.7	82.0	81.7	81.3
2003	79.3	78.7	78.9	80.5	82.0	81.6	81.7	81.8	81.9	82.3	82.1	82.0	81.1

Employment by Industry: Minnesota—*Continued*

(Numbers in thousands. Not seasonally adjusted.)

Industry	January	February	March	April	May	June	July	August	September	October	November	December	Annual Average
ST. CLOUD—*Continued*													
Goods-producing													
1990	13.8	13.8	13.8	14.2	14.8	15.5	15.7	15.6	15.6	15.7	15.4	14.8	14.8
1991	14.0	13.9	13.5	14.5	15.3	15.9	16.9	17.0	16.8	16.8	16.4	16.0	15.5
1992	15.5	15.4	15.7	16.0	16.9	17.6	17.5	17.5	17.4	17.1	16.9	16.6	16.6
1993	15.8	15.8	16.1	16.7	17.3	17.6	17.9	18.1	17.9	17.6	17.4	17.2	17.1
1994	16.5	16.7	16.9	17.4	17.9	18.6	18.6	18.7	18.7	18.3	18.2	18.1	17.8
1995	17.4	17.5	17.9	18.2	18.7	19.0	19.3	19.2	19.1	19.3	19.0	18.7	18.6
1996	18.0	18.1	18.3	18.5	19.1	19.6	19.6	19.6	19.2	18.7	18.4	18.2	18.7
1997	17.5	17.9	18.4	18.8	19.5	20.0	20.4	20.4	20.2	20.1	19.8	19.7	19.3
1998	19.3	19.4	19.5	20.1	20.6	21.1	21.5	21.6	21.4	20.6	20.4	20.5	20.5
1999	20.0	20.2	20.4	21.0	21.4	21.9	22.4	22.4	22.0	22.0	21.9	21.6	21.4
2000	20.9	21.0	21.3	21.9	22.6	22.9	23.5	23.4	22.9	22.6	20.9	22.0	22.1
2001	21.4	21.3	21.4	21.5	22.3	22.5	22.4	22.5	22.4	22.0	21.8	21.2	21.9
2002	20.2	20.3	20.5	20.8	21.7	22.3	22.5	22.6	22.4	22.0	21.8	21.3	21.5
2003	20.6	20.2	20.5	21.0	21.9	22.2	22.6	22.6	22.2	22.1	21.7	21.3	21.6
Construction and mining													
1990	2.4	2.3	2.3	2.7	3.1	3.4	3.5	3.5	3.5	3.5	3.3	2.8	3.0
1991	2.2	2.2	2.2	2.6	3.0	3.4	3.5	3.6	3.5	3.4	3.1	2.7	2.9
1992	2.3	2.2	2.3	2.6	3.2	3.5	3.6	3.6	3.6	3.5	3.3	2.9	3.0
1993	2.4	2.3	2.4	2.8	3.3	3.5	3.7	3.8	3.7	3.6	3.4	3.1	3.1
1994	2.5	2.5	2.6	3.0	3.3	3.7	3.8	3.8	3.8	3.6	3.4	3.1	3.2
1995	2.6	2.5	2.7	3.0	3.5	3.8	4.0	4.0	4.0	3.9	3.6	3.3	3.4
1996	2.9	2.8	2.8	3.1	3.7	4.0	4.2	4.2	4.1	3.9	3.8	3.5	3.5
1997	3.0	2.9	3.0	3.4	4.0	4.3	4.4	4.5	4.4	4.4	4.1	3.8	3.8
1998	3.4	3.3	3.4	3.6	4.0	4.3	4.3	4.3	4.2	4.2	4.0	3.9	3.9
1999	3.2	3.3	3.5	3.9	4.2	4.5	4.7	4.7	4.5	4.4	4.2	4.0	4.0
2000	3.4	3.4	3.6	4.0	4.5	4.8	4.9	4.9	4.7	4.5	4.3	4.0	4.2
2001	3.6	3.6	3.7	3.9	4.7	5.0	5.1	5.2	5.0	5.0	4.8	4.4	4.5
2002	3.9	3.8	3.9	4.3	4.9	5.3	5.5	5.6	5.4	5.2	5.0	4.6	4.8
2003	4.1	3.9	4.0	4.5	5.1	5.4	5.6	5.6	5.4	5.4	5.1	4.7	4.9
Manufacturing													
1990	11.4	11.5	11.5	11.5	11.7	12.1	12.2	12.1	12.1	12.2	12.1	12.0	11.8
1991	11.8	11.7	11.3	11.9	12.3	12.5	13.4	13.4	13.3	13.4	13.3	13.3	12.6
1992	13.2	13.2	13.4	13.4	13.7	14.1	13.9	13.9	13.8	13.6	13.6	13.7	13.6
1993	13.4	13.5	13.7	13.9	14.0	14.1	14.2	14.3	14.2	14.0	14.0	14.1	13.9
1994	14.0	14.2	14.3	14.4	14.6	14.9	14.8	14.9	14.9	14.7	14.8	15.0	14.6
1995	14.8	15.0	15.2	15.2	15.2	15.2	15.3	15.2	15.1	15.4	15.4	15.4	15.2
1996	15.1	15.3	15.5	15.4	15.4	15.6	15.4	15.4	15.1	14.8	14.6	14.7	15.1
1997	14.5	15.0	15.4	15.4	15.5	15.7	16.0	15.9	15.8	15.7	15.7	15.9	15.5
1998	15.9	16.1	16.1	16.5	16.6	16.8	17.2	17.3	17.2	16.4	16.4	16.6	16.5
1999	16.8	16.9	16.9	17.1	17.2	17.4	17.7	17.7	17.5	17.6	17.7	17.6	17.3
2000	17.5	17.6	17.7	17.9	18.1	18.1	18.6	18.5	18.2	18.1	16.6	18.0	17.9
2001	17.8	17.7	17.7	17.6	17.6	17.5	17.3	17.3	17.4	17.0	17.0	16.8	17.4
2002	16.3	16.5	16.6	16.5	16.8	17.0	17.0	17.0	17.0	16.8	16.8	16.7	16.8
2003	16.5	16.3	16.5	16.5	16.8	16.8	17.0	17.0	16.8	16.7	16.6	16.6	16.7
Service-providing													
1990	53.8	54.4	53.4	54.2	55.3	52.9	51.7	52.3	55.4	57.1	58.0	58.1	54.7
1991	56.4	56.8	56.2	57.2	57.9	55.1	53.0	53.4	56.6	57.7	58.2	58.6	56.4
1992	56.8	56.7	57.2	57.1	57.9	56.0	54.8	55.3	58.2	59.6	60.7	60.5	57.5
1993	59.2	59.4	59.3	60.3	60.8	57.9	56.7	56.1	59.6	61.1	61.6	62.1	59.5
1994	59.9	60.3	60.6	61.9	62.7	60.0	58.8	58.8	61.8	63.3	64.3	64.8	61.4
1995	63.2	63.3	64.1	64.2	64.7	62.3	61.1	60.9	64.3	65.7	66.1	66.7	63.8
1996	64.9	64.8	65.5	66.2	66.9	63.7	62.0	61.7	65.3	66.5	67.5	67.3	65.1
1997	64.5	64.9	65.0	65.8	66.6	63.7	62.6	62.2	65.5	67.1	67.5	68.1	65.2
1998	65.4	66.5	66.4	67.6	68.4	66.5	63.7	64.2	67.1	69.5	70.0	70.3	67.1
1999	68.1	69.1	69.3	71.2	70.8	69.6	68.3	67.8	69.8	73.1	73.6	74.1	70.4
2000	70.8	72.3	72.9	73.3	73.1	71.1	70.2	69.6	71.9	74.2	75.0	75.5	72.4
2001	71.5	72.6	73.4	74.0	74.2	72.2	70.5	70.8	73.4	75.2	76.1	76.3	73.4
2002	72.9	74.0	74.2	74.5	74.8	71.3	70.3	70.9	73.3	73.7	74.3	74.7	73.2
2003	72.3	72.5	72.4	73.5	73.6	71.9	70.6	70.5	72.9	74.2	74.5	74.9	72.8
Trade, transportation, and utilities													
1990	18.2	18.1	17.7	17.4	17.5	17.8	18.1	18.2	18.5	18.4	19.1	19.2	18.1
1991	18.4	18.2	18.1	18.4	18.7	18.5	18.8	19.0	19.4	19.6	20.2	20.1	18.9
1992	19.4	19.2	19.1	19.0	19.3	19.3	18.8	19.3	19.6	20.1	20.7	20.7	19.5
1993	20.0	19.7	19.5	19.9	20.1	19.8	19.8	19.7	20.2	20.7	20.9	20.8	20.0
1994	20.1	19.9	19.8	20.3	20.6	20.4	20.6	20.8	21.2	21.7	22.5	22.7	20.8
1995	22.1	21.7	21.8	21.9	21.9	21.5	22.1	21.9	22.3	22.7	23.2	23.2	22.1
1996	22.4	22.1	22.0	22.5	22.5	22.1	21.6	21.8	22.1	22.0	22.3	22.3	22.1
1997	21.4	21.1	21.0	21.4	21.6	21.2	21.3	21.3	21.6	21.7	22.0	22.4	21.5
1998	21.3	21.4	21.3	21.7	22.0	22.0	21.7	21.8	22.1	22.6	22.8	23.1	21.9
1999	21.9	21.9	21.7	22.4	22.6	22.7	22.8	22.9	22.8	23.5	24.0	24.3	22.7
2000	23.4	23.5	23.4	23.5	23.4	23.0	23.2	23.1	23.1	23.1	23.6	23.6	23.3
2001	22.3	22.0	21.9	22.2	22.4	22.1	21.9	22.0	22.1	22.4	22.9	23.2	22.3
2002	21.8	21.7	21.7	21.7	21.6	21.1	21.1	21.1	21.3	20.8	21.5	21.7	21.4
2003	20.9	20.4	20.3	20.7	20.8	20.8	20.7	20.8	20.8	20.9	21.4	21.6	20.8

Employment by Industry: Minnesota—*Continued*

(Numbers in thousands. Not seasonally adjusted.)

Industry	January	February	March	April	May	June	July	August	September	October	November	December	Annual Average
ST. CLOUD—*Continued*													
Wholesale trade													
1990	2.8	2.9	2.9	2.9	3.0	3.0	3.0	3.0	3.0	3.0	3.0	3.0	2.9
1991	2.9	3.0	3.0	2.9	3.0	3.0	3.1	3.1	3.1	3.1	3.0	3.0	3.0
1992	3.2	3.2	3.2	3.2	3.3	3.4	3.2	3.2	3.3	3.3	3.3	3.4	3.2
1993	3.4	3.4	3.4	3.5	3.5	3.5	3.5	3.5	3.5	3.4	3.4	3.4	3.4
1994	3.4	3.4	3.4	3.5	3.6	3.6	3.6	3.6	3.6	3.5	3.5	3.5	3.5
1995	3.8	3.8	3.8	3.9	3.9	3.9	3.9	3.9	3.9	3.9	3.9	3.8	3.8
1996	3.9	3.9	3.9	4.0	4.1	4.0	4.0	4.0	4.0	4.1	4.0	4.0	3.9
1997	4.0	4.0	4.0	4.2	4.3	4.2	4.3	4.2	4.2	4.2	4.2	4.2	4.1
1998	4.1	4.2	4.2	4.4	4.4	4.5	4.2	4.2	4.2	4.2	4.2	4.2	4.2
1999	4.2	4.2	4.2	4.3	4.3	4.3	4.6	4.6	4.5	4.5	4.5	4.5	4.3
2000	4.5	4.6	4.6	4.6	4.6	4.5	4.6	4.5	4.5	4.4	4.4	4.4	4.5
2001	4.4	4.4	4.4	4.5	4.5	4.5	4.5	4.5	4.5	4.4	4.4	4.5	4.5
2002	4.3	4.3	4.3	4.4	4.4	4.4	4.5	4.4	4.4	4.4	4.4	4.4	4.4
2003	4.4	4.4	4.4	4.5	4.5	4.5	4.6	4.5	4.5	4.5	4.5	4.5	4.5
Retail trade													
1990	13.1	12.9	12.5	12.1	12.1	12.4	12.7	12.8	13.0	12.9	13.6	13.7	12.8
1991	13.0	12.7	12.6	12.9	13.0	12.9	13.2	13.4	13.6	13.9	14.5	14.4	13.3
1992	13.6	13.4	13.3	13.3	13.4	13.4	13.2	13.6	13.7	14.2	14.8	14.7	13.7
1993	14.1	13.8	13.6	13.8	14.0	13.7	13.8	13.7	14.0	14.5	14.8	14.7	14.0
1994	14.1	13.8	13.7	14.1	14.2	14.0	14.4	14.6	14.9	15.5	16.3	16.5	14.6
1995	15.7	15.3	15.4	15.4	15.4	15.1	15.7	15.5	15.8	16.1	16.6	16.7	15.7
1996	15.8	15.5	15.4	15.8	15.7	15.4	15.0	15.2	15.4	15.2	15.7	15.7	15.4
1997	14.8	14.5	14.5	14.6	14.7	14.4	14.4	14.5	14.7	14.7	15.0	15.3	14.6
1998	14.4	14.4	14.3	14.5	14.7	14.7	14.7	14.9	15.0	15.4	15.6	15.9	14.8
1999	14.8	14.8	14.6	14.9	15.1	15.3	15.1	15.3	15.2	15.9	16.4	16.7	15.3
2000	15.9	15.8	15.7	15.7	15.6	15.4	15.5	15.5	15.4	15.5	16.0	16.0	15.6
2001	14.9	14.6	14.4	14.6	14.8	14.6	14.5	14.6	14.6	14.9	15.4	15.6	14.8
2002	14.6	14.5	14.5	14.3	14.2	13.8	13.7	13.8	13.8	13.3	14.0	14.3	14.1
2003	13.5	13.1	12.9	13.1	13.2	13.2	13.1	13.3	13.2	13.3	13.8	14.0	13.3
Transportation and utilities													
1990	2.3	2.3	2.3	2.4	2.4	2.4	2.4	2.4	2.5	2.5	2.5	2.5	2.4
1991	2.5	2.5	2.5	2.6	2.7	2.6	2.5	2.5	2.7	2.6	2.7	2.7	2.5
1992	2.6	2.6	2.6	2.5	2.6	2.5	2.4	2.5	2.6	2.6	2.6	2.6	2.5
1993	2.5	2.5	2.5	2.6	2.6	2.6	2.5	2.5	2.7	2.8	2.7	2.7	2.6
1994	2.6	2.7	2.7	2.7	2.8	2.8	2.6	2.6	2.7	2.7	2.7	2.7	2.6
1995	2.6	2.6	2.6	2.6	2.6	2.5	2.5	2.5	2.6	2.7	2.7	2.7	2.6
1996	2.7	2.7	2.7	2.7	2.7	2.7	2.6	2.6	2.7	2.7	2.6	2.6	2.6
1997	2.6	2.6	2.5	2.6	2.6	2.6	2.6	2.6	2.7	2.8	2.8	2.9	2.6
1998	2.8	2.8	2.8	2.8	2.9	2.8	2.8	2.7	2.9	3.0	3.0	3.0	2.8
1999	2.9	2.9	2.9	3.2	3.2	3.1	3.1	3.0	3.1	3.1	3.1	3.1	3.0
2000	3.0	3.1	3.1	3.2	3.2	3.1	3.1	3.1	3.2	3.2	3.2	3.2	3.1
2001	3.0	3.0	3.1	3.1	3.1	3.0	2.9	2.9	3.0	3.1	3.1	3.1	3.0
2002	2.9	2.9	2.9	3.0	3.0	2.9	2.9	2.9	3.1	3.1	3.1	3.0	3.0
2003	3.0	2.9	3.0	3.1	3.1	3.1	3.0	3.0	3.1	3.1	3.1	3.1	3.1
Information													
1990	1.0	1.0	1.0	1.1	1.2	1.1	1.2	1.1	1.1	1.2	1.2	1.2	1.1
1991	1.1	1.1	1.1	1.1	1.1	1.1	1.1	1.1	1.1	1.1	1.2	1.2	1.1
1992	1.1	1.1	1.1	1.1	1.1	1.1	1.1	1.1	1.1	1.1	1.1	1.1	1.1
1993	1.0	1.0	1.0	1.0	1.0	1.0	1.0	1.0	1.0	1.0	1.0	1.0	1.0
1994	1.0	1.0	1.0	1.0	1.1	1.1	1.0	1.0	1.0	1.1	1.1	1.1	1.0
1995	1.1	1.1	1.1	1.1	1.1	1.1	1.2	1.1	1.2	1.1	1.1	1.2	1.1
1996	1.2	1.2	1.2	1.1	1.2	1.1	1.2	1.2	1.1	1.2	1.2	1.2	1.1
1997	1.2	1.2	1.3	1.2	1.2	1.2	1.2	1.2	1.2	1.2	1.2	1.2	1.2
1998	1.2	1.3	1.3	1.2	1.2	1.2	1.2	1.2	1.2	1.3	1.3	1.3	1.2
1999	1.3	1.2	1.2	1.3	1.3	1.3	1.3	1.2	1.2	1.3	1.3	1.3	1.2
2000	1.3	1.3	1.3	1.3	1.3	1.4	1.4	1.4	1.4	1.3	1.3	1.4	1.3
2001	1.4	1.4	1.4	1.4	1.4	1.5	1.5	1.6	1.6	1.6	1.7	1.7	1.5
2002	1.7	1.7	1.7	1.7	1.7	1.7	1.7	1.6	1.6	1.5	1.5	1.4	1.6
2003	1.5	1.4	1.4	1.4	1.4	1.4	1.4	1.4	1.4	1.4	1.4	1.4	1.4
Financial activities													
1990	2.3	2.3	2.3	2.3	2.3	2.3	2.4	2.4	2.4	2.4	2.4	2.4	2.3
1991	2.3	2.3	2.3	2.4	2.4	2.4	2.5	2.5	2.5	2.5	2.5	2.5	2.4
1992	2.4	2.4	2.5	2.4	2.4	2.4	2.4	2.4	2.4	2.5	2.5	2.5	2.4
1993	2.5	2.5	2.6	2.5	2.5	2.5	2.6	2.6	2.6	2.7	2.7	2.9	2.6
1994	2.6	2.7	2.7	2.7	2.7	2.7	2.7	2.8	2.8	2.8	2.8	2.8	2.7
1995	2.8	2.8	2.8	2.7	2.7	2.8	2.8	2.9	2.9	2.9	2.9	2.9	2.8
1996	2.9	2.9	3.0	3.0	3.1	3.1	3.1	3.1	3.1	3.2	3.2	3.2	3.0
1997	3.1	3.1	3.1	3.2	3.2	3.2	3.3	3.3	3.3	3.3	3.3	3.4	3.2
1998	3.3	3.3	3.3	3.4	3.5	3.5	3.4	3.4	3.4	3.5	3.5	3.4	3.4
1999	3.3	3.4	3.4	3.6	3.6	3.6	3.5	3.5	3.5	3.5	3.5	3.5	3.4
2000	3.4	3.4	3.4	3.4	3.5	3.5	3.5	3.5	3.5	3.5	3.5	3.5	3.4
2001	3.5	3.5	3.5	3.6	3.6	3.7	3.7	3.7	3.7	3.7	3.7	3.7	3.6
2002	3.7	3.6	3.6	4.0	4.0	4.0	4.0	4.0	4.0	4.0	4.0	4.0	3.9
2003	3.9	4.0	4.0	4.1	4.1	4.1	4.1	4.1	4.1	4.0	4.0	4.1	4.1

Employment by Industry: Minnesota—*Continued*

(Numbers in thousands. Not seasonally adjusted.)

Industry	January	February	March	April	May	June	July	August	September	October	November	December	Annual Average
ST. CLOUD—*Continued*													
Professional and business services													
1990	3.6	3.7	3.7	3.8	3.9	4.0	4.1	4.0	4.1	4.4	4.5	4.6	4.0
1991	4.1	4.1	4.1	4.0	3.9	4.0	2.9	3.0	3.0	3.2	3.2	3.4	3.5
1992	2.9	2.9	3.1	3.2	3.4	3.5	3.6	3.8	3.7	3.7	3.7	3.7	3.4
1993	3.6	3.6	3.6	3.8	3.6	3.6	3.9	3.5	3.5	3.7	3.8	3.9	3.6
1994	3.6	3.6	3.8	3.8	3.8	4.0	4.0	4.0	4.0	3.9	3.9	3.9	3.8
1995	3.7	3.8	4.0	4.2	4.1	4.3	4.2	4.3	4.2	4.2	4.2	4.2	4.1
1996	4.0	4.0	4.2	4.4	4.5	4.7	4.7	4.6	4.7	4.7	4.9	4.8	4.5
1997	4.3	4.4	4.4	4.5	4.6	4.7	4.7	4.6	4.6	4.9	5.0	4.9	4.6
1998	4.5	4.6	4.7	5.1	5.0	5.0	4.9	5.1	5.2	5.3	5.4	5.3	5.0
1999	5.2	5.4	5.6	6.0	5.9	6.1	6.2	6.1	6.1	6.5	6.6	6.5	6.0
2000	6.3	6.2	6.5	6.6	6.4	6.6	6.7	6.7	6.7	7.1	7.1	7.2	6.6
2001	6.5	6.4	6.9	7.0	6.9	6.9	7.1	7.2	7.2	7.1	7.2	7.0	7.0
2002	6.3	6.4	6.5	6.7	6.7	6.5	6.6	6.9	7.1	7.0	6.9	6.8	6.7
2003	6.7	6.7	6.8	6.9	7.1	7.2	7.2	7.2	7.2	7.2	7.1	7.0	7.0
Educational and health services													
1990	8.3	8.4	8.6	8.8	9.1	8.0	7.9	8.0	8.9	9.3	9.4	9.5	8.6
1991	9.1	9.3	9.4	9.5	9.6	8.7	8.5	8.6	9.4	9.6	9.6	9.7	9.2
1992	9.4	9.6	9.7	9.6	9.8	8.8	8.8	8.7	9.6	9.9	10.0	10.1	9.5
1993	9.8	9.9	10.0	10.1	10.3	9.2	9.0	9.0	9.8	10.1	10.2	10.2	9.8
1994	9.8	10.0	10.1	10.3	10.4	9.4	9.2	9.2	10.1	10.4	10.4	10.4	9.9
1995	10.0	10.2	10.5	10.6	10.7	9.8	9.6	9.6	10.5	10.9	10.9	11.1	10.3
1996	10.8	10.7	11.1	11.1	11.2	9.7	9.6	9.6	10.6	11.0	11.1	11.2	10.6
1997	10.6	10.9	11.0	11.2	11.4	10.1	9.9	9.9	10.9	11.5	11.5	11.6	10.8
1998	11.2	11.6	11.7	11.8	12.0	11.0	10.3	10.3	11.3	12.0	12.2	12.2	11.4
1999	12.1	12.4	12.6	12.7	12.8	11.5	11.3	11.3	12.4	12.9	12.9	13.0	12.3
2000	12.5	12.8	12.9	12.9	13.1	11.8	11.7	11.6	12.9	13.7	13.8	13.9	12.8
2001	13.6	13.8	14.0	14.1	14.3	13.0	12.6	12.7	13.5	14.3	14.4	14.4	13.7
2002	13.9	14.4	14.5	14.2	14.5	12.7	12.7	12.8	13.4	13.8	13.9	14.0	13.7
2003	13.4	13.7	13.6	13.9	13.9	13.1	13.0	13.0	13.5	14.0	14.0	14.0	13.6
Leisure and hospitality													
1990	5.5	5.5	5.6	5.7	5.9	5.8	5.6	5.6	5.9	5.9	5.8	5.8	5.7
1991	5.9	5.9	6.0	6.1	6.1	6.0	6.0	6.0	6.2	6.0	5.8	5.9	5.9
1992	5.8	5.7	5.8	6.0	6.1	6.1	5.9	6.0	6.0	6.1	6.0	6.0	5.9
1993	5.9	6.1	6.1	6.2	6.4	6.5	6.3	6.4	6.4	6.3	6.2	6.3	6.2
1994	6.3	6.3	6.3	6.6	6.8	6.8	6.5	6.5	6.6	6.7	6.5	6.6	6.5
1995	6.4	6.5	6.7	6.5	6.7	6.7	6.4	6.6	6.5	6.7	6.6	6.8	6.5
1996	6.6	6.7	6.8	6.9	7.1	6.9	6.8	7.0	7.0	7.2	7.1	7.1	6.9
1997	6.8	6.9	7.0	7.0	7.2	7.2	7.1	7.3	7.4	7.3	7.2	7.2	7.1
1998	7.1	7.2	7.2	7.2	7.4	7.3	7.0	7.4	7.4	7.4	7.2	7.2	7.2
1999	7.0	7.1	7.2	7.5	7.7	7.7	7.4	7.7	7.5	7.7	7.4	7.5	7.4
2000	7.1	7.3	7.4	7.6	7.8	7.6	7.6	7.8	7.7	7.5	7.3	7.3	7.5
2001	7.1	7.3	7.4	7.4	7.7	7.7	7.6	7.8	7.7	7.7	7.5	7.7	7.6
2002	7.7	7.7	7.7	7.8	8.3	8.1	8.0	8.1	8.1	8.1	7.9	8.0	8.0
2003	7.9	7.9	7.9	8.1	8.3	8.3	8.2	8.2	8.2	8.2	8.0	8.1	8.1
Other services													
1990	3.1	3.2	3.2	3.2	3.2	3.3	3.3	3.3	3.3	3.3	3.3	3.3	3.2
1991	3.3	3.3	3.4	3.4	3.5	3.5	3.4	3.5	3.5	3.5	3.5	3.5	3.4
1992	3.5	3.5	3.5	3.5	3.5	3.6	3.7	3.7	3.7	3.7	3.7	3.7	3.6
1993	3.7	3.8	3.8	3.9	3.8	3.8	3.8	3.8	3.8	3.7	3.8	3.8	3.7
1994	3.7	3.8	3.8	3.8	3.9	3.8	3.9	3.9	3.9	3.9	3.9	4.0	3.8
1995	3.9	3.9	4.0	3.9	4.0	4.0	4.0	4.0	4.0	4.1	4.0	4.0	3.9
1996	3.9	3.9	4.0	4.0	4.0	4.0	4.0	3.9	3.9	3.9	4.0	4.0	3.9
1997	3.9	4.0	4.0	4.0	4.0	4.1	4.0	4.0	4.0	4.1	4.1	4.1	4.0
1998	3.9	3.9	3.9	4.0	4.0	4.0	4.0	4.0	3.9	4.0	4.0	4.1	3.9
1999	4.0	4.0	4.0	4.0	4.1	4.1	4.1	4.1	4.1	4.2	4.2	4.2	4.0
2000	4.1	4.1	4.1	4.2	4.1	4.2	4.2	4.2	4.2	4.2	4.2	4.3	4.1
2001	4.1	4.1	4.2	4.2	4.2	4.3	4.3	4.3	4.3	4.3	4.3	4.3	4.2
2002	4.3	4.3	4.3	4.4	4.4	4.4	4.5	4.5	4.5	4.5	4.5	4.5	4.4
2003	4.4	4.4	4.4	4.4	4.5	4.5	4.5	4.5	4.5	4.5	4.5	4.5	4.5
Government													
1990	11.8	12.2	11.3	11.9	12.2	10.6	9.1	9.7	11.2	12.2	12.3	12.1	11.3
1991	12.2	12.6	11.8	12.3	12.6	10.9	9.8	9.7	11.5	12.2	12.2	12.3	11.6
1992	12.3	12.3	12.4	12.3	12.3	11.2	10.5	10.3	12.1	12.5	13.0	12.7	11.9
1993	12.7	12.8	12.7	12.9	13.1	11.5	10.3	10.1	12.3	12.9	13.0	13.2	12.2
1994	12.8	13.0	13.1	13.4	13.4	11.8	10.9	10.6	12.2	12.8	13.2	13.3	12.5
1995	13.2	13.3	13.2	13.3	13.5	12.1	10.8	10.5	12.7	13.1	13.2	13.3	12.6
1996	13.1	13.3	13.2	13.2	13.3	12.1	11.0	10.5	12.8	13.3	13.7	13.5	12.7
1997	13.2	13.3	13.2	13.3	13.4	12.0	11.1	10.6	12.5	13.1	13.2	13.3	12.6
1998	12.9	13.2	13.0	13.2	13.3	12.5	11.2	11.0	12.6	13.4	13.6	13.7	12.8
1999	13.3	13.7	13.6	13.7	12.8	12.6	11.7	11.0	12.2	13.5	13.7	13.8	12.9
2000	12.7	13.7	13.9	13.8	13.5	13.0	11.9	11.3	12.4	13.8	14.2	14.3	13.2
2001	13.0	14.1	14.1	14.1	13.7	13.0	11.8	11.5	13.3	14.1	14.4	14.3	13.5
2002	13.5	14.2	14.2	14.0	13.6	12.8	11.7	11.9	13.3	14.0	14.1	14.3	13.5
2003	13.6	14.0	14.0	14.0	13.5	12.5	11.5	11.3	13.2	14.0	14.1	14.2	13.3

Employment by Industry: Minnesota—*Continued*

(Numbers in thousands. Not seasonally adjusted.)

Industry	January	February	March	April	May	June	July	August	September	October	November	December	Annual Average
ST. CLOUD—*Continued*													
Federal government													
1990	1.6	1.6	1.6	1.6	1.8	1.6	1.8	1.8	1.7	1.7	1.7	1.7	1.6
1991	1.7	1.7	1.7	1.7	1.7	1.8	1.8	1.8	1.8	1.7	1.7	1.8	1.7
1992	1.6	1.6	1.6	1.6	1.6	1.6	1.6	1.6	1.6	1.6	1.6	1.6	1.6
1993	1.6	1.6	1.6	1.6	1.6	1.6	1.6	1.6	1.6	1.6	1.6	1.7	1.6
1994	1.6	1.6	1.6	1.6	1.5	1.5	1.6	1.6	1.6	1.6	1.6	1.7	1.5
1995	1.6	1.6	1.6	1.6	1.6	1.6	1.6	1.6	1.6	1.6	1.6	1.7	1.6
1996	1.6	1.6	1.6	1.6	1.6	1.6	1.6	1.6	1.6	1.6	1.6	1.7	1.6
1997	1.6	1.6	1.6	1.6	1.6	1.6	1.6	1.6	1.6	1.6	1.6	1.6	1.6
1998	1.5	1.5	1.5	1.6	1.6	1.6	1.5	1.6	1.6	1.6	1.6	1.6	1.5
1999	1.6	1.6	1.6	1.6	1.6	1.6	1.6	1.5	1.5	1.5	1.5	1.6	1.5
2000	1.5	1.5	1.6	1.6	1.8	1.8	1.6	1.6	1.5	1.6	1.6	1.7	1.6
2001	1.6	1.6	1.6	1.6	1.6	1.6	1.6	1.6	1.6	1.6	1.6	1.6	1.6
2002	1.5	1.5	1.6	1.6	1.5	1.6	1.5	1.5	1.5	1.5	1.5	1.5	1.5
2003	1.5	1.5	1.5	1.5	1.5	1.5	1.5	1.5	1.5	1.5	1.5	1.5	1.5
State government													
1990	4.3	4.4	3.7	4.2	4.2	2.9	2.3	2.8	4.3	4.4	4.3	4.2	3.8
1991	4.3	4.3	3.7	4.2	4.2	2.9	2.8	2.8	4.2	4.2	4.2	4.2	3.8
1992	3.8	3.7	3.8	3.7	3.7	2.5	2.5	2.3	3.7	3.9	4.0	3.8	3.4
1993	3.9	3.9	3.8	3.8	3.9	2.5	2.4	2.3	4.0	4.0	4.0	3.9	3.5
1994	3.9	3.9	3.9	3.9	3.9	2.6	2.6	2.5	3.9	3.9	4.0	4.0	3.5
1995	4.0	4.0	3.9	3.9	4.0	2.5	2.6	2.6	4.0	4.0	4.0	3.8	3.6
1996	3.9	3.9	3.8	3.9	3.9	2.6	2.6	2.3	3.8	4.0	4.0	3.9	3.5
1997	3.9	3.9	3.8	3.9	3.9	2.5	2.6	2.5	3.7	3.8	3.7	3.8	3.5
1998	3.8	3.8	3.7	3.8	3.8	3.1	3.0	2.9	3.9	4.0	4.1	4.1	3.6
1999	3.9	4.1	4.0	4.1	3.1	2.9	2.7	2.7	3.4	4.0	4.1	4.1	3.5
2000	3.2	4.1	4.1	4.1	3.6	2.9	3.0	2.8	3.5	4.2	4.3	4.3	3.6
2001	3.3	4.3	4.3	4.3	3.7	3.0	2.9	2.8	4.1	4.3	4.3	4.3	3.8
2002	3.7	4.3	4.3	4.3	3.6	3.0	2.9	2.9	3.9	4.1	4.2	4.2	3.8
2003	3.7	4.0	4.0	4.0	3.4	2.7	2.6	2.5	4.1	4.3	4.3	4.3	3.7
Local government													
1990	7.7	8.0	7.8	8.0	8.1	7.9	6.7	6.7	7.2	8.2	8.5	8.3	7.7
1991	8.3	8.6	8.6	8.5	8.8	8.2	7.1	6.9	7.6	8.4	8.5	8.6	8.1
1992	6.9	7.0	7.0	7.0	7.0	7.1	6.4	6.4	6.8	7.0	7.4	7.3	6.9
1993	7.2	7.3	7.3	7.5	7.6	7.4	6.3	6.2	6.7	7.3	7.4	7.6	7.1
1994	7.3	7.5	7.6	7.9	8.0	7.7	6.7	6.5	6.7	7.3	7.6	7.6	7.3
1995	7.6	7.7	7.7	7.8	7.9	8.0	6.6	6.3	7.1	7.5	7.6	7.8	7.4
1996	7.6	7.8	7.8	7.7	7.8	7.9	6.8	6.6	7.4	7.7	8.1	7.9	7.5
1997	7.7	7.8	7.8	7.8	7.9	7.9	6.9	6.5	7.2	7.7	7.9	7.9	7.5
1998	7.6	7.9	7.8	7.8	7.9	7.8	6.7	6.5	7.1	7.8	7.9	8.0	7.5
1999	7.8	8.0	8.0	8.0	8.1	8.1	7.4	6.8	7.3	8.0	8.1	8.1	7.8
2000	8.0	8.1	8.2	8.1	8.1	8.3	7.3	6.9	7.4	8.0	8.3	8.3	7.9
2001	8.1	8.2	8.2	8.2	8.4	8.4	7.3	7.1	7.6	8.2	8.5	8.4	8.1
2002	8.3	8.4	8.3	8.1	8.5	8.2	7.3	7.5	7.9	8.4	8.4	8.6	8.2
2003	8.4	8.5	8.5	8.5	8.6	8.3	7.4	7.3	7.6	8.2	8.3	8.4	8.2

Average Weekly Hours by Industry: Minnesota

(Not seasonally adjusted.)

Industry	January	February	March	April	May	June	July	August	September	October	November	December	Annual Average
STATEWIDE													
Construction													
2001	36.8	35.9	35.8	35.7	38.8	38.8	40.5	39.9	39.9	39.3	38.4	37.9	38.4
2002	36.3	35.2	34.8	35.5	38.2	40.2	38.2	40.4	39.8	39.6	38.0	37.3	38.0
2003	34.7	33.7	35.5	36.2	36.4	39.1	38.1	39.4	39.9	39.2	37.0	35.4	37.3
Manufacturing													
2001	39.8	39.6	40.1	39.8	39.6	39.3	38.8	39.3	40.4	39.5	39.3	40.0	39.6
2002	39.0	39.4	38.6	39.1	39.0	40.0	39.4	40.1	40.2	40.0	40.6	41.2	39.7
2003	39.2	39.5	39.9	39.2	39.4	40.3	39.4	40.8	41.5	40.6	41.8	40.3	40.2
Trade, transportation, and utilities													
2001	30.2	30.4	30.7	31.0	31.1	31.9	31.5	31.8	31.0	30.6	29.7	30.7	30.9
2002	28.8	29.1	29.1	28.9	29.7	30.7	31.1	30.5	30.3	29.6	29.9	31.2	29.9
2003	29.6	30.8	30.8	30.8	31.6	32.2	32.0	31.8	31.2	31.7	31.6	31.6	31.3
Wholesale trade													
2001	37.4	37.5	37.4	37.7	38.0	38.1	37.2	36.5	38.3	38.4	37.9	37.7	37.7
2002	36.7	36.5	37.6	36.6	37.9	38.4	36.9	37.2	37.9	37.4	37.5	36.7	37.3
2003	35.7	38.3	38.5	37.4	38.9	39.1	38.0	39.6	39.1	40.2	39.4	38.5	38.6
Retail trade													
2001	26.7	26.5	26.9	27.2	27.1	28.0	28.2	28.4	27.6	27.3	26.4	27.8	27.3
2002	25.6	25.7	25.2	25.4	26.0	27.0	27.5	27.0	26.8	25.7	26.3	28.3	26.4
2003	26.0	26.2	26.2	26.5	27.1	27.8	27.8	26.9	26.1	26.3	25.8	26.4	26.6
Information													
2001	38.1	37.1	37.9	38.6	37.7	37.5	38.0	36.6	38.3	37.7	37.2	38.1	37.7
2002	36.4	36.4	37.0	36.5	37.3	38.5	38.1	39.4	40.2	38.0	37.9	39.3	38.0
2003	37.4	38.8	39.1	38.1	38.5	39.6	39.2	40.1	39.4	37.9	37.2	36.6	38.5
MINNEAPOLIS-ST. PAUL													
Construction													
2001	36.4	34.2	33.7	33.2	37.1	36.8	39.0	38.2	37.9	37.1	37.0	36.4	36.6
2002	35.7	34.2	33.0	33.2	35.7	37.0	36.3	37.4	37.4	37.2	35.6	35.6	35.8
2003	34.6	33.1	33.5	34.0	34.5	35.0	34.8	35.7	36.7	35.6	34.9	34.2	34.8
Manufacturing													
2001	40.2	40.2	41.1	40.8	40.7	40.2	39.6	39.5	40.3	39.9	39.1	40.2	40.1
2002	39.3	39.9	39.2	39.5	39.3	40.1	39.3	40.4	40.0	40.0	40.8	41.1	39.9
2003	40.7	40.2	40.6	40.0	40.2	40.7	39.9	41.0	41.4	41.2	41.8	41.3	40.7
Trade, transportation, and utilities													
2001	28.6	29.2	29.9	29.7	29.7	30.3	29.7	30.4	29.0	28.5	27.5	28.9	29.3
2002	26.5	27.1	26.8	26.8	28.1	28.9	28.7	28.4	28.4	27.3	27.5	27.5	27.7
2003	27.0	27.3	27.4	27.9	28.2	28.6	28.7	28.5	28.4	28.4	28.3	28.9	28.1
Wholesale trade													
2001	36.5	36.9	37.2	37.2	37.4	38.4	37.3	36.0	37.6	37.5	38.3	37.2	37.3
2002	36.1	36.3	37.1	36.9	39.4	38.8	37.0	36.7	37.6	37.3	37.2	35.1	37.1
2003	36.1	36.3	35.9	36.4	36.8	36.4	35.7	36.4	36.1	37.3	37.3	36.2	36.4
Retail trade													
2001	26.3	26.1	26.7	26.8	26.9	27.1	26.7	27.5	26.8	26.8	25.1	27.6	26.7
2002	24.4	24.8	24.0	24.1	24.7	25.6	25.8	25.7	25.8	24.3	24.8	25.1	24.9
2003	23.9	23.9	24.3	24.7	25.0	25.6	26.1	25.3	25.0	24.5	24.3	25.2	24.8
Transportation and utilities													
2001	27.3	29.9	31.0	29.8	29.6	30.8	30.2	32.4	26.5	24.7	23.8	24.7	28.4
2002	23.1	24.3	24.5	24.4	26.6	28.4	28.7	27.6	26.1	25.7	25.7	26.5	26.0
2003	25.9	27.2	26.7	27.4	27.9	28.4	27.8	28.8	29.4	29.6	30.2	31.3	28.4
Information													
2001	37.6	36.1	36.7	38.6	37.3	37.4	38.4	36.2	38.2	35.6	35.6	37.7	37.1
2002	36.2	36.1	36.9	36.4	37.0	38.7	39.0	39.5	40.3	37.8	37.4	39.1	37.9
2003	38.0	38.3	39.2	38.4	38.2	38.9	39.2	39.1	39.7	39.1	39.3	38.8	38.9

Average Hourly Earnings by Industry: Minnesota

(Dollars, not seasonally adjusted.)

Industry	January	February	March	April	May	June	July	August	September	October	November	December	Annual Average
STATEWIDE													
Construction													
2001	21.79	21.83	21.79	21.74	21.30	22.51	22.67	23.26	23.37	22.82	22.82	22.92	22.49
2002	23.21	23.20	23.20	22.86	22.32	22.42	22.46	22.78	22.80	22.56	22.29	22.91	22.70
2003	23.56	24.37	23.73	23.21	22.87	22.21	22.64	22.94	22.76	22.64	22.74	23.89	23.03
Manufacturing													
2001	14.66	14.56	14.54	14.72	14.65	14.65	14.71	14.74	14.85	14.99	15.00	15.07	14.76
2002	14.94	14.89	14.91	15.12	15.07	14.98	14.94	15.18	15.19	15.14	15.13	15.24	15.06
2003	15.35	15.34	15.35	15.49	15.47	15.56	15.32	15.30	15.39	15.27	15.47	15.81	15.43
Trade, transportation, and utilities													
2001	14.15	14.27	14.44	14.49	14.26	14.18	14.05	14.14	14.38	14.29	14.43	14.50	14.30
2002	14.48	14.65	14.61	14.69	14.88	14.84	14.60	14.66	14.75	14.66	14.82	14.66	14.69
2003	14.66	15.09	15.09	14.95	14.60	14.56	14.64	14.62	14.85	14.63	14.63	14.50	14.73
Wholesale trade													
2001	18.60	18.47	18.79	18.99	18.40	18.68	18.32	18.39	18.51	18.25	18.54	18.56	18.54
2002	18.54	18.88	18.27	18.94	19.26	19.96	19.63	19.55	19.56	19.12	19.52	19.19	19.21
2003	18.92	19.56	19.92	19.62	18.26	18.23	18.79	18.54	18.79	18.75	18.60	18.44	18.86
Retail trade													
2001	11.53	11.75	11.74	11.74	11.74	11.57	11.57	11.71	11.84	11.88	12.04	12.02	11.76
2002	12.00	12.04	12.24	12.10	12.23	11.92	11.81	11.93	11.96	12.01	12.05	12.00	12.02
2003	11.83	12.08	11.85	11.86	11.87	11.86	11.78	11.85	11.90	11.64	11.64	11.52	11.80
Information													
2001	18.80	17.81	17.61	18.24	18.25	18.33	18.43	18.72	18.89	19.24	19.56	19.47	18.61
2002	19.75	18.57	18.39	19.71	18.75	18.53	19.58	19.16	20.39	20.87	21.55	21.45	19.77
2003	21.47	21.23	20.99	20.83	20.44	20.54	20.34	20.12	19.59	19.91	19.22	19.32	20.30
MINNEAPOLIS-ST. PAUL													
Construction													
2001	24.23	24.40	24.10	24.02	23.75	24.36	24.06	24.94	25.07	24.21	24.00	23.89	24.27
2002	24.23	24.63	24.48	24.16	24.00	24.29	23.99	24.60	24.75	24.68	24.52	25.17	24.46
2003	25.90	26.29	26.33	25.89	25.52	25.29	25.41	25.78	25.34	25.05	24.99	25.70	25.57
Manufacturing													
2001	15.81	15.56	15.51	15.86	15.75	15.74	15.98	16.09	16.21	16.13	16.30	16.39	15.94
2002	16.16	16.06	15.92	16.23	16.33	16.35	16.44	16.60	16.52	16.40	16.27	16.36	16.31
2003	16.70	16.53	16.63	16.68	16.60	16.78	16.70	16.75	16.78	16.71	16.87	16.91	16.72
Trade, transportation, and utilities													
2001	16.27	16.31	16.32	16.63	16.55	16.74	16.27	16.40	17.09	16.98	17.52	17.14	16.68
2002	17.55	17.17	17.07	17.34	17.51	17.30	16.93	16.78	16.72	16.57	16.97	16.75	17.05
2003	16.52	16.54	16.71	16.65	16.90	16.96	16.90	16.85	16.97	16.78	16.31	16.11	16.68
Wholesale trade													
2001	22.22	21.96	22.40	22.54	22.25	22.99	21.41	22.54	23.77	23.53	24.28	23.68	22.80
2002	24.35	23.42	22.05	22.97	23.26	23.77	23.17	22.60	22.83	22.60	23.32	23.63	23.16
2003	22.26	22.16	22.62	22.19	22.70	22.83	23.13	22.89	23.15	22.89	21.44	21.29	22.46
Retail trade													
2001	13.78	14.11	13.87	14.23	14.30	14.30	14.14	14.36	14.30	14.24	14.53	14.49	14.22
2002	14.56	14.23	14.70	14.74	14.99	14.72	14.51	14.46	14.05	13.89	14.22	13.81	14.40
2003	13.58	13.62	13.62	13.80	13.90	13.96	13.63	13.70	13.73	13.38	13.38	13.13	13.62
Transportation and utilities													
2001	15.02	14.66	14.74	15.11	15.01	14.93	15.11	14.34	15.34	15.39	16.01	15.86	15.08
2002	15.97	16.25	16.15	16.22	15.93	15.16	14.95	15.03	15.11	14.91	15.33	15.55	15.53
2003	15.66	15.55	15.75	15.79	15.94	16.12	16.27	16.02	16.11	16.27	16.29	16.42	16.03
Information													
2001	19.80	19.86	19.95	20.18	20.05	20.24	20.27	20.85	20.71	20.97	21.37	20.82	20.41
2002	20.46	20.45	20.11	21.71	20.18	19.88	20.34	19.99	20.60	20.85	21.24	21.18	20.59
2003	20.70	21.12	20.87	21.14	20.72	20.89	21.18	21.41	20.95	21.29	20.76	20.58	20.97

Average Weekly Earnings by Industry: Minnesota

(Dollars, not seasonally adjusted.)

Industry	January	February	March	April	May	June	July	August	September	October	November	December	Annual Average
STATEWIDE													
Construction													
2001	801.87	783.70	780.08	776.12	826.44	873.39	918.14	928.07	932.46	896.83	876.29	868.67	863.62
2002	842.52	816.64	807.36	811.53	852.62	901.28	857.97	920.31	907.44	893.38	847.02	854.54	862.60
2003	817.53	821.27	842.42	840.20	832.47	868.41	862.58	903.84	908.12	887.49	841.38	845.71	859.02
Manufacturing													
2001	583.47	576.58	583.05	585.86	580.14	575.75	570.75	579.28	599.94	592.11	589.50	602.80	584.50
2002	582.66	586.67	575.53	591.19	587.73	599.20	588.64	608.72	610.64	605.60	614.28	627.89	597.88
2003	601.72	605.93	612.47	607.21	609.52	627.07	603.61	624.24	638.69	619.96	646.65	637.14	620.29
Trade, transportation, and utilities													
2001	427.33	433.81	443.31	449.19	443.49	452.34	442.58	449.65	445.78	437.27	428.57	445.15	441.87
2002	417.02	426.32	425.15	424.54	441.94	455.59	454.06	447.13	446.93	433.94	443.12	457.39	439.23
2003	433.94	464.77	464.77	460.46	461.36	468.83	468.48	464.92	463.32	463.77	462.31	458.20	461.05
Wholesale trade													
2001	695.64	692.63	702.75	715.92	699.20	711.71	681.50	671.24	708.93	700.80	702.67	699.71	698.96
2002	680.42	689.12	686.95	693.20	729.95	766.46	724.35	727.26	741.32	715.09	732.00	704.27	716.53
2003	675.44	749.15	766.92	733.79	710.31	712.79	714.02	734.18	734.69	753.75	732.84	709.94	728.00
Retail trade													
2001	307.85	311.38	315.81	319.33	318.15	323.96	326.27	332.56	326.78	324.32	317.86	334.16	321.05
2002	307.20	309.43	308.45	307.34	317.98	321.84	324.78	322.11	320.53	308.66	316.92	339.60	317.33
2003	307.58	316.50	310.47	314.29	321.68	329.71	327.48	318.77	310.59	306.13	300.31	304.13	313.88
Information													
2001	716.28	660.75	667.42	704.06	688.03	687.38	700.34	685.15	723.49	725.35	727.63	741.81	701.60
2002	718.90	675.95	680.43	719.42	699.38	713.41	746.00	754.90	819.68	793.06	816.75	842.99	751.26
2003	802.98	823.72	820.71	793.62	786.94	813.38	797.33	806.81	771.85	754.59	714.98	707.11	781.55
MINNEAPOLIS-ST. PAUL													
Construction													
2001	881.97	834.48	812.17	797.46	881.13	896.45	938.34	952.71	950.15	898.19	888.00	869.60	888.28
2002	865.01	842.35	807.84	802.11	856.80	898.73	870.84	920.04	925.65	918.10	872.91	896.05	875.67
2003	896.14	870.20	882.06	880.26	880.44	885.15	884.27	920.35	929.98	891.78	872.15	878.94	889.84
Manufacturing													
2001	635.56	625.51	637.46	647.09	641.03	632.75	632.81	635.56	653.26	643.59	637.33	658.88	639.19
2002	635.09	640.79	624.06	641.09	641.77	655.64	646.09	670.64	660.80	656.00	663.82	672.40	650.77
2003	679.69	664.51	675.18	667.20	667.32	682.95	666.33	686.75	694.69	688.45	705.17	698.38	680.50
Trade, transportation, and utilities													
2001	465.32	476.25	487.97	493.91	491.54	507.22	483.22	498.56	495.61	483.93	481.80	495.35	488.72
2002	465.08	465.31	457.48	464.71	492.03	499.97	485.89	476.55	474.85	452.36	466.68	460.63	472.29
2003	446.04	451.54	457.85	464.54	476.58	485.06	485.03	480.23	481.95	476.55	461.57	465.58	468.71
Wholesale trade													
2001	811.03	810.32	833.28	838.49	832.15	882.82	798.59	811.44	893.75	882.38	929.92	880.90	850.44
2002	879.04	850.15	818.06	847.59	916.44	922.28	857.29	829.42	858.41	842.98	867.50	829.41	859.24
2003	803.59	804.41	812.06	807.72	835.36	831.01	825.74	833.20	835.72	853.80	799.71	770.70	817.54
Retail trade													
2001	362.41	368.27	370.33	381.36	384.67	387.53	377.54	394.90	383.24	381.63	364.70	399.92	379.67
2002	355.26	352.90	352.80	355.23	370.25	376.83	374.36	371.62	362.49	337.53	352.66	346.63	358.56
2003	324.56	325.52	330.97	340.86	347.50	357.38	355.74	346.61	343.25	327.81	325.13	330.88	337.78
Transportation and utilities													
2001	410.05	438.33	456.94	450.28	444.30	459.84	456.32	464.62	406.51	380.13	381.04	391.74	428.27
2002	368.91	394.88	395.68	395.77	423.74	430.54	429.07	414.83	394.37	383.19	393.98	412.08	403.78
2003	405.59	422.96	420.53	432.65	444.73	457.81	452.31	461.38	473.63	481.59	491.96	513.95	455.25
Information													
2001	744.48	716.95	732.17	778.95	747.87	756.98	778.37	754.77	791.12	746.53	760.77	784.91	757.21
2002	740.65	738.25	742.06	790.24	746.66	769.36	793.26	789.61	830.18	788.13	794.38	828.14	780.36
2003	786.60	808.90	818.10	811.78	791.50	812.62	830.26	837.13	831.72	832.44	815.87	798.50	815.73

MISSISSIPPI AT A GLANCE

(Population and total nonfarm employment numbers in thousands)

Population, Census 2000:	2,844.7
Total nonfarm employment, 2003:	1,116.6
Change in total nonfarm employment	
(Number)	
1990–2003:	180.1
1990–2001:	193.4
2001–2003:	-13.3
(Compound annual rate of change)	
1990–2003:	1.4%
1990–2001:	1.7%
2001–2003:	-0.6%
Unemployment rate	
1990:	7.7%
2001:	5.6%
2003:	6.4%

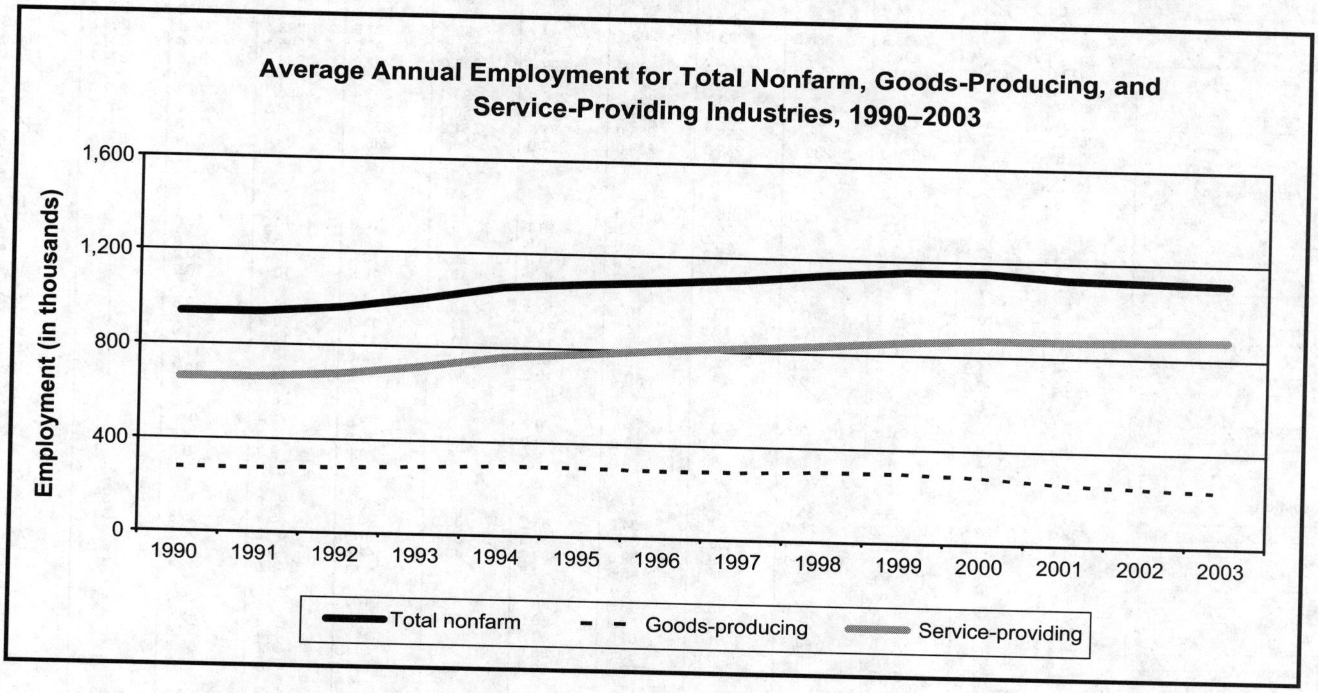

Nonfarm payroll employment rose steadily throughout the 1990–2003 period, albeit with a slowed period of job growth during the 1990–1991 recession and a moderate dip from 2001 to 2003. The drop was a result of a decline in goods-producing employment each year since 1998 accompanied by a sluggish performance in the service-providing industries. Educational and health services had the most rapid growth from 2000 to 2003, rising 9.5 percent.

Employment by Industry: Mississippi

(Numbers in thousands. Not seasonally adjusted.)

Industry	January	February	March	April	May	June	July	August	September	October	November	December	Annual Average
STATEWIDE													
Total nonfarm													
1990	916.5	919.7	928.6	935.8	943.3	941.9	931.4	930.8	948.1	948.2	948.5	945.5	936.5
1991	924.1	921.7	926.2	932.7	935.5	938.7	927.4	934.5	950.9	952.5	953.5	952.7	937.5
1992	936.6	940.1	945.9	954.9	960.7	961.1	951.9	962.9	970.8	977.1	979.2	981.6	960.2
1993	966.0	973.3	980.4	992.7	1000.7	1002.5	990.1	1004.6	1017.5	1027.5	1032.6	1038.3	1002.1
1994	1021.6	1026.6	1038.0	1046.3	1055.8	1064.5	1055.4	1067.2	1075.5	1066.9	1073.0	1075.9	1055.5
1995	1057.9	1063.6	1066.5	1072.5	1078.7	1079.3	1058.2	1079.7	1087.9	1082.0	1082.7	1085.4	1074.5
1996	1065.9	1069.3	1078.5	1088.0	1095.3	1096.8	1078.4	1095.3	1101.9	1094.6	1099.6	1102.8	1088.8
1997	1079.9	1085.9	1095.4	1102.8	1111.6	1105.9	1094.6	1112.2	1117.8	1122.5	1125.5	1131.3	1107.1
1998	1109.5	1115.4	1119.6	1132.0	1137.8	1135.8	1126.0	1139.3	1143.3	1146.2	1147.3	1151.8	1133.6
1999	1127.4	1132.3	1143.5	1155.4	1159.5	1161.3	1149.3	1161.5	1165.9	1158.1	1160.6	1163.5	1153.1
2000	1144.1	1145.0	1153.8	1158.3	1166.7	1164.0	1147.2	1157.0	1155.3	1149.8	1150.7	1150.7	1153.5
2001	1128.8	1128.8	1131.1	1136.3	1138.2	1135.1	1120.8	1131.7	1130.9	1124.9	1126.6	1126.1	1129.9
2002	1111.0	1113.8	1120.3	1127.8	1131.7	1133.2	1119.6	1128.3	1130.6	1122.1	1121.5	1123.2	1123.6
2003	1107.2	1108.7	1112.1	1116.9	1119.2	1115.9	1109.9	1115.6	1117.8	1124.9	1125.6	1125.9	1116.6
Total private													
1990	712.4	714.3	721.7	728.8	733.2	744.7	739.5	739.7	741.9	740.7	741.1	739.7	733.1
1991	718.9	716.0	720.5	726.7	729.4	740.0	738.0	738.4	743.9	743.3	744.1	744.2	733.6
1992	728.6	731.0	736.8	744.6	750.6	756.1	757.5	759.6	761.3	765.4	766.7	770.3	752.3
1993	755.7	761.4	768.5	781.3	788.1	798.0	796.8	798.9	804.5	812.2	816.5	823.0	792.0
1994	806.6	810.6	822.0	830.3	839.6	854.5	855.3	856.8	860.2	850.8	855.2	860.0	841.8
1995	842.7	846.5	848.8	854.9	860.6	867.1	858.1	866.0	870.5	866.4	866.4	870.4	859.8
1996	849.1	851.5	859.8	869.3	875.9	882.7	875.8	880.5	883.1	874.9	879.1	882.6	872.0
1997	861.2	865.6	875.4	882.0	891.0	892.2	888.1	893.2	896.5	900.0	903.0	908.8	888.0
1998	887.7	892.2	897.7	908.1	913.0	917.3	913.5	916.4	917.0	917.3	918.9	923.7	910.2
1999	901.6	904.5	916.1	927.0	930.7	936.1	932.5	934.8	936.3	928.5	931.1	934.1	926.1
2000	913.9	913.8	920.3	923.9	927.5	931.6	920.1	924.3	920.2	914.0	913.8	913.6	919.7
2001	891.6	890.5	892.6	897.2	899.0	898.8	890.4	895.5	892.3	885.9	887.8	887.3	892.4
2002	872.8	874.5	880.7	887.1	890.6	893.7	886.0	889.4	888.4	879.4	878.7	880.4	883.5
2003	865.9	866.5	869.0	873.2	875.3	873.7	872.2	873.9	872.6	877.9	879.0	878.9	873.2
Goods-producing													
1990	267.4	269.1	271.6	274.0	277.1	280.5	277.1	280.3	281.3	281.8	280.6	276.8	276.4
1991	269.3	267.5	267.5	270.6	271.0	275.9	275.1	279.0	280.9	281.9	282.3	280.3	275.1
1992	273.3	274.1	275.6	280.6	282.7	284.4	281.7	283.8	285.0	284.8	284.6	283.7	281.1
1993	278.3	281.2	283.9	286.4	287.5	289.8	286.3	289.1	292.1	295.6	295.5	295.5	288.4
1994	290.2	290.9	294.5	294.5	296.3	300.9	298.2	300.5	302.9	298.9	300.2	300.9	297.4
1995	296.6	297.8	297.0	299.2	299.5	300.4	293.0	298.7	297.6	295.6	292.3	292.7	296.7
1996	285.8	287.8	287.8	291.7	293.1	294.5	290.1	291.9	291.4	288.0	288.2	287.2	289.7
1997	282.7	283.8	286.8	288.8	293.0	293.1	289.7	292.5	291.9	293.4	294.4	294.6	290.3
1998	291.9	294.1	294.3	299.2	301.2	303.5	299.2	301.2	302.8	305.1	304.4	304.0	300.0
1999	298.1	298.0	299.6	299.8	300.4	303.2	299.4	298.6	297.9	296.0	295.8	294.7	298.4
2000	289.9	289.2	290.3	290.2	290.7	291.2	286.8	286.0	283.4	282.2	279.3	277.3	286.3
2001	269.0	266.8	264.3	265.9	265.0	264.9	260.1	260.9	259.8	258.3	257.6	255.1	262.3
2002	252.8	253.2	254.0	253.0	253.7	255.0	251.5	251.2	250.3	246.6	244.3	243.1	250.7
2003	239.8	239.6	239.3	239.1	239.0	238.0	237.0	236.3	236.6	238.4	237.9	237.9	238.2
Natural resources and mining													
1990	9.9	9.9	10.0	10.3	10.4	10.5	10.5	10.6	10.5	10.6	10.6	10.5	10.3
1991	10.1	10.1	10.2	9.9	9.7	10.0	10.1	10.2	10.3	10.2	10.0	9.8	10.0
1992	9.0	9.3	9.6	9.6	9.7	9.6	9.8	9.7	9.7	9.8	9.6	9.6	9.5
1993	9.3	9.4	9.6	9.7	9.7	9.9	10.0	10.2	10.2	10.3	10.2	10.3	9.9
1994	9.9	10.0	10.0	9.8	9.8	9.9	10.2	10.4	10.5	10.0	10.2	10.3	10.0
1995	10.0	10.0	10.1	10.1	10.2	10.4	10.4	10.5	10.6	10.5	10.5	10.4	10.3
1996	10.2	10.2	10.4	10.5	10.8	10.8	11.1	11.1	11.3	10.8	11.0	10.9	10.7
1997	10.7	10.8	10.9	11.0	11.5	11.6	11.5	11.6	11.8	11.6	11.7	11.9	11.3
1998	11.4	11.6	11.7	12.0	12.2	12.3	12.1	12.3	12.5	12.1	11.8	11.5	11.9
1999	10.9	10.8	10.4	10.2	10.1	10.3	10.0	10.2	10.3	10.4	10.4	10.4	10.3
2000	9.2	9.3	9.4	9.2	9.3	9.4	9.4	9.3	9.4	9.6	9.5	9.5	9.3
2001	9.3	9.3	9.6	9.7	9.6	9.7	9.7	9.8	9.8	9.6	9.6	9.6	9.6
2002	8.9	8.9	9.0	8.9	9.0	9.0	9.0	9.0	9.0	8.8	8.7	8.5	8.9
2003	8.3	8.3	8.5	8.7	8.8	8.8	8.8	8.7	8.7	8.9	9.0	8.9	8.7
Construction													
1990	34.4	34.4	35.6	36.2	37.3	38.0	37.5	38.2	38.4	38.9	39.0	37.1	37.0
1991	32.0	32.8	34.2	35.1	34.6	34.8	35.2	36.0	35.5	35.8	35.8	33.8	34.6
1992	31.4	31.9	33.0	34.9	36.5	37.4	37.5	37.8	37.6	37.2	36.8	36.3	35.6
1993	33.9	35.4	36.6	38.0	39.2	39.8	39.7	40.4	41.6	43.5	42.6	41.9	39.3
1994	38.9	38.9	41.1	42.7	44.1	45.6	44.7	44.5	46.1	43.0	43.4	43.1	43.0
1995	41.7	42.2	42.1	44.8	45.6	46.5	46.7	47.7	47.7	46.2	45.4	45.8	45.2
1996	44.5	45.3	47.3	48.6	49.7	50.4	50.5	50.0	49.7	48.5	48.4	47.5	48.3
1997	45.2	46.1	47.8	49.3	51.4	51.7	52.6	52.8	52.7	52.7	52.4	52.2	50.5
1998	49.8	51.1	51.3	53.5	53.9	55.5	56.0	56.0	55.9	56.8	55.8	55.7	54.2
1999	53.0	54.0	55.3	55.3	56.0	57.0	56.4	56.0	55.8	54.6	54.7	53.9	55.1
2000	53.4	54.1	55.0	54.5	55.3	56.4	55.9	55.6	54.4	53.9	52.9	52.3	54.4
2001	48.6	49.6	49.9	51.3	51.7	52.4	52.2	53.2	53.0	53.4	54.2	53.7	51.9
2002	53.3	53.2	53.9	53.6	54.3	55.7	54.8	54.9	54.7	53.3	52.7	52.4	53.9
2003	51.0	51.1	50.8	51.0	50.9	50.8	51.1	51.9	51.7	52.4	51.7	50.7	51.3

Employment by Industry: Mississippi—*Continued*

(Numbers in thousands. Not seasonally adjusted.)

Industry	January	February	March	April	May	June	July	August	September	October	November	December	Annual Average
STATEWIDE—*Continued*													
Manufacturing													
1990	223.1	224.8	226.0	227.5	229.4	232.0	229.1	231.5	232.4	232.3	231.0	229.2	229.0
1991	227.2	224.6	223.1	225.6	226.7	231.1	229.8	232.8	235.1	235.9	236.5	236.7	230.4
1992	232.9	232.9	233.0	236.1	236.5	237.4	234.4	236.3	237.7	237.8	238.2	237.8	235.9
1993	235.1	236.4	237.7	238.7	238.6	240.1	236.6	238.5	240.3	241.8	242.7	243.3	239.1
1994	241.4	242.0	243.4	242.0	242.4	245.4	243.3	245.6	246.3	245.9	246.6	247.5	244.3
1995	244.9	245.6	244.8	244.3	243.7	243.5	235.9	240.5	239.3	238.9	236.4	236.5	241.1
1996	231.1	232.3	230.1	232.6	232.6	233.3	228.5	230.8	230.4	228.7	228.8	228.8	230.6
1997	226.8	226.9	228.1	228.5	230.1	229.8	225.6	228.1	227.4	229.1	230.3	230.5	228.4
1998	230.7	231.4	231.3	233.7	235.1	235.7	231.1	232.9	234.4	236.2	236.8	236.8	233.8
1999	234.2	233.2	233.9	234.3	234.3	235.9	233.0	232.4	231.8	231.0	230.7	230.4	232.9
2000	227.3	225.8	225.9	226.5	226.1	225.4	221.5	221.1	219.6	218.7	216.9	215.5	222.5
2001	211.1	207.9	204.8	204.9	203.7	202.8	198.2	197.9	197.0	195.3	193.8	191.8	200.8
2002	190.6	191.1	191.1	190.5	190.4	190.3	187.7	187.3	186.6	184.5	182.9	182.2	187.9
2003	180.5	180.2	180.0	179.4	179.3	178.4	177.1	175.7	176.2	177.1	177.2	178.3	178.3
Service-providing													
1990	649.1	650.6	657.0	661.8	666.2	661.4	654.3	650.5	666.8	666.4	667.9	668.7	660.0
1991	654.8	654.2	658.7	662.1	664.5	662.8	652.3	655.5	670.0	670.6	671.2	672.4	662.4
1992	663.3	666.0	670.3	674.3	678.0	676.7	670.2	679.1	685.8	692.3	694.6	697.9	679.0
1993	687.7	692.1	696.5	706.3	713.2	712.7	703.8	715.5	725.4	731.9	737.1	742.8	713.7
1994	731.4	735.7	743.5	751.8	759.5	763.6	757.2	766.7	772.6	768.0	772.8	775.0	758.1
1995	761.3	765.8	769.5	773.3	779.2	778.9	765.2	781.0	790.3	786.4	790.4	792.7	777.8
1996	780.1	781.5	790.7	796.3	802.2	802.3	788.3	803.4	810.5	806.6	811.4	815.6	799.0
1997	797.2	802.1	808.6	814.0	818.6	812.8	804.9	819.7	825.9	829.1	831.1	836.7	816.7
1998	817.6	821.3	825.3	832.8	836.6	832.3	826.8	838.1	840.5	841.1	842.9	847.8	833.5
1999	829.3	834.3	843.9	855.6	859.1	858.1	849.9	862.9	868.0	862.1	864.8	868.8	854.7
2000	854.2	855.8	863.5	868.1	876.0	872.8	860.4	871.0	871.9	867.6	871.4	873.4	867.1
2001	859.8	862.0	866.8	870.4	873.2	870.2	860.7	870.8	871.1	866.6	869.0	871.0	867.6
2002	858.2	860.6	866.3	874.8	878.0	878.2	868.1	877.1	880.3	875.5	877.2	880.1	872.9
2003	867.4	869.1	872.8	877.8	880.2	877.9	872.9	879.3	881.2	886.5	887.7	888.0	878.4
Trade, transportation, and utilities													
1990	183.9	182.9	184.6	186.2	187.0	188.3	188.5	190.4	190.3	189.2	190.7	192.3	187.8
1991	184.5	182.2	183.5	183.3	184.0	185.0	183.9	184.9	185.4	184.8	186.2	188.6	184.6
1992	180.6	179.8	180.9	183.4	184.8	185.6	186.1	187.6	187.6	188.9	190.6	193.4	185.7
1993	185.3	184.8	185.7	188.4	188.6	190.5	190.9	192.2	192.3	194.8	197.2	200.1	190.9
1994	191.9	192.1	194.8	195.2	197.4	200.3	200.3	201.2	202.4	202.4	205.7	208.0	199.3
1995	201.2	199.9	200.7	201.7	203.4	206.2	205.5	207.3	209.6	210.1	213.7	215.7	206.2
1996	207.9	206.3	208.9	208.8	210.3	211.2	209.9	211.3	211.6	211.3	214.4	217.7	210.8
1997	208.8	207.9	210.2	210.8	212.7	213.3	213.2	213.5	216.1	217.9	220.5	224.5	214.1
1998	214.9	213.8	215.4	216.7	217.4	218.9	218.4	218.5	218.9	220.2	223.2	226.4	218.5
1999	218.8	219.0	221.0	222.4	223.6	225.1	224.9	226.0	227.5	228.3	231.3	233.9	225.1
2000	225.1	224.5	225.7	226.1	227.8	228.5	226.1	227.4	227.3	226.5	229.1	231.4	227.1
2001	223.2	221.4	223.0	222.7	223.6	224.2	221.3	222.3	221.8	222.2	225.4	227.0	223.2
2002	218.1	217.3	218.3	219.9	221.1	222.9	221.5	221.9	222.0	220.9	223.4	225.9	221.1
2003	217.7	217.1	216.9	216.6	218.4	218.8	219.3	219.6	218.4	220.8	222.3	223.7	219.1
Wholesale trade													
1990	32.7	32.7	32.9	33.0	33.1	33.6	33.6	34.0	33.7	33.2	33.1	33.0	33.2
1991	31.9	31.8	32.0	31.8	32.0	32.2	31.9	32.2	32.2	32.2	32.2	32.3	32.0
1992	32.0	31.9	32.0	32.3	32.5	32.7	32.7	32.9	32.8	32.9	32.7	32.9	32.5
1993	32.4	32.4	32.5	32.8	32.9	33.1	33.1	33.2	33.3	33.4	33.4	33.4	32.9
1994	32.9	32.8	33.1	33.4	33.4	33.7	34.0	34.2	34.3	34.2	34.2	34.4	33.7
1995	34.3	34.4	34.5	34.6	34.6	35.0	35.1	35.3	35.4	35.1	35.0	35.2	34.8
1996	34.4	34.6	34.8	34.8	35.0	35.2	35.2	35.3	35.2	35.0	34.9	35.0	34.9
1997	34.5	34.8	35.0	35.0	35.4	35.6	35.7	36.2	36.1	36.0	35.8	36.1	35.5
1998	36.2	36.6	36.6	36.9	37.0	37.3	37.0	37.3	37.0	36.8	36.7	36.8	36.8
1999	36.3	36.4	36.3	36.4	36.6	36.7	36.9	37.2	37.1	36.6	36.4	36.4	36.6
2000	36.9	37.0	37.0	36.9	36.9	37.2	37.0	37.4	37.2	36.7	36.5	36.6	36.9
2001	35.9	35.4	35.5	35.2	35.1	35.4	35.4	35.7	35.5	35.0	34.8	35.2	35.3
2002	34.9	34.9	34.9	34.9	34.8	35.1	35.1	35.5	35.4	35.0	34.8	35.1	35.0
2003	34.7	34.6	34.5	34.7	34.9	35.3	35.0	35.1	35.2	35.7	35.8	35.9	35.1
Retail trade													
1990	115.2	113.9	114.6	115.3	115.9	115.9	116.5	117.7	117.5	117.0	118.7	120.8	116.5
1991	114.9	112.8	113.1	113.4	113.9	114.4	113.4	114.1	114.2	113.3	115.0	117.7	114.1
1992	112.4	111.9	112.8	114.2	115.2	115.4	116.1	117.0	116.8	117.8	119.8	122.6	116.0
1993	116.5	116.0	116.4	118.1	118.1	119.4	119.6	120.7	120.4	121.4	124.2	127.5	119.8
1994	120.7	120.7	122.5	122.5	123.8	125.8	125.5	126.1	127.0	126.5	129.9	132.9	125.3
1995	127.0	125.7	126.1	126.9	128.4	130.8	129.7	130.8	132.1	132.1	135.9	138.3	130.3
1996	131.9	130.1	132.3	132.2	133.5	134.2	132.9	133.7	133.8	133.6	136.9	140.4	133.7
1997	133.4	132.1	133.9	134.0	134.6	134.9	134.5	135.5	136.4	137.9	140.7	145.1	136.0
1998	136.1	134.7	136.0	136.9	137.5	138.5	138.4	138.0	138.7	139.5	142.6	145.9	138.5
1999	139.4	139.5	141.5	142.3	143.1	143.9	143.3	143.6	145.2	146.0	149.2	151.9	144.0
2000	143.7	142.9	144.0	144.2	145.5	145.8	143.9	144.6	144.7	144.6	147.6	150.0	145.1
2001	141.9	140.7	142.1	141.6	142.4	142.8	140.2	140.7	140.5	141.1	144.8	146.1	142.1
2002	138.5	137.7	138.9	140.0	140.6	141.8	140.6	140.0	140.2	139.3	142.1	144.6	140.4
2003	137.5	136.8	137.1	136.5	137.6	137.7	138.3	138.8	138.3	140.2	141.8	143.7	138.7

Employment by Industry: Mississippi—*Continued*

(Numbers in thousands. Not seasonally adjusted.)

Industry	January	February	March	April	May	June	July	August	September	October	November	December	Annual Average
STATEWIDE—*Continued*													
Transportation and utilities													
1990	36.0	36.3	37.1	37.9	38.0	38.8	38.4	38.7	39.1	39.0	38.9	38.5	38.0
1991	37.7	37.6	38.4	38.1	38.1	38.4	38.6	38.6	39.0	39.3	39.0	38.6	38.4
1992	36.2	36.0	36.1	36.9	37.1	37.5	37.3	37.7	38.0	38.2	38.1	37.9	37.2
1993	36.4	36.4	36.8	37.5	37.6	38.0	38.2	38.3	38.6	40.0	39.6	39.2	38.0
1994	38.3	38.6	39.2	39.3	40.2	40.8	40.8	40.9	41.1	41.7	41.6	40.7	40.2
1995	39.9	39.8	40.1	40.2	40.4	40.4	40.7	41.2	42.1	42.9	42.8	42.2	41.0
1996	41.6	41.6	41.8	41.8	41.8	41.8	41.8	42.3	42.6	42.7	42.6	42.3	42.0
1997	40.9	41.0	41.3	41.8	42.7	42.8	43.0	41.8	43.6	44.0	44.0	43.3	42.5
1998	42.6	42.5	42.8	42.9	42.9	43.1	43.0	43.2	43.2	43.9	43.9	43.7	43.1
1999	43.1	43.1	43.2	43.7	43.9	44.5	44.7	45.2	45.2	45.7	45.7	45.6	44.4
2000	44.5	44.6	44.7	45.0	45.4	45.5	45.2	45.4	45.4	45.2	45.0	44.8	45.0
2001	45.4	45.3	45.4	45.9	46.1	46.0	45.7	45.9	45.8	46.1	45.8	45.7	45.8
2002	44.7	44.7	44.5	45.0	45.7	46.0	45.8	46.4	46.4	46.6	46.5	46.2	45.7
2003	45.5	45.7	45.3	45.4	45.9	45.8	46.0	45.7	44.9	44.9	44.7	44.1	45.3
Information													
1990	13.3	13.3	13.6	13.7	13.8	13.9	14.0	14.2	14.0	14.0	14.0	14.0	13.8
1991	13.7	13.7	13.8	12.9	12.9	13.0	13.2	13.2	13.2	13.1	13.0	13.1	13.2
1992	12.7	12.7	12.8	12.5	12.6	12.7	12.9	12.9	12.8	13.1	12.8	12.8	12.7
1993	12.7	12.7	12.7	13.0	13.1	13.2	13.3	13.3	13.0	13.3	13.2	13.2	13.0
1994	13.2	13.2	13.3	13.4	13.7	13.8	13.7	13.8	13.7	13.5	13.7	13.8	13.5
1995	13.9	13.9	13.9	13.9	14.0	14.3	14.4	14.4	14.6	14.6	14.7	14.4	14.2
1996	14.1	14.1	14.5	15.0	15.2	16.7	14.8	14.8	14.7	14.8	15.1	14.8	14.8
1997	15.1	15.0	15.1	15.3	15.2	15.3	15.5	15.5	15.2	15.4	15.3	15.4	15.2
1998	15.2	15.3	15.3	15.4	15.7	15.9	16.2	16.4	16.1	16.0	16.0	16.1	15.8
1999	15.9	15.8	16.0	16.2	16.4	16.7	16.8	16.9	16.9	16.8	16.8	17.0	16.5
2000	16.8	16.8	17.0	16.9	17.1	17.5	17.7	17.7	17.6	17.6	17.8	17.9	17.3
2001	17.6	17.5	17.4	17.1	17.1	17.3	17.0	16.7	16.5	16.4	16.5	16.5	17.0
2002	16.5	16.4	16.3	16.3	16.3	16.2	16.1	16.0	15.8	15.7	15.8	15.7	16.1
2003	15.5	15.3	15.3	15.1	15.1	15.0	14.7	14.9	14.9	14.8	14.6	14.8	15.0
Financial activities													
1990	41.4	41.2	41.1	41.0	41.1	41.4	41.2	41.2	40.8	40.8	40.8	40.9	41.0
1991	39.9	39.9	40.1	40.2	40.3	40.6	40.5	40.6	40.6	40.3	40.3	40.5	40.3
1992	39.7	39.5	39.6	39.7	39.9	40.0	40.4	40.4	40.0	39.8	39.8	40.1	39.9
1993	39.7	39.7	39.8	40.2	40.3	40.7	40.8	40.9	40.9	40.9	41.0	41.3	40.5
1994	40.9	41.1	41.3	41.3	41.3	41.6	41.6	41.5	41.4	41.1	41.1	41.4	41.3
1995	40.8	40.8	40.8	40.9	41.2	41.6	41.7	42.0	42.0	41.8	41.9	42.5	41.5
1996	42.2	42.2	42.5	42.9	43.1	43.6	43.3	43.2	42.9	42.7	42.8	43.1	42.8
1997	42.7	42.8	43.0	43.3	43.6	44.0	43.9	43.9	43.6	43.5	43.7	44.2	43.5
1998	44.3	44.1	44.5	44.8	45.0	45.1	45.0	44.9	44.7	44.9	44.9	45.2	44.7
1999	44.9	45.0	45.4	45.7	45.7	45.3	46.2	46.2	46.0	45.9	45.9	46.2	45.7
2000	45.8	45.8	45.9	45.9	46.0	46.5	46.1	45.9	46.0	45.6	45.7	46.0	45.9
2001	45.3	45.5	45.5	45.6	45.8	46.2	46.1	46.3	46.0	45.8	45.8	46.1	45.8
2002	45.6	45.4	45.5	45.7	45.7	46.1	45.8	45.8	45.6	45.7	46.0	46.0	45.7
2003	45.8	45.7	45.8	45.8	46.0	46.3	46.2	46.6	46.4	46.4	46.3	46.6	46.2
Professional and business services													
1990	49.3	49.9	50.6	51.2	51.0	51.9	51.5	51.9	51.9	51.8	51.5	51.7	51.1
1991	49.6	49.6	50.3	52.0	51.8	52.5	52.9	53.1	53.4	53.4	52.9	52.6	52.0
1992	54.2	55.0	55.2	55.3	55.5	55.2	55.7	56.2	56.4	57.6	57.2	58.3	55.9
1993	58.2	59.4	59.9	62.6	62.5	63.2	63.3	63.9	63.9	65.5	65.1	64.8	62.6
1994	64.0	64.9	66.0	67.1	67.3	68.2	69.8	70.1	69.9	68.9	68.6	68.9	67.8
1995	68.4	69.2	69.6	69.8	69.4	70.1	69.3	70.1	69.9	69.5	69.4	69.2	69.4
1996	69.9	71.0	71.9	73.2	73.6	75.2	74.0	75.9	76.7	76.3	76.1	76.5	74.1
1997	73.6	75.4	76.3	77.7	78.0	78.5	78.3	80.1	79.4	79.0	78.6	79.2	77.8
1998	75.1	76.0	76.3	78.3	78.7	80.0	80.7	80.4	79.5	79.3	78.6	79.6	78.5
1999	75.1	76.4	77.4	80.2	80.6	81.7	81.6	82.0	81.7	79.5	79.4	79.3	79.5
2000	78.5	78.7	79.4	79.9	80.0	80.5	79.0	80.6	80.3	78.3	78.7	78.2	79.3
2001	76.2	77.1	76.9	77.2	76.8	76.7	77.0	77.6	77.1	76.0	75.8	76.4	76.7
2002	75.8	76.5	77.1	78.5	78.0	79.0	78.3	79.4	78.6	77.2	76.5	77.1	77.7
2003	76.9	77.1	77.0	78.8	78.2	78.2	78.9	80.5	81.3	81.6	82.4	81.1	79.3
Educational and health services													
1990	73.0	73.2	73.6	74.3	74.2	78.2	77.4	71.6	74.4	75.9	76.2	76.5	74.8
1991	76.6	76.9	77.1	77.7	78.1	79.9	80.4	75.2	79.3	80.0	80.1	80.4	78.4
1992	80.3	80.9	81.6	81.9	82.1	83.5	85.6	81.7	82.6	84.0	84.1	84.5	82.7
1993	84.0	84.4	84.7	85.6	85.6	87.3	88.5	84.7	86.6	88.0	87.9	88.5	86.3
1994	87.9	88.3	88.9	89.7	90.2	94.2	93.6	89.7	93.0	93.6	94.0	94.8	91.4
1995	94.6	95.0	95.5	96.0	96.2	95.6	96.1	94.1	98.4	98.9	99.3	99.5	96.6
1996	98.1	98.3	98.9	99.1	99.5	97.4	97.1	96.1	100.5	100.5	100.8	101.3	98.9
1997	101.6	102.3	102.7	102.5	102.9	100.1	100.4	99.7	103.9	104.7	105.0	105.3	102.5
1998	103.9	105.0	105.5	105.4	104.7	101.9	101.8	102.3	104.6	104.5	104.6	104.9	104.0
1999	102.9	102.9	103.3	104.4	103.9	101.8	100.6	101.7	104.3	103.8	103.6	103.6	103.0
2000	104.0	104.3	104.8	105.1	105.3	103.1	102.6	104.3	106.2	106.8	107.1	107.5	105.0
2001	108.0	108.7	109.3	109.8	110.2	107.6	107.6	110.0	111.4	111.8	112.2	112.6	109.9
2002	111.6	111.9	112.6	113.5	113.6	110.6	109.9	111.8	114.2	114.6	114.9	115.2	112.9
2003	114.3	114.7	115.2	116.0	116.3	113.7	113.5	113.7	114.8	115.8	115.9	116.0	115.0

Employment by Industry: Mississippi—*Continued*

(Numbers in thousands. Not seasonally adjusted.)

Industry	January	February	March	April	May	June	July	August	September	October	November	December	Annual Average
STATEWIDE—*Continued*													
Leisure and hospitality													
1990	53.2	53.9	55.5	57.1	57.6	58.8	58.2	58.6	57.6	55.7	55.8	56.2	56.5
1991	54.6	55.4	57.0	58.6	59.7	61.2	60.1	60.6	59.3	58.0	57.9	57.5	58.3
1992	56.7	57.9	59.6	59.4	60.9	62.4	62.6	64.7	64.5	64.5	64.9	65.2	61.9
1993	65.3	66.8	69.2	72.2	77.4	79.9	80.0	81.3	82.1	80.7	83.3	86.2	77.0
1994	85.3	86.9	89.6	95.6	99.5	101.3	103.8	105.7	102.9	98.8	98.2	98.4	97.1
1995	93.6	96.2	97.2	99.0	102.5	103.8	103.1	104.5	103.9	101.5	100.7	101.8	100.6
1996	97.3	97.8	101.0	104.1	106.3	108.8	111.2	111.8	110.0	106.0	106.4	106.6	105.6
1997	101.0	102.5	105.0	107.1	109.0	110.9	110.4	111.6	110.2	110.1	109.8	110.0	108.1
1998	107.4	108.9	111.4	113.3	115.0	116.4	116.9	117.9	115.9	112.9	112.8	113.1	113.4
1999	111.9	113.2	119.1	123.5	125.2	126.9	127.8	128.5	127.1	123.3	123.3	124.2	122.8
2000	118.9	119.3	121.6	124.1	124.8	127.9	125.8	126.6	123.6	121.6	120.7	119.8	122.8
2001	116.2	117.3	119.8	122.3	123.6	124.4	124.1	124.5	122.5	118.5	117.6	116.6	120.6
2002	115.6	116.9	119.6	122.7	124.6	125.9	125.4	126.0	124.6	121.6	120.7	120.3	122.0
2003	118.7	119.7	121.5	123.8	124.6	125.7	125.4	125.5	123.3	123.3	122.4	122.4	123.0
Other services													
1990	30.9	30.8	31.1	31.3	31.4	31.7	31.6	31.5	31.6	31.5	31.5	31.3	31.3
1991	30.7	30.8	31.2	31.4	31.6	31.9	31.9	31.8	31.8	31.8	31.4	31.2	31.4
1992	31.1	31.1	31.5	31.8	32.1	32.3	32.5	32.3	32.4	32.7	32.7	32.3	32.0
1993	32.2	32.4	32.6	32.9	33.1	33.4	33.7	33.5	33.6	33.4	33.3	33.4	33.1
1994	33.2	33.2	33.6	33.5	33.9	34.2	34.3	34.3	34.0	33.6	33.7	33.8	33.7
1995	33.6	33.7	34.1	34.4	34.4	35.1	35.0	34.9	34.5	34.4	34.4	34.6	34.4
1996	33.8	34.0	34.3	34.5	34.8	35.3	35.4	35.5	35.3	35.3	35.3	35.4	34.9
1997	35.7	35.9	36.3	36.5	36.6	37.0	36.7	36.4	36.2	36.0	35.7	35.6	36.2
1998	35.0	35.0	35.0	35.0	35.3	35.6	35.3	34.8	34.5	34.4	34.4	34.4	34.8
1999	34.0	34.2	34.3	34.8	34.9	35.4	35.2	34.9	34.9	34.9	35.0	35.2	34.8
2000	34.9	35.2	35.6	35.7	35.8	36.4	36.0	35.8	35.8	35.4	35.4	35.5	35.6
2001	36.1	36.2	36.4	36.6	36.9	37.5	37.2	37.2	37.2	36.9	36.9	37.0	36.8
2002	36.8	36.9	37.3	37.5	37.6	38.0	37.5	37.3	37.3	37.1	37.1	37.1	37.3
2003	37.2	37.3	38.0	38.0	37.7	38.0	37.2	36.8	36.9	36.8	37.2	36.4	37.3
Government													
1990	204.1	205.4	206.9	207.0	210.1	197.2	191.9	191.1	206.2	207.5	207.4	205.8	203.3
1991	205.2	205.7	205.7	206.0	206.1	198.7	189.4	196.1	207.0	209.2	209.4	208.5	203.9
1992	208.0	209.1	209.1	210.3	210.1	205.0	194.4	203.3	209.5	211.7	212.5	211.3	207.8
1993	210.3	211.9	211.9	211.4	212.6	204.5	193.3	205.7	213.0	215.3	216.1	215.3	210.1
1994	215.0	216.0	216.0	216.0	216.2	210.0	200.1	210.4	215.3	216.1	217.8	215.9	213.7
1995	215.2	217.1	217.7	217.6	218.1	212.2	200.1	213.7	217.4	215.6	216.3	215.0	214.6
1996	216.8	217.8	218.7	218.7	219.4	214.1	202.6	214.8	218.8	219.7	220.5	220.2	216.8
1997	218.7	220.3	220.0	220.8	220.6	213.7	206.5	219.0	221.3	222.5	222.5	222.5	219.0
1998	221.8	223.2	221.9	223.9	224.8	218.5	212.5	222.9	226.3	228.9	228.4	228.1	223.4
1999	225.8	227.8	227.4	228.4	228.8	225.2	216.8	226.7	229.6	229.6	229.5	229.4	227.0
2000	230.2	231.2	233.5	234.4	239.2	232.4	227.1	232.7	235.1	235.8	236.9	237.1	233.8
2001	237.2	238.3	238.5	239.1	239.2	236.3	230.4	236.2	238.6	239.0	238.8	238.8	237.5
2002	238.2	239.3	239.6	240.7	241.1	239.5	233.6	238.9	242.2	242.7	242.8	242.8	240.1
2003	241.3	242.2	243.1	243.7	243.9	242.2	237.7	241.7	245.2	247.0	246.6	247.0	243.5
Federal government													
1990	27.2	27.0	28.5	28.2	31.7	29.2	29.7	28.3	27.9	27.7	27.2	27.4	28.3
1991	26.9	26.9	27.0	27.2	27.4	28.0	28.3	28.3	28.2	28.3	28.0	27.7	27.6
1992	27.6	27.6	27.7	27.9	28.0	28.2	28.3	28.5	28.4	28.5	28.2	28.0	28.0
1993	27.5	27.5	27.5	27.4	27.5	27.8	28.0	28.1	27.5	28.0	27.8	27.8	27.7
1994	27.0	27.1	27.1	27.3	27.3	27.6	27.9	27.8	27.5	27.4	27.2	27.2	27.3
1995	26.7	26.7	26.8	26.9	27.2	27.4	27.5	27.5	27.1	26.9	26.8	26.5	27.0
1996	26.5	26.4	26.3	26.4	26.4	26.5	26.6	26.7	26.4	26.0	26.2	26.2	26.3
1997	25.9	25.8	25.9	26.0	26.0	26.2	26.3	26.4	26.3	26.1	26.3	26.2	26.1
1998	25.7	25.6	25.6	25.6	25.9	26.1	26.4	26.5	26.2	26.6	26.8	26.9	26.1
1999	25.9	26.1	25.7	25.9	25.8	26.2	26.2	26.2	26.0	26.0	26.0	26.0	26.0
2000	25.8	25.8	27.3	26.9	31.6	28.9	28.5	27.1	26.1	25.9	26.0	26.0	27.1
2001	25.9	25.7	25.8	25.7	25.8	26.4	26.5	26.3	26.1	26.0	25.9	25.9	26.0
2002	25.6	25.4	25.4	25.4	25.5	26.1	26.2	25.9	25.8	25.9	26.0	26.1	25.8
2003	25.8	25.7	25.7	25.6	25.7	25.9	25.9	26.0	25.9	25.7	25.6	26.1	25.8
State government													
1990	54.5	54.9	54.9	55.1	54.2	52.5	53.2	53.4	55.8	55.6	55.5	55.3	54.5
1991	55.4	55.3	55.1	55.3	54.7	53.0	52.9	53.1	55.3	55.4	55.4	55.4	54.6
1992	56.3	56.7	56.4	56.4	56.2	56.7	55.8	55.9	56.2	56.1	56.0	56.0	56.2
1993	55.8	56.0	56.1	56.2	56.7	56.9	56.6	56.4	57.4	57.3	57.2	57.0	56.6
1994	57.2	57.4	57.1	57.1	56.9	57.1	56.5	56.7	56.6	56.2	55.9	55.6	56.6
1995	56.0	56.4	56.4	56.5	56.3	56.5	56.0	56.5	56.0	55.8	55.6	55.4	56.1
1996	55.7	55.9	56.0	56.0	56.1	57.0	56.6	56.2	56.1	56.4	56.3	56.1	56.2
1997	56.1	56.6	56.4	56.7	56.6	57.8	57.8	57.8	57.1	57.4	57.0	56.9	57.0
1998	57.1	57.5	57.6	57.8	58.1	58.2	58.4	58.1	58.7	59.2	58.1	58.1	58.0
1999	57.3	57.6	57.8	58.6	58.7	59.9	59.6	60.2	59.9	59.4	59.2	59.2	58.9
2000	61.1	61.3	61.6	62.0	61.9	62.4	62.5	62.5	62.5	62.0	61.9	61.7	61.9
2001	62.3	62.4	62.4	62.7	62.4	62.8	62.0	62.2	62.4	61.6	61.3	61.3	62.2
2002	61.7	61.9	62.1	62.7	62.3	62.6	61.6	61.9	62.0	62.1	61.9	62.0	62.1
2003	62.0	62.2	62.4	62.8	62.6	63.4	63.3	62.9	63.0	63.2	63.1	62.4	62.8

Employment by Industry: Mississippi—*Continued*

(Numbers in thousands. Not seasonally adjusted.)

Industry	January	February	March	April	May	June	July	August	September	October	November	December	Annual Average
STATEWIDE—*Continued*													
Local government													
1990	122.5	123.4	123.6	123.8	124.1	115.4	109.1	109.4	122.6	124.3	124.8	123.2	120.5
1991	122.9	123.5	123.6	123.5	124.0	117.7	108.2	114.7	123.5	125.5	126.0	125.4	121.5
1992	124.1	124.8	125.0	126.0	125.9	120.1	110.3	118.9	124.9	127.1	128.3	127.3	123.5
1993	127.0	128.4	128.3	127.8	128.4	119.8	108.7	121.2	128.1	130.0	131.1	130.5	125.7
1994	130.8	131.5	131.8	131.6	132.0	125.3	115.7	125.9	131.2	132.5	134.7	133.1	129.6
1995	132.5	134.0	134.5	134.2	134.6	128.3	116.6	129.7	134.3	132.9	133.9	133.1	131.5
1996	134.6	135.5	136.4	136.3	136.9	130.6	119.4	131.9	136.3	137.3	138.0	137.9	134.2
1997	136.7	137.9	137.7	138.1	138.0	129.7	122.4	134.8	137.9	139.0	139.2	139.4	135.9
1998	139.0	140.1	138.7	140.5	140.8	134.2	127.7	138.3	141.4	143.1	143.5	143.1	139.2
1999	142.6	144.1	143.9	143.9	144.3	139.1	131.0	140.3	143.7	144.2	144.3	144.2	142.1
2000	143.3	144.1	144.6	145.5	145.7	141.1	136.1	143.1	146.5	147.9	149.0	149.4	144.6
2001	149.0	150.2	150.3	150.7	151.0	147.1	141.9	147.7	150.1	151.4	151.6	151.6	149.4
2002	150.9	152.0	152.1	152.6	153.3	150.8	145.8	151.1	154.4	154.7	154.9	154.7	152.3
2003	153.5	154.3	155.0	155.3	155.6	152.9	148.5	152.8	156.3	158.1	157.9	158.5	154.9
JACKSON													
Total nonfarm													
1990	182.4	183.4	184.6	186.2	187.3	187.2	185.4	185.3	188.1	187.3	188.4	187.9	186.1
1991	184.1	183.9	184.3	184.9	186.0	186.3	185.2	185.9	187.9	188.2	190.1	190.7	186.4
1992	187.5	187.4	188.2	188.9	189.5	190.9	189.1	190.2	192.4	192.4	192.6	193.2	190.1
1993	190.1	191.5	192.6	194.6	195.9	196.7	193.9	195.7	197.0	199.5	200.4	201.6	195.7
1994	198.8	200.6	202.2	202.6	204.5	206.6	204.2	205.2	206.5	205.7	207.9	209.0	204.4
1995	205.3	206.2	207.2	208.2	209.7	210.1	207.2	211.3	212.1	212.4	213.5	213.3	209.7
1996	211.4	212.1	214.8	215.0	216.2	217.4	213.1	215.6	216.4	215.3	216.8	217.9	215.1
1997	215.6	217.2	218.5	219.7	221.0	221.2	218.9	221.3	222.9	223.1	223.5	225.5	220.7
1998	221.9	223.7	224.6	225.9	226.6	227.9	226.4	228.5	229.2	229.1	228.7	229.1	226.8
1999	225.3	226.4	228.1	230.4	230.6	231.5	228.2	229.1	229.6	229.0	228.1	228.5	228.7
2000	227.9	228.2	229.5	230.6	231.6	232.5	229.4	230.9	230.2	230.3	231.2	232.2	230.3
2001	229.0	230.2	230.9	228.8	229.2	230.0	227.7	229.7	228.8	228.2	228.6	229.7	229.2
2002	228.0	229.2	230.4	231.0	231.7	232.6	230.2	231.2	230.5	229.6	230.2	231.1	230.5
2003	227.7	228.4	230.2	230.8	232.1	233.4	233.6	234.5	234.5	235.0	235.4	235.2	232.6
Total private													
1990	140.7	141.1	142.1	143.8	144.5	145.9	146.5	146.8	146.2	145.2	146.2	147.0	144.6
1991	143.0	142.8	143.1	144.1	145.0	146.5	147.6	148.2	147.8	147.2	149.0	149.9	146.1
1992	146.3	146.0	146.7	147.9	148.6	150.8	151.4	151.3	151.2	150.9	151.1	151.5	149.4
1993	148.5	149.4	150.5	152.3	153.3	155.3	155.2	155.3	155.0	156.9	157.3	158.7	153.9
1994	155.7	157.2	158.9	159.6	161.4	163.8	163.3	163.3	163.4	162.2	163.9	165.2	161.4
1995	161.4	161.9	162.7	163.9	165.3	166.5	166.1	167.9	167.7	167.6	168.4	168.6	165.6
1996	166.3	166.7	168.9	169.5	170.5	172.6	171.1	171.5	170.9	169.4	170.7	171.8	169.9
1997	170.4	171.8	173.1	174.3	175.9	177.2	176.6	176.6	177.2	177.0	177.7	179.3	175.5
1998	175.8	177.2	178.1	179.2	180.0	181.9	181.4	182.2	181.8	181.0	181.2	181.5	180.1
1999	177.2	178.2	179.8	181.7	182.0	183.3	181.7	181.5	180.9	180.3	179.9	180.1	180.5
2000	179.3	179.5	180.4	181.5	181.8	183.7	181.7	182.6	181.5	181.2	182.0	182.9	181.5
2001	179.9	180.8	181.2	178.5	178.7	180.0	179.1	180.5	179.1	178.0	178.5	179.4	179.5
2002	178.1	179.0	179.8	180.7	181.4	182.7	181.2	181.7	180.6	179.4	180.2	180.8	180.5
2003	177.4	177.9	179.3	179.9	181.1	182.6	184.1	185.0	184.7	185.1	185.4	185.3	182.3
Goods-producing													
1990	25.9	26.1	26.5	26.6	27.1	27.6	27.9	27.9	27.9	27.8	27.6	27.5	27.2
1991	27.1	26.9	26.4	26.8	27.0	27.5	28.0	28.3	28.3	28.0	28.4	28.4	27.5
1992	27.7	27.3	27.3	27.9	27.9	28.3	28.3	28.2	28.4	28.1	27.9	27.7	27.9
1993	27.1	27.3	27.5	27.8	27.7	27.9	28.1	28.2	28.2	28.7	28.7	28.7	27.9
1994	28.0	28.4	28.7	28.9	29.3	29.7	29.5	29.8	30.2	29.7	29.9	29.8	29.3
1995	29.2	29.3	29.5	29.8	30.2	30.4	29.6	30.4	30.3	30.0	29.7	29.6	29.8
1996	30.0	29.9	30.3	30.5	30.7	31.1	30.5	30.7	30.7	30.5	30.5	30.3	30.4
1997	30.1	30.2	30.6	30.5	31.2	31.3	31.3	31.6	31.2	31.4	31.4	31.2	31.0
1998	30.4	30.5	30.5	30.9	31.4	31.7	31.2	32.0	32.0	31.7	31.4	31.0	31.2
1999	30.7	30.7	31.3	30.9	31.2	31.7	31.3	31.3	31.0	30.4	30.2	30.3	30.9
2000	30.2	30.2	30.3	30.5	30.5	30.9	30.1	30.3	30.1	30.1	30.0	30.3	30.2
2001	29.3	29.3	29.4	29.1	29.2	29.9	29.8	30.0	30.1	30.0	30.0	29.9	29.7
2002	29.3	29.3	29.5	29.5	29.6	29.7	29.2	29.1	28.9	28.6	28.1	28.0	29.1
2003	27.9	28.0	28.5	29.0	29.7	30.2	30.5	31.2	31.1	31.4	31.2	31.0	30.0
Natural resources and mining													
1990	0.9	0.8	0.9	0.8	0.8	0.8	0.8	0.8	0.8	0.8	0.8	0.8	0.8
1991	0.8	0.8	0.8	0.8	0.8	0.8	0.8	0.8	0.7	0.7	0.7	0.7	0.7
1992	0.7	0.7	0.7	0.7	0.7	0.7	0.9	0.9	0.9	0.8	0.8	0.8	0.7
1993	0.9	0.8	0.8	0.9	0.8	0.8	0.8	0.8	0.8	0.9	0.8	0.9	0.8
1994	0.8	0.8	0.8	0.8	0.8	0.8	0.9	0.9	0.9	0.9	0.9	0.9	0.8
1995	0.9	0.9	0.9	0.8	0.9	0.8	0.9	0.9	0.8	0.8	0.8	0.8	0.8
1996	0.8	0.8	0.9	0.9	0.9	0.9	1.0	1.0	1.0	1.0	1.0	1.0	0.9
1997	1.0	1.0	1.0	0.9	1.1	1.1	1.1	1.2	1.1	1.2	1.2	1.2	1.0
1998	1.3	1.2	1.2	1.2	1.2	1.2	1.3	1.3	1.3	1.2	1.1	1.1	1.2
1999	1.0	1.0	1.0	0.9	0.9	0.9	0.9	0.9	0.9	0.9	0.9	0.9	0.9
2000	0.8	0.9	0.9	0.8	0.8	0.8	0.9	0.9	0.9	1.0	1.0	1.1	0.9
2001	1.1	1.1	1.2	1.0	0.9	0.9	0.9	0.9	0.9	0.9	0.9	0.9	1.0
2002	0.8	0.8	0.8	0.8	0.8	0.8	0.7	0.7	0.6	0.6	0.6	0.6	0.7
2003	0.6	0.6	0.7	0.7	0.7	0.7	0.7	0.7	0.7	0.7	0.7	0.7	0.7

Employment by Industry: Mississippi—*Continued*

(Numbers in thousands. Not seasonally adjusted.)

Industry	January	February	March	April	May	June	July	August	September	October	November	December	Annual Average
JACKSON—*Continued*													
Construction													
1990	7.0	6.9	7.1	7.1	7.3	7.6	7.6	7.7	7.6	7.5	7.5	7.4	7.3
1991	7.0	7.1	7.0	7.0	6.9	7.2	7.4	7.5	7.3	7.3	7.3	7.3	7.1
1992	7.0	6.9	7.0	7.3	7.5	7.7	7.8	7.7	7.8	7.7	7.7	7.7	7.4
1993	7.4	7.6	7.8	8.0	8.1	8.3	8.5	8.6	8.6	8.9	8.8	8.9	8.2
1994	8.5	8.7	8.9	9.3	9.5	9.7	9.5	9.6	9.7	9.6	9.6	9.6	9.3
1995	9.2	9.3	9.5	9.9	10.1	10.3	10.3	10.4	10.4	10.1	10.0	10.1	9.9
1996	10.2	10.2	10.5	10.5	10.9	11.3	11.1	11.0	11.0	10.8	10.8	10.7	10.7
1997	10.6	10.9	11.2	11.3	11.6	11.6	11.6	11.6	11.4	11.3	11.2	11.2	11.2
1998	10.4	10.6	10.6	10.9	11.1	11.4	11.5	11.4	11.3	11.1	11.0	11.2	11.0
1999	11.0	11.0	11.2	11.3	11.4	11.8	11.8	11.5	11.4	11.1	11.0	11.0	11.2
2000	11.0	11.1	11.2	11.4	11.5	11.7	11.4	11.4	11.3	11.2	11.2	11.3	11.3
2001	10.4	10.8	10.8	10.8	11.0	11.3	11.3	11.5	11.6	11.7	11.8	11.8	11.2
2002	11.6	11.6	11.8	11.8	11.8	11.7	11.6	11.4	11.3	11.0	11.0	11.0	11.5
2003	10.7	10.7	10.9	11.2	11.4	11.6	11.7	12.1	11.7	11.8	11.4	11.0	11.4
Manufacturing													
1990	18.0	18.4	18.5	18.7	19.0	19.2	19.5	19.4	19.5	19.5	19.3	19.3	19.0
1991	19.3	19.0	18.6	19.0	19.3	19.5	19.8	20.0	20.3	20.0	20.4	20.4	19.6
1992	20.0	19.7	19.6	19.9	19.7	19.9	19.6	19.6	19.7	19.6	19.4	19.2	19.6
1993	18.8	18.9	18.9	18.9	18.8	18.8	18.8	18.8	18.8	18.9	19.1	18.9	18.8
1994	18.7	18.9	19.0	18.8	19.0	19.2	19.1	19.3	19.6	19.2	19.4	19.3	19.1
1995	19.1	19.1	19.1	19.1	19.2	19.3	18.4	19.1	19.1	19.1	18.9	18.7	19.0
1996	19.0	18.9	18.9	19.1	18.9	18.9	18.4	18.7	18.7	18.7	18.7	18.6	18.7
1997	18.5	18.3	18.4	18.3	18.5	18.6	18.6	18.8	18.7	18.9	19.0	18.8	18.6
1998	18.7	18.7	18.7	18.8	19.1	19.1	18.4	19.3	19.4	19.4	19.3	18.7	18.9
1999	18.7	18.7	19.1	18.7	18.9	19.0	18.6	18.9	18.7	18.4	18.3	18.4	18.7
2000	18.4	18.2	18.2	18.3	18.2	18.4	17.8	18.0	17.9	17.9	17.8	17.9	18.0
2001	17.8	17.4	17.4	17.3	17.3	17.7	17.6	17.6	17.6	17.4	17.3	17.2	17.5
2002	16.9	16.9	16.9	16.9	17.0	17.2	16.9	17.0	17.0	17.0	16.5	16.4	16.9
2003	16.6	16.7	16.9	17.1	17.6	17.9	18.1	18.4	18.7	18.9	19.1	19.3	17.9
Service-providing													
1990	156.5	157.3	158.1	159.6	160.2	159.6	157.5	157.4	160.2	159.5	160.8	160.4	158.9
1991	157.0	157.0	157.9	158.1	159.0	158.8	157.2	157.6	159.6	160.2	161.7	162.3	158.8
1992	159.8	160.1	160.9	161.0	161.6	162.6	160.8	162.0	164.0	164.3	164.7	165.5	162.2
1993	163.0	164.2	165.1	166.8	168.2	168.8	165.8	167.5	168.8	170.8	171.7	172.9	167.8
1994	170.8	172.2	173.5	173.7	175.2	176.9	174.7	175.4	176.3	176.0	178.0	179.2	175.1
1995	176.1	176.9	177.7	178.4	179.5	179.7	177.6	180.9	181.8	182.4	183.8	183.7	179.8
1996	181.4	182.2	184.5	184.5	185.5	186.3	182.6	184.9	185.7	184.8	186.3	187.6	184.6
1997	185.5	187.0	187.9	189.2	189.8	189.9	187.6	189.7	191.7	191.7	192.1	194.3	189.7
1998	191.5	193.2	194.1	195.0	195.2	196.2	195.2	196.5	197.2	197.4	197.3	198.1	195.5
1999	194.6	195.7	196.8	199.5	199.4	199.8	196.9	197.8	198.6	198.6	197.9	198.2	197.8
2000	197.7	198.0	199.2	200.1	201.1	201.6	199.3	200.6	200.1	200.2	201.2	201.9	200.0
2001	199.7	200.9	201.5	199.7	200.0	200.1	197.9	199.7	198.7	198.2	198.6	199.8	199.6
2002	198.7	199.9	200.9	201.5	202.1	202.9	201.0	202.1	201.6	201.0	202.1	203.1	201.4
2003	199.8	200.4	201.7	201.8	202.4	203.2	203.1	203.3	203.4	203.6	204.2	204.2	202.6
Trade, transportation, and utilities													
1990	41.0	40.8	41.0	41.2	41.3	41.4	41.4	41.5	41.6	41.4	42.2	42.7	41.4
1991	41.3	40.9	41.0	41.0	41.1	41.1	41.2	41.4	41.4	41.1	42.2	43.0	41.3
1992	40.8	40.4	40.4	40.5	40.7	41.1	41.2	41.2	41.5	41.4	42.1	42.7	41.1
1993	41.4	41.1	41.3	42.0	42.0	42.3	42.2	42.5	42.4	43.0	43.8	44.7	42.3
1994	42.7	42.7	43.0	42.7	43.4	44.0	44.1	44.1	44.2	44.0	45.3	45.9	43.8
1995	44.5	44.2	44.3	44.2	44.8	44.7	44.8	45.4	45.7	45.9	47.0	47.6	45.2
1996	46.4	46.2	46.8	46.4	46.6	46.9	46.4	46.6	46.6	46.9	48.0	49.3	46.9
1997	47.0	47.0	47.1	47.4	47.9	48.1	47.9	47.5	48.9	48.8	49.5	50.9	48.1
1998	49.0	49.2	49.2	48.6	48.6	49.3	49.0	49.0	49.0	49.0	49.9	50.6	49.2
1999	49.2	49.8	50.1	50.2	50.3	50.5	50.0	50.1	50.3	50.9	51.1	51.5	50.3
2000	50.2	49.9	49.9	49.8	50.2	50.3	50.0	50.1	49.9	50.1	50.8	51.3	50.2
2001	50.0	50.0	50.1	48.6	48.6	48.6	48.4	48.5	48.2	48.0	48.5	49.0	48.9
2002	47.6	47.6	47.9	48.2	48.3	49.1	49.0	49.0	49.1	48.8	49.7	50.6	48.7
2003	48.6	48.4	48.5	48.1	48.2	48.4	48.4	48.3	48.3	48.5	49.0	49.8	48.5
Wholesale trade													
1990	10.0	10.0	10.0	10.0	10.0	10.0	9.9	9.9	9.9	9.7	9.8	9.8	9.9
1991	9.8	9.8	9.8	9.8	9.9	9.8	9.9	10.0	9.9	10.0	10.1	10.1	9.9
1992	9.9	9.8	9.9	9.8	9.9	10.0	10.0	10.0	10.0	10.0	10.0	10.0	9.9
1993	9.9	9.9	10.0	10.1	10.2	10.3	10.3	10.2	10.2	10.2	10.2	10.2	10.1
1994	10.3	10.3	10.4	10.4	10.4	10.5	10.6	10.6	10.5	10.5	10.5	10.6	10.4
1995	10.7	10.8	10.9	11.0	11.0	10.9	10.9	10.9	11.0	10.9	10.9	10.9	10.9
1996	10.8	10.8	10.9	10.8	10.9	11.0	10.9	11.0	11.0	10.9	11.0	11.1	10.9
1997	11.2	11.3	11.3	11.4	11.5	11.6	11.4	11.5	11.5	11.6	11.6	11.8	11.4
1998	11.9	12.2	12.2	12.3	12.4	12.6	12.5	12.6	12.5	12.4	12.4	12.4	12.3
1999	12.4	12.4	12.3	12.4	12.3	12.3	12.4	12.4	12.2	12.0	11.9	11.8	12.2
2000	12.6	12.6	12.6	12.6	12.6	12.6	12.6	12.7	12.6	12.4	12.4	12.3	12.5
2001	12.7	12.4	12.4	12.0	11.9	12.0	12.1	12.0	11.9	11.8	11.7	11.8	12.1
2002	11.8	11.9	11.9	11.9	11.9	12.0	12.0	12.0	12.0	11.9	11.8	11.8	11.9
2003	11.5	11.5	11.5	11.5	11.5	11.6	11.5	11.6	11.6	11.6	11.6	11.6	11.6

Employment by Industry: Mississippi—*Continued*

(Numbers in thousands. Not seasonally adjusted.)

Industry	January	February	March	April	May	June	July	August	September	October	November	December	Annual Average
JACKSON—*Continued*													
Retail trade													
1990	23.0	22.6	22.5	22.6	22.7	22.7	22.9	23.0	23.0	23.1	23.7	24.2	23.0
1991	22.8	22.5	22.5	22.6	22.6	22.7	22.6	22.7	22.7	22.6	23.5	24.2	22.8
1992	22.7	22.5	22.6	22.7	22.8	23.0	23.1	23.0	23.3	23.5	24.1	24.5	23.1
1993	23.7	23.4	23.4	24.0	23.9	24.0	23.9	24.3	24.2	24.7	25.5	26.4	24.2
1994	24.5	24.4	24.6	24.5	24.6	24.9	24.9	24.9	25.0	24.9	26.2	26.8	25.0
1995	25.6	25.1	25.1	24.8	25.2	25.3	25.3	25.7	25.9	26.1	27.1	27.8	25.7
1996	26.5	26.2	26.5	26.4	26.4	26.6	26.3	26.4	26.4	26.5	27.5	28.7	26.7
1997	26.7	26.6	26.6	26.7	26.8	26.8	26.8	27.0	27.5	27.4	28.1	29.2	27.1
1998	27.2	27.1	27.2	26.7	26.6	26.9	26.7	26.6	26.7	26.8	27.5	28.2	27.0
1999	26.7	27.2	27.5	27.6	27.8	28.0	27.5	27.5	27.9	28.5	29.0	29.5	27.8
2000	27.4	27.1	27.1	26.9	27.2	27.3	27.1	27.2	27.1	27.6	28.3	28.9	27.4
2001	27.4	27.8	27.9	26.6	26.7	26.6	26.4	26.5	26.4	26.3	27.0	27.4	26.9
2002	26.3	26.1	26.3	26.6	26.7	27.2	27.1	27.0	27.2	27.0	28.0	28.8	27.0
2003	27.1	26.9	27.1	26.7	26.8	26.9	27.1	26.9	27.0	27.3	27.9	28.5	27.2
Transportation and utilities													
1990	8.0	8.2	8.5	8.6	8.6	8.7	8.6	8.6	8.7	8.6	8.7	8.7	8.5
1991	8.7	8.6	8.7	8.6	8.6	8.6	8.7	8.7	8.8	8.5	8.6	8.7	8.6
1992	8.2	8.1	7.9	8.0	8.0	8.1	8.1	8.2	8.2	7.9	8.0	8.2	8.0
1993	7.8	7.8	7.9	7.9	7.9	8.0	8.0	8.0	8.0	8.1	8.1	8.1	7.9
1994	7.9	8.0	8.0	7.8	8.4	8.6	8.6	8.6	8.7	8.6	8.6	8.5	8.3
1995	8.2	8.3	8.3	8.4	8.6	8.5	8.6	8.8	8.8	8.9	9.0	8.9	8.6
1996	9.1	9.2	9.4	9.2	9.3	9.3	9.2	9.2	9.2	9.5	9.5	9.5	9.3
1997	9.1	9.1	9.2	9.3	9.6	9.7	9.7	9.0	9.9	9.8	9.8	9.9	9.5
1998	9.9	9.9	9.8	9.6	9.6	9.8	9.8	9.8	9.8	9.8	10.0	10.0	9.8
1999	10.1	10.2	10.3	10.2	10.2	10.2	10.1	10.2	10.2	10.4	10.2	10.2	10.2
2000	10.2	10.2	10.2	10.3	10.4	10.4	10.3	10.2	10.2	10.1	10.1	10.1	10.2
2001	9.9	9.8	9.8	10.0	10.0	10.0	9.9	10.0	9.9	9.9	9.8	9.8	9.9
2002	9.5	9.6	9.7	9.7	9.7	9.9	9.9	10.0	9.9	9.9	9.9	10.0	9.8
2003	10.0	10.0	9.9	9.9	9.9	9.9	9.8	9.8	9.7	9.6	9.5	9.7	9.8
Information													
1990	4.6	4.6	4.9	5.0	5.0	5.1	5.1	5.1	5.1	5.1	5.2	5.1	4.9
1991	5.1	5.1	5.2	4.4	4.4	4.4	4.5	4.5	4.5	4.5	4.5	4.5	4.6
1992	4.3	4.3	4.3	4.1	4.1	4.2	4.2	4.2	4.1	4.1	4.1	4.1	4.1
1993	4.1	4.1	4.2	4.4	4.4	4.5	4.5	4.4	4.4	4.5	4.5	4.5	4.3
1994	4.5	4.5	4.5	4.6	4.7	4.8	4.7	4.8	4.8	4.5	4.6	4.7	4.6
1995	4.9	4.9	4.9	4.9	5.0	5.1	5.4	5.4	5.6	5.6	5.7	5.4	5.2
1996	5.4	5.5	5.9	5.7	5.7	5.9	5.8	5.8	5.8	5.6	5.7	5.6	5.7
1997	5.6	5.6	5.6	5.7	5.7	5.8	5.8	5.9	5.8	5.9	5.8	5.8	5.7
1998	5.9	6.1	6.1	6.2	6.3	6.3	6.4	6.4	6.4	6.6	6.6	6.6	6.3
1999	6.4	6.3	6.4	6.6	6.6	6.7	6.7	6.7	6.7	6.8	6.8	6.8	6.6
2000	6.7	6.7	6.8	6.9	7.0	7.2	7.2	7.2	7.2	7.3	7.4	7.4	7.0
2001	8.0	8.0	7.8	7.3	7.2	7.3	7.2	7.1	7.0	6.9	6.9	6.9	7.3
2002	7.1	7.1	7.0	6.6	6.6	6.5	6.4	6.3	6.1	6.1	6.1	6.0	6.5
2003	5.9	5.9	5.8	5.7	5.7	5.6	5.6	5.7	5.6	5.6	5.6	5.6	5.7
Financial activities													
1990	14.7	14.7	14.4	14.4	14.3	14.3	14.1	14.0	14.0	14.0	14.1	14.2	14.2
1991	14.3	14.4	14.4	14.4	14.5	14.4	14.4	14.5	14.6	14.6	14.7	14.8	14.5
1992	14.5	14.2	14.2	14.1	14.2	14.2	14.2	14.2	14.1	14.0	14.0	14.1	14.1
1993	14.1	14.1	14.1	14.2	14.2	14.4	14.4	14.5	14.4	14.3	14.5	14.6	14.3
1994	14.3	14.5	14.6	14.3	14.3	14.4	14.4	14.3	14.3	14.3	14.4	14.5	14.3
1995	14.3	14.3	14.3	14.2	14.2	14.3	14.5	14.6	14.6	14.6	14.6	14.7	14.4
1996	14.8	14.8	15.0	14.9	15.0	15.2	15.0	15.0	14.9	14.9	14.9	15.0	14.9
1997	15.0	14.9	14.9	15.0	15.0	15.0	14.9	14.9	15.0	14.9	15.1	15.3	14.9
1998	15.2	15.3	15.4	15.7	15.7	15.6	15.6	15.6	15.6	15.6	15.6	15.7	15.5
1999	15.8	15.7	15.7	15.7	15.7	15.7	15.9	15.9	15.8	15.6	15.6	15.7	15.7
2000	15.7	15.8	15.9	15.9	15.9	15.9	15.5	15.4	15.4	15.3	15.3	15.4	15.6
2001	15.6	15.8	15.9	15.3	15.3	15.5	15.4	15.4	15.4	15.4	15.4	15.5	15.5
2002	15.5	15.5	15.5	15.5	15.6	15.6	15.5	15.4	15.5	15.7	15.9	15.8	15.6
2003	15.6	15.6	15.6	15.5	15.6	15.7	15.8	16.1	16.1	16.2	16.2	16.2	15.9
Professional and business services													
1990	17.4	17.6	17.7	18.1	18.3	18.6	18.5	18.6	18.7	18.4	18.2	18.3	18.2
1991	16.9	17.0	17.2	18.2	18.2	18.3	18.5	18.3	18.5	18.6	18.7	18.8	18.1
1992	19.7	20.1	20.4	20.6	20.6	20.7	20.8	20.8	20.9	21.1	21.0	21.2	20.6
1993	20.2	20.6	20.8	20.7	20.9	21.2	21.3	21.4	21.5	22.3	22.1	22.0	21.2
1994	22.8	23.3	23.6	24.1	24.2	24.6	24.9	24.9	24.8	24.8	24.9	25.0	24.3
1995	24.3	24.6	24.7	25.0	24.8	25.1	24.8	25.2	25.0	25.0	25.1	24.9	24.8
1996	24.5	24.7	25.3	25.6	25.8	26.1	26.1	26.7	26.3	25.6	25.6	25.5	25.6
1997	25.6	26.1	26.4	27.0	27.2	27.4	27.3	27.5	27.4	27.2	27.3	27.4	26.9
1998	26.8	26.9	27.0	27.6	27.7	28.1	28.2	28.2	28.3	28.1	27.8	28.0	27.7
1999	25.4	25.5	25.6	26.1	26.1	26.2	25.7	25.5	25.2	25.2	25.1	25.2	25.5
2000	25.2	25.2	25.2	25.4	25.2	25.7	25.7	26.0	26.0	25.4	25.5	25.5	25.5
2001	24.9	24.8	24.5	25.0	24.7	24.6	24.6	25.1	24.7	24.4	24.5	24.7	24.7
2002	24.7	25.2	24.8	25.1	25.1	25.1	24.9	25.3	24.9	24.9	24.7	24.7	25.0
2003	24.8	25.0	25.3	25.7	25.6	25.6	26.3	26.5	26.5	26.1	26.3	25.9	25.8

Employment by Industry: Mississippi—*Continued*

(Numbers in thousands. Not seasonally adjusted.)

Industry	January	February	March	April	May	June	July	August	September	October	November	December	Annual Average
JACKSON—*Continued*													
Educational and health services													
1990	18.4	18.5	18.6	18.7	18.8	18.8	19.6	19.8	19.1	19.0	19.1	19.4	18.9
1991	19.0	19.0	19.1	19.3	19.5	20.1	20.2	20.3	19.7	20.0	20.1	20.1	19.7
1992	19.7	19.8	19.9	20.0	20.0	20.2	20.7	20.8	20.3	20.4	20.5	20.5	20.2
1993	20.5	20.7	20.8	20.8	20.9	21.4	21.3	20.9	21.1	21.3	21.2	21.5	21.0
1994	21.3	21.4	21.6	21.8	21.8	22.3	22.0	21.6	21.8	21.7	21.7	22.0	21.7
1995	21.9	22.1	22.2	22.5	22.5	22.6	22.7	22.5	22.7	22.9	22.9	23.0	22.5
1996	23.0	23.1	23.5	23.5	23.6	23.8	23.8	23.5	23.9	23.9	24.0	24.2	23.6
1997	23.9	24.2	24.4	24.5	24.5	24.5	24.3	24.2	24.4	24.2	24.2	24.3	24.3
1998	24.7	25.0	25.2	25.0	24.8	24.9	25.1	25.0	25.2	25.1	25.1	25.0	25.0
1999	24.7	24.8	24.9	25.6	25.3	25.1	24.7	24.9	25.2	25.2	25.2	24.9	25.0
2000	25.6	25.6	25.7	26.1	25.9	25.5	25.3	25.7	25.7	26.1	26.2	26.2	25.8
2001	26.0	26.2	26.4	26.5	26.6	26.5	26.3	26.8	27.0	27.2	27.2	27.3	26.7
2002	27.6	27.6	27.8	28.0	28.0	28.0	27.8	28.0	28.2	27.9	27.9	28.0	27.9
2003	27.5	27.8	27.9	28.0	28.1	28.4	28.6	28.9	28.6	28.9	28.6	28.4	28.3
Leisure and hospitality													
1990	11.4	11.6	11.8	12.5	12.4	12.7	12.5	12.5	12.2	11.9	12.1	12.3	12.1
1991	12.0	12.2	12.4	12.5	12.8	13.0	13.1	13.1	12.9	12.6	12.7	12.7	12.6
1992	12.3	12.6	12.8	13.2	13.5	14.1	14.1	14.1	13.9	13.5	13.2	13.2	13.3
1993	13.4	13.8	14.0	14.6	15.3	15.6	15.4	15.4	15.0	14.8	14.5	14.7	14.7
1994	14.1	14.4	14.8	15.1	15.4	15.6	15.3	15.5	15.2	15.0	14.9	15.1	15.0
1995	14.3	14.5	14.7	15.2	15.7	16.0	15.9	16.1	15.8	15.6	15.4	15.4	15.3
1996	14.6	14.8	14.3	15.1	15.2	15.6	15.4	15.1	14.7	14.0	14.0	13.9	14.7
1997	15.3	15.8	16.1	16.0	16.3	16.8	16.9	16.9	16.5	16.7	16.5	16.5	16.3
1998	15.8	16.2	16.7	17.2	17.4	17.9	17.8	17.9	17.3	16.9	16.8	16.7	17.0
1999	16.9	17.2	17.6	18.3	18.5	19.0	19.1	18.8	18.4	17.9	17.6	17.4	18.0
2000	17.4	17.7	18.1	18.4	18.5	19.4	19.2	19.2	18.5	18.3	18.2	18.1	18.4
2001	17.6	18.2	18.5	18.1	18.4	18.8	18.7	18.9	18.1	17.5	17.5	17.5	18.2
2002	17.9	18.2	18.8	19.2	19.6	20.0	19.8	20.0	19.4	19.0	19.3	19.2	19.2
2003	18.6	18.7	19.1	19.3	19.6	20.1	20.3	19.8	19.9	19.8	19.9	19.9	19.6
Other services													
1990	7.3	7.2	7.2	7.3	7.3	7.4	7.4	7.4	7.6	7.6	7.7	7.5	7.4
1991	7.3	7.3	7.4	7.5	7.5	7.7	7.7	7.8	7.9	7.8	7.7	7.6	7.6
1992	7.3	7.3	7.4	7.5	7.6	8.0	7.9	7.8	8.0	8.3	8.3	8.0	7.7
1993	7.7	7.7	7.8	7.8	7.9	8.0	8.0	8.0	8.0	8.0	8.0	8.0	7.9
1994	8.0	8.0	8.1	8.1	8.3	8.4	8.4	8.3	8.1	8.2	8.2	8.2	8.1
1995	8.0	8.0	8.1	8.1	8.1	8.3	8.4	8.3	8.0	8.0	8.0	8.0	8.1
1996	7.6	7.7	7.8	7.8	7.9	8.0	8.1	8.1	8.0	8.0	8.0	8.0	7.9
1997	7.9	8.0	8.0	8.2	8.1	8.3	8.2	8.1	8.0	7.9	7.9	7.9	8.0
1998	8.0	8.0	8.0	8.0	8.1	8.1	8.1	8.1	8.0	8.0	8.0	7.9	8.0
1999	8.1	8.2	8.2	8.3	8.3	8.4	8.3	8.3	8.3	8.3	8.3	8.3	8.2
2000	8.3	8.4	8.5	8.5	8.6	8.8	8.7	8.7	8.7	8.6	8.6	8.7	8.5
2001	8.5	8.5	8.6	8.6	8.7	8.8	8.7	8.7	8.6	8.6	8.5	8.6	8.6
2002	8.4	8.5	8.5	8.6	8.6	8.7	8.6	8.6	8.5	8.4	8.5	8.5	8.5
2003	8.5	8.5	8.6	8.6	8.6	8.6	8.6	8.5	8.6	8.6	8.6	8.5	8.6
Government													
1990	41.7	42.3	42.5	42.4	42.8	41.3	38.9	38.5	41.9	42.1	42.2	40.9	41.4
1991	41.1	41.1	41.2	40.8	41.0	39.8	37.6	37.7	40.1	41.0	41.1	40.8	40.2
1992	41.2	41.4	41.5	41.0	40.9	40.1	37.7	38.9	41.2	41.5	41.5	41.7	40.7
1993	41.6	42.1	42.1	42.3	42.6	41.4	38.7	40.4	42.0	42.6	43.1	42.9	41.8
1994	43.1	43.4	43.3	43.0	43.1	42.8	40.9	41.9	43.1	43.5	44.0	43.8	42.9
1995	43.9	44.3	44.5	44.3	44.4	43.6	41.1	43.4	44.4	44.8	45.1	44.7	44.0
1996	45.1	45.4	45.9	45.5	45.7	44.8	42.0	44.1	45.5	45.9	46.1	46.1	45.1
1997	45.2	45.4	45.4	45.4	45.1	44.0	42.3	44.7	45.7	46.1	45.8	46.2	45.1
1998	46.1	46.5	46.5	46.7	46.6	46.0	45.0	46.3	47.4	48.1	47.5	47.6	46.6
1999	48.1	48.2	48.3	48.7	48.6	48.2	46.5	47.6	48.7	48.7	48.2	48.4	48.1
2000	48.6	48.7	49.1	49.1	49.8	48.8	47.7	48.3	48.7	49.1	49.2	49.3	48.8
2001	49.1	49.4	49.7	50.3	50.5	50.0	48.6	49.2	49.7	50.2	50.1	50.3	49.8
2002	49.9	50.2	50.6	50.3	50.3	49.9	49.0	49.5	49.9	50.2	50.0	50.3	50.0
2003	50.3	50.5	50.9	50.9	51.0	50.8	49.5	49.5	49.8	49.9	50.0	49.9	50.3
Federal government													
1990	5.8	5.8	5.9	6.0	6.3	6.0	6.0	5.7	5.7	5.7	5.6	5.6	5.8
1991	5.6	5.7	5.7	5.6	5.6	5.6	5.6	5.6	5.5	5.4	5.4	5.3	5.5
1992	5.3	5.3	5.4	5.3	5.3	5.3	5.3	5.3	5.3	5.3	5.3	5.3	5.3
1993	5.3	5.3	5.3	5.3	5.3	5.4	5.4	5.3	5.3	5.3	5.3	5.3	5.3
1994	5.3	5.3	5.3	5.3	5.2	5.2	5.3	5.2	5.2	5.4	5.3	5.4	5.2
1995	5.3	5.3	5.4	5.4	5.4	5.5	5.5	5.5	5.4	5.4	5.4	5.4	5.4
1996	5.5	5.5	5.5	5.5	5.5	5.5	5.5	5.5	5.5	5.5	5.4	5.5	5.4
1997	5.3	5.3	5.3	5.3	5.3	5.3	5.4	5.4	5.4	5.4	5.4	5.5	5.3
1998	5.4	5.3	5.3	5.4	5.4	5.4	5.4	5.4	5.4	5.4	5.4	5.5	5.3
1999	5.5	5.4	5.4	5.4	5.4	5.4	5.4	5.4	5.4	5.4	5.3	5.4	5.4
2000	5.3	5.3	5.4	5.5	6.1	5.9	5.4	5.4	5.3	5.3	5.3	5.3	5.4
2001	5.3	5.3	5.3	5.3	5.3	5.4	5.4	5.3	5.4	5.3	5.3	5.4	5.3
2002	5.3	5.3	5.3	5.2	5.2	5.3	5.3	5.2	5.2	5.3	5.3	5.4	5.3
2003	5.4	5.4	5.4	5.4	5.4	5.4	5.4	5.3	5.3	5.4	5.4	5.4	5.4

Employment by Industry: Mississippi—*Continued*

(Numbers in thousands. Not seasonally adjusted.)

Industry	January	February	March	April	May	June	July	August	September	October	November	December	Annual Average
JACKSON—*Continued*													
State government													
1990	19.5	19.8	19.8	19.7	19.6	19.2	19.1	19.1	19.7	19.5	19.5	19.4	19.4
1991	19.6	19.5	19.5	19.3	19.4	18.9	18.8	18.6	19.4	19.5	19.5	19.6	19.3
1992	19.8	19.9	20.0	19.6	19.5	19.5	19.6	19.5	19.8	19.8	19.7	19.9	19.7
1993	19.9	20.1	20.1	20.0	20.0	20.0	19.9	19.8	20.1	20.3	20.3	20.4	20.0
1994	20.6	20.8	20.7	20.6	20.7	20.6	20.7	20.7	20.9	20.8	20.8	20.9	20.7
1995	21.2	21.3	21.3	21.2	21.2	21.2	21.3	21.4	21.5	21.7	21.7	21.6	21.3
1996	22.0	22.0	22.0	22.0	22.0	22.3	22.1	21.9	22.1	22.2	22.2	22.3	22.0
1997	22.5	22.6	22.6	22.5	22.2	22.3	22.5	22.4	22.6	22.9	22.7	22.7	22.5
1998	23.0	23.2	23.3	23.3	23.2	23.2	23.5	23.3	23.5	24.4	23.6	23.7	23.4
1999	23.9	23.9	24.1	24.4	24.4	24.7	24.5	24.2	24.3	24.4	24.4	24.4	24.3
2000	24.8	24.8	25.1	25.1	25.2	25.3	25.5	25.2	25.4	25.6	25.6	25.6	25.2
2001	25.6	25.6	25.6	26.3	26.3	26.4	26.1	25.9	26.1	26.1	26.1	26.0	26.0
2002	26.1	26.2	26.3	26.4	26.2	26.2	25.9	25.8	26.0	26.1	26.0	26.0	26.1
2003	26.7	26.7	26.8	27.1	27.0	27.2	26.0	25.9	26.2	26.2	26.4	26.3	26.5
Local government													
1990	16.4	16.8	16.8	16.8	16.9	16.2	13.7	13.7	16.6	16.9	17.1	15.8	16.1
1991	15.9	15.9	16.0	15.9	16.0	15.3	13.2	13.5	15.2	16.1	16.2	15.9	15.4
1992	16.1	16.2	16.1	16.1	16.1	15.3	12.8	14.1	16.1	16.4	16.5	16.5	15.6
1993	16.4	16.7	16.7	17.0	17.3	16.0	13.4	15.3	16.6	17.0	17.5	17.2	16.4
1994	17.2	17.3	17.3	17.1	17.2	17.0	14.9	16.0	17.0	17.3	17.9	17.5	16.9
1995	17.4	17.7	17.8	17.7	17.8	16.9	14.3	16.5	17.5	17.7	18.0	17.7	17.2
1996	17.6	17.9	18.4	18.0	18.2	17.0	14.4	16.7	17.9	18.2	18.5	18.3	17.5
1997	17.4	17.5	17.5	17.6	17.6	16.4	14.4	16.9	17.7	17.8	17.7	18.0	17.2
1998	17.7	18.0	17.9	18.0	18.0	17.4	16.1	17.6	18.5	18.3	18.5	18.4	17.8
1999	18.7	18.9	18.8	18.9	18.8	18.1	16.6	18.0	19.0	18.9	18.5	18.6	18.4
2000	18.5	18.6	18.6	18.5	18.5	17.6	16.8	17.7	18.0	18.2	18.3	18.4	18.1
2001	18.2	18.5	18.8	18.7	18.9	18.2	17.1	18.0	18.2	18.8	18.7	18.9	18.4
2002	18.5	18.7	19.0	18.7	18.9	18.4	17.8	18.5	18.7	18.8	18.7	18.9	18.6
2003	18.2	18.4	18.7	18.4	18.6	18.2	18.1	18.3	18.3	18.3	18.2	18.2	18.3

Average Weekly Hours by Industry: Mississippi

(Not seasonally adjusted.)

Industry	January	February	March	April	May	June	July	August	September	October	November	December	Annual Average
STATEWIDE													
Manufacturing													
2001	40.1	39.4	39.5	38.3	39.3	39.4	39.7	39.9	40.2	39.4	39.7	41.8	39.7
2002	41.1	41.1	41.3	40.8	41.0	41.2	40.1	40.5	40.7	39.3	39.2	41.5	40.6
2003	40.3	40.2	39.6	38.2	38.5	39.5	39.2	40.2	40.5	40.5	40.5	41.0	39.9
JACKSON													
Manufacturing													
2001	39.3	38.1	37.0	38.1	39.1	38.5	38.2	38.4	39.1	38.2	39.8	38.9	38.6
2002	38.9	40.8	39.2	39.6	41.1	40.4	40.3	40.1	40.8	40.5	40.7	39.9	40.2
2003	40.1	40.1	39.6	38.7	39.4	40.1	39.2	38.7	39.0	39.0	39.5	39.8	39.4

Average Hourly Earnings by Industry: Mississippi

(Dollars, not seasonally adjusted.)

Industry	January	February	March	April	May	June	July	August	September	October	November	December	Annual Average
STATEWIDE													
Manufacturing													
2001	11.93	11.85	11.80	11.87	11.87	11.86	11.88	11.94	11.92	11.96	12.06	12.28	11.93
2002	12.16	12.30	12.24	12.30	12.21	12.26	12.14	12.31	12.39	12.41	12.48	12.62	12.32
2003	12.72	12.83	12.77	12.73	12.77	12.83	12.79	12.87	12.97	13.03	13.07	13.19	12.88
JACKSON													
Manufacturing													
2001	12.69	12.59	12.45	12.66	12.50	12.49	12.39	12.22	12.15	12.42	12.61	12.68	12.49
2002	12.44	12.97	12.85	12.92	12.83	12.76	12.49	12.95	12.98	12.95	13.10	13.04	12.86
2003	13.20	13.52	13.48	13.68	13.69	13.79	14.01	14.29	14.57	14.76	14.55	14.81	14.07

Average Weekly Earnings by Industry: Mississippi

(Dollars, not seasonally adjusted.)

Industry	January	February	March	April	May	June	July	August	September	October	November	December	Annual Average
STATEWIDE													
Manufacturing													
2001	478.39	466.89	466.10	454.62	466.49	467.28	471.64	476.41	479.18	471.22	478.78	513.30	473.62
2002	499.78	505.53	505.51	501.84	500.61	505.11	486.81	498.56	504.27	487.71	489.22	523.73	500.19
2003	512.62	515.77	505.69	486.29	491.65	506.79	501.37	517.37	525.29	527.72	529.34	540.79	513.91
JACKSON													
Manufacturing													
2001	498.72	479.68	460.65	482.35	488.75	480.87	473.30	469.25	475.07	474.44	501.88	493.25	482.11
2002	483.92	529.18	503.72	511.63	527.31	515.50	503.35	519.30	529.58	524.48	533.17	520.30	516.97
2003	529.32	542.15	533.81	529.42	539.39	552.98	549.19	553.02	568.23	575.64	574.73	589.44	554.36

MISSOURI AT A GLANCE

(Population and total nonfarm employment numbers in thousands)

Population, Census 2000:	5,595.2
Total nonfarm employment, 2003:	2,676.0
Change in total nonfarm employment	
(Number)	
1990–2003:	331.0
1990–2001:	381.4
2001–2003:	-50.4
(Compound annual rate of change)	
1990–2003:	1.0%
1990–2001:	1.4%
2001–2003:	-0.9%
Unemployment rate	
1990:	5.8%
2001:	4.5%
2003:	5.6%

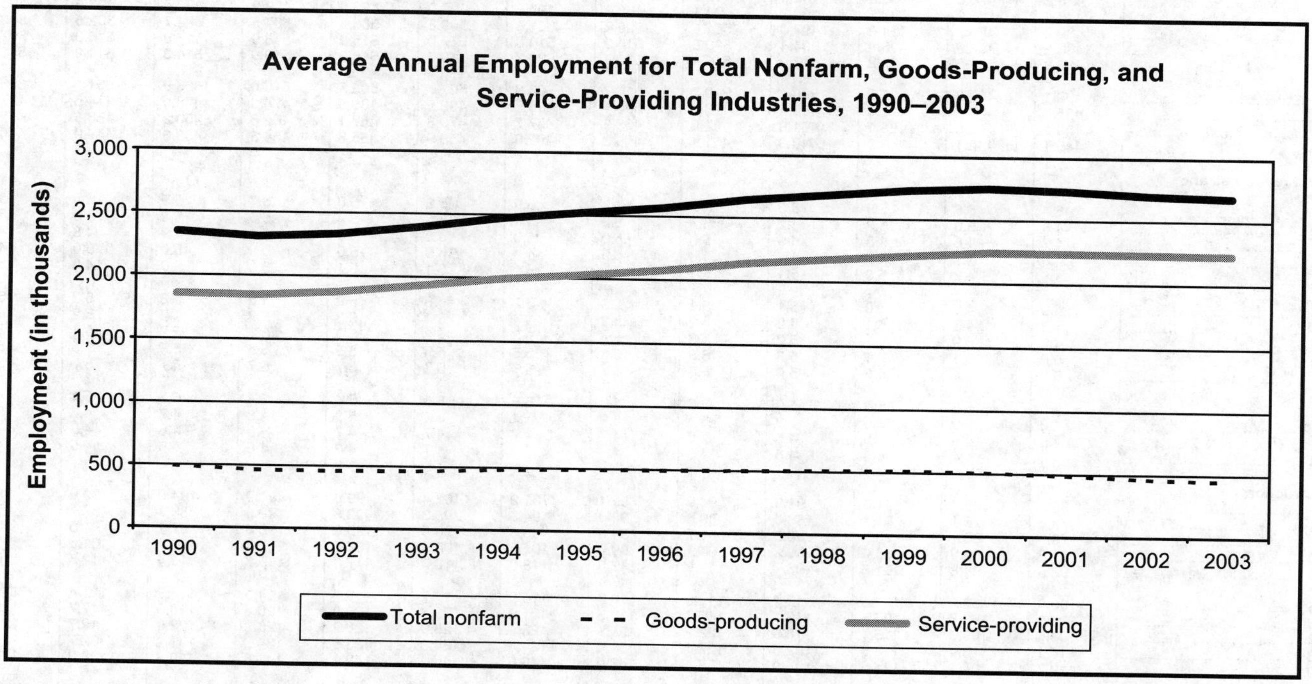

Employment in goods-producing industries declined dramatically in both recessions. In 2003, goods-producing employment remained below its 1990 level due to a loss of approximately 76,500 jobs in manufacturing over that period. In the service-providing sector, employment grew from 1992 to 2000 before beginning a gradual decline in 2001. By 2003, no recovery was yet evident, and total nonfarm employment was at its lowest since 1997.

Employment by Industry: Missouri

(Numbers in thousands. Not seasonally adjusted.)

Industry	January	February	March	April	May	June	July	August	September	October	November	December	Annual Average
STATEWIDE													
Total nonfarm													
1990	2287.1	2301.9	2323.4	2341.7	2367.8	2371.4	2344.5	2353.8	2374.8	2362.2	2356.7	2355.1	2345.0
1991	2252.8	2261.8	2285.7	2298.8	2318.6	2321.8	2308.8	2318.5	2342.8	2335.8	2330.0	2334.2	2309.1
1992	2257.8	2276.5	2300.2	2332.9	2352.9	2351.0	2337.2	2337.8	2364.9	2367.0	2362.8	2363.1	2333.6
1993	2296.4	2321.1	2343.5	2388.8	2412.4	2412.9	2394.1	2394.1	2429.9	2441.7	2446.8	2453.6	2394.6
1994	2376.5	2390.2	2422.5	2457.2	2478.8	2490.8	2471.4	2479.2	2508.5	2516.9	2522.1	2531.6	2470.4
1995	2437.1	2462.8	2498.7	2521.9	2534.3	2539.6	2507.9	2518.2	2555.1	2552.1	2557.2	2565.9	2520.9
1996	2483.0	2502.6	2538.2	2570.2	2587.3	2580.3	2553.1	2561.4	2589.2	2606.3	2617.7	2620.6	2567.4
1997	2544.6	2572.2	2610.3	2637.0	2658.1	2662.6	2631.8	2641.6	2669.1	2675.1	2682.3	2687.3	2639.3
1998	2593.9	2627.8	2646.0	2681.1	2711.8	2717.1	2679.6	2680.7	2714.1	2710.7	2713.3	2732.1	2684.0
1999	2636.1	2665.2	2691.9	2729.4	2745.3	2747.5	2721.9	2714.1	2759.5	2763.1	2767.8	2779.6	2726.8
2000	2691.1	2701.1	2735.0	2758.5	2774.3	2786.0	2729.8	2733.4	2763.1	2771.8	2774.5	2766.2	2748.7
2001	2688.3	2700.8	2727.1	2751.7	2765.9	2775.1	2683.3	2693.5	2738.2	2730.3	2731.9	2730.4	2726.4
2002	2660.5	2667.2	2690.7	2705.7	2720.2	2727.9	2635.8	2653.9	2719.1	2716.1	2720.5	2720.0	2694.8
2003	2640.4	2643.1	2664.8	2693.4	2705.4	2712.4	2616.1	2623.2	2695.9	2707.3	2709.7	2700.1	2676.0
Total private													
1990	1922.9	1927.5	1945.4	1962.5	1983.2	2007.6	1998.1	2010.6	2005.9	1986.4	1976.3	1977.4	1975.3
1991	1882.0	1881.4	1905.1	1916.5	1938.0	1955.5	1963.8	1976.2	1973.3	1960.1	1951.9	1957.6	1938.4
1992	1890.1	1900.6	1920.6	1951.4	1972.9	1987.7	1989.7	1992.8	1995.7	1989.3	1982.1	1983.2	1963.0
1993	1926.1	1940.2	1960.2	1998.6	2025.2	2042.0	2043.8	2047.2	2051.8	2056.8	2056.6	2064.8	2017.7
1994	1992.3	2001.6	2032.2	2061.4	2085.8	2110.6	2110.0	2121.2	2123.5	2124.4	2126.9	2136.5	2085.5
1995	2053.4	2069.8	2100.8	2123.9	2136.3	2155.9	2143.0	2157.7	2162.8	2151.5	2154.2	2161.9	2130.9
1996	2088.5	2098.1	2129.1	2159.1	2179.3	2184.6	2180.7	2192.8	2189.2	2194.8	2198.3	2206.3	2166.7
1997	2143.8	2156.7	2190.4	2212.5	2233.3	2251.0	2243.4	2257.8	2254.9	2253.6	2258.0	2262.8	2226.5
1998	2188.2	2205.9	2222.8	2256.8	2286.4	2300.1	2295.7	2302.4	2295.6	2289.7	2290.5	2304.9	2269.9
1999	2218.2	2239.9	2263.9	2299.7	2312.6	2329.7	2329.6	2333.5	2330.7	2331.5	2332.7	2343.5	2305.5
2000	2265.6	2267.4	2294.5	2325.0	2336.2	2355.5	2336.2	2340.1	2338.6	2342.4	2338.6	2330.9	2322.6
2001	2260.2	2265.4	2290.2	2314.3	2327.4	2341.0	2317.3	2324.5	2305.8	2293.7	2292.5	2287.9	2301.7
2002	2224.6	2228.1	2250.0	2264.7	2277.2	2294.2	2271.2	2287.0	2287.6	2275.9	2277.3	2275.9	2267.8
2003	2203.0	2200.5	2221.4	2246.2	2257.0	2271.8	2255.1	2262.5	2263.8	2268.4	2270.7	2261.2	2248.5
Goods-producing													
1990	483.2	484.4	485.2	489.3	493.6	501.1	495.6	499.9	496.7	490.0	482.2	480.7	490.1
1991	446.9	449.3	455.9	461.3	466.3	469.0	469.4	473.9	472.4	468.3	464.5	464.3	463.4
1992	445.0	447.1	451.0	457.4	463.0	465.7	464.0	464.2	466.8	463.3	461.0	459.9	459.0
1993	445.1	449.0	452.8	456.4	462.7	468.9	468.6	468.0	469.8	473.3	471.9	472.2	463.2
1994	453.6	456.5	465.3	471.2	477.3	486.2	484.8	490.6	490.9	489.2	487.5	489.4	478.5
1995	473.2	476.6	486.2	492.2	492.7	500.2	495.5	498.6	498.0	494.2	493.5	495.5	491.3
1996	478.4	481.0	488.5	491.2	494.1	498.6	496.6	499.0	496.9	499.2	497.5	496.9	493.1
1997	483.2	486.7	494.0	497.0	501.6	506.4	501.6	509.8	506.4	507.5	504.7	502.5	500.1
1998	488.2	492.9	493.8	504.4	510.8	514.2	510.3	517.0	515.9	516.0	513.0	516.0	507.7
1999	495.8	502.8	507.2	513.9	516.4	520.8	520.7	519.7	518.3	516.9	514.3	514.2	513.4
2000	499.1	497.8	501.9	506.1	510.2	516.7	506.3	507.7	505.5	510.0	506.9	501.2	505.8
2001	485.6	487.2	492.0	496.4	498.1	500.1	485.8	492.5	486.5	478.3	478.0	474.5	487.9
2002	459.2	459.8	463.1	461.8	462.9	468.5	457.7	470.8	467.1	462.8	460.2	458.5	462.7
2003	445.1	442.1	446.2	448.3	451.4	455.3	452.3	458.9	455.5	454.5	453.3	447.9	450.9
Natural resources and mining													
1990	5.4	5.5	5.5	5.6	5.7	5.9	5.9	5.9	5.8	5.7	5.7	5.6	5.6
1991	4.8	5.0	5.2	5.2	5.3	5.3	5.4	5.5	5.4	5.3	5.2	5.0	5.2
1992	4.7	4.8	4.8	4.9	5.0	5.0	5.0	5.0	5.0	5.0	4.9	4.8	4.9
1993	4.5	4.7	4.7	4.7	4.8	4.9	4.9	5.0	5.0	5.0	5.0	5.0	4.8
1994	4.8	4.8	5.0	5.1	5.2	5.2	5.1	5.1	5.1	5.0	5.0	4.9	5.0
1995	4.9	4.9	5.0	5.1	5.1	5.3	5.2	5.3	5.2	5.3	5.2	5.2	5.1
1996	4.8	4.9	5.1	5.2	5.2	5.2	5.4	5.4	5.3	5.3	5.2	5.2	5.1
1997	4.9	4.9	5.1	5.2	5.3	5.4	5.3	5.3	5.3	5.2	5.2	5.1	5.1
1998	5.0	5.1	5.1	5.3	5.3	5.4	5.5	5.5	5.5	5.5	5.5	5.5	5.3
1999	5.2	5.4	5.5	5.6	5.6	5.7	5.7	5.7	5.7	5.7	5.7	5.7	5.6
2000	5.5	5.5	5.6	6.0	6.0	6.0	5.5	5.5	5.4	5.4	5.3	5.1	5.6
2001	4.8	4.9	5.0	5.2	5.1	5.2	5.1	5.2	5.0	4.8	4.7	4.6	5.0
2002	4.5	4.5	4.5	4.5	4.6	4.7	4.7	4.7	4.7	4.6	4.6	4.5	4.6
2003	4.4	4.4	4.4	4.5	4.6	4.7	4.7	4.7	4.8	4.6	4.5	4.5	4.6
Construction													
1990	90.5	89.4	91.5	91.9	94.9	99.1	101.2	102.4	99.0	96.9	94.0	90.6	95.1
1991	73.6	76.1	81.1	86.0	89.6	93.0	94.5	95.3	92.8	92.6	88.7	87.7	87.5
1992	79.5	80.1	83.3	88.3	91.7	94.5	96.3	96.5	95.6	96.0	92.1	91.0	90.4
1993	81.6	83.3	86.0	90.2	94.1	99.0	101.6	102.8	102.5	105.3	103.1	101.6	95.9
1994	93.0	94.8	101.7	106.7	111.6	117.0	118.6	118.7	117.0	115.7	113.4	112.5	110.0
1995	100.3	102.2	107.6	112.1	112.0	116.7	116.9	117.7	116.7	114.5	113.3	111.4	111.7
1996	100.2	102.5	107.9	113.1	115.7	119.5	121.9	122.8	120.0	120.6	118.3	117.7	115.0
1997	108.4	109.7	115.1	118.9	122.9	125.9	128.4	128.0	126.2	126.2	122.9	119.7	121.0
1998	110.1	113.4	113.8	122.5	127.1	130.4	134.8	134.3	133.5	134.3	131.1	132.7	126.5
1999	119.7	124.1	127.6	134.0	137.1	140.9	143.8	143.4	142.2	141.5	139.3	138.3	136.0
2000	129.0	128.5	132.8	136.6	139.5	143.9	143.4	144.6	144.1	142.9	140.1	135.1	138.4
2001	128.2	129.2	134.8	140.6	144.0	149.0	148.1	148.1	144.7	143.0	141.1	138.3	140.8
2002	129.8	129.0	132.1	131.8	134.0	139.0	142.4	141.7	138.8	137.4	135.1	133.8	135.4
2003	125.3	123.1	126.4	131.8	134.9	138.5	141.3	141.3	139.2	136.6	134.6	129.9	133.6

Employment by Industry: Missouri—*Continued*

(Numbers in thousands. Not seasonally adjusted.)

Industry	January	February	March	April	May	June	July	August	September	October	November	December	Annual Average
STATEWIDE—*Continued*													
Manufacturing													
1990	387.3	389.5	388.2	391.8	393.0	396.1	388.5	391.6	391.9	387.4	382.5	384.5	389.3
1991	368.5	368.2	369.6	370.1	371.4	370.7	369.5	373.1	374.2	370.4	370.6	371.6	370.6
1992	360.8	362.2	362.9	364.2	366.3	366.2	362.7	362.7	366.2	362.3	364.0	364.1	363.7
1993	359.0	361.0	362.1	361.5	363.8	365.0	362.1	360.2	362.3	363.0	363.8	365.6	362.4
1994	355.8	356.9	358.6	359.4	360.5	364.0	361.1	366.8	368.8	368.5	369.1	372.0	363.4
1995	368.0	369.5	373.6	375.0	375.6	378.2	373.4	375.6	376.1	374.4	375.0	378.9	374.4
1996	373.4	373.6	375.5	372.9	373.2	373.9	369.3	370.8	371.6	373.3	374.0	374.0	372.9
1997	369.9	372.1	373.8	372.9	373.4	375.1	367.9	376.5	374.9	376.1	376.6	377.7	373.9
1998	373.1	374.4	374.9	376.6	378.4	378.4	370.0	377.2	376.9	376.2	376.4	377.8	375.8
1999	370.9	373.3	374.1	374.3	373.7	374.2	371.2	370.6	370.4	369.7	369.3	370.2	371.8
2000	364.6	363.8	363.5	363.5	364.7	366.8	357.4	357.6	356.0	361.7	361.5	361.0	361.8
2001	352.6	353.1	352.2	350.6	349.0	345.9	332.6	339.2	336.8	330.5	332.2	331.6	342.2
2002	324.9	326.3	326.5	325.5	324.3	324.8	310.6	324.4	323.6	320.8	320.5	320.2	322.7
2003	315.4	314.6	315.4	312.0	311.9	312.1	306.3	312.9	311.5	313.3	314.2	313.5	312.8
Service-providing													
1990	1803.9	1817.5	1838.2	1852.4	1874.2	1870.3	1848.9	1853.9	1878.1	1872.2	1874.5	1874.4	1854.8
1991	1805.9	1812.5	1829.8	1837.5	1852.3	1852.8	1839.4	1844.6	1870.4	1867.5	1865.5	1869.9	1845.6
1992	1812.8	1829.4	1849.2	1875.5	1889.9	1885.3	1873.2	1873.6	1898.1	1903.7	1901.8	1903.2	1874.6
1993	1851.3	1872.1	1890.7	1932.4	1949.7	1944.0	1925.5	1926.1	1960.1	1968.4	1974.9	1981.4	1931.3
1994	1922.9	1933.7	1957.2	1986.0	2001.5	2004.6	1986.6	1988.6	2017.6	2027.7	2034.6	2042.2	1991.9
1995	1963.9	1986.2	2012.5	2029.7	2041.6	2039.4	2012.4	2019.6	2057.1	2057.9	2063.7	2070.4	2029.5
1996	2004.6	2021.6	2049.7	2079.0	2093.2	2081.7	2056.5	2062.4	2092.3	2107.1	2120.2	2123.7	2074.3
1997	2061.4	2085.5	2116.3	2140.0	2156.5	2156.2	2130.2	2131.8	2162.7	2167.6	2177.6	2184.8	2139.2
1998	2105.7	2134.9	2152.2	2176.7	2201.0	2202.9	2169.3	2163.7	2198.2	2194.7	2200.3	2216.1	2176.3
1999	2140.3	2162.4	2184.7	2215.5	2228.9	2226.7	2201.2	2194.4	2241.2	2246.2	2253.5	2265.4	2213.4
2000	2192.0	2203.3	2233.1	2252.4	2264.1	2269.3	2223.5	2225.7	2257.6	2261.8	2267.6	2265.0	2243.0
2001	2202.7	2213.6	2235.1	2255.3	2267.8	2275.0	2222.6	2224.5	2251.7	2252.0	2253.9	2255.9	2242.5
2002	2201.3	2207.4	2227.6	2243.9	2257.3	2259.4	2203.4	2206.8	2252.0	2253.3	2260.3	2261.5	2236.2
2003	2195.3	2201.0	2218.6	2245.1	2254.0	2257.1	2192.5	2193.2	2240.4	2252.8	2256.4	2252.2	2229.9
Trade, transportation, and utilities													
1990	500.6	495.6	499.9	499.8	504.4	507.1	504.2	506.3	508.1	507.7	512.1	515.8	505.1
1991	493.9	485.4	489.2	487.5	492.9	494.7	495.1	497.2	498.6	499.7	504.5	507.7	495.5
1992	486.8	485.4	488.6	490.6	495.1	495.4	494.6	494.1	496.6	500.0	503.6	507.8	494.8
1993	484.0	483.6	486.1	491.5	495.7	497.8	495.0	496.5	501.0	504.7	511.6	517.8	497.1
1994	500.0	498.2	503.5	499.7	505.5	507.3	507.8	509.6	515.4	521.1	529.2	536.7	511.1
1995	507.4	506.6	511.4	512.1	515.4	516.8	512.9	516.4	520.5	526.6	534.5	540.2	518.4
1996	513.3	510.9	515.3	518.3	522.3	521.3	517.8	521.2	523.7	529.9	539.2	545.8	523.2
1997	523.7	519.9	524.4	525.4	529.6	531.3	532.0	533.1	537.2	539.1	548.5	556.5	533.3
1998	529.1	525.7	529.4	534.8	541.8	543.5	542.0	541.7	544.7	547.3	558.6	567.7	542.1
1999	538.5	538.9	544.3	547.9	550.1	552.5	550.6	551.5	555.2	563.0	570.2	578.5	553.4
2000	550.8	547.5	552.2	554.2	556.3	555.0	552.6	552.3	558.4	561.6	571.0	576.8	557.4
2001	544.1	538.8	541.3	542.4	544.6	545.7	541.8	541.5	542.7	544.8	553.4	556.2	544.8
2002	535.9	530.9	535.1	533.6	537.9	539.7	540.3	539.7	542.5	540.7	549.8	554.0	540.0
2003	529.4	524.8	527.6	530.0	531.9	531.7	530.3	531.5	532.0	535.7	542.6	544.3	532.7
Wholesale trade													
1990	117.3	117.4	118.2	117.5	118.1	119.0	119.5	119.6	119.5	119.8	119.1	118.8	118.6
1991	114.5	114.4	115.4	114.7	115.6	116.1	116.0	116.2	116.4	116.8	117.2	117.3	115.8
1992	114.7	115.0	116.2	115.8	116.2	117.1	116.8	116.5	116.1	117.4	116.9	117.1	116.3
1993	112.9	113.6	114.3	115.1	115.7	116.0	116.1	116.1	116.0	116.8	117.1	117.5	115.6
1994	115.1	115.6	116.6	115.7	116.0	116.4	117.3	117.8	118.2	118.7	119.1	120.2	117.2
1995	116.3	117.1	118.3	118.8	119.2	120.0	118.7	119.7	119.9	119.8	120.1	120.6	119.0
1996	117.9	119.0	119.7	120.3	120.6	120.3	118.9	119.8	119.9	120.5	121.2	121.8	119.9
1997	120.4	121.1	122.4	120.9	121.3	121.6	122.0	121.9	122.5	122.9	123.4	124.1	122.0
1998	121.6	122.1	123.0	123.9	124.6	125.5	123.3	122.9	123.1	123.0	123.2	123.9	123.3
1999	121.2	122.0	122.8	122.8	122.9	123.3	122.8	122.6	122.3	123.1	122.8	123.7	122.7
2000	120.5	121.0	121.9	121.4	121.4	121.9	121.4	121.1	122.1	122.1	122.6	123.2	121.7
2001	120.8	121.0	121.2	121.1	121.1	121.6	121.1	120.6	120.3	119.6	118.9	119.2	120.5
2002	119.3	119.2	119.8	119.4	119.5	120.3	121.0	120.0	119.5	118.8	118.8	118.7	119.5
2003	117.8	117.9	118.1	118.6	118.7	119.0	118.9	119.0	117.9	118.8	117.8	118.1	118.4
Retail trade													
1990	273.0	267.3	269.7	269.6	272.7	275.0	273.5	274.4	273.3	273.9	279.0	283.2	273.7
1991	268.4	260.3	262.3	262.4	266.2	268.2	270.2	270.9	269.3	269.4	274.3	279.1	268.4
1992	262.9	260.8	261.8	264.9	268.4	268.5	269.5	269.3	269.1	271.2	277.0	281.4	268.7
1993	264.6	262.4	263.4	267.7	270.6	272.5	271.7	272.8	274.0	277.4	284.2	289.7	272.5
1994	275.0	272.2	275.5	275.7	278.3	280.0	280.9	282.7	284.3	288.4	296.0	302.2	282.6
1995	281.9	279.5	282.1	282.6	285.0	286.7	286.3	288.0	289.5	293.9	301.6	306.9	288.6
1996	287.2	283.0	286.0	288.8	291.9	292.1	291.1	292.3	292.8	298.1	306.7	313.1	293.5
1997	293.7	289.2	291.9	293.8	296.7	298.2	300.2	300.5	301.0	302.4	311.6	318.4	299.8
1998	296.1	292.4	294.5	297.7	302.7	304.3	306.3	305.2	305.9	308.3	319.7	327.3	305.0
1999	304.8	303.2	307.2	309.5	310.9	312.2	311.6	311.2	312.3	317.0	324.4	331.4	313.0
2000	310.0	305.8	308.6	310.4	311.9	311.9	310.3	310.2	312.4	314.9	324.2	329.8	313.4
2001	310.6	305.1	306.7	308.0	310.0	311.9	308.9	308.4	309.3	312.3	321.5	325.0	311.5
2002	308.6	304.1	307.3	306.0	309.2	311.1	310.1	310.3	312.9	311.5	320.9	326.4	311.5
2003	305.3	300.7	303.7	306.3	308.4	309.3	308.5	310.0	310.6	313.1	323.2	324.3	310.3

Employment by Industry: Missouri—*Continued*

(Numbers in thousands. Not seasonally adjusted.)

Industry	January	February	March	April	May	June	July	August	September	October	November	December	Annual Average
STATEWIDE—*Continued*													
Transportation and utilities													
1990	110.3	110.9	112.0	112.7	113.6	113.1	111.2	112.3	115.3	114.0	114.0	113.8	112.7
1991	111.0	110.7	111.5	110.4	111.1	110.4	108.9	110.1	112.9	113.5	113.0	111.3	111.2
1992	109.2	109.6	110.6	109.9	110.5	109.8	108.3	108.3	111.4	111.4	109.7	109.3	109.8
1993	106.5	107.6	108.4	108.7	109.4	109.3	107.2	107.6	111.0	110.5	110.3	110.6	108.9
1994	109.9	110.4	111.4	108.3	111.2	110.9	109.6	109.1	112.9	114.0	114.1	114.3	111.3
1995	109.2	110.0	111.0	110.7	111.2	110.1	107.9	108.7	111.1	112.9	112.8	112.7	110.6
1996	108.2	108.9	109.6	109.2	109.8	108.9	107.8	109.1	111.0	111.3	111.3	110.9	109.6
1997	109.6	109.6	110.1	110.7	111.6	111.5	109.8	110.7	113.7	113.8	113.5	114.0	111.5
1998	111.4	111.2	111.9	113.2	114.5	113.7	112.4	113.6	115.7	116.0	115.7	116.5	113.8
1999	112.5	113.7	114.3	115.6	116.3	117.0	116.2	117.7	120.6	122.9	123.0	123.4	117.8
2000	120.3	120.7	121.7	122.4	123.0	121.2	120.9	121.0	123.9	124.6	124.2	123.8	122.3
2001	112.7	112.7	113.4	113.3	113.5	112.2	111.8	112.5	113.1	112.9	113.0	112.0	112.8
2002	108.0	107.6	108.0	108.2	109.2	108.3	109.2	109.4	110.1	110.4	110.1	108.9	109.0
2003	106.3	106.2	105.8	105.1	104.8	103.4	102.9	102.5	103.5	103.8	101.6	101.9	104.0
Information													
1990	66.8	66.5	66.8	66.7	66.7	67.5	67.5	66.9	66.7	66.2	66.6	67.1	66.8
1991	63.1	63.0	63.6	62.3	62.7	62.9	63.4	63.5	63.2	62.9	63.9	64.4	63.2
1992	61.7	61.9	61.9	61.7	62.0	62.1	62.3	62.4	62.3	61.3	61.4	61.9	61.9
1993	61.6	61.9	62.1	62.6	63.0	63.4	63.2	63.5	63.2	64.4	64.4	65.1	63.2
1994	63.0	63.3	63.6	62.8	63.2	64.0	64.5	64.6	64.3	64.1	64.7	65.1	63.9
1995	65.1	65.0	65.9	67.3	67.6	68.3	66.3	66.8	66.9	66.4	66.8	68.0	66.7
1996	66.9	66.4	67.1	68.2	68.4	68.7	69.7	69.9	69.8	70.5	71.2	73.0	69.1
1997	71.3	71.9	72.5	72.5	73.0	73.6	73.9	74.2	74.0	72.7	73.1	73.7	73.0
1998	73.4	73.5	73.4	73.5	74.1	74.7	75.0	74.7	74.0	74.0	74.7	74.6	74.1
1999	74.1	74.3	74.7	74.2	74.8	75.3	75.0	75.5	75.5	75.3	76.1	77.3	75.2
2000	77.0	76.8	76.7	76.7	76.5	76.4	76.2	76.1	76.0	75.9	75.9	75.7	76.3
2001	74.8	75.3	75.6	75.1	74.9	75.4	74.9	74.6	74.1	73.1	73.1	71.9	74.4
2002	72.8	72.8	72.4	70.9	71.1	71.2	69.6	69.4	68.7	66.9	67.4	67.6	70.1
2003	68.0	68.5	68.6	67.3	66.9	67.4	66.4	66.1	65.7	64.9	65.5	65.6	66.7
Financial activities													
1990	137.3	137.8	138.9	138.8	139.8	141.3	141.7	141.8	140.9	139.4	138.7	139.3	139.6
1991	136.0	135.9	136.2	133.7	135.0	136.3	137.9	138.3	137.3	136.2	135.7	136.9	136.2
1992	135.1	135.7	136.3	137.9	139.0	140.2	139.6	139.4	138.8	138.0	137.0	137.7	137.8
1993	137.2	137.6	137.8	139.3	140.5	141.8	142.9	143.6	142.9	143.5	143.6	144.9	141.3
1994	142.3	142.2	143.1	144.3	144.6	145.5	145.5	145.5	143.9	142.6	142.6	143.2	143.7
1995	138.5	139.0	139.9	140.3	140.3	141.6	141.4	142.1	141.4	139.8	140.1	141.2	140.4
1996	138.7	139.4	140.5	142.4	143.6	144.4	145.1	145.3	143.8	144.5	144.7	145.5	143.1
1997	144.0	144.3	145.0	146.6	147.3	148.1	150.3	150.9	150.3	149.4	149.6	151.0	148.0
1998	152.9	154.7	154.8	152.7	154.4	156.3	157.6	157.7	156.7	156.8	157.0	158.3	155.8
1999	156.7	157.1	157.8	157.9	158.5	159.5	159.9	159.9	157.9	158.7	158.6	159.5	158.5
2000	155.3	155.5	156.1	157.5	157.7	159.6	159.9	159.5	158.8	159.3	159.7	160.6	158.3
2001	158.2	158.3	159.0	159.8	161.0	162.4	162.4	162.3	160.6	159.6	159.7	160.2	160.3
2002	158.5	158.4	160.7	160.3	160.8	161.6	162.1	162.4	160.8	160.8	161.1	162.0	160.8
2003	160.5	160.4	160.8	162.1	162.8	164.2	164.0	164.3	162.5	163.2	163.0	163.0	162.6
Professional and business services													
1990	214.1	216.6	218.3	218.5	219.4	221.8	221.7	222.9	223.2	220.7	219.1	219.8	219.6
1991	216.4	217.5	220.5	220.9	220.2	221.8	223.0	224.3	224.8	224.0	222.3	222.4	221.5
1992	220.1	223.3	226.3	230.3	230.8	233.4	234.5	236.2	237.2	235.8	234.9	236.4	231.6
1993	232.9	236.1	239.8	247.6	249.5	251.3	254.7	254.9	257.6	256.4	256.8	258.0	249.6
1994	246.6	249.1	253.8	257.5	258.5	262.5	263.0	265.1	265.9	268.7	269.3	268.6	260.7
1995	260.1	264.7	268.4	271.7	271.9	274.7	271.0	274.0	275.0	273.5	274.4	275.2	271.2
1996	271.2	273.9	278.2	282.6	284.2	284.1	282.6	288.0	287.4	285.3	286.4	286.4	282.5
1997	282.1	285.6	290.2	294.4	294.6	298.5	298.3	299.7	297.5	298.4	298.7	298.9	294.7
1998	288.2	294.5	295.9	304.3	305.1	309.3	309.2	310.1	307.8	307.6	306.2	308.0	303.8
1999	300.9	304.9	309.9	315.2	313.0	315.4	316.6	318.5	316.7	316.8	316.4	316.7	313.4
2000	310.6	311.5	316.0	321.8	319.8	325.8	322.6	323.7	323.2	321.0	320.0	317.7	319.5
2001	315.5	317.5	321.0	321.6	319.8	321.4	316.4	317.8	314.5	312.8	310.5	311.4	316.7
2002	302.1	305.2	307.4	309.0	307.5	308.9	307.9	309.4	308.2	309.7	310.2	309.4	307.9
2003	299.2	299.7	302.4	304.3	302.9	305.6	304.4	305.7	305.8	305.2	306.6	303.8	303.8
Educational and health services													
1990	247.7	251.1	252.3	253.3	254.2	253.9	254.3	257.0	259.5	262.4	263.3	264.5	256.1
1991	256.8	259.3	261.3	261.8	263.5	263.1	263.8	265.5	269.9	272.4	273.1	275.8	265.5
1992	269.4	272.2	274.3	276.0	276.0	275.8	276.7	275.4	278.9	281.6	282.4	283.6	276.8
1993	282.2	284.9	286.1	288.5	289.0	288.5	288.3	288.5	291.8	293.3	293.7	294.4	289.1
1994	288.8	291.3	292.5	303.1	302.7	302.0	300.8	300.7	304.8	305.5	306.3	306.3	300.4
1995	300.8	305.4	305.9	306.1	304.7	304.3	302.5	303.0	307.9	308.9	308.9	309.5	305.6
1996	306.3	309.8	311.8	312.6	312.4	309.3	310.0	308.8	313.6	315.9	316.5	317.2	312.0
1997	313.1	318.0	320.3	320.6	321.7	320.7	316.4	316.7	322.1	326.8	328.6	329.3	321.1
1998	325.2	327.9	328.6	328.6	328.9	326.8	323.4	322.1	324.0	323.0	321.9	321.6	325.1
1999	317.5	319.6	318.7	322.5	322.3	322.7	323.4	324.1	328.3	328.6	330.1	331.7	324.1
2000	328.6	333.0	335.6	338.4	336.9	336.7	335.9	336.0	336.7	337.2	338.2	338.0	335.9
2001	336.4	339.1	340.8	342.8	342.9	342.7	342.8	343.0	345.2	346.7	348.3	348.4	343.3
2002	345.6	348.4	348.8	349.7	350.5	348.0	338.3	339.1	353.2	352.8	354.1	354.4	348.6
2003	349.7	352.0	353.1	353.6	352.6	351.6	340.2	339.9	354.3	359.9	360.1	359.9	352.2

Employment by Industry: Missouri—*Continued*

(Numbers in thousands. Not seasonally adjusted.)

Industry	January	February	March	April	May	June	July	August	September	October	November	December	Annual Average
STATEWIDE—*Continued*													
Leisure and hospitality													
1990	184.4	186.2	193.7	205.6	214.0	221.7	220.1	222.8	218.5	207.3	202.2	198.3	206.2
1991	180.3	182.0	188.5	199.0	206.7	215.8	218.7	220.8	216.0	204.9	197.2	194.8	202.0
1992	183.1	185.8	192.2	205.7	214.9	221.6	223.1	226.5	220.7	213.9	206.9	200.5	207.9
1993	189.0	192.4	199.5	215.5	227.3	231.5	231.3	232.9	226.8	221.5	215.2	212.1	216.2
1994	199.2	201.3	209.6	221.6	232.8	241.3	241.5	243.2	237.0	231.4	225.7	225.0	225.8
1995	209.3	212.8	222.0	233.2	242.5	247.4	251.3	254.4	251.6	240.5	234.5	229.9	235.7
1996	213.5	215.7	225.5	240.6	250.4	253.8	253.8	255.9	249.6	244.8	238.1	236.3	239.8
1997	222.6	225.7	238.0	249.8	258.6	264.6	262.9	265.6	260.2	252.1	247.4	242.6	249.1
1998	225.6	230.2	239.6	250.5	262.4	265.4	267.9	268.8	262.6	254.8	248.9	247.2	251.9
1999	226.1	232.2	239.8	255.6	265.0	269.7	270.2	270.6	264.8	258.2	252.9	251.0	254.7
2000	231.3	232.0	241.7	255.5	263.6	269.5	267.3	269.1	263.8	261.0	250.6	244.2	254.1
2001	230.2	233.3	243.0	258.0	267.0	272.8	273.7	273.3	264.0	260.8	251.8	247.5	256.3
2002	234.9	236.5	245.6	261.8	268.6	277.0	276.4	277.5	269.4	264.6	257.2	252.7	260.2
2003	235.5	237.0	245.8	262.9	270.5	276.8	278.2	277.3	270.9	267.1	261.4	258.7	261.8
Other services													
1990	88.8	89.3	90.3	90.5	91.1	93.2	93.0	93.0	92.3	92.7	92.1	91.9	91.5
1991	88.6	89.0	89.9	90.0	90.7	91.9	92.5	92.7	91.1	91.7	90.7	91.3	90.8
1992	88.9	89.2	90.0	91.8	92.1	93.5	94.9	94.6	94.4	95.4	94.9	95.4	92.9
1993	94.1	94.7	96.0	97.2	97.5	98.8	99.8	99.3	98.7	99.7	99.4	100.3	97.9
1994	98.8	99.7	100.8	101.2	101.2	101.8	102.1	101.9	101.3	101.8	101.6	102.2	101.2
1995	99.0	99.7	101.1	101.0	101.2	102.6	102.1	102.4	101.5	101.6	101.5	102.4	101.3
1996	100.2	101.0	102.2	103.2	103.9	104.4	105.1	104.7	104.4	104.7	104.7	105.2	103.6
1997	103.8	104.6	106.0	106.2	106.9	107.8	108.0	107.8	107.2	107.6	107.4	108.3	106.8
1998	105.6	106.5	107.3	108.0	108.9	109.9	110.3	110.3	109.9	110.2	110.2	111.5	109.0
1999	108.6	110.1	111.5	112.5	112.5	113.8	113.2	113.7	114.0	114.0	114.1	114.6	112.7
2000	112.9	113.3	114.3	114.8	115.2	115.8	115.4	115.7	116.2	116.4	116.3	116.7	115.3
2001	115.4	115.9	117.5	118.2	119.1	120.5	119.5	119.5	118.2	117.6	117.7	117.8	118.1
2002	115.6	116.1	116.9	117.6	117.9	119.3	118.9	118.7	117.7	117.6	117.3	117.3	117.6
2003	115.6	116.0	116.9	117.7	118.0	119.2	119.3	118.8	117.1	117.9	118.2	118.0	117.7
Government													
1990	364.2	374.4	378.0	379.2	384.6	363.8	346.4	343.2	368.9	375.8	380.4	377.7	369.7
1991	370.8	380.4	380.6	382.3	380.6	366.3	345.0	342.3	369.5	375.7	378.1	376.6	370.6
1992	367.7	375.9	379.6	381.5	380.0	363.3	347.5	345.0	369.2	377.7	380.7	379.9	370.6
1993	370.3	380.9	383.3	390.2	387.2	370.9	350.3	346.9	378.1	384.9	390.2	388.8	376.8
1994	384.2	388.6	390.3	395.8	393.0	380.2	361.4	358.0	385.0	392.5	395.2	395.1	384.9
1995	383.7	393.0	397.9	398.0	398.0	383.7	364.9	360.5	392.3	400.6	403.0	404.0	389.9
1996	394.5	404.5	409.1	411.1	408.0	395.7	372.4	368.6	400.0	411.5	419.4	414.3	400.7
1997	400.8	415.5	419.9	424.5	424.8	411.6	388.4	383.8	414.2	421.5	424.3	424.5	412.8
1998	405.7	421.9	423.2	424.3	425.4	417.0	383.9	378.3	418.5	421.0	422.8	427.2	414.1
1999	417.9	425.3	428.0	429.7	432.7	417.8	392.3	380.6	428.8	431.6	435.1	436.1	421.3
2000	425.5	433.7	440.5	433.5	438.1	430.5	393.6	393.3	424.5	429.4	435.9	435.3	426.2
2001	428.1	435.4	436.9	437.4	438.5	434.1	366.0	369.0	432.4	436.6	439.4	442.5	424.7
2002	435.9	439.1	440.7	441.0	443.0	433.7	364.6	366.9	431.5	440.2	443.2	444.1	427.0
2003	437.4	442.6	443.4	447.2	448.4	440.6	361.0	360.7	432.1	438.9	439.0	438.9	427.5
Federal government													
1990	71.3	72.1	74.8	75.3	79.6	75.8	75.8	73.5	72.8	71.9	71.8	71.9	73.8
1991	72.8	73.3	73.4	73.1	72.4	72.9	70.8	70.5	70.0	69.8	69.6	69.1	71.4
1992	70.1	71.0	71.1	71.7	71.4	70.7	69.0	68.8	68.5	68.4	67.9	68.4	69.7
1993	68.1	69.2	69.4	69.8	69.7	69.7	68.0	67.7	67.7	66.4	66.1	67.1	68.2
1994	66.7	67.6	67.8	69.1	69.1	68.5	68.1	68.3	67.0	65.7	65.4	66.0	67.4
1995	65.6	66.7	67.1	67.0	66.1	66.1	64.0	63.5	63.1	62.9	61.0	61.9	64.5
1996	63.5	64.7	64.8	65.6	64.0	63.9	61.8	61.5	60.7	60.1	60.1	60.7	62.6
1997	60.5	63.8	64.5	65.6	64.6	63.8	62.8	61.5	59.8	58.8	59.2	60.0	62.0
1998	55.7	58.1	58.7	58.0	57.2	57.2	56.4	56.3	55.8	55.8	56.1	57.7	56.9
1999	56.2	57.4	57.5	58.0	57.1	57.0	56.9	56.6	56.3	56.6	56.8	57.9	57.0
2000	57.1	58.4	60.9	60.0	65.8	65.8	61.4	61.8	56.0	55.5	55.7	56.6	59.6
2001	56.5	56.8	56.9	57.3	56.7	56.7	57.0	55.9	55.6	55.2	55.2	56.0	56.3
2002	55.7	56.4	56.9	56.7	56.1	56.7	56.8	55.8	55.3	55.5	55.4	56.4	56.1
2003	55.4	56.1	55.7	57.1	56.6	55.7	55.9	54.5	54.1	54.8	53.8	54.4	55.3
State government													
1990	88.7	90.5	91.1	90.5	90.1	85.9	84.1	84.9	90.7	91.6	92.5	91.9	89.3
1991	90.2	91.4	91.4	91.4	91.0	86.4	84.5	85.1	90.6	91.5	91.7	91.9	89.7
1992	88.2	90.7	91.5	91.3	90.9	86.9	86.7	86.9	91.4	92.7	93.0	93.5	90.3
1993	89.3	92.4	93.2	93.3	93.7	89.3	86.1	87.4	94.8	93.9	94.3	94.6	91.8
1994	93.7	94.8	95.0	95.3	95.6	92.8	90.3	90.4	98.1	97.3	97.7	97.0	94.8
1995	91.9	96.1	97.9	96.8	96.5	93.6	92.3	92.8	98.0	99.6	100.4	99.3	96.2
1996	96.2	100.3	101.4	100.7	98.0	95.1	93.0	93.7	99.4	101.8	102.1	101.5	98.6
1997	95.8	101.0	101.2	102.9	102.0	97.6	95.2	95.0	101.4	104.8	104.8	104.2	100.4
1998	98.1	103.3	102.7	103.3	102.5	98.2	96.1	95.8	103.5	102.4	102.8	104.0	101.0
1999	101.6	104.1	104.6	106.8	106.6	100.6	100.1	100.4	107.8	109.1	109.8	109.4	105.1
2000	105.8	109.3	110.9	110.7	108.6	103.6	102.9	103.8	109.7	110.7	111.7	110.8	108.2
2001	109.5	110.5	110.5	110.1	110.3	107.3	99.1	99.7	110.2	109.9	109.7	110.6	108.1
2002	108.0	108.5	108.1	107.7	108.2	104.6	95.5	95.2	106.6	109.8	110.3	110.6	106.1
2003	109.6	110.6	110.6	112.2	112.2	109.5	98.3	97.7	110.1	109.4	109.4	108.6	108.2

Employment by Industry: Missouri—*Continued*

(Numbers in thousands. Not seasonally adjusted.)

Industry	January	February	March	April	May	June	July	August	September	October	November	December	Annual Average
STATEWIDE—*Continued*													
Local government													
1990	204.2	211.8	212.1	213.4	214.9	202.1	186.5	184.8	205.4	212.3	216.1	213.9	206.4
1991	207.8	215.7	215.8	217.8	217.2	207.0	189.7	186.7	208.9	214.4	216.8	215.6	209.4
1992	209.4	214.2	217.0	218.5	217.7	205.7	191.8	189.3	209.3	216.6	219.8	218.0	210.6
1993	212.9	219.3	220.7	227.1	223.8	211.9	196.2	191.8	215.6	224.6	229.8	227.1	216.7
1994	223.8	226.2	227.5	231.4	228.3	218.9	203.0	199.3	219.9	229.5	232.1	232.1	222.6
1995	226.2	230.2	232.9	234.2	235.4	224.0	208.6	204.2	231.2	238.1	241.6	242.8	229.1
1996	234.8	239.5	242.9	244.8	246.0	236.7	217.6	213.4	239.9	249.6	257.2	252.1	239.5
1997	244.5	250.7	254.2	256.0	258.2	250.2	230.4	227.3	253.0	257.9	260.3	260.3	250.2
1998	251.9	260.5	261.8	263.0	265.7	261.6	231.4	226.2	259.2	262.8	263.9	265.5	256.1
1999	260.1	263.8	265.9	264.9	269.0	260.2	235.3	223.6	264.7	265.9	268.5	268.8	259.2
2000	262.6	266.0	268.7	262.8	263.7	261.1	229.3	227.7	258.8	263.2	268.5	267.9	258.4
2001	262.1	268.1	269.5	270.0	271.5	270.1	235.0	236.9	266.6	271.5	274.5	275.9	260.3
2002	272.2	274.2	275.7	276.6	278.7	272.4	237.6	239.6	269.6	274.9	277.5	277.1	264.8
2003	272.4	275.9	277.1	277.9	279.6	275.4	235.5	237.4	267.9	274.7	275.8	275.9	264.0
KANSAS CITY													
Total nonfarm													
1990	766.2	771.6	781.0	784.5	792.9	799.5	788.6	791.6	792.8	790.0	791.9	793.5	787.0
1991	759.8	762.1	773.9	776.7	780.0	789.0	784.6	786.0	790.0	785.5	788.3	789.2	780.4
1992	768.4	773.5	781.6	791.9	795.0	800.0	793.1	795.6	797.4	796.6	796.4	798.7	790.6
1993	778.2	786.1	793.6	807.2	814.2	820.4	815.5	813.8	819.9	822.6	824.5	829.9	810.4
1994	807.7	814.6	824.7	834.8	842.9	851.8	845.6	846.9	851.4	852.1	857.2	860.3	840.8
1995	836.9	843.6	852.8	856.5	862.8	870.9	858.6	858.5	873.9	867.5	871.5	879.1	861.0
1996	852.6	857.7	867.5	873.7	881.2	887.7	880.4	881.1	890.6	895.7	902.7	906.4	881.4
1997	886.3	892.3	903.9	910.6	921.6	927.9	920.3	920.4	927.7	924.9	930.2	932.2	916.5
1998	915.7	922.7	927.8	939.0	947.1	954.6	942.0	949.4	956.1	954.8	957.5	965.0	944.3
1999	938.5	943.6	951.4	964.2	968.4	975.0	966.3	967.7	969.7	974.5	978.5	986.3	965.3
2000	961.5	962.5	970.3	978.5	986.2	995.5	979.6	983.1	986.8	991.6	992.4	991.1	981.6
2001	954.9	958.0	965.5	971.8	974.1	983.0	967.3	967.9	969.4	968.7	967.8	967.5	968.0
2002	942.5	945.1	950.9	959.7	961.9	968.8	940.9	944.1	948.5	952.0	955.3	954.7	952.0
2003	928.3	928.6	933.0	942.7	947.2	953.6	936.7	939.7	944.4	948.9	946.4	945.4	941.2
Total private													
1990	648.0	649.4	659.1	661.4	667.9	676.8	672.9	674.6	671.7	667.1	665.5	669.7	665.3
1991	638.2	636.3	647.7	649.3	655.4	664.0	667.8	669.8	668.5	662.2	663.3	665.2	657.3
1992	646.0	648.8	654.7	664.3	669.1	675.3	675.0	677.5	674.8	671.6	671.0	673.8	666.8
1993	656.2	660.6	666.3	679.5	685.7	692.6	693.9	696.8	694.8	695.5	697.3	702.2	685.1
1994	683.0	687.1	695.7	705.5	712.6	722.3	723.1	725.3	724.8	724.3	728.4	732.3	713.7
1995	710.7	713.8	721.6	725.4	731.3	740.0	736.6	741.4	745.7	738.3	742.1	749.3	733.0
1996	726.0	728.1	736.0	743.8	750.9	758.4	759.2	762.8	762.5	766.3	771.2	776.9	753.5
1997	758.5	761.1	771.3	777.2	787.7	795.7	795.5	799.5	796.7	793.8	798.2	799.8	786.3
1998	783.0	786.7	791.5	802.8	811.1	818.6	813.9	824.1	822.6	821.1	825.4	831.7	811.0
1999	807.4	808.6	815.4	826.4	831.3	839.0	838.7	843.1	837.1	839.4	842.5	849.7	831.6
2000	826.9	825.1	831.4	838.8	844.9	854.3	848.8	854.6	852.0	854.0	853.6	852.1	844.7
2001	822.0	821.9	828.9	834.2	837.8	847.3	836.7	839.9	833.2	831.3	829.8	828.7	832.6
2002	804.9	805.3	810.3	819.6	822.3	829.6	810.6	816.3	812.4	815.0	817.8	817.4	815.1
2003	791.5	789.2	792.6	801.9	806.3	814.1	804.9	810.9	807.8	810.3	808.2	807.0	803.7
Goods-producing													
1990	121.6	123.1	125.8	125.8	126.8	129.4	129.2	128.6	128.0	127.0	124.0	123.2	126.0
1991	113.8	115.1	117.8	119.2	120.7	122.4	123.5	123.4	123.3	122.9	121.5	120.5	120.3
1992	116.5	117.0	118.5	121.0	121.7	123.2	123.0	123.5	123.2	122.7	121.2	120.4	120.9
1993	115.8	116.8	117.9	119.3	121.3	123.5	124.2	124.3	124.1	125.0	124.0	123.8	121.6
1994	119.6	121.1	124.2	127.3	129.6	132.8	130.6	132.1	132.9	133.1	132.0	131.6	128.9
1995	126.2	126.5	128.7	131.3	131.9	134.3	133.2	134.1	134.3	132.7	132.3	132.9	131.5
1996	128.7	129.5	132.1	133.9	134.9	137.6	138.0	138.5	137.5	137.6	136.9	136.2	135.1
1997	132.1	132.7	135.4	136.6	139.3	141.5	142.0	142.1	140.3	140.2	139.2	137.3	138.2
1998	134.5	136.0	135.7	139.5	141.9	141.9	141.2	146.4	146.4	146.1	145.2	145.8	141.7
1999	136.5	137.2	138.9	145.1	146.0	147.4	147.6	147.5	146.2	146.0	145.3	144.7	144.0
2000	141.1	139.5	141.1	143.7	146.3	148.4	144.3	148.3	147.3	147.2	145.2	142.8	144.6
2001	134.2	134.0	136.0	137.9	139.2	140.9	134.3	137.9	136.1	134.8	134.0	132.7	136.0
2002	126.7	128.3	129.5	131.2	131.7	133.9	124.1	130.3	128.7	131.4	130.9	130.5	129.8
2003	126.8	127.0	128.8	128.9	131.0	132.2	127.9	132.7	132.0	132.7	132.7	130.1	130.2
Construction and mining													
1990	29.7	29.5	30.8	31.7	32.7	34.3	34.2	34.4	33.3	32.5	31.6	30.5	32.1
1991	25.8	26.6	28.0	29.8	31.0	32.2	33.7	33.6	32.8	32.6	31.0	30.1	30.6
1992	27.3	27.7	29.1	31.8	32.5	33.5	34.2	34.4	34.0	33.8	32.6	31.7	31.8
1993	27.6	28.6	30.1	30.9	32.7	34.6	35.4	35.8	35.5	36.5	35.6	34.8	33.1
1994	31.4	32.0	34.8	36.9	38.9	41.4	42.9	42.6	41.6	40.6	39.8	39.0	38.4
1995	35.2	35.4	37.4	39.1	39.6	41.6	41.7	41.8	41.7	40.9	40.5	40.3	39.6
1996	36.8	37.5	39.6	41.7	42.4	44.6	45.8	45.6	44.7	44.8	43.7	43.1	42.5
1997	39.7	40.0	42.5	44.0	46.3	47.7	48.0	47.8	46.7	46.5	45.8	43.9	44.9
1998	41.0	42.3	42.0	46.0	47.9	49.2	50.3	50.6	50.3	50.0	49.4	49.7	47.4
1999	45.8	46.7	47.9	51.1	52.3	53.6	55.3	55.1	54.4	53.9	53.4	52.7	51.9
2000	49.6	49.3	50.7	52.8	53.9	55.5	56.2	56.4	55.8	55.3	54.0	51.4	53.4
2001	47.4	47.1	49.4	52.0	53.3	54.5	53.5	53.5	51.7	51.4	51.2	49.9	51.2
2002	46.9	46.4	47.9	49.2	49.9	51.8	51.3	51.0	49.9	50.8	50.4	50.1	49.6
2003	46.4	46.3	47.6	49.8	50.4	51.4	51.9	51.8	51.4	50.8	50.6	48.1	49.7

Employment by Industry: Missouri—*Continued*

(Numbers in thousands. Not seasonally adjusted.)

Industry	January	February	March	April	May	June	July	August	September	October	November	December	Annual Average
KANSAS CITY—*Continued*													
Manufacturing													
1990	91.9	93.6	95.0	94.1	94.1	95.1	95.0	94.2	94.7	94.5	92.4	92.7	93.9
1991	88.0	88.5	89.8	89.4	89.7	90.2	89.8	89.8	90.5	90.3	90.5	90.4	89.7
1992	89.2	89.3	89.4	89.2	89.2	89.7	88.8	89.1	89.2	88.9	88.6	88.7	89.1
1993	88.2	88.2	87.8	88.4	88.6	88.9	88.8	88.5	88.6	88.5	88.4	89.0	88.4
1994	88.2	89.1	89.4	90.4	90.7	91.4	87.7	89.5	91.3	92.5	92.2	92.6	90.4
1995	91.0	91.1	91.3	92.2	92.3	92.7	91.5	92.3	92.6	91.8	91.8	92.6	91.9
1996	91.9	92.0	92.5	92.2	92.5	93.0	92.2	92.9	92.8	92.8	93.2	93.1	92.6
1997	92.4	92.7	92.9	92.6	93.0	93.8	94.0	94.3	93.6	93.7	93.4	93.4	93.3
1998	93.5	93.7	93.7	93.5	94.0	92.7	90.9	95.8	96.1	96.1	95.8	96.1	94.3
1999	90.7	90.5	91.0	94.0	93.7	93.8	92.3	92.4	91.8	92.1	91.9	92.0	92.2
2000	91.5	90.2	90.4	90.9	92.4	92.9	88.1	91.9	91.5	91.9	91.2	91.4	91.2
2001	86.8	86.9	86.6	85.9	85.9	86.4	80.8	84.4	84.4	83.4	82.8	82.8	84.8
2002	79.8	81.9	81.6	82.0	81.8	82.1	72.8	79.3	78.8	80.6	80.5	80.4	80.1
2003	80.4	80.7	81.2	79.1	80.6	80.8	76.0	80.9	80.6	81.9	82.1	82.0	80.5
Service-providing													
1990	644.6	648.5	655.2	658.7	666.1	670.1	659.4	663.0	664.8	663.0	667.9	670.3	660.9
1991	646.0	647.0	656.1	657.5	659.3	666.6	661.1	662.6	666.7	662.6	666.8	668.7	660.0
1992	651.9	656.5	663.1	670.9	673.3	676.8	670.1	672.1	674.2	673.9	675.2	678.3	669.6
1993	662.4	669.3	675.7	687.9	692.9	696.9	691.3	689.5	695.8	697.6	700.5	706.1	688.8
1994	688.1	693.5	700.5	707.5	713.3	719.0	715.0	714.8	718.5	719.0	725.2	728.7	711.9
1995	710.7	717.1	724.1	725.2	730.9	736.6	725.4	724.4	739.6	734.8	739.2	746.2	729.5
1996	723.9	728.2	735.4	739.8	746.3	750.1	742.4	742.6	753.1	758.1	765.8	770.2	746.3
1997	754.2	759.6	768.5	774.0	782.3	786.4	778.3	778.3	787.4	784.7	791.0	794.9	778.3
1998	781.2	786.7	792.1	799.5	805.2	812.7	800.8	803.0	809.7	808.7	812.3	819.2	802.6
1999	802.0	806.4	812.5	819.1	822.4	827.6	818.7	820.2	823.5	828.5	833.2	841.6	821.3
2000	820.4	823.0	829.2	834.8	839.9	847.1	835.3	834.8	839.5	844.4	847.2	848.3	837.0
2001	820.7	824.0	829.5	833.9	834.9	842.1	833.0	830.0	833.3	833.9	833.8	834.8	832.0
2002	815.8	816.8	821.4	828.5	830.2	834.9	816.8	813.8	819.8	820.6	824.4	824.2	822.3
2003	801.5	801.6	804.2	813.8	816.2	821.4	808.8	807.0	812.4	816.2	813.7	815.3	811.0
Trade, transportation, and utilities													
1990	186.2	183.8	185.7	184.4	185.8	186.7	184.8	185.2	186.0	185.9	188.0	190.6	186.0
1991	181.4	177.6	179.6	180.0	181.9	182.8	181.2	181.9	182.4	182.1	185.2	187.5	181.9
1992	177.2	176.2	177.7	179.1	179.9	180.2	180.4	180.3	181.1	181.3	183.5	186.0	180.2
1993	177.3	177.2	177.8	179.3	180.0	180.3	180.1	180.2	181.9	182.1	184.7	187.9	180.7
1994	182.2	181.9	183.4	183.0	184.8	185.7	186.9	187.0	188.5	190.3	194.1	196.9	187.0
1995	188.0	186.8	187.5	186.7	188.4	188.7	189.5	190.3	192.9	194.5	198.5	201.4	191.1
1996	192.7	191.3	191.9	191.8	192.9	194.1	193.0	194.0	194.8	197.2	201.6	204.6	195.0
1997	198.0	196.5	197.2	197.9	199.6	200.7	201.5	202.3	203.4	203.8	207.7	210.5	201.6
1998	203.1	202.4	202.5	203.9	205.3	206.5	204.6	205.5	204.9	207.2	212.4	216.0	206.2
1999	207.2	205.7	206.4	206.2	207.2	208.7	208.4	208.6	207.9	211.4	214.8	219.1	209.3
2000	208.9	206.9	206.8	206.2	206.6	207.5	207.0	206.8	207.1	208.7	212.6	215.0	208.3
2001	207.2	204.6	204.5	205.1	205.5	205.5	204.8	204.5	204.2	206.4	209.5	211.0	206.1
2002	203.6	200.8	201.7	202.3	203.1	202.8	200.0	199.3	199.4	201.0	204.5	206.0	202.0
2003	195.0	193.3	193.6	194.5	194.6	195.5	194.2	196.0	197.2	197.9	198.7	200.2	195.9
Wholesale trade													
1990	46.9	46.6	46.8	47.1	47.4	47.6	48.0	47.7	47.6	48.4	48.1	47.9	47.5
1991	45.3	44.9	45.4	45.4	45.8	46.0	45.7	45.7	45.6	45.6	46.3	46.3	45.6
1992	44.5	44.5	44.7	44.9	45.1	45.5	46.0	45.9	45.6	45.7	45.7	45.6	45.3
1993	44.6	44.9	45.1	45.7	46.0	46.3	46.4	46.1	46.2	46.6	46.8	47.0	45.9
1994	45.9	45.9	46.1	45.9	46.1	46.4	47.3	47.3	47.4	47.5	47.7	48.3	46.8
1995	47.4	47.5	47.6	47.6	48.0	48.3	48.8	48.5	48.4	48.4	48.5	49.1	48.1
1996	48.4	48.6	48.9	48.8	49.1	49.6	49.1	49.1	49.3	49.5	49.9	50.3	49.2
1997	51.1	51.4	51.8	51.1	51.6	51.9	51.7	51.7	52.0	51.5	51.7	51.9	51.6
1998	51.7	51.8	52.1	52.6	53.0	53.1	52.9	53.3	53.2	53.4	53.4	53.6	52.8
1999	52.7	52.7	52.8	52.7	52.7	53.1	52.8	53.3	52.9	52.9	52.8	53.1	52.9
2000	52.3	52.3	52.5	51.1	51.3	51.4	51.9	51.7	51.6	51.4	51.2	51.0	51.6
2001	50.1	50.1	50.1	49.8	49.8	50.1	50.0	49.5	49.3	49.0	48.7	48.7	49.6
2002	48.5	48.5	48.5	49.0	49.0	49.3	48.6	48.6	48.2	48.4	48.3	48.0	48.6
2003	46.3	46.5	46.5	46.8	46.8	47.0	46.3	46.4	46.1	46.1	46.3	47.1	46.5
Retail trade													
1990	96.8	94.7	95.6	94.0	94.5	95.5	93.5	94.0	93.7	93.9	96.4	98.4	95.0
1991	93.9	90.8	92.0	92.3	93.6	94.6	94.8	95.2	94.5	94.7	97.3	98.8	94.3
1992	91.4	90.1	90.3	91.9	92.3	92.3	93.0	93.3	93.3	94.1	96.9	98.9	93.1
1993	91.6	90.8	90.9	91.4	91.2	91.1	91.5	92.0	92.1	92.9	95.3	98.0	92.4
1994	92.5	91.8	92.6	93.5	94.0	94.8	95.7	96.1	96.5	97.8	101.5	103.8	95.8
1995	96.9	95.6	96.2	95.5	96.2	96.8	97.3	98.2	99.8	100.9	104.7	106.9	98.7
1996	99.5	97.9	98.2	98.3	99.1	99.8	99.3	100.3	100.8	103.0	107.0	109.6	101.1
1997	102.2	100.4	100.7	102.1	103.3	104.2	105.2	106.0	106.8	107.7	111.4	114.0	105.3
1998	106.8	106.0	105.8	106.7	107.7	108.8	107.1	107.6	107.0	109.1	114.3	117.7	108.7
1999	109.9	108.4	109.0	108.9	109.9	111.0	111.1	110.8	110.4	113.8	117.4	121.4	111.8
2000	112.1	110.1	109.8	110.5	110.8	111.6	110.7	110.7	111.0	112.8	116.9	119.5	112.2
2001	108.8	106.5	106.7	107.3	107.8	108.6	107.8	107.2	107.0	109.2	112.7	114.7	108.7
2002	108.1	105.3	106.1	105.9	106.4	107.6	105.9	105.9	106.4	107.0	110.8	112.9	107.4
2003	105.1	103.4	103.8	104.4	104.7	105.5	105.8	106.8	107.4	108.2	109.0	109.4	106.1

Employment by Industry: Missouri—*Continued*

(Numbers in thousands. Not seasonally adjusted.)

Industry	January	February	March	April	May	June	July	August	September	October	November	December	Annual Average
KANSAS CITY—*Continued*													
Transportation and utilities													
1990	42.5	42.5	43.3	43.3	43.9	43.6	43.3	43.5	44.7	43.6	43.5	44.3	43.5
1991	42.2	41.9	42.2	42.3	42.5	42.2	40.7	41.0	42.3	41.8	41.6	42.4	41.9
1992	41.3	41.6	42.7	42.3	42.5	42.4	41.4	41.1	42.2	41.5	40.9	41.5	41.7
1993	41.1	41.5	41.8	42.2	42.8	42.9	42.2	42.1	43.6	42.6	42.6	42.9	42.3
1994	43.8	44.2	44.7	43.6	44.7	44.5	43.9	43.6	44.6	45.0	44.9	44.8	44.3
1995	43.7	43.7	43.7	43.6	44.2	43.6	43.4	43.6	44.7	45.2	45.3	45.4	44.1
1996	44.8	44.8	44.8	44.7	44.7	44.7	44.6	44.6	44.7	44.7	44.7	44.7	44.7
1997	44.7	44.7	44.7	44.7	44.7	44.6	44.6	44.6	44.6	44.6	44.6	44.6	44.6
1998	44.6	44.6	44.6	44.6	44.6	44.6	44.6	44.6	44.7	44.7	44.7	44.7	44.6
1999	44.6	44.6	44.6	44.6	44.6	44.6	44.5	44.5	44.6	44.7	44.6	44.6	44.6
2000	44.5	44.5	44.5	44.6	44.5	44.5	44.4	44.4	44.5	44.5	44.5	44.5	44.5
2001	48.3	48.0	47.7	48.0	47.9	46.8	47.0	47.8	47.9	48.2	48.1	47.6	47.8
2002	47.0	47.0	47.1	47.4	47.7	45.9	45.5	44.8	44.8	45.6	45.4	45.1	46.1
2003	43.6	43.4	43.3	43.3	43.1	43.0	42.1	42.8	43.7	43.6	43.4	43.7	43.3
Information													
1990	34.6	34.4	34.6	34.8	34.9	35.2	35.3	35.2	35.0	34.4	34.8	34.8	34.8
1991	35.7	35.2	35.5	34.6	35.0	35.4	35.8	35.9	35.7	34.9	35.2	35.3	35.3
1992	35.1	35.3	35.3	34.9	34.9	35.2	35.4	36.0	35.6	34.5	34.6	35.0	35.1
1993	35.8	35.9	36.1	36.9	37.1	37.7	37.9	38.2	37.9	38.6	38.5	38.9	37.4
1994	37.5	37.6	37.6	37.9	38.3	38.8	40.3	40.1	39.6	39.7	40.0	40.4	38.9
1995	40.0	40.0	40.2	41.0	41.4	41.9	41.1	41.3	41.5	41.1	41.3	42.2	41.0
1996	40.9	40.9	41.0	42.0	42.4	43.0	44.1	44.3	44.3	44.5	45.1	45.7	43.2
1997	45.5	45.9	46.5	46.8	47.4	47.8	48.2	48.2	48.1	47.6	47.9	48.4	47.4
1998	48.9	48.9	49.0	48.4	48.8	49.1	50.0	50.3	50.2	49.1	49.4	49.1	49.3
1999	51.3	51.3	51.4	51.1	51.5	52.1	53.0	53.9	53.3	53.9	54.2	54.6	52.6
2000	54.8	55.0	55.0	57.1	57.2	57.9	58.5	58.8	58.8	57.7	58.3	57.3	57.2
2001	56.4	56.5	56.4	54.8	54.8	55.5	55.4	55.3	55.2	54.5	54.3	52.2	55.1
2002	53.5	53.0	52.5	52.7	52.4	52.6	52.0	51.7	51.1	50.0	50.0	50.0	51.8
2003	49.3	48.7	48.5	48.9	48.6	48.9	47.5	47.4	46.8	46.9	46.8	46.4	47.9
Financial activities													
1990	60.1	60.4	61.0	60.8	61.4	62.0	62.3	62.1	61.6	61.3	61.2	61.6	61.3
1991	60.4	60.5	60.9	58.9	59.5	60.4	61.4	61.2	60.5	59.3	59.4	59.8	60.1
1992	60.2	60.5	60.8	60.9	61.7	62.3	62.6	62.6	61.5	61.1	61.0	61.2	61.3
1993	61.2	61.4	61.6	61.9	62.0	62.6	62.9	62.9	62.6	62.8	63.0	63.2	62.3
1994	63.4	63.3	63.3	63.1	63.2	63.3	63.6	63.5	62.7	62.9	63.0	63.3	63.2
1995	61.1	61.4	61.5	61.4	61.5	62.0	62.2	62.3	61.9	60.9	61.0	61.7	61.5
1996	60.4	60.6	60.9	61.4	61.7	62.1	62.2	62.4	62.0	62.4	62.5	62.7	61.8
1997	62.2	62.2	62.5	63.0	63.3	63.9	63.9	64.3	63.8	63.6	63.8	64.5	63.4
1998	67.1	67.5	67.5	67.0	67.4	68.2	69.2	69.5	69.2	69.4	69.7	70.5	68.5
1999	70.4	70.4	70.7	70.8	70.9	71.4	71.4	71.8	70.8	71.4	71.5	71.9	71.1
2000	70.2	70.2	70.1	70.2	70.4	71.0	71.2	71.2	70.7	71.6	71.7	72.1	70.9
2001	68.4	68.6	68.9	69.3	69.6	70.5	71.0	71.1	70.5	70.3	70.4	70.8	70.0
2002	70.2	70.3	70.5	70.7	70.9	71.5	71.1	71.1	70.5	70.8	71.2	71.4	70.9
2003	69.8	69.9	69.9	70.4	70.5	70.8	70.3	70.6	70.0	70.3	70.2	70.4	70.3
Professional and business services													
1990	79.1	80.1	81.9	82.3	82.8	83.9	83.7	83.9	83.7	83.2	82.2	83.1	82.4
1991	80.1	80.6	83.2	82.8	83.2	84.4	85.7	85.9	86.2	85.7	85.7	85.5	84.0
1992	85.6	86.8	87.8	90.1	90.1	91.4	91.2	91.7	91.9	90.9	90.6	91.3	89.9
1993	90.0	91.1	92.4	95.6	96.2	96.7	98.0	99.1	98.2	98.5	98.8	99.5	96.1
1994	94.4	95.8	97.3	100.3	100.8	102.3	103.8	104.3	104.9	103.0	103.5	103.7	101.1
1995	102.5	103.9	105.7	105.3	105.9	107.5	106.1	107.6	107.8	106.7	107.1	108.5	106.2
1996	105.5	106.6	109.1	110.1	110.9	111.5	111.5	112.9	113.7	114.1	115.1	116.0	111.4
1997	111.8	113.1	115.7	117.4	118.6	120.5	121.3	122.3	122.5	121.2	121.6	121.8	119.0
1998	117.9	119.7	121.4	123.3	124.0	126.9	125.4	127.7	127.8	129.9	130.2	130.3	125.4
1999	125.9	126.7	128.8	130.8	130.2	131.9	131.9	133.5	133.1	132.8	133.3	134.5	131.1
2000	132.4	132.2	133.9	133.6	134.4	136.5	133.5	134.6	134.6	134.5	134.8	134.7	134.1
2001	128.7	129.9	131.1	130.5	130.2	132.6	130.1	130.6	130.3	127.7	126.4	127.4	129.6
2002	121.2	122.9	123.8	124.5	124.0	125.8	123.5	123.4	123.0	122.0	122.4	121.9	123.2
2003	118.3	117.9	117.5	120.6	120.6	122.7	121.3	121.2	120.9	120.7	120.7	121.2	120.3
Educational and health services													
1990	73.4	74.2	74.7	74.7	75.4	75.7	75.2	76.2	75.4	76.2	76.6	76.9	75.3
1991	75.2	75.7	76.7	76.9	77.4	77.8	78.7	78.7	79.2	79.5	79.9	80.3	78.0
1992	78.8	79.6	79.9	80.3	80.6	80.8	81.2	80.6	81.0	81.9	81.9	82.2	80.7
1993	82.0	83.0	83.2	84.6	84.8	84.9	84.6	84.1	85.0	85.0	85.4	85.5	84.3
1994	86.1	86.8	87.2	87.8	87.7	87.5	86.6	86.2	86.7	86.2	86.7	86.7	86.8
1995	87.3	88.4	88.8	89.5	89.7	89.9	88.8	88.9	90.3	89.2	89.4	90.0	89.1
1996	89.1	90.1	90.4	90.4	90.7	91.0	91.3	91.4	92.5	92.9	93.1	93.1	91.3
1997	91.8	93.0	93.8	94.1	94.8	94.7	93.1	93.1	94.1	96.1	96.5	96.7	94.3
1998	94.3	94.4	94.7	95.3	95.4	94.9	94.4	94.4	95.1	94.1	94.4	94.8	94.7
1999	94.8	95.0	95.1	94.4	94.7	95.0	95.0	95.4	96.0	96.6	96.5	97.0	95.5
2000	95.7	97.1	97.4	98.3	97.9	98.4	99.0	98.7	99.6	100.6	101.2	100.9	98.7
2001	102.6	103.5	104.1	104.4	104.4	105.1	104.9	104.2	104.4	104.2	104.9	104.8	104.3
2002	103.9	104.5	104.6	105.5	106.1	106.3	104.9	105.2	105.5	106.9	107.0	107.2	105.6
2003	105.8	106.0	105.9	107.6	107.9	107.4	107.4	106.6	107.1	108.9	108.4	108.6	107.3

Employment by Industry: Missouri—*Continued*

(Numbers in thousands. Not seasonally adjusted.)

Industry	January	February	March	April	May	June	July	August	September	October	November	December	Annual Average
KANSAS CITY—*Continued*													
Leisure and hospitality													
1990	62.3	62.6	64.2	67.1	69.0	71.4	70.0	71.2	70.0	67.1	67.0	67.6	67.4
1991	60.9	60.9	62.9	65.7	66.4	69.1	69.6	70.9	69.8	66.1	64.8	64.6	65.9
1992	61.6	62.3	63.4	66.4	68.4	69.9	69.0	70.5	68.4	66.8	65.9	65.2	66.4
1993	62.1	63.1	64.7	69.0	71.3	73.3	72.4	74.3	71.6	69.9	69.3	69.6	69.2
1994	66.5	67.2	68.9	72.0	74.0	77.2	76.5	77.5	75.0	74.5	74.5	75.0	73.2
1995	71.8	72.8	75.0	76.1	78.2	80.6	80.6	81.5	81.9	78.4	77.5	77.2	77.6
1996	73.9	74.1	75.3	78.8	81.7	83.0	83.0	83.1	81.8	81.4	80.6	82.2	79.9
1997	81.1	81.5	83.5	84.5	87.4	89.0	87.8	89.7	87.1	84.0	84.0	82.9	85.2
1998	79.8	80.1	82.8	87.1	89.8	92.0	90.2	91.1	90.0	86.4	85.2	85.8	86.7
1999	81.8	82.7	84.2	87.6	90.2	91.3	90.1	91.2	89.1	87.2	86.9	87.5	87.5
2000	83.5	83.8	86.2	88.8	91.0	93.3	92.6	93.5	91.5	91.5	87.7	86.9	89.2
2001	81.6	81.8	84.6	88.7	90.3	92.8	92.0	92.3	89.0	89.9	86.8	86.1	88.0
2002	82.5	82.3	84.4	88.9	90.4	92.5	91.2	91.6	90.8	89.4	88.5	87.0	88.3
2003	84.0	84.0	85.8	88.4	90.3	93.1	92.7	93.0	91.8	91.4	89.6	88.8	89.4
Other services													
1990	30.7	30.8	31.2	31.5	31.8	32.5	32.4	32.2	32.0	32.0	31.7	31.9	31.7
1991	30.7	30.7	31.1	31.2	31.3	31.7	31.9	31.9	31.4	31.7	31.6	31.7	31.4
1992	31.0	31.1	31.3	31.6	31.8	32.3	32.2	32.3	32.1	32.4	32.3	32.5	31.9
1993	32.0	32.1	32.6	32.9	33.0	33.6	33.8	33.7	33.5	33.6	33.6	33.8	33.1
1994	33.3	33.4	33.8	34.1	34.2	34.7	34.8	34.6	34.5	34.6	34.6	34.7	34.2
1995	33.8	34.0	34.2	34.1	34.3	35.1	35.1	35.4	35.1	34.8	35.0	35.4	34.6
1996	34.8	35.0	35.3	35.4	35.7	36.1	36.1	36.2	35.9	36.2	36.3	36.4	35.8
1997	36.0	36.2	36.7	36.9	37.3	37.6	37.7	37.5	37.4	37.3	37.5	37.7	37.2
1998	37.4	37.7	37.9	38.3	38.5	39.1	38.9	39.2	39.0	38.9	38.9	39.4	38.6
1999	39.5	39.6	39.9	40.4	40.6	41.2	41.3	41.2	40.7	40.1	40.0	40.4	40.4
2000	40.3	40.4	40.9	40.9	41.1	41.3	42.7	42.7	42.4	42.2	42.1	42.4	41.6
2001	42.9	43.0	43.3	43.5	43.8	44.4	44.2	44.0	43.5	43.5	43.5	43.7	43.6
2002	43.3	43.2	43.3	43.8	43.7	44.2	43.8	43.7	43.4	43.5	43.3	43.4	43.6
2003	42.5	42.4	42.6	42.6	42.8	43.5	43.6	43.4	42.0	41.5	41.1	41.3	42.4
Government													
1990	118.2	122.2	121.9	123.1	125.0	122.7	115.7	117.0	121.1	122.9	126.4	123.8	121.6
1991	121.6	125.8	126.2	127.4	124.6	125.0	116.8	116.2	121.5	123.3	125.0	124.0	123.1
1992	122.4	124.7	126.9	127.6	125.9	124.7	118.1	118.1	122.6	125.0	125.4	124.9	123.8
1993	122.0	125.5	127.3	127.7	128.5	127.8	121.6	117.0	125.1	127.1	127.2	127.7	125.3
1994	124.7	127.5	129.0	129.3	130.3	129.5	122.5	121.6	126.6	127.8	128.8	128.0	127.1
1995	126.2	129.8	131.2	131.1	131.5	130.9	122.0	117.1	128.2	129.2	129.4	129.8	128.0
1996	126.6	129.6	131.5	129.9	130.3	129.3	121.2	118.3	128.1	129.4	131.5	129.5	127.9
1997	127.8	131.2	132.6	133.4	133.9	132.2	124.8	120.9	131.0	131.1	132.0	132.4	130.3
1998	132.7	136.0	136.3	136.2	136.0	136.0	128.1	125.3	133.5	133.7	132.1	133.3	133.3
1999	131.1	135.0	136.0	137.8	137.1	136.0	127.6	124.6	132.6	135.1	136.0	136.6	133.8
2000	134.6	137.4	138.9	139.7	141.3	141.2	130.8	128.5	134.8	137.6	138.8	139.0	136.9
2001	132.9	136.1	136.6	137.6	136.3	135.7	130.6	128.0	136.2	137.4	138.0	138.8	135.4
2002	137.6	139.8	140.6	140.1	139.6	139.2	130.3	127.8	136.1	137.0	137.5	137.3	136.9
2003	136.8	139.4	140.4	140.8	140.9	139.5	131.8	128.8	136.6	138.6	138.2	138.4	137.5
Federal government													
1990	31.8	32.7	33.3	33.6	34.0	33.9	33.2	32.8	32.5	32.1	32.2	32.7	32.9
1991	32.8	33.4	33.7	33.7	32.7	32.5	31.8	31.7	31.5	31.4	31.4	31.4	32.3
1992	31.8	32.4	32.7	33.0	32.7	31.9	30.7	30.6	31.2	31.2	31.3	31.5	31.7
1993	30.9	32.4	32.9	33.5	33.9	33.5	33.3	32.6	32.2	32.1	31.7	32.3	32.6
1994	31.5	32.4	33.3	33.6	33.6	33.1	33.0	32.1	31.5	30.7	30.3	30.9	32.1
1995	30.0	31.2	31.8	32.1	31.9	31.6	31.8	31.3	30.1	30.0	29.5	30.1	30.9
1996	29.5	30.7	31.6	31.3	30.8	30.2	29.7	28.9	28.4	28.3	28.2	28.5	29.7
1997	29.0	30.2	30.4	31.2	31.0	30.8	30.5	29.5	29.1	28.7	28.8	29.3	29.9
1998	30.9	31.7	31.7	31.0	30.0	30.5	30.0	29.5	29.0	28.8	29.1	29.8	30.2
1999	29.3	30.8	31.1	31.6	31.3	31.2	30.2	29.7	29.1	29.0	29.5	30.0	30.2
2000	29.8	30.9	31.9	32.2	33.9	34.1	31.6	31.3	29.3	29.8	30.1	30.6	31.3
2001	27.9	28.4	28.5	28.9	28.3	28.3	28.3	27.3	27.2	26.7	26.7	27.0	27.8
2002	27.5	28.3	28.7	28.8	28.1	28.2	27.9	27.0	26.7	26.5	26.4	26.8	27.6
2003	27.2	28.1	28.1	28.8	28.2	27.4	27.7	26.4	26.2	26.7	25.8	26.2	27.2
State government													
1990	17.5	17.7	17.7	17.9	18.0	17.7	17.9	17.7	17.9	17.8	17.8	17.8	17.7
1991	17.8	17.8	17.9	17.8	17.9	17.7	17.6	17.3	17.8	17.6	17.7	17.9	17.7
1992	17.7	17.9	18.1	18.0	18.0	17.9	18.0	17.9	18.0	18.0	18.1	18.3	17.9
1993	17.9	18.1	18.3	18.3	18.4	18.5	18.3	18.4	18.6	18.5	18.6	18.7	18.3
1994	18.3	18.5	18.5	18.5	18.6	18.7	18.6	18.6	19.1	19.0	18.8	18.8	18.6
1995	18.7	19.0	19.0	19.0	19.1	18.8	18.8	18.8	19.1	19.0	19.1	19.0	18.9
1996	18.4	18.8	19.0	18.8	18.9	18.4	18.4	18.2	18.7	18.5	18.6	18.6	18.6
1997	18.1	18.4	18.6	18.6	18.5	18.1	18.1	18.0	18.5	18.6	18.4	18.4	18.4
1998	18.1	18.5	18.8	18.7	18.7	18.4	18.2	18.0	18.6	18.4	16.3	16.4	18.1
1999	16.0	16.3	16.4	16.4	16.3	16.1	16.2	16.1	16.7	16.7	16.7	16.6	16.4
2000	16.3	16.4	16.4	16.5	16.5	15.9	16.3	16.0	16.4	16.6	16.7	16.5	16.4
2001	14.9	15.1	15.1	15.1	15.1	15.0	15.1	15.1	15.1	15.1	15.1	15.1	15.1
2002	15.0	15.0	15.0	14.9	15.0	14.8	14.3	14.3	14.2	15.2	15.2	15.2	14.2
2003	15.3	15.3	15.2	15.1	15.1	14.9	15.1	15.1	15.1	15.1	15.1	15.2	15.1

Employment by Industry: Missouri—*Continued*

(Numbers in thousands. Not seasonally adjusted.)

Industry	January	February	March	April	May	June	July	August	September	October	November	December	Annual Average
KANSAS CITY—*Continued*													
Local government													
1990	68.9	71.8	70.9	71.6	73.0	71.1	64.6	66.5	70.7	73.0	76.4	73.3	70.9
1991	71.0	74.6	74.6	75.9	74.0	74.8	67.4	67.2	72.2	74.3	75.9	74.7	73.0
1992	72.9	74.4	76.1	76.6	75.2	74.9	69.4	69.6	73.4	75.8	76.0	75.1	74.1
1993	73.2	75.0	76.1	75.9	76.2	75.8	70.0	66.0	74.3	76.5	76.9	76.7	74.3
1994	74.9	76.6	77.2	77.2	78.1	77.7	70.9	70.9	76.0	78.1	79.7	78.3	76.3
1995	77.5	79.6	80.4	80.0	80.5	80.5	71.4	67.0	79.0	80.2	80.8	80.7	78.1
1996	78.7	80.1	80.9	79.8	80.6	80.7	73.1	71.2	81.0	82.6	84.7	82.4	79.7
1997	80.7	82.6	83.6	83.6	84.4	83.3	76.2	73.4	83.4	83.8	84.8	84.7	82.0
1998	83.7	85.8	85.8	86.5	87.3	87.1	79.9	77.8	85.9	86.5	86.7	87.1	85.0
1999	85.8	87.9	88.5	89.8	89.5	88.7	81.2	78.8	86.8	89.4	89.8	90.0	87.2
2000	88.5	90.1	90.6	91.0	90.9	91.2	82.9	81.2	89.1	91.2	92.0	91.9	89.2
2001	90.0	92.5	92.9	93.5	92.8	92.3	81.5	81.0	93.8	95.5	96.1	96.6	91.5
2002	95.0	96.4	96.8	96.4	96.5	96.2	84.2	84.7	95.2	95.3	95.9	95.3	94.0
2003	94.3	96.0	97.1	96.9	97.6	97.2	81.5	80.9	95.3	96.8	97.3	97.0	94.0
ST. LOUIS													
Total nonfarm													
1990	1170.7	1176.3	1182.5	1187.0	1195.4	1199.1	1193.7	1190.3	1203.6	1195.1	1191.2	1193.0	1189.8
1991	1152.0	1151.8	1162.9	1163.4	1171.8	1172.3	1165.4	1166.5	1180.1	1178.5	1175.8	1180.3	1168.4
1992	1138.9	1149.2	1159.4	1171.9	1177.2	1175.6	1167.7	1165.5	1181.5	1183.0	1185.0	1185.4	1170.0
1993	1150.3	1159.9	1167.6	1188.2	1195.6	1194.4	1187.6	1182.1	1203.0	1208.6	1210.7	1218.1	1188.8
1994	1178.5	1188.4	1203.1	1218.2	1224.3	1230.3	1222.5	1225.0	1241.3	1245.3	1250.8	1258.2	1223.8
1995	1210.6	1220.7	1234.1	1245.9	1248.4	1250.8	1238.6	1240.2	1257.6	1255.9	1260.6	1265.9	1244.1
1996	1227.6	1237.2	1250.8	1264.9	1274.4	1268.2	1259.1	1265.0	1278.7	1283.1	1293.5	1294.2	1266.4
1997	1256.3	1265.5	1281.7	1293.8	1295.5	1301.1	1282.3	1288.7	1302.1	1304.3	1309.5	1313.4	1291.2
1998	1279.8	1290.0	1295.1	1303.7	1314.9	1312.1	1300.1	1305.1	1317.7	1318.8	1322.0	1331.8	1307.6
1999	1282.6	1294.4	1303.7	1322.6	1329.4	1328.6	1327.3	1323.1	1337.7	1340.6	1345.2	1354.3	1324.1
2000	1309.1	1312.0	1323.5	1339.7	1347.4	1352.2	1332.2	1325.7	1335.4	1344.5	1344.4	1339.6	1333.8
2001	1295.3	1305.2	1319.3	1332.5	1339.4	1346.4	1308.7	1311.7	1326.3	1322.3	1327.4	1327.3	1321.8
2002	1293.5	1294.8	1302.6	1312.3	1318.8	1327.2	1282.7	1294.6	1310.7	1311.4	1312.5	1315.4	1306.4
2003	1276.9	1275.6	1284.1	1296.8	1302.4	1308.2	1280.3	1283.2	1296.3	1297.7	1302.6	1304.1	1292.4
Total private													
1990	1027.0	1029.6	1034.4	1036.2	1044.7	1055.5	1058.1	1057.9	1058.1	1046.9	1040.2	1044.8	1044.4
1991	1006.6	1002.9	1013.0	1012.1	1021.0	1029.2	1031.3	1035.8	1034.4	1028.9	1024.1	1030.1	1022.4
1992	992.8	999.8	1008.8	1019.4	1026.0	1034.0	1034.9	1034.5	1036.1	1031.9	1030.1	1032.8	1023.4
1993	1002.5	1008.3	1015.2	1031.0	1040.3	1049.5	1051.8	1049.1	1053.3	1056.0	1056.2	1064.0	1039.7
1994	1029.1	1034.9	1048.6	1059.0	1069.7	1082.9	1083.9	1087.9	1090.6	1090.6	1093.6	1101.5	1072.7
1995	1059.0	1066.1	1078.4	1090.6	1093.7	1103.8	1099.4	1103.9	1105.2	1100.7	1103.4	1108.7	1092.7
1996	1075.5	1080.9	1092.0	1105.2	1115.3	1116.5	1116.7	1124.7	1122.3	1124.8	1126.9	1134.5	1111.3
1997	1100.2	1106.8	1121.8	1131.8	1138.6	1148.9	1138.3	1146.9	1145.6	1146.4	1149.3	1154.2	1135.7
1998	1123.0	1129.6	1134.0	1145.3	1156.3	1162.7	1159.6	1165.8	1161.3	1159.8	1161.8	1171.2	1152.5
1999	1127.6	1136.1	1144.0	1161.8	1167.1	1179.1	1184.3	1183.5	1179.0	1179.4	1183.3	1191.3	1168.0
2000	1151.1	1150.7	1160.6	1176.8	1181.1	1194.4	1186.0	1182.8	1174.7	1183.3	1181.6	1176.3	1175.0
2001	1135.6	1143.0	1156.4	1169.3	1175.3	1182.0	1167.7	1169.3	1164.7	1159.3	1162.8	1162.1	1162.3
2002	1131.1	1131.2	1138.5	1148.0	1153.0	1164.2	1142.6	1151.1	1148.9	1147.1	1147.0	1150.2	1146.1
2003	1114.6	1111.8	1120.0	1131.6	1136.2	1144.6	1139.9	1139.2	1135.8	1133.5	1137.7	1138.4	1131.9
Goods-producing													
1990	253.8	253.9	252.9	256.8	259.1	263.5	260.4	261.4	258.9	255.8	250.5	250.2	256.4
1991	229.7	230.9	234.2	239.5	240.8	242.2	241.1	241.8	241.4	239.1	237.4	236.3	237.8
1992	224.0	223.8	226.4	229.2	232.5	234.0	233.3	232.4	233.8	230.7	230.3	229.8	230.0
1993	221.0	222.3	223.7	225.2	227.2	231.0	230.2	227.8	228.5	229.4	228.3	229.1	226.9
1994	215.5	216.4	220.6	223.7	227.3	232.3	234.0	235.8	235.1	233.8	233.1	234.8	228.5
1995	227.7	228.3	234.4	236.8	237.7	242.2	240.4	240.5	239.6	237.3	237.4	237.5	236.7
1996	229.0	229.8	233.4	234.1	235.8	239.6	239.5	241.6	240.0	239.9	238.8	238.1	236.6
1997	229.5	231.1	234.1	237.9	240.2	242.4	236.1	243.2	240.4	242.3	241.8	241.0	238.3
1998	233.9	235.2	236.5	241.1	243.7	244.6	240.8	246.5	245.3	248.2	246.2	249.0	242.6
1999	236.9	239.4	241.1	244.3	246.4	250.1	252.1	251.5	249.4	248.7	248.8	249.1	246.5
2000	241.2	241.6	243.9	246.5	248.7	252.0	247.8	245.1	242.1	247.0	245.5	239.4	245.1
2001	229.8	235.5	239.1	241.3	242.1	243.1	238.4	241.6	240.0	233.8	236.3	233.6	237.9
2002	224.3	225.0	226.8	227.9	228.0	231.3	222.8	229.9	228.4	226.4	225.3	224.9	226.8
2003	215.6	213.7	216.5	218.1	219.6	222.3	221.7	224.1	222.5	221.9	221.6	219.5	219.8
Construction and mining													
1990	54.5	53.2	54.0	54.9	56.6	58.9	60.6	60.6	58.2	57.8	56.3	54.3	56.6
1991	43.4	45.2	48.2	51.5	53.2	55.2	54.9	55.2	54.4	54.2	51.8	51.4	51.5
1992	45.9	45.5	47.0	49.2	51.3	53.5	54.0	53.8	53.6	54.5	52.4	51.7	51.0
1993	46.3	47.4	48.8	51.3	52.7	55.5	55.8	56.1	56.3	57.6	56.1	55.9	53.3
1994	51.5	52.0	55.5	57.1	59.7	62.8	64.1	64.3	63.6	62.5	61.8	60.9	59.7
1995	54.4	55.8	58.5	59.7	60.1	63.1	63.3	63.4	62.8	61.7	61.2	60.3	60.4
1996	53.6	55.0	57.9	60.7	62.2	64.5	66.3	67.5	66.4	65.9	65.0	64.7	62.5
1997	58.9	59.9	62.3	64.9	66.9	68.4	69.2	68.8	67.9	68.2	66.9	65.8	65.7
1998	59.5	60.8	61.6	66.0	68.4	69.5	72.3	72.0	71.6	72.3	70.6	71.9	68.0
1999	63.5	66.6	68.4	71.5	73.4	76.4	77.6	78.0	77.0	77.2	75.9	75.5	73.4
2000	70.5	70.6	73.2	75.7	77.5	79.7	79.2	79.8	79.5	78.8	77.1	74.4	76.3
2001	69.9	70.7	74.1	77.0	78.7	82.2	82.1	82.0	80.9	80.0	79.4	77.1	77.8
2002	72.6	72.4	74.1	75.7	76.4	79.4	80.3	79.8	78.7	78.6	77.3	76.5	76.8
2003	70.9	69.3	71.5	74.5	76.1	78.4	80.9	80.4	79.5	78.8	77.3	75.1	76.1

Employment by Industry: Missouri—*Continued*

(Numbers in thousands. Not seasonally adjusted.)

Industry	January	February	March	April	May	June	July	August	September	October	November	December	Annual Average
ST. LOUIS—*Continued*													
Manufacturing													
1990	199.3	200.7	198.9	201.9	202.5	204.6	199.8	200.8	200.7	198.0	194.2	195.9	199.7
1991	186.3	185.7	186.0	188.0	187.6	187.0	186.2	186.6	187.0	184.9	185.6	184.9	186.3
1992	178.1	178.3	179.4	180.0	181.2	180.5	179.3	178.6	180.2	176.2	177.9	178.1	178.9
1993	174.7	174.9	174.9	173.9	174.5	175.5	174.4	171.7	172.2	171.8	172.2	173.2	173.6
1994	164.0	164.4	165.1	166.6	167.6	169.5	169.9	171.5	171.5	171.3	171.3	173.9	168.9
1995	173.3	172.5	175.9	177.1	177.6	179.1	177.1	177.1	176.8	175.6	176.2	177.2	176.3
1996	175.4	174.8	175.5	173.4	173.6	175.1	173.2	174.1	173.6	174.0	173.8	173.4	174.2
1997	170.6	171.2	171.8	173.0	173.3	174.0	166.9	174.4	172.5	174.1	174.9	175.2	172.7
1998	174.4	174.4	174.9	175.1	175.3	175.1	168.5	174.5	173.7	175.9	175.6	177.1	174.5
1999	173.4	172.8	172.7	172.8	173.0	173.7	174.5	173.5	172.4	171.5	172.9	173.6	173.1
2000	170.7	171.0	170.7	170.8	171.2	172.3	168.6	165.3	162.6	168.2	168.4	165.0	168.7
2001	159.9	164.8	165.0	164.3	163.4	160.9	156.3	159.6	159.1	153.8	156.9	156.5	160.0
2002	151.7	152.6	152.7	152.2	151.6	151.9	142.5	150.1	149.7	147.8	148.0	148.4	149.9
2003	144.7	144.4	145.0	143.6	143.5	143.9	140.8	143.7	143.0	143.1	144.3	144.4	143.7
Service-providing													
1990	916.9	922.4	929.6	930.2	936.3	935.6	933.3	928.9	944.7	939.3	940.7	942.8	933.3
1991	922.3	920.9	928.7	923.9	931.0	930.1	924.3	924.7	938.7	939.4	938.4	944.0	930.5
1992	914.9	925.4	933.0	942.7	944.7	941.6	934.4	933.1	947.7	952.3	954.7	955.6	940.0
1993	929.3	937.6	943.9	963.0	968.4	963.4	957.4	954.3	974.5	979.2	982.4	989.0	961.8
1994	963.0	972.0	982.5	994.5	997.0	998.0	988.5	989.2	1006.2	1011.5	1017.7	1023.4	995.3
1995	982.9	992.4	999.7	1009.1	1010.7	1008.6	998.2	999.7	1018.0	1018.6	1023.2	1028.4	1007.5
1996	998.6	1007.4	1017.4	1030.8	1038.6	1028.6	1019.6	1023.4	1038.7	1043.2	1054.7	1056.1	1029.8
1997	1026.8	1034.4	1047.6	1055.9	1055.3	1058.7	1046.2	1045.5	1061.7	1062.0	1067.7	1072.4	1052.9
1998	1045.9	1054.8	1058.6	1062.6	1071.2	1067.5	1059.3	1058.6	1072.4	1070.6	1075.8	1082.8	1065.0
1999	1045.7	1055.0	1062.6	1078.3	1083.0	1078.5	1075.2	1071.6	1088.3	1091.9	1096.4	1105.2	1077.6
2000	1067.9	1070.4	1079.6	1093.2	1098.7	1100.2	1084.4	1080.6	1093.3	1097.5	1098.9	1100.2	1088.7
2001	1065.5	1069.7	1080.2	1091.2	1097.3	1103.3	1070.3	1070.1	1086.3	1088.5	1091.1	1093.7	1083.9
2002	1069.2	1069.8	1075.8	1084.4	1090.8	1095.9	1059.9	1064.7	1082.3	1085.0	1087.2	1090.5	1079.6
2003	1061.3	1061.9	1067.6	1078.7	1082.8	1085.9	1058.6	1059.1	1073.8	1075.8	1081.0	1084.6	1072.6
Trade, transportation, utilities													
1990	252.7	249.0	250.6	249.8	252.2	253.7	252.8	253.4	253.6	255.0	258.5	260.9	253.5
1991	249.1	243.8	244.8	242.5	244.1	245.3	245.6	246.4	247.0	247.4	250.9	254.7	246.8
1992	239.5	236.8	237.6	236.9	239.4	240.4	238.1	238.0	238.3	242.4	245.3	248.7	240.1
1993	234.3	232.3	233.4	237.0	238.8	241.2	238.2	239.1	240.1	244.0	249.0	252.8	240.0
1994	240.5	238.6	240.1	241.0	243.5	244.1	244.6	245.2	246.8	250.3	254.4	259.2	245.7
1995	244.4	241.5	242.5	244.7	246.0	247.0	243.8	245.4	246.3	248.5	253.7	257.6	246.8
1996	243.9	241.1	242.6	243.5	245.8	246.0	244.6	246.3	246.6	249.4	254.6	259.4	247.0
1997	248.8	245.9	247.7	246.8	248.2	249.8	249.3	249.3	250.5	252.9	257.8	263.1	250.8
1998	250.6	246.9	248.7	247.3	249.9	250.6	251.0	250.4	250.8	251.8	257.0	264.0	251.6
1999	250.9	249.2	250.5	251.7	252.1	254.3	254.2	254.8	255.4	258.8	263.6	268.3	255.3
2000	256.4	252.9	254.8	256.0	257.0	257.7	256.1	255.1	255.1	256.9	260.4	263.5	256.8
2001	257.0	253.0	254.2	255.3	255.4	256.2	253.7	252.5	253.3	255.5	260.4	263.5	255.8
2002	254.9	250.8	251.8	252.0	253.5	256.0	253.3	252.8	253.4	254.2	258.7	262.3	254.5
2003	251.3	247.5	247.8	247.6	248.1	247.8	248.5	247.4	246.2	245.4	249.1	250.7	248.1
Wholesale trade													
1990	59.1	59.2	59.3	59.2	59.5	60.3	60.3	60.5	60.0	59.9	59.7	59.6	59.7
1991	57.7	57.7	58.0	57.5	57.7	58.2	57.9	57.9	57.7	57.7	57.6	57.7	57.7
1992	55.3	55.1	55.4	55.6	56.1	56.9	56.0	56.1	55.2	56.3	56.1	56.5	55.8
1993	54.7	54.8	55.1	56.0	56.2	56.5	56.3	56.3	55.5	56.0	56.2	56.5	55.8
1994	54.7	54.9	55.2	55.0	55.3	55.5	56.5	57.1	56.7	57.2	57.4	58.1	56.1
1995	56.1	56.2	56.6	57.2	57.6	58.2	57.3	58.1	57.6	56.8	56.9	57.2	57.2
1996	56.0	56.2	56.6	55.9	56.3	56.4	56.0	56.9	56.3	56.3	56.5	56.9	56.4
1997	56.0	56.2	56.9	56.7	56.8	57.3	57.1	57.2	57.1	57.2	57.2	57.6	56.9
1998	56.4	56.5	57.0	57.3	57.4	57.9	57.7	57.8	57.5	57.3	57.2	58.1	57.3
1999	56.8	57.1	57.3	57.4	57.6	58.0	58.2	58.3	58.0	58.2	58.1	58.5	57.8
2000	57.1	57.3	57.7	58.1	58.2	58.9	58.6	58.5	58.3	58.3	58.2	58.4	58.1
2001	58.2	58.2	58.2	58.8	58.9	59.1	58.9	58.9	58.3	57.9	57.6	57.9	58.4
2002	56.9	56.8	57.0	56.6	56.7	57.0	56.1	55.3	54.8	55.0	54.8	54.6	56.0
2003	54.6	54.5	54.5	56.2	56.2	56.4	57.0	57.1	56.2	56.3	55.7	55.4	55.8
Retail trade													
1990	141.4	137.3	138.2	137.4	138.9	139.8	139.9	139.8	139.3	140.8	144.2	147.1	140.3
1991	137.9	132.9	133.3	132.7	133.9	135.1	136.0	136.4	135.4	135.6	139.3	142.9	135.9
1992	132.5	129.9	130.2	129.1	130.8	131.6	131.4	131.1	130.4	133.1	136.8	139.5	132.2
1993	129.3	127.0	127.3	129.8	131.0	133.1	131.3	131.7	131.6	134.4	139.0	142.5	132.3
1994	133.2	131.1	132.0	133.7	134.5	135.4	135.4	135.9	135.7	137.9	142.1	146.0	136.1
1995	136.9	133.8	134.2	135.4	136.5	137.4	136.5	136.7	136.7	138.6	143.6	147.1	137.8
1996	137.2	134.2	135.3	136.7	138.2	138.7	138.6	138.9	139.0	141.5	146.4	150.8	139.6
1997	141.9	138.9	139.5	139.0	140.1	141.2	142.1	141.8	141.2	142.9	147.9	152.9	142.5
1998	143.3	140.0	141.1	139.1	141.0	142.0	143.1	142.0	141.7	143.2	149.1	154.5	143.3
1999	143.6	141.3	142.2	143.0	143.0	144.7	145.1	145.1	144.5	147.0	151.8	156.1	145.6
2000	146.3	142.6	143.9	143.9	144.7	145.7	145.0	144.3	143.6	145.1	149.4	152.8	145.6
2001	144.1	140.2	140.8	141.4	141.6	143.2	141.1	140.1	140.8	143.0	148.2	151.6	143.0
2002	144.3	140.9	141.5	141.6	142.8	144.5	142.7	143.1	143.8	143.8	149.0	153.4	144.3
2003	143.4	140.0	140.9	142.3	143.2	143.9	143.4	143.8	143.3	142.3	148.6	151.0	143.8

Employment by Industry: Missouri—*Continued*

(Numbers in thousands. Not seasonally adjusted.)

Industry	January	February	March	April	May	June	July	August	September	October	November	December	Annual Average
ST. LOUIS—*Continued*													
Transportation and utilities													
1990	52.2	52.5	53.1	53.2	53.8	53.6	52.6	53.1	54.3	54.3	54.6	54.2	53.4
1991	53.5	53.2	53.5	52.3	52.5	52.0	51.7	52.1	53.9	54.1	54.0	54.1	53.0
1992	51.7	51.8	52.0	52.2	52.5	51.9	50.7	50.8	52.7	53.0	52.4	52.7	52.0
1993	50.3	50.5	51.0	51.2	51.6	51.6	50.6	51.1	53.0	53.6	53.8	53.8	51.8
1994	52.6	52.6	52.9	52.3	53.7	53.2	52.7	52.2	54.4	55.2	54.9	55.1	53.5
1995	51.4	51.5	51.7	52.1	51.9	51.4	50.0	50.6	52.0	53.1	53.2	53.3	51.9
1996	50.7	50.7	50.7	50.9	51.3	50.9	50.0	50.5	51.3	51.6	51.7	51.7	51.0
1997	50.9	50.8	51.3	51.1	51.3	51.3	50.1	50.3	52.2	52.8	52.7	52.6	51.5
1998	50.9	50.4	50.6	50.9	51.5	50.7	50.2	50.6	51.6	51.3	50.7	51.4	50.9
1999	50.5	50.8	51.0	51.3	51.5	51.6	50.9	51.4	52.9	53.6	53.7	53.7	51.9
2000	53.0	53.0	53.2	54.0	54.1	53.1	52.5	52.3	53.2	53.5	52.8	52.3	53.1
2001	54.7	54.6	55.2	55.1	54.9	53.9	53.7	53.5	54.2	54.6	54.6	54.0	54.4
2002	53.7	53.1	53.3	53.8	54.0	54.5	54.5	54.4	54.8	55.4	54.9	54.3	54.2
2003	53.3	53.0	52.4	49.1	48.7	47.5	48.1	46.5	46.7	46.8	44.8	44.3	48.4
Information													
1990	31.6	31.4	31.6	31.5	31.4	31.8	31.6	31.2	31.1	31.2	31.3	31.5	31.4
1991	27.5	27.3	27.8	27.0	27.1	27.2	27.2	27.2	27.1	27.2	28.1	28.2	27.4
1992	26.2	26.1	26.3	26.3	26.6	26.7	26.6	26.5	26.4	26.3	26.2	26.4	26.3
1993	25.5	25.5	25.6	26.1	26.3	26.4	25.8	25.8	25.6	25.3	25.3	25.5	25.7
1994	25.1	25.1	25.2	25.1	25.2	25.6	25.3	25.4	25.3	25.3	25.5	25.6	25.3
1995	26.0	25.7	26.2	26.7	26.8	27.1	26.5	26.7	26.8	26.7	26.9	27.3	26.6
1996	27.5	26.7	27.0	27.1	27.3	27.4	27.7	27.9	27.9	28.1	28.4	29.4	27.7
1997	28.6	28.7	29.0	28.7	29.1	29.2	29.2	29.3	29.1	28.5	28.6	28.9	28.9
1998	29.2	28.9	28.7	29.0	29.0	29.3	29.7	29.9	29.4	30.7	30.9	31.4	29.7
1999	30.7	30.6	30.7	30.2	30.4	31.0	30.9	31.0	31.3	31.7	32.1	32.9	31.1
2000	32.9	32.9	32.9	32.9	32.9	32.9	33.0	33.0	32.8	32.8	32.8	32.8	32.9
2001	31.7	32.0	32.2	32.0	32.1	32.2	32.1	32.1	31.7	31.2	31.1	30.4	31.7
2002	30.8	30.7	30.5	30.2	30.3	30.3	29.4	29.5	28.9	28.9	28.9	29.0	29.8
2003	30.5	30.7	30.6	29.0	28.8	29.0	28.8	28.6	28.2	28.3	28.1	28.6	29.1
Financial activities													
1990	72.3	72.5	73.0	73.0	73.5	74.2	73.9	74.0	73.5	72.8	72.5	72.9	73.1
1991	71.8	71.5	71.4	70.2	70.7	71.3	71.5	71.6	71.0	70.8	70.4	70.9	71.0
1992	70.8	70.8	71.0	70.9	71.4	72.0	71.9	71.8	71.3	71.1	70.9	71.3	71.2
1993	70.7	70.7	70.7	71.6	72.3	73.2	74.2	74.6	73.8	74.4	74.4	75.8	73.0
1994	71.5	71.4	71.8	73.7	73.8	74.3	74.6	74.5	73.6	71.6	71.8	72.1	72.9
1995	70.1	70.2	70.7	71.3	71.3	72.0	72.2	72.6	72.2	71.3	71.7	72.3	71.5
1996	71.4	71.6	72.2	72.9	73.7	74.5	74.9	75.0	74.2	74.1	74.5	74.9	73.7
1997	74.2	74.3	74.6	75.9	76.2	76.3	77.0	77.4	77.1	76.9	77.0	77.6	76.2
1998	78.5	79.5	79.3	78.5	79.2	80.0	79.6	79.6	78.5	78.7	78.5	79.9	79.2
1999	78.5	78.3	78.8	78.3	78.7	79.3	80.3	79.8	78.8	78.7	78.5	78.9	78.9
2000	77.0	77.0	76.9	77.5	77.7	78.9	78.5	78.2	77.3	77.2	76.9	77.0	77.5
2001	74.3	74.3	74.7	75.5	76.0	76.7	76.6	76.4	75.6	75.2	75.4	75.8	75.5
2002	74.8	74.7	75.1	75.2	75.5	75.9	75.1	75.2	74.5	75.2	75.4	76.1	75.2
2003	76.1	76.0	76.4	77.7	78.1	78.9	79.1	79.5	78.5	78.7	78.8	78.4	78.0
Professional and business services													
1990	139.2	139.8	140.7	141.3	142.3	143.9	145.1	146.0	146.0	143.9	143.5	143.8	142.9
1991	142.0	141.7	143.3	145.3	144.6	146.1	146.2	146.9	147.5	145.9	144.9	144.7	144.9
1992	139.7	141.0	143.1	146.0	146.7	148.5	148.6	149.5	149.6	149.9	150.0	150.7	146.9
1993	145.9	147.7	150.2	155.7	156.4	158.1	161.4	160.4	163.0	160.9	161.6	162.5	156.9
1994	152.8	154.5	158.2	162.3	162.8	165.0	165.6	167.0	167.4	168.1	169.5	169.7	163.6
1995	161.9	164.0	165.9	168.4	167.8	170.6	169.8	170.5	171.3	169.2	169.8	170.2	168.3
1996	168.4	170.0	172.1	175.0	176.2	176.7	175.9	179.6	178.7	175.3	176.7	176.5	175.1
1997	173.0	173.9	176.3	179.3	178.8	181.1	180.0	180.5	176.9	178.1	178.1	178.6	177.9
1998	176.8	179.6	179.5	182.3	182.4	185.0	186.0	185.4	182.8	181.5	179.7	182.6	182.0
1999	179.2	180.1	182.7	187.0	185.6	188.2	189.5	191.0	189.6	188.6	189.3	190.8	186.8
2000	187.0	187.2	190.0	194.8	193.8	198.0	197.1	197.6	193.4	193.6	193.4	192.6	193.2
2001	186.9	188.7	191.9	192.9	192.5	193.9	191.3	191.9	188.6	188.4	187.3	187.5	190.2
2002	182.4	183.1	184.1	184.4	183.8	185.1	182.5	183.5	182.5	182.4	183.0	183.0	183.3
2003	176.8	177.4	178.9	180.4	179.6	181.0	180.0	180.2	178.7	178.1	179.5	180.2	179.2
Educational and health services													
1990	135.2	137.9	138.2	137.2	137.1	135.9	137.7	137.6	140.7	141.7	141.5	142.6	138.6
1991	141.5	142.8	143.5	142.0	142.8	142.5	142.6	143.0	146.2	147.7	147.2	148.6	144.2
1992	146.6	149.4	150.1	151.4	150.3	150.0	151.2	150.4	152.4	152.4	152.6	153.3	150.8
1993	153.6	155.3	155.7	155.8	155.3	154.9	155.3	155.1	157.6	158.7	158.3	158.7	156.1
1994	155.7	157.8	158.4	166.5	165.8	165.3	165.2	165.1	168.4	169.1	169.4	169.1	164.7
1995	164.9	168.1	168.0	167.9	166.3	165.4	164.9	164.9	168.0	168.6	168.2	168.3	167.0
1996	166.7	169.4	169.9	170.0	169.0	166.2	168.7	167.9	171.2	173.7	174.1	175.3	170.2
1997	171.7	175.3	176.3	175.8	176.4	175.9	173.3	173.5	177.2	179.8	180.4	181.1	176.4
1998	179.2	180.6	180.6	182.0	182.1	181.5	179.5	179.4	181.2	180.7	180.9	179.9	180.6
1999	176.9	179.1	178.5	181.3	180.8	181.0	183.2	182.7	185.2	184.4	185.5	185.9	182.0
2000	183.8	185.0	185.6	187.0	186.9	186.4	181.7	181.4	187.5	187.6	187.6	187.1	185.6
2001	181.5	183.1	183.7	185.2	185.2	184.6	180.8	181.0	186.9	187.1	188.0	188.3	184.6
2002	186.7	188.6	188.8	189.8	190.7	189.5	184.0	184.6	190.8	190.6	191.1	191.3	188.9
2003	188.0	189.2	189.7	190.0	189.6	189.3	184.2	184.0	190.0	192.2	193.9	195.3	189.6

Employment by Industry: Missouri—*Continued*

(Numbers in thousands. Not seasonally adjusted.)

Industry	January	February	March	April	May	June	July	August	September	October	November	December	Annual Average
ST. LOUIS—*Continued*													
Leisure and hospitality													
1990	96.7	97.1	100.0	103.6	106.8	110.7	111.2	111.7	109.8	104.1	102.2	100.5	104.5
1991	95.6	95.8	98.0	101.4	104.7	109.9	109.5	111.3	108.3	103.7	101.0	100.4	103.3
1992	96.7	96.5	99.4	103.2	106.7	110.8	110.2	111.8	108.8	107.1	104.6	101.8	104.8
1993	98.1	99.4	101.4	107.3	112.9	115.3	116.4	115.0	111.7	109.7	106.6	106.7	108.3
1994	102.8	103.4	105.3	110.4	116.4	120.8	121.4	120.8	117.8	115.0	112.2	113.4	113.3
1995	109.3	110.6	113.3	117.6	122.2	123.7	126.4	127.3	124.5	119.8	117.4	116.3	119.0
1996	111.3	112.6	115.9	122.5	126.6	129.8	128.3	129.8	126.0	123.0	118.8	118.7	121.9
1997	114.1	115.9	121.7	126.4	129.3	133.5	130.9	131.5	129.3	125.5	123.4	121.4	125.2
1998	118.4	120.7	123.4	125.3	130.5	132.2	134.4	135.4	131.1	127.9	125.1	126.5	127.6
1999	117.7	120.3	121.9	130.4	135.2	138.1	137.1	136.7	133.4	130.0	127.9	128.0	129.7
2000	120.9	121.1	123.9	129.7	133.9	137.8	135.8	136.8	132.6	132.0	126.9	123.4	129.6
2001	118.5	119.7	122.9	129.2	133.7	136.4	136.9	135.8	131.2	131.0	126.6	125.3	128.9
2002	121.1	121.3	123.9	130.8	133.6	138.3	137.7	138.0	133.3	132.8	128.0	126.9	130.5
2003	120.6	121.0	123.1	130.9	134.0	137.3	138.8	137.1	134.5	132.5	129.8	129.0	130.7
Other services													
1990	45.5	48.0	47.4	43.0	42.3	41.8	45.4	42.6	44.5	42.4	40.2	42.4	43.7
1991	49.4	49.1	50.0	44.2	46.2	44.7	47.6	47.6	45.9	47.1	44.2	46.3	46.8
1992	49.3	55.4	54.9	55.5	52.4	51.6	55.0	54.1	55.5	52.0	50.2	50.8	53.0
1993	53.4	55.1	54.5	52.3	51.1	49.4	50.3	51.3	53.0	53.6	52.7	52.9	52.4
1994	65.2	67.7	69.0	56.3	54.9	55.5	53.2	54.1	56.2	57.4	57.7	57.6	58.7
1995	54.7	57.7	57.4	57.2	55.6	55.8	55.4	56.0	56.5	59.3	58.3	59.2	56.9
1996	57.3	59.7	58.9	60.1	60.9	56.3	57.1	56.6	57.7	61.3	61.0	62.2	59.1
1997	60.3	61.7	62.1	61.0	60.4	60.7	62.5	62.2	65.1	62.4	62.2	62.5	61.9
1998	56.4	58.2	57.3	59.8	59.5	59.5	58.6	59.2	62.2	60.3	63.5	57.9	59.4
1999	56.8	59.1	59.8	58.6	57.9	57.1	57.0	56.0	55.9	58.5	57.6	57.4	57.6
2000	51.9	53.0	52.6	52.4	50.2	50.7	56.0	55.6	53.9	56.2	58.1	60.5	54.3
2001	55.9	56.7	57.7	57.9	58.3	58.9	57.9	58.0	57.4	57.1	57.7	57.7	57.6
2002	56.1	57.0	57.5	57.7	57.6	57.8	57.8	57.6	57.1	56.6	56.6	56.7	57.2
2003	55.7	56.3	57.0	57.9	58.4	59.0	58.8	58.3	57.2	56.4	56.9	56.7	57.4
Government													
1990	143.7	146.7	148.1	150.8	150.7	143.6	135.6	132.4	145.5	148.2	151.0	148.2	145.3
1991	145.4	148.9	149.9	151.3	150.8	143.1	134.1	130.7	145.7	149.6	151.7	150.2	145.9
1992	146.1	149.4	150.6	152.5	151.2	141.6	132.8	131.0	145.4	151.1	154.9	152.6	146.6
1993	147.8	151.6	152.4	157.2	155.3	144.9	135.8	133.0	149.7	152.6	154.5	154.1	149.0
1994	149.4	153.5	154.5	159.2	154.6	147.4	138.6	137.1	150.7	154.7	157.2	156.7	151.1
1995	151.6	154.6	155.7	155.3	154.7	147.0	139.2	136.3	152.4	155.2	157.2	157.2	151.4
1996	152.1	156.3	158.8	159.7	159.1	151.7	142.4	140.3	156.4	158.3	166.6	159.7	155.1
1997	156.1	158.7	159.9	162.0	156.9	152.2	144.0	141.8	156.5	157.9	160.2	159.2	155.5
1998	156.8	160.4	161.1	158.4	158.6	149.4	140.5	139.3	156.4	159.0	160.2	160.6	155.1
1999	155.0	158.3	159.7	160.8	162.3	149.5	143.0	139.6	158.7	161.2	161.9	163.0	156.1
2000	158.0	161.3	162.9	162.9	166.3	157.8	146.2	142.9	160.7	161.2	162.8	163.3	158.9
2001	159.7	162.2	162.9	163.2	164.1	164.4	141.0	142.4	161.6	163.0	164.6	165.2	159.5
2002	162.4	163.6	164.1	164.3	165.8	163.0	140.1	143.5	161.8	164.3	165.5	165.2	160.3
2003	162.3	163.8	164.1	165.2	166.2	163.6	140.4	144.0	160.5	164.2	164.9	165.7	160.4
Federal government													
1990	37.1	37.1	37.2	37.6	39.2	37.7	38.0	37.2	36.6	36.4	36.3	36.1	37.2
1991	36.5	36.8	36.5	36.5	36.3	36.5	36.1	36.3	36.2	36.2	36.1	36.2	36.3
1992	36.3	36.2	36.3	36.5	36.5	36.6	36.0	35.8	35.7	35.8	35.4	35.5	36.0
1993	35.2	35.1	35.1	35.3	35.3	35.5	35.5	35.4	35.2	34.4	34.4	34.6	35.0
1994	34.4	34.3	34.3	34.3	34.4	34.4	34.0	34.0	34.1	33.7	33.7	33.9	34.1
1995	34.0	34.0	33.9	33.1	33.0	33.1	33.1	32.9	32.9	32.6	32.6	32.9	33.2
1996	33.2	33.2	33.1	33.3	33.2	33.3	32.6	32.6	32.9	32.2	32.3	32.8	32.9
1997	33.1	32.7	32.5	32.3	32.0	31.9	31.4	30.9	29.0	28.9	28.9	29.5	31.1
1998	29.5	29.5	29.3	27.6	27.4	27.5	27.4	27.4	27.4	27.5	27.5	28.1	28.0
1999	27.0	26.9	26.9	27.1	27.0	27.0	27.3	27.5	27.3	27.4	27.3	28.0	27.2
2000	27.5	27.5	27.7	28.1	30.6	31.2	29.0	29.2	26.8	26.6	26.8	27.2	28.2
2001	26.8	26.7	26.7	26.8	26.8	27.0	27.1	26.9	26.7	26.7	26.8	27.1	26.8
2002	26.8	26.7	26.7	26.6	26.6	26.8	26.8	26.7	26.5	27.3	27.2	27.6	26.9
2003	26.4	26.2	25.9	26.7	26.8	26.7	26.6	26.3	26.0	26.1	25.9	26.2	26.3
State government													
1990	20.0	20.2	20.3	20.0	20.1	20.0	19.8	19.4	19.9	20.1	19.9	19.8	19.9
1991	19.8	19.8	19.8	19.9	19.8	19.4	19.2	19.2	19.5	19.6	19.8	19.9	19.6
1992	19.5	19.8	19.6	19.5	19.4	19.3	19.1	19.1	19.2	19.5	19.7	19.8	19.4
1993	19.3	19.7	19.8	19.8	19.8	19.6	18.9	19.1	20.0	19.8	19.9	20.0	19.6
1994	19.6	20.0	20.1	20.1	19.6	19.2	19.3	19.0	19.7	20.0	20.1	19.7	19.7
1995	19.6	20.0	20.1	20.2	19.7	19.3	19.6	19.3	20.3	20.3	20.5	20.3	19.9
1996	19.9	20.4	20.5	20.6	20.1	20.1	19.9	19.8	20.7	20.8	20.9	20.7	20.4
1997	20.3	20.8	20.9	20.8	20.1	20.1	19.9	20.0	20.8	20.9	20.9	20.7	20.5
1998	20.7	21.0	21.0	21.0	20.5	19.9	20.2	20.7	21.0	20.7	20.9	21.0	20.7
1999	20.7	20.9	21.0	21.3	21.5	19.9	20.8	20.9	21.8	21.7	21.7	21.9	21.2
2000	21.1	21.2	21.1	21.4	21.4	20.6	20.9	20.9	21.6	21.4	21.5	21.5	21.2
2001	21.1	21.2	21.2	21.1	21.2	20.5	19.6	19.5	20.8	21.0	20.9	20.9	20.8
2002	20.4	20.4	20.3	20.2	20.3	19.9	18.2	18.3	19.5	20.1	20.2	20.2	19.8
2003	20.6	20.6	20.6	20.6	20.6	20.5	18.7	18.9	21.0	21.0	21.2	21.2	20.5

Employment by Industry: Missouri—*Continued*

(Numbers in thousands. Not seasonally adjusted.)

Industry	January	February	March	April	May	June	July	August	September	October	November	December	Annual Average
ST. LOUIS—*Continued*													
Local government													
1990	86.6	89.4	90.6	93.2	91.4	85.9	77.8	75.8	89.0	91.7	94.8	92.3	88.2
1991	89.1	92.3	93.6	94.9	94.7	87.2	78.8	75.2	90.0	93.8	95.8	94.1	89.9
1992	90.3	93.4	94.7	96.5	95.3	85.7	77.7	76.1	90.5	95.8	99.8	97.3	91.0
1993	93.3	96.8	97.5	102.1	100.2	89.8	81.4	78.5	94.5	98.4	100.2	99.5	94.3
1994	95.4	99.2	100.1	104.8	100.6	93.8	85.3	84.1	96.9	101.0	103.4	103.1	97.3
1995	98.0	100.6	101.7	102.0	102.0	94.6	86.5	84.1	99.2	102.3	104.1	104.0	98.3
1996	99.0	102.7	105.2	105.8	105.8	98.3	89.9	87.9	102.8	105.3	113.4	106.2	101.9
1997	102.7	105.2	106.5	108.9	104.8	100.2	92.7	90.9	106.7	108.1	110.4	109.0	103.8
1998	106.6	109.9	110.8	109.8	110.7	102.0	92.9	91.2	108.0	110.8	111.8	111.5	106.3
1999	107.3	110.5	111.8	112.4	113.8	102.6	94.9	91.2	109.6	112.1	112.9	113.1	107.7
2000	109.4	112.6	114.1	113.4	114.3	106.0	96.3	92.8	112.3	113.2	114.5	114.6	109.5
2001	111.8	114.3	115.0	115.3	116.1	116.9	94.3	96.0	114.1	115.3	116.9	117.2	111.9
2002	115.2	116.5	117.1	117.5	118.9	116.3	95.1	98.5	115.8	116.9	118.1	117.4	113.6
2003	115.3	117.0	117.6	117.9	118.8	116.4	95.1	98.8	113.5	117.1	117.8	118.3	112.8
SPRINGFIELD													
Total nonfarm													
1990	122.5	123.5	124.9	125.1	125.8	125.1	12[illegible].0	124.6	127.4	127.3	127.3	127.1	125.3
1991	122.7	124.2	125.7	125.8	126.8	127.5	125.2	125.8	129.0	129.8	130.2	130.8	126.9
1992	128.4	129.0	130.5	131.6	132.1	131.6	130.2	129.9	133.7	134.3	134.3	135.4	131.7
1993	131.8	133.2	134.9	137.2	138.3	137.0	136.2	136.0	140.7	141.2	142.7	143.7	137.7
1994	140.0	142.0	143.6	145.1	146.4	145.8	144.6	145.2	149.5	150.3	150.9	150.7	146.1
1995	145.0	148.2	150.6	150.9	151.2	150.3	150.1	150.3	153.4	154.6	155.6	155.9	151.3
1996	150.8	152.5	155.0	155.8	157.1	156.5	154.1	153.6	157.0	157.6	158.6	158.4	155.5
1997	153.4	155.7	155.9	160.3	161.2	161.1	157.9	159.1	162.1	164.6	166.0	166.4	160.3
1998	158.9	161.3	160.9	164.3	164.8	164.2	159.1	159.4	164.0	165.5	166.2	168.1	163.1
1999	162.5	165.2	165.6	168.6	168.7	167.9	162.9	163.3	169.0	170.5	171.4	173.1	167.4
2000	168.2	168.8	170.7	171.3	171.8	172.8	168.9	168.3	171.6	170.7	170.9	170.1	170.3
2001	165.4	166.9	167.9	169.1	169.2	168.7	166.5	165.4	168.0	168.1	168.7	168.9	167.7
2002	163.8	164.8	166.4	167.5	168.5	168.3	166.1	166.0	169.2	169.3	170.6	170.9	167.6
2003	166.5	168.4	169.8	171.6	171.8	171.8	169.4	169.4	171.8	172.2	172.4	171.8	170.6
Total private													
1990	106.7	107.0	108.2	108.4	108.8	109.7	109.2	110.8	111.3	110.6	110.4	110.1	109.2
1991	106.5	107.3	108.8	108.9	109.9	110.6	110.9	112.0	113.3	113.0	113.1	113.5	110.6
1992	111.4	111.8	113.2	114.1	114.7	115.1	115.3	115.6	116.6	116.8	116.6	117.6	114.9
1993	114.7	115.6	117.0	119.2	120.4	120.1	120.8	121.0	122.9	123.4	124.3	125.1	120.3
1994	122.3	123.6	125.3	126.6	128.0	128.4	129.0	130.1	131.6	131.8	131.6	131.9	128.3
1995	128.5	130.2	131.9	132.6	133.0	133.0	133.0	133.9	135.8	135.8	136.2	136.7	133.3
1996	132.7	133.3	135.5	136.2	137.4	137.7	137.4	137.1	138.2	138.0	138.6	138.4	136.7
1997	134.6	136.1	137.7	140.2	141.0	141.4	141.0	142.3	143.0	144.5	145.5	145.7	141.0
1998	140.0	140.8	142.2	143.7	144.2	143.6	144.1	144.2	144.3	144.5	144.8	146.3	143.6
1999	142.5	144.2	144.8	147.3	147.5	147.8	147.7	148.2	148.8	149.1	149.8	151.2	147.4
2000	147.4	148.1	148.9	149.6	149.4	150.1	149.0	149.6	149.1	148.5	148.5	148.0	148.9
2001	146.2	147.0	148.0	148.9	149.1	148.8	148.0	148.2	148.2	147.9	148.2	148.4	148.1
2002	143.8	144.8	146.4	146.9	147.8	148.2	147.2	147.6	148.9	148.5	149.5	149.8	147.5
2003	146.3	147.5	148.9	150.5	150.4	150.9	149.6	150.3	151.1	150.9	151.3	150.6	149.9
Goods-producing													
1990	25.7	25.7	25.7	25.7	25.7	26.3	26.4	26.8	26.8	26.3	26.0	25.7	26.0
1991	24.7	25.1	25.3	25.2	25.6	25.9	25.8	25.7	26.3	26.5	26.0	26.0	25.6
1992	25.5	25.4	25.2	25.6	25.3	25.3	25.1	24.8	25.6	25.5	25.1	25.4	25.3
1993	24.3	24.6	25.0	25.6	25.7	25.6	26.1	25.6	26.6	26.6	26.5	26.4	25.7
1994	25.1	25.2	25.6	26.8	27.2	27.5	27.8	28.2	28.5	28.2	28.2	28.2	27.2
1995	27.8	28.0	28.2	28.3	28.2	28.5	28.2	28.4	28.4	28.1	28.0	28.1	28.1
1996	27.4	27.7	28.3	28.5	28.9	29.3	29.3	29.1	29.5	29.1	29.1	28.6	28.7
1997	27.9	28.3	28.7	29.0	29.2	29.5	29.5	29.4	29.5	29.6	29.4	29.2	29.1
1998	28.4	28.7	28.8	29.4	29.6	29.6	30.0	29.7	29.5	29.1	29.0	28.9	29.2
1999	28.2	28.8	28.8	29.4	29.5	29.6	29.9	29.7	30.0	29.9	29.9	30.3	29.5
2000	29.8	29.7	29.7	29.6	29.6	29.8	29.9	30.0	29.8	29.4	29.1	28.5	29.6
2001	28.4	28.5	28.6	28.9	28.8	28.8	28.4	28.1	27.6	27.1	26.8	26.8	28.1
2002	26.2	26.0	26.3	26.4	26.4	26.6	26.4	26.5	26.5	26.3	26.3	26.2	26.3
2003	25.7	25.7	25.9	26.1	26.3	26.5	26.0	25.9	25.7	25.5	25.4	24.8	25.8
Construction and mining													
1990	4.5	4.4	4.5	4.5	4.5	4.7	4.8	5.1	4.9	4.8	4.7	4.4	4.6
1991	3.7	4.0	4.3	4.5	4.7	4.9	5.0	5.0	4.9	4.9	4.7	4.7	4.6
1992	4.6	4.6	4.7	5.0	4.9	5.0	5.1	5.2	5.1	5.2	5.0	5.0	4.9
1993	4.7	5.0	5.2	5.8	5.8	5.9	6.2	6.2	6.3	6.3	6.2	6.1	5.8
1994	5.7	5.8	6.1	6.5	6.7	6.8	6.9	7.0	7.1	6.9	6.8	6.8	6.5
1995	6.5	6.4	6.7	6.6	6.5	6.6	6.7	6.8	6.8	6.6	6.5	6.2	6.5
1996	5.8	5.9	6.1	6.4	6.7	6.9	6.9	7.0	6.8	6.6	6.5	6.4	6.5
1997	6.1	6.2	6.5	6.5	6.6	6.8	6.9	6.9	6.8	6.9	6.7	6.5	6.6
1998	6.4	6.5	6.5	6.9	7.1	7.2	7.5	7.4	7.3	7.2	7.2	7.2	7.0
1999	6.8	6.9	7.0	7.4	7.5	7.6	7.8	7.7	7.8	7.6	7.5	7.5	7.4
2000	7.2	7.1	7.2	7.2	7.2	7.4	7.5	7.6	7.6	7.3	7.2	7.0	7.3
2001	7.1	7.4	7.7	8.1	8.2	8.4	8.2	8.2	8.0	7.9	7.8	7.9	7.9
2002	7.3	7.3	7.5	7.8	7.9	8.2	8.3	8.4	8.3	8.1	8.1	8.0	7.9
2003	7.7	7.7	7.8	8.2	8.4	8.6	8.4	8.4	8.3	8.1	8.0	7.8	8.1

Employment by Industry: Missouri—*Continued*

(Numbers in thousands. Not seasonally adjusted.)

Industry	January	February	March	April	May	June	July	August	September	October	November	December	Annual Average
SPRINGFIELD—*Continued*													
Manufacturing													
1990	21.2	21.3	21.2	21.2	21.2	21.6	21.6	21.7	21.9	21.5	21.3	21.3	21.4
1991	21.0	21.1	21.0	20.7	20.9	21.0	20.8	20.7	21.4	21.6	21.3	21.3	21.0
1992	20.9	20.8	20.5	20.6	20.4	20.3	20.0	19.6	20.5	20.3	20.1	20.4	20.3
1993	19.6	19.6	19.8	19.8	19.9	19.7	19.9	19.4	20.3	20.3	20.3	20.3	19.9
1994	19.4	19.4	19.5	20.3	20.5	20.7	20.9	21.2	21.4	21.3	21.4	21.4	20.6
1995	21.3	21.6	21.5	21.7	21.7	21.9	21.5	21.6	21.6	21.5	21.5	21.9	21.6
1996	21.6	21.8	22.2	22.1	22.2	22.4	22.4	22.1	22.7	22.5	22.6	22.2	22.2
1997	21.8	22.1	22.2	22.5	22.6	22.7	22.6	22.5	22.7	22.7	22.7	22.7	22.4
1998	22.0	22.2	22.3	22.5	22.5	22.4	22.5	22.3	22.2	21.9	21.8	21.7	22.2
1999	21.4	21.9	21.8	22.0	22.0	22.0	22.1	22.0	22.2	22.3	22.4	22.8	22.1
2000	22.6	22.6	22.5	22.4	22.4	22.4	22.4	22.4	22.2	22.1	21.9	21.5	22.3
2001	21.3	21.1	20.9	20.8	20.6	20.4	20.2	19.9	19.6	19.2	19.0	18.9	20.2
2002	18.9	18.7	18.8	18.6	18.5	18.4	18.1	18.1	18.2	18.2	18.2	18.2	18.4
2003	18.0	18.0	18.1	17.9	17.9	17.9	17.6	17.5	17.4	17.4	17.4	17.0	17.7
Service-providing													
1990	96.8	97.8	99.2	99.4	100.1	98.8	96.6	97.8	100.6	101.0	101.3	101.4	99.2
1991	98.0	99.1	100.4	100.6	101.2	101.6	99.4	100.1	102.7	103.3	104.2	104.8	101.2
1992	102.9	103.6	105.3	106.0	106.8	106.3	105.1	105.1	108.1	108.8	109.2	110.0	106.4
1993	107.5	108.6	109.9	111.6	112.6	111.4	110.1	110.4	114.1	114.6	116.2	117.3	112.0
1994	114.9	116.8	118.0	118.3	119.2	118.3	116.8	117.0	121.0	122.1	122.7	122.5	118.9
1995	117.2	120.2	122.4	122.6	123.0	121.8	121.9	121.9	125.0	126.5	127.6	127.8	123.1
1996	123.4	124.8	126.7	127.3	128.2	127.2	124.8	124.5	127.5	128.5	129.5	129.8	126.8
1997	125.5	127.4	127.2	131.3	132.0	131.6	128.4	129.7	132.6	135.0	136.6	137.2	131.2
1998	130.5	132.6	132.1	134.9	135.2	134.6	129.1	129.7	134.5	136.4	137.2	139.2	133.8
1999	134.3	136.4	136.8	139.2	139.2	138.3	133.0	133.6	139.0	140.6	141.5	142.8	137.9
2000	138.4	139.1	141.0	141.7	142.2	143.0	139.0	138.3	141.8	141.3	141.8	141.6	140.8
2001	137.0	138.4	139.3	140.2	140.4	139.9	138.1	137.3	140.4	141.0	141.9	142.1	139.7
2002	137.6	138.8	140.1	141.1	142.1	141.7	139.7	139.5	142.7	143.0	144.3	144.7	141.3
2003	140.8	142.7	143.9	145.5	145.5	145.3	143.4	143.5	146.1	146.7	147.0	147.0	144.8
Trade, transportation, and utilities													
1990	31.4	31.2	31.5	31.3	31.4	31.4	31.5	31.7	31.8	31.7	32.3	32.1	31.6
1991	31.2	30.8	31.3	31.7	31.9	31.9	32.0	32.1	32.4	32.5	33.1	33.2	32.0
1992	32.3	32.3	32.9	32.7	33.1	33.0	32.8	32.9	32.7	33.0	33.3	33.6	32.8
1993	32.9	33.0	33.2	33.5	34.1	33.8	34.2	34.3	34.7	35.4	36.2	36.7	34.3
1994	35.2	35.6	36.1	35.9	36.4	36.2	36.5	36.5	37.5	38.1	38.4	38.8	36.7
1995	36.8	37.5	38.2	38.3	38.5	38.0	38.2	38.3	39.2	39.8	40.4	40.6	38.6
1996	38.7	38.3	38.7	38.9	39.4	39.2	39.3	39.3	39.6	39.8	40.6	40.7	39.3
1997	38.8	38.8	39.0	39.4	39.5	39.4	39.4	39.7	40.1	40.2	41.1	41.5	39.7
1998	39.8	39.6	40.0	40.3	40.5	40.2	40.2	40.3	40.4	40.7	41.6	42.5	40.5
1999	40.5	40.7	41.2	41.3	41.3	41.4	41.0	41.3	41.6	42.2	43.2	44.1	41.7
2000	42.2	42.1	42.3	41.9	42.0	41.9	41.5	41.7	41.7	41.5	42.3	42.7	42.0
2001	41.1	40.9	41.2	40.9	41.0	40.9	40.7	41.2	41.3	41.2	42.1	42.3	41.2
2002	40.6	40.7	41.1	40.7	41.1	41.2	41.0	41.2	41.3	41.5	42.1	42.4	41.2
2003	40.5	40.5	40.7	41.4	41.5	41.4	41.1	41.4	41.6	41.8	42.5	42.8	41.4
Wholesale trade													
1990	7.7	7.7	7.8	7.6	7.6	7.6	7.8	7.9	8.0	7.9	7.9	7.8	7.7
1991	7.8	7.7	7.9	8.0	8.0	8.0	8.2	8.2	8.2	8.2	8.2	8.3	8.0
1992	8.6	8.6	9.1	8.8	8.8	8.9	8.9	8.8	8.7	8.9	8.9	9.0	8.8
1993	8.6	8.7	8.6	8.5	8.5	8.5	8.6	8.8	8.7	8.8	8.8	8.8	8.6
1994	8.8	8.9	9.0	8.8	8.8	8.9	8.9	8.9	9.1	9.0	9.0	9.1	8.9
1995	8.9	9.1	9.2	9.3	9.4	9.3	9.3	9.2	9.5	9.5	9.5	9.5	9.3
1996	9.5	9.5	9.5	9.5	9.5	9.5	9.5	9.5	9.5	9.5	9.5	9.5	9.5
1997	9.5	9.6	9.5	9.8	9.7	9.7	9.7	9.7	9.7	9.8	9.7	9.7	9.6
1998	9.6	9.7	9.7	9.7	9.8	9.7	9.7	9.7	9.8	9.8	9.8	9.8	9.7
1999	9.7	9.6	9.7	9.6	9.6	9.6	9.5	9.5	9.5	9.6	9.7	9.8	9.6
2000	9.9	9.9	9.9	9.5	9.4	9.2	9.2	9.1	9.0	8.8	8.8	8.8	9.3
2001	8.8	8.8	8.8	8.8	8.7	8.7	8.8	8.8	8.8	8.8	8.8	8.8	8.8
2002	8.8	8.9	9.1	8.8	8.8	8.8	8.9	8.8	8.8	8.8	8.8	8.8	8.8
2003	8.8	8.8	8.8	9.0	9.0	9.1	9.1	9.0	9.1	9.1	9.1	9.2	9.0
Retail trade													
1990	15.7	15.4	15.6	15.8	15.9	16.0	15.9	15.9	15.9	16.0	16.3	16.3	15.8
1991	15.6	15.4	15.5	15.8	16.1	16.1	16.1	16.1	16.3	16.5	16.9	17.0	16.1
1992	16.0	16.0	16.2	16.4	16.9	16.8	16.7	16.9	17.0	17.2	17.5	17.8	16.7
1993	17.8	17.7	17.8	18.1	18.7	18.6	18.8	18.8	19.0	19.5	20.3	20.6	18.8
1994	19.6	19.7	20.0	20.1	20.5	20.3	20.4	20.5	21.1	21.8	22.0	22.2	20.6
1995	20.6	20.9	21.3	21.3	21.5	21.2	21.3	21.4	21.8	22.3	22.8	23.0	21.6
1996	21.5	21.1	21.3	21.5	21.9	21.7	21.8	21.7	21.9	22.3	23.0	23.3	21.9
1997	21.3	21.2	21.4	21.5	21.7	21.6	21.7	21.9	22.2	22.1	23.0	23.3	21.9
1998	21.9	21.7	21.8	22.0	22.1	22.0	22.1	22.1	22.1	22.3	23.1	23.9	22.3
1999	22.3	22.4	22.7	22.8	22.8	23.0	22.7	22.8	23.0	23.3	24.0	24.6	23.0
2000	22.9	22.8	22.8	22.9	23.0	22.8	22.5	22.7	22.8	22.9	23.6	23.9	23.0
2001	22.9	22.7	22.9	22.7	22.8	22.7	22.4	22.7	22.8	22.8	23.6	23.7	22.9
2002	22.5	22.4	22.6	22.5	22.7	22.7	22.6	22.9	23.1	23.2	23.8	24.0	22.9
2003	22.5	22.2	22.4	22.8	22.9	22.8	22.5	22.8	22.9	23.1	23.7	23.9	22.9

Employment by Industry: Missouri—*Continued*

(Numbers in thousands. Not seasonally adjusted.)

Industry	January	February	March	April	May	June	July	August	September	October	November	December	Annual Average
SPRINGFIELD—*Continued*													
Transportation and utilities													
1990	8.0	8.1	8.1	7.9	7.9	7.8	7.8	7.9	7.9	7.8	8.1	8.0	7.9
1991	7.8	7.7	7.9	7.9	7.8	7.8	7.7	7.8	7.9	7.8	8.0	7.9	7.8
1992	7.7	7.7	7.6	7.5	7.4	7.3	7.2	7.2	7.0	6.9	6.9	6.8	7.2
1993	6.5	6.6	6.8	6.9	6.9	6.7	6.8	6.7	7.0	7.1	7.1	7.3	6.8
1994	6.8	7.0	7.1	7.0	7.1	7.0	7.2	7.1	7.3	7.3	7.4	7.5	7.1
1995	7.3	7.5	7.7	7.7	7.6	7.5	7.6	7.7	7.9	8.0	8.1	8.1	7.7
1996	7.7	7.7	7.9	7.9	8.0	8.0	8.0	8.1	8.2	8.0	8.1	7.9	7.9
1997	8.0	8.0	8.1	8.1	8.1	8.1	8.0	8.1	8.2	8.3	8.4	8.5	8.1
1998	8.3	8.2	8.5	8.6	8.6	8.5	8.4	8.5	8.5	8.6	8.7	8.8	8.5
1999	8.5	8.7	8.8	8.9	8.9	8.8	8.8	9.0	9.1	9.3	9.5	9.7	9.0
2000	9.4	9.4	9.6	9.5	9.6	9.9	9.8	9.9	9.9	9.8	9.9	10.0	9.7
2001	9.4	9.4	9.5	9.4	9.5	9.5	9.5	9.7	9.7	9.6	9.7	9.8	9.6
2002	9.3	9.4	9.4	9.4	9.6	9.7	9.5	9.5	9.4	9.5	9.5	9.6	9.5
2003	9.2	9.5	9.5	9.6	9.6	9.5	9.5	9.6	9.6	9.6	9.7	9.7	9.6
Information													
1990	2.4	2.4	2.5	2.4	2.4	2.4	2.3	2.3	2.4	2.4	2.4	2.5	2.4
1991	2.5	2.5	2.5	2.4	2.4	2.4	2.4	2.4	2.4	2.5	2.5	2.5	2.4
1992	2.5	2.4	2.5	2.5	2.5	2.5	2.6	2.5	2.6	2.6	2.6	2.7	2.5
1993	2.5	2.6	2.6	2.6	2.6	2.6	2.7	2.7	2.8	2.7	2.7	2.8	2.6
1994	2.7	2.8	2.8	2.7	2.7	2.8	2.8	2.8	2.8	2.8	2.8	2.8	2.7
1995	2.8	2.8	2.9	2.9	2.9	2.9	2.9	2.9	2.9	2.9	2.9	3.0	2.8
1996	3.0	3.0	3.1	3.1	3.1	3.2	3.1	3.1	3.1	3.1	3.1	3.1	3.0
1997	3.0	3.1	3.0	3.1	3.1	3.2	3.2	3.2	3.2	3.2	3.3	3.3	3.1
1998	3.2	3.2	3.2	3.1	3.0	3.1	3.0	3.0	3.0	3.0	3.0	3.1	3.1
1999	3.0	3.0	3.0	3.0	3.0	3.0	2.9	3.0	3.0	3.0	3.1	3.1	3.0
2000	3.1	3.0	3.0	3.2	3.1	3.1	3.2	3.2	3.2	3.3	3.3	3.3	3.2
2001	3.5	3.5	3.5	3.5	3.5	3.5	3.6	3.6	3.6	3.7	3.7	3.7	3.6
2002	3.7	3.8	3.7	3.8	4.0	4.1	4.0	4.0	4.1	4.0	4.3	4.5	4.0
2003	4.5	4.8	4.8	4.7	4.6	4.7	4.6	4.6	4.9	4.9	4.9	4.9	4.7
Financial activities													
1990	6.1	6.2	6.2	6.2	6.2	6.2	6.3	6.3	6.4	6.3	6.3	6.4	6.2
1991	6.3	6.3	6.3	6.3	6.3	6.4	6.5	6.5	6.5	6.4	6.5	6.5	6.4
1992	6.4	6.4	6.5	6.7	6.7	6.8	6.9	6.9	6.9	6.8	6.8	6.8	6.7
1993	6.7	6.6	6.7	6.9	6.9	6.9	7.0	7.0	7.1	7.1	7.2	7.2	6.9
1994	7.3	7.3	7.3	7.3	7.3	7.3	7.3	7.4	7.4	7.3	7.3	7.4	7.3
1995	7.3	7.4	7.4	7.4	7.4	7.5	7.3	7.3	7.5	7.6	7.7	7.7	7.4
1996	7.6	7.6	7.7	7.8	7.8	7.8	7.9	7.9	7.9	8.1	8.1	8.2	7.8
1997	8.0	8.0	8.1	8.3	8.3	8.3	8.3	8.4	8.3	8.3	8.4	8.4	8.2
1998	8.7	8.8	9.0	8.8	8.8	8.8	8.9	8.9	8.9	9.2	9.3	9.4	9.0
1999	9.8	9.8	9.7	9.9	10.0	10.0	9.8	9.9	9.9	9.9	9.9	9.9	9.9
2000	9.8	9.9	9.9	10.0	9.9	10.0	10.0	10.1	10.0	9.9	9.9	10.0	10.0
2001	9.9	9.9	9.9	9.7	9.8	9.8	10.1	10.1	10.0	10.0	10.0	10.1	9.9
2002	9.7	9.8	9.9	10.0	10.1	10.1	10.3	10.3	10.3	10.3	10.3	10.4	10.1
2003	10.3	10.3	10.4	10.6	10.6	10.6	10.5	10.5	10.5	10.5	10.3	10.4	10.5
Professional and business services													
1990	7.9	7.9	8.0	8.5	8.4	8.3	7.9	8.3	8.2	8.2	8.1	8.0	8.1
1991	8.0	8.1	8.3	8.2	8.2	8.5	8.6	8.7	8.9	8.7	8.7	8.7	8.4
1992	8.8	9.0	9.3	9.5	9.5	9.5	9.6	9.7	9.9	9.4	9.2	9.5	9.4
1993	10.5	10.6	10.8	11.0	11.1	11.0	10.9	11.0	11.1	11.0	10.9	11.1	10.9
1994	11.1	11.3	11.5	11.8	11.9	12.2	12.4	12.6	12.6	13.0	12.5	12.3	12.1
1995	12.4	12.6	12.6	12.7	12.8	12.6	12.6	12.8	12.9	12.4	12.6	12.7	12.6
1996	13.0	13.2	13.5	13.4	13.3	13.4	13.3	13.3	13.3	13.0	13.0	13.3	13.2
1997	13.6	14.0	14.3	14.6	14.7	14.8	14.8	15.4	15.3	16.2	16.2	16.3	15.0
1998	13.9	14.1	14.4	14.8	14.8	14.6	14.9	15.0	15.2	15.4	15.0	15.1	14.8
1999	14.9	15.2	15.3	16.0	15.8	15.8	16.0	16.0	16.0	15.9	15.6	15.4	15.7
2000	15.0	15.4	15.7	15.9	15.6	16.1	15.5	15.6	15.3	14.9	14.8	14.6	15.4
2001	13.8	14.1	14.1	14.6	14.2	14.2	13.8	13.9	13.7	13.5	13.4	13.4	13.9
2002	12.3	12.6	13.1	12.8	12.8	13.0	13.0	12.9	13.2	13.2	13.4	13.2	13.0
2003	13.0	13.1	13.4	13.5	13.6	13.7	13.7	13.9	13.9	13.9	14.1	14.1	13.7
Educational and health services													
1990	16.8	17.0	17.2	16.9	17.0	17.2	17.2	17.4	17.8	17.8	17.9	18.0	17.3
1991	17.7	18.0	18.3	18.2	18.4	18.4	18.4	18.9	19.1	19.2	19.3	19.6	18.6
1992	19.2	19.4	19.7	19.5	19.6	19.7	20.0	20.0	20.3	20.6	20.8	20.9	19.9
1993	20.2	20.3	20.5	20.6	20.6	20.6	20.5	20.6	20.8	21.0	21.1	21.1	20.6
1994	21.3	21.5	21.6	21.5	21.5	21.4	21.1	21.2	21.6	21.8	21.9	21.8	21.5
1995	21.6	21.9	22.0	21.9	22.0	21.9	21.7	21.9	22.3	22.6	22.6	22.7	22.0
1996	22.5	22.6	22.8	22.7	22.7	22.6	22.4	22.3	22.8	22.9	23.0	22.9	22.6
1997	22.9	23.0	23.1	23.7	23.7	23.7	23.4	23.6	24.0	24.2	24.4	24.5	23.6
1998	24.5	24.6	24.7	24.7	24.8	24.8	24.8	24.8	24.9	24.9	25.0	25.1	24.8
1999	25.1	25.2	25.2	25.3	25.4	25.4	25.5	25.5	25.6	25.8	25.9	26.1	25.5
2000	26.1	26.2	26.3	26.4	26.4	26.4	26.5	26.5	26.6	26.8	26.8	26.9	26.5
2001	27.3	27.5	27.6	27.6	27.7	27.5	27.3	27.2	27.9	28.6	28.6	28.7	27.8
2002	28.7	28.8	28.9	29.0	28.9	28.6	28.2	28.4	29.1	29.2	29.4	29.5	28.9
2003	29.2	29.8	29.8	29.8	29.2	29.1	29.1	29.2	29.7	29.9	30.0	30.0	29.6

Employment by Industry: Missouri—*Continued*

(Numbers in thousands. Not seasonally adjusted.)

Industry	January	February	March	April	May	June	July	August	September	October	November	December	Annual Average
SPRINGFIELD—*Continued*													
Leisure and hospitality													
1990	10.7	10.9	11.4	11.7	12.0	12.0	11.7	12.0	11.9	11.9	11.5	11.5	11.6
1991	10.3	10.5	10.8	10.9	11.1	11.1	11.1	11.5	11.7	11.2	11.0	11.0	11.0
1992	10.7	10.9	11.1	11.5	11.8	12.0	12.0	12.3	12.2	12.5	12.4	12.2	11.8
1993	11.3	11.5	11.7	12.4	12.8	13.0	13.0	13.1	13.2	13.0	12.9	12.9	12.5
1994	12.8	12.8	13.3	13.8	14.1	14.1	14.0	14.3	14.1	13.6	13.4	13.5	13.6
1995	13.0	13.2	13.7	14.1	14.3	14.6	15.1	15.2	15.6	15.4	15.1	14.8	14.5
1996	13.6	13.9	14.4	14.8	15.1	15.2	14.9	15.0	14.8	14.8	14.6	14.4	14.6
1997	13.2	13.6	14.2	14.7	15.1	15.1	14.9	15.2	15.1	15.3	15.3	15.0	14.7
1998	14.1	14.3	14.6	15.1	15.2	15.2	14.9	15.2	15.0	14.7	14.4	14.4	14.8
1999	13.7	14.1	14.2	14.9	15.0	15.1	15.2	15.3	15.3	15.0	14.8	14.8	14.8
2000	14.1	14.4	14.6	15.2	15.4	15.4	15.1	15.2	15.2	15.3	14.9	14.6	15.0
2001	14.1	14.4	14.8	15.3	15.6	15.7	15.8	15.9	15.8	15.6	15.4	15.2	15.3
2002	14.5	14.9	15.2	15.9	16.2	16.3	16.1	16.2	16.2	15.8	15.6	15.5	15.7
2003	14.9	15.0	15.5	16.2	16.4	16.7	16.5	16.7	16.7	16.3	16.0	15.7	16.1
Other services													
1990	5.7	5.7	5.7	5.7	5.7	5.9	5.9	6.0	6.0	6.0	5.9	5.9	5.8
1991	5.8	6.0	6.0	6.0	6.0	6.0	6.1	6.2	6.0	6.0	6.0	6.0	6.0
1992	6.0	6.0	6.0	6.1	6.2	6.3	6.3	6.5	6.4	6.4	6.4	6.5	6.2
1993	6.3	6.4	6.5	6.6	6.6	6.6	6.4	6.7	6.6	6.6	6.8	6.9	6.5
1994	6.8	7.1	7.1	6.8	6.9	6.9	7.1	7.1	7.1	7.0	7.1	7.1	7.0
1995	6.8	6.8	6.9	7.0	6.9	7.0	7.0	7.1	7.0	7.0	6.9	7.1	6.9
1996	6.9	7.0	7.0	7.0	7.1	7.0	7.2	7.1	7.2	7.2	7.1	7.2	7.0
1997	7.2	7.3	7.3	7.4	7.4	7.4	7.5	7.4	7.5	7.5	7.4	7.5	7.4
1998	7.4	7.5	7.5	7.5	7.5	7.3	7.4	7.3	7.4	7.5	7.5	7.8	7.5
1999	7.3	7.4	7.4	7.5	7.5	7.5	7.4	7.5	7.4	7.4	7.4	7.5	7.4
2000	7.3	7.4	7.4	7.4	7.4	7.4	7.3	7.3	7.3	7.4	7.4	7.4	7.4
2001	8.1	8.2	8.3	8.4	8.5	8.4	8.3	8.2	8.3	8.2	8.2	8.2	8.3
2002	8.1	8.2	8.2	8.3	8.3	8.3	8.2	8.1	8.2	8.2	8.1	8.1	8.2
2003	8.2	8.3	8.4	8.2	8.2	8.2	8.1	8.1	8.1	8.1	8.1	7.9	8.2
Government													
1990	15.8	16.5	16.7	16.7	17.0	15.4	13.8	13.8	16.1	16.7	16.9	17.0	16.0
1991	16.2	16.9	16.9	16.9	16.9	16.9	14.3	13.8	15.7	16.8	17.1	17.3	16.3
1992	17.0	17.2	17.3	17.5	17.4	16.5	14.9	14.3	17.1	17.5	17.7	17.8	16.8
1993	17.1	17.6	17.9	18.0	17.9	16.9	15.4	15.0	17.8	17.8	18.4	18.6	17.3
1994	17.7	18.4	18.3	18.5	18.4	17.4	15.6	15.1	17.9	18.5	19.3	18.8	17.8
1995	16.5	18.0	18.7	18.3	18.2	17.3	17.1	16.4	17.6	18.8	19.4	19.2	17.9
1996	18.1	19.2	19.5	19.6	19.7	18.8	16.7	16.5	18.8	19.6	20.0	20.0	18.8
1997	18.8	19.6	18.2	20.1	20.2	19.7	16.9	16.8	19.1	20.1	20.5	20.7	19.2
1998	18.9	20.5	18.7	20.6	20.6	20.6	15.0	15.2	19.7	21.0	21.4	21.8	19.5
1999	20.0	21.0	20.8	21.3	21.2	20.1	15.2	15.1	20.2	21.4	21.6	21.9	20.0
2000	20.8	20.7	21.8	21.7	22.4	22.7	19.9	18.7	22.5	22.2	22.4	22.1	21.5
2001	19.2	19.9	19.9	20.2	20.1	19.9	18.5	17.2	19.8	20.2	20.5	20.5	19.7
2002	20.0	20.0	20.0	20.6	20.7	20.1	18.9	18.4	20.3	20.8	21.1	21.1	20.2
2003	20.2	20.9	20.9	21.1	21.4	20.9	19.8	19.1	20.7	21.3	21.1	21.2	20.7
Federal government													
1990	2.1	2.1	2.2	2.3	2.4	2.2	2.2	2.1	2.1	2.1	2.1	2.1	2.1
1991	2.2	2.2	2.2	2.2	2.2	2.2	2.2	2.2	2.2	2.2	2.2	2.3	2.2
1992	2.2	2.3	2.2	2.2	2.2	2.2	2.2	2.2	2.2	2.2	2.2	2.3	2.2
1993	2.2	2.2	2.2	2.2	2.2	2.2	2.3	2.3	2.3	2.3	2.3	2.4	2.2
1994	2.3	2.3	2.3	2.3	2.3	2.3	2.3	2.3	2.3	2.3	2.3	2.4	2.3
1995	2.3	2.3	2.3	2.3	2.3	2.3	2.4	2.4	2.4	2.4	2.4	2.5	2.3
1996	2.3	2.3	2.3	2.4	2.4	2.4	2.4	2.4	2.4	2.4	2.4	2.5	2.3
1997	2.4	2.3	2.3	2.3	2.3	2.3	2.3	2.4	2.4	2.4	2.4	2.5	2.3
1998	2.6	2.5	2.5	2.4	2.4	2.4	2.4	2.4	2.4	2.4	2.5	2.5	2.5
1999	2.4	2.4	2.4	2.4	2.4	2.4	2.4	2.4	2.4	2.4	2.4	2.6	2.4
2000	2.5	2.6	3.1	2.7	3.6	3.6	3.2	3.3	2.4	2.4	2.4	2.5	2.9
2001	2.4	2.4	2.4	2.4	2.4	2.4	2.4	2.4	2.4	2.4	2.4	2.5	2.4
2002	2.4	2.4	2.4	2.4	2.4	2.4	2.5	2.5	2.4	2.4	2.5	2.6	2.4
2003	2.4	2.4	2.4	2.5	2.5	2.5	2.5	2.4	2.4	2.5	2.5	2.5	2.5
State government													
1990	4.7	5.3	5.4	5.2	5.3	4.1	4.0	4.0	5.0	5.4	5.5	5.5	4.9
1991	4.9	5.4	5.4	5.3	5.3	5.4	4.1	4.1	4.7	5.4	5.6	5.7	5.1
1992	5.4	5.4	5.6	5.6	5.4	4.5	4.3	4.2	5.6	5.7	5.8	5.8	5.2
1993	5.2	5.7	5.9	5.9	5.8	4.8	4.5	4.5	5.7	5.4	6.0	6.0	5.4
1994	5.4	5.9	5.7	5.9	5.8	4.8	4.4	4.4	5.6	5.9	6.0	6.0	5.4
1995	3.9	5.3	5.9	5.3	5.3	4.4	4.4	4.6	4.9	5.6	6.1	6.0	5.1
1996	5.1	6.0	6.1	6.1	6.2	5.2	4.8	4.8	5.3	5.9	6.1	6.2	5.6
1997	5.2	6.0	4.7	6.3	6.2	6.1	4.9	4.8	5.4	6.0	6.2	6.3	5.6
1998	5.3	6.1	4.6	6.2	6.3	6.3	5.0	5.1	5.6	6.5	6.7	6.9	5.9
1999	5.6	6.5	6.5	6.5	6.6	5.3	5.2	5.1	5.8	6.5	6.7	6.8	6.1
2000	5.8	5.6	6.0	5.9	5.9	6.0	6.1	5.9	6.8	6.9	6.9	6.6	6.2
2001	4.1	4.4	4.4	4.5	4.5	4.3	4.4	4.3	4.5	4.5	4.6	4.6	4.4
2002	4.2	4.4	4.4	4.5	4.5	4.2	4.3	4.2	4.5	4.6	4.6	4.6	4.4
2003	4.4	4.7	4.6	4.7	4.7	4.2	4.6	4.4	4.7	4.6	4.6	4.6	4.6

Employment by Industry: Missouri—*Continued*

(Numbers in thousands. Not seasonally adjusted.)

Industry	January	February	March	April	May	June	July	August	September	October	November	December	Annual Average
SPRINGFIELD—*Continued*													
Local government													
1990	9.0	9.1	9.1	9.2	9.3	9.1	7.6	7.7	9.0	9.2	9.3	9.4	8.9
1991	9.1	9.3	9.3	9.4	9.4	9.3	8.0	7.5	8.8	9.2	9.3	9.3	8.9
1992	9.4	9.5	9.5	9.7	9.8	9.8	8.4	7.9	9.3	9.6	9.7	9.7	9.3
1993	9.7	9.7	9.8	9.9	9.9	9.9	8.6	8.2	9.8	10.1	10.1	10.2	9.6
1994	10.0	10.2	10.3	10.3	10.3	10.3	8.9	8.4	10.0	10.3	11.0	10.4	10.0
1995	10.3	10.4	10.5	10.7	10.6	10.6	10.3	9.4	10.3	10.8	10.9	10.7	10.4
1996	10.7	10.9	11.1	11.1	11.1	11.2	9.5	9.3	11.1	11.3	11.5	11.3	10.8
1997	11.2	11.3	11.2	11.5	11.7	11.3	9.7	9.6	11.3	11.7	11.9	11.9	11.1
1998	11.0	11.9	11.6	12.0	11.9	11.9	7.6	7.7	11.7	12.1	12.2	12.4	11.2
1999	12.0	12.1	11.9	12.4	12.2	12.4	7.6	7.6	12.0	12.5	12.5	12.5	11.5
2000	12.5	12.5	12.7	13.1	12.9	13.1	10.6	9.5	13.3	12.9	13.1	13.0	12.4
2001	12.7	13.1	13.1	13.3	13.2	13.2	11.7	10.5	12.9	13.3	13.5	13.4	12.4
2002	13.4	13.2	13.2	13.7	13.8	13.5	12.1	11.7	13.4	13.8	14.0	13.9	12.8
2003	13.4	13.8	13.9	13.9	14.2	14.2	12.7	12.3	13.6	14.2	14.0	14.1	13.2

Average Weekly Hours by Industry: Missouri

(Not seasonally adjusted.)

Industry	January	February	March	April	May	June	July	August	September	October	November	December	Annual Average
STATEWIDE													
Goods-producing													
2001	39.0	38.2	38.6	37.9	39.4	39.6	38.1	39.8	40.5	39.0	38.9	39.1	39.0
2002	38.9	38.7	38.9	38.9	38.2	38.1	37.3	37.1	37.5	36.2	37.4	38.6	38.0
2003	38.5	39.1	39.7	38.3	38.6	39.4	39.5	40.1	39.2	39.4	38.9	38.4	39.1
Construction													
2001	36.2	33.3	35.2	35.0	36.4	37.8	36.2	37.6	38.0	35.2	34.0	34.1	35.8
2002	35.4	34.5	35.7	35.0	33.4	34.5	34.9	34.5	36.3	36.0	34.1	35.2	35.0
2003	34.2	34.0	36.6	36.8	37.1	37.3	38.6	38.6	36.1	36.1	34.8	33.7	36.2
Manufacturing													
2001	40.0	40.0	39.9	39.0	40.6	40.1	38.7	40.5	41.4	40.6	40.9	41.2	40.3
2002	40.3	40.3	40.1	40.5	40.3	39.6	38.3	38.2	37.9	36.2	39.0	40.2	39.3
2003	40.4	41.4	41.1	38.9	39.3	40.5	40.0	40.8	40.9	41.1	41.0	40.7	40.5
Trade, transportation, and utilities													
2001	33.2	33.4	33.8	33.9	33.6	34.4	34.8	34.1	34.2	35.9	36.0	36.8	34.5
2002	37.7	35.9	36.3	36.2	36.4	37.4	37.0	36.7	36.8	35.5	35.3	35.7	36.4
2003	34.0	34.9	34.6	34.6	34.4	35.1	34.9	34.8	35.2	34.8	34.6	34.7	34.7
Wholesale trade													
2001	39.8	40.6	40.6	40.7	40.2	39.9	40.0	40.4	40.7	39.5	40.4	40.8	40.3
2002	39.0	39.5	40.8	40.3	41.6	41.2	40.1	41.6	41.2	39.4	38.5	39.7	40.2
2003	37.9	39.3	39.1	39.4	38.4	39.5	39.6	40.4	40.0	40.0	41.7	40.0	39.6
Retail trade													
2001	29.7	29.2	29.8	29.8	30.0	30.6	30.9	30.1	30.3	34.1	33.7	35.0	31.1
2002	37.2	33.6	34.5	34.5	34.2	35.6	35.5	34.3	34.2	32.8	32.7	33.2	34.3
2003	31.1	31.8	31.7	31.6	32.0	32.7	32.8	32.8	32.7	32.3	31.6	32.4	32.1
Transportation and utilities													
2001	36.5	38.0	38.4	38.7	36.9	39.8	40.7	38.7	38.4	37.2	38.3	38.2	38.3
2002	37.8	38.8	36.7	36.7	37.4	38.7	38.0	38.4	39.8	39.3	40.0	39.6	38.4
2003	38.3	39.6	38.7	38.4	37.5	38.0	36.4	35.3	37.9	37.0	37.1	36.8	37.6
Financial activities													
2001	36.8	35.8	35.5	38.4	35.6	35.9	38.2	36.9	36.3	37.0	36.3	37.6	36.7
2002	38.8	37.2	36.8	37.7	36.1	37.9	37.4	37.7	37.8	37.2	37.4	37.8	37.5
2003	37.1	38.1	38.2	37.0	37.0	38.6	37.5	36.7	36.4	36.2	36.5	35.6	37.1
KANSAS CITY													
Goods-producing													
2001	38.3	39.5	39.5	39.6	40.5	41.5	38.8	42.9	42.8	41.5	41.8	41.7	40.7
2002	41.8	40.1	40.6	40.2	39.3	39.3	38.0	37.5	39.2	40.3	41.3	41.5	39.9
2003	40.4	40.8	40.6	42.2	41.3	41.5	41.9	43.1	40.8	41.5	40.9	36.9	41.0
Construction and mining													
2001	37.2	36.1	36.3	36.2	36.5	38.9	36.9	41.3	40.0	38.5	40.5	37.2	38.0
2002	38.0	35.0	36.7	35.3	33.3	35.3	33.8	31.4	37.2	37.2	37.9	38.3	35.7
2003	36.9	37.6	38.6	40.8	40.2	41.3	42.9	43.7	39.5	38.1	38.2	30.2	39.1
Manufacturing													
2001	39.0	41.4	41.4	41.7	43.0	43.1	40.1	44.0	44.6	43.4	42.6	44.4	42.4
2002	44.1	43.0	42.8	43.2	42.9	41.9	41.0	41.6	40.5	42.3	43.5	43.5	42.6
2003	42.5	42.7	41.8	43.2	42.0	41.6	41.2	42.7	41.7	43.7	42.8	41.2	42.2
Trade, transportation, and utilities													
2001	30.9	32.0	32.0	32.8	32.8	33.8	33.5	33.7	34.1	33.4	32.0	33.6	32.9
2002	31.7	32.2	32.9	33.0	32.9	33.9	33.6	33.3	33.5	33.9	33.8	34.0	33.2
2003	32.3	33.9	33.3	33.4	32.8	33.6	33.1	33.8	33.4	33.6	33.8	34.2	33.4
Wholesale trade													
2001	39.3	39.4	39.0	39.1	39.0	38.7	38.7	38.5	38.4	37.0	37.8	39.6	38.7
2002	39.3	40.2	41.2	41.4	41.4	40.2	39.8	41.6	41.1	40.2	38.9	39.5	40.4
2003	38.8	38.5	38.9	38.8	38.2	39.1	39.6	40.2	39.9	41.4	41.8	40.6	39.6
Retail trade													
2001	27.0	26.8	27.3	28.3	28.7	29.1	29.0	28.6	29.1	28.5	27.7	29.1	28.3
2002	27.7	28.3	28.5	28.4	27.6	29.5	29.2	29.0	28.6	29.3	29.6	29.9	28.8
2003	28.4	30.5	29.8	29.6	30.6	31.5	31.0	31.1	30.9	30.6	30.3	30.3	30.4
Transportation and utilities													
2001	33.2	38.3	37.4	38.3	37.4	41.4	40.4	42.0	42.6	42.4	38.1	40.7	39.4
2002	35.1	35.1	36.7	37.1	38.9	39.5	39.2	36.5	39.3	40.1	40.5	40.0	38.1
2003	36.2	38.5	37.2	38.5	33.7	34.3	32.7	35.6	34.6	34.8	36.0	38.6	35.9
Financial activities													
2001	34.3	33.9	33.3	35.7	34.0	34.8	36.0	34.9	36.5	33.7	34.1	35.6	34.7
2002	34.3	34.5	35.1	33.8	34.7	37.3	35.5	35.7	34.5	35.9	34.9	34.9	35.1
2003	33.2	33.1	32.8	32.1	32.2	33.2	33.2	33.6	33.2	33.5	33.9	34.0	33.2

Average Weekly Hours by Industry: Missouri—*Continued*

(Not seasonally adjusted.)

Industry	January	February	March	April	May	June	July	August	September	October	November	December	Annual Average
ST. LOUIS													
Goods-producing													
2001	38.3	37.7	38.9	38.0	39.9	39.0	39.1	39.1	40.3	38.9	37.5	39.0	38.8
2002	39.6	38.6	38.9	39.3	39.0	38.0	38.4	39.2	39.2	38.9	37.2	39.2	38.8
2003	40.3	39.6	39.8	38.9	39.5	38.7	38.9	39.4	38.0	38.0	38.0	38.9	39.0
Construction and mining													
2001	36.1	32.7	35.1	34.4	36.9	36.4	36.3	36.1	37.8	33.9	30.2	34.8	35.1
2002	35.5	35.0	36.3	35.6	35.0	36.0	36.1	36.3	37.2	35.9	31.7	33.9	35.4
2003	35.0	32.4	35.1	35.4	35.3	34.0	36.0	36.1	33.7	33.4	31.7	34.1	34.4
Manufacturing													
2001	39.5	40.3	41.0	40.2	41.8	40.8	40.9	41.0	41.8	42.0	42.0	41.6	41.1
2002	42.0	40.7	40.4	41.4	41.3	39.2	39.9	40.9	40.3	40.7	40.4	42.2	40.8
2003	43.2	43.5	42.4	40.9	42.1	41.6	40.9	41.5	40.9	41.0	42.0	41.9	41.8
Trade, transportation, and utilities													
2001	31.0	31.3	31.1	31.7	31.5	31.6	32.3	31.6	31.5	31.2	31.4	32.2	31.5
2002	31.1	31.0	31.4	31.6	31.7	32.3	32.8	32.4	32.8	32.4	32.0	33.0	32.0
2003	31.7	33.4	33.3	33.2	33.0	33.7	33.5	34.3	33.9	34.0	34.0	33.5	33.5
Wholesale trade													
2001	36.7	37.6	37.3	38.3	37.1	37.0	37.3	37.1	39.2	36.8	37.9	38.0	37.5
2002	37.1	37.2	38.0	37.6	37.8	39.8	38.2	38.0	38.4	36.5	36.7	37.3	37.7
2003	35.5	38.2	37.5	36.5	36.6	37.8	35.9	37.5	37.3	37.3	38.8	36.0	37.1
Retail trade													
2001	27.5	27.6	27.5	27.9	28.2	28.7	29.1	28.2	27.4	28.2	28.1	29.2	28.1
2002	27.6	27.6	28.3	28.8	28.6	29.0	30.1	29.5	30.0	29.8	29.3	30.5	29.1
2003	29.3	30.5	30.5	30.8	30.7	31.1	32.2	32.4	31.8	31.8	30.8	31.5	31.1
Transportation and utilities													
2001	35.5	35.3	35.0	35.9	35.4	34.8	36.4	35.7	35.3	34.3	34.7	35.9	35.3
2002	35.2	34.5	33.5	33.4	34.5	34.0	35.4	35.6	35.5	35.7	35.6	36.5	34.9
2003	35.0	36.8	36.9	37.1	36.4	37.5	35.1	36.8	36.9	37.4	39.6	37.9	36.9
Financial activities													
2001	33.9	33.6	34.1	34.0	34.0	33.5	33.4	32.5	33.6	33.5	32.9	35.1	33.7
2002	34.7	33.3	33.3	34.3	35.3	34.7	34.4	34.0	34.7	34.5	33.1	33.7	34.2
2003	32.5	33.7	35.0	33.8	33.9	34.5	34.0	33.5	33.8	33.4	33.3	33.3	33.7
SPRINGFIELD													
Trade, transportation, and utilities													
2001	31.4	30.5	32.1	31.6	31.9	33.6	33.7	33.3	32.1	32.5	32.0	32.2	32.3
2002	31.4	30.4	31.8	31.5	31.5	32.2	32.5	32.1	32.1	31.9	32.3	32.7	31.9
2003	30.6	31.1	31.7	31.8	32.3	33.3	34.1	33.8	32.9	32.3	31.8	32.6	32.4
Retail trade													
2001	31.4	30.5	32.1	31.7	31.9	33.7	33.7	33.3	32.0	32.5	32.1	32.3	32.2
2002	31.4	30.4	31.8	31.5	31.5	32.2	32.5	32.1	32.1	31.9	32.3	32.7	31.9
2003	30.6	31.1	31.7	31.8	32.3	33.3	34.1	33.8	32.9	32.3	31.8	32.6	32.4

Average Hourly Earnings by Industry: Missouri

(Dollars, not seasonally adjusted.)

Industry	January	February	March	April	May	June	July	August	September	October	November	December	Annual Average
STATEWIDE													
Goods-producing													
2001	17.26	17.23	17.63	17.86	17.86	17.91	18.00	18.40	18.24	18.03	18.20	18.19	17.90
2002	18.15	17.96	18.14	18.63	18.33	18.68	18.35	18.12	18.20	18.64	19.36	19.51	18.50
2003	19.50	19.33	19.26	19.37	19.55	19.81	19.60	19.75	19.39	19.38	19.62	19.52	19.51
Construction													
2001	22.42	22.04	22.28	22.01	22.12	22.78	22.97	22.65	22.17	22.70	22.41	22.65	22.45
2002	22.18	22.21	22.26	22.86	22.06	22.84	23.15	23.01	23.14	22.94	22.66	22.95	22.70
2003	22.26	21.84	21.87	22.09	22.40	22.55	22.96	22.57	21.99	21.94	22.75	22.39	22.32
Manufacturing													
2001	15.44	15.68	15.97	16.23	16.14	15.72	15.69	16.53	16.56	16.14	16.61	16.56	16.11
2002	16.71	16.50	16.62	17.09	16.99	17.06	16.16	15.92	15.93	16.56	17.95	18.07	16.80
2003	18.48	18.40	18.14	18.00	18.09	18.39	17.69	18.27	18.14	18.19	18.25	18.38	18.21
Trade, transportation, and utilities													
2001	12.52	13.07	13.03	13.38	13.40	13.18	13.67	13.89	13.98	13.96	13.57	13.33	13.42
2002	13.98	14.86	15.29	14.96	15.02	14.62	14.80	14.76	14.64	14.69	14.57	13.89	14.67
2003	13.84	14.12	14.03	14.11	13.98	14.11	14.58	14.51	14.60	14.17	14.34	14.15	14.21
Wholesale trade													
2001	15.88	17.84	17.87	18.84	19.43	18.67	20.28	20.89	20.94	19.73	18.07	17.49	18.83
2002	17.59	17.66	18.24	18.55	18.47	16.34	18.06	17.89	17.94	18.45	18.42	17.73	17.94
2003	18.66	18.10	17.39	18.06	18.16	19.20	20.61	19.84	20.08	17.82	18.75	18.62	18.78
Retail trade													
2001	9.75	9.76	9.69	9.91	9.88	9.92	10.04	9.99	10.00	11.06	11.10	11.01	10.21
2002	12.20	13.70	14.24	13.52	13.50	13.69	13.31	13.26	13.06	12.87	12.85	11.81	13.16
2003	11.20	11.81	11.86	11.73	11.55	11.41	11.33	11.24	11.13	11.05	10.81	10.68	11.31
Transportation and utilities													
2001	15.19	15.00	15.05	14.97	14.68	14.63	14.80	14.69	15.15	15.11	15.08	15.09	14.95
2002	15.04	14.69	14.65	14.60	15.00	15.12	15.20	15.16	15.11	15.26	15.02	15.31	15.02
2003	15.16	15.36	15.76	15.78	15.84	15.69	16.63	17.57	17.83	18.49	18.96	19.01	16.81
Financial activities													
2001	13.00	13.94	13.24	12.77	13.32	13.05	12.76	12.45	12.75	12.82	13.20	13.29	13.04
2002	12.91	13.49	13.49	13.70	13.72	13.36	13.45	13.63	13.69	13.76	13.79	14.02	13.59
2003	13.56	13.62	13.54	13.97	14.16	13.86	14.07	14.07	14.42	14.37	14.43	14.45	14.04
KANSAS CITY													
Goods-producing													
2001	18.99	19.42	19.10	19.70	19.54	19.76	19.10	20.17	20.58	20.61	20.68	21.16	19.92
2002	20.30	20.06	20.23	20.89	20.61	20.63	20.32	20.65	20.96	20.97	20.79	21.00	20.62
2003	20.81	20.72	20.85	20.87	21.03	21.22	21.28	21.49	21.18	21.44	21.46	21.32	21.15
Construction and mining													
2001	21.75	22.23	21.46	21.44	21.25	21.46	21.60	21.90	22.38	22.05	22.14	23.37	21.92
2002	22.03	21.50	21.97	22.49	22.54	22.38	22.56	23.15	23.25	22.82	22.49	22.80	22.51
2003	22.51	22.29	22.82	22.69	23.02	23.23	23.37	23.15	22.93	23.39	23.44	23.34	23.03
Manufacturing													
2001	17.50	18.08	17.91	18.77	18.65	18.78	17.52	19.12	19.58	19.81	19.81	20.02	18.82
2002	19.42	19.42	19.36	20.10	19.69	19.67	18.97	19.37	19.59	19.92	19.83	20.00	19.62
2003	19.93	19.92	19.78	19.75	19.80	19.86	19.71	20.35	20.05	20.33	20.29	20.38	20.02
Trade, transportation and utilities													
2001	14.35	14.48	14.58	14.51	14.59	14.38	14.77	14.69	14.82	14.38	14.73	14.56	14.57
2002	14.89	14.96	14.98	14.84	14.72	14.49	14.49	14.62	14.70	14.54	14.43	14.44	14.67
2003	14.50	14.22	14.30	14.44	14.40	14.27	14.35	14.41	14.50	14.62	14.72	14.72	14.46
Whloesale trade													
2001	19.94	20.14	20.13	21.14	21.40	20.02	21.42	20.92	21.61	20.95	21.43	21.11	20.85
2002	21.22	20.88	20.67	20.67	20.32	21.21	20.71	20.35	20.29	20.43	20.33	20.33	20.62
2003	20.51	20.21	20.58	20.77	20.81	20.56	20.70	20.64	20.58	20.56	20.69	20.41	20.58
Retail trade													
2001	10.22	10.39	10.15	10.20	10.30	10.48	10.31	10.42	10.82	10.51	10.42	10.38	10.39
2002	10.54	10.79	11.15	10.72	10.67	10.68	10.51	10.65	10.87	10.58	10.72	10.78	10.72
2003	10.89	10.56	10.56	10.45	10.70	10.70	10.80	10.86	10.94	11.12	10.94	11.09	10.80
Transportation and utilities													
2001	16.95	16.39	17.37	16.30	16.48	16.53	17.04	16.75	16.15	15.80	17.04	17.02	16.64
2002	17.31	17.40	16.83	16.95	16.65	15.54	16.16	16.67	16.50	16.64	16.46	16.57	16.63
2003	15.66	16.19	16.12	16.76	16.71	16.50	16.41	16.56	16.95	16.74	16.92	16.82	16.52
Financial activities													
2001	15.01	15.15	14.47	14.37	14.22	14.38	14.30	14.58	14.70	14.64	14.55	14.77	14.59
2002	15.30	15.32	15.20	15.02	14.89	14.51	14.77	14.86	14.93	15.10	15.15	15.32	15.03
2003	15.18	15.66	15.74	15.69	15.74	15.88	15.86	15.63	15.71	15.46	15.43	15.47	15.62

Average Hourly Earnings by Industry: Missouri—*Continued*

(Dollars, not seasonally adjusted.)

Industry	January	February	March	April	May	June	July	August	September	October	November	December	Annual Average
ST. LOUIS													
Goods-producing													
2001	21.29	21.22	21.76	21.84	21.68	21.49	22.01	22.47	21.84	21.72	22.20	21.98	21.80
2002	21.84	21.92	21.92	22.29	22.04	22.77	22.24	22.75	22.67	22.42	22.57	22.37	22.32
2003	22.15	22.21	21.90	21.91	22.15	22.07	21.67	22.07	21.92	21.95	22.13	22.44	22.05
Construction and mining													
2001	24.59	24.11	24.56	24.20	23.93	24.87	25.19	25.08	23.64	25.26	25.08	24.90	24.62
2002	24.35	24.33	24.44	24.55	23.67	24.99	25.46	24.85	25.26	24.76	24.83	24.63	24.69
2003	24.60	24.89	24.94	24.75	25.82	25.45	25.06	25.44	25.22	25.23	25.83	26.03	25.28
Manufacturing													
2001	19.59	19.95	20.39	20.64	20.46	19.50	20.12	20.99	20.84	19.91	20.93	20.53	20.33
2002	20.62	20.77	20.63	21.17	21.22	21.52	20.28	21.61	21.24	21.19	21.54	21.32	21.10
2003	21.08	21.16	20.51	20.47	20.29	20.36	19.66	20.18	20.13	20.20	20.37	20.64	20.43
Trade, transportation, and utilities													
2001	13.25	13.92	13.99	14.55	14.49	14.62	15.16	15.41	15.72	15.48	15.15	14.81	14.72
2002	15.12	15.13	15.65	15.39	15.34	15.13	15.35	15.77	15.64	15.58	15.57	15.69	15.45
2003	16.73	16.95	16.78	16.83	16.92	17.27	17.23	17.14	17.43	16.56	16.52	16.28	16.89
Wholesale trade													
2001	17.54	20.15	20.82	22.20	22.51	22.50	24.21	25.27	25.35	24.94	23.07	22.97	22.67
2002	22.49	23.14	24.53	24.53	24.02	22.19	23.59	24.51	23.55	23.13	22.73	23.10	23.46
2003	24.16	23.21	22.38	23.38	23.31	24.71	24.29	23.30	23.91	20.87	21.61	22.00	23.10
Retail trade													
2001	10.32	10.41	10.34	10.55	10.77	10.97	11.09	10.87	11.14	11.16	11.49	11.11	10.86
2002	11.43	11.54	11.65	11.27	11.29	11.37	11.44	11.87	12.21	12.32	12.41	12.46	11.78
2003	13.51	14.21	14.28	13.98	14.13	14.18	14.20	14.18	14.25	13.78	13.34	13.01	13.92
Transportation and utilities													
2001	15.34	15.00	14.74	15.14	14.47	14.82	15.01	14.80	14.81	15.28	15.11	15.15	14.97
2002	15.72	14.54	15.00	15.05	15.43	16.02	16.03	16.14	15.89	16.05	16.33	16.80	15.76
2003	16.90	16.81	16.97	17.00	17.17	17.09	18.02	18.55	19.04	19.38	19.54	19.85	17.99
Financial activities													
2001	12.99	13.13	12.86	13.31	13.36	13.42	12.65	12.36	12.48	12.93	13.41	13.28	13.02
2002	13.26	13.44	13.31	14.60	13.02	13.02	13.17	13.24	13.20	12.80	13.07	13.44	13.29
2003	13.08	13.20	12.68	13.52	13.36	13.90	13.80	13.67	14.33	14.07	14.33	14.62	13.71
SPRINGFIELD													
Trade, transportation, and utilities													
2001	9.02	9.01	8.86	8.85	9.01	8.96	9.61	9.52	9.49	9.45	9.54	9.48	9.24
2002	9.47	9.51	9.90	9.57	9.61	9.64	9.51	9.33	9.31	9.27	9.31	9.23	9.47
2003	9.02	9.09	9.05	9.11	9.06	9.58	9.64	9.74	9.67	9.65	9.52	9.34	9.38
Retail trade													
2001	9.02	9.01	8.86	8.85	9.01	8.96	9.61	9.52	9.49	9.45	9.54	9.48	9.24
2002	9.47	9.51	9.90	9.57	9.61	9.64	9.51	9.33	9.31	9.27	9.31	9.23	9.47
2003	9.02	9.09	9.05	9.11	9.06	9.58	9.64	9.74	9.67	9.65	9.52	9.34	9.38

Average Weekly Earnings by Industry: Missouri

(Dollars, not seasonally adjusted.)

Industry	January	February	March	April	May	June	July	August	September	October	November	December	Annual Average
STATEWIDE													
Goods-producing													
2001	673.14	658.19	680.52	676.89	703.68	709.24	685.80	732.32	738.72	703.17	707.98	711.23	698.10
2002	706.04	695.05	705.65	724.71	700.21	711.71	684.46	672.25	682.50	674.77	724.06	753.09	703.00
2003	750.75	755.80	764.62	741.87	754.63	780.51	774.20	791.98	760.09	763.57	763.22	749.57	762.84
Construction													
2001	811.60	733.93	784.26	770.35	805.17	861.08	831.51	851.64	842.46	799.04	761.94	772.37	803.71
2002	785.17	766.25	794.68	800.10	736.80	787.98	807.94	793.85	839.98	825.84	772.71	807.84	794.50
2003	761.29	742.56	800.44	812.91	831.04	841.12	886.26	871.20	793.84	792.03	791.70	754.54	807.98
Manufacturing													
2001	617.60	627.20	637.20	632.97	655.28	630.37	607.20	669.47	685.58	655.28	679.35	682.27	649.23
2002	673.41	664.95	666.46	692.15	684.70	675.58	618.93	608.14	603.75	599.47	700.05	726.41	660.24
2003	746.59	761.76	745.55	700.20	710.94	744.80	707.60	745.42	741.93	747.61	748.25	748.07	737.51
Trade, transportation, and utilities													
2001	415.66	436.54	440.41	453.58	450.24	453.39	475.72	473.65	478.12	501.16	488.52	490.54	462.99
2002	527.05	533.47	555.03	541.55	546.73	546.79	547.60	541.69	538.75	521.50	514.32	495.87	533.99
2003	470.56	492.79	485.44	488.21	480.91	495.26	508.84	504.95	513.92	493.12	496.16	491.01	493.09
Wholesale trade													
2001	632.02	724.30	725.52	766.79	781.09	744.93	811.20	843.96	852.26	779.34	730.03	713.59	758.85
2002	686.01	697.57	744.19	747.57	768.35	673.21	724.21	744.22	739.13	726.93	709.17	703.88	721.19
2003	707.21	711.33	679.95	711.56	697.34	758.40	816.16	801.54	803.20	712.80	781.88	744.80	743.69
Retail trade													
2001	289.58	284.99	288.76	295.32	296.40	303.55	310.24	300.70	303.00	377.15	374.07	385.35	317.53
2002	453.84	460.32	491.28	466.44	461.70	487.36	472.51	454.82	446.65	422.14	420.20	392.09	451.39
2003	348.32	375.56	375.96	370.67	369.60	373.11	371.62	368.67	363.95	356.92	341.60	346.03	363.05
Transportation and utilities													
2001	554.44	570.00	577.92	579.34	541.69	582.27	602.36	568.50	581.76	562.09	577.56	576.44	572.59
2002	568.51	569.97	537.66	535.82	561.00	585.14	577.60	582.14	601.38	599.72	600.80	606.28	576.77
2003	580.63	608.26	609.91	605.95	594.00	596.22	605.33	620.22	675.76	684.13	703.42	699.57	632.06
Financial activities													
2001	478.40	499.05	470.02	490.37	474.19	468.50	487.43	459.41	462.83	474.34	479.16	499.70	478.57
2002	500.91	501.83	496.43	516.49	495.29	506.34	503.03	513.85	517.48	511.87	515.75	529.96	509.63
2003	503.08	518.92	517.23	516.89	523.92	535.00	527.63	516.37	524.89	520.19	526.70	514.42	520.88
KANSAS CITY													
Goods-producing													
2001	727.32	767.09	754.45	780.12	791.37	820.04	741.08	865.29	880.82	855.32	864.42	882.37	810.74
2002	848.54	804.41	821.34	839.78	809.97	810.76	772.16	774.38	821.63	845.09	858.63	871.50	822.74
2003	840.72	845.38	846.51	880.71	868.54	880.63	891.63	926.22	864.14	889.76	877.71	786.71	867.15
Construction and mining													
2001	809.10	802.50	779.00	776.13	775.63	834.79	797.04	904.47	895.20	848.93	896.67	869.36	832.96
2002	837.14	752.50	806.30	793.90	750.58	790.01	762.53	726.91	864.90	848.90	852.37	873.24	803.61
2003	830.62	838.10	880.85	925.75	925.40	959.40	1002.57	1011.66	905.74	891.16	895.41	704.87	900.47
Manufacturing													
2001	682.50	748.51	741.47	782.71	801.95	809.42	702.55	841.28	873.27	859.75	843.91	888.89	797.97
2002	856.42	835.06	828.61	868.32	844.70	824.17	777.77	805.79	793.40	842.62	862.61	870.00	835.81
2003	847.03	850.58	826.80	853.20	831.60	826.18	812.05	868.95	836.09	888.42	868.41	839.66	844.84
Trade, transportation and utilities													
2001	443.42	463.36	466.56	475.93	478.55	486.04	494.80	495.05	505.36	480.29	471.36	489.22	479.35
2002	472.01	481.71	492.84	489.72	484.29	491.21	486.86	486.85	492.45	492.91	487.73	490.96	487.04
2003	468.35	482.06	476.19	482.30	472.32	479.47	474.99	487.06	484.30	491.23	497.54	503.42	482.96
Whloesale trade													
2001	783.64	793.52	785.07	826.57	834.60	774.77	828.95	805.42	829.82	775.15	810.05	835.96	806.90
2002	833.95	839.38	851.60	855.74	841.25	852.64	824.26	846.56	833.92	821.29	790.84	803.04	833.05
2003	795.79	778.09	800.56	805.88	794.94	803.90	819.72	829.73	821.14	851.18	864.84	828.65	814.97
Retail trade													
2001	275.94	278.45	277.10	288.66	295.61	304.97	298.99	298.01	314.86	299.54	288.63	302.06	294.04
2002	291.96	305.36	317.78	304.45	294.49	315.06	306.89	308.85	310.88	309.99	317.31	322.32	308.74
2003	309.28	322.08	314.69	309.32	327.42	337.05	334.80	337.75	338.05	340.27	331.48	336.03	328.32
Transportation and utilities													
2001	562.74	627.74	649.64	624.29	616.35	684.34	688.42	703.50	687.99	669.92	649.22	692.71	655.62
2002	607.58	610.74	617.66	628.85	647.69	613.83	633.47	608.46	648.45	667.26	666.63	662.80	633.60
2003	566.89	623.32	599.66	645.26	563.13	565.95	536.61	589.54	586.47	582.55	609.12	649.25	593.07
Financial activities													
2001	514.84	513.59	481.85	513.01	483.48	500.42	514.80	508.84	536.55	493.37	496.16	525.81	506.27
2002	524.79	528.54	533.52	507.68	516.68	541.22	524.34	530.50	515.09	542.09	528.74	534.67	527.55
2003	503.98	518.35	516.27	503.65	506.83	527.22	526.55	525.17	521.57	517.91	523.08	525.98	518.58

Average Weekly Earnings by Industry: Missouri—*Continued*

(Dollars, not seasonally adjusted.)

Industry	January	February	March	April	May	June	July	August	September	October	November	December	Annual Average
ST. LOUIS													
Goods-producing													
2001	815.41	799.99	846.46	829.92	865.03	838.11	860.59	878.58	880.15	844.91	832.50	857.22	845.84
2002	864.86	846.11	852.69	876.00	859.56	865.26	854.02	891.80	888.66	872.14	839.60	876.90	866.02
2003	892.65	879.52	871.62	852.30	874.93	854.11	842.96	869.56	832.96	834.10	840.94	872.92	859.95
Construction and mining													
2001	887.70	788.40	862.06	832.48	883.02	905.27	914.40	905.39	893.59	856.31	757.42	866.52	864.16
2002	864.43	851.55	887.17	873.98	828.45	899.64	919.11	902.06	939.67	888.88	787.11	834.96	874.03
2003	861.00	806.44	875.39	876.15	911.45	865.30	902.16	918.38	849.91	842.68	818.81	887.62	869.63
Manufacturing													
2001	773.81	803.99	835.99	829.73	855.23	795.60	822.91	860.59	871.11	836.22	879.06	854.05	835.56
2002	866.04	845.34	833.45	876.44	876.39	843.58	809.17	883.85	855.97	862.43	870.22	899.70	860.88
2003	910.66	920.46	869.62	837.22	854.21	846.98	804.09	837.47	823.32	828.20	855.54	864.82	853.97
Trade, transportation, and utilities													
2001	410.75	435.70	435.09	461.24	456.44	461.99	489.67	486.96	495.18	482.98	475.71	476.88	463.68
2002	470.23	469.03	491.41	486.32	486.28	488.70	503.48	510.95	512.99	504.79	498.24	517.77	494.40
2003	530.34	566.13	558.77	558.76	558.36	582.00	577.21	587.90	590.88	563.04	561.68	545.38	565.82
Wholesale trade													
2001	643.72	757.64	776.59	850.26	835.12	832.50	903.03	937.52	993.72	917.79	874.35	872.86	850.13
2002	834.38	860.81	932.14	922.33	907.96	883.16	901.14	931.38	904.32	844.25	834.19	861.63	884.44
2003	857.68	886.62	839.25	853.37	853.15	934.04	872.01	873.75	891.84	778.45	838.47	792.00	857.01
Retail trade													
2001	283.80	287.32	284.35	294.35	303.71	314.84	322.72	306.53	305.24	314.71	322.87	324.41	305.17
2002	315.47	318.50	329.70	324.58	322.89	329.73	344.34	350.17	366.30	367.14	363.61	380.03	342.80
2003	395.84	433.41	435.54	430.58	433.79	441.00	457.24	459.43	453.15	438.20	410.87	409.82	432.91
Transportation and utilities													
2001	544.57	529.50	515.90	543.53	512.24	515.74	546.36	528.36	522.79	524.10	524.32	543.89	528.44
2002	553.34	501.63	502.50	502.67	532.34	544.68	567.46	574.58	564.10	572.99	581.35	613.20	550.02
2003	591.50	618.61	626.19	630.70	624.99	640.88	632.50	682.64	702.58	724.81	773.78	752.32	663.83
Financial activities													
2001	440.36	441.17	438.53	452.54	454.24	449.57	422.51	401.70	419.33	433.16	441.19	466.13	438.77
2002	460.12	447.55	443.22	500.78	459.61	451.79	453.05	450.16	458.04	441.60	432.62	452.93	454.52
2003	425.10	444.84	443.80	456.98	452.90	479.55	469.20	457.95	484.35	469.94	477.19	486.85	462.03
SPRINGFIELD													
Trade, transportation, and utilities													
2001	283.23	274.81	284.41	279.66	287.42	301.06	323.86	317.02	304.63	307.13	305.28	305.26	298.45
2002	297.36	289.10	314.82	301.46	302.72	310.41	309.08	299.49	298.85	295.71	300.71	301.82	302.09
2003	276.01	282.70	286.89	289.70	292.64	319.01	328.72	329.21	318.14	311.70	302.74	304.48	303.91
Retail trade													
2001	283.23	274.81	284.41	280.55	287.42	301.95	323.86	317.02	303.68	307.13	306.23	306.20	297.53
2002	297.36	289.10	314.82	301.46	302.72	310.41	309.08	299.49	298.85	295.71	300.71	301.82	302.09
2003	276.01	282.70	286.89	289.70	292.64	319.01	328.72	329.21	318.14	311.70	302.74	304.48	303.91

MONTANA AT A GLANCE

(Population and total nonfarm employment numbers in thousands)

Population, Census 2000:	902.2
Total nonfarm employment, 2003:	400.1
Change in total nonfarm employment	
(Number)	
1990–2003:	102.9
1990–2001:	94.5
2001–2003:	8.4
(Compound annual rate of change)	
1990–2003:	2.3%
1990–2001:	2.5%
2001–2003:	1.1%
Unemployment rate	
1990:	6.0%
2001:	4.5%
2003:	4.4%

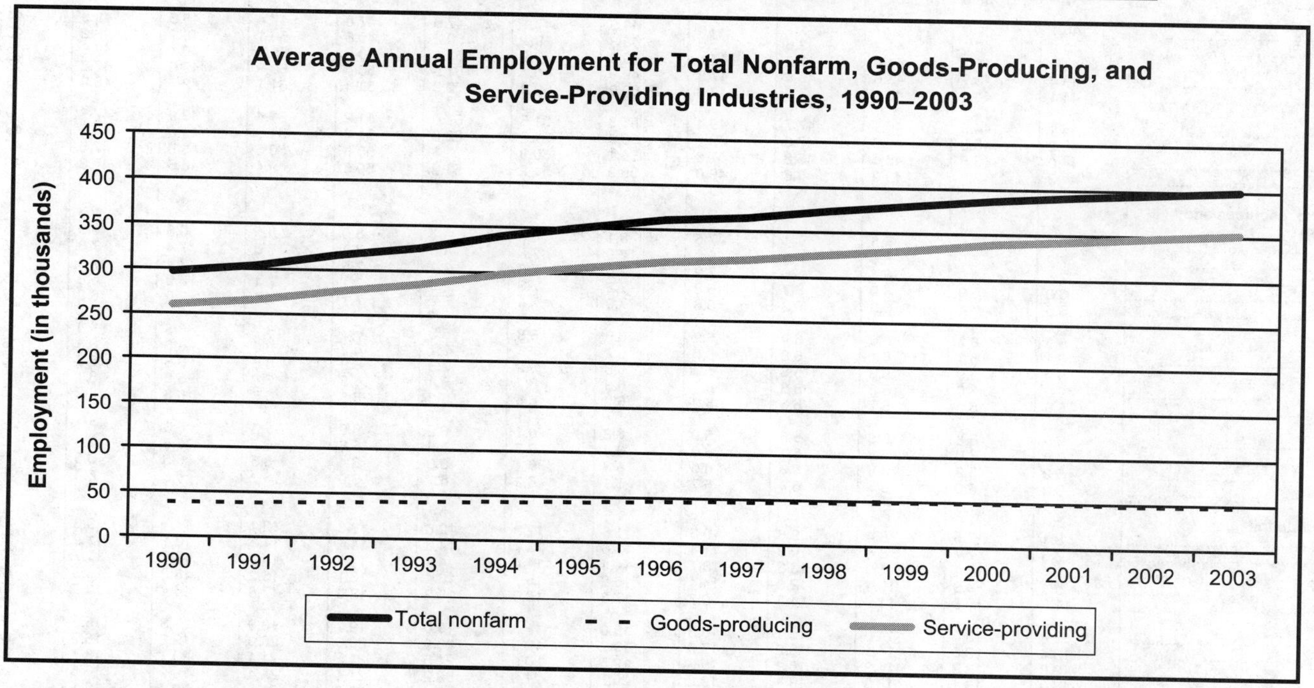

Unlike most states, Montana had a relatively smooth gain in employment over the 1990–2003 period, albeit with some bursts of growth and subsequent slowdowns. The goods-producing sector weakened in the 2001 recession, but rebounded in 2003 due to an increase in construction employment. Growth slowed in the service-providing sector beginning in 2001, as several service industries experienced employment losses or no growth. Educational and health services helped counteract this trend, as employment increased by 7 percent from 2001 to 2003.

Employment by Industry: Montana

(Numbers in thousands. Not seasonally adjusted.)

Industry	January	February	March	April	May	June	July	August	September	October	November	December	Annual Average
STATEWIDE													
Total nonfarm													
1990	283.9	284.1	288.5	294.2	299.9	306.0	298.3	301.1	304.3	305.1	302.1	299.6	297.2
1991	289.7	289.9	292.1	296.9	303.6	310.0	304.7	310.0	314.3	312.3	310.4	310.2	303.6
1992	301.8	302.8	306.7	313.1	319.4	325.3	318.6	321.7	324.9	322.6	322.4	319.8	316.5
1993	308.4	311.0	314.2	322.2	327.3	334.3	327.6	333.3	334.7	333.8	330.6	330.5	325.6
1994	321.1	322.4	326.0	334.1	341.0	346.4	343.6	350.4	354.3	349.5	347.7	345.7	340.1
1995	335.6	337.5	341.0	343.9	350.3	357.1	355.2	358.6	362.2	358.6	355.1	353.8	350.7
1996	343.7	346.2	349.6	355.8	362.7	366.8	364.0	368.1	370.3	368.5	365.7	362.5	360.3
1997	349.8	352.3	354.5	359.3	367.6	369.7	367.9	371.2	374.3	373.1	370.0	369.7	364.9
1998	357.1	359.7	362.3	368.0	374.8	377.9	377.4	380.2	382.8	381.1	378.4	377.4	373.0
1999	364.0	366.8	371.5	377.2	382.1	386.4	385.1	386.9	389.0	386.5	384.4	383.5	380.2
2000	373.0	374.8	381.9	383.7	392.5	395.0	391.9	394.4	396.0	391.2	389.6	386.4	387.5
2001	379.8	381.1	385.1	388.0	396.1	400.6	395.3	397.3	397.4	395.3	392.7	391.1	391.7
2002	381.7	383.3	385.6	390.7	398.9	404.7	400.4	402.0	404.1	401.5	399.7	399.7	396.0
2003	386.4	388.7	390.4	396.9	403.9	407.3	404.2	407.5	407.1	403.6	403.0	402.5	400.1
Total private													
1990	213.8	213.1	216.1	220.4	225.3	232.9	233.6	235.3	233.3	231.2	228.6	227.0	225.8
1991	217.8	217.2	218.9	223.0	229.1	237.7	241.3	244.6	242.3	237.7	235.5	236.7	231.8
1992	228.7	228.2	231.9	237.5	242.7	249.6	251.6	253.3	250.1	246.3	244.5	244.1	242.3
1993	234.7	235.9	238.7	246.2	251.2	260.0	261.3	264.3	260.9	256.8	253.8	254.4	251.5
1994	246.6	246.3	249.8	256.8	263.2	271.2	274.9	277.0	275.0	269.6	267.7	268.0	263.8
1995	259.0	259.6	262.6	264.9	271.1	281.2	284.7	287.3	284.9	279.0	275.9	275.9	273.8
1996	268.0	268.4	271.0	276.3	283.0	292.1	294.2	297.0	292.7	288.7	285.0	283.4	283.3
1997	272.2	273.2	275.2	279.7	287.8	296.0	298.0	300.3	296.4	292.5	289.4	289.9	287.5
1998	278.9	280.3	282.2	287.5	294.0	301.7	305.5	307.4	303.4	299.9	296.6	296.9	294.5
1999	285.9	287.7	290.5	295.6	300.6	310.0	312.5	314.5	309.8	305.0	302.5	302.8	301.4
2000	294.0	294.3	298.8	301.5	308.0	316.8	318.0	319.4	314.9	308.5	307.1	305.5	307.2
2001	295.7	295.8	299.1	302.3	308.6	316.5	317.3	319.0	313.5	309.5	307.3	306.2	307.6
2002	298.1	298.2	299.9	304.9	311.3	319.6	321.1	322.9	318.6	315.2	312.3	312.0	311.2
2003	303.3	303.0	304.4	309.0	315.0	322.7	324.1	326.3	320.7	315.9	314.8	315.0	314.5
Goods-producing													
1990	34.5	33.7	34.7	35.8	37.7	39.4	40.9	41.4	41.2	40.8	39.4	37.4	38.0
1991	33.7	33.4	32.7	34.7	37.2	39.6	41.0	42.0	41.9	41.5	40.2	39.0	38.0
1992	36.1	36.1	37.0	39.6	40.8	42.3	42.5	42.8	42.0	42.3	41.0	39.2	40.1
1993	35.6	36.2	37.0	39.5	41.4	43.7	43.9	44.8	44.2	44.6	42.5	40.2	41.1
1994	37.4	36.8	37.7	41.2	43.2	45.4	46.7	46.4	46.3	46.1	44.5	42.6	42.8
1995	39.7	39.7	40.7	41.7	43.5	46.3	47.1	47.6	47.8	47.4	45.5	43.5	44.2
1996	40.8	40.6	41.4	43.6	45.5	48.3	49.1	50.2	49.8	50.1	48.1	45.2	46.0
1997	41.1	41.1	41.4	43.6	47.2	49.0	50.2	51.1	50.6	50.4	49.1	47.5	46.8
1998	43.4	43.7	43.6	45.6	47.8	49.3	50.7	51.3	50.5	50.5	49.0	47.3	47.7
1999	44.1	44.1	45.0	47.9	48.9	50.9	52.2	52.3	51.4	51.1	49.7	48.2	48.8
2000	45.1	44.9	46.1	47.7	49.4	51.3	51.5	52.0	51.2	51.4	49.9	47.9	49.0
2001	45.3	45.0	45.6	47.0	49.1	50.9	51.8	52.3	51.4	51.0	49.3	47.5	48.9
2002	44.0	43.5	43.4	45.3	47.8	50.1	50.9	51.6	50.6	50.5	49.0	47.5	47.9
2003	44.3	43.7	43.9	46.6	49.0	50.9	51.2	51.2	50.6	49.4	48.5	47.3	48.1
Natural resources and mining													
1990	7.6	7.6	7.5	7.1	7.6	8.1	8.5	8.7	8.6	8.5	8.3	8.0	8.0
1991	7.2	7.0	6.6	6.5	6.8	7.5	7.8	8.0	7.8	7.6	7.4	7.3	7.2
1992	7.0	7.0	6.7	6.6	7.2	7.5	7.6	7.7	7.5	7.4	7.4	7.3	7.2
1993	6.9	6.9	6.9	6.7	6.8	7.2	7.3	7.3	7.1	7.1	6.9	6.8	6.9
1994	6.5	6.4	6.3	6.3	6.6	7.0	7.4	7.2	7.1	7.1	7.0	6.9	6.8
1995	6.5	6.3	6.0	6.0	6.2	6.6	6.8	6.8	6.7	6.7	6.5	6.4	6.4
1996	6.1	6.1	6.1	5.8	6.0	6.7	7.1	7.1	6.9	6.8	6.6	6.4	6.4
1997	5.9	5.9	5.8	5.8	6.3	6.8	6.9	7.0	6.8	6.5	6.3	6.2	6.3
1998	6.0	6.0	5.8	5.8	6.1	6.3	6.4	6.4	6.5	6.4	6.3	6.1	6.1
1999	5.8	5.8	5.7	5.6	5.9	6.2	6.6	6.6	6.5	6.5	6.3	6.2	6.1
2000	5.9	5.8	5.8	5.6	5.9	6.3	6.1	6.2	6.0	6.3	6.3	6.1	6.0
2001	6.0	6.0	5.8	5.7	6.0	6.4	6.5	6.5	6.5	6.7	6.5	6.3	6.2
2002	5.9	5.9	5.8	5.8	6.0	6.3	6.4	6.5	6.4	6.5	6.3	6.3	6.2
2003	6.0	5.9	5.7	5.4	5.7	6.1	6.2	6.1	6.0	6.2	6.3	6.3	6.0
Construction													
1990	8.1	7.6	8.4	9.6	10.8	11.6	12.3	12.6	12.8	12.1	11.1	9.6	10.5
1991	7.6	7.7	8.4	10.3	11.4	12.6	13.7	14.3	14.4	14.1	13.1	11.9	11.6
1992	10.1	10.1	11.0	13.3	13.7	14.4	14.4	14.7	14.0	14.3	13.1	11.7	12.9
1993	9.1	9.5	10.3	12.8	14.4	15.8	15.7	16.4	16.1	16.2	15.2	13.3	13.7
1994	11.2	10.8	11.9	14.3	15.7	17.0	18.0	18.2	18.0	17.6	16.4	14.7	15.3
1995	12.8	13.0	14.0	15.1	16.3	18.0	18.6	19.0	19.1	18.8	17.3	15.5	16.4
1996	13.4	13.5	14.1	16.2	17.6	19.2	19.6	20.4	20.5	20.9	19.2	16.7	17.6
1997	13.8	13.9	14.2	16.2	18.6	19.5	20.9	21.5	21.2	21.1	20.1	18.7	18.3
1998	16.0	16.1	16.3	18.4	19.8	20.7	21.8	22.2	21.4	21.4	19.9	18.6	19.3
1999	16.3	16.4	17.3	20.0	20.7	22.1	22.6	22.7	22.0	21.4	20.4	19.1	20.0
2000	17.0	16.9	18.0	19.9	21.1	22.4	22.7	23.0	22.3	22.2	20.7	19.4	20.4
2001	17.7	17.4	18.4	20.2	21.9	23.1	23.7	24.0	23.4	22.8	21.9	20.4	21.2
2002	18.2	18.0	18.1	19.9	21.9	23.5	24.1	24.5	24.0	23.7	22.7	21.5	21.7
2003	19.2	19.0	19.4	22.4	24.1	25.5	25.8	26.1	25.8	24.5	23.4	22.3	23.1

Employment by Industry: Montana—*Continued*

(Numbers in thousands. Not seasonally adjusted.)

Industry	January	February	March	April	May	June	July	August	September	October	November	December	Annual Average
STATEWIDE—*Continued*													
Manufacturing													
1990	18.8	18.5	18.8	19.1	19.3	19.7	20.1	20.1	19.8	20.2	20.0	19.8	19.5
1991	18.9	18.7	17.7	17.9	19.0	19.5	19.5	19.7	19.7	19.8	19.7	19.8	19.1
1992	19.0	19.0	19.3	19.7	19.9	20.4	20.5	20.4	20.5	20.6	20.5	20.2	20.0
1993	19.6	19.8	19.8	20.0	20.2	20.7	20.9	21.1	21.0	21.3	20.4	20.1	20.4
1994	19.7	19.6	19.5	20.6	20.9	21.4	21.3	21.0	21.2	21.4	21.1	21.0	20.7
1995	20.4	20.4	20.7	20.6	21.0	21.7	21.7	21.8	22.0	21.9	21.7	21.6	21.2
1996	21.3	21.0	21.2	21.6	21.9	22.4	22.4	22.7	22.4	22.4	22.3	22.1	21.9
1997	21.4	21.3	21.4	21.6	22.3	22.7	22.4	22.6	22.6	22.8	22.7	22.6	22.2
1998	21.4	21.6	21.5	21.4	21.9	22.3	22.5	22.7	22.6	22.7	22.8	22.6	22.1
1999	22.0	21.9	22.0	22.3	22.3	22.6	23.0	23.0	22.9	23.2	23.0	22.9	22.5
2000	22.2	22.2	22.3	22.2	22.4	22.6	22.7	22.8	22.9	22.9	22.9	22.4	22.5
2001	21.6	21.6	21.4	21.1	21.2	21.4	21.6	21.8	21.5	21.5	20.9	20.8	21.4
2002	19.9	19.6	19.5	19.6	19.9	20.3	20.4	20.6	20.2	20.3	20.0	19.7	20.0
2003	19.1	18.8	18.8	18.8	19.2	19.3	19.2	19.0	18.8	18.7	18.8	18.7	18.9
Service-providing													
1990	249.4	250.4	253.8	258.4	262.2	266.6	257.4	259.7	263.1	264.3	262.7	262.2	259.1
1991	256.0	256.5	259.4	262.2	266.4	270.4	263.7	268.0	272.4	270.8	270.2	271.2	265.6
1992	265.7	266.7	269.7	273.5	278.6	283.0	276.1	278.9	282.9	280.3	281.4	280.6	276.4
1993	272.8	274.8	277.2	282.7	285.9	290.6	283.7	288.5	290.5	289.2	288.1	290.3	284.5
1994	283.7	285.6	288.3	292.9	297.8	301.0	296.9	304.0	308.0	303.4	303.2	303.1	297.3
1995	295.9	297.8	300.3	302.2	306.8	310.8	308.1	311.0	314.4	311.2	309.6	310.3	306.5
1996	302.9	305.6	308.2	312.2	317.2	318.5	314.9	317.9	320.5	318.4	317.6	317.3	314.2
1997	308.7	311.2	313.1	315.7	320.4	320.7	317.7	320.1	323.7	322.7	320.9	322.2	318.0
1998	313.7	316.0	318.7	322.4	327.0	328.6	326.7	328.9	332.3	330.6	329.4	330.1	325.3
1999	319.9	322.7	326.5	329.3	333.2	335.5	332.9	334.6	337.6	335.4	334.7	335.3	331.4
2000	327.9	329.9	335.8	336.0	343.1	343.7	340.4	342.4	344.8	339.8	339.7	338.5	338.5
2001	334.5	336.1	339.5	341.0	347.0	349.7	343.5	345.0	346.0	344.3	343.4	343.6	342.8
2002	337.7	339.8	342.2	345.4	351.1	354.6	349.5	350.4	353.5	351.0	350.7	352.2	348.2
2003	342.1	345.0	346.5	350.3	354.9	356.4	353.0	356.3	356.5	354.2	354.5	355.2	352.1
Trade, transportation, and utilities													
1990	67.9	67.5	68.1	69.1	70.4	71.7	71.3	72.0	71.6	71.8	72.1	72.6	70.5
1991	69.4	68.8	69.3	70.0	71.1	72.4	72.9	73.9	73.7	73.0	73.7	74.7	71.9
1992	71.7	70.9	71.4	72.5	74.0	75.0	75.0	75.2	74.9	74.8	75.1	76.1	73.8
1993	73.1	72.8	73.2	75.6	76.4	77.8	77.5	77.6	77.4	77.4	77.9	79.1	76.3
1994	75.8	75.4	76.3	76.5	78.3	79.4	80.1	80.9	80.6	79.8	80.7	81.7	78.7
1995	78.7	77.7	78.2	79.6	81.3	83.1	83.3	84.1	82.9	82.6	82.6	83.3	81.4
1996	80.1	79.8	80.3	81.3	82.6	83.9	83.7	84.3	83.6	83.9	84.7	84.9	82.7
1997	81.7	81.3	81.4	81.7	82.6	83.7	84.7	84.6	84.4	84.2	85.2	86.1	83.4
1998	82.8	82.7	83.0	84.0	85.4	86.1	86.0	86.4	85.7	85.9	86.7	87.7	85.2
1999	83.6	83.5	83.9	85.3	85.8	87.1	86.8	87.2	86.8	86.5	87.1	87.6	85.9
2000	84.5	83.9	84.4	85.3	86.6	88.0	87.7	88.2	87.1	86.1	86.9	87.5	86.3
2001	83.9	83.0	83.5	84.6	85.9	86.5	86.2	86.3	85.2	85.0	85.6	85.9	85.1
2002	82.6	82.1	82.6	83.9	85.2	86.0	86.3	86.1	85.4	85.3	85.8	86.4	84.8
2003	82.5	81.8	82.2	82.9	84.4	85.3	85.1	85.6	85.1	84.9	85.8	86.5	84.3
Wholesale trade													
1990	12.9	12.9	13.1	13.3	13.5	13.6	13.5	13.6	13.5	13.8	13.7	13.6	13.4
1991	13.2	13.1	13.3	13.4	13.5	13.6	13.7	13.8	13.7	13.8	13.9	13.7	13.5
1992	13.4	13.3	13.5	13.7	13.8	13.9	13.9	13.9	13.8	13.9	13.9	13.8	13.7
1993	13.3	13.4	13.6	14.4	14.5	14.7	14.7	14.7	14.6	14.7	14.6	14.6	14.3
1994	14.2	14.3	14.5	14.7	14.9	14.9	15.1	15.2	15.1	14.6	14.7	14.7	14.7
1995	14.7	14.7	14.9	14.9	15.0	15.2	15.3	15.3	15.2	15.2	15.1	15.1	15.0
1996	14.7	14.8	14.9	15.1	15.4	15.4	15.3	15.3	15.1	15.2	15.2	15.2	15.1
1997	14.8	14.9	15.0	15.2	15.5	15.6	15.7	15.6	15.5	15.4	15.3	15.5	15.3
1998	15.2	15.3	15.5	15.8	16.0	15.9	15.8	15.8	15.6	15.8	15.8	15.8	15.6
1999	15.6	15.7	15.8	16.0	16.1	16.2	16.0	15.9	15.8	15.6	15.6	15.7	15.8
2000	15.5	15.5	15.6	15.9	16.0	16.1	15.9	15.8	15.7	15.4	15.3	15.4	15.6
2001	15.2	15.0	15.2	15.5	15.7	15.8	15.6	15.6	15.3	15.3	15.3	15.2	15.4
2002	14.9	14.8	14.9	15.3	15.5	15.6	15.7	15.6	15.4	15.4	15.4	15.5	15.3
2003	15.0	14.9	15.0	15.4	15.6	15.7	15.6	15.6	15.5	15.5	15.4	15.3	15.4
Retail trade													
1990	39.6	39.2	39.5	40.2	41.1	42.0	42.1	42.5	42.0	41.7	42.0	42.6	41.2
1991	40.4	39.9	40.3	40.8	41.7	42.8	43.4	44.1	43.6	43.0	43.7	44.5	42.3
1992	42.4	41.8	42.2	42.9	44.0	45.0	45.4	45.7	45.0	44.9	45.3	46.2	44.2
1993	44.0	43.5	43.7	45.1	45.8	46.8	47.1	47.3	46.7	46.3	46.9	48.0	45.9
1994	45.8	45.3	45.9	46.0	47.2	48.1	48.7	49.2	48.7	48.4	49.2	50.1	47.7
1995	47.5	46.8	47.0	48.4	49.6	51.1	51.5	52.0	50.5	50.4	50.5	51.1	49.7
1996	49.1	48.7	49.1	49.7	50.7	51.8	52.0	52.5	51.9	52.3	53.2	53.4	51.2
1997	50.7	50.1	50.1	50.1	50.4	51.3	52.7	52.9	52.2	52.3	53.2	53.7	51.6
1998	51.1	50.8	50.9	51.7	52.9	53.4	53.7	54.1	53.4	53.1	53.9	54.7	52.8
1999	51.5	51.2	51.4	52.4	52.9	54.0	54.3	54.6	54.0	53.8	54.3	54.9	53.2
2000	52.4	51.8	52.2	52.6	53.5	54.9	55.0	55.4	54.5	53.6	54.6	55.1	53.8
2001	52.6	51.9	52.0	52.6	53.5	54.2	54.6	54.8	53.9	53.5	54.3	54.6	53.5
2002	52.0	51.6	51.9	52.8	53.7	54.4	54.7	54.6	54.1	53.9	54.7	55.1	53.6
2003	52.2	51.7	52.0	52.3	53.4	54.1	54.3	54.6	54.1	54.0	54.9	55.4	53.6

Employment by Industry: Montana—*Continued*

(Numbers in thousands. Not seasonally adjusted.)

Industry	January	February	March	April	May	June	July	August	September	October	November	December	Annual Average
STATEWIDE—*Continued*													
Transportation and utilities													
1990	15.4	15.4	15.5	15.6	15.8	16.1	15.7	15.9	16.1	16.3	16.4	16.4	15.8
1991	15.8	15.8	15.7	15.8	15.9	16.0	15.8	16.0	16.4	16.2	16.1	16.5	16.0
1992	15.9	15.8	15.7	15.9	16.2	16.1	15.7	15.6	16.1	16.0	15.9	16.1	15.9
1993	15.8	15.9	15.9	16.1	16.1	16.3	15.7	15.6	16.1	16.4	16.4	16.5	16.0
1994	15.8	15.8	15.9	15.8	16.2	16.4	16.3	16.5	16.8	16.8	16.8	16.9	16.3
1995	16.5	16.2	16.3	16.3	16.7	16.8	16.5	16.8	17.2	17.0	17.0	17.1	16.7
1996	16.3	16.3	16.3	16.5	16.5	16.7	16.4	16.5	16.6	16.4	16.3	16.3	16.4
1997	16.2	16.3	16.3	16.4	16.7	16.8	16.3	16.1	16.7	16.5	16.7	16.9	16.4
1998	16.5	16.6	16.6	16.5	16.5	16.8	16.5	16.5	16.7	17.0	17.0	17.2	16.7
1999	16.5	16.6	16.7	16.9	16.8	16.9	16.5	16.7	17.0	17.1	17.2	17.0	16.8
2000	16.6	16.6	16.6	16.8	17.1	17.0	16.8	17.0	16.9	17.1	17.0	17.0	16.8
2001	16.1	16.1	16.3	16.5	16.7	16.5	16.0	15.9	16.0	16.2	16.0	16.1	16.2
2002	15.7	15.7	15.8	15.8	16.0	16.0	15.9	15.9	15.9	16.0	15.7	15.8	15.9
2003	15.3	15.2	15.2	15.2	15.4	15.5	15.2	15.4	15.5	15.4	15.5	15.8	15.4
Information													
1990	6.4	6.4	6.3	6.3	6.4	6.9	6.4	6.4	6.4	6.4	6.4	6.4	6.4
1991	6.4	6.1	6.2	6.4	6.9	7.3	7.3	7.1	6.8	6.5	6.5	6.8	6.6
1992	6.3	6.3	6.3	6.3	6.4	6.4	6.6	6.5	6.5	6.3	6.3	6.4	6.3
1993	6.2	6.1	6.1	6.3	6.4	6.5	6.6	6.6	6.4	6.2	6.2	6.3	6.3
1994	6.2	6.2	6.3	6.3	6.4	6.5	6.5	6.5	6.4	6.2	6.3	6.4	6.3
1995	6.3	6.3	6.4	6.4	6.5	6.7	6.8	6.8	6.6	6.6	6.7	6.7	6.5
1996	6.6	6.5	6.5	6.5	6.8	6.8	7.1	7.0	7.0	6.9	6.9	6.9	6.7
1997	6.7	6.8	6.8	7.1	7.3	7.4	7.4	7.5	7.2	7.4	7.3	7.2	7.1
1998	7.2	7.3	7.4	7.4	7.4	7.5	7.6	7.6	7.6	7.6	7.6	7.7	7.4
1999	7.6	7.7	7.6	7.7	7.8	7.9	7.9	8.0	7.9	8.0	8.0	8.0	7.8
2000	7.9	7.9	8.0	8.0	8.1	8.1	7.8	7.8	7.8	8.0	8.0	8.0	7.9
2001	7.9	8.0	7.9	7.8	7.9	8.0	7.9	8.0	7.8	7.9	8.0	7.8	7.9
2002	7.8	7.8	7.8	7.8	7.9	7.9	8.0	7.9	7.8	7.7	7.8	7.8	7.8
2003	7.7	7.8	7.7	7.5	7.6	7.6	7.6	7.7	7.6	7.4	7.4	7.5	7.6
Financial activities													
1990	13.5	13.5	13.7	13.8	13.8	14.0	14.0	14.0	14.0	13.7	13.9	14.0	13.8
1991	13.9	13.8	14.0	14.0	14.0	14.3	14.6	14.6	14.5	14.3	14.4	14.8	14.2
1992	14.5	14.3	14.5	14.4	14.5	14.7	14.9	14.9	14.9	14.7	14.7	15.1	14.6
1993	14.9	14.9	15.0	15.0	15.0	15.4	15.4	15.4	15.3	15.4	15.4	15.8	15.2
1994	15.7	15.7	15.8	16.0	16.0	16.3	16.2	16.3	16.1	16.1	16.1	16.1	16.0
1995	15.9	15.9	16.0	15.9	16.0	16.3	16.5	16.5	16.5	16.2	16.1	16.3	16.1
1996	16.2	16.2	16.3	16.3	16.5	16.9	16.9	17.0	16.8	16.7	16.6	16.9	16.6
1997	16.4	16.4	16.5	16.9	17.2	17.4	17.5	17.6	17.4	17.3	17.2	17.5	17.1
1998	17.1	17.2	17.3	17.5	17.6	17.9	18.0	18.1	17.8	17.9	17.8	18.1	17.6
1999	17.9	18.0	18.0	18.0	18.2	18.4	18.5	18.5	18.1	18.2	18.1	18.3	18.1
2000	18.1	18.2	18.3	18.5	18.7	19.0	19.0	19.0	18.7	18.4	18.4	18.6	18.5
2001	18.4	18.3	18.4	18.5	18.8	19.1	19.3	19.2	19.1	18.8	18.8	19.0	18.8
2002	18.8	18.9	19.0	19.2	19.4	19.6	19.3	19.3	19.1	19.6	19.6	19.9	19.3
2003	19.9	19.9	20.0	19.9	20.0	20.4	20.6	20.8	20.5	20.3	20.3	20.4	20.3
Professional and business services													
1990	14.6	14.6	14.9	15.4	15.6	16.2	16.1	16.1	15.8	15.9	15.8	15.9	15.5
1991	15.4	15.7	15.8	16.1	16.2	16.7	16.5	16.9	16.8	16.7	16.4	16.8	16.3
1992	16.8	16.9	17.3	18.3	17.9	18.3	18.3	18.4	18.1	17.8	17.6	18.1	17.8
1993	17.6	18.0	18.4	19.4	19.2	19.8	20.5	20.8	20.4	19.3	19.1	19.7	19.3
1994	19.5	19.8	20.1	20.9	20.9	21.7	21.9	22.2	22.1	22.2	21.6	22.3	21.2
1995	21.8	22.2	22.4	23.0	22.8	23.5	24.3	24.6	24.5	23.8	23.7	23.5	23.3
1996	23.3	23.9	24.1	24.9	25.4	26.3	26.5	26.8	26.2	26.0	25.3	25.3	25.3
1997	24.1	24.3	24.9	25.6	26.0	26.8	26.2	26.8	26.4	26.0	25.7	25.9	25.7
1998	24.6	25.1	25.4	26.0	26.6	27.1	27.8	28.0	27.7	28.0	27.2	27.3	26.7
1999	26.3	26.9	27.4	28.5	28.9	29.6	29.7	29.6	29.3	29.3	29.1	29.5	28.6
2000	28.6	29.1	29.9	30.2	30.7	31.7	31.9	31.9	31.6	31.6	31.8	31.3	30.8
2001	30.4	31.0	31.4	31.7	32.1	32.8	32.4	32.6	32.0	31.8	31.6	31.7	31.8
2002	31.3	31.6	31.7	31.9	32.0	32.8	33.0	33.4	33.3	32.9	32.3	31.7	32.3
2003	31.2	31.3	31.7	32.7	33.2	33.6	33.6	34.0	33.0	33.4	32.9	32.8	32.8
Educational and health services													
1990	34.3	34.5	34.7	35.1	35.1	35.0	34.2	34.4	35.2	35.6	35.7	35.9	34.9
1991	35.4	35.6	36.1	36.3	36.5	36.3	36.0	36.4	37.1	36.8	37.2	37.3	36.4
1992	37.2	37.3	37.7	38.1	38.3	38.2	38.0	38.2	38.9	39.2	39.5	39.3	38.3
1993	39.0	39.3	39.4	39.5	39.4	39.3	38.9	39.0	39.9	39.9	40.1	40.4	39.5
1994	40.1	40.5	40.7	41.3	41.4	41.0	41.0	41.1	42.0	41.8	42.3	42.6	41.3
1995	42.1	42.6	42.8	42.3	42.3	42.2	42.2	42.4	43.3	43.2	43.3	43.5	42.6
1996	43.5	43.8	44.0	44.2	44.2	44.0	43.3	43.3	44.2	44.5	44.6	44.9	44.0
1997	44.8	45.1	45.2	45.2	45.3	44.9	44.1	44.1	44.8	45.3	45.4	45.7	44.9
1998	45.3	45.8	45.8	46.1	46.1	46.2	45.5	45.6	46.4	46.9	47.0	47.3	46.1
1999	47.0	47.5	47.5	47.5	47.4	47.3	47.0	47.5	48.0	48.1	48.6	49.1	47.7
2000	48.6	49.0	49.2	48.9	49.2	48.9	48.2	48.6	49.2	49.1	49.5	49.6	49.0
2001	48.4	48.7	49.3	49.5	49.6	49.4	48.7	49.3	50.0	50.4	51.1	51.4	49.7
2002	51.4	51.6	51.9	52.2	52.4	51.9	50.6	50.9	51.8	52.8	53.3	53.3	52.0
2003	53.2	53.6	53.5	53.5	53.5	52.7	51.6	52.2	52.9	53.8	53.9	54.2	53.2

Employment by Industry: Montana—*Continued*

(Numbers in thousands. Not seasonally adjusted.)

Industry	January	February	March	April	May	June	July	August	September	October	November	December	Annual Average
STATEWIDE—*Continued*													
Leisure and hospitality													
1990	31.4	31.6	32.3	33.4	34.7	37.9	38.9	39.2	37.4	35.4	33.7	33.2	34.9
1991	32.5	32.6	33.6	34.1	35.6	39.4	41.1	42.0	39.9	37.2	35.4	35.6	36.5
1992	34.6	34.9	36.1	36.6	39.0	42.6	43.8	44.8	42.5	38.8	38.0	37.4	39.0
1993	36.3	36.4	37.4	38.4	40.8	44.7	45.5	47.1	44.6	41.4	40.0	40.1	41.0
1994	39.3	39.3	40.2	41.8	43.9	47.6	49.2	50.3	48.2	44.1	42.9	42.9	44.1
1995	41.3	41.9	42.7	43.0	45.6	49.9	51.1	51.9	49.8	45.8	44.6	45.5	46.0
1996	44.0	44.0	44.8	46.0	48.3	52.0	53.5	54.3	51.1	46.4	44.6	44.9	47.8
1997	43.4	44.1	44.8	45.5	48.0	52.5	53.6	54.4	51.2	47.4	45.0	45.4	47.9
1998	44.2	44.1	45.3	46.3	48.3	52.7	54.9	55.5	52.8	48.1	46.3	46.4	48.7
1999	44.8	45.2	46.2	45.7	48.4	53.4	55.0	56.1	53.0	48.5	46.6	46.8	49.1
2000	46.2	46.2	47.5	47.4	49.7	54.2	56.4	56.6	53.8	48.7	47.3	47.4	50.1
2001	45.9	46.2	47.1	47.1	48.9	53.3	54.9	55.3	51.9	48.7	47.0	46.9	49.4
2002	46.7	47.1	47.8	48.7	50.5	55.0	56.7	57.4	54.3	50.2	48.3	49.1	51.0
2003	48.6	49.0	49.4	49.8	51.2	56.1	58.3	58.8	54.9	50.8	50.0	50.0	52.2
Other services													
1990	11.2	11.3	11.4	11.5	11.6	11.8	11.8	11.8	11.7	11.6	11.6	11.6	11.5
1991	11.1	11.2	11.2	11.4	11.6	11.7	11.9	11.7	11.6	11.7	11.7	11.7	11.5
1992	11.5	11.5	11.6	11.7	11.8	12.1	12.5	12.5	12.3	12.4	12.3	12.5	12.0
1993	12.0	12.2	12.2	12.5	12.6	12.8	13.0	13.0	12.7	12.6	12.6	12.8	12.5
1994	12.6	12.6	12.7	12.8	13.1	13.3	13.3	13.3	13.3	13.3	13.3	13.4	13.0
1995	13.2	13.3	13.4	13.0	13.1	13.2	13.4	13.4	13.5	13.4	13.4	13.6	13.3
1996	13.5	13.6	13.6	13.5	13.7	13.9	14.1	14.1	14.0	14.2	14.2	14.4	13.9
1997	14.0	14.1	14.2	14.1	14.2	14.3	14.3	14.2	14.4	14.5	14.5	14.6	14.2
1998	14.3	14.4	14.4	14.6	14.8	14.9	15.0	14.9	14.9	15.0	15.0	15.1	14.7
1999	14.6	14.8	14.9	15.0	15.2	15.4	15.4	15.3	15.3	15.3	15.3	15.3	15.1
2000	15.0	15.1	15.4	15.5	15.6	15.6	15.5	15.3	15.5	15.2	15.3	15.2	15.3
2001	15.5	15.6	15.9	16.1	16.3	16.5	16.1	16.0	16.1	15.9	15.9	16.0	16.0
2002	15.5	15.6	15.7	15.9	16.1	16.3	16.3	16.3	16.3	16.2	16.2	16.3	16.1
2003	15.9	15.9	16.0	16.1	16.1	16.1	16.1	16.0	16.1	15.9	16.0	16.3	16.0
Government													
1990	70.1	71.0	72.4	73.8	74.6	73.1	64.7	65.8	71.0	73.9	73.5	72.6	71.3
1991	71.9	72.7	73.2	73.9	74.5	72.3	63.4	65.4	72.0	74.6	74.9	73.5	71.8
1992	73.1	74.6	74.8	75.6	76.7	75.7	67.0	68.4	74.8	76.3	77.9	75.7	74.2
1993	73.7	75.1	75.5	76.0	76.1	74.3	66.3	69.0	73.8	77.0	76.8	76.1	74.1
1994	74.5	76.1	76.2	77.3	77.8	75.2	68.7	73.4	79.3	79.9	80.0	77.7	76.3
1995	76.6	77.9	78.4	79.0	79.2	75.9	70.5	71.3	77.3	79.6	79.2	77.9	76.9
1996	75.7	77.8	78.6	79.5	79.7	74.7	69.8	71.1	77.6	79.8	80.7	79.1	77.0
1997	77.6	79.1	79.3	79.6	79.8	73.7	69.9	70.9	77.9	80.6	80.6	79.8	77.4
1998	78.2	79.4	80.1	80.5	80.8	76.2	71.9	72.8	79.4	81.2	81.8	80.5	78.5
1999	78.1	79.1	81.0	81.6	81.5	76.4	72.6	72.4	79.2	81.5	81.9	80.7	78.8
2000	79.0	80.5	83.1	82.2	84.5	78.2	73.9	75.0	81.1	82.7	82.5	80.9	80.3
2001	84.1	85.3	86.0	85.7	87.5	84.1	78.0	78.3	83.9	85.8	85.4	84.9	84.1
2002	83.6	85.1	85.7	85.8	87.6	85.1	79.3	79.1	85.5	86.3	87.4	87.7	84.9
2003	83.1	85.7	86.0	87.9	88.9	84.6	80.1	81.2	86.4	87.7	88.2	87.5	85.6
Federal government													
1990	12.7	12.6	12.9	14.4	14.8	14.8	15.6	15.0	14.8	14.1	13.1	13.5	14.0
1991	12.5	12.4	12.4	12.6	12.9	13.6	14.3	14.2	13.8	13.4	13.1	12.5	13.1
1992	12.3	12.4	12.5	13.0	13.4	14.3	15.0	14.9	14.4	13.8	13.0	12.9	13.4
1993	12.3	12.3	12.3	13.0	13.5	14.6	14.9	14.8	14.3	14.0	13.1	12.9	13.5
1994	12.6	12.6	12.6	12.9	13.5	14.2	15.0	15.0	15.0	14.0	13.1	12.7	13.6
1995	12.5	12.4	12.4	12.6	13.3	14.2	14.5	14.5	13.9	13.6	12.5	12.3	13.2
1996	12.0	12.0	12.0	12.4	13.2	13.9	14.1	14.1	13.7	12.8	12.2	12.1	12.8
1997	11.8	11.8	11.8	12.0	13.0	13.5	14.0	14.0	13.5	12.5	12.1	11.9	12.6
1998	11.8	11.6	11.7	12.1	13.0	13.6	13.9	14.6	13.9	12.6	12.2	12.0	12.7
1999	11.7	11.6	11.7	12.1	12.8	13.5	14.0	13.9	13.6	13.2	12.6	12.1	12.7
2000	12.0	12.2	13.7	13.4	15.1	14.4	14.8	14.5	13.8	13.2	12.5	12.0	13.4
2001	12.2	12.1	12.3	12.4	13.2	14.7	15.0	14.9	14.6	13.6	13.1	12.7	13.4
2002	12.4	12.4	12.6	12.6	13.4	15.0	15.4	15.1	15.0	13.9	13.6	14.0	13.8
2003	12.1	12.1	12.3	13.3	14.0	15.3	15.6	15.4	14.9	14.0	13.7	13.6	13.9
State government													
1990	20.8	21.1	21.6	21.5	21.3	20.5	19.5	18.4	20.4	21.8	21.8	21.0	20.8
1991	22.1	22.2	22.2	22.2	21.7	21.3	18.7	19.4	21.4	22.3	22.6	21.8	21.4
1992	22.1	22.4	22.4	22.3	22.1	20.1	19.0	20.4	22.8	22.7	22.9	22.5	21.8
1993	22.5	22.8	22.8	22.7	21.8	19.1	19.0	20.3	22.3	22.6	22.7	22.5	21.7
1994	22.0	22.5	22.5	22.7	22.1	19.3	19.1	23.2	25.5	24.1	23.1	22.7	22.4
1995	22.9	23.4	23.6	23.3	22.4	19.9	19.5	20.1	23.2	23.7	23.6	23.0	22.3
1996	22.2	23.3	23.6	23.6	22.7	20.1	20.1	20.9	23.9	24.5	24.4	23.8	22.7
1997	23.4	24.4	24.3	24.1	23.0	20.2	19.8	20.5	24.1	24.7	24.7	24.1	23.1
1998	23.6	23.9	24.3	24.2	23.6	20.8	20.8	21.0	24.4	25.2	25.0	24.6	23.4
1999	24.2	23.9	25.2	25.1	23.9	21.1	21.0	21.3	24.5	25.3	25.4	24.8	23.8
2000	24.1	24.5	25.1	24.8	24.3	21.6	21.6	22.9	25.8	25.5	25.3	24.9	24.2
2001	24.5	24.8	25.2	25.0	24.6	22.3	21.1	21.4	23.6	24.6	24.6	24.5	23.9
2002	24.2	24.8	24.8	25.1	24.8	23.4	21.4	21.4	25.0	25.1	25.5	25.6	24.3
2003	23.8	25.4	25.3	25.9	25.1	21.9	22.2	23.4	26.1	26.1	26.0	25.6	24.7

Employment by Industry: Montana—*Continued*

(Numbers in thousands. Not seasonally adjusted.)

Industry	January	February	March	April	May	June	July	August	September	October	November	December	Annual Average
STATEWIDE—*Continued*													
Local government													
1990	36.6	37.3	37.9	37.9	38.5	37.8	29.6	32.4	35.8	38.0	38.6	38.1	36.5
1991	37.3	38.1	38.6	39.1	39.9	37.4	30.4	31.8	36.8	38.9	39.2	39.2	37.2
1992	38.7	39.8	39.9	40.3	41.2	41.3	33.0	33.1	37.6	39.8	42.0	40.3	38.9
1993	38.9	40.0	40.4	40.3	40.8	40.6	32.4	33.9	37.2	40.4	41.0	40.7	38.8
1994	39.9	41.0	41.1	41.7	42.2	41.7	34.6	35.2	38.8	41.8	43.8	42.3	40.3
1995	41.2	42.1	42.4	43.1	43.5	41.8	36.5	36.7	40.2	42.3	43.1	42.6	41.2
1996	41.5	42.5	43.0	43.5	43.8	40.7	35.6	36.1	40.0	42.5	44.1	43.2	41.3
1997	42.4	42.9	43.2	43.5	43.8	40.0	36.1	36.4	40.3	43.4	43.8	43.8	41.6
1998	42.8	43.9	44.1	44.2	44.2	41.8	37.2	37.2	41.1	43.4	44.6	43.9	42.3
1999	42.2	43.6	44.1	44.4	44.8	41.8	37.6	37.2	41.1	43.0	43.9	43.8	42.2
2000	42.9	43.8	44.3	44.0	45.1	42.2	37.5	37.6	41.5	44.0	44.7	44.0	42.6
2001	47.4	48.4	48.5	48.3	49.7	47.1	41.9	42.0	45.7	47.6	47.7	47.7	46.8
2002	47.0	47.9	48.3	48.1	49.4	46.7	42.5	42.6	45.5	47.3	48.3	48.1	46.8
2003	47.2	48.2	48.4	48.7	49.8	47.4	42.3	42.4	45.4	47.6	48.5	48.3	47.0
BILLINGS													
Total nonfarm													
1999	62.7	63.7	64.2	65.1	65.6	65.6	64.7	64.8	65.4	65.5	65.6	66.0	64.9
2000	64.5	64.9	65.8	65.8	67.3	67.1	66.3	67.3	66.9	65.3	64.8	65.0	65.9
2001	65.1	65.3	66.2	67.1	68.4	68.6	67.2	68.1	67.9	67.8	68.1	67.8	67.3
2002	66.4	67.2	67.7	68.4	69.2	69.6	69.1	69.5	69.5	68.8	68.7	69.0	68.6
2003	67.5	67.9	67.8	69.8	70.7	70.4	69.4	70.1	70.7	70.2	70.2	70.1	69.6
Total private													
1999	54.2	54.9	55.6	56.4	56.8	57.4	57.5	57.6	57.2	56.9	56.8	57.1	56.5
2000	55.5	55.7	56.5	57.0	58.1	58.7	58.9	59.5	58.6	56.7	56.5	56.5	57.3
2001	57.0	56.7	57.5	58.5	59.6	60.3	60.1	60.5	59.8	59.4	59.6	59.3	59.0
2002	58.2	58.6	59.1	59.8	60.5	61.3	61.6	61.9	61.2	60.2	60.1	60.2	60.2
2003	59.1	59.1	59.1	60.9	61.7	62.0	62.0	62.5	62.3	61.4	61.4	61.3	61.1
Goods-producing													
1999	6.5	6.7	6.9	7.4	7.6	7.7	7.6	7.5	7.5	7.4	7.0	6.7	7.2
2000	6.5	6.5	6.6	6.8	7.2	7.3	7.2	7.4	7.2	7.2	6.9	6.5	6.9
2001	6.5	6.4	6.6	7.0	7.3	7.5	7.5	7.5	7.3	7.3	7.1	6.8	7.1
2002	6.6	6.6	6.6	6.7	6.9	7.1	7.4	7.5	7.2	7.1	6.8	6.6	6.9
2003	6.6	6.7	6.7	7.5	7.9	7.9	7.9	8.0	8.0	7.7	7.5	7.1	7.5
Construction and mining													
1999	3.2	3.3	3.5	4.0	4.1	4.3	4.2	4.1	4.1	3.9	3.5	3.3	3.7
2000	3.1	3.1	3.3	3.5	3.8	4.0	3.9	4.1	3.9	3.9	3.6	3.2	3.6
2001	3.1	3.0	3.3	3.7	4.0	4.2	4.2	4.2	4.1	4.1	3.9	3.6	3.8
2002	3.4	3.4	3.5	3.6	3.8	4.0	4.2	4.3	4.1	4.0	3.8	3.6	3.8
2003	3.5	3.5	3.5	4.3	4.6	4.6	4.6	4.7	4.7	4.4	4.2	3.8	4.2
Manufacturing													
1999	3.3	3.4	3.4	3.4	3.5	3.4	3.4	3.4	3.4	3.5	3.5	3.4	3.4
2000	3.4	3.4	3.3	3.3	3.4	3.3	3.3	3.3	3.3	3.3	3.3	3.3	3.3
2001	3.4	3.4	3.3	3.3	3.3	3.3	3.3	3.3	3.2	3.2	3.2	3.2	3.3
2002	3.2	3.2	3.1	3.1	3.1	3.1	3.2	3.2	3.1	3.1	3.0	3.0	3.1
2003	3.1	3.2	3.2	3.2	3.3	3.3	3.3	3.3	3.3	3.3	3.3	3.3	3.3
Service-providing													
1999	56.2	57.0	57.3	57.7	58.0	57.9	57.1	57.3	57.9	58.1	58.6	59.3	57.7
2000	58.0	58.4	59.2	59.0	60.1	59.8	59.1	59.9	59.7	58.1	57.9	58.5	58.9
2001	58.6	58.9	59.6	60.1	61.1	61.1	59.7	60.6	60.6	60.5	61.0	61.0	60.2
2002	59.8	60.6	61.1	61.7	62.3	62.5	61.7	62.0	62.3	61.7	61.9	62.4	61.7
2003	60.9	61.2	61.1	62.3	62.8	62.5	61.5	62.1	62.7	62.5	62.7	63.0	62.1
Trade, transportation, and utilities													
1999	17.3	17.4	17.4	17.5	17.4	17.4	17.4	17.3	17.2	17.2	17.5	17.8	17.4
2000	17.2	17.1	17.2	17.3	17.5	17.6	17.6	17.7	17.4	16.9	17.1	17.5	17.3
2001	17.9	17.6	17.8	18.0	18.3	18.2	18.2	18.2	18.2	18.2	18.4	18.4	18.1
2002	17.5	17.4	17.5	17.9	18.1	18.1	18.5	18.2	18.3	18.2	18.3	18.6	18.1
2003	17.9	17.7	17.6	17.9	18.1	18.2	18.1	18.2	18.2	18.1	18.4	18.5	18.1
Wholesale trade													
1999	5.1	5.2	5.2	5.2	5.2	5.2	5.2	5.1	5.1	5.0	5.0	5.1	5.1
2000	5.1	5.1	5.1	5.2	5.2	5.2	5.2	5.2	5.1	5.0	5.0	5.1	5.1
2001	5.0	5.0	5.0	5.1	5.2	5.2	5.2	5.2	5.2	5.2	5.2	5.1	5.1
2002	5.0	5.0	5.0	5.0	5.1	5.1	5.3	5.2	5.2	5.0	5.0	5.1	5.1
2003	4.9	4.9	4.9	5.0	5.0	5.1	5.1	5.1	5.0	4.9	4.9	5.0	5.0
Retail trade													
1999	9.1	9.1	9.1	9.2	9.1	9.2	9.2	9.2	9.1	9.2	9.4	9.6	9.2
2000	9.1	9.0	9.1	9.1	9.2	9.4	9.3	9.4	9.2	8.8	9.1	9.3	9.1
2001	9.4	9.2	9.3	9.4	9.5	9.5	9.5	9.5	9.4	9.4	9.6	9.6	9.4
2002	9.0	8.9	8.9	9.3	9.4	9.4	9.5	9.4	9.4	9.5	9.7	9.8	9.4
2003	9.4	9.3	9.2	9.3	9.5	9.5	9.4	9.5	9.5	9.5	9.8	9.8	9.5
Transportation and utilities													
1999	3.1	3.1	3.1	3.1	3.1	3.0	3.0	3.0	3.0	3.0	3.1	3.1	3.0
2000	3.0	3.0	3.0	3.0	3.1	3.0	3.1	3.1	3.1	3.1	3.0	3.1	3.0
2001	3.5	3.4	3.5	3.5	3.6	3.5	3.5	3.5	3.6	3.6	3.6	3.7	3.5
2002	3.5	3.5	3.6	3.6	3.6	3.6	3.7	3.6	3.7	3.7	3.6	3.7	3.6
2003	3.6	3.5	3.5	3.6	3.6	3.6	3.6	3.6	3.7	3.7	3.7	3.7	3.6
Information													
1999	1.2	1.1	1.1	1.1	1.1	1.1	1.1	1.1	1.1	1.1	1.2	1.2	1.1
2000	1.2	1.2	1.2	1.2	1.2	1.2	1.1	1.1	1.1	1.1	1.1	1.1	1.1
2001	1.1	1.1	1.1	1.1	1.1	1.1	1.1	1.2	1.2	1.2	1.2	1.2	1.1
2002	1.2	1.2	1.2	1.2	1.2	1.2	1.2	1.2	1.2	1.1	1.2	1.2	1.2
2003	1.2	1.2	1.2	1.2	1.2	1.2	1.2	1.3	1.3	1.2	1.2	1.2	1.2

Employment by Industry: Montana—*Continued*

(Numbers in thousands. Not seasonally adjusted.)

Industry	January	February	March	April	May	June	July	August	September	October	November	December	Annual Average
BILLINGS—*Continued*													
Financial activities													
1999	3.2	3.3	3.3	3.3	3.4	3.4	3.4	3.4	3.4	3.4	3.3	3.4	3.3
2000	3.3	3.3	3.4	3.4	3.5	3.5	3.5	3.5	3.5	3.3	3.3	3.3	3.4
2001	3.4	3.4	3.4	3.5	3.6	3.6	3.6	3.7	3.7	3.6	3.6	3.7	3.6
2002	3.5	3.6	3.6	3.7	3.7	3.8	3.8	3.7	3.7	3.7	3.7	3.7	3.7
2003	3.8	3.8	3.8	3.7	3.7	3.7	3.8	3.8	3.8	3.8	3.8	3.8	3.8
Professional and business services													
1999	6.7	7.0	7.2	7.3	7.3	7.5	7.7	7.7	7.7	7.8	7.7	7.8	7.4
2000	7.5	7.7	7.8	7.9	7.9	8.1	8.4	8.4	8.2	8.4	8.2	8.2	8.0
2001	8.0	8.1	8.1	8.2	8.3	8.4	8.3	8.4	8.2	8.2	8.1	8.1	8.2
2002	8.2	8.3	8.4	8.3	8.4	8.5	8.6	8.9	8.7	8.4	8.3	8.2	8.4
2003	7.9	7.9	8.0	8.4	8.4	8.4	8.5	8.6	8.5	8.6	8.6	8.6	8.4
Educational and health services													
1999	8.9	8.9	8.9	8.9	8.9	8.9	8.9	9.0	9.1	9.1	9.3	9.4	9.0
2000	9.4	9.4	9.5	9.4	9.4	9.5	9.4	9.4	9.5	9.1	9.2	9.3	9.3
2001	9.4	9.4	9.5	9.6	9.6	9.8	9.5	9.6	9.7	9.7	9.9	9.9	9.6
2002	10.1	10.2	10.2	10.1	10.1	10.1	9.9	10.0	10.1	10.2	10.3	10.3	10.1
2003	10.4	10.5	10.4	10.4	10.4	10.3	10.2	10.2	10.3	10.3	10.3	10.4	10.3
Leisure and hospitality													
1999	7.3	7.4	7.7	7.7	7.9	8.2	8.2	8.4	8.0	7.7	7.6	7.6	7.8
2000	7.3	7.4	7.6	7.8	8.1	8.3	8.5	8.8	8.5	7.5	7.5	7.5	7.9
2001	7.6	7.6	7.8	7.9	8.2	8.5	8.7	8.7	8.3	8.1	8.1	8.0	8.1
2002	7.9	8.1	8.4	8.7	8.9	9.3	9.0	9.2	8.8	8.3	8.2	8.3	8.6
2003	8.1	8.1	8.2	8.6	8.7	9.0	9.1	9.2	8.9	8.4	8.3	8.4	8.6
Other services													
1999	3.1	3.1	3.1	3.2	3.2	3.2	3.2	3.2	3.2	3.2	3.2	3.2	3.1
2000	3.1	3.1	3.2	3.2	3.3	3.2	3.2	3.2	3.2	3.2	3.2	3.1	3.1
2001	3.1	3.1	3.2	3.2	3.2	3.2	3.2	3.2	3.2	3.1	3.2	3.2	3.2
2002	3.2	3.2	3.2	3.2	3.2	3.2	3.2	3.2	3.2	3.2	3.3	3.3	3.2
2003	3.2	3.2	3.2	3.2	3.3	3.3	3.2	3.2	3.3	3.3	3.3	3.3	3.3
Government													
1999	8.5	8.8	8.6	8.7	8.8	8.2	7.2	7.2	8.2	8.6	8.8	8.9	8.3
2000	9.0	9.2	9.3	8.8	9.2	8.4	7.4	7.8	8.3	8.6	8.3	8.5	8.5
2001	8.1	8.6	8.7	8.6	8.8	8.3	7.1	7.6	8.1	8.4	8.5	8.5	8.3
2002	8.2	8.6	8.6	8.6	8.7	8.3	7.5	7.6	8.3	8.6	8.6	8.8	8.4
2003	8.4	8.8	8.7	8.9	9.0	8.4	7.4	7.6	8.4	8.8	8.8	8.8	8.5
Federal government													
2001	1.8	1.8	1.8	1.8	1.8	1.8	1.8	1.9	1.8	1.8	1.8	1.8	1.8
2002	1.8	1.8	1.8	1.8	1.8	1.9	1.9	1.8	1.9	1.9	1.9	2.0	1.9
2003	1.9	1.9	1.9	1.9	1.9	1.9	1.9	1.9	1.9	1.9	1.8	1.9	1.9
State government													
2001	1.3	1.7	1.7	1.7	1.6	1.3	1.3	1.3	1.6	1.6	1.6	1.6	1.5
2002	1.3	1.6	1.6	1.6	1.6	1.3	1.4	1.4	1.6	1.6	1.7	1.7	1.5
2003	1.4	1.7	1.7	1.7	1.7	1.4	1.4	1.4	1.6	1.7	1.7	1.7	1.6
Local government													
2001	5.0	5.1	5.2	5.1	5.4	5.2	4.0	4.4	4.7	5.0	5.1	5.1	4.9
2002	5.1	5.2	5.2	5.2	5.3	5.1	4.2	4.4	4.8	5.1	5.0	5.1	5.0
2003	5.1	5.2	5.1	5.3	5.4	5.1	4.1	4.3	4.9	5.2	5.3	5.2	5.0

Average Weekly Hours by Industry: Montana

(Not seasonally adjusted.)

Industry	January	February	March	April	May	June	July	August	September	October	November	December	Annual Average
STATEWIDE													
Manufacturing													
2001	38.6	38.7	38.3	37.8	38.3	39.5	38.1	39.1	38.8	38.3	39.9	39.2	38.8
2002	37.1	37.1	37.7	38.3	38.1	39.3	36.0	38.4	38.6	39.0	39.5	39.5	38.2
2003	39.1	38.4	37.9	38.7	38.5	39.1	37.4	38.3	38.2	38.3	38.3	38.4	38.4

Average Hourly Earnings by Industry: Montana

(Dollars, not seasonally adjusted.)

Industry	January	February	March	April	May	June	July	August	September	October	November	December	Annual Average
STATEWIDE													
Manufacturing													
2001	13.81	13.73	14.00	13.88	13.80	13.88	14.18	13.95	14.13	14.43	14.20	14.41	14.03
2002	14.54	14.45	14.61	14.53	14.46	14.42	14.45	14.35	14.33	14.30	14.44	14.31	14.43
2003	14.20	14.07	14.21	14.13	13.73	13.75	13.87	14.05	13.94	14.05	14.16	14.16	14.02

Average Weekly Earnings by Industry: Montana

(Dollars, not seasonally adjusted.)

Industry	January	February	March	April	May	June	July	August	September	October	November	December	Annual Average
MONTANA													
Manufacturing													
2001	533.07	531.35	536.20	524.66	528.54	548.26	540.26	545.45	548.24	552.67	566.58	564.87	544.3[illegible]
2002	539.43	536.10	550.80	556.50	550.93	566.71	520.20	551.04	553.14	557.70	570.38	565.25	551.2[illegible]
2003	555.22	540.29	538.56	546.83	528.61	537.63	518.74	538.12	532.51	538.12	542.33	543.74	538.3[illegible]

NEBRASKA AT A GLANCE

(Population and total nonfarm employment numbers in thousands)

Population, Census 2000:	1,711.3
Total nonfarm employment, 2003:	903.8
Change in total nonfarm employment	
(Number)	
1990–2003:	173.7
1990–2001:	183.1
2001–2003:	-9.4
(Compound annual rate of change)	
1990–2003:	1.7%
1990–2001:	2.1%
2001–2003:	-0.5%
Unemployment rate	
1990:	2.3%
2001:	3.1%
2003:	4.0%

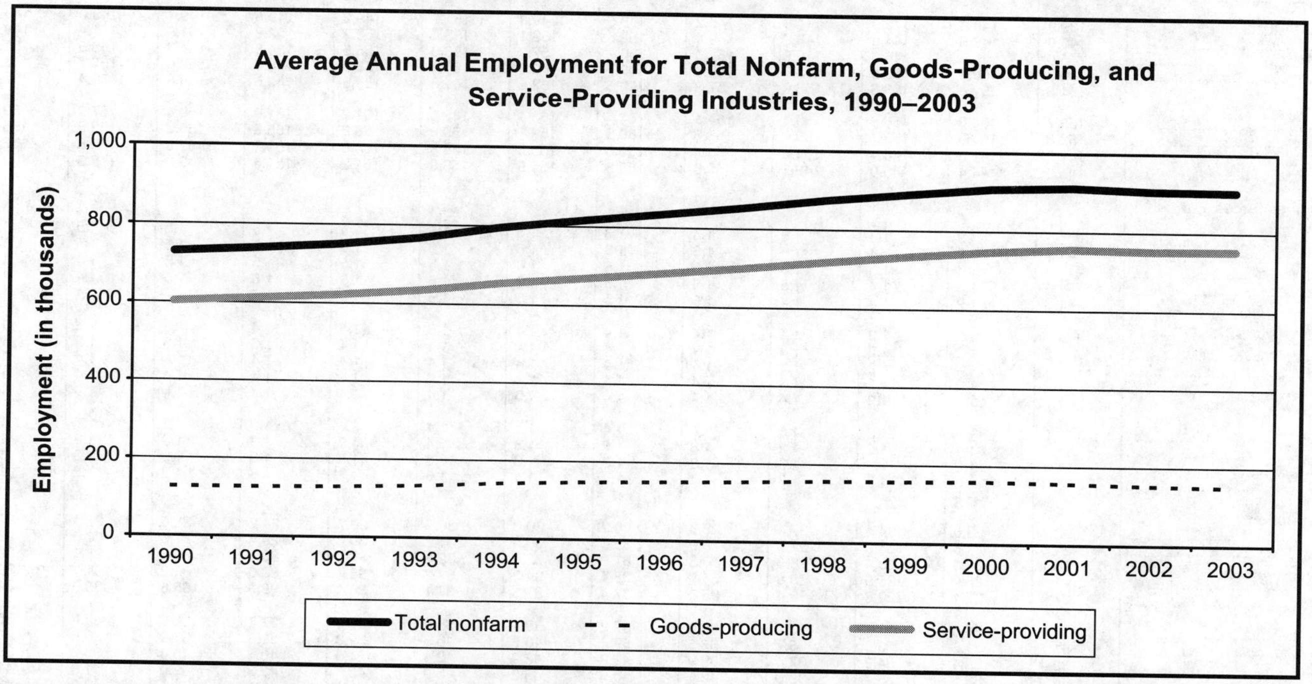

As in several other states, total nonfarm payroll employment in Nebraska grew significantly during the mid to late 1990s and declined during the 2001 recession. The goods-producing industry suffered a loss of over 10,000 jobs between 2000 and 2003 despite employment gains in natural resources and mining and construction. Employment in manufacturing declined by nearly 11 percent during this time. In comparison, employment in service-providing industries recovered in 2003 after declining in 2002. Educational and health services added the largest number of jobs, 7,500 from 2000 to 2003.

Employment by Industry: Nebraska

(Numbers in thousands. Not seasonally adjusted.)

Industry	January	February	March	April	May	June	July	August	September	October	November	December	Annual Average
STATEWIDE													
Total nonfarm													
1990	704.4	709.8	716.6	727.7	738.3	741.7	730.2	732.1	737.1	736.9	744.3	741.9	730.1
1991	720.4	723.8	730.5	735.4	742.9	746.1	741.2	743.3	749.9	745.7	744.2	746.6	739.2
1992	728.8	733.0	738.3	744.8	757.5	759.6	748.4	748.5	757.1	761.7	762.7	761.0	750.1
1993	739.0	744.1	750.8	763.1	772.3	775.6	764.6	769.6	775.4	782.5	784.4	785.1	767.2
1994	766.4	772.0	778.2	788.9	802.9	806.4	797.1	796.0	803.9	808.2	818.1	814.5	796.1
1995	792.3	797.8	805.0	811.6	818.1	824.1	813.3	821.7	820.8	828.1	831.5	831.8	816.3
1996	811.6	817.2	824.1	830.5	839.4	843.2	831.0	835.8	839.3	846.0	849.3	850.3	834.8
1997	827.2	831.5	843.1	847.4	859.4	863.2	855.3	853.9	861.2	865.2	869.5	873.4	854.2
1998	847.6	854.0	857.8	871.4	880.1	884.3	881.0	876.9	882.9	888.3	892.3	896.4	876.1
1999	866.0	873.3	877.6	888.0	894.6	902.8	898.0	893.7	898.2	902.9	907.0	910.6	892.7
2000	886.8	890.2	899.7	906.4	914.7	923.7	909.2	910.7	912.3	913.3	916.8	917.2	908.4
2001	895.3	896.5	903.1	912.2	922.4	927.4	911.8	914.9	915.8	916.7	922.5	920.3	913.2
2002	887.8	891.7	898.9	907.6	913.5	916.8	901.8	902.4	910.7	910.3	912.9	913.4	905.7
2003	891.9	892.0	895.6	905.0	910.0	913.0	901.2	899.1	904.9	911.4	912.2	909.5	903.8
Total private													
1990	565.1	567.2	572.3	581.9	587.7	594.8	594.9	597.2	594.6	592.9	595.3	596.0	586.7
1991	579.5	579.5	584.9	588.7	594.3	599.1	599.8	602.2	602.4	597.4	596.2	598.4	593.5
1992	584.3	586.3	590.2	596.1	603.6	608.2	609.2	610.0	610.8	612.3	609.1	609.6	602.5
1993	592.6	595.6	600.9	610.2	618.1	625.0	624.0	629.7	627.1	630.8	632.0	632.8	618.2
1994	617.6	620.9	626.2	636.9	644.8	652.6	654.9	653.7	653.3	654.5	658.1	660.3	644.5
1995	642.1	645.6	651.7	658.4	663.5	671.3	670.9	679.1	672.4	675.7	677.6	678.8	665.6
1996	662.5	665.4	671.6	676.7	682.9	689.7	688.1	692.1	688.6	693.0	693.8	696.7	683.4
1997	676.3	679.3	689.6	693.5	703.5	709.1	709.2	709.2	710.1	711.2	714.0	718.5	702.0
1998	696.9	700.8	703.7	718.4	724.9	731.8	738.2	734.9	733.6	736.2	739.6	743.5	725.2
1999	716.4	721.4	724.9	735.4	739.9	749.3	752.3	750.0	747.5	749.3	752.6	756.4	741.3
2000	734.0	736.2	743.2	750.6	755.3	765.5	760.7	762.4	759.0	759.1	760.9	761.3	754.0
2001	742.5	741.2	746.5	754.5	761.7	767.2	761.7	763.6	758.6	758.2	761.5	760.2	756.5
2002	731.4	732.2	738.7	747.1	750.7	755.1	750.2	751.5	752.8	748.7	750.7	751.8	746.7
2003	732.2	731.3	734.7	742.9	746.4	750.4	747.9	748.2	746.8	748.5	749.1	747.1	743.8
Goods-producing													
1990	119.8	120.2	121.7	125.2	126.8	129.9	130.8	131.5	129.9	129.8	129.6	127.6	126.9
1991	123.4	123.4	124.4	125.3	127.6	129.1	129.2	130.3	129.8	128.2	126.4	125.5	126.9
1992	122.4	122.9	123.8	125.9	129.3	131.6	132.3	132.0	131.0	131.4	129.6	128.3	128.4
1993	124.5	124.7	126.4	128.8	132.2	135.0	135.7	137.7	136.6	137.3	136.6	135.4	132.6
1994	131.6	131.6	134.0	138.3	141.6	145.0	146.0	145.1	144.8	145.4	145.5	144.1	141.1
1995	139.9	140.6	142.9	144.8	146.2	148.5	149.3	151.7	149.2	149.8	149.1	148.0	146.7
1996	143.0	142.5	144.3	146.9	149.4	152.5	153.1	153.9	152.2	152.8	151.9	151.4	149.5
1997	145.0	145.5	148.3	150.8	152.9	156.7	157.7	156.9	155.6	154.8	154.3	153.5	152.7
1998	149.6	150.3	150.4	155.6	158.4	160.7	162.3	161.1	159.5	158.8	157.6	157.7	156.8
1999	151.3	152.8	153.6	156.0	157.3	160.5	162.2	161.6	159.8	159.6	158.8	158.4	157.7
2000	153.7	154.0	156.9	159.1	161.1	164.4	163.1	162.8	161.2	161.0	159.4	157.7	159.5
2001	152.6	151.9	152.7	156.0	158.3	160.3	159.7	159.3	156.8	156.2	155.2	153.8	156.1
2002	148.1	147.3	148.4	151.0	153.1	155.5	155.6	155.3	154.0	153.1	152.0	150.8	152.0
2003	145.5	144.4	145.0	148.1	150.6	152.6	151.9	153.3	151.2	151.4	149.9	148.2	149.3
Natural resources and mining													
1990	1.3	1.3	1.4	1.5	1.5	1.6	1.6	1.6	1.5	1.5	1.5	1.5	1.5
1991	1.3	1.3	1.4	1.5	1.6	1.6	1.6	1.6	1.6	1.5	1.5	1.5	1.5
1992	1.4	1.4	1.5	1.5	1.6	1.6	1.6	1.5	1.5	1.5	1.5	1.4	1.5
1993	1.3	1.3	1.4	1.5	1.5	1.6	1.6	1.6	1.6	1.6	1.5	1.4	1.5
1994	1.3	1.2	1.4	1.4	1.5	1.5	1.5	1.5	1.5	1.5	1.4	1.4	1.4
1995	1.2	1.2	1.3	1.4	1.4	1.4	1.4	1.5	1.4	1.4	1.3	1.3	1.4
1996	1.2	1.2	1.2	1.3	1.4	1.4	1.4	1.4	1.4	1.3	1.3	1.3	1.3
1997	1.1	1.2	1.2	1.3	1.4	1.4	1.4	1.4	1.4	1.4	1.4	1.4	1.3
1998	1.2	1.2	1.2	1.3	1.4	1.4	1.4	1.4	1.4	1.4	1.4	1.4	1.3
1999	1.2	1.2	1.2	1.4	1.4	1.4	1.5	1.4	1.4	1.4	1.4	1.3	1.4
2000	1.2	1.2	1.3	1.3	1.4	1.4	1.4	1.4	1.4	1.3	1.3	1.3	1.3
2001	1.1	1.1	1.2	1.2	1.3	1.3	1.3	1.4	1.3	1.3	1.3	1.3	1.3
2002	1.2	1.2	1.2	1.3	1.3	1.3	1.3	1.3	1.3	1.3	1.3	1.3	1.3
2003	1.3	1.3	1.3	1.3	1.4	1.4	1.4	1.5	1.4	1.5	1.2	1.2	1.4
Construction													
1990	22.7	23.0	24.4	27.4	28.8	30.2	30.8	30.9	29.7	29.2	28.6	27.1	27.7
1991	24.5	24.6	25.9	27.4	29.2	30.5	30.8	31.2	30.3	29.4	27.5	26.6	28.2
1992	24.1	24.3	25.4	28.0	30.3	31.9	32.5	32.1	31.2	30.6	29.5	28.1	29.0
1993	24.9	25.0	25.9	28.8	31.7	33.4	34.0	34.2	33.0	33.0	32.2	31.1	30.6
1994	27.9	27.4	29.6	33.4	35.8	37.4	37.8	37.1	36.1	36.0	35.8	33.9	34.0
1995	30.8	31.0	32.1	33.7	35.0	37.2	38.1	38.8	37.8	37.7	36.9	35.6	35.4
1996	31.7	31.5	33.0	35.7	37.5	39.4	40.2	40.5	39.3	39.3	37.9	36.6	36.9
1997	32.4	32.4	34.9	37.4	39.9	42.2	42.9	42.4	41.0	40.5	39.4	38.2	38.6
1998	35.3	35.5	35.7	39.5	42.1	43.7	45.2	45.0	43.7	43.3	42.0	41.8	41.1
1999	36.9	37.5	38.3	41.6	43.5	45.7	47.0	46.9	45.4	44.8	44.1	43.3	42.9
2000	39.5	39.4	41.2	43.6	45.2	47.2	46.8	47.0	45.8	45.3	43.6	41.8	43.9
2001	38.6	38.3	39.4	42.9	45.4	47.2	47.3	47.5	46.1	45.9	45.3	44.0	44.0
2002	40.0	39.6	41.2	44.0	45.9	47.5	47.9	47.7	46.9	46.5	45.6	44.5	44.8
2003	41.4	40.6	41.4	44.6	47.0	48.9	48.6	49.9	48.3	48.3	46.9	45.1	45.9

Employment by Industry: Nebraska—*Continued*

(Numbers in thousands. Not seasonally adjusted.)

Industry	January	February	March	April	May	June	July	August	September	October	November	December	Annual Average
STATEWIDE—*Continued*													
Manufacturing													
1990	95.8	95.9	95.9	96.3	96.5	98.1	98.4	99.0	98.7	99.1	99.5	99.0	97.7
1991	97.6	97.5	97.1	96.4	96.8	97.0	96.8	97.5	97.9	97.3	97.4	97.4	97.2
1992	96.9	97.2	96.9	96.4	97.4	98.1	98.2	98.4	98.3	99.3	98.6	98.8	97.9
1993	98.3	98.4	99.1	98.5	99.0	100.0	100.1	101.9	102.0	102.7	102.9	102.9	100.5
1994	102.4	103.0	103.0	103.5	104.3	106.1	106.7	106.5	107.2	107.9	108.3	108.8	105.6
1995	107.9	108.4	109.5	109.7	109.8	109.9	109.8	111.4	110.0	110.7	110.9	111.1	109.9
1996	110.1	109.8	110.1	109.9	110.5	111.7	111.5	112.0	111.5	112.2	112.7	113.5	111.3
1997	111.5	111.9	112.2	112.1	111.6	113.1	113.4	113.1	113.2	112.9	113.5	113.9	112.7
1998	113.1	113.6	113.5	114.8	114.9	115.6	115.7	114.7	114.4	114.1	114.2	114.5	114.4
1999	113.2	114.1	114.1	113.0	112.4	113.4	113.7	113.3	113.0	113.4	113.3	113.8	113.4
2000	113.0	113.4	114.4	114.2	114.5	115.8	114.9	114.4	114.0	114.4	114.5	114.6	114.3
2001	112.9	112.5	112.1	111.9	111.6	111.8	111.1	110.4	109.4	109.0	108.6	108.5	110.8
2002	106.9	106.5	106.0	105.7	105.9	106.7	106.4	106.3	105.8	105.3	105.1	105.0	106.0
2003	102.8	102.5	102.3	102.2	102.2	102.3	101.9	101.9	101.5	101.6	101.8	101.9	102.1
Service-providing													
1990	584.6	589.6	594.9	602.5	611.5	611.8	599.4	600.6	607.2	607.1	614.7	614.3	603.2
1991	597.0	600.4	606.1	610.1	615.3	617.0	612.0	613.0	620.1	617.5	617.8	621.1	612.3
1992	606.4	610.1	614.5	618.9	628.2	628.0	616.1	616.5	626.1	630.3	633.1	632.7	621.7
1993	614.5	619.4	624.4	634.3	640.1	640.6	628.9	631.9	638.8	645.2	647.8	649.7	634.6
1994	634.8	640.4	644.2	650.6	661.3	661.4	651.1	650.9	659.1	662.8	672.6	670.4	655.0
1995	652.4	657.2	662.1	666.8	671.9	675.6	664.0	670.0	671.6	678.3	682.4	683.8	669.7
1996	668.6	674.7	679.8	683.6	690.0	690.7	677.9	681.9	687.1	693.2	697.4	698.9	685.3
1997	682.2	686.0	694.8	696.6	706.5	706.5	697.6	697.0	705.6	710.4	715.2	719.9	701.5
1998	698.0	703.7	707.4	715.8	721.7	723.6	718.7	715.8	723.4	729.5	734.7	738.7	719.3
1999	714.7	720.5	724.0	732.0	737.3	742.3	735.8	732.1	738.4	743.3	748.2	752.2	735.1
2000	733.1	736.2	742.8	747.3	753.6	759.3	746.1	747.9	751.1	752.3	757.4	759.5	748.9
2001	742.7	744.6	750.4	756.2	764.1	767.1	752.1	755.6	759.0	760.5	767.3	766.5	757.2
2002	739.7	744.4	750.5	756.6	760.4	761.3	746.2	747.1	756.7	757.2	760.9	762.6	753.6
2003	746.4	747.6	750.6	756.9	759.4	760.4	749.3	745.8	753.7	760.0	762.3	761.3	754.5
Trade, transportation, and utilities													
1990	165.2	163.8	165.0	167.0	168.5	169.8	170.2	170.4	170.1	170.1	171.9	173.5	168.8
1991	167.6	165.3	166.6	167.7	169.4	170.0	170.1	171.0	169.9	170.5	172.0	173.5	169.5
1992	166.8	166.0	166.9	168.1	170.2	170.2	170.8	170.7	171.0	172.3	173.4	175.1	170.1
1993	167.6	167.2	167.7	169.9	171.4	172.7	172.8	174.7	173.6	175.4	178.0	179.7	172.6
1994	172.6	171.8	172.5	174.4	175.7	177.6	178.4	178.5	178.8	180.1	183.0	185.4	177.4
1995	177.2	176.4	175.2	175.8	176.7	180.7	180.5	180.5	180.9	183.3	185.4	186.8	180.0
1996	180.0	178.8	179.6	180.3	182.4	182.9	183.2	184.5	184.2	186.5	189.1	191.2	183.6
1997	183.2	181.2	183.8	184.4	187.9	188.1	188.3	188.4	189.6	191.1	193.9	196.5	188.0
1998	187.9	186.8	186.8	189.7	191.8	193.2	193.2	192.8	193.8	196.2	200.5	202.6	192.9
1999	194.2	192.4	192.8	195.0	195.9	197.7	198.3	197.6	196.9	198.8	202.0	204.9	197.2
2000	196.2	194.8	195.5	196.7	197.6	199.5	197.9	198.2	197.5	199.2	202.4	204.5	198.3
2001	196.6	194.6	195.2	196.8	198.8	199.0	197.5	197.5	196.9	197.2	200.7	202.2	197.8
2002	194.4	191.9	192.6	193.8	195.5	195.6	194.5	194.5	194.8	194.1	197.7	199.7	194.9
2003	192.6	191.1	192.0	193.0	194.4	194.9	193.5	194.4	194.9	193.8	197.0	197.5	194.1
Wholesale trade													
1990	38.0	38.1	38.7	39.2	39.4	39.8	40.1	39.8	39.6	39.4	39.3	39.1	39.2
1991	37.7	37.5	38.0	38.8	39.3	39.8	39.6	39.4	39.2	38.6	38.2	38.2	38.7
1992	37.6	37.8	38.4	38.4	39.0	39.1	39.2	38.9	38.5	38.6	38.1	38.4	38.5
1993	37.4	37.6	38.0	38.5	39.0	39.5	39.3	39.5	38.6	38.7	38.4	38.6	38.6
1994	37.8	38.0	38.4	39.2	39.5	40.2	40.6	40.1	39.7	39.4	39.3	39.2	39.3
1995	38.0	38.6	39.4	39.6	39.9	40.1	40.2	40.7	39.5	39.6	39.5	39.6	39.6
1996	39.2	39.5	39.8	40.1	40.5	40.7	40.8	40.9	40.7	40.9	40.7	40.9	40.4
1997	39.8	40.0	40.6	40.8	41.4	41.8	42.0	41.8	41.6	41.6	41.4	41.4	41.2
1998	40.9	41.0	41.3	41.9	42.3	42.7	42.9	42.8	42.6	42.2	42.4	42.8	42.2
1999	41.4	41.7	41.9	42.7	42.9	43.4	43.5	43.1	42.6	42.4	42.2	42.5	42.5
2000	41.9	42.0	42.1	41.8	41.9	42.2	42.3	42.3	41.8	41.6	41.5	41.4	41.9
2001	42.1	42.1	42.3	42.6	43.1	43.3	43.2	42.8	42.3	42.2	42.0	41.9	42.5
2002	41.1	40.9	41.3	41.6	42.0	42.2	42.5	42.0	41.6	41.0	41.0	41.1	41.5
2003	40.4	40.3	40.5	40.9	41.2	41.5	41.2	41.0	40.8	39.7	40.2	40.2	40.7
Retail trade													
1990	93.5	91.9	92.4	93.9	94.8	95.5	95.9	95.8	95.6	95.4	97.6	99.2	95.1
1991	94.9	93.1	93.8	94.1	95.0	95.1	95.4	96.2	95.6	96.6	98.7	100.5	95.8
1992	94.3	93.1	93.5	94.0	95.1	95.2	95.7	95.9	96.1	97.0	98.8	100.1	95.7
1993	94.5	93.7	93.8	95.3	96.4	96.9	97.3	98.8	98.4	100.0	102.9	104.2	97.7
1994	98.3	97.2	97.4	98.3	99.5	99.9	100.4	100.7	101.1	102.4	105.4	107.7	100.7
1995	101.7	100.3	97.5	97.6	98.0	102.1	102.4	101.2	103.3	105.0	107.5	108.6	102.1
1996	102.7	101.2	101.4	101.9	103.3	103.6	103.7	104.6	104.7	106.9	109.7	111.1	104.6
1997	104.3	101.9	102.4	102.6	104.5	104.5	104.4	104.6	105.4	106.7	109.6	112.1	105.3
1998	105.1	103.6	103.3	105.0	106.4	107.0	106.7	106.7	107.6	109.7	113.5	115.2	107.5
1999	109.6	106.8	106.8	107.9	108.5	109.7	110.3	110.0	109.6	111.4	114.6	117.1	110.2
2000	109.9	108.5	108.9	109.8	110.9	112.4	110.4	110.5	110.2	112.0	115.2	117.4	111.3
2001	109.7	107.6	107.8	108.7	110.2	110.4	109.0	109.5	109.3	109.9	113.4	114.8	110.0
2002	108.0	105.8	106.1	106.9	108.2	108.3	107.5	107.7	108.6	108.7	111.9	113.8	108.5
2003	106.3	104.6	105.1	105.9	106.8	107.2	106.2	106.8	107.4	107.5	110.2	110.6	107.1

Employment by Industry: Nebraska—*Continued*

(Numbers in thousands. Not seasonally adjusted.)

Industry	January	February	March	April	May	June	July	August	September	October	November	December	Annual Average
STATEWIDE—*Continued*													
Transportation and utilities													
1990	33.7	33.8	33.9	33.9	34.3	34.5	34.2	34.8	34.9	35.3	35.0	35.2	34.5
1991	35.0	34.7	34.8	34.8	35.1	35.1	35.1	35.4	35.1	35.3	35.1	34.8	35.0
1992	34.9	35.1	35.0	35.7	36.1	35.9	35.9	35.9	36.4	36.7	36.5	36.6	35.9
1993	35.7	35.9	35.9	36.1	36.0	36.3	36.2	36.4	36.6	36.7	36.7	36.9	36.3
1994	36.5	36.6	36.7	36.9	36.7	37.5	37.4	37.7	38.0	38.3	38.3	38.5	37.4
1995	37.5	37.5	38.3	38.6	38.8	38.5	37.9	38.6	38.1	38.7	38.4	38.6	38.3
1996	38.1	38.1	38.4	38.3	38.6	38.6	38.7	39.0	38.8	38.7	38.7	39.2	38.6
1997	39.1	39.3	40.8	41.0	42.0	41.8	41.9	42.0	42.6	42.8	42.9	43.0	41.6
1998	41.9	42.2	42.2	42.8	43.1	43.5	43.6	43.3	43.6	44.3	44.6	44.6	43.3
1999	43.2	43.9	44.1	44.4	44.5	44.6	44.5	44.5	44.7	45.0	45.2	45.3	44.5
2000	44.4	44.3	44.5	45.1	44.8	44.9	45.2	45.4	45.5	45.6	45.7	45.7	45.1
2001	44.8	44.9	45.1	45.5	45.5	45.3	45.3	45.2	45.3	45.1	45.3	45.5	45.2
2002	45.3	45.2	45.2	45.3	45.3	45.1	44.5	44.8	44.6	44.4	44.8	44.8	44.9
2003	45.9	46.2	46.4	46.2	46.4	46.2	46.1	46.6	46.7	46.6	46.6	46.7	46.4
Information													
1990	22.0	22.0	21.8	21.8	22.0	22.3	22.4	22.5	22.5	21.9	22.0	22.2	22.1
1991	21.5	21.5	21.5	22.0	22.1	22.1	22.0	22.0	22.0	21.8	21.8	21.8	21.8
1992	21.6	21.5	21.4	21.3	21.4	21.5	21.8	21.8	21.8	21.4	21.3	21.5	21.5
1993	21.6	21.7	21.8	21.7	22.0	22.1	22.0	22.3	22.0	21.9	21.9	21.9	21.9
1994	21.5	21.6	21.7	21.8	21.9	22.3	22.6	22.6	22.9	22.6	22.9	23.2	22.3
1995	22.6	22.7	22.9	22.9	22.8	23.0	22.9	23.2	22.9	22.9	23.2	23.0	22.9
1996	22.5	22.9	23.0	23.1	23.2	23.6	23.7	23.9	23.8	23.9	24.2	24.5	23.5
1997	24.5	24.5	24.7	24.6	24.9	25.0	25.1	25.2	25.1	25.3	25.7	26.0	25.1
1998	25.5	25.7	25.9	26.0	26.1	26.3	26.6	26.5	26.3	26.6	26.7	27.0	26.3
1999	26.4	26.7	26.6	26.7	26.8	27.0	27.5	27.5	27.4	27.6	27.6	27.8	27.1
2000	27.6	27.2	26.8	27.3	26.9	27.1	27.1	26.8	26.5	26.5	26.7	26.7	26.9
2001	26.3	26.2	26.3	26.5	26.2	26.3	25.8	25.4	25.2	25.2	25.2	25.3	25.8
2002	24.9	24.8	24.8	24.8	24.9	24.9	24.7	24.7	24.4	24.4	24.5	24.5	24.7
2003	21.5	21.5	21.5	21.4	21.4	21.6	21.8	21.4	21.3	21.2	21.4	21.4	21.5
Financial activities													
1990	48.3	48.6	48.6	48.7	49.1	49.5	49.4	49.3	49.0	48.7	48.8	49.3	48.9
1991	48.5	48.7	49.0	48.7	49.0	49.5	49.6	49.7	49.6	49.1	49.1	49.5	49.2
1992	48.8	48.8	48.9	49.2	49.6	49.9	50.1	50.2	49.9	49.7	49.6	50.0	49.6
1993	49.0	49.1	49.4	49.6	50.1	50.9	51.0	51.5	50.9	50.8	50.7	51.1	50.3
1994	50.8	51.0	51.3	51.4	51.8	52.4	52.6	52.4	52.0	51.8	51.8	52.3	51.8
1995	51.9	52.2	52.8	53.2	53.5	53.8	53.8	54.6	53.7	53.5	53.5	54.1	53.4
1996	53.4	53.6	53.7	53.4	53.9	54.4	53.9	54.4	54.0	54.0	54.1	54.6	54.0
1997	54.0	54.4	55.1	55.2	55.8	56.0	56.1	56.1	56.1	56.0	56.1	56.9	55.7
1998	56.5	56.8	57.2	58.2	58.0	59.0	60.0	59.8	59.5	59.7	59.9	60.7	58.8
1999	59.3	59.8	60.1	60.7	60.8	61.6	61.7	61.4	60.8	61.2	61.2	61.8	60.9
2000	60.6	60.4	60.3	60.5	60.6	61.1	60.5	60.5	60.3	60.1	60.3	60.6	60.5
2001	59.1	59.2	59.3	59.7	60.1	61.0	60.8	60.8	60.5	60.3	60.5	61.0	60.2
2002	60.6	60.7	60.9	61.0	61.3	61.9	61.8	61.7	61.3	61.5	61.6	62.1	61.4
2003	61.7	61.8	62.0	61.8	62.1	62.6	62.6	61.9	61.6	61.7	61.4	61.6	61.9
Professional and business services													
1990	59.4	59.8	60.6	61.4	61.6	63.2	62.2	62.2	62.6	63.1	63.2	63.9	61.9
1991	61.5	61.7	62.4	62.3	61.9	63.2	64.2	64.0	64.3	63.8	63.8	65.0	63.2
1992	62.7	63.3	63.6	65.1	65.2	65.7	65.6	65.9	66.3	67.0	65.9	65.6	65.2
1993	64.4	65.3	66.1	68.0	68.5	69.1	68.7	68.2	68.4	70.3	70.5	70.2	68.1
1994	70.1	70.6	70.9	72.6	72.5	74.4	75.3	75.2	74.4	75.6	75.9	76.3	73.7
1995	75.2	76.2	77.4	78.0	78.4	79.7	81.1	82.7	80.5	82.0	82.4	83.0	79.7
1996	83.5	85.0	86.1	86.4	85.7	86.1	85.2	85.1	83.8	85.3	84.9	85.0	85.2
1997	83.6	84.8	86.0	85.9	86.8	87.9	88.1	88.5	88.7	89.6	90.3	91.7	87.7
1998	87.7	88.7	89.6	91.9	91.7	93.0	94.4	93.2	92.5	91.2	90.7	91.1	91.3
1999	87.6	87.7	88.0	90.3	90.9	92.7	94.2	93.9	94.2	94.1	94.4	95.1	91.9
2000	92.4	93.0	94.1	95.8	96.1	98.1	97.8	98.0	97.6	98.2	98.7	99.1	96.6
2001	95.8	96.1	96.7	97.2	97.9	99.2	98.2	98.8	97.4	96.4	96.7	95.8	97.2
2002	89.0	89.8	91.4	92.9	92.7	93.1	91.3	91.2	90.8	90.9	90.9	90.5	91.2
2003	88.3	89.0	89.6	91.2	90.8	91.6	90.8	91.2	92.4	93.4	92.7	92.8	91.2
Educational and health services													
1990	72.6	74.0	74.2	74.1	73.7	73.3	73.1	74.3	75.1	75.9	76.5	76.4	74.4
1991	74.7	75.9	76.0	76.0	75.5	74.8	75.0	75.0	77.2	77.5	77.6	77.6	76.1
1992	77.5	78.6	78.7	78.2	77.6	77.4	77.2	77.4	79.5	80.3	80.6	80.3	78.6
1993	79.1	80.4	81.1	80.9	80.4	80.2	79.6	80.2	81.7	82.9	83.1	83.0	81.1
1994	81.6	83.3	83.5	83.9	84.3	83.3	82.4	82.7	84.0	84.5	85.2	85.5	83.7
1995	84.0	84.9	85.9	85.5	85.5	84.2	83.4	84.7	85.8	87.0	87.3	86.8	85.4
1996	86.7	87.9	88.4	88.5	88.0	88.0	87.5	88.1	90.2	91.2	91.4	91.8	89.0
1997	90.4	92.0	92.5	92.5	91.9	91.4	90.7	90.7	93.3	94.5	94.8	94.5	92.4
1998	93.0	94.7	95.0	95.2	94.5	94.3	96.5	96.9	98.5	101.4	102.5	102.4	97.1
1999	98.7	101.5	101.9	102.5	102.0	101.9	100.9	101.0	103.5	103.7	104.8	104.5	102.2
2000	102.8	105.0	105.7	104.6	104.1	104.6	104.6	105.7	107.2	107.4	107.9	108.1	105.6
2001	106.7	107.4	108.5	108.1	107.5	107.2	106.3	107.7	110.6	113.6	114.7	114.0	109.4
2002	109.8	112.0	113.7	112.7	110.4	109.1	107.7	108.4	114.2	113.8	114.3	114.4	111.7
2003	114.4	115.1	114.6	114.9	112.3	111.2	111.1	110.8	111.6	113.1	113.9	114.0	113.1

Employment by Industry: Nebraska—*Continued*

(Numbers in thousands. Not seasonally adjusted.)

Industry	January	February	March	April	May	June	July	August	September	October	November	December	Annual Average
STATEWIDE—*Continued*													
Leisure and hospitality													
1990	55.0	55.8	57.3	60.1	62.4	63.0	62.9	63.4	61.8	59.8	59.9	59.7	60.1
1991	59.4	59.7	61.6	63.1	65.1	66.4	65.9	66.4	66.0	62.9	62.1	61.8	63.4
1992	60.8	61.3	62.9	64.3	66.2	67.3	66.9	67.6	67.2	65.7	64.4	64.2	64.9
1993	62.0	62.5	63.5	66.4	68.5	69.6	68.9	69.8	68.6	67.0	66.1	66.2	66.6
1994	64.0	65.5	66.5	68.6	70.8	71.2	71.3	71.2	70.5	68.6	67.7	67.3	68.6
1995	64.7	65.8	67.6	71.0	73.3	74.0	72.7	74.5	72.3	70.0	69.6	69.6	70.4
1996	66.0	67.2	68.7	70.1	72.4	74.1	73.4	74.1	72.4	71.4	70.2	70.3	70.9
1997	68.1	69.1	71.0	72.0	75.0	75.6	74.9	75.1	73.6	71.6	70.6	71.0	72.3
1998	68.4	69.3	70.2	72.7	75.3	76.1	75.9	75.8	74.6	73.2	72.7	72.9	73.1
1999	70.1	71.3	72.4	75.0	76.9	78.1	78.1	77.9	75.7	74.9	74.5	74.5	75.0
2000	71.7	72.6	74.4	77.1	79.2	80.8	80.1	80.8	79.3	77.2	76.0	75.2	77.0
2001	72.5	72.7	74.4	76.9	79.3	80.5	79.6	80.4	77.9	75.8	75.0	74.7	76.6
2002	71.8	72.5	73.7	76.7	78.6	80.7	80.1	81.5	79.3	76.9	75.9	75.9	77.0
2003	73.8	73.9	75.2	77.6	79.9	80.8	80.7	80.7	79.1	79.0	77.7	76.7	77.9
Other services													
1990	22.8	23.0	23.1	23.6	23.6	23.8	23.9	23.6	23.6	23.6	23.4	23.4	23.5
1991	22.9	23.3	23.4	23.6	23.7	24.0	23.8	23.8	23.6	23.6	23.4	23.7	23.6
1992	23.7	23.9	24.0	24.0	24.1	24.6	24.5	24.4	24.1	24.5	24.3	24.6	24.2
1993	24.4	24.7	24.9	24.9	25.0	25.4	25.3	25.3	25.3	25.2	25.1	25.3	25.1
1994	25.4	25.5	25.8	25.9	26.2	26.4	26.3	26.0	25.9	25.9	26.1	26.2	26.0
1995	26.6	26.8	27.0	27.2	27.1	27.4	27.2	27.2	27.1	27.2	27.1	27.5	27.1
1996	27.4	27.5	27.8	28.0	27.9	28.1	28.1	28.1	28.0	27.9	28.0	27.9	27.9
1997	27.5	27.8	28.2	28.1	28.3	28.4	28.3	28.3	28.1	28.3	28.3	28.4	28.2
1998	28.3	28.5	28.6	29.1	29.1	29.2	29.3	28.8	28.9	29.1	29.0	29.1	28.9
1999	28.8	29.2	29.5	29.2	29.3	29.8	29.4	29.1	29.2	29.4	29.3	29.4	29.3
2000	29.0	29.2	29.5	29.5	29.7	29.9	29.6	29.6	29.4	29.5	29.5	29.4	29.5
2001	32.9	33.1	33.4	33.3	33.6	33.7	33.8	33.7	33.3	33.5	33.5	33.4	33.4
2002	32.8	33.2	33.2	34.2	34.2	34.3	34.5	34.2	34.0	34.0	33.8	33.9	33.9
2003	34.4	34.5	34.8	34.9	34.9	35.1	35.5	34.5	34.7	34.9	35.1	34.9	34.9
Government													
1990	139.3	142.6	144.3	145.8	150.6	146.9	135.3	134.9	142.5	144.0	149.0	145.9	143.4
1991	140.9	144.3	145.6	146.7	148.6	147.0	141.4	141.1	147.5	148.3	148.0	148.2	145.6
1992	144.5	146.7	148.1	148.7	153.9	151.4	139.2	138.5	146.3	149.4	153.6	151.4	147.6
1993	146.4	148.5	149.9	152.9	154.2	150.6	140.6	139.9	148.3	151.7	152.4	152.3	149.0
1994	148.8	151.1	152.0	152.0	158.1	153.8	142.2	142.3	150.6	153.7	160.0	154.2	151.6
1995	150.2	152.2	153.3	153.2	154.6	152.8	142.4	142.6	148.4	152.4	153.9	153.0	150.8
1996	149.1	151.8	152.5	153.8	156.5	153.5	142.9	143.7	150.7	153.0	155.5	153.6	151.4
1997	150.9	152.2	153.5	153.9	155.9	154.1	146.1	144.7	151.1	154.0	155.5	154.9	152.2
1998	150.7	153.2	154.1	153.0	155.2	152.5	142.8	142.0	149.3	152.1	152.7	152.9	150.9
1999	149.6	151.9	152.7	152.6	154.7	153.5	145.7	143.7	150.7	153.6	154.4	154.2	151.4
2000	152.8	154.0	156.5	155.8	159.4	158.2	148.5	148.3	153.3	154.2	155.9	155.9	154.4
2001	152.8	155.3	156.6	157.7	160.7	160.2	150.1	151.3	157.2	158.5	161.0	160.1	156.8
2002	156.4	159.5	160.2	160.5	162.8	161.7	151.6	150.9	157.9	161.6	162.2	161.6	158.9
2003	159.7	160.7	160.9	162.1	163.6	162.6	153.3	150.9	158.1	162.9	163.1	162.4	160.0
Federal government													
1990	17.7	17.7	18.2	19.4	19.4	18.3	18.1	17.9	17.8	17.3	17.4	17.4	18.1
1991	17.2	17.2	17.4	17.3	17.2	17.7	17.6	17.6	17.5	17.4	17.4	17.5	17.4
1992	17.4	17.2	17.3	17.2	17.0	17.2	17.0	16.9	16.8	16.9	16.8	17.1	17.1
1993	17.1	17.1	17.1	17.2	17.2	17.5	17.4	17.4	17.5	17.3	17.4	17.6	17.3
1994	17.3	17.3	17.3	17.4	17.4	17.5	17.2	17.1	17.1	17.0	17.0	17.0	17.2
1995	16.6	16.6	16.6	16.6	16.5	16.5	16.4	16.3	16.2	16.1	16.3	16.2	16.4
1996	15.8	15.8	15.8	16.2	16.0	16.1	16.1	16.1	16.0	15.9	15.9	16.2	16.0
1997	16.1	16.1	16.1	16.1	16.0	16.3	16.4	16.2	16.1	15.7	15.8	16.1	16.1
1998	16.1	16.1	16.0	15.8	15.8	16.0	16.0	16.0	16.0	15.8	16.0	16.2	16.0
1999	15.9	15.7	15.8	15.8	15.8	15.9	16.0	16.0	15.9	15.8	15.9	16.1	15.9
2000	16.1	16.2	18.1	16.4	18.8	16.2	16.3	16.4	15.8	15.9	16.0	16.5	16.6
2001	15.9	15.8	15.8	15.8	15.9	16.1	16.2	16.2	16.0	16.0	16.2	16.6	16.0
2002	16.1	16.1	15.9	16.1	16.1	16.5	16.6	16.4	16.2	16.4	16.5	16.9	16.3
2003	16.6	16.6	16.6	16.5	16.5	16.8	16.9	16.9	16.8	16.8	16.4	16.7	16.7
State government													
1990	34.7	36.8	37.4	37.1	37.7	35.5	34.6	35.5	38.2	38.0	38.6	38.2	36.9
1991	35.7	37.9	38.3	38.0	38.7	36.6	35.5	36.0	38.7	39.2	39.0	38.9	37.7
1992	37.1	38.4	38.7	38.6	40.4	38.3	36.1	36.7	39.2	39.9	39.7	39.4	38.5
1993	37.7	39.2	39.5	39.5	39.5	37.1	36.1	36.4	39.7	40.1	40.3	40.3	38.8
1994	38.2	39.6	40.2	39.4	40.2	37.4	36.8	37.6	40.7	40.4	40.6	40.3	39.3
1995	38.5	40.0	40.6	39.9	40.4	37.9	37.4	38.6	40.4	40.5	40.6	40.6	39.6
1996	38.7	40.5	40.6	40.1	40.5	38.0	37.7	38.6	41.3	40.8	41.3	41.1	39.9
1997	39.6	40.3	40.6	40.0	40.5	38.3	38.0	38.3	41.1	41.1	42.7	42.2	40.2
1998	38.7	40.5	40.9	39.6	40.5	37.7	36.4	36.7	39.2	39.0	38.8	39.1	38.9
1999	36.4	38.2	38.5	37.9	39.0	37.2	37.1	36.6	38.7	38.9	39.1	39.0	38.1
2000	37.9	38.6	39.1	38.6	39.2	39.4	38.6	39.1	39.6	38.6	38.9	38.8	38.9
2001	37.4	38.9	40.1	39.8	40.9	38.6	37.8	39.4	41.2	41.0	42.2	40.9	39.9
2002	38.4	40.1	40.9	40.1	40.4	37.9	37.6	37.4	40.5	40.4	40.2	39.4	39.4
2003	39.1	39.4	39.3	39.3	39.6	37.2	36.6	36.8	38.8	40.0	39.9	39.8	38.8

Employment by Industry: Nebraska—*Continued*

(Numbers in thousands. Not seasonally adjusted.)

Industry	January	February	March	April	May	June	July	August	September	October	November	December	Annual Average
STATEWIDE—*Continued*													
Local government													
1990	86.9	88.1	88.7	89.3	93.5	93.1	82.6	81.5	86.5	88.7	93.0	90.3	88.5
1991	88.0	89.2	89.9	91.4	92.7	92.7	88.3	87.5	91.3	91.7	91.6	91.8	90.5
1992	90.0	91.1	92.1	92.9	96.5	95.9	86.1	84.9	90.3	92.6	97.1	94.9	92.0
1993	91.6	92.2	93.3	96.2	97.5	96.0	87.1	86.1	91.1	94.3	94.7	94.4	92.9
1994	93.3	94.2	94.5	95.2	100.5	98.9	88.2	87.6	92.8	96.3	102.4	96.9	95.1
1995	95.1	95.6	96.1	96.7	97.7	98.4	88.6	87.7	91.8	95.8	97.0	96.2	94.7
1996	94.6	95.5	96.1	97.5	100.0	99.4	89.1	89.0	93.4	96.3	98.3	96.3	95.5
1997	95.2	95.8	96.8	97.8	99.4	99.5	91.7	90.2	93.9	97.2	97.0	96.6	95.9
1998	95.9	96.6	97.2	97.6	98.9	98.8	90.4	89.3	94.1	97.3	97.9	97.6	96.0
1999	97.3	98.0	98.4	98.9	99.9	100.4	92.6	91.1	96.1	98.9	99.4	99.1	97.5
2000	98.8	99.2	99.3	100.8	101.4	102.6	93.6	92.8	97.9	99.7	101.0	100.6	99.0
2001	99.5	100.6	100.7	102.1	103.9	105.5	96.1	95.7	100.0	101.5	102.6	102.6	100.9
2002	101.9	103.3	103.4	104.3	106.3	107.3	97.4	97.1	101.2	104.8	105.5	105.3	103.2
2003	104.0	104.7	105.0	106.3	107.5	108.6	99.8	97.2	102.5	106.1	106.8	105.9	104.5
LINCOLN													
Total nonfarm													
1990	117.9	119.7	120.9	121.2	124.2	121.0	118.9	120.5	123.4	123.7	125.8	124.0	121.7
1991	120.3	122.4	123.6	123.6	124.9	123.7	120.6	121.9	124.6	125.5	125.4	125.9	123.5
1992	122.3	123.5	124.4	125.1	127.3	126.9	123.8	124.6	127.7	128.8	129.6	128.6	126.0
1993	123.9	125.2	126.9	128.2	129.2	129.0	126.9	128.9	131.5	131.5	131.6	131.4	128.6
1994	128.0	129.5	131.0	131.6	134.3	133.6	131.9	133.1	134.9	135.1	137.0	134.5	132.8
1995	132.8	134.4	135.7	136.4	136.9	138.1	135.7	137.8	138.8	139.8	140.8	141.0	137.3
1996	137.9	140.0	141.3	141.2	143.4	141.8	140.5	142.6	144.1	145.7	147.1	146.0	142.6
1997	141.4	142.2	144.1	145.2	146.5	145.5	144.0	145.2	146.2	147.6	149.7	148.7	145.5
1998	142.5	144.5	145.2	146.3	148.3	147.9	148.3	148.1	150.7	151.1	151.6	151.7	148.0
1999	147.1	148.3	149.1	151.1	152.5	153.3	152.7	152.6	154.6	155.0	155.5	155.9	152.3
2000	149.1	150.5	152.5	153.6	155.4	156.4	154.3	155.1	155.5	155.7	156.5	156.9	154.2
2001	155.4	156.1	157.8	159.2	161.2	160.9	158.5	160.1	161.6	160.2	161.8	160.3	159.4
2002	153.8	155.2	157.0	160.4	160.9	161.0	158.3	159.2	162.7	161.6	162.2	162.2	159.5
2003	157.3	158.6	160.3	158.6	159.2	158.2	156.5	156.7	156.6	158.4	158.7	158.5	158.1
Total private													
1990	87.0	87.4	88.2	88.7	89.0	88.7	88.5	89.4	90.5	90.5	91.1	91.0	89.1
1991	88.6	89.4	90.4	90.4	90.7	90.9	89.7	90.5	91.2	91.6	91.3	91.8	90.5
1992	89.9	90.2	90.9	91.9	92.6	92.5	91.6	92.7	93.6	94.7	94.5	94.8	92.4
1993	91.2	91.6	92.6	93.9	94.9	95.1	94.0	94.9	95.9	97.1	97.2	97.0	94.6
1994	95.3	95.9	96.8	97.9	99.0	99.5	98.5	99.7	100.2	100.8	101.6	100.5	98.8
1995	99.0	99.8	100.8	101.4	102.0	103.2	102.6	103.7	104.4	104.9	105.9	106.1	102.8
1996	104.3	105.1	106.4	106.6	107.0	107.6	106.8	107.6	108.0	108.9	109.4	109.7	107.2
1997	106.1	106.6	107.9	109.5	110.2	111.0	110.6	111.5	111.5	112.7	114.1	114.0	110.4
1998	110.5	111.4	111.9	113.8	114.8	115.9	116.2	116.3	116.7	117.4	117.7	117.9	115.0
1999	114.6	114.9	115.4	117.7	118.3	119.7	119.9	120.1	120.4	120.9	121.0	121.6	118.7
2000	115.4	116.3	117.7	119.1	120.1	120.6	119.8	120.3	120.3	121.4	121.6	122.0	119.5
2001	121.1	121.3	122.0	123.8	124.7	125.1	124.5	124.8	124.8	124.0	124.5	123.8	123.7
2002	119.0	119.3	120.6	124.2	123.9	124.8	124.3	124.5	126.4	124.9	125.3	125.2	123.5
2003	122.0	122.4	123.6	122.8	123.0	123.3	122.9	123.2	121.6	122.3	122.5	122.1	122.6
Goods-producing													
1990	17.1	16.9	17.2	17.7	17.8	17.8	17.7	18.2	18.3	18.3	18.3	18.1	17.7
1991	17.6	17.9	18.2	18.2	18.3	18.6	18.0	18.3	18.4	18.2	17.9	18.1	18.1
1992	17.3	17.4	17.7	18.1	18.4	18.6	18.6	18.9	19.1	18.9	18.7	18.9	18.3
1993	18.0	18.1	18.3	19.0	19.0	19.4	19.1	19.5	19.4	19.3	19.3	19.2	18.9
1994	18.8	19.0	19.4	20.0	20.3	20.6	20.5	20.8	20.7	21.0	20.9	20.4	20.2
1995	19.9	19.9	20.4	20.9	21.2	21.5	21.7	21.8	21.9	21.8	21.9	21.6	21.2
1996	20.7	20.7	21.0	21.5	21.9	22.2	22.3	22.2	22.0	22.1	21.9	21.7	21.6
1997	20.7	21.0	21.2	21.8	21.3	22.3	22.6	22.7	22.6	23.0	23.1	22.9	22.1
1998	22.5	22.7	22.6	23.2	23.9	24.2	24.7	24.8	24.7	24.9	24.4	24.4	23.9
1999	23.6	23.8	23.7	24.7	24.8	25.3	25.5	25.6	25.5	25.4	25.2	25.2	24.8
2000	23.9	23.9	24.1	24.3	24.9	25.2	25.1	25.1	24.8	24.9	24.8	24.7	24.6
2001	25.0	24.9	24.9	25.6	26.0	26.0	26.0	25.9	25.6	25.5	25.3	24.9	25.5
2002	24.0	23.9	24.2	24.8	25.1	25.3	25.3	25.2	25.1	24.8	24.4	24.2	24.7
2003	23.2	23.0	23.3	23.7	23.6	23.8	23.8	23.8	23.7	23.9	23.9	23.2	23.6
Construction and mining													
1990	3.7	3.7	4.0	4.3	4.5	4.7	4.8	4.8	4.8	4.8	4.7	4.5	4.4
1991	4.0	4.3	4.6	4.7	4.9	5.1	4.9	4.9	4.8	4.7	4.4	4.4	4.6
1992	4.0	4.1	4.3	4.7	5.0	5.1	5.4	5.4	5.4	5.1	4.9	4.8	4.8
1993	4.2	4.3	4.5	4.9	5.2	5.4	5.4	5.4	5.3	5.3	5.2	5.0	5.0
1994	4.6	4.6	5.0	5.4	5.7	5.8	5.8	5.8	5.6	5.6	5.5	5.1	5.3
1995	4.7	4.7	4.9	5.3	5.5	5.9	5.9	5.9	6.0	5.9	5.9	5.7	5.5
1996	5.1	5.2	5.4	5.9	6.2	6.4	6.5	6.5	6.3	6.3	6.1	5.9	5.9
1997	5.3	5.4	5.8	6.4	6.5	6.8	6.9	6.9	6.7	6.7	6.6	6.3	6.3
1998	5.9	5.9	5.9	6.4	6.8	7.1	7.4	7.4	7.3	7.5	7.0	6.9	6.7
1999	6.2	6.4	6.5	7.3	7.5	7.9	8.1	8.1	8.0	7.9	7.7	7.6	7.4
2000	6.7	6.7	7.0	7.3	7.7	7.9	7.9	7.9	7.6	7.5	7.3	7.0	7.3
2001	6.9	7.0	7.1	7.9	8.4	8.5	8.6	8.6	8.4	8.3	8.2	7.8	8.0
2002	7.1	7.1	7.4	8.0	8.4	8.6	8.6	8.6	8.5	8.5	8.3	8.2	8.1
2003	7.5	7.4	7.6	7.9	8.2	8.4	8.4	8.4	8.4	8.4	8.5	7.9	8.1

Employment by Industry: Nebraska—*Continued*

(Numbers in thousands. Not seasonally adjusted.)

Industry	January	February	March	April	May	June	July	August	September	October	November	December	Annual Average
LINCOLN—*Continued*													
Manufacturing													
1990	13.4	13.2	13.2	13.4	13.3	13.1	12.9	13.4	13.5	13.5	13.6	13.6	13.3
1991	13.6	13.6	13.6	13.5	13.4	13.5	13.1	13.4	13.6	13.5	13.5	13.7	13.5
1992	13.3	13.3	13.4	13.4	13.4	13.5	13.2	13.5	13.7	13.8	13.8	14.1	13.5
1993	13.8	13.8	13.8	14.1	13.8	14.0	13.7	14.1	14.1	14.0	14.1	14.2	13.9
1994	14.2	14.4	14.4	14.6	14.6	14.8	14.7	15.0	15.1	15.4	15.4	15.3	14.8
1995	15.2	15.2	15.5	15.6	15.7	15.6	15.8	15.9	15.9	15.9	16.0	15.9	15.6
1996	15.6	15.5	15.6	15.6	15.7	15.8	15.8	15.7	15.7	15.8	15.8	15.8	15.7
1997	15.4	15.6	15.4	15.4	14.8	15.5	15.7	15.8	15.9	16.3	16.5	16.6	15.7
1998	16.6	16.8	16.7	16.8	17.1	17.1	17.3	17.4	17.4	17.4	17.4	17.5	17.1
1999	17.4	17.4	17.2	17.4	17.3	17.4	17.4	17.5	17.5	17.5	17.5	17.6	17.4
2000	17.2	17.2	17.1	17.0	17.2	17.3	17.2	17.2	17.2	17.4	17.5	17.7	17.2
2001	18.1	17.9	17.8	17.7	17.6	17.5	17.4	17.3	17.2	17.2	17.1	17.1	17.5
2002	16.9	16.8	16.8	16.8	16.7	16.7	16.7	16.6	16.6	16.3	16.1	16.0	16.6
2003	15.7	15.6	15.7	15.8	15.4	15.4	15.4	15.4	15.3	15.5	15.4	15.3	15.5
Service-providing													
1990	100.8	102.8	103.7	103.5	106.4	103.2	101.2	102.3	105.1	105.4	107.5	105.9	103.9
1991	102.7	104.5	105.4	105.4	106.6	105.1	102.6	103.6	106.2	107.3	107.5	107.8	105.3
1992	105.0	106.1	106.7	107.0	108.9	108.3	105.2	105.7	108.6	109.9	110.9	109.7	107.6
1993	105.9	107.1	108.6	109.2	110.2	109.6	107.8	109.4	112.1	112.2	112.3	112.2	109.7
1994	109.2	110.5	111.6	111.6	114.0	113.0	111.4	112.3	114.2	114.1	116.1	114.1	112.6
1995	112.9	114.5	115.3	115.5	115.7	116.6	114.0	116.0	116.9	118.0	118.9	119.4	116.1
1996	117.2	119.3	120.3	119.7	121.5	119.6	118.2	120.4	122.1	123.6	125.2	124.3	120.9
1997	120.7	121.2	122.9	123.4	125.2	123.2	121.4	122.5	123.6	124.6	126.6	125.8	123.4
1998	120.0	121.8	122.6	123.1	124.4	123.7	123.6	123.3	126.0	126.2	127.2	127.3	124.1
1999	123.5	124.5	125.4	126.4	127.7	128.0	127.2	127.0	129.1	129.6	130.3	130.7	127.4
2000	125.2	126.6	128.4	129.3	130.5	131.2	129.2	130.0	130.7	130.8	131.7	132.2	129.6
2001	130.4	131.2	132.9	133.6	135.2	134.9	132.5	134.2	136.0	134.7	136.5	135.4	134.0
2002	129.8	131.3	132.8	135.6	135.8	135.7	133.0	134.0	137.6	136.8	137.8	138.0	134.9
2003	134.1	135.6	137.0	134.9	135.6	134.4	132.7	132.9	132.9	134.5	134.8	135.3	134.6
Trade, transportation, and utilities													
1990	22.1	21.9	22.1	22.1	22.2	22.2	22.2	22.4	22.7	22.6	23.0	23.2	22.3
1991	22.4	22.2	22.4	22.3	22.6	22.4	22.4	22.6	22.5	22.9	23.0	23.4	22.5
1992	22.6	22.5	22.5	22.9	23.0	23.0	22.7	23.0	23.0	23.5	23.8	24.0	23.0
1993	22.8	22.7	22.8	22.8	23.1	23.0	22.5	22.5	23.0	23.6	24.0	24.1	23.0
1994	23.3	23.1	23.2	23.3	23.8	23.9	23.7	24.0	24.1	24.3	24.7	24.8	23.8
1995	23.7	23.8	24.0	23.7	23.8	24.0	23.7	23.9	24.1	24.2	24.6	24.9	24.0
1996	24.5	24.4	24.5	24.3	24.6	24.6	24.3	24.5	24.5	25.2	25.8	26.1	24.7
1997	25.4	24.9	25.0	25.3	25.7	25.7	25.2	25.3	25.4	25.7	26.5	26.8	25.5
1998	25.3	25.2	25.3	25.4	25.7	26.1	25.9	25.7	26.0	26.3	26.8	27.1	25.9
1999	25.7	25.5	25.6	26.0	26.2	26.5	26.3	26.2	26.4	26.9	27.3	27.7	26.3
2000	25.8	26.0	26.2	26.5	26.8	26.8	26.6	26.6	26.6	27.0	27.4	27.8	26.6
2001	27.7	27.5	27.5	27.5	27.9	28.0	27.7	27.6	27.8	27.6	28.2	28.3	27.8
2002	27.0	27.0	26.9	27.3	27.4	27.5	27.5	27.2	27.3	27.2	27.9	28.1	27.4
2003	27.3	27.4	27.6	26.9	27.2	27.4	27.1	27.3	27.2	27.1	27.5	27.7	27.3
Wholesale trade													
1990	3.9	3.8	3.8	3.9	3.9	3.9	3.9	4.0	4.0	4.0	4.1	4.1	3.9
1991	3.9	3.9	3.9	3.9	4.0	4.0	3.9	3.9	3.9	3.9	3.8	3.9	3.9
1992	3.9	3.9	3.9	3.9	3.9	3.9	3.9	3.9	3.7	3.8	3.8	3.8	3.8
1993	3.6	3.5	3.6	3.5	3.7	3.7	3.6	3.6	3.6	3.6	3.6	3.6	3.6
1994	3.7	3.7	3.8	3.7	3.8	3.8	3.8	3.8	3.7	3.8	3.8	3.8	3.7
1995	3.8	3.8	3.8	3.8	3.9	3.9	3.9	3.8	3.8	3.8	3.9	4.0	3.8
1996	4.0	4.0	4.0	4.1	4.2	4.2	4.2	4.1	4.1	4.1	4.2	4.2	4.1
1997	4.2	4.1	4.1	4.1	4.3	4.3	4.2	4.2	4.1	4.1	4.1	4.1	4.1
1998	4.1	4.0	4.1	4.2	4.3	4.4	4.4	4.4	4.4	4.3	4.3	4.4	4.2
1999	4.2	4.2	4.3	4.4	4.5	4.6	4.5	4.5	4.4	4.4	4.5	4.5	4.4
2000	4.2	4.2	4.2	4.3	4.3	4.4	4.3	4.3	4.2	4.2	4.2	4.3	4.2
2001	4.5	4.6	4.6	4.5	4.8	4.9	4.8	4.7	4.8	4.5	4.5	4.5	4.6
2002	4.4	4.4	4.4	4.5	4.5	4.7	4.8	4.6	4.6	4.5	4.6	4.6	4.6
2003	4.4	4.3	4.4	4.0	4.1	4.2	4.1	4.2	4.1	4.0	4.0	4.0	4.2
Retail trade													
1990	13.9	13.8	13.9	13.9	14.0	13.9	14.0	14.0	14.2	14.2	14.5	14.6	14.0
1991	13.6	13.5	13.6	13.6	13.8	13.6	13.6	13.8	13.8	14.1	14.3	14.6	13.8
1992	13.9	13.8	13.8	13.6	13.5	13.5	13.4	13.5	13.6	13.9	14.3	14.4	13.7
1993	13.7	13.7	13.7	13.6	13.7	13.5	13.3	13.3	13.7	14.1	14.5	14.6	13.7
1994	13.9	13.7	13.7	14.0	14.1	14.0	13.9	14.0	14.1	14.3	14.8	14.9	14.1
1995	13.8	13.8	13.9	13.7	13.6	13.8	13.9	14.1	14.3	14.3	14.6	14.8	14.0
1996	14.4	14.3	14.3	14.0	14.1	14.1	13.9	14.0	14.1	14.6	15.1	15.3	14.3
1997	15.0	14.6	14.6	14.7	14.9	14.8	14.5	14.5	14.7	14.9	15.6	15.9	14.8
1998	14.8	14.7	14.7	14.8	15.0	15.2	15.0	15.2	15.5	15.8	16.3	16.5	15.2
1999	15.5	15.3	15.3	15.5	15.5	15.7	15.6	15.5	15.8	16.2	16.5	16.8	15.7
2000	15.5	15.6	15.7	15.8	16.0	16.0	15.7	15.7	15.9	16.3	16.7	17.0	15.9
2001	16.5	16.2	16.2	16.3	16.4	16.4	16.1	16.2	16.3	16.4	16.9	17.1	16.4
2002	16.1	15.9	15.9	16.1	16.3	16.3	16.2	16.4	16.5	16.4	17.0	17.2	16.4
2003	16.1	16.2	16.3	16.2	16.4	16.5	16.3	16.5	16.6	16.5	16.9	17.1	16.5

Employment by Industry: Nebraska—*Continued*

(Numbers in thousands. Not seasonally adjusted.)

Industry	January	February	March	April	May	June	July	August	September	October	November	December	Annual Average
LINCOLN—*Continued*													
Transportation and utilities													
1990	4.3	4.3	4.4	4.3	4.3	4.4	4.3	4.4	4.5	4.4	4.4	4.5	4.3
1991	4.9	4.8	4.9	4.8	4.8	4.8	4.9	4.9	4.8	4.9	4.9	4.9	4.8
1992	4.8	4.8	4.8	5.4	5.6	5.6	5.4	5.6	5.7	5.8	5.7	5.8	5.4
1993	5.5	5.5	5.5	5.7	5.7	5.8	5.6	5.6	5.7	5.9	5.9	5.9	5.6
1994	5.7	5.7	5.7	5.6	5.9	6.1	6.0	6.2	6.3	6.2	6.1	6.1	5.9
1995	6.1	6.2	6.3	6.2	6.3	6.3	5.9	6.0	6.0	6.1	6.1	6.1	6.1
1996	6.1	6.1	6.2	6.2	6.3	6.3	6.2	6.4	6.3	6.5	6.5	6.6	6.3
1997	6.2	6.2	6.3	6.5	6.5	6.6	6.5	6.6	6.6	6.7	6.8	6.8	6.5
1998	6.4	6.5	6.5	6.4	6.4	6.5	6.5	6.1	6.1	6.2	6.2	6.2	6.3
1999	6.0	6.0	6.0	6.1	6.2	6.2	6.2	6.2	6.2	6.3	6.3	6.4	6.1
2000	6.1	6.2	6.3	6.4	6.5	6.4	6.6	6.6	6.5	6.5	6.5	6.5	6.4
2001	6.7	6.7	6.7	6.7	6.7	6.7	6.8	6.7	6.7	6.7	6.8	6.7	6.7
2002	6.5	6.7	6.6	6.7	6.6	6.5	6.5	6.2	6.2	6.3	6.3	6.3	6.5
2003	6.8	6.9	6.9	6.7	6.7	6.7	6.7	6.6	6.5	6.6	6.6	6.6	6.7
Information													
1990	3.7	3.7	3.7	3.8	3.8	3.7	3.8	3.8	3.8	3.7	3.7	3.8	3.7
1991	3.6	3.7	3.7	3.8	3.8	3.8	3.7	3.8	3.8	3.7	3.7	3.7	3.7
1992	3.7	3.6	3.6	3.7	3.6	3.6	3.6	3.7	3.7	3.7	3.7	3.8	3.6
1993	3.6	3.6	3.7	3.7	3.6	3.6	3.6	3.6	3.6	3.7	3.7	3.7	3.6
1994	3.7	3.7	3.7	3.7	3.5	3.5	3.5	3.6	3.6	3.6	3.6	3.5	3.6
1995	3.5	3.6	3.6	3.6	3.5	3.6	3.5	3.5	3.6	3.6	3.6	3.6	3.5
1996	3.4	3.4	3.5	3.5	3.4	3.4	3.4	3.4	3.5	3.5	3.5	3.5	3.4
1997	3.3	3.4	3.4	3.5	3.4	3.4	3.4	3.4	3.4	3.5	3.6	3.6	3.4
1998	3.4	3.4	3.4	3.6	3.6	3.5	3.6	3.6	3.6	3.6	3.7	3.7	3.5
1999	3.6	3.6	3.6	3.6	3.7	3.7	3.6	3.6	3.6	3.7	3.7	3.6	3.6
2000	3.4	3.6	3.5	3.5	3.5	3.5	3.5	3.5	3.5	3.6	3.6	3.6	3.5
2001	3.8	3.8	3.7	3.8	3.7	3.7	3.7	3.3	3.3	3.4	3.4	3.4	3.6
2002	3.3	3.3	3.3	3.4	3.3	3.3	3.3	3.4	3.4	3.5	3.5	3.4	3.4
2003	3.4	3.5	3.5	3.4	3.4	3.4	3.3	3.3	3.3	3.4	3.4	3.4	3.4
Financial activities													
1990	7.5	7.6	7.6	7.7	7.7	7.7	7.7	7.7	7.7	7.8	7.8	7.8	7.6
1991	7.7	7.7	7.7	7.5	7.5	7.5	7.5	7.5	7.5	7.6	7.6	7.6	7.5
1992	7.4	7.4	7.4	7.5	7.5	7.6	7.7	7.7	7.6	7.6	7.6	7.6	7.5
1993	7.2	7.2	7.1	7.1	7.2	7.2	7.3	7.3	7.3	7.3	7.3	7.3	7.2
1994	7.1	7.2	7.3	7.4	7.5	7.6	7.5	7.5	7.5	7.5	7.6	7.5	7.4
1995	7.5	7.5	7.6	7.7	7.7	7.9	7.8	7.9	7.9	7.9	7.9	8.0	7.7
1996	8.0	8.1	7.8	7.8	7.8	7.9	7.8	8.0	8.0	8.0	8.1	8.2	7.9
1997	7.8	7.9	8.1	8.3	8.4	8.5	8.5	8.6	8.6	8.5	8.6	8.7	8.3
1998	8.5	8.7	8.7	8.9	8.9	9.1	9.3	9.4	9.3	9.4	9.4	9.5	9.0
1999	9.3	9.4	9.5	9.6	9.7	9.8	9.8	9.7	9.6	9.8	9.7	9.8	9.6
2000	9.6	9.7	9.8	10.0	10.1	10.1	10.1	10.1	10.0	10.0	10.0	10.1	9.9
2001	9.7	9.8	9.8	10.4	10.5	10.6	10.6	10.6	10.6	10.3	10.3	10.4	10.3
2002	10.4	10.4	10.5	10.6	10.7	10.9	10.9	10.9	11.0	11.0	11.0	11.1	10.8
2003	11.0	11.0	11.1	11.0	11.1	11.2	11.1	11.0	10.9	10.9	10.9	11.0	11.0
Professional and business services													
1990	9.9	9.9	10.1	10.0	10.0	10.2	10.0	10.2	10.3	10.3	10.4	10.3	10.1
1991	10.2	10.3	10.3	10.3	10.2	10.3	10.2	10.2	10.2	10.3	10.2	10.3	10.2
1992	10.2	10.1	10.3	10.5	10.8	10.5	10.4	10.6	10.8	10.9	10.8	10.8	10.5
1993	11.1	11.1	11.2	11.6	12.1	12.0	12.1	12.3	12.3	12.4	12.3	12.1	11.8
1994	12.3	12.4	12.5	12.6	12.7	12.7	12.8	13.1	13.0	13.1	13.1	12.9	12.7
1995	13.5	13.7	13.6	13.7	14.1	14.2	14.1	14.5	14.2	14.6	14.7	14.7	14.1
1996	15.1	15.4	15.7	15.7	15.5	15.2	15.0	15.1	15.1	15.2	15.2	15.1	15.2
1997	15.1	15.1	15.4	15.4	15.8	15.8	15.9	16.2	16.1	16.1	16.3	16.2	15.7
1998	15.8	16.1	16.3	16.5	16.3	16.5	16.2	16.2	16.1	15.8	15.9	15.8	16.1
1999	15.7	15.8	15.9	16.2	16.2	16.6	17.1	17.4	17.3	16.9	16.9	17.0	16.5
2000	16.3	16.3	16.6	16.8	16.8	16.7	16.4	16.5	16.4	17.0	16.9	17.0	16.6
2001	16.5	16.8	17.0	17.2	17.3	17.5	17.6	17.9	17.9	17.4	17.2	16.8	17.3
2002	15.6	15.6	15.9	16.5	16.5	16.5	16.4	16.5	16.9	16.4	16.6	16.5	16.3
2003	15.8	15.8	15.9	15.7	15.6	15.8	15.7	15.6	15.0	15.3	15.4	15.1	15.6
Educational and health services													
1990	11.3	11.5	11.6	11.2	11.3	11.2	11.2	11.2	11.4	11.5	11.6	11.6	11.3
1991	11.5	11.7	11.8	11.8	11.7	11.7	11.6	11.6	11.9	12.1	12.1	12.1	11.8
1992	12.2	12.5	12.5	12.3	12.3	12.3	12.1	12.1	12.3	12.5	12.6	12.6	12.3
1993	12.4	12.4	12.7	12.4	12.4	12.4	12.3	12.4	12.6	13.1	13.1	12.8	12.5
1994	12.8	13.0	13.1	13.2	13.4	13.3	13.0	13.1	13.4	13.5	13.7	13.6	13.2
1995	13.9	14.0	14.1	14.1	14.1	14.1	14.0	14.2	14.4	14.6	14.8	14.9	14.2
1996	14.7	14.9	15.1	15.1	15.2	15.3	15.1	15.3	15.6	15.8	16.0	16.2	15.3
1997	15.9	16.2	16.5	16.7	16.9	16.7	16.3	16.5	16.7	17.0	17.1	17.0	16.6
1998	16.6	16.7	16.8	16.7	16.7	16.7	16.7	16.6	16.9	17.2	17.3	17.3	16.8
1999	16.8	16.9	17.1	17.3	17.3	17.2	17.1	17.2	17.5	17.6	17.8	17.8	17.3
2000	17.2	17.5	17.7	17.9	18.0	18.2	18.2	18.4	18.6	18.5	18.7	18.8	18.1
2001	18.5	18.5	18.7	18.6	18.6	18.4	18.0	18.3	18.4	19.0	19.3	19.2	18.6
2002	18.9	18.9	19.5	20.6	20.1	19.8	19.6	19.6	21.0	20.5	20.4	20.4	19.9
2003	20.3	20.5	20.6	20.3	20.1	19.7	19.9	19.9	19.8	20.0	19.8	19.9	20.1

Employment by Industry: Nebraska—*Continued*

(Numbers in thousands. Not seasonally adjusted.)

Industry	January	February	March	April	May	June	July	August	September	October	November	December	Annual Average
LINCOLN—*Continued*													
Leisure and hospitality													
1990	10.0	10.4	10.4	10.6	10.6	10.3	10.3	10.4	10.6	10.6	10.7	10.7	10.4
1991	10.0	10.1	10.6	10.9	11.0	11.0	10.7	10.9	11.2	11.2	11.2	11.0	10.8
1992	10.8	10.9	11.1	11.1	11.1	11.0	10.7	11.0	11.4	11.7	11.5	11.3	11.1
1993	10.6	11.0	11.2	11.7	11.8	11.7	11.4	11.6	11.9	12.0	11.8	12.0	11.5
1994	11.5	11.7	11.7	11.9	12.0	12.1	11.7	11.8	12.0	12.0	12.1	11.9	11.8
1995	11.3	11.6	11.8	11.9	11.8	12.1	12.0	12.1	12.4	12.3	12.4	12.3	12.0
1996	12.1	12.4	12.8	12.7	12.6	12.9	12.8	13.0	13.2	13.1	12.9	13.0	12.7
1997	12.1	12.3	12.5	12.6	12.8	12.8	12.8	12.8	12.7	12.9	12.8	12.6	12.6
1998	12.3	12.6	12.7	13.3	13.5	13.6	13.5	13.7	13.8	13.9	14.0	13.9	13.4
1999	13.7	13.7	13.8	14.1	14.1	14.2	14.3	14.3	14.2	14.4	14.2	14.3	14.1
2000	13.3	13.3	13.7	14.0	13.9	13.9	13.8	14.0	14.2	14.3	14.1	13.9	13.8
2001	14.0	14.1	14.4	14.7	14.7	14.8	14.7	14.9	14.9	14.7	14.6	14.7	14.6
2002	13.9	14.2	14.3	14.8	14.7	15.2	15.0	15.4	15.2	15.0	15.0	14.9	14.8
2003	14.5	14.6	14.9	15.1	15.3	15.3	15.3	15.5	15.3	15.2	15.2	15.5	15.1
Other services													
1990	5.4	5.5	5.5	5.6	5.6	5.6	5.6	5.5	5.7	5.7	5.6	5.5	5.5
1991	5.6	5.8	5.7	5.6	5.6	5.6	5.6	5.6	5.7	5.6	5.6	5.6	5.6
1992	5.7	5.8	5.8	5.8	5.9	5.9	5.8	5.7	5.7	5.9	5.8	5.8	5.8
1993	5.5	5.5	5.6	5.6	5.7	5.8	5.7	5.7	5.8	5.7	5.7	5.8	5.6
1994	5.8	5.8	5.9	5.8	5.8	5.8	5.8	5.8	5.9	5.8	5.9	5.9	5.8
1995	5.7	5.7	5.7	5.8	5.8	5.8	5.8	5.8	5.9	5.9	6.0	6.1	5.8
1996	5.8	5.8	6.0	6.0	6.0	6.1	6.1	6.1	6.1	6.0	6.0	5.9	5.9
1997	5.8	5.8	5.8	5.9	5.9	5.8	5.9	6.0	6.0	6.0	6.1	6.2	5.9
1998	6.1	6.0	6.1	6.2	6.2	6.2	6.3	6.3	6.3	6.3	6.2	6.2	6.2
1999	6.2	6.2	6.2	6.2	6.3	6.4	6.2	6.1	6.3	6.2	6.2	6.2	6.2
2000	5.9	6.0	6.1	6.1	6.1	6.2	6.1	6.1	6.2	6.1	6.1	6.1	6.0
2001	5.9	5.9	6.0	6.0	6.0	6.1	6.2	6.3	6.3	6.1	6.2	6.1	6.1
2002	5.9	6.0	6.0	6.2	6.1	6.3	6.3	6.3	6.5	6.5	6.5	6.6	6.3
2003	6.5	6.6	6.7	6.7	6.7	6.7	6.7	6.8	6.4	6.5	6.4	6.3	6.6
Government													
1990	30.9	32.3	32.7	32.5	35.2	32.3	30.4	31.1	32.9	33.2	34.7	33.0	32.6
1991	31.7	33.0	33.2	33.2	34.2	32.8	30.9	31.4	33.4	33.9	34.1	34.1	32.9
1992	32.4	33.3	33.5	33.2	34.7	34.4	32.2	31.9	34.1	34.1	35.1	33.8	33.5
1993	32.7	33.6	34.3	34.3	34.3	33.9	32.9	34.0	35.6	34.4	34.4	34.4	34.0
1994	32.7	33.6	34.2	33.7	35.3	34.1	33.4	33.4	34.7	34.3	35.4	34.0	34.0
1995	33.8	34.6	34.9	35.0	34.9	34.9	33.1	34.1	34.4	34.9	34.9	34.9	34.5
1996	33.6	34.9	34.9	34.6	36.4	34.2	33.7	35.0	36.1	36.8	37.7	36.3	35.3
1997	35.3	35.6	36.2	35.7	36.3	34.5	33.4	33.7	34.7	34.9	35.6	34.7	35.0
1998	32.0	33.1	33.3	32.5	33.5	32.0	32.1	31.8	34.0	33.7	33.9	33.8	32.9
1999	32.5	33.4	33.7	33.4	34.2	33.6	32.8	32.5	34.2	34.1	34.5	34.3	33.6
2000	33.7	34.2	34.8	34.5	35.3	35.8	34.5	34.8	35.2	34.3	34.9	34.9	34.7
2001	34.3	34.8	35.8	35.4	36.5	35.8	34.0	35.3	36.8	36.2	37.3	36.5	35.7
2002	34.8	35.9	36.4	36.2	37.0	36.2	34.0	34.7	36.3	36.7	36.9	37.0	36.0
2003	35.3	36.2	36.7	35.8	36.2	34.9	33.6	33.5	35.0	36.1	36.2	36.4	35.5
Federal government													
1990	2.6	2.6	2.7	2.8	2.8	2.8	2.7	2.7	2.7	2.6	2.6	2.6	2.6
1991	2.6	2.6	2.6	2.6	2.6	2.7	2.7	2.7	2.7	2.6	2.7	2.7	2.6
1992	2.7	2.7	2.7	2.7	2.7	2.8	2.8	2.8	2.8	2.9	2.9	3.0	2.7
1993	2.8	2.8	2.8	2.8	2.8	2.8	2.8	2.8	2.8	2.8	2.8	2.8	2.8
1994	2.5	2.5	2.5	2.7	2.7	2.7	2.6	2.6	2.6	2.6	2.6	2.6	2.6
1995	2.5	2.5	2.5	2.5	2.5	2.6	2.5	2.5	2.5	2.5	2.4	2.5	2.5
1996	2.5	2.4	2.4	2.4	2.4	2.5	2.5	2.5	2.5	2.5	2.5	2.6	2.4
1997	2.5	2.5	2.5	2.5	2.5	2.5	2.5	2.5	2.5	2.5	2.6	2.6	2.5
1998	2.6	2.6	2.6	2.5	2.5	2.6	2.6	2.5	2.6	2.6	2.6	2.6	2.5
1999	2.6	2.5	2.5	2.5	2.5	2.5	2.5	2.5	2.5	2.5	2.5	2.6	2.5
2000	2.7	2.7	2.8	2.9	3.2	2.9	2.9	2.9	2.8	2.8	2.8	2.9	2.8
2001	2.9	2.8	2.8	2.8	2.9	2.9	3.0	3.0	3.0	3.0	3.0	3.0	2.9
2002	2.7	2.7	2.7	2.7	2.7	2.8	2.8	2.8	2.8	2.8	2.9	2.9	2.8
2003	2.8	2.8	2.7	2.7	2.7	2.8	2.8	2.8	2.8	2.8	2.9	2.9	2.8
State government													
1990	16.7	17.5	17.9	17.7	18.2	16.8	16.4	17.1	18.3	18.2	18.6	18.1	17.6
1991	17.1	18.0	18.2	18.0	18.6	17.2	16.6	17.1	18.4	18.8	18.7	18.5	17.9
1992	17.5	18.0	18.2	18.1	19.8	18.8	17.0	17.5	18.6	19.1	19.0	18.7	18.3
1993	17.8	18.4	18.7	18.7	18.8	17.6	17.5	18.0	19.9	19.2	19.3	19.4	18.6
1994	18.1	18.8	19.2	18.7	19.4	17.9	17.6	18.1	19.6	19.4	19.6	19.3	18.8
1995	18.4	19.0	19.4	19.1	19.6	18.2	17.8	18.7	19.4	19.4	19.5	19.5	19.0
1996	18.3	19.3	19.3	19.1	19.7	18.1	18.0	18.6	19.9	19.5	19.8	19.6	19.1
1997	18.8	18.9	19.1	18.8	19.2	18.1	17.7	18.1	19.5	19.6	21.2	20.4	19.1
1998	18.1	19.0	19.1	18.4	19.3	17.4	18.5	18.4	19.9	19.7	19.7	19.7	18.9
1999	18.3	19.2	19.4	19.0	19.8	18.9	18.8	18.7	19.8	19.8	20.0	19.7	19.2
2000	19.2	19.5	19.8	19.4	19.9	20.3	20.1	20.4	20.4	19.7	19.8	19.7	19.8
2001	19.1	19.5	20.4	20.2	20.9	19.8	19.2	20.4	21.3	21.0	21.7	20.8	20.4
2002	19.4	20.3	20.7	20.5	21.0	20.0	19.2	19.7	21.1	21.1	21.1	21.1	20.4
2003	19.7	20.6	21.0	19.9	20.3	18.7	18.5	18.6	19.8	20.5	20.5	20.6	19.9

Employment by Industry: Nebraska—*Continued*

(Numbers in thousands. Not seasonally adjusted.)

Industry	January	February	March	April	May	June	July	August	September	October	November	December	Annual Average
LINCOLN—*Continued*													
Local government													
1990	11.6	12.2	12.1	12.0	14.2	12.7	11.3	11.3	11.9	12.4	13.5	12.3	12.2
1991	12.0	12.4	12.4	12.6	13.0	12.9	11.6	11.6	12.3	12.5	12.7	12.9	12.4
1992	12.2	12.6	12.6	12.4	12.2	12.8	12.4	11.6	12.7	12.1	13.2	12.1	12.4
1993	12.1	12.4	12.8	12.8	12.7	13.5	12.6	13.2	12.9	12.4	12.3	12.2	12.6
1994	12.1	12.3	12.5	12.3	13.2	13.5	13.2	12.7	12.5	12.3	13.2	12.1	12.6
1995	12.9	13.1	13.0	13.4	12.8	14.1	12.8	12.9	12.5	13.0	13.0	12.9	13.0
1996	12.8	13.2	13.2	13.1	14.3	13.6	13.2	13.9	13.7	14.8	15.4	14.1	13.7
1997	14.0	14.2	14.6	14.4	14.6	13.9	13.2	13.1	12.7	12.8	11.8	11.7	13.4
1998	11.3	11.5	11.6	11.6	11.7	12.0	11.0	10.9	11.5	11.4	11.6	11.5	11.4
1999	11.6	11.7	11.8	11.9	11.9	12.2	11.5	11.3	11.9	11.8	12.0	12.0	11.8
2000	11.8	12.0	12.2	12.2	12.2	12.6	11.5	11.5	12.0	11.8	12.3	12.3	12.0
2001	12.3	12.5	12.6	12.4	12.7	13.1	11.8	11.9	12.5	12.2	12.6	12.7	12.4
2002	12.7	12.9	13.0	13.0	13.3	13.4	12.0	12.2	12.4	12.8	12.9	13.0	12.8
2003	12.8	12.8	13.0	13.2	13.2	13.4	12.3	12.1	12.4	12.8	12.8	12.9	12.8
OMAHA													
Total nonfarm													
1990	323.5	324.2	326.3	332.5	335.8	338.7	336.1	337.1	338.1	336.7	339.0	338.8	333.9
1991	329.6	329.4	331.4	333.1	334.9	337.2	336.5	337.7	339.1	338.8	338.0	339.5	335.4
1992	327.5	328.5	329.9	333.1	339.9	342.3	340.7	339.7	342.9	344.9	345.3	343.6	338.2
1993	335.1	336.3	338.9	344.2	347.8	349.4	348.2	348.3	350.3	353.7	355.7	355.3	346.9
1994	349.1	350.7	352.8	356.8	361.3	364.5	361.2	363.4	366.1	366.7	369.7	370.6	361.1
1995	362.7	364.8	368.0	370.1	372.2	375.9	374.3	376.8	375.5	379.4	381.7	383.1	373.7
1996	375.8	377.5	381.3	382.9	385.3	389.7	385.7	385.4	387.5	391.7	393.6	395.3	386.0
1997	384.6	386.4	391.3	391.7	395.7	398.6	395.1	394.6	398.5	400.2	402.1	405.7	395.4
1998	392.6	394.2	394.7	401.3	405.4	410.0	410.2	409.0	409.7	412.6	415.8	418.5	406.2
1999	402.7	405.1	406.9	412.3	415.6	421.1	419.7	419.3	419.4	421.9	424.2	426.3	416.2
2000	414.2	414.7	417.9	421.0	424.3	430.3	425.7	425.7	425.7	424.4	425.5	425.9	422.9
2001	427.1	425.9	428.0	434.8	438.2	442.4	436.8	437.6	436.8	436.7	439.9	438.4	435.2
2002	421.8	422.5	424.7	432.0	433.9	436.4	430.5	431.9	435.6	434.5	437.3	436.8	431.5
2003	424.3	424.0	425.4	422.3	424.2	426.5	425.1	423.5	425.1	426.8	428.4	425.6	425.1
Total private													
1990	275.6	275.9	277.9	283.6	286.0	290.2	288.5	290.9	290.0	287.9	289.8	290.2	285.5
1991	281.0	280.3	282.4	283.8	285.2	287.7	288.9	289.9	290.3	288.4	288.2	289.7	286.3
1992	279.1	279.8	281.0	283.4	289.9	292.5	292.6	292.1	294.2	294.3	294.0	293.4	288.9
1993	285.5	286.5	288.7	292.5	296.0	299.3	299.9	300.3	301.1	303.0	304.7	304.8	296.9
1994	298.8	300.1	302.4	306.3	310.1	313.7	312.9	314.8	315.8	315.4	317.8	319.3	310.6
1995	312.1	313.9	317.1	319.6	321.4	325.0	325.9	328.4	326.5	328.2	330.0	332.1	323.4
1996	325.4	326.5	330.4	331.4	333.7	338.5	337.3	337.9	338.6	341.2	342.8	344.8	335.7
1997	333.8	335.5	340.6	340.2	343.5	346.8	344.5	344.9	347.6	348.5	350.0	353.5	344.1
1998	340.5	341.8	342.4	349.2	352.9	357.7	362.4	361.3	360.5	362.5	365.8	368.6	355.5
1999	353.2	355.1	357.0	362.2	364.9	370.7	370.8	371.1	369.7	371.0	373.5	375.8	366.3
2000	363.5	363.9	367.2	370.0	372.4	378.9	376.1	376.6	375.4	373.2	374.0	374.6	372.2
2001	376.0	374.7	376.8	382.6	385.5	389.5	385.9	386.9	384.9	384.1	386.9	385.5	383.3
2002	369.2	369.3	371.6	378.9	380.5	383.1	379.2	381.0	382.8	380.2	383.0	383.0	378.5
2003	370.5	369.8	371.4	367.8	369.5	372.0	372.3	372.6	371.9	371.9	373.5	371.4	371.2
Goods-producing													
1990	48.5	48.2	48.7	50.6	50.9	52.3	52.4	52.6	52.2	51.9	51.8	51.0	50.9
1991	48.8	48.9	49.3	49.6	50.5	50.8	51.2	51.6	51.7	51.1	49.9	49.6	50.3
1992	46.3	46.6	47.5	47.9	50.1	50.8	50.7	50.8	50.7	50.9	50.5	49.7	49.4
1993	47.2	46.5	47.1	48.4	49.7	50.7	51.0	51.4	51.4	51.6	51.4	50.9	49.8
1994	49.1	48.8	49.5	51.2	52.2	53.4	53.4	53.2	53.2	53.1	53.2	52.3	51.9
1995	51.6	51.6	51.7	52.7	52.5	53.9	54.5	54.6	54.3	53.9	53.8	53.7	53.2
1996	51.9	51.4	52.7	54.1	55.0	56.5	56.2	56.3	55.8	56.0	55.8	55.5	54.8
1997	53.0	53.3	54.4	55.0	56.3	57.7	57.5	57.3	56.9	56.2	55.8	55.8	55.8
1998	53.9	54.2	53.7	56.5	57.8	59.1	60.1	60.0	59.5	58.7	58.7	58.7	57.6
1999	56.3	56.3	56.9	58.1	59.0	59.9	60.5	60.5	59.8	59.9	59.5	59.0	58.8
2000	56.4	56.6	57.9	58.9	59.6	60.8	60.5	60.3	60.1	59.5	58.5	57.6	58.9
2001	56.5	56.1	56.5	58.8	59.7	60.5	60.3	60.0	59.0	58.7	58.2	57.4	58.5
2002	54.4	54.1	54.4	56.3	56.9	58.2	58.4	58.5	58.1	57.8	57.6	56.7	56.8
2003	54.3	53.8	54.0	55.0	56.4	57.2	57.4	57.4	57.2	57.2	56.0	54.9	55.9
Construction and mining													
1990	11.7	11.7	12.1	13.9	14.6	15.4	15.4	15.5	15.1	14.9	14.8	13.8	14.1
1991	12.1	12.2	12.7	13.6	14.3	14.7	15.1	15.4	15.1	14.9	13.7	13.4	13.9
1992	11.6	11.6	12.3	13.4	14.5	15.1	15.3	15.3	15.2	15.4	15.1	14.3	14.1
1993	12.0	12.1	12.5	13.9	15.3	15.9	16.1	16.3	16.1	16.2	15.9	15.1	14.8
1994	13.8	13.5	14.5	16.4	17.4	18.4	18.3	18.2	18.0	17.8	17.6	16.6	16.7
1995	15.6	15.5	15.7	16.8	16.9	18.1	18.5	18.4	18.1	17.8	17.6	17.1	17.2
1996	15.1	15.0	15.9	17.3	18.2	19.1	19.1	19.0	18.6	18.6	18.0	17.5	17.6
1997	15.8	15.7	16.9	18.0	19.1	20.2	20.0	20.0	19.7	19.6	19.1	18.7	18.6
1998	17.3	17.4	17.3	19.8	21.1	21.8	22.5	22.3	21.9	21.5	21.5	21.4	20.5
1999	19.0	19.3	19.7	21.1	21.8	22.7	23.4	23.2	22.7	22.4	22.1	21.7	21.6
2000	19.9	19.9	20.7	21.9	22.4	23.2	23.3	23.5	23.1	23.1	22.1	21.2	22.0
2001	20.5	20.3	20.8	23.1	24.3	25.0	25.0	25.0	24.6	24.6	24.3	23.4	23.4
2002	20.8	20.7	21.5	23.5	24.1	25.0	25.2	25.2	24.9	24.9	24.7	23.8	23.7
2003	22.2	21.6	22.0	23.1	24.3	25.0	25.2	25.5	25.3	25.4	24.1	23.1	23.9

Employment by Industry: Nebraska—*Continued*

(Numbers in thousands. Not seasonally adjusted.)

Industry	January	February	March	April	May	June	July	August	September	October	November	December	Annual Average
OMAHA—*Continued*													
Manufacturing													
1990	36.8	36.5	36.6	36.7	36.3	36.9	37.0	37.1	37.1	37.0	37.0	37.2	36.9
1991	36.7	36.7	36.6	36.0	36.2	36.1	36.1	36.2	36.6	36.2	36.2	36.2	36.3
1992	34.7	35.0	35.2	34.5	35.6	35.7	35.4	35.5	35.5	35.5	35.4	35.4	35.3
1993	35.2	34.4	34.6	34.5	34.4	34.8	34.9	35.1	35.3	35.4	35.5	35.8	35.0
1994	35.3	35.3	35.0	34.8	34.8	35.0	35.1	35.0	35.2	35.3	35.6	35.7	35.2
1995	36.0	36.1	36.0	35.9	35.6	35.8	36.0	36.2	36.2	36.1	36.2	36.6	36.1
1996	36.8	36.4	36.8	36.8	36.8	37.4	37.1	37.3	37.2	37.4	37.8	38.0	37.2
1997	37.2	37.6	37.5	37.0	37.2	37.5	37.5	37.3	37.2	36.6	36.7	37.1	37.2
1998	36.6	36.8	36.4	36.7	36.7	37.3	37.6	37.7	37.6	37.2	37.2	37.3	37.1
1999	37.3	37.0	37.2	37.0	37.2	37.2	37.1	37.3	37.1	37.5	37.4	37.3	37.2
2000	36.5	36.7	37.2	37.0	37.2	37.6	37.2	36.8	37.0	36.4	36.4	36.4	36.9
2001	36.0	35.8	35.7	35.7	35.4	35.5	35.3	35.0	34.4	34.1	33.9	34.0	35.1
2002	33.6	33.4	32.9	32.8	32.8	33.2	33.2	33.3	33.2	32.9	32.9	32.9	33.1
2003	32.1	32.2	32.0	31.9	32.1	32.2	32.2	31.9	31.9	31.8	31.9	31.8	32.0
Service-providing													
1990	275.0	276.0	277.6	281.9	284.9	286.4	283.7	284.5	285.9	284.8	287.2	287.8	283.0
1991	280.8	280.5	282.1	283.5	284.4	286.4	285.3	286.1	287.4	287.7	288.1	289.9	285.2
1992	281.2	281.9	282.4	285.2	289.8	291.5	290.0	288.9	292.2	294.0	294.8	293.9	288.8
1993	287.9	289.8	291.8	295.8	298.1	298.7	297.2	296.9	298.9	302.1	304.3	304.4	297.2
1994	300.0	301.9	303.3	305.6	309.1	311.1	307.8	310.2	312.9	313.6	316.5	318.3	309.2
1995	311.1	313.2	316.3	317.4	319.7	322.0	319.8	322.2	321.2	325.5	327.9	329.4	320.5
1996	323.9	326.1	328.6	328.8	330.3	333.2	329.5	329.1	331.7	335.7	337.8	339.8	331.2
1997	331.6	333.1	336.9	336.7	339.4	340.9	337.6	337.3	341.6	344.0	346.3	349.9	339.6
1998	338.7	340.0	341.0	344.8	347.6	350.9	350.1	349.0	350.2	353.9	357.1	359.8	348.6
1999	346.4	348.8	350.0	354.2	356.6	361.2	359.2	358.8	359.6	362.0	364.7	367.3	357.4
2000	357.8	358.1	360.0	362.1	364.7	369.5	365.2	365.4	365.6	364.9	367.0	368.3	364.1
2001	370.6	369.8	371.5	376.0	378.5	381.9	376.5	377.6	377.8	378.0	381.7	381.0	376.7
2002	367.4	368.4	370.3	375.7	377.0	378.2	372.1	373.4	377.5	376.7	379.7	380.1	374.7
2003	370.0	370.2	371.4	367.3	367.8	369.3	367.7	366.1	367.9	369.6	372.4	370.7	369.2
Trade, transportation, and utilities													
1990	71.6	71.1	71.2	72.4	72.6	73.4	72.7	72.9	73.0	72.9	74.5	74.9	72.8
1991	73.1	71.6	72.4	72.6	72.8	73.2	73.2	74.0	73.8	74.5	75.7	76.5	73.6
1992	72.2	71.8	72.0	72.3	74.0	74.0	74.3	74.3	74.2	75.3	76.4	77.2	74.0
1993	73.8	73.5	73.8	74.8	75.4	75.8	76.8	77.2	77.6	77.8	79.7	80.5	76.4
1994	77.9	77.7	77.8	77.8	79.1	80.0	79.8	81.1	81.8	82.2	83.9	85.4	80.4
1995	82.3	82.1	82.5	82.4	83.1	83.4	83.6	85.2	85.0	86.1	87.7	88.7	84.3
1996	84.8	83.7	83.9	83.3	84.2	84.0	84.4	85.1	86.3	87.6	89.3	90.7	85.6
1997	86.6	85.9	86.8	86.8	87.8	88.0	87.8	88.1	89.6	90.9	92.5	93.9	88.7
1998	88.3	87.0	86.4	88.3	89.4	90.6	90.7	91.0	91.5	94.4	97.3	98.9	91.2
1999	91.8	91.5	91.5	92.5	92.8	95.4	94.0	95.3	95.0	96.1	98.1	99.5	94.5
2000	94.4	93.6	93.6	94.4	95.0	96.0	95.1	95.0	94.9	95.9	97.6	98.9	95.4
2001	98.9	97.6	97.8	98.7	99.2	99.5	98.7	99.3	99.9	100.6	103.2	104.1	99.8
2002	98.0	96.8	97.0	97.2	98.4	98.4	97.2	98.0	98.5	98.3	100.7	101.9	98.4
2003	97.0	96.0	96.8	93.3	94.0	94.4	94.2	94.6	94.8	94.6	96.3	96.2	95.2
Wholesale trade													
1990	17.8	17.9	18.0	18.4	18.3	18.5	18.6	18.5	18.5	18.2	18.3	18.4	18.3
1991	17.9	17.8	18.0	18.0	18.0	18.2	18.3	18.3	18.3	18.3	18.2	18.3	18.1
1992	17.8	17.9	17.9	17.8	18.4	18.5	18.5	18.5	18.3	18.6	18.3	18.3	18.2
1993	17.9	18.0	18.2	18.4	18.4	18.4	18.4	18.3	18.3	18.4	18.3	18.3	18.3
1994	18.0	18.1	18.2	18.5	18.6	18.7	18.6	18.7	18.8	18.5	18.6	18.6	18.5
1995	18.7	18.8	18.9	18.8	18.8	18.9	18.9	18.9	18.9	18.7	18.7	18.8	18.8
1996	18.4	18.5	18.6	18.5	18.7	18.8	19.0	19.0	19.0	19.2	19.2	19.4	18.9
1997	18.8	18.9	19.2	19.0	19.2	19.1	19.4	19.5	19.5	19.6	19.6	19.7	19.3
1998	19.7	19.6	19.5	19.6	19.7	19.9	19.9	20.0	20.0	19.9	20.0	20.2	19.8
1999	19.6	19.7	19.7	19.8	20.0	20.1	20.0	20.0	19.9	20.2	20.1	20.1	19.9
2000	20.0	20.0	20.0	19.9	19.8	19.9	19.9	19.8	19.8	19.6	19.5	19.5	19.8
2001	20.8	20.9	20.9	20.9	21.0	21.0	20.9	20.8	20.7	20.8	20.7	20.6	20.8
2002	20.1	20.2	20.3	20.3	20.4	20.5	20.4	20.5	20.3	20.2	20.2	20.3	20.3
2003	20.2	20.2	20.4	18.7	18.7	18.9	19.0	19.0	18.7	18.7	18.8	18.7	19.2
Retail trade													
1990	37.2	36.3	36.4	37.3	37.3	37.8	37.6	37.6	37.4	37.3	38.9	39.2	37.5
1991	38.0	36.8	37.3	37.5	37.6	37.9	37.9	38.3	38.1	38.9	40.2	41.2	38.3
1992	37.7	37.2	37.3	37.5	38.3	38.5	38.8	38.7	38.5	39.3	40.6	41.6	38.7
1993	39.0	38.5	38.5	39.5	40.2	40.3	41.1	41.6	41.9	42.3	44.3	45.0	41.0
1994	42.3	41.9	41.9	42.1	42.8	43.4	43.4	44.3	44.7	45.3	47.0	48.4	44.0
1995	45.6	45.2	45.3	45.2	45.7	45.9	46.2	47.5	47.3	48.4	50.1	50.9	46.9
1996	48.2	47.0	46.9	46.6	47.1	47.0	47.0	47.6	48.5	49.9	51.6	52.6	48.3
1997	48.5	47.1	47.6	47.4	48.1	48.4	47.9	48.4	49.3	50.5	52.1	53.3	49.1
1998	48.1	46.9	46.4	47.4	48.1	49.2	49.3	49.5	49.6	52.2	54.7	55.9	49.8
1999	50.4	49.8	49.6	50.2	50.2	52.8	51.6	52.8	52.5	53.2	55.2	56.6	52.1
2000	52.1	51.3	51.2	51.9	52.7	53.5	52.6	52.5	52.5	53.6	55.5	56.7	53.0
2001	54.3	52.8	53.0	53.6	54.0	54.4	53.7	54.4	55.0	55.7	58.2	59.0	54.8
2002	53.5	52.3	52.2	52.4	53.0	53.1	52.6	52.7	53.4	53.5	55.4	56.5	53.4
2003	51.8	50.6	51.0	50.3	50.8	51.0	50.6	51.0	51.4	51.5	53.1	53.1	51.4

Employment by Industry: Nebraska—*Continued*

(Numbers in thousands. Not seasonally adjusted.)

Industry	January	February	March	April	May	June	July	August	September	October	November	December	Annual Average
OMAHA—*Continued*													
Transportation and utilities													
1990	16.6	16.9	16.8	16.7	17.0	17.1	16.5	16.8	17.1	17.4	17.3	17.3	17.0
1991	17.2	17.0	17.1	17.1	17.2	17.1	17.0	17.4	17.4	17.3	17.3	17.0	17.2
1992	16.7	16.7	16.8	17.0	17.3	17.0	17.0	17.1	17.4	17.4	17.5	17.3	17.1
1993	16.9	17.0	17.1	16.9	16.8	17.1	17.3	17.3	17.4	17.1	17.1	17.2	17.1
1994	17.6	17.7	17.7	17.2	17.7	17.9	17.8	18.1	18.3	18.4	18.3	18.4	17.9
1995	18.0	18.1	18.3	18.4	18.6	18.6	18.5	18.8	18.8	19.0	18.9	19.0	18.6
1996	18.2	18.2	18.4	18.2	18.4	18.2	18.4	18.5	18.8	18.5	18.5	18.7	18.4
1997	19.3	19.9	20.0	20.4	20.5	20.5	20.5	20.2	20.8	20.8	20.8	20.9	20.4
1998	20.5	20.5	20.5	21.3	21.6	21.5	21.5	21.5	21.9	22.3	22.6	22.8	21.5
1999	21.8	22.0	22.2	22.5	22.6	22.5	22.4	22.5	22.6	22.7	22.8	22.8	22.5
2000	22.3	22.3	22.4	22.6	22.5	22.6	22.6	22.7	22.6	22.7	22.6	22.7	22.6
2001	23.8	23.9	23.9	24.2	24.2	24.1	24.1	24.1	24.2	24.1	24.3	24.5	24.1
2002	24.4	24.3	24.5	24.5	25.0	24.8	24.2	24.8	24.8	24.6	25.1	25.1	24.7
2003	25.0	25.2	25.4	24.3	24.5	24.5	24.6	24.6	24.7	24.4	24.4	24.4	24.7
Information													
1990	9.4	9.5	9.2	8.9	9.1	9.4	9.3	9.4	9.5	9.1	9.1	9.2	9.3
1991	10.0	9.9	9.9	10.3	10.4	10.4	10.5	10.4	10.4	10.5	10.5	10.7	10.3
1992	12.3	12.2	12.2	12.0	12.2	12.4	12.6	12.5	12.5	12.2	12.2	12.3	12.3
1993	12.3	12.4	12.6	12.5	13.0	13.0	13.0	13.2	13.1	12.8	12.9	13.0	12.8
1994	13.6	13.6	13.7	13.7	14.0	14.3	14.6	14.7	15.1	14.8	15.1	15.3	14.4
1995	14.8	14.9	15.0	14.9	14.9	15.2	15.3	15.4	15.2	15.2	15.4	15.4	15.1
1996	15.4	15.4	15.5	15.3	15.5	15.6	15.7	15.8	15.7	15.5	15.9	15.9	15.6
1997	15.7	15.7	16.0	16.0	16.1	16.2	16.0	16.1	16.1	16.2	16.7	17.0	16.2
1998	17.4	17.5	17.5	17.7	17.9	18.2	18.3	18.2	18.1	18.3	18.4	18.5	18.0
1999	18.2	18.2	18.2	18.3	18.3	18.4	19.0	19.0	19.0	19.2	19.1	19.3	18.7
2000	19.4	19.0	18.3	18.8	18.5	19.2	18.2	18.2	18.0	18.0	18.1	18.0	18.5
2001	18.3	18.2	18.3	18.5	18.4	18.3	17.9	17.8	17.7	17.6	17.7	17.6	18.0
2002	17.2	17.1	17.1	17.1	17.2	17.1	17.1	17.1	16.8	16.7	16.8	16.8	17.0
2003	13.8	13.8	13.8	13.6	13.6	13.7	13.9	13.7	13.7	13.6	13.7	13.6	13.7
Financial activities													
1990	30.2	30.4	30.7	30.7	30.9	31.2	30.9	31.0	30.9	30.5	30.4	30.8	30.7
1991	29.8	30.0	30.1	29.8	30.0	30.2	30.1	30.3	30.2	30.0	30.0	30.2	30.1
1992	29.3	29.4	29.2	29.5	30.1	30.5	30.5	30.5	30.4	30.1	30.2	30.4	30.0
1993	29.9	30.1	30.3	30.3	30.7	31.2	31.2	31.3	30.9	30.8	30.7	30.8	30.7
1994	30.6	30.7	30.8	30.9	31.4	31.7	31.4	31.4	31.2	30.9	30.9	31.1	31.1
1995	31.5	31.5	31.7	32.0	32.2	32.9	32.6	32.7	32.5	32.3	32.4	32.8	32.3
1996	32.2	32.3	32.5	32.0	32.4	32.7	32.5	32.6	32.6	32.6	32.7	33.1	32.5
1997	33.0	33.1	33.5	32.9	33.2	33.5	33.6	33.7	33.8	33.8	33.7	34.3	33.5
1998	33.6	33.8	33.9	34.4	34.5	35.1	35.6	35.5	35.3	35.3	35.4	35.9	34.9
1999	35.3	35.2	35.5	35.6	35.8	36.1	36.3	36.2	35.9	35.9	35.7	36.0	35.8
2000	35.6	35.6	35.9	35.7	35.9	36.2	35.9	36.0	36.1	36.1	36.0	36.2	35.9
2001	36.3	36.3	36.3	36.6	36.9	37.4	37.4	37.3	37.2	37.0	37.0	36.9	36.9
2002	36.8	36.9	37.0	37.2	37.3	37.6	37.6	37.5	37.1	37.4	37.5	37.7	37.3
2003	37.5	37.6	37.6	36.5	36.6	36.8	36.7	36.6	36.4	36.3	36.5	36.6	36.8
Professional and business services													
1990	41.1	41.0	41.5	42.5	42.7	43.3	43.3	43.8	44.1	43.8	43.7	44.0	42.9
1991	41.9	41.8	42.1	41.8	41.4	42.3	43.3	43.0	43.3	42.1	42.1	42.8	42.3
1992	39.9	40.3	40.1	41.5	42.0	42.5	42.6	42.0	43.4	43.3	42.6	42.0	41.9
1993	41.8	42.2	42.3	43.0	43.3	43.8	43.0	42.6	42.8	44.9	45.1	44.7	43.3
1994	43.5	43.8	44.5	45.3	45.1	45.4	45.9	45.8	46.4	47.4	47.5	48.0	45.7
1995	46.4	47.2	47.8	48.1	48.2	49.6	50.8	50.9	49.9	50.5	50.5	50.9	49.2
1996	52.0	52.9	53.7	53.6	53.1	54.0	53.0	52.6	52.1	53.2	53.1	53.5	53.1
1997	51.8	52.5	53.4	52.8	52.9	53.5	52.9	53.2	53.8	54.8	55.2	56.4	53.6
1998	52.7	53.2	54.6	55.2	54.8	55.5	55.7	55.5	55.0	53.9	53.9	54.5	54.5
1999	53.2	54.3	54.4	55.8	56.2	56.7	56.6	56.3	56.3	56.7	57.4	58.2	56.0
2000	55.7	56.0	57.1	58.5	58.3	60.0	59.7	59.9	59.4	58.5	58.8	59.5	58.5
2001	63.0	62.7	62.7	63.9	64.3	64.9	63.7	64.1	63.1	62.0	62.4	62.3	63.3
2002	58.7	59.3	60.1	60.8	60.6	60.9	59.2	59.3	58.5	59.0	59.2	59.0	59.6
2003	57.6	58.3	58.6	57.8	57.6	58.0	57.4	57.4	57.5	57.9	58.3	58.6	57.9
Educational and health services													
1990	36.8	37.9	38.0	38.1	37.7	37.6	37.4	38.7	39.3	39.9	40.4	40.3	38.5
1991	38.5	39.1	39.1	39.1	38.4	38.0	37.7	37.8	39.4	39.9	40.0	39.9	38.9
1992	38.8	39.2	39.3	39.2	38.8	38.6	38.5	38.5	40.3	40.7	40.9	40.5	39.4
1993	39.3	40.6	40.8	40.5	39.9	39.7	39.6	39.4	41.0	41.4	41.6	41.5	40.4
1994	40.5	41.7	41.7	42.1	41.9	41.0	40.2	41.1	41.6	42.0	42.3	42.5	41.6
1995	41.6	41.9	42.2	41.6	41.4	40.6	40.5	40.6	41.9	42.8	42.9	43.0	41.8
1996	42.0	43.2	43.3	43.5	43.0	43.2	42.7	42.9	44.4	45.4	45.7	45.8	43.8
1997	44.4	45.2	45.7	45.2	44.6	43.9	43.1	43.2	45.1	45.7	45.5	44.8	44.7
1998	44.5	45.3	45.2	44.8	44.6	44.5	47.1	47.1	48.0	49.9	50.5	50.4	46.8
1999	48.5	49.2	49.8	49.8	49.3	49.5	49.3	49.2	50.4	50.5	51.2	51.3	49.8
2000	50.3	51.1	51.5	49.9	49.7	50.2	50.4	51.2	52.0	51.8	52.1	52.0	51.0
2001	51.4	51.9	52.4	52.2	51.7	52.3	51.9	52.3	53.9	55.2	55.8	55.1	53.0
2002	53.2	54.0	54.2	56.5	55.1	54.4	53.3	53.8	58.6	57.3	57.8	57.7	55.5
2003	58.1	58.3	57.8	58.1	56.6	56.1	56.2	56.9	57.1	57.9	58.9	58.6	57.6

Employment by Industry: Nebraska—*Continued*

(Numbers in thousands. Not seasonally adjusted.)

Industry	January	February	March	April	May	June	July	August	September	October	November	December	Annual Average
OMAHA—*Continued*													
Leisure and hospitality													
1990	25.9	25.8	26.5	28.1	29.8	30.4	29.9	30.0	28.8	27.6	27.8	27.8	28.2
1991	27.1	27.1	27.5	28.6	29.6	30.4	30.5	30.5	29.5	28.2	28.0	27.9	28.7
1992	27.6	27.6	27.9	28.3	29.8	30.7	30.5	30.7	30.3	29.2	28.7	28.8	29.2
1993	28.0	27.9	28.4	29.7	30.7	31.6	31.7	31.8	31.0	30.4	30.0	30.1	30.1
1994	29.8	29.9	30.4	31.2	32.3	33.6	33.4	33.4	32.5	31.0	30.9	30.7	31.6
1995	29.9	30.6	31.9	33.6	34.7	34.9	34.0	34.3	32.8	32.4	32.3	32.8	32.9
1996	32.5	32.9	33.6	34.5	35.4	37.2	37.6	37.4	36.6	36.2	35.7	35.7	35.4
1997	34.9	35.3	36.1	36.8	37.9	38.9	38.4	38.1	37.2	35.8	35.5	36.0	36.7
1998	34.9	35.4	35.7	36.7	38.3	39.1	39.2	38.6	37.9	36.9	36.7	36.8	37.2
1999	35.2	35.7	36.1	37.4	38.6	39.6	40.1	39.7	38.5	37.7	37.6	37.6	37.8
2000	36.9	37.1	37.9	39.0	40.4	41.4	41.2	41.0	40.2	38.7	38.2	37.7	39.1
2001	37.1	37.4	38.1	39.2	40.4	41.5	41.1	41.2	39.6	38.2	37.8	37.4	39.1
2002	36.4	36.5	37.2	38.6	39.8	41.2	40.9	41.5	40.2	38.7	38.4	38.2	39.0
2003	37.4	37.3	37.9	38.8	40.0	40.9	41.4	40.8	39.8	39.6	38.8	38.2	39.2
Other services													
1990	12.1	12.0	12.1	12.3	12.3	12.6	12.6	12.5	12.2	12.2	12.1	12.2	12.3
1991	11.8	11.9	12.0	12.0	12.1	12.4	12.4	12.3	12.0	12.1	12.0	12.1	12.1
1992	12.7	12.7	12.8	12.7	12.9	13.0	12.9	12.8	12.4	12.6	12.5	12.5	12.7
1993	13.2	13.3	13.4	13.3	13.3	13.5	13.6	13.4	13.3	13.3	13.3	13.3	13.4
1994	13.8	13.9	14.0	14.1	14.1	14.3	14.2	14.1	14.0	14.0	14.0	14.0	14.0
1995	14.0	14.1	14.3	14.3	14.4	14.5	14.6	14.7	14.9	15.0	15.0	14.8	14.6
1996	14.6	14.7	15.2	15.1	15.1	15.3	15.2	15.2	15.1	14.7	14.6	14.6	15.0
1997	14.4	14.5	14.7	14.7	14.7	15.1	15.2	15.2	15.1	15.1	15.1	15.3	14.9
1998	15.2	15.4	15.4	15.6	15.6	15.6	15.7	15.4	15.2	15.1	14.9	14.9	15.3
1999	14.7	14.7	14.6	14.7	14.9	15.1	15.0	14.9	14.8	15.0	14.9	14.9	14.9
2000	14.8	14.9	15.0	14.8	15.0	15.1	15.1	15.0	14.7	14.7	14.7	14.7	14.9
2001	14.5	14.5	14.7	14.7	14.9	15.1	14.9	14.9	14.5	14.8	14.8	14.7	14.8
2002	14.5	14.6	14.6	15.2	15.2	15.3	15.5	15.3	15.0	15.0	15.0	15.0	15.0
2003	14.8	14.7	14.9	14.7	14.7	14.9	15.1	15.2	15.4	14.8	15.0	14.7	14.9
Government													
1990	47.9	48.3	48.4	48.9	49.8	48.5	47.6	46.2	48.1	48.8	49.2	48.6	48.4
1991	48.6	49.1	49.0	49.3	49.7	49.5	47.6	47.8	48.8	50.4	49.8	49.8	49.1
1992	48.4	48.7	48.9	49.7	50.0	49.8	48.1	47.6	48.7	50.6	51.3	50.2	49.3
1993	49.6	49.8	50.2	51.7	51.8	50.1	48.3	48.0	49.2	50.7	51.0	50.5	50.1
1994	50.3	50.6	50.4	50.5	51.2	50.8	48.3	48.6	50.3	51.3	51.9	51.3	50.5
1995	50.6	50.9	50.9	50.5	50.8	50.9	48.4	48.4	49.0	51.2	51.7	51.0	50.4
1996	50.4	51.0	50.9	51.5	51.6	51.2	48.4	47.5	48.9	50.5	50.8	50.5	50.3
1997	50.8	50.9	50.7	51.5	52.2	51.8	50.6	49.7	50.9	51.7	52.1	52.2	51.3
1998	52.1	52.4	52.3	52.1	52.5	52.3	47.8	47.7	49.2	50.1	50.0	49.9	50.7
1999	49.5	50.0	49.9	50.1	50.7	50.4	48.9	48.2	49.7	50.9	50.7	50.5	50.0
2000	50.7	50.8	50.7	51.0	51.9	51.4	49.6	49.1	50.3	51.2	51.5	51.3	50.8
2001	51.1	51.2	51.2	52.2	52.7	52.9	50.9	50.7	51.9	52.6	53.0	52.9	51.9
2002	52.6	53.2	53.1	53.1	53.4	53.3	51.3	50.9	52.8	54.3	54.3	53.8	53.0
2003	53.8	54.2	54.0	54.5	54.7	54.5	52.8	50.9	53.2	54.9	54.9	54.2	53.9
Federal government													
1990	9.5	9.5	9.6	9.8	10.4	9.7	9.9	9.8	9.8	9.5	9.5	9.5	9.7
1991	9.4	9.4	9.5	9.4	9.4	9.5	9.6	9.6	9.6	9.6	9.5	9.6	9.5
1992	9.4	9.3	9.4	9.3	9.1	9.1	8.9	8.9	8.9	9.1	9.0	9.2	9.1
1993	8.9	8.8	8.8	8.7	8.7	8.8	8.9	8.9	9.0	8.9	8.9	9.2	8.9
1994	9.0	9.0	8.9	8.9	8.9	9.0	8.8	8.8	8.8	8.8	8.7	8.9	8.9
1995	8.7	8.6	8.6	8.5	8.5	8.5	8.5	8.5	8.4	8.4	8.5	8.6	8.5
1996	8.4	8.4	8.4	8.5	8.4	8.5	8.1	8.0	7.9	8.1	8.2	8.4	8.3
1997	8.6	8.6	8.5	8.6	8.6	8.8	8.7	8.7	8.7	8.5	8.5	8.7	8.6
1998	8.7	8.7	8.6	8.5	8.5	8.7	8.7	8.6	8.5	8.4	8.5	8.7	8.6
1999	8.4	8.4	8.4	8.5	8.5	8.6	8.5	8.5	8.4	8.4	8.4	8.6	8.5
2000	8.4	8.4	8.5	8.5	9.4	8.5	8.5	8.5	8.3	8.3	8.3	8.6	8.5
2001	8.4	8.3	8.3	8.2	8.3	8.4	8.5	8.5	8.4	8.3	8.4	8.7	8.4
2002	8.4	8.4	8.4	8.4	8.4	8.6	8.5	8.4	8.3	8.5	8.5	8.6	8.5
2003	8.6	8.6	8.7	8.7	8.7	8.8	8.8	8.8	8.8	8.8	8.8	8.9	8.8
State government													
1990	9.2	9.5	9.6	9.5	9.6	9.1	9.8	9.3	9.7	9.7	9.8	9.8	9.6
1991	9.6	9.8	9.9	9.8	10.0	9.5	9.6	9.7	10.1	10.2	10.1	10.2	9.9
1992	9.9	10.0	10.1	9.9	10.1	9.5	9.7	9.8	10.1	10.3	10.3	10.3	10.0
1993	10.1	10.3	10.4	10.4	10.3	9.9	9.9	10.0	10.4	10.4	10.4	10.4	10.2
1994	10.2	10.4	10.5	10.3	10.4	9.9	9.8	10.0	10.5	10.5	10.4	10.5	10.3
1995	10.2	10.4	10.6	10.4	10.4	10.1	10.0	10.3	10.5	10.6	10.5	10.6	10.4
1996	10.3	10.6	10.6	10.5	10.5	10.1	10.1	9.7	9.9	10.0	10.0	10.1	10.2
1997	10.0	10.0	10.0	10.5	10.6	10.1	10.4	10.5	10.7	10.5	10.7	11.0	10.4
1998	10.6	10.8	11.0	10.5	10.7	10.3	7.7	8.1	8.3	8.3	8.0	8.2	9.4
1999	7.9	8.1	8.1	8.0	8.2	7.8	8.0	7.9	8.0	8.1	8.2	8.2	8.0
2000	8.2	8.2	8.2	8.0	7.9	7.9	7.9	7.9	8.0	8.0	8.0	8.0	8.0
2001	7.8	7.8	7.9	8.5	8.6	8.1	8.1	8.3	8.5	8.6	8.7	8.7	8.3
2002	8.5	8.6	8.7	8.7	8.7	8.3	8.7	8.8	9.2	9.3	9.2	9.2	8.8
2003	9.2	9.3	9.2	9.0	9.1	8.6	8.7	8.8	9.0	9.2	9.1	9.1	9.0

Employment by Industry: Nebraska—*Continued*

(Numbers in thousands. Not seasonally adjusted.)

Industry	January	February	March	April	May	June	July	August	September	October	November	December	Annual Average
OMAHA—*Continued*													
Local government													
1990	29.2	29.3	29.2	29.6	29.8	29.7	27.9	27.1	28.6	29.6	29.9	29.3	29.1
1991	29.6	29.9	29.6	30.1	30.3	30.5	28.4	28.5	29.1	30.6	30.2	30.0	29.7
1992	29.1	29.4	29.4	30.5	30.8	31.2	29.5	28.9	29.7	31.2	32.0	30.7	30.2
1993	30.6	30.7	31.0	32.6	32.8	31.4	29.5	29.1	29.8	31.4	31.7	30.9	31.0
1994	31.1	31.2	31.0	31.3	31.9	31.9	29.7	29.8	31.0	32.0	32.8	31.9	31.3
1995	31.7	31.9	31.7	31.6	31.9	32.3	29.9	29.6	30.1	32.2	32.7	31.8	31.5
1996	31.7	32.0	31.9	32.5	32.7	32.6	30.2	29.8	31.1	32.4	32.6	32.0	31.8
1997	32.2	32.3	32.2	32.4	33.0	32.9	31.5	30.5	31.5	32.7	32.9	32.5	32.2
1998	32.8	32.9	32.7	33.1	33.3	33.3	31.4	31.0	32.4	33.4	33.5	33.0	32.7
1999	33.2	33.5	33.4	33.6	34.0	34.0	32.4	31.8	33.3	34.4	34.1	33.7	33.5
2000	34.1	34.2	34.0	34.5	34.6	35.0	33.2	32.7	34.0	34.9	35.2	34.7	34.3
2001	34.9	35.1	35.0	35.5	35.8	36.4	34.3	33.9	35.0	35.7	35.9	35.5	35.3
2002	35.7	36.2	36.0	36.0	36.3	36.4	34.1	33.7	35.3	36.5	36.6	36.0	35.7
2003	36.0	36.3	36.1	36.8	36.9	37.1	35.3	33.3	35.4	36.9	37.0	36.2	36.1

Average Weekly Hours by Industry: Nebraska

(Not seasonally adjusted.)

Industry	January	February	March	April	May	June	July	August	September	October	November	December	Annual Average
STATEWIDE													
Manufacturing													
2001	40.6	39.8	40.9	39.3	41.6	40.7	41.3	42.1	42.0	41.6	41.8	43.2	41.2
2002	41.8	41.5	42.1	41.8	41.9	43.2	42.5	42.6	41.9	40.8	41.4	41.7	41.9
2003	41.3	41.4	41.8	40.9	40.9	42.1	41.8	42.0	41.8	41.7	42.0	41.6	41.6
Professional and business services													
2001	34.0	33.9	34.7	35.1	35.5	36.1	36.4	35.5	35.4	35.3	35.6	35.7	35.3
2002	35.0	35.2	35.0	35.3	35.1	36.3	34.6	35.1	35.3	34.4	35.3	35.9	35.2
2003	33.7	34.6	34.3	32.8	33.2	34.4	33.4	33.5	32.4	32.8	32.5	31.9	33.3
LINCOLN													
Manufacturing													
2001	40.7	39.9	40.0	39.4	40.4	38.5	38.2	40.0	41.6	39.7	39.1	41.6	40.0
2002	39.8	39.8	39.7	40.0	40.0	40.8	39.1	40.8	41.3	40.2	40.3	39.8	40.1
2003	41.4	39.9	40.4	40.0	39.8	39.7	40.8	42.5	43.7	42.7	43.5	43.7	41.5
Professional and business services													
2001	37.5	34.1	35.8	35.5	36.4	37.9	38.3	37.9	37.8	36.9	37.2	38.8	37.0
2002	36.4	35.5	35.1	36.3	36.3	38.5	36.9	36.9	36.5	35.2	35.4	34.9	36.2
2003	33.9	35.2	34.8	28.0	30.4	31.9	31.6	31.3	31.3	32.2	31.6	31.6	32.0
OMAHA													
Manufacturing													
2001	42.9	40.5	41.8	40.7	41.9	40.9	43.4	44.0	43.2	44.3	44.9	45.6	42.8
2002	45.6	44.0	44.8	45.1	43.2	44.3	43.6	43.1	41.5	40.3	42.4	41.7	43.3
2003	41.4	42.0	41.8	41.8	41.1	41.8	41.2	42.2	41.3	42.3	41.3	42.3	41.7
Professional and business services													
2001	34.7	34.9	35.3	36.2	36.0	36.5	36.4	35.5	35.4	34.7	34.6	34.5	35.4
2002	34.0	33.8	34.2	34.3	34.5	35.3	33.9	33.9	34.7	33.8	36.2	36.4	34.6
2003	36.0	36.6	35.9	35.2	35.3	36.2	34.8	35.3	34.3	34.3	34.9	33.0	35.2
Leisure and hospitality													
2001	22.8	23.3	22.3	22.1	21.9	21.9	23.0	21.9	21.4	21.0	20.8	22.4	22.0
2002	20.5	20.9	21.1	21.0	22.4	23.1	22.2	22.5	21.4	21.2	21.2	21.9	21.7
2003	19.5	21.2	21.5	21.2	21.7	22.4	22.1	22.8	22.2	22.9	22.9	22.5	21.9

Average Hourly Earnings by Industry: Nebraska

(Dollars, not seasonally adjusted.)

Industry	January	February	March	April	May	June	July	August	September	October	November	December	Annual Average
STATEWIDE													
Manufacturing													
2001	13.59	13.52	13.33	13.48	13.46	13.58	13.50	13.50	13.68	14.02	14.09	13.84	13.64
2002	13.78	13.72	13.74	14.03	13.99	14.08	14.26	14.13	14.06	14.17	14.13	14.50	14.05
2003	14.61	14.49	14.61	14.70	14.65	14.63	14.93	14.84	14.87	15.29	15.09	15.60	14.86
Professional and business services													
2001	14.99	15.09	15.16	15.53	15.58	15.40	15.50	15.59	15.95	15.94	16.36	16.69	15.65
2002	17.01	17.07	17.16	17.23	17.32	16.78	16.74	16.57	16.51	16.16	16.38	16.54	16.79
2003	16.68	16.49	16.45	16.54	16.43	16.30	16.26	16.00	16.11	15.88	16.02	15.85	16.25
LINCOLN													
Manufacturing													
2001	14.02	14.10	14.05	13.99	14.23	14.41	14.27	14.44	14.55	14.89	14.79	14.32	14.33
2002	14.64	14.54	14.56	14.91	14.62	14.64	14.56	14.93	14.79	14.94	14.80	14.84	14.73
2003	15.05	15.12	15.44	15.20	15.10	15.35	15.53	15.48	15.49	16.64	16.84	16.46	15.66
Professional and business services													
2001	14.51	13.94	14.35	14.26	14.71	14.34	14.59	14.35	14.68	14.47	14.29	14.99	14.46
2002	14.93	14.99	14.84	14.69	14.52	14.15	14.23	14.42	14.69	14.37	14.81	14.83	14.61
2003	15.00	14.85	14.98	14.89	15.10	15.11	15.10	15.44	16.08	15.59	16.11	16.14	15.35
OMAHA													
Manufacturing													
2001	15.27	15.34	15.12	14.85	15.38	15.69	15.20	15.16	15.22	15.85	16.04	16.25	15.45
2002	15.81	15.55	15.93	15.73	15.96	15.83	16.18	15.88	15.97	16.36	16.18	17.34	16.05
2003	17.41	16.82	17.11	17.63	17.28	17.04	17.86	17.62	17.62	18.22	17.36	17.75	17.48
Professional and business services													
2001	15.74	15.95	16.01	16.45	16.42	16.32	16.46	16.51	16.87	17.01	17.40	17.79	16.57
2002	18.09	18.26	18.18	18.38	18.82	18.34	18.32	18.29	18.52	18.08	18.60	18.88	18.40
2003	18.41	18.31	18.21	18.36	18.17	18.13	18.08	17.57	17.87	17.83	17.88	17.90	18.07
Leisure and hospitality													
2001	7.44	7.33	7.43	7.50	7.55	7.33	7.48	7.47	7.51	7.60	7.56	7.80	7.50
2002	7.81	8.01	7.82	7.72	7.82	7.72	7.89	8.08	8.16	8.14	8.20	8.28	7.97
2003	8.22	8.22	8.25	8.07	8.15	8.06	8.01	8.06	7.85	7.83	8.03	7.92	8.05

Average Weekly Earnings by Industry: Nebraska

(Dollars, not seasonally adjusted.)

Industry	January	February	March	April	May	June	July	August	September	October	November	December	Annual Average
STATEWIDE													
Manufacturing													
2001	551.75	538.10	545.20	529.76	559.94	552.71	557.55	568.35	574.56	583.23	588.96	597.89	561.97
2002	576.00	569.38	578.45	586.45	586.18	608.26	606.05	601.94	589.11	578.14	584.98	604.65	588.70
2003	603.39	599.89	610.70	601.23	599.19	615.92	624.07	623.28	621.57	637.59	633.78	648.96	618.18
Professional and business services													
2001	509.66	511.55	526.05	545.10	553.09	555.94	564.20	553.45	564.63	562.68	582.42	595.83	552.45
2002	595.35	600.86	600.60	608.22	607.93	609.11	579.20	581.61	582.80	555.90	578.21	593.79	591.01
2003	562.12	570.55	564.24	542.51	545.48	560.72	543.08	536.00	521.96	520.86	520.65	505.62	541.13
LINCOLN													
Manufacturing													
2001	570.61	562.59	562.00	551.21	574.89	554.79	545.11	577.60	605.28	591.13	578.29	595.71	573.20
2002	582.67	578.69	578.03	596.40	584.80	597.31	569.30	609.14	610.83	600.59	596.44	590.63	590.67
2003	623.07	603.29	623.78	608.00	600.98	609.40	633.62	657.90	676.91	710.53	732.54	719.30	649.89
Professional and business services													
2001	544.13	475.35	513.73	506.23	535.44	543.49	558.80	543.87	554.90	533.94	531.59	581.61	535.02
2002	543.45	532.15	520.88	533.25	527.08	544.78	525.09	532.10	536.19	505.82	524.27	517.57	528.88
2003	508.50	522.72	521.30	416.92	459.04	482.01	477.16	483.27	503.30	502.00	509.08	510.02	491.20
OMAHA													
Manufacturing													
2001	655.08	621.27	632.02	604.40	644.42	641.72	659.68	667.04	657.50	702.16	720.20	741.00	661.26
2002	720.94	684.20	713.66	709.42	689.47	701.27	705.45	684.43	662.76	659.31	686.03	723.08	694.97
2003	720.77	706.44	715.20	736.93	710.21	712.27	735.83	743.56	727.71	770.71	716.97	750.83	728.92
Professional and business services													
2001	546.18	556.66	565.15	595.49	591.12	595.68	599.14	586.11	597.20	590.25	602.04	613.76	586.58
2002	615.06	617.19	621.76	630.43	649.29	647.40	621.05	620.03	642.64	611.10	673.32	687.23	636.64
2003	662.76	670.15	653.74	646.27	641.40	656.31	629.18	620.22	612.94	611.57	624.01	590.70	636.06
Leisure and hospitality													
2001	169.63	170.79	165.69	165.75	165.35	160.53	172.04	163.59	160.71	159.60	157.25	174.72	165.00
2002	160.11	167.41	165.00	162.12	175.17	178.33	175.16	181.80	174.62	172.57	173.84	181.33	172.95
2003	160.29	174.26	177.38	171.08	176.86	180.54	177.02	183.77	174.27	179.31	183.89	178.20	176.30

NEVADA AT A GLANCE

(Population and total nonfarm employment numbers in thousands)

Population, Census 2000:	1,998.3
Total nonfarm employment, 2003:	1,087.4
Change in total nonfarm employment	
(Number)	
1990–2003:	466.5
1990–2001:	430.5
2001–2003:	36.0
(Compound annual rate of change)	
1990–2003:	4.4%
1990–2001:	4.9%
2001–2003:	1.7%
Unemployment rate	
1990:	5.1%
2001:	5.3%
2003:	5.1%

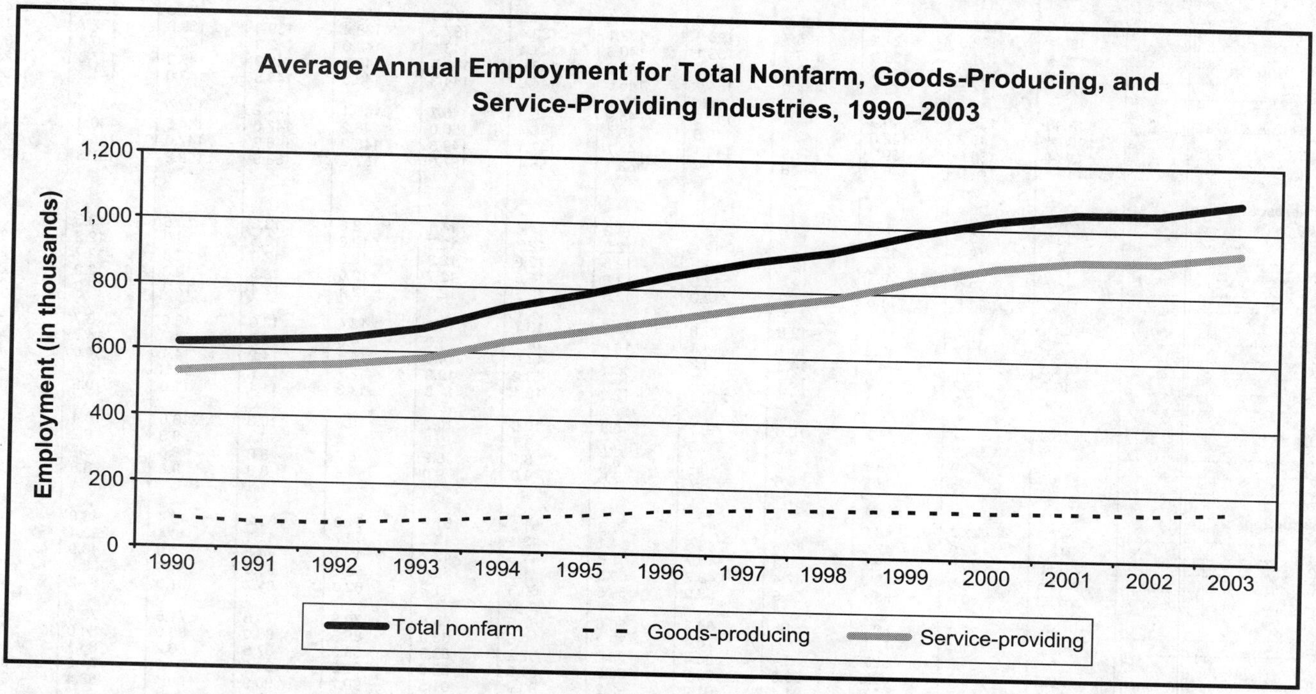

Nonfarm payroll employment rose steadily throughout the 1990–2003 period, with some slackening during the 1990–1991 and 2001 recessions. The slowdown was particularly evident during the latter contraction, as employment increased by only 600 from 2001 to 2002. In contrast, nearly 44,000 jobs were added from 1999 to 2000, and more than 24,000 jobs from 2000 to 2001. However, total nonfarm employment recovered in 2003, adding over 35,000 jobs, up from 3.4 percent from 2002.

Employment by Industry: Nevada

(Numbers in thousands. Not seasonally adjusted.)

Industry	January	February	March	April	May	June	July	August	September	October	November	December	Annual Average
STATEWIDE													
Total nonfarm													
1990	595.9	598.2	606.4	612.0	619.5	625.1	627.1	631.9	634.5	633.9	636.4	630.9	620.9
1991	614.9	617.2	621.6	625.5	632.2	635.0	628.5	632.4	637.9	634.2	632.5	631.7	628.6
1992	614.6	618.5	624.6	631.3	640.4	638.4	639.0	643.6	654.8	650.0	657.4	651.5	638.6
1993	639.2	643.4	652.0	658.2	665.5	672.2	668.7	675.0	682.4	694.5	700.5	706.9	671.5
1994	697.0	704.7	714.8	725.3	734.1	737.5	740.9	749.5	759.0	759.1	767.6	767.3	738.0
1995	747.2	756.3	770.2	773.6	781.1	787.1	786.9	793.6	804.8	806.1	813.5	812.2	786.0
1996	799.3	809.2	818.6	829.4	837.7	843.4	846.0	852.6	862.6	864.3	877.9	873.9	842.9
1997	859.1	867.7	876.5	878.1	887.8	891.9	890.9	896.3	904.7	908.4	913.1	914.3	890.7
1998	886.5	894.3	903.6	912.7	921.7	928.1	925.1	932.7	941.1	950.0	956.8	958.0	925.8
1999	941.0	950.4	966.0	974.9	981.5	984.5	980.7	987.8	997.0	1007.0	1012.4	1013.3	983.0
2000	991.6	997.5	1007.4	1014.8	1028.0	1027.7	1024.8	1038.3	1043.6	1046.7	1051.1	1051.3	1026.9
2001	1033.8	1043.2	1051.7	1053.1	1060.2	1062.4	1052.3	1058.6	1063.1	1048.0	1047.0	1043.4	1051.4
2002	1019.1	1025.9	1037.4	1046.2	1055.6	1053.6	1049.2	1057.5	1063.6	1070.5	1072.2	1072.7	1052.0
2003	1053.5	1062.9	1071.8	1073.9	1084.3	1083.7	1083.6	1093.1	1103.2	1109.5	1114.4	1115.3	1087.4
Total private													
1990	522.4	523.6	530.9	536.1	543.1	549.9	555.6	561.3	558.3	555.2	556.9	551.0	545.3
1991	537.1	536.7	540.2	543.6	549.5	554.8	552.5	555.2	555.5	549.6	547.5	546.1	547.3
1992	531.8	532.5	538.1	545.0	553.0	557.4	558.4	562.0	564.1	562.1	564.7	562.6	552.6
1993	553.3	555.5	562.5	568.8	575.5	582.7	586.0	590.8	593.3	603.2	608.8	615.1	582.9
1994	608.5	612.9	621.9	632.3	640.4	649.2	654.6	661.7	664.5	663.4	670.1	670.6	645.8
1995	653.9	659.5	671.7	675.2	682.6	693.4	696.0	704.4	707.3	706.2	712.0	711.7	689.4
1996	700.9	708.6	716.7	728.4	736.1	746.5	750.1	758.3	759.8	759.0	768.4	768.0	741.7
1997	756.2	761.5	769.2	770.8	780.0	786.4	790.1	796.6	797.4	798.6	801.8	802.1	784.2
1998	778.8	783.0	791.4	800.1	809.9	817.9	819.9	826.0	826.9	834.4	839.8	841.4	814.1
1999	826.5	832.6	846.2	855.1	861.7	869.7	870.9	877.9	880.3	885.1	890.7	890.7	865.6
2000	874.0	876.6	884.7	891.7	900.8	910.5	910.2	920.1	922.2	920.9	925.1	925.4	905.1
2001	911.0	915.9	923.6	923.5	931.5	936.9	933.5	939.3	934.4	917.9	916.3	912.0	924.7
2002	893.2	895.0	905.4	914.4	922.9	924.3	926.5	934.5	932.5	934.3	935.4	935.5	921.2
2003	922.1	926.4	934.5	936.8	946.3	950.0	956.8	966.5	968.2	971.1	975.6	975.6	952.5
Goods-producing													
1990	84.1	84.4	86.7	87.5	89.4	90.5	89.9	90.6	89.8	88.7	86.6	84.7	87.7
1991	79.0	78.4	78.1	79.4	80.6	81.6	80.8	81.6	80.6	78.4	77.3	76.8	79.3
1992	73.1	73.6	75.3	77.0	78.9	80.7	81.3	82.8	83.5	84.6	84.2	83.7	79.8
1993	80.3	82.9	85.5	88.1	90.1	92.4	94.1	95.2	95.1	95.9	95.4	96.0	90.9
1994	92.4	93.1	96.3	99.8	102.6	104.8	105.9	107.0	108.2	108.2	107.7	108.1	102.8
1995	103.0	105.3	108.4	109.6	112.2	115.4	116.5	118.3	120.2	121.1	121.8	122.7	114.5
1996	120.1	122.0	124.2	126.7	128.8	132.1	133.4	137.3	138.9	139.8	139.8	137.7	131.7
1997	132.5	134.1	136.0	136.6	139.1	140.6	141.4	143.4	143.0	142.3	140.9	140.8	139.2
1998	132.7	133.2	135.9	139.0	142.5	145.2	146.0	146.5	146.6	148.0	147.3	147.6	142.5
1999	144.4	144.5	145.5	144.0	144.1	145.5	144.0	144.3	143.3	143.6	143.0	141.2	143.9
2000	137.3	137.9	140.4	141.1	142.9	145.9	145.8	146.7	145.1	144.2	144.0	143.9	142.9
2001	139.4	140.2	142.0	143.0	145.5	148.4	148.4	150.0	148.2	147.0	144.5	140.9	144.8
2002	136.1	136.6	139.0	141.9	144.1	144.7	147.1	149.6	148.2	148.2	147.0	145.6	144.0
2003	142.4	144.0	146.7	147.8	150.7	153.1	155.1	157.6	157.3	158.5	158.2	157.3	152.4
Natural resources and mining													
1990	13.3	13.4	13.5	14.0	14.1	14.2	14.4	14.1	13.8	13.6	13.5	13.5	13.7
1991	12.8	12.4	12.2	12.5	12.6	12.8	12.7	12.7	12.6	12.5	12.3	12.3	12.5
1992	11.9	12.0	12.0	12.3	12.3	12.5	12.8	12.8	12.8	12.9	12.8	12.7	12.4
1993	12.5	12.6	12.6	12.4	12.5	12.6	12.8	12.7	12.6	12.3	12.3	12.2	12.5
1994	11.9	11.8	11.8	11.9	12.0	12.3	12.5	12.3	12.4	12.4	12.3	12.3	12.1
1995	12.4	12.5	12.7	12.8	12.8	13.3	13.7	13.6	13.4	13.6	13.6	13.7	13.1
1996	13.6	13.7	13.9	14.1	14.4	14.8	14.9	15.0	14.8	14.7	14.7	14.7	14.4
1997	14.4	14.4	14.4	14.3	14.3	14.5	14.6	14.6	14.4	14.2	14.1	14.0	14.3
1998	13.3	13.2	13.2	13.1	13.1	13.4	13.2	12.9	12.7	12.7	12.5	12.5	12.9
1999	12.4	12.3	12.4	12.1	12.1	12.2	12.1	11.8	11.3	11.1	11.0	10.8	11.8
2000	10.9	11.2	11.2	10.6	10.7	10.8	10.8	10.7	10.6	10.6	10.5	10.4	10.7
2001	9.9	9.9	9.8	9.6	9.8	9.7	9.7	9.6	9.4	9.4	9.3	9.2	9.6
2002	9.0	8.9	8.8	8.8	8.8	8.9	8.9	8.9	8.8	8.8	8.6	8.7	8.8
2003	8.2	8.6	8.7	8.6	8.7	8.9	9.0	9.0	8.8	8.8	8.8	8.8	8.7
Construction													
1990	47.7	47.7	49.3	49.5	51.0	51.9	51.2	51.9	51.3	50.2	48.4	46.6	49.7
1991	42.1	42.0	42.0	42.6	43.5	44.1	43.1	43.5	42.7	41.1	40.1	39.4	42.1
1992	36.8	36.8	38.1	39.3	40.7	41.8	41.8	43.2	43.7	44.8	44.6	43.9	41.2
1993	40.6	42.8	45.0	47.4	48.7	50.3	51.5	52.4	52.2	53.3	52.9	53.2	49.1
1994	50.2	50.9	53.4	55.9	58.0	59.5	60.3	61.2	62.0	61.7	61.3	61.2	57.9
1995	56.1	58.0	60.6	61.8	64.2	66.5	67.0	68.8	70.5	70.8	71.5	72.0	65.6
1996	69.6	71.4	72.9	75.0	76.4	79.2	80.6	83.9	85.5	86.0	86.0	84.0	79.2
1997	79.9	81.2	82.8	83.4	85.4	86.6	87.2	88.9	88.5	87.6	86.2	86.1	85.3
1998	79.8	80.2	82.6	85.9	88.9	90.8	91.8	92.6	92.9	94.6	94.0	94.0	89.0
1999	91.8	91.9	92.6	91.4	91.2	92.2	90.9	91.5	90.7	90.9	90.1	88.4	91.1
2000	84.7	84.8	87.0	88.4	89.9	92.3	92.1	93.0	91.5	90.1	89.8	89.5	89.4
2001	85.7	86.4	88.0	89.3	91.5	94.0	94.2	95.9	94.7	94.0	92.0	88.7	91.2
2002	85.0	85.6	88.1	90.8	92.6	92.9	94.8	97.3	96.1	95.7	94.7	93.3	92.2
2003	91.2	92.4	94.9	96.1	98.5	100.6	102.3	104.5	104.7	105.5	104.9	103.9	100.0

Employment by Industry: Nevada—*Continued*

(Numbers in thousands. Not seasonally adjusted.)

Industry	January	February	March	April	May	June	July	August	September	October	November	December	Annual Average
STATEWIDE—*Continued*													
Manufacturing													
1990	23.1	23.3	23.9	24.0	24.3	24.4	24.3	24.6	24.7	24.9	24.7	24.6	24.2
1991	24.1	24.0	23.9	24.3	24.5	24.7	25.0	25.4	25.3	24.8	24.9	25.1	24.6
1992	24.4	24.8	25.2	25.4	25.9	26.4	26.7	26.8	27.0	26.9	26.8	27.1	26.1
1993	27.2	27.5	27.9	28.3	28.9	29.5	29.8	30.1	30.3	30.3	30.2	30.6	29.2
1994	30.3	30.4	31.1	32.0	32.6	33.0	33.1	33.5	33.8	34.1	34.1	34.6	32.7
1995	34.5	34.8	35.1	35.0	35.2	35.6	35.8	35.9	36.3	36.7	36.7	37.0	35.7
1996	36.9	36.9	37.4	37.6	38.0	38.1	37.9	38.4	38.6	39.1	39.1	39.0	38.0
1997	38.2	38.5	38.8	38.9	39.4	39.5	39.6	39.9	40.1	40.5	40.6	40.7	39.5
1998	39.6	39.8	40.1	40.0	40.5	41.0	41.0	41.0	41.0	40.7	40.8	41.1	40.5
1999	40.2	40.3	40.5	40.5	40.8	41.1	41.0	41.0	41.3	41.6	41.9	42.0	41.0
2000	41.7	41.9	42.2	42.1	42.3	42.8	42.9	43.0	43.0	43.5	43.7	44.0	42.7
2001	43.8	43.9	44.2	44.1	44.2	44.7	44.5	44.5	44.1	43.6	43.2	43.0	44.0
2002	42.1	42.1	42.1	42.3	42.7	42.9	43.4	43.4	43.3	43.7	43.7	43.6	42.9
2003	43.0	43.0	43.1	43.1	43.5	43.6	43.8	44.1	43.8	44.2	44.5	44.6	43.7
Service-providing													
1990	511.8	513.8	519.7	524.5	530.1	534.6	537.2	541.3	544.7	545.2	549.8	546.2	533.2
1991	535.9	538.8	543.5	546.1	551.6	553.4	547.7	550.8	557.3	555.8	555.2	554.9	549.2
1992	541.5	544.9	549.3	554.3	561.5	557.7	557.7	560.8	571.3	565.4	573.2	567.8	558.7
1993	558.9	560.5	566.5	570.1	575.4	579.8	574.6	579.8	587.3	598.6	605.1	610.9	580.6
1994	604.6	611.6	618.5	625.5	631.5	632.7	635.0	642.5	650.8	650.9	659.9	659.2	635.2
1995	644.2	651.0	661.8	664.0	668.9	671.7	670.4	675.3	684.6	685.0	691.7	689.5	671.5
1996	679.2	687.2	694.4	702.7	708.9	711.3	712.6	715.3	723.7	724.5	738.1	736.2	711.1
1997	726.6	733.6	740.5	741.5	748.7	751.3	749.5	752.9	761.7	766.1	772.2	773.5	751.5
1998	753.8	761.1	767.7	773.7	779.2	782.9	779.1	786.2	794.5	802.0	809.5	810.4	783.3
1999	796.6	805.9	820.5	830.9	837.4	839.0	836.7	843.5	853.7	863.4	869.4	872.1	839.0
2000	854.3	859.6	867.0	873.7	885.1	881.8	879.0	891.6	898.5	902.5	907.1	907.4	883.9
2001	894.4	903.0	909.7	910.1	914.7	914.0	903.9	908.6	914.9	901.0	902.5	902.5	906.6
2002	883.0	889.3	898.4	904.3	911.5	908.9	902.1	907.9	915.4	922.3	925.2	927.1	908.0
2003	911.1	918.9	925.1	926.1	933.6	930.6	928.5	935.5	945.9	951.0	956.2	958.0	935.0
Trade, transportation, and utilities													
1990	107.3	106.6	108.1	108.9	109.8	110.7	111.7	113.1	113.3	113.7	115.9	118.1	111.4
1991	113.9	112.8	113.2	112.7	114.3	116.0	115.3	116.1	116.1	115.6	117.4	119.4	115.2
1992	112.5	111.1	112.0	113.4	115.0	116.2	115.9	116.7	116.7	116.9	119.0	120.8	115.5
1993	117.1	116.0	116.5	116.4	117.5	118.4	118.1	118.2	118.9	120.8	123.1	125.7	118.8
1994	120.3	120.7	122.0	123.9	125.7	126.5	129.2	130.0	130.6	132.0	135.7	137.8	127.8
1995	133.2	132.4	133.9	134.8	135.6	137.0	137.8	138.9	140.2	141.4	144.8	147.1	138.0
1996	141.5	141.3	143.2	143.1	145.4	146.9	147.8	148.9	149.4	151.1	155.1	157.4	147.5
1997	149.7	149.4	151.0	151.9	153.9	155.4	156.9	157.5	158.9	161.7	163.8	166.8	156.4
1998	159.7	158.9	159.9	161.1	162.8	163.6	164.9	165.8	166.1	167.7	171.5	174.2	164.6
1999	166.2	166.0	167.3	169.4	171.6	173.0	174.6	175.6	177.0	179.9	182.9	186.4	174.1
2000	179.4	178.7	178.9	180.8	181.9	183.4	184.1	186.6	188.2	189.6	193.7	197.1	185.2
2001	188.2	186.5	186.8	188.1	189.6	191.0	191.3	191.9	191.7	191.8	193.8	194.9	190.5
2002	187.5	185.6	186.4	188.9	190.1	190.7	191.4	191.4	192.0	194.6	197.0	199.3	191.2
2003	190.2	189.7	191.3	190.4	191.7	192.9	194.1	195.9	197.3	199.7	203.3	205.5	195.2
Wholesale trade													
1990	20.0	20.2	20.6	20.8	21.1	21.4	21.3	21.4	21.3	21.2	21.2	21.3	20.9
1991	20.6	20.5	20.7	20.4	20.7	20.8	20.4	20.3	20.1	20.1	20.2	20.3	20.4
1992	20.0	19.7	19.9	19.9	20.1	20.2	20.2	20.3	20.2	20.4	20.4	20.5	20.1
1993	20.3	20.4	20.5	20.5	20.7	20.9	20.7	20.7	20.7	20.9	21.0	21.2	20.7
1994	21.3	21.4	21.8	22.2	22.4	22.6	23.2	23.5	23.6	23.8	23.8	24.0	22.8
1995	23.8	24.1	24.4	24.8	25.0	25.2	25.4	25.6	26.0	26.0	26.3	26.7	25.2
1996	26.6	26.9	27.2	27.2	27.6	27.9	27.9	27.9	27.9	28.1	28.3	28.5	27.6
1997	28.1	28.5	28.9	28.9	29.4	29.6	29.9	30.2	30.2	30.3	30.4	30.6	29.5
1998	30.2	30.3	30.5	30.6	30.8	30.7	30.9	31.1	31.1	31.2	31.4	31.6	30.8
1999	31.0	31.2	31.5	31.7	32.0	32.3	32.5	32.6	32.8	33.1	33.0	33.2	32.2
2000	32.6	32.8	33.1	33.4	33.8	34.1	34.2	34.4	34.5	34.5	35.0	35.3	33.9
2001	34.5	34.7	34.8	35.0	35.2	35.5	35.3	35.3	35.2	35.1	34.9	34.9	35.0
2002	34.4	34.6	35.0	35.0	35.0	35.1	34.9	34.9	34.7	34.7	34.6	34.7	34.8
2003	34.0	34.2	34.2	34.1	34.1	34.3	34.4	34.4	34.3	34.3	34.4	34.4	34.3
Retail trade													
1990	64.5	63.6	64.3	65.1	65.7	66.2	67.0	68.1	68.0	68.6	70.7	72.4	67.0
1991	68.5	67.4	67.4	67.2	68.3	69.6	69.4	70.2	70.5	70.1	71.9	73.6	69.5
1992	67.9	67.0	67.9	68.9	70.0	70.7	70.3	70.9	71.1	70.9	72.6	74.1	70.1
1993	70.8	69.6	69.7	69.5	70.1	70.7	70.3	70.5	71.0	72.3	74.3	76.8	71.3
1994	71.8	71.6	72.2	73.6	74.9	75.2	76.4	76.6	76.9	77.9	81.0	83.0	75.9
1995	78.9	78.0	78.7	79.0	79.5	80.5	81.0	81.8	82.5	83.2	85.8	87.8	81.3
1996	83.2	82.7	83.8	83.7	85.5	86.4	86.9	87.6	88.2	89.0	92.6	94.9	87.0
1997	88.8	87.9	88.5	88.9	90.1	91.0	92.1	92.8	93.3	95.4	97.8	100.6	92.2
1998	94.7	93.5	93.9	94.8	96.2	96.8	97.6	98.0	98.4	99.5	102.7	105.2	97.6
1999	98.8	98.1	99.0	100.3	101.5	102.5	103.2	103.9	104.8	106.5	109.4	112.6	103.3
2000	106.8	105.8	105.3	106.4	107.3	108.0	108.3	110.2	111.3	112.0	115.3	118.3	109.5
2001	112.3	110.4	110.3	111.0	111.9	113.0	113.3	114.0	114.1	114.5	117.1	118.3	113.4
2002	112.3	110.6	111.1	112.5	113.7	114.3	114.3	114.1	114.9	117.0	120.7	123.2	114.9
2003	115.4	114.5	115.8	115.2	116.4	117.3	118.5	120.2	121.3	123.3	126.5	128.6	119.4

Employment by Industry: Nevada—*Continued*

(Numbers in thousands. Not seasonally adjusted.)

Industry	January	February	March	April	May	June	July	August	September	October	November	December	Annual Average
STATEWIDE—*Continued*													
Transportation and utilities													
1990	22.8	22.8	23.2	23.0	23.0	23.1	23.4	23.6	24.0	23.9	24.0	24.4	23.4
1991	24.8	24.9	25.1	25.1	25.3	25.6	25.5	25.6	25.5	25.4	25.3	25.5	25.3
1992	24.6	24.4	24.2	24.6	24.9	25.3	25.4	25.5	25.4	25.6	26.0	26.2	25.1
1993	26.0	26.0	26.3	26.4	26.7	26.8	27.1	27.0	27.2	27.6	27.8	27.7	26.8
1994	27.2	27.7	28.0	28.1	28.4	28.7	29.6	29.9	30.1	30.3	30.9	30.8	29.1
1995	30.5	30.3	30.8	31.0	31.1	31.3	31.4	31.5	31.7	32.2	32.7	32.6	31.4
1996	31.7	31.7	32.2	32.2	32.3	32.6	33.0	33.4	33.3	34.0	34.2	34.0	32.8
1997	32.8	33.0	33.6	34.1	34.4	34.8	34.9	34.5	35.4	36.0	35.6	35.6	34.5
1998	34.8	35.1	35.5	35.7	35.8	36.1	36.4	36.7	36.6	37.0	37.4	37.4	36.2
1999	36.4	36.7	36.8	37.4	38.1	38.2	38.9	39.1	39.4	40.3	40.5	40.6	38.5
2000	40.0	40.1	40.5	41.0	40.8	41.3	41.6	42.0	42.4	43.1	43.4	43.5	41.6
2001	41.4	41.4	41.7	42.1	42.5	42.5	42.7	42.6	42.4	42.2	41.8	41.7	42.1
2002	40.8	40.4	40.3	41.4	41.4	41.3	42.2	42.4	42.4	42.9	41.7	41.4	41.6
2003	40.8	41.0	41.3	41.1	41.2	41.3	41.2	41.3	41.7	42.1	42.4	42.5	41.5
Information													
1990	10.9	11.2	11.9	10.8	11.0	11.2	11.1	10.9	10.8	10.6	10.6	10.8	10.9
1991	10.5	10.5	10.6	10.3	10.3	10.5	11.3	11.8	12.1	10.5	10.6	10.9	10.8
1992	10.6	10.8	10.9	10.5	10.8	11.1	10.6	10.6	10.5	10.4	10.5	10.6	10.6
1993	10.5	10.8	10.9	10.4	10.5	10.8	11.1	11.0	11.1	11.2	11.3	11.4	10.9
1994	11.2	10.5	10.7	11.2	11.3	11.7	12.2	11.9	12.2	13.4	14.1	14.1	12.0
1995	12.8	12.9	12.4	12.0	12.0	12.4	11.9	11.4	11.5	12.5	12.8	12.8	12.2
1996	12.3	12.5	12.5	13.3	13.0	12.8	13.4	13.1	12.7	13.1	13.5	14.0	13.0
1997	13.1	13.3	13.6	13.3	13.5	13.6	14.1	14.6	14.5	14.6	14.5	14.5	13.9
1998	14.3	14.3	14.4	14.8	14.8	15.0	15.0	15.2	15.3	15.6	15.9	16.2	15.0
1999	16.2	16.3	16.4	16.7	16.6	17.0	17.2	17.4	17.7	18.0	18.2	18.8	17.2
2000	19.1	18.6	19.0	18.7	19.5	19.4	19.1	19.5	19.3	19.7	19.8	19.2	19.2
2001	19.9	21.5	21.3	19.8	19.7	19.0	18.0	17.7	17.3	17.7	18.0	17.6	19.0
2002	17.5	17.3	17.1	17.1	17.3	16.9	16.7	16.8	16.7	16.4	16.5	16.5	16.9
2003	16.1	16.0	15.8	15.8	16.1	16.0	15.7	15.6	15.5	15.4	15.6	15.6	15.8
Financial activities													
1990	30.1	30.5	30.6	31.5	31.7	32.2	32.7	32.7	32.5	31.9	32.3	32.4	31.7
1991	31.5	31.6	31.6	31.7	32.1	33.0	33.3	33.6	33.4	33.4	33.3	33.5	32.6
1992	32.7	33.2	33.3	33.8	33.8	34.1	34.2	34.2	34.3	33.9	34.2	34.5	33.8
1993	34.2	34.5	35.0	35.3	35.7	36.1	36.2	36.5	36.8	36.9	37.2	37.4	35.9
1994	37.5	38.0	38.6	39.3	39.4	39.6	39.2	39.4	39.4	39.4	39.8	40.2	39.1
1995	39.1	39.6	40.1	40.4	40.7	41.1	41.3	41.8	42.0	42.4	42.7	43.0	41.1
1996	42.7	43.3	43.7	43.8	44.1	44.6	44.3	44.8	44.9	45.0	45.6	45.7	44.3
1997	45.6	46.0	46.5	45.9	46.6	47.0	47.6	47.9	47.8	47.9	47.7	48.0	47.0
1998	47.0	47.4	47.9	48.3	48.9	49.4	49.4	49.9	50.3	50.4	50.8	51.2	49.2
1999	50.4	50.5	50.7	50.8	51.0	51.5	51.2	51.5	51.1	51.4	51.9	52.0	51.1
2000	51.0	51.2	51.6	51.8	52.1	52.7	53.1	53.3	53.2	53.0	53.6	54.1	52.5
2001	53.9	54.3	54.8	54.7	54.8	55.4	55.3	55.8	55.9	55.4	55.2	55.8	55.1
2002	54.4	55.1	55.4	55.5	55.6	55.8	55.9	56.3	56.0	56.5	57.0	57.2	55.9
2003	56.6	56.9	57.0	57.7	58.4	58.5	59.1	59.1	59.4	59.6	60.1	60.3	58.6
Professional and business services													
1990	57.0	55.9	57.0	57.4	58.7	59.1	59.1	60.3	60.2	61.0	62.7	59.2	58.9
1991	59.6	60.1	60.4	60.7	61.2	61.2	59.3	58.7	59.6	59.5	59.0	59.0	59.8
1992	58.9	58.4	59.8	60.5	61.5	61.4	61.4	62.6	62.8	63.0	64.0	61.7	61.3
1993	61.7	62.4	62.8	62.6	63.2	63.2	63.4	65.0	65.4	66.9	68.9	67.7	64.4
1994	68.6	69.0	69.7	70.9	72.1	73.4	72.6	73.5	74.8	74.1	77.1	74.5	72.5
1995	73.2	74.4	77.0	76.1	76.8	77.4	75.7	79.6	79.7	78.3	80.7	77.0	77.1
1996	77.5	79.3	78.8	79.8	80.5	80.8	79.8	82.7	83.9	83.9	87.6	84.7	81.6
1997	85.2	86.1	86.9	86.8	87.7	87.7	87.0	89.6	90.1	90.8	92.6	90.9	88.4
1998	88.5	89.5	89.6	90.2	91.3	92.7	92.9	95.7	95.2	97.1	99.4	97.3	93.2
1999	95.0	96.9	99.3	99.9	99.6	100.6	99.8	102.1	103.2	104.4	107.1	105.0	101.0
2000	104.5	105.4	106.3	108.3	110.2	111.2	108.7	111.5	115.1	114.4	115.0	113.3	110.3
2001	113.4	115.1	116.1	114.3	115.1	114.8	111.8	113.9	112.6	111.0	111.6	109.6	113.3
2002	110.7	110.7	112.6	112.5	113.5	112.6	112.5	116.3	116.8	116.5	117.5	116.2	114.0
2003	117.4	117.8	118.1	118.6	119.2	118.1	120.1	123.8	124.2	124.1	125.5	124.2	120.9
Educational and health services													
1990	33.3	34.0	34.2	34.6	34.8	35.2	34.5	35.0	35.5	35.5	36.2	36.9	34.9
1991	37.1	38.0	38.5	38.2	38.5	38.7	38.3	38.6	39.1	39.0	39.3	38.7	38.5
1992	39.3	39.8	40.1	39.8	39.9	39.3	40.1	40.1	40.6	40.8	41.0	41.4	40.1
1993	41.7	42.0	42.4	42.2	42.3	42.7	42.4	42.4	43.0	43.5	43.8	44.2	42.7
1994	43.9	44.5	45.0	44.9	44.9	45.6	45.2	45.4	46.0	46.0	46.2	46.6	45.3
1995	45.9	46.5	47.1	47.2	47.5	47.9	47.3	47.9	48.4	48.3	48.9	49.6	47.7
1996	49.1	50.0	50.4	50.0	50.3	50.4	50.0	50.2	50.8	50.7	51.0	51.3	50.3
1997	51.5	52.0	52.4	52.3	53.0	53.2	52.8	53.4	53.8	54.6	54.4	54.8	53.1
1998	53.8	54.2	54.5	54.8	55.3	55.6	55.2	55.6	55.9	56.2	56.2	56.6	55.3
1999	56.9	57.7	58.1	58.3	58.8	59.2	59.2	59.1	59.8	60.2	60.5	61.0	59.0
2000	60.6	61.4	62.3	62.1	62.3	63.0	62.9	63.2	64.1	64.8	65.3	66.0	63.1
2001	66.1	66.7	67.4	67.2	67.9	68.3	67.8	68.7	69.0	69.2	69.6	70.0	68.2
2002	69.1	70.0	70.7	71.5	72.1	72.0	71.6	72.3	72.6	73.4	73.8	74.0	71.9
2003	73.5	74.4	74.7	74.9	75.3	75.0	74.7	75.4	76.1	76.8	77.3	77.5	75.5

Employment by Industry: Nevada—*Continued*

(Numbers in thousands. Not seasonally adjusted.)

Industry	January	February	March	April	May	June	July	August	September	October	November	December	Annual Average
STATEWIDE—*Continued*													
Leisure and hospitality													
1990	183.7	185.0	186.1	189.0	191.1	194.0	199.4	201.3	198.9	196.8	195.6	192.1	192.7
1991	188.7	188.4	190.8	193.6	195.3	196.4	196.6	197.1	197.1	196.0	193.6	190.9	193.7
1992	188.0	189.0	189.9	193.1	196.0	197.2	197.6	197.7	198.3	195.2	194.5	192.7	194.1
1993	190.7	189.4	191.5	196.0	198.2	200.8	202.4	204.0	204.6	209.6	210.7	214.3	201.0
1994	216.5	218.9	221.3	223.6	225.5	228.4	230.8	234.9	233.7	230.8	230.0	229.7	227.0
1995	227.4	228.6	232.7	235.1	237.5	241.7	244.7	245.5	244.4	241.5	239.6	238.8	238.1
1996	237.1	238.9	242.2	249.9	252.0	256.5	259.0	258.7	256.6	252.9	253.5	254.9	251.0
1997	256.0	257.5	259.4	260.4	262.2	264.6	265.7	265.4	264.7	262.3	263.8	262.2	262.0
1998	259.2	261.6	264.9	267.4	269.6	271.4	271.6	272.1	272.3	274.1	273.6	273.1	269.2
1999	272.7	275.7	283.5	290.1	293.7	296.3	298.2	301.2	301.4	301.1	300.6	299.8	292.8
2000	296.2	297.2	299.5	302.1	304.8	307.4	309.0	311.7	309.6	307.8	306.4	304.4	304.6
2001	302.2	303.4	306.5	307.1	309.1	309.5	311.0	311.2	309.6	296.3	294.5	294.0	304.5
2002	288.9	290.3	294.3	297.1	300.0	301.1	301.6	302.0	300.8	299.4	297.4	297.6	297.5
2003	296.5	298.0	300.9	301.8	304.7	305.4	307.0	308.1	307.6	306.4	305.0	304.6	303.8
Other services													
1990	16.0	16.0	16.3	16.4	16.6	17.0	17.2	17.4	17.3	17.0	17.0	16.8	16.7
1991	16.8	16.9	17.0	17.0	17.2	17.4	17.6	17.7	17.5	17.2	17.0	16.9	17.1
1992	16.7	16.6	16.8	16.9	17.1	17.4	17.3	17.3	17.4	17.3	17.3	17.2	17.1
1993	17.1	17.5	17.9	17.8	18.0	18.3	18.3	18.5	18.4	18.4	18.4	18.4	18.0
1994	18.1	18.2	18.3	18.7	18.9	19.2	19.5	19.6	19.6	19.5	19.5	19.6	19.0
1995	19.3	19.8	20.1	20.0	20.3	20.5	20.8	21.0	20.9	20.7	20.7	20.7	20.4
1996	20.6	21.3	21.7	21.8	22.0	22.4	22.4	22.6	22.6	22.5	22.3	22.3	22.0
1997	22.6	23.1	23.4	23.6	24.0	24.3	24.6	24.8	24.6	24.4	24.1	24.1	23.9
1998	23.6	23.9	24.3	24.5	24.7	25.0	24.9	25.2	25.2	25.3	25.1	25.2	24.7
1999	24.7	25.0	25.4	25.9	26.3	26.6	26.7	26.7	26.8	26.5	26.5	26.5	26.1
2000	25.9	26.2	26.7	26.8	27.1	27.5	27.5	27.6	27.6	27.4	27.3	27.4	27.0
2001	27.9	28.2	28.7	29.3	29.8	30.5	29.9	30.1	30.1	29.5	29.1	29.2	29.4
2002	29.0	29.4	29.9	29.9	30.2	30.5	29.7	29.8	29.4	29.3	29.2	29.1	29.6
2003	29.4	29.6	30.0	29.8	30.2	31.0	31.0	31.0	30.8	30.6	30.6	30.6	30.4
Government													
1990	73.5	74.6	75.5	75.9	76.4	75.2	71.5	70.6	76.2	78.7	79.5	79.9	75.6
1991	77.8	80.5	81.4	81.9	82.7	80.2	76.0	77.2	82.4	84.6	85.0	85.6	81.2
1992	82.8	86.0	86.5	86.3	87.4	81.0	80.6	81.6	90.7	87.9	92.7	88.9	86.0
1993	85.9	87.9	89.5	89.4	90.0	89.5	82.7	84.2	89.1	91.3	91.7	91.8	88.5
1994	88.5	91.8	92.9	93.0	93.7	88.3	86.3	87.8	94.5	95.7	97.5	96.7	92.2
1995	93.3	96.8	98.5	98.4	98.5	93.7	90.9	89.2	97.5	99.9	101.5	100.5	96.5
1996	98.4	100.6	101.9	101.0	101.6	96.9	95.9	94.3	102.8	105.3	109.5	105.9	101.1
1997	102.9	106.2	107.3	107.3	107.8	105.5	100.8	99.7	107.3	109.8	111.3	112.2	106.5
1998	107.7	111.3	112.2	112.6	111.8	110.2	105.2	106.7	114.2	115.6	117.0	116.6	111.7
1999	114.5	117.8	119.8	119.8	119.8	114.8	109.8	109.9	116.7	121.9	121.7	122.6	117.4
2000	117.6	120.9	122.7	123.1	127.2	117.2	114.6	118.2	121.4	125.8	126.0	125.9	121.7
2001	122.8	127.3	128.1	129.6	128.7	125.5	118.8	119.3	128.7	130.1	130.7	131.4	126.8
2002	125.9	130.9	132.0	131.8	132.7	129.3	122.7	123.0	131.1	136.2	136.8	137.2	130.8
2003	131.4	136.5	137.3	137.1	138.0	133.7	126.8	126.6	135.0	138.4	138.8	139.7	134.9
Federal government													
1990	11.8	11.8	12.0	12.7	12.6	13.5	13.4	12.3	12.0	11.9	12.0	12.0	12.3
1991	11.9	11.9	12.0	12.3	12.4	12.7	12.8	12.8	12.8	12.7	12.7	12.8	12.4
1992	12.7	12.7	12.7	12.9	13.0	13.3	13.5	13.4	13.4	13.1	12.9	13.2	13.0
1993	12.9	12.9	12.9	13.0	13.1	13.4	13.8	13.8	13.7	13.5	13.4	13.4	13.3
1994	13.3	13.3	13.3	13.3	13.3	13.5	13.5	13.7	13.7	13.7	13.6	13.8	13.5
1995	13.6	13.5	13.5	13.5	13.6	13.8	13.8	13.9	13.9	13.6	13.5	13.6	13.6
1996	13.3	13.3	13.3	13.4	13.5	13.7	13.7	13.7	13.6	13.3	13.4	13.6	13.4
1997	13.2	13.1	13.1	13.3	13.4	13.7	13.8	13.8	13.8	13.6	13.6	13.9	13.5
1998	13.7	13.8	13.6	13.6	13.7	13.9	14.1	14.4	14.2	14.3	14.3	14.4	14.0
1999	13.9	13.8	13.9	14.2	14.1	14.5	14.4	14.5	14.4	14.4	14.4	14.8	14.2
2000	14.4	14.5	15.7	15.4	18.5	15.1	15.9	14.8	14.6	14.6	14.6	14.9	15.2
2001	14.4	14.3	14.4	14.4	14.7	15.1	15.1	15.2	15.2	15.0	14.9	15.3	14.8
2002	14.7	14.6	14.7	14.8	15.1	15.6	15.8	15.8	15.7	16.5	16.6	17.2	15.6
2003	16.4	16.4	16.5	16.4	16.6	16.9	17.0	16.9	16.8	16.5	16.3	16.8	16.6
State government													
1990	19.7	20.3	21.0	20.9	20.7	18.8	18.7	19.0	20.2	21.8	22.0	22.4	20.4
1991	20.0	22.1	23.0	23.0	23.1	20.3	20.0	20.0	21.7	23.2	23.1	23.4	21.9
1992	20.9	22.9	23.4	23.2	23.5	21.2	20.8	20.5	22.2	23.4	23.7	23.8	22.4
1993	21.0	22.9	24.0	23.7	23.8	21.1	20.3	20.6	21.9	23.7	23.9	24.0	22.5
1994	21.1	23.2	24.3	24.3	24.3	21.6	22.0	21.7	23.2	24.7	24.9	25.1	23.3
1995	21.8	24.4	26.0	25.8	25.3	23.6	22.3	22.0	24.4	25.8	27.0	26.1	24.5
1996	23.9	25.6	26.8	26.8	26.8	23.6	23.4	23.6	25.5	27.6	28.0	27.8	25.7
1997	24.9	27.7	28.3	28.3	28.0	25.0	24.9	25.0	26.8	28.3	29.2	29.8	27.1
1998	25.6	28.4	29.5	29.7	28.2	25.8	25.8	27.0	28.8	29.4	30.3	29.9	28.2
1999	27.8	30.4	31.9	31.2	31.1	28.5	26.4	26.9	29.4	31.7	31.2	31.3	29.8
2000	27.0	29.5	29.9	30.5	30.6	27.0	26.4	27.3	29.7	31.6	31.5	31.5	29.3
2001	27.6	31.5	32.2	32.3	32.1	28.5	27.5	28.0	31.5	32.5	32.9	32.7	30.8
2002	28.5	32.4	33.0	33.0	32.6	28.8	28.3	28.8	31.8	33.5	33.6	33.5	31.5
2003	29.1	32.9	33.6	33.6	33.5	29.2	28.7	29.0	31.8	34.1	34.5	34.6	32.1

Employment by Industry: Nevada—*Continued*

(Numbers in thousands. Not seasonally adjusted.)

Industry	January	February	March	April	May	June	July	August	September	October	November	December	Annual Average
STATEWIDE—*Continued*													
Local government													
1990	42.0	42.5	42.5	42.3	43.1	42.9	39.4	39.3	44.0	45.0	45.5	45.5	42.8
1991	45.9	46.5	46.4	46.6	47.2	47.2	43.2	44.4	47.9	48.7	49.2	49.4	46.8
1992	49.2	50.4	50.4	50.2	50.9	46.5	46.3	47.7	55.1	51.4	56.1	51.9	50.5
1993	52.0	52.1	52.6	52.7	53.1	55.0	48.6	49.8	53.5	54.1	54.4	54.4	52.6
1994	54.1	55.3	55.3	55.4	56.1	53.2	50.8	52.4	57.6	57.3	59.0	57.8	55.3
1995	57.9	58.9	59.0	59.1	59.6	56.3	54.8	53.3	59.2	60.5	61.0	60.8	58.3
1996	61.2	61.7	61.8	60.8	61.3	59.6	58.8	57.0	63.7	64.4	68.1	64.5	61.9
1997	64.8	65.4	65.9	65.7	66.4	66.8	62.1	60.9	66.7	67.9	68.5	68.5	65.8
1998	68.4	69.1	69.1	69.3	69.9	70.5	65.3	65.3	71.2	71.9	72.4	72.3	69.5
1999	72.8	73.6	74.0	74.4	74.6	71.8	69.0	68.5	72.9	75.8	76.1	76.5	73.3
2000	76.2	76.9	77.1	77.2	78.1	75.1	72.3	76.1	77.1	79.6	79.9	79.5	77.0
2001	80.8	81.5	81.5	82.9	81.9	81.9	76.2	76.1	82.0	82.6	82.9	83.4	81.1
2002	82.7	83.9	84.3	84.0	85.0	84.9	78.6	78.4	83.6	86.2	86.6	86.5	83.7
2003	85.9	87.2	87.2	87.1	87.9	87.6	81.1	80.7	86.4	87.8	88.0	88.3	86.3
LAS VEGAS													
Total nonfarm													
1990	396.3	398.2	404.2	406.5	411.2	412.9	413.8	418.3	421.4	422.8	426.6	423.1	412.9
1991	416.5	418.2	421.5	422.2	425.6	425.0	419.0	420.7	425.4	425.5	425.1	424.7	422.4
1992	414.1	416.6	420.5	425.1	431.1	425.7	426.8	430.4	438.5	435.7	442.9	439.1	428.8
1993	434.1	436.6	443.0	447.1	449.9	453.8	446.6	453.3	459.2	469.9	476.3	482.9	454.3
1994	482.1	487.1	493.8	500.0	504.9	504.1	506.4	515.0	521.2	520.4	527.6	528.6	507.6
1995	518.4	523.6	533.8	538.0	543.0	543.9	541.4	545.8	554.9	559.0	566.7	565.7	544.5
1996	560.0	569.1	576.7	583.7	587.5	588.4	589.3	597.1	605.6	608.3	621.4	619.5	592.2
1997	611.5	618.3	623.0	623.0	628.8	630.0	626.9	632.6	639.8	644.3	648.8	650.2	631.4
1998	635.1	640.8	646.2	653.2	659.3	661.5	657.8	665.7	672.2	682.3	690.0	692.3	663.0
1999	682.3	689.6	699.2	707.3	711.9	710.8	706.8	714.8	722.7	733.2	740.0	740.8	713.2
2000	728.0	731.2	738.9	744.2	754.2	750.9	747.4	756.2	763.6	766.5	772.3	772.3	752.1
2001	771.7	779.3	785.5	785.6	790.3	788.8	781.6	787.6	792.0	779.0	780.1	778.5	783.3
2002	766.9	771.8	781.8	787.0	793.3	787.9	784.7	790.1	795.8	802.4	805.2	806.1	789.4
2003	797.8	803.2	811.1	812.0	818.5	814.9	814.8	821.7	830.4	835.6	840.4	840.9	820.1
Total private													
1990	352.9	354.7	359.9	362.1	366.7	370.1	373.3	378.1	376.6	376.3	379.7	376.0	368.8
1991	370.3	370.6	373.0	373.6	376.6	378.0	375.1	375.3	376.6	374.7	374.2	373.7	374.3
1992	364.6	365.1	368.9	373.5	378.6	379.0	378.8	381.1	383.9	382.9	387.2	385.8	377.4
1993	382.4	384.0	389.0	393.2	395.5	399.6	398.2	402.7	405.4	414.4	420.7	427.3	401.0
1994	428.2	431.7	437.6	443.5	448.2	453.3	455.5	461.9	464.7	462.0	469.1	469.8	452.1
1995	461.1	464.6	473.8	478.3	483.1	489.4	487.3	492.6	495.6	497.7	504.0	503.9	485.9
1996	499.8	507.6	514.5	522.3	525.9	531.0	531.8	539.5	542.4	543.0	553.9	553.9	530.4
1997	547.5	552.5	557.0	556.6	562.4	565.6	566.2	571.1	572.8	575.7	579.3	579.8	565.5
1998	566.7	570.6	575.6	582.0	588.9	592.8	591.9	597.4	599.4	609.1	615.4	617.3	592.2
1999	609.0	614.7	623.1	631.1	635.7	639.3	637.4	644.8	648.2	654.4	660.9	661.4	638.3
2000	650.7	652.8	659.3	664.1	670.7	675.8	672.8	681.9	684.2	684.4	689.3	689.3	672.9
2001	690.8	696.1	701.7	700.2	706.2	707.2	703.8	709.4	706.8	692.9	693.7	692.0	700.1
2002	683.3	685.2	694.2	700.0	705.9	704.0	703.9	708.8	709.1	711.6	713.8	714.1	702.8
2003	709.8	712.2	719.6	720.7	726.9	727.2	730.4	737.8	740.4	743.1	747.3	747.7	730.3
Goods-producing													
1990	51.6	52.7	54.2	54.1	55.0	55.6	54.8	55.5	54.8	54.0	52.5	51.3	53.8
1991	48.4	48.1	47.8	48.0	48.4	48.8	48.1	48.1	47.1	45.5	44.9	44.8	47.3
1992	43.0	43.4	44.4	45.3	46.4	47.2	47.2	48.1	48.9	49.6	49.8	50.1	46.9
1993	49.1	50.9	52.8	54.2	55.1	56.7	56.8	57.7	57.5	57.6	57.3	58.3	55.3
1994	56.2	57.0	58.9	60.3	61.6	63.0	63.5	64.6	65.8	65.3	65.8	66.5	62.3
1995	62.8	64.3	66.5	67.9	69.9	71.7	70.9	72.1	73.8	75.0	76.0	77.2	70.6
1996	76.2	78.5	80.4	81.2	81.7	83.2	83.5	86.7	88.6	89.8	90.8	90.1	84.2
1997	87.0	87.9	89.3	89.2	90.9	91.6	91.4	92.8	92.4	92.0	90.6	91.6	90.5
1998	86.8	87.4	89.2	92.4	94.6	95.7	95.9	96.6	97.0	98.4	98.5	99.5	94.3
1999	98.2	99.1	98.3	97.0	96.3	96.3	94.6	95.1	94.7	95.6	95.9	95.1	96.3
2000	92.3	92.6	94.8	95.6	96.7	98.8	98.3	98.8	97.6	96.9	97.5	97.8	96.4
2001	95.9	96.9	98.2	98.3	99.9	101.5	101.7	103.2	102.5	101.7	100.6	99.2	100.0
2002	95.7	96.6	98.5	100.5	101.8	101.5	102.5	104.1	103.5	103.8	103.1	102.4	101.2
2003	101.4	101.8	104.3	105.2	106.7	107.5	108.6	110.6	111.1	112.1	112.0	111.5	107.7
Natural resources and mining													
1990	2.2	2.2	2.2	2.3	2.3	2.3	2.3	2.3	2.2	2.2	2.2	2.2	2.2
1991	2.0	2.0	1.9	2.0	2.0	2.0	2.1	2.0	2.0	1.9	1.9	1.9	1.9
1992	1.8	1.8	1.8	1.9	1.9	1.9	1.9	1.8	1.8	1.8	1.8	1.8	1.8
1993	1.8	1.9	1.8	1.8	1.9	1.8	1.8	1.8	1.7	1.7	1.7	1.7	1.7
1994	1.6	1.6	1.6	1.6	1.6	1.6	1.6	1.6	1.8	1.8	1.8	1.8	1.6
1995	1.9	1.9	1.9	1.9	2.0	2.1	2.1	2.0	2.0	2.1	2.1	2.1	2.0
1996	2.1	2.1	2.2	2.2	2.2	2.3	2.2	2.3	2.3	2.3	2.3	2.2	2.2
1997	2.3	2.2	2.2	2.3	2.3	2.3	2.2	2.2	2.2	2.2	2.1	2.1	2.2
1998	2.0	2.0	2.0	2.1	2.1	2.1	2.0	1.9	1.9	2.0	1.9	1.8	1.9
1999	1.9	1.9	1.9	1.9	1.9	1.8	1.8	1.8	1.8	1.8	1.8	1.8	1.8
2000	1.7	1.7	1.8	1.7	1.8	1.8	1.8	1.8	1.7	1.8	1.7	1.7	1.7
2001	1.7	1.6	1.6	1.6	1.6	1.5	1.5	1.5	1.5	1.4	1.3	1.3	1.5
2002	1.3	1.3	1.4	1.3	1.3	1.3	1.3	1.3	1.3	1.3	1.3	1.3	1.3
2003	1.3	1.3	1.3	1.3	1.3	1.3	1.3	1.3	1.2	1.3	1.3	1.3	1.3

Employment by Industry: Nevada—*Continued*

(Numbers in thousands. Not seasonally adjusted.)

Industry	January	February	March	April	May	June	July	August	September	October	November	December	Annual Average
LAS VEGAS—*Continued*													
Construction													
1990	37.4	38.1	39.5	39.1	39.8	40.3	39.5	40.1	39.5	38.7	37.2	36.2	38.7
1991	33.5	33.2	33.0	33.0	33.3	33.6	32.6	32.4	31.6	30.3	29.7	29.6	32.1
1992	28.2	28.4	29.2	29.7	30.6	31.2	31.0	32.0	32.6	33.5	33.7	33.8	31.1
1993	32.6	34.1	35.9	37.2	37.7	39.1	39.2	39.9	39.7	40.2	39.9	40.6	38.0
1994	38.7	39.4	41.0	42.1	43.1	44.1	44.6	45.3	46.1	45.6	46.0	46.8	43.5
1995	43.2	44.6	46.5	48.0	49.6	51.1	50.2	51.4	52.9	53.9	54.8	56.0	50.1
1996	54.8	56.9	58.4	59.0	59.3	60.6	61.0	64.0	65.7	66.7	67.4	66.9	61.7
1997	64.1	64.9	66.1	66.0	67.4	68.0	68.1	69.2	68.7	68.0	66.9	67.8	67.1
1998	63.7	64.4	66.0	69.0	71.0	71.9	72.2	72.8	73.1	74.6	74.6	75.5	70.7
1999	74.5	75.2	74.3	72.7	71.8	71.7	70.1	70.6	70.2	70.7	70.8	69.9	71.8
2000	67.6	67.8	69.6	70.6	71.5	73.5	73.2	73.6	72.5	71.5	72.2	72.3	71.3
2001	70.4	71.3	72.6	72.7	74.1	75.6	75.9	77.2	76.6	76.1	75.1	73.8	74.3
2002	70.6	71.4	73.2	75.2	76.2	75.9	76.7	78.2	77.6	77.4	76.7	75.9	75.4
2003	75.3	75.7	78.1	78.9	80.3	80.9	81.9	83.6	84.2	84.8	84.6	84.1	81.0
Manufacturing													
1990	12.0	12.4	12.5	12.7	12.9	13.0	13.0	13.1	13.1	13.1	13.1	12.9	12.8
1991	12.9	12.9	12.9	13.0	13.1	13.2	13.4	13.7	13.5	13.3	13.3	13.3	13.2
1992	13.0	13.2	13.4	13.7	13.9	14.1	14.3	14.3	14.5	14.3	14.3	14.5	13.9
1993	14.7	14.9	15.1	15.2	15.5	15.8	15.8	16.0	16.1	15.7	15.7	16.0	15.5
1994	15.9	16.0	16.3	16.6	16.9	17.3	17.3	17.7	17.9	17.9	18.0	17.9	17.1
1995	17.7	17.8	18.1	18.0	18.3	18.5	18.6	18.7	18.9	19.0	19.1	19.1	18.4
1996	19.3	19.5	19.8	20.0	20.2	20.3	20.3	20.4	20.6	20.8	21.1	21.0	20.2
1997	20.6	20.8	21.0	20.9	21.2	21.3	21.1	21.4	21.5	21.8	21.6	21.7	21.2
1998	21.1	21.0	21.2	21.3	21.5	21.7	21.7	21.9	22.0	21.8	22.0	22.2	21.6
1999	21.8	22.0	22.1	22.4	22.6	22.8	22.7	22.7	22.7	23.1	23.3	23.4	22.6
2000	23.0	23.1	23.4	23.3	23.4	23.5	23.3	23.4	23.4	23.6	23.6	23.8	23.4
2001	23.8	24.0	24.0	24.0	24.2	24.4	24.3	24.5	24.4	24.2	24.2	24.1	24.2
2002	23.8	23.9	23.9	24.0	24.3	24.3	24.5	24.6	24.6	25.1	25.1	25.2	24.4
2003	24.8	24.8	24.9	25.0	25.1	25.3	25.4	25.7	25.7	26.0	26.1	26.1	25.4
Service-providing													
1990	344.7	345.5	350.0	352.4	356.2	357.3	359.0	362.8	366.6	368.8	374.1	371.8	359.1
1991	368.1	370.1	373.7	374.2	377.2	376.2	370.9	372.6	378.3	380.0	380.2	379.9	375.1
1992	371.1	373.2	376.1	379.8	384.7	378.5	379.6	382.3	389.6	386.1	393.1	389.0	381.9
1993	385.0	385.7	390.2	392.9	394.8	397.1	389.8	395.6	401.7	412.3	419.0	424.6	399.0
1994	425.9	430.1	434.9	439.7	443.3	441.1	442.9	450.4	455.4	455.1	461.8	462.1	445.2
1995	455.6	459.3	467.3	470.1	473.1	472.2	470.5	473.7	481.1	484.0	490.7	488.5	473.8
1996	483.8	490.6	496.3	502.5	505.8	505.2	505.8	510.4	517.0	518.5	530.6	529.4	507.9
1997	524.5	530.4	533.7	533.8	537.9	538.4	535.5	539.8	547.4	552.3	558.2	558.6	540.8
1998	548.3	553.4	557.0	560.8	564.7	565.8	561.9	569.1	575.2	583.9	591.5	592.8	568.7
1999	584.1	590.5	600.9	610.3	615.6	614.5	612.2	619.7	628.0	637.6	644.1	645.7	616.9
2000	635.7	638.6	644.1	648.6	657.5	652.1	649.1	657.4	666.0	669.6	674.8	674.5	655.6
2001	675.8	682.4	687.3	687.3	690.4	687.3	679.9	684.4	689.5	677.3	679.5	679.3	683.4
2002	671.2	675.2	683.3	686.5	691.5	686.4	682.2	686.0	692.3	698.6	702.1	703.7	688.3
2003	696.4	701.4	706.8	706.8	711.8	707.4	706.2	711.1	719.3	723.5	728.4	729.4	712.4
Trade, transportation, and utilities													
1990	71.3	70.9	72.3	72.6	73.0	73.5	74.0	74.8	75.3	76.1	78.1	79.5	74.2
1991	76.2	75.6	75.9	75.6	76.6	77.5	77.3	77.3	77.7	77.5	78.8	80.1	77.1
1992	75.4	74.6	75.4	76.5	77.8	78.2	78.2	78.5	78.8	78.6	80.4	81.1	77.7
1993	79.5	78.8	79.0	78.9	78.9	79.7	78.8	79.1	79.8	81.0	82.8	84.8	80.0
1994	81.6	82.3	83.2	84.2	85.2	85.6	87.4	88.0	88.5	88.9	91.7	93.3	86.6
1995	90.7	90.1	91.1	92.4	92.7	93.8	94.0	95.0	95.8	96.5	99.2	100.9	94.3
1996	97.6	98.1	99.6	99.6	100.6	101.4	102.4	103.0	103.6	104.7	108.2	109.4	102.3
1997	104.4	104.4	105.8	106.9	107.8	108.7	109.3	109.9	111.0	113.1	114.7	116.8	109.4
1998	112.4	112.2	112.9	113.5	114.7	115.1	116.0	116.9	117.2	118.8	121.6	123.7	116.2
1999	118.5	117.9	118.6	120.1	121.6	122.4	123.0	124.2	125.0	128.0	130.7	133.6	123.6
2000	128.7	128.3	128.0	129.3	130.2	130.9	131.1	133.3	134.4	136.1	138.8	141.3	132.5
2001	138.2	137.2	137.4	138.5	139.5	140.3	140.3	140.6	140.4	140.3	142.3	143.3	139.9
2002	138.5	137.4	138.3	140.6	140.8	141.0	141.2	141.3	142.0	144.1	146.0	148.2	141.6
2003	141.8	141.7	143.2	142.8	143.4	144.0	144.6	146.1	147.3	149.2	151.8	153.8	145.8
Wholesale trade													
1990	11.4	11.5	11.8	11.8	11.8	12.0	12.0	12.0	12.0	12.1	12.1	12.2	11.8
1991	12.0	12.0	12.1	11.9	12.1	12.2	12.0	11.8	11.6	11.7	11.7	11.8	11.9
1992	11.8	11.4	11.6	11.6	11.8	11.9	11.8	11.9	11.8	11.9	11.9	11.9	11.7
1993	11.8	11.8	11.8	11.7	11.8	11.9	11.5	11.6	11.6	11.7	11.8	11.9	11.7
1994	12.1	12.3	12.5	12.8	12.9	13.0	13.5	13.7	13.7	13.7	13.7	13.9	13.1
1995	13.6	13.9	14.1	14.5	14.6	14.8	14.9	15.1	15.4	15.3	15.5	15.8	14.7
1996	15.7	15.8	16.0	16.2	16.5	16.7	16.9	16.9	16.9	16.9	17.0	17.1	16.5
1997	16.9	17.3	17.5	17.6	17.7	17.8	17.8	18.0	18.1	18.2	18.2	18.3	17.7
1998	18.0	18.1	18.1	18.4	18.5	18.5	18.7	18.8	18.8	18.9	19.0	19.1	18.5
1999	18.8	18.8	19.0	19.1	19.2	19.3	19.4	19.5	19.6	19.9	19.9	20.0	19.3
2000	19.3	19.3	19.5	19.9	20.1	20.2	20.1	20.2	20.2	20.1	20.3	20.5	19.9
2001	21.3	21.4	21.6	21.9	22.2	22.4	22.2	22.3	22.2	22.1	22.1	22.1	22.0
2002	21.7	21.9	22.2	22.3	22.3	22.4	22.3	22.4	22.4	22.4	22.4	22.5	22.3
2003	22.0	22.0	22.1	22.1	22.0	22.1	22.2	22.1	22.2	22.2	22.3	22.3	22.1

Employment by Industry: Nevada—*Continued*

(Numbers in thousands. Not seasonally adjusted.)

Industry	January	February	March	April	May	June	July	August	September	October	November	December	Annual Average
LAS VEGAS—*Continued*													
Retail trade													
1990	45.4	44.9	45.7	46.0	46.4	46.6	47.0	47.7	48.0	48.7	50.4	51.5	47.3
1991	48.3	47.7	47.9	47.6	48.2	48.8	48.7	49.0	49.6	49.4	50.8	52.0	49.0
1992	47.9	47.5	48.2	49.1	50.0	50.1	50.0	50.2	50.7	50.3	51.8	52.5	49.8
1993	51.0	50.2	50.3	50.1	50.1	50.6	50.0	50.1	50.6	51.3	52.8	54.8	50.9
1994	51.9	52.1	52.6	53.3	54.0	54.1	54.7	54.8	55.2	55.5	57.6	59.2	54.5
1995	57.1	56.4	56.9	57.4	57.6	58.4	58.4	59.0	59.5	59.9	61.9	63.5	58.8
1996	60.6	60.8	61.8	61.6	62.2	62.7	63.1	63.5	64.2	64.8	67.8	69.3	63.5
1997	65.3	64.8	65.7	66.3	66.9	67.4	67.9	68.4	69.1	70.4	72.2	74.3	68.2
1998	70.7	70.1	70.6	71.0	71.9	72.2	72.7	73.2	73.6	74.5	77.0	79.0	73.0
1999	74.4	73.6	74.1	75.0	75.9	76.5	76.8	77.5	77.9	79.9	82.4	85.1	77.4
2000	81.1	80.6	79.7	80.8	81.6	82.0	82.0	83.8	84.5	85.8	88.0	90.4	83.3
2001	87.1	85.8	85.7	86.3	86.8	87.4	87.5	87.8	87.9	88.1	90.4	91.5	87.7
2002	87.4	86.3	86.8	88.1	88.5	88.8	88.6	88.5	89.0	90.8	93.9	96.2	89.4
2003	90.4	90.0	91.2	90.8	91.7	92.2	92.6	94.1	94.9	96.6	98.8	100.7	93.7
Transportation and utilities													
1990	14.5	14.5	14.8	14.8	14.8	14.9	15.0	15.1	15.3	15.3	15.6	15.8	15.0
1991	15.9	15.9	15.9	16.1	16.3	16.5	16.6	16.5	16.5	16.4	16.3	16.3	16.2
1992	15.7	15.7	15.6	15.8	16.0	16.2	16.4	16.4	16.3	16.4	16.7	16.7	16.1
1993	16.7	16.8	16.9	17.1	17.0	17.2	17.3	17.4	17.6	18.0	18.2	18.1	17.3
1994	17.6	17.9	18.1	18.1	18.3	18.5	19.2	19.5	19.6	19.7	20.4	20.2	18.9
1995	20.0	19.8	20.1	20.5	20.5	20.6	20.7	20.9	20.9	21.3	21.8	21.6	20.7
1996	21.3	21.5	21.8	21.8	21.9	22.0	22.4	22.6	22.5	23.0	23.4	23.0	22.2
1997	22.2	22.3	22.6	23.0	23.2	23.5	23.6	23.5	23.8	24.5	24.3	24.2	23.3
1998	23.7	24.0	24.2	24.1	24.3	24.4	24.6	24.9	24.8	25.4	25.6	25.6	24.6
1999	25.3	25.5	25.5	26.0	26.5	26.6	26.8	27.2	27.5	28.2	28.4	28.5	26.8
2000	28.3	28.4	28.8	28.6	28.5	28.7	29.0	29.3	29.7	30.2	30.5	30.4	29.2
2001	29.8	30.0	30.1	30.3	30.5	30.5	30.6	30.5	30.3	30.1	29.8	29.7	30.2
2002	29.4	29.2	29.3	30.2	30.0	29.8	30.3	30.4	30.6	30.9	29.7	29.5	29.9
2003	29.4	29.7	29.9	29.9	29.7	29.7	29.8	29.9	30.2	30.4	30.7	30.8	30.0
Information													
1990	6.5	6.6	7.1	6.8	6.9	7.1	6.9	7.0	6.9	6.9	6.9	6.9	6.8
1991	6.6	6.7	6.7	6.5	6.5	6.6	6.5	6.5	6.5	6.4	6.5	6.8	6.5
1992	6.6	6.6	6.6	6.5	6.5	6.7	6.8	6.8	6.7	6.8	6.9	6.9	6.7
1993	6.9	7.0	7.0	6.8	6.9	7.1	7.2	7.2	7.1	7.2	7.3	7.3	7.0
1994	6.7	6.8	6.8	7.5	7.5	7.8	7.9	7.9	8.1	8.5	8.8	8.8	7.7
1995	8.6	8.5	8.5	8.5	8.5	8.9	8.6	8.1	8.2	9.1	9.3	9.4	8.6
1996	8.9	9.1	9.1	9.6	9.3	9.1	9.1	9.2	9.1	9.4	9.7	10.0	9.3
1997	9.2	9.4	9.7	9.4	9.5	9.7	10.0	10.2	10.4	10.5	10.4	10.4	9.9
1998	10.3	10.2	10.3	10.8	10.7	10.9	10.9	11.1	11.2	11.5	11.8	12.0	10.9
1999	11.9	12.0	12.1	12.5	12.6	12.9	13.2	13.3	13.6	13.9	14.1	14.7	13.0
2000	14.8	14.4	14.8	14.7	15.5	15.2	14.9	15.2	15.0	15.4	15.5	14.9	15.0
2001	15.9	17.6	17.4	15.9	15.9	15.2	14.2	13.9	13.5	13.9	14.3	13.9	15.1
2002	13.9	13.7	13.5	13.5	13.6	13.2	13.0	13.0	12.9	12.7	12.8	12.7	13.2
2003	12.3	12.1	12.0	12.2	12.4	12.4	12.0	11.9	11.9	11.8	11.9	11.9	12.1
Financial activities													
1990	21.0	21.4	21.5	21.8	22.0	22.4	22.7	22.7	22.6	22.3	22.7	22.8	22.1
1991	22.1	22.3	22.2	22.4	22.7	23.5	23.8	24.0	24.0	23.9	23.7	24.0	23.2
1992	23.6	24.0	24.0	24.4	24.5	24.5	24.7	24.7	24.8	24.5	24.7	25.2	24.4
1993	24.8	25.1	25.6	25.9	26.1	26.4	26.2	26.6	26.8	26.8	27.1	27.4	26.2
1994	27.8	28.3	28.8	29.3	29.3	29.6	29.2	29.3	29.4	29.4	29.7	30.1	29.1
1995	29.3	30.2	30.7	30.9	31.3	31.6	31.7	32.1	32.1	32.2	32.6	32.6	31.4
1996	33.1	33.6	33.9	33.5	33.8	34.0	33.8	34.2	34.2	34.1	34.7	34.7	33.9
1997	34.3	34.6	34.9	34.5	35.0	34.8	35.6	35.8	35.8	35.7	35.5	35.6	35.1
1998	34.9	35.2	35.6	36.2	36.6	37.0	36.8	37.2	37.5	37.8	38.2	38.4	36.7
1999	37.9	38.0	38.0	38.2	38.4	38.7	38.4	38.7	38.6	38.9	39.3	39.2	38.5
2000	38.5	38.6	39.0	39.0	39.1	39.5	39.9	40.1	40.2	39.9	40.5	40.8	39.5
2001	41.5	41.8	42.3	42.1	42.3	42.7	42.7	43.3	43.5	43.0	42.8	43.4	42.6
2002	42.1	42.6	42.9	43.1	43.1	43.3	43.4	43.3	43.2	43.7	44.2	44.2	43.3
2003	44.1	44.3	44.6	44.9	45.6	45.7	46.1	46.1	46.4	46.5	47.0	47.2	45.7
Professional and business services													
1990	42.3	41.1	41.8	41.6	42.7	42.8	42.7	43.7	43.5	43.8	45.9	43.8	42.9
1991	44.9	45.0	45.3	45.7	45.9	45.5	43.6	43.0	43.9	43.7	43.5	43.3	44.4
1992	43.4	42.8	43.9	44.1	45.0	44.6	44.6	45.5	45.8	45.6	46.8	44.7	44.7
1993	44.9	45.3	45.5	45.0	44.8	44.7	44.6	45.9	46.0	46.3	48.2	47.2	45.7
1994	50.5	50.4	50.6	51.1	51.9	52.6	51.4	52.3	53.4	52.7	55.6	52.7	52.1
1995	53.6	54.5	56.4	55.7	56.0	56.7	54.2	56.8	57.2	56.8	58.5	55.7	56.0
1996	57.0	58.8	58.4	59.6	59.8	59.8	58.4	61.4	62.2	62.3	66.0	63.1	60.5
1997	63.7	64.5	64.4	64.3	64.8	64.9	63.8	65.9	66.2	67.0	68.7	66.8	65.4
1998	65.8	66.5	65.7	66.2	67.1	67.9	67.6	70.0	69.8	71.8	73.7	71.6	68.6
1999	70.7	72.0	73.6	74.1	73.9	74.2	73.0	75.3	76.8	77.3	79.4	77.0	74.7
2000	77.9	78.8	79.5	80.8	82.1	82.3	79.5	82.1	85.1	83.9	85.1	82.9	81.6
2001	87.5	89.1	89.4	87.3	88.5	87.5	85.2	87.5	86.5	84.9	85.4	83.4	86.9
2002	87.2	86.8	88.5	87.8	88.8	87.5	87.2	89.7	90.4	89.8	90.6	89.1	88.6
2003	92.4	92.6	92.6	92.0	92.6	90.9	92.5	95.2	95.2	94.7	95.4	93.8	93.3

Employment by Industry: Nevada—*Continued*

(Numbers in thousands. Not seasonally adjusted.)

Industry	January	February	March	April	May	June	July	August	September	October	November	December	Annual Average
LAS VEGAS—*Continued*													
Educational and health services													
1990	21.5	21.9	22.0	22.3	22.6	22.7	22.5	22.9	23.2	23.5	23.9	24.3	22.7
1991	24.3	25.1	25.6	25.1	25.3	25.4	25.4	25.6	26.0	26.0	26.3	26.6	25.5
1992	26.5	26.8	27.0	26.8	26.8	26.8	26.8	26.7	27.2	27.5	27.8	28.1	27.0
1993	28.4	28.8	29.0	28.9	29.0	29.3	29.1	29.1	29.6	29.9	30.1	30.3	29.2
1994	30.2	30.6	31.0	30.8	31.1	31.2	31.1	31.2	31.5	31.8	32.0	32.3	31.2
1995	31.7	32.2	32.8	33.1	33.2	33.5	33.2	33.7	34.2	34.2	34.7	35.2	33.4
1996	35.1	35.7	36.1	35.6	35.9	35.8	35.6	35.7	36.1	36.1	36.2	36.5	35.8
1997	36.9	37.2	37.5	37.2	37.8	37.9	37.4	38.2	38.6	39.5	39.2	39.7	38.0
1998	38.5	39.1	39.3	39.2	39.7	40.0	39.7	39.7	39.8	39.7	39.8	40.0	39.5
1999	40.3	40.9	40.9	41.4	41.7	42.0	42.2	42.0	42.5	42.8	43.1	43.4	41.9
2000	44.1	44.6	45.0	45.3	45.5	45.7	45.9	46.1	46.9	47.5	47.8	48.4	46.0
2001	48.7	49.2	49.7	49.9	50.4	50.6	50.4	51.4	51.5	51.5	51.8	52.2	50.6
2002	51.8	52.4	52.9	53.2	53.8	53.5	53.5	53.9	54.2	54.9	55.2	55.3	53.7
2003	54.9	55.6	55.8	56.1	56.4	56.2	55.9	56.2	56.9	57.3	57.7	57.9	56.4
Leisure and hospitality													
1990	126.8	128.2	129.0	130.9	132.4	133.7	137.3	138.9	137.8	137.1	137.2	135.0	133.6
1991	135.1	135.0	136.6	137.6	138.4	137.7	137.3	137.6	138.4	138.8	137.7	135.3	137.1
1992	133.5	134.3	134.9	137.2	138.7	138.0	137.7	138.0	138.9	137.5	137.8	136.9	136.9
1993	136.0	135.1	137.0	140.5	141.6	142.4	142.3	143.7	145.2	152.1	154.3	158.4	144.0
1994	161.8	162.8	164.6	166.3	167.4	169.2	170.6	174.2	173.5	171.1	171.2	171.8	168.7
1995	170.1	170.1	172.9	175.0	176.4	178.0	179.5	179.4	178.8	178.5	178.2	177.4	176.1
1996	176.5	178.2	181.1	187.1	188.5	191.2	192.5	192.5	191.8	189.8	191.6	193.4	187.8
1997	195.2	197.3	197.9	197.5	198.7	199.9	200.5	200.0	200.2	199.8	202.3	201.1	199.2
1998	200.4	202.3	204.7	205.7	207.3	207.9	206.8	207.4	208.3	212.3	213.1	213.3	207.4
1999	213.1	216.2	222.6	228.4	231.5	233.0	233.1	236.2	236.9	238.0	238.5	238.4	230.4
2000	235.0	235.8	238.1	239.3	241.2	242.7	242.6	245.6	244.3	244.0	243.4	242.5	241.2
2001	242.3	243.2	245.8	246.2	247.3	246.6	247.0	246.9	246.3	235.7	234.9	234.9	243.1
2002	232.1	233.4	236.8	238.7	241.1	241.0	240.5	240.8	240.4	240.2	239.7	239.9	238.7
2003	240.4	241.4	244.1	245.0	247.0	247.2	247.5	248.4	248.4	248.4	248.4	248.5	246.2
Other services													
1990	11.9	11.9	12.0	12.0	12.1	12.3	12.4	12.6	12.5	12.6	12.5	12.4	12.2
1991	12.7	12.8	12.9	12.7	12.8	13.0	13.1	13.2	13.0	12.9	12.8	12.8	12.8
1992	12.6	12.6	12.7	12.7	12.9	13.0	12.8	12.8	12.8	12.8	13.0	12.8	12.7
1993	12.8	13.0	13.1	13.0	13.1	13.3	13.2	13.4	13.4	13.5	13.6	13.6	13.2
1994	13.4	13.5	13.7	14.0	14.2	14.3	14.4	14.4	14.5	14.3	14.3	14.3	14.1
1995	14.3	14.7	14.9	14.8	15.1	15.2	15.2	15.4	15.5	15.4	15.5	15.5	15.1
1996	15.4	15.6	15.9	16.1	16.3	16.5	16.5	16.8	16.8	16.8	16.7	16.7	16.3
1997	16.8	17.2	17.5	17.6	17.9	18.1	18.2	18.3	18.2	18.1	17.9	17.8	17.8
1998	17.6	17.7	17.9	18.0	18.2	18.3	18.2	18.5	18.6	18.8	18.7	18.8	18.2
1999	18.4	18.6	19.0	19.4	19.7	19.8	19.9	20.0	20.1	19.9	19.9	20.0	19.5
2000	19.4	19.7	20.1	20.1	20.4	20.7	20.6	20.7	20.7	20.7	20.7	20.7	20.3
2001	20.8	21.1	21.5	22.0	22.4	22.8	22.3	22.6	22.6	21.9	21.6	21.7	21.9
2002	22.0	22.3	22.8	22.6	22.9	23.0	22.6	22.7	22.5	22.4	22.2	22.3	22.5
2003	22.5	22.7	23.0	22.5	22.8	23.3	23.2	23.3	23.2	23.1	23.1	23.1	23.0
Government													
1990	43.4	43.5	44.3	44.4	44.5	42.8	40.5	40.2	44.8	46.5	46.9	47.1	44.0
1991	46.2	47.6	48.5	48.6	49.0	47.0	43.9	45.4	48.8	50.8	50.9	51.0	48.1
1992	49.5	51.5	51.6	51.6	52.5	46.7	48.0	49.3	54.6	52.8	55.7	53.3	51.4
1993	51.7	52.6	54.0	53.9	54.4	54.2	48.4	50.6	53.8	55.5	55.6	55.6	53.3
1994	53.9	55.4	56.2	56.5	56.7	50.8	50.9	53.1	56.5	58.4	58.5	58.8	55.4
1995	57.3	59.0	60.0	59.7	59.9	54.5	54.1	53.2	59.3	61.3	62.7	61.8	58.5
1996	60.2	61.5	62.2	61.4	61.6	57.4	57.5	57.6	63.2	65.3	67.5	65.6	61.7
1997	64.0	65.8	66.0	66.4	66.4	64.4	60.7	61.5	67.0	68.6	69.5	70.4	65.8
1998	68.4	70.2	70.6	71.2	70.4	68.7	65.9	68.3	72.8	73.2	74.6	75.0	70.7
1999	73.3	74.9	76.1	76.2	76.2	71.5	69.4	70.0	74.5	78.8	79.1	79.4	74.9
2000	77.3	78.4	79.6	80.1	83.5	75.1	74.6	74.3	79.4	82.1	83.0	83.0	79.2
2001	80.9	83.2	83.8	85.4	84.1	81.6	77.8	78.2	85.2	86.1	86.4	86.5	83.3
2002	83.6	86.6	87.6	87.0	87.4	83.9	80.8	81.3	86.7	90.8	91.4	92.0	86.6
2003	88.0	91.0	91.5	91.3	91.6	87.7	84.4	83.9	90.0	92.5	93.1	93.2	89.9
Federal government													
1990	7.2	7.3	7.4	7.8	7.6	8.4	8.2	7.5	7.4	7.4	7.3	7.3	7.5
1991	7.4	7.4	7.5	7.5	7.6	7.6	7.7	7.7	7.8	7.8	7.8	7.9	7.6
1992	7.9	7.9	7.8	7.9	7.9	8.1	8.2	8.1	8.1	8.0	8.0	8.2	8.0
1993	8.0	8.0	8.0	8.1	8.1	8.2	8.5	8.5	8.5	8.4	8.4	8.4	8.2
1994	8.3	8.3	8.2	8.3	8.2	8.2	8.2	8.4	8.4	8.5	8.6	8.7	8.3
1995	8.6	8.5	8.5	8.5	8.6	8.7	8.6	8.6	8.7	8.6	8.6	8.7	8.6
1996	8.5	8.5	8.5	8.6	8.6	8.7	8.8	8.7	8.7	8.6	8.6	8.8	8.6
1997	8.7	8.7	8.6	8.7	8.7	8.8	8.9	8.9	8.9	8.9	8.9	9.1	8.8
1998	8.9	9.0	8.8	8.9	9.0	9.1	9.2	9.2	9.1	9.0	9.1	9.4	9.0
1999	9.2	9.2	9.2	9.3	9.3	9.5	9.4	9.5	9.4	9.5	9.6	9.9	9.4
2000	9.6	9.7	10.5	10.4	12.9	10.1	10.7	9.9	9.7	9.8	9.8	10.1	10.2
2001	9.7	9.6	9.7	9.7	9.8	10.0	9.9	10.0	10.0	10.0	10.0	10.2	9.9
2002	9.9	9.9	10.0	10.0	10.1	10.3	10.5	10.5	10.5	11.2	11.4	11.9	10.5
2003	11.3	11.3	11.4	11.3	11.4	11.5	11.6	11.6	11.4	11.3	11.3	11.6	11.4

Employment by Industry: Nevada—*Continued*

(Numbers in thousands. Not seasonally adjusted.)

Industry	January	February	March	April	May	June	July	August	September	October	November	December	Annual Average
LAS VEGAS—*Continued*													
State government													
1990	8.3	8.0	8.5	8.3	8.2	7.1	7.3	7.4	8.0	8.9	9.0	9.1	8.1
1991	7.8	8.7	9.3	9.4	9.4	7.8	7.7	7.7	8.5	9.5	9.4	9.5	8.7
1992	8.3	9.3	9.6	9.4	9.7	8.5	8.2	7.9	8.9	9.7	9.8	9.9	9.1
1993	8.4	9.3	9.9	9.6	9.8	8.5	8.0	8.3	8.8	10.0	10.2	10.2	9.2
1994	8.7	9.5	10.1	10.2	10.1	8.7	9.3	8.8	9.4	10.5	10.4	10.6	9.6
1995	8.8	10.0	10.6	10.7	10.5	9.1	8.8	8.6	9.7	10.8	12.0	11.2	10.0
1996	9.5	10.5	11.3	11.2	11.4	9.6	9.4	9.4	10.4	11.9	12.1	12.1	10.7
1997	10.5	11.8	12.0	12.1	11.9	10.5	10.5	10.3	11.1	12.0	12.4	13.1	11.5
1998	11.2	12.5	13.0	13.4	11.8	11.0	11.0	12.1	12.5	12.6	13.5	13.8	12.3
1999	11.7	12.5	13.4	13.1	13.1	12.3	10.7	10.9	12.3	14.1	13.7	13.7	12.6
2000	11.9	12.7	12.9	13.5	13.7	11.5	11.1	11.5	12.8	14.1	14.1	14.0	12.8
2001	11.8	13.7	14.2	14.4	14.3	12.1	11.8	11.9	14.1	14.6	15.0	14.7	13.6
2002	12.5	14.6	14.9	14.9	14.7	12.2	12.3	12.3	14.0	15.3	15.4	15.3	14.0
2003	12.7	14.8	15.3	15.4	15.1	12.5	12.5	12.4	14.0	15.9	16.3	16.1	14.4
Local government													
1990	27.9	28.2	28.4	28.3	28.7	27.3	25.0	25.3	29.4	30.2	30.6	30.7	28.3
1991	31.0	31.5	31.7	31.7	32.0	31.6	28.5	30.0	32.5	33.5	33.7	33.6	31.7
1992	33.3	34.3	34.2	34.3	34.9	30.1	31.6	33.3	37.6	35.1	37.9	35.2	34.3
1993	35.3	35.3	36.1	36.2	36.5	37.5	31.9	33.8	36.5	37.1	37.0	37.0	35.8
1994	36.9	37.6	37.9	38.0	38.4	33.9	33.4	35.9	38.7	39.4	39.5	39.5	37.4
1995	39.9	40.5	40.9	40.5	40.8	36.7	36.7	36.0	40.9	41.9	42.1	41.9	39.9
1996	42.2	42.5	42.4	41.6	41.6	39.1	39.3	39.5	44.1	44.8	46.8	44.7	42.3
1997	44.8	45.3	45.4	45.6	45.8	45.1	41.3	42.3	47.0	47.7	48.2	48.2	45.5
1998	48.3	48.7	48.8	48.9	49.6	48.6	45.7	47.0	51.2	51.6	52.0	51.8	49.3
1999	52.4	53.2	53.5	53.8	53.8	49.7	49.3	49.6	52.8	55.2	55.8	55.8	52.9
2000	55.8	56.0	56.2	56.2	56.9	53.5	52.8	52.9	56.9	58.2	59.1	58.9	56.1
2001	59.4	59.9	59.9	61.3	60.0	59.5	56.1	56.3	61.1	61.5	61.4	61.6	59.8
2002	61.2	62.1	62.7	62.1	62.6	61.4	58.0	58.5	62.2	64.3	64.6	64.8	62.0
2003	64.0	64.9	64.8	64.6	65.1	63.7	60.3	59.9	64.6	65.3	65.5	65.5	64.0
RENO													
Total nonfarm													
1990	139.3	139.8	140.8	142.7	144.5	145.6	145.1	146.0	146.3	146.3	145.5	144.5	143.8
1991	138.6	139.2	140.5	141.9	143.6	144.5	143.4	144.2	145.5	144.7	144.1	143.7	142.8
1992	139.4	140.4	141.6	143.7	145.6	146.7	145.8	146.7	148.8	148.7	148.7	147.0	145.2
1993	142.0	143.8	146.3	147.6	149.5	150.9	150.5	151.6	153.9	155.0	155.2	155.6	150.1
1994	149.4	151.3	153.0	156.2	158.4	160.0	159.6	160.0	162.5	162.4	163.2	162.6	158.2
1995	155.8	158.5	160.6	162.6	164.3	166.4	168.2	170.0	171.5	170.5	170.2	170.5	165.7
1996	165.9	166.9	168.3	170.1	172.3	174.2	174.5	174.0	175.8	175.7	176.2	175.0	172.4
1997	170.0	171.9	174.4	176.0	178.1	178.6	179.7	179.0	180.9	180.5	180.9	181.0	177.5
1998	174.4	175.4	178.4	180.3	182.4	183.1	183.9	184.9	186.5	186.7	186.8	187.0	182.4
1999	179.5	180.8	184.5	185.0	186.8	187.9	187.6	187.9	189.5	190.2	190.4	191.1	186.7
2000	184.9	186.4	188.4	191.0	193.2	194.4	194.6	195.1	196.9	197.6	197.8	198.0	193.1
2001	192.9	194.8	197.0	198.1	199.4	200.5	198.7	199.5	200.7	199.5	200.2	199.0	198.4
2002	189.9	191.4	193.0	195.3	196.7	197.0	195.7	196.4	197.1	199.1	199.3	199.8	195.9
2003	192.3	194.6	196.8	197.4	199.2	199.3	199.6	201.5	202.7	204.5	205.1	205.2	199.9
Total private													
1990	121.7	121.4	122.3	124.2	125.7	127.4	128.0	129.0	128.2	127.4	126.6	125.3	125.6
1991	120.4	120.1	121.3	122.6	124.0	125.8	125.7	126.7	126.2	125.0	124.4	123.7	123.8
1992	120.3	120.3	121.5	123.6	125.5	127.2	127.6	128.7	128.6	128.6	128.0	126.8	125.5
1993	122.9	123.7	125.8	127.1	129.1	131.2	132.0	133.4	133.8	134.6	134.9	135.0	130.2
1994	129.7	130.6	132.0	135.3	137.3	139.7	140.6	141.3	141.2	141.1	141.1	140.9	137.5
1995	135.5	136.9	138.4	140.5	142.6	144.7	148.1	150.3	149.7	148.4	148.1	148.4	144.3
1996	144.3	144.6	145.6	147.3	149.5	152.3	153.1	153.8	153.2	152.8	152.4	152.0	150.0
1997	148.1	148.8	150.9	152.6	154.5	155.9	157.8	157.8	157.7	157.1	156.9	157.0	154.5
1998	151.8	151.6	154.2	156.2	158.3	159.9	162.1	163.1	162.5	162.3	162.2	162.7	158.9
1999	156.4	156.5	160.0	160.5	162.3	164.4	166.1	166.1	165.6	165.9	166.1	166.3	163.0
2000	161.8	161.8	163.4	165.9	167.8	170.4	172.1	172.5	172.7	172.6	172.8	172.9	168.8
2001	168.8	169.1	171.2	172.3	173.6	175.6	175.7	176.2	175.5	173.9	174.1	172.5	173.2
2002	165.1	165.2	166.6	169.0	170.3	171.6	172.0	172.5	171.3	172.3	172.5	172.8	170.1
2003	166.5	167.6	169.4	170.4	172.0	173.3	175.4	177.0	176.5	177.6	178.0	177.8	173.5
Goods-producing													
1990	16.3	15.8	16.1	16.4	16.8	17.1	17.2	17.4	17.5	17.5	17.2	16.8	16.8
1991	15.7	15.7	15.8	16.3	16.7	16.7	16.9	17.1	17.2	16.8	16.5	16.1	16.4
1992	15.1	15.3	15.7	16.4	16.8	17.3	17.8	17.9	17.8	18.1	17.7	17.1	16.9
1993	15.6	16.3	17.1	17.9	18.3	18.6	19.2	19.4	19.4	19.8	19.9	19.7	18.4
1994	19.0	19.1	19.7	21.3	21.9	22.4	22.6	22.7	22.6	22.7	22.0	21.7	21.4
1995	20.6	20.9	21.2	21.9	22.5	23.0	24.2	24.6	24.5	24.3	24.3	24.2	23.0
1996	23.0	23.0	23.1	24.1	24.7	25.8	26.1	26.6	26.4	26.5	25.9	25.1	25.0
1997	24.0	24.4	24.5	25.2	25.5	25.7	25.9	26.2	26.3	26.4	26.5	25.9	25.5
1998	24.5	24.4	24.9	25.3	26.4	27.1	27.8	28.2	28.2	28.4	28.0	27.7	26.7
1999	26.3	25.7	26.7	26.5	27.3	27.9	27.9	27.9	27.7	27.8	27.3	26.8	27.1
2000	26.1	26.0	26.3	27.4	28.0	29.0	29.0	29.3	29.2	29.4	29.0	29.1	28.1
2001	28.4	28.5	29.0	29.8	30.3	31.0	30.8	31.2	30.8	30.6	29.9	28.7	29.9
2002	27.6	27.7	28.5	29.0	29.4	29.8	30.2	30.6	30.0	30.3	29.9	29.5	29.4
2003	28.5	28.9	29.6	29.8	30.4	31.0	31.6	32.1	31.7	31.9	31.7	31.4	30.7

Employment by Industry: Nevada—*Continued*

(Numbers in thousands. Not seasonally adjusted.)

Industry	January	February	March	April	May	June	July	August	September	October	November	December	Annual Average
RENO—*Continued*													
Natural resources and mining													
1990	1.0	1.0	1.0	1.1	1.1	1.1	1.2	1.2	1.1	1.1	1.1	1.1	1.0
1991	0.9	0.8	0.8	0.7	0.7	0.7	0.7	0.7	0.7	0.7	0.6	0.6	0.7
1992	0.5	0.6	0.6	0.6	0.7	0.7	0.7	0.7	0.7	0.7	0.7	0.6	0.6
1993	0.5	0.5	0.5	0.5	0.5	0.5	0.6	0.6	0.6	0.6	0.6	0.5	0.5
1994	0.5	0.5	0.5	0.6	0.6	0.6	0.6	0.6	0.6	0.6	0.6	0.6	0.5
1995	0.5	0.5	0.5	0.5	0.5	0.5	0.5	0.5	0.5	0.5	0.5	0.5	0.5
1996	0.5	0.5	0.5	0.5	0.5	0.5	0.5	0.5	0.5	0.6	0.6	0.6	0.5
1997	0.5	0.6	0.6	0.6	0.6	0.6	0.6	0.6	0.6	0.6	0.6	0.6	0.5
1998	0.5	0.5	0.5	0.4	0.5	0.5	0.5	0.5	0.5	0.4	0.4	0.4	0.4
1999	0.4	0.4	0.4	0.4	0.4	0.4	0.4	0.4	0.4	0.4	0.4	0.4	0.4
2000	0.4	0.4	0.4	0.4	0.4	0.4	0.4	0.4	0.4	0.4	0.4	0.4	0.4
2001	0.4	0.4	0.4	0.4	0.4	0.4	0.4	0.4	0.4	0.4	0.4	0.4	0.4
2002	0.3	0.3	0.3	0.3	0.3	0.4	0.4	0.4	0.4	0.4	0.4	0.4	0.4
2003	0.4	0.4	0.4	0.4	0.3	0.3	0.3	0.3	0.3	0.3	0.3	0.3	0.3
Construction													
1990	7.8	7.4	7.5	7.7	8.0	8.3	8.3	8.4	8.5	8.4	8.1	7.7	8.0
1991	6.9	7.0	7.1	7.5	7.8	7.8	7.9	8.0	8.1	7.8	7.5	7.1	7.5
1992	6.3	6.3	6.5	7.0	7.2	7.5	7.9	8.0	7.8	8.0	7.6	7.1	7.2
1993	5.8	6.3	6.9	7.6	7.9	8.0	8.4	8.4	8.3	8.5	8.5	8.4	7.7
1994	7.8	7.8	8.2	9.1	9.6	10.1	10.4	10.5	10.4	10.3	9.7	9.3	9.4
1995	8.5	8.8	9.1	9.7	10.4	10.8	11.7	12.1	12.0	11.5	11.5	11.2	10.6
1996	10.2	10.1	10.2	11.3	11.8	12.9	13.1	13.4	13.1	12.9	12.4	11.6	11.9
1997	10.9	11.1	11.2	11.7	12.1	12.3	12.4	12.8	12.8	12.8	12.7	12.0	12.0
1998	11.0	10.8	11.3	11.7	12.6	13.2	13.8	14.2	14.2	14.5	14.2	13.7	12.9
1999	12.7	12.2	13.2	13.4	14.1	14.7	14.6	14.6	14.4	14.4	13.8	13.3	13.7
2000	12.6	12.5	12.9	14.0	14.5	15.2	15.1	15.4	15.2	15.1	14.7	14.6	14.3
2001	14.0	14.1	14.5	15.4	16.0	16.6	16.5	16.9	16.6	16.6	16.1	15.0	15.7
2002	14.2	14.4	15.1	15.5	15.9	16.1	16.4	16.8	16.3	16.4	16.0	15.7	15.7
2003	14.9	15.3	15.9	16.1	16.8	17.4	17.9	18.3	18.0	18.1	17.9	17.5	17.0
Manufacturing													
1990	7.5	7.4	7.6	7.6	7.7	7.7	7.7	7.8	7.9	8.0	8.0	8.0	7.7
1991	7.9	7.9	7.9	8.1	8.2	8.2	8.3	8.4	8.4	8.3	8.4	8.4	8.2
1992	8.3	8.4	8.6	8.8	8.9	9.1	9.2	9.2	9.3	9.4	9.4	9.4	9.0
1993	9.3	9.5	9.7	9.8	9.9	10.1	10.2	10.4	10.5	10.7	10.8	10.8	10.1
1994	10.7	10.8	11.0	11.6	11.7	11.7	11.6	11.6	11.6	11.8	11.7	11.8	11.4
1995	11.6	11.6	11.6	11.7	11.6	11.7	12.0	12.0	12.0	12.3	12.3	12.5	11.9
1996	12.3	12.4	12.4	12.3	12.4	12.4	12.5	12.7	12.8	13.0	12.9	12.9	12.5
1997	12.6	12.7	12.7	12.9	12.8	12.8	12.9	12.8	12.9	13.0	13.2	13.3	12.8
1998	13.0	13.1	13.1	13.2	13.3	13.4	13.5	13.5	13.5	13.5	13.4	13.6	13.3
1999	13.2	13.1	13.1	12.7	12.8	12.8	12.9	12.9	12.9	13.0	13.1	13.1	12.9
2000	13.1	13.1	13.0	13.0	13.1	13.4	13.5	13.5	13.6	13.9	13.9	14.1	13.4
2001	14.0	14.0	14.1	14.0	13.9	14.0	13.9	13.9	13.8	13.6	13.4	13.3	13.8
2002	13.1	13.0	13.1	13.2	13.2	13.3	13.4	13.4	13.3	13.5	13.5	13.4	13.3
2003	13.2	13.2	13.3	13.3	13.3	13.3	13.4	13.5	13.4	13.5	13.5	13.6	13.4
Service-providing													
1990	123.0	124.0	124.7	126.3	127.7	128.5	127.9	128.6	128.8	128.8	128.3	127.7	127.0
1991	122.9	123.5	124.7	125.6	126.9	127.8	126.5	127.1	128.3	127.9	127.6	127.6	126.3
1992	124.3	125.1	125.9	127.3	128.8	129.4	128.0	128.8	131.0	130.6	131.0	129.9	128.3
1993	126.4	127.5	129.2	129.7	131.2	132.3	131.3	132.2	134.5	135.2	135.3	135.9	131.7
1994	130.4	132.2	133.3	134.9	136.5	137.6	137.0	137.3	139.9	139.7	141.2	140.9	136.7
1995	135.2	137.6	139.4	140.7	141.8	143.4	144.0	145.4	147.0	146.2	145.9	146.3	142.7
1996	142.9	143.9	145.2	146.0	147.6	148.4	148.4	147.4	149.4	149.2	150.3	149.9	147.3
1997	146.0	147.5	149.9	150.8	152.6	152.9	153.8	152.8	154.6	154.1	154.4	155.1	152.0
1998	149.9	151.0	153.5	155.0	156.0	156.0	156.1	156.7	158.3	158.3	158.8	159.3	155.7
1999	153.2	155.1	157.8	158.5	159.5	160.0	159.7	160.0	161.8	162.4	163.1	164.3	159.6
2000	158.8	160.4	162.1	163.6	165.2	165.4	165.6	165.8	167.7	168.2	168.8	168.9	165.0
2001	164.5	166.3	168.0	168.3	169.1	169.5	167.9	168.3	169.9	168.9	170.3	170.3	168.4
2002	162.3	163.7	164.5	166.3	167.3	167.2	165.5	165.8	167.1	168.8	169.4	170.3	166.5
2003	163.8	165.7	167.2	167.6	168.8	168.3	168.0	169.4	171.0	172.6	173.4	173.8	169.1
Trade, transportation, and utilities													
1990	32.5	32.1	32.3	32.5	32.9	33.1	33.3	33.7	33.7	33.4	33.9	34.3	33.1
1991	32.6	32.1	32.2	31.8	32.1	32.5	32.0	32.5	32.4	32.3	32.7	33.0	32.3
1992	31.8	31.1	31.4	31.4	31.9	32.1	31.9	32.5	32.3	32.8	33.4	34.1	32.2
1993	31.9	31.6	31.8	32.1	32.6	32.6	32.8	33.0	33.1	33.6	34.3	35.0	32.8
1994	33.4	33.0	33.1	33.8	34.2	34.6	35.0	35.1	35.1	35.7	36.4	37.2	34.7
1995	35.5	35.5	35.7	35.7	36.2	36.3	36.7	36.9	37.3	37.8	38.4	38.9	36.7
1996	37.1	36.7	37.0	36.8	37.7	38.0	37.9	38.1	38.0	38.5	39.2	39.8	37.9
1997	37.7	37.5	37.8	37.9	38.5	39.0	39.4	39.1	39.4	40.2	40.7	41.3	39.0
1998	39.2	38.5	38.8	39.2	39.5	39.3	39.5	39.8	39.8	40.5	41.5	42.2	39.8
1999	39.6	39.5	39.9	40.1	40.6	41.0	41.5	41.6	41.8	41.9	42.4	43.2	41.0
2000	41.5	41.1	41.3	41.3	41.4	41.8	42.3	42.3	42.6	43.0	43.8	44.5	42.2
2001	42.6	42.2	42.3	42.2	42.5	42.8	43.0	43.2	43.3	43.7	44.1	44.1	43.0
2002	42.0	41.6	41.5	41.6	42.0	42.2	42.5	42.4	42.4	42.9	43.4	43.6	42.3
2003	41.7	41.4	41.8	41.8	42.1	42.4	42.6	42.8	43.1	43.7	44.2	44.3	42.7

Employment by Industry: Nevada—*Continued*

(Numbers in thousands. Not seasonally adjusted.)

Industry	January	February	March	April	May	June	July	August	September	October	November	December	Annual Average
RENO—*Continued*													
Wholesale trade													
1990	7.4	7.5	7.6	7.7	7.9	8.0	7.9	8.0	7.8	7.7	7.7	7.6	7.7
1991	7.3	7.2	7.3	7.2	7.2	7.3	7.1	7.2	7.1	7.1	7.1	7.0	7.1
1992	7.0	7.0	7.1	7.0	7.1	7.1	7.1	7.1	7.1	7.2	7.2	7.2	7.1
1993	6.9	6.9	7.0	7.1	7.2	7.2	7.4	7.4	7.3	7.4	7.4	7.5	7.2
1994	7.5	7.4	7.4	7.6	7.6	7.7	7.7	7.8	7.8	8.0	8.0	8.1	7.7
1995	8.0	8.1	8.2	8.3	8.4	8.4	8.5	8.5	8.6	8.8	8.8	8.9	8.4
1996	8.9	9.0	9.0	8.9	9.0	9.1	9.0	9.0	8.9	9.1	9.1	9.1	9.0
1997	8.8	8.9	9.1	9.1	9.4	9.5	9.6	9.6	9.5	9.5	9.6	9.7	9.3
1998	9.5	9.5	9.6	9.5	9.5	9.4	9.4	9.5	9.5	9.7	9.7	9.8	9.5
1999	9.6	9.7	9.8	9.8	10.0	10.2	10.3	10.3	10.3	10.4	10.3	10.4	10.0
2000	10.3	10.4	10.5	10.6	10.7	10.9	11.0	11.1	11.1	11.3	11.5	11.5	10.9
2001	11.6	11.6	11.6	11.5	11.5	11.5	11.5	11.5	11.4	11.3	11.2	11.2	11.5
2002	11.1	11.1	11.1	11.0	11.0	11.0	10.9	10.8	10.7	10.7	10.6	10.6	10.9
2003	10.5	10.5	10.5	10.6	10.6	10.7	10.7	10.8	10.8	10.8	10.7	10.7	10.7
Retail trade													
1990	17.8	17.3	17.2	17.4	17.6	17.8	18.1	18.3	18.3	18.5	18.9	19.3	18.0
1991	17.5	17.0	17.0	16.8	17.1	17.4	17.3	17.5	17.5	17.5	17.9	18.1	17.3
1992	17.1	16.6	16.8	16.8	17.1	17.3	17.1	17.5	17.3	17.6	18.1	18.6	17.3
1993	17.0	16.7	16.8	16.9	17.1	17.1	17.1	17.3	17.5	17.9	18.5	19.2	17.4
1994	17.5	17.2	17.2	17.7	17.9	18.2	18.4	18.4	18.4	18.6	19.3	19.8	18.2
1995	18.3	18.1	18.1	18.0	18.4	18.4	18.7	18.8	19.0	19.2	19.8	20.2	18.7
1996	18.9	18.4	18.6	18.6	19.4	19.6	19.4	19.6	19.6	19.7	20.4	21.0	19.4
1997	19.4	19.1	19.0	18.9	19.2	19.4	19.7	19.8	19.7	20.4	20.9	21.5	19.7
1998	19.6	19.0	19.0	19.4	19.8	19.8	19.8	19.9	20.0	20.5	21.4	22.0	20.0
1999	20.1	19.9	20.2	20.3	20.6	20.8	20.9	21.0	21.2	21.2	21.6	22.2	20.8
2000	20.9	20.5	20.5	20.8	20.8	20.9	21.2	21.1	21.3	21.3	21.9	22.4	21.1
2001	20.7	20.4	20.4	20.3	20.5	20.8	20.9	21.2	21.4	21.6	22.2	22.2	21.1
2002	20.8	20.4	20.5	20.5	20.8	20.9	21.2	21.1	21.3	21.6	22.2	22.5	21.2
2003	20.9	20.7	20.9	20.9	21.2	21.4	21.7	21.8	22.0	22.4	23.0	23.2	21.7
Transportation and utilities													
1990	7.3	7.3	7.5	7.4	7.4	7.3	7.3	7.4	7.6	7.2	7.3	7.4	7.3
1991	7.8	7.9	7.9	7.8	7.8	7.8	7.6	7.8	7.8	7.7	7.7	7.9	7.7
1992	7.7	7.5	7.5	7.6	7.7	7.7	7.7	7.9	7.9	8.0	8.1	8.3	7.8
1993	8.0	8.0	8.0	8.1	8.3	8.3	8.3	8.3	8.3	8.3	8.4	8.3	8.2
1994	8.4	8.4	8.5	8.5	8.7	8.7	8.9	8.9	8.9	9.1	9.1	9.3	8.7
1995	9.2	9.3	9.4	9.4	9.4	9.5	9.5	9.6	9.7	9.8	9.8	9.8	9.5
1996	9.3	9.3	9.4	9.3	9.3	9.3	9.5	9.5	9.5	9.7	9.7	9.7	9.4
1997	9.5	9.5	9.7	9.9	9.9	10.1	10.1	9.7	10.2	10.3	10.2	10.1	9.9
1998	10.1	10.0	10.2	10.3	10.2	10.1	10.3	10.4	10.3	10.3	10.4	10.4	10.2
1999	9.9	9.9	9.9	10.0	10.0	10.0	10.3	10.3	10.3	10.3	10.5	10.6	10.1
2000	10.3	10.2	10.3	9.9	9.9	10.0	10.1	10.1	10.2	10.4	10.4	10.6	10.2
2001	10.3	10.2	10.3	10.4	10.5	10.5	10.6	10.5	10.5	10.8	10.7	10.7	10.5
2002	10.1	10.1	9.9	10.1	10.2	10.3	10.4	10.5	10.4	10.6	10.6	10.5	10.3
2003	10.3	10.2	10.4	10.3	10.3	10.3	10.2	10.2	10.3	10.5	10.5	10.4	10.3
Information													
1990	3.8	3.8	3.7	3.7	3.7	3.7	3.7	3.6	3.4	3.5	3.5	3.6	3.6
1991	3.5	3.5	3.5	3.5	3.5	3.6	3.5	3.6	3.5	3.5	3.5	3.5	3.5
1992	3.4	3.4	3.4	3.4	3.5	3.5	3.4	3.4	3.4	3.3	3.3	3.3	3.3
1993	3.3	3.3	3.3	3.3	3.3	3.4	3.4	3.3	3.4	3.3	3.3	3.4	3.3
1994	3.3	3.3	3.3	3.3	3.3	3.4	3.4	3.3	3.3	3.2	3.2	3.2	3.2
1995	3.2	3.2	3.2	3.1	3.1	3.1	3.0	3.0	3.0	3.0	3.0	3.1	3.0
1996	3.0	3.0	3.0	3.0	3.0	3.0	3.1	3.1	3.1	3.2	3.2	3.2	3.0
1997	3.2	3.2	3.2	3.3	3.3	3.3	3.2	3.2	3.2	3.3	3.3	3.3	3.2
1998	3.4	3.4	3.4	3.5	3.6	3.6	3.5	3.5	3.5	3.5	3.5	3.6	3.5
1999	3.6	3.6	3.6	3.6	3.4	3.5	3.4	3.4	3.4	3.6	3.6	3.6	3.5
2000	3.6	3.6	3.6	3.6	3.6	3.6	3.7	3.7	3.7	3.7	3.7	3.7	3.6
2001	3.7	3.7	3.8	3.7	3.7	3.6	3.6	3.6	3.5	3.5	3.5	3.5	3.6
2002	3.5	3.4	3.4	3.4	3.5	3.5	3.4	3.3	3.3	3.2	3.2	3.2	3.4
2003	3.2	3.3	3.3	3.2	3.2	3.2	3.2	3.2	3.2	3.2	3.3	3.3	3.2
Financial activities													
1990	7.8	7.9	8.1	8.4	8.5	8.6	8.6	8.6	8.5	8.3	8.2	8.1	8.3
1991	8.0	8.0	8.0	8.0	8.0	8.1	8.1	8.2	8.0	8.1	8.1	8.1	8.0
1992	7.8	7.8	7.9	8.0	7.9	8.0	7.9	8.0	8.1	8.0	8.0	8.0	7.9
1993	7.9	7.9	8.0	8.0	8.0	8.2	8.3	8.4	8.5	8.6	8.6	8.4	8.2
1994	8.3	8.3	8.4	8.5	8.5	8.5	8.4	8.5	8.3	8.2	8.2	8.3	8.3
1995	8.0	7.7	7.7	7.9	8.1	8.2	8.3	8.4	8.4	8.5	8.5	8.6	8.1
1996	8.2	8.3	8.4	8.4	8.4	8.6	8.5	8.6	8.6	8.7	8.7	8.7	8.5
1997	8.9	8.9	9.0	8.9	9.0	9.0	9.1	9.2	9.2	9.2	9.2	9.3	9.0
1998	9.2	9.2	9.3	9.3	9.4	9.5	9.6	9.7	9.7	9.7	9.7	9.8	9.5
1999	9.4	9.4	9.5	9.4	9.5	9.6	9.7	9.6	9.4	9.4	9.5	9.6	9.5
2000	9.7	9.8	9.9	10.0	10.1	10.3	10.3	10.3	10.3	10.3	10.3	10.4	10.1
2001	10.2	10.2	10.3	10.3	10.3	10.4	10.4	10.3	10.2	10.3	10.3	10.3	10.3
2002	10.2	10.2	10.2	10.3	10.3	10.3	10.3	10.3	10.3	10.4	10.4	10.4	10.3
2003	10.1	10.2	10.2	10.4	10.4	10.5	10.5	10.7	10.6	10.7	10.7	10.8	10.5

Employment by Industry: Nevada—*Continued*

(Numbers in thousands. Not seasonally adjusted.)

Industry	January	February	March	April	May	June	July	August	September	October	November	December	Annual Average
RENO—*Continued*													
Professional and business services													
1990	9.2	9.4	9.6	9.9	10.1	10.3	10.4	10.7	10.6	11.0	10.8	10.5	10.2
1991	9.8	10.0	10.0	10.1	10.2	10.4	10.6	10.5	10.4	10.6	10.4	10.4	10.2
1992	10.1	10.1	10.2	10.7	10.8	11.0	10.9	11.2	11.1	11.6	11.4	11.1	10.8
1993	11.5	11.8	12.1	12.0	12.5	12.7	12.6	12.8	12.9	13.7	13.9	13.7	12.6
1994	12.2	12.6	12.7	13.5	13.6	14.2	14.4	14.5	14.7	14.9	14.9	14.9	13.9
1995	13.5	13.6	14.1	14.4	14.6	14.7	15.0	15.9	15.3	15.2	15.3	15.1	14.7
1996	14.7	14.9	15.0	14.8	15.1	15.3	15.5	15.5	15.8	15.8	15.6	15.7	15.3
1997	15.4	15.5	16.1	16.3	16.5	16.5	16.6	16.8	16.9	16.8	16.9	16.9	16.4
1998	16.3	16.5	17.0	17.4	17.4	17.8	18.1	18.3	18.0	18.5	18.5	18.7	17.7
1999	17.6	17.9	18.5	18.9	18.8	19.2	19.6	19.5	19.2	19.5	20.2	20.5	19.1
2000	18.7	18.6	19.0	19.6	20.1	20.6	20.6	21.0	21.2	21.0	21.4	21.5	20.2
2001	20.6	20.7	21.1	21.3	21.1	21.4	21.2	20.8	20.5	20.3	20.9	20.9	20.9
2002	19.3	19.4	19.4	20.1	20.2	20.3	20.2	20.4	20.1	20.8	21.5	21.7	20.3
2003	19.6	19.7	20.0	20.6	20.7	21.2	21.5	21.9	22.1	22.8	23.5	23.8	21.5
Educational and health services													
1990	11.2	11.4	11.5	11.5	11.5	11.6	11.3	11.3	11.4	11.4	11.6	11.6	11.4
1991	12.2	12.2	12.4	12.4	12.4	12.5	12.3	12.3	12.5	12.5	12.5	12.5	12.3
1992	12.3	12.5	12.6	12.5	12.6	12.7	12.7	12.8	12.9	12.8	12.8	12.8	12.6
1993	12.8	12.8	13.0	13.0	13.0	13.1	12.9	13.0	13.1	13.4	13.4	13.5	13.0
1994	13.2	13.3	13.3	13.6	13.6	13.8	13.5	13.6	13.7	13.3	13.4	13.4	13.4
1995	13.1	13.3	13.2	13.1	13.2	13.4	13.1	13.2	13.3	13.2	13.3	13.4	13.2
1996	13.3	13.5	13.5	13.4	13.6	13.6	13.5	13.5	13.6	13.7	13.8	13.8	13.5
1997	13.7	13.8	13.9	13.8	14.0	14.1	14.1	13.9	14.0	13.9	14.0	14.2	13.9
1998	13.8	13.9	14.1	14.3	14.3	14.4	14.2	14.2	14.4	14.5	14.5	14.7	14.2
1999	14.8	15.0	15.2	15.0	15.1	15.1	15.0	15.0	15.2	15.4	15.5	15.7	15.1
2000	15.5	15.6	15.8	15.7	15.7	15.8	15.9	15.8	16.0	16.2	16.3	16.4	15.8
2001	16.5	16.6	16.8	16.9	17.0	17.1	16.9	17.1	17.2	17.3	17.5	17.5	17.0
2002	17.4	17.7	17.8	18.0	18.2	18.2	17.8	18.0	18.1	18.4	18.4	18.5	18.0
2003	18.4	18.5	18.5	18.5	18.6	18.4	18.5	18.6	18.7	19.0	19.1	19.1	18.7
Leisure and hospitality													
1990	36.8	36.9	36.8	37.6	37.9	38.6	39.1	39.3	38.8	38.1	37.2	36.3	37.7
1991	34.6	34.5	35.3	36.4	36.9	37.7	38.0	38.2	38.0	37.1	36.6	36.1	36.6
1992	35.7	36.0	36.2	37.0	37.8	38.3	38.7	38.6	38.7	37.7	37.2	36.3	37.3
1993	35.7	35.7	36.1	36.4	37.0	38.1	38.4	39.0	38.9	37.9	37.2	37.0	37.2
1994	36.1	36.8	37.2	37.0	37.9	38.4	38.8	39.1	39.0	38.7	38.6	37.8	37.9
1995	37.1	38.1	38.7	39.7	40.2	41.2	42.8	43.3	43.0	41.6	40.6	40.4	40.5
1996	40.2	40.3	40.6	41.9	42.1	42.9	43.5	43.3	42.7	41.6	41.1	40.8	41.7
1997	40.2	40.4	41.2	42.0	42.4	42.9	44.0	43.9	43.3	42.1	41.2	41.0	42.0
1998	40.1	40.3	41.1	41.6	42.1	42.5	43.7	43.8	43.3	41.7	41.0	40.5	41.8
1999	39.6	39.8	41.0	41.4	41.9	42.3	43.2	43.3	43.2	42.7	42.1	41.4	41.8
2000	41.1	41.4	41.7	42.5	43.1	43.5	44.3	44.2	43.8	43.1	42.5	41.5	42.7
2001	40.8	41.0	41.7	41.8	42.3	42.7	43.2	43.5	43.4	41.7	41.4	41.0	42.0
2002	38.6	38.7	39.3	40.1	40.1	40.7	40.9	40.9	40.6	39.8	39.2	39.4	39.9
2003	38.5	39.1	39.5	39.6	40.0	39.9	40.7	40.9	40.5	39.6	38.8	38.5	39.6
Other services													
1990	4.1	4.1	4.2	4.2	4.3	4.4	4.4	4.4	4.3	4.2	4.2	4.1	4.2
1991	4.0	4.1	4.1	4.1	4.2	4.3	4.3	4.3	4.2	4.1	4.1	4.0	4.1
1992	4.1	4.1	4.1	4.2	4.2	4.3	4.3	4.3	4.3	4.3	4.2	4.1	4.2
1993	4.2	4.3	4.4	4.4	4.4	4.5	4.4	4.5	4.5	4.3	4.3	4.3	4.3
1994	4.2	4.2	4.3	4.3	4.3	4.4	4.5	4.5	4.5	4.4	4.4	4.4	4.3
1995	4.5	4.6	4.6	4.7	4.7	4.8	5.0	5.0	4.9	4.8	4.7	4.7	4.7
1996	4.8	4.9	5.0	4.9	4.9	5.1	5.0	5.1	5.0	4.8	4.9	4.9	4.9
1997	5.0	5.1	5.2	5.2	5.3	5.4	5.5	5.5	5.4	5.2	5.1	5.1	5.2
1998	5.3	5.4	5.6	5.6	5.6	5.7	5.7	5.6	5.6	5.5	5.5	5.5	5.5
1999	5.5	5.6	5.6	5.6	5.7	5.8	5.8	5.8	5.7	5.6	5.5	5.5	5.6
2000	5.6	5.7	5.8	5.8	5.8	5.8	6.0	5.9	5.9	5.9	5.8	5.8	5.8
2001	6.0	6.2	6.2	6.3	6.4	6.6	6.6	6.5	6.6	6.5	6.5	6.5	6.4
2002	6.5	6.5	6.5	6.5	6.6	6.6	6.7	6.6	6.5	6.5	6.5	6.5	6.5
2003	6.5	6.5	6.5	6.5	6.6	6.7	6.8	6.8	6.6	6.7	6.7	6.6	6.6
Government													
1990	17.6	18.4	18.5	18.5	18.8	18.2	17.1	17.0	18.1	18.9	18.9	19.2	18.2
1991	18.2	19.1	19.2	19.3	19.6	18.7	17.7	17.5	19.3	19.7	19.7	20.0	19.0
1992	19.1	20.1	20.1	20.1	20.1	19.5	18.2	18.0	20.2	20.1	20.7	20.2	19.7
1993	19.1	20.1	20.5	20.5	20.4	19.7	18.5	18.2	20.1	20.4	20.3	20.6	19.8
1994	19.7	20.7	21.0	20.9	21.1	20.3	19.0	18.7	21.3	21.3	22.1	21.7	20.6
1995	20.3	21.6	22.2	22.1	21.7	21.7	20.1	19.7	21.8	22.1	22.1	22.1	21.4
1996	21.6	22.3	22.7	22.8	22.8	21.9	21.4	20.2	22.6	22.9	23.8	23.0	22.3
1997	21.9	23.1	23.5	23.4	23.6	22.7	21.9	21.2	23.2	23.4	24.0	24.0	22.9
1998	22.6	23.8	24.2	24.1	24.1	23.2	21.8	21.8	24.0	24.4	24.6	24.3	23.5
1999	23.1	24.3	24.5	24.5	24.5	23.5	21.5	21.8	23.9	24.3	24.3	24.8	23.7
2000	23.1	24.6	25.0	25.1	25.4	24.0	22.5	22.6	24.2	25.0	25.0	25.1	24.3
2001	24.1	25.7	25.8	25.8	25.8	24.9	23.0	23.3	25.2	25.6	26.1	26.5	25.2
2002	24.8	26.2	26.4	26.3	26.4	25.4	23.7	23.9	25.8	26.8	26.8	27.0	25.8
2003	25.8	27.0	27.4	27.0	27.2	26.0	24.2	24.5	26.2	26.9	27.1	27.4	26.4

Employment by Industry: Nevada—*Continued*

(Numbers in thousands. Not seasonally adjusted.)

Industry	January	February	March	April	May	June	July	August	September	October	November	December	Annual Average
RENO—*Continued*													
Federal government													
1990	3.0	3.0	3.1	3.2	3.4	3.3	3.3	3.1	3.1	3.1	3.1	3.1	3.1
1991	3.0	3.0	3.0	3.1	3.1	3.1	3.1	3.1	3.1	3.1	3.1	3.1	3.0
1992	3.1	3.1	3.1	3.2	3.2	3.2	3.2	3.2	3.2	3.1	3.1	3.2	3.1
1993	3.1	3.1	3.1	3.1	3.1	3.2	3.2	3.2	3.2	3.2	3.1	3.2	3.1
1994	3.2	3.1	3.1	3.2	3.2	3.2	3.2	3.2	3.1	3.2	3.2	3.2	3.1
1995	3.1	3.1	3.1	3.1	3.1	3.2	3.2	3.2	3.2	3.1	3.1	3.1	3.1
1996	3.0	3.0	3.0	3.0	3.0	3.0	2.9	2.8	2.9	2.8	2.8	2.9	2.9
1997	2.8	2.8	2.8	3.0	3.1	3.1	3.1	3.1	3.1	3.1	3.1	3.2	3.0
1998	3.2	3.1	3.1	3.1	3.2	3.2	3.2	3.2	3.2	3.2	3.3	3.3	3.1
1999	3.2	3.2	3.2	3.2	3.2	3.2	3.2	3.2	3.2	3.2	3.2	3.3	3.2
2000	3.2	3.2	3.4	3.3	3.8	3.3	3.4	3.2	3.2	3.2	3.2	3.3	3.3
2001	3.2	3.2	3.2	3.2	3.2	3.3	3.3	3.3	3.3	3.3	3.3	3.3	3.3
2002	3.2	3.2	3.2	3.2	3.2	3.3	3.3	3.3	3.3	3.5	3.4	3.5	3.3
2003	3.5	3.5	3.5	3.4	3.4	3.4	3.4	3.4	3.4	3.4	3.4	3.4	3.4
State government													
1990	5.5	6.1	6.2	6.2	6.1	5.5	5.2	5.4	5.7	6.3	6.4	6.7	5.9
1991	5.6	6.4	6.6	6.6	6.7	5.7	5.7	5.8	6.5	6.8	6.8	6.9	6.3
1992	6.0	6.8	6.9	6.9	6.8	6.0	5.9	6.0	6.5	6.9	6.9	6.9	6.5
1993	5.8	6.6	7.0	7.0	6.9	5.9	5.8	5.9	6.5	6.8	6.8	6.8	6.4
1994	5.9	6.8	7.1	6.9	6.9	6.0	6.0	6.1	6.8	7.1	7.2	7.2	6.6
1995	6.0	7.0	7.7	7.5	7.2	7.0	6.4	6.3	7.3	7.5	7.5	7.4	7.0
1996	6.9	7.5	7.8	7.9	7.7	6.7	6.7	6.9	7.5	8.0	8.2	8.0	7.4
1997	6.9	7.9	8.2	8.1	8.0	7.0	6.9	7.2	8.1	8.2	8.6	8.5	7.8
1998	7.1	8.3	8.7	8.6	8.5	7.4	7.4	7.5	8.5	8.8	8.8	8.3	8.1
1999	7.3	8.4	8.6	8.6	8.6	7.3	7.1	7.2	8.2	8.5	8.5	8.5	8.0
2000	7.2	8.3	8.5	8.5	8.3	7.3	7.2	7.6	8.3	8.9	8.7	8.7	8.1
2001	7.4	8.7	8.8	8.9	8.7	7.7	7.2	7.6	8.5	8.9	8.9	9.0	8.4
2002	7.6	8.8	9.0	9.0	8.9	7.8	7.5	7.9	8.8	9.2	9.3	9.2	8.6
2003	7.9	8.9	9.2	9.1	9.2	7.9	7.8	8.2	9.0	9.2	9.3	9.5	8.8
Local government													
1990	9.1	9.3	9.2	9.1	9.3	9.4	8.6	8.5	9.3	9.5	9.4	9.4	9.1
1991	9.6	9.7	9.6	9.6	9.8	9.9	8.9	8.6	9.7	9.8	9.8	10.0	9.5
1992	10.0	10.2	10.1	10.0	10.1	10.3	9.1	8.8	10.5	10.1	10.7	10.1	10.0
1993	10.2	10.4	10.4	10.4	10.4	10.6	9.5	9.1	10.4	10.4	10.4	10.6	10.2
1994	10.6	10.8	10.8	10.8	11.0	11.1	9.8	9.4	11.4	11.0	11.7	11.3	10.8
1995	11.2	11.5	11.4	11.5	11.4	11.5	10.5	10.2	11.3	11.5	11.5	11.6	11.2
1996	11.7	11.8	11.9	11.9	12.1	12.2	11.8	10.5	12.2	12.1	12.8	12.1	11.9
1997	12.2	12.4	12.5	12.3	12.5	12.6	11.9	10.9	12.0	12.1	12.3	12.3	12.1
1998	12.3	12.4	12.4	12.4	12.4	12.6	11.2	11.1	12.3	12.4	12.5	12.7	12.2
1999	12.6	12.7	12.7	12.7	12.7	13.0	11.2	11.4	12.5	12.6	12.6	13.0	12.4
2000	12.7	13.1	13.1	13.3	13.3	13.4	11.9	11.8	12.7	12.9	13.1	13.1	12.8
2001	13.5	13.8	13.8	13.7	13.9	13.9	12.5	12.4	13.4	13.4	13.9	14.2	13.5
2002	14.0	14.2	14.2	14.1	14.3	14.3	12.9	12.7	13.7	14.1	14.1	14.3	13.9
2003	14.4	14.6	14.7	14.5	14.6	14.7	13.0	12.9	13.8	14.3	14.4	14.5	14.2

Average Weekly Hours by Industry: Nevada

(Not seasonally adjusted.)

Industry	January	February	March	April	May	June	July	August	September	October	November	December	Annual Average
STATEWIDE													
Construction													
2001	34.9	36.3	38.0	38.5	38.3	38.1	38.3	39.2	38.3	38.4	36.7	37.4	37.7
2002	37.1	38.1	37.9	38.2	38.6	39.7	38.8	40.1	39.3	39.4	37.6	38.7	38.7
2003	37.6	36.0	37.7	38.8	38.4	38.9	38.6	39.6	38.4	37.4	36.2	35.9	37.8
Manufacturing													
2001	38.5	39.1	39.0	38.1	39.4	39.4	38.3	38.8	38.6	38.4	38.2	38.1	38.7
2002	37.9	39.5	39.8	39.6	39.8	39.5	38.5	39.7	37.9	37.4	38.3	38.1	38.8
2003	38.0	37.5	38.7	38.3	39.0	39.4	40.0	40.3	39.8	39.3	39.3	38.7	39.0
Wholesale trade													
2001	38.9	38.2	38.8	40.5	40.3	41.3	42.8	41.1	42.4	39.8	41.3	40.1	40.5
2002	38.3	38.0	37.5	37.9	36.9	37.9	38.1	39.0	38.4	38.5	37.2	38.2	38.0
2003	38.5	37.7	36.5	37.1	37.1	36.8	37.4	35.4	36.1	36.9	36.7	36.4	36.9
Retail trade													
2001	28.9	28.1	27.6	27.5	27.6	28.4	28.8	29.2	30.6	30.6	31.5	31.7	29.2
2002	30.7	30.8	31.3	32.0	31.6	32.6	32.8	32.0	31.6	31.3	31.0	31.7	31.6
2003	31.2	32.1	32.4	32.4	32.2	33.4	32.5	33.0	33.3	34.6	35.3	36.4	33.3
LAS VEGAS													
Construction													
2001	34.7	36.2	36.5	37.1	37.1	37.1	36.6	37.2	36.7	36.0	34.8	36.7	36.4
2002	36.3	37.6	37.5	37.9	38.6	39.8	38.9	39.7	38.0	39.4	37.7	38.1	38.3
2003	37.7	36.5	38.3	39.0	39.0	39.3	39.1	39.5	38.6	37.8	36.1	37.2	38.2
Manufacturing													
2001	38.7	39.3	39.3	38.5	39.8	40.4	40.1	40.6	40.7	40.2	39.6	40.6	39.8
2002	39.6	40.5	40.1	40.7	40.6	39.2	39.3	39.9	40.5	39.2	40.5	39.6	40.0
2003	39.2	38.2	40.5	40.2	41.0	40.1	41.0	42.3	43.0	42.6	41.7	40.6	40.9
Wholesale trade													
2001	38.9	40.6	40.1	41.6	39.6	40.2	41.2	40.4	41.1	39.8	41.8	39.6	40.4
2002	38.2	38.5	37.4	37.6	36.8	37.1	37.3	38.8	37.6	38.6	37.3	38.2	37.8
2003	37.6	38.1	37.5	37.7	37.9	37.1	36.1	37.0	37.3	37.9	37.9	38.3	37.5
Retail trade													
2001	28.3	27.8	26.6	27.0	27.2	27.5	28.5	29.0	29.3	29.7	31.3	31.9	28.7
2002	30.9	30.5	31.5	32.1	32.1	32.4	33.1	31.3	31.0	31.2	31.9	32.6	31.7
2003	31.4	32.1	32.2	32.6	32.3	33.3	32.4	32.8	33.1	33.7	34.8	35.6	33.1

Average Hourly Earnings by Industry: Nevada

(Dollars, not seasonally adjusted.)

Industry	January	February	March	April	May	June	July	August	September	October	November	December	Annual Average
STATEWIDE													
Construction													
2001	21.07	20.76	20.87	20.84	20.84	20.59	20.51	20.88	21.02	20.86	20.52	20.53	20.77
2002	20.56	20.55	20.91	21.02	21.36	21.15	21.45	21.29	21.39	21.38	20.98	21.48	21.14
2003	21.09	21.40	21.69	21.77	21.98	22.17	21.89	22.03	21.57	21.03	20.91	21.06	21.55
Manufacturing													
2001	13.85	13.77	13.99	14.08	13.94	13.97	13.55	13.38	13.44	13.65	13.81	14.12	13.79
2002	14.42	14.30	14.35	14.46	14.67	14.36	14.85	15.07	14.80	14.93	14.73	14.53	14.62
2003	14.65	14.46	14.28	14.50	14.68	14.46	14.70	14.93	14.99	14.86	14.58	14.38	14.63
Wholesale trade													
2001	15.98	16.12	15.75	16.05	15.32	14.92	15.11	14.93	15.26	15.36	14.75	15.08	15.37
2002	14.80	14.83	14.62	14.52	14.76	14.91	15.35	15.77	15.54	15.65	15.76	15.96	15.21
2003	16.54	17.09	17.48	17.05	17.43	17.86	17.95	17.64	17.13	16.86	16.70	16.77	17.20
Retail trade													
2001	11.23	11.55	11.43	11.50	11.50	11.52	11.43	11.76	11.76	11.55	11.59	11.57	11.54
2002	11.74	11.58	11.79	12.10	11.99	11.88	12.03	12.03	12.24	12.16	12.19	12.37	12.02
2003	12.52	12.79	12.40	12.70	12.81	12.92	12.78	12.62	12.44	12.17	12.03	11.83	12.48
LAS VEGAS													
Construction													
2001	20.20	20.64	20.93	20.82	20.97	20.63	20.68	20.90	21.25	21.21	21.05	20.90	20.85
2002	20.76	20.84	21.20	21.30	21.40	21.37	21.62	21.58	21.53	21.48	21.08	21.46	21.32
2003	21.04	21.37	21.61	21.76	21.98	22.46	22.02	22.06	21.65	21.28	21.32	21.48	21.68
Manufacturing													
2001	13.11	13.34	13.22	13.38	12.84	12.88	12.50	12.49	12.43	12.82	12.83	13.13	12.90
2002	13.65	13.98	14.12	13.76	13.69	13.84	13.65	13.26	13.31	13.66	13.98	13.63	13.71
2003	13.36	13.77	13.51	13.11	13.35	13.38	13.57	13.93	14.25	14.50	14.29	14.50	13.81
Wholesale trade													
2001	16.18	16.42	15.84	16.33	15.97	15.94	15.76	15.38	15.18	14.74	14.34	14.01	15.50
2002	13.95	14.05	14.22	13.94	14.15	14.54	15.02	15.39	15.15	15.39	15.10	15.17	14.68
2003	15.57	16.07	16.29	16.69	16.78	16.53	16.64	16.73	16.97	16.88	16.85	17.05	16.59
Retail trade													
2001	11.03	11.36	11.45	11.52	11.59	11.59	11.39	11.74	11.56	11.22	11.31	11.34	11.42
2002	11.59	11.30	11.75	11.91	11.87	11.79	11.87	11.91	12.16	11.98	12.06	12.16	11.87
2003	12.23	12.55	12.49	12.47	12.65	13.01	12.82	12.64	12.52	12.45	12.60	12.34	12.56

Average Weekly Earnings by Industry: Nevada

(Dollars, not seasonally adjusted.)

Industry	January	February	March	April	May	June	July	August	September	October	November	December	Annual Average
STATEWIDE													
Construction													
2001	735.34	753.59	793.06	802.34	798.17	784.48	785.53	818.50	805.07	801.02	753.08	767.82	783.03
2002	762.78	782.96	792.49	802.96	824.50	839.66	832.26	853.73	840.63	842.37	788.85	831.28	818.12
2003	792.98	770.40	817.71	844.68	844.03	862.41	844.95	872.39	828.29	786.52	756.94	756.05	814.59
Manufacturing													
2001	533.23	538.41	545.61	536.45	549.24	550.42	518.97	519.14	518.78	524.16	527.54	537.97	533.67
2002	546.52	564.85	571.13	572.62	583.87	567.22	571.73	598.28	560.92	558.38	564.16	553.59	567.26
2003	556.70	542.25	552.64	555.35	572.52	569.72	588.00	601.68	596.60	584.00	572.99	556.51	570.57
Wholesale trade													
2001	621.62	615.78	611.10	650.03	617.40	616.20	646.71	613.62	647.02	611.33	609.18	604.71	622.49
2002	566.84	563.54	548.25	550.31	544.64	565.09	584.84	615.03	596.74	602.53	586.27	609.67	577.98
2003	636.79	644.29	638.02	632.56	646.65	657.25	671.33	624.46	618.39	622.13	612.89	610.43	634.68
Retail trade													
2001	324.55	324.56	315.47	316.25	317.40	327.17	329.18	343.39	359.86	353.43	365.09	366.77	336.97
2002	360.42	356.66	369.03	387.20	378.88	387.29	394.58	384.96	386.78	380.61	377.89	392.13	379.83
2003	390.62	410.56	401.76	411.48	412.48	431.53	415.35	416.46	414.25	421.08	424.66	430.61	415.58
LAS VEGAS													
Construction													
2001	700.94	747.17	763.95	772.42	777.99	765.37	756.89	777.48	779.88	763.56	732.54	767.03	758.94
2002	753.59	783.58	795.00	807.27	826.04	850.53	841.02	856.73	818.14	846.31	794.72	817.63	816.56
2003	793.21	780.01	827.66	848.64	857.22	882.68	860.98	871.37	835.69	804.38	769.65	799.06	828.18
Manufacturing													
2001	507.36	524.26	519.55	515.13	511.03	520.35	501.25	507.09	505.90	515.36	508.07	533.08	513.42
2002	540.54	566.19	566.21	560.03	555.81	542.53	536.45	529.07	539.06	535.47	566.19	539.75	548.40
2003	523.71	526.01	547.16	527.02	547.35	536.54	556.37	589.24	612.75	617.70	595.89	588.70	564.83
Wholesale trade													
2001	629.40	666.65	635.18	679.33	632.41	640.79	649.31	621.35	623.90	586.65	599.41	554.80	626.20
2002	532.89	540.93	531.83	524.14	520.72	539.43	560.25	597.13	569.64	594.05	563.23	579.49	554.90
2003	585.43	612.27	610.88	629.21	635.96	613.26	600.70	619.01	632.98	639.75	638.62	653.02	622.13
Retail trade													
2001	312.15	315.81	304.57	311.04	315.25	318.73	324.62	340.46	338.71	333.23	354.00	361.75	327.75
2002	358.13	344.65	370.13	382.31	381.03	382.00	392.90	372.78	376.96	373.78	384.71	396.42	376.28
2003	384.02	402.86	402.18	406.52	408.60	433.23	415.37	414.59	414.41	419.57	438.48	439.30	415.74

NEW HAMPSHIRE AT A GLANCE

(Population and total nonfarm employment numbers in thousands)

Population, Census 2000:	1,235.8
Total nonfarm employment, 2003:	616.6
Change in total nonfarm employment	
(Number)	
1990–2003:	108.6
1990–2001:	119.2
2001–2003:	-10.6
(Compound annual rate of change)	
1990–2003:	1.5%
1990–2001:	1.9%
2001–2003:	-0.8%
Unemployment rate	
1990:	5.6%
2001:	3.4%
2003:	4.5%

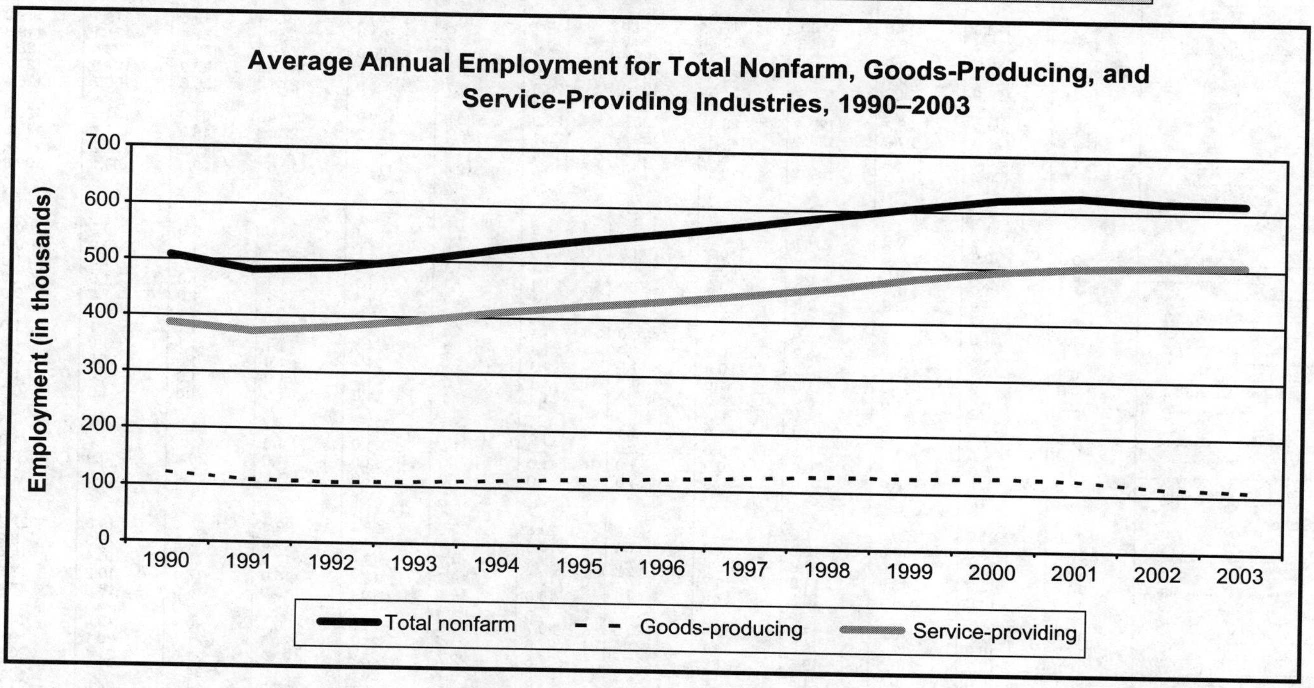

Cyclical trends were evident in New Hampshire as total nonfarm payroll employment fell in both the 1990–1991 and 2001 recessions. Sharp declines in goods-producing employment accentuated this trend. Employment in this sector dropped by over 18,000 jobs from 2000 to 2003, even though construction added nearly 4,000 jobs. In contrast, the service-providing sector showed modest gains, adding over 13,000 jobs from 2000 to 2003. Educational and health services and government added the most jobs during this period.

Employment by Industry: New Hampshire

(Numbers in thousands. Not seasonally adjusted.)

Industry	January	February	March	April	May	June	July	August	September	October	November	December	Annual Average
STATEWIDE													
Total nonfarm													
1990	508.4	505.8	507.3	505.7	511.2	517.0	506.4	509.9	514.5	506.6	502.1	501.8	508.0
1991	478.6	474.7	474.4	473.5	480.5	486.8	477.2	483.9	488.4	488.7	487.8	490.2	482.0
1992	472.1	471.3	473.2	479.0	488.3	494.3	486.8	489.4	496.5	497.5	495.7	499.8	486.9
1993	483.6	485.1	486.2	492.7	501.1	508.9	506.0	510.1	515.3	512.1	511.4	516.9	502.4
1994	501.4	504.0	507.5	513.3	520.1	530.0	525.2	530.8	536.1	534.3	534.7	539.9	523.1
1995	520.2	522.7	526.8	531.3	537.8	547.5	538.8	544.5	550.6	551.0	550.4	555.7	539.7
1996	535.3	537.9	540.7	544.4	552.6	562.3	555.3	559.6	562.9	562.2	563.0	567.5	553.6
1997	550.1	551.3	554.1	559.1	570.3	578.2	573.2	576.0	581.0	581.3	581.6	586.2	570.2
1998	571.0	573.6	577.7	581.2	589.1	595.7	590.9	592.4	596.1	597.2	598.4	604.6	588.9
1999	587.2	590.0	592.5	599.2	605.4	613.8	608.7	610.7	613.3	614.6	613.7	620.4	605.7
2000	603.3	605.6	609.6	615.8	623.4	631.4	625.1	624.6	628.9	628.6	631.5	637.1	622.0
2001	622.1	622.8	623.6	625.3	633.4	638.4	627.4	627.4	628.3	626.0	624.6	627.4	627.2
2002	608.3	607.7	610.7	613.9	620.7	626.9	621.1	621.9	623.7	621.0	620.4	624.2	618.4
2003	603.6	602.6	605.1	608.5	617.0	624.8	618.7	621.2	622.2	624.3	623.7	627.6	616.6
Total private													
1990	436.8	431.9	432.4	430.3	435.6	445.1	442.5	444.9	440.6	432.1	426.7	425.6	435.3
1991	406.8	400.3	399.3	399.0	406.1	414.5	414.0	419.9	416.2	414.0	412.1	413.4	409.6
1992	398.8	396.5	397.2	403.7	412.6	421.9	423.9	426.8	423.0	421.2	418.7	421.9	413.8
1993	411.4	409.6	409.3	416.0	424.8	435.5	438.8	443.4	439.6	435.6	434.4	438.8	428.1
1994	427.3	426.8	429.4	435.0	442.7	455.3	456.5	462.4	459.6	455.4	454.1	458.7	446.9
1995	445.7	444.2	447.8	453.0	460.6	472.9	471.3	477.8	473.6	470.9	470.4	474.3	463.5
1996	459.4	458.2	460.1	463.8	473.4	485.8	485.1	490.2	484.3	481.8	480.7	485.6	475.7
1997	472.1	470.6	472.9	477.5	489.9	501.2	501.6	505.9	501.8	499.7	498.7	504.6	491.3
1998	492.3	492.2	495.5	498.6	507.3	517.4	519.7	522.7	515.6	514.2	514.4	521.0	509.2
1999	506.8	506.7	508.8	515.2	522.0	533.8	535.8	538.6	531.5	529.9	527.7	534.5	524.2
2000	520.7	519.7	522.9	529.4	536.2	549.3	550.7	551.7	544.9	542.6	544.3	550.5	538.5
2001	537.4	535.0	535.2	537.7	545.1	554.2	552.8	553.2	540.8	535.7	533.5	536.1	541.4
2002	521.4	517.4	519.6	523.9	531.6	540.2	541.9	543.7	535.1	528.7	526.8	530.5	530.1
2003	514.9	510.4	512.4	516.4	526.3	536.2	538.3	541.6	532.8	530.7	529.1	533.2	526.9
Goods-producing													
1990	123.9	122.3	121.6	122.5	123.7	125.0	121.4	123.1	122.3	120.2	118.0	116.5	121.7
1991	110.9	108.1	108.1	108.2	110.2	111.7	108.2	111.2	111.7	111.8	111.1	109.2	110.0
1992	104.5	103.0	102.8	105.1	106.8	108.3	107.4	108.5	108.8	108.7	108.1	107.4	106.6
1993	105.1	104.5	104.3	106.9	108.8	110.5	109.7	112.0	112.0	111.2	110.9	110.9	108.9
1994	108.4	108.0	108.8	110.6	112.7	114.8	112.1	115.4	115.3	115.5	115.4	115.7	112.7
1995	113.5	112.8	114.2	116.1	117.7	119.3	116.1	119.3	119.4	119.4	119.8	119.1	117.2
1996	116.2	115.7	116.7	118.2	119.7	122.0	119.4	122.7	122.3	122.3	121.4	121.1	119.8
1997	118.4	118.0	118.8	120.7	123.5	125.4	122.8	126.4	126.0	126.6	126.4	126.6	123.3
1998	125.6	125.1	126.0	127.2	128.8	130.2	127.8	129.6	128.7	128.4	127.9	127.9	127.7
1999	124.8	123.9	124.5	126.4	127.3	128.8	126.5	127.7	127.0	127.1	126.6	126.7	126.4
2000	124.8	124.2	125.2	127.1	128.4	130.0	129.3	130.8	129.9	130.4	131.0	131.3	128.5
2001	128.4	128.0	127.6	128.4	129.3	129.1	126.1	126.4	123.7	122.0	119.8	118.7	125.6
2002	114.5	113.2	113.2	114.4	115.5	115.5	114.4	114.9	113.7	112.8	111.6	112.2	113.8
2003	108.3	106.7	107.3	109.0	110.8	112.1	110.6	112.4	111.2	110.5	109.3	109.1	109.8
Natural resources and mining													
1990	0.9	0.9	0.9	0.8	0.8	0.9	1.0	1.0	1.1	1.0	1.0	0.9	0.9
1991	0.9	0.9	0.9	0.8	0.9	1.0	1.0	1.0	1.0	1.1	1.0	0.9	0.9
1992	0.9	0.9	0.9	0.9	0.9	1.1	1.1	1.1	1.1	1.1	1.1	1.1	1.0
1993	1.0	1.0	1.0	0.9	0.9	1.0	1.1	1.1	1.1	1.1	1.0	1.0	1.0
1994	0.9	0.9	0.9	0.8	0.9	1.0	1.1	1.1	1.1	1.1	1.0	1.0	0.9
1995	1.0	1.0	1.0	0.9	1.0	1.0	1.1	1.1	1.1	1.1	1.1	1.1	1.0
1996	1.0	0.9	0.9	0.9	0.9	1.0	1.1	1.1	1.1	1.1	1.1	1.0	1.0
1997	0.9	0.9	0.9	0.9	0.9	1.0	1.1	1.0	1.1	1.0	1.0	1.0	0.9
1998	0.9	0.9	1.0	1.0	1.0	1.0	1.1	1.1	1.1	1.0	1.0	1.0	1.0
1999	0.9	0.9	1.0	0.9	1.0	1.0	1.1	1.1	1.0	1.0	1.0	1.0	0.9
2000	1.0	1.0	1.0	0.9	1.0	1.1	1.1	1.1	1.1	1.1	1.1	1.1	1.0
2001	1.0	1.0	1.0	0.9	1.0	1.0	1.0	1.0	1.0	1.0	1.0	1.0	1.0
2002	0.9	0.9	0.9	0.9	0.9	1.0	1.0	1.0	1.0	1.0	0.9	0.9	0.9
2003	0.9	0.8	0.9	0.9	0.9	1.0	1.0	1.0	1.0	1.0	1.0	1.0	1.0
Construction													
1990	22.6	21.2	20.9	21.9	23.1	23.8	23.6	23.6	23.1	22.3	21.1	19.6	22.2
1991	16.4	15.0	14.8	15.6	17.3	17.9	18.0	18.4	18.3	18.0	17.4	16.3	16.9
1992	13.8	13.0	13.0	14.6	16.0	17.0	17.4	17.7	17.6	17.8	17.1	16.4	15.9
1993	13.7	13.3	13.4	14.8	16.7	17.7	18.7	19.3	19.0	18.0	17.4	16.6	16.5
1994	14.5	14.0	14.1	16.3	17.9	19.0	19.3	19.5	19.4	19.0	18.5	18.0	17.4
1995	16.1	15.6	16.2	17.9	19.4	20.5	20.7	20.8	20.6	20.5	20.7	19.4	19.0
1996	17.2	16.9	17.2	18.6	20.1	21.4	21.6	22.2	21.7	21.5	21.1	20.1	19.9
1997	18.2	17.7	18.0	19.5	21.6	22.4	22.5	22.7	22.2	22.2	21.8	21.1	20.8
1998	20.1	19.6	20.1	21.8	23.2	24.3	24.9	25.2	24.6	24.9	24.4	24.1	23.1
1999	21.7	21.3	21.6	23.8	24.9	25.7	26.0	25.8	25.5	25.0	24.7	24.4	24.2
2000	22.4	21.8	22.5	24.0	25.1	26.3	26.7	26.8	26.2	26.1	26.0	25.5	24.9
2001	23.8	23.5	23.8	25.8	27.7	28.8	29.6	29.7	28.8	28.7	28.3	28.1	27.2
2002	26.2	25.4	25.7	27.4	28.9	29.0	28.8	29.4	28.8	28.9	28.2	28.0	27.9
2003	25.7	24.9	25.2	27.4	29.4	30.4	31.2	31.5	30.7	30.3	29.5	29.1	28.8

Employment by Industry: New Hampshire—*Continued*

(Numbers in thousands. Not seasonally adjusted.)

Industry	January	February	March	April	May	June	July	August	September	October	November	December	Annual Average
STATEWIDE—*Continued*													
Manufacturing													
1990	100.4	100.2	99.8	99.8	99.8	100.3	96.8	98.5	98.1	96.9	95.9	96.0	98.5
1991	93.6	92.2	92.4	91.8	92.0	92.8	89.2	91.8	92.4	92.7	92.7	92.0	92.1
1992	89.8	89.1	88.9	89.6	89.9	90.2	88.9	89.7	90.1	89.8	89.9	89.9	89.6
1993	90.4	90.2	89.9	91.2	91.2	91.8	89.9	91.6	91.9	92.1	92.5	93.3	91.3
1994	93.0	93.1	93.8	93.5	93.9	94.8	91.7	94.8	94.8	95.4	95.9	96.7	94.2
1995	96.4	96.2	97.0	97.3	97.3	97.8	94.3	97.4	97.7	97.8	98.0	98.6	97.1
1996	98.0	97.9	98.6	98.7	98.7	99.6	96.7	99.4	99.5	99.7	99.2	100.0	98.8
1997	99.3	99.4	99.9	100.3	101.0	102.0	99.2	102.7	102.7	103.4	103.6	104.5	101.5
1998	104.6	104.6	104.9	104.4	104.6	104.9	101.8	103.3	103.0	102.5	102.5	102.8	103.6
1999	102.2	101.7	101.9	101.7	101.4	102.1	99.4	100.8	100.5	101.1	100.9	101.3	101.2
2000	101.4	101.4	101.7	102.2	102.3	102.6	101.5	102.9	102.6	103.2	103.9	104.7	102.5
2001	103.6	103.5	102.8	101.7	100.6	99.3	95.5	95.7	93.9	92.3	90.5	89.6	97.4
2002	87.4	86.9	86.6	86.1	85.7	85.5	84.6	84.5	83.9	82.9	82.5	83.3	85.0
2003	81.7	81.0	81.2	80.7	80.5	80.7	78.4	79.9	79.5	79.2	78.8	79.0	80.1
Service-providing													
1990	384.5	383.5	385.7	383.2	387.5	392.0	385.0	386.8	392.2	386.4	384.1	385.3	386.3
1991	367.7	366.6	366.3	365.3	370.3	375.1	369.0	372.7	376.7	376.9	376.7	381.0	372.0
1992	367.6	368.3	370.4	373.9	381.5	386.0	379.4	380.9	387.7	388.8	387.6	392.4	380.3
1993	378.5	380.6	381.9	385.8	392.3	398.4	396.3	398.1	403.3	400.9	400.5	406.0	393.5
1994	393.0	396.0	398.7	402.7	407.4	415.2	413.1	415.4	420.8	418.8	419.3	424.2	410.3
1995	406.7	409.9	412.6	415.2	420.1	428.2	422.7	425.2	431.2	431.6	430.6	436.6	422.5
1996	419.1	422.2	424.0	426.2	432.9	440.3	435.9	436.9	440.6	439.9	441.6	446.4	433.8
1997	431.7	433.3	435.3	438.4	446.8	452.8	450.4	449.6	455.0	454.7	455.2	459.6	446.9
1998	445.4	448.5	451.7	454.0	460.3	465.5	463.1	462.8	467.4	468.8	470.5	476.7	461.2
1999	462.4	466.1	468.0	472.8	478.1	485.0	482.2	483.0	486.3	487.5	487.1	493.7	479.3
2000	478.5	481.4	484.4	488.7	495.0	501.4	495.8	493.8	499.0	498.2	500.5	505.8	493.5
2001	493.7	494.8	496.0	496.9	504.1	509.3	501.3	501.0	504.6	504.0	504.8	508.7	501.6
2002	493.8	494.5	497.5	499.5	505.2	511.4	506.7	507.0	510.0	508.2	508.8	512.0	504.6
2003	495.3	495.9	497.8	499.5	506.2	512.7	508.1	508.8	511.0	513.8	514.4	518.5	506.8
Trade, transportation, and utilities													
1990	111.6	108.9	108.9	107.2	108.2	110.8	110.0	110.1	109.5	108.5	109.1	109.9	109.3
1991	103.0	100.0	98.9	98.6	99.6	100.9	101.3	102.3	102.2	102.3	104.0	106.4	101.6
1992	101.4	99.8	99.9	100.5	102.8	105.2	104.0	105.0	104.8	105.1	107.4	110.4	103.8
1993	105.2	103.7	103.4	105.0	106.8	108.9	108.9	110.1	109.9	111.2	113.1	116.0	108.5
1994	109.8	107.9	108.1	110.3	111.5	114.0	113.0	114.6	114.9	115.6	118.0	120.4	113.1
1995	115.0	112.9	112.8	113.8	115.3	118.1	117.5	118.1	118.1	118.6	121.7	124.2	117.1
1996	117.2	115.0	114.5	114.9	117.1	119.4	118.3	118.9	118.3	120.0	123.6	126.7	118.6
1997	119.9	117.2	117.2	117.7	120.1	122.8	122.2	121.4	123.0	124.1	126.5	129.8	121.8
1998	123.0	120.7	121.6	121.9	124.1	126.5	126.3	127.5	127.1	128.6	132.4	136.4	126.3
1999	130.1	128.3	129.2	130.3	131.8	134.3	133.7	134.4	134.0	135.5	138.5	142.9	133.5
2000	135.6	133.0	133.3	134.8	136.3	138.6	137.0	137.1	136.3	137.4	141.0	144.8	137.1
2001	137.3	134.2	133.7	134.8	136.7	138.6	137.4	137.6	136.4	137.7	140.6	143.1	137.3
2002	137.1	133.6	134.3	135.9	137.3	139.5	138.6	139.2	138.9	138.7	141.0	144.6	138.2
2003	136.0	133.3	134.3	135.3	137.1	139.4	138.9	139.9	139.3	140.5	143.6	146.4	138.7
Wholesale trade													
1990	20.2	20.2	20.2	20.1	20.2	20.4	20.1	20.1	20.0	20.0	19.7	19.5	20.0
1991	18.6	18.5	18.3	18.3	18.4	18.4	18.5	18.4	18.4	18.5	18.5	18.5	18.4
1992	18.5	18.4	18.5	18.5	18.7	18.9	18.9	19.1	19.1	19.2	19.1	19.2	18.8
1993	18.5	18.5	18.6	18.9	19.2	19.5	19.6	19.7	19.5	19.6	19.5	19.7	19.2
1994	19.0	19.0	19.2	19.6	19.8	20.0	19.9	20.2	20.3	20.4	20.4	20.7	19.8
1995	20.3	20.2	20.3	20.5	20.7	21.1	21.0	21.3	21.3	21.2	21.3	21.5	20.8
1996	20.9	20.9	21.0	21.2	21.5	21.9	21.9	22.0	22.0	22.0	22.3	22.4	21.6
1997	22.1	22.1	22.3	22.6	22.8	23.2	23.1	23.3	23.1	23.1	23.2	23.4	22.8
1998	23.0	23.0	23.2	23.2	23.4	23.6	23.8	24.0	23.6	23.5	23.7	24.0	23.5
1999	23.8	23.9	24.1	24.5	24.6	25.0	24.8	24.9	24.7	24.4	24.4	24.7	24.4
2000	24.5	24.6	24.8	24.9	25.8	26.2	26.3	26.4	26.2	26.3	26.4	26.7	25.7
2001	26.3	26.3	26.3	26.5	26.6	26.9	27.0	26.9	26.7	26.9	26.6	26.8	26.7
2002	26.5	26.4	26.5	26.4	26.4	26.7	26.7	26.7	26.6	26.8	26.6	26.8	26.6
2003	26.2	26.1	26.0	26.4	26.6	27.0	27.1	27.3	27.0	27.2	27.3	27.5	26.8
Retail trade													
1990	79.4	76.5	76.4	75.1	75.7	77.6	77.6	77.6	76.8	76.0	77.0	77.9	76.9
1991	72.3	69.3	68.6	68.5	69.2	70.4	71.0	72.0	71.4	71.5	73.5	75.7	71.1
1992	71.0	69.4	69.5	70.0	71.7	73.2	73.0	73.9	73.1	73.3	75.7	78.4	72.6
1993	73.7	72.2	71.8	73.3	74.6	76.0	76.3	77.4	77.0	77.8	79.9	82.4	76.0
1994	77.4	75.4	75.4	76.7	77.6	79.3	79.2	80.4	80.4	80.7	83.4	85.9	79.3
1995	80.8	78.9	78.7	79.8	81.0	82.9	83.0	83.5	82.9	83.3	86.4	88.6	82.4
1996	82.8	80.6	80.1	80.3	81.8	83.5	83.3	83.9	82.7	84.3	87.7	90.4	83.4
1997	83.6	81.0	80.7	80.7	82.5	84.4	84.7	84.6	84.9	85.8	88.4	91.4	84.3
1998	85.2	83.0	83.6	83.8	85.5	87.1	87.1	87.8	87.1	88.9	92.4	95.5	87.2
1999	90.2	88.2	88.8	89.3	90.6	92.5	92.7	93.3	92.4	93.7	96.9	100.4	92.4
2000	94.2	91.7	91.9	93.1	93.7	95.2	94.6	94.6	93.3	94.0	97.8	101.2	94.6
2001	95.4	92.2	91.9	92.5	94.0	95.5	95.0	95.4	93.7	94.8	98.2	100.5	94.9
2002	95.3	92.0	92.5	93.7	94.9	96.6	96.2	96.9	96.3	95.8	98.4	101.6	95.9
2003	94.1	91.8	92.7	93.3	94.6	96.4	96.6	97.6	96.2	97.2	100.5	103.0	96.2

Employment by Industry: New Hampshire—*Continued*

(Numbers in thousands. Not seasonally adjusted.)

Industry	January	February	March	April	May	June	July	August	September	October	November	December	Annual Average
STATEWIDE—*Continued*													
Transportation and utilities													
1990	12.0	12.2	12.3	12.0	12.3	12.8	12.3	12.4	12.7	12.5	12.4	12.5	12.3
1991	12.1	12.2	12.0	11.8	12.0	12.1	11.8	11.9	12.4	12.3	12.0	12.2	12.0
1992	11.9	12.0	11.9	12.0	12.4	13.1	12.1	12.0	12.6	12.6	12.6	12.8	12.3
1993	13.0	13.0	13.0	12.8	13.0	13.4	13.0	13.0	13.4	13.8	13.7	13.9	13.2
1994	13.4	13.5	13.5	14.0	14.1	14.7	13.9	14.0	14.2	14.5	14.2	13.8	13.9
1995	13.9	13.8	13.8	13.5	13.6	14.1	13.5	13.3	13.9	14.1	14.0	14.1	13.8
1996	13.5	13.5	13.4	13.4	13.8	14.0	13.1	13.0	13.6	13.7	13.6	13.9	13.5
1997	14.2	14.1	14.2	14.4	14.8	15.2	14.4	13.5	15.0	15.2	14.9	15.0	14.5
1998	14.8	14.7	14.8	14.9	15.2	15.8	15.4	15.7	16.4	16.2	16.3	16.9	15.5
1999	16.1	16.2	16.3	16.5	16.6	16.8	16.2	16.2	16.9	17.4	17.2	17.8	16.6
2000	16.9	16.7	16.6	16.8	16.8	17.2	16.1	16.1	16.8	17.1	16.8	16.9	16.7
2001	15.6	15.7	15.5	15.8	16.1	16.2	15.4	15.3	16.0	16.0	15.8	15.8	15.8
2002	15.3	15.2	15.3	15.8	16.0	16.2	15.7	15.6	16.0	16.1	16.0	16.2	15.8
2003	15.7	15.4	15.6	15.6	15.9	16.0	15.2	15.0	16.1	16.1	15.8	15.9	15.7
Information													
1990	10.7	10.5	10.5	10.5	10.5	10.5	10.6	10.6	10.4	10.4	10.4	10.4	10.5
1991	10.0	9.7	9.6	9.4	9.4	9.3	9.2	9.0	8.9	8.6	8.5	8.4	9.1
1992	8.4	8.4	8.5	8.4	8.6	8.6	8.5	8.5	8.4	8.5	8.6	8.6	8.5
1993	8.5	8.4	8.5	8.8	8.9	9.0	8.9	8.8	8.7	8.8	9.0	9.2	8.7
1994	9.1	9.2	9.2	9.3	9.5	9.6	9.7	9.7	9.7	9.7	9.8	9.9	9.5
1995	9.9	10.0	10.5	10.6	10.7	10.9	10.7	10.7	10.6	10.6	10.6	10.8	10.5
1996	10.7	10.8	10.9	10.9	10.9	11.1	11.0	11.0	10.9	10.8	11.0	11.2	10.9
1997	11.1	11.3	11.3	11.4	11.5	11.6	11.8	11.9	11.8	11.9	11.9	12.2	11.6
1998	12.0	12.1	12.2	12.4	12.3	12.4	12.5	12.5	12.4	12.8	13.0	13.0	12.4
1999	12.5	12.6	12.5	12.7	12.8	12.9	13.3	13.5	13.3	13.4	13.6	13.6	13.0
2000	13.3	13.3	13.4	13.7	14.0	14.2	14.2	13.6	14.1	14.5	14.6	14.6	13.9
2001	14.3	14.2	14.1	13.8	13.7	13.8	13.7	13.6	13.5	13.4	13.4	13.4	13.7
2002	13.4	13.3	13.1	13.0	12.9	12.9	12.8	12.7	12.7	12.7	12.7	12.6	12.9
2003	12.7	12.4	12.4	12.1	12.1	12.3	11.8	11.7	11.5	11.5	11.5	11.7	12.0
Financial activities													
1990	33.2	32.9	32.9	33.1	33.4	33.7	33.5	33.4	32.8	32.3	32.1	32.2	32.9
1991	31.1	30.8	30.8	30.2	30.5	31.2	31.1	31.2	30.4	30.5	30.7	31.1	30.8
1992	29.2	29.2	29.1	29.5	30.0	30.3	29.8	29.8	29.5	29.2	29.0	29.3	29.4
1993	28.2	28.4	28.6	27.9	28.3	28.8	28.7	28.7	28.3	28.1	28.2	28.7	28.4
1994	28.2	28.2	28.2	28.0	28.2	28.8	29.3	29.4	29.2	28.8	28.8	29.3	28.7
1995	28.9	28.9	29.0	28.8	29.2	29.8	29.5	29.7	29.5	29.2	29.2	29.6	29.2
1996	29.2	29.1	29.2	29.5	29.7	30.1	30.4	30.4	30.3	30.5	30.7	31.0	30.0
1997	31.1	31.3	31.6	31.4	31.8	32.1	32.3	32.5	32.0	31.8	32.2	32.4	31.8
1998	32.0	31.9	31.9	31.7	31.9	32.5	32.7	32.6	32.2	32.4	32.5	33.0	32.2
1999	33.5	33.6	33.6	34.0	34.4	34.9	34.6	34.5	34.4	34.1	34.2	34.4	34.1
2000	34.1	33.9	33.8	33.7	33.8	34.3	34.3	34.4	34.1	34.1	34.4	34.8	34.1
2001	34.9	35.1	35.3	35.4	35.7	36.1	36.1	36.3	35.8	35.6	35.8	36.3	35.7
2002	36.3	36.2	36.2	36.1	36.3	36.7	36.8	37.0	36.8	36.7	36.7	36.8	36.6
2003	36.8	36.8	36.7	37.0	37.2	37.4	37.6	37.7	37.2	37.1	37.3	37.4	37.2
Professional and business services													
1990	36.2	36.1	36.5	37.1	37.1	37.6	37.4	37.4	37.2	36.0	35.5	35.1	36.6
1991	34.9	34.6	34.6	35.0	35.6	36.3	35.8	36.4	36.5	36.7	36.8	36.7	35.8
1992	35.8	36.1	36.3	38.1	38.6	39.8	40.5	40.7	41.1	41.5	40.5	40.8	39.1
1993	40.4	40.8	41.0	41.4	42.8	43.9	43.3	43.9	44.1	43.7	43.1	43.4	42.6
1994	42.3	43.3	43.6	44.8	45.4	46.4	46.0	46.4	46.6	46.2	46.0	45.9	45.2
1995	43.8	44.0	44.2	45.3	46.0	46.7	46.7	47.7	47.6	48.0	48.0	48.1	46.3
1996	46.8	47.0	47.4	48.4	49.6	50.4	50.2	50.4	50.6	50.1	50.1	50.4	49.2
1997	48.1	48.5	48.8	50.4	51.6	52.2	51.2	51.5	51.3	51.2	51.7	52.0	50.7
1998	50.7	51.5	52.2	53.2	53.3	54.4	54.0	54.0	53.4	53.7	53.7	54.5	53.2
1999	53.3	53.6	53.9	55.4	55.2	56.0	56.4	57.0	56.3	56.3	56.0	56.9	55.5
2000	55.4	56.1	57.1	58.1	58.4	59.8	59.4	60.0	59.3	59.5	60.0	60.3	58.6
2001	57.4	56.9	57.1	57.3	58.0	58.5	57.7	57.9	56.6	55.6	55.2	55.2	57.0
2002	53.0	52.8	53.1	53.9	54.7	55.0	55.4	55.7	55.0	54.5	54.6	53.9	54.3
2003	52.3	52.0	52.1	53.9	54.3	55.1	54.8	55.2	54.6	54.2	54.0	54.4	53.9
Educational and health services													
1990	60.8	61.0	61.5	61.1	61.0	61.0	60.1	60.3	62.2	63.0	63.1	63.4	61.5
1991	61.8	62.2	62.3	62.7	62.7	62.4	61.1	61.2	63.0	63.4	63.8	64.2	62.5
1992	63.2	63.7	63.9	64.6	64.7	64.4	63.3	63.1	64.3	65.2	65.4	65.5	64.2
1993	65.7	65.6	65.7	66.6	66.6	66.3	65.8	65.7	67.2	67.5	68.2	68.8	66.6
1994	68.9	69.6	70.1	69.7	70.1	70.0	70.0	69.8	71.7	71.9	72.1	72.8	70.5
1995	71.4	72.1	72.6	73.4	73.6	73.5	72.4	72.4	74.3	74.8	75.1	75.8	73.4
1996	73.6	74.4	74.8	75.8	75.7	75.5	74.4	74.4	76.4	76.5	77.1	77.4	75.5
1997	76.5	77.3	78.1	78.5	78.9	78.2	77.8	77.6	79.3	80.0	80.3	80.5	78.5
1998	79.7	80.8	81.3	81.1	81.3	80.1	79.5	79.3	80.7	81.1	81.6	81.2	80.6
1999	79.1	80.3	80.5	81.9	82.0	81.8	80.6	80.4	82.2	82.6	83.1	83.3	81.4
2000	81.8	82.8	83.3	84.3	84.1	84.2	83.2	83.4	85.1	84.8	85.4	85.5	83.9
2001	86.9	88.3	88.4	88.3	88.2	88.4	88.3	88.6	89.6	90.2	91.0	91.5	89.0
2002	90.4	91.5	92.2	92.1	92.4	92.1	91.0	91.0	92.4	91.8	92.4	92.3	91.8
2003	92.1	92.9	93.2	92.8	93.0	92.9	92.7	92.5	93.1	94.0	94.7	94.8	93.2

Employment by Industry: New Hampshire—*Continued*

(Numbers in thousands. Not seasonally adjusted.)

Industry	January	February	March	April	May	June	July	August	September	October	November	December	Annual Average
STATEWIDE—*Continued*													
Leisure and hospitality													
1990	42.7	42.6	42.8	41.2	44.1	48.7	51.6	52.1	48.5	44.1	41.0	40.7	45.0
1991	38.8	38.7	38.8	38.7	41.8	46.2	50.7	51.7	47.0	44.3	40.9	41.0	43.2
1992	39.3	39.3	39.6	40.2	43.6	47.7	52.5	53.2	48.6	45.4	42.1	42.1	44.4
1993	40.7	40.5	40.1	41.4	44.4	49.7	54.7	55.4	50.8	46.7	43.4	43.3	45.9
1994	42.4	42.3	43.0	43.7	46.6	52.6	57.2	57.7	53.2	48.8	45.0	45.6	48.1
1995	44.5	44.6	45.1	45.8	48.8	54.9	58.9	60.2	54.7	51.1	46.7	47.2	50.2
1996	46.5	46.8	47.2	46.7	51.2	57.5	61.3	62.3	55.9	52.2	47.5	48.4	51.9
1997	47.8	48.1	48.1	48.2	53.0	59.0	63.4	64.4	58.3	54.1	49.6	50.9	53.7
1998	49.2	49.9	49.9	50.5	54.6	59.8	65.2	65.3	59.4	55.3	51.3	52.7	55.2
1999	51.6	52.3	52.1	51.9	55.6	61.8	67.1	67.4	60.9	57.4	52.2	53.0	56.9
2000	52.3	52.9	53.2	53.9	57.2	63.8	68.8	68.3	61.8	57.9	53.8	55.1	58.2
2001	54.4	54.6	54.5	55.4	59.1	65.4	69.5	69.4	62.3	58.7	55.1	55.6	59.5
2002	54.8	54.9	55.7	56.6	60.4	66.3	70.9	71.1	64.1	60.6	57.1	57.5	60.8
2003	56.3	56.0	55.9	55.9	61.1	66.2	71.4	72.0	66.1	63.4	59.1	59.8	61.9
Other services													
1990	17.7	17.6	17.7	17.6	17.6	17.8	17.9	17.9	17.7	17.6	17.5	17.4	17.6
1991	16.3	16.2	16.2	16.2	16.3	16.5	16.6	16.9	16.5	16.4	16.3	16.4	16.4
1992	17.0	17.0	17.1	17.3	17.5	17.6	17.9	18.0	17.5	17.6	17.6	17.8	17.4
1993	17.6	17.7	17.7	18.0	18.2	18.4	18.8	18.8	18.6	18.4	18.5	18.5	18.2
1994	18.2	18.3	18.4	18.6	18.7	19.1	19.2	19.4	19.0	18.9	19.0	19.1	18.8
1995	18.7	18.9	19.4	19.2	19.3	19.7	19.5	19.7	19.4	19.2	19.3	19.5	19.3
1996	19.2	19.4	19.4	19.4	19.5	19.8	20.1	20.1	19.6	19.4	19.3	19.4	19.5
1997	19.2	18.9	19.0	19.2	19.5	19.9	20.1	20.2	20.1	20.0	20.1	20.2	19.7
1998	20.1	20.2	20.4	20.6	21.0	21.5	21.7	21.9	21.7	21.9	22.0	22.3	21.2
1999	21.9	22.1	22.5	22.6	22.9	23.3	23.6	23.7	23.4	23.5	23.5	23.7	23.0
2000	23.4	23.5	23.6	23.8	24.0	24.4	24.5	24.1	24.3	24.0	24.1	24.1	23.9
2001	23.8	23.7	24.5	24.3	24.4	24.3	24.0	23.4	22.9	22.5	22.6	22.3	23.6
2002	21.9	21.9	21.8	21.9	22.1	22.2	22.0	22.1	21.5	20.9	20.7	20.6	21.6
2003	20.4	20.3	20.5	20.4	20.7	20.8	20.5	20.2	19.8	19.5	19.6	19.6	20.2
Government													
1990	71.6	73.9	74.9	75.4	75.6	71.9	63.9	65.0	73.9	74.5	75.4	76.2	72.6
1991	71.8	74.4	75.1	74.5	74.4	72.3	63.2	64.0	72.2	74.7	75.7	76.8	72.4
1992	73.3	74.8	76.0	75.3	75.7	72.4	62.9	62.6	73.5	76.3	77.0	77.9	73.1
1993	72.2	75.5	76.9	76.7	76.3	73.4	67.2	66.7	75.7	76.5	77.0	78.1	74.3
1994	74.1	77.2	78.1	78.3	77.4	74.7	68.7	68.4	76.5	78.9	80.6	81.2	76.1
1995	74.5	78.5	79.0	78.3	77.2	74.6	67.5	66.7	77.0	80.1	80.0	81.4	76.2
1996	75.9	79.7	80.6	80.6	79.2	76.5	70.2	69.4	78.6	80.4	82.3	81.9	77.9
1997	78.0	80.7	81.2	81.6	80.4	77.0	71.6	70.1	79.2	81.6	82.9	81.6	78.8
1998	78.7	81.4	82.2	82.6	81.8	78.3	71.2	69.7	80.5	83.0	84.0	83.6	79.7
1999	80.4	83.3	83.7	84.0	83.4	80.0	72.9	72.1	81.8	84.7	86.0	85.9	81.5
2000	82.6	85.9	86.7	86.4	87.2	82.1	74.4	72.9	84.0	86.0	87.2	86.6	83.5
2001	84.7	87.8	88.4	87.6	88.3	84.2	74.6	74.2	87.5	90.3	91.1	91.3	85.8
2002	86.9	90.3	91.1	90.0	89.1	86.7	79.2	78.2	88.6	92.3	93.6	93.7	88.3
2003	88.7	92.2	92.7	92.1	90.7	88.6	80.4	79.6	89.4	93.6	94.6	94.4	89.8
Federal government													
1990	8.6	8.5	8.7	9.9	10.3	9.3	8.8	8.5	8.4	8.1	8.1	8.5	8.8
1991	8.2	8.1	8.0	7.8	7.8	7.9	7.9	7.9	7.8	7.8	7.8	8.1	7.9
1992	7.9	7.7	7.8	7.8	7.8	7.9	7.8	7.8	7.8	7.6	7.5	7.8	7.7
1993	7.5	7.4	7.4	7.6	7.6	7.7	7.6	7.7	7.7	7.7	7.6	8.0	7.6
1994	7.7	7.7	7.7	8.0	8.0	8.1	7.9	7.8	7.8	7.6	7.5	7.9	7.8
1995	7.6	7.7	7.6	7.7	7.7	7.9	8.0	8.0	8.0	8.0	7.9	8.6	7.8
1996	8.1	8.0	8.0	8.3	8.3	8.3	8.1	8.2	8.1	7.9	8.0	8.4	8.1
1997	8.1	8.1	8.1	8.1	8.1	8.1	8.1	8.1	8.1	8.1	8.2	8.8	8.1
1998	8.2	8.1	8.1	8.1	8.2	8.2	7.9	8.0	8.0	8.1	8.2	8.2	8.1
1999	7.9	7.9	7.8	8.1	7.9	8.0	7.9	8.0	8.0	7.9	7.9	8.1	7.9
2000	7.9	8.0	8.9	8.5	9.8	8.6	8.4	7.9	7.7	7.6	7.6	7.7	8.2
2001	8.2	8.1	8.1	8.0	8.1	8.2	8.2	8.2	8.1	8.1	8.1	8.2	8.1
2002	8.1	7.9	7.9	7.8	7.9	8.1	8.1	8.2	8.0	8.0	8.1	8.7	8.1
2003	8.1	8.0	8.0	8.0	7.9	8.0	8.0	8.0	7.9	7.9	7.9	8.0	8.0
State government													
1990	17.4	19.7	20.1	19.6	19.4	17.1	16.9	18.1	20.0	20.6	20.6	20.5	19.1
1991	18.3	20.7	21.3	20.7	20.5	17.9	17.1	17.9	19.6	20.7	20.8	20.9	19.7
1992	19.3	20.4	21.0	20.6	20.8	17.9	17.5	17.8	20.2	21.9	21.3	20.9	19.9
1993	18.5	21.1	21.9	21.5	21.0	18.4	18.4	18.5	21.6	21.2	21.0	21.0	20.3
1994	19.4	22.1	22.4	22.4	21.5	19.0	19.5	19.3	21.7	23.0	23.0	23.1	21.3
1995	19.2	22.2	22.5	21.8	20.6	18.8	19.0	18.9	21.6	22.3	21.9	21.7	20.8
1996	18.6	21.5	21.9	22.2	20.7	18.4	18.5	18.6	21.2	22.1	22.3	21.4	20.6
1997	19.7	21.9	21.7	22.4	21.2	18.4	19.5	18.3	21.5	22.1	22.3	19.9	20.7
1998	19.4	21.5	21.2	22.6	21.6	18.9	19.2	18.8	21.2	22.4	22.2	21.1	20.8
1999	19.7	22.2	22.0	22.7	21.9	19.0	19.2	19.0	21.6	22.7	22.6	21.5	21.1
2000	20.0	22.7	22.3	23.0	22.2	19.5	19.7	19.4	21.5	22.9	22.8	21.5	21.4
2001	20.4	23.2	23.5	23.4	23.4	20.6	20.1	20.0	23.4	24.2	23.9	23.7	22.5
2002	20.4	23.4	23.8	23.8	22.3	20.5	21.1	20.8	23.1	24.5	24.5	23.2	22.6
2003	21.3	24.2	24.4	24.2	22.7	20.4	20.6	20.9	21.8	24.6	24.7	24.5	22.9

Employment by Industry: New Hampshire—*Continued*

(Numbers in thousands. Not seasonally adjusted.)

Industry	January	February	March	April	May	June	July	August	September	October	November	December	Annual Average
STATEWIDE—*Continued*													
Local government													
1990	45.6	45.7	46.1	45.9	45.9	45.5	38.2	38.4	45.5	45.8	46.7	47.2	44.7
1991	45.3	45.6	45.8	46.0	46.1	46.5	38.2	38.2	44.8	46.2	47.1	47.8	44.8
1992	46.1	46.7	47.2	46.9	47.1	46.6	37.6	37.0	45.5	46.8	48.2	49.2	45.4
1993	46.2	47.0	47.6	47.6	47.7	47.3	41.2	40.5	46.4	47.6	48.4	49.1	46.3
1994	47.0	47.4	48.0	47.9	47.9	47.6	41.3	41.3	47.0	48.3	50.1	50.2	47.0
1995	47.7	48.6	48.9	48.8	48.9	47.9	40.5	39.8	47.4	49.8	50.2	51.1	47.4
1996	49.2	50.2	50.7	50.1	50.2	49.8	43.6	42.6	49.3	50.4	52.0	52.1	49.1
1997	50.2	50.7	51.4	51.1	51.1	50.5	44.0	43.7	49.6	51.4	52.4	52.9	49.9
1998	51.1	51.8	52.9	51.9	52.0	51.2	44.1	42.9	51.3	52.5	53.6	54.3	50.8
1999	52.8	53.2	53.9	53.2	53.6	53.0	45.8	45.1	52.2	54.1	55.5	56.3	52.3
2000	54.7	55.2	55.5	54.9	55.2	54.0	46.3	45.6	54.8	55.5	56.8	57.4	53.8
2001	56.1	56.5	56.8	56.2	56.8	55.4	46.3	46.0	56.0	58.0	59.1	59.4	55.2
2002	58.4	59.0	59.4	58.4	58.9	58.1	50.0	49.2	57.5	59.8	61.0	61.8	57.6
2003	59.3	60.0	60.3	59.9	60.1	60.2	51.8	50.7	59.7	61.1	62.0	61.9	58.9
MANCHESTER													
Total nonfarm													
1990	89.0	87.3	89.6	87.9	88.2	88.7	86.6	86.7	87.4	86.4	86.1	86.2	87.5
1991	83.3	82.8	82.4	82.6	82.4	83.6	81.9	82.3	83.7	84.1	84.9	85.2	83.3
1992	80.1	79.8	79.9	81.4	82.1	82.1	81.0	81.5	82.8	83.3	83.7	84.3	81.8
1993	82.4	82.4	82.2	83.4	84.2	85.1	84.2	85.1	85.8	86.0	86.3	87.1	84.5
1994	85.9	85.7	86.2	87.5	88.4	89.2	87.4	88.0	89.4	90.2	90.7	91.7	88.4
1995	89.1	88.7	89.3	90.9	91.9	92.4	90.2	90.8	91.9	93.0	93.4	93.7	91.3
1996	92.0	92.1	92.4	92.7	93.4	94.2	92.1	92.7	93.5	94.4	95.9	96.9	93.5
1997	94.7	94.4	95.0	95.5	96.5	97.3	95.1	95.6	97.2	98.5	99.8	101.0	96.7
1998	98.1	98.2	98.7	99.7	100.1	100.4	98.9	99.1	100.2	100.9	102.4	102.9	100.0
1999	100.7	100.8	101.6	103.5	103.4	103.9	102.1	102.0	103.5	104.6	105.4	106.6	103.2
2000	105.0	104.6	105.2	106.7	106.7	107.6	105.9	105.4	107.1	107.6	109.1	109.8	106.7
2001	109.1	108.3	108.3	108.7	109.6	109.4	107.3	107.5	108.2	108.3	108.9	109.4	108.6
2002	107.1	106.6	107.1	107.8	108.0	108.4	106.2	106.9	107.6	109.1	110.0	110.1	107.9
2003	107.3	107.1	107.5	109.5	109.9	110.8	109.2	109.0	110.3	110.4	111.1	111.9	109.5
Total private													
1990	79.2	77.6	79.9	78.2	78.5	78.9	77.7	77.9	77.4	76.9	76.5	76.4	77.9
1991	73.7	73.1	72.8	73.1	72.8	74.1	73.3	73.7	74.2	74.6	75.2	75.3	73.8
1992	70.4	70.1	70.2	71.8	72.5	72.7	72.3	72.9	73.2	73.5	73.7	74.2	72.3
1993	72.5	72.4	72.2	73.5	74.2	75.3	75.0	75.8	75.9	76.1	76.2	76.7	74.7
1994	75.8	75.6	76.0	77.1	78.0	78.9	78.1	78.7	79.2	80.0	80.4	80.9	78.2
1995	78.8	78.3	79.0	80.5	81.5	82.2	80.9	81.4	81.6	82.4	83.2	83.2	81.1
1996	81.6	81.5	81.8	82.2	82.9	83.8	82.6	83.4	83.1	83.7	84.9	85.6	83.1
1997	84.0	83.7	84.3	84.9	85.8	86.7	85.6	86.0	86.5	87.5	88.6	89.3	86.1
1998	87.1	87.0	87.5	88.6	89.0	89.4	89.0	89.6	89.2	89.8	91.1	91.5	89.1
1999	89.4	89.5	90.1	92.2	92.2	92.9	92.3	92.6	92.3	93.2	93.8	94.7	92.1
2000	93.3	92.7	93.3	94.9	94.8	96.1	95.5	95.3	95.6	95.9	97.3	98.2	95.2
2001	97.4	96.3	96.4	96.9	97.7	97.9	96.6	96.9	96.3	96.2	96.6	97.3	96.9
2002	95.0	94.1	94.6	95.4	95.6	96.3	95.8	96.7	95.8	96.6	97.3	97.5	95.9
2003	95.1	94.5	94.9	97.0	97.3	98.4	98.1	98.1	97.8	97.7	98.2	99.1	97.2
Goods-producing													
1990	16.3	15.8	16.1	16.0	16.1	16.1	15.8	15.8	15.5	15.2	14.8	14.6	15.7
1991	13.9	13.7	13.6	13.9	14.0	14.2	13.7	14.1	14.1	14.4	14.2	13.9	14.0
1992	13.0	12.7	12.7	13.4	13.5	13.8	13.2	13.6	13.5	13.5	13.5	13.5	13.3
1993	13.1	13.0	13.0	13.3	13.4	13.7	13.9	14.1	14.2	14.1	14.0	13.9	13.6
1994	13.7	13.7	13.7	14.1	14.4	14.8	14.7	15.1	15.2	15.3	15.3	15.4	14.6
1995	15.1	15.0	15.2	15.7	16.0	16.3	16.0	16.4	16.3	16.2	16.3	16.2	15.9
1996	16.1	16.1	16.2	16.8	17.1	17.4	17.3	17.7	17.6	17.7	17.8	17.9	17.1
1997	17.6	17.5	17.8	17.9	18.3	18.6	18.2	18.6	18.5	18.7	18.8	18.9	18.3
1998	18.7	18.5	18.7	19.1	19.3	19.5	19.3	19.4	19.2	19.1	19.1	19.1	19.1
1999	18.6	18.3	18.5	19.1	19.2	19.4	19.0	19.0	19.0	19.3	19.4	19.3	19.0
2000	19.2	18.9	19.2	19.5	19.6	19.6	19.7	19.7	19.6	19.6	19.8	19.9	19.5
2001	19.5	19.1	19.2	19.4	19.5	19.4	18.8	18.9	18.6	18.5	18.3	18.2	19.0
2002	18.0	17.9	17.9	18.0	18.1	18.2	18.0	18.0	17.9	18.1	17.7	17.7	18.0
2003	17.3	17.1	17.3	17.6	17.8	18.1	18.0	18.0	17.9	17.8	17.8	17.7	17.7
Construction and mining													
1990	4.4	4.1	4.1	4.2	4.4	4.4	4.4	4.4	4.2	4.1	3.9	3.8	4.2
1991	3.2	3.1	3.0	3.2	3.3	3.4	3.4	3.4	3.4	3.6	3.4	3.3	3.3
1992	2.8	2.6	2.6	2.9	3.0	3.2	3.3	3.4	3.2	3.2	3.1	3.0	3.0
1993	2.5	2.4	2.4	2.8	2.9	3.1	3.3	3.4	3.4	3.2	3.1	3.0	3.0
1994	2.7	2.7	2.6	2.9	3.1	3.3	3.5	3.6	3.6	3.6	3.5	3.5	3.2
1995	3.2	3.1	3.2	3.5	3.8	3.9	4.1	4.1	4.0	3.9	3.9	3.7	3.7
1996	3.4	3.4	3.4	3.7	3.9	4.0	4.1	4.2	4.1	4.2	4.2	4.1	3.9
1997	3.8	3.7	3.9	4.1	4.3	4.5	4.5	4.6	4.5	4.5	4.4	4.4	4.3
1998	4.2	4.0	4.1	4.5	4.6	4.8	4.8	4.9	4.8	4.8	4.7	4.7	4.6
1999	4.3	4.2	4.3	4.8	5.0	5.1	5.2	5.2	5.1	4.9	4.9	4.8	4.8
2000	4.6	4.4	4.6	4.8	5.0	5.1	5.2	5.2	5.1	5.1	5.1	5.1	4.9
2001	4.9	4.8	4.9	5.2	5.5	5.6	5.8	5.9	5.8	5.8	5.8	5.8	5.5
2002	5.8	5.7	5.7	5.9	6.1	6.3	6.4	6.3	6.1	6.4	6.1	6.0	6.1
2003	5.6	5.4	5.5	5.9	6.2	6.4	6.5	6.5	6.4	6.3	6.3	6.2	6.1

Employment by Industry: New Hampshire—*Continued*

(Numbers in thousands. Not seasonally adjusted.)

Industry	January	February	March	April	May	June	July	August	September	October	November	December	Annual Average
MANCHESTER—*Continued*													
Manufacturing													
1990	11.9	11.7	12.0	11.8	11.7	11.7	11.4	11.4	11.3	11.1	10.9	10.8	11.5
1991	10.7	10.6	10.6	10.7	10.7	10.8	10.3	10.7	10.7	10.8	10.8	10.6	10.7
1992	10.2	10.1	10.1	10.5	10.5	10.6	9.9	10.2	10.3	10.3	10.4	10.5	10.3
1993	10.6	10.6	10.6	10.5	10.5	10.6	10.6	10.7	10.8	10.9	10.9	10.9	10.7
1994	11.0	11.0	11.1	11.2	11.3	11.5	11.2	11.5	11.6	11.7	11.8	11.9	11.4
1995	11.9	11.9	12.0	12.2	12.2	12.4	11.9	12.3	12.3	12.3	12.4	12.5	12.2
1996	12.7	12.7	12.8	13.1	13.2	13.4	13.2	13.5	13.5	13.5	13.6	13.8	13.3
1997	13.8	13.8	13.9	13.8	14.0	14.1	13.7	14.0	14.0	14.2	14.4	14.5	14.0
1998	14.5	14.5	14.6	14.6	14.7	14.7	14.5	14.5	14.4	14.3	14.4	14.4	14.5
1999	14.3	14.1	14.2	14.3	14.2	14.3	13.8	13.8	13.9	14.4	14.5	14.5	14.2
2000	14.6	14.5	14.6	14.7	14.6	14.5	14.5	14.5	14.5	14.5	14.7	14.8	14.6
2001	14.6	14.3	14.3	14.2	14.0	13.8	13.0	13.0	12.8	12.7	12.5	12.4	13.5
2002	12.2	12.2	12.2	12.1	12.0	11.9	11.6	11.7	11.8	11.7	11.6	11.7	11.9
2003	11.7	11.7	11.8	11.7	11.6	11.7	11.5	11.5	11.5	11.5	11.5	11.5	11.6
Service-providing													
1990	72.7	71.5	73.5	71.9	72.1	72.6	70.8	70.9	71.9	71.2	71.3	71.6	71.8
1991	69.4	69.1	68.8	68.7	68.4	69.4	68.2	68.2	69.6	69.7	70.7	71.3	69.3
1992	67.1	67.1	67.2	68.0	68.6	68.3	67.8	67.9	69.3	69.8	70.2	70.8	68.5
1993	69.3	69.4	69.2	70.1	70.8	71.4	70.3	71.0	71.6	71.9	72.3	73.2	70.9
1994	72.2	72.0	72.5	73.4	74.0	74.4	72.7	72.9	74.2	74.9	75.4	76.3	73.7
1995	74.0	73.7	74.1	75.2	75.9	76.1	74.2	74.4	75.6	76.8	77.1	77.5	75.4
1996	75.9	76.0	76.2	75.9	76.3	76.8	74.8	75.0	75.9	76.7	78.1	79.0	76.4
1997	77.1	76.9	77.2	77.6	78.2	78.7	76.9	77.0	78.7	79.8	81.0	82.1	78.4
1998	79.4	79.7	80.0	80.6	80.8	80.9	79.6	79.7	81.0	81.8	83.3	83.8	80.9
1999	82.1	82.5	83.1	84.4	84.2	84.5	83.1	83.0	84.5	85.3	86.0	87.3	84.2
2000	85.8	85.7	86.0	87.2	87.1	88.0	86.2	85.7	87.5	88.0	89.3	89.9	87.2
2001	89.6	89.2	89.1	89.3	90.1	90.0	88.5	88.6	89.6	89.8	90.6	91.2	89.6
2002	89.1	88.7	89.2	89.8	89.9	90.2	88.2	88.9	89.7	91.0	92.3	92.4	90.0
2003	90.0	90.0	90.2	91.9	92.1	92.7	91.2	91.0	92.4	92.6	93.3	94.2	91.8
Trade, transportation, and utilities													
1990	21.6	20.9	21.5	20.7	20.6	21.1	20.8	20.8	20.6	20.5	20.6	20.9	20.9
1991	19.8	19.3	19.1	19.5	19.4	19.6	19.5	19.9	19.9	20.0	20.5	20.9	19.8
1992	18.5	18.2	18.3	18.1	18.4	18.6	18.4	18.3	18.4	18.7	19.1	19.5	18.5
1993	18.3	17.9	17.8	17.9	18.0	18.3	18.0	18.1	18.2	18.6	19.1	19.6	18.3
1994	19.1	18.7	18.7	19.2	19.3	19.5	19.0	19.1	19.3	19.8	20.1	20.7	19.4
1995	19.8	19.4	19.6	19.9	20.2	20.5	20.3	20.3	20.4	20.8	21.4	21.7	20.4
1996	20.4	19.9	19.9	20.1	20.3	20.7	20.5	20.7	20.5	21.0	21.6	22.1	20.6
1997	21.1	20.8	20.8	20.9	21.0	21.4	21.1	21.0	21.4	22.0	22.4	22.9	21.4
1998	21.5	21.2	21.2	21.1	21.2	21.3	21.2	21.6	21.4	21.8	22.5	22.8	21.6
1999	22.1	21.8	22.0	22.1	22.2	22.5	22.4	22.5	22.3	22.6	23.2	23.8	22.5
2000	22.8	22.3	22.2	22.7	22.9	23.2	22.9	22.9	23.0	23.1	23.9	24.4	23.0
2001	23.9	23.4	23.3	23.3	23.7	23.6	23.2	23.4	23.2	23.6	24.3	24.7	23.6
2002	23.7	23.0	23.0	23.3	23.6	23.8	23.5	23.8	23.4	23.8	24.7	25.0	23.7
2003	23.9	23.6	23.7	24.0	24.2	24.4	24.4	24.4	24.5	24.5	25.1	25.7	24.4
Wholesale trade													
1990	5.2	5.2	5.3	5.1	5.1	5.1	5.1	5.1	5.0	5.0	5.0	5.0	5.1
1991	4.6	4.6	4.4	4.5	4.5	4.5	4.5	4.5	4.5	4.5	4.5	4.5	4.5
1992	4.3	4.3	4.2	4.1	4.1	4.2	4.2	4.2	4.2	4.3	4.2	4.3	4.2
1993	4.3	4.3	4.3	4.3	4.3	4.3	4.4	4.4	4.4	4.4	4.4	4.4	4.4
1994	4.4	4.4	4.4	4.6	4.6	4.7	4.7	4.7	4.7	4.7	4.7	4.8	4.6
1995	4.7	4.8	4.8	5.0	5.1	5.1	5.1	5.1	5.1	5.2	5.2	5.3	5.0
1996	5.1	5.1	5.1	5.2	5.1	5.4	5.4	5.5	5.4	5.4	5.5	5.5	5.3
1997	5.4	5.4	5.4	5.5	5.5	5.6	5.6	5.7	5.6	5.7	5.7	5.7	5.6
1998	5.5	5.5	5.6	5.4	5.4	5.4	5.4	5.5	5.4	5.4	5.5	5.5	5.5
1999	5.4	5.4	5.4	5.6	5.6	5.7	5.9	5.9	5.9	5.8	5.7	5.8	5.7
2000	5.8	5.8	5.8	5.9	6.0	6.1	6.1	6.1	6.1	6.0	6.0	6.0	6.0
2001	6.0	6.0	6.0	6.0	6.0	6.0	6.1	6.1	6.1	6.1	6.1	6.1	6.1
2002	6.0	6.0	6.0	6.0	6.1	6.1	6.1	6.1	5.9	6.2	6.2	6.1	6.1
2003	6.2	6.2	6.1	6.2	6.2	6.2	6.3	6.2	6.2	6.2	6.2	6.2	6.2
Retail trade													
1990	13.6	12.9	13.2	12.7	12.6	13.0	12.8	12.7	12.6	12.5	12.6	12.9	12.8
1991	12.5	12.0	12.0	12.0	11.9	12.1	12.1	12.4	12.3	12.4	12.9	13.3	12.3
1992	11.3	11.0	11.2	11.1	11.4	11.5	11.4	11.3	11.2	11.3	11.8	12.1	11.4
1993	11.1	10.7	10.6	10.7	10.8	11.1	10.8	10.9	10.9	11.1	11.6	12.1	11.0
1994	11.7	11.3	11.3	11.6	11.6	11.8	11.6	11.7	11.8	12.1	12.4	12.9	11.8
1995	12.2	11.8	11.9	11.9	12.2	12.5	12.2	12.2	12.2	12.4	13.0	13.1	12.3
1996	12.5	12.0	11.9	12.0	12.2	12.3	12.2	12.3	12.1	12.5	13.0	13.4	12.4
1997	12.6	12.3	12.3	12.2	12.3	12.5	12.4	12.5	12.6	13.0	13.4	13.9	12.7
1998	12.9	12.6	12.5	12.4	12.5	12.6	12.5	12.7	12.5	12.9	13.5	13.8	12.8
1999	13.2	12.8	13.0	13.0	13.1	13.2	13.1	13.1	12.8	13.2	13.9	14.4	13.2
2000	13.4	13.0	13.0	13.3	13.4	13.5	13.4	13.3	13.3	13.5	14.3	14.8	13.5
2001	14.2	13.7	13.7	13.6	13.9	13.9	13.5	13.7	13.4	13.6	14.3	14.7	13.9
2002	14.0	13.4	13.4	13.4	13.6	13.8	13.6	13.9	13.6	13.7	14.5	15.0	13.8
2003	13.9	13.6	13.8	13.9	14.0	14.2	14.3	14.4	14.3	14.5	15.2	15.8	14.3

Employment by Industry: New Hampshire—*Continued*

(Numbers in thousands. Not seasonally adjusted.)

Industry	January	February	March	April	May	June	July	August	September	October	November	December	Annual Average
MANCHESTER—*Continued*													
Transportation and utilities													
1990	2.8	2.8	3.0	2.9	2.9	3.0	2.9	3.0	3.0	3.0	3.0	3.0	2.9
1991	2.7	2.7	2.7	3.0	3.0	3.0	2.9	3.0	3.1	3.1	3.1	3.1	3.0
1992	2.9	2.9	2.9	2.9	2.9	2.9	2.8	2.8	3.0	3.1	3.1	3.1	2.9
1993	2.9	2.9	2.9	2.9	2.9	2.9	2.8	2.8	2.9	3.1	3.1	3.1	2.9
1994	3.0	3.0	3.0	3.0	3.1	3.0	2.7	2.7	2.8	3.0	3.0	3.0	2.9
1995	2.9	2.8	2.9	3.0	2.9	2.9	3.0	3.0	3.1	3.2	3.2	3.3	3.0
1996	2.8	2.8	2.9	2.9	3.0	3.0	2.9	2.9	3.0	3.1	3.1	3.2	3.0
1997	3.1	3.1	3.1	3.2	3.2	3.3	3.1	2.8	3.2	3.3	3.3	3.3	3.2
1998	3.1	3.1	3.1	3.3	3.3	3.3	3.3	3.4	3.5	3.5	3.5	3.5	3.3
1999	3.5	3.6	3.6	3.5	3.5	3.6	3.4	3.5	3.6	3.6	3.6	3.6	3.6
2000	3.6	3.5	3.4	3.5	3.5	3.6	3.4	3.5	3.6	3.6	3.6	3.6	3.5
2001	3.7	3.7	3.6	3.7	3.8	3.7	3.6	3.6	3.7	3.9	3.9	3.9	3.7
2002	3.7	3.6	3.6	3.9	3.9	3.9	3.8	3.8	3.9	3.9	4.0	3.9	3.8
2003	3.8	3.8	3.8	3.9	4.0	4.0	3.8	3.8	4.0	3.8	3.7	3.7	3.8
Information													
1990	1.9	1.9	1.9	2.0	1.9	1.9	2.0	2.0	2.0	1.9	1.9	1.9	1.9
1991	1.8	1.8	1.8	1.7	1.7	1.7	1.8	1.7	1.7	1.7	1.7	1.9	1.8
1992	2.1	2.1	2.1	2.1	2.2	2.2	2.1	2.1	2.1	2.1	2.1	2.1	2.1
1993	2.1	2.1	2.1	2.1	2.1	2.2	2.0	2.0	1.9	2.0	2.0	2.0	2.1
1994	2.1	2.1	2.1	2.2	2.2	2.2	2.3	2.3	2.3	2.3	2.3	2.4	2.2
1995	2.5	2.5	2.5	2.7	2.7	2.7	2.7	2.7	2.6	2.6	2.6	2.6	2.6
1996	2.6	2.6	2.6	2.6	2.6	2.6	2.4	2.4	2.4	2.4	2.4	2.5	2.5
1997	2.6	2.6	2.6	2.6	2.6	2.6	2.7	2.7	2.7	2.9	2.9	2.9	2.7
1998	2.7	2.7	2.7	2.8	2.7	2.7	2.8	2.8	2.8	2.9	3.0	3.0	2.8
1999	2.8	2.9	2.8	3.0	3.0	3.0	3.2	3.2	3.1	3.2	3.2	3.2	3.1
2000	3.1	3.1	3.2	3.4	3.4	3.5	3.3	3.1	3.4	3.6	3.6	3.6	3.4
2001	3.8	3.6	3.5	3.3	3.3	3.3	3.3	3.2	3.2	3.2	3.2	3.2	3.3
2002	3.2	3.2	3.2	3.2	3.2	3.2	3.2	3.1	3.0	3.0	3.0	3.0	3.1
2003	3.0	3.0	3.0	3.0	2.9	3.1	3.0	3.0	3.0	3.1	3.1	3.1	3.0
Financial activities													
1990	8.5	8.5	8.7	8.2	8.3	8.3	8.2	8.3	8.2	8.2	8.1	8.2	8.3
1991	7.8	7.8	7.8	7.6	7.6	7.8	7.9	7.8	7.7	7.2	7.6	7.5	7.7
1992	7.1	7.1	6.9	7.5	7.5	7.2	7.1	7.1	7.1	7.0	7.0	7.0	7.1
1993	6.8	7.0	7.0	6.6	6.6	6.7	6.7	6.8	6.7	6.7	6.7	6.7	6.8
1994	6.5	6.5	6.6	6.5	6.5	6.5	7.1	7.1	7.0	6.9	6.9	6.9	6.8
1995	6.7	6.6	6.6	7.0	7.0	7.2	7.1	7.1	7.1	7.1	7.1	7.2	7.0
1996	7.4	7.4	7.4	7.5	7.6	7.6	7.5	7.5	7.4	7.4	7.4	7.4	7.5
1997	7.5	7.5	7.6	7.9	7.9	7.9	7.5	7.5	7.4	7.0	7.3	7.2	7.5
1998	7.3	7.2	7.2	7.3	7.3	7.4	7.3	7.3	7.2	7.1	7.2	7.2	7.3
1999	7.6	7.6	7.6	7.8	7.9	8.0	7.9	7.9	7.9	7.8	7.8	7.9	7.8
2000	7.7	7.7	7.6	7.5	7.5	7.5	7.5	7.5	7.4	7.4	7.5	7.6	7.5
2001	7.6	7.7	7.8	7.9	7.9	7.9	7.9	7.9	7.9	8.0	8.1	8.4	7.9
2002	8.4	8.5	8.5	8.5	8.5	8.5	8.6	8.7	8.7	8.7	8.7	8.8	8.6
2003	8.8	8.8	8.8	8.9	8.9	8.9	8.8	8.7	8.6	8.5	8.6	8.7	8.8
Professional and business services													
1990	11.3	11.2	11.6	11.6	11.8	11.7	11.4	11.4	11.4	11.3	11.3	11.2	11.4
1991	11.2	11.2	11.2	11.0	10.8	11.2	11.1	11.0	11.1	11.2	11.2	11.1	11.1
1992	10.2	10.3	10.3	10.6	10.6	10.8	11.3	11.5	11.7	11.6	11.5	11.5	11.0
1993	11.4	11.6	11.6	12.4	12.9	13.1	13.0	13.3	13.2	13.3	12.9	12.8	12.6
1994	13.0	13.2	13.3	13.4	13.6	13.8	12.8	12.9	13.0	13.1	13.1	12.7	13.2
1995	12.3	12.3	12.5	12.6	12.7	12.7	12.7	12.9	13.0	13.2	13.0	12.9	12.7
1996	12.3	12.3	12.4	12.0	12.1	12.2	11.8	11.9	11.8	11.7	12.0	12.1	12.1
1997	11.7	11.7	11.8	11.7	11.9	12.2	12.0	12.2	12.1	12.1	12.3	12.4	12.0
1998	12.5	12.6	12.8	13.0	12.9	13.2	13.2	13.3	13.2	13.2	13.2	13.4	13.0
1999	13.2	13.3	13.4	14.1	13.8	13.9	13.9	14.1	14.0	13.7	13.5	13.7	13.7
2000	13.8	13.7	13.8	14.4	14.3	14.8	14.5	14.4	14.5	14.4	14.4	14.6	14.3
2001	14.3	13.9	13.9	14.1	14.2	14.4	14.2	14.3	14.1	13.8	13.6	13.6	14.0
2002	12.9	12.7	12.7	12.6	12.7	12.9	13.2	13.5	13.6	13.5	13.6	13.5	13.1
2003	13.3	13.2	13.1	14.0	14.1	14.2	14.4	14.4	14.5	14.3	14.2	14.3	14.0
Educational and health services													
1990	10.5	10.4	10.8	10.6	10.5	10.4	10.4	10.6	10.7	10.8	10.8	10.8	10.6
1991	10.6	10.8	10.8	10.9	10.7	10.6	10.4	10.2	10.7	10.9	10.9	10.9	10.7
1992	10.5	10.7	10.8	10.7	10.7	10.6	10.4	10.4	10.7	10.8	10.8	10.8	10.7
1993	10.9	10.9	10.9	11.0	10.9	10.8	10.9	10.9	11.2	11.2	11.2	11.3	11.0
1994	11.3	11.4	11.5	11.6	11.7	11.7	11.5	11.4	11.9	12.0	12.1	12.1	11.7
1995	11.9	12.0	12.0	12.2	12.1	12.0	11.5	11.4	11.8	12.1	12.3	12.2	12.0
1996	12.7	12.9	12.9	12.8	12.6	12.5	12.5	12.6	13.1	13.2	13.3	13.2	12.9
1997	13.1	13.4	13.4	13.4	13.2	13.0	13.0	12.9	13.3	13.7	13.8	13.8	13.3
1998	13.4	13.7	13.8	13.8	13.8	13.3	13.2	13.1	13.7	13.7	13.8	13.7	13.6
1999	13.2	13.7	13.7	13.9	13.6	13.5	13.2	13.1	13.5	13.9	14.1	14.2	13.6
2000	14.4	14.7	14.9	14.9	14.7	14.7	14.6	14.8	15.1	15.3	15.4	15.4	14.9
2001	15.6	15.9	15.9	15.8	15.9	15.9	15.8	15.9	16.1	16.2	16.2	16.2	16.0
2002	16.2	16.3	16.5	16.4	16.2	16.2	15.8	16.0	16.2	16.4	16.4	16.2	16.2
2003	16.4	16.4	16.4	16.6	16.3	16.5	16.3	16.4	16.5	16.7	16.7	16.6	16.5

Employment by Industry: New Hampshire—*Continued*

(Numbers in thousands. Not seasonally adjusted.)

Industry	January	February	March	April	May	June	July	August	September	October	November	December	Annual Average
MANCHESTER—*Continued*													
Leisure and hospitality													
1990	5.7	5.6	5.9	5.8	6.0	6.1	5.8	5.8	5.8	5.8	5.8	5.6	5.8
1991	5.4	5.3	5.3	5.3	5.5	5.8	5.8	5.9	5.8	6.0	5.9	5.9	5.7
1992	5.5	5.5	5.5	5.9	6.1	6.0	6.3	6.3	6.2	6.2	6.1	6.1	6.0
1993	6.1	6.1	6.0	6.3	6.4	6.6	6.7	6.7	6.6	6.3	6.4	6.5	6.4
1994	6.2	6.0	6.1	6.2	6.4	6.4	6.8	6.8	6.5	6.6	6.6	6.7	6.4
1995	6.5	6.5	6.5	6.5	6.8	6.8	6.8	6.8	6.5	6.5	6.6	6.5	6.6
1996	6.2	6.4	6.5	6.5	6.7	6.9	6.7	6.8	6.5	6.5	6.5	6.5	6.6
1997	6.5	6.4	6.5	6.7	7.0	7.1	7.2	7.2	7.1	7.1	7.1	7.2	6.9
1998	7.1	7.1	7.1	7.4	7.6	7.7	7.8	7.8	7.5	7.7	7.9	7.9	7.6
1999	7.5	7.5	7.6	7.7	7.9	8.0	8.0	8.1	7.7	8.0	7.9	7.9	7.8
2000	7.6	7.7	7.8	7.9	7.9	8.2	8.4	8.4	8.1	8.1	8.3	8.3	8.1
2001	8.3	8.2	8.3	8.5	8.7	8.8	8.8	8.8	8.7	8.4	8.4	8.5	8.5
2002	8.2	8.2	8.4	8.9	8.9	9.1	9.1	9.2	8.8	8.9	9.0	9.1	8.8
2003	8.2	8.2	8.3	8.6	8.8	8.9	8.9	8.9	8.6	8.5	8.4	8.7	8.6
Other services													
1990	3.4	3.3	3.4	3.3	3.3	3.3	3.3	3.2	3.2	3.2	3.2	3.2	3.3
1991	3.2	3.2	3.2	3.2	3.1	3.2	3.1	3.1	3.2	3.2	3.2	3.2	3.2
1992	3.5	3.5	3.6	3.5	3.5	3.5	3.5	3.6	3.5	3.6	3.6	3.7	3.6
1993	3.8	3.8	3.8	3.9	3.9	3.9	3.8	3.9	3.9	3.9	3.9	3.9	3.9
1994	3.9	4.0	4.0	3.9	3.9	4.0	3.9	4.0	4.0	4.0	4.0	4.0	4.0
1995	4.0	4.0	4.1	3.9	4.0	4.0	3.8	3.8	3.9	3.9	3.9	3.9	3.9
1996	3.9	3.9	3.9	3.9	3.9	3.9	3.9	3.8	3.8	3.8	3.9	3.9	3.9
1997	3.9	3.8	3.8	3.8	3.9	3.9	3.9	3.9	4.0	4.0	4.0	4.0	3.9
1998	3.9	4.0	4.0	4.1	4.2	4.3	4.2	4.3	4.2	4.3	4.4	4.4	4.2
1999	4.4	4.4	4.5	4.5	4.6	4.6	4.7	4.7	4.8	4.7	4.7	4.7	4.6
2000	4.7	4.6	4.6	4.6	4.5	4.6	4.6	4.5	4.5	4.4	4.4	4.4	4.5
2001	4.4	4.5	4.5	4.6	4.5	4.6	4.6	4.5	4.5	4.5	4.5	4.5	4.5
2002	4.4	4.3	4.4	4.5	4.4	4.4	4.4	4.4	4.2	4.2	4.2	4.2	4.3
2003	4.2	4.2	4.3	4.3	4.3	4.3	4.3	4.3	4.2	4.3	4.3	4.3	4.3
Government													
1990	9.8	9.7	9.7	9.7	9.7	9.8	8.9	8.8	10.0	9.5	9.6	9.8	9.6
1991	9.6	9.7	9.6	9.5	9.6	9.5	8.6	8.6	9.5	9.5	9.7	9.9	9.4
1992	9.7	9.7	9.7	9.6	9.6	9.4	8.7	8.6	9.6	9.8	10.0	10.1	9.5
1993	9.9	10.0	10.0	9.9	10.0	9.8	9.2	9.3	9.9	9.9	10.1	10.4	9.9
1994	10.1	10.1	10.2	10.4	10.4	10.3	9.3	9.3	10.2	10.2	10.3	10.8	10.1
1995	10.3	10.4	10.3	10.4	10.4	10.2	9.3	9.4	10.3	10.6	10.2	10.5	10.2
1996	10.4	10.6	10.6	10.5	10.5	10.4	9.5	9.3	10.4	10.7	11.0	11.3	10.4
1997	10.7	10.7	10.7	10.6	10.7	10.6	9.5	9.6	10.7	11.0	11.2	11.7	10.6
1998	11.0	11.2	11.2	11.1	11.1	11.0	9.9	9.5	11.0	11.1	11.3	11.4	10.9
1999	11.3	11.3	11.5	11.3	11.2	11.0	9.8	9.4	11.2	11.4	11.6	11.9	11.1
2000	11.7	11.9	11.9	11.8	11.9	11.5	10.4	10.1	11.5	11.7	11.8	11.6	11.5
2001	11.7	12.0	11.9	11.8	11.9	11.5	10.7	10.6	11.9	12.1	12.3	12.1	11.7
2002	12.1	12.5	12.5	12.4	12.4	12.1	10.4	10.2	11.8	12.5	12.7	12.6	12.0
2003	12.2	12.6	12.6	12.5	12.6	12.4	11.1	10.9	12.5	12.7	12.9	12.8	12.3
Federal government													
1990	2.5	2.5	2.5	2.5	2.5	2.6	2.6	2.6	2.6	2.5	2.5	2.7	2.6
1991	2.6	2.6	2.6	2.6	2.6	2.6	2.6	2.6	2.6	2.6	2.6	2.7	2.6
1992	2.7	2.6	2.6	2.6	2.6	2.6	2.6	2.6	2.6	2.5	2.5	2.7	2.6
1993	2.5	2.5	2.5	2.5	2.5	2.5	2.5	2.6	2.6	2.5	2.5	2.8	2.5
1994	2.5	2.5	2.5	2.5	2.5	2.6	2.6	2.5	2.5	2.5	2.5	2.9	2.6
1995	2.6	2.6	2.6	2.6	2.6	2.6	2.6	2.6	2.6	2.6	2.6	3.0	2.6
1996	2.6	2.6	2.6	2.6	2.6	2.6	2.6	2.6	2.6	2.6	2.6	3.0	2.6
1997	2.6	2.5	2.5	2.5	2.5	2.5	2.5	2.5	2.5	2.6	2.7	3.2	2.6
1998	2.6	2.6	2.6	2.6	2.6	2.6	2.6	2.6	2.6	2.6	2.7	2.8	2.6
1999	2.6	2.6	2.6	2.7	2.6	2.6	2.6	2.6	2.6	2.6	2.6	2.8	2.6
2000	2.6	2.7	2.7	2.7	2.8	2.7	2.7	2.6	2.6	2.6	2.6	2.7	2.7
2001	2.6	2.6	2.6	2.6	2.5	2.5	2.5	2.5	2.5	2.5	2.5	2.6	2.5
2002	2.5	2.5	2.5	2.5	2.5	2.5	2.5	2.6	2.6	2.6	2.6	2.7	2.6
2003	2.6	2.6	2.6	2.6	2.6	2.6	2.6	2.5	2.5	2.5	2.5	2.5	2.6
State government													
1990	0.9	0.9	0.9	0.8	0.8	0.8	0.8	0.8	0.8	0.8	0.8	0.8	0.8
1991	0.9	0.9	0.9	0.9	0.9	0.9	0.9	0.9	0.9	0.9	0.9	0.9	0.9
1992	0.9	0.9	0.9	0.9	0.9	0.9	0.9	0.9	1.0	1.0	0.9	0.9	0.9
1993	1.1	1.2	1.4	1.2	1.3	1.2	1.2	1.2	1.3	1.3	1.3	1.3	1.3
1994	1.1	1.1	1.2	1.2	1.2	1.1	1.1	1.1	1.2	1.2	1.2	1.2	1.2
1995	1.1	1.1	1.1	1.1	1.1	1.1	1.0	1.1	1.2	1.1	1.1	1.1	1.1
1996	1.1	1.1	1.1	1.1	1.2	1.1	1.1	1.0	1.1	1.1	1.1	1.2	1.1
1997	1.1	1.2	1.2	1.1	1.2	1.1	1.1	1.1	1.2	1.2	1.2	1.2	1.2
1998	1.1	1.2	1.2	1.2	1.2	1.1	1.1	1.1	1.2	1.2	1.2	1.2	1.2
1999	1.2	1.2	1.3	1.2	1.2	1.2	1.2	1.1	1.2	1.3	1.3	1.2	1.2
2000	1.2	1.3	1.3	1.2	1.2	1.2	1.2	1.1	1.3	1.3	1.3	1.2	1.2
2001	1.1	1.3	1.3	1.2	1.3	1.2	1.2	1.2	1.3	1.4	1.4	1.3	1.3
2002	1.2	1.4	1.4	1.4	1.4	1.3	1.3	1.2	1.3	1.3	1.3	1.3	1.3
2003	1.3	1.4	1.4	1.4	1.4	1.3	1.5	1.5	1.4	1.6	1.5	1.5	1.4

Employment by Industry: New Hampshire—*Continued*

(Numbers in thousands. Not seasonally adjusted.)

Industry	January	February	March	April	May	June	July	August	September	October	November	December	Annual Average
MANCHESTER—*Continued*													
Local government													
1990	6.4	6.3	6.3	6.4	6.4	6.4	5.5	5.4	6.6	6.2	6.3	6.3	6.2
1991	6.1	6.2	6.1	6.0	6.1	6.0	5.1	5.1	6.0	6.0	6.2	6.3	5.9
1992	6.1	6.2	6.2	6.1	6.1	5.9	5.2	5.1	6.0	6.3	6.6	6.5	6.0
1993	6.3	6.3	6.1	6.2	6.2	6.1	5.5	5.5	6.0	6.1	6.3	6.3	6.1
1994	6.5	6.5	6.5	6.7	6.7	6.6	5.6	5.7	6.5	6.5	6.6	6.7	6.4
1995	6.6	6.7	6.6	6.7	6.7	6.5	5.7	5.7	6.5	6.9	6.5	6.4	6.5
1996	6.7	6.9	6.9	6.8	6.7	6.7	5.8	5.7	6.7	7.0	7.3	7.1	6.7
1997	7.0	7.0	7.0	7.0	7.0	7.0	5.9	6.0	7.0	7.2	7.3	7.3	6.9
1998	7.3	7.4	7.4	7.3	7.3	7.3	6.2	5.8	7.2	7.3	7.4	7.4	7.1
1999	7.5	7.5	7.6	7.4	7.4	7.2	6.0	5.7	7.4	7.5	7.7	7.9	7.2
2000	7.9	7.9	7.9	7.9	7.9	7.6	6.5	6.4	7.6	7.8	7.9	7.7	7.6
2001	8.0	8.1	8.0	8.0	8.1	7.8	7.0	6.9	8.1	8.2	8.4	8.2	7.9
2002	8.4	8.6	8.6	8.5	8.5	8.3	6.6	6.4	7.9	8.6	8.8	8.6	8.2
2003	8.3	8.6	8.6	8.5	8.6	8.5	7.0	6.9	8.6	8.6	8.9	8.8	8.3
PORTSMOUTH-DOVER-ROCHESTER													
Total nonfarm													
1990	103.3	103.0	103.6	104.6	106.1	107.6	104.4	105.5	107.0	104.0	103.7	102.5	104.6
1991	95.5	96.5	97.1	97.8	100.1	101.3	98.1	100.5	102.1	100.8	100.5	101.0	99.3
1992	96.9	96.7	97.3	99.7	101.8	101.6	99.4	100.7	103.0	101.7	101.7	101.5	100.2
1993	96.4	98.4	99.1	101.6	102.9	103.7	103.6	104.2	106.7	104.5	104.8	104.2	102.5
1994	99.5	101.7	102.3	105.3	106.2	107.5	107.1	108.1	109.8	108.1	108.2	108.3	106.0
1995	103.5	105.4	106.2	107.9	109.1	111.4	111.3	112.0	113.6	112.6	112.6	113.4	109.9
1996	106.2	107.4	108.4	110.3	112.3	114.1	113.1	114.0	113.9	114.5	114.2	115.0	112.0
1997	109.1	110.5	111.2	115.4	117.7	118.6	115.8	116.3	117.0	116.4	116.2	116.7	115.1
1998	112.4	114.2	114.3	115.8	118.0	118.0	117.0	118.0	118.9	118.3	117.7	118.3	116.7
1999	113.2	114.9	114.9	118.5	120.4	121.3	121.3	121.9	122.6	122.2	122.0	122.2	119.6
2000	118.5	120.2	121.3	124.4	126.5	126.2	125.4	125.0	126.1	125.4	126.1	125.9	124.3
2001	123.6	124.1	123.7	125.7	128.0	128.1	127.8	127.7	126.5	126.3	126.0	125.2	126.1
2002	120.3	121.5	122.4	124.9	126.3	126.4	126.9	126.9	127.0	125.8	125.8	125.8	125.0
2003	119.5	121.1	121.8	123.1	125.3	125.8	125.1	125.6	125.5	126.4	126.3	126.4	124.3
Total private													
1990	77.5	76.8	76.9	77.6	79.2	81.9	81.4	82.1	80.9	77.7	76.8	76.0	78.7
1991	71.5	70.3	70.6	71.9	74.4	76.7	76.0	77.9	77.2	75.2	74.3	74.8	74.2
1992	71.6	70.8	71.2	74.0	76.2	78.3	78.0	79.0	78.7	76.9	76.8	76.6	75.7
1993	74.6	74.3	74.5	76.9	78.9	81.6	82.2	83.2	82.2	81.1	81.5	81.8	79.4
1994	78.5	78.9	79.4	82.3	83.8	86.5	87.5	88.8	88.1	86.0	85.9	86.0	84.3
1995	83.2	83.2	84.1	86.6	88.5	91.2	92.2	93.0	92.2	89.9	89.9	90.6	88.7
1996	85.6	85.7	86.4	88.4	90.9	93.4	92.9	93.9	91.7	91.3	90.7	91.4	90.2
1997	88.2	88.4	89.1	92.6	95.2	98.1	95.2	97.0	95.9	94.4	94.0	95.2	93.6
1998	91.7	92.2	92.6	93.7	96.0	98.0	97.9	98.8	97.4	96.1	95.4	96.5	95.5
1999	92.1	92.6	92.8	96.0	98.0	100.8	101.8	102.5	101.1	99.8	99.3	100.2	98.1
2000	96.7	97.1	98.2	100.9	102.7	105.2	105.5	105.4	103.9	102.1	102.3	103.1	101.9
2001	101.0	100.6	100.4	102.0	104.3	106.1	107.0	107.3	103.6	102.3	101.8	101.4	103.2
2002	97.7	97.2	98.0	100.5	102.3	104.0	105.3	105.8	103.2	101.1	100.5	101.0	101.4
2003	96.2	96.0	96.7	98.1	100.9	103.2	103.9	104.4	102.4	101.0	100.7	100.9	100.4
Goods-producing													
1990	19.5	19.6	19.4	19.5	19.7	20.0	18.9	19.8	19.5	19.1	18.8	18.7	19.4
1991	17.9	17.4	17.4	17.6	18.2	18.7	17.1	18.5	18.6	18.3	18.0	18.2	18.0
1992	17.0	16.8	16.7	17.3	17.6	17.7	16.7	17.6	17.7	17.7	17.6	17.4	17.3
1993	17.1	16.9	16.9	17.2	17.7	18.0	17.3	17.8	17.7	18.3	18.4	18.4	17.6
1994	17.7	17.7	17.7	17.9	18.2	18.5	18.1	18.7	18.8	19.0	19.2	19.2	18.4
1995	19.0	18.9	19.2	19.5	19.8	20.1	19.2	19.7	19.9	19.6	19.7	19.8	19.5
1996	18.7	18.7	18.8	18.8	19.0	19.4	18.6	19.5	19.3	19.2	19.0	19.1	19.0
1997	18.9	18.8	19.0	19.7	20.0	20.4	18.2	19.9	19.9	19.8	19.6	20.0	19.5
1998	19.4	19.5	19.6	19.9	20.2	20.4	19.5	20.6	20.6	20.6	20.4	20.3	20.1
1999	19.4	19.3	19.4	19.9	20.3	20.6	20.0	20.5	20.6	20.7	20.7	20.6	20.2
2000	20.4	20.4	20.7	20.9	21.1	21.3	21.1	21.5	21.5	21.1	21.1	21.4	21.0
2001	21.2	21.2	21.2	21.3	21.4	21.2	20.6	20.9	20.5	20.0	19.7	19.1	20.7
2002	18.3	18.2	18.2	18.2	18.2	18.2	18.1	18.3	17.8	17.6	17.4	17.6	18.0
2003	16.8	16.5	16.6	16.8	17.0	17.3	17.0	17.4	17.2	16.9	16.8	16.6	16.9
Construction and mining													
1990	3.2	3.0	3.0	3.2	3.4	3.5	3.6	3.6	3.5	3.3	3.2	2.9	3.3
1991	2.4	2.2	2.2	2.3	2.5	2.7	2.7	2.7	2.7	2.6	2.5	2.4	2.5
1992	2.1	2.0	1.9	2.2	2.4	2.5	2.6	2.6	2.6	2.6	2.5	2.4	2.4
1993	2.0	2.0	1.9	2.2	2.4	2.6	2.8	2.7	2.6	2.7	2.6	2.5	2.4
1994	2.1	2.0	2.0	2.4	2.6	2.8	3.0	3.0	3.0	2.9	2.9	2.8	2.6
1995	2.5	2.4	2.6	2.9	3.1	3.4	3.4	3.3	3.3	3.2	3.2	3.1	3.0
1996	2.7	2.7	2.7	2.9	3.1	3.3	3.4	3.5	3.3	3.3	3.2	3.1	3.1
1997	2.9	2.8	2.9	3.1	3.3	3.5	3.5	3.5	3.5	3.4	3.3	3.3	3.3
1998	3.1	3.1	3.2	3.5	3.8	4.0	4.2	4.3	4.2	4.3	4.1	4.0	3.8
1999	3.4	3.4	3.5	3.8	4.2	4.3	4.2	4.2	4.1	4.1	4.1	3.9	3.9
2000	3.7	3.7	3.8	3.8	3.9	4.1	4.2	4.2	4.1	3.9	3.9	4.0	3.9
2001	3.8	3.8	3.8	4.0	4.2	4.3	4.5	4.4	4.3	4.3	4.3	4.3	4.2
2002	4.2	4.1	4.1	4.3	4.4	4.5	4.5	4.6	4.4	4.4	4.4	4.4	4.4
2003	4.0	3.9	4.0	4.2	4.4	4.7	4.8	4.8	4.7	4.6	4.6	4.5	4.4

Employment by Industry: New Hampshire—*Continued*

(Numbers in thousands. Not seasonally adjusted.)

Industry	January	February	March	April	May	June	July	August	September	October	November	December	Annual Average
PORTSMOUTH-DOVER-ROCHESTER—*Continued*													
Manufacturing													
1990	16.3	16.6	16.4	16.3	16.3	16.5	15.3	16.2	16.0	15.8	15.6	15.8	16.1
1991	15.5	15.2	15.2	15.3	15.7	16.0	14.4	15.8	15.9	15.7	15.5	15.8	15.5
1992	14.9	14.8	14.8	15.1	15.2	15.2	14.1	15.0	15.1	15.1	15.1	15.0	15.0
1993	15.1	14.9	15.0	15.0	15.3	15.4	14.5	15.1	15.1	15.6	15.8	15.9	15.2
1994	15.6	15.7	15.7	15.5	15.6	15.7	15.1	15.7	15.8	16.1	16.3	16.4	15.8
1995	16.5	16.5	16.6	16.6	16.7	16.7	15.8	16.4	16.6	16.4	16.5	16.7	16.5
1996	16.0	16.0	16.1	15.9	15.9	16.1	15.2	16.0	16.0	15.9	15.8	16.0	15.9
1997	16.0	16.0	16.1	16.6	16.7	16.9	14.7	16.4	16.4	16.4	16.3	16.7	16.3
1998	16.3	16.4	16.4	16.4	16.4	16.4	15.3	16.3	16.4	16.3	16.3	16.3	16.3
1999	16.0	15.9	15.9	16.1	16.1	16.3	15.8	16.3	16.5	16.6	16.6	16.7	16.2
2000	16.7	16.7	16.9	17.1	17.2	17.2	16.9	17.3	17.4	17.2	17.2	17.4	17.1
2001	17.4	17.4	17.4	17.3	17.2	16.9	16.1	16.5	16.2	15.7	15.4	14.8	16.5
2002	14.1	14.1	14.1	13.9	13.8	13.7	13.6	13.7	13.4	13.2	13.0	13.2	13.7
2003	12.8	12.6	12.6	12.6	12.6	12.6	12.2	12.6	12.5	12.3	12.2	12.1	12.5
Service-providing													
1990	83.8	83.4	84.2	85.1	86.4	87.6	85.5	85.7	87.5	84.9	84.9	83.8	85.2
1991	77.6	79.1	79.7	80.2	81.9	82.6	81.0	82.0	83.5	82.5	82.5	82.8	81.3
1992	79.9	79.9	80.6	82.4	84.2	83.9	82.7	83.1	85.3	84.0	84.1	84.1	82.9
1993	79.3	81.5	82.2	84.4	85.2	85.7	86.3	86.4	89.0	86.2	86.4	85.8	84.9
1994	81.8	84.0	84.6	87.4	88.0	89.0	89.0	89.4	91.0	89.1	89.0	89.1	87.6
1995	84.5	86.5	87.0	88.4	89.3	91.3	92.1	92.3	93.7	93.0	92.9	93.6	90.4
1996	87.5	88.7	89.6	91.5	93.3	94.7	94.5	94.5	94.6	95.3	95.2	95.9	92.9
1997	90.2	91.7	92.2	95.7	97.7	98.2	97.6	96.4	97.1	96.6	96.6	96.7	95.6
1998	93.0	94.7	94.7	95.9	97.8	97.6	97.5	97.4	98.3	97.7	97.3	98.0	96.7
1999	93.8	95.6	95.5	98.6	100.1	100.7	101.3	101.4	102.0	101.5	101.3	101.6	99.5
2000	98.1	99.8	100.6	103.5	105.4	104.9	104.3	103.5	104.6	104.3	105.0	104.5	103.2
2001	102.4	102.9	102.5	104.4	106.6	106.9	107.2	106.8	106.0	106.3	106.3	106.1	105.4
2002	102.0	103.3	104.2	106.7	108.1	108.2	108.8	108.6	109.2	108.2	108.4	108.2	107.0
2003	102.7	104.6	105.2	106.3	108.3	108.5	108.1	108.2	108.3	109.5	109.5	109.8	107.4
Trade, transportation, and utilities													
1990	20.3	19.5	19.4	19.2	19.5	20.2	20.3	20.3	20.1	19.6	19.8	19.7	19.8
1991	18.3	17.5	17.5	17.3	17.9	18.3	18.7	19.0	18.7	18.5	18.6	19.1	18.3
1992	18.0	17.5	17.5	18.0	18.5	18.9	19.3	19.5	19.5	19.1	19.6	20.0	18.8
1993	18.9	18.5	18.6	18.9	19.1	19.9	20.2	20.4	20.2	20.1	20.6	20.8	19.7
1994	19.5	19.4	19.4	20.7	21.0	21.5	21.7	22.1	21.9	21.6	22.1	21.8	21.1
1995	20.9	20.5	20.6	21.1	21.3	22.0	22.1	22.1	22.1	22.0	22.6	23.1	21.7
1996	21.9	21.7	21.6	21.9	22.3	22.8	22.7	22.6	22.3	22.8	23.4	23.9	22.5
1997	22.2	22.0	22.0	22.8	23.4	23.9	23.4	23.2	23.4	23.4	24.0	24.3	23.2
1998	22.8	22.5	22.6	22.6	23.0	23.2	23.4	23.6	23.4	23.7	24.3	25.0	23.3
1999	23.6	23.6	23.6	23.9	24.3	24.9	25.1	25.2	25.1	25.1	25.6	26.3	24.7
2000	24.8	24.5	24.5	25.6	25.6	26.0	25.7	25.6	25.5	25.5	26.2	26.7	25.5
2001	25.5	25.2	25.0	25.4	25.9	26.2	26.2	26.3	25.9	26.1	26.4	26.8	25.9
2002	25.5	25.0	25.1	25.8	26.0	26.3	26.5	26.6	26.1	25.8	26.1	26.7	26.0
2003	24.7	24.4	24.6	24.8	25.3	25.6	25.5	25.5	25.4	25.3	26.1	26.7	25.3
Wholesale trade													
1990	3.5	3.5	3.5	3.5	3.5	3.6	3.6	3.6	3.5	3.4	3.4	3.3	3.5
1991	3.0	3.0	3.0	2.9	2.9	2.9	2.9	2.9	2.9	3.0	3.0	3.0	3.0
1992	2.8	2.8	2.8	2.9	3.0	3.1	3.0	3.1	3.1	3.1	3.1	3.1	3.0
1993	2.9	2.9	2.9	3.0	3.0	3.1	3.1	3.2	3.2	3.1	3.1	3.1	3.1
1994	3.0	3.1	3.1	3.4	3.5	3.6	3.6	3.6	3.6	3.5	3.5	3.5	3.4
1995	3.4	3.4	3.4	3.7	3.7	3.7	3.7	3.7	3.7	3.7	3.7	3.8	3.6
1996	3.8	3.8	3.9	3.8	3.9	4.0	4.0	4.0	3.9	4.1	4.1	4.1	4.0
1997	4.0	4.1	4.1	4.2	4.3	4.4	4.2	4.2	4.2	4.2	4.2	4.2	4.2
1998	4.1	4.1	4.1	4.0	4.1	4.0	4.1	4.1	4.0	4.0	4.0	4.1	4.1
1999	4.1	4.2	4.2	4.2	4.2	4.3	4.4	4.4	4.4	4.3	4.3	4.4	4.3
2000	4.2	4.2	4.2	4.5	4.7	4.8	4.8	4.7	4.8	4.7	4.8	4.8	4.6
2001	4.8	4.8	4.8	4.9	5.0	5.0	5.0	5.0	4.8	4.8	4.6	4.6	4.8
2002	4.5	4.5	4.5	4.5	4.3	4.3	4.3	4.3	4.2	4.2	4.2	4.2	4.3
2003	4.1	4.2	4.2	4.3	4.3	4.4	4.3	4.4	4.4	4.3	4.3	4.4	4.3
Retail trade													
1990	15.1	14.3	14.2	14.0	14.2	14.7	14.9	14.9	14.8	14.6	14.8	14.8	14.6
1991	13.7	12.9	12.9	12.8	13.2	13.5	13.8	14.1	13.9	13.8	14.0	14.4	13.6
1992	13.6	13.1	13.1	13.5	13.8	14.1	14.4	14.5	14.5	14.3	14.8	15.2	14.1
1993	14.2	13.8	13.8	14.0	14.2	14.6	14.8	14.9	14.9	14.8	15.3	15.5	14.6
1994	14.5	14.2	14.2	14.6	14.8	15.0	15.1	15.4	15.4	15.3	15.8	16.0	15.0
1995	15.1	14.7	14.8	15.0	15.2	15.7	15.8	15.9	15.8	15.7	16.3	16.7	15.6
1996	15.7	15.5	15.4	15.7	15.9	16.3	16.2	16.2	16.0	16.3	16.9	17.4	16.1
1997	16.0	15.7	15.7	16.3	16.7	17.1	16.9	16.8	16.8	16.9	17.5	17.8	16.7
1998	16.4	16.1	16.2	16.3	16.6	16.8	16.9	17.1	17.0	17.3	17.9	18.4	16.9
1999	17.1	17.0	17.0	17.2	17.5	17.9	18.1	18.2	18.0	18.1	18.6	19.2	17.8
2000	17.9	17.6	17.6	18.4	18.2	18.4	18.3	18.3	18.0	18.1	18.7	19.3	18.2
2001	18.2	17.8	17.6	17.9	18.2	18.4	18.5	18.6	18.5	18.7	19.2	19.7	18.4
2002	18.5	18.0	18.1	18.7	19.0	19.3	19.5	19.6	19.1	19.0	19.4	20.0	19.0
2003	18.2	17.8	18.0	18.0	18.4	18.6	18.7	18.6	18.5	18.6	19.4	19.9	18.6

Employment by Industry: New Hampshire—*Continued*

(Numbers in thousands. Not seasonally adjusted.)

Industry	January	February	March	April	May	June	July	August	September	October	November	December	Annual Average
PORTSMOUTH-DOVER-ROCHESTER—*Continued*													
Transportation and utilities													
1990	1.7	1.7	1.7	1.7	1.8	1.9	1.8	1.8	1.8	1.6	1.6	1.6	1.7
1991	1.6	1.6	1.6	1.6	1.8	1.9	2.0	2.0	1.9	1.7	1.6	1.7	1.8
1992	1.6	1.6	1.6	1.6	1.7	1.7	1.9	1.9	1.9	1.7	1.7	1.7	1.7
1993	1.8	1.8	1.9	1.9	1.9	2.2	2.3	2.3	2.1	2.2	2.2	2.2	2.1
1994	2.0	2.1	2.1	2.7	2.7	2.9	3.0	3.1	2.9	2.8	2.8	2.3	2.6
1995	2.4	2.4	2.4	2.4	2.4	2.6	2.6	2.5	2.6	2.6	2.6	2.6	2.5
1996	2.4	2.4	2.3	2.4	2.5	2.5	2.5	2.4	2.4	2.4	2.4	2.4	2.4
1997	2.2	2.2	2.2	2.3	2.4	2.4	2.3	2.2	2.4	2.3	2.3	2.3	2.3
1998	2.3	2.3	2.3	2.3	2.3	2.4	2.4	2.4	2.4	2.4	2.4	2.5	2.4
1999	2.4	2.4	2.4	2.5	2.6	2.7	2.6	2.6	2.7	2.7	2.7	2.7	2.6
2000	2.7	2.7	2.7	2.7	2.7	2.8	2.6	2.6	2.7	2.7	2.7	2.6	2.7
2001	2.5	2.6	2.6	2.6	2.7	2.8	2.7	2.7	2.6	2.6	2.6	2.5	2.6
2002	2.5	2.5	2.5	2.6	2.7	2.7	2.7	2.7	2.8	2.6	2.5	2.5	2.6
2003	2.4	2.4	2.4	2.5	2.6	2.6	2.5	2.5	2.5	2.4	2.4	2.4	2.5
Information													
1990	1.3	1.3	1.3	1.3	1.4	1.4	1.4	1.4	1.3	1.4	1.4	1.3	1.4
1991	1.3	1.3	1.3	1.3	1.3	1.3	1.3	1.3	1.3	1.3	1.3	1.3	1.3
1992	1.4	1.4	1.4	1.4	1.5	1.5	1.5	1.4	1.5	1.5	1.5	1.5	1.5
1993	1.5	1.5	1.4	1.5	1.5	1.5	1.5	1.5	1.5	1.7	1.7	1.7	1.5
1994	1.6	1.7	1.7	1.8	1.8	1.8	1.8	1.8	1.8	1.8	1.9	1.9	1.8
1995	1.9	2.1	2.3	2.3	2.4	2.4	2.4	2.4	2.4	2.5	2.5	2.6	2.4
1996	2.5	2.5	2.5	2.6	2.7	2.7	2.7	2.7	2.7	2.7	2.7	2.8	2.7
1997	2.9	2.9	2.9	3.0	3.1	3.1	3.0	3.0	3.0	2.9	2.9	3.2	3.0
1998	3.3	3.3	3.3	3.3	3.3	3.3	3.2	3.2	3.2	3.3	3.2	3.2	3.3
1999	3.1	3.1	3.1	3.2	3.2	3.2	3.3	3.4	3.4	3.4	3.5	3.5	3.3
2000	3.4	3.5	3.6	3.5	3.6	3.7	3.6	3.4	3.6	3.5	3.5	3.5	3.5
2001	3.5	3.5	3.6	3.4	3.4	3.4	3.4	3.4	3.3	3.3	3.3	3.3	3.4
2002	3.3	3.3	3.3	3.3	3.3	3.2	3.2	3.2	3.2	3.2	3.3	3.2	3.3
2003	3.3	3.3	3.3	3.0	3.0	3.0	2.9	2.9	2.9	2.9	2.9	2.9	3.0
Financial activities													
1990	6.8	6.8	6.8	6.9	6.9	6.9	6.8	6.8	6.7	6.7	6.7	6.7	6.8
1991	6.5	6.5	6.5	6.5	6.6	6.7	6.6	6.6	6.5	6.5	6.5	6.6	6.6
1992	6.4	6.4	6.4	6.3	6.4	6.5	6.4	6.4	6.4	6.4	6.4	6.4	6.4
1993	6.4	6.4	6.4	6.4	6.5	6.5	6.5	6.5	6.4	6.4	6.4	6.4	6.4
1994	6.3	6.3	6.3	6.4	6.4	6.4	6.4	6.4	6.3	6.2	6.1	6.2	6.3
1995	6.2	6.2	6.1	6.1	6.2	6.3	6.3	6.2	6.2	6.1	6.1	6.2	6.2
1996	6.0	6.0	6.1	6.0	6.1	6.1	6.1	6.1	6.0	6.1	6.1	6.1	6.1
1997	6.2	6.3	6.3	6.5	6.6	6.7	6.6	6.7	6.5	6.6	6.5	6.6	6.5
1998	6.5	6.5	6.5	6.4	6.5	6.6	6.7	6.7	6.6	6.6	6.5	6.6	6.6
1999	6.7	6.7	6.7	6.8	6.8	7.0	7.1	7.1	7.0	6.8	6.7	6.8	6.9
2000	6.8	6.7	6.8	6.7	6.8	6.9	7.0	7.0	7.0	6.9	6.9	7.0	6.9
2001	7.0	6.9	6.9	7.0	7.0	7.1	7.2	7.3	7.0	7.0	7.1	7.1	7.1
2002	7.2	7.2	7.2	7.2	7.3	7.4	7.4	7.4	7.4	7.3	7.4	7.4	7.3
2003	7.5	7.6	7.6	7.6	7.6	7.8	7.7	7.6	7.6	7.5	7.6	7.6	7.6
Professional and business services													
1990	7.3	7.2	7.3	7.3	7.4	7.6	7.7	7.7	7.7	7.4	7.3	7.2	7.4
1991	6.6	6.6	6.7	6.8	7.0	7.0	7.0	7.2	7.3	7.1	7.1	6.9	6.9
1992	6.6	6.5	6.6	7.0	7.2	7.5	7.1	7.1	7.2	7.4	7.3	7.4	7.1
1993	7.6	7.9	8.0	8.1	8.4	8.7	8.7	8.8	9.0	8.7	8.7	8.9	8.5
1994	8.5	8.8	9.0	9.0	8.8	9.2	9.2	9.3	9.4	9.3	9.3	9.6	9.1
1995	9.7	9.8	9.3	9.4	9.5	9.7	9.7	10.1	10.0	10.0	10.2	10.3	9.8
1996	10.2	10.2	10.3	10.6	10.8	10.7	10.6	10.7	10.6	10.7	10.5	10.5	10.5
1997	10.1	10.2	10.2	10.8	10.8	10.8	10.7	10.8	10.9	10.9	11.1	11.2	10.7
1998	11.0	11.2	11.3	11.6	11.6	11.9	11.4	11.3	11.3	11.0	10.9	11.2	11.3
1999	10.7	10.8	10.7	11.2	11.1	11.3	11.4	11.5	11.5	11.5	11.5	11.7	11.2
2000	11.5	11.8	11.9	12.1	12.1	12.1	12.1	12.2	12.1	12.1	12.2	12.3	12.0
2001	12.4	12.2	12.1	12.1	12.4	12.5	12.5	12.5	12.0	11.9	11.8	11.7	12.2
2002	11.2	11.4	11.4	11.9	12.0	12.0	12.2	12.4	12.2	12.2	12.0	11.9	11.9
2003	11.5	11.5	11.5	12.1	12.3	12.5	12.8	13.0	13.0	12.9	12.6	12.6	12.4
Educational and health services													
1990	10.7	10.8	10.8	11.0	11.0	11.0	10.9	11.0	11.3	11.2	11.2	11.2	11.0
1991	10.8	10.8	10.8	10.9	11.0	11.0	10.9	10.9	11.1	11.1	11.1	11.2	11.0
1992	11.3	11.4	11.5	11.8	11.8	11.9	11.6	11.6	11.7	11.8	11.9	11.8	11.7
1993	12.0	12.0	12.0	12.3	12.3	12.3	12.4	12.3	12.5	12.5	12.7	12.8	12.3
1994	12.8	13.0	13.1	13.0	13.1	13.3	13.6	13.7	14.0	13.7	13.7	13.8	13.4
1995	13.2	13.2	13.5	14.1	14.2	14.1	14.6	14.6	15.0	14.6	14.6	14.8	14.2
1996	13.4	13.5	13.7	14.2	14.2	14.2	14.0	14.0	14.1	14.3	14.4	14.5	14.0
1997	14.4	14.5	14.7	14.9	15.0	15.1	14.6	14.8	14.9	14.7	14.8	14.9	14.8
1998	14.8	14.9	14.9	14.7	14.8	14.7	14.6	14.6	14.8	14.7	14.7	14.9	14.8
1999	14.2	14.4	14.6	15.1	15.2	15.1	15.3	15.3	15.4	15.5	15.6	15.7	15.1
2000	15.4	15.7	15.9	16.2	16.4	16.4	16.1	16.2	16.5	16.5	16.7	16.8	16.2
2001	16.7	16.9	16.8	16.8	16.9	16.9	16.9	17.0	17.1	17.1	17.2	17.3	17.0
2002	17.3	17.3	17.5	17.6	17.7	17.7	17.5	17.6	17.8	17.8	17.9	17.9	17.6
2003	17.7	17.9	18.0	17.9	18.1	18.1	18.0	18.1	18.2	18.3	18.4	18.5	18.1

Employment by Industry: New Hampshire—*Continued*

(Numbers in thousands. Not seasonally adjusted.)

Industry	January	February	March	April	May	June	July	August	September	October	November	December	Annual Average
PORTSMOUTH-DOVER-ROCHESTER—*Continued*													
Leisure and hospitality													
1990	8.1	8.1	8.4	8.9	9.8	11.3	12.1	11.9	11.2	9.2	8.6	8.3	9.7
1991	7.3	7.4	7.5	8.6	9.5	10.7	11.4	11.4	10.7	9.5	8.8	8.6	9.3
1992	7.8	7.8	8.0	9.0	10.0	11.0	12.1	12.1	11.4	9.8	9.3	8.9	9.8
1993	8.0	8.0	8.0	9.3	10.1	11.4	12.3	12.5	11.6	10.1	9.7	9.5	10.0
1994	8.8	8.7	8.9	10.2	11.1	12.3	13.2	13.3	12.5	11.0	10.2	10.1	10.9
1995	9.0	9.2	9.5	10.4	11.4	12.8	14.1	14.1	12.9	11.4	10.5	10.1	11.3
1996	9.3	9.5	9.8	10.7	12.1	13.7	14.5	14.6	13.0	11.8	11.0	10.9	11.7
1997	9.9	10.2	10.4	11.1	12.5	14.2	14.9	14.8	13.5	12.3	11.3	11.2	12.2
1998	9.9	10.3	10.4	11.1	12.5	13.9	15.1	14.8	13.5	12.1	11.3	11.2	12.2
1999	10.5	10.7	10.7	11.8	13.0	14.6	15.5	15.4	14.0	12.8	11.7	11.6	12.7
2000	10.5	10.6	10.9	11.9	13.1	14.7	15.9	15.6	13.7	12.6	11.8	11.5	12.7
2001	10.8	10.9	10.9	12.0	13.2	14.7	16.1	15.9	13.9	13.0	12.4	12.2	13.0
2002	11.1	11.0	11.5	12.6	13.8	15.2	16.4	16.2	14.6	13.3	12.6	12.5	13.4
2003	11.0	11.1	11.3	12.1	13.7	15.0	16.1	16.0	14.2	13.3	12.4	12.1	13.2
Other services													
1990	3.5	3.5	3.5	3.5	3.5	3.5	3.3	3.2	3.1	3.1	3.0	2.9	3.3
1991	2.8	2.8	2.9	2.9	2.9	3.0	3.0	3.0	3.0	2.9	2.9	2.9	2.9
1992	3.1	3.0	3.1	3.2	3.2	3.3	3.3	3.3	3.3	3.2	3.2	3.2	3.2
1993	3.1	3.1	3.2	3.2	3.3	3.3	3.3	3.4	3.3	3.3	3.3	3.3	3.3
1994	3.3	3.3	3.3	3.3	3.4	3.5	3.5	3.5	3.4	3.4	3.4	3.4	3.4
1995	3.3	3.3	3.6	3.7	3.7	3.8	3.8	3.8	3.7	3.7	3.7	3.7	3.7
1996	3.6	3.6	3.6	3.6	3.7	3.8	3.7	3.7	3.7	3.7	3.6	3.6	3.7
1997	3.6	3.5	3.6	3.8	3.8	3.9	3.8	3.8	3.8	3.8	3.8	3.8	3.8
1998	4.0	4.0	4.0	4.1	4.1	4.0	4.0	4.0	4.0	4.1	4.1	4.1	4.0
1999	3.9	4.0	4.0	4.1	4.1	4.1	4.1	4.1	4.1	4.0	4.0	4.0	4.0
2000	3.9	3.9	3.9	4.0	4.0	4.1	4.0	3.9	4.0	3.9	3.9	3.9	4.0
2001	3.9	3.8	3.9	4.0	4.1	4.1	4.1	4.0	3.9	3.9	3.9	3.9	4.0
2002	3.8	3.8	3.8	3.9	4.0	4.0	4.0	4.1	4.1	3.9	3.8	3.8	3.9
2003	3.7	3.7	3.8	3.8	3.9	3.9	3.9	3.9	3.9	3.9	3.9	3.9	3.9
Government													
1990	25.8	26.2	26.7	27.0	26.9	25.7	23.0	23.4	26.1	26.3	26.9	26.5	25.9
1991	24.0	26.2	26.5	25.9	25.7	24.6	22.1	22.6	24.9	25.6	26.2	26.2	25.0
1992	25.3	25.9	26.1	25.7	25.6	23.3	21.4	21.7	24.3	24.8	24.9	24.9	24.5
1993	21.8	24.1	24.6	24.7	24.0	22.1	21.4	21.0	24.5	23.4	23.3	22.4	23.1
1994	21.0	22.8	22.9	23.0	22.4	21.0	19.6	19.3	21.7	22.1	22.3	22.3	21.7
1995	20.3	22.2	22.1	21.3	20.6	20.2	19.1	19.0	21.4	22.7	22.7	22.8	21.2
1996	20.6	21.7	22.0	21.9	21.4	20.7	20.2	20.1	22.2	23.2	23.5	23.6	21.8
1997	20.9	22.1	22.1	22.8	22.5	20.5	20.6	19.3	21.1	22.0	22.2	21.5	21.5
1998	20.7	22.0	21.7	22.1	22.0	20.0	19.1	19.2	21.5	22.2	22.3	21.8	21.2
1999	21.1	22.3	22.1	22.5	22.4	20.5	19.5	19.4	21.5	22.4	22.7	22.0	21.5
2000	21.8	23.1	23.1	23.5	23.8	21.0	19.9	19.6	22.2	23.3	23.8	22.8	22.3
2001	22.6	23.5	23.3	23.7	23.7	22.0	20.8	20.4	22.9	24.0	24.2	23.8	22.9
2002	22.6	24.3	24.4	24.4	24.0	22.4	21.6	21.1	23.8	24.7	25.3	24.8	23.6
2003	23.3	25.1	25.1	25.0	24.4	22.6	21.2	21.2	23.1	25.4	25.6	25.5	24.0
Federal government													
1990	11.0	10.6	10.6	11.0	11.1	10.7	10.2	10.1	10.0	9.7	9.7	9.7	10.4
1991	9.3	9.4	9.5	8.9	8.8	8.8	8.6	8.6	8.7	8.5	8.6	8.7	8.9
1992	8.6	8.6	8.5	8.6	8.5	7.9	7.9	7.9	7.9	7.8	7.8	7.9	8.2
1993	7.7	7.7	7.7	7.7	7.2	7.2	7.1	7.1	7.1	7.0	6.8	6.5	7.2
1994	6.4	6.4	6.4	6.4	6.3	6.3	6.2	5.7	5.7	5.4	5.4	5.5	6.0
1995	5.6	5.7	5.6	5.6	5.5	5.5	5.4	5.4	5.4	5.4	5.4	5.5	5.5
1996	5.4	5.3	5.2	5.3	5.3	5.3	5.3	5.3	5.4	5.4	5.5	5.6	5.4
1997	5.4	5.4	5.4	5.4	5.3	5.3	5.3	5.2	5.2	5.1	5.1	5.2	5.3
1998	5.1	5.1	5.1	5.1	5.2	5.2	4.9	5.2	5.1	5.1	5.1	5.2	5.1
1999	5.1	5.1	5.1	5.2	5.2	5.2	5.2	5.3	5.2	5.2	5.2	5.3	5.2
2000	5.3	5.4	5.8	5.7	6.3	5.7	5.7	5.6	5.4	5.5	5.5	5.5	5.6
2001	5.6	5.5	5.5	5.5	5.5	5.6	5.7	5.7	5.7	5.7	5.7	5.7	5.6
2002	5.8	5.8	5.7	5.7	5.7	5.8	5.8	5.8	5.8	5.9	5.9	6.0	5.8
2003	5.9	6.1	6.1	6.0	5.9	5.9	5.9	5.9	5.9	6.0	5.9	6.0	6.0
State government													
1990	4.4	5.0	5.4	5.0	4.8	3.8	3.9	4.4	5.7	6.1	6.1	6.1	5.1
1991	4.2	6.1	6.4	6.2	6.2	4.8	4.5	5.1	6.2	6.6	6.8	6.8	5.8
1992	6.1	6.5	6.7	6.6	6.6	4.8	4.8	5.2	6.8	7.1	6.9	6.8	6.2
1993	4.5	6.8	7.1	7.0	6.7	4.8	5.4	5.3	7.6	7.1	7.0	6.4	6.3
1994	5.1	6.8	6.8	7.0	6.5	5.1	5.1	5.2	6.7	7.1	7.0	6.9	6.3
1995	5.2	6.8	6.8	6.3	5.8	5.2	5.4	5.4	6.9	7.6	7.5	7.4	6.4
1996	5.5	6.4	6.9	6.6	6.1	5.2	5.4	5.5	7.0	7.6	7.5	7.5	6.4
1997	5.5	6.5	6.4	6.6	6.3	4.6	5.7	4.7	6.0	6.6	6.5	5.8	5.9
1998	5.4	6.5	6.2	6.5	6.2	4.4	5.1	5.0	6.0	6.5	6.4	5.7	5.8
1999	5.4	6.4	6.2	6.5	6.2	4.4	4.7	4.6	5.8	6.4	6.4	5.7	5.7
2000	5.6	6.6	6.3	6.6	6.3	4.8	5.1	4.9	5.7	6.6	6.7	5.8	5.9
2001	5.7	6.6	6.3	6.7	6.5	4.8	5.2	5.0	5.9	6.7	6.7	6.2	6.0
2002	5.1	6.7	6.8	6.9	6.4	5.0	5.5	5.3	6.1	6.9	7.0	6.6	6.2
2003	5.5	6.9	6.9	7.0	6.4	5.0	5.0	5.2	5.9	7.5	7.6	7.5	6.4

Employment by Industry: New Hampshire—*Continued*

(Numbers in thousands. Not seasonally adjusted.)

Industry	January	February	March	April	May	June	July	August	September	October	November	December	Annual Average
PORTSMOUTH-DOVER-ROCHESTER—*Continued*													
Local government													
1990	10.4	10.6	10.7	11.0	11.0	11.2	8.9	8.9	10.4	10.5	11.1	10.7	10.5
1991	10.5	10.7	10.6	10.8	10.7	11.0	9.0	8.9	10.0	10.5	10.8	10.7	10.4
1992	10.6	10.8	10.9	10.5	10.5	10.6	8.7	8.6	9.6	9.9	10.2	10.2	10.1
1993	9.6	9.6	9.8	10.0	10.1	10.1	8.9	8.6	9.8	9.3	9.5	9.5	9.6
1994	9.5	9.6	9.7	9.6	9.6	9.6	8.3	8.4	9.3	9.6	9.9	9.9	9.4
1995	9.5	9.7	9.7	9.4	9.3	9.5	8.3	8.2	9.1	9.7	9.8	9.9	9.3
1996	9.7	10.0	9.9	10.0	10.0	10.2	9.5	9.3	9.8	10.2	10.5	10.5	10.0
1997	10.0	10.2	10.3	10.8	10.9	10.6	9.6	9.4	9.9	10.3	10.6	10.5	10.3
1998	10.2	10.4	10.4	10.5	10.6	10.4	9.1	9.0	10.4	10.6	10.8	10.9	10.3
1999	10.6	10.8	10.8	10.8	11.0	10.9	9.6	9.5	10.5	10.8	11.1	11.0	10.6
2000	10.9	11.1	11.0	11.2	11.2	10.5	9.1	9.1	11.1	11.2	11.6	11.5	10.8
2001	11.3	11.4	11.5	11.5	11.7	11.6	9.9	9.7	11.3	11.6	11.8	11.9	11.3
2002	11.7	11.8	11.9	11.8	11.9	11.6	10.3	10.0	11.9	11.9	12.4	12.2	11.6
2003	11.9	12.1	12.1	12.0	12.1	11.7	10.3	10.1	11.3	11.9	12.1	12.0	11.6

Average Weekly Hours by Industry: New Hampshire

(Not seasonally adjusted.)

Industry	January	February	March	April	May	June	July	August	September	October	November	December	Annual Average
STATEWIDE													
Manufacturing													
2001	41.7	41.7	41.9	40.1	40.0	40.0	39.8	40.4	40.6	40.3	40.2	40.5	40.6
2002	39.7	40.1	40.6	39.8	39.3	39.8	39.1	39.0	40.0	39.7	40.0	40.5	39.8
2003	40.0	40.4	40.5	39.9	39.8	40.0	39.4	39.4	40.2	39.6	40.5	40.6	40.0
MANCHESTER													
Manufacturing													
2001	39.5	39.9	39.3	38.3	38.2	39.0	39.1	40.7	39.6	39.6	39.5	40.4	39.4
2002	39.7	39.4	39.9	38.7	39.3	39.7	38.3	37.5	37.8	38.6	38.4	39.7	38.9
2003	38.6	39.3	39.6	38.8	38.9	39.4	39.6	39.8	40.5	39.7	38.4	37.6	39.2
PORTSMOUTH-DOVER-ROCHESTER													
Manufacturing													
2001	43.3	44.1	45.2	43.4	42.9	43.7	42.6	41.9	42.7	42.2	41.2	41.6	42.9
2002	42.2	43.6	44.2	42.4	43.0	43.1	40.9	42.3	43.1	42.6	42.1	43.7	42.8
2003	42.5	44.0	44.3	42.9	42.9	43.9	40.7	41.2	38.7	37.9	38.8	38.3	41.3

Average Hourly Earnings by Industry: New Hampshire

(Dollars, not seasonally adjusted.)

Industry	January	February	March	April	May	June	July	August	September	October	November	December	Annual Average
STATEWIDE													
Manufacturing													
2001	13.87	13.87	13.86	14.01	14.06	14.09	14.02	14.02	14.00	13.95	14.07	13.97	13.98
2002	13.94	13.91	13.84	13.98	13.96	14.02	14.01	14.27	14.60	14.53	14.59	14.87	14.21
2003	14.94	14.71	14.89	14.94	14.87	14.83	14.96	14.63	14.65	14.79	14.89	15.11	14.85
MANCHESTER													
Manufacturing													
2001	16.19	16.03	15.84	15.50	15.60	15.66	15.56	15.69	15.54	15.68	15.74	15.85	15.74
2002	16.06	16.03	15.87	15.76	15.87	16.05	15.54	15.61	15.99	15.96	15.73	15.76	15.86
2003	15.61	15.82	15.79	15.67	15.84	15.84	15.61	15.99	15.98	15.96	15.73	16.04	15.82
PORTSMOUTH-DOVER-ROCHESTER													
Manufacturing													
2001	14.64	14.56	14.57	14.71	14.76	14.93	15.05	14.97	15.01	15.12	15.58	15.27	14.91
2002	15.45	15.55	15.27	15.45	15.31	15.62	15.95	15.55	15.66	15.43	15.45	15.72	15.53
2003	16.02	15.24	15.10	15.28	15.01	15.13	14.88	14.63	14.81	14.92	15.25	15.41	15.14

Average Weekly Earnings by Industry: New Hampshire

(Dollars, not seasonally adjusted.)

Industry	January	February	March	April	May	June	July	August	September	October	November	December	Annual Average
STATEWIDE													
Manufacturing													
2001	578.38	578.38	580.73	561.80	562.40	563.60	558.00	566.41	568.40	562.19	565.61	565.79	567.59
2002	553.42	557.79	561.90	556.40	548.63	558.00	547.79	556.53	584.00	576.84	583.60	602.24	565.56
2003	597.60	594.28	603.05	596.11	591.83	593.20	589.42	576.42	588.93	585.68	603.05	613.47	594.00
MANCHESTER													
Manufacturing													
2001	639.51	639.60	622.51	593.65	595.92	610.74	608.40	638.58	615.38	620.93	621.73	640.34	620.16
2002	637.58	631.58	633.21	609.91	623.69	637.19	595.18	585.38	604.42	616.06	604.03	625.67	616.95
2003	602.55	621.73	625.28	608.00	616.18	624.10	618.16	636.40	647.19	633.61	604.03	603.10	620.14
PORTSMOUTH-DOVER-ROCHESTER													
Manufacturing													
2001	633.91	642.10	658.56	638.41	633.20	652.44	641.13	627.24	640.93	638.06	641.90	635.23	639.64
2002	651.99	677.98	674.93	655.08	658.33	673.22	652.36	657.77	674.95	657.32	650.45	686.96	664.68
2003	680.85	670.56	668.93	655.51	643.93	664.21	605.62	602.76	573.15	565.47	591.70	590.20	625.28

NEW JERSEY AT A GLANCE

(Population and total nonfarm employment numbers in thousands)

Population, Census 2000:	8,414.4
Total nonfarm employment, 2003:	3,980.3
Change in total nonfarm employment	
(Number)	
1990–2003:	345.2
1990–2001:	362.0
2001–2003:	-16.8
(Compound annual rate of change)	
1990–2003:	0.7%
1990–2001:	0.9%
2001–2003:	-0.2%
Unemployment rate	
1990:	5.1%
2001:	4.3%
2003:	5.9%

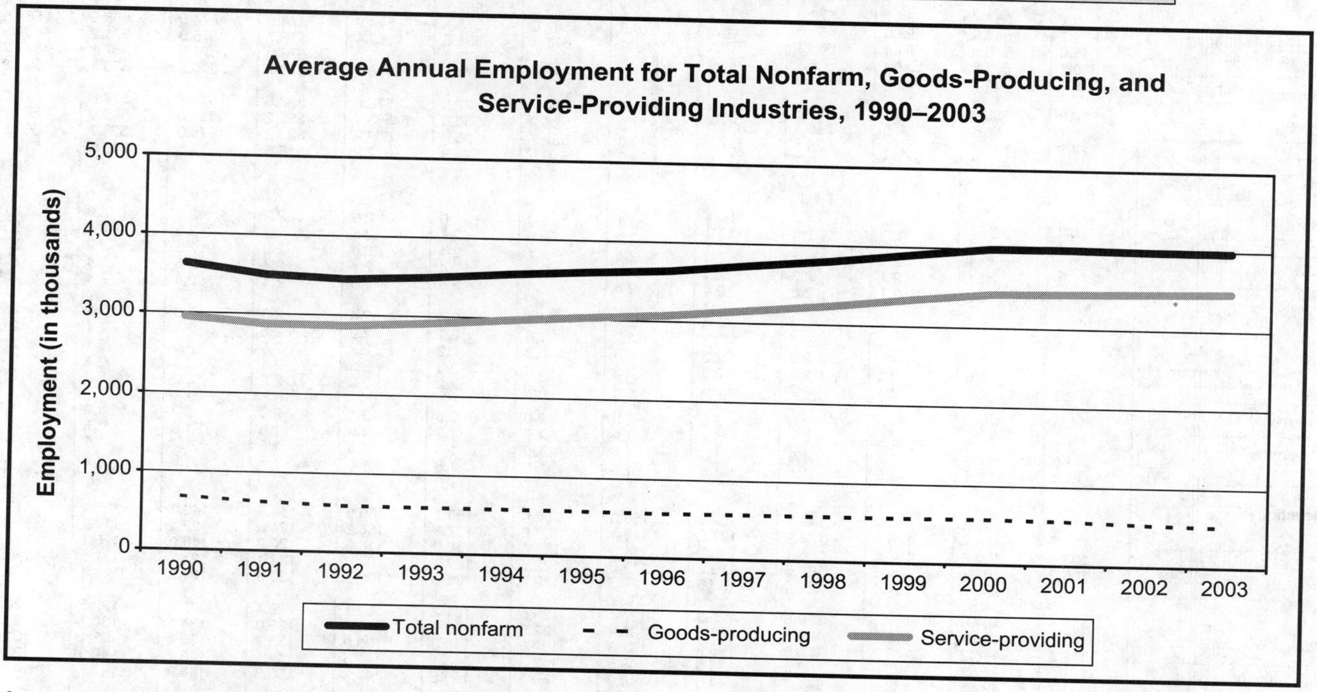

After a recovery from the 1990–1991 recession, total nonfarm payroll employment reached a plateau in 2001 and experienced small declines through 2003. This can be attributed to a drop in goods-producing industries and a sluggish performance in the service-providing sector. In the goods-producing sector, employment dropped from 573,000 in 2000 to 512,600 in 2003. During the same period, growth lagged in the service-providing sector, increasing by only 46,300 jobs.

Employment by Industry: New Jersey

(Numbers in thousands. Not seasonally adjusted.)

Industry	January	February	March	April	May	June	July	August	September	October	November	December	Annual Average
STATEWIDE													
Total nonfarm													
1990	3615.7	3620.2	3650.7	3642.7	3666.2	3711.3	3665.8	3653.1	3622.7	3599.2	3591.2	3582.4	3635.1
1991	3469.7	3464.6	3483.9	3493.3	3514.7	3551.4	3511.2	3502.2	3493.0	3493.6	3505.2	3501.4	3498.6
1992	3388.5	3392.4	3410.1	3428.3	3456.4	3503.9	3489.1	3480.3	3466.3	3486.0	3496.0	3496.9	3457.8
1993	3411.1	3419.2	3431.9	3466.0	3497.9	3545.9	3512.5	3510.5	3507.1	3527.1	3539.7	3547.2	3493.0
1994	3433.8	3430.6	3476.8	3523.3	3560.1	3611.2	3586.2	3588.9	3588.1	3599.3	3614.2	3620.8	3552.7
1995	3515.2	3520.8	3555.0	3580.5	3610.2	3653.0	3615.0	3621.0	3623.5	3630.4	3639.3	3643.1	3600.5
1996	3511.0	3547.2	3580.7	3599.6	3646.5	3699.5	3667.1	3666.0	3667.6	3676.1	3697.2	3708.8	3638.9
1997	3605.7	3622.6	3658.8	3688.4	3727.9	3781.4	3754.1	3741.2	3757.6	3769.6	3785.0	3801.8	3724.5
1998	3695.6	3707.9	3737.6	3771.5	3813.5	3857.2	3822.1	3812.0	3820.5	3844.1	3856.2	3877.1	3801.2
1999	3780.6	3802.9	3839.1	3876.1	3901.2	3954.0	3931.0	3919.3	3918.8	3943.2	3962.0	3985.0	3901.1
2000	3887.9	3896.4	3942.9	3975.9	4006.9	4060.6	4020.0	4002.5	4014.9	4017.6	4042.4	4066.5	3994.5
2001	3922.5	3931.9	3957.0	3994.2	4026.2	4073.3	4008.6	3990.9	3995.1	4010.2	4023.7	4032.5	3997.1
2002	3932.8	3940.2	3968.8	3982.7	4007.4	4042.7	3982.8	3970.8	3974.7	3983.2	4006.5	4014.6	3983.9
2003	3908.0	3898.5	3922.2	3956.4	3992.8	4031.8	4002.8	3983.7	3986.9	4014.8	4029.2	4036.4	3980.3
Total private													
1990	3048.9	3043.9	3071.4	3057.8	3078.0	3119.7	3094.3	3090.8	3062.3	3023.6	3009.8	2999.8	3058.3
1991	2899.2	2886.9	2902.4	2912.7	2935.5	2973.3	2950.0	2950.5	2940.2	2922.9	2927.7	2924.2	2927.1
1992	2822.1	2817.0	2830.8	2848.7	2882.0	2925.5	2919.2	2917.0	2913.1	2916.1	2919.3	2921.2	2886.0
1993	2843.9	2843.3	2851.7	2887.7	2923.2	2968.4	2955.8	2958.5	2953.8	2954.2	2959.3	2968.0	2922.3
1994	2866.7	2858.3	2898.4	2943.9	2982.4	3029.1	3021.6	3031.8	3029.7	3023.1	3031.6	3036.4	2979.4
1995	2944.9	2942.8	2973.2	2998.1	3030.2	3071.3	3053.5	3066.2	3065.7	3056.3	3060.2	3063.9	3027.1
1996	2946.0	2972.8	3001.7	3020.6	3070.9	3118.8	3105.3	3114.4	3110.6	3105.0	3120.7	3133.3	3068.3
1997	3041.2	3050.4	3083.6	3112.2	3153.0	3202.4	3196.1	3193.1	3199.0	3194.6	3204.9	3220.6	3154.2
1998	3126.6	3131.6	3157.4	3192.8	3237.8	3279.9	3267.2	3265.6	3259.0	3267.0	3275.1	3295.1	3229.5
1999	3209.8	3222.7	3254.8	3290.8	3319.6	3371.5	3370.1	3369.0	3352.5	3357.2	3370.8	3393.5	3323.5
2000	3307.4	3306.1	3346.9	3379.8	3406.3	3463.7	3451.2	3444.9	3439.0	3421.2	3439.2	3462.4	3405.6
2001	3330.1	3326.5	3350.1	3385.9	3419.5	3465.1	3431.4	3421.9	3400.4	3394.7	3400.8	3408.4	3394.5
2002	3320.8	3317.8	3343.0	3358.9	3384.4	3421.7	3397.7	3395.3	3376.2	3362.9	3378.7	3387.5	3370.4
2003	3291.6	3271.1	3291.4	3324.7	3361.6	3401.1	3399.2	3393.9	3377.7	3379.3	3385.8	3394.0	3356.0
Goods-producing													
1990	685.8	686.7	690.9	685.6	689.1	694.2	684.1	686.1	681.4	670.5	660.4	648.6	680.2
1991	617.3	614.4	617.5	625.0	630.0	635.9	624.8	629.2	629.6	626.2	621.4	609.7	623.4
1992	578.8	575.6	577.7	582.8	588.8	597.4	592.2	597.5	595.1	596.3	592.9	586.1	588.4
1993	565.2	563.7	566.2	573.0	581.3	588.9	585.8	590.9	593.6	593.7	590.3	585.7	581.5
1994	553.1	550.4	560.4	573.8	583.6	590.8	586.1	594.3	598.0	595.2	591.6	583.1	580.0
1995	560.1	557.7	564.1	572.5	577.3	585.7	575.8	582.3	584.6	583.3	578.4	569.1	574.2
1996	538.7	544.8	553.6	559.4	568.0	576.9	567.2	573.1	574.9	574.5	574.0	568.9	564.5
1997	545.6	546.8	554.4	565.1	572.5	581.4	577.1	581.5	582.4	578.7	575.8	571.2	569.3
1998	550.2	551.2	557.3	568.1	574.3	579.5	569.7	573.4	575.5	576.0	571.2	567.1	567.7
1999	549.1	551.7	556.3	566.0	570.2	577.4	572.5	574.2	576.2	576.7	575.5	573.1	568.2
2000	556.8	555.3	565.1	573.8	577.5	583.6	574.7	577.5	578.0	578.5	578.6	577.6	573.0
2001	554.7	556.1	560.5	566.4	571.3	574.5	564.2	566.0	563.4	559.2	554.6	549.9	561.7
2002	527.3	526.6	529.5	534.1	537.7	540.0	532.7	535.9	533.9	530.2	528.0	523.7	531.6
2003	503.7	498.3	501.0	510.7	517.0	520.9	519.5	520.3	517.9	516.6	514.5	510.6	512.6
Natural resources and mining													
1990	3.1	3.1	3.2	3.2	3.1	3.1	3.0	3.0	2.9	2.9	2.9	2.9	3.0
1991	2.4	2.4	2.5	2.6	2.6	2.6	2.5	2.5	2.5	2.5	2.5	2.4	2.5
1992	2.1	2.1	2.1	2.3	2.4	2.4	2.4	2.4	2.4	2.3	2.3	2.2	2.2
1993	2.1	2.1	2.1	2.3	2.4	2.4	2.4	2.4	2.4	2.4	2.5	2.4	2.3
1994	2.1	2.0	2.1	2.3	2.4	2.4	2.4	2.5	2.5	2.4	2.4	2.4	2.3
1995	2.1	2.0	2.1	2.3	2.4	2.4	2.4	2.4	2.4	2.3	2.3	2.2	2.2
1996	1.8	1.9	2.0	2.1	2.2	2.2	2.0	2.1	2.2	2.2	2.1	2.1	2.0
1997	1.9	1.9	2.0	2.2	2.3	2.3	2.2	2.2	2.3	2.3	2.3	2.1	2.1
1998	2.0	2.0	2.1	2.3	2.3	2.3	2.3	2.3	2.3	2.4	2.4	2.4	2.2
1999	2.1	2.1	2.1	2.2	2.3	2.3	2.2	2.2	2.2	2.2	2.2	2.2	2.1
2000	1.9	1.7	1.8	2.0	2.0	2.0	2.0	2.0	2.1	2.0	2.0	1.9	1.9
2001	1.6	1.5	1.6	1.8	1.8	1.9	1.9	1.9	1.9	1.8	1.8	1.8	1.7
2002	1.6	1.6	1.7	1.5	1.5	1.6	1.5	1.5	1.5	1.6	1.7	1.7	1.6
2003	1.4	1.4	1.5	1.5	1.6	1.6	1.6	1.6	1.6	1.6	1.6	1.6	1.6
Construction													
1990	144.3	143.5	148.0	149.1	152.8	156.0	156.0	153.1	150.0	144.7	140.3	135.1	147.7
1991	116.3	113.7	116.3	123.9	127.2	129.4	127.2	127.3	126.2	124.5	122.1	117.2	122.6
1992	103.5	100.8	102.6	106.6	110.5	114.5	117.4	118.0	118.0	120.0	118.0	115.1	112.0
1993	105.2	103.3	104.6	109.6	115.2	119.0	122.5	123.9	122.8	124.4	123.2	121.5	116.2
1994	102.0	98.6	104.4	117.4	123.6	127.3	129.7	131.8	132.5	133.6	131.9	128.0	121.7
1995	113.6	107.8	113.1	120.8	125.3	129.1	129.6	131.2	130.1	129.4	127.4	122.6	123.3
1996	103.0	106.4	112.1	120.9	127.2	130.9	132.9	133.6	133.4	135.0	134.1	130.7	125.0
1997	117.2	116.2	120.7	128.9	133.9	137.6	139.6	140.0	138.9	138.7	136.4	133.4	131.7
1998	121.2	121.1	125.6	133.3	136.9	140.5	142.3	143.1	142.5	144.1	142.2	140.9	136.1
1999	128.1	129.6	132.8	141.7	144.8	148.9	150.5	150.5	149.3	150.3	148.9	147.7	143.5
2000	138.2	135.3	143.2	148.7	151.6	154.7	153.9	155.1	154.8	153.6	153.6	152.0	149.5
2001	141.8	142.6	147.0	155.2	160.5	163.7	164.5	166.4	165.1	167.7	166.2	164.4	158.7
2002	153.0	152.2	155.2	160.7	164.1	166.9	167.5	169.2	167.5	166.9	165.7	161.8	162.6
2003	149.1	144.3	147.1	156.9	162.8	165.5	167.2	167.5	165.7	164.0	162.1	159.6	159.3

Employment by Industry: New Jersey—*Continued*

(Numbers in thousands. Not seasonally adjusted.)

Industry	January	February	March	April	May	June	July	August	September	October	November	December	Annual Average
STATEWIDE—*Continued*													
Manufacturing													
1990	538.4	540.1	539.7	533.3	533.2	535.1	525.1	530.0	528.5	522.9	517.2	510.6	529.5
1991	498.6	498.3	498.7	498.5	500.2	503.9	495.1	499.4	500.9	499.2	496.8	490.1	498.3
1992	473.2	472.7	473.0	473.9	475.9	480.5	472.4	477.1	474.7	474.0	472.6	468.8	474.0
1993	457.9	458.3	459.5	461.1	463.7	467.5	460.9	464.6	468.4	466.9	464.6	461.8	462.9
1994	449.0	449.8	453.9	454.1	457.6	461.1	454.0	460.0	463.0	459.2	457.3	452.7	455.9
1995	444.4	447.9	448.9	449.4	449.6	454.2	443.8	448.7	452.1	451.6	448.7	444.3	448.6
1996	433.9	436.5	439.5	436.4	438.6	443.8	432.3	437.4	439.3	437.3	437.8	436.1	437.4
1997	426.5	428.7	431.7	434.0	436.3	441.5	435.3	439.3	441.2	437.7	437.1	435.7	435.4
1998	427.0	428.1	429.6	432.5	435.1	436.7	425.1	428.0	430.7	429.5	426.6	423.8	429.3
1999	418.9	420.0	421.4	422.1	423.1	426.2	419.8	421.5	424.7	424.2	424.4	423.2	422.4
2000	416.7	418.3	420.1	423.1	423.9	426.9	418.8	420.4	421.1	422.9	423.0	423.7	421.5
2001	411.3	412.0	411.9	409.4	409.0	408.9	397.8	397.7	396.4	389.7	386.6	383.7	401.2
2002	372.7	372.8	372.6	371.9	372.1	371.5	363.7	365.2	364.9	361.7	360.6	360.2	367.5
2003	353.2	352.6	352.4	352.3	352.6	353.8	350.7	351.2	350.6	351.0	350.8	349.4	351.7
Service-providing													
1990	2929.9	2933.5	2959.8	2957.1	2977.1	3017.1	2981.7	2967.0	2941.3	2928.7	2930.8	2933.8	2954.8
1991	2852.4	2850.2	2866.4	2868.3	2884.7	2915.5	2886.4	2873.0	2863.4	2867.4	2883.8	2891.7	2875.2
1992	2809.7	2816.8	2832.4	2845.5	2867.6	2906.5	2896.9	2882.8	2871.2	2889.7	2903.1	2910.8	2869.4
1993	2845.9	2855.5	2865.7	2893.0	2916.6	2957.0	2926.7	2919.6	2913.5	2933.4	2949.4	2961.5	2911.4
1994	2880.7	2880.2	2916.4	2949.5	2976.5	3020.4	3000.1	2994.6	2990.1	3004.1	3022.6	3037.7	2972.7
1995	2955.1	2963.1	2990.9	3008.0	3032.9	3067.3	3039.2	3038.7	3038.9	3047.1	3060.9	3074.0	3026.3
1996	2972.3	3002.4	3027.1	3040.2	3078.5	3122.6	3099.9	3092.9	3092.7	3101.6	3123.2	3139.9	3074.4
1997	3060.1	3075.8	3104.4	3123.3	3155.4	3200.0	3177.0	3159.7	3175.2	3190.9	3209.2	3230.6	3155.1
1998	3145.4	3156.7	3180.3	3203.4	3239.2	3277.7	3252.4	3238.6	3245.0	3268.1	3285.0	3310.0	3233.4
1999	3231.5	3251.2	3282.8	3310.1	3331.0	3376.6	3358.5	3345.1	3342.6	3366.5	3386.5	3411.9	3332.8
2000	3331.1	3341.1	3377.8	3402.1	3429.4	3477.0	3445.3	3425.0	3436.9	3439.1	3463.8	3488.9	3421.4
2001	3367.8	3375.8	3396.5	3427.8	3454.9	3498.8	3444.4	3424.9	3431.7	3451.0	3469.1	3482.6	3435.4
2002	3405.5	3413.6	3439.3	3448.6	3469.7	3502.7	3450.1	3434.9	3440.8	3453.0	3478.5	3490.9	3452.3
2003	3404.3	3400.2	3421.2	3445.7	3475.8	3510.9	3483.3	3463.4	3469.0	3498.2	3514.7	3525.8	3467.7
Trade, transportation, and utilities													
1990	846.2	833.1	837.2	827.9	832.8	840.4	829.2	829.5	826.8	826.2	830.4	839.4	833.2
1991	799.9	786.2	786.1	787.6	789.6	798.1	785.7	786.3	791.4	793.8	806.5	817.2	794.0
1992	781.9	769.6	769.1	767.1	773.2	781.3	774.7	772.2	778.8	788.1	798.9	809.8	780.3
1993	776.4	767.3	766.2	768.5	775.2	786.8	776.9	776.1	780.7	789.9	802.8	816.9	781.9
1994	786.0	775.2	782.3	787.5	797.2	809.7	799.9	802.7	808.6	814.4	829.2	841.1	802.8
1995	808.3	798.8	802.8	808.7	815.9	811.7	811.2	812.5	818.0	824.8	836.8	850.1	816.6
1996	809.8	806.7	809.1	807.8	818.6	829.2	817.3	818.5	825.7	832.0	846.4	860.7	823.4
1997	825.2	818.2	821.9	821.4	827.5	838.6	828.1	818.7	836.7	844.9	859.5	874.5	834.6
1998	838.8	828.3	830.2	833.4	843.3	850.4	841.9	842.0	848.5	856.6	871.4	885.9	847.5
1999	855.9	850.3	856.6	859.6	865.1	876.2	872.2	873.3	875.3	882.6	898.7	918.1	873.6
2000	885.2	876.5	882.5	887.9	892.7	899.8	896.9	896.5	900.5	905.8	922.7	941.1	899.0
2001	895.2	881.3	883.1	887.5	891.9	899.7	886.1	883.0	883.5	886.0	899.6	911.3	890.6
2002	879.3	869.5	874.8	873.0	877.3	887.4	875.0	873.2	877.8	882.3	896.1	910.7	881.4
2003	873.8	863.9	865.2	867.7	875.0	883.1	873.1	871.3	875.4	884.5	897.0	909.4	878.3
Wholesale trade													
1990	231.5	231.1	232.5	230.7	230.3	231.3	228.5	228.8	227.1	225.7	224.5	223.4	228.7
1991	217.9	217.1	217.3	216.8	216.8	218.0	215.5	215.6	215.3	214.6	214.8	214.5	216.1
1992	213.9	213.4	214.0	211.6	212.9	214.4	212.6	212.2	212.1	212.9	212.3	212.6	212.9
1993	206.2	206.5	207.2	208.0	208.4	209.9	209.0	209.1	208.6	209.0	210.1	210.6	208.5
1994	207.3	207.5	208.9	209.9	210.3	214.3	212.5	213.5	213.3	214.0	214.8	215.2	211.7
1995	212.3	213.5	214.8	214.0	214.4	217.0	215.6	216.4	216.8	216.8	217.5	218.0	215.5
1996	212.9	215.7	217.0	216.8	217.4	219.4	218.1	218.3	217.9	219.0	220.0	221.3	217.8
1997	217.5	219.3	221.1	220.2	220.9	223.0	222.2	222.5	222.2	223.9	226.3	227.9	222.2
1998	223.9	224.7	225.8	226.2	227.3	229.2	228.5	227.9	227.3	227.8	228.4	228.9	227.1
1999	230.3	231.3	232.6	233.4	233.4	234.7	234.4	234.7	234.8	235.4	235.6	237.5	234.0
2000	237.3	237.7	239.0	240.9	242.5	241.2	244.1	243.2	243.6	242.8	242.9	245.2	241.7
2001	241.7	242.1	242.7	243.5	243.3	244.1	242.7	242.1	241.7	239.5	239.4	239.5	241.8
2002	238.5	238.2	239.3	237.8	237.7	238.1	235.5	234.8	234.4	234.8	234.5	234.9	236.5
2003	232.3	232.0	232.1	233.4	233.5	234.3	233.5	231.8	231.3	230.6	230.5	231.3	232.2
Retail trade													
1990	449.8	437.2	437.9	431.7	435.3	440.8	437.8	437.4	433.4	433.1	439.0	448.2	438.4
1991	420.7	408.5	407.6	408.9	410.4	416.4	413.0	413.1	413.2	414.0	426.2	436.4	415.7
1992	410.7	398.6	397.1	397.3	400.0	404.9	403.7	402.5	402.8	410.1	421.1	431.4	406.6
1993	409.6	400.7	398.5	398.5	402.7	411.5	407.4	407.1	406.1	411.0	422.9	436.7	409.3
1994	413.1	401.5	404.6	408.9	415.2	422.5	417.0	418.7	419.4	421.8	436.1	447.6	418.8
1995	422.4	411.5	413.1	419.0	425.3	417.9	423.3	424.9	424.0	427.2	439.7	452.5	425.0
1996	424.0	415.5	415.4	415.9	423.6	430.7	426.5	427.7	428.0	432.2	445.9	458.4	428.6
1997	431.1	420.9	421.9	420.7	425.4	432.4	430.1	431.0	432.0	435.1	448.0	460.9	432.4
1998	433.8	422.3	422.4	423.9	429.6	434.2	432.9	433.8	433.4	439.7	454.4	467.0	435.6
1999	442.2	433.8	437.8	438.6	443.3	451.4	450.5	452.2	449.8	451.6	466.6	482.8	450.0
2000	457.9	448.7	452.7	453.8	457.5	464.8	463.2	465.2	462.0	463.8	479.9	495.4	463.7
2001	465.5	451.0	452.4	455.3	459.3	466.9	460.2	460.2	454.9	459.1	475.2	487.5	462.2
2002	461.2	451.7	455.7	455.1	459.4	468.1	464.3	464.4	461.9	462.8	477.1	491.9	464.5
2003	461.9	453.3	454.1	457.3	463.8	470.9	467.5	469.0	465.9	474.8	487.5	499.2	468.8

Employment by Industry: New Jersey—*Continued*

(Numbers in thousands. Not seasonally adjusted.)

Industry	January	February	March	April	May	June	July	August	September	October	November	December	Annual Average
STATEWIDE—*Continued*													
Transportation and utilities													
1990	164.9	164.8	166.8	165.5	167.2	168.3	162.9	163.3	166.3	167.4	166.9	167.8	166.0
1991	161.3	160.6	161.2	161.9	162.4	163.7	157.2	157.6	162.9	165.2	165.5	166.3	162.1
1992	157.3	157.6	158.0	158.2	160.3	162.0	158.4	157.5	163.9	165.1	165.5	165.8	160.8
1993	160.6	160.1	160.5	162.0	164.1	165.4	160.5	159.9	166.0	169.9	169.8	169.6	164.0
1994	165.6	166.2	168.8	168.7	171.7	172.9	170.4	170.5	175.9	178.6	178.3	178.3	172.1
1995	173.6	173.8	174.9	175.7	176.2	176.8	172.3	171.2	177.2	180.8	179.6	179.6	175.9
1996	172.9	175.5	176.7	175.1	177.6	179.1	172.7	172.5	179.8	180.8	180.5	181.0	177.0
1997	176.6	178.0	178.9	180.5	181.2	183.2	175.8	165.2	182.5	185.9	185.2	185.7	179.8
1998	181.1	181.3	182.0	183.3	186.4	187.0	180.5	180.3	187.8	189.1	188.6	190.0	184.7
1999	183.4	185.2	186.2	187.6	188.4	190.1	187.3	186.4	190.7	195.6	196.5	197.8	189.6
2000	190.0	190.1	190.8	193.2	192.7	193.8	189.6	188.1	194.9	199.2	199.9	200.5	193.5
2001	188.0	188.2	188.0	188.7	189.3	188.7	183.2	180.7	186.9	187.4	185.0	184.3	186.5
2002	179.6	179.6	179.8	180.1	180.2	181.2	175.2	174.0	181.5	184.7	184.5	183.9	180.4
2003	179.6	178.6	179.0	177.0	177.7	177.9	172.1	170.5	178.2	179.1	179.0	178.9	177.3
Information													
1990	124.1	122.3	122.7	120.2	119.2	120.6	122.3	121.4	120.7	117.2	117.7	117.6	120.5
1991	116.2	116.5	116.9	115.1	115.0	115.8	116.0	115.7	115.3	113.5	113.8	113.8	115.3
1992	113.1	113.4	113.6	111.8	112.3	114.2	114.3	114.1	114.1	114.3	114.7	115.1	113.7
1993	111.4	111.2	111.8	111.2	111.4	113.2	112.7	112.3	112.0	111.5	112.0	112.1	111.9
1994	111.1	111.4	112.4	113.4	113.7	114.7	115.8	116.1	114.4	117.9	119.4	120.1	115.0
1995	120.4	119.0	120.3	119.5	120.1	121.4	118.7	120.0	120.0	118.4	118.4	119.2	119.6
1996	117.0	115.1	115.9	114.7	116.4	118.1	117.2	118.2	117.7	118.5	119.8	121.0	117.4
1997	120.0	120.5	122.0	121.1	121.7	123.3	123.6	124.4	123.6	122.7	123.2	124.1	122.5
1998	118.6	119.4	120.2	117.8	118.4	119.4	118.2	118.5	118.1	118.8	119.3	120.1	118.9
1999	121.0	120.8	121.4	121.8	123.1	124.6	124.1	124.4	123.8	122.5	124.6	124.2	123.0
2000	126.6	126.3	127.4	126.2	126.8	128.5	128.0	123.7	127.4	126.2	127.4	128.6	126.9
2001	127.2	127.8	128.4	127.0	127.3	128.1	126.1	123.5	126.3	124.5	125.3	125.3	126.4
2002	121.0	120.3	120.3	116.3	116.5	115.7	111.4	111.0	109.4	104.6	106.1	105.6	113.2
2003	102.8	102.4	102.8	102.1	102.2	102.6	102.7	103.0	101.8	101.1	101.6	102.1	102.3
Financial activities													
1990	237.9	237.7	238.3	236.3	236.0	238.3	237.8	236.1	231.5	228.3	226.6	226.6	234.2
1991	227.1	225.7	225.7	225.6	226.6	229.1	227.7	226.0	221.6	220.0	219.4	220.1	224.5
1992	220.7	221.2	221.7	221.9	223.1	226.7	227.4	226.1	223.4	222.6	223.1	223.6	223.4
1993	223.1	222.5	223.1	223.6	223.8	226.8	227.3	228.1	224.5	224.0	224.9	226.0	224.8
1994	228.6	228.7	229.8	229.3	229.9	233.0	233.0	232.5	230.9	227.4	227.2	228.1	229.8
1995	226.7	226.2	227.3	226.1	226.6	230.4	232.3	232.5	229.4	229.4	230.6	231.8	229.1
1996	228.0	229.0	229.3	228.1	229.2	233.2	234.3	234.2	232.5	231.3	231.9	233.8	231.2
1997	233.3	233.1	234.0	233.6	235.9	238.2	241.7	242.4	239.8	240.2	241.0	245.1	238.1
1998	243.8	243.4	243.6	245.5	247.1	250.0	252.8	253.2	250.2	250.5	251.2	252.6	248.6
1999	256.1	255.5	256.2	259.6	260.1	263.2	265.6	265.2	261.5	261.2	261.5	263.4	260.7
2000	262.5	263.0	264.1	264.9	266.1	271.1	272.4	271.6	268.8	265.8	265.4	266.7	266.8
2001	262.0	261.9	262.2	265.5	267.1	271.1	270.0	269.1	266.8	280.9	279.9	281.3	269.8
2002	277.3	276.2	275.1	275.7	276.1	277.7	279.4	278.9	276.6	275.1	275.8	276.4	276.7
2003	274.5	273.8	274.3	273.9	274.8	277.8	280.6	280.4	277.5	278.2	279.2	279.6	277.1
Professional and business services													
1990	435.7	437.6	441.4	438.8	439.3	445.0	444.5	444.9	440.2	432.9	430.1	428.3	438.2
1991	418.3	417.7	422.8	421.1	420.3	424.7	424.2	424.6	421.9	418.6	418.0	418.0	420.8
1992	404.1	406.1	411.0	414.6	416.4	421.9	425.4	425.3	424.3	424.3	423.6	422.2	418.2
1993	419.6	424.3	428.2	439.7	443.7	447.9	447.6	449.1	447.4	449.7	449.1	448.1	441.2
1994	428.6	431.4	438.3	448.0	450.5	454.1	457.3	459.4	459.2	459.0	459.2	458.5	450.2
1995	446.8	451.3	458.5	458.9	462.3	468.5	465.9	470.5	472.2	473.6	474.3	473.0	464.6
1996	457.8	468.2	473.0	479.7	486.8	490.7	498.1	503.4	502.1	501.3	504.6	506.0	489.3
1997	492.8	497.4	505.3	514.3	519.1	526.6	530.0	534.4	533.2	536.9	538.7	540.5	522.4
1998	526.3	531.3	539.7	548.3	552.4	561.3	562.6	563.2	559.9	565.5	566.2	571.3	554.0
1999	549.4	557.1	567.0	575.7	576.8	587.0	587.8	590.2	586.8	589.5	590.4	591.5	579.1
2000	575.8	579.3	591.6	595.6	597.6	610.9	608.7	610.3	608.5	598.7	601.0	604.3	598.5
2001	580.7	582.0	590.9	597.3	599.8	607.5	599.2	599.6	595.0	588.9	586.3	582.4	592.4
2002	569.0	570.8	581.0	584.2	583.6	588.2	584.9	587.8	582.2	580.1	581.9	579.9	581.1
2003	562.2	559.0	565.2	571.2	573.4	578.5	577.1	580.4	580.2	578.7	578.3	578.5	573.6
Educational and health services													
1990	355.6	359.6	362.6	362.2	361.2	362.5	356.3	355.4	362.6	366.9	370.3	370.3	362.1
1991	365.9	370.4	372.8	373.6	375.5	373.5	368.9	367.3	375.2	380.1	382.7	383.5	374.1
1992	376.9	381.3	383.4	385.6	388.3	386.7	382.2	380.6	388.3	394.3	395.7	396.8	386.6
1993	392.9	395.7	397.5	399.0	400.8	399.3	395.7	392.7	400.6	405.5	406.6	406.9	399.4
1994	403.0	405.9	409.9	412.5	413.8	411.7	408.3	406.6	414.8	418.7	420.5	422.8	412.3
1995	416.4	420.4	423.2	424.0	424.4	426.7	422.0	420.0	428.3	429.5	431.6	433.0	424.9
1996	423.8	430.8	433.8	435.0	437.4	436.1	430.7	428.9	436.4	442.1	445.9	446.0	435.5
1997	442.1	448.1	451.1	450.9	452.7	451.9	447.8	446.0	454.6	457.6	459.7	459.6	451.8
1998	454.1	458.5	460.9	465.2	468.4	467.2	463.4	461.3	468.0	474.1	475.1	476.5	466.0
1999	472.2	477.2	481.0	480.5	481.9	480.4	476.3	473.2	478.7	487.7	489.7	491.7	480.8
2000	484.3	488.2	490.7	494.2	494.7	496.8	493.3	491.0	497.9	503.1	506.2	509.2	495.8
2001	492.6	496.4	499.3	504.4	507.8	511.1	503.6	501.6	505.8	510.3	514.3	517.1	505.3
2002	517.6	522.9	524.4	526.2	528.8	529.4	524.7	522.0	526.6	531.3	535.6	536.2	527.1
2003	532.3	532.5	536.2	537.6	541.4	540.9	538.0	533.7	538.4	544.8	547.2	547.9	539.2

Employment by Industry: New Jersey—*Continued*

(Numbers in thousands. Not seasonally adjusted.)

Industry	January	February	March	April	May	June	July	August	September	October	November	December	Annual Average
STATEWIDE—*Continued*													
Leisure and hospitality													
1990	244.0	247.5	257.9	266.6	279.5	296.5	297.6	295.6	279.7	263.8	257.5	252.6	269.9
1991	239.3	241.3	245.4	250.6	263.4	279.5	284.5	284.2	270.1	255.6	250.9	247.0	259.3
1992	233.6	236.2	240.4	250.8	264.4	280.2	284.6	283.4	272.6	259.0	253.2	250.3	259.0
1993	239.9	242.7	242.4	255.0	268.0	285.0	287.8	287.9	276.6	261.4	254.8	253.5	262.9
1994	240.6	239.8	248.1	260.5	273.6	293.8	297.2	295.8	282.0	268.5	262.2	259.8	268.4
1995	247.5	249.7	256.5	267.2	281.7	302.3	302.1	302.8	290.7	273.7	266.4	263.3	275.3
1996	248.8	254.5	261.7	269.9	287.4	305.0	310.4	308.6	293.8	277.4	269.9	268.2	279.6
1997	256.9	260.5	267.8	277.6	294.3	311.1	315.1	313.6	299.0	284.5	277.9	275.7	286.1
1998	266.5	270.7	276.3	283.6	301.3	317.7	322.5	318.6	305.9	292.6	287.3	287.6	294.2
1999	273.7	277.0	282.3	291.6	305.1	322.8	329.9	327.6	311.9	297.6	290.4	290.3	300.0
2000	278.0	278.5	285.1	295.4	308.3	328.1	330.8	329.3	315.5	301.5	296.3	292.6	303.2
2001	278.9	281.6	285.4	296.0	310.6	327.2	334.2	332.4	315.6	299.1	294.6	294.2	304.1
2002	283.3	285.0	290.8	302.2	316.0	333.2	338.8	336.5	322.4	310.8	306.8	306.0	311.0
2003	293.7	292.7	297.3	310.3	325.6	342.7	352.3	349.7	333.6	322.0	314.4	312.2	320.5
Other services													
1990	119.6	119.4	120.4	120.2	120.9	122.2	122.5	121.8	119.4	117.8	116.8	116.4	119.7
1991	115.2	114.7	115.2	114.1	115.1	116.7	118.2	117.2	115.1	115.1	115.0	114.9	115.5
1992	113.0	113.6	113.9	114.1	115.5	117.1	118.4	117.8	116.5	117.2	117.2	117.3	115.9
1993	115.4	115.9	116.3	117.7	119.0	120.5	122.0	121.4	118.4	118.5	118.8	118.8	118.5
1994	115.7	115.5	117.2	118.9	120.1	121.3	124.0	124.4	121.8	122.0	122.3	122.9	120.5
1995	118.7	119.7	120.5	121.2	121.9	124.6	125.5	125.6	122.5	123.6	123.7	124.4	122.6
1996	122.1	123.7	125.3	126.0	127.1	129.6	130.1	129.5	127.5	127.9	128.2	128.7	127.1
1997	125.3	125.8	127.1	128.2	129.3	131.3	132.7	132.1	129.7	129.1	129.1	129.9	129.1
1998	128.3	128.8	129.2	130.9	132.6	134.4	136.1	135.4	132.9	132.9	133.4	134.0	132.4
1999	132.4	133.1	134.0	136.0	137.3	139.9	141.7	140.9	138.3	139.4	140.0	141.2	137.8
2000	138.2	139.0	140.4	141.8	142.6	144.9	146.4	145.0	142.4	141.6	141.6	142.3	142.1
2001	138.8	139.4	140.3	141.8	143.7	145.9	148.0	146.7	144.0	145.8	146.2	146.9	143.9
2002	146.0	146.5	147.1	147.2	148.4	150.1	150.8	150.0	147.3	148.5	148.4	149.0	148.3
2003	148.6	148.5	149.4	151.2	152.2	154.6	155.9	155.1	152.9	153.4	153.6	153.7	152.4
Government													
1990	566.8	576.3	579.3	584.9	588.2	591.6	571.5	562.3	560.4	575.6	581.4	582.6	576.7
1991	570.5	577.7	581.5	580.6	579.2	578.1	561.2	551.7	552.8	570.7	577.5	577.2	571.5
1992	566.4	575.4	579.3	579.6	574.4	578.4	569.9	563.3	553.2	569.9	576.7	575.7	571.8
1993	567.2	575.9	580.2	578.3	574.7	577.5	556.7	552.0	553.3	572.9	580.4	579.2	570.6
1994	567.1	572.3	578.4	579.4	577.7	582.1	564.6	557.1	558.4	576.2	582.6	584.4	573.3
1995	570.3	578.0	581.8	582.4	580.0	581.7	561.5	554.8	557.8	574.1	579.1	579.2	573.3
1996	565.0	574.4	579.0	579.0	575.6	580.7	561.8	551.6	557.0	571.1	576.5	575.5	570.6
1997	564.5	572.2	575.2	576.2	574.9	579.0	558.0	548.1	558.6	575.0	580.1	581.2	570.2
1998	569.0	576.3	580.2	578.7	575.7	577.3	554.9	546.4	561.5	577.1	581.1	582.0	571.6
1999	570.8	580.2	584.3	585.3	581.6	582.5	560.9	550.3	566.3	586.0	591.2	591.5	577.5
2000	580.5	590.3	596.0	596.1	600.6	596.9	568.8	557.6	575.9	596.4	603.2	604.1	588.8
2001	592.4	605.4	606.9	608.3	606.7	608.2	577.2	569.0	594.7	615.5	622.9	624.1	602.6
2002	612.0	622.4	625.8	623.8	623.0	621.0	585.1	575.5	598.5	620.3	627.8	627.1	613.5
2003	616.4	627.4	630.8	631.7	631.2	630.7	603.6	589.8	609.2	635.5	643.4	642.4	624.3
Federal government													
1990	79.0	79.0	79.5	81.3	86.4	86.3	84.9	80.4	78.9	78.1	78.1	78.4	80.8
1991	77.4	77.3	77.3	77.4	77.5	77.4	78.0	77.7	77.4	77.4	77.3	78.2	77.5
1992	77.0	76.6	76.9	76.6	76.4	76.8	77.0	76.0	74.7	74.1	73.7	73.8	75.8
1993	73.6	73.3	73.1	72.0	72.1	72.3	72.3	72.0	71.7	71.6	71.7	72.7	72.3
1994	71.7	71.5	71.3	71.2	71.1	71.9	72.5	72.3	72.2	71.9	72.0	72.9	71.8
1995	71.4	70.7	70.7	70.7	70.7	70.9	70.9	70.7	70.2	70.2	70.2	71.2	70.7
1996	69.9	69.9	70.0	70.3	70.3	70.5	70.2	70.1	69.8	69.4	69.3	70.3	70.0
1997	68.9	68.8	68.5	68.5	68.5	68.5	68.4	68.2	68.0	67.4	67.3	68.4	68.2
1998	66.7	66.3	66.3	66.2	66.0	66.6	66.6	66.6	66.4	66.3	66.7	68.0	66.5
1999	66.7	66.2	66.3	66.8	65.5	65.4	66.1	66.4	66.2	65.8	65.8	67.1	66.1
2000	65.7	66.0	67.5	68.8	78.9	73.4	71.1	67.0	65.5	65.3	65.3	65.9	68.3
2001	65.9	65.9	65.8	65.8	65.7	65.9	66.1	65.9	65.4	65.2	65.3	66.1	65.7
2002	64.9	63.9	64.2	63.0	62.8	63.3	63.3	63.6	63.6	63.7	63.7	64.8	63.7
2003	64.3	63.9	63.6	63.4	63.1	63.4	63.9	63.6	63.2	62.8	62.9	63.6	63.5
State government													
1990	126.4	131.1	131.4	133.0	130.9	129.8	129.7	128.9	129.0	132.6	133.8	133.6	130.8
1991	127.8	132.0	134.1	133.8	131.5	127.1	126.5	125.1	125.5	128.8	129.1	128.9	129.1
1992	123.2	127.9	129.9	130.7	129.3	127.7	127.4	126.7	126.8	129.9	130.2	127.5	128.1
1993	122.3	127.9	129.0	129.6	126.8	125.8	123.5	124.4	125.3	129.4	130.1	128.6	126.8
1994	123.1	128.2	129.4	129.5	126.2	125.3	125.3	124.4	124.9	129.3	129.5	128.4	126.9
1995	130.4	136.2	137.4	138.0	136.5	133.0	132.1	131.7	131.8	135.7	135.4	133.4	134.3
1996	128.8	134.2	134.8	135.6	131.0	130.2	130.2	127.9	130.4	133.7	133.8	132.1	131.8
1997	128.2	132.3	133.5	134.8	131.1	130.8	130.3	128.7	131.7	135.4	135.2	134.8	132.2
1998	130.4	135.2	135.5	136.4	133.0	130.7	129.3	128.3	133.0	136.2	135.9	134.4	133.1
1999	128.6	134.7	135.8	136.6	133.1	129.7	129.8	129.2	132.7	137.3	137.5	136.1	133.4
2000	129.5	136.1	136.7	138.2	134.0	130.0	131.4	129.8	135.5	140.5	141.7	140.9	135.3
2001	134.4	141.7	141.6	142.6	139.8	135.9	136.3	136.1	139.9	144.6	145.6	145.6	140.3
2002	138.8	144.5	145.0	145.1	142.1	137.5	134.4	134.3	137.7	141.9	143.7	142.6	140.6
2003	136.8	143.7	145.1	145.2	145.1	138.3	139.4	138.2	142.8	147.6	148.7	147.6	143.2

Employment by Industry: New Jersey—*Continued*

(Numbers in thousands. Not seasonally adjusted.)

Industry	January	February	March	April	May	June	July	August	September	October	November	December	Annual Average
STATEWIDE—*Continued*													
Local government													
1990	361.4	366.2	368.4	370.6	370.9	375.5	356.9	353.0	352.5	364.9	369.5	370.6	365.0
1991	365.3	368.4	370.1	369.5	370.4	373.8	357.1	349.3	350.4	365.0	371.7	370.8	365.1
1992	366.2	370.9	372.5	372.3	368.7	373.9	365.5	360.6	351.7	365.9	372.8	374.4	367.9
1993	371.3	374.7	378.1	376.7	375.8	379.4	360.9	355.6	356.3	371.9	378.6	377.9	371.4
1994	372.3	372.6	377.7	378.7	380.4	384.9	366.8	360.4	361.7	375.0	381.1	383.1	374.5
1995	368.5	371.1	373.7	373.7	372.8	377.8	358.5	352.4	355.8	368.2	373.5	374.6	368.3
1996	366.3	370.3	374.2	373.1	374.3	380.0	361.4	353.6	356.8	368.0	373.4	373.1	368.7
1997	367.4	371.1	373.2	372.9	375.3	379.7	359.3	351.2	358.9	372.2	377.6	378.0	369.7
1998	371.9	374.8	378.4	376.1	376.7	380.0	359.0	351.5	362.1	374.6	378.5	379.6	371.9
1999	375.5	379.3	382.2	381.9	383.0	387.4	365.0	354.7	367.4	382.9	387.9	388.3	377.9
2000	385.3	388.2	391.8	389.1	387.7	393.5	366.3	360.8	374.9	390.6	396.2	397.3	385.1
2001	392.1	397.8	399.5	399.9	401.2	406.4	374.8	367.0	389.4	405.7	412.0	412.4	396.5
2002	408.3	414.0	416.6	415.7	418.1	420.2	387.4	377.6	397.2	414.7	420.4	419.7	409.2
2003	415.3	419.8	422.1	423.1	423.0	429.0	400.3	388.0	403.2	425.1	431.8	431.2	417.7
ATLANTIC CITY													
Total nonfarm													
1990	161.5	163.2	169.9	171.9	177.3	189.1	191.4	190.3	179.2	170.2	166.7	163.2	174.4
1991	157.5	157.0	157.8	162.4	168.3	177.5	182.5	181.9	174.0	165.9	162.5	160.4	167.3
1992	155.3	155.4	156.8	159.9	166.5	177.6	183.2	182.8	175.7	165.6	162.9	161.4	166.9
1993	155.6	156.3	156.3	162.7	169.0	179.7	183.7	183.5	177.1	166.0	163.2	162.0	167.9
1994	156.7	156.5	159.4	165.3	172.1	183.0	187.5	187.1	179.7	170.2	166.7	165.2	170.7
1995	160.8	160.3	162.7	168.4	174.0	185.5	190.2	190.1	182.4	171.9	168.2	166.8	173.4
1996	159.2	160.7	163.5	167.7	177.3	188.9	193.8	193.2	186.1	176.4	172.7	172.0	175.9
1997	166.5	166.6	169.1	173.7	181.7	191.9	197.4	197.6	189.8	180.9	176.9	175.8	180.6
1998	169.8	170.5	172.5	176.1	182.4	192.4	197.2	197.3	190.2	182.0	178.1	178.0	182.2
1999	171.9	173.4	175.0	180.3	186.3	196.6	203.1	202.6	194.5	185.6	182.3	180.2	185.9
2000	174.4	173.6	176.7	182.0	188.8	198.2	203.1	202.8	196.6	188.1	185.6	181.3	187.6
2001	176.7	177.7	179.4	185.4	192.7	201.5	205.2	205.0	198.6	188.0	185.2	184.7	190.0
2002	176.8	177.4	179.3	182.3	188.5	197.2	204.5	202.5	196.7	188.2	185.5	185.0	188.7
2003	177.6	177.4	178.8	183.6	190.7	199.8	208.7	206.5	199.8	194.4	192.0	190.2	191.6
Total private													
1990	134.4	135.5	142.1	144.2	149.1	160.2	163.4	162.4	151.8	143.0	138.9	135.2	146.6
1991	130.2	129.2	129.8	134.3	140.0	148.4	154.4	154.2	145.6	137.6	134.2	132.0	139.1
1992	127.6	127.1	128.3	131.6	138.3	148.3	154.1	154.0	146.9	137.2	134.3	132.7	138.3
1993	127.5	127.4	127.6	134.1	140.4	150.5	155.5	155.6	147.8	137.1	134.1	133.1	139.2
1994	128.5	127.9	130.5	136.3	143.0	153.2	159.1	159.0	150.2	141.5	137.8	136.4	141.9
1995	132.3	131.6	133.8	139.5	144.9	155.7	161.1	161.5	152.9	142.9	139.3	138.0	144.4
1996	131.2	132.5	135.0	139.1	148.4	158.8	164.8	164.7	156.6	147.5	144.1	143.2	147.1
1997	138.3	138.3	140.6	145.3	153.0	162.6	168.5	169.0	160.6	152.1	148.1	147.0	151.9
1998	142.1	142.1	143.9	147.6	154.1	163.1	168.2	168.3	160.7	153.2	149.3	149.2	153.4
1999	143.7	144.5	145.9	151.2	157.4	166.8	173.7	173.4	165.4	156.2	152.8	150.9	156.8
2000	145.6	144.2	147.0	152.1	158.6	167.8	173.1	172.9	166.8	158.2	155.8	151.4	157.7
2001	147.4	147.5	149.3	155.0	162.3	170.2	175.1	174.8	167.5	157.0	154.2	153.6	159.4
2002	146.3	146.2	147.9	151.6	157.6	165.4	174.0	172.6	165.7	156.6	154.0	153.3	157.6
2003	147.0	145.8	147.1	151.7	158.4	167.4	177.1	175.5	168.0	162.1	159.4	157.6	159.8
Goods-producing													
1990	15.4	15.6	16.0	15.7	15.7	16.0	15.4	15.1	14.3	13.9	13.7	13.2	15.0
1991	11.9	11.8	12.0	12.5	12.7	13.3	12.6	12.7	12.5	12.6	12.5	12.3	12.4
1992	11.5	11.3	11.5	11.7	12.2	12.6	12.5	12.5	12.2	11.9	11.9	11.7	11.9
1993	11.3	11.3	11.4	12.1	12.7	13.1	13.2	13.3	12.7	12.5	12.3	12.2	12.3
1994	11.3	11.2	11.8	12.7	13.4	13.8	13.6	13.5	13.3	13.3	13.1	13.2	12.8
1995	12.1	11.9	12.5	12.9	13.2	13.6	13.2	13.2	13.1	12.7	12.6	12.5	12.7
1996	11.4	11.8	12.6	13.1	13.6	14.0	13.4	13.5	13.4	13.1	12.9	12.9	12.9
1997	12.2	12.0	12.3	13.3	13.4	13.7	13.1	13.7	13.4	13.2	12.9	13.0	13.0
1998	12.1	12.0	12.3	12.8	13.0	13.4	13.0	13.0	12.7	12.7	12.4	12.7	12.6
1999	11.8	12.1	12.2	12.8	13.0	13.5	13.4	13.2	12.8	12.7	12.5	12.4	12.7
2000	12.0	11.8	12.3	13.1	13.3	13.8	13.6	13.8	13.7	13.5	13.4	13.6	13.1
2001	13.5	13.6	14.0	14.2	14.6	14.8	14.7	15.1	14.6	14.5	14.3	14.3	14.3
2002	13.4	13.6	14.0	14.6	14.8	15.3	15.1	15.0	14.7	14.2	14.3	14.2	14.4
2003	13.9	13.5	14.0	14.6	15.2	15.4	15.1	15.2	14.9	14.5	14.4	14.3	14.6
Construction and mining													
1990	8.5	8.5	8.8	8.4	8.4	8.6	8.2	7.8	7.2	7.0	6.8	6.5	7.8
1991	5.5	5.3	5.4	5.8	6.0	6.2	6.0	5.9	5.7	5.7	5.7	5.6	5.7
1992	5.2	5.0	5.1	5.3	5.6	5.7	5.7	5.6	5.4	5.5	5.3	5.2	5.3
1993	4.8	4.8	4.9	5.4	5.7	5.8	5.9	5.9	5.7	5.6	5.5	5.4	5.4
1994	4.7	4.6	5.1	6.0	6.4	6.6	6.5	6.4	6.2	6.3	6.2	6.3	5.9
1995	5.5	5.2	5.7	6.1	6.3	6.4	6.0	6.0	6.0	6.1	6.2	6.1	5.9
1996	5.0	5.4	6.0	6.5	6.8	6.9	6.6	6.7	6.7	6.7	6.7	6.7	6.3
1997	6.2	6.1	6.5	7.2	7.2	7.2	7.2	7.2	7.0	6.9	6.9	6.8	6.8
1998	6.2	6.1	6.3	6.7	6.8	6.9	6.6	6.6	6.4	6.6	6.6	6.8	6.5
1999	6.3	6.5	6.7	7.1	7.2	7.4	7.4	7.1	6.9	7.0	7.0	6.9	6.9
2000	6.5	6.4	6.7	7.1	7.3	7.5	7.5	7.6	7.4	7.4	7.4	7.5	7.1
2001	7.7	7.9	8.2	8.3	8.6	8.7	8.7	9.0	8.8	9.0	8.9	9.0	8.5
2002	8.4	8.4	8.8	9.1	9.3	9.6	9.2	9.2	9.1	8.8	8.9	8.8	9.0
2003	8.6	8.3	8.7	9.1	9.6	9.6	9.2	9.3	9.2	8.8	8.7	8.7	9.0

Employment by Industry: New Jersey—*Continued*

(Numbers in thousands. Not seasonally adjusted.)

Industry	January	February	March	April	May	June	July	August	September	October	November	December	Annual Average
ATLANTIC CITY—*Continued*													
Manufacturing													
1990	6.9	7.1	7.2	7.3	7.3	7.4	7.2	7.3	7.1	6.9	6.9	6.7	7.1
1991	6.4	6.5	6.6	6.7	6.7	7.1	6.6	6.8	6.8	6.9	6.8	6.7	6.7
1992	6.3	6.3	6.4	6.4	6.6	6.9	6.8	6.9	6.8	6.4	6.6	6.5	6.5
1993	6.5	6.5	6.5	6.7	7.0	7.3	7.3	7.4	7.0	6.9	6.8	6.8	6.8
1994	6.6	6.6	6.7	6.7	7.0	7.2	7.1	7.1	7.1	7.0	6.9	6.9	6.9
1995	6.6	6.7	6.8	6.8	6.9	7.2	7.2	7.2	7.1	6.6	6.4	6.4	6.8
1996	6.4	6.4	6.6	6.6	6.8	7.1	6.8	6.8	6.7	6.4	6.2	6.2	6.5
1997	6.0	5.9	5.8	6.1	6.2	6.5	5.9	6.5	6.4	6.3	6.0	6.2	6.1
1998	5.9	5.9	6.0	6.1	6.2	6.5	6.4	6.4	6.3	6.1	5.8	5.9	6.1
1999	5.5	5.6	5.5	5.7	5.8	6.1	6.0	6.1	5.9	5.7	5.5	5.5	5.7
2000	5.5	5.4	5.6	6.0	6.0	6.3	6.1	6.2	6.3	6.1	6.0	6.1	5.9
2001	5.8	5.7	5.8	5.9	6.0	6.1	6.0	6.1	5.8	5.5	5.4	5.3	5.7
2002	5.0	5.2	5.2	5.5	5.5	5.7	5.9	5.8	5.6	5.4	5.4	5.4	5.5
2003	5.3	5.2	5.3	5.5	5.6	5.8	5.9	5.9	5.7	5.7	5.7	5.6	5.6
Service-providing													
1990	146.1	147.6	153.9	156.2	161.6	173.1	176.0	175.2	164.9	156.3	153.0	150.0	159.4
1991	145.6	145.2	145.8	149.9	155.6	164.2	169.9	169.2	161.5	153.3	150.0	148.1	154.8
1992	143.8	144.1	145.3	148.2	154.3	165.0	170.7	170.3	163.5	153.7	151.0	149.7	154.9
1993	144.3	145.0	144.9	150.6	156.3	166.6	170.5	170.2	164.4	153.5	150.9	149.8	155.5
1994	145.4	145.3	147.6	152.6	158.7	169.2	173.9	173.6	166.4	156.9	153.6	152.0	157.9
1995	148.7	148.4	150.2	155.5	160.8	171.9	177.0	176.9	169.3	159.2	155.6	154.3	160.6
1996	147.8	148.9	150.9	154.6	163.7	174.9	180.4	179.7	172.7	163.3	159.8	159.1	162.9
1997	154.3	154.6	156.8	160.4	168.3	178.2	184.3	183.9	176.4	167.7	164.0	162.8	167.6
1998	157.7	158.5	160.2	163.3	169.4	179.0	184.2	184.3	177.5	169.3	165.7	165.3	169.5
1999	160.1	161.3	162.8	167.5	173.3	183.1	189.7	189.4	181.7	172.9	169.8	167.8	173.2
2000	162.4	161.8	164.4	168.9	175.5	184.4	189.5	189.0	182.9	174.6	172.2	167.7	174.4
2001	163.2	164.1	165.4	171.2	178.1	186.7	190.5	189.9	184.0	173.5	170.9	170.4	175.6
2002	163.4	163.8	165.3	167.7	173.7	181.9	189.4	187.5	182.0	174.0	171.2	170.8	174.2
2003	163.7	163.9	164.8	169.0	175.5	184.4	193.6	191.3	184.9	179.9	177.6	175.9	177.0
Trade, transportation, and utilities													
1990	26.5	25.7	26.2	26.3	27.5	29.3	29.9	29.8	27.9	26.5	26.3	26.4	27.3
1991	24.7	24.0	24.3	24.6	25.7	27.7	28.5	28.6	27.1	25.8	25.6	25.9	26.0
1992	24.3	23.9	24.1	24.2	25.2	26.8	28.1	27.8	26.5	25.0	24.7	24.8	25.4
1993	23.5	23.1	23.2	24.0	25.1	27.0	27.4	27.6	26.1	24.5	24.5	24.8	25.0
1994	23.5	23.1	23.4	24.4	25.6	27.6	28.4	28.5	27.0	25.6	25.5	26.0	25.7
1995	24.2	23.7	23.9	24.8	25.4	27.4	28.6	28.5	27.1	25.8	25.9	26.1	25.9
1996	23.6	23.3	23.6	24.2	25.8	27.7	29.1	29.0	27.8	26.5	26.1	26.2	26.0
1997	24.7	24.5	24.6	25.6	27.1	28.8	29.7	29.9	28.7	27.8	27.6	27.8	27.2
1998	26.0	25.5	25.6	25.6	26.9	28.6	29.5	29.7	28.2	27.3	27.3	27.7	27.3
1999	26.4	26.1	26.4	27.0	28.2	30.1	31.3	31.4	29.7	28.5	28.7	28.7	28.5
2000	27.6	27.0	27.6	28.4	29.4	31.2	32.2	32.0	30.6	28.8	28.6	29.3	29.3
2001	28.0	27.5	27.8	28.6	29.8	31.5	31.9	31.7	30.0	28.9	29.0	29.3	29.5
2002	27.2	26.8	27.2	27.3	28.3	30.3	31.6	31.4	29.7	28.6	28.4	28.9	28.8
2003	26.7	26.3	26.5	27.4	28.3	30.2	31.9	31.7	30.0	29.9	30.0	30.2	29.1
Wholesale trade													
1990	3.1	3.1	3.2	3.1	3.2	3.3	3.3	3.3	3.1	3.0	2.9	2.9	3.1
1991	2.8	2.8	2.8	2.8	2.9	3.1	3.1	3.2	3.0	3.0	2.9	2.9	2.9
1992	2.8	2.8	2.8	2.7	2.8	2.8	2.9	2.8	2.8	2.7	2.5	2.4	2.7
1993	2.3	2.3	2.4	2.3	2.4	2.5	2.5	2.5	2.4	2.3	2.3	2.2	2.3
1994	2.2	2.1	2.2	2.3	2.5	2.6	2.6	2.6	2.6	2.6	2.6	2.6	2.4
1995	2.3	2.4	2.4	2.6	2.6	2.7	2.8	2.8	2.7	2.5	2.5	2.5	2.5
1996	2.4	2.4	2.4	2.6	2.7	2.8	2.8	2.8	2.7	2.7	2.6	2.6	2.6
1997	2.4	2.5	2.5	2.6	2.7	2.8	3.0	3.0	2.9	2.8	2.7	2.7	2.7
1998	2.7	2.7	2.7	2.6	2.8	2.9	2.9	2.9	2.8	2.7	2.7	2.7	2.7
1999	2.8	2.8	2.8	2.9	3.0	3.0	3.0	3.0	2.9	2.9	2.9	2.9	2.9
2000	2.9	2.9	2.9	3.1	3.1	3.2	3.4	3.5	3.4	3.0	2.9	2.9	3.1
2001	3.1	3.1	3.2	3.3	3.4	3.5	3.6	3.5	3.5	3.3	3.2	3.2	3.3
2002	3.0	3.0	3.1	3.1	3.2	3.3	3.3	3.3	3.1	3.0	2.9	2.9	3.1
2003	2.7	2.7	2.7	2.8	2.9	2.9	3.2	3.1	3.0	3.0	3.0	3.0	2.9
Retail trade													
1990	19.5	18.7	19.0	19.2	20.2	21.8	22.6	22.6	20.9	19.6	19.5	19.6	20.2
1991	18.2	17.5	17.8	18.0	18.9	20.6	21.5	21.5	20.1	18.9	18.9	19.2	19.2
1992	17.8	17.4	17.5	17.6	18.4	19.9	21.2	21.1	19.7	18.4	18.4	18.6	18.8
1993	17.5	17.1	17.1	17.9	18.8	20.4	20.9	21.1	19.6	18.2	18.3	18.7	18.8
1994	17.5	17.1	17.3	17.9	18.8	20.5	21.5	21.5	20.1	18.8	18.9	19.5	19.1
1995	18.2	17.7	17.8	18.4	18.9	20.7	22.0	22.0	20.6	19.5	19.7	20.0	19.6
1996	17.9	17.6	17.8	18.3	19.6	21.3	22.4	22.4	21.1	20.1	19.9	20.0	19.8
1997	18.7	18.3	18.4	19.0	20.2	21.7	22.7	22.8	21.4	20.7	20.6	20.9	20.4
1998	19.3	18.8	18.9	19.1	20.0	21.6	22.6	22.5	21.1	20.4	20.5	20.9	20.4
1999	19.6	19.2	19.5	20.0	21.0	22.8	23.9	23.8	22.2	21.1	21.3	21.3	21.3
2000	20.1	19.5	20.0	20.5	21.4	23.0	23.9	23.7	22.2	20.9	20.9	21.6	21.4
2001	20.6	20.1	20.3	20.9	21.9	23.5	24.0	24.0	22.3	21.6	21.9	22.2	21.9
2002	20.2	19.8	20.1	20.5	21.4	23.2	24.6	24.4	22.8	21.7	21.7	22.2	21.9
2003	20.4	20.1	20.3	21.0	21.8	23.5	24.9	24.8	23.1	23.0	23.1	23.4	22.5

Employment by Industry: New Jersey—*Continued*

(Numbers in thousands. Not seasonally adjusted.)

Industry	January	February	March	April	May	June	July	August	September	October	November	December	Annual Average
ATLANTIC CITY—*Continued*													
Transportation and utilities													
1990	3.9	3.9	4.0	4.0	4.1	4.2	4.0	3.9	3.9	3.9	3.9	3.9	3.9
1991	3.7	3.7	3.7	3.8	3.9	4.0	3.9	3.9	4.0	3.9	3.8	3.8	3.8
1992	3.7	3.7	3.8	3.9	4.0	4.1	4.0	3.9	4.0	3.9	3.8	3.8	3.8
1993	3.7	3.7	3.7	3.8	3.9	4.1	4.0	4.0	4.1	4.0	3.9	3.9	3.9
1994	3.8	3.9	3.9	4.2	4.3	4.5	4.3	4.4	4.3	4.2	4.0	3.9	4.1
1995	3.7	3.6	3.7	3.8	3.9	4.0	3.8	3.7	3.8	3.8	3.7	3.6	3.7
1996	3.3	3.3	3.4	3.3	3.5	3.6	3.9	3.8	4.0	3.7	3.6	3.6	3.5
1997	3.6	3.7	3.7	4.0	4.2	4.3	4.0	4.1	4.4	4.3	4.3	4.2	4.0
1998	4.0	4.0	4.0	3.9	4.1	4.1	4.0	4.3	4.3	4.2	4.1	4.1	4.0
1999	4.0	4.1	4.1	4.1	4.2	4.3	4.4	4.6	4.6	4.5	4.5	4.5	4.3
2000	4.6	4.6	4.7	4.8	4.9	5.0	4.9	4.8	5.0	4.9	4.8	4.8	4.8
2001	4.3	4.3	4.3	4.4	4.5	4.5	4.3	4.2	4.2	4.0	3.9	3.9	4.2
2002	4.0	4.0	4.0	3.7	3.7	3.8	3.7	3.7	3.8	3.9	3.8	3.8	3.8
2003	3.6	3.5	3.5	3.6	3.6	3.8	3.8	3.8	3.9	3.9	3.9	3.8	3.7
Information													
1990	2.3	2.3	2.3	2.3	2.3	2.4	2.3	2.3	2.2	2.2	2.2	2.2	2.2
1991	2.2	2.2	2.2	2.5	2.5	2.6	2.5	2.5	2.4	2.4	2.4	2.4	2.4
1992	2.4	2.4	2.3	2.4	2.4	2.5	2.6	2.5	2.4	2.4	2.4	2.4	2.4
1993	2.3	2.3	2.3	2.3	2.4	2.5	2.5	2.5	2.4	2.4	2.4	2.4	2.3
1994	2.4	2.3	2.3	2.3	2.3	2.4	2.5	2.5	2.4	2.5	2.4	2.4	2.3
1995	2.5	2.4	2.4	2.5	2.5	2.6	2.7	2.7	2.5	2.4	2.4	2.4	2.5
1996	2.4	2.4	2.4	2.2	2.2	2.3	2.4	2.4	2.3	2.2	2.2	2.2	2.3
1997	2.2	2.1	2.1	2.1	2.1	2.2	2.2	2.2	2.1	2.1	2.1	2.1	2.1
1998	2.1	2.1	2.1	2.2	2.2	2.2	2.2	2.2	2.1	2.1	2.2	2.3	2.1
1999	2.1	2.1	2.1	2.1	2.1	2.2	2.2	2.2	2.2	2.2	2.2	2.2	2.1
2000	2.2	2.2	2.2	2.0	2.0	2.0	2.0	1.8	1.9	1.9	2.0	2.0	2.0
2001	2.0	2.0	1.9	2.0	2.0	2.1	2.1	2.0	2.1	2.1	2.0	2.1	2.0
2002	2.0	2.0	1.9	1.9	1.9	1.9	2.0	2.0	1.8	1.8	1.8	1.8	1.9
2003	1.7	1.7	1.7	1.6	1.6	1.7	1.7	1.6	1.7	1.7	1.7	1.7	1.7
Financial activities													
1990	7.1	7.1	7.2	6.9	7.1	7.2	7.2	7.2	7.0	6.8	6.7	6.6	7.0
1991	6.5	6.5	6.5	6.6	6.6	6.7	6.7	6.7	6.4	6.2	5.9	5.9	6.4
1992	5.8	5.8	5.9	6.0	6.1	6.3	6.6	6.6	6.4	6.1	6.0	5.9	6.1
1993	5.6	5.6	5.6	5.8	5.9	6.1	6.1	6.1	5.9	5.8	5.8	5.8	5.8
1994	5.8	5.9	5.9	6.0	6.2	6.3	6.4	6.4	6.3	5.9	5.9	5.9	6.0
1995	5.8	5.8	5.9	6.1	6.1	6.4	6.5	6.5	6.3	5.9	5.9	5.9	6.0
1996	5.9	5.9	6.0	6.1	6.2	6.4	6.5	6.6	6.4	6.2	6.1	6.1	6.2
1997	6.0	6.1	6.1	6.2	6.3	6.6	6.8	6.8	6.6	6.4	6.2	6.1	6.3
1998	5.7	5.7	5.9	6.1	6.1	6.4	6.7	6.6	6.3	6.0	5.8	5.9	6.1
1999	5.7	5.5	5.5	5.8	5.9	6.1	6.4	6.3	6.0	5.8	5.7	5.8	5.8
2000	5.6	5.7	5.7	5.9	6.1	6.3	6.6	6.5	6.3	5.9	5.8	5.9	6.0
2001	5.6	5.6	5.7	5.8	5.9	6.1	6.3	6.2	6.0	5.8	5.7	5.8	5.8
2002	5.6	5.6	5.7	5.7	5.8	6.0	6.4	6.4	6.2	5.9	5.9	5.9	5.9
2003	5.8	5.8	5.9	6.0	6.1	6.4	6.6	6.7	6.4	6.2	6.1	6.1	6.2
Professional and business services													
1990	8.5	8.6	8.7	8.5	8.7	8.8	8.7	8.7	8.6	8.4	8.3	8.1	8.5
1991	8.0	7.9	8.1	8.3	8.4	8.7	8.7	8.7	8.6	8.4	8.3	8.3	8.3
1992	8.1	8.2	8.3	8.2	8.3	8.4	8.5	8.5	8.5	8.4	8.2	8.2	8.3
1993	8.0	8.1	8.3	9.0	9.2	9.5	9.5	9.6	9.5	9.5	9.4	9.4	9.0
1994	8.8	8.9	9.2	9.2	9.3	9.6	9.5	9.6	9.6	9.4	9.2	9.0	9.2
1995	8.7	8.9	9.1	9.2	9.3	9.7	9.5	9.6	9.5	9.4	9.3	9.2	9.2
1996	8.7	9.2	9.4	10.1	10.2	10.5	10.2	10.4	10.2	10.4	10.6	10.5	10.0
1997	10.4	10.4	10.9	10.8	11.0	11.3	11.3	11.3	11.2	11.1	11.1	11.1	10.9
1998	11.0	11.1	11.3	11.7	11.5	11.8	11.9	12.0	11.9	11.9	12.0	12.0	11.6
1999	11.5	11.8	12.2	12.9	13.0	13.2	13.1	13.2	13.0	12.9	12.8	12.6	12.6
2000	11.8	11.9	12.2	12.6	12.6	12.9	12.4	12.1	12.4	12.1	12.2	12.0	12.2
2001	12.0	12.1	12.4	12.6	12.9	13.0	12.6	12.5	12.7	12.5	12.4	12.3	12.4
2002	11.9	12.0	12.0	12.2	12.1	12.0	12.1	11.8	11.7	11.7	11.7	11.5	11.9
2003	11.4	11.4	11.6	12.1	12.2	12.4	12.5	12.4	12.3	12.0	11.9	11.8	12.0
Educational and health services													
1990	14.3	14.3	14.5	14.2	14.5	14.5	14.6	14.7	14.9	14.8	14.8	14.8	14.5
1991	14.4	14.5	14.6	14.2	14.2	14.4	14.8	14.8	14.8	14.8	14.9	14.9	14.6
1992	14.8	14.6	14.8	15.1	15.1	15.2	15.2	15.3	15.3	15.6	15.7	15.6	15.1
1993	15.4	15.6	15.6	15.9	16.1	16.2	16.2	16.2	16.4	16.3	16.3	16.3	16.0
1994	16.8	16.9	17.0	17.2	17.4	17.4	17.0	16.9	17.1	17.1	17.1	17.1	17.0
1995	17.3	17.4	17.3	18.0	18.0	18.0	17.8	17.7	17.9	17.8	17.9	17.9	17.7
1996	17.3	17.4	17.5	17.6	17.9	18.1	17.9	18.0	18.3	18.3	18.3	18.4	17.9
1997	17.9	18.1	18.3	18.3	18.5	18.6	18.2	18.2	18.3	18.4	18.6	18.6	18.3
1998	18.5	18.6	18.7	18.6	18.6	18.6	18.4	18.5	18.7	18.6	18.7	18.8	18.6
1999	19.3	19.4	19.5	19.7	19.8	19.8	19.8	19.7	19.9	19.7	19.7	19.7	19.6
2000	19.3	19.3	19.3	19.6	19.7	19.8	19.9	19.8	19.9	19.9	20.0	20.1	19.7
2001	19.3	19.4	19.5	19.7	19.8	19.9	19.6	19.8	20.0	20.2	20.4	20.5	19.8
2002	20.8	20.8	20.8	21.0	21.0	21.0	20.7	20.9	21.3	21.2	21.3	21.3	21.0
2003	21.3	21.3	21.4	21.1	21.2	21.3	21.3	21.3	21.6	21.8	21.7	21.8	21.4

Employment by Industry: New Jersey—*Continued*

(Numbers in thousands. Not seasonally adjusted.)

Industry	January	February	March	April	May	June	July	August	September	October	November	December	Annual Average
ATLANTIC CITY—*Continued*													
Leisure and hospitality													
1990	55.3	56.9	62.2	65.3	68.2	76.6	79.6	79.0	71.6	65.5	62.2	59.3	66.8
1991	57.8	57.7	57.4	61.1	65.2	70.1	75.4	75.0	68.8	62.7	60.0	57.7	64.0
1992	56.3	56.4	56.9	59.5	64.3	71.6	75.5	75.6	70.5	63.0	60.7	59.5	64.1
1993	56.9	56.9	56.7	60.3	64.2	71.0	75.3	75.1	69.7	61.3	58.7	57.6	63.6
1994	55.5	55.2	56.4	59.9	64.0	70.9	76.3	76.2	69.3	62.9	59.9	58.1	63.7
1995	57.2	57.0	58.1	61.2	65.5	72.8	77.5	77.9	71.3	64.0	60.5	59.2	65.1
1996	57.2	57.7	58.7	60.9	67.4	74.4	79.8	79.3	72.8	65.7	62.9	61.9	66.5
1997	60.1	60.3	61.3	63.8	69.2	75.7	81.5	81.2	74.8	67.8	64.3	63.1	68.5
1998	61.6	61.9	62.7	65.4	70.3	76.3	80.5	80.3	75.0	69.2	65.6	64.4	69.4
1999	61.7	62.3	62.8	65.5	69.7	75.8	81.2	81.2	75.7	68.5	65.5	63.8	69.4
2000	61.6	60.9	62.2	64.9	69.6	75.7	80.1	80.7	76.0	70.3	68.1	62.8	69.4
2001	62.0	62.3	62.9	67.0	71.9	77.0	81.9	81.6	76.3	67.5	65.0	63.9	69.9
2002	60.3	60.2	61.1	63.7	68.3	73.2	80.2	79.2	74.6	67.7	65.2	64.2	68.2
2003	60.9	60.5	60.6	63.3	68.0	73.9	81.7	80.4	75.1	70.2	67.8	66.0	69.0
Other services													
1990	5.0	5.0	5.0	5.0	5.1	5.4	5.7	5.6	5.3	4.9	4.7	4.6	5.1
1991	4.7	4.6	4.7	4.5	4.7	4.9	5.2	5.2	5.0	4.7	4.6	4.6	4.7
1992	4.4	4.5	4.5	4.5	4.7	4.9	5.1	5.2	5.1	4.8	4.7	4.6	4.7
1993	4.5	4.5	4.5	4.7	4.8	5.1	5.3	5.2	5.1	4.8	4.7	4.6	4.8
1994	4.4	4.4	4.5	4.6	4.8	5.2	5.4	5.4	5.2	4.8	4.7	4.7	4.8
1995	4.5	4.5	4.6	4.8	4.9	5.2	5.3	5.4	5.2	4.9	4.8	4.8	4.9
1996	4.7	4.8	4.8	4.9	5.1	5.4	5.5	5.5	5.4	5.1	5.0	5.0	5.1
1997	4.8	4.8	5.0	5.2	5.4	5.7	5.7	5.7	5.5	5.3	5.3	5.2	5.3
1998	5.1	5.2	5.3	5.2	5.5	5.8	6.0	6.0	5.8	5.4	5.3	5.4	5.5
1999	5.2	5.2	5.2	5.4	5.7	6.1	6.3	6.2	6.1	5.9	5.7	5.7	5.7
2000	5.5	5.4	5.5	5.6	5.9	6.1	6.3	6.2	6.0	5.8	5.7	5.7	5.8
2001	5.0	5.0	5.1	5.1	5.4	5.8	6.0	5.9	5.8	5.5	5.4	5.4	5.4
2002	5.1	5.2	5.2	5.2	5.4	5.7	5.9	5.9	5.7	5.5	5.4	5.5	5.5
2003	5.3	5.3	5.4	5.6	5.8	6.1	6.3	6.2	6.0	5.8	5.8	5.7	5.8
Government													
1990	27.1	27.7	27.8	27.7	28.2	28.9	28.0	27.9	27.4	27.2	27.8	28.0	27.8
1991	27.3	27.8	28.0	28.1	28.3	29.1	28.1	27.7	28.4	28.3	28.3	28.4	28.1
1992	27.7	28.3	28.5	28.3	28.2	29.3	29.1	28.8	28.8	28.4	28.6	28.7	28.5
1993	28.1	28.9	28.7	28.6	28.6	29.2	28.2	27.9	29.3	28.9	29.1	28.9	28.7
1994	28.2	28.6	28.9	29.0	29.1	29.8	28.4	28.1	29.5	28.7	28.9	28.8	28.8
1995	28.5	28.7	28.9	28.9	29.1	29.8	29.1	28.6	29.5	29.0	28.9	28.8	28.9
1996	28.0	28.2	28.5	28.6	28.9	30.1	29.0	28.5	29.5	28.9	28.6	28.8	28.8
1997	28.2	28.3	28.5	28.4	28.7	29.3	28.9	28.6	29.2	28.8	28.8	28.8	28.7
1998	27.7	28.4	28.6	28.5	28.3	29.3	29.0	29.0	29.5	28.8	28.8	28.8	28.7
1999	28.2	28.9	29.1	29.1	28.9	29.8	29.4	29.2	29.1	29.4	29.5	29.3	29.1
2000	28.8	29.4	29.7	29.9	30.2	30.4	30.0	29.9	29.8	29.9	29.8	29.9	29.8
2001	29.3	30.2	30.1	30.4	30.4	31.3	30.1	30.2	31.1	31.0	31.0	31.1	30.5
2002	30.5	31.2	31.4	30.7	30.9	31.8	30.5	29.9	31.0	31.6	31.5	31.7	31.1
2003	30.6	31.6	31.7	31.9	32.3	32.4	31.6	31.0	31.8	32.3	32.6	32.6	31.9
Federal government													
1990	3.0	3.0	3.0	3.0	3.4	3.4	3.3	3.1	3.0	3.0	3.0	3.0	3.1
1991	2.9	3.0	2.9	3.0	3.0	3.0	3.1	3.1	3.1	3.1	3.1	3.1	3.0
1992	3.1	3.1	3.2	3.2	3.2	3.3	3.3	3.3	3.1	3.1	3.1	3.2	3.1
1993	3.2	3.2	3.2	3.2	3.2	3.1	3.2	3.2	3.0	3.1	3.1	3.1	3.1
1994	3.1	3.1	3.1	3.2	3.1	3.1	3.1	3.1	3.0	3.0	3.0	3.1	3.0
1995	3.0	3.0	3.0	3.0	3.0	3.0	3.1	3.0	3.0	3.0	3.0	3.0	3.0
1996	3.0	2.9	3.0	2.9	3.0	3.0	3.0	3.0	3.0	2.9	2.9	3.0	2.9
1997	2.9	2.9	2.9	2.9	2.9	2.9	2.9	2.9	2.9	2.9	2.9	2.9	2.9
1998	2.8	2.8	2.9	2.9	3.0	3.0	3.0	3.0	2.9	2.9	2.9	2.9	2.9
1999	2.9	2.9	2.9	2.9	2.9	2.9	2.9	2.9	2.9	2.9	2.9	2.9	2.9
2000	2.9	2.9	3.1	3.0	3.6	3.1	3.1	3.0	2.9	2.9	2.9	2.9	3.0
2001	2.9	2.9	2.9	2.9	2.9	2.9	3.0	3.0	2.9	3.0	3.0	3.1	2.9
2002	3.1	3.3	3.4	3.1	3.1	3.1	3.2	3.2	3.3	3.3	3.3	3.3	3.2
2003	3.3	3.3	3.3	3.4	3.3	3.3	3.3	3.3	3.3	3.3	3.3	3.3	3.3
State government													
1990	5.5	5.7	5.6	5.6	5.4	5.6	5.4	5.6	5.3	5.6	5.8	5.8	5.5
1991	5.4	5.6	5.6	5.6	5.6	5.3	5.4	5.3	5.4	5.5	5.5	5.5	5.4
1992	5.2	5.4	5.5	5.4	5.3	5.2	5.4	5.2	5.2	5.4	5.4	5.3	5.3
1993	5.0	5.4	5.3	5.3	5.2	5.1	5.2	5.2	5.3	5.5	5.4	5.3	5.2
1994	5.0	5.3	5.4	5.5	5.5	5.2	5.2	5.2	5.3	5.5	5.4	5.3	5.3
1995	5.5	5.8	5.9	5.9	6.0	5.8	6.0	5.9	5.7	5.8	5.8	5.8	5.8
1996	5.7	5.7	5.9	6.0	5.8	6.0	6.0	5.9	5.9	6.0	5.8	5.9	5.8
1997	5.8	5.7	5.9	5.9	5.7	5.8	5.9	5.9	6.0	6.2	6.1	6.0	5.9
1998	5.4	6.0	6.0	6.0	5.6	5.8	5.9	6.0	6.2	6.2	6.1	6.1	5.9
1999	5.4	5.9	6.1	6.1	5.7	5.7	5.9	5.9	6.0	6.1	6.1	6.0	5.9
2000	5.5	6.1	6.2	6.3	5.8	5.8	5.9	5.9	6.1	6.3	6.2	6.2	6.0
2001	5.6	6.2	6.2	6.3	6.1	6.0	6.0	6.0	6.2	6.3	6.2	6.2	6.1
2002	5.9	6.1	6.1	6.1	5.8	5.8	5.8	5.8	5.9	6.1	6.1	6.1	6.0
2003	5.7	6.2	6.2	6.1	6.2	5.6	5.8	5.7	6.0	6.2	6.2	6.2	6.0

Employment by Industry: New Jersey—*Continued*

(Numbers in thousands. Not seasonally adjusted.)

Industry	January	February	March	April	May	June	July	August	September	October	November	December	Annual Average
ATLANTIC CITY—*Continued*													
Local government													
1990	18.6	19.0	19.2	19.1	19.4	19.9	19.3	19.2	19.1	18.6	19.0	19.2	19.1
1991	19.0	19.2	19.5	19.5	19.7	20.8	19.6	19.3	19.9	19.7	19.7	19.8	19.6
1992	19.4	19.8	19.8	19.7	19.7	20.8	20.4	20.3	20.5	19.9	20.1	20.2	20.0
1993	19.9	20.3	20.2	20.1	20.2	21.0	19.8	19.5	21.0	20.3	20.6	20.5	20.2
1994	20.1	20.2	20.4	20.3	20.5	21.5	20.1	19.8	21.2	20.2	20.5	20.4	20.4
1995	20.0	19.9	20.0	20.0	20.1	21.0	20.0	19.7	20.8	20.2	20.1	20.0	20.1
1996	19.3	19.6	19.6	19.7	20.1	21.1	20.0	19.6	20.6	20.0	19.9	19.9	19.9
1997	19.5	19.7	19.7	19.6	20.1	20.6	20.1	19.8	20.3	19.7	19.8	19.9	19.9
1998	19.5	19.6	19.7	19.6	19.7	20.5	20.1	20.0	20.4	19.7	19.8	19.8	19.8
1999	19.9	20.1	20.1	20.1	20.3	21.2	20.6	20.4	20.2	20.4	20.5	20.4	20.3
2000	20.4	20.4	20.4	20.6	20.8	21.5	21.0	21.0	20.8	20.7	20.7	20.8	20.7
2001	20.8	21.1	21.0	21.2	21.4	22.4	21.1	21.2	22.0	21.7	21.8	21.8	21.4
2002	21.5	21.8	21.9	21.5	22.0	22.9	21.5	20.9	21.8	22.2	22.1	22.3	21.9
2003	21.6	22.1	22.2	22.4	22.8	23.5	22.5	22.0	22.5	22.8	23.1	23.1	22.6
BERGEN-PASSAIC													
Total nonfarm													
1990	652.3	651.1	655.8	649.8	651.9	657.4	645.6	642.8	643.6	642.7	642.9	640.5	648.0
1991	616.4	613.4	616.4	614.3	616.2	620.8	608.3	608.6	612.1	615.7	619.3	617.0	614.8
1992	595.4	595.1	597.1	596.0	600.4	605.4	597.3	597.5	599.1	603.6	605.8	607.0	599.9
1993	593.9	593.7	595.7	602.0	605.5	613.3	601.8	604.1	605.7	612.5	615.9	617.5	605.1
1994	594.2	591.9	599.8	606.3	610.2	618.4	611.9	613.0	616.6	621.8	626.7	626.0	611.4
1995	608.2	608.4	613.6	617.6	619.7	625.6	613.4	616.3	620.4	623.8	627.7	627.7	618.5
1996	605.5	612.4	617.0	621.4	626.4	632.8	621.6	624.1	628.4	633.6	639.9	641.8	625.4
1997	620.0	621.6	628.6	633.3	637.2	646.1	635.6	636.2	643.2	648.1	652.5	656.9	638.2
1998	639.5	640.1	644.7	649.0	654.6	662.4	650.5	649.7	654.0	659.7	662.5	664.7	652.6
1999	647.3	649.4	656.4	660.7	662.6	670.1	660.6	658.9	663.3	667.5	672.0	676.1	662.0
2000	659.3	661.4	668.4	672.4	674.6	682.5	670.0	666.5	673.7	673.3	678.7	684.1	672.0
2001	658.0	659.4	662.3	666.9	668.2	674.8	659.4	654.8	660.4	660.6	665.9	668.9	663.3
2002	652.8	652.5	657.4	658.3	661.3	665.9	651.3	649.1	655.6	660.6	666.9	671.3	658.6
2003	644.9	644.0	647.1	651.9	655.7	659.9	650.9	647.5	651.8	656.4	661.0	664.0	652.9
Total private													
1990	581.7	580.0	584.2	577.6	579.6	583.7	575.3	574.8	574.6	571.8	570.5	567.8	576.8
1991	545.4	542.4	544.3	542.5	544.6	549.7	541.1	542.8	544.9	544.9	547.4	545.9	544.6
1992	525.9	524.5	525.8	524.0	528.9	532.9	527.8	528.9	530.6	532.8	534.1	535.7	529.3
1993	523.5	522.3	523.6	529.3	533.7	539.9	532.7	534.9	537.0	540.3	541.9	543.9	533.5
1994	522.7	520.0	527.9	533.5	537.6	544.8	539.9	542.9	547.5	549.4	552.9	552.8	539.3
1995	536.9	535.9	541.0	544.2	547.4	552.3	543.4	547.0	551.4	550.8	553.9	554.3	546.5
1996	534.2	540.2	544.0	548.1	554.0	559.9	551.0	555.3	559.2	561.5	566.8	569.2	553.6
1997	549.7	550.3	556.7	560.8	565.9	573.2	565.9	568.5	573.9	575.4	579.0	583.5	566.9
1998	567.3	567.7	571.9	577.8	584.8	591.3	582.6	583.8	585.2	588.9	590.8	593.9	582.1
1999	577.5	578.2	584.4	588.9	591.7	598.4	591.4	592.3	593.6	595.1	599.1	602.6	591.1
2000	586.7	587.4	593.7	597.8	599.8	607.3	598.7	598.4	602.3	598.8	603.2	608.6	598.5
2001	584.3	584.0	586.9	591.2	593.3	598.9	587.4	584.9	586.6	584.4	588.5	591.3	588.4
2002	577.3	575.2	580.0	580.4	583.6	588.2	578.0	578.9	581.1	582.9	588.2	592.4	582.2
2003	568.4	565.6	568.6	572.5	576.9	581.3	575.9	575.0	575.3	575.5	579.0	582.1	574.7
Goods-producing													
1990	146.6	147.1	147.8	146.7	148.0	148.7	147.1	147.5	147.2	145.9	143.7	140.8	146.4
1991	134.7	133.8	133.8	131.9	133.3	134.8	132.3	134.3	134.9	133.8	132.7	130.7	133.4
1992	124.6	123.7	123.8	122.7	123.9	125.3	123.3	125.2	125.9	125.1	124.1	122.4	124.1
1993	118.0	118.3	118.8	119.8	121.3	123.3	121.3	123.7	123.7	123.4	121.8	120.4	121.1
1994	114.1	113.6	115.7	118.1	119.6	121.6	119.5	122.7	124.1	124.3	123.6	121.0	119.8
1995	117.4	116.9	118.3	119.8	120.8	121.9	118.9	121.7	122.5	122.2	121.2	118.6	120.0
1996	113.5	115.5	116.3	118.8	120.0	121.4	117.8	120.7	121.2	122.2	121.9	120.4	119.1
1997	116.3	116.2	117.5	118.8	120.0	121.9	119.7	121.9	123.0	123.0	122.4	121.6	120.1
1998	118.7	118.5	119.1	119.9	121.5	122.1	119.6	121.2	122.0	122.3	121.6	120.4	120.5
1999	116.1	116.6	117.3	118.0	118.6	119.8	117.6	119.1	120.1	120.0	119.7	119.0	118.4
2000	114.4	114.4	115.8	116.8	117.4	118.1	115.1	115.8	116.8	116.8	116.7	116.0	116.1
2001	109.5	109.8	110.1	111.8	112.2	112.5	108.1	108.7	108.9	107.5	107.0	106.2	109.3
2002	103.9	103.4	103.3	103.4	103.8	104.2	102.5	103.9	104.2	103.9	103.3	102.5	103.5
2003	98.3	97.4	97.5	98.5	99.0	99.5	99.0	98.8	99.1	99.1	98.6	98.1	98.6
Construction and mining													
1990	25.4	25.3	25.9	26.8	27.7	28.2	28.4	28.2	27.6	26.5	25.7	24.9	26.7
1991	20.9	20.3	20.8	21.2	21.9	22.3	22.3	22.5	22.3	21.9	21.4	20.4	21.5
1992	17.9	17.3	17.6	18.1	18.8	19.4	19.6	19.9	19.9	19.9	19.4	18.8	18.8
1993	17.0	16.6	16.8	18.1	19.1	20.0	20.5	21.1	20.7	20.8	20.6	20.2	19.2
1994	16.6	16.0	17.0	19.2	20.3	21.0	21.5	21.9	22.1	22.4	22.4	21.7	20.1
1995	18.9	17.9	18.9	20.3	21.1	21.7	21.3	21.7	21.5	21.8	21.4	20.4	20.5
1996	17.0	17.5	18.3	19.7	20.7	21.3	21.9	22.2	21.9	22.3	22.0	21.4	20.5
1997	19.3	18.9	19.4	20.5	21.3	21.9	22.3	22.6	22.6	22.8	22.8	22.4	21.4
1998	20.0	20.0	20.6	21.7	22.5	23.1	23.5	23.8	23.7	23.9	23.7	23.3	22.4
1999	20.9	21.0	21.3	22.7	23.2	23.9	24.8	24.9	25.3	25.4	25.0	24.8	23.6
2000	22.7	22.2	23.3	24.0	24.5	24.9	25.0	25.0	25.2	25.0	24.9	24.8	24.2
2001	23.7	23.7	24.2	25.7	26.4	26.8	26.7	26.7	26.9	27.2	27.1	26.9	26.0
2002	26.0	25.8	25.9	26.5	27.1	27.5	27.7	27.8	27.6	27.4	27.3	26.6	26.9
2003	24.9	24.3	24.6	26.1	27.1	27.3	27.5	27.5	27.3	27.2	26.9	26.7	26.5

Employment by Industry: New Jersey—*Continued*

(Numbers in thousands. Not seasonally adjusted.)

Industry	January	February	March	April	May	June	July	August	September	October	November	December	Annual Average
BERGEN-PASSAIC *—Continued*													
Manufacturing													
1990	121.2	121.8	121.9	119.9	120.3	120.5	118.7	119.3	119.6	119.4	118.0	115.9	119.7
1991	113.8	113.5	113.0	110.7	111.4	112.5	110.0	111.8	112.6	111.9	111.3	110.3	111.9
1992	106.7	106.4	106.2	104.6	105.1	105.9	103.7	105.3	106.0	105.2	104.7	103.6	105.2
1993	101.0	101.7	102.0	101.7	102.2	103.3	100.8	102.6	103.0	102.6	101.2	100.2	101.8
1994	97.5	97.6	98.7	98.9	99.3	100.6	98.0	100.8	102.0	101.9	101.2	99.3	99.6
1995	98.5	99.0	99.4	99.5	99.7	100.2	97.6	100.0	101.0	100.4	99.8	98.2	99.4
1996	96.5	98.0	98.0	99.1	99.3	100.1	95.9	98.5	99.3	99.9	99.9	99.0	98.6
1997	97.0	97.3	98.1	98.3	98.7	100.0	97.4	99.3	100.4	100.2	99.6	99.2	98.7
1998	98.7	98.5	98.5	98.2	99.0	99.0	96.1	97.4	98.3	98.4	97.9	97.1	98.0
1999	95.2	95.6	96.0	95.3	95.4	95.9	92.8	94.2	94.8	94.6	94.7	94.2	94.8
2000	91.7	92.2	92.5	92.8	92.9	93.2	90.1	90.8	91.6	91.8	91.8	91.2	91.8
2001	85.8	86.1	85.9	86.1	85.8	85.7	81.4	82.0	82.0	80.3	79.9	79.3	83.3
2002	77.9	77.6	77.4	76.9	76.7	76.7	74.8	76.1	76.6	76.5	76.0	75.9	76.6
2003	73.4	73.1	72.9	72.4	71.9	72.2	71.5	71.3	71.8	71.9	71.7	71.4	72.1
Service-providing													
1990	505.7	504.0	508.0	503.1	503.9	508.7	498.5	495.3	496.4	496.8	499.2	499.7	501.6
1991	481.7	479.6	482.6	482.4	482.9	486.0	476.0	474.3	477.2	481.9	486.6	486.3	481.4
1992	470.8	471.4	473.3	473.3	476.5	480.1	474.0	472.3	473.2	478.5	481.7	484.6	475.8
1993	475.9	475.4	476.9	482.2	484.2	490.0	480.5	480.4	482.0	489.1	494.1	497.1	483.9
1994	480.1	478.3	484.1	488.2	490.6	496.8	492.4	490.3	492.5	497.5	503.1	505.0	491.5
1995	490.8	491.5	495.3	497.8	498.9	503.7	494.5	494.6	497.9	501.6	506.5	509.1	498.5
1996	492.0	496.9	500.7	502.6	506.4	511.4	503.8	503.4	507.2	511.4	518.0	521.4	506.2
1997	503.7	505.4	511.1	514.5	517.2	524.2	515.9	514.3	520.2	525.1	530.1	535.3	518.0
1998	520.8	521.6	525.6	529.1	533.1	540.3	530.9	528.5	532.0	537.4	540.9	544.3	532.0
1999	531.2	532.8	539.1	542.7	544.0	550.3	543.0	539.8	543.2	547.5	552.3	557.1	543.5
2000	544.9	547.0	552.6	555.6	557.2	564.4	554.9	550.7	556.9	556.5	562.0	568.1	555.9
2001	548.5	549.6	552.2	555.1	556.0	562.3	551.3	546.1	551.5	553.1	558.9	562.7	553.9
2002	548.9	549.1	554.1	554.9	557.5	561.7	548.8	545.2	551.4	556.7	563.6	568.8	555.1
2003	546.6	546.6	549.6	553.4	556.7	560.4	551.9	548.7	552.7	557.3	562.4	565.9	554.4
Trade, transportation, and utilities													
1990	174.9	172.0	172.9	168.1	168.5	169.7	166.2	166.6	166.8	167.3	168.4	169.1	169.2
1991	161.3	158.4	158.0	158.2	157.8	159.0	155.7	155.6	157.2	159.5	162.8	163.9	158.9
1992	155.1	153.0	152.9	151.6	152.9	153.6	151.7	151.5	152.7	154.6	156.5	158.7	153.7
1993	154.4	152.5	152.3	152.0	152.7	154.2	151.7	151.4	153.3	155.4	158.0	160.8	154.0
1994	153.2	150.9	152.1	152.7	153.9	155.2	154.5	154.7	156.7	158.4	161.2	163.7	155.6
1995	158.3	156.0	156.3	156.0	156.8	157.2	155.2	155.3	157.1	157.3	160.3	163.0	157.4
1996	156.7	155.6	155.6	155.8	156.9	158.4	155.7	156.0	158.1	158.6	162.7	164.8	157.9
1997	158.4	156.4	157.1	157.2	158.0	159.7	157.3	157.2	159.5	161.0	163.9	167.1	159.4
1998	159.7	157.5	157.7	158.2	159.8	161.2	158.8	158.6	159.9	161.6	164.1	166.5	160.3
1999	160.8	158.9	160.4	160.8	161.5	163.0	160.9	161.0	162.2	163.0	166.4	170.1	162.4
2000	164.5	162.8	163.6	165.0	165.2	166.2	164.2	163.7	165.5	166.9	169.9	174.5	166.0
2001	166.7	163.7	163.6	164.1	164.4	165.5	163.0	161.7	163.0	162.3	165.0	167.6	164.2
2002	161.1	159.1	159.9	160.1	160.4	161.9	159.5	157.9	159.0	160.9	164.1	167.4	160.9
2003	160.1	158.6	158.6	157.9	158.7	160.0	157.6	156.9	158.0	159.0	162.4	164.9	159.4
Wholesale trade													
1990	65.3	65.2	66.0	63.1	62.9	63.1	61.6	61.7	61.5	61.6	61.3	60.9	62.8
1991	60.2	59.7	59.8	59.1	58.9	59.1	58.7	58.7	58.3	57.8	58.4	58.2	58.9
1992	56.7	56.7	56.8	56.2	56.6	56.7	56.0	55.9	55.9	56.2	56.3	56.5	56.3
1993	55.2	55.4	55.6	54.8	54.6	54.9	54.7	54.8	54.9	54.9	54.9	55.1	54.9
1994	54.3	54.4	54.8	55.3	55.3	55.4	56.4	56.4	56.6	56.2	56.1	56.4	55.6
1995	55.6	56.0	56.4	56.5	56.2	56.3	55.5	55.4	55.6	54.9	55.0	55.3	55.7
1996	54.5	55.1	55.4	55.2	55.0	55.3	55.0	54.6	54.6	55.0	55.6	55.6	55.0
1997	54.6	55.0	55.5	55.3	55.6	55.9	55.5	55.4	55.6	55.4	55.8	56.4	55.5
1998	54.0	54.1	54.4	54.7	54.9	55.3	54.9	54.9	54.7	54.7	54.8	54.8	54.6
1999	55.9	56.0	56.3	56.4	56.5	56.7	56.7	56.7	56.9	57.1	57.4	57.7	56.6
2000	57.5	57.7	57.9	57.8	57.7	58.0	57.6	57.7	58.0	57.7	57.9	59.3	57.9
2001	60.5	60.5	60.6	60.6	60.4	60.4	59.8	59.4	59.4	58.5	58.5	58.4	59.7
2002	57.5	57.2	57.6	57.6	57.4	57.4	56.8	56.5	56.4	56.6	56.6	57.0	57.1
2003	56.0	56.0	56.0	56.0	56.0	56.1	55.3	55.0	54.8	54.8	55.1	55.5	55.6
Retail trade													
1990	86.6	84.0	83.8	81.8	82.3	83.1	81.8	81.9	82.2	82.5	83.9	85.1	83.2
1991	79.0	76.8	76.1	76.6	76.3	77.0	76.5	76.4	77.5	79.5	82.2	83.5	78.1
1992	77.0	74.7	74.5	74.0	74.0	74.6	74.0	73.9	74.4	75.8	77.7	79.6	75.3
1993	77.0	75.1	74.5	74.3	75.0	76.1	74.8	74.5	75.3	76.9	79.4	82.1	76.2
1994	76.3	73.8	74.4	73.9	75.0	76.1	75.1	75.5	76.2	78.5	81.5	83.7	76.6
1995	79.2	76.6	76.4	76.0	77.0	77.4	77.4	77.5	78.0	78.5	81.4	83.8	78.2
1996	78.6	76.5	76.2	76.4	77.6	78.8	77.9	78.5	79.3	79.5	82.8	85.0	78.9
1997	80.2	77.7	77.8	77.5	77.9	79.1	77.9	77.9	78.8	80.1	82.7	85.3	79.4
1998	80.2	77.9	77.7	78.0	78.9	79.8	79.2	79.2	79.6	80.9	83.4	86.0	80.0
1999	81.0	79.1	80.1	80.1	80.5	81.7	80.5	80.6	80.8	80.8	83.8	87.3	81.3
2000	82.4	80.6	80.9	82.5	82.7	83.5	82.6	82.5	82.6	83.8	86.6	90.0	83.3
2001	82.8	79.8	79.6	80.1	80.5	81.8	80.7	80.4	80.7	81.1	83.9	86.6	81.4
2002	82.1	80.2	80.6	80.7	81.3	82.7	81.8	81.2	81.2	82.5	85.6	88.6	82.4
2003	82.9	81.7	81.7	81.8	82.5	83.6	82.3	82.2	82.3	83.7	86.7	89.2	83.4

Employment by Industry: New Jersey—*Continued*

(Numbers in thousands. Not seasonally adjusted.)

Industry	January	February	March	April	May	June	July	August	September	October	November	December	Annual Average
BERGEN-PASSAIC *—Continued*													
Transportation and utilities													
1990	23.0	22.8	23.1	23.2	23.3	23.5	22.8	23.0	23.1	23.2	23.2	23.1	23.1
1991	22.1	21.9	22.1	22.5	22.6	22.9	20.5	20.5	21.4	22.2	22.2	22.2	21.9
1992	21.4	21.6	21.6	21.4	22.3	22.3	21.7	21.7	22.4	22.6	22.5	22.6	22.0
1993	22.2	22.0	22.2	22.9	23.1	23.2	22.2	22.1	23.1	23.6	23.7	23.6	22.8
1994	22.6	22.7	22.9	23.5	23.6	23.7	23.0	22.8	23.9	23.7	23.6	23.6	23.3
1995	23.5	23.4	23.5	23.5	23.6	23.5	22.3	22.4	23.5	23.9	23.9	23.9	23.4
1996	23.6	24.0	24.0	24.2	24.3	24.3	22.8	22.9	24.2	24.1	24.3	24.2	23.9
1997	23.6	23.7	23.8	24.4	24.5	24.7	23.9	23.9	25.1	25.5	25.4	25.4	24.4
1998	25.5	25.5	25.6	25.5	26.0	26.1	24.7	24.5	25.6	26.0	25.9	25.7	25.5
1999	23.9	23.8	24.0	24.3	24.5	24.6	23.7	23.7	24.5	25.1	25.2	25.1	24.3
2000	24.6	24.5	24.8	24.7	24.8	24.7	24.0	23.5	24.9	25.4	25.4	25.2	24.7
2001	23.4	23.4	23.4	23.4	23.5	23.3	22.5	21.9	22.9	22.7	22.6	22.6	22.9
2002	21.5	21.7	21.7	21.8	21.7	21.8	20.9	20.2	21.4	21.8	21.9	21.8	21.5
2003	21.2	20.9	20.9	20.1	20.2	20.3	20.0	19.7	20.9	20.5	20.6	20.2	20.5
Information													
1990	21.5	21.9	21.9	21.6	21.7	21.8	21.6	21.4	21.4	22.2	22.3	22.1	21.7
1991	21.8	21.6	21.6	21.9	21.9	22.2	21.8	21.6	21.6	20.9	20.9	21.1	21.5
1992	21.5	21.6	21.4	21.1	21.1	21.5	21.7	21.6	21.9	22.0	21.9	22.0	21.6
1993	20.6	20.2	20.4	19.9	19.8	20.2	20.2	19.9	19.9	19.6	19.8	19.9	20.0
1994	20.1	20.4	20.8	20.9	21.1	21.5	21.2	21.3	21.3	21.3	21.5	21.4	21.0
1995	21.5	21.5	21.6	21.6	21.7	21.7	21.8	22.1	21.9	22.3	22.2	22.6	21.8
1996	22.7	22.8	22.9	23.0	23.1	23.6	23.6	23.6	23.6	24.3	24.4	24.7	23.5
1997	23.3	23.8	25.0	23.9	23.9	24.2	24.3	24.5	24.6	23.3	23.5	23.7	24.0
1998	23.6	23.8	24.3	24.5	24.7	24.9	24.4	24.5	24.4	24.4	24.5	24.7	24.3
1999	23.6	23.5	23.6	23.6	23.7	23.9	24.0	24.0	24.0	23.6	23.7	23.7	23.7
2000	22.0	22.0	22.0	22.3	22.4	22.9	22.6	22.1	22.6	22.4	22.7	22.9	22.4
2001	25.4	25.5	25.6	25.4	25.1	25.3	25.0	24.5	24.7	24.4	24.8	24.4	25.0
2002	23.5	23.5	23.4	22.1	21.9	21.9	20.9	20.8	20.4	19.5	19.8	19.7	21.5
2003	15.6	15.5	15.7	15.6	15.7	15.9	15.8	15.8	15.5	14.5	14.7	14.9	15.4
Financial activities													
1990	38.2	38.2	38.2	39.2	38.8	39.4	38.8	38.7	38.2	37.9	37.9	38.0	38.4
1991	37.9	37.7	37.7	37.4	37.5	38.1	37.9	37.7	37.0	36.7	36.7	36.6	37.4
1992	36.3	36.3	36.5	36.0	36.2	36.7	36.3	36.2	35.9	35.8	35.6	35.9	36.1
1993	36.0	35.9	36.2	35.8	36.0	36.7	36.0	35.9	35.3	35.5	35.5	35.7	35.8
1994	35.4	35.6	35.9	35.4	35.5	36.1	36.0	35.9	35.9	35.5	35.6	35.6	35.7
1995	36.0	35.8	36.0	35.4	35.3	35.6	35.8	36.0	35.8	34.8	35.0	35.1	35.5
1996	34.5	34.8	35.1	34.1	34.4	35.0	34.5	34.5	34.4	34.6	34.8	35.2	34.6
1997	34.2	34.4	34.7	34.4	34.7	35.4	35.7	35.8	35.6	35.7	35.9	36.4	35.2
1998	37.1	37.2	37.4	36.9	37.4	38.2	38.7	38.5	37.9	37.5	37.3	37.5	37.6
1999	37.9	37.9	37.8	39.0	39.4	39.7	39.6	39.5	38.5	38.4	38.5	39.0	38.7
2000	39.0	38.8	38.9	39.1	39.3	40.0	39.7	39.9	39.5	38.5	38.7	38.9	39.1
2001	36.0	36.1	36.0	36.2	36.5	37.1	36.4	36.2	36.1	36.7	37.2	38.0	36.5
2002	36.9	36.8	36.9	36.4	36.8	37.1	37.0	37.1	37.0	37.2	37.3	37.6	37.0
2003	37.1	37.1	37.4	37.3	37.6	38.0	38.1	37.8	37.6	38.1	38.5	38.3	37.7
Professional and business services													
1990	87.6	87.8	88.7	86.7	86.5	87.2	87.1	87.2	86.3	83.9	83.5	83.0	86.2
1991	78.6	78.8	79.9	78.4	77.8	78.5	78.1	78.5	78.2	77.0	76.8	76.2	78.0
1992	74.2	74.4	75.1	75.8	76.5	76.7	77.7	77.4	76.7	76.8	77.0	77.3	76.3
1993	76.8	77.4	77.9	81.1	81.6	82.0	82.5	82.8	82.5	83.3	83.6	83.2	81.2
1994	78.9	79.4	80.7	82.0	82.1	83.0	83.4	84.0	84.1	83.7	84.4	84.1	82.4
1995	79.3	80.7	82.0	84.0	84.3	85.0	84.2	84.2	84.7	85.5	86.1	85.7	83.8
1996	80.8	83.1	84.3	86.0	87.3	87.7	88.6	89.6	89.3	88.4	89.0	89.2	86.9
1997	87.2	88.0	89.8	93.2	93.8	94.9	95.4	95.9	95.8	96.7	96.7	97.1	93.7
1998	93.8	94.6	96.1	99.4	99.9	101.5	100.0	100.1	99.3	100.3	100.4	100.9	98.8
1999	98.1	99.5	101.6	102.4	102.2	104.1	103.2	103.1	102.6	102.4	102.6	102.7	102.0
2000	101.8	103.1	105.4	104.1	104.2	106.4	105.1	105.3	105.0	103.8	104.4	104.9	104.4
2001	101.9	102.8	104.3	104.8	104.6	106.1	105.1	105.1	105.3	104.4	104.6	104.5	104.4
2002	100.9	100.4	103.3	103.3	104.0	104.8	102.4	103.2	103.9	102.8	103.4	104.2	103.1
2003	99.3	99.4	100.0	101.6	102.6	103.0	100.8	102.1	102.1	101.6	101.5	102.0	101.3
Educational and health services													
1990	58.8	59.2	59.9	59.5	59.6	59.3	57.9	57.9	59.3	60.0	60.3	60.5	59.3
1991	59.8	60.5	61.1	61.7	61.9	62.0	60.4	60.2	61.7	63.1	63.7	64.1	61.6
1992	63.4	64.0	64.4	64.3	64.7	64.8	63.3	63.3	64.2	65.6	65.9	66.1	64.5
1993	65.7	65.7	66.3	65.9	66.1	66.2	65.2	64.7	66.2	66.9	67.0	67.2	66.0
1994	66.8	66.8	68.0	68.2	68.1	68.0	66.7	66.1	67.9	69.0	69.3	69.5	67.8
1995	69.7	69.7	70.7	70.9	70.9	71.5	70.3	70.2	72.2	71.8	72.5	72.4	71.0
1996	71.5	72.8	73.5	72.7	73.3	73.5	70.8	70.6	72.9	74.2	74.6	75.4	72.9
1997	73.4	74.0	74.5	74.8	75.3	75.4	73.3	72.7	75.2	75.6	76.6	76.9	74.8
1998	76.1	76.9	77.3	79.0	79.3	79.5	78.5	78.4	79.8	81.3	81.2	81.5	79.0
1999	81.3	81.7	82.3	82.2	82.3	82.2	81.0	80.6	82.0	83.8	84.3	84.0	82.3
2000	82.9	83.6	84.2	85.4	85.4	86.0	85.4	84.9	87.1	86.7	87.1	87.5	85.5
2001	82.3	82.8	83.5	84.4	85.0	85.5	83.5	83.2	84.4	85.0	85.7	86.3	84.3
2002	87.3	87.9	88.4	88.7	89.2	89.3	87.8	88.0	89.5	90.8	92.1	92.4	89.3
2003	91.4	91.2	92.1	92.5	92.6	92.7	92.0	91.3	92.3	93.3	93.4	93.8	92.4

Employment by Industry: New Jersey—*Continued*

(Numbers in thousands. Not seasonally adjusted.)

Industry	January	February	March	April	May	June	July	August	September	October	November	December	Annual Average
BERGEN-PASSAIC *—Continued*													
Leisure and hospitality													
1990	32.4	32.2	33.0	33.8	34.5	35.4	34.6	33.7	33.9	33.5	33.4	33.4	33.6
1991	30.8	31.2	31.8	32.5	33.7	34.2	33.5	33.6	33.6	33.3	33.3	32.7	32.8
1992	30.4	31.0	31.2	31.9	32.8	33.3	32.8	32.7	32.8	32.2	32.3	32.4	32.1
1993	31.5	31.9	31.3	34.1	35.2	35.9	34.4	35.1	35.4	35.4	35.4	35.6	34.2
1994	34.0	33.2	34.2	35.3	36.3	38.0	36.8	36.5	36.3	36.0	35.9	36.1	35.7
1995	33.8	34.4	35.1	35.3	36.4	37.8	35.7	35.9	36.1	35.5	35.1	35.2	35.5
1996	33.4	34.2	34.7	35.8	36.9	37.7	37.3	37.5	37.4	36.6	36.8	36.9	36.2
1997	34.7	35.2	35.7	36.1	37.5	38.6	37.0	37.1	37.3	37.1	37.1	37.6	36.7
1998	35.5	36.5	37.2	36.9	38.8	40.2	38.6	38.6	38.4	38.0	38.3	38.9	37.9
1999	36.5	36.9	37.9	39.1	39.9	41.3	40.0	40.0	39.8	38.9	38.8	38.8	38.9
2000	37.3	37.7	38.6	39.5	40.3	41.6	40.2	40.3	40.1	38.8	38.8	39.0	39.3
2001	37.7	38.3	38.7	39.2	40.1	41.2	40.5	40.0	39.2	38.7	38.9	39.0	39.2
2002	38.2	38.8	39.5	41.2	42.1	43.6	42.5	42.7	42.5	42.6	43.0	43.4	41.7
2003	41.6	41.5	42.2	43.7	45.1	46.4	46.3	46.2	45.2	44.5	44.5	44.5	44.3
Other services													
1990	21.7	21.6	21.8	22.0	22.0	22.2	22.0	21.8	21.5	21.1	21.0	20.9	21.6
1991	20.5	20.4	20.4	20.5	20.7	20.9	21.4	21.3	20.7	20.6	20.5	20.6	20.7
1992	20.4	20.5	20.5	20.6	20.8	21.0	21.0	21.0	20.5	20.7	20.8	20.9	20.7
1993	20.5	20.4	20.4	20.7	21.0	21.4	21.4	21.4	20.7	20.8	20.8	21.1	20.8
1994	20.2	20.1	20.5	20.9	21.0	21.4	21.8	21.7	21.2	21.2	21.4	21.4	21.0
1995	20.9	20.9	21.0	21.2	21.2	21.6	21.5	21.6	21.1	21.4	21.5	21.7	21.3
1996	21.1	21.4	21.6	21.9	22.1	22.6	22.7	22.8	22.3	22.6	22.6	22.6	22.1
1997	22.2	22.3	22.4	22.4	22.7	23.1	23.2	23.4	22.9	23.0	22.9	23.1	22.8
1998	22.8	22.7	22.8	23.0	23.4	23.7	24.0	23.9	23.5	23.5	23.4	23.5	23.3
1999	23.2	23.2	23.5	23.8	24.1	24.4	25.1	25.0	24.4	25.0	25.1	25.3	24.3
2000	24.8	25.0	25.2	25.6	25.6	26.1	26.4	26.4	25.7	24.9	24.9	24.9	25.4
2001	24.8	25.0	25.1	25.3	25.4	25.7	25.8	25.5	25.0	25.4	25.3	25.3	25.3
2002	25.5	25.3	25.3	25.2	25.4	25.4	25.4	25.3	24.6	25.2	25.2	25.2	25.3
2003	25.0	24.9	25.1	25.4	25.6	25.8	26.3	26.1	25.5	25.4	25.4	25.6	25.5
Government													
1990	70.6	71.1	71.6	72.2	72.3	73.7	70.3	68.0	69.0	70.9	72.4	72.7	71.2
1991	71.0	71.0	72.1	71.8	71.6	71.1	67.2	65.8	67.2	70.8	71.9	71.1	70.2
1992	69.5	70.6	71.3	72.0	71.5	72.5	69.5	68.6	68.5	70.8	71.7	71.3	70.6
1993	70.4	71.4	72.1	72.7	71.8	73.4	69.1	69.2	68.7	72.2	74.0	73.6	71.5
1994	71.5	71.9	71.9	72.8	72.6	73.6	72.0	70.1	69.1	72.4	73.8	73.2	72.0
1995	71.3	72.5	72.6	73.4	72.3	73.3	70.0	69.3	69.0	73.0	73.8	73.4	71.9
1996	71.3	72.2	73.0	73.3	72.4	72.9	70.6	68.8	69.2	72.1	73.1	72.6	71.7
1997	70.3	71.3	71.9	72.5	71.3	72.9	69.7	67.7	69.3	72.7	73.5	73.4	71.3
1998	72.2	72.4	72.8	71.2	69.8	71.1	67.9	65.9	68.8	70.8	71.7	70.8	70.4
1999	69.8	71.2	72.0	71.8	70.9	71.7	69.2	66.6	69.7	72.4	72.9	73.5	70.9
2000	72.6	74.0	74.7	74.6	74.8	75.2	71.3	68.1	71.4	74.5	75.5	75.5	73.5
2001	73.7	75.4	75.4	75.7	74.9	75.9	72.0	69.9	73.8	76.2	77.4	77.6	74.8
2002	75.5	77.3	77.4	77.9	77.7	77.7	73.3	70.2	74.5	77.7	78.7	78.9	76.4
2003	76.5	78.4	78.5	79.4	78.8	78.6	75.0	72.5	76.5	80.9	82.0	81.9	78.3
Federal government													
2002	5.1	5.0	5.1	5.0	5.0	5.0	5.0	5.0	5.0	5.1	5.0	5.0	5.0
2003	5.0	4.9	4.9	4.9	4.9	4.9	4.9	4.9	4.8	4.8	4.8	4.8	4.8
State government													
2002	10.2	11.5	11.3	11.4	11.4	10.3	10.3	9.9	10.8	11.0	11.3	11.2	10.8
2003	9.8	11.3	11.4	11.4	11.3	10.0	10.0	9.9	11.4	11.8	11.9	11.9	11.0
Local government													
2002	60.2	60.8	61.0	61.5	61.3	62.4	58.0	55.3	58.7	61.6	62.4	62.7	60.4
2003	61.7	62.2	62.2	63.1	62.6	63.7	60.1	57.7	60.3	64.3	65.3	65.2	62.3
CAMDEN													
Total nonfarm													
1990	445.8	446.3	447.9	447.6	451.3	454.8	444.5	443.2	442.0	442.6	443.6	444.5	446.1
1991	429.6	427.0	428.5	431.4	434.2	434.8	428.7	425.1	426.5	426.9	429.3	431.6	429.4
1992	418.1	417.7	419.5	421.2	424.2	428.4	423.4	422.3	422.9	428.4	431.7	433.4	424.2
1993	421.7	421.9	423.8	427.4	431.1	433.4	427.6	428.0	429.6	435.5	437.9	441.4	429.9
1994	428.6	427.3	433.4	440.7	444.7	448.1	441.0	440.8	445.2	449.3	453.1	456.4	442.3
1995	442.3	442.0	445.6	448.6	452.1	454.4	447.3	448.4	451.9	455.6	459.2	460.3	450.6
1996	441.6	445.8	450.3	453.9	458.6	464.2	454.7	455.8	459.3	463.5	467.2	470.1	457.0
1997	456.7	459.0	464.0	466.1	470.2	474.3	467.3	466.8	473.1	476.6	479.8	483.0	469.7
1998	471.8	472.2	476.4	480.3	484.8	489.6	482.1	481.4	485.3	488.2	492.2	495.6	483.3
1999	482.5	485.4	490.4	494.3	496.5	502.2	494.5	493.4	495.3	501.2	504.4	508.0	495.6
2000	492.3	491.4	497.9	500.2	501.7	505.9	499.0	498.4	501.1	502.4	507.5	511.2	500.7
2001	495.2	494.4	498.3	503.7	505.9	510.8	502.7	502.4	504.2	508.1	512.9	515.9	504.5
2002	504.9	504.8	508.9	510.4	512.0	518.4	507.8	507.9	510.0	514.1	518.0	520.2	511.5
2003	508.3	506.0	511.4	518.3	520.6	525.9	518.2	516.0	519.6	526.1	530.0	532.3	519.4

Employment by Industry: New Jersey—*Continued*

(Numbers in thousands. Not seasonally adjusted.)

Industry	January	February	March	April	May	June	July	August	September	October	November	December	Annual Average
CAMDEN—*Continued*													
Total private													
1990	369.1	368.6	370.5	369.7	372.4	375.3	370.6	370.2	368.2	365.3	365.1	365.8	369.2
1991	352.1	349.3	350.9	352.2	354.7	356.7	353.6	352.2	351.9	349.5	350.4	352.9	352.2
1992	340.8	339.6	340.7	342.5	345.9	349.5	348.3	348.0	348.4	351.2	353.1	355.1	346.9
1993	344.6	343.7	344.9	349.3	353.1	356.0	355.2	356.3	356.1	357.3	359.3	362.5	353.1
1994	351.8	350.2	354.8	361.3	365.3	369.1	367.0	368.2	370.4	371.0	373.8	376.3	364.9
1995	364.3	363.3	366.4	369.2	372.9	376.0	374.5	375.8	376.5	376.6	379.0	379.9	372.8
1996	363.6	366.4	370.5	374.0	379.9	384.9	381.8	383.5	384.1	384.5	387.0	390.1	379.1
1997	378.6	379.5	384.1	386.5	391.3	395.3	393.9	393.8	396.3	396.6	399.0	402.2	391.4
1998	392.0	391.4	395.0	398.6	404.4	409.3	408.2	408.4	407.9	407.2	410.4	414.2	403.9
1999	402.5	403.5	408.5	412.1	415.6	421.5	420.9	420.5	417.5	419.4	422.0	426.1	415.8
2000	411.9	409.0	414.6	416.7	418.5	423.7	423.5	422.4	421.4	419.5	423.8	428.3	419.4
2001	413.1	409.8	414.0	419.3	422.6	427.1	426.6	426.6	422.5	422.8	426.5	429.7	421.7
2002	419.0	417.8	421.8	423.6	425.9	432.8	430.3	430.8	427.8	427.9	430.9	433.7	426.9
2003	423.1	419.8	424.5	431.2	434.5	439.7	438.5	438.1	437.1	439.5	441.4	443.8	434.3
Goods-producing													
1990	84.2	84.2	85.0	84.4	85.0	85.3	84.5	84.1	83.2	80.6	79.0	77.9	83.1
1991	74.9	73.8	74.0	75.3	75.6	75.7	75.0	75.0	75.0	74.8	74.3	73.9	74.7
1992	69.4	68.8	69.0	69.8	70.6	71.8	71.5	71.4	71.2	71.1	70.9	70.4	70.4
1993	68.9	68.7	68.9	70.3	71.4	72.1	72.4	73.0	73.1	72.5	72.5	72.5	71.3
1994	69.5	68.4	69.7	72.1	73.4	74.5	74.1	75.3	75.9	76.1	76.3	75.9	73.4
1995	72.8	71.8	72.9	73.9	74.9	75.6	74.9	75.7	75.5	75.8	75.4	74.2	74.4
1996	69.5	70.1	71.8	73.0	73.9	75.2	75.0	75.4	75.2	74.9	75.1	74.7	73.6
1997	72.3	72.0	72.9	74.0	74.3	75.2	75.8	76.1	76.0	75.5	75.3	75.1	74.5
1998	73.1	72.9	73.5	75.1	75.5	76.2	76.1	76.1	75.9	75.6	75.5	75.2	75.0
1999	72.8	73.2	73.8	75.2	75.7	76.5	77.1	77.4	77.4	77.5	77.3	77.1	75.9
2000	74.7	74.0	75.6	76.6	76.6	77.2	77.0	77.0	76.8	76.6	76.6	76.6	76.2
2001	74.6	74.1	74.9	75.4	75.8	76.1	76.6	76.4	75.9	75.5	74.7	74.3	75.3
2002	71.7	71.6	72.0	72.3	73.2	73.6	72.9	73.6	72.9	72.6	72.2	71.5	72.5
2003	69.1	67.9	68.7	70.6	71.4	72.0	71.6	72.0	71.9	71.5	71.5	71.2	70.8
Construction and mining													
1990	21.1	21.1	21.9	22.2	22.7	23.1	23.1	22.6	22.3	21.1	20.2	19.5	21.7
1991	17.9	17.1	17.5	18.2	18.6	18.9	19.0	18.7	18.4	18.5	18.2	17.4	18.2
1992	15.7	15.3	15.5	16.0	16.6	17.3	17.8	17.9	17.6	17.2	17.1	16.7	16.7
1993	15.8	15.6	15.6	16.4	17.2	17.7	18.0	18.2	18.1	18.2	18.1	17.8	17.2
1994	15.7	14.8	15.7	17.5	18.5	19.2	19.7	20.0	20.0	20.5	20.5	20.1	18.5
1995	18.2	17.3	18.0	18.8	19.3	20.0	20.1	20.3	20.0	20.1	19.8	18.9	19.2
1996	15.7	16.4	17.8	18.8	19.6	20.4	20.6	20.9	20.6	20.9	21.2	20.7	19.4
1997	18.9	18.6	19.4	20.3	21.2	21.6	22.2	22.4	22.2	22.1	21.8	21.3	21.0
1998	20.1	20.0	20.4	21.6	21.8	22.4	22.4	22.6	22.3	22.3	22.4	22.2	21.7
1999	19.9	20.2	20.6	21.7	22.2	22.6	23.0	23.1	22.8	23.1	22.8	22.5	22.0
2000	20.8	19.9	21.4	22.2	22.4	22.7	22.5	22.7	22.6	22.4	22.4	22.3	22.0
2001	21.2	21.2	22.0	23.0	23.6	23.9	24.6	24.7	24.3	24.5	24.3	23.9	23.4
2002	22.4	22.4	23.0	23.4	24.1	24.5	24.6	25.0	24.5	24.5	24.2	23.6	23.9
2003	22.1	21.0	21.7	23.6	24.4	24.9	25.0	25.1	25.0	24.8	24.5	24.1	23.9
Manufacturing													
1990	63.1	63.1	63.1	62.2	62.3	62.2	61.4	61.5	60.9	59.5	58.8	58.4	61.3
1991	57.0	56.7	56.5	57.1	57.0	56.8	56.0	56.3	56.6	56.3	56.1	56.5	56.5
1992	53.7	53.5	53.5	53.8	54.0	54.5	53.7	53.5	53.6	53.9	53.8	53.7	53.7
1993	53.1	53.1	53.3	53.9	54.2	54.4	54.4	54.8	55.0	54.3	54.4	54.7	54.1
1994	53.8	53.6	54.0	54.6	54.9	55.3	54.4	55.3	55.9	55.6	55.8	55.8	54.9
1995	54.6	54.5	54.9	55.1	55.6	55.6	54.8	55.4	55.5	55.7	55.6	55.3	55.2
1996	53.8	53.7	54.0	54.2	54.3	54.8	54.4	54.5	54.6	54.0	53.9	54.0	54.1
1997	53.4	53.4	53.5	53.7	53.1	53.6	53.6	53.7	53.8	53.4	53.5	53.8	53.5
1998	53.0	52.9	53.1	53.5	53.7	53.8	53.7	53.5	53.6	53.3	53.1	53.0	53.3
1999	52.9	53.0	53.2	53.5	53.5	53.9	54.1	54.3	54.6	54.4	54.5	54.6	53.8
2000	53.9	54.1	54.2	54.4	54.2	54.5	54.5	54.3	54.2	54.2	54.2	54.3	54.2
2001	53.4	52.9	52.9	52.4	52.2	52.2	52.0	51.7	51.6	51.0	50.4	50.4	51.9
2002	49.3	49.2	49.0	48.9	49.1	49.1	48.3	48.6	48.4	48.1	48.0	47.9	48.7
2003	47.0	46.9	47.0	47.0	47.0	47.1	46.6	46.9	46.9	46.7	47.0	47.1	46.9
Service-providing													
1990	361.6	362.1	362.9	363.2	366.3	369.5	360.0	359.1	358.8	362.0	364.6	366.6	363.0
1991	354.7	353.2	354.5	356.1	358.6	359.1	353.7	350.1	351.5	352.1	355.0	357.7	354.6
1992	348.7	348.9	350.5	351.4	353.6	356.6	351.9	350.9	351.7	357.3	360.8	363.0	353.7
1993	352.8	353.2	354.9	357.1	359.7	361.3	355.2	355.0	356.5	363.0	365.4	368.9	358.5
1994	359.1	358.9	363.7	368.6	371.3	373.6	366.9	365.5	369.3	373.2	376.8	380.5	368.9
1995	369.5	370.2	372.7	374.7	377.2	378.8	372.4	372.7	376.4	379.8	383.8	386.1	376.1
1996	372.1	375.7	378.5	380.9	384.7	389.0	379.7	380.4	384.1	388.6	392.1	395.4	383.4
1997	384.4	387.0	391.1	392.1	395.9	399.1	391.5	390.7	397.1	401.1	404.5	407.9	395.2
1998	398.7	399.3	402.9	405.2	409.3	413.4	406.0	405.3	409.4	412.6	416.7	420.4	408.2
1999	409.7	412.2	416.6	419.1	420.8	425.7	417.4	416.0	417.9	423.7	427.1	430.9	419.7
2000	417.6	417.4	422.3	423.6	425.1	428.7	422.0	421.4	424.3	425.8	430.9	434.6	424.4
2001	420.6	420.3	423.4	428.3	430.1	434.7	426.1	426.0	428.3	432.6	438.2	441.6	429.1
2002	433.2	433.2	436.9	438.1	438.8	444.8	434.9	434.3	437.1	441.5	445.8	448.7	438.9
2003	439.2	438.1	442.7	447.7	449.2	453.9	446.6	444.0	447.7	454.6	458.5	461.1	448.6

Employment by Industry: New Jersey—*Continued*

(Numbers in thousands. Not seasonally adjusted.)

Industry	January	February	March	April	May	June	July	August	September	October	November	December	Annual Average
CAMDEN—*Continued*													
Trade, transportation, and utilities													
1990	108.7	106.8	106.5	105.3	105.6	106.0	104.7	105.0	104.6	105.9	107.4	109.6	106.3
1991	102.7	100.3	99.9	100.8	101.2	101.6	100.0	99.7	100.7	100.4	102.1	104.3	101.1
1992	100.0	98.0	97.9	97.9	98.2	98.7	98.1	98.3	99.4	101.1	103.6	105.8	99.7
1993	100.6	98.8	98.6	98.9	99.5	100.1	99.3	99.4	99.7	101.8	103.9	106.3	100.5
1994	103.1	101.3	102.2	103.7	104.5	105.5	104.7	104.9	106.2	107.5	110.4	112.4	105.5
1995	107.4	106.0	105.9	107.1	107.8	108.2	107.9	108.1	109.5	110.5	112.9	114.7	108.8
1996	109.0	107.9	108.3	109.1	110.4	111.5	109.9	110.6	112.0	112.9	114.9	117.1	111.1
1997	111.8	110.8	111.3	110.8	111.3	111.3	110.6	109.0	111.6	112.9	115.3	117.8	112.0
1998	113.1	111.3	111.5	111.7	112.9	114.6	115.0	115.0	116.3	116.0	118.6	121.5	114.7
1999	116.3	115.4	116.5	117.6	118.2	119.5	119.2	119.9	119.7	121.3	124.3	127.7	119.6
2000	120.5	119.0	119.7	120.6	121.1	121.9	121.4	122.0	121.8	122.0	124.8	128.3	121.9
2001	121.7	119.3	119.9	121.3	121.5	122.2	120.5	120.0	118.8	120.6	124.1	125.9	121.3
2002	119.9	118.5	119.6	119.6	119.7	121.2	119.4	119.8	120.3	120.8	123.1	125.8	120.6
2003	121.0	119.2	120.0	121.2	121.6	122.5	121.4	121.1	121.9	124.3	126.5	128.3	122.4
Wholesale trade													
1990	26.2	26.3	26.1	25.7	25.6	25.6	25.3	25.4	25.2	25.1	25.1	24.9	25.5
1991	23.8	23.5	23.5	23.7	23.7	23.7	23.3	23.1	23.2	23.3	23.2	23.4	23.4
1992	23.1	23.1	22.9	23.0	23.0	23.2	23.3	23.2	23.1	23.2	23.2	23.3	23.1
1993	23.1	23.0	23.1	23.4	23.5	23.6	23.8	23.8	23.5	23.5	23.5	23.7	23.4
1994	23.4	23.3	23.6	23.8	23.8	24.0	24.0	24.2	24.2	24.8	25.0	25.2	24.1
1995	25.0	25.1	25.2	25.1	25.1	25.2	25.6	25.7	25.9	26.1	26.2	26.1	25.5
1996	25.4	25.9	26.1	26.2	26.5	26.7	26.5	26.6	26.6	26.9	26.8	27.1	26.4
1997	26.5	26.7	27.1	27.5	27.6	27.7	27.7	27.7	27.5	27.5	27.6	27.9	27.4
1998	27.2	27.2	27.4	27.3	27.3	27.6	28.2	28.2	28.1	28.0	28.1	28.3	27.7
1999	27.8	28.0	28.2	28.7	28.8	29.0	29.1	29.4	29.2	29.6	29.6	29.9	28.9
2000	29.4	29.5	29.8	29.8	29.9	30.1	30.6	30.5	30.4	30.3	30.4	30.7	30.1
2001	31.8	31.8	32.1	32.8	32.7	32.9	33.0	32.8	32.8	32.9	33.0	33.3	32.6
2002	32.1	32.0	32.1	32.3	32.3	32.4	32.2	32.2	32.2	32.4	32.5	32.9	32.3
2003	32.6	32.7	33.0	33.1	32.8	33.1	32.9	32.7	32.8	32.5	32.3	32.6	32.8
Retail trade													
1990	67.4	65.1	64.9	64.4	64.5	64.8	64.4	64.6	64.0	65.0	66.4	68.6	65.3
1991	64.1	61.9	61.4	61.9	62.1	62.4	61.8	61.9	62.2	62.3	64.1	66.0	62.6
1992	62.5	60.6	60.4	60.1	60.2	60.6	60.2	60.6	60.9	62.9	65.3	67.1	61.7
1993	61.9	60.1	59.8	60.1	60.3	60.5	60.8	60.9	60.6	62.0	64.2	66.4	61.4
1994	63.7	62.2	62.4	63.8	64.3	65.0	64.4	64.6	65.2	65.8	68.6	70.3	65.0
1995	65.9	64.2	64.0	64.9	65.5	65.8	65.9	66.4	66.9	66.9	69.3	71.2	66.4
1996	66.7	65.0	65.0	65.7	66.3	67.2	66.4	67.3	67.7	68.3	70.2	72.0	67.3
1997	66.3	65.1	64.6	64.6	65.2	65.5	65.6	65.6	65.8	66.7	68.9	71.0	66.2
1998	67.1	65.4	65.4	65.4	66.2	67.4	67.6	67.7	68.2	67.9	70.5	72.5	67.6
1999	68.5	67.4	68.2	68.2	68.8	69.7	69.2	69.7	69.5	69.9	72.8	75.2	69.7
2000	69.9	68.4	68.9	69.4	70.1	70.7	70.5	71.1	70.2	70.1	72.8	74.9	70.5
2001	70.1	67.8	68.1	68.5	68.8	69.5	68.5	68.6	66.8	68.4	71.7	73.2	69.1
2002	68.9	67.8	68.6	68.3	68.5	69.9	69.1	69.5	69.2	69.3	71.6	73.9	69.6
2003	69.5	67.6	68.0	68.7	69.4	70.1	69.7	69.8	69.7	72.1	74.5	75.9	70.4
Transportation and utilities													
1990	15.1	15.4	15.5	15.2	15.5	15.6	15.0	15.0	15.4	15.8	15.9	16.1	15.4
1991	14.8	14.9	15.0	15.2	15.4	15.5	14.9	14.7	15.3	14.8	14.8	14.9	15.0
1992	14.4	14.3	14.6	14.8	15.0	14.9	14.6	14.5	15.4	15.0	15.1	15.4	14.8
1993	15.6	15.7	15.7	15.4	15.7	16.0	14.7	14.7	15.6	16.3	16.2	16.2	15.6
1994	16.0	15.8	16.2	16.1	16.4	16.5	16.3	16.1	16.8	16.9	16.8	16.9	16.4
1995	16.5	16.7	16.7	17.1	17.2	17.2	16.4	16.0	16.7	17.5	17.4	17.4	16.9
1996	16.9	17.0	17.2	17.2	17.6	17.6	17.0	16.7	17.7	17.7	17.9	18.0	17.3
1997	19.0	19.0	19.6	18.7	18.5	18.1	17.3	15.7	18.3	18.7	18.8	18.9	18.3
1998	18.8	18.7	18.7	19.0	19.4	19.6	19.2	19.1	20.0	20.1	20.0	20.7	19.4
1999	20.0	20.0	20.1	20.7	20.6	20.8	20.9	20.8	21.0	21.8	21.9	22.6	20.9
2000	21.2	21.1	21.0	21.4	21.1	21.1	20.3	20.4	21.2	21.6	21.6	22.7	21.2
2001	19.8	19.7	19.7	20.0	20.0	19.8	19.0	18.6	19.2	19.3	19.4	19.4	19.4
2002	18.9	18.7	18.9	19.0	18.9	18.9	18.1	18.1	18.9	19.1	19.0	19.0	18.8
2003	18.9	18.9	19.0	19.4	19.4	19.3	18.8	18.6	19.4	19.7	19.7	19.8	19.2
Information													
1990	10.7	10.7	10.6	10.5	10.6	10.9	10.3	10.3	10.2	10.0	10.0	10.0	10.4
1991	10.0	9.9	10.0	9.8	9.8	9.8	9.8	9.7	9.6	9.6	9.6	9.6	9.7
1992	9.2	9.2	9.2	8.9	9.0	9.2	9.1	9.1	9.0	9.1	9.1	9.1	9.1
1993	8.8	8.8	8.8	8.5	8.5	8.5	8.5	8.6	8.6	8.6	8.7	8.6	8.6
1994	8.5	8.6	8.6	8.6	8.5	8.7	8.6	8.6	8.4	8.4	8.4	8.6	8.5
1995	8.8	8.8	8.8	8.4	8.4	8.6	8.4	8.5	8.4	8.3	8.3	8.3	8.5
1996	8.2	8.2	8.2	8.1	8.2	8.2	8.0	8.0	8.0	8.2	8.3	8.4	8.1
1997	8.3	8.4	8.4	8.3	8.5	8.7	8.7	8.7	8.5	8.5	8.5	8.6	8.5
1998	8.6	8.8	8.7	8.7	8.7	8.8	8.8	9.0	8.9	8.4	8.5	8.6	8.7
1999	8.4	8.4	8.6	8.6	8.6	8.7	8.7	8.8	8.7	8.8	8.8	8.9	8.6
2000	8.8	8.8	9.0	8.6	8.6	8.7	8.7	8.2	8.7	8.7	8.8	9.0	8.7
2001	8.7	8.8	8.8	8.8	9.0	9.0	8.9	8.6	8.7	8.7	8.9	9.0	8.8
2002	9.0	8.9	8.9	8.5	8.8	8.7	8.5	8.5	8.4	8.2	8.4	8.4	8.6
2003	8.0	7.9	7.9	7.8	7.8	7.9	7.9	7.9	7.7	7.8	7.9	8.0	7.9

Employment by Industry: New Jersey—*Continued*

(Numbers in thousands. Not seasonally adjusted.)

Industry	January	February	March	April	May	June	July	August	September	October	November	December	Annual Average
CAMDEN—*Continued*													
Financial activities													
1990	26.3	26.3	26.5	26.6	26.7	27.0	26.4	26.3	25.9	25.7	25.6	25.5	26.2
1991	25.4	25.4	25.4	25.1	25.2	25.5	25.2	24.8	24.4	23.6	23.7	23.8	24.7
1992	24.3	24.3	24.4	24.5	24.6	25.0	24.7	24.7	24.4	24.3	24.2	24.4	24.4
1993	24.4	24.3	24.4	24.8	24.9	25.2	25.2	25.5	25.3	25.3	25.4	25.7	25.0
1994	25.7	25.8	26.0	25.9	25.8	26.1	25.6	25.6	25.6	25.5	25.5	25.6	25.7
1995	24.6	24.6	24.7	24.9	25.0	25.3	25.3	25.3	25.0	25.0	25.2	25.3	25.0
1996	24.5	24.6	24.8	24.6	24.9	25.3	25.3	25.4	25.4	25.0	25.3	25.6	25.0
1997	24.9	25.0	25.3	25.7	26.1	26.5	26.6	26.9	26.8	26.6	26.8	27.2	26.2
1998	27.1	27.3	27.7	28.0	28.4	28.8	28.8	28.9	28.6	29.4	29.7	30.2	28.5
1999	30.6	30.9	31.3	31.5	31.8	32.1	32.2	32.2	31.7	31.4	31.4	31.4	31.5
2000	31.3	31.3	31.2	30.9	31.1	31.6	31.5	31.5	31.0	31.1	31.3	31.6	31.2
2001	31.0	31.2	31.4	31.1	31.3	31.9	32.0	32.0	31.4	31.5	31.6	32.0	31.5
2002	32.0	32.0	32.0	32.3	32.3	32.8	33.1	33.2	33.0	33.1	33.4	33.7	32.7
2003	33.5	33.7	34.1	34.7	35.0	35.7	36.3	36.5	36.0	36.1	36.5	36.7	35.4
Professional and business services													
1990	47.5	47.8	48.4	48.5	48.7	49.2	49.6	49.6	48.6	47.8	47.7	47.6	48.4
1991	45.9	45.9	46.8	46.5	46.7	46.8	46.2	45.9	45.5	45.2	44.9	45.3	45.9
1992	43.2	44.0	44.5	45.1	45.4	45.9	45.9	46.1	46.3	46.3	46.5	46.5	45.4
1993	45.0	46.0	46.4	47.7	48.5	48.5	48.3	49.0	48.8	49.0	48.7	48.8	47.8
1994	45.9	46.7	47.7	49.0	49.3	49.4	49.4	49.6	49.9	49.3	48.9	49.4	48.7
1995	47.9	48.4	49.3	49.1	49.2	49.3	50.3	50.8	50.7	50.7	50.7	50.5	49.7
1996	48.9	50.4	51.1	52.3	52.9	53.5	53.4	54.1	53.8	54.1	53.8	54.1	52.7
1997	53.5	54.2	55.4	55.6	56.4	57.5	57.7	58.6	58.9	59.3	58.9	58.7	57.0
1998	56.6	57.0	58.6	59.1	59.8	60.9	60.4	60.2	59.8	60.3	60.4	60.7	59.4
1999	58.6	59.2	60.4	60.7	61.0	62.3	61.9	61.1	60.2	60.1	59.8	59.8	60.4
2000	59.0	58.4	59.8	58.7	58.3	59.7	59.8	59.3	59.2	58.8	59.5	59.5	59.1
2001	58.7	57.8	59.2	60.5	61.0	61.6	62.0	63.4	62.8	61.8	62.1	62.2	61.0
2002	61.0	61.0	62.1	62.6	62.4	64.3	63.9	64.2	62.2	62.8	63.0	63.5	62.8
2003	62.9	63.1	64.0	65.5	65.7	66.1	66.2	65.4	66.6	66.3	66.0	66.0	65.3
Educational and health services													
1990	47.2	47.8	48.1	47.8	47.9	48.1	47.3	47.4	48.8	49.2	49.5	49.6	48.2
1991	48.8	49.5	49.7	50.1	50.2	50.2	50.0	49.9	50.7	51.0	51.3	51.4	50.2
1992	51.9	52.3	52.4	52.3	52.7	52.7	53.2	53.1	53.6	54.2	54.3	54.4	53.0
1993	54.0	53.9	54.3	54.2	54.3	54.3	54.3	54.0	54.6	55.8	55.8	56.0	54.6
1994	55.8	55.9	56.4	56.2	56.7	56.7	56.8	56.6	57.2	57.3	57.6	57.6	56.7
1995	58.0	58.5	58.8	58.7	58.9	59.0	58.0	57.9	58.4	58.7	59.1	59.3	58.6
1996	58.7	59.3	59.6	59.9	60.5	60.8	60.2	60.2	60.3	61.3	61.5	61.9	60.3
1997	61.3	62.1	62.7	62.9	63.4	63.5	63.3	63.5	63.9	64.6	65.1	65.4	63.4
1998	64.4	64.7	65.1	65.5	66.1	66.3	65.8	66.1	65.8	66.3	66.7	66.8	65.8
1999	66.0	66.3	66.9	66.6	66.8	66.5	66.9	66.6	66.1	67.5	67.7	67.8	66.8
2000	65.9	65.9	66.3	66.7	67.0	67.4	68.8	68.7	68.7	68.4	68.7	69.1	67.6
2001	65.6	65.8	66.3	67.6	67.9	68.6	68.3	68.2	67.9	68.6	69.2	69.9	67.8
2002	70.5	70.8	71.1	71.1	71.1	71.6	72.9	72.3	72.3	72.3	72.7	72.7	71.8
2003	71.8	71.7	72.2	72.3	72.4	72.9	73.3	73.3	72.7	73.3	73.7	74.1	72.8
Leisure and hospitality													
1990	29.5	29.9	30.3	31.4	32.5	33.2	32.4	32.3	31.8	31.0	30.9	30.6	31.3
1991	28.9	29.1	29.6	30.2	31.5	32.3	32.3	32.5	31.4	30.2	30.0	30.1	30.6
1992	28.4	28.4	28.7	29.5	30.8	31.5	31.2	30.9	30.0	30.3	29.7	29.7	29.9
1993	28.4	28.6	28.7	29.9	31.1	32.1	31.8	31.6	31.1	29.6	29.5	29.7	30.1
1994	28.3	28.3	29.0	30.3	31.5	32.4	31.9	31.8	31.1	30.9	30.7	30.6	30.5
1995	29.2	29.5	30.1	31.1	32.7	33.8	33.6	33.4	33.0	31.2	31.0	31.2	31.6
1996	28.5	29.3	29.9	30.2	32.2	33.3	32.9	32.8	32.3	31.0	30.8	31.0	31.1
1997	29.4	29.8	30.7	32.0	33.9	35.0	33.6	33.4	33.1	31.8	31.5	31.7	32.1
1998	31.5	31.7	32.2	32.3	34.5	35.2	34.7	34.5	34.2	32.7	32.6	32.8	33.2
1999	31.4	31.7	32.4	33.1	34.6	36.6	35.8	35.4	34.9	33.7	33.5	34.1	33.9
2000	32.8	32.5	33.7	35.2	36.2	37.6	36.7	36.2	35.8	34.1	34.3	34.4	34.9
2001	32.7	32.7	33.3	34.1	35.5	37.0	37.1	37.0	36.2	34.9	34.6	35.0	35.0
2002	33.8	33.8	34.8	35.6	36.8	38.7	37.7	37.5	37.0	36.4	36.3	36.2	36.2
2003	35.1	34.5	35.7	37.1	38.4	40.1	39.6	39.7	38.3	38.0	36.9	37.0	37.5
Other services													
1990	15.0	15.1	15.1	15.2	15.4	15.6	15.4	15.2	15.1	15.1	15.0	15.0	15.1
1991	15.5	15.4	15.5	14.4	14.5	14.8	15.1	14.7	14.6	14.7	14.5	14.5	14.8
1992	14.4	14.6	14.6	14.5	14.6	14.7	14.6	14.4	14.5	14.8	14.8	14.8	14.6
1993	14.5	14.6	14.8	15.0	14.9	15.2	15.4	15.2	14.9	14.7	14.8	14.9	14.9
1994	15.0	15.2	15.2	15.5	15.6	15.8	15.9	15.8	16.1	16.0	16.0	16.2	15.6
1995	15.6	15.7	15.9	16.0	16.0	16.2	16.1	16.1	16.0	16.4	16.4	16.4	16.0
1996	16.3	16.6	16.8	16.8	16.9	17.1	17.1	17.0	17.1	17.1	17.3	17.3	16.9
1997	17.1	17.2	17.4	17.2	17.4	17.6	17.6	17.6	17.5	17.4	17.6	17.7	17.4
1998	17.6	17.7	17.7	18.2	18.5	18.5	18.6	18.6	18.4	18.5	18.4	18.4	18.2
1999	18.4	18.4	18.6	18.8	18.9	19.3	19.1	19.1	18.8	19.1	19.2	19.3	18.9
2000	18.9	19.1	19.3	19.4	19.6	19.6	19.6	19.5	19.4	19.8	19.8	19.8	19.4
2001	20.1	20.1	20.2	20.5	20.6	20.7	21.2	21.0	20.8	21.2	21.3	21.4	20.7
2002	21.1	21.2	21.3	21.6	21.6	21.9	21.9	21.7	21.7	21.7	21.8	21.9	21.6
2003	21.7	21.8	21.9	22.0	22.2	22.5	22.2	22.2	22.0	22.2	22.4	22.5	22.1

Employment by Industry: New Jersey—*Continued*

(Numbers in thousands. Not seasonally adjusted.)

Industry	January	February	March	April	May	June	July	August	September	October	November	December	Annual Average
CAMDEN—*Continued*													
Government													
1990	76.7	77.7	77.4	77.9	78.9	79.5	73.9	73.0	73.8	77.3	78.5	78.7	76.9
1991	77.5	77.7	77.6	79.2	79.5	78.1	75.1	72.9	74.6	77.4	78.9	78.7	77.2
1992	77.3	78.1	78.8	78.7	78.3	78.9	75.1	74.3	74.5	77.2	78.6	78.3	77.3
1993	77.1	78.2	78.9	78.1	78.0	77.4	72.4	71.7	73.5	78.2	78.6	78.9	76.7
1994	76.8	77.1	78.6	79.4	79.4	79.0	74.0	72.6	74.8	78.3	79.3	80.1	77.4
1995	78.0	78.7	79.2	79.4	79.2	78.4	72.8	72.6	75.4	79.0	80.2	80.4	77.7
1996	78.0	79.4	79.8	79.9	78.7	79.3	72.9	72.3	75.2	79.0	80.2	80.0	77.8
1997	78.1	79.5	79.9	79.6	78.9	79.0	73.4	73.0	76.8	80.0	80.8	80.8	78.3
1998	79.8	80.8	81.4	81.7	80.4	80.3	73.9	73.0	77.4	81.0	81.8	81.4	79.4
1999	80.0	81.9	81.9	82.2	80.9	80.7	73.6	72.9	77.8	81.8	82.4	81.9	79.8
2000	80.4	82.4	83.3	83.5	83.2	82.2	75.5	76.0	79.7	82.9	83.7	82.9	81.3
2001	82.1	84.6	84.3	84.4	83.3	83.7	76.1	75.8	81.7	85.3	86.4	86.2	82.8
2002	85.9	87.0	87.1	86.8	86.1	85.6	77.5	77.1	82.2	86.2	87.1	86.5	84.6
2003	85.2	86.2	86.9	87.1	86.1	86.2	79.7	77.9	82.5	86.6	88.6	88.5	85.1
Federal government													
1990	10.2	10.2	10.1	10.3	10.8	11.5	10.9	10.3	10.2	10.0	10.1	9.9	10.3
1991	9.9	10.0	9.8	10.0	10.2	10.1	10.1	10.1	10.0	10.1	10.1	10.3	10.0
1992	10.1	10.1	10.1	10.0	10.0	10.0	10.0	9.9	9.5	9.3	9.4	9.5	9.8
1993	9.5	9.4	9.4	9.3	9.4	9.5	9.4	9.3	9.1	9.3	9.4	9.9	9.4
1994	9.6	9.6	9.5	9.6	9.6	9.7	9.8	9.8	9.7	9.7	9.7	10.1	9.7
1995	9.6	9.5	9.5	9.5	9.6	9.6	9.7	9.7	9.6	9.6	9.6	9.9	9.6
1996	9.5	9.5	9.5	9.5	9.5	9.6	9.6	9.6	9.5	9.5	9.6	9.8	9.5
1997	9.4	9.4	9.4	9.4	9.5	9.5	9.6	9.7	9.9	9.8	9.9	10.2	9.6
1998	9.9	9.8	9.8	9.8	9.8	9.9	10.0	9.9	9.8	9.8	9.8	10.0	9.8
1999	9.8	9.9	9.7	9.8	9.7	9.7	9.8	9.9	9.7	9.7	9.7	9.9	9.7
2000	9.6	9.6	9.8	10.1	11.4	10.6	10.5	10.0	9.7	9.7	9.6	9.8	10.0
2001	10.2	10.1	10.1	10.1	10.1	10.2	10.3	10.2	10.0	10.0	10.1	10.3	10.1
2002	10.5	10.1	10.1	10.0	10.0	10.1	10.1	10.2	10.2	10.1	10.1	10.3	10.2
2003	10.1	10.1	10.0	9.9	9.9	10.0	10.1	10.0	10.0	9.9	10.1	10.2	10.0
State government													
1990	14.1	14.3	14.0	13.9	13.9	13.4	13.4	13.5	13.4	13.9	13.9	13.8	13.7
1991	13.6	13.8	13.8	13.9	13.5	12.8	12.9	12.6	12.3	12.4	12.6	12.5	13.0
1992	12.0	12.2	12.5	12.4	12.2	12.1	12.3	12.1	12.1	12.0	11.9	11.8	12.1
1993	11.5	12.0	12.1	12.1	11.8	11.2	11.4	11.2	11.5	12.0	12.0	11.7	11.7
1994	10.9	11.6	11.7	11.8	11.6	11.1	11.2	11.2	11.2	11.7	11.8	11.8	11.4
1995	12.4	12.9	13.0	13.0	12.8	12.1	12.3	12.4	12.8	13.3	13.5	13.2	12.8
1996	12.7	13.3	13.3	13.4	12.3	12.3	12.4	12.3	12.6	13.2	13.4	13.1	12.8
1997	12.7	13.2	13.2	13.3	12.4	12.3	12.4	12.3	12.7	13.2	13.1	13.2	12.8
1998	12.8	13.5	13.6	13.5	12.4	12.4	12.3	12.3	13.1	13.4	13.4	13.2	12.9
1999	12.5	13.2	13.3	13.4	12.4	12.3	12.3	12.2	12.4	13.4	13.4	13.2	12.8
2000	12.1	13.4	13.5	13.7	12.7	12.4	12.3	12.3	13.3	13.9	13.9	13.4	13.0
2001	12.5	13.8	13.5	13.6	12.8	12.6	12.8	12.8	13.8	14.3	14.4	14.3	13.4
2002	13.9	14.6	14.3	14.2	13.5	12.8	12.7	12.5	13.1	13.8	13.9	13.7	13.6
2003	13.1	13.6	13.6	13.7	13.3	12.6	12.5	12.7	13.3	13.9	14.6	14.4	13.4
Local government													
1990	52.4	53.2	53.3	53.7	54.2	54.6	49.6	49.2	50.2	53.4	54.5	55.0	52.7
1991	54.0	53.9	54.0	55.3	55.8	55.2	52.1	50.2	52.3	54.9	56.2	55.9	54.1
1992	55.2	55.8	56.2	56.3	56.1	56.8	52.8	52.3	52.9	55.9	57.3	57.0	55.3
1993	56.1	56.8	57.4	56.7	56.8	56.7	51.6	51.2	52.9	56.9	57.2	57.3	55.6
1994	56.3	55.9	57.4	58.0	58.2	58.2	53.0	51.6	53.9	56.9	57.8	58.2	56.2
1995	56.0	56.3	56.7	56.9	56.8	56.7	50.8	50.5	53.0	56.1	57.1	57.3	55.3
1996	55.8	56.6	57.0	57.0	56.9	57.4	50.9	50.4	53.1	56.3	57.2	57.1	55.4
1997	56.0	56.9	57.3	56.9	57.0	57.2	51.4	51.0	54.2	57.0	57.8	57.4	55.8
1998	57.1	57.5	58.0	58.4	58.2	58.0	51.6	50.8	54.5	57.8	58.6	58.2	56.5
1999	57.7	58.8	58.9	59.0	58.8	58.7	51.5	50.8	55.7	58.7	59.3	58.8	57.2
2000	58.7	59.4	60.0	59.7	59.1	59.2	52.7	53.7	56.7	59.3	60.2	59.7	58.2
2001	59.4	60.7	60.7	60.7	60.4	60.9	53.0	52.8	57.9	61.0	61.9	61.6	59.2
2002	61.5	62.3	62.7	62.6	62.6	62.7	54.7	54.4	58.9	62.3	63.1	62.5	60.9
2003	62.0	62.5	63.3	63.5	62.9	63.6	57.1	55.2	59.2	62.8	63.9	63.9	61.7
JERSEY CITY													
Total nonfarm													
1990	243.5	244.5	246.6	244.8	247.4	248.3	246.8	246.9	247.7	245.4	245.6	244.2	245.9
1991	232.4	233.0	234.7	233.9	234.7	237.0	232.8	234.6	235.7	236.5	237.0	236.0	234.8
1992	224.1	225.5	226.9	226.3	227.5	228.3	228.4	228.8	229.0	231.7	232.6	230.8	228.3
1993	223.9	224.2	225.5	227.9	228.5	231.6	230.9	233.0	233.1	235.8	236.9	235.6	230.5
1994	228.0	229.4	232.0	234.0	236.5	238.2	236.8	238.8	240.7	241.8	242.7	241.5	236.7
1995	233.5	234.9	235.8	236.1	236.8	237.9	236.5	238.1	240.4	241.7	240.8	240.5	237.7
1996	232.4	235.4	236.3	236.7	238.2	240.4	237.9	238.0	241.0	241.8	242.9	242.6	238.6
1997	235.3	236.4	237.9	238.9	239.4	241.5	240.5	238.0	243.0	244.2	246.1	247.5	240.7
1998	239.4	240.8	242.5	242.1	243.6	245.3	245.1	244.8	246.2	246.6	247.0	248.9	244.3
1999	243.2	244.3	246.0	248.1	248.2	249.5	248.1	247.6	249.2	251.3	253.7	254.7	248.6
2000	249.5	250.9	253.0	254.2	255.6	257.3	258.4	256.7	260.1	261.9	263.1	264.5	257.1
2001	250.2	251.0	251.7	252.4	254.0	253.4	251.4	250.1	253.7	265.1	265.4	265.0	255.2
2002	261.4	260.8	261.0	257.8	257.2	254.9	251.2	250.3	253.3	254.8	256.3	255.7	256.2
2003	248.3	248.7	248.7	247.6	248.1	247.3	244.2	244.0	248.3	249.5	250.6	250.8	248.0

Employment by Industry: New Jersey—*Continued*

(Numbers in thousands. Not seasonally adjusted.)

Industry	January	February	March	April	May	June	July	August	September	October	November	December	Annual Average
JERSEY CITY—*Continued*													
Total private													
1990	202.9	203.5	205.0	203.1	204.8	205.6	204.3	205.2	206.5	204.2	204.1	202.4	204.3
1991	191.5	191.8	193.6	192.9	194.1	196.6	191.9	193.7	196.2	196.3	196.7	195.1	194.2
1992	183.7	184.8	186.1	185.5	187.0	187.9	185.7	187.1	189.6	191.3	192.2	190.0	187.5
1993	183.7	183.9	184.7	187.7	188.6	191.7	188.7	191.4	193.7	195.5	196.2	194.7	190.0
1994	187.7	188.9	191.2	193.6	196.1	197.8	195.7	198.3	200.9	201.3	202.2	200.3	196.1
1995	193.1	194.1	194.9	195.4	196.3	197.4	196.2	197.4	201.1	202.0	200.9	200.4	197.4
1996	192.5	195.4	196.1	196.7	198.1	200.1	197.7	199.1	201.8	202.6	203.5	203.4	198.9
1997	196.6	197.6	198.9	200.1	200.3	202.5	200.5	199.2	204.6	205.4	206.9	208.0	201.7
1998	201.4	202.5	203.9	203.7	205.2	207.1	206.4	207.2	209.2	208.5	208.7	210.2	206.1
1999	205.2	205.9	207.2	208.8	209.5	211.2	209.5	209.8	211.4	213.0	214.7	215.5	210.1
2000	211.4	212.3	213.8	215.9	216.4	218.9	220.4	220.2	222.4	223.0	223.7	224.9	218.6
2001	212.0	211.7	212.4	213.5	214.7	215.0	213.2	213.7	215.3	223.9	223.5	222.8	215.9
2002	220.5	219.5	219.6	217.4	216.7	216.4	213.1	213.5	214.8	215.1	216.0	215.2	216.5
2003	208.9	208.5	208.4	207.6	207.5	207.7	206.0	206.9	209.0	208.8	209.4	209.5	208.2
Goods-producing													
1990	38.6	39.3	39.9	39.2	40.1	41.0	40.3	40.9	41.3	40.3	40.0	38.1	39.9
1991	33.7	33.8	34.5	35.5	36.8	37.7	36.5	37.3	37.5	37.5	37.2	35.2	36.1
1992	31.2	31.3	31.7	32.5	33.2	34.0	33.8	34.5	34.8	34.7	34.5	32.4	33.2
1993	32.1	32.2	32.6	34.2	35.1	36.2	35.0	36.1	36.4	36.6	36.1	34.7	34.7
1994	31.6	31.8	32.4	33.5	34.7	35.3	34.0	35.1	35.5	35.6	34.9	33.2	33.9
1995	30.9	31.2	31.4	30.7	31.2	31.8	30.5	31.5	32.4	32.7	31.9	30.7	31.4
1996	28.3	28.9	29.2	29.2	29.7	30.6	30.7	30.6	30.9	30.7	30.8	29.8	29.9
1997	28.1	28.1	28.8	29.5	30.1	30.8	30.3	31.1	31.5	30.9	30.8	30.1	30.0
1998	27.9	28.3	28.8	29.1	30.0	30.6	29.6	30.2	30.2	29.2	28.5	27.7	29.1
1999	26.9	26.9	27.4	27.7	28.1	28.7	27.6	28.1	28.6	28.7	28.6	28.0	27.9
2000	27.6	27.8	28.3	28.5	28.7	29.3	28.7	29.1	29.3	28.5	28.2	27.8	28.4
2001	26.5	26.4	26.7	26.4	26.5	26.9	25.9	26.4	26.7	26.0	25.7	25.2	26.2
2002	23.0	22.7	23.1	23.2	23.4	23.4	22.9	23.1	23.2	22.9	22.5	21.8	22.9
2003	20.7	20.4	20.4	20.7	21.0	21.0	20.4	20.7	20.8	20.4	20.2	19.9	20.6
Construction and mining													
1990	6.2	6.2	6.4	6.4	6.5	6.7	6.4	6.2	6.3	5.9	5.8	5.5	6.2
1991	4.7	4.5	4.7	5.0	5.0	5.0	5.1	5.1	5.0	4.9	4.8	4.6	4.8
1992	4.0	3.8	3.9	4.0	4.0	4.1	4.3	4.4	4.4	4.6	4.7	4.4	4.2
1993	3.9	3.8	3.9	4.2	4.4	4.6	4.6	4.8	4.8	4.8	4.7	4.6	4.4
1994	3.7	3.7	3.7	4.3	4.6	4.7	4.5	4.6	4.6	4.4	4.4	4.3	4.2
1995	3.9	3.7	3.8	3.8	4.0	4.0	4.0	4.0	4.0	4.0	4.0	3.9	3.9
1996	3.5	3.5	3.6	3.9	4.0	4.2	4.2	4.4	4.4	4.4	4.4	4.3	4.0
1997	3.9	3.8	3.9	4.4	4.5	4.7	4.9	5.0	5.0	5.1	5.1	5.1	4.6
1998	4.5	4.7	4.9	5.2	5.4	5.6	5.7	5.9	5.6	5.3	5.3	5.3	5.2
1999	5.1	5.1	5.4	5.5	5.6	5.9	5.8	5.7	5.7	5.7	5.7	5.6	5.5
2000	5.5	5.5	5.8	5.8	6.0	6.1	6.0	6.1	6.0	5.9	5.8	5.8	5.8
2001	5.4	5.4	5.4	5.6	5.7	5.9	6.0	6.2	6.3	6.3	6.2	6.2	5.8
2002	5.7	5.6	5.7	6.1	6.2	6.2	6.4	6.5	6.5	6.7	6.7	6.5	6.2
2003	5.8	5.5	5.6	5.9	6.0	6.0	6.0	6.0	6.0	6.0	5.9	5.8	5.9
Manufacturing													
1990	32.4	33.1	33.5	32.8	33.6	34.3	33.9	34.7	35.0	34.4	34.2	32.6	33.7
1991	29.0	29.3	29.8	30.5	31.8	32.7	31.4	32.2	32.5	32.6	32.4	30.6	31.2
1992	27.2	27.5	27.8	28.5	29.2	29.9	29.5	30.1	30.4	30.1	29.8	28.0	29.0
1993	28.2	28.4	28.7	30.0	30.7	31.6	30.4	31.3	31.6	31.8	31.4	30.1	30.3
1994	27.9	28.1	28.7	29.2	30.1	30.6	29.5	30.5	30.9	31.2	30.5	28.9	29.6
1995	27.0	27.5	27.6	26.9	27.2	27.8	26.5	27.5	28.4	28.7	27.9	26.8	27.4
1996	24.8	25.4	25.6	25.3	25.7	26.4	26.5	26.2	26.5	26.3	26.4	25.5	25.8
1997	24.2	24.3	24.9	25.1	25.6	26.1	25.4	26.1	26.5	25.8	25.7	25.0	25.3
1998	23.4	23.6	23.9	23.9	24.6	25.0	23.9	24.3	24.6	23.9	23.2	22.4	23.8
1999	21.8	21.8	22.0	22.2	22.5	22.8	21.8	22.4	22.9	23.0	22.9	22.4	22.3
2000	22.1	22.3	22.5	22.7	22.7	23.2	22.7	23.0	23.3	22.6	22.4	22.0	22.6
2001	21.1	21.0	21.3	20.8	20.8	21.0	19.9	20.2	20.4	19.7	19.5	19.0	20.3
2002	17.3	17.1	17.4	17.1	17.2	17.2	16.5	16.6	16.7	16.2	15.8	15.3	16.7
2003	14.9	14.9	14.8	14.8	15.0	15.0	14.4	14.7	14.8	14.4	14.3	14.1	14.7
Service-providing													
1990	204.9	205.2	206.7	205.6	207.3	207.3	206.5	206.0	206.4	205.1	205.6	206.1	206.0
1991	198.7	199.2	200.2	198.4	197.9	199.3	196.3	197.3	198.2	199.0	199.8	200.8	198.7
1992	192.9	194.2	195.2	193.8	194.3	194.3	194.6	194.3	194.2	197.0	198.1	198.4	195.1
1993	191.8	192.0	192.9	193.7	193.4	195.4	195.9	196.9	196.7	199.2	200.8	200.9	195.8
1994	196.4	197.6	199.6	200.5	201.8	202.9	202.8	203.7	205.2	206.2	207.8	208.3	202.7
1995	202.6	203.7	204.4	205.4	205.6	206.1	206.0	206.6	208.0	209.0	208.9	209.8	206.3
1996	204.1	206.5	207.1	207.5	208.5	209.8	207.2	207.4	210.1	211.1	212.1	212.8	208.6
1997	207.2	208.3	209.1	209.4	209.3	210.7	210.2	206.9	211.5	213.3	215.3	217.4	210.7
1998	211.5	212.5	213.7	213.0	213.6	214.7	215.5	214.6	216.0	217.4	218.5	221.2	215.1
1999	216.3	217.4	218.6	220.4	220.1	220.8	220.5	219.5	220.6	222.6	225.1	226.7	220.7
2000	221.9	223.1	224.7	225.7	226.9	228.0	229.7	227.6	230.8	233.4	234.9	236.7	228.6
2001	223.7	224.6	225.0	226.0	227.5	226.5	225.5	223.7	227.0	239.1	239.7	239.8	229.0
2002	238.4	238.1	237.9	234.6	233.8	231.5	228.3	227.2	230.1	231.9	233.8	233.9	233.3
2003	227.6	228.3	228.3	226.9	227.1	226.3	223.8	223.3	227.5	229.1	230.4	230.9	227.5

Employment by Industry: New Jersey—*Continued*

(Numbers in thousands. Not seasonally adjusted.)

Industry	January	February	March	April	May	June	July	August	September	October	November	December	Annual Average
JERSEY CITY—*Continued*													
Trade, transportation, and utilities													
1990	79.4	78.8	79.2	78.6	78.7	78.8	78.3	78.6	79.1	78.9	78.9	79.4	78.8
1991	75.2	75.0	75.6	75.0	74.8	75.7	74.3	75.2	76.3	76.4	77.0	77.3	75.6
1992	72.8	72.7	72.7	72.0	71.9	72.2	71.3	71.5	72.7	73.5	74.0	74.1	72.6
1993	68.1	67.8	67.8	68.6	68.2	69.4	69.3	69.6	70.5	71.3	71.8	71.9	69.5
1994	70.4	70.7	71.4	71.2	72.2	72.7	72.3	73.0	74.4	74.2	74.6	74.3	72.6
1995	71.1	70.9	71.2	71.9	71.8	71.9	71.9	71.7	73.1	72.9	72.6	73.1	72.0
1996	70.0	70.6	70.2	70.6	70.8	71.4	69.2	69.9	71.0	72.5	72.7	73.0	70.9
1997	69.9	70.0	70.2	68.9	68.7	69.7	69.0	66.5	70.7	72.1	73.3	74.3	70.2
1998	72.1	71.9	72.0	70.6	70.8	71.3	70.5	70.3	71.9	72.2	72.9	74.2	71.7
1999	72.4	72.4	72.8	72.0	71.9	72.2	72.2	71.8	72.6	73.8	75.1	75.6	72.9
2000	73.4	73.5	73.4	72.8	72.4	72.5	72.6	72.3	73.5	74.4	75.1	75.8	73.4
2001	70.3	69.7	69.7	69.5	69.6	69.0	67.8	68.1	69.1	69.6	69.8	69.8	69.3
2002	67.8	67.5	67.3	66.7	66.3	66.6	65.4	65.7	66.6	67.2	67.7	68.1	66.9
2003	65.5	65.6	65.6	64.7	64.9	65.0	64.3	64.7	66.1	66.4	66.7	67.0	65.5
Wholesale trade													
1990	24.3	24.3	24.6	23.6	23.5	23.6	23.7	23.8	23.8	23.6	23.6	23.6	23.8
1991	22.4	22.6	23.0	22.9	22.7	23.3	22.4	22.7	23.1	22.7	22.5	22.2	22.7
1992	22.4	22.4	22.7	22.8	22.7	22.8	22.7	22.7	22.8	22.8	22.8	22.8	22.7
1993	19.2	19.2	19.2	19.2	19.2	19.5	19.3	19.4	19.4	19.9	20.0	20.1	19.4
1994	19.7	20.0	20.1	20.3	20.4	20.6	20.6	21.0	21.0	20.7	20.8	20.7	20.4
1995	19.4	19.7	19.8	19.3	19.2	19.5	19.3	19.7	20.0	19.9	19.9	19.9	19.6
1996	19.0	19.2	19.2	20.1	20.0	20.4	18.9	19.1	19.0	19.4	19.3	19.3	19.4
1997	19.8	20.1	20.2	18.4	18.2	18.4	18.0	18.2	18.2	18.3	18.8	18.9	18.7
1998	18.5	18.6	18.6	18.1	18.2	18.4	18.5	18.4	18.3	18.2	18.4	18.6	18.4
1999	18.6	18.6	18.8	18.6	18.3	18.2	18.2	18.4	18.4	18.3	18.5	18.6	18.4
2000	18.4	18.4	18.3	17.7	17.6	17.6	17.6	17.5	17.8	17.4	17.3	17.3	17.7
2001	17.8	17.8	17.9	17.4	17.3	17.1	16.7	16.8	16.8	16.7	16.4	16.3	17.0
2002	16.3	16.3	16.3	16.2	16.1	16.2	15.9	16.1	16.2	16.5	16.5	16.6	16.3
2003	16.3	16.3	16.3	16.3	16.3	16.4	16.4	16.6	16.7	16.7	16.5	16.5	16.4
Retail trade													
1990	27.6	27.1	27.2	28.0	28.2	28.3	27.8	27.9	28.1	27.7	27.9	28.2	27.8
1991	26.6	26.2	26.4	25.7	25.8	25.7	25.4	25.7	26.3	26.0	26.8	27.3	26.1
1992	24.8	24.4	24.1	23.8	23.9	23.8	23.2	23.3	23.8	24.3	24.9	25.2	24.1
1993	23.8	23.5	23.3	23.7	23.3	24.0	24.1	24.2	24.5	24.7	25.3	25.8	24.1
1994	24.6	24.3	24.5	25.2	25.6	25.8	25.5	25.8	26.3	26.4	26.9	27.1	25.6
1995	25.5	25.1	25.1	25.3	25.6	25.5	25.2	25.0	25.4	25.1	25.4	26.0	25.3
1996	25.1	24.8	24.3	24.6	25.0	25.0	24.8	25.2	25.5	26.1	26.5	26.7	25.3
1997	24.6	24.1	24.1	24.1	24.1	24.5	24.7	24.9	25.1	25.8	26.5	27.2	24.9
1998	25.9	25.5	25.5	25.1	25.3	25.4	24.6	24.6	25.2	25.7	26.6	27.3	25.5
1999	25.4	24.7	24.6	24.5	24.7	24.9	24.7	24.8	25.2	24.8	26.0	26.5	25.0
2000	25.3	25.0	25.3	24.9	24.7	24.9	24.6	24.7	25.0	25.3	26.1	26.7	25.2
2001	24.5	23.9	23.9	24.0	24.1	24.1	23.7	24.0	24.2	24.5	25.4	26.2	24.3
2002	23.9	23.6	23.7	23.3	23.2	23.4	22.9	23.0	23.1	23.0	23.7	24.3	23.4
2003	22.9	22.6	22.5	22.5	22.8	22.8	22.8	23.1	23.3	23.3	23.7	24.2	23.0
Transportation and utilities													
1990	27.5	27.4	27.4	27.0	27.0	26.9	26.8	26.9	27.2	27.6	27.4	27.6	27.2
1991	26.2	26.2	26.2	26.4	26.3	26.7	26.5	26.8	26.9	27.7	27.7	27.8	26.7
1992	25.6	25.9	25.9	25.4	25.3	25.6	25.4	25.5	26.1	26.4	26.3	26.1	25.7
1993	25.1	25.1	25.3	25.7	25.7	25.9	25.9	26.0	26.6	26.7	26.5	26.0	25.8
1994	26.1	26.4	26.8	25.7	26.2	26.3	26.2	26.2	27.1	27.1	26.9	26.5	26.4
1995	26.2	26.1	26.3	27.3	27.0	26.9	27.4	27.0	27.7	27.9	27.3	27.2	27.0
1996	25.9	26.6	26.7	25.9	25.8	26.0	25.5	25.6	26.5	27.0	26.9	27.0	26.2
1997	25.5	25.8	25.9	26.4	26.4	26.8	26.3	23.4	27.4	28.0	28.0	28.2	26.5
1998	27.7	27.8	27.9	27.4	27.3	27.5	27.4	27.3	28.4	28.3	27.9	28.3	27.7
1999	28.4	29.1	29.4	28.9	28.9	29.1	29.3	28.6	29.0	30.7	30.6	30.5	29.3
2000	29.7	30.1	29.8	30.2	30.1	30.0	30.4	30.1	30.7	31.7	31.7	31.8	30.5
2001	28.0	28.0	27.9	28.1	28.2	27.8	27.4	27.3	28.1	28.4	28.0	27.3	27.8
2002	27.6	27.6	27.3	27.2	27.0	27.0	26.6	26.6	27.3	27.7	27.5	27.2	27.2
2003	26.3	26.7	26.8	25.9	25.8	25.8	25.1	25.0	26.1	26.4	26.5	26.3	26.1
Information													
1990	6.2	6.3	6.3	6.6	6.7	6.6	6.7	6.7	6.7	6.6	6.7	6.6	6.5
1991	6.5	6.5	6.5	5.9	5.8	6.1	6.3	6.3	6.3	6.3	6.3	6.4	6.2
1992	6.2	6.1	6.1	5.9	5.9	5.9	6.1	6.0	6.0	6.1	6.2	6.3	6.0
1993	6.2	6.1	6.1	6.0	6.0	6.1	6.0	5.9	6.0	6.0	6.0	6.0	6.0
1994	5.8	5.9	5.9	6.0	6.0	6.1	6.1	6.1	6.2	6.3	6.4	6.5	6.1
1995	6.2	6.2	6.2	6.3	6.4	6.5	6.7	6.7	6.7	6.6	6.7	6.7	6.4
1996	6.5	6.6	6.7	6.7	6.9	7.0	6.9	7.0	7.0	7.1	7.3	7.4	6.9
1997	7.8	7.7	7.6	7.5	7.6	7.7	7.7	7.7	7.7	7.7	7.7	7.9	7.6
1998	7.7	7.7	7.7	8.1	8.0	8.1	8.0	8.1	8.4	8.4	8.4	8.5	8.0
1999	9.6	9.5	9.4	9.3	9.3	9.5	9.5	9.6	9.5	9.1	9.3	9.3	9.4
2000	9.4	9.4	9.5	9.6	9.7	9.8	9.9	9.9	10.0	10.1	10.2	10.3	9.8
2001	8.7	8.7	8.7	8.6	8.7	8.6	8.5	8.3	8.9	9.0	9.1	9.3	8.7
2002	9.8	9.7	9.4	9.0	9.1	9.1	8.4	8.3	8.6	8.5	8.7	8.8	9.0
2003	8.4	8.3	8.1	8.3	8.3	8.2	8.2	8.3	8.1	8.0	8.0	8.2	8.2

Employment by Industry: New Jersey—*Continued*

(Numbers in thousands. Not seasonally adjusted.)

Industry	January	February	March	April	May	June	July	August	September	October	November	December	Annual Average
JERSEY CITY—*Continued*													
Financial activities													
1990	13.8	14.0	14.0	14.0	14.1	14.1	14.1	14.0	13.8	13.8	13.8	13.8	13.9
1991	13.4	13.5	13.6	13.6	13.7	13.8	13.7	13.7	13.6	13.7	13.7	13.8	13.6
1992	15.3	15.8	16.3	16.5	16.6	16.6	16.1	16.1	16.1	16.3	16.4	16.5	16.2
1993	16.6	16.5	16.7	16.7	16.8	17.2	17.2	18.4	18.3	18.4	18.5	18.6	17.4
1994	18.5	18.6	18.7	19.1	19.2	19.9	20.4	20.4	20.4	20.1	20.9	21.0	19.7
1995	21.0	21.0	21.1	21.1	21.1	21.2	21.2	21.2	21.3	21.4	21.7	21.8	21.2
1996	21.8	22.0	22.0	21.8	22.0	22.4	22.8	22.9	23.0	22.7	22.8	22.9	22.4
1997	24.4	24.4	24.4	24.4	24.4	24.7	24.8	24.9	24.7	24.7	24.6	24.8	24.6
1998	24.2	24.4	24.4	24.6	24.8	25.2	26.0	26.1	25.9	25.6	25.8	26.0	25.2
1999	27.0	27.3	27.5	27.9	28.0	28.5	29.3	29.4	29.1	29.0	29.3	29.5	28.4
2000	30.1	30.6	31.1	31.5	32.1	33.1	34.2	34.1	33.9	33.7	33.7	34.0	32.6
2001	32.3	32.3	32.2	32.5	32.4	32.7	33.6	33.4	32.5	41.1	40.9	41.1	34.7
2002	43.3	42.6	41.9	40.7	39.9	39.2	39.7	39.0	38.2	37.9	37.5	37.3	39.8
2003	36.2	35.9	35.5	34.8	34.2	34.4	34.3	34.1	33.7	34.0	34.0	34.2	34.6
Professional and business services													
1990	26.8	26.9	27.2	27.0	27.1	27.3	26.6	26.8	26.7	26.7	26.7	26.7	26.8
1991	25.1	25.2	25.3	24.9	24.8	25.2	23.9	24.3	24.4	24.6	24.6	24.7	24.7
1992	21.9	22.2	22.3	21.6	21.9	22.0	22.1	22.6	22.6	22.9	23.1	22.6	22.3
1993	23.2	23.5	23.6	24.1	24.2	24.4	23.6	23.9	24.2	24.3	24.6	24.2	23.9
1994	22.9	23.3	23.9	24.1	24.1	23.9	23.7	24.3	24.2	24.5	25.0	24.7	24.0
1995	24.3	24.7	24.6	24.2	24.0	24.4	23.8	24.4	25.0	25.5	25.0	25.0	24.5
1996	25.1	25.9	26.3	25.8	25.7	25.8	26.4	27.0	27.5	27.1	27.4	27.9	26.4
1997	24.7	25.3	25.4	26.2	25.6	25.7	25.2	25.5	26.0	26.7	27.0	27.1	25.8
1998	26.3	26.7	27.0	26.9	27.2	27.4	28.2	28.6	28.6	29.5	29.4	29.6	27.9
1999	26.3	26.5	26.6	28.0	27.9	27.9	27.0	27.5	27.5	28.0	27.9	28.4	27.4
2000	27.3	27.4	27.6	28.5	28.2	28.7	29.9	30.2	30.4	30.0	30.1	30.0	29.0
2001	30.2	30.3	30.5	31.2	31.6	31.6	32.0	32.5	32.6	32.1	31.9	31.1	31.4
2002	30.8	30.7	31.3	30.5	30.2	30.2	30.0	30.9	31.1	31.3	32.1	31.6	30.9
2003	31.1	31.1	31.2	31.1	30.6	30.5	30.8	31.5	31.6	31.0	30.9	30.9	31.0
Educational and health services													
1990	20.9	21.0	21.1	20.5	20.7	20.5	20.8	20.8	21.2	21.2	21.3	21.2	20.9
1991	21.3	21.5	21.7	21.4	21.5	21.3	20.5	20.3	21.1	21.2	21.3	21.4	21.2
1992	20.6	20.9	21.1	21.0	21.2	21.0	20.3	20.2	20.7	20.9	21.1	21.2	20.8
1993	21.2	21.3	21.4	21.5	21.6	21.6	21.2	21.2	21.7	22.2	22.4	22.4	21.6
1994	21.8	21.9	22.0	22.3	22.4	22.1	21.7	21.8	22.3	22.4	22.4	22.5	22.1
1995	22.3	22.5	22.7	23.0	23.4	23.1	23.4	23.3	23.7	23.8	23.8	24.0	23.2
1996	22.7	23.1	23.3	24.0	24.2	24.0	23.0	23.2	23.6	23.9	23.8	23.8	23.5
1997	23.5	23.9	24.1	25.2	25.4	25.2	24.9	24.9	25.4	24.6	24.7	24.7	24.7
1998	24.4	24.5	24.9	25.2	25.2	25.2	25.3	25.3	25.5	25.1	25.1	25.2	25.0
1999	24.9	25.0	25.2	25.2	25.3	25.1	25.0	24.7	25.3	25.5	25.6	25.6	25.2
2000	25.2	25.2	25.4	25.7	25.8	25.9	25.6	25.4	25.8	26.6	26.6	26.9	25.8
2001	26.9	27.2	27.4	27.7	27.8	27.9	27.3	27.1	27.4	27.7	27.7	27.9	27.5
2002	27.6	28.0	28.2	28.6	28.7	28.6	28.2	28.0	28.1	28.4	28.5	28.6	28.3
2003	28.0	28.1	28.4	28.5	28.6	28.6	28.6	28.3	28.9	29.3	29.8	29.7	28.7
Leisure and hospitality													
1990	9.8	9.9	9.9	10.1	10.4	10.4	10.3	10.3	10.6	9.8	9.8	9.8	10.0
1991	9.5	9.5	9.6	9.7	9.8	9.8	9.9	9.9	10.2	10.0	10.0	9.9	9.8
1992	9.6	9.6	9.7	9.8	10.0	9.9	9.7	9.7	9.9	10.1	10.1	10.1	9.8
1993	9.7	9.8	9.8	9.9	10.1	10.3	9.9	9.9	10.2	10.3	10.3	10.4	10.0
1994	10.2	10.2	10.3	10.8	10.9	11.2	10.9	11.0	11.2	11.5	11.3	11.4	10.9
1995	10.8	10.9	10.9	11.3	11.5	11.5	11.5	11.5	11.8	12.0	12.0	11.9	11.4
1996	11.0	11.1	11.2	11.4	11.5	11.5	11.3	11.1	11.4	11.2	11.2	11.1	11.2
1997	10.8	10.9	11.0	11.0	11.1	11.1	11.1	11.1	11.2	11.3	11.4	11.5	11.1
1998	11.5	11.6	11.7	11.8	11.7	11.7	11.3	11.1	11.2	11.1	11.2	11.5	11.4
1999	10.6	10.7	10.7	11.1	11.4	11.6	11.3	11.2	11.3	11.4	11.4	11.4	11.1
2000	10.9	10.9	11.0	11.5	11.8	11.8	11.7	11.5	11.7	11.9	12.0	12.1	11.5
2001	10.6	10.7	10.7	10.9	11.3	11.5	11.2	11.1	11.2	11.5	11.5	11.4	11.1
2002	11.3	11.3	11.4	11.7	12.0	12.1	11.4	11.4	11.9	11.8	11.8	11.7	11.7
2003	11.8	11.9	12.0	12.2	12.5	12.6	12.2	12.1	12.5	12.5	12.5	12.3	12.3
Other services													
1990	7.4	7.3	7.4	7.1	7.0	6.9	7.2	7.1	7.1	6.9	6.9	6.8	7.0
1991	6.8	6.8	6.8	6.9	6.9	7.0	6.8	6.7	6.8	6.6	6.6	6.4	6.7
1992	6.1	6.2	6.2	6.2	6.3	6.3	6.3	6.5	6.8	6.8	6.8	6.8	6.4
1993	6.6	6.7	6.7	6.7	6.6	6.5	6.5	6.4	6.4	6.4	6.5	6.5	6.5
1994	6.5	6.5	6.6	6.6	6.6	6.6	6.6	6.6	6.7	6.7	6.7	6.7	6.6
1995	6.5	6.7	6.8	6.9	6.9	7.0	7.2	7.1	7.1	7.1	7.2	7.2	6.9
1996	7.1	7.2	7.2	7.2	7.3	7.4	7.4	7.4	7.4	7.4	7.5	7.5	7.3
1997	7.4	7.3	7.4	7.4	7.4	7.6	7.5	7.5	7.4	7.4	7.4	7.6	7.4
1998	7.3	7.4	7.4	7.4	7.5	7.6	7.5	7.5	7.5	7.4	7.4	7.5	7.4
1999	7.5	7.6	7.6	7.6	7.6	7.7	7.6	7.5	7.5	7.5	7.5	7.7	7.5
2000	7.5	7.5	7.5	7.8	7.7	7.8	7.8	7.7	7.8	7.8	7.8	8.0	7.7
2001	6.5	6.4	6.5	6.7	6.8	6.8	6.9	6.8	6.9	6.9	6.9	7.0	6.7
2002	6.9	7.0	7.0	7.0	7.1	7.2	7.1	7.1	7.1	7.1	7.2	7.3	7.1
2003	7.2	7.2	7.2	7.3	7.4	7.4	7.2	7.2	7.3	7.2	7.3	7.3	7.3

Employment by Industry: New Jersey—*Continued*

(Numbers in thousands. Not seasonally adjusted.)

Industry	January	February	March	April	May	June	July	August	September	October	November	December	Annual Average
JERSEY CITY—*Continued*													
Government													
1990	40.6	41.0	41.6	41.7	42.6	42.7	42.5	41.7	41.2	41.2	41.5	41.8	41.6
1991	40.9	41.2	41.1	41.0	40.6	40.4	40.9	40.9	39.5	40.2	40.3	40.9	40.6
1992	40.4	40.7	40.8	40.8	40.5	40.4	42.7	41.7	39.4	40.4	40.4	40.8	40.7
1993	40.2	40.3	40.8	40.2	39.9	39.9	42.2	41.6	39.4	40.3	40.7	40.9	40.5
1994	40.3	40.5	40.8	40.4	40.4	40.4	41.1	40.5	39.8	40.5	40.5	41.2	40.5
1995	40.4	40.8	40.9	40.7	40.5	40.5	40.3	40.7	39.3	39.7	39.9	40.1	40.3
1996	39.9	40.0	40.2	40.0	40.1	40.3	40.2	38.9	39.2	39.2	39.4	39.2	39.7
1997	38.7	38.8	39.0	38.8	39.1	39.0	40.0	38.8	38.4	38.8	39.2	39.5	39.0
1998	38.0	38.3	38.6	38.4	38.4	38.2	38.7	37.6	37.0	38.1	38.3	38.7	38.1
1999	38.0	38.4	38.8	39.3	38.7	38.3	38.6	37.8	37.8	38.3	39.0	39.2	38.5
2000	38.1	38.6	39.2	38.3	39.2	38.4	38.0	36.5	37.7	38.9	39.4	39.6	38.4
2001	38.2	39.3	39.3	38.9	39.3	38.4	38.2	36.4	38.4	41.2	41.9	42.2	39.3
2002	40.9	41.3	41.4	40.4	40.5	38.5	38.1	36.8	38.5	39.7	40.3	40.5	39.7
2003	39.4	40.2	40.3	40.0	40.6	39.6	38.2	37.1	39.3	40.7	41.2	41.3	39.8
Federal government													
1990	11.5	11.5	11.5	11.6	12.5	12.3	11.9	11.4	11.4	11.3	11.2	11.3	11.6
1991	11.3	11.3	11.3	11.3	11.2	11.2	11.2	11.2	11.1	11.0	11.0	11.0	11.1
1992	11.0	10.9	10.8	10.8	10.8	10.8	11.0	10.7	10.6	10.6	10.4	10.5	10.7
1993	10.5	10.5	10.5	10.3	10.3	10.3	10.3	10.2	10.3	10.2	10.3	10.4	10.3
1994	10.4	10.3	10.3	10.2	10.3	10.3	10.4	10.4	10.7	10.7	10.6	10.8	10.4
1995	10.6	10.6	10.6	10.7	10.6	10.6	10.6	10.5	10.5	10.5	10.6	10.8	10.6
1996	10.6	10.6	10.6	10.5	10.5	10.5	10.5	10.5	10.5	10.1	10.0	10.1	10.4
1997	9.7	9.7	9.7	9.5	9.6	9.5	9.5	9.4	9.2	9.0	9.0	9.1	9.4
1998	8.4	8.3	8.3	8.2	8.2	8.3	8.3	8.2	8.2	8.1	8.2	8.4	8.2
1999	8.2	8.0	8.0	8.5	7.9	7.8	7.8	7.8	7.8	7.6	7.7	7.9	7.9
2000	7.6	7.6	7.7	7.9	8.8	8.2	7.8	7.4	7.4	7.4	7.6	7.7	7.7
2001	7.7	7.7	7.7	7.6	7.7	7.5	7.5	7.5	7.5	7.6	7.7	8.0	7.6
2002	7.6	7.2	7.2	7.1	7.1	7.0	7.0	7.2	7.0	6.9	6.9	7.2	7.1
2003	7.0	6.9	6.9	6.9	6.9	6.9	6.9	6.9	6.8	6.8	6.8	7.0	6.9
State government													
1990	3.0	3.2	3.5	3.5	3.3	3.3	2.9	2.6	3.2	3.5	3.5	3.6	3.2
1991	3.2	3.5	3.5	3.5	3.1	2.7	2.7	2.7	2.8	3.2	3.2	3.2	3.1
1992	2.8	3.0	3.1	3.2	2.9	2.8	2.8	2.8	2.9	3.3	3.3	3.3	3.0
1993	3.2	3.4	3.5	3.4	3.1	3.0	3.0	3.1	3.2	3.6	3.6	3.6	3.3
1994	3.2	3.4	3.5	3.5	3.3	3.3	3.0	3.0	3.2	3.5	3.5	3.5	3.3
1995	4.1	4.3	4.3	4.3	4.3	4.3	3.6	3.6	3.8	4.1	4.1	4.0	4.0
1996	3.9	4.0	4.1	4.1	4.0	4.0	3.4	3.4	3.5	4.0	4.0	3.8	3.8
1997	3.7	3.9	4.0	4.0	4.0	3.9	3.7	3.7	3.9	4.3	4.3	4.3	3.9
1998	3.9	4.3	4.3	4.3	4.3	3.8	3.7	3.7	4.0	4.3	4.3	4.3	4.1
1999	3.8	4.3	4.4	4.4	4.3	3.8	3.8	3.8	3.7	4.2	4.3	4.2	4.0
2000	3.7	4.1	4.3	4.2	4.1	3.7	3.6	3.6	3.9	4.2	4.2	4.1	3.9
2001	3.5	4.0	4.0	4.0	3.9	3.4	3.4	3.2	3.6	3.8	3.8	3.8	3.7
2002	3.2	3.6	3.6	3.7	3.6	3.1	3.0	3.1	3.4	3.7	3.8	3.8	3.5
2003	3.1	3.7	3.7	3.8	3.8	3.0	3.2	3.2	3.6	4.0	4.1	4.1	3.6
Local government													
1990	26.1	26.3	26.6	26.6	26.8	27.1	27.7	27.7	26.6	26.4	26.8	26.9	26.8
1991	26.4	26.4	26.3	26.2	26.3	26.5	27.0	27.0	25.6	26.0	26.1	26.7	26.3
1992	26.6	26.8	26.9	26.8	26.8	26.8	28.9	28.2	25.9	26.5	26.7	27.0	26.9
1993	26.5	26.4	26.8	26.5	26.5	26.6	28.9	28.3	25.9	26.5	26.8	26.9	26.8
1994	26.7	26.8	27.0	26.7	26.8	26.8	27.7	27.1	25.9	26.3	26.4	26.9	26.7
1995	25.7	25.9	26.0	25.7	25.6	25.6	26.1	25.6	25.0	25.1	25.2	25.3	25.5
1996	25.4	25.4	25.5	25.4	25.6	25.8	26.3	25.0	25.2	25.1	25.4	25.3	25.4
1997	25.3	25.2	25.3	25.3	25.5	25.6	26.8	25.7	25.3	25.5	25.9	26.1	25.6
1998	25.7	25.7	26.0	25.9	25.9	26.1	26.7	25.7	24.8	25.7	25.8	26.0	25.8
1999	26.0	26.1	26.4	26.4	26.5	26.7	27.0	26.2	26.3	26.5	27.0	27.1	26.5
2000	26.8	26.9	27.2	26.2	26.3	26.5	26.6	25.5	26.4	27.3	27.6	27.8	26.7
2001	27.0	27.6	27.6	27.3	27.7	27.5	27.3	25.7	27.3	29.8	30.4	30.4	27.9
2002	30.1	30.5	30.6	29.6	29.8	28.4	28.1	26.5	28.1	29.1	29.6	29.5	29.2
2003	29.3	29.6	29.7	29.3	29.9	29.7	28.1	27.0	28.9	29.9	30.3	30.2	29.3
MIDDLESEX-SOMERSET-HUNTERDON													
Total nonfarm													
1990	543.4	541.1	546.2	545.7	548.5	551.5	542.3	542.9	538.4	539.9	539.4	538.9	543.1
1991	525.2	525.2	528.1	529.5	531.9	535.2	530.1	531.0	532.0	533.9	537.9	536.3	531.3
1992	521.3	523.2	527.3	531.3	533.7	539.1	534.6	533.5	534.4	541.8	545.1	547.5	534.4
1993	532.8	534.6	535.1	542.5	546.3	551.7	545.2	543.1	546.5	553.0	557.0	559.2	545.5
1994	543.2	543.4	551.3	556.3	559.2	563.5	556.9	558.7	560.7	566.3	570.4	573.0	558.5
1995	557.3	559.0	563.9	565.0	568.8	572.8	566.5	566.7	572.6	576.7	579.9	581.7	569.2
1996	561.0	568.5	573.1	575.2	579.8	585.0	585.4	584.0	588.8	592.7	600.8	604.1	583.2
1997	587.0	591.9	597.0	602.2	607.3	612.0	606.4	603.8	610.5	616.3	621.5	624.8	606.7
1998	605.0	608.6	612.3	617.3	622.5	625.1	621.3	616.6	623.0	632.3	635.3	639.2	621.5
1999	624.1	629.7	636.1	638.5	642.1	646.7	646.7	645.3	648.4	656.5	661.7	666.5	645.1
2000	651.3	654.2	662.4	663.7	667.7	672.6	665.1	663.5	665.6	670.8	675.4	680.7	666.0
2001	661.5	664.1	668.7	673.5	676.5	679.4	662.7	659.9	663.3	667.2	667.7	666.1	667.5
2002	648.8	650.3	656.7	655.9	658.2	661.4	650.5	649.0	649.1	649.8	653.7	654.7	653.2
2003	632.5	631.9	635.1	637.5	641.3	643.2	636.5	635.1	635.2	642.7	645.5	647.3	638.7

Employment by Industry: New Jersey—*Continued*

(Numbers in thousands. Not seasonally adjusted.)

Industry	January	February	March	April	May	June	July	August	September	October	November	December	Annual Average
MIDDLESEX-SOMERSET-HUNTERDON—*Continued*													
Total private													
1990	469.7	466.7	470.3	468.7	470.5	473.9	468.4	468.6	465.3	462.6	462.1	461.6	467.3
1991	450.0	447.7	450.2	451.8	454.5	459.3	456.5	458.4	458.8	457.3	460.2	459.0	455.3
1992	446.9	446.2	449.4	453.7	456.7	463.1	459.6	459.6	461.0	465.0	467.7	469.9	458.2
1993	458.0	457.3	457.5	464.2	468.5	474.8	471.5	470.1	472.5	475.0	477.8	480.6	468.9
1994	467.9	465.7	472.7	477.8	481.9	486.7	482.8	485.5	486.6	488.2	491.6	494.3	481.8
1995	482.4	481.3	485.3	486.8	491.0	496.6	492.6	494.3	497.4	499.0	501.9	503.6	492.6
1996	486.4	490.6	495.0	497.2	503.3	508.8	511.6	512.4	513.9	515.0	522.5	526.1	506.9
1997	511.3	513.9	519.1	523.8	529.6	535.4	533.0	532.7	536.2	537.7	542.1	545.4	530.0
1998	528.2	529.1	532.6	537.7	543.4	547.5	547.7	545.1	547.5	552.5	554.8	558.8	543.7
1999	546.7	549.4	554.7	557.0	561.3	568.0	570.7	570.6	570.9	574.4	578.5	583.4	565.4
2000	571.3	571.8	579.1	579.6	583.6	591.0	587.0	586.7	586.6	586.8	590.1	595.6	584.1
2001	579.6	579.4	583.3	587.6	590.6	595.4	583.9	582.5	582.4	580.7	579.9	578.6	583.6
2002	564.8	563.5	568.8	569.1	572.6	576.8	570.4	570.3	568.4	564.3	566.8	568.3	568.7
2003	549.7	546.1	548.3	550.7	554.9	559.0	556.8	556.2	553.4	556.1	557.6	560.0	554.1
Goods-producing													
1990	114.3	114.5	115.2	114.6	114.4	115.3	112.6	113.3	111.6	111.3	110.3	108.6	113.0
1991	105.4	105.5	106.3	107.2	108.5	109.7	108.0	107.6	108.2	107.3	106.4	103.9	107.0
1992	100.6	100.5	101.0	101.8	102.5	103.8	102.8	102.4	101.7	102.5	102.0	101.9	101.9
1993	98.1	98.0	98.1	99.4	100.5	101.6	101.5	101.6	102.4	102.7	102.6	102.5	100.7
1994	97.3	97.0	98.7	99.6	100.6	101.8	100.9	101.9	101.9	100.6	100.4	100.0	100.0
1995	97.7	97.2	98.1	100.1	100.6	101.7	101.0	100.8	101.7	102.2	102.1	101.5	100.3
1996	96.2	97.8	99.1	98.7	99.6	101.2	101.2	100.5	100.4	100.6	100.7	100.6	99.7
1997	96.9	97.4	98.5	101.2	102.0	103.4	104.0	102.8	102.9	103.6	104.0	103.7	101.7
1998	100.1	99.2	99.9	102.2	103.3	104.1	103.8	102.8	104.0	105.0	104.4	103.2	102.6
1999	102.8	102.8	104.0	104.1	105.1	106.3	105.8	104.8	105.5	105.8	105.8	106.1	104.9
2000	104.9	105.4	106.7	106.2	107.5	108.2	109.3	107.5	107.6	107.6	107.8	108.4	107.2
2001	103.8	104.8	105.3	106.7	107.9	107.7	105.8	105.8	105.4	104.6	104.0	103.1	105.4
2002	100.4	100.1	100.8	102.5	103.3	103.5	101.6	101.2	100.6	100.0	99.8	99.8	101.1
2003	96.8	95.8	95.2	96.6	98.0	98.3	98.4	98.5	97.3	97.1	97.0	97.1	97.2
Construction and mining													
1990	19.6	19.6	20.0	20.2	20.7	21.2	21.2	20.7	20.6	20.4	19.9	19.4	20.2
1991	16.6	16.2	16.6	18.4	19.1	19.7	18.6	18.5	18.2	17.7	17.3	16.6	17.7
1992	14.7	14.2	14.6	15.3	15.9	16.6	16.6	16.6	16.6	17.1	16.8	16.5	15.9
1993	14.6	14.3	14.4	15.7	16.5	17.1	17.8	17.9	17.6	17.8	17.7	17.4	16.5
1994	14.6	14.2	15.1	16.9	17.9	18.4	18.8	19.1	19.1	18.7	18.5	18.1	17.4
1995	16.1	15.4	16.2	17.4	18.0	18.6	18.8	19.0	18.7	18.8	18.6	18.1	17.8
1996	15.0	15.4	16.4	17.6	18.5	19.0	19.5	19.4	19.1	18.9	18.8	18.6	18.0
1997	16.8	16.8	17.5	19.0	19.5	20.1	20.4	20.4	20.2	20.2	19.8	19.3	19.1
1998	17.4	17.3	18.1	19.6	20.3	20.7	21.3	21.3	21.2	21.4	21.2	20.9	20.0
1999	18.5	18.5	19.2	20.5	21.1	21.8	22.3	22.4	22.0	22.3	22.0	22.0	21.0
2000	20.2	19.7	20.9	21.6	22.4	22.7	23.1	23.4	23.3	23.5	23.3	23.1	22.2
2001	22.0	22.1	22.9	24.2	25.2	26.0	26.2	26.3	26.2	26.4	26.1	25.7	24.9
2002	23.5	23.4	24.1	25.0	25.4	25.8	26.0	26.0	25.8	25.5	25.1	24.7	25.0
2003	22.3	21.5	21.6	23.0	24.1	24.5	24.8	24.7	24.5	24.4	24.2	24.2	23.7
Manufacturing													
1990	94.7	94.9	95.2	94.4	93.7	94.1	91.4	92.6	91.0	90.9	90.4	89.2	92.7
1991	88.8	89.3	89.7	88.8	89.4	90.0	89.4	89.1	90.0	89.6	89.1	87.3	89.2
1992	85.9	86.3	86.4	86.5	86.6	87.2	86.2	85.8	85.1	85.4	85.2	85.4	86.0
1993	83.5	83.7	83.7	83.7	84.0	84.5	83.7	83.7	84.8	84.9	84.9	85.1	84.1
1994	82.7	82.8	83.6	82.7	82.7	83.4	82.1	82.8	82.8	81.9	81.9	81.9	82.6
1995	81.6	81.8	81.9	82.7	82.6	83.1	82.2	81.8	83.0	83.4	83.5	83.4	82.5
1996	81.2	82.4	82.7	81.1	81.1	82.2	81.7	81.1	81.3	81.7	81.9	82.0	81.7
1997	80.1	80.6	81.0	82.2	82.5	83.3	83.6	82.4	82.7	83.4	84.2	84.4	82.5
1998	82.7	81.9	81.8	82.6	83.0	83.4	82.5	81.5	82.8	83.6	83.2	82.3	82.6
1999	84.3	84.3	84.8	83.6	84.0	84.5	83.5	82.4	83.5	83.5	83.8	84.1	83.8
2000	84.7	85.7	85.8	84.6	85.1	85.5	86.2	84.1	84.3	84.1	84.5	85.3	84.9
2001	81.8	82.7	82.4	82.5	82.7	81.7	79.6	79.5	79.2	78.2	77.9	77.4	80.4
2002	76.9	76.7	76.7	77.5	77.9	77.7	75.6	75.2	74.8	74.5	74.7	75.1	76.1
2003	74.5	74.3	73.6	73.6	73.9	73.8	73.6	73.8	72.8	72.7	72.8	72.9	73.5
Service-providing													
1990	429.1	426.6	431.0	431.1	434.1	436.2	429.7	429.6	426.8	428.6	429.1	430.3	430.1
1991	419.8	419.7	421.8	422.3	423.4	425.5	422.1	423.4	423.8	426.6	431.5	432.4	424.3
1992	420.7	422.7	426.3	429.5	431.2	435.3	431.8	431.1	432.7	439.3	443.1	445.6	432.4
1993	434.7	436.6	437.0	443.1	445.8	450.1	443.7	441.5	444.1	450.3	454.4	456.7	444.8
1994	445.9	446.4	452.6	456.7	458.6	461.7	456.0	456.8	458.8	465.7	470.0	473.0	458.5
1995	459.6	461.8	465.8	464.9	468.2	471.1	465.5	465.9	470.9	474.5	477.8	480.2	468.8
1996	464.8	470.7	474.0	476.5	480.2	483.8	484.2	483.5	488.4	492.1	500.1	503.5	483.4
1997	490.1	494.5	498.5	501.0	505.3	508.6	502.4	501.0	507.6	512.7	517.5	521.1	505.0
1998	504.9	509.4	512.4	515.1	519.2	521.0	517.5	513.8	519.0	527.3	530.9	536.0	518.8
1999	521.3	526.9	532.1	534.4	537.0	540.4	540.9	540.5	542.9	550.7	555.9	560.4	540.2
2000	546.4	548.8	555.7	557.5	560.2	564.4	555.8	556.0	558.0	563.2	567.6	572.3	558.8
2001	557.7	559.3	563.4	566.8	568.6	571.7	556.9	554.1	557.9	562.6	563.7	563.0	562.1
2002	548.4	550.2	555.9	553.4	554.9	557.9	548.9	547.8	548.5	549.8	553.9	554.9	552.0
2003	535.7	536.1	539.9	540.9	543.3	544.9	538.1	536.6	537.9	545.6	548.5	550.2	541.5

Employment by Industry: New Jersey—*Continued*

(Numbers in thousands. Not seasonally adjusted.)

Industry	January	February	March	April	May	June	July	August	September	October	November	December	Annual Average
MIDDLESEX-SOMERSET-HUNTERDON—*Continued*													
Trade, transportation, and utilities													
1990	129.5	127.0	127.4	126.2	127.4	127.8	125.0	125.1	126.0	125.4	126.5	128.1	126.7
1991	121.4	119.4	119.5	118.4	118.5	119.7	118.0	118.8	119.9	121.6	124.3	126.1	120.4
1992	121.6	119.4	119.7	120.1	120.6	121.3	119.5	119.3	121.0	122.3	125.4	126.8	121.4
1993	120.9	119.1	118.7	119.6	120.4	122.1	119.9	119.5	121.0	122.0	124.2	127.1	121.2
1994	123.6	121.0	122.5	121.6	122.9	123.7	121.2	122.1	123.6	125.3	128.5	130.3	123.8
1995	123.6	122.1	122.5	124.1	124.5	125.8	124.6	124.9	125.1	128.0	130.3	131.9	125.6
1996	125.1	125.2	125.9	126.2	127.2	127.5	126.4	126.6	127.7	130.1	133.3	135.8	128.0
1997	131.1	130.2	131.1	131.3	131.9	133.5	131.4	129.8	133.5	135.1	138.0	140.0	133.0
1998	135.4	133.1	133.2	132.9	134.1	135.2	134.7	134.7	137.1	139.5	141.8	143.3	136.2
1999	137.6	136.7	137.3	138.8	139.4	140.8	139.2	139.4	140.9	143.6	146.0	149.7	140.7
2000	147.2	145.8	147.4	146.6	146.1	146.9	145.2	145.7	146.0	149.8	153.0	156.1	147.9
2001	152.1	149.6	149.5	149.9	149.9	150.7	148.1	148.1	149.4	150.5	152.3	154.3	150.3
2002	148.5	147.1	148.0	146.7	146.9	147.9	145.1	145.0	146.1	146.3	148.1	149.9	147.1
2003	144.0	142.4	142.4	143.4	144.5	145.3	144.1	143.5	143.6	145.9	149.2	151.8	145.0
Wholesale trade													
1990	38.8	38.7	38.6	39.6	39.6	39.7	39.1	39.2	38.6	38.1	37.8	37.6	38.7
1991	36.6	36.5	36.5	36.5	36.6	36.8	36.3	36.3	36.1	36.2	36.0	36.0	36.3
1992	36.2	36.1	36.2	36.5	36.5	36.7	35.9	35.9	36.0	35.6	35.5	35.2	36.0
1993	34.5	34.6	34.4	34.8	35.0	35.5	35.0	34.8	34.5	34.3	34.5	34.5	34.7
1994	34.8	34.6	34.7	34.4	34.3	34.6	34.9	35.1	35.1	35.0	35.3	35.2	34.8
1995	35.3	35.6	35.6	35.6	35.8	36.2	36.7	36.7	36.5	36.6	37.0	37.0	36.2
1996	36.2	36.8	37.0	37.3	37.4	37.4	37.8	37.9	37.7	37.5	38.0	38.1	37.4
1997	38.0	38.6	39.1	39.2	39.3	39.8	40.3	40.5	40.4	40.7	41.0	41.0	39.8
1998	41.4	41.7	41.9	41.5	41.8	42.5	42.6	42.4	42.5	42.8	42.4	42.3	42.1
1999	41.9	42.1	42.3	43.5	43.4	43.9	44.0	43.8	44.1	44.1	44.1	44.8	43.5
2000	45.9	46.2	46.8	47.2	47.3	47.7	47.3	47.5	47.3	47.7	48.0	48.5	47.2
2001	50.6	50.7	50.8	51.2	51.2	51.5	51.2	51.3	51.4	51.4	51.3	51.1	51.1
2002	50.4	50.5	50.7	50.0	49.7	49.6	48.9	48.6	48.4	48.3	48.1	47.7	49.2
2003	47.5	47.4	47.2	47.7	47.6	47.7	48.4	47.8	46.9	46.9	47.1	47.2	47.5
Retail trade													
1990	64.7	62.5	62.9	61.0	61.7	61.9	60.9	61.0	61.4	61.4	62.7	64.3	62.2
1991	59.5	57.8	57.8	56.8	56.9	57.7	57.4	57.9	58.3	59.3	62.1	63.6	58.7
1992	60.7	58.8	58.7	59.0	59.3	59.7	59.5	59.3	59.7	61.2	64.0	65.8	60.4
1993	61.7	59.9	59.6	59.6	60.2	61.2	60.3	60.3	60.8	62.0	63.9	66.8	61.3
1994	63.2	60.7	61.7	60.7	61.5	62.1	60.5	61.0	61.8	62.8	65.8	67.9	62.4
1995	62.3	60.5	60.7	61.0	61.5	62.3	61.0	61.4	61.9	62.3	64.3	66.4	62.1
1996	61.9	60.8	61.0	60.8	61.6	61.8	60.9	61.1	61.3	63.6	66.1	68.4	62.4
1997	64.1	62.5	62.9	62.9	63.2	64.1	62.8	63.0	63.8	64.7	67.2	69.3	64.2
1998	64.9	62.8	62.5	61.8	62.5	62.6	62.8	63.0	64.0	66.5	69.1	70.9	64.4
1999	67.6	66.1	66.4	65.9	66.5	67.3	66.5	66.9	67.3	69.7	72.1	74.9	68.1
2000	72.5	71.2	72.0	69.9	70.4	70.7	69.9	70.2	70.5	72.1	74.9	77.7	71.8
2001	73.0	70.4	70.1	70.1	70.6	71.0	69.6	69.8	69.7	70.6	72.7	75.0	71.0
2002	70.6	69.2	69.8	69.5	70.0	70.7	69.4	69.6	69.5	69.7	71.8	74.1	70.3
2003	68.7	67.7	67.8	68.3	69.2	69.7	68.8	69.1	69.3	71.4	74.3	76.6	70.1
Transportation and utilities													
1990	26.0	25.8	25.9	25.6	26.1	26.2	25.0	24.9	26.0	25.9	26.0	26.2	25.8
1991	25.3	25.1	25.2	25.1	25.0	25.2	24.3	24.6	25.5	26.1	26.2	26.5	25.3
1992	24.7	24.5	24.8	24.6	24.8	24.9	24.1	24.1	25.3	25.5	25.9	25.8	24.9
1993	24.7	24.6	24.7	25.2	25.2	25.4	24.6	24.4	25.7	25.7	25.8	25.8	25.1
1994	25.6	25.7	26.1	26.5	27.1	27.0	25.8	26.0	26.7	27.5	27.4	27.2	26.5
1995	26.0	26.0	26.2	27.5	27.2	27.3	26.9	26.8	26.7	29.1	29.0	28.5	27.2
1996	27.0	27.6	27.9	28.1	28.2	28.3	27.7	27.6	28.7	29.0	29.2	29.3	28.2
1997	29.0	29.1	29.1	29.2	29.4	29.6	28.3	26.3	29.3	29.7	29.8	29.7	29.0
1998	29.1	28.6	28.8	29.6	29.8	30.1	29.3	29.3	30.6	30.2	30.3	30.1	29.6
1999	28.1	28.5	28.6	29.4	29.5	29.6	28.7	28.7	29.5	29.8	29.8	30.0	29.1
2000	28.8	28.4	28.6	29.5	28.4	28.5	28.0	28.0	28.2	30.0	30.1	29.9	28.8
2001	28.5	28.5	28.6	28.6	28.1	28.2	27.3	27.0	28.3	28.5	28.3	28.2	28.1
2002	27.5	27.4	27.5	27.2	27.2	27.6	26.8	26.8	28.2	28.3	28.2	28.1	27.6
2003	27.8	27.3	27.4	27.4	27.7	27.9	26.9	26.6	27.4	27.6	27.8	28.0	27.5
Information													
1990	26.7	25.7	26.2	25.9	25.4	25.7	26.5	26.2	26.1	25.4	25.5	25.7	25.9
1991	26.6	26.8	26.9	27.3	27.5	27.6	28.1	28.3	28.2	27.4	27.5	27.5	27.4
1992	27.4	27.7	27.9	28.0	28.2	28.8	28.7	28.8	28.9	29.3	29.5	29.6	28.5
1993	28.0	28.2	28.2	28.6	28.7	29.1	29.4	29.0	29.1	28.8	28.8	28.8	28.7
1994	28.0	28.1	28.4	29.1	29.2	29.3	29.3	29.5	28.9	31.0	31.6	31.7	29.5
1995	31.0	30.9	31.5	32.1	32.1	32.4	30.8	31.6	32.2	31.5	31.5	31.6	31.6
1996	30.2	27.2	27.6	29.8	30.4	30.8	31.1	31.3	31.5	31.8	32.2	32.5	30.5
1997	33.1	33.1	33.2	32.0	32.1	32.4	32.0	32.3	32.2	31.6	31.8	31.9	32.3
1998	26.4	26.6	26.8	27.0	27.1	27.3	26.1	26.1	26.1	25.7	25.8	25.8	26.4
1999	26.9	27.0	27.1	26.7	27.3	27.7	27.1	27.4	27.5	27.5	28.3	27.8	27.3
2000	28.4	28.3	28.7	28.6	28.6	28.7	29.0	28.4	28.7	29.3	29.5	29.5	28.8
2001	29.3	29.5	29.8	29.3	29.3	29.6	28.7	28.5	29.1	28.4	28.5	28.5	29.0
2002	28.6	28.0	28.2	27.8	27.7	27.7	26.6	27.4	27.1	25.2	25.4	25.3	27.1
2003	25.6	25.5	25.7	24.8	24.6	24.6	24.6	24.5	24.1	24.4	24.6	24.6	24.8

Employment by Industry: New Jersey—*Continued*

(Numbers in thousands. Not seasonally adjusted.)

Industry	January	February	March	April	May	June	July	August	September	October	November	December	Annual Average
MIDDLESEX-SOMERSET-HUNTERDON—*Continued*													
Financial activities													
1990	38.7	38.7	38.7	38.9	39.2	39.3	39.1	38.9	38.2	37.3	37.2	37.2	38.4
1991	38.5	37.5	37.4	38.1	38.2	38.5	38.9	39.0	38.5	37.8	37.7	37.8	38.1
1992	37.2	37.3	37.4	38.7	39.1	39.8	40.3	40.2	39.8	40.5	40.5	40.8	39.3
1993	39.9	39.7	39.8	40.0	39.7	40.2	41.0	40.9	40.5	40.2	40.3	40.3	40.2
1994	40.7	40.7	41.0	40.6	40.5	41.2	41.2	41.2	40.6	40.2	39.9	39.8	40.6
1995	39.9	39.7	40.1	39.4	39.7	40.3	40.4	40.4	40.1	39.9	40.1	40.2	40.0
1996	39.8	40.1	40.1	39.5	39.6	40.3	40.8	40.9	40.5	40.2	40.4	40.5	40.2
1997	41.6	41.7	41.9	42.2	42.8	43.1	43.3	43.5	43.1	43.9	44.0	44.1	42.9
1998	44.5	44.4	44.2	44.9	44.8	45.2	46.3	46.3	45.8	45.2	44.7	44.8	45.0
1999	46.5	45.9	45.8	46.4	46.2	46.5	48.8	48.8	48.3	48.6	48.5	49.0	47.4
2000	48.1	48.0	48.0	48.6	48.6	49.3	49.3	49.2	48.6	46.0	45.5	45.7	47.9
2001	45.7	45.5	45.5	45.8	45.6	46.0	43.7	43.6	44.2	47.0	46.2	45.3	45.3
2002	43.0	42.5	42.2	42.2	42.3	42.9	42.4	42.4	42.2	42.0	42.2	42.6	42.4
2003	42.6	42.6	42.5	42.0	42.2	42.5	42.3	42.3	42.1	41.9	41.9	41.8	42.2
Professional and business services													
1990	75.6	75.8	76.6	76.3	76.4	77.8	77.3	77.2	76.0	75.0	74.7	74.3	76.0
1991	73.7	73.4	74.7	75.9	75.9	76.8	78.2	78.8	77.9	77.2	77.9	77.6	76.5
1992	76.0	75.9	77.3	77.3	77.7	79.3	79.7	79.8	79.5	79.7	79.5	79.6	78.4
1993	81.5	82.3	83.1	85.6	86.6	88.0	87.5	87.3	86.9	87.3	87.8	87.4	85.9
1994	87.4	87.7	89.0	93.1	94.0	95.2	96.0	96.5	96.7	96.5	96.7	97.2	93.8
1995	96.6	96.8	97.8	95.9	97.1	98.5	99.2	100.3	101.1	100.4	101.2	100.9	98.8
1996	99.0	102.0	102.8	102.3	103.7	105.3	109.0	110.7	110.8	109.7	112.4	112.7	106.7
1997	106.7	108.5	110.2	112.1	114.3	115.3	115.8	117.6	117.5	115.9	116.7	118.2	114.0
1998	115.5	117.7	119.8	121.7	122.9	124.3	126.1	125.7	125.1	126.0	126.9	129.7	123.4
1999	121.9	124.7	127.2	127.3	128.3	131.1	133.8	135.0	135.2	134.5	135.2	135.4	130.8
2000	130.3	131.2	134.1	134.5	136.4	139.5	136.6	138.5	138.8	136.5	136.7	137.8	135.9
2001	139.0	139.5	141.6	142.9	143.2	144.9	141.7	140.7	139.6	135.9	134.1	132.2	139.6
2002	130.3	130.8	133.5	133.2	134.1	135.3	136.5	137.0	135.8	133.9	133.9	133.4	134.0
2003	124.0	123.3	125.0	125.1	124.8	126.0	125.8	127.1	126.4	126.3	125.3	125.1	125.4
Educational and health services													
1990	41.1	41.2	41.6	41.1	41.2	41.2	41.1	41.1	41.5	42.5	42.7	42.7	41.5
1991	42.1	42.6	42.8	42.3	42.5	42.4	41.5	41.7	42.2	42.7	43.1	42.9	42.4
1992	42.3	42.9	43.2	43.3	43.3	43.4	42.9	42.9	43.9	44.7	44.9	45.1	43.5
1993	44.6	44.9	45.0	45.6	45.9	45.9	45.5	45.2	46.2	46.7	46.9	47.0	45.7
1994	46.2	46.5	47.0	46.4	46.4	46.4	45.6	45.7	46.7	46.8	46.9	47.3	46.4
1995	46.8	47.6	47.8	47.9	48.2	48.3	47.9	47.8	49.0	49.2	49.5	50.0	48.3
1996	48.9	50.1	50.4	50.7	51.4	51.3	51.4	51.0	52.0	52.8	53.4	53.8	51.4
1997	52.8	53.5	53.8	53.8	54.1	54.3	53.4	53.2	54.0	55.0	55.3	55.0	54.0
1998	54.4	55.2	55.5	55.0	55.6	55.0	54.5	54.2	54.8	56.6	56.8	57.1	55.3
1999	57.0	57.6	57.9	58.0	58.2	58.0	57.3	57.2	57.3	58.2	58.8	59.1	57.8
2000	59.5	59.8	60.3	60.5	60.9	61.3	61.0	60.8	61.5	62.7	63.0	63.3	61.2
2001	56.2	56.6	56.9	57.7	58.0	58.4	57.8	57.6	58.1	58.2	58.6	58.9	57.7
2002	58.3	59.1	59.5	59.3	59.7	60.1	59.5	59.0	60.0	60.3	60.9	60.8	59.7
2003	60.6	60.4	60.8	61.0	61.6	61.8	61.1	60.4	61.0	62.0	61.9	62.2	61.2
Leisure and hospitality													
1990	29.4	29.5	30.2	30.8	31.7	32.0	32.0	32.0	31.4	31.1	30.8	30.7	30.9
1991	28.3	28.4	28.5	28.3	29.0	29.9	29.6	29.9	29.8	29.0	29.0	28.9	29.0
1992	27.4	28.0	28.4	29.8	30.4	31.6	30.6	31.1	31.1	30.8	30.8	30.9	30.0
1993	29.6	29.8	29.3	29.7	30.9	31.8	30.6	30.4	30.5	31.4	31.2	31.4	30.5
1994	29.1	28.9	30.0	31.2	32.1	32.7	32.3	32.2	32.1	31.4	31.2	31.6	31.2
1995	30.8	30.9	31.5	31.3	32.5	33.1	32.4	32.2	32.1	31.5	30.8	30.8	31.6
1996	30.7	31.5	32.2	33.0	34.3	34.9	34.3	34.1	33.9	32.5	32.8	32.8	33.0
1997	31.6	32.0	32.7	33.6	34.7	35.4	35.0	35.4	35.2	34.6	34.4	34.5	34.0
1998	33.6	34.5	34.8	35.6	37.0	37.9	37.3	36.5	36.0	36.0	36.0	36.5	35.9
1999	35.0	35.5	36.0	36.3	37.2	37.7	38.8	38.0	36.4	36.0	35.6	36.0	36.5
2000	33.0	33.4	33.9	34.8	35.6	36.7	36.0	36.1	35.1	34.7	34.5	34.6	34.8
2001	33.4	33.6	34.2	34.8	35.9	37.1	36.8	36.9	35.7	35.2	35.2	35.3	35.3
2002	34.7	34.8	35.3	36.1	37.1	37.9	37.1	36.9	35.6	35.4	35.4	35.2	36.0
2003	34.8	34.7	35.2	36.1	37.4	38.4	38.3	37.9	37.3	36.7	35.9	35.8	36.5
Other services													
1990	14.4	14.3	14.4	14.9	14.8	14.8	14.8	14.8	14.5	14.6	14.4	14.3	14.5
1991	14.0	14.1	14.1	14.3	14.4	14.7	14.2	14.3	14.1	14.3	14.3	14.3	14.2
1992	14.4	14.5	14.5	14.7	14.9	15.1	15.1	15.1	15.1	15.2	15.1	15.2	14.9
1993	15.4	15.3	15.3	15.7	15.8	16.1	16.1	16.2	15.9	15.9	16.0	16.1	15.8
1994	15.6	15.8	16.1	16.2	16.2	16.4	16.3	16.4	16.1	16.4	16.4	16.4	16.1
1995	16.0	16.1	16.0	16.0	16.3	16.5	16.3	16.3	16.1	16.3	16.4	16.7	16.2
1996	16.5	16.7	16.9	17.0	17.1	17.5	17.4	17.3	17.1	17.3	17.3	17.4	17.1
1997	17.5	17.5	17.7	17.6	17.7	18.0	18.1	18.1	17.8	18.0	17.9	18.0	17.8
1998	18.3	18.4	18.4	18.4	18.6	18.5	18.9	18.8	18.6	18.5	18.4	18.4	18.5
1999	19.0	19.2	19.4	19.4	19.6	19.9	19.9	20.0	19.8	20.2	20.3	20.3	19.7
2000	19.9	19.9	20.0	19.8	19.9	20.4	20.6	20.5	20.3	20.2	20.1	20.2	20.1
2001	20.1	20.3	20.5	20.5	20.8	21.0	21.3	21.3	20.9	20.9	21.0	21.0	20.8
2002	21.0	21.1	21.3	21.3	21.5	21.5	21.6	21.4	21.0	21.2	21.1	21.3	21.3
2003	21.3	21.4	21.5	21.7	21.8	22.1	22.2	22.0	21.6	21.8	21.8	21.6	21.7

Employment by Industry: New Jersey—*Continued*

(Numbers in thousands. Not seasonally adjusted.)

Industry	January	February	March	April	May	June	July	August	September	October	November	December	Annual Average
MIDDLESEX-SOMERSET-HUNTERDON—*Continued*													
Government													
1990	73.7	74.4	75.9	77.0	78.0	77.6	73.9	74.3	73.1	77.3	77.3	77.3	75.8
1991	75.2	77.5	77.9	77.7	77.4	75.9	73.6	72.6	73.2	76.6	77.7	77.3	76.0
1992	74.4	77.0	77.9	77.6	77.0	76.0	75.0	73.9	73.4	76.8	77.4	77.6	76.1
1993	74.8	77.3	77.6	78.3	77.8	76.9	73.7	73.0	74.0	78.0	79.2	78.6	76.6
1994	75.3	77.7	78.6	78.5	77.3	76.8	74.1	73.2	74.1	78.1	78.8	78.7	76.7
1995	74.9	77.7	78.6	78.2	77.8	76.2	73.9	72.4	75.2	77.7	78.0	78.1	76.5
1996	74.6	77.9	78.1	78.0	76.5	76.2	73.8	71.6	74.9	77.7	78.3	78.0	76.3
1997	75.7	78.0	77.9	78.4	77.7	76.6	73.4	71.1	74.3	78.6	79.4	79.4	76.7
1998	76.8	79.5	79.7	79.6	79.1	77.6	73.6	71.5	75.5	79.8	80.5	80.4	77.8
1999	77.4	80.3	81.4	81.5	80.8	78.7	76.0	74.7	77.5	82.1	83.2	83.1	79.7
2000	80.0	82.4	83.3	84.1	84.1	81.6	78.1	76.8	79.0	84.0	85.3	85.1	81.9
2001	81.9	84.7	85.4	85.9	85.9	84.0	78.8	77.4	80.9	86.5	87.8	87.5	83.8
2002	84.0	86.8	87.9	86.8	85.6	84.6	80.1	78.7	80.7	85.5	86.9	86.4	84.5
2003	82.8	85.8	86.8	86.8	86.4	84.2	79.7	78.9	81.8	86.6	87.9	87.3	84.6
Federal government													
1990	7.0	7.1	7.2	7.7	8.3	8.4	8.1	7.5	7.4	7.4	7.4	7.5	7.5
1991	7.5	7.5	7.5	7.6	7.6	7.6	7.7	7.7	7.7	7.5	7.5	7.6	7.5
1992	7.6	7.6	7.6	7.7	7.7	7.7	7.7	7.8	7.8	7.7	7.6	7.7	7.6
1993	7.5	7.5	7.5	7.5	7.5	7.5	7.5	7.5	7.5	7.4	7.4	7.5	7.4
1994	7.4	7.4	7.3	7.3	7.3	7.3	7.3	7.3	7.2	7.1	7.1	7.1	7.2
1995	7.0	6.9	6.9	6.9	6.6	6.6	6.6	6.6	6.6	6.5	6.5	6.7	6.7
1996	6.6	6.6	6.6	6.6	6.5	6.5	6.6	6.6	6.5	6.5	6.4	6.6	6.5
1997	6.5	6.5	6.5	6.6	6.5	6.5	6.5	6.5	6.5	6.3	6.4	6.5	6.4
1998	6.5	6.5	6.5	6.5	6.5	6.5	6.5	6.5	6.5	6.5	6.5	6.7	6.5
1999	6.8	6.8	7.0	6.8	6.8	6.9	6.9	7.0	7.1	7.2	7.1	7.2	6.9
2000	7.2	7.1	7.2	7.6	8.4	8.2	7.8	7.5	7.3	7.3	7.3	7.3	7.5
2001	7.3	7.3	7.3	7.2	7.1	7.1	7.1	7.1	7.0	7.0	6.9	6.9	7.1
2002	6.6	6.6	6.7	5.9	5.8	5.9	5.9	5.8	5.8	4.7	4.7	4.7	5.8
2003	4.7	4.7	4.6	4.7	4.6	4.6	4.6	4.6	4.6	4.6	4.6	4.6	4.6
State government													
1990	23.4	23.7	24.8	25.1	25.3	24.3	23.6	25.4	24.5	26.1	25.8	25.8	24.8
1991	24.0	26.0	26.4	26.3	25.9	24.4	24.3	24.2	24.5	26.0	26.2	26.0	25.3
1992	23.5	25.6	26.3	26.1	26.0	24.4	24.6	24.4	24.6	26.2	26.4	26.1	25.3
1993	23.7	26.0	26.2	26.5	26.1	24.6	24.5	24.7	25.6	27.3	27.3	26.8	25.7
1994	24.1	26.6	26.9	26.8	25.6	24.8	24.9	24.8	25.1	27.3	27.4	27.1	25.9
1995	24.9	27.5	27.7	27.7	27.5	25.5	25.8	25.2	26.9	27.8	27.7	27.5	26.8
1996	25.0	27.8	27.5	27.7	26.3	25.3	25.1	24.6	26.3	27.7	27.8	27.1	26.5
1997	25.4	27.4	27.1	27.5	26.5	24.9	24.8	24.3	26.3	27.6	27.8	27.2	26.4
1998	25.6	27.8	27.7	27.8	27.1	24.8	24.7	24.1	26.3	27.8	27.8	27.5	26.5
1999	25.1	27.6	27.6	27.8	27.0	24.9	24.9	24.8	26.2	27.9	28.3	28.1	26.6
2000	25.5	27.7	27.7	28.1	27.4	25.0	25.1	25.2	26.2	28.4	28.7	28.5	26.9
2001	26.0	28.2	28.3	28.9	28.3	26.1	26.0	25.8	26.7	29.2	29.6	29.2	27.6
2002	26.7	28.7	29.2	29.1	27.4	26.2	25.7	25.8	26.7	28.7	29.2	28.6	27.7
2003	25.9	28.4	28.9	28.9	28.7	26.1	26.1	26.0	27.4	29.2	29.4	28.9	27.8
Local government													
1990	43.3	43.6	43.9	44.2	44.4	44.9	42.2	41.4	41.2	43.8	44.1	44.0	43.4
1991	43.7	44.0	44.0	43.8	43.9	43.9	41.6	40.7	41.0	43.1	44.0	43.7	43.1
1992	43.3	43.8	44.0	43.8	43.3	43.9	42.7	41.7	41.0	42.9	43.4	43.8	43.1
1993	43.6	43.8	43.9	44.3	44.2	44.8	41.7	40.8	40.9	43.3	44.5	44.3	43.3
1994	43.8	43.7	44.4	44.4	44.4	44.7	41.9	41.1	41.8	43.7	44.3	44.5	43.5
1995	43.0	43.3	44.0	43.6	43.7	44.1	41.5	40.6	41.7	43.4	43.8	43.9	43.0
1996	43.0	43.5	44.0	43.7	43.7	44.4	42.1	40.4	42.1	43.5	44.1	44.3	43.2
1997	43.8	44.1	44.3	44.3	44.7	45.2	42.1	40.3	41.5	44.7	45.2	45.7	43.8
1998	44.7	45.2	45.5	45.3	45.5	46.3	42.4	40.9	42.7	45.5	46.2	46.2	44.7
1999	45.5	45.9	46.8	46.9	47.0	46.9	44.2	42.9	44.2	47.0	47.8	47.8	46.0
2000	47.3	47.6	48.4	48.4	48.3	48.4	45.2	44.1	45.5	48.3	49.3	49.3	47.5
2001	48.6	49.2	49.8	49.8	50.5	50.8	45.7	44.5	47.2	50.3	51.3	51.4	49.0
2002	50.7	51.5	52.0	51.8	52.4	52.5	48.5	47.1	48.2	52.1	53.0	53.1	51.1
2003	52.2	52.7	53.3	53.2	53.1	53.5	49.0	48.3	49.8	52.8	53.9	53.8	52.1
MONMOUTH-OCEAN													
Total nonfarm													
1990	323.5	323.3	327.7	329.0	335.0	346.7	344.2	343.1	332.6	326.3	322.5	321.3	331.2
1991	311.6	311.0	315.5	319.5	325.8	337.2	334.2	332.1	323.6	318.2	318.6	317.2	322.0
1992	306.6	306.9	310.0	314.7	321.1	333.1	334.4	333.9	326.3	322.9	322.6	321.6	321.1
1993	316.8	317.9	321.0	325.5	333.2	345.3	344.8	344.3	337.2	334.4	333.9	333.6	332.3
1994	322.1	321.5	328.2	335.9	343.3	356.2	357.0	356.9	347.7	341.7	342.4	342.4	341.2
1995	331.3	330.5	337.1	342.1	349.1	361.8	361.5	361.2	352.7	348.6	348.0	348.1	347.6
1996	333.7	337.8	344.6	347.1	358.0	370.0	369.2	368.5	357.8	353.6	354.0	354.4	354.0
1997	343.2	344.6	350.1	356.3	365.1	378.1	378.7	375.5	366.9	363.9	362.3	363.5	362.3
1998	352.8	354.3	358.5	364.5	371.5	379.4	381.0	378.1	369.5	368.6	367.9	367.8	367.8
1999	359.7	361.6	366.5	374.1	379.3	391.2	393.3	391.6	381.5	379.2	380.6	382.5	378.4
2000	371.1	370.6	378.3	387.6	394.1	406.5	407.0	404.8	395.1	391.3	394.4	396.8	391.4
2001	380.7	380.6	385.7	391.4	399.0	411.8	412.1	411.3	401.5	397.0	398.5	399.7	397.4
2002	388.5	388.4	393.4	400.0	406.8	418.2	414.8	415.0	406.9	405.2	406.6	408.0	404.3
2003	393.3	390.9	394.4	402.8	410.8	421.1	420.1	419.6	411.7	410.7	411.7	412.7	408.3

Employment by Industry: New Jersey—*Continued*

(Numbers in thousands. Not seasonally adjusted.)

Industry	January	February	March	April	May	June	July	August	September	October	November	December	Annual Average
MONMOUTH-OCEAN —*Continued*													
Total private													
1990	258.9	258.1	261.8	262.5	267.3	277.5	278.8	278.5	267.7	261.5	257.3	255.8	265.4
1991	246.9	245.9	249.4	253.6	259.7	268.3	269.0	268.1	260.2	254.3	253.5	252.4	256.7
1992	242.3	242.1	244.9	250.0	256.6	266.4	270.1	269.9	263.9	260.3	259.1	258.0	256.9
1993	254.1	255.1	257.0	262.2	269.0	279.3	281.8	281.9	275.4	271.8	270.7	270.8	269.0
1994	259.5	259.1	264.6	272.8	279.2	289.5	292.9	293.3	285.0	279.5	279.3	278.7	277.7
1995	268.5	267.8	273.5	279.2	285.7	295.5	298.0	298.3	290.9	286.5	285.1	285.0	284.5
1996	271.7	275.4	281.1	283.8	293.4	303.4	305.0	305.1	296.3	291.0	290.9	291.3	290.7
1997	280.8	281.9	286.4	292.6	300.4	311.0	314.5	312.1	304.3	300.0	298.0	299.1	298.4
1998	289.1	290.2	293.6	299.7	306.0	313.0	317.3	315.2	306.6	305.0	304.2	304.1	303.6
1999	296.8	298.1	302.6	310.3	314.7	324.8	328.5	327.5	318.6	315.5	316.1	318.1	314.3
2000	307.2	306.6	312.7	322.5	327.2	338.5	341.2	340.2	331.5	326.4	328.6	330.8	326.1
2001	315.3	314.7	319.0	325.1	331.9	342.8	346.3	345.4	335.7	330.3	331.0	332.3	330.8
2002	321.8	321.3	325.4	332.7	338.4	348.1	349.5	350.1	340.5	337.3	338.2	339.6	336.9
2003	325.5	322.8	325.9	334.2	341.8	350.0	353.6	354.0	344.4	342.0	341.9	343.2	339.9
Goods-producing													
1990	42.3	42.2	42.9	41.9	41.6	42.3	41.7	41.5	40.4	40.4	39.5	38.7	41.2
1991	35.6	35.3	35.4	36.0	36.7	37.3	36.6	36.8	36.4	35.5	34.8	34.2	35.8
1992	31.9	31.6	32.1	32.9	33.9	34.8	34.8	35.3	34.9	35.3	35.3	34.9	33.9
1993	33.7	33.7	34.0	34.4	35.2	35.8	35.9	36.2	35.8	36.5	36.2	36.0	35.2
1994	32.9	32.6	33.7	35.7	36.5	37.4	37.6	37.8	37.5	36.4	36.1	35.9	35.8
1995	33.8	33.4	34.3	35.7	36.2	36.6	36.9	36.8	36.4	36.5	36.0	35.4	35.6
1996	32.5	33.6	34.6	35.7	36.9	37.9	36.8	36.9	36.2	36.3	36.0	35.7	35.7
1997	33.0	33.7	34.8	36.0	36.8	37.8	37.7	37.7	37.5	37.3	36.6	36.2	36.2
1998	34.0	34.1	35.2	36.0	36.5	36.8	37.4	37.3	36.9	36.6	36.2	36.0	36.0
1999	35.0	35.5	36.4	37.6	38.0	38.9	38.5	38.8	38.6	39.0	39.2	39.2	37.8
2000	38.1	38.1	39.2	40.5	40.5	40.8	40.7	40.8	40.6	40.4	40.4	39.9	40.0
2001	37.8	38.3	39.0	40.2	41.2	42.1	42.2	42.6	42.0	41.8	41.4	40.4	40.7
2002	39.3	39.1	39.8	41.0	41.4	41.8	41.9	42.2	41.8	41.5	41.4	41.0	41.0
2003	38.3	37.7	38.1	39.9	40.8	41.3	41.2	41.6	41.0	41.0	40.8	40.3	40.2
Construction and mining													
1990	16.1	15.8	16.3	16.0	16.0	16.5	16.2	15.8	15.1	15.6	14.9	14.3	15.7
1991	12.1	11.9	11.9	12.8	13.3	13.7	13.4	13.6	13.6	13.0	12.8	12.3	12.8
1992	10.7	10.6	11.1	11.7	12.4	13.0	13.1	13.3	13.3	13.6	13.4	13.2	12.4
1993	12.3	12.2	12.4	13.0	13.8	14.3	14.4	14.6	14.3	14.9	14.8	14.6	13.8
1994	12.5	12.2	13.0	14.8	15.6	16.3	16.6	16.7	16.8	16.8	16.7	16.4	15.3
1995	14.8	14.1	14.9	16.1	16.5	16.9	17.3	17.2	17.0	17.0	16.5	16.0	16.1
1996	13.8	14.3	15.1	16.2	17.1	17.8	17.8	17.9	17.7	17.8	17.5	17.1	16.6
1997	14.9	14.9	15.8	16.9	17.4	18.1	18.5	18.3	18.3	18.2	17.7	17.4	17.2
1998	16.0	16.1	16.8	17.6	17.9	18.3	18.8	18.8	18.7	18.9	18.7	18.6	17.9
1999	17.4	17.8	18.5	19.7	20.1	20.8	20.8	21.0	20.7	21.0	21.0	20.9	19.9
2000	20.1	19.9	20.9	22.1	22.2	22.6	22.7	22.8	22.5	22.2	22.2	21.5	21.8
2001	20.3	20.7	21.3	22.4	23.4	24.1	24.4	24.7	24.4	24.6	24.4	24.1	23.2
2002	22.0	21.9	22.5	23.6	24.0	24.3	24.8	25.0	24.7	24.5	24.3	24.0	23.8
2003	21.6	20.9	21.4	23.0	23.8	24.3	24.2	24.6	24.2	24.0	23.8	23.5	23.3
Manufacturing													
1990	26.2	26.4	26.6	25.9	25.6	25.8	25.5	25.7	25.3	24.8	24.6	24.4	25.5
1991	23.5	23.4	23.5	23.2	23.4	23.6	23.2	23.2	22.8	22.5	22.0	21.9	23.0
1992	21.2	21.0	21.0	21.2	21.5	21.8	21.7	22.0	21.6	21.7	21.9	21.7	21.5
1993	21.4	21.5	21.6	21.4	21.4	21.5	21.5	21.6	21.5	21.6	21.4	21.4	21.4
1994	20.4	20.4	20.7	20.9	20.9	21.1	21.0	21.1	20.7	19.6	19.4	19.5	20.4
1995	19.0	19.3	19.4	19.6	19.7	19.7	19.6	19.6	19.4	19.5	19.5	19.4	19.4
1996	18.7	19.3	19.5	19.5	19.8	20.1	19.0	19.0	18.5	18.5	18.5	18.6	19.0
1997	18.1	18.8	19.0	19.1	19.4	19.7	19.2	19.4	19.2	19.1	18.9	18.8	19.0
1998	18.0	18.0	18.4	18.4	18.6	18.5	18.6	18.5	18.2	17.7	17.5	17.4	18.1
1999	17.6	17.7	17.9	17.9	17.9	18.1	17.7	17.8	17.9	18.0	18.2	18.3	17.9
2000	18.0	18.2	18.3	18.4	18.3	18.2	18.0	18.0	18.1	18.2	18.2	18.4	18.1
2001	17.5	17.6	17.7	17.8	17.8	18.0	17.8	17.9	17.6	17.2	17.0	16.3	17.5
2002	17.3	17.2	17.3	17.4	17.4	17.5	17.1	17.2	17.1	17.0	17.1	17.0	17.2
2003	16.7	16.8	16.7	16.9	17.0	17.0	17.0	17.0	16.8	17.0	17.0	16.8	16.9
Service-providing													
1990	281.2	281.1	284.8	287.1	293.4	304.4	302.5	301.6	292.2	285.9	283.0	282.6	289.9
1991	276.0	275.7	280.1	283.5	289.1	299.9	297.6	295.3	287.2	282.7	283.8	283.0	286.1
1992	274.7	275.3	277.9	281.8	287.2	298.3	299.6	298.6	291.4	287.6	287.3	286.7	287.2
1993	283.1	284.2	287.0	291.1	298.0	309.5	308.9	308.1	301.4	297.9	297.7	297.6	297.0
1994	289.2	288.9	294.5	300.2	306.8	318.8	319.4	319.1	310.2	305.3	306.3	306.5	305.4
1995	297.5	297.1	302.8	306.4	312.9	325.2	324.6	324.4	316.3	312.1	312.0	312.7	312.0
1996	301.2	304.2	310.0	311.4	321.1	332.1	332.4	331.6	321.6	317.3	318.0	318.7	318.3
1997	310.2	310.9	315.3	320.3	328.3	340.3	341.0	337.8	329.4	326.6	325.7	327.3	326.0
1998	318.8	320.2	323.3	328.5	335.0	342.6	343.6	340.8	332.6	332.0	331.7	331.8	331.7
1999	324.7	326.1	330.1	336.5	341.3	352.3	354.8	352.8	342.9	340.2	341.4	343.3	340.5
2000	333.0	332.5	339.1	347.1	353.6	365.7	366.3	364.0	354.5	350.9	354.0	356.9	351.4
2001	342.9	342.3	346.7	351.2	357.8	369.7	369.9	368.7	359.5	355.2	357.1	359.3	356.6
2002	349.2	349.3	353.6	359.0	365.4	376.4	372.9	372.8	365.1	363.7	365.2	367.0	363.3
2003	355.0	353.2	356.3	362.9	370.0	379.8	378.9	378.0	370.7	369.7	370.9	372.4	368.2

Employment by Industry: New Jersey—*Continued*

(Numbers in thousands. Not seasonally adjusted.)

Industry	January	February	March	April	May	June	July	August	September	October	November	December	Annual Average
MONMCUTH-OCEAN *—Continued*													
Trade, transportation, and utilities													
1990	74.7	73.3	73.7	73.0	74.0	75.7	75.6	75.6	73.7	73.5	74.0	74.9	74.3
1991	71.6	69.8	69.8	69.8	71.0	72.6	72.2	72.2	71.7	70.8	72.2	73.4	71.4
1992	70.0	68.4	68.1	68.7	69.9	71.8	71.7	71.4	71.3	72.0	73.2	74.4	70.9
1993	72.7	71.3	71.2	71.0	72.6	75.2	74.5	74.4	73.8	75.2	76.5	78.0	73.8
1994	74.6	72.9	73.6	74.9	76.5	78.1	77.7	78.0	77.7	77.6	79.3	80.6	76.7
1995	76.7	74.8	75.5	75.8	77.2	78.9	79.2	79.0	78.7	79.3	80.5	82.4	78.1
1996	78.6	77.3	77.8	77.1	79.1	80.8	80.8	81.2	81.1	81.3	82.5	84.8	80.2
1997	79.7	78.1	78.2	79.4	80.6	82.4	82.4	81.3	81.5	81.1	82.9	85.3	81.0
1998	79.7	78.2	78.1	78.8	80.0	80.9	80.8	80.5	80.4	82.1	83.7	85.6	80.7
1999	82.3	81.3	81.9	83.1	83.7	85.7	85.3	85.2	84.4	84.9	86.9	89.1	84.4
2000	84.4	83.1	84.6	85.8	86.5	88.9	87.5	87.6	86.7	86.8	89.6	91.8	86.9
2001	86.7	84.5	85.2	85.9	87.0	88.7	87.8	87.1	86.3	86.5	88.7	90.4	87.0
2002	86.6	84.8	85.7	86.5	87.7	89.7	88.9	88.9	88.3	88.7	90.9	93.1	88.3
2003	88.0	86.5	86.8	87.9	89.7	91.0	89.8	90.2	89.5	90.7	91.8	94.0	89.7
Wholesale trade													
1990	9.1	9.2	9.4	9.1	9.0	9.2	9.0	8.9	8.8	8.7	8.6	8.5	8.9
1991	8.4	8.4	8.3	8.1	8.2	8.2	8.2	8.2	8.2	8.1	8.2	8.1	8.2
1992	7.7	7.7	7.8	8.2	8.4	8.7	8.7	8.8	8.6	8.7	8.7	8.7	8.3
1993	8.8	8.8	8.9	9.0	9.1	9.4	9.3	9.4	9.2	9.4	9.4	9.4	9.1
1994	9.2	9.3	9.3	9.9	9.9	10.1	10.0	10.1	10.0	10.0	10.1	10.1	9.8
1995	9.7	9.7	9.9	10.1	10.2	10.2	10.4	10.5	10.3	10.3	10.2	10.2	10.1
1996	9.9	10.1	10.2	10.1	10.2	10.5	10.8	10.7	10.6	10.3	10.3	10.4	10.3
1997	10.3	10.4	10.4	10.7	10.8	11.0	11.0	11.0	11.0	10.9	10.9	11.0	10.7
1998	11.0	11.2	11.1	11.1	11.1	11.1	11.2	11.1	11.1	11.2	11.1	11.3	11.1
1999	11.2	11.2	11.3	11.3	11.3	11.4	11.1	11.1	11.0	11.2	11.2	11.3	11.2
2000	11.3	11.3	11.5	11.6	11.7	11.8	11.7	11.8	12.1	12.1	12.0	12.0	11.7
2001	12.2	12.2	12.3	12.6	12.6	12.6	12.6	12.7	12.6	12.4	12.5	12.5	12.4
2002	12.7	12.7	12.8	13.0	13.0	13.0	13.0	13.0	12.8	13.1	13.0	13.0	12.9
2003	12.6	12.5	12.5	12.8	12.9	13.0	12.8	12.8	12.7	12.9	12.9	12.9	12.8
Retail trade													
1990	56.4	54.8	54.9	54.6	55.5	56.9	57.3	57.4	55.3	55.0	55.7	56.7	55.8
1991	53.9	52.0	52.0	51.9	52.8	54.5	54.6	54.7	53.6	52.9	54.1	55.4	53.5
1992	52.7	51.1	50.7	51.0	51.9	53.2	53.8	53.6	52.8	53.4	54.4	55.5	52.8
1993	54.0	52.6	52.4	52.2	53.4	55.4	55.5	55.5	54.5	55.2	56.5	57.9	54.5
1994	55.3	53.6	54.1	54.7	56.0	57.4	57.9	58.1	57.2	56.6	58.3	59.7	56.5
1995	56.4	54.5	54.8	55.1	56.2	57.7	58.5	58.4	57.5	57.6	59.1	60.9	57.2
1996	57.9	56.2	56.5	56.0	57.8	59.8	59.5	60.0	59.2	59.4	60.9	63.0	58.8
1997	58.8	57.2	57.3	57.9	58.8	60.3	61.1	60.8	59.6	59.4	60.9	63.0	59.5
1998	57.6	56.0	56.0	56.8	57.8	58.7	59.2	59.2	58.1	59.3	61.1	62.9	58.5
1999	60.0	59.0	59.6	60.4	61.0	62.8	63.6	63.5	62.0	61.8	64.0	66.2	61.9
2000	61.9	60.6	61.8	62.5	63.1	65.1	64.9	65.2	63.6	63.6	66.5	68.6	63.9
2001	63.7	61.5	62.0	62.4	63.2	64.8	64.6	64.0	62.5	62.9	65.1	66.7	63.6
2002	63.2	61.5	62.3	62.7	63.8	65.7	65.8	65.9	64.5	64.2	66.5	68.5	64.6
2003	63.9	62.6	62.9	63.9	65.3	66.7	66.6	66.9	65.3	66.3	68.4	69.8	65.7
Transportation and utilities													
1990	9.2	9.3	9.4	9.3	9.5	9.6	9.3	9.3	9.6	9.8	9.7	9.7	9.4
1991	9.3	9.4	9.5	9.8	10.0	9.9	9.4	9.3	9.9	9.8	9.9	9.9	9.6
1992	9.6	9.6	9.6	9.5	9.6	9.9	9.2	9.0	9.9	9.9	10.1	10.2	9.6
1993	9.9	9.9	9.9	9.8	10.1	10.4	9.7	9.5	10.1	10.6	10.6	10.7	10.1
1994	10.1	10.0	10.2	10.3	10.6	10.6	9.8	9.8	10.5	11.0	10.9	10.8	10.3
1995	10.6	10.6	10.8	10.6	10.8	11.0	10.3	10.1	10.9	11.4	11.2	11.3	10.8
1996	10.8	11.0	11.1	11.0	11.1	10.5	10.5	10.5	11.3	11.6	11.3	11.4	11.0
1997	10.6	10.5	10.5	10.8	11.0	11.1	10.3	9.5	10.9	10.8	11.1	11.3	10.7
1998	11.1	11.0	11.0	10.9	11.1	11.1	10.4	10.2	11.2	11.6	11.5	11.4	11.0
1999	11.1	11.1	11.0	11.4	11.4	11.5	10.6	10.6	11.4	11.9	11.7	11.6	11.2
2000	11.2	11.2	11.3	11.7	11.7	12.0	10.9	10.6	11.0	11.1	11.1	11.2	11.2
2001	10.8	10.8	10.9	10.9	11.2	11.3	10.6	10.4	11.2	11.2	11.1	11.2	10.9
2002	10.7	10.6	10.6	10.8	10.9	11.0	10.1	10.0	11.0	11.4	11.4	11.6	10.8
2003	11.5	11.4	11.4	11.2	11.5	11.3	10.4	10.5	11.5	11.5	10.5	11.3	11.2
Information													
1990	11.0	10.2	10.3	9.9	9.9	10.0	10.4	10.3	10.1	10.0	9.9	10.0	10.1
1991	10.0	10.0	10.0	9.7	9.7	9.8	9.7	9.7	9.6	9.4	9.3	9.2	9.6
1992	9.4	9.4	9.7	9.6	9.6	9.6	9.8	9.9	9.8	9.7	9.9	10.0	9.7
1993	10.2	10.2	10.3	10.3	10.3	10.5	10.7	10.7	10.6	10.7	10.7	10.7	10.4
1994	10.7	10.7	10.8	10.8	10.9	11.1	11.2	11.2	11.1	10.9	11.0	11.1	10.9
1995	11.2	11.0	11.1	10.5	10.6	10.7	10.9	10.9	10.8	10.9	10.8	10.9	10.8
1996	10.8	10.8	10.8	10.9	11.0	11.1	10.8	11.2	11.0	11.0	11.0	11.1	10.9
1997	11.1	11.0	10.9	11.1	11.2	11.5	11.7	11.7	11.4	11.5	11.4	11.4	11.3
1998	11.8	11.9	11.8	11.9	11.9	12.0	11.9	11.8	11.5	11.8	12.0	12.1	11.8
1999	12.3	12.1	12.1	12.1	12.2	12.4	12.9	12.9	12.7	12.5	13.0	12.8	12.5
2000	13.4	13.4	13.5	13.2	13.2	13.4	13.8	13.1	13.3	13.6	13.7	13.6	13.4
2001	13.0	13.0	13.1	12.8	12.8	13.0	12.9	12.6	12.8	12.6	12.8	12.9	12.8
2002	11.6	11.5	11.6	10.8	11.0	11.1	10.8	10.6	10.4	9.9	10.2	10.2	10.8
2003	9.9	9.7	9.8	10.1	10.2	10.3	10.2	10.1	9.9	10.0	10.3	10.3	10.1

Employment by Industry: New Jersey—*Continued*

(Numbers in thousands. Not seasonally adjusted.)

Industry	January	February	March	April	May	June	July	August	September	October	November	December	Annual Average
MONMOUTH-OCEAN *—Continued*													
Financial activities													
1990	18.3	18.3	18.3	18.2	18.3	18.6	18.6	18.5	17.9	17.6	17.4	17.4	18.1
1991	17.5	17.4	17.4	17.5	17.7	18.0	18.1	18.0	17.9	17.4	17.4	17.4	17.6
1992	17.2	17.2	17.2	17.2	17.4	17.8	18.0	17.8	17.6	17.6	17.6	17.7	17.5
1993	17.6	17.6	17.6	17.5	17.6	18.0	18.0	18.0	17.7	17.7	17.8	17.9	17.7
1994	17.9	18.1	18.2	18.2	18.3	18.6	18.4	18.4	18.0	17.9	17.6	17.7	18.1
1995	17.7	17.6	17.8	17.7	17.9	18.1	18.2	18.1	17.6	17.8	17.9	18.0	17.8
1996	17.7	17.9	18.0	18.0	18.3	18.7	18.7	18.6	18.5	18.2	18.3	18.5	18.2
1997	18.3	18.3	18.3	18.4	18.7	19.2	19.5	19.4	19.0	18.8	18.7	18.8	18.7
1998	19.0	18.9	18.8	19.1	19.2	19.3	19.8	19.6	19.2	18.9	18.8	19.0	19.1
1999	19.6	19.7	19.7	19.6	19.7	20.2	20.2	20.3	19.9	20.0	20.0	20.1	19.9
2000	19.8	19.7	19.7	20.0	20.3	20.7	21.0	20.8	20.5	20.4	20.6	20.6	20.3
2001	19.9	19.9	20.0	20.3	20.6	20.9	21.0	20.9	20.6	20.5	20.6	20.9	20.5
2002	21.4	21.6	21.6	22.4	22.6	22.9	22.9	22.9	22.7	22.5	22.6	22.6	22.4
2003	23.0	23.0	23.2	23.2	23.4	23.7	24.6	24.5	24.3	24.2	24.3	24.2	23.8
Professional and business services													
1990	32.6	32.7	33.0	33.3	33.4	33.9	34.2	34.5	34.0	33.0	32.4	31.9	33.2
1991	31.9	31.9	32.4	33.1	33.4	33.3	33.2	33.1	32.5	32.9	32.7	32.3	32.7
1992	31.1	31.2	31.5	32.3	32.6	33.5	33.5	33.6	33.0	33.5	33.1	32.7	32.6
1993	33.1	33.8	34.1	35.3	35.6	36.0	36.3	36.3	36.2	36.9	36.2	35.8	35.4
1994	33.7	34.1	34.5	35.5	35.7	36.3	36.1	36.4	36.2	36.4	36.3	36.2	35.6
1995	35.5	35.7	36.8	38.0	38.4	38.6	37.4	38.0	37.7	38.0	37.8	37.4	37.4
1996	35.3	36.3	37.4	38.1	39.2	39.6	39.9	40.1	39.6	39.2	39.2	39.1	38.5
1997	38.5	38.6	39.1	39.9	40.5	41.6	41.6	41.8	41.4	41.7	41.4	41.8	40.6
1998	40.7	41.5	42.2	43.7	44.2	44.9	44.6	44.6	44.2	44.3	43.3	41.7	43.3
1999	39.9	40.6	41.5	42.8	42.7	43.6	43.2	43.2	42.6	42.9	42.6	42.3	42.3
2000	40.7	40.8	42.2	44.2	44.5	45.4	45.8	46.2	45.8	45.7	46.1	46.4	44.4
2001	45.0	45.1	46.0	46.6	46.9	47.9	47.9	48.1	47.5	46.5	46.2	45.8	46.6
2002	43.8	44.1	45.0	46.1	45.9	46.6	45.6	46.0	45.5	45.3	45.3	45.3	45.4
2003	43.0	42.3	43.0	43.7	44.0	44.5	44.6	44.5	44.1	43.7	43.7	43.4	43.7
Educational and health services													
1990	42.9	43.4	43.8	44.0	43.9	44.4	44.2	44.0	44.5	45.1	44.9	45.2	44.1
1991	44.7	45.0	45.6	45.7	45.5	45.7	45.6	45.5	46.3	47.1	47.3	47.4	45.9
1992	46.3	47.2	47.3	47.1	47.3	47.6	47.8	47.6	48.3	49.2	49.3	49.4	47.8
1993	48.6	49.2	49.5	50.0	50.2	50.0	50.5	50.2	50.8	51.5	51.6	51.1	50.2
1994	50.6	51.1	51.5	52.5	52.8	52.6	52.4	52.5	52.9	53.7	53.9	53.8	52.5
1995	53.1	53.5	54.0	54.2	54.2	53.9	54.9	54.8	55.2	56.1	55.7	56.2	54.6
1996	55.0	56.3	56.6	56.2	56.8	56.8	56.5	56.2	56.4	56.9	57.6	57.0	56.5
1997	57.4	58.2	58.6	58.2	58.3	58.5	59.1	58.8	59.2	60.2	59.4	59.5	58.7
1998	59.5	60.1	60.1	60.3	60.6	60.3	60.8	60.6	60.3	60.8	61.2	61.5	60.5
1999	62.4	63.2	63.6	63.5	63.5	63.6	63.7	63.1	63.5	64.2	65.0	65.1	63.7
2000	63.9	64.2	64.6	65.5	65.5	65.9	65.9	65.6	65.4	65.6	66.1	66.6	65.4
2001	64.4	64.8	65.2	65.6	66.2	66.7	66.7	66.7	66.4	67.6	68.2	68.4	66.4
2002	68.2	68.7	68.6	69.4	69.8	70.0	69.3	70.0	70.0	71.2	71.5	71.2	69.8
2003	70.5	70.9	71.3	71.4	71.9	71.9	71.8	71.8	72.1	72.8	73.3	73.4	71.9
Leisure and hospitality													
1990	25.5	26.4	28.0	30.7	34.5	40.6	41.9	41.8	35.4	30.5	27.9	26.5	32.4
1991	24.2	25.2	27.5	30.4	34.1	39.7	41.4	40.7	34.2	29.6	28.2	27.0	31.8
1992	24.9	25.5	27.3	30.4	33.9	39.1	41.9	41.5	36.7	30.9	28.6	26.9	32.3
1993	26.1	27.2	28.1	31.4	35.1	41.2	42.8	42.9	37.8	30.6	29.1	28.6	33.4
1994	26.4	26.9	29.4	32.2	35.4	42.0	45.6	45.0	38.3	33.2	31.7	30.0	34.6
1995	27.3	28.6	30.7	33.7	37.5	44.6	46.1	46.3	40.9	34.0	32.6	30.9	36.1
1996	28.0	29.3	31.8	33.8	37.9	43.9	46.5	46.0	39.3	33.8	32.1	30.8	36.1
1997	29.2	30.3	32.7	35.7	40.1	45.6	47.4	46.6	40.1	35.3	33.6	31.8	37.3
1998	30.4	31.4	33.3	35.5	39.2	44.3	47.1	45.9	39.8	35.9	34.4	33.6	37.5
1999	30.9	31.3	32.8	36.8	40.0	45.2	49.0	48.4	42.0	37.3	34.6	34.5	38.5
2000	32.3	32.6	34.0	37.9	41.2	47.7	50.3	49.9	43.6	38.7	36.7	36.5	40.1
2001	33.1	33.7	34.8	37.9	41.1	47.0	50.9	50.5	43.7	38.5	36.7	36.9	40.4
2002	34.4	34.9	36.4	39.7	43.1	48.8	52.4	51.7	44.6	40.5	39.1	39.0	42.1
2003	35.6	35.5	36.4	40.3	44.0	49.1	52.7	52.3	45.2	41.1	39.1	38.9	42.5
Other services													
1990	11.6	11.6	11.8	11.5	11.7	12.0	12.2	12.3	11.7	11.4	11.3	11.2	11.6
1991	11.4	11.3	11.3	11.4	11.6	11.9	12.2	12.1	11.6	11.6	11.6	11.5	11.6
1992	11.5	11.6	11.7	11.8	12.0	12.2	12.6	12.8	12.3	12.1	12.1	12.0	12.0
1993	12.1	12.1	12.2	12.3	12.4	12.6	13.1	13.2	12.7	12.7	12.6	12.7	12.5
1994	12.7	12.7	12.9	13.0	13.1	13.4	13.9	14.0	13.3	13.4	13.4	13.4	13.2
1995	13.2	13.2	13.3	13.6	13.7	14.1	14.4	14.4	13.6	13.9	13.8	13.8	13.7
1996	13.8	13.9	14.1	14.0	14.2	14.6	15.0	14.9	14.2	14.3	14.2	14.3	14.2
1997	13.6	13.7	13.8	13.9	14.2	14.4	15.1	14.8	14.2	14.1	14.0	14.3	14.1
1998	14.0	14.1	14.1	14.4	14.4	14.5	14.9	14.9	14.3	14.6	14.6	14.6	14.4
1999	14.4	14.4	14.6	14.8	14.9	15.2	15.7	15.6	14.9	14.7	14.8	15.0	14.9
2000	14.6	14.7	14.9	15.4	15.5	15.7	16.2	16.2	15.6	15.2	15.4	15.4	15.4
2001	15.4	15.4	15.7	15.8	16.1	16.5	16.9	16.9	16.4	16.3	16.4	16.6	16.1
2002	16.5	16.6	16.7	16.8	16.9	17.2	17.7	17.8	17.2	17.7	17.2	17.2	17.1
2003	17.2	17.2	17.3	17.7	17.8	18.2	18.7	19.0	18.3	18.5	18.6	18.7	18.1

Employment by Industry: New Jersey—*Continued*

(Numbers in thousands. Not seasonally adjusted.)

Industry	January	February	March	April	May	June	July	August	September	October	November	December	Annual Average
MONMOUTH-OCEAN *—Continued*													
Government													
1990	64.6	65.2	65.9	66.5	67.7	69.2	65.4	64.6	64.9	64.8	65.2	65.5	65.7
1991	64.7	65.1	66.1	65.9	66.1	68.9	65.2	64.0	63.4	63.9	65.1	64.8	65.2
1992	64.3	64.8	65.1	64.7	64.5	66.7	64.3	64.0	62.4	62.6	63.5	63.6	64.2
1993	62.7	62.8	64.0	63.3	64.2	66.0	63.0	62.4	61.8	62.6	63.2	62.8	63.2
1994	62.6	62.4	63.6	63.1	64.1	66.7	64.1	63.6	62.7	62.2	63.1	63.7	63.4
1995	62.8	62.7	63.6	62.9	63.4	66.3	63.5	62.9	61.8	62.1	62.9	63.1	63.1
1996	62.0	62.4	63.5	63.3	64.6	66.6	64.2	63.4	61.5	62.6	63.1	63.1	63.3
1997	62.4	62.7	63.7	63.7	64.7	67.1	64.2	63.4	62.6	63.9	64.3	64.4	63.9
1998	63.7	64.1	64.9	64.8	65.5	66.4	63.7	62.9	62.9	63.6	63.7	63.7	64.1
1999	62.9	63.5	63.9	63.8	64.6	66.4	64.8	64.1	62.9	63.7	64.5	64.4	64.1
2000	63.9	64.0	65.6	65.1	66.9	68.0	65.8	64.6	63.6	64.9	65.8	66.0	65.3
2001	65.4	65.9	66.7	66.3	67.1	69.0	65.8	65.9	65.8	66.7	67.5	67.4	66.6
2002	66.7	67.1	68.0	67.3	68.4	70.1	65.3	64.9	66.4	67.9	68.4	68.4	67.4
2003	67.8	68.1	68.5	68.6	69.0	71.1	66.5	65.6	67.3	68.7	69.8	69.5	68.4
Federal government													
1990	16.1	16.0	16.1	16.7	17.9	17.0	17.2	16.2	16.1	15.5	15.4	15.4	16.3
1991	15.2	15.2	15.3	15.3	15.4	15.5	15.4	15.3	15.2	15.3	15.2	15.2	15.2
1992	14.5	14.3	14.4	14.3	14.2	14.2	14.2	14.1	13.6	13.5	13.4	13.2	13.9
1993	13.0	13.0	12.9	12.5	12.4	12.5	12.5	12.5	12.4	12.4	12.4	12.4	12.5
1994	12.3	12.3	12.3	12.3	12.4	12.6	12.6	12.4	12.4	12.3	12.2	12.3	12.3
1995	12.2	11.8	11.7	11.7	11.8	11.9	11.8	11.8	11.7	11.6	11.6	11.7	11.7
1996	11.6	11.6	11.5	11.6	11.8	11.6	11.6	11.5	11.5	11.7	11.7	11.8	11.6
1997	11.7	11.7	11.6	11.9	11.9	12.0	12.3	12.3	12.2	12.3	12.2	12.3	12.0
1998	12.3	12.2	12.2	12.2	12.0	12.1	12.0	12.0	12.0	11.9	11.8	11.9	12.0
1999	11.9	11.8	11.8	11.7	11.6	11.7	11.9	11.9	11.8	11.6	11.6	11.7	11.7
2000	11.6	11.5	12.0	12.0	13.6	12.4	12.4	11.9	11.6	11.5	11.5	11.5	11.9
2001	11.5	11.5	11.5	11.5	11.5	11.6	11.7	11.7	11.7	11.5	11.5	11.6	11.5
2002	11.5	11.3	11.4	11.3	11.3	11.6	11.5	11.5	11.4	11.4	11.2	11.4	11.4
2003	11.2	11.2	11.1	10.9	10.9	11.1	11.2	11.2	11.1	11.0	11.0	11.1	11.1
State government													
1990	4.9	5.0	5.0	5.3	5.4	6.5	6.6	6.5	5.9	4.8	4.9	5.0	5.4
1991	4.9	5.0	5.0	5.2	5.2	6.6	6.7	6.8	5.7	4.9	5.0	5.0	5.5
1992	5.0	5.1	5.1	5.0	5.3	6.0	6.2	6.2	5.3	4.7	4.8	4.9	5.3
1993	4.8	4.9	5.0	5.1	5.2	6.3	6.3	6.3	5.3	4.8	4.9	4.9	5.3
1994	4.9	5.0	5.0	5.1	5.0	6.3	6.3	6.2	5.3	4.8	4.9	4.9	5.3
1995	5.8	5.9	6.0	6.0	6.0	7.3	7.2	7.1	6.0	5.5	5.5	5.5	6.1
1996	5.5	5.5	5.5	5.6	5.7	6.9	6.8	6.7	5.8	5.3	5.3	5.3	5.8
1997	5.0	5.0	5.1	5.1	5.3	6.4	6.4	6.3	5.5	5.1	4.9	5.0	5.4
1998	5.0	5.0	5.0	5.0	5.2	5.6	5.8	5.7	5.0	4.9	4.5	4.4	5.0
1999	4.4	4.4	4.4	4.5	4.6	5.1	5.3	5.3	4.7	4.6	4.5	4.4	4.6
2000	4.3	4.3	4.4	4.4	4.5	4.9	5.1	5.0	4.5	4.4	4.4	4.5	4.5
2001	4.4	4.5	4.5	4.5	4.6	5.0	5.1	5.1	4.6	4.4	4.4	4.3	4.6
2002	4.2	4.2	4.2	4.1	4.7	4.6	4.5	4.7	4.4	4.0	4.1	4.0	4.3
2003	3.9	3.9	3.9	3.9	4.4	4.5	4.5	4.7	4.4	4.1	4.0	4.0	4.2
Local government													
1990	43.6	44.2	44.8	44.5	44.4	45.7	41.6	41.9	42.9	44.5	44.9	45.1	44.0
1991	44.6	44.9	45.8	45.5	45.7	47.0	43.4	42.3	43.0	44.3	45.5	45.3	44.7
1992	44.8	45.4	45.6	45.4	45.0	46.5	43.9	43.7	43.5	44.4	45.3	45.5	44.9
1993	44.9	44.9	46.1	45.7	46.6	47.2	44.2	43.6	44.1	45.4	45.9	45.5	45.3
1994	45.4	45.1	46.3	45.7	46.7	47.8	45.2	45.0	45.0	45.1	46.0	46.5	45.8
1995	44.8	45.0	45.9	45.2	45.6	47.1	44.5	44.0	44.1	45.0	45.8	45.9	45.2
1996	44.9	45.3	46.5	46.1	47.1	48.1	45.8	45.2	44.2	45.6	46.1	46.0	45.9
1997	45.7	46.0	47.0	46.7	47.5	48.7	45.5	44.8	44.9	46.5	47.2	47.1	46.4
1998	46.4	46.9	47.7	47.6	48.3	48.7	45.9	45.2	45.9	46.8	47.4	47.4	47.0
1999	46.6	47.3	47.7	47.6	48.4	49.6	47.6	46.9	46.4	47.5	48.4	48.3	47.6
2000	48.0	48.2	49.2	48.7	48.8	50.7	48.3	47.7	47.5	49.0	49.9	50.0	48.8
2001	49.5	49.9	50.7	50.3	51.0	52.4	49.0	49.1	49.5	50.8	51.6	51.5	50.4
2002	51.0	51.6	52.4	51.9	52.4	53.9	49.3	48.7	50.6	52.5	53.1	53.0	51.7
2003	52.7	53.0	53.5	53.8	53.7	55.5	50.8	49.7	51.8	53.6	54.8	54.4	53.1
NEWARK													
Total nonfarm													
1990	970.6	970.2	975.5	969.0	969.4	976.8	965.9	961.6	957.3	953.5	953.5	952.3	964.6
1991	922.3	922.0	926.0	925.1	925.9	931.3	923.9	919.2	918.9	921.4	924.8	926.8	923.9
1992	898.6	899.7	902.7	902.7	906.4	913.1	911.1	907.6	904.3	911.9	914.1	915.5	907.3
1993	891.3	894.2	896.9	901.9	907.4	913.7	906.9	903.8	907.0	913.8	917.8	921.1	906.3
1994	889.3	890.0	900.0	908.0	915.0	925.1	920.0	919.5	920.8	927.7	931.9	935.0	915.1
1995	911.6	913.5	921.8	924.4	930.1	937.1	927.0	927.5	928.0	933.8	937.4	939.5	927.6
1996	909.3	916.3	922.2	923.6	931.0	941.2	932.4	931.4	931.6	938.3	941.5	944.9	930.3
1997	925.6	929.8	936.7	939.4	946.7	957.4	952.5	948.7	952.0	957.7	964.0	967.4	948.1
1998	942.7	945.7	952.2	962.2	971.2	979.4	970.2	969.9	971.6	978.2	982.9	987.0	967.7
1999	971.7	977.3	983.4	990.5	994.7	1004.0	996.7	992.2	995.9	1006.7	1011.9	1019.1	995.3
2000	998.1	1000.1	1008.4	1017.3	1024.2	1034.7	1020.4	1012.3	1021.8	1025.6	1032.5	1040.2	1019.6
2001	1002.7	1004.7	1008.0	1016.3	1021.9	1030.5	1011.3	1004.9	1010.3	1016.7	1019.7	1022.4	1014.1
2002	997.7	1002.3	1006.6	1010.5	1014.1	1018.5	1005.6	1001.4	1004.6	1011.1	1017.5	1019.2	1009.1
2003	998.8	995.4	999.7	1005.4	1012.5	1018.7	1012.0	1006.2	1010.3	1021.4	1024.4	1026.2	1010.9

Employment by Industry: New Jersey—*Continued*

(Numbers in thousands. Not seasonally adjusted.)

Industry	January	February	March	April	May	June	July	August	September	October	November	December	Annual Average
NEWARK—*Continued*													
Total private													
1990	828.7	825.8	830.1	822.5	823.9	832.0	822.6	820.1	817.5	810.3	808.4	807.5	820.7
1991	781.4	778.0	781.3	780.8	782.7	789.6	782.8	780.4	781.9	779.0	780.9	782.5	781.7
1992	757.3	755.6	758.4	759.2	764.3	770.9	767.1	765.3	766.9	768.8	769.2	770.6	764.4
1993	748.1	749.5	751.5	756.8	764.1	770.9	766.3	765.2	768.7	770.8	772.9	776.1	763.4
1994	747.6	746.7	755.8	763.2	771.8	780.8	778.2	779.3	781.1	782.6	785.1	787.9	771.6
1995	767.0	767.3	775.0	777.2	783.2	790.8	783.3	785.7	788.5	790.0	791.7	794.2	782.8
1996	766.9	771.7	777.0	778.8	787.2	796.4	789.3	790.3	792.4	795.3	797.3	800.7	786.9
1997	783.4	785.5	792.4	795.3	803.0	812.9	811.3	809.7	813.2	815.6	820.5	823.5	805.5
1998	801.8	803.6	809.0	819.0	828.2	835.5	829.8	831.2	831.6	835.0	838.4	841.7	825.4
1999	829.1	833.6	838.6	845.4	850.5	859.3	857.4	856.6	855.8	861.8	865.9	873.0	852.2
2000	854.6	854.8	862.5	870.6	877.0	888.4	881.1	877.3	881.2	880.4	885.7	893.0	875.5
2001	858.2	857.7	861.0	868.6	875.1	883.9	870.3	866.8	865.7	868.2	869.4	871.6	868.0
2002	848.8	850.4	854.1	858.4	862.4	867.1	860.2	858.1	857.6	859.2	863.7	865.3	858.8
2003	845.9	840.2	844.3	849.8	857.3	863.3	860.3	858.3	859.4	863.9	866.1	867.9	856.4
Goods-producing													
1990	196.4	195.6	195.5	194.5	194.9	197.5	194.8	194.8	193.9	190.6	188.5	185.8	193.5
1991	177.0	176.8	177.6	180.8	180.9	182.2	179.6	180.2	180.9	178.5	177.8	175.7	179.0
1992	168.3	167.3	167.3	167.2	167.9	169.6	167.6	167.9	168.6	168.5	168.0	166.7	167.9
1993	159.6	159.2	160.2	161.2	163.2	164.6	163.2	164.2	166.5	166.2	165.7	164.5	163.1
1994	155.9	155.8	158.5	161.0	163.9	166.6	165.1	166.6	167.4	166.3	166.3	165.0	163.2
1995	159.1	158.6	160.1	162.2	163.4	164.2	160.6	161.9	162.2	163.2	162.1	160.3	161.4
1996	151.2	153.4	155.2	155.5	157.5	159.6	157.1	158.5	159.4	158.9	158.7	157.8	156.9
1997	151.7	152.2	153.8	156.7	158.4	160.8	160.3	161.0	161.4	161.3	160.2	159.3	158.0
1998	152.5	153.1	155.0	158.8	160.3	161.3	157.7	161.0	162.2	161.8	160.7	159.9	158.6
1999	155.4	156.2	156.6	159.7	160.8	162.3	161.4	162.1	162.9	162.8	162.4	161.7	160.3
2000	156.6	156.1	158.1	160.0	161.6	163.3	160.7	162.4	163.0	162.6	162.9	162.2	160.7
2001	152.8	153.1	153.9	155.4	156.3	157.7	154.0	154.7	154.4	154.1	152.8	151.8	154.2
2002	143.4	144.1	144.4	144.8	145.1	145.0	143.7	144.3	144.4	143.0	142.2	141.2	143.8
2003	135.9	135.2	136.0	138.4	140.3	141.2	141.2	141.1	141.0	140.1	140.0	138.1	139.0
Construction and mining													
1990	36.0	35.6	36.7	37.7	38.5	39.5	39.5	39.1	38.6	37.0	36.2	34.7	37.4
1991	30.1	29.0	29.6	32.3	33.1	33.8	33.4	33.8	33.7	33.4	32.3	31.2	32.1
1992	27.4	26.8	27.1	27.9	28.6	29.4	30.7	30.5	30.5	31.0	30.6	29.9	29.2
1993	26.9	26.1	26.3	27.9	29.4	30.1	31.2	31.4	31.5	32.0	31.6	31.3	29.6
1994	25.8	25.1	26.3	29.5	31.2	32.5	33.0	33.4	33.1	33.3	33.0	32.1	30.6
1995	28.4	27.1	28.5	30.9	32.2	33.1	33.2	33.5	33.1	32.8	32.2	30.9	31.3
1996	25.7	26.3	27.5	29.7	31.1	31.9	32.3	32.4	32.3	32.8	32.5	31.8	30.5
1997	28.7	28.6	29.4	31.5	32.8	33.9	34.5	34.2	34.1	34.4	33.4	32.8	32.3
1998	29.3	29.3	30.6	32.8	33.9	34.8	35.3	35.5	35.7	35.9	35.4	35.1	33.6
1999	32.1	32.5	33.0	36.0	36.8	37.8	37.8	37.7	37.5	37.2	36.8	36.4	35.9
2000	34.0	33.3	34.7	37.2	38.0	38.7	38.5	38.8	39.2	38.2	38.3	37.5	37.2
2001	35.0	35.0	36.0	39.0	40.2	41.0	40.5	41.0	41.1	42.3	42.0	41.4	39.5
2002	38.0	37.8	38.3	39.3	40.1	40.8	40.9	41.4	41.5	41.3	40.9	39.8	40.0
2003	36.4	35.5	36.0	38.3	39.9	40.5	41.4	41.2	41.1	40.3	39.8	38.6	39.1
Manufacturing													
1990	160.4	160.0	158.8	156.8	156.4	158.0	155.3	155.7	155.3	153.6	152.3	151.1	156.1
1991	146.9	147.8	148.0	148.5	147.8	148.4	146.2	146.4	147.2	145.1	145.5	144.5	146.8
1992	140.9	140.5	140.2	139.3	139.3	140.2	136.9	137.4	138.1	137.5	137.4	136.8	138.7
1993	132.7	133.1	133.9	133.3	133.8	134.5	132.0	132.8	135.0	134.2	134.1	133.2	133.5
1994	130.1	130.7	132.2	131.5	132.7	134.1	132.1	133.2	134.3	133.0	133.3	132.9	132.5
1995	130.7	131.5	131.6	131.3	131.2	131.1	127.4	128.4	129.1	130.4	129.9	129.4	130.1
1996	125.5	127.1	127.7	125.8	126.4	127.7	124.8	126.1	127.1	126.1	126.2	126.0	126.3
1997	123.0	123.6	124.4	125.2	125.6	126.9	125.8	126.8	127.3	126.9	126.8	126.5	125.7
1998	123.2	123.8	124.4	126.0	126.4	126.5	122.4	125.5	126.5	125.9	125.3	124.8	125.0
1999	123.3	123.7	123.6	123.7	124.0	124.5	123.6	124.4	125.4	125.6	125.6	125.3	124.3
2000	122.6	122.8	123.4	122.8	123.6	124.6	122.2	123.6	123.8	124.4	124.6	124.7	123.5
2001	117.8	118.1	117.9	116.4	116.1	116.7	113.5	113.7	113.3	111.8	110.8	110.4	114.7
2002	105.4	106.3	106.1	105.5	105.0	104.2	102.8	102.9	102.9	101.7	101.3	101.4	103.8
2003	99.5	99.7	100.0	100.1	100.4	100.7	99.8	99.9	99.9	99.8	100.2	99.5	100.0
Service-providing													
1990	774.2	774.6	780.0	774.5	774.5	779.3	771.1	766.8	763.4	762.9	765.0	766.5	771.0
1991	745.3	745.2	748.4	744.3	745.0	749.1	744.3	739.0	738.0	742.9	747.0	751.1	744.9
1992	730.3	732.4	735.4	735.5	738.5	743.5	743.5	739.7	735.7	743.4	746.1	748.8	739.4
1993	731.7	735.0	736.7	740.7	744.2	749.1	743.7	739.6	740.5	747.6	752.1	756.6	743.1
1994	733.4	734.2	741.5	747.0	751.1	758.5	754.9	752.9	753.4	761.4	765.6	770.0	751.9
1995	752.5	754.9	761.7	762.2	766.7	772.9	766.4	765.6	765.8	770.6	775.3	779.2	766.1
1996	758.1	762.9	767.0	768.1	773.5	781.6	775.3	772.9	772.2	779.4	782.8	787.1	773.4
1997	773.9	777.6	782.9	782.7	788.3	796.6	792.2	787.7	790.6	796.4	803.8	808.1	790.0
1998	790.2	792.6	797.2	803.4	810.9	818.1	812.5	808.9	809.4	816.4	822.2	827.1	809.0
1999	816.3	821.1	826.8	830.8	833.9	841.7	835.3	830.1	833.0	843.9	849.5	857.4	834.9
2000	841.5	844.0	850.3	857.3	862.6	871.4	859.7	849.9	858.8	863.0	869.6	878.0	858.8
2001	849.9	851.6	854.1	860.9	865.6	872.8	857.3	850.2	855.9	862.6	866.9	870.6	859.8
2002	854.3	858.2	862.2	865.7	869.0	873.5	861.9	857.1	860.2	868.1	875.3	878.0	865.3
2003	862.9	860.2	863.7	867.0	872.2	877.5	870.8	865.1	869.3	881.3	884.4	888.1	871.9

Employment by Industry: New Jersey—*Continued*

(Numbers in thousands. Not seasonally adjusted.)

Industry	January	February	March	April	May	June	July	August	September	October	November	December	Annual Average
NEWARK—*Continued*													
Trade, transportation, and utilities													
1990	204.9	202.3	204.0	200.2	200.7	202.2	198.6	198.1	198.6	198.0	198.8	200.6	200.5
1991	194.0	190.7	190.5	190.4	190.3	191.7	190.3	189.8	191.2	191.2	193.6	195.9	191.6
1992	188.8	185.7	185.4	184.5	185.6	186.5	185.4	184.8	186.0	187.7	189.2	191.9	186.7
1993	184.4	183.0	182.8	183.6	185.4	187.4	185.6	185.2	187.0	188.3	191.4	194.8	186.5
1994	185.5	183.9	185.7	186.6	188.6	190.2	188.9	189.4	190.5	193.4	196.3	199.1	189.8
1995	193.1	191.8	192.3	192.8	194.3	195.9	193.3	193.7	196.2	196.8	199.0	202.4	195.1
1996	193.1	193.5	193.7	191.7	193.8	196.2	191.7	192.5	194.8	196.9	199.5	203.4	195.0
1997	196.4	195.5	196.7	194.4	196.0	198.8	194.8	192.6	196.7	199.8	203.0	206.5	197.6
1998	199.3	198.6	199.4	202.4	204.6	205.9	202.5	202.8	204.7	207.7	211.5	214.3	204.4
1999	208.4	208.2	208.8	209.3	210.7	212.8	212.2	212.6	213.5	215.7	219.7	224.8	213.0
2000	217.6	215.9	217.2	217.4	218.3	220.4	218.1	217.6	220.2	222.6	226.7	231.1	220.2
2001	220.5	218.4	218.6	219.3	219.7	220.9	217.2	216.1	216.9	217.6	219.8	222.5	218.9
2002	218.0	216.0	216.9	216.5	217.5	219.0	215.9	214.9	217.2	218.9	222.5	225.4	218.2
2003	218.4	215.6	215.8	214.8	215.8	217.1	213.4	212.1	214.1	217.0	218.3	221.2	216.1
Wholesale trade													
1990	52.3	52.1	52.4	51.1	51.0	51.2	50.8	50.7	50.5	50.3	50.1	49.7	51.0
1991	48.8	48.5	48.3	48.6	48.4	48.3	48.1	47.9	48.1	47.8	47.7	47.5	48.1
1992	47.3	47.2	47.5	46.5	46.7	46.9	46.5	46.5	46.4	46.4	46.2	46.6	46.7
1993	45.6	45.7	46.0	47.1	47.1	47.3	47.0	47.0	47.2	47.4	47.7	47.9	46.9
1994	46.6	46.5	47.0	47.6	47.7	47.7	48.0	48.1	48.0	49.0	49.3	49.4	47.9
1995	49.6	49.7	50.1	50.6	50.9	51.5	51.1	51.3	51.5	51.7	51.8	51.9	50.9
1996	50.0	50.7	50.8	49.9	50.0	50.6	50.5	50.7	50.6	51.0	51.3	51.7	50.6
1997	50.1	50.1	50.7	50.0	49.9	50.4	50.7	50.8	50.7	50.7	51.3	51.6	50.5
1998	51.7	51.8	52.4	52.5	52.6	52.9	52.9	53.0	52.8	53.3	53.7	53.5	52.7
1999	52.8	53.1	53.2	53.2	53.3	53.8	53.6	53.7	53.5	54.0	54.2	54.7	53.5
2000	53.6	53.6	53.9	54.7	54.9	55.3	55.3	55.1	55.5	55.6	55.5	56.2	54.9
2001	56.0	56.2	56.1	56.6	56.5	56.6	56.5	56.2	56.2	55.9	56.2	56.5	56.2
2002	57.4	57.3	57.4	56.8	56.9	56.9	56.5	56.5	56.6	56.3	56.5	56.4	56.8
2003	55.9	55.8	55.9	55.7	55.8	55.9	55.4	54.7	55.2	54.9	54.4	54.8	55.4
Retail trade													
1990	100.3	98.0	98.3	96.4	96.7	97.3	95.8	95.1	95.1	94.9	96.0	98.1	96.8
1991	93.4	90.9	90.6	90.7	90.8	91.9	90.9	90.5	90.8	91.0	93.4	95.7	91.7
1992	90.6	87.6	87.2	87.5	87.7	87.8	87.2	86.7	86.9	88.2	89.8	91.9	88.2
1993	87.3	86.1	85.7	85.1	85.9	87.4	86.0	85.8	86.1	86.7	89.4	92.1	86.9
1994	86.2	84.3	84.8	85.2	86.1	87.0	86.2	86.3	86.9	87.1	89.5	91.6	86.7
1995	87.4	86.0	85.9	86.2	87.0	88.2	86.3	86.8	87.9	87.9	90.1	92.9	87.7
1996	88.3	87.5	87.2	87.0	88.1	89.1	87.2	87.4	88.0	89.2	91.9	94.9	88.8
1997	90.6	89.0	89.5	87.6	88.8	89.9	87.9	88.1	88.8	90.5	93.2	96.1	90.0
1998	91.6	89.6	89.8	91.4	92.6	93.6	92.7	92.5	92.8	94.4	97.5	99.9	93.2
1999	96.0	94.7	95.3	95.0	95.7	96.7	96.4	97.0	96.8	98.0	100.7	104.7	97.2
2000	100.7	98.7	99.4	99.5	100.3	101.2	99.7	99.8	100.4	101.7	105.2	108.4	101.2
2001	101.1	98.6	99.2	99.4	99.6	100.8	98.4	98.3	98.2	99.2	102.4	105.2	100.0
2002	101.9	99.9	100.6	100.4	101.0	102.0	100.6	100.0	100.7	101.7	104.9	108.2	101.8
2003	102.8	100.7	100.6	100.3	101.3	102.3	101.0	101.0	100.8	103.3	104.7	107.6	102.2
Transportation and utilities													
1990	52.3	52.2	53.3	52.7	53.0	53.7	52.0	52.3	53.0	52.8	52.7	52.8	52.7
1991	51.8	51.3	51.6	51.1	51.1	51.5	51.3	51.4	52.3	52.4	52.5	52.7	51.7
1992	50.9	50.9	50.7	50.5	51.2	51.8	51.7	51.6	52.7	53.1	53.2	53.4	51.8
1993	51.5	51.2	51.1	51.4	52.4	52.7	52.6	52.4	53.7	54.2	54.3	54.8	52.6
1994	52.7	53.1	53.9	53.8	54.8	55.5	54.7	55.0	55.6	57.3	57.5	58.1	55.1
1995	56.1	56.1	56.3	56.0	56.4	56.2	55.9	55.6	56.8	57.2	57.1	57.6	56.4
1996	54.8	55.3	55.7	54.8	55.7	56.5	54.0	54.4	56.2	56.7	56.3	56.8	55.6
1997	55.7	56.4	56.5	56.8	57.3	58.5	56.2	53.7	57.2	58.6	58.5	58.8	57.0
1998	56.0	57.2	57.2	58.5	59.4	59.4	56.9	57.3	59.1	60.0	60.3	60.9	58.5
1999	59.6	60.4	60.3	61.1	61.7	62.3	62.2	61.9	63.2	63.7	64.8	65.4	62.2
2000	63.3	63.6	63.9	63.2	63.1	63.9	63.1	62.7	64.3	65.3	66.0	66.5	64.0
2001	63.4	63.6	63.3	63.3	63.6	63.5	62.3	61.6	62.5	62.5	61.2	60.8	62.6
2002	58.7	58.8	58.9	59.3	59.6	60.1	58.8	58.4	59.9	60.9	61.1	60.8	59.6
2003	59.7	59.1	59.3	58.8	58.7	58.9	57.0	56.4	58.1	58.8	59.2	58.8	58.6
Information													
1990	33.6	33.2	33.2	33.2	32.7	33.0	32.9	32.6	32.5	31.4	31.3	31.6	32.6
1991	30.5	30.3	30.4	30.7	30.4	30.4	30.3	30.2	30.1	29.9	30.2	30.0	30.2
1992	29.6	29.7	29.7	28.8	29.0	29.3	29.2	29.2	29.1	28.7	28.9	28.9	29.1
1993	28.1	28.1	28.3	28.2	28.3	28.6	28.4	28.5	28.3	28.2	28.4	28.4	28.3
1994	28.3	28.2	28.3	28.5	28.5	28.8	28.8	28.7	28.2	28.6	28.9	29.1	28.5
1995	29.9	29.0	29.4	29.5	29.5	29.6	29.8	30.0	30.0	29.1	29.1	29.2	29.5
1996	28.9	26.2	26.3	26.8	27.2	27.5	27.3	27.2	27.0	26.4	26.8	27.0	27.0
1997	27.4	27.5	27.5	28.8	28.9	29.1	29.3	29.5	29.3	29.8	29.9	30.0	28.9
1998	29.3	29.3	29.0	28.6	29.1	29.3	28.6	28.7	28.3	28.5	28.7	28.7	28.8
1999	29.1	29.4	29.6	30.2	30.4	30.8	30.4	30.4	30.2	30.0	30.5	30.5	30.1
2000	31.3	31.2	31.5	30.9	31.2	31.6	31.6	30.0	31.6	31.4	31.7	32.4	31.3
2001	31.2	31.3	31.5	31.2	31.3	31.4	30.9	30.2	31.1	30.5	30.3	30.1	30.9
2002	28.0	27.7	27.7	27.6	27.7	27.9	27.1	26.9	26.8	26.0	26.6	26.5	27.2
2003	25.8	25.7	25.8	25.7	25.8	25.9	26.4	26.9	26.7	26.5	26.5	26.5	26.2

Employment by Industry: New Jersey—*Continued*

(Numbers in thousands. Not seasonally adjusted.)

Industry	January	February	March	April	May	June	July	August	September	October	November	December	Annual Average
NEWARK—*Continued*													
Financial activities													
1990	80.1	79.8	80.0	78.3	77.7	78.5	78.7	78.0	76.3	74.9	74.3	74.0	77.5
1991	73.8	73.5	73.2	72.5	72.7	73.5	73.5	72.7	70.9	71.7	71.4	71.7	72.5
1992	71.2	71.2	70.8	70.1	70.2	71.2	71.4	70.9	69.6	69.7	69.2	69.1	70.3
1993	70.0	70.0	69.8	69.7	69.7	70.6	71.0	70.5	69.4	68.7	69.3	69.8	69.8
1994	69.3	69.3	69.6	69.9	69.9	70.9	71.9	71.7	71.5	68.8	68.5	68.9	70.0
1995	69.0	69.2	69.5	69.1	69.0	70.0	70.9	71.1	69.8	69.8	70.3	70.8	69.8
1996	71.2	71.5	71.3	71.6	71.8	72.8	72.9	72.7	71.9	71.6	71.6	72.1	71.9
1997	73.6	72.9	73.0	71.4	71.9	72.7	73.8	74.0	73.4	73.5	74.1	74.2	73.2
1998	75.1	75.0	74.6	74.4	74.9	75.4	76.6	76.0	75.3	75.0	75.2	75.2	75.2
1999	76.6	76.4	76.6	76.0	75.6	76.3	76.1	75.9	75.4	74.9	75.0	75.4	75.8
2000	75.7	75.9	76.0	75.6	75.7	76.6	76.8	76.4	76.1	76.6	76.8	76.8	76.2
2001	76.5	76.2	76.4	77.5	78.3	79.5	79.6	79.7	79.2	80.1	79.9	80.3	78.6
2002	76.6	76.4	76.2	76.9	76.9	77.6	78.4	78.4	78.1	77.7	77.7	77.9	77.4
2003	77.3	77.0	76.9	77.1	77.3	77.9	78.8	79.1	78.5	78.7	78.9	79.2	78.1
Professional and business services													
1990	129.9	130.1	130.4	128.7	128.3	129.7	130.0	130.3	129.0	128.7	128.3	127.9	129.2
1991	124.4	123.3	124.5	123.0	122.8	124.5	123.6	123.4	123.0	122.0	121.5	121.8	123.1
1992	118.3	118.6	120.7	122.3	122.1	123.9	125.6	125.5	125.2	124.1	123.9	123.5	122.8
1993	120.8	121.7	122.6	124.5	125.8	126.9	127.6	127.7	126.8	126.5	126.5	126.6	125.3
1994	121.8	121.7	122.9	124.1	124.6	126.6	126.7	126.6	126.4	126.7	126.7	126.4	125.1
1995	122.5	123.8	125.8	125.2	126.0	127.7	127.1	128.1	128.4	128.7	128.8	129.0	126.7
1996	126.4	127.4	127.9	129.7	130.9	132.0	133.7	134.1	133.4	134.3	135.1	134.7	131.6
1997	133.1	133.6	134.9	136.3	137.0	139.6	140.9	142.1	141.0	140.6	141.9	142.0	138.5
1998	140.0	140.2	141.4	143.4	144.0	145.9	146.1	145.9	144.2	144.8	144.9	145.1	143.8
1999	145.1	146.2	147.6	148.5	148.4	150.1	150.5	151.2	149.2	151.2	151.3	152.5	149.3
2000	150.9	151.4	153.6	158.2	158.7	161.6	161.8	161.5	160.1	156.1	156.2	157.2	157.2
2001	157.8	157.5	158.2	160.4	161.0	163.6	160.5	160.2	158.3	159.0	158.7	157.9	159.4
2002	154.9	156.3	157.7	159.6	159.5	159.8	159.7	160.7	158.7	159.9	160.5	159.6	158.9
2003	156.0	154.5	155.6	156.8	158.3	159.8	160.3	161.3	161.3	162.3	163.4	163.7	159.4
Educational and health services													
1990	100.8	101.7	102.8	102.0	101.9	101.7	99.7	98.9	101.3	102.3	103.2	103.8	101.6
1991	101.4	102.8	103.4	102.0	102.3	101.7	100.0	99.2	101.7	102.6	103.2	103.9	102.0
1992	101.7	103.1	103.7	104.1	105.1	104.6	102.6	102.1	104.7	106.2	106.4	107.1	104.2
1993	105.7	106.9	107.4	107.0	107.6	107.1	104.7	103.8	107.2	107.9	108.4	109.0	106.8
1994	108.2	109.0	110.2	110.1	110.8	110.1	109.2	108.2	110.8	112.6	113.1	113.8	110.5
1995	110.8	112.2	113.3	112.9	113.4	113.6	112.6	111.9	114.7	115.5	116.3	116.6	113.6
1996	113.6	115.5	116.8	116.5	116.6	116.2	115.1	114.7	117.2	118.2	119.0	118.8	116.5
1997	118.1	119.6	120.5	120.1	120.6	119.7	119.3	118.4	121.1	121.3	122.6	122.6	120.3
1998	120.9	121.8	122.6	123.2	123.6	123.3	122.0	121.2	123.7	125.3	125.5	125.8	123.2
1999	124.7	126.5	127.7	128.6	128.9	128.4	127.4	126.1	128.7	131.2	131.4	132.1	128.4
2000	129.3	130.6	131.4	132.7	133.1	133.1	131.2	130.2	132.3	134.0	135.0	136.0	132.4
2001	128.2	129.5	130.0	131.1	132.0	132.4	129.8	128.5	130.3	131.4	132.2	133.1	130.7
2002	133.3	134.8	135.2	135.6	136.2	135.7	133.4	132.1	133.0	134.4	135.1	135.4	134.5
2003	135.1	134.9	136.0	136.5	137.1	136.5	135.5	134.0	135.4	137.0	137.6	137.5	136.1
Leisure and hospitality													
1990	48.7	48.9	49.8	51.3	53.1	54.5	53.0	52.9	51.8	50.5	50.2	50.1	51.2
1991	46.1	46.4	47.4	47.7	49.4	51.4	50.8	50.6	50.5	49.1	49.1	49.3	48.9
1992	45.9	46.6	47.4	48.8	50.6	51.6	50.7	50.5	50.1	50.0	49.5	49.4	49.2
1993	46.2	46.9	46.7	48.8	49.9	51.2	50.8	50.6	49.7	50.9	48.9	48.8	49.1
1994	45.2	45.3	46.9	49.4	51.6	53.2	52.3	52.4	51.8	51.3	50.5	50.7	50.0
1995	48.1	48.3	49.7	50.6	52.6	54.0	53.0	53.1	52.2	51.7	50.8	50.4	51.2
1996	47.7	48.9	50.1	51.0	53.1	55.4	54.7	54.2	52.7	53.1	50.6	50.7	51.8
1997	48.2	49.1	50.4	52.0	54.3	56.0	56.3	55.8	54.5	53.6	52.8	52.8	52.9
1998	49.8	50.4	51.7	52.4	55.5	57.5	58.9	58.3	56.7	55.4	55.0	55.5	54.7
1999	54.0	54.7	55.6	56.3	58.6	60.9	61.0	60.3	58.5	58.5	57.8	58.0	57.8
2000	55.7	56.0	56.7	57.7	59.9	62.6	61.5	60.6	59.8	58.9	58.2	58.8	58.8
2001	54.0	54.5	54.9	55.5	57.7	59.0	58.6	58.2	57.0	56.3	56.1	56.1	56.4
2002	54.4	54.7	55.4	56.9	58.7	60.7	60.5	59.8	59.0	58.5	57.9	58.1	57.9
2003	56.4	56.5	57.1	58.7	60.9	62.5	62.1	61.8	60.6	60.0	59.4	59.4	59.6
Other services													
1990	34.3	34.2	34.4	34.3	34.6	34.9	34.9	34.5	34.1	33.9	33.8	33.7	34.3
1991	34.2	34.2	34.3	33.7	33.9	34.2	34.7	34.3	33.6	34.0	34.1	34.2	34.1
1992	33.5	33.4	33.4	33.4	33.8	34.2	34.6	34.4	33.6	33.9	34.1	34.0	33.8
1993	33.3	33.7	33.7	33.8	34.2	34.5	35.0	34.7	33.8	34.1	34.3	34.2	34.1
1994	33.4	33.5	33.7	33.6	33.9	34.4	35.3	35.7	34.5	34.9	34.8	34.9	34.3
1995	34.5	34.4	34.9	34.9	35.0	35.8	36.0	35.9	35.0	35.2	35.3	35.5	35.2
1996	34.8	35.3	35.7	36.0	36.3	36.7	36.8	36.4	36.0	35.9	36.0	36.2	36.0
1997	34.9	35.1	35.6	35.6	35.9	36.2	36.6	36.3	35.8	35.7	36.0	36.1	35.8
1998	34.9	35.2	35.3	35.8	36.2	36.9	37.4	37.3	36.5	36.5	36.9	37.2	36.3
1999	35.8	36.0	36.1	36.8	37.1	37.7	38.4	38.0	37.4	37.5	37.8	38.0	37.2
2000	37.5	37.7	38.0	38.1	38.5	39.2	39.4	38.6	38.1	38.2	38.2	38.5	38.3
2001	37.2	37.2	37.5	38.2	38.8	39.4	39.7	39.2	38.5	39.2	39.6	39.8	38.7
2002	40.2	40.4	40.6	40.5	40.8	41.4	41.5	41.0	40.4	40.8	41.2	41.2	40.8
2003	41.0	40.8	41.1	41.8	41.8	42.4	42.6	42.0	41.8	42.3	42.0	42.3	41.8

Employment by Industry: New Jersey—*Continued*

(Numbers in thousands. Not seasonally adjusted.)

Industry	January	February	March	April	May	June	July	August	September	October	November	December	Annual Average
NEWARK—*Continued*													
Government													
1990	141.9	144.4	145.4	146.5	145.5	144.8	143.3	141.5	139.8	143.2	145.1	144.8	143.8
1991	140.9	144.0	144.7	144.3	143.2	141.7	141.1	138.8	137.0	142.4	143.9	144.3	142.1
1992	141.3	144.1	144.3	143.5	142.1	142.2	144.0	142.3	137.4	143.1	144.9	144.9	142.8
1993	143.2	144.7	145.4	145.1	143.3	142.8	140.6	138.6	138.3	143.0	144.9	145.0	142.9
1994	141.7	143.3	144.2	144.8	143.2	144.3	141.8	140.2	139.7	145.1	146.8	147.1	143.5
1995	144.6	146.2	146.8	147.2	146.9	146.3	143.7	141.8	139.5	143.8	145.7	145.3	144.8
1996	142.4	144.6	145.2	144.8	143.8	144.8	143.1	141.1	139.2	143.0	144.2	144.2	143.3
1997	142.2	144.3	144.3	144.1	143.7	144.5	141.2	139.0	138.8	142.1	143.5	143.9	142.6
1998	140.9	142.1	143.2	143.2	143.0	143.9	140.4	138.7	140.0	143.2	144.5	145.3	142.3
1999	142.6	143.7	144.8	145.1	144.2	144.7	139.3	135.6	140.1	144.9	146.0	146.1	143.0
2000	143.5	145.3	145.9	146.7	147.2	146.3	139.3	135.0	140.6	145.2	146.8	147.2	144.0
2001	144.5	147.0	147.0	147.7	146.8	146.6	141.0	138.1	144.6	148.5	150.3	150.8	146.0
2002	148.9	151.9	152.5	152.1	151.7	151.4	145.4	143.3	147.0	151.9	153.8	153.9	150.3
2003	152.9	155.2	155.4	155.6	155.2	155.4	151.7	147.9	150.9	157.5	158.3	158.3	154.5
Federal government													
1990	21.1	21.0	21.1	21.3	21.6	21.6	21.8	21.3	21.0	20.6	20.6	20.7	21.1
1991	20.4	20.3	20.3	20.3	20.3	20.4	20.3	20.2	20.1	20.3	20.2	20.5	20.3
1992	20.9	20.7	20.7	20.6	20.6	20.8	20.9	20.5	20.3	20.3	20.0	20.0	20.5
1993	19.9	19.9	20.0	19.8	19.8	19.8	19.7	19.6	19.7	19.6	19.6	19.8	19.7
1994	19.3	19.2	19.2	19.1	19.0	19.3	19.6	19.7	19.6	19.7	19.6	19.7	19.4
1995	19.4	19.3	19.3	19.3	19.4	19.4	19.4	19.3	19.2	19.1	19.1	19.2	19.2
1996	19.0	18.9	18.9	18.9	18.8	18.9	18.9	18.9	18.8	18.7	18.7	18.8	18.8
1997	18.6	18.6	18.5	18.2	18.1	18.1	18.0	17.8	17.8	17.7	17.5	17.7	18.0
1998	17.4	17.3	17.4	17.4	17.4	17.5	17.5	17.5	17.4	17.4	17.4	17.6	17.4
1999	17.5	17.4	17.7	17.6	17.5	17.5	17.5	17.6	17.6	17.6	17.5	17.8	17.5
2000	17.6	17.7	18.0	18.3	20.5	19.7	19.1	17.8	17.4	17.3	17.3	17.3	18.1
2001	17.3	17.3	17.2	17.2	17.2	17.3	17.4	17.3	17.3	17.1	17.1	17.1	17.2
2002	17.0	16.9	17.0	16.5	16.6	16.8	17.0	17.1	17.3	18.5	18.7	18.9	17.4
2003	19.0	18.9	18.9	19.1	18.9	18.9	19.0	19.0	18.9	18.8	18.7	18.6	18.9
State government													
1990	21.9	23.5	24.3	24.9	24.3	23.2	21.7	22.0	22.7	24.1	24.6	24.4	23.4
1991	22.7	24.4	25.3	25.3	24.5	22.1	21.9	21.4	22.8	24.4	24.6	25.1	23.7
1992	26.1	27.5	28.0	27.7	27.1	26.4	26.2	25.9	26.5	28.0	28.1	27.8	27.1
1993	27.7	28.0	28.3	28.2	27.4	26.5	26.5	26.2	26.7	28.0	28.3	28.0	27.4
1994	27.1	28.3	28.6	28.5	27.0	26.6	26.4	26.4	26.9	28.3	28.6	28.6	27.6
1995	30.1	31.0	31.2	31.3	31.2	29.3	29.8	29.4	29.4	30.2	30.5	30.1	30.2
1996	29.4	30.6	30.7	30.8	29.9	29.2	29.8	29.2	29.9	30.6	30.8	30.9	30.1
1997	30.0	31.0	31.2	31.5	30.5	30.2	30.1	30.0	30.1	30.8	30.9	30.9	30.6
1998	29.7	30.5	30.7	30.7	30.6	30.3	29.8	29.8	30.1	30.6	30.8	30.8	30.3
1999	29.6	30.4	30.5	30.6	29.9	29.2	28.8	28.3	29.4	30.1	30.3	29.9	29.7
2000	28.9	29.9	30.1	30.4	29.4	27.9	28.1	27.6	28.7	29.5	29.9	30.0	29.2
2001	28.7	29.6	29.8	30.0	29.0	28.2	28.2	28.1	28.5	29.7	30.2	30.5	29.2
2002	29.0	30.4	30.8	30.6	29.8	29.0	29.0	28.8	29.3	30.5	30.7	30.7	29.9
2003	29.8	30.9	31.0	31.0	30.7	29.7	29.7	29.4	30.5	31.7	31.5	31.3	30.6
Local government													
1990	91.5	92.5	92.5	92.9	92.2	92.4	92.6	91.0	88.4	90.9	92.2	92.0	91.7
1991	90.1	91.5	91.3	91.0	90.6	91.3	91.2	89.5	86.3	90.0	91.3	91.0	90.4
1992	94.3	95.9	95.6	95.2	94.4	95.0	96.9	95.9	90.6	94.8	96.8	97.1	95.2
1993	95.6	96.8	97.1	97.1	96.1	96.5	94.4	92.8	91.9	95.4	97.0	97.2	95.6
1994	95.3	95.8	96.4	97.2	97.2	98.4	95.8	94.1	93.2	97.1	98.6	98.8	96.4
1995	95.1	95.9	96.3	96.6	96.3	97.6	94.5	93.1	90.9	94.5	96.1	96.0	95.2
1996	94.0	95.1	95.6	95.1	95.1	96.7	94.4	93.0	90.5	93.7	94.7	94.5	94.3
1997	93.6	94.7	94.6	94.4	95.1	96.2	93.1	91.2	90.9	93.6	95.1	95.3	93.9
1998	93.8	94.3	95.1	95.1	95.0	96.1	93.1	91.4	92.5	95.2	96.3	96.9	94.5
1999	95.5	95.9	96.6	96.9	96.8	98.0	93.0	89.7	93.1	97.2	98.2	98.4	95.7
2000	97.0	97.7	97.8	98.0	97.3	98.7	92.1	89.6	94.5	98.4	99.6	99.9	96.7
2001	98.5	100.1	100.0	100.5	100.6	101.1	95.4	92.7	98.8	101.7	103.0	103.2	99.6
2002	102.9	104.6	104.7	105.0	105.3	105.6	99.4	97.4	100.4	102.9	104.4	104.3	103.1
2003	104.1	105.4	105.5	105.5	105.6	106.8	103.0	99.5	101.5	107.0	108.1	108.4	105.0
TRENTON													
Total nonfarm													
1990	197.3	199.0	199.9	199.4	199.6	200.6	195.7	194.5	196.2	198.2	197.7	197.9	198.0
1991	193.4	192.6	194.5	194.1	194.5	195.8	190.7	190.5	191.6	193.7	193.6	194.2	193.2
1992	190.9	191.0	192.4	193.3	194.6	195.4	192.3	191.5	191.4	195.0	195.9	195.5	193.2
1993	192.8	193.8	194.8	194.9	195.4	196.4	191.9	190.9	191.6	196.2	196.3	197.4	194.3
1994	192.7	193.1	195.0	196.5	197.8	198.2	194.8	193.3	194.7	198.4	197.4	199.0	195.9
1995	194.5	195.9	197.4	197.7	198.1	196.6	192.6	191.9	192.9	195.8	195.4	195.9	195.3
1996	189.9	192.2	194.4	194.5	195.8	195.7	192.3	191.1	191.8	195.4	196.8	197.9	193.9
1997	192.9	194.2	196.6	198.0	198.6	199.2	195.1	194.5	197.5	199.6	200.8	201.3	197.3
1998	195.5	196.4	198.3	198.8	200.0	200.3	197.2	196.3	198.4	201.8	202.4	203.5	199.0
1999	199.7	201.5	203.6	206.7	207.8	209.2	206.5	206.3	207.7	212.1	213.1	214.8	207.4
2000	210.0	211.6	214.0	215.9	216.7	219.2	214.5	215.1	217.7	220.6	222.7	224.4	216.8
2001	218.2	218.8	221.0	222.2	223.9	224.9	221.0	219.8	221.2	224.8	225.4	227.2	222.3
2002	221.8	222.0	223.7	225.0	226.3	226.6	219.4	219.0	220.5	222.5	224.8	225.3	223.1
2003	223.1	223.0	224.8	226.5	228.6	229.7	227.2	225.2	227.5	227.9	228.9	229.8	226.9

Employment by Industry: New Jersey—*Continued*

(Numbers in thousands. Not seasonally adjusted.)

Industry	January	February	March	April	May	June	July	August	September	October	November	December	Annual Average
TRENTON—*Continued*													
Total private													
1990	141.0	142.3	143.0	142.4	142.5	143.3	140.1	139.2	140.1	141.8	141.2	141.3	141.5
1991	137.3	136.8	138.0	138.1	138.3	139.4	136.6	136.9	138.0	139.4	139.0	139.5	138.1
1992	136.5	136.3	137.0	137.4	138.9	139.5	138.0	137.4	137.9	141.3	142.1	141.7	138.6
1993	139.2	139.5	139.6	140.1	140.9	141.9	140.3	139.1	139.2	143.4	142.9	144.0	140.8
1994	139.2	139.4	140.4	142.2	143.5	143.9	142.2	141.5	142.1	144.7	143.8	145.3	142.3
1995	141.4	142.4	143.4	143.3	144.4	143.1	141.1	141.0	141.1	143.4	143.0	143.4	142.5
1996	137.9	139.5	141.0	140.7	142.6	142.6	140.9	140.7	140.6	143.3	144.4	145.4	141.6
1997	141.2	142.0	143.8	144.9	145.5	146.4	144.5	144.3	145.6	147.1	147.7	148.2	145.1
1998	143.2	143.9	145.6	146.2	147.5	148.5	147.0	146.4	146.8	148.9	149.2	149.9	146.9
1999	146.6	148.0	149.8	152.6	154.0	155.5	153.9	154.0	154.2	157.7	158.2	159.6	153.6
2000	155.0	156.1	158.3	160.7	161.3	163.2	160.7	161.1	161.4	163.0	164.4	165.4	160.8
2001	159.4	159.2	161.2	162.6	164.1	165.1	163.0	161.6	161.2	163.7	164.1	165.2	162.5
2002	160.4	160.9	162.1	163.5	164.6	165.3	161.4	161.1	161.1	161.7	163.3	163.9	162.4
2003	161.0	160.5	161.9	163.5	165.4	166.6	165.3	163.8	165.3	165.1	166.0	166.9	164.3
Goods-producing													
1990	25.6	25.9	26.1	25.9	25.6	25.7	25.3	25.0	25.0	24.9	24.6	24.4	25.3
1991	23.5	23.1	23.3	23.2	23.3	23.4	22.9	22.9	22.9	23.2	22.4	22.3	23.0
1992	21.8	21.6	21.6	22.3	22.4	22.7	22.5	22.6	22.6	22.9	22.9	22.6	22.3
1993	22.2	22.1	21.6	21.6	21.7	21.9	22.1	21.7	21.7	22.2	22.2	22.4	21.9
1994	21.4	21.3	21.3	21.8	22.0	22.4	22.7	22.4	22.7	22.8	22.2	22.0	22.0
1995	20.8	21.4	21.3	21.6	21.8	21.5	20.7	20.9	20.5	21.2	20.9	20.6	21.1
1996	18.5	18.6	18.7	18.4	18.7	18.7	18.3	18.5	18.3	18.3	18.2	18.0	18.4
1997	17.3	17.2	17.3	17.7	17.5	17.8	17.7	18.4	18.3	17.9	17.9	17.7	17.7
1998	16.1	15.8	16.1	16.3	16.6	16.7	16.7	16.7	16.5	16.4	16.3	16.2	16.3
1999	15.1	15.0	15.1	15.5	15.9	16.0	15.9	16.0	15.8	16.1	16.0	16.0	15.7
2000	16.1	16.1	16.6	17.1	17.3	17.6	17.7	17.9	17.9	17.8	17.9	18.0	17.3
2001	17.5	17.2	17.5	17.7	17.9	17.7	17.4	17.2	17.1	17.0	16.9	16.7	17.3
2002	14.8	14.6	14.7	15.1	15.2	15.3	14.5	14.8	14.7	14.5	14.6	14.3	14.8
2003	14.0	14.0	14.0	14.3	14.3	14.5	14.6	14.3	14.4	14.3	14.3	14.2	14.3
Construction and mining													
1990	4.1	4.0	4.0	4.5	4.5	4.7	4.7	4.7	4.6	4.6	4.5	4.3	4.4
1991	3.7	3.6	3.7	4.0	4.2	4.2	4.2	4.1	4.1	4.0	3.9	3.7	3.9
1992	3.3	3.1	3.1	3.5	3.7	3.9	4.0	4.2	4.2	4.3	4.3	4.0	3.8
1993	3.7	3.6	3.5	3.6	3.7	3.9	4.1	4.0	3.9	4.1	4.0	4.0	3.8
1994	3.4	3.3	3.5	4.1	4.3	4.4	4.6	4.7	4.7	4.8	4.6	4.6	4.2
1995	4.0	3.9	3.9	4.1	4.3	4.4	4.4	4.4	4.2	4.3	4.3	4.2	4.2
1996	3.6	3.7	3.7	3.9	4.2	4.3	4.4	4.4	4.3	4.3	4.3	4.2	4.1
1997	3.8	3.7	3.8	4.1	4.3	4.6	4.7	4.7	4.6	4.5	4.6	4.4	4.3
1998	4.1	4.1	4.3	4.4	4.6	4.8	4.9	4.9	4.9	4.8	4.8	4.9	4.6
1999	4.4	4.4	4.5	4.8	5.0	5.1	5.1	5.1	5.0	5.1	5.0	5.0	4.8
2000	4.7	4.6	5.0	5.1	5.2	5.4	5.4	5.5	5.5	5.4	5.4	5.4	5.2
2001	5.1	5.0	5.1	5.3	5.5	5.5	5.6	5.6	5.5	5.5	5.6	5.4	5.4
2002	5.2	5.1	5.2	5.6	5.7	5.8	5.7	5.8	5.7	5.6	5.7	5.6	5.6
2003	5.3	5.3	5.3	5.5	5.6	5.7	5.9	5.8	5.7	5.6	5.6	5.4	5.6
Manufacturing													
1990	21.5	21.9	22.1	21.4	21.1	21.0	20.6	20.3	20.4	20.3	20.1	20.1	20.9
1991	19.8	19.5	19.6	19.2	19.1	19.2	18.7	18.8	18.8	19.2	18.5	18.6	19.0
1992	18.5	18.5	18.5	18.8	18.7	18.8	18.5	18.4	18.4	18.6	18.6	18.6	18.5
1993	18.5	18.5	18.1	18.0	18.0	18.0	18.0	17.7	17.8	18.1	18.2	18.4	18.1
1994	18.0	18.0	17.8	17.7	17.7	18.0	18.1	17.7	18.0	18.0	17.6	17.4	17.8
1995	16.8	17.5	17.4	17.5	17.5	17.1	16.3	16.5	16.3	16.9	16.6	16.4	16.9
1996	14.9	14.9	15.0	14.5	14.5	14.4	13.9	14.1	14.0	14.0	13.9	13.8	14.3
1997	13.5	13.5	13.5	13.6	13.2	13.2	13.0	13.7	13.7	13.4	13.3	13.3	13.4
1998	12.0	11.7	11.8	11.9	12.0	11.9	11.8	11.8	11.6	11.6	11.5	11.3	11.7
1999	10.7	10.6	10.6	10.7	10.9	10.9	10.8	10.9	10.8	11.0	11.0	11.0	10.8
2000	11.4	11.5	11.6	12.0	12.1	12.2	12.3	12.4	12.4	12.4	12.5	12.6	12.1
2001	12.4	12.2	12.4	12.4	12.4	12.2	11.8	11.6	11.6	11.5	11.3	11.3	11.9
2002	9.6	9.5	9.5	9.5	9.5	9.5	8.8	9.0	9.0	8.9	8.9	8.7	9.2
2003	8.7	8.7	8.7	8.8	8.7	8.8	8.7	8.5	8.7	8.7	8.7	8.8	8.7
Service-providing													
1990	171.7	173.1	173.8	173.5	174.0	174.9	170.4	169.5	171.2	173.3	173.1	173.5	172.6
1991	169.9	169.5	171.2	170.9	171.2	172.4	167.8	167.6	168.7	170.5	171.2	171.9	170.2
1992	169.1	169.4	170.8	171.0	172.2	172.7	169.8	168.9	168.8	172.1	173.0	172.9	170.8
1993	170.6	171.7	173.2	173.3	173.7	174.5	169.8	169.2	169.9	174.0	174.1	175.0	172.4
1994	171.3	171.8	173.7	174.7	175.8	175.8	172.1	170.9	172.0	175.6	175.2	177.0	173.8
1995	173.7	174.5	176.1	176.1	176.3	175.1	171.9	171.0	172.4	174.6	174.5	175.3	174.2
1996	171.4	173.6	175.7	176.1	177.1	177.0	174.0	172.6	173.5	177.1	178.6	179.9	175.5
1997	175.6	177.0	179.3	180.3	181.1	181.4	177.4	176.1	179.2	181.7	182.9	183.6	179.6
1998	179.4	180.6	182.2	182.5	183.4	183.6	180.5	179.6	181.9	185.4	186.1	187.3	182.7
1999	184.6	186.5	188.5	191.2	191.9	193.2	190.6	190.3	191.9	196.0	197.1	198.8	191.7
2000	193.9	195.5	197.4	198.8	199.4	201.6	196.8	197.2	199.8	202.8	204.8	206.4	199.5
2001	200.7	201.6	203.5	204.5	206.0	207.2	203.6	202.6	204.1	207.8	208.5	210.5	205.0
2002	207.0	207.4	209.0	209.9	211.1	211.3	204.9	204.2	205.8	208.0	210.2	211.0	208.3
2003	209.1	209.0	210.8	212.2	214.3	215.2	212.6	210.9	213.1	213.6	214.6	215.6	212.6

Employment by Industry: New Jersey—*Continued*

(Numbers in thousands. Not seasonally adjusted.)

Industry	January	February	March	April	May	June	July	August	September	October	November	December	Annual Average
TRENTON—*Continued*													
Trade, transportation and utilities													
1990	27.7	27.4	27.2	27.2	27.6	27.8	27.1	27.1	27.1	27.7	28.0	28.4	27.5
1991	26.7	26.0	26.3	26.4	26.5	26.8	25.7	25.8	26.0	26.3	26.6	27.2	26.3
1992	26.1	25.5	25.5	24.9	25.5	25.6	25.1	24.9	25.2	26.2	26.9	27.4	25.7
1993	27.0	26.4	26.3	26.2	26.5	26.7	26.0	25.5	25.9	26.5	27.1	27.9	26.5
1994	25.9	25.4	25.6	25.4	25.7	25.7	25.1	25.2	25.4	26.4	26.6	27.5	25.8
1995	26.5	26.2	26.3	26.2	26.5	26.5	26.0	26.1	26.3	26.7	27.0	27.6	26.4
1996	26.2	26.2	26.4	26.4	27.0	27.0	26.1	25.9	26.3	27.0	27.6	28.4	26.7
1997	27.1	26.5	26.5	26.4	26.6	26.8	25.9	25.8	26.7	27.0	27.5	28.0	26.7
1998	27.0	26.6	26.9	26.7	27.0	27.0	26.5	26.4	26.3	27.4	27.8	28.5	27.0
1999	27.3	27.3	27.4	27.1	27.5	27.9	27.5	27.6	27.9	28.9	29.5	30.2	28.0
2000	29.1	28.7	28.8	29.3	29.2	29.4	28.5	29.0	28.8	29.0	30.4	30.8	29.2
2001	31.5	31.0	31.1	30.6	31.3	31.7	31.7	31.5	31.6	32.0	33.0	33.7	31.7
2002	32.1	31.6	31.8	31.8	31.9	32.2	30.8	30.9	31.2	31.8	32.7	33.5	31.9
2003	32.1	31.8	32.0	32.2	32.8	33.0	32.3	32.3	32.8	33.1	33.7	34.3	32.7
Wholesale trade													
1990	5.2	5.2	5.2	5.4	5.5	5.5	5.3	5.3	5.3	5.3	5.2	5.2	5.3
1991	5.5	5.4	5.5	5.6	5.6	5.7	5.5	5.6	5.5	5.5	5.5	5.5	5.5
1992	5.6	5.5	5.5	5.3	5.6	5.6	5.5	5.5	5.5	5.7	5.7	5.6	5.5
1993	5.9	5.9	5.9	6.0	6.0	6.0	5.9	5.8	5.9	5.9	5.9	5.9	5.9
1994	5.5	5.5	5.5	5.3	5.3	5.2	5.3	5.4	5.3	5.4	5.3	5.4	5.3
1995	5.3	5.4	5.5	5.2	5.2	5.1	5.3	5.3	5.3	5.3	5.2	5.2	5.2
1996	5.1	5.2	5.3	5.4	5.4	5.4	5.4	5.3	5.3	5.2	5.2	5.3	5.2
1997	5.1	5.1	5.2	5.3	5.4	5.4	5.3	5.4	5.3	5.3	5.3	5.4	5.2
1998	5.5	5.5	5.6	5.4	5.4	5.4	5.3	5.3	5.2	5.3	5.3	5.4	5.3
1999	5.4	5.5	5.5	5.3	5.4	5.4	5.3	5.3	5.3	5.3	5.4	5.4	5.3
2000	5.7	5.6	5.7	5.7	5.7	5.7	5.7	5.7	5.7	5.7	5.8	5.8	5.7
2001	7.0	6.9	7.0	6.4	6.5	6.5	6.9	6.8	6.7	6.5	6.5	6.6	6.7
2002	6.5	6.5	6.6	6.7	6.6	6.6	6.4	6.2	6.2	6.1	6.2	6.1	6.4
2003	6.2	6.2	6.2	6.4	6.4	6.5	6.4	6.4	6.4	6.4	6.4	6.5	6.4
Retail trade													
1990	18.0	17.6	17.5	17.3	17.4	17.7	17.5	17.5	17.3	17.9	18.3	18.7	17.7
1991	17.1	16.5	16.7	16.7	16.7	16.8	16.2	16.3	16.3	16.5	16.8	17.4	16.6
1992	16.3	15.8	15.8	15.4	15.6	15.6	15.4	15.4	15.4	16.1	16.8	17.4	15.9
1993	16.7	16.2	16.0	16.0	16.2	16.4	15.9	15.7	15.7	16.1	16.7	17.4	16.2
1994	16.2	15.6	15.8	15.7	15.9	16.0	15.6	15.6	15.5	16.3	16.7	17.5	16.0
1995	16.8	16.4	16.4	16.5	16.9	17.0	16.6	16.7	16.6	16.7	17.2	17.8	16.8
1996	17.0	16.6	16.6	16.5	17.0	17.0	16.5	16.5	16.6	17.1	17.7	18.5	16.9
1997	17.6	17.0	16.9	16.7	16.7	16.9	16.5	16.7	17.0	17.1	17.6	18.1	17.0
1998	17.3	16.9	17.0	17.0	17.2	17.3	17.0	16.9	17.0	17.6	18.1	18.7	17.3
1999	17.7	17.5	17.6	17.5	17.8	18.1	18.0	18.1	18.3	19.0	19.5	20.2	18.2
2000	18.8	18.5	18.5	18.8	18.9	19.1	18.5	19.0	18.7	18.6	19.8	20.3	18.9
2001	19.9	19.5	19.5	19.6	20.0	20.3	20.2	20.1	19.9	20.4	21.4	21.9	20.2
2002	20.5	19.9	20.0	19.8	20.0	20.3	19.8	20.1	20.0	20.3	21.1	22.0	20.3
2003	20.8	20.5	20.6	20.8	21.2	21.4	21.0	21.1	21.1	21.4	22.0	22.5	21.2
Transportation and utilities													
1990	4.5	4.6	4.5	4.5	4.7	4.6	4.3	4.3	4.5	4.5	4.5	4.5	4.5
1991	4.1	4.1	4.1	4.1	4.2	4.3	4.0	3.9	4.2	4.3	4.3	4.3	4.1
1992	4.2	4.2	4.2	4.2	4.3	4.4	4.2	4.0	4.3	4.4	4.4	4.4	4.2
1993	4.4	4.3	4.4	4.2	4.3	4.3	4.2	4.0	4.3	4.5	4.5	4.6	4.3
1994	4.2	4.3	4.3	4.4	4.5	4.5	4.2	4.2	4.6	4.7	4.6	4.6	4.4
1995	4.4	4.4	4.4	4.5	4.4	4.4	4.1	4.1	4.4	4.7	4.6	4.6	4.4
1996	4.1	4.4	4.5	4.5	4.6	4.6	4.2	4.1	4.4	4.7	4.7	4.6	4.4
1997	4.4	4.4	4.4	4.4	4.5	4.5	4.1	3.7	4.4	4.6	4.6	4.5	4.3
1998	4.2	4.2	4.3	4.3	4.4	4.3	4.2	4.2	4.1	4.5	4.4	4.4	4.2
1999	4.2	4.3	4.3	4.3	4.3	4.4	4.2	4.2	4.3	4.6	4.6	4.6	4.3
2000	4.6	4.6	4.6	4.8	4.6	4.6	4.3	4.3	4.4	4.7	4.8	4.7	4.5
2001	4.6	4.6	4.6	4.6	4.8	4.9	4.6	4.6	5.0	5.1	5.1	5.2	4.8
2002	5.1	5.2	5.2	5.3	5.3	5.3	4.6	4.6	5.0	5.4	5.4	5.4	5.2
2003	5.1	5.1	5.2	5.0	5.2	5.1	4.9	4.8	5.3	5.3	5.3	5.3	5.1
Information													
1990	7.1	7.1	7.0	6.9	6.9	6.9	7.0	6.9	6.9	6.8	6.7	6.7	6.9
1991	6.7	6.7	6.7	6.8	6.8	6.8	6.8	6.7	6.8	6.9	6.8	6.8	6.7
1992	6.7	6.7	6.7	6.8	6.9	6.9	6.8	6.8	6.6	6.7	6.7	6.7	6.7
1993	6.4	6.4	6.4	6.7	6.7	6.7	6.5	6.5	6.3	6.6	6.5	6.4	6.5
1994	6.5	6.5	6.6	6.4	6.4	6.5	6.8	6.8	6.6	6.8	6.8	6.8	6.6
1995	6.2	6.2	6.3	6.2	6.3	6.3	6.3	6.3	6.2	6.0	5.9	6.0	6.1
1996	5.8	5.7	5.7	5.8	5.9	5.9	5.8	5.9	5.9	5.9	5.9	6.0	5.8
1997	5.8	5.9	5.9	5.9	6.0	6.1	6.2	6.3	6.2	6.3	6.4	6.4	6.1
1998	6.4	6.5	6.6	6.6	6.7	6.6	6.7	6.6	6.6	6.6	6.5	6.5	6.5
1999	6.4	6.5	6.5	6.7	6.9	7.0	7.1	7.0	6.8	6.6	6.6	6.7	6.7
2000	6.7	6.8	6.8	7.1	7.2	7.4	7.1	6.9	7.1	7.5	7.5	7.6	7.1
2001	7.7	7.6	7.7	7.5	7.6	7.7	7.7	7.4	7.5	7.4	7.5	7.6	7.5
2002	7.3	7.7	7.8	7.5	7.7	7.6	7.5	7.5	7.3	7.1	7.1	7.0	7.4
2003	6.8	7.0	6.9	6.9	6.9	6.9	6.8	6.8	6.7	6.6	6.6	6.5	6.8

Employment by Industry: New Jersey—*Continued*

(Numbers in thousands. Not seasonally adjusted.)

Industry	January	February	March	April	May	June	July	August	September	October	November	December	Annual Average
TRENTON—*Continued*													
Financial activities													
1990	11.7	11.8	11.9	11.7	11.7	11.8	11.8	11.8	11.5	11.6	11.5	11.6	11.7
1991	11.5	11.6	11.6	10.8	10.8	11.1	11.2	11.3	11.0	10.8	10.8	10.8	11.1
1992	10.7	10.7	10.7	10.5	10.7	10.9	11.0	10.9	10.7	10.8	10.8	10.8	10.7
1993	10.6	10.6	10.7	10.8	10.8	11.0	11.0	10.9	10.4	10.6	10.6	10.6	10.7
1994	11.1	11.1	11.2	11.7	11.7	12.0	11.4	11.4	11.0	11.2	11.0	11.1	11.3
1995	11.2	11.1	11.2	11.1	11.1	11.2	11.4	11.4	11.0	11.1	11.1	11.1	11.1
1996	10.9	11.1	11.2	11.2	11.3	11.5	12.0	12.0	11.8	11.6	11.7	11.8	11.5
1997	11.8	11.8	11.9	12.4	12.4	12.1	12.3	12.3	11.9	11.9	11.8	11.8	12.0
1998	11.6	11.5	11.5	11.6	11.6	11.8	11.9	12.0	11.7	11.8	11.8	11.9	11.7
1999	11.8	11.8	12.0	12.4	12.5	12.6	12.7	12.6	12.4	12.7	12.8	12.9	12.4
2000	13.2	13.4	12.8	12.9	12.9	13.1	13.0	13.0	12.7	13.1	12.9	12.9	12.9
2001	12.3	12.3	12.4	13.6	13.7	14.0	14.5	14.3	14.1	15.3	14.8	14.9	13.8
2002	15.7	15.8	15.7	16.0	16.2	16.3	16.5	16.3	16.2	16.2	16.3	16.3	16.1
2003	16.5	16.3	16.3	16.2	16.3	16.4	16.7	16.5	16.3	16.2	16.4	16.4	16.4
Professional and business services													
1990	20.5	20.8	21.1	21.4	21.4	21.8	21.6	21.5	21.4	21.7	21.5	21.4	21.3
1991	20.3	20.4	20.5	21.1	21.1	21.4	21.4	21.6	21.4	21.2	20.9	21.1	21.0
1992	20.2	20.4	20.7	20.7	20.8	21.0	21.3	21.3	21.0	21.5	21.5	21.4	20.9
1993	21.3	21.8	22.0	21.6	21.9	22.0	22.1	22.0	21.6	22.6	22.1	22.4	21.9
1994	21.4	21.6	22.0	22.5	23.0	22.9	23.0	23.1	22.8	23.0	22.9	22.9	22.5
1995	23.2	23.6	23.9	23.6	24.3	23.9	23.6	23.8	23.6	23.9	23.8	23.7	23.7
1996	24.0	24.4	24.7	24.7	25.1	25.2	25.1	25.2	24.8	25.6	25.9	26.2	25.0
1997	25.4	25.7	26.4	26.8	26.9	27.5	27.9	27.5	27.6	27.9	28.1	28.1	27.1
1998	27.1	27.8	28.4	28.8	29.1	30.1	30.6	30.7	30.6	30.8	30.6	30.6	29.6
1999	30.6	31.0	31.7	33.6	33.8	34.4	35.0	35.2	35.0	35.8	35.5	35.3	33.9
2000	33.7	34.1	35.2	35.2	35.5	36.2	36.2	36.1	36.0	35.9	36.2	36.4	35.5
2001	33.6	33.5	34.5	34.1	34.2	34.4	32.8	32.6	31.7	32.1	32.0	32.0	33.1
2002	31.2	31.0	31.7	32.5	32.2	32.4	31.9	31.9	31.3	30.7	30.8	30.5	31.5
2003	29.7	29.5	30.2	30.6	30.8	31.3	31.3	31.3	31.2	30.7	30.8	31.0	30.7
Educational and health services													
1990	32.0	32.4	32.5	32.6	32.4	32.3	31.2	31.0	32.0	33.1	33.1	33.1	32.3
1991	33.9	34.2	34.4	34.8	34.7	34.7	33.4	33.4	34.5	35.5	36.0	35.8	34.6
1992	36.2	36.4	36.8	37.1	37.1	36.8	35.9	35.7	36.6	37.4	37.5	37.2	36.7
1993	36.6	36.9	37.2	37.8	37.7	37.5	36.9	36.4	37.3	38.3	38.1	38.2	37.4
1994	37.3	37.7	37.9	38.0	37.9	37.7	37.2	36.9	37.9	38.2	38.1	38.6	37.7
1995	38.2	38.4	38.4	38.2	37.9	37.4	37.1	36.5	37.3	37.9	37.8	37.8	37.7
1996	36.7	37.1	37.5	37.3	37.5	37.2	36.8	36.6	37.0	38.0	38.1	37.9	37.3
1997	37.8	38.5	38.8	38.6	38.5	38.5	37.3	37.1	37.9	38.8	38.8	38.9	38.2
1998	37.9	38.4	38.7	38.6	38.5	38.3	37.0	36.8	37.8	38.5	38.8	38.8	38.1
1999	38.4	39.0	39.6	39.4	39.3	39.2	37.7	37.6	38.6	39.7	39.8	40.3	39.0
2000	38.2	39.0	39.5	40.1	40.1	39.9	38.9	38.9	39.9	40.9	40.9	41.0	39.7
2001	38.6	39.1	39.2	39.8	39.8	39.8	39.2	39.2	40.1	40.4	40.4	40.7	39.6
2002	40.1	40.9	40.9	40.8	41.1	41.0	40.6	40.1	40.7	41.1	41.3	41.6	40.9
2003	41.6	41.7	41.9	42.1	42.9	42.7	42.2	41.3	42.3	43.0	43.1	43.2	42.3
Leisure and hospitality													
1990	9.3	9.7	9.9	9.9	10.0	10.1	9.4	9.2	9.4	9.3	9.1	9.0	9.5
1991	8.1	8.3	8.6	8.5	8.6	8.7	8.6	8.6	8.8	8.9	8.8	8.8	8.6
1992	8.2	8.4	8.4	8.4	8.7	8.8	8.7	8.6	8.6	8.9	8.9	8.8	8.6
1993	8.4	8.6	8.6	8.7	9.0	9.1	8.9	8.8	8.8	9.2	9.0	8.9	8.8
1994	8.4	8.6	8.7	9.1	9.4	9.4	9.1	8.8	8.9	9.3	9.1	9.4	9.0
1995	8.6	8.8	9.1	9.5	9.6	9.5	9.2	9.1	9.3	9.7	9.6	9.7	9.3
1996	8.9	9.4	9.7	9.8	10.0	10.0	9.8	9.6	9.6	9.8	9.8	9.9	9.6
1997	9.3	9.7	10.1	10.4	10.8	10.8	10.5	10.2	10.3	10.5	10.4	10.5	10.2
1998	10.3	10.6	10.7	10.8	11.2	11.3	10.8	10.5	10.7	10.5	10.5	10.5	10.7
1999	9.9	10.2	10.3	10.5	10.7	11.1	10.8	10.8	10.6	10.7	10.7	10.8	10.5
2000	11.1	11.1	11.5	11.7	11.8	12.3	12.0	11.9	11.8	11.6	11.5	11.4	11.6
2001	11.0	11.3	11.6	12.0	12.2	12.4	12.2	12.0	11.8	12.1	12.1	12.1	11.9
2002	11.9	12.0	12.2	12.4	12.9	13.1	12.2	12.2	12.5	13.0	13.1	13.3	12.6
2003	12.8	12.8	13.2	13.7	13.9	14.1	13.7	13.6	13.8	13.6	13.5	13.7	13.5
Other services													
1990	7.1	7.2	7.3	6.8	6.9	6.9	6.7	6.7	6.8	6.7	6.7	6.7	6.8
1991	6.6	6.5	6.6	6.5	6.5	6.5	6.6	6.6	6.6	6.6	6.7	6.7	6.5
1992	6.6	6.6	6.6	6.7	6.8	6.8	6.7	6.6	6.6	6.9	6.9	6.8	6.7
1993	6.7	6.7	6.8	6.7	6.6	7.0	6.8	7.3	7.2	7.4	7.3	7.2	6.9
1994	7.2	7.2	7.1	7.3	7.4	7.3	6.9	6.9	6.8	7.0	7.1	7.0	7.1
1995	6.7	6.7	6.9	6.9	6.9	6.8	6.8	6.9	6.9	6.9	6.9	6.9	6.8
1996	6.9	7.0	7.1	7.1	7.1	7.1	7.0	7.0	6.9	7.1	7.2	7.2	7.0
1997	6.7	6.7	6.9	6.7	6.8	6.8	6.7	6.7	6.7	6.8	6.8	6.8	6.7
1998	6.8	6.7	6.7	6.8	6.8	6.7	6.8	6.7	6.6	6.9	6.9	6.9	6.7
1999	7.1	7.2	7.2	7.4	7.4	7.3	7.2	7.2	7.1	7.2	7.3	7.4	7.2
2000	6.9	6.9	7.1	7.3	7.3	7.3	7.3	7.4	7.2	7.2	7.1	7.3	7.1
2001	7.2	7.2	7.2	7.3	7.4	7.4	7.5	7.4	7.3	7.4	7.4	7.5	7.3
2002	7.3	7.3	7.3	7.4	7.4	7.4	7.4	7.4	7.2	7.3	7.4	7.4	7.4
2003	7.5	7.4	7.4	7.5	7.5	7.7	7.7	7.7	7.8	7.6	7.6	7.6	7.6

Employment by Industry: New Jersey—*Continued*

(Numbers in thousands. Not seasonally adjusted.)

Industry	January	February	March	April	May	June	July	August	September	October	November	December	Annual Average
TRENTON—*Continued*													
Government													
1990	56.3	56.7	56.9	57.0	57.1	57.3	55.6	55.3	56.1	56.4	56.5	56.6	56.4
1991	56.1	55.8	56.5	56.0	56.2	56.4	54.1	53.6	53.6	54.3	54.6	54.7	55.1
1992	54.4	54.7	55.4	55.9	55.7	55.9	54.3	54.1	53.5	53.7	53.8	53.8	54.6
1993	53.6	54.3	55.2	54.8	54.5	54.5	51.6	51.8	52.4	52.8	53.4	53.4	53.5
1994	53.5	53.7	54.6	54.3	54.3	54.3	52.6	51.8	52.6	53.7	53.6	53.7	53.5
1995	53.1	53.5	54.0	54.4	53.7	53.5	51.5	50.9	51.8	52.4	52.4	52.5	52.8
1996	52.0	52.7	53.4	53.8	53.2	53.1	51.4	50.4	51.2	52.1	52.4	52.5	52.3
1997	51.7	52.2	52.8	53.1	53.1	52.8	50.6	50.2	51.9	52.5	53.1	53.1	52.2
1998	52.3	52.5	52.7	52.6	52.5	51.8	50.2	49.9	51.6	52.9	53.2	53.6	52.1
1999	53.1	53.5	53.8	54.1	53.8	53.7	52.6	52.3	53.5	54.4	54.9	55.2	53.7
2000	55.0	55.5	55.7	55.2	55.4	56.0	53.8	54.0	56.3	57.6	58.3	59.0	55.9
2001	58.8	59.6	59.8	59.6	59.8	59.8	58.0	58.2	60.0	61.1	61.3	62.0	59.8
2002	61.4	61.1	61.6	61.5	61.7	61.3	58.0	57.9	59.4	60.8	61.5	61.4	60.6
2003	62.1	62.5	62.9	63.0	63.2	63.1	61.9	61.4	62.2	62.8	62.9	62.9	62.6
Federal government													
1990	3.6	3.6	3.6	3.7	3.8	3.9	3.9	3.6	3.6	3.5	3.5	3.6	3.6
1991	3.5	3.4	3.5	3.4	3.4	3.6	3.6	3.6	3.6	3.5	3.5	3.6	3.5
1992	3.5	3.5	3.5	3.5	3.4	3.5	3.5	3.5	3.4	3.5	3.4	3.4	3.4
1993	3.4	3.4	3.4	3.3	3.3	3.3	3.3	3.3	3.3	3.2	3.3	3.4	3.3
1994	3.4	3.3	3.4	3.4	3.3	3.4	3.4	3.4	3.4	3.4	3.4	3.5	3.3
1995	3.4	3.4	3.3	3.3	3.3	3.3	3.3	3.5	3.4	3.4	3.4	3.4	3.3
1996	3.4	3.5	3.7	4.0	3.9	4.0	3.9	3.9	3.9	3.9	4.0	4.0	3.8
1997	3.9	3.9	3.8	3.7	3.7	3.6	3.4	3.4	3.5	3.4	3.5	3.6	3.6
1998	3.3	3.3	3.2	3.1	3.1	3.1	3.1	3.1	3.1	3.2	3.3	3.5	3.2
1999	3.2	3.1	3.0	3.4	3.0	2.9	2.9	2.9	2.9	2.9	3.0	3.1	3.0
2000	2.9	2.9	3.0	3.1	3.4	3.5	3.3	3.1	3.0	3.0	3.0	3.1	3.1
2001	3.0	3.0	3.0	3.0	3.0	2.9	2.9	2.9	2.9	2.9	2.9	3.1	2.9
2002	2.9	2.9	2.9	2.9	3.0	3.0	3.0	3.0	3.0	3.0	3.0	3.1	3.0
2003	3.1	2.9	2.9	2.9	2.9	2.9	2.9	2.8	2.8	2.8	2.8	2.9	2.9
State government													
1990	36.2	36.6	36.7	36.7	36.7	36.6	36.6	36.6	36.2	36.0	36.0	36.0	36.4
1991	36.1	35.7	36.3	36.2	36.2	36.0	35.7	35.3	34.4	34.4	34.4	34.4	35.4
1992	34.4	34.4	34.9	35.5	35.5	35.6	35.2	34.7	33.9	33.4	33.0	33.1	34.4
1993	33.2	33.7	34.3	34.2	34.1	34.1	32.8	32.9	32.7	32.7	32.9	33.0	33.3
1994	33.4	33.2	33.7	33.7	33.6	33.6	33.2	32.9	32.9	33.0	32.7	32.6	33.2
1995	32.8	33.2	33.4	33.6	33.0	32.9	32.3	32.0	31.9	32.1	31.9	31.8	32.5
1996	31.9	32.3	32.4	32.4	32.0	31.8	31.6	31.2	31.1	31.3	31.2	31.3	31.7
1997	31.2	31.4	31.9	32.1	32.1	32.1	31.9	31.7	31.8	32.1	32.3	32.2	31.9
1998	32.2	32.2	32.3	32.2	32.1	31.8	31.6	31.6	32.1	32.6	32.6	32.7	32.1
1999	32.9	33.0	33.2	33.3	33.3	33.6	33.9	34.0	34.2	34.2	34.4	34.5	33.7
2000	34.7	34.9	34.9	34.5	34.7	34.9	35.2	35.5	36.3	36.9	37.4	37.9	35.6
2001	38.2	38.6	38.7	38.4	38.6	38.5	39.0	39.1	39.7	40.0	40.0	40.5	39.1
2002	40.4	40.0	40.0	40.0	40.0	39.8	38.0	38.2	38.4	39.0	39.4	39.4	39.4
2003	40.3	40.6	40.9	41.1	41.1	41.1	41.1	41.1	41.6	41.1	41.1	41.0	41.0
Local government													
1990	16.5	16.5	16.6	16.6	16.6	16.8	15.1	15.1	16.3	16.9	17.0	17.0	16.4
1991	16.5	16.7	16.7	16.4	16.6	16.8	14.8	14.7	15.6	16.4	16.7	16.7	16.2
1992	16.5	16.8	17.0	16.9	16.8	16.8	15.6	15.9	16.2	16.8	17.4	17.3	16.6
1993	17.0	17.2	17.5	17.3	17.1	17.1	15.5	15.6	16.4	16.9	17.2	17.0	16.8
1994	16.7	17.2	17.5	17.2	17.4	17.3	16.0	15.5	16.3	17.3	17.5	17.6	16.9
1995	16.9	16.9	17.3	17.5	17.4	17.3	15.9	15.4	16.5	16.9	17.1	17.3	16.8
1996	16.7	16.9	17.3	17.4	17.3	17.3	15.9	15.3	16.2	16.9	17.2	17.2	16.8
1997	16.6	16.9	17.1	17.3	17.3	17.1	15.3	15.1	16.6	17.0	17.3	17.3	16.7
1998	16.8	17.0	17.2	17.3	17.3	16.9	15.5	15.2	16.4	17.1	17.3	17.4	16.7
1999	17.0	17.4	17.6	17.4	17.5	17.2	15.8	15.4	16.4	17.3	17.5	17.6	17.0
2000	17.4	17.7	17.8	17.6	17.3	17.6	15.3	15.4	17.0	17.7	17.9	18.0	17.2
2001	17.6	18.0	18.1	18.2	18.2	18.4	16.1	16.2	17.4	18.2	18.4	18.4	17.7
2002	18.1	18.2	18.7	18.6	18.7	18.5	17.0	16.7	18.0	18.8	19.1	18.9	18.3
2003	18.7	19.0	19.1	19.0	19.2	19.1	17.9	17.5	17.8	18.9	19.0	19.0	18.7
VINELAND-MILLVILLE-BRIDGETON													
Total nonfarm													
1990	58.4	58.7	58.8	59.3	60.3	60.7	60.0	60.0	60.1	60.1	59.8	59.0	59.6
1991	57.1	57.1	57.3	57.8	57.7	58.6	56.9	56.9	57.7	57.5	57.1	56.3	57.3
1992	55.6	55.6	56.0	56.8	57.0	57.4	56.9	56.5	57.0	56.8	56.7	56.3	56.5
1993	54.4	54.6	54.8	55.8	55.8	55.9	55.1	54.7	55.9	55.9	56.0	56.1	55.4
1994	55.2	55.0	55.8	56.6	57.1	57.8	56.6	56.3	57.2	57.4	57.4	57.3	56.6
1995	55.8	55.9	56.5	57.5	57.5	58.6	56.7	56.7	57.7	57.8	57.6	57.5	57.1
1996	55.4	55.7	56.5	56.3	57.5	58.1	56.4	56.7	57.9	58.2	57.9	58.0	57.0
1997	56.4	56.3	57.1	57.5	58.4	59.2	58.3	58.4	59.8	59.8	59.6	59.3	58.3
1998	57.8	57.6	58.0	59.0	59.9	60.0	58.7	59.1	59.8	59.8	59.9	60.1	59.1
1999	59.2	59.0	59.8	60.0	60.9	61.8	60.1	60.1	60.6	61.1	61.1	60.9	60.3
2000	60.0	60.0	60.4	60.5	61.4	61.2	59.4	59.3	60.9	60.8	60.9	60.3	60.4
2001	58.7	58.7	59.6	60.4	61.1	61.6	59.0	59.0	60.2	60.0	59.9	59.8	59.8
2002	58.8	59.2	60.1	60.1	60.7	61.2	58.4	58.9	60.8	60.3	60.3	59.9	59.9
2003	59.4	59.1	59.9	60.7	61.5	62.1	60.0	60.6	61.9	61.8	61.9	61.2	60.8

Employment by Industry: New Jersey—*Continued*

(Numbers in thousands. Not seasonally adjusted.)

Industry	January	February	March	April	May	June	July	August	September	October	November	December	Annual Average
VINELAND-MILLVILLE-BRIDGETON—*Continued*													
Total private													
1990	46.0	46.1	46.1	46.5	47.5	47.8	47.5	47.7	47.7	47.3	46.8	46.0	46.9
1991	44.2	44.2	44.4	44.9	44.8	45.8	44.5	44.7	45.4	44.9	44.6	43.8	44.6
1992	43.1	42.9	43.2	43.9	44.2	44.5	44.3	44.1	44.7	44.2	43.9	43.5	43.8
1993	41.7	41.8	42.0	42.9	43.0	43.0	43.1	42.8	43.3	43.2	43.1	43.1	42.7
1994	42.3	42.2	42.9	43.5	44.0	44.7	44.4	44.1	44.7	44.7	44.5	44.3	43.8
1995	43.1	43.1	43.4	44.5	44.6	45.6	44.4	44.5	45.2	45.0	44.8	44.6	44.4
1996	42.7	42.9	43.6	43.4	44.5	45.1	44.2	44.6	45.2	45.5	45.2	45.2	44.3
1997	43.7	43.5	44.2	44.4	45.2	46.0	46.0	46.2	46.8	46.4	46.0	45.6	45.3
1998	44.3	43.9	43.9	44.7	45.5	45.9	45.7	46.1	46.1	45.7	45.8	45.9	45.2
1999	45.1	44.7	45.3	45.4	46.3	47.2	46.6	46.5	46.5	46.4	46.4	46.1	46.0
2000	45.6	45.3	45.5	45.7	46.4	46.5	46.5	46.7	46.9	46.3	46.3	45.7	46.1
2001	44.3	44.1	44.9	45.7	46.4	46.9	46.1	46.2	46.0	45.3	45.0	44.7	45.4
2002	44.0	44.1	44.8	44.8	45.3	45.9	45.3	45.8	46.1	45.2	44.9	44.7	45.1
2003	44.5	43.9	44.7	45.4	46.2	46.8	46.4	47.2	47.0	46.4	46.4	45.7	45.9
Goods-producing													
1990	17.1	17.4	17.3	17.4	17.8	17.8	17.7	18.1	18.1	17.7	17.5	17.0	17.5
1991	15.9	16.0	16.0	16.3	16.0	16.6	16.1	16.3	16.6	16.8	16.6	16.0	16.2
1992	15.3	15.3	15.4	15.7	15.9	16.0	16.1	16.1	16.2	15.9	15.4	15.1	15.7
1993	14.4	14.6	14.8	15.2	15.3	15.4	15.6	15.5	15.7	15.7	15.5	15.3	15.2
1994	15.0	15.0	15.3	15.7	16.1	16.6	16.5	16.5	16.5	16.2	16.0	15.5	15.9
1995	14.9	14.9	15.0	15.6	15.4	15.8	15.4	15.5	15.6	15.5	15.2	14.9	15.3
1996	13.8	14.1	14.4	14.6	15.0	15.3	14.9	15.3	15.4	15.6	15.3	15.1	14.9
1997	14.1	14.4	14.8	14.7	15.4	15.7	15.7	16.0	15.9	15.4	15.2	14.9	15.1
1998	14.4	14.4	14.3	14.7	14.8	15.0	15.3	15.5	15.4	15.0	14.9	14.9	14.8
1999	14.5	14.5	14.6	14.6	14.6	14.9	15.0	14.9	14.7	14.5	14.4	14.4	14.6
2000	14.5	14.5	14.6	14.4	14.7	14.6	14.9	14.8	14.8	14.6	14.5	14.4	14.6
2001	13.6	13.6	13.7	13.9	14.0	14.1	13.9	13.9	13.7	13.4	13.2	13.1	13.6
2002	12.8	12.9	13.0	13.0	13.1	13.3	13.2	13.2	13.1	12.9	12.8	12.8	13.0
2003	12.5	12.2	12.4	12.6	12.8	13.0	12.9	13.1	12.8	12.7	12.9	12.5	12.7
Construction and mining													
1990	2.3	2.4	2.5	2.6	2.7	2.6	2.7	2.8	2.7	2.5	2.5	2.4	2.5
1991	1.9	1.9	1.9	2.1	2.2	2.3	2.3	2.3	2.4	2.3	2.3	2.1	2.1
1992	2.0	1.9	2.0	2.1	2.2	2.3	2.3	2.3	2.3	2.2	2.1	2.0	2.1
1993	1.8	1.8	1.9	2.0	2.1	2.1	2.2	2.2	2.2	2.2	2.2	2.2	2.0
1994	1.8	1.7	1.9	2.1	2.2	2.3	2.3	2.4	2.3	2.3	2.2	2.2	2.1
1995	2.0	1.9	2.0	2.2	2.2	2.4	2.2	2.3	2.3	2.3	2.2	2.1	2.1
1996	1.7	1.8	2.0	2.2	2.3	2.4	2.4	2.4	2.4	2.5	2.4	2.4	2.2
1997	2.1	2.1	2.3	2.3	2.5	2.6	2.5	2.5	2.5	2.4	2.4	2.3	2.3
1998	2.2	2.2	2.1	2.4	2.4	2.5	2.6	2.6	2.6	2.5	2.5	2.5	2.4
1999	2.1	2.1	2.2	2.4	2.4	2.5	2.5	2.4	2.3	2.3	2.3	2.3	2.3
2000	2.2	2.2	2.3	2.4	2.6	2.5	2.6	2.6	2.5	2.5	2.4	2.4	2.4
2001	2.1	2.2	2.3	2.4	2.5	2.5	2.6	2.6	2.4	2.3	2.2	2.2	2.3
2002	2.1	2.1	2.2	2.2	2.3	2.4	2.6	2.6	2.6	2.6	2.6	2.6	2.4
2003	2.5	2.3	2.5	2.7	2.8	2.9	3.1	3.2	3.0	2.9	2.9	2.7	2.8
Manufacturing													
1990	14.8	15.0	14.8	14.8	15.1	15.2	15.0	15.3	15.4	15.2	15.0	14.6	15.0
1991	14.0	14.1	14.1	14.2	13.8	14.3	13.8	14.0	14.2	14.5	14.3	13.9	14.1
1992	13.3	13.4	13.4	13.6	13.7	13.7	13.8	13.8	13.9	13.7	13.3	13.1	13.5
1993	12.6	12.8	12.9	13.2	13.2	13.3	13.4	13.3	13.5	13.5	13.3	13.1	13.1
1994	13.2	13.3	13.4	13.6	13.9	14.3	14.2	14.1	14.2	13.9	13.8	13.3	13.7
1995	12.9	13.0	13.0	13.4	13.2	13.4	13.2	13.2	13.3	13.2	13.0	12.8	13.1
1996	12.1	12.3	12.4	12.4	12.7	12.9	12.5	12.9	13.0	13.1	12.9	12.7	12.6
1997	12.0	12.3	12.5	12.4	12.9	13.1	13.2	13.5	13.4	13.0	12.8	12.6	12.8
1998	12.2	12.2	12.2	12.3	12.4	12.5	12.7	12.9	12.8	12.5	12.4	12.4	12.4
1999	12.4	12.4	12.4	12.2	12.2	12.4	12.5	12.5	12.4	12.2	12.1	12.1	12.3
2000	12.3	12.3	12.3	12.0	12.1	12.1	12.3	12.2	12.3	12.1	12.1	12.0	12.1
2001	11.5	11.4	11.4	11.5	11.5	11.6	11.3	11.3	11.3	11.1	11.0	10.9	11.3
2002	10.7	10.8	10.8	10.8	10.8	10.9	10.6	10.6	10.5	10.3	10.2	10.2	10.6
2003	10.0	9.9	9.9	9.9	10.0	10.1	9.8	9.9	9.8	9.8	10.0	9.8	9.9
Service-providing													
1990	41.3	41.3	41.5	41.9	42.5	42.9	42.3	41.9	42.0	42.4	42.3	42.0	42.0
1991	41.2	41.1	41.3	41.5	41.7	42.0	40.8	40.6	41.1	40.7	40.5	40.3	41.0
1992	40.3	40.3	40.6	41.1	41.1	41.4	40.8	40.4	40.8	40.9	41.3	41.2	40.8
1993	40.0	40.0	40.0	40.6	40.5	40.5	39.5	39.2	40.2	40.2	40.5	40.8	40.1
1994	40.2	40.0	40.5	40.9	41.0	41.2	40.1	39.8	40.7	41.2	41.4	41.8	40.7
1995	40.9	41.0	41.5	41.9	42.1	42.8	41.3	41.2	42.1	42.3	42.4	42.6	41.8
1996	41.6	41.6	42.1	41.7	42.5	42.8	41.5	41.4	42.5	42.6	42.6	42.9	42.1
1997	42.3	41.9	42.3	42.8	43.0	43.5	42.6	42.4	43.9	44.4	44.4	44.4	43.1
1998	43.4	43.2	43.7	44.3	45.1	45.0	43.4	43.6	44.4	44.8	45.0	45.2	44.2
1999	44.7	44.5	45.2	45.4	46.3	46.9	45.1	45.2	45.9	46.6	46.7	46.5	45.7
2000	45.5	45.5	45.8	46.1	46.7	46.6	44.5	44.5	46.1	46.2	46.4	45.9	45.8
2001	45.1	45.1	45.9	46.5	47.1	47.5	45.1	45.1	46.5	46.6	46.7	46.7	46.1
2002	46.0	46.3	47.1	47.1	47.6	47.9	45.2	45.7	47.7	47.4	47.5	47.1	46.9
2003	46.9	46.9	47.5	48.1	48.7	49.1	47.1	47.5	49.1	49.1	49.0	48.7	48.1

Employment by Industry: New Jersey—*Continued*

(Numbers in thousands. Not seasonally adjusted.)

Industry	January	February	March	April	May	June	July	August	September	October	November	December	Annual Average
VINELAND-MILLVILLE-BRIDGETON—*Continued*													
Trade, transportation, and utilities													
1990	11.4	11.1	11.2	11.3	11.4	11.6	11.5	11.4	11.3	11.4	11.5	11.4	11.3
1991	10.8	10.7	10.8	10.6	10.7	10.8	10.3	10.5	10.5	10.5	10.5	10.5	10.6
1992	10.6	10.4	10.5	10.6	10.5	10.7	10.5	10.6	10.7	10.8	10.9	11.1	10.6
1993	10.5	10.5	10.4	10.5	10.6	10.5	10.3	10.3	10.4	10.6	10.6	10.9	10.5
1994	10.2	10.1	10.2	10.4	10.6	10.7	10.5	10.5	10.8	10.9	11.2	11.4	10.6
1995	11.4	11.2	11.3	11.2	11.3	11.6	11.3	11.2	11.7	11.6	11.7	11.7	11.4
1996	11.4	11.3	11.4	11.3	11.7	11.9	11.6	11.7	11.8	11.9	12.1	12.1	11.6
1997	11.9	11.6	11.7	11.6	11.8	12.0	11.9	11.8	12.3	12.6	12.6	12.5	12.0
1998	11.8	11.6	11.7	11.8	12.1	12.0	11.6	11.7	11.8	12.0	12.4	12.4	11.9
1999	12.1	11.9	12.1	12.2	12.8	13.0	12.6	12.7	12.9	12.9	13.1	13.0	12.6
2000	12.2	12.0	12.2	12.2	12.6	12.8	12.5	13.0	13.1	12.8	12.9	12.8	12.5
2001	12.3	12.0	12.4	12.7	13.1	13.3	12.6	12.8	12.9	12.6	12.6	12.3	12.6
2002	11.8	11.7	12.1	12.0	12.2	12.4	12.1	12.6	13.1	12.6	12.4	12.2	12.3
2003	12.0	11.8	12.1	12.2	12.6	12.6	12.6	13.2	13.4	13.0	12.8	12.7	12.6
Wholesale trade													
1990	1.9	1.9	1.9	1.9	2.0	2.0	1.9	2.0	1.9	1.9	1.9	1.8	1.9
1991	1.8	1.8	1.8	1.9	1.9	2.0	1.8	1.9	1.8	1.9	1.8	1.7	1.8
1992	2.0	1.9	1.9	2.0	2.0	2.0	2.0	2.0	2.0	2.0	2.0	2.0	1.9
1993	1.9	1.8	1.9	1.9	1.9	1.9	1.9	1.9	1.9	2.0	1.9	1.9	1.9
1994	1.6	1.6	1.6	1.7	1.7	1.8	1.8	1.8	1.8	1.8	1.8	1.7	1.7
1995	1.7	1.7	1.7	1.6	1.7	1.8	1.8	1.8	1.8	1.7	1.7	1.7	1.7
1996	1.6	1.6	1.6	1.6	1.7	1.8	1.8	1.8	1.8	1.8	1.8	1.7	1.7
1997	1.9	1.8	1.9	1.9	2.0	2.1	2.1	2.0	2.0	2.1	2.0	2.0	1.9
1998	1.9	2.0	2.0	2.1	2.2	2.2	2.1	2.1	2.1	2.2	2.2	2.1	2.1
1999	2.1	2.1	2.1	2.2	2.3	2.3	2.3	2.3	2.3	2.3	2.3	2.1	2.2
2000	2.1	2.1	2.2	2.2	2.3	2.3	2.4	2.3	2.4	2.2	2.2	2.1	2.2
2001	2.2	2.2	2.3	2.3	2.4	2.4	2.3	2.3	2.3	2.2	2.1	2.0	2.2
2002	1.9	2.0	2.1	2.1	2.2	2.2	2.3	2.3	2.3	2.3	2.3	2.2	2.2
2003	2.2	2.1	2.2	2.4	2.5	2.4	2.4	2.4	2.4	2.4	2.4	2.4	2.4
Retail trade													
1990	6.7	6.5	6.6	6.7	6.7	6.8	6.9	6.8	6.7	6.7	6.8	6.9	6.7
1991	6.3	6.2	6.3	6.1	6.2	6.2	6.1	6.2	6.2	6.1	6.2	6.3	6.2
1992	6.1	6.0	6.1	6.1	6.1	6.2	6.1	6.2	6.1	6.3	6.4	6.6	6.1
1993	6.2	6.3	6.1	6.2	6.2	6.2	6.1	6.1	6.1	6.1	6.2	6.4	6.1
1994	6.1	6.0	6.1	6.1	6.2	6.2	6.2	6.2	6.3	6.2	6.5	6.8	6.2
1995	6.9	6.7	6.7	6.6	6.6	6.7	6.7	6.6	6.8	6.8	7.0	7.0	6.7
1996	6.7	6.6	6.6	6.6	6.7	6.8	6.9	6.9	6.9	7.1	7.3	7.4	6.8
1997	7.1	6.9	6.9	7.0	7.0	7.1	7.2	7.2	7.5	7.8	7.8	7.7	7.2
1998	7.2	6.9	7.0	7.0	7.0	7.0	6.7	6.8	6.7	6.8	7.2	7.3	6.9
1999	7.1	6.9	7.2	7.4	7.9	8.0	7.9	8.0	8.1	8.0	8.1	8.2	7.7
2000	7.8	7.7	7.7	7.6	7.9	8.1	8.1	8.7	8.3	8.2	8.3	8.3	8.0
2001	7.9	7.6	7.8	8.1	8.4	8.6	8.1	8.5	8.3	8.1	8.2	8.0	8.1
2002	7.7	7.5	7.7	7.6	7.7	7.9	7.8	8.3	8.5	8.1	7.9	7.8	7.9
2003	7.7	7.6	7.7	7.7	8.0	8.1	8.4	9.0	8.9	8.5	8.3	8.2	8.2
Transportation and utilities													
1990	2.8	2.7	2.7	2.7	2.7	2.8	2.7	2.6	2.7	2.8	2.8	2.7	2.7
1991	2.7	2.7	2.7	2.6	2.6	2.6	2.4	2.4	2.5	2.5	2.5	2.5	2.5
1992	2.5	2.5	2.5	2.5	2.4	2.5	2.4	2.4	2.6	2.5	2.5	2.5	2.4
1993	2.4	2.4	2.4	2.4	2.5	2.4	2.3	2.3	2.4	2.5	2.5	2.6	2.4
1994	2.5	2.5	2.5	2.6	2.7	2.7	2.5	2.5	2.7	2.9	2.9	2.9	2.6
1995	2.8	2.8	2.9	3.0	3.0	3.1	2.8	2.8	3.1	3.1	3.0	3.0	2.9
1996	3.1	3.1	3.2	3.1	3.3	3.3	2.9	3.0	3.1	3.0	3.0	3.0	3.0
1997	2.9	2.9	2.9	2.7	2.8	2.8	2.6	2.6	2.8	2.7	2.8	2.8	2.7
1998	2.7	2.7	2.7	2.7	2.9	2.8	2.8	2.8	3.0	3.0	3.0	3.0	2.8
1999	2.9	2.9	2.8	2.6	2.6	2.7	2.4	2.4	2.5	2.6	2.7	2.7	2.6
2000	2.3	2.2	2.3	2.4	2.4	2.4	2.0	2.0	2.4	2.4	2.4	2.4	2.3
2001	2.2	2.2	2.3	2.3	2.3	2.3	2.2	2.0	2.3	2.3	2.3	2.3	2.2
2002	2.2	2.2	2.3	2.3	2.3	2.3	2.0	2.0	2.3	2.2	2.2	2.2	2.2
2003	2.1	2.1	2.2	2.1	2.1	2.1	1.8	1.8	2.1	2.1	2.1	2.1	2.1
Information													
1990	0.7	0.7	0.7	0.7	0.8	0.8	0.8	0.8	0.8	0.8	0.7	0.7	0.7
1991	0.7	0.7	0.7	0.7	0.7	0.7	0.7	0.7	0.7	0.7	0.7	0.7	0.7
1992	0.7	0.7	0.7	0.7	0.7	0.7	0.7	0.7	0.7	0.7	0.7	0.7	0.7
1993	0.6	0.6	0.6	0.6	0.6	0.6	0.6	0.6	0.6	0.6	0.6	0.6	0.6
1994	0.6	0.6	0.6	0.6	0.6	0.6	0.6	0.6	0.6	0.6	0.6	0.6	0.6
1995	0.6	0.6	0.6	0.6	0.6	0.6	0.6	0.6	0.6	0.6	0.6	0.6	0.6
1996	0.6	0.6	0.6	0.6	0.6	0.6	0.6	0.6	0.6	0.6	0.7	0.7	0.6
1997	0.7	0.7	0.7	0.7	0.7	0.7	0.7	0.7	0.7	0.7	0.6	0.7	0.6
1998	0.7	0.8	0.7	0.8	0.8	0.8	0.8	0.8	0.8	0.7	0.8	0.8	0.7
1999	0.8	0.8	0.8	0.8	0.8	0.9	0.9	0.9	0.9	0.9	0.9	0.9	0.8
2000	1.0	1.0	1.0	0.8	0.8	0.8	0.9	0.8	0.8	1.1	1.1	1.1	0.9
2001	1.0	1.0	1.1	1.1	1.1	1.1	1.2	1.1	1.1	1.1	1.1	1.1	1.0
2002	1.1	1.1	1.1	1.1	1.1	1.0	1.0	1.0	1.0	1.0	1.0	1.0	1.0
2003	1.0	1.0	1.0	1.0	1.0	1.0	1.0	1.0	1.0	1.0	1.0	1.0	1.0

Employment by Industry: New Jersey—*Continued*

(Numbers in thousands. Not seasonally adjusted.)

Industry	January	February	March	April	May	June	July	August	September	October	November	December	Annual Average
VINELAND-MILLVILLE-BRIDGETON—*Continued*													
Financial activities													
1990	4.2	4.2	4.2	4.4	4.5	4.5	4.5	4.4	4.4	4.5	4.5	4.4	4.3
1991	4.1	4.1	4.1	4.3	4.3	4.3	4.3	4.2	4.1	4.1	4.0	3.9	4.1
1992	4.0	4.0	3.9	4.0	4.0	4.0	4.0	3.9	3.9	3.8	3.8	3.7	3.9
1993	3.4	3.4	3.4	3.4	3.4	3.4	3.5	3.4	3.4	3.4	3.5	3.5	3.4
1994	3.6	3.6	3.6	3.4	3.3	3.3	3.4	3.3	3.4	3.4	3.4	3.4	3.4
1995	3.2	3.2	3.2	3.2	3.3	3.2	3.3	3.3	3.2	3.2	3.2	3.2	3.2
1996	3.2	3.2	3.2	3.1	3.1	3.2	3.2	3.1	3.1	3.2	3.1	3.1	3.1
1997	2.9	2.9	2.9	2.9	2.8	2.8	2.9	2.9	2.9	2.9	2.9	2.9	2.8
1998	2.7	2.5	2.5	2.5	2.5	2.5	2.6	2.5	2.5	2.5	2.4	2.4	2.5
1999	2.4	2.3	2.3	2.4	2.4	2.4	2.4	2.4	2.3	2.3	2.2	2.2	2.3
2000	2.1	2.1	2.0	2.2	2.2	2.2	2.1	2.1	2.1	2.0	2.0	2.0	2.0
2001	1.8	1.9	1.8	1.9	1.9	1.9	1.9	1.9	1.9	2.1	2.1	2.1	1.9
2002	2.1	2.1	2.1	2.1	2.1	2.1	2.0	2.1	2.0	1.9	1.9	1.9	2.0
2003	1.8	1.8	1.8	1.9	1.9	2.0	2.0	2.0	2.0	2.0	2.0	2.0	1.9
Professional and business services													
1990	2.3	2.3	2.3	2.3	2.4	2.4	2.4	2.4	2.4	2.3	2.2	2.2	2.3
1991	2.4	2.2	2.3	2.3	2.2	2.3	2.4	2.3	2.4	2.1	2.1	2.0	2.2
1992	2.0	2.0	2.0	2.1	2.0	2.1	2.1	2.1	2.1	2.0	2.0	2.0	2.0
1993	2.0	1.9	1.9	2.0	2.0	2.0	2.0	2.0	2.0	2.0	2.0	2.0	1.9
1994	1.9	1.9	2.0	2.0	2.0	2.0	2.0	2.0	2.0	2.0	2.0	2.0	1.9
1995	2.0	2.0	2.0	2.1	2.1	2.2	2.1	2.2	2.2	2.1	2.1	2.1	2.1
1996	2.1	2.1	2.1	2.1	2.1	2.1	2.1	2.2	2.2	2.3	2.3	2.3	2.1
1997	2.4	2.3	2.4	2.3	2.3	2.5	2.6	2.7	2.6	2.7	2.7	2.6	2.5
1998	2.6	2.5	2.5	2.5	2.6	2.7	2.7	2.8	2.7	2.8	2.7	2.7	2.6
1999	2.7	2.6	2.7	2.6	2.7	2.8	2.8	2.9	2.8	2.8	2.8	2.8	2.7
2000	2.8	2.7	2.7	2.7	2.7	2.7	2.9	2.8	2.7	2.7	2.7	2.5	2.7
2001	2.8	2.8	2.9	2.8	2.9	2.9	3.1	3.1	3.1	3.0	2.9	2.9	2.9
2002	2.9	3.0	3.0	3.0	3.0	3.1	3.2	3.3	3.2	3.3	3.3	3.2	3.1
2003	3.4	3.4	3.4	3.5	3.4	3.5	3.5	3.5	3.4	3.4	3.4	3.3	3.4
Educational and health services													
1990	6.0	6.1	6.1	6.0	6.0	6.1	5.9	5.9	6.1	6.2	6.1	6.1	6.0
1991	6.2	6.4	6.4	6.4	6.4	6.5	6.4	6.3	6.6	6.5	6.5	6.5	6.4
1992	6.6	6.6	6.7	6.7	6.8	6.7	6.5	6.5	6.8	6.7	6.9	6.8	6.6
1993	6.8	6.8	6.9	6.9	6.9	6.8	6.7	6.6	6.9	6.8	6.8	6.8	6.8
1994	6.9	6.9	7.0	7.1	7.1	7.0	7.0	6.9	7.1	7.3	7.2	7.2	7.0
1995	7.0	7.1	7.1	7.2	7.3	7.4	7.1	7.1	7.4	7.4	7.5	7.5	7.2
1996	7.3	7.4	7.5	7.3	7.4	7.4	7.2	7.2	7.5	7.5	7.5	7.5	7.3
1997	7.4	7.4	7.4	7.6	7.5	7.5	7.5	7.5	7.7	7.6	7.7	7.7	7.5
1998	7.8	7.8	7.9	7.9	8.0	7.9	7.7	7.8	8.0	7.9	7.9	8.0	7.8
1999	8.0	8.0	8.1	7.9	7.9	8.1	7.9	7.9	8.0	8.1	8.2	8.1	8.0
2000	8.3	8.3	8.2	8.4	8.3	8.3	8.0	8.1	8.2	8.1	8.1	8.1	8.2
2001	8.1	8.1	8.1	8.3	8.3	8.4	8.3	8.3	8.4	8.3	8.3	8.4	8.2
2002	8.5	8.5	8.6	8.6	8.6	8.7	8.6	8.5	8.7	8.6	8.6	8.7	8.6
2003	8.8	8.8	8.9	8.9	9.0	9.0	8.9	8.9	9.0	9.1	9.2	9.2	9.0
Leisure and hospitality													
1990	2.5	2.5	2.5	2.7	2.8	2.9	2.9	3.0	2.9	2.7	2.7	2.6	2.7
1991	2.5	2.5	2.5	2.7	2.8	2.9	2.6	2.7	2.8	2.5	2.5	2.5	2.6
1992	2.3	2.3	2.4	2.5	2.7	2.7	2.6	2.6	2.7	2.6	2.5	2.4	2.5
1993	2.4	2.4	2.4	2.6	2.6	2.6	2.6	2.6	2.6	2.5	2.5	2.4	2.5
1994	2.4	2.4	2.5	2.6	2.6	2.7	2.6	2.6	2.5	2.5	2.3	2.3	2.5
1995	2.3	2.4	2.4	2.8	2.8	3.0	2.8	2.8	2.7	2.8	2.7	2.8	2.6
1996	2.5	2.4	2.6	2.6	2.8	2.8	2.7	2.7	2.7	2.5	2.4	2.5	2.6
1997	2.5	2.4	2.5	2.7	2.8	2.9	2.7	2.7	2.8	2.6	2.5	2.5	2.6
1998	2.5	2.5	2.5	2.6	2.8	3.0	2.9	3.0	2.9	2.9	2.8	2.8	2.7
1999	2.7	2.7	2.8	3.0	3.1	3.1	2.9	2.8	2.9	2.9	2.8	2.8	2.8
2000	2.8	2.8	2.8	3.0	3.1	3.1	3.1	3.1	3.2	3.0	3.0	2.9	2.9
2001	2.9	2.9	3.1	3.2	3.3	3.3	3.2	3.3	3.1	3.0	3.0	3.0	3.1
2002	2.9	2.9	3.0	3.1	3.2	3.3	3.2	3.2	3.2	3.1	3.1	3.1	3.1
2003	3.2	3.1	3.3	3.5	3.6	3.7	3.6	3.6	3.5	3.3	3.2	3.1	3.4
Other services													
1990	1.8	1.8	1.8	1.7	1.8	1.7	1.8	1.7	1.7	1.7	1.6	1.6	1.7
1991	1.6	1.6	1.6	1.6	1.7	1.7	1.7	1.7	1.7	1.7	1.7	1.7	1.6
1992	1.6	1.6	1.6	1.6	1.6	1.6	1.8	1.6	1.6	1.7	1.7	1.7	1.6
1993	1.6	1.6	1.6	1.7	1.6	1.7	1.8	1.8	1.7	1.6	1.6	1.6	1.6
1994	1.7	1.7	1.7	1.7	1.7	1.8	1.8	1.7	1.8	1.8	1.8	1.9	1.7
1995	1.7	1.7	1.8	1.8	1.8	1.8	1.8	1.8	1.8	1.8	1.8	1.8	1.7
1996	1.8	1.8	1.8	1.8	1.8	1.8	1.9	1.8	1.9	1.9	1.8	1.9	1.8
1997	1.8	1.8	1.8	1.9	1.9	1.9	2.0	1.9	1.9	1.9	1.8	1.8	1.8
1998	1.8	1.8	1.8	1.9	1.9	2.0	2.1	2.0	2.0	1.9	1.9	1.9	1.9
1999	1.9	1.9	1.9	1.9	2.0	2.0	2.1	2.0	2.0	2.0	2.0	1.9	1.9
2000	1.9	1.9	2.0	2.0	2.0	2.0	2.1	2.0	2.0	2.0	2.0	1.9	1.9
2001	1.8	1.8	1.8	1.8	1.8	1.9	1.9	1.8	1.8	1.8	1.8	1.8	1.8
2002	1.9	1.9	1.9	1.9	2.0	2.0	2.0	1.9	1.8	1.8	1.8	1.8	1.9
2003	1.8	1.8	1.8	1.8	1.9	2.0	1.9	1.9	1.9	1.9	1.9	1.9	1.9

Employment by Industry: New Jersey—*Continued*

(Numbers in thousands. Not seasonally adjusted.)

Industry	January	February	March	April	May	June	July	August	September	October	November	December	Annual Average
VINELAND-MILLVILLE-BRIDGETON—*Continued*													
Government													
1990	12.4	12.6	12.7	12.8	12.8	12.9	12.5	12.3	12.4	12.8	13.0	13.0	12.6
1991	12.9	12.9	12.9	12.9	12.9	12.8	12.4	12.2	12.3	12.6	12.5	12.5	12.6
1992	12.5	12.7	12.8	12.9	12.8	12.9	12.6	12.4	12.3	12.6	12.8	12.8	12.6
1993	12.7	12.8	12.8	12.9	12.8	12.9	12.0	11.9	12.6	12.7	12.9	13.0	12.6
1994	12.9	12.8	12.9	13.1	13.1	13.1	12.2	12.2	12.5	12.7	12.9	13.0	12.7
1995	12.7	12.8	13.1	13.0	12.9	13.0	12.3	12.2	12.5	12.8	12.8	12.9	12.7
1996	12.7	12.8	12.9	12.9	13.0	13.0	12.2	12.1	12.7	12.7	12.7	12.8	12.7
1997	12.7	12.8	12.9	13.1	13.2	13.2	12.3	12.2	13.0	13.4	13.6	13.7	13.0
1998	13.5	13.7	14.1	14.3	14.4	14.1	13.0	13.0	13.7	14.1	14.1	14.2	13.8
1999	14.1	14.3	14.5	14.6	14.6	14.6	13.5	13.6	14.1	14.7	14.7	14.8	14.3
2000	14.4	14.7	14.9	14.8	15.0	14.7	12.9	12.6	14.0	14.5	14.6	14.6	14.3
2001	14.4	14.6	14.7	14.7	14.7	14.7	12.9	12.8	14.2	14.7	14.9	15.1	14.3
2002	14.8	15.1	15.3	15.3	15.4	15.3	13.1	13.1	14.7	15.1	15.4	15.2	14.8
2003	14.9	15.2	15.2	15.3	15.3	15.3	13.6	13.4	14.9	15.4	15.5	15.5	15.0
Federal government													
1990	0.7	0.8	0.8	0.8	0.8	0.8	0.8	0.7	0.7	0.7	0.7	0.7	0.7
1991	0.7	0.7	0.7	0.7	0.7	0.7	0.7	0.7	0.7	0.7	0.7	0.7	0.7
1992	0.7	0.8	0.8	0.8	0.8	0.8	0.8	0.8	0.7	0.7	0.8	0.8	0.7
1993	0.8	0.8	0.8	0.8	0.8	0.8	0.8	0.8	0.8	0.8	0.8	0.8	0.8
1994	0.8	0.8	0.8	0.8	0.8	0.8	0.8	0.8	0.7	0.7	0.7	0.7	0.7
1995	0.7	0.7	0.8	0.8	0.8	0.8	0.8	0.8	0.8	0.8	0.8	0.8	0.7
1996	0.8	0.8	0.8	0.8	0.8	0.8	0.8	0.8	0.8	0.8	0.8	0.8	0.8
1997	0.8	0.8	0.8	0.8	0.8	0.8	0.8	0.8	0.8	0.8	0.8	0.8	0.8
1998	0.8	0.7	0.8	0.8	0.8	0.8	0.8	0.8	0.8	0.7	0.7	0.7	0.7
1999	0.8	0.8	0.8	0.8	0.8	0.7	0.8	0.8	0.8	0.8	0.8	0.8	0.7
2000	0.8	0.8	1.0	0.9	1.2	1.0	0.9	0.8	0.8	0.8	0.8	0.8	0.8
2001	0.8	0.8	0.8	0.8	0.8	0.8	0.8	0.8	0.8	0.8	0.8	0.8	0.7
2002	0.8	0.8	0.8	0.8	0.8	0.8	0.8	0.8	0.8	0.8	0.8	0.8	0.8
2003	0.7	0.7	0.7	0.7	0.7	0.7	0.7	0.7	0.7	0.7	0.7	0.7	0.7
State government													
1990	4.5	4.5	4.6	4.6	4.6	4.6	4.7	4.7	4.7	4.7	4.8	4.8	4.6
1991	4.8	4.7	4.7	4.7	4.6	4.5	4.5	4.4	4.3	4.3	4.2	4.2	4.4
1992	4.2	4.2	4.3	4.3	4.3	4.3	4.3	4.3	4.2	4.2	4.2	4.1	4.2
1993	4.1	4.1	4.1	4.1	4.1	4.1	4.1	4.2	4.2	4.2	4.2	4.2	4.1
1994	4.2	4.1	4.1	4.2	4.2	4.2	4.2	4.2	4.2	4.2	4.2	4.2	4.1
1995	4.3	4.3	4.4	4.4	4.4	4.4	4.4	4.4	4.3	4.3	4.3	4.3	4.3
1996	4.3	4.3	4.3	4.3	4.3	4.3	4.3	4.3	4.2	4.1	4.1	4.1	4.2
1997	4.2	4.2	4.3	4.4	4.4	4.5	4.5	4.5	4.6	4.7	4.8	4.9	4.5
1998	4.9	5.1	5.2	5.3	5.3	5.1	5.1	5.1	5.1	5.1	5.1	5.1	5.1
1999	5.0	5.0	5.1	5.2	5.2	5.2	5.3	5.3	5.3	5.2	5.1	5.2	5.1
2000	5.1	5.1	5.1	5.0	5.0	5.0	5.0	5.0	5.0	5.0	5.0	4.9	5.0
2001	5.0	5.0	5.0	5.0	5.0	5.0	5.0	5.0	5.0	5.0	5.0	5.1	5.0
2002	5.1	5.1	5.2	5.2	5.2	5.2	5.1	5.1	5.1	5.1	5.2	5.2	5.2
2003	5.2	5.2	5.2	5.2	5.2	5.3	5.2	5.2	5.3	5.3	5.3	5.3	5.2
Local government													
1990	7.2	7.3	7.3	7.4	7.4	7.5	7.0	6.9	7.0	7.4	7.5	7.5	7.2
1991	7.4	7.5	7.5	7.5	7.6	7.6	7.2	7.1	7.3	7.6	7.6	7.6	7.4
1992	7.6	7.7	7.7	7.8	7.7	7.8	7.5	7.3	7.4	7.7	7.8	7.9	7.6
1993	7.8	7.9	7.9	8.0	7.9	8.0	7.1	6.9	7.6	7.7	7.9	8.0	7.7
1994	7.9	7.9	8.0	8.1	8.1	8.1	7.2	7.2	7.6	7.8	8.0	8.1	7.8
1995	7.7	7.8	7.9	7.8	7.7	7.8	7.1	7.0	7.4	7.7	7.7	7.8	7.6
1996	7.6	7.7	7.8	7.8	7.9	7.9	7.1	7.0	7.7	7.8	7.8	7.9	7.6
1997	7.7	7.8	7.8	7.9	8.0	7.9	7.0	6.9	7.6	7.9	8.0	8.0	7.7
1998	7.8	7.9	8.1	8.2	8.3	8.2	7.1	7.1	7.8	8.3	8.3	8.4	7.9
1999	8.3	8.5	8.6	8.6	8.6	8.7	7.4	7.5	8.0	8.7	8.8	8.8	8.3
2000	8.5	8.8	8.8	8.9	8.8	8.7	7.0	6.8	8.2	8.7	8.8	8.9	8.4
2001	8.6	8.8	8.9	8.9	8.9	8.9	7.1	7.0	8.4	8.9	9.1	9.2	8.5
2002	8.9	9.2	9.3	9.3	9.4	9.3	7.2	7.2	8.8	9.2	9.4	9.2	8.9
2003	9.0	9.3	9.3	9.4	9.4	9.3	7.7	7.5	8.9	9.4	9.5	9.5	9.0

Average Weekly Hours by Industry: New Jersey

(Not seasonally adjusted.)

Industry	January	February	March	April	May	June	July	August	September	October	November	December	Annual Average
STATEWIDE													
Manufacturing													
2001	40.2	40.5	40.6	40.1	40.7	40.9	40.6	41.0	40.5	40.8	40.6	41.3	40.6
2002	40.3	40.3	40.9	40.5	40.7	41.4	40.7	41.1	41.1	41.3	41.3	41.5	40.9
2003	40.2	39.9	40.6	40.7	41.1	41.3	40.9	40.9	41.2	41.3	41.4	42.5	41.0
Information													
2002	. . .	. . .	. . .	35.6	35.0	37.9	35.6	37.8	38.3	37.6	37.6	38.2	36.8
2003	37.5	37.5	37.4	37.2	37.4	38.2	37.7	37.7	37.5	37.4	37.9	36.7	37.5

. . . = Not available.

Average Hourly Earnings by Industry: New Jersey

(Dollars, not seasonally adjusted.)

Industry	January	February	March	April	May	June	July	August	September	October	November	December	Annual Average
STATEWIDE													
Manufacturing													
2001	14.48	14.67	14.68	14.78	14.80	14.49	14.58	14.66	14.82	14.82	14.88	15.22	14.74
2002	14.99	15.02	14.95	15.12	15.10	15.02	15.29	15.12	15.22	15.52	15.49	15.48	15.19
2003	15.09	15.02	15.13	15.25	15.47	15.56	15.69	15.61	15.75	15.59	15.70	15.60	15.46
Information													
2002	. . .	. . .	. . .	20.32	20.81	21.12	23.01	24.87	25.49	25.58	27.29	27.96	23.20
2003	27.11	27.31	26.97	26.79	27.30	28.42	27.23	29.02	29.04	28.66	28.81	28.49	27.96

. . . = Not available.

Average Weekly Earnings by Industry: New Jersey

(Dollars, not seasonally adjusted.)

Industry	January	February	March	April	May	June	July	August	September	October	November	December	Annual Average
STATEWIDE													
Manufacturing													
2001	582.10	594.14	596.01	592.68	602.36	592.64	591.95	601.06	600.21	604.66	604.13	628.59	598.44
2002	604.10	605.31	611.46	612.36	614.57	621.83	622.30	621.43	625.54	640.98	639.74	642.42	621.27
2003	606.62	599.30	614.28	620.68	635.82	642.63	641.72	638.45	648.90	643.87	649.98	663.00	633.86
Information													
2002	. . .	. . .	. . .	723.39	728.35	800.45	819.16	940.09	976.27	961.81	1026.10	1068.07	853.76
2003	1016.63	1024.13	1008.68	996.59	1021.02	1085.64	1026.57	1094.05	1089.00	1071.88	1091.90	1045.58	1048.50

. . . = Not available.

NEW MEXICO AT A GLANCE

(Population and total nonfarm employment numbers in thousands)

Population, Census 2000:	1,819.0
Total nonfarm employment, 2003:	775.5
Change in total nonfarm employment	
(Number)	
1990–2003:	195.1
1990–2001:	176.8
2001–2003:	18.3
(Compound annual rate of change)	
1990–2003:	2.3%
1990–2001:	2.4%
2001–2003:	1.2%
Unemployment rate	
1990:	6.8%
2001:	4.9%
2003:	5.9%

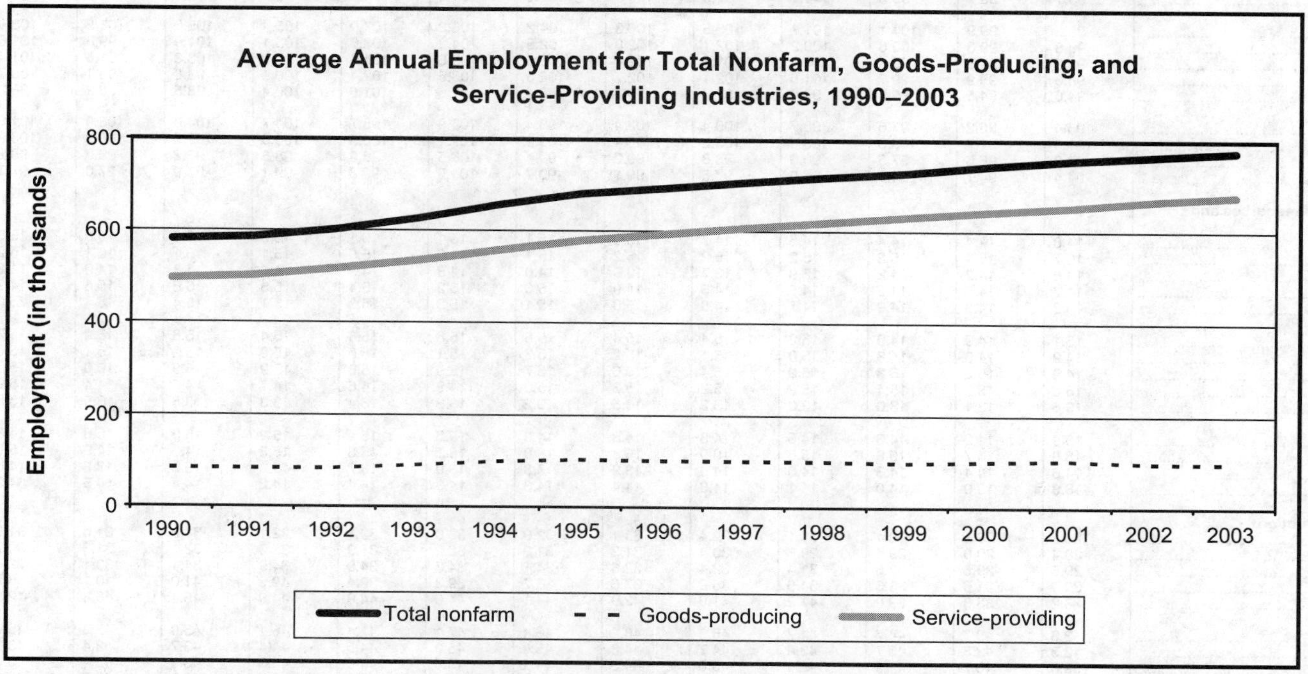

Total nonfarm payroll employment grew rapidly following the 1990–1991 recession, but slowed in the mid-1990s when employment in the goods-producing sector dropped and growth in the service-providing sector slowed. Between 1995 and 1999, over 5,000 jobs were lost in the goods-producing industries. Construction accounted for 2,100 of the losses and natural resources and mining for 2,000. A modest recovery in nonfarm employment began in 2001 and continued through 2003 due to an increase in employment in the service-providing sector. However, goods-producing employment continued to decline in 2002 and 2003 after small increases in 2000 and 2001.

Employment by Industry: New Mexico

(Numbers in thousands. Not seasonally adjusted.)

Industry	January	February	March	April	May	June	July	August	September	October	November	December	Annual Average
STATEWIDE													
Total nonfarm													
1990	561.2	565.9	572.0	578.8	586.1	587.7	579.0	582.8	587.6	587.1	590.4	586.2	580.4
1991	570.8	575.9	578.8	582.1	587.8	585.8	584.3	588.2	595.2	591.7	591.4	592.9	585.4
1992	579.7	584.6	590.5	596.4	601.7	603.8	600.4	603.9	611.7	613.6	617.3	614.5	601.5
1993	600.0	607.2	613.6	621.7	624.6	626.2	622.5	628.1	639.8	642.4	641.9	646.3	626.1
1994	630.8	638.2	644.0	648.9	654.0	659.2	658.1	661.1	669.9	669.6	675.1	678.7	657.3
1995	665.2	673.1	676.4	676.4	683.4	686.9	679.0	684.6	691.5	689.2	690.8	692.6	682.4
1996	675.4	683.6	686.9	690.3	696.7	698.1	692.6	695.7	701.1	702.7	704.3	707.2	694.5
1997	685.9	694.5	698.8	702.1	709.9	711.7	708.3	712.0	716.8	719.1	719.3	723.5	708.4
1998	702.1	711.0	716.2	719.1	723.4	724.8	718.3	721.1	726.0	724.3	724.9	728.7	719.9
1999	710.1	716.4	722.6	726.7	730.6	733.3	727.4	733.3	740.1	738.1	738.1	740.0	729.7
2000	722.5	730.2	738.0	741.0	747.3	746.2	742.3	748.3	754.9	752.3	755.5	759.1	744.8
2001	739.8	748.1	755.1	756.4	762.3	762.5	754.7	759.6	763.9	759.9	761.1	762.6	757.2
2002	748.5	754.1	760.9	764.2	770.0	769.4	763.7	768.3	774.1	770.6	773.7	776.2	766.1
2003	759.5	765.2	769.9	772.8	777.8	776.8	772.4	777.4	781.8	782.5	784.1	786.1	775.5
Total private													
1990	416.9	415.3	420.3	425.6	432.7	439.3	436.2	440.3	437.1	434.5	434.8	435.4	430.7
1991	423.8	422.8	425.8	427.2	432.1	436.4	438.3	442.1	440.3	435.9	435.2	437.8	433.1
1992	428.3	427.9	433.5	438.2	443.0	447.2	452.2	455.9	454.2	454.7	453.7	456.3	445.4
1993	445.3	447.2	453.3	459.0	462.0	468.9	471.1	477.1	478.3	479.1	479.5	484.0	467.0
1994	471.8	474.1	479.6	484.0	489.1	497.1	501.1	506.2	505.6	503.1	506.9	512.2	494.2
1995	503.3	505.1	508.5	508.5	514.6	523.1	518.7	524.2	523.7	519.3	520.4	522.0	515.9
1996	509.9	511.9	515.2	517.6	523.8	528.6	527.4	530.6	527.8	526.6	527.4	529.9	523.0
1997	514.2	517.0	521.8	523.7	530.2	536.3	536.1	540.6	538.2	539.1	538.9	541.9	531.5
1998	526.5	529.7	533.5	538.8	542.9	547.9	546.0	548.9	548.2	544.0	543.8	548.2	541.5
1999	534.4	536.3	540.6	544.3	548.3	555.4	553.6	557.6	557.6	554.7	553.6	556.9	549.4
2000	543.8	546.3	551.4	554.5	559.3	566.9	565.1	570.8	570.8	567.6	570.8	573.5	561.7
2001	560.5	562.5	567.7	568.8	574.2	578.4	576.2	579.6	574.6	571.6	572.6	573.8	571.7
2002	563.4	563.4	568.8	572.1	576.9	579.1	579.2	582.5	580.3	576.7	579.0	581.0	575.2
2003	569.0	569.9	573.4	575.5	581.2	583.2	584.4	588.3	585.0	583.4	584.2	585.8	580.3
Goods-producing													
1990	81.2	80.3	81.6	82.8	85.0	86.3	86.1	87.5	87.1	87.0	86.3	85.1	84.6
1991	81.7	81.8	82.0	82.0	83.1	84.2	84.7	85.6	85.6	85.1	84.4	83.3	83.6
1992	79.8	79.4	80.8	81.5	82.5	83.1	85.2	87.1	87.8	88.5	87.4	86.2	84.1
1993	82.7	83.4	85.3	87.2	88.8	91.2	92.7	95.0	95.8	97.9	97.3	96.3	91.1
1994	93.1	93.7	95.3	96.7	97.5	100.1	101.8	103.5	104.1	103.1	103.0	102.7	99.5
1995	99.5	99.9	101.1	101.7	103.5	106.3	104.2	106.2	107.0	105.4	105.0	103.5	103.6
1996	98.8	99.3	100.6	100.2	102.1	102.8	102.8	104.2	103.6	103.1	101.9	99.9	101.6
1997	95.9	97.3	98.8	99.0	101.0	102.4	102.6	105.6	104.6	105.1	103.3	101.6	101.4
1998	98.3	98.9	99.7	101.0	102.1	102.7	102.3	103.6	102.4	100.9	98.6	98.1	100.7
1999	94.6	94.5	95.3	96.9	97.5	99.4	100.1	101.5	101.6	100.4	98.5	98.2	98.2
2000	95.4	96.2	97.6	98.7	100.4	102.4	103.4	105.9	105.7	104.7	104.0	103.9	101.5
2001	101.6	101.7	103.3	103.8	105.2	106.4	105.9	107.1	105.3	103.6	102.3	100.9	103.9
2002	97.6	96.6	97.5	98.0	98.8	99.2	99.4	100.5	98.9	98.5	97.2	96.3	98.2
2003	94.4	94.1	94.9	96.0	97.6	99.1	99.7	101.0	99.8	99.1	97.8	97.0	97.5
Natural resources and mining													
1990	14.8	14.4	14.4	14.5	14.7	15.0	15.1	15.1	15.1	15.6	16.0	16.0	15.0
1991	15.7	15.4	15.3	15.2	15.2	15.2	15.1	15.0	15.0	15.1	15.1	15.1	15.2
1992	14.6	14.2	14.2	13.9	13.7	13.9	14.0	14.3	14.3	14.6	14.8	14.9	14.2
1993	14.7	14.5	14.5	14.5	14.5	14.9	15.0	15.2	15.4	15.5	15.5	15.6	14.9
1994	15.2	14.9	14.9	14.7	14.8	15.0	15.1	15.3	15.3	15.1	15.4	15.4	15.0
1995	15.1	14.9	14.9	15.2	15.4	15.4	15.8	15.8	15.6	15.4	15.5	15.2	15.3
1996	14.9	14.9	14.8	15.0	15.1	15.2	15.3	15.1	15.0	15.0	15.2	15.1	15.0
1997	14.9	15.2	15.3	15.2	15.4	15.6	15.7	15.9	15.8	15.9	15.9	16.0	15.5
1998	15.6	15.5	15.4	15.2	15.2	15.3	15.0	14.9	14.6	14.7	14.6	14.4	15.0
1999	13.6	13.1	13.0	13.0	13.2	13.5	13.2	13.3	13.4	13.3	13.5	13.5	13.3
2000	13.9	14.2	14.3	14.6	14.8	14.8	14.9	15.3	15.4	15.2	15.3	15.6	14.8
2001	15.6	15.7	15.8	15.8	16.0	15.8	16.0	16.1	15.8	15.3	14.9	14.9	15.6
2002	14.6	14.4	14.3	14.0	14.0	13.9	13.8	13.9	13.7	13.9	13.8	13.8	14.0
2003	13.8	13.9	14.0	14.1	14.3	14.4	14.3	14.3	14.4	14.2	14.4	14.5	14.2
Construction													
1990	29.8	29.5	30.4	31.1	32.4	33.1	32.9	33.0	32.1	32.1	31.8	31.0	31.6
1991	28.4	29.0	29.4	29.3	30.4	31.3	31.9	32.2	31.9	32.3	32.1	31.3	30.7
1992	29.5	29.6	30.6	31.4	32.4	32.6	34.1	34.3	34.0	34.9	34.1	33.1	32.5
1993	30.9	31.6	33.3	34.9	36.2	37.6	38.7	39.3	39.4	40.9	41.0	40.1	36.9
1994	38.2	38.8	39.9	41.2	41.6	42.9	44.1	44.6	44.9	44.9	45.4	45.8	42.6
1995	43.3	43.7	44.7	44.7	46.0	48.1	46.4	47.1	47.4	46.1	45.9	45.3	45.7
1996	42.3	42.8	43.7	43.3	44.7	44.8	45.0	45.0	44.5	44.4	43.7	42.4	43.8
1997	39.8	40.7	41.9	42.4	43.6	44.3	44.2	45.0	44.0	44.8	43.9	42.4	43.0
1998	40.5	41.1	42.0	43.5	44.4	44.7	44.9	44.8	43.9	43.2	42.2	42.2	43.1
1999	40.5	40.8	41.9	43.3	43.6	44.8	45.4	45.4	45.5	45.2	43.9	43.5	43.6
2000	41.1	41.4	42.5	43.4	44.4	45.7	46.4	47.2	47.0	46.7	46.5	46.3	44.8
2001	44.5	44.7	45.9	46.7	47.9	49.4	49.1	49.4	48.2	47.6	48.0	46.9	47.4
2002	44.7	44.3	45.1	45.8	46.3	46.5	46.1	46.8	45.8	46.2	46.0	45.6	45.8
2003	44.4	44.2	44.9	46.1	47.3	48.2	48.6	49.1	48.1	48.3	47.6	47.1	47.0

Employment by Industry: New Mexico—*Continued*

(Numbers in thousands. Not seasonally adjusted.)

Industry	January	February	March	April	May	June	July	August	September	October	November	December	Annual Average
STATEWIDE—*Continued*													
Manufacturing													
1990	36.6	36.4	36.8	37.2	37.9	38.2	38.1	39.4	39.9	39.3	38.5	38.1	38.0
1991	37.6	37.4	37.3	37.5	37.5	37.7	37.7	38.4	38.7	37.7	37.2	36.9	37.6
1992	35.7	35.6	36.0	36.2	36.4	36.6	37.1	38.5	39.5	39.0	38.5	38.2	37.2
1993	37.1	37.3	37.5	37.8	38.1	38.7	39.0	40.5	41.0	41.5	40.8	40.6	39.1
1994	39.7	40.0	40.5	40.8	41.1	42.2	42.6	43.6	43.9	43.1	42.2	41.5	41.7
1995	41.1	41.3	41.5	41.8	42.1	42.8	42.0	43.3	44.0	43.9	43.6	43.0	42.5
1996	41.6	41.6	42.1	41.9	42.3	42.8	42.5	44.1	44.1	43.7	43.0	42.4	42.6
1997	41.2	41.4	41.6	41.4	42.0	42.5	42.7	44.7	44.8	44.4	43.5	43.2	42.7
1998	42.2	42.3	42.3	42.3	42.5	42.7	42.4	43.9	43.9	43.0	41.8	41.5	42.5
1999	40.5	40.6	40.4	40.6	40.7	41.1	41.5	42.8	42.7	41.9	41.1	41.2	41.2
2000	40.4	40.6	40.8	40.7	41.2	41.9	42.1	43.4	43.3	42.8	42.2	42.0	41.7
2001	41.5	41.3	41.6	41.3	41.3	41.2	40.8	41.6	41.3	40.7	39.4	39.1	40.9
2002	38.3	37.9	38.1	38.2	38.5	38.8	39.5	39.8	39.4	38.4	37.4	36.9	38.4
2003	36.2	36.0	36.0	35.8	36.0	36.5	36.8	37.6	37.3	36.6	35.8	35.4	36.3
Service-providing													
1990	480.0	485.6	490.4	496.0	501.1	501.4	492.9	495.3	500.5	500.1	504.1	501.1	495.7
1991	489.1	494.1	496.8	500.1	504.7	501.6	499.6	502.6	509.6	506.6	507.0	509.6	501.7
1992	499.9	505.2	509.7	514.9	519.2	520.7	515.2	516.8	523.9	525.1	529.9	528.3	517.4
1993	517.3	523.8	528.3	534.5	535.8	535.0	529.8	533.1	544.0	544.5	544.6	550.0	535.0
1994	537.7	544.5	548.7	552.2	556.5	559.1	556.3	557.6	565.8	566.5	572.1	576.0	557.7
1995	565.7	573.2	575.3	574.7	579.9	580.6	574.8	578.4	584.5	583.8	585.8	589.1	578.8
1996	576.6	584.3	586.3	590.1	594.6	595.3	589.8	591.5	597.5	599.6	602.4	607.3	592.9
1997	590.0	597.2	600.0	603.1	608.9	609.3	605.7	606.4	612.2	614.0	616.0	621.9	607.0
1998	603.8	612.1	616.5	618.1	621.3	622.1	616.0	617.5	623.6	623.4	626.3	630.6	619.2
1999	615.5	621.9	627.3	629.8	633.1	633.9	627.3	631.8	638.5	637.7	639.6	641.8	631.5
2000	627.1	634.0	640.4	642.3	646.9	643.8	638.9	642.4	649.2	647.6	651.5	655.2	643.2
2001	638.2	646.4	651.8	652.6	657.1	656.1	648.8	652.5	658.6	656.3	658.8	661.7	653.2
2002	650.9	657.5	663.4	666.2	671.2	670.2	664.3	667.8	675.2	672.1	676.5	679.9	667.9
2003	665.1	671.1	675.0	676.8	680.2	677.7	672.7	676.4	682.0	683.4	686.3	689.1	678.0
Trade, transportation, and utilities													
1990	116.2	115.1	115.6	116.0	117.8	118.1	117.0	118.0	118.1	118.1	119.7	120.8	117.5
1991	114.4	112.5	113.0	113.1	114.3	114.3	114.2	115.1	115.5	115.5	116.9	118.6	114.7
1992	114.8	114.0	114.2	116.0	117.4	117.6	118.0	118.8	119.5	120.5	121.9	124.2	118.0
1993	119.9	119.2	119.7	120.7	120.7	120.8	121.3	122.4	122.8	123.7	125.8	128.5	122.1
1994	123.1	122.5	123.1	122.8	125.0	125.3	125.4	126.6	127.2	127.9	131.2	134.4	126.2
1995	129.4	129.1	129.9	128.9	130.4	131.2	130.6	132.0	132.3	133.7	135.0	137.0	131.6
1996	130.6	129.8	130.3	130.6	132.3	132.0	132.2	133.8	133.4	133.7	136.4	137.8	132.7
1997	133.0	131.9	132.2	131.9	132.8	133.4	133.7	134.3	134.9	136.4	138.7	140.7	134.4
1998	134.8	134.2	134.8	134.9	135.5	136.3	135.1	135.4	136.0	136.3	138.1	140.5	135.9
1999	135.0	134.3	135.2	134.7	135.6	135.9	134.9	135.8	136.4	136.8	138.7	140.4	136.1
2000	134.8	134.0	134.4	135.5	137.1	137.7	136.3	137.6	137.8	138.4	141.2	142.3	137.2
2001	136.4	134.4	134.7	134.3	135.5	135.4	135.0	135.8	134.8	134.7	137.0	138.5	135.5
2002	133.9	132.7	133.1	133.7	135.3	135.7	135.0	136.0	135.8	135.9	138.2	139.9	135.4
2003	134.1	133.3	134.1	134.2	135.4	135.0	134.9	136.1	135.7	135.7	138.3	140.0	135.6
Wholesale trade													
1990	21.7	21.7	21.8	22.0	22.2	22.3	21.8	22.0	21.8	22.0	22.0	22.0	21.9
1991	20.7	20.7	20.6	20.4	20.5	20.6	20.9	20.8	21.0	21.2	21.1	21.3	20.8
1992	20.9	20.9	21.1	21.3	21.5	21.7	21.7	21.7	21.7	21.9	22.0	22.1	21.5
1993	21.6	21.6	21.8	22.0	22.1	22.4	22.4	22.4	22.4	22.7	22.8	23.0	22.2
1994	22.6	22.6	22.8	22.9	23.1	23.5	23.6	23.7	23.6	23.7	23.9	24.2	23.3
1995	23.5	23.7	23.9	23.8	23.9	24.2	23.9	24.1	24.0	23.9	24.0	23.9	23.9
1996	23.5	23.3	23.5	23.6	23.8	24.0	23.7	23.7	23.7	23.4	23.6	23.6	23.6
1997	23.2	23.3	23.5	23.6	23.8	23.9	23.7	23.7	23.6	23.6	23.6	23.6	23.5
1998	23.2	23.3	23.4	23.3	23.2	23.3	23.0	22.8	22.6	22.7	22.6	22.6	23.0
1999	22.3	22.3	22.4	22.7	22.7	22.9	22.4	22.3	22.2	22.2	22.2	22.2	22.4
2000	21.9	22.0	22.3	22.6	22.9	23.0	22.8	22.9	22.9	22.9	22.8	22.8	22.6
2001	22.7	22.7	22.8	22.7	22.9	23.1	23.0	23.0	23.0	22.7	22.7	22.7	22.8
2002	22.5	22.5	22.5	22.5	22.6	22.8	22.9	22.8	22.5	22.5	22.5	22.5	22.6
2003	21.9	21.9	22.2	22.2	22.2	22.2	22.3	22.4	22.1	21.8	22.0	22.0	22.1
Retail trade													
1990	72.3	71.2	71.5	72.1	73.7	74.5	73.8	74.3	73.9	73.7	75.2	76.2	73.5
1991	71.8	69.9	70.5	70.8	71.9	72.4	72.6	73.4	72.4	72.7	74.2	75.4	72.3
1992	72.1	71.2	71.3	73.1	74.1	74.7	75.2	75.5	75.6	76.3	77.3	78.9	74.6
1993	75.8	74.9	75.1	76.3	76.0	76.7	77.6	78.3	77.9	78.1	79.8	82.0	77.3
1994	78.7	78.0	78.3	78.8	79.7	80.4	80.7	81.3	81.2	81.4	83.7	86.1	80.6
1995	82.3	81.5	81.9	81.7	83.1	84.3	84.3	85.3	84.8	86.0	87.3	89.2	84.3
1996	85.1	84.0	84.4	84.7	86.1	86.7	87.3	88.1	87.5	87.4	89.9	91.1	86.8
1997	87.3	85.8	85.8	85.7	86.3	87.6	88.2	88.6	88.0	89.2	91.5	93.3	88.1
1998	88.4	87.6	88.0	88.3	88.7	90.1	89.6	89.6	89.8	89.9	91.8	94.0	89.6
1999	89.3	88.7	89.3	88.6	89.4	90.0	90.2	90.5	90.4	90.8	92.8	94.6	90.3
2000	89.7	88.7	88.9	89.2	90.2	91.2	90.6	91.1	90.7	91.2	94.1	95.2	90.9
2001	90.2	88.7	88.8	88.7	89.6	90.1	90.0	90.1	88.7	88.8	91.3	92.7	89.8
2002	88.7	87.6	88.2	88.5	89.9	90.8	90.1	90.4	90.2	90.1	92.4	94.1	90.1
2003	89.5	88.7	89.2	89.2	90.3	90.4	90.4	91.0	90.5	90.7	93.2	94.9	90.7

Employment by Industry: New Mexico—*Continued*

(Numbers in thousands. Not seasonally adjusted.)

Industry	January	February	March	April	May	June	July	August	September	October	November	December	Annual Average
STATEWIDE—*Continued*													
Transportation and utilities													
1990	22.2	22.2	22.3	21.9	21.9	21.3	21.4	21.7	22.4	22.4	22.5	22.6	22.0
1991	21.9	21.9	21.9	21.9	21.9	21.3	20.7	20.9	22.1	21.6	21.6	21.9	21.6
1992	21.8	21.9	21.8	21.6	21.8	21.2	21.1	21.6	22.2	22.3	22.6	23.2	21.9
1993	22.5	22.7	22.8	22.4	22.6	21.7	21.3	21.7	22.5	22.9	23.2	23.5	22.4
1994	21.8	21.9	22.0	21.1	22.2	21.4	21.1	21.6	22.4	22.8	23.6	24.1	22.1
1995	23.6	23.9	24.1	23.4	23.4	22.7	22.4	22.6	23.5	23.8	23.7	23.9	23.4
1996	22.0	22.5	22.4	22.3	22.4	21.3	21.2	22.0	22.2	22.9	22.9	23.1	22.2
1997	22.5	22.8	22.9	22.6	22.7	21.9	21.8	22.0	23.3	23.6	23.6	23.8	22.7
1998	23.2	23.3	23.4	23.3	23.6	22.9	22.5	23.0	23.6	23.7	23.7	23.9	23.3
1999	23.4	23.3	23.5	23.4	23.5	23.0	22.3	23.0	23.8	23.8	23.7	23.6	23.3
2000	23.2	23.3	23.2	23.7	24.0	23.5	22.9	23.6	24.2	24.3	24.3	24.3	23.7
2001	23.5	23.0	23.1	22.9	23.0	22.2	22.0	22.7	23.1	23.2	23.0	23.1	22.9
2002	22.7	22.6	22.4	22.7	22.8	22.1	22.0	22.8	23.1	23.3	23.3	23.3	22.8
2003	22.7	22.7	22.7	22.8	22.9	22.4	22.2	22.7	23.1	23.2	23.1	23.1	22.8
Information													
1990	10.7	10.7	10.6	10.6	10.7	10.7	10.9	10.9	10.8	10.4	10.4	10.5	10.6
1991	10.0	9.9	10.1	10.0	10.1	10.2	10.3	10.5	10.4	10.3	10.1	10.2	10.1
1992	10.1	10.0	10.1	10.1	10.1	10.3	10.4	10.4	10.3	10.4	10.4	10.6	10.2
1993	10.4	10.4	10.5	10.6	10.8	10.7	10.8	11.2	11.2	10.9	11.1	10.8	10.7
1994	11.8	12.0	12.1	12.0	12.2	12.7	12.8	12.8	12.7	12.6	12.9	13.0	12.4
1995	12.4	12.4	12.6	12.5	12.7	12.9	12.3	12.4	12.5	12.4	12.5	12.9	12.5
1996	12.8	13.0	13.0	12.7	12.8	13.3	13.3	12.6	12.4	12.6	12.8	13.0	12.8
1997	12.5	12.5	12.8	12.7	13.1	13.4	13.4	13.4	13.3	13.7	14.1	14.5	13.2
1998	13.9	13.9	14.0	13.8	14.0	14.1	14.3	14.8	15.1	14.6	15.2	15.4	14.4
1999	15.1	15.1	15.3	15.7	16.1	16.8	16.3	16.4	16.4	16.1	16.3	16.8	16.0
2000	16.3	16.3	16.4	16.3	16.4	16.7	16.9	17.2	17.3	16.7	16.7	17.2	16.7
2001	17.3	17.6	17.5	16.9	17.1	17.0	16.8	16.9	17.0	16.9	17.0	17.0	17.1
2002	16.8	17.1	17.2	17.0	17.0	16.8	17.0	16.8	16.6	16.4	16.8	16.8	16.9
2003	16.3	16.1	16.3	15.9	16.1	16.1	16.0	15.8	15.8	15.6	15.6	15.9	16.0
Financial activities													
1990	27.5	27.2	27.4	27.3	27.5	27.9	27.8	27.8	27.6	27.9	27.8	27.9	27.6
1991	27.4	27.2	27.3	27.2	27.3	27.6	28.1	28.3	28.0	27.2	27.2	27.6	27.5
1992	27.6	27.6	27.8	27.8	28.0	28.3	28.6	28.8	28.6	28.5	28.4	28.7	28.2
1993	28.7	28.8	28.9	29.3	29.2	29.6	29.9	30.0	29.6	29.9	29.9	30.3	29.5
1994	29.8	30.0	30.0	30.1	30.3	30.5	30.7	30.8	30.5	30.4	30.5	31.0	30.3
1995	30.2	30.1	30.2	30.8	30.9	30.9	30.6	30.8	30.5	31.2	31.4	31.5	30.7
1996	31.0	31.1	31.4	31.6	31.8	32.0	32.4	32.5	32.3	32.1	32.1	32.5	31.9
1997	31.9	32.0	32.3	32.6	32.6	32.9	33.2	33.3	32.9	32.8	32.9	33.2	32.7
1998	32.7	32.9	33.0	33.1	33.2	33.6	33.7	33.8	33.9	33.8	34.1	34.4	33.5
1999	34.2	34.1	34.3	33.9	34.0	34.3	34.4	34.2	34.1	33.7	33.6	34.0	34.0
2000	33.5	33.5	33.6	33.3	33.4	33.5	33.4	33.3	33.2	33.3	33.5	33.8	33.4
2001	33.1	33.3	33.4	33.3	33.3	33.5	33.5	33.4	33.1	33.1	33.1	33.5	33.3
2002	33.4	33.3	33.4	33.3	33.3	33.4	33.7	33.9	33.6	33.4	33.5	33.8	33.5
2003	33.3	33.4	33.4	33.5	33.7	34.1	34.3	34.5	34.2	34.1	34.0	34.1	33.9
Professional and business services													
1990	54.5	54.4	55.4	57.3	57.7	59.2	57.9	58.0	58.0	57.8	57.4	58.4	57.1
1991	59.2	59.9	60.3	60.1	60.6	61.1	60.5	61.1	61.5	61.7	60.7	60.9	60.6
1992	60.4	60.5	61.7	62.1	62.2	63.3	64.3	63.9	63.1	62.2	61.9	61.8	62.2
1993	61.5	61.9	63.3	63.4	63.7	65.2	64.6	64.9	65.7	65.5	65.2	66.1	64.2
1994	64.2	65.2	66.2	66.9	67.0	68.6	69.2	69.9	70.4	70.3	70.6	71.1	68.3
1995	71.8	72.8	73.4	72.8	73.5	75.0	74.2	74.6	74.4	72.8	73.1	73.5	73.4
1996	73.6	74.0	73.6	75.0	75.6	76.4	75.5	75.5	75.5	75.2	75.3	75.9	75.0
1997	73.5	73.9	74.1	75.7	76.2	77.0	76.8	76.5	76.7	76.7	76.0	76.2	75.7
1998	75.5	76.3	76.9	78.0	78.3	79.4	78.9	79.8	79.8	79.7	79.4	80.4	78.5
1999	78.2	79.0	80.1	80.3	81.0	82.4	82.4	83.4	83.7	84.0	83.8	84.1	81.8
2000	82.7	83.4	84.1	85.4	85.3	86.7	86.5	87.0	87.7	87.6	88.6	89.0	86.1
2001	86.4	87.4	88.4	88.7	88.9	89.7	89.3	89.4	88.3	89.1	88.4	88.6	88.6
2002	87.7	87.8	88.9	88.6	89.0	89.2	90.1	90.0	89.9	89.3	89.7	90.2	89.2
2003	87.7	88.6	88.8	88.5	88.7	88.5	88.8	89.1	88.5	88.6	88.8	88.9	88.6
Educational and health services													
1990	49.2	49.7	50.4	50.3	50.6	49.8	49.7	50.4	51.8	52.3	52.7	52.8	50.8
1991	52.2	52.8	53.2	52.9	53.2	51.8	52.9	53.6	55.3	55.7	55.9	56.6	53.8
1992	56.0	56.7	57.3	57.2	57.5	55.8	56.3	56.9	58.3	58.9	59.3	59.7	57.4
1993	58.3	59.2	59.5	59.9	59.9	58.5	58.4	59.3	61.5	61.8	61.9	62.5	60.0
1994	61.5	62.0	62.4	63.2	63.3	62.4	62.1	62.5	64.5	65.1	65.5	66.1	63.3
1995	66.1	66.7	67.1	67.3	67.9	66.4	65.9	66.6	69.0	69.0	69.4	69.6	67.5
1996	69.7	70.3	70.5	70.8	71.3	69.8	69.4	69.7	72.2	72.6	72.7	73.1	71.0
1997	72.7	73.7	74.3	74.5	75.0	73.1	72.5	73.3	75.5	76.0	76.3	76.4	74.4
1998	75.6	76.5	76.8	78.7	78.7	76.2	75.1	75.2	77.8	78.5	79.3	79.2	77.3
1999	78.7	79.8	80.1	80.3	80.0	78.0	77.1	77.6	80.8	81.0	81.3	81.3	79.6
2000	81.2	82.3	82.8	82.4	82.2	80.5	78.8	79.7	83.1	83.5	84.4	84.6	82.1
2001	85.1	86.6	87.2	87.5	88.0	85.3	84.9	86.1	89.5	89.8	91.0	91.2	87.7
2002	91.7	92.6	93.5	94.6	94.6	91.3	90.4	91.7	95.9	96.4	97.6	97.3	94.0
2003	97.7	98.5	98.6	99.1	99.2	95.6	95.3	96.2	100.1	101.3	101.9	101.8	98.8

Employment by Industry: New Mexico—*Continued*

(Numbers in thousands. Not seasonally adjusted.)

Industry	January	February	March	April	May	June	July	August	September	October	November	December	Annual Average
STATEWIDE—*Continued*													
Leisure and hospitality													
1990	56.8	57.0	58.2	60.2	61.9	64.0	63.5	64.3	61.9	59.3	58.9	58.3	60.3
1991	57.6	57.4	58.4	60.3	61.7	63.8	64.4	65.0	62.4	59.0	58.5	59.1	60.6
1992	58.5	58.6	60.3	61.8	63.5	65.1	65.8	66.6	64.6	63.4	62.1	62.8	62.7
1993	61.7	61.9	63.8	65.1	65.9	68.2	68.4	69.6	67.5	66.2	65.2	66.2	65.8
1994	65.1	65.3	67.1	68.5	69.8	72.2	72.4	73.5	71.4	69.3	68.7	69.4	69.3
1995	69.2	69.4	71.3	71.6	72.6	75.5	75.4	76.3	74.2	71.2	70.4	70.4	72.2
1996	70.0	70.8	72.1	72.8	73.7	76.3	75.7	76.1	73.9	72.3	71.2	72.6	73.1
1997	70.1	70.7	72.1	72.4	74.3	76.7	76.1	76.7	74.3	72.3	71.6	72.7	73.3
1998	69.8	70.9	72.0	72.8	74.3	76.3	77.0	77.0	75.7	72.8	71.7	72.7	73.5
1999	71.4	72.1	72.9	75.0	76.3	78.6	78.5	79.1	77.5	76.0	74.8	75.3	75.6
2000	73.4	73.8	75.7	76.1	77.3	80.2	80.6	81.1	79.4	77.0	75.9	76.2	77.2
2001	74.8	75.3	76.8	77.9	79.5	81.9	81.5	82.1	79.7	77.8	77.1	77.3	78.5
2002	75.7	76.3	78.0	79.6	81.3	83.6	83.6	83.9	81.9	79.1	78.4	79.1	80.0
2003	78.0	78.3	79.6	80.8	82.6	84.6	84.9	85.3	82.6	80.8	79.6	80.0	81.4
Other services													
1990	20.8	20.9	21.1	21.1	21.5	23.3	23.3	23.4	21.8	21.7	21.6	21.6	21.8
1991	21.3	21.3	21.5	21.6	21.8	23.4	23.2	22.9	21.6	21.4	21.5	21.5	21.9
1992	21.1	21.1	21.3	21.7	21.8	23.7	23.6	23.4	22.0	22.3	22.3	22.3	22.2
1993	22.1	22.4	22.3	22.8	23.0	24.7	25.0	24.7	24.2	23.2	23.1	23.3	23.4
1994	23.2	23.4	23.4	23.8	24.0	25.3	26.7	26.6	24.8	24.4	24.5	24.5	24.5
1995	24.7	24.7	22.9	22.9	23.1	24.9	25.5	25.3	23.8	23.6	23.6	23.6	24.0
1996	23.4	23.6	23.7	23.9	24.2	26.0	26.1	26.2	24.5	25.0	25.0	25.1	24.7
1997	24.6	25.0	25.2	24.9	25.2	27.4	27.8	27.5	26.0	26.1	26.0	26.6	26.0
1998	25.9	26.1	26.3	26.5	26.8	29.3	29.6	29.3	27.5	27.4	27.4	27.5	27.4
1999	27.2	27.4	27.4	27.5	27.8	30.0	29.9	29.6	27.1	26.7	26.6	26.8	27.8
2000	26.5	26.8	26.8	26.8	27.2	29.2	29.2	29.0	26.6	26.4	26.5	26.5	27.2
2001	25.8	26.2	26.4	26.4	26.7	29.2	29.3	28.8	26.9	26.6	26.7	26.8	27.2
2002	26.6	27.0	27.2	27.3	27.6	29.9	30.0	29.7	27.7	27.7	27.6	27.6	28.0
2003	27.5	27.6	27.7	27.5	27.9	30.2	30.5	30.3	28.3	28.2	28.2	28.1	28.5
Government													
1990	144.3	150.6	151.7	153.2	153.4	148.4	142.8	142.5	150.5	152.6	155.6	150.8	149.7
1991	147.0	153.1	153.0	154.9	155.7	149.4	146.0	146.1	154.9	155.8	156.2	155.1	152.2
1992	151.4	156.7	157.0	158.2	158.7	156.6	148.2	148.0	157.5	158.9	163.6	158.2	156.0
1993	154.7	160.0	160.3	162.7	162.6	157.3	151.4	151.0	161.5	163.3	162.4	162.3	159.1
1994	159.0	164.1	164.4	164.9	164.9	162.1	157.0	154.9	164.3	166.5	168.2	166.5	163.0
1995	161.9	168.0	167.9	167.9	168.8	163.8	160.3	160.4	167.8	169.9	170.4	170.6	166.4
1996	165.5	171.7	171.7	172.7	172.9	169.5	165.2	165.1	173.3	176.1	176.9	177.3	171.4
1997	171.7	177.5	177.0	178.4	179.7	175.4	172.2	171.4	178.6	180.0	180.4	181.6	176.9
1998	175.6	181.3	182.7	180.3	180.5	176.9	172.3	172.2	177.8	180.3	181.1	180.5	178.4
1999	175.7	180.1	182.0	182.4	182.3	177.9	173.8	175.7	182.5	183.4	184.5	183.1	180.2
2000	178.7	183.9	186.6	186.5	188.0	179.3	177.2	177.5	184.1	184.7	184.7	185.6	183.0
2001	179.3	185.6	187.4	187.6	188.1	184.1	178.5	180.0	189.3	188.3	188.5	188.8	185.5
2002	185.1	190.7	192.1	192.1	193.1	190.3	184.5	185.8	193.8	193.9	194.7	195.2	190.9
2003	190.5	195.3	196.5	197.3	196.6	193.6	188.0	189.1	196.8	199.1	199.9	200.3	195.3
Federal government													
1990	31.0	30.9	31.3	33.0	34.1	32.8	33.4	32.4	31.5	31.1	30.8	30.7	31.9
1991	30.5	30.5	30.7	30.9	31.6	32.1	32.3	32.3	32.1	31.7	31.5	31.6	31.4
1992	31.5	31.3	31.4	31.7	32.1	32.5	32.9	32.7	32.4	31.8	31.7	31.7	31.9
1993	31.2	31.4	31.4	31.5	31.9	32.2	32.4	32.3	31.8	31.8	31.4	31.7	31.7
1994	31.5	31.5	31.5	31.7	31.9	32.2	32.2	32.0	32.0	31.4	31.1	31.2	31.6
1995	30.7	30.7	30.8	31.1	31.6	31.9	31.9	31.8	31.5	31.1	30.7	30.7	31.2
1996	30.3	30.2	30.2	30.5	30.8	29.6	29.0	29.9	30.6	30.5	30.3	30.5	30.2
1997	29.9	29.8	29.8	30.2	30.5	29.7	30.1	30.8	30.8	29.9	29.7	30.0	30.1
1998	29.9	29.7	29.7	29.9	30.2	29.5	30.2	30.7	30.7	30.5	30.3	30.1	30.1
1999	29.4	29.2	29.3	29.7	29.8	29.5	29.5	29.9	29.9	29.8	29.9	29.9	29.6
2000	29.4	29.4	31.8	31.5	34.0	30.5	31.1	30.2	29.6	29.2	29.0	29.5	30.4
2001	28.8	28.6	28.9	29.1	29.7	30.6	29.5	30.3	30.3	29.7	29.5	30.0	29.6
2002	29.3	29.1	29.4	29.5	30.1	31.0	29.9	30.7	30.7	29.9	29.6	30.3	30.0
2003	29.5	29.4	29.8	29.8	30.3	31.0	29.5	30.2	30.1	29.7	29.5	30.0	29.9
State government													
1990	48.4	54.0	54.3	53.0	51.7	47.1	48.1	48.9	53.9	54.5	54.1	52.7	51.7
1991	50.2	54.5	54.6	55.9	55.1	50.2	50.1	50.9	56.4	56.3	56.1	54.7	53.7
1992	51.9	56.0	56.2	56.8	56.2	51.1	50.6	51.4	57.6	58.1	58.0	56.8	55.0
1993	54.4	57.7	58.0	59.3	58.5	53.6	52.2	52.8	59.1	59.6	58.6	58.0	56.8
1994	55.2	59.0	59.1	59.2	58.8	53.7	53.1	53.8	59.3	60.3	59.8	59.3	57.5
1995	56.4	59.9	60.4	59.8	59.4	53.9	52.7	53.6	58.7	59.1	59.0	58.1	57.5
1996	54.7	58.5	58.4	58.7	58.2	54.4	53.5	54.2	60.3	60.9	61.3	61.4	57.8
1997	57.4	61.5	60.1	61.5	60.9	56.7	55.5	55.7	60.8	61.8	61.9	61.6	59.6
1998	57.7	62.0	62.5	61.8	61.4	57.0	55.4	56.8	60.9	61.3	61.6	61.1	59.9
1999	57.7	61.3	62.2	62.1	61.6	57.3	56.4	58.2	63.4	63.5	63.7	62.8	60.8
2000	59.4	63.0	63.6	63.8	62.6	57.8	58.6	59.7	64.8	64.5	64.2	64.1	62.1
2001	59.5	64.6	65.3	65.1	64.1	58.4	58.5	60.5	64.5	65.2	64.5	63.7	62.8
2002	61.4	65.5	65.8	65.6	65.0	60.2	60.2	62.2	65.9	66.7	67.0	66.7	64.4
2003	63.8	67.5	68.3	68.3	66.9	62.0	62.0	64.2	68.1	68.9	69.0	68.5	66.5

Employment by Industry: New Mexico—*Continued*

(Numbers in thousands. Not seasonally adjusted.)

Industry	January	February	March	April	May	June	July	August	September	October	November	December	Annual Average
STATEWIDE—*Continued*													
Local government													
1990	64.9	65.7	66.1	67.2	67.6	68.5	61.3	61.2	65.1	67.0	70.7	67.4	66.0
1991	66.3	68.1	67.7	68.1	69.0	67.1	63.6	62.9	66.4	67.8	68.6	68.8	67.0
1992	68.0	69.4	69.4	69.7	70.4	73.0	64.7	63.9	67.5	69.0	73.9	69.7	69.0
1993	69.1	70.9	70.9	71.9	72.2	71.5	66.8	65.9	70.6	71.9	72.4	72.6	70.5
1994	72.3	73.6	73.8	74.0	74.2	76.2	71.7	69.1	73.0	74.8	77.3	76.0	73.8
1995	74.8	77.4	76.7	77.0	77.8	78.0	75.7	75.0	77.6	79.7	80.7	81.8	77.6
1996	80.5	83.0	83.1	83.5	83.9	85.5	82.7	81.0	82.4	84.7	85.3	85.4	83.4
1997	84.4	86.2	87.1	86.7	88.3	89.0	86.6	84.9	87.0	88.3	88.8	90.0	87.2
1998	88.0	89.6	90.5	88.6	88.9	90.4	86.7	84.7	86.2	88.5	89.2	89.3	88.3
1999	88.6	89.6	90.5	90.6	90.9	91.1	87.9	87.6	89.2	90.1	90.9	90.4	89.7
2000	89.9	91.5	91.2	91.2	91.4	91.0	87.5	87.6	89.7	91.0	91.5	92.0	90.4
2001	91.0	92.4	93.2	93.4	94.3	95.1	90.5	89.2	94.5	93.4	94.5	95.1	93.1
2002	94.4	96.1	96.9	97.0	98.0	99.1	94.4	92.9	97.2	97.3	98.1	98.2	96.6
2003	97.2	98.4	98.4	99.2	99.4	100.6	96.5	94.7	98.6	100.5	101.4	101.8	98.9
ALBUQUERQUE													
Total nonfarm													
1990	256.6	258.9	262.2	265.5	268.7	268.0	265.7	266.6	269.3	267.5	266.1	265.5	265.0
1991	258.9	261.4	263.2	264.3	265.9	265.7	266.7	268.0	271.9	271.6	270.3	272.2	266.6
1992	265.0	268.2	270.9	273.3	275.9	275.9	276.9	278.5	281.5	282.3	281.9	283.1	276.1
1993	276.7	280.3	283.4	285.9	287.5	289.5	289.7	290.8	296.2	296.9	297.9	299.3	289.5
1994	293.1	295.8	299.2	301.4	305.3	307.9	309.0	309.4	315.4	314.6	316.7	318.9	307.2
1995	312.6	317.3	318.9	317.7	320.8	321.4	318.2	320.0	323.8	322.3	324.2	325.4	320.2
1996	316.9	321.0	322.1	324.2	326.2	327.1	326.3	326.9	329.5	330.3	332.0	333.6	326.3
1997	323.4	327.0	328.0	331.8	335.1	336.0	334.3	334.4	336.4	337.2	338.0	339.9	333.4
1998	331.0	334.5	335.6	338.5	340.4	341.4	338.6	336.8	340.2	339.7	341.3	343.5	338.4
1999	334.0	337.3	339.9	341.3	343.7	346.0	343.1	344.6	348.3	349.8	350.3	352.1	344.2
2000	343.4	346.5	350.1	352.5	355.9	356.5	354.3	355.8	360.0	359.1	361.7	363.1	354.9
2001	353.3	356.7	359.3	359.9	361.7	362.5	358.6	358.9	358.8	358.5	360.0	361.2	359.1
2002	352.1	353.6	356.4	357.4	359.9	360.7	358.5	358.8	361.2	358.7	360.9	362.9	358.4
2003	353.3	356.1	358.8	359.5	361.4	361.3	359.4	361.2	363.3	362.8	364.2	365.7	360.6
Total private													
1990	204.2	204.2	207.2	210.0	213.2	214.6	212.6	213.6	213.6	211.6	210.8	210.5	210.5
1991	205.2	206.2	207.7	209.1	210.8	212.1	212.6	213.9	215.0	214.5	213.7	215.3	211.3
1992	209.8	210.8	213.6	216.0	218.9	220.6	221.8	223.2	223.5	223.5	223.8	225.5	219.2
1993	220.5	221.9	224.8	227.1	228.9	231.1	231.7	234.2	236.5	236.3	237.9	239.4	230.8
1994	235.3	236.0	239.1	241.1	245.4	248.8	250.2	252.0	254.1	253.2	255.7	257.9	247.4
1995	254.3	256.3	257.6	256.2	259.4	261.3	259.4	261.0	261.3	260.1	262.1	263.2	259.3
1996	257.0	258.5	259.5	261.4	263.6	264.7	265.7	266.7	266.1	266.7	268.6	269.6	264.0
1997	261.4	263.0	265.2	267.0	269.5	271.5	271.5	272.1	271.2	272.1	272.6	274.3	269.2
1998	267.1	268.6	269.8	272.2	274.1	274.8	273.6	273.5	274.0	273.5	274.6	276.7	272.7
1999	269.4	270.7	272.9	274.3	276.9	279.9	278.7	280.5	281.2	281.9	281.8	283.9	277.6
2000	277.6	278.4	281.3	283.7	286.3	289.8	287.8	289.8	291.5	290.9	293.2	294.6	287.0
2001	287.5	288.1	290.3	290.5	292.1	293.5	291.1	291.7	289.1	288.7	289.6	289.8	290.2
2002	283.4	282.4	284.9	285.9	288.4	288.7	288.0	288.7	289.0	287.1	288.9	290.3	287.1
2003	283.6	283.9	286.0	286.8	289.0	289.9	289.6	291.2	290.9	290.1	291.1	292.3	288.7
Goods-producing													
1990	35.4	35.4	36.0	36.1	37.0	37.3	37.0	37.2	37.2	36.7	35.7	35.0	36.3
1991	33.9	34.3	34.7	35.1	35.3	36.1	36.1	36.2	36.1	36.2	36.1	36.0	35.5
1992	34.6	35.1	35.5	36.7	37.4	38.0	38.7	39.3	39.6	39.9	39.7	39.6	37.8
1993	38.2	39.0	39.6	40.4	41.0	42.0	42.9	43.8	44.3	45.3	45.9	46.0	42.3
1994	45.0	45.2	46.3	47.1	47.6	49.1	50.0	50.5	50.8	51.0	51.2	51.2	48.7
1995	49.7	50.2	50.5	50.2	50.6	51.4	50.6	51.1	51.2	50.5	50.7	50.6	50.6
1996	48.6	49.2	49.6	49.2	49.9	50.3	50.8	51.0	50.7	50.1	50.0	49.4	49.9
1997	47.8	48.4	49.2	49.3	50.0	50.3	50.7	51.6	50.5	50.8	50.0	49.5	49.8
1998	48.5	48.7	49.1	49.2	49.3	49.3	49.2	49.2	48.6	47.7	47.0	46.7	48.5
1999	45.8	46.0	46.6	47.4	47.7	48.4	49.0	49.2	49.3	48.7	48.1	48.1	47.8
2000	47.1	47.7	48.4	48.8	50.1	50.9	52.0	52.8	53.1	52.8	53.0	53.0	50.8
2001	52.3	52.4	52.9	52.4	52.7	53.2	52.2	52.2	51.1	50.5	50.1	49.6	51.8
2002	48.1	47.5	47.9	48.1	48.1	48.6	48.7	48.8	48.0	47.4	47.1	47.1	48.0
2003	46.4	46.3	46.6	46.8	47.4	47.8	48.4	48.8	48.3	47.7	47.6	47.3	47.5
Construction and mining													
1990	14.4	14.4	14.8	14.7	15.3	15.5	15.1	15.0	14.9	14.6	14.0	13.6	14.6
1991	12.5	12.9	13.1	13.3	13.3	13.8	13.6	13.7	13.6	13.9	13.9	13.8	13.4
1992	13.1	13.5	13.9	13.9	14.4	14.8	15.2	15.3	15.3	16.1	15.7	15.6	14.7
1993	14.8	15.3	15.7	16.6	17.1	17.8	18.3	18.8	19.2	19.5	20.0	19.8	17.7
1994	19.4	19.4	20.0	20.6	20.8	21.8	22.5	22.7	22.8	22.9	23.5	23.8	21.6
1995	22.6	22.9	23.1	22.8	23.0	23.6	22.9	23.2	23.2	22.3	22.4	22.3	22.8
1996	21.5	22.0	22.3	21.8	22.4	22.4	22.9	22.9	22.8	22.5	22.3	21.8	22.3
1997	20.9	21.3	21.9	22.1	22.5	22.5	22.4	22.8	22.0	22.0	21.4	21.0	21.9
1998	20.4	20.6	21.3	21.4	21.5	21.5	21.7	21.5	21.2	20.9	20.3	20.2	21.0
1999	19.5	19.7	20.3	21.1	21.4	22.0	22.3	22.4	22.5	22.1	21.6	21.5	21.3
2000	20.6	21.0	21.6	21.9	22.9	23.5	24.0	24.7	25.0	24.8	25.1	24.9	23.3
2001	24.3	24.3	24.7	24.6	25.0	25.7	25.4	25.5	24.8	24.5	24.6	24.2	24.8
2002	23.2	22.8	23.2	23.3	23.3	23.6	23.5	23.7	23.1	23.0	23.1	23.1	23.2
2003	22.8	22.7	23.0	23.3	23.9	24.3	24.7	25.0	24.6	24.5	24.6	24.4	24.0

Employment by Industry: New Mexico—*Continued*

(Numbers in thousands. Not seasonally adjusted.)

Industry	January	February	March	April	May	June	July	August	September	October	November	December	Annual Average
ALBUQUERQUE—*Continued*													
Manufacturing													
1990	21.0	21.0	21.2	21.4	21.7	21.8	21.9	22.2	22.3	22.1	21.7	21.4	21.6
1991	21.4	21.4	21.6	21.8	22.0	22.3	22.5	22.5	22.5	22.3	22.2	22.2	22.0
1992	21.5	21.6	21.6	22.8	23.0	23.2	23.5	24.0	24.3	23.8	24.0	24.0	23.1
1993	23.4	23.7	23.9	23.8	23.9	24.2	24.6	25.0	25.1	25.8	25.9	26.2	24.6
1994	25.6	25.8	26.3	26.5	26.8	27.3	27.5	27.8	28.0	28.1	27.7	27.4	27.0
1995	27.1	27.3	27.4	27.4	27.6	27.8	27.7	27.9	28.0	28.2	28.3	28.3	27.7
1996	27.1	27.2	27.3	27.4	27.5	27.9	27.9	28.1	27.9	27.6	27.7	27.6	27.6
1997	26.9	27.1	27.3	27.2	27.5	27.8	28.3	28.8	28.5	28.8	28.6	28.5	27.9
1998	28.1	28.1	27.8	27.8	27.8	27.8	27.5	27.7	27.4	26.8	26.7	26.5	27.5
1999	26.3	26.3	26.3	26.3	26.3	26.4	26.7	26.8	26.8	26.6	26.5	26.6	26.4
2000	26.5	26.7	26.8	26.9	27.2	27.4	28.0	28.1	28.1	28.0	27.9	28.1	27.4
2001	28.0	28.1	28.2	27.8	27.7	27.5	26.8	26.7	26.3	26.0	25.5	25.4	27.0
2002	24.9	24.7	24.7	24.8	24.8	25.0	25.2	25.1	24.9	24.4	24.0	24.0	24.7
2003	23.6	23.6	23.6	23.5	23.5	23.5	23.7	23.8	23.7	23.2	23.0	22.9	23.5
Service-providing													
1990	221.2	223.5	226.2	229.4	231.7	230.7	228.7	229.4	232.1	230.8	230.4	230.5	228.7
1991	225.0	227.1	228.5	229.2	230.6	229.6	230.6	231.8	235.8	235.4	234.2	236.2	231.1
1992	230.4	233.1	235.4	236.6	238.5	237.9	238.2	239.2	241.9	242.4	242.2	243.5	238.2
1993	238.5	241.3	243.8	245.5	246.5	247.5	246.8	247.0	251.9	251.6	252.0	253.3	247.1
1994	248.1	250.6	252.9	254.3	257.7	258.8	259.0	258.9	264.6	263.6	265.5	267.7	258.4
1995	262.9	267.1	268.4	267.5	270.2	270.0	267.6	268.9	272.6	271.8	273.5	274.8	269.6
1996	268.3	271.8	272.5	275.0	276.3	276.8	275.5	275.9	278.8	280.2	282.0	284.2	276.4
1997	275.6	278.6	278.8	282.5	285.1	285.7	283.6	282.8	285.9	286.4	288.0	290.4	283.6
1998	282.5	285.8	286.5	289.3	291.1	292.1	289.4	287.6	291.6	292.0	294.3	296.8	289.9
1999	288.2	291.3	293.3	293.9	296.0	297.6	294.1	295.4	299.0	301.1	302.2	304.0	296.3
2000	296.3	298.8	301.7	303.7	305.8	305.6	302.3	303.0	306.9	306.3	308.7	310.1	304.1
2001	301.0	304.3	306.4	307.5	309.0	309.3	306.4	306.7	307.7	308.0	309.9	311.6	307.3
2002	304.0	306.1	308.5	309.3	311.8	312.1	309.8	310.0	313.2	311.3	313.8	315.8	310.5
2003	306.9	309.8	312.2	312.7	314.0	313.5	311.0	312.4	315.0	315.1	316.6	318.4	313.1
Trade, transportation, and utilities													
1990	54.9	54.5	55.1	54.9	55.5	55.5	54.5	54.6	55.0	54.8	56.0	56.2	55.1
1991	53.1	52.5	52.6	52.6	53.0	53.1	52.8	53.0	53.4	53.5	54.5	55.4	53.2
1992	53.7	53.3	53.6	54.1	54.8	54.9	55.0	55.4	55.7	56.2	57.1	58.5	55.1
1993	56.5	56.0	56.3	56.3	56.4	56.4	56.7	57.2	57.5	57.6	59.0	60.2	57.1
1994	57.5	57.1	57.2	56.7	58.2	58.4	58.4	58.8	59.4	59.7	61.5	63.2	58.8
1995	60.4	60.3	60.3	60.1	60.9	60.8	60.4	61.0	61.4	62.5	63.6	64.5	61.3
1996	61.2	60.6	60.6	60.8	61.2	61.0	61.8	62.7	62.6	63.0	65.0	65.8	62.1
1997	63.7	63.3	63.3	62.8	63.2	63.6	63.7	63.8	64.1	64.8	66.7	68.4	64.2
1998	65.1	64.6	64.7	65.1	65.3	65.4	64.8	64.4	64.5	65.1	66.8	68.1	65.3
1999	65.1	64.6	64.9	64.4	64.7	64.7	64.3	64.6	64.3	65.3	66.4	67.6	65.0
2000	64.7	64.1	64.3	65.2	65.9	65.8	65.1	65.9	66.1	66.6	69.0	69.5	66.0
2001	66.5	65.1	65.0	64.6	65.0	64.8	64.4	65.0	64.6	64.7	66.3	67.1	65.3
2002	64.8	63.7	63.7	64.1	65.0	64.7	64.5	64.9	65.1	65.3	67.1	68.2	65.1
2003	64.8	64.3	64.7	64.5	64.8	64.6	64.1	64.9	64.5	64.6	66.3	67.2	64.9
Wholesale trade													
1990	13.0	13.1	13.1	13.2	13.2	13.2	12.9	12.8	12.8	12.7	12.8	12.7	12.9
1991	12.0	12.0	12.0	12.0	12.0	12.0	12.0	12.0	12.2	12.3	12.4	12.5	12.1
1992	12.2	12.2	12.3	12.4	12.5	12.6	12.6	12.6	12.6	12.7	12.7	12.8	12.5
1993	12.7	12.7	12.8	12.8	13.0	13.1	13.1	13.0	13.0	12.9	13.0	13.1	12.9
1994	13.1	13.0	13.1	13.3	13.5	13.7	13.7	13.7	13.8	13.8	14.0	14.0	13.5
1995	13.8	13.9	13.9	13.8	14.0	14.0	13.8	13.8	13.9	13.9	13.9	13.9	13.8
1996	13.6	13.5	13.5	13.5	13.5	13.5	13.6	13.5	13.5	13.4	13.4	13.5	13.5
1997	13.6	13.7	13.8	14.1	14.3	14.3	14.2	14.2	14.1	14.0	13.9	14.0	14.0
1998	13.7	13.7	13.7	13.8	13.8	13.8	13.6	13.5	13.5	13.6	13.6	13.6	13.6
1999	13.5	13.5	13.6	14.1	14.1	14.2	13.7	13.7	13.6	13.6	13.6	13.7	13.7
2000	13.4	13.5	13.6	14.1	14.2	14.1	14.0	14.2	14.2	14.0	14.1	14.0	13.9
2001	13.9	13.9	13.9	13.8	13.9	13.8	13.7	13.7	13.7	13.5	13.5	13.5	13.7
2002	13.5	13.4	13.4	13.3	13.4	13.3	13.4	13.3	13.3	13.3	13.4	13.3	13.4
2003	12.9	12.9	13.2	13.1	13.0	13.0	12.9	13.1	13.0	12.8	12.9	12.9	13.0
Retail trade													
1990	31.9	31.4	31.7	31.9	32.4	32.5	32.0	32.1	32.1	32.1	33.2	33.5	32.2
1991	31.1	30.5	30.6	30.7	31.1	31.3	31.2	31.4	31.1	31.6	32.4	33.1	31.3
1992	31.3	30.9	31.0	31.6	32.1	32.2	32.3	32.4	32.5	33.0	33.7	34.5	32.2
1993	33.1	32.5	32.6	32.9	32.8	33.0	33.5	33.9	33.9	34.0	35.0	35.9	33.5
1994	34.5	34.1	34.1	34.4	34.8	35.0	35.1	35.3	35.5	35.7	37.0	38.4	35.3
1995	36.1	35.7	35.6	35.8	36.4	36.6	36.6	37.0	37.0	37.9	38.9	39.9	36.9
1996	37.9	37.3	37.4	37.7	38.1	38.2	39.0	39.5	39.5	39.6	41.5	42.1	38.9
1997	40.1	39.3	39.2	38.7	38.8	39.5	39.8	39.9	39.7	40.5	42.4	43.7	40.1
1998	41.2	40.6	40.7	40.8	40.9	41.2	40.8	40.2	40.3	40.6	42.2	43.3	41.0
1999	40.5	40.0	40.2	39.5	39.8	39.9	40.1	40.1	39.7	40.6	41.8	42.9	40.4
2000	40.1	39.5	39.6	39.8	40.3	40.6	40.2	40.6	40.7	41.3	43.5	44.2	40.8
2001	41.6	40.7	40.7	40.4	40.7	41.0	40.7	40.8	40.4	40.6	42.3	43.1	41.1
2002	40.9	39.9	40.1	40.5	41.3	41.3	41.0	41.1	41.3	41.4	43.0	44.1	41.3
2003	41.5	41.0	41.1	41.0	41.4	41.3	41.0	41.3	41.1	41.3	42.9	43.8	41.6

Employment by Industry: New Mexico—*Continued*

(Numbers in thousands. Not seasonally adjusted.)

Industry	January	February	March	April	May	June	July	August	September	October	November	December	Annual Average
ALBUQUERQUE—*Continued*													
Transportation and utilities													
1990	10.0	10.0	10.3	9.8	9.9	9.8	9.6	9.7	10.1	10.0	10.0	10.0	9.9
1991	10.0	10.0	10.0	9.9	9.9	9.8	9.6	9.6	10.1	9.6	9.7	9.8	9.8
1992	10.2	10.2	10.3	10.1	10.2	10.1	10.1	10.4	10.6	10.5	10.7	11.2	10.3
1993	10.7	10.8	10.9	10.6	10.6	10.3	10.1	10.3	10.6	10.7	11.0	11.2	10.6
1994	9.9	10.0	10.0	9.0	9.9	9.7	9.6	9.8	10.1	10.2	10.5	10.8	9.9
1995	10.5	10.7	10.8	10.5	10.5	10.2	10.0	10.2	10.5	10.7	10.8	10.7	10.5
1996	9.7	9.8	9.7	9.6	9.6	9.3	9.2	9.7	9.6	10.0	10.1	10.2	9.7
1997	10.0	10.3	10.3	10.0	10.1	9.8	9.7	9.7	10.3	10.3	10.4	10.7	10.1
1998	10.2	10.3	10.3	10.5	10.6	10.4	10.4	10.7	10.7	10.9	11.0	11.2	10.6
1999	11.1	11.1	11.1	10.8	10.8	10.6	10.5	10.8	11.0	11.1	11.0	11.0	10.9
2000	11.2	11.1	11.1	11.3	11.4	11.1	10.9	11.1	11.2	11.3	11.4	11.3	11.2
2001	11.0	10.5	10.4	10.4	10.4	10.0	10.0	10.5	10.5	10.6	10.5	10.5	10.4
2002	10.4	10.4	10.2	10.3	10.3	10.1	10.1	10.5	10.5	10.6	10.7	10.8	10.4
2003	10.4	10.4	10.4	10.4	10.4	10.3	10.2	10.5	10.4	10.5	10.5	10.5	10.4
Information													
1990	5.9	6.0	5.9	5.8	5.8	5.8	5.9	5.9	5.8	5.6	5.6	5.6	5.8
1991	5.1	5.1	5.2	5.2	5.2	5.3	5.4	5.4	5.4	5.2	5.2	5.2	5.2
1992	5.2	5.2	5.2	5.1	5.1	5.2	5.1	5.2	5.1	5.1	5.1	5.2	5.1
1993	5.2	5.2	5.2	5.4	5.5	5.4	5.4	5.8	5.9	5.5	5.7	5.4	5.4
1994	6.7	6.8	6.8	6.7	6.9	7.1	7.3	7.2	7.1	7.0	7.3	7.3	7.0
1995	7.0	7.1	7.1	7.0	7.0	7.0	6.9	7.0	7.1	6.8	6.9	7.1	7.0
1996	7.0	7.3	7.2	7.1	7.0	7.1	7.2	7.0	6.8	6.8	7.1	7.2	7.0
1997	7.3	7.3	7.5	7.3	7.5	7.6	7.7	7.7	7.7	7.7	8.1	8.4	7.6
1998	8.6	8.6	8.6	8.5	8.6	8.6	8.7	9.0	9.1	9.2	9.7	9.8	8.9
1999	9.6	9.7	9.7	10.1	10.4	10.4	10.5	10.6	10.6	10.7	10.8	11.1	10.3
2000	11.1	10.9	11.1	11.0	11.0	11.1	10.9	11.0	11.1	11.0	11.0	11.4	11.0
2001	11.5	11.7	11.6	11.2	11.2	11.2	11.4	11.5	11.6	11.4	11.5	11.5	11.4
2002	11.2	11.4	11.5	11.3	11.4	11.1	10.9	10.7	10.4	10.5	10.8	10.8	11.0
2003	10.5	10.5	10.5	10.3	10.3	10.3	10.3	10.0	10.2	10.0	10.0	10.2	10.3
Financial activities													
1990	15.0	14.8	14.9	15.0	15.1	15.4	15.4	15.3	15.3	15.4	15.4	15.3	15.1
1991	14.9	14.9	15.1	15.0	15.0	15.2	15.3	15.4	15.4	15.1	14.9	15.2	15.1
1992	15.0	15.1	15.2	15.1	15.3	15.4	15.5	15.6	15.5	15.4	15.3	15.5	15.3
1993	15.6	15.6	15.7	15.9	15.9	16.1	16.2	16.2	16.1	16.3	16.3	16.3	16.0
1994	15.9	16.0	16.0	16.2	16.4	16.4	16.4	16.4	16.3	16.1	16.2	16.5	16.2
1995	16.2	16.1	16.1	16.6	16.7	16.6	16.5	16.5	16.3	16.8	17.0	17.0	16.5
1996	16.5	16.7	16.8	17.0	17.0	17.1	17.5	17.5	17.4	17.3	17.3	17.5	17.1
1997	17.1	17.2	17.5	17.7	17.6	17.8	17.9	17.9	17.7	17.9	17.9	17.9	17.6
1998	17.4	17.6	17.5	17.6	17.8	18.0	18.2	18.3	18.4	18.6	18.9	19.0	18.1
1999	19.2	19.3	19.5	19.4	19.5	19.7	19.7	19.7	19.7	19.6	19.6	19.7	19.5
2000	19.2	19.2	19.2	19.4	19.4	19.4	19.4	19.3	19.4	19.5	19.6	19.7	19.3
2001	19.4	19.5	19.7	19.8	19.7	19.8	19.7	19.6	19.4	19.3	19.2	19.4	19.5
2002	18.6	18.5	18.6	18.6	18.7	18.8	18.9	19.0	18.9	18.9	18.8	18.9	18.8
2003	18.4	18.5	18.6	18.7	18.8	18.9	19.1	19.2	19.1	19.0	19.0	19.1	18.9
Professional and business services													
1990	35.6	35.6	36.4	38.0	38.1	39.3	38.6	38.6	38.7	38.2	37.7	38.8	37.8
1991	40.0	40.7	40.8	41.0	41.2	41.5	41.5	42.0	42.6	43.0	41.9	41.9	41.5
1992	40.7	40.7	41.6	41.8	42.0	42.7	43.5	43.1	42.5	41.8	41.6	41.6	41.9
1993	41.4	41.7	42.9	42.8	43.2	44.1	43.4	43.5	44.3	44.1	43.9	44.2	43.2
1994	43.2	43.7	44.6	45.2	45.9	46.8	47.2	47.6	48.3	47.9	48.1	48.2	46.3
1995	49.4	50.1	50.4	49.6	50.2	51.1	51.0	51.3	51.1	50.1	50.4	50.7	50.4
1996	51.1	51.4	51.2	52.5	52.5	53.2	52.5	52.4	52.6	52.7	52.7	53.2	52.3
1997	51.0	51.3	51.2	53.3	53.5	54.3	53.8	53.4	53.7	53.3	52.6	52.8	52.8
1998	52.1	52.6	52.9	54.1	54.2	54.8	54.2	54.9	55.0	54.6	54.3	55.1	54.0
1999	53.2	53.8	54.5	54.5	55.2	56.5	56.4	57.1	57.4	57.4	57.2	57.7	55.9
2000	56.3	56.5	57.1	58.3	58.5	59.3	58.8	59.2	59.6	58.9	58.7	59.2	58.3
2001	57.0	57.6	58.1	58.3	58.5	59.1	58.5	58.5	57.2	58.0	57.8	57.5	58.0
2002	56.6	56.5	57.2	56.5	57.1	57.3	57.5	57.4	57.9	57.2	57.3	57.8	57.2
2003	56.2	56.6	57.0	56.3	56.6	57.1	57.0	57.1	57.2	57.6	57.2	57.7	57.0
Educational and health services													
1990	23.6	23.7	24.1	24.1	24.3	23.7	24.0	24.3	24.7	24.9	25.0	24.9	24.2
1991	24.7	25.1	25.2	25.1	25.2	24.6	25.4	25.7	26.5	27.0	27.0	27.3	25.7
1992	27.1	27.5	27.8	27.5	27.6	27.1	27.3	27.6	28.4	28.6	28.9	29.1	27.8
1993	28.0	28.3	28.5	28.4	28.5	27.9	27.8	28.0	28.9	28.8	28.9	28.9	28.4
1994	28.9	28.9	29.1	29.3	29.4	29.1	28.9	29.0	30.1	30.3	30.5	30.7	29.5
1995	31.0	31.4	31.5	31.1	31.6	30.9	30.8	30.8	31.7	32.0	32.2	32.3	31.4
1996	32.2	32.3	32.5	32.6	32.9	32.2	32.3	32.1	32.9	33.5	33.6	33.7	32.7
1997	33.5	34.0	34.4	34.2	34.5	33.8	34.0	33.9	34.8	35.0	35.0	35.1	34.3
1998	34.7	35.0	35.1	35.3	35.6	35.0	34.7	34.3	35.1	35.7	35.8	36.0	35.1
1999	35.4	35.8	35.9	36.0	36.1	36.0	35.3	35.4	36.7	37.0	36.9	37.0	36.1
2000	37.4	37.7	37.9	37.4	37.3	37.7	36.1	35.9	37.2	37.5	37.7	37.8	37.3
2001	38.2	38.6	39.0	39.1	39.3	38.9	38.6	38.6	39.7	39.9	40.1	40.3	39.2
2002	40.7	41.0	41.3	41.3	41.5	40.7	40.1	40.4	41.7	41.7	42.0	41.8	41.2
2003	42.3	42.5	42.8	42.9	43.0	42.2	41.6	42.1	43.5	43.8	44.0	44.0	42.9

Employment by Industry: New Mexico—*Continued*

(Numbers in thousands. Not seasonally adjusted.)

Industry	January	February	March	April	May	June	July	August	September	October	November	December	Annual Average
ALBUQUERQUE—*Continued*													
Leisure and hospitality													
1990	24.7	25.0	25.6	26.9	28.0	27.9	27.7	28.1	27.6	26.7	26.2	25.6	26.6
1991	24.8	24.8	25.2	26.2	26.9	27.0	26.9	27.1	26.6	25.6	25.3	25.4	25.9
1992	24.7	25.0	25.8	26.7	27.6	27.9	27.3	27.8	27.6	27.2	26.8	26.7	26.7
1993	26.3	26.7	27.3	28.5	28.9	29.4	29.4	30.1	29.9	29.1	28.7	28.8	28.5
1994	28.4	28.6	29.4	30.0	31.0	31.6	31.5	32.1	31.9	30.8	30.5	30.4	30.5
1995	30.2	30.7	31.3	31.3	32.0	33.0	32.5	32.8	32.2	31.1	31.0	30.8	31.5
1996	30.4	30.9	31.4	31.9	32.7	33.1	32.8	33.2	32.5	32.7	32.4	32.3	32.1
1997	30.5	30.9	31.5	31.8	32.6	33.3	32.8	33.0	32.1	31.8	31.7	31.5	31.9
1998	30.2	31.0	31.4	31.7	32.6	32.8	32.9	32.5	32.6	31.9	31.4	31.3	31.8
1999	30.5	30.9	31.2	31.8	32.5	33.1	32.5	32.9	32.5	32.6	32.2	32.1	32.0
2000	31.1	31.5	32.5	32.9	33.3	34.4	34.3	34.6	34.2	33.7	33.2	33.0	33.2
2001	32.2	32.4	33.0	34.0	34.5	34.9	34.8	34.9	34.4	33.9	33.6	33.3	33.8
2002	32.5	32.7	33.5	34.6	35.2	35.7	35.6	35.7	35.4	34.6	34.3	34.2	34.5
2003	33.5	33.7	34.2	35.8	36.5	37.0	37.0	37.1	36.3	35.7	35.3	35.1	35.6
Other services													
1990	9.1	9.2	9.2	9.2	9.4	9.7	9.5	9.6	9.3	9.3	9.2	9.1	9.3
1991	8.7	8.8	8.9	8.9	9.0	9.3	9.2	9.1	9.0	8.9	8.8	8.9	8.9
1992	8.8	8.9	8.9	9.0	9.1	9.4	9.4	9.2	9.1	9.3	9.3	9.3	9.1
1993	9.3	9.4	9.3	9.4	9.5	9.8	9.9	9.6	9.6	9.6	9.5	9.6	9.5
1994	9.7	9.7	9.7	9.9	10.0	10.3	10.5	10.4	10.2	10.4	10.4	10.4	10.1
1995	10.4	10.4	10.4	10.3	10.4	10.5	10.7	10.5	10.3	10.3	10.3	10.2	10.3
1996	10.0	10.1	10.2	10.3	10.4	10.7	10.8	10.8	10.6	10.6	10.5	10.5	10.4
1997	10.5	10.6	10.6	10.6	10.6	10.8	10.9	10.8	10.6	10.8	10.6	10.7	10.6
1998	10.5	10.5	10.5	10.7	10.7	10.9	10.9	10.9	10.7	10.7	10.7	10.7	10.7
1999	10.6	10.6	10.6	10.7	10.8	11.1	11.0	11.0	10.7	10.6	10.6	10.6	10.7
2000	10.7	10.8	10.8	10.7	10.8	11.2	11.2	11.1	10.8	10.9	11.0	11.0	10.9
2001	10.4	10.8	11.0	11.1	11.2	11.6	11.5	11.4	11.1	11.0	11.0	11.1	11.1
2002	10.9	11.1	11.2	11.4	11.4	11.8	11.8	11.8	11.6	11.5	11.5	11.5	11.5
2003	11.5	11.5	11.6	11.5	11.6	12.0	12.1	12.0	11.8	11.7	11.7	11.7	11.7
Government													
1990	52.4	54.7	55.0	55.5	55.5	53.4	53.1	53.0	55.7	55.9	55.3	55.0	54.5
1991	53.7	55.2	55.5	55.2	55.1	53.6	54.1	54.1	56.9	57.1	56.6	56.9	55.3
1992	55.2	57.4	57.3	57.3	57.0	55.3	55.1	55.3	58.0	58.8	58.1	57.6	56.8
1993	56.2	58.4	58.6	58.8	58.6	58.4	58.0	56.6	59.7	60.6	60.0	59.9	58.6
1994	57.8	59.8	60.1	60.3	59.9	59.1	58.8	57.4	61.3	61.4	61.0	61.0	59.8
1995	58.3	61.0	61.3	61.5	61.4	60.1	58.8	59.0	62.5	62.2	62.1	62.2	60.8
1996	59.9	62.5	62.6	62.8	62.6	62.4	60.6	60.2	63.4	63.6	63.4	64.0	62.3
1997	62.0	64.0	62.8	64.8	65.6	64.5	62.8	62.3	65.2	65.1	65.4	65.6	64.1
1998	63.9	65.9	65.8	66.3	66.3	66.6	65.0	63.3	66.2	66.2	66.7	66.8	65.7
1999	64.6	66.6	67.0	67.0	66.8	66.1	64.4	64.1	67.1	67.9	68.5	68.2	66.5
2000	65.8	68.1	68.8	68.8	69.6	66.7	66.5	66.0	68.5	68.2	68.5	68.5	67.8
2001	65.8	68.6	69.0	69.4	69.6	69.0	67.5	67.2	69.7	69.8	70.4	71.4	69.0
2002	68.7	71.2	71.5	71.5	71.5	72.0	70.5	70.1	72.2	71.6	72.0	72.6	71.3
2003	69.7	72.2	72.8	72.7	72.4	71.4	69.8	70.0	72.4	72.7	73.1	73.4	71.9
Federal government													
1990	14.0	14.2	14.2	14.7	15.4	14.8	14.9	14.5	14.3	14.1	14.0	13.9	14.4
1991	14.1	14.2	14.2	14.1	14.2	14.4	14.5	14.6	14.5	14.4	14.4	14.6	14.3
1992	14.5	14.4	14.5	14.5	14.6	14.8	15.0	14.9	14.8	14.6	14.7	14.6	14.6
1993	14.4	14.6	14.6	14.7	14.9	15.0	14.9	15.0	14.7	14.8	14.8	15.0	14.7
1994	14.7	14.7	14.7	14.7	14.7	14.8	14.9	14.8	14.9	14.5	14.4	14.6	14.7
1995	14.2	14.3	14.3	14.4	14.5	14.6	14.5	14.5	14.4	14.2	14.1	14.4	14.3
1996	14.2	14.1	14.1	14.1	14.0	14.1	14.0	14.0	13.9	14.1	14.0	14.2	14.0
1997	14.1	14.0	14.0	14.1	14.2	14.3	14.1	14.0	14.0	13.9	13.8	14.0	14.0
1998	14.0	13.9	13.8	14.1	14.1	14.3	14.2	14.1	14.0	13.9	13.9	14.2	14.0
1999	13.9	13.7	13.7	13.8	13.7	13.7	13.7	13.8	13.7	13.9	14.2	14.2	13.8
2000	13.8	13.7	14.0	14.1	15.2	14.0	14.2	14.0	13.7	13.5	13.6	13.9	13.9
2001	13.4	13.4	13.4	13.6	13.7	14.0	13.8	13.9	13.9	13.8	13.8	14.0	13.7
2002	13.7	13.6	13.7	13.7	13.9	14.2	14.0	14.2	14.1	14.0	13.9	14.2	13.9
2003	13.9	13.9	14.0	14.0	14.1	14.2	13.7	13.9	13.9	13.8	13.7	13.9	13.9
State government													
1990	13.5	15.5	15.6	15.7	14.9	13.0	12.9	14.0	16.6	16.6	16.0	15.8	15.0
1991	14.5	15.9	16.0	15.9	15.7	13.6	13.7	14.8	17.4	17.3	16.7	16.6	15.6
1992	15.2	17.1	16.9	16.8	16.4	14.3	14.2	15.4	17.7	18.1	17.2	16.8	16.3
1993	15.7	17.4	17.3	17.4	17.1	14.8	14.8	15.9	18.4	18.6	17.8	17.5	16.8
1994	16.0	17.8	18.0	18.1	17.8	15.6	15.5	16.6	19.0	19.1	18.5	18.3	17.5
1995	16.4	18.4	18.6	18.6	18.3	15.8	15.7	16.8	19.3	18.8	18.7	18.4	17.8
1996	16.3	18.6	18.5	18.9	19.1	17.3	17.1	18.3	21.2	20.9	21.1	21.7	19.0
1997	19.9	21.6	20.0	21.7	21.6	19.5	19.1	19.9	22.2	21.8	21.9	21.9	20.9
1998	20.1	22.1	22.0	22.0	21.9	20.2	19.5	19.7	22.2	21.7	21.9	21.7	21.2
1999	19.8	21.8	22.1	22.0	21.9	20.2	19.7	20.2	23.0	22.6	22.7	22.4	21.5
2000	20.4	22.5	22.8	22.7	22.5	20.3	20.8	21.2	23.5	23.0	22.9	22.9	22.1
2001	20.5	22.9	22.9	22.7	22.6	20.9	20.6	21.4	23.4	23.0	23.1	23.4	22.3
2002	21.2	23.4	23.4	23.4	23.0	21.4	21.2	21.9	23.6	23.7	23.8	23.9	22.8
2003	21.5	23.7	24.0	24.0	23.6	21.9	21.7	22.9	24.3	24.4	24.4	24.5	23.4

Employment by Industry: New Mexico—*Continued*

(Numbers in thousands. Not seasonally adjusted.)

Industry	January	February	March	April	May	June	July	August	September	October	November	December	Annual Average
ALBUQUERQUE—*Continued*													
Local government													
1990	24.9	25.0	25.2	25.1	25.2	25.6	25.3	24.5	24.8	25.2	25.3	25.3	25.1
1991	25.1	25.1	25.3	25.2	25.2	25.6	25.9	24.7	25.0	25.4	25.5	25.7	25.3
1992	25.5	25.9	25.9	26.0	26.0	26.2	25.9	25.0	25.5	26.1	26.2	26.2	25.8
1993	26.1	26.4	26.7	26.7	26.6	28.6	28.3	25.7	26.6	27.2	27.4	27.4	26.9
1994	27.1	27.3	27.4	27.5	27.4	28.7	28.4	26.0	27.4	27.8	28.1	28.1	27.6
1995	27.7	28.3	28.4	28.5	28.6	29.7	28.6	27.7	28.8	29.2	29.3	29.4	28.6
1996	29.4	29.8	30.0	29.8	29.5	31.0	29.5	27.9	28.3	28.6	28.3	28.1	29.1
1997	28.0	28.4	28.8	29.0	29.8	30.7	29.6	28.4	29.0	29.4	29.7	29.7	29.2
1998	29.8	29.9	30.0	30.2	30.3	32.1	31.3	29.5	30.0	30.6	30.9	30.9	30.4
1999	30.9	31.1	31.2	31.2	31.2	32.2	31.0	30.1	30.4	31.4	31.6	31.6	31.1
2000	31.6	31.9	32.0	32.0	31.9	32.4	31.5	30.8	31.3	31.7	32.0	31.7	31.7
2001	31.9	32.3	32.7	33.1	33.3	34.1	33.1	31.9	32.4	33.0	33.5	34.0	32.9
2002	33.8	34.2	34.4	34.4	34.6	36.4	35.3	34.0	34.5	33.9	34.3	34.5	34.5
2003	34.3	34.6	34.8	34.7	34.7	35.3	34.4	33.2	34.2	34.5	35.0	35.0	34.6
LAS CRUCES													
Total nonfarm													
1990	43.5	44.1	44.0	44.5	45.2	43.4	41.2	42.3	44.0	44.4	44.7	44.8	43.8
1991	42.5	43.2	43.5	43.7	43.6	42.4	41.8	42.1	44.1	44.7	45.1	45.2	43.4
1992	43.7	44.4	44.6	44.8	44.7	43.3	43.1	43.2	45.3	45.8	45.9	46.0	44.5
1993	45.2	45.7	45.8	46.1	46.1	45.9	43.4	44.0	46.2	46.8	47.5	47.6	45.8
1994	45.9	46.4	46.6	47.3	47.1	46.2	44.3	45.5	47.6	48.0	48.7	49.3	46.9
1995	48.0	48.4	48.6	48.5	48.7	47.9	46.3	46.8	49.0	49.7	50.2	50.1	48.5
1996	49.4	49.9	50.3	50.2	50.2	48.9	48.0	48.8	50.5	50.8	50.7	51.0	49.8
1997	49.9	50.4	50.2	50.9	51.5	50.1	49.2	50.0	51.6	52.7	53.2	53.3	51.0
1998	51.8	52.1	52.6	52.5	52.8	51.5	49.8	53.0	53.2	53.7	53.9	53.9	52.5
1999	53.7	54.0	54.8	55.1	55.1	54.1	52.3	55.6	56.0	56.4	56.7	56.9	55.0
2000	56.9	57.0	57.2	56.9	57.4	55.1	54.1	56.9	57.5	58.3	58.6	58.0	56.9
2001	56.6	57.5	58.4	58.6	59.5	56.3	55.0	57.2	58.2	58.5	58.3	58.1	57.7
2002	58.1	58.8	59.6	60.0	60.3	58.1	57.2	60.6	60.5	61.1	61.3	60.8	59.7
2003	60.3	60.8	61.3	62.0	62.5	59.9	59.3	61.8	62.2	62.6	63.0	62.7	61.5
Total private													
1990	25.8	25.5	25.4	25.8	26.5	26.1	26.0	26.5	26.7	26.6	26.7	26.9	26.2
1991	25.4	25.4	25.5	25.6	25.6	25.5	25.6	26.4	26.6	26.6	26.6	26.7	25.9
1992	25.6	25.9	26.2	26.3	26.3	26.1	26.6	27.1	27.3	27.2	27.2	27.4	26.6
1993	27.0	27.2	27.1	27.6	27.5	27.4	27.4	28.3	28.8	28.5	29.1	29.1	27.9
1994	27.8	28.0	28.1	28.7	28.5	28.3	28.2	29.2	29.7	29.5	29.8	30.3	28.8
1995	29.3	29.4	29.6	29.3	29.6	29.7	29.5	30.2	30.5	30.5	30.7	30.6	29.9
1996	30.3	30.7	30.8	30.7	30.6	30.3	30.4	31.2	31.4	31.0	30.8	31.0	30.7
1997	30.3	30.4	30.3	30.8	31.2	31.1	31.2	32.0	32.4	32.5	32.9	33.0	31.5
1998	31.7	31.9	32.1	33.8	34.0	33.9	34.0	34.9	35.1	35.0	35.0	35.2	33.8
1999	35.2	35.6	36.0	36.3	36.5	36.5	36.3	37.1	37.2	37.2	37.0	37.7	36.5
2000	37.5	37.6	37.6	37.5	37.9	37.6	37.5	38.4	38.7	38.8	38.9	38.6	38.0
2001	37.5	37.7	38.1	38.1	39.1	38.8	38.6	38.9	38.7	38.5	38.2	38.5	38.4
2002	38.5	38.6	39.2	39.8	39.9	40.1	40.2	41.0	40.7	40.7	40.9	40.8	40.0
2003	40.2	40.1	40.4	41.1	41.7	41.5	41.4	42.2	41.7	41.7	42.0	42.0	41.3
Goods-producing													
1990	4.8	4.9	4.8	4.9	5.1	5.1	5.1	5.5	5.4	5.4	5.3	5.2	5.1
1991	4.7	4.7	4.8	4.6	4.7	4.7	4.6	5.1	5.1	5.0	4.8	4.7	4.7
1992	4.6	4.7	4.9	4.8	4.9	4.8	4.9	5.2	5.2	4.9	4.9	4.8	4.8
1993	4.7	4.7	4.7	4.9	4.8	4.8	4.8	5.3	5.4	4.9	5.0	4.9	4.9
1994	4.7	4.8	4.9	4.9	5.0	5.1	5.1	5.6	5.7	5.4	5.6	5.5	5.1
1995	5.5	5.5	5.6	5.5	5.5	5.6	5.5	6.0	6.0	5.8	5.8	5.7	5.6
1996	5.6	5.7	5.8	5.8	5.8	5.7	5.6	6.0	6.0	5.8	5.7	5.7	5.7
1997	5.3	5.5	5.5	5.5	5.6	5.6	5.5	5.9	6.0	5.8	5.9	5.7	5.6
1998	5.4	5.5	5.6	5.7	5.7	5.7	6.0	6.3	6.4	6.3	6.1	6.1	5.9
1999	6.3	6.4	6.4	6.3	6.3	6.5	6.4	6.7	6.6	6.5	6.3	6.3	6.4
2000	6.3	6.2	6.3	6.3	6.5	6.5	6.5	6.7	6.7	6.7	6.6	6.5	6.4
2001	6.2	6.1	6.1	6.2	6.4	6.4	6.3	6.4	6.5	6.5	6.3	6.2	6.3
2002	6.1	6.0	6.2	6.3	6.3	6.5	6.5	6.6	6.7	6.7	6.8	6.7	6.5
2003	6.5	6.4	6.5	6.6	6.7	6.8	6.8	6.9	6.9	6.9	7.0	6.9	6.7
Construction and mining													
1990	2.1	2.2	2.2	2.2	2.3	2.3	2.3	2.4	2.2	2.2	2.2	2.1	2.2
1991	2.0	2.0	2.1	2.1	2.2	2.1	2.1	2.2	2.1	2.1	2.1	2.1	2.1
1992	2.2	2.2	2.4	2.4	2.5	2.4	2.4	2.4	2.3	2.3	2.3	2.3	2.3
1993	2.3	2.4	2.5	2.6	2.6	2.6	2.6	2.6	2.7	2.5	2.6	2.5	2.5
1994	2.5	2.6	2.7	2.7	2.8	2.8	2.9	2.9	3.0	3.0	3.1	3.1	2.8
1995	3.1	3.1	3.3	3.1	3.1	3.2	3.2	3.3	3.2	3.1	3.1	3.2	3.1
1996	3.3	3.3	3.4	3.4	3.4	3.3	3.2	3.3	3.2	3.1	3.0	3.0	3.2
1997	2.8	3.0	3.0	3.0	3.1	3.1	3.1	3.1	3.1	3.2	3.2	3.1	3.0
1998	2.9	3.0	3.0	3.1	3.1	3.1	3.2	3.1	3.1	3.1	3.1	3.1	3.0
1999	3.2	3.3	3.4	3.3	3.3	3.5	3.4	3.4	3.3	3.3	3.2	3.3	3.3
2000	3.2	3.2	3.3	3.3	3.4	3.4	3.4	3.4	3.3	3.3	3.3	3.2	3.3
2001	3.0	3.0	3.0	3.1	3.3	3.3	3.2	3.2	3.2	3.1	3.2	3.1	3.1
2002	3.1	3.1	3.3	3.4	3.4	3.5	3.5	3.5	3.5	3.5	3.5	3.5	3.4
2003	3.5	3.5	3.6	3.7	3.8	3.8	3.7	3.7	3.7	3.7	3.7	3.7	3.7

Employment by Industry: New Mexico—*Continued*

(Numbers in thousands. Not seasonally adjusted.)

Industry	January	February	March	April	May	June	July	August	September	October	November	December	Annual Average
LAS CRUCES—*Continued*													
Manufacturing													
1990	2.7	2.7	2.6	2.7	2.8	2.8	2.8	3.1	3.2	3.2	3.1	3.1	2.9
1991	2.7	2.7	2.7	2.5	2.5	2.6	2.5	2.9	3.0	2.9	2.7	2.6	2.6
1992	2.4	2.5	2.5	2.4	2.4	2.4	2.5	2.8	2.9	2.6	2.6	2.5	2.5
1993	2.4	2.3	2.2	2.3	2.2	2.2	2.2	2.7	2.7	2.4	2.4	2.4	2.3
1994	2.2	2.2	2.2	2.2	2.2	2.3	2.2	2.7	2.7	2.4	2.5	2.4	2.3
1995	2.4	2.4	2.3	2.4	2.4	2.4	2.3	2.7	2.8	2.7	2.7	2.5	2.5
1996	2.3	2.4	2.4	2.4	2.4	2.4	2.4	2.7	2.8	2.7	2.7	2.7	2.5
1997	2.5	2.5	2.5	2.5	2.5	2.5	2.4	2.8	2.9	2.6	2.7	2.6	2.5
1998	2.5	2.5	2.6	2.6	2.6	2.6	2.8	3.2	3.3	3.2	3.0	3.0	2.8
1999	3.1	3.1	3.0	3.0	3.0	3.0	3.0	3.3	3.3	3.2	3.1	3.0	3.0
2000	3.1	3.0	3.0	3.0	3.1	3.1	3.1	3.3	3.4	3.4	3.3	3.3	3.1
2001	3.2	3.1	3.1	3.1	3.1	3.1	3.1	3.2	3.3	3.4	3.1	3.1	3.2
2002	3.0	2.9	2.9	2.9	2.9	3.0	3.0	3.1	3.2	3.2	3.3	3.2	3.1
2003	3.0	2.9	2.9	2.9	2.9	3.0	3.1	3.2	3.2	3.2	3.3	3.2	3.1
Service-providing													
1990	38.7	39.2	39.2	39.6	40.1	38.3	36.1	36.8	38.6	39.0	39.4	39.6	38.7
1991	37.8	38.5	38.7	39.1	38.9	37.7	37.2	37.0	39.0	39.7	40.3	40.5	38.7
1992	39.1	39.7	39.7	40.0	39.8	38.5	38.2	38.0	40.1	40.9	41.0	41.2	39.6
1993	40.5	41.0	41.1	41.2	41.3	41.1	38.6	38.7	40.8	41.9	42.5	42.7	40.9
1994	41.2	41.6	41.7	42.4	42.1	41.1	39.2	39.9	41.9	42.6	43.1	43.8	41.7
1995	42.5	42.9	43.0	43.0	43.2	42.3	40.8	40.8	43.0	43.9	44.4	44.4	42.8
1996	43.8	44.2	44.5	44.4	44.4	43.2	42.4	42.8	44.5	45.0	45.0	45.3	44.1
1997	44.6	44.9	44.7	45.4	45.9	44.5	43.7	44.1	45.6	46.9	47.3	47.6	45.4
1998	46.4	46.6	47.0	46.8	47.1	45.8	43.8	46.7	46.8	47.4	47.8	47.8	46.6
1999	47.4	47.6	48.4	48.8	48.8	47.6	45.9	48.9	49.4	49.9	50.4	50.6	48.6
2000	50.6	50.8	50.9	50.6	50.9	48.6	47.6	50.2	50.8	51.6	52.0	51.5	50.5
2001	50.4	51.4	52.3	52.4	53.1	49.9	48.7	50.8	51.7	52.0	52.0	51.9	51.4
2002	52.0	52.8	53.4	53.7	54.0	51.6	50.7	54.0	53.8	54.4	54.5	54.1	53.3
2003	53.8	54.4	54.8	55.4	55.8	53.1	52.5	54.9	55.3	55.7	56.0	55.8	54.8
Trade, transportation, and utilities													
1990	7.3	6.9	6.9	6.9	7.4	7.2	7.0	7.1	7.4	7.4	7.7	7.9	7.2
1991	7.1	7.0	6.9	7.1	7.0	6.8	6.9	7.0	7.2	7.3	7.4	7.5	7.1
1992	7.0	7.1	7.0	7.1	7.1	7.0	7.0	7.0	7.2	7.3	7.4	7.6	7.1
1993	7.3	7.4	7.2	7.4	7.3	7.2	7.2	7.4	7.5	7.7	8.0	8.1	7.4
1994	7.5	7.5	7.5	7.7	7.7	7.5	7.6	7.7	8.0	7.8	8.0	8.2	7.7
1995	7.8	7.7	7.8	7.7	8.0	7.9	7.9	7.9	8.1	8.2	8.4	8.4	7.9
1996	8.3	8.3	8.3	8.1	8.1	7.9	8.0	8.2	8.2	8.2	8.3	8.5	8.2
1997	8.2	8.2	8.1	8.0	8.2	8.2	8.3	8.6	8.7	8.9	9.1	9.1	8.4
1998	8.7	8.6	8.6	8.4	8.5	8.5	8.4	8.7	8.6	8.6	8.7	8.8	8.5
1999	8.7	8.7	8.7	8.6	8.7	8.8	8.6	8.7	8.9	8.8	8.9	9.1	8.7
2000	8.8	8.8	8.8	8.9	9.0	9.0	8.8	9.0	9.1	9.1	9.3	9.4	9.0
2001	9.0	8.9	8.9	8.8	9.2	9.1	9.0	9.0	8.9	8.9	8.9	9.1	9.0
2002	8.7	8.7	8.8	8.9	9.0	9.0	9.1	9.4	9.1	9.1	9.3	9.3	9.0
2003	8.9	8.8	8.9	8.8	9.1	9.1	9.1	9.6	9.4	9.4	9.6	9.7	9.2
Wholesale trade													
1990	0.8	0.7	0.7	0.7	0.8	0.8	0.7	0.7	0.7	0.9	1.0	1.0	0.7
1991	0.9	0.8	0.7	0.7	0.7	0.7	0.8	0.8	0.8	0.8	0.8	0.8	0.7
1992	0.7	0.7	0.7	0.8	0.8	0.8	0.8	0.8	0.8	0.9	0.9	0.9	0.8
1993	0.8	0.8	0.7	0.7	0.7	0.8	0.8	0.8	0.8	0.9	1.0	0.9	0.8
1994	0.8	0.8	0.8	0.8	0.8	0.8	0.9	1.0	1.0	0.8	0.8	0.8	0.8
1995	0.8	0.8	0.8	0.8	0.8	0.9	0.9	0.9	0.9	0.9	0.9	0.8	0.8
1996	0.9	0.9	0.9	0.9	0.9	0.9	0.9	0.9	0.9	0.9	0.9	0.9	0.9
1997	1.0	1.0	0.9	0.8	0.9	0.9	0.9	0.9	0.9	0.9	0.9	0.9	0.9
1998	0.8	0.8	0.8	0.8	0.8	0.8	0.8	0.9	0.8	0.8	0.8	0.8	0.8
1999	0.8	0.8	0.8	0.9	0.9	0.9	1.0	0.9	0.9	0.9	0.9	0.9	0.8
2000	0.9	0.9	0.9	1.0	1.0	1.1	1.0	1.0	1.1	1.1	1.1	1.1	1.0
2001	1.1	1.1	1.2	1.1	1.2	1.3	1.3	1.3	1.2	1.1	1.0	1.0	1.2
2002	1.0	1.0	1.0	1.1	1.1	1.1	1.2	1.2	1.1	1.0	1.1	1.0	1.1
2003	1.0	1.0	1.0	1.0	1.1	1.1	1.1	1.1	1.1	1.0	1.1	1.0	1.1
Retail trade													
1990	5.4	5.2	5.2	5.2	5.5	5.5	5.5	5.5	5.6	5.5	5.7	5.8	5.4
1991	5.3	5.3	5.2	5.3	5.3	5.3	5.3	5.4	5.4	5.5	5.6	5.6	5.3
1992	5.4	5.4	5.4	5.4	5.4	5.4	5.4	5.4	5.4	5.4	5.5	5.7	5.4
1993	5.5	5.6	5.5	5.7	5.6	5.6	5.6	5.7	5.7	5.8	5.9	6.1	5.6
1994	5.7	5.7	5.7	5.8	5.8	5.8	5.8	5.8	5.9	5.9	6.1	6.3	5.8
1995	5.9	5.8	5.9	5.8	6.0	6.0	6.0	6.0	6.0	6.1	6.3	6.4	6.0
1996	6.2	6.2	6.2	6.0	6.0	6.0	6.0	6.1	6.1	6.1	6.2	6.3	6.1
1997	6.0	6.0	6.0	6.0	6.1	6.3	6.4	6.6	6.6	6.7	6.9	6.9	6.3
1998	6.5	6.4	6.4	6.3	6.3	6.4	6.4	6.5	6.4	6.4	6.5	6.6	6.4
1999	6.5	6.5	6.5	6.3	6.4	6.5	6.4	6.4	6.6	6.5	6.6	6.8	6.5
2000	6.4	6.4	6.4	6.4	6.5	6.5	6.4	6.4	6.4	6.4	6.6	6.6	6.4
2001	6.4	6.3	6.2	6.3	6.4	6.5	6.4	6.3	6.3	6.3	6.4	6.5	6.4
2002	6.2	6.2	6.3	6.3	6.4	6.5	6.5	6.6	6.5	6.6	6.7	6.8	6.5
2003	6.4	6.3	6.4	6.3	6.5	6.5	6.7	6.9	6.8	6.8	6.9	7.1	6.6

Employment by Industry: New Mexico—*Continued*

(Numbers in thousands. Not seasonally adjusted.)

Industry	January	February	March	April	May	June	July	August	September	October	November	December	Annual Average
LAS CRUCES—*Continued*													
Transportation and utilities													
1990	1.1	1.0	1.0	1.0	1.1	0.9	0.8	0.9	1.1	1.0	1.0	1.1	1.0
1991	0.9	0.9	1.0	1.1	1.0	0.8	0.8	0.8	1.0	1.0	1.0	1.1	0.9
1992	0.9	1.0	0.9	0.9	0.9	0.8	0.8	0.8	1.0	1.0	1.0	1.0	0.9
1993	1.0	1.0	1.0	1.0	1.0	0.8	0.8	0.9	1.0	1.0	1.1	1.1	0.9
1994	1.0	1.0	1.0	1.1	1.1	0.9	0.9	0.9	1.1	1.1	1.1	1.1	1.0
1995	1.1	1.1	1.1	1.1	1.2	1.0	1.0	1.0	1.2	1.2	1.2	1.2	1.1
1996	1.2	1.2	1.2	1.2	1.2	1.0	1.1	1.2	1.2	1.2	1.2	1.3	1.1
1997	1.2	1.2	1.2	1.2	1.2	1.0	1.0	1.1	1.2	1.3	1.3	1.3	1.1
1998	1.4	1.4	1.4	1.3	1.4	1.3	1.2	1.3	1.4	1.4	1.4	1.4	1.3
1999	1.4	1.4	1.4	1.4	1.4	1.4	1.2	1.4	1.4	1.4	1.4	1.4	1.3
2000	1.5	1.5	1.5	1.5	1.5	1.4	1.4	1.6	1.6	1.6	1.6	1.7	1.5
2001	1.5	1.5	1.5	1.4	1.6	1.3	1.3	1.4	1.4	1.5	1.5	1.6	1.5
2002	1.5	1.5	1.5	1.5	1.5	1.4	1.4	1.6	1.5	1.5	1.5	1.5	1.5
2003	1.5	1.5	1.5	1.5	1.5	1.5	1.3	1.6	1.5	1.6	1.6	1.6	1.5
Information													
1990	0.8	0.8	0.8	0.8	0.8	0.8	0.8	0.8	0.8	0.8	0.8	0.8	0.8
1991	0.8	0.8	0.8	0.8	0.8	0.8	0.8	0.8	0.8	0.9	0.9	0.9	0.8
1992	0.9	0.9	0.9	0.9	0.9	1.0	1.0	1.0	1.0	1.0	1.0	1.0	0.9
1993	1.0	1.0	1.0	0.9	0.9	0.9	1.0	1.0	1.0	1.0	1.0	1.0	0.9
1994	1.0	1.0	1.0	1.0	1.0	1.0	1.0	1.0	1.0	1.0	1.0	1.0	1.0
1995	1.0	1.0	0.9	0.9	0.9	0.9	0.9	0.9	0.9	0.9	0.9	0.9	0.9
1996	0.9	0.9	0.9	0.9	0.9	0.9	0.9	0.9	0.9	0.9	0.9	0.9	0.9
1997	0.8	0.8	0.8	0.8	0.9	0.9	0.8	0.8	0.8	0.8	0.8	0.8	0.8
1998	0.8	0.8	0.8	0.8	0.8	0.8	0.8	0.8	0.8	0.8	0.8	0.8	0.8
1999	0.8	0.8	0.8	0.8	0.8	0.8	0.8	0.8	0.8	0.8	0.8	0.8	0.8
2000	0.8	0.8	0.8	0.8	0.8	0.8	0.8	0.8	0.8	0.8	0.8	0.8	0.8
2001	0.8	0.8	0.8	0.9	1.0	1.0	0.9	0.9	0.9	0.9	0.9	0.9	0.9
2002	0.9	1.0	1.1	1.2	1.1	1.0	1.0	1.0	1.0	1.0	1.0	1.0	1.0
2003	1.0	1.0	1.0	1.2	1.2	1.2	1.2	1.2	1.2	1.2	1.2	1.2	1.2
Financial activities													
1990	1.7	1.7	1.7	1.7	1.7	1.7	1.7	1.7	1.7	1.8	1.7	1.7	1.7
1991	1.7	1.7	1.7	1.8	1.8	1.8	1.9	1.9	1.9	1.8	1.8	1.8	1.8
1992	1.8	1.8	1.8	1.8	1.8	1.8	1.8	1.9	1.9	1.9	1.9	1.9	1.8
1993	2.0	2.0	2.0	2.0	2.0	2.0	2.1	2.1	2.1	2.0	2.1	2.1	2.0
1994	2.0	2.0	2.0	2.0	2.1	2.1	2.0	2.1	2.0	2.0	2.0	2.1	2.0
1995	2.0	2.0	2.0	1.9	1.9	2.0	2.0	2.0	2.0	2.0	2.0	2.0	1.9
1996	2.0	2.0	2.0	2.0	2.0	2.0	2.0	2.0	2.0	2.0	2.0	2.0	2.0
1997	1.9	1.9	1.9	1.9	1.9	1.9	2.1	2.1	2.1	2.1	2.1	2.1	2.0
1998	2.0	2.1	2.1	2.2	2.2	2.2	2.2	2.2	2.3	2.2	2.2	2.2	2.1
1999	2.2	2.2	2.2	2.2	2.2	2.2	2.2	2.2	2.2	2.2	2.2	2.2	2.2
2000	2.1	2.1	2.1	2.0	2.1	2.0	2.1	2.1	2.0	2.1	2.1	2.1	2.0
2001	2.1	2.1	2.1	2.0	2.0	2.0	2.0	2.0	2.0	2.0	1.9	2.0	2.0
2002	2.2	2.2	2.2	2.2	2.2	2.2	2.2	2.2	2.2	2.2	2.2	2.1	2.2
2003	2.2	2.1	2.1	2.2	2.3	2.3	2.3	2.3	2.3	2.3	2.3	2.2	2.2
Professional and business services													
1990	2.7	2.7	2.7	2.7	2.7	2.7	2.8	2.7	2.7	2.7	2.6	2.7	2.7
1991	2.8	2.8	2.8	2.6	2.6	2.7	2.6	2.6	2.6	2.7	2.7	2.9	2.7
1992	2.7	2.7	2.7	2.7	2.7	2.7	2.8	2.8	2.8	2.8	2.8	2.9	2.7
1993	2.8	2.7	2.7	2.7	2.8	2.8	2.7	2.7	2.8	2.8	2.9	2.9	2.7
1994	2.8	2.8	2.8	2.8	2.4	2.4	2.4	2.5	2.6	2.6	2.5	2.8	2.6
1995	2.6	2.7	2.7	2.6	2.5	2.6	2.5	2.6	2.6	2.6	2.6	2.6	2.6
1996	2.6	2.6	2.6	2.6	2.6	2.6	2.5	2.5	2.5	2.7	2.6	2.6	2.5
1997	2.8	2.8	2.8	3.1	3.0	3.1	3.4	3.4	3.4	3.6	3.7	3.8	3.2
1998	3.8	3.7	3.8	4.0	4.0	4.1	4.1	4.1	4.2	4.3	4.3	4.4	4.0
1999	3.9	4.1	4.3	4.7	4.7	4.7	4.8	5.0	5.1	5.2	5.1	5.1	4.7
2000	5.2	5.3	5.1	5.1	5.1	5.1	5.1	5.2	5.3	5.3	5.4	5.1	5.1
2001	5.3	5.5	5.7	5.6	5.7	5.6	5.6	5.7	5.5	5.4	5.3	5.3	5.5
2002	5.4	5.3	5.3	5.4	5.4	5.6	5.7	5.6	5.3	5.3	5.1	5.0	5.4
2003	5.1	5.1	5.1	5.3	5.4	5.3	5.2	5.2	5.2	5.2	5.2	5.2	5.2
Educational and health services													
1990	2.9	2.8	2.8	2.9	2.9	2.8	2.9	3.0	3.0	3.0	3.0	3.1	2.9
1991	3.0	3.0	3.1	3.1	3.1	3.0	2.9	3.1	3.2	3.1	3.2	3.2	3.0
1992	3.1	3.1	3.2	3.3	3.3	3.2	3.3	3.4	3.4	3.5	3.4	3.4	3.3
1993	3.6	3.7	3.8	3.8	3.9	3.9	3.8	4.0	4.1	4.1	4.2	4.2	3.9
1994	4.0	4.1	4.1	4.1	4.1	4.1	4.0	4.2	4.2	4.4	4.4	4.4	4.1
1995	4.4	4.5	4.5	4.5	4.6	4.5	4.5	4.6	4.7	4.7	4.7	4.7	4.5
1996	4.8	4.9	5.0	4.9	4.9	4.8	5.0	5.2	5.5	5.2	5.1	5.0	5.0
1997	5.0	5.0	5.0	5.0	5.1	4.9	4.9	5.0	5.1	5.1	5.2	5.2	5.0
1998	5.0	5.1	5.1	6.5	6.6	6.4	6.2	6.4	6.5	6.5	6.6	6.5	6.1
1999	6.8	6.8	6.9	6.9	7.0	6.8	6.8	7.0	7.0	7.0	7.0	7.2	6.9
2000	7.3	7.4	7.4	7.3	7.3	7.2	7.2	7.5	7.6	7.6	7.6	7.6	7.4
2001	7.2	7.3	7.4	7.5	7.6	7.6	7.7	7.9	7.9	7.7	7.8	7.9	7.6
2002	8.1	8.2	8.3	8.5	8.4	8.4	8.3	8.8	8.8	8.9	9.0	9.0	8.6
2003	9.0	9.1	9.0	9.0	9.1	9.0	9.2	9.4	9.1	9.1	9.1	9.1	9.1

Employment by Industry: New Mexico—*Continued*

(Numbers in thousands. Not seasonally adjusted.)

Industry	January	February	March	April	May	June	July	August	September	October	November	December	Annual Average
LAS CRUCES—*Continued*													
Leisure and hospitality													
1990	4.5	4.5	4.5	4.7	4.6	4.5	4.3	4.4	4.4	4.2	4.3	4.3	4.4
1991	4.1	4.1	4.1	4.3	4.2	4.3	4.4	4.5	4.5	4.5	4.5	4.4	4.3
1992	4.2	4.3	4.4	4.4	4.3	4.2	4.4	4.5	4.5	4.5	4.5	4.5	4.3
1993	4.3	4.4	4.4	4.5	4.4	4.4	4.4	4.4	4.5	4.6	4.5	4.5	4.4
1994	4.5	4.5	4.5	4.8	4.8	4.6	4.6	4.7	4.8	4.9	4.9	4.9	4.7
1995	4.6	4.6	4.7	4.8	4.8	4.7	4.6	4.7	4.8	4.8	4.8	4.8	4.7
1996	4.7	4.8	4.8	4.9	4.8	4.8	4.8	4.8	4.8	4.7	4.7	4.8	4.7
1997	4.8	4.7	4.7	5.0	4.9	4.9	4.5	4.6	4.7	4.6	4.6	4.7	4.7
1998	4.4	4.5	4.5	4.6	4.6	4.5	4.6	4.7	4.7	4.7	4.7	4.9	4.6
1999	4.9	5.0	5.1	5.2	5.2	5.1	5.1	5.1	5.1	5.2	5.2	5.5	5.1
2000	5.5	5.5	5.6	5.6	5.6	5.5	5.5	5.6	5.7	5.7	5.6	5.6	5.5
2001	5.4	5.5	5.6	5.6	5.7	5.6	5.6	5.6	5.6	5.7	5.7	5.7	5.6
2002	5.7	5.8	5.9	5.9	6.0	6.0	5.9	6.0	6.2	6.0	6.1	6.3	6.0
2003	6.1	6.2	6.3	6.5	6.4	6.3	6.1	6.2	6.2	6.2	6.2	6.3	6.3
Other services													
1990	1.1	1.2	1.2	1.2	1.3	1.3	1.4	1.3	1.3	1.3	1.3	1.2	1.2
1991	1.2	1.3	1.3	1.3	1.4	1.4	1.5	1.4	1.3	1.3	1.3	1.3	1.3
1992	1.3	1.3	1.3	1.3	1.3	1.4	1.4	1.3	1.3	1.3	1.3	1.3	1.3
1993	1.3	1.3	1.3	1.4	1.4	1.4	1.4	1.4	1.4	1.4	1.4	1.4	1.3
1994	1.3	1.3	1.3	1.4	1.4	1.5	1.5	1.4	1.4	1.4	1.4	1.4	1.3
1995	1.4	1.4	1.4	1.4	1.4	1.5	1.6	1.5	1.4	1.5	1.5	1.5	1.4
1996	1.4	1.5	1.4	1.5	1.5	1.6	1.6	1.6	1.5	1.5	1.5	1.5	1.5
1997	1.5	1.5	1.5	1.5	1.6	1.6	1.7	1.6	1.6	1.6	1.5	1.6	1.5
1998	1.6	1.6	1.6	1.6	1.6	1.7	1.7	1.7	1.6	1.6	1.6	1.5	1.6
1999	1.6	1.6	1.6	1.6	1.6	1.6	1.6	1.6	1.5	1.5	1.5	1.5	1.5
2000	1.5	1.5	1.5	1.5	1.5	1.5	1.5	1.5	1.5	1.5	1.5	1.5	1.5
2001	1.5	1.5	1.5	1.5	1.5	1.5	1.5	1.4	1.4	1.4	1.4	1.4	1.5
2002	1.4	1.4	1.4	1.4	1.5	1.4	1.5	1.4	1.4	1.5	1.4	1.4	1.4
2003	1.4	1.4	1.5	1.5	1.5	1.5	1.5	1.4	1.4	1.4	1.4	1.4	1.4
Government													
1990	17.7	18.6	18.6	18.7	18.7	17.3	15.2	15.8	17.3	17.8	18.0	17.9	17.6
1991	17.1	17.8	18.0	18.1	18.0	16.9	16.2	15.7	17.5	18.1	18.5	18.5	17.5
1992	18.1	18.5	18.4	18.5	18.4	17.2	16.5	16.1	18.0	18.6	18.7	18.6	17.9
1993	18.2	18.5	18.7	18.5	18.6	18.5	16.0	15.7	17.4	18.3	18.4	18.5	17.9
1994	18.1	18.4	18.5	18.6	18.6	17.9	16.1	16.3	17.9	18.5	18.9	19.0	18.0
1995	18.7	19.0	19.0	19.2	19.1	18.2	16.8	16.6	18.5	19.2	19.5	19.5	18.6
1996	19.1	19.2	19.5	19.5	19.6	18.6	17.6	17.6	19.1	19.8	19.9	20.0	19.1
1997	19.6	20.0	19.9	20.1	20.3	19.0	18.0	18.0	19.2	20.2	20.3	20.3	19.5
1998	20.1	20.2	20.5	18.7	18.8	17.6	15.8	18.1	18.1	18.7	18.9	18.7	18.6
1999	18.5	18.4	18.8	18.8	18.6	17.6	16.0	18.5	18.8	19.2	19.7	19.2	18.5
2000	19.4	19.4	19.6	19.4	19.5	17.5	16.6	18.5	18.8	19.5	19.7	19.4	18.9
2001	19.1	19.8	20.3	20.5	20.4	17.5	16.4	18.3	19.5	20.0	20.1	19.6	19.3
2002	19.6	20.2	20.4	20.2	20.4	18.0	17.0	19.6	19.8	20.4	20.4	20.0	19.7
2003	20.1	20.7	20.9	20.9	20.8	18.4	17.9	19.6	20.5	20.9	21.0	20.7	20.2
Federal government													
1990	4.7	4.7	4.7	4.8	4.9	4.8	4.9	4.7	4.6	4.5	4.5	4.5	4.6
1991	4.5	4.5	4.5	4.5	4.5	4.6	4.6	4.6	4.5	4.4	4.5	4.5	4.5
1992	4.5	4.5	4.5	4.5	4.5	4.5	4.5	4.5	4.3	4.3	4.3	4.3	4.4
1993	4.2	4.2	4.2	3.9	3.9	3.9	3.9	3.8	3.7	3.7	3.7	3.7	3.9
1994	3.7	3.7	3.7	3.7	3.7	3.7	3.8	3.7	3.7	3.7	3.7	3.7	3.7
1995	3.7	3.7	3.7	3.7	3.7	3.7	3.8	3.7	3.7	3.7	3.7	3.7	3.7
1996	3.7	3.7	3.7	3.7	3.8	3.9	3.9	3.8	3.9	3.9	3.8	3.9	3.8
1997	3.8	3.8	3.8	3.8	3.8	3.8	3.8	3.8	3.8	3.8	3.8	3.8	3.8
1998	3.8	3.8	3.8	3.6	3.6	3.6	3.6	3.6	3.6	3.5	3.5	3.5	3.6
1999	3.5	3.5	3.5	3.5	3.5	3.5	3.5	3.5	3.5	3.5	3.5	3.5	3.5
2000	3.5	3.5	3.7	3.6	3.8	3.6	3.7	3.5	3.5	3.4	3.4	3.4	3.5
2001	3.4	3.4	3.4	3.4	3.4	3.5	3.5	3.5	3.4	3.5	3.5	3.5	3.5
2002	3.4	3.4	3.4	3.4	3.5	3.6	3.6	3.6	3.5	3.5	3.5	3.5	3.5
2003	3.5	3.5	3.5	3.5	3.5	3.6	3.6	3.6	3.5	3.5	3.5	3.6	3.5
State government													
1990	7.1	7.8	7.9	7.8	7.6	6.3	5.3	5.8	6.7	7.1	7.2	7.1	6.9
1991	6.5	7.0	7.1	7.2	7.1	5.9	5.4	5.3	6.7	7.2	7.4	7.3	6.6
1992	7.1	7.3	7.3	7.4	7.3	6.0	5.7	5.7	7.2	7.7	7.7	7.6	7.0
1993	7.4	7.4	7.6	7.7	7.8	7.7	5.9	5.7	7.1	7.8	7.9	7.8	7.3
1994	7.6	7.6	7.8	7.9	7.8	6.6	6.0	5.9	7.2	7.8	8.0	8.0	7.3
1995	7.7	7.7	7.9	8.0	7.9	6.9	5.9	5.9	7.4	7.9	8.1	8.0	7.4
1996	7.6	7.6	7.9	7.8	7.9	6.7	5.9	5.9	7.4	7.9	8.1	8.0	7.3
1997	7.7	7.9	7.9	8.1	8.1	6.9	6.0	5.9	7.2	8.0	8.1	8.1	7.4
1998	7.8	7.8	8.2	8.0	8.1	7.0	6.1	7.6	7.7	8.1	8.3	8.1	7.7
1999	7.8	7.7	7.9	8.0	7.8	6.8	6.1	7.7	7.9	8.3	8.5	8.1	7.7
2000	8.5	8.5	8.4	8.4	8.2	6.4	6.7	7.8	8.0	8.6	8.8	8.5	8.0
2001	8.2	8.9	9.3	9.5	9.4	6.4	6.6	8.0	8.5	8.7	8.8	8.2	8.4
2002	8.4	8.9	9.1	8.9	9.0	6.6	6.9	8.2	8.4	8.9	8.8	8.4	8.4
2003	8.6	9.1	9.3	9.4	9.1	6.9	7.2	8.2	9.0	9.3	9.3	8.8	8.7

Employment by Industry: New Mexico—*Continued*

(Numbers in thousands. Not seasonally adjusted.)

Industry	January	February	March	April	May	June	July	August	September	October	November	December	Annual Average
LAS CRUCES—*Continued*													
Local government													
1990	5.9	6.1	6.0	6.1	6.2	6.2	5.0	5.3	6.0	6.2	6.3	6.3	5.9
1991	6.1	6.3	6.4	6.4	6.4	6.4	6.2	5.8	6.3	6.5	6.6	6.7	6.3
1992	6.5	6.7	6.6	6.6	6.6	6.7	6.3	5.9	6.5	6.6	6.7	6.7	6.5
1993	6.6	6.9	6.9	6.9	6.9	6.9	6.2	6.2	6.6	6.8	6.8	7.0	6.7
1994	6.8	7.1	7.0	7.0	7.1	7.6	6.3	6.7	7.0	7.0	7.2	7.3	7.0
1995	7.3	7.6	7.4	7.5	7.5	7.6	7.1	7.0	7.4	7.6	7.7	7.8	7.4
1996	7.8	7.9	7.9	8.0	7.9	8.0	7.8	7.9	7.8	8.0	8.0	8.1	7.9
1997	8.1	8.3	8.2	8.2	8.4	8.3	8.2	8.3	8.2	8.4	8.4	8.4	8.2
1998	8.5	8.6	8.5	7.1	7.1	7.0	6.1	6.9	6.8	7.1	7.1	7.1	7.3
1999	7.2	7.2	7.4	7.3	7.3	7.3	6.4	7.3	7.4	7.4	7.7	7.6	7.2
2000	7.4	7.4	7.5	7.4	7.5	7.5	6.2	7.2	7.3	7.5	7.5	7.5	7.3
2001	7.5	7.5	7.6	7.6	7.6	7.6	6.3	6.8	7.6	7.8	7.8	7.9	7.5
2002	7.8	7.9	7.9	7.9	7.9	7.8	6.5	7.8	7.9	8.0	8.1	8.1	7.8
2003	8.0	8.1	8.1	8.0	8.2	7.9	7.1	7.8	8.0	8.1	8.2	8.3	8.0
SANTA FE													
Total nonfarm													
1990	57.7	58.5	59.2	60.3	61.4	63.1	63.0	63.0	62.0	62.0	62.5	61.9	61.2
1991	60.6	61.4	61.8	62.0	62.7	64.1	63.9	64.3	63.1	63.3	63.3	63.3	62.8
1992	61.3	62.2	62.5	63.2	63.7	65.1	65.9	65.9	65.8	65.1	65.4	65.1	64.2
1993	63.7	64.8	65.7	66.0	66.3	68.2	67.9	68.5	67.5	68.1	67.2	67.1	66.7
1994	65.5	66.6	67.3	67.6	68.3	70.3	70.4	69.7	69.7	69.7	70.1	70.3	68.7
1995	68.9	69.8	70.4	70.2	70.9	72.1	71.7	71.8	70.7	69.6	69.4	69.2	70.3
1996	67.6	68.4	68.7	69.1	70.3	71.2	71.3	71.2	70.5	69.9	70.3	70.8	69.9
1997	68.7	70.1	70.7	70.2	70.8	72.1	72.7	72.4	72.2	71.2	71.2	71.3	71.1
1998	69.3	70.7	71.3	72.4	72.8	73.4	74.0	73.9	73.5	73.2	73.3	73.0	72.5
1999	70.7	71.5	72.2	73.2	73.5	76.2	75.4	75.9	75.4	74.8	74.8	75.4	74.0
2000	72.9	73.6	74.7	74.9	75.8	76.4	76.7	76.3	75.8	75.0	74.6	74.9	75.1
2001	73.3	74.3	75.2	74.8	75.7	77.1	77.5	77.3	76.2	76.3	76.2	76.4	75.9
2002	74.2	75.1	76.0	76.7	77.4	78.8	79.1	79.7	78.5	78.1	78.7	78.6	77.6
2003	76.9	77.6	78.0	78.1	78.9	80.0	80.3	80.1	79.7	79.2	79.7	79.9	79.0
Total private													
1990	34.2	34.6	35.3	36.4	37.2	38.8	38.8	39.1	37.9	37.8	38.4	37.8	37.1
1991	36.4	36.6	37.1	37.6	38.3	39.6	39.9	40.4	39.2	39.2	39.2	39.2	38.5
1992	37.3	37.7	38.0	39.0	39.6	40.8	41.7	41.8	41.5	40.7	40.9	40.6	39.9
1993	39.3	39.8	40.5	41.2	41.6	43.6	43.5	44.0	42.9	42.9	43.0	43.2	42.1
1994	41.7	42.0	42.9	43.3	43.9	45.8	45.9	45.8	45.2	45.1	45.0	45.5	44.3
1995	44.4	44.6	45.1	45.4	45.9	47.3	47.1	47.4	46.5	45.3	45.1	45.0	45.7
1996	43.9	44.0	44.7	45.1	46.1	47.0	46.8	47.0	46.0	45.2	45.3	45.8	45.5
1997	44.3	44.7	45.2	45.4	46.1	47.4	47.5	47.4	47.2	46.5	46.5	46.6	46.2
1998	45.0	45.6	46.3	47.2	47.5	48.3	48.8	49.0	48.3	47.9	48.0	47.8	47.4
1999	45.7	45.9	46.7	47.4	47.8	50.2	49.7	50.4	49.7	49.0	49.0	49.2	48.3
2000	46.9	47.6	48.1	48.5	49.3	50.3	50.6	50.6	49.9	49.2	48.8	49.2	49.0
2001	47.7	48.2	48.9	48.9	49.6	51.2	51.3	51.4	49.9	49.8	49.9	50.0	49.7
2002	48.4	48.7	49.4	50.1	50.4	52.1	52.2	52.8	51.4	51.0	51.4	51.5	50.8
2003	50.1	50.4	50.7	50.8	51.6	52.8	53.2	53.2	52.4	51.9	52.3	52.5	51.8
Goods-producing													
1990	4.5	4.5	4.8	4.9	5.1	5.2	5.2	5.1	5.0	5.2	5.2	5.0	4.9
1991	4.4	4.5	4.5	4.6	4.7	4.8	4.8	4.8	4.8	5.0	4.9	4.8	4.7
1992	4.3	4.3	4.3	4.5	4.6	4.8	4.9	4.8	4.9	5.0	4.9	4.9	4.6
1993	4.7	4.7	4.8	4.8	5.0	5.4	5.3	5.3	5.2	5.5	5.4	5.3	5.1
1994	5.2	5.1	5.3	5.3	5.5	5.7	5.7	5.7	5.6	5.8	5.8	5.9	5.5
1995	5.6	5.6	5.6	5.7	5.8	6.0	5.8	5.9	5.8	5.4	5.6	5.5	5.6
1996	5.2	5.3	5.5	5.4	5.5	5.5	5.4	5.5	5.4	5.3	5.3	5.3	5.3
1997	5.0	5.1	5.2	5.2	5.3	5.5	5.5	5.5	5.6	5.5	5.5	5.3	5.3
1998	5.0	5.0	5.2	5.5	5.8	5.8	5.8	5.8	5.7	5.8	5.8	5.7	5.5
1999	5.5	5.5	5.7	5.9	5.9	6.1	6.3	6.4	6.3	6.4	6.3	6.2	6.0
2000	5.8	5.9	5.9	6.2	6.3	6.4	6.5	6.5	6.3	6.3	6.2	6.1	6.2
2001	5.9	6.0	6.2	6.3	6.3	6.5	6.5	6.5	6.4	6.3	6.2	6.1	6.3
2002	6.0	6.0	6.1	6.1	6.2	6.2	6.1	6.2	6.0	6.0	6.0	5.8	6.1
2003	5.8	5.8	5.8	5.9	6.1	6.3	6.3	6.3	6.1	6.1	6.0	5.9	6.0
Construction and mining													
1990	3.0	3.0	3.2	3.3	3.5	3.5	3.5	3.4	3.3	3.5	3.5	3.3	3.3
1991	2.8	2.9	2.9	3.0	3.1	3.1	3.1	3.1	3.1	3.3	3.2	3.1	3.0
1992	2.7	2.7	2.7	2.9	3.0	3.2	3.3	3.2	3.2	3.3	3.2	3.1	3.0
1993	3.0	3.0	3.2	3.3	3.5	3.8	3.7	3.7	3.6	3.8	3.7	3.7	3.5
1994	3.6	3.5	3.7	3.7	3.8	4.0	4.0	4.0	4.0	4.1	4.1	4.1	3.8
1995	3.9	3.9	3.9	4.0	4.1	4.3	4.1	4.2	4.1	3.8	3.9	3.8	4.0
1996	3.5	3.6	3.8	3.7	3.8	3.8	3.8	3.9	3.8	3.7	3.7	3.7	3.7
1997	3.4	3.5	3.6	3.6	3.7	3.9	3.9	3.9	4.0	3.9	3.9	3.7	3.7
1998	3.5	3.5	3.6	3.9	4.2	4.2	4.2	4.2	4.2	4.2	4.2	4.1	4.0
1999	4.0	4.0	4.2	4.4	4.4	4.6	4.8	4.8	4.8	4.8	4.7	4.6	4.5
2000	4.3	4.4	4.4	4.7	4.7	4.9	5.0	5.0	4.8	4.8	4.7	4.6	4.6
2001	4.4	4.5	4.7	4.8	4.9	5.1	5.1	5.1	5.0	4.9	4.8	4.7	4.8
2002	4.7	4.7	4.8	4.8	4.9	4.9	4.8	4.9	4.7	4.7	4.7	4.5	4.8
2003	4.6	4.6	4.6	4.7	4.9	5.1	5.1	5.1	4.9	4.9	4.8	4.7	4.8

Employment by Industry: New Mexico—*Continued*

(Numbers in thousands. Not seasonally adjusted.)

Industry	January	February	March	April	May	June	July	August	September	October	November	December	Annual Average
SANTA FE—*Continued*													
Manufacturing													
1990	1.5	1.5	1.6	1.6	1.6	1.7	1.7	1.7	1.7	1.7	1.7	1.7	1.6
1991	1.6	1.6	1.6	1.6	1.6	1.7	1.7	1.7	1.7	1.7	1.7	1.7	1.6
1992	1.6	1.6	1.6	1.6	1.6	1.6	1.6	1.6	1.7	1.7	1.7	1.8	1.6
1993	1.7	1.7	1.6	1.5	1.5	1.6	1.6	1.6	1.6	1.7	1.7	1.6	1.6
1994	1.6	1.6	1.6	1.6	1.7	1.7	1.7	1.7	1.6	1.7	1.7	1.8	1.6
1995	1.7	1.7	1.7	1.7	1.7	1.7	1.7	1.7	1.7	1.6	1.7	1.7	1.6
1996	1.7	1.7	1.7	1.7	1.7	1.7	1.6	1.6	1.6	1.6	1.6	1.6	1.6
1997	1.6	1.6	1.6	1.6	1.6	1.6	1.6	1.6	1.6	1.6	1.6	1.6	1.6
1998	1.5	1.5	1.6	1.6	1.6	1.6	1.6	1.6	1.5	1.6	1.6	1.6	1.5
1999	1.5	1.5	1.5	1.5	1.5	1.5	1.5	1.6	1.5	1.6	1.6	1.6	1.5
2000	1.5	1.5	1.5	1.5	1.6	1.5	1.5	1.5	1.5	1.5	1.5	1.5	1.5
2001	1.5	1.5	1.5	1.5	1.4	1.4	1.4	1.4	1.4	1.4	1.4	1.4	1.4
2002	1.3	1.3	1.3	1.3	1.3	1.3	1.3	1.3	1.3	1.3	1.3	1.3	1.3
2003	1.2	1.2	1.2	1.2	1.2	1.2	1.2	1.2	1.2	1.2	1.2	1.2	1.2
Service-providing													
1990	53.2	54.0	54.4	55.4	56.3	57.9	57.8	57.9	57.0	56.8	57.3	56.9	56.2
1991	56.2	56.9	57.3	57.4	58.0	59.3	59.1	59.5	58.3	58.3	58.4	58.5	58.1
1992	57.0	57.9	58.2	58.7	59.1	60.3	61.0	61.1	60.9	60.1	60.5	60.2	59.5
1993	59.0	60.1	60.9	61.2	61.3	62.8	62.6	63.2	62.3	62.6	61.8	61.8	61.6
1994	60.3	61.5	62.0	62.3	62.8	64.6	64.7	64.0	64.1	63.9	64.3	64.4	63.2
1995	63.3	64.2	64.8	64.5	65.1	66.1	65.9	65.9	64.9	64.2	63.8	63.7	64.7
1996	62.4	63.1	63.2	63.7	64.8	65.7	65.9	65.7	65.1	64.6	65.0	65.5	64.5
1997	63.7	65.0	65.5	65.0	65.5	66.6	67.2	66.9	66.6	65.7	65.7	66.0	65.7
1998	64.3	65.7	66.1	66.9	67.0	67.6	68.2	68.1	67.8	67.4	67.5	67.3	66.9
1999	65.2	66.0	66.5	67.3	67.6	70.1	69.1	69.5	69.1	68.4	68.5	69.2	68.0
2000	67.1	67.7	68.8	68.7	69.5	70.0	70.2	69.8	69.5	68.7	68.4	68.8	68.9
2001	67.4	68.3	69.0	68.5	69.4	70.6	71.0	70.8	69.8	70.0	70.0	70.3	69.6
2002	68.2	69.1	69.9	70.6	71.2	72.6	73.0	73.5	72.5	72.1	72.7	72.8	71.5
2003	71.1	71.8	72.2	72.2	72.8	73.7	74.0	73.8	73.6	73.1	73.7	74.0	73.0
Trade, transportation, and utilities													
1990	7.6	7.4	7.6	7.8	8.2	8.3	8.2	8.4	8.2	8.2	8.4	8.6	8.0
1991	8.1	7.9	8.1	8.2	8.5	8.6	8.7	8.9	8.7	8.7	8.8	8.9	8.5
1992	8.6	8.5	8.5	8.6	8.9	9.1	9.2	9.3	9.3	9.2	9.5	9.4	9.0
1993	8.9	8.9	9.0	9.3	9.3	9.5	9.5	9.7	9.5	9.5	9.7	10.0	9.4
1994	9.6	9.4	9.5	9.6	9.7	10.0	10.1	10.1	10.1	10.0	10.1	10.4	9.8
1995	9.9	9.8	9.9	10.0	10.2	10.2	10.5	10.7	10.5	10.4	10.5	10.7	10.2
1996	10.2	10.0	10.0	10.1	10.3	10.3	10.3	10.4	10.3	10.3	10.6	10.7	10.2
1997	10.1	9.9	9.9	9.9	10.0	10.1	10.2	10.1	10.3	10.5	10.5	10.6	10.1
1998	9.9	9.9	10.1	10.1	10.1	10.2	10.2	10.3	10.3	10.5	10.6	10.9	10.2
1999	10.0	9.9	10.1	10.1	10.2	10.3	10.3	10.5	10.6	10.5	10.8	11.1	10.3
2000	10.5	10.4	10.4	10.4	10.6	10.6	10.8	10.8	10.7	10.6	10.7	10.9	10.6
2001	10.4	10.3	10.3	10.3	10.6	10.6	10.6	10.7	10.5	10.6	10.7	10.8	10.5
2002	10.3	10.2	10.2	10.5	10.6	10.9	10.8	11.0	11.0	10.9	11.0	11.1	10.7
2003	10.5	10.4	10.4	10.5	10.7	10.7	10.8	10.9	10.8	10.7	10.9	11.1	10.7
Wholesale trade													
1990	0.7	0.7	0.7	0.7	0.8	0.8	0.8	0.8	0.8	0.8	0.8	0.9	0.7
1991	0.9	0.9	0.9	0.9	1.0	1.0	1.0	1.0	1.0	1.0	1.0	1.0	0.9
1992	1.0	1.0	1.0	1.0	1.0	1.0	1.0	1.0	1.0	1.0	1.0	0.9	0.9
1993	0.9	0.9	0.9	0.9	0.9	0.9	0.9	0.9	0.9	0.9	0.9	0.9	0.9
1994	0.9	0.9	0.9	0.9	0.9	1.0	0.9	0.9	0.9	0.9	0.9	0.9	0.9
1995	0.9	0.9	1.0	0.9	0.9	0.9	1.0	1.0	0.9	0.9	0.9	0.9	0.9
1996	0.9	0.9	0.9	0.9	0.9	0.9	0.9	0.9	0.9	0.9	0.9	0.9	0.9
1997	0.9	0.8	0.8	0.8	0.8	0.8	0.8	0.8	0.8	0.8	0.8	0.8	0.8
1998	0.8	0.9	0.9	0.9	0.9	0.9	0.9	0.9	0.9	0.9	1.0	0.9	0.9
1999	0.9	0.9	0.9	0.9	0.9	0.9	0.9	0.9	0.9	0.9	0.9	1.0	0.9
2000	0.9	0.9	0.9	0.9	0.9	0.9	0.9	0.9	0.9	0.9	0.9	0.9	0.9
2001	0.9	0.9	0.9	0.9	1.0	1.0	1.0	1.0	1.0	1.0	1.0	1.0	1.0
2002	1.0	1.0	1.0	1.0	1.0	1.1	1.0	1.1	1.1	1.1	1.0	1.0	1.0
2003	1.0	1.0	1.0	1.1	1.1	1.1	1.1	1.1	1.1	1.0	1.0	1.1	1.1
Retail trade													
1990	6.3	6.1	6.3	6.5	6.8	6.9	6.8	7.0	6.8	6.8	7.0	7.0	6.6
1991	6.6	6.4	6.6	6.7	6.9	7.0	7.1	7.2	7.0	7.0	7.1	7.2	6.9
1992	6.9	6.8	6.8	6.9	7.2	7.4	7.5	7.6	7.6	7.5	7.8	7.8	7.3
1993	7.3	7.3	7.4	7.7	7.7	7.9	7.9	8.1	7.9	7.9	8.1	8.4	7.8
1994	8.0	7.9	7.9	8.0	8.1	8.3	8.5	8.5	8.5	8.4	8.5	8.8	8.2
1995	8.3	8.2	8.2	8.4	8.6	8.7	8.8	9.0	8.9	8.8	8.9	9.1	8.6
1996	8.6	8.4	8.4	8.5	8.7	8.7	8.7	8.8	8.7	8.7	9.0	9.1	8.6
1997	8.5	8.4	8.4	8.4	8.5	8.6	8.7	8.7	8.8	9.0	9.0	9.1	8.6
1998	8.4	8.3	8.5	8.5	8.5	8.6	8.6	8.7	8.7	8.8	8.9	9.2	8.6
1999	8.4	8.3	8.5	8.5	8.6	8.7	8.8	9.0	9.0	8.9	9.2	9.4	8.7
2000	8.9	8.8	8.8	8.9	9.0	9.1	9.2	9.2	9.1	9.0	9.1	9.3	9.0
2001	8.7	8.6	8.6	8.7	8.8	8.9	8.9	9.0	8.8	8.9	9.0	9.1	8.8
2002	8.6	8.5	8.5	8.7	8.8	9.0	9.0	9.1	9.1	9.0	9.2	9.3	8.9
2003	8.8	8.7	8.7	8.7	8.9	8.9	9.0	9.1	9.0	8.9	9.1	9.2	8.9

Employment by Industry: New Mexico—*Continued*

(Numbers in thousands. Not seasonally adjusted.)

Industry	January	February	March	April	May	June	July	August	September	October	November	December	Annual Average
SANTA FE—*Continued*													
Transportation and utilities													
1990	0.6	0.6	0.6	0.6	0.6	0.6	0.6	0.6	0.6	0.6	0.6	0.7	0.6
1991	0.6	0.6	0.6	0.6	0.6	0.6	0.6	0.7	0.7	0.7	0.7	0.7	0.6
1992	0.7	0.7	0.7	0.7	0.7	0.7	0.7	0.7	0.7	0.7	0.7	0.7	0.7
1993	0.7	0.7	0.7	0.7	0.7	0.7	0.7	0.7	0.7	0.7	0.7	0.7	0.7
1994	0.7	0.6	0.7	0.7	0.7	0.7	0.7	0.7	0.7	0.7	0.7	0.7	0.6
1995	0.7	0.7	0.7	0.7	0.7	0.6	0.7	0.7	0.7	0.7	0.7	0.7	0.6
1996	0.7	0.7	0.7	0.7	0.7	0.7	0.7	0.7	0.7	0.7	0.7	0.7	0.7
1997	0.7	0.7	0.7	0.7	0.7	0.7	0.7	0.6	0.7	0.7	0.7	0.7	0.6
1998	0.7	0.7	0.7	0.7	0.7	0.7	0.7	0.7	0.7	0.8	0.7	0.8	0.7
1999	0.7	0.7	0.7	0.7	0.7	0.7	0.6	0.6	0.7	0.7	0.7	0.7	0.6
2000	0.7	0.7	0.7	0.6	0.7	0.6	0.7	0.7	0.7	0.7	0.7	0.7	0.6
2001	0.8	0.8	0.8	0.7	0.8	0.7	0.7	0.7	0.7	0.7	0.7	0.7	0.7
2002	0.7	0.7	0.7	0.8	0.8	0.8	0.8	0.8	0.8	0.8	0.8	0.8	0.8
2003	0.7	0.7	0.7	0.7	0.7	0.7	0.7	0.7	0.7	0.8	0.8	0.8	0.7
Information													
1990	0.9	0.9	0.9	0.9	0.9	0.9	0.9	0.9	0.9	0.9	0.9	0.9	0.9
1991	0.9	0.9	0.9	0.9	0.9	1.0	1.0	1.1	1.1	1.2	1.0	1.0	0.9
1992	1.0	0.9	0.9	1.0	1.0	1.0	1.1	1.1	1.0	1.0	1.0	1.0	1.0
1993	1.0	1.0	1.0	1.1	1.1	1.1	1.1	1.1	1.1	1.0	1.0	1.1	1.0
1994	1.1	1.1	1.2	1.1	1.1	1.3	1.3	1.3	1.3	1.3	1.2	1.2	1.2
1995	1.2	1.1	1.1	1.1	1.1	1.2	1.0	1.0	1.1	1.1	1.1	1.1	1.1
1996	1.1	1.1	1.1	1.1	1.2	1.2	1.2	1.2	1.2	1.2	1.2	1.2	1.1
1997	1.1	1.1	1.1	1.2	1.2	1.2	1.2	1.2	1.2	1.2	1.3	1.3	1.1
1998	1.2	1.2	1.2	1.3	1.3	1.2	1.2	1.4	1.3	1.3	1.3	1.2	1.2
1999	1.3	1.2	1.2	1.2	1.2	2.0	1.3	1.3	1.2	1.2	1.3	1.4	1.3
2000	1.2	1.2	1.2	1.2	1.2	1.3	1.2	1.2	1.2	1.2	1.2	1.2	1.2
2001	1.1	1.1	1.1	1.1	1.2	1.1	1.0	1.0	1.0	1.0	1.0	1.0	1.1
2002	1.0	1.0	1.0	1.0	1.0	1.0	1.0	1.0	1.0	1.0	1.1	1.1	1.0
2003	1.1	1.1	1.0	1.0	1.1	1.1	1.1	1.0	1.1	1.1	1.1	1.1	1.1
Financial activities													
1990	2.2	2.2	2.2	2.3	2.3	2.4	2.4	2.4	2.3	2.3	2.3	2.3	2.3
1991	2.2	2.2	2.2	2.2	2.2	2.3	2.3	2.3	2.3	2.3	2.3	2.3	2.2
1992	2.3	2.4	2.4	2.3	2.4	2.4	2.4	2.4	2.4	2.4	2.4	2.4	2.3
1993	2.4	2.4	2.4	2.5	2.5	2.6	2.6	2.6	2.5	2.6	2.6	2.6	2.5
1994	2.6	2.7	2.7	2.7	2.7	2.8	2.9	2.8	2.8	2.8	2.8	2.9	2.7
1995	2.9	2.9	2.9	2.9	2.9	3.0	2.9	2.9	2.9	2.9	2.9	2.9	2.9
1996	3.0	2.9	2.9	3.0	3.0	3.0	3.1	3.1	3.0	3.0	3.0	3.1	3.0
1997	3.1	3.1	3.1	3.1	3.1	3.1	3.2	3.1	3.0	3.1	3.2	3.2	3.1
1998	3.2	3.2	3.2	3.3	3.3	3.4	3.4	3.3	3.3	3.4	3.4	3.4	3.3
1999	3.2	3.2	3.2	3.2	3.2	3.3	3.3	3.3	3.2	3.2	3.2	3.2	3.2
2000	3.2	3.2	3.2	3.1	3.1	3.1	3.2	3.2	3.2	3.2	3.2	3.2	3.1
2001	3.1	3.2	3.2	3.2	3.2	3.3	3.3	3.3	3.2	3.2	3.2	3.3	3.2
2002	3.2	3.2	3.3	3.3	3.3	3.3	3.2	3.3	3.2	3.3	3.3	3.4	3.3
2003	3.3	3.4	3.4	3.3	3.4	3.5	3.4	3.5	3.4	3.5	3.5	3.5	3.4
Professional and business services													
1990	5.3	5.5	5.5	5.8	5.9	6.0	6.0	6.1	6.1	6.0	6.2	6.0	5.8
1991	5.7	5.8	5.8	5.9	5.8	5.9	5.7	5.8	5.8	6.0	6.1	6.0	5.8
1992	5.8	5.9	6.0	6.0	6.0	6.1	6.3	6.3	6.4	6.2	6.3	6.2	6.1
1993	6.1	6.2	6.2	6.3	6.3	6.5	6.5	6.6	6.6	6.5	6.5	6.6	6.4
1994	6.3	6.5	6.6	6.5	6.5	6.7	6.7	6.7	6.7	6.9	6.8	6.8	6.6
1995	6.5	6.6	6.7	6.7	6.7	6.8	6.7	6.7	6.7	6.3	6.4	6.4	6.6
1996	6.4	6.4	6.5	6.7	6.8	6.8	6.8	6.9	6.8	6.8	6.9	6.9	6.7
1997	6.8	6.8	6.9	7.0	6.9	7.0	7.1	7.1	7.1	7.1	7.0	7.1	6.9
1998	7.2	7.3	7.5	7.4	7.5	7.6	7.7	7.7	7.7	7.8	7.9	7.8	7.5
1999	7.4	7.4	7.5	7.7	7.7	7.9	7.8	7.9	7.9	8.1	8.1	8.0	7.7
2000	7.7	7.8	7.9	8.0	8.0	8.2	8.2	8.2	8.2	8.2	8.2	8.3	8.0
2001	8.0	8.0	8.0	8.1	8.0	8.2	8.3	8.3	8.3	8.3	8.3	8.3	8.2
2002	8.1	8.0	8.2	8.3	8.4	8.5	8.6	8.7	8.8	8.7	8.7	8.9	8.5
2003	8.5	8.5	8.7	8.7	8.7	8.8	8.9	9.0	9.0	8.9	8.9	9.1	8.8
Educational and health services													
1990	5.3	5.6	5.7	5.5	5.5	5.2	5.1	5.1	5.5	5.6	5.7	5.6	5.4
1991	5.7	6.1	6.2	6.1	6.1	5.8	6.0	6.1	6.3	6.4	6.4	6.5	6.1
1992	6.1	6.5	6.5	6.6	6.6	6.1	6.1	6.2	6.7	6.7	6.7	6.7	6.4
1993	6.4	6.8	6.8	6.7	6.6	6.3	6.3	6.4	7.0	7.0	7.1	7.0	6.7
1994	6.7	6.9	7.0	6.9	6.9	6.8	6.5	6.5	7.1	7.2	7.3	7.3	6.9
1995	7.2	7.5	7.5	7.6	7.6	7.3	7.0	7.0	7.6	7.4	7.4	7.3	7.3
1996	7.3	7.6	7.7	7.6	7.7	7.4	6.9	6.9	7.4	7.3	7.3	7.3	7.3
1997	7.3	7.6	7.5	7.6	7.7	7.5	7.1	7.2	7.7	7.7	7.8	7.7	7.5
1998	7.5	7.9	7.8	7.9	7.7	7.3	7.2	7.2	7.7	7.7	7.7	7.5	7.5
1999	7.4	7.7	7.8	7.8	7.7	7.3	7.1	7.2	7.7	7.6	7.6	7.5	7.5
2000	7.3	7.8	7.9	7.9	7.9	7.3	7.2	7.3	7.8	7.9	7.9	7.8	7.6
2001	7.8	8.2	8.3	8.3	8.3	7.9	7.8	7.9	8.4	8.5	8.6	8.5	8.2
2002	8.1	8.6	8.7	8.8	8.7	8.3	8.3	8.3	8.8	8.9	9.0	8.8	8.6
2003	8.6	9.1	9.1	9.2	9.2	8.7	8.6	8.5	9.2	9.2	9.4	9.3	9.0

Employment by Industry: New Mexico—*Continued*

(Numbers in thousands. Not seasonally adjusted.)

Industry	January	February	March	April	May	June	July	August	September	October	November	December	Annual Average
SANTA FE—*Continued*													
Leisure and hospitality													
1990	6.7	6.7	6.8	7.3	7.4	8.5	8.7	8.7	7.8	7.6	7.7	7.4	7.6
1991	7.5	7.3	7.4	7.7	8.0	8.8	9.0	9.0	8.1	7.6	7.7	7.7	7.9
1992	7.3	7.2	7.4	8.0	8.1	8.9	9.3	9.3	8.7	8.2	8.1	8.1	8.2
1993	7.9	7.8	8.2	8.5	8.7	9.6	9.7	9.8	8.9	8.7	8.7	8.6	8.7
1994	8.2	8.2	8.5	9.1	9.3	9.9	10.0	10.0	9.4	8.9	8.9	9.0	9.1
1995	9.0	9.0	9.2	9.1	9.2	9.9	10.3	10.4	9.5	9.4	8.9	8.8	9.3
1996	8.4	8.4	8.6	8.9	9.2	9.9	10.1	10.1	9.5	8.8	8.6	8.9	9.1
1997	8.6	8.7	9.0	9.0	9.4	10.0	10.2	10.3	9.8	8.9	8.8	9.0	9.3
1998	8.6	8.7	8.8	9.2	9.2	9.7	10.1	10.2	9.7	8.8	8.7	8.8	9.2
1999	8.4	8.5	8.6	8.9	9.2	9.9	10.2	10.5	10.1	9.4	9.1	9.2	9.3
2000	8.6	8.7	8.9	9.0	9.3	9.9	10.0	10.0	9.7	9.0	8.7	9.0	9.2
2001	8.7	8.7	9.0	8.9	9.2	10.0	10.2	10.2	9.2	9.0	9.0	9.2	9.3
2002	8.9	8.9	9.0	9.2	9.3	10.1	10.4	10.5	9.5	9.1	9.2	9.4	9.5
2003	9.3	9.1	9.3	9.1	9.3	9.8	10.2	10.2	9.5	9.1	9.2	9.3	9.5
Other services													
1990	1.7	1.8	1.8	1.9	1.9	2.3	2.3	2.4	2.1	2.0	2.0	2.0	2.0
1991	1.9	1.9	2.0	2.0	2.1	2.4	2.4	2.4	2.1	2.0	2.0	2.0	2.1
1992	1.9	2.0	2.0	2.0	2.0	2.4	2.4	2.4	2.1	2.0	2.0	1.9	2.0
1993	1.9	2.0	2.1	2.0	2.1	2.6	2.5	2.5	2.1	2.1	2.0	2.0	2.1
1994	2.0	2.1	2.1	2.1	2.2	2.6	2.7	2.7	2.2	2.2	2.1	2.0	2.2
1995	2.1	2.1	2.2	2.3	2.4	2.9	2.9	2.8	2.4	2.4	2.3	2.3	2.4
1996	2.3	2.3	2.4	2.3	2.4	2.9	3.0	2.9	2.4	2.5	2.4	2.4	2.5
1997	2.3	2.4	2.5	2.4	2.5	3.0	3.0	2.9	2.5	2.5	2.4	2.4	2.5
1998	2.4	2.4	2.5	2.5	2.6	3.1	3.2	3.1	2.6	2.6	2.6	2.5	2.6
1999	2.5	2.5	2.6	2.6	2.7	3.4	3.4	3.3	2.7	2.6	2.6	2.6	2.7
2000	2.6	2.6	2.7	2.7	2.9	3.5	3.5	3.4	2.8	2.8	2.7	2.7	2.9
2001	2.7	2.7	2.8	2.7	2.8	3.6	3.6	3.5	2.9	2.9	2.9	2.8	3.0
2002	2.8	2.8	2.9	2.9	2.9	3.8	3.8	3.8	3.1	3.1	3.1	3.0	3.2
2003	3.0	3.0	3.0	3.1	3.1	3.9	3.9	3.8	3.3	3.3	3.3	3.2	3.3
Government													
1990	23.5	23.9	23.9	23.9	24.2	24.3	24.2	23.9	24.1	24.2	24.1	24.1	24.0
1991	24.2	24.8	24.7	24.4	24.4	24.5	24.0	23.9	23.9	24.1	24.1	24.1	24.2
1992	24.0	24.5	24.5	24.2	24.1	24.3	24.2	24.1	24.3	24.4	24.5	24.5	24.3
1993	24.4	25.0	25.2	24.8	24.7	24.6	24.4	24.5	24.6	25.2	24.2	23.9	24.6
1994	23.8	24.6	24.4	24.3	24.4	24.5	24.5	23.9	24.5	24.6	25.1	24.8	24.4
1995	24.5	25.2	25.3	24.8	25.0	24.8	24.6	24.4	24.2	24.3	24.3	24.2	24.6
1996	23.7	24.4	24.0	24.0	24.2	24.2	24.5	24.2	24.5	24.7	25.0	25.0	24.3
1997	24.4	25.4	25.5	24.8	24.7	24.7	25.2	25.0	25.0	24.7	24.7	24.7	24.9
1998	24.3	25.1	25.0	25.2	25.3	25.1	25.2	24.9	25.2	25.3	25.3	25.2	25.0
1999	25.0	25.6	25.5	25.8	25.7	26.0	25.7	25.5	25.7	25.8	25.8	26.2	25.6
2000	26.0	26.0	26.6	26.4	26.5	26.1	26.1	25.7	25.9	25.8	25.8	25.7	26.0
2001	25.6	26.1	26.3	25.9	26.1	25.9	26.2	25.9	26.3	26.5	26.3	26.4	26.1
2002	25.8	26.4	26.6	26.6	27.0	26.7	26.9	26.9	27.1	27.1	27.3	27.1	26.8
2003	26.8	27.2	27.3	27.3	27.3	27.2	27.1	26.9	27.3	27.3	27.4	27.4	27.2
Federal government													
1990	1.6	1.6	1.6	1.7	1.9	1.8	1.8	1.7	1.7	1.7	1.6	1.6	1.6
1991	1.5	1.6	1.6	1.6	1.7	1.8	1.7	1.7	1.7	1.7	1.7	1.7	1.6
1992	1.7	1.7	1.7	1.7	1.7	1.8	1.8	1.7	1.7	1.7	1.7	1.7	1.7
1993	1.7	1.7	1.7	1.7	1.7	1.7	1.7	1.7	1.7	1.7	1.7	1.7	1.7
1994	1.7	1.7	1.7	1.7	1.7	1.7	1.7	1.6	1.6	1.6	1.6	1.6	1.6
1995	1.6	1.6	1.6	1.6	1.7	1.7	1.6	1.6	1.6	1.6	1.6	1.6	1.6
1996	1.5	1.5	1.5	1.5	1.5	1.5	1.6	1.5	1.5	1.5	1.5	1.5	1.5
1997	1.5	1.5	1.5	1.5	1.5	1.5	1.5	1.5	1.5	1.5	1.5	1.4	1.4
1998	1.4	1.4	1.4	1.5	1.5	1.5	1.5	1.5	1.5	1.5	1.5	1.5	1.4
1999	1.4	1.4	1.4	1.4	1.4	1.5	1.5	1.5	1.5	1.5	1.5	1.5	1.4
2000	1.5	1.5	1.9	1.8	2.1	1.6	1.7	1.5	1.5	1.4	1.4	1.4	1.6
2001	1.5	1.5	1.6	1.5	1.6	1.6	1.6	1.6	1.6	1.6	1.5	1.6	1.6
2002	1.5	1.5	1.5	1.5	1.6	1.6	1.6	1.6	1.6	1.5	1.5	1.5	1.5
2003	1.5	1.4	1.5	1.5	1.5	1.6	1.5	1.5	1.5	1.4	1.4	1.5	1.5
State government													
1990	17.6	17.9	17.8	17.7	17.8	18.0	18.1	17.9	18.0	18.0	18.0	17.8	17.8
1991	18.1	18.5	18.5	18.2	18.0	18.1	18.0	17.9	17.6	17.6	17.6	17.6	17.9
1992	17.6	18.0	18.0	17.7	17.8	17.8	17.8	17.9	18.0	17.9	18.0	18.0	17.8
1993	18.0	18.5	18.6	18.2	18.1	18.0	18.2	18.2	18.3	18.4	17.5	17.5	18.1
1994	17.5	18.0	17.7	17.7	17.7	17.9	17.9	17.9	17.9	17.9	18.0	18.1	17.8
1995	18.0	18.4	18.5	18.0	18.0	17.9	17.8	17.8	17.5	17.4	17.3	17.1	17.8
1996	17.0	17.4	17.0	16.9	17.0	16.9	17.0	16.8	16.9	16.9	16.9	16.9	16.9
1997	16.7	17.2	17.2	16.6	16.5	16.5	16.5	16.5	16.4	16.4	16.4	16.4	16.6
1998	16.4	16.8	16.8	16.9	17.0	16.8	16.8	16.8	16.8	16.8	16.8	16.8	16.7
1999	16.6	17.1	17.2	17.1	17.0	17.3	17.1	17.1	17.3	17.3	17.3	17.3	17.1
2000	17.3	17.2	17.4	17.2	17.1	17.2	17.2	17.2	17.1	17.0	17.0	17.1	17.1
2001	17.0	17.3	17.4	17.2	17.2	17.2	17.4	17.4	17.5	17.5	17.3	17.4	17.3
2002	17.3	17.7	17.7	17.7	17.9	17.9	18.0	18.1	18.2	18.2	18.3	18.3	17.9
2003	18.2	18.4	18.4	18.4	18.3	18.3	18.2	18.2	18.3	18.3	18.4	18.4	18.3

Employment by Industry: New Mexico—*Continued*

(Numbers in thousands. Not seasonally adjusted.)

Industry	January	February	March	April	May	June	July	August	September	October	November	December	Annual Average
SANTA FE—*Continued*													
Local government													
1990	4.3	4.4	4.5	4.5	4.5	4.5	4.3	4.3	4.4	4.5	4.5	4.7	4.4
1991	4.6	4.7	4.6	4.6	4.7	4.6	4.3	4.3	4.6	4.8	4.8	4.8	4.6
1992	4.7	4.8	4.8	4.8	4.6	4.7	4.6	4.5	4.6	4.8	4.8	4.8	4.7
1993	4.7	4.8	4.9	4.9	4.9	4.9	4.5	4.6	4.6	5.1	5.0	4.7	4.8
1994	4.6	4.9	5.0	4.9	5.0	4.9	4.9	4.4	5.0	5.1	5.5	5.1	4.9
1995	4.9	5.2	5.2	5.2	5.3	5.2	5.2	5.0	5.1	5.3	5.4	5.5	5.2
1996	5.2	5.5	5.5	5.6	5.7	5.8	5.9	5.9	6.1	6.3	6.6	6.6	5.8
1997	6.2	6.7	6.8	6.7	6.7	6.7	7.2	7.0	7.1	6.8	6.8	6.9	6.8
1998	6.5	6.9	6.8	6.8	6.8	6.8	6.9	6.6	6.9	7.0	7.0	6.9	6.8
1999	7.0	7.1	6.9	7.3	7.3	7.2	7.1	6.9	6.9	7.0	7.0	7.4	7.0
2000	7.2	7.3	7.3	7.4	7.3	7.3	7.2	7.0	7.3	7.4	7.4	7.2	7.2
2001	7.1	7.3	7.3	7.2	7.3	7.1	7.2	6.9	7.2	7.4	7.5	7.4	7.2
2002	7.0	7.2	7.4	7.4	7.5	7.2	7.3	7.2	7.3	7.4	7.5	7.3	7.3
2003	7.1	7.4	7.4	7.4	7.5	7.3	7.4	7.2	7.5	7.6	7.6	7.5	7.4

Average Weekly Hours by Industry: New Mexico

(Not seasonally adjusted.)

Industry	January	February	March	April	May	June	July	August	September	October	November	December	Annual Average
STATEWIDE													
Natural resources and mining													
2001	43.1	42.9	43.6	44.0	43.8	43.0	42.9	43.7	45.5	47.1	45.9	45.2	44.3
2002	42.8	44.0	44.6	44.9	44.6	44.4	43.9	44.8	43.9	44.2	43.8	44.1	44.2
2003	43.9	45.1	45.5	44.7	44.6	44.1	43.9	43.7	43.5	42.9	43.1	43.2	44.0
Construction													
2001	38.7	39.2	39.1	37.9	39.0	39.1	38.5	39.5	39.0	39.5	38.1	38.0	38.8
2002	39.2	39.0	38.1	39.8	39.4	39.3	39.1	39.9	39.0	39.5	39.7	39.4	39.3
2003	39.8	38.9	39.7	39.5	39.1	39.6	39.8	39.7	39.7	40.0	39.9	40.0	39.7
Manufacturing													
2001	37.8	38.8	38.6	38.2	38.8	39.1	38.6	39.6	39.6	39.4	39.9	40.2	39.0
2002	38.8	39.7	39.3	39.9	40.1	41.0	39.8	40.1	40.3	39.7	40.2	39.7	39.9
2003	38.5	39.1	39.3	39.2	40.0	39.8	39.7	39.6	39.5	39.5	39.4	39.2	39.4
Wholesale trade													
2001	30.9	31.9	32.3	32.3	31.4	32.2	32.3	32.4	32.7	31.9	32.9	33.1	32.2
2002	32.4	33.2	32.6	32.4	33.4	33.9	34.1	35.0	34.9	34.4	35.1	35.0	33.9
2003	34.1	34.7	35.4	35.6	35.7	34.9	35.2	35.7	35.6	35.9	36.0	36.1	35.4
Retail trade													
2001	32.0	31.8	31.8	32.1	31.6	32.1	32.6	32.7	31.9	32.1	31.7	32.6	32.1
2002	31.7	31.9	32.2	32.0	32.2	32.8	33.1	32.6	32.0	31.8	31.5	31.8	32.1
2003	31.6	31.7	31.8	31.6	32.0	32.4	33.0	33.1	32.3	32.0	31.8	32.2	32.1
Financial activities													
2001	34.5	35.0	34.7	35.5	35.3	35.2	36.1	35.1	36.2	35.7	35.4	36.8	35.4
2002	35.2	35.1	35.3	35.6	34.7	35.4	34.9	35.1	36.0	36.5	35.7	36.6	35.5
2003	35.9	36.4	36.8	37.4	36.9	36.8	36.6	36.8	36.4	36.1	36.1	36.0	36.5
ALBUQUERQUE													
Manufacturing													
2001	37.3	38.5	37.8	37.3	38.4	38.8	37.2	38.3	38.5	38.7	38.8	39.0	38.2
2002	38.1	39.1	39.2	40.5	40.8	41.1	39.6	39.8	40.6	38.9	39.8	39.1	39.7
2003	37.2	38.4	38.7	38.8	41.1	40.6	38.7	38.8	38.3	38.2	39.2	39.0	38.9

Average Hourly Earnings by Industry: New Mexico

(Dollars, not seasonally adjusted.)

Industry	January	February	March	April	May	June	July	August	September	October	November	December	Annual Average
STATEWIDE													
Natural resources and mining													
2001	16.74	16.42	16.44	16.63	16.60	16.88	16.86	16.33	16.59	16.25	16.10	16.45	16.52
2002	16.51	17.08	16.87	16.49	16.72	16.83	16.23	16.76	16.98	17.15	16.89	17.17	16.81
2003	17.16	17.06	17.56	17.34	17.17	17.12	17.18	17.11	17.14	17.17	17.19	17.21	17.20
Construction													
2001	15.06	15.12	15.14	15.13	14.94	15.12	14.87	14.93	14.82	14.94	14.78	14.85	14.97
2002	14.49	14.66	14.56	14.43	14.40	14.58	14.44	14.56	14.52	14.74	14.73	15.03	14.59
2003	15.03	15.08	15.18	15.13	15.14	14.99	15.05	15.02	15.06	15.08	15.08	15.11	15.08
Manufacturing													
2001	12.85	13.16	13.29	13.54	13.28	13.49	13.15	13.09	13.09	13.03	13.63	13.62	13.27
2002	13.50	13.82	13.84	13.37	13.70	13.49	13.28	13.22	13.12	13.12	13.26	13.25	13.41
2003	13.14	13.33	13.49	13.31	13.40	13.25	13.19	13.10	13.03	13.00	13.04	13.05	13.19
Wholesale trade													
2001	13.74	13.69	13.44	13.59	13.88	13.99	14.26	14.02	14.29	14.03	13.85	14.25	13.92
2002	14.08	14.08	14.45	14.42	14.62	14.87	14.49	14.21	14.34	14.38	14.52	14.28	14.40
2003	14.74	14.85	14.87	14.83	14.68	14.54	14.49	14.42	14.38	14.41	14.43	14.44	14.59
Retail trade													
2001	9.49	9.60	9.59	9.67	9.65	9.62	9.64	9.74	9.86	9.78	9.74	9.63	9.67
2002	9.62	9.61	9.84	9.56	9.72	9.63	9.62	9.63	9.64	9.65	9.75	9.98	9.69
2003	10.14	10.11	10.21	10.26	10.32	10.41	10.35	10.36	10.44	10.37	10.39	10.41	10.32
Financial activities													
2001	13.15	13.27	13.58	13.38	13.16	13.32	13.23	13.01	13.84	13.63	13.41	13.44	13.37
2002	13.15	13.33	13.55	13.32	13.61	13.42	13.33	13.20	13.56	13.23	13.45	13.38	13.38
2003	13.60	13.46	13.87	13.78	13.62	13.57	13.49	13.43	13.47	13.42	13.45	13.46	13.55
ALBUQUERQUE													
Manufacturing													
2001	14.40	14.66	14.81	15.17	14.51	14.95	13.96	14.34	14.80	14.67	15.58	15.26	14.75
2002	14.95	15.51	15.49	14.89	15.76	15.34	15.02	15.07	14.83	15.35	15.46	14.51	15.18
2003	14.65	14.42	14.58	14.15	15.05	14.91	14.70	14.61	13.88	14.54	14.38	14.47	14.53

Average Weekly Earnings by Industry: New Mexico

(Dollars, not seasonally adjusted.)

Industry	January	February	March	April	May	June	July	August	September	October	November	December	Annual Average
STATEWIDE													
Natural resources and mining													
2001	721.49	704.42	716.78	731.72	727.08	725.84	723.29	713.62	754.85	765.38	738.99	743.54	731.84
2002	706.63	751.52	752.40	740.40	745.71	747.25	712.50	750.85	745.42	758.03	739.78	757.20	743.00
2003	753.32	769.41	798.98	775.10	765.78	754.99	754.20	747.71	745.59	736.59	740.89	743.47	756.80
Construction													
2001	582.82	592.70	591.97	573.43	582.66	591.19	572.50	589.74	577.98	590.13	563.12	564.30	580.84
2002	568.01	571.74	554.74	574.31	567.36	572.99	564.60	580.94	566.28	582.23	584.78	592.18	573.39
2003	598.19	586.61	602.65	597.64	591.97	593.60	598.99	596.29	597.88	603.20	601.69	604.40	598.68
Manufacturing													
2001	485.73	510.61	512.99	517.23	515.26	527.46	507.59	518.36	518.36	513.38	543.84	547.52	517.53
2002	523.80	548.65	543.91	533.46	549.37	553.09	528.54	530.12	528.74	520.86	533.05	526.03	535.06
2003	505.89	521.20	530.16	521.75	536.00	527.35	523.64	518.76	514.69	513.50	513.78	511.56	519.69
Wholesale trade													
2001	424.57	436.71	434.11	438.96	435.83	450.48	460.60	454.25	467.28	447.56	455.67	471.68	448.22
2002	456.19	467.46	471.07	467.21	488.31	504.09	494.11	497.35	500.47	494.67	509.65	499.80	488.16
2003	502.63	515.30	526.40	527.95	524.08	507.45	510.05	514.79	511.93	517.32	519.48	521.28	516.49
Retail trade													
2001	303.68	305.28	304.96	310.41	304.94	308.80	314.26	318.50	314.53	313.94	308.76	313.94	310.41
2002	304.95	306.56	316.85	305.92	312.98	315.86	318.42	313.94	308.48	306.87	307.13	317.36	311.05
2003	320.42	320.49	324.68	324.22	330.24	337.28	341.55	342.92	337.21	331.84	330.40	335.20	331.27
Financial activities													
2001	453.68	464.45	471.23	474.99	464.55	468.86	477.60	456.65	501.01	486.59	474.71	494.59	473.30
2002	462.88	467.88	478.32	474.19	472.27	475.07	465.22	463.32	488.16	482.90	480.17	489.71	474.99
2003	488.24	489.94	510.42	515.37	502.58	499.38	493.73	494.22	490.31	484.46	485.55	484.56	494.58
ALBUQUERQUE													
Manufacturing													
2001	537.12	564.41	559.82	565.84	557.18	580.06	519.31	549.22	569.80	567.73	604.50	595.14	563.45
2002	569.60	606.44	607.21	603.05	643.01	630.47	594.79	599.79	602.10	597.12	615.31	567.34	602.65
2003	544.98	553.73	564.25	549.02	618.56	605.35	568.89	566.87	531.60	555.43	563.70	564.33	565.22

NEW YORK AT A GLANCE

(Population and total nonfarm employment numbers in thousands)

Population, Census 2000:	18,976.5
Total nonfarm employment, 2003:	8,403.5
Change in total nonfarm employment	
(Number)	
1990–2003:	191.2
1990–2001:	379.4
2001–2003:	-188.2
(Compound annual rate of change)	
1990–2003:	0.2%
1990–2001:	0.4%
2001–2003:	-1.1%
Unemployment rate	
1990:	5.3%
2001:	4.9%
2003:	6.4%

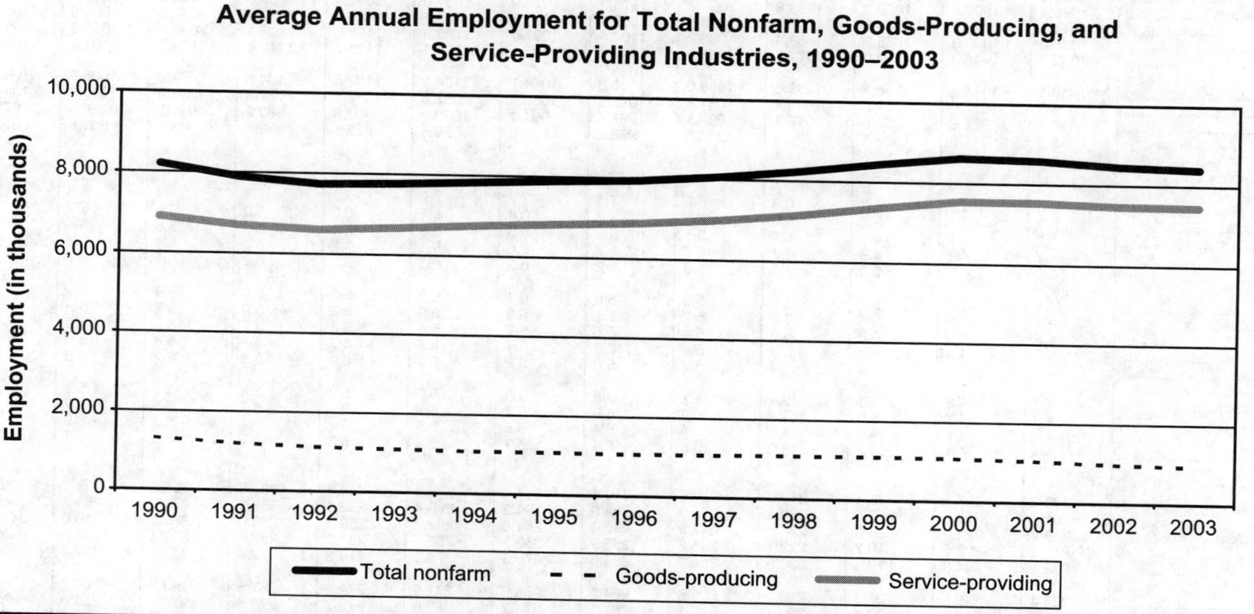

Total nonfarm payroll employment dropped significantly during both the 1990–1991 and 2001 recessions. Between the two contractions overall employment expanded smoothly. The decline following the latter recession was not nearly as pronounced as in the decade before. However, total nonfarm employment still declined by over 230,000 jobs from 2000 to 2003. Manufacturing employment continued to drop throughout the period. In the service-providing sector, financial activities and professional and business services weathered the strains of the 1990–1991 recession before recovering mid-decade only to slump again in the 2001–2003 period.

Employment by Industry: New York

(Numbers in thousands. Not seasonally adjusted.)

Industry	January	February	March	April	May	June	July	August	September	October	November	December	Annual Average
STATEWIDE													
Total nonfarm													
1990	8101.7	8130.0	8189.5	8196.4	8291.8	8342.1	8211.1	8214.3	8221.9	8219.6	8219.3	8210.1	8212.3
1991	7849.7	7847.1	7878.6	7887.3	7943.0	7994.8	7841.6	7842.4	7852.5	7894.7	7912.2	7896.7	7886.7
1992	7605.1	7619.6	7656.2	7709.9	7769.9	7811.7	7731.9	7721.6	7734.3	7789.2	7798.6	7815.4	7730.3
1993	7571.3	7607.3	7639.2	7698.4	7781.5	7838.9	7787.1	7772.7	7784.2	7850.4	7880.3	7905.3	7759.7
1994	7618.3	7652.3	7715.3	7773.0	7851.3	7911.2	7838.7	7844.6	7863.1	7938.5	7978.9	7990.8	7831.3
1995	7730.0	7765.7	7825.9	7859.3	7917.9	7973.8	7876.4	7884.8	7903.3	7958.7	7997.9	8012.8	7892.2
1996	7708.4	7786.8	7842.7	7876.7	7968.6	8021.8	7925.8	7928.7	7958.5	8045.0	8088.1	8112.7	7938.7
1997	7823.7	7876.3	7958.9	7995.7	8072.7	8123.1	8072.3	8060.3	8105.7	8200.9	8238.2	8277.3	8067.1
1998	7988.3	8058.6	8124.3	8163.0	8259.7	8307.9	8240.1	8239.6	8256.1	8357.4	8403.5	8442.6	8236.8
1999	8212.0	8277.3	8329.4	8407.3	8473.0	8521.2	8464.7	8461.1	8452.4	8572.0	8628.6	8671.4	8455.9
2000	8391.5	8443.1	8517.7	8588.0	8673.3	8716.6	8645.3	8603.2	8663.6	8751.2	8798.0	8831.4	8635.2
2001	8521.1	8557.6	8602.6	8605.3	8685.6	8718.1	8584.9	8549.4	8550.9	8547.7	8582.0	8595.3	8591.7
2002	8291.3	8339.0	8392.3	8428.0	8508.0	8537.3	8456.2	8441.2	8443.8	8526.2	8560.9	8583.2	8459.0
2003	8264.6	8297.7	8341.4	8365.3	8449.1	8477.2	8382.6	8359.5	8388.2	8474.7	8514.4	8527.3	8403.5
Total private													
1990	6645.1	6655.9	6702.5	6703.5	6779.5	6836.6	6766.6	6786.4	6789.0	6744.9	6732.5	6724.9	6739.0
1991	6392.9	6373.2	6401.7	6414.6	6466.4	6526.3	6441.2	6456.0	6459.4	6454.6	6462.0	6451.4	6441.6
1992	6190.6	6183.8	6212.6	6261.5	6323.4	6374.3	6328.7	6330.1	6340.8	6357.2	6352.3	6371.6	6302.2
1993	6157.0	6174.0	6194.1	6257.0	6334.5	6396.6	6355.5	6374.9	6388.4	6412.6	6425.3	6447.2	6326.4
1994	6191.3	6202.1	6258.6	6317.5	6389.4	6461.8	6431.6	6457.9	6477.7	6496.7	6521.3	6538.4	6395.4
1995	6310.5	6325.8	6386.0	6416.5	6482.0	6545.9	6483.5	6515.2	6537.4	6547.3	6570.0	6588.5	6475.7
1996	6318.3	6371.3	6421.3	6454.5	6543.3	6607.2	6556.9	6580.7	6602.6	6637.2	6668.1	6695.1	6538.0
1997	6440.0	6467.5	6541.7	6578.3	6649.9	6712.9	6691.3	6699.5	6733.0	6771.2	6798.1	6839.3	6660.2
1998	6596.2	6630.3	6683.8	6726.4	6817.2	6879.5	6836.8	6856.2	6871.8	6919.3	6948.5	6987.0	6812.8
1999	6789.6	6829.3	6871.9	6951.3	7011.8	7072.4	7032.2	7049.8	7043.8	7113.2	7157.9	7203.2	7010.5
2000	6945.9	6978.4	7038.5	7095.7	7159.5	7236.3	7191.1	7192.0	7236.6	7273.9	7312.2	7350.3	7167.5
2001	7068.1	7084.7	7123.8	7117.1	7200.8	7242.7	7157.7	7146.0	7110.3	7060.9	7078.8	7095.8	7123.9
2002	6814.2	6836.8	6881.9	6926.4	6998.1	7031.4	6985.5	6992.6	6990.0	7028.5	7046.3	7064.5	6966.4
2003	6785.3	6794.8	6834.3	6864.6	6945.4	6975.1	6928.3	6928.2	6942.2	6983.4	7007.7	7022.9	6917.7
Goods-producing													
1990	1292.2	1294.7	1308.4	1309.9	1331.4	1349.5	1328.2	1336.0	1336.3	1315.3	1289.3	1260.7	1312.7
1991	1171.7	1165.2	1168.5	1190.3	1204.3	1222.9	1203.6	1215.2	1215.8	1206.5	1190.9	1160.7	1193.0
1992	1096.4	1091.2	1096.5	1110.1	1128.0	1144.0	1135.4	1143.5	1142.8	1135.2	1122.9	1103.6	1120.8
1993	1048.2	1049.4	1054.3	1069.2	1094.0	1109.7	1098.7	1109.2	1115.7	1108.5	1099.1	1079.5	1086.3
1994	1013.9	1013.5	1027.3	1051.7	1075.5	1094.8	1088.9	1103.5	1107.7	1103.2	1097.3	1078.7	1071.3
1995	1023.6	1025.0	1039.5	1056.0	1075.4	1091.1	1078.1	1096.4	1099.1	1088.3	1079.6	1062.2	1067.9
1996	998.8	1009.4	1022.3	1033.8	1057.3	1078.2	1072.9	1089.0	1092.9	1089.0	1080.2	1064.6	1057.4
1997	1014.5	1016.9	1033.8	1048.6	1068.1	1083.1	1081.7	1095.6	1099.5	1098.6	1092.5	1081.6	1067.9
1998	1036.3	1043.3	1053.2	1068.4	1086.7	1104.4	1087.0	1103.9	1108.5	1103.1	1098.0	1086.5	1081.6
1999	1042.7	1046.3	1052.0	1077.3	1095.0	1110.9	1102.1	1111.1	1111.7	1112.4	1109.5	1101.1	1089.3
2000	1046.4	1044.7	1058.3	1069.5	1086.0	1103.6	1094.7	1104.9	1107.5	1104.8	1097.4	1085.6	1083.6
2001	1035.6	1033.8	1039.8	1046.4	1061.8	1073.9	1056.6	1057.8	1047.3	1037.8	1026.2	1011.9	1044.1
2002	956.1	952.6	960.5	972.4	987.5	997.4	991.1	1000.0	993.9	990.2	981.8	966.8	979.2
2003	918.8	911.8	921.1	928.3	946.0	956.2	949.8	955.6	953.5	952.1	946.2	931.8	939.3
Natural resources and mining													
1990	6.0	6.0	6.2	6.6	6.9	7.1	7.2	7.2	7.1	7.1	6.9	6.5	6.7
1991	5.2	5.1	5.2	5.6	6.0	6.2	6.4	6.1	6.0	6.0	5.8	5.4	5.8
1992	4.7	4.7	4.9	5.1	5.6	5.9	5.9	5.9	5.9	5.9	5.8	5.5	5.5
1993	4.7	4.8	4.8	5.2	5.6	5.9	6.0	6.1	6.2	6.2	6.1	5.7	5.6
1994	4.8	4.8	5.0	5.3	5.8	6.2	6.2	6.3	6.2	6.2	6.1	5.7	5.7
1995	4.6	4.7	5.1	5.4	5.9	6.0	6.1	6.2	6.0	5.9	5.6	5.1	5.6
1996	4.4	4.6	4.7	5.3	5.7	6.1	6.0	6.0	6.0	5.9	5.7	5.3	5.5
1997	4.6	4.6	4.9	5.0	5.4	5.6	5.7	5.8	5.8	5.7	5.5	5.0	5.3
1998	4.5	4.6	4.8	5.3	5.6	5.8	5.7	5.7	5.7	5.7	5.6	5.3	5.4
1999	4.6	4.7	4.9	5.4	5.7	5.8	5.9	6.0	5.9	5.8	5.7	5.2	5.5
2000	4.7	4.6	5.1	5.4	5.7	5.9	5.9	6.0	6.0	5.8	5.7	5.2	5.5
2001	4.6	4.7	5.0	5.2	5.6	5.6	5.7	5.7	5.5	5.7	5.5	5.2	5.3
2002	4.4	4.4	4.6	5.0	5.4	5.4	5.5	5.5	5.4	5.4	5.3	4.9	5.1
2003	4.4	4.4	4.6	5.0	5.5	5.6	5.7	5.8	5.8	5.7	5.6	5.1	5.3
Construction													
1990	300.2	297.4	305.1	313.9	330.3	340.1	341.3	345.3	342.3	331.2	321.2	305.5	322.8
1991	261.4	253.5	256.4	270.3	283.9	294.0	294.2	295.4	292.0	286.1	276.7	263.7	277.3
1992	229.2	222.4	224.3	234.6	247.9	256.4	261.0	262.7	260.3	258.0	250.1	240.3	245.6
1993	213.5	208.6	210.7	229.1	246.2	255.9	262.2	265.7	267.5	265.4	259.1	248.0	244.3
1994	209.1	204.8	212.8	233.5	252.7	263.6	270.5	276.2	276.3	273.4	268.9	257.0	249.9
1995	226.4	219.2	227.5	242.8	255.6	264.2	266.6	271.5	271.4	267.5	261.2	250.2	252.0
1996	213.7	216.3	223.8	239.1	255.1	267.1	274.2	280.0	279.7	278.5	272.7	261.0	255.1
1997	230.5	227.7	237.2	250.6	265.1	274.8	284.0	288.7	287.8	286.0	280.9	272.3	265.5
1998	247.1	248.2	254.0	269.6	284.1	294.3	301.3	304.7	304.5	305.8	303.0	296.4	284.4
1999	270.7	272.0	276.0	299.3	313.7	324.4	328.9	333.4	332.2	331.9	328.5	321.9	311.1
2000	289.5	286.9	299.6	312.3	327.4	338.5	343.3	348.1	349.3	349.0	346.3	337.6	327.3
2001	302.2	300.3	306.4	322.0	339.2	348.0	347.7	349.3	342.8	341.9	337.6	328.8	330.5
2002	293.8	291.5	297.1	311.3	323.9	332.0	338.4	342.7	338.5	337.4	332.7	323.2	321.9
2003	291.4	286.3	293.2	307.4	323.3	331.4	337.3	339.3	336.1	334.9	331.1	321.0	319.4

Employment by Industry: New York—*Continued*

(Numbers in thousands. Not seasonally adjusted.)

Industry	January	February	March	April	May	June	July	August	September	October	November	December	Annual Average
STATEWIDE—*Continued*													
Manufacturing													
1990	986.0	991.3	997.1	989.4	994.2	1002.3	979.7	983.5	986.9	977.0	961.2	948.7	983.1
1991	905.1	906.6	906.9	914.4	914.4	922.7	903.0	913.7	917.8	914.4	908.4	891.6	909.9
1992	862.5	864.1	867.3	870.4	874.5	881.7	868.5	874.9	876.6	871.3	867.0	857.8	869.7
1993	830.0	836.0	838.8	834.9	842.2	847.9	830.5	837.4	842.0	836.9	833.9	825.8	836.4
1994	800.0	803.9	809.5	812.9	817.0	825.0	812.2	821.0	825.2	823.6	822.3	816.0	815.7
1995	792.6	801.1	806.9	807.8	813.9	820.9	805.4	818.7	821.7	814.9	812.8	806.9	810.3
1996	780.7	788.5	793.8	789.4	796.5	805.0	792.7	803.0	807.2	804.6	801.8	798.3	796.8
1997	779.4	784.6	791.7	793.0	797.6	802.7	792.0	801.1	805.9	806.9	806.1	804.3	797.1
1998	784.7	790.5	794.4	793.5	797.0	804.3	780.0	793.5	798.3	791.6	789.4	784.8	791.8
1999	767.4	769.6	771.1	772.6	775.6	780.7	767.3	771.7	773.6	774.7	775.3	774.0	772.8
2000	752.2	753.2	753.6	751.8	752.9	759.2	745.5	750.8	752.2	750.0	745.4	742.8	750.8
2001	728.8	728.8	728.4	719.2	717.0	720.3	703.2	702.8	699.0	690.2	683.1	677.9	708.2
2002	657.9	656.7	658.8	656.1	658.2	660.0	647.2	651.8	650.0	647.4	643.8	638.7	652.2
2003	623.0	621.1	623.3	615.9	617.2	619.2	606.8	610.5	611.6	611.5	609.5	605.7	614.6
Service-providing													
1990	6809.5	6835.3	6881.1	6886.5	6960.4	6992.6	6882.9	6878.3	6885.6	6904.3	6930.0	6949.4	6899.7
1991	6678.0	6681.9	6710.1	6697.0	6738.7	6771.9	6638.0	6627.2	6636.7	6688.2	6721.3	6736.0	6693.8
1992	6508.7	6528.4	6559.7	6599.8	6641.9	6667.7	6596.5	6578.1	6591.5	6654.0	6675.7	6711.8	6609.5
1993	6523.1	6557.9	6584.9	6629.2	6687.5	6729.2	6688.4	6663.5	6668.5	6741.9	6781.2	6825.8	6673.4
1994	6604.4	6638.8	6688.0	6721.3	6775.8	6816.4	6749.8	6741.1	6755.4	6835.3	6881.6	6912.1	6760.0
1995	6706.4	6740.7	6786.4	6803.3	6842.5	6882.7	6798.3	6788.4	6804.2	6870.4	6918.3	6950.6	6824.4
1996	6709.6	6777.4	6820.4	6842.9	6911.3	6943.6	6852.9	6839.7	6865.6	6956.0	7007.9	7048.1	6881.3
1997	6809.2	6859.4	6925.1	6947.1	7004.6	7040.0	6990.6	6964.7	7006.2	7102.3	7145.7	7195.7	6999.2
1998	6952.0	7015.3	7071.1	7094.6	7173.0	7203.5	7153.1	7135.7	7147.6	7254.3	7305.5	7356.1	7155.2
1999	7169.3	7231.0	7277.4	7330.0	7378.0	7410.3	7362.6	7350.0	7340.7	7459.6	7519.1	7570.3	7366.5
2000	7345.1	7398.4	7459.4	7518.5	7587.3	7613.0	7550.6	7498.3	7556.1	7646.4	7700.6	7745.8	7551.6
2001	7485.5	7523.8	7562.8	7558.9	7623.8	7644.2	7528.3	7491.6	7503.6	7509.9	7555.8	7583.4	7547.6
2002	7335.2	7386.4	7431.8	7455.6	7520.5	7539.9	7465.1	7441.2	7449.9	7536.0	7579.1	7616.4	7479.8
2003	7345.8	7385.9	7420.3	7437.0	7503.1	7521.0	7432.8	7403.9	7434.7	7522.6	7568.2	7595.5	7464.2
Trade, transportation, and utilities													
1990	1584.3	1563.9	1568.1	1556.9	1571.7	1584.6	1559.4	1564.2	1572.2	1574.4	1590.1	1607.4	1574.8
1991	1504.7	1474.4	1472.4	1471.4	1481.9	1497.3	1465.6	1469.6	1477.8	1483.5	1508.4	1519.3	1485.5
1992	1446.4	1421.3	1419.5	1424.2	1438.6	1449.8	1424.8	1426.4	1434.2	1452.5	1468.6	1492.3	1441.6
1993	1425.3	1407.8	1403.3	1404.4	1420.0	1435.5	1417.1	1422.4	1427.7	1448.4	1468.3	1494.1	1431.2
1994	1414.4	1394.7	1399.0	1400.6	1416.8	1434.0	1419.6	1426.1	1440.6	1455.6	1482.1	1506.0	1432.5
1995	1439.4	1421.0	1425.6	1427.0	1439.1	1456.0	1432.4	1437.6	1455.0	1465.9	1493.0	1516.0	1450.7
1996	1431.1	1415.7	1420.3	1419.7	1438.2	1453.0	1431.7	1433.9	1452.9	1464.3	1497.0	1523.9	1448.5
1997	1447.0	1424.0	1434.6	1430.8	1444.5	1459.3	1439.4	1431.9	1460.1	1473.7	1502.3	1530.5	1456.5
1998	1457.8	1438.4	1442.8	1438.7	1460.8	1475.4	1452.0	1455.4	1470.7	1489.4	1516.6	1545.4	1470.3
1999	1483.1	1465.4	1469.9	1482.4	1494.1	1508.4	1485.1	1494.4	1503.1	1527.3	1561.3	1592.2	1505.6
2000	1524.8	1508.2	1514.6	1515.2	1528.8	1548.6	1527.7	1534.8	1547.9	1559.1	1588.7	1618.7	1543.1
2001	1533.9	1511.8	1513.8	1502.5	1519.2	1533.3	1501.0	1497.9	1498.6	1499.1	1522.3	1543.6	1514.8
2002	1467.3	1447.0	1455.7	1457.0	1471.9	1489.0	1466.1	1467.2	1481.0	1491.1	1514.8	1541.6	1479.1
2003	1464.5	1445.7	1449.5	1450.1	1466.3	1481.5	1458.0	1460.4	1471.9	1485.0	1508.5	1531.4	1472.7
Wholesale trade													
1990	414.3	414.6	416.6	415.1	416.9	419.1	415.3	415.3	414.0	411.0	409.8	408.8	414.2
1991	393.0	390.4	390.6	391.4	391.5	393.9	389.3	389.8	389.5	389.0	388.9	388.3	390.5
1992	379.1	377.8	378.0	381.9	383.6	385.0	382.2	381.6	380.9	383.1	382.2	382.1	381.5
1993	372.3	372.4	372.5	365.2	367.6	370.0	368.8	369.5	367.8	369.6	369.6	369.9	369.6
1994	357.0	357.8	360.6	362.0	363.6	366.1	365.5	366.8	367.7	367.3	368.7	369.3	364.4
1995	361.9	362.8	365.1	364.2	365.7	369.6	364.3	365.3	366.3	365.8	367.4	368.5	365.6
1996	355.6	358.1	360.5	359.0	361.1	363.4	360.6	362.3	363.2	362.5	364.5	365.9	361.4
1997	354.1	355.3	358.4	359.0	361.0	362.9	362.4	363.7	364.2	365.5	367.4	369.4	361.9
1998	359.7	361.4	363.2	363.5	365.9	368.1	364.0	364.8	364.7	365.9	367.4	368.2	364.7
1999	364.7	365.2	366.9	369.4	371.6	373.6	370.6	373.1	372.4	374.4	377.4	378.2	371.5
2000	376.5	377.7	380.4	377.1	378.9	382.1	379.8	380.9	381.6	381.8	382.2	384.2	380.3
2001	370.0	370.8	371.2	367.8	369.0	370.9	367.3	366.6	364.7	363.4	362.7	363.2	367.3
2002	353.3	353.5	354.5	354.0	355.7	357.2	354.1	355.9	355.4	357.7	358.4	359.3	355.8
2003	351.0	350.8	352.2	350.9	353.5	354.9	352.8	352.9	351.9	353.6	353.7	354.2	352.7
Retail trade													
1990	870.5	849.2	850.0	841.1	850.2	857.8	847.4	851.0	850.2	856.0	873.2	890.8	857.3
1991	821.7	798.5	797.0	791.8	799.9	809.9	795.2	799.1	798.0	803.5	827.4	844.2	807.2
1992	784.2	761.0	757.9	759.4	768.9	775.8	767.1	769.2	767.8	779.6	796.6	818.4	775.5
1993	770.4	753.2	748.0	754.9	764.6	775.8	769.2	774.4	774.4	787.5	806.9	832.4	776.0
1994	778.4	757.9	759.4	762.9	771.0	782.7	779.5	784.8	789.2	801.1	828.4	851.0	787.2
1995	800.4	781.0	782.6	788.9	796.3	807.3	802.7	806.7	811.1	817.6	844.0	865.0	808.6
1996	805.4	786.3	787.1	789.0	802.1	812.5	805.5	808.3	814.0	820.0	851.0	876.2	813.1
1997	820.0	797.3	802.7	797.8	807.2	818.9	809.6	813.5	817.8	827.6	854.7	879.4	820.5
1998	830.1	808.7	810.8	806.0	820.8	832.1	822.5	825.6	829.5	844.4	870.9	897.0	833.2
1999	848.2	829.4	831.4	839.1	845.6	856.0	847.5	853.4	852.1	869.8	899.7	928.0	858.4
2000	871.7	854.1	856.7	860.2	869.5	883.9	874.8	881.3	881.3	888.4	918.2	944.4	882.0
2001	880.9	858.6	859.6	854.1	863.3	874.6	859.1	861.2	853.2	856.9	885.7	907.7	867.9
2002	850.1	830.7	837.7	837.8	847.9	862.1	854.2	856.8	857.1	862.0	886.5	912.0	857.9
2003	848.6	830.9	832.1	836.8	847.6	860.5	851.8	854.9	854.7	864.0	888.8	909.7	856.7

Employment by Industry: New York—*Continued*

(Numbers in thousands. Not seasonally adjusted.)

Industry	January	February	March	April	May	June	July	August	September	October	November	December	Annual Average
STATEWIDE—*Continued*													
Transportation and utilities													
1990	299.5	300.1	301.5	300.7	304.6	307.7	296.7	297.9	308.0	307.4	307.1	307.8	303.3
1991	290.0	285.5	284.8	288.2	290.5	293.5	281.1	280.7	290.3	291.0	292.1	286.8	287.9
1992	283.1	282.5	283.6	282.9	286.1	289.0	275.5	275.6	285.5	289.8	289.8	291.8	284.6
1993	282.6	282.2	282.8	284.3	287.8	289.7	279.1	278.5	285.5	291.3	291.8	291.8	285.6
1994	279.0	279.0	279.0	275.7	282.2	285.2	274.6	274.5	283.7	287.2	285.0	285.7	280.9
1995	277.1	277.2	277.9	273.9	277.1	279.1	265.4	265.6	277.6	282.5	281.6	282.5	276.5
1996	270.1	271.3	272.7	271.7	275.0	277.1	265.6	263.3	275.7	281.8	281.5	281.8	274.0
1997	272.9	271.4	273.5	274.0	276.3	277.5	267.4	254.7	278.1	280.6	280.2	281.7	274.0
1998	268.0	268.3	268.8	269.2	274.1	275.2	265.5	265.0	276.5	279.1	278.3	280.2	272.4
1999	270.2	270.8	271.6	273.9	276.9	278.8	267.0	267.9	278.6	283.1	284.2	286.0	275.8
2000	276.6	276.4	277.5	277.9	280.4	282.6	273.1	272.6	285.0	288.9	288.3	290.1	280.8
2001	283.0	282.4	283.0	280.6	286.9	287.8	274.6	270.1	280.7	278.8	273.9	272.7	279.5
2002	263.9	262.8	263.5	265.2	268.3	269.7	257.8	254.5	268.5	271.4	269.9	270.3	265.5
2003	264.9	264.0	265.2	262.4	265.2	266.1	253.4	252.6	265.3	267.4	266.0	267.5	263.3
Information													
1990	284.4	284.5	283.6	285.0	288.1	287.8	288.4	288.7	288.3	284.3	284.7	287.2	286.3
1991	274.7	274.0	277.6	273.6	275.1	277.5	271.3	271.9	268.5	269.6	269.3	272.4	273.0
1992	262.4	261.2	265.3	259.8	260.7	260.8	262.6	261.4	265.1	261.5	262.0	263.3	262.2
1993	256.3	256.4	258.7	259.9	260.4	263.2	263.1	264.1	263.9	261.7	262.3	264.9	261.2
1994	255.8	257.2	262.4	260.0	261.0	264.5	261.0	262.0	262.2	262.6	264.1	265.6	261.5
1995	259.9	260.6	264.4	263.8	266.0	267.5	266.2	269.2	267.2	267.7	271.1	269.5	266.1
1996	266.5	267.2	267.3	266.7	268.7	269.8	271.4	273.7	272.1	273.7	278.3	277.3	271.1
1997	270.2	272.9	275.8	271.8	276.9	279.5	279.7	282.0	280.0	283.3	284.8	287.5	278.7
1998	281.0	282.5	287.1	287.8	290.9	291.0	287.2	289.2	286.3	289.4	293.4	294.2	288.3
1999	287.7	292.0	293.1	292.9	293.4	296.1	301.1	301.8	299.3	301.2	304.4	308.7	297.6
2000	304.1	308.7	312.0	315.0	319.1	323.7	323.0	301.6	327.0	329.5	332.2	333.6	319.1
2001	326.8	329.7	330.2	327.6	330.4	330.5	326.3	324.1	318.4	316.6	319.7	317.5	324.8
2002	299.4	303.3	299.0	298.4	305.2	302.7	292.2	294.4	288.9	290.0	292.2	290.6	296.4
2003	277.0	281.0	278.1	274.9	283.1	276.3	272.9	279.8	272.8	275.2	277.2	278.3	277.2
Financial activities													
1990	782.5	783.3	783.7	779.0	779.9	785.7	784.1	784.4	777.9	771.2	770.2	771.4	779.4
1991	750.0	747.5	749.0	745.3	746.5	751.4	750.0	749.4	745.4	741.7	742.1	745.8	747.0
1992	720.9	720.5	721.7	724.1	725.6	731.9	728.9	727.8	723.0	719.6	718.6	722.8	723.8
1993	712.6	714.7	714.1	716.8	720.0	727.1	728.3	729.0	724.3	725.6	727.5	731.7	722.6
1994	721.7	724.3	726.4	727.0	728.3	737.0	736.6	737.7	733.9	725.6	727.2	731.4	729.8
1995	717.7	720.3	721.1	714.0	715.4	722.8	722.0	722.1	720.2	716.9	717.3	721.9	719.3
1996	706.4	711.4	713.4	710.4	713.8	721.7	721.7	722.6	717.8	713.5	715.7	721.4	715.8
1997	705.2	708.8	713.6	712.5	714.9	723.7	726.8	729.3	725.0	724.1	725.5	730.9	720.0
1998	723.8	724.3	726.2	725.6	729.5	738.8	743.2	743.4	736.5	730.7	731.5	734.3	732.3
1999	736.2	737.1	736.2	736.2	738.6	746.0	746.3	747.7	739.4	740.4	742.4	746.2	741.1
2000	738.9	740.9	742.4	740.7	742.8	754.6	752.4	752.9	748.2	747.4	748.4	753.6	746.9
2001	739.9	740.2	742.4	737.7	738.0	747.2	745.4	742.4	733.3	704.1	701.7	707.8	731.7
2002	705.5	705.5	705.4	703.4	703.7	710.2	710.5	709.5	699.6	700.3	700.7	703.4	704.8
2003	692.2	690.1	689.7	690.5	694.2	702.1	705.6	704.5	697.0	697.8	699.7	701.7	697.1
Professional and business services													
1990	841.0	845.3	852.8	858.6	861.9	869.7	864.0	866.4	861.6	854.2	852.6	850.8	856.6
1991	814.4	815.4	820.4	815.9	816.9	824.3	815.1	811.7	809.2	806.4	806.6	806.0	813.5
1992	786.9	789.5	794.3	805.9	808.1	817.3	816.9	815.0	809.8	815.4	812.1	817.4	807.4
1993	797.9	806.1	812.6	834.0	835.2	847.8	844.0	843.6	843.2	847.0	848.4	852.6	834.4
1994	831.2	837.8	845.6	850.7	854.1	863.7	866.5	870.0	863.9	873.2	874.2	874.7	858.8
1995	850.8	857.0	866.0	872.7	877.7	888.2	880.8	884.3	881.8	887.9	887.8	893.2	877.4
1996	867.3	880.9	890.7	900.0	907.8	920.1	917.0	921.3	920.6	928.9	933.2	939.6	910.6
1997	908.9	919.6	933.2	945.6	950.8	966.9	971.0	975.7	972.7	980.5	982.3	989.7	958.1
1998	955.3	964.7	976.8	992.3	997.8	1016.0	1020.9	1024.2	1018.9	1031.8	1035.8	1043.3	1006.5
1999	1014.3	1027.3	1037.6	1054.4	1057.2	1075.6	1082.1	1084.9	1078.5	1088.6	1093.3	1102.7	1066.4
2000	1065.2	1076.7	1088.9	1101.7	1112.4	1129.7	1132.0	1139.7	1137.7	1143.3	1145.0	1148.8	1118.4
2001	1100.4	1104.5	1107.8	1102.7	1108.6	1116.4	1108.9	1106.4	1095.6	1076.1	1074.3	1075.0	1098.1
2002	1031.8	1035.7	1041.4	1050.9	1055.1	1065.4	1062.3	1062.7	1057.1	1060.8	1062.0	1062.6	1054.0
2003	1018.7	1018.5	1028.1	1038.6	1042.4	1053.0	1049.3	1049.3	1046.5	1048.2	1049.6	1051.6	1041.2
Educational and health services													
1990	1051.9	1069.5	1079.1	1075.7	1078.7	1070.5	1054.3	1054.4	1079.8	1094.7	1103.1	1106.6	1076.5
1991	1092.6	1107.6	1116.1	1115.0	1113.6	1102.4	1089.3	1089.1	1114.5	1131.5	1139.4	1142.7	1112.8
1992	1125.0	1140.3	1147.2	1149.9	1147.3	1137.3	1120.3	1117.0	1144.2	1164.4	1170.8	1175.1	1144.9
1993	1158.7	1172.3	1179.4	1179.5	1178.7	1168.8	1155.0	1153.7	1177.0	1198.4	1208.0	1211.3	1178.4
1994	1185.0	1202.3	1211.4	1217.8	1217.1	1206.0	1191.4	1188.9	1218.5	1237.6	1246.6	1252.6	1214.6
1995	1227.1	1244.6	1256.4	1254.9	1250.5	1238.0	1219.3	1215.9	1243.4	1264.9	1270.9	1274.3	1246.7
1996	1248.2	1275.1	1283.2	1283.0	1281.5	1266.6	1243.8	1238.3	1264.6	1295.0	1301.8	1302.3	1273.6
1997	1271.3	1293.3	1303.1	1304.1	1298.4	1281.0	1268.9	1261.5	1289.0	1316.2	1323.2	1325.8	1294.7
1998	1296.7	1318.1	1327.9	1330.5	1331.0	1312.0	1298.2	1293.0	1320.1	1351.1	1359.0	1362.4	1325.0
1999	1341.8	1365.0	1372.4	1373.2	1369.0	1347.9	1331.0	1323.3	1347.2	1378.4	1386.9	1389.4	1360.5
2000	1356.3	1376.3	1387.0	1395.4	1386.8	1365.3	1345.1	1338.5	1370.1	1398.8	1416.8	1422.9	1379.9
2001	1397.7	1422.1	1435.4	1437.8	1439.6	1413.7	1392.1	1387.4	1425.9	1458.1	1468.1	1472.1	1429.2
2002	1429.5	1457.5	1471.0	1474.1	1472.4	1442.5	1431.1	1425.3	1466.8	1500.0	1508.2	1509.5	1465.7
2003	1470.7	1498.6	1509.5	1509.1	1505.7	1476.6	1455.8	1447.0	1492.4	1524.4	1533.0	1533.7	1496.4

Employment by Industry: New York—*Continued*

(Numbers in thousands. Not seasonally adjusted.)

Industry	January	February	March	April	May	June	July	August	September	October	November	December	Annual Average
STATEWIDE—*Continued*													
Leisure and hospitality													
1990	536.7	540.1	549.9	561.1	587.2	606.5	607.8	611.5	594.0	571.7	563.6	561.8	574.3
1991	516.5	520.0	526.9	531.6	553.9	575.7	575.3	578.8	558.8	545.8	535.2	533.7	546.0
1992	489.1	493.4	500.5	517.4	542.4	559.9	567.1	567.7	551.1	534.6	523.9	522.7	530.8
1993	490.2	498.1	501.1	517.6	547.5	565.6	571.8	576.7	561.2	544.7	533.4	533.9	536.8
1994	498.9	499.9	511.5	530.7	555.3	578.7	584.7	587.2	569.3	555.2	545.4	544.7	546.8
1995	512.1	515.7	528.2	542.2	569.5	592.4	596.8	602.0	583.0	565.9	559.5	559.2	560.5
1996	518.3	526.1	535.4	550.5	581.8	602.5	604.9	609.0	588.0	576.9	565.7	568.3	569.0
1997	532.4	539.0	550.2	565.9	594.8	617.2	622.2	623.6	605.8	591.8	583.7	587.3	584.5
1998	546.1	556.7	564.5	577.4	611.9	632.4	637.3	637.1	621.3	609.1	597.4	601.8	599.4
1999	566.8	576.4	588.3	607.2	633.7	656.0	655.0	658.3	638.1	630.3	623.3	625.6	621.6
2000	581.7	591.1	600.2	621.4	644.5	670.4	676.6	680.4	658.0	647.6	639.7	641.5	637.8
2001	594.8	601.1	610.4	619.2	656.8	679.0	681.8	685.2	650.1	625.9	621.0	621.3	637.2
2002	584.3	592.8	603.8	624.0	653.4	674.0	683.3	686.0	656.9	646.2	635.2	638.0	639.8
2003	598.8	603.4	610.1	624.2	655.7	676.0	687.0	684.0	661.4	651.0	642.7	643.6	644.8
Other services													
1990	272.1	274.6	276.9	277.3	280.6	282.3	280.4	280.8	278.9	279.1	278.9	279.0	278.4
1991	268.3	269.1	270.8	271.5	274.2	274.8	271.0	270.3	269.4	269.6	270.1	270.8	270.8
1992	263.5	266.4	267.6	270.1	272.7	273.3	272.7	271.3	270.6	274.0	273.4	274.4	270.8
1993	267.8	269.2	270.6	275.6	278.7	278.9	277.5	276.2	275.4	278.3	278.3	279.2	275.5
1994	270.4	272.4	275.0	279.0	281.3	283.1	282.9	282.5	281.6	283.7	284.4	284.7	280.1
1995	279.9	281.6	284.8	285.9	288.4	289.9	287.9	287.7	287.7	289.8	290.8	292.2	287.2
1996	281.7	285.5	288.7	290.4	294.2	295.3	293.5	292.9	293.7	295.9	296.2	297.7	292.1
1997	290.5	293.0	297.4	299.0	301.5	302.2	301.6	299.9	300.9	303.0	303.8	306.0	299.9
1998	299.2	302.3	305.3	305.7	308.6	309.5	311.0	310.0	309.5	314.7	316.8	319.1	309.3
1999	317.0	319.8	322.4	327.7	330.8	331.5	329.5	328.3	326.5	334.6	336.8	337.3	328.5
2000	328.5	331.8	335.1	336.8	339.1	340.4	339.6	339.2	340.2	343.4	344.0	345.6	338.6
2001	339.0	341.5	344.0	343.2	346.4	348.7	345.6	344.8	341.1	343.2	345.5	346.6	344.1
2002	340.3	342.4	345.1	346.2	348.9	350.2	348.9	347.5	345.8	349.9	351.4	352.0	347.4
2003	344.6	345.7	348.2	348.9	352.0	353.4	349.9	347.6	346.7	349.7	350.8	350.8	349.0
Government													
1990	1456.6	1474.1	1487.0	1492.9	1512.3	1505.5	1444.5	1427.9	1432.9	1474.7	1486.8	1485.2	1473.4
1991	1456.8	1473.9	1476.9	1472.7	1476.6	1468.5	1400.4	1386.4	1393.1	1440.1	1450.2	1445.3	1445.1
1992	1414.5	1435.8	1443.6	1448.4	1446.5	1437.4	1403.2	1391.5	1393.5	1432.0	1446.3	1443.8	1428.0
1993	1414.3	1433.3	1445.1	1441.4	1447.0	1442.3	1431.6	1397.8	1395.8	1437.8	1455.0	1458.1	1433.3
1994	1427.0	1450.2	1456.7	1455.5	1461.9	1449.4	1407.1	1386.7	1385.4	1441.8	1457.6	1452.4	1436.0
1995	1419.5	1439.9	1439.9	1442.8	1435.9	1427.9	1392.9	1369.6	1365.9	1411.4	1427.9	1424.3	1416.5
1996	1390.1	1415.5	1421.4	1422.2	1425.3	1414.6	1368.9	1348.0	1355.9	1407.8	1420.0	1417.6	1400.6
1997	1383.7	1408.8	1417.2	1417.4	1422.8	1410.2	1381.0	1360.8	1372.7	1429.7	1440.1	1438.0	1406.9
1998	1392.1	1428.3	1440.5	1436.6	1442.5	1428.4	1403.3	1383.4	1384.3	1438.1	1455.0	1455.6	1424.0
1999	1422.4	1448.0	1457.5	1456.0	1461.2	1448.8	1432.5	1411.3	1408.6	1458.8	1470.7	1468.2	1445.3
2000	1445.6	1464.7	1479.2	1492.3	1513.8	1480.3	1454.2	1411.2	1427.0	1477.3	1485.8	1481.1	1467.7
2001	1453.0	1472.9	1478.8	1488.2	1484.8	1475.4	1427.2	1403.4	1440.6	1486.8	1503.2	1499.5	1467.8
2002	1477.1	1502.2	1510.4	1501.6	1509.9	1505.9	1470.7	1448.6	1453.8	1497.7	1514.6	1518.7	1492.6
2003	1479.3	1502.9	1507.1	1500.7	1503.7	1502.1	1454.3	1431.3	1446.0	1491.3	1506.7	1504.4	1485.8
Federal government													
1990	163.3	163.6	164.2	169.8	186.7	182.7	177.3	167.8	162.0	159.7	159.4	161.6	168.2
1991	157.4	157.7	157.7	157.8	158.1	159.1	159.7	158.3	157.2	156.8	157.0	159.0	158.0
1992	157.4	157.2	157.2	156.8	156.5	156.9	156.4	155.8	154.4	153.5	151.6	153.1	155.6
1993	151.0	151.8	152.2	151.3	151.4	152.2	150.6	150.7	148.8	147.9	147.7	150.4	150.5
1994	148.0	148.4	149.2	149.0	149.3	149.8	149.0	148.9	148.2	147.1	147.1	148.9	148.6
1995	146.2	147.0	147.1	147.3	147.4	147.9	147.0	146.3	145.4	144.0	143.8	145.6	146.3
1996	143.7	144.8	145.1	146.2	145.9	146.3	145.1	145.0	144.0	142.6	142.9	146.7	144.9
1997	142.3	142.7	142.7	143.1	142.1	142.5	141.5	141.5	141.0	139.7	140.1	143.5	141.9
1998	139.6	140.3	140.3	139.4	139.5	140.2	139.7	140.7	140.4	139.2	140.3	142.7	140.2
1999	140.0	140.9	142.1	143.9	142.0	140.6	141.0	140.3	140.2	139.1	139.4	142.5	141.0
2000	139.9	141.9	148.8	152.4	181.9	155.1	151.2	140.8	137.4	137.3	137.4	139.5	147.0
2001	138.0	138.5	138.6	138.7	138.3	138.9	139.1	138.6	137.8	137.2	137.0	138.2	138.2
2002	138.3	138.8	139.8	138.5	137.6	138.1	137.6	136.9	137.2	137.6	138.9	139.4	138.2
2003	136.7	136.8	137.3	136.9	136.0	135.2	135.3	134.6	133.7	134.1	134.6	136.3	135.6
State government													
1990	284.5	287.4	289.4	289.3	289.3	286.1	283.4	280.8	285.8	287.2	287.1	285.1	286.3
1991	280.2	282.2	281.1	277.5	275.8	272.1	267.5	266.7	267.2	271.5	271.3	270.0	273.6
1992	270.1	272.4	273.1	273.6	272.5	266.1	266.7	267.2	274.1	274.7	273.7	272.6	271.4
1993	268.4	270.7	273.0	272.0	271.6	266.9	265.7	266.5	271.0	272.2	271.2	272.7	270.2
1994	267.1	274.2	274.7	275.1	275.7	270.4	272.0	273.7	278.8	276.7	277.6	277.2	274.4
1995	274.0	279.8	277.7	276.1	269.9	260.0	260.1	257.5	268.2	267.9	267.9	263.6	268.6
1996	259.3	266.9	266.9	267.1	265.2	256.0	252.8	250.2	262.1	262.7	263.3	254.9	260.6
1997	252.2	261.0	261.3	261.8	260.3	249.5	251.1	249.9	261.2	262.3	263.1	254.6	257.4
1998	249.3	261.3	261.8	261.8	261.0	249.1	250.8	250.1	259.6	261.1	261.8	252.9	256.7
1999	250.1	261.6	262.0	262.0	261.7	250.3	253.1	253.0	263.5	265.0	266.0	257.3	258.8
2000	253.9	264.9	265.0	265.1	264.8	252.5	255.2	255.0	266.1	268.3	269.4	260.4	261.7
2001	256.4	270.4	270.6	269.4	268.8	254.5	256.7	256.8	270.1	272.7	274.1	263.5	265.3
2002	259.1	273.5	273.6	270.2	269.6	261.4	262.1	262.7	269.9	271.1	270.6	269.2	267.8
2003	264.2	268.7	268.9	265.2	264.5	256.1	256.2	256.9	265.1	266.5	266.5	257.5	263.0

Employment by Industry: New York—*Continued*

(Numbers in thousands. Not seasonally adjusted.)

Industry	January	February	March	April	May	June	July	August	September	October	November	December	Annual Average
STATEWIDE—*Continued*													
Local government													
1990	1008.9	1023.1	1033.4	1033.9	1036.3	1036.7	983.7	979.2	985.0	1027.7	1040.3	1038.6	1018.9
1991	1019.2	1034.0	1038.1	1037.4	1042.7	1037.3	973.2	961.4	968.7	1011.7	1021.9	1016.3	1013.5
1992	987.1	1006.2	1013.2	1017.9	1017.5	1014.3	980.1	968.4	965.0	1003.8	1021.1	1018.2	1001.1
1993	994.8	1010.8	1019.8	1018.1	1024.0	1023.2	1015.2	980.6	975.9	1017.7	1036.1	1034.9	1012.6
1994	1011.9	1027.6	1032.9	1031.3	1036.9	1029.3	986.0	964.1	958.4	1018.0	1032.9	1026.3	1013.0
1995	999.3	1012.4	1015.1	1019.4	1018.7	1020.0	985.8	965.8	952.3	999.5	1016.1	1015.1	1001.6
1996	987.0	1003.9	1009.3	1008.8	1014.2	1012.4	971.0	952.8	949.8	1002.5	1013.8	1016.0	995.1
1997	989.2	1005.0	1013.3	1012.5	1020.4	1018.2	988.3	969.4	970.5	1027.7	1037.0	1039.9	1007.6
1998	1003.2	1026.7	1038.4	1035.4	1042.0	1039.1	1012.8	992.6	984.3	1037.8	1052.9	1060.0	1027.1
1999	1032.3	1045.5	1053.4	1050.1	1057.5	1057.9	1038.4	1018.0	1004.9	1054.7	1065.3	1068.4	1045.5
2000	1051.8	1057.9	1065.4	1074.8	1067.1	1072.7	1047.8	1015.4	1023.5	1071.7	1079.0	1081.2	1059.0
2001	1058.6	1064.0	1069.6	1080.1	1077.7	1082.0	1031.4	1008.0	1032.7	1076.9	1092.1	1097.8	1064.2
2002	1079.7	1089.9	1097.0	1092.9	1102.7	1106.4	1071.0	1049.0	1046.7	1089.0	1105.1	1110.1	1086.6
2003	1078.4	1097.4	1100.9	1098.6	1103.2	1110.8	1062.8	1039.8	1047.2	1090.7	1105.6	1110.6	1087.2
ALBANY-SCHENECTADY-TROY													
Total nonfarm													
1990	418.4	420.9	424.4	427.8	433.8	437.1	427.9	430.1	431.2	433.1	432.4	431.3	429.0
1991	416.9	417.0	419.0	419.2	421.3	426.0	416.7	419.8	418.4	423.1	424.0	420.4	420.2
1992	406.6	410.1	411.7	414.7	419.0	422.5	416.8	419.9	418.9	425.2	424.5	423.7	417.8
1993	409.6	412.7	415.2	418.8	426.1	429.2	423.1	424.2	424.4	430.5	432.0	432.3	423.2
1994	417.3	420.7	421.6	425.4	430.3	433.9	429.8	432.5	433.0	438.3	439.8	437.9	430.0
1995	424.7	427.9	429.5	432.8	433.4	433.3	423.5	425.2	427.5	430.1	432.3	432.0	429.4
1996	416.3	422.1	424.0	427.3	428.5	428.8	418.4	421.7	425.2	428.6	433.5	431.6	425.5
1997	417.4	423.5	427.9	430.8	434.9	436.3	428.8	430.7	433.4	438.5	441.6	441.7	432.1
1998	425.7	431.6	432.8	437.4	442.3	444.4	436.7	438.4	440.3	445.3	449.4	448.9	439.4
1999	436.9	441.6	443.6	451.6	454.3	456.2	446.2	447.9	451.4	455.0	458.3	458.2	450.1
2000	444.8	448.0	450.4	455.8	459.9	463.2	454.9	455.1	459.2	464.0	467.2	468.1	457.6
2001	453.0	455.0	457.3	460.6	465.4	467.4	459.8	463.1	460.9	463.7	467.0	467.1	461.7
2002	448.2	452.8	456.1	460.2	462.8	464.1	456.9	459.7	461.6	464.2	465.7	464.6	459.7
2003	448.8	452.4	453.8	457.3	461.5	462.5	456.0	458.6	460.7	465.9	466.0	465.4	459.1
Total private													
1990	306.1	306.5	308.4	310.8	314.9	319.3	316.9	320.3	318.8	318.6	317.8	316.9	314.6
1991	303.7	302.0	304.5	305.6	308.1	312.8	309.2	312.4	310.7	311.8	312.0	309.4	308.5
1992	297.2	298.0	299.7	302.0	307.0	310.9	309.9	313.2	310.0	313.8	312.4	312.4	307.2
1993	300.5	302.1	303.2	306.8	313.6	317.9	316.0	318.4	315.4	319.0	319.8	319.5	312.7
1994	306.8	307.5	308.3	311.8	316.6	320.7	320.0	323.3	321.7	324.4	325.1	323.7	317.5
1995	313.0	314.1	316.9	320.5	322.7	324.4	318.9	322.5	318.9	320.3	321.7	322.3	319.7
1996	307.6	310.4	312.5	315.0	316.4	319.1	315.2	318.8	317.5	318.2	322.4	322.0	316.3
1997	310.2	313.1	317.4	319.6	323.4	326.4	324.6	326.6	325.6	328.4	330.2	331.5	323.1
1998	318.8	321.2	322.6	326.1	330.5	334.0	332.1	334.3	331.2	334.7	337.6	337.9	330.1
1999	328.7	330.0	332.0	339.2	342.3	345.1	340.1	342.5	340.9	343.2	345.7	346.4	339.7
2000	335.9	336.6	339.0	343.6	347.0	350.7	348.6	349.7	349.1	352.3	354.4	356.2	346.9
2001	342.6	341.9	344.5	347.0	351.9	355.0	352.1	355.0	350.1	350.8	352.8	353.8	349.8
2002	337.0	338.6	341.9	345.5	348.2	350.2	349.4	352.8	349.2	350.4	351.3	350.4	347.1
2003	336.8	338.2	340.0	344.3	348.6	350.4	350.0	353.3	350.4	353.8	353.5	353.0	347.7
Goods-producing													
1990	57.5	57.0	57.6	59.4	61.3	62.9	61.9	62.6	62.2	61.6	60.0	58.5	60.2
1991	54.3	52.9	53.6	55.6	56.9	58.5	58.4	59.1	58.8	58.8	57.2	54.8	56.6
1992	51.4	50.8	51.0	52.4	54.3	55.4	55.5	56.0	55.9	56.0	54.6	53.1	53.9
1993	50.1	49.6	50.1	51.7	53.5	54.9	54.7	55.3	54.7	54.9	53.9	52.0	53.0
1994	49.2	48.4	48.7	50.5	52.6	54.2	54.0	54.8	54.7	55.0	54.1	52.5	52.4
1995	49.2	48.6	48.9	50.3	51.4	52.0	50.9	51.9	51.3	51.1	50.2	48.8	50.4
1996	45.8	45.3	45.9	47.2	48.1	49.1	48.5	50.1	50.0	49.9	49.6	48.2	48.1
1997	45.3	45.1	45.8	47.4	48.9	50.2	49.5	50.2	50.0	50.2	49.8	49.0	48.5
1998	46.7	46.6	46.9	48.8	50.1	51.4	51.2	51.9	51.8	51.5	51.0	50.0	49.8
1999	47.3	47.2	47.6	50.2	51.4	52.5	51.9	52.8	52.4	52.3	52.0	50.8	50.7
2000	48.8	48.1	48.9	50.5	52.1	52.9	52.6	53.0	52.4	52.6	52.2	51.3	51.3
2001	48.5	48.0	48.1	49.6	51.3	52.3	51.9	52.2	51.4	50.8	50.0	48.5	50.2
2002	44.9	44.2	44.8	46.1	47.3	48.1	48.5	48.8	48.3	47.7	47.2	45.4	46.8
2003	43.0	42.1	42.4	43.4	45.1	46.3	46.7	47.4	46.8	46.6	46.0	45.1	45.1
Construction and mining													
1990	17.3	16.7	16.9	18.4	20.1	21.0	21.3	21.5	20.9	20.3	19.0	17.6	19.3
1991	15.1	14.1	14.5	16.0	17.0	18.1	19.2	19.6	19.0	18.8	17.5	15.4	17.0
1992	13.2	12.6	12.7	14.0	15.5	16.3	17.0	17.4	17.1	17.0	15.7	14.4	15.2
1993	12.4	11.7	11.9	13.5	15.1	16.1	16.8	17.1	16.8	16.9	16.1	14.6	14.9
1994	12.0	11.5	11.7	13.4	15.6	16.9	17.3	17.6	17.5	17.6	16.8	15.7	15.3
1995	13.2	12.4	12.7	14.4	15.6	16.2	16.2	16.6	16.2	16.0	15.2	13.7	14.9
1996	11.7	11.6	11.8	13.1	14.0	15.0	15.3	16.2	16.0	16.0	15.4	14.3	14.2
1997	12.5	12.1	12.6	13.9	15.4	16.3	16.8	17.2	17.0	16.7	16.3	15.4	15.2
1998	13.7	13.4	13.5	15.4	16.5	17.4	18.1	18.4	18.0	17.9	17.6	16.7	16.4
1999	14.8	14.6	14.7	16.7	17.9	18.8	19.1	19.5	19.4	19.1	18.9	17.7	17.6
2000	15.9	15.4	16.0	17.3	18.8	19.5	19.8	20.1	19.7	19.4	19.1	18.0	18.3
2001	16.2	15.9	16.1	17.5	19.2	20.0	20.3	20.6	20.2	19.8	19.2	17.9	18.6
2002	15.8	15.3	15.8	17.3	18.5	19.1	19.8	20.0	19.6	19.2	19.0	17.7	18.0
2003	16.0	15.4	15.6	16.7	18.4	19.4	20.2	20.6	20.0	19.9	19.5	18.2	18.3

Employment by Industry: New York—*Continued*

(Numbers in thousands. Not seasonally adjusted.)

Industry	January	February	March	April	May	June	July	August	September	October	November	December	Annual Average
ALBANY-SCHENECTADY-TROY—*Continued*													
Manufacturing													
1990	40.2	40.3	40.7	41.0	41.2	41.9	40.6	41.1	41.3	41.3	41.0	40.9	41.0
1991	39.2	38.8	39.1	39.6	39.9	40.4	39.2	39.5	39.8	40.0	39.7	39.4	39.6
1992	38.2	38.2	38.3	38.4	38.8	39.1	38.5	38.6	38.8	39.0	38.9	38.7	38.6
1993	37.7	37.9	38.2	38.2	38.4	38.8	37.9	38.2	37.9	38.0	37.8	37.4	38.0
1994	37.2	36.9	37.0	37.1	37.0	37.3	36.7	37.2	37.2	37.4	37.3	36.8	37.1
1995	36.0	36.2	36.2	35.9	35.8	35.8	34.7	35.3	35.1	35.1	35.0	35.1	35.5
1996	34.1	33.7	34.1	34.1	34.1	34.1	33.2	33.9	34.0	33.9	34.2	33.9	33.9
1997	32.8	33.0	33.2	33.5	33.5	33.9	32.7	33.0	33.0	33.5	33.5	33.6	33.3
1998	33.0	33.2	33.4	33.4	33.6	34.0	33.1	33.5	33.8	33.6	33.4	33.3	33.4
1999	32.5	32.6	32.9	33.5	33.5	33.7	32.8	33.3	33.0	33.2	33.1	33.1	33.1
2000	32.9	32.7	32.9	33.2	33.3	33.4	32.8	32.9	32.7	33.2	33.1	33.3	33.0
2001	32.2	32.1	32.0	32.0	32.1	32.3	31.5	31.5	31.2	31.0	30.8	30.6	31.6
2002	29.1	28.9	29.0	28.8	28.8	29.0	28.7	28.8	28.7	28.5	28.2	27.7	28.7
2003	27.0	26.7	26.8	26.7	26.7	26.9	26.5	26.8	26.8	26.7	26.5	26.9	26.8
Service-providing													
1990	360.9	363.9	366.8	368.4	372.5	374.2	366.0	367.5	369.0	371.5	372.4	372.8	368.8
1991	362.6	364.1	365.4	363.6	364.4	367.5	358.3	360.7	359.6	364.3	366.8	365.6	363.6
1992	355.2	359.3	360.7	362.3	364.7	367.1	361.3	363.9	363.0	369.2	369.9	370.6	363.9
1993	359.5	363.1	365.1	367.1	372.6	374.3	368.4	368.9	369.7	375.6	378.1	380.3	370.2
1994	368.1	372.3	372.9	374.9	377.7	379.7	375.8	377.7	378.3	383.3	385.7	385.4	377.7
1995	375.5	379.3	380.6	382.5	382.0	381.3	372.6	373.3	376.2	379.0	382.1	383.2	379.0
1996	370.5	376.8	378.1	380.1	380.4	379.7	369.9	371.6	375.2	378.7	383.9	383.4	377.4
1997	372.1	378.4	382.1	383.4	386.0	386.1	379.3	380.5	383.4	388.3	391.8	392.7	383.7
1998	379.0	385.0	385.9	388.6	392.2	393.0	385.5	386.5	388.5	393.8	398.4	398.9	389.6
1999	389.6	394.4	396.0	401.4	402.9	403.7	394.3	395.1	399.0	402.7	406.3	407.4	399.4
2000	396.0	399.9	401.5	405.3	407.8	410.3	402.3	402.1	406.8	411.4	415.0	416.8	406.3
2001	404.5	407.0	409.2	411.0	414.1	415.1	407.9	410.9	409.5	412.9	417.0	418.6	411.5
2002	403.3	408.6	411.3	414.1	415.5	416.0	408.4	410.9	413.3	416.5	418.5	419.2	413.0
2003	405.8	410.3	411.4	413.9	416.4	416.2	409.3	411.2	413.9	419.3	420.0	420.3	414.0
Trade, transportation, and utilities													
1990	78.2	76.9	76.9	76.0	77.0	78.1	76.9	77.3	77.6	78.1	79.8	80.7	77.8
1991	76.3	74.4	74.4	74.0	74.3	75.3	73.2	73.7	73.9	74.9	76.6	77.0	74.8
1992	72.5	71.5	71.3	71.0	71.9	72.9	71.7	72.0	72.0	73.5	74.6	76.0	72.6
1993	72.2	71.2	71.0	71.2	72.1	73.1	72.3	73.0	73.4	75.2	76.9	78.6	73.4
1994	74.9	73.9	73.7	73.9	74.9	75.5	74.9	75.5	76.2	77.2	79.0	80.0	75.8
1995	76.8	75.7	76.0	76.7	77.3	77.9	76.9	77.5	77.7	79.1	80.9	82.1	77.9
1996	76.8	76.1	76.0	76.1	76.6	77.6	76.4	76.7	77.0	78.0	80.6	82.1	77.5
1997	78.1	76.9	77.9	77.9	78.5	79.4	78.3	78.0	79.0	79.6	81.7	83.3	79.1
1998	78.1	77.1	77.0	77.1	78.1	78.8	77.2	77.5	77.8	79.1	81.4	82.9	78.5
1999	80.1	78.9	79.1	79.7	80.1	80.7	78.6	80.0	79.9	81.0	83.1	85.2	80.5
2000	80.9	79.8	80.1	80.3	81.4	82.2	82.0	83.1	83.0	84.3	86.6	88.3	82.7
2001	82.4	81.2	81.0	80.4	81.3	82.3	81.0	81.3	80.5	81.7	84.4	85.3	81.9
2002	80.5	79.2	79.6	80.0	80.5	81.5	80.7	80.8	80.7	81.2	83.1	84.7	81.0
2003	80.7	79.7	79.9	80.0	80.8	81.9	81.0	81.4	81.3	82.9	84.1	85.1	81.6
Wholesale trade													
1990	16.1	16.2	16.3	16.5	16.5	16.8	16.5	16.6	16.5	16.4	16.4	16.4	16.4
1991	16.2	16.1	16.2	16.4	16.4	16.6	16.5	16.5	16.3	16.4	16.4	16.2	16.4
1992	16.1	16.1	16.2	15.8	15.9	16.1	16.0	16.0	15.8	15.9	15.8	15.8	16.0
1993	15.2	15.3	15.3	15.3	15.4	15.6	15.5	15.4	15.3	15.5	15.5	15.6	15.4
1994	15.4	15.3	15.4	15.2	15.4	15.5	15.2	15.3	15.1	15.2	15.3	15.2	15.3
1995	15.1	15.2	15.3	15.5	15.6	15.6	15.3	15.2	15.2	15.4	15.5	15.5	15.4
1996	14.9	15.2	15.3	15.3	15.2	15.3	15.2	15.3	15.2	15.3	15.4	15.5	15.3
1997	15.1	15.2	15.4	15.5	15.6	15.7	16.0	16.0	15.9	16.1	16.1	16.2	15.7
1998	15.6	15.7	15.8	15.8	16.0	16.1	15.6	15.7	15.5	15.7	15.9	15.9	15.8
1999	16.1	16.1	16.2	16.4	16.5	16.6	15.9	16.3	16.2	16.3	16.4	16.5	16.3
2000	16.6	16.6	16.8	16.9	17.0	17.0	17.0	17.1	17.0	16.9	17.1	17.1	16.9
2001	16.7	16.7	16.6	16.8	16.9	17.1	17.2	17.1	17.0	16.7	16.7	16.7	16.9
2002	16.7	16.6	16.6	16.6	16.7	16.7	16.8	16.7	16.6	16.6	16.7	16.7	16.7
2003	16.9	16.9	17.0	17.0	17.0	17.0	17.0	17.0	16.9	17.0	17.0	17.0	17.0
Retail trade													
1990	50.3	49.2	49.1	48.2	49.0	49.4	48.8	48.9	49.1	49.8	51.3	52.2	49.6
1991	48.4	46.9	46.8	46.2	46.5	47.1	45.6	46.2	46.2	46.9	48.4	48.9	47.0
1992	45.4	44.4	44.1	44.2	44.7	45.3	44.8	45.1	45.0	46.1	47.3	48.4	45.4
1993	45.7	44.7	44.4	44.6	45.2	45.9	45.6	46.5	46.7	47.9	49.6	51.0	46.5
1994	48.2	47.3	46.9	47.4	48.0	48.4	48.3	48.9	49.4	49.9	51.8	52.8	48.9
1995	50.0	48.9	49.1	49.5	50.0	50.6	50.3	50.8	50.8	51.5	53.2	54.4	50.8
1996	50.3	49.3	49.0	49.1	49.7	50.6	50.0	50.2	50.2	50.4	52.9	54.2	50.5
1997	50.8	49.7	50.4	50.3	50.8	51.5	50.5	50.8	50.9	51.1	53.1	54.6	51.2
1998	50.4	49.3	49.2	49.3	49.9	50.5	49.6	49.8	49.9	51.0	52.9	54.4	50.5
1999	52.3	51.1	51.2	51.2	51.3	51.8	50.8	51.5	51.1	51.9	53.6	55.6	52.0
2000	51.8	50.6	50.6	50.6	51.1	51.8	51.9	52.7	52.5	53.6	55.6	57.2	52.5
2001	51.9	50.8	50.7	49.8	50.3	51.1	50.3	50.5	49.6	50.9	53.6	54.5	51.2
2002	50.5	49.4	49.9	50.2	50.4	51.3	50.9	51.0	50.6	50.9	52.7	54.3	51.0
2003	50.4	49.3	49.4	49.7	50.4	51.5	51.1	51.4	51.0	52.3	53.6	54.6	51.2

Employment by Industry: New York—*Continued*

(Numbers in thousands. Not seasonally adjusted.)

Industry	January	February	March	April	May	June	July	August	September	October	November	December	Annual Average
ALBANY-SCHENECTADY-TROY—*Continued*													
Transportation and utilities													
1990	11.8	11.5	11.5	11.3	11.5	11.9	11.6	11.8	12.0	11.9	12.1	12.1	11.8
1991	11.7	11.4	11.4	11.4	11.4	11.6	11.1	11.0	11.4	11.6	11.8	11.9	11.5
1992	11.0	11.0	11.0	11.0	11.3	11.5	10.9	10.9	11.2	11.5	11.5	11.8	11.2
1993	11.3	11.2	11.3	11.3	11.5	11.6	11.2	11.1	11.4	11.8	11.8	12.0	11.5
1994	11.3	11.3	11.4	11.3	11.5	11.6	11.4	11.3	11.7	12.1	11.9	12.0	11.6
1995	11.7	11.6	11.6	11.7	11.7	11.7	11.3	11.5	11.7	12.2	12.2	12.2	11.8
1996	11.6	11.6	11.7	11.7	11.7	11.7	11.2	11.2	11.6	12.3	12.3	12.4	11.8
1997	12.2	12.0	12.1	12.1	12.1	12.2	11.8	11.2	12.2	12.4	12.5	12.5	12.1
1998	12.1	12.1	12.0	12.0	12.2	12.2	12.0	12.0	12.4	12.4	12.6	12.6	12.2
1999	11.7	11.7	11.7	12.1	12.3	12.3	11.9	12.2	12.6	12.8	13.1	13.1	12.3
2000	12.5	12.6	12.7	12.8	13.3	13.4	13.1	13.3	13.5	13.8	13.9	14.0	13.2
2001	13.8	13.7	13.7	13.8	14.1	14.1	13.5	13.7	13.9	14.1	14.1	14.1	13.9
2002	13.3	13.2	13.1	13.2	13.4	13.5	13.0	13.1	13.5	13.7	13.7	13.7	13.4
2003	13.4	13.5	13.5	13.3	13.4	13.4	12.9	13.0	13.4	13.6	13.5	13.5	13.4
Information													
1990	11.4	11.5	11.5	11.3	11.3	11.2	11.1	11.1	11.2	11.2	11.2	11.2	11.3
1991	11.3	11.4	11.5	11.6	11.6	11.7	11.8	11.7	11.6	11.3	11.3	11.8	11.6
1992	12.0	12.1	12.2	12.4	12.6	12.7	12.8	12.6	12.5	12.6	12.6	12.6	12.5
1993	12.3	12.5	12.6	12.7	12.8	12.8	12.7	12.7	12.7	12.6	12.6	12.5	12.6
1994	11.6	11.7	12.1	12.4	12.3	12.3	12.1	12.1	12.3	12.2	12.3	12.2	12.1
1995	12.2	12.4	12.5	12.2	11.9	12.0	11.8	11.9	11.9	11.9	12.0	12.1	12.1
1996	11.8	12.0	12.1	11.9	11.8	11.8	11.8	11.9	11.9	12.0	12.2	12.2	12.0
1997	12.2	12.5	12.7	12.6	12.7	12.8	12.7	12.7	12.6	12.7	12.8	12.8	12.7
1998	12.0	12.1	12.3	12.7	12.7	12.8	12.2	12.1	12.0	12.1	12.2	12.1	12.3
1999	11.9	12.0	12.2	12.2	12.4	12.5	12.2	12.3	12.2	12.2	12.3	12.5	12.2
2000	12.1	12.2	12.3	12.6	12.6	12.8	12.6	11.0	12.6	12.3	12.4	12.5	12.3
2001	12.5	12.4	12.5	12.5	12.6	12.7	12.4	12.4	12.4	12.3	12.3	12.3	12.4
2002	12.2	12.2	12.3	12.3	12.4	12.4	12.2	12.2	12.1	12.2	12.3	12.3	12.3
2003	12.1	12.2	12.5	12.6	12.7	12.5	12.5	12.6	12.4	12.3	12.2	12.2	12.4
Financial activities													
1990	23.9	24.0	24.1	24.2	24.2	24.7	24.3	24.3	24.1	23.9	23.8	23.9	24.1
1991	23.7	23.6	23.8	23.7	23.9	24.4	24.5	24.5	24.1	23.9	24.0	24.0	24.0
1992	24.3	24.3	24.6	24.6	24.8	25.3	25.2	25.3	25.1	24.9	24.9	25.1	24.9
1993	24.8	24.9	25.1	25.2	25.4	26.0	26.1	26.0	25.5	25.4	25.4	25.5	25.4
1994	24.9	25.0	25.0	24.8	24.8	25.3	25.0	24.9	24.7	24.7	24.6	24.8	24.9
1995	24.4	24.6	24.7	24.7	24.8	25.1	25.1	25.1	24.9	24.5	24.6	24.8	24.8
1996	24.1	24.3	24.4	24.6	24.5	24.7	24.6	24.5	24.4	24.3	24.3	24.3	24.4
1997	23.6	24.1	24.5	24.5	24.5	24.7	24.5	24.5	24.6	24.6	24.6	24.9	24.5
1998	24.4	24.7	25.0	24.7	24.8	25.1	25.2	25.3	25.0	25.0	25.2	25.3	25.0
1999	24.7	24.8	24.9	25.1	25.1	25.3	25.1	25.3	25.1	24.8	24.9	25.1	25.0
2000	25.3	25.4	25.4	25.6	25.7	26.0	25.9	26.0	25.6	25.5	25.6	26.0	25.7
2001	25.2	25.3	25.4	25.1	25.3	25.8	25.7	25.7	25.4	25.5	25.5	25.6	25.5
2002	24.9	25.2	25.4	25.3	25.6	25.9	25.5	25.8	25.3	25.7	25.8	25.9	25.5
2003	25.9	25.9	26.0	26.1	26.3	26.7	26.8	26.7	26.3	26.3	26.4	26.7	26.3
Professional and business services													
1990	38.8	38.8	39.3	41.0	41.3	41.9	42.1	42.8	42.3	41.9	41.6	41.4	41.1
1991	39.2	39.5	39.8	39.9	40.1	40.9	40.5	40.9	40.3	40.3	40.4	39.8	40.1
1992	37.8	38.7	39.0	39.8	40.1	40.6	41.2	41.3	40.8	42.1	41.7	41.7	40.4
1993	41.5	41.9	42.3	42.6	44.3	45.3	44.1	43.7	43.0	44.1	43.9	44.0	43.4
1994	43.3	43.8	43.8	44.2	44.2	45.0	44.8	45.5	44.2	44.7	44.3	44.0	44.3
1995	43.1	43.7	44.2	45.0	44.4	44.8	42.6	42.6	40.8	40.8	40.6	40.7	42.8
1996	41.0	41.1	41.6	42.0	42.2	42.5	41.8	41.7	41.4	41.0	41.5	41.7	41.6
1997	40.8	41.6	42.3	42.3	42.7	43.4	44.4	44.7	44.2	44.8	44.9	45.0	43.4
1998	45.1	45.4	45.4	46.4	46.7	47.9	48.5	48.5	47.3	47.3	48.0	48.1	47.1
1999	47.2	47.4	47.6	49.6	49.9	50.9	50.7	50.4	49.7	50.3	50.6	50.6	49.6
2000	50.7	50.7	51.0	52.0	52.3	53.1	52.8	53.2	52.4	53.0	53.2	53.4	52.3
2001	52.6	52.9	52.8	53.5	54.2	54.6	54.4	54.6	53.3	53.0	52.8	54.2	53.6
2002	50.3	50.2	50.5	51.2	51.0	51.9	51.7	52.0	51.2	51.2	50.6	50.3	51.0
2003	48.5	48.4	48.7	50.0	50.4	51.1	51.0	51.0	50.5	50.6	51.3	50.7	50.2
Educational and health services													
1990	55.5	56.6	56.8	56.2	55.9	56.1	55.8	55.9	57.0	57.8	58.2	58.2	56.7
1991	58.0	58.6	59.1	58.4	57.8	57.8	56.9	56.7	58.7	59.6	60.1	60.2	58.5
1992	59.9	60.6	61.2	61.0	61.0	61.0	60.4	60.5	60.9	62.6	62.8	62.8	61.2
1993	61.6	62.5	62.9	62.8	62.9	62.6	62.7	62.5	63.4	64.2	64.9	65.0	63.2
1994	63.6	64.6	64.5	64.4	64.4	64.3	64.1	63.4	64.4	66.0	66.4	66.3	64.7
1995	65.3	66.4	66.9	67.1	66.8	66.0	65.1	65.3	66.3	67.9	68.4	68.7	66.7
1996	65.7	67.7	67.7	67.6	66.6	66.1	65.0	64.8	66.3	67.3	68.4	68.1	66.8
1997	67.1	68.8	69.2	68.7	68.5	67.5	67.3	66.9	68.0	69.6	70.2	70.1	68.5
1998	68.8	70.2	70.4	70.0	69.8	69.0	68.9	68.4	68.9	71.5	72.1	71.9	70.0
1999	71.6	72.9	73.3	73.3	72.7	71.9	71.4	71.4	72.1	73.3	74.1	73.7	72.6
2000	72.5	74.3	74.6	74.4	73.9	73.1	72.6	72.8	73.9	76.5	76.7	76.9	74.4
2001	75.2	76.1	78.0	77.9	77.1	75.2	75.2	75.1	77.5	78.7	79.2	79.2	77.0
2002	76.8	79.7	80.4	80.5	79.3	77.4	77.7	77.7	80.0	81.2	81.4	81.5	79.5
2003	78.7	81.6	81.7	82.1	81.5	79.2	78.4	78.1	80.8	83.4	82.9	82.9	80.9

Employment by Industry: New York—*Continued*

(Numbers in thousands. Not seasonally adjusted.)

Industry	January	February	March	April	May	June	July	August	September	October	November	December	Annual Average
ALBANY-SCHENECTADY-TROY—*Continued*													
Leisure and hospitality													
1990	26.9	27.6	28.0	28.5	29.6	30.0	30.3	31.7	30.1	29.6	28.8	28.6	29.1
1991	26.7	27.4	28.0	28.0	28.9	29.5	29.2	31.0	28.9	28.5	27.9	27.3	28.4
1992	25.2	25.9	26.3	26.9	28.3	28.9	28.8	31.2	28.9	27.7	27.0	26.8	27.7
1993	24.4	25.8	25.4	26.6	28.5	29.1	29.1	30.9	28.7	28.2	27.8	27.4	27.7
1994	25.3	25.8	26.2	27.0	28.6	29.2	30.3	32.1	30.2	29.7	29.4	28.9	28.6
1995	27.3	27.7	28.5	29.4	30.8	31.3	31.1	32.7	30.4	29.5	29.4	29.4	29.8
1996	27.3	28.4	29.4	30.0	31.0	31.8	31.7	33.6	31.0	29.8	29.8	29.4	30.3
1997	27.3	28.0	28.8	29.7	31.0	31.8	31.6	33.3	30.9	30.2	29.5	29.5	30.1
1998	27.5	28.6	29.0	29.8	31.5	32.1	32.3	34.0	31.9	31.3	30.8	30.5	30.8
1999	29.1	29.6	30.0	31.3	32.8	33.6	32.6	32.6	31.9	31.4	30.6	30.3	31.3
2000	28.3	28.7	29.2	30.4	31.2	32.6	32.3	32.7	31.5	30.1	29.5	29.5	30.5
2001	28.3	28.1	28.7	30.2	32.1	33.8	33.7	35.8	31.7	30.8	30.4	30.4	31.2
2002	29.4	29.7	30.5	31.5	33.4	34.3	34.6	37.0	33.1	32.4	31.8	31.3	32.4
2003	29.0	29.4	29.9	31.2	32.8	33.5	34.4	36.8	33.0	33.0	31.7	31.5	32.2
Other services													
1990	13.9	14.1	14.2	14.2	14.3	14.4	14.5	14.6	14.3	14.5	14.4	14.4	14.3
1991	14.2	14.2	14.3	14.4	14.6	14.7	14.7	14.8	14.4	14.5	14.5	14.5	14.5
1992	14.1	14.1	14.1	13.9	14.0	14.1	14.3	14.3	13.9	14.4	14.2	14.3	14.1
1993	13.6	13.7	13.8	14.0	14.1	14.1	14.3	14.3	14.0	14.4	14.4	14.5	14.1
1994	14.0	14.3	14.3	14.6	14.8	14.9	14.8	15.0	15.0	14.9	15.0	15.0	14.7
1995	14.7	15.0	15.2	15.1	15.3	15.3	15.4	15.5	15.6	15.5	15.6	15.7	15.3
1996	15.1	15.5	15.4	15.6	15.6	15.5	15.4	15.5	15.5	15.9	16.0	16.0	15.6
1997	15.8	16.1	16.2	16.5	16.6	16.6	16.3	16.3	16.3	16.7	16.7	16.9	16.4
1998	16.2	16.5	16.6	16.6	16.8	16.9	16.6	16.6	16.5	16.9	16.9	17.1	16.7
1999	16.8	17.2	17.3	17.8	17.9	17.7	17.6	17.7	17.6	17.9	18.1	18.2	17.7
2000	17.3	17.4	17.5	17.8	17.8	18.0	17.8	17.9	17.7	18.0	18.2	18.3	17.8
2001	17.9	17.9	18.0	17.8	18.0	18.3	17.8	17.9	17.9	18.0	18.2	18.3	18.0
2002	18.0	18.2	18.4	18.6	18.7	18.7	18.5	18.5	18.5	18.8	19.1	19.0	18.6
2003	18.9	18.9	18.9	18.9	19.0	19.2	19.2	19.3	19.3	18.7	18.9	18.8	19.0
Government													
1990	112.3	114.4	116.0	117.0	118.9	117.8	111.0	109.8	112.4	114.5	114.6	114.4	114.4
1991	113.2	115.0	114.5	113.6	113.2	113.2	107.5	107.4	107.7	111.3	112.0	111.0	111.6
1992	109.4	112.1	112.0	112.7	112.0	111.6	106.9	106.7	108.9	111.4	112.1	111.3	110.6
1993	109.1	110.6	112.0	112.0	112.5	111.3	107.1	105.8	109.0	111.5	112.2	112.8	110.5
1994	110.5	113.2	113.3	113.6	113.7	113.2	109.8	109.2	111.3	113.9	114.7	114.2	112.6
1995	111.7	113.8	112.6	112.3	110.7	108.9	104.6	102.7	108.6	109.8	110.6	109.7	109.7
1996	108.7	111.7	111.5	112.3	112.1	109.7	103.2	102.9	107.7	110.4	111.1	109.6	109.2
1997	107.2	110.4	110.5	111.2	111.5	109.9	104.2	104.1	107.8	110.1	111.4	110.2	109.0
1998	106.9	110.4	110.2	111.3	111.8	110.4	104.6	104.1	109.1	110.6	111.8	111.0	109.4
1999	108.2	111.6	111.6	112.4	112.0	111.1	106.1	105.4	110.5	111.8	112.6	111.8	110.4
2000	108.9	111.4	111.4	112.2	112.9	112.5	106.3	105.4	110.1	111.7	112.8	111.9	110.6
2001	110.4	113.1	112.8	113.6	113.5	112.4	107.7	108.1	110.8	112.9	114.2	113.3	111.9
2002	111.2	114.2	114.2	114.7	114.6	113.9	107.5	106.9	112.4	113.8	114.4	114.2	112.7
2003	112.0	114.2	113.8	113.0	112.9	112.1	106.0	105.3	110.3	112.1	112.5	112.4	111.4
Federal government													
1990	9.9	9.9	10.5	11.3	12.4	11.7	11.5	10.6	10.7	10.6	10.4	10.6	10.8
1991	10.0	9.7	9.6	9.5	9.5	9.8	9.6	9.5	9.4	9.4	9.4	9.4	9.6
1992	9.3	9.3	9.3	9.2	9.2	9.3	9.2	9.1	9.1	9.1	9.0	9.0	9.2
1993	9.0	9.0	9.0	9.0	9.0	9.1	9.0	9.0	8.9	8.9	8.9	9.0	9.0
1994	9.0	8.9	8.9	8.8	8.8	8.8	8.8	9.0	8.9	8.8	8.8	8.5	8.8
1995	8.5	8.4	8.3	8.3	8.3	8.3	8.7	8.6	8.8	8.7	8.7	8.7	8.5
1996	8.6	8.8	8.9	9.0	8.8	8.7	8.8	8.7	8.6	8.5	8.5	8.6	8.7
1997	9.0	9.0	8.9	8.9	8.9	8.9	8.8	8.8	8.7	8.7	8.7	8.8	8.8
1998	8.7	8.8	8.7	8.6	8.5	8.6	8.5	8.5	8.4	8.4	8.4	8.5	8.6
1999	8.3	8.3	8.3	8.5	8.2	8.3	8.3	8.3	8.2	8.2	8.2	8.2	8.3
2000	8.1	8.1	8.4	8.3	9.2	8.7	8.7	8.1	8.0	8.0	8.0	8.1	8.3
2001	7.8	7.8	7.8	7.8	7.8	7.9	8.0	7.9	7.8	7.8	7.8	7.8	7.8
2002	7.7	7.6	7.6	7.6	7.6	7.8	7.8	7.8	7.9	7.9	8.0	8.1	7.8
2003	8.0	7.9	7.9	7.9	7.8	7.8	7.8	7.7	7.7	7.7	7.6	7.4	7.8
State government													
1990	61.0	62.0	63.0	62.7	63.0	62.3	60.5	59.9	60.6	60.4	60.2	59.7	61.3
1991	59.9	60.7	60.9	60.1	59.7	59.5	58.4	58.0	57.5	58.2	58.3	57.8	59.1
1992	58.1	59.0	59.0	59.2	59.0	58.5	58.1	57.9	58.5	58.5	58.4	58.0	58.5
1993	57.6	57.7	58.8	59.0	59.0	57.9	58.3	57.5	58.4	58.3	58.1	59.2	58.3
1994	58.7	60.0	60.3	60.3	60.2	59.5	59.8	59.7	60.4	60.3	60.2	60.2	60.0
1995	59.1	60.1	59.4	58.5	57.2	55.4	56.1	55.1	56.6	55.8	55.8	54.9	57.0
1996	55.8	57.2	57.2	57.2	57.0	55.3	54.8	54.1	55.6	55.5	55.7	54.2	55.8
1997	53.9	55.4	55.6	55.8	55.5	54.1	54.1	54.3	54.9	54.7	55.0	53.9	54.8
1998	53.2	55.1	55.0	55.0	55.0	53.3	53.4	53.6	54.7	54.8	55.3	54.2	54.4
1999	53.7	55.5	55.5	55.7	55.6	53.9	54.1	54.3	55.5	55.5	55.9	54.9	55.0
2000	53.6	55.1	55.2	55.3	55.3	53.5	53.7	54.0	55.1	55.2	55.7	54.6	54.7
2001	54.4	56.1	56.1	56.1	56.0	54.2	54.3	54.6	55.8	56.0	56.5	55.4	55.5
2002	54.3	56.0	56.1	55.8	55.9	54.5	54.4	54.7	55.6	55.6	55.6	55.4	55.3
2003	54.9	55.2	55.3	54.2	54.2	53.0	52.9	53.2	54.0	54.1	54.1	54.1	54.1

Employment by Industry: New York—*Continued*

(Numbers in thousands. Not seasonally adjusted.)

Industry	January	February	March	April	May	June	July	August	September	October	November	December	Annual Average
ALBANY-SCHENECTADY-TROY—*Continued*													
Local government													
1990	41.4	42.5	42.6	43.0	43.5	43.8	39.0	39.2	41.2	43.5	43.9	44.1	42.3
1991	43.2	44.6	44.0	44.0	44.0	43.9	39.4	39.8	40.8	43.7	44.3	43.8	43.0
1992	41.9	43.8	43.7	44.3	43.8	43.8	39.6	39.7	41.3	43.8	44.7	44.3	42.9
1993	42.6	43.9	44.1	44.0	44.5	44.4	39.9	39.3	41.7	44.3	45.2	44.6	43.2
1994	42.9	44.3	44.1	44.6	44.7	44.9	41.1	40.6	42.0	44.8	45.8	45.5	43.8
1995	44.1	45.3	44.9	45.5	45.2	45.2	39.8	39.0	43.2	45.3	46.1	46.2	44.2
1996	44.3	45.7	45.4	46.1	46.3	45.7	39.6	40.1	43.6	46.3	46.9	46.8	44.7
1997	44.4	46.0	46.0	46.5	47.2	46.9	41.3	41.0	44.1	46.7	47.7	47.5	45.4
1998	45.0	46.5	46.5	47.7	48.3	48.5	42.7	42.0	46.0	47.4	48.1	48.3	46.4
1999	46.2	47.8	47.8	48.2	48.2	48.9	43.7	42.8	46.8	48.1	48.5	48.7	47.1
2000	47.2	48.2	47.8	48.6	48.4	50.3	43.9	43.3	47.0	48.5	49.1	49.2	47.6
2001	48.2	49.2	48.9	49.7	49.7	50.3	45.4	45.6	47.2	49.1	49.9	50.1	48.6
2002	49.2	50.6	50.5	51.3	51.1	51.6	45.3	44.4	48.9	50.3	50.8	50.7	49.6
2003	49.1	51.1	50.6	50.9	50.9	51.3	45.3	44.4	48.6	50.3	50.8	50.9	49.5
BUFFALO													
Total nonfarm													
1990	528.3	537.7	542.5	544.2	553.2	557.5	547.3	549.4	552.5	554.8	555.0	553.0	547.9
1991	526.7	525.1	528.1	530.0	538.2	539.7	531.1	532.6	533.5	538.5	538.6	539.0	533.4
1992	516.3	518.7	519.1	524.1	533.7	536.0	529.0	529.1	533.2	533.8	534.2	536.2	528.6
1993	515.1	517.2	518.2	520.5	530.9	534.6	526.9	526.5	531.6	536.2	537.5	539.0	527.8
1994	517.9	521.3	523.7	527.0	537.7	539.7	534.7	535.0	541.5	544.7	545.6	545.8	534.5
1995	526.1	528.9	533.1	536.2	542.3	545.3	536.9	538.0	542.9	547.0	548.5	547.6	539.4
1996	526.4	528.3	530.9	530.5	542.6	546.2	537.8	538.5	543.6	548.0	549.3	550.4	539.3
1997	529.1	532.6	536.9	540.1	548.7	550.7	543.3	542.7	547.9	553.1	553.5	554.1	544.3
1998	532.4	537.1	539.8	540.8	549.5	551.0	537.8	545.3	548.4	554.3	554.5	555.9	545.5
1999	536.0	542.2	545.0	550.8	559.4	561.4	553.2	553.8	555.8	563.6	565.1	564.6	554.2
2000	545.5	548.4	550.8	555.0	561.4	563.1	557.3	558.2	560.8	566.6	567.6	564.8	558.2
2001	547.2	548.6	550.3	546.9	556.5	558.5	546.5	546.4	547.1	550.6	551.1	549.5	549.9
2002	537.5	539.5	541.5	543.4	551.2	553.7	546.5	548.4	549.5	554.8	555.1	556.0	548.1
2003	536.0	537.8	540.5	542.8	548.9	551.4	541.8	542.2	548.3	553.5	554.0	553.4	545.9
Total private													
1990	439.8	448.0	452.0	453.9	462.0	466.3	459.3	462.3	466.5	464.2	463.8	461.6	458.3
1991	438.1	434.7	437.7	441.6	448.6	450.1	444.9	447.1	449.2	450.6	449.8	450.3	445.2
1992	430.7	430.3	430.7	436.0	445.1	448.4	444.3	445.4	448.1	446.6	446.3	448.5	441.7
1993	430.0	430.4	430.9	433.8	443.2	447.2	443.1	444.5	446.3	447.9	448.5	449.7	441.2
1994	431.2	432.2	434.5	439.4	447.9	450.8	448.9	450.5	454.0	455.1	454.7	455.4	446.2
1995	438.1	438.9	442.7	446.7	452.8	456.8	453.1	455.0	456.8	458.1	459.1	458.1	451.3
1996	439.6	439.7	442.2	443.1	453.2	457.9	453.6	455.9	457.5	459.8	460.4	461.9	452.0
1997	442.9	444.4	448.2	452.9	459.8	463.8	459.6	460.0	462.3	464.3	464.3	465.7	457.3
1998	446.7	449.1	450.9	453.2	460.2	463.8	453.6	461.2	462.0	464.9	464.4	466.4	458.0
1999	449.0	452.8	454.9	462.7	468.9	473.2	468.0	469.1	468.9	472.4	473.2	473.6	465.5
2000	456.0	457.0	458.6	462.6	468.0	472.4	469.9	471.5	472.1	472.9	473.7	473.2	467.3
2001	456.5	455.7	457.3	454.2	463.0	466.9	459.5	459.6	456.8	457.2	457.2	456.3	458.4
2002	445.4	445.2	446.7	450.3	457.0	460.8	457.0	458.8	458.8	460.2	460.3	461.0	455.1
2003	442.6	441.9	443.2	447.0	452.7	456.0	451.6	452.2	454.9	456.4	456.9	456.3	451.0
Goods-producing													
1990	111.3	112.3	113.4	114.3	117.0	118.7	117.9	118.9	120.2	117.9	115.4	111.7	115.7
1991	106.2	103.0	103.5	106.5	108.9	110.4	109.9	110.4	111.2	110.1	107.9	106.7	107.8
1992	102.6	101.5	101.7	103.3	106.1	107.5	106.6	106.4	107.4	106.5	105.1	103.9	104.8
1993	99.3	98.3	97.9	100.2	103.3	104.6	104.0	104.7	105.4	105.0	104.3	102.7	102.4
1994	97.9	97.4	98.3	100.0	102.8	104.4	104.2	104.2	105.9	105.4	104.7	103.1	102.3
1995	101.1	100.3	101.5	103.3	105.6	107.6	107.6	108.4	108.5	108.5	107.1	105.0	105.3
1996	101.6	101.2	101.7	102.4	105.5	108.5	108.6	109.7	109.2	108.5	107.0	105.7	105.8
1997	101.4	100.8	101.7	103.3	105.9	107.4	106.9	107.4	107.4	106.8	105.4	104.7	104.9
1998	101.1	101.3	101.4	102.8	105.0	106.9	99.9	106.9	107.0	106.3	105.3	104.3	104.0
1999	100.1	100.4	100.5	103.0	105.1	106.9	107.1	107.2	106.8	106.2	105.2	104.1	104.3
2000	101.2	100.7	101.3	103.2	105.1	106.6	106.2	107.2	106.6	106.4	105.6	103.7	104.4
2001	99.0	98.0	98.0	98.7	99.3	101.4	101.2	100.3	99.8	98.9	97.8	96.3	99.1
2002	89.9	89.4	89.9	92.1	94.1	95.1	95.1	94.9	94.0	94.3	93.8	91.5	92.8
2003	87.7	86.3	87.1	87.4	89.4	90.4	90.3	90.5	90.2	89.3	88.3	86.4	88.6
Construction and mining													
1990	18.7	18.4	19.4	20.3	23.0	24.2	25.2	25.5	25.5	24.4	23.1	21.2	22.4
1991	17.3	16.3	16.5	18.6	21.1	22.4	22.9	23.2	23.0	22.4	20.6	19.1	20.2
1992	16.0	15.4	15.6	17.4	19.9	20.8	21.1	21.3	21.1	20.6	19.4	18.0	18.8
1993	15.7	15.0	15.1	17.4	19.7	20.5	21.2	21.3	21.3	21.0	19.9	18.2	18.8
1994	14.7	14.5	15.2	17.0	19.4	20.3	21.1	21.2	21.2	20.9	20.3	18.5	18.6
1995	16.1	15.4	16.2	17.8	20.0	21.3	22.4	22.8	22.5	22.0	20.8	18.8	19.6
1996	16.5	16.3	16.8	18.3	20.7	22.2	23.0	23.5	23.1	22.4	21.1	19.4	20.2
1997	16.5	16.0	16.6	18.2	20.3	21.3	22.1	22.2	22.0	21.8	20.3	18.8	19.6
1998	16.3	16.3	16.4	17.9	19.8	20.8	21.3	21.5	21.3	21.2	20.2	18.9	19.3
1999	16.2	16.5	16.6	19.3	21.4	22.2	23.0	22.9	22.5	22.5	21.6	20.2	20.4
2000	17.7	17.2	17.9	19.7	21.4	22.2	23.0	23.4	22.9	22.4	21.7	19.6	20.7
2001	17.6	17.3	17.8	19.5	21.5	22.5	23.2	23.3	22.7	22.3	21.6	20.6	20.8
2002	17.1	16.7	17.4	19.4	21.2	22.0	22.9	23.1	22.4	22.4	21.7	20.2	20.5
2003	17.3	16.6	16.9	18.3	20.2	21.0	21.9	22.4	21.8	21.3	20.5	19.1	19.8

Employment by Industry: New York—*Continued*

(Numbers in thousands. Not seasonally adjusted.)

Industry	January	February	March	April	May	June	July	August	September	October	November	December	Annual Average
BUFFALO—*Continued*													
Manufacturing													
1990	92.6	93.9	94.0	94.0	94.0	94.5	92.7	93.4	94.7	93.5	92.3	90.5	93.3
1991	88.9	86.7	87.0	87.9	87.8	88.0	87.0	87.2	88.2	87.7	87.3	87.6	87.6
1992	86.6	86.1	86.1	85.9	86.2	86.7	85.5	85.1	86.3	85.9	85.7	85.9	86.0
1993	83.6	83.3	82.8	82.8	83.6	84.1	82.8	83.4	84.1	84.0	84.4	84.5	83.6
1994	83.2	82.9	83.1	83.0	83.4	84.1	83.1	83.0	84.7	84.5	84.4	84.6	83.6
1995	85.0	84.9	85.3	85.5	85.6	86.3	85.2	85.6	86.0	86.5	86.3	86.2	85.7
1996	85.1	84.9	84.9	84.1	84.8	86.3	85.6	86.2	86.1	86.1	85.9	86.3	85.5
1997	84.9	84.8	85.1	85.1	85.6	86.1	84.8	85.2	85.4	85.0	85.1	85.9	85.2
1998	84.8	85.0	85.0	84.9	85.2	86.1	78.6	85.4	85.7	85.1	85.1	85.4	84.6
1999	83.9	83.9	83.9	83.7	83.7	84.7	84.1	84.3	84.3	83.7	83.6	83.9	83.9
2000	83.5	83.5	83.4	83.5	83.7	84.4	83.2	83.8	83.7	84.0	83.9	84.1	83.7
2001	81.4	80.7	80.2	79.2	77.8	78.9	78.0	77.0	77.1	76.6	76.2	75.7	78.2
2002	72.8	72.7	72.5	72.7	72.9	73.1	72.2	71.8	71.6	71.9	72.1	71.3	72.3
2003	70.4	69.7	70.2	69.1	69.2	69.4	68.4	68.1	68.4	68.0	67.8	67.3	68.8
Service-providing													
1990	417.0	425.4	429.1	429.9	436.2	438.8	429.4	430.5	432.3	436.9	439.6	441.3	432.2
1991	420.5	422.1	424.6	423.5	429.3	429.3	421.2	422.2	422.3	428.4	430.7	432.3	425.5
1992	413.7	417.2	417.4	420.8	427.6	428.5	422.4	422.7	425.8	427.3	429.1	432.3	423.7
1993	415.8	418.9	420.3	420.3	427.6	430.0	422.9	421.8	426.2	431.2	433.2	436.3	425.3
1994	420.0	423.9	425.4	427.0	434.9	435.3	430.5	430.8	435.6	439.3	440.9	442.7	432.1
1995	425.0	428.6	431.6	432.9	436.7	437.7	429.3	429.6	434.4	438.5	441.4	442.6	434.0
1996	424.8	427.1	429.2	428.1	437.1	437.7	429.2	428.8	434.4	439.5	442.3	444.7	433.5
1997	427.7	431.8	435.2	436.8	442.8	443.3	436.4	435.3	440.5	446.3	448.1	449.4	439.4
1998	431.3	435.8	438.4	438.0	444.5	444.1	437.9	438.4	441.4	448.0	449.2	451.6	441.5
1999	435.9	441.8	444.5	447.8	454.3	454.5	446.1	446.6	449.0	457.4	459.9	460.5	449.8
2000	444.3	447.7	449.5	451.8	456.3	456.5	451.1	451.0	454.2	460.2	462.0	461.1	453.8
2001	448.2	450.6	452.3	448.2	457.2	457.1	445.3	446.1	447.3	451.7	453.3	453.2	450.9
2002	447.6	450.1	451.6	451.3	457.1	458.6	451.4	453.5	455.5	460.5	461.3	464.5	455.3
2003	448.3	451.5	453.4	455.4	459.5	461.0	451.5	451.7	458.1	464.2	465.7	467.0	457.3
Trade, transportation, and utilities													
1990	112.1	112.8	113.3	113.1	114.5	115.6	112.7	113.4	114.4	114.8	117.6	119.4	114.4
1991	109.8	107.4	108.0	107.4	108.6	109.2	106.8	107.6	108.1	110.0	113.3	115.0	109.2
1992	107.0	105.6	105.3	105.8	107.8	108.8	106.7	107.6	107.9	108.1	110.1	112.0	107.7
1993	107.4	106.0	106.0	105.4	106.7	107.4	105.7	106.0	106.6	108.2	110.2	112.7	107.3
1994	106.1	104.5	104.1	104.3	106.5	107.6	106.2	107.2	108.6	109.7	111.7	113.4	107.4
1995	107.2	105.5	105.7	106.7	107.4	108.5	107.0	107.2	108.7	109.6	112.1	113.4	108.2
1996	107.4	105.3	105.3	104.3	106.4	106.9	105.7	105.4	106.4	108.5	111.2	113.1	107.1
1997	107.3	105.3	105.5	105.6	106.8	107.9	106.6	105.7	107.6	108.9	110.9	112.6	107.5
1998	106.5	105.3	104.8	104.6	106.3	107.1	106.0	105.9	106.3	107.1	109.1	110.9	106.6
1999	104.2	103.5	103.8	105.2	106.7	107.6	105.7	106.5	106.8	109.5	112.0	114.0	107.1
2000	107.9	106.6	106.5	105.8	107.1	108.6	107.1	108.1	108.3	108.6	111.2	112.8	108.2
2001	110.1	108.1	108.2	105.9	107.7	108.6	106.0	105.8	105.6	106.2	108.2	109.5	107.5
2002	105.2	103.1	103.2	103.1	104.3	105.9	103.9	104.0	104.4	105.2	106.6	108.0	104.7
2003	102.4	100.4	100.5	100.8	102.1	103.4	102.1	102.3	103.0	103.6	106.1	107.6	102.9
Wholesale trade													
1990	23.2	23.7	23.8	23.8	23.8	24.3	24.1	24.2	24.0	23.9	24.1	24.2	23.9
1991	23.4	23.1	23.2	23.1	23.2	23.6	23.6	23.7	23.4	23.5	23.6	23.7	23.4
1992	23.1	23.0	23.1	23.3	23.7	24.2	24.3	24.4	24.3	24.0	23.9	24.0	23.7
1993	24.3	24.3	24.2	23.9	24.2	24.6	24.6	24.7	24.5	24.5	24.5	24.8	24.4
1994	23.2	23.1	23.0	22.8	23.1	23.5	23.8	23.9	23.7	23.8	23.6	23.7	23.4
1995	23.3	23.2	23.1	23.3	23.3	23.7	23.6	23.6	23.6	23.6	23.7	23.9	23.4
1996	23.3	23.2	23.4	23.2	23.5	23.2	23.1	23.1	23.0	23.0	23.3	23.5	23.2
1997	23.3	23.3	23.4	23.7	23.8	23.9	24.0	24.1	24.0	24.3	24.4	24.5	23.8
1998	23.8	23.7	23.8	24.0	24.1	24.3	24.0	24.0	23.9	24.0	24.0	24.1	23.9
1999	23.2	23.3	23.5	23.2	23.3	23.4	23.2	23.2	22.9	23.2	23.5	23.2	23.2
2000	23.4	23.5	23.2	22.7	22.7	22.8	22.8	22.8	22.5	22.4	22.5	22.5	22.8
2001	24.0	24.0	24.0	23.8	23.9	24.1	23.9	23.7	23.5	23.6	23.5	23.5	23.8
2002	23.2	23.2	23.1	23.0	23.1	23.3	23.2	23.1	23.1	23.3	23.3	23.3	23.2
2003	22.5	22.4	22.5	22.4	22.7	22.6	22.8	22.7	22.6	22.6	22.7	22.4	22.6
Retail trade													
1990	70.5	70.3	70.4	70.2	71.2	71.5	70.2	70.9	70.8	71.1	73.8	75.4	71.3
1991	68.1	66.2	66.5	65.6	66.3	66.3	65.3	65.9	65.9	67.6	70.8	72.1	67.2
1992	65.4	64.0	63.6	63.8	65.1	65.3	64.3	64.9	64.4	64.9	67.0	68.6	65.1
1993	64.6	63.3	63.3	62.9	63.4	63.7	63.2	63.3	63.2	64.5	66.7	68.8	64.2
1994	64.3	62.9	62.6	63.4	64.1	64.5	64.0	64.6	65.2	65.8	68.2	70.1	64.9
1995	64.8	63.3	63.5	64.1	64.6	65.1	64.8	65.0	65.6	66.0	68.6	69.8	65.4
1996	65.4	63.4	63.2	62.2	63.5	64.1	64.2	64.1	64.1	66.0	68.6	70.4	64.9
1997	65.7	63.8	63.8	63.4	64.2	64.8	64.5	64.5	64.6	65.6	67.6	69.2	65.1
1998	64.8	63.4	63.1	62.5	63.5	64.1	64.0	63.7	63.4	64.2	66.3	68.1	64.2
1999	63.1	62.3	62.3	63.3	64.3	64.8	63.8	64.4	64.3	66.2	68.5	70.8	64.8
2000	65.3	64.0	64.2	63.8	64.7	65.8	65.4	66.2	65.9	65.9	68.5	70.1	65.8
2001	65.8	64.1	64.1	62.7	63.8	64.4	63.1	63.2	62.5	63.0	65.2	66.5	64.0
2002	62.9	61.2	61.6	61.3	62.0	63.1	62.2	62.3	61.9	62.5	64.0	65.4	62.5
2003	61.2	59.6	59.6	60.0	60.7	61.9	61.2	61.5	61.4	61.8	64.3	66.1	61.6

Employment by Industry: New York—*Continued*

(Numbers in thousands. Not seasonally adjusted.)

Industry	January	February	March	April	May	June	July	August	September	October	November	December	Annual Average
BUFFALO—*Continued*													
Transportation and utilities													
1990	18.4	18.8	19.1	19.1	19.5	19.8	18.4	18.3	19.6	19.8	19.7	19.8	19.1
1991	18.3	18.1	18.3	18.7	19.1	19.3	17.9	18.0	18.8	18.9	18.9	19.2	18.6
1992	18.5	18.6	18.6	18.7	19.0	19.3	18.1	18.3	19.2	19.2	19.2	19.4	18.8
1993	18.5	18.4	18.5	18.6	19.1	19.1	17.9	18.0	18.9	19.2	19.0	19.1	18.6
1994	18.6	18.5	18.5	18.1	19.3	19.6	18.4	18.7	19.7	20.1	19.9	19.6	19.0
1995	19.1	19.0	19.1	19.3	19.5	19.7	18.6	18.6	19.5	20.0	19.8	19.7	19.3
1996	18.7	18.7	18.7	18.9	19.4	19.6	18.4	18.2	19.3	19.5	19.3	19.2	18.9
1997	18.3	18.2	18.3	18.5	18.8	19.2	18.1	17.1	19.0	19.0	18.9	18.9	18.5
1998	17.9	18.2	17.9	18.1	18.7	18.7	18.0	18.2	19.0	18.9	18.8	18.7	18.4
1999	17.9	17.9	18.0	18.7	19.1	19.4	18.7	18.9	19.6	20.1	20.0	20.0	19.0
2000	19.2	19.1	19.1	19.3	19.7	20.0	18.9	19.1	19.9	20.3	20.2	20.2	19.5
2001	20.3	20.0	20.1	19.4	20.0	20.1	19.0	18.9	19.6	19.6	19.5	19.5	19.7
2002	19.1	18.7	18.5	18.8	19.2	19.5	18.5	18.6	19.4	19.4	19.3	19.3	19.0
2003	18.7	18.4	18.4	18.4	18.7	18.9	18.1	18.1	19.0	19.2	19.1	19.1	18.7
Information													
1990	10.6	10.7	10.7	10.6	10.7	10.7	10.8	10.7	10.8	10.9	10.9	10.9	10.7
1991	10.4	10.4	10.5	10.5	10.4	10.4	10.4	10.4	10.5	10.3	10.2	10.2	10.3
1992	9.8	9.8	9.8	9.9	10.1	10.2	10.2	10.1	10.2	10.0	10.0	10.1	10.0
1993	10.1	10.1	10.2	10.4	10.6	10.6	10.7	10.9	10.8	10.5	10.4	10.4	10.4
1994	10.2	10.1	10.2	10.2	10.1	10.2	10.3	10.4	10.5	10.5	10.5	10.7	10.3
1995	10.1	10.1	10.2	10.1	10.2	10.4	10.2	10.3	10.3	10.2	10.2	10.3	10.2
1996	9.6	9.6	9.7	9.6	9.7	9.8	9.8	9.8	9.9	10.0	10.1	10.2	9.8
1997	10.1	10.1	10.1	9.9	10.0	10.1	10.1	10.2	10.1	10.1	10.2	10.3	10.1
1998	10.0	10.1	10.1	10.1	10.1	10.2	10.4	10.5	10.7	10.5	10.5	10.6	10.3
1999	10.2	10.3	10.3	10.3	10.5	10.6	10.2	10.4	10.4	10.4	10.4	10.6	10.3
2000	9.7	9.8	9.7	10.0	10.1	10.1	10.2	9.0	10.3	10.1	10.1	10.2	9.9
2001	11.0	11.0	11.1	11.0	11.2	11.3	11.0	10.8	10.7	10.4	10.4	10.5	10.9
2002	10.4	10.5	10.6	10.6	10.9	10.9	10.7	10.9	10.9	10.8	10.2	10.3	10.6
2003	9.8	9.9	9.9	9.8	9.9	9.8	9.8	10.0	9.8	9.8	9.8	9.8	9.8
Financial activities													
1990	30.1	30.6	30.8	30.7	30.8	31.0	30.6	30.6	30.3	29.8	29.7	29.8	30.4
1991	29.4	29.3	29.4	29.2	29.3	29.3	29.6	29.4	29.0	28.4	28.3	28.5	29.0
1992	28.5	28.7	28.6	28.6	28.7	29.0	28.9	28.8	28.5	28.5	28.5	28.7	28.6
1993	28.0	28.0	28.0	28.3	28.4	28.7	28.7	28.7	28.2	28.3	28.3	28.3	28.3
1994	28.6	28.9	28.9	28.9	29.0	29.2	29.1	29.1	28.7	28.6	28.6	28.7	28.8
1995	28.3	28.5	28.7	28.6	28.7	28.9	28.8	28.9	28.5	28.6	28.6	28.7	28.6
1996	28.3	28.4	28.5	28.5	28.6	29.0	29.3	29.2	29.1	29.1	29.1	29.2	28.8
1997	28.5	28.6	29.0	29.2	29.4	29.7	29.8	29.7	29.8	29.3	29.1	29.4	29.2
1998	29.5	29.4	29.6	29.1	29.1	29.4	29.9	29.7	29.3	28.8	28.7	29.0	29.2
1999	29.5	29.5	29.5	29.7	29.8	30.1	29.9	30.0	29.6	29.6	29.6	29.6	29.7
2000	29.3	29.3	29.5	29.4	29.8	30.3	30.3	30.3	30.1	30.0	30.2	30.3	29.9
2001	30.2	30.2	30.5	30.3	30.8	30.9	31.5	31.6	31.6	32.1	31.9	32.5	31.2
2002	33.1	33.1	32.9	32.8	32.9	33.3	33.4	33.3	32.9	33.4	33.7	33.8	33.2
2003	33.2	32.8	32.4	33.3	33.4	33.7	33.9	34.0	33.8	33.9	34.1	34.3	33.6
Professional and business services													
1990	45.2	46.2	46.7	47.0	48.0	48.3	48.6	49.0	48.8	48.8	48.8	48.4	47.8
1991	45.7	45.8	46.2	46.5	47.1	47.7	47.1	47.3	46.8	47.5	47.4	46.9	46.8
1992	45.5	45.6	45.9	46.5	47.5	48.7	48.9	49.1	48.9	48.1	47.8	47.9	47.5
1993	46.2	46.1	46.3	47.1	47.9	48.8	48.9	49.4	49.2	49.3	49.2	49.2	48.1
1994	48.3	48.8	48.9	49.5	49.9	50.8	51.4	51.8	50.9	50.9	50.3	50.1	50.1
1995	48.3	48.8	49.2	49.5	49.9	50.6	50.1	50.6	50.3	50.3	50.1	50.1	49.8
1996	47.7	48.0	48.6	49.1	50.3	51.2	51.4	52.7	52.0	51.4	51.2	51.4	50.4
1997	50.0	50.9	51.5	53.1	53.6	55.1	55.0	55.4	54.4	55.9	55.7	55.4	53.8
1998	53.0	53.5	54.3	55.5	56.0	56.9	57.0	57.2	56.1	58.9	58.6	58.9	56.3
1999	57.9	58.4	58.7	60.4	60.2	61.8	62.1	62.0	61.3	61.5	62.0	61.4	60.6
2000	59.5	60.1	60.2	60.8	61.6	62.2	62.9	63.0	62.3	62.3	61.7	60.8	61.4
2001	59.6	59.8	60.0	60.6	62.0	62.2	62.0	62.5	61.4	61.0	60.2	59.4	60.9
2002	59.6	59.7	59.6	60.2	61.2	62.3	62.7	63.5	63.6	63.3	63.2	63.0	61.8
2003	60.6	61.3	61.2	62.5	62.7	63.6	64.1	63.9	63.9	64.4	63.7	63.1	62.9
Educational and health services													
1990	69.6	72.2	72.9	73.2	73.5	73.3	70.1	70.0	73.2	74.4	74.7	74.9	72.6
1991	72.8	73.8	74.6	74.7	74.8	73.6	73.2	73.5	75.8	77.0	77.3	77.3	74.8
1992	74.4	75.5	75.7	76.6	77.1	76.6	75.5	75.7	77.6	79.0	79.6	80.1	76.9
1993	77.7	79.1	79.5	78.8	79.1	78.8	77.1	77.0	79.0	80.1	80.5	80.8	78.9
1994	78.3	79.9	80.1	80.8	81.0	79.4	78.8	78.7	81.0	82.2	82.5	82.6	80.4
1995	80.9	82.3	82.8	82.8	83.1	82.0	80.9	80.5	82.6	83.5	83.9	84.2	82.4
1996	82.1	83.5	83.7	83.8	84.3	82.7	80.5	80.4	83.2	84.6	85.1	85.3	83.2
1997	82.9	84.2	84.9	84.5	85.1	83.7	81.3	81.2	83.9	84.9	85.1	85.3	83.9
1998	82.8	83.9	84.1	84.1	84.4	83.0	79.9	79.9	83.1	83.8	84.1	84.0	83.0
1999	82.8	84.0	84.6	85.0	85.1	83.5	82.0	81.4	84.0	85.0	84.5	84.1	83.8
2000	82.7	83.3	83.4	83.9	83.8	82.7	81.7	81.3	83.5	85.6	85.1	85.4	83.5
2001	80.3	80.7	80.4	80.3	80.8	79.7	78.1	78.0	80.2	81.4	81.8	81.5	80.3
2002	80.5	81.7	82.0	81.9	81.8	80.5	79.0	79.0	82.1	83.4	83.7	83.9	81.6
2003	81.5	83.2	83.8	83.6	83.2	81.8	79.9	79.8	83.6	85.2	85.5	85.1	83.0

Employment by Industry: New York—*Continued*

(Numbers in thousands. Not seasonally adjusted.)

Industry	January	February	March	April	May	June	July	August	September	October	November	December	Annual Average
BUFFALO—*Continued*													
Leisure and hospitality													
1990	42.6	44.2	44.9	46.0	48.4	49.8	49.7	50.7	49.7	48.1	47.4	47.4	47.4
1991	45.3	46.1	46.5	47.7	50.4	50.9	49.1	49.8	48.6	47.7	46.0	46.3	47.8
1992	44.0	44.5	44.6	46.0	48.2	48.5	48.2	48.5	47.8	46.4	45.3	46.0	46.5
1993	42.1	43.3	43.1	43.7	46.9	48.5	48.3	48.3	47.4	46.6	45.7	45.9	45.8
1994	42.4	43.0	44.0	45.4	48.1	48.9	48.5	48.8	48.0	47.1	45.8	46.2	46.3
1995	42.2	43.1	44.1	45.1	47.2	48.0	47.8	48.5	47.1	46.2	46.1	45.4	45.9
1996	42.6	43.0	43.7	44.6	47.1	48.4	47.0	47.5	46.6	46.2	45.2	45.4	45.6
1997	42.0	43.3	43.9	45.6	46.8	47.9	48.0	48.4	47.4	46.5	45.9	46.2	45.9
1998	42.5	44.0	44.6	45.1	47.2	48.2	48.1	48.8	47.3	47.0	45.6	45.9	46.1
1999	42.3	44.0	44.3	46.0	48.2	49.3	48.0	48.5	47.2	47.3	46.7	46.9	46.5
2000	43.4	44.5	44.9	46.2	47.3	48.7	48.1	49.1	48.0	46.8	46.8	46.7	46.7
2001	43.0	44.4	45.3	43.9	47.4	48.6	46.5	47.3	44.5	43.9	43.5	42.9	45.1
2002	43.9	44.6	45.1	46.3	48.5	49.5	49.1	50.1	48.2	47.1	46.2	47.5	47.2
2003	44.7	45.1	45.2	46.2	48.5	49.7	48.3	48.9	47.7	47.1	46.2	46.7	47.0
Other services													
1990	18.3	19.0	19.3	19.0	19.1	18.9	18.9	19.0	19.1	19.5	19.3	19.1	19.0
1991	18.5	18.9	19.0	19.1	19.1	18.6	18.8	18.7	19.2	19.6	19.4	19.4	19.0
1992	18.9	19.1	19.1	19.3	19.6	19.1	19.3	19.2	19.8	20.0	19.9	19.8	19.4
1993	19.2	19.5	19.9	19.9	20.3	19.8	19.7	19.5	19.7	19.9	19.9	19.7	19.7
1994	19.4	19.6	20.0	20.3	20.5	20.3	20.4	20.3	20.4	20.7	20.6	20.6	20.2
1995	20.0	20.3	20.5	20.6	20.7	20.8	20.7	20.6	20.8	21.2	21.0	21.0	20.6
1996	20.3	20.7	21.0	20.8	21.3	21.4	21.3	21.2	21.1	21.5	21.5	21.6	21.1
1997	20.7	21.2	21.6	21.7	22.2	22.0	21.9	22.0	21.7	21.9	22.0	21.8	21.7
1998	21.3	21.6	22.0	21.9	22.1	22.1	22.4	22.3	22.2	22.5	22.5	22.8	22.1
1999	22.0	22.7	23.2	23.1	23.3	23.4	23.0	23.1	22.8	22.9	22.8	22.9	22.9
2000	22.3	22.7	23.1	23.3	23.2	23.2	23.4	23.5	23.0	23.1	23.0	23.3	23.0
2001	23.3	23.5	23.8	23.5	23.8	24.2	23.2	23.3	23.0	23.3	23.4	23.7	23.5
2002	22.8	23.1	23.4	23.3	23.3	23.3	23.1	23.1	22.7	22.7	22.9	23.0	23.1
2003	22.7	22.9	23.1	23.4	23.5	23.6	23.2	22.8	22.9	23.1	23.2	23.3	23.1
Government													
1990	88.5	89.7	90.5	90.3	91.2	91.2	88.0	87.1	86.0	90.6	91.2	91.4	89.6
1991	88.6	90.4	90.4	88.4	89.6	89.6	86.2	85.5	84.3	87.9	88.8	88.7	88.2
1992	85.6	88.4	88.4	88.1	88.6	87.6	84.7	83.7	85.1	87.2	87.9	87.7	86.9
1993	85.1	86.8	87.3	86.7	87.7	87.4	83.8	82.0	85.3	88.3	89.0	89.3	86.5
1994	86.7	89.1	89.2	87.6	89.8	88.9	85.8	84.5	87.5	89.6	90.9	90.4	88.3
1995	88.0	90.0	90.4	89.5	89.5	88.5	83.8	83.0	86.1	88.9	89.4	89.5	88.0
1996	86.8	88.6	88.7	87.4	89.4	88.3	84.2	82.6	86.1	88.2	88.9	88.5	87.3
1997	86.2	88.2	88.7	87.2	88.9	86.9	83.7	82.7	85.6	88.8	89.2	88.4	87.0
1998	85.7	88.0	88.9	87.6	89.3	87.2	84.2	84.1	86.4	89.4	90.1	89.5	87.5
1999	87.0	89.4	90.1	88.1	90.5	88.2	85.2	84.7	86.9	91.2	91.9	91.0	88.6
2000	89.5	91.4	92.2	92.4	93.4	90.7	87.4	86.7	88.7	93.7	93.9	91.6	90.9
2001	90.7	92.9	93.0	92.7	93.5	91.6	87.0	86.8	90.3	93.4	93.9	93.2	91.6
2002	92.1	94.3	94.8	93.1	94.2	92.9	89.5	89.6	90.7	94.6	94.8	95.0	93.0
2003	93.4	95.9	97.3	95.8	96.2	95.4	90.2	90.0	93.4	97.1	97.1	97.1	94.9
Federal government													
1990	10.9	10.7	10.7	11.1	11.8	11.3	11.3	10.8	10.6	10.4	10.4	10.4	10.8
1991	10.3	10.3	10.4	10.3	10.3	10.4	10.7	10.7	10.6	10.5	10.6	10.8	10.4
1992	10.6	10.5	10.5	10.5	10.5	10.5	10.7	10.7	10.5	10.3	10.3	10.5	10.5
1993	10.3	10.3	10.3	10.3	10.3	10.5	10.6	10.6	10.6	10.4	10.4	10.7	10.4
1994	10.4	10.4	10.4	10.3	10.3	10.3	10.4	10.4	10.3	10.2	10.3	10.5	10.3
1995	10.2	10.2	10.2	10.2	10.2	10.4	10.4	10.4	10.2	10.2	10.1	10.4	10.2
1996	10.3	10.3	10.3	10.3	10.3	10.4	10.5	10.4	10.3	10.2	10.2	10.3	10.3
1997	10.6	10.6	10.6	10.5	10.5	10.5	10.6	10.6	10.4	10.4	10.4	10.8	10.5
1998	10.4	10.4	10.3	10.3	10.3	10.4	10.5	10.5	10.4	10.2	10.4	10.7	10.4
1999	10.4	10.3	10.3	10.3	10.2	10.3	10.5	10.4	10.3	10.3	10.4	10.7	10.3
2000	10.4	10.5	10.8	11.3	12.6	10.9	11.0	10.5	10.3	10.3	10.4	10.6	10.8
2001	10.2	10.2	10.2	10.3	10.3	10.4	10.5	10.6	10.4	10.4	10.4	10.7	10.4
2002	10.5	10.5	10.5	10.4	10.4	10.5	10.6	10.6	10.4	10.8	10.7	10.9	10.6
2003	10.6	10.6	10.6	10.4	10.3	10.3	10.5	10.5	10.4	10.7	10.6	10.8	10.5
State government													
1990	22.8	22.5	23.0	23.2	23.3	23.4	21.9	21.9	21.8	23.6	23.5	23.5	22.8
1991	22.8	22.8	22.6	22.1	22.1	22.0	19.7	20.1	19.8	21.2	21.1	20.8	21.4
1992	20.6	20.7	20.8	20.8	20.9	19.6	19.1	19.1	20.6	20.8	20.9	20.8	20.3
1993	20.1	20.5	20.8	20.8	20.9	19.5	18.7	18.9	20.5	20.9	20.8	20.8	20.2
1994	20.6	21.4	21.4	21.4	21.7	20.4	19.9	20.0	21.8	21.9	21.9	21.7	21.1
1995	21.6	22.0	21.8	21.8	21.4	19.9	19.3	20.0	21.2	21.3	21.2	21.0	21.0
1996	20.1	20.6	20.6	20.7	20.8	19.6	18.6	18.4	20.6	20.7	20.7	20.2	20.1
1997	19.9	20.5	20.5	20.7	20.8	18.6	18.6	18.5	20.5	21.1	21.0	20.1	20.0
1998	19.9	20.6	20.6	20.7	20.9	18.8	19.0	19.5	20.9	21.4	21.4	20.3	20.3
1999	20.0	20.7	20.6	20.6	20.8	18.7	18.9	19.5	21.0	21.5	21.6	20.6	20.3
2000	20.6	21.3	21.3	21.3	21.5	19.3	19.5	20.0	21.5	22.0	22.1	20.9	20.9
2001	21.5	22.2	22.2	22.1	22.2	19.9	20.0	20.6	22.3	22.8	23.0	21.7	21.7
2002	22.3	23.2	23.2	22.9	22.7	21.1	20.9	21.6	23.0	23.4	23.4	23.1	22.6
2003	23.0	23.4	23.5	23.0	22.7	21.1	20.8	21.5	23.1	23.6	23.5	23.3	22.7

Employment by Industry: New York—*Continued*

(Numbers in thousands. Not seasonally adjusted.)

Industry	January	February	March	April	May	June	July	August	September	October	November	December	Annual Average
BUFFALO—*Continued*													
Local government													
1990	54.8	56.5	56.8	56.0	56.0	56.5	54.9	54.5	53.7	56.6	57.3	57.5	55.9
1991	55.5	57.3	57.4	55.9	57.2	57.2	55.7	54.7	53.8	56.2	57.1	57.1	56.2
1992	54.4	57.1	57.1	56.9	57.2	57.5	54.9	53.9	54.0	56.1	56.8	56.4	56.0
1993	54.7	56.0	56.2	55.7	56.4	57.4	54.5	52.5	54.2	57.0	57.8	57.7	55.8
1994	55.7	57.3	57.4	55.8	57.8	58.2	55.5	54.1	55.4	57.6	58.7	58.1	56.8
1995	56.1	57.8	58.4	57.4	57.9	58.3	54.1	52.7	54.6	57.5	58.1	58.1	56.7
1996	56.3	57.7	57.9	56.4	58.3	58.4	55.1	53.8	55.2	57.3	58.1	58.0	56.8
1997	55.6	57.1	57.7	56.0	57.6	57.7	54.6	53.6	54.7	57.3	57.8	57.5	56.4
1998	55.4	57.0	58.0	56.6	58.1	58.0	54.7	54.1	55.1	57.8	58.3	58.5	56.8
1999	56.6	58.4	59.2	57.2	59.5	59.2	55.8	54.8	55.6	59.4	59.9	59.7	57.9
2000	58.5	59.6	60.1	59.8	59.3	60.5	56.9	56.2	56.9	61.4	61.4	60.1	59.2
2001	59.0	60.5	60.6	60.3	61.0	61.3	56.5	55.6	57.6	60.2	60.5	60.8	59.5
2002	59.3	60.6	61.1	59.8	61.1	61.3	58.0	57.4	57.3	60.4	60.7	61.0	59.8
2003	59.8	61.9	63.2	62.4	63.2	64.0	58.9	58.0	59.9	62.8	63.0	63.0	61.7
NASSAU-SUFFOLK													
Total nonfarm													
1990	1110.2	1108.2	1119.4	1122.6	1137.1	1149.8	1123.0	1117.0	1121.2	1123.5	1125.2	1125.3	1123.5
1991	1067.7	1065.3	1072.2	1075.2	1086.4	1095.9	1067.4	1060.9	1066.2	1074.5	1077.6	1080.4	1074.1
1992	1032.6	1031.2	1037.9	1048.1	1056.1	1067.4	1045.4	1039.3	1047.7	1057.8	1061.3	1063.3	1049.0
1993	1026.2	1026.5	1034.9	1048.8	1064.5	1078.0	1056.1	1056.7	1064.6	1075.8	1079.5	1084.0	1058.0
1994	1038.0	1034.9	1051.4	1065.7	1079.4	1094.7	1073.8	1074.0	1083.1	1094.6	1100.9	1105.2	1074.6
1995	1065.4	1066.9	1079.8	1087.5	1098.2	1112.9	1091.9	1090.8	1099.5	1102.9	1108.5	1112.8	1093.1
1996	1058.6	1066.9	1080.6	1089.5	1108.4	1123.6	1097.6	1098.3	1106.8	1120.7	1127.9	1134.4	1101.1
1997	1083.5	1085.1	1102.3	1113.0	1124.2	1138.3	1119.3	1117.7	1126.0	1139.1	1147.7	1155.9	1121.0
1998	1107.7	1115.5	1130.6	1136.1	1153.4	1167.7	1146.9	1143.2	1151.2	1168.7	1175.1	1184.3	1148.4
1999	1150.7	1156.6	1168.1	1186.7	1197.3	1209.2	1188.9	1187.3	1189.2	1207.0	1215.6	1225.4	1190.2
2000	1174.3	1180.2	1194.9	1213.6	1226.8	1236.3	1216.5	1210.2	1228.7	1237.3	1243.5	1253.8	1218.0
2001	1192.6	1196.9	1208.6	1210.5	1228.2	1241.0	1219.4	1215.0	1213.3	1225.9	1231.3	1240.1	1218.6
2002	1183.7	1187.5	1201.5	1211.1	1222.9	1233.3	1213.0	1207.8	1217.9	1229.9	1235.6	1241.3	1215.5
2003	1188.6	1191.1	1206.0	1216.6	1229.9	1242.4	1222.2	1215.4	1226.2	1239.1	1244.9	1249.6	1222.7
Total private													
1990	925.3	920.1	930.2	932.4	946.0	957.4	947.8	946.6	944.7	937.3	937.0	937.8	938.6
1991	884.6	879.5	886.0	888.3	899.3	909.2	897.0	896.8	895.8	895.2	896.6	899.8	894.0
1992	857.6	853.9	859.6	869.0	878.1	889.0	882.7	880.9	879.9	883.0	884.2	886.8	875.4
1993	854.1	851.9	857.2	870.5	885.4	899.1	891.4	895.1	895.7	898.2	899.1	904.0	883.5
1994	862.7	855.7	870.0	883.6	896.1	911.4	905.5	909.6	910.2	913.6	917.4	922.8	896.6
1995	887.1	885.4	896.5	902.3	914.2	928.2	922.2	924.2	925.9	921.6	924.1	929.9	913.5
1996	881.3	884.6	897.7	905.2	923.3	938.7	931.5	935.0	934.4	938.5	944.6	951.4	922.2
1997	908.3	905.2	920.7	929.2	940.4	954.5	950.2	953.5	953.0	957.5	963.6	971.5	942.3
1998	930.6	930.3	943.7	951.3	967.5	981.8	974.3	975.7	974.3	983.3	987.7	995.2	966.3
1999	967.1	968.9	978.8	996.6	1006.4	1019.8	1013.1	1016.9	1008.9	1018.0	1024.6	1034.5	1004.5
2000	987.2	989.4	1001.8	1017.0	1029.1	1041.2	1037.8	1036.9	1042.3	1043.8	1048.6	1059.0	1027.8
2001	1002.0	1001.9	1012.6	1014.1	1030.5	1042.1	1034.8	1033.0	1024.2	1028.4	1031.6	1038.4	1024.5
2002	987.4	987.1	999.9	1010.0	1021.3	1032.8	1028.4	1028.3	1026.9	1031.7	1035.7	1040.3	1019.2
2003	991.2	989.1	1002.0	1013.6	1026.7	1039.3	1034.1	1032.3	1031.1	1037.4	1042.0	1046.0	1023.7
Goods-producing													
1990	190.8	190.5	192.2	191.0	192.1	193.4	189.7	189.3	188.1	184.9	182.0	179.2	188.6
1991	164.9	164.2	164.4	167.0	168.8	169.1	165.0	165.5	165.6	164.5	162.6	159.7	165.1
1992	149.7	148.4	149.1	151.2	151.8	152.9	151.3	152.1	152.1	152.9	152.0	150.7	151.2
1993	143.9	143.9	145.0	147.8	149.5	150.9	148.2	149.7	150.2	151.3	150.5	148.2	148.3
1994	136.4	135.0	137.8	142.7	145.1	147.2	145.8	146.9	147.9	148.1	148.7	146.4	144.0
1995	137.3	138.0	140.4	142.7	145.1	147.3	145.1	146.7	147.4	146.7	146.5	145.0	144.0
1996	135.4	137.9	140.8	142.9	145.6	148.1	147.9	149.7	151.2	151.8	151.3	150.5	146.1
1997	142.7	142.6	145.5	148.0	149.3	151.4	150.8	152.7	153.2	153.6	153.9	153.3	149.8
1998	146.4	147.6	150.3	153.6	155.7	158.2	156.2	157.5	158.0	158.7	159.3	158.5	155.0
1999	155.7	156.2	157.8	162.2	164.3	165.9	163.3	164.8	165.2	167.1	167.5	168.3	163.2
2000	158.5	158.4	161.8	164.8	166.8	168.8	167.6	168.8	170.4	170.6	171.0	170.3	166.5
2001	157.6	157.8	159.2	161.3	163.1	164.2	162.3	163.0	162.7	162.0	161.3	160.1	161.2
2002	151.5	151.5	153.2	155.5	156.7	157.8	157.7	159.2	158.9	159.1	158.7	156.7	156.4
2003	147.7	146.5	148.4	151.3	153.3	154.6	153.9	154.3	155.0	156.1	155.2	153.1	152.5
Construction and mining													
1990	49.8	49.6	51.4	53.0	54.4	55.1	54.6	54.7	54.0	52.1	51.3	49.6	52.5
1991	42.1	41.7	42.6	45.7	46.6	47.2	45.8	45.5	45.3	44.1	43.2	41.7	44.3
1992	35.5	34.7	35.9	37.6	38.7	39.4	39.8	39.9	40.0	40.4	39.8	39.0	38.4
1993	34.5	34.6	35.3	38.9	40.6	41.7	41.5	42.0	42.3	42.9	42.4	41.4	39.8
1994	33.6	33.2	35.4	40.1	42.2	43.8	44.4	45.2	45.5	44.9	44.7	43.7	41.4
1995	37.7	37.3	39.8	42.3	43.5	44.8	44.7	45.2	45.3	45.0	44.4	43.3	42.8
1996	36.4	37.5	39.6	42.6	44.7	46.2	47.2	48.1	48.5	48.7	48.4	46.9	44.6
1997	41.8	41.5	43.4	46.4	47.7	48.9	49.9	50.3	50.5	50.4	50.2	49.3	47.5
1998	44.3	44.8	46.8	50.2	51.9	53.6	53.7	54.3	54.2	54.4	54.7	54.0	51.4
1999	50.9	51.3	52.5	56.7	58.5	59.6	59.3	59.8	59.8	60.4	60.5	60.7	57.5
2000	54.0	53.8	57.0	59.8	61.7	63.1	63.1	63.2	64.1	64.1	64.3	63.8	61.0
2001	56.1	56.6	58.1	61.5	63.6	64.9	64.8	65.2	64.3	64.5	64.7	64.1	62.4
2002	58.2	58.4	60.2	63.3	64.7	65.6	67.1	67.9	67.0	67.2	66.6	65.1	64.3
2003	58.6	57.6	59.6	62.8	65.0	66.1	67.1	67.2	67.1	67.8	66.9	65.1	64.2

Employment by Industry: New York—*Continued*

(Numbers in thousands. Not seasonally adjusted.)

Industry	January	February	March	April	May	June	July	August	September	October	November	December	Annual Average
NASSAU-SUFFOLK *—Continued*													
Manufacturing													
1990	141.0	140.9	140.8	138.0	137.7	138.3	135.1	134.6	134.1	132.8	130.7	129.6	136.1
1991	122.8	122.5	121.8	121.3	122.2	121.9	119.2	120.0	120.3	120.4	119.4	118.0	120.8
1992	114.2	113.7	113.2	113.6	113.1	113.5	111.5	112.2	112.1	112.5	112.2	111.7	112.8
1993	109.4	109.3	109.7	108.9	108.9	109.2	106.7	107.7	107.9	108.4	108.1	106.8	108.4
1994	102.8	101.8	102.4	102.6	102.9	103.4	101.4	101.7	102.4	103.2	104.0	102.7	102.6
1995	99.6	100.7	100.6	100.4	101.6	102.5	100.4	101.5	102.1	101.7	102.1	101.7	101.2
1996	99.0	100.4	101.2	100.3	100.9	101.9	100.7	101.6	102.7	103.1	102.9	103.6	101.5
1997	100.9	101.1	102.1	101.6	101.6	102.5	100.9	102.4	102.7	103.2	103.7	104.0	102.2
1998	102.1	102.8	103.5	103.4	103.8	104.6	102.5	103.2	103.8	104.3	104.6	104.5	103.6
1999	104.8	104.9	105.3	105.5	105.8	106.3	104.0	105.0	105.4	106.7	107.0	107.6	105.7
2000	104.5	104.6	104.8	105.0	105.1	105.7	104.5	105.6	106.3	106.5	106.7	106.5	105.5
2001	101.5	101.2	101.1	99.8	99.5	99.3	97.5	97.8	98.4	97.5	96.6	96.0	98.9
2002	93.3	93.1	93.0	92.2	92.0	92.2	90.6	91.3	91.9	91.9	92.1	91.6	92.1
2003	89.1	88.9	88.8	88.5	88.3	88.5	86.8	87.1	87.9	88.3	88.3	88.0	88.2
Service-providing													
1990	919.4	917.7	927.2	931.6	945.0	956.4	933.3	927.7	933.1	938.6	943.2	946.1	934.9
1991	902.8	901.1	907.8	908.2	917.6	926.8	902.4	895.4	900.6	910.0	915.0	920.7	909.0
1992	882.9	882.8	888.8	896.9	904.3	914.5	894.1	887.2	895.6	904.9	909.3	912.6	897.8
1993	882.3	882.6	889.9	901.0	915.0	927.1	907.9	907.0	914.4	924.5	929.0	935.8	909.7
1994	901.6	899.9	913.6	923.0	934.3	947.5	928.0	927.1	935.2	946.5	952.2	958.8	930.6
1995	928.1	928.9	939.4	944.8	953.1	965.6	946.8	944.1	952.1	956.2	962.0	967.8	949.1
1996	923.2	929.0	939.8	946.6	962.8	975.5	949.7	948.6	955.6	968.9	976.6	983.9	955.0
1997	940.8	942.5	956.8	965.0	974.9	986.9	968.5	965.0	972.8	985.5	993.8	1002.6	971.3
1998	961.3	967.9	980.3	982.5	997.7	1009.5	990.7	985.7	993.2	1010.0	1015.8	1025.8	993.4
1999	995.0	1000.4	1010.3	1024.5	1033.0	1043.3	1025.6	1022.5	1024.0	1039.9	1048.1	1057.1	1027.0
2000	1015.8	1021.8	1033.1	1048.8	1060.0	1067.5	1048.9	1041.4	1058.3	1066.7	1072.5	1083.5	1051.5
2001	1035.0	1039.1	1049.4	1049.2	1065.1	1076.8	1057.1	1052.0	1050.6	1063.9	1070.0	1080.0	1057.4
2002	1032.2	1036.0	1048.3	1055.6	1066.2	1075.5	1055.3	1048.6	1059.0	1070.8	1076.9	1084.6	1059.1
2003	1040.9	1044.6	1057.6	1065.3	1076.6	1087.8	1068.3	1061.1	1071.2	1083.0	1089.7	1096.5	1070.2
Trade, transportation, and utilities													
1990	267.1	260.8	262.0	260.7	262.8	265.7	260.8	261.0	263.4	264.6	268.3	271.9	264.1
1991	253.6	247.1	247.9	248.1	250.3	252.7	246.2	246.4	249.1	250.7	256.5	261.3	250.8
1992	249.4	244.6	244.4	245.1	247.3	248.5	243.0	243.1	245.1	249.3	253.2	258.0	247.6
1993	244.8	239.2	238.6	240.1	243.5	247.3	242.7	245.0	246.6	249.9	252.8	259.6	245.8
1994	246.5	239.6	241.4	241.7	244.7	249.4	246.3	247.1	250.5	254.3	260.9	267.8	249.2
1995	254.7	249.2	249.5	251.4	253.6	256.6	252.5	252.6	256.2	255.8	262.2	268.3	255.2
1996	252.4	246.2	247.6	249.7	253.5	257.0	251.7	253.0	256.6	256.8	264.6	271.6	255.1
1997	260.6	253.0	255.0	254.2	256.8	260.9	255.9	256.2	260.8	265.0	270.6	278.1	260.6
1998	263.6	257.6	258.2	257.3	260.9	264.2	259.3	260.1	263.0	268.7	273.8	281.1	264.0
1999	264.4	259.8	261.3	263.5	264.1	267.7	264.1	266.0	266.6	269.0	275.5	283.2	267.1
2000	267.8	265.4	267.1	269.6	271.1	274.7	270.2	270.9	272.8	275.6	282.0	289.7	273.1
2001	273.8	269.6	270.3	267.8	271.5	274.7	269.5	268.0	268.9	270.5	275.7	281.9	271.9
2002	265.1	261.1	263.8	263.0	264.7	269.0	264.7	264.1	267.5	269.2	275.3	282.1	267.5
2003	267.0	263.6	265.3	266.4	268.9	273.0	267.7	267.4	269.7	272.6	277.7	284.2	270.3
Wholesale trade													
1990	69.1	68.8	69.3	69.8	70.1	70.3	69.6	69.8	69.3	68.6	68.2	68.2	69.3
1991	65.8	65.4	65.7	66.0	66.0	66.0	65.0	65.0	64.8	65.4	65.4	65.7	65.5
1992	63.8	63.7	63.9	63.8	64.0	64.1	63.5	63.4	63.4	64.1	64.0	63.9	63.8
1993	63.7	64.0	64.1	64.7	65.3	65.5	65.1	65.2	65.0	65.1	65.2	65.4	64.9
1994	63.1	63.5	64.3	64.5	64.9	65.6	65.4	65.5	65.7	65.7	65.7	66.1	65.0
1995	64.2	64.3	64.9	64.8	64.9	65.5	65.0	65.3	65.6	65.5	65.5	65.9	65.1
1996	63.8	64.4	65.0	65.2	65.8	66.2	65.6	66.1	66.0	65.9	66.0	66.1	65.5
1997	64.4	65.0	65.6	66.0	66.2	66.4	65.9	66.4	66.1	66.5	66.6	67.1	66.0
1998	66.2	66.7	67.3	67.4	67.8	68.5	68.3	68.5	68.4	68.9	69.1	69.1	68.0
1999	70.0	70.0	70.4	70.9	71.2	71.4	71.1	71.6	71.4	71.2	71.6	71.9	71.1
2000	69.8	70.3	70.7	71.0	71.2	71.9	71.7	71.8	72.1	72.1	72.2	72.6	71.5
2001	74.6	74.9	75.1	73.4	73.8	74.2	73.6	73.5	73.2	73.6	73.3	73.6	73.9
2002	71.4	71.6	72.0	71.6	71.9	72.3	72.1	72.5	72.6	73.0	73.1	73.7	72.3
2003	72.0	72.2	72.7	72.6	72.8	73.4	72.9	72.9	72.8	73.6	73.7	74.2	73.0
Retail trade													
1990	150.9	147.1	147.4	146.2	147.5	149.5	148.6	148.9	148.6	149.0	151.8	154.3	149.2
1991	143.6	138.9	139.2	138.2	140.0	142.2	140.0	140.3	140.1	140.7	145.2	148.2	141.4
1992	137.6	134.0	133.8	134.4	136.1	137.2	135.4	135.7	135.5	137.3	141.7	144.6	136.9
1993	134.7	130.7	129.9	130.4	132.4	135.6	134.6	136.9	136.5	138.8	140.9	146.1	135.6
1994	137.8	132.5	133.2	133.9	135.6	138.8	137.6	138.7	139.6	141.8	147.4	152.2	139.1
1995	143.7	140.2	139.9	140.8	142.3	144.5	144.2	144.5	145.3	144.2	149.2	154.3	144.4
1996	143.3	138.4	139.4	140.9	143.2	146.1	144.0	145.7	146.4	145.6	151.9	157.3	145.2
1997	147.3	141.9	143.4	142.5	144.2	147.4	145.5	147.1	146.9	149.7	154.3	160.0	147.5
1998	151.4	146.8	147.6	146.6	148.9	151.3	148.9	149.6	150.0	152.8	157.6	163.1	151.2
1999	157.2	152.5	153.2	154.5	154.5	157.5	156.6	158.2	156.7	159.0	164.8	171.3	158.0
2000	160.0	157.1	157.9	159.7	160.8	163.3	161.7	162.5	161.3	163.4	169.6	176.2	162.8
2001	162.1	157.7	158.1	158.8	159.8	162.3	160.3	160.0	157.9	158.6	164.4	170.3	160.9
2002	157.8	153.7	155.7	155.2	156.5	159.9	158.5	158.5	158.4	159.0	165.0	171.1	159.1
2003	159.0	155.6	156.4	157.9	159.6	163.1	161.2	161.3	160.6	162.1	167.2	172.9	161.4

Employment by Industry: New York—*Continued*

(Numbers in thousands. Not seasonally adjusted.)

Industry	January	February	March	April	May	June	July	August	September	October	November	December	Annual Average
NASSAU-SUFFOLK *—Continued*													
Transportation and utilities													
1990	47.1	44.9	45.3	44.7	45.2	45.9	42.6	42.3	45.5	47.0	48.3	49.4	45.7
1991	44.2	42.8	43.0	43.9	44.3	44.5	41.2	41.1	44.2	44.6	45.9	47.4	43.9
1992	48.0	46.9	46.7	46.9	47.2	47.2	44.1	44.0	46.2	47.9	47.5	49.5	46.8
1993	46.4	44.5	44.6	45.0	45.8	46.2	43.0	42.9	45.1	46.0	46.7	48.1	45.4
1994	45.6	43.6	43.9	43.3	44.2	45.0	43.3	42.9	45.2	46.8	47.8	49.5	45.1
1995	46.8	44.7	44.7	45.8	46.4	46.6	43.3	42.8	45.3	46.1	47.5	48.1	45.7
1996	45.3	43.4	43.2	43.6	44.5	44.7	42.1	41.2	44.2	45.3	46.7	48.2	44.4
1997	48.9	46.1	46.0	45.7	46.4	47.1	44.5	42.7	47.8	48.8	49.7	51.0	47.1
1998	46.0	44.1	43.3	43.3	44.2	44.4	42.1	42.0	44.6	47.0	47.1	48.9	44.8
1999	37.2	37.3	37.7	38.1	38.4	38.8	36.4	36.2	38.5	38.8	39.1	40.0	38.0
2000	38.0	38.0	38.5	38.9	39.1	39.5	36.8	36.6	39.4	40.1	40.2	40.9	38.8
2001	37.1	37.0	37.1	35.6	37.9	38.2	35.6	34.5	37.8	38.3	38.0	38.0	37.1
2002	35.9	35.8	36.1	36.2	36.3	36.8	34.1	33.1	36.5	37.2	37.2	37.3	36.0
2003	36.0	35.8	36.2	35.9	36.5	36.5	33.6	33.2	36.3	36.9	36.8	37.1	35.9
Information													
1990	32.7	32.1	31.5	31.4	31.8	32.4	32.1	31.6	31.5	31.8	31.8	31.9	31.9
1991	32.0	31.3	31.1	30.5	30.4	30.7	31.0	30.2	30.1	29.8	29.6	29.8	30.5
1992	29.4	30.3	29.0	28.3	28.6	28.7	29.3	28.6	28.3	28.5	28.5	28.7	28.9
1993	28.9	28.7	28.2	27.9	27.9	28.2	28.7	28.4	28.3	28.5	28.8	28.8	28.4
1994	27.3	26.8	26.9	26.8	26.8	27.1	26.7	26.5	26.4	26.5	26.7	26.7	26.8
1995	26.5	26.4	26.5	26.1	26.5	27.0	26.8	26.9	27.1	26.2	26.3	26.5	26.6
1996	25.9	26.0	26.2	26.1	26.3	26.5	27.8	27.4	27.1	27.4	27.8	28.1	26.9
1997	27.3	27.6	27.9	28.2	28.3	28.6	29.0	29.1	28.6	28.5	28.7	29.0	28.4
1998	29.3	29.3	29.8	30.0	30.0	30.3	30.5	30.4	30.0	30.0	30.1	30.3	30.0
1999	30.7	30.9	30.8	30.0	30.4	30.8	30.7	30.9	30.5	30.7	31.0	31.1	30.7
2000	31.2	31.3	31.6	31.5	31.7	32.3	32.5	28.2	32.8	32.6	33.0	33.4	31.8
2001	33.0	33.0	33.1	33.0	33.1	33.4	33.0	33.1	32.4	32.4	32.8	32.9	32.9
2002	33.1	32.9	32.8	33.2	33.5	33.4	32.7	32.6	31.5	31.7	31.3	31.1	32.5
2003	29.6	29.6	29.5	29.0	29.5	29.2	29.0	29.5	28.7	28.5	28.7	28.8	29.1
Financial activitiess													
1990	85.3	85.5	86.0	85.9	86.0	86.8	86.1	86.2	85.2	84.5	84.4	84.6	85.5
1991	82.3	82.4	83.1	82.9	83.0	83.7	83.2	83.0	82.6	81.6	81.8	82.4	82.7
1992	81.2	81.2	81.4	80.7	80.6	81.5	81.3	80.8	80.0	79.7	79.6	80.0	80.7
1993	80.0	80.6	81.0	80.9	81.7	82.7	82.5	82.2	81.5	81.3	81.5	81.9	81.5
1994	81.2	81.6	81.7	82.1	82.6	83.6	83.0	83.1	82.4	81.3	80.9	81.6	82.1
1995	80.2	80.7	80.8	79.8	80.1	80.9	80.7	80.7	80.7	79.7	79.6	80.5	80.4
1996	78.4	79.0	79.8	79.5	80.1	80.9	81.2	81.0	80.2	79.7	79.9	80.2	80.0
1997	78.6	79.1	79.9	79.7	80.2	80.8	81.1	81.5	79.9	80.9	80.7	81.1	80.3
1998	78.9	78.9	79.3	80.7	81.4	82.1	82.3	82.2	80.9	81.8	81.4	81.8	81.0
1999	83.7	83.9	84.0	85.0	85.3	86.5	86.9	86.9	85.6	85.8	85.9	86.2	85.5
2000	84.4	84.1	84.2	84.1	84.3	85.1	84.5	84.4	83.6	83.9	83.6	84.6	84.2
2001	80.3	80.7	81.0	80.9	81.3	82.3	82.4	82.2	80.9	81.5	81.2	82.5	81.4
2002	80.9	81.0	81.4	82.2	82.2	82.8	82.7	82.7	81.7	81.9	81.9	82.4	82.0
2003	80.7	80.9	81.7	82.4	82.9	84.2	84.1	84.2	83.2	83.6	84.1	84.4	83.0
Professional and business services													
1990	108.7	109.5	111.9	114.5	115.8	116.7	116.4	115.8	116.3	115.4	114.8	114.5	114.2
1991	109.6	109.4	109.4	108.9	109.9	111.1	111.8	111.4	111.6	111.2	110.8	110.6	110.5
1992	106.9	106.9	108.2	110.8	111.3	114.0	113.6	113.2	113.2	113.0	112.7	112.5	111.4
1993	110.5	111.6	112.9	115.8	117.4	119.9	119.5	119.4	119.4	120.3	120.0	120.3	117.3
1994	117.4	119.6	121.8	124.3	125.2	126.6	126.7	127.0	126.0	128.3	127.2	127.2	124.8
1995	123.7	124.7	127.1	128.2	128.8	130.1	131.0	131.0	130.4	130.4	129.6	130.0	128.8
1996	123.8	125.9	128.1	129.5	132.0	134.4	133.3	133.0	133.0	135.0	134.8	134.8	131.5
1997	128.2	129.4	132.1	134.8	135.9	139.1	139.2	140.3	139.4	139.2	139.0	140.0	136.4
1998	133.4	134.8	137.5	138.9	140.3	144.5	142.9	143.9	142.8	143.4	143.7	144.3	140.9
1999	139.8	141.6	143.4	147.8	148.6	151.3	151.1	151.8	150.5	152.0	152.7	154.2	148.7
2000	147.7	148.8	150.5	153.6	156.0	157.8	157.5	158.8	159.1	159.0	158.7	159.6	155.6
2001	153.6	154.7	157.2	158.2	160.1	161.5	160.6	160.1	157.9	156.5	156.0	156.5	157.7
2002	147.6	147.8	150.2	152.6	154.4	156.2	155.0	154.7	154.9	154.9	154.8	154.4	153.1
2003	145.5	145.9	148.7	151.5	153.1	155.3	153.9	153.8	153.4	154.8	154.2	153.8	152.0
Educational and health services													
1990	129.5	130.9	132.9	132.7	133.6	132.4	132.8	133.1	133.5	135.5	137.3	138.8	133.6
1991	135.0	137.1	139.1	138.8	138.9	138.0	135.9	136.0	136.8	141.0	141.7	143.0	138.4
1992	139.2	140.5	142.6	144.0	143.7	142.5	142.0	141.9	142.7	145.6	147.6	147.9	143.4
1993	144.3	145.5	148.0	149.1	149.3	148.4	147.1	148.0	148.9	151.3	153.0	153.0	148.8
1994	149.0	149.6	152.2	153.3	154.3	153.0	151.1	152.0	154.0	155.6	157.3	158.2	153.3
1995	155.5	157.4	159.6	159.3	158.4	157.4	157.0	156.8	158.0	161.7	162.1	162.5	158.8
1996	157.6	161.2	163.3	162.3	163.2	162.1	161.2	161.5	161.7	166.1	167.1	167.5	162.9
1997	160.1	162.7	165.0	165.8	165.4	163.2	163.3	162.7	163.8	167.0	168.6	168.4	164.7
1998	165.9	168.1	170.9	170.8	171.2	168.8	168.0	167.8	168.0	174.0	175.1	174.8	170.3
1999	171.1	174.2	176.1	178.3	177.9	175.0	173.3	172.8	172.5	178.4	179.1	178.7	175.6
2000	173.3	176.3	178.2	179.6	179.6	176.2	176.9	176.2	179.4	181.2	181.8	183.5	178.5
2001	175.3	177.4	180.6	180.4	181.0	179.2	178.0	178.2	180.6	185.9	186.3	187.5	180.9
2002	181.1	184.1	186.7	187.4	187.4	184.5	184.9	185.0	187.2	193.2	193.6	194.4	187.5
2003	189.0	191.3	194.0	194.2	193.5	191.7	189.5	189.2	192.3	196.6	198.3	199.2	193.2

Employment by Industry: New York—*Continued*

(Numbers in thousands. Not seasonally adjusted.)

Industry	January	February	March	April	May	June	July	August	September	October	November	December	Annual Average
NASSAU-SUFFOLK *—Continued*													
Leisure and hospitality													
1990	73.1	72.3	74.8	77.2	84.4	90.1	90.5	90.1	87.3	81.9	79.6	78.1	81.6
1991	69.5	70.2	72.9	73.8	79.2	84.8	85.2	85.6	81.3	78.0	75.3	74.9	77.6
1992	64.4	64.5	67.2	70.4	76.0	81.6	83.1	82.3	79.1	74.6	71.6	70.0	73.7
1993	64.1	64.6	65.4	70.2	77.0	82.2	83.3	83.0	81.2	76.1	73.1	72.7	74.4
1994	65.9	64.3	68.4	72.5	76.5	83.4	85.0	86.0	81.6	77.3	73.6	72.6	75.6
1995	67.5	67.2	70.2	72.7	79.1	85.6	86.6	86.7	83.0	78.0	74.8	73.8	77.1
1996	66.5	66.7	69.4	72.2	78.7	85.4	84.7	85.6	80.6	77.7	74.9	74.5	76.4
1997	68.1	68.0	71.4	74.1	79.7	85.4	86.2	86.5	82.4	78.2	76.9	76.2	77.8
1998	69.2	69.8	72.7	74.7	82.1	87.4	88.8	87.6	85.0	79.6	76.9	76.8	79.2
1999	73.1	73.5	76.0	79.2	84.5	90.8	92.5	92.5	86.8	83.3	80.9	80.6	82.8
2000	74.0	74.3	77.0	82.1	87.3	94.0	96.5	97.5	91.5	87.8	85.3	84.6	86.0
2001	79.6	79.6	81.8	83.6	90.6	96.7	99.2	98.6	90.7	89.6	88.2	86.8	88.8
2002	79.4	79.8	82.5	86.7	92.4	98.6	100.3	99.6	94.2	90.7	89.1	88.2	90.1
2003	82.1	81.6	84.5	88.2	94.4	100.2	104.6	102.7	97.5	94.2	92.5	91.1	92.8
Other services													
1990	38.1	38.5	38.9	39.0	39.5	39.9	39.4	39.5	39.4	38.7	38.8	38.8	39.0
1991	37.7	37.8	38.1	38.3	38.8	39.1	38.7	38.7	38.7	38.4	38.3	38.1	38.4
1992	37.4	37.5	37.7	38.5	38.8	39.3	39.1	38.9	39.4	39.4	39.0	39.0	38.7
1993	37.6	37.8	38.1	38.7	39.1	39.5	39.4	39.4	39.6	39.5	39.4	39.5	39.0
1994	39.0	39.2	39.8	40.2	40.9	41.1	40.9	41.0	41.4	42.2	42.1	42.3	40.8
1995	41.7	41.8	42.4	42.1	42.6	43.3	42.5	42.8	43.1	43.1	43.0	43.3	42.6
1996	41.3	41.7	42.5	43.0	43.9	44.3	43.7	43.8	44.0	44.0	44.2	44.2	43.4
1997	42.7	42.8	43.9	44.4	44.8	45.1	44.7	44.5	44.9	45.1	45.2	45.4	44.5
1998	43.9	44.2	45.0	45.3	45.9	46.3	46.3	46.2	46.6	47.1	47.4	47.6	46.0
1999	48.6	48.8	49.4	50.6	51.3	51.8	51.2	51.2	51.2	51.7	52.0	52.2	50.8
2000	50.3	50.8	51.4	51.7	52.3	52.3	52.1	52.1	52.7	53.1	53.2	53.3	52.1
2001	48.8	49.1	49.4	48.9	49.8	50.1	49.8	49.8	50.1	50.0	50.1	50.2	49.7
2002	48.7	48.9	49.3	49.4	50.0	50.5	50.4	50.4	51.0	51.0	51.0	51.0	50.1
2003	49.6	49.7	49.9	50.6	51.1	51.1	51.4	51.2	51.3	51.0	51.3	51.4	50.8
Government													
1990	184.9	188.1	189.2	190.2	191.1	192.4	175.2	170.4	176.5	186.2	188.2	187.5	185.0
1991	183.1	185.8	186.2	186.9	187.1	186.7	170.4	164.1	170.4	179.3	181.0	180.6	180.1
1992	175.0	177.3	178.3	179.1	178.0	178.4	162.7	158.4	167.8	174.8	177.1	176.5	173.6
1993	172.1	174.6	177.7	178.3	179.1	178.9	164.7	161.6	168.9	177.6	180.4	180.0	174.5
1994	175.3	179.2	181.4	182.1	183.3	183.3	168.3	164.4	172.9	181.0	183.5	182.4	178.1
1995	178.3	181.5	183.3	185.2	184.0	184.7	169.7	166.6	173.6	181.3	184.4	182.9	179.6
1996	177.3	182.3	182.9	184.3	185.1	184.9	166.1	163.3	172.4	182.2	183.3	183.0	178.9
1997	175.2	179.9	181.6	183.8	183.8	183.8	169.1	164.2	173.0	181.6	184.1	184.4	178.7
1998	177.1	185.2	186.9	184.8	185.9	185.9	172.6	167.5	176.9	185.4	187.4	189.1	182.1
1999	183.6	187.7	189.3	190.1	190.9	189.4	175.8	170.4	180.3	189.0	191.0	190.9	185.7
2000	187.1	190.8	193.1	196.6	197.7	195.1	178.7	173.3	186.4	193.5	194.9	194.8	190.2
2001	190.6	195.0	196.0	196.4	197.7	198.9	184.6	182.0	189.1	197.5	199.7	201.7	194.1
2002	196.3	200.4	201.6	201.1	201.6	200.5	184.6	179.5	191.0	198.2	199.9	201.0	196.3
2003	197.4	202.0	204.0	203.0	203.2	203.1	188.1	183.1	195.1	201.7	202.9	203.6	198.9
Federal government													
1990	21.2	21.9	22.1	22.7	24.2	24.1	22.8	22.5	21.6	20.8	20.7	20.8	22.1
1991	20.3	21.2	21.3	21.6	21.5	21.2	21.1	20.5	20.5	20.5	20.5	20.6	20.9
1992	20.4	21.0	21.3	21.4	21.3	21.2	20.2	20.3	20.2	19.8	19.5	19.7	20.5
1993	19.4	20.3	20.6	20.7	20.8	20.8	19.8	19.9	19.3	19.1	19.0	19.4	19.9
1994	19.4	20.1	20.5	20.7	20.6	20.6	20.0	20.0	20.0	19.4	19.5	19.6	20.0
1995	19.6	20.4	20.5	20.9	20.7	20.8	20.2	20.2	20.0	19.6	19.6	19.7	20.2
1996	19.9	20.7	20.9	21.2	21.2	21.2	20.2	20.2	20.2	19.8	19.9	20.6	20.5
1997	20.1	20.7	20.9	21.3	20.6	20.5	20.0	19.6	19.6	19.1	19.2	19.2	20.1
1998	19.5	20.5	20.7	20.0	20.0	20.1	20.0	19.9	19.9	19.6	19.6	19.7	20.0
1999	20.2	21.1	21.3	21.7	21.3	21.0	20.8	20.6	20.2	19.9	19.7	20.0	20.7
2000	20.1	21.2	22.2	23.0	25.3	22.5	21.6	20.3	19.9	19.7	19.5	19.6	21.2
2001	20.6	21.4	21.6	22.2	21.7	21.6	21.3	21.0	20.9	20.7	20.7	21.1	21.2
2002	21.9	22.8	23.4	22.7	22.1	21.6	21.5	20.8	20.7	20.7	20.5	20.6	21.6
2003	20.8	21.0	21.7	21.6	21.4	20.7	20.8	20.5	20.1	20.1	19.6	19.8	20.7
State government													
1990	30.6	30.9	31.2	31.2	31.0	30.3	30.4	29.8	30.9	30.9	30.7	30.4	30.7
1991	29.4	29.5	29.5	29.5	29.4	28.6	28.1	28.0	27.7	28.6	28.5	28.5	28.8
1992	28.0	28.3	28.3	28.4	28.5	27.4	27.7	28.0	28.7	28.4	28.4	28.2	28.2
1993	27.9	28.0	28.3	28.3	28.3	27.9	28.1	28.8	28.5	28.7	28.7	28.8	28.4
1994	27.5	28.3	28.3	28.5	28.7	27.9	28.2	28.2	29.4	28.4	28.4	28.4	28.4
1995	27.3	28.3	28.5	28.4	27.6	26.5	26.1	25.7	27.0	27.0	27.1	26.5	27.2
1996	25.8	27.0	27.1	27.2	26.8	25.5	25.1	24.7	26.2	26.3	26.3	25.5	26.1
1997	25.0	26.0	26.2	26.3	25.9	24.6	25.3	25.0	26.3	26.2	26.3	25.4	25.7
1998	24.6	25.9	26.1	26.3	26.0	24.6	25.2	24.9	26.1	26.2	26.2	25.5	25.6
1999	24.6	25.9	26.0	26.1	25.8	24.7	25.4	25.1	26.1	26.1	26.0	25.2	25.6
2000	24.6	26.0	26.2	26.2	26.1	24.9	25.5	25.2	26.5	26.6	26.7	26.0	25.9
2001	26.2	27.9	28.4	27.8	27.7	25.3	25.9	26.5	28.1	28.3	28.3	29.1	27.5
2002	25.1	26.6	26.5	25.5	25.5	24.3	25.0	24.9	26.0	26.0	25.9	26.0	25.6
2003	25.1	25.8	25.7	25.1	25.2	23.9	24.1	24.0	25.7	25.1	25.1	25.2	25.0

Employment by Industry: New York—*Continued*

(Numbers in thousands. Not seasonally adjusted.)

Industry	January	February	March	April	May	June	July	August	September	October	November	December	Annual Average
NASSAU-SUFFOLK *—Continued*													
Local government													
1990	133.2	135.3	135.9	136.2	135.9	138.0	122.0	118.2	124.1	134.5	136.8	136.3	132.2
1991	133.3	135.1	135.4	135.8	136.2	136.9	121.1	115.5	122.2	130.2	132.0	131.5	130.4
1992	126.6	128.0	128.6	129.4	128.3	129.8	114.7	110.1	118.9	126.6	129.2	128.5	124.9
1993	124.8	126.3	128.8	129.3	130.1	130.2	116.8	112.9	121.1	129.8	132.7	131.8	126.2
1994	128.4	130.9	132.6	132.9	134.0	134.7	120.0	116.1	123.5	133.1	135.6	134.4	129.7
1995	131.4	132.8	134.3	135.9	135.7	137.5	123.4	120.8	126.6	134.7	137.7	136.7	132.3
1996	131.6	134.7	134.8	135.8	137.1	138.2	120.9	118.3	126.0	136.1	137.1	136.9	132.3
1997	130.1	133.2	134.5	136.2	137.4	138.6	123.8	119.6	127.2	136.3	138.6	139.9	133.0
1998	133.0	138.8	140.1	138.5	139.9	141.2	127.4	122.7	130.9	139.6	141.6	143.9	136.5
1999	138.8	140.7	142.0	142.3	143.8	143.7	129.6	124.7	134.0	143.0	145.3	145.7	139.5
2000	142.4	143.6	144.7	147.4	146.3	147.7	131.6	127.8	140.0	147.2	148.7	149.2	143.1
2001	143.8	145.7	146.0	146.4	148.3	152.0	137.4	134.5	140.1	148.5	150.7	151.5	145.4
2002	149.3	151.0	151.7	152.9	154.0	154.6	138.1	133.8	144.3	151.5	153.5	154.4	149.1
2003	151.5	155.2	156.6	156.3	156.6	158.5	143.2	138.6	149.3	156.5	158.2	158.6	153.3
NEW YORK PMSA													
Total nonfarm													
1990	4074.2	4082.0	4112.7	4103.4	4134.5	4146.1	4083.7	4084.8	4084.7	4067.1	4073.5	4078.7	4093.8
1991	3888.4	3884.8	3907.4	3898.7	3904.8	3919.8	3845.2	3839.1	3843.4	3860.2	3876.6	3876.3	3878.7
1992	3741.0	3738.8	3766.3	3780.5	3788.3	3797.0	3771.7	3756.8	3753.9	3778.7	3791.2	3810.7	3772.9
1993	3702.2	3720.4	3743.7	3763.3	3778.4	3796.4	3799.9	3779.4	3777.2	3809.0	3835.2	3859.5	3780.4
1994	3731.8	3747.1	3786.5	3804.9	3821.1	3837.8	3814.8	3808.8	3803.2	3849.1	3877.2	3895.4	3814.8
1995	3769.5	3783.5	3816.5	3822.7	3841.3	3858.5	3834.9	3830.6	3826.0	3858.4	3891.4	3908.1	3836.8
1996	3762.9	3807.5	3837.6	3847.2	3874.1	3896.1	3870.2	3864.3	3861.1	3914.0	3947.0	3970.9	3871.1
1997	3846.2	3864.1	3907.6	3915.3	3933.3	3958.6	3965.3	3954.7	3959.6	4012.4	4038.6	4073.9	3952.5
1998	3943.2	3967.4	4004.6	4017.4	4038.7	4059.8	4069.2	4056.9	4040.4	4100.0	4137.3	4165.7	4050.1
1999	4061.1	4084.9	4113.3	4128.1	4138.1	4163.6	4177.7	4165.8	4138.4	4208.3	4248.6	4283.4	4159.3
2000	4159.8	4181.1	4219.9	4252.2	4284.5	4301.9	4284.9	4253.8	4273.5	4326.9	4362.5	4389.2	4274.2
2001	4243.5	4252.7	4277.0	4266.3	4282.0	4291.2	4274.8	4246.8	4204.5	4175.9	4206.7	4217.9	4244.9
2002	4075.3	4096.8	4121.5	4128.4	4156.1	4165.7	4138.3	4116.8	4106.0	4151.7	4181.2	4198.5	4136.4
2003	4044.7	4055.0	4072.6	4071.8	4097.5	4103.6	4074.6	4052.5	4056.8	4098.0	4128.7	4147.4	4083.6
Total private													
1990	3389.4	3395.2	3417.9	3406.8	3427.6	3441.8	3392.0	3397.8	3407.5	3380.8	3382.3	3388.0	3402.3
1991	3207.6	3203.0	3220.9	3211.4	3216.9	3236.6	3173.7	3172.8	3189.3	3192.7	3205.5	3206.9	3203.1
1992	3079.5	3076.4	3097.2	3109.8	3118.0	3131.0	3093.7	3083.2	3105.5	3118.9	3123.5	3142.2	3106.6
1993	3041.6	3056.1	3074.8	3095.7	3111.1	3130.0	3096.9	3100.6	3124.5	3147.2	3164.2	3185.4	3110.7
1994	3066.1	3079.1	3114.5	3134.2	3150.6	3176.4	3145.8	3152.5	3177.3	3194.1	3218.6	3237.9	3153.9
1995	3124.0	3138.9	3170.3	3175.3	3195.2	3214.1	3169.3	3178.9	3208.9	3227.9	3253.2	3269.0	3193.8
1996	3137.8	3179.8	3205.2	3215.6	3243.2	3266.2	3227.1	3233.2	3255.3	3292.4	3320.1	3338.5	3242.9
1997	3220.9	3239.7	3278.2	3285.8	3303.1	3329.5	3308.6	3309.8	3344.0	3373.5	3397.4	3428.4	3318.2
1998	3310.3	3329.6	3358.9	3372.9	3393.8	3417.5	3401.4	3401.7	3420.9	3458.3	3486.8	3510.5	3405.2
1999	3418.2	3441.7	3465.8	3478.7	3488.9	3515.0	3486.5	3490.8	3504.3	3557.4	3594.0	3625.1	3505.5
2000	3508.5	3532.6	3565.0	3588.3	3606.6	3640.3	3597.9	3592.3	3638.6	3673.3	3708.2	3732.6	3615.4
2001	3594.3	3610.6	3629.5	3610.3	3633.3	3643.0	3585.7	3573.1	3569.6	3525.8	3548.3	3558.4	3590.2
2002	3417.5	3440.6	3460.7	3469.1	3493.4	3500.6	3457.9	3449.9	3463.8	3497.4	3517.5	3532.5	3475.1
2003	3394.1	3404.2	3421.8	3419.9	3445.1	3448.3	3410.4	3400.7	3425.7	3455.0	3478.9	3494.6	3433.2
Goods-producing													
1990	455.1	460.7	468.8	464.5	470.4	474.6	461.7	467.9	468.6	458.3	449.5	437.6	461.5
1991	398.7	402.2	407.1	407.1	409.8	415.4	404.8	412.0	414.7	411.6	407.1	396.0	407.2
1992	367.4	370.2	375.2	378.2	381.5	384.4	377.6	381.3	384.8	380.6	377.8	370.0	377.4
1993	347.3	353.4	359.0	365.2	371.6	376.0	368.4	374.0	380.8	376.2	373.6	366.1	367.6
1994	336.8	341.9	351.8	360.3	365.4	369.6	365.5	374.5	378.1	374.3	372.0	365.3	363.0
1995	342.3	347.8	355.6	359.4	362.6	366.0	359.1	367.0	371.6	367.0	365.3	358.5	360.2
1996	325.7	336.8	343.8	346.4	354.0	359.8	354.9	362.8	367.3	365.5	363.3	356.6	353.1
1997	333.9	339.0	348.4	352.4	356.6	360.6	358.3	365.5	370.3	369.1	369.1	364.7	357.3
1998	343.0	349.7	354.9	356.5	362.1	366.9	363.3	367.8	371.9	369.4	368.5	362.4	361.4
1999	346.9	351.1	356.3	362.0	366.8	372.7	368.0	373.5	377.8	378.5	377.8	372.9	367.0
2000	349.3	353.2	361.9	363.6	367.3	373.1	367.0	372.1	375.5	374.8	373.4	369.6	366.7
2001	342.2	344.9	349.2	349.3	353.5	357.8	346.7	348.4	345.3	343.2	340.7	336.3	346.5
2002	312.6	315.8	319.3	321.1	325.3	328.3	323.5	326.3	326.8	324.5	321.5	318.1	321.9
2003	298.9	299.5	304.8	304.5	308.2	310.7	305.9	307.0	309.4	307.2	304.0	299.4	304.9
Construction and mining													
1990	140.7	140.5	143.6	143.0	145.5	147.2	145.5	146.6	146.4	142.6	141.3	137.9	143.4
1991	121.1	119.3	120.3	121.9	123.2	125.3	123.7	123.5	123.7	121.4	120.3	117.3	121.8
1992	104.6	102.8	103.4	104.5	106.1	107.3	107.7	107.8	107.6	106.5	106.1	104.8	105.8
1993	95.8	95.2	96.8	101.4	104.2	106.5	107.2	108.5	111.3	110.2	110.1	109.2	104.7
1994	95.5	94.9	99.1	105.5	108.6	110.5	113.0	115.7	116.8	115.7	115.5	114.0	108.7
1995	103.8	102.6	106.1	109.6	111.4	112.7	112.8	115.1	116.5	116.0	115.7	114.0	111.4
1996	97.7	101.2	104.5	109.5	112.9	116.2	117.9	120.2	120.7	121.0	120.6	117.9	113.4
1997	105.7	105.6	110.3	113.2	115.3	117.9	120.8	123.4	124.5	123.7	124.6	123.8	117.4
1998	114.2	115.9	119.0	122.1	125.5	128.9	131.1	132.6	133.7	135.2	135.7	134.9	127.4
1999	127.1	128.5	131.4	137.2	140.5	144.6	145.9	148.7	150.1	150.5	150.7	150.6	142.2
2000	138.3	138.8	144.5	147.1	150.6	153.9	154.8	157.5	159.5	161.4	162.5	161.8	152.6
2001	148.1	148.5	151.2	154.7	158.2	160.4	156.9	157.4	155.4	157.5	157.4	156.1	155.2
2002	140.7	141.6	143.2	145.7	147.9	150.2	150.4	151.8	152.3	151.8	151.2	150.8	148.1
2003	138.2	137.5	141.4	144.6	147.8	149.8	149.4	150.2	151.1	149.4	148.2	145.5	146.0

Employment by Industry: New York—*Continued*

(Numbers in thousands. Not seasonally adjusted.)

Industry	January	February	March	April	May	June	July	August	September	October	November	December	Annual Average
NEW YORK PMSA *—Continued*													
Manufacturing													
1990	314.4	320.2	325.2	321.5	324.9	327.4	316.2	321.3	322.2	315.7	308.2	299.7	318.1
1991	277.6	282.9	286.8	285.2	286.6	290.1	281.1	288.5	291.0	290.2	286.8	278.7	285.5
1992	262.8	267.4	271.8	273.7	275.4	277.1	269.9	273.5	277.2	274.1	271.7	265.2	271.7
1993	251.5	258.2	262.2	263.8	267.4	269.5	261.2	265.5	269.5	266.0	263.5	256.9	262.9
1994	241.3	247.0	252.7	254.8	256.8	259.1	252.5	258.8	261.3	258.6	256.5	251.3	254.2
1995	238.5	245.2	249.5	249.8	251.2	253.3	246.3	251.9	255.1	251.0	249.6	244.5	248.8
1996	228.0	235.6	239.3	236.9	241.1	243.6	237.0	242.6	246.6	244.5	242.7	238.7	239.7
1997	228.2	233.4	238.1	239.2	241.3	242.7	237.5	242.1	245.8	245.4	244.5	240.9	239.9
1998	228.8	233.8	235.9	234.4	236.6	238.0	232.2	235.2	238.2	234.2	232.8	227.5	234.0
1999	219.8	222.6	224.9	224.8	226.3	228.1	222.1	224.8	227.7	228.0	227.1	222.3	224.9
2000	211.0	214.4	217.4	216.5	216.7	219.2	212.2	214.6	216.0	213.4	210.9	207.8	214.2
2001	194.1	196.4	198.0	194.6	195.3	197.4	189.8	191.0	189.9	185.7	183.3	180.2	191.3
2002	171.9	174.2	176.1	175.4	177.4	178.1	173.1	174.5	174.5	172.7	170.3	167.3	173.8
2003	160.7	162.0	163.4	159.9	160.4	160.9	156.5	156.8	158.3	157.8	155.8	153.9	158.8
Service-providing													
1990	3619.1	3621.3	3643.9	3638.9	3664.1	3671.5	3622.0	3616.9	3616.1	3608.8	3624.0	3641.1	3632.3
1991	3489.7	3482.6	3500.3	3491.6	3495.0	3504.4	3440.4	3427.1	3428.7	3448.6	3469.5	3480.3	3471.5
1992	3373.6	3368.6	3391.1	3402.3	3406.8	3412.6	3394.1	3375.5	3369.1	3398.1	3413.4	3440.7	3395.5
1993	3354.9	3367.0	3384.7	3398.1	3406.8	3420.4	3431.5	3405.4	3396.4	3432.8	3461.6	3493.4	3412.8
1994	3395.0	3405.2	3434.7	3444.6	3455.7	3468.2	3449.3	3434.3	3425.1	3474.8	3505.2	3530.1	3451.9
1995	3427.2	3435.7	3460.9	3463.3	3478.7	3492.5	3475.8	3463.6	3454.4	3491.4	3526.1	3549.6	3476.6
1996	3437.2	3470.7	3493.8	3500.8	3520.1	3536.3	3515.3	3501.5	3493.8	3548.5	3583.7	3614.3	3518.0
1997	3512.3	3525.1	3559.2	3562.9	3576.7	3598.0	3607.0	3589.2	3589.3	3643.3	3669.5	3709.2	3595.1
1998	3600.2	3617.7	3649.7	3660.9	3676.6	3692.9	3705.9	3689.1	3668.5	3730.6	3768.8	3803.3	3688.7
1999	3714.2	3733.8	3757.0	3766.1	3771.3	3790.9	3809.7	3792.3	3760.6	3829.8	3870.8	3910.5	3792.3
2000	3810.5	3827.9	3858.0	3888.6	3917.2	3928.8	3917.9	3881.7	3898.0	3952.1	3989.1	4019.6	3907.5
2001	3901.3	3907.8	3927.8	3917.0	3928.5	3933.4	3928.1	3898.4	3859.2	3832.7	3866.0	3881.6	3898.5
2002	3762.7	3781.0	3802.2	3807.3	3830.8	3837.4	3814.8	3790.5	3779.2	3827.2	3859.7	3880.4	3814.4
2003	3745.8	3755.5	3767.8	3767.3	3789.3	3792.9	3768.7	3745.5	3747.4	3790.8	3824.7	3848.0	3778.6
Trade, transportation, and utilities													
1990	721.4	712.6	714.5	707.4	713.3	716.3	704.0	704.6	710.7	707.9	712.9	721.0	712.2
1991	674.6	663.4	661.4	661.0	662.6	667.6	651.0	651.0	657.0	659.5	668.4	669.6	662.3
1992	643.0	633.4	633.6	633.3	635.4	638.3	624.1	621.4	627.1	634.6	639.1	650.4	634.5
1993	622.3	617.6	617.6	621.0	625.0	628.6	620.3	619.8	624.3	635.4	643.4	654.7	627.5
1994	619.5	613.7	616.8	618.0	621.6	626.0	617.7	618.6	627.1	632.6	644.6	656.0	626.0
1995	629.9	624.5	628.3	626.1	630.9	636.4	623.1	624.4	636.4	641.9	653.6	663.3	634.9
1996	625.6	623.0	625.8	624.6	630.2	636.3	625.5	624.9	637.1	643.4	658.6	669.9	635.4
1997	637.2	629.3	634.6	631.1	635.1	640.9	628.5	624.3	641.9	648.2	661.3	675.8	640.7
1998	643.7	636.7	639.7	636.4	642.4	647.4	636.9	637.2	647.7	655.9	668.6	681.8	647.9
1999	651.7	650.4	652.7	655.4	658.1	664.1	650.8	652.7	660.5	673.1	689.3	703.4	663.5
2000	671.7	665.5	668.3	669.0	673.0	680.7	667.5	669.3	679.7	684.3	699.7	713.3	678.5
2001	678.8	673.0	673.5	666.2	669.9	673.3	656.9	654.8	659.1	654.3	660.6	670.2	665.9
2002	638.1	632.5	636.9	637.2	641.4	646.4	634.2	633.0	644.9	651.0	662.0	674.6	644.4
2003	639.6	634.2	635.9	632.5	637.8	641.1	628.5	629.0	639.2	645.6	658.2	670.4	640.9
Wholesale trade													
1990	215.8	216.1	217.0	214.6	215.9	216.9	214.5	214.6	214.6	212.1	211.4	211.0	214.5
1991	203.1	202.2	202.0	200.1	199.4	200.2	197.4	197.8	197.8	198.0	197.7	197.0	199.4
1992	191.6	191.2	191.1	193.3	193.3	193.2	191.1	190.0	189.5	191.0	190.7	190.6	191.4
1993	184.3	184.9	185.4	186.3	186.5	187.1	185.4	185.4	185.1	186.5	186.5	186.6	185.8
1994	180.1	180.6	182.0	183.1	183.3	184.0	183.1	183.9	184.7	184.6	185.5	186.4	183.4
1995	182.7	183.5	184.8	184.3	184.9	186.2	182.4	183.2	184.1	184.0	185.2	185.7	184.3
1996	177.7	179.0	180.0	179.1	179.9	181.3	179.8	180.9	181.8	181.8	183.2	183.5	180.7
1997	177.2	177.9	179.5	179.2	180.1	181.5	180.1	180.8	181.5	182.9	184.2	185.3	180.9
1998	178.0	178.5	179.5	178.8	179.5	180.1	178.3	178.6	178.8	179.4	180.4	180.7	179.2
1999	178.3	178.2	178.9	180.1	181.1	182.2	180.0	181.3	181.4	183.1	184.9	185.4	181.2
2000	177.9	178.4	179.9	178.6	179.3	181.1	179.3	180.3	180.7	181.1	181.9	182.7	180.1
2001	183.8	184.6	184.8	182.4	182.5	183.1	180.6	180.4	179.9	179.3	179.0	179.4	181.7
2002	173.5	174.0	175.0	174.2	174.5	174.7	172.3	173.3	173.5	175.3	175.7	176.0	174.3
2003	172.2	172.5	173.2	171.8	173.0	173.5	171.1	171.3	171.7	172.9	172.5	172.9	172.3
Retail trade													
1990	330.2	325.5	326.3	321.7	324.5	325.4	320.5	320.5	322.5	324.6	329.6	335.8	325.6
1991	309.8	303.2	302.4	300.2	301.7	304.1	295.9	296.1	298.6	300.4	307.1	313.5	302.8
1992	294.7	288.9	287.9	286.5	287.7	289.1	283.8	282.8	284.5	288.5	292.9	301.2	289.0
1993	285.9	282.4	281.2	283.3	286.4	288.6	285.4	285.9	289.4	295.0	301.6	311.2	289.7
1994	290.3	285.9	287.8	288.4	290.4	292.7	290.1	290.3	294.1	298.3	307.3	315.6	294.3
1995	298.0	294.2	296.3	295.7	297.7	301.2	297.9	298.2	303.5	306.9	315.7	323.8	302.4
1996	299.9	297.5	298.4	299.4	303.0	306.3	302.1	301.6	307.2	312.6	324.3	333.4	307.1
1997	311.0	306.3	308.9	306.0	307.8	312.0	305.8	307.0	312.2	315.3	325.6	336.1	312.8
1998	319.7	315.4	316.6	314.4	317.9	321.6	317.2	318.2	322.5	328.6	338.5	349.9	323.4
1999	328.1	326.5	327.6	328.8	329.2	333.6	328.6	329.7	332.1	340.1	353.6	366.7	335.4
2000	345.4	338.8	339.9	341.9	344.4	349.3	342.6	344.6	348.0	350.5	364.8	377.0	348.9
2001	345.1	338.1	338.1	333.9	336.0	339.0	331.4	332.8	332.7	331.5	342.1	352.2	337.7
2002	328.7	322.7	325.6	325.8	328.4	333.1	328.9	329.4	333.7	337.1	348.4	359.9	333.5
2003	330.5	324.7	324.9	325.2	327.9	330.7	326.3	327.4	331.3	336.6	348.7	359.9	332.8

Employment by Industry: New York—*Continued*

(Numbers in thousands. Not seasonally adjusted.)

Industry	January	February	March	April	May	June	July	August	September	October	November	December	Annual Average
NEW YORK PMSA *—Continued*													
Transportation and utilities													
1990	175.4	171.0	171.2	171.1	172.9	174.0	169.0	169.5	173.6	171.2	171.9	174.2	172.1
1991	161.7	158.0	157.0	160.7	161.5	163.3	157.7	157.1	160.6	161.1	163.6	159.1	160.1
1992	156.7	153.3	154.6	153.5	154.4	156.0	149.2	148.6	153.1	155.1	155.5	158.6	154.1
1993	152.1	150.3	151.0	151.4	152.1	152.9	149.5	148.5	149.8	153.9	155.3	156.9	152.0
1994	149.1	147.2	147.0	146.5	147.9	149.3	144.5	144.4	148.3	149.7	151.8	154.0	148.3
1995	149.2	146.8	147.2	146.1	148.3	149.0	142.8	143.0	148.8	151.0	152.7	153.8	148.2
1996	148.0	146.5	147.4	146.1	147.3	148.7	143.6	142.4	148.1	149.0	151.1	153.0	147.6
1997	149.0	145.1	146.2	145.9	147.2	147.4	142.6	136.5	148.2	150.0	151.5	154.4	147.0
1998	146.0	142.8	143.6	143.2	145.0	145.7	141.4	140.4	146.4	147.9	149.7	151.2	145.3
1999	145.3	145.7	146.2	146.5	147.8	148.3	142.2	141.7	147.0	149.9	150.8	151.3	146.9
2000	148.4	148.3	148.5	148.5	149.3	150.3	145.6	144.4	151.0	152.7	153.0	153.6	149.5
2001	149.9	150.3	150.6	149.9	151.4	151.2	144.9	141.6	146.5	143.5	139.5	138.6	146.5
2002	135.9	135.8	136.3	137.2	138.5	138.6	133.0	130.3	137.7	138.6	137.9	138.7	136.5
2003	136.9	137.0	137.8	135.5	136.9	136.9	131.1	130.3	136.2	136.1	137.0	137.6	135.7
Information													
1990	189.4	190.3	189.3	190.3	192.7	191.8	192.4	193.0	192.6	190.7	189.2	191.2	191.1
1991	180.0	180.5	183.6	181.8	183.3	184.8	178.6	179.5	178.0	179.6	179.5	181.9	180.9
1992	172.9	171.3	175.1	171.4	171.8	171.4	172.4	172.0	175.6	172.6	172.9	173.4	172.7
1993	167.2	167.4	170.1	170.4	170.6	173.1	173.1	173.9	174.3	171.9	172.0	174.8	171.6
1994	167.7	168.4	171.7	170.1	171.1	173.6	170.6	171.8	172.0	172.2	173.9	174.4	171.5
1995	168.0	168.7	170.4	170.1	173.1	173.2	172.3	174.2	174.5	175.3	177.6	177.6	172.9
1996	175.9	176.2	176.5	175.8	177.0	178.5	178.0	180.1	177.9	178.8	181.4	181.4	178.1
1997	176.5	178.2	179.7	176.2	180.8	182.6	182.7	184.9	183.0	186.1	186.5	188.8	182.2
1998	180.8	182.2	184.4	184.2	186.8	186.0	184.4	186.8	183.9	186.0	188.4	187.7	185.1
1999	184.2	188.1	188.0	188.2	188.0	190.3	194.4	195.7	193.5	193.3	195.3	197.9	191.4
2000	196.2	199.6	201.4	204.9	207.6	211.1	210.2	198.1	212.9	214.2	216.6	216.2	207.4
2001	222.6	225.5	225.5	223.2	225.4	224.5	222.1	220.6	216.5	215.0	217.7	215.1	221.1
2002	198.4	202.5	197.9	197.4	203.2	200.9	191.8	194.1	190.6	191.8	194.7	193.1	196.4
2003	181.6	185.1	181.9	179.4	186.5	180.6	179.3	185.0	180.1	182.9	184.8	186.0	182.7
Financial activities													
1990	561.7	561.2	560.8	558.1	558.1	561.6	560.2	560.0	556.4	550.9	549.7	551.3	557.5
1991	533.6	531.3	532.0	528.5	528.1	530.8	528.7	528.1	525.4	519.7	520.9	524.0	527.6
1992	504.1	503.4	504.0	504.2	505.1	508.6	507.9	507.4	505.1	502.7	501.6	504.9	504.9
1993	494.5	496.3	496.4	490.9	492.9	497.0	497.9	499.8	498.1	499.2	500.9	504.2	497.3
1994	497.1	498.5	500.3	501.3	501.6	507.8	508.0	509.3	507.8	501.9	503.7	507.0	503.7
1995	497.2	498.8	499.4	496.0	496.4	500.8	499.9	499.9	499.4	496.8	497.5	500.3	498.5
1996	488.8	493.0	493.6	491.5	494.4	500.3	499.2	500.4	496.8	494.5	496.8	500.7	495.8
1997	490.9	492.8	495.9	495.5	497.0	504.6	506.9	509.1	506.9	506.1	507.7	511.3	502.1
1998	507.4	507.1	507.6	506.5	508.1	514.8	518.5	519.1	514.0	511.8	512.8	514.8	511.9
1999	514.2	513.8	513.1	510.8	512.1	516.8	517.7	518.5	513.2	515.5	517.8	520.9	515.4
2000	516.8	518.8	519.1	518.7	519.6	528.6	526.7	527.3	524.5	524.3	526.4	529.7	523.4
2001	519.1	518.7	519.8	515.6	513.9	519.6	518.1	515.3	509.8	480.3	481.7	482.1	507.8
2002	482.9	482.8	482.1	477.0	476.9	481.7	482.0	480.5	474.6	474.9	474.6	476.4	478.9
2003	468.6	467.1	465.8	464.8	465.9	470.2	472.5	471.2	466.9	466.8	467.9	468.1	467.9
Professional and business services													
1990	525.9	526.4	529.5	529.8	529.3	533.1	527.3	527.2	523.8	517.2	516.8	517.8	525.3
1991	493.6	492.7	494.8	488.9	486.8	488.6	480.5	476.4	476.6	474.4	475.6	476.4	483.8
1992	465.7	464.9	468.0	471.0	470.1	472.8	471.3	468.1	465.5	470.2	469.2	474.0	469.2
1993	465.0	469.0	473.1	480.9	476.9	483.1	480.8	479.0	480.1	480.9	482.6	487.3	478.2
1994	478.8	482.6	487.9	487.6	489.0	492.9	495.0	495.7	494.4	499.0	501.4	503.7	492.3
1995	488.5	491.4	496.2	498.1	501.1	506.8	501.9	503.7	503.2	508.0	509.6	514.4	501.9
1996	504.8	514.8	518.4	521.6	523.2	530.0	528.5	530.0	529.6	535.7	541.2	546.9	527.1
1997	531.4	536.8	543.3	548.4	548.3	556.0	560.7	562.5	561.4	565.9	568.3	575.0	554.8
1998	560.3	565.4	572.7	581.7	580.5	590.2	597.2	597.2	594.4	600.7	604.4	610.4	587.9
1999	594.4	601.5	607.8	609.8	609.8	620.7	623.3	624.3	622.4	630.5	633.5	642.0	618.3
2000	621.3	629.8	636.9	643.7	648.2	659.2	659.4	662.9	661.8	665.6	670.5	675.2	652.9
2001	658.9	661.5	661.6	654.4	654.6	658.6	655.4	653.0	649.8	633.4	634.8	634.3	650.9
2002	612.1	614.4	617.2	619.9	619.9	623.5	619.6	618.1	615.1	618.8	620.0	622.1	618.4
2003	596.9	596.6	601.9	603.6	604.3	609.2	605.3	604.2	604.1	605.3	607.7	611.1	604.1
Educational and health services													
1990	549.0	556.8	561.7	560.6	561.7	557.8	548.0	547.2	556.7	563.5	569.5	571.9	558.7
1991	561.4	568.2	573.7	574.3	573.7	569.7	561.1	559.6	569.3	578.5	582.7	585.2	571.5
1992	576.8	583.5	587.4	590.0	589.0	586.3	576.3	573.6	586.0	594.6	598.2	601.9	587.0
1993	594.6	599.2	605.2	604.2	604.2	599.8	591.2	588.9	598.7	614.0	619.7	622.6	603.5
1994	609.0	616.8	623.2	625.0	624.7	622.6	612.9	610.6	622.4	636.3	641.8	647.0	624.4
1995	632.9	640.0	646.9	644.5	644.3	639.5	628.2	625.9	636.9	650.6	654.6	657.0	641.8
1996	644.7	658.5	663.9	664.2	663.6	658.1	644.1	639.5	649.0	670.9	673.9	673.7	658.7
1997	661.2	670.4	675.3	676.1	671.6	666.4	658.1	652.7	664.2	681.8	684.5	688.2	670.9
1998	671.0	680.9	687.0	690.6	688.1	681.7	674.5	670.2	681.8	701.1	706.6	709.6	686.9
1999	705.0	711.8	716.9	713.5	709.7	701.9	691.8	686.4	695.4	714.0	720.8	724.0	707.6
2000	713.6	721.1	726.7	729.1	726.6	716.3	700.9	698.3	717.1	736.7	742.1	746.5	722.9
2001	714.3	724.8	731.3	731.5	735.0	724.7	711.7	707.2	718.6	740.8	748.5	751.0	728.3
2002	730.0	743.1	749.9	751.0	753.0	742.2	733.5	726.8	742.7	760.5	766.4	766.8	747.2
2003	751.8	761.9	768.0	767.2	768.0	757.0	746.1	738.1	756.0	773.1	778.1	779.8	762.0

Employment by Industry: New York—*Continued*

(Numbers in thousands. Not seasonally adjusted.)

Industry	January	February	March	April	May	June	July	August	September	October	November	December	Annual Average
NEW YORK PMSA *—Continued*													
Leisure and hospitality													
1990	245.8	245.7	250.8	253.9	258.5	261.8	256.1	255.8	256.4	250.3	252.3	254.4	253.5
1991	229.1	228.0	230.5	232.3	234.3	241.0	234.3	232.6	233.4	234.4	235.5	236.7	233.5
1992	215.2	215.4	218.8	225.6	228.3	232.3	229.4	226.0	227.4	227.0	228.2	229.7	225.3
1993	215.7	217.8	217.0	224.5	230.3	233.0	228.2	229.2	231.3	231.1	233.0	235.7	227.2
1994	221.6	220.7	225.3	233.1	237.7	243.4	237.7	234.7	237.4	238.3	240.8	243.5	234.5
1995	227.4	228.9	233.3	240.2	244.9	249.4	244.8	244.4	246.3	246.2	251.8	253.7	242.6
1996	233.1	236.1	240.3	247.9	255.7	257.8	253.6	252.9	253.6	257.3	258.1	261.2	250.6
1997	245.0	247.2	252.7	257.9	264.8	268.7	265.3	263.9	267.1	265.8	268.7	271.9	261.6
1998	253.8	256.0	259.9	264.4	272.5	276.9	273.4	270.9	274.0	277.1	279.0	283.8	270.1
1999	262.3	264.9	269.4	276.2	280.6	284.6	279.2	279.6	280.7	285.3	290.2	294.3	278.9
2000	273.5	277.4	282.1	290.4	294.5	301.0	297.7	297.0	297.4	301.2	306.0	307.9	293.8
2001	289.5	292.0	297.0	298.6	308.3	311.1	304.7	304.4	302.3	289.6	293.5	297.6	299.1
2002	274.2	279.2	285.6	293.5	300.3	303.9	301.9	301.3	298.8	302.5	304.0	306.5	296.0
2003	286.1	288.5	291.0	295.5	301.0	305.5	302.5	297.9	300.6	303.0	305.3	308.1	298.7
Other services													
1990	141.1	141.5	142.5	142.2	143.6	144.8	142.3	142.1	142.3	142.0	142.4	142.8	142.5
1991	136.6	136.7	137.8	137.5	138.3	138.7	134.7	133.6	134.9	135.0	135.8	137.1	136.4
1992	134.4	134.3	135.1	136.1	136.8	136.9	134.7	133.4	134.0	136.6	136.5	137.9	135.6
1993	135.0	135.4	136.4	138.6	139.6	139.4	137.0	136.0	136.9	138.5	139.0	140.0	137.7
1994	135.6	136.5	137.5	138.8	139.5	140.5	138.4	137.3	138.1	139.5	140.4	141.0	138.6
1995	137.8	138.8	140.2	140.9	141.9	142.0	140.0	139.4	140.6	142.1	143.2	144.2	140.9
1996	139.2	141.4	142.9	143.6	145.1	145.4	143.3	142.6	144.0	146.3	146.8	148.1	144.1
1997	144.8	146.0	148.3	148.2	148.9	149.7	148.1	146.9	149.2	150.5	151.3	152.7	148.7
1998	150.3	151.6	152.7	152.6	153.3	153.6	153.2	152.5	153.2	156.3	158.5	160.0	154.0
1999	159.5	160.1	161.6	162.8	163.8	163.9	161.3	160.1	160.8	167.2	169.3	169.7	163.3
2000	166.1	167.2	168.6	168.9	169.8	170.3	168.5	167.3	169.7	172.2	173.5	174.2	169.7
2001	168.9	170.2	171.6	171.5	172.7	173.4	170.1	169.4	168.2	169.2	170.8	171.8	170.7
2002	169.2	170.3	171.8	172.0	173.4	173.7	171.4	169.8	170.3	173.4	174.3	174.9	172.0
2003	170.6	171.3	172.5	172.4	173.4	174.0	170.3	168.3	169.4	171.1	172.9	171.7	171.4
Government													
1990	684.8	686.8	694.8	696.6	706.9	704.3	691.7	687.0	677.2	686.3	691.2	690.7	691.5
1991	680.8	681.8	686.5	687.3	687.9	683.2	671.5	666.3	654.1	667.5	671.1	669.4	675.6
1992	661.5	662.4	669.1	670.7	670.3	666.0	678.0	673.6	648.4	659.8	667.7	668.5	666.3
1993	660.6	664.3	668.9	667.6	667.3	666.4	703.0	678.8	652.7	661.8	671.0	674.1	669.7
1994	665.7	668.0	672.0	670.7	670.5	661.4	669.0	656.3	625.9	655.0	658.6	657.5	660.9
1995	645.5	644.6	646.2	647.4	646.1	644.4	665.6	651.7	617.1	630.5	638.2	639.1	643.0
1996	625.1	627.7	632.4	631.6	630.9	629.9	643.1	631.1	605.8	621.6	626.9	632.4	628.2
1997	625.3	624.4	629.4	629.5	630.2	629.1	656.7	644.9	615.6	638.9	641.2	645.5	634.2
1998	632.9	637.8	645.7	644.5	644.9	642.3	667.8	655.2	619.5	641.7	650.5	655.2	644.8
1999	642.9	643.2	647.5	649.4	649.2	648.6	691.2	675.0	634.1	650.9	654.6	658.3	653.7
2000	651.3	648.5	654.9	663.9	677.9	661.6	687.0	661.5	634.9	653.6	654.3	656.6	658.8
2001	649.2	642.1	647.5	656.0	648.7	648.2	689.1	673.7	634.9	650.1	658.4	659.5	654.8
2002	657.8	656.2	660.8	659.3	662.7	665.1	680.4	666.9	642.2	654.3	663.7	666.0	661.3
2003	650.6	650.8	650.8	651.9	652.4	655.3	664.2	651.8	631.1	643.0	649.8	652.8	650.3
NEW YORK CITY													
Total nonfarm													
1990	3555.7	3563.1	3588.8	3578.2	3601.6	3605.9	3549.5	3553.9	3556.2	3540.2	3548.4	3553.2	3566.2
1991	3389.5	3387.8	3407.6	3394.9	3396.7	3406.0	3339.9	3335.5	3341.8	3357.2	3370.9	3370.4	3374.9
1992	3258.6	3258.1	3282.0	3289.2	3292.5	3296.3	3276.9	3265.8	3264.2	3285.7	3297.0	3314.9	3281.8
1993	3224.7	3241.4	3264.0	3278.4	3286.8	3298.5	3307.7	3289.0	3287.5	3316.6	3338.9	3360.6	3291.2
1994	3255.5	3271.1	3304.8	3316.8	3326.4	3336.1	3319.4	3313.8	3308.9	3349.9	3374.2	3390.6	3322.3
1995	3284.3	3298.1	3324.7	3329.5	3341.3	3351.8	3336.5	3331.5	3328.8	3357.2	3386.4	3401.2	3339.3
1996	3279.2	3318.7	3343.9	3350.4	3369.9	3384.1	3365.5	3361.3	3360.2	3406.7	3435.5	3455.1	3369.2
1997	3353.9	3369.4	3406.6	3412.3	3425.0	3441.4	3452.4	3441.9	3446.1	3492.5	3515.4	3545.6	3441.9
1998	3436.2	3457.8	3490.3	3500.4	3515.5	3529.5	3543.0	3533.9	3519.2	3573.5	3606.1	3630.1	3528.0
1999	3538.1	3558.6	3583.6	3591.7	3598.4	3616.9	3636.9	3628.0	3600.0	3664.4	3701.3	3730.4	3620.7
2000	3627.4	3647.5	3679.0	3706.2	3731.6	3742.2	3731.4	3704.2	3719.8	3767.7	3798.6	3821.4	3723.1
2001	3698.9	3707.1	3728.1	3715.6	3724.4	3728.4	3721.8	3696.3	3655.7	3621.8	3648.9	3657.7	3692.1
2002	3535.9	3555.7	3574.5	3578.2	3600.3	3604.8	3584.7	3566.4	3553.7	3593.1	3620.5	3634.2	3583.5
2003	3505.2	3514.3	3524.9	3521.5	3541.2	3541.7	3518.9	3498.8	3501.7	3534.7	3562.2	3577.4	3528.5
Total private													
1990	2953.9	2959.9	2977.9	2966.1	2980.4	2988.9	2940.4	2948.2	2960.4	2938.0	2942.1	2947.6	2958.7
1991	2792.6	2790.2	2805.4	2791.9	2793.5	2807.7	2750.0	2748.8	2767.2	2772.1	2783.1	2784.0	2782.2
1992	2678.1	2677.4	2695.4	2701.7	2705.5	2713.9	2679.0	2671.1	2695.1	2707.3	2712.9	2729.3	2697.2
1993	2645.4	2659.5	2677.5	2693.5	2703.0	2716.2	2685.7	2689.9	2714.0	2736.8	2751.9	2769.5	2703.6
1994	2670.9	2684.9	2715.3	2729.2	2739.9	2759.2	2731.2	2738.2	2763.5	2777.9	2800.5	2817.4	2744.0
1995	2721.4	2737.1	2762.0	2766.2	2779.5	2792.6	2752.0	2760.4	2791.8	2809.4	2832.5	2845.5	2779.2
1996	2735.4	2773.9	2795.1	2801.9	2822.8	2838.4	2802.3	2809.2	2833.5	2867.3	2892.2	2906.1	2823.2
1997	2810.1	2828.2	2860.5	2865.7	2878.2	2896.9	2877.1	2877.0	2911.7	2936.6	2958.0	2984.3	2890.4
1998	2885.3	2903.7	2928.7	2940.0	2955.5	2972.5	2957.2	2959.0	2980.5	3015.1	3040.5	3059.7	2966.5
1999	2978.9	3000.6	3021.2	3027.5	3035.2	3055.0	3032.3	3038.4	3051.3	3101.4	3135.8	3161.0	3053.2
2000	3063.6	3087.9	3113.6	3132.2	3145.4	3172.0	3132.4	3129.7	3172.9	3203.6	3235.2	3254.6	3153.6
2001	3138.5	3155.0	3170.1	3149.5	3166.4	3171.1	3118.4	3107.2	3108.4	3062.4	3082.9	3090.1	3126.7
2002	2970.2	2993.2	3007.4	3011.7	3032.1	3035.2	2994.0	2988.2	3001.6	3032.1	3051.4	3062.3	3015.0
2003	2946.5	2957.7	2968.5	2963.7	2983.3	2982.1	2945.9	2937.7	2962.3	2986.3	3008.4	3019.5	2971.8

Employment by Industry: New York—*Continued*

(Numbers in thousands. Not seasonally adjusted.)

Industry	January	February	March	April	May	June	July	August	September	October	November	December	Annual Average
NEW YORK CITY—*Continued*													
Goods-producing													
1990	374.8	380.2	387.1	381.5	386.1	389.2	377.3	384.0	385.6	377.5	371.5	360.7	379.6
1991	328.3	332.8	337.9	336.5	337.9	342.6	332.4	339.4	342.2	339.4	335.6	326.1	335.9
1992	302.2	305.8	310.2	312.4	314.6	316.8	310.2	314.5	318.5	314.8	312.6	305.3	311.5
1993	286.2	292.2	298.0	302.5	307.9	311.5	304.1	309.5	315.3	311.4	308.9	302.1	304.1
1994	278.2	283.6	292.0	298.3	301.9	305.4	301.2	309.7	312.6	308.6	306.7	300.4	299.9
1995	281.7	287.9	294.3	297.0	299.1	302.0	296.2	303.7	308.0	303.6	302.2	295.6	297.6
1996	268.0	278.0	283.9	285.2	290.8	296.1	292.7	300.3	304.7	302.7	300.3	293.7	291.4
1997	275.3	280.9	289.4	291.3	294.3	297.2	294.2	301.0	305.2	303.7	303.6	299.2	294.6
1998	281.9	288.3	292.6	292.8	297.5	301.7	298.6	302.6	306.5	303.8	303.0	297.1	297.2
1999	283.7	287.3	291.2	294.8	298.7	303.5	299.7	305.1	308.1	308.7	307.8	303.0	299.3
2000	283.6	288.0	294.3	295.2	297.5	302.7	297.5	301.8	304.7	303.0	301.6	298.1	297.3
2001	275.0	277.5	281.0	280.6	283.5	286.8	277.1	279.0	276.5	274.1	272.0	267.9	277.6
2002	249.1	252.0	254.2	255.1	258.5	260.9	256.1	258.5	258.3	256.1	253.4	250.1	255.2
2003	235.2	236.5	239.9	239.2	241.8	243.2	238.9	240.0	242.0	239.5	236.2	231.8	238.7
Natural resources and mining													
1990	0.2	0.2	0.2	0.2	0.1	0.1	0.1	0.1	0.1	0.2	0.1	0.1	0.1
1991	0.1	0.1	0.1	0.1	0.1	0.1	0.1	0.1	0.1	0.1	0.1	0.1	0.1
1992	0.2	0.2	0.2	0.2	0.2	0.2	0.2	0.2	0.2	0.2	0.2	0.2	0.2
1993	0.2	0.2	0.2	0.2	0.2	0.2	0.2	0.2	0.2	0.2	0.2	0.2	0.2
1994	0.3	0.3	0.3	0.3	0.2	0.2	0.2	0.2	0.2	0.2	0.2	0.2	0.2
1995	0.2	0.2	0.2	0.2	0.2	0.2	0.2	0.2	0.2	0.2	0.2	0.2	0.2
1996	0.2	0.2	0.2	0.2	0.2	0.2	0.2	0.2	0.2	0.2	0.2	0.2	0.2
1997	0.2	0.2	0.2	0.2	0.2	0.2	0.2	0.2	0.2	0.2	0.2	0.2	0.2
1998	0.2	0.2	0.2	0.2	0.2	0.2	0.2	0.2	0.2	0.2	0.2	0.2	0.2
1999	0.2	0.2	0.2	0.2	0.2	0.2	0.2	0.2	0.2	0.2	0.2	0.2	0.2
2000	0.1	0.1	0.1	0.1	0.1	0.1	0.1	0.1	0.1	0.1	0.1	0.1	0.1
2001	0.1	0.1	0.1	0.1	0.1	0.1	0.1	0.1	0.1	0.1	0.1	0.1	0.1
2002	0.1	0.1	0.1	0.1	0.1	0.1	0.1	0.1	0.1	0.1	0.1	0.1	0.1
2003	0.1	0.1	0.1	0.1	0.1	0.1	0.1	0.1	0.1	0.1	0.1	0.1	0.1
Construction													
1990	113.9	113.8	116.0	114.2	115.5	116.2	114.4	115.4	115.7	113.5	112.6	110.1	114.3
1991	98.5	97.3	98.1	98.4	98.7	100.1	98.8	98.7	99.1	97.4	96.7	95.2	98.1
1992	86.7	85.3	85.4	85.2	85.8	86.5	86.3	86.3	86.5	85.4	85.2	84.6	85.8
1993	78.4	78.1	79.5	82.7	84.2	85.9	85.9	87.0	89.3	88.4	88.4	88.4	84.7
1994	78.8	78.5	81.7	85.8	87.5	88.9	90.6	92.9	93.7	92.2	92.3	91.4	87.9
1995	84.6	84.0	86.5	88.6	89.5	90.3	90.0	91.9	93.3	92.7	92.8	91.5	89.6
1996	79.3	82.2	84.5	87.9	89.9	92.5	93.8	95.5	96.3	96.6	96.1	94.0	90.7
1997	85.2	85.6	89.6	90.6	91.7	93.4	95.0	97.3	98.2	97.0	98.0	97.4	93.3
1998	90.9	92.3	94.5	96.1	98.8	101.8	103.8	105.2	106.4	107.7	108.2	107.8	101.1
1999	101.4	102.4	104.4	108.1	110.5	113.4	114.7	117.3	118.5	118.8	119.0	119.0	112.3
2000	109.8	110.7	114.5	116.2	118.4	121.1	122.2	124.2	125.8	126.8	128.0	127.6	120.4
2001	117.2	117.4	119.7	121.9	124.3	125.8	122.6	123.2	121.8	123.6	123.7	122.6	122.0
2002	111.5	112.1	112.8	114.3	115.8	117.7	116.9	117.7	117.9	117.5	117.2	116.8	115.7
2003	107.5	107.2	109.6	111.4	113.6	114.9	114.7	115.4	116.3	114.3	113.0	110.8	112.4
Manufacturing													
1990	260.7	266.2	270.9	267.1	270.5	272.9	262.8	268.5	269.8	263.8	258.8	250.5	265.2
1991	229.7	235.4	239.7	238.0	239.1	242.4	233.5	240.6	243.0	241.9	238.8	230.8	237.7
1992	215.3	220.3	224.6	227.0	228.6	230.1	223.7	228.0	231.8	229.2	227.2	220.5	225.5
1993	207.6	213.9	218.3	219.6	223.5	225.4	218.0	222.3	225.8	222.8	220.3	213.5	219.3
1994	199.1	204.8	210.0	212.2	214.2	216.3	210.4	216.6	218.7	216.2	214.2	208.8	211.8
1995	196.9	203.7	207.6	208.2	209.4	211.5	206.0	211.6	214.5	210.7	209.2	203.9	207.8
1996	188.5	195.6	199.2	197.1	200.7	203.4	198.7	204.6	208.2	205.9	204.0	199.5	200.5
1997	189.9	195.1	199.6	200.5	202.4	203.6	199.0	203.5	206.8	206.5	205.4	201.6	201.2
1998	190.8	195.8	197.9	196.5	198.5	199.7	194.6	197.2	199.9	195.9	194.6	189.1	195.9
1999	182.1	184.7	186.6	186.5	188.0	189.9	184.8	187.6	189.4	189.7	188.6	183.8	186.8
2000	173.7	177.2	179.7	178.9	179.0	181.5	175.2	177.5	178.8	176.1	173.5	170.4	176.8
2001	157.7	160.0	161.2	158.6	159.1	160.9	154.4	155.7	154.6	150.4	148.2	145.2	155.5
2002	137.5	139.8	141.3	140.7	142.6	143.1	139.1	140.7	140.3	138.5	136.1	133.2	139.4
2003	127.6	129.2	130.2	127.7	128.1	128.2	124.1	124.5	125.6	125.1	123.1	120.9	126.2
Service-providing													
1990	3180.9	3182.9	3201.7	3196.7	3215.5	3216.7	3172.2	3169.9	3170.6	3162.7	3176.9	3192.5	3186.6
1991	3061.2	3055.0	3069.7	3058.4	3058.8	3063.4	3007.5	2996.1	2999.6	3017.8	3035.3	3044.3	3038.9
1992	2956.4	2952.3	2971.8	2976.8	2977.9	2979.5	2966.7	2951.3	2945.7	2970.9	2984.4	3009.6	2970.3
1993	2938.5	2949.2	2966.0	2975.9	2978.9	2987.0	3003.6	2979.5	2972.2	3005.2	3030.0	3058.5	2987.0
1994	2977.3	2987.5	3012.8	3018.5	3024.5	3030.7	3018.2	3004.1	2996.3	3041.3	3067.5	3090.2	3022.4
1995	3002.6	3010.2	3030.4	3032.5	3042.2	3049.8	3040.3	3027.8	3020.8	3053.6	3084.2	3105.6	3041.7
1996	3011.2	3040.7	3060.0	3065.2	3079.1	3088.0	3072.8	3061.0	3055.5	3104.0	3135.2	3161.4	3077.8
1997	3078.6	3088.5	3117.2	3121.0	3130.7	3144.2	3158.2	3140.9	3140.9	3188.8	3211.8	3246.4	3147.3
1998	3154.3	3169.5	3197.7	3207.6	3218.0	3227.8	3244.4	3231.3	3212.7	3269.7	3303.1	3333.0	3230.8
1999	3254.4	3271.3	3292.4	3296.9	3299.7	3313.4	3337.2	3322.9	3291.9	3355.7	3393.5	3427.4	3321.4
2000	3343.8	3359.5	3384.7	3411.0	3434.1	3439.5	3433.9	3402.4	3415.1	3464.7	3497.0	3523.3	3425.8
2001	3423.9	3429.6	3447.1	3435.0	3440.9	3441.6	3444.7	3417.3	3379.2	3347.7	3376.9	3389.8	3414.5
2002	3286.8	3303.7	3320.3	3323.1	3341.8	3343.9	3328.6	3307.9	3295.4	3337.0	3367.1	3384.1	3328.3
2003	3270.0	3277.8	3285.0	3282.3	3299.4	3298.5	3280.0	3258.8	3259.7	3295.2	3326.0	3345.6	3289.9

Employment by Industry: New York—*Continued*

(Numbers in thousands. Not seasonally adjusted.)

Industry	January	February	March	April	May	June	July	August	September	October	November	December	Annual Average
NEW YORK CITY—*Continued*													
Trade, transportation, and utilities													
1990	609.1	602.5	604.1	597.8	602.6	604.7	594.6	595.2	600.5	598.3	602.2	608.3	601.7
1991	569.6	560.5	558.9	558.7	560.0	563.6	549.7	549.6	554.9	556.5	563.1	561.9	558.9
1992	542.4	534.5	535.1	533.4	534.6	536.5	525.5	523.3	528.5	534.9	537.8	546.8	534.4
1993	523.7	520.3	520.7	523.5	525.7	528.2	521.9	521.5	524.9	534.2	540.2	548.6	527.8
1994	520.1	515.6	518.2	519.3	521.4	524.8	518.9	519.7	527.1	531.3	540.5	549.4	525.5
1995	528.5	524.4	526.9	525.5	529.0	533.0	522.7	524.1	534.7	538.6	547.8	555.1	532.5
1996	524.4	522.8	525.4	523.8	528.5	532.8	524.2	524.2	534.7	540.5	552.8	561.4	533.0
1997	535.8	529.4	533.5	531.6	534.7	538.8	529.0	524.1	539.2	543.8	554.0	565.6	538.3
1998	538.1	532.5	534.5	533.3	537.6	541.0	533.0	533.5	542.5	549.2	559.2	569.4	542.0
1999	543.8	544.6	547.0	549.2	552.0	556.5	546.0	548.0	554.3	565.0	578.7	589.9	556.3
2000	564.5	559.6	561.9	561.3	564.8	571.0	560.7	562.2	570.8	574.2	586.7	596.9	569.6
2001	568.4	564.7	565.3	559.8	562.1	564.1	550.6	548.8	551.8	546.0	549.9	557.0	557.4
2002	530.7	526.8	530.5	530.3	534.1	537.6	528.2	527.6	536.8	542.4	551.5	561.4	536.5
2003	533.4	529.5	530.4	527.0	530.8	532.8	523.0	523.6	531.5	535.9	546.5	555.9	533.4
Wholesale trade													
1990	184.2	184.4	185.2	182.8	184.0	184.7	183.0	183.3	183.4	181.1	180.6	179.9	183.1
1991	172.7	171.7	171.6	170.5	169.9	170.6	168.2	168.6	168.9	169.0	168.8	167.8	169.9
1992	163.8	163.5	163.5	164.2	164.2	163.9	162.7	162.0	161.6	163.1	162.8	162.6	163.2
1993	157.5	157.9	158.5	159.4	159.3	159.6	158.1	158.2	158.0	159.0	159.0	158.9	158.6
1994	154.4	154.7	156.1	157.0	157.1	157.9	157.1	157.8	158.8	158.7	159.3	159.8	157.4
1995	156.7	157.6	158.7	157.9	158.4	159.5	155.9	156.7	157.6	157.3	158.1	158.4	157.7
1996	150.9	152.1	152.9	151.8	152.4	153.5	152.2	153.3	154.2	154.3	155.7	155.7	153.3
1997	151.3	151.8	153.1	153.4	154.3	155.4	154.4	154.9	155.8	156.7	157.9	159.0	154.8
1998	152.2	152.6	153.3	152.8	153.4	154.0	152.5	152.7	153.1	153.5	154.3	154.4	153.2
1999	152.6	152.6	153.4	154.4	155.3	156.2	154.4	155.6	155.7	157.5	159.2	159.5	155.5
2000	153.3	153.8	154.9	153.6	154.3	155.8	154.3	155.2	155.6	155.9	156.7	157.2	155.1
2001	158.2	158.7	158.9	156.9	156.9	157.2	155.1	154.9	154.3	153.4	153.2	153.4	155.9
2002	148.3	148.8	149.6	148.9	149.2	149.2	146.9	148.1	148.4	150.2	150.6	150.8	149.1
2003	147.5	147.8	148.3	146.8	147.8	148.2	146.1	146.4	146.7	147.3	146.9	147.3	147.3
Retail trade													
1990	265.8	263.2	263.9	260.3	262.3	262.9	258.7	258.6	260.5	262.4	266.2	271.0	263.0
1991	251.4	246.5	246.0	243.2	244.3	245.6	238.8	238.8	241.4	242.7	247.3	251.9	244.8
1992	238.3	234.0	233.4	231.6	232.3	233.2	229.3	228.3	230.5	233.2	236.2	242.5	233.6
1993	230.6	228.5	227.6	228.9	230.8	232.3	229.9	230.2	233.5	238.1	242.9	250.0	233.6
1994	233.4	230.4	231.8	232.3	233.3	234.6	233.1	233.2	236.7	240.1	246.7	253.2	236.6
1995	239.1	236.7	237.8	237.6	238.8	241.3	239.3	239.7	244.6	247.1	253.9	260.0	243.0
1996	241.7	240.3	241.2	242.0	244.9	246.9	243.6	243.4	248.5	253.6	262.6	269.4	248.2
1997	252.0	248.7	250.6	248.7	249.9	252.8	247.4	247.7	252.1	254.6	262.3	270.2	253.1
1998	257.0	253.9	254.4	253.3	255.9	258.0	255.0	256.0	259.7	264.9	272.4	281.2	260.1
1999	262.1	262.6	263.8	264.8	265.5	268.5	264.7	265.8	268.3	274.3	285.5	295.9	270.2
2000	279.2	274.0	275.1	275.7	277.8	281.5	276.0	277.9	281.0	282.7	294.2	303.4	281.5
2001	277.7	273.2	273.3	269.9	271.3	273.1	266.6	267.8	268.3	266.5	274.5	282.2	272.0
2002	263.5	259.3	261.7	261.6	263.9	267.3	264.1	264.7	268.4	271.5	280.9	290.0	268.1
2003	266.8	262.5	262.4	262.3	264.1	265.7	262.1	262.9	266.4	270.6	280.7	289.4	268.0
Transportation and utilities													
1990	159.1	154.9	155.0	154.7	156.3	157.1	152.9	153.3	156.6	154.8	155.4	157.4	155.6
1991	145.5	142.3	141.3	145.0	145.8	147.4	142.7	142.2	144.6	144.8	147.0	142.2	144.2
1992	140.3	137.0	138.2	137.6	138.1	139.4	133.5	133.0	136.4	138.6	138.8	141.7	137.7
1993	135.6	133.9	134.6	135.2	135.6	136.3	133.9	133.1	133.4	137.1	138.3	139.7	135.6
1994	132.3	130.5	130.3	130.0	131.0	132.3	128.7	128.7	131.6	132.5	134.5	136.4	131.6
1995	132.7	130.1	130.4	130.0	131.8	132.2	127.5	127.7	132.5	134.2	135.8	136.7	131.8
1996	131.8	130.4	131.3	130.0	131.2	132.4	128.4	127.5	132.0	132.6	134.5	136.3	131.5
1997	132.5	128.9	129.8	129.5	130.5	130.6	127.2	121.5	131.3	132.5	133.8	136.4	130.4
1998	128.9	126.0	126.8	127.2	128.3	129.0	125.5	124.8	129.7	130.8	132.5	133.8	128.6
1999	129.1	129.4	129.8	130.0	131.2	131.8	126.9	126.6	130.3	133.2	134.0	134.5	130.6
2000	132.0	131.8	131.9	132.0	132.7	133.7	130.4	129.1	134.2	135.6	135.8	136.3	133.0
2001	132.5	132.8	133.1	133.0	133.9	133.8	128.9	126.1	129.2	126.1	122.2	121.4	129.4
2002	118.9	118.7	119.2	119.8	121.0	121.1	117.2	114.8	120.0	120.7	120.0	120.6	119.3
2003	119.1	119.2	119.7	117.9	118.9	118.9	114.8	114.3	118.4	118.0	118.9	119.2	118.1
Information													
1990	167.5	168.3	167.5	168.4	170.7	169.6	170.3	171.0	170.6	168.9	167.5	169.5	169.2
1991	158.8	159.3	162.4	160.6	162.1	163.5	157.3	158.2	156.8	158.9	158.9	161.4	159.9
1992	152.7	151.3	154.9	151.3	151.7	151.3	152.1	152.1	155.7	152.6	153.2	153.5	152.7
1993	147.4	147.8	150.2	150.8	151.0	153.3	153.2	154.0	154.7	152.2	152.5	155.0	151.8
1994	148.3	149.2	152.4	151.0	152.0	154.3	151.5	152.8	153.0	153.3	155.0	155.9	152.4
1995	149.4	150.3	152.0	151.6	154.5	154.5	153.9	155.7	156.2	156.9	159.0	159.0	154.4
1996	157.1	157.4	157.6	157.1	158.0	159.3	158.8	160.7	158.6	159.2	161.8	161.6	158.9
1997	157.4	158.9	160.1	156.9	161.4	162.9	162.9	165.2	163.5	166.5	166.9	168.8	162.6
1998	161.9	163.3	165.7	165.5	168.1	167.2	165.5	168.1	165.4	167.5	170.0	169.2	166.5
1999	165.8	169.6	169.6	169.8	169.6	171.7	175.7	177.1	174.8	174.7	176.4	178.3	172.8
2000	176.1	179.8	181.7	185.1	187.5	190.5	189.5	179.8	192.3	193.8	195.9	195.3	187.3
2001	201.2	204.3	204.1	202.1	204.3	203.1	201.6	200.0	196.4	195.1	197.5	195.0	200.4
2002	178.2	182.4	178.1	177.7	183.5	181.3	172.5	174.8	171.6	172.8	175.6	174.0	176.9
2003	162.7	166.4	163.2	160.8	167.9	162.1	160.7	166.3	161.7	164.3	166.2	167.1	164.1

Employment by Industry: New York—*Continued*

(Numbers in thousands. Not seasonally adjusted.)

Industry	January	February	March	April	May	June	July	August	September	October	November	December	Annual Average
NEW YORK CITY—*Continued*													
Financial activities													
1990	526.4	525.7	525.2	522.2	522.1	525.1	523.9	524.2	520.7	515.4	514.4	515.8	521.8
1991	500.1	498.2	498.6	495.3	494.6	496.9	495.1	494.5	491.9	486.9	487.9	490.8	494.2
1992	470.6	470.2	470.8	470.5	471.2	474.2	473.9	473.6	471.5	469.2	468.4	471.4	471.3
1993	462.6	464.3	464.4	458.8	460.4	463.8	464.8	466.9	465.6	466.9	468.6	471.6	464.9
1994	465.3	466.7	468.3	469.6	469.7	475.2	476.0	477.1	475.9	470.5	472.1	475.2	471.8
1995	466.3	467.8	468.2	465.3	465.2	469.1	468.4	468.3	468.1	465.6	466.0	468.6	467.2
1996	457.7	461.9	462.2	460.4	463.0	468.1	467.1	468.3	465.3	462.7	465.1	468.7	464.2
1997	457.9	459.6	462.3	461.9	463.0	469.7	471.6	473.9	472.1	471.5	473.0	476.4	467.7
1998	472.7	472.5	473.2	472.3	473.7	479.7	483.3	484.0	479.7	477.3	478.6	480.1	477.3
1999	479.6	479.2	478.2	476.1	477.4	481.7	483.0	484.2	479.1	482.1	484.6	487.2	481.0
2000	482.7	484.6	485.0	484.6	485.1	493.6	491.7	492.2	489.7	489.7	491.7	494.6	488.8
2001	484.9	484.4	485.5	481.5	479.9	485.2	483.5	480.6	475.7	446.4	447.8	448.1	473.6
2002	449.2	449.3	448.5	443.5	443.3	447.7	447.9	446.6	441.0	441.1	440.7	442.2	445.1
2003	435.6	433.9	432.5	431.6	432.4	436.0	438.1	436.6	432.6	432.6	433.8	433.9	434.1
Professional and business services													
1990	469.9	470.0	471.9	472.0	470.8	474.0	468.0	468.2	464.8	458.2	458.2	460.0	467.2
1991	438.2	437.3	438.1	431.2	428.9	430.2	423.3	419.4	419.9	418.5	419.7	421.6	427.2
1992	413.7	413.0	415.3	416.8	415.6	417.7	415.9	413.0	411.0	415.6	415.0	419.8	415.2
1993	413.3	416.5	420.1	427.1	422.9	428.3	427.0	425.3	426.6	427.6	429.1	433.4	424.8
1994	425.8	429.4	434.4	432.2	432.9	436.4	438.5	439.1	437.7	442.4	445.3	447.6	436.8
1995	433.7	436.7	440.1	441.6	443.6	448.8	444.6	445.9	445.1	449.7	451.5	456.4	444.8
1996	449.7	458.9	461.5	464.1	465.0	470.7	469.0	469.7	469.6	475.6	481.0	486.5	468.4
1997	473.6	478.7	484.0	488.0	487.0	493.9	499.3	500.2	499.3	502.8	505.3	512.3	493.7
1998	501.0	505.8	512.0	519.0	517.4	525.7	532.9	533.3	530.9	537.0	540.6	546.2	525.2
1999	530.8	537.4	543.1	544.3	543.6	553.9	557.0	558.7	557.0	565.2	568.1	576.2	552.9
2000	558.2	566.2	571.8	578.1	582.1	592.0	592.2	595.6	594.5	597.6	602.7	607.0	586.5
2001	592.6	595.0	594.9	585.5	584.7	587.9	585.5	583.0	580.5	563.1	564.8	564.7	581.9
2002	546.0	548.2	549.9	551.1	550.9	554.1	551.2	549.9	546.7	550.3	551.5	554.4	550.4
2003	531.0	531.0	534.8	534.8	535.2	539.5	536.1	534.9	534.7	535.5	537.9	541.2	535.6
Educational and health services													
1990	468.6	475.3	479.6	479.0	479.6	476.1	465.7	464.9	474.4	480.2	485.8	487.8	476.4
1991	479.3	484.8	489.6	488.8	488.6	484.9	477.0	475.5	484.6	493.1	496.7	498.5	486.8
1992	492.1	498.0	501.5	503.9	503.0	500.5	490.5	488.6	499.3	506.6	510.2	513.8	500.7
1993	508.4	511.8	517.7	516.8	516.6	512.4	504.2	502.2	511.3	526.0	531.2	534.2	516.1
1994	523.1	529.9	535.7	537.0	537.2	534.3	524.7	523.1	534.9	546.5	551.4	556.2	536.2
1995	544.6	550.6	556.5	555.0	554.6	549.6	538.2	535.7	546.6	559.3	563.0	565.3	551.6
1996	554.7	566.4	571.0	571.3	570.7	564.9	550.9	546.6	556.8	576.3	578.5	577.7	565.5
1997	568.8	576.5	580.6	581.6	577.8	572.6	564.0	558.7	570.2	585.2	587.5	590.6	576.2
1998	575.1	583.2	589.0	592.3	589.8	583.6	576.9	572.9	584.7	601.7	606.3	609.3	588.7
1999	605.7	610.4	614.8	610.3	607.4	599.8	591.3	586.2	594.5	611.1	617.6	619.8	605.7
2000	613.1	619.6	624.1	626.6	623.7	614.0	598.9	596.6	614.6	632.0	636.8	640.7	620.1
2001	614.4	623.5	628.9	629.3	632.7	624.0	611.0	606.9	618.3	639.7	646.9	649.1	627.1
2002	631.6	643.0	648.5	649.7	651.7	642.1	632.9	626.5	642.3	657.4	663.3	662.7	646.0
2003	651.2	659.9	664.8	664.3	664.8	655.9	644.7	637.2	653.5	667.8	672.1	672.9	659.1
Leisure and hospitality													
1990	213.8	213.7	217.6	220.4	222.6	223.4	216.3	216.4	219.4	215.2	217.8	220.2	218.1
1991	198.6	197.6	199.2	200.6	200.5	205.0	198.0	196.0	199.3	201.2	202.8	204.2	200.3
1992	186.9	187.3	189.5	194.8	195.6	197.6	193.8	190.0	193.9	194.5	196.7	198.4	193.3
1993	186.1	188.5	187.3	193.1	196.9	197.5	191.6	192.6	196.8	198.0	200.5	202.9	194.3
1994	191.9	191.6	194.6	200.8	203.3	206.4	199.9	197.1	202.0	204.0	207.4	210.1	200.8
1995	197.1	198.6	202.0	207.6	210.1	212.2	206.6	206.0	210.9	212.2	218.3	220.0	208.5
1996	202.6	205.4	209.0	215.2	220.7	220.2	215.0	215.4	218.7	223.4	225.3	227.9	216.6
1997	215.2	217.6	222.0	225.5	230.5	231.7	227.4	226.1	232.4	232.1	236.0	238.6	227.9
1998	223.8	226.1	228.8	232.1	238.0	240.3	234.0	232.1	237.9	242.6	244.8	249.2	235.8
1999	231.2	233.4	237.2	242.1	244.9	246.3	239.6	240.3	244.5	249.5	255.5	259.4	243.7
2000	240.9	244.6	248.1	254.6	257.2	260.4	255.7	256.1	259.3	263.8	269.3	270.9	256.7
2001	254.5	257.2	260.8	261.3	268.7	269.0	260.6	261.4	263.0	250.7	255.3	258.7	260.1
2002	238.2	243.2	248.2	254.7	259.1	260.3	255.8	256.3	257.0	261.4	263.9	265.6	255.3
2003	248.9	251.6	253.0	256.4	259.9	261.9	256.4	253.0	259.3	262.1	265.6	267.8	258.0
Other services													
1990	123.8	124.2	124.9	124.8	125.9	126.8	124.3	124.3	124.4	124.3	124.7	125.3	124.8
1991	119.7	119.7	120.7	120.2	120.9	121.0	117.2	116.2	117.6	117.6	118.4	119.5	119.1
1992	117.5	117.3	118.1	118.6	119.2	119.3	117.1	116.0	116.7	119.1	119.0	120.3	118.2
1993	117.7	118.1	119.1	120.9	121.6	121.2	118.9	117.9	118.8	120.5	120.9	121.7	119.8
1994	118.2	118.9	119.7	121.0	121.5	122.4	120.5	119.6	120.3	121.3	122.1	122.6	120.7
1995	120.1	120.8	122.0	122.6	123.4	123.4	121.4	121.0	122.2	123.5	124.7	125.5	122.6
1996	121.2	123.1	124.5	124.8	126.1	126.3	124.6	124.0	125.1	126.9	127.4	128.6	125.2
1997	126.1	126.6	128.6	128.9	129.5	130.1	128.7	127.8	129.8	131.0	131.7	132.8	129.3
1998	130.8	132.0	132.9	132.7	133.4	133.3	133.0	132.5	132.9	136.0	138.0	139.2	133.9
1999	138.3	138.7	140.1	140.9	141.6	141.6	140.0	138.8	139.0	145.1	147.1	147.2	141.5
2000	144.5	145.5	146.7	146.7	147.5	147.8	146.2	145.4	147.0	149.5	150.5	151.1	147.4
2001	147.5	148.4	149.6	149.4	150.5	151.0	148.5	147.5	146.2	147.3	148.7	149.6	148.7
2002	147.2	148.3	149.5	149.6	151.0	151.2	149.4	148.0	147.9	150.6	151.5	151.9	149.7
2003	148.5	148.9	149.9	149.6	150.5	150.7	148.0	146.1	147.0	148.6	150.1	148.9	148.9

Employment by Industry: New York—*Continued*

(Numbers in thousands. Not seasonally adjusted.)

Industry	January	February	March	April	May	June	July	August	September	October	November	December	Annual Average
NEW YORK CITY—*Continued*													
Government													
1990	601.8	603.2	610.9	612.1	621.2	617.0	609.1	605.7	595.8	602.2	606.3	605.6	607.6
1991	596.9	597.6	602.2	603.0	603.2	598.3	589.9	586.7	574.6	585.1	587.8	586.4	592.6
1992	580.5	580.7	586.6	587.5	587.0	582.4	597.9	594.7	569.1	578.4	584.1	585.6	584.5
1993	579.3	581.9	586.5	584.9	583.8	582.3	622.0	599.1	573.5	579.8	587.0	591.1	587.6
1994	584.6	586.2	589.5	587.6	586.5	576.9	588.2	575.6	545.4	572.0	573.7	573.2	578.3
1995	562.9	561.0	562.7	563.3	561.8	559.2	584.5	571.1	537.0	547.8	553.9	555.7	560.1
1996	543.8	544.8	548.8	548.5	547.1	545.7	563.2	552.1	526.7	539.4	543.3	549.0	546.0
1997	543.8	541.2	546.1	546.6	546.8	544.5	575.3	564.9	534.4	555.9	557.4	561.3	551.5
1998	550.9	554.1	561.6	560.4	560.0	557.0	585.8	574.9	538.7	558.4	565.6	570.4	561.5
1999	559.2	558.0	562.4	564.2	563.2	561.9	604.6	589.6	548.7	563.0	565.5	569.4	567.5
2000	563.8	559.6	565.4	574.0	586.2	570.2	599.0	574.5	546.9	564.1	563.4	566.8	569.5
2001	560.4	552.1	558.0	566.1	558.0	557.3	603.4	589.1	547.3	559.4	566.0	567.6	565.4
2002	565.7	562.5	567.1	566.5	568.2	569.6	590.7	578.2	552.1	561.0	569.1	571.9	568.6
2003	558.7	556.6	556.4	557.8	557.9	559.6	573.0	561.1	539.4	548.4	553.8	557.9	556.7
Federal government													
1990	76.5	76.1	75.7	76.9	86.3	85.7	82.7	78.6	75.6	74.9	74.7	76.4	78.3
1991	74.0	73.9	73.9	73.8	73.6	73.9	74.2	73.8	73.4	73.1	73.1	74.5	73.8
1992	73.6	73.2	73.2	72.8	72.6	72.5	72.8	72.6	72.2	71.9	70.9	71.5	72.5
1993	70.7	70.6	70.6	69.7	69.6	69.6	68.9	69.0	68.8	68.1	68.1	69.5	69.4
1994	68.2	68.1	68.3	68.1	68.3	68.5	68.6	68.5	68.4	68.2	68.1	69.4	68.4
1995	67.8	67.9	68.0	68.0	68.0	68.4	68.1	67.8	67.6	67.0	67.2	68.4	67.9
1996	64.8	64.8	65.0	65.2	65.2	65.3	65.1	65.2	65.0	64.4	64.5	66.9	65.1
1997	63.6	63.5	63.4	63.5	63.4	63.5	63.1	63.3	63.3	62.8	62.9	65.3	63.5
1998	63.9	64.0	63.8	63.8	63.9	63.9	63.8	64.0	63.9	63.7	64.0	66.0	64.1
1999	64.5	64.5	64.4	65.0	64.4	64.3	64.6	64.5	65.1	64.5	64.7	66.7	64.8
2000	65.1	65.5	66.7	70.2	87.9	73.5	69.9	64.8	63.4	63.3	63.1	64.4	68.2
2001	64.5	64.3	64.3	63.9	64.0	64.1	64.4	64.3	64.2	64.0	63.7	64.2	64.2
2002	63.5	63.4	63.8	62.5	61.9	61.6	61.2	61.1	61.7	60.9	61.4	61.8	62.1
2003	60.2	60.2	60.2	60.4	59.9	59.6	59.4	59.2	59.1	59.0	58.2	59.1	59.5
State government													
1990	56.3	56.6	56.7	56.6	56.6	57.0	57.1	57.1	56.7	56.7	56.8	56.4	56.7
1991	55.4	55.6	55.4	55.2	54.7	54.7	54.5	54.5	54.0	53.9	53.9	54.0	54.7
1992	53.8	53.9	54.2	54.2	54.1	54.1	54.3	54.3	54.1	54.0	54.1	54.2	54.1
1993	54.2	54.3	54.4	54.1	53.9	53.8	54.2	54.4	54.0	53.9	53.8	53.8	54.1
1994	54.4	54.7	54.7	54.7	54.8	54.9	55.1	55.8	54.9	54.8	55.1	55.1	54.9
1995	54.7	54.4	54.3	54.1	53.3	53.0	53.5	53.2	52.5	52.2	52.1	51.9	53.3
1996	51.6	51.6	51.5	51.7	51.5	51.6	51.2	50.9	50.5	50.3	50.3	49.8	51.0
1997	49.5	49.6	49.7	49.8	49.7	49.8	50.1	49.6	49.2	49.2	49.4	49.0	49.6
1998	49.1	49.2	49.3	49.2	49.3	49.6	50.1	49.7	49.2	49.1	49.5	48.9	49.4
1999	49.0	49.1	49.3	49.3	49.4	49.7	50.1	49.7	49.4	49.2	49.7	49.2	49.4
2000	49.1	49.5	49.6	49.5	49.5	49.9	50.4	50.0	49.4	49.4	49.7	49.1	49.6
2001	50.2	50.6	50.7	50.3	50.4	50.7	51.1	50.8	50.3	50.2	50.5	50.0	50.5
2002	50.1	50.5	50.6	50.5	50.5	50.7	50.5	50.3	50.1	49.9	49.8	49.7	50.3
2003	49.5	49.6	49.6	49.6	49.6	49.8	49.8	49.8	49.5	49.5	49.4	49.3	49.6
Local government													
1990	469.0	470.4	478.5	478.5	478.3	474.3	469.4	469.9	463.4	470.6	474.8	472.8	472.5
1991	467.4	468.2	472.9	474.1	474.9	469.7	461.2	458.4	447.2	458.1	460.7	457.9	464.2
1992	453.0	453.5	459.2	460.5	460.4	455.8	470.8	467.7	442.7	452.4	459.1	459.9	457.9
1993	454.5	457.0	461.5	461.1	460.3	458.9	498.8	475.7	450.6	457.8	465.1	467.8	464.1
1994	461.9	463.5	466.5	464.7	463.5	453.5	464.5	451.3	422.1	449.0	450.5	448.8	455.0
1995	440.5	438.6	440.3	441.2	440.5	437.8	463.0	450.1	417.0	428.5	434.6	435.4	439.0
1996	427.5	428.5	432.3	431.6	430.4	428.8	446.9	436.0	411.2	424.7	428.5	432.3	429.9
1997	430.6	428.0	432.9	433.3	433.7	431.2	462.1	451.9	421.8	443.8	445.0	447.0	438.4
1998	437.9	440.9	448.5	447.4	446.8	443.5	471.9	461.2	425.6	445.6	452.1	455.5	448.1
1999	445.7	444.4	448.7	449.9	449.4	447.9	489.9	475.4	434.2	449.3	451.1	453.5	453.3
2000	449.6	444.6	449.1	454.3	448.8	446.8	478.7	459.7	434.1	451.4	450.6	453.3	451.8
2001	445.7	437.2	443.0	451.9	443.6	442.5	487.9	474.0	432.8	445.2	451.8	453.4	450.8
2002	452.1	448.6	452.7	453.5	455.8	457.3	479.0	466.8	440.3	450.2	457.9	460.4	456.2
2003	449.0	446.8	446.6	447.8	448.4	450.2	463.8	452.1	430.8	439.9	446.2	449.5	447.6
ROCHESTER													
Total nonfarm													
1990	501.2	504.9	506.9	509.7	519.4	522.0	512.1	512.6	518.2	521.1	521.2	518.2	514.0
1991	499.5	502.2	502.8	507.5	515.0	518.3	508.9	509.1	514.1	517.1	516.6	510.7	510.2
1992	497.0	499.6	499.3	505.1	511.4	513.3	503.6	504.4	508.6	518.0	518.5	518.4	508.1
1993	504.5	506.3	505.3	511.2	520.3	524.6	515.9	517.1	518.8	522.4	523.0	523.2	516.1
1994	505.2	507.4	508.0	513.8	520.7	524.7	516.1	516.3	521.2	524.6	527.5	525.5	517.6
1995	510.1	514.2	516.8	520.0	526.0	530.9	520.0	522.6	529.9	531.7	533.1	532.6	524.0
1996	516.9	520.7	521.4	524.0	531.7	535.2	524.3	524.1	528.0	532.3	533.5	532.2	527.0
1997	513.3	519.5	522.6	526.8	536.0	539.2	530.5	527.7	533.1	543.4	543.8	542.2	531.5
1998	525.8	529.7	531.7	534.3	543.4	547.0	535.7	536.7	543.4	548.6	548.9	550.0	539.6
1999	532.8	537.9	538.9	547.2	555.3	558.2	548.1	546.2	548.8	554.1	555.2	556.2	548.2
2000	538.3	542.2	545.6	552.8	558.3	562.5	553.2	553.0	557.7	557.7	558.7	559.6	553.3
2001	543.6	545.9	547.2	549.5	556.6	559.9	546.5	545.5	548.4	549.2	550.2	548.7	549.3
2002	527.2	529.0	531.0	534.5	541.7	543.3	534.4	535.3	536.9	540.4	541.4	541.5	536.4
2003	523.4	525.0	527.4	528.6	539.1	539.9	533.3	534.1	537.4	544.4	543.0	539.6	534.6

Employment by Industry: New York—*Continued*

(Numbers in thousands. Not seasonally adjusted.)

Industry	January	February	March	April	May	June	July	August	September	October	November	December	Annual Average
ROCHESTER—*Continued*													
Total private													
1990	428.9	430.2	432.1	434.0	442.9	446.9	445.4	446.0	447.6	445.5	444.2	440.9	440.4
1991	425.3	425.5	426.8	430.8	437.9	442.4	441.5	442.1	443.7	441.1	439.9	433.8	435.9
1992	424.2	423.0	423.0	427.9	434.8	437.4	435.2	436.8	437.8	441.7	441.3	441.3	433.7
1993	429.4	428.8	427.6	433.2	441.7	446.4	445.3	447.5	445.6	444.4	443.5	443.7	439.8
1994	429.1	428.4	429.3	434.6	440.7	445.4	445.0	445.9	446.8	445.4	445.7	445.0	440.1
1995	433.0	433.2	436.4	439.0	445.7	451.5	449.1	452.9	455.3	452.0	452.3	452.1	446.0
1996	440.2	440.3	441.0	442.7	450.3	455.6	453.2	454.5	453.2	452.0	451.8	452.4	448.9
1997	437.7	438.4	441.5	445.3	454.7	460.3	459.6	458.0	455.8	461.0	460.7	460.4	452.8
1998	447.5	446.7	448.3	451.1	460.3	465.2	462.5	464.6	464.1	464.9	464.4	465.6	458.8
1999	452.2	453.1	453.4	462.5	470.6	474.2	471.8	471.1	468.4	470.3	470.1	471.9	465.8
2000	456.8	457.1	459.5	466.5	472.2	478.3	477.0	476.9	475.8	473.3	472.7	473.8	470.0
2001	460.3	458.9	460.0	462.3	469.8	474.2	468.6	467.4	464.0	461.3	460.8	458.9	463.9
2002	442.5	440.2	441.4	446.5	453.2	455.6	455.1	456.0	452.9	452.2	452.0	450.9	449.9
2003	436.8	435.3	437.1	439.7	449.3	451.3	452.9	453.9	452.4	454.2	451.8	449.5	447.0
Goods-producing													
1990	146.8	146.4	146.3	147.2	150.2	152.3	152.3	152.0	151.1	150.2	148.2	145.7	149.1
1991	140.5	139.8	139.8	141.9	144.7	147.5	146.3	145.8	144.3	144.5	142.7	136.9	142.9
1992	135.1	134.1	133.7	135.2	137.1	139.7	139.8	140.3	139.2	139.7	138.4	136.7	137.4
1993	133.4	132.1	131.5	132.1	134.6	136.9	138.4	139.0	137.8	136.2	135.2	134.3	135.1
1994	131.3	130.0	130.2	130.7	132.5	135.8	136.5	136.8	135.3	135.5	135.3	134.3	133.7
1995	131.0	130.3	130.9	130.9	132.9	136.5	137.4	138.6	137.7	136.2	135.8	134.5	134.4
1996	131.9	131.0	131.0	132.1	134.0	136.8	136.4	137.2	135.4	135.2	134.6	133.6	134.1
1997	130.8	130.6	131.2	132.8	135.0	137.5	139.4	140.5	138.9	139.3	138.1	136.8	135.9
1998	134.3	133.0	132.8	133.4	134.2	136.4	135.1	137.1	136.1	134.9	133.9	132.2	134.5
1999	129.4	128.6	127.8	129.4	130.8	132.6	131.9	131.9	130.1	129.1	128.6	127.2	129.8
2000	124.7	123.4	123.6	124.2	125.4	127.9	128.4	128.7	127.9	126.9	126.1	124.8	126.0
2001	121.8	120.3	119.8	120.2	121.5	122.3	122.6	122.4	120.3	117.9	116.0	114.2	119.9
2002	111.4	109.0	108.8	109.5	110.5	111.1	111.5	112.2	110.0	109.6	108.9	106.8	109.9
2003	103.6	101.8	101.8	101.7	104.1	105.0	106.8	107.3	105.9	105.9	104.7	102.2	104.2
Natural resources and mining													
1990	0.8	0.7	0.8	0.9	0.9	1.0	1.0	1.0	0.9	0.9	0.9	0.9	0.9
1991	0.7	0.7	0.8	0.8	0.9	0.9	1.0	0.9	0.9	0.9	0.9	0.8	0.9
1992	0.7	0.7	0.7	0.7	0.8	0.8	0.8	0.8	0.9	0.8	0.8	0.8	0.8
1993	0.7	0.7	0.7	0.8	0.8	0.9	0.8	0.9	1.0	0.9	0.9	0.9	0.8
1994	0.7	0.7	0.7	0.9	0.9	1.0	1.0	1.0	1.0	0.9	0.9	0.9	0.9
1995	0.6	0.6	0.7	0.7	0.7	0.8	0.8	0.8	0.7	0.6	0.6	0.5	0.7
1996	0.5	0.5	0.5	0.6	0.7	0.7	0.6	0.6	0.6	0.6	0.5	0.5	0.6
1997	0.4	0.4	0.4	0.5	0.5	0.6	0.6	0.6	0.6	0.5	0.5	0.5	0.5
1998	0.3	0.3	0.4	0.5	0.5	0.5	0.5	0.5	0.5	0.5	0.5	0.4	0.5
1999	0.3	0.4	0.4	0.5	0.5	0.5	0.5	0.5	0.5	0.5	0.5	0.4	0.5
2000	0.4	0.4	0.4	0.5	0.5	0.5	0.5	0.5	0.5	0.5	0.5	0.4	0.5
2001	0.4	0.4	0.4	0.5	0.5	0.6	0.6	0.6	0.6	0.6	0.6	0.6	0.5
2002	0.5	0.5	0.5	0.6	0.7	0.7	0.7	0.7	0.6	0.6	0.6	0.5	0.6
2003	0.5	0.5	0.5	0.5	0.6	0.6	0.6	0.7	0.6	0.7	0.6	0.6	0.6
Construction													
1990	16.6	16.4	16.5	17.9	19.6	20.9	21.5	21.7	21.2	20.3	18.9	17.5	19.1
1991	15.5	15.1	15.3	16.9	18.4	19.4	19.4	19.4	18.5	18.2	17.4	16.4	17.5
1992	14.4	13.7	13.5	14.4	15.6	16.8	17.6	17.9	17.7	17.5	16.9	15.9	16.0
1993	13.5	12.8	12.6	13.9	15.7	16.9	18.0	18.4	18.1	17.5	16.6	15.6	15.8
1994	13.2	12.5	12.7	14.1	15.7	16.9	17.6	17.8	17.4	17.3	16.9	15.6	15.6
1995	13.7	13.0	13.2	14.3	15.7	17.1	17.9	18.3	18.0	17.3	16.6	15.4	15.9
1996	13.7	13.3	13.6	14.4	15.9	17.1	17.6	18.1	17.5	17.3	16.8	15.8	15.9
1997	14.1	13.7	14.3	15.2	17.1	18.2	19.2	19.7	19.0	18.9	18.0	17.0	17.0
1998	15.9	15.7	15.9	17.0	18.4	19.3	20.1	20.4	19.8	19.8	19.0	18.2	18.3
1999	16.4	16.1	16.1	18.0	19.5	20.6	21.5	21.7	20.7	20.1	19.6	18.4	19.1
2000	16.8	16.3	16.6	17.9	19.2	20.5	21.2	21.7	20.9	20.6	20.3	19.4	19.3
2001	18.0	17.5	17.8	18.9	20.7	21.6	22.2	22.2	21.2	20.3	19.4	18.2	19.8
2002	16.3	15.6	15.8	17.0	18.2	19.2	20.0	20.6	19.9	19.6	18.9	17.5	18.2
2003	15.5	15.0	15.2	16.1	17.9	18.8	20.2	20.6	20.1	20.1	19.8	18.5	18.2
Manufacturing													
1990	129.4	129.3	129.0	128.4	129.7	130.4	129.8	129.3	129.0	129.0	128.4	127.3	129.1
1991	124.3	124.0	123.7	124.2	125.4	127.2	125.9	125.5	124.9	125.4	124.4	119.7	124.6
1992	120.0	119.7	119.5	120.1	120.7	122.1	121.4	121.6	120.6	121.4	120.7	120.0	120.7
1993	119.2	118.6	118.2	117.4	118.1	119.1	119.6	119.7	118.7	117.8	117.7	117.8	118.5
1994	117.4	116.8	116.8	115.7	115.9	117.9	117.9	118.0	116.9	117.3	117.5	117.8	117.2
1995	116.7	116.7	117.0	115.9	116.5	118.6	118.7	119.5	119.0	118.3	118.6	118.6	117.8
1996	117.7	117.2	116.9	117.1	117.4	119.0	118.2	118.5	117.3	117.3	117.3	117.3	117.6
1997	116.3	116.5	116.5	117.1	117.4	118.7	119.6	120.2	119.3	119.9	119.6	119.3	118.4
1998	118.1	117.0	116.5	115.9	115.3	116.6	114.5	116.2	115.8	114.6	114.4	113.6	115.7
1999	112.7	112.1	111.3	110.9	110.8	111.5	109.9	109.7	108.9	108.5	108.5	108.4	110.3
2000	107.5	106.7	106.6	105.8	105.7	106.9	106.7	106.5	106.5	105.8	105.3	105.0	106.3
2001	103.4	102.4	101.6	100.8	100.3	100.1	99.8	99.6	98.5	97.0	96.0	95.4	99.6
2002	94.6	92.9	92.5	91.9	91.6	91.2	90.8	90.9	89.5	89.4	89.4	88.8	91.1
2003	87.6	86.3	86.1	85.1	85.6	85.6	86.0	86.0	85.2	85.1	84.3	83.1	85.5

Employment by Industry: New York—*Continued*

(Numbers in thousands. Not seasonally adjusted.)

Industry	January	February	March	April	May	June	July	August	September	October	November	December	Annual Average
ROCHESTER—*Continued*													
Service-providing													
1990	354.4	358.5	360.6	362.5	369.2	369.7	359.8	360.6	367.1	370.9	373.0	372.5	364.9
1991	359.0	362.4	363.0	365.6	370.3	370.8	362.6	363.3	369.8	372.6	373.9	373.8	367.3
1992	361.9	365.5	365.6	369.9	374.3	373.6	363.8	364.1	369.4	378.3	380.1	381.7	370.7
1993	371.1	374.2	373.8	379.1	385.7	387.7	377.5	378.1	381.0	386.2	387.8	388.9	380.9
1994	373.9	377.4	377.8	383.1	388.2	388.9	379.6	379.5	385.9	389.1	392.2	391.2	383.9
1995	379.1	383.9	385.9	389.1	393.1	394.4	382.6	384.0	392.2	395.5	397.3	398.1	389.6
1996	385.0	389.7	390.4	391.9	397.7	398.4	387.9	386.9	392.6	397.1	398.9	398.6	392.9
1997	382.5	388.9	391.4	394.0	401.0	401.7	391.1	387.2	394.2	404.1	405.7	405.4	395.6
1998	391.5	396.7	398.9	400.9	409.2	410.6	400.6	399.6	407.3	413.7	415.0	417.8	405.2
1999	403.4	409.3	411.1	417.8	424.5	425.6	416.2	414.3	418.7	425.0	426.6	429.0	418.5
2000	413.6	418.8	422.0	428.6	432.9	434.6	424.8	424.3	429.8	430.8	432.6	434.8	427.3
2001	421.8	425.6	427.4	429.3	435.1	437.6	423.9	423.1	428.1	431.3	434.2	434.5	429.3
2002	415.8	420.0	422.2	425.0	431.2	432.2	422.9	423.1	426.9	430.8	432.5	434.7	426.4
2003	419.8	423.2	425.6	426.9	435.0	434.9	426.5	426.8	431.5	438.5	438.3	437.4	430.4
Trade, transportation, and utilities													
1990	89.6	88.2	88.4	87.6	88.7	89.6	88.8	89.3	88.9	89.1	90.5	91.6	89.2
1991	87.6	85.8	85.9	85.0	85.9	87.7	87.2	87.9	87.7	88.2	89.7	90.8	87.5
1992	86.0	83.3	83.0	84.1	85.5	86.5	85.5	86.1	85.5	87.8	89.5	91.7	86.2
1993	86.2	84.8	85.0	86.0	87.4	88.4	87.1	87.4	86.3	87.1	88.9	90.5	87.1
1994	87.5	85.1	85.4	85.2	86.7	88.5	87.3	87.8	87.5	87.8	89.4	90.4	87.4
1995	87.0	85.1	85.3	85.4	86.5	88.1	86.6	87.4	87.5	88.4	90.4	91.0	87.4
1996	87.3	85.7	85.5	84.5	86.4	87.3	85.9	86.4	86.5	88.0	89.4	90.9	87.0
1997	86.5	85.1	85.5	84.9	86.7	88.0	87.1	85.9	86.1	88.4	89.9	91.1	87.1
1998	88.0	86.2	86.8	86.9	89.4	90.6	89.6	89.5	89.3	90.1	91.7	94.4	89.4
1999	89.8	88.5	88.4	89.8	91.4	91.7	91.2	92.0	91.9	93.4	95.3	97.5	91.7
2000	92.9	91.1	91.2	91.4	92.6	93.4	92.3	93.0	92.4	92.8	94.5	96.3	92.8
2001	94.1	91.6	91.7	92.3	93.5	94.7	92.5	92.6	91.6	92.4	94.2	95.1	93.0
2002	91.2	89.0	88.8	88.9	90.4	91.4	90.2	90.6	89.6	89.8	91.2	92.3	90.3
2003	89.3	87.4	87.4	87.6	89.4	90.3	88.7	89.2	88.8	89.5	90.5	91.5	89.1
Wholesale trade													
1990	17.6	17.5	17.7	17.7	17.8	17.9	17.9	17.9	17.8	18.0	17.9	17.8	17.8
1991	17.6	17.6	17.6	17.5	17.6	17.8	17.8	17.8	17.7	17.4	17.5	17.5	17.6
1992	17.3	17.1	17.1	17.5	17.7	17.8	18.0	17.9	17.7	17.8	17.7	17.8	17.6
1993	17.6	17.5	17.7	18.0	18.2	18.5	18.3	18.3	17.9	17.9	17.9	18.0	18.0
1994	18.3	18.1	18.2	18.3	18.5	18.9	18.7	18.8	18.8	18.7	18.9	19.0	18.6
1995	19.1	18.9	19.0	19.0	19.1	19.7	19.7	19.8	19.6	19.0	19.0	18.8	19.2
1996	18.3	18.3	18.3	17.8	18.0	18.4	18.2	18.2	18.0	17.9	17.8	17.7	18.1
1997	17.5	17.4	17.6	17.6	17.8	18.0	18.1	17.9	17.6	18.0	18.0	17.9	17.8
1998	18.0	18.3	18.5	18.8	19.0	19.2	18.9	18.9	18.7	18.8	18.7	18.9	18.7
1999	18.6	18.6	18.7	18.8	19.0	19.2	19.3	19.3	19.0	18.8	18.9	19.0	18.9
2000	18.8	18.6	18.7	18.9	19.0	19.2	19.3	19.3	19.0	19.0	19.1	19.1	19.0
2001	20.3	20.2	20.2	20.3	20.5	20.8	20.5	20.3	19.9	19.9	19.9	19.8	20.2
2002	19.7	19.6	19.4	19.7	19.8	19.9	19.9	19.8	19.5	19.2	19.2	19.2	19.6
2003	19.0	18.8	18.8	18.9	19.1	19.3	19.4	19.3	18.9	18.7	18.7	18.7	19.0
Retail trade													
1990	61.2	59.9	59.9	59.1	60.0	60.7	60.2	60.6	59.8	60.0	61.5	62.9	60.5
1991	59.4	57.5	57.5	56.7	57.4	58.8	58.5	59.2	58.7	59.6	61.2	62.1	58.9
1992	57.2	54.7	54.4	55.1	56.2	57.1	56.6	57.3	56.2	58.3	60.1	62.1	57.1
1993	57.0	55.7	55.7	56.3	57.3	58.0	57.5	57.8	56.6	57.3	59.1	60.7	57.4
1994	57.6	55.5	55.8	55.7	56.7	58.0	57.7	58.1	57.2	57.6	59.1	60.0	57.4
1995	56.9	55.1	55.2	55.3	56.2	57.1	56.3	56.7	56.6	57.5	59.5	60.4	56.9
1996	57.7	56.0	55.8	55.2	56.8	57.2	56.8	57.4	57.0	58.4	59.9	61.5	57.5
1997	58.5	57.2	57.3	56.7	58.2	59.3	58.7	58.3	57.8	59.3	60.9	61.7	58.7
1998	59.1	56.9	57.3	56.8	58.9	59.9	59.7	59.5	59.1	59.9	61.7	63.7	59.4
1999	60.2	58.9	58.7	59.9	61.2	61.3	61.0	61.7	61.4	63.1	64.9	66.3	61.6
2000	63.0	61.4	61.4	61.2	62.3	62.9	62.3	63.0	62.0	62.4	64.0	65.0	62.6
2001	63.0	60.8	60.8	61.3	62.0	62.9	61.5	61.8	60.8	61.3	63.2	64.3	62.0
2002	61.6	59.5	59.6	59.4	60.7	61.5	61.0	61.4	60.2	60.5	62.0	63.1	60.9
2003	60.3	58.7	58.7	58.8	60.4	61.3	60.2	60.7	60.1	61.0	62.2	63.1	60.5
Transportation and utilities													
1990	10.8	10.8	10.8	10.8	10.9	11.0	10.7	10.8	11.3	11.1	11.1	10.9	10.9
1991	10.6	10.7	10.8	10.8	10.9	11.1	10.9	10.9	11.3	11.2	11.0	11.2	11.0
1992	11.5	11.5	11.5	11.5	11.6	11.6	10.9	10.9	11.6	11.7	11.7	11.8	11.5
1993	11.6	11.6	11.6	11.7	11.9	11.9	11.3	11.3	11.8	11.9	11.9	11.8	11.7
1994	11.6	11.5	11.4	11.2	11.5	11.6	10.9	10.9	11.5	11.5	11.4	11.4	11.4
1995	11.0	11.1	11.1	11.1	11.2	11.3	10.6	10.9	11.3	11.9	11.9	11.8	11.3
1996	11.3	11.4	11.4	11.5	11.6	11.7	10.9	10.8	11.5	11.7	11.7	11.7	11.4
1997	10.5	10.5	10.6	10.6	10.7	10.7	10.3	9.7	10.7	11.1	11.0	11.5	10.7
1998	10.9	11.0	11.0	11.3	11.5	11.5	11.0	11.1	11.5	11.4	11.3	11.8	11.3
1999	11.0	11.0	11.0	11.1	11.2	11.2	10.9	11.0	11.5	11.5	11.5	12.2	11.3
2000	11.1	11.1	11.1	11.3	11.3	11.3	10.7	10.7	11.4	11.4	11.4	12.2	11.3
2001	10.8	10.6	10.7	10.7	11.0	11.0	10.5	10.5	10.9	11.2	11.1	11.0	10.8
2002	9.9	9.9	9.8	9.8	9.9	10.0	9.3	9.4	9.9	10.1	10.0	10.0	9.8
2003	10.0	9.9	9.9	9.9	9.9	9.7	9.1	9.2	9.8	9.8	9.6	9.7	9.7

Employment by Industry: New York—*Continued*

(Numbers in thousands. Not seasonally adjusted.)

Industry	January	February	March	April	May	June	July	August	September	October	November	December	Annual Average
ROCHESTER—*Continued*													
Information													
1990	10.1	10.1	10.1	10.1	10.1	10.3	10.4	10.4	10.2	10.2	10.3	10.3	10.2
1991	9.7	9.8	9.9	9.7	9.7	9.8	10.1	10.0	9.9	9.9	9.9	9.9	9.9
1992	10.1	10.1	10.2	10.2	10.3	10.5	10.3	10.4	10.3	10.3	10.3	10.4	10.3
1993	10.0	9.9	10.0	9.9	9.9	10.0	10.0	10.0	9.8	9.8	9.9	9.9	9.9
1994	9.9	9.9	10.0	10.0	9.9	10.1	10.2	10.2	9.9	9.9	9.9	10.0	10.0
1995	10.2	10.2	10.3	10.3	10.4	10.5	10.6	10.7	10.6	10.5	10.5	10.6	10.5
1996	11.0	11.2	11.2	11.1	11.1	11.1	11.2	11.3	11.3	11.3	11.4	11.4	11.2
1997	11.3	11.3	11.3	10.9	10.8	10.8	10.7	10.7	10.5	10.4	10.4	10.6	10.8
1998	10.7	10.8	10.8	10.8	10.8	10.9	11.2	11.2	11.1	11.1	11.2	11.2	11.0
1999	11.3	11.4	11.5	11.7	11.7	11.8	11.9	11.8	11.8	12.0	12.1	12.2	11.8
2000	12.3	12.4	12.5	12.6	12.7	12.9	12.9	13.0	13.1	13.2	13.3	13.5	12.9
2001	14.2	14.3	14.4	14.2	14.4	14.5	14.4	14.3	14.1	14.4	14.5	14.6	14.4
2002	14.8	14.4	14.6	14.3	14.4	14.3	14.1	14.0	13.9	13.8	13.8	13.9	14.2
2003	13.6	13.6	13.5	13.6	13.8	13.8	13.7	13.8	13.6	14.1	14.0	14.1	13.8
Financial activities													
1990	23.9	23.8	23.9	24.1	24.3	24.6	24.9	25.0	24.5	24.3	24.4	24.2	24.3
1991	23.6	23.6	23.7	23.9	24.1	24.6	24.8	25.0	24.4	24.2	24.3	24.3	24.2
1992	23.3	23.2	23.2	23.4	23.7	24.1	24.1	24.1	23.6	23.4	23.4	23.5	23.6
1993	24.7	24.3	24.1	24.4	24.6	25.1	25.3	25.2	24.6	24.6	24.6	24.7	24.7
1994	24.6	24.7	24.6	24.4	24.7	25.2	25.1	25.1	24.7	24.4	24.4	24.5	24.7
1995	24.3	24.1	24.1	24.0	24.3	24.9	24.9	25.0	24.5	24.6	24.5	24.5	24.5
1996	24.3	24.5	24.3	24.3	24.5	25.1	25.3	25.3	24.7	24.4	24.5	24.6	24.7
1997	23.7	23.2	22.6	22.6	22.7	23.1	23.1	22.9	22.2	22.5	22.4	22.6	22.8
1998	21.9	21.9	22.1	21.9	22.2	22.5	22.8	22.7	22.0	21.8	21.9	21.8	22.1
1999	21.8	21.7	21.7	21.8	21.9	22.5	22.7	22.6	21.9	21.7	21.6	21.9	22.0
2000	21.9	22.0	21.9	22.3	22.4	23.0	22.7	22.5	21.9	22.1	22.1	22.1	22.2
2001	22.0	22.2	22.1	22.0	22.2	22.8	22.6	22.6	22.0	21.9	21.9	21.8	22.2
2002	21.3	21.3	21.2	21.2	21.5	21.9	22.3	22.4	21.7	21.7	21.7	21.7	21.7
2003	21.6	21.5	21.5	21.8	22.3	22.8	23.1	23.1	22.7	22.7	22.5	22.6	22.4
Professional and business services													
1990	40.9	41.3	41.9	41.7	42.3	42.8	42.7	43.2	43.1	42.3	42.3	41.5	42.2
1991	41.7	42.6	42.9	43.8	44.6	45.5	45.3	45.6	46.0	45.7	45.6	45.3	44.6
1992	43.7	43.8	44.0	44.9	45.5	46.2	46.1	46.3	46.4	46.9	46.9	46.4	45.6
1993	44.8	44.8	45.1	47.4	48.7	49.7	49.0	49.2	49.3	49.4	49.6	49.1	48.0
1994	45.0	45.2	45.3	45.2	45.5	46.4	46.5	46.4	46.1	47.8	47.6	47.1	46.2
1995	45.3	45.5	46.0	45.7	46.6	47.7	47.8	48.6	48.3	48.7	49.0	49.1	47.4
1996	47.5	48.1	48.3	48.8	49.7	50.3	50.7	50.9	50.8	51.5	51.2	50.9	49.9
1997	49.7	49.9	50.6	51.6	53.0	54.4	53.7	53.9	53.4	54.6	54.5	54.1	52.8
1998	51.8	51.6	51.9	52.6	53.8	55.2	56.2	56.5	56.7	57.3	57.1	57.0	54.8
1999	56.2	56.1	56.5	58.7	59.5	61.0	62.6	62.1	60.6	61.7	61.6	61.2	59.8
2000	59.1	59.3	59.7	60.4	61.0	62.8	63.7	63.5	62.7	62.2	61.8	61.3	61.5
2001	60.5	60.2	60.9	59.5	60.2	61.4	61.1	60.9	60.1	59.1	58.6	58.0	60.0
2002	54.7	54.8	54.9	56.8	57.6	58.8	58.7	58.6	58.4	57.8	58.1	57.8	57.3
2003	55.6	55.4	55.9	57.2	57.8	58.7	59.0	59.2	59.1	59.1	58.1	57.1	57.7
Educational and health services													
1990	68.0	70.3	70.5	70.2	70.8	69.3	68.7	68.1	73.4	75.4	75.0	75.0	71.2
1991	72.3	74.3	73.9	74.4	74.0	70.8	71.8	71.5	76.7	76.4	76.4	76.0	74.0
1992	77.2	79.3	79.0	78.4	78.0	74.6	73.3	73.2	77.7	79.7	79.6	79.5	77.5
1993	80.3	82.4	81.9	80.7	80.3	78.7	78.0	78.7	81.5	82.7	82.8	82.5	80.9
1994	80.8	83.0	82.8	85.8	85.4	81.3	80.5	80.4	86.7	85.5	85.5	85.2	83.6
1995	83.3	85.7	86.5	88.3	87.8	83.7	82.0	82.0	87.7	86.9	86.9	87.0	85.7
1996	84.5	86.4	86.4	86.8	86.1	83.9	82.2	81.8	85.2	85.7	85.9	86.0	85.1
1997	82.8	85.3	86.2	86.7	86.6	84.3	83.3	82.7	86.2	88.3	88.8	88.1	85.8
1998	86.1	88.4	88.4	88.6	88.6	85.9	84.3	84.5	88.1	89.9	90.5	90.1	87.8
1999	87.6	90.5	90.9	91.7	91.4	88.3	86.7	86.4	90.2	91.9	92.0	92.5	90.0
2000	89.6	91.9	93.0	95.9	94.7	92.1	91.3	90.6	95.5	94.8	95.3	95.9	93.4
2001	93.1	95.2	95.4	96.7	96.6	93.9	90.7	90.2	95.1	96.1	97.0	96.7	94.7
2002	93.6	95.8	96.6	96.5	95.9	93.2	92.5	92.5	97.0	98.7	99.1	99.3	95.9
2003	96.1	98.8	99.2	99.1	98.2	95.5	94.8	94.8	98.8	101.3	101.7	101.5	98.3
Leisure and hospitality													
1990	33.7	34.0	34.9	36.7	39.8	41.3	41.0	41.3	39.6	37.2	36.6	35.7	37.7
1991	33.8	33.4	34.4	35.8	38.5	39.9	39.8	40.0	38.4	36.1	35.2	34.6	36.7
1992	33.1	33.4	34.1	35.6	38.4	39.5	39.9	40.1	38.7	37.3	36.7	36.5	36.9
1993	33.9	34.4	33.9	36.4	39.7	40.9	41.2	41.7	40.1	38.4	36.2	36.4	37.8
1994	34.2	34.6	35.2	36.8	39.3	41.3	41.9	42.2	39.8	38.2	37.2	37.2	38.2
1995	35.3	35.8	36.5	37.5	40.1	42.8	42.7	43.5	41.9	39.4	37.8	38.0	39.3
1996	36.2	36.1	36.9	38.0	41.2	43.5	43.6	43.5	41.4	39.2	38.0	38.2	39.7
1997	36.3	36.4	37.4	39.0	42.9	45.2	45.2	44.5	41.8	40.8	39.7	40.3	40.8
1998	37.9	38.1	38.6	40.0	44.2	46.4	46.0	45.8	43.6	42.3	40.5	41.2	42.1
1999	38.1	38.3	38.6	41.3	45.7	48.1	46.6	46.3	44.0	42.4	40.7	41.1	42.6
2000	38.1	38.7	39.2	41.1	44.6	47.1	46.9	46.7	43.8	42.6	40.9	41.1	42.6
2001	36.6	36.9	37.4	39.0	42.9	45.7	45.9	45.6	42.4	40.9	39.7	39.7	41.1
2002	36.7	37.0	37.6	40.0	43.5	45.4	46.2	45.9	42.7	41.0	39.3	39.2	41.2
2003	37.4	37.2	38.0	38.9	43.6	45.1	46.6	46.4	43.5	41.4	40.2	40.4	41.6

Employment by Industry: New York—*Continued*

(Numbers in thousands. Not seasonally adjusted.)

Industry	January	February	March	April	May	June	July	August	September	October	November	December	Annual Average
ROCHESTER—*Continued*													
Other services													
1990	15.9	16.1	16.1	16.4	16.7	16.7	16.6	16.7	16.8	16.8	16.9	16.9	16.6
1991	16.1	16.2	16.3	16.3	16.4	16.6	16.2	16.3	16.3	16.1	16.1	16.0	16.2
1992	15.7	15.8	15.8	16.1	16.3	16.3	16.2	16.3	16.4	16.6	16.5	16.6	16.2
1993	16.1	16.1	16.1	16.3	16.5	16.7	16.3	16.3	16.2	16.2	16.3	16.3	16.3
1994	15.8	15.9	15.8	16.5	16.7	16.8	17.0	17.0	16.8	16.3	16.4	16.3	16.4
1995	16.6	16.5	16.8	16.9	17.1	17.3	17.1	17.1	17.1	17.3	17.4	17.4	17.1
1996	17.5	17.3	17.4	17.1	17.3	17.6	17.9	18.1	17.9	16.7	16.8	16.8	17.4
1997	16.6	16.6	16.7	16.8	17.0	17.0	17.1	16.9	16.7	16.7	16.9	16.8	16.8
1998	16.8	16.7	16.9	16.9	17.1	17.3	17.3	17.3	17.2	17.5	17.6	17.7	17.2
1999	18.0	18.0	18.0	18.1	18.2	18.2	18.2	18.0	17.9	18.1	18.2	18.3	18.1
2000	18.2	18.3	18.4	18.6	18.8	19.1	18.8	18.9	18.5	18.7	18.7	18.8	18.7
2001	18.0	18.2	18.3	18.4	18.5	18.9	18.8	18.8	18.4	18.6	18.9	18.8	18.6
2002	18.8	18.9	18.9	19.3	19.4	19.5	19.6	19.8	19.6	19.8	19.9	19.9	19.5
2003	19.6	19.6	19.8	19.8	20.1	20.1	20.2	20.1	20.0	20.2	20.1	20.1	20.0
Government													
1990	72.3	74.7	74.8	75.7	76.5	75.1	66.7	66.6	70.6	75.6	77.0	77.3	73.6
1991	74.2	76.7	76.0	76.7	77.1	75.9	67.4	67.0	70.4	76.0	76.7	76.9	74.3
1992	72.8	76.6	76.3	77.2	76.6	75.9	68.4	67.6	70.8	76.3	77.2	77.1	74.4
1993	75.1	77.5	77.7	78.0	78.6	78.2	70.6	69.6	73.2	78.0	79.5	79.5	76.3
1994	76.1	79.0	78.7	79.2	80.0	79.3	71.1	70.4	74.4	79.2	81.8	80.5	77.5
1995	77.1	81.0	80.4	81.0	80.3	79.4	70.9	69.7	74.6	79.7	80.8	80.5	78.0
1996	76.7	80.4	80.4	81.3	81.4	79.6	71.1	69.6	74.8	80.3	81.7	79.8	78.1
1997	75.6	81.1	81.1	81.5	81.3	78.9	70.9	69.7	77.3	82.4	83.1	81.8	78.7
1998	78.3	83.0	83.4	83.2	83.1	81.8	73.2	72.1	79.3	83.7	84.5	84.4	80.8
1999	80.6	84.8	85.5	84.7	84.7	84.0	76.3	75.1	80.4	83.8	85.1	84.3	82.4
2000	81.5	85.1	86.1	86.3	86.1	84.2	76.2	76.1	81.9	84.4	86.0	85.8	83.3
2001	83.3	87.0	87.2	87.2	86.8	85.7	77.9	78.1	84.4	87.9	89.4	89.8	85.4
2002	84.7	88.8	89.6	88.0	88.5	87.7	79.3	79.3	84.0	88.2	89.4	90.6	86.5
2003	86.6	89.7	90.3	88.9	89.8	88.6	80.4	80.2	85.0	90.2	91.2	90.1	87.6
Federal government													
1990	5.8	5.9	5.9	6.5	7.1	6.5	6.4	5.9	5.8	5.7	5.7	5.7	6.1
1991	5.7	5.7	5.7	5.7	5.7	5.8	5.9	5.8	5.8	5.7	5.7	5.8	5.8
1992	5.8	5.8	5.8	5.8	5.8	5.9	5.9	5.8	5.8	5.7	5.7	5.8	5.8
1993	5.7	5.6	5.6	5.7	5.7	5.8	5.8	5.8	5.8	5.8	5.8	5.9	5.8
1994	5.9	5.9	5.9	5.9	5.9	5.9	5.9	5.9	5.8	5.8	5.8	5.9	5.9
1995	5.7	5.7	5.7	5.8	5.8	5.9	5.9	5.8	5.8	5.8	5.8	5.9	5.8
1996	5.8	5.8	5.8	5.8	5.8	5.9	5.8	5.8	5.8	5.7	5.7	5.8	5.8
1997	5.7	5.7	5.7	5.7	5.7	5.7	5.7	5.7	5.6	5.5	5.5	5.7	5.7
1998	5.5	5.5	5.5	5.6	5.6	5.5	5.5	5.5	5.5	5.6	5.5	5.7	5.5
1999	5.5	5.6	5.6	5.5	5.5	5.5	5.6	5.5	5.6	5.5	5.5	5.6	5.5
2000	5.6	5.6	5.7	6.1	7.0	5.8	6.0	5.5	5.5	5.4	5.5	5.5	5.8
2001	5.5	5.4	5.4	5.4	5.3	5.4	5.4	5.3	5.3	5.3	5.3	5.3	5.4
2002	5.3	5.3	5.3	5.3	5.3	5.5	5.5	5.5	5.4	5.5	5.5	5.8	5.4
2003	5.6	5.6	5.5	5.5	5.5	5.5	5.5	5.5	5.5	5.6	5.6	6.0	5.6
State government													
1990	13.6	13.6	13.7	13.7	13.8	13.2	13.0	13.0	13.9	13.9	14.2	14.3	13.7
1991	13.9	13.9	13.8	13.6	13.7	13.0	12.7	12.6	13.4	13.5	13.5	13.7	13.4
1992	13.7	13.7	13.6	13.7	13.2	13.2	13.0	13.0	13.5	13.9	13.8	13.8	13.5
1993	14.1	14.1	14.2	14.2	14.2	14.1	13.1	13.2	14.2	14.3	14.3	14.3	14.0
1994	13.2	13.9	13.9	14.0	13.9	13.4	13.2	13.4	13.9	13.9	14.0	13.9	13.7
1995	13.7	14.7	14.5	14.4	13.9	12.9	12.5	12.4	14.2	14.2	14.3	13.4	13.8
1996	13.3	14.4	14.1	14.3	14.0	12.9	12.4	12.2	13.9	14.0	14.1	12.5	13.5
1997	12.8	14.0	14.0	14.1	13.8	12.3	12.3	12.2	14.0	14.1	14.2	12.6	13.4
1998	12.4	14.0	14.1	14.2	13.9	12.3	12.2	12.2	13.9	14.1	14.1	13.2	13.4
1999	12.4	14.0	14.1	14.2	13.9	12.3	12.3	12.3	14.2	14.3	14.5	13.4	13.5
2000	12.6	14.2	14.4	14.4	14.2	12.5	12.5	12.5	14.3	14.5	14.7	13.6	13.7
2001	13.0	14.7	14.9	14.8	14.5	12.7	12.7	12.7	14.7	14.9	15.0	13.9	14.0
2002	13.1	14.9	15.1	14.9	14.7	13.9	13.9	13.8	14.8	14.9	14.9	14.8	14.5
2003	14.3	14.7	14.7	14.5	14.4	13.5	13.6	13.5	14.4	14.7	14.7	13.7	14.2
Local government													
1990	52.9	55.3	55.2	55.5	55.7	55.4	47.3	47.7	50.9	56.0	57.2	57.3	53.9
1991	54.6	57.1	56.5	57.4	57.7	57.1	48.8	48.6	51.2	56.7	57.5	57.5	55.1
1992	53.3	57.1	56.9	57.7	57.5	56.8	49.6	48.8	51.5	56.7	57.7	57.6	55.1
1993	55.4	57.7	58.0	58.1	58.6	58.3	51.7	50.6	53.3	57.9	59.4	59.3	56.5
1994	57.1	59.2	58.9	59.3	60.3	60.0	52.1	51.1	54.6	59.5	61.9	60.7	57.9
1995	57.7	60.5	60.2	60.9	60.5	60.6	52.6	51.4	54.6	59.7	60.7	61.1	58.4
1996	57.6	60.3	60.5	61.1	61.6	60.8	52.8	51.6	55.2	60.6	61.9	61.5	58.8
1997	57.0	61.3	61.4	61.7	61.8	60.9	52.9	51.8	57.6	62.8	63.4	63.6	59.7
1998	60.4	63.5	63.8	63.4	63.6	64.0	55.5	54.4	59.9	64.0	64.9	65.5	61.9
1999	62.7	65.2	65.8	65.0	65.3	66.2	58.4	57.3	60.6	64.0	65.1	65.3	63.4
2000	63.3	65.3	66.0	65.8	64.9	65.9	57.7	58.1	62.1	64.5	65.8	66.7	63.8
2001	64.8	66.9	66.9	67.0	67.0	67.6	59.8	60.1	64.4	67.7	69.1	70.6	66.0
2002	66.3	68.6	69.2	67.8	68.5	68.3	59.9	60.0	63.8	67.8	69.0	70.0	66.6
2003	66.7	69.4	70.1	68.9	69.9	69.6	61.3	61.2	65.1	69.9	70.9	70.4	67.8

Employment by Industry: New York—*Continued*

(Numbers in thousands. Not seasonally adjusted.)

Industry	January	February	March	April	May	June	July	August	September	October	November	December	Annual Average
SYRACUSE													
Total nonfarm													
1990	333.8	335.8	337.4	339.6	343.1	345.7	340.8	341.6	345.7	350.0	347.5	347.2	342.4
1991	329.9	330.7	329.0	332.5	333.3	335.8	329.5	331.8	332.5	336.2	336.2	335.9	332.8
1992	321.5	323.9	323.6	327.0	329.7	333.6	327.6	328.8	333.3	335.8	335.4	335.3	329.6
1993	322.4	324.2	323.9	327.6	331.3	334.3	329.0	328.6	333.5	335.2	335.0	333.6	329.9
1994	320.4	323.3	323.9	328.0	330.3	333.2	329.7	331.5	336.1	338.2	338.0	337.1	330.8
1995	326.7	329.2	329.9	332.6	334.0	335.5	327.8	328.9	334.4	336.2	336.9	336.3	332.4
1996	324.4	327.5	329.4	331.8	333.1	336.1	332.0	331.0	338.6	339.7	339.5	338.5	333.5
1997	326.9	329.2	332.1	336.4	337.2	338.1	333.7	331.4	338.6	341.9	342.5	342.1	335.8
1998	330.2	333.7	334.8	338.1	340.3	342.6	338.1	339.0	344.5	345.9	346.5	347.5	340.1
1999	338.1	341.2	341.5	347.6	350.9	351.2	345.7	346.3	351.6	353.5	354.5	353.3	348.0
2000	342.3	344.9	347.0	352.1	354.7	355.1	349.5	347.9	354.9	357.2	357.3	356.4	351.6
2001	343.2	346.7	347.1	351.2	355.6	355.2	347.1	345.0	347.8	351.7	351.7	350.4	349.4
2002	338.1	339.5	341.4	343.1	347.5	347.8	341.9	345.1	348.9	350.7	350.8	349.7	345.4
2003	337.4	339.6	340.7	342.6	347.4	346.7	339.8	341.7	346.7	350.9	350.7	350.0	344.5
Total private													
1990	275.5	276.4	277.7	279.4	282.3	284.8	284.1	285.6	288.4	289.8	286.9	286.4	283.1
1991	271.0	270.2	268.9	272.3	273.2	275.7	273.3	276.1	276.0	277.0	276.4	276.3	273.9
1992	264.1	264.6	264.2	267.3	270.3	274.3	271.8	273.6	276.1	275.9	274.9	275.2	271.0
1993	264.3	265.0	264.4	268.4	271.9	275.0	273.0	274.1	276.5	275.5	275.0	273.6	271.4
1994	261.9	262.8	263.1	267.1	269.2	272.1	272.2	273.8	277.8	277.3	276.4	275.5	270.8
1995	266.7	267.5	268.5	270.7	272.7	274.8	270.8	273.2	276.3	275.2	274.9	274.9	272.2
1996	264.9	266.5	268.4	270.6	272.2	275.5	275.1	275.2	279.3	278.8	277.8	277.3	273.5
1997	267.1	267.6	270.4	274.3	275.1	276.8	275.9	275.0	278.1	279.0	279.2	279.1	274.8
1998	270.2	271.6	272.6	275.6	277.4	280.0	279.3	281.4	283.3	285.0	285.0	286.5	279.0
1999	278.5	279.9	280.3	286.2	289.7	290.2	288.4	290.3	291.1	291.7	292.0	291.4	287.5
2000	281.4	282.2	284.2	288.3	290.6	292.1	290.2	290.2	292.5	294.0	293.0	292.9	289.3
2001	282.2	283.2	284.0	287.6	291.6	291.7	287.3	286.4	286.8	287.9	287.4	286.7	286.9
2002	275.5	274.6	276.6	278.4	282.5	283.4	280.1	284.9	286.6	286.2	285.7	284.7	281.6
2003	275.3	275.2	276.3	278.4	282.8	282.3	279.5	282.1	283.7	286.2	285.7	284.9	281.0
Goods-producing													
1990	63.8	63.5	63.8	65.6	66.9	68.7	68.7	69.2	69.3	67.8	64.9	64.2	66.4
1991	60.4	59.3	57.7	60.2	61.4	62.7	62.8	63.4	62.7	62.6	61.9	60.7	61.3
1992	59.0	58.4	58.2	59.0	60.3	62.1	62.0	62.6	62.2	61.4	60.3	59.3	60.4
1993	56.7	56.4	56.4	57.9	59.8	61.1	61.2	61.7	61.4	60.5	59.6	58.1	59.2
1994	54.7	54.4	54.7	56.4	58.4	60.1	60.5	60.8	60.7	60.0	59.3	57.7	58.1
1995	55.2	54.9	55.2	57.5	58.7	60.2	58.4	60.0	59.8	59.3	58.9	57.9	58.0
1996	56.0	55.5	56.1	57.3	58.8	60.4	60.8	61.3	60.8	60.2	59.1	58.1	58.7
1997	56.2	55.8	56.3	58.1	59.4	60.5	60.8	61.3	60.6	61.0	60.7	59.9	59.2
1998	58.0	58.1	58.7	60.5	61.2	62.7	63.0	63.7	63.5	63.9	64.0	63.4	61.7
1999	61.1	60.8	60.2	62.6	64.2	65.2	64.8	65.5	64.7	64.1	63.8	62.7	63.3
2000	60.1	59.6	60.0	61.9	63.3	64.6	64.2	64.5	63.8	63.4	62.4	61.5	62.4
2001	57.4	57.9	58.0	58.6	59.8	60.8	59.7	59.2	58.6	58.3	57.4	56.3	58.5
2002	53.9	53.5	53.9	54.2	55.4	56.2	54.1	56.3	55.6	54.8	54.2	53.0	54.6
2003	51.2	50.6	50.8	51.5	52.7	53.6	52.3	53.9	53.0	52.9	52.4	51.6	52.2
Construction and mining													
1990	14.6	14.1	14.0	15.1	16.7	17.9	18.6	19.3	19.3	18.1	17.0	15.5	16.7
1991	13.3	12.5	12.5	13.6	14.8	15.5	16.3	16.3	15.6	15.3	14.4	13.4	14.5
1992	12.3	11.9	11.8	12.4	13.8	14.7	15.1	15.6	15.4	15.0	14.2	13.2	13.8
1993	11.4	10.7	10.8	12.1	13.9	14.8	15.8	16.1	16.0	15.5	14.5	13.1	13.7
1994	10.7	10.2	10.5	12.1	13.8	14.9	15.4	15.6	15.4	15.0	14.3	12.7	13.4
1995	10.9	10.3	10.6	11.5	12.7	13.4	13.8	14.0	13.6	13.5	12.8	11.8	12.4
1996	10.1	9.7	10.1	10.9	12.2	13.2	14.1	14.3	14.0	13.8	12.9	12.0	12.3
1997	10.2	10.0	10.4	11.4	12.8	13.6	14.4	14.5	13.9	13.8	13.2	12.4	12.6
1998	11.2	11.1	11.1	12.3	13.3	14.1	14.5	14.8	14.5	14.5	14.3	13.5	13.3
1999	11.7	11.5	11.3	13.0	14.1	14.8	15.3	15.5	15.2	15.2	14.9	13.7	13.9
2000	11.4	11.1	11.5	13.0	14.1	15.1	15.6	15.7	15.3	15.0	14.4	13.3	13.8
2001	12.1	11.7	11.7	12.8	14.4	15.2	15.8	15.8	15.5	14.9	14.4	13.3	14.0
2002	11.6	11.3	11.6	12.3	13.6	14.4	15.1	15.2	14.6	14.5	14.1	13.0	13.4
2003	11.6	11.2	11.3	12.6	13.8	14.5	15.2	15.4	14.7	14.7	14.1	13.4	13.5
Manufacturing													
1990	49.2	49.4	49.8	50.5	50.2	50.8	50.1	49.9	50.0	49.7	47.9	48.7	49.7
1991	47.1	46.8	45.2	46.6	46.6	47.2	46.5	47.1	47.1	47.3	47.5	47.3	46.9
1992	46.7	46.5	46.4	46.6	46.5	47.4	46.9	47.0	46.8	46.4	46.1	46.1	46.6
1993	45.3	45.7	45.6	45.8	45.9	46.3	45.4	45.6	45.4	45.0	45.1	45.0	45.5
1994	44.0	44.2	44.2	44.3	44.6	45.2	45.1	45.2	45.3	45.0	45.0	45.0	44.8
1995	44.3	44.6	44.6	46.0	46.0	46.8	44.6	46.0	46.2	45.8	46.1	46.1	45.6
1996	45.9	45.8	46.0	46.4	46.6	47.2	46.7	47.0	46.8	46.4	46.2	46.1	46.4
1997	46.0	45.8	45.9	46.7	46.6	46.9	46.4	46.8	46.7	47.2	47.5	47.5	46.7
1998	46.8	47.0	47.6	48.2	47.9	48.6	48.5	48.9	49.0	49.4	49.7	49.9	48.5
1999	49.4	49.3	48.9	49.6	50.1	50.4	49.5	50.0	49.5	48.9	48.9	49.0	49.5
2000	48.7	48.5	48.5	48.9	49.2	49.5	48.6	48.8	48.5	48.4	48.0	48.2	48.7
2001	45.3	46.2	46.3	45.8	45.4	45.6	43.9	43.4	43.1	43.4	43.0	43.0	44.5
2002	42.3	42.2	42.3	41.9	41.8	41.8	39.0	41.1	41.0	40.3	40.1	40.0	41.2
2003	39.6	39.4	39.5	38.9	38.9	39.1	37.1	38.5	38.3	38.2	38.3	38.2	38.7

Employment by Industry: New York—*Continued*

(Numbers in thousands. Not seasonally adjusted.)

Industry	January	February	March	April	May	June	July	August	September	October	November	December	Annual Average
SYRACUSE—*Continued*													
Service-providing													
1990	270.0	272.3	273.6	274.0	276.2	277.0	272.1	272.4	276.4	282.2	282.6	283.0	276.0
1991	269.5	271.4	271.3	272.3	271.9	273.1	266.7	268.4	269.8	273.6	274.3	275.2	271.5
1992	262.5	265.5	265.4	268.0	269.4	271.5	265.6	266.2	271.1	274.4	275.1	276.0	269.2
1993	265.7	267.8	267.5	269.7	271.5	273.2	267.8	266.9	272.1	274.7	275.4	275.5	270.7
1994	265.7	268.9	269.2	271.6	271.9	273.1	269.2	270.7	275.4	278.2	278.7	279.4	272.7
1995	271.5	274.3	274.7	275.1	275.3	275.3	269.4	268.9	274.6	276.9	278.0	278.4	274.4
1996	268.4	272.0	273.3	274.5	274.3	275.7	271.2	269.7	277.8	279.5	280.4	280.4	274.8
1997	270.7	273.4	275.8	278.3	277.8	277.6	272.9	270.1	278.0	280.9	281.8	282.2	276.6
1998	272.2	275.6	276.1	277.6	279.1	279.9	275.1	275.3	281.0	282.0	282.5	284.1	278.4
1999	277.0	280.4	281.3	285.0	286.7	286.0	280.9	280.8	286.9	289.4	290.7	290.6	284.6
2000	282.2	285.3	287.0	290.2	291.4	290.5	285.3	283.4	291.1	293.8	294.9	294.9	289.2
2001	285.8	288.8	289.1	292.6	295.8	294.4	287.4	285.8	289.2	293.4	294.3	294.1	290.9
2002	284.2	286.0	287.5	288.9	292.1	291.6	287.8	288.8	293.3	295.9	296.6	296.7	290.8
2003	286.2	289.0	289.9	291.1	294.7	293.1	287.5	287.8	293.7	298.0	298.3	298.4	292.3
Trade, trasnportation, and utilities													
1990	79.8	79.1	79.1	77.9	78.1	79.1	78.5	79.1	79.1	81.2	82.2	82.8	79.7
1991	77.3	75.7	75.8	75.8	76.1	77.1	75.9	76.8	75.9	76.5	77.4	78.0	76.5
1992	72.5	71.4	71.2	71.3	72.2	73.2	72.1	72.6	72.4	73.7	74.6	75.5	72.7
1993	72.0	71.0	70.3	70.5	71.4	72.3	71.3	71.9	71.8	72.4	73.4	74.0	71.9
1994	70.3	69.6	69.4	69.6	70.0	70.7	70.4	71.2	71.9	72.9	73.5	74.4	71.2
1995	71.8	71.3	71.3	71.7	71.8	72.1	70.8	71.0	71.4	72.0	73.4	74.4	71.9
1996	70.4	69.6	69.6	69.6	70.0	71.1	70.5	70.4	71.3	71.6	72.9	73.7	70.9
1997	70.6	69.5	70.0	70.2	70.4	71.3	70.8	69.8	70.7	71.3	72.9	73.4	70.9
1998	70.0	68.7	68.5	68.7	69.8	71.2	69.5	69.8	69.4	70.7	72.0	73.1	70.1
1999	70.7	69.8	69.8	70.6	71.7	72.4	71.8	72.3	72.1	73.0	74.3	75.0	72.0
2000	72.4	71.5	72.0	72.1	73.1	74.1	73.5	74.1	73.5	74.2	75.2	76.0	73.5
2001	74.1	72.3	72.6	73.5	74.2	75.2	73.1	73.1	72.4	72.7	73.7	74.4	73.4
2002	72.0	69.9	70.3	70.7	72.1	73.5	72.2	73.3	73.0	73.4	73.9	74.7	72.4
2003	70.9	69.2	69.3	69.8	70.7	71.9	71.3	71.5	71.0	72.3	73.0	73.3	71.2
Wholesale trade													
1990	21.2	21.2	21.2	21.0	20.9	21.2	21.0	20.8	20.6	20.7	20.6	20.4	20.9
1991	19.4	19.2	19.2	19.4	19.3	19.5	19.3	19.3	18.9	18.9	18.7	18.6	19.1
1992	17.5	17.4	17.2	17.1	17.2	17.4	17.3	17.1	16.9	17.0	17.0	16.9	17.2
1993	16.5	16.5	16.4	16.3	16.5	16.7	16.7	16.7	16.5	16.8	16.9	16.9	16.6
1994	16.4	16.5	16.6	16.6	16.6	16.7	16.8	16.9	17.0	16.8	16.9	16.9	16.7
1995	16.5	16.6	16.8	16.6	16.6	16.4	16.5	16.5	16.5	16.4	16.4	16.4	16.5
1996	16.1	16.1	16.2	16.1	16.2	16.4	16.3	16.3	16.5	16.4	16.4	16.5	16.3
1997	16.0	16.0	16.0	16.1	16.3	16.4	16.4	16.5	16.4	16.5	16.6	16.7	16.3
1998	16.2	16.2	16.1	16.2	16.3	16.6	15.6	15.7	15.6	15.7	15.8	15.9	16.0
1999	15.7	15.7	15.6	15.7	16.0	16.2	16.1	16.1	16.1	16.1	16.1	16.0	16.0
2000	16.1	16.1	16.3	16.3	16.5	16.5	16.8	16.8	16.7	16.7	16.8	16.9	16.5
2001	17.5	17.5	17.4	17.6	17.6	17.7	17.5	17.4	17.2	17.1	17.0	17.0	17.4
2002	16.6	16.3	16.3	16.6	16.8	17.1	16.8	17.1	17.0	17.0	17.0	17.1	16.8
2003	16.4	16.2	16.2	16.3	16.6	16.7	16.4	16.3	16.0	16.1	16.3	16.4	16.3
Retail trade													
1990	42.0	41.1	41.0	40.3	40.5	40.9	40.5	41.1	41.4	43.4	44.4	45.2	41.8
1991	41.1	39.8	39.7	39.6	39.9	40.4	40.0	40.8	40.2	40.5	41.5	42.0	40.5
1992	38.7	37.6	37.4	37.6	38.2	38.7	38.1	38.6	38.5	39.6	40.4	41.3	38.7
1993	39.0	37.9	37.4	37.7	38.2	38.9	38.3	38.8	38.8	39.0	39.9	40.8	38.7
1994	38.1	37.3	37.2	37.5	37.5	38.3	38.1	38.8	39.1	40.2	41.2	42.2	38.8
1995	40.2	39.5	39.5	40.0	40.0	40.4	39.4	39.7	40.0	40.3	41.7	42.8	40.3
1996	40.0	39.3	39.0	39.1	39.5	40.2	39.9	40.0	40.3	40.3	41.7	42.5	40.2
1997	39.9	38.8	39.1	39.0	39.2	39.9	39.7	39.7	39.5	39.8	41.1	41.7	39.8
1998	39.3	38.0	37.9	37.7	38.5	39.5	39.0	39.2	38.8	40.0	41.1	42.1	39.3
1999	40.3	39.3	39.4	39.7	40.5	40.9	40.6	41.1	40.6	41.3	42.5	43.4	40.8
2000	41.1	40.0	40.2	40.5	41.3	42.2	41.6	42.0	41.2	41.9	42.9	43.6	41.5
2001	40.8	39.2	39.5	39.6	40.2	41.1	39.8	40.0	39.2	39.6	40.8	41.6	40.1
2002	39.8	38.3	38.4	38.5	39.4	40.3	39.8	40.6	39.9	40.4	40.8	41.7	39.8
2003	39.4	38.1	38.2	38.4	39.1	40.0	40.1	40.3	39.7	40.6	41.1	41.5	39.7
Transportation and utilities													
1990	16.6	16.8	16.9	16.6	16.7	17.0	17.0	17.2	17.1	17.1	17.2	17.2	17.0
1991	16.8	16.7	16.9	16.8	16.9	17.2	16.6	16.7	16.8	17.1	17.2	17.4	16.9
1992	16.3	16.4	16.6	16.6	16.8	17.1	16.7	16.9	17.0	17.1	17.2	17.3	16.8
1993	16.5	16.6	16.5	16.5	16.7	16.7	16.3	16.4	16.5	16.6	16.6	16.3	16.5
1994	15.8	15.8	15.6	15.5	15.9	15.7	15.5	15.5	15.8	15.9	15.4	15.3	15.6
1995	15.1	15.2	15.0	15.1	15.2	15.3	14.9	14.8	14.9	15.3	15.3	15.2	15.1
1996	14.3	14.2	14.4	14.4	14.3	14.5	14.3	14.1	14.5	14.9	14.8	14.7	14.5
1997	14.7	14.7	14.9	15.1	14.9	15.0	14.7	13.6	14.8	15.0	15.2	15.0	14.8
1998	14.5	14.5	14.5	14.8	15.0	15.1	14.9	14.9	15.0	15.0	15.1	15.1	14.9
1999	14.7	14.8	14.8	15.2	15.2	15.3	15.1	15.1	15.4	15.6	15.7	15.6	15.2
2000	15.2	15.4	15.5	15.3	15.3	15.4	15.1	15.3	15.6	15.6	15.5	15.5	15.4
2001	15.8	15.6	15.7	16.3	16.4	16.4	15.8	15.7	16.0	16.0	15.9	15.8	16.0
2002	15.6	15.3	15.6	15.6	15.9	16.1	15.6	15.6	16.1	16.0	16.1	15.9	15.8
2003	15.1	14.9	14.9	15.1	15.0	15.2	14.8	14.9	15.3	15.6	15.6	15.4	15.2

Employment by Industry: New York—*Continued*

(Numbers in thousands. Not seasonally adjusted.)

Industry	January	February	March	April	May	June	July	August	September	October	November	December	Annual Average
SYRACUSE—*Continued*													
Information													
1990	8.0	8.0	8.1	8.0	8.0	7.9	7.9	7.8	7.9	8.0	8.0	7.9	8.0
1991	7.8	7.7	7.6	7.6	7.6	7.7	7.5	7.5	7.5	7.4	7.4	7.3	7.6
1992	6.8	6.8	6.8	6.9	6.9	6.9	7.0	6.9	6.8	6.9	6.9	6.9	6.9
1993	6.7	6.7	6.6	6.6	6.6	6.7	6.6	6.6	6.6	6.6	6.6	6.7	6.6
1994	6.5	6.6	6.4	6.4	6.4	6.5	6.5	6.5	6.5	6.6	6.7	6.5	6.5
1995	6.7	6.6	6.7	6.7	6.7	6.8	6.7	6.7	6.7	6.7	6.8	6.6	6.7
1996	6.5	6.5	6.6	6.5	6.4	6.6	6.6	6.6	6.7	6.7	6.7	6.7	6.6
1997	7.2	7.1	7.1	6.9	7.0	7.2	7.0	6.9	6.9	6.9	6.9	7.0	7.0
1998	7.0	7.0	7.0	7.1	7.0	7.2	7.2	7.1	7.1	7.2	7.1	7.2	7.1
1999	7.3	7.4	7.4	7.6	7.6	7.7	7.6	7.7	7.7	7.7	7.8	7.9	7.6
2000	7.7	7.7	7.8	8.0	8.0	8.1	8.3	7.5	8.3	8.3	8.4	8.5	8.1
2001	8.6	8.7	8.6	8.6	8.5	8.7	8.7	8.4	8.3	8.2	8.2	8.1	8.5
2002	7.3	7.3	7.3	7.4	7.4	7.5	7.5	7.5	7.4	7.4	7.4	7.5	7.4
2003	7.3	7.2	7.1	7.2	7.2	7.2	7.2	7.3	7.2	7.2	7.3	7.3	7.2
Financial activities													
1990	21.1	21.3	21.3	21.1	21.1	21.2	21.4	21.4	21.4	21.4	21.6	21.8	21.3
1991	21.1	21.1	21.3	21.4	21.3	21.5	21.4	21.4	21.1	21.0	21.0	21.1	21.2
1992	20.4	20.5	20.5	20.5	20.4	20.7	20.6	20.6	20.5	20.3	20.3	20.2	20.5
1993	19.8	19.9	19.9	19.8	19.9	20.1	20.2	20.1	20.0	19.8	19.8	19.9	19.9
1994	19.3	19.5	19.4	19.4	19.4	19.5	19.5	19.6	19.6	19.5	19.6	19.6	19.5
1995	19.0	18.9	19.0	18.5	18.5	18.7	18.8	18.9	18.8	18.3	18.4	18.5	18.7
1996	18.1	18.1	18.1	18.1	18.0	18.3	18.4	18.3	18.1	18.1	18.2	18.2	18.2
1997	18.0	18.1	18.2	18.1	18.1	18.3	18.3	18.2	18.0	17.9	17.9	18.0	18.1
1998	18.1	17.9	18.0	18.6	18.5	18.8	18.8	18.8	18.7	18.5	18.5	18.6	18.5
1999	18.6	18.6	18.6	18.9	18.9	19.2	19.2	19.1	18.7	18.7	18.8	18.8	18.8
2000	18.4	18.2	18.4	18.3	18.4	18.5	18.5	18.5	18.3	18.0	18.0	18.2	18.3
2001	18.2	18.2	18.2	18.2	18.4	18.7	18.4	18.5	18.1	18.3	18.2	18.3	18.3
2002	17.9	17.8	17.9	17.9	17.9	18.1	18.4	18.4	18.0	17.8	17.7	17.7	18.0
2003	17.8	17.8	17.8	17.7	17.9	18.1	18.2	18.2	18.0	17.7	17.7	17.7	17.9
Professional and business services													
1990	27.2	27.5	27.7	28.1	28.8	28.4	28.6	28.8	30.2	30.7	29.9	29.0	28.7
1991	27.9	28.1	27.8	28.0	26.5	27.2	26.4	26.8	27.6	28.0	27.5	27.9	27.5
1992	27.2	27.5	27.4	28.8	28.1	29.4	29.0	29.2	30.9	30.4	29.9	30.4	29.0
1993	29.3	30.0	30.4	30.4	29.9	31.1	30.0	30.0	31.6	31.7	31.4	31.0	30.6
1994	30.1	30.1	30.0	30.4	29.4	29.9	30.0	29.8	31.1	31.0	30.7	30.7	30.3
1995	30.6	30.7	30.5	30.9	30.0	30.4	30.3	30.3	30.5	30.4	30.0	29.7	30.4
1996	29.2	29.5	30.0	30.6	30.8	31.3	31.4	31.4	31.6	31.6	31.2	30.9	30.8
1997	29.2	29.4	29.8	30.1	30.1	30.6	31.1	30.9	30.8	31.0	30.6	30.4	30.3
1998	30.2	30.7	30.6	30.1	30.6	31.3	31.4	32.0	31.6	31.6	31.3	31.7	31.1
1999	30.3	30.7	30.8	31.2	31.4	32.2	32.4	32.4	32.0	31.8	31.6	31.8	31.6
2000	30.8	30.9	31.1	31.2	31.4	31.8	31.3	31.7	31.2	32.2	32.1	31.6	31.4
2001	30.8	30.8	30.7	31.3	31.7	31.9	31.7	31.4	30.8	31.3	30.9	31.0	31.2
2002	29.7	29.7	29.8	30.5	30.8	31.8	32.3	32.6	32.1	32.1	32.2	31.9	31.3
2003	32.6	32.5	32.8	33.7	34.2	34.5	34.9	35.5	35.0	35.5	35.4	35.0	34.3
Educational and health services													
1990	40.7	41.7	42.1	41.7	41.7	41.0	40.8	41.0	42.8	43.3	43.5	43.7	42.0
1991	42.0	43.3	43.6	43.9	43.6	42.4	42.1	42.3	44.2	45.1	45.3	45.6	43.6
1992	44.6	46.1	46.2	45.9	45.6	44.6	43.9	44.0	46.1	46.8	47.1	47.1	45.7
1993	45.8	47.0	47.2	47.7	47.4	46.4	45.9	46.0	47.7	48.3	48.1	48.1	47.1
1994	47.3	48.4	48.8	49.0	48.6	47.5	47.0	47.2	49.6	49.9	49.7	49.9	48.6
1995	48.5	49.8	50.1	49.5	49.2	48.5	47.8	47.8	51.4	51.5	51.4	51.5	49.8
1996	50.5	52.2	52.5	52.5	51.0	49.9	49.1	49.0	52.9	53.4	53.5	53.7	51.7
1997	51.2	52.6	53.3	54.1	52.3	50.5	49.2	49.3	53.0	53.2	53.3	53.4	52.1
1998	51.7	53.3	53.7	53.3	51.9	49.9	49.7	50.2	54.2	54.2	54.3	54.3	52.6
1999	53.4	54.9	55.0	55.1	54.2	51.5	50.7	50.3	53.8	54.8	54.8	54.7	53.6
2000	52.9	54.4	54.8	55.2	53.5	51.7	51.0	50.5	54.1	55.2	55.1	55.4	53.7
2001	54.3	55.5	55.9	56.3	56.0	52.9	52.4	52.3	55.7	56.9	57.4	57.4	55.3
2002	55.8	57.2	57.5	56.7	56.4	53.2	52.3	53.2	57.0	58.3	58.7	58.7	56.3
2003	56.0	58.0	58.1	57.8	57.1	53.7	52.1	52.4	56.7	58.0	57.7	58.3	56.3
Leisure and hospitality													
1990	24.4	24.8	25.0	26.3	27.0	27.6	27.1	27.3	26.9	26.5	25.8	26.0	26.2
1991	23.8	24.2	24.3	24.5	25.8	26.1	26.2	26.9	26.2	25.4	24.8	24.6	25.2
1992	22.7	22.9	22.9	24.0	25.7	26.1	26.0	26.5	26.1	25.3	24.6	24.7	24.8
1993	23.1	22.9	22.5	24.2	25.5	25.8	26.3	26.3	25.9	24.5	24.4	24.1	24.6
1994	22.4	22.6	22.8	24.0	25.2	26.0	26.1	26.6	26.3	25.2	24.6	24.4	24.7
1995	23.0	23.4	23.6	23.9	25.7	26.0	25.9	26.5	25.8	25.0	24.1	24.3	24.8
1996	22.6	23.2	23.5	23.9	25.2	25.9	26.2	26.1	25.8	24.8	23.9	23.7	24.6
1997	22.7	22.9	23.3	24.4	25.5	26.1	26.3	26.3	25.7	25.0	24.3	24.3	24.7
1998	22.9	23.3	23.4	24.5	25.7	26.2	26.8	26.9	26.0	26.0	25.0	25.2	25.2
1999	24.0	24.5	24.8	26.1	27.5	27.8	27.6	28.6	27.7	27.1	26.4	26.0	26.5
2000	25.0	25.6	25.7	27.0	28.4	28.9	28.9	29.1	28.9	28.0	27.3	27.1	27.5
2001	24.9	25.7	25.9	27.3	29.3	29.7	29.4	29.8	29.2	28.0	27.4	27.0	27.8
2002	25.1	25.3	25.9	27.1	28.6	29.0	29.3	29.5	29.5	28.2	27.3	26.9	27.6
2003	25.3	25.7	26.1	26.6	28.8	29.2	29.7	29.5	29.1	28.4	27.9	27.5	27.8

Employment by Industry: New York—*Continued*

(Numbers in thousands. Not seasonally adjusted.)

Industry	January	February	March	April	May	June	July	August	September	October	November	December	Annual Average
SYRACUSE—*Continued*													
Other services													
1990	10.5	10.5	10.6	10.7	10.7	10.9	11.1	11.0	10.8	10.9	11.0	11.0	10.8
1991	10.7	10.8	10.8	10.9	10.9	11.0	11.0	11.0	10.8	11.0	11.1	11.1	10.9
1992	10.9	11.0	11.0	10.9	11.1	11.3	11.2	11.2	11.1	11.1	11.2	11.1	11.1
1993	10.9	11.1	11.1	11.3	11.4	11.5	11.5	11.5	11.5	11.7	11.7	11.7	11.4
1994	11.3	11.6	11.6	11.9	11.8	11.9	12.2	12.1	12.1	12.2	12.3	12.3	11.9
1995	11.9	11.9	12.1	12.0	12.1	12.1	12.1	12.0	11.9	12.0	11.9	12.0	12.0
1996	11.6	11.9	12.0	12.1	12.0	12.0	12.1	12.1	12.1	12.4	12.3	12.3	12.1
1997	12.0	12.2	12.4	12.4	12.3	12.3	12.4	12.3	12.4	12.7	12.6	12.7	12.4
1998	12.3	12.6	12.7	12.8	12.7	12.7	12.9	12.9	12.8	12.9	12.8	13.0	12.8
1999	13.1	13.2	13.7	14.1	14.2	14.2	14.3	14.4	14.4	14.5	14.5	14.5	14.1
2000	14.1	14.3	14.4	14.6	14.5	14.4	14.5	14.3	14.4	14.7	14.5	14.6	14.4
2001	13.9	14.1	14.1	13.8	13.7	13.8	13.9	13.7	13.7	14.2	14.2	14.2	13.9
2002	13.8	13.9	14.0	13.9	13.9	14.1	14.0	14.1	14.0	14.2	14.3	14.3	14.0
2003	14.2	14.2	14.3	14.1	14.2	14.1	13.8	13.8	13.7	14.2	14.3	14.2	14.1
Government													
1990	58.3	59.4	59.7	60.2	60.8	60.9	56.7	56.0	57.3	60.2	60.6	60.8	59.2
1991	58.9	60.5	60.1	60.2	60.1	60.1	56.2	55.7	56.5	59.2	59.8	59.6	58.9
1992	57.4	59.3	59.4	59.7	59.4	59.3	55.8	55.2	57.2	59.9	60.5	60.1	58.6
1993	58.1	59.2	59.5	59.2	59.4	59.3	56.0	54.5	57.0	59.7	60.0	60.0	58.5
1994	58.5	60.5	60.8	60.9	61.1	61.1	57.5	57.7	58.3	60.9	61.6	61.6	60.0
1995	60.0	61.7	61.4	61.9	61.3	60.7	57.0	55.7	58.1	61.0	62.0	61.4	60.2
1996	59.5	61.0	61.0	61.2	60.9	60.6	56.9	55.8	59.3	60.9	61.7	61.2	60.0
1997	59.8	61.6	61.7	62.1	62.1	61.3	57.8	56.4	60.5	62.9	63.3	63.0	61.0
1998	60.0	62.1	62.2	62.5	62.9	62.6	58.8	57.6	61.2	60.9	61.5	61.0	61.1
1999	59.6	61.3	61.2	61.4	61.2	61.0	57.3	56.0	60.5	61.8	62.5	61.9	60.5
2000	60.9	62.7	62.8	63.8	64.1	63.0	59.3	57.7	62.4	63.2	64.3	63.5	62.3
2001	61.0	63.5	63.1	63.6	64.0	63.5	59.8	58.6	61.0	63.8	64.3	63.7	62.5
2002	62.6	64.9	64.8	64.7	65.0	64.4	61.8	60.2	62.3	64.5	65.1	65.0	63.8
2003	62.1	64.4	64.4	64.2	64.6	64.4	60.3	59.6	63.0	64.7	65.0	65.1	63.5
Federal government													
1990	4.5	4.5	4.6	4.9	5.4	5.1	5.1	4.7	4.5	4.4	4.5	4.5	4.7
1991	4.4	4.4	4.3	4.3	4.4	4.5	4.6	4.6	4.5	4.5	4.6	4.6	4.5
1992	4.5	4.5	4.5	4.5	4.5	4.5	4.5	4.5	4.5	4.5	4.4	4.6	4.5
1993	4.5	4.5	4.5	4.5	4.5	4.5	4.6	4.6	4.5	4.5	4.5	4.6	4.5
1994	4.7	4.7	4.7	4.7	4.7	4.7	4.6	4.6	4.6	4.6	4.6	4.6	4.7
1995	4.7	4.7	4.7	4.7	4.7	4.7	4.6	4.6	4.6	4.6	4.6	4.6	4.7
1996	5.0	5.0	5.0	4.9	4.9	5.0	5.0	5.1	5.0	5.0	5.0	5.0	5.0
1997	4.9	4.9	4.9	4.9	4.9	5.0	4.9	5.0	5.0	5.0	5.1	5.1	5.0
1998	5.0	4.9	5.0	5.0	5.0	5.0	4.9	4.9	4.9	5.0	5.1	5.2	5.0
1999	5.1	5.1	5.0	5.1	5.0	5.0	5.0	5.0	5.0	5.0	5.1	5.1	5.0
2000	5.0	5.0	5.2	5.5	6.0	5.4	5.4	5.1	5.0	5.1	5.2	5.3	5.3
2001	4.9	4.8	4.8	4.8	4.8	4.9	4.8	4.8	4.7	4.7	4.7	4.7	4.8
2002	4.8	4.8	4.8	4.8	4.7	4.7	4.7	4.8	4.8	4.8	4.8	4.9	4.8
2003	4.9	4.9	4.9	4.9	4.9	4.9	4.9	4.9	4.9	4.8	4.8	4.8	4.9
State government													
1990	14.3	14.5	14.5	14.6	14.6	14.4	14.3	14.3	14.8	14.9	14.8	14.8	14.6
1991	14.3	14.5	14.4	14.4	14.2	14.0	13.9	13.9	14.3	14.3	14.3	14.3	14.2
1992	14.3	14.5	14.3	14.5	14.2	14.1	14.3	14.4	14.8	14.9	14.8	14.6	14.5
1993	14.3	14.5	14.5	14.4	14.1	13.9	13.7	13.8	14.5	14.5	14.5	14.5	14.3
1994	13.9	14.6	14.7	14.7	14.8	14.3	14.4	14.5	15.1	15.0	15.0	15.1	14.7
1995	14.9	15.4	15.2	15.3	14.9	14.2	14.3	14.2	15.1	15.3	15.3	15.0	14.9
1996	14.7	15.2	15.2	15.2	15.0	14.5	14.4	14.4	15.3	15.4	15.4	14.9	15.0
1997	14.6	15.3	15.2	15.3	15.1	14.4	14.5	14.4	15.3	15.5	15.6	15.0	15.0
1998	14.4	15.3	15.2	15.4	15.3	14.7	14.7	14.7	15.5	15.5	15.5	14.7	15.1
1999	14.3	15.2	15.1	15.3	15.1	14.6	14.7	14.7	15.5	15.4	15.4	14.6	15.0
2000	14.7	15.6	15.5	15.7	15.7	15.0	15.1	15.1	16.0	16.0	16.1	15.2	15.5
2001	14.7	15.8	15.7	15.9	15.8	15.0	15.1	15.1	16.1	16.2	16.3	15.3	15.6
2002	15.4	16.6	16.5	15.7	15.7	15.4	15.4	15.4	15.8	15.9	15.9	15.7	15.8
2003	15.1	15.5	15.5	15.4	15.5	15.2	15.1	15.1	15.6	15.5	15.5	15.5	15.4
Local government													
1990	39.5	40.4	40.6	40.7	40.8	41.4	37.2	37.0	38.1	40.9	41.4	41.4	40.0
1991	40.1	41.6	41.3	41.4	41.4	41.5	37.6	37.1	37.7	40.3	41.0	40.7	40.1
1992	38.6	40.3	40.6	40.7	40.7	40.7	37.0	36.3	37.9	40.5	41.3	40.8	39.6
1993	39.3	40.2	40.5	40.2	40.9	40.9	37.7	36.2	38.0	40.6	41.0	40.9	39.7
1994	39.9	41.2	41.4	41.5	41.6	42.1	38.5	38.5	38.7	41.3	42.1	41.9	40.7
1995	40.4	41.6	41.5	41.9	41.7	41.7	38.1	37.0	38.4	41.2	42.0	41.8	40.6
1996	39.8	40.8	40.8	41.1	41.0	41.1	37.4	36.3	39.1	40.5	41.3	41.3	40.0
1997	40.3	41.5	41.6	41.9	42.0	42.0	38.4	37.0	40.3	42.4	42.7	42.9	41.1
1998	40.6	41.9	42.0	42.1	42.6	42.9	39.2	38.0	40.8	40.4	40.9	41.1	41.0
1999	40.2	41.0	41.1	41.0	41.1	41.4	37.6	36.3	40.0	41.4	42.0	42.2	40.4
2000	41.2	42.1	42.1	42.6	42.4	42.6	38.8	37.5	41.4	42.1	43.0	43.0	41.6
2001	41.4	42.9	42.6	42.9	43.4	43.6	39.9	38.7	40.2	42.9	43.3	43.7	42.1
2002	42.4	43.5	43.5	44.2	44.6	44.3	41.7	40.0	41.7	43.8	44.4	44.4	43.2
2003	42.1	44.0	44.0	43.9	44.2	44.3	40.3	39.6	42.5	44.4	44.7	44.8	43.2

Employment by Industry: New York—*Continued*

(Numbers in thousands. Not seasonally adjusted.)

Industry	January	February	March	April	May	June	July	August	September	October	November	December	Annual Average
WESTCHESTER COUNTY													
Total nonfarm													
1990	400.2	401.2	404.6	405.3	410.6	416.5	412.5	408.1	407.5	406.2	403.9	404.0	406.7
1991	383.1	381.7	383.6	387.5	391.2	395.2	389.6	387.4	386.7	387.0	389.0	389.7	387.6
1992	369.9	368.6	371.1	376.9	380.5	384.2	379.2	375.3	375.0	378.2	378.6	379.4	376.4
1993	364.2	364.9	365.8	369.4	374.3	379.2	374.1	372.0	372.3	374.6	377.9	379.7	372.4
1994	361.9	362.2	366.5	371.3	376.4	381.9	376.4	376.2	376.3	380.2	383.1	383.8	374.7
1995	368.7	369.2	374.8	376.2	380.9	385.9	379.6	379.7	378.9	382.9	386.5	388.0	379.3
1996	370.4	373.9	377.2	380.4	385.9	391.8	384.6	383.1	381.6	386.9	390.8	393.7	383.4
1997	375.1	377.0	381.9	383.2	388.2	394.7	391.5	391.0	391.5	396.5	399.0	403.1	389.4
1998	386.6	387.4	390.6	392.9	397.6	402.6	398.2	395.7	394.4	398.3	402.0	404.9	395.9
1999	394.1	396.9	400.2	406.0	408.6	413.9	410.4	407.4	408.7	414.1	417.1	420.4	408.2
2000	403.4	405.2	410.6	414.5	419.4	424.3	419.7	416.2	418.9	425.0	428.8	431.1	418.1
2001	412.1	413.0	416.2	417.1	422.4	425.6	418.3	415.4	414.4	419.2	421.8	423.4	418.2
2002	406.1	407.6	412.5	414.3	418.0	421.2	415.8	413.1	414.4	419.8	420.9	423.6	415.6
2003	404.4	405.7	411.8	413.7	418.0	421.4	416.9	415.4	416.0	422.0	423.7	426.1	416.3
Total private													
1990	342.6	343.0	346.5	346.9	351.5	355.8	354.2	350.8	350.9	348.0	345.1	345.1	348.4
1991	324.6	323.0	325.1	328.9	332.3	336.1	331.9	331.0	331.0	329.1	330.4	331.2	329.6
1992	312.5	310.5	313.1	318.3	321.8	325.3	322.4	319.4	319.4	320.7	319.8	321.1	318.7
1993	307.0	307.1	307.8	311.5	315.9	320.5	316.9	315.8	317.3	317.5	319.2	321.5	314.8
1994	304.9	304.5	308.5	312.9	317.4	322.3	319.2	318.8	319.8	321.7	323.0	324.2	316.4
1995	310.3	310.2	316.0	317.0	321.6	326.0	322.1	322.7	323.0	324.3	326.5	328.7	320.7
1996	312.6	315.0	318.0	321.3	326.3	332.0	327.5	326.3	325.8	328.2	331.0	334.4	324.9
1997	317.1	317.8	322.6	324.3	328.9	334.5	332.6	333.0	333.7	337.4	339.2	342.9	330.3
1998	327.9	327.6	330.4	332.5	336.7	341.4	338.7	337.3	336.8	338.8	341.2	344.0	336.1
1999	333.9	335.7	339.0	344.8	346.9	351.9	346.9	344.8	347.0	350.3	352.2	356.2	345.8
2000	339.7	340.4	346.0	349.5	352.9	358.2	355.3	352.4	355.6	360.1	362.7	366.2	353.3
2001	348.0	347.9	351.5	352.2	357.1	360.5	356.1	353.9	351.1	352.7	354.1	356.2	353.4
2002	339.4	339.4	344.3	347.1	349.6	352.6	351.0	348.4	349.6	351.9	352.0	355.1	348.4
2003	337.6	336.9	342.8	345.1	349.2	352.3	350.6	349.0	349.9	353.9	354.6	357.7	348.3
Goods-producing													
1990	58.2	58.3	59.4	59.8	60.8	61.6	61.1	60.3	60.0	58.5	55.5	54.5	59.0
1991	49.6	48.9	48.7	50.1	51.1	51.6	51.3	51.5	51.5	51.1	50.5	49.5	50.5
1992	45.2	44.5	45.2	46.1	46.8	47.3	47.1	46.4	46.3	46.0	45.4	44.9	45.9
1993	42.2	42.0	42.0	43.4	44.2	45.0	44.8	44.8	45.6	45.6	45.4	45.0	44.2
1994	40.3	40.3	41.6	43.4	44.6	45.1	45.3	45.6	46.1	46.5	46.4	45.8	44.3
1995	42.6	42.2	43.2	44.4	45.2	45.5	44.7	45.0	45.4	45.4	45.2	44.9	44.5
1996	41.4	42.1	42.7	44.2	45.5	45.6	44.1	44.3	44.2	44.7	44.8	44.7	44.0
1997	41.1	40.7	41.5	43.1	43.8	44.6	45.5	45.7	46.1	46.4	46.4	46.3	44.3
1998	42.8	42.7	43.5	44.9	45.6	46.1	45.9	46.3	46.6	46.6	46.7	46.3	45.3
1999	44.3	44.8	45.9	47.9	48.7	49.2	48.8	48.9	49.9	50.0	50.1	49.9	48.2
2000	46.5	46.3	48.3	48.7	49.5	49.9	49.1	49.7	50.4	50.8	50.9	50.7	49.2
2001	47.2	47.1	47.6	48.1	49.2	49.6	48.5	48.3	47.9	47.9	47.6	47.1	48.0
2002	43.5	43.7	44.7	45.4	45.9	46.3	46.4	46.7	47.3	47.1	46.8	46.7	45.9
2003	43.3	43.0	44.6	45.3	46.0	46.8	46.1	46.1	46.4	46.5	46.5	46.2	45.6
Construction and mining													
1990	21.0	21.0	21.8	22.8	23.7	24.4	24.6	24.4	24.3	22.8	22.6	21.8	22.9
1991	17.7	17.3	17.5	18.5	19.5	19.8	19.4	19.4	19.2	18.6	18.3	17.2	18.5
1992	13.8	13.6	14.0	15.1	15.8	16.2	16.4	16.6	16.4	16.4	16.2	15.6	15.5
1993	13.4	13.2	13.4	14.7	15.5	16.1	16.6	16.7	17.1	17.0	16.9	16.3	15.6
1994	12.7	12.5	13.4	15.3	16.5	16.8	17.4	17.7	17.9	18.3	18.1	17.5	16.2
1995	14.8	14.3	15.1	16.3	16.9	17.3	17.5	17.7	17.8	18.0	17.7	17.4	16.7
1996	14.2	14.7	15.4	16.8	17.8	18.3	18.5	18.9	18.7	18.9	18.9	18.4	17.5
1997	15.5	15.2	15.8	17.4	18.1	18.8	20.0	20.1	20.2	20.5	20.4	20.2	18.5
1998	17.7	17.7	18.5	19.9	20.5	20.7	21.1	21.1	21.1	21.3	21.3	20.8	20.1
1999	19.4	19.8	20.6	22.5	23.1	23.9	24.1	24.3	24.4	24.4	24.5	24.3	22.9
2000	21.8	21.5	23.1	23.8	24.7	25.2	25.1	25.6	26.1	26.7	26.6	26.5	24.7
2001	23.9	23.9	24.2	25.3	26.3	26.7	26.3	26.1	25.7	25.8	25.7	25.4	25.4
2002	22.2	22.4	23.2	24.0	24.5	24.8	25.5	26.1	26.4	26.2	26.0	26.0	24.8
2003	23.2	22.9	24.3	25.4	26.1	26.7	26.4	26.5	26.5	26.8	26.9	26.4	25.7
Manufacturing													
1990	37.2	37.3	37.6	37.0	37.1	37.2	36.5	35.9	35.7	35.7	32.9	32.7	36.1
1991	31.9	31.6	31.2	31.6	31.6	31.8	31.9	32.1	32.3	32.5	32.2	32.3	31.9
1992	31.4	30.9	31.2	31.0	31.0	31.1	30.7	29.8	29.9	29.6	29.2	29.3	30.4
1993	28.8	28.8	28.6	28.7	28.7	28.9	28.2	28.1	28.5	28.6	28.5	28.7	28.6
1994	27.6	27.8	28.2	28.1	28.1	28.3	27.9	27.9	28.2	28.2	28.3	28.3	28.1
1995	27.8	27.9	28.1	28.1	28.3	28.2	27.2	27.3	27.6	27.4	27.5	27.5	27.7
1996	27.2	27.4	27.3	27.4	27.7	27.3	25.6	25.4	25.5	25.8	25.9	26.3	26.6
1997	25.6	25.5	25.7	25.7	25.7	25.8	25.5	25.6	25.9	25.9	26.0	26.1	25.8
1998	25.1	25.0	25.0	25.0	25.1	25.4	24.8	25.2	25.5	25.3	25.4	25.5	25.2
1999	24.9	25.0	25.3	25.4	25.6	25.3	24.7	24.6	25.5	25.6	25.6	25.6	25.3
2000	24.7	24.8	25.2	24.9	24.8	24.7	24.0	24.1	24.3	24.1	24.3	24.2	24.5
2001	23.3	23.2	23.4	22.8	22.9	22.9	22.2	22.2	22.2	22.1	21.9	21.7	22.6
2002	21.3	21.3	21.5	21.4	21.4	21.5	20.9	20.6	20.9	20.9	20.8	20.7	21.1
2003	20.1	20.1	20.3	19.9	19.9	20.1	19.7	19.6	19.9	19.7	19.6	19.8	19.9

Employment by Industry: New York—*Continued*

(Numbers in thousands. Not seasonally adjusted.)

Industry	January	February	March	April	May	June	July	August	September	October	November	December	Annual Average
WESTCHESTER COUNTY *—Continued*													
Service-providing													
1990	342.0	342.9	345.2	345.5	349.8	354.9	351.4	347.8	347.5	347.7	348.4	349.5	347.7
1991	333.5	332.8	334.9	337.4	340.1	343.6	338.3	335.9	335.2	335.9	338.5	340.2	337.2
1992	324.7	324.1	325.9	330.8	333.7	336.9	332.1	328.9	328.7	332.2	333.2	334.5	330.5
1993	322.0	322.9	323.8	326.0	330.1	334.2	329.3	327.2	326.7	329.0	332.5	334.7	328.2
1994	321.6	321.9	324.9	327.9	331.8	336.8	331.1	330.6	330.2	333.7	336.7	338.0	330.4
1995	326.1	327.0	331.6	331.8	335.7	340.4	334.9	334.7	333.5	337.5	341.3	343.1	334.8
1996	329.0	331.8	334.5	336.2	340.4	346.2	340.5	338.8	337.4	342.2	346.0	349.0	339.3
1997	334.0	336.3	340.4	340.1	344.4	350.1	346.0	345.3	345.4	350.1	352.6	356.8	345.1
1998	343.8	344.7	347.1	348.0	352.0	356.5	352.3	349.4	347.8	351.7	355.3	358.6	350.6
1999	349.8	352.1	354.3	358.1	359.9	364.7	361.6	358.5	358.8	364.1	367.0	370.5	360.0
2000	356.9	358.9	362.3	365.8	369.9	374.4	370.6	366.5	368.5	374.2	377.9	380.4	368.9
2001	364.9	365.9	368.6	369.0	373.2	376.0	369.8	367.1	366.5	371.3	374.2	376.3	370.2
2002	362.6	363.9	367.8	368.9	372.1	374.9	369.4	366.4	367.1	372.7	374.1	376.9	369.7
2003	361.1	362.7	367.2	368.4	372.0	374.6	370.8	369.3	369.6	375.5	377.2	379.9	370.7
Trade, transportation, and utilities													
1990	87.5	86.0	86.1	85.7	86.4	86.9	85.1	84.6	85.4	85.1	85.8	87.3	86.0
1991	81.1	79.6	79.3	79.5	79.9	80.8	78.6	78.7	79.2	79.9	81.6	83.8	80.2
1992	78.1	76.9	76.5	77.9	78.5	79.1	76.5	76.1	76.5	77.6	78.7	80.4	77.7
1993	76.1	75.0	74.8	75.4	76.8	77.7	76.4	76.1	76.9	78.3	79.9	82.0	77.1
1994	76.8	75.7	76.2	76.1	77.1	77.8	76.0	75.9	77.1	78.1	79.9	81.8	77.4
1995	77.9	77.2	78.5	77.9	78.7	79.5	77.6	77.6	78.5	79.7	81.7	83.7	79.0
1996	78.4	77.7	77.9	78.1	79.0	80.4	78.5	77.8	79.3	79.6	82.1	84.3	79.4
1997	78.1	76.8	77.7	76.5	77.4	78.4	76.4	76.6	78.9	80.3	82.4	85.0	78.7
1998	81.3	80.0	79.9	78.4	79.4	80.6	78.3	78.1	79.3	80.5	82.5	84.6	80.2
1999	81.0	79.7	79.9	80.3	80.2	81.4	78.9	78.5	79.9	82.0	84.0	86.0	81.0
2000	80.8	79.9	80.6	81.3	81.8	82.9	80.8	81.0	82.3	83.6	85.7	87.9	82.4
2001	83.1	81.6	81.7	80.3	81.3	82.6	80.3	79.9	81.0	81.9	83.9	85.8	82.0
2002	81.2	80.0	80.4	80.6	80.7	81.6	79.7	79.1	81.1	81.5	82.9	84.7	81.1
2003	79.4	78.2	78.8	78.7	79.6	80.5	78.6	78.6	80.2	81.7	83.3	85.4	80.3
Wholesale trade													
1990	26.0	26.0	26.0	26.1	26.2	26.3	25.8	25.4	25.4	25.2	25.0	25.2	25.7
1991	24.9	24.9	24.9	24.6	24.4	24.5	24.1	24.0	23.9	23.8	23.6	23.9	24.3
1992	22.6	22.6	22.6	23.9	23.8	23.9	23.1	22.8	22.8	22.6	22.6	22.7	23.0
1993	21.6	21.8	21.9	21.9	22.0	22.3	22.1	22.0	21.9	22.0	22.1	22.2	22.0
1994	20.8	20.7	20.9	20.9	20.9	20.8	20.7	20.7	20.7	20.7	20.8	21.0	20.8
1995	20.7	20.7	21.0	21.0	21.0	21.1	21.3	21.2	21.2	21.3	21.5	21.8	21.2
1996	21.3	21.6	21.8	22.1	22.1	22.4	22.2	22.3	22.2	22.1	22.1	22.3	22.0
1997	20.6	20.7	21.0	20.4	20.5	20.5	20.3	20.4	20.3	20.6	20.6	20.7	20.6
1998	20.5	20.7	20.7	20.7	20.7	20.7	20.5	20.5	20.3	20.6	20.6	20.8	20.6
1999	20.1	20.0	20.2	20.4	20.3	20.5	20.1	20.1	20.1	20.3	20.4	20.5	20.3
2000	19.1	19.2	19.6	19.4	19.6	19.8	19.6	19.6	19.5	19.8	19.7	19.8	19.6
2001	19.7	19.9	20.0	19.6	19.7	19.9	19.6	19.6	19.6	19.9	19.8	20.0	19.8
2002	19.5	19.5	19.6	19.5	19.5	19.6	19.5	19.4	19.3	19.2	19.2	19.2	19.4
2003	18.9	18.8	18.9	19.0	19.1	19.1	18.9	18.8	18.8	19.3	19.3	19.3	19.0
Retail trade													
1990	49.1	47.8	47.8	47.1	47.5	47.7	47.0	46.8	47.2	47.6	48.5	49.5	47.8
1991	44.1	42.9	42.6	43.2	43.6	44.3	43.1	43.3	43.4	44.0	45.7	47.2	44.0
1992	42.9	41.9	41.5	41.9	42.3	42.7	41.5	41.4	41.1	42.4	43.4	44.7	42.3
1993	42.0	40.9	40.6	41.2	42.3	42.8	42.3	42.3	42.6	43.5	44.7	46.6	42.7
1994	43.4	42.4	42.7	42.7	43.4	44.1	43.3	43.3	43.7	44.4	46.0	47.4	43.9
1995	44.4	43.6	44.5	44.7	45.0	45.6	44.4	44.6	44.7	45.5	47.1	48.6	45.2
1996	44.4	43.6	43.6	43.7	44.4	45.4	44.5	44.1	44.7	44.9	47.2	49.0	45.0
1997	44.8	43.8	44.2	43.6	44.2	45.0	44.3	44.8	45.5	46.1	48.1	50.2	45.4
1998	47.8	46.7	46.5	45.3	46.0	47.1	45.7	45.6	46.1	46.7	48.6	50.5	46.9
1999	48.7	47.5	47.3	47.5	47.3	48.4	47.3	47.0	47.3	48.9	50.8	52.7	48.4
2000	49.3	48.2	48.4	49.5	49.7	50.6	49.7	49.9	50.2	50.8	52.9	55.0	50.4
2001	50.1	48.3	48.3	47.7	48.1	49.2	48.2	48.1	47.9	48.3	50.3	52.0	48.9
2002	48.4	47.1	47.4	47.4	47.5	48.3	47.6	47.4	48.0	48.3	49.7	51.4	48.2
2003	46.6	45.6	45.9	46.1	46.6	47.5	46.9	47.2	47.6	48.3	49.9	51.8	47.5
Transportation and utilities													
1990	12.4	12.2	12.3	12.5	12.7	12.9	12.3	12.4	12.8	12.3	12.3	12.6	12.5
1991	12.1	11.8	11.8	11.7	11.9	12.0	11.4	11.4	11.9	12.1	12.3	12.7	11.9
1992	12.6	12.4	12.4	12.1	12.4	12.5	11.9	11.9	12.6	12.6	12.7	13.0	12.4
1993	12.5	12.3	12.3	12.3	12.5	12.6	12.0	11.8	12.4	12.8	13.1	13.2	12.5
1994	12.6	12.6	12.6	12.5	12.8	12.9	12.0	11.9	12.7	13.0	13.1	13.4	12.7
1995	12.8	12.9	13.0	12.2	12.7	12.8	11.9	11.8	12.6	12.9	13.1	13.3	12.7
1996	12.7	12.5	12.5	12.3	12.5	12.6	11.8	11.4	12.4	12.6	12.8	13.0	12.4
1997	12.7	12.3	12.5	12.5	12.7	12.9	11.8	11.4	13.1	13.6	13.7	14.1	12.8
1998	13.0	12.6	12.7	12.4	12.7	12.8	12.1	12.0	12.9	13.2	13.3	13.3	12.8
1999	12.2	12.2	12.4	12.4	12.6	12.5	11.5	11.4	12.5	12.8	12.8	12.8	12.3
2000	12.4	12.5	12.6	12.4	12.5	12.5	11.5	11.5	12.6	13.0	13.1	13.1	12.5
2001	13.3	13.4	13.4	13.0	13.5	13.5	12.5	12.2	13.5	13.7	13.8	13.8	13.3
2002	13.3	13.4	13.4	13.7	13.7	13.7	12.6	12.3	13.8	14.0	14.0	14.1	13.5
2003	13.9	13.8	14.0	13.6	13.9	13.9	12.8	12.6	13.8	14.1	14.1	14.3	13.7

Employment by Industry: New York—*Continued*

(Numbers in thousands. Not seasonally adjusted.)

Industry	January	February	March	April	May	June	July	August	September	October	November	December	Annual Average
WESTCHESTER COUNTY *—Continued*													
Information													
1990	18.3	18.5	18.4	18.3	18.5	18.6	18.6	18.4	18.3	18.0	18.0	18.0	18.3
1991	17.8	17.6	17.7	17.5	17.5	17.6	17.6	17.6	17.5	17.2	17.1	17.0	17.5
1992	16.5	16.4	16.5	16.3	16.4	16.4	16.5	16.3	16.2	16.3	16.2	16.3	16.4
1993	16.2	16.1	16.2	16.1	16.2	16.3	16.2	16.3	16.0	16.0	16.1	16.1	16.2
1994	15.6	15.5	15.6	15.5	15.5	15.7	15.5	15.5	15.4	15.2	15.3	15.0	15.4
1995	14.9	14.9	14.9	14.9	15.1	15.3	14.9	14.9	14.9	14.9	15.0	15.1	15.0
1996	15.3	15.3	15.3	15.4	15.4	15.6	15.4	15.5	15.5	15.6	15.6	15.8	15.5
1997	15.3	15.4	15.6	15.4	15.5	15.7	15.6	15.6	15.4	15.5	15.5	15.7	15.5
1998	15.4	15.4	15.4	15.2	15.2	15.2	14.9	14.8	14.7	14.6	14.7	14.8	15.0
1999	14.6	14.7	14.7	14.7	14.7	14.9	15.1	15.1	15.1	15.1	15.4	15.7	15.0
2000	16.1	16.0	16.0	16.3	16.5	16.9	17.0	15.0	16.9	16.7	16.9	17.1	16.5
2001	17.3	17.2	17.4	17.1	17.0	17.2	16.4	16.4	16.0	15.9	16.1	16.1	16.7
2002	16.2	16.1	15.9	15.8	15.8	15.7	15.4	15.3	15.1	15.1	15.1	15.1	15.6
2003	14.8	14.7	14.7	14.6	14.6	14.5	14.5	14.6	14.4	14.6	14.6	14.9	14.6
Financial activities													
1990	29.6	29.8	29.9	30.2	30.3	30.7	30.4	30.1	29.9	29.6	29.6	29.7	30.0
1991	28.4	28.1	28.3	28.0	28.2	28.6	28.4	28.4	28.4	27.8	28.0	28.1	28.2
1992	28.5	28.1	28.2	28.4	28.6	29.0	28.7	28.6	28.2	27.9	27.8	28.0	28.3
1993	26.9	26.8	26.7	26.7	26.9	27.4	27.3	27.3	26.9	26.8	26.7	26.9	26.9
1994	26.3	26.3	26.5	26.2	26.3	26.8	26.5	26.5	26.5	26.1	26.1	26.3	26.4
1995	25.8	25.8	26.0	25.6	25.9	26.4	26.2	26.2	26.0	26.0	26.2	26.5	26.1
1996	25.7	25.7	25.9	25.9	26.1	26.5	26.7	26.5	26.0	26.2	26.2	26.4	26.2
1997	27.6	27.8	28.0	28.0	28.4	29.1	29.3	29.3	28.9	29.0	29.1	29.2	28.6
1998	28.7	28.7	28.6	28.5	28.6	29.0	29.0	29.1	28.5	28.5	28.4	28.5	28.7
1999	28.5	28.4	28.6	28.6	28.6	28.9	28.8	28.6	28.4	28.0	28.1	28.3	28.5
2000	28.1	28.2	28.3	28.5	28.6	29.2	29.0	29.1	28.8	28.5	28.7	29.0	28.7
2001	28.0	28.1	28.2	28.0	28.1	28.5	28.7	28.8	28.3	28.2	28.2	28.3	28.3
2002	27.9	27.8	27.9	27.7	27.8	28.2	28.3	28.1	27.9	28.0	28.1	28.4	28.0
2003	27.3	27.5	27.6	27.7	27.9	28.4	28.6	28.8	28.6	28.5	28.3	28.3	28.1
Professional and business services													
1990	47.3	47.8	48.4	48.9	49.3	50.1	50.1	49.9	49.9	49.9	49.5	48.8	49.2
1991	46.6	46.7	47.5	48.6	48.9	49.3	48.3	48.0	47.8	47.1	47.2	46.1	47.7
1992	43.2	43.2	43.8	45.2	45.5	46.0	46.2	45.9	45.4	45.7	45.2	45.1	45.0
1993	42.8	43.4	43.8	44.1	44.5	45.2	44.1	44.0	43.7	43.5	43.6	43.8	43.9
1994	43.8	43.9	44.2	45.6	46.1	46.6	46.3	46.4	46.5	46.2	45.9	45.6	45.6
1995	44.6	44.5	45.9	46.1	46.8	47.4	46.3	46.8	47.1	47.4	47.3	46.9	46.4
1996	45.0	45.6	46.5	46.5	47.3	48.3	48.1	49.0	48.7	48.7	48.8	48.7	47.6
1997	47.1	47.7	48.5	49.5	50.4	51.0	50.5	51.0	50.9	51.6	51.2	51.0	50.0
1998	48.2	48.2	49.0	50.6	51.1	52.1	51.8	51.6	51.3	51.3	51.0	51.2	50.6
1999	49.7	50.0	50.7	51.2	51.5	52.4	52.0	51.5	51.5	51.7	51.5	51.8	51.3
2000	49.9	50.5	51.6	52.0	52.5	53.2	53.1	53.2	53.1	54.7	54.6	54.6	52.8
2001	54.2	54.2	54.5	56.2	57.1	57.7	56.8	56.8	56.3	57.1	56.9	56.5	56.2
2002	53.8	53.9	54.8	56.0	56.1	56.4	55.3	55.2	55.4	55.6	55.5	54.8	55.2
2003	53.7	53.6	54.9	55.9	56.2	56.6	56.2	56.3	56.4	57.0	56.8	56.8	55.9
Educational and health services													
1990	63.1	64.2	64.8	64.2	64.4	64.1	63.9	63.5	64.5	65.5	65.8	66.1	64.5
1991	64.4	65.4	66.0	67.3	67.1	66.8	65.7	65.3	66.4	67.0	67.4	68.0	66.4
1992	66.1	66.8	67.4	67.2	67.0	66.9	66.6	65.7	67.6	68.6	68.8	68.8	67.3
1993	67.1	68.1	68.3	67.9	67.8	67.6	66.5	66.2	67.9	68.3	68.7	68.6	67.8
1994	66.0	67.0	67.3	67.8	67.5	67.9	67.1	66.7	67.3	68.9	69.4	69.6	67.7
1995	67.7	68.5	69.5	68.8	68.7	68.8	68.6	68.6	69.4	70.4	70.7	70.9	69.2
1996	69.3	70.7	71.4	71.6	71.5	72.0	70.8	70.5	70.9	72.8	73.5	73.9	71.6
1997	70.6	71.9	72.5	72.2	71.9	71.9	71.2	71.1	71.7	73.8	74.2	74.6	72.3
1998	73.4	74.6	74.8	74.8	74.9	74.8	73.5	72.8	73.6	75.6	76.4	76.5	74.6
1999	75.6	77.5	77.8	79.0	78.5	78.5	76.1	75.7	77.2	79.0	79.2	80.1	77.9
2000	76.9	77.6	78.1	78.4	78.5	78.1	77.6	77.0	77.9	80.0	80.4	80.8	78.4
2001	75.6	77.0	77.8	77.5	77.6	76.0	75.3	74.6	75.1	75.6	75.9	76.2	76.2
2002	73.3	74.5	75.6	75.6	75.5	74.5	74.5	74.0	74.6	76.5	76.4	77.3	75.2
2003	74.8	75.8	76.8	76.6	76.8	75.3	75.1	74.3	76.1	78.2	78.6	79.3	76.5
Leisure and hospitality													
1990	25.0	24.8	25.6	26.1	27.9	29.7	30.7	30.0	28.8	27.6	27.1	27.0	27.5
1991	23.4	23.3	24.1	24.2	25.8	27.5	28.1	27.8	26.4	25.2	24.8	24.8	25.5
1992	21.6	21.2	22.2	23.5	25.2	26.8	27.0	26.8	25.6	24.8	23.9	23.8	24.4
1993	22.2	22.1	22.4	23.9	25.3	27.0	27.4	27.0	25.9	24.8	24.5	24.8	24.8
1994	22.4	22.0	23.1	24.4	26.2	28.2	28.6	28.3	26.9	26.4	25.6	25.7	25.7
1995	23.0	23.0	23.8	25.1	26.8	28.8	29.5	29.5	27.3	26.1	26.0	26.2	26.3
1996	23.6	23.7	24.0	25.0	26.9	28.8	29.5	28.5	26.6	25.6	24.9	25.4	26.0
1997	22.6	22.3	23.3	24.6	26.4	28.6	29.0	29.0	26.7	25.7	25.3	25.7	25.8
1998	23.1	22.9	23.9	24.8	26.5	28.0	30.0	29.5	27.5	26.0	25.7	26.1	26.2
1999	24.0	24.2	24.9	26.3	27.7	29.6	30.7	30.2	28.1	27.6	26.9	27.2	27.3
2000	24.9	25.3	26.2	27.2	28.4	30.9	31.8	30.8	28.9	28.4	27.9	28.4	28.3
2001	26.4	26.2	27.6	28.4	30.2	32.2	34.1	32.8	30.1	29.8	29.2	29.8	29.7
2002	27.2	27.1	28.5	29.5	31.3	33.3	35.2	34.0	31.6	31.2	30.4	31.1	30.9
2003	28.1	27.8	28.9	29.7	31.3	33.1	35.2	34.1	31.4	31.1	30.0	30.4	30.9

Employment by Industry: New York—*Continued*

(Numbers in thousands. Not seasonally adjusted.)

Industry	January	February	March	April	May	June	July	August	September	October	November	December	Annual Average
WESTCHESTER COUNTY *—Continued*													
Other services													
1990	13.6	13.6	13.9	13.7	13.9	14.1	14.3	14.0	14.1	13.8	13.8	13.7	13.9
1991	13.3	13.4	13.5	13.7	13.8	13.9	13.9	13.7	13.8	13.8	13.8	13.9	13.7
1992	13.3	13.4	13.3	13.7	13.8	13.8	13.8	13.6	13.6	13.8	13.8	13.8	13.6
1993	13.5	13.6	13.6	14.0	14.2	14.3	14.2	14.1	14.4	14.2	14.3	14.3	14.1
1994	13.7	13.8	14.0	13.9	14.1	14.2	13.9	13.9	14.0	14.3	14.4	14.4	14.1
1995	13.8	14.1	14.2	14.2	14.4	14.3	14.3	14.1	14.4	14.4	14.4	14.5	14.3
1996	13.9	14.2	14.3	14.6	14.6	14.8	14.4	14.2	14.6	15.0	15.1	15.2	14.6
1997	14.7	15.2	15.5	15.0	15.1	15.2	15.1	14.7	15.1	15.1	15.1	15.4	15.1
1998	15.0	15.1	15.3	15.3	15.4	15.6	15.3	15.1	15.3	15.7	15.8	16.0	15.4
1999	16.2	16.4	16.5	16.8	17.0	17.0	16.5	16.3	16.9	16.9	17.0	17.2	16.7
2000	16.5	16.6	16.9	17.1	17.1	17.1	16.9	16.6	17.3	17.4	17.6	17.7	17.1
2001	16.2	16.5	16.7	16.6	16.6	16.7	16.0	16.3	16.4	16.3	16.3	16.4	16.4
2002	16.3	16.3	16.5	16.5	16.5	16.6	16.2	16.0	16.6	16.9	16.8	17.0	16.5
2003	16.2	16.3	16.5	16.6	16.8	17.1	16.3	16.2	16.4	16.3	16.5	16.4	16.5
Government													
1990	57.6	58.2	58.1	58.4	59.1	60.7	58.3	57.3	56.6	58.2	58.8	58.9	58.4
1991	58.5	58.7	58.5	58.6	58.9	59.1	57.7	56.4	55.7	57.9	58.6	58.5	58.1
1992	57.4	58.1	58.0	58.6	58.7	58.9	56.8	55.9	55.6	57.5	58.8	58.3	57.7
1993	57.2	57.8	58.0	57.9	58.4	58.7	57.2	56.2	55.0	57.1	58.7	58.2	57.5
1994	57.0	57.7	58.0	58.4	59.0	59.6	57.2	57.4	56.5	58.5	60.1	59.6	58.3
1995	58.4	59.0	58.8	59.2	59.3	59.9	57.5	57.0	55.9	58.6	60.0	59.3	58.6
1996	57.8	58.9	59.2	59.1	59.6	59.8	57.1	56.8	55.8	58.7	59.8	59.3	58.5
1997	58.0	59.2	59.3	58.9	59.3	60.2	58.9	58.0	57.8	59.1	59.8	60.2	59.1
1998	58.7	59.8	60.2	60.4	60.9	61.2	59.5	58.4	57.6	59.5	60.8	60.9	59.8
1999	60.2	61.2	61.2	61.2	61.7	62.0	63.5	62.6	61.7	63.8	64.9	64.2	62.4
2000	63.7	64.8	64.6	65.0	66.5	66.1	64.4	63.8	63.3	64.9	66.1	64.9	64.8
2001	64.1	65.1	64.7	64.9	65.3	65.1	62.2	61.5	63.3	66.5	67.7	67.2	64.8
2002	66.7	68.2	68.2	67.2	68.4	68.6	64.8	64.7	64.8	67.9	68.9	68.5	67.2
2003	66.8	68.8	69.0	68.6	68.8	69.1	66.3	66.4	66.1	68.1	69.1	68.4	68.0
Federal government													
1990	6.5	6.4	6.5	6.7	7.0	7.5	7.0	6.5	6.4	6.4	6.3	6.5	6.6
1991	6.2	6.1	6.1	6.0	6.0	6.0	6.0	6.0	6.0	6.0	6.0	6.2	6.1
1992	6.1	6.0	6.0	6.0	5.9	5.9	5.9	5.8	5.8	5.9	5.8	6.0	5.9
1993	5.8	5.8	5.9	5.8	5.9	6.0	5.9	5.9	5.9	5.9	5.9	6.1	5.9
1994	5.9	5.9	6.0	5.9	5.9	5.9	5.9	5.9	5.9	5.9	5.9	6.1	5.9
1995	5.9	5.9	5.9	5.8	5.9	5.9	5.9	5.9	5.9	5.9	6.0	6.2	5.9
1996	5.9	6.0	6.0	5.9	5.9	5.8	5.7	5.7	5.7	5.7	5.8	6.0	5.8
1997	5.8	5.8	5.8	5.7	5.7	5.7	5.7	5.8	5.8	5.7	5.7	6.1	5.8
1998	5.7	5.8	5.8	5.7	5.7	5.7	5.7	5.7	5.7	5.7	5.7	6.1	5.8
1999	5.7	5.8	5.8	5.9	5.7	5.7	5.7	5.7	5.7	5.7	5.7	5.8	5.7
2000	5.7	5.7	5.7	5.9	6.9	6.3	5.9	5.6	5.5	5.5	5.5	5.6	5.8
2001	5.7	5.7	5.7	5.7	5.7	5.6	5.5	5.5	5.5	5.5	5.4	5.5	5.6
2002	5.5	5.5	5.5	5.5	5.5	5.5	5.5	5.5	5.5	5.5	5.5	5.5	5.5
2003	5.5	5.5	5.5	5.5	5.5	5.4	5.4	5.4	5.4	5.4	5.3	5.3	5.4
State government													
1990	8.5	8.6	8.5	8.6	8.6	8.6	8.9	8.8	8.9	8.9	8.7	8.6	8.7
1991	8.6	8.5	8.6	8.8	8.7	8.5	8.6	8.5	8.6	8.9	8.9	8.9	8.7
1992	8.7	8.8	8.9	8.9	8.8	8.6	8.6	8.6	8.8	8.9	8.9	8.8	8.8
1993	8.6	8.6	8.7	8.7	8.7	8.6	8.5	8.5	8.5	8.6	8.6	8.6	8.6
1994	8.6	8.7	8.7	8.8	8.8	8.7	8.8	8.8	8.9	8.9	9.0	9.0	8.8
1995	8.8	9.0	8.9	9.0	8.8	8.6	8.7	8.5	8.7	8.9	8.9	8.8	8.8
1996	8.6	8.8	8.8	8.9	8.7	8.6	8.5	8.5	8.6	8.7	8.8	8.6	8.7
1997	8.3	8.6	8.6	8.6	8.6	8.4	8.4	8.4	8.6	8.8	8.8	8.5	8.6
1998	8.2	8.5	8.6	8.6	8.6	8.4	8.4	8.3	8.5	8.6	8.7	8.6	8.5
1999	8.3	8.6	8.5	8.6	8.7	8.4	8.4	8.3	8.5	8.7	8.7	8.5	8.5
2000	8.3	8.6	8.6	8.7	8.8	8.5	8.5	8.4	8.6	8.9	9.0	8.8	8.6
2001	7.8	8.2	8.2	8.2	8.2	7.9	7.9	7.9	8.1	8.3	8.3	8.1	8.1
2002	7.9	8.3	8.3	8.2	8.3	8.1	8.0	8.0	8.2	8.2	8.2	8.2	8.2
2003	8.1	8.3	8.3	8.2	8.3	8.0	7.9	7.9	8.1	8.1	8.1	8.1	8.1
Local government													
1990	42.6	43.2	43.1	43.2	43.6	44.6	42.4	42.0	41.2	43.0	43.8	43.8	43.0
1991	43.7	44.0	43.9	43.8	44.1	44.7	43.1	41.9	41.1	43.1	43.7	43.4	43.4
1992	42.6	43.3	43.2	43.8	43.9	44.4	42.3	41.4	41.0	42.7	44.2	43.4	43.0
1993	42.7	43.4	43.4	43.4	43.9	44.2	42.7	41.8	40.6	42.7	44.2	43.5	43.0
1994	42.6	43.1	43.3	43.6	44.3	45.0	42.5	42.7	41.7	43.7	45.2	44.5	43.5
1995	43.7	44.2	43.9	44.4	44.6	45.4	42.9	42.6	41.3	43.7	45.1	44.4	43.9
1996	43.3	44.1	44.4	44.3	45.0	45.3	42.9	42.6	41.5	44.2	45.2	44.7	44.0
1997	44.0	44.8	45.0	44.6	45.0	46.0	44.8	43.7	43.4	44.6	45.3	45.5	44.7
1998	44.8	45.5	45.8	46.1	46.6	47.1	45.4	44.4	43.4	45.2	46.4	46.2	45.6
1999	46.2	46.8	46.9	46.7	47.3	47.9	49.4	48.6	47.5	49.4	50.5	49.9	48.1
2000	49.7	50.5	50.3	50.4	50.8	51.3	50.0	49.8	49.2	50.5	51.6	50.5	50.4
2001	50.6	51.2	50.8	51.0	51.4	51.6	48.8	48.1	49.7	52.7	54.0	53.6	51.1
2002	53.3	54.4	54.4	53.5	54.6	55.0	51.3	51.2	51.1	54.2	55.2	54.8	53.6
2003	53.2	55.0	55.2	54.9	55.0	55.7	53.0	53.1	52.6	54.6	55.7	55.0	54.4

Average Weekly Hours by Industry: New York

(Not seasonally adjusted.)

Industry	January	February	March	April	May	June	July	August	September	October	November	December	Annual Average
STATEWIDE													
Construction													
2001	38.4	38.0	37.6	37.9	39.2	38.7	38.4	38.5	37.0	40.0	39.4	39.3	38.6
2002	38.5	38.7	38.8	38.9	38.4	38.9	38.6	39.2	38.3	36.9	37.5	37.5	38.3
2003	37.7	35.3	37.4	37.3	38.9	39.1	38.4	39.0	38.4	37.4	37.6	36.1	37.8
Manufacturing													
2001	40.3	39.9	40.0	38.2	39.8	39.6	39.1	39.6	39.6	39.9	40.4	40.9	39.8
2002	39.8	40.3	40.6	40.2	40.5	40.3	39.6	40.0	40.6	40.4	40.6	41.1	40.3
2003	40.3	40.3	40.3	39.9	40.1	40.0	39.0	38.9	40.2	40.1	40.2	40.4	40.0
NEW YORK CITY													
Construction													
2001	38.9	38.7	37.6	38.1	39.3	39.0	37.7	37.6	34.6	40.8	40.7	40.2	38.6
2002	39.0	40.3	39.7	39.7	39.2	39.2	37.6	38.0	37.2	35.2	36.1	37.4	38.2
2003	36.5	34.5	37.6	36.0	38.0	37.2	36.4	36.9	37.2	34.2	37.4	36.1	36.5
Manufacturing													
2001	38.4	38.1	38.2	36.5	36.8	37.0	35.8	36.2	36.0	37.3	38.1	38.2	37.2
2002	36.6	36.8	37.3	36.8	36.7	37.6	38.0	37.8	37.6	36.5	37.3	38.7	37.3
2003	38.4	37.4	37.0	36.3	36.9	36.9	36.1	34.6	36.4	36.3	36.4	36.1	36.6

Average Hourly Earnings by Industry: New York

(Dollars, not seasonally adjusted.)

Industry	January	February	March	April	May	June	July	August	September	October	November	December	Annual Average
STATEWIDE													
Construction													
2001	25.35	25.29	25.64	25.18	25.33	24.80	24.72	24.96	24.77	26.01	25.66	26.33	25.33
2002	25.72	26.64	26.44	26.43	26.46	26.18	26.06	25.55	26.37	25.64	26.05	26.36	26.15
2003	26.61	26.70	27.19	26.88	27.18	27.14	27.36	27.17	27.34	27.21	27.83	27.75	27.21
Manufacturing													
2001	15.89	15.88	15.86	16.03	16.00	15.98	16.14	16.42	16.60	16.52	16.72	16.93	16.24
2002	16.65	16.81	16.84	17.00	16.71	16.62	16.39	16.64	16.77	16.68	17.00	16.85	16.75
2003	16.79	16.70	16.74	16.69	16.70	16.60	16.57	16.88	16.89	16.71	16.91	17.21	16.78
NEW YORK CITY													
Construction													
2001	30.60	30.60	31.13	30.74	31.73	30.63	30.41	30.81	30.70	31.85	31.06	32.60	31.09
2002	30.91	31.75	30.99	30.77	32.05	31.79	31.26	30.95	32.94	31.74	31.69	31.90	31.56
2003	30.94	31.75	33.14	32.27	33.92	33.89	34.38	34.14	33.54	33.94	34.22	33.71	33.36
Manufacturing													
2001	12.51	12.07	12.04	12.27	12.27	12.04	12.62	12.59	12.40	13.03	12.95	13.15	12.49
2002	13.00	12.74	12.92	13.43	13.32	12.74	12.73	13.00	12.97	13.40	13.31	13.26	13.07
2003	13.53	12.94	13.68	13.83	13.67	13.66	14.36	14.22	14.37	13.49	13.99	14.08	13.81

Average Weekly Earnings by Industry: New York

(Dollars, not seasonally adjusted.)

Industry	January	February	March	April	May	June	July	August	September	October	November	December	Annual Average
STATEWIDE													
Construction													
2001	973.44	961.02	964.06	954.32	992.94	959.76	949.25	960.96	916.49	1040.40	1011.00	1034.77	977.74
2002	990.22	1030.97	1025.87	1028.13	1016.06	1018.40	1005.92	1001.56	1009.97	946.12	976.88	988.50	1001.55
2003	1003.20	942.51	1016.91	1002.62	1057.30	1061.17	1050.62	1059.63	1049.86	1017.65	1046.41	1001.78	1028.54
Manufacturing													
2001	640.37	633.61	634.40	612.35	636.80	632.81	631.07	650.23	657.36	659.15	675.49	692.44	646.35
2002	662.67	677.44	683.70	683.40	676.76	669.79	649.04	665.60	680.86	673.87	690.20	692.54	675.03
2003	676.64	673.01	674.62	665.93	669.67	664.00	646.23	656.63	678.98	670.07	679.78	695.28	671.20
NEW YORK CITY													
Construction													
2001	1190.34	1184.22	1170.49	1171.19	1246.99	1194.57	1146.46	1158.46	1062.22	1299.48	1264.14	1310.52	1200.07
2002	1205.49	1279.53	1230.30	1221.57	1256.36	1246.17	1175.38	1176.10	1225.37	1117.25	1144.01	1193.06	1205.59
2003	1129.31	1095.38	1246.06	1161.72	1288.96	1260.71	1251.43	1259.77	1247.69	1160.75	1279.83	1216.93	1217.64
Manufacturing													
2001	480.38	459.87	459.93	447.86	451.54	445.48	451.80	455.76	446.40	486.02	493.40	502.33	464.63
2002	475.80	468.83	481.92	494.22	488.84	479.02	483.74	491.40	487.67	489.10	496.46	513.16	487.51
2003	519.55	483.96	506.16	502.03	504.42	504.05	518.40	492.01	523.07	489.69	509.24	508.29	505.45

NORTH CAROLINA AT A GLANCE

(Population and total nonfarm employment numbers in thousands)

Population, Census 2000:	8,049.3
Total nonfarm employment, 2003:	3,803.1
Change in total nonfarm employment	
(Number)	
1990–2003:	685.5
1990–2001:	781.1
2001–2003:	-95.6
(Compound annual rate of change)	
1990–2003:	1.5%
1990–2001:	2.1%
2001–2003:	-1.2%
Unemployment rate	
1990:	4.2%
2001:	5.6%
2003:	6.5%

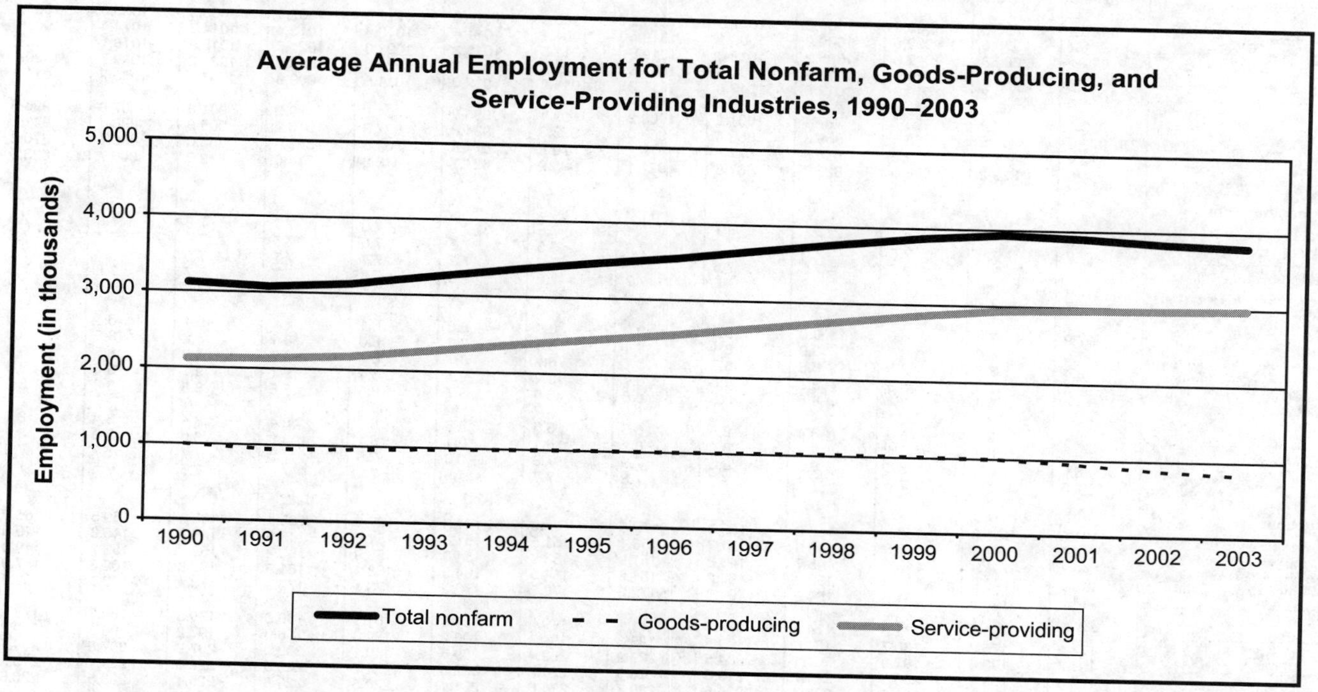

After declining in the 1990–1991 recession, total nonfarm payroll employment followed the pattern of most other states by expanding through the 1990s until being slowed by the 2001 contraction. Goods-producing industries led the decline, as employment fell sharply in 2001. From 2001 to 2003, nearly 100,000 jobs were lost in manufacturing alone, and another 17,000 jobs were lost in construction. Employment in the service-providing sector eased, but never declined. In 2003, total nonfarm employment was still well below its 2000 peak.

Employment by Industry: North Carolina

(Numbers in thousands. Not seasonally adjusted.)

Industry	January	February	March	April	May	June	July	August	September	October	November	December	Annual Average
STATEWIDE													
Total nonfarm													
1990	3065.6	3086.6	3109.6	3120.3	3138.5	3156.7	3091.8	3112.6	3137.1	3129.5	3138.5	3124.8	3117.6
1991	3035.3	3031.7	3039.8	3050.0	3070.7	3083.5	3036.5	3070.7	3100.0	3115.8	3118.1	3114.0	3072.1
1992	3049.8	3058.2	3084.6	3087.5	3124.0	3157.7	3101.5	3131.0	3158.0	3177.2	3184.7	3190.5	3125.3
1993	3142.2	3161.4	3179.5	3216.5	3240.5	3269.9	3230.2	3254.1	3285.0	3302.3	3324.2	3330.3	3244.6
1994	3250.4	3266.0	3302.1	3330.8	3355.2	3390.2	3327.1	3363.7	3409.6	3421.6	3441.8	3447.4	3358.8
1995	3375.0	3390.0	3422.1	3436.5	3454.3	3485.3	3420.4	3450.1	3496.9	3516.2	3529.8	3538.5	3459.5
1996	3429.1	3467.2	3500.8	3518.2	3558.8	3587.6	3503.0	3542.9	3582.7	3603.3	3625.9	3638.2	3546.4
1997	3556.7	3577.7	3615.5	3639.8	3671.2	3694.5	3617.5	3657.9	3713.7	3722.1	3741.0	3749.7	3663.1
1998	3657.0	3678.9	3711.6	3752.1	3779.2	3800.9	3739.3	3789.3	3828.6	3837.2	3851.3	3858.9	3773.6
1999	3778.2	3808.1	3836.2	3857.8	3869.6	3878.8	3831.7	3883.5	3904.3	3922.1	3931.8	3942.3	3870.3
2000	3841.3	3862.2	3908.0	3930.6	3960.3	3979.4	3902.1	3952.1	3969.4	3961.2	3969.8	3968.1	3933.7
2001	3904.3	3910.6	3928.3	3923.4	3933.3	3925.0	3846.4	3888.5	3891.4	3886.6	3878.5	3867.7	3898.7
2002	3783.2	3799.7	3828.4	3853.0	3875.3	3858.2	3792.8	3843.1	3853.1	3858.4	3853.8	3846.7	3837.1
2003	3750.6	3753.5	3776.9	3795.9	3833.4	3808.6	3764.1	3811.5	3824.9	3852.1	3839.1	3827.1	3803.1
Total private													
1990	2578.8	2592.1	2608.9	2619.2	2631.9	2654.6	2640.8	2658.5	2649.5	2627.1	2627.2	2619.6	2625.6
1991	2534.9	2524.3	2528.5	2538.2	2561.8	2578.8	2578.9	2605.6	2600.7	2600.1	2597.2	2596.5	2570.4
1992	2537.4	2539.4	2562.4	2585.8	2615.2	2646.0	2648.0	2666.8	2663.7	2668.4	2666.0	2676.1	2622.9
1993	2615.7	2630.8	2645.3	2683.0	2708.2	2739.0	2747.9	2763.0	2758.6	2762.1	2773.0	2784.7	2717.6
1994	2712.9	2724.0	2755.6	2783.8	2808.4	2845.0	2842.9	2866.6	2869.5	2867.2	2877.4	2889.3	2820.2
1995	2823.1	2832.2	2859.8	2876.0	2897.4	2929.6	2921.9	2945.1	2945.8	2950.2	2958.1	2969.0	2909.0
1996	2869.7	2900.5	2930.0	2946.6	2987.4	3017.2	3001.2	3025.3	3017.9	3026.3	3041.9	3057.4	2985.1
1997	2981.6	2997.0	3031.2	3052.7	3087.3	3112.5	3102.0	3120.2	3133.5	3128.3	3142.2	3153.0	3086.7
1998	3067.5	3081.1	3110.7	3150.0	3179.9	3212.8	3207.6	3226.4	3224.5	3221.3	3234.8	3244.3	3180.0
1999	3171.0	3190.8	3216.1	3245.8	3260.9	3288.8	3291.6	3300.4	3293.0	3302.9	3309.8	3322.2	3266.1
2000	3230.3	3244.0	3280.5	3300.6	3324.2	3357.7	3340.0	3344.0	3338.0	3322.1	3327.8	3328.9	3311.5
2001	3269.7	3269.2	3283.6	3282.7	3290.0	3307.6	3271.2	3273.3	3248.1	3228.2	3217.6	3211.2	3262.7
2002	3137.6	3147.1	3171.4	3198.2	3219.0	3234.9	3215.1	3226.9	3209.5	3198.1	3196.3	3193.7	3195.7
2003	3108.6	3106.1	3125.1	3145.8	3180.1	3185.2	3184.4	3191.9	3172.7	3175.0	3168.1	3159.9	3158.6
Goods-producing													
1990	997.9	1005.3	1007.4	1005.5	1005.0	1011.0	1000.9	1004.8	999.9	986.8	984.6	975.6	998.7
1991	945.8	939.4	934.5	932.8	937.4	942.6	938.7	949.4	949.2	946.1	943.9	941.6	941.7
1992	929.6	929.0	933.4	939.6	948.7	959.5	959.3	967.3	967.5	965.5	964.9	967.6	952.6
1993	958.8	963.7	967.3	970.9	976.2	987.6	986.5	988.5	987.4	983.5	987.3	987.5	978.7
1994	969.8	972.5	979.1	980.2	987.9	999.0	996.1	1004.6	1006.3	1005.9	1007.0	1008.0	993.0
1995	997.2	997.6	1005.4	1004.3	1007.6	1014.2	1005.6	1012.6	1011.0	1007.5	1005.3	1005.0	1006.1
1996	981.2	990.6	992.9	1000.2	1009.1	1018.4	1004.1	1011.6	1010.6	1013.4	1014.3	1014.4	1005.0
1997	999.4	1002.3	1007.6	1005.2	1012.0	1019.0	1011.5	1015.3	1021.0	1021.8	1018.9	1018.1	1012.6
1998	1005.6	1009.0	1014.0	1017.4	1021.5	1031.6	1022.8	1027.7	1028.0	1023.2	1021.2	1019.7	1020.1
1999	1009.3	1009.2	1012.5	1012.6	1013.6	1019.2	1014.8	1012.0	1011.5	1009.8	1007.7	1006.7	1011.5
2000	989.4	990.3	998.7	997.4	1001.2	1008.2	1002.1	998.8	1001.5	989.5	991.6	987.8	996.3
2001	972.9	968.5	965.4	959.8	953.4	953.0	938.3	934.8	927.3	916.2	905.6	898.4	941.1
2002	879.4	878.8	879.3	876.8	877.6	875.7	870.2	871.8	866.5	860.9	855.0	850.1	870.2
2003	834.6	829.2	830.0	827.7	837.6	827.1	823.9	821.7	818.2	814.0	812.2	809.7	823.8
Natural resources and mining													
1990	7.8	7.9	8.0	8.1	8.1	8.1	7.8	7.9	7.8	7.7	7.8	7.8	7.9
1991	7.7	7.6	7.6	7.5	7.5	7.6	7.5	7.5	7.5	7.5	7.5	7.4	7.5
1992	7.4	7.4	7.5	7.5	7.6	7.7	7.7	7.7	7.7	7.7	7.6	7.6	7.5
1993	7.4	7.5	7.6	7.6	7.6	7.7	7.8	7.8	7.8	7.7	7.7	7.8	7.6
1994	7.7	7.7	7.8	7.7	7.8	7.8	7.9	7.9	7.9	7.9	7.9	7.9	7.8
1995	7.9	7.9	8.0	8.0	8.0	8.0	8.0	8.0	8.1	8.1	8.1	8.1	8.0
1996	7.9	8.0	8.1	8.0	8.1	8.1	8.1	8.1	8.0	8.1	8.2	8.2	8.0
1997	8.4	8.5	8.5	8.6	8.7	8.7	8.7	8.7	8.7	8.9	8.8	8.7	8.6
1998	8.4	8.4	8.5	8.7	8.8	8.7	9.2	9.1	9.1	9.1	9.1	9.0	8.8
1999	8.8	8.8	8.7	8.8	8.8	8.8	8.6	8.7	8.5	8.6	8.6	8.6	8.6
2000	8.4	8.3	8.5	8.4	8.5	8.5	8.5	8.5	8.5	8.4	8.4	8.4	8.4
2001	8.2	8.1	8.1	8.2	8.2	8.2	8.1	8.1	8.1	8.0	8.0	8.0	8.1
2002	8.0	8.0	8.1	8.0	8.0	7.9	7.8	7.8	7.8	7.8	7.7	7.7	7.9
2003	7.6	7.5	7.6	7.7	7.7	7.8	7.7	7.9	7.9	7.8	7.6	7.5	7.7
Construction													
1990	161.5	164.3	167.9	167.2	169.3	172.6	171.6	171.2	167.8	165.1	163.9	160.5	166.9
1991	148.2	147.3	147.8	149.9	151.7	153.1	151.5	151.8	151.0	149.0	147.3	145.8	149.5
1992	140.1	141.4	143.8	145.7	148.8	151.9	153.7	154.3	153.9	153.2	152.7	152.7	149.3
1993	145.3	148.0	150.9	153.8	157.2	161.8	164.5	164.5	163.1	161.9	161.8	162.8	157.9
1994	154.3	156.7	161.6	164.9	167.9	172.3	172.2	172.5	173.1	172.8	173.1	172.7	167.8
1995	167.4	165.9	172.3	174.6	177.1	181.1	179.6	181.8	181.5	180.6	179.9	180.6	176.8
1996	171.2	175.3	180.7	184.8	190.5	195.3	194.3	196.2	194.3	196.0	197.2	196.5	189.3
1997	191.8	193.4	197.9	201.1	204.5	207.2	209.4	209.5	210.1	209.0	207.9	207.5	204.1
1998	199.3	198.9	203.3	211.7	215.8	220.9	221.7	222.3	221.7	222.5	222.0	221.1	215.1
1999	215.3	217.1	220.5	225.7	226.6	230.7	231.6	231.1	230.5	229.8	229.1	228.5	226.3
2000	220.0	219.3	227.4	228.1	231.2	235.2	233.8	235.2	235.0	232.4	232.0	230.7	230.0
2001	223.6	224.7	230.0	230.3	233.1	235.8	233.1	232.6	230.0	227.4	224.9	222.3	229.0
2002	214.4	214.4	216.9	221.0	223.3	224.1	222.7	223.3	220.1	217.2	214.5	213.7	218.8
2003	206.1	204.6	206.8	209.6	214.0	215.2	217.6	216.1	214.3	212.8	212.9	211.7	211.8

Employment by Industry: North Carolina—*Continued*

(Numbers in thousands. Not seasonally adjusted.)

Industry	January	February	March	April	May	June	July	August	September	October	November	December	Annual Average
STATEWIDE—*Continued*													
Manufacturing													
1990	828.6	833.1	831.5	830.2	827.6	830.3	821.5	825.7	824.3	814.0	812.9	807.3	823.9
1991	789.9	784.5	779.1	775.4	778.2	781.9	779.7	790.1	790.7	789.6	789.1	788.4	784.7
1992	782.1	780.2	782.1	786.4	792.3	799.9	797.9	805.3	805.9	804.6	804.6	807.3	795.7
1993	806.1	808.2	808.8	809.5	811.4	818.1	814.2	816.2	816.5	813.9	817.8	816.9	813.1
1994	807.8	808.1	809.7	807.6	812.2	818.9	816.0	824.2	825.3	825.2	826.0	827.4	817.3
1995	821.9	823.8	825.1	821.7	822.5	825.1	818.0	822.8	821.4	818.8	817.3	816.3	821.2
1996	802.1	807.3	804.1	807.4	810.5	815.0	801.7	807.3	808.3	809.3	808.9	809.7	807.6
1997	799.2	800.4	801.2	795.5	798.8	803.1	793.4	797.1	802.2	803.9	802.2	801.9	799.9
1998	797.9	801.7	802.2	797.0	796.9	802.0	791.9	796.3	797.2	791.6	790.1	789.6	796.2
1999	785.2	783.3	783.3	778.1	778.2	779.7	774.6	772.2	772.5	771.4	770.0	769.6	776.5
2000	761.0	762.7	762.8	760.9	761.5	764.5	759.8	755.1	758.0	748.7	751.2	748.7	757.9
2001	741.1	735.7	727.3	721.3	712.1	709.0	697.1	694.1	689.2	680.8	672.7	668.1	704.0
2002	657.0	656.4	654.3	647.8	646.3	643.7	639.7	640.7	638.6	635.9	632.8	628.7	643.5
2003	620.9	617.1	615.6	610.4	615.9	604.1	598.6	597.7	596.0	593.4	591.7	590.5	604.3
Service-providing													
1990	2067.7	2081.3	2102.2	2114.8	2133.5	2145.7	2090.9	2107.8	2137.2	2142.7	2153.9	2149.2	2118.9
1991	2089.5	2092.3	2105.3	2117.2	2133.3	2140.9	2097.8	2121.3	2150.8	2169.7	2174.2	2172.4	2130.3
1992	2120.2	2129.2	2151.2	2147.9	2175.3	2198.2	2142.2	2163.7	2190.5	2211.7	2219.8	2222.9	2172.7
1993	2183.4	2197.7	2212.2	2245.6	2264.3	2282.3	2243.7	2265.6	2297.6	2318.8	2336.9	2342.8	2265.9
1994	2280.6	2293.5	2323.0	2350.6	2367.3	2391.2	2331.0	2359.1	2403.3	2415.7	2434.8	2439.4	2365.7
1995	2377.8	2392.4	2416.7	2432.2	2446.7	2471.1	2414.8	2437.5	2485.9	2508.7	2524.5	2533.5	2453.4
1996	2447.9	2476.6	2507.9	2518.0	2549.7	2569.2	2498.9	2531.3	2572.1	2589.9	2611.6	2623.8	2541.4
1997	2557.3	2575.4	2607.9	2634.6	2659.2	2675.5	2606.0	2642.6	2692.7	2700.3	2722.1	2731.6	2650.4
1998	2651.4	2669.9	2697.6	2734.7	2757.7	2769.3	2716.5	2761.6	2800.6	2814.0	2830.1	2839.2	2753.5
1999	2768.9	2798.9	2823.7	2845.2	2856.0	2859.6	2816.9	2871.5	2892.8	2912.3	2924.1	2935.6	2858.7
2000	2851.9	2871.9	2909.3	2933.2	2959.1	2971.2	2900.0	2953.3	2967.9	2971.7	2978.2	2980.3	2937.3
2001	2931.4	2942.1	2962.9	2963.6	2979.9	2972.0	2908.1	2953.7	2964.1	2970.4	2972.9	2969.3	2957.6
2002	2903.8	2920.9	2949.1	2976.2	2997.7	2982.5	2922.6	2971.3	2986.6	2997.5	2998.8	2996.6	2967.0
2003	2916.0	2924.3	2946.9	2968.2	2995.8	2981.5	2940.2	2989.8	3006.7	3038.1	3026.9	3017.4	2979.3
Trade, transportation, and utilities													
1990	626.3	626.5	629.6	625.7	628.0	630.9	626.9	631.8	632.9	632.5	639.0	644.4	631.2
1991	619.6	612.2	612.4	614.3	619.9	621.6	619.3	626.1	624.2	629.0	633.3	637.6	622.4
1992	606.4	602.1	607.3	609.6	614.5	621.2	623.0	629.5	630.4	631.8	637.4	645.3	621.5
1993	616.7	613.4	615.3	624.8	629.1	634.9	638.1	643.0	641.3	647.4	655.4	665.0	635.3
1994	634.8	631.5	636.9	637.6	644.2	651.9	650.4	655.9	658.0	661.7	671.7	682.2	651.4
1995	655.9	652.4	657.1	660.7	668.2	672.6	677.9	685.2	687.6	694.6	704.4	715.6	677.6
1996	681.5	680.2	685.5	681.3	689.8	694.9	691.3	695.5	694.4	699.4	713.3	724.8	694.3
1997	696.1	691.6	699.8	699.8	706.4	710.7	709.9	713.7	716.7	723.5	738.4	745.1	712.6
1998	699.0	696.0	702.0	709.0	714.0	722.4	717.0	721.9	724.4	726.4	739.1	748.7	718.3
1999	715.3	715.4	722.2	726.0	730.7	736.8	740.1	749.5	748.7	747.4	760.7	771.7	738.7
2000	735.4	734.6	741.8	746.9	753.2	759.2	751.1	753.8	752.6	755.6	765.1	772.7	751.8
2001	746.2	740.9	745.0	742.6	745.6	748.4	739.8	738.9	737.3	735.4	742.0	746.3	742.4
2002	715.3	710.2	716.6	720.1	723.8	728.4	725.0	727.4	724.9	725.2	738.2	745.0	725.0
2003	710.8	707.9	710.5	711.9	716.1	720.6	720.9	724.7	725.5	725.7	736.2	739.0	720.8
Wholesale trade													
1990	137.8	139.0	140.5	139.0	138.5	140.3	140.0	141.4	141.5	141.0	140.1	139.4	139.8
1991	143.2	143.1	143.9	143.9	144.0	144.4	142.4	144.1	143.7	145.1	144.2	143.7	143.8
1992	139.5	139.6	140.0	139.9	140.5	141.1	144.1	145.5	145.6	144.9	143.7	141.2	142.1
1993	137.9	138.6	139.2	139.8	140.0	140.7	141.3	142.7	142.8	143.9	143.5	142.4	141.0
1994	139.5	139.9	140.8	141.3	142.1	143.4	144.2	146.2	146.8	146.3	145.7	146.3	143.5
1995	143.9	144.8	146.0	146.6	147.6	148.5	148.9	149.9	150.2	150.7	150.1	150.7	148.1
1996	147.9	149.3	150.6	145.2	146.2	146.8	147.2	148.6	148.3	148.3	148.4	149.3	148.0
1997	147.0	148.4	150.1	150.3	151.4	151.7	152.0	153.2	154.2	155.2	155.1	154.8	151.9
1998	152.3	153.0	154.3	156.4	157.4	159.0	158.9	160.2	159.3	160.2	159.9	160.1	157.5
1999	158.0	158.7	159.4	161.1	161.7	162.3	163.5	164.0	163.4	165.0	165.3	165.6	162.3
2000	160.7	161.6	162.9	163.9	164.6	165.7	165.2	165.8	165.6	166.1	165.3	166.1	164.4
2001	162.1	162.1	162.8	161.6	162.0	162.8	163.0	162.8	162.8	162.6	161.9	162.0	162.4
2002	160.1	160.1	160.7	162.3	162.7	163.6	163.4	163.4	163.6	164.0	164.2	164.2	162.7
2003	162.0	161.9	162.8	162.9	163.2	163.7	164.0	165.1	164.7	164.5	163.7	164.1	163.6
Retail trade													
1990	377.4	375.0	376.0	374.2	376.7	378.1	375.9	377.9	377.3	377.2	385.2	390.4	378.4
1991	364.3	357.3	357.3	357.9	362.2	363.4	361.6	364.8	363.2	366.9	372.6	377.8	364.1
1992	353.9	348.9	352.5	354.1	357.3	362.2	359.5	362.5	362.0	365.0	372.3	382.0	361.0
1993	359.2	355.4	356.6	362.8	366.4	370.5	371.7	373.9	372.8	376.4	385.0	395.3	370.5
1994	372.2	367.4	371.4	373.0	376.7	382.1	378.9	381.8	383.8	387.7	399.3	409.3	381.9
1995	386.8	382.9	386.0	389.4	395.0	398.7	395.9	400.3	402.4	407.9	418.8	428.7	399.4
1996	401.9	397.6	401.2	402.0	408.7	413.0	409.6	411.7	410.6	414.5	428.7	439.0	411.5
1997	415.4	409.3	415.1	415.1	419.9	423.8	423.0	425.0	427.3	430.4	445.5	453.7	425.2
1998	419.7	416.7	420.7	421.9	425.6	430.7	425.1	427.8	431.3	432.5	445.5	454.0	429.2
1999	426.9	426.2	432.0	432.2	436.6	441.5	442.4	451.2	451.6	445.7	458.7	469.4	442.8
2000	442.4	440.1	445.1	448.3	453.5	457.5	450.2	451.9	450.7	451.6	463.0	470.3	452.0
2001	448.9	442.8	446.1	444.5	447.1	449.4	442.5	443.0	442.3	441.5	451.0	455.6	446.2
2002	431.0	426.5	431.8	433.6	436.2	438.6	434.9	436.5	434.7	433.7	446.4	453.4	436.4
2003	424.7	421.2	423.6	425.3	428.8	432.5	433.0	434.8	434.9	434.6	446.8	449.9	432.5

Employment by Industry: North Carolina—*Continued*

(Numbers in thousands. Not seasonally adjusted.)

Industry	January	February	March	April	May	June	July	August	September	October	November	December	Annual Average
STATEWIDE—*Continued*													
Transportation and utilities													
1990	111.1	112.5	113.1	112.5	112.8	112.5	111.0	112.5	114.1	114.3	113.7	114.6	112.8
1991	112.1	111.8	111.2	112.5	113.7	113.8	115.3	117.2	117.3	117.0	116.5	116.1	114.5
1992	113.0	113.6	114.8	115.6	116.7	117.9	119.4	121.5	122.8	121.9	121.4	122.1	118.3
1993	119.6	119.4	119.5	122.2	122.7	123.7	125.1	126.4	125.7	127.1	126.9	127.3	123.8
1994	123.1	124.2	124.7	123.3	125.4	126.4	127.3	127.9	127.4	127.7	126.7	126.6	125.8
1995	125.2	124.7	125.1	124.7	125.6	125.4	133.1	135.0	135.0	136.0	135.5	136.2	130.1
1996	131.7	133.3	133.7	134.1	134.9	135.1	134.5	135.2	135.5	136.6	136.2	136.5	134.7
1997	133.7	133.9	134.6	134.4	135.1	135.2	134.9	135.5	135.2	137.9	137.8	136.6	135.4
1998	127.0	126.3	127.0	130.7	131.0	132.7	133.0	133.9	133.8	133.7	133.7	134.6	131.4
1999	130.4	130.5	130.8	132.7	132.4	133.0	134.2	134.3	133.7	136.7	136.7	136.7	133.5
2000	132.3	132.9	133.8	134.7	135.1	136.0	135.7	136.1	136.3	137.9	136.8	136.3	135.3
2001	135.2	136.0	136.1	136.5	136.5	136.2	134.3	133.1	132.2	131.3	129.1	128.7	133.8
2002	124.2	123.6	124.1	124.2	124.9	126.2	126.7	127.5	126.6	127.5	127.6	127.4	125.9
2003	124.1	124.8	124.1	123.7	124.1	124.4	123.9	124.8	125.9	126.6	125.7	125.0	124.8
Information													
1990	55.8	56.4	56.8	57.4	57.6	58.2	58.3	58.2	58.6	57.9	58.2	58.5	57.6
1991	56.7	56.6	56.9	53.9	53.9	54.0	58.6	59.0	58.5	55.3	54.9	55.1	56.1
1992	53.7	53.7	54.0	53.8	54.3	54.8	55.0	55.0	55.1	55.8	56.0	56.5	54.8
1993	55.6	56.0	58.1	58.1	58.3	58.9	58.9	59.3	59.4	59.9	60.3	60.4	58.6
1994	56.8	57.1	57.6	60.6	61.0	61.7	61.6	61.8	62.1	62.5	63.0	63.3	60.7
1995	62.1	62.4	62.8	62.4	63.0	63.8	63.3	63.9	64.4	64.3	64.6	65.2	63.5
1996	64.1	64.4	64.5	64.4	65.1	65.9	66.4	66.9	66.8	67.5	68.2	68.7	66.0
1997	67.5	68.0	68.2	69.6	70.4	70.9	68.6	69.2	69.2	70.7	70.8	71.6	69.5
1998	70.3	71.0	70.9	72.4	72.9	73.7	74.0	74.1	73.9	74.2	75.7	75.8	73.2
1999	74.8	75.1	75.6	76.7	77.3	77.9	78.2	78.2	78.2	77.7	78.3	78.0	77.1
2000	78.1	78.5	79.3	80.8	81.2	82.4	82.9	83.4	83.4	83.8	84.4	84.3	81.8
2001	82.7	84.0	83.8	82.3	82.7	82.4	81.4	81.5	79.8	79.6	80.1	78.9	81.6
2002	79.6	79.4	79.6	79.3	79.5	79.4	78.6	78.2	77.5	77.7	77.7	77.9	78.7
2003	76.2	76.1	75.8	74.5	75.0	75.5	75.3	75.5	76.1	76.1	76.0	75.2	75.6
Financial activities													
1990	134.0	135.4	136.1	136.7	137.1	138.7	138.6	138.8	138.4	137.1	136.8	136.9	137.0
1991	135.0	134.6	135.0	136.0	136.7	137.7	137.8	138.3	137.2	135.5	135.4	135.7	136.2
1992	135.0	135.1	135.4	136.6	137.6	139.2	140.3	140.7	140.0	139.7	139.3	140.4	138.2
1993	138.7	139.1	139.9	141.3	141.2	142.4	143.5	143.6	142.1	142.1	141.7	142.3	141.4
1994	139.3	139.7	140.8	142.1	142.8	144.5	145.4	145.9	145.3	143.9	143.6	144.5	143.1
1995	140.9	141.5	142.6	144.0	145.0	147.3	147.7	148.6	148.1	147.7	148.3	149.4	145.9
1996	148.5	150.5	151.9	153.6	155.6	158.7	160.8	162.6	161.8	161.9	163.0	164.6	157.7
1997	162.5	163.8	165.7	166.9	168.6	170.1	171.7	172.7	172.8	172.4	172.6	174.5	169.5
1998	171.0	171.7	173.8	178.4	179.3	182.3	184.2	185.9	185.6	175.8	175.5	176.7	178.3
1999	174.3	175.4	175.9	177.5	177.4	178.8	179.5	179.3	178.0	179.4	178.4	179.0	177.7
2000	175.4	176.2	177.4	177.4	178.8	181.2	181.4	181.7	180.6	179.1	178.7	179.7	178.9
2001	184.5	185.1	186.0	186.3	187.1	189.1	189.2	189.4	187.9	187.3	187.2	187.4	187.2
2002	185.3	185.9	187.1	186.5	187.2	189.5	190.5	191.0	190.1	190.4	189.6	190.1	188.6
2003	187.1	187.7	188.9	190.0	191.4	193.2	194.8	195.3	192.8	192.7	192.0	192.2	191.5
Professional and business services													
1990	229.1	223.9	227.3	231.4	233.5	235.6	235.6	238.5	237.9	239.0	237.8	235.7	233.7
1991	224.1	225.0	226.5	228.2	229.0	230.9	232.2	236.9	239.8	244.8	244.5	243.1	233.7
1992	238.8	240.7	244.6	248.9	250.8	255.5	258.8	262.3	263.6	267.9	266.2	266.5	255.3
1993	261.2	267.1	269.0	275.9	278.5	280.5	280.6	283.8	285.1	285.8	285.9	285.1	278.2
1994	280.5	283.5	288.9	297.7	297.1	301.4	301.7	307.2	307.8	308.9	309.1	308.9	299.3
1995	300.0	304.8	308.2	310.0	305.7	310.2	309.0	314.7	316.7	320.6	320.8	320.8	311.7
1996	306.7	317.1	323.6	326.9	331.1	335.8	336.9	343.7	343.7	345.4	346.3	346.8	333.6
1997	335.2	341.9	348.6	356.1	358.9	362.8	365.8	371.9	375.1	373.5	374.0	374.6	361.5
1998	359.2	364.1	368.2	385.7	390.5	397.4	399.0	403.4	403.3	414.2	415.7	416.0	393.0
1999	405.5	414.0	418.3	425.9	426.2	431.7	429.7	432.2	431.6	440.4	439.2	439.2	427.8
2000	426.1	430.8	437.7	441.7	441.9	446.7	445.0	448.4	447.5	446.6	444.4	442.7	441.6
2001	427.0	426.2	427.7	424.7	422.0	424.1	414.7	417.6	414.2	414.8	410.9	411.3	419.6
2002	400.8	407.1	411.6	416.9	420.8	424.0	418.1	424.8	424.7	422.3	419.6	419.0	417.5
2003	407.8	409.4	414.6	419.7	422.8	423.7	423.9	427.2	427.5	427.9	426.9	422.7	421.2
Educational and health services													
1990	217.0	220.4	221.8	222.9	223.2	223.7	224.2	227.4	230.0	231.1	232.5	233.4	225.6
1991	232.7	234.3	235.5	236.1	237.0	236.9	237.0	239.3	242.9	244.1	245.4	246.5	238.9
1992	246.0	248.4	250.0	251.4	254.0	255.3	251.7	253.7	257.8	266.1	267.6	270.2	256.0
1993	268.8	273.1	275.2	275.9	275.7	275.2	275.5	276.5	280.4	282.1	282.7	283.6	277.0
1994	278.5	281.2	283.2	285.5	286.3	287.1	285.9	287.4	292.5	293.5	295.4	296.6	287.7
1995	293.0	296.3	298.9	299.6	301.5	302.4	299.8	301.6	306.6	309.3	311.6	312.8	302.7
1996	306.7	310.9	314.8	314.9	317.5	316.5	315.7	318.2	321.6	325.0	327.6	329.4	318.2
1997	326.9	331.5	334.5	335.8	337.5	337.1	336.5	337.6	344.0	341.3	343.3	344.4	337.5
1998	345.8	348.9	350.9	350.9	352.3	343.9	349.3	351.6	355.6	358.1	360.3	360.5	352.3
1999	357.2	361.2	363.0	365.0	364.4	363.7	363.2	364.6	368.7	371.4	372.5	373.6	365.7
2000	368.0	371.9	374.1	374.9	375.8	377.0	377.2	379.0	381.1	382.4	384.0	384.8	377.5
2001	387.5	391.1	394.0	396.6	398.1	398.8	398.7	402.3	403.9	406.1	408.1	409.5	399.6
2002	407.5	411.4	413.1	418.2	418.9	417.5	414.5	418.0	419.9	423.3	424.5	424.6	417.6
2003	420.3	423.4	425.4	426.7	427.9	427.1	424.8	429.0	428.7	435.6	435.0	435.3	428.3

Employment by Industry: North Carolina—*Continued*

(Numbers in thousands. Not seasonally adjusted.)

Industry	January	February	March	April	May	June	July	August	September	October	November	December	Annual Average
STATEWIDE—*Continued*													
Leisure and hospitality													
1990	214.2	218.5	223.4	232.3	239.7	247.6	247.2	249.6	243.5	235.6	230.8	227.8	234.1
1991	215.4	216.4	221.5	230.3	240.6	246.4	246.5	247.6	240.3	236.9	231.2	228.1	233.4
1992	221.1	223.7	230.1	238.2	249.5	255.9	257.4	259.4	254.3	248.6	244.2	241.3	243.6
1993	231.8	236.5	240.9	252.7	261.9	267.2	269.4	270.2	262.8	258.3	253.4	250.8	254.6
1994	241.6	243.3	249.8	260.0	268.4	276.7	278.7	280.8	275.4	268.4	264.9	262.5	264.2
1995	252.4	255.4	261.3	271.2	281.6	291.6	291.7	292.2	286.0	280.2	276.8	273.3	276.1
1996	260.4	264.5	273.3	281.5	293.6	299.3	298.4	299.7	292.9	287.2	282.2	281.2	284.5
1997	271.5	275.0	282.9	293.7	306.1	312.2	307.6	309.1	304.1	293.7	292.0	291.0	294.9
1998	283.0	286.0	294.4	298.3	309.7	318.2	317.9	318.9	311.2	306.3	302.8	301.1	303.9
1999	289.1	293.8	300.4	311.4	319.4	325.7	330.3	329.1	321.7	320.4	315.9	315.4	314.3
2000	300.4	302.5	310.8	320.2	329.8	338.5	335.9	335.4	328.4	322.6	317.2	314.4	321.3
2001	306.6	309.9	317.1	326.1	335.0	343.2	340.1	340.6	330.5	322.0	316.5	312.3	325.0
2002	305.6	309.3	318.2	332.4	342.5	350.3	350.5	350.6	343.0	334.3	329.0	326.9	332.7
2003	313.2	313.5	320.8	333.2	345.2	351.6	353.7	353.5	341.8	340.3	327.9	325.1	335.0
Other services													
1990	104.5	105.7	106.5	107.3	107.8	108.9	109.1	109.4	108.3	107.1	107.5	107.3	107.4
1991	105.6	105.8	106.2	106.6	107.3	108.7	108.8	109.0	108.6	108.4	108.6	108.8	107.7
1992	106.8	106.7	107.6	107.7	105.8	104.6	102.5	98.9	95.0	93.0	90.4	88.3	100.6
1993	84.1	81.9	79.6	83.4	87.3	92.3	95.4	98.1	100.1	103.0	106.3	110.0	93.4
1994	111.6	115.2	119.3	120.1	120.7	122.7	123.1	123.0	122.1	122.4	122.7	123.3	120.5
1995	121.6	121.8	123.5	123.8	124.8	127.5	126.9	126.3	125.4	126.0	126.3	126.9	125.0
1996	120.6	122.3	123.5	123.8	125.6	127.7	127.6	127.1	126.1	126.5	127.0	127.5	125.4
1997	122.5	122.9	123.9	125.6	127.4	129.7	130.4	130.7	130.6	131.4	132.2	133.7	128.4
1998	133.6	134.4	136.5	137.9	139.7	143.3	143.4	142.9	142.5	143.1	144.5	145.8	140.6
1999	145.5	146.7	148.2	150.7	151.9	155.0	155.8	155.5	154.6	156.4	157.1	158.6	153.0
2000	157.5	159.2	160.7	161.3	162.3	164.5	164.4	163.5	162.9	162.5	162.4	162.5	161.9
2001	162.3	163.5	164.6	164.3	166.1	168.6	169.0	168.2	167.2	166.8	167.2	167.1	166.2
2002	164.1	165.0	165.9	168.0	168.7	170.1	167.7	165.1	162.9	164.0	162.7	160.1	165.4
2003	158.6	158.9	159.1	162.1	164.1	166.4	167.1	165.0	162.1	162.7	161.9	160.7	162.4
Government													
1990	486.8	494.5	500.7	501.1	506.6	502.1	451.0	454.1	487.6	502.4	511.3	505.2	491.9
1991	500.4	507.4	511.3	511.8	508.9	504.7	457.6	465.1	499.3	515.7	520.9	517.5	501.7
1992	512.4	518.8	522.2	501.7	508.8	511.7	453.5	464.2	494.3	508.8	518.7	514.4	502.4
1993	526.5	530.6	534.2	533.5	532.3	530.9	482.3	491.1	526.4	540.2	551.2	545.6	527.0
1994	537.5	542.0	546.5	547.0	546.8	545.2	484.2	497.1	540.1	554.4	564.4	558.1	538.6
1995	551.9	557.8	562.3	560.5	556.9	555.7	498.5	505.0	551.1	566.0	571.7	569.5	550.5
1996	559.4	566.7	570.8	571.6	571.4	570.4	501.8	517.6	564.8	577.0	584.0	580.8	561.3
1997	575.1	580.7	584.3	587.1	583.9	582.0	515.5	537.7	580.2	593.8	598.8	596.7	576.3
1998	589.5	597.8	600.9	602.1	599.3	588.1	531.7	562.9	604.1	615.9	616.5	614.6	593.6
1999	607.2	617.3	620.1	612.0	608.7	590.0	540.1	583.1	611.3	619.2	622.0	620.1	604.2
2000	611.0	618.2	627.5	630.0	636.1	621.7	562.1	608.1	631.4	639.1	642.0	639.2	622.2
2001	634.6	641.4	644.7	640.7	643.3	617.4	575.2	615.2	643.3	658.4	660.9	656.5	636.0
2002	645.6	652.6	657.0	654.8	656.3	623.3	577.7	616.2	643.6	660.3	657.5	653.0	641.5
2003	642.0	647.4	651.8	650.1	653.3	623.4	579.7	619.6	652.2	677.1	671.0	667.2	644.6
Federal government													
1990	55.7	55.9	58.9	58.0	64.3	62.5	60.7	58.1	56.4	56.3	56.2	55.4	58.2
1991	55.5	56.2	56.6	56.5	57.2	58.0	58.3	58.4	58.1	57.9	57.9	58.3	57.4
1992	57.5	57.1	57.5	57.8	57.8	58.1	58.4	58.3	57.9	57.8	57.6	58.1	57.8
1993	57.6	57.5	57.5	57.9	57.9	58.2	58.8	59.0	59.0	58.8	59.1	59.6	58.4
1994	59.0	58.9	58.9	59.5	59.8	60.1	59.9	60.2	60.7	60.8	60.5	60.9	59.9
1995	60.5	60.5	60.6	60.5	60.7	61.0	61.1	61.0	61.3	61.5	61.7	62.4	61.0
1996	61.7	61.6	61.6	62.2	62.2	62.6	62.1	62.4	61.9	61.5	61.4	61.8	61.9
1997	60.7	60.4	60.4	60.8	61.3	61.9	61.8	62.2	61.9	61.4	62.6	63.3	61.5
1998	61.4	61.2	61.1	61.2	61.7	61.8	61.8	62.0	61.8	61.7	62.1	63.2	61.7
1999	62.1	62.0	61.2	61.9	61.2	61.2	61.4	61.8	61.7	61.8	62.4	63.5	61.8
2000	61.8	62.2	66.9	65.1	74.5	80.3	70.2	73.4	62.1	62.0	62.2	63.7	67.0
2001	62.2	61.8	62.0	61.6	61.9	62.1	62.1	62.2	61.8	61.8	61.9	63.0	62.0
2002	61.3	61.1	61.3	61.2	61.4	62.3	61.8	61.9	62.4	62.4	62.8	63.5	62.0
2003	62.2	61.7	61.4	61.3	61.3	61.4	61.4	61.1	61.1	61.3	61.1	62.3	61.5
State government													
1990	138.0	144.3	145.8	145.8	140.8	135.8	128.1	131.2	138.1	146.1	149.4	145.2	140.7
1991	140.2	145.5	147.6	147.6	143.1	137.4	130.9	134.9	142.9	150.5	152.8	150.0	143.6
1992	145.9	151.9	153.6	132.3	133.7	132.8	129.1	130.8	133.1	136.2	136.4	136.5	137.6
1993	153.6	156.9	158.2	157.0	154.4	148.1	142.8	146.6	152.5	158.3	163.0	160.0	154.2
1994	155.3	158.7	161.2	160.9	155.9	150.3	143.4	151.2	157.1	162.7	165.3	161.3	156.9
1995	158.5	163.3	165.7	163.5	160.1	154.0	148.0	151.5	159.9	166.6	169.1	165.4	160.4
1996	159.3	166.1	167.4	166.2	163.7	159.0	150.6	155.8	162.7	169.9	171.5	167.7	163.3
1997	164.8	169.5	170.9	172.5	166.8	162.2	154.0	157.5	165.9	172.8	174.4	171.1	166.8
1998	166.0	172.1	173.6	175.1	169.8	163.5	156.5	160.0	170.6	178.9	178.7	176.3	170.0
1999	170.9	177.6	179.6	176.5	172.6	167.4	159.4	164.5	172.2	178.5	177.3	174.2	172.5
2000	170.4	176.3	177.7	180.8	176.7	171.5	165.3	168.6	182.2	187.4	189.1	185.0	177.5
2001	180.1	184.6	186.5	185.7	186.8	183.7	177.0	180.9	185.4	189.2	188.9	188.3	184.8
2002	182.0	185.7	189.0	187.8	187.7	182.4	174.6	177.7	181.5	182.4	182.4	181.0	182.9
2003	174.6	177.9	180.1	178.3	179.7	177.5	169.0	173.8	181.3	187.9	190.6	187.7	179.9

Employment by Industry: North Carolina—*Continued*

(Numbers in thousands. Not seasonally adjusted.)

Industry	January	February	March	April	May	June	July	August	September	October	November	December	Annual Average
STATEWIDE—*Continued*													
Local government													
1990	293.1	294.3	296.0	297.3	301.5	303.8	262.2	264.8	293.1	300.0	305.7	304.6	293.0
1991	304.7	305.7	307.1	307.7	308.6	309.3	268.4	271.8	298.3	307.3	310.2	309.2	300.6
1992	309.0	309.8	311.1	311.6	317.3	320.8	266.0	275.1	303.3	314.8	324.7	319.8	306.9
1993	315.3	316.2	318.5	318.6	320.0	324.6	280.7	285.5	314.9	323.1	329.1	326.0	314.3
1994	323.2	324.4	326.4	326.6	331.1	334.8	280.9	285.7	322.3	330.9	338.6	335.9	321.7
1995	332.9	334.0	336.0	336.5	336.1	340.7	289.4	292.5	329.9	337.9	340.9	341.7	329.0
1996	338.4	339.0	341.8	343.2	345.5	348.8	289.1	299.4	340.2	345.6	351.1	351.3	336.1
1997	349.6	350.8	353.0	353.8	355.8	357.9	299.7	318.0	352.4	359.6	361.8	362.3	347.8
1998	362.1	364.5	366.2	365.8	367.8	362.8	313.4	340.9	371.7	375.3	375.7	375.1	361.7
1999	374.2	377.7	379.3	373.6	374.9	361.4	319.3	356.8	377.4	378.9	382.3	382.4	369.8
2000	378.8	379.7	382.9	384.1	384.9	369.9	326.6	366.1	387.1	389.7	390.7	390.5	377.5
2001	392.3	395.0	396.2	393.5	394.7	371.6	336.0	372.1	396.1	407.5	410.1	405.3	389.2
2002	402.3	405.8	406.7	405.8	407.2	378.6	341.3	376.6	399.7	415.5	412.3	408.5	396.7
2003	405.2	407.8	410.3	410.5	412.3	384.5	349.3	384.7	409.8	427.9	419.3	417.2	403.2
CHARLOTTE-GASTONIA-ROCK HILL													
Total nonfarm													
1990	615.2	621.5	626.7	626.4	629.7	632.2	620.2	623.0	628.9	626.7	627.2	626.8	625.3
1991	607.1	606.4	609.2	610.0	613.2	613.2	606.6	611.9	617.5	619.9	618.5	619.3	612.7
1992	606.2	608.2	614.9	618.8	624.0	625.6	616.4	624.9	629.9	637.9	639.9	643.4	624.1
1993	629.2	632.8	637.5	645.9	651.2	656.4	649.1	652.3	659.6	668.5	672.5	677.5	652.7
1994	660.2	665.3	672.9	677.5	681.6	688.6	681.1	682.9	695.1	697.0	701.1	705.9	684.1
1995	692.7	697.0	704.3	708.1	710.8	714.9	702.4	707.6	717.4	719.0	723.6	727.6	710.4
1996	706.7	715.7	722.7	724.7	732.1	734.9	719.6	727.3	736.9	740.8	746.9	752.7	730.0
1997	733.7	739.1	748.4	751.6	758.5	761.2	743.2	753.9	763.2	758.5	763.3	769.2	753.6
1998	754.1	759.8	764.7	771.9	779.6	783.8	776.0	785.6	791.4	791.3	793.7	797.7	779.1
1999	793.8	802.5	807.6	809.2	813.0	813.1	809.2	819.6	825.9	829.2	831.0	836.3	815.8
2000	824.2	826.9	836.1	843.2	849.3	855.2	835.9	840.7	845.2	849.9	851.9	852.8	842.6
2001	830.4	833.8	834.4	836.6	836.1	836.6	818.6	828.6	830.3	834.6	833.1	830.2	831.9
2002	810.5	817.3	823.9	825.8	828.1	829.1	815.6	827.3	831.6	834.0	834.1	832.3	825.8
2003	814.2	814.4	821.0	821.1	828.0	824.4	812.3	819.1	825.4	834.5	832.9	833.6	823.4
Total private													
1990	546.1	551.3	555.9	554.7	557.5	560.1	556.6	557.5	558.2	553.7	553.9	553.2	554.8
1991	535.0	533.5	535.7	537.5	541.0	541.7	542.1	546.3	546.1	546.0	544.3	544.6	541.1
1992	532.7	533.4	539.5	543.4	548.6	551.7	554.0	555.3	557.5	561.9	562.7	566.1	550.5
1993	553.7	556.8	560.5	569.2	574.1	579.8	579.9	582.7	584.1	591.0	593.4	597.9	576.9
1994	582.1	586.6	593.8	598.9	603.0	609.6	610.1	613.9	617.6	617.2	620.4	623.5	606.3
1995	612.9	616.9	623.0	626.0	629.1	634.2	630.4	634.2	635.3	635.9	638.3	641.2	629.7
1996	622.5	630.3	636.6	638.8	646.0	649.8	647.3	651.3	651.7	654.5	658.9	664.1	645.9
1997	645.7	650.4	659.1	662.6	669.2	672.8	665.4	669.9	674.3	667.9	672.3	677.5	665.5
1998	663.1	667.7	672.6	679.6	687.3	694.1	694.9	698.6	698.7	695.9	698.6	701.9	687.7
1999	699.6	706.9	711.9	714.1	718.3	722.4	724.5	727.6	728.8	732.2	733.3	738.0	721.4
2000	726.8	729.1	736.5	743.7	748.2	755.6	748.9	745.9	747.5	747.9	750.5	751.6	744.3
2001	731.9	733.8	734.1	735.6	735.2	740.0	732.9	734.8	730.8	730.5	726.9	725.5	732.7
2002	707.8	713.0	718.7	721.5	723.8	729.0	725.9	730.4	728.4	726.4	726.4	726.1	723.1
2003	709.6	708.8	714.8	716.8	723.1	724.6	720.4	719.2	719.3	722.0	722.1	723.3	718.7
Goods-producing													
1990	185.0	186.2	186.9	186.9	187.8	188.5	187.0	186.0	185.4	183.1	183.5	181.7	185.6
1991	177.0	176.5	175.2	174.9	175.0	175.4	174.3	174.9	174.4	172.7	171.3	170.2	174.3
1992	167.7	167.9	168.7	169.4	171.1	172.3	172.4	173.0	173.3	173.6	173.5	174.0	171.4
1993	172.8	173.9	174.1	175.4	177.0	178.8	178.0	178.2	178.5	178.5	179.0	179.0	176.9
1994	176.7	177.8	179.6	180.1	181.0	182.8	182.7	183.3	184.3	185.2	186.1	185.9	182.1
1995	184.6	185.5	187.0	187.3	190.0	191.4	187.2	188.0	187.6	187.0	186.4	185.6	187.3
1996	181.7	184.7	184.7	185.8	187.3	188.1	186.0	187.2	186.6	186.9	186.8	186.5	186.0
1997	182.2	183.6	185.3	185.5	186.2	187.3	184.7	185.8	187.1	185.2	185.2	185.7	185.3
1998	186.4	187.0	187.4	187.6	188.6	189.4	186.6	187.8	187.0	183.5	183.6	183.5	186.5
1999	185.7	186.4	186.7	186.1	186.2	187.4	187.2	187.5	187.2	186.7	185.7	186.2	186.5
2000	184.2	184.1	185.3	187.9	188.7	190.2	187.5	182.6	185.5	181.2	183.6	183.1	185.3
2001	181.6	181.8	178.1	181.3	178.5	181.4	179.8	179.9	179.8	177.6	175.8	174.7	179.2
2002	167.0	169.7	170.1	168.4	168.5	169.5	168.1	168.8	167.7	166.7	165.3	163.4	167.8
2003	161.3	160.5	161.4	159.1	159.6	159.7	156.5	154.7	155.1	153.7	153.1	153.8	157.4
Natural resources and mining													
2002	0.8	0.9	0.9	0.8	0.8	0.8	0.8	0.8	0.8	0.9	0.9	0.9	0.8
2003	0.9	0.8	0.8	0.9	0.9	0.9	0.8	0.8	0.9	0.9	0.9	0.9	0.9
Construction													
2002	52.4	52.1	53.0	53.5	54.1	54.5	54.5	54.6	53.6	52.6	52.1	51.8	53.2
2003	50.2	49.9	50.5	49.1	50.1	50.6	50.8	50.4	51.0	50.6	50.3	50.7	50.4

Employment by Industry: North Carolina—*Continued*

(Numbers in thousands. Not seasonally adjusted.)

Industry	January	February	March	April	May	June	July	August	September	October	November	December	Annual Average
CHARLOTTE-GASTONIA-ROCK HILL—*Continued*													
Manufacturing													
1990	148.9	149.6	149.8	149.9	150.0	150.3	148.8	147.9	147.7	145.5	146.4	145.3	148.3
1991	143.2	143.1	141.8	141.4	141.5	141.9	141.3	142.1	142.0	140.6	139.8	139.0	141.4
1992	137.5	137.8	138.1	138.3	139.2	139.9	139.7	140.1	140.6	140.7	140.8	141.1	139.4
1993	141.2	142.0	141.9	142.0	142.9	143.7	142.6	142.5	142.8	142.7	143.2	142.9	142.5
1994	142.4	143.0	143.5	143.1	143.7	144.7	144.8	145.3	145.9	146.4	146.8	146.5	144.6
1995	145.4	146.5	147.2	147.0	148.9	149.8	146.4	146.5	146.1	145.5	145.0	144.2	146.5
1996	142.4	143.8	143.3	143.2	143.4	143.2	141.6	142.3	142.0	141.8	141.6	141.3	142.4
1997	138.7	139.6	140.2	139.9	139.8	140.3	137.4	138.4	139.5	138.6	138.4	138.8	139.1
1998	139.9	140.6	140.3	138.6	138.6	139.1	135.6	136.9	136.3	133.2	133.1	133.2	137.1
1999	136.1	136.3	136.0	134.1	133.8	134.5	133.6	133.8	133.6	133.5	132.7	133.1	134.2
2000	132.6	132.4	132.2	133.7	133.8	134.5	132.1	126.9	129.9	125.9	128.5	128.2	130.8
2001	125.4	125.5	120.5	123.6	120.3	122.5	120.4	120.5	120.5	119.6	118.6	118.2	121.3
2002	113.8	116.7	116.2	114.1	113.6	114.2	112.8	113.4	113.3	113.2	112.3	110.7	113.7
2003	110.2	109.8	110.1	109.1	108.6	108.2	104.9	103.5	103.2	102.2	101.9	102.2	106.2
Service-providing													
1990	430.2	435.3	439.8	439.5	441.9	443.7	433.2	437.0	443.5	443.6	443.7	445.1	439.7
1991	430.1	429.9	434.0	435.1	438.2	437.8	432.3	437.0	443.1	447.2	447.2	449.1	438.4
1992	438.5	440.3	446.2	449.4	452.9	453.3	444.0	451.9	456.6	464.3	466.4	469.4	452.7
1993	456.4	458.9	463.4	470.5	474.2	477.6	471.1	474.1	481.1	490.0	493.5	498.5	475.7
1994	483.5	487.5	493.3	497.4	500.6	505.8	498.4	499.6	510.8	511.8	515.0	520.0	501.9
1995	508.1	511.5	517.3	520.8	520.8	523.5	515.2	519.6	529.8	532.0	537.2	542.0	523.1
1996	525.0	531.0	538.0	538.9	544.8	546.8	533.6	540.1	550.3	553.9	560.1	566.2	544.0
1997	551.5	555.5	563.1	566.1	572.3	573.9	558.5	568.1	576.1	573.3	578.1	583.5	568.3
1998	567.7	572.8	577.3	584.3	591.0	594.4	589.4	597.8	604.4	607.8	610.1	614.2	592.6
1999	608.1	616.1	620.9	623.1	626.8	625.7	622.0	632.1	638.7	642.5	645.3	650.1	629.2
2000	640.0	642.8	650.8	655.3	660.6	665.0	648.4	658.1	659.7	668.7	668.3	669.7	657.2
2001	648.7	652.1	656.3	655.3	657.5	655.1	638.9	648.7	650.5	657.0	658.3	655.4	652.8
2002	643.5	647.6	653.8	657.4	659.6	659.6	647.5	658.5	663.9	667.3	668.8	668.9	658.0
2003	652.9	653.9	659.6	662.0	668.4	664.7	655.8	664.4	670.3	680.8	679.8	679.8	666.0
Trade, transportation, and utilities													
1990	148.8	148.9	149.7	147.7	147.9	147.7	146.7	147.2	147.4	147.4	149.0	150.3	148.2
1991	141.4	139.3	140.0	140.3	141.4	141.1	142.9	144.6	144.2	142.8	143.8	144.9	142.2
1992	139.4	138.0	139.1	141.3	142.4	143.1	143.8	144.5	145.2	146.5	148.2	151.0	143.5
1993	143.6	143.2	143.6	145.1	145.3	146.4	147.3	148.0	148.0	150.7	152.9	155.3	147.4
1994	148.4	148.5	149.3	149.6	151.4	153.0	153.8	154.7	155.3	155.9	158.4	161.1	153.2
1995	156.9	156.6	157.2	158.1	160.7	161.0	166.0	167.0	168.2	168.9	171.5	173.9	163.8
1996	166.9	166.0	167.1	167.0	168.3	168.6	167.8	168.6	169.1	170.6	174.0	177.1	169.2
1997	171.2	170.3	171.5	172.1	173.1	173.8	171.8	172.2	172.5	171.4	174.6	176.5	172.5
1998	166.1	165.3	165.8	168.3	169.7	171.4	171.3	172.4	173.4	169.1	172.1	174.2	169.9
1999	170.5	170.9	172.1	173.7	175.2	175.7	176.8	177.9	178.7	179.6	182.4	185.4	176.5
2000	179.9	180.0	181.4	181.0	182.2	183.9	183.4	183.6	183.7	184.7	187.2	188.8	183.3
2001	181.6	180.8	181.5	180.5	180.9	181.5	179.3	179.3	179.0	179.7	181.1	182.0	180.6
2002	175.4	174.1	175.3	174.4	174.5	175.3	174.9	175.8	175.3	175.5	178.9	180.5	175.8
2003	172.5	172.2	172.3	171.7	172.0	172.7	172.4	172.4	174.2	174.7	177.4	178.2	173.6
Wholesale trade													
1990	39.3	39.7	40.1	39.1	39.0	39.1	39.2	39.1	39.0	39.0	39.0	39.0	39.2
1991	38.4	38.2	38.5	38.3	38.4	38.3	38.9	39.0	38.9	39.4	39.4	39.3	38.7
1992	38.6	38.4	38.5	39.5	39.5	39.6	39.6	39.8	39.9	40.7	40.6	41.0	39.6
1993	39.9	40.2	40.4	40.6	40.6	40.8	41.0	41.1	41.2	41.7	41.8	41.9	40.9
1994	41.2	41.5	41.8	42.7	42.8	43.3	43.6	43.8	43.9	43.5	43.8	44.1	43.0
1995	43.7	44.1	44.4	44.5	45.1	45.2	44.6	44.6	44.7	45.0	45.3	45.3	44.7
1996	44.4	45.1	45.5	45.2	45.5	45.4	45.5	45.6	45.5	45.7	46.1	46.6	45.5
1997	45.8	46.2	46.4	46.2	46.5	46.4	46.1	46.4	46.6	46.4	46.4	46.3	46.3
1998	46.8	46.9	47.2	48.1	48.3	48.9	49.2	49.3	48.9	48.4	48.8	48.8	48.3
1999	49.3	49.5	49.7	50.4	50.4	50.5	51.3	51.6	51.4	51.6	51.9	52.1	50.8
2000	51.9	52.2	52.6	51.1	51.5	51.9	51.7	51.8	51.9	51.9	52.1	52.3	51.9
2001	52.7	52.8	53.1	50.9	50.7	50.8	50.6	50.4	50.3	49.9	49.7	49.4	50.9
2002	48.7	48.6	48.8	48.6	48.4	48.3	48.4	48.3	48.3	48.2	48.3	48.2	48.4
2003	47.6	47.7	47.6	47.4	47.3	47.4	47.6	47.2	47.7	47.7	47.5	47.7	47.5
Retail trade													
1990	74.3	73.8	74.1	73.5	73.7	73.6	73.4	73.9	74.0	73.8	75.5	77.0	74.2
1991	69.9	68.5	68.6	68.1	68.9	68.6	69.4	70.4	70.1	70.6	71.7	73.0	69.8
1992	68.1	66.7	67.4	68.2	69.0	69.5	69.1	69.4	69.5	70.7	72.6	75.0	69.6
1993	69.6	68.6	68.8	69.9	70.1	70.6	70.5	70.8	70.8	72.6	75.0	77.2	71.2
1994	72.6	71.6	72.0	72.6	73.1	74.0	74.2	74.7	75.5	76.6	78.8	81.3	74.7
1995	76.9	75.8	76.5	76.8	78.3	78.6	77.3	78.0	79.0	80.6	83.0	85.5	78.8
1996	79.6	78.2	78.7	78.7	79.6	80.2	79.4	80.0	80.4	81.1	83.9	86.6	80.5
1997	82.3	80.9	81.6	82.2	83.0	83.9	83.2	83.5	84.0	83.3	86.4	88.7	83.5
1998	84.2	83.8	84.2	83.9	84.8	85.3	84.8	85.5	86.8	84.5	87.0	89.1	85.3
1999	84.9	85.0	86.0	85.7	87.2	87.8	87.8	88.5	89.4	90.0	92.6	95.1	88.3
2000	90.2	89.8	90.3	90.9	91.7	92.8	90.9	90.8	90.7	90.9	93.6	95.1	91.4
2001	90.6	89.1	89.9	90.1	90.6	91.3	89.3	89.4	89.3	89.5	91.7	93.0	90.3
2002	88.3	87.3	88.2	87.9	88.0	88.5	87.7	88.2	88.0	88.4	91.7	93.3	88.8
2003	87.0	86.3	87.0	87.0	87.3	87.9	87.3	87.9	88.7	88.9	91.6	92.5	88.3

Employment by Industry: North Carolina—*Continued*

(Numbers in thousands. Not seasonally adjusted.)

Industry	January	February	March	April	May	June	July	August	September	October	November	December	Annual Average
CHARLOTTE-GASTONIA-ROCK HILL—*Continued*													
Transportation and utilities													
1990	35.2	35.4	35.5	35.1	35.2	35.0	34.1	34.2	34.4	34.6	34.5	34.3	34.7
1991	33.1	32.6	32.9	33.9	34.1	34.2	34.6	35.2	35.2	32.8	32.7	32.6	33.6
1992	32.7	32.9	33.2	33.6	33.9	34.0	35.1	35.3	35.8	35.1	35.0	35.0	34.3
1993	34.1	34.4	34.4	34.6	34.6	35.0	35.8	36.1	36.0	36.4	36.1	36.2	35.3
1994	34.6	35.4	35.5	34.3	35.5	35.7	36.0	36.2	35.9	35.8	35.8	35.7	35.5
1995	36.3	36.7	36.3	36.8	37.3	37.2	44.1	44.4	44.5	43.3	43.2	43.1	40.2
1996	42.9	42.7	42.9	43.1	43.2	43.0	42.9	43.0	43.2	43.8	44.0	43.9	43.2
1997	43.1	43.2	43.5	43.7	43.6	43.5	42.5	42.3	41.9	41.7	41.8	41.5	42.6
1998	35.1	34.6	34.4	36.3	36.6	37.2	37.3	37.6	37.7	36.2	36.3	36.3	36.3
1999	36.3	36.4	36.4	37.6	37.6	37.4	37.7	37.8	37.9	38.0	37.9	38.2	37.4
2000	37.8	38.0	38.5	39.0	39.0	39.2	40.8	41.0	41.1	41.9	41.5	41.4	39.9
2001	38.3	38.9	38.5	39.5	39.6	39.4	39.4	39.5	39.4	40.3	39.7	39.6	39.3
2002	38.4	38.2	38.3	37.9	38.1	38.5	38.8	39.3	39.0	38.9	38.9	39.0	38.6
2003	37.9	38.2	37.7	37.3	37.4	37.4	37.5	37.3	37.8	38.1	38.3	38.0	37.7
Information													
1990	16.6	16.7	16.8	16.9	16.9	16.9	17.0	16.9	17.3	17.6	17.6	17.6	17.0
1991	17.2	17.2	17.4	16.8	16.6	16.5	16.8	16.9	17.4	17.0	17.2	17.3	17.0
1992	16.6	16.7	16.8	16.5	16.6	16.6	16.5	16.6	16.8	17.2	17.2	17.2	16.7
1993	17.2	17.3	17.7	17.5	17.5	17.7	17.5	17.8	18.1	18.7	18.8	18.9	17.8
1994	18.1	18.2	18.4	19.2	19.2	19.2	19.7	19.8	20.2	20.5	20.6	20.6	19.4
1995	20.3	20.4	20.4	20.5	20.8	20.7	20.0	20.2	20.6	20.3	20.3	20.5	20.4
1996	18.7	18.9	18.9	18.8	18.9	19.3	19.4	19.6	19.8	20.1	20.5	20.7	19.4
1997	20.1	20.2	20.3	20.4	20.5	20.8	20.6	20.8	21.1	21.1	21.2	21.5	20.7
1998	21.7	21.9	21.6	22.9	22.9	23.3	23.0	23.1	23.4	23.4	23.6	23.7	22.8
1999	24.0	24.3	24.6	25.0	25.0	25.2	25.6	25.6	25.8	25.2	25.4	25.2	25.0
2000	25.3	25.4	25.5	25.6	25.3	25.5	25.5	25.6	25.7	25.8	26.2	25.9	25.6
2001	25.5	25.6	25.7	24.9	24.9	25.0	25.0	24.7	24.1	24.7	24.7	24.4	24.9
2002	24.6	24.5	24.7	24.3	24.3	24.5	24.4	24.3	24.2	24.5	24.5	24.7	24.5
2003	24.1	23.8	23.9	23.6	23.5	23.8	23.9	24.1	24.9	25.5	25.5	24.9	24.3
Financial activities													
1990	39.1	39.6	39.6	39.6	39.7	40.0	39.9	39.8	39.7	39.6	39.8	39.8	39.6
1991	39.4	39.4	39.4	40.3	40.4	40.6	40.3	40.4	40.1	40.8	40.8	41.2	40.2
1992	39.4	39.4	39.7	39.6	40.0	40.4	40.6	40.7	40.5	41.0	41.2	41.4	40.3
1993	40.7	40.7	41.1	41.7	41.9	42.2	42.2	42.6	42.3	42.9	42.9	43.2	42.0
1994	40.9	41.3	41.5	41.3	41.5	41.9	42.3	42.3	42.6	42.5	42.5	42.8	41.9
1995	41.5	41.6	42.0	42.2	42.7	43.3	42.9	43.1	43.1	43.1	43.4	43.7	42.7
1996	44.3	45.2	45.7	46.7	47.0	47.9	48.9	49.4	49.2	49.5	50.0	50.3	47.8
1997	50.0	50.3	50.8	51.1	51.8	51.5	52.6	52.9	53.0	52.6	52.7	53.5	51.9
1998	54.0	54.3	54.7	48.8	49.1	49.7	50.9	51.5	51.4	51.1	51.1	51.4	51.5
1999	52.1	52.6	52.6	52.5	52.3	52.4	52.4	52.4	52.2	52.3	52.4	52.7	52.4
2000	52.5	52.8	52.8	54.0	54.5	55.3	54.9	55.1	54.9	55.1	55.2	55.5	54.3
2001	61.2	61.5	61.7	62.0	62.1	62.3	62.9	63.3	63.2	63.1	63.6	63.7	62.6
2002	64.0	64.3	64.8	65.2	65.4	66.0	67.0	67.3	67.3	67.8	68.3	68.4	66.3
2003	67.8	68.1	68.3	68.2	68.4	68.8	70.4	70.2	69.0	68.9	69.7	70.3	69.0
Professional and business services													
1990	58.3	59.6	60.7	60.4	61.1	61.6	61.9	62.3	62.7	61.6	60.7	60.5	60.9
1991	59.7	59.7	59.9	60.6	61.2	61.1	61.2	62.1	62.9	65.0	64.9	64.5	61.9
1992	64.6	65.1	66.0	66.5	67.2	67.6	69.1	69.7	70.5	72.5	72.3	72.3	68.6
1993	71.7	72.8	73.5	75.6	76.1	77.3	77.2	78.1	78.8	80.2	80.1	80.7	76.8
1994	80.7	81.5	82.8	85.5	85.6	86.6	86.2	88.4	89.2	87.0	87.0	87.1	85.6
1995	85.7	86.8	87.6	87.8	82.2	83.4	82.1	83.2	83.7	84.6	84.9	85.3	84.7
1996	82.1	83.9	85.3	84.9	86.0	86.6	86.7	88.1	88.7	88.9	89.6	90.6	86.7
1997	86.6	88.2	90.6	91.5	92.4	93.2	92.9	95.5	97.2	96.5	96.8	97.4	93.2
1998	91.7	93.7	94.4	101.8	103.6	105.6	107.4	107.9	108.1	116.7	116.4	116.4	105.3
1999	115.5	118.6	119.5	120.8	121.4	123.0	123.4	124.8	125.9	127.5	127.3	127.9	122.9
2000	125.6	126.6	128.9	132.8	132.7	133.6	132.6	133.5	133.5	134.8	133.3	133.3	131.7
2001	120.7	121.2	122.2	120.2	119.8	118.8	117.2	117.4	116.2	116.3	113.9	114.2	118.2
2002	113.2	115.3	115.9	116.2	117.2	117.7	116.8	119.2	119.2	117.8	116.7	115.9	116.8
2003	114.9	114.4	116.1	119.0	119.9	119.5	119.6	119.7	120.2	121.7	119.7	119.5	118.7
Educational and health services													
1990	34.9	35.3	35.5	35.3	35.4	35.4	35.3	36.1	36.7	36.5	36.7	36.8	35.8
1991	37.2	37.5	37.7	38.0	38.2	37.9	38.1	38.4	39.0	39.9	40.1	40.4	38.5
1992	39.8	40.5	40.7	41.1	41.6	41.5	41.5	41.5	42.4	43.4	43.7	44.0	41.8
1993	44.1	44.8	45.3	45.7	45.6	45.4	45.5	45.4	46.1	47.6	47.6	47.8	45.9
1994	45.8	46.1	46.2	46.5	46.5	46.4	46.1	45.9	47.4	47.7	48.2	48.4	46.7
1995	47.8	48.6	49.0	49.2	49.6	49.2	48.0	48.5	49.5	50.2	50.6	51.0	49.2
1996	49.0	49.9	50.6	50.8	51.3	51.0	50.4	50.7	51.5	52.3	52.6	52.9	51.0
1997	52.6	53.4	53.9	54.2	54.5	54.2	53.1	53.3	54.6	54.8	55.1	55.4	54.0
1998	55.5	56.5	57.0	56.6	56.6	56.2	56.2	56.5	57.3	57.0	57.3	57.2	56.6
1999	57.3	57.8	58.0	57.6	57.4	57.0	56.7	57.2	57.9	58.9	58.8	58.7	57.7
2000	58.4	59.0	59.2	59.2	59.1	59.0	58.7	59.1	60.0	61.1	61.4	61.4	59.6
2001	60.0	60.8	61.4	59.3	59.4	59.9	59.2	59.9	60.3	61.0	61.4	61.3	60.3
2002	60.1	60.9	61.0	62.7	63.1	63.4	63.6	64.5	65.2	65.8	66.1	67.0	63.6
2003	66.4	66.8	67.2	67.1	67.5	67.4	67.1	67.9	68.4	70.3	71.1	71.3	68.2

Employment by Industry: North Carolina—*Continued*

(Numbers in thousands. Not seasonally adjusted.)

Industry	January	February	March	April	May	June	July	August	September	October	November	December	Annual Average
CHARLOTTE-GASTONIA-ROCK HILL—*Continued*													
Leisure and hospitality													
1990	40.8	42.0	43.6	44.8	45.5	46.5	45.6	46.0	45.8	44.7	43.4	43.1	44.3
1991	40.9	41.5	43.5	43.9	45.5	46.1	45.6	45.9	45.1	44.7	43.1	42.9	44.0
1992	42.4	42.9	45.4	46.3	47.4	48.2	48.4	48.6	48.6	47.6	46.9	46.8	46.6
1993	45.3	46.2	47.8	49.9	51.5	51.9	51.6	51.5	50.7	50.0	49.1	49.3	49.5
1994	47.8	48.7	50.8	51.4	52.6	54.0	53.4	53.7	52.9	52.5	51.5	51.4	51.7
1995	50.3	51.5	53.4	54.4	56.3	57.9	57.3	57.3	55.9	55.1	54.5	54.3	54.8
1996	53.4	54.8	57.3	57.6	59.7	60.7	60.3	59.9	59.2	58.5	57.6	58.1	58.0
1997	56.4	57.7	60.0	61.0	63.6	64.4	62.3	62.0	61.2	58.6	58.8	59.1	60.4
1998	58.7	59.7	61.9	63.4	66.3	67.4	68.3	68.3	66.9	64.3	63.5	64.1	64.4
1999	63.0	64.5	66.4	66.1	68.2	68.7	69.3	69.1	67.8	68.3	67.5	67.9	67.2
2000	66.8	66.8	68.7	68.4	70.8	72.7	71.0	71.2	69.1	69.5	67.9	67.7	69.2
2001	65.7	66.2	66.9	70.8	71.9	73.2	71.6	72.1	69.9	69.6	67.9	66.3	69.3
2002	64.1	64.7	67.0	70.5	71.5	72.9	72.4	72.3	71.4	70.2	68.7	69.1	69.6
2003	66.1	66.7	69.2	71.1	74.8	75.2	73.8	73.5	71.3	70.7	69.7	69.3	71.0
Other services													
1990	22.6	23.0	23.1	23.1	23.2	23.5	23.2	23.2	23.2	23.2	23.2	23.4	23.1
1991	22.2	22.4	22.6	22.7	22.7	23.0	22.9	23.1	23.0	23.1	23.1	23.2	22.8
1992	22.8	22.9	23.1	22.7	22.3	22.0	21.7	20.7	20.2	20.1	19.7	19.4	21.4
1993	18.3	17.9	17.4	18.3	19.2	20.1	20.6	21.1	21.6	22.4	23.0	23.7	20.3
1994	23.7	24.5	25.2	25.3	25.2	25.7	25.9	25.8	25.7	25.9	26.1	26.2	25.4
1995	25.8	25.9	26.4	26.5	26.8	27.3	26.9	26.9	26.7	26.7	26.7	26.9	26.6
1996	26.4	26.9	27.0	27.2	27.5	27.6	27.8	27.8	27.6	27.7	27.8	27.9	27.4
1997	26.6	26.7	26.7	26.8	27.1	27.6	27.4	27.4	27.6	27.7	27.9	28.4	27.3
1998	29.0	29.3	29.8	30.2	30.5	31.1	31.2	31.1	31.2	30.8	31.0	31.4	30.5
1999	31.5	31.8	32.0	32.3	32.6	33.0	33.1	33.1	33.3	33.7	33.8	34.0	32.8
2000	34.1	34.4	34.7	34.8	34.9	35.4	35.3	35.2	35.1	35.7	35.7	35.9	35.1
2001	35.5	36.0	36.5	36.7	37.4	37.9	37.9	38.2	38.3	38.5	38.7	38.9	37.5
2002	39.4	39.5	39.9	39.8	39.3	39.7	38.7	38.2	38.1	38.1	37.9	37.1	38.8
2003	36.5	36.3	36.4	37.0	37.4	37.5	36.7	36.7	36.2	36.5	35.9	36.0	36.6
Government													
1990	69.1	70.2	70.8	71.7	72.2	72.1	63.6	65.5	70.7	73.0	73.3	73.6	70.4
1991	72.1	72.9	73.5	72.5	72.2	71.5	64.5	65.6	71.4	73.9	74.2	74.7	71.5
1992	73.5	74.8	75.4	75.4	75.4	73.9	62.4	69.6	72.4	76.0	77.2	77.3	73.6
1993	75.5	76.0	77.0	76.7	77.1	76.6	69.2	69.6	75.5	77.5	79.1	79.6	75.7
1994	78.1	78.7	79.1	78.6	78.6	79.0	71.0	69.0	77.5	79.8	80.7	82.4	77.7
1995	79.8	80.1	81.3	82.1	81.7	80.7	72.0	73.4	82.1	83.1	85.3	86.4	80.6
1996	84.2	85.4	86.1	85.9	86.1	85.1	72.3	76.0	85.2	86.3	88.0	88.6	84.1
1997	88.0	88.7	89.3	89.0	89.3	88.4	77.8	84.0	88.9	90.6	91.0	91.7	88.0
1998	91.0	92.1	92.1	92.3	92.3	89.7	81.1	87.0	92.7	95.4	95.1	95.8	91.3
1999	94.2	95.6	95.7	95.1	94.7	90.7	84.7	92.0	97.1	97.0	97.7	98.3	94.4
2000	97.4	97.8	99.6	99.5	101.1	99.6	87.0	94.8	97.7	102.0	101.4	101.2	98.2
2001	98.5	100.0	100.4	101.0	100.8	96.5	85.7	93.8	99.5	104.1	106.2	104.7	99.3
2002	102.7	104.3	105.2	104.3	104.3	100.1	89.7	96.9	103.2	107.6	107.7	106.2	102.7
2003	104.6	105.6	106.2	104.3	104.9	99.8	91.9	99.9	106.1	112.5	110.8	110.3	104.7
Federal government													
1990	6.7	6.7	6.9	7.2	8.0	8.0	7.5	7.1	6.8	6.9	6.8	6.7	7.1
1991	6.8	7.2	7.2	6.7	6.8	6.8	6.8	6.7	6.6	6.6	6.6	6.6	6.7
1992	6.7	6.6	6.6	6.6	6.6	6.6	6.6	6.5	6.5	6.6	6.5	6.6	6.5
1993	6.5	6.5	6.5	6.6	6.7	6.7	6.8	6.8	6.9	6.9	6.9	7.0	6.7
1994	6.9	6.9	6.9	6.9	6.9	7.0	7.0	7.0	7.0	7.0	7.0	7.2	6.9
1995	7.0	7.0	7.1	7.1	7.1	7.1	7.3	7.3	7.3	7.3	7.4	7.6	7.2
1996	7.4	7.3	7.3	7.4	7.4	7.4	7.4	7.3	7.3	7.3	7.3	7.4	7.3
1997	7.4	7.4	7.4	7.5	7.6	7.6	7.7	7.7	7.7	7.6	7.7	7.9	7.6
1998	7.7	7.7	7.7	7.8	7.8	7.8	7.8	7.9	7.9	8.0	8.1	8.2	7.8
1999	8.0	8.0	8.0	8.0	7.9	7.9	8.0	8.1	8.1	8.0	8.2	8.4	8.0
2000	8.3	8.4	9.0	9.0	10.8	12.4	9.6	10.6	8.2	8.1	8.1	8.4	9.2
2001	8.2	8.2	8.2	8.1	8.1	8.1	8.1	8.1	8.1	8.1	8.1	8.3	8.1
2002	8.1	8.1	8.1	8.0	7.9	8.1	8.0	8.0	8.2	8.5	8.5	8.6	8.2
2003	8.4	8.4	8.3	8.3	8.3	8.2	8.2	8.3	8.3	8.3	8.2	8.4	8.3
State government													
1990	10.2	11.4	11.5	11.5	11.0	9.7	9.3	9.4	11.1	11.5	11.6	11.5	10.8
1991	10.6	11.8	11.9	11.7	11.4	9.9	9.7	10.0	11.4	12.2	12.5	12.6	11.3
1992	11.7	12.8	12.9	12.9	12.8	11.3	11.0	11.0	11.7	12.9	13.1	13.1	12.2
1993	12.3	12.7	13.1	13.1	13.1	11.6	11.2	11.0	11.9	12.3	13.4	13.4	12.4
1994	12.4	12.3	12.6	12.6	12.6	11.9	11.0	11.0	11.4	12.4	12.7	12.7	12.1
1995	12.3	12.4	12.7	13.2	13.2	11.8	11.1	11.2	11.9	12.6	13.6	13.6	12.4
1996	12.7	13.7	13.8	13.7	13.6	12.3	11.5	11.8	12.6	13.6	14.1	13.9	13.1
1997	13.0	13.5	13.7	13.8	13.9	12.5	11.3	11.4	12.2	13.0	13.2	12.9	12.8
1998	12.4	12.6	12.7	13.5	13.5	12.5	11.4	11.5	12.4	13.6	13.6	13.7	12.7
1999	13.1	13.3	13.6	13.5	13.4	12.8	11.7	11.9	12.6	13.5	13.6	13.7	13.0
2000	12.9	13.3	13.6	13.6	13.5	12.6	11.6	11.4	12.3	13.8	14.1	13.7	13.0
2001	12.0	12.5	12.4	12.5	12.5	11.4	9.6	9.9	10.8	12.6	12.9	12.8	11.8
2002	12.1	12.6	13.0	13.1	13.2	12.3	11.6	11.8	12.5	13.0	13.0	13.2	12.6
2003	12.7	13.1	13.1	11.4	11.4	11.1	9.9	10.2	11.4	13.1	13.4	13.7	12.0

Employment by Industry: North Carolina—*Continued*

(Numbers in thousands. Not seasonally adjusted.)

Industry	January	February	March	April	May	June	July	August	September	October	November	December	Annual Average
CHARLOTTE-GASTONIA-ROCK HILL—*Continued*													
Local government													
1990	52.2	52.1	52.4	53.0	53.2	54.4	46.8	49.0	52.8	54.6	54.9	55.4	52.5
1991	54.7	53.9	54.4	54.1	54.0	54.8	48.0	48.9	53.4	55.1	55.1	55.5	53.4
1992	55.1	55.4	55.9	55.9	56.0	56.0	44.8	52.1	54.2	56.5	57.6	57.6	54.7
1993	56.7	56.8	57.4	57.0	57.3	58.3	51.2	51.8	56.7	58.3	58.8	59.2	56.6
1994	58.8	59.5	59.6	59.1	59.1	60.1	53.0	51.0	59.1	60.4	61.0	62.5	58.6
1995	60.5	60.7	61.5	61.8	61.4	61.8	53.6	54.9	62.9	63.2	64.3	65.2	60.9
1996	64.1	64.4	65.0	64.8	65.1	65.4	53.4	56.9	65.3	65.4	66.6	67.3	63.6
1997	67.6	67.8	68.2	67.7	67.8	68.3	58.8	64.9	69.0	70.0	70.1	70.9	67.5
1998	70.9	71.8	71.7	71.0	71.0	69.4	61.9	67.6	72.4	73.8	73.4	73.9	70.7
1999	73.1	74.3	74.1	73.6	73.4	70.0	65.0	72.0	76.4	75.5	75.9	76.2	73.2
2000	76.2	76.1	77.0	76.9	76.8	74.6	65.8	72.8	77.2	80.1	79.2	79.1	75.9
2001	78.3	79.3	79.8	80.4	80.3	77.1	68.0	75.8	80.6	83.4	85.1	83.6	79.3
2002	82.5	83.6	84.1	83.2	83.2	79.7	70.1	77.1	82.5	86.1	86.2	84.4	81.9
2003	83.5	84.1	84.8	84.6	85.2	80.5	73.8	81.4	86.4	91.1	89.2	88.2	84.4
GREENSBORO-WINSTON-SALEM-HIGH POINT													
Total nonfarm													
1990	545.6	548.6	551.3	553.2	554.9	556.8	547.4	550.5	550.6	553.2	554.5	551.5	551.5
1991	538.6	537.4	537.8	538.5	539.9	542.4	534.8	540.5	543.5	548.3	550.8	550.7	541.9
1992	540.4	539.6	543.4	549.3	552.4	554.7	546.4	549.6	556.1	563.4	566.4	567.4	552.4
1993	554.7	556.5	559.7	566.1	568.7	571.9	566.3	569.6	573.9	580.6	584.2	586.2	569.8
1994	572.7	572.4	578.6	585.4	590.6	596.4	583.2	587.1	594.4	599.5	605.8	607.4	589.4
1995	594.7	595.7	600.7	603.2	604.6	609.6	594.9	601.4	609.3	613.6	617.2	619.6	605.3
1996	600.6	605.0	611.4	614.9	619.3	623.3	610.0	616.7	623.2	625.7	630.8	633.3	617.8
1997	621.1	622.3	628.3	630.9	635.1	637.8	624.2	628.0	637.5	635.8	640.9	646.7	632.3
1998	628.7	632.2	637.7	644.4	647.2	651.5	642.3	650.5	654.4	658.6	662.4	664.0	647.8
1999	648.4	653.4	660.1	663.2	662.8	663.5	648.5	656.6	660.9	670.3	673.2	676.1	661.4
2000	656.1	659.1	665.2	671.3	674.6	673.7	661.5	668.6	671.4	672.0	674.3	676.3	668.6
2001	667.8	667.6	667.6	661.6	662.0	658.9	647.7	651.2	653.5	651.7	652.4	649.7	657.6
2002	641.8	642.7	646.6	648.9	651.3	645.0	636.2	643.5	646.1	648.3	649.8	649.3	645.8
2003	630.8	631.3	635.7	637.7	637.6	633.5	624.3	630.3	630.6	635.3	636.4	634.9	633.2
Total private													
1990	485.0	487.6	490.2	490.7	491.5	493.9	490.7	494.1	491.8	492.0	490.8	488.7	490.5
1991	476.9	475.6	475.3	475.9	477.7	481.2	481.3	486.1	484.9	486.6	487.8	487.9	481.4
1992	478.3	477.7	480.4	485.9	488.2	491.6	492.7	494.4	496.1	499.4	500.0	502.2	490.5
1993	492.5	494.5	496.7	502.7	505.9	509.4	511.8	513.7	513.4	516.6	518.6	521.4	508.1
1994	509.7	509.6	515.0	520.2	525.1	530.3	529.0	530.8	532.2	534.2	537.6	540.7	526.2
1995	529.5	530.8	534.9	537.0	539.9	544.4	540.5	545.6	546.0	547.5	550.1	552.6	541.5
1996	535.1	539.7	544.9	548.3	552.9	556.7	555.1	559.7	557.9	559.0	562.2	565.3	553.0
1997	553.8	555.3	559.9	562.1	566.7	570.0	568.1	569.7	571.8	568.5	572.2	576.7	566.2
1998	560.6	563.1	567.8	574.4	578.1	582.7	582.7	585.6	584.7	585.7	589.2	590.7	578.7
1999	577.7	581.9	587.5	591.0	592.0	592.9	590.2	591.8	591.8	597.4	599.6	602.2	591.3
2000	585.0	587.7	592.5	597.5	600.2	601.7	599.3	599.8	599.5	599.1	600.7	602.2	597.1
2001	596.2	595.7	595.5	589.3	589.3	589.6	587.2	586.3	583.3	579.1	578.4	576.4	587.2
2002	569.3	569.6	572.5	574.8	577.1	576.6	575.1	575.7	574.4	574.0	575.2	575.3	574.1
2003	558.7	558.6	562.0	563.8	563.3	563.8	562.1	562.2	558.6	560.9	561.7	560.3	561.3
Goods-producing													
1990	187.0	188.0	188.1	188.9	187.4	187.4	185.1	185.9	184.3	182.7	180.5	179.5	185.4
1991	177.8	177.2	175.8	176.4	176.2	177.1	175.7	176.9	176.2	173.6	173.8	173.8	175.8
1992	172.1	172.1	172.8	175.6	176.3	178.0	178.6	178.6	179.3	179.9	180.5	180.2	177.0
1993	178.9	179.4	179.9	179.1	179.4	181.1	180.8	180.7	180.1	180.1	180.2	180.5	180.0
1994	177.6	178.2	179.1	177.0	180.2	182.1	181.2	181.9	181.7	181.8	181.7	182.6	180.4
1995	180.8	181.4	182.0	181.8	181.8	183.1	182.3	182.9	182.1	181.6	181.7	182.0	181.9
1996	178.4	179.4	179.7	181.3	182.3	183.8	182.4	183.1	182.1	182.0	182.4	182.8	181.6
1997	181.8	181.1	181.5	180.6	181.9	182.9	181.9	181.9	182.1	180.4	180.5	181.3	181.4
1998	180.2	180.9	181.4	183.5	184.4	188.3	186.2	186.3	186.0	185.6	185.1	184.9	184.4
1999	183.5	183.9	184.7	184.8	184.6	185.1	183.8	183.6	183.3	182.8	182.6	183.0	183.8
2000	179.2	179.7	180.5	181.1	181.7	181.8	182.1	181.4	181.2	180.2	180.1	179.7	180.7
2001	184.0	182.8	180.3	173.8	172.9	171.9	171.9	170.8	169.4	167.3	166.3	164.0	173.0
2002	161.3	160.5	160.7	159.5	160.1	158.6	160.6	160.1	160.5	159.9	159.3	158.9	160.0
2003	154.7	153.9	153.9	153.3	152.8	152.2	150.6	149.8	149.2	149.5	148.5	147.2	151.3
Natural resources and mining													
2002	0.6	0.6	0.6	0.6	0.6	0.6	0.6	0.6	0.6	0.6	0.7	0.7	0.6
2003	0.7	0.7	0.7	0.7	0.7	0.7	0.7	0.7	0.7	0.7	0.7	0.7	0.7
Construction													
2002	30.3	30.2	30.5	31.1	31.4	31.9	32.2	32.4	32.2	31.7	31.4	31.2	31.3
2003	29.5	29.4	29.8	29.9	30.5	30.6	30.3	29.8	30.0	30.2	30.0	29.6	30.0

Employment by Industry: North Carolina—*Continued*

(Numbers in thousands. Not seasonally adjusted.)

Industry	January	February	March	April	May	June	July	August	September	October	November	December	Annual Average
GREENSBORO-WINSTON-SALEM-HIGH POINT *—Continued*													
Manufacturing													
1990	160.7	161.2	161.0	161.7	160.1	159.6	157.3	158.1	157.1	156.2	154.5	153.8	158.4
1991	153.7	153.2	151.9	152.4	151.9	152.6	151.0	152.2	152.0	149.8	150.1	150.1	151.7
1992	149.1	149.0	149.3	151.8	152.3	153.6	153.9	154.0	154.6	155.1	155.6	155.4	152.8
1993	154.8	155.3	155.4	154.6	154.5	155.6	155.1	155.1	154.6	154.6	154.8	155.0	154.9
1994	153.3	153.7	153.8	151.1	153.8	155.2	154.2	155.0	154.9	155.2	155.2	155.9	154.2
1995	155.0	155.8	155.6	155.0	154.7	155.5	154.7	155.0	154.5	153.9	154.0	154.0	154.8
1996	152.0	152.5	152.0	152.7	153.0	153.8	152.3	152.7	152.2	152.1	152.7	153.0	152.5
1997	152.8	152.0	151.8	150.3	151.2	151.7	150.5	150.3	150.4	149.1	149.3	150.0	150.7
1998	149.9	150.3	150.4	151.4	151.6	154.5	152.3	152.3	152.0	151.6	151.4	151.0	151.5
1999	150.6	150.6	151.0	150.6	150.1	149.8	148.9	148.6	148.4	148.1	148.1	148.4	149.4
2000	146.5	147.1	147.1	147.7	147.9	147.7	147.9	147.0	146.7	145.9	145.8	145.4	146.8
2001	148.2	147.0	143.6	139.2	138.1	136.8	136.9	135.9	135.0	133.6	132.9	132.3	138.3
2002	130.4	129.7	129.6	127.8	128.1	126.1	127.8	127.1	127.7	127.6	127.2	127.0	128.0
2003	124.5	123.8	123.4	122.7	121.6	120.9	119.6	119.3	118.5	118.6	117.8	116.9	120.6
Service-providing													
1990	358.6	360.6	363.2	364.3	367.5	369.4	362.3	364.6	366.3	370.5	374.0	372.0	366.1
1991	360.8	360.2	362.0	362.1	363.7	365.3	359.1	363.6	367.3	374.7	377.0	376.9	366.0
1992	368.3	367.5	370.6	373.7	376.1	376.7	367.8	371.0	376.8	383.5	385.9	387.2	375.4
1993	375.8	377.1	379.8	387.0	389.3	390.8	385.5	388.9	393.8	400.5	404.0	405.7	389.8
1994	395.1	394.2	399.5	408.4	410.4	414.3	402.0	405.2	412.7	417.7	424.1	424.8	409.0
1995	413.9	414.3	418.7	421.4	422.8	426.5	412.6	418.5	427.2	432.0	435.5	437.6	423.4
1996	422.2	425.6	431.7	433.6	437.0	439.5	427.6	433.6	441.1	443.7	448.4	450.5	436.2
1997	439.3	441.2	446.8	450.3	453.2	454.9	442.3	446.1	455.4	455.4	460.4	465.4	450.8
1998	448.5	451.3	456.3	460.9	462.8	463.2	456.1	464.2	468.4	473.0	477.3	479.1	463.4
1999	464.9	469.5	475.4	478.4	478.2	478.4	464.7	473.0	477.6	487.5	490.6	493.1	477.6
2000	476.9	479.4	484.7	490.2	492.9	491.9	479.4	487.2	490.2	491.8	494.2	496.6	487.9
2001	483.9	484.8	487.4	487.9	488.9	487.1	475.8	480.4	484.0	484.4	486.1	485.7	484.7
2002	480.5	482.2	485.9	489.4	491.2	486.4	475.6	483.4	485.6	488.4	490.5	490.4	485.8
2003	476.1	477.4	481.8	484.4	484.8	481.3	473.7	480.5	481.4	485.8	487.9	487.7	481.9
Trade, transportation, and utilities													
1990	110.7	110.3	110.8	109.7	110.4	110.4	109.7	110.4	109.8	111.7	113.0	113.8	110.8
1991	110.8	109.3	109.3	110.2	110.8	111.4	111.6	112.1	111.6	113.8	114.9	115.9	111.8
1992	110.3	109.4	109.7	110.6	111.3	112.3	111.0	112.0	112.7	114.1	115.6	117.7	112.2
1993	113.4	112.4	112.8	115.0	115.5	115.7	116.3	116.9	116.8	118.6	119.9	122.0	116.2
1994	117.0	116.2	116.7	118.2	118.9	119.5	119.7	120.1	120.8	121.4	123.9	126.4	119.9
1995	122.3	121.6	122.6	122.2	122.7	122.9	123.0	124.5	125.0	127.0	128.7	131.5	124.5
1996	125.3	124.9	125.6	126.4	127.6	127.7	127.2	127.5	127.0	127.6	130.1	132.2	127.4
1997	126.8	125.3	126.8	127.1	127.8	128.4	128.5	128.8	129.6	130.8	133.2	135.1	129.0
1998	127.1	126.5	127.8	129.4	129.3	131.8	129.0	129.8	130.6	130.6	133.6	135.7	130.1
1999	129.8	130.0	131.3	132.9	133.4	133.0	132.9	133.5	133.4	135.4	138.0	140.1	133.6
2000	133.4	133.1	134.4	135.9	136.7	136.5	135.6	136.2	136.2	137.8	140.0	141.3	136.4
2001	136.7	136.1	136.4	135.9	136.2	135.7	133.9	133.6	133.3	132.7	133.7	134.4	134.9
2002	129.0	127.5	128.1	127.8	128.0	128.5	127.4	127.5	126.9	127.3	130.2	131.7	128.3
2003	125.7	125.0	125.7	125.6	125.5	125.9	126.5	126.5	126.2	125.9	128.6	129.1	126.4
Wholesale trade													
1990	25.8	25.9	26.1	25.0	25.2	25.1	26.0	26.2	25.9	26.2	26.0	25.9	25.7
1991	25.6	25.7	25.7	26.3	26.2	26.4	25.9	25.9	25.8	25.9	25.8	25.9	25.9
1992	24.7	24.8	24.8	25.4	25.3	25.3	24.3	24.3	24.3	24.3	24.1	24.2	24.6
1993	23.9	24.0	24.2	24.1	24.1	24.2	24.3	24.5	24.7	24.6	24.5	24.7	24.3
1994	24.5	24.6	24.7	25.2	25.3	25.5	25.6	25.8	26.1	25.9	25.8	26.0	25.4
1995	25.7	25.7	26.0	25.9	26.0	26.1	26.0	26.3	26.3	26.3	26.3	26.5	26.0
1996	26.2	26.3	26.6	26.7	26.8	26.8	26.8	27.0	26.9	26.7	26.9	26.9	26.7
1997	26.7	27.0	27.2	28.4	28.5	28.7	28.6	28.6	28.6	28.6	28.8	28.8	28.2
1998	28.2	28.3	28.4	27.6	27.8	28.3	28.1	28.2	28.1	28.2	28.3	28.3	28.1
1999	28.1	28.3	28.4	28.7	28.8	28.8	28.9	29.0	28.9	29.3	29.4	29.4	28.8
2000	28.7	28.9	29.2	29.6	29.8	29.7	29.9	29.9	29.8	29.9	29.8	29.9	29.5
2001	29.4	29.5	29.5	29.4	29.4	29.3	29.2	29.2	28.9	28.7	28.4	28.3	29.1
2002	29.0	29.1	29.1	29.2	29.2	29.3	29.3	29.2	29.1	29.1	29.3	29.3	29.2
2003	28.8	28.9	29.0	29.0	28.9	29.0	29.2	29.4	29.0	28.9	29.4	29.6	29.1
Retail trade													
1990	63.4	62.3	62.4	62.2	62.6	62.7	61.4	61.8	61.7	62.9	64.5	65.4	62.7
1991	62.6	61.1	60.9	60.6	61.1	61.4	61.1	61.5	61.2	62.6	63.8	64.5	61.8
1992	60.9	59.8	60.1	59.9	60.4	60.9	60.4	61.1	61.4	62.3	64.0	65.7	61.4
1993	62.0	60.8	60.9	61.3	61.6	61.6	62.0	62.3	62.1	63.1	64.5	66.1	62.3
1994	62.3	61.4	61.8	62.2	62.6	62.9	62.6	63.1	63.5	64.0	66.7	68.9	63.5
1995	65.4	64.9	65.6	65.3	65.6	65.9	65.7	66.9	67.4	68.3	70.1	72.3	66.9
1996	67.6	67.0	67.4	67.4	68.5	68.7	67.9	68.0	68.0	68.4	71.0	73.0	68.5
1997	68.9	67.4	68.3	67.4	67.9	68.4	68.4	68.7	69.6	69.5	71.9	73.8	69.1
1998	67.9	67.5	68.2	68.8	68.9	70.3	67.9	68.5	69.3	69.5	72.5	74.1	69.4
1999	69.7	69.9	71.1	71.0	71.5	71.2	71.3	71.7	71.9	72.2	74.7	76.6	71.9
2000	72.4	71.8	72.6	72.7	73.3	73.2	71.8	72.3	72.4	73.3	75.6	76.7	73.1
2001	73.4	72.4	72.7	71.9	72.4	72.4	71.4	71.6	72.0	72.1	74.0	75.1	72.6
2002	70.4	69.4	70.0	69.5	69.8	70.1	69.3	69.5	69.1	69.2	71.8	73.4	70.1
2003	68.7	67.8	68.2	67.9	68.0	68.0	68.0	67.8	68.0	67.9	70.2	70.5	68.4

Employment by Industry: North Carolina—*Continued*

(Numbers in thousands. Not seasonally adjusted.)

Industry	January	February	March	April	May	June	July	August	September	October	November	December	Annual Average
GREENSBORO-WINSTON-SALEM-HIGH POINT *—Continued*													
Transportation and utilities													
1990	21.5	22.1	22.3	22.5	22.6	22.6	22.3	22.4	22.2	22.6	22.5	22.5	22.3
1991	22.6	22.5	22.7	23.3	23.5	23.6	24.6	24.7	24.6	25.3	25.3	25.5	24.0
1992	24.7	24.8	24.8	25.3	25.6	26.1	26.3	26.6	27.0	27.5	27.5	27.8	26.1
1993	27.5	27.6	27.7	29.6	29.8	29.9	30.0	30.1	30.0	30.9	30.9	31.2	29.6
1994	30.2	30.2	30.2	30.8	31.0	31.1	31.5	31.2	31.2	31.5	31.4	31.5	30.9
1995	31.2	31.0	31.0	31.0	31.1	30.9	31.3	31.3	31.3	32.4	32.3	32.7	31.4
1996	31.5	31.6	31.6	32.3	32.3	32.2	32.5	32.5	32.1	32.5	32.2	32.3	32.1
1997	31.2	30.9	31.3	31.3	31.4	31.3	31.5	31.5	31.4	32.7	32.5	32.5	31.6
1998	31.0	30.7	31.2	33.0	32.6	33.2	33.0	33.1	33.2	32.9	32.8	33.3	32.5
1999	32.0	31.8	31.8	33.2	33.1	33.0	32.7	32.8	32.6	33.9	33.9	34.1	32.9
2000	32.3	32.4	32.6	33.6	33.6	33.6	33.9	34.0	34.0	34.6	34.6	34.7	33.6
2001	33.9	34.2	34.2	34.6	34.4	34.0	33.3	32.8	32.4	31.9	31.3	31.0	33.2
2002	29.6	29.0	29.0	29.1	29.0	29.1	28.8	28.8	28.7	29.0	29.1	29.0	29.0
2003	28.2	28.3	28.5	28.7	28.6	28.9	29.3	29.3	29.2	29.1	29.0	29.0	28.8
Information													
1990	9.8	9.8	9.9	9.8	10.0	10.2	10.1	10.2	10.2	10.3	10.4	10.4	10.0
1991	10.2	10.3	10.4	10.0	10.1	10.1	10.1	10.0	9.8	9.7	9.6	9.6	9.9
1992	8.9	8.9	8.9	9.0	9.0	9.1	9.3	9.3	9.2	9.2	9.3	9.4	9.1
1993	9.3	9.4	9.4	9.5	9.5	9.7	9.7	9.8	9.8	9.8	9.9	9.9	9.6
1994	9.8	9.7	9.8	9.9	9.9	10.2	10.1	10.1	9.9	9.9	10.0	10.0	9.9
1995	10.1	10.1	10.3	10.2	10.4	10.6	10.8	10.9	10.9	10.7	10.7	10.8	10.5
1996	10.5	10.7	10.7	10.8	10.8	11.0	11.2	11.2	11.0	11.1	11.2	11.3	10.9
1997	11.4	11.5	11.4	11.3	11.5	11.6	11.6	11.6	11.6	11.6	11.7	11.7	11.5
1998	11.4	11.3	11.6	11.5	11.6	11.9	11.9	12.0	11.9	12.0	12.0	12.0	11.7
1999	12.2	12.2	12.3	10.9	11.0	11.1	11.1	11.1	11.1	11.2	11.3	11.5	11.4
2000	11.3	11.2	11.3	12.8	12.9	13.1	13.4	13.4	13.3	13.2	13.2	13.2	12.6
2001	12.9	13.0	13.0	13.0	13.0	13.1	13.0	12.8	12.7	12.2	12.2	12.2	12.8
2002	11.9	11.8	11.8	11.9	11.9	11.7	11.3	11.1	10.9	10.9	10.8	10.7	11.4
2003	10.5	10.4	10.4	10.4	10.5	10.5	10.4	10.4	10.2	10.2	10.2	10.1	10.4
Financial activities													
1990	27.0	27.1	27.3	27.4	27.5	27.9	28.1	27.9	28.0	27.9	27.7	27.7	27.6
1991	27.7	27.7	27.7	27.3	27.2	27.6	28.0	28.0	27.8	27.1	27.1	27.2	27.5
1992	27.7	27.7	27.2	27.7	27.6	27.9	28.6	28.5	28.6	28.7	28.5	28.9	28.1
1993	28.9	28.9	29.1	29.6	29.3	29.5	29.7	29.7	29.6	29.8	29.7	29.9	29.4
1994	30.1	29.9	30.0	30.6	30.5	30.7	30.9	31.0	30.9	30.9	30.8	31.0	30.6
1995	30.9	30.9	31.0	31.0	31.0	31.3	31.4	31.5	31.4	31.5	31.6	31.7	31.2
1996	31.3	31.5	31.7	32.4	32.5	32.9	33.2	33.6	33.6	33.8	33.8	34.1	32.8
1997	33.3	33.5	33.8	34.5	34.6	34.8	34.9	35.0	35.1	35.2	35.2	35.5	34.6
1998	34.7	34.8	35.0	36.0	36.1	36.9	36.5	36.7	36.7	37.1	37.0	37.2	36.2
1999	36.6	36.7	36.8	37.4	37.3	37.2	36.9	36.8	36.7	36.8	36.9	37.2	36.9
2000	36.5	36.6	36.8	36.0	36.0	36.1	36.2	36.1	35.9	36.0	35.9	36.2	36.1
2001	34.8	34.8	35.0	35.4	35.3	35.4	35.5	35.5	35.3	35.0	34.9	34.8	35.1
2002	37.2	37.2	37.3	37.1	37.0	37.2	36.7	36.7	36.6	37.0	36.9	37.1	37.0
2003	36.5	36.5	36.8	37.1	37.0	37.1	36.9	36.5	34.8	34.6	34.7	35.1	36.1
Professional and business services													
1990	45.1	45.8	46.6	46.9	48.1	48.8	49.1	49.7	49.9	50.3	49.9	48.3	48.2
1991	43.3	43.6	43.7	43.2	43.5	44.3	46.2	48.4	48.9	51.3	51.4	50.6	46.5
1992	49.4	49.5	50.4	50.3	50.5	50.7	51.4	52.3	52.8	53.7	52.7	52.7	51.3
1993	50.8	52.1	52.8	54.9	55.9	56.2	57.9	58.6	58.5	58.6	58.2	57.5	56.0
1994	55.6	55.0	56.8	58.5	58.5	59.4	59.0	59.1	60.0	61.2	61.7	60.8	58.8
1995	58.5	59.2	60.2	61.1	61.8	62.6	61.2	63.3	63.8	64.1	64.0	62.6	61.8
1996	60.3	62.4	63.6	63.8	64.1	65.3	66.0	68.1	68.3	68.4	68.8	68.1	65.6
1997	67.4	68.7	69.0	70.9	71.5	72.1	72.1	72.5	72.9	70.7	71.0	71.1	70.8
1998	66.4	67.2	67.9	71.0	72.1	74.1	74.9	75.8	74.9	75.6	75.7	74.8	72.5
1999	72.1	73.4	75.2	76.2	76.6	77.2	77.1	78.2	78.2	81.2	81.1	80.0	77.2
2000	76.8	78.2	79.3	79.7	80.1	80.6	79.3	80.2	80.4	79.0	78.6	78.7	79.2
2001	75.4	75.3	75.7	75.1	74.5	75.0	73.8	74.4	74.5	73.8	73.1	72.6	74.4
2002	71.4	72.4	73.3	73.9	74.3	74.2	72.6	74.1	74.2	74.0	73.1	72.7	73.4
2003	70.0	70.8	71.8	71.7	71.4	71.0	70.8	72.5	72.4	73.1	72.6	71.7	71.7
Educational and health services													
1990	47.8	48.5	48.8	48.9	49.0	48.9	48.9	49.3	49.7	49.6	49.9	49.9	49.1
1991	49.9	50.1	50.3	50.3	50.4	50.7	50.8	51.5	52.0	52.6	52.7	52.8	51.1
1992	53.1	53.2	53.6	53.6	54.0	54.0	54.6	54.9	55.6	56.2	56.3	56.8	54.6
1993	57.0	57.7	58.1	57.6	57.7	57.6	57.6	57.5	58.1	59.2	59.3	59.5	58.0
1994	58.6	59.1	59.5	61.0	61.0	61.2	61.2	61.4	62.1	62.7	63.0	63.2	61.1
1995	62.6	62.9	63.4	63.9	64.0	64.2	63.1	63.6	64.3	64.8	65.0	65.4	63.9
1996	63.2	63.7	64.7	64.8	65.0	64.7	64.7	65.3	65.6	66.3	66.7	67.1	65.1
1997	67.0	68.0	68.5	68.4	68.6	68.4	68.6	68.9	69.8	70.2	70.6	71.0	69.0
1998	70.4	70.8	71.0	71.2	71.4	64.6	70.7	71.1	71.8	72.1	72.7	72.7	70.8
1999	71.5	72.6	73.0	72.9	72.8	72.2	71.6	72.0	73.1	73.7	74.0	74.3	72.8
2000	74.1	74.8	75.2	74.6	74.7	75.0	74.7	75.2	75.8	76.3	77.1	77.1	75.3
2001	76.8	77.5	77.8	78.2	78.3	78.6	78.8	79.3	79.6	80.0	80.5	80.8	78.9
2002	81.1	81.9	82.2	83.0	83.3	83.3	83.3	83.8	84.0	84.6	84.9	84.8	83.4
2003	84.0	84.8	85.2	85.7	85.4	85.4	84.7	84.9	85.2	87.3	87.6	87.0	85.6

Employment by Industry: North Carolina—*Continued*

(Numbers in thousands. Not seasonally adjusted.)

Industry	January	February	March	April	May	June	July	August	September	October	November	December	Annual Average
GREENSBORO-WINSTON-SALEM-HIGH POINT *—Continued*													
Leisure and hospitality													
1990	38.9	39.3	39.8	40.0	40.1	40.9	40.5	41.4	40.8	40.5	40.4	40.1	40.2
1991	38.6	38.7	39.3	39.9	40.7	41.1	39.9	40.3	39.5	39.5	39.2	38.9	39.6
1992	38.1	38.3	39.2	40.3	41.1	41.4	41.4	41.7	41.5	41.5	41.4	41.1	40.5
1993	39.5	40.3	40.6	42.3	43.3	43.5	43.3	43.7	43.2	42.5	42.7	42.7	42.3
1994	41.1	41.1	41.9	43.7	44.7	45.6	45.2	45.7	45.3	44.8	44.8	45.0	44.0
1995	43.0	43.4	43.9	45.3	46.5	47.5	46.6	46.9	46.6	45.7	46.2	46.2	45.6
1996	44.5	45.0	46.6	46.7	48.3	48.8	47.7	48.2	47.8	47.3	46.5	46.8	47.0
1997	44.5	45.3	46.8	47.1	48.4	49.1	47.8	48.2	48.0	46.7	47.0	47.8	47.2
1998	47.2	48.2	49.4	47.7	48.6	49.9	48.5	48.9	48.1	48.0	48.1	48.2	48.4
1999	46.8	47.6	48.3	49.7	49.9	50.3	49.8	49.7	49.3	49.2	48.5	48.7	48.9
2000	46.5	46.6	47.3	49.4	49.9	50.5	49.9	49.3	48.8	48.7	47.9	48.1	48.5
2001	47.4	48.1	48.8	49.7	50.5	51.4	51.6	51.4	50.2	49.9	49.5	49.5	49.8
2002	48.5	49.2	50.0	52.1	53.3	53.9	54.0	53.9	53.3	52.0	51.9	52.0	52.0
2003	50.7	50.5	51.6	53.1	53.9	54.6	54.9	55.0	53.9	53.6	53.1	53.7	53.2
Other services													
1990	18.7	18.8	18.9	19.1	19.0	19.4	19.2	19.3	19.1	19.0	19.0	19.0	19.0
1991	18.6	18.7	18.8	18.6	18.8	18.9	19.0	18.9	19.1	19.0	19.1	19.1	18.8
1992	18.7	18.6	18.6	18.8	18.4	18.2	17.8	17.1	16.4	16.1	15.7	15.4	17.4
1993	14.7	14.3	14.0	14.7	15.3	16.1	16.5	16.8	17.3	18.0	18.7	19.4	16.3
1994	19.9	20.4	21.2	21.3	21.4	21.6	21.7	21.5	21.5	21.5	21.7	21.7	21.2
1995	21.3	21.3	21.5	21.5	21.7	22.2	22.1	22.0	21.9	22.1	22.2	22.4	21.8
1996	21.6	22.1	22.3	22.1	22.3	22.5	22.7	22.7	22.5	22.5	22.7	22.9	22.4
1997	21.6	21.9	22.1	22.2	22.4	22.7	22.7	22.8	22.7	22.9	23.0	23.2	22.5
1998	23.2	23.4	23.7	24.1	24.6	25.2	25.0	25.0	24.7	24.7	25.0	25.2	24.4
1999	25.2	25.5	25.9	26.2	26.4	26.8	27.0	26.9	26.7	27.1	27.2	27.4	26.5
2000	27.2	27.5	27.7	28.0	28.2	28.1	28.1	28.0	27.9	27.9	27.9	27.9	27.8
2001	28.3	28.4	28.6	28.3	28.4	28.6	28.7	28.5	28.3	28.2	28.2	28.2	28.4
2002	28.9	29.1	29.1	29.5	29.2	29.2	29.2	28.5	28.0	28.3	28.1	27.4	28.7
2003	26.6	26.7	26.6	26.9	26.8	27.1	27.3	26.6	26.7	26.7	26.4	26.4	26.7
Government													
1990	60.6	61.0	61.1	62.5	63.4	62.9	56.7	56.4	58.8	61.2	63.7	62.8	60.9
1991	61.7	61.8	62.5	62.6	62.2	61.2	53.5	54.4	58.6	61.7	63.0	62.8	60.5
1992	62.1	61.9	63.0	63.4	64.2	63.1	53.7	55.2	60.0	64.0	66.4	65.2	61.8
1993	62.2	62.0	63.0	63.4	62.8	62.5	54.5	55.9	60.5	64.0	65.6	64.8	61.7
1994	63.0	62.8	63.6	65.2	65.5	66.1	54.2	56.3	62.2	65.3	68.2	66.7	63.2
1995	65.2	64.9	65.8	66.2	64.7	65.2	54.4	55.8	63.3	66.1	67.1	67.0	63.8
1996	65.5	65.3	66.5	66.6	66.4	66.6	54.9	57.0	65.3	66.7	68.6	68.0	64.7
1997	67.3	67.0	68.4	68.8	68.4	67.8	56.1	58.3	65.7	67.3	68.7	70.0	66.1
1998	68.1	69.1	69.9	70.0	69.1	68.8	59.6	64.9	69.7	72.9	73.2	73.3	69.0
1999	70.7	71.5	72.6	72.2	70.8	70.6	58.3	64.8	69.1	72.9	73.6	73.9	70.0
2000	71.1	71.4	72.7	73.8	74.4	72.0	62.2	68.8	71.9	72.9	73.6	74.1	71.5
2001	71.6	71.9	72.1	72.3	72.7	69.3	60.4	64.9	70.1	72.6	74.1	73.4	70.5
2002	72.5	73.1	74.1	74.1	74.2	68.4	61.1	67.8	71.7	74.3	74.6	74.0	71.7
2003	72.1	72.7	73.7	73.9	74.3	69.7	62.2	68.1	72.0	74.4	74.7	74.6	71.9
Federal government													
1992	5.3	5.3	5.3	5.3	5.3	5.3	5.3	5.3	5.3	5.3	5.2	5.4	5.3
1993	5.2	5.2	5.3	5.3	5.3	5.3	5.4	5.4	5.5	5.5	5.6	5.7	5.3
1994	5.5	5.5	5.5	5.6	5.8	5.9	5.9	6.0	6.2	6.1	6.2	6.4	5.8
1995	6.3	6.3	6.3	6.3	6.3	6.2	6.2	6.2	6.3	6.3	6.4	6.6	6.3
1996	6.3	6.4	6.3	6.4	6.4	6.4	6.4	6.5	6.3	6.2	6.3	6.5	6.3
1997	6.4	6.4	6.3	6.3	6.4	6.5	6.5	6.4	6.5	5.9	6.3	6.4	6.3
1998	6.4	6.3	6.3	6.3	6.3	6.3	6.3	6.3	6.4	6.3	6.5	6.8	6.3
1999	6.5	6.4	6.4	6.7	6.4	6.3	6.3	6.4	6.3	6.3	6.4	6.7	6.4
2000	6.4	6.4	6.8	6.8	8.4	8.9	7.6	7.8	6.3	6.3	6.4	6.9	7.0
2001	6.4	6.4	6.3	6.2	6.2	6.2	6.1	6.1	6.0	6.1	6.1	6.5	6.2
2002	6.2	6.2	6.2	6.0	6.0	6.1	6.0	6.0	6.0	6.1	6.1	6.3	6.1
2003	6.1	6.0	6.0	6.0	5.9	5.9	5.9	5.8	5.8	5.8	5.8	6.0	5.9
State government													
1992	13.6	13.3	14.1	14.3	13.9	13.0	11.0	11.8	12.6	14.4	14.6	14.7	13.4
1993	14.2	14.0	14.6	14.7	14.2	13.1	11.6	11.9	12.6	14.4	15.0	15.0	13.7
1994	14.3	14.1	14.7	15.1	14.5	13.8	11.7	12.0	13.0	14.7	15.4	15.0	14.0
1995	14.6	14.3	15.0	15.2	14.1	13.5	11.9	11.8	13.5	15.0	15.6	15.3	14.1
1996	14.5	14.3	15.2	14.9	14.5	14.0	12.1	12.3	13.3	15.0	15.7	15.5	14.2
1997	14.9	14.6	15.7	15.7	14.9	13.7	12.2	12.4	12.6	13.7	14.3	15.6	14.1
1998	13.9	14.7	15.1	15.2	14.2	13.5	12.7	12.7	14.2	15.2	15.6	15.5	14.3
1999	14.0	14.7	15.2	15.3	14.4	13.5	12.3	12.8	14.1	14.9	15.1	15.0	14.2
2000	14.6	14.7	15.2	16.4	15.2	13.9	12.9	12.8	14.5	15.5	15.7	15.7	14.7
2001	14.5	14.6	14.7	15.0	15.0	14.4	13.5	13.9	14.3	15.0	15.2	15.1	14.6
2002	14.3	14.6	15.3	15.3	15.3	14.6	13.9	14.0	14.4	15.1	15.2	15.2	14.8
2003	14.3	14.7	15.2	15.4	15.4	15.1	13.8	14.0	14.6	15.3	15.4	15.2	14.9

Employment by Industry: North Carolina—*Continued*

(Numbers in thousands. Not seasonally adjusted.)

Industry	January	February	March	April	May	June	July	August	September	October	November	December	Annual Average
GREENSBORO-WINSTON-SALEM-HIGH POINT *—Continued*													
Local government													
1992	43.2	43.3	43.6	43.8	45.0	44.8	37.4	38.1	42.1	44.3	46.6	45.1	43.1
1993	42.8	42.8	43.1	43.4	43.3	44.1	37.5	38.6	42.4	44.1	45.0	44.1	42.6
1994	43.2	43.2	43.4	44.5	45.2	46.4	36.6	38.3	43.0	44.5	46.6	45.3	43.3
1995	44.3	44.3	44.5	44.7	44.3	45.5	36.3	37.8	43.5	44.8	45.1	45.1	43.3
1996	44.7	44.6	45.0	45.3	45.5	46.2	36.4	38.2	45.7	45.5	46.6	46.0	44.1
1997	46.0	46.0	46.4	46.8	47.1	47.6	37.4	39.5	46.6	47.7	48.1	48.0	45.6
1998	47.8	48.1	48.5	48.5	48.6	49.0	40.6	45.9	49.1	51.4	51.1	51.0	48.3
1999	50.2	50.4	51.0	50.2	50.0	50.8	39.7	45.6	48.7	51.7	52.1	52.2	49.3
2000	50.1	50.3	50.7	50.6	50.8	49.2	41.7	48.2	51.1	51.1	51.5	51.5	49.7
2001	50.7	50.9	51.1	51.1	51.5	48.7	40.8	44.9	49.8	51.5	52.8	51.8	49.6
2002	52.0	52.3	52.6	52.8	52.9	47.7	41.2	47.8	51.3	53.1	53.3	52.5	50.8
2003	51.7	52.0	52.5	52.5	53.0	48.7	42.5	48.3	51.6	53.3	53.5	53.4	51.1
RALEIGH-DURHAM													
Total nonfarm													
1990	456.8	465.0	467.5	468.4	467.3	469.9	463.8	467.1	472.2	475.1	475.9	476.6	468.8
1991	460.7	466.3	468.2	470.8	469.0	469.7	463.9	468.6	475.8	482.7	484.9	486.3	472.2
1992	474.9	480.3	484.1	484.4	487.4	488.7	486.0	488.7	495.8	502.5	504.8	507.2	490.4
1993	497.5	503.6	503.6	508.0	509.5	512.2	509.1	513.9	518.7	514.1	525.0	525.6	511.7
1994	526.9	530.5	535.9	536.7	536.3	540.4	523.3	532.5	536.6	540.7	547.0	548.0	536.2
1995	539.4	544.4	548.8	548.9	551.9	557.8	551.5	555.5	565.2	573.0	578.2	575.8	557.5
1996	559.9	572.0	577.2	577.9	581.2	584.6	577.7	582.7	589.9	597.1	603.7	602.3	583.8
1997	589.8	598.2	603.4	612.8	612.4	616.2	605.0	609.5	618.1	629.5	635.7	634.3	613.7
1998	624.1	632.7	637.5	648.1	648.3	650.3	636.8	640.9	651.0	655.8	659.4	659.6	645.3
1999	647.0	656.4	661.5	669.2	669.3	674.1	663.8	669.3	675.1	680.3	682.9	685.1	669.5
2000	663.6	670.2	677.9	681.3	683.1	688.9	668.7	673.1	678.6	679.3	683.8	686.3	677.9
2001	683.1	684.0	689.5	695.6	696.4	700.3	690.4	690.1	686.5	686.2	683.9	684.7	689.2
2002	672.9	676.3	680.8	685.2	688.6	687.4	678.0	682.4	684.6	686.0	685.3	684.8	682.7
2003	668.4	670.9	674.4	677.6	683.5	684.5	678.1	681.7	685.9	687.8	688.2	687.3	680.7
Total private													
1990	359.5	363.9	365.5	365.9	366.5	370.2	368.7	370.3	371.5	371.6	372.1	374.1	368.3
1991	360.2	361.0	362.7	365.4	366.2	368.3	368.5	370.5	370.8	374.9	377.2	379.4	368.7
1992	368.5	370.4	373.8	376.9	380.8	383.2	385.5	385.2	387.5	390.9	391.7	396.0	382.5
1993	386.2	390.3	390.2	396.0	398.2	401.9	403.4	405.5	406.7	399.6	407.6	410.7	399.6
1994	413.8	415.3	419.7	422.4	423.1	427.5	417.7	421.0	421.3	423.3	427.8	431.4	422.0
1995	423.6	426.2	429.8	431.9	435.8	442.9	443.6	447.0	450.6	454.1	458.3	458.0	441.8
1996	444.7	453.5	458.8	460.5	464.6	468.5	470.3	472.6	472.6	476.7	482.5	482.6	467.3
1997	470.3	476.3	481.8	489.5	492.3	495.8	493.9	496.4	497.9	504.0	509.9	510.8	493.2
1998	500.2	504.1	508.0	519.4	522.9	527.0	525.8	526.9	527.3	527.2	531.8	533.6	521.1
1999	524.2	528.9	533.4	542.2	544.4	549.3	547.9	548.6	548.3	552.0	555.5	559.5	544.5
2000	537.8	540.6	548.1	552.9	555.7	560.2	554.4	555.6	555.6	560.1	563.5	565.6	554.1
2001	563.4	562.6	566.5	569.0	569.0	573.6	567.4	564.7	556.6	556.3	553.3	555.7	563.2
2002	545.2	546.1	550.7	556.0	558.5	558.4	555.2	555.8	553.3	552.8	553.1	552.6	553.1
2003	538.3	539.4	542.2	545.5	550.4	551.7	550.3	551.6	549.9	549.2	550.9	551.0	547.5
Goods-producing													
1990	93.7	94.4	94.3	93.6	93.7	94.7	93.9	94.2	93.7	92.3	91.9	91.6	93.5
1991	83.1	82.9	82.9	83.5	83.7	84.3	84.7	85.0	84.5	88.3	88.6	88.4	84.9
1992	86.4	87.1	87.4	87.4	88.3	89.0	91.6	91.3	91.4	90.3	90.0	91.1	89.2
1993	89.7	90.6	90.5	91.4	92.0	93.3	94.7	95.2	94.7	90.5	94.0	94.4	92.5
1994	95.9	95.4	96.2	96.6	96.9	97.6	96.2	96.7	96.4	97.6	98.3	98.6	96.8
1995	99.3	99.4	99.8	100.2	101.7	103.5	104.0	104.8	104.7	105.0	105.0	104.6	102.6
1996	102.5	104.3	105.0	109.7	110.6	111.7	111.6	112.2	111.8	112.0	112.8	112.0	109.6
1997	111.1	112.2	113.9	114.1	115.0	115.9	115.4	115.9	115.5	120.1	120.4	120.1	115.8
1998	117.9	118.2	119.4	122.1	123.0	124.4	124.2	124.1	123.5	122.3	122.4	122.4	121.9
1999	122.3	123.0	125.6	124.2	124.9	126.2	125.2	124.9	124.5	124.1	124.1	124.0	124.4
2000	121.1	121.3	123.7	124.3	125.3	126.8	126.3	126.9	126.8	127.1	127.6	127.5	125.3
2001	127.0	127.7	129.2	129.0	129.4	129.8	129.0	127.8	124.1	124.8	122.1	121.7	126.8
2002	117.1	116.7	117.2	114.9	115.0	114.6	114.4	113.7	112.6	111.8	111.0	110.5	114.1
2003	108.0	107.7	108.6	107.1	108.0	108.7	108.2	108.4	107.5	106.8	107.2	106.9	107.8
Natural resources and mining													
2002	1.3	1.4	1.3	1.4	1.4	1.4	1.4	1.4	1.4	1.4	1.4	1.4	1.3
2003	1.1	1.1	1.1	1.1	1.1	1.2	1.2	1.2	1.2	1.1	1.0	1.1	1.1
Construction													
2002	38.5	38.8	39.1	39.3	39.9	39.7	39.7	39.7	38.8	38.5	37.9	37.3	38.9
2003	36.4	36.4	36.7	36.6	37.6	38.2	38.3	38.7	38.0	37.7	37.9	37.8	37.5

Employment by Industry: North Carolina—*Continued*

(Numbers in thousands. Not seasonally adjusted.)

Industry	January	February	March	April	May	June	July	August	September	October	November	December	Annual Average
RALEIGH-DURHAM *—Continued*													
Manufacturing													
1990	68.9	68.9	68.4	67.9	67.9	68.3	67.7	67.9	67.9	67.3	67.1	67.4	67.9
1991	60.8	60.4	60.2	60.6	60.5	60.8	61.1	61.4	61.2	65.1	65.5	65.7	61.9
1992	64.7	65.2	65.1	64.5	65.1	65.3	67.1	67.0	67.1	66.8	66.8	67.6	66.0
1993	67.0	67.5	67.0	67.3	67.5	68.4	69.3	69.9	69.6	66.0	69.5	69.7	68.2
1994	72.0	71.5	71.6	71.6	71.2	71.1	69.9	70.3	70.0	70.9	71.4	71.6	71.0
1995	72.6	73.0	72.5	72.2	72.8	73.7	73.9	74.6	74.5	74.8	75.0	74.7	73.6
1996	74.4	75.1	75.0	79.7	79.8	80.2	80.1	80.3	80.6	80.3	80.9	80.3	78.8
1997	79.4	80.1	81.2	80.1	80.4	80.7	79.8	80.3	80.2	84.1	84.5	84.2	81.2
1998	83.8	84.0	84.2	84.7	84.8	85.1	84.5	84.2	84.0	83.1	83.2	83.2	84.0
1999	83.8	83.8	85.5	82.7	83.1	83.4	82.6	82.3	82.2	82.7	82.9	83.2	83.1
2000	82.0	82.3	83.5	83.1	83.5	84.0	84.0	84.2	84.3	84.7	85.1	85.3	83.8
2001	86.5	86.7	87.1	86.5	85.8	85.5	85.2	84.0	81.0	82.0	81.1	80.5	84.3
2002	77.3	76.5	76.8	74.2	73.7	73.5	73.3	72.6	72.4	71.9	71.7	71.8	73.8
2003	70.5	70.2	70.8	69.4	69.3	69.3	68.7	68.5	68.3	68.0	68.3	68.0	69.1
Service-providing													
1990	363.1	370.6	373.2	374.8	373.6	375.2	369.9	372.9	378.5	382.8	384.0	385.0	375.3
1991	377.6	383.4	385.3	387.3	385.3	385.4	379.2	383.6	391.3	394.4	396.3	397.9	387.2
1992	388.5	393.2	396.7	397.0	399.1	399.7	394.4	397.4	404.4	412.2	414.8	416.1	401.1
1993	407.8	413.0	413.1	416.6	417.5	418.9	414.4	418.7	424.0	423.6	431.0	431.2	419.1
1994	431.0	435.1	439.7	440.1	439.4	442.8	427.1	435.8	440.2	443.1	448.7	449.4	439.3
1995	440.1	445.0	449.0	448.7	450.2	454.3	447.5	450.7	460.5	468.0	473.2	471.2	454.8
1996	457.4	467.7	472.2	468.2	470.6	472.9	466.1	470.5	478.1	485.1	490.9	490.3	474.1
1997	478.7	486.0	489.5	498.7	497.4	500.3	489.6	493.6	502.6	509.4	515.3	514.2	497.9
1998	506.2	514.5	518.1	526.0	525.3	525.9	512.6	516.8	527.5	533.5	537.0	537.2	523.3
1999	524.7	533.4	535.9	545.0	544.4	547.9	538.6	544.4	550.6	556.2	558.8	561.1	545.0
2000	542.5	548.9	554.2	557.0	557.8	562.1	542.4	546.2	551.8	552.2	556.2	558.8	552.5
2001	555.9	556.3	560.3	566.5	567.0	570.4	561.4	562.3	562.4	561.4	561.8	564.4	562.5
2002	555.8	559.6	563.6	570.3	573.6	572.8	563.6	568.7	572.0	574.2	574.3	574.3	568.6
2003	560.4	563.2	565.8	570.5	575.5	575.8	569.9	573.3	578.4	581.0	581.0	580.4	572.9
Trade, transportation, and utilities													
1990	85.3	85.4	85.6	85.0	84.3	85.0	84.0	84.2	85.3	86.5	87.6	89.3	85.6
1991	90.6	89.9	89.6	90.2	90.4	90.4	89.9	91.1	91.5	92.1	93.4	94.8	91.1
1992	89.9	89.6	89.7	89.8	90.5	91.1	92.3	92.4	93.5	93.2	94.4	96.6	91.9
1993	93.0	92.8	92.6	92.2	92.4	92.4	93.0	93.8	94.3	94.3	96.5	98.0	93.7
1994	96.5	96.0	96.3	95.7	95.7	96.5	94.0	94.7	95.2	96.5	99.1	101.2	96.4
1995	97.8	97.3	97.7	96.6	95.5	95.0	94.4	95.7	97.3	99.8	102.3	103.7	97.7
1996	98.5	98.9	99.4	97.6	98.8	99.6	99.6	100.3	100.5	102.5	105.5	106.7	100.6
1997	101.1	101.6	102.4	103.1	103.4	103.8	103.9	104.7	105.4	109.3	112.8	113.3	105.4
1998	105.7	105.8	106.3	110.1	110.8	111.4	110.4	111.0	112.0	113.4	116.0	117.7	110.8
1999	112.3	112.3	112.3	113.0	113.4	114.6	115.0	115.4	115.9	117.7	120.0	122.8	115.3
2000	114.3	113.5	114.6	115.7	116.5	117.4	113.1	113.5	113.6	115.4	117.4	119.5	115.3
2001	116.1	115.0	115.7	116.4	116.2	117.0	115.5	115.1	115.1	113.8	114.7	115.6	115.5
2002	112.2	111.8	112.9	113.3	113.3	113.3	112.3	113.0	112.9	112.9	115.1	116.5	113.3
2003	110.5	110.0	110.6	111.1	112.0	113.0	112.7	114.4	114.2	113.4	116.0	116.6	112.9
Wholesale trade													
1990	18.0	18.3	18.5	18.8	17.9	18.6	17.6	17.5	17.7	18.1	17.8	17.7	18.0
1991	24.0	24.0	24.1	24.1	24.1	24.1	24.0	24.2	24.1	23.8	23.7	23.6	23.9
1992	23.2	23.5	23.5	23.9	23.9	24.0	24.6	24.7	24.9	24.9	24.8	24.9	24.2
1993	24.1	24.3	24.2	24.2	24.2	24.3	24.5	24.6	24.5	24.5	24.7	24.1	24.3
1994	24.2	24.2	24.2	24.2	24.1	24.1	23.7	24.0	24.1	24.1	24.0	24.3	24.1
1995	24.0	24.1	24.1	22.8	20.5	19.3	19.2	19.4	19.7	19.7	19.7	19.7	21.0
1996	19.5	19.8	19.9	20.0	20.1	20.4	20.6	20.9	21.1	21.2	21.2	21.2	20.4
1997	21.0	21.8	22.0	22.2	22.4	22.5	22.6	22.8	23.0	23.6	23.6	23.6	22.5
1998	22.9	23.0	23.3	24.2	24.4	24.6	24.4	24.8	24.8	24.4	24.4	24.4	24.1
1999	24.3	24.4	24.3	24.6	24.6	24.8	24.9	25.0	25.0	25.3	25.2	25.4	24.8
2000	23.9	23.9	24.0	24.0	24.1	24.4	24.1	24.2	24.1	24.5	24.3	24.3	24.1
2001	24.4	24.5	24.6	24.3	24.1	24.2	24.3	24.1	24.0	23.8	23.5	23.4	24.1
2002	26.2	26.2	26.2	26.6	26.6	26.6	26.6	26.5	26.5	26.7	26.6	26.5	26.5
2003	26.5	26.4	26.9	26.5	26.6	26.8	27.1	27.4	27.5	27.2	27.5	27.2	27.0
Retail trade													
1990	49.4	49.0	48.8	49.0	49.2	49.1	49.4	49.6	50.2	50.8	52.1	53.7	50.0
1991	49.1	48.2	47.5	48.3	48.4	48.3	47.7	48.3	48.8	50.2	51.6	52.9	49.1
1992	48.3	47.5	47.5	47.2	47.7	48.0	48.5	48.6	49.3	49.2	50.5	52.4	48.7
1993	49.9	49.5	49.5	49.7	49.9	49.8	50.0	50.6	51.3	51.8	53.3	55.5	50.9
1994	54.1	53.3	53.8	53.2	53.5	54.3	52.4	52.8	53.5	54.7	57.6	59.6	54.4
1995	56.3	55.7	55.9	56.3	57.4	58.3	57.7	58.2	59.4	61.4	63.8	65.4	58.8
1996	61.3	61.0	61.2	60.1	61.1	61.5	61.3	61.6	61.8	63.3	66.5	68.0	62.3
1997	62.8	62.4	63.2	63.7	63.8	64.3	64.2	64.7	65.3	67.8	71.3	72.0	65.4
1998	65.2	65.2	65.3	67.0	67.5	68.0	66.9	67.2	68.2	69.7	72.1	73.8	68.0
1999	69.5	69.4	69.5	69.9	70.4	71.3	71.1	71.5	72.2	73.2	75.6	78.0	71.8
2000	71.5	70.7	71.6	73.1	73.7	74.2	72.4	72.8	73.0	74.0	76.4	78.6	73.5
2001	74.8	73.7	74.1	74.8	74.8	75.7	74.1	74.2	74.4	75.2	77.1	78.0	75.1
2002	72.2	71.8	72.8	72.6	72.6	72.6	71.5	72.5	72.7	72.5	75.0	76.6	73.0
2003	70.8	70.3	70.4	71.2	72.1	72.9	72.5	73.6	73.7	73.4	75.9	76.5	72.8

Employment by Industry: North Carolina—*Continued*

(Numbers in thousands. Not seasonally adjusted.)

Industry	January	February	March	April	May	June	July	August	September	October	November	December	Annual Average
RALEIGH-DURHAM *—Continued*													
Transportation and utilities													
1990	17.9	18.1	18.3	17.2	17.2	17.3	17.0	17.1	17.4	17.6	17.7	17.9	17.5
1991	17.5	17.7	18.0	17.8	17.9	18.0	18.2	18.6	18.6	18.1	18.1	18.3	18.0
1992	18.4	18.6	18.7	18.7	18.9	19.1	19.2	19.1	19.3	19.1	19.1	19.3	18.9
1993	19.0	19.0	18.9	18.3	18.3	18.3	18.5	18.6	18.5	18.0	18.5	18.4	18.5
1994	18.2	18.5	18.3	18.3	18.1	18.1	17.9	17.9	17.6	17.7	17.5	17.3	17.9
1995	17.5	17.5	17.7	17.5	17.6	17.4	17.5	18.1	18.2	18.7	18.8	18.6	17.9
1996	17.7	18.1	18.3	17.5	17.6	17.7	17.7	17.8	17.6	18.0	17.8	17.5	17.7
1997	17.3	17.4	17.2	17.2	17.2	17.0	17.1	17.2	17.1	17.9	17.9	17.7	17.3
1998	17.6	17.6	17.7	18.9	18.9	18.8	19.1	19.0	19.0	19.3	19.5	19.5	18.7
1999	18.5	18.5	18.5	18.5	18.4	18.5	19.0	18.9	18.7	19.2	19.2	19.4	18.7
2000	18.9	18.9	19.0	18.6	18.7	18.8	16.6	16.5	16.5	16.9	16.7	16.6	17.7
2001	16.9	16.8	17.0	17.3	17.3	17.1	17.1	16.8	16.7	14.8	14.1	14.2	16.3
2002	13.8	13.8	13.9	14.1	14.1	14.1	14.2	14.0	13.7	13.7	13.5	13.4	13.9
2003	13.2	13.3	13.3	13.4	13.3	13.3	13.1	13.4	13.0	12.8	12.6	12.9	13.1
Information													
1990	10.8	10.9	11.0	10.6	10.6	10.8	10.9	10.9	10.9	10.9	11.0	11.0	10.8
1991	10.4	10.4	10.5	10.0	10.0	10.0	10.5	10.4	10.4	10.0	10.1	10.1	10.2
1992	10.1	10.0	10.1	10.3	10.4	10.5	10.9	10.8	10.9	11.0	11.0	11.7	10.6
1993	11.6	11.8	11.8	13.2	13.2	13.4	13.4	13.3	13.3	13.2	13.4	13.5	12.9
1994	13.6	13.7	13.8	13.9	13.9	14.0	13.8	13.7	13.8	13.7	13.8	14.0	13.8
1995	13.9	14.0	14.1	13.9	14.1	14.6	14.7	14.9	15.1	15.2	15.4	15.5	14.6
1996	17.2	17.3	17.4	17.0	16.6	16.9	17.3	17.3	17.6	17.6	17.8	17.9	17.3
1997	17.7	17.7	18.0	18.8	19.0	19.4	17.5	17.6	17.7	18.5	18.3	18.5	18.2
1998	18.3	18.4	18.5	19.2	19.2	19.2	19.7	19.3	19.1	18.8	19.4	19.2	19.0
1999	19.4	19.5	19.6	21.4	21.7	22.0	21.6	21.8	21.8	21.8	22.0	21.7	21.1
2000	22.1	22.3	22.8	22.6	22.9	23.5	23.4	23.5	23.4	24.2	24.3	24.3	23.2
2001	24.3	25.0	25.0	24.6	24.6	24.4	24.0	24.4	24.0	23.7	23.6	23.2	24.2
2002	23.6	23.4	23.8	23.4	23.4	23.4	22.9	22.8	22.7	22.6	22.5	22.4	23.1
2003	22.2	22.3	22.2	22.1	22.1	22.1	22.1	21.9	21.7	21.7	21.4	21.7	22.0
Financial activities													
1990	22.4	22.7	22.8	22.7	22.7	23.0	22.7	22.7	22.9	22.9	22.9	23.0	22.7
1991	22.4	22.6	22.7	23.2	23.2	23.3	23.5	23.5	23.2	22.2	22.1	22.3	22.8
1992	22.8	22.9	23.0	23.0	23.2	23.4	23.5	23.5	23.7	23.4	23.4	23.5	23.2
1993	23.0	23.2	23.3	23.3	23.3	23.5	23.4	23.3	23.3	23.5	23.6	23.8	23.3
1994	24.1	24.4	24.4	24.4	24.5	24.8	24.0	24.2	24.1	23.9	23.9	24.2	24.2
1995	23.1	23.3	23.6	23.9	24.1	24.6	24.8	24.9	25.1	25.0	25.2	25.2	24.4
1996	25.3	25.7	25.9	25.5	25.7	26.0	26.8	27.1	27.1	27.5	27.8	27.8	26.5
1997	27.3	27.8	28.0	27.8	27.9	28.0	28.2	28.3	28.4	29.0	29.1	29.2	28.2
1998	28.2	28.5	28.5	29.5	29.6	29.9	29.9	30.2	30.2	30.3	30.3	30.4	29.6
1999	30.1	30.5	30.5	31.1	31.1	31.4	31.6	31.6	31.5	31.8	31.8	31.9	31.2
2000	30.7	30.9	31.2	31.5	31.7	31.9	31.1	31.3	31.4	31.7	31.7	31.9	31.4
2001	30.7	30.6	30.7	30.7	30.8	30.9	30.5	30.4	30.3	30.5	30.6	30.7	30.6
2002	31.4	31.7	31.9	32.6	32.7	32.8	32.7	32.8	32.6	32.4	32.1	31.9	32.3
2003	31.7	31.8	31.9	32.2	32.5	32.6	32.3	32.7	32.5	32.2	31.9	31.7	32.2
Professional and business services													
1990	48.6	50.2	50.7	52.0	52.3	52.9	52.6	52.8	53.2	54.8	54.2	54.1	52.3
1991	51.3	51.9	52.6	54.1	53.8	54.1	54.6	54.8	55.3	54.2	54.7	55.2	53.8
1992	52.9	52.9	54.3	56.4	56.7	57.6	58.8	59.1	59.4	60.5	60.5	61.1	57.5
1993	58.8	59.7	60.0	62.5	62.9	63.4	63.1	63.0	63.5	62.3	63.3	63.5	62.1
1994	64.4	65.1	66.0	68.2	68.0	69.0	67.8	68.5	67.9	69.6	70.2	70.5	67.9
1995	67.9	69.3	70.4	72.3	73.3	75.0	76.1	76.9	77.2	77.7	78.4	78.3	74.4
1996	77.3	80.4	82.7	82.5	83.2	84.0	84.7	84.4	84.5	85.4	86.1	86.2	83.4
1997	83.4	85.4	86.7	89.5	90.1	90.5	91.5	91.8	92.2	92.5	93.3	93.8	90.0
1998	92.4	93.9	95.0	95.6	95.7	96.1	96.2	96.4	96.6	96.1	96.9	97.4	95.6
1999	95.3	96.2	97.3	101.7	101.8	102.5	101.1	100.9	100.9	101.4	102.0	102.6	100.3
2000	98.5	99.5	101.3	103.8	103.7	104.6	104.9	105.9	105.6	106.6	107.3	107.6	104.1
2001	109.7	107.2	107.5	107.6	106.3	107.2	104.5	104.0	102.7	102.8	102.7	103.1	105.4
2002	99.8	100.1	101.0	102.4	102.9	103.4	102.5	102.6	102.2	101.9	101.9	101.9	101.9
2003	98.9	99.1	99.8	102.3	102.9	103.3	103.0	101.6	102.0	102.4	103.2	102.4	101.7
Educational and health services													
1990	44.5	45.0	45.4	45.7	45.4	45.4	45.6	46.0	46.8	47.0	47.3	47.8	45.9
1991	47.0	47.5	47.9	47.8	47.6	47.5	47.2	47.6	48.7	49.0	49.2	49.4	48.0
1992	49.0	49.6	50.0	50.3	50.6	50.4	46.6	46.8	48.2	53.6	54.0	54.4	50.2
1993	53.9	55.1	55.1	55.4	54.9	54.8	54.5	55.0	56.3	55.1	55.2	55.5	55.0
1994	56.0	56.6	57.0	56.7	56.6	56.6	55.1	55.7	56.4	55.9	56.3	56.4	56.2
1995	56.3	57.0	57.6	57.7	58.3	58.9	58.7	59.1	60.4	60.7	61.2	60.7	58.8
1996	60.0	60.9	61.7	61.0	61.3	61.1	61.2	61.9	62.5	63.2	64.0	63.9	61.8
1997	62.8	63.6	64.2	65.1	65.0	65.2	64.7	65.1	66.0	61.7	62.3	62.3	64.0
1998	65.9	66.8	67.1	67.8	68.3	68.2	67.8	68.5	69.3	70.2	70.4	70.3	68.3
1999	69.6	70.5	70.6	71.0	71.0	70.4	71.1	71.8	72.3	72.1	72.4	72.7	71.2
2000	70.8	71.4	71.7	71.6	71.4	71.0	71.0	70.5	71.0	72.1	71.8	71.7	71.3
2001	72.3	72.4	72.8	73.5	73.6	73.3	74.5	74.6	74.3	74.8	74.5	75.0	73.8
2002	74.7	75.4	75.5	78.8	78.8	78.6	78.6	79.4	80.1	80.9	81.4	81.0	78.6
2003	80.4	81.4	81.6	81.7	81.9	81.2	81.1	81.5	83.1	83.6	83.8	84.0	82.1

Employment by Industry: North Carolina—*Continued*

(Numbers in thousands. Not seasonally adjusted.)

Industry	January	February	March	April	May	June	July	August	September	October	November	December	Annual Average
RALEIGH-DURHAM *—Continued*													
Leisure and hospitality													
1990	34.6	35.4	35.6	36.2	37.2	37.9	38.1	38.4	38.2	36.9	36.8	37.0	36.8
1991	35.4	35.6	36.2	36.2	37.1	37.5	36.9	36.8	36.4	38.1	38.1	38.0	36.8
1992	36.4	37.2	38.0	38.4	40.1	40.3	40.5	40.6	40.7	39.8	39.8	39.5	39.2
1993	38.4	39.6	39.8	40.5	41.3	41.5	41.1	41.3	40.9	40.0	40.3	40.0	40.3
1994	40.5	40.7	41.7	42.5	43.0	43.9	42.7	43.3	43.5	42.0	42.1	42.3	42.3
1995	41.0	41.6	42.1	42.5	43.8	45.6	45.3	45.3	45.3	44.8	44.9	44.3	43.8
1996	42.1	43.6	44.3	44.9	45.8	46.2	46.0	46.3	45.7	45.2	45.2	45.0	45.0
1997	44.1	45.0	45.5	47.3	47.9	48.5	48.2	48.5	48.1	47.6	48.3	47.9	47.2
1998	46.6	47.1	47.5	49.0	50.0	50.8	50.8	50.7	50.0	49.1	49.2	48.9	49.1
1999	47.8	49.2	49.6	51.5	52.1	53.3	53.3	53.2	52.4	53.7	53.8	54.0	51.9
2000	51.2	52.2	53.1	53.2	53.9	54.4	54.2	53.9	53.8	52.6	52.9	52.7	53.1
2001	52.1	53.3	54.0	56.4	57.2	58.1	57.3	56.9	55.8	54.7	54.1	54.4	55.4
2002	52.4	53.1	54.4	57.3	58.5	58.8	58.2	58.5	57.6	57.4	56.9	57.0	56.7
2003	55.1	55.3	55.9	57.3	58.6	58.4	58.9	59.1	58.1	57.9	56.4	56.6	57.3
Other services													
1990	19.6	19.9	20.1	20.1	20.3	20.5	20.9	21.1	20.5	20.3	20.4	20.3	20.3
1991	20.0	20.2	20.3	20.4	20.4	21.2	21.2	21.3	20.8	21.0	21.0	21.2	20.7
1992	21.0	21.1	21.3	21.3	21.0	20.9	21.3	20.7	19.7	19.1	18.6	18.1	20.3
1993	17.8	17.5	17.1	17.5	18.2	19.6	20.2	20.6	20.4	20.7	21.3	22.0	19.4
1994	22.8	23.4	24.3	24.4	24.5	25.1	24.1	24.2	24.0	24.1	24.1	24.2	24.1
1995	24.3	24.3	24.5	24.8	25.0	25.7	25.6	25.4	25.5	25.9	25.9	25.7	25.2
1996	21.8	22.4	22.4	22.3	22.6	23.0	23.1	23.1	22.9	23.3	23.3	23.1	22.7
1997	22.8	23.0	23.1	23.8	24.0	24.5	24.5	24.5	24.6	25.3	25.4	25.7	24.2
1998	25.2	25.4	25.7	26.1	26.3	27.0	26.8	26.7	26.6	27.0	27.2	27.3	26.4
1999	27.4	27.7	27.9	28.3	28.4	28.9	29.0	29.0	29.0	29.4	29.4	29.8	28.6
2000	29.1	29.5	29.7	30.2	30.3	30.6	30.4	30.1	30.0	30.4	30.5	30.4	30.1
2001	31.1	31.4	31.5	30.8	30.8	32.8	32.3	31.2	30.4	31.2	30.9	32.0	31.4
2002	34.0	33.9	34.0	33.3	33.9	33.5	33.6	33.0	32.6	32.9	32.2	31.4	33.2
2003	31.5	31.8	31.6	31.7	32.4	32.4	32.0	32.0	30.8	31.2	31.0	31.1	31.6
Government													
1990	97.3	101.1	102.0	102.5	100.8	99.7	95.1	96.8	100.7	103.5	103.8	102.5	100.4
1991	100.5	105.3	105.5	105.4	102.8	101.4	95.4	98.1	105.0	107.8	107.7	106.9	103.4
1992	106.4	109.9	110.3	107.5	106.6	105.5	100.5	103.5	108.3	111.6	113.1	111.2	107.8
1993	111.3	113.3	113.4	112.0	111.3	110.3	105.7	108.4	112.0	114.5	117.4	114.9	112.0
1994	113.1	115.2	116.2	114.3	113.2	112.9	105.6	111.5	115.3	117.4	119.2	116.6	114.2
1995	115.8	118.2	119.0	117.0	116.1	114.9	107.9	108.5	114.6	118.9	119.9	117.8	115.7
1996	115.2	118.5	118.4	117.4	116.6	116.1	107.4	110.1	117.3	120.4	121.2	119.7	116.5
1997	119.5	121.9	121.6	123.3	120.1	120.4	111.1	113.1	120.2	125.5	125.8	123.5	120.5
1998	123.9	128.6	129.5	128.7	125.4	123.3	111.0	114.0	123.7	128.6	127.6	126.0	124.1
1999	122.8	127.5	128.1	127.0	124.9	124.8	115.9	120.7	126.8	128.3	127.4	125.6	124.9
2000	125.8	129.6	129.8	128.4	127.4	128.7	114.3	117.5	123.0	119.2	120.3	120.7	123.7
2001	119.6	121.5	122.9	126.7	127.5	126.7	122.9	125.5	129.8	130.0	130.6	130.4	126.2
2002	127.7	130.2	130.1	129.2	130.1	129.0	122.8	126.6	131.3	133.2	132.2	132.2	129.6
2003	130.1	131.5	132.2	132.1	133.1	132.8	127.8	130.1	136.0	138.6	137.3	136.3	133.2
Federal government													
1990	8.3	8.3	8.4	8.5	9.2	9.3	8.9	8.5	8.4	8.4	8.4	8.3	8.5
1991	8.3	8.3	8.4	8.4	8.5	8.6	8.6	8.6	8.6	8.6	8.6	8.7	8.5
1992	8.7	8.7	8.7	8.8	8.8	8.8	8.9	8.9	8.8	8.8	8.8	8.9	8.8
1993	8.8	8.8	8.8	8.7	8.7	8.7	8.7	8.7	8.7	8.7	8.7	8.8	8.7
1994	8.7	8.7	8.7	8.7	8.6	8.6	8.7	8.6	8.6	8.6	8.6	8.7	8.6
1995	8.7	8.7	8.7	8.7	8.7	8.8	8.7	8.7	8.7	8.8	8.8	8.9	8.7
1996	8.8	8.8	8.8	8.9	8.9	8.9	8.9	9.0	9.1	9.2	9.2	9.4	8.9
1997	9.3	9.3	9.2	9.3	9.4	9.5	9.6	9.6	9.4	9.4	9.7	9.8	9.4
1998	9.5	9.4	9.5	9.4	9.5	9.6	9.6	9.6	9.6	9.6	9.7	10.0	9.5
1999	9.6	9.6	9.7	9.8	9.8	9.9	10.0	9.9	9.9	10.0	10.2	10.3	9.8
2000	10.0	10.0	10.4	10.7	11.4	13.0	11.1	11.7	9.8	9.8	9.8	10.1	10.6
2001	9.9	9.9	9.9	9.9	9.9	10.0	10.1	10.1	10.0	10.0	10.0	10.2	10.0
2002	10.0	10.0	10.0	9.9	9.9	10.1	10.1	10.3	10.5	10.4	10.5	10.7	10.2
2003	10.4	10.3	10.3	10.3	10.3	10.3	10.4	10.3	10.3	10.4	10.4	10.5	10.4
State government													
1990	52.2	55.7	56.1	56.0	53.1	51.7	51.1	52.9	54.6	56.8	56.6	55.3	54.3
1991	53.1	57.6	57.8	58.0	54.9	52.9	53.0	55.5	57.5	60.0	59.1	58.0	56.4
1992	57.7	60.8	60.9	58.3	57.1	55.5	55.5	58.7	59.9	61.7	61.5	60.6	59.0
1993	60.5	62.5	62.4	60.9	60.1	58.6	58.2	61.1	61.4	63.1	64.9	62.9	61.3
1994	61.6	63.4	63.9	62.3	60.8	59.9	59.0	64.2	63.8	64.7	65.4	63.5	62.7
1995	62.8	65.2	65.8	63.7	62.8	60.7	60.1	62.0	64.2	65.3	66.1	64.0	63.5
1996	61.8	65.0	64.6	63.4	62.4	61.2	59.5	62.5	64.0	65.7	65.8	64.1	63.3
1997	64.1	66.2	65.6	67.0	63.3	62.9	61.3	63.2	64.7	67.7	67.8	65.3	64.9
1998	66.8	71.4	72.0	71.2	67.5	64.5	59.6	61.8	65.2	69.6	68.7	67.1	67.1
1999	65.8	70.1	70.1	68.7	66.5	65.8	62.8	65.9	67.6	69.4	68.0	66.1	67.2
2000	66.9	70.5	70.0	67.9	66.0	65.2	58.3	60.4	62.0	58.9	59.6	59.6	63.7
2001	58.7	59.9	60.4	64.7	65.1	65.7	63.8	65.1	65.9	66.0	65.8	66.0	63.9
2002	63.6	65.6	66.4	65.6	66.2	66.1	64.0	65.9	67.0	66.6	66.6	66.5	65.8
2003	65.0	66.3	67.0	66.9	67.6	67.9	67.3	69.3	71.4	71.0	71.1	70.0	68.4

Employment by Industry: North Carolina—*Continued*

(Numbers in thousands. Not seasonally adjusted.)

Industry	January	February	March	April	May	June	July	August	September	October	November	December	Annual Average
RALEIGH-DURHAM *—Continued*													
Local government													
1990	36.9	37.2	37.6	38.0	38.4	38.7	35.2	35.3	37.7	38.3	38.8	38.9	37.5
1991	39.2	39.4	39.4	39.0	39.4	39.9	33.8	34.1	38.9	39.3	40.0	40.3	38.5
1992	40.0	40.4	40.7	40.4	40.7	41.2	36.1	35.9	39.6	41.1	42.8	41.7	40.0
1993	42.0	42.0	42.2	42.4	42.5	43.0	38.8	38.6	41.9	42.7	43.8	43.2	41.9
1994	42.8	43.1	43.6	43.3	43.8	44.4	37.9	38.7	42.9	44.1	45.2	44.4	42.8
1995	44.3	44.3	44.5	44.6	44.6	45.4	39.1	37.8	41.7	44.8	45.0	44.9	43.4
1996	44.6	44.7	45.0	45.1	45.3	46.0	39.0	38.6	44.2	45.5	46.2	46.2	44.2
1997	46.1	46.4	46.8	47.0	47.4	48.0	40.2	40.3	46.1	48.4	48.3	48.4	46.1
1998	47.6	47.8	48.0	48.1	48.4	49.2	41.8	42.6	48.9	49.4	49.2	48.9	47.4
1999	47.4	47.8	48.3	48.5	48.6	49.1	43.1	44.9	49.3	48.9	49.2	49.2	47.8
2000	48.9	49.1	49.4	49.8	50.0	50.5	44.9	45.4	51.2	50.5	50.9	51.0	49.3
2001	51.0	51.7	52.6	52.1	52.5	51.0	49.0	50.3	53.9	54.0	54.8	54.2	52.3
2002	54.1	54.6	53.7	53.7	54.0	52.8	48.7	50.4	53.8	56.2	55.1	55.0	53.5
2003	54.7	54.9	54.9	54.9	55.2	54.6	50.1	50.5	54.3	57.2	55.8	55.8	54.4

Average Weekly Hours by Industry: North Carolina

(Not seasonally adjusted.)

Industry	January	February	March	April	May	June	July	August	September	October	November	December	Annual Average
STATEWIDE													
Manufacturing													
2001	40.0	39.3	39.5	38.4	39.5	39.7	38.5	39.7	39.9	39.7	39.2	39.8	39.4
2002	39.8	39.7	40.1	40.5	40.2	40.8	39.0	41.3	40.8	39.6	39.7	41.1	40.2
2003	39.3	39.5	39.8	39.3	39.3	39.8	38.8	39.7	40.2	40.1	40.7	40.5	39.8
CHARLOTTE-GASTONIA-ROCK HILL													
Manufacturing													
2001	40.9	39.1	39.7	38.4	39.6	39.7	37.5	39.0	39.5	40.2	39.0	39.3	39.3
2002	39.1	39.2	39.5	40.6	40.3	40.7	39.0	40.3	39.8	38.7	38.3	39.8	39.6
2003	39.5	39.2	39.5	39.4	39.3	40.0	39.5	39.7	39.2	39.7	39.8	40.4	39.6
GREENSBORO-WINSTON-SALEM-HIGH POINT													
Manufacturing													
2001	39.8	40.3	40.2	39.2	39.7	39.7	37.9	40.7	40.2	39.9	39.2	39.9	39.7
2002	40.4	40.7	41.2	41.0	40.4	41.7	40.6	42.5	41.4	40.2	40.6	40.2	40.9
2003	39.0	39.0	39.6	38.8	38.3	39.4	37.8	38.6	39.3	38.4	39.6	39.2	38.9
RALEIGH-DURHAM													
Manufacturing													
2001	41.0	39.9	38.3	38.7	39.2	38.5	38.5	38.1	39.8	39.8	39.0	40.0	39.2
2002	41.2	40.6	39.9	39.9	40.9	40.2	39.7	41.5	43.0	42.2	40.8	42.3	41.0
2003	40.4	40.0	40.9	41.5	41.6	42.2	41.6	40.9	40.8	41.9	43.0	42.2	41.4

Average Hourly Earnings by Industry: North Carolina

(Dollars, not seasonally adjusted.)

Industry	January	February	March	April	May	June	July	August	September	October	November	December	Annual Average
STATEWIDE													
Manufacturing													
2001	12.65	12.65	12.65	12.79	12.74	12.75	12.90	12.79	12.87	12.82	13.02	13.07	12.81
2002	13.08	13.08	13.11	13.13	13.22	13.26	13.31	13.10	13.11	13.17	13.17	13.38	13.18
2003	13.50	13.44	13.49	13.59	13.55	13.55	13.63	13.67	13.84	13.77	13.86	14.09	13.66
CHARLOTTE-GASTONIA-ROCK HILL													
Manufacturing													
2001	13.42	13.46	13.31	13.58	13.29	13.46	13.63	13.32	13.56	13.35	13.64	13.95	13.49
2002	13.43	13.77	13.83	13.77	14.07	14.20	14.05	14.22	13.78	13.97	13.83	13.83	13.90
2003	14.24	14.34	14.36	14.40	14.38	14.38	14.55	14.54	14.85	14.81	14.85	14.89	14.54
GREENSBORO-WINSTON-SALEM-HIGH POINT													
Manufacturing													
2001	13.18	13.06	13.12	13.09	13.11	13.06	13.28	13.14	13.22	13.12	13.32	13.27	13.16
2002	13.29	13.24	13.24	13.23	13.29	13.30	13.43	13.15	13.20	13.17	13.00	13.27	13.23
2003	12.94	13.12	13.17	13.22	13.31	13.31	13.61	13.54	13.69	13.89	13.97	14.17	13.49
RALEIGH-DURHAM													
Manufacturing													
2001	12.93	13.00	13.16	13.42	13.35	13.31	13.61	13.71	13.68	13.92	14.15	14.08	13.52
2002	14.11	13.77	13.74	13.66	13.83	13.83	14.07	14.22	14.69	14.92	15.02	15.13	14.24
2003	14.63	14.61	14.76	14.33	14.14	13.93	14.27	14.48	14.66	14.72	14.86	15.02	14.53

Average Weekly Earnings by Industry: North Carolina

(Dollars, not seasonally adjusted.)

Industry	January	February	March	April	May	June	July	August	September	October	November	December	Annual Average
STATEWIDE													
Manufacturing													
2001	506.00	497.15	499.68	491.14	503.23	506.18	496.65	507.76	513.51	508.95	510.38	520.19	504.71
2002	520.58	519.28	525.71	531.77	531.44	541.01	519.09	541.03	534.89	521.53	522.85	549.92	529.84
2003	530.55	530.88	536.90	534.09	532.52	539.29	528.84	542.70	556.37	552.18	564.10	570.65	543.67
CHARLOTTE-GASTONIA-ROCK HILL													
Manufacturing													
2001	548.88	526.29	528.41	521.47	526.28	534.36	511.13	519.48	535.62	536.67	531.96	548.24	530.16
2002	525.11	539.78	546.29	559.06	567.02	577.94	547.95	573.07	548.44	540.64	529.69	550.43	550.44
2003	562.48	562.13	567.22	567.36	565.13	575.20	574.73	577.24	582.12	587.96	591.03	601.56	575.78
GREENSBORO-WINSTON-SALEM-HIGH POINT													
Manufacturing													
2001	524.56	526.32	527.42	513.13	520.47	518.48	503.31	534.80	531.44	523.49	522.14	529.47	522.45
2002	536.92	538.87	545.49	542.43	536.92	554.61	545.26	558.88	546.48	529.43	527.80	533.45	541.11
2003	504.66	511.68	521.53	512.94	509.77	524.41	514.46	522.64	538.02	533.38	553.21	555.46	524.76
RALEIGH-DURHAM													
Manufacturing													
2001	530.13	518.70	504.03	519.35	523.32	512.44	523.99	522.35	544.46	554.02	551.85	563.20	529.98
2002	581.33	559.06	548.23	545.03	565.65	555.97	558.58	590.13	631.67	629.62	612.82	640.00	583.84
2003	591.05	584.40	603.68	594.70	588.22	587.85	593.63	592.23	598.13	616.77	638.98	633.84	601.54

NORTH DAKOTA AT A GLANCE

(Population and total nonfarm employment numbers in thousands)

Population, Census 2000:	642.2
Total nonfarm employment, 2003:	332.6
Change in total nonfarm employment	
(Number)	
1990–2003:	66.8
1990–2001:	63.9
2001–2003:	2.9
(Compound annual rate of change)	
1990–2003:	1.7%
1990–2001:	2.0%
2001–2003:	0.4%
Unemployment rate	
1990:	4.0%
2001:	2.8%
2003:	3.6%

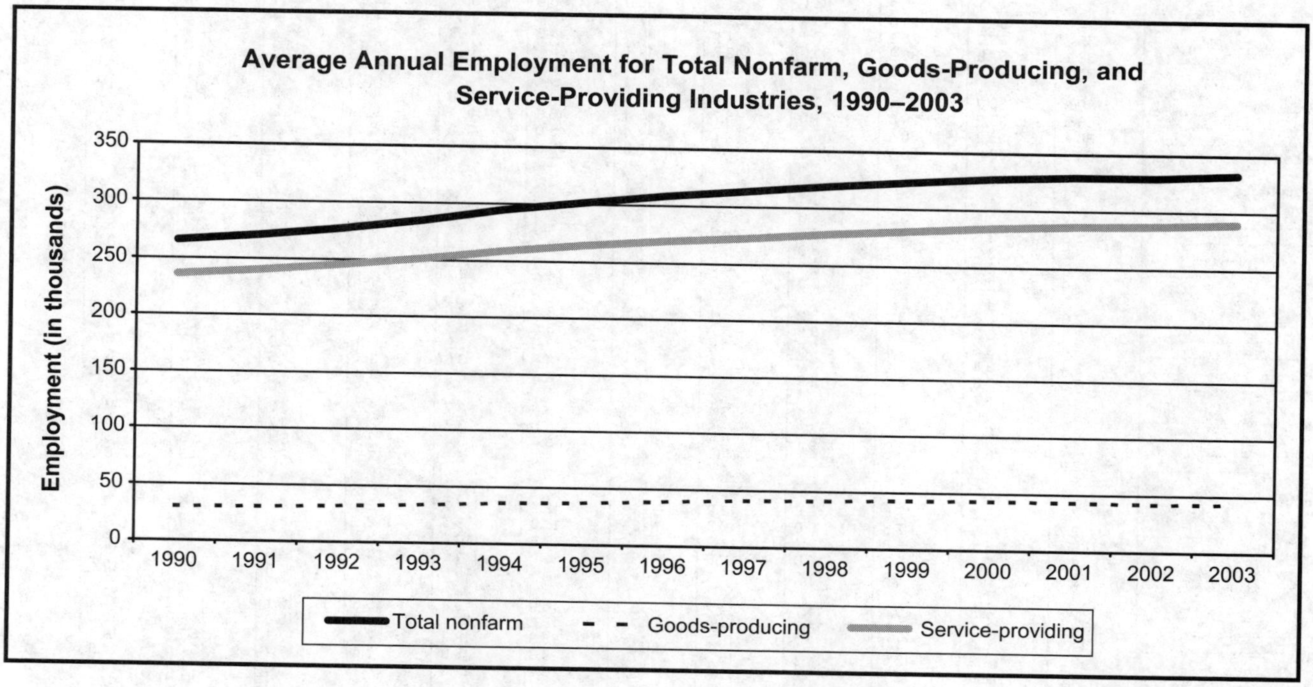

Turbulence in the national economy seemed to have passed over North Dakota, where total nonfarm payroll employment grew steadily during the 1990–2003 period. The growth in private sector jobs slackened in 2001, but overall employment did not decline because of moderate employment growth in financial activities, educational and health services, and government.

Employment by Industry: North Dakota

(Numbers in thousands. Not seasonally adjusted.)

Industry	January	February	March	April	May	June	July	August	September	October	November	December	Annual Average
STATEWIDE													
Total nonfarm													
1990	256.7	257.6	259.5	264.2	269.5	269.8	266.1	265.7	268.5	271.5	270.6	270.3	265.8
1991	261.9	263.0	264.6	268.2	272.3	273.6	270.9	270.5	275.6	277.0	275.0	274.6	270.6
1992	267.5	268.8	270.9	275.1	278.9	279.6	277.8	278.0	280.4	284.2	282.0	282.7	277.1
1993	275.2	275.7	277.9	281.9	287.8	287.0	286.1	285.6	289.2	291.3	290.4	290.1	284.8
1994	281.6	283.5	286.7	291.8	296.8	297.4	296.2	296.5	300.2	302.4	302.5	301.9	294.7
1995	291.7	293.2	296.2	299.3	305.0	304.8	302.2	303.5	305.3	306.7	307.3	305.8	301.7
1996	297.4	300.1	301.5	305.1	312.0	312.5	309.7	310.3	312.8	315.7	314.0	312.7	308.6
1997	303.1	306.0	306.8	310.1	315.9	315.1	313.2	313.9	319.2	322.6	321.4	321.5	314.0
1998	311.3	312.9	314.9	317.8	323.6	319.0	318.1	317.2	321.8	327.5	325.7	323.8	319.4
1999	313.5	315.1	315.6	323.4	327.6	325.9	322.2	322.9	329.2	330.7	330.3	330.0	323.8
2000	319.2	320.4	323.2	327.1	332.8	329.0	327.6	327.2	331.5	332.9	330.9	330.9	327.7
2001	322.5	324.2	326.3	330.1	335.3	333.6	324.9	325.5	333.9	335.0	333.2	332.1	329.7
2002	322.6	323.9	323.9	328.6	333.8	333.4	325.1	327.0	334.2	335.5	334.5	334.5	329.8
2003	324.0	325.3	327.2	331.6	336.8	335.4	327.5	330.6	338.5	340.0	337.8	336.6	332.6
Total private													
1990	190.9	190.9	192.7	196.6	201.5	203.9	203.7	204.9	205.2	205.9	204.7	204.1	200.4
1991	196.7	197.0	198.2	201.7	204.9	208.0	208.3	209.6	210.0	209.9	207.6	207.0	204.9
1992	201.0	201.2	203.1	207.1	211.5	213.7	214.4	215.0	214.3	215.9	213.5	214.0	210.3
1993	207.3	207.0	209.4	213.4	218.7	221.0	222.3	223.0	222.4	223.6	222.9	222.0	217.7
1994	214.7	215.1	218.4	223.4	227.9	231.2	232.3	233.2	233.2	234.1	234.0	233.3	227.5
1995	220.2	220.6	223.5	226.8	232.1	234.5	235.0	236.5	234.7	234.8	235.3	233.6	230.6
1996	227.0	228.4	229.9	233.2	239.7	242.7	243.0	243.5	241.8	243.3	241.6	239.9	237.8
1997	232.3	233.5	234.4	238.0	243.1	247.6	248.5	249.2	247.6	249.4	248.2	248.0	243.3
1998	239.3	239.8	242.0	244.7	250.3	251.5	254.2	253.3	250.4	253.7	251.8	249.7	248.3
1999	241.2	241.4	241.9	249.2	254.0	257.8	257.3	258.2	256.6	256.1	255.7	254.7	252.0
2000	245.7	245.3	247.7	251.8	256.9	259.6	260.6	260.4	258.1	258.1	256.2	255.5	254.6
2001	248.0	248.6	250.6	254.3	259.8	262.4	261.2	260.9	259.0	258.7	257.1	255.6	256.4
2002	247.5	247.8	247.9	252.3	257.3	261.3	260.7	261.0	258.6	258.3	257.2	256.2	255.5
2003	248.6	247.8	249.3	253.3	258.3	262.5	262.0	263.5	261.5	261.5	259.6	258.0	257.2
Goods-producing													
1990	25.8	25.8	26.4	27.6	30.5	31.6	32.1	32.4	32.3	33.3	31.6	29.8	29.9
1991	27.4	27.4	27.4	28.5	30.2	32.0	33.0	33.3	33.5	33.5	31.1	29.6	30.5
1992	27.6	27.3	27.8	30.0	31.8	33.4	34.6	34.6	34.4	34.9	32.7	31.3	31.7
1993	29.0	28.8	29.4	30.9	33.7	35.1	36.1	36.3	36.2	36.9	34.9	33.2	33.3
1994	30.9	30.8	31.6	33.5	35.7	37.7	38.4	39.0	39.1	39.1	38.0	35.9	35.8
1995	32.5	32.4	33.2	34.9	37.7	39.0	39.4	39.9	39.3	39.4	38.4	36.3	36.8
1996	34.6	34.3	35.0	36.4	39.8	41.9	42.4	42.6	41.9	42.3	39.9	37.7	39.0
1997	35.2	35.3	35.8	37.7	41.4	43.6	44.8	44.9	43.8	44.1	42.3	40.8	40.8
1998	38.1	37.9	38.2	39.9	42.7	44.1	45.1	44.9	43.5	44.3	41.9	40.0	41.7
1999	37.3	37.1	37.3	40.6	43.1	46.0	46.9	47.4	46.3	45.8	43.8	42.1	42.8
2000	39.0	38.8	39.4	41.4	44.5	46.5	47.0	46.8	45.8	45.1	42.5	40.9	43.1
2001	38.9	38.5	39.6	41.0	43.7	45.4	46.3	46.1	46.2	45.2	43.1	41.1	42.9
2002	38.4	38.2	38.4	40.2	42.7	44.4	45.0	45.3	44.2	43.7	42.4	40.9	42.0
2003	38.5	38.0	38.4	40.1	43.1	45.3	45.8	46.3	45.8	45.4	43.2	41.8	42.6
Natural resources and mining													
1990	3.4	3.5	3.5	3.6	3.8	3.9	3.9	3.9	3.9	4.0	3.9	3.8	3.7
1991	3.6	3.6	3.7	3.6	3.6	3.7	3.8	3.7	3.6	3.5	3.4	3.3	3.5
1992	3.2	3.2	3.2	3.3	3.4	3.4	3.4	3.4	3.4	3.4	3.3	3.2	3.3
1993	3.0	3.0	3.1	3.1	3.3	3.4	3.5	3.5	3.5	3.5	3.4	3.2	3.2
1994	2.9	2.9	2.9	3.0	3.2	3.3	3.3	3.4	3.4	3.3	3.4	3.2	3.1
1995	2.8	2.8	3.0	3.2	3.4	3.5	3.5	3.6	3.7	3.7	3.7	3.5	3.3
1996	3.4	3.3	3.5	3.5	3.7	3.8	3.8	3.8	3.8	3.9	3.8	3.6	3.6
1997	3.4	3.4	3.4	3.5	3.8	3.8	3.9	3.9	3.8	3.9	3.8	3.7	3.6
1998	3.4	3.4	3.4	3.5	3.7	3.8	3.8	3.6	3.5	3.5	3.3	3.2	3.5
1999	3.0	2.8	2.8	2.9	3.1	3.2	3.3	3.4	3.3	3.4	3.4	3.2	3.1
2000	3.0	3.0	3.0	3.1	3.4	3.4	3.6	3.7	3.7	3.5	3.3	3.2	3.3
2001	3.1	3.1	3.3	3.3	3.5	3.7	3.8	3.7	3.7	3.7	3.5	3.3	3.5
2002	2.9	2.8	2.9	3.1	3.3	3.4	3.4	3.4	3.3	3.4	3.3	3.1	3.2
2003	2.9	2.9	3.0	3.2	3.4	3.5	3.6	3.5	3.5	3.4	3.3	3.2	3.3
Construction													
1990	7.5	7.3	7.5	8.8	11.2	11.8	12.4	12.7	12.1	12.2	10.8	9.4	10.3
1991	7.7	7.6	7.6	9.0	10.8	12.2	13.0	13.5	12.9	12.6	10.9	9.7	10.6
1992	8.4	8.1	8.3	10.1	11.9	13.1	13.9	14.2	13.4	13.1	11.6	10.5	11.3
1993	8.6	8.4	8.7	10.0	12.6	13.6	14.2	14.5	14.1	14.3	12.7	11.3	11.9
1994	9.4	9.3	9.8	11.2	13.1	14.5	15.4	15.5	15.2	14.8	13.8	12.1	12.8
1995	9.9	9.8	10.4	11.7	14.2	15.2	16.0	16.4	15.5	15.1	14.0	12.7	13.4
1996	11.2	10.9	11.4	12.7	15.5	17.5	18.5	18.4	17.3	16.9	14.9	12.8	14.8
1997	11.0	10.9	11.0	12.7	15.7	17.4	18.3	18.4	17.5	17.1	15.7	14.4	15.0
1998	12.1	11.9	12.1	14.1	16.5	17.6	18.8	18.8	17.4	17.7	16.0	14.5	15.6
1999	12.0	12.0	12.2	15.0	17.0	19.4	20.7	21.0	20.1	19.0	17.2	15.8	16.7
2000	13.2	12.9	13.3	14.9	17.2	18.6	19.0	18.7	17.4	17.0	14.9	13.5	15.8
2001	12.1	11.8	12.5	13.8	16.0	17.3	18.1	18.4	17.8	17.4	15.8	14.1	15.4
2002	12.4	12.2	12.2	13.6	15.7	16.9	17.6	17.8	17.1	16.4	15.3	14.2	15.1
2003	12.4	12.2	12.4	13.9	16.3	18.0	18.4	19.0	18.8	18.3	16.4	15.0	15.9

Employment by Industry: North Dakota—*Continued*

(Numbers in thousands. Not seasonally adjusted.)

Industry	January	February	March	April	May	June	July	August	September	October	November	December	Annual Average
STATEWIDE—*Continued*													
Manufacturing													
1990	14.9	15.0	15.4	15.2	15.5	15.9	15.8	15.8	16.3	17.1	16.9	16.6	15.8
1991	16.1	16.2	16.1	15.9	15.8	16.1	16.2	16.1	17.0	17.4	16.8	16.6	16.3
1992	16.0	16.0	16.3	16.6	16.5	16.9	17.3	17.0	17.6	18.4	17.8	17.6	17.0
1993	17.4	17.4	17.6	17.8	17.8	18.1	18.4	18.3	18.6	19.1	18.8	18.7	18.1
1994	18.6	18.6	18.9	19.3	19.4	19.9	19.7	20.1	20.5	21.0	20.8	20.6	19.7
1995	19.8	19.8	19.8	20.0	20.1	20.3	19.9	19.9	20.1	20.6	20.7	20.1	20.0
1996	20.0	20.1	20.1	20.2	20.6	20.6	20.1	20.4	20.8	21.5	21.2	21.3	20.5
1997	20.8	21.0	21.4	21.5	21.9	22.4	22.6	22.6	22.5	23.1	22.8	22.7	22.1
1998	22.6	22.6	22.7	22.3	22.5	22.7	22.5	22.5	22.6	23.1	22.6	22.3	22.5
1999	22.3	22.3	22.3	22.7	23.0	23.4	22.9	23.0	22.9	23.4	23.2	23.1	22.8
2000	22.8	22.9	23.1	23.4	23.9	24.5	24.4	24.4	24.7	24.6	24.3	24.2	23.9
2001	23.7	23.6	23.8	23.9	24.2	24.4	24.4	24.0	24.7	24.1	23.8	23.7	24.0
2002	23.1	23.2	23.3	23.5	23.7	24.1	24.0	24.1	23.8	23.9	23.8	23.6	23.7
2003	23.2	22.9	23.0	23.0	23.4	23.8	23.8	23.8	23.5	23.7	23.5	23.6	23.4
Service-providing													
1990	230.9	231.8	233.1	236.6	239.0	238.2	234.0	233.3	236.2	238.2	239.0	240.5	235.9
1991	234.5	235.6	237.2	239.7	242.1	241.6	237.9	237.2	242.1	243.5	243.9	245.0	240.0
1992	239.9	241.5	243.1	245.1	247.1	246.2	243.2	243.4	246.0	249.3	249.3	251.4	245.4
1993	246.2	246.9	248.5	251.0	254.1	251.9	250.0	249.3	253.0	254.4	255.5	256.9	251.4
1994	250.7	252.7	255.1	258.3	261.1	259.7	257.8	257.5	261.1	263.3	264.5	266.0	258.9
1995	259.2	260.8	263.0	264.4	267.3	265.8	262.8	263.6	266.0	267.3	268.9	269.5	264.8
1996	262.8	265.8	266.5	268.7	272.2	270.6	267.3	267.7	270.9	273.4	274.1	275.0	269.5
1997	267.9	270.7	271.0	272.4	274.5	271.5	268.4	269.0	275.4	278.5	279.1	280.7	273.2
1998	273.2	275.0	276.7	277.9	280.9	274.9	273.0	272.3	278.3	283.2	283.8	283.8	277.7
1999	276.2	278.0	278.3	282.8	284.5	279.9	275.3	275.5	282.9	284.9	286.5	287.9	281.0
2000	280.2	281.6	283.8	285.7	288.3	282.5	280.6	280.4	285.7	287.8	288.4	290.0	284.5
2001	283.6	285.7	286.7	289.1	291.6	288.2	278.6	279.4	287.7	289.8	290.1	291.0	286.8
2002	284.2	285.7	285.5	288.4	291.1	289.0	280.1	281.7	290.0	291.8	292.1	293.6	287.8
2003	285.5	287.3	288.8	291.5	293.7	290.1	281.7	284.3	292.7	294.6	294.6	294.8	290.0
Trade, transportation, and utilities													
1990	62.9	62.3	62.5	63.6	64.5	64.8	64.2	64.6	64.6	65.0	66.2	67.0	64.3
1991	64.3	63.7	63.9	64.7	65.3	65.4	65.1	65.5	65.4	65.6	66.4	67.1	65.2
1992	64.8	64.4	64.6	65.4	66.5	66.5	66.2	66.4	66.1	66.7	67.3	68.0	66.0
1993	65.4	65.0	65.4	66.7	67.8	67.9	68.0	68.5	68.1	68.9	70.4	71.0	67.7
1994	68.4	68.2	69.0	70.1	71.1	71.3	71.4	71.5	71.0	71.8	73.0	73.7	70.8
1995	69.2	68.6	69.0	69.2	70.3	70.7	70.4	70.7	70.1	71.0	72.2	72.6	70.3
1996	69.6	69.4	69.5	70.1	71.4	71.0	70.7	70.8	70.2	71.4	72.4	72.5	70.7
1997	69.7	69.3	68.8	69.9	70.7	71.2	70.9	71.0	70.6	72.1	73.3	74.1	70.9
1998	71.3	70.8	71.2	71.5	72.6	71.9	72.6	71.9	71.2	72.4	73.3	73.4	72.0
1999	70.3	69.7	69.4	70.9	71.7	71.7	71.1	71.0	70.5	71.2	72.4	73.2	71.0
2000	70.3	69.5	69.6	70.7	71.4	71.0	70.7	70.9	70.6	71.5	72.4	73.1	70.9
2001	71.4	70.8	71.1	72.0	73.2	72.8	72.1	72.0	71.4	71.8	72.9	73.3	72.0
2002	71.0	70.3	70.3	70.9	72.2	72.4	71.7	71.5	71.2	71.8	72.9	73.6	71.7
2003	70.9	70.2	70.4	71.5	72.3	72.4	71.7	71.9	71.7	72.5	73.4	73.7	71.9
Wholesale trade													
1990	15.6	15.5	15.7	16.0	16.3	16.4	16.2	16.2	16.0	16.2	16.1	16.0	16.0
1991	15.5	15.5	15.6	15.9	16.0	16.1	16.0	16.0	15.9	15.9	15.9	15.9	15.8
1992	15.5	15.5	15.6	16.0	16.3	16.3	16.2	16.2	16.0	16.2	16.1	16.2	16.0
1993	15.9	15.8	16.1	16.4	16.7	16.6	16.5	16.6	16.2	16.3	16.4	16.4	16.3
1994	16.2	16.2	16.5	17.0	17.4	17.4	17.3	17.3	17.1	17.3	17.4	17.5	17.0
1995	16.8	16.8	17.0	17.4	17.8	18.0	17.7	17.7	17.4	17.6	17.7	17.7	17.4
1996	17.4	17.4	17.5	17.7	18.4	18.4	18.0	18.0	17.8	18.0	18.0	17.9	17.8
1997	17.7	17.8	17.8	18.1	18.8	19.0	18.5	18.4	18.2	18.3	18.3	18.2	18.2
1998	17.9	17.8	18.0	18.4	18.9	18.7	18.8	18.6	18.3	18.5	18.5	18.4	18.4
1999	18.1	18.0	18.1	18.7	19.2	19.0	18.7	18.6	18.3	18.5	18.5	18.5	18.5
2000	18.2	18.0	18.1	18.6	18.8	18.7	18.4	18.4	18.2	18.3	18.3	18.3	18.3
2001	18.0	18.0	18.2	18.4	19.1	18.9	18.6	18.5	18.1	18.2	18.1	18.1	18.3
2002	17.8	17.7	17.7	18.0	18.4	18.6	18.2	18.1	17.8	18.0	17.9	17.8	18.0
2003	17.5	17.3	17.4	18.1	18.4	18.5	18.3	18.1	17.9	18.1	18.0	17.9	18.0
Retail trade													
1990	35.0	34.4	34.4	35.1	35.7	35.8	35.5	35.9	35.8	35.9	37.3	38.0	35.7
1991	36.4	35.9	36.0	36.6	36.9	36.9	36.7	37.0	36.8	36.9	37.8	38.4	36.8
1992	36.6	36.2	36.4	36.8	37.5	37.5	37.3	37.5	37.3	37.6	38.4	38.9	37.3
1993	37.0	36.7	36.7	37.3	37.8	37.8	37.8	37.9	37.7	37.9	39.0	39.5	37.7
1994	37.3	36.9	37.1	37.8	38.4	38.7	39.0	39.2	38.9	39.4	40.7	41.4	38.7
1995	38.5	38.1	38.3	38.3	38.9	39.1	39.3	39.4	39.2	39.6	40.7	41.1	39.2
1996	38.8	38.5	38.6	39.2	39.9	39.7	39.9	40.0	39.7	40.6	41.8	42.1	39.9
1997	40.1	39.6	39.3	39.9	39.8	40.0	40.3	40.3	39.9	40.9	41.9	42.6	40.3
1998	40.5	39.9	39.9	40.3	40.9	40.6	41.2	41.0	40.6	41.6	42.6	43.0	41.0
1999	40.6	40.2	40.0	40.8	40.9	41.2	41.1	40.9	40.8	41.1	42.3	43.1	41.0
2000	40.8	40.3	40.2	40.7	41.1	41.0	41.1	41.1	40.9	41.4	42.4	43.1	41.1
2001	40.4	39.9	40.1	40.5	41.1	40.8	40.5	40.5	40.3	40.6	41.7	42.1	40.7
2002	40.3	39.8	39.8	40.0	40.8	40.8	40.5	40.5	40.4	40.7	41.9	42.6	40.7
2003	40.3	39.9	39.9	40.4	40.9	41.0	40.6	41.0	40.7	41.2	42.2	42.5	40.9

Employment by Industry: North Dakota—*Continued*

(Numbers in thousands. Not seasonally adjusted.)

Industry	January	February	March	April	May	June	July	August	September	October	November	December	Annual Average
STATEWIDE—*Continued*													
Transportation and utilities													
1990	12.3	12.4	12.4	12.5	12.5	12.6	12.5	12.5	12.8	12.9	12.8	13.0	12.6
1991	12.4	12.3	12.3	12.2	12.4	12.4	12.4	12.5	12.7	12.8	12.7	12.8	12.4
1992	12.7	12.7	12.6	12.6	12.7	12.7	12.7	12.7	12.8	12.9	12.8	12.9	12.7
1993	12.5	12.5	12.6	13.0	13.3	13.5	13.7	14.0	14.2	14.7	15.0	15.1	13.6
1994	14.9	15.1	15.4	15.3	15.3	15.2	15.1	15.0	15.0	15.1	14.9	14.8	15.0
1995	13.9	13.7	13.7	13.5	13.6	13.6	13.4	13.6	13.5	13.8	13.8	13.8	13.6
1996	13.4	13.5	13.4	13.2	13.1	12.9	12.8	12.8	12.7	12.8	12.6	12.5	12.9
1997	11.9	11.9	11.7	11.9	12.1	12.2	12.1	12.3	12.5	12.9	13.1	13.3	12.3
1998	12.9	13.1	13.3	12.8	12.8	12.6	12.6	12.3	12.3	12.3	12.2	12.0	12.6
1999	11.6	11.5	11.3	11.4	11.6	11.5	11.3	11.5	11.4	11.6	11.6	11.6	11.4
2000	11.3	11.2	11.3	11.4	11.5	11.3	11.2	11.4	11.5	11.8	11.7	11.7	11.4
2001	13.0	12.9	12.8	13.1	13.0	13.1	13.0	13.0	13.0	13.0	13.1	13.1	13.0
2002	12.9	12.8	12.8	12.9	13.0	13.0	13.0	12.9	13.0	13.1	13.1	13.2	13.0
2003	13.1	13.0	13.1	13.0	13.0	12.9	12.8	12.8	13.1	13.2	13.2	13.3	13.0
Information													
1990	6.1	6.2	6.1	6.1	6.1	6.2	6.1	6.1	6.1	6.0	6.0	6.0	6.0
1991	6.0	6.1	6.1	6.2	6.2	6.3	6.2	6.2	6.2	6.3	6.3	6.3	6.2
1992	6.2	6.2	6.2	6.2	6.2	6.3	6.3	6.2	6.2	6.3	6.3	6.3	6.2
1993	6.4	6.3	6.4	6.3	6.4	6.4	6.5	6.5	6.5	6.4	6.4	6.5	6.4
1994	6.4	6.4	6.4	6.5	6.5	6.6	6.6	6.6	6.7	6.7	6.8	6.9	6.5
1995	6.6	6.7	6.7	6.9	7.0	7.1	7.2	7.3	7.3	6.9	7.0	7.1	6.9
1996	6.9	7.0	7.0	7.0	7.1	7.1	7.2	7.1	7.1	7.1	7.1	7.1	7.0
1997	7.1	7.1	7.2	7.2	7.2	7.3	7.3	7.4	7.4	7.5	7.5	7.6	7.3
1998	7.5	7.5	7.6	7.6	7.7	7.7	7.8	7.8	7.8	8.1	8.3	8.2	7.8
1999	8.0	8.0	8.0	8.1	8.2	8.2	8.3	8.4	8.3	8.3	8.4	8.5	8.2
2000	8.4	8.4	8.5	8.5	8.5	8.5	8.5	8.4	8.5	8.5	8.5	8.6	8.4
2001	8.4	8.4	8.4	8.4	8.5	8.6	8.5	8.5	8.5	8.6	8.5	8.4	8.5
2002	8.0	8.0	7.9	7.9	8.0	8.0	8.0	7.9	7.8	7.8	7.8	7.9	7.9
2003	7.7	7.6	7.7	7.7	7.7	7.7	7.7	7.7	7.7	7.7	7.8	7.8	7.7
Financial activities													
1990	12.7	12.7	12.8	12.8	13.0	13.2	13.1	13.1	13.0	13.0	12.9	13.0	12.9
1991	12.9	13.0	13.0	13.0	13.1	13.2	13.1	13.2	13.1	13.1	13.1	13.2	13.0
1992	13.2	13.2	13.2	13.3	13.3	13.4	13.4	13.5	13.4	13.5	13.5	13.7	13.3
1993	13.6	13.7	13.7	13.7	13.8	13.8	14.0	14.1	13.9	13.9	14.0	14.2	13.8
1994	13.9	13.9	14.0	14.1	14.2	14.3	14.4	14.4	14.3	14.3	14.3	14.6	14.2
1995	14.1	14.1	14.2	14.2	14.2	14.3	14.2	14.4	14.4	14.5	14.5	14.7	14.3
1996	14.6	14.7	14.7	14.7	14.9	15.0	15.1	15.1	14.7	14.7	14.7	14.9	14.8
1997	14.7	14.7	14.7	14.8	14.9	15.0	14.9	15.0	15.0	15.2	15.2	15.5	14.9
1998	14.9	14.9	15.1	15.6	15.7	15.9	16.1	16.1	16.0	16.0	16.2	16.2	15.7
1999	16.0	15.9	16.1	16.1	16.3	16.3	16.3	16.5	16.3	16.5	16.8	17.2	16.3
2000	16.9	16.9	16.8	16.6	16.8	16.8	16.9	16.9	16.9	16.9	16.9	17.1	16.8
2001	16.8	16.8	16.8	16.8	16.9	17.0	16.9	17.0	16.9	17.0	16.9	17.0	16.9
2002	17.7	17.8	17.8	17.8	17.9	18.1	18.1	18.3	18.1	18.3	18.3	18.4	18.1
2003	18.2	18.1	18.3	18.2	18.3	18.5	18.4	18.5	18.5	18.5	18.5	18.7	18.4
Professional and business services													
1990	11.7	11.6	11.7	12.0	12.0	12.3	12.4	12.5	12.7	12.6	12.3	12.1	12.1
1991	12.0	12.0	12.1	12.6	12.4	12.6	12.6	12.7	12.9	12.9	12.6	12.5	12.4
1992	12.3	12.3	12.5	12.8	12.8	12.9	12.9	13.2	13.2	13.3	13.1	13.3	12.8
1993	13.1	13.0	13.3	13.8	14.2	14.3	14.0	14.0	14.4	14.7	14.7	14.3	13.9
1994	13.8	14.1	14.5	14.9	15.2	15.6	15.9	16.2	16.3	16.3	16.2	16.0	15.4
1995	15.3	15.6	16.2	16.3	16.6	17.0	16.8	17.1	17.1	17.2	17.2	16.8	16.6
1996	16.9	17.8	17.7	18.2	18.2	18.5	19.1	19.0	19.6	20.1	19.8	19.9	18.7
1997	20.0	20.6	20.7	20.7	21.2	21.6	21.0	21.1	21.0	21.1	21.2	21.3	20.9
1998	21.0	21.2	21.4	21.4	21.9	22.5	22.6	22.8	22.3	23.3	23.0	23.0	22.2
1999	22.6	23.1	23.3	24.0	24.3	24.6	24.2	24.2	24.4	24.3	24.4	24.1	23.9
2000	23.3	23.8	24.4	24.7	24.9	25.4	25.8	25.5	25.2	25.4	25.3	25.4	24.9
2001	24.5	25.5	25.1	25.5	25.6	26.1	25.4	25.3	25.0	25.2	25.1	25.0	25.3
2002	23.1	23.5	23.6	24.1	24.1	25.0	24.6	24.7	24.7	24.4	24.0	23.8	24.1
2003	23.2	23.5	23.3	23.5	23.5	24.0	23.7	24.2	24.0	24.1	23.9	23.5	23.7
Educational and health services													
1990	35.7	36.0	36.1	36.6	36.7	36.8	36.8	36.9	37.3	37.4	37.5	37.9	36.8
1991	37.4	37.8	37.9	38.0	38.2	38.5	38.4	38.5	38.9	39.2	39.2	39.4	38.4
1992	39.1	39.5	39.7	39.7	39.9	40.2	40.0	39.8	40.1	40.7	40.6	41.1	40.0
1993	40.9	40.9	41.1	41.1	41.1	41.4	41.2	40.9	41.0	41.2	41.3	41.5	41.1
1994	40.9	41.2	41.5	41.4	41.4	41.7	41.7	41.5	42.1	42.3	42.6	43.0	41.7
1995	41.4	41.8	42.0	42.2	42.2	42.6	42.6	42.6	42.6	42.7	43.1	43.2	42.4
1996	42.5	42.9	42.9	42.8	43.2	43.5	42.8	43.1	43.0	43.4	43.8	43.7	43.1
1997	43.1	43.4	43.5	43.4	43.4	43.9	43.9	43.6	44.1	44.6	44.9	44.7	43.8
1998	44.3	44.8	45.2	44.7	44.9	44.7	44.5	44.3	44.6	45.1	45.1	45.4	44.8
1999	44.7	45.1	45.1	45.2	45.2	45.1	45.1	44.8	45.0	45.0	45.2	45.1	45.0
2000	44.9	44.9	45.2	45.1	45.3	45.6	45.7	45.8	45.6	46.1	46.3	46.4	45.5
2001	45.5	45.8	45.9	45.8	46.0	46.2	46.3	46.2	45.8	46.1	46.4	46.6	46.1
2002	46.2	46.3	46.0	46.4	46.6	46.9	46.9	46.9	46.7	47.0	47.1	47.2	46.7
2003	46.9	47.0	47.1	47.4	47.5	48.1	48.2	47.9	47.6	47.6	47.8	47.5	47.6

Employment by Industry: North Dakota—*Continued*

(Numbers in thousands. Not seasonally adjusted.)

Industry	January	February	March	April	May	June	July	August	September	October	November	December	Annual Average
STATEWIDE—*Continued*													
Leisure and hospitality													
1990	23.1	23.4	24.1	24.7	25.5	25.9	26.0	26.2	25.9	25.2	24.8	24.8	24.9
1991	23.6	23.8	24.5	25.3	26.1	26.6	26.6	26.9	26.6	25.8	25.3	25.2	25.5
1992	24.4	24.8	25.4	26.0	27.2	27.3	27.3	27.6	27.0	26.5	26.1	26.2	26.3
1993	25.0	25.4	26.1	26.8	27.5	28.0	28.4	28.5	28.0	27.2	26.7	26.8	27.0
1994	25.9	26.0	26.7	28.0	28.9	29.1	29.1	29.2	28.8	28.4	27.9	27.9	27.9
1995	26.4	26.7	27.3	28.1	29.0	29.2	29.8	29.9	29.3	28.5	28.2	28.0	28.3
1996	27.3	27.7	28.4	29.2	30.2	30.8	30.8	30.9	30.3	29.2	28.7	28.8	29.3
1997	27.6	28.0	28.5	29.1	29.2	29.9	30.6	31.1	30.4	29.3	28.4	28.4	29.2
1998	27.3	27.8	28.2	28.9	29.6	29.6	30.4	30.5	30.0	29.3	28.7	28.2	29.0
1999	27.1	27.2	27.4	28.9	29.8	30.5	30.0	30.4	30.2	29.5	29.2	29.0	29.1
2000	27.8	27.8	28.4	29.4	30.1	30.5	30.7	30.8	30.2	29.2	28.9	28.6	29.3
2001	27.5	27.7	28.5	29.4	30.5	31.0	30.6	30.6	29.9	29.5	28.9	28.8	29.4
2002	28.0	28.4	28.6	29.6	30.4	31.1	31.2	31.2	30.7	30.1	29.4	29.2	29.8
2003	28.1	28.2	28.9	29.6	30.6	31.3	31.2	31.5	30.6	30.4	29.7	29.7	30.0
Other services													
1990	12.9	12.9	13.0	13.2	13.2	13.1	13.0	13.1	13.3	13.4	13.4	13.5	13.1
1991	13.1	13.2	13.3	13.4	13.4	13.4	13.3	13.3	13.4	13.5	13.6	13.7	13.3
1992	13.4	13.5	13.7	13.7	13.8	13.7	13.7	13.7	13.9	14.0	13.9	14.1	13.7
1993	13.9	13.9	14.0	14.1	14.2	14.1	14.1	14.2	14.3	14.4	14.5	14.5	14.1
1994	14.5	14.5	14.7	14.9	14.9	14.9	14.8	14.8	14.9	15.2	15.2	15.3	14.8
1995	14.7	14.7	14.9	15.0	15.1	14.6	14.6	14.6	14.6	14.6	14.7	14.9	14.7
1996	14.6	14.6	14.7	14.8	14.9	14.9	14.9	14.9	15.0	15.1	15.2	15.3	14.9
1997	14.9	15.1	15.2	15.2	15.1	15.1	15.1	15.1	15.3	15.5	15.4	15.6	15.2
1998	14.9	14.9	15.1	15.1	15.2	15.1	15.1	15.0	15.0	15.2	15.3	15.3	15.1
1999	15.2	15.3	15.3	15.4	15.4	15.4	15.4	15.5	15.6	15.5	15.5	15.5	15.4
2000	15.1	15.2	15.4	15.4	15.4	15.3	15.3	15.3	15.3	15.4	15.4	15.4	15.3
2001	15.0	15.1	15.2	15.4	15.4	15.3	15.1	15.2	15.3	15.3	15.3	15.4	15.3
2002	15.1	15.3	15.3	15.4	15.4	15.4	15.2	15.2	15.2	15.2	15.3	15.2	15.3
2003	15.1	15.2	15.2	15.3	15.3	15.2	15.3	15.5	15.6	15.3	15.3	15.3	15.3
Government													
1990	65.8	66.7	66.8	67.6	68.0	65.9	62.4	60.8	63.3	65.6	65.9	66.2	65.4
1991	65.2	66.0	66.4	66.5	67.4	65.6	62.6	60.9	65.6	67.1	67.4	67.6	65.6
1992	66.5	67.6	67.8	68.0	67.4	65.9	63.4	63.0	66.1	68.3	68.5	68.7	66.7
1993	67.9	68.7	68.5	68.5	69.1	66.0	63.8	62.6	66.8	67.7	67.5	68.1	67.1
1994	66.9	68.4	68.3	68.4	68.9	66.2	63.9	63.3	67.0	68.3	68.5	68.6	67.2
1995	71.5	72.6	72.7	72.5	72.9	70.3	67.2	67.0	70.6	71.9	72.0	72.2	71.1
1996	70.4	71.7	71.6	71.9	72.3	69.8	66.7	66.8	71.0	72.4	72.4	72.8	70.8
1997	70.8	72.5	72.4	72.1	72.8	67.5	64.7	64.7	71.6	73.2	73.2	73.5	70.7
1998	72.0	73.1	72.9	73.1	73.3	67.5	63.9	63.9	71.4	73.8	73.9	74.1	71.0
1999	72.3	73.7	73.7	74.2	73.6	68.1	64.9	64.7	72.6	74.6	74.6	75.3	71.8
2000	73.5	75.1	75.5	75.3	75.9	69.4	67.0	66.8	73.4	74.8	74.7	75.4	73.0
2001	74.5	75.6	75.7	75.8	75.5	71.2	63.7	64.6	74.9	76.3	76.1	76.5	73.4
2002	75.1	76.1	76.0	76.3	76.5	72.1	64.4	66.0	75.6	77.2	77.3	78.3	74.2
2003	75.4	77.5	77.9	78.3	78.5	72.9	65.5	67.1	77.0	78.5	78.2	78.6	75.5
Federal government													
1990	10.4	10.3	10.6	11.3	11.0	10.9	10.6	10.4	10.3	9.9	9.9	10.1	10.4
1991	9.9	9.8	9.9	10.0	10.1	10.2	10.2	10.2	10.2	10.0	10.0	10.0	10.0
1992	10.0	10.1	10.1	10.1	9.9	10.0	10.1	10.2	10.0	10.0	9.9	9.9	10.0
1993	9.8	9.8	9.7	9.7	9.8	9.7	9.7	9.8	9.8	9.8	9.7	9.7	9.7
1994	9.7	9.8	9.7	9.7	9.6	9.6	9.7	9.6	9.6	9.5	9.4	9.4	9.6
1995	9.3	9.3	9.3	9.3	9.4	9.4	9.4	9.4	9.2	9.3	9.2	9.2	9.3
1996	9.0	8.9	8.9	9.0	9.0	8.9	9.1	9.1	9.0	9.1	9.0	9.0	9.0
1997	8.9	8.9	8.9	8.9	9.1	9.2	9.2	9.2	9.2	9.0	9.0	9.0	9.0
1998	8.9	8.9	8.9	8.9	9.0	9.1	9.0	9.1	9.0	8.9	9.0	9.0	8.9
1999	8.9	8.8	8.9	9.0	9.1	9.0	9.1	9.1	9.2	9.3	9.3	9.5	9.1
2000	9.4	9.4	10.2	9.7	10.4	9.4	9.8	9.5	9.4	9.3	9.4	9.5	9.6
2001	9.9	9.8	9.8	9.8	9.9	10.2	10.0	10.0	10.1	9.8	9.8	9.9	9.9
2002	9.7	9.6	9.6	9.7	9.8	10.2	10.1	10.1	10.0	9.9	10.0	10.3	9.9
2003	9.8	9.8	9.9	10.0	10.1	10.3	10.4	10.4	10.3	10.2	10.1	10.3	10.1
State government													
1990	19.8	20.3	20.3	20.3	20.5	18.7	17.8	17.3	18.6	20.3	20.3	20.2	19.5
1991	19.9	20.4	20.6	20.5	20.6	19.2	18.4	17.6	20.0	20.8	21.0	20.9	19.9
1992	20.3	20.8	20.9	20.9	20.1	19.2	18.5	18.6	20.2	21.5	21.7	21.5	20.3
1993	21.2	21.5	21.5	21.5	21.4	19.1	19.1	18.3	20.8	20.9	20.7	20.9	20.5
1994	20.2	20.9	21.0	21.0	21.1	19.1	18.8	19.0	20.9	21.4	21.6	21.2	20.5
1995	20.5	21.1	21.4	21.4	20.9	19.0	18.4	18.9	20.4	21.2	21.2	20.9	20.4
1996	20.1	20.9	20.8	21.1	20.4	18.6	18.4	18.9	20.8	21.2	21.2	21.2	20.3
1997	20.5	21.2	21.2	21.0	20.4	18.7	18.6	18.5	20.5	21.0	21.0	20.8	20.2
1998	20.4	20.8	20.9	21.0	20.0	18.3	18.3	18.4	21.2	21.4	21.4	21.2	20.2
1999	20.5	21.1	21.1	21.3	19.8	18.2	18.0	18.3	20.3	21.0	21.3	20.9	20.1
2000	20.5	21.3	21.2	21.3	20.4	18.6	18.4	18.7	20.9	21.4	21.4	21.3	20.4
2001	20.7	21.3	21.4	21.9	20.6	18.8	18.7	18.9	21.4	22.0	22.0	21.8	20.7
2002	21.4	21.8	21.8	21.9	21.0	19.7	18.7	19.1	21.6	22.2	22.3	22.4	21.2
2003	21.0	22.5	22.5	22.8	21.9	19.8	19.6	20.1	22.4	23.0	22.9	22.6	21.8

Employment by Industry: North Dakota—*Continued*

(Numbers in thousands. Not seasonally adjusted.)

Industry	January	February	March	April	May	June	July	August	September	October	November	December	Annual Average
STATEWIDE—*Continued*													
Local government													
1990	35.6	36.1	35.9	36.0	36.5	36.3	34.0	33.1	34.4	35.4	35.7	35.9	35.4
1991	35.4	35.8	35.9	36.0	36.7	36.2	34.0	33.1	35.4	36.3	36.4	36.7	35.6
1992	36.2	36.7	36.8	37.0	37.4	36.7	34.8	34.2	35.9	36.8	36.9	37.3	36.3
1993	36.9	37.4	37.3	37.3	37.9	37.2	35.0	34.5	36.2	37.0	37.1	37.5	36.7
1994	37.0	37.7	37.6	37.7	38.2	37.5	35.4	34.7	36.5	37.4	37.5	38.0	37.1
1995	41.7	42.2	42.0	41.8	42.6	41.9	39.4	38.7	41.0	41.4	41.6	42.1	41.3
1996	41.3	41.9	41.9	41.8	42.9	42.3	39.2	38.8	41.2	42.1	42.2	42.6	41.5
1997	41.4	42.4	42.3	42.2	43.3	39.6	36.9	37.0	41.9	43.2	43.2	43.7	41.4
1998	42.7	43.4	43.1	43.2	44.3	40.1	36.6	36.4	41.2	43.5	43.5	43.9	41.8
1999	42.9	43.8	43.7	43.9	44.7	40.9	37.8	37.3	43.1	44.3	44.0	44.9	42.6
2000	43.6	44.4	44.1	44.3	45.1	41.4	38.8	38.6	43.1	44.1	43.9	44.6	43.0
2001	43.9	44.5	44.5	44.1	45.0	42.2	35.0	35.7	43.4	44.5	44.3	44.8	42.6
2002	44.0	44.7	44.6	44.7	45.7	42.2	35.6	36.8	44.0	45.1	45.0	45.6	43.2
2003	44.6	45.2	45.5	45.5	46.5	42.8	35.5	36.6	44.3	45.3	45.2	45.7	43.6
BISMARCK													
Total nonfarm													
1990	38.2	38.5	38.8	40.0	40.9	40.8	39.8	40.1	40.5	40.5	40.8	40.7	39.9
1991	39.5	39.8	40.3	40.8	40.9	41.2	40.9	41.7	41.9	41.8	41.8	41.9	41.0
1992	40.8	40.9	41.3	42.3	43.0	43.5	43.2	43.2	43.1	43.5	43.0	43.7	42.6
1993	42.6	42.4	42.5	43.4	44.0	44.0	43.9	44.0	44.6	44.7	44.8	45.0	43.8
1994	43.4	43.5	44.1	44.8	45.4	45.5	45.5	45.5	45.8	45.7	45.8	46.2	45.1
1995	44.9	44.9	45.2	46.1	47.4	47.1	46.6	46.0	46.7	46.9	46.7	46.6	46.2
1996	45.6	45.8	46.1	46.7	48.1	47.8	47.3	47.3	47.6	48.0	47.9	47.8	47.1
1997	47.0	47.3	47.3	47.9	49.3	49.7	48.9	49.1	49.4	49.6	49.5	49.3	48.6
1998	47.9	48.1	48.2	49.2	50.2	50.9	49.7	49.6	49.9	50.7	50.8	51.1	49.6
1999	49.5	49.8	49.8	50.8	51.6	52.0	51.0	50.8	51.6	51.9	52.0	51.7	51.0
2000	50.4	50.4	51.0	51.6	52.6	52.3	52.0	51.6	51.7	51.9	52.3	52.1	51.6
2001	51.1	51.4	51.7	52.0	52.6	53.0	52.3	51.9	52.6	52.2	52.2	52.2	52.1
2002	51.0	51.4	51.5	52.2	53.4	53.7	53.0	52.2	53.0	53.1	52.9	52.8	52.5
2003	52.4	52.4	52.5	53.5	54.1	54.8	53.7	53.5	54.3	54.4	53.8	53.9	53.6
Total private													
1990	29.6	29.7	29.9	31.1	31.9	31.7	31.3	31.6	31.8	31.7	32.0	31.8	31.1
1991	30.5	30.8	31.2	31.7	31.8	31.9	32.2	32.8	32.7	32.7	32.5	32.7	31.9
1992	31.6	31.6	32.0	32.9	33.6	33.8	33.9	33.9	33.8	33.9	33.5	34.0	33.2
1993	32.9	32.7	32.7	33.5	34.2	34.5	34.6	34.9	35.0	35.1	35.2	35.3	34.2
1994	33.9	33.7	34.2	34.9	35.6	35.8	36.1	36.2	36.2	36.1	36.1	36.4	35.4
1995	34.9	34.9	35.1	36.0	37.2	37.0	37.0	37.1	36.9	36.9	36.7	36.7	36.3
1996	35.7	35.8	36.1	36.8	37.9	38.0	38.2	38.3	37.9	38.0	37.8	37.7	37.3
1997	36.9	37.0	37.2	37.8	38.9	39.5	39.3	39.4	39.1	39.2	39.0	38.9	38.5
1998	37.5	37.6	37.7	38.7	39.6	40.0	40.0	40.1	39.6	40.1	40.2	40.3	39.2
1999	38.6	38.9	39.0	40.1	40.8	41.4	41.3	41.2	41.1	41.0	41.1	40.8	40.4
2000	39.6	39.4	39.9	40.5	41.4	41.9	41.9	41.8	41.1	41.0	41.4	41.1	40.9
2001	40.2	40.3	40.5	40.9	41.6	42.0	42.1	42.2	41.6	41.3	41.2	41.3	41.2
2002	40.0	40.3	40.4	41.1	42.0	42.6	42.5	42.3	42.1	42.0	41.7	41.5	41.5
2003	41.1	41.1	41.2	42.0	42.6	43.6	43.3	43.4	43.3	43.2	42.6	42.6	42.5
Goods-producing													
1990	3.1	3.2	3.3	3.8	4.6	4.1	4.1	4.1	4.2	4.1	4.0	3.7	3.8
1991	3.3	3.3	3.3	3.7	3.8	3.9	4.2	4.2	4.2	4.2	3.9	3.8	3.8
1992	3.4	3.5	3.7	4.0	4.2	4.5	4.6	4.6	4.3	4.4	4.0	3.9	4.0
1993	3.6	3.6	3.5	3.9	4.3	4.4	4.5	4.6	4.5	4.4	4.3	4.0	4.1
1994	3.7	3.7	3.8	4.1	4.4	4.6	4.8	4.9	4.9	4.8	4.6	4.3	4.3
1995	4.0	3.9	4.0	4.6	5.3	5.0	5.1	5.1	4.9	4.9	4.6	4.4	4.6
1996	4.1	4.0	4.1	4.4	4.9	5.2	5.4	5.3	5.1	5.1	4.8	4.5	4.7
1997	4.2	4.2	4.2	4.6	5.1	5.4	5.6	5.6	5.4	5.4	5.2	5.0	4.9
1998	4.4	4.4	4.4	4.9	5.4	5.6	5.8	5.7	5.5	5.5	5.3	5.1	5.1
1999	4.5	4.5	4.5	5.1	5.6	6.0	6.0	5.9	5.9	5.7	5.6	5.3	5.3
2000	4.9	4.8	5.0	5.3	5.9	6.1	6.1	6.0	5.7	5.7	5.4	5.1	5.5
2001	4.8	4.8	4.9	5.3	5.7	6.0	6.1	6.1	6.0	5.8	5.6	5.3	5.5
2002	5.0	4.9	5.0	5.3	5.9	6.2	6.3	6.2	6.1	6.0	5.7	5.4	5.7
2003	5.0	4.9	5.0	5.5	5.8	6.2	6.2	6.2	6.3	6.2	5.9	5.7	5.7
Construction and mining													
1990	1.2	1.2	1.3	1.8	2.5	1.9	2.0	2.0	2.0	2.0	1.9	1.7	1.7
1991	1.3	1.3	1.3	1.6	1.7	1.8	2.0	2.0	2.1	2.1	1.8	1.7	1.7
1992	1.4	1.5	1.6	1.9	2.1	2.3	2.4	2.4	2.2	2.2	1.9	1.8	1.9
1993	1.5	1.5	1.5	1.8	2.1	2.2	2.3	2.4	2.4	2.4	2.3	2.0	2.0
1994	1.6	1.6	1.7	1.9	2.2	2.3	2.5	2.6	2.6	2.5	2.3	2.1	2.1
1995	1.8	1.7	1.8	2.3	3.0	2.6	2.7	2.7	2.6	2.6	2.4	2.2	2.3
1996	1.9	1.8	1.9	2.1	2.5	2.8	2.9	2.8	2.7	2.8	2.6	2.3	2.4
1997	2.0	2.0	1.9	2.3	2.7	2.9	3.1	3.1	3.0	3.0	2.8	2.6	2.6
1998	2.1	2.1	2.1	2.5	2.9	3.0	3.2	3.1	3.0	3.0	2.8	2.6	2.7
1999	2.0	2.0	2.0	2.5	2.9	3.2	3.2	3.1	3.1	3.0	2.8	2.6	2.7
2000	2.2	2.1	2.3	2.6	3.0	3.1	3.1	3.0	2.9	2.9	2.6	2.4	2.6
2001	2.1	2.1	2.2	2.4	2.8	3.0	3.1	3.2	3.1	3.1	2.9	2.6	2.7
2002	2.4	2.3	2.4	2.7	3.2	3.4	3.5	3.4	3.4	3.3	3.0	2.8	3.0
2003	2.4	2.3	2.4	2.8	3.1	3.4	3.4	3.4	3.5	3.4	3.2	3.0	3.0

Employment by Industry: North Dakota—*Continued*

(Numbers in thousands. Not seasonally adjusted.)

Industry	January	February	March	April	May	June	July	August	September	October	November	December	Annual Average
BISMARCK—*Continued*													
Manufacturing													
1990	1.9	2.0	2.0	2.0	2.1	2.2	2.1	2.1	2.2	2.1	2.1	2.0	2.0
1991	2.0	2.0	2.0	2.1	2.1	2.1	2.2	2.2	2.1	2.1	2.1	2.1	2.0
1992	2.0	2.0	2.1	2.1	2.1	2.2	2.2	2.2	2.1	2.2	2.1	2.1	2.1
1993	2.1	2.1	2.0	2.1	2.2	2.2	2.2	2.2	2.1	2.0	2.0	2.0	2.1
1994	2.1	2.1	2.1	2.2	2.2	2.3	2.3	2.3	2.3	2.3	2.3	2.2	2.2
1995	2.2	2.2	2.2	2.3	2.3	2.4	2.4	2.4	2.3	2.3	2.2	2.2	2.2
1996	2.2	2.2	2.2	2.3	2.4	2.4	2.5	2.5	2.4	2.3	2.2	2.2	2.3
1997	2.2	2.2	2.3	2.3	2.4	2.5	2.5	2.5	2.4	2.4	2.4	2.4	2.3
1998	2.3	2.3	2.3	2.4	2.5	2.6	2.6	2.6	2.5	2.5	2.5	2.5	2.4
1999	2.5	2.5	2.5	2.6	2.7	2.8	2.8	2.8	2.8	2.7	2.8	2.7	2.6
2000	2.7	2.7	2.7	2.7	2.9	3.0	3.0	3.0	2.8	2.8	2.8	2.7	2.8
2001	2.7	2.7	2.7	2.9	2.9	3.0	3.0	2.9	2.9	2.7	2.7	2.7	2.8
2002	2.6	2.6	2.6	2.6	2.7	2.8	2.8	2.8	2.7	2.7	2.7	2.6	2.7
2003	2.6	2.6	2.6	2.7	2.7	2.8	2.8	2.8	2.8	2.8	2.7	2.7	2.7
Service-providing													
1990	35.1	35.3	35.5	36.2	36.3	36.7	35.7	36.0	36.3	36.4	36.8	37.0	36.1
1991	36.2	36.5	37.0	37.1	37.1	37.3	36.7	37.5	37.7	37.6	37.9	38.1	37.2
1992	37.4	37.4	37.6	38.3	38.8	39.0	38.6	38.6	38.8	39.1	39.0	39.8	38.5
1993	39.0	38.8	39.0	39.5	39.7	39.6	39.4	39.4	40.1	40.3	40.5	41.0	39.6
1994	39.7	39.8	40.3	40.7	41.0	40.9	40.7	40.6	40.9	40.9	41.2	41.9	40.7
1995	40.9	41.0	41.2	41.5	42.1	42.1	41.5	40.9	41.8	42.0	42.1	42.2	41.6
1996	41.5	41.8	42.0	42.3	43.2	42.6	41.9	42.0	42.5	42.9	43.1	43.3	42.4
1997	42.8	43.1	43.1	43.3	44.2	44.3	43.3	43.5	44.0	44.2	44.3	44.3	43.7
1998	43.5	43.7	43.8	44.3	44.8	45.3	43.9	43.9	44.4	45.2	45.5	46.0	44.5
1999	45.0	45.3	45.3	45.7	46.0	46.0	45.0	44.9	45.7	46.2	46.4	46.4	45.6
2000	45.5	45.6	46.0	46.3	46.7	46.2	45.9	45.6	46.0	46.2	46.9	47.0	46.1
2001	46.3	46.6	46.8	46.7	46.9	47.0	46.2	45.8	46.6	46.4	46.6	46.9	46.5
2002	46.0	46.5	46.5	46.9	47.5	47.5	46.7	46.0	46.9	47.1	47.2	47.4	46.9
2003	47.4	47.5	47.5	48.0	48.3	48.6	47.5	47.3	48.0	48.2	47.9	48.2	47.9
Trade, transportation, and utilities													
1990	9.2	9.1	9.1	9.3	9.3	9.3	9.2	9.3	9.3	9.4	9.8	9.9	9.3
1991	9.4	9.4	9.4	9.5	9.5	9.5	9.5	9.7	9.6	9.6	9.8	9.9	9.5
1992	9.5	9.3	9.4	9.6	9.7	9.7	9.8	9.7	9.7	9.8	9.9	10.1	9.6
1993	9.7	9.6	9.6	9.8	9.9	10.0	10.1	10.1	10.3	10.5	10.6	10.8	10.0
1994	10.2	10.1	10.2	10.2	10.3	10.4	10.6	10.5	10.5	10.6	10.8	10.9	10.4
1995	10.2	10.1	10.1	10.2	10.3	10.7	10.7	10.6	10.5	10.7	10.8	10.9	10.4
1996	10.4	10.4	10.3	10.3	10.7	10.6	10.5	10.5	10.3	10.4	10.7	10.7	10.4
1997	10.3	10.2	10.2	10.3	10.6	10.6	10.6	10.6	10.5	10.7	10.9	11.0	10.5
1998	10.5	10.4	10.4	10.4	10.5	10.5	10.5	10.4	10.2	10.4	10.6	10.8	10.4
1999	10.1	10.2	10.2	10.5	10.5	10.5	10.6	10.5	10.5	10.5	10.7	10.8	10.4
2000	10.5	10.5	10.4	10.5	10.6	10.7	10.8	10.7	10.6	10.5	10.9	10.9	10.6
2001	10.9	10.7	10.8	10.8	10.9	11.1	11.0	11.0	10.7	10.8	11.0	11.2	10.9
2002	10.7	10.7	10.7	10.8	10.9	11.0	11.0	11.0	10.8	11.1	11.2	11.3	10.9
2003	10.9	10.8	10.8	11.1	11.1	11.2	11.2	11.3	11.1	11.1	11.2	11.3	11.1
Wholesale trade													
1990	1.6	1.6	1.6	1.6	1.6	1.6	1.6	1.6	1.6	1.7	1.7	1.7	1.6
1991	1.6	1.6	1.6	1.6	1.6	1.6	1.6	1.6	1.6	1.6	1.6	1.6	1.6
1992	1.6	1.6	1.6	1.6	1.6	1.6	1.7	1.7	1.7	1.7	1.7	1.7	1.6
1993	1.7	1.7	1.7	1.7	1.7	1.7	1.7	1.7	1.7	1.7	1.7	1.7	1.7
1994	1.7	1.7	1.7	1.7	1.7	1.8	1.8	1.8	1.8	1.8	1.8	1.8	1.7
1995	1.8	1.8	1.8	1.8	1.8	1.9	1.9	1.9	1.8	1.9	1.9	1.9	1.8
1996	1.9	1.9	1.8	1.8	1.9	1.9	1.8	1.8	1.8	1.9	1.9	1.9	1.8
1997	1.9	1.9	1.9	1.9	1.9	1.9	1.9	1.9	1.9	1.9	1.9	1.9	1.9
1998	1.9	1.9	1.9	1.9	2.0	1.9	1.9	1.9	1.9	1.9	1.9	2.0	1.9
1999	1.9	1.9	1.9	2.0	2.0	2.0	2.0	2.0	2.0	2.0	2.0	2.0	1.9
2000	2.0	2.0	2.0	2.1	2.1	2.1	2.1	2.1	2.1	2.0	2.1	2.1	2.0
2001	2.1	2.1	2.1	2.1	2.1	2.1	2.1	2.1	2.0	2.1	2.0	2.1	2.0
2002	2.0	2.0	2.0	2.0	2.0	2.0	2.0	2.0	2.0	2.1	2.1	2.1	2.0
2003	2.0	2.0	2.0	2.1	2.1	2.1	2.1	2.1	2.1	2.1	2.1	2.1	2.1
Retail trade													
1990	5.9	5.8	5.8	5.9	5.9	5.9	5.8	5.9	5.9	5.9	6.3	6.4	5.9
1991	6.0	6.0	6.0	6.1	6.1	6.1	6.1	6.2	6.1	6.1	6.3	6.4	6.1
1992	6.0	5.9	6.0	6.1	6.2	6.2	6.2	6.1	6.1	6.2	6.3	6.4	6.1
1993	6.1	6.0	6.0	6.2	6.2	6.3	6.3	6.3	6.4	6.5	6.6	6.8	6.3
1994	6.2	6.1	6.1	6.2	6.3	6.3	6.4	6.4	6.4	6.5	6.7	6.8	6.3
1995	6.3	6.2	6.2	6.3	6.4	6.6	6.7	6.6	6.6	6.6	6.7	6.8	6.5
1996	6.4	6.4	6.4	6.5	6.7	6.7	6.7	6.7	6.6	6.6	6.9	6.9	6.6
1997	6.6	6.5	6.5	6.6	6.8	6.8	6.8	6.8	6.7	6.8	7.0	7.1	6.7
1998	6.6	6.5	6.5	6.7	6.7	6.7	6.8	6.7	6.6	6.8	7.0	7.1	6.7
1999	6.6	6.7	6.7	6.8	6.8	6.8	6.9	6.8	6.8	6.8	7.0	7.1	6.8
2000	6.8	6.8	6.7	6.7	6.8	6.8	6.9	6.8	6.7	6.7	7.0	7.0	6.8
2001	6.7	6.5	6.6	6.7	6.8	6.9	6.8	6.8	6.7	6.7	7.0	7.1	6.7
2002	6.7	6.7	6.7	6.8	6.9	7.0	7.0	7.0	6.8	6.9	7.0	7.1	6.9
2003	6.8	6.8	6.7	6.9	7.0	7.1	7.1	7.2	7.0	7.0	7.1	7.2	7.0

Employment by Industry: North Dakota—*Continued*

(Numbers in thousands. Not seasonally adjusted.)

Industry	January	February	March	April	May	June	July	August	September	October	November	December	Annual Average
BISMARCK—*Continued*													
Transportation and utilities													
1990	1.7	1.7	1.7	1.8	1.8	1.8	1.8	1.8	1.8	1.8	1.8	1.8	1.7
1991	1.8	1.8	1.8	1.8	1.8	1.8	1.8	1.9	1.9	1.9	1.9	1.9	1.8
1992	1.9	1.8	1.8	1.9	1.9	1.9	1.9	1.9	1.9	1.9	1.9	2.0	1.8
1993	1.9	1.9	1.9	1.9	2.0	2.0	2.1	2.1	2.2	2.3	2.3	2.3	2.0
1994	2.3	2.3	2.4	2.3	2.3	2.3	2.4	2.3	2.3	2.3	2.3	2.3	2.3
1995	2.1	2.1	2.1	2.1	2.1	2.2	2.1	2.1	2.1	2.2	2.2	2.2	2.1
1996	2.1	2.1	2.1	2.0	2.1	2.0	2.0	2.0	1.9	1.9	1.9	1.9	2.0
1997	1.8	1.8	1.8	1.8	1.9	1.9	1.9	1.9	1.9	2.0	2.0	2.0	1.8
1998	2.0	2.0	2.0	1.8	1.8	1.9	1.8	1.8	1.7	1.7	1.7	1.7	1.8
1999	1.6	1.6	1.6	1.7	1.7	1.7	1.7	1.7	1.7	1.7	1.7	1.7	1.6
2000	1.7	1.7	1.7	1.7	1.7	1.8	1.8	1.8	1.8	1.8	1.8	1.8	1.7
2001	2.1	2.1	2.1	2.0	2.0	2.1	2.1	2.1	2.0	2.0	2.0	2.0	2.0
2002	2.0	2.0	2.0	2.0	2.0	2.0	2.0	2.0	2.0	2.1	2.1	2.1	2.0
2003	2.1	2.0	2.1	2.1	2.0	2.0	2.0	2.0	2.0	2.0	2.0	2.0	2.0
Information													
1990	0.9	0.9	0.9	0.9	0.9	0.9	0.9	0.9	0.9	0.9	0.9	0.9	0.9
1991	1.0	1.0	1.0	1.0	1.0	1.0	0.9	0.9	0.9	1.0	1.0	1.0	0.9
1992	1.0	1.0	1.0	1.0	1.0	1.0	1.0	1.0	1.0	1.0	0.9	1.0	0.9
1993	1.0	1.0	1.0	1.0	1.0	1.0	1.0	1.0	1.0	1.0	1.0	1.0	1.0
1994	1.0	1.0	1.0	1.0	1.0	1.0	1.0	1.0	1.0	1.0	1.0	1.0	1.0
1995	1.0	1.0	1.0	1.0	1.0	1.0	1.0	1.0	1.1	1.0	1.0	1.0	1.0
1996	1.1	1.1	1.1	1.1	1.1	1.1	1.1	1.1	1.1	1.1	1.1	1.1	1.1
1997	1.2	1.2	1.2	1.2	1.2	1.3	1.3	1.3	1.3	1.3	1.3	1.3	1.2
1998	1.3	1.3	1.3	1.3	1.3	1.3	1.3	1.3	1.3	1.3	1.3	1.3	1.3
1999	1.4	1.4	1.4	1.4	1.4	1.4	1.4	1.4	1.4	1.4	1.4	1.4	1.4
2000	1.4	1.4	1.4	1.3	1.3	1.3	1.4	1.4	1.3	1.4	1.4	1.4	1.3
2001	1.4	1.4	1.4	1.4	1.4	1.4	1.4	1.4	1.4	1.4	1.4	1.4	1.4
2002	1.3	1.3	1.3	1.4	1.4	1.4	1.4	1.4	1.4	1.4	1.4	1.4	1.4
2003	1.4	1.4	1.4	1.4	1.4	1.4	1.4	1.4	1.4	1.4	1.4	1.4	1.4
Financial activities													
1990	1.5	1.4	1.4	1.5	1.5	1.6	1.5	1.5	1.5	1.6	1.6	1.6	1.5
1991	1.6	1.6	1.7	1.7	1.7	1.7	1.7	1.7	1.7	1.7	1.7	1.7	1.6
1992	1.7	1.7	1.7	1.8	1.8	1.8	1.8	1.8	1.8	1.8	1.8	1.9	1.7
1993	1.9	1.8	1.8	1.8	1.8	1.9	1.9	1.9	1.9	1.9	1.9	2.0	1.8
1994	2.0	2.0	2.1	2.1	2.1	2.1	2.1	2.1	2.1	2.1	2.1	2.2	2.0
1995	2.1	2.1	2.1	2.1	2.2	2.2	2.2	2.2	2.2	2.3	2.3	2.3	2.1
1996	2.3	2.2	2.3	2.3	2.3	2.2	2.3	2.3	2.3	2.3	2.2	2.2	2.2
1997	2.3	2.3	2.3	2.3	2.3	2.3	2.3	2.3	2.3	2.3	2.3	2.3	2.3
1998	2.3	2.3	2.2	2.5	2.5	2.5	2.5	2.5	2.5	2.6	2.6	2.6	2.4
1999	2.5	2.5	2.5	2.5	2.6	2.6	2.5	2.5	2.5	2.5	2.5	2.5	2.5
2000	2.5	2.5	2.5	2.6	2.7	2.7	2.6	2.7	2.6	2.7	2.6	2.7	2.6
2001	2.6	2.6	2.6	2.5	2.5	2.5	2.5	2.5	2.5	2.5	2.5	2.5	2.5
2002	2.5	2.5	2.5	2.5	2.5	2.5	2.5	2.6	2.6	2.7	2.7	2.7	2.6
2003	2.8	2.8	2.8	2.8	2.8	2.9	2.9	2.9	2.9	3.0	2.9	3.0	2.9
Professional and business services													
1990	2.5	2.5	2.5	2.6	2.6	2.6	2.6	2.6	2.6	2.6	2.6	2.5	2.5
1991	2.4	2.5	2.6	2.6	2.6	2.6	2.6	2.7	2.7	2.7	2.6	2.6	2.6
1992	2.6	2.6	2.6	2.7	2.8	2.7	2.8	2.8	2.8	2.8	2.7	2.8	2.7
1993	2.7	2.7	2.8	2.9	3.0	3.1	3.1	3.2	3.1	3.1	3.1	3.1	2.9
1994	3.0	3.0	3.1	3.2	3.4	3.4	3.4	3.4	3.4	3.4	3.3	3.4	3.2
1995	3.3	3.4	3.4	3.5	3.5	3.4	3.3	3.4	3.4	3.4	3.3	3.3	3.3
1996	3.3	3.5	3.5	3.6	3.7	3.7	3.8	3.8	3.8	3.9	3.8	4.0	3.7
1997	3.8	3.9	4.0	4.0	4.1	4.2	4.0	4.0	3.9	3.9	3.8	3.7	3.9
1998	3.8	3.9	3.9	3.9	4.2	4.2	4.2	4.3	4.2	4.3	4.3	4.3	4.1
1999	4.4	4.5	4.5	4.7	4.8	4.9	4.9	4.9	4.8	4.8	4.9	4.8	4.7
2000	4.7	4.7	4.8	4.9	5.0	5.0	5.0	4.9	4.9	4.9	5.0	4.9	4.8
2001	4.8	4.9	4.7	4.6	4.7	4.6	4.7	4.7	4.6	4.5	4.5	4.5	4.6
2002	4.5	4.5	4.5	4.5	4.5	4.7	4.5	4.4	4.5	4.3	4.3	4.3	4.5
2003	4.5	4.6	4.5	4.5	4.7	4.8	4.6	4.6	4.5	4.5	4.4	4.4	4.6
Educational and health services													
1990	6.2	6.3	6.4	6.5	6.4	6.4	6.4	6.5	6.6	6.7	6.7	6.8	6.4
1991	6.6	6.7	6.7	6.7	6.7	6.6	6.6	6.8	6.9	6.9	6.9	7.0	6.7
1992	6.9	7.0	7.1	7.2	7.2	7.2	7.0	7.0	7.3	7.3	7.3	7.4	7.1
1993	7.3	7.3	7.2	7.2	7.2	7.2	7.0	7.0	7.2	7.2	7.3	7.3	7.2
1994	7.2	7.2	7.2	7.3	7.3	7.2	7.1	7.2	7.4	7.3	7.4	7.6	7.2
1995	7.4	7.4	7.5	7.5	7.5	7.5	7.4	7.4	7.6	7.6	7.7	7.7	7.5
1996	7.6	7.6	7.7	7.8	7.8	7.8	7.7	7.8	7.9	7.9	7.9	7.9	7.7
1997	7.8	7.9	7.9	7.9	7.8	7.9	7.8	7.8	8.0	8.2	8.2	8.2	7.9
1998	8.0	8.0	8.1	8.2	8.1	8.2	8.0	8.1	8.2	8.3	8.3	8.4	8.1
1999	8.2	8.3	8.3	8.2	8.0	8.0	8.0	8.0	8.1	8.2	8.2	8.2	8.1
2000	8.1	8.0	8.1	8.1	8.0	8.1	8.0	8.1	8.2	8.2	8.4	8.4	8.1
2001	8.2	8.3	8.4	8.4	8.4	8.4	8.4	8.4	8.5	8.6	8.6	8.7	8.4
2002	8.6	8.8	8.8	8.8	8.9	8.9	8.9	8.9	9.0	8.9	8.9	8.9	8.9
2003	9.0	9.1	9.1	9.0	9.0	9.1	9.0	9.0	9.1	9.2	9.1	9.0	9.1

Employment by Industry: North Dakota—*Continued*

(Numbers in thousands. Not seasonally adjusted.)

Industry	January	February	March	April	May	June	July	August	September	October	November	December	Annual Average
BISMARCK—*Continued*													
Leisure and hospitality													
1990	3.7	3.8	3.8	3.9	4.0	4.2	4.1	4.1	4.1	3.8	3.8	3.8	3.9
1991	3.7	3.8	3.9	3.9	3.9	4.0	4.1	4.2	4.1	4.0	4.0	4.1	3.9
1992	3.9	3.9	3.9	4.0	4.2	4.2	4.2	4.3	4.2	4.1	4.2	4.2	4.1
1993	4.1	4.1	4.2	4.3	4.4	4.3	4.4	4.4	4.3	4.3	4.3	4.4	4.2
1994	4.2	4.1	4.2	4.3	4.4	4.4	4.4	4.4	4.3	4.2	4.2	4.3	4.2
1995	4.2	4.3	4.3	4.3	4.4	4.5	4.6	4.7	4.5	4.3	4.4	4.4	4.4
1996	4.3	4.4	4.5	4.6	4.7	4.7	4.7	4.7	4.7	4.6	4.6	4.6	4.5
1997	4.6	4.6	4.7	4.7	4.9	4.9	4.9	5.0	4.9	4.6	4.5	4.6	4.7
1998	4.5	4.6	4.6	4.7	4.8	4.8	4.9	4.9	4.9	4.8	4.9	4.9	4.7
1999	4.6	4.6	4.7	4.8	5.0	5.1	5.0	5.1	5.0	5.0	4.9	4.9	4.8
2000	4.7	4.7	4.8	4.9	4.9	5.0	5.0	5.1	4.9	4.7	4.8	4.8	4.8
2001	4.7	4.8	4.9	5.1	5.2	5.2	5.1	5.2	5.0	4.9	4.8	4.9	4.9
2002	4.6	4.7	4.8	4.9	5.0	5.0	5.0	5.0	4.9	4.8	4.7	4.7	4.8
2003	4.7	4.7	4.8	4.9	5.0	5.2	5.1	5.1	4.9	4.9	4.8	4.9	4.9
Other services													
1990	2.5	2.5	2.5	2.6	2.6	2.6	2.5	2.6	2.6	2.6	2.6	2.6	2.5
1991	2.5	2.5	2.6	2.6	2.6	2.6	2.6	2.6	2.6	2.6	2.6	2.6	2.5
1992	2.6	2.6	2.6	2.6	2.7	2.7	2.7	2.7	2.7	2.7	2.7	2.7	2.6
1993	2.6	2.6	2.6	2.6	2.6	2.6	2.6	2.7	2.7	2.7	2.7	2.7	2.6
1994	2.6	2.6	2.6	2.7	2.7	2.7	2.7	2.7	2.6	2.7	2.7	2.7	2.6
1995	2.7	2.7	2.7	2.8	3.0	2.7	2.7	2.7	2.7	2.7	2.6	2.7	2.7
1996	2.6	2.6	2.6	2.7	2.7	2.7	2.7	2.8	2.7	2.7	2.7	2.7	2.6
1997	2.7	2.7	2.7	2.8	2.9	2.9	2.8	2.8	2.8	2.8	2.8	2.8	2.7
1998	2.7	2.7	2.8	2.8	2.8	2.9	2.8	2.9	2.8	2.9	2.9	2.9	2.8
1999	2.9	2.9	2.9	2.9	2.9	2.9	2.9	2.9	2.9	2.9	2.9	2.9	2.9
2000	2.8	2.8	2.9	2.9	3.0	3.0	3.0	2.9	2.9	2.9	2.9	2.9	2.9
2001	2.8	2.8	2.8	2.8	2.8	2.8	2.9	2.9	2.9	2.8	2.8	2.8	2.8
2002	2.8	2.9	2.8	2.9	2.9	2.9	2.9	2.8	2.8	2.8	2.8	2.8	2.8
2003	2.8	2.8	2.8	2.8	2.8	2.8	2.9	2.9	3.1	2.9	2.9	2.9	2.9
Government													
1990	8.6	8.8	8.9	8.9	9.0	9.1	8.5	8.5	8.7	8.8	8.8	8.9	8.7
1991	9.0	9.0	9.1	9.1	9.1	9.3	8.7	8.9	9.2	9.1	9.3	9.2	9.0
1992	9.2	9.3	9.3	9.4	9.4	9.7	9.3	9.3	9.3	9.6	9.5	9.7	9.4
1993	9.7	9.7	9.8	9.9	9.8	9.5	9.3	9.1	9.6	9.6	9.6	9.7	9.6
1994	9.5	9.8	9.9	9.9	9.8	9.7	9.4	9.3	9.6	9.6	9.7	9.8	9.6
1995	10.0	10.0	10.1	10.1	10.2	10.1	9.6	8.9	9.8	10.0	10.0	9.9	9.8
1996	9.9	10.0	10.0	9.9	10.2	9.8	9.1	9.0	9.7	10.0	10.1	10.1	9.8
1997	10.1	10.3	10.1	10.1	10.4	10.2	9.6	9.7	10.3	10.4	10.5	10.4	10.1
1998	10.4	10.5	10.5	10.5	10.6	10.9	9.7	9.5	10.3	10.6	10.6	10.8	10.4
1999	10.9	10.9	10.8	10.7	10.8	10.6	9.7	9.6	10.5	10.9	10.9	10.9	10.6
2000	10.8	11.0	11.1	11.1	11.2	10.4	10.1	9.8	10.6	10.9	10.9	11.0	10.7
2001	10.9	11.1	11.2	11.1	11.0	11.0	10.2	9.7	11.0	10.9	11.0	10.9	10.8
2002	11.0	11.1	11.1	11.1	11.4	11.1	10.5	9.9	10.9	11.1	11.2	11.3	11.0
2003	11.3	11.3	11.3	11.5	11.5	11.2	10.4	10.1	11.0	11.2	11.2	11.3	11.1
Federal government													
1990	1.1	1.1	1.2	1.2	1.2	1.2	1.2	1.1	1.1	1.1	1.1	1.1	1.1
1991	1.1	1.1	1.1	1.1	1.1	1.1	1.1	1.2	1.1	1.1	1.1	1.1	1.1
1992	1.1	1.1	1.1	1.1	1.1	1.2	1.2	1.2	1.1	1.1	1.1	1.1	1.1
1993	1.1	1.1	1.1	1.1	1.1	1.1	1.1	1.1	1.1	1.1	1.1	1.1	1.1
1994	1.1	1.1	1.1	1.1	1.1	1.1	1.1	1.1	1.1	1.1	1.1	1.1	1.1
1995	1.1	1.1	1.1	1.1	1.1	1.1	1.2	1.1	1.1	1.1	1.1	1.1	1.1
1996	1.1	1.1	1.1	1.1	1.1	1.1	1.1	1.1	1.0	1.0	1.0	1.0	1.0
1997	1.0	1.1	1.0	1.0	1.1	1.1	1.1	1.1	1.1	1.0	1.0	1.0	1.0
1998	1.0	1.0	1.0	1.0	1.0	1.1	1.0	1.0	1.0	1.0	1.0	1.0	1.0
1999	1.0	1.0	1.0	1.0	1.0	1.0	1.0	1.0	1.1	1.1	1.1	1.1	1.0
2000	1.1	1.1	1.2	1.2	1.3	1.1	1.2	1.2	1.1	1.1	1.1	1.1	1.1
2001	1.1	1.1	1.1	1.1	1.1	1.2	1.2	1.2	1.2	1.1	1.1	1.1	1.1
2002	1.1	1.1	1.1	1.1	1.2	1.2	1.2	1.2	1.1	1.1	1.1	1.2	1.1
2003	1.1	1.1	1.1	1.1	1.2	1.2	1.2	1.2	1.2	1.2	1.2	1.2	1.2
State government													
1990	3.9	4.0	4.0	4.0	4.1	4.0	4.0	4.0	4.0	4.1	4.0	4.1	4.0
1991	4.2	4.2	4.2	4.3	4.2	4.3	4.2	4.2	4.3	4.2	4.3	4.2	4.2
1992	4.3	4.3	4.3	4.4	4.4	4.5	4.5	4.5	4.5	4.5	4.5	4.6	4.4
1993	4.6	4.6	4.6	4.8	4.7	4.6	4.6	4.5	4.6	4.5	4.5	4.5	4.5
1994	4.5	4.6	4.7	4.7	4.6	4.7	4.6	4.6	4.6	4.5	4.5	4.6	4.6
1995	4.6	4.6	4.7	4.7	4.7	4.7	4.5	4.5	4.6	4.6	4.6	4.4	4.6
1996	4.5	4.5	4.6	4.5	4.7	4.7	4.5	4.5	4.6	4.6	4.6	4.6	4.5
1997	4.7	4.7	4.7	4.7	4.8	4.8	4.8	4.9	4.9	4.9	4.9	4.8	4.8
1998	4.8	4.8	4.9	5.0	5.0	5.0	5.0	4.8	5.0	5.0	5.0	5.1	4.9
1999	5.1	5.2	5.1	5.1	5.0	4.9	4.9	4.9	4.9	5.0	5.0	5.0	5.0
2000	5.0	5.1	5.1	5.1	5.1	5.1	5.0	5.0	5.0	5.1	5.1	5.1	5.0
2001	5.1	5.2	5.3	5.2	5.1	5.1	5.1	5.0	5.1	5.1	5.2	5.1	5.1
2002	5.2	5.2	5.2	5.2	5.3	5.2	5.3	5.1	5.2	5.2	5.2	5.1	5.2
2003	5.2	5.2	5.2	5.4	5.3	5.2	5.2	5.1	5.1	5.2	5.2	5.2	5.2

Employment by Industry: North Dakota—*Continued*

(Numbers in thousands. Not seasonally adjusted.)

Industry	January	February	March	April	May	June	July	August	September	October	November	December	Annual Average
BISMARCK—*Continued*													
Local government													
1990	3.6	3.7	3.7	3.7	3.7	3.9	3.3	3.4	3.6	3.6	3.7	3.7	3.6
1991	3.7	3.7	3.8	3.7	3.8	3.9	3.4	3.5	3.8	3.8	3.9	3.9	3.7
1992	3.8	3.9	3.9	3.9	3.9	4.0	3.6	3.6	3.7	4.0	3.9	4.0	3.8
1993	4.0	4.0	4.1	4.0	4.0	3.8	3.6	3.5	3.9	4.0	4.0	4.1	3.9
1994	3.9	4.1	4.1	4.1	4.1	3.9	3.7	3.6	3.9	4.0	4.1	4.1	3.9
1995	4.3	4.3	4.3	4.3	4.4	4.3	3.9	3.3	4.1	4.3	4.3	4.4	4.1
1996	4.3	4.4	4.3	4.3	4.4	4.0	3.5	3.4	4.1	4.4	4.5	4.5	4.1
1997	4.4	4.5	4.4	4.4	4.5	4.3	3.7	3.7	4.3	4.5	4.6	4.6	4.3
1998	4.6	4.7	4.6	4.5	4.6	4.8	3.7	3.7	4.3	4.6	4.6	4.7	4.4
1999	4.8	4.7	4.7	4.6	4.8	4.7	3.8	3.7	4.5	4.8	4.8	4.8	4.5
2000	4.7	4.8	4.8	4.8	4.8	4.2	3.9	3.6	4.5	4.7	4.7	4.8	4.5
2001	4.7	4.8	4.8	4.8	4.8	4.7	3.9	3.5	4.7	4.7	4.7	4.7	4.5
2002	4.7	4.8	4.8	4.8	4.9	4.7	4.0	3.6	4.6	4.8	4.9	5.0	4.6
2003	5.0	5.0	5.0	5.0	5.0	4.8	4.0	3.8	4.7	4.8	4.8	4.9	4.7
FARGO-MOORHEAD													
Total nonfarm													
1990	75.4	75.3	76.0	77.2	78.9	77.8	76.2	76.4	77.9	80.0	80.3	80.0	77.6
1991	78.2	78.0	77.7	79.0	80.7	79.4	78.2	78.7	80.7	82.9	82.3	82.0	79.8
1992	79.9	80.3	80.3	81.9	83.0	82.3	80.8	81.5	83.7	84.7	84.3	84.6	82.2
1993	81.8	82.5	82.4	83.7	85.0	84.1	83.4	83.3	85.6	86.6	86.7	86.1	84.2
1994	82.5	83.2	83.7	85.7	87.2	86.2	86.1	86.0	88.3	89.9	90.4	90.1	86.6
1995	87.1	87.6	88.5	88.6	89.6	88.9	87.1	87.7	89.7	91.6	91.7	91.4	89.1
1996	88.4	89.6	89.8	90.8	92.7	92.0	90.2	90.5	93.2	95.5	95.7	94.8	91.9
1997	92.3	93.2	93.6	95.2	96.3	95.1	95.1	95.9	97.1	99.6	99.2	99.5	96.0
1998	96.4	97.0	97.7	99.3	99.2	98.8	98.6	98.3	99.3	101.6	101.4	101.0	99.0
1999	98.0	98.6	98.9	101.1	100.9	100.9	99.5	99.4	102.2	103.5	103.2	103.2	100.7
2000	100.4	101.0	101.8	102.0	102.2	102.0	101.8	102.1	104.7	105.3	105.3	104.8	102.7
2001	103.2	103.3	103.9	103.7	104.1	103.6	102.8	102.8	105.7	105.5	105.2	104.9	104.0
2002	102.3	102.8	102.2	104.0	104.5	103.3	103.6	104.5	106.7	106.6	106.6	106.5	104.5
2003	103.3	103.8	103.8	105.9	106.7	106.0	105.0	106.1	108.0	108.0	107.9	107.4	106.0
Total private													
1990	60.0	59.9	60.6	61.9	63.5	63.4	63.4	63.4	63.7	64.7	64.9	64.7	62.8
1991	62.9	62.6	62.4	63.7	65.1	64.9	65.1	65.8	65.9	67.1	66.5	66.1	64.8
1992	64.0	64.2	64.4	66.0	67.1	67.5	67.5	68.0	68.2	68.8	68.4	68.7	66.9
1993	66.0	66.1	66.5	67.6	68.9	69.3	69.6	69.9	70.4	70.7	70.8	70.2	68.8
1994	67.9	68.4	69.0	70.9	72.3	72.7	73.5	73.7	74.1	74.9	75.5	75.0	72.3
1995	72.5	72.7	73.7	74.1	75.2	75.5	75.2	75.5	75.9	77.0	77.1	76.7	75.0
1996	74.2	74.9	75.1	76.2	78.2	78.7	78.6	78.6	78.7	80.8	81.0	80.2	77.9
1997	77.8	78.3	78.7	79.8	81.9	82.4	82.7	83.2	82.8	83.9	83.6	83.8	81.5
1998	81.0	81.2	82.1	83.5	84.3	84.8	85.8	85.8	85.0	86.0	85.8	85.2	84.2
1999	82.2	82.5	82.8	85.0	85.8	86.7	86.6	86.8	86.7	87.4	87.1	87.1	85.5
2000	84.4	84.4	85.3	85.5	86.5	87.2	88.7	88.9	89.1	89.1	89.1	88.5	87.2
2001	87.2	86.8	87.6	87.3	88.8	89.1	89.9	89.7	89.9	89.1	89.0	88.6	88.5
2002	86.1	86.4	86.0	87.4	88.5	89.1	90.5	91.1	90.6	90.0	90.1	89.9	88.8
2003	87.3	87.3	87.4	89.3	90.7	91.4	91.5	92.1	91.4	91.1	91.0	90.6	90.1
Goods-producing													
1990	7.8	7.8	8.1	8.4	9.3	9.8	10.0	10.1	10.1	10.6	10.2	9.3	9.2
1991	8.5	8.4	8.4	8.7	9.4	9.9	10.2	10.6	10.5	10.9	10.0	9.3	9.5
1992	8.6	8.5	8.5	9.4	9.8	10.6	10.9	11.1	10.9	11.0	10.3	9.4	9.9
1993	8.8	8.7	8.7	9.4	10.2	10.7	11.3	11.3	11.3	11.3	11.1	10.2	10.2
1994	9.6	9.4	9.7	10.3	11.1	11.7	11.9	12.0	11.9	12.1	11.9	11.1	11.0
1995	10.4	10.4	10.5	10.9	11.9	12.5	12.5	12.7	12.7	12.8	12.6	11.7	11.8
1996	11.0	10.8	10.9	11.5	12.6	13.3	13.3	13.4	13.1	13.6	13.0	12.3	12.4
1997	11.7	11.6	11.9	12.3	13.3	14.0	14.5	14.7	14.2	14.2	13.6	13.0	13.2
1998	12.3	12.3	12.6	12.9	13.8	14.2	14.8	14.8	14.2	14.1	13.6	13.0	13.5
1999	12.2	12.2	12.3	13.3	14.0	15.0	15.0	15.1	14.6	14.8	14.3	13.5	13.8
2000	12.6	12.6	12.9	13.3	14.1	14.6	15.1	15.0	15.0	14.6	14.0	13.4	13.9
2001	13.0	12.7	13.0	13.4	14.2	14.8	15.2	14.8	15.0	14.6	14.0	13.3	14.0
2002	12.7	12.6	12.7	13.2	14.0	14.6	15.0	15.2	15.0	14.6	14.3	13.8	14.0
2003	13.1	13.1	13.1	13.6	14.7	15.3	15.7	15.9	15.1	14.8	14.3	13.9	14.4
Construction and mining													
1990	2.7	2.7	2.8	3.1	3.8	4.3	4.4	4.4	4.2	4.3	3.9	3.3	3.6
1991	2.7	2.7	2.8	3.2	3.9	4.3	4.5	4.7	4.4	4.5	4.0	3.5	3.7
1992	3.1	3.0	3.0	3.7	4.2	4.7	5.0	5.1	4.8	4.6	4.2	3.6	4.0
1993	3.2	3.1	3.1	3.6	4.4	4.8	5.1	5.2	5.1	4.9	4.6	4.0	4.2
1994	3.6	3.5	3.7	4.0	4.7	5.3	5.5	5.5	5.3	5.1	4.8	4.2	4.6
1995	3.6	3.6	3.6	3.9	4.7	5.3	5.6	5.8	5.6	5.3	5.0	4.5	4.7
1996	4.0	3.8	3.9	4.3	5.3	6.0	6.2	6.2	5.8	5.7	5.3	4.6	5.0
1997	4.1	4.0	4.2	4.5	5.4	6.0	6.4	6.6	6.2	6.0	5.5	5.0	5.3
1998	4.3	4.3	4.6	5.1	6.0	6.3	6.9	6.9	6.3	6.2	5.7	5.3	5.6
1999	4.5	4.5	4.6	5.6	6.2	6.9	7.2	7.2	6.8	6.8	6.3	5.6	6.0
2000	4.8	4.7	4.9	5.4	6.0	6.4	6.9	7.0	6.6	6.3	5.7	5.2	5.8
2001	4.8	4.6	4.8	5.2	6.0	6.5	6.9	6.9	6.6	6.3	5.8	5.1	5.7
2002	4.6	4.5	4.5	5.0	5.8	6.2	6.6	6.7	6.5	6.2	5.9	5.5	5.7
2003	4.9	4.9	4.9	5.4	6.3	6.9	7.2	7.4	6.9	6.5	6.1	5.7	6.1

Employment by Industry: North Dakota—*Continued*

(Numbers in thousands. Not seasonally adjusted.)

Industry	January	February	March	April	May	June	July	August	September	October	November	December	Annual Average
FARGO-MOORHEAD *—Continued*													
Manufacturing													
1990	5.1	5.1	5.3	5.3	5.5	5.5	5.6	5.7	5.9	6.3	6.3	6.0	5.6
1991	5.8	5.7	5.6	5.5	5.5	5.6	5.7	5.9	6.1	6.4	6.0	5.8	5.8
1992	5.5	5.5	5.5	5.7	5.6	5.9	5.9	6.0	6.1	6.4	6.1	5.8	5.8
1993	5.6	5.6	5.6	5.8	5.8	5.9	6.2	6.1	6.2	6.4	6.5	6.2	5.9
1994	6.0	5.9	6.0	6.3	6.4	6.4	6.4	6.5	6.6	7.0	7.1	6.9	6.4
1995	6.8	6.8	6.9	7.0	7.2	7.2	6.9	6.9	7.1	7.5	7.6	7.2	7.0
1996	7.0	7.0	7.0	7.2	7.3	7.3	7.1	7.2	7.3	7.9	7.7	7.7	7.3
1997	7.6	7.6	7.7	7.8	7.9	8.0	8.1	8.1	8.0	8.2	8.1	8.0	7.9
1998	8.0	8.0	8.0	7.8	7.8	7.9	7.9	7.9	7.9	7.9	7.9	7.7	7.8
1999	7.7	7.7	7.7	7.7	7.8	8.1	7.8	7.9	7.8	8.0	8.0	7.9	7.8
2000	7.8	7.9	8.0	7.9	8.1	8.2	8.2	8.0	8.4	8.3	8.3	8.2	8.1
2001	8.2	8.1	8.2	8.2	8.2	8.3	8.3	7.9	8.4	8.3	8.2	8.2	8.2
2002	8.1	8.1	8.2	8.2	8.2	8.4	8.4	8.5	8.5	8.4	8.4	8.3	8.3
2003	8.2	8.2	8.2	8.2	8.4	8.4	8.5	8.5	8.2	8.3	8.2	8.2	8.3
Service-providing													
1990	67.6	67.5	67.9	68.8	69.6	68.0	66.2	66.3	67.8	69.4	70.1	70.7	68.3
1991	69.7	69.6	69.3	70.3	71.3	69.5	68.0	68.1	70.2	72.0	72.3	72.7	70.2
1992	71.3	71.8	71.8	72.5	73.2	71.7	69.9	70.4	72.8	73.7	74.0	75.2	72.3
1993	73.0	73.8	73.7	74.3	74.8	73.4	72.1	72.0	74.3	75.3	75.6	75.9	74.0
1994	72.9	73.8	74.0	75.4	76.1	74.5	74.2	74.0	76.4	77.8	78.5	79.0	75.5
1995	76.7	77.2	78.0	77.7	77.7	76.4	74.6	75.0	77.0	78.8	79.1	79.7	77.3
1996	77.4	78.8	78.9	79.3	80.1	78.7	76.9	77.1	80.1	81.9	82.7	82.5	79.5
1997	80.6	81.6	81.7	82.9	83.0	81.1	80.6	81.2	82.9	85.4	85.6	86.5	82.7
1998	84.1	84.7	85.1	86.4	85.4	84.6	83.8	83.5	85.1	87.5	87.8	88.0	85.5
1999	85.8	86.4	86.6	87.8	86.9	85.9	84.5	84.3	87.6	88.7	88.9	89.7	86.9
2000	87.8	88.4	88.9	88.7	88.1	87.4	86.7	87.1	89.7	90.7	91.3	91.4	88.8
2001	90.2	90.6	90.9	90.3	89.9	88.8	87.6	88.0	90.7	90.9	91.2	91.6	90.0
2002	89.6	90.2	89.5	90.8	90.5	88.7	88.6	89.3	91.7	92.0	92.3	92.7	90.5
2003	90.2	90.7	90.7	92.3	92.0	90.7	89.3	90.2	92.9	93.2	93.6	93.5	91.6
Trade, transportation, and utilities													
1990	18.8	18.6	18.7	19.2	19.5	19.2	19.0	19.0	19.1	19.4	19.9	20.4	19.2
1991	19.9	19.6	19.5	19.8	20.0	19.7	19.7	19.8	19.8	20.1	20.5	20.5	19.9
1992	19.9	19.8	19.9	20.1	20.5	20.4	20.2	20.4	20.5	20.7	20.9	21.2	20.3
1993	20.3	20.2	20.4	20.4	20.8	20.7	20.6	20.6	20.9	21.2	21.4	21.9	20.7
1994	21.0	21.1	21.2	21.6	22.1	22.0	22.1	22.2	22.3	22.6	23.1	23.3	22.0
1995	22.5	22.4	22.6	22.6	22.9	22.5	22.4	22.4	22.6	23.1	23.4	23.7	22.7
1996	22.6	22.4	22.6	22.9	23.2	22.9	22.9	22.9	23.1	23.7	24.2	24.1	23.1
1997	23.2	23.1	23.0	23.4	23.7	23.5	23.4	23.6	23.7	24.2	24.7	25.1	23.7
1998	24.1	24.0	24.1	24.4	24.3	24.1	24.2	24.2	24.2	24.6	24.9	25.0	24.3
1999	23.8	23.7	23.6	24.1	24.2	24.1	23.9	23.9	24.0	24.3	24.6	24.9	24.0
2000	24.1	23.8	23.7	23.9	24.0	24.0	23.9	24.0	24.2	24.4	24.8	24.9	24.1
2001	24.8	24.5	24.7	24.4	24.6	24.3	24.3	24.5	24.5	24.5	24.6	24.8	24.5
2002	24.1	23.9	23.9	23.9	24.1	24.1	24.1	24.1	24.4	24.4	25.0	25.1	24.3
2003	24.2	24.1	24.1	24.6	24.7	24.7	24.5	24.7	24.7	24.7	25.2	25.2	24.6
Wholesale trade													
1990	5.0	5.0	5.1	5.2	5.2	5.3	5.2	5.2	5.2	5.2	5.2	5.3	5.1
1991	5.2	5.1	5.2	5.3	5.4	5.3	5.3	5.3	5.2	5.3	5.3	5.2	5.2
1992	5.2	5.2	5.2	5.3	5.4	5.4	5.5	5.5	5.4	5.4	5.3	5.3	5.3
1993	5.4	5.5	5.6	5.6	5.7	5.7	5.7	5.7	5.6	5.6	5.6	5.7	5.6
1994	5.7	5.7	5.8	5.9	6.0	6.0	6.0	6.0	5.9	6.0	6.0	6.1	5.9
1995	6.0	6.1	6.2	6.2	6.3	6.2	6.2	6.2	6.1	6.2	6.2	6.2	6.1
1996	6.2	6.2	6.3	6.4	6.6	6.6	6.5	6.5	6.4	6.6	6.6	6.5	6.4
1997	6.5	6.5	6.5	6.6	6.8	6.8	6.7	6.7	6.6	6.7	6.7	6.7	6.6
1998	6.7	6.7	6.8	7.0	7.0	7.0	7.0	7.0	6.9	6.9	6.9	6.9	6.9
1999	6.8	6.8	6.8	7.0	7.1	7.1	6.9	6.9	6.8	7.0	6.9	6.9	6.9
2000	6.9	6.8	6.8	6.9	6.9	6.9	6.9	6.9	6.8	6.9	6.9	6.9	6.8
2001	7.1	7.1	7.2	7.1	7.2	7.1	7.1	7.1	6.9	6.9	6.7	6.7	7.0
2002	6.7	6.7	6.7	6.7	6.8	6.9	6.9	6.8	6.8	6.8	6.8	6.7	6.8
2003	6.6	6.6	6.6	6.9	6.9	7.0	7.0	7.0	6.9	6.8	6.8	6.8	6.8
Retail trade													
1990	10.7	10.5	10.4	10.8	11.0	10.7	10.7	10.7	10.8	11.0	11.5	11.8	10.8
1991	11.6	11.4	11.2	11.3	11.4	11.2	11.3	11.3	11.4	11.5	11.9	12.0	11.4
1992	11.4	11.3	11.4	11.6	11.8	11.6	11.4	11.5	11.7	11.9	12.2	12.4	11.6
1993	11.6	11.4	11.5	11.4	11.6	11.4	11.4	11.3	11.6	11.7	11.9	12.2	11.5
1994	11.4	11.4	11.4	11.7	12.0	12.0	12.1	12.2	12.3	12.5	13.0	13.2	12.1
1995	12.6	12.5	12.6	12.6	12.7	12.5	12.5	12.5	12.7	13.0	13.3	13.6	12.7
1996	12.6	12.4	12.5	12.7	12.8	12.6	12.8	12.8	13.1	13.5	14.0	14.0	12.9
1997	13.2	13.1	13.0	13.2	13.3	13.2	13.2	13.3	13.4	13.7	14.2	14.5	13.4
1998	13.7	13.6	13.5	13.7	13.7	13.5	13.6	13.7	13.7	14.1	14.4	14.6	13.8
1999	13.7	13.6	13.5	13.8	13.8	13.7	13.7	13.7	13.8	13.8	14.3	14.5	13.8
2000	13.9	13.7	13.6	13.7	13.8	13.7	13.7	13.7	13.9	14.0	14.4	14.6	13.8
2001	13.9	13.6	13.7	13.6	13.7	13.5	13.5	13.7	13.9	13.9	14.2	14.4	13.7
2002	13.9	13.7	13.6	13.7	13.7	13.7	13.7	13.7	14.0	14.0	14.6	14.8	13.9
2003	14.0	13.9	13.8	14.1	14.1	14.1	14.0	14.1	14.2	14.3	14.7	14.8	14.2

Employment by Industry: North Dakota—*Continued*

(Numbers in thousands. Not seasonally adjusted.)

Industry	January	February	March	April	May	June	July	August	September	October	November	December	Annual Average
FARGO-MOORHEAD —*Continued*													
Transportation and utilities													
1990	3.1	3.1	3.2	3.2	3.3	3.2	3.1	3.1	3.1	3.2	3.2	3.3	3.1
1991	3.1	3.1	3.1	3.2	3.2	3.2	3.1	3.2	3.2	3.3	3.3	3.3	3.1
1992	3.3	3.3	3.3	3.2	3.3	3.4	3.3	3.4	3.4	3.4	3.4	3.5	3.3
1993	3.3	3.3	3.3	3.4	3.5	3.6	3.5	3.6	3.7	3.9	3.9	4.0	3.5
1994	3.9	4.0	4.0	4.0	4.1	4.0	4.0	4.0	4.1	4.1	4.1	4.0	4.0
1995	3.9	3.8	3.8	3.8	3.9	3.8	3.7	3.7	3.8	3.9	3.9	3.9	3.8
1996	3.8	3.8	3.8	3.8	3.8	3.7	3.6	3.6	3.6	3.6	3.6	3.6	3.6
1997	3.5	3.5	3.5	3.6	3.6	3.5	3.5	3.6	3.7	3.8	3.8	3.9	3.6
1998	3.7	3.7	3.8	3.7	3.6	3.6	3.6	3.5	3.6	3.6	3.6	3.5	3.6
1999	3.3	3.3	3.3	3.3	3.3	3.3	3.3	3.3	3.4	3.5	3.4	3.5	3.3
2000	3.3	3.3	3.3	3.3	3.3	3.4	3.3	3.4	3.5	3.5	3.5	3.4	3.3
2001	3.8	3.8	3.8	3.7	3.7	3.7	3.7	3.7	3.7	3.7	3.7	3.7	3.7
2002	3.5	3.5	3.6	3.5	3.6	3.5	3.5	3.6	3.6	3.6	3.6	3.6	3.6
2003	3.6	3.6	3.7	3.6	3.7	3.6	3.5	3.6	3.6	3.6	3.7	3.6	3.6
Information													
1990	2.3	2.3	2.4	2.4	2.4	2.4	2.3	2.3	2.3	2.2	2.3	2.3	2.3
1991	2.3	2.3	2.3	2.3	2.3	2.3	2.3	2.3	2.3	2.3	2.3	2.4	2.3
1992	2.3	2.3	2.3	2.3	2.3	2.3	2.3	2.3	2.3	2.4	2.4	2.5	2.3
1993	2.4	2.4	2.4	2.4	2.4	2.4	2.5	2.5	2.5	2.3	2.3	2.3	2.4
1994	2.4	2.4	2.4	2.5	2.5	2.5	2.5	2.5	2.5	2.5	2.5	2.5	2.4
1995	2.5	2.6	2.6	2.6	2.5	2.5	2.5	2.5	2.6	2.5	2.5	2.6	2.5
1996	2.5	2.5	2.5	2.5	2.5	2.5	2.5	2.5	2.5	2.5	2.6	2.6	2.5
1997	2.5	2.5	2.5	2.4	2.4	2.4	2.5	2.5	2.5	2.6	2.7	2.7	2.5
1998	2.7	2.7	2.7	2.7	2.7	2.6	2.8	2.8	2.8	2.9	2.9	2.9	2.7
1999	2.9	2.9	2.9	2.9	3.0	3.0	3.0	3.1	3.1	3.2	3.1	3.2	3.0
2000	3.2	3.2	3.2	3.3	3.3	3.4	3.4	3.4	3.3	3.3	3.3	3.4	3.3
2001	3.4	3.4	3.4	3.2	3.3	3.3	3.3	3.3	3.3	3.4	3.4	3.4	3.3
2002	3.3	3.3	3.3	3.3	3.3	3.3	3.3	3.3	3.2	3.2	3.2	3.2	3.3
2003	3.2	3.2	3.2	3.2	3.2	3.2	3.2	3.2	3.2	3.2	3.2	3.2	3.2
Financial activities													
1990	4.8	4.8	4.9	5.0	5.0	5.0	5.0	5.0	4.9	5.0	5.0	5.0	4.9
1991	5.1	5.0	5.0	5.0	5.1	5.1	5.1	5.1	5.0	5.1	5.1	5.1	5.0
1992	5.1	5.2	5.2	5.2	5.2	5.2	5.1	5.2	5.2	5.3	5.3	5.4	5.2
1993	5.4	5.4	5.5	5.5	5.5	5.4	5.5	5.5	5.4	5.5	5.5	5.6	5.4
1994	5.4	5.5	5.5	5.6	5.6	5.6	5.6	5.6	5.6	5.6	5.7	5.7	5.5
1995	5.7	5.6	5.7	5.6	5.6	5.5	5.6	5.6	5.7	5.8	5.7	5.8	5.6
1996	5.8	5.9	5.9	6.0	6.1	6.1	6.1	5.9	5.7	5.8	5.8	5.9	5.9
1997	5.6	5.6	5.7	5.7	5.7	5.8	5.7	5.8	5.8	6.0	6.0	6.1	5.7
1998	5.8	5.8	5.9	6.4	6.4	6.4	6.4	6.5	6.5	6.5	6.5	6.5	6.3
1999	6.4	6.4	6.5	6.4	6.5	6.5	6.4	6.5	6.5	6.5	6.5	6.5	6.4
2000	6.5	6.5	6.5	6.3	6.4	6.4	6.7	6.7	6.7	6.7	6.8	6.8	6.5
2001	7.0	7.0	7.0	6.8	6.8	6.9	6.9	6.9	6.9	7.0	6.9	7.0	6.9
2002	7.9	8.0	8.0	8.0	8.0	8.1	8.1	8.1	8.1	8.2	8.1	8.1	8.1
2003	8.0	7.9	8.0	8.0	8.0	8.1	8.1	8.1	8.0	8.1	8.1	8.2	8.1
Professional and business services													
1990	4.3	4.2	4.3	4.4	4.4	4.4	4.4	4.4	4.5	4.6	4.5	4.5	4.4
1991	4.5	4.5	4.4	4.6	4.6	4.5	4.5	4.6	4.7	4.9	4.8	4.8	4.6
1992	4.6	4.5	4.5	4.7	4.6	4.7	4.7	4.9	5.0	5.1	5.0	5.2	4.7
1993	5.0	5.0	5.0	5.1	5.2	5.3	5.1	5.2	5.6	5.7	5.8	5.4	5.2
1994	5.2	5.4	5.5	5.8	5.9	6.0	6.3	6.3	6.4	6.4	6.5	6.4	6.0
1995	6.1	6.2	6.4	6.5	6.5	6.6	6.5	6.7	6.9	7.2	7.2	7.0	6.6
1996	7.1	7.6	7.3	7.4	7.5	7.6	7.9	8.0	8.5	8.7	8.7	8.4	7.8
1997	8.7	8.9	8.9	9.0	9.3	9.1	9.0	9.1	9.3	9.4	9.3	9.4	9.1
1998	9.0	9.1	9.2	9.4	9.4	9.7	9.7	10.0	9.9	10.4	10.3	10.2	9.6
1999	9.8	10.0	10.3	10.5	10.3	10.3	10.0	9.9	10.3	10.2	10.0	10.2	10.1
2000	9.7	9.8	10.1	10.1	10.1	10.2	10.6	10.7	10.7	10.5	10.4	10.3	10.2
2001	10.3	10.4	10.4	10.5	10.4	10.7	10.5	10.3	10.4	10.4	10.5	10.4	10.4
2002	8.9	9.1	9.1	9.3	9.3	9.6	9.6	9.8	9.8	9.7	9.5	9.6	9.4
2003	9.0	9.2	9.1	9.2	9.2	9.5	9.5	9.6	9.7	9.7	9.6	9.5	9.4
Educational and health services													
1990	10.4	10.5	10.5	10.6	10.6	10.7	10.7	10.7	10.8	10.8	10.9	11.0	10.6
1991	10.9	11.0	11.0	11.2	11.3	11.3	11.4	11.4	11.5	11.5	11.6	11.6	11.3
1992	11.4	11.6	11.6	11.7	11.8	11.7	11.8	11.8	11.6	11.7	11.9	12.1	11.7
1993	11.7	11.8	11.8	11.9	11.9	11.9	11.9	12.1	11.9	11.8	11.8	11.9	11.8
1994	11.7	11.9	11.8	11.8	11.8	11.7	11.9	12.0	12.1	12.1	12.1	12.2	11.9
1995	12.0	12.1	12.1	12.1	12.2	12.5	12.2	12.2	11.9	12.0	12.1	12.1	12.1
1996	11.8	12.0	12.0	11.9	12.0	12.3	12.0	12.0	11.7	12.2	12.3	12.4	12.0
1997	12.2	12.4	12.4	12.6	12.8	13.2	13.3	13.1	12.7	13.1	13.1	13.1	12.8
1998	12.9	13.0	13.1	12.9	12.9	13.2	13.2	12.8	12.6	12.8	12.8	12.9	12.9
1999	12.7	12.8	12.8	13.1	13.0	13.0	13.8	13.5	13.2	13.4	13.3	13.3	13.1
2000	13.4	13.5	13.6	13.5	13.5	13.7	14.1	14.0	13.7	14.3	14.5	14.5	13.8
2001	14.1	14.3	14.5	14.4	14.5	14.2	15.1	15.3	15.0	14.4	14.7	14.7	14.6
2002	14.7	14.9	14.3	14.7	14.8	14.4	15.4	15.4	14.8	14.9	15.0	15.0	14.9
2003	14.9	15.0	15.0	15.2	15.2	14.8	15.1	15.1	15.0	15.2	15.3	15.3	15.1

Employment by Industry: North Dakota—*Continued*

(Numbers in thousands. Not seasonally adjusted.)

Industry	January	February	March	April	May	June	July	August	September	October	November	December	Annual Average
FARGO-MOORHEAD *—Continued*													
Leisure and hospitality													
1990	7.7	7.8	7.8	8.0	8.3	8.0	8.1	8.0	8.1	8.1	8.1	8.2	8.0
1991	7.8	7.8	7.8	8.1	8.4	8.2	8.0	8.1	8.1	8.2	8.1	8.2	8.0
1992	8.1	8.2	8.3	8.5	8.7	8.5	8.4	8.3	8.5	8.4	8.4	8.6	8.4
1993	8.2	8.3	8.4	8.6	8.6	8.7	8.5	8.6	8.6	8.6	8.6	8.6	8.5
1994	8.5	8.6	8.7	9.0	9.0	8.9	8.9	8.9	9.0	9.2	9.3	9.3	8.9
1995	8.9	9.0	9.3	9.3	9.2	9.1	9.1	9.0	9.1	9.2	9.2	9.3	9.1
1996	8.9	9.2	9.4	9.4	9.7	9.4	9.4	9.4	9.5	9.6	9.6	9.7	9.4
1997	9.3	9.5	9.6	9.7	10.0	9.7	9.6	9.7	9.8	9.6	9.4	9.5	9.6
1998	9.4	9.5	9.7	9.9	9.9	9.7	9.9	9.9	10.0	9.9	9.9	9.8	9.7
1999	9.6	9.6	9.6	9.9	10.0	10.1	9.8	10.0	10.2	10.0	10.3	10.5	9.9
2000	10.1	10.1	10.3	10.3	10.4	10.3	10.3	10.5	10.7	10.5	10.5	10.4	10.3
2001	10.3	10.2	10.3	10.4	10.8	10.8	10.5	10.5	10.6	10.5	10.6	10.7	10.5
2002	10.3	10.4	10.4	10.7	10.7	10.8	10.8	10.9	10.9	10.6	10.5	10.6	10.6
2003	10.3	10.1	10.3	10.8	11.0	11.2	11.0	11.0	11.0	10.8	10.6	10.7	10.7
Other services													
1990	3.9	3.9	3.9	3.9	4.0	3.9	3.9	3.9	3.9	4.0	4.0	4.0	3.9
1991	3.9	4.0	4.0	4.0	4.0	3.9	3.9	3.9	4.0	4.1	4.1	4.2	4.0
1992	4.0	4.1	4.1	4.1	4.2	4.1	4.1	4.0	4.2	4.2	4.2	4.3	4.1
1993	4.2	4.3	4.3	4.3	4.3	4.2	4.2	4.1	4.2	4.3	4.3	4.3	4.2
1994	4.1	4.1	4.2	4.3	4.3	4.3	4.3	4.2	4.3	4.4	4.4	4.5	4.2
1995	4.4	4.4	4.5	4.5	4.4	4.3	4.4	4.4	4.4	4.4	4.4	4.5	4.4
1996	4.5	4.5	4.5	4.6	4.6	4.6	4.5	4.5	4.6	4.7	4.8	4.8	4.6
1997	4.6	4.7	4.7	4.7	4.7	4.7	4.7	4.7	4.8	4.8	4.8	4.9	4.7
1998	4.8	4.8	4.8	4.9	4.9	4.9	4.8	4.8	4.8	4.8	4.9	4.9	4.8
1999	4.8	4.9	4.8	4.8	4.8	4.7	4.7	4.8	4.8	5.0	5.0	5.0	4.8
2000	4.8	4.9	5.0	4.8	4.7	4.6	4.6	4.6	4.8	4.8	4.8	4.8	4.7
2001	4.3	4.3	4.3	4.2	4.2	4.1	4.1	4.1	4.2	4.3	4.3	4.3	4.2
2002	4.2	4.2	4.3	4.3	4.3	4.2	4.2	4.3	4.4	4.4	4.5	4.5	4.3
2003	4.6	4.7	4.6	4.7	4.7	4.6	4.4	4.5	4.7	4.6	4.7	4.6	4.6
Government													
1990	15.4	15.4	15.4	15.3	15.4	14.4	12.8	13.0	14.2	15.3	15.4	15.3	14.7
1991	15.3	15.4	15.3	15.3	15.6	14.5	13.1	12.9	14.8	15.8	15.8	15.9	14.9
1992	15.9	16.1	15.9	15.9	15.9	14.8	13.3	13.5	15.5	15.9	15.9	15.9	15.3
1993	15.8	16.4	15.9	16.1	16.1	14.8	13.8	13.4	15.2	15.9	15.9	15.9	15.4
1994	14.6	14.8	14.7	14.8	14.9	13.5	12.6	12.3	14.2	15.0	14.9	15.1	14.2
1995	14.6	14.9	14.8	14.5	14.4	13.4	11.9	12.2	13.8	14.6	14.6	14.7	14.0
1996	14.2	14.7	14.7	14.6	14.5	13.3	11.6	11.9	14.5	14.7	14.7	14.6	14.0
1997	14.5	14.9	14.9	15.4	14.4	12.7	12.4	12.7	14.3	15.7	15.6	15.7	14.4
1998	15.4	15.8	15.6	15.8	14.9	14.0	12.8	12.5	14.3	15.6	15.6	15.8	14.8
1999	15.8	16.1	16.1	16.1	15.1	14.2	12.9	12.6	15.5	16.1	16.1	16.1	15.2
2000	16.0	16.6	16.5	16.5	15.7	14.8	13.1	13.2	15.6	16.2	16.2	16.3	15.5
2001	16.0	16.5	16.3	16.4	15.3	14.5	12.9	13.1	15.8	16.4	16.2	16.3	15.4
2002	16.2	16.4	16.2	16.6	16.0	14.2	13.1	13.4	16.1	16.6	16.5	16.6	15.7
2003	16.0	16.5	16.4	16.6	16.0	14.6	13.5	14.0	16.6	16.9	16.9	16.8	15.9
Federal government													
1990	2.3	2.3	2.4	2.4	2.4	2.4	2.4	2.3	2.3	2.2	2.3	2.3	2.3
1991	2.3	2.2	2.2	2.3	2.3	2.3	2.3	2.3	2.3	2.3	2.3	2.4	2.2
1992	2.3	2.3	2.3	2.3	2.3	2.3	2.3	2.4	2.3	2.3	2.3	2.3	2.3
1993	2.2	2.2	2.2	2.3	2.3	2.3	2.3	2.3	2.3	2.3	2.3	2.3	2.2
1994	2.3	2.3	2.3	2.3	2.3	2.3	2.3	2.3	2.3	2.3	2.2	2.3	2.2
1995	2.2	2.2	2.2	2.2	2.2	2.2	2.2	2.2	2.2	2.2	2.2	2.2	2.2
1996	2.2	2.2	2.2	2.1	2.1	2.1	2.2	2.2	2.2	2.2	2.2	2.2	2.1
1997	2.2	2.2	2.2	2.1	2.2	2.2	2.2	2.2	2.2	2.2	2.1	2.2	2.1
1998	2.1	2.1	2.1	2.2	2.2	2.2	2.2	2.2	2.2	2.2	2.2	2.2	2.1
1999	2.2	2.2	2.2	2.2	2.2	2.2	2.2	2.2	2.2	2.2	2.2	2.3	2.2
2000	2.3	2.4	2.4	2.5	2.6	2.5	2.4	2.4	2.2	2.2	2.2	2.3	2.3
2001	2.3	2.3	2.3	2.3	2.3	2.3	2.3	2.3	2.3	2.3	2.2	2.2	2.2
2002	2.2	2.2	2.2	2.3	2.3	2.3	2.3	2.3	2.3	2.3	2.3	2.3	2.3
2003	2.2	2.2	2.2	2.3	2.3	2.3	2.3	2.3	2.3	2.3	2.3	2.3	2.3
State government													
1990	6.3	6.3	6.3	6.2	6.3	5.4	4.6	5.1	5.7	6.4	6.4	6.3	5.9
1991	6.3	6.4	6.3	6.3	6.4	5.5	4.9	4.8	6.1	6.6	6.6	6.5	6.0
1992	6.6	6.7	6.6	6.5	6.5	5.6	5.0	5.2	6.4	6.7	6.7	6.5	6.2
1993	6.5	6.9	6.5	6.7	6.6	5.5	5.3	5.1	6.3	6.5	6.5	6.4	6.2
1994	5.2	5.3	5.2	5.3	5.3	4.1	4.0	3.9	5.1	5.4	5.4	5.3	4.9
1995	5.1	5.3	5.2	5.2	5.0	4.1	3.5	3.9	4.8	5.3	5.2	5.2	4.8
1996	4.8	5.2	5.2	5.2	5.0	4.0	3.9	4.0	4.9	5.3	5.3	5.1	4.8
1997	5.1	5.3	5.3	6.0	4.8	4.7	4.5	4.6	5.8	6.1	6.0	5.9	5.3
1998	5.8	6.0	6.0	6.0	5.0	4.6	4.9	4.6	5.7	6.0	6.0	6.0	5.5
1999	5.9	6.0	6.0	6.1	5.0	4.6	4.8	4.5	5.8	6.1	6.1	5.9	5.5
2000	5.8	6.2	6.2	6.1	5.1	4.6	4.7	4.5	5.9	6.2	6.2	6.1	5.6
2001	5.8	6.1	6.0	6.2	5.3	4.4	4.6	4.6	5.9	6.2	6.2	6.2	5.6
2002	6.1	6.2	6.1	6.3	5.4	4.5	4.7	4.7	6.1	6.4	6.3	6.3	5.8
2003	6.0	6.2	6.1	6.3	5.5	4.7	4.9	5.1	6.5	6.7	6.7	6.5	5.9

Employment by Industry: North Dakota—*Continued*

(Numbers in thousands. Not seasonally adjusted.)

Industry	January	February	March	April	May	June	July	August	September	October	November	December	Annual Average
FARGO-MOORHEAD *—Continued*													
Local government													
1990	6.8	6.8	6.7	6.7	6.7	6.6	5.8	5.6	6.2	6.7	6.7	6.7	6.5
1991	6.7	6.8	6.8	6.7	6.9	6.7	5.9	5.8	6.4	6.9	6.9	7.0	6.6
1992	7.0	7.1	7.0	7.1	7.1	6.9	6.0	5.9	6.8	6.9	6.9	7.1	6.8
1993	7.1	7.3	7.2	7.1	7.2	7.0	6.2	6.0	6.6	7.1	7.1	7.2	6.9
1994	7.1	7.2	7.2	7.2	7.3	7.1	6.3	6.1	6.8	7.3	7.3	7.5	7.0
1995	7.3	7.4	7.4	7.1	7.2	7.1	6.2	6.1	6.8	7.1	7.2	7.3	7.0
1996	7.2	7.3	7.3	7.3	7.4	7.2	5.5	5.7	7.4	7.2	7.2	7.3	7.0
1997	7.2	7.4	7.4	7.3	7.4	5.8	5.7	5.9	6.3	7.4	7.5	7.6	6.9
1998	7.5	7.7	7.5	7.6	7.7	7.2	5.7	5.7	6.4	7.4	7.4	7.6	7.1
1999	7.7	7.9	7.9	7.8	7.9	7.4	5.9	5.9	7.5	7.8	7.8	7.9	7.4
2000	7.9	8.0	7.9	7.9	8.0	7.7	6.0	6.3	7.5	7.8	7.8	7.9	7.5
2001	7.9	8.1	8.0	7.9	7.7	7.8	6.0	6.2	7.6	7.9	7.8	7.9	7.5
2002	7.9	8.0	7.9	8.0	8.3	7.4	6.1	6.4	7.7	7.9	7.9	8.0	7.6
2003	7.8	8.1	8.1	8.0	8.2	7.6	6.3	6.6	7.8	7.9	7.9	8.0	7.7
GRAND FORKS													
Total nonfarm													
1990	40.5	40.9	41.1	40.9	41.5	40.8	40.6	40.2	41.6	43.3	42.7	42.9	41.4
1991	41.0	41.8	41.8	42.0	42.5	41.8	41.4	41.3	43.4	44.2	43.5	43.8	42.3
1992	42.1	42.7	42.6	43.3	42.8	43.0	42.7	42.3	43.6	45.4	45.3	45.5	43.4
1993	43.9	44.0	44.0	44.7	45.3	44.4	44.2	43.2	45.8	46.1	46.9	46.4	44.9
1994	44.6	45.2	45.4	46.0	46.8	46.1	45.8	45.8	47.7	48.3	48.5	47.7	46.4
1995	46.3	46.6	47.1	47.3	47.9	47.1	46.9	46.5	47.9	49.2	49.7	48.8	47.6
1996	47.2	47.8	47.9	48.2	48.5	47.8	47.3	47.3	48.6	49.9	49.1	48.9	48.2
1997	46.2	47.2	47.1	47.5	44.7	46.3	46.5	46.5	48.6	49.4	49.4	49.1	47.3
1998	47.4	47.6	48.0	48.6	48.7	47.8	47.3	47.1	48.7	49.0	49.3	48.6	48.1
1999	47.1	47.6	47.8	48.0	47.8	47.9	47.2	47.7	49.5	50.2	50.3	50.1	48.4
2000	47.8	48.6	48.8	48.7	49.4	48.6	47.2	47.7	49.3	49.8	49.5	49.6	48.7
2001	48.2	49.5	49.6	49.5	49.5	48.7	46.3	47.0	49.4	50.9	50.4	50.2	49.1
2002	48.6	48.7	48.6	49.3	48.7	48.0	46.5	47.0	49.6	50.8	51.5	51.1	49.0
2003	48.9	49.1	49.2	50.0	49.8	48.6	47.5	48.3	50.4	51.3	52.4	51.9	49.8
Total private													
1990	28.4	28.4	28.5	28.5	29.0	29.7	30.0	29.6	30.4	30.8	30.0	30.2	29.4
1991	28.9	29.2	29.1	29.5	29.8	30.5	30.6	30.7	31.3	31.7	30.9	31.0	30.2
1992	30.1	30.1	30.1	30.8	31.1	32.0	32.1	31.7	32.3	32.6	32.1	32.5	31.4
1993	31.1	31.1	31.2	32.0	32.6	33.0	33.2	32.6	33.3	33.4	34.1	33.4	32.5
1994	32.0	32.1	32.5	33.2	33.9	34.5	34.6	34.5	35.0	35.3	35.1	34.5	33.9
1995	33.8	33.7	34.1	34.5	35.6	36.1	36.2	35.6	36.3	36.8	37.0	36.1	35.4
1996	35.2	35.3	35.5	35.9	36.5	36.9	36.7	36.5	36.6	37.3	36.5	36.1	36.2
1997	34.5	34.6	34.6	34.9	32.4	34.9	35.1	35.0	35.5	36.6	36.3	35.9	35.0
1998	34.7	34.8	35.1	35.7	36.3	36.5	36.3	36.0	36.2	36.1	36.1	35.6	35.7
1999	34.7	34.6	35.1	35.6	36.1	36.6	36.5	36.5	37.1	37.1	37.0	36.8	36.1
2000	35.0	35.3	35.6	35.7	36.8	37.0	36.5	36.4	36.9	36.8	36.4	36.4	36.2
2001	35.5	36.4	36.5	36.3	37.1	36.9	36.4	36.5	36.9	37.8	37.1	36.8	36.6
2002	35.7	35.5	35.4	36.0	36.3	36.6	36.5	36.5	36.9	37.6	37.7	37.3	36.5
2003	35.8	35.8	35.9	36.3	36.9	36.7	36.9	37.3	37.5	37.7	38.4	37.9	36.9
Goods-producing													
1990	3.5	3.4	3.5	3.2	3.5	3.8	3.9	3.8	4.2	4.6	4.0	3.9	3.7
1991	3.5	3.5	3.6	3.4	3.7	4.0	4.0	4.1	4.5	4.7	4.1	3.9	3.9
1992	3.7	3.7	3.7	3.9	4.0	4.2	4.3	4.4	4.7	5.0	4.5	4.4	4.2
1993	4.0	4.0	4.0	4.2	4.3	4.6	4.7	4.6	5.2	5.1	5.4	4.6	4.5
1994	4.2	4.3	4.4	4.6	4.8	5.0	5.0	5.3	5.7	6.0	5.8	5.1	5.0
1995	4.9	4.9	5.0	5.1	5.5	5.6	5.6	5.6	5.9	6.3	6.3	5.4	5.5
1996	5.2	5.1	5.2	5.3	5.8	5.7	5.5	5.8	6.0	6.7	5.8	5.4	5.6
1997	5.1	5.2	5.1	5.4	5.7	6.3	6.3	6.3	6.4	7.0	6.4	6.0	5.9
1998	5.7	5.6	5.8	6.1	6.5	6.7	6.5	6.5	6.6	6.6	6.0	5.6	6.1
1999	5.5	5.6	5.7	6.0	6.5	6.9	6.8	6.9	7.0	7.2	6.9	6.5	6.4
2000	6.1	5.9	6.1	6.2	6.8	7.1	6.8	6.9	6.9	6.6	6.3	6.1	6.4
2001	5.8	5.7	5.8	5.9	6.3	6.5	6.5	6.7	6.7	6.6	6.3	5.9	6.2
2002	5.7	5.5	5.5	5.5	5.8	6.0	6.0	6.0	5.9	6.2	6.0	5.8	5.8
2003	5.3	5.2	5.2	5.3	5.9	6.0	6.3	6.2	6.2	6.2	6.2	5.8	5.8
Construction and mining													
1990	1.1	1.0	1.0	1.1	1.4	1.7	1.8	1.9	1.7	1.6	1.4	1.3	1.4
1991	1.0	0.9	1.0	1.2	1.4	1.7	1.8	1.9	1.7	1.7	1.5	1.3	1.4
1992	1.1	1.1	1.1	1.3	1.7	1.9	2.0	2.1	1.9	1.8	1.7	1.5	1.6
1993	1.2	1.2	1.2	1.4	1.8	2.1	2.2	2.2	2.2	2.1	2.0	1.7	1.7
1994	1.4	1.4	1.5	1.7	2.1	2.4	2.6	2.5	2.4	2.3	2.2	1.9	2.0
1995	1.6	1.6	1.7	1.8	2.2	2.6	2.7	2.7	2.5	2.4	2.3	1.9	2.1
1996	1.8	1.7	1.8	1.9	2.3	2.6	2.7	2.7	2.6	2.7	2.4	2.0	2.2
1997	1.7	1.7	1.7	2.0	2.6	3.2	3.3	3.3	3.1	3.0	2.8	2.7	2.5
1998	2.4	2.3	2.4	2.7	3.1	3.4	3.5	3.5	3.2	3.1	2.9	2.6	2.9
1999	2.2	2.2	2.2	2.5	2.9	3.3	3.5	3.5	3.3	3.3	3.2	2.8	2.9
2000	2.5	2.3	2.4	2.6	3.0	3.2	3.1	3.1	2.8	2.7	2.4	2.3	2.7
2001	2.2	2.1	2.2	2.3	2.6	3.0	3.1	3.2	3.0	2.8	2.7	2.4	2.6
2002	2.2	2.1	2.1	2.1	2.5	2.7	2.8	2.8	2.7	2.7	2.6	2.4	2.5
2003	2.1	2.0	2.0	2.1	2.6	2.8	3.0	3.0	2.9	2.9	2.8	2.5	2.6

Employment by Industry: North Dakota—*Continued*

(Numbers in thousands. Not seasonally adjusted.)

Industry	January	February	March	April	May	June	July	August	September	October	November	December	Annual Average
GRAND FORKS—*Continued*													
Manufacturing													
1990	2.4	2.4	2.5	2.1	2.1	2.1	2.1	1.9	2.5	3.0	2.6	2.6	2.3
1991	2.5	2.6	2.6	2.2	2.3	2.3	2.2	2.2	2.8	3.0	2.6	2.6	2.4
1992	2.6	2.6	2.6	2.6	2.3	2.3	2.3	2.3	2.8	3.2	2.8	2.9	2.6
1993	2.8	2.8	2.8	2.8	2.5	2.5	2.5	2.4	3.0	3.0	3.4	2.9	2.7
1994	2.8	2.9	2.9	2.9	2.7	2.6	2.4	2.8	3.3	3.7	3.6	3.2	2.9
1995	3.3	3.3	3.3	3.3	3.3	3.0	2.9	2.9	3.4	3.9	4.0	3.5	3.3
1996	3.4	3.4	3.4	3.4	3.5	3.1	2.8	3.1	3.4	4.0	3.4	3.4	3.3
1997	3.4	3.5	3.4	3.4	3.1	3.1	3.0	3.0	3.3	4.0	3.6	3.3	3.3
1998	3.3	3.3	3.4	3.4	3.4	3.3	3.0	3.0	3.4	3.5	3.1	3.0	3.2
1999	3.3	3.4	3.5	3.5	3.6	3.6	3.3	3.4	3.7	3.9	3.7	3.7	3.5
2000	3.6	3.6	3.7	3.6	3.8	3.9	3.7	3.8	4.1	3.9	3.9	3.8	3.7
2001	3.6	3.6	3.6	3.6	3.7	3.5	3.4	3.5	3.7	3.8	3.6	3.5	3.5
2002	3.5	3.4	3.4	3.4	3.3	3.3	3.2	3.2	3.2	3.5	3.4	3.4	3.4
2003	3.2	3.2	3.2	3.2	3.3	3.2	3.3	3.2	3.3	3.3	3.4	3.3	3.3
Service-providing													
1990	37.0	37.5	37.6	37.7	38.0	37.0	36.7	36.4	37.4	38.7	38.7	39.0	37.6
1991	37.5	38.3	38.2	38.6	38.8	37.8	37.4	37.2	38.9	39.5	39.4	39.9	38.4
1992	38.4	39.0	38.9	39.4	38.8	38.8	38.4	37.9	38.9	40.4	40.8	41.1	39.2
1993	39.9	40.0	40.0	40.5	41.0	39.8	39.5	38.6	40.6	41.0	41.5	41.8	40.3
1994	40.4	40.9	41.0	41.4	42.0	41.1	40.8	40.5	42.0	42.3	42.7	42.6	41.4
1995	41.4	41.7	42.1	42.2	42.4	41.5	41.3	40.9	42.0	42.9	43.4	43.4	42.1
1996	42.0	42.7	42.7	42.9	42.7	42.1	41.8	41.5	42.6	43.2	43.3	43.5	42.5
1997	41.1	42.0	42.0	42.1	39.0	40.0	40.2	40.2	42.2	42.4	43.0	43.1	41.4
1998	41.7	42.0	42.2	42.5	42.2	41.1	40.8	40.6	42.1	42.4	43.3	43.0	41.9
1999	41.6	42.0	42.1	42.0	41.3	41.0	40.4	40.8	42.5	43.0	43.4	43.6	41.9
2000	41.7	42.7	42.7	42.5	42.6	41.5	40.4	40.8	42.4	43.2	43.2	43.5	42.2
2001	42.4	43.8	43.8	43.6	43.2	42.2	39.8	40.3	42.7	44.3	44.1	44.3	42.8
2002	42.9	43.2	43.1	43.8	42.9	42.0	40.5	41.0	43.7	44.6	45.5	45.3	43.2
2003	43.6	43.9	44.0	44.7	43.9	42.6	41.2	42.1	44.2	45.1	46.2	46.1	44.0
Trade, transportation, and utilities													
1990	9.5	9.4	9.4	9.4	9.5	9.6	9.6	9.7	9.7	9.9	10.0	10.2	9.6
1991	9.7	9.7	9.5	9.8	9.7	9.7	9.7	9.8	9.9	10.0	10.1	10.3	9.8
1992	9.8	9.6	9.6	9.7	9.8	9.9	9.9	9.7	9.9	10.0	10.2	10.3	9.8
1993	9.8	9.7	9.7	9.9	10.1	9.9	10.0	10.0	10.0	10.2	10.6	10.6	10.0
1994	10.1	10.0	10.1	10.1	10.2	10.2	10.2	10.3	10.3	10.6	10.7	10.7	10.2
1995	10.4	10.2	10.3	10.2	10.3	10.3	10.3	10.2	10.5	10.6	10.8	10.9	10.4
1996	10.4	10.4	10.3	10.4	10.4	10.4	10.2	10.2	10.3	10.5	10.8	10.9	10.4
1997	10.2	9.9	10.0	10.1	9.5	9.8	9.9	10.0	10.1	10.5	10.7	10.9	10.1
1998	10.3	10.2	10.2	10.3	10.4	10.4	10.3	10.2	10.4	10.2	10.6	10.6	10.3
1999	10.1	9.8	10.0	10.2	10.1	10.1	9.9	9.9	10.2	10.4	10.6	10.9	10.1
2000	10.1	10.2	10.2	10.2	10.4	10.3	10.1	10.2	10.5	10.7	10.8	10.9	10.3
2001	10.8	11.0	10.9	10.9	11.0	10.7	10.7	10.6	10.6	11.2	11.4	11.4	10.9
2002	10.8	10.6	10.6	10.7	10.7	10.6	10.5	10.6	10.6	10.9	11.2	11.3	10.8
2003	10.7	10.6	10.5	10.7	10.8	10.7	10.6	10.7	10.8	10.9	11.2	11.3	10.8
Wholesale trade													
1990	2.0	2.0	2.0	2.0	2.1	2.1	2.1	2.1	2.1	2.1	2.0	2.0	2.0
1991	2.0	2.0	2.0	2.1	2.1	2.1	1.9	1.9	1.9	1.9	1.9	1.9	1.9
1992	1.9	1.8	1.9	1.9	2.0	2.0	2.0	1.9	1.9	1.9	1.9	1.9	1.9
1993	1.9	1.9	1.9	2.0	2.1	2.0	2.0	2.0	1.9	1.9	2.0	2.0	1.9
1994	1.9	1.9	1.9	2.0	2.1	2.1	2.0	2.1	2.0	2.1	2.1	2.0	2.0
1995	2.0	2.0	2.0	2.1	2.1	2.2	2.1	2.1	2.1	2.1	2.1	2.1	2.0
1996	2.0	2.1	2.1	2.1	2.2	2.3	2.1	2.1	2.1	2.1	2.1	2.1	2.1
1997	2.0	2.0	2.1	2.1	2.2	2.2	2.1	2.1	2.1	2.1	2.1	2.1	2.1
1998	2.0	2.0	2.0	2.0	2.1	2.1	2.0	2.0	2.0	2.0	2.1	2.0	2.0
1999	2.0	1.9	2.0	2.1	2.1	2.1	2.0	2.0	2.0	2.0	2.0	2.0	2.0
2000	1.9	1.9	2.0	2.0	2.1	2.0	1.9	1.9	2.0	2.0	1.9	1.9	1.9
2001	1.9	2.0	2.0	2.0	2.1	2.1	2.1	2.0	2.0	2.1	2.1	2.0	2.0
2002	1.9	1.9	1.9	2.0	2.0	2.1	2.0	2.0	2.0	2.0	2.0	2.0	2.0
2003	1.9	1.9	1.9	2.0	2.0	2.0	2.0	2.0	2.0	2.0	2.0	2.0	2.0
Retail trade													
1990	6.0	5.9	5.9	6.0	6.1	6.1	6.1	6.2	6.2	6.2	6.4	6.6	6.1
1991	6.2	6.2	6.1	6.3	6.3	6.3	6.4	6.5	6.4	6.4	6.5	6.7	6.3
1992	6.3	6.2	6.1	6.2	6.3	6.3	6.3	6.3	6.3	6.4	6.6	6.7	6.3
1993	6.3	6.2	6.2	6.3	6.4	6.3	6.4	6.4	6.4	6.4	6.7	6.7	6.3
1994	6.4	6.3	6.3	6.4	6.4	6.4	6.5	6.5	6.5	6.7	6.9	7.0	6.5
1995	6.7	6.5	6.6	6.5	6.6	6.6	6.7	6.6	6.7	6.8	7.0	7.1	6.7
1996	6.7	6.6	6.6	6.7	6.7	6.7	6.7	6.7	6.7	6.9	7.2	7.3	6.7
1997	6.8	6.6	6.6	6.6	5.9	6.3	6.5	6.6	6.6	6.9	7.1	7.3	6.6
1998	6.8	6.7	6.7	6.7	6.8	6.8	6.8	6.7	6.8	6.7	7.0	7.1	6.8
1999	6.8	6.6	6.7	6.7	6.7	6.7	6.7	6.7	6.8	7.0	7.2	7.5	6.8
2000	6.9	7.0	6.9	6.9	7.0	7.0	7.0	7.1	7.1	7.3	7.5	7.6	7.1
2001	7.3	7.4	7.3	7.3	7.3	7.1	7.1	7.1	7.1	7.4	7.6	7.7	7.3
2002	7.3	7.1	7.1	7.2	7.2	7.0	7.0	7.1	7.1	7.2	7.5	7.6	7.2
2003	7.1	7.0	7.0	7.0	7.1	7.1	7.0	7.1	7.2	7.3	7.6	7.7	7.2

Employment by Industry: North Dakota—*Continued*

(Numbers in thousands. Not seasonally adjusted.)

Industry	January	February	March	April	May	June	July	August	September	October	November	December	Annual Average
GRAND FORKS—*Continued*													
Transportation and utilities													
1990	1.5	1.5	1.5	1.4	1.3	1.4	1.4	1.4	1.4	1.6	1.6	1.6	1.4
1991	1.5	1.5	1.4	1.4	1.3	1.3	1.4	1.4	1.6	1.7	1.7	1.7	1.4
1992	1.6	1.6	1.6	1.6	1.5	1.6	1.6	1.5	1.7	1.7	1.7	1.7	1.6
1993	1.6	1.6	1.6	1.6	1.6	1.6	1.6	1.6	1.7	1.9	1.9	1.9	1.6
1994	1.8	1.8	1.9	1.7	1.7	1.7	1.7	1.7	1.8	1.8	1.7	1.7	1.7
1995	1.7	1.7	1.7	1.6	1.6	1.5	1.5	1.5	1.7	1.7	1.7	1.7	1.6
1996	1.7	1.7	1.6	1.6	1.5	1.4	1.4	1.4	1.5	1.5	1.5	1.5	1.5
1997	1.4	1.3	1.3	1.4	1.4	1.3	1.3	1.3	1.4	1.5	1.5	1.5	1.3
1998	1.5	1.5	1.5	1.6	1.5	1.5	1.5	1.5	1.6	1.5	1.5	1.5	1.5
1999	1.3	1.3	1.3	1.4	1.3	1.3	1.2	1.2	1.4	1.4	1.4	1.4	1.3
2000	1.3	1.3	1.3	1.3	1.3	1.3	1.2	1.2	1.4	1.4	1.4	1.4	1.3
2001	1.6	1.6	1.6	1.6	1.6	1.5	1.5	1.5	1.5	1.7	1.7	1.7	1.5
2002	1.6	1.6	1.6	1.5	1.5	1.5	1.5	1.5	1.5	1.7	1.7	1.7	1.6
2003	1.7	1.7	1.6	1.7	1.7	1.6	1.6	1.6	1.6	1.6	1.6	1.6	1.6
Information													
1990	0.9	0.9	0.8	0.8	0.8	0.9	0.8	0.8	0.8	0.8	0.8	0.8	0.8
1991	0.8	0.8	0.8	0.8	0.8	0.8	0.8	0.8	0.8	0.8	0.8	0.8	0.8
1992	0.8	0.8	0.8	0.8	0.8	0.8	0.8	0.8	0.8	0.8	0.8	0.9	0.8
1993	0.8	0.8	0.8	0.8	0.8	0.8	0.8	0.8	0.8	0.8	0.8	0.8	0.8
1994	0.8	0.8	0.8	0.8	0.9	0.9	0.9	0.9	0.9	0.9	0.9	0.9	0.8
1995	0.8	0.8	0.8	0.9	0.9	0.9	0.9	0.9	0.9	0.9	0.9	0.9	0.8
1996	0.8	0.8	0.8	0.8	0.8	0.8	0.8	0.8	0.8	0.8	0.8	0.8	0.8
1997	0.8	0.8	0.8	0.8	0.7	0.8	0.8	0.8	0.8	0.8	0.8	0.8	0.7
1998	0.8	0.8	0.8	0.8	0.8	0.8	0.8	0.8	0.8	0.8	0.8	0.8	0.8
1999	0.8	0.8	0.8	0.8	0.8	0.8	0.8	0.8	0.8	0.8	0.8	0.8	0.8
2000	0.8	0.8	0.8	0.8	0.8	0.8	0.8	0.7	0.7	0.7	0.7	0.7	0.7
2001	0.8	0.8	0.8	0.8	0.8	0.8	0.8	0.8	0.8	0.8	0.7	0.7	0.7
2002	0.7	0.7	0.7	0.7	0.7	0.7	0.7	0.7	0.7	0.7	0.7	0.7	0.7
2003	0.7	0.7	0.7	0.7	0.7	0.7	0.7	0.7	0.7	0.7	0.7	0.7	0.7
Financial activities													
1990	1.6	1.6	1.6	1.6	1.6	1.6	1.6	1.6	1.6	1.6	1.6	1.6	1.6
1991	1.6	1.6	1.6	1.6	1.6	1.6	1.6	1.6	1.6	1.6	1.6	1.7	1.6
1992	1.6	1.6	1.6	1.7	1.7	1.7	1.7	1.7	1.7	1.7	1.7	1.7	1.6
1993	1.7	1.7	1.7	1.7	1.7	1.7	1.7	1.7	1.7	1.7	1.7	1.7	1.7
1994	1.7	1.7	1.7	1.7	1.8	1.8	1.8	1.8	1.8	1.7	1.7	1.8	1.7
1995	1.7	1.7	1.7	1.7	1.7	1.7	1.7	1.6	1.6	1.7	1.7	1.7	1.6
1996	1.7	1.7	1.7	1.7	1.7	1.7	1.7	1.8	1.7	1.8	1.8	1.8	1.7
1997	1.7	1.7	1.7	1.7	1.7	1.8	1.7	1.7	1.7	1.7	1.7	1.7	1.7
1998	1.6	1.6	1.6	1.6	1.6	1.6	1.6	1.6	1.6	1.6	1.6	1.6	1.6
1999	1.6	1.5	1.6	1.6	1.6	1.6	1.6	1.6	1.6	1.6	1.6	1.6	1.5
2000	1.6	1.6	1.6	1.5	1.6	1.6	1.6	1.5	1.5	1.6	1.6	1.6	1.5
2001	1.6	1.6	1.6	1.6	1.6	1.6	1.6	1.6	1.6	1.6	1.5	1.5	1.5
2002	1.5	1.5	1.5	1.6	1.6	1.6	1.6	1.6	1.6	1.6	1.6	1.6	1.6
2003	1.6	1.6	1.6	1.6	1.6	1.6	1.6	1.6	1.6	1.6	1.6	1.6	1.6
Professional and business services													
1990	1.6	1.6	1.6	1.7	1.7	1.7	1.8	1.8	1.9	1.8	1.7	1.7	1.7
1991	1.7	1.7	1.7	1.8	1.8	1.8	1.8	1.8	1.9	1.9	1.8	1.8	1.7
1992	1.8	1.8	1.8	1.8	1.9	1.9	1.9	1.9	2.0	1.9	1.8	1.9	1.8
1993	1.8	1.8	1.8	1.9	2.0	2.0	2.0	1.9	2.0	2.0	1.9	1.9	1.9
1994	1.8	1.8	1.9	2.0	2.0	2.0	2.1	2.1	2.1	2.1	2.0	2.0	1.9
1995	2.0	2.1	2.1	2.2	2.4	2.4	2.4	2.4	2.4	2.4	2.4	2.4	2.3
1996	2.5	2.5	2.6	2.6	2.5	2.6	2.7	2.6	2.6	2.6	2.5	2.4	2.5
1997	2.4	2.5	2.5	2.4	2.3	2.5	2.5	2.5	2.5	2.5	2.5	2.6	2.4
1998	2.5	2.5	2.5	2.5	2.5	2.6	2.6	2.5	2.4	2.5	2.5	2.6	2.5
1999	2.6	2.6	2.5	2.6	2.6	2.7	2.9	2.8	2.8	2.6	2.6	2.5	2.6
2000	2.3	2.4	2.4	2.4	2.5	2.5	2.6	2.6	2.5	2.5	2.4	2.5	2.4
2001	2.4	3.1	3.0	2.6	2.6	2.7	2.5	2.6	2.7	2.8	2.6	2.6	2.6
2002	2.4	2.5	2.5	2.6	2.5	2.5	2.8	2.7	2.9	3.0	2.9	2.7	2.7
2003	2.6	2.6	2.7	2.8	2.5	2.6	2.7	2.9	2.8	2.9	3.1	2.9	2.8
Educational and health services													
1990	5.2	5.3	5.3	5.3	5.3	5.3	5.4	5.3	5.4	5.4	5.3	5.3	5.3
1991	5.3	5.4	5.3	5.4	5.4	5.4	5.5	5.5	5.5	5.6	5.6	5.6	5.4
1992	5.7	5.8	5.8	5.8	5.8	6.0	6.1	5.9	5.9	6.0	6.0	6.1	5.9
1993	6.0	6.0	6.1	6.1	6.1	6.3	6.3	6.1	6.1	6.2	6.3	6.3	6.1
1994	6.3	6.4	6.4	6.5	6.5	6.6	6.7	6.4	6.5	6.5	6.5	6.5	6.4
1995	6.5	6.5	6.6	6.6	6.7	7.0	7.2	7.2	7.0	7.0	7.0	7.0	6.8
1996	6.9	7.0	7.0	7.0	7.1	7.2	7.2	7.2	7.0	7.3	7.3	7.3	7.1
1997	7.2	7.3	7.3	7.1	6.7	7.2	7.2	6.9	6.9	7.0	7.2	7.0	7.0
1998	7.0	7.1	7.2	7.3	7.3	7.3	7.4	7.3	7.2	7.3	7.5	7.4	7.2
1999	7.3	7.4	7.5	7.3	7.2	7.4	7.3	7.2	7.2	7.2	7.3	7.3	7.3
2000	7.3	7.4	7.5	7.4	7.5	7.7	7.5	7.4	7.5	7.5	7.5	7.5	7.4
2001	7.4	7.4	7.4	7.4	7.5	7.6	7.6	7.5	7.5	7.6	7.6	7.7	7.5
2002	7.7	7.7	7.7	7.7	7.7	7.9	7.9	7.9	8.0	8.0	8.0	8.0	7.9
2003	8.0	8.0	8.1	8.1	8.1	8.1	8.1	8.1	8.1	8.0	8.0	8.0	8.1

Employment by Industry: North Dakota—*Continued*

(Numbers in thousands. Not seasonally adjusted.)

Industry	January	February	March	April	May	June	July	August	September	October	November	December	Annual Average
GRAND FORKS—*Continued*													
Leisure and hospitality													
1990	4.3	4.4	4.4	4.6	4.7	4.6	4.7	4.8	4.9	4.8	4.7	4.8	4.6
1991	4.4	4.5	4.6	4.7	4.9	4.8	4.8	4.9	4.9	4.9	4.8	4.8	4.7
1992	4.6	4.7	4.7	4.9	5.0	4.9	4.8	4.9	5.0	5.0	4.9	5.0	4.8
1993	4.8	4.9	4.9	5.1	5.2	5.1	5.0	5.0	5.1	5.0	5.0	5.1	5.0
1994	4.8	4.8	4.9	5.1	5.2	5.2	5.1	5.2	5.3	5.1	5.1	5.1	5.0
1995	5.1	5.1	5.2	5.3	5.5	5.3	5.3	5.3	5.5	5.4	5.4	5.4	5.3
1996	5.3	5.4	5.5	5.7	5.8	5.7	5.6	5.7	5.7	5.4	5.3	5.3	5.5
1997	5.0	5.1	5.1	5.2	4.0	4.6	4.8	4.9	5.1	5.0	4.9	4.8	4.8
1998	4.7	4.9	4.9	5.0	5.1	5.0	5.0	5.0	5.1	4.9	4.9	4.8	4.9
1999	4.6	4.7	4.7	4.9	5.1	4.9	4.9	5.0	5.1	5.1	5.0	5.0	4.9
2000	4.7	4.8	4.8	5.0	5.1	4.9	5.0	5.0	5.1	5.0	4.9	4.9	4.9
2001	4.7	4.8	5.0	5.2	5.3	5.1	4.9	4.9	5.1	5.3	5.1	5.1	5.0
2002	5.0	5.1	5.0	5.3	5.4	5.4	5.1	5.1	5.3	5.3	5.4	5.3	5.2
2003	5.0	5.2	5.2	5.2	5.3	5.1	5.0	5.1	5.3	5.5	5.6	5.6	5.3
Other services													
1990	1.8	1.8	1.9	1.9	1.9	2.2	2.2	1.8	1.9	1.9	1.9	1.9	1.9
1991	1.9	2.0	2.0	2.0	1.9	2.4	2.4	2.2	2.2	2.2	2.1	2.1	2.1
1992	2.1	2.1	2.1	2.2	2.1	2.6	2.6	2.4	2.3	2.2	2.2	2.2	2.2
1993	2.2	2.2	2.2	2.3	2.4	2.6	2.7	2.5	2.4	2.4	2.4	2.4	2.3
1994	2.3	2.3	2.3	2.4	2.5	2.8	2.8	2.5	2.4	2.4	2.4	2.4	2.4
1995	2.4	2.4	2.4	2.5	2.6	2.9	2.8	2.4	2.5	2.5	2.5	2.4	2.5
1996	2.4	2.4	2.4	2.4	2.4	2.8	3.0	2.4	2.5	2.2	2.2	2.2	2.4
1997	2.1	2.1	2.1	2.2	1.8	1.9	1.9	1.9	2.0	2.1	2.1	2.1	2.0
1998	2.1	2.1	2.1	2.1	2.1	2.1	2.1	2.1	2.1	2.2	2.2	2.2	2.1
1999	2.2	2.2	2.3	2.2	2.2	2.2	2.3	2.3	2.4	2.2	2.2	2.2	2.2
2000	2.1	2.2	2.2	2.2	2.1	2.1	2.1	2.1	2.2	2.2	2.2	2.2	2.1
2001	2.0	2.0	2.0	1.9	2.0	1.9	1.8	1.8	1.9	1.9	1.9	1.9	1.9
2002	1.9	1.9	1.9	1.9	1.9	1.9	1.9	1.9	1.9	1.9	1.9	1.9	1.9
2003	1.9	1.9	1.9	1.9	2.0	1.9	1.9	2.0	2.0	1.9	2.0	2.0	1.9
Government													
1990	12.1	12.5	12.6	12.4	12.5	11.1	10.6	10.6	11.2	12.5	12.7	12.7	11.9
1991	12.1	12.6	12.7	12.5	12.7	11.3	10.8	10.6	12.1	12.5	12.6	12.8	12.1
1992	12.0	12.6	12.5	12.5	11.7	11.0	10.6	10.6	11.3	12.8	13.2	13.0	11.9
1993	12.8	12.9	12.8	12.7	12.7	11.4	11.0	10.6	12.5	12.7	12.8	13.0	12.3
1994	12.6	13.1	12.9	12.8	12.9	11.6	11.2	11.3	12.7	13.0	13.4	13.2	12.5
1995	12.5	12.9	13.0	12.8	12.3	11.0	10.7	10.9	11.6	12.4	12.7	12.7	12.1
1996	12.0	12.5	12.4	12.3	12.0	10.9	10.6	10.8	12.0	12.6	12.6	12.8	11.9
1997	11.7	12.6	12.5	12.6	12.3	11.4	11.4	11.5	13.1	12.8	13.1	13.2	12.3
1998	12.7	12.8	12.9	12.9	12.4	11.3	11.0	11.1	12.5	12.9	13.2	13.0	12.3
1999	12.4	13.0	12.7	12.4	11.7	11.3	10.7	11.2	12.4	13.1	13.3	13.3	12.2
2000	12.8	13.3	13.2	13.0	12.6	11.6	10.7	11.3	12.4	13.0	13.1	13.2	12.5
2001	12.7	13.1	13.1	13.2	12.4	11.8	9.9	10.5	12.5	13.1	13.3	13.4	12.4
2002	12.9	13.2	13.2	13.3	12.4	11.4	10.0	10.5	12.7	13.2	13.8	13.8	12.5
2003	13.1	13.3	13.3	13.7	12.9	11.9	10.6	11.0	12.9	13.6	14.0	14.0	12.9
Federal government													
1990	1.7	1.7	1.7	1.7	1.7	1.8	1.7	1.7	1.7	1.7	1.7	1.7	1.7
1991	1.7	1.7	1.7	1.7	1.7	1.7	1.7	1.7	1.7	1.6	1.6	1.7	1.6
1992	1.6	1.6	1.6	1.6	1.6	1.6	1.6	1.6	1.6	1.6	1.6	1.6	1.6
1993	1.6	1.6	1.6	1.6	1.6	1.6	1.6	1.6	1.6	1.6	1.6	1.6	1.6
1994	1.6	1.7	1.6	1.6	1.6	1.6	1.6	1.5	1.6	1.5	1.5	1.5	1.5
1995	1.5	1.5	1.5	1.5	1.5	1.5	1.5	1.5	1.4	1.5	1.5	1.5	1.4
1996	1.5	1.5	1.5	1.4	1.4	1.4	1.4	1.4	1.4	1.4	1.4	1.5	1.4
1997	1.4	1.4	1.4	1.5	1.5	1.6	1.5	1.5	1.5	1.4	1.5	1.5	1.4
1998	1.4	1.4	1.4	1.4	1.4	1.4	1.4	1.4	1.4	1.4	1.4	1.4	1.4
1999	1.4	1.4	1.4	1.4	1.4	1.4	1.4	1.4	1.4	1.4	1.4	1.4	1.4
2000	1.4	1.4	1.4	1.4	1.6	1.5	1.5	1.5	1.4	1.4	1.4	1.4	1.4
2001	1.4	1.4	1.4	1.4	1.4	1.5	1.5	1.4	1.4	1.4	1.4	1.4	1.4
2002	1.4	1.4	1.4	1.4	1.4	1.4	1.5	1.5	1.4	1.4	1.5	1.5	1.4
2003	1.5	1.5	1.5	1.5	1.5	1.5	1.5	1.5	1.5	1.5	1.5	1.5	1.5
State government													
1990	5.9	6.2	6.3	6.2	6.2	4.8	4.9	4.9	5.2	6.3	6.3	6.3	5.7
1991	5.8	6.2	6.3	6.2	6.3	4.9	5.0	4.8	6.1	6.2	6.2	6.2	5.8
1992	5.7	6.1	6.1	6.1	5.2	4.5	4.7	4.7	5.2	6.3	6.4	6.2	5.6
1993	6.2	6.2	6.2	6.2	6.2	4.9	5.0	4.6	6.0	6.1	6.0	6.2	5.8
1994	5.8	6.2	6.1	6.2	6.2	5.0	4.8	5.2	6.1	6.3	6.5	6.3	5.8
1995	5.8	6.1	6.2	6.2	5.6	4.9	4.6	5.0	5.6	6.0	6.1	6.0	5.6
1996	5.4	5.9	5.9	5.9	5.5	4.7	4.6	5.1	5.9	6.1	6.0	6.0	5.5
1997	5.3	6.0	6.0	6.0	5.6	4.9	5.4	5.6	6.5	6.3	6.3	6.3	5.8
1998	6.1	6.2	6.3	6.4	5.7	5.2	4.8	5.1	6.2	6.3	6.4	6.2	5.9
1999	5.7	6.1	5.9	6.0	5.2	4.8	4.5	5.1	6.1	6.5	6.6	6.5	5.7
2000	6.0	6.4	6.3	6.2	5.6	4.8	4.5	5.1	5.9	6.3	6.3	6.3	5.8
2001	5.9	6.2	6.3	6.5	5.6	5.1	4.7	5.2	6.1	6.4	6.5	6.5	5.9
2002	6.2	6.4	6.4	6.6	5.7	5.2	4.8	5.3	6.3	6.5	6.8	6.8	6.1
2003	6.1	6.4	6.4	6.8	6.0	5.5	5.2	5.6	6.3	6.7	7.0	7.0	6.3

Employment by Industry: North Dakota—*Continued*

(Numbers in thousands. Not seasonally adjusted.)

Industry	January	February	March	April	May	June	July	August	September	October	November	December	Annual Average
GRAND FORKS—*Continued*													
Local government													
1990	4.5	4.6	4.6	4.5	4.6	4.5	4.0	4.0	4.3	4.5	4.7	4.7	4.4
1991	4.6	4.7	4.7	4.6	4.7	4.7	4.1	4.1	4.3	4.7	4.8	4.9	4.5
1992	4.7	4.9	4.8	4.8	4.9	4.9	4.3	4.3	4.5	4.9	5.2	5.2	4.7
1993	5.0	5.1	5.0	4.9	4.9	4.9	4.4	4.4	4.9	5.0	5.2	5.2	4.9
1994	5.2	5.2	5.2	5.0	5.1	5.0	4.8	4.6	5.0	5.2	5.4	5.4	5.0
1995	5.2	5.3	5.3	5.1	5.2	4.6	4.6	4.4	4.6	4.9	5.1	5.2	4.9
1996	5.1	5.1	5.0	5.0	5.1	4.8	4.6	4.3	4.7	5.1	5.2	5.3	4.9
1997	5.0	5.2	5.1	5.1	5.2	4.9	4.5	4.4	5.1	5.1	5.3	5.4	5.0
1998	5.2	5.2	5.2	5.1	5.3	4.7	4.8	4.6	4.9	5.2	5.4	5.4	5.0
1999	5.3	5.5	5.4	5.0	5.1	5.1	4.8	4.7	4.9	5.2	5.3	5.4	5.1
2000	5.4	5.5	5.5	5.4	5.4	5.3	4.7	4.7	5.1	5.3	5.4	5.5	5.2
2001	5.4	5.5	5.4	5.3	5.4	5.2	3.7	3.9	5.0	5.3	5.4	5.5	5.0
2002	5.3	5.4	5.4	5.3	5.3	4.8	3.7	3.7	5.0	5.3	5.5	5.5	5.0
2003	5.5	5.4	5.4	5.4	5.4	4.9	3.9	3.9	5.1	5.4	5.5	5.5	5.1

Average Weekly Hours by Industry: North Dakota

(Not seasonally adjusted.)

Industry	January	February	March	April	May	June	July	August	September	October	November	December	Annual Average
STATEWIDE													
Manufacturing													
2001	39.1	40.7	40.5	39.4	41.4	42.3	41.8	41.6	41.1	41.7	40.8	41.0	40.9
2002	39.1	39.3	38.9	39.8	40.5	41.9	39.5	40.8	40.8	41.4	39.5	41.3	40.2
2003	38.0	39.8	40.1	39.7	39.2	40.6	41.3	40.9	39.5	40.5	40.3	40.6	40.0
FARGO-MOORHEAD													
Manufacturing													
2001	39.5	40.1	41.1	40.0	40.8	40.9	41.3	41.8	41.2	41.5	41.9	41.8	40.9
2002	41.3	41.8	42.4	41.4	41.9	41.6	41.0	41.3	41.3	40.8	40.5	39.8	41.3
2003	39.7	39.8	40.0	39.5	39.8	41.5	41.0	39.7	39.9	39.8	39.1	38.6	39.9

Average Hourly Earnings by Industry: North Dakota

(Dollars, not seasonally adjusted.)

Industry	January	February	March	April	May	June	July	August	September	October	November	December	Annual Average
STATEWIDE													
Manufacturing													
2001	12.68	12.42	12.55	12.88	12.69	12.56	12.62	12.81	12.91	13.06	12.96	13.06	12.77
2002	13.36	13.25	13.32	13.43	12.98	12.91	13.19	13.04	13.05	12.90	13.16	13.52	13.17
2003	14.08	13.58	13.59	13.70	14.02	13.80	13.66	14.39	14.46	14.39	14.24	14.53	14.04
FARGO-MOORHEAD													
Manufacturing													
2001	13.68	13.47	13.29	13.53	13.12	13.00	13.01	13.33	13.37	13.59	13.40	13.51	13.36
2002	13.99	13.68	13.78	13.91	13.64	13.44	13.52	13.45	13.33	13.66	13.55	13.36	13.61
2003	13.84	13.43	13.35	13.61	13.30	13.20	13.53	13.93	13.71	13.66	13.84	13.87	13.60

Average Weekly Earnings by Industry: North Dakota

(Dollars, not seasonally adjusted.)

Industry	January	February	March	April	May	June	July	August	September	October	November	December	Annual Average
STATEWIDE													
Manufacturing													
2001	495.79	505.49	508.28	507.47	525.37	531.29	527.52	532.90	530.60	544.60	528.77	535.46	522.29
2002	522.38	520.73	518.15	534.51	525.69	540.93	521.01	532.03	532.44	534.06	519.82	558.38	529.43
2003	535.04	540.48	544.96	543.89	549.58	560.28	564.16	588.55	571.17	582.80	573.87	589.92	561.60
FARGO-MOORHEAD													
Manufacturing													
2001	540.36	540.15	546.22	541.20	535.30	531.70	537.31	557.19	550.84	563.99	561.46	564.72	546.42
2002	577.79	571.82	584.27	575.87	571.52	559.10	554.32	555.49	550.53	557.33	548.78	531.73	562.09
2003	549.45	534.51	534.00	537.60	529.34	547.80	554.73	553.02	547.03	543.67	541.14	535.38	542.64

OHIO AT A GLANCE

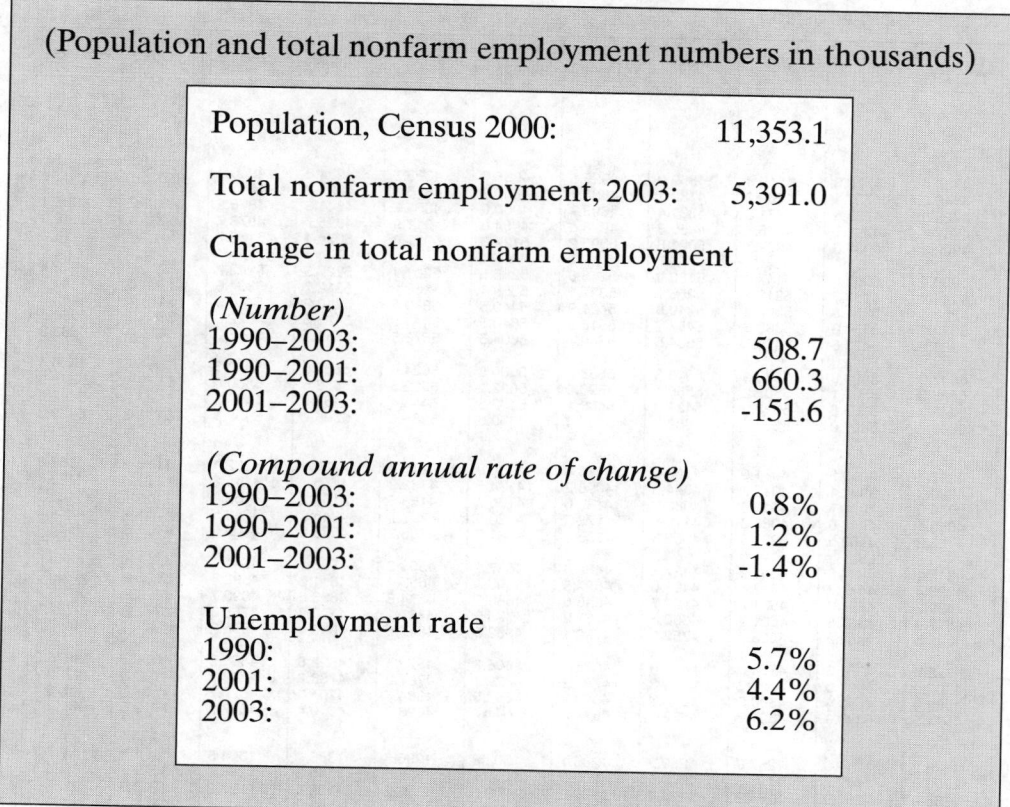

(Population and total nonfarm employment numbers in thousands)

Population, Census 2000:	11,353.1
Total nonfarm employment, 2003:	5,391.0
Change in total nonfarm employment	
(Number)	
1990–2003:	508.7
1990–2001:	660.3
2001–2003:	-151.6
(Compound annual rate of change)	
1990–2003:	0.8%
1990–2001:	1.2%
2001–2003:	-1.4%
Unemployment rate	
1990:	5.7%
2001:	4.4%
2003:	6.2%

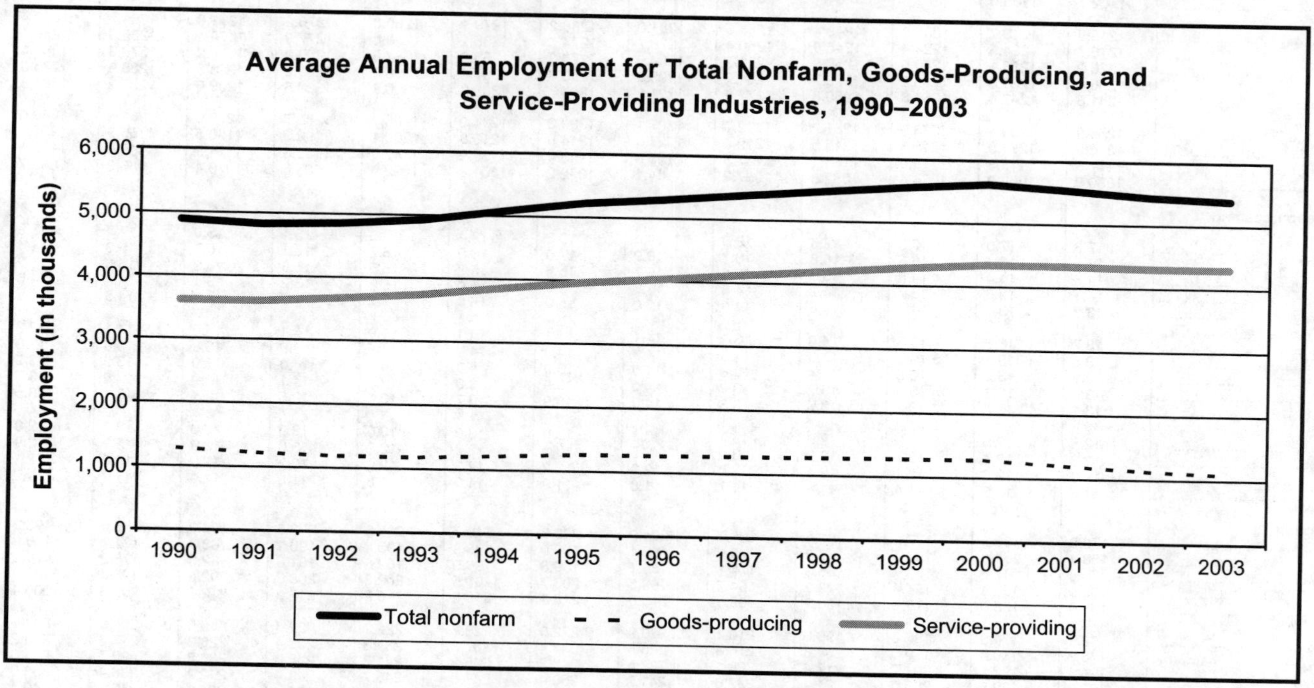

Total nonfarm payroll employment declined in both the 1990–1991 and 2001 recessions. However, the latter contraction had a greater impact on employment in Ohio. The number of jobs in the goods-producing sector continued to decline through 2003, as the recession particularly impacted the manufacturing industry. From 2000 to 2003, employment in manufacturing declined by over 175,000. In the service-providing sector, weakness was evident in the 2001–2003 period, though financial activities, educational and health services, leisure and hospitality, and government all experienced gains in employment over the period.

Employment by Industry: Ohio

(Numbers in thousands. Not seasonally adjusted.)

Industry	January	February	March	April	May	June	July	August	September	October	November	December	Annual Average
STATEWIDE													
Total nonfarm													
1990	4738.4	4770.3	4819.8	4859.0	4925.8	4955.7	4895.7	4904.3	4940.4	4933.5	4926.2	4918.5	4882.3
1991	4745.6	4726.1	4760.7	4782.1	4836.1	4856.7	4816.2	4820.3	4861.5	4867.8	4879.2	4871.1	4818.6
1992	4725.5	4735.6	4771.8	4831.4	4893.7	4900.0	4851.2	4844.6	4876.9	4918.0	4908.1	4915.3	4847.6
1993	4787.1	4798.7	4818.6	4859.3	4928.6	4954.5	4911.9	4925.7	4978.7	5005.6	5019.0	5032.2	4918.3
1994	4902.1	4933.8	4987.7	5021.8	5093.2	5122.8	5057.6	5074.4	5136.7	5170.1	5193.7	5217.9	5075.9
1995	5060.4	5087.5	5147.6	5188.0	5245.6	5286.5	5201.1	5227.9	5283.2	5290.6	5310.5	5324.0	5221.0
1996	5145.4	5183.5	5213.5	5256.7	5327.1	5359.1	5288.2	5312.7	5334.6	5358.6	5381.7	5396.0	5296.4
1997	5233.1	5254.8	5306.2	5349.8	5421.9	5449.5	5389.6	5410.2	5440.0	5465.7	5482.7	5506.4	5392.4
1998	5336.2	5359.6	5398.6	5452.7	5518.9	5540.5	5449.5	5493.6	5522.3	5554.1	5569.6	5589.3	5482.0
1999	5381.9	5433.5	5469.1	5534.5	5580.7	5604.5	5576.5	5581.7	5607.0	5635.0	5663.9	5694.8	5563.5
2000	5503.9	5524.9	5573.4	5610.8	5668.2	5690.3	5624.0	5629.5	5643.3	5661.2	5680.4	5686.0	5624.6
2001	5488.3	5501.1	5532.2	5560.1	5596.3	5612.1	5529.5	5533.5	5530.6	5539.3	5546.9	5541.5	5542.6
2002	5348.7	5363.6	5398.0	5429.2	5480.1	5492.5	5443.4	5456.6	5469.5	5479.1	5492.6	5486.2	5445.0
2003	5309.8	5307.0	5339.4	5389.7	5439.4	5439.6	5385.6	5395.7	5408.1	5424.4	5429.6	5424.2	5391.0
Total private													
1990	4022.6	4040.3	4081.5	4123.9	4175.8	4230.9	4215.7	4237.4	4232.1	4198.6	4183.8	4178.2	4160.0
1991	4020.7	3987.1	4017.7	4044.3	4090.2	4134.5	4132.2	4150.1	4145.3	4123.3	4123.7	4119.2	4090.6
1992	3988.0	3986.7	4019.8	4080.3	4136.6	4166.2	4163.5	4165.2	4157.8	4168.1	4155.3	4164.0	4112.6
1993	4049.1	4048.6	4065.0	4110.3	4172.7	4220.3	4227.4	4245.8	4258.5	4251.4	4264.2	4279.7	4182.7
1994	4166.2	4183.5	4233.9	4267.3	4335.0	4381.6	4366.9	4390.2	4402.5	4409.9	4428.7	4454.0	4334.9
1995	4315.1	4327.6	4381.2	4427.1	4480.3	4537.5	4503.3	4536.1	4541.4	4525.1	4540.0	4553.8	4472.3
1996	4398.4	4417.7	4442.6	4493.0	4554.5	4603.7	4585.4	4611.2	4598.4	4593.6	4608.0	4623.4	4544.1
1997	4479.2	4484.2	4531.2	4583.7	4646.6	4688.0	4674.8	4699.6	4693.7	4697.9	4706.3	4730.2	4634.6
1998	4577.4	4587.5	4621.7	4680.8	4737.2	4775.5	4731.1	4779.9	4766.3	4777.8	4785.0	4803.9	4718.6
1999	4625.5	4653.2	4683.2	4752.2	4792.1	4832.5	4847.5	4860.4	4838.7	4846.7	4867.5	4897.7	4791.4
2000	4728.7	4734.3	4778.0	4814.6	4856.1	4906.7	4879.5	4892.8	4865.9	4861.7	4875.2	4881.8	4839.6
2001	4702.0	4697.6	4724.2	4754.3	4788.2	4822.7	4781.2	4788.2	4742.2	4728.3	4729.7	4724.3	4748.6
2002	4553.9	4550.4	4580.5	4615.3	4663.4	4697.5	4684.8	4704.0	4677.7	4667.0	4673.4	4668.8	4644.7
2003	4511.5	4493.9	4521.8	4573.0	4619.2	4641.7	4623.3	4640.4	4617.5	4612.6	4612.8	4606.3	4589.5
Goods-producing													
1990	1228.2	1244.6	1257.8	1269.2	1285.1	1303.2	1296.5	1305.1	1304.5	1291.2	1270.7	1253.4	1275.7
1991	1206.0	1187.0	1193.8	1200.0	1212.9	1230.7	1228.7	1240.3	1238.9	1229.8	1222.8	1207.8	1216.5
1992	1166.6	1161.9	1164.2	1174.4	1189.2	1200.3	1196.2	1196.0	1197.2	1200.0	1188.8	1180.7	1184.6
1993	1146.4	1143.0	1143.9	1158.4	1176.1	1192.5	1198.6	1202.7	1209.1	1203.2	1201.3	1197.2	1181.0
1994	1162.7	1165.0	1181.7	1194.1	1216.9	1234.9	1231.6	1241.0	1247.4	1251.7	1251.3	1247.2	1218.7
1995	1215.9	1216.7	1235.9	1249.4	1263.5	1281.0	1266.2	1279.1	1280.8	1276.2	1271.8	1264.7	1258.4
1996	1218.7	1224.5	1224.4	1245.8	1260.4	1278.7	1274.6	1286.1	1283.0	1277.9	1270.4	1265.5	1259.1
1997	1226.9	1226.1	1240.0	1256.6	1271.3	1284.9	1270.3	1290.3	1287.8	1283.8	1279.2	1276.8	1266.1
1998	1236.4	1239.3	1246.2	1270.7	1281.7	1293.0	1258.8	1297.6	1298.3	1300.2	1293.5	1288.9	1275.3
1999	1241.8	1247.4	1254.8	1269.8	1277.8	1291.5	1294.7	1303.2	1300.8	1300.5	1299.6	1297.2	1281.5
2000	1258.9	1259.4	1273.0	1281.2	1292.7	1307.1	1290.3	1294.2	1285.7	1280.7	1276.0	1261.8	1280.0
2001	1216.9	1211.9	1215.5	1216.5	1219.6	1227.9	1214.5	1216.8	1200.1	1190.3	1180.5	1166.9	1206.5
2002	1117.8	1113.3	1118.0	1125.1	1137.5	1150.8	1143.4	1155.9	1147.0	1138.8	1131.9	1119.6	1133.3
2003	1080.0	1069.0	1074.4	1082.8	1097.2	1104.1	1092.2	1101.8	1092.4	1085.6	1079.4	1068.9	1085.7
Natural resources and mining													
1990	17.3	17.0	17.3	17.8	18.0	18.4	18.5	18.4	18.3	18.1	18.0	17.5	17.8
1991	16.7	16.1	16.5	16.8	16.7	16.9	17.0	16.9	16.7	16.1	15.7	15.3	16.4
1992	14.8	14.4	14.8	15.3	15.6	15.7	15.6	15.7	15.5	15.5	15.2	15.0	15.2
1993	14.1	13.6	13.7	14.2	14.6	14.8	15.2	15.0	15.2	15.2	15.1	14.9	14.6
1994	13.9	13.7	14.1	14.6	14.9	15.0	15.0	15.0	15.1	14.9	14.7	14.5	14.6
1995	13.7	13.5	13.8	14.0	13.9	14.1	14.1	14.1	14.0	14.1	14.0	14.1	13.9
1996	13.2	13.1	13.5	13.8	14.0	14.3	14.3	14.4	14.1	13.9	13.8	13.6	13.8
1997	13.2	13.2	13.5	13.4	13.8	14.0	13.9	14.0	14.0	14.0	13.9	13.9	13.7
1998	13.4	13.3	13.5	13.7	13.8	14.0	13.9	13.9	13.9	14.1	14.0	13.9	13.7
1999	13.1	13.3	13.3	13.7	13.8	14.0	13.9	13.7	13.6	13.5	13.4	13.1	13.5
2000	12.5	12.5	12.8	12.9	13.1	13.3	13.0	13.0	13.0	13.0	13.0	12.8	12.9
2001	12.2	12.4	12.7	12.8	13.0	13.3	13.3	13.3	13.3	13.0	12.9	12.7	12.9
2002	12.0	12.0	12.1	12.4	12.0	12.3	12.2	12.3	12.2	12.2	12.0	11.9	12.1
2003	11.5	11.3	11.4	11.6	11.7	11.8	11.9	11.9	11.8	11.8	11.9	11.7	11.7
Construction													
1990	170.0	169.3	177.2	186.1	196.7	204.9	208.8	210.7	208.3	203.5	198.3	185.6	193.2
1991	158.4	154.0	158.4	167.8	175.2	183.1	193.0	195.3	193.4	190.1	183.4	171.7	176.9
1992	150.6	147.6	153.7	165.3	177.1	185.1	189.8	190.9	189.8	191.0	182.8	175.2	174.9
1993	155.9	153.4	154.4	172.2	184.7	193.5	203.7	203.5	202.3	208.3	202.6	195.4	185.8
1994	166.0	165.6	176.6	190.2	205.5	215.0	218.1	218.5	216.5	217.9	212.3	203.6	200.4
1995	178.1	174.3	187.2	199.6	210.1	220.9	222.0	223.7	222.2	222.3	216.0	207.9	207.0
1996	178.2	180.4	190.3	204.8	216.8	228.5	234.4	237.3	234.3	233.4	226.8	217.5	215.2
1997	194.1	192.7	201.7	217.4	229.1	237.5	243.5	245.3	241.5	238.9	230.8	222.7	224.6
1998	199.6	199.6	203.9	221.1	232.6	241.7	250.4	249.8	246.7	248.4	242.2	235.4	230.9
1999	203.9	210.8	216.6	229.1	237.8	247.0	261.1	260.1	258.5	258.4	254.2	247.3	240.4
2000	220.7	219.5	232.7	242.8	253.6	263.6	264.3	263.2	257.0	252.8	247.6	235.8	246.1
2001	212.5	213.1	221.4	232.6	243.1	252.8	258.7	260.3	253.8	252.3	247.8	238.1	240.5
2002	212.2	210.4	216.8	226.3	236.9	246.5	253.8	255.7	250.8	249.0	243.4	232.2	236.2
2003	207.5	200.8	207.5	223.6	233.7	241.8	245.6	248.3	244.3	242.6	236.5	225.4	229.8

Employment by Industry: Ohio—*Continued*

(Numbers in thousands. Not seasonally adjusted.)

Industry	January	February	March	April	May	June	July	August	September	October	November	December	Annual Average
STATEWIDE—*Continued*													
Manufacturing													
1990	1040.9	1058.3	1063.3	1065.3	1070.4	1079.9	1069.2	1076.0	1077.9	1069.6	1054.4	1050.3	1064.6
1991	1030.9	1016.9	1018.9	1015.4	1021.0	1030.7	1018.7	1028.1	1028.8	1023.6	1023.7	1020.8	1023.1
1992	1001.2	999.9	995.7	993.8	996.5	999.5	990.8	989.4	991.9	993.5	990.8	990.5	994.4
1993	976.4	976.0	975.8	972.0	976.8	984.2	979.7	984.2	991.6	979.7	983.6	986.9	980.5
1994	982.8	985.7	991.0	989.3	996.5	1004.9	998.5	1007.5	1015.8	1018.9	1024.3	1029.1	1003.6
1995	1024.1	1028.9	1034.9	1035.8	1039.5	1046.0	1030.1	1041.3	1044.6	1039.8	1041.8	1042.7	1037.4
1996	1027.3	1031.0	1020.6	1027.2	1029.6	1035.9	1025.9	1034.4	1034.6	1030.6	1029.8	1034.4	1030.1
1997	1019.6	1020.2	1024.8	1025.8	1028.4	1033.4	1012.9	1031.0	1032.3	1030.9	1034.5	1040.2	1027.8
1998	1023.4	1026.4	1028.8	1035.9	1035.3	1037.3	994.5	1033.9	1037.7	1037.7	1037.3	1039.6	1030.6
1999	1024.8	1023.3	1024.9	1027.0	1026.2	1030.5	1019.7	1029.4	1028.7	1028.6	1032.0	1036.8	1027.6
2000	1025.7	1027.4	1027.5	1025.5	1026.0	1030.2	1013.0	1018.0	1015.7	1014.9	1015.4	1013.2	1021.0
2001	992.2	986.4	981.4	971.1	963.5	961.8	942.5	943.2	933.0	925.0	919.8	916.1	953.0
2002	893.6	890.9	889.1	886.4	888.6	892.0	877.4	887.9	884.0	877.6	876.5	875.5	885.0
2003	861.0	856.9	855.5	847.6	851.8	850.5	834.7	841.6	836.3	831.2	831.0	831.8	844.2
Service-providing													
1990	3510.2	3525.7	3562.0	3589.8	3640.7	3652.5	3599.2	3599.2	3635.9	3642.3	3655.5	3665.1	3606.5
1991	3539.6	3539.1	3566.9	3582.1	3623.2	3626.0	3587.5	3580.0	3622.6	3638.0	3656.4	3663.3	3602.0
1992	3558.9	3573.7	3607.6	3657.0	3704.5	3699.7	3655.0	3648.6	3679.7	3718.0	3719.3	3734.6	3663.0
1993	3640.7	3655.7	3674.7	3700.9	3752.5	3762.0	3713.3	3723.0	3769.6	3802.4	3817.7	3835.0	3737.2
1994	3739.4	3768.8	3806.0	3827.7	3876.3	3887.9	3826.0	3833.4	3889.3	3918.4	3942.4	3970.7	3857.1
1995	3844.5	3870.8	3911.7	3938.6	3982.1	4005.5	3934.9	3948.8	4002.4	4014.4	4038.7	4059.3	3962.6
1996	3926.7	3959.0	3989.1	4010.9	4066.7	4080.4	4013.6	4026.6	4051.6	4080.7	4111.3	4130.5	4037.2
1997	4006.2	4028.7	4066.2	4093.2	4150.6	4164.6	4119.3	4119.9	4152.2	4181.9	4203.5	4229.6	4126.3
1998	4099.8	4120.3	4152.4	4182.0	4237.2	4247.5	4190.7	4196.0	4224.0	4253.9	4276.1	4300.4	4206.6
1999	4140.1	4186.1	4214.3	4264.7	4302.9	4313.0	4281.8	4278.5	4306.2	4334.5	4364.3	4397.6	4282.0
2000	4245.0	4265.5	4300.4	4329.6	4375.5	4383.2	4333.7	4335.3	4357.6	4380.5	4404.4	4424.2	4344.5
2001	4271.4	4289.2	4316.7	4343.6	4376.7	4384.2	4315.0	4316.7	4330.5	4349.0	4366.4	4374.6	4336.2
2002	4230.9	4250.3	4280.0	4304.1	4342.6	4341.7	4300.0	4300.7	4322.5	4340.3	4360.7	4366.6	4311.7
2003	4229.8	4238.0	4265.0	4306.9	4342.2	4335.5	4293.4	4293.9	4315.7	4338.8	4350.2	4355.3	4305.4
Trade, transportation, and utilities													
1990	956.4	947.1	952.8	958.3	966.7	974.2	969.7	974.2	971.7	970.1	982.9	997.0	968.4
1991	946.5	926.8	933.2	936.6	945.6	949.6	949.2	951.6	950.6	954.9	970.6	983.0	949.8
1992	938.8	928.1	935.8	939.9	948.4	950.7	948.9	949.8	948.8	960.9	974.1	989.7	951.1
1993	944.4	931.9	934.9	939.4	951.1	958.8	958.4	963.7	965.8	973.1	989.6	1007.8	959.9
1994	971.0	967.2	975.3	976.0	990.3	998.1	991.9	998.2	1006.3	1017.8	1037.6	1060.9	999.2
1995	1009.1	999.7	1006.4	1011.6	1020.2	1027.9	1022.3	1028.3	1029.8	1037.5	1060.1	1078.4	1027.6
1996	1028.0	1017.2	1021.2	1028.9	1040.9	1047.8	1045.7	1051.5	1050.9	1060.5	1085.0	1104.9	1048.5
1997	1055.8	1042.4	1046.9	1052.1	1062.8	1068.9	1067.8	1065.6	1069.8	1080.5	1101.2	1122.1	1069.6
1998	1069.8	1058.6	1061.3	1068.2	1079.9	1084.8	1083.6	1087.2	1084.3	1094.8	1117.6	1135.4	1085.4
1999	1077.3	1072.6	1077.5	1087.4	1096.0	1101.8	1103.8	1103.9	1100.1	1113.7	1136.4	1160.4	1102.5
2000	1107.9	1097.0	1100.2	1101.8	1107.7	1113.5	1107.4	1108.6	1103.9	1123.9	1145.8	1165.8	1115.2
2001	1105.8	1089.5	1091.8	1094.0	1098.7	1102.3	1088.2	1086.3	1081.2	1087.4	1107.2	1117.0	1095.8
2002	1058.2	1045.3	1050.2	1053.2	1060.1	1064.7	1061.5	1061.5	1053.5	1057.7	1077.5	1089.2	1061.1
2003	1034.7	1023.7	1026.8	1036.3	1043.1	1045.7	1043.3	1045.6	1043.6	1049.9	1068.7	1079.5	1045.1
Wholesale trade													
1990	208.5	209.8	211.3	212.2	213.0	214.4	214.6	214.7	214.1	213.5	212.7	213.4	212.6
1991	207.4	205.4	206.9	207.6	208.3	209.5	208.9	208.4	208.2	208.8	208.4	208.8	208.0
1992	204.3	204.1	207.2	210.3	212.8	213.0	213.2	212.3	211.1	214.2	213.0	213.7	210.7
1993	211.5	212.1	212.9	213.6	215.1	216.7	216.3	216.4	216.7	216.4	217.0	218.5	215.2
1994	216.0	216.6	219.2	219.1	220.7	222.4	221.1	221.0	221.4	222.3	223.2	225.1	220.6
1995	220.7	222.2	224.0	224.2	225.5	227.1	226.5	227.8	227.7	227.7	228.7	230.0	226.0
1996	226.6	228.1	229.2	229.5	231.0	232.3	232.7	232.6	231.5	232.5	233.5	234.5	231.1
1997	230.9	232.2	233.9	235.4	237.4	239.1	238.6	238.7	238.0	239.0	238.9	240.5	236.8
1998	237.3	237.9	239.0	239.0	240.3	241.1	240.9	240.9	239.9	241.8	242.4	243.0	240.2
1999	238.8	240.2	241.0	243.4	245.3	246.4	247.4	247.0	245.4	245.7	246.1	247.5	244.5
2000	244.2	244.9	246.1	246.4	247.6	249.2	248.0	247.8	247.2	248.5	248.7	250.0	247.3
2001	247.6	247.6	248.4	248.2	248.8	249.3	247.9	247.1	244.6	243.8	242.8	243.1	246.6
2002	238.4	237.7	238.6	239.3	240.2	240.9	240.7	240.2	238.3	237.7	237.6	238.3	239.0
2003	233.7	233.5	234.1	234.8	235.8	236.4	236.8	236.1	234.6	235.0	234.7	235.0	235.0
Retail trade													
1990	596.4	585.8	589.1	592.7	598.4	603.5	599.5	603.5	601.9	600.8	614.7	629.0	601.2
1991	591.1	574.9	578.9	581.1	588.2	590.3	589.8	591.9	590.9	592.7	608.3	621.4	591.6
1992	585.8	575.6	578.9	579.3	583.7	584.9	581.5	582.9	582.5	590.6	605.2	619.4	587.5
1993	581.0	568.1	569.9	572.0	580.4	584.8	583.5	588.5	589.2	594.4	610.3	626.9	587.4
1994	595.3	589.9	593.8	594.5	602.6	606.9	601.2	607.2	613.2	620.8	639.9	661.1	610.5
1995	617.9	606.8	610.3	613.4	619.4	624.8	620.6	625.4	626.6	631.8	653.6	671.2	626.8
1996	630.1	618.2	620.1	625.5	634.5	639.7	637.0	641.6	642.2	649.0	673.1	693.0	642.0
1997	649.7	635.2	636.8	638.3	645.8	650.2	649.1	651.6	649.0	656.3	677.7	697.2	653.0
1998	653.5	642.1	643.0	646.4	655.0	658.8	656.1	657.3	655.0	662.3	685.0	702.4	659.7
1999	653.4	647.3	650.4	653.8	659.3	663.8	662.2	663.5	660.7	669.5	693.0	715.8	666.0
2000	669.8	658.8	661.1	660.0	664.2	668.5	663.5	664.9	660.4	675.2	697.0	715.9	671.6
2001	665.9	651.0	652.6	652.8	656.8	660.4	648.7	647.5	645.4	651.5	673.3	684.4	657.5
2002	637.4	626.1	630.3	631.1	635.8	639.8	635.8	634.9	629.4	631.3	650.7	662.9	637.1
2003	618.8	609.4	612.3	619.8	624.6	627.3	624.9	627.4	626.6	631.0	649.1	660.9	627.7

Employment by Industry: Ohio—*Continued*

(Numbers in thousands. Not seasonally adjusted.)

Industry	January	February	March	April	May	June	July	August	September	October	November	December	Annual Average
STATEWIDE—*Continued*													
Transportation and utilities													
1990	151.5	151.5	152.4	153.4	155.3	156.3	155.6	156.0	155.7	155.8	155.5	154.6	154.4
1991	148.0	146.5	147.4	147.9	149.1	149.8	150.5	151.3	151.5	153.4	153.9	152.8	150.1
1992	148.7	148.4	149.7	150.3	151.9	152.8	154.2	154.6	155.2	156.1	155.9	156.6	152.8
1993	151.9	151.7	152.1	153.8	155.6	157.3	158.6	158.8	159.9	162.3	162.3	162.4	157.2
1994	159.7	160.7	162.3	162.4	167.0	168.8	169.6	170.0	171.7	174.7	174.5	174.7	168.0
1995	170.5	170.7	172.1	174.0	175.3	176.0	175.2	175.1	175.5	178.0	177.8	177.2	174.7
1996	171.3	170.9	171.9	173.9	175.4	175.8	176.0	177.3	177.2	179.0	178.4	177.4	175.3
1997	175.2	175.0	176.2	178.4	179.6	179.6	180.1	175.3	182.8	185.2	184.6	184.4	179.7
1998	179.0	178.6	179.3	182.8	184.6	184.9	186.6	189.0	189.4	190.7	190.2	190.0	185.4
1999	185.1	185.1	186.1	190.2	191.4	191.6	194.2	193.4	194.0	198.5	197.3	197.1	192.0
2000	193.9	193.3	193.0	195.4	195.9	195.8	195.9	195.9	196.3	200.2	200.1	199.9	196.3
2001	192.3	190.9	190.8	193.0	193.1	192.6	191.6	191.7	191.2	192.1	191.1	189.5	191.7
2002	182.4	181.5	181.3	182.8	184.1	184.0	185.0	186.4	185.8	188.7	189.2	188.0	184.9
2003	182.2	180.8	180.4	181.7	182.7	182.0	181.6	182.1	182.4	183.9	184.9	183.6	182.4
Information													
1990	99.9	99.9	100.2	101.0	101.4	102.6	102.8	102.9	102.6	102.4	102.7	102.9	101.7
1991	101.5	101.1	100.9	99.7	99.8	100.1	100.8	100.5	99.8	99.6	99.9	100.1	100.3
1992	99.0	99.4	98.7	98.4	98.8	98.8	98.7	98.2	97.9	97.8	97.2	97.8	98.3
1993	96.1	96.3	96.2	94.8	95.7	96.7	96.3	97.0	96.3	95.1	95.9	96.4	96.0
1994	95.6	95.7	95.8	94.5	95.4	95.7	95.8	96.0	95.6	95.0	96.0	96.8	95.6
1995	95.0	95.6	95.3	95.4	96.1	97.2	97.4	97.8	98.1	97.1	98.0	98.7	96.8
1996	97.8	98.4	99.1	98.3	99.1	100.0	99.9	100.3	99.8	98.9	100.2	100.8	99.3
1997	99.4	100.1	100.6	100.3	101.4	102.5	102.7	102.7	101.8	102.0	102.6	103.6	101.6
1998	103.4	104.0	104.0	103.2	103.8	104.7	104.9	105.3	104.8	104.8	105.0	104.8	104.3
1999	104.9	105.1	105.4	105.1	105.5	106.5	107.2	107.2	106.2	106.4	107.0	107.6	106.1
2000	106.7	106.8	107.6	106.4	106.6	107.7	107.1	107.6	106.8	107.2	107.8	108.5	107.2
2001	108.4	108.3	108.0	106.1	106.4	107.3	106.8	106.3	104.8	104.3	104.4	104.6	106.3
2002	103.5	102.5	102.2	101.9	101.7	101.9	101.3	100.8	99.5	98.4	99.1	99.2	101.0
2003	98.2	97.7	97.7	97.6	98.1	98.1	98.2	97.7	96.3	95.9	96.1	96.4	97.3
Financial activities													
1990	247.9	249.4	250.9	250.9	252.5	256.0	256.1	256.6	254.9	252.4	252.1	252.5	252.6
1991	248.7	248.7	249.4	248.8	250.8	253.6	253.8	254.1	253.2	250.9	250.8	252.0	251.2
1992	248.6	249.5	250.6	253.0	255.7	258.1	257.5	256.4	254.9	255.1	254.6	255.7	254.1
1993	251.7	252.3	254.1	253.3	256.2	259.4	260.6	261.4	261.1	260.2	262.2	264.3	258.0
1994	259.9	261.8	263.7	263.0	264.5	267.4	269.0	271.1	269.8	267.8	268.8	269.6	266.3
1995	266.5	267.9	269.3	267.7	268.8	271.3	271.1	271.8	271.6	268.8	270.3	272.0	269.7
1996	269.2	271.4	273.1	273.3	275.1	278.4	278.8	279.3	277.8	277.6	278.0	279.6	275.9
1997	275.9	278.2	280.2	281.5	283.2	285.5	287.9	288.3	286.1	286.8	288.0	290.2	284.3
1998	285.7	286.7	288.8	289.2	291.5	294.5	296.5	297.1	295.0	295.3	296.2	298.6	292.9
1999	296.5	298.2	299.1	301.9	303.5	306.1	307.3	307.0	304.7	304.9	305.4	307.2	303.4
2000	304.2	304.1	304.5	304.7	305.2	307.4	305.9	305.9	304.6	303.2	305.3	307.7	305.2
2001	302.6	303.8	304.9	305.5	306.9	310.8	310.4	310.7	307.7	306.5	308.3	309.4	307.3
2002	305.6	306.9	307.5	306.4	307.5	309.6	310.7	310.3	307.9	308.0	309.6	311.1	308.4
2003	307.9	308.7	309.6	309.5	311.6	314.3	315.5	315.2	313.3	312.6	312.9	313.3	312.0
Professional and business services													
1990	415.2	418.5	424.8	434.0	439.2	445.3	446.7	450.1	449.1	449.4	446.5	441.9	438.3
1991	424.1	424.0	427.7	430.0	431.7	436.5	435.4	437.1	438.6	438.2	435.9	431.4	432.5
1992	419.5	422.9	429.0	451.7	456.0	461.5	464.6	466.1	466.0	468.9	465.6	465.5	453.1
1993	455.8	462.7	466.4	476.0	479.2	486.5	486.9	489.6	495.2	498.1	496.5	495.6	482.3
1994	486.0	493.1	501.4	506.4	510.3	516.3	516.8	521.4	524.1	524.9	526.2	526.6	512.7
1995	510.8	517.4	526.1	535.3	538.5	546.9	543.7	553.3	555.2	554.6	554.1	551.3	540.6
1996	530.1	535.4	539.9	546.8	553.0	560.9	557.5	563.3	561.5	564.9	565.7	562.5	553.4
1997	549.1	554.9	564.7	575.6	583.4	591.4	596.4	602.1	603.1	610.6	610.1	609.3	587.5
1998	587.8	591.2	599.4	605.6	610.3	619.5	620.0	625.4	625.3	630.2	629.0	629.9	614.4
1999	607.2	611.7	617.3	628.9	630.3	638.5	640.5	643.9	640.3	644.9	646.3	648.3	633.1
2000	618.5	622.4	630.9	642.7	645.4	655.2	653.3	657.6	656.0	654.1	653.0	649.5	644.8
2001	621.3	622.0	628.0	633.5	635.3	640.2	636.0	636.6	629.8	625.9	620.8	618.7	629.0
2002	596.8	597.0	603.2	610.5	613.8	618.9	621.4	626.3	625.4	627.1	625.2	621.5	615.6
2003	597.8	597.4	602.2	609.2	610.4	612.9	610.2	613.8	611.0	611.7	607.1	602.9	607.2
Educational and health services													
1990	532.3	535.6	538.3	539.0	538.9	539.8	537.6	540.1	548.3	553.3	555.9	557.5	543.0
1991	549.0	552.9	555.8	557.5	559.4	558.8	557.6	559.7	568.2	572.7	575.5	577.5	562.0
1992	568.3	573.7	577.9	582.6	582.7	579.3	579.1	579.4	585.0	590.3	592.4	594.2	582.0
1993	591.6	596.2	598.2	597.4	598.9	598.3	598.5	600.2	607.4	608.8	612.6	614.0	601.8
1994	603.4	608.7	611.2	612.2	613.7	611.5	609.9	610.9	618.1	622.8	625.6	628.5	614.7
1995	616.1	623.3	626.5	626.1	626.4	623.7	620.3	621.5	630.0	635.3	638.1	639.9	627.2
1996	625.8	634.1	636.1	635.5	635.9	631.1	628.4	628.8	637.2	643.1	645.2	646.3	635.6
1997	632.5	637.8	640.2	640.0	641.1	636.6	637.0	637.7	646.5	651.5	654.5	656.1	642.6
1998	647.2	654.0	656.7	659.8	659.7	656.0	650.4	651.0	658.6	665.1	667.1	668.2	657.8
1999	655.4	663.5	664.1	671.2	669.1	664.4	663.9	664.9	673.1	677.3	679.7	681.1	668.9
2000	666.9	674.9	677.9	677.8	677.3	677.5	676.0	679.3	685.6	687.0	690.4	693.4	680.3
2001	680.1	690.2	691.7	696.2	693.5	688.6	680.3	683.6	695.4	706.7	710.5	711.2	694.0
2002	698.2	708.9	709.8	711.8	710.6	703.2	697.2	700.2	714.0	724.7	728.7	728.9	711.4
2003	719.1	725.2	727.2	729.6	725.9	718.1	713.1	714.5	729.9	740.2	741.3	740.9	727.1

Employment by Industry: Ohio—*Continued*

(Numbers in thousands. Not seasonally adjusted.)

Industry	January	February	March	April	May	June	July	August	September	October	November	December	Annual Average
STATEWIDE—*Continued*													
Leisure and hospitality													
1990	371.2	372.4	382.0	395.6	414.3	429.0	427.0	428.0	419.7	398.9	390.7	389.9	401.5
1991	365.4	365.9	374.1	387.9	404.2	418.0	421.7	421.5	412.3	392.2	382.9	381.8	393.9
1992	365.0	367.7	377.7	393.4	416.8	427.5	429.2	430.6	420.6	406.7	395.3	393.0	401.9
1993	377.5	380.7	384.7	402.9	426.5	437.9	438.5	440.9	434.0	421.4	413.3	411.1	414.1
1994	395.8	399.3	410.0	425.6	446.8	459.8	457.0	455.8	445.5	431.1	424.1	423.8	431.2
1995	405.4	409.9	421.5	438.1	461.3	480.4	476.2	476.2	467.0	445.6	437.6	437.2	446.3
1996	419.4	425.3	435.5	450.4	473.3	488.4	483.5	483.9	471.8	453.5	446.0	445.4	456.3
1997	425.0	428.7	440.9	458.4	481.9	496.0	491.9	491.5	479.1	464.6	453.4	453.8	463.7
1998	430.1	435.0	445.4	463.9	488.9	501.3	497.4	496.0	482.1	468.2	458.6	460.0	468.9
1999	430.5	440.0	449.4	469.4	489.4	501.5	510.3	510.0	494.0	479.0	472.9	474.5	476.7
2000	446.7	448.7	460.8	476.8	496.8	512.9	515.2	515.4	499.6	482.1	473.4	471.3	483.3
2001	443.8	447.6	458.5	474.7	498.0	514.6	515.4	516.6	495.2	478.5	469.0	467.3	481.6
2002	448.2	449.9	461.1	477.9	502.0	516.7	519.4	518.4	502.5	484.5	473.9	471.2	485.5
2003	449.1	447.1	456.7	480.4	503.9	519.1	522.3	523.8	505.2	490.3	481.1	478.2	488.1
Other services													
1990	171.5	172.8	174.7	175.9	177.7	180.8	179.3	180.4	181.3	180.9	182.3	183.1	178.3
1991	179.5	180.7	182.8	183.8	185.8	187.2	185.0	185.3	183.7	185.0	185.3	185.6	184.1
1992	182.2	183.5	185.9	186.9	189.0	190.0	189.3	188.7	187.4	188.4	187.3	187.4	187.1
1993	185.6	185.5	186.6	188.1	189.0	190.2	189.6	190.3	189.6	191.5	192.8	193.3	189.3
1994	191.8	192.7	194.8	195.5	197.1	197.9	194.9	195.8	195.7	198.8	199.1	200.6	196.2
1995	196.3	197.1	200.2	203.5	205.5	209.1	206.1	208.1	208.9	210.0	210.0	211.6	205.5
1996	209.4	211.4	213.3	214.0	216.8	218.4	217.0	218.0	216.4	217.2	217.5	218.4	215.6
1997	214.6	216.0	217.7	219.2	221.5	222.2	220.8	221.4	219.5	218.1	217.3	218.3	218.8
1998	217.0	218.7	219.9	220.2	221.4	221.7	219.5	220.3	217.9	219.2	218.0	218.1	219.3
1999	211.9	214.7	215.6	218.5	220.5	222.2	219.8	220.3	219.5	220.0	220.2	221.4	218.7
2000	218.9	221.0	223.1	223.2	224.4	225.4	224.3	224.2	223.7	223.5	223.5	223.8	223.2
2001	223.1	224.3	225.8	227.8	229.8	231.0	229.6	231.3	228.0	228.7	229.0	229.2	228.1
2002	225.6	226.6	228.5	228.5	230.2	231.7	229.9	230.6	227.9	227.8	227.5	228.1	228.6
2003	224.7	225.1	227.2	227.6	229.0	229.4	228.5	228.0	225.8	226.4	226.2	226.2	227.0
Government													
1990	715.8	730.0	738.3	735.1	750.0	724.8	680.0	666.9	708.3	734.9	742.4	740.3	722.2
1991	724.9	739.0	743.0	737.8	745.9	722.2	684.0	670.2	716.2	744.5	755.5	751.9	727.9
1992	737.5	748.9	752.0	751.1	757.1	733.8	687.7	679.4	719.1	749.9	752.8	751.3	735.0
1993	738.0	750.1	753.6	749.0	755.9	734.2	684.5	679.9	720.2	754.2	754.8	752.5	735.5
1994	735.9	750.3	753.8	754.5	758.2	741.2	690.7	684.2	734.2	760.2	765.0	763.9	741.0
1995	745.3	759.9	766.4	760.9	765.3	749.0	697.8	691.8	741.8	765.5	770.5	770.2	748.7
1996	747.0	765.8	770.9	763.7	772.6	755.4	702.8	701.5	736.2	765.0	773.7	772.6	752.2
1997	753.9	770.6	775.0	766.1	775.3	761.5	714.8	710.6	746.3	767.8	776.4	776.2	757.8
1998	758.8	772.1	776.9	771.9	781.7	765.0	718.4	713.7	756.0	776.3	784.6	785.4	763.4
1999	756.4	780.3	785.9	782.3	788.6	772.0	729.0	721.3	768.3	788.3	796.4	797.1	772.1
2000	775.2	790.6	795.4	796.2	812.1	783.6	744.5	736.7	777.4	799.5	805.2	804.2	785.0
2001	786.3	803.5	808.0	805.8	808.1	789.4	748.3	745.3	788.4	811.0	817.2	817.2	794.0
2002	794.8	813.2	817.5	813.9	816.7	795.0	758.6	752.6	791.8	812.1	819.2	817.4	800.2
2003	798.3	813.1	817.6	816.7	820.2	797.9	762.3	755.3	790.6	811.8	816.8	817.9	801.5
Federal government													
1990	96.9	96.5	97.7	99.9	107.7	100.9	100.1	96.9	95.4	94.7	94.5	95.1	98.0
1991	94.1	94.2	94.4	94.5	94.5	94.9	95.3	95.2	95.0	94.6	94.5	95.3	94.7
1992	94.8	94.2	94.1	94.3	94.2	94.3	93.8	93.4	93.3	93.3	92.4	93.3	93.7
1993	91.9	91.7	91.4	90.1	90.1	90.1	90.4	90.2	90.1	89.6	89.6	91.1	90.5
1994	89.3	89.8	89.4	89.5	89.6	90.0	90.1	90.2	90.2	92.3	92.1	93.8	90.5
1995	91.1	90.8	91.2	91.0	90.9	91.2	91.1	90.6	90.4	90.5	90.5	92.5	90.9
1996	89.6	89.3	89.3	89.0	87.8	87.9	87.7	88.1	87.6	86.9	88.2	89.9	88.4
1997	87.8	87.4	87.2	85.0	84.8	84.9	84.9	85.1	84.8	84.0	85.1	87.2	85.6
1998	83.9	83.8	83.8	83.4	83.5	83.8	83.9	84.0	83.9	83.7	84.5	87.2	84.1
1999	83.6	83.8	83.7	84.7	83.6	83.6	83.9	83.9	83.7	83.5	84.2	86.3	84.0
2000	83.5	84.1	85.6	88.4	100.4	91.6	91.9	85.4	83.7	83.2	83.7	85.4	87.2
2001	83.4	82.7	82.5	82.3	82.3	82.6	83.1	82.8	82.4	82.1	81.9	83.5	82.6
2002	81.9	80.9	80.9	80.5	80.5	81.2	81.0	81.4	80.9	81.0	81.0	81.9	81.1
2003	80.4	79.8	79.6	79.6	79.4	79.6	79.9	79.6	78.9	78.6	78.5	79.7	79.5
State government													
1990	158.5	167.3	170.4	169.4	169.1	160.0	144.4	144.2	154.4	169.4	173.2	171.2	162.6
1991	162.6	171.7	173.8	172.8	173.2	158.1	146.2	144.1	154.7	170.0	174.8	173.1	164.5
1992	165.3	171.9	172.8	172.4	173.2	156.2	145.7	143.9	152.5	170.7	169.5	169.1	163.6
1993	162.6	168.7	169.3	171.2	170.2	156.4	145.2	144.9	154.1	172.4	171.5	171.0	163.1
1994	162.8	170.4	171.7	173.9	171.7	158.9	146.5	146.0	161.5	173.0	173.5	173.4	165.2
1995	164.5	172.3	174.8	173.3	172.2	160.3	146.6	146.0	160.8	171.7	173.1	172.5	165.6
1996	161.6	171.2	172.9	170.8	170.7	158.1	144.8	147.2	152.0	167.7	171.0	169.9	163.1
1997	162.9	169.9	170.7	168.9	168.8	157.7	147.4	147.5	156.8	166.6	170.0	169.8	163.0
1998	165.8	168.9	170.4	169.2	169.3	156.1	147.9	146.6	159.8	169.2	171.1	171.0	163.7
1999	162.6	169.4	171.2	169.8	169.6	156.8	148.1	146.7	160.5	169.6	171.6	171.7	163.9
2000	162.8	170.4	171.2	169.5	168.2	157.5	147.6	147.0	159.4	170.0	171.6	169.7	163.7
2001	163.7	171.7	172.4	171.6	167.9	160.0	149.4	148.7	161.1	171.1	172.9	171.2	165.1
2002	164.3	170.7	172.0	170.4	166.5	156.3	147.7	147.0	160.3	170.2	173.1	171.0	164.1
2003	164.9	170.3	171.3	171.3	169.6	155.4	148.8	148.6	162.6	171.2	173.4	173.5	165.1

Employment by Industry: Ohio—*Continued*

(Numbers in thousands. Not seasonally adjusted.)

Industry	January	February	March	April	May	June	July	August	September	October	November	December	Annual Average
STATEWIDE—*Continued*													
Local government													
1990	460.4	466.2	470.2	465.8	473.2	464.0	435.5	425.8	458.5	470.7	474.7	473.9	461.5
1991	468.2	473.1	474.8	470.5	478.2	469.1	442.5	430.9	466.6	480.0	486.2	483.5	468.6
1992	477.4	482.8	485.1	484.4	489.7	483.3	448.2	442.1	473.3	485.9	490.9	488.9	477.6
1993	483.5	489.7	492.9	487.7	495.6	487.7	448.9	444.8	476.0	492.2	493.7	490.4	481.9
1994	483.8	490.1	492.7	491.1	496.9	492.3	454.1	448.0	482.5	494.9	499.4	496.7	485.2
1995	489.7	496.8	500.4	496.6	502.2	497.5	460.1	455.2	490.6	503.3	506.9	505.2	492.0
1996	495.8	505.3	508.7	503.9	514.1	509.4	470.3	466.2	496.6	510.4	514.5	512.8	500.6
1997	503.2	513.3	517.1	512.2	521.7	518.9	482.5	478.0	504.7	517.2	521.3	519.2	509.1
1998	509.1	519.4	522.7	519.3	528.9	525.1	486.6	483.1	512.3	523.4	529.0	527.2	515.5
1999	510.2	527.1	531.0	527.8	535.4	531.6	497.0	490.7	524.1	535.2	540.6	539.1	524.1
2000	528.9	536.1	538.6	538.3	543.5	534.5	505.0	504.3	534.3	546.3	549.9	549.1	534.0
2001	539.2	549.1	553.1	551.9	557.9	546.8	515.8	513.8	544.9	557.8	562.4	562.5	546.3
2002	548.6	561.6	564.6	563.0	569.7	557.5	529.9	524.2	550.6	560.9	565.1	564.5	555.0
2003	553.0	563.0	566.7	565.8	571.2	562.9	533.6	527.1	549.1	562.0	564.9	564.7	557.0
AKRON													
Total nonfarm													
1990	274.1	278.8	282.1	284.4	288.8	285.2	282.6	284.7	290.3	289.9	290.4	289.3	285.0
1991	275.6	277.6	280.4	282.1	286.6	281.5	281.2	281.0	288.4	288.3	289.0	288.9	283.3
1992	278.3	280.1	281.3	286.6	290.9	284.8	284.6	284.7	290.6	293.6	291.5	292.3	286.6
1993	283.6	285.6	287.2	290.0	294.0	289.1	288.7	289.6	296.8	299.6	300.9	301.4	292.2
1994	292.3	295.5	299.6	299.0	305.8	302.2	301.3	301.3	310.3	310.7	312.4	313.2	303.6
1995	301.8	305.6	308.8	310.9	315.7	311.4	311.5	312.6	319.4	318.7	318.9	320.0	312.9
1996	309.0	311.6	314.1	316.1	322.1	316.7	315.3	317.6	323.8	326.4	326.7	326.3	318.8
1997	312.1	316.2	318.0	320.4	325.5	321.9	320.1	320.8	326.1	327.9	327.6	328.8	322.1
1998	316.9	318.2	320.7	325.3	329.1	324.1	321.2	321.1	326.6	329.5	330.1	332.5	324.6
1999	317.6	322.4	324.9	330.7	334.7	331.0	329.9	329.4	334.9	336.6	338.1	339.0	330.7
2000	324.3	327.8	330.9	334.0	338.0	334.6	332.3	330.8	334.2	336.4	337.0	335.6	332.9
2001	324.1	325.9	328.0	330.7	332.4	332.7	327.3	327.8	331.0	332.4	333.2	332.4	329.8
2002	319.0	320.0	322.6	323.1	324.3	325.8	324.4	323.9	328.7	329.5	328.6	328.2	324.8
2003	315.4	316.4	318.5	326.2	328.7	326.0	324.5	323.7	328.5	330.2	329.4	330.4	324.8
Total private													
1990	232.4	232.3	235.1	237.8	241.4	244.3	243.4	245.2	244.4	242.9	242.9	242.3	240.3
1991	233.6	230.7	233.0	235.1	239.1	242.6	242.0	242.2	242.9	241.4	240.8	241.2	238.7
1992	233.4	233.0	233.8	239.4	243.4	246.2	245.6	246.5	245.8	246.9	244.9	245.9	242.0
1993	239.5	239.7	240.0	243.0	246.9	249.6	249.5	250.9	252.0	251.6	253.1	253.9	247.4
1994	248.3	249.3	252.2	252.0	258.2	262.1	262.0	262.1	263.5	262.4	263.9	264.9	258.4
1995	256.6	257.8	260.4	262.9	266.9	271.0	270.9	272.5	272.1	269.9	270.1	271.4	266.8
1996	263.1	263.3	265.0	267.7	272.8	275.5	274.7	276.4	276.1	277.2	277.1	277.0	272.1
1997	265.9	267.1	268.7	271.4	275.8	279.0	277.8	279.3	278.1	278.9	277.9	279.2	274.9
1998	268.9	269.3	271.3	276.0	279.3	281.0	279.2	279.8	278.8	280.4	280.7	282.6	277.2
1999	272.3	273.4	275.1	281.0	284.1	286.8	288.1	288.0	286.4	286.8	287.6	288.7	283.1
2000	277.8	277.4	280.5	283.4	286.3	290.5	289.3	289.4	286.6	286.6	286.9	287.2	285.1
2001	276.3	275.8	276.9	279.8	284.5	287.8	283.8	285.7	282.5	282.2	282.4	283.1	281.7
2002	271.3	270.0	271.7	272.3	276.4	280.0	280.8	281.7	279.5	278.4	277.0	277.4	276.4
2003	267.1	265.9	267.0	273.6	277.7	279.5	279.1	278.8	277.8	278.0	276.8	277.7	274.9
Goods-producing													
1990	70.4	70.7	71.8	72.5	73.7	74.5	74.1	75.0	74.5	73.9	73.1	72.1	73.0
1991	69.4	67.4	68.4	68.9	70.0	70.9	70.7	70.3	70.7	71.0	70.3	70.1	69.8
1992	66.6	66.5	66.8	68.4	69.9	70.9	70.7	71.1	71.4	71.7	70.9	70.7	69.6
1993	68.5	68.6	68.5	69.4	70.4	71.2	71.7	72.1	72.4	71.8	72.1	71.9	70.7
1994	69.3	69.6	70.5	71.6	73.5	74.4	75.1	75.3	75.9	75.7	75.9	75.6	73.5
1995	72.8	73.2	74.0	74.9	75.8	76.5	76.4	76.8	77.2	77.1	76.4	75.9	75.5
1996	73.2	73.7	74.0	75.1	76.1	77.2	76.6	77.1	76.9	77.5	76.8	76.5	75.8
1997	73.1	73.5	73.8	75.0	75.7	76.5	75.5	76.7	76.4	77.8	77.2	76.9	75.6
1998	73.8	74.0	74.5	76.5	77.3	77.6	76.6	77.2	77.6	77.3	77.0	77.2	76.3
1999	74.9	75.1	74.9	76.7	77.8	78.7	78.1	78.8	78.5	78.4	78.1	77.7	77.3
2000	75.4	75.3	75.9	77.1	77.9	78.9	78.0	77.7	76.7	76.7	76.4	75.4	76.7
2001	72.1	71.7	71.7	72.1	72.7	73.1	71.3	72.2	71.0	70.4	69.7	69.4	71.5
2002	62.1	61.6	62.0	62.2	63.7	64.4	65.2	65.4	64.8	64.3	63.7	63.1	63.5
2003	61.5	61.4	61.8	63.4	64.0	64.3	64.2	64.8	65.0	64.5	64.2	63.5	63.6
Construction and mining													
1990	9.0	8.9	9.4	10.2	10.8	11.2	11.3	11.4	11.1	11.0	10.7	9.8	10.4
1991	8.6	8.3	8.5	9.3	9.8	10.2	10.6	10.7	10.4	10.6	10.2	9.7	9.7
1992	8.5	8.2	8.4	9.4	10.2	10.8	10.9	11.0	11.0	11.2	10.7	10.1	10.0
1993	8.8	8.6	8.5	9.6	10.5	11.0	11.6	11.7	11.6	11.9	11.4	10.8	10.5
1994	9.3	9.2	9.7	10.9	11.9	12.5	13.1	12.9	12.9	12.9	12.6	12.0	11.6
1995	10.0	9.9	10.5	11.3	12.1	12.8	13.0	13.0	12.9	12.9	12.4	11.8	11.8
1996	10.4	10.5	11.1	12.2	13.0	13.7	13.9	14.1	14.0	14.2	13.6	12.8	12.7
1997	11.2	11.2	11.6	12.7	13.5	14.1	14.6	14.8	14.6	14.6	13.9	13.2	13.3
1998	11.9	11.8	12.1	13.4	14.2	14.8	14.9	14.9	14.7	14.9	14.5	14.1	13.8
1999	11.9	12.3	12.4	13.6	14.5	15.2	15.8	15.7	15.4	15.5	15.2	14.5	14.3
2000	12.8	12.8	13.6	14.6	15.3	15.8	15.7	15.6	15.5	15.3	14.9	14.0	14.6
2001	12.5	12.5	13.1	13.9	14.9	15.5	15.8	15.8	15.3	15.2	14.7	14.1	14.4
2002	12.3	12.1	12.5	12.7	13.9	14.6	15.2	15.4	15.0	14.6	14.2	13.5	13.8
2003	12.1	11.7	12.2	13.5	14.3	14.7	15.0	15.6	15.8	15.2	14.9	14.2	14.1

Employment by Industry: Ohio—*Continued*

(Numbers in thousands. Not seasonally adjusted.)

Industry	January	February	March	April	May	June	July	August	September	October	November	December	Annual Average
AKRON—*Continued*													
Manufacturing													
1990	61.4	61.8	62.4	62.3	62.9	63.3	62.8	63.6	63.4	62.9	62.4	62.3	62.6
1991	60.8	59.1	59.9	59.6	60.2	60.7	60.1	59.6	60.3	60.4	60.1	60.4	60.1
1992	58.1	58.3	58.4	59.0	59.7	60.1	59.8	60.1	60.4	60.5	60.2	60.6	59.6
1993	59.7	60.0	60.0	59.8	59.9	60.2	60.1	60.4	60.8	59.9	60.7	61.1	60.2
1994	60.0	60.4	60.8	60.7	61.6	61.9	62.0	62.4	63.0	62.8	63.3	63.6	61.8
1995	62.8	63.3	63.5	63.6	63.7	63.7	63.4	63.8	64.3	64.2	64.0	64.1	63.7
1996	62.8	63.2	62.9	62.9	63.1	63.5	62.7	63.0	62.9	63.3	63.2	63.7	63.1
1997	61.9	62.3	62.2	62.3	62.2	62.4	60.9	61.9	61.8	63.2	63.3	63.7	62.3
1998	61.9	62.2	62.4	63.1	63.1	62.8	61.7	62.3	62.9	62.4	62.5	63.1	62.5
1999	63.0	62.8	62.5	63.1	63.3	63.5	62.3	63.1	63.1	62.9	62.9	63.2	62.9
2000	62.6	62.5	62.3	62.5	62.6	63.1	62.3	62.1	61.2	61.4	61.5	61.4	62.1
2001	59.6	59.2	58.6	58.2	57.8	57.6	55.5	56.4	55.7	55.2	55.0	55.3	57.0
2002	49.8	49.5	49.5	49.5	49.8	49.8	50.0	50.0	49.8	49.7	49.5	49.6	49.7
2003	49.4	49.7	49.6	49.9	49.7	49.6	49.2	49.2	49.2	49.3	49.3	49.3	49.5
Service-providing													
1990	203.7	208.1	210.3	211.9	215.1	210.7	208.5	209.7	215.8	216.0	217.3	217.2	212.0
1991	206.2	210.2	212.0	213.2	216.6	210.6	210.5	210.7	217.7	217.3	218.7	218.8	213.5
1992	211.7	213.6	214.5	218.2	221.0	213.9	213.9	213.6	219.2	221.9	220.6	221.6	216.9
1993	215.1	217.0	218.7	220.6	223.6	217.9	217.0	217.5	224.4	227.8	228.8	229.5	221.4
1994	223.0	225.9	229.1	227.4	232.3	227.8	226.2	226.0	234.4	235.0	236.5	237.6	230.1
1995	229.0	232.4	234.8	236.0	239.9	234.9	235.1	235.8	242.2	241.6	242.5	244.1	237.3
1996	235.8	237.9	240.1	241.0	246.0	239.5	238.7	240.5	246.9	248.9	249.9	249.8	242.9
1997	239.0	242.7	244.2	245.4	249.8	245.4	244.6	244.1	249.7	250.1	250.4	251.9	246.4
1998	243.1	244.2	246.2	248.8	251.8	246.5	244.6	243.9	249.0	252.2	253.1	255.3	248.2
1999	242.7	247.3	250.0	254.0	256.9	252.3	251.8	250.6	256.4	258.2	260.0	261.3	253.4
2000	248.9	252.5	255.0	256.9	260.1	255.7	254.3	253.1	257.5	259.7	260.6	260.2	256.2
2001	252.0	254.2	256.3	258.6	259.7	259.6	256.0	255.6	260.0	262.0	263.5	263.0	258.4
2002	256.9	258.4	260.6	260.9	260.6	261.4	259.2	258.5	263.9	265.2	264.9	265.1	261.3
2003	253.9	255.0	256.7	262.8	264.7	261.7	260.3	258.9	263.5	265.7	265.2	266.9	261.3
Trade, transportation, and utilities													
1990	56.8	55.9	56.0	56.7	57.2	57.4	57.1	57.8	57.7	57.4	58.3	59.1	57.2
1991	56.5	55.2	55.6	55.6	55.8	56.1	56.0	56.6	56.7	56.8	57.6	58.4	56.4
1992	55.7	54.9	54.9	54.8	54.8	55.1	55.0	55.0	55.0	55.3	55.6	56.5	55.2
1993	54.2	53.3	53.1	53.2	53.9	54.2	54.1	54.5	55.0	55.2	55.9	56.9	54.4
1994	55.6	55.0	55.4	55.4	56.3	56.9	56.5	56.5	56.7	57.9	58.7	59.6	56.7
1995	56.9	56.5	56.5	57.2	57.5	58.4	59.0	59.5	59.4	60.2	61.4	62.5	58.7
1996	60.0	59.4	59.7	60.8	61.1	61.8	61.8	62.3	62.5	62.8	64.0	65.0	61.7
1997	62.5	61.4	61.5	62.2	62.7	62.9	63.3	63.3	63.3	63.1	64.4	65.4	63.0
1998	62.4	61.7	61.9	62.3	63.1	63.2	63.3	63.5	63.5	64.4	65.4	66.6	63.4
1999	63.5	62.9	63.2	64.5	65.0	65.6	66.0	65.6	65.6	65.9	67.5	68.9	65.3
2000	66.0	65.4	65.7	66.2	66.7	67.1	66.8	67.2	67.1	68.1	69.5	70.3	67.1
2001	69.8	68.8	68.8	69.3	69.8	70.1	68.8	68.6	68.1	68.4	69.0	69.7	69.1
2002	68.1	67.1	67.3	67.3	67.6	67.9	67.6	67.8	67.2	67.5	68.5	69.0	67.7
2003	63.5	62.7	63.0	64.5	65.0	65.2	64.8	64.7	64.8	65.7	66.1	66.9	64.7
Wholesale trade													
1990	12.2	12.2	12.3	12.4	12.4	12.4	12.4	12.5	12.4	12.4	12.5	12.6	12.3
1991	12.1	12.0	12.0	11.9	11.9	11.9	12.0	12.0	12.0	12.0	11.9	11.9	11.9
1992	11.6	11.6	11.5	11.7	11.8	11.9	11.9	11.8	11.7	11.7	11.7	11.7	11.7
1993	11.8	11.9	11.9	11.8	11.9	12.0	12.1	12.1	12.1	12.3	12.3	12.4	12.0
1994	12.7	12.7	12.7	12.8	13.0	13.1	13.1	13.1	12.9	13.0	13.1	13.2	12.9
1995	13.0	13.2	13.3	13.8	13.9	14.0	14.3	14.3	14.2	14.3	14.3	14.7	13.9
1996	14.7	14.7	14.9	15.2	15.4	15.6	15.4	15.4	15.4	15.5	15.6	15.7	15.2
1997	15.3	15.3	15.4	16.0	16.1	16.1	16.2	16.2	16.1	16.0	16.0	16.1	15.9
1998	15.6	15.6	15.6	15.8	15.9	15.8	15.9	15.9	15.7	15.8	15.8	16.0	15.7
1999	15.7	15.7	15.8	16.0	16.1	16.3	16.2	16.2	16.2	16.1	16.2	16.5	16.0
2000	16.2	16.2	16.3	16.3	16.4	16.5	16.5	16.5	16.4	16.4	16.4	16.4	16.3
2001	17.2	17.1	17.1	17.0	17.3	17.3	17.0	17.0	16.8	16.7	16.6	16.7	17.0
2002	16.5	16.3	16.4	16.3	16.1	16.0	15.9	15.8	15.7	15.6	15.5	15.6	16.0
2003	15.3	15.3	15.3	16.1	16.1	16.1	15.9	16.1	15.9	16.1	16.1	16.3	15.9
Retail trade													
1990	34.5	33.6	33.5	34.0	34.5	34.6	34.4	34.8	34.8	34.6	35.4	36.2	34.5
1991	34.6	33.5	33.8	33.9	33.9	34.1	34.0	34.4	34.6	34.7	35.5	36.3	34.4
1992	34.2	33.5	33.6	33.6	34.1	34.3	34.2	34.4	34.4	34.8	35.1	35.9	34.3
1993	33.8	32.9	32.8	32.8	33.3	33.4	33.1	33.4	33.8	33.7	34.4	35.2	33.5
1994	33.6	33.1	33.4	33.4	34.0	34.3	34.0	34.1	34.6	35.3	36.1	36.9	34.4
1995	34.8	34.3	34.1	34.2	34.4	35.0	35.2	35.6	35.6	35.8	36.9	37.6	35.2
1996	35.5	34.8	34.8	35.7	35.8	36.2	36.4	36.8	37.1	37.4	38.5	39.5	36.5
1997	37.7	36.6	36.6	36.5	36.8	37.0	37.2	37.3	37.2	37.1	38.3	39.2	37.2
1998	37.0	36.2	36.3	36.2	36.8	37.0	37.0	37.1	37.2	37.9	38.9	39.9	37.2
1999	37.4	36.9	37.0	38.0	38.3	38.6	38.7	38.8	38.8	38.9	40.4	41.5	38.6
2000	39.4	39.0	39.1	39.0	39.3	39.7	39.1	39.4	39.3	39.8	41.2	41.9	39.6
2001	40.0	39.4	39.3	39.7	39.9	40.1	39.3	39.1	38.8	39.3	40.2	40.8	39.7
2002	38.5	37.9	38.0	38.0	38.3	38.6	38.3	38.5	38.3	38.8	39.9	40.5	38.6
2003	37.7	37.3	37.5	37.9	38.3	38.4	38.6	38.5	38.6	39.2	39.7	39.8	38.5

Employment by Industry: Ohio—*Continued*

(Numbers in thousands. Not seasonally adjusted.)

Industry	January	February	March	April	May	June	July	August	September	October	November	December	Annual Average
AKRON—*Continued*													
Transportation and utilities													
1990	10.1	10.1	10.2	10.3	10.3	10.4	10.3	10.5	10.5	10.4	10.4	10.3	10.3
1991	9.8	9.7	9.8	9.8	10.0	10.1	10.0	10.2	10.1	10.1	10.2	10.2	10.0
1992	9.9	9.8	9.8	9.5	8.9	8.9	8.9	8.8	8.9	8.8	8.8	8.9	9.1
1993	8.6	8.5	8.4	8.6	8.7	8.8	8.9	9.0	9.1	9.2	9.2	9.3	8.8
1994	9.3	9.2	9.3	9.2	9.3	9.5	9.4	9.3	9.2	9.6	9.5	9.5	9.3
1995	9.1	9.0	9.1	9.2	9.2	9.4	9.5	9.6	9.6	10.1	10.2	10.2	9.5
1996	9.8	9.9	10.0	9.9	9.9	10.0	10.0	10.1	10.0	9.9	9.9	9.8	9.9
1997	9.5	9.5	9.5	9.7	9.8	9.8	9.9	9.8	10.0	10.0	10.1	10.1	9.8
1998	9.8	9.9	10.0	10.3	10.4	10.4	10.4	10.5	10.6	10.7	10.7	10.7	10.3
1999	10.4	10.3	10.4	10.5	10.6	10.7	11.1	10.6	10.6	10.9	10.9	10.9	10.6
2000	10.4	10.2	10.3	10.9	11.0	10.9	11.2	11.3	11.4	11.9	11.9	12.0	11.1
2001	12.6	12.3	12.4	12.6	12.6	12.7	12.5	12.5	12.5	12.4	12.2	12.2	12.5
2002	13.1	12.9	12.9	13.0	13.2	13.3	13.4	13.5	13.2	13.1	13.1	12.9	13.1
2003	10.5	10.1	10.2	10.5	10.6	10.7	10.3	10.1	10.3	10.4	10.3	10.8	10.4
Information													
1990	4.8	4.8	4.8	4.8	4.8	4.9	5.0	4.9	4.9	4.9	4.9	4.9	4.8
1991	4.8	4.8	4.8	4.7	4.7	4.8	4.8	4.8	4.7	4.7	4.7	4.8	4.7
1992	4.7	4.7	4.7	4.6	4.7	4.6	4.6	4.6	4.6	4.5	4.5	4.5	4.6
1993	4.6	4.6	4.6	4.5	4.5	4.5	4.5	4.5	4.4	4.3	4.4	4.4	4.4
1994	4.5	4.5	4.6	4.7	4.8	4.9	4.9	4.8	4.8	4.7	4.8	4.9	4.7
1995	4.9	4.8	4.7	4.8	4.8	4.7	4.7	4.7	4.7	4.5	4.6	4.5	4.7
1996	4.5	4.6	4.6	4.6	4.7	4.7	4.6	4.6	4.6	4.5	4.7	4.7	4.6
1997	4.7	4.8	4.8	4.7	4.7	4.8	4.9	4.9	4.8	4.7	4.7	4.7	4.7
1998	4.6	4.7	4.7	4.7	4.7	4.8	4.8	4.8	4.8	4.7	4.7	4.7	4.7
1999	4.9	5.0	5.1	5.0	5.1	5.2	5.2	5.2	5.2	5.2	5.2	5.2	5.1
2000	4.9	5.0	5.0	5.1	5.0	5.1	5.2	5.2	5.3	5.3	5.3	5.3	5.1
2001	5.0	5.1	5.0	4.9	4.9	4.9	4.9	5.0	4.9	5.0	5.0	5.0	5.0
2002	5.5	5.5	5.4	5.3	5.3	5.4	5.5	5.5	5.5	5.5	5.5	5.6	5.5
2003	5.5	5.5	5.5	5.6	5.7	5.7	5.7	5.7	5.7	5.7	5.7	5.8	5.7
Financial activities													
1990	11.2	11.3	11.3	11.4	11.4	11.5	11.4	11.5	11.4	11.5	11.4	11.5	11.4
1991	11.5	11.5	11.5	11.4	11.6	11.7	11.8	11.8	11.8	11.8	11.8	11.9	11.6
1992	11.5	11.5	11.6	11.9	12.0	12.1	12.3	12.3	12.3	12.3	12.3	12.3	12.0
1993	11.6	11.7	11.7	11.7	11.9	12.0	12.0	12.0	12.1	11.9	12.1	12.2	11.9
1994	12.1	12.1	12.2	12.2	12.4	12.5	12.4	12.4	12.4	12.3	12.4	12.5	12.3
1995	12.3	12.4	12.4	12.2	12.3	12.5	12.6	12.6	12.7	12.4	12.4	13.0	12.4
1996	13.1	13.1	13.3	13.3	13.5	13.5	13.6	13.6	13.6	13.6	13.7	13.9	13.4
1997	13.6	13.8	13.9	13.9	14.0	14.2	14.0	14.0	13.9	13.7	13.8	14.0	13.9
1998	13.6	13.7	13.9	13.8	13.9	14.1	13.9	14.0	13.9	13.9	14.0	14.2	13.9
1999	13.6	13.8	13.9	13.8	13.9	14.0	14.1	14.1	14.0	14.0	14.0	14.1	13.9
2000	14.1	14.1	14.3	14.0	14.3	14.6	14.4	14.5	14.5	14.3	14.3	14.4	14.3
2001	13.9	14.2	14.3	14.2	14.3	14.6	14.5	14.6	14.5	14.4	14.4	14.4	14.4
2002	14.1	14.2	14.2	13.9	14.1	14.2	14.2	14.3	14.3	14.3	14.3	14.4	14.2
2003	14.2	14.2	14.3	14.5	14.6	14.7	14.6	14.5	14.4	14.4	14.3	14.3	14.4
Professional and business services													
1990	24.7	24.8	25.4	26.0	26.4	26.8	26.6	26.7	26.7	27.0	26.9	26.5	26.2
1991	25.0	25.0	25.2	25.9	26.2	26.6	26.6	26.8	26.9	26.8	26.7	26.3	26.1
1992	26.8	26.8	27.0	28.2	28.9	29.3	28.5	28.9	28.7	29.6	29.2	28.9	28.4
1993	29.4	29.6	30.2	31.4	31.8	32.3	31.9	32.3	32.4	33.3	33.4	33.3	31.7
1994	32.5	33.2	33.5	33.2	33.6	34.4	34.3	34.2	34.6	33.9	34.3	34.0	33.8
1995	33.2	33.5	34.5	34.9	35.5	35.9	36.2	36.4	35.9	35.7	35.8	35.5	35.2
1996	34.3	33.8	34.2	34.2	35.0	35.3	35.3	35.8	35.9	37.0	36.9	36.2	35.3
1997	33.7	34.1	34.8	34.2	34.9	35.6	35.9	36.0	36.2	36.5	35.9	35.8	35.3
1998	34.4	34.5	34.7	35.8	36.0	36.5	36.0	36.3	35.9	36.1	36.4	36.4	35.7
1999	35.4	35.9	36.4	36.8	37.1	37.7	38.3	37.9	37.6	38.4	38.6	38.1	37.3
2000	36.4	36.2	37.1	38.3	37.9	38.7	38.5	38.6	38.5	38.4	37.8	37.4	37.8
2001	35.6	35.5	35.9	36.8	38.1	38.8	38.3	38.9	39.3	40.1	40.7	40.6	38.2
2002	38.7	38.7	39.2	39.0	39.1	39.6	40.0	40.5	40.8	41.0	40.1	40.1	39.7
2003	39.2	39.3	39.0	40.7	41.3	41.3	41.2	41.5	41.3	41.6	40.7	40.7	40.7
Educational and health services													
1990	29.5	29.6	29.8	29.6	29.8	29.9	29.6	29.8	30.4	30.8	31.0	31.1	30.0
1991	30.5	30.7	31.1	31.2	31.4	31.6	31.4	31.5	32.1	32.4	32.5	32.6	31.5
1992	32.2	32.4	32.6	33.1	33.4	33.3	33.3	33.3	33.7	34.2	34.3	34.4	33.3
1993	34.1	34.5	34.5	34.0	34.0	33.9	33.9	33.9	34.5	35.2	35.5	35.5	34.4
1994	35.1	35.3	35.6	35.0	35.6	35.4	35.3	35.3	36.0	36.5	36.5	36.7	35.6
1995	36.2	36.6	36.7	36.7	36.9	36.7	36.3	36.4	36.8	37.3	37.6	37.7	36.8
1996	37.1	37.4	37.5	37.5	37.7	37.3	37.1	37.3	37.6	37.9	37.7	37.7	37.4
1997	37.3	37.9	37.9	38.0	38.1	37.9	37.4	37.6	37.8	38.3	38.2	38.3	37.8
1998	38.1	38.5	38.7	37.9	37.8	37.8	37.4	37.5	37.9	38.8	38.9	39.2	38.2
1999	38.3	38.5	38.8	39.2	39.2	38.9	38.7	38.7	39.3	39.6	39.6	39.7	39.0
2000	39.0	39.3	39.6	38.8	39.0	38.9	39.1	39.3	39.6	40.1	40.3	40.5	39.4
2001	38.3	38.6	38.9	39.1	39.3	39.3	38.9	39.3	39.7	39.9	40.2	40.6	39.3
2002	40.3	40.6	40.8	40.6	40.7	40.5	40.5	40.6	41.0	41.2	41.5	41.6	40.8
2003	41.2	41.2	41.2	41.1	41.3	41.1	41.7	41.4	41.5	42.0	42.4	42.9	41.6

Employment by Industry: Ohio—*Continued*

(Numbers in thousands. Not seasonally adjusted.)

Industry	January	February	March	April	May	June	July	August	September	October	November	December	Annual Average
AKRON—*Continued*													
Leisure and hospitality													
1990	24.4	24.6	25.3	25.9	27.0	28.0	28.3	28.1	27.5	26.1	25.8	25.6	26.3
1991	24.7	24.8	25.0	25.9	27.8	29.1	28.8	28.7	28.4	26.3	25.6	25.4	26.7
1992	24.5	24.7	24.6	26.4	27.5	28.5	28.8	29.0	28.0	27.0	25.8	25.9	26.7
1993	24.3	24.6	24.6	26.0	27.5	28.4	28.4	28.6	28.2	26.8	26.5	26.4	26.6
1994	26.0	26.4	26.9	26.6	28.5	29.9	30.0	30.1	29.7	27.8	27.7	27.8	28.1
1995	27.0	27.4	28.0	28.6	30.4	32.3	31.8	32.1	31.5	28.8	28.0	28.3	29.5
1996	27.1	27.4	27.6	28.2	30.8	31.7	31.4	31.4	30.9	29.7	29.1	28.8	29.5
1997	27.2	27.6	27.9	29.2	31.3	32.6	32.3	32.3	31.4	30.7	29.6	30.0	30.1
1998	28.1	28.1	28.7	30.9	32.3	32.7	33.0	32.4	31.2	31.1	30.2	30.2	30.7
1999	27.9	28.2	28.7	31.3	32.5	33.1	34.3	34.4	33.0	32.0	31.4	31.6	31.5
2000	28.6	28.6	29.3	30.6	32.1	33.5	33.7	33.5	31.5	30.4	30.0	30.4	31.0
2001	27.7	27.9	28.3	29.3	31.2	32.7	32.8	32.8	30.9	29.9	29.4	29.3	30.2
2002	28.6	28.4	28.8	29.9	31.7	33.6	33.6	33.5	31.9	30.6	29.5	29.6	30.8
2003	28.1	27.7	28.2	29.8	31.7	32.9	33.1	32.5	31.3	30.4	29.9	30.0	30.5
Other services													
1990	10.6	10.6	10.7	10.9	11.1	11.3	11.3	11.4	11.3	11.3	11.5	11.5	11.1
1991	11.2	11.3	11.4	11.5	11.6	11.8	11.9	11.7	11.6	11.6	11.6	11.7	11.5
1992	11.4	11.5	11.6	12.0	12.2	12.4	12.4	12.3	12.1	12.3	12.3	12.7	12.1
1993	12.8	12.8	12.8	12.8	12.9	13.1	13.0	13.0	13.0	13.1	13.2	13.3	12.9
1994	13.2	13.2	13.5	13.3	13.5	13.7	13.5	13.5	13.4	13.6	13.6	13.8	13.4
1995	13.3	13.4	13.6	13.6	13.7	14.0	13.9	14.0	13.9	13.9	13.9	14.0	13.7
1996	13.8	13.9	14.1	14.0	13.9	14.0	14.3	14.3	14.1	14.2	14.2	14.2	14.0
1997	13.8	14.0	14.1	14.2	14.4	14.5	14.5	14.5	14.3	14.1	14.1	14.1	14.2
1998	13.9	14.1	14.2	14.1	14.2	14.3	14.2	14.1	14.0	14.1	14.1	14.1	14.1
1999	13.8	14.0	14.1	13.7	13.5	13.6	13.4	13.3	13.2	13.3	13.2	13.4	13.5
2000	13.4	13.5	13.6	13.3	13.4	13.7	13.6	13.4	13.4	13.3	13.3	13.5	13.4
2001	13.9	14.0	14.0	14.1	14.2	14.3	14.3	14.3	14.1	14.1	14.0	14.1	14.1
2002	13.9	13.9	14.0	14.1	14.2	14.4	14.2	14.1	14.0	14.0	13.9	14.0	14.1
2003	13.9	13.9	14.0	14.0	14.1	14.3	13.8	13.7	13.8	13.7	13.5	13.6	13.9
Government													
1990	41.7	46.5	47.0	46.6	47.4	40.9	39.2	39.5	45.9	47.0	47.5	47.0	44.6
1991	42.0	46.9	47.4	47.0	47.5	38.9	39.2	38.8	45.5	46.9	48.2	47.7	44.6
1992	44.9	47.1	47.5	47.2	47.5	38.6	39.0	38.2	44.8	46.7	46.6	46.4	44.5
1993	44.1	45.9	47.2	47.0	47.1	39.5	39.2	38.7	44.8	48.0	47.8	47.5	44.7
1994	44.0	46.2	47.4	47.0	47.6	40.1	39.3	39.2	46.8	48.3	48.5	48.3	45.2
1995	45.2	47.8	48.4	48.0	48.8	40.4	40.6	40.1	47.3	48.8	48.8	48.6	46.0
1996	45.9	48.3	49.1	48.4	49.3	41.2	40.6	41.2	47.7	49.2	49.6	49.3	46.6
1997	46.2	49.1	49.3	49.0	49.7	42.9	42.3	41.5	48.0	49.0	49.7	49.6	47.1
1998	48.0	48.9	49.4	49.3	49.8	43.1	42.0	41.3	47.8	49.1	49.4	49.9	47.3
1999	45.3	49.0	49.8	49.7	50.6	44.2	41.8	41.4	48.5	49.8	50.5	50.3	47.5
2000	46.5	50.4	50.4	50.6	51.7	44.1	43.0	41.4	47.6	49.8	50.1	48.4	47.8
2001	47.8	50.1	51.1	50.9	47.9	44.9	43.5	42.1	48.5	50.2	50.8	49.3	48.1
2002	47.7	50.0	50.9	50.8	47.9	45.8	43.6	42.2	49.2	51.1	51.6	50.8	48.5
2003	48.3	50.5	51.5	52.6	51.0	46.5	45.4	44.9	50.7	52.2	52.6	52.7	49.9
Federal government													
1990	2.4	2.4	2.5	2.6	3.0	2.6	2.6	2.4	2.4	2.4	2.4	2.4	2.5
1991	2.4	2.4	2.4	2.4	2.4	2.4	2.4	2.4	2.4	2.4	2.4	2.4	2.4
1992	2.4	2.4	2.4	2.4	2.3	2.3	2.4	2.3	2.3	2.3	2.3	2.4	2.3
1993	2.3	2.3	2.3	2.3	2.2	2.3	2.3	2.2	2.2	2.3	2.3	2.5	2.2
1994	2.5	2.5	2.4	2.5	2.5	2.6	2.8	2.9	2.9	2.9	2.9	3.2	2.7
1995	2.9	2.9	2.9	2.9	2.9	2.9	3.0	3.0	3.2	3.1	3.1	3.2	3.0
1996	3.0	3.0	3.1	3.1	3.2	3.3	3.2	3.3	3.2	3.2	3.3	3.4	3.1
1997	3.4	3.2	3.2	3.2	3.2	3.2	3.2	3.1	3.1	3.1	3.3	3.5	3.2
1998	3.1	3.1	3.0	3.0	3.0	3.1	3.0	3.0	3.0	3.1	3.1	3.3	3.0
1999	3.0	3.0	3.0	3.2	3.0	2.9	2.9	2.9	2.9	3.0	3.1	3.2	3.0
2000	2.9	3.0	3.0	3.1	3.8	3.4	3.3	3.1	3.0	3.1	3.1	3.2	3.1
2001	3.1	3.1	3.1	3.1	3.1	3.1	3.1	3.1	3.1	3.1	3.2	3.3	3.1
2002	3.2	3.1	3.1	3.1	3.1	3.2	3.1	3.3	3.3	3.3	3.2	3.4	3.2
2003	3.2	3.2	3.3	3.2	3.2	3.2	3.2	3.1	3.1	3.0	2.9	3.0	3.1
State government													
1990	13.0	17.4	17.7	17.4	17.3	12.2	11.5	12.1	17.1	17.8	18.1	17.7	15.7
1991	13.3	17.7	17.9	17.7	17.8	10.2	11.4	11.2	16.4	17.0	18.1	17.7	15.5
1992	14.9	17.3	17.5	17.3	17.4	9.6	11.1	10.6	15.4	16.6	16.5	16.4	15.0
1993	14.0	16.1	16.4	16.3	16.1	9.5	10.8	10.5	15.1	16.7	16.6	16.5	14.5
1994	14.0	16.0	16.4	16.5	16.1	9.4	10.6	10.3	16.0	16.2	16.2	16.1	14.4
1995	13.7	15.8	16.3	16.0	15.9	9.3	10.4	10.3	14.9	15.9	15.8	15.8	14.1
1996	13.3	15.4	15.9	15.5	15.4	9.0	10.1	10.1	14.8	15.6	15.6	15.6	13.8
1997	12.5	15.5	15.6	15.5	15.4	9.9	10.6	10.3	14.8	15.4	15.5	15.5	13.8
1998	14.1	15.4	15.6	15.4	15.3	10.2	10.5	10.1	14.6	15.4	15.5	15.7	13.9
1999	11.9	15.2	15.6	15.6	15.4	10.2	9.9	10.2	14.6	15.4	15.6	15.7	13.7
2000	11.8	15.2	15.5	15.4	15.3	9.9	10.0	8.7	12.7	14.2	14.2	12.6	12.9
2001	12.2	14.1	15.2	15.0	11.7	10.2	10.5	9.3	13.1	14.5	14.6	12.9	12.8
2002	11.8	13.4	14.4	14.4	11.1	9.8	10.4	9.3	13.2	14.6	14.6	13.7	12.6
2003	12.0	13.6	14.6	15.8	14.1	10.8	11.1	10.9	15.4	16.1	16.1	16.0	13.9

Employment by Industry: Ohio—*Continued*

(Numbers in thousands. Not seasonally adjusted.)

Industry	January	February	March	April	May	June	July	August	September	October	November	December	Annual Average
AKRON—*Continued*													
Local government													
1990	26.3	26.7	26.8	26.6	27.1	26.1	25.1	25.0	26.4	26.8	27.1	26.9	26.4
1991	26.3	26.9	27.1	26.9	27.4	26.3	25.4	25.2	26.8	27.6	27.8	27.6	26.7
1992	27.6	27.4	27.6	27.5	27.8	26.7	25.5	25.3	27.1	27.8	27.8	27.6	27.1
1993	27.8	27.5	28.5	28.4	28.8	27.7	26.1	26.0	27.5	29.0	28.9	28.5	27.8
1994	27.5	27.7	28.6	28.0	29.0	28.1	25.9	26.0	27.9	29.2	29.4	29.0	28.0
1995	28.6	29.1	29.2	29.1	30.0	28.2	27.2	26.8	29.2	29.8	29.9	29.6	28.8
1996	29.6	29.9	30.1	29.8	30.7	28.9	27.3	27.8	29.7	30.4	30.7	30.3	29.6
1997	30.3	30.4	30.5	30.3	31.1	29.8	28.5	28.1	30.1	30.5	30.9	30.6	30.0
1998	30.8	30.4	30.8	30.9	31.5	29.8	28.5	28.2	30.2	30.6	30.8	30.9	30.2
1999	30.4	30.8	31.2	30.9	32.2	31.1	29.0	28.3	31.0	31.4	31.8	31.4	30.7
2000	31.8	32.2	31.9	32.1	32.6	30.8	29.7	29.6	31.9	32.5	32.8	32.6	31.7
2001	32.5	32.9	32.8	32.8	33.1	31.6	29.9	29.7	32.3	32.6	33.0	33.1	32.2
2002	32.7	33.5	33.4	33.3	33.7	32.8	30.1	29.6	32.7	33.2	33.8	33.7	32.7
2003	33.1	33.7	33.6	33.6	33.7	32.5	31.1	30.9	32.2	33.1	33.6	33.7	32.9
CANTON													
Total nonfarm													
1990	162.1	161.4	163.0	164.5	167.7	169.0	169.1	169.9	170.4	169.9	170.2	169.3	167.2
1991	163.8	162.7	163.4	165.3	167.6	166.9	166.8	167.2	167.9	166.6	167.4	166.8	166.0
1992	162.1	161.5	162.7	164.7	166.9	167.5	166.6	166.7	166.6	168.4	168.0	168.4	165.8
1993	163.3	163.0	163.0	164.9	166.6	166.7	167.1	167.5	168.3	168.4	168.9	169.4	166.4
1994	165.1	165.4	167.1	168.2	170.7	172.0	170.3	170.4	172.0	172.4	173.6	174.2	170.1
1995	169.0	170.3	172.2	173.6	175.7	177.1	175.2	176.9	178.5	177.8	178.0	178.9	175.2
1996	173.1	173.7	175.3	176.7	178.6	180.0	179.1	179.8	181.1	180.8	181.6	181.7	178.4
1997	175.6	177.0	178.2	179.3	181.9	182.5	181.4	181.1	182.4	182.3	182.7	183.8	180.6
1998	178.7	180.1	180.9	182.5	184.9	184.8	184.1	184.6	185.6	186.6	186.7	187.3	183.9
1999	179.2	181.3	181.7	183.6	184.8	185.7	184.7	184.5	185.2	185.5	187.2	188.1	184.2
2000	183.5	183.7	185.7	187.6	189.1	190.3	187.8	187.3	188.1	187.9	189.2	189.7	187.4
2001	183.5	183.6	184.3	187.3	188.4	190.0	187.5	186.3	187.1	186.4	186.4	186.8	186.5
2002	179.5	179.8	181.3	182.0	183.3	183.1	182.6	181.7	182.8	182.4	182.7	183.0	182.0
2003	174.1	174.1	175.4	178.1	179.1	179.4	177.8	177.6	177.6	177.8	178.6	178.3	177.3
Total private													
1990	142.8	141.9	143.5	144.9	147.7	149.8	150.6	151.6	151.3	150.5	150.7	149.8	147.9
1991	144.3	143.1	143.9	146.2	148.1	148.4	148.2	149.0	148.8	147.1	147.4	147.0	146.7
1992	142.5	141.8	143.0	145.1	147.3	148.6	148.5	148.8	147.7	148.8	148.1	148.5	146.5
1993	143.6	143.3	143.4	145.5	147.2	148.1	149.3	149.9	149.6	149.0	149.2	149.8	147.3
1994	146.1	146.4	148.2	149.2	151.4	153.6	152.7	153.0	153.4	153.4	154.6	155.2	151.4
1995	150.6	151.5	153.3	154.6	156.7	158.6	157.5	159.4	159.6	158.8	158.8	159.4	156.5
1996	154.1	154.1	155.5	157.1	158.8	160.8	160.8	161.8	161.6	161.0	161.5	161.7	159.0
1997	156.6	157.0	158.2	159.4	161.7	162.8	162.4	163.0	162.6	162.1	162.3	163.6	160.9
1998	159.4	159.9	160.8	162.5	164.5	165.1	165.6	166.1	165.6	166.0	165.9	166.5	163.9
1999	159.6	160.5	160.9	163.0	163.9	165.5	165.6	165.7	164.8	164.3	165.7	166.7	163.8
2000	163.1	162.6	164.5	166.3	167.2	169.8	168.1	168.4	167.7	166.9	168.0	168.5	166.7
2001	163.1	162.3	163.0	166.0	167.0	169.3	167.6	166.9	166.1	164.9	164.7	164.8	165.5
2002	158.5	158.0	159.4	160.2	161.2	161.9	162.2	161.6	161.2	160.5	160.9	161.4	160.6
2003	153.2	152.5	153.6	156.3	157.3	158.1	157.7	157.7	156.3	156.1	156.7	156.4	156.0
Goods-producing													
1990	51.8	51.6	52.1	52.2	53.5	54.2	55.2	55.8	55.7	55.9	55.5	54.1	53.9
1991	51.9	50.9	51.3	51.8	52.3	52.6	52.4	52.7	52.4	51.7	51.6	50.8	51.8
1992	49.7	49.2	49.7	50.2	50.7	51.7	51.7	51.7	51.3	51.3	50.6	50.6	50.7
1993	49.2	49.1	48.8	49.6	50.3	50.9	51.7	51.6	51.8	51.4	51.3	51.0	50.5
1994	49.8	49.8	50.5	51.0	51.9	53.2	53.5	54.0	54.2	53.9	54.1	54.0	52.4
1995	53.1	53.1	53.7	54.3	55.0	55.8	55.7	56.0	56.0	55.2	54.7	54.5	54.7
1996	53.1	53.2	53.3	53.7	54.1	54.9	55.3	55.8	55.7	55.2	55.1	54.8	54.5
1997	53.2	53.2	53.4	54.1	54.8	55.4	55.3	55.7	55.6	55.5	55.4	55.6	54.7
1998	54.7	55.1	55.0	55.8	56.1	56.7	57.1	57.4	57.5	58.0	57.4	57.3	56.5
1999	54.7	55.1	55.1	55.0	55.1	55.8	56.3	56.3	56.4	55.7	55.8	55.7	55.5
2000	54.6	54.3	54.8	55.0	55.2	55.9	55.3	54.7	54.3	54.0	54.2	53.7	54.6
2001	50.9	50.4	50.7	51.6	52.1	52.6	52.4	52.2	51.6	51.5	50.7	50.3	51.4
2002	47.8	47.7	47.8	48.1	48.4	48.8	48.8	48.4	48.0	47.5	47.1	46.8	47.9
2003	42.9	42.5	42.9	43.4	43.5	43.6	43.7	43.3	42.5	42.2	42.0	41.7	42.9
Construction and mining													
1990	6.8	6.7	7.1	7.9	8.1	8.2	8.4	8.5	8.4	8.9	8.7	7.7	7.9
1991	6.5	6.3	6.6	7.1	7.3	7.6	8.1	8.2	8.1	8.0	7.7	7.2	7.3
1992	6.3	6.0	6.3	6.8	7.2	7.7	7.9	8.0	7.7	7.9	7.4	7.1	7.1
1993	6.4	6.2	6.2	7.2	7.8	8.0	8.5	8.3	8.4	8.5	8.2	8.0	7.6
1994	6.6	6.4	7.0	7.5	8.0	8.5	8.6	8.8	8.5	8.5	8.5	8.4	7.9
1995	7.2	6.9	7.4	8.1	8.6	9.1	9.3	9.4	9.3	9.0	8.6	8.3	8.4
1996	7.1	7.3	7.7	8.1	8.4	9.0	9.4	9.5	9.2	9.1	8.8	8.5	8.5
1997	7.4	7.5	7.7	8.4	8.9	9.2	9.5	9.5	9.3	9.3	9.1	8.9	8.7
1998	8.3	8.3	8.3	8.9	9.2	9.5	9.9	9.9	9.8	10.2	9.7	9.5	9.2
1999	7.6	8.0	8.1	8.5	8.9	9.3	10.1	10.0	9.8	9.7	9.6	9.3	9.0
2000	8.4	8.1	8.7	9.1	9.4	9.8	10.0	9.9	9.8	9.6	9.4	8.9	9.2
2001	8.1	8.2	8.5	9.0	9.5	9.7	10.0	10.1	9.7	9.7	9.4	9.0	9.2
2002	8.1	8.1	8.4	8.6	8.9	9.3	9.7	9.6	9.5	9.5	9.3	9.0	9.0
2003	8.3	7.9	8.3	9.1	9.4	9.8	10.1	10.2	10.0	9.9	9.6	9.1	9.3

Employment by Industry: Ohio—*Continued*

(Numbers in thousands. Not seasonally adjusted.)

Industry	January	February	March	April	May	June	July	August	September	October	November	December	Annual Average
CANTON—*Continued*													
Manufacturing													
1990	45.0	44.9	45.0	44.3	45.4	46.0	46.8	47.3	47.3	47.0	46.8	46.4	46.0
1991	45.4	44.6	44.7	44.7	45.0	45.0	44.3	44.5	44.3	43.7	43.9	43.6	44.4
1992	43.4	43.2	43.4	43.4	43.5	44.0	43.8	43.7	43.6	43.4	43.2	43.5	43.5
1993	42.8	42.9	42.6	42.4	42.5	42.9	43.2	43.3	43.4	42.9	43.1	43.0	42.9
1994	43.2	43.4	43.5	43.5	43.9	44.7	44.9	45.2	45.7	45.4	45.6	45.6	44.5
1995	45.9	46.2	46.3	46.2	46.4	46.7	46.4	46.6	46.7	46.2	46.1	46.2	46.3
1996	46.0	45.9	45.6	45.6	45.7	45.9	45.9	46.3	46.5	46.1	46.3	46.3	46.0
1997	45.8	45.7	45.7	45.7	45.9	46.2	45.8	46.2	46.3	46.2	46.3	46.7	46.0
1998	46.4	46.8	46.7	46.9	46.9	47.2	47.2	47.5	47.7	47.8	47.7	47.8	47.2
1999	47.1	47.1	47.0	46.5	46.2	46.5	46.2	46.3	46.6	46.0	46.2	46.4	46.5
2000	46.2	46.2	46.1	45.9	45.8	46.1	45.3	44.8	44.5	44.4	44.8	44.8	45.4
2001	42.8	42.2	42.2	42.6	42.6	42.9	42.4	42.1	41.9	41.8	41.3	41.3	42.2
2002	39.7	39.6	39.4	39.5	39.5	39.5	39.1	38.8	38.5	38.0	37.8	37.8	38.9
2003	34.6	34.6	34.6	34.3	34.1	33.8	33.6	33.1	32.5	32.3	32.4	32.6	33.5
Service-providing													
1990	110.3	109.8	110.9	112.3	114.2	114.8	113.9	114.1	114.7	114.0	114.7	115.2	113.2
1991	111.9	111.8	112.1	113.5	115.3	114.3	114.4	114.5	115.5	114.9	115.8	116.0	114.1
1992	112.4	112.3	113.0	114.5	116.2	115.8	114.9	115.0	115.3	117.1	117.4	117.8	115.1
1993	114.1	113.9	114.2	115.3	116.3	115.8	115.4	115.9	116.5	117.0	117.6	118.4	115.8
1994	115.3	115.6	116.6	117.2	118.8	118.8	116.8	116.4	117.8	118.5	119.5	120.2	117.6
1995	115.9	117.2	118.5	119.3	120.7	121.3	119.5	120.9	122.5	122.6	123.3	124.4	120.5
1996	120.0	120.5	122.0	123.0	124.5	125.1	123.8	124.0	125.4	125.6	126.5	126.9	123.9
1997	122.4	123.8	124.8	125.2	127.1	127.1	126.1	125.4	126.8	126.8	127.3	128.2	125.9
1998	124.0	125.0	125.9	126.7	128.8	128.1	127.0	127.2	128.1	128.6	129.3	130.0	127.3
1999	124.5	126.2	126.6	128.6	129.7	129.9	128.4	128.2	128.8	129.8	131.4	132.4	128.7
2000	128.9	129.4	130.9	132.6	133.9	134.4	132.5	132.6	133.8	133.9	135.0	136.0	132.8
2001	132.6	133.2	133.6	135.7	136.3	137.4	135.1	134.1	135.5	134.9	135.7	136.5	135.1
2002	131.7	132.1	133.5	133.9	134.9	134.3	133.8	133.3	134.8	134.9	135.6	136.2	134.1
2003	131.2	131.6	132.5	134.7	135.6	135.8	134.1	134.3	135.1	135.6	136.6	136.6	134.5
Trade, transportation, and utilities													
1990	32.2	31.4	31.6	31.9	32.4	32.7	32.7	32.7	32.6	32.2	32.6	33.1	32.3
1991	32.2	31.6	31.8	32.1	32.4	32.5	32.7	32.7	32.5	32.4	32.9	33.4	32.4
1992	31.8	31.3	31.4	31.8	32.4	32.4	32.5	32.4	32.0	32.4	32.8	33.3	32.2
1993	31.5	31.0	31.1	31.5	31.7	31.7	32.0	32.0	32.0	31.7	32.5	33.1	31.8
1994	31.6	31.5	31.5	31.4	31.8	32.0	32.0	32.0	32.0	32.2	32.8	33.4	32.0
1995	32.0	31.5	31.8	32.3	32.7	33.1	32.6	32.9	32.9	33.3	33.9	34.6	32.8
1996	32.4	32.1	32.5	33.0	33.2	33.6	34.0	34.1	34.2	34.5	35.3	35.7	33.7
1997	34.1	33.7	33.8	33.7	34.2	34.4	34.4	34.4	34.1	34.5	35.0	35.7	34.3
1998	34.4	33.9	33.9	33.4	33.9	34.0	34.1	34.1	33.9	34.1	34.9	35.2	34.1
1999	33.2	33.0	33.1	33.5	33.9	34.2	33.8	33.7	33.4	33.7	34.6	35.3	33.7
2000	33.9	33.3	33.8	34.2	34.5	35.3	35.2	35.2	34.8	35.1	35.8	36.5	34.8
2001	35.4	34.9	35.1	35.3	35.4	35.9	35.9	35.8	35.7	35.7	36.3	36.7	35.7
2002	34.9	34.4	34.7	34.8	34.9	35.1	35.1	35.0	34.7	34.6	35.5	36.0	35.0
2003	34.4	34.2	34.3	35.0	35.1	35.3	35.1	35.4	35.2	35.2	35.9	36.2	35.1
Wholesale trade													
1990	7.3	7.3	7.4	7.5	7.6	7.7	7.8	7.8	7.7	7.7	7.7	7.6	7.5
1991	7.9	7.8	7.8	8.0	8.0	8.0	8.0	7.9	7.8	7.9	7.9	7.9	7.9
1992	7.6	7.6	7.6	7.7	7.8	7.9	8.0	7.8	7.7	7.9	8.0	8.0	7.8
1993	7.6	7.6	7.6	7.7	7.7	7.8	8.0	7.9	7.9	7.8	8.0	8.0	7.8
1994	7.8	7.9	7.9	7.8	7.9	7.9	8.0	7.9	7.9	8.0	8.1	8.1	7.9
1995	8.0	7.9	8.0	8.1	8.2	8.2	8.2	8.2	8.1	8.3	8.4	8.4	8.1
1996	8.0	8.1	8.2	8.3	8.3	8.3	8.5	8.4	8.4	8.5	8.5	8.5	8.3
1997	8.3	8.3	8.4	8.4	8.5	8.6	8.6	8.4	8.4	8.4	8.5	8.5	8.4
1998	8.3	8.2	8.3	8.1	8.2	8.2	8.3	8.3	8.2	8.3	8.5	8.4	8.2
1999	8.2	8.2	8.2	8.3	8.3	8.4	8.3	8.2	8.1	8.1	8.1	8.1	8.2
2000	8.1	8.0	8.2	8.1	8.2	8.3	8.4	8.3	8.2	8.3	8.3	8.6	8.2
2001	8.6	8.6	8.7	8.7	8.7	8.9	9.1	8.9	8.9	9.0	9.0	9.0	8.8
2002	8.8	8.8	8.9	8.8	8.7	8.5	8.6	8.5	8.4	8.2	8.4	8.4	8.6
2003	8.1	8.3	8.4	8.5	8.3	8.4	8.5	8.4	8.4	8.4	8.4	8.4	8.4
Retail trade													
1990	21.2	20.4	20.5	20.8	21.1	21.3	21.2	21.2	21.2	20.8	21.2	21.8	21.0
1991	20.8	20.3	20.5	20.7	20.9	21.0	21.2	21.3	21.2	20.9	21.4	21.9	21.0
1992	20.8	20.3	20.4	20.6	21.1	20.9	20.8	20.9	20.6	20.8	21.1	21.6	20.8
1993	20.3	19.8	19.8	20.1	20.3	20.2	20.3	20.4	20.4	20.2	20.8	21.4	20.3
1994	20.2	20.0	20.0	20.0	20.3	20.5	20.4	20.5	20.5	20.6	21.1	21.7	20.4
1995	20.5	20.1	20.3	20.6	20.9	21.2	20.8	21.0	21.1	21.3	21.8	22.5	21.0
1996	20.7	20.3	20.5	21.0	21.2	21.5	21.8	22.1	22.2	22.4	23.2	23.7	21.7
1997	22.6	22.2	22.2	22.1	22.4	22.6	22.6	22.7	22.4	22.8	23.3	23.9	22.6
1998	23.0	22.6	22.5	22.3	22.6	22.7	22.7	22.6	22.5	22.5	23.2	23.6	22.7
1999	22.0	21.7	21.8	22.1	22.4	22.6	22.4	22.4	22.2	22.4	23.3	24.0	22.4
2000	22.7	22.2	22.5	23.1	23.2	23.9	23.7	23.8	23.5	23.6	24.4	24.8	23.4
2001	23.4	22.9	23.0	23.2	23.3	23.6	23.4	23.4	23.3	23.2	23.8	24.2	23.4
2002	22.8	22.3	22.5	22.6	22.8	23.2	23.1	23.0	22.8	22.8	23.5	24.0	23.0
2003	22.6	22.3	22.3	22.8	23.2	23.2	22.9	23.3	23.1	23.1	23.8	24.1	23.1

Employment by Industry: Ohio—*Continued*

(Numbers in thousands. Not seasonally adjusted.)

Industry	January	February	March	April	May	June	July	August	September	October	November	December	Annual Average
CANTON—*Continued*													
Transportation and utilities													
1990	3.7	3.7	3.7	3.6	3.7	3.7	3.7	3.7	3.7	3.7	3.7	3.7	3.6
1991	3.5	3.5	3.5	3.4	3.5	3.5	3.5	3.5	3.5	3.6	3.6	3.6	3.5
1992	3.4	3.4	3.4	3.5	3.5	3.6	3.7	3.7	3.7	3.7	3.7	3.7	3.5
1993	3.6	3.6	3.7	3.7	3.7	3.7	3.7	3.7	3.7	3.7	3.7	3.7	3.6
1994	3.6	3.6	3.6	3.6	3.6	3.6	3.6	3.6	3.6	3.6	3.6	3.6	3.6
1995	3.5	3.5	3.5	3.6	3.6	3.7	3.6	3.7	3.7	3.7	3.7	3.7	3.6
1996	3.7	3.7	3.8	3.7	3.7	3.8	3.7	3.6	3.6	3.6	3.6	3.5	3.6
1997	3.2	3.2	3.2	3.2	3.3	3.2	3.2	3.3	3.3	3.3	3.2	3.3	3.2
1998	3.1	3.1	3.1	3.0	3.1	3.1	3.1	3.2	3.2	3.3	3.2	3.2	3.1
1999	3.0	3.1	3.1	3.1	3.2	3.2	3.1	3.1	3.1	3.2	3.2	3.2	3.1
2000	3.1	3.1	3.1	3.0	3.1	3.1	3.1	3.1	3.1	3.2	3.1	3.1	3.1
2001	3.4	3.4	3.4	3.4	3.4	3.4	3.4	3.5	3.5	3.5	3.5	3.5	3.4
2002	3.3	3.3	3.3	3.4	3.4	3.4	3.4	3.5	3.5	3.6	3.6	3.6	3.4
2003	3.7	3.6	3.6	3.7	3.6	3.7	3.7	3.7	3.7	3.7	3.7	3.7	3.7
Information													
1990	2.4	2.4	2.4	2.4	2.4	2.4	2.4	2.4	2.4	2.4	2.4	2.4	2.4
1991	2.4	2.4	2.4	2.3	2.3	2.3	2.3	2.3	2.3	2.3	2.3	2.3	2.3
1992	2.3	2.3	2.3	2.3	2.4	2.4	2.3	2.3	2.3	2.4	2.4	2.4	2.3
1993	2.5	2.5	2.5	2.5	2.5	2.5	2.5	2.5	2.5	2.4	2.4	2.4	2.4
1994	2.4	2.4	2.3	2.2	2.2	2.2	2.2	2.2	2.2	2.2	2.2	2.2	2.2
1995	2.1	2.2	2.2	2.1	2.1	2.1	2.1	2.1	2.1	2.1	2.1	2.2	2.1
1996	2.1	2.1	2.2	2.2	2.2	2.2	2.2	2.2	2.2	2.2	2.2	2.3	2.1
1997	2.3	2.3	2.3	2.3	2.3	2.5	2.5	2.5	2.4	2.4	2.4	2.5	2.3
1998	2.5	2.5	2.5	2.5	2.5	2.5	2.4	2.4	2.3	2.4	2.4	2.4	2.4
1999	2.4	2.3	2.3	2.4	2.4	2.4	2.4	2.4	2.4	2.4	2.4	2.5	2.3
2000	2.4	2.4	2.4	2.4	2.4	2.4	2.4	2.4	2.4	2.4	2.4	2.4	2.4
2001	2.4	2.4	2.4	2.4	2.4	2.4	2.4	2.4	2.3	2.3	2.4	2.4	2.4
2002	2.3	2.3	2.3	2.3	2.3	2.4	2.3	2.3	2.3	2.3	2.3	2.3	2.3
2003	2.3	2.3	2.3	2.3	2.3	2.3	2.3	2.3	2.2	2.3	2.3	2.3	2.3
Financial activities													
1990	6.7	6.7	6.8	6.9	6.8	6.9	6.8	6.8	6.7	6.7	6.7	6.7	6.7
1991	6.6	6.6	6.5	6.4	6.4	6.4	6.2	6.3	6.3	6.2	6.2	6.2	6.3
1992	6.2	6.2	6.3	6.3	6.4	6.4	6.3	6.3	6.2	6.3	6.3	6.4	6.3
1993	6.3	6.3	6.3	6.3	6.3	6.3	6.3	6.4	6.3	6.4	6.5	6.6	6.3
1994	6.5	6.5	6.6	6.6	6.7	6.8	6.7	6.7	6.7	6.6	6.6	6.6	6.6
1995	6.5	6.5	6.6	6.4	6.2	6.3	6.3	6.4	6.3	6.3	6.3	6.3	6.3
1996	6.4	6.4	6.4	6.4	6.5	6.5	6.4	6.5	6.4	6.4	6.5	6.5	6.4
1997	6.3	6.4	6.4	6.5	6.5	6.6	6.5	6.5	6.5	6.4	6.5	6.6	6.4
1998	6.5	6.5	6.6	6.8	6.8	6.9	6.9	6.9	6.8	6.9	6.9	7.0	6.7
1999	6.8	6.9	6.9	7.1	7.2	7.3	7.3	7.3	7.2	7.2	7.3	7.4	7.1
2000	7.3	7.4	7.4	7.5	7.5	7.6	7.6	7.6	7.6	7.4	7.4	7.5	7.4
2001	7.2	7.2	7.2	7.3	7.4	7.5	7.5	7.5	7.5	7.5	7.5	7.6	7.4
2002	7.4	7.4	7.6	7.6	7.6	7.7	7.9	7.9	7.9	7.9	7.8	7.9	7.7
2003	7.6	7.6	7.6	7.8	7.8	7.9	7.9	7.8	7.8	7.8	7.8	7.8	7.8
Professional and business services													
1990	9.7	9.8	9.9	9.9	10.1	10.3	10.3	10.4	10.3	10.4	10.4	10.3	10.1
1991	9.5	9.6	9.6	10.2	10.2	10.2	10.0	10.2	10.4	10.6	10.6	10.5	10.1
1992	9.7	10.0	9.9	10.2	10.3	10.2	10.4	10.5	10.7	10.9	10.5	10.3	10.3
1993	10.1	10.2	10.1	10.5	10.7	10.5	10.8	11.0	11.2	11.4	11.0	11.0	10.7
1994	10.8	11.0	11.2	11.6	11.7	11.9	11.4	11.4	11.6	11.8	11.9	11.9	11.5
1995	11.6	12.0	12.1	12.1	12.2	12.4	12.3	13.0	13.1	13.2	13.4	13.2	12.5
1996	12.4	12.5	12.7	12.9	13.1	13.4	13.2	13.6	13.9	13.3	13.3	13.3	13.1
1997	12.2	12.4	12.7	13.4	13.7	13.8	13.8	13.9	14.1	13.8	13.9	14.0	13.4
1998	13.0	13.3	13.5	13.3	13.6	13.8	13.9	14.1	14.0	13.8	13.8	13.9	13.6
1999	13.2	13.3	13.3	14.0	13.8	14.0	13.9	13.9	13.8	14.0	14.3	14.5	13.8
2000	14.1	14.3	14.2	15.3	15.5	16.0	15.5	15.9	16.1	15.4	15.6	15.5	15.2
2001	15.4	15.6	15.9	16.1	15.6	16.0	17.1	16.4	16.6	15.7	15.7	15.7	16.0
2002	15.3	15.1	15.3	15.0	14.9	14.9	15.5	15.3	15.7	15.6	15.8	15.8	15.4
2003	14.4	14.3	14.5	14.7	14.9	15.0	14.7	14.6	14.7	14.8	14.8	14.8	14.7
Educational and health services													
1990	20.1	20.1	20.2	20.6	20.8	20.8	20.8	21.0	21.2	21.4	21.5	21.6	20.8
1991	21.0	21.2	21.3	21.6	22.0	21.5	21.4	21.6	22.0	22.1	22.2	22.2	21.6
1992	21.7	21.8	22.0	22.2	22.3	22.2	22.2	22.3	22.4	22.8	22.9	22.9	22.3
1993	22.0	22.0	22.2	22.1	22.2	22.0	22.1	22.3	22.3	22.5	22.6	22.7	22.2
1994	22.7	22.8	23.0	22.7	22.9	22.8	22.6	22.7	23.0	23.2	23.5	23.6	22.9
1995	23.0	23.6	23.8	23.8	24.0	23.9	23.7	23.9	24.1	24.4	24.4	24.5	23.9
1996	24.2	24.4	24.5	24.6	24.7	24.6	24.3	24.4	24.7	25.3	25.2	25.2	24.6
1997	25.0	25.3	25.4	25.3	25.4	25.1	25.0	25.1	25.4	25.6	25.6	25.7	25.3
1998	25.9	26.1	26.3	26.7	26.9	26.4	26.2	26.3	26.6	26.7	26.7	26.7	26.4
1999	26.6	27.0	26.8	26.5	26.5	26.2	26.2	26.4	26.3	26.8	26.9	26.8	26.5
2000	27.0	27.2	27.5	27.2	27.1	27.0	27.0	27.3	27.8	27.8	28.1	28.3	27.4
2001	27.5	27.8	27.2	28.3	28.4	28.4	26.0	26.1	26.5	26.7	26.8	26.7	27.2
2002	26.2	26.5	26.7	26.9	26.8	26.4	26.1	26.2	26.6	26.9	27.1	27.2	26.6
2003	26.7	26.9	27.0	27.2	27.0	26.7	26.7	26.9	27.1	27.4	27.6	27.4	27.1

Employment by Industry: Ohio—*Continued*

(Numbers in thousands. Not seasonally adjusted.)

Industry	January	February	March	April	May	June	July	August	September	October	November	December	Annual Average
CANTON—*Continued*													
Leisure and hospitality													
1990	13.4	13.3	13.8	14.2	14.8	15.2	15.2	15.4	15.3	14.5	14.5	14.4	14.5
1991	13.7	13.7	13.8	14.6	15.2	15.5	15.8	15.8	15.6	14.6	14.3	14.2	14.7
1992	13.9	13.7	14.1	14.7	15.4	15.7	15.6	15.8	15.4	15.2	15.1	15.1	14.9
1993	14.4	14.3	14.4	15.1	15.6	16.1	15.9	16.0	15.6	15.3	15.0	14.9	15.2
1994	14.4	14.4	15.0	15.6	16.0	16.4	16.2	16.0	15.7	15.5	15.3	15.2	15.4
1995	14.4	14.6	15.0	15.6	16.3	16.6	16.5	16.7	16.6	16.0	15.7	15.7	15.8
1996	15.1	15.0	15.4	16.1	16.8	17.2	17.0	16.8	16.3	15.8	15.6	15.5	16.0
1997	15.3	15.4	15.8	15.6	16.3	16.5	16.5	16.4	16.1	15.5	15.2	15.2	15.8
1998	14.4	14.5	14.9	15.6	16.3	16.4	16.6	16.5	16.2	15.8	15.6	15.7	15.7
1999	14.7	14.8	15.3	16.1	16.6	17.0	17.3	17.2	16.9	16.2	16.0	16.1	16.1
2000	15.4	15.3	15.9	16.2	16.4	16.9	16.6	16.8	16.2	16.2	15.9	16.0	16.1
2001	14.9	14.7	15.0	15.5	16.0	16.6	16.7	16.8	16.4	15.8	15.7	15.7	15.8
2002	15.1	15.0	15.3	15.8	16.5	16.8	16.8	16.9	16.3	16.2	15.7	15.8	16.0
2003	15.4	15.2	15.4	16.4	17.1	17.5	17.7	17.8	17.2	16.8	16.8	16.6	16.7
Other services													
1990	6.5	6.6	6.7	6.8	6.9	7.3	7.2	7.1	7.1	7.0	7.1	7.2	6.9
1991	7.0	7.1	7.2	7.2	7.3	7.4	7.4	7.4	7.3	7.2	7.3	7.4	7.2
1992	7.2	7.3	7.3	7.4	7.4	7.6	7.5	7.5	7.4	7.5	7.5	7.5	7.4
1993	7.6	7.9	8.0	7.9	7.9	8.1	8.0	8.1	7.9	7.9	7.9	8.1	7.9
1994	7.9	8.0	8.1	8.1	8.2	8.3	8.1	8.0	8.0	8.0	8.2	8.3	8.1
1995	7.9	8.0	8.1	8.0	8.2	8.4	8.3	8.4	8.5	8.3	8.3	8.4	8.2
1996	8.4	8.4	8.5	8.2	8.2	8.4	8.4	8.4	8.2	8.3	8.3	8.4	8.3
1997	8.2	8.3	8.4	8.5	8.5	8.5	8.4	8.5	8.4	8.4	8.3	8.3	8.3
1998	8.0	8.0	8.1	8.4	8.4	8.4	8.4	8.4	8.3	8.3	8.2	8.3	8.2
1999	8.0	8.1	8.1	8.4	8.4	8.6	8.4	8.5	8.4	8.3	8.4	8.4	8.3
2000	8.4	8.4	8.5	8.5	8.6	8.7	8.5	8.5	8.5	8.6	8.6	8.6	8.5
2001	9.4	9.3	9.5	9.5	9.7	9.9	9.6	9.7	9.5	9.7	9.6	9.7	9.6
2002	9.5	9.6	9.7	9.7	9.8	9.8	9.7	9.6	9.7	9.5	9.6	9.6	9.7
2003	9.5	9.5	9.6	9.5	9.6	9.8	9.6	9.6	9.6	9.6	9.5	9.6	9.6
Government													
1990	19.3	19.5	19.5	19.6	20.0	19.2	18.5	18.3	19.1	19.4	19.5	19.5	19.2
1991	19.5	19.6	19.5	19.1	19.5	18.5	18.6	18.2	19.1	19.5	20.0	19.8	19.2
1992	19.6	19.7	19.7	19.6	19.6	18.9	18.1	17.9	18.9	19.6	19.9	19.9	19.2
1993	19.7	19.7	19.6	19.4	19.4	18.6	17.8	17.6	18.7	19.4	19.7	19.6	19.1
1994	19.0	19.0	18.9	19.0	19.3	18.4	17.6	17.4	18.6	19.0	19.0	19.0	18.6
1995	18.4	18.8	18.9	19.0	19.0	18.5	17.7	17.5	18.9	19.0	19.2	19.5	18.7
1996	19.0	19.6	19.8	19.6	19.8	19.2	18.3	18.0	19.5	19.8	20.1	20.0	19.3
1997	19.0	20.0	20.0	19.9	20.2	19.7	19.0	18.1	19.8	20.2	20.4	20.2	19.7
1998	19.3	20.2	20.1	20.0	20.4	19.7	18.5	18.5	20.0	20.6	20.8	20.8	19.9
1999	19.6	20.8	20.8	20.6	20.9	20.2	19.1	18.8	20.4	21.2	21.5	21.4	20.4
2000	20.4	21.1	21.2	21.3	21.9	20.5	19.7	18.9	20.4	21.0	21.2	21.2	20.7
2001	20.4	21.3	21.3	21.3	21.4	20.7	19.9	19.4	21.0	21.5	21.7	22.0	21.0
2002	21.0	21.8	21.9	21.8	22.1	21.2	20.4	20.1	21.6	21.9	21.8	21.6	21.4
2003	20.9	21.6	21.8	21.8	21.8	21.3	20.1	19.9	21.3	21.7	21.9	21.9	21.3
Federal government													
2001	1.3	1.3	1.3	1.3	1.3	1.3	1.3	1.3	1.3	1.3	1.3	1.4	1.3
2002	1.3	1.3	1.3	1.3	1.3	1.3	1.3	1.3	1.3	1.3	1.2	1.3	1.3
2003	1.3	1.2	1.3	1.2	1.2	1.2	1.2	1.2	1.2	1.2	1.2	1.2	1.2
State government													
2001	1.4	1.4	1.5	1.5	1.3	1.3	1.4	1.3	1.4	1.5	1.4	1.5	1.4
2002	1.4	1.4	1.4	1.5	1.3	1.3	1.3	1.3	1.4	1.4	1.4	1.3	1.4
2003	1.4	1.4	1.4	1.4	1.3	1.3	1.3	1.3	1.4	1.4	1.4	1.6	1.4
Local government													
1990	16.3	16.4	16.3	16.3	16.3	15.9	15.2	15.2	15.9	16.2	16.4	16.3	16.0
1991	16.5	16.5	16.3	16.0	16.4	15.5	15.5	15.2	16.1	16.5	16.8	16.6	16.1
1992	16.6	16.6	16.6	16.5	16.6	16.1	15.1	15.1	16.0	16.7	17.0	17.0	16.3
1993	16.9	16.8	16.7	16.5	16.5	15.9	15.0	14.8	16.0	16.5	17.0	16.7	16.2
1994	16.2	16.2	16.1	16.1	16.4	15.7	14.8	14.7	15.8	16.1	16.1	16.0	15.8
1995	15.6	16.0	16.1	16.1	16.1	15.8	15.0	14.8	16.1	16.2	16.4	16.6	15.9
1996	16.3	16.8	17.0	16.8	17.0	16.6	15.6	15.3	16.7	17.0	17.3	17.1	16.6
1997	16.3	17.2	17.2	17.2	17.5	17.1	16.4	15.5	17.1	17.5	17.6	17.4	17.0
1998	16.7	17.5	17.4	17.3	17.7	17.0	15.9	15.8	17.3	17.8	18.0	17.9	17.1
1999	16.9	18.0	18.0	17.8	18.1	17.6	16.4	16.2	17.6	18.4	18.6	18.4	17.6
2000	17.6	18.3	18.3	18.3	18.5	17.7	16.9	16.2	17.7	18.3	18.4	18.3	17.8
2001	17.7	18.6	18.5	18.5	18.8	18.1	17.2	16.8	18.3	18.7	19.0	19.1	18.3
2002	18.3	19.1	19.2	19.0	19.5	18.6	17.8	17.5	18.9	19.2	19.2	19.0	18.8
2003	18.2	19.0	19.1	19.2	19.3	18.8	17.6	17.4	18.7	19.1	19.3	19.1	18.7

Employment by Industry: Ohio—*Continued*

(Numbers in thousands. Not seasonally adjusted.)

Industry	January	February	March	April	May	June	July	August	September	October	November	December	Annual Average
CINCINNATI													
Total nonfarm													
1990	734.5	737.9	745.7	751.1	760.3	764.5	760.6	763.9	766.6	765.1	767.5	770.5	757.3
1991	740.3	738.7	744.5	748.4	755.0	759.7	752.9	753.6	759.5	756.7	758.5	761.9	752.4
1992	736.0	738.6	744.1	756.4	762.5	766.3	760.7	760.0	762.3	764.1	761.6	766.4	756.5
1993	744.2	746.3	749.5	759.5	767.0	771.4	767.9	769.4	775.0	775.0	776.4	779.7	765.1
1994	757.8	764.2	773.9	779.3	788.1	792.4	783.3	787.9	793.2	796.4	799.7	805.3	785.1
1995	776.9	781.2	791.7	799.6	806.5	814.1	803.5	807.9	811.0	813.1	814.9	821.6	803.5
1996	796.8	803.5	809.5	817.6	826.3	832.0	823.6	827.4	829.0	830.5	840.3	845.0	823.4
1997	819.1	821.1	831.2	836.6	847.1	852.3	847.2	850.0	851.3	851.5	856.8	861.2	843.7
1998	835.0	839.2	848.4	856.8	866.9	870.7	862.8	865.5	866.2	871.0	873.4	877.8	861.1
1999	847.6	854.5	861.3	871.0	876.1	880.8	881.1	881.9	884.2	883.7	888.1	895.5	875.4
2000	865.1	871.0	879.5	881.4	890.5	896.5	891.1	890.5	890.4	891.9	894.2	898.5	886.7
2001	874.3	876.1	881.2	881.9	888.3	892.6	883.5	883.7	879.8	876.4	876.0	877.7	881.0
2002	857.7	859.2	865.8	864.5	868.8	870.9	865.0	867.5	864.2	865.9	868.5	869.7	865.6
2003	850.9	849.0	856.9	870.7	875.9	878.6	873.5	873.5	872.0	874.9	877.9	876.8	869.2
Total private													
1990	638.5	639.3	646.4	652.0	659.3	667.7	668.6	672.6	671.5	668.4	668.1	670.8	660.2
1991	642.4	638.6	644.3	648.6	655.2	662.0	661.6	662.9	661.9	657.8	658.6	661.8	654.6
1992	636.8	637.2	642.8	654.6	660.6	667.0	667.5	667.8	664.9	665.1	662.2	666.9	657.7
1993	645.3	645.2	648.4	658.8	666.3	672.4	674.1	675.9	676.4	674.0	675.2	678.3	665.8
1994	658.4	662.2	671.7	676.7	685.8	692.3	689.6	693.7	693.9	694.4	697.8	703.3	684.9
1995	676.4	678.0	688.0	696.1	703.4	713.0	708.7	713.0	711.8	711.0	713.9	719.6	702.7
1996	696.2	700.1	706.0	713.8	722.7	730.0	728.0	732.6	728.9	729.5	737.3	742.6	722.3
1997	721.4	720.8	729.8	734.3	745.0	752.4	753.4	755.4	752.7	752.9	756.0	760.1	744.5
1998	736.3	737.7	745.4	753.6	762.7	769.9	768.7	770.3	765.9	769.5	770.6	775.6	760.5
1999	748.0	752.3	757.5	767.1	772.3	779.1	785.0	785.8	783.3	781.3	785.2	793.0	774.1
2000	764.4	766.8	774.3	776.0	783.1	791.9	792.4	793.0	789.5	788.8	790.4	794.4	783.7
2001	771.2	770.6	775.2	775.2	780.8	787.3	783.8	783.8	776.2	771.0	769.9	771.2	776.4
2002	752.3	751.4	757.0	755.8	759.7	764.0	763.2	764.3	759.0	758.2	760.5	762.1	759.0
2003	745.1	741.9	749.2	762.3	767.4	772.0	772.9	771.9	767.1	767.0	769.5	768.4	762.9
Goods-producing													
1990	163.4	163.9	165.4	165.5	167.4	169.3	170.2	170.8	170.6	168.7	168.8	167.1	167.5
1991	160.5	158.9	160.1	160.0	162.2	163.5	163.6	164.7	164.8	164.1	163.3	162.4	162.3
1992	156.3	155.6	157.8	159.5	159.8	160.9	161.6	161.7	161.5	161.3	160.1	159.3	159.6
1993	154.4	153.6	154.4	157.3	158.1	159.2	159.2	160.1	160.9	160.2	159.4	158.2	157.9
1994	152.3	152.5	155.1	155.6	158.7	160.2	160.0	161.0	161.2	161.7	162.3	161.6	158.5
1995	155.9	156.2	158.9	160.1	161.3	163.4	163.0	163.6	163.7	163.8	163.5	162.6	161.3
1996	155.9	156.1	157.6	159.7	161.4	163.9	164.7	166.2	165.8	164.7	164.7	164.2	162.0
1997	160.6	160.4	162.6	163.2	164.9	166.6	166.7	167.4	167.1	165.6	165.8	165.3	164.6
1998	160.3	160.2	161.9	161.6	163.7	166.1	166.8	167.3	166.5	166.9	166.4	166.1	164.4
1999	161.7	163.0	164.0	164.7	165.0	166.1	168.2	168.1	167.8	168.0	167.8	167.7	166.0
2000	163.3	164.0	165.8	165.7	167.4	168.0	168.4	167.8	167.1	166.4	165.8	164.9	166.2
2001	159.4	159.5	160.2	160.9	161.9	162.4	161.4	161.9	160.1	158.9	157.5	156.1	160.0
2002	149.9	149.1	149.4	148.3	148.3	149.4	149.6	150.4	149.8	149.6	149.3	147.9	149.3
2003	146.0	144.8	146.5	148.8	149.5	150.0	150.4	150.3	150.0	149.4	148.8	147.4	148.5
Construction and mining													
1990	31.1	31.3	32.3	32.9	34.4	34.9	35.6	35.6	35.2	34.2	34.1	32.5	33.6
1991	28.7	28.3	29.2	30.6	31.6	32.5	33.8	34.2	34.2	33.7	33.0	31.8	31.8
1992	28.6	28.7	30.7	31.5	33.0	33.7	33.9	33.9	33.5	33.1	31.7	30.8	31.9
1993	28.3	28.4	28.8	31.7	33.3	34.2	35.2	35.5	35.7	36.3	35.6	34.8	33.1
1994	30.1	30.3	32.2	34.4	36.6	37.8	37.7	37.9	37.6	37.6	37.1	36.0	35.4
1995	32.6	32.3	34.2	35.0	36.1	37.5	37.2	37.5	37.2	37.3	36.9	36.2	35.8
1996	31.6	32.3	33.7	35.7	37.0	38.6	39.4	40.3	40.0	39.4	38.9	38.0	37.0
1997	35.4	35.5	37.0	38.9	40.3	41.3	42.0	42.4	41.9	40.9	39.9	38.8	39.5
1998	35.7	35.6	36.5	38.5	39.8	41.2	42.2	42.0	41.3	41.4	41.1	40.5	39.6
1999	36.7	37.8	38.7	40.0	40.7	41.7	43.8	43.7	43.4	43.6	43.4	42.9	41.3
2000	39.9	40.0	41.4	41.7	42.9	44.0	44.3	44.2	43.3	42.7	42.1	41.2	42.3
2001	39.1	39.3	40.3	41.9	43.0	44.2	44.6	44.7	44.0	43.7	43.2	42.2	42.5
2002	38.7	38.6	39.2	39.2	39.3	40.5	41.0	41.4	40.9	40.4	40.2	38.9	39.9
2003	37.3	36.6	38.1	40.5	41.4	42.2	43.0	43.3	42.7	42.4	42.3	40.5	40.9
Manufacturing													
1990	132.3	132.6	133.1	132.6	133.0	134.4	134.6	135.2	135.4	134.5	134.7	134.6	133.9
1991	131.8	130.6	130.9	129.4	130.6	131.0	129.8	130.5	130.6	130.4	130.3	130.6	130.5
1992	127.7	126.9	127.1	128.0	126.8	127.2	127.7	127.8	128.0	128.2	128.4	128.5	127.6
1993	126.1	125.2	125.6	125.6	124.8	125.0	124.0	124.6	125.2	123.9	123.8	123.4	124.7
1994	122.2	122.2	122.9	121.2	122.1	122.4	122.3	123.1	123.6	124.1	125.2	125.6	123.0
1995	123.3	123.9	124.7	125.1	125.2	125.9	125.8	126.1	126.5	126.5	126.6	126.4	125.5
1996	124.3	123.8	123.9	124.0	124.4	125.3	125.3	125.9	125.8	125.3	125.8	126.2	125.0
1997	125.2	124.9	125.6	124.3	124.6	125.3	124.7	125.0	125.2	124.7	125.9	126.5	125.1
1998	124.6	124.6	125.4	123.1	123.9	124.9	124.6	125.3	125.2	125.5	125.3	125.6	124.8
1999	125.0	125.2	125.3	124.7	124.3	124.4	124.4	124.4	124.4	124.4	124.4	124.8	124.6
2000	123.4	124.0	124.4	124.0	124.5	124.0	124.1	123.6	123.8	123.7	123.7	123.7	123.9
2001	120.3	120.2	119.9	119.0	118.9	118.2	116.8	117.2	116.1	115.2	114.3	113.9	117.5
2002	111.2	110.5	110.2	109.1	109.0	108.9	108.6	109.0	108.9	109.2	109.1	109.0	109.4
2003	108.7	108.2	108.4	108.3	108.1	107.8	107.4	107.0	107.3	107.0	106.5	106.9	107.6

Employment by Industry: Ohio—*Continued*

(Numbers in thousands. Not seasonally adjusted.)

Industry	January	February	March	April	May	June	July	August	September	October	November	December	Annual Average
CINCINNATI—*Continued*													
Service-providing													
1990	571.1	574.0	580.3	585.6	592.9	595.2	590.4	593.1	596.0	596.4	598.7	603.4	589.7
1991	579.8	579.8	584.4	588.4	592.8	596.2	589.3	588.9	594.7	592.6	595.2	599.5	590.1
1992	579.7	583.0	586.3	596.9	602.7	605.4	599.1	598.3	600.8	602.8	601.5	607.1	596.9
1993	589.8	592.7	595.1	602.2	608.9	612.2	608.7	609.3	614.1	614.8	617.0	621.5	607.1
1994	605.5	611.7	618.8	623.7	629.4	632.2	623.3	626.9	632.0	634.7	637.4	643.7	626.6
1995	621.0	625.0	632.8	639.5	645.2	650.7	640.5	644.3	647.3	649.3	651.4	659.0	642.1
1996	640.9	647.4	651.9	657.9	664.9	668.1	658.9	661.2	663.2	665.8	675.6	680.8	661.3
1997	658.5	660.7	668.6	673.4	682.2	685.7	680.5	682.6	684.2	685.9	691.0	695.9	679.1
1998	674.7	679.0	686.5	695.2	703.2	704.6	696.0	698.2	699.7	704.1	707.0	711.7	696.6
1999	685.9	691.5	697.3	706.3	711.1	714.7	712.9	713.8	716.4	715.7	720.3	727.8	709.4
2000	701.8	707.0	713.7	715.7	723.1	728.5	722.7	722.7	723.3	725.5	728.4	733.6	720.5
2001	714.9	716.6	721.0	721.0	726.4	730.2	722.1	721.8	719.7	717.5	718.5	721.6	720.9
2002	707.8	710.1	716.4	716.2	720.5	721.5	715.4	717.1	714.4	716.3	719.2	721.8	716.4
2003	704.9	704.2	710.4	721.9	726.4	728.6	723.1	723.2	722.0	725.5	729.1	729.4	720.7
Trade, transportation and utilities													
1990	160.1	158.1	159.7	159.4	159.9	160.6	161.3	163.0	163.0	162.9	165.0	167.9	161.7
1991	159.3	156.3	157.7	157.6	159.0	159.2	158.9	159.2	159.8	159.5	162.6	165.6	159.5
1992	157.2	156.0	156.6	157.4	158.6	159.0	159.2	158.6	158.8	160.9	162.8	165.6	159.2
1993	158.5	156.7	157.0	157.6	159.6	161.1	160.1	161.1	161.0	163.0	165.7	169.1	160.8
1994	163.5	163.5	164.9	164.2	166.2	167.5	166.3	167.1	169.0	170.1	173.5	177.8	167.8
1995	167.7	165.7	166.7	166.1	167.5	168.6	167.5	168.4	168.8	170.2	174.0	178.4	169.1
1996	170.9	169.1	169.2	170.5	172.0	172.9	171.8	173.4	173.3	175.7	180.1	184.4	173.6
1997	176.2	173.2	173.7	173.6	175.6	176.5	176.2	176.6	177.8	179.2	182.8	186.5	177.3
1998	178.5	176.6	177.7	179.5	180.7	181.6	182.0	183.1	182.5	183.0	187.7	191.1	182.0
1999	178.6	177.1	177.9	179.0	180.4	182.2	181.7	182.9	182.3	184.1	187.3	191.3	182.0
2000	182.0	180.8	181.5	181.8	183.0	184.1	182.6	182.9	182.3	186.1	189.2	192.9	184.1
2001	187.4	184.7	184.9	180.8	181.9	182.4	183.1	183.0	182.6	183.6	186.4	188.7	184.1
2002	180.6	178.8	179.5	178.2	178.5	178.7	177.2	176.7	175.4	176.4	179.9	182.7	178.6
2003	174.4	173.1	174.0	176.7	177.4	177.8	178.6	179.2	178.8	179.2	183.5	184.7	178.1
Wholesale trade													
1990	39.6	39.4	39.5	39.3	39.3	39.6	39.6	40.1	39.9	39.9	40.0	40.3	39.7
1991	39.5	39.3	39.4	39.2	39.3	39.3	39.4	39.3	39.1	39.4	39.6	39.7	39.3
1992	38.7	38.6	38.6	38.7	39.1	39.4	39.6	39.4	39.3	39.5	39.2	39.5	39.1
1993	38.9	38.9	39.0	39.2	39.3	39.5	39.4	39.3	39.2	39.0	39.4	39.6	39.2
1994	39.6	39.8	40.2	40.0	40.5	40.9	41.1	41.2	41.2	41.3	41.5	41.7	40.7
1995	41.3	41.7	41.8	41.2	41.4	42.0	41.7	41.8	41.6	41.9	42.0	42.3	41.7
1996	42.7	42.9	43.0	42.7	42.8	43.2	43.5	43.5	43.5	43.6	43.9	44.3	43.3
1997	43.6	43.6	44.0	44.1	44.4	44.8	44.9	45.1	45.0	44.9	45.0	45.3	44.5
1998	43.7	43.6	43.8	44.3	44.4	45.0	45.0	45.1	44.8	45.2	45.4	45.6	44.6
1999	44.7	44.5	44.4	44.5	44.8	45.5	45.4	45.4	45.2	45.2	45.2	45.5	45.0
2000	44.1	44.3	44.4	44.6	44.7	45.3	44.8	44.8	44.6	45.1	45.2	45.5	44.7
2001	47.0	47.1	47.0	46.3	46.4	46.4	46.3	46.2	45.9	45.9	45.8	46.1	46.4
2002	45.4	45.3	45.2	45.2	45.1	45.2	45.0	44.5	43.9	43.8	43.7	43.6	44.7
2003	43.2	43.2	43.3	45.7	45.8	46.2	46.5	46.7	46.7	46.8	46.6	46.7	45.6
Retail trade													
1990	91.1	89.2	90.4	90.4	90.6	90.7	91.1	91.9	92.2	92.0	94.3	97.0	91.7
1991	89.9	87.6	88.5	88.0	89.0	89.0	88.6	88.8	89.3	88.7	91.6	94.4	89.4
1992	88.4	87.1	87.7	88.0	88.7	88.7	88.6	88.3	88.5	89.7	92.1	94.5	89.1
1993	88.9	87.4	87.6	87.8	89.3	90.3	89.1	90.0	89.7	91.0	93.6	96.9	90.1
1994	91.5	91.1	91.8	91.6	92.7	93.7	93.0	93.6	95.3	96.1	99.5	103.4	94.4
1995	94.8	92.6	93.3	93.2	93.9	94.6	93.7	94.4	94.4	94.7	98.5	102.4	95.0
1996	96.1	93.9	93.8	95.0	96.2	96.7	96.4	97.5	97.4	98.0	102.0	105.6	97.3
1997	99.0	96.5	96.4	96.1	97.6	98.2	97.8	98.3	98.0	98.9	102.0	105.2	98.6
1998	100.3	98.6	99.3	99.2	100.1	100.6	100.7	101.0	100.3	99.9	104.2	107.7	100.9
1999	96.8	95.7	96.5	97.0	97.9	99.2	99.3	99.9	99.1	99.9	103.2	106.7	99.2
2000	99.3	98.2	98.6	98.3	99.1	100.0	99.1	99.3	98.6	101.2	104.4	107.7	100.3
2001	100.6	98.0	98.5	97.9	98.8	100.0	98.2	98.2	97.7	98.2	101.6	103.9	99.3
2002	97.6	96.2	96.8	95.7	96.2	97.0	96.1	96.0	95.3	95.1	98.7	101.4	96.8
2003	94.5	93.1	93.6	93.8	94.5	95.1	95.5	95.7	95.1	95.2	99.9	101.4	95.6
Transportation and utilities													
1990	29.4	29.5	29.8	29.7	30.0	30.3	30.6	31.0	30.9	31.0	30.7	30.6	30.2
1991	29.9	29.4	29.8	30.4	30.7	30.9	30.9	31.1	31.4	31.4	31.4	31.5	30.7
1992	30.1	30.3	30.3	30.7	30.8	30.9	31.0	30.9	31.0	31.7	31.5	31.6	30.9
1993	30.7	30.4	30.4	30.6	31.0	31.3	31.6	31.8	32.1	33.0	32.7	32.6	31.5
1994	32.4	32.6	32.9	32.6	33.0	32.9	32.2	32.3	32.5	32.7	32.5	32.7	32.6
1995	31.6	31.4	31.6	31.7	32.2	32.0	32.1	32.2	32.8	33.6	33.5	33.7	32.3
1996	32.1	32.3	32.4	32.8	33.0	33.0	31.9	32.4	32.4	34.1	34.2	34.5	32.9
1997	33.6	33.1	33.3	33.4	33.6	33.5	33.5	33.2	34.8	35.4	35.8	36.0	34.1
1998	34.5	34.4	34.6	36.0	36.2	36.0	36.3	37.0	37.4	37.9	38.1	37.8	36.3
1999	37.1	36.9	37.0	37.5	37.7	37.5	37.0	37.6	38.0	39.0	38.9	39.1	37.7
2000	38.6	38.3	38.5	38.9	39.2	38.8	38.7	38.8	39.1	39.8	39.6	39.7	39.0
2001	39.8	39.6	39.4	36.6	36.7	36.0	38.6	38.6	39.0	39.5	39.0	38.7	38.5
2002	37.6	37.3	37.5	37.3	37.2	36.5	36.1	36.2	36.2	37.5	37.5	37.7	37.1
2003	36.7	36.8	37.1	37.2	37.1	36.5	36.6	36.8	37.0	37.2	37.0	36.6	36.9

Employment by Industry: Ohio—*Continued*

(Numbers in thousands. Not seasonally adjusted.)

Industry	January	February	March	April	May	June	July	August	September	October	November	December	Annual Average
CINCINNATI—*Continued*													
Information													
1990	17.8	17.8	17.8	17.9	17.9	18.0	18.2	18.2	18.1	18.0	17.9	17.9	17.9
1991	18.1	18.0	17.9	17.8	17.8	17.8	18.0	17.9	17.8	17.7	17.7	17.7	17.8
1992	17.3	17.1	17.0	17.1	17.1	17.3	17.0	17.1	16.8	16.8	16.8	17.0	17.0
1993	16.3	16.2	16.2	16.1	16.1	16.3	16.4	16.5	16.3	16.2	16.2	16.2	16.2
1994	15.9	16.0	16.1	16.1	16.3	16.4	16.4	16.6	16.4	16.2	16.5	16.4	16.2
1995	15.7	15.7	15.8	16.1	16.1	16.3	16.4	16.4	16.3	16.0	16.2	16.4	16.1
1996	16.4	16.4	16.6	16.5	16.5	16.8	17.0	17.1	16.9	16.8	17.0	17.1	16.7
1997	17.0	17.4	17.7	17.4	17.7	18.1	18.3	18.1	17.9	18.3	18.2	18.4	17.8
1998	18.5	18.7	18.8	19.4	19.6	19.7	19.6	19.8	19.7	19.6	19.6	19.7	19.3
1999	19.6	19.6	19.7	19.5	19.5	19.7	19.8	19.8	19.6	19.5	19.3	19.8	19.6
2000	19.3	19.1	19.6	19.3	19.4	19.5	18.9	19.1	18.8	18.9	18.7	18.8	19.1
2001	19.1	18.9	19.0	18.8	19.0	19.2	18.8	18.6	18.3	18.3	18.2	18.1	18.7
2002	17.8	17.6	17.5	17.0	16.8	16.4	16.3	16.0	15.5	15.2	15.5	15.4	16.4
2003	15.6	15.5	15.6	15.5	15.7	15.6	15.6	15.5	15.5	15.3	15.3	15.3	15.5
Financial activities													
1990	41.1	41.2	41.5	41.7	42.0	42.8	42.9	43.2	42.6	41.9	42.0	42.3	42.1
1991	41.3	41.2	41.4	41.1	41.5	42.0	42.1	42.2	42.0	41.8	42.0	42.2	41.7
1992	41.4	41.5	41.6	41.6	42.1	42.9	42.5	42.2	41.9	41.1	41.0	41.3	41.7
1993	41.2	41.1	41.8	41.8	41.9	42.4	43.0	42.9	42.8	41.7	42.1	42.8	42.1
1994	42.8	42.9	43.3	43.3	43.4	43.7	43.8	43.8	43.8	43.1	43.4	43.6	43.4
1995	42.8	43.2	43.8	42.8	43.4	44.5	44.1	44.2	43.8	43.8	44.1	44.5	43.7
1996	44.8	45.3	45.7	45.7	46.2	46.9	47.0	47.1	46.8	46.3	46.5	46.7	46.2
1997	46.6	46.7	47.3	47.2	47.7	48.5	48.7	49.0	48.4	48.5	48.7	49.2	48.0
1998	49.2	49.2	49.6	49.7	50.1	50.6	51.7	51.7	51.1	51.4	51.6	51.9	50.6
1999	50.7	50.9	50.9	51.6	51.9	52.5	53.0	52.7	52.3	52.4	52.6	53.0	52.0
2000	53.1	53.1	53.0	53.0	53.2	53.7	53.4	53.4	53.0	53.1	53.4	54.0	53.2
2001	54.2	54.3	54.1	54.6	54.7	55.2	55.1	55.4	55.2	55.1	55.2	55.7	54.9
2002	55.1	55.2	55.2	55.2	55.2	55.4	55.7	55.7	55.2	55.4	55.6	56.0	55.4
2003	56.1	56.1	56.2	56.0	56.3	56.5	56.9	56.5	56.3	56.8	56.7	56.5	56.4
Professional and business services													
1990	83.5	84.0	85.6	86.3	87.5	88.5	88.3	88.7	88.4	89.7	88.9	88.6	87.3
1991	86.4	85.9	86.8	87.3	87.5	88.5	88.3	88.4	88.7	88.1	88.5	88.2	87.7
1992	86.4	86.9	87.7	90.1	89.9	91.5	92.2	92.6	92.1	93.0	92.5	92.8	90.6
1993	89.5	90.4	90.6	92.3	92.6	94.0	94.0	93.9	95.0	95.5	95.3	94.8	93.1
1994	91.8	93.2	95.4	95.9	96.5	97.8	97.4	98.3	99.1	101.2	101.2	101.5	97.4
1995	98.1	99.4	101.5	104.0	104.7	106.7	105.3	107.6	108.0	107.9	108.3	108.6	105.0
1996	106.0	107.5	108.8	109.6	111.1	111.8	110.4	110.8	110.1	112.4	113.6	113.6	110.4
1997	111.4	111.9	113.8	114.4	115.7	117.4	118.8	119.7	118.8	120.5	120.5	119.6	116.8
1998	116.1	117.4	119.1	120.5	120.5	122.6	122.4	123.1	122.6	123.7	122.7	122.4	121.0
1999	119.8	120.9	122.0	124.1	123.9	125.2	127.0	127.2	127.4	128.0	128.5	129.4	125.2
2000	125.2	125.7	127.7	127.3	127.8	130.7	131.3	131.9	131.5	131.6	131.4	130.6	129.3
2001	131.9	132.4	133.1	134.1	133.9	134.6	132.6	132.6	131.7	129.2	127.6	126.8	131.7
2002	127.2	127.1	128.4	128.1	127.9	128.5	129.0	130.8	131.0	131.7	131.4	130.4	129.3
2003	128.2	127.5	128.7	131.6	131.3	132.0	132.2	132.0	131.6	131.1	130.4	130.4	130.6
Educational and health services													
1990	83.9	84.9	85.5	85.7	86.2	86.4	85.9	86.6	88.0	88.7	89.2	89.4	86.7
1991	86.9	88.2	88.9	89.0	89.3	89.0	88.7	89.0	90.2	91.0	91.5	91.8	89.4
1992	88.8	89.9	90.5	91.9	92.1	91.7	91.0	91.6	92.3	93.8	94.1	94.6	91.8
1993	92.3	92.9	93.2	93.8	93.9	93.0	93.6	93.6	95.0	94.9	95.6	96.1	93.9
1994	94.3	95.5	96.1	96.5	96.7	95.8	95.2	95.8	97.1	97.1	97.5	98.3	96.3
1995	96.3	97.7	98.2	98.4	98.0	97.1	96.5	97.0	98.6	99.3	99.6	99.9	98.0
1996	97.8	99.6	99.8	99.3	99.5	98.5	98.4	99.0	100.4	100.9	101.8	102.0	99.7
1997	100.4	101.4	102.0	101.1	101.6	100.3	101.1	101.1	102.6	103.5	104.1	104.3	101.9
1998	101.6	102.7	103.2	103.5	103.5	102.0	102.6	102.6	103.9	105.4	105.6	106.0	103.5
1999	104.1	105.9	106.2	107.1	107.1	105.8	106.3	106.7	108.1	108.1	108.5	108.5	106.8
2000	105.0	106.7	107.0	107.3	107.9	107.2	107.9	108.0	109.4	109.1	109.7	110.1	107.9
2001	105.3	106.6	106.8	107.4	106.9	106.5	106.1	106.1	107.3	108.4	108.6	108.6	107.1
2002	107.0	107.9	108.0	108.2	108.2	107.6	107.0	107.7	109.2	110.1	110.7	110.7	108.5
2003	110.2	110.4	110.8	111.1	111.0	110.3	110.0	110.9	111.2	112.9	112.8	112.4	111.2
Leisure and hospitality													
1990	62.5	62.9	64.1	68.8	71.4	74.7	74.5	74.8	73.6	71.3	68.9	70.0	69.7
1991	63.1	62.9	64.1	68.2	70.0	73.5	73.8	73.4	70.8	67.8	65.1	66.0	68.2
1992	62.3	62.7	64.0	68.4	72.2	74.8	75.2	75.4	73.3	70.0	66.9	68.3	69.4
1993	64.7	65.1	66.1	70.2	74.2	76.2	77.3	77.3	75.1	72.5	70.5	70.5	71.6
1994	67.1	67.8	69.4	73.5	76.2	78.7	78.3	78.8	75.3	72.8	71.3	71.7	73.4
1995	68.2	68.5	70.6	74.8	78.2	81.5	81.3	81.1	78.0	75.3	73.4	74.1	75.4
1996	69.4	70.7	72.5	76.9	80.2	82.8	82.5	82.7	79.8	76.8	77.7	78.4	77.5
1997	73.5	74.1	76.5	81.0	84.8	87.6	86.2	86.1	83.2	80.4	79.1	79.6	81.0
1998	75.1	75.7	77.6	82.4	87.4	89.8	86.0	85.4	82.8	83.0	80.7	81.9	82.3
1999	76.9	78.1	79.8	83.6	86.9	89.4	91.1	90.9	88.6	84.2	84.4	86.3	85.0
2000	80.0	80.5	82.7	84.5	86.9	90.8	92.1	92.4	90.0	86.4	85.0	85.7	86.4
2001	78.8	78.9	81.5	83.1	86.5	90.7	90.8	90.2	85.8	82.3	81.1	82.0	84.3
2002	79.3	80.1	83.1	84.8	88.6	91.3	91.9	90.7	87.4	84.5	82.8	83.6	85.7
2003	79.5	79.0	81.4	86.4	89.6	93.2	92.3	91.1	87.8	86.5	85.9	85.8	86.5

Employment by Industry: Ohio—*Continued*

(Numbers in thousands. Not seasonally adjusted.)

Industry	January	February	March	April	May	June	July	August	September	October	November	December	Annual Average
CINCINNATI—*Continued*													
Other services													
1990	26.2	26.5	26.8	26.7	27.0	27.4	27.3	27.3	27.2	27.2	27.4	27.6	27.0
1991	26.8	27.2	27.4	27.6	27.9	28.5	28.2	28.1	27.8	27.8	27.9	27.9	27.7
1992	27.1	27.5	27.6	28.6	28.8	28.9	28.8	28.6	28.2	28.2	28.0	28.0	28.1
1993	28.4	29.2	29.1	29.7	29.9	30.2	30.5	30.5	30.3	30.0	30.4	30.6	29.9
1994	30.7	30.8	31.4	31.6	31.8	32.2	32.2	32.3	32.0	32.2	32.1	32.4	31.8
1995	31.7	31.6	32.5	33.8	34.2	34.9	34.6	34.7	34.6	34.7	34.8	35.1	33.9
1996	35.0	35.4	35.8	35.6	35.8	36.4	36.2	36.3	35.8	35.9	35.9	36.2	35.8
1997	35.7	35.7	36.2	36.4	37.0	37.4	37.4	37.4	36.9	36.9	36.8	37.2	36.7
1998	37.0	37.2	37.5	37.0	37.2	37.5	37.6	37.3	36.8	36.5	36.3	36.5	37.0
1999	36.6	36.8	37.0	37.5	37.6	38.2	37.9	37.5	37.2	37.0	36.8	37.0	37.2
2000	36.5	36.9	37.0	37.1	37.5	37.9	37.8	37.5	37.4	37.2	37.2	37.4	37.2
2001	35.1	35.3	35.6	35.5	36.0	36.3	35.9	36.0	35.2	35.2	35.3	35.2	35.6
2002	35.4	35.6	35.9	36.0	36.2	36.7	36.5	36.3	35.5	35.3	35.3	35.4	35.8
2003	35.1	35.5	36.0	36.2	36.6	36.6	36.9	36.4	35.9	35.8	36.1	35.9	36.1
Government													
1990	96.0	98.6	99.3	99.1	101.0	96.8	92.0	91.3	95.1	96.7	99.4	99.7	97.0
1991	97.9	100.1	100.2	99.8	99.8	97.7	91.3	90.7	97.6	98.9	99.9	100.1	97.8
1992	99.2	101.4	101.3	101.8	101.9	99.3	93.2	92.2	97.4	99.0	99.4	99.5	98.8
1993	98.9	101.1	101.1	100.7	100.7	99.0	93.8	93.5	98.6	101.0	101.2	101.4	99.2
1994	99.4	102.0	102.2	102.6	102.3	100.1	93.7	94.2	99.3	102.0	101.9	102.0	100.1
1995	100.5	103.2	103.7	103.5	103.1	101.1	94.8	94.9	99.2	102.1	101.0	102.0	100.7
1996	100.6	103.4	103.5	103.8	103.6	102.0	95.6	94.8	100.1	101.0	103.0	102.4	101.1
1997	97.7	100.3	101.4	102.3	102.1	99.9	93.8	94.6	98.6	98.6	100.8	101.1	99.2
1998	98.7	101.5	103.0	103.2	104.2	100.8	94.1	95.2	100.3	101.5	102.8	102.2	100.6
1999	99.6	102.2	103.8	103.9	103.8	101.7	96.1	96.1	100.9	102.4	102.9	102.5	101.3
2000	100.7	104.2	105.2	105.4	107.4	104.6	98.7	97.5	100.9	103.1	103.8	104.1	102.9
2001	103.1	105.5	106.0	106.7	107.5	105.3	99.7	99.9	103.6	105.4	106.1	106.5	104.6
2002	105.4	107.8	108.8	108.7	109.1	106.9	101.8	103.2	105.2	107.7	108.0	107.6	106.7
2003	105.8	107.1	107.7	108.4	108.5	106.6	100.6	101.6	104.9	107.9	108.4	108.4	106.3
Federal government													
1990	16.2	17.4	17.6	17.7	18.2	16.7	16.3	15.7	15.3	15.2	15.2	15.7	16.4
1991	15.6	17.0	17.0	17.1	16.2	16.0	15.5	15.8	15.8	15.4	15.5	15.8	16.0
1992	16.7	17.5	17.5	17.6	17.5	17.5	16.3	16.4	16.4	15.7	15.6	15.9	16.7
1993	16.2	17.1	17.1	16.6	16.4	16.1	15.7	16.0	15.8	15.6	15.6	16.0	16.1
1994	15.7	17.0	17.1	17.3	16.6	16.4	15.4	15.5	15.4	15.4	14.9	15.4	16.0
1995	15.9	17.1	17.2	17.5	16.4	16.5	15.8	15.6	15.2	15.2	14.6	15.4	16.0
1996	15.6	17.2	17.2	17.7	16.5	16.1	15.0	15.0	15.0	14.5	14.9	15.3	15.8
1997	15.4	16.6	17.1	17.5	16.4	16.2	15.3	15.4	15.2	14.6	14.9	15.3	15.8
1998	15.2	16.8	16.9	17.3	17.4	16.1	15.3	15.1	15.0	14.8	15.1	15.6	15.8
1999	15.4	16.9	17.0	17.4	16.7	16.5	16.1	15.8	15.5	15.4	15.1	15.4	16.1
2000	15.6	17.5	17.9	18.8	19.9	18.2	18.0	16.7	15.9	15.6	15.9	16.2	17.1
2001	17.1	17.9	17.8	17.9	17.5	17.4	17.6	16.9	16.7	16.4	16.5	16.7	17.2
2002	17.4	17.8	18.2	18.3	17.8	17.7	17.9	17.5	17.5	17.6	17.6	17.6	17.7
2003	17.3	17.7	17.8	17.8	17.6	17.2	17.1	16.7	16.4	16.8	16.9	17.0	17.2
State government													
1990	21.3	21.7	21.8	21.7	21.7	21.1	19.6	19.8	20.1	20.2	22.3	22.4	21.1
1991	22.4	22.3	22.4	22.3	21.9	21.6	20.6	20.0	20.8	22.2	22.4	22.4	21.7
1992	22.1	22.5	22.4	22.4	22.1	21.6	20.5	19.9	20.8	21.9	22.0	22.2	21.7
1993	21.3	21.9	21.8	21.8	21.6	21.1	20.0	19.8	20.5	21.7	22.1	22.0	21.3
1994	21.8	22.4	22.4	22.4	22.1	21.5	20.4	20.2	20.9	22.2	22.5	22.1	21.7
1995	21.7	22.3	22.1	22.1	22.1	21.1	19.4	19.6	20.3	22.0	21.6	21.9	21.3
1996	21.6	21.8	21.7	21.8	21.4	21.3	19.2	19.4	20.0	20.4	21.7	21.6	20.9
1997	17.7	18.3	18.4	18.6	18.2	17.4	15.8	16.3	16.9	16.8	18.5	18.5	17.6
1998	17.3	17.9	18.6	18.3	18.2	17.4	15.3	16.3	17.1	18.0	18.5	18.3	17.6
1999	17.3	17.6	18.4	18.3	17.9	17.1	15.6	15.7	16.9	17.9	18.5	18.3	17.4
2000	17.5	18.4	18.5	17.5	17.8	17.5	15.7	16.3	16.7	18.1	18.4	18.4	17.5
2001	17.7	18.2	18.2	18.3	18.4	17.5	15.7	16.8	17.0	17.6	18.0	18.1	17.6
2002	17.6	18.0	18.0	17.7	17.8	17.4	16.1	17.1	16.8	18.5	18.8	18.9	17.7
2003	18.8	19.0	18.7	18.6	18.6	17.3	16.6	16.4	17.2	18.8	19.1	19.3	18.2
Local government													
1990	54.9	55.9	56.3	56.1	57.5	55.4	52.7	52.4	56.1	57.6	58.2	57.9	55.9
1991	56.3	57.1	57.1	56.8	58.0	56.6	52.0	51.7	57.3	57.5	58.2	58.2	56.4
1992	60.4	61.4	61.4	61.8	62.3	60.2	56.4	55.9	60.2	61.4	61.8	61.4	60.3
1993	61.4	62.1	62.2	62.3	62.7	61.8	58.1	57.7	62.3	63.7	63.5	63.4	61.7
1994	61.9	62.6	62.7	62.9	63.6	62.2	57.9	58.5	63.0	64.4	64.5	64.5	62.3
1995	62.9	63.8	64.4	63.9	64.6	63.5	59.6	59.7	63.7	64.9	64.8	64.7	63.3
1996	63.4	64.4	64.6	64.3	65.7	64.6	61.4	60.4	65.1	66.1	66.4	65.5	64.3
1997	64.6	65.4	65.9	66.2	67.5	66.3	62.7	62.9	66.5	67.2	67.4	67.3	65.8
1998	66.2	66.8	67.5	67.6	68.6	67.3	63.5	63.8	68.2	68.7	69.2	68.3	67.1
1999	66.9	67.7	68.4	68.2	69.2	68.1	64.4	64.6	68.5	69.1	69.3	68.8	67.7
2000	67.6	68.3	68.8	69.1	69.7	68.9	65.0	64.5	68.3	69.4	69.5	69.5	68.2
2001	68.3	69.4	70.0	70.5	71.6	70.4	66.4	66.2	69.9	71.4	71.6	71.7	69.8
2002	70.4	72.0	72.6	72.7	73.5	71.8	67.8	68.6	70.9	71.6	71.6	71.1	71.2
2003	69.7	70.4	71.2	72.0	72.3	72.1	66.9	68.5	71.3	72.3	72.4	72.1	70.9

Employment by Industry: Ohio—*Continued*

(Numbers in thousands. Not seasonally adjusted.)

Industry	January	February	March	April	May	June	July	August	September	October	November	December	Annual Average
CLEVELAND													
Total nonfarm													
1990	1041.1	1049.0	1060.1	1065.2	1079.0	1091.0	1081.6	1074.5	1077.6	1074.1	1069.8	1069.9	1069.4
1991	1028.6	1022.4	1036.2	1036.0	1046.5	1056.0	1051.8	1044.6	1048.5	1049.1	1053.2	1050.6	1043.6
1992	1016.3	1016.9	1026.2	1033.4	1046.4	1053.9	1043.3	1043.3	1047.4	1051.4	1052.5	1055.0	1040.5
1993	1023.6	1025.9	1029.6	1036.1	1049.9	1059.1	1051.2	1050.8	1057.5	1062.9	1063.2	1068.5	1048.1
1994	1042.2	1049.0	1059.3	1066.3	1079.2	1089.5	1078.5	1079.4	1085.0	1092.7	1099.5	1104.2	1077.0
1995	1071.4	1077.4	1088.0	1094.5	1107.0	1120.3	1106.6	1104.4	1113.0	1115.7	1121.9	1125.3	1103.7
1996	1086.9	1096.1	1104.8	1108.5	1123.9	1136.2	1120.4	1123.2	1125.8	1129.5	1132.3	1136.6	1118.6
1997	1101.0	1107.6	1117.9	1126.9	1140.1	1151.7	1142.2	1145.3	1147.6	1150.7	1156.9	1160.3	1137.3
1998	1123.4	1129.1	1136.7	1148.0	1160.9	1170.7	1154.7	1158.9	1161.0	1168.6	1170.5	1173.8	1154.6
1999	1138.7	1145.4	1151.9	1162.8	1173.4	1182.0	1175.2	1175.5	1174.8	1178.7	1185.4	1189.5	1169.4
2000	1155.4	1159.8	1168.4	1172.5	1184.9	1192.4	1179.0	1178.3	1176.8	1175.6	1178.5	1180.7	1175.1
2001	1147.7	1150.1	1156.8	1157.1	1164.8	1169.1	1154.9	1153.2	1144.1	1143.2	1143.0	1140.9	1152.1
2002	1100.4	1102.6	1108.7	1108.1	1117.3	1121.0	1111.0	1111.1	1113.1	1115.4	1114.8	1113.4	1111.4
2003	1085.5	1086.3	1091.9	1108.0	1119.2	1121.3	1115.4	1114.8	1117.7	1121.1	1121.2	1120.2	1110.2
Total private													
1990	904.4	910.5	919.9	925.8	936.8	949.1	944.7	946.1	942.5	936.7	931.5	931.8	931.6
1991	892.2	884.7	897.5	898.0	907.3	916.3	914.9	915.5	911.1	908.8	911.0	908.9	905.5
1992	876.2	875.4	883.4	891.3	903.1	910.4	910.8	912.5	910.1	911.2	912.0	914.4	900.9
1993	882.9	882.6	886.0	892.8	905.8	914.9	917.7	919.5	919.8	919.2	921.5	926.6	907.4
1994	901.7	906.2	916.3	923.2	935.2	944.0	943.2	945.8	946.7	948.7	954.5	959.5	935.4
1995	929.2	933.5	943.6	951.6	962.7	974.2	969.2	970.3	973.7	972.6	977.8	980.4	961.5
1996	944.9	951.8	959.7	965.3	978.9	989.5	983.7	988.0	984.5	984.8	986.1	990.8	975.6
1997	958.4	962.2	972.0	984.2	995.2	1005.0	1006.0	1009.7	1007.3	1007.1	1012.3	1015.7	994.5
1998	981.6	985.2	992.4	1004.5	1015.7	1024.5	1018.2	1022.9	1018.3	1023.7	1024.3	1027.6	1011.5
1999	996.6	999.7	1005.5	1017.3	1026.2	1034.9	1036.6	1037.1	1030.5	1031.4	1037.0	1040.9	1024.4
2000	1010.3	1012.1	1019.7	1024.4	1032.4	1044.1	1037.2	1037.5	1030.4	1026.9	1029.0	1030.6	1027.8
2001	1001.3	1000.8	1006.1	1007.0	1014.0	1020.5	1012.3	1010.6	995.0	991.7	990.9	988.3	1003.2
2002	952.7	950.8	956.0	956.6	964.7	970.6	969.4	970.9	964.1	963.4	962.3	961.5	961.9
2003	937.5	935.4	939.9	956.3	967.5	972.2	973.8	975.7	970.8	970.5	969.9	968.3	961.5
Goods-producing													
1990	260.7	267.6	270.0	271.7	274.2	278.2	277.8	277.2	275.8	274.2	267.5	265.4	271.6
1991	252.5	248.0	254.6	254.3	255.8	257.7	258.4	258.1	255.7	255.5	254.6	249.9	254.5
1992	240.3	240.7	243.5	241.2	243.5	246.4	245.1	245.6	245.5	245.5	245.0	243.4	243.8
1993	235.2	234.5	234.2	235.6	239.2	242.0	242.8	243.4	243.3	243.9	243.6	243.5	240.1
1994	234.8	235.7	238.2	240.8	244.5	247.9	248.7	249.9	251.3	252.4	253.1	253.1	245.8
1995	246.0	247.3	250.6	252.7	255.9	259.3	257.5	257.5	258.8	257.2	257.5	256.2	254.7
1996	244.0	248.8	251.2	252.5	256.6	259.7	259.2	260.5	259.7	258.7	257.3	257.1	255.4
1997	247.3	247.7	250.3	253.5	256.1	259.2	259.3	261.3	260.0	258.2	258.1	257.6	255.7
1998	248.0	250.7	251.5	255.3	256.9	259.3	255.4	258.8	258.5	260.1	258.8	257.6	255.9
1999	248.6	249.7	250.6	253.6	254.9	257.1	258.9	258.5	257.7	257.0	258.9	258.4	255.3
2000	251.2	252.6	255.1	254.7	256.7	259.7	257.2	257.3	255.0	254.1	253.5	250.3	254.7
2001	241.9	240.5	240.5	239.0	239.9	240.6	238.5	237.7	232.3	229.7	228.8	226.0	236.3
2002	214.8	213.0	214.0	213.0	215.4	217.6	217.7	218.3	216.4	215.9	214.4	211.8	215.2
2003	205.4	204.3	205.3	207.0	209.8	211.1	211.4	212.3	210.5	209.6	208.4	206.0	208.4
Construction and mining													
1990	35.1	35.4	36.9	38.8	40.9	43.4	44.3	45.0	43.8	43.4	42.6	39.9	40.7
1991	33.6	32.1	32.8	34.8	36.3	38.3	39.8	40.0	39.2	38.8	36.6	33.9	36.3
1992	29.9	29.3	30.8	33.0	35.8	37.5	38.1	38.7	38.5	38.6	37.2	35.6	35.2
1993	31.7	31.2	31.2	34.8	37.7	39.4	41.4	41.6	41.3	42.8	41.9	40.2	37.9
1994	33.2	32.9	34.4	37.3	40.0	41.8	42.8	43.0	43.0	42.8	42.1	40.5	39.4
1995	34.9	34.8	36.9	39.1	41.5	43.9	44.2	44.3	44.3	44.1	42.7	40.8	40.9
1996	35.5	35.5	37.5	39.9	42.9	45.3	46.5	47.1	47.0	46.2	44.3	43.2	42.5
1997	38.1	37.6	39.3	42.9	44.9	47.5	49.6	50.5	48.8	48.0	46.7	44.9	44.9
1998	39.3	39.4	39.8	43.9	46.0	47.7	50.0	50.1	49.2	49.4	48.4	46.7	45.8
1999	39.7	40.8	41.4	44.4	46.6	48.3	51.8	51.8	51.1	51.4	49.9	48.5	47.1
2000	42.7	42.5	45.0	46.4	48.7	51.1	51.4	51.3	49.7	49.2	48.4	45.6	47.6
2001	41.3	41.1	42.3	44.7	47.4	49.2	50.5	51.0	49.2	49.1	47.9	45.8	46.6
2002	39.9	39.2	40.4	41.3	43.8	45.7	47.3	47.7	46.8	46.9	45.7	43.3	44.0
2003	39.2	38.3	39.5	42.5	45.3	47.1	48.3	49.1	48.4	48.3	47.1	45.1	44.9
Manufacturing													
1990	225.6	232.2	233.1	232.9	233.3	234.8	233.5	232.2	232.0	230.8	224.9	225.5	230.9
1991	218.9	215.9	221.8	219.5	219.5	219.4	218.6	218.1	216.5	216.7	218.0	216.0	218.2
1992	210.4	211.4	212.7	208.2	207.7	208.9	207.0	206.9	207.0	206.9	207.8	207.8	208.5
1993	203.5	203.3	203.0	200.8	201.5	202.6	201.4	201.8	202.0	201.1	201.7	203.3	202.1
1994	201.6	202.8	203.8	203.5	204.5	206.1	205.9	206.9	208.3	209.6	211.0	212.6	206.3
1995	211.1	212.5	213.7	213.6	214.4	215.4	213.3	213.2	214.5	213.1	214.8	215.4	213.7
1996	208.5	213.3	213.7	212.6	213.7	214.4	212.7	213.4	212.7	212.5	213.0	213.9	212.8
1997	209.2	210.1	211.0	210.6	211.2	211.7	209.7	210.8	211.2	210.2	211.4	212.7	210.8
1998	208.7	211.3	211.7	211.4	210.9	211.6	205.4	208.7	209.3	210.7	210.4	210.9	210.0
1999	208.9	208.9	209.2	209.2	208.3	208.8	207.1	206.7	206.6	205.6	209.0	209.9	208.1
2000	208.5	210.1	210.1	208.3	208.0	208.6	205.8	206.0	205.3	204.9	205.1	204.7	207.1
2001	200.6	199.4	198.2	194.3	192.5	191.4	188.0	186.7	183.1	180.6	180.9	180.2	189.7
2002	174.9	173.8	173.6	171.7	171.6	171.9	170.4	170.6	169.6	169.0	168.7	168.5	171.2
2003	166.2	166.0	165.8	164.5	164.5	164.0	163.1	163.2	162.1	161.3	161.3	160.9	163.6

Employment by Industry: Ohio—*Continued*

(Numbers in thousands. Not seasonally adjusted.)

Industry	January	February	March	April	May	June	July	August	September	October	November	December	Annual Average
CLEVELAND—*Continued*													
Service-providing													
1990	780.4	781.4	790.1	793.5	804.8	812.8	803.8	797.3	801.8	799.9	802.3	804.5	797.7
1991	776.1	774.4	781.6	781.7	790.7	798.3	793.4	786.5	792.8	793.6	798.6	800.7	789.0
1992	776.0	776.2	782.7	792.2	802.9	807.5	798.2	797.7	801.9	805.9	807.5	811.6	796.6
1993	788.4	791.4	795.4	800.5	810.7	817.1	808.4	807.4	814.2	819.0	819.6	825.0	808.0
1994	807.4	813.3	821.1	825.5	834.7	841.6	829.8	829.5	833.7	840.3	846.4	851.1	831.2
1995	825.4	830.1	837.4	841.8	851.1	861.0	849.1	846.9	854.2	858.5	864.4	869.1	849.0
1996	842.9	847.3	853.6	856.0	867.3	876.5	861.2	862.7	866.1	870.8	875.0	879.5	863.2
1997	853.7	859.9	867.6	873.4	884.0	892.5	882.9	884.0	887.6	892.5	898.8	902.7	881.6
1998	875.4	878.4	885.2	892.7	904.0	911.4	899.3	900.1	902.5	908.5	911.7	916.2	898.7
1999	890.1	895.7	901.3	909.2	918.5	924.9	916.3	917.0	917.1	921.7	926.5	931.1	914.1
2000	904.2	907.2	913.3	917.8	928.2	932.7	921.8	921.0	921.8	921.5	925.0	930.4	920.4
2001	905.8	909.6	916.3	918.1	924.9	928.5	916.4	915.5	911.8	913.5	914.2	914.9	915.8
2002	885.6	889.6	894.7	895.1	901.9	903.4	893.3	892.8	896.7	899.5	900.4	901.6	896.2
2003	880.1	882.0	886.6	901.0	909.4	910.2	904.0	902.5	907.2	911.5	912.8	914.2	901.8
Trade, transportation, and utilities													
1990	210.2	207.1	208.7	209.5	211.7	213.7	211.9	212.6	211.4	210.5	213.3	216.5	211.4
1991	205.0	200.7	202.1	201.5	203.1	204.4	203.2	203.4	202.2	202.8	205.8	209.2	203.6
1992	200.2	197.3	198.1	200.0	202.5	203.6	204.2	204.5	204.3	206.1	208.6	212.6	203.5
1993	198.5	196.3	196.7	197.0	199.2	200.4	200.4	200.5	200.3	201.0	204.2	208.9	200.2
1994	198.2	197.9	199.1	200.5	202.4	204.0	201.9	202.3	202.7	205.4	209.4	213.8	203.1
1995	204.3	202.4	203.6	204.5	206.3	208.0	207.5	207.7	208.5	211.0	216.3	219.7	208.3
1996	210.6	208.8	210.2	210.5	213.2	214.7	214.0	214.8	214.2	217.5	221.5	225.6	214.6
1997	214.3	212.2	212.8	212.9	215.8	218.1	217.6	216.3	217.6	219.2	223.9	228.1	217.4
1998	217.9	214.7	215.6	216.4	219.5	220.3	220.8	221.1	220.0	221.9	225.6	229.2	220.2
1999	219.8	217.8	218.6	218.5	219.8	221.1	220.7	219.7	218.1	220.4	224.4	229.1	220.6
2000	220.6	218.2	218.7	218.2	219.6	221.1	219.0	218.9	217.9	220.5	224.3	228.6	220.4
2001	220.4	217.2	217.8	217.3	218.0	218.6	215.5	214.6	212.5	213.3	216.2	217.5	216.6
2002	207.7	204.5	205.6	203.9	205.5	206.2	205.8	205.8	203.8	205.3	207.6	210.2	206.0
2003	203.7	201.0	200.3	206.6	208.5	209.5	209.6	209.7	208.1	209.5	211.9	213.8	207.7
Wholesale trade													
1990	54.4	54.4	54.8	55.1	55.1	55.6	55.8	55.9	55.5	54.9	54.6	54.6	55.0
1991	53.2	52.6	52.8	53.1	53.2	53.5	53.3	53.3	52.9	52.8	52.8	52.8	53.0
1992	51.8	51.7	51.6	52.3	52.9	53.0	53.8	53.8	53.4	53.9	53.6	53.8	52.9
1993	52.0	52.0	52.3	52.3	52.5	52.7	52.6	52.5	52.0	52.2	52.3	52.9	52.3
1994	51.8	52.0	52.4	52.6	52.9	53.3	52.9	53.0	53.1	53.6	54.0	54.6	53.0
1995	53.8	54.1	54.4	54.0	54.2	54.6	54.3	54.2	54.5	54.3	54.7	54.9	54.3
1996	54.8	55.3	55.5	56.1	56.6	56.7	57.1	57.2	56.9	57.1	57.3	57.5	56.5
1997	56.3	56.8	57.0	56.7	57.2	57.7	57.8	58.0	57.7	57.9	58.2	58.5	57.4
1998	58.1	58.2	58.4	58.1	58.4	58.5	58.9	58.8	58.4	58.7	58.8	58.9	58.5
1999	58.1	58.2	58.2	58.1	58.2	58.5	59.1	58.7	58.1	58.1	58.1	58.3	58.3
2000	57.8	57.9	58.0	57.4	57.5	57.8	57.3	57.1	57.1	57.3	57.2	57.7	57.5
2001	59.4	59.6	60.0	59.5	59.3	59.5	58.7	58.4	57.6	57.3	57.1	56.6	58.6
2002	56.4	56.1	56.4	55.9	55.9	55.6	55.6	55.3	54.6	54.5	54.2	54.5	55.4
2003	52.4	52.2	52.0	55.7	56.2	56.1	56.1	55.8	55.0	54.9	54.5	54.2	54.6
Retail trade													
1990	124.3	121.5	122.2	122.5	124.1	125.8	123.7	124.5	123.7	123.7	126.9	130.0	124.4
1991	121.3	118.2	119.0	118.4	119.6	120.5	119.5	119.5	118.8	119.6	122.6	125.8	120.2
1992	119.3	116.7	117.1	118.0	119.6	120.3	119.9	120.2	120.3	122.0	124.8	128.3	120.5
1993	117.4	115.4	115.1	115.4	117.2	117.6	117.2	118.1	118.3	118.6	121.7	125.6	118.1
1994	117.0	116.4	116.7	117.1	118.4	119.5	118.4	119.0	119.5	121.5	125.1	129.0	119.8
1995	121.4	119.5	120.4	121.0	122.0	122.9	122.6	122.9	123.3	125.4	130.1	133.1	123.7
1996	124.8	122.8	123.2	122.9	124.7	126.0	124.9	125.7	125.5	128.4	132.3	136.4	126.4
1997	126.7	124.6	124.9	124.6	126.5	128.2	127.6	127.8	127.5	128.5	132.9	136.9	128.0
1998	128.1	125.4	125.6	126.5	128.7	129.3	129.0	128.9	128.1	129.4	133.0	136.6	129.0
1999	129.7	127.7	128.3	127.6	128.7	129.5	127.9	127.4	126.3	128.0	132.3	136.9	129.1
2000	129.5	127.2	127.5	127.0	128.2	129.3	127.8	128.1	127.1	128.9	132.9	136.7	129.1
2001	126.7	123.8	123.9	123.4	123.9	124.4	122.5	122.1	121.1	122.2	126.2	128.6	124.1
2002	120.4	117.4	118.4	116.8	118.1	119.0	118.6	118.7	117.5	118.5	121.3	124.0	119.1
2003	117.7	115.8	115.7	117.7	118.7	119.7	119.7	119.9	119.3	120.3	123.4	125.5	119.5
Transportation and utilities													
1990	31.5	31.2	31.7	31.9	32.5	32.3	32.4	32.2	32.2	31.9	31.8	31.9	31.9
1991	30.5	29.9	30.3	30.0	30.3	30.4	30.4	30.6	30.5	30.4	30.4	30.6	30.3
1992	29.1	28.9	29.4	29.7	30.0	30.3	30.5	30.5	30.6	30.2	30.2	30.5	29.9
1993	29.1	28.9	29.3	29.3	29.5	30.1	30.6	29.9	30.0	30.2	30.2	30.4	29.7
1994	29.4	29.5	30.0	30.8	31.1	31.2	30.6	30.3	30.1	30.3	30.3	30.2	30.3
1995	29.1	28.8	28.8	29.5	30.1	30.5	30.6	30.6	30.7	31.3	31.5	31.7	30.2
1996	31.0	30.7	31.5	31.5	31.9	32.0	32.0	31.9	31.8	32.0	31.9	31.7	31.6
1997	31.3	30.8	30.9	31.6	32.1	32.2	32.2	30.5	32.4	32.8	32.8	32.7	31.8
1998	31.7	31.1	31.6	31.8	32.4	32.5	32.9	33.4	33.5	33.8	33.8	33.7	32.6
1999	32.0	31.9	32.1	32.8	32.9	33.1	33.7	33.6	33.7	34.3	34.0	33.9	33.1
2000	33.3	33.1	33.2	33.8	33.9	34.0	33.9	33.7	33.7	34.3	34.2	34.2	33.7
2001	34.3	33.8	33.9	34.4	34.8	34.7	34.3	34.1	33.8	33.8	32.9	32.3	33.9
2002	30.9	31.0	30.8	31.2	31.5	31.6	31.6	31.8	31.7	32.3	32.1	31.7	31.5
2003	33.6	33.0	32.6	33.2	33.6	33.7	33.8	34.0	33.8	34.3	34.0	34.1	33.6

Employment by Industry: Ohio—*Continued*

(Numbers in thousands. Not seasonally adjusted.)

Industry	January	February	March	April	May	June	July	August	September	October	November	December	Annual Average
CLEVELAND—*Continued*													
Information													
1990	26.7	26.6	26.8	26.9	27.1	27.7	27.5	27.4	27.3	27.6	27.8	27.8	27.2
1991	26.8	26.5	26.5	26.3	26.4	26.4	26.4	26.4	26.2	25.9	26.1	26.1	26.3
1992	25.5	25.4	25.4	25.4	25.6	25.3	25.2	25.1	25.1	25.1	25.0	24.9	25.2
1993	23.8	23.9	23.9	23.8	24.0	24.2	24.1	24.0	23.9	23.6	23.7	23.8	23.8
1994	23.6	23.7	23.7	23.4	23.4	23.3	23.6	23.6	23.6	23.7	23.8	24.0	23.6
1995	23.9	24.2	24.0	23.8	24.1	24.2	24.6	24.5	24.5	24.1	24.4	24.5	24.2
1996	24.3	24.5	24.6	24.3	24.4	24.7	24.7	24.8	24.6	24.6	24.7	24.8	24.5
1997	24.0	24.1	24.1	24.0	24.2	24.3	24.6	24.5	24.5	24.3	24.6	24.7	24.3
1998	24.5	24.6	24.7	24.7	24.8	25.0	24.9	24.9	24.9	24.8	24.9	24.8	24.7
1999	25.1	25.0	25.0	24.8	24.8	25.1	25.2	25.0	24.8	24.8	25.2	25.1	24.9
2000	24.5	24.4	24.5	24.1	23.9	24.2	23.9	23.9	23.7	23.5	23.6	23.7	23.9
2001	25.0	25.0	25.1	24.9	24.8	24.9	24.8	24.5	24.1	23.9	23.9	23.9	24.6
2002	23.9	23.6	23.5	22.7	22.5	22.5	22.3	22.1	21.8	21.7	21.7	21.6	22.5
2003	21.6	21.5	21.5	21.6	21.6	21.5	21.3	21.2	21.1	21.0	21.1	21.0	21.3
Financial activities													
1990	65.5	65.7	66.4	66.1	66.7	67.5	68.1	68.1	67.6	66.9	66.8	66.8	66.8
1991	65.6	65.7	65.9	65.6	66.4	67.5	68.3	68.6	68.1	67.6	67.8	68.0	67.0
1992	67.0	67.2	67.1	67.2	67.2	68.0	67.5	67.3	67.0	66.9	67.2	67.3	67.2
1993	66.0	66.2	66.6	66.7	67.5	68.5	68.0	68.2	68.0	68.2	68.8	69.2	67.6
1994	69.3	69.5	69.9	69.7	69.8	70.0	69.9	69.7	69.3	68.6	69.0	68.9	69.4
1995	68.4	68.9	69.4	69.8	69.4	69.8	70.0	70.0	69.5	69.8	70.6	70.7	69.6
1996	70.3	70.2	69.9	69.9	70.2	71.1	71.1	71.5	71.2	71.1	71.1	71.5	70.7
1997	71.3	72.1	72.6	72.6	72.8	73.3	74.5	74.8	74.0	73.8	74.8	74.8	73.4
1998	73.6	73.8	74.8	75.7	76.6	77.8	77.8	78.2	77.7	77.9	77.6	78.1	76.6
1999	77.3	77.6	78.1	78.9	79.5	80.4	81.4	81.2	81.0	80.8	80.8	81.0	79.8
2000	80.5	80.1	80.5	79.7	79.4	80.2	79.7	79.9	79.8	79.1	79.8	80.4	79.9
2001	80.1	80.4	80.6	80.5	80.7	81.8	81.7	81.8	80.7	80.5	81.2	81.6	81.0
2002	80.4	80.7	80.7	80.6	80.5	80.4	80.3	80.1	79.3	79.1	79.8	80.2	80.2
2003	79.5	79.7	79.9	80.6	81.2	82.2	82.1	82.3	81.6	81.5	81.7	82.1	81.2
Professional and business services													
1990	102.1	103.5	104.8	106.2	107.8	109.4	109.0	109.4	109.3	108.8	108.0	106.4	107.0
1991	101.8	102.6	104.0	103.6	104.4	106.5	105.7	105.9	106.1	106.5	106.3	105.2	104.8
1992	99.7	100.0	101.3	106.5	107.7	109.2	110.1	111.1	110.5	110.1	109.5	109.8	107.1
1993	107.0	107.7	109.2	110.7	111.6	113.8	115.1	116.2	117.4	117.1	116.2	115.4	113.1
1994	114.5	116.0	118.4	120.0	121.3	122.6	123.5	124.1	124.3	124.2	123.7	123.3	121.3
1995	117.7	119.3	121.3	124.0	124.6	127.0	126.5	128.3	128.1	129.0	128.2	127.6	125.1
1996	120.7	121.7	122.5	126.0	128.2	129.8	128.4	129.6	128.6	128.2	128.1	127.7	126.6
1997	124.8	126.9	129.4	134.4	135.5	137.3	138.6	139.8	139.6	141.0	141.0	140.2	135.7
1998	135.3	136.4	137.5	139.7	140.7	143.2	142.1	143.1	142.3	144.6	144.4	143.9	141.1
1999	140.2	141.8	143.3	145.2	146.0	148.1	147.3	149.3	147.8	148.9	148.5	148.0	146.2
2000	141.4	142.0	143.1	147.8	148.5	150.9	150.1	150.5	149.4	148.4	147.5	146.7	147.1
2001	142.2	142.1	143.7	144.0	144.5	145.3	144.1	143.5	139.7	138.7	136.8	135.6	141.7
2002	131.1	131.4	132.8	133.0	133.1	134.6	134.1	134.9	133.0	134.7	133.4	132.5	133.2
2003	128.7	128.7	130.0	133.0	134.1	135.5	136.1	135.3	134.6	135.6	133.9	132.8	133.2
Educational and health services													
1990	126.5	127.0	127.9	128.1	127.8	127.8	126.4	126.8	128.5	129.6	130.0	130.4	128.0
1991	128.0	128.8	129.6	129.8	130.3	130.4	129.7	130.3	132.4	133.3	134.2	134.2	130.9
1992	132.1	133.4	134.1	133.9	134.6	133.9	134.1	134.4	135.6	137.7	137.7	137.7	134.9
1993	136.0	137.3	137.8	137.6	138.0	137.6	138.5	138.6	139.5	140.0	140.6	140.7	138.5
1994	138.9	140.6	141.6	142.1	142.3	142.0	142.1	142.4	144.0	145.1	146.1	146.2	142.7
1995	143.5	145.3	145.8	145.5	145.8	145.6	144.3	143.7	146.3	147.4	148.0	148.1	145.7
1996	144.5	146.2	146.9	147.6	148.1	147.0	144.8	145.0	147.2	148.4	148.7	149.0	146.9
1997	144.9	146.3	146.8	147.9	147.5	146.8	145.4	146.1	148.1	149.6	150.8	151.0	147.6
1998	147.9	149.5	150.6	152.5	152.1	151.7	150.4	150.1	151.8	153.0	153.4	153.5	151.3
1999	150.9	152.2	152.5	154.9	155.3	154.5	153.7	153.6	155.5	156.5	156.9	156.9	154.4
2000	154.9	157.0	157.8	157.4	157.4	157.8	156.1	156.3	157.4	157.6	158.3	158.9	157.2
2001	156.8	160.3	160.9	161.5	160.8	159.9	158.1	158.5	162.0	164.5	165.2	165.5	161.2
2002	161.8	165.1	165.2	165.2	164.7	163.3	162.2	162.5	165.8	167.3	167.9	168.1	164.9
2003	166.0	168.1	168.6	168.8	168.6	166.3	166.9	167.3	170.9	172.8	173.0	173.4	169.2
Leisure and hospitality													
1990	74.9	74.9	76.7	78.4	82.3	84.8	84.5	84.7	82.8	79.3	78.0	78.1	79.9
1991	73.2	73.1	74.9	76.8	80.3	82.5	82.6	82.5	80.4	77.1	75.9	75.9	77.9
1992	72.0	72.0	74.0	76.8	81.4	83.1	83.6	83.7	81.5	79.7	78.7	78.4	78.7
1993	75.6	74.7	75.4	78.9	83.6	85.4	85.4	85.6	84.5	82.1	80.9	81.4	81.1
1994	78.0	78.2	80.4	81.9	86.2	88.7	89.1	89.2	87.0	84.2	84.1	84.5	84.2
1995	80.2	80.7	82.9	85.1	89.9	93.4	92.1	91.7	90.8	86.8	85.5	86.0	87.0
1996	83.6	84.4	86.8	87.5	92.1	95.9	95.1	95.3	92.8	90.3	88.7	88.8	90.1
1997	86.4	87.1	89.8	92.7	96.6	99.0	98.8	99.5	96.4	94.2	92.2	92.3	93.7
1998	88.1	88.9	90.7	93.4	98.0	99.9	99.7	99.7	96.7	94.8	93.3	94.1	94.7
1999	89.3	90.0	91.6	94.9	99.2	101.4	102.6	103.0	99.3	96.5	95.7	95.7	96.6
2000	90.2	90.5	92.4	95.3	99.4	102.5	103.6	103.2	99.7	96.2	94.5	94.3	96.8
2001	89.1	89.4	91.6	93.5	98.7	102.2	102.4	102.6	96.9	94.7	92.3	91.6	95.4
2002	87.1	86.6	88.0	92.1	96.7	99.2	100.4	100.8	98.0	94.1	92.3	92.0	93.9
2003	87.6	87.1	89.0	93.3	98.2	100.3	100.8	101.7	98.5	95.6	95.4	95.1	95.2

Employment by Industry: Ohio—*Continued*

(Numbers in thousands. Not seasonally adjusted.)

Industry	January	February	March	April	May	June	July	August	September	October	November	December	Annual Average
CLEVELAND—*Continued*													
Other services													
1990	37.8	38.1	38.6	38.9	39.2	40.0	39.5	39.9	39.8	39.8	40.1	40.4	39.3
1991	39.3	39.3	39.9	40.1	40.6	40.9	40.6	40.3	40.0	40.1	40.3	40.4	40.1
1992	39.4	39.4	39.9	40.3	40.6	40.9	41.0	40.8	40.6	40.1	40.3	40.3	40.3
1993	40.8	42.0	42.2	42.5	42.7	43.0	43.4	43.0	42.9	43.3	43.5	43.7	42.7
1994	44.4	44.6	45.0	44.8	45.3	45.5	44.4	44.6	44.5	45.1	45.3	45.7	44.9
1995	45.2	45.4	46.0	46.2	46.7	46.9	46.7	46.9	47.2	47.3	47.3	47.6	46.6
1996	46.9	47.2	47.6	47.0	46.1	46.6	46.4	46.5	46.2	46.0	46.0	46.3	46.5
1997	45.4	45.8	46.2	46.2	46.7	47.0	47.2	47.4	47.1	46.8	46.9	47.0	46.6
1998	46.3	46.6	47.0	46.8	47.1	47.3	47.1	47.0	46.4	46.6	46.3	46.4	46.7
1999	45.4	45.6	45.8	46.5	46.7	47.2	46.8	46.8	46.3	46.5	46.6	46.7	46.4
2000	47.0	47.3	47.6	47.2	47.5	47.7	47.6	47.5	47.5	47.5	47.5	47.7	47.4
2001	45.8	45.9	45.9	46.3	46.6	47.2	47.2	47.4	46.8	46.4	46.5	46.6	46.6
2002	45.9	45.9	46.2	46.1	46.3	46.8	46.6	46.4	46.0	45.3	45.2	45.1	46.0
2003	45.0	45.0	45.3	45.4	45.5	45.8	45.6	45.9	45.5	44.9	44.5	44.1	45.2
Government													
1990	136.7	138.5	140.2	139.4	142.2	141.9	136.9	128.4	135.1	137.4	138.3	138.1	137.7
1991	136.4	137.7	138.7	138.0	139.2	139.7	136.9	129.1	137.4	140.3	142.2	141.7	138.1
1992	140.1	141.5	142.8	142.1	143.3	143.5	132.5	130.8	137.3	140.2	140.5	140.6	139.6
1993	140.7	143.3	143.6	143.3	144.1	144.2	133.5	131.3	137.7	143.7	141.7	141.9	140.7
1994	140.5	142.8	143.0	143.1	144.0	145.5	135.3	133.6	138.3	144.0	145.0	144.7	141.6
1995	142.2	143.9	144.4	142.9	144.3	146.1	137.4	134.1	139.3	143.1	144.1	144.9	142.2
1996	142.0	144.3	145.1	143.2	145.0	146.7	136.7	135.2	141.3	144.7	146.2	145.8	143.0
1997	142.6	145.4	145.9	142.7	144.9	146.7	136.2	135.6	140.3	143.6	144.6	144.6	142.7
1998	141.8	143.9	144.3	143.5	145.2	146.2	136.5	136.0	142.7	144.9	146.2	146.2	143.1
1999	142.1	145.7	146.4	145.5	147.2	147.1	138.6	138.4	144.3	147.3	148.4	148.6	144.9
2000	145.1	147.7	148.7	148.1	152.5	148.3	141.8	140.8	146.4	148.7	149.5	150.1	147.3
2001	146.4	149.3	150.7	150.1	150.8	148.6	142.6	142.6	149.1	151.5	152.1	152.6	148.9
2002	147.7	151.8	152.7	151.5	152.6	150.4	141.6	140.2	149.0	152.0	152.5	151.9	149.5
2003	148.0	150.9	152.0	151.7	151.7	149.1	141.6	139.1	146.9	150.6	151.3	151.9	148.7
Federal government													
1990	20.5	20.3	20.5	20.7	22.2	21.1	20.9	20.2	19.9	19.5	19.4	19.6	20.4
1991	19.4	19.5	19.5	19.5	19.5	19.6	19.8	19.8	19.9	19.8	19.9	20.2	19.7
1992	21.7	21.4	21.4	21.4	21.4	21.4	21.3	21.2	21.3	21.5	21.3	21.6	21.4
1993	21.4	21.4	21.4	21.2	21.1	21.0	21.1	21.1	21.0	20.7	20.6	21.2	21.1
1994	21.1	21.1	21.0	21.5	21.4	21.3	21.3	21.3	21.3	23.1	23.0	23.1	21.7
1995	23.0	23.0	22.7	22.6	22.6	22.5	23.0	22.6	22.6	22.6	22.6	23.0	22.7
1996	22.9	22.9	22.9	22.1	21.9	21.9	22.0	21.9	21.8	21.6	21.9	22.5	22.1
1997	21.8	21.7	21.5	19.7	19.7	19.8	19.7	19.7	19.7	19.6	19.9	20.5	20.2
1998	20.0	20.0	20.1	20.0	20.0	20.1	20.1	20.1	20.1	20.2	20.2	20.6	20.1
1999	20.3	20.4	20.3	20.4	20.3	20.4	20.3	20.3	20.3	20.3	20.3	20.7	20.3
2000	20.4	20.5	20.6	21.0	24.4	21.9	22.0	20.3	20.1	20.0	19.9	20.4	20.9
2001	19.6	19.5	19.5	19.3	19.3	19.3	19.5	19.3	19.3	19.3	19.2	19.5	19.4
2002	19.3	18.7	18.8	18.7	18.7	18.8	18.8	19.2	19.5	19.5	19.2	19.2	19.0
2003	19.2	18.9	18.7	18.8	18.8	18.7	18.8	18.8	18.6	18.7	18.6	19.2	18.8
State government													
1990	7.9	8.3	8.5	8.5	8.1	8.7	7.9	8.0	7.8	8.4	8.3	8.6	8.2
1991	8.1	8.6	8.8	9.0	8.6	9.0	8.2	8.3	8.1	8.2	8.9	8.8	8.5
1992	9.8	10.0	10.2	10.3	10.5	10.0	9.4	9.2	9.2	9.8	9.8	9.7	9.8
1993	9.6	9.7	9.7	10.2	9.9	9.7	9.2	9.1	8.9	9.7	9.5	9.6	9.5
1994	9.5	9.7	9.8	10.2	9.9	9.8	9.2	9.1	9.3	9.7	9.9	9.9	9.6
1995	9.7	9.7	10.0	10.0	9.9	9.8	9.1	9.0	9.2	9.6	9.6	9.6	9.6
1996	9.2	9.5	9.5	9.4	9.5	9.3	8.7	8.7	8.6	9.3	9.3	9.2	9.1
1997	9.0	9.3	9.3	9.2	9.3	9.2	8.7	8.5	8.3	9.1	9.2	9.2	9.0
1998	9.2	9.2	9.3	9.3	9.3	9.2	8.7	8.5	9.1	9.2	9.4	9.4	9.1
1999	8.6	9.3	9.4	9.4	9.5	9.4	8.7	8.4	9.2	9.2	9.4	9.4	9.1
2000	8.5	9.3	9.4	9.4	9.5	9.4	8.7	8.4	9.2	9.3	9.3	9.2	9.1
2001	8.4	9.2	9.4	9.4	9.2	9.4	8.6	8.3	9.0	9.0	9.2	9.2	9.0
2002	8.3	9.1	9.2	9.2	9.1	9.2	8.4	8.2	8.9	8.9	9.1	9.0	8.9
2003	8.5	8.6	8.7	8.8	8.6	8.1	8.1	7.9	8.6	8.6	8.7	8.8	8.5
Local government													
1990	90.0	91.3	92.3	91.3	92.1	92.6	90.2	83.0	89.0	90.6	91.4	90.8	90.3
1991	90.0	90.5	91.1	90.6	92.0	91.8	91.1	84.1	91.2	93.6	94.5	93.7	91.1
1992	108.6	110.1	111.2	110.4	111.4	112.1	101.8	100.4	106.8	108.9	109.4	109.3	108.3
1993	109.7	112.2	112.5	111.9	113.1	113.5	103.2	101.1	107.8	113.3	111.6	111.1	110.0
1994	109.9	112.0	112.2	111.4	112.7	114.4	104.8	103.2	107.7	111.2	112.1	111.7	110.2
1995	109.5	111.2	111.7	110.3	111.8	113.8	105.3	102.5	107.5	110.9	111.9	112.3	109.8
1996	109.9	111.9	112.7	111.7	113.6	115.5	106.0	104.6	110.9	113.8	115.0	114.1	111.6
1997	111.8	114.4	115.1	113.8	115.9	117.7	107.8	107.4	112.3	114.9	115.5	114.9	113.4
1998	112.6	114.7	114.9	114.2	115.9	116.9	107.7	107.4	113.5	115.5	116.6	116.2	113.8
1999	113.2	116.0	116.7	115.7	117.4	117.3	109.6	109.7	114.8	117.8	118.7	118.5	115.4
2000	116.2	117.9	118.7	117.7	118.6	117.0	111.1	112.1	117.1	119.4	120.3	120.5	117.2
2001	118.4	120.6	121.8	121.4	122.3	119.9	114.5	115.0	120.8	123.2	123.7	123.9	120.5
2002	120.1	124.0	124.7	123.6	124.8	122.4	114.4	112.8	120.6	123.6	124.2	123.7	121.6
2003	120.3	123.4	124.6	124.1	124.3	122.3	114.7	112.4	119.7	123.3	124.0	123.9	121.4

Employment by Industry: Ohio—*Continued*

(Numbers in thousands. Not seasonally adjusted.)

Industry	January	February	March	April	May	June	July	August	September	October	November	December	Annual Average
COLUMBUS													
Total nonfarm													
1990	683.4	685.5	690.3	697.3	704.9	712.8	701.7	704.2	706.3	712.5	714.4	716.0	702.4
1991	691.7	690.1	693.9	695.4	701.1	705.7	696.0	698.5	702.4	706.7	711.2	711.0	700.3
1992	693.0	694.1	699.0	708.3	717.2	720.0	713.2	713.7	714.8	725.6	726.7	728.1	712.8
1993	708.3	711.6	714.1	718.6	726.4	732.8	725.7	730.2	734.2	741.8	744.1	748.0	727.9
1994	729.9	735.0	740.8	745.3	754.9	760.3	749.6	754.4	760.8	773.3	779.2	786.3	755.8
1995	761.6	766.4	773.5	777.8	783.4	791.3	777.4	784.0	789.9	793.6	799.2	803.2	783.4
1996	775.3	781.4	786.1	792.2	799.2	803.6	797.4	799.8	796.0	802.2	807.8	811.6	796.0
1997	791.0	794.4	801.1	810.1	819.4	825.4	821.6	823.5	822.1	829.5	836.4	843.0	818.1
1998	816.7	819.7	823.6	832.2	840.2	846.7	838.9	845.2	843.4	851.1	859.2	863.5	840.0
1999	836.2	842.7	845.8	856.3	861.3	866.7	871.5	871.1	869.0	880.0	888.4	897.3	865.5
2000	867.8	871.5	876.4	882.6	887.9	895.5	892.6	892.6	888.8	896.8	904.3	907.9	888.7
2001	887.9	889.6	893.2	894.6	897.5	900.3	892.1	890.2	884.8	891.6	896.3	897.8	893.0
2002	874.8	875.0	879.3	880.3	883.6	886.4	880.0	879.9	877.8	882.7	886.6	886.4	881.1
2003	861.9	860.0	862.6	871.2	876.8	879.5	876.4	875.3	873.7	878.3	882.0	880.8	873.2
Total private													
1990	557.5	558.6	561.7	568.0	573.7	581.3	581.3	585.2	584.0	583.3	583.9	584.7	575.2
1991	562.9	559.4	562.8	564.6	569.1	573.5	574.4	577.8	577.9	576.1	578.4	577.7	571.2
1992	562.0	561.8	566.5	575.3	582.9	586.3	589.0	589.8	588.4	591.8	592.9	593.4	581.6
1993	576.6	578.2	580.2	584.6	592.6	598.6	601.8	605.7	606.7	607.4	609.8	612.7	596.2
1994	597.4	600.8	606.5	610.5	620.5	625.6	624.9	629.8	631.4	637.3	642.8	649.2	623.0
1995	627.9	631.0	636.9	641.2	647.3	654.5	652.3	658.9	659.6	658.1	663.4	667.2	649.8
1996	642.5	646.5	650.2	656.7	663.5	668.0	668.3	671.1	668.6	668.3	673.1	676.8	662.8
1997	654.7	657.3	663.3	673.6	682.1	687.2	687.3	689.2	688.6	692.5	698.3	704.4	681.5
1998	678.9	681.7	685.0	694.0	701.3	707.2	704.3	710.6	708.1	713.5	720.0	723.3	702.3
1999	697.2	703.0	706.0	716.3	721.4	726.5	735.2	736.1	733.1	741.1	747.7	755.6	726.6
2000	727.9	730.5	734.9	741.1	746.1	752.1	752.8	754.8	749.3	754.5	761.0	763.6	747.3
2001	746.8	746.7	749.5	751.1	753.2	755.6	750.6	750.0	742.5	745.8	749.5	750.4	749.3
2002	728.8	728.5	732.7	734.2	737.2	739.0	737.3	738.1	734.5	736.8	738.9	738.4	735.4
2003	715.0	712.5	715.3	724.3	729.0	731.6	732.3	732.5	730.5	731.9	734.6	732.7	726.9
Goods-producing													
1990	109.4	109.5	111.2	112.5	113.8	116.0	116.9	117.6	117.1	115.6	114.7	112.9	113.9
1991	107.2	106.2	106.9	108.1	109.5	111.0	112.7	113.9	113.7	112.2	111.4	109.5	110.1
1992	105.8	105.3	106.2	108.5	109.9	110.9	111.2	111.2	111.4	111.5	110.5	109.4	109.3
1993	106.2	106.4	106.5	107.8	109.7	111.7	113.1	113.5	114.1	113.0	112.9	112.1	110.5
1994	108.7	109.4	111.4	112.7	115.5	117.4	116.8	117.7	118.1	118.7	118.8	118.3	115.2
1995	115.4	115.2	117.3	118.9	120.3	121.9	120.7	122.1	122.0	121.0	120.2	119.4	119.5
1996	112.8	113.5	114.8	117.3	118.6	120.2	120.2	120.8	120.4	120.6	120.2	119.1	118.2
1997	116.9	117.0	117.9	120.9	123.2	124.1	124.3	125.3	124.5	124.5	124.2	123.8	122.2
1998	119.5	119.9	120.9	124.1	125.1	126.4	123.6	127.9	127.4	128.4	128.4	127.6	124.9
1999	121.5	121.9	122.5	125.5	126.9	128.4	130.5	130.8	130.6	131.8	131.9	131.4	127.8
2000	127.2	127.3	129.2	130.4	132.0	134.1	134.0	134.0	132.7	132.2	131.4	129.9	131.2
2001	124.7	124.7	125.5	126.3	126.8	127.9	128.4	128.2	125.9	124.5	123.1	121.4	125.6
2002	116.2	115.6	116.4	116.8	117.4	119.0	118.6	119.9	119.3	118.0	116.2	114.8	117.4
2003	110.4	108.7	109.1	110.8	111.8	112.8	114.8	114.8	114.7	113.9	113.9	111.9	112.3
Construction and mining													
1990	25.4	25.3	26.4	27.2	28.6	29.9	30.9	31.2	30.7	29.8	29.2	27.7	28.5
1991	23.3	22.9	23.5	24.6	25.6	26.6	28.2	28.6	28.3	27.4	26.8	25.6	25.9
1992	23.0	22.6	23.3	25.3	26.7	27.5	28.4	28.7	28.7	28.5	27.8	26.9	26.4
1993	23.9	23.8	23.7	25.5	26.8	27.9	29.7	29.5	29.5	30.0	29.3	28.3	27.3
1994	25.1	25.1	26.6	28.3	30.2	31.5	31.8	32.2	32.1	32.5	32.1	31.1	29.8
1995	28.2	27.8	29.5	31.0	32.4	33.8	33.5	34.1	33.9	33.6	33.0	32.4	31.9
1996	28.5	28.9	30.3	31.9	33.4	34.8	35.6	35.8	35.3	35.1	34.6	33.7	33.1
1997	31.0	31.1	32.3	34.7	36.3	37.3	37.8	38.0	37.6	37.3	36.5	35.7	35.4
1998	31.8	32.2	32.9	35.6	37.2	38.4	39.2	39.3	39.0	39.4	39.2	38.4	36.8
1999	34.9	35.0	35.7	37.7	39.1	40.5	42.6	42.5	42.3	42.6	42.3	41.3	39.7
2000	37.7	37.6	39.5	41.5	42.8	44.2	44.5	44.4	43.6	42.5	41.8	40.3	41.7
2001	38.0	38.4	39.7	41.8	43.0	44.7	45.7	46.0	44.9	43.8	43.1	41.9	42.6
2002	37.8	37.4	38.5	39.7	40.0	41.2	42.1	42.3	41.8	41.4	40.8	39.4	40.2
2003	36.2	35.1	35.8	38.4	39.5	40.7	42.8	42.0	42.4	41.8	41.8	40.3	39.7
Manufacturing													
1990	84.0	84.2	84.8	85.3	85.2	86.1	86.0	86.4	86.4	85.8	85.5	85.2	85.4
1991	83.9	83.3	83.4	83.5	83.9	84.4	84.5	85.3	85.4	84.8	84.6	83.9	84.2
1992	82.8	82.7	82.9	83.2	83.2	83.4	82.8	82.5	82.7	83.0	82.7	82.5	82.8
1993	82.3	82.6	82.8	82.3	82.9	83.8	83.4	84.0	84.6	83.0	83.6	83.8	83.2
1994	83.6	84.3	84.8	84.4	85.3	85.9	85.0	85.5	86.0	86.2	86.7	87.2	85.4
1995	87.2	87.4	87.8	87.9	87.9	88.1	87.2	88.0	88.1	87.4	87.2	87.0	87.6
1996	84.3	84.6	84.5	85.4	85.2	85.4	84.6	85.0	85.1	85.5	85.6	85.4	85.0
1997	85.9	85.9	85.6	86.2	86.9	86.8	86.5	87.3	86.9	87.2	87.7	88.1	86.7
1998	87.7	87.7	88.0	88.5	87.9	88.0	84.4	88.6	88.4	89.0	89.2	89.2	88.0
1999	86.6	86.9	86.8	87.8	87.8	87.9	87.9	88.3	88.3	89.2	89.6	90.1	88.1
2000	89.5	89.7	89.7	88.9	89.2	89.9	89.5	89.6	89.1	89.7	89.6	89.6	89.5
2001	86.7	86.3	85.8	84.5	83.8	83.2	82.7	82.2	81.0	80.7	80.0	79.5	83.0
2002	78.4	78.2	77.9	77.1	77.4	77.8	76.5	77.6	77.5	76.6	75.4	75.4	77.2
2003	74.2	73.6	73.3	72.4	72.3	72.1	72.0	72.8	72.3	72.1	72.1	71.6	72.6

Employment by Industry: Ohio—*Continued*

(Numbers in thousands. Not seasonally adjusted.)

Industry	January	February	March	April	May	June	July	August	September	October	November	December	Annual Average
COLUMBUS—*Continued*													
Service-providing													
1990	574.0	576.0	579.1	584.8	591.1	596.8	584.8	586.6	589.2	596.9	599.7	603.1	588.5
1991	584.5	583.9	587.0	587.3	591.6	594.7	583.3	584.6	588.7	594.5	599.8	601.5	590.1
1992	587.2	588.8	592.8	599.8	607.3	609.1	602.0	602.5	603.4	614.1	616.2	618.7	603.4
1993	602.1	605.2	607.6	610.8	616.7	621.1	612.6	616.7	620.1	628.8	631.2	635.9	617.4
1994	621.2	625.6	629.4	632.6	639.4	642.9	632.8	636.7	642.7	654.6	660.4	668.0	640.5
1995	646.2	651.2	656.2	658.9	663.1	669.4	656.7	661.9	667.9	672.6	679.0	683.8	663.9
1996	662.5	667.9	671.3	674.9	680.6	683.4	677.2	679.0	675.6	681.6	687.6	692.5	677.8
1997	674.1	677.4	683.2	689.2	696.2	701.3	697.3	698.2	697.6	705.0	712.2	719.2	695.9
1998	697.2	699.8	702.7	708.1	715.1	720.3	715.3	717.3	716.0	722.7	730.8	735.9	715.1
1999	714.7	720.8	723.3	730.8	734.4	738.3	741.0	740.3	738.4	748.2	756.5	765.9	737.7
2000	740.6	744.2	747.2	752.2	755.9	761.4	758.6	758.6	756.1	764.6	772.9	778.0	757.5
2001	763.2	764.9	767.7	768.3	770.7	772.4	763.7	762.0	758.9	767.1	773.2	776.4	767.4
2002	758.6	759.4	762.9	763.5	766.2	767.4	761.4	760.0	758.5	764.7	770.4	771.6	763.7
2003	751.5	751.3	753.5	760.4	765.0	766.7	761.6	760.5	759.0	764.4	768.1	768.9	760.9
Trade, transportation, and utilities													
1990	144.1	142.7	142.6	143.5	144.6	145.8	144.8	145.9	145.6	147.2	148.6	150.8	145.5
1991	143.9	140.9	142.2	141.8	142.6	142.4	142.4	143.8	144.5	146.5	149.7	150.7	144.2
1992	145.0	143.5	144.1	145.4	146.6	147.1	148.0	148.7	149.2	150.3	153.8	155.5	148.1
1993	147.4	146.3	146.7	145.9	148.1	149.3	149.3	150.6	151.2	153.9	156.9	160.1	150.4
1994	153.8	153.3	154.0	152.9	156.0	156.9	156.0	158.2	160.4	164.8	169.6	174.8	159.2
1995	164.1	162.7	163.5	163.9	164.5	166.1	165.2	167.1	166.9	168.5	173.8	177.8	167.0
1996	168.1	166.4	166.2	167.2	168.4	168.8	169.5	170.5	169.7	170.9	176.2	181.7	170.3
1997	171.0	169.5	170.2	172.6	173.9	174.5	174.5	174.0	174.9	178.6	184.2	189.7	175.6
1998	175.9	174.3	174.0	176.0	177.3	178.4	177.9	178.5	178.1	181.3	187.0	190.8	179.1
1999	179.1	178.0	178.2	181.1	182.1	181.9	183.6	183.5	183.9	188.4	193.9	200.7	184.5
2000	187.3	185.7	185.4	187.2	187.6	188.2	188.7	188.9	187.8	192.8	200.0	204.6	190.3
2001	195.6	191.5	191.5	191.4	191.2	191.1	188.5	187.9	187.8	191.1	196.6	199.9	192.0
2002	187.7	185.6	186.4	185.9	186.3	185.7	185.4	185.0	184.2	185.4	188.2	190.4	186.4
2003	177.4	175.3	175.9	178.0	178.7	179.0	178.3	180.2	180.4	181.5	185.6	187.9	179.9
Wholesale trade													
1990	28.0	28.7	28.7	28.8	29.0	29.1	28.6	28.6	28.7	28.6	27.9	28.2	28.5
1991	27.7	27.2	27.8	27.9	27.9	28.1	27.5	27.7	27.8	27.6	27.5	27.4	27.6
1992	27.4	27.5	27.5	27.8	28.5	28.4	28.3	28.2	28.5	28.7	28.7	28.5	28.1
1993	27.6	27.7	27.8	27.7	27.9	28.1	28.4	28.5	28.5	28.5	28.4	28.5	28.1
1994	28.6	28.7	29.0	28.8	29.0	29.2	29.1	29.2	29.5	29.6	29.7	30.0	29.2
1995	29.5	29.8	30.0	30.1	30.2	30.5	30.2	30.5	30.4	30.3	30.4	30.5	30.2
1996	29.6	30.0	30.2	30.2	30.3	30.5	30.2	30.2	30.1	30.0	30.1	30.2	30.1
1997	30.1	30.6	31.0	31.5	31.8	32.1	31.7	32.1	32.2	32.1	32.1	32.4	31.6
1998	32.0	32.3	32.5	32.5	32.7	32.7	32.3	32.4	32.4	32.6	32.6	32.7	32.4
1999	32.8	33.1	33.3	33.6	34.0	33.9	34.0	34.0	33.9	34.4	34.4	34.9	33.8
2000	34.3	34.7	34.8	35.2	35.3	35.7	35.8	35.9	36.0	35.7	35.8	35.8	35.4
2001	38.8	38.9	39.2	39.4	39.4	39.4	39.2	39.1	38.7	38.8	38.6	39.0	39.0
2002	38.5	38.5	38.7	38.2	38.2	38.1	38.2	38.2	38.0	38.0	38.0	38.1	38.2
2003	35.1	35.1	35.3	35.6	35.9	36.2	36.5	36.9	37.2	37.6	38.0	38.1	36.5
Retail trade													
1990	95.7	93.7	94.0	94.4	95.2	96.1	95.5	96.2	96.0	97.5	99.5	101.7	96.2
1991	95.7	93.4	93.9	93.5	94.1	93.8	94.2	95.3	95.7	97.6	100.7	102.1	95.8
1992	96.8	95.3	95.9	96.2	96.3	96.7	97.1	97.8	98.1	98.8	102.3	104.4	97.9
1993	97.7	96.5	96.6	95.4	97.0	97.8	97.8	98.9	99.3	101.2	104.2	107.1	99.1
1994	101.0	100.1	100.5	99.5	101.6	102.1	100.8	102.7	104.4	108.1	112.9	118.0	104.3
1995	107.6	106.0	106.5	106.3	106.7	107.7	107.3	108.9	108.9	110.0	114.7	118.7	109.1
1996	109.4	107.2	106.8	107.8	108.7	109.1	109.8	110.7	110.3	111.3	116.8	122.5	110.8
1997	112.6	110.6	110.9	111.9	112.8	113.3	113.4	114.1	113.3	116.2	121.7	126.8	114.8
1998	114.5	112.7	112.3	112.5	113.4	114.2	113.4	113.6	113.3	115.7	121.7	125.4	115.2
1999	114.6	113.2	113.3	113.7	114.9	115.2	115.4	115.6	116.1	118.6	124.3	130.7	117.1
2000	118.5	116.6	116.7	117.1	117.6	118.0	117.8	118.0	116.9	120.9	128.0	132.8	119.9
2001	121.1	117.3	117.5	116.7	116.7	116.9	114.0	113.6	114.1	116.5	122.2	125.5	117.7
2002	114.2	112.5	113.2	113.5	113.9	113.3	112.0	111.3	110.9	111.5	114.2	116.4	113.1
2003	107.5	105.4	105.9	107.2	107.6	107.8	107.2	108.0	107.7	108.6	111.9	114.4	108.3
Transportation and utilities													
1990	20.4	20.3	19.9	20.3	20.4	20.6	20.7	21.1	20.9	21.1	21.2	20.9	20.6
1991	20.5	20.3	20.5	20.4	20.6	20.5	20.7	20.8	21.0	21.3	21.5	21.2	20.7
1992	20.8	20.7	20.7	21.4	21.8	22.0	22.6	22.7	22.6	22.8	22.8	22.6	21.9
1993	22.1	22.1	22.3	22.8	23.2	23.4	23.1	23.2	23.4	24.2	24.3	24.5	23.2
1994	24.2	24.5	24.5	24.6	25.4	25.6	26.1	26.3	26.5	27.1	27.0	26.8	25.7
1995	27.0	26.9	27.0	27.5	27.6	27.9	27.7	27.7	27.6	28.2	28.7	28.6	27.7
1996	29.1	29.2	29.2	29.2	29.4	29.2	29.5	29.6	29.3	29.6	29.3	29.0	29.3
1997	28.3	28.3	28.3	29.2	29.3	29.1	29.4	27.8	29.4	30.3	30.4	30.5	29.1
1998	29.4	29.3	29.2	31.0	31.2	31.5	32.2	32.5	32.4	33.0	32.7	32.7	31.4
1999	31.7	31.7	31.6	33.8	33.2	32.8	34.2	33.9	33.9	35.4	35.2	35.1	33.5
2000	34.5	34.4	33.9	34.9	34.7	34.5	35.1	35.0	34.9	36.2	36.2	36.0	35.0
2001	35.7	35.3	34.8	35.3	35.1	34.8	35.3	35.2	35.0	35.8	35.8	35.4	35.3
2002	35.0	34.6	34.5	34.2	34.2	34.3	35.2	35.5	35.3	35.9	36.0	35.9	35.1
2003	34.8	34.8	34.7	35.2	35.2	35.0	34.6	35.3	35.5	35.3	35.7	35.4	35.1

Employment by Industry: Ohio—*Continued*

(Numbers in thousands. Not seasonally adjusted.)

Industry	January	February	March	April	May	June	July	August	September	October	November	December	Annual Average
COLUMBUS—*Continued*													
Information													
1990	18.2	18.3	18.3	18.4	18.4	18.5	18.7	18.8	18.8	18.7	18.9	18.9	18.5
1991	19.0	19.0	19.1	18.6	18.6	18.7	18.8	18.8	18.6	18.5	18.5	18.4	18.7
1992	18.3	18.3	18.3	18.2	18.2	18.2	18.3	18.0	17.9	18.1	18.0	18.1	18.1
1993	18.5	18.6	18.5	18.1	18.3	18.4	18.1	18.6	18.5	18.3	18.5	18.6	18.4
1994	17.6	17.7	17.9	17.7	17.9	17.9	18.3	18.4	18.4	18.3	18.7	18.9	18.1
1995	18.2	18.5	18.4	18.5	18.6	18.8	19.0	19.3	19.4	19.4	19.7	19.7	18.9
1996	19.3	19.4	19.5	19.5	19.7	19.9	19.8	19.9	19.7	19.5	19.8	19.8	19.6
1997	19.9	19.9	19.9	19.9	20.0	20.2	20.2	20.3	20.2	20.3	20.3	20.6	20.1
1998	20.4	20.6	20.3	20.2	20.3	20.7	20.4	20.5	20.5	20.5	20.7	20.7	20.4
1999	21.1	21.2	21.2	21.1	21.1	21.3	21.4	21.7	21.7	21.9	22.2	22.4	21.5
2000	22.6	22.8	22.9	22.6	22.8	23.0	23.1	23.3	23.2	23.7	23.7	23.7	23.1
2001	24.0	23.9	23.6	22.6	22.7	22.8	22.4	22.4	21.9	21.6	21.6	21.4	22.6
2002	21.7	21.4	21.4	21.0	21.0	21.1	21.2	21.3	21.2	21.0	21.1	21.1	21.2
2003	20.7	20.7	20.4	20.7	20.7	20.8	20.6	20.4	20.2	20.1	20.3	20.4	20.5
Financial activities													
1990	56.3	56.4	56.4	56.9	57.2	57.8	58.0	58.0	57.9	57.5	57.4	57.5	57.2
1991	56.8	56.8	56.9	57.0	57.4	58.1	57.7	57.6	57.5	56.4	56.2	56.5	57.0
1992	56.1	56.3	56.4	57.1	57.5	57.0	57.1	57.2	56.7	56.3	56.3	56.5	56.7
1993	55.3	55.3	55.8	55.5	56.4	57.3	58.2	58.6	58.3	57.6	57.6	57.8	56.9
1994	59.0	59.2	59.8	59.6	60.2	60.9	61.7	61.9	61.5	61.7	62.0	62.1	60.8
1995	61.6	61.8	61.9	61.5	61.8	62.5	62.6	63.0	62.8	62.9	63.2	63.6	62.4
1996	63.7	64.1	64.4	63.8	64.2	65.1	65.1	65.0	64.8	64.7	64.9	65.2	64.5
1997	64.9	66.0	66.4	67.5	67.5	67.6	68.1	67.9	67.6	68.0	68.4	68.1	67.3
1998	66.4	66.6	66.9	68.3	68.8	69.2	70.4	70.4	69.9	69.2	70.4	71.8	69.0
1999	72.1	72.6	72.7	73.3	73.6	73.9	73.6	73.7	73.2	73.3	73.9	74.3	73.3
2000	73.3	73.4	73.1	72.8	73.0	73.4	73.3	73.1	73.0	73.1	73.6	74.2	73.2
2001	75.3	75.6	76.1	76.1	76.1	76.7	76.1	75.9	75.6	74.9	75.2	75.5	75.8
2002	74.9	75.2	75.3	75.2	74.9	74.6	74.6	74.5	74.2	74.8	75.2	75.3	74.9
2003	75.0	75.5	75.5	75.9	76.2	76.6	76.6	76.6	76.3	76.2	76.6	76.3	76.1
Professional and business services													
1990	79.4	80.2	80.9	82.1	83.0	84.0	84.8	86.1	85.7	86.1	85.8	85.8	83.6
1991	82.3	81.7	81.9	81.6	81.7	82.1	81.8	82.0	81.9	82.4	82.5	82.6	82.0
1992	80.2	80.7	81.7	84.2	84.5	86.2	85.7	85.7	85.6	86.7	86.7	87.2	84.5
1993	85.9	87.0	87.5	90.1	90.0	90.2	91.7	91.7	92.6	93.3	93.0	93.4	90.5
1994	91.6	92.6	93.3	93.6	93.5	94.0	94.0	95.0	94.4	95.7	95.5	95.9	94.0
1995	93.0	94.6	95.9	96.7	97.5	98.6	97.8	99.8	100.2	100.8	100.8	100.9	98.0
1996	97.6	98.5	99.6	102.0	103.4	103.7	104.0	105.1	104.3	105.6	105.7	104.6	102.8
1997	102.7	103.8	104.9	107.5	109.1	110.8	110.9	112.5	112.4	114.2	114.3	114.1	109.7
1998	112.7	112.8	113.6	113.4	114.8	115.6	116.0	116.9	116.6	118.1	117.8	117.4	115.4
1999	116.0	117.5	118.7	119.5	120.0	121.3	125.0	125.1	124.2	125.6	125.9	126.6	122.1
2000	122.9	124.1	125.3	126.0	126.3	127.6	128.2	128.6	128.5	129.1	128.9	128.6	127.0
2001	129.7	130.1	130.4	130.5	129.3	128.9	128.8	128.5	127.0	127.8	127.0	126.9	128.7
2002	125.2	125.4	125.6	125.4	124.4	124.6	124.6	124.9	124.1	125.0	125.6	125.2	125.0
2003	123.7	123.4	123.8	124.4	123.9	123.4	122.6	121.6	121.3	121.9	121.4	120.4	122.7
Educational and health services													
1990	65.5	66.3	66.5	66.9	66.7	67.1	67.0	67.2	68.1	69.2	69.9	70.6	67.5
1991	69.5	69.7	69.8	70.1	70.1	70.4	70.1	70.4	71.2	71.9	72.5	72.6	70.6
1992	72.0	72.3	72.7	74.3	74.7	74.5	74.8	74.9	75.1	76.3	76.8	77.0	74.6
1993	75.9	76.4	76.8	76.6	76.6	76.6	76.1	76.6	77.1	77.1	77.3	77.7	76.7
1994	76.3	77.3	77.3	78.0	78.0	78.0	78.3	78.4	78.9	79.5	80.1	80.9	78.4
1995	79.2	80.2	80.8	80.3	80.0	79.9	80.2	80.3	81.3	82.4	83.0	83.6	80.9
1996	80.7	82.0	82.4	82.4	82.1	81.9	82.0	81.8	82.9	83.2	83.5	82.6	82.2
1997	80.8	81.9	82.5	82.6	82.5	82.0	82.4	82.1	83.2	83.3	83.8	83.9	82.5
1998	84.1	85.5	86.0	86.3	86.6	86.3	86.1	86.6	87.7	88.6	88.8	88.3	86.7
1999	86.3	87.7	87.6	87.9	86.9	86.5	87.0	87.3	88.1	88.9	89.0	89.0	87.6
2000	87.3	88.3	88.3	88.7	88.6	88.2	87.9	89.0	89.0	89.7	90.0	90.5	88.7
2001	88.4	90.1	90.6	90.5	90.8	90.6	89.3	89.5	89.6	92.2	92.9	93.0	90.6
2002	91.6	92.7	93.0	93.0	93.1	92.2	91.5	91.4	92.5	94.8	95.2	95.2	93.0
2003	94.0	95.1	95.3	96.1	96.4	95.3	94.4	94.2	95.7	97.7	97.7	97.9	95.8
Leisure and hospitality													
1990	58.7	59.2	59.8	61.2	63.2	65.0	64.2	64.5	63.5	61.7	61.2	60.8	61.9
1991	57.4	58.0	58.7	59.8	61.4	62.7	63.2	63.5	62.7	60.7	60.1	59.9	60.6
1992	57.2	57.9	59.1	59.4	62.7	63.5	64.8	64.9	63.5	63.5	62.1	61.1	61.6
1993	58.3	59.1	59.3	61.5	64.6	66.0	65.9	66.5	65.6	64.7	64.0	63.6	63.2
1994	60.9	61.7	63.0	66.2	69.4	70.4	69.9	70.1	69.4	68.0	67.3	67.5	66.9
1995	65.8	67.1	68.1	70.2	73.0	74.9	75.2	75.2	74.9	71.1	70.5	70.0	71.3
1996	68.3	70.3	70.9	73.2	75.6	77.0	76.1	76.1	75.3	72.1	71.2	72.2	73.1
1997	66.9	67.3	69.3	70.4	73.2	75.3	74.3	74.4	73.7	71.0	70.8	71.6	71.5
1998	67.7	69.4	70.8	73.0	75.4	77.5	77.2	77.0	75.4	74.8	74.3	74.4	73.9
1999	69.8	72.2	73.2	74.9	77.2	79.3	80.7	80.4	77.9	77.7	77.0	77.0	76.4
2000	73.2	74.3	75.9	78.2	80.4	82.0	82.0	82.2	79.8	78.7	78.2	77.0	78.4
2001	75.6	76.9	77.7	79.1	81.4	82.6	82.2	82.6	80.2	79.1	78.2	77.5	79.4
2002	77.1	77.8	79.6	81.4	84.2	85.6	85.4	85.0	83.2	82.2	81.7	80.6	82.0
2003	78.0	77.8	79.1	82.0	84.8	86.9	88.3	87.7	85.5	84.5	83.2	81.8	83.3

Employment by Industry: Ohio—*Continued*

(Numbers in thousands. Not seasonally adjusted.)

Industry	January	February	March	April	May	June	July	August	September	October	November	December	Annual Average
COLUMBUS—*Continued*													
Other services													
1990	25.9	26.0	26.0	26.5	26.8	27.1	26.9	27.1	27.3	27.3	27.4	27.4	26.8
1991	26.8	27.1	27.3	27.6	27.8	28.1	27.7	27.8	27.8	27.5	27.5	27.5	27.5
1992	27.4	27.5	28.0	28.2	28.8	28.9	29.1	29.2	29.0	29.1	28.7	28.6	28.5
1993	29.1	29.1	29.1	29.1	28.9	29.1	29.4	29.6	29.3	29.5	29.6	29.4	29.2
1994	29.5	29.6	29.8	29.8	30.0	30.1	29.9	30.1	30.3	30.6	30.8	30.8	30.1
1995	30.6	30.9	31.0	31.2	31.6	31.8	31.6	32.1	32.1	32.0	32.2	32.2	31.6
1996	32.0	32.3	32.4	31.3	31.5	31.4	31.6	31.9	31.5	31.7	31.6	31.6	31.7
1997	31.6	31.9	32.2	32.2	32.7	32.7	32.6	32.7	32.1	32.6	32.3	32.6	32.3
1998	32.2	32.6	32.5	32.7	33.0	33.1	32.7	32.8	32.5	32.6	32.6	32.3	32.6
1999	31.3	31.9	31.9	33.0	33.6	33.9	33.4	33.6	33.5	33.5	33.9	34.2	33.1
2000	34.1	34.6	34.8	35.2	35.4	35.6	35.6	35.7	35.3	35.2	35.2	35.1	35.1
2001	33.5	33.9	34.1	34.6	34.9	35.0	34.9	35.0	34.5	34.6	34.9	34.8	34.6
2002	34.4	34.8	35.0	35.5	35.9	36.2	36.0	36.1	35.8	35.6	35.7	35.8	35.6
2003	35.8	36.0	36.2	36.4	36.5	36.8	36.7	37.0	36.4	36.1	35.9	36.1	36.3
Government													
1990	125.9	126.9	128.6	129.3	131.2	131.5	120.4	119.0	122.3	129.2	130.5	131.3	127.1
1991	128.8	130.7	131.1	130.8	132.0	132.2	121.6	120.7	124.5	130.6	132.8	133.3	129.0
1992	131.0	132.3	132.5	133.0	134.3	133.7	124.2	123.9	126.4	133.8	133.8	134.7	131.1
1993	131.7	133.4	133.9	134.0	133.8	134.2	123.9	124.5	127.5	134.4	134.3	135.3	131.7
1994	132.5	134.2	134.3	134.8	134.4	134.7	124.7	124.6	129.4	136.0	136.4	137.1	132.7
1995	133.7	135.4	136.6	136.6	136.1	136.8	125.1	125.1	130.3	135.5	135.8	136.0	133.5
1996	132.8	134.9	135.9	135.5	135.7	135.6	129.1	128.7	127.4	133.9	134.7	134.8	133.2
1997	136.3	137.1	137.8	136.5	137.3	138.2	134.3	134.3	133.5	137.0	138.1	138.6	136.5
1998	137.8	138.0	138.6	138.2	138.9	139.5	134.6	134.6	135.3	137.6	139.2	140.2	137.7
1999	139.0	139.7	139.8	140.0	139.9	140.2	136.3	135.0	135.9	138.9	140.7	141.7	138.9
2000	139.9	141.0	141.5	141.5	141.8	143.4	139.8	137.8	139.5	142.3	143.3	144.3	141.3
2001	141.1	142.9	143.7	143.5	144.3	144.7	141.5	140.2	142.3	145.8	146.8	147.4	143.7
2002	146.0	146.5	146.6	146.1	146.4	147.4	142.7	141.8	143.3	145.9	147.7	148.0	145.7
2003	146.9	147.5	147.3	146.9	147.8	147.9	144.1	142.8	143.2	146.4	147.4	148.1	146.4
Federal government													
1990	16.4	16.3	16.7	17.3	19.1	17.5	17.4	16.7	16.4	16.6	16.4	16.6	16.9
1991	16.5	16.5	16.6	16.6	16.6	16.6	16.7	16.6	16.6	16.4	16.5	16.6	16.5
1992	16.5	16.4	16.4	16.4	16.4	16.3	16.0	16.0	16.0	16.2	16.0	16.1	16.2
1993	15.8	15.7	15.7	15.3	15.2	15.2	15.2	15.1	15.0	15.0	15.1	15.3	15.3
1994	15.1	15.6	15.4	14.9	15.0	14.9	14.9	15.0	14.9	15.5	15.6	15.9	15.2
1995	15.2	15.1	15.6	15.6	15.5	15.5	15.0	14.8	14.8	14.8	14.7	14.9	15.1
1996	14.6	14.6	14.6	14.6	14.4	14.2	14.0	13.9	13.7	13.2	13.3	13.4	14.0
1997	15.5	15.5	15.5	15.5	15.5	15.5	15.5	15.5	15.3	15.1	15.1	15.4	15.4
1998	14.8	14.8	14.8	14.7	14.7	14.7	14.7	14.7	14.6	14.5	14.5	15.0	14.7
1999	14.4	14.4	14.3	14.3	14.2	14.2	14.2	14.3	14.3	14.1	14.3	14.6	14.3
2000	14.2	14.2	14.3	14.6	16.2	15.2	15.4	14.3	14.2	14.1	14.2	14.5	14.6
2001	14.1	13.9	13.9	13.8	13.8	13.8	13.8	13.9	13.8	13.7	13.6	13.9	13.8
2002	13.7	13.5	13.6	13.5	13.5	13.6	13.6	13.8	13.7	13.7	13.7	13.9	13.7
2003	13.7	13.5	13.4	13.3	13.3	13.3	13.3	13.3	13.2	13.1	13.1	13.5	13.3
State government													
1990	55.6	56.2	57.0	56.9	56.9	58.6	52.8	52.9	52.3	57.6	58.5	58.8	56.1
1991	56.6	58.0	58.2	57.9	58.4	58.3	53.6	53.2	52.7	57.2	58.7	58.7	56.7
1992	56.4	57.7	57.8	57.7	58.4	57.6	53.8	54.4	52.2	57.8	57.3	58.1	56.6
1993	56.4	57.7	58.0	58.9	58.5	58.6	54.2	55.2	53.8	58.9	58.4	59.1	57.3
1994	57.1	58.6	58.8	59.7	58.8	59.0	54.8	55.5	54.7	59.1	59.2	60.0	57.9
1995	57.4	59.0	59.7	59.5	58.9	59.5	55.0	55.5	54.8	58.5	58.8	59.3	57.9
1996	56.9	58.4	59.0	58.6	58.5	58.7	54.6	55.9	53.4	58.3	58.7	59.0	57.5
1997	58.7	59.1	59.4	58.6	58.7	59.1	57.1	58.0	56.7	58.6	59.1	59.3	58.5
1998	59.3	59.1	59.1	58.7	58.8	59.0	57.0	58.1	56.7	58.5	59.0	59.4	58.5
1999	59.6	59.2	59.1	58.6	58.7	59.0	57.2	57.6	56.5	58.4	58.8	59.4	58.5
2000	59.1	59.0	59.2	58.7	56.9	58.9	58.0	58.3	57.4	59.3	59.7	60.0	58.7
2001	58.8	59.7	59.5	59.1	59.2	59.3	58.3	58.4	58.6	60.7	61.0	61.4	59.5
2002	60.6	60.7	60.5	60.1	59.9	60.2	58.6	59.5	58.5	59.9	60.7	60.8	60.0
2003	60.2	60.5	60.2	59.8	60.1	60.1	59.0	59.3	58.6	60.2	61.0	61.1	60.0
Local government													
1990	55.9	56.3	56.9	57.2	57.2	57.4	52.2	51.4	55.6	57.0	57.8	58.0	56.0
1991	57.8	58.4	58.5	58.5	59.3	59.5	53.5	53.0	57.5	59.2	59.9	60.3	57.9
1992	58.1	58.2	58.3	58.9	59.5	59.8	54.4	53.5	58.2	59.8	60.5	60.5	58.3
1993	59.5	60.0	60.2	59.8	60.1	60.4	54.5	54.2	58.7	60.5	60.8	60.9	59.1
1994	60.3	60.0	60.1	60.2	60.6	60.8	55.0	54.1	59.8	61.4	61.6	61.2	59.5
1995	61.1	61.3	61.3	61.5	61.7	61.8	55.1	54.8	60.7	62.2	62.3	61.8	60.4
1996	61.3	61.9	62.3	62.3	62.8	62.7	60.5	58.9	60.3	62.4	62.7	62.4	61.7
1997	62.1	62.5	62.9	62.4	63.1	63.6	61.7	60.8	61.5	63.3	63.9	63.9	62.6
1998	63.7	64.1	64.7	64.8	65.4	65.8	62.9	61.8	64.0	64.6	65.7	65.8	64.4
1999	65.0	66.1	66.4	67.1	67.0	67.0	64.9	63.1	65.1	66.4	67.6	67.7	66.1
2000	66.6	67.8	68.0	68.2	68.7	69.3	66.4	65.2	67.9	68.9	69.4	69.8	68.0
2001	68.2	69.3	70.3	70.6	71.3	71.6	69.4	67.9	69.9	71.4	72.2	72.1	70.4
2002	71.7	72.3	72.5	72.5	73.0	73.6	70.5	68.5	71.1	72.3	73.3	73.3	72.1
2003	73.0	73.5	73.7	73.8	74.4	74.5	71.8	70.2	71.4	73.1	73.3	73.5	73.0

Employment by Industry: Ohio—*Continued*

(Numbers in thousands. Not seasonally adjusted.)

Industry	January	February	March	April	May	June	July	August	September	October	November	December	Annual Average
HAMILTON-MIDDLETOWN													
Total nonfarm													
1993	98.1	98.9	98.8	99.3	100.4	97.9	97.0	97.0	101.3	103.1	103.9	103.6	99.9
1994	100.4	101.4	103.2	104.0	105.1	103.3	101.2	102.1	107.7	108.3	109.4	110.2	104.6
1995	106.2	108.0	109.3	111.1	111.4	110.5	108.5	109.1	113.4	112.2	112.7	113.4	110.4
1996	108.0	111.3	112.2	112.7	113.6	111.5	108.9	110.8	111.3	115.2	116.5	116.8	112.4
1997	115.2	116.1	117.2	118.3	119.2	117.7	115.8	117.5	120.4	122.0	123.2	124.1	118.8
1998	119.5	120.8	122.4	123.0	125.3	124.2	122.2	122.9	126.4	126.8	128.0	129.0	124.2
1999	123.5	126.0	127.2	128.5	129.1	127.9	126.3	127.8	131.3	132.2	133.6	134.4	128.9
2000	129.8	130.9	132.1	132.9	134.0	132.1	129.0	130.5	133.7	134.7	135.8	136.1	132.6
2001	131.6	132.7	133.8	135.2	135.6	133.6	130.4	132.2	134.8	135.0	135.5	134.8	133.8
2002	130.0	131.8	133.0	133.1	134.0	130.9	129.5	130.2	134.0	134.2	135.1	134.9	132.6
2003	131.1	132.0	133.0	134.6	135.4	133.9	132.5	133.7	136.5	137.8	137.9	137.8	134.7
Total private													
1993	79.8	79.5	79.4	79.8	80.9	81.9	82.5	82.5	83.2	83.3	84.0	84.0	81.7
1994	82.0	82.1	83.6	84.3	85.7	86.9	86.6	87.3	88.2	88.3	89.0	90.2	86.1
1995	87.3	88.0	89.0	90.9	92.3	93.2	92.8	93.6	93.6	92.1	92.3	92.8	91.4
1996	89.6	90.9	91.5	92.3	93.2	93.8	93.1	93.7	93.5	94.6	95.6	96.0	93.1
1997	95.0	95.0	96.0	97.3	98.3	99.2	99.5	100.0	100.2	101.0	101.9	102.8	98.8
1998	99.0	99.3	100.8	101.5	103.7	105.2	105.3	105.2	105.9	105.6	106.6	107.6	103.8
1999	103.2	104.6	105.6	107.1	107.9	108.8	109.2	109.5	109.8	110.0	111.2	112.3	108.2
2000	108.5	108.6	109.7	110.1	110.9	111.7	111.0	112.0	112.1	112.0	112.7	113.0	111.0
2001	109.8	109.8	110.6	111.9	112.5	112.9	112.1	113.1	112.3	111.6	111.7	111.2	111.6
2002	107.4	108.1	109.1	109.3	109.9	110.4	110.5	110.6	111.3	110.5	111.1	111.1	109.9
2003	108.6	108.1	109.0	110.8	111.4	113.4	113.9	114.5	114.3	114.1	114.2	114.1	112.2
Goods-producing													
1993	22.4	22.0	21.9	22.1	22.4	22.8	23.0	23.0	23.0	23.4	23.6	23.3	22.7
1994	22.4	22.3	22.9	23.3	23.9	24.4	24.6	24.8	25.1	24.9	25.2	25.4	24.1
1995	24.1	24.2	24.6	25.0	25.2	25.6	25.8	26.0	26.2	25.5	25.2	25.3	25.2
1996	23.7	23.9	24.2	24.8	25.1	25.5	25.6	25.8	25.8	25.7	25.9	25.7	25.1
1997	25.5	25.5	25.9	26.6	26.8	27.2	27.5	27.8	27.7	27.8	27.8	27.8	26.9
1998	27.2	27.3	27.8	28.1	28.7	29.3	29.9	29.6	29.8	29.6	29.8	30.0	28.9
1999	28.7	29.1	29.3	30.3	30.4	30.9	30.8	30.6	30.7	30.7	30.9	30.6	30.2
2000	29.7	29.5	30.0	29.5	29.9	30.4	30.3	30.6	30.4	30.3	30.2	30.0	30.0
2001	28.6	28.6	29.0	29.3	29.5	29.6	29.3	29.5	29.2	28.9	28.5	28.1	29.0
2002	27.2	27.1	27.4	27.6	27.7	28.1	28.0	28.1	28.1	28.1	27.9	27.6	27.7
2003	26.8	26.5	26.8	27.5	27.7	28.4	28.5	28.6	28.3	28.1	27.9	27.5	27.7
Construction and mining													
1993	4.8	4.5	4.4	4.7	4.9	5.1	5.2	5.3	5.3	5.6	5.5	5.2	5.0
1994	4.3	4.3	4.8	4.9	5.3	5.7	6.0	6.0	6.1	5.9	5.9	5.8	5.4
1995	5.0	4.9	5.3	5.6	5.7	6.0	6.3	6.5	6.5	6.1	6.0	6.0	5.8
1996	4.7	4.8	5.1	5.7	5.9	6.2	6.5	6.6	6.5	6.5	6.6	6.3	5.9
1997	5.6	5.8	6.1	6.7	6.8	7.1	7.3	7.4	7.1	7.0	6.9	6.8	6.7
1998	5.8	5.9	6.2	6.7	7.3	7.7	8.6	8.4	8.1	8.0	8.0	8.0	7.3
1999	7.0	7.2	7.4	8.1	8.2	8.6	8.9	8.7	8.6	8.6	8.7	8.4	8.2
2000	7.4	7.2	7.8	7.8	8.1	8.5	8.5	8.6	8.4	8.4	8.4	8.2	8.1
2001	7.2	7.3	7.8	8.1	8.4	8.6	8.7	8.8	8.6	8.5	8.3	8.0	8.2
2002	7.1	7.2	7.5	7.7	7.9	8.3	8.4	8.4	8.3	8.5	8.3	8.0	8.0
2003	7.3	7.0	7.2	7.9	8.1	8.7	8.9	8.9	8.7	8.6	8.4	8.0	8.1
Manufacturing													
1993	17.6	17.5	17.5	17.4	17.5	17.7	17.8	17.7	17.7	17.8	18.1	18.1	17.7
1994	18.1	18.0	18.1	18.4	18.6	18.7	18.6	18.8	19.0	19.0	19.3	19.6	18.6
1995	19.1	19.3	19.3	19.4	19.5	19.6	19.5	19.5	19.7	19.4	19.2	19.3	19.4
1996	19.0	19.1	19.1	19.1	19.2	19.3	19.1	19.2	19.3	19.2	19.3	19.4	19.1
1997	19.9	19.7	19.8	19.9	20.0	20.1	20.2	20.4	20.6	20.8	20.9	21.0	20.2
1998	21.4	21.4	21.6	21.4	21.4	21.6	21.3	21.2	21.7	21.6	21.8	22.0	21.5
1999	21.7	21.9	21.9	22.2	22.2	22.3	21.9	21.9	22.1	22.1	22.2	22.2	22.0
2000	22.3	22.3	22.2	21.7	21.8	21.9	21.8	22.0	22.0	21.9	21.8	21.8	21.9
2001	21.4	21.3	21.2	21.2	21.1	21.0	20.6	20.7	20.6	20.4	20.2	20.1	20.8
2002	20.1	19.9	19.9	19.9	19.8	19.8	19.6	19.7	19.8	19.6	19.6	19.6	19.8
2003	19.5	19.5	19.6	19.6	19.6	19.7	19.6	19.7	19.6	19.5	19.5	19.5	19.6
Service-providing													
1993	75.7	76.9	76.9	77.2	78.0	75.1	74.0	74.0	78.3	79.7	80.3	80.3	77.2
1994	78.0	79.1	80.3	80.7	81.2	78.9	76.6	77.3	82.6	83.4	84.2	84.8	80.5
1995	82.1	83.8	84.7	86.1	86.2	84.9	82.7	83.1	87.2	86.7	87.5	88.1	85.2
1996	84.3	87.4	88.0	87.9	88.5	86.0	83.3	85.0	85.5	89.5	90.6	91.1	87.2
1997	89.7	90.6	91.3	91.7	92.4	90.5	88.3	89.7	92.7	94.2	95.4	96.3	91.9
1998	92.3	93.5	94.6	94.9	96.6	94.9	92.3	93.3	96.6	97.2	98.2	99.0	95.2
1999	94.8	96.9	97.9	98.2	98.7	97.0	95.5	97.2	100.6	101.5	102.7	103.8	98.7
2000	100.1	101.4	102.1	103.4	104.1	101.7	98.7	99.9	103.3	104.4	105.6	106.1	102.5
2001	103.0	104.1	104.8	105.9	106.1	104.0	101.1	102.7	105.6	106.1	107.0	106.7	104.8
2002	102.8	104.7	105.6	105.5	106.3	102.8	101.5	102.1	105.9	106.1	107.2	107.3	104.8
2003	104.3	105.5	106.2	107.1	107.7	105.5	104.0	105.1	108.2	109.7	110.0	110.3	107.0

Employment by Industry: Ohio—*Continued*

(Numbers in thousands. Not seasonally adjusted.)

Industry	January	February	March	April	May	June	July	August	September	October	November	December	Annual Average
HAMILTON-MIDDLETOWN *—Continued*													
Trade, transportation, and utilities													
1993	19.2	19.1	19.1	19.2	19.6	20.0	20.3	20.2	20.4	20.3	20.7	20.9	19.9
1994	20.6	20.6	20.9	21.1	21.5	21.7	21.5	21.8	22.1	22.2	22.6	23.2	21.6
1995	22.0	21.9	22.2	23.4	23.8	23.7	23.5	23.7	23.8	23.9	24.4	24.9	23.4
1996	24.3	24.3	24.3	24.3	24.4	24.4	24.1	24.3	24.4	25.3	25.8	26.2	24.6
1997	26.0	25.7	25.7	26.0	26.1	26.1	26.2	26.3	26.4	26.6	27.0	27.4	26.2
1998	26.6	26.4	26.4	26.6	26.9	26.8	26.8	26.7	26.7	27.1	27.7	28.2	26.9
1999	27.1	27.2	27.4	27.5	27.5	27.6	27.6	27.7	27.8	28.1	28.9	30.0	27.8
2000	28.8	28.6	28.9	28.9	29.1	29.1	29.0	29.0	29.2	29.4	30.2	30.8	29.2
2001	30.5	30.3	30.4	30.5	30.4	30.4	30.4	30.7	30.7	31.2	31.9	31.9	30.8
2002	30.9	31.0	31.0	30.6	30.6	30.4	30.6	30.4	30.6	30.3	31.0	31.3	30.7
2003	30.6	30.3	30.3	30.6	30.9	31.1	31.3	31.6	31.6	31.9	32.4	32.5	31.3
Wholesale trade													
1993	5.3	5.4	5.4	5.5	5.6	5.7	5.6	5.6	5.6	5.6	5.6	5.6	5.5
1994	5.6	5.6	5.6	5.5	5.6	5.6	5.7	5.7	5.7	5.8	5.8	5.9	5.6
1995	5.8	5.8	5.9	6.1	6.2	6.2	6.1	6.1	6.1	6.1	6.1	6.2	6.0
1996	6.2	6.3	6.2	6.3	6.3	6.3	6.4	6.3	6.3	6.4	6.4	6.5	6.3
1997	6.8	6.8	6.8	7.0	7.1	7.1	7.1	7.1	7.0	7.1	7.1	7.2	7.0
1998	7.2	7.1	7.1	7.4	7.4	7.4	7.4	7.5	7.5	7.6	7.7	7.8	7.4
1999	7.7	7.8	7.9	8.0	8.1	8.2	8.3	8.5	8.5	8.8	9.0	9.2	8.3
2000	9.2	9.2	9.3	9.6	9.7	9.7	9.7	9.7	9.8	9.8	9.9	10.1	9.6
2001	10.8	10.8	10.9	10.8	10.8	10.8	10.8	10.9	10.8	11.0	11.0	10.9	10.9
2002	11.0	11.0	11.0	10.6	10.6	10.5	10.7	10.6	10.6	10.4	10.4	10.4	10.7
2003	10.3	10.3	10.3	10.4	10.5	10.6	10.7	10.8	10.9	11.0	11.2	11.2	10.7
Retail trade													
1993	10.9	10.7	10.8	10.8	11.0	11.2	11.5	11.5	11.6	11.5	11.8	12.0	11.2
1994	11.6	11.6	11.8	11.9	12.1	12.2	11.9	12.1	12.4	12.4	12.8	13.3	12.1
1995	12.4	12.2	12.5	13.3	13.5	13.4	13.4	13.6	13.6	13.6	14.2	14.6	13.3
1996	14.0	13.9	13.9	13.8	13.9	13.9	13.6	13.9	14.0	14.8	15.4	15.7	14.2
1997	15.1	14.8	14.7	14.9	14.9	14.9	14.9	15.0	15.1	15.2	15.6	15.9	15.0
1998	15.3	15.2	15.2	15.1	15.4	15.2	15.1	15.1	15.1	15.3	15.8	16.1	15.3
1999	15.2	15.1	15.1	15.0	14.8	14.8	14.6	14.5	14.6	14.5	15.0	15.7	14.9
2000	14.7	14.5	14.6	14.3	14.3	14.3	14.3	14.3	14.4	14.6	15.1	15.6	14.5
2001	14.6	14.5	14.6	14.7	14.6	14.6	14.6	14.7	14.7	14.8	15.4	15.4	14.8
2002	14.6	14.7	14.8	14.8	14.8	14.8	14.8	14.7	14.7	14.5	15.0	15.2	14.8
2003	14.3	14.1	14.1	14.3	14.4	14.6	14.7	14.8	14.7	14.8	15.1	15.2	14.6
Transportation and utilities													
1993	3.0	3.0	2.9	2.9	3.0	3.1	3.2	3.1	3.2	3.2	3.3	3.3	3.1
1994	3.4	3.4	3.5	3.7	3.8	3.9	3.9	4.0	4.0	4.0	4.0	4.0	3.8
1995	3.8	3.9	3.8	4.0	4.1	4.1	4.0	4.0	4.1	4.2	4.1	4.1	4.0
1996	4.1	4.1	4.2	4.2	4.2	4.2	4.1	4.1	4.1	4.1	4.0	4.0	4.1
1997	4.1	4.1	4.2	4.1	4.1	4.1	4.2	4.2	4.3	4.3	4.3	4.3	4.1
1998	4.1	4.1	4.1	4.1	4.1	4.2	4.3	4.1	4.1	4.2	4.2	4.3	4.1
1999	4.2	4.3	4.4	4.5	4.6	4.6	4.7	4.7	4.7	4.8	4.9	5.1	4.6
2000	4.9	4.9	5.0	5.0	5.1	5.1	5.0	5.0	5.0	5.0	5.2	5.1	5.0
2001	5.1	5.0	4.9	5.0	5.0	5.0	5.0	5.1	5.2	5.4	5.5	5.6	5.2
2002	5.3	5.3	5.2	5.2	5.2	5.1	5.1	5.1	5.3	5.4	5.6	5.7	5.3
2003	6.0	5.9	5.9	5.9	6.0	5.9	5.9	6.0	6.0	6.1	6.1	6.1	6.0
Information													
1993	0.8	0.8	0.7	0.7	0.7	0.7	0.8	0.8	0.8	0.8	0.8	0.8	0.7
1994	0.8	0.8	0.8	0.7	0.7	0.8	0.7	0.7	0.7	0.8	0.8	0.8	0.7
1995	0.8	0.8	0.8	0.8	0.8	0.8	0.8	0.8	0.8	0.8	0.8	0.9	0.8
1996	1.0	1.0	1.0	1.0	1.0	1.0	1.0	1.0	1.0	0.9	0.9	0.9	0.9
1997	0.9	0.9	0.9	0.9	0.9	0.9	0.9	0.9	0.9	0.9	0.9	0.9	0.9
1998	0.9	0.9	0.9	0.9	0.9	0.9	0.8	0.8	0.8	0.9	0.9	0.9	0.8
1999	1.0	1.0	1.1	1.0	1.0	1.0	1.0	1.0	1.0	1.0	1.0	1.0	1.0
2000	1.1	1.1	1.1	1.2	1.2	1.2	1.2	1.2	1.2	1.2	1.2	1.2	1.1
2001	1.2	1.2	1.1	1.1	1.1	1.1	0.9	0.9	0.9	0.9	0.9	0.8	1.0
2002	0.8	0.8	0.8	0.7	0.7	0.7	0.7	0.7	0.7	0.7	0.8	0.8	0.7
2003	0.8	0.8	0.8	0.7	0.8	0.8	0.8	0.8	0.7	0.8	0.8	0.8	0.8
Financial activities													
1993	6.6	6.6	6.6	6.6	6.6	6.7	6.6	6.6	6.7	6.6	6.7	6.7	6.6
1994	6.8	6.8	6.8	6.6	6.7	6.8	6.8	6.8	6.8	6.8	6.8	6.8	6.7
1995	6.9	6.9	6.9	6.9	6.9	7.0	7.0	7.0	6.9	6.9	6.9	6.9	6.9
1996	6.9	6.9	7.0	7.0	7.1	7.1	7.1	7.2	7.1	7.2	7.2	7.2	7.0
1997	7.3	7.3	7.3	7.2	7.4	7.5	7.5	7.5	7.5	7.5	7.5	7.6	7.4
1998	7.3	7.3	7.4	7.5	7.6	7.8	7.8	7.8	7.8	7.8	7.9	8.1	7.6
1999	7.9	8.0	8.0	8.1	8.1	8.2	8.4	8.4	8.4	8.7	8.7	8.7	8.3
2000	8.5	8.6	8.5	8.4	8.4	8.3	8.5	8.5	8.4	8.6	8.6	8.6	8.4
2001	8.4	8.5	8.5	8.6	8.7	8.8	8.9	9.0	8.9	8.9	9.0	9.0	8.8
2002	9.0	9.1	9.1	9.1	9.1	9.2	9.0	9.0	9.1	9.1	9.2	9.3	9.1
2003	9.3	9.4	9.3	9.6	9.6	9.7	9.7	9.7	9.9	9.8	9.7	9.9	9.6

Employment by Industry: Ohio—*Continued*

(Numbers in thousands. Not seasonally adjusted.)

Industry	January	February	March	April	May	June	July	August	September	October	November	December	Annual Average
HAMILTON-MIDDLETOWN *—Continued*													
Professional and business services													
1993	7.6	7.6	7.7	7.6	7.6	7.6	7.7	7.8	8.1	8.0	8.0	8.1	7.7
1994	7.5	7.6	7.8	7.9	7.9	8.0	8.2	8.3	8.5	8.4	8.4	8.5	8.0
1995	8.4	8.7	8.7	8.9	9.1	9.3	9.1	9.5	9.5	9.2	9.2	9.0	9.0
1996	8.5	8.8	8.8	9.1	9.3	9.5	9.2	9.3	9.1	9.3	9.4	9.5	9.1
1997	8.9	9.0	9.4	9.4	9.7	9.8	9.8	9.9	10.0	10.4	11.1	11.2	9.8
1998	10.3	10.2	10.9	11.0	11.5	11.9	11.6	11.8	11.9	12.0	11.9	11.8	11.4
1999	11.1	11.4	11.8	11.8	12.3	12.3	12.2	12.6	12.6	12.6	12.5	12.4	12.1
2000	11.7	11.8	12.0	12.3	12.3	12.6	12.1	12.6	12.7	12.3	12.1	11.9	12.2
2001	11.9	11.8	12.2	12.1	12.2	12.3	11.8	11.9	11.8	11.1	10.9	10.7	11.7
2002	9.7	9.8	10.2	10.4	10.4	10.4	10.3	10.2	10.4	10.3	10.2	10.2	10.2
2003	9.9	10.0	10.2	10.3	10.3	10.4	10.4	10.4	10.4	10.3	10.2	10.1	10.2
Educational and health services													
1993	11.7	11.6	11.5	11.7	11.9	12.0	12.0	11.9	12.1	12.1	12.2	12.2	11.9
1994	12.0	12.0	12.0	11.9	12.0	12.1	11.9	11.9	11.9	11.9	11.9	12.0	11.9
1995	11.9	12.1	12.2	12.1	12.2	12.2	12.0	11.9	11.8	11.7	12.0	11.9	12.0
1996	11.6	12.0	11.9	11.8	11.8	11.7	11.6	11.6	11.6	12.0	12.1	12.1	11.8
1997	12.1	12.2	12.2	12.3	12.3	12.3	12.4	12.4	12.5	12.8	12.9	13.0	12.4
1998	12.5	12.6	12.7	12.7	12.9	12.9	12.9	13.0	13.1	13.2	13.3	13.4	12.9
1999	13.1	13.1	13.1	13.3	13.3	13.2	13.5	13.6	13.6	13.6	13.7	13.8	13.4
2000	13.4	13.5	13.6	13.7	13.8	13.9	13.6	13.8	13.8	14.0	14.1	14.1	13.7
2001	13.2	13.3	13.3	13.5	13.5	13.5	13.7	13.7	13.7	13.8	13.8	14.0	13.6
2002	13.8	13.9	13.9	14.1	14.2	14.2	14.2	14.3	14.4	14.5	14.5	14.6	14.2
2003	14.4	14.4	14.5	14.6	14.5	14.6	14.6	14.6	14.7	14.9	15.0	15.0	14.7
Leisure and hospitality													
1993	7.8	8.1	8.2	8.1	8.3	8.3	8.3	8.4	8.3	8.2	8.1	8.1	8.1
1994	8.0	8.1	8.5	8.8	9.0	9.1	8.8	8.9	9.0	9.0	9.1	9.3	8.8
1995	9.1	9.2	9.4	9.4	9.8	10.0	10.2	10.2	10.1	9.6	9.4	9.5	9.6
1996	9.1	9.5	9.7	9.8	10.0	10.1	10.0	10.0	10.0	9.7	9.8	9.9	9.8
1997	9.7	9.8	10.0	10.2	10.4	10.7	10.6	10.5	10.6	10.2	10.0	10.2	10.2
1998	9.7	10.0	10.1	10.3	10.7	11.1	11.0	11.0	11.3	10.5	10.6	10.7	10.5
1999	9.9	10.3	10.4	10.6	10.8	11.1	11.2	11.1	11.1	10.7	10.9	11.2	10.7
2000	10.7	10.9	11.0	11.2	11.3	11.4	11.5	11.5	11.6	11.4	11.4	11.6	11.2
2001	11.3	11.4	11.4	11.9	12.2	12.3	12.3	12.4	12.2	11.8	11.8	11.7	11.9
2002	11.1	11.4	11.7	11.8	12.1	12.3	12.7	12.9	13.0	12.5	12.5	12.4	12.2
2003	11.8	11.7	12.0	12.5	12.6	13.3	13.6	13.8	13.7	13.3	13.3	13.3	12.9
Other services													
1993	3.7	3.7	3.7	3.8	3.8	3.8	3.8	3.8	3.8	3.9	3.9	3.9	3.8
1994	3.9	3.9	3.9	4.0	4.0	4.0	4.1	4.1	4.1	4.3	4.2	4.2	4.0
1995	4.1	4.2	4.2	4.4	4.5	4.6	4.4	4.5	4.5	4.5	4.4	4.4	4.3
1996	4.5	4.5	4.6	4.5	4.5	4.5	4.5	4.5	4.5	4.5	4.5	4.5	4.5
1997	4.6	4.6	4.6	4.7	4.7	4.7	4.6	4.7	4.6	4.8	4.7	4.7	4.6
1998	4.5	4.6	4.6	4.4	4.5	4.5	4.5	4.5	4.5	4.5	4.5	4.5	4.5
1999	4.4	4.5	4.5	4.5	4.5	4.5	4.5	4.5	4.6	4.6	4.6	4.6	4.5
2000	4.6	4.6	4.6	4.9	4.9	4.8	4.8	4.8	4.8	4.8	4.9	4.8	4.7
2001	4.7	4.7	4.7	4.9	4.9	4.9	4.8	5.0	4.9	5.0	4.9	5.0	4.9
2002	4.9	5.0	5.0	5.0	5.1	5.1	5.0	5.0	5.0	5.0	5.0	4.9	5.0
2003	5.0	5.0	5.1	5.0	5.0	5.1	5.0	5.0	5.0	5.0	4.9	5.0	5.0
Government													
1993	18.3	19.4	19.4	19.5	19.5	16.0	14.5	14.5	18.1	19.8	19.9	19.6	18.2
1994	18.4	19.3	19.6	19.7	19.4	16.4	14.6	14.8	19.5	20.0	20.4	20.0	18.5
1995	18.9	20.0	20.3	20.2	19.1	17.3	15.7	15.5	19.8	20.1	20.4	20.6	18.9
1996	18.4	20.4	20.7	20.4	20.4	17.7	15.8	17.1	17.8	20.6	20.9	20.8	19.2
1997	20.2	21.1	21.2	21.0	20.9	18.5	16.3	17.5	20.2	21.0	21.3	21.3	20.0
1998	20.5	21.5	21.6	21.5	21.6	19.0	16.9	17.7	20.5	21.2	21.4	21.4	20.4
1999	20.3	21.4	21.6	21.4	21.2	19.1	17.1	18.3	21.5	22.2	22.4	22.1	20.7
2000	21.3	22.3	22.4	22.8	23.1	20.4	18.0	18.5	21.6	22.7	23.1	23.1	21.6
2001	21.8	22.9	23.2	23.3	23.1	20.7	18.3	19.1	22.5	23.4	23.8	23.6	22.1
2002	22.6	23.7	23.9	23.8	24.1	20.5	19.0	19.6	22.7	23.7	24.0	23.8	22.6
2003	22.5	23.9	24.0	23.8	24.0	20.5	18.6	19.2	22.2	23.7	23.7	23.7	22.5
Federal government													
2001	0.6	0.6	0.6	0.6	0.6	0.6	0.6	0.6	0.6	0.6	0.6	0.6	0.6
2002	0.6	0.6	0.6	0.6	0.6	0.6	0.6	0.6	0.6	0.5	0.5	0.6	0.6
2003	0.5	0.5	0.5	0.5	0.5	0.6	0.5	0.5	0.5	0.5	0.5	0.5	0.5

Employment by Industry: Ohio—*Continued*

(Numbers in thousands. Not seasonally adjusted.)

Industry	January	February	March	April	May	June	July	August	September	October	November	December	Annual Average
HAMILTON-MIDDLETOWN *—Continued*													
State government													
1993	7.0	7.9	7.9	7.9	7.5	4.4	4.0	4.2	7.2	8.3	8.2	8.0	6.8
1994	7.1	8.1	8.2	8.2	7.9	5.5	4.2	4.5	8.4	8.4	8.4	8.2	7.2
1995	7.4	8.4	8.6	8.4	7.4	5.8	4.4	4.4	8.4	8.4	8.5	8.5	7.3
1996	6.9	8.5	8.7	8.5	8.2	5.9	4.6	6.1	6.1	8.6	8.7	8.5	7.4
1997	8.0	8.8	8.8	8.7	8.4	6.1	4.6	6.1	8.3	8.7	8.7	8.6	7.8
1998	8.1	8.8	8.8	8.7	8.4	5.8	4.7	5.8	8.4	8.7	8.7	8.6	7.7
1999	7.9	8.7	8.6	8.6	8.0	5.8	4.7	5.8	8.4	8.7	8.7	8.6	7.7
2000	7.9	8.7	8.6	8.6	8.6	6.3	5.1	6.0	7.9	8.6	8.8	8.9	7.8
2001	7.8	8.7	8.9	8.8	8.7	6.4	5.3	6.1	8.3	8.9	9.3	9.1	8.0
2002	8.3	9.1	9.2	9.1	9.2	5.8	5.4	6.1	8.4	9.1	9.4	9.2	8.2
2003	8.4	9.3	9.4	9.2	9.3	5.9	5.4	6.1	8.4	9.4	9.3	9.3	8.3
Local government													
1993	10.8	11.0	11.0	11.1	11.5	11.1	10.0	9.8	10.4	11.0	11.2	11.1	10.8
1994	10.8	10.7	10.9	11.0	11.0	10.4	9.9	9.8	10.6	11.1	11.5	11.2	10.7
1995	11.0	11.1	11.2	11.2	11.1	10.9	10.7	10.6	10.9	11.2	11.4	11.5	11.0
1996	11.0	11.4	11.4	11.3	11.6	11.2	10.6	10.4	11.1	11.4	11.6	11.7	11.2
1997	11.7	11.8	11.8	11.7	11.9	11.8	11.1	10.8	11.3	11.8	12.1	12.1	11.6
1998	11.8	12.1	12.2	12.2	12.6	12.6	11.6	11.3	11.5	11.9	12.1	12.2	12.0
1999	11.8	12.1	12.4	12.2	12.6	12.7	11.8	11.9	12.5	12.9	13.1	12.9	12.4
2000	12.8	13.0	13.1	13.4	13.5	13.3	12.2	11.9	13.1	13.6	13.7	13.6	13.1
2001	13.4	13.6	13.7	13.9	13.8	13.7	12.4	12.4	13.6	13.9	13.9	13.9	13.5
2002	13.7	14.0	14.1	14.1	14.3	14.1	13.0	12.9	13.7	14.1	14.1	14.0	13.8
2003	13.6	14.1	14.1	14.1	14.2	14.0	12.7	12.6	13.3	13.8	13.9	13.9	13.7
STEUBENVILLE-WEIRTON													
Total nonfarm													
1993	48.4	48.4	48.9	49.3	49.8	50.2	49.1	48.8	49.2	50.0	49.9	49.4	49.2
1994	48.9	48.9	49.1	49.6	51.0	51.1	50.3	49.3	50.2	50.0	50.8	50.9	50.0
1995	48.5	49.1	49.7	50.6	51.2	51.4	50.4	50.7	51.1	51.1	51.1	51.1	50.5
1996	49.9	49.5	50.3	51.0	52.1	52.1	51.2	51.5	51.0	48.7	48.8	48.8	50.4
1997	47.3	47.1	47.4	48.2	49.1	49.3	48.6	49.2	50.2	50.6	50.9	50.9	49.0
1998	50.1	50.0	50.8	52.0	52.5	52.8	51.5	51.3	51.1	51.9	51.6	52.0	51.4
1999	49.6	49.7	50.8	50.8	51.2	51.4	50.5	50.3	50.4	51.1	51.8	52.2	50.8
2000	49.8	49.5	50.3	50.2	50.9	50.3	50.4	50.0	49.9	50.5	49.6	49.7	50.0
2001	47.6	49.1	50.1	50.7	50.4	50.4	50.0	49.5	49.4	49.7	49.5	49.3	49.6
2002	47.4	48.2	48.7	49.4	50.4	50.9	50.3	50.2	50.7	49.9	50.8	50.0	49.7
2003	49.0	49.5	50.3	50.5	51.0	50.7	49.5	49.5	49.4	49.1	49.3	48.2	49.7
Total private													
1993	42.3	42.2	42.6	42.9	43.4	43.7	43.2	43.0	43.2	43.9	43.8	43.4	43.1
1994	43.0	43.0	43.1	43.5	44.8	44.8	44.4	43.5	44.3	43.9	44.3	44.7	43.9
1995	42.6	42.8	43.5	44.4	44.8	45.0	44.4	44.7	45.1	44.9	44.9	44.9	44.3
1996	43.7	43.3	44.0	44.7	45.3	45.5	45.1	45.5	44.9	42.5	42.5	42.5	44.1
1997	41.0	40.8	41.0	41.8	42.6	42.7	42.3	43.1	43.8	44.2	44.5	44.5	42.6
1998	43.6	43.5	44.3	45.5	45.9	46.1	45.2	45.1	44.8	45.5	45.2	45.6	45.0
1999	43.4	43.3	44.3	44.3	44.6	44.7	44.2	44.1	43.9	44.6	45.3	45.6	44.3
2000	43.4	43.0	43.6	43.6	43.8	43.6	44.0	43.7	43.5	44.0	43.1	43.2	43.5
2001	41.2	42.6	43.4	44.0	43.7	43.6	43.7	43.3	43.1	43.2	43.0	42.8	43.1
2002	41.1	41.7	42.2	42.9	43.8	44.2	43.8	43.8	44.3	43.9	44.2	43.6	43.3
2003	42.8	43.2	43.9	44.1	44.5	44.1	43.1	43.2	43.2	42.8	43.1	41.9	43.3
Goods-producing													
1993	16.6	16.6	16.9	16.9	17.0	17.2	17.0	16.8	16.9	17.2	17.2	16.9	16.9
1994	16.7	16.5	16.5	16.5	17.1	16.9	17.0	16.4	16.8	16.6	16.9	16.9	16.7
1995	15.9	16.0	16.2	16.1	16.3	16.2	16.0	16.1	16.4	16.5	16.5	16.4	16.2
1996	16.1	15.8	16.0	16.1	16.3	16.4	16.2	16.2	16.0	13.4	13.3	13.3	15.4
1997	13.0	12.9	13.0	13.2	13.2	13.3	13.4	14.5	15.2	15.7	15.8	15.7	14.0
1998	15.4	15.3	15.6	15.9	15.7	15.7	15.7	15.6	15.6	16.0	15.8	15.9	15.6
1999	15.2	15.1	15.4	15.1	15.1	15.2	15.1	15.0	14.8	15.4	15.9	16.0	15.2
2000	15.1	15.0	15.2	14.7	14.8	14.8	14.8	14.8	14.7	14.9	14.3	14.3	14.7
2001	13.6	14.6	14.8	14.4	13.9	14.1	14.1	13.9	13.6	13.7	13.6	13.5	14.0
2002	13.3	13.5	13.6	13.9	14.0	14.2	14.4	14.2	14.4	14.1	14.2	13.6	14.0
2003	13.7	13.6	13.7	13.2	13.0	12.9	13.0	13.0	12.7	12.5	12.6	11.6	13.0
Construction and mining													
1993	1.8	1.8	1.9	2.1	2.3	2.5	2.6	2.5	2.5	2.7	2.8	2.6	2.3
1994	2.3	2.2	2.3	2.4	2.7	2.6	2.7	2.6	2.6	2.4	2.3	2.2	2.4
1995	1.9	1.9	2.0	2.0	2.1	2.1	2.1	2.1	2.2	2.3	2.3	2.2	2.1
1996	1.9	1.8	1.8	2.0	2.1	2.3	2.1	2.1	2.1	2.2	2.1	2.1	2.0
1997	1.9	1.8	1.9	2.0	2.0	2.1	2.2	2.3	2.4	2.4	2.4	2.2	2.1
1998	2.0	2.0	2.0	2.4	2.2	2.2	2.3	2.3	2.2	2.3	2.3	2.2	2.2
1999	2.0	1.9	2.0	2.2	2.2	2.3	2.2	2.2	2.1	2.4	2.6	2.6	2.2
2000	1.8	1.8	1.9	1.9	2.1	2.2	2.2	2.1	2.2	2.3	2.1	2.2	2.0
2001	2.2	2.5	2.7	2.6	2.0	2.1	2.2	2.2	2.1	2.1	2.1	2.1	2.2
2002	1.9	2.0	2.1	2.4	2.4	2.5	2.7	2.7	2.9	2.6	2.6	2.2	2.4
2003	2.7	2.6	2.7	2.3	2.2	2.1	2.2	2.2	2.2	2.1	2.1	2.0	2.3

Employment by Industry: Ohio—*Continued*

(Numbers in thousands. Not seasonally adjusted.)

Industry	January	February	March	April	May	June	July	August	September	October	November	December	Annual Average
STEUBENVILLE-WEIRTON *—Continued*													
Manufacturing													
1993	14.8	14.8	15.0	14.8	14.7	14.7	14.4	14.3	14.4	14.5	14.4	14.3	14.5
1994	14.4	14.3	14.2	14.1	14.4	14.3	14.3	13.8	14.2	14.2	14.6	14.7	14.2
1995	14.0	14.1	14.2	14.1	14.2	14.1	13.9	14.0	14.2	14.2	14.2	14.2	14.1
1996	14.2	14.0	14.2	14.1	14.2	14.1	14.1	14.1	13.9	11.2	11.2	11.2	13.3
1997	11.1	11.1	11.1	11.2	11.2	11.2	11.2	12.2	12.8	13.3	13.4	13.5	11.9
1998	13.4	13.3	13.6	13.5	13.5	13.5	13.4	13.3	13.4	13.7	13.5	13.7	13.4
1999	13.2	13.2	13.4	12.9	12.9	12.9	12.9	12.8	12.7	13.0	13.3	13.4	13.0
2000	13.3	13.2	13.3	12.8	12.7	12.6	12.6	12.7	12.5	12.6	12.2	12.1	12.7
2001	11.4	12.1	12.1	11.8	11.9	12.0	11.9	11.7	11.5	11.6	11.5	11.4	11.7
2002	11.4	11.5	11.5	11.5	11.6	11.7	11.7	11.5	11.5	11.5	11.6	11.4	11.5
2003	11.0	11.0	11.0	10.9	10.8	10.8	10.8	10.8	10.5	10.4	10.5	9.6	10.7
Service-providing													
1993	31.8	31.8	32.0	32.4	32.8	33.0	32.1	32.0	32.3	32.8	32.7	32.5	32.3
1994	32.2	32.4	32.6	33.1	33.9	34.2	33.3	32.9	33.4	33.4	33.9	34.0	33.2
1995	32.6	33.1	33.5	34.5	34.9	35.2	34.4	34.6	34.7	34.6	34.6	34.7	34.2
1996	33.8	33.7	34.3	34.9	35.8	35.7	35.0	35.3	35.0	35.3	35.5	35.5	34.9
1997	34.3	34.2	34.4	35.0	35.9	36.0	35.2	34.7	35.0	34.9	35.1	35.2	34.9
1998	34.7	34.7	35.2	36.1	36.8	37.1	35.8	35.7	35.5	35.9	35.8	36.1	35.7
1999	34.4	34.6	35.4	35.7	36.1	36.2	35.4	35.3	35.6	35.7	35.9	36.2	35.5
2000	34.7	34.5	35.1	35.5	36.1	35.5	35.6	35.2	35.2	35.6	35.3	35.4	35.3
2001	34.0	34.5	35.3	36.3	36.5	36.3	35.9	35.6	35.8	36.0	35.9	35.8	35.7
2002	34.1	34.7	35.1	35.5	36.4	36.7	35.9	36.0	36.3	35.8	36.6	36.4	35.8
2003	35.3	35.9	36.6	37.3	38.0	37.8	36.5	36.5	36.7	36.6	36.7	36.6	36.7
Trade, transportation, and utilities													
1993	9.6	9.5	9.5	9.5	9.6	9.6	9.5	9.5	9.5	9.8	9.9	10.0	9.6
1994	9.8	9.9	10.0	9.9	10.1	10.2	10.1	9.8	10.0	9.7	9.9	10.0	9.9
1995	9.5	9.4	9.4	9.4	9.5	9.5	9.4	9.5	9.5	9.6	9.7	9.7	9.5
1996	9.5	9.4	9.6	9.6	9.7	9.8	9.7	9.9	9.8	9.8	10.0	9.8	9.7
1997	9.3	9.2	9.3	9.4	9.5	9.5	9.4	9.2	9.1	9.1	9.3	9.3	9.3
1998	8.9	8.8	8.8	9.1	9.3	9.3	8.9	8.9	8.8	9.0	9.2	9.3	9.0
1999	8.6	8.6	8.8	8.8	8.9	9.0	8.7	8.7	8.7	8.9	9.1	9.1	8.8
2000	8.7	8.5	8.6	8.7	8.7	8.7	8.9	8.7	8.6	8.7	8.8	8.9	8.7
2001	8.7	8.6	8.6	8.7	8.8	8.8	8.9	8.8	8.7	8.6	8.7	8.8	8.7
2002	8.3	8.2	8.2	8.2	8.5	8.5	8.7	8.8	8.6	8.6	8.7	8.8	8.5
2003	8.6	8.6	8.6	8.7	8.8	8.8	8.7	8.8	8.7	8.7	8.9	8.9	8.7
Wholesale trade													
1993	1.0	1.0	1.0	1.1	1.1	1.0	1.1	1.1	1.0	1.0	1.0	1.1	1.0
1994	1.1	1.1	1.1	1.0	1.1	1.1	1.1	1.0	1.1	1.0	1.0	1.0	1.0
1995	1.0	1.0	1.0	1.0	1.0	1.0	1.0	1.0	1.0	1.0	1.0	1.0	1.0
1996	1.0	1.0	1.0	1.0	1.0	1.1	1.1	1.1	1.1	1.1	1.1	1.0	1.0
1997	1.0	1.0	1.0	1.1	1.1	1.1	1.1	1.0	1.0	1.1	1.1	1.1	1.0
1998	1.0	1.0	1.0	1.1	1.1	1.1	1.0	1.0	1.0	1.0	1.0	1.0	1.0
1999	1.0	1.0	1.1	1.1	1.1	1.1	1.0	1.0	1.0	1.1	1.1	1.1	1.0
2000	1.0	1.0	1.0	1.1	1.0	1.0	1.1	1.1	1.1	1.0	1.0	1.0	1.0
2001	1.0	1.0	1.0	1.0	1.1	1.1	1.1	1.1	1.1	1.0	1.0	1.1	1.1
2002	1.0	1.0	1.0	1.0	1.0	1.0	1.0	1.0	1.0	1.0	1.0	1.0	1.0
2003	1.1	1.1	1.1	1.1	1.1	1.1	1.1	1.1	1.1	1.1	1.1	1.1	1.1
Retail trade													
1993	5.9	5.8	5.8	5.7	5.8	5.9	5.8	5.8	5.9	6.1	6.2	6.3	5.9
1994	6.1	6.1	6.2	6.2	6.3	6.4	6.3	6.2	6.3	6.1	6.3	6.4	6.2
1995	6.0	5.9	5.9	6.0	6.1	6.1	6.0	6.1	6.1	6.2	6.3	6.4	6.0
1996	6.2	6.1	6.2	6.2	6.3	6.3	6.3	6.5	6.4	6.4	6.5	6.5	6.3
1997	6.1	6.0	6.0	6.0	6.1	6.1	6.0	5.9	5.8	5.8	6.0	6.0	5.9
1998	5.7	5.6	5.6	5.7	5.9	6.0	5.8	5.8	5.8	5.9	6.1	6.2	5.8
1999	5.7	5.7	5.8	5.8	5.9	6.0	5.9	5.8	5.8	5.9	6.1	6.1	5.8
2000	5.7	5.5	5.6	5.6	5.7	5.7	5.8	5.7	5.6	5.8	5.9	6.0	5.7
2001	5.6	5.5	5.5	5.6	5.6	5.6	5.6	5.5	5.4	5.5	5.6	5.6	5.6
2002	5.3	5.2	5.2	5.2	5.4	5.4	5.6	5.7	5.6	5.6	5.7	5.8	5.5
2003	5.5	5.5	5.5	5.6	5.7	5.7	5.6	5.7	5.6	5.6	5.8	5.8	5.6
Transportation and utilities													
1993	2.7	2.7	2.7	2.7	2.7	2.7	2.6	2.6	2.6	2.7	2.7	2.6	2.6
1994	2.6	2.7	2.7	2.7	2.7	2.7	2.7	2.6	2.6	2.6	2.6	2.6	2.6
1995	2.5	2.5	2.5	2.4	2.4	2.4	2.4	2.4	2.4	2.4	2.4	2.3	2.4
1996	2.3	2.3	2.4	2.4	2.4	2.4	2.3	2.3	2.3	2.3	2.4	2.3	2.3
1997	2.2	2.2	2.3	2.3	2.3	2.3	2.3	2.3	2.3	2.2	2.2	2.2	2.2
1998	2.2	2.2	2.2	2.3	2.3	2.2	2.1	2.1	2.0	2.1	2.1	2.1	2.1
1999	1.9	1.9	1.9	1.9	1.9	1.9	1.8	1.9	1.9	1.9	1.9	1.9	1.8
2000	2.0	2.0	2.0	2.0	2.0	2.0	2.0	1.9	1.9	1.9	1.9	1.9	1.9
2001	2.1	2.1	2.1	2.1	2.1	2.1	2.2	2.2	2.2	2.1	2.1	2.1	2.1
2002	2.0	2.0	2.0	2.0	2.1	2.1	2.1	2.1	2.0	2.0	2.0	2.0	2.0
2003	2.0	2.0	2.0	2.0	2.0	2.0	2.0	2.0	2.0	2.0	2.0	2.0	2.0

Employment by Industry: Ohio—*Continued*

(Numbers in thousands. Not seasonally adjusted.)

Industry	January	February	March	April	May	June	July	August	September	October	November	December	Annual Average
STEUBENVILLE-WEIRTON *—Continued*													
Information													
1993	0.5	0.5	0.5	0.4	0.5	0.5	0.5	0.5	0.5	0.5	0.5	0.5	0.4
1994	0.5	0.5	0.5	0.5	0.5	0.5	0.5	0.5	0.5	0.5	0.5	0.5	0.5
1995	0.5	0.5	0.5	0.6	0.6	0.6	0.6	0.6	0.6	0.6	0.6	0.6	0.5
1996	0.6	0.6	0.6	0.6	0.6	0.6	0.6	0.6	0.6	0.6	0.6	0.6	0.6
1997	0.7	0.6	0.6	0.6	0.7	0.7	0.7	0.7	0.7	0.6	0.6	0.6	0.6
1998	0.6	0.6	0.6	0.6	0.6	0.7	0.8	0.8	0.8	0.7	0.7	0.7	0.6
1999	0.8	0.8	0.8	0.8	0.8	0.8	0.8	0.8	0.8	0.8	0.8	0.8	0.8
2000	0.8	0.8	0.8	0.8	0.9	0.8	0.8	0.9	0.9	0.9	0.8	0.8	0.8
2001	0.8	0.8	0.8	0.8	0.8	0.8	0.9	0.8	0.8	0.8	0.8	0.8	0.8
2002	0.7	0.7	0.7	0.7	0.7	0.7	0.7	0.8	0.7	0.7	0.7	0.7	0.7
2003	0.7	0.7	0.7	0.7	0.8	0.8	0.8	0.7	0.7	0.8	0.8	0.8	0.8
Financial activities													
1993	1.7	1.7	1.7	1.7	1.7	1.7	1.7	1.7	1.7	1.7	1.6	1.6	1.6
1994	1.6	1.6	1.6	1.6	1.6	1.7	1.6	1.6	1.6	1.6	1.6	1.6	1.6
1995	1.6	1.6	1.6	1.6	1.6	1.6	1.6	1.6	1.6	1.6	1.6	1.6	1.6
1996	1.6	1.6	1.6	1.6	1.6	1.6	1.6	1.6	1.5	1.6	1.6	1.6	1.5
1997	1.5	1.5	1.5	1.5	1.6	1.6	1.6	1.6	1.6	1.6	1.6	1.7	1.5
1998	1.6	1.6	1.6	1.6	1.7	1.7	1.7	1.6	1.6	1.6	1.6	1.6	1.6
1999	1.6	1.6	1.6	1.6	1.6	1.6	1.6	1.6	1.6	1.6	1.6	1.7	1.6
2000	1.6	1.6	1.6	1.6	1.6	1.6	1.6	1.6	1.5	1.6	1.6	1.6	1.5
2001	1.5	1.5	1.4	1.5	1.5	1.5	1.5	1.4	1.4	1.5	1.5	1.5	1.5
2002	1.4	1.4	1.4	1.4	1.4	1.5	1.5	1.4	1.4	1.4	1.4	1.4	1.4
2003	1.4	1.4	1.4	1.4	1.5	1.5	1.5	1.5	1.4	1.5	1.5	1.5	1.5
Professional and business services													
1993	1.8	1.8	1.8	2.0	1.9	1.9	1.8	1.8	1.8	2.0	1.9	1.9	1.8
1994	1.9	1.9	1.9	1.9	2.0	2.0	1.9	1.9	1.9	2.0	2.0	2.0	1.9
1995	1.9	2.0	2.1	2.2	2.2	2.3	2.2	2.2	2.2	2.1	2.1	2.1	2.1
1996	2.1	2.0	2.0	2.1	2.2	2.2	2.2	2.2	2.1	2.2	2.2	2.5	2.1
1997	2.4	2.4	2.5	2.5	2.6	2.6	2.5	2.4	2.4	2.5	2.5	2.5	2.4
1998	2.6	2.6	2.8	2.9	3.0	3.1	2.9	2.9	2.9	3.1	3.1	3.1	2.9
1999	2.7	2.7	2.8	2.8	2.8	2.6	2.6	2.5	2.5	2.5	2.6	2.6	2.6
2000	2.4	2.4	2.3	2.4	2.2	2.3	2.3	2.2	2.3	2.3	2.3	2.3	2.3
2001	2.3	2.3	2.3	2.4	2.5	2.5	2.5	2.5	2.3	2.3	2.1	2.1	2.3
2002	2.1	2.1	2.1	2.2	2.4	2.5	2.4	2.5	2.6	2.6	2.7	2.8	2.4
2003	2.7	2.8	3.0	3.0	3.0	3.0	3.0	3.0	2.9	2.9	2.9	2.8	2.9
Educational and health services													
1993	6.7	6.7	6.7	6.7	6.7	6.8	6.6	6.6	6.8	6.8	6.9	6.8	6.7
1994	6.9	7.0	6.9	7.0	7.1	7.1	7.0	7.0	7.2	7.1	7.1	7.2	7.0
1995	7.1	7.2	7.3	7.5	7.5	7.5	7.3	7.4	7.5	7.6	7.6	7.6	7.4
1996	7.4	7.4	7.4	7.4	7.4	7.3	7.3	7.3	7.3	7.6	7.6	7.6	7.4
1997	7.4	7.5	7.5	7.5	7.6	7.5	7.3	7.3	7.4	7.4	7.4	7.4	7.4
1998	7.4	7.4	7.5	7.6	7.6	7.6	7.4	7.4	7.5	7.6	7.5	7.5	7.5
1999	7.6	7.6	7.7	7.8	7.7	7.7	7.6	7.6	7.7	7.8	7.8	7.9	7.7
2000	7.7	7.7	7.8	7.7	7.8	7.7	7.7	7.7	7.8	7.9	7.9	8.0	7.7
2001	8.0	8.3	8.9	9.2	9.1	8.6	8.5	8.5	9.0	9.3	9.3	9.2	8.8
2002	8.6	9.1	9.3	9.2	9.2	9.0	8.3	8.3	9.0	9.0	9.1	9.0	8.9
2003	8.7	9.2	9.5	9.6	9.7	9.3	8.3	8.4	9.1	8.9	8.9	8.9	9.0
Leisure and hospitality													
1993	3.4	3.4	3.4	3.6	3.9	3.9	4.0	4.0	3.9	3.8	3.7	3.6	3.7
1994	3.5	3.5	3.6	3.9	4.2	4.2	4.1	4.1	4.1	4.1	4.0	4.2	3.9
1995	3.9	3.9	4.2	4.7	4.8	5.0	5.0	5.0	5.0	4.6	4.5	4.5	4.5
1996	4.1	4.2	4.4	4.8	5.0	5.0	5.0	5.2	5.1	4.8	4.7	4.6	4.7
1997	4.3	4.3	4.2	4.6	4.8	4.9	4.8	4.8	4.8	4.6	4.6	4.6	4.6
1998	4.5	4.6	4.8	5.1	5.3	5.3	5.1	5.2	5.0	4.8	4.6	4.7	4.9
1999	4.3	4.3	4.5	4.7	4.9	5.0	5.0	5.1	5.0	4.8	4.7	4.7	4.7
2000	4.3	4.3	4.5	4.8	4.9	4.9	5.0	5.0	4.9	4.8	4.6	4.5	4.7
2001	4.4	4.6	4.7	5.1	5.2	5.3	5.4	5.5	5.4	5.1	5.1	5.0	5.1
2002	4.9	4.9	5.1	5.4	5.7	5.9	5.9	5.9	5.8	5.6	5.5	5.4	5.5
2003	5.2	5.1	5.2	5.6	5.8	5.9	5.9	5.9	5.8	5.6	5.6	5.5	5.6
Other services													
1993	2.0	2.0	2.1	2.1	2.1	2.1	2.1	2.1	2.1	2.1	2.1	2.1	2.0
1994	2.1	2.1	2.1	2.2	2.2	2.2	2.2	2.2	2.2	2.3	2.3	2.3	2.2
1995	2.2	2.2	2.2	2.3	2.3	2.3	2.3	2.3	2.3	2.3	2.3	2.4	2.2
1996	2.3	2.3	2.4	2.5	2.5	2.6	2.5	2.5	2.5	2.5	2.5	2.5	2.4
1997	2.4	2.4	2.4	2.5	2.6	2.6	2.6	2.6	2.6	2.7	2.7	2.7	2.5
1998	2.6	2.6	2.6	2.7	2.7	2.7	2.7	2.7	2.6	2.7	2.7	2.8	2.6
1999	2.6	2.6	2.7	2.7	2.8	2.8	2.8	2.8	2.8	2.8	2.8	2.8	2.7
2000	2.8	2.7	2.8	2.9	2.9	2.8	2.9	2.8	2.8	2.9	2.8	2.8	2.8
2001	1.9	1.9	1.9	1.9	1.9	2.0	1.9	1.9	1.9	1.9	1.9	1.9	1.9
2002	1.8	1.8	1.8	1.9	1.9	1.9	1.9	1.9	1.8	1.9	1.9	1.9	1.9
2003	1.8	1.8	1.8	1.9	1.9	1.9	1.9	1.9	1.9	1.9	1.9	1.9	1.9

Employment by Industry: Ohio—*Continued*

(Numbers in thousands. Not seasonally adjusted.)

Industry	January	February	March	April	May	June	July	August	September	October	November	December	Annual Average
STEUBENVILLE-WEIRTON —*Continued*													
Government													
1993	6.1	6.2	6.3	6.4	6.4	6.5	5.9	5.8	6.0	6.1	6.1	6.0	6.1
1994	5.9	5.9	6.0	6.1	6.2	6.3	5.9	5.8	5.9	6.1	6.5	6.2	6.0
1995	5.9	6.3	6.2	6.2	6.4	6.4	6.0	6.0	6.0	6.2	6.2	6.2	6.1
1996	6.2	6.2	6.3	6.3	6.8	6.6	6.1	6.0	6.1	6.2	6.3	6.3	6.2
1997	6.3	6.3	6.4	6.4	6.5	6.6	6.3	6.1	6.4	6.4	6.4	6.4	6.3
1998	6.5	6.5	6.5	6.5	6.6	6.7	6.3	6.2	6.3	6.4	6.4	6.4	6.4
1999	6.2	6.4	6.5	6.5	6.6	6.7	6.3	6.2	6.5	6.5	6.5	6.6	6.4
2000	6.4	6.5	6.7	6.6	7.1	6.7	6.4	6.3	6.4	6.5	6.5	6.5	6.5
2001	6.4	6.5	6.7	6.7	6.7	6.8	6.3	6.2	6.3	6.5	6.5	6.5	6.5
2002	6.3	6.5	6.5	6.5	6.6	6.7	6.5	6.4	6.4	6.0	6.6	6.4	6.5
2003	6.2	6.3	6.4	6.4	6.5	6.6	6.4	6.3	6.2	6.3	6.2	6.3	6.3
Local government													
1993	5.4	5.5	5.5	5.6	5.6	5.7	5.1	5.0	5.2	5.4	5.4	5.3	5.3
1994	5.2	5.2	5.3	5.3	5.4	5.5	5.1	5.0	5.2	5.4	5.8	5.5	5.3
1995	5.2	5.6	5.5	5.5	5.6	5.6	5.2	5.2	5.3	5.5	5.5	5.5	5.4
1996	5.5	5.5	5.6	5.6	6.0	5.8	5.2	5.2	5.3	5.5	5.6	5.6	5.5
1997	5.6	5.6	5.7	5.7	5.7	5.8	5.5	5.3	5.6	5.7	5.7	5.7	5.6
1998	5.8	5.8	5.8	5.8	5.9	5.9	5.5	5.4	5.5	5.7	5.7	5.7	5.7
1999	5.5	5.7	5.8	5.8	5.8	5.9	5.5	5.4	5.7	5.8	5.8	5.8	5.7
2000	5.7	5.8	5.9	5.8	6.2	5.8	5.5	5.5	5.7	5.8	5.8	5.8	5.7
2001	5.7	5.8	6.0	6.0	6.0	6.0	5.6	5.5	5.6	5.7	5.8	5.8	5.8
2002	5.6	5.8	5.8	5.8	5.9	6.0	5.7	5.6	5.7	5.3	5.9	5.7	5.7
2003	5.5	5.6	5.7	5.7	5.8	5.9	5.7	5.6	5.5	5.6	5.6	5.6	5.7
YOUNGSTOWN-WARREN													
Total nonfarm													
1990	218.6	224.6	227.4	228.6	232.6	233.1	224.5	229.4	233.3	232.9	230.3	231.9	228.9
1991	222.2	222.2	223.9	224.0	227.6	228.3	226.9	227.6	230.0	229.6	229.6	228.0	226.6
1992	221.9	221.6	222.8	225.2	228.0	229.2	226.6	225.6	226.5	229.7	228.7	228.9	226.2
1993	223.8	223.8	224.3	225.2	228.5	228.9	226.3	226.3	228.3	230.7	231.3	232.7	227.5
1994	227.0	228.5	230.3	231.7	235.3	237.0	227.3	230.7	235.2	238.2	239.4	239.5	233.3
1995	233.6	234.6	238.1	240.5	243.3	245.9	239.8	241.2	243.0	243.0	245.2	244.5	241.0
1996	236.1	236.8	233.6	240.4	244.4	244.9	240.5	241.3	244.7	245.2	246.1	245.3	241.6
1997	239.3	240.2	243.3	244.3	248.7	250.7	244.6	245.5	248.2	247.9	248.7	248.9	245.8
1998	241.8	242.5	243.8	247.1	251.3	251.8	238.8	248.4	250.0	250.2	249.9	249.7	247.1
1999	239.9	241.4	243.5	248.0	250.7	251.7	249.7	250.8	251.8	252.0	252.4	252.6	248.7
2000	243.0	242.8	244.8	248.0	250.5	251.6	247.6	248.3	250.9	247.5	248.2	247.5	247.5
2001	237.4	237.6	239.2	240.5	242.0	243.2	237.9	239.2	241.5	239.5	240.4	239.3	239.8
2002	228.9	229.6	231.5	230.3	233.4	233.6	230.3	232.0	233.3	232.0	233.4	233.3	231.8
2003	226.0	227.0	228.4	225.6	232.5	232.2	228.1	229.9	232.3	232.2	231.9	232.2	229.9
Total private													
1990	189.8	195.6	197.9	199.8	202.6	205.3	199.3	204.3	205.3	203.2	200.8	201.7	200.4
1991	193.1	192.4	193.9	195.0	197.4	199.7	200.8	201.7	202.1	199.9	199.3	197.8	197.7
1992	192.6	191.7	192.8	195.5	198.3	200.4	200.9	200.0	198.6	199.8	198.4	198.7	197.3
1993	194.7	193.9	194.0	195.5	198.0	199.5	200.7	200.7	201.7	201.1	201.1	202.4	198.6
1994	197.9	198.2	199.7	201.4	204.5	207.3	200.5	204.4	206.3	207.3	207.8	208.0	203.6
1995	203.4	203.3	206.7	209.5	211.9	216.1	213.3	214.5	213.7	212.1	213.7	213.2	210.9
1996	205.8	205.6	202.0	209.4	212.6	215.2	213.5	214.7	215.4	214.4	214.8	214.5	211.4
1997	208.6	208.7	211.2	213.5	216.9	219.6	216.9	218.1	218.6	216.8	216.7	217.1	215.2
1998	210.8	210.8	211.7	215.4	218.9	220.2	209.9	220.0	219.6	218.2	217.4	217.3	215.8
1999	209.0	209.5	210.9	215.8	217.8	219.5	220.2	222.1	220.8	219.4	219.4	219.6	217.0
2000	211.2	210.2	211.6	215.0	216.5	218.6	217.5	218.4	217.8	214.5	214.6	214.0	214.9
2001	205.5	204.6	205.9	207.7	208.8	211.1	208.4	209.8	208.6	206.3	206.6	205.7	207.4
2002	196.9	196.5	197.9	197.3	200.1	201.8	200.3	202.3	200.9	199.3	199.9	200.1	199.4
2003	194.4	194.0	194.9	192.9	199.3	200.7	198.4	200.4	200.3	199.9	199.0	199.3	197.8
Goods-producing													
1990	57.9	64.2	64.7	65.1	66.3	67.9	61.7	66.8	67.7	66.7	63.7	64.1	64.7
1991	60.4	60.7	61.1	62.1	63.0	64.0	64.9	65.5	65.8	65.0	63.8	62.2	63.2
1992	60.2	59.5	59.6	60.5	61.9	63.0	62.9	62.7	61.9	63.6	62.6	62.8	61.7
1993	61.3	61.0	60.9	61.4	62.6	63.5	64.1	64.4	64.7	64.1	63.5	63.4	62.9
1994	62.8	62.6	63.5	64.8	66.2	67.1	61.0	64.4	65.1	66.9	66.9	66.6	64.8
1995	66.3	65.8	67.2	68.7	69.1	70.8	70.1	70.8	69.0	68.8	69.5	69.0	68.7
1996	67.1	66.8	62.2	67.9	68.9	70.1	70.3	71.1	71.2	70.7	70.0	69.5	68.8
1997	67.6	67.4	68.1	68.4	69.2	70.4	69.8	70.8	70.5	70.2	69.7	69.2	69.2
1998	66.6	66.3	66.4	67.4	68.1	68.8	58.6	68.8	68.8	68.0	67.2	66.6	66.8
1999	63.6	63.8	63.7	64.9	65.6	66.4	66.1	67.2	66.1	66.7	66.3	65.7	65.5
2000	63.7	63.3	63.6	64.4	64.9	65.7	64.7	64.8	63.9	63.1	62.5	61.5	63.8
2001	58.4	57.7	58.1	57.9	58.3	59.1	57.9	58.7	58.2	57.8	57.4	56.2	58.0
2002	53.5	53.4	53.3	53.0	53.9	54.6	53.2	55.3	54.5	53.7	53.9	53.4	53.8
2003	51.7	51.0	51.1	47.1	51.8	52.3	50.7	52.4	51.8	51.2	50.5	50.4	51.0

Employment by Industry: Ohio—*Continued*

(Numbers in thousands. Not seasonally adjusted.)

Industry	January	February	March	April	May	June	July	August	September	October	November	December	Annual Average
YOUNGSTOWN-WARREN —*Continued*													
Construction and mining													
1990	8.1	7.6	7.9	8.2	8.8	9.4	9.7	10.0	9.8	9.5	9.2	8.6	8.9
1991	7.5	7.1	7.4	8.0	8.5	9.0	9.8	9.9	9.7	9.7	9.2	8.4	8.6
1992	7.5	7.0	7.0	7.5	8.3	8.9	9.7	9.8	9.7	9.4	8.5	8.0	8.4
1993	7.0	6.9	6.9	7.8	8.6	9.2	9.5	9.7	9.4	9.5	8.7	8.4	8.4
1994	7.3	7.3	7.8	8.8	9.8	10.4	11.1	11.0	10.6	10.5	10.0	9.4	9.5
1995	8.1	7.6	8.4	9.5	10.0	10.5	10.8	11.0	10.9	10.7	10.1	9.5	9.7
1996	8.0	8.0	8.5	9.2	10.2	11.0	11.2	11.4	11.2	10.9	10.5	10.0	10.0
1997	8.9	8.7	9.1	9.8	10.5	11.1	11.2	11.2	11.1	11.2	10.6	10.1	10.2
1998	9.1	9.1	9.2	10.2	10.9	11.4	11.8	11.8	11.8	11.7	11.2	10.8	10.7
1999	9.1	9.4	9.7	10.6	11.2	11.8	12.2	12.3	12.3	12.3	11.9	11.4	11.1
2000	9.8	9.7	10.2	11.0	11.5	11.9	12.2	12.2	11.6	11.3	11.0	10.2	11.0
2001	9.3	9.3	9.7	10.4	11.0	11.4	11.8	11.8	11.6	11.5	11.3	10.6	10.8
2002	9.5	9.3	9.5	9.8	10.4	10.8	11.4	11.5	11.0	10.8	10.7	10.1	10.4
2003	9.2	8.6	8.9	9.9	10.3	10.8	11.1	11.1	10.9	10.9	10.5	10.0	10.2
Manufacturing													
1990	49.8	56.6	56.8	56.9	57.5	58.5	52.0	56.8	57.9	57.2	54.5	55.5	55.8
1991	52.9	53.6	53.7	54.1	54.5	55.0	55.1	55.6	56.1	55.3	54.6	53.8	54.5
1992	52.7	52.5	52.6	53.0	53.6	54.1	53.2	52.9	52.2	54.2	54.1	54.8	53.3
1993	54.3	54.1	54.0	53.6	54.0	54.3	54.6	54.7	55.3	54.6	54.8	55.0	54.4
1994	55.5	55.3	55.7	56.0	56.4	56.7	49.9	53.4	54.5	56.4	56.9	57.2	55.3
1995	58.2	58.2	58.8	59.2	59.1	60.3	59.3	59.8	58.1	58.1	59.4	59.5	59.0
1996	59.1	58.8	53.7	58.7	58.7	59.1	59.1	59.7	60.0	59.8	59.5	59.5	58.8
1997	58.7	58.7	59.0	58.6	58.7	59.3	58.6	59.6	59.4	59.0	59.1	59.1	58.9
1998	57.5	57.2	57.2	57.2	57.2	57.4	46.8	57.0	57.0	56.3	56.0	55.8	56.0
1999	54.5	54.4	54.0	54.3	54.4	54.6	53.9	54.9	53.8	54.4	54.4	54.3	54.3
2000	53.9	53.6	53.4	53.4	53.4	53.8	52.5	52.6	52.3	51.8	51.5	51.3	52.7
2001	49.1	48.4	48.4	47.5	47.3	47.7	46.1	46.9	46.6	46.3	46.1	45.6	47.2
2002	44.0	44.1	43.8	43.2	43.5	43.8	41.8	43.8	43.5	42.9	43.2	43.3	43.4
2003	42.5	42.4	42.2	37.2	41.5	41.5	39.6	41.3	40.9	40.3	40.0	40.4	40.8
Service-providing													
1990	160.7	160.4	162.7	163.5	166.3	165.2	162.8	162.6	165.6	166.2	166.6	167.8	164.2
1991	161.8	161.5	162.8	161.9	164.6	164.3	162.0	162.1	164.2	164.6	165.8	165.8	163.4
1992	161.7	162.1	163.2	164.7	166.1	166.2	163.7	162.9	164.6	166.1	166.1	166.1	164.4
1993	162.5	162.8	163.4	163.8	165.9	165.4	162.2	161.9	163.6	166.6	167.8	169.3	164.6
1994	164.2	165.9	166.8	166.9	169.1	169.9	166.3	166.3	170.1	171.3	172.5	172.9	168.5
1995	167.3	168.8	170.9	171.8	174.2	175.1	169.7	170.4	174.0	174.2	175.7	175.5	172.3
1996	169.0	170.0	171.4	172.5	175.5	174.8	170.2	170.2	173.5	174.5	176.1	175.8	172.7
1997	171.7	172.8	175.2	175.9	179.5	180.3	174.8	174.7	177.7	177.7	179.0	179.7	176.5
1998	175.2	176.2	177.4	179.7	183.2	183.0	180.2	179.6	181.2	182.2	182.7	183.1	180.3
1999	176.3	177.6	179.8	183.1	185.1	185.3	183.6	183.6	185.7	185.3	186.1	186.9	183.2
2000	179.3	179.5	181.2	183.6	185.6	185.9	182.9	183.5	187.0	184.4	185.7	186.0	183.7
2001	179.0	179.9	181.1	182.6	183.7	184.1	180.0	180.5	183.3	181.7	183.0	183.1	181.8
2002	175.4	176.2	178.2	177.3	179.5	179.0	177.1	176.7	178.8	178.3	179.5	179.9	178.0
2003	174.3	176.0	177.3	178.5	180.7	179.9	177.4	177.5	180.5	181.0	181.4	181.8	178.9
Trade, transportation, and utilities													
1990	48.6	48.0	48.5	48.9	49.3	49.6	49.4	49.5	49.1	49.4	50.2	51.1	49.3
1991	48.6	47.5	48.0	47.8	48.0	48.4	48.9	49.1	48.7	48.3	49.4	49.7	48.5
1992	48.2	47.3	47.9	48.7	49.1	49.3	49.1	48.9	48.1	48.1	48.5	49.1	48.5
1993	47.1	46.7	46.7	46.8	47.1	47.2	46.7	46.7	46.6	47.3	48.3	49.4	47.2
1994	47.3	46.8	47.2	47.7	48.1	48.6	47.9	48.1	48.7	48.9	49.6	50.2	48.2
1995	47.8	47.4	48.0	48.4	49.0	49.5	48.7	48.9	49.2	49.3	50.4	50.8	48.9
1996	48.3	47.7	48.1	48.5	49.1	49.5	48.7	48.8	48.8	49.5	50.5	51.3	49.0
1997	49.0	48.4	49.0	48.8	49.1	49.8	49.0	49.0	48.9	49.1	50.1	50.7	49.2
1998	49.6	49.3	49.6	49.7	50.5	50.7	50.3	50.2	50.2	50.9	51.5	51.7	50.3
1999	49.5	48.9	49.3	50.4	50.5	50.9	51.1	51.5	51.2	52.4	53.3	53.8	51.0
2000	51.0	50.1	50.2	50.9	51.2	51.7	51.8	52.0	51.8	52.0	52.8	53.6	51.5
2001	51.4	50.6	50.6	50.6	50.9	51.3	49.9	49.7	49.4	49.3	50.1	50.5	50.4
2002	47.7	46.8	47.1	47.1	47.5	48.0	47.8	47.4	47.1	46.8	47.6	47.9	47.4
2003	46.3	46.5	47.0	48.1	48.3	48.5	48.2	47.9	48.3	48.8	49.1	49.3	48.0
Wholesale trade													
1990	9.8	9.8	10.0	9.9	10.0	10.0	10.0	10.0	10.0	10.1	10.0	10.2	9.9
1991	10.1	10.0	10.3	10.3	10.2	10.3	10.4	10.4	10.3	10.2	10.4	10.3	10.2
1992	10.0	9.9	10.0	10.2	10.3	10.4	10.0	9.8	9.5	9.2	9.1	9.2	9.8
1993	9.1	9.1	9.0	9.0	9.0	9.1	9.1	9.1	9.1	9.1	9.1	9.1	9.0
1994	8.9	8.8	9.0	8.9	9.0	9.1	9.1	9.0	9.1	8.9	8.8	8.8	8.9
1995	8.5	8.5	8.6	8.7	8.8	8.9	8.8	8.7	8.7	8.6	8.6	8.6	8.6
1996	8.6	8.5	8.5	8.6	8.7	8.8	8.6	8.6	8.5	8.5	8.5	8.5	8.5
1997	8.2	8.3	8.3	8.2	8.3	8.4	8.3	8.3	8.3	8.3	8.4	8.4	8.3
1998	8.3	8.2	8.3	8.4	8.5	8.5	8.7	8.8	8.7	8.6	8.6	8.6	8.5
1999	8.5	8.4	8.4	8.6	8.6	8.7	8.8	8.8	8.7	8.8	8.9	8.9	8.6
2000	8.9	8.8	8.8	8.8	8.9	9.0	9.1	9.1	8.9	8.7	8.7	8.7	8.8
2001	8.8	8.8	8.8	8.7	8.7	8.8	8.7	8.5	8.4	8.3	8.2	8.2	8.6
2002	7.9	7.8	7.9	8.0	8.1	8.1	8.1	8.1	8.0	8.0	8.0	8.0	8.0
2003	7.9	7.9	7.9	8.4	8.5	8.6	8.7	8.8	8.6	8.7	8.6	8.6	8.4

Employment by Industry: Ohio—*Continued*

(Numbers in thousands. Not seasonally adjusted.)

Industry	January	February	March	April	May	June	July	August	September	October	November	December	Annual Average
YOUNGSTOWN-WARREN *—Continued*													
Retail trade													
1990	32.9	32.2	32.5	33.0	33.3	33.6	33.5	33.6	33.3	33.5	34.3	34.9	33.3
1991	32.8	31.8	31.9	31.8	32.1	32.4	32.9	33.0	32.7	32.5	33.3	33.8	32.5
1992	32.5	31.8	32.2	32.7	33.0	33.1	33.1	33.0	32.6	32.7	33.2	33.7	32.8
1993	31.4	30.9	30.9	31.0	31.3	31.3	31.0	30.9	30.7	31.3	32.2	33.2	31.3
1994	31.6	31.1	31.2	31.5	31.7	32.0	31.5	31.9	32.2	32.5	33.4	34.0	32.0
1995	32.0	31.6	32.0	32.1	32.6	33.0	32.5	32.7	32.7	32.9	33.9	34.3	32.6
1996	32.0	31.5	31.9	32.1	32.6	32.9	32.7	32.8	32.8	33.3	34.3	35.0	32.8
1997	33.3	32.7	33.2	33.3	33.5	34.1	33.4	33.5	33.3	33.5	34.4	35.0	33.6
1998	34.0	33.7	33.7	33.7	34.3	34.6	34.2	33.9	33.8	34.7	35.3	35.4	34.2
1999	33.6	33.2	33.5	34.4	34.4	34.7	35.0	35.4	35.1	36.1	36.9	37.3	34.9
2000	34.5	33.8	33.8	34.5	34.7	35.1	35.0	35.1	35.1	35.3	36.0	36.8	34.9
2001	33.9	33.2	33.2	33.2	33.5	33.8	32.9	32.7	32.5	32.5	33.4	33.8	33.2
2002	31.9	31.2	31.3	31.3	31.6	32.1	32.0	31.6	31.3	31.1	31.9	32.2	31.6
2003	30.7	30.9	31.4	31.9	32.0	32.1	31.7	31.4	31.8	32.1	32.6	32.9	31.8
Transportation and utilities													
1990	5.9	6.0	6.0	6.0	6.0	6.0	5.9	5.9	5.8	5.8	5.9	6.0	5.9
1991	5.7	5.7	5.8	5.7	5.7	5.7	5.6	5.7	5.7	5.6	5.7	5.6	5.6
1992	5.7	5.6	5.7	5.8	5.8	5.8	6.0	6.1	6.0	6.2	6.2	6.2	5.9
1993	6.6	6.7	6.8	6.8	6.8	6.8	6.6	6.7	6.8	6.9	7.0	7.1	6.8
1994	6.8	6.9	7.0	7.3	7.4	7.5	7.3	7.2	7.4	7.5	7.4	7.4	7.2
1995	7.3	7.3	7.4	7.6	7.6	7.6	7.4	7.5	7.8	7.8	7.9	7.9	7.5
1996	7.7	7.7	7.7	7.8	7.8	7.8	7.4	7.4	7.5	7.7	7.7	7.8	7.6
1997	7.5	7.4	7.5	7.3	7.3	7.3	7.3	7.2	7.3	7.3	7.3	7.3	7.3
1998	7.3	7.4	7.6	7.6	7.7	7.6	7.4	7.5	7.7	7.6	7.6	7.7	7.5
1999	7.4	7.3	7.4	7.4	7.5	7.5	7.3	7.3	7.4	7.5	7.5	7.6	7.4
2000	7.6	7.5	7.6	7.6	7.6	7.6	7.7	7.8	7.8	8.0	8.1	8.1	7.7
2001	8.7	8.6	8.6	8.7	8.7	8.7	8.3	8.5	8.5	8.5	8.5	8.5	8.6
2002	7.9	7.8	7.9	7.8	7.8	7.8	7.7	7.7	7.8	7.7	7.7	7.7	7.8
2003	7.7	7.7	7.7	7.8	7.8	7.8	7.8	7.7	7.9	8.0	7.9	7.8	7.8
Information													
1990	3.4	3.3	3.3	3.3	3.3	3.4	3.5	3.5	3.5	3.5	3.5	3.6	3.4
1991	3.5	3.5	3.5	3.4	3.4	3.4	3.6	3.6	3.5	3.6	3.7	3.8	3.5
1992	3.7	3.7	3.6	3.6	3.6	3.6	3.6	3.5	3.5	3.6	3.5	3.5	3.5
1993	3.5	3.3	3.3	3.2	3.3	3.3	3.3	3.4	3.3	3.3	3.3	3.4	3.3
1994	3.4	3.3	3.3	3.3	3.3	3.3	3.3	3.3	3.3	3.2	3.2	3.3	3.2
1995	3.4	3.4	3.3	3.3	3.3	3.4	3.4	3.4	3.4	3.3	3.3	3.3	3.3
1996	3.3	3.3	3.4	3.5	3.5	3.5	3.5	3.6	3.5	3.5	3.6	3.7	3.4
1997	3.6	3.6	3.6	3.8	3.8	3.9	3.7	3.7	3.7	3.7	3.7	3.7	3.7
1998	3.7	3.6	3.5	3.6	3.6	3.6	3.6	3.6	3.5	3.5	3.4	3.5	3.5
1999	3.4	3.4	3.4	3.4	3.4	3.3	3.4	3.4	3.3	3.3	3.2	3.2	3.3
2000	3.3	3.2	3.3	3.2	3.3	3.3	3.3	3.3	3.2	3.1	3.2	3.2	3.2
2001	3.3	3.3	3.3	3.3	3.3	3.3	3.3	3.3	3.3	3.3	3.3	3.4	3.3
2002	3.5	3.5	3.5	3.2	3.3	3.3	3.3	3.3	3.3	3.3	3.4	3.5	3.4
2003	3.5	3.6	3.6	3.7	3.7	3.8	3.8	3.8	3.8	3.8	3.8	3.8	3.7
Financial activities													
1990	9.3	9.3	9.3	9.3	9.4	9.5	9.5	9.5	9.4	9.4	9.4	9.4	9.3
1991	9.5	9.5	9.5	9.3	9.4	9.6	9.5	9.5	9.5	9.4	9.4	9.5	9.4
1992	9.7	9.8	9.8	9.8	9.8	10.0	9.8	9.8	9.7	9.7	9.7	9.8	9.7
1993	9.8	9.7	9.8	9.2	9.2	9.4	9.5	9.5	9.5	9.3	9.3	9.4	9.4
1994	9.3	9.2	9.3	9.2	9.4	9.5	9.5	9.5	9.4	9.0	9.0	9.1	9.2
1995	8.9	8.8	8.9	8.8	8.8	8.9	8.8	8.8	8.8	8.8	8.7	8.7	8.8
1996	8.7	8.7	8.7	8.5	8.5	8.7	8.7	8.7	8.6	8.6	8.6	8.6	8.6
1997	8.8	8.7	8.8	8.9	9.0	9.1	9.0	9.0	8.9	8.7	8.6	8.6	8.8
1998	8.5	8.5	8.6	9.0	9.1	9.2	9.1	9.1	8.9	8.9	8.8	8.9	8.8
1999	8.8	8.8	8.9	9.0	9.1	9.2	9.4	9.3	9.2	9.0	9.0	9.1	9.0
2000	9.1	9.1	9.2	9.3	9.3	9.4	9.2	9.2	9.2	8.9	9.0	8.9	9.1
2001	8.7	8.6	8.7	8.7	8.8	9.1	9.1	9.1	8.9	8.8	8.9	8.9	8.9
2002	8.7	8.7	8.8	8.7	8.7	8.9	8.8	8.9	8.8	8.8	8.8	8.8	8.8
2003	8.7	8.7	8.7	8.8	8.9	9.0	9.2	9.2	9.3	9.3	9.3	9.4	9.0
Professional and business services													
1990	12.9	13.0	13.2	13.8	14.2	14.2	14.2	14.2	14.0	14.0	13.9	13.6	13.7
1991	12.9	13.0	13.0	13.6	13.5	13.7	13.7	13.7	13.7	13.5	13.1	12.9	13.3
1992	12.8	12.9	13.1	13.3	13.3	13.4	13.8	13.6	13.3	13.6	13.1	12.9	13.2
1993	13.4	13.5	13.5	14.2	14.2	14.4	15.3	15.3	15.3	15.5	15.3	15.3	14.6
1994	15.0	15.4	15.5	15.5	15.5	15.7	16.0	16.3	16.5	16.7	16.8	16.6	15.9
1995	16.5	16.7	17.2	17.3	17.5	18.1	18.0	18.2	18.1	17.7	17.7	17.5	17.5
1996	16.3	16.6	17.0	17.3	17.6	18.1	18.0	18.1	18.3	18.1	18.3	17.9	17.6
1997	17.5	18.2	18.7	20.2	21.1	21.2	21.2	21.2	21.6	20.9	20.8	21.2	20.3
1998	19.5	19.5	19.8	21.0	21.6	22.0	22.2	22.6	22.8	22.0	22.0	22.2	21.4
1999	21.0	21.2	21.4	22.7	22.7	22.8	22.8	23.0	23.3	21.8	21.8	22.0	22.2
2000	20.3	20.3	20.7	21.6	21.6	21.9	21.7	22.3	22.0	21.8	21.8	21.6	21.4
2001	20.2	20.3	20.6	21.6	21.5	21.8	21.7	21.2	20.6	20.4	20.4	20.5	20.9
2002	19.4	19.4	19.8	19.5	19.7	19.7	20.1	20.3	20.1	19.9	19.6	19.6	19.8
2003	18.1	18.1	17.9	17.8	18.1	18.4	18.2	18.2	18.3	18.3	18.0	18.0	18.1

Employment by Industry: Ohio—*Continued*

(Numbers in thousands. Not seasonally adjusted.)

Industry	January	February	March	April	May	June	July	August	September	October	November	December	Annual Average
YOUNGSTOWN-WARREN *—Continued*													
Educational and health services													
1990	30.0	30.1	30.3	30.3	30.3	30.4	30.6	30.6	30.8	31.1	31.2	31.2	30.5
1991	30.9	31.0	31.2	31.1	31.2	31.3	31.0	31.1	31.4	31.4	31.5	31.7	31.2
1992	31.5	31.6	31.7	32.0	32.1	32.1	32.6	32.6	32.6	32.9	33.1	33.2	32.3
1993	32.7	32.6	32.7	32.5	32.4	32.2	32.5	32.3	32.4	32.5	32.6	32.8	32.5
1994	32.5	32.7	32.6	32.2	32.4	32.6	32.4	32.4	32.6	32.7	32.8	32.9	32.5
1995	32.4	32.5	32.6	32.8	32.9	32.9	32.6	32.5	32.7	32.8	32.9	32.9	32.7
1996	32.0	32.2	32.3	32.5	32.3	32.2	32.2	32.2	32.3	32.6	32.8	32.8	32.3
1997	32.1	32.1	32.1	31.9	32.0	32.0	31.6	31.7	31.9	32.3	32.2	32.3	32.0
1998	32.4	32.6	32.5	33.0	33.2	33.1	33.2	33.2	33.3	33.6	33.8	34.0	33.1
1999	33.7	33.8	34.0	34.0	34.1	34.0	34.1	34.2	34.3	34.4	34.5	34.5	34.1
2000	33.5	33.8	33.9	34.2	34.1	34.1	33.9	33.9	34.3	34.3	34.3	34.4	34.0
2001	32.8	33.2	33.2	33.4	32.8	32.9	33.3	34.2	34.5	34.4	34.7	34.7	33.7
2002	34.0	34.3	34.5	34.5	34.7	34.5	34.2	34.2	34.5	35.1	35.4	35.5	34.6
2003	35.7	35.7	35.7	35.6	35.6	35.3	35.3	35.6	35.7	35.5	35.5	35.8	35.6
Leisure and hospitality													
1990	19.0	19.1	19.8	20.3	21.0	21.5	21.5	21.3	21.9	20.3	20.1	19.9	20.4
1991	18.9	18.7	19.1	19.2	20.0	20.4	20.6	20.7	21.0	19.8	19.4	19.2	19.7
1992	17.9	18.0	18.3	18.4	19.1	19.7	19.8	19.8	20.4	19.1	18.7	18.3	18.9
1993	17.6	17.7	17.6	18.8	19.6	20.0	20.1	20.0	20.7	19.8	19.4	19.3	19.2
1994	18.4	18.8	18.9	19.3	20.0	20.9	21.2	21.1	21.4	20.6	20.1	19.9	20.0
1995	18.8	19.3	19.9	20.5	21.5	22.5	22.1	22.2	22.6	21.3	21.1	20.8	21.0
1996	20.0	20.0	20.1	21.1	22.3	22.7	22.0	22.0	22.5	21.1	20.6	20.3	21.2
1997	19.8	20.0	20.4	21.0	21.9	22.5	22.3	22.4	22.8	21.5	21.1	21.0	21.3
1998	20.2	20.5	20.9	21.1	22.0	22.3	22.5	22.2	21.7	20.9	20.2	20.0	21.2
1999	19.0	19.3	20.0	20.9	21.8	22.2	22.9	23.0	22.9	21.4	20.9	20.8	21.2
2000	20.2	20.2	20.5	21.1	21.7	22.2	22.8	22.8	23.2	21.2	20.8	20.6	21.4
2001	19.7	19.8	20.2	21.0	21.9	22.4	22.2	22.5	22.6	21.2	20.7	20.5	21.2
2002	19.7	19.9	20.4	20.7	21.6	22.1	22.3	22.3	21.9	20.9	20.4	20.5	21.1
2003	19.7	19.7	20.1	20.9	21.8	22.4	22.2	22.5	22.3	22.2	22.1	21.9	21.5
Other services													
1990	8.7	8.6	8.8	8.8	8.8	8.8	8.9	8.9	8.9	8.8	8.8	8.8	8.8
1991	8.4	8.5	8.5	8.5	8.9	8.9	8.6	8.5	8.5	8.9	9.0	8.8	8.6
1992	8.6	8.9	8.8	9.2	9.4	9.3	9.3	9.1	9.1	9.2	9.2	9.1	9.1
1993	9.3	9.4	9.5	9.4	9.6	9.5	9.2	9.1	9.2	9.3	9.4	9.4	9.3
1994	9.2	9.4	9.4	9.4	9.6	9.6	9.2	9.3	9.3	9.3	9.4	9.4	9.3
1995	9.3	9.4	9.6	9.7	9.8	10.0	9.6	9.7	9.9	10.1	10.1	10.2	9.7
1996	10.1	10.3	10.2	10.1	10.4	10.4	10.1	10.2	10.2	10.3	10.4	10.4	10.2
1997	10.2	10.3	10.5	10.5	10.8	10.7	10.3	10.3	10.3	10.4	10.5	10.4	10.4
1998	10.3	10.5	10.4	10.6	10.8	10.5	10.4	10.3	10.4	10.4	10.5	10.4	10.4
1999	10.0	10.3	10.2	10.5	10.6	10.7	10.4	10.5	10.5	10.4	10.4	10.5	10.4
2000	10.1	10.2	10.2	10.3	10.4	10.3	10.1	10.1	10.2	10.1	10.2	10.2	10.2
2001	11.0	11.1	11.2	11.2	11.3	11.2	11.0	11.1	11.1	11.1	11.1	11.0	11.1
2002	10.4	10.5	10.5	10.6	10.7	10.7	10.6	10.6	10.7	10.8	10.8	10.9	10.7
2003	10.7	10.7	10.8	10.9	11.1	11.0	10.8	10.8	10.8	10.8	10.7	10.7	10.8
Government													
1990	28.8	29.0	29.5	28.8	30.0	27.8	25.2	25.1	28.0	29.7	29.5	30.2	28.4
1991	29.1	29.8	30.0	29.0	30.2	28.6	26.1	25.9	27.9	29.7	30.3	30.2	28.9
1992	29.3	29.9	30.0	29.7	29.7	28.8	25.7	25.6	27.9	29.9	30.3	30.2	28.9
1993	29.1	29.9	30.3	29.7	30.5	29.4	25.6	25.6	26.6	29.6	30.2	30.3	28.9
1994	29.1	30.3	30.6	30.3	30.8	29.7	26.8	26.3	28.9	30.9	31.6	31.5	29.7
1995	30.2	31.3	31.4	31.0	31.4	29.8	26.5	26.7	29.3	30.9	31.5	31.3	30.1
1996	30.3	31.2	31.6	31.0	31.8	29.7	27.0	26.6	29.3	30.8	31.3	30.8	30.1
1997	30.7	31.5	32.1	30.8	31.8	31.1	27.7	27.4	29.6	31.1	32.0	31.8	30.6
1998	31.0	31.7	32.1	31.7	32.4	31.6	28.9	28.4	30.4	32.0	32.5	32.4	31.2
1999	30.9	31.9	32.6	32.2	32.9	32.2	29.5	28.7	31.0	32.6	33.0	33.0	31.7
2000	31.8	32.6	33.2	33.0	34.0	33.0	30.1	29.9	33.1	33.0	33.6	33.5	32.5
2001	31.9	33.0	33.3	32.8	33.2	32.1	29.5	29.4	32.9	33.2	33.8	33.6	32.4
2002	32.0	33.1	33.6	33.0	33.3	31.8	30.0	29.7	32.4	32.7	33.5	33.2	32.4
2003	31.6	33.0	33.5	32.7	33.2	31.5	29.7	29.5	32.0	32.3	32.9	32.9	32.1
Federal government													
2001	2.6	2.6	2.6	2.6	2.6	2.6	2.6	2.6	2.6	2.6	2.6	2.6	2.6
2002	2.6	2.6	2.6	2.6	2.6	2.6	2.6	2.6	2.5	2.6	2.6	2.6	2.6
2003	2.5	2.5	2.5	2.5	2.5	2.4	2.5	2.5	2.4	2.5	2.4	2.5	2.5

Employment by Industry: Ohio—*Continued*

(Numbers in thousands. Not seasonally adjusted.)

Industry	January	February	March	April	May	June	July	August	September	October	November	December	Annual Average
YOUNGSTOWN-WARREN *—Continued*													
State government													
1990	4.2	4.6	4.7	4.3	4.6	4.7	3.6	3.5	3.6	4.8	4.4	4.8	4.3
1991	4.1	4.7	4.8	4.4	4.7	4.6	3.4	3.4	3.6	4.8	4.8	4.7	4.3
1992	4.4	5.0	5.0	4.9	4.6	4.5	3.7	3.7	3.8	5.1	5.0	5.0	4.5
1993	4.4	5.0	5.0	4.8	5.1	4.8	4.1	4.1	4.2	5.5	5.4	5.4	4.8
1994	4.6	5.2	5.3	5.1	5.3	5.0	4.2	4.0	4.4	5.2	5.5	5.5	4.9
1995	4.8	5.4	5.4	5.1	5.4	5.1	4.2	4.1	4.5	5.1	5.5	5.4	5.0
1996	4.7	5.3	5.3	5.1	5.4	5.1	4.2	4.0	4.2	4.9	5.2	5.2	4.8
1997	4.7	5.2	5.3	4.9	5.3	5.0	4.3	4.1	4.2	5.0	5.4	5.4	4.9
1998	5.1	5.4	5.5	5.3	5.5	5.3	4.8	4.4	4.6	5.4	5.7	5.7	5.2
1999	5.1	5.6	5.7	5.4	5.7	5.4	4.8	4.4	4.6	5.4	5.8	5.8	5.3
2000	5.2	5.7	5.8	5.4	5.7	5.6	4.6	4.5	5.6	5.3	5.8	5.7	5.4
2001	4.8	5.7	5.8	5.4	5.6	4.9	4.5	4.4	5.6	5.4	5.8	5.7	5.3
2002	4.8	5.6	5.8	5.4	5.5	4.5	4.5	4.4	5.6	5.5	6.0	5.8	5.3
2003	4.9	5.9	6.0	5.5	5.7	4.6	4.6	4.6	5.8	5.6	6.1	6.0	5.4
Local government													
1990	18.3	18.0	18.3	18.0	18.4	16.8	15.6	15.7	18.0	18.5	18.6	18.8	17.7
1991	18.6	18.6	18.7	18.2	18.8	17.7	16.6	16.4	18.0	18.5	18.9	18.8	18.1
1992	22.6	22.7	22.8	22.6	22.9	22.1	19.7	19.7	21.9	22.6	23.1	23.0	22.1
1993	22.5	22.7	23.1	22.8	23.3	22.4	19.3	19.3	20.2	22.0	22.6	22.7	21.9
1994	22.3	22.9	23.1	23.0	23.3	22.5	20.4	20.1	22.3	23.5	23.8	23.7	22.5
1995	23.2	23.6	23.7	23.6	23.7	22.4	20.0	20.3	22.5	23.5	23.7	23.6	22.8
1996	23.3	23.6	24.0	23.6	24.1	22.3	20.5	20.3	22.8	23.6	23.7	23.2	22.9
1997	23.1	23.3	23.8	23.4	23.9	23.6	20.8	20.7	22.8	23.5	24.0	23.7	23.0
1998	23.3	23.7	24.0	23.8	24.2	23.6	21.4	21.3	23.1	23.9	24.1	23.9	23.3
1999	23.1	23.6	24.2	24.1	24.5	24.1	22.0	21.6	23.7	24.5	24.5	24.4	23.6
2000	23.9	24.2	24.5	24.7	24.8	24.4	22.5	22.6	24.8	25.1	25.2	25.1	24.3
2001	24.5	24.7	24.9	24.8	25.0	24.6	22.4	22.4	24.7	25.2	25.4	25.3	24.5
2002	24.6	24.9	25.2	25.0	25.2	24.7	22.9	22.7	24.3	24.6	24.9	24.8	24.5
2003	24.2	24.6	25.0	24.7	25.0	24.5	22.6	22.4	23.8	24.2	24.4	24.4	24.2

Average Weekly Hours by Industry: Ohio

(Not seasonally adjusted.)

Industry	January	February	March	April	May	June	July	August	September	October	November	December	Annual Average
STATEWIDE													
Goods-producing													
2001	41.1	40.6	40.6	39.8	40.9	41.2	40.8	41.2	41.5	40.9	41.7	41.9	41.0
2002	40.5	40.5	41.2	41.0	41.2	41.4	40.4	41.2	41.5	41.2	40.9	41.3	41.0
2003	40.9	40.4	40.9	40.4	40.6	40.2	39.0	40.2	41.1	41.1	40.9	40.7	40.5
Service-providing													
2001	30.8	31.0	31.1	31.2	31.1	31.4	31.5	31.3	31.4	30.9	31.2	31.5	31.2
2002	30.8	31.1	31.0	30.9	31.2	31.7	31.3	31.3	31.2	30.9	31.1	31.7	31.2
2003	30.6	30.8	31.0	30.9	31.1	31.3	31.2	31.2	31.1	31.1	31.2	31.0	31.1
Natural resources and mining													
2001	46.2	46.4	46.6	45.3	46.9	48.6	47.9	48.3	48.2	48.0	48.7	46.8	47.4
2002	44.3	44.5	44.2	45.8	45.2	45.6	46.8	46.8	46.2	46.1	46.4	44.5	45.6
2003	44.9	44.0	47.4	47.8	47.8	46.6	46.6	47.1	47.5	47.3	45.8	41.9	46.2
Construction													
2001	39.5	38.5	38.8	38.2	39.8	41.0	40.7	40.7	40.9	40.4	41.8	39.6	40.0
2002	39.4	39.0	39.9	39.2	39.6	40.1	40.3	40.1	40.0	40.3	39.5	38.2	39.7
2003	38.0	36.9	38.5	38.5	38.4	38.5	37.2	40.4	40.0	39.8	39.3	37.2	38.6
Manufacturing													
2001	41.3	40.9	40.9	40.2	41.2	41.1	40.7	41.2	41.6	40.9	41.6	42.4	41.2
2002	40.7	40.8	41.5	41.4	41.7	41.7	40.4	41.5	41.9	41.4	41.2	42.1	41.4
2003	41.5	41.1	41.4	40.8	41.1	40.6	39.4	40.1	41.3	41.4	41.3	41.7	41.0
Trade, transportation and utilities													
2001	31.3	31.5	31.8	32.4	32.2	32.6	32.6	32.3	32.2	31.8	32.2	32.7	32.1
2002	31.6	31.8	32.0	31.9	32.3	32.9	33.0	32.7	32.6	32.2	32.3	33.4	32.4
2003	31.6	31.9	32.0	32.2	32.7	32.8	33.2	32.9	33.2	33.1	33.0	32.9	32.6
Wholesale trade													
2001	36.7	37.0	37.4	37.6	37.4	37.0	37.1	36.8	37.1	36.5	36.7	37.2	37.0
2002	36.6	35.8	35.8	35.9	36.1	36.9	37.6	37.6	38.0	37.0	37.3	38.1	36.9
2003	36.2	36.6	36.6	36.5	36.8	36.4	37.3	36.2	37.4	38.1	37.2	36.5	36.8
Retail trade													
2001	28.2	28.1	28.3	28.9	28.9	29.1	29.5	29.2	29.0	28.7	28.6	29.7	28.9
2002	28.1	28.7	29.0	29.2	29.5	29.8	30.1	29.6	29.3	29.0	29.0	30.8	29.3
2003	28.7	29.1	29.4	29.7	30.1	30.4	30.3	30.4	30.1	29.8	29.8	30.3	29.8
Transportation and utilities													
2001	35.6	36.4	36.7	37.8	37.0	39.2	37.5	37.5	37.4	36.7	39.7	38.4	37.5
2002	37.9	38.0	37.9	36.6	37.6	38.7	37.3	37.8	37.8	37.5	38.2	37.5	37.7
2003	36.2	35.8	35.7	35.7	37.0	37.1	38.2	37.9	39.2	39.0	39.4	38.1	37.5
Financial activities													
2001	35.0	34.9	35.2	36.0	35.1	35.9	35.8	35.2	36.2	35.2	37.1	36.6	35.7
2002	35.3	35.6	35.4	35.2	35.9	36.5	35.7	35.6	36.3	35.2	35.4	36.0	35.7
2003	34.9	35.9	36.2	35.2	35.3	36.2	35.3	35.9	36.0	36.2	36.1	35.2	35.7
AKRON													
Manufacturing													
2001	40.1	40.5	40.2	39.6	40.2	39.3	38.8	38.8	39.3	39.1	40.3	40.4	39.7
2002	38.4	39.0	40.5	40.0	40.9	40.9	38.9	40.1	40.6	41.1	41.2	40.0	40.1
2003	41.1	41.5	41.0	41.3	40.9	40.2	39.7	39.7	40.4	40.8	41.4	41.9	40.8
Wholesale trade													
2001	34.7	34.6	34.7	35.1	34.6	34.3	34.3	35.0	35.4	35.9	36.7	38.1	35.3
2002	36.6	35.4	35.1	37.2	37.2	38.3	35.2	33.2	35.5	34.1	34.6	35.0	35.7
2003	33.4	36.5	35.5	35.0	32.9	36.3	35.7	35.8	35.6	36.5	37.7	37.9	35.7
Retail trade													
2001	27.9	27.8	27.5	28.7	28.7	28.8	29.0	28.6	28.4	29.4	28.6	30.1	28.6
2002	28.8	28.6	28.7	28.3	28.2	28.7	29.1	29.1	28.7	28.1	29.0	30.9	28.9
2003	28.0	28.1	28.5	27.7	27.5	28.1	27.6	30.0	28.7	28.2	28.5	30.1	28.4
Financial activities													
2001	42.6	43.0	42.5	43.1	39.9	42.9	41.2	41.3	42.6	39.1	44.4	41.5	42.1
2002	38.4	39.4	40.6	39.8	41.3	40.2	41.2	42.3	42.8	41.4	41.2	42.9	41.0
2003	43.1	42.8	40.7	40.9	42.9	41.0	41.5	41.5	40.2	40.8	40.5	40.0	41.3
CANTON													
Manufacturing													
2001	38.6	38.4	38.5	38.9	39.3	39.4	38.6	39.6	40.3	39.3	38.7	41.7	39.3
2002	38.5	40.0	39.7	40.0	40.6	40.8	40.8	40.3	39.3	38.5	39.7	40.5	39.9
2003	38.4	38.9	38.9	38.6	39.2	39.1	38.5	38.2	38.5	38.4	38.5	39.2	38.7
Retail trade													
2001	28.6	28.7	28.1	28.4	27.1	28.4	28.7	29.5	29.4	29.2	29.6	29.3	28.7
2002	28.3	29.1	29.0	30.0	29.3	29.1	29.6	29.2	28.9	29.6	29.1	30.7	29.3
2003	30.1	28.9	29.3	30.1	30.3	30.5	30.8	30.2	30.2	30.5	29.8	30.2	30.1
CINCINNATI													
Manufacturing													
2001	42.1	42.1	42.2	41.8	41.9	41.6	40.7	41.5	42.9	41.0	41.0	41.4	41.7
2002	40.6	40.2	41.0	40.2	41.1	40.7	39.4	41.1	42.0	42.2	42.3	44.1	41.3
2003	41.7	41.7	42.5	41.4	42.1	41.4	40.1	41.0	41.3	41.5	41.9	42.2	41.6
Trade, transportation, and utilities													
2001	33.6	33.0	32.8	33.0	32.5	32.5	32.6	32.7	32.8	33.2	32.7	34.0	32.9
2002	32.6	32.5	33.2	33.3	34.3	34.5	34.5	34.3	33.8	33.3	32.7	33.6	33.6
2003	33.1	34.0	33.9	32.9	33.4	33.6	33.4	34.7	34.2	33.6	33.6	33.7	33.7

Average Weekly Hours by Industry: Ohio—*Continued*

(Not seasonally adjusted.)

Industry	January	February	March	April	May	June	July	August	September	October	November	December	Annual Average
CINCINNATI—*Continued*													
Wholesale trade													
2001	39.7	39.5	39.3	39.4	38.6	37.5	38.7	38.1	38.3	36.8	37.9	39.4	38.6
2002	35.7	34.8	37.2	35.9	37.7	37.9	38.7	38.4	38.4	39.4	38.6	39.9	37.7
2003	39.5	39.5	39.2	37.0	37.7	38.7	39.8	39.9	40.0	40.0	40.2	41.9	39.4
Retail trade													
2001	29.0	28.7	29.4	29.2	28.9	29.2	29.0	29.3	29.4	29.6	28.7	30.0	29.2
2002	29.3	29.8	30.3	30.0	31.3	32.0	31.9	31.5	29.9	28.7	29.4	29.8	30.3
2003	28.8	29.9	29.9	29.0	29.5	29.6	29.2	30.4	29.3	29.0	28.7	29.3	29.4
Financial activities													
2001	36.8	37.2	38.6	38.7	38.7	39.2	38.8	38.5	38.9	37.7	38.1	39.0	38.4
2002	38.0	38.5	38.4	38.1	37.9	37.6	37.2	36.7	38.1	37.0	37.0	37.2	37.6
2003	36.2	36.4	37.0	36.6	36.6	37.4	36.6	37.1	37.7	38.2	38.5	38.6	37.2
CLEVELAND													
Manufacturing													
2001	41.2	40.6	40.0	39.0	40.8	40.4	40.5	40.1	40.8	39.9	40.8	41.7	40.5
2002	40.1	40.6	41.9	41.2	41.7	41.9	40.7	42.3	42.5	41.8	42.0	42.3	41.6
2003	41.7	42.1	42.1	41.9	41.5	41.2	40.7	39.6	40.9	40.9	41.4	41.8	41.3
Trade, transportation, and utilities													
2001	30.6	29.8	30.2	32.1	32.0	32.0	32.3	31.5	32.3	30.8	30.7	31.8	31.4
2002	30.0	30.0	30.0	30.1	30.8	31.2	30.6	30.3	31.2	30.5	30.8	32.2	30.6
2003	29.8	30.9	30.4	30.8	30.9	30.8	30.9	30.8	32.0	32.1	32.0	32.8	31.2
Wholesale trade													
2001	39.9	37.9	38.6	38.1	38.4	39.9	39.5	37.6	38.3	36.2	35.7	36.2	38.0
2002	36.5	33.0	34.7	34.9	35.6	36.6	35.3	36.1	38.5	36.2	36.9	37.8	36.0
2003	36.0	36.7	37.9	35.6	37.7	35.8	37.5	35.7	37.0	38.8	38.3	37.1	37.0
Retail trade													
2001	25.8	25.3	25.9	26.9	26.8	26.5	27.1	26.9	27.6	26.5	26.5	28.3	26.7
2002	26.2	27.4	27.4	27.0	27.3	27.8	27.9	26.8	27.3	26.9	27.4	28.9	27.4
2003	25.4	26.9	26.1	26.9	27.2	27.4	27.1	27.9	28.6	28.1	28.2	29.8	27.5
Financial activities													
2001	33.7	34.0	34.6	35.5	34.8	34.5	35.1	34.9	33.8	33.1	32.6	33.4	34.2
2002	33.0	33.2	32.7	33.1	33.6	34.6	33.1	35.8	36.0	34.7	35.3	37.0	34.3
2003	35.9	36.7	36.9	36.5	36.0	35.7	35.6	36.8	38.6	37.1	38.2	37.7	36.8
COLUMBUS													
Manufacturing													
2001	39.8	39.9	40.1	39.8	41.0	40.8	40.7	40.9	41.0	40.3	40.6	41.8	40.5
2002	39.9	39.5	39.3	39.9	40.2	40.6	39.2	40.0	40.6	40.1	40.7	40.9	40.1
2003	40.1	39.9	40.8	39.1	40.0	38.9	38.4	39.1	39.8	39.8	40.5	39.9	39.7
Trade, transportation, and utilities													
2001	28.7	29.2	29.4	29.2	29.8	29.8	29.8	29.7	30.0	30.0	29.9	31.3	29.7
2002	29.8	30.1	29.9	30.2	30.3	30.8	31.0	30.9	31.4	31.8	31.3	32.5	30.8
2003	31.9	31.4	32.3	32.2	32.9	33.0	33.7	33.3	33.6	32.8	34.4	34.2	33.0
Wholesale trade													
2001	31.6	32.7	32.9	33.0	34.7	32.9	33.1	32.9	33.3	34.6	33.8	34.4	33.3
2002	33.4	33.0	33.2	33.4	34.1	34.3	33.4	32.1	32.8	33.9	33.7	33.6	33.4
2003	32.0	32.0	31.8	30.7	31.5	31.1	33.7	32.8	33.7	32.0	35.7	32.3	32.4
Retail trade													
2001	27.0	27.3	27.5	27.5	27.9	28.4	28.5	27.9	28.3	27.7	27.9	29.9	28.0
2002	27.5	28.1	27.4	27.7	27.5	28.1	28.5	28.5	29.4	29.8	28.9	30.8	28.5
2003	30.8	30.6	31.5	31.6	32.1	33.0	32.8	32.3	32.3	31.7	31.9	34.1	32.1
Transportation and utilities													
2001	30.8	31.1	31.3	30.4	30.4	31.0	30.2	31.9	32.1	32.2	32.6	33.1	31.4
2002	33.4	33.1	34.6	34.9	35.3	35.6	36.1	36.9	36.2	36.0	36.7	37.1	35.5
2003	35.4	33.3	35.2	35.5	36.4	34.9	36.5	36.9	37.5	37.2	41.0	36.3	36.3
Financial activities													
2001	34.7	35.1	35.3	36.4	36.1	36.3	36.4	36.9	37.2	37.0	37.1	37.3	36.3
2002	37.4	37.3	37.9	38.9	38.2	38.4	37.5	37.9	39.4	38.5	37.1	37.0	38.0
2003	36.7	37.2	37.3	36.5	36.4	38.6	38.0	37.5	37.1	37.8	39.1	36.2	37.4
YOUNGSTOWN-WARREN													
Manufacturing													
2001	41.2	40.4	40.9	41.5	41.5	41.4	41.3	41.7	40.7	41.1	40.4	41.1	41.1
2002	40.0	40.8	40.3	41.7	41.6	40.3	38.8	40.1	41.2	42.1	40.8	42.1	40.8
2003	40.1	40.0	39.6	39.3	39.7	40.0	36.8	38.6	39.8	41.4	41.2	41.9	39.9
Retail trade													
2001	32.0	31.8	31.8	33.3	33.0	33.0	34.4	32.9	33.0	32.2	32.3	34.0	32.8
2002	31.6	31.9	32.0	33.1	34.1	33.1	33.5	31.4	31.2	31.3	30.7	32.8	32.2
2003	29.4	30.4	29.6	28.7	29.4	30.1	31.1	31.0	29.7	29.6	29.7	30.2	29.9
Financial activities													
2001	35.4	36.1	34.2	35.8	35.4	34.0	34.7	33.8	33.8	33.9	33.3	32.6	34.4
2002	31.2	32.3	32.1	32.4	34.0	34.1	33.2	33.1	34.3	31.7	33.1	34.4	33.0
2003	34.9	35.6	35.7	34.8	35.2	34.2	33.0	34.0	34.6	34.7	36.0	35.8	34.9

Average Hourly Earnings by Industry: Ohio

(Dollars, not seasonally adjusted.)

Industry	January	February	March	April	May	June	July	August	September	October	November	December	Annual Average
STATEWIDE													
Goods-producing													
2001	16.96	16.96	17.07	17.12	17.34	17.42	17.33	17.51	17.64	17.62	17.84	17.95	17.40
2002	17.81	17.85	17.92	17.97	18.06	18.04	17.93	18.06	18.23	18.32	18.31	18.47	18.08
2003	18.36	18.35	18.38	18.21	18.25	18.29	18.43	18.75	18.82	18.50	18.42	18.53	18.44
Service-providing													
2001	13.09	13.28	13.47	13.49	13.30	13.28	13.39	13.29	13.30	13.27	13.33	13.38	13.32
2002	13.37	13.35	13.40	13.32	13.16	13.28	13.26	13.24	13.42	13.50	13.54	13.67	13.38
2003	13.81	13.88	13.90	13.80	13.74	13.69	13.73	13.66	13.78	13.72	13.81	13.82	13.78
Natural resources and mining													
2001	15.13	15.29	15.41	15.45	15.78	15.42	15.45	15.58	15.83	15.69	15.70	15.85	15.56
2002	15.71	15.21	15.34	15.34	15.20	15.22	15.16	15.29	15.58	15.21	15.20	15.54	15.33
2003	15.84	15.54	15.85	16.16	16.01	16.28	16.43	16.65	16.84	17.06	17.40	17.17	16.46
Construction													
2001	19.61	19.68	19.81	19.60	19.69	19.62	19.71	19.87	20.15	20.20	20.73	20.23	19.92
2002	20.44	20.81	20.65	20.64	20.60	20.36	20.59	20.47	20.64	20.62	20.03	20.27	20.51
2003	20.17	20.46	20.20	20.21	20.41	20.06	20.19	20.48	20.61	20.33	20.31	20.06	20.30
Manufacturing													
2001	16.45	16.44	16.50	16.57	16.77	16.85	16.68	16.87	16.97	16.92	17.07	17.41	16.79
2002	17.23	17.22	17.32	17.35	17.44	17.45	17.17	17.41	17.59	17.71	17.89	18.08	17.49
2003	18.00	17.96	18.01	17.74	17.72	17.83	17.97	18.27	18.34	18.00	17.92	18.17	18.00
Trade, transportation and utilities													
2001	12.54	12.70	12.90	12.99	12.94	12.94	13.04	12.91	12.84	12.81	12.84	12.77	12.85
2002	12.52	12.72	12.73	12.55	12.47	12.61	12.56	12.62	12.66	12.74	12.74	12.76	12.64
2003	12.87	12.92	13.03	12.88	12.96	12.99	12.96	12.97	13.04	12.95	12.97	12.89	12.95
Wholesale trade													
2001	14.30	14.31	14.42	14.72	14.68	14.48	14.74	14.60	14.54	14.68	14.69	14.55	14.56
2002	14.77	15.04	14.99	14.89	14.86	15.00	14.98	14.75	15.13	15.11	15.20	15.33	15.00
2003	15.15	15.08	15.07	14.70	14.84	14.78	14.70	14.66	14.66	14.75	14.80	14.76	14.83
Retail trade													
2001	10.61	10.88	11.02	11.04	10.96	11.03	11.19	10.96	10.94	10.77	10.85	10.96	10.93
2002	10.96	11.16	11.18	10.95	10.91	11.03	10.91	11.02	10.95	11.05	11.02	11.11	11.02
2003	11.23	11.25	11.40	11.23	11.21	11.21	11.16	11.28	11.33	11.20	11.19	11.22	11.24
Transportation and utilities													
2001	15.68	15.55	15.98	15.98	16.11	16.08	15.95	16.06	15.85	16.09	15.97	15.84	15.93
2002	13.95	14.11	14.22	14.17	13.92	14.09	14.22	14.39	14.27	14.49	14.56	14.58	14.25
2003	14.69	14.96	15.17	15.41	15.70	16.03	15.95	15.76	15.80	15.57	15.80	15.66	15.55
Financial activities													
2001	15.08	15.07	15.42	15.17	15.33	15.39	15.44	15.14	15.18	14.97	15.32	15.20	15.23
2002	15.22	15.26	15.16	15.33	15.27	15.42	15.40	15.39	15.15	15.32	15.24	15.25	15.29
2003	15.36	15.63	15.48	15.73	15.59	15.71	15.55	15.62	15.63	15.63	15.67	15.51	15.59
AKRON													
Manufacturing													
2001	13.80	13.93	13.89	13.78	13.75	13.83	13.77	13.72	14.14	14.15	14.34	14.49	13.96
2002	14.50	14.87	14.78	15.00	15.02	15.15	15.44	15.34	15.14	15.34	15.07	15.46	15.09
2003	15.56	15.70	15.59	15.55	15.53	15.78	16.09	15.85	15.28	15.10	15.09	14.75	15.49
Wholesale trade													
2001	13.78	13.68	13.80	14.11	14.22	14.68	15.05	14.76	14.86	14.63	14.67	14.69	14.42
2002	15.11	15.24	15.34	15.44	15.48	15.62	15.33	15.23	15.30	15.73	15.86	15.63	15.43
2003	16.17	15.71	15.73	15.89	16.17	15.72	16.24	15.79	16.41	15.88	15.81	15.74	15.93
Retail trade													
2001	10.63	10.26	10.28	10.84	10.17	10.65	10.38	10.48	10.75	10.81	11.54	11.24	10.68
2002	11.07	11.00	11.22	11.69	12.00	11.81	11.67	11.49	11.56	11.32	11.05	11.06	11.41
2003	11.07	11.11	11.03	10.82	10.72	10.66	10.64	10.71	11.07	10.84	10.70	10.37	10.81
Financial activities													
2001	16.57	16.71	16.36	17.01	16.96	16.82	16.80	16.32	16.07	15.71	15.43	15.90	16.38
2002	15.80	15.49	14.99	14.54	14.37	14.60	14.81	14.29	14.80	14.56	14.29	14.27	14.73
2003	13.97	13.42	13.86	13.74	13.68	13.92	13.85	13.95	14.38	14.08	14.40	14.12	13.94
CANTON													
Manufacturing													
2001	13.72	13.78	14.05	13.84	13.86	13.95	14.63	14.84	14.94	14.77	14.68	14.94	14.34
2002	14.44	14.63	14.79	14.53	14.49	14.76	14.76	14.52	14.82	14.83	14.81	14.84	14.68
2003	15.28	15.03	15.20	15.35	15.28	15.35	15.29	15.48	15.56	15.41	15.38	15.27	15.32
Retail trade													
2001	9.09	9.23	9.69	9.41	9.19	9.32	9.50	9.23	9.46	9.23	9.14	8.92	9.28
2002	8.93	8.80	8.96	8.67	8.67	8.50	8.56	8.57	8.65	8.56	8.43	8.44	8.64
2003	8.51	8.25	8.58	8.97	8.75	8.94	9.24	9.38	9.44	9.55	10.12	10.52	9.21
CINCINNATI													
Manufacturing													
2001	16.73	16.69	17.26	17.20	17.52	17.44	17.30	17.58	17.50	17.55	17.79	17.82	17.36
2002	17.76	18.07	17.90	17.92	17.75	17.36	17.12	17.42	17.51	17.82	17.89	18.05	17.72
2003	18.18	17.98	18.20	17.88	17.82	18.36	17.83	18.25	18.06	18.02	18.43	18.46	18.12
Trade, transportation, and utilities													
2001	15.06	15.27	15.55	16.36	15.84	15.95	16.17	15.60	16.25	15.73	16.10	16.29	15.84
2002	16.56	16.94	16.39	16.32	16.54	16.59	16.21	16.06	15.80	15.85	16.46	16.01	16.31
2003	16.69	16.61	16.37	16.31	16.22	16.09	16.46	16.52	16.81	16.97	16.26	16.16	16.45

Average Hourly Earnings by Industry: Ohio—*Continued*

(Dollars, not seasonally adjusted.)

Industry	January	February	March	April	May	June	July	August	September	October	November	December	Annual Average
CINCINNATI—*Continued*													
Wholesale trade													
2001	17.68	17.69	17.77	19.79	18.18	18.27	18.65	17.57	17.70	17.73	17.70	17.41	18.02
2002	18.92	18.62	17.81	17.88	17.84	18.01	18.05	18.00	17.90	17.95	18.64	18.58	18.18
2003	18.65	18.81	18.14	18.18	18.02	17.94	18.14	17.58	18.11	18.02	18.70	18.64	18.24
Retail trade													
2001	14.17	14.46	14.45	15.10	14.83	15.23	15.41	14.85	16.02	15.32	15.92	16.33	15.19
2002	15.98	16.77	16.29	16.37	16.68	16.69	15.68	15.52	15.27	15.27	15.44	14.97	15.92
2003	15.55	15.70	15.45	15.23	15.00	14.75	14.97	15.27	15.43	15.38	14.80	14.47	15.16
Financial activities													
2001	15.15	15.92	16.47	15.05	15.12	15.42	14.97	15.24	15.29	15.53	15.55	15.53	15.43
2002	15.32	15.55	15.65	15.45	15.38	15.24	15.15	15.49	14.88	15.16	14.92	15.42	15.30
2003	16.29	15.85	15.71	16.10	16.60	17.01	17.43	17.67	17.51	16.74	16.83	17.08	16.74
CLEVELAND													
Manufacturing													
2001	16.50	16.27	16.42	16.66	16.75	16.89	16.79	17.03	16.92	16.53	16.99	17.17	16.74
2002	16.99	17.11	17.10	17.07	17.21	17.33	17.04	17.01	17.31	17.06	17.37	17.47	17.17
2003	17.18	17.28	17.30	17.17	17.06	17.02	16.79	17.50	17.71	17.25	17.76	18.30	17.36
Trade, transportation, and utilities													
2001	11.70	11.88	12.07	12.22	12.32	12.37	12.41	12.27	12.21	12.39	12.33	11.94	12.18
2002	12.20	12.23	12.60	12.40	12.53	12.52	12.64	12.54	12.89	12.75	12.77	12.55	12.55
2003	12.63	12.67	13.00	12.87	13.09	13.00	13.16	13.03	12.93	12.83	12.95	12.77	12.91
Wholesale trade													
2001	14.05	14.46	14.48	14.78	14.99	15.00	15.19	14.62	14.41	14.91	14.98	15.13	14.75
2002	15.03	15.44	15.92	15.96	15.83	15.67	15.65	15.60	16.00	15.85	16.19	16.08	15.77
2003	15.92	15.92	15.84	15.90	16.07	15.96	15.95	15.34	15.38	15.07	15.46	15.45	15.69
Retail trade													
2001	10.39	10.42	10.66	10.67	10.70	10.53	10.71	10.81	10.85	10.75	10.92	10.45	10.65
2002	10.65	10.52	10.67	10.57	10.77	10.88	10.98	10.86	11.14	11.22	11.08	10.85	10.85
2003	10.94	11.02	11.55	11.33	11.43	11.46	11.51	11.84	11.50	11.34	11.41	11.30	11.39
Financial activities													
2001	15.66	15.63	16.03	16.06	16.08	16.03	16.29	16.18	16.09	16.33	16.22	16.70	16.11
2002	16.22	16.05	15.87	15.79	15.82	15.76	15.80	15.63	15.59	15.67	15.70	15.70	15.80
2003	16.24	16.58	16.33	16.90	16.68	17.11	17.34	18.32	18.65	18.48	17.71	17.55	17.33
COLUMBUS													
Manufacturing													
2001	13.97	14.14	14.44	14.45	14.62	15.01	14.78	15.04	15.11	15.15	15.23	15.37	14.77
2002	15.26	15.30	15.55	15.53	15.45	15.74	15.94	16.06	16.48	16.38	16.55	16.75	15.92
2003	16.72	16.90	17.13	17.18	17.31	17.35	17.05	17.27	17.23	17.09	17.20	17.53	17.16
Trade, transportation, and utilities													
2001	14.24	14.64	14.63	14.29	14.37	14.51	14.95	14.85	14.45	14.58	14.50	14.62	14.55
2002	13.72	13.66	13.47	13.29	13.40	13.43	13.58	13.80	13.82	13.84	13.75	13.61	13.61
2003	13.64	13.94	13.45	13.40	13.55	13.44	13.48	13.32	13.27	13.32	12.92	13.65	13.44
Wholesale trade													
2001	15.75	16.01	16.01	16.31	15.64	16.55	16.30	16.26	16.39	16.81	16.36	16.67	16.26
2002	16.40	16.47	16.26	16.28	16.47	16.62	16.80	16.37	16.71	16.59	16.81	16.61	16.53
2003	16.32	15.83	15.46	15.42	15.62	15.62	15.35	15.80	15.20	15.78	14.46	14.77	15.47
Retail trade													
2001	11.86	12.17	12.25	11.54	11.95	11.86	12.59	11.96	11.98	11.92	12.06	12.30	12.04
2002	12.25	12.17	11.94	11.63	11.60	11.57	11.65	12.16	12.09	12.12	11.90	12.11	11.93
2003	12.26	12.67	12.10	12.03	12.15	12.06	12.01	11.80	11.82	11.75	11.69	12.68	12.09
Transportation and utilities													
2001	18.98	19.58	19.47	19.64	19.71	19.88	20.18	20.91	19.05	19.18	19.35	19.58	19.62
2002	14.80	14.78	14.59	14.66	14.90	15.00	15.31	15.41	15.52	15.68	15.70	14.97	15.12
2003	15.07	15.76	15.40	15.45	15.58	15.55	15.92	15.26	15.43	15.40	14.65	15.61	15.41
Financial activities													
2001	17.64	17.90	17.98	18.15	18.84	18.98	19.42	18.87	19.10	18.82	19.24	19.09	18.67
2002	19.23	19.20	19.05	19.25	19.32	19.52	19.71	19.79	19.74	19.92	19.74	19.62	19.51
2003	19.65	19.68	19.58	19.90	19.76	20.02	20.29	19.68	19.81	19.73	19.59	19.33	19.75
YOUNGSTOWN-WARREN													
Manufacturing													
2001	18.27	18.56	18.66	18.97	19.33	19.18	18.83	19.43	19.68	19.45	19.38	19.93	19.13
2002	20.39	20.05	20.29	21.15	21.14	20.36	20.15	20.59	21.04	22.29	22.84	22.99	21.12
2003	22.82	22.80	22.64	21.52	22.11	22.57	22.96	22.62	23.09	22.05	21.80	21.89	22.41
Retail trade													
2001	9.32	9.36	9.36	9.38	9.48	9.45	9.36	9.33	9.65	9.68	9.48	9.61	9.46
2002	9.80	9.76	9.79	9.61	9.46	9.47	9.49	9.56	9.52	9.42	9.39	9.38	9.55
2003	9.36	9.09	9.16	9.21	9.42	9.02	9.29	9.53	9.52	9.58	9.45	9.62	9.36
Financial activities													
2001	9.85	9.91	10.30	10.12	10.29	10.23	9.92	10.01	10.07	9.76	10.29	10.34	10.09
2002	10.67	10.85	10.64	10.71	10.82	11.14	10.57	10.88	11.34	11.63	12.19	12.88	11.21
2003	12.68	12.72	12.60	12.10	12.15	12.03	11.91	11.75	11.99	11.27	11.55	11.85	12.04

Average Weekly Earnings by Industry: Ohio

(Dollars, not seasonally adjusted.)

Industry	January	February	March	April	May	June	July	August	September	October	November	December	Annual Average
STATEWIDE													
Goods-producing													
2001	697.06	688.58	693.04	681.38	709.21	717.70	707.06	721.41	732.06	720.66	743.93	752.11	713.40
2002	721.31	722.93	738.30	736.77	744.07	746.86	724.37	744.07	756.55	754.78	748.88	762.81	741.28
2003	750.92	741.34	751.74	735.68	740.95	735.26	718.77	753.75	773.50	760.35	753.38	754.17	746.82
Service-providing													
2001	403.17	411.68	418.92	420.89	413.63	416.99	421.79	415.98	417.62	410.04	415.90	421.47	415.58
2002	411.80	415.19	415.40	411.59	410.59	420.98	415.04	414.41	418.70	417.15	421.09	433.34	417.46
2003	422.59	427.50	430.90	426.42	427.31	428.50	428.38	426.19	428.56	426.69	430.87	428.42	428.56
Natural resources and mining													
2001	699.01	709.46	718.11	699.89	740.08	749.41	740.06	752.51	763.01	753.12	764.59	741.78	737.54
2002	695.95	676.85	678.03	702.57	687.04	694.03	709.49	715.57	719.80	701.18	705.28	691.53	699.05
2003	711.22	683.76	751.29	772.45	765.28	758.65	765.64	784.22	799.90	806.94	796.92	719.42	760.45
Construction													
2001	774.60	757.68	768.63	748.72	783.66	804.42	802.20	808.71	824.14	816.08	866.51	801.11	796.80
2002	805.34	811.59	823.94	809.09	815.76	816.44	829.78	820.85	825.60	830.99	791.19	774.31	814.25
2003	766.46	754.97	777.70	778.09	783.74	772.31	751.07	827.39	824.40	809.13	798.18	746.23	783.58
Manufacturing													
2001	679.39	672.40	674.85	666.11	690.92	692.54	678.88	695.04	705.95	692.03	710.11	738.18	691.75
2002	701.26	702.58	718.78	718.29	727.25	727.67	693.67	722.52	737.02	733.19	737.07	761.17	724.09
2003	747.00	738.16	745.61	723.79	728.29	723.90	708.02	732.63	757.44	745.20	740.10	757.69	738.00
Trade, transportation and utilities													
2001	392.50	400.05	410.22	420.88	416.67	421.84	425.10	416.99	413.45	407.36	413.45	417.58	412.49
2002	395.63	404.50	407.36	400.35	402.78	414.87	414.48	412.67	412.72	410.23	411.50	426.18	409.54
2003	406.69	412.15	416.96	414.74	423.79	426.07	430.27	426.71	432.93	428.65	428.01	424.08	422.17
Wholesale trade													
2001	524.81	529.47	539.31	553.47	549.03	535.76	546.85	537.28	539.43	535.82	539.12	541.26	538.72
2002	540.58	538.43	536.64	534.55	536.45	553.50	563.25	554.60	574.94	559.07	566.96	584.07	553.50
2003	548.43	551.93	551.56	536.55	546.11	537.99	548.31	530.69	548.28	561.98	550.56	538.74	545.74
Retail trade													
2001	299.20	305.73	311.87	319.06	316.74	320.97	330.11	320.03	317.26	309.10	310.31	325.51	315.88
2002	307.98	320.29	324.22	319.74	321.85	328.69	328.39	326.19	320.84	320.45	319.58	342.19	322.89
2003	322.30	327.38	335.16	333.53	337.42	340.78	338.15	342.91	341.03	333.76	333.46	339.97	334.95
Transportation and utilities													
2001	558.21	566.02	586.47	604.04	596.07	630.34	598.13	602.25	592.79	590.50	634.01	608.26	597.38
2002	528.71	536.18	538.94	518.62	523.39	545.28	530.41	543.94	539.41	543.38	556.19	546.75	537.23
2003	531.78	535.57	541.57	550.14	580.90	594.71	609.29	597.30	619.36	607.23	622.52	596.65	583.13
Financial activities													
2001	527.80	525.94	542.78	546.12	538.08	552.50	552.75	532.93	549.52	526.94	568.37	556.32	543.71
2002	537.27	543.26	536.66	539.62	548.19	562.83	549.78	547.88	549.95	539.26	539.50	549.00	545.85
2003	536.06	561.12	560.38	553.70	550.33	568.70	548.92	560.76	562.68	565.81	565.69	545.95	556.56
AKRON													
Manufacturing													
2001	553.38	564.17	558.38	545.69	552.75	543.52	534.28	532.34	555.70	553.27	577.90	585.40	554.21
2002	556.80	579.93	598.59	600.00	614.32	619.64	600.62	615.13	614.68	630.47	620.88	618.40	605.11
2003	639.52	651.55	639.19	642.22	635.18	634.36	638.77	629.25	617.31	616.08	624.73	618.03	631.99
Wholesale trade													
2001	478.17	473.33	478.86	495.26	492.01	503.52	516.22	516.60	526.04	525.22	538.39	559.69	509.03
2002	553.03	539.50	538.43	574.37	575.86	598.25	539.62	505.64	543.15	536.39	548.76	547.05	550.85
2003	540.08	573.42	558.42	556.15	531.99	570.64	579.77	565.28	584.20	579.62	596.04	596.55	568.70
Retail trade													
2001	296.58	285.23	282.70	311.11	291.88	306.72	301.02	299.73	305.30	317.81	330.04	338.32	305.45
2002	318.82	314.60	322.01	330.83	338.40	338.95	339.60	334.36	331.77	318.09	320.45	341.75	329.75
2003	309.96	312.19	314.36	299.71	294.80	299.55	293.66	321.30	317.71	305.69	304.95	312.14	307.00
Financial activities													
2001	705.88	718.53	695.30	733.13	676.70	721.58	692.16	674.02	684.58	614.26	685.09	659.85	689.60
2002	606.72	610.31	608.59	578.69	593.48	586.92	610.17	604.47	633.44	602.78	588.75	612.18	603.93
2003	602.11	574.38	564.10	561.97	586.87	570.72	574.78	578.93	578.08	574.46	583.20	564.80	575.72
CANTON													
Manufacturing													
2001	529.59	529.15	540.93	538.38	544.70	549.63	564.72	587.66	602.08	580.46	568.12	623.00	563.56
2002	555.94	585.20	587.16	581.20	588.29	602.21	602.21	585.16	582.43	570.96	587.96	601.02	585.73
2003	586.75	584.67	591.28	592.51	598.98	600.19	588.67	591.34	599.06	591.74	592.13	598.58	592.88
Retail trade													
2001	259.97	264.90	272.29	267.24	249.05	264.69	272.65	272.29	278.12	269.52	270.54	261.36	266.34
2002	252.72	256.08	259.84	260.10	254.03	247.35	253.38	250.24	249.99	253.38	245.31	259.11	253.15
2003	256.15	238.43	251.39	270.00	265.13	272.67	284.59	283.28	285.09	291.28	301.58	317.70	277.22
CINCINNATI													
Manufacturing													
2001	704.33	702.65	728.37	718.96	734.09	725.50	704.11	729.57	750.75	719.55	729.39	737.75	723.91
2002	721.06	726.41	733.90	720.38	729.53	706.55	674.53	715.96	735.42	752.00	756.75	796.01	731.84
2003	758.11	749.77	773.50	740.23	750.22	760.10	714.98	748.25	745.88	747.83	772.22	779.01	753.79
Trade, transportation, and utilities													
2001	506.02	503.91	510.04	539.88	514.80	518.38	527.14	510.12	533.00	522.24	526.47	553.86	521.14
2002	539.86	550.55	544.15	543.46	567.32	572.36	559.25	550.86	534.04	527.81	538.24	537.94	548.02
2003	552.44	564.74	554.94	536.60	541.75	540.62	549.76	573.24	574.90	570.19	546.34	544.59	554.37

Average Weekly Earnings by Industry: Ohio—*Continued*

(Dollars, not seasonally adjusted.)

Industry	January	February	March	April	May	June	July	August	September	October	November	December	Annual Average
CINCINNATI—*Continued*													
Wholesale trade													
2001	701.90	698.76	698.36	779.73	701.75	685.13	721.76	669.42	677.91	652.46	670.83	685.95	695.57
2002	675.44	647.98	662.53	641.89	672.57	682.58	698.54	691.20	687.36	707.23	719.50	741.34	685.39
2003	736.68	743.00	711.09	672.66	679.35	694.28	721.97	701.44	724.40	720.80	751.74	781.02	718.66
Retail trade													
2001	410.93	415.00	424.83	440.92	428.59	444.72	446.89	435.11	470.99	453.47	456.90	489.90	443.55
2002	468.21	499.75	493.59	491.10	522.08	534.08	500.19	488.88	456.57	438.25	453.94	446.11	482.38
2003	447.84	469.43	461.96	441.67	442.50	436.60	437.12	464.21	452.10	446.02	424.76	423.97	445.70
Financial activities													
2001	557.52	592.22	635.74	582.44	585.14	604.46	580.84	586.74	594.78	585.48	592.46	605.67	592.51
2002	582.16	598.68	600.96	588.65	582.90	573.02	563.58	568.48	566.93	560.92	552.04	573.62	575.28
2003	589.70	576.94	581.27	589.26	607.56	636.17	637.94	655.56	660.13	639.47	647.96	659.29	622.73
CLEVELAND													
Manufacturing													
2001	679.80	660.56	656.80	649.74	683.40	682.36	680.00	682.90	690.34	659.55	693.19	715.99	677.97
2002	681.30	694.67	716.49	703.28	717.66	726.13	693.53	719.52	735.68	713.11	729.54	738.98	714.27
2003	716.41	727.49	728.33	719.42	707.99	701.22	683.35	693.00	724.34	705.53	735.26	764.94	716.97
Trade, transportation, and utilities													
2001	358.02	354.02	364.51	392.26	394.24	395.84	400.84	386.51	394.38	381.61	378.53	379.69	382.45
2002	366.00	366.90	378.00	373.24	385.92	390.62	386.78	379.96	402.17	388.88	393.32	404.11	384.03
2003	376.37	391.50	395.20	396.40	404.48	400.40	406.64	401.32	413.76	411.84	414.40	418.86	402.79
Wholesale trade													
2001	560.60	548.03	558.93	563.12	575.62	598.50	600.01	549.71	551.90	539.74	534.79	547.71	560.50
2002	548.60	509.52	552.42	557.00	563.55	573.52	552.45	563.16	616.00	573.77	597.41	607.82	567.72
2003	573.12	584.26	600.34	566.04	605.84	571.37	598.13	547.64	569.06	584.72	592.12	573.20	580.53
Retail trade													
2001	268.06	263.63	276.09	287.02	286.76	279.05	290.24	290.79	299.46	284.88	289.38	295.74	284.36
2002	279.03	288.25	292.36	285.39	294.02	302.46	306.34	291.05	304.12	301.82	303.59	313.57	297.29
2003	277.88	296.44	301.46	304.78	310.90	314.00	311.92	330.34	328.90	318.65	321.76	336.74	313.23
Financial activities													
2001	527.74	531.42	554.64	570.13	559.58	553.04	571.78	564.68	543.84	540.52	528.77	557.78	550.96
2002	535.26	532.86	518.95	522.65	531.55	545.30	522.98	559.55	561.24	543.75	554.21	580.90	541.94
2003	583.02	608.49	602.58	616.85	600.48	610.83	617.30	674.18	719.89	685.61	676.52	661.64	637.74
COLUMBUS													
Manufacturing													
2001	556.01	564.19	579.04	575.11	599.42	612.41	601.55	615.14	619.51	610.55	618.34	642.47	598.19
2002	608.87	604.35	611.12	619.65	621.09	639.04	624.85	642.40	669.09	656.84	673.59	685.08	638.39
2003	670.47	674.31	698.90	671.74	692.40	674.92	654.72	675.26	685.75	680.18	696.60	699.45	681.25
Trade, transportation, and utilities													
2001	408.69	427.49	430.12	417.27	428.23	432.40	445.51	441.05	433.50	437.40	433.55	457.61	432.14
2002	408.86	411.17	402.75	401.36	406.02	413.64	420.98	426.42	433.95	440.11	430.38	442.33	419.19
2003	435.12	437.72	434.44	431.48	445.80	443.52	454.28	443.56	445.87	436.90	444.45	466.83	443.52
Wholesale trade													
2001	497.70	523.53	526.73	538.23	542.71	544.50	539.53	534.95	545.79	581.63	552.97	573.45	541.46
2002	547.76	543.51	539.83	543.75	561.63	570.07	561.12	525.48	548.09	562.40	566.50	558.10	552.10
2003	522.24	506.56	491.63	473.39	492.03	485.78	517.30	518.24	512.24	504.96	516.22	477.07	501.23
Retail trade													
2001	320.22	332.24	336.88	317.35	333.41	336.82	358.82	333.68	339.03	330.18	336.47	367.77	337.12
2002	336.88	341.98	327.16	322.15	319.00	325.12	332.03	346.56	355.45	361.18	343.91	372.99	340.01
2003	377.61	387.70	381.15	380.15	390.02	397.98	393.93	381.14	381.79	372.48	372.91	432.39	388.09
Transportation and utilities													
2001	584.58	608.94	609.41	597.06	599.18	616.28	609.44	667.03	611.51	617.60	630.81	648.10	616.07
2002	494.32	489.22	504.81	511.63	525.97	534.00	552.69	568.63	561.82	564.48	576.19	555.39	536.76
2003	533.48	524.81	542.08	548.48	567.11	542.70	581.08	563.09	578.63	572.88	600.65	566.64	559.38
Financial activities													
2001	612.11	628.29	634.69	660.66	680.12	688.97	706.89	696.30	710.52	696.34	713.80	712.06	677.72
2002	719.20	716.16	722.00	748.83	738.02	749.57	739.13	750.04	777.76	766.92	732.35	725.94	741.38
2003	721.16	732.10	730.33	726.35	719.26	772.77	771.02	738.00	734.95	745.79	765.97	699.75	738.65
YOUNGSTOWN-WARREN													
Manufacturing													
2001	752.72	749.82	763.19	787.26	802.20	794.05	777.68	810.23	800.98	799.40	782.95	819.12	786.24
2002	815.60	818.04	817.69	881.96	879.42	820.51	781.82	825.66	866.85	938.41	931.87	967.88	861.70
2003	915.08	912.00	896.54	845.74	877.77	902.80	844.93	873.13	918.98	912.87	898.16	917.19	894.16
Retail trade													
2001	298.24	297.65	297.65	312.35	312.84	311.85	321.98	306.96	318.45	311.70	306.20	326.74	310.29
2002	309.68	311.34	313.28	318.09	322.59	313.46	317.92	300.18	297.02	294.85	288.27	307.66	307.51
2003	275.18	276.34	271.14	264.33	276.95	271.50	288.92	295.43	282.74	283.57	280.67	290.52	279.86
Financial activities													
2001	348.69	357.75	352.26	362.30	364.27	347.82	344.22	338.34	340.37	330.86	342.66	337.08	347.10
2002	332.90	350.46	341.54	347.00	367.88	379.87	350.92	360.13	388.96	368.67	403.49	443.07	369.93
2003	442.53	452.83	449.82	421.08	427.68	411.43	393.03	399.50	414.85	391.07	415.80	424.23	420.20

OKLAHOMA AT A GLANCE

(Population and total nonfarm employment numbers in thousands)

Population, Census 2000:	3,450.7
Total nonfarm employment, 2003:	1,450.6
Change in total nonfarm employment	
(Number)	
1990–2003:	254.8
1990–2001:	311.0
2001–2003:	-56.2
(Compound annual rate of change)	
1990–2003:	1.5%
1990–2001:	2.1%
2001–2003:	-1.9%
Unemployment rate	
1990:	5.7%
2001:	3.7%
2003:	5.6%

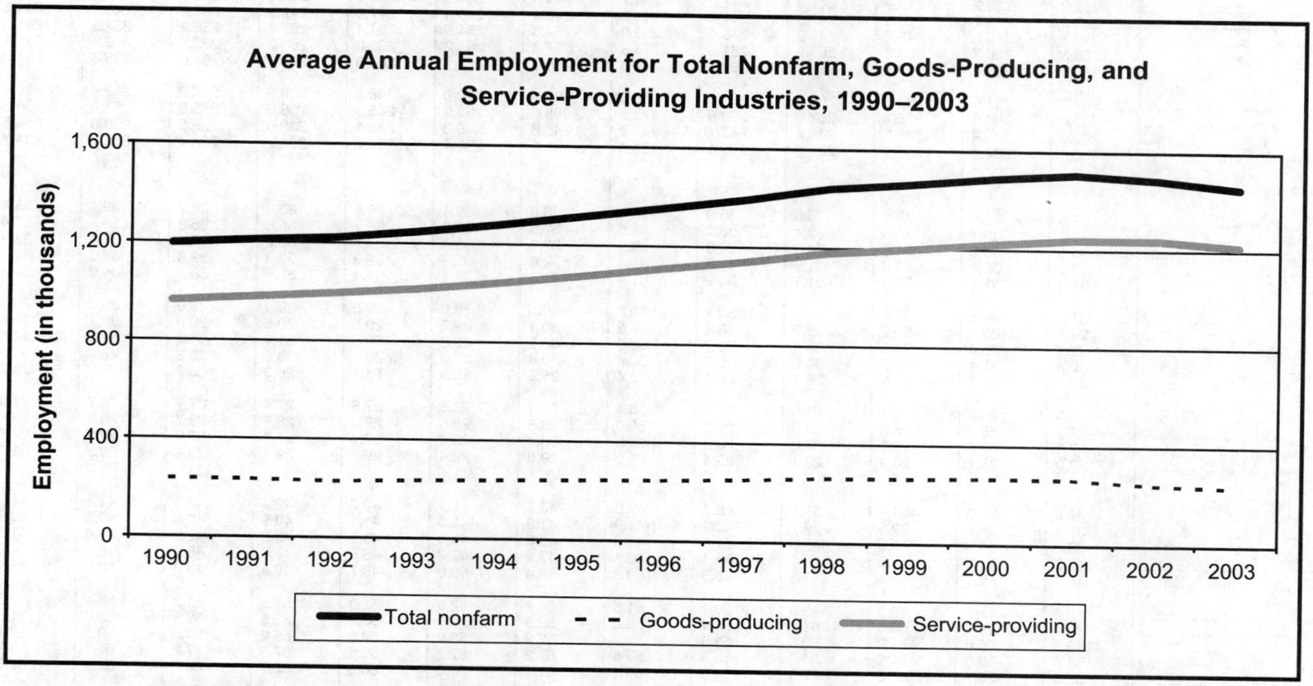

Total nonfarm payroll employment grew steadily throughout the 1990–2001 period, but declined significantly following the 2001 recession. While much of this was accounted for by a fall in goods-producing jobs, employment in service-providing industries also deteriorated. Retail trade was particularly impacted by the recession, losing 10,000 jobs from 2000 to 2003. Professional and business services lost another 8,800 jobs during this time. As a result, the total nonfarm job count in 2003 remained well below its 2001 peak.

Employment by Industry: Oklahoma

(Numbers in thousands. Not seasonally adjusted.)

Industry	January	February	March	April	May	June	July	August	September	October	November	December	Annual Average
STATEWIDE													
Total nonfarm													
1990	1163.6	1174.2	1183.7	1190.4	1200.2	1204.3	1189.5	1197.3	1213.3	1208.8	1211.3	1213.2	1195.8
1991	1185.7	1195.5	1205.8	1213.4	1220.9	1218.5	1197.5	1203.3	1219.3	1222.2	1223.9	1225.8	1210.9
1992	1200.8	1202.4	1210.0	1219.7	1228.1	1221.5	1212.3	1214.0	1231.3	1239.0	1238.8	1241.7	1221.6
1993	1216.7	1226.1	1235.1	1242.3	1247.9	1250.7	1243.2	1244.4	1257.0	1262.9	1264.6	1272.2	1246.9
1994	1245.0	1250.4	1261.8	1272.8	1280.0	1283.9	1277.5	1279.4	1296.4	1295.2	1301.4	1310.0	1279.4
1995	1281.2	1291.7	1301.7	1308.4	1317.8	1319.5	1306.1	1312.2	1327.5	1334.2	1340.4	1347.0	1315.6
1996	1315.8	1324.7	1340.8	1345.1	1361.0	1358.5	1344.7	1356.5	1366.1	1371.0	1375.5	1381.7	1353.4
1997	1351.2	1363.3	1376.4	1377.3	1392.3	1394.6	1384.7	1390.2	1405.6	1420.3	1424.0	1430.6	1392.5
1998	1404.0	1415.6	1427.1	1437.6	1451.0	1446.1	1433.4	1438.0	1450.2	1458.4	1462.5	1470.1	1441.1
1999	1432.8	1444.6	1452.9	1458.4	1466.9	1462.4	1453.8	1458.1	1471.9	1474.8	1479.8	1486.3	1461.9
2000	1447.4	1456.6	1473.0	1483.4	1499.7	1497.9	1480.0	1488.9	1504.6	1507.8	1516.9	1516.9	1489.4
2001	1480.4	1493.0	1506.7	1516.1	1525.2	1519.9	1493.9	1501.8	1512.1	1505.8	1514.8	1511.4	1506.8
2002	1468.5	1476.8	1487.6	1496.7	1508.8	1493.7	1474.1	1482.8	1488.4	1484.5	1489.3	1486.7	1486.5
2003	1449.0	1452.9	1456.4	1459.6	1467.4	1451.5	1426.0	1433.6	1444.8	1455.6	1456.3	1454.3	1450.6
Total private													
1990	902.2	906.7	916.1	925.4	933.7	948.7	945.0	951.1	951.1	940.6	943.0	943.6	933.9
1991	922.0	927.1	935.6	943.6	951.3	961.5	952.4	956.5	953.2	949.1	949.9	950.6	946.0
1992	930.6	928.5	934.6	944.8	952.4	957.2	958.7	961.1	961.7	962.0	962.1	964.2	951.4
1993	943.9	949.2	958.9	966.6	971.5	983.8	987.4	990.1	990.9	992.5	992.8	998.5	977.1
1994	975.3	977.3	987.1	998.6	1005.2	1017.0	1021.0	1023.5	1026.4	1020.9	1026.2	1033.5	1009.3
1995	1012.3	1017.9	1027.2	1035.2	1043.2	1054.2	1050.6	1056.7	1058.3	1059.9	1065.1	1070.9	1045.9
1996	1046.0	1050.5	1064.5	1069.2	1083.4	1092.1	1087.9	1098.5	1096.2	1094.2	1098.1	1103.8	1082.0
1997	1078.3	1085.5	1097.1	1098.3	1110.9	1124.0	1122.7	1126.9	1128.4	1136.8	1141.1	1146.1	1116.3
1998	1128.5	1135.3	1145.6	1157.1	1167.7	1173.9	1169.6	1172.5	1171.0	1173.4	1177.5	1183.1	1162.9
1999	1154.4	1159.7	1166.5	1171.6	1179.1	1185.1	1185.9	1187.7	1188.1	1186.0	1190.9	1196.7	1179.3
2000	1164.5	1167.8	1180.5	1192.1	1201.8	1212.9	1210.0	1217.8	1217.8	1213.3	1220.7	1221.3	1201.7
2001	1188.4	1194.5	1206.3	1216.0	1222.3	1230.3	1216.1	1221.2	1214.2	1201.4	1207.7	1205.5	1210.3
2002	1170.2	1172.8	1181.9	1190.8	1199.3	1198.2	1189.8	1196.0	1188.6	1177.9	1182.0	1179.5	1185.6
2003	1153.9	1151.8	1155.6	1159.7	1166.7	1163.0	1155.6	1160.8	1156.2	1160.9	1161.5	1158.4	1158.7
Goods-producing													
1990	227.6	229.1	231.7	234.2	236.4	240.8	240.9	240.1	240.0	239.6	238.2	236.9	236.2
1991	230.3	233.5	234.2	235.2	236.4	239.5	236.6	237.3	234.6	232.7	231.7	231.1	234.4
1992	227.8	223.1	223.8	226.8	227.8	228.2	229.9	230.9	230.2	231.1	229.8	230.0	228.2
1993	226.9	227.9	229.2	230.7	231.9	235.3	237.2	237.8	236.5	237.6	237.3	237.4	233.8
1994	233.4	232.5	234.3	235.3	237.1	240.6	241.6	241.9	242.2	240.1	241.0	242.5	238.5
1995	238.9	239.2	240.9	241.8	242.6	244.7	244.0	244.8	243.0	242.2	242.0	242.7	242.2
1996	238.8	239.1	240.8	241.9	244.6	246.8	246.4	248.3	247.2	247.0	247.4	248.1	244.7
1997	245.1	246.5	248.5	246.2	248.9	253.0	254.3	254.8	254.4	257.3	256.9	257.5	251.9
1998	256.3	258.7	259.8	259.9	261.3	264.3	261.3	264.2	263.0	263.2	262.8	263.4	261.5
1999	260.9	260.8	260.9	260.0	262.3	264.6	265.0	265.1	264.8	264.2	264.0	265.6	263.2
2000	261.3	261.6	264.1	263.5	265.6	268.5	268.6	270.0	268.8	266.9	267.6	269.4	266.3
2001	263.0	264.6	266.7	267.0	268.9	272.3	268.0	266.9	265.5	258.9	258.9	257.4	264.8
2002	246.3	245.9	246.3	245.4	247.7	248.2	246.6	246.3	243.1	240.6	239.5	239.0	244.6
2003	236.4	234.8	235.3	234.6	235.1	234.0	235.0	236.1	234.2	234.2	234.4	232.7	234.7
Natural resources and mining													
1990	37.6	37.4	37.4	38.0	38.0	39.1	38.8	39.1	38.5	38.8	38.7	39.4	38.4
1991	38.3	38.1	38.3	38.4	38.2	38.5	37.5	37.3	36.7	36.0	35.8	35.8	37.4
1992	35.3	35.2	34.8	34.5	34.3	33.5	33.7	33.4	33.1	33.2	33.0	33.4	33.9
1993	32.9	32.4	32.2	31.9	31.8	32.4	32.6	32.7	32.3	32.3	32.3	32.9	32.3
1994	31.9	31.2	31.3	31.1	30.9	31.4	31.5	31.4	31.4	30.6	30.7	30.9	31.1
1995	31.0	30.5	30.5	30.4	30.4	30.3	30.5	30.8	30.5	29.9	29.9	30.2	30.4
1996	29.8	29.8	29.9	29.7	30.2	30.2	30.1	29.9	29.6	29.5	29.8	30.1	29.8
1997	29.9	30.4	30.5	30.0	30.2	30.8	30.9	30.8	30.5	31.4	31.3	31.6	30.6
1998	30.9	31.4	31.7	30.2	30.3	30.6	30.4	30.3	30.1	28.5	28.3	28.3	30.0
1999	28.5	27.8	27.5	26.1	26.4	26.4	25.6	25.8	25.7	26.3	26.3	26.7	26.6
2000	26.6	26.7	26.7	25.6	26.1	26.4	27.3	27.5	27.6	27.4	27.7	28.7	27.0
2001	27.9	28.5	28.8	28.6	29.1	30.0	29.6	29.6	29.0	28.7	28.7	28.5	28.9
2002	27.8	27.7	27.7	27.8	28.3	28.5	28.4	28.4	27.7	27.3	27.2	27.3	27.8
2003	28.0	28.1	28.2	28.1	28.4	29.0	29.0	29.4	29.2	29.4	29.9	29.5	28.9
Construction													
1990	38.5	38.0	38.4	39.7	40.7	42.6	43.7	44.4	42.7	42.7	42.6	41.1	41.2
1991	37.5	38.9	39.8	39.7	40.3	41.9	41.8	42.1	41.1	40.9	40.4	40.3	40.3
1992	38.9	38.9	40.3	40.5	41.0	41.5	43.2	44.0	43.2	43.2	42.2	41.6	41.5
1993	40.2	41.2	42.3	43.4	44.1	46.1	47.2	47.2	46.6	46.8	46.9	46.7	44.8
1994	45.1	45.1	46.3	47.5	48.5	50.3	50.4	50.0	49.7	49.4	49.6	50.0	48.4
1995	47.6	47.7	48.3	49.5	50.1	51.6	51.7	52.0	51.3	51.5	51.2	51.1	50.3
1996	49.4	49.3	50.0	51.1	52.4	53.2	52.8	53.7	53.1	52.6	52.3	52.0	51.8
1997	49.9	50.0	51.3	50.6	51.6	52.7	52.9	52.9	52.8	55.2	54.6	53.5	52.3
1998	51.8	53.0	54.2	54.6	55.9	57.5	57.2	57.2	56.5	57.3	57.2	57.1	55.7
1999	56.5	56.7	57.3	57.9	58.8	60.1	61.1	61.0	60.8	60.7	60.2	60.2	59.3
2000	58.3	58.3	59.9	61.3	62.4	63.4	63.0	63.8	63.1	63.3	62.7	62.4	61.8
2001	60.6	62.5	65.0	66.3	67.6	69.4	68.9	69.5	67.6	66.3	65.1	64.4	66.1
2002	63.1	63.3	63.7	63.6	65.2	65.9	66.5	66.4	64.8	64.0	63.3	63.1	64.4
2003	61.9	61.2	61.8	63.4	64.2	65.6	64.8	64.5	63.2	62.1	61.6	60.5	62.9

Employment by Industry: Oklahoma—*Continued*

(Numbers in thousands. Not seasonally adjusted.)

Industry	January	February	March	April	May	June	July	August	September	October	November	December	Annual Average
STATEWIDE—*Continued*													
Manufacturing													
1990	151.5	153.7	155.9	156.5	157.7	159.1	158.4	156.6	158.8	158.1	156.9	156.4	156.6
1991	154.5	156.5	156.1	157.1	157.9	159.1	157.3	157.9	156.8	155.8	155.5	155.0	156.6
1992	153.6	149.0	148.7	151.8	152.5	153.2	153.0	153.5	153.9	154.7	154.6	155.0	152.7
1993	153.8	154.3	154.7	155.4	156.0	156.8	157.4	157.9	157.6	158.5	158.1	157.8	156.5
1994	156.4	156.2	156.7	156.7	157.7	158.9	159.7	160.5	161.1	160.1	160.7	161.6	158.8
1995	160.3	161.0	162.1	161.9	162.1	162.8	161.8	162.0	161.2	160.8	160.9	161.4	161.5
1996	159.6	160.0	160.9	161.1	162.0	163.4	163.5	164.7	164.5	164.9	165.3	166.0	162.9
1997	165.3	166.1	166.7	165.6	167.1	169.5	170.5	171.1	171.1	170.7	171.0	172.4	168.9
1998	173.6	174.3	173.9	175.1	175.1	176.2	173.7	176.7	176.4	177.4	177.3	178.0	175.6
1999	175.9	176.3	176.1	176.0	177.1	178.1	178.3	178.3	178.3	177.2	177.5	178.7	177.3
2000	176.4	176.6	177.5	176.6	177.1	178.7	178.3	178.7	178.1	176.2	177.2	178.3	177.5
2001	174.5	173.6	172.9	172.1	172.2	172.9	169.5	167.8	168.9	163.9	165.1	164.5	169.8
2002	155.4	154.9	154.9	154.0	154.2	153.8	151.7	151.5	150.6	149.3	149.0	148.6	152.3
2003	146.5	145.5	145.3	143.1	142.5	139.4	141.2	142.2	141.8	142.7	142.9	142.7	143.0
Service-providing													
1990	936.0	945.1	952.0	956.2	963.8	963.5	948.6	957.2	973.3	969.2	973.1	976.3	959.5
1991	955.4	962.0	971.6	978.2	984.5	979.0	960.9	966.0	984.7	989.5	992.2	994.7	976.5
1992	973.0	979.3	986.2	992.9	1000.3	993.3	982.4	983.1	1001.1	1007.9	1009.0	1011.7	993.3
1993	989.8	998.2	1005.9	1011.6	1016.0	1015.4	1006.0	1006.6	1020.5	1025.3	1027.3	1034.8	1013.1
1994	1011.6	1017.9	1027.5	1037.5	1042.9	1043.3	1035.9	1037.5	1054.2	1055.1	1060.4	1067.5	1040.9
1995	1042.3	1052.5	1060.8	1066.6	1075.2	1074.8	1062.1	1067.4	1084.5	1092.0	1098.4	1104.3	1073.4
1996	1077.0	1085.6	1100.0	1103.2	1116.4	1111.7	1098.3	1108.2	1118.9	1124.0	1128.1	1133.6	1108.7
1997	1106.1	1116.8	1127.9	1131.1	1143.4	1141.6	1130.4	1135.4	1151.2	1163.0	1167.1	1173.1	1140.5
1998	1147.7	1156.9	1167.3	1177.7	1189.7	1181.8	1172.1	1173.8	1187.2	1195.2	1199.7	1206.7	1179.6
1999	1171.9	1183.8	1192.0	1198.4	1204.6	1197.8	1188.8	1193.0	1207.1	1210.6	1215.8	1220.7	1198.7
2000	1186.1	1195.0	1208.9	1219.9	1234.1	1229.4	1211.4	1218.9	1235.8	1240.9	1249.3	1247.5	1223.1
2001	1217.4	1228.4	1240.0	1249.1	1256.3	1247.6	1225.9	1234.9	1246.6	1246.9	1255.9	1254.0	1241.9
2002	1222.2	1230.9	1241.3	1251.3	1261.1	1245.5	1227.5	1236.5	1245.3	1243.9	1249.8	1247.7	1241.9
2003	1212.6	1218.1	1221.1	1225.0	1232.3	1217.5	1191.0	1197.5	1210.6	1221.4	1221.9	1221.6	1215.9
Trade, transportation, and utilities													
1990	244.1	242.3	243.5	244.2	246.5	250.6	249.2	251.4	250.1	249.1	252.7	255.2	248.2
1991	244.6	241.5	242.9	244.6	247.7	249.8	249.1	248.5	248.1	249.7	252.8	255.3	247.8
1992	247.1	244.7	245.4	246.9	249.7	251.5	250.9	250.4	249.9	251.1	254.4	257.0	249.9
1993	246.8	244.7	246.7	247.9	249.5	252.8	255.3	256.4	256.1	258.6	261.9	265.3	253.5
1994	253.8	253.0	254.6	256.7	258.6	261.2	261.8	261.8	261.5	261.3	265.6	269.8	259.9
1995	260.9	259.3	260.1	261.8	262.9	266.1	265.4	266.4	266.4	268.9	273.4	276.8	265.7
1996	267.6	264.9	268.0	267.7	271.5	273.2	271.6	274.0	272.6	274.4	280.0	284.0	272.4
1997	272.0	270.4	273.5	272.6	275.4	278.4	278.6	280.2	279.5	282.4	287.6	291.7	278.5
1998	281.8	280.4	282.6	284.7	287.0	288.1	286.5	287.6	286.9	292.1	296.0	299.1	287.7
1999	285.1	283.4	285.5	285.8	287.3	288.6	289.3	290.0	290.1	291.1	295.8	299.7	289.3
2000	288.0	286.0	287.4	289.9	292.7	295.2	293.3	295.8	295.8	296.8	303.0	305.3	294.1
2001	290.7	287.8	289.3	289.9	291.2	292.4	288.1	288.7	286.7	287.0	291.5	293.3	289.7
2002	283.8	281.7	284.3	284.3	285.5	285.4	283.0	283.6	282.4	281.3	286.1	287.9	284.1
2003	276.6	274.5	275.6	276.3	277.9	277.0	274.3	275.6	275.2	278.2	280.9	283.7	277.2
Wholesale trade													
1990	48.8	48.8	49.2	49.7	50.1	51.4	51.5	51.8	51.4	50.9	51.0	50.7	50.4
1991	48.7	48.7	49.1	49.7	50.0	50.3	49.8	49.9	49.9	50.4	50.4	50.4	49.7
1992	49.2	48.9	49.0	49.5	49.9	50.5	49.8	49.5	49.5	49.8	50.0	49.8	49.6
1993	48.7	48.7	49.1	49.3	49.5	50.2	50.1	49.8	49.7	50.8	50.9	50.8	49.8
1994	49.6	49.2	49.5	49.9	50.0	50.9	50.6	50.6	50.9	51.0	51.2	51.3	50.3
1995	50.7	50.9	51.3	51.5	51.9	52.8	52.3	52.3	52.5	52.5	52.8	52.7	52.0
1996	51.7	51.8	52.3	52.1	52.8	53.3	53.1	53.1	53.0	53.6	53.6	53.7	52.8
1997	53.1	53.3	53.7	53.0	53.5	54.3	54.5	54.3	54.1	55.0	55.0	55.1	54.0
1998	55.0	55.1	55.3	55.2	55.8	56.3	56.2	56.3	56.0	57.3	57.4	57.6	56.1
1999	56.6	56.8	57.3	57.2	57.2	57.7	56.7	56.4	56.2	56.6	56.8	56.7	56.9
2000	55.9	56.0	56.4	56.4	56.7	58.3	57.2	57.7	57.6	57.5	57.5	57.6	57.1
2001	56.0	55.9	56.4	56.6	56.9	57.7	57.0	57.1	56.9	56.8	56.7	57.0	56.7
2002	56.4	56.1	56.5	56.2	56.6	57.0	56.8	56.9	56.6	56.0	56.1	56.1	56.4
2003	54.9	54.5	54.9	54.6	55.0	55.3	54.5	54.3	54.5	54.2	53.9	54.7	54.6
Retail trade													
1990	144.3	142.2	142.8	142.7	143.9	145.4	144.3	146.3	145.6	144.9	148.1	150.5	145.0
1991	144.8	141.6	142.5	143.6	145.9	146.9	145.9	145.2	145.0	146.5	149.6	151.6	145.7
1992	144.5	142.8	143.4	144.5	146.6	147.4	147.9	148.0	147.9	148.0	151.1	154.0	147.1
1993	146.0	144.0	145.5	146.7	147.6	149.6	150.6	151.5	151.5	152.1	155.3	158.3	149.8
1994	150.7	149.9	151.0	152.6	153.8	155.2	155.9	156.8	156.4	156.2	160.3	163.9	155.2
1995	156.8	154.9	155.1	156.4	157.3	158.9	158.9	159.9	159.7	161.2	165.1	168.4	159.3
1996	159.2	156.4	158.8	158.7	161.3	162.1	162.3	164.5	163.9	164.3	169.6	173.3	162.8
1997	162.9	160.9	162.7	163.0	164.8	165.9	166.2	167.7	167.6	168.9	173.0	176.8	166.7
1998	167.9	166.2	167.8	170.2	171.3	171.7	170.1	171.0	170.9	174.3	179.3	182.5	171.9
1999	171.6	169.9	171.8	171.6	172.9	173.5	174.7	175.5	175.8	176.7	181.5	185.2	175.1
2000	175.4	173.5	174.5	176.0	178.2	178.6	178.0	179.8	180.2	181.0	187.2	189.4	179.3
2001	176.2	173.6	174.5	174.6	175.5	175.9	172.8	173.4	172.5	173.2	177.9	179.8	174.9
2002	172.0	170.2	172.2	172.5	173.2	172.5	170.2	170.9	170.1	169.7	174.7	176.9	172.1
2003	167.6	165.8	166.6	168.0	169.1	168.5	166.8	168.2	167.9	171.5	174.7	176.7	169.3

Employment by Industry: Oklahoma—*Continued*

(Numbers in thousands. Not seasonally adjusted.)

Industry	January	February	March	April	May	June	July	August	September	October	November	December	Annual Average
STATEWIDE—*Continued*													
Transportation and utilities													
1990	51.0	51.3	51.5	51.8	52.5	53.8	53.4	53.3	53.1	53.3	53.6	54.0	52.7
1991	51.1	51.2	51.3	51.3	51.8	52.6	53.4	53.4	53.2	52.8	52.8	53.3	52.3
1992	53.4	53.0	53.0	52.9	53.2	53.6	53.2	52.9	52.5	53.3	53.3	53.2	53.1
1993	52.1	52.0	52.1	51.9	52.4	53.0	54.6	55.1	54.9	55.7	55.7	56.2	53.8
1994	53.5	53.9	54.1	54.2	54.8	55.1	55.3	54.4	54.2	54.1	54.1	54.6	54.3
1995	53.4	53.5	53.7	53.9	53.7	54.4	54.2	54.2	54.2	55.2	55.5	55.7	54.3
1996	56.7	56.7	56.9	56.9	57.4	57.8	56.2	56.4	55.7	56.5	56.8	57.0	56.7
1997	56.0	56.2	57.1	56.6	57.1	58.2	57.9	58.2	57.8	58.5	59.6	59.8	57.7
1998	58.9	59.1	59.5	59.3	59.9	60.1	60.2	60.3	60.0	60.5	59.3	59.0	59.6
1999	56.9	56.7	56.4	57.0	57.2	57.4	57.9	58.1	58.1	57.8	57.5	57.8	57.4
2000	56.7	56.5	56.5	57.5	57.8	58.3	58.1	58.3	58.0	58.3	58.3	58.3	57.7
2001	58.5	58.3	58.4	58.7	58.8	58.8	58.3	58.2	57.3	57.0	56.9	56.5	57.9
2002	55.4	55.4	55.6	55.6	55.7	55.9	56.0	55.8	55.7	55.6	55.3	54.9	55.6
2003	54.1	54.2	54.1	53.7	53.8	53.2	53.0	53.1	52.8	52.5	52.3	52.3	53.3
Information													
1990	22.6	22.5	22.5	22.7	22.9	23.2	23.1	23.2	23.1	23.0	23.0	23.0	22.9
1991	22.6	22.8	23.0	22.9	23.2	23.3	23.2	23.3	23.2	22.9	22.9	23.0	23.0
1992	22.5	22.6	22.7	22.8	23.0	23.1	23.0	23.0	23.1	22.8	22.8	23.1	22.8
1993	23.0	22.9	23.1	23.1	23.3	23.7	23.7	23.7	23.7	23.2	23.2	23.6	23.3
1994	23.4	23.5	23.6	23.9	24.0	24.3	24.3	24.3	24.4	24.2	24.4	24.8	24.0
1995	24.4	24.5	24.7	25.0	25.2	25.5	25.9	25.7	25.8	25.7	25.9	26.3	25.3
1996	26.1	26.3	26.7	27.0	27.3	27.6	28.2	28.4	28.4	28.8	28.9	29.2	27.7
1997	29.2	29.3	29.4	29.7	30.0	30.4	30.3	30.3	30.3	30.4	30.8	31.0	30.0
1998	31.2	31.3	31.2	31.1	31.5	31.6	31.6	31.9	31.9	32.0	32.6	32.8	31.7
1999	32.1	33.1	32.5	32.1	32.4	33.4	32.9	33.1	33.2	33.0	33.2	33.5	32.9
2000	34.0	34.5	34.6	34.9	35.1	35.7	36.1	36.3	36.7	36.2	36.6	36.8	35.6
2001	36.7	37.0	36.5	36.9	36.7	36.4	36.6	37.4	37.5	37.5	38.0	37.8	37.0
2002	36.8	36.9	36.4	35.6	35.4	35.1	35.0	34.9	34.5	34.3	34.4	34.0	35.3
2003	33.5	33.2	32.9	32.7	32.8	32.5	31.9	31.6	31.4	30.7	30.6	30.3	32.0
Financial activities													
1990	66.8	66.9	67.2	68.0	68.5	69.2	68.8	69.2	68.5	67.2	67.5	67.7	67.9
1991	66.9	66.7	67.3	67.8	68.4	69.1	68.9	68.9	68.3	67.8	67.7	67.9	67.9
1992	66.2	66.5	66.5	66.8	67.5	68.0	67.6	67.5	67.0	67.6	67.5	67.8	67.2
1993	66.5	66.7	67.1	68.1	68.4	68.9	69.4	69.2	68.8	68.9	68.5	69.3	68.3
1994	69.0	69.2	69.9	70.4	71.0	71.7	71.8	71.4	71.3	70.5	70.5	71.1	70.6
1995	70.3	70.8	71.2	72.0	72.8	74.1	74.5	75.0	75.2	75.2	75.9	76.9	73.6
1996	75.7	76.4	77.8	77.8	78.4	78.9	78.7	78.8	78.0	78.0	77.7	78.0	77.8
1997	76.7	76.5	76.5	77.0	77.7	78.9	79.8	79.6	79.2	78.4	78.3	78.7	78.1
1998	78.8	79.0	79.7	79.9	80.6	81.6	81.7	81.6	81.0	81.1	81.4	82.0	80.7
1999	80.1	80.5	80.9	81.0	81.7	82.3	82.7	82.6	81.9	81.2	81.4	81.8	81.5
2000	80.4	80.6	80.7	81.3	81.9	83.0	82.1	82.5	82.2	81.9	81.8	82.3	81.7
2001	80.8	81.2	81.7	82.3	82.8	83.6	83.3	83.7	83.1	82.7	82.6	82.6	82.5
2002	82.9	82.6	82.6	82.7	83.3	84.0	83.8	83.8	82.9	82.4	82.5	82.5	83.0
2003	81.6	81.7	82.0	82.4	82.9	83.5	84.2	84.5	84.1	84.3	84.2	84.0	83.3
Professional and business services													
1990	93.0	94.1	95.9	96.8	97.2	99.6	99.5	100.6	101.7	97.2	97.9	98.0	97.6
1991	97.5	99.2	100.9	101.6	101.9	103.7	101.3	103.2	101.8	101.6	101.5	100.9	101.2
1992	98.7	99.8	100.6	102.5	102.6	103.5	104.8	105.6	105.7	104.8	104.7	103.9	103.1
1993	103.1	104.9	106.5	106.9	106.9	109.5	110.3	110.0	109.9	109.8	109.2	109.4	108.0
1994	107.2	108.1	110.4	112.5	112.6	114.9	115.9	117.8	118.0	117.6	118.6	118.7	114.3
1995	114.9	117.6	119.9	120.2	121.0	122.9	122.2	124.5	125.1	124.3	125.4	125.4	121.9
1996	122.2	124.8	127.1	127.5	130.4	132.0	133.3	136.3	136.0	135.1	134.3	134.5	131.1
1997	130.2	133.1	135.5	138.4	140.5	142.1	144.8	145.6	147.0	146.9	147.0	147.6	141.5
1998	145.5	148.2	151.1	154.5	158.0	159.8	159.9	157.8	158.6	158.2	157.1	157.8	155.5
1999	156.5	157.0	159.1	160.6	162.7	164.4	162.8	162.5	163.0	163.6	162.7	163.2	161.5
2000	155.4	156.5	160.1	163.3	164.8	166.8	167.5	169.2	168.8	168.7	168.8	167.6	164.8
2001	160.8	163.1	166.0	168.7	169.1	171.1	168.2	168.9	167.1	163.9	164.0	163.6	166.2
2002	156.5	158.3	160.7	163.9	165.6	165.1	162.2	164.2	163.5	161.4	160.7	160.5	161.9
2003	154.3	154.8	154.8	156.3	157.8	157.9	156.5	157.1	157.2	157.0	155.1	153.6	156.0
Educational and health services													
1990	110.0	111.4	112.3	111.8	111.8	112.2	112.3	113.8	115.4	116.0	116.5	116.4	113.3
1991	116.6	117.9	118.7	119.2	119.8	119.0	118.5	119.4	121.6	122.2	122.6	123.1	119.8
1992	123.0	124.0	124.7	124.0	124.1	123.8	124.0	124.6	127.8	127.8	127.7	128.2	125.3
1993	128.0	129.5	130.3	129.2	128.8	128.9	129.0	129.5	132.6	132.0	132.1	133.4	130.2
1994	131.3	132.2	132.7	133.6	133.5	133.5	134.0	134.8	137.7	138.8	139.1	140.5	135.1
1995	139.2	140.5	141.6	141.8	142.2	142.3	141.5	143.2	146.6	148.3	149.0	149.5	143.8
1996	146.6	148.3	149.8	150.5	151.1	151.6	149.4	151.1	153.4	153.2	153.9	155.0	151.1
1997	153.1	155.5	156.1	155.2	156.0	156.2	155.1	155.6	157.9	160.2	161.2	160.5	156.8
1998	162.7	163.3	164.2	163.9	163.4	161.3	163.0	163.1	164.1	164.2	166.0	166.3	163.7
1999	160.6	162.9	162.4	161.9	160.6	158.6	159.6	159.7	161.3	160.1	161.2	161.0	160.8
2000	157.7	159.7	160.6	162.8	163.1	162.7	162.7	163.5	165.6	164.7	166.8	166.0	163.0
2001	163.2	164.8	165.9	167.1	166.9	165.4	164.8	167.2	169.1	169.1	171.1	170.9	167.1
2002	169.2	170.8	171.1	173.1	172.6	171.2	171.6	174.8	176.3	175.3	178.4	177.3	173.5
2003	176.2	176.8	176.6	176.6	176.1	173.9	171.6	173.1	174.1	175.8	176.5	176.4	175.3

Employment by Industry: Oklahoma—*Continued*

(Numbers in thousands. Not seasonally adjusted.)

Industry	January	February	March	April	May	June	July	August	September	October	November	December	Annual Average
STATEWIDE—*Continued*													
Leisure and hospitality													
1990	87.2	89.6	91.7	96.0	98.3	100.1	98.7	99.9	99.8	96.5	95.3	94.0	95.5
1991	91.0	92.9	95.5	99.0	100.1	102.4	100.5	101.7	101.7	98.6	97.3	96.0	98.0
1992	92.6	95.1	97.8	101.4	103.5	104.2	104.0	104.4	103.5	102.2	100.7	99.3	100.7
1993	95.2	97.9	100.7	104.9	106.6	107.8	106.2	107.2	107.3	106.3	104.7	104.3	104.0
1994	101.1	102.5	104.9	109.1	111.2	112.6	112.9	113.3	113.5	110.8	109.6	108.6	109.1
1995	106.5	108.6	110.9	114.1	117.1	118.0	117.0	116.5	115.8	114.7	112.5	112.0	113.6
1996	108.0	109.3	112.1	114.2	117.1	117.9	116.8	117.9	117.4	114.7	112.8	111.8	114.1
1997	109.8	111.7	114.8	116.0	118.6	120.1	115.6	116.6	116.4	117.4	115.7	115.4	115.6
1998	110.0	111.9	114.2	119.4	121.2	121.4	119.5	120.1	119.0	116.0	114.6	113.9	116.7
1999	112.7	114.8	117.3	121.5	123.2	123.9	123.7	124.9	124.5	123.6	123.4	122.7	121.4
2000	119.4	120.5	124.0	126.5	128.3	129.8	129.1	129.9	129.1	127.7	125.7	123.1	126.1
2001	119.2	121.4	124.6	129.3	131.3	132.6	131.0	132.0	129.3	126.5	125.9	124.3	127.2
2002	120.2	121.8	125.2	128.1	131.3	131.1	130.2	131.3	129.4	127.4	125.4	123.5	127.1
2003	120.9	121.4	123.8	127.4	130.2	129.8	128.4	129.5	127.1	127.4	124.8	122.8	126.1
Other services													
1990	50.9	50.8	51.3	51.7	52.1	53.0	52.5	52.9	52.5	52.0	51.9	52.4	52.0
1991	52.5	52.6	53.1	53.3	53.8	54.7	54.3	54.2	53.9	53.6	53.4	53.3	53.5
1992	52.7	52.7	53.1	53.6	54.2	54.9	54.5	54.7	54.5	54.6	54.5	54.9	54.0
1993	54.4	54.7	55.3	55.8	56.1	56.9	56.3	56.3	56.0	56.1	55.9	55.8	55.8
1994	56.1	56.3	56.7	57.1	57.2	58.2	58.7	58.2	57.8	57.6	57.4	57.5	57.4
1995	57.2	57.4	57.9	58.5	59.4	60.6	60.1	60.6	60.4	60.6	61.0	61.3	59.5
1996	61.0	61.4	62.2	62.6	63.0	64.1	63.5	63.7	63.2	63.0	63.1	63.2	62.8
1997	62.2	62.5	62.8	63.2	63.8	64.9	64.2	64.2	63.7	63.8	63.6	63.7	63.5
1998	62.2	62.5	62.8	63.7	64.7	65.8	66.1	66.2	66.5	66.6	67.0	67.8	65.1
1999	66.4	67.2	67.9	68.7	68.9	69.3	69.9	69.8	69.3	69.2	69.2	69.2	68.8
2000	68.3	68.4	69.0	69.9	70.3	71.2	70.6	70.6	70.8	70.4	70.4	70.8	70.1
2001	74.0	74.6	75.6	74.8	75.4	76.5	76.1	76.4	75.9	75.8	75.7	75.6	75.5
2002	74.5	74.8	75.3	77.7	77.9	78.1	77.4	77.1	76.5	75.2	75.0	74.8	76.2
2003	74.4	74.6	74.6	73.4	73.9	74.4	73.7	73.3	72.9	73.3	75.0	74.9	74.0
Government													
1990	261.4	267.5	267.6	265.0	266.5	255.6	244.5	246.2	262.2	268.2	268.3	269.6	261.8
1991	263.7	268.4	270.2	269.8	269.6	257.0	245.1	246.8	266.1	273.1	274.0	275.2	264.9
1992	270.2	273.9	275.4	274.9	275.7	264.3	253.6	252.9	269.6	277.0	276.7	277.5	270.1
1993	272.8	276.9	276.2	275.7	276.4	266.9	255.8	254.3	266.1	270.4	271.8	273.7	269.7
1994	269.7	273.1	274.7	274.2	274.8	266.9	256.5	255.9	270.0	274.3	275.2	276.5	270.1
1995	268.9	273.8	274.5	273.2	274.6	265.3	255.5	255.5	269.2	274.3	275.3	276.1	269.6
1996	269.8	274.2	276.3	275.9	277.6	266.4	256.8	258.0	269.9	276.8	277.4	277.9	271.4
1997	272.9	277.8	279.3	279.0	281.4	270.6	262.0	263.3	277.2	283.5	282.9	284.5	276.2
1998	275.5	280.3	281.5	280.5	283.3	272.2	263.8	265.5	279.2	285.0	285.0	287.0	278.2
1999	278.4	284.9	286.4	286.8	287.8	277.3	267.9	270.4	283.8	288.8	288.9	289.6	282.6
2000	282.9	288.8	292.5	291.3	297.9	285.0	270.0	271.1	286.8	294.5	296.2	295.6	287.7
2001	292.0	298.5	300.4	300.1	302.9	289.6	277.8	280.6	297.9	304.4	307.1	305.9	296.4
2002	298.3	304.0	305.7	305.9	309.5	295.5	284.3	286.8	299.8	306.6	307.3	307.2	300.9
2003	295.1	301.1	300.8	299.9	300.7	288.5	270.4	272.8	288.6	294.7	294.8	295.9	291.9
Federal government													
1990	51.4	51.1	50.9	50.8	50.9	51.4	51.5	51.4	50.8	50.2	49.6	49.7	50.8
1991	49.5	49.4	49.4	49.5	49.4	49.9	49.8	49.7	49.5	49.6	49.8	50.0	49.6
1992	49.7	49.7	49.5	49.7	49.8	50.3	50.4	50.3	49.6	49.8	49.4	49.7	49.8
1993	49.4	49.4	48.2	48.0	48.1	48.1	47.6	47.1	45.6	45.4	45.3	45.5	47.3
1994	45.2	45.2	45.2	45.5	45.4	45.5	45.3	45.1	44.9	44.4	44.3	44.6	45.0
1995	43.4	43.5	43.5	43.4	43.5	43.8	43.9	43.9	43.5	43.3	43.4	43.5	43.5
1996	43.1	43.2	43.4	43.7	43.8	44.0	43.9	43.9	43.8	44.2	44.1	44.4	43.7
1997	44.5	44.5	44.5	44.6	44.6	44.7	44.8	44.7	44.7	44.6	44.5	45.1	44.6
1998	44.5	44.5	44.4	44.6	44.8	45.0	44.9	44.9	45.0	44.9	45.4	46.2	44.9
1999	44.7	45.0	44.9	45.1	44.9	45.0	45.4	45.6	45.9	46.0	46.0	46.5	45.4
2000	46.1	46.0	48.2	47.2	52.6	51.0	49.2	49.4	46.0	46.1	46.1	46.3	47.9
2001	46.0	45.9	46.2	46.1	46.2	46.6	46.5	46.3	46.3	46.3	46.3	46.3	46.2
2002	45.9	45.7	45.9	46.0	46.1	46.6	46.3	46.4	46.2	46.7	46.7	47.0	46.3
2003	46.1	46.0	45.9	45.7	45.9	46.3	43.4	43.4	43.2	43.3	43.4	43.7	44.7
State government													
1990	72.6	76.8	77.4	77.1	77.3	72.5	70.3	71.2	76.1	78.5	78.6	78.3	75.5
1991	74.9	78.4	78.7	78.5	78.4	73.8	71.0	72.0	78.1	79.8	79.7	79.5	76.9
1992	76.8	80.2	80.8	80.4	80.5	74.6	72.8	71.5	77.9	80.4	79.8	80.3	78.0
1993	76.7	78.7	78.9	79.1	78.2	72.5	70.6	69.5	77.0	78.2	78.6	78.3	76.3
1994	75.3	77.5	78.2	78.4	78.0	73.5	71.5	71.3	77.8	78.8	79.2	79.4	76.5
1995	75.5	78.3	78.5	77.8	78.0	72.7	70.1	70.1	76.8	78.2	78.7	78.3	76.0
1996	74.4	77.3	78.2	78.4	78.4	73.0	70.3	71.5	76.9	79.2	79.8	79.7	76.4
1997	75.8	78.5	79.5	79.3	80.0	74.1	72.3	72.7	79.2	81.2	80.9	80.9	77.8
1998	75.2	77.8	78.7	77.8	78.8	72.7	71.4	72.8	78.2	80.6	80.3	80.7	77.0
1999	76.3	80.1	80.8	81.2	80.0	75.8	72.0	73.3	79.0	81.5	80.8	80.7	78.5
2000	76.6	80.3	81.2	80.8	81.0	74.3	71.6	71.8	80.7	82.1	82.1	81.2	78.6
2001	76.7	81.5	82.1	82.6	82.8	75.5	73.8	75.8	82.4	84.0	84.5	83.8	80.4
2002	78.8	83.6	84.2	84.1	84.2	76.2	74.4	75.7	82.7	84.0	84.3	84.2	81.4
2003	76.9	82.4	82.2	82.3	82.3	74.5	73.0	73.6	81.0	83.2	82.8	84.0	79.9

Employment by Industry: Oklahoma—*Continued*

(Numbers in thousands. Not seasonally adjusted.)

Industry	January	February	March	April	May	June	July	August	September	October	November	December	Annual Average
STATEWIDE—*Continued*													
Local government													
1990	137.4	139.6	139.3	137.1	138.3	131.7	122.7	123.6	135.3	139.5	140.1	141.6	135.5
1991	139.3	140.6	142.1	141.8	141.8	133.3	124.3	125.1	138.5	143.7	144.5	145.7	138.3
1992	143.7	144.0	145.1	144.8	145.4	139.4	130.4	131.1	142.1	146.8	147.5	147.5	142.3
1993	146.7	148.8	149.1	148.6	150.1	146.3	137.6	137.7	143.5	146.8	147.9	149.9	146.0
1994	149.2	150.4	151.3	150.3	151.4	147.9	139.7	139.5	147.3	151.1	151.7	152.5	148.5
1995	150.0	152.0	152.5	152.0	153.1	148.8	141.5	141.5	148.9	152.8	153.2	154.3	150.0
1996	152.3	153.7	154.7	153.8	155.4	149.4	142.6	142.6	149.2	153.4	153.5	153.8	151.2
1997	152.6	154.8	155.3	155.1	156.8	151.8	144.9	145.9	153.3	157.7	157.5	158.5	153.6
1998	155.8	158.0	158.4	158.1	159.7	154.5	147.5	147.8	156.0	159.5	159.3	160.1	156.2
1999	157.4	159.8	160.7	160.5	162.9	156.5	150.5	151.5	158.9	161.3	162.1	162.4	158.7
2000	160.2	162.5	163.1	163.3	164.3	159.7	149.2	149.9	160.1	166.3	168.0	168.1	161.2
2001	169.3	171.1	172.1	171.4	173.9	167.5	157.5	158.5	169.2	174.1	176.3	175.8	169.7
2002	173.6	174.7	175.6	175.8	179.2	172.7	163.6	164.7	170.9	175.9	176.3	176.0	173.3
2003	172.1	172.7	172.7	171.9	172.5	167.7	154.0	155.8	164.4	168.2	168.6	168.2	167.4
LAWTON													
Total nonfarm													
1990	35.3	35.3	35.3	34.9	35.2	35.6	34.8	35.0	35.4	35.6	35.6	35.7	35.3
1991	35.4	35.2	34.9	34.7	35.6	34.8	34.6	35.0	35.5	35.7	36.2	36.4	35.3
1992	36.0	36.4	36.8	37.1	37.4	37.2	36.5	37.0	37.6	38.1	38.2	38.7	37.2
1993	37.2	37.7	37.8	38.0	37.5	37.2	36.2	36.4	37.0	36.6	36.9	37.5	37.1
1994	36.6	37.2	37.6	37.2	37.4	37.4	36.7	37.2	37.2	37.1	37.0	36.9	37.1
1995	35.6	35.9	36.1	36.2	37.1	37.1	36.6	37.2	37.2	37.5	37.3	37.7	36.7
1996	36.6	37.1	37.3	37.5	38.6	38.1	37.0	37.1	37.4	37.4	37.5	37.4	37.4
1997	36.8	37.0	37.4	37.2	37.5	37.7	36.9	37.1	37.5	37.9	38.6	38.3	37.4
1998	37.6	37.5	38.0	37.7	37.9	38.2	36.8	37.1	37.5	38.0	38.3	38.5	37.7
1999	37.5	37.8	38.1	38.1	38.8	38.5	38.1	38.7	38.8	39.1	39.0	39.3	38.4
2000	38.2	38.3	38.6	38.9	39.5	39.2	38.0	38.5	38.9	38.9	38.8	39.0	38.7
2001	37.5	37.9	38.1	38.9	38.6	38.7	37.1	37.7	38.0	38.0	38.2	38.4	38.1
2002	37.7	38.4	38.7	39.1	39.7	39.8	38.5	39.3	39.4	39.8	40.0	40.1	39.2
2003	39.3	39.6	39.7	40.0	40.1	39.3	38.3	38.9	38.7	39.2	39.5	39.4	39.3
Total private													
1990	23.3	23.1	23.0	22.8	23.1	23.5	23.8	24.0	23.9	23.5	23.5	23.6	23.4
1991	23.3	23.1	23.1	22.7	23.4	23.6	23.5	23.9	23.9	23.6	24.0	24.2	23.5
1992	23.9	23.9	24.0	24.5	24.6	24.4	24.9	25.3	25.4	25.2	25.3	25.5	24.7
1993	24.4	24.8	25.0	25.4	25.0	24.7	25.0	25.4	25.4	24.9	25.2	25.5	25.0
1994	24.7	24.9	25.4	25.3	25.5	25.7	25.5	25.7	25.6	25.5	25.5	25.3	25.3
1995	24.3	24.3	24.5	24.6	25.2	25.5	25.7	26.1	26.0	25.8	25.6	25.9	25.2
1996	25.1	25.5	25.6	25.8	26.6	26.3	26.1	26.1	26.0	25.7	25.8	25.8	25.8
1997	25.2	25.4	25.7	25.3	25.6	25.8	25.7	25.9	25.8	25.7	26.5	26.3	25.7
1998	25.6	25.5	25.9	25.9	26.1	26.3	26.1	26.1	26.1	26.0	26.4	26.6	26.0
1999	25.9	25.9	26.1	26.2	26.5	26.6	27.2	27.5	27.3	27.4	27.3	27.5	26.7
2000	26.8	26.7	27.0	27.2	27.6	27.4	27.4	27.5	27.5	27.0	27.0	27.0	27.1
2001	26.0	26.1	26.2	26.8	26.8	26.9	26.4	26.6	26.4	26.2	26.3	26.5	26.4
2002	26.1	26.5	26.7	27.3	27.6	27.9	27.9	28.1	27.9	28.0	28.3	28.3	27.6
2003	27.8	27.7	27.9	28.3	28.7	28.5	28.4	28.7	28.0	28.0	28.3	28.1	28.2
Goods-producing													
1990	4.6	4.5	4.5	4.4	4.5	4.6	4.6	4.7	4.6	4.5	4.5	4.4	4.5
1991	4.4	4.4	4.5	4.4	4.6	4.8	4.6	4.7	4.7	4.6	4.8	4.8	4.6
1992	4.6	4.6	4.6	4.8	4.9	4.9	5.1	5.2	5.3	5.4	5.4	5.4	5.0
1993	5.2	5.3	5.4	5.5	5.3	5.4	5.3	5.3	5.3	5.2	5.3	5.3	5.3
1994	5.2	5.1	5.2	5.2	5.4	5.3	5.3	5.3	5.3	5.0	5.1	5.1	5.2
1995	4.9	4.8	4.8	4.9	4.9	5.0	4.9	5.0	5.1	5.2	5.2	5.1	4.9
1996	5.0	5.0	5.0	5.0	5.1	5.1	5.1	5.1	5.1	5.0	4.9	5.0	5.0
1997	4.9	4.8	4.8	4.6	4.8	4.7	4.7	4.8	4.7	4.8	4.9	4.9	4.7
1998	4.9	4.8	5.1	5.1	5.1	5.2	5.2	5.2	5.2	5.2	5.2	5.3	5.1
1999	5.3	5.3	5.3	5.3	5.3	5.4	5.6	5.6	5.5	5.4	5.4	5.5	5.4
2000	5.4	5.4	5.4	5.4	5.6	5.6	5.6	5.6	5.7	5.6	5.5	5.6	5.5
2001	5.3	5.3	5.4	5.4	5.3	5.4	5.3	5.4	5.4	5.3	5.3	5.3	5.3
2002	5.2	5.2	5.3	5.4	5.5	5.5	5.5	5.5	5.4	5.5	5.5	5.5	5.4
2003	5.5	5.3	5.3	5.3	5.3	5.3	5.1	5.2	5.1	4.9	5.0	5.0	5.2
Natural resources and mining													
1990	0.1	0.1	0.1	0.1	0.1	0.1	0.1	0.1	0.1	0.1	0.1	0.1	0.1
1991	0.1	0.1	0.1	0.1	0.1	0.1	0.1	0.1	0.1	0.1	0.1	0.1	0.1
1992	0.1	0.1	0.1	0.1	0.1	0.1	0.1	0.1	0.1	0.1	0.1	0.1	0.1
1993	0.1	0.1	0.1	0.1	0.1	0.1	0.1	0.1	0.1	0.1	0.1	0.1	0.1
1994	0.1	0.1	0.1	0.1	0.1	0.1	0.1	0.1	0.1	0.1	0.1	0.1	0.1
1995	0.1	0.1	0.1	0.1	0.1	0.1	0.1	0.1	0.1	0.1	0.1	0.1	0.1
1996	0.1	0.1	0.1	0.1	0.1	0.1	0.1	0.1	0.1	0.1	0.1	0.1	0.1
1997	0.1	0.1	0.1	0.1	0.1	0.1	0.1	0.1	0.1	0.1	0.1	0.1	0.1
1998	0.1	0.1	0.1	0.1	0.1	0.1	0.1	0.1	0.1	0.1	0.1	0.1	0.1
1999	0.1	0.1	0.1	0.1	0.1	0.1	0.1	0.1	0.1	0.1	0.1	0.1	0.1
2000	0.1	0.1	0.1	0.1	0.1	0.1	0.1	0.1	0.1	0.1	0.1	0.1	0.1
2001	0.1	0.1	0.1	0.1	0.1	0.1	0.1	0.1	0.1	0.1	0.1	0.1	0.1
2002	0.1	0.1	0.1	0.1	0.1	0.1	0.1	0.1	0.1	0.1	0.1	0.1	0.1
2003	0.2	0.1	0.1	0.1	0.1	0.1	0.1	0.1	0.1	0.1	0.1	0.1	0.1

Employment by Industry: Oklahoma—*Continued*

(Numbers in thousands. Not seasonally adjusted.)

Industry	January	February	March	April	May	June	July	August	September	October	November	December	Annual Average
LAWTON—*Continued*													
Construction													
1990	1.0	0.9	0.9	0.9	1.0	1.1	1.1	1.1	1.0	1.0	1.0	1.0	1.0
1991	1.0	1.0	1.1	1.0	1.0	1.1	1.0	1.0	1.0	1.0	1.1	1.1	1.0
1992	1.1	1.1	1.1	1.1	1.2	1.3	1.4	1.5	1.6	1.6	1.6	1.5	1.3
1993	1.4	1.5	1.5	1.5	1.4	1.5	1.4	1.4	1.4	1.4	1.4	1.4	1.4
1994	1.4	1.3	1.4	1.5	1.6	1.6	1.6	1.5	1.5	1.3	1.3	1.3	1.4
1995	1.3	1.2	1.2	1.3	1.3	1.4	1.3	1.4	1.4	1.5	1.5	1.5	1.3
1996	1.4	1.4	1.4	1.4	1.5	1.5	1.5	1.5	1.5	1.4	1.4	1.3	1.4
1997	1.3	1.2	1.2	1.1	1.2	1.1	1.1	1.2	1.1	1.2	1.3	1.3	1.1
1998	1.3	1.3	1.4	1.4	1.4	1.5	1.5	1.4	1.4	1.4	1.4	1.5	1.4
1999	1.5	1.5	1.5	1.5	1.5	1.6	1.7	1.7	1.7	1.6	1.6	1.6	1.5
2000	1.6	1.6	1.6	1.6	1.7	1.7	1.7	1.7	1.7	1.7	1.6	1.6	1.6
2001	1.5	1.5	1.6	1.6	1.6	1.6	1.6	1.6	1.5	1.5	1.5	1.5	1.5
2002	1.5	1.5	1.6	1.6	1.7	1.7	1.7	1.7	1.6	1.6	1.6	1.6	1.6
2003	1.6	1.5	1.5	1.6	1.6	1.6	1.5	1.5	1.5	1.4	1.4	1.4	1.5
Manufacturing													
1990	3.5	3.5	3.5	3.4	3.4	3.4	3.4	3.5	3.5	3.4	3.4	3.3	3.4
1991	3.3	3.3	3.3	3.3	3.5	3.6	3.5	3.6	3.6	3.5	3.6	3.6	3.4
1992	3.4	3.4	3.4	3.6	3.6	3.5	3.6	3.6	3.6	3.7	3.7	3.8	3.5
1993	3.7	3.7	3.8	3.9	3.8	3.8	3.8	3.8	3.8	3.7	3.8	3.8	3.7
1994	3.7	3.7	3.7	3.6	3.7	3.6	3.6	3.7	3.7	3.6	3.7	3.7	3.6
1995	3.5	3.5	3.5	3.5	3.5	3.5	3.5	3.5	3.6	3.6	3.6	3.5	3.5
1996	3.5	3.5	3.5	3.5	3.5	3.5	3.5	3.5	3.5	3.5	3.4	3.6	3.5
1997	3.5	3.5	3.5	3.4	3.5	3.5	3.5	3.5	3.5	3.5	3.5	3.5	3.4
1998	3.5	3.4	3.6	3.6	3.6	3.6	3.6	3.7	3.7	3.7	3.7	3.7	3.6
1999	3.7	3.7	3.7	3.7	3.7	3.7	3.8	3.8	3.7	3.7	3.7	3.8	3.7
2000	3.7	3.7	3.7	3.7	3.8	3.8	3.8	3.8	3.9	3.8	3.8	3.9	3.7
2001	3.7	3.7	3.7	3.7	3.6	3.7	3.6	3.7	3.8	3.7	3.7	3.7	3.6
2002	3.6	3.6	3.6	3.7	3.7	3.7	3.7	3.7	3.7	3.8	3.8	3.8	3.7
2003	3.7	3.7	3.7	3.6	3.6	3.6	3.5	3.6	3.5	3.4	3.5	3.5	3.6
Service-providing													
1990	30.7	30.8	30.8	30.5	30.7	31.0	30.2	30.3	30.8	31.1	31.1	31.3	30.7
1991	31.0	30.8	30.4	30.3	31.0	30.0	30.0	30.3	30.8	31.1	31.4	31.6	30.7
1992	31.4	31.8	32.2	32.3	32.5	32.3	31.4	31.8	32.3	32.7	32.8	33.3	32.2
1993	32.0	32.4	32.4	32.5	32.2	31.8	30.9	31.1	31.7	31.4	31.6	32.2	31.8
1994	31.4	32.1	32.4	32.0	32.0	32.1	31.4	31.9	31.9	32.1	31.9	31.8	31.9
1995	30.7	31.1	31.3	31.3	32.2	32.1	31.7	32.2	32.1	32.3	32.1	32.6	31.8
1996	31.6	32.1	32.3	32.5	33.5	33.0	31.9	32.0	32.3	32.4	32.6	32.4	32.3
1997	31.9	32.2	32.6	32.6	32.7	33.0	32.2	32.3	32.8	33.1	33.7	33.4	32.7
1998	32.7	32.7	32.9	32.6	32.8	33.0	31.6	31.9	32.3	32.8	33.1	33.2	32.6
1999	32.2	32.5	32.8	32.8	33.5	33.1	32.5	33.1	33.3	33.7	33.6	33.8	33.0
2000	32.8	32.9	33.2	33.5	33.9	33.6	32.4	32.9	33.2	33.3	33.3	33.4	33.2
2001	32.2	32.6	32.7	33.5	33.3	33.3	31.8	32.3	32.6	32.7	32.9	33.1	32.8
2002	32.5	33.2	33.4	33.7	34.2	34.3	33.0	33.8	34.0	34.3	34.5	34.6	33.8
2003	33.8	34.3	34.4	34.7	34.8	34.0	33.2	33.7	33.6	34.3	34.5	34.4	34.1
Trade, transportation, and utilities													
1990	7.2	7.1	7.0	6.9	7.0	7.2	7.1	7.2	7.3	7.0	7.0	7.3	7.1
1991	6.8	6.7	6.6	6.4	6.7	6.6	6.7	6.8	6.9	6.8	7.1	7.2	6.7
1992	6.7	6.6	6.6	6.7	6.8	6.7	6.8	6.9	6.8	7.0	7.2	7.3	6.8
1993	6.8	6.8	6.8	6.8	6.8	6.7	6.7	6.9	6.9	6.7	6.9	7.0	6.8
1994	6.6	6.7	6.9	6.8	6.9	6.9	6.9	7.0	6.9	7.0	7.1	7.1	6.9
1995	6.8	6.7	6.7	6.6	6.9	6.9	6.9	7.0	7.0	6.8	6.9	7.1	6.8
1996	6.7	6.7	6.7	6.6	6.8	6.8	6.8	6.8	6.8	6.7	6.9	7.0	6.7
1997	6.6	6.6	6.6	6.6	6.8	6.9	6.8	6.8	6.7	6.6	7.0	6.9	6.7
1998	6.5	6.8	6.7	6.7	6.7	6.7	6.6	6.5	6.5	6.6	6.9	6.9	6.6
1999	6.6	6.6	6.7	6.7	6.9	6.9	7.0	7.0	6.9	7.1	7.1	7.2	6.8
2000	6.8	6.8	6.9	7.0	7.0	7.0	6.9	6.9	6.9	6.8	7.0	7.0	6.9
2001	6.6	6.5	6.5	6.5	6.6	6.6	6.4	6.5	6.4	6.5	6.6	6.6	6.5
2002	6.3	6.3	6.3	6.5	6.5	6.5	6.4	6.4	6.4	6.5	6.6	6.7	6.5
2003	6.4	6.6	6.9	6.8	6.9	6.9	7.0	7.0	6.8	7.0	7.1	7.1	6.9
Wholesale trade													
1990	0.7	0.7	0.6	0.6	0.7	0.7	0.7	0.7	0.7	0.7	0.7	0.7	0.6
1991	0.7	0.7	0.7	0.6	0.7	0.6	0.6	0.6	0.7	0.6	0.7	0.6	0.6
1992	0.6	0.6	0.6	0.6	0.6	0.6	0.6	0.6	0.6	0.6	0.6	0.6	0.6
1993	0.6	0.6	0.6	0.6	0.6	0.6	0.6	0.7	0.7	0.6	0.6	0.6	0.6
1994	0.5	0.5	0.6	0.6	0.6	0.6	0.6	0.6	0.6	0.6	0.6	0.5	0.5
1995	0.5	0.5	0.5	0.5	0.5	0.6	0.6	0.6	0.6	0.5	0.5	0.5	0.5
1996	0.5	0.5	0.5	0.5	0.5	0.5	0.5	0.5	0.5	0.5	0.5	0.5	0.5
1997	0.5	0.5	0.5	0.5	0.5	0.5	0.5	0.5	0.5	0.5	0.5	0.5	0.5
1998	0.5	0.5	0.5	0.5	0.5	0.5	0.5	0.5	0.5	0.5	0.5	0.5	0.5
1999	0.5	0.5	0.5	0.5	0.5	0.5	0.5	0.5	0.5	0.5	0.5	0.5	0.5
2000	0.5	0.5	0.6	0.5	0.5	0.5	0.5	0.5	0.5	0.5	0.5	0.5	0.5
2001	0.5	0.5	0.5	0.5	0.5	0.5	0.5	0.5	0.5	0.5	0.5	0.5	0.5
2002	0.5	0.5	0.5	0.5	0.5	0.5	0.5	0.5	0.5	0.5	0.5	0.5	0.5
2003	0.5	0.5	0.5	0.5	0.6	0.6	0.6	0.6	0.5	0.5	0.5	0.5	0.5

Employment by Industry: Oklahoma—*Continued*

(Numbers in thousands. Not seasonally adjusted.)

Industry	January	February	March	April	May	June	July	August	September	October	November	December	Annual Average
LAWTON—*Continued*													
Retail trade													
1990	4.9	4.9	4.9	4.7	4.7	4.8	4.8	4.9	4.9	4.8	4.9	4.9	4.8
1991	4.6	4.5	4.5	4.4	4.6	4.6	4.6	4.7	4.7	4.7	4.9	5.1	4.6
1992	4.8	4.7	4.7	4.7	4.8	4.7	4.8	4.9	4.8	5.0	5.2	5.3	4.8
1993	4.8	4.8	4.8	4.9	4.9	4.8	4.8	4.9	4.9	4.8	5.0	5.0	4.8
1994	4.8	4.8	4.9	4.8	4.9	4.9	4.9	5.0	5.0	5.0	5.1	5.2	4.9
1995	5.0	4.9	4.9	4.8	5.0	4.9	4.9	5.0	5.0	4.9	5.0	5.2	4.9
1996	4.8	4.8	4.8	4.8	4.9	4.9	4.9	4.9	4.9	4.8	5.0	5.1	4.8
1997	4.8	4.8	4.8	4.8	5.0	5.0	4.9	4.9	4.8	4.8	5.2	5.1	4.9
1998	4.8	5.1	5.0	4.9	4.9	4.9	4.8	4.8	4.8	4.9	5.2	5.2	4.9
1999	4.9	4.9	5.0	5.0	5.1	5.1	5.2	5.2	5.1	5.2	5.3	5.3	5.1
2000	5.0	5.0	5.0	5.1	5.1	5.1	5.0	5.0	5.0	5.0	5.2	5.2	5.0
2001	4.8	4.7	4.7	4.6	4.7	4.7	4.6	4.7	4.6	4.7	4.8	4.8	4.6
2002	4.6	4.6	4.6	4.7	4.7	4.7	4.7	4.7	4.8	4.8	4.9	5.0	4.7
2003	4.7	4.8	5.1	5.1	5.1	5.1	5.1	5.1	5.1	5.2	5.3	5.3	5.1
Transportation and utilities													
1990	1.6	1.5	1.5	1.6	1.6	1.7	1.6	1.6	1.7	1.5	1.4	1.7	1.5
1991	1.5	1.5	1.4	1.4	1.4	1.4	1.5	1.5	1.5	1.5	1.5	1.5	1.4
1992	1.3	1.3	1.3	1.4	1.4	1.4	1.4	1.4	1.4	1.4	1.4	1.4	1.3
1993	1.4	1.4	1.4	1.3	1.3	1.3	1.3	1.3	1.3	1.3	1.3	1.4	1.3
1994	1.3	1.4	1.4	1.4	1.4	1.4	1.4	1.4	1.3	1.4	1.4	1.4	1.3
1995	1.3	1.3	1.3	1.3	1.4	1.4	1.4	1.4	1.4	1.4	1.4	1.4	1.3
1996	1.4	1.4	1.4	1.3	1.4	1.4	1.4	1.4	1.4	1.4	1.4	1.4	1.3
1997	1.3	1.3	1.3	1.3	1.3	1.4	1.4	1.4	1.4	1.3	1.3	1.3	1.3
1998	1.2	1.2	1.2	1.3	1.3	1.3	1.3	1.2	1.2	1.2	1.2	1.2	1.2
1999	1.2	1.2	1.2	1.2	1.3	1.3	1.3	1.3	1.3	1.4	1.3	1.4	1.2
2000	1.3	1.3	1.3	1.4	1.4	1.4	1.4	1.4	1.4	1.3	1.3	1.3	1.3
2001	1.3	1.3	1.3	1.4	1.4	1.4	1.3	1.3	1.3	1.3	1.3	1.3	1.3
2002	1.2	1.2	1.2	1.3	1.3	1.3	1.2	1.2	1.1	1.2	1.2	1.2	1.2
2003	1.2	1.3	1.3	1.2	1.2	1.2	1.3	1.3	1.2	1.3	1.3	1.3	1.3
Information													
1990	0.7	0.7	0.7	0.7	0.7	0.7	0.7	0.7	0.7	0.7	0.7	0.7	0.7
1991	0.7	0.7	0.6	0.6	0.6	0.6	0.6	0.6	0.6	0.6	0.6	0.6	0.6
1992	0.6	0.6	0.6	0.6	0.6	0.6	0.6	0.6	0.6	0.6	0.6	0.6	0.6
1993	0.6	0.6	0.6	0.7	0.7	0.6	0.6	0.6	0.6	0.6	0.6	0.6	0.6
1994	0.6	0.6	0.6	0.7	0.6	0.7	0.6	0.6	0.6	0.7	0.7	0.6	0.6
1995	0.6	0.6	0.7	0.6	0.7	0.7	0.7	0.7	0.7	0.7	0.6	0.6	0.6
1996	0.6	0.6	0.6	0.6	0.6	0.6	0.6	0.6	0.6	0.6	0.6	0.6	0.6
1997	0.6	0.6	0.6	0.6	0.6	0.6	0.6	0.6	0.6	0.6	0.6	0.6	0.6
1998	0.6	0.6	0.6	0.6	0.6	0.6	0.6	0.6	0.6	0.6	0.6	0.6	0.6
1999	0.7	0.6	0.6	0.6	0.6	0.6	0.6	0.6	0.6	0.6	0.6	0.6	0.6
2000	0.6	0.6	0.6	0.6	0.6	0.6	0.6	0.6	0.6	0.6	0.6	0.6	0.6
2001	0.5	0.5	0.5	0.5	0.5	0.5	0.5	0.5	0.5	0.5	0.5	0.5	0.5
2002	0.5	0.5	0.5	0.5	0.5	0.5	0.5	0.5	0.5	0.5	0.5	0.5	0.5
2003	0.5	0.5	0.5	0.5	0.5	0.5	0.5	0.5	0.5	0.5	0.5	0.5	0.5
Financial activities													
1990	1.9	1.9	1.9	2.0	2.0	2.0	2.0	2.0	2.0	1.9	1.9	1.9	1.9
1991	1.9	1.8	1.9	1.8	1.9	1.9	1.9	1.9	1.9	1.9	1.9	1.9	1.8
1992	1.8	1.8	1.9	1.7	1.7	1.7	1.8	1.8	1.8	1.8	1.7	1.8	1.7
1993	1.7	1.8	1.8	1.8	1.8	1.8	1.8	1.8	1.8	1.8	1.8	1.8	1.7
1994	1.8	1.8	1.8	1.8	1.8	1.8	1.8	1.8	1.8	1.8	1.8	1.8	1.8
1995	1.7	1.7	1.7	1.8	1.8	1.8	1.9	1.9	1.9	1.9	1.9	1.9	1.8
1996	1.9	2.0	1.9	1.9	2.0	1.9	1.9	1.9	1.9	1.8	1.8	1.8	1.8
1997	1.7	1.7	1.7	1.7	1.7	1.8	1.7	1.8	1.8	1.8	1.8	1.8	1.7
1998	1.8	1.7	1.8	1.7	1.7	1.7	1.7	1.7	1.7	1.8	1.7	1.7	1.7
1999	1.7	1.7	1.7	1.7	1.7	1.8	1.8	1.8	1.8	1.8	1.8	1.8	1.7
2000	1.8	1.8	1.8	1.8	1.8	1.8	1.8	1.8	1.8	1.7	1.7	1.7	1.7
2001	1.7	1.7	1.8	1.8	1.8	1.9	1.9	1.9	1.9	1.9	1.9	2.0	1.8
2002	2.0	2.0	2.0	2.0	2.0	2.1	2.1	2.1	2.1	2.2	2.3	2.3	2.1
2003	2.3	2.3	2.3	2.3	2.4	2.4	2.4	2.4	2.3	2.4	2.4	2.3	2.4
Professional and business services													
1990	1.5	1.5	1.6	1.6	1.5	1.6	1.7	1.7	1.7	1.8	1.8	1.8	1.6
1991	1.9	1.8	1.8	1.9	1.9	1.9	1.9	1.9	1.9	1.8	1.8	1.8	1.8
1992	2.5	2.5	2.5	2.5	2.5	2.4	2.4	2.5	2.6	2.1	2.0	2.0	2.3
1993	2.1	2.1	2.1	2.0	1.9	1.9	2.0	2.1	2.2	2.1	2.1	2.2	2.0
1994	2.1	2.2	2.2	2.2	2.1	2.2	2.1	2.1	2.2	2.1	2.0	2.0	2.1
1995	2.0	2.1	2.1	2.1	2.2	2.3	2.3	2.4	2.3	2.2	2.2	2.2	2.2
1996	2.2	2.3	2.4	2.6	2.8	2.7	2.6	2.6	2.5	2.6	2.6	2.6	2.5
1997	2.5	2.6	2.6	2.3	2.3	2.3	2.4	2.4	2.4	2.5	2.7	2.7	2.4
1998	2.7	2.6	2.5	2.6	2.6	2.8	2.9	2.8	2.8	2.7	2.8	2.8	2.7
1999	2.8	2.8	2.8	3.0	3.0	3.0	3.1	3.1	3.0	3.1	3.1	3.2	3.0
2000	3.3	3.2	3.3	3.2	3.2	3.2	3.4	3.4	3.4	3.1	3.1	3.1	3.2
2001	2.9	3.0	2.9	3.2	3.2	3.2	3.2	3.1	3.1	3.0	2.9	3.0	3.0
2002	3.2	3.3	3.3	3.4	3.5	3.7	3.6	3.7	3.8	3.8	3.9	3.7	3.6
2003	3.7	3.6	3.4	3.6	3.7	3.6	3.6	3.5	3.5	3.5	3.5	3.5	3.6

Employment by Industry: Oklahoma—*Continued*

(Numbers in thousands. Not seasonally adjusted.)

Industry	January	February	March	April	May	June	July	August	September	October	November	December	Annual Average
LAWTON—*Continued*													
Educational and health services													
1990	2.2	2.2	2.2	2.2	2.3	2.3	2.4	2.4	2.4	2.3	2.4	2.4	2.3
1991	2.5	2.5	2.5	2.4	2.5	2.5	2.5	2.6	2.5	2.7	2.6	2.7	2.5
1992	2.7	2.7	2.7	2.7	2.7	2.7	2.7	2.7	2.8	2.7	2.8	2.8	2.7
1993	2.6	2.7	2.7	2.8	2.8	2.7	2.8	2.8	2.8	2.7	2.8	2.9	2.7
1994	3.0	3.0	3.1	3.1	3.1	3.1	3.1	3.2	3.2	3.3	3.3	3.3	3.1
1995	3.1	3.1	3.1	3.1	3.1	3.1	3.2	3.3	3.3	3.3	3.3	3.4	3.2
1996	3.3	3.4	3.4	3.5	3.5	3.4	3.4	3.4	3.4	3.4	3.4	3.3	3.4
1997	3.4	3.4	3.4	3.5	3.5	3.5	3.5	3.6	3.6	3.6	3.7	3.7	3.5
1998	3.7	3.7	3.8	3.5	3.6	3.5	3.4	3.5	3.5	3.4	3.4	3.5	3.5
1999	3.2	3.3	3.3	3.2	3.2	3.0	2.9	3.0	3.1	3.1	3.1	3.1	3.1
2000	2.8	2.9	2.9	3.1	3.2	3.1	3.0	3.1	3.0	3.2	3.2	3.2	3.0
2001	3.0	3.1	3.0	3.1	3.1	3.0	3.0	3.1	3.1	3.1	3.2	3.2	3.1
2002	3.3	3.4	3.4	3.5	3.5	3.5	3.6	3.7	3.6	3.5	3.5	3.6	3.5
2003	3.6	3.6	3.6	3.7	3.7	3.7	3.6	3.7	3.6	3.6	3.7	3.7	3.7
Leisure and hospitality													
1990	3.5	3.5	3.4	3.3	3.4	3.4	3.6	3.6	3.5	3.5	3.4	3.3	3.4
1991	3.3	3.4	3.3	3.4	3.3	3.4	3.4	3.5	3.5	3.4	3.4	3.3	3.3
1992	3.2	3.3	3.3	3.6	3.5	3.5	3.6	3.6	3.6	3.7	3.7	3.7	3.5
1993	3.6	3.6	3.7	3.8	3.8	3.7	3.8	3.9	3.8	3.9	3.8	3.8	3.7
1994	3.6	3.7	3.8	3.7	3.8	3.9	3.8	3.9	3.8	3.8	3.7	3.6	3.7
1995	3.5	3.5	3.6	3.7	3.8	3.8	3.9	3.9	3.8	3.8	3.6	3.7	3.7
1996	3.6	3.6	3.7	3.7	3.8	3.8	3.8	3.8	3.8	3.7	3.7	3.6	3.7
1997	3.6	3.8	4.0	4.1	4.0	4.0	4.0	4.0	4.1	3.9	3.9	3.8	3.9
1998	3.6	3.5	3.6	3.8	3.8	3.8	3.8	3.9	3.9	3.8	3.9	3.9	3.7
1999	3.6	3.6	3.7	3.7	3.8	3.9	4.1	4.3	4.3	4.2	4.1	4.0	3.9
2000	4.0	3.9	4.0	4.0	4.1	4.0	4.0	4.0	4.0	4.0	3.9	3.8	3.9
2001	3.8	3.8	3.9	4.1	4.1	4.1	3.9	3.9	3.8	3.7	3.7	3.7	3.8
2002	3.5	3.6	3.7	3.8	3.8	3.8	3.9	4.0	3.9	3.8	3.8	3.8	3.8
2003	3.6	3.6	3.7	3.8	3.9	3.8	3.9	4.1	4.0	3.9	3.8	3.8	3.8
Other services													
1990	1.7	1.7	1.7	1.7	1.7	1.7	1.7	1.7	1.7	1.8	1.8	1.8	1.7
1991	1.8	1.8	1.9	1.8	1.9	1.9	1.9	1.9	1.9	1.8	1.8	1.9	1.8
1992	1.8	1.8	1.8	1.9	1.9	1.9	1.9	2.0	1.9	1.9	1.9	1.9	1.8
1993	1.8	1.9	1.9	2.0	1.9	1.9	2.0	2.0	2.0	1.9	1.9	1.9	1.9
1994	1.8	1.8	1.8	1.8	1.8	1.8	1.9	1.8	1.8	1.8	1.8	1.8	1.8
1995	1.7	1.8	1.8	1.8	1.8	1.9	1.9	1.9	1.9	1.9	1.9	1.9	1.8
1996	1.8	1.9	1.9	1.9	2.0	2.0	1.9	1.9	1.9	1.9	1.9	1.9	1.9
1997	1.9	1.9	2.0	1.9	1.9	2.0	2.0	1.9	1.9	1.9	1.9	1.9	1.9
1998	1.8	1.8	1.8	1.9	2.0	2.0	1.9	1.9	1.9	1.9	1.9	1.9	1.8
1999	2.0	2.0	2.0	2.0	2.0	2.0	2.1	2.1	2.1	2.1	2.1	2.1	2.0
2000	2.1	2.1	2.1	2.1	2.1	2.1	2.1	2.1	2.1	2.0	2.0	2.0	2.0
2001	2.2	2.2	2.2	2.2	2.2	2.2	2.2	2.2	2.2	2.2	2.2	2.2	2.2
2002	2.1	2.2	2.2	2.2	2.3	2.3	2.3	2.2	2.2	2.2	2.2	2.2	2.2
2003	2.2	2.2	2.2	2.3	2.3	2.3	2.3	2.3	2.2	2.2	2.3	2.2	2.3
Government													
1990	12.0	12.2	12.3	12.1	12.1	12.1	11.0	11.0	11.5	12.1	12.1	12.1	11.8
1991	12.1	12.1	11.8	12.0	12.2	11.2	11.1	11.1	11.6	12.1	12.2	12.2	11.8
1992	12.1	12.5	12.8	12.6	12.8	12.8	11.6	11.7	12.2	12.9	12.9	13.2	12.5
1993	12.8	12.9	12.8	12.6	12.5	12.5	11.2	11.0	11.6	11.7	11.7	12.0	12.1
1994	11.9	12.3	12.2	11.9	11.9	11.7	11.2	11.5	11.6	11.6	11.5	11.6	11.7
1995	11.3	11.6	11.6	11.6	11.9	11.6	10.9	11.1	11.2	11.7	11.7	11.8	11.5
1996	11.5	11.6	11.7	11.7	12.0	11.8	10.9	11.0	11.4	11.7	11.7	11.6	11.5
1997	11.6	11.6	11.7	11.9	11.9	11.9	11.2	11.2	11.7	12.2	12.1	12.0	11.7
1998	12.0	12.0	12.1	11.8	11.8	11.9	10.7	11.0	11.4	12.0	11.9	11.9	11.7
1999	11.6	11.9	12.0	11.9	12.3	11.9	10.9	11.2	11.5	11.7	11.7	11.8	11.7
2000	11.4	11.6	11.6	11.7	11.9	11.8	10.6	11.0	11.4	11.9	11.8	12.0	11.5
2001	11.5	11.8	11.9	12.1	11.8	11.8	10.7	11.1	11.6	11.8	11.9	11.9	11.6
2002	11.6	11.9	12.0	11.8	12.1	11.9	10.6	11.2	11.5	11.8	11.7	11.8	11.7
2003	11.5	11.9	11.8	11.7	11.4	10.8	9.9	10.2	10.7	11.2	11.2	11.3	11.1
Federal government													
1990	5.4	5.4	5.4	5.4	5.4	5.5	5.5	5.5	5.4	5.2	5.3	5.2	5.3
1991	5.2	5.3	5.3	5.3	5.4	5.5	5.5	5.4	5.3	5.1	5.2	5.2	5.3
1992	5.2	5.2	5.3	5.3	5.4	5.5	5.6	5.6	5.4	5.5	5.4	5.4	5.4
1993	5.3	5.2	5.2	5.0	4.9	4.9	4.8	4.6	4.4	4.3	4.3	4.4	4.7
1994	4.5	4.6	4.6	4.3	4.4	4.4	4.4	4.4	4.3	4.1	4.1	4.1	4.3
1995	3.9	4.0	4.0	4.0	4.1	4.2	4.3	4.2	4.1	4.0	4.0	3.9	4.0
1996	3.9	3.9	3.9	4.0	4.1	4.1	4.1	4.0	3.9	4.0	3.9	3.8	3.9
1997	3.8	3.8	3.8	3.8	3.7	3.7	3.9	3.9	3.9	3.9	3.8	3.8	3.8
1998	3.8	3.8	3.8	3.8	3.8	3.9	3.9	3.9	3.9	3.8	3.7	3.7	3.8
1999	3.6	3.6	3.7	3.7	3.8	3.8	3.8	3.8	3.8	3.7	3.7	3.7	3.7
2000	3.6	3.6	3.6	3.6	3.9	3.8	3.8	3.7	3.7	3.6	3.6	3.6	3.6
2001	3.5	3.5	3.6	3.6	3.5	3.6	3.4	3.4	3.4	3.3	3.3	3.3	3.4
2002	3.3	3.3	3.3	3.3	3.3	3.4	3.2	3.3	3.3	3.3	3.3	3.3	3.3
2003	3.2	3.2	3.2	3.2	3.2	3.3	2.8	2.8	2.8	2.8	2.8	2.8	3.0

Employment by Industry: Oklahoma—*Continued*

(Numbers in thousands. Not seasonally adjusted.)

Industry	January	February	March	April	May	June	July	August	September	October	November	December	Annual Average
LAWTON—*Continued*													
State government													
1990	1.3	1.3	1.4	1.3	1.4	1.2	1.2	1.0	1.2	1.4	1.3	1.3	1.2
1991	1.2	1.3	1.3	1.2	1.3	1.1	1.1	1.0	1.2	1.3	1.2	1.2	1.2
1992	1.2	1.5	1.6	1.5	1.6	1.4	1.4	1.2	1.4	1.6	1.5	1.7	1.4
1993	1.5	1.6	1.5	1.5	1.5	1.4	1.4	1.1	1.4	1.5	1.4	1.5	1.4
1994	1.4	1.5	1.4	1.5	1.4	1.3	1.3	1.2	1.3	1.4	1.4	1.4	1.3
1995	1.4	1.4	1.4	1.4	1.5	1.4	1.3	1.2	1.2	1.4	1.4	1.5	1.3
1996	1.4	1.4	1.4	1.4	1.5	1.4	1.3	1.2	1.3	1.3	1.5	1.5	1.3
1997	1.5	1.4	1.5	1.5	1.5	1.5	1.4	1.2	1.3	1.5	1.5	1.5	1.4
1998	1.5	1.4	1.5	1.5	1.5	1.5	1.4	1.3	1.3	1.5	1.5	1.6	1.4
1999	1.4	1.5	1.5	1.5	1.7	1.4	1.4	1.3	1.4	1.5	1.5	1.6	1.4
2000	1.4	1.5	1.5	1.6	1.5	1.4	1.4	1.3	1.4	1.5	1.4	1.6	1.4
2001	1.4	1.5	1.5	1.7	1.4	1.4	1.4	1.3	1.4	1.5	1.5	1.6	1.4
2002	1.4	1.4	1.5	1.4	1.6	1.4	1.4	1.3	1.4	1.5	1.4	1.5	1.4
2003	1.3	1.5	1.4	1.6	1.4	1.4	1.4	1.2	1.3	1.6	1.6	1.7	1.5
Local government													
1990	5.3	5.5	5.5	5.4	5.3	5.4	4.3	4.5	4.9	5.5	5.5	5.6	5.2
1991	5.7	5.5	5.2	5.5	5.5	4.6	4.5	4.7	5.1	5.7	5.8	5.8	5.3
1992	5.7	5.8	5.9	5.8	5.8	5.9	4.6	4.9	5.4	5.8	6.0	6.1	5.6
1993	6.0	6.1	6.1	6.1	6.1	6.2	5.0	5.3	5.8	5.9	6.0	6.1	5.8
1994	6.0	6.2	6.2	6.1	6.1	6.0	5.5	5.9	6.0	6.1	6.0	6.1	6.0
1995	6.0	6.1	6.2	6.2	6.3	6.0	5.3	5.7	5.9	6.3	6.3	6.4	6.0
1996	6.2	6.3	6.4	6.3	6.4	6.3	5.5	5.8	6.2	6.4	6.3	6.3	6.2
1997	6.3	6.4	6.4	6.6	6.7	6.7	5.9	6.1	6.5	6.8	6.8	6.7	6.4
1998	6.7	6.8	6.8	6.5	6.5	6.5	5.4	5.8	6.2	6.7	6.7	6.6	6.4
1999	6.6	6.8	6.8	6.7	6.8	6.7	5.7	6.1	6.3	6.5	6.5	6.5	6.5
2000	6.4	6.5	6.5	6.5	6.5	6.6	5.4	6.0	6.3	6.8	6.8	6.8	6.4
2001	6.6	6.8	6.8	6.8	6.9	6.8	5.9	6.4	6.8	7.0	7.1	7.0	6.7
2002	6.9	7.2	7.2	7.1	7.2	7.1	6.0	6.6	6.8	7.0	7.0	7.0	6.9
2003	7.0	7.2	7.2	6.9	6.8	6.1	5.7	6.2	6.6	6.8	6.8	6.8	6.7
OKLAHOMA CITY													
Total nonfarm													
1990	418.9	424.1	429.0	431.9	434.6	435.7	425.2	426.4	437.2	435.1	435.1	434.5	430.6
1991	424.7	429.8	432.9	435.7	436.7	438.4	426.5	429.1	436.5	437.5	438.5	439.0	433.7
1992	429.7	429.6	433.2	438.1	440.2	440.2	428.9	431.9	440.7	445.2	446.9	448.4	437.7
1993	440.5	443.4	445.3	447.8	448.4	448.2	438.3	439.4	449.8	451.5	451.9	454.7	446.6
1994	446.9	450.5	453.8	457.8	461.2	462.1	455.9	453.8	467.5	466.2	469.7	472.7	459.8
1995	464.8	469.0	471.5	473.8	476.1	477.0	469.9	473.0	481.7	485.4	488.7	491.6	476.8
1996	478.4	481.4	489.7	490.4	495.6	495.5	485.4	491.1	496.4	498.5	500.5	502.5	492.1
1997	487.9	492.5	497.1	494.7	498.7	500.9	493.5	495.2	505.7	509.1	509.7	513.0	499.8
1998	500.8	504.8	508.1	513.7	517.9	517.9	507.8	511.8	520.1	524.5	526.2	529.5	515.2
1999	517.0	521.9	526.2	524.9	527.4	528.9	523.1	525.8	533.6	535.3	538.1	542.5	528.7
2000	526.8	530.1	535.6	537.5	542.1	542.2	533.7	539.0	547.7	547.3	550.5	549.9	540.2
2001	539.7	542.0	546.9	550.2	552.9	553.2	539.3	544.5	550.7	547.7	551.5	550.5	547.4
2002	530.8	536.2	541.0	542.7	546.3	542.4	532.1	537.0	543.5	541.6	544.2	543.1	540.1
2003	527.0	530.5	532.4	534.3	537.6	531.4	523.5	526.8	532.6	534.0	534.2	535.5	531.7
Total private													
1990	317.1	320.5	324.6	328.3	330.3	333.3	331.8	329.9	334.4	330.4	331.0	330.5	328.5
1991	322.3	325.8	328.4	331.4	332.3	336.3	333.8	334.4	333.4	332.8	333.4	333.4	331.4
1992	325.1	323.6	326.2	331.9	333.7	335.7	335.2	335.6	336.4	338.2	339.7	340.8	333.5
1993	334.3	336.4	339.3	342.1	342.3	345.7	346.9	346.6	347.7	348.9	348.9	351.4	344.2
1994	344.6	347.4	350.1	353.6	356.4	360.3	361.6	361.0	364.4	362.6	365.4	367.5	357.9
1995	362.7	365.5	368.0	370.7	372.3	376.1	376.4	378.5	380.2	382.5	385.4	388.1	375.5
1996	376.7	378.3	386.1	386.9	391.3	395.1	392.5	396.8	396.1	395.5	397.3	399.0	390.9
1997	386.3	389.1	393.2	391.1	394.5	399.8	399.0	399.2	401.8	403.7	404.6	407.4	397.4
1998	399.8	402.3	405.2	410.9	413.8	416.6	413.2	415.7	416.6	419.4	421.8	424.0	413.2
1999	413.8	417.1	420.6	419.6	422.5	424.9	427.8	428.6	429.1	429.2	432.3	435.9	425.1
2000	422.3	424.0	428.1	430.2	433.2	436.9	436.7	439.3	440.7	439.1	441.0	441.5	434.4
2001	432.7	433.3	437.4	441.1	443.1	446.2	440.0	441.1	440.8	435.9	438.5	438.0	439.0
2002	421.6	425.0	429.0	430.8	434.1	434.2	432.4	434.5	433.0	429.0	431.2	430.4	430.4
2003	418.7	419.2	421.8	423.3	426.6	423.6	423.6	426.1	425.9	425.7	425.3	426.5	423.9
Goods-producing													
1990	65.4	67.6	69.1	68.9	69.3	69.6	69.8	66.9	69.4	69.0	68.0	67.3	68.3
1991	64.6	67.3	66.8	68.4	68.6	69.3	68.7	68.8	68.1	67.1	66.8	66.6	67.5
1992	65.2	61.6	61.8	65.1	65.3	65.2	66.1	66.2	66.2	66.6	66.8	67.2	65.2
1993	66.4	66.6	66.7	67.0	67.1	67.8	68.7	68.7	68.3	68.6	68.5	68.7	67.7
1994	67.6	67.9	68.4	69.1	69.4	70.9	71.9	71.9	72.1	71.4	72.1	72.4	70.4
1995	71.7	72.1	72.7	72.7	72.9	73.6	73.5	73.8	73.1	72.9	72.9	73.3	72.9
1996	71.5	71.7	72.9	73.2	74.0	74.5	74.9	75.8	75.1	74.6	74.7	74.4	73.9
1997	72.9	73.2	74.0	72.9	73.7	75.1	75.5	75.7	75.7	76.3	75.8	76.1	74.7
1998	77.1	77.4	77.3	77.2	77.8	78.9	75.9	78.4	78.0	78.7	78.6	78.9	77.8
1999	78.1	78.1	78.2	77.6	78.7	79.6	81.2	81.4	81.2	80.4	80.2	80.4	79.5
2000	78.4	78.7	79.3	78.8	79.3	80.2	80.1	80.8	80.6	80.1	80.3	80.6	79.8
2001	78.1	77.8	78.5	78.4	79.3	79.8	78.5	76.7	77.6	75.0	75.8	75.1	77.5
2002	68.4	69.6	69.7	68.8	70.0	70.2	70.2	69.9	69.3	68.2	68.0	67.7	69.2
2003	66.7	66.6	67.0	67.1	67.4	65.3	68.1	68.4	68.0	67.3	67.1	66.6	67.1

Employment by Industry: Oklahoma—*Continued*

(Numbers in thousands. Not seasonally adjusted.)

Industry	January	February	March	April	May	June	July	August	September	October	November	December	Annual Average
OKLAHOMA CITY *—Continued*													
Natural resources and mining													
1990	8.2	8.0	8.0	8.0	8.0	8.0	8.0	8.0	7.9	8.1	8.2	8.3	8.0
1991	7.8	7.7	7.7	7.9	8.0	8.0	7.5	7.4	7.3	7.2	7.1	7.0	7.5
1992	6.7	6.6	6.6	6.3	6.3	5.9	6.0	6.0	6.0	6.1	6.2	6.4	6.2
1993	6.5	6.3	6.1	6.0	6.0	6.1	6.1	6.1	6.0	6.1	6.1	6.2	6.1
1994	6.0	6.0	6.0	5.9	5.9	6.0	6.1	6.1	6.1	5.8	5.9	5.9	5.9
1995	5.8	5.7	5.7	5.7	5.7	5.6	5.8	5.8	5.8	5.7	5.7	5.7	5.7
1996	5.8	5.8	5.9	5.9	6.0	6.0	6.1	6.0	5.9	5.9	6.0	6.0	5.9
1997	6.0	6.1	6.2	6.4	6.4	6.7	6.6	6.6	6.7	6.7	6.6	6.7	6.4
1998	6.4	6.4	6.6	5.9	5.9	6.0	5.9	5.9	5.8	5.2	5.1	5.2	5.8
1999	5.5	5.4	5.3	5.0	5.0	5.1	4.8	4.8	4.8	5.1	5.1	5.1	5.0
2000	5.1	5.3	5.3	5.4	5.4	5.5	5.7	5.9	5.9	6.1	6.2	6.5	5.7
2001	6.2	6.3	6.5	6.5	6.5	6.7	6.7	6.7	6.5	6.5	6.4	6.4	6.5
2002	6.4	6.5	6.5	6.3	6.5	6.5	6.6	6.5	6.5	6.4	6.4	6.4	6.5
2003	6.5	6.5	6.5	6.7	6.7	6.8	7.1	7.2	7.2	7.2	7.3	7.2	6.9
Construction													
1990	11.9	12.0	12.2	12.7	13.0	13.5	13.9	14.0	13.7	13.5	13.3	13.0	13.0
1991	12.6	13.0	13.4	13.5	13.6	14.0	13.9	14.0	13.7	13.6	13.4	13.4	13.5
1992	13.3	13.5	13.7	14.0	14.2	14.3	14.7	14.7	14.7	14.8	14.6	14.5	14.2
1993	14.0	14.4	14.7	15.2	15.2	15.7	16.3	16.1	16.0	16.2	16.1	16.0	15.4
1994	15.7	16.0	16.2	16.6	16.8	17.6	17.8	17.7	17.6	17.3	17.6	17.7	17.0
1995	17.1	17.2	17.5	18.0	18.1	18.6	18.7	18.9	18.5	18.3	18.2	18.4	18.1
1996	17.3	17.5	17.9	18.3	18.9	19.2	19.1	19.5	19.5	19.0	18.8	18.5	18.6
1997	17.9	18.1	18.6	18.1	18.5	18.9	19.1	19.2	19.0	19.6	19.2	18.9	18.7
1998	18.7	19.1	19.4	19.3	19.8	20.4	20.2	20.1	19.9	20.6	20.5	20.5	19.8
1999	20.4	20.6	20.7	20.8	21.0	21.5	22.0	21.8	21.8	22.2	22.0	22.1	21.4
2000	21.4	21.3	21.8	22.1	22.6	23.1	22.8	23.1	22.9	23.0	22.6	22.3	22.4
2001	21.6	22.0	22.6	23.2	23.8	24.4	24.0	24.2	23.5	23.0	22.4	22.0	23.0
2002	21.3	21.2	21.4	21.4	21.9	22.3	22.5	22.4	22.0	21.8	21.6	21.6	21.8
2003	21.2	21.1	21.4	21.8	22.5	23.3	23.1	23.2	22.8	22.5	22.2	21.7	22.2
Manufacturing													
1990	45.3	47.6	48.9	48.2	48.3	48.1	47.9	44.9	47.8	47.4	46.5	46.0	47.2
1991	44.2	46.6	45.7	47.0	47.0	47.3	47.3	47.4	47.1	46.3	46.3	46.2	46.5
1992	45.2	41.5	41.5	44.8	44.8	45.0	45.4	45.5	45.5	45.7	46.0	46.3	44.7
1993	45.9	45.9	45.9	45.8	45.9	46.0	46.3	46.5	46.3	46.3	46.3	46.5	46.1
1994	45.9	45.9	46.2	46.6	46.7	47.3	48.0	48.1	48.4	48.3	48.6	48.8	47.4
1995	48.8	49.2	49.5	49.0	49.1	49.4	49.0	49.1	48.8	48.9	49.0	49.2	49.0
1996	48.4	48.4	49.1	49.0	49.1	49.3	49.7	50.3	49.7	49.7	49.9	49.9	49.3
1997	49.0	49.0	49.2	48.4	48.8	49.5	49.8	49.9	50.0	50.0	50.0	50.5	49.5
1998	52.0	51.9	51.3	52.0	52.1	52.5	49.8	52.4	52.3	52.9	53.0	53.2	52.1
1999	52.2	52.1	52.2	51.8	52.7	53.0	54.4	54.8	54.6	53.1	53.1	53.2	53.1
2000	51.9	52.1	52.2	51.3	51.3	51.6	51.6	51.8	51.8	51.0	51.5	51.8	51.7
2001	50.3	49.5	49.4	48.7	49.0	48.7	47.8	45.8	47.6	45.5	47.0	46.7	48.0
2002	40.7	41.9	41.8	41.1	41.6	41.4	41.1	41.0	40.8	40.0	40.0	39.7	40.9
2003	39.0	39.0	39.1	38.6	38.2	35.2	37.9	38.0	38.0	37.6	37.6	37.7	38.0
Service-providing													
1990	353.5	356.5	359.9	363.0	365.3	366.1	355.4	359.5	367.8	366.1	367.1	367.2	362.2
1991	360.1	362.5	366.1	367.3	368.1	369.1	357.8	360.3	368.4	370.4	371.7	372.4	366.1
1992	364.5	368.0	371.4	373.0	374.9	375.0	362.8	365.7	374.5	378.6	380.1	381.2	372.4
1993	374.1	376.8	378.6	380.8	381.3	380.4	369.6	370.7	381.5	382.9	383.4	386.0	378.8
1994	379.3	382.6	385.4	388.7	391.8	391.2	384.0	381.9	395.4	394.8	397.6	400.3	389.4
1995	393.1	396.9	398.8	401.1	403.2	403.4	396.4	399.2	408.6	412.5	415.8	418.3	403.9
1996	406.9	409.7	416.8	417.2	421.6	421.0	410.5	415.3	421.3	423.9	425.8	428.1	418.1
1997	415.0	419.3	423.1	421.8	425.0	425.8	418.0	419.5	430.0	432.8	433.9	436.9	425.0
1998	423.7	427.4	430.8	436.5	440.1	439.0	431.9	433.4	442.1	445.8	447.6	450.6	437.4
1999	438.9	443.8	448.0	447.3	448.7	449.3	441.9	444.4	452.4	454.9	457.9	462.1	449.1
2000	448.4	451.4	456.3	458.7	462.8	462.0	453.6	458.2	467.1	467.2	470.2	469.3	460.4
2001	461.6	464.2	468.4	471.8	473.6	473.4	460.8	467.8	473.1	472.7	475.7	475.4	469.8
2002	462.4	466.6	471.3	473.9	476.3	472.2	461.9	467.1	474.2	473.4	476.2	475.4	470.9
2003	460.3	463.9	465.4	467.2	470.2	466.1	455.4	458.4	464.6	466.7	467.1	468.9	464.5
Trade, transportation, and utilities													
1990	83.0	81.9	82.2	82.4	82.5	83.3	83.2	83.7	83.6	83.6	84.9	85.5	83.3
1991	81.2	80.1	80.7	82.1	83.0	83.7	83.8	83.6	83.7	84.8	86.3	87.5	83.3
1992	84.4	83.6	83.7	84.1	84.7	85.5	85.0	85.0	85.1	85.6	87.2	88.3	85.1
1993	85.1	84.2	85.0	84.8	84.9	85.5	86.6	86.9	86.8	87.6	89.1	90.9	86.4
1994	87.8	87.5	87.7	88.3	89.3	90.2	89.8	89.5	89.5	89.6	91.9	93.3	89.5
1995	90.1	89.1	89.1	89.8	90.0	91.2	91.3	92.0	92.1	94.2	96.3	98.1	91.9
1996	93.9	92.4	94.3	94.4	95.4	95.9	95.6	96.4	95.8	95.9	98.5	100.2	95.7
1997	94.6	93.9	95.0	94.1	94.4	95.5	96.2	96.6	96.8	97.3	99.7	101.7	96.3
1998	96.4	95.7	96.3	98.2	98.3	98.9	97.9	98.1	98.5	101.2	103.0	104.3	98.9
1999	99.2	98.3	98.8	98.5	98.8	99.2	100.6	100.5	100.5	101.8	104.3	106.5	100.5
2000	101.8	100.4	100.3	100.2	100.8	101.7	100.9	101.7	101.6	102.2	104.8	106.3	101.9
2001	101.6	99.8	100.0	100.4	100.5	100.7	99.5	99.6	99.2	100.0	101.9	102.9	100.5
2002	99.0	98.1	99.2	98.6	98.8	98.8	98.6	99.0	98.7	97.8	100.4	101.2	99.0
2003	96.4	95.3	95.8	95.8	96.3	96.3	95.6	96.3	96.5	97.4	97.7	98.9	96.5

Employment by Industry: Oklahoma—*Continued*

(Numbers in thousands. Not seasonally adjusted.)

Industry	January	February	March	April	May	June	July	August	September	October	November	December	Annual Average
OKLAHOMA CITY *—Continued*													
Wholesale trade													
1990	17.7	17.6	17.8	18.2	18.1	18.4	18.9	19.1	19.0	18.6	18.4	18.4	18.3
1991	17.7	17.6	17.8	18.0	18.1	18.2	18.2	18.2	18.2	18.8	18.9	19.0	18.2
1992	18.6	18.5	18.5	18.9	19.0	19.2	18.8	18.8	18.9	18.9	19.0	19.0	18.8
1993	18.9	18.8	19.0	18.9	18.9	19.0	19.0	19.0	18.9	19.0	19.0	19.2	18.9
1994	19.3	19.2	19.1	19.6	19.7	19.9	19.9	19.9	20.0	19.7	19.9	19.9	19.6
1995	19.9	19.8	19.9	20.0	20.4	20.6	20.6	20.6	20.7	20.8	20.9	21.0	20.4
1996	20.5	20.5	20.8	20.7	20.9	20.9	20.8	20.9	20.8	20.9	21.1	21.2	20.8
1997	20.8	20.7	20.8	20.1	20.2	20.4	20.9	20.7	20.6	20.6	20.6	20.7	20.5
1998	20.8	21.0	21.0	20.9	21.1	21.2	21.1	21.0	21.1	22.1	22.4	22.5	21.3
1999	22.2	22.3	22.6	22.9	22.7	22.8	22.5	22.4	22.3	22.6	22.8	22.6	22.5
2000	22.4	22.3	22.3	21.6	21.6	22.6	21.8	22.0	21.9	21.6	21.7	21.8	22.0
2001	21.0	21.0	21.1	21.1	21.2	21.6	21.5	21.6	21.5	21.4	21.4	21.6	21.3
2002	21.1	21.0	21.1	20.9	21.1	21.2	21.4	21.3	21.3	21.0	21.1	21.0	21.1
2003	20.9	20.8	20.9	20.7	20.7	20.7	20.5	20.5	20.6	20.8	20.8	20.5	20.7
Retail trade													
1990	50.0	49.0	49.1	49.6	49.8	50.1	49.6	50.1	50.1	50.4	51.8	52.5	50.1
1991	49.7	48.7	49.0	50.0	50.6	51.1	50.8	50.7	50.7	51.2	52.6	53.3	50.7
1992	50.5	49.9	50.0	50.0	50.5	51.0	51.2	51.4	51.5	51.8	53.3	54.4	51.2
1993	51.6	50.7	51.4	51.4	51.4	51.8	51.9	52.2	52.3	52.4	54.0	55.5	52.2
1994	52.7	52.4	52.6	53.3	53.8	54.4	54.2	54.3	54.2	54.5	56.5	57.9	54.2
1995	55.1	54.2	54.1	54.5	54.4	54.9	54.8	55.4	55.4	56.9	58.8	60.4	55.7
1996	56.4	54.9	56.1	55.9	56.4	56.9	56.8	57.8	57.9	57.6	59.9	61.5	57.3
1997	56.7	55.9	56.7	56.6	56.7	57.3	58.1	58.7	59.1	59.2	60.5	62.4	58.1
1998	58.4	57.3	58.0	58.1	58.0	58.5	57.8	58.0	58.4	59.7	62.2	63.5	58.9
1999	60.2	59.4	59.7	59.0	59.6	59.9	60.9	60.9	60.9	62.2	64.6	66.7	61.1
2000	62.7	61.5	61.5	61.8	62.2	62.2	62.3	62.9	62.9	63.7	66.2	67.6	63.1
2001	63.4	61.9	62.0	61.8	61.9	62.0	60.8	60.8	60.7	61.8	63.7	64.7	62.1
2002	61.9	61.2	62.1	61.6	61.6	61.5	60.9	61.4	61.3	61.0	63.6	64.8	61.9
2003	60.4	59.4	59.7	60.1	60.5	60.6	60.1	60.8	61.0	61.6	62.1	63.7	60.8
Transportation and utilities													
1990	15.3	15.3	15.3	14.6	14.6	14.8	14.7	14.5	14.5	14.6	14.7	14.6	14.7
1991	13.8	13.8	13.9	14.1	14.3	14.4	14.8	14.7	14.8	14.8	14.8	15.2	14.4
1992	15.3	15.2	15.2	15.2	15.2	15.3	15.0	14.8	14.7	14.9	14.9	14.9	15.0
1993	14.6	14.7	14.6	14.5	14.6	14.7	15.7	15.7	15.6	16.2	16.1	16.2	15.2
1994	15.8	15.9	16.0	15.4	15.8	15.9	15.7	15.3	15.3	15.4	15.5	15.5	15.6
1995	15.1	15.1	15.1	15.3	15.2	15.7	15.9	16.0	16.0	16.5	16.6	16.7	15.7
1996	17.0	17.0	17.4	17.8	18.1	18.1	18.0	17.7	17.1	17.4	17.5	17.5	17.5
1997	17.1	17.3	17.5	17.4	17.5	17.8	17.2	17.2	17.1	17.5	18.6	18.6	17.5
1998	17.2	17.4	17.3	19.2	19.2	19.2	19.0	19.1	19.0	19.4	18.4	18.3	18.5
1999	16.8	16.6	16.5	16.6	16.5	16.5	17.2	17.2	17.3	17.0	16.9	17.2	16.8
2000	16.7	16.6	16.5	16.8	17.0	16.9	16.8	16.8	16.8	16.9	16.9	16.9	16.8
2001	17.2	16.9	16.9	17.5	17.4	17.1	17.2	17.2	17.0	16.8	16.8	16.6	17.0
2002	16.0	15.9	16.0	16.1	16.1	16.1	16.3	16.3	16.1	15.8	15.7	15.4	16.0
2003	15.1	15.1	15.2	15.0	15.1	15.0	15.0	15.0	14.9	15.0	14.8	14.7	15.0
Information													
1990	9.2	9.2	9.2	8.8	8.9	9.0	9.0	9.0	9.0	8.9	8.8	8.8	8.9
1991	8.8	8.8	8.9	8.8	8.8	8.9	8.8	8.9	8.8	8.7	8.7	8.7	8.8
1992	8.7	8.7	8.8	8.8	8.8	8.9	8.8	8.9	8.9	8.9	8.9	8.9	8.8
1993	9.0	9.0	9.0	9.2	9.2	9.5	9.5	9.5	9.5	9.4	9.3	9.3	9.2
1994	9.4	9.4	9.4	9.5	9.6	9.5	9.7	9.6	9.6	9.6	9.7	9.8	9.5
1995	9.5	9.6	9.6	9.9	9.9	10.0	10.5	10.1	10.1	10.1	10.2	10.3	9.9
1996	10.4	10.5	10.7	10.7	10.8	10.9	11.2	11.4	11.4	11.6	11.7	11.9	11.1
1997	11.7	11.7	11.8	11.8	12.0	12.1	12.0	11.9	11.9	12.0	12.1	12.1	11.9
1998	11.5	11.5	11.5	11.6	11.7	11.7	11.2	11.5	11.3	11.5	11.7	11.8	11.5
1999	12.1	12.3	12.3	12.2	12.2	12.1	12.1	12.1	12.1	12.2	12.6	12.8	12.2
2000	13.2	13.6	13.7	14.3	14.2	14.4	14.6	14.6	14.8	14.8	14.8	14.8	14.3
2001	15.0	15.2	15.2	14.9	14.9	15.0	14.7	14.4	14.5	14.5	14.4	14.4	14.7
2002	14.5	14.5	14.3	14.2	14.3	14.2	14.1	14.1	13.9	13.8	14.0	13.9	14.2
2003	13.7	13.6	13.7	13.6	13.7	13.6	13.5	13.5	13.4	13.0	13.0	12.8	13.4
Financial activities													
1990	27.8	27.8	27.9	28.6	28.7	28.7	28.8	28.9	28.8	28.1	28.3	28.3	28.3
1991	27.5	27.4	27.7	28.0	28.1	28.4	28.3	28.2	27.7	27.5	27.4	27.4	27.8
1992	26.9	27.0	27.0	27.2	27.5	27.7	27.3	27.2	27.1	27.6	27.7	27.7	27.3
1993	27.9	28.0	28.2	27.8	27.9	28.1	28.3	28.1	28.0	27.8	27.6	28.0	27.9
1994	27.8	28.1	28.3	28.7	28.9	29.2	29.0	28.8	28.9	28.5	28.6	28.7	28.6
1995	28.3	28.5	28.6	29.0	29.2	29.5	29.7	29.8	29.7	29.6	29.7	30.0	29.3
1996	29.4	29.8	30.5	30.8	31.1	31.2	31.1	31.1	30.8	30.9	30.8	30.9	30.7
1997	30.6	30.6	30.6	30.7	31.1	31.4	31.5	31.3	31.3	31.2	31.0	31.2	31.0
1998	31.1	31.3	31.5	31.4	31.8	32.2	32.7	32.5	32.2	32.7	33.0	33.3	32.1
1999	32.8	33.1	33.2	33.1	33.2	33.5	33.8	33.6	33.4	33.6	33.6	33.8	33.3
2000	33.0	33.2	33.2	33.1	33.1	33.2	33.2	33.4	33.3	33.3	33.4	33.5	33.2
2001	32.8	33.0	33.1	33.4	33.5	33.8	33.8	34.0	33.8	33.8	33.8	33.7	33.5
2002	33.6	33.6	33.6	33.6	33.8	34.2	34.2	34.3	34.1	33.9	34.0	34.1	33.9
2003	33.9	34.0	34.2	34.2	34.4	34.6	35.1	35.3	35.2	33.8	33.7	34.0	34.4

Employment by Industry: Oklahoma—*Continued*

(Numbers in thousands. Not seasonally adjusted.)

Industry	January	February	March	April	May	June	July	August	September	October	November	December	Annual Average
OKLAHOMA CITY *—Continued*													
Professional and business services													
1990	37.3	37.7	38.4	39.1	39.3	40.6	40.0	40.4	41.4	39.6	40.5	40.8	39.5
1991	40.9	41.5	42.0	40.6	40.4	41.0	40.5	41.2	40.2	40.0	40.3	40.1	40.7
1992	39.9	40.5	41.2	42.2	42.0	42.4	43.2	43.5	43.5	43.1	43.0	43.1	42.3
1993	42.3	42.6	42.9	43.6	43.6	44.8	44.4	44.1	44.1	44.0	43.5	43.8	43.6
1994	42.2	42.8	43.5	44.1	44.4	45.1	45.3	46.0	46.6	45.9	46.4	46.4	44.8
1995	46.7	47.9	48.5	48.8	48.7	49.7	49.4	50.6	51.0	50.9	52.0	51.7	49.6
1996	51.4	52.2	53.1	52.3	53.2	53.7	52.9	54.2	53.9	54.1	53.6	53.6	53.1
1997	52.4	53.5	54.3	55.5	55.9	56.5	56.5	56.4	57.6	57.5	57.4	58.2	55.9
1998	57.5	58.5	58.8	60.5	61.4	62.3	62.9	62.2	63.0	61.5	61.5	61.9	61.0
1999	60.9	62.3	63.5	63.3	64.3	65.4	64.6	65.4	65.7	65.3	65.5	66.5	64.3
2000	63.6	64.4	65.9	66.8	67.5	68.8	69.4	69.3	70.0	68.6	68.3	68.7	67.6
2001	66.5	67.1	68.3	69.6	69.4	70.9	69.0	70.6	71.0	68.5	68.3	68.5	68.9
2002	66.3	67.8	69.1	70.4	70.4	70.4	68.7	69.3	69.3	67.8	67.5	67.6	68.7
2003	64.2	64.6	64.9	65.8	66.7	66.3	65.5	66.0	66.5	67.0	66.2	66.5	65.9
Educational and health services													
1990	40.0	40.4	40.7	40.5	40.7	40.6	40.5	40.8	41.7	42.0	41.9	42.0	40.9
1991	41.8	42.3	42.6	42.9	43.2	43.2	42.9	43.1	43.6	44.0	43.9	44.0	43.1
1992	43.4	44.0	44.2	44.1	44.1	44.2	44.0	44.1	45.2	45.4	45.5	45.5	44.4
1993	45.6	46.3	46.5	47.1	46.7	46.5	46.6	46.7	48.0	48.2	48.3	48.6	47.0
1994	48.2	48.8	49.0	48.8	48.8	48.6	49.4	49.3	50.7	51.3	51.5	51.9	49.6
1995	51.9	52.5	52.9	52.8	53.0	53.1	53.1	53.8	55.3	55.6	55.8	56.2	53.8
1996	54.1	54.8	55.9	55.9	56.2	57.5	56.0	56.5	57.4	57.8	58.1	58.2	56.5
1997	55.7	56.7	56.9	55.5	55.9	56.6	55.6	55.6	56.6	58.0	57.8	57.6	56.5
1998	59.2	59.9	60.6	61.2	60.9	59.9	61.0	61.0	61.9	62.3	62.8	62.8	61.1
1999	60.9	62.1	62.2	61.3	61.1	60.3	60.8	60.7	61.5	60.9	60.9	60.9	61.1
2000	59.4	60.0	60.4	61.0	61.6	61.1	61.3	61.8	62.6	62.1	62.3	62.1	61.3
2001	62.6	63.2	63.7	63.3	63.6	63.0	62.7	63.8	64.3	65.0	64.8	64.9	63.7
2002	63.7	64.5	64.9	65.1	65.5	64.7	64.9	66.0	66.2	66.3	67.0	66.8	65.5
2003	65.9	66.8	67.3	66.7	66.6	66.2	64.8	65.6	66.3	66.7	68.0	68.5	66.6
Leisure and hospitality													
1990	34.4	35.9	36.8	39.5	40.1	40.4	39.6	39.3	39.7	38.7	38.2	37.4	38.3
1991	37.0	37.8	38.9	39.8	39.3	40.6	39.4	39.4	40.1	39.4	38.8	38.1	39.0
1992	36.2	37.8	39.0	39.8	40.4	40.7	39.9	39.7	39.5	39.9	39.5	39.0	39.2
1993	36.9	38.5	39.5	40.9	41.2	41.4	40.4	40.3	40.6	40.9	40.3	39.9	40.0
1994	38.4	39.6	40.4	41.6	42.4	43.0	42.7	42.2	43.3	42.7	41.7	41.5	41.6
1995	41.0	42.3	43.0	43.7	44.4	44.5	44.4	43.7	44.1	44.2	43.3	43.2	43.4
1996	41.0	41.8	43.1	43.9	44.7	45.1	44.8	45.2	45.7	44.7	43.9	43.6	43.9
1997	42.7	43.7	44.7	45.0	45.6	46.3	45.4	45.4	45.7	45.6	45.0	44.5	44.9
1998	42.6	43.4	44.4	46.1	46.6	47.0	46.0	46.3	45.8	45.4	44.8	44.2	45.2
1999	44.0	44.8	46.1	46.9	47.4	47.9	47.5	47.8	47.7	47.7	48.1	47.7	46.9
2000	46.3	47.1	48.5	48.9	49.5	50.1	50.0	50.4	50.3	50.7	49.8	48.1	49.1
2001	47.6	48.6	49.7	52.3	52.9	53.5	52.7	52.9	51.6	50.6	51.0	50.1	51.1
2002	48.7	49.4	50.6	51.6	52.7	53.1	53.3	53.5	53.2	53.1	52.3	51.1	51.9
2003	49.9	50.2	50.8	52.2	53.4	53.1	53.0	53.2	52.5	52.9	52.9	52.0	52.2
Other services													
1990	20.0	20.0	20.3	20.5	20.8	21.1	20.9	20.9	20.8	20.5	20.4	20.4	20.5
1991	20.5	20.6	20.8	20.8	20.9	21.2	21.4	21.2	21.2	21.3	21.2	21.0	21.0
1992	20.4	20.4	20.5	20.6	20.9	21.1	20.9	21.0	20.9	21.1	21.1	21.1	20.8
1993	21.1	21.2	21.5	21.7	21.7	22.1	22.4	22.3	22.4	22.4	22.3	22.2	21.9
1994	23.2	23.3	23.4	23.5	23.6	23.8	23.8	23.7	23.7	23.6	23.5	23.5	23.5
1995	23.5	23.5	23.6	24.0	24.2	24.5	24.5	24.7	24.8	25.0	25.2	25.3	24.4
1996	25.0	25.1	25.6	25.7	25.9	26.3	26.0	26.2	26.0	25.9	26.0	26.2	25.8
1997	25.7	25.8	25.9	25.6	25.9	26.3	26.3	26.3	26.2	25.8	25.8	26.0	25.9
1998	24.4	24.6	24.8	24.7	25.3	25.7	25.6	25.7	25.9	26.1	26.4	26.8	25.5
1999	25.8	26.1	26.3	26.7	26.8	26.9	27.2	27.1	27.0	27.3	27.1	27.3	26.8
2000	26.6	26.6	26.8	27.1	27.2	27.4	27.2	27.3	27.5	27.3	27.3	27.4	27.1
2001	28.5	28.6	28.9	28.8	29.0	29.5	29.1	29.1	28.8	28.5	28.5	28.4	28.7
2002	27.4	27.5	27.6	28.5	28.6	28.6	28.4	28.4	28.3	28.1	28.0	28.0	28.1
2003	28.0	28.1	28.1	27.9	28.1	28.2	28.0	27.8	27.5	27.6	26.7	27.2	27.8
Government													
1990	101.8	103.6	104.4	103.6	104.3	102.4	93.4	96.5	102.8	104.7	104.1	104.0	102.1
1991	102.4	104.0	104.5	104.3	104.4	102.1	92.7	94.7	103.1	104.7	105.1	105.6	102.3
1992	104.6	106.0	107.0	106.2	106.5	104.5	93.7	96.3	104.3	107.0	107.2	107.6	104.2
1993	106.2	107.0	106.0	105.7	106.1	102.5	91.4	92.8	102.1	102.6	103.0	103.3	102.3
1994	102.3	103.1	103.7	104.2	104.8	101.8	94.3	92.8	103.1	103.6	104.3	105.2	101.9
1995	102.1	103.5	103.5	103.1	103.8	100.9	93.5	94.5	101.5	102.9	103.3	103.5	101.3
1996	101.7	103.1	103.6	103.5	104.3	100.4	92.9	94.3	100.3	103.0	103.2	103.5	101.1
1997	101.6	103.4	103.9	103.6	104.2	101.1	94.5	96.0	103.9	105.4	105.1	105.6	102.3
1998	101.0	102.5	102.9	102.8	104.1	101.3	94.6	96.1	103.5	105.1	104.4	105.5	101.9
1999	103.2	104.8	105.6	105.3	104.9	104.0	95.3	97.2	104.5	106.1	105.8	106.6	103.6
2000	104.5	106.1	107.5	107.3	108.9	105.3	97.0	99.7	107.0	108.2	109.5	108.4	105.8
2001	107.0	108.7	109.5	109.1	109.8	107.0	99.3	103.4	109.9	111.8	113.0	112.5	108.4
2002	109.2	111.2	112.0	111.9	112.2	108.2	99.7	102.5	110.5	112.6	113.0	112.7	109.6
2003	108.3	111.3	110.6	111.0	111.0	107.8	99.9	100.7	106.7	108.3	108.9	109.0	107.8

Employment by Industry: Oklahoma—*Continued*

(Numbers in thousands. Not seasonally adjusted.)

Industry	January	February	March	April	May	June	July	August	September	October	November	December	Annual Average
OKLAHOMA CITY *—Continued*													
Federal government													
1990	30.2	30.1	30.2	30.1	30.1	30.3	30.2	30.1	29.7	29.7	28.9	28.9	29.8
1991	28.6	28.5	28.5	28.6	28.2	28.4	28.2	28.2	28.1	28.0	28.0	27.9	28.2
1992	28.1	28.0	27.9	27.8	27.8	27.9	27.9	27.9	27.7	27.9	27.8	27.9	27.8
1993	27.8	27.7	26.6	26.7	26.7	26.7	26.4	26.2	25.1	24.7	24.5	24.6	26.1
1994	24.6	24.6	24.6	24.7	24.6	24.4	24.4	24.3	24.3	24.0	24.0	24.2	24.3
1995	23.4	23.4	23.4	23.5	23.6	23.5	23.6	23.6	23.6	23.5	23.5	23.5	23.5
1996	23.5	23.6	23.6	23.9	24.2	24.5	24.5	24.6	24.6	25.0	25.2	25.4	24.3
1997	25.4	25.4	25.4	25.5	25.5	25.5	25.5	25.5	25.5	25.5	25.4	25.6	25.4
1998	25.4	25.3	25.3	25.4	25.5	25.6	25.6	25.5	25.6	25.6	25.6	25.7	25.5
1999	25.5	25.5	25.7	25.7	25.7	25.7	25.9	26.1	26.3	26.4	26.5	26.7	25.9
2000	26.5	26.5	27.0	27.0	28.7	28.2	27.4	27.8	26.8	26.9	26.9	27.1	27.2
2001	26.9	27.0	27.1	27.0	27.0	27.2	27.2	27.1	27.1	27.2	27.1	27.1	27.0
2002	27.0	26.9	26.9	27.0	27.0	27.1	27.1	27.2	27.1	27.5	27.5	27.5	27.2
2003	27.1	27.0	26.8	26.7	26.6	26.7	25.8	25.8	25.8	25.9	25.9	26.1	26.4
State government													
1990	34.8	35.8	36.3	36.4	36.3	35.5	34.6	35.5	36.5	37.1	37.1	37.0	36.0
1991	36.2	37.1	37.3	37.5	37.5	36.6	35.0	36.0	37.9	38.2	38.3	38.2	37.1
1992	37.1	38.0	38.5	38.1	38.1	36.6	35.1	36.2	37.5	38.3	38.2	38.4	37.5
1993	37.7	37.8	37.8	37.5	37.2	35.4	34.8	34.1	36.9	37.0	37.1	37.1	36.7
1994	36.3	36.5	36.8	37.4	37.5	35.7	35.2	35.1	37.4	38.0	38.2	38.3	36.8
1995	37.2	38.2	37.7	37.6	37.9	36.2	34.7	35.1	37.2	37.7	37.9	37.7	37.0
1996	36.5	37.4	37.7	37.8	37.9	35.9	34.6	34.9	36.8	37.7	37.6	37.8	36.8
1997	36.1	37.2	37.5	37.4	37.9	35.8	34.8	35.1	37.7	38.4	38.2	38.5	37.0
1998	34.6	35.5	35.9	35.5	36.4	34.5	33.6	34.4	36.6	37.5	36.7	37.4	35.7
1999	35.9	37.1	37.4	37.2	36.7	36.6	33.7	34.3	36.7	37.4	36.6	37.2	36.4
2000	35.9	36.9	37.6	37.3	37.7	35.2	33.8	35.0	37.9	38.2	38.3	37.2	36.8
2001	36.4	38.2	38.6	38.7	38.7	36.4	35.6	37.4	39.0	39.7	39.7	39.5	38.1
2002	37.0	39.5	39.8	39.7	39.4	36.9	35.8	37.2	39.2	39.4	39.7	39.5	38.6
2003	36.2	39.1	38.9	39.0	38.8	36.2	35.5	36.2	38.8	39.5	39.6	39.8	38.1
Local government													
1990	36.8	37.7	37.9	37.1	37.9	36.6	28.6	30.9	36.6	37.9	38.1	38.1	36.1
1991	37.6	38.4	38.7	38.2	38.7	37.1	29.5	30.5	37.1	38.5	38.8	39.5	36.8
1992	39.4	40.0	40.6	40.3	40.6	40.0	30.7	32.2	39.1	40.8	41.2	41.3	38.8
1993	40.7	41.5	41.6	41.5	42.2	40.4	30.2	32.5	40.1	40.9	41.4	41.6	39.5
1994	41.4	42.0	42.3	42.1	42.7	41.7	34.7	33.4	41.4	41.6	42.1	42.7	40.6
1995	41.5	41.9	42.4	42.0	42.3	41.2	35.2	35.8	40.7	41.7	41.9	42.3	40.7
1996	41.7	42.1	42.3	41.8	42.2	40.0	33.8	34.8	38.9	40.3	40.4	40.3	39.8
1997	40.1	40.8	41.0	40.7	40.8	39.8	34.2	35.4	40.7	41.5	41.5	41.5	39.8
1998	41.0	41.7	41.7	41.9	42.2	41.2	35.4	36.2	41.3	42.0	42.1	42.4	40.7
1999	41.8	42.2	42.5	42.4	42.5	41.7	35.7	36.8	41.5	42.3	42.7	42.7	41.2
2000	42.1	42.7	42.9	43.0	42.5	41.9	35.8	36.9	42.3	43.1	44.3	44.1	41.8
2001	43.7	43.5	43.8	43.4	44.1	43.4	36.5	38.9	43.8	44.9	46.2	45.9	43.1
2002	45.2	44.8	45.3	45.2	45.8	44.2	36.8	38.1	44.2	45.7	45.8	45.7	43.9
2003	45.0	45.2	44.9	45.3	45.6	44.9	38.6	38.7	42.1	42.9	43.4	43.1	43.3
TULSA													
Total nonfarm													
1990	311.9	312.0	314.6	315.4	317.8	322.6	315.7	319.3	324.4	323.9	325.5	327.6	319.2
1991	318.8	320.7	323.1	323.6	325.5	327.9	321.2	323.6	327.2	329.4	328.1	328.0	324.7
1992	322.6	323.1	324.5	327.3	328.3	328.2	323.4	324.5	330.9	331.7	330.5	330.9	327.1
1993	325.2	326.9	329.6	329.4	330.7	333.3	326.4	329.5	334.5	336.5	336.4	338.9	331.4
1994	334.2	334.8	337.4	340.2	341.7	343.7	342.3	344.8	347.5	346.7	347.5	350.6	342.6
1995	342.8	344.1	347.6	346.9	350.4	352.6	347.9	350.1	351.9	352.8	354.3	356.5	349.8
1996	350.5	351.9	355.2	356.8	361.0	362.4	360.8	363.7	365.3	365.7	365.8	368.2	360.6
1997	362.1	364.8	367.4	368.1	371.6	373.5	373.2	374.9	377.7	381.8	383.4	386.2	373.7
1998	380.0	383.3	386.7	389.9	394.2	393.9	392.8	392.9	395.7	396.9	396.9	399.9	391.9
1999	387.5	388.6	390.2	393.2	396.3	396.9	396.7	395.8	397.8	398.0	399.6	400.8	395.1
2000	391.2	392.2	396.9	400.9	405.1	408.1	404.4	407.1	407.9	408.0	409.8	410.6	403.5
2001	397.7	401.0	404.1	407.9	409.8	411.3	407.4	409.0	407.5	405.8	407.5	407.6	406.4
2002	399.0	399.0	400.1	402.0	404.4	400.4	394.2	395.5	393.8	392.6	393.2	393.3	397.3
2003	383.7	383.3	383.8	384.9	385.3	382.2	376.8	377.4	377.0	379.6	383.1	380.2	381.4
Total private													
1990	274.0	273.2	276.0	277.7	279.6	283.9	283.9	286.3	286.4	285.4	286.8	288.2	281.7
1991	279.7	280.9	283.2	283.8	286.2	289.1	287.8	289.1	287.8	288.2	287.4	287.4	285.8
1992	282.3	281.9	283.3	286.3	287.2	288.4	289.1	289.5	290.0	289.5	289.3	289.3	287.1
1993	284.1	285.2	287.8	288.0	288.9	292.1	292.1	293.8	294.6	294.7	294.7	297.1	291.0
1994	293.7	294.0	296.3	298.9	300.4	303.1	303.3	305.6	305.8	304.7	305.7	308.5	301.6
1995	301.7	302.4	305.9	305.6	309.0	311.7	309.3	310.8	311.4	311.0	312.6	314.5	308.8
1996	309.1	310.2	312.6	314.7	318.5	320.9	321.2	323.6	323.8	323.2	323.7	326.0	318.9
1997	320.7	322.5	324.9	325.8	328.9	332.4	334.0	335.4	335.6	338.6	340.5	342.7	331.8
1998	337.9	340.2	343.5	347.0	350.8	352.3	353.4	353.4	352.8	353.1	353.2	355.7	349.4
1999	345.3	345.5	346.7	349.1	352.0	354.5	356.4	355.3	355.2	354.1	354.7	356.3	352.1
2000	347.8	348.1	352.0	356.1	358.7	362.8	362.1	364.2	364.4	362.8	364.8	365.0	359.1
2001	354.0	356.1	359.1	362.9	364.2	366.6	364.8	366.3	362.8	359.7	361.3	361.2	361.5
2002	353.8	352.9	353.7	355.4	356.9	354.8	350.8	351.9	349.1	346.2	347.0	346.9	351.6
2003	339.2	338.2	338.6	340.0	340.5	338.9	335.2	336.5	334.3	334.6	338.2	335.1	337.4

Employment by Industry: Oklahoma—*Continued*

(Numbers in thousands. Not seasonally adjusted.)

Industry	January	February	March	April	May	June	July	August	September	October	November	December	Annual Average
TULSA—*Continued*													
Goods-producing													
1990	73.7	73.2	73.7	74.6	74.9	76.3	76.1	76.7	76.3	76.6	76.6	76.8	75.4
1991	74.0	74.1	74.6	74.1	74.7	75.7	74.8	74.7	73.6	74.0	73.5	73.1	74.2
1992	72.6	72.1	72.5	72.6	72.5	72.9	72.5	72.6	72.4	72.6	72.0	71.9	72.4
1993	71.6	71.7	72.3	72.0	72.2	73.1	73.2	73.3	72.9	73.4	73.2	72.9	72.6
1994	71.8	71.6	72.0	72.1	72.8	73.2	73.0	73.5	73.7	72.9	72.9	73.4	72.7
1995	73.0	73.1	73.5	73.3	73.5	74.2	73.7	73.8	73.4	72.7	72.5	72.4	73.2
1996	72.2	72.3	72.6	73.1	74.0	74.9	74.7	74.8	74.6	74.6	74.7	74.8	73.9
1997	74.5	75.2	75.6	75.3	75.6	76.6	77.8	77.7	77.6	78.5	78.7	78.9	76.8
1998	78.0	79.0	79.6	80.7	81.3	82.1	82.3	82.5	82.5	82.2	82.1	82.1	81.2
1999	80.3	80.3	80.3	79.5	80.4	81.5	81.0	80.1	79.9	79.9	79.5	80.1	80.2
2000	79.0	78.9	79.6	78.9	79.2	80.1	80.3	80.8	80.4	79.4	79.6	79.9	79.7
2001	77.7	78.3	79.1	79.6	80.3	81.3	80.6	81.0	79.9	78.8	78.8	78.7	79.5
2002	77.6	76.4	76.2	75.8	75.9	75.5	74.3	74.2	72.7	71.8	71.4	71.5	74.4
2003	70.5	69.8	69.9	70.0	70.1	70.6	70.0	69.8	69.2	67.8	67.3	66.8	69.3
Natural resources and mining													
1990	10.8	10.8	10.8	10.7	10.7	11.0	11.0	11.1	10.8	10.6	10.6	10.9	10.8
1991	10.1	10.2	10.3	10.2	10.1	10.3	10.1	10.1	10.0	9.8	9.8	9.8	10.0
1992	9.6	9.6	9.5	9.5	9.5	9.5	9.4	9.4	9.2	8.9	8.8	8.8	9.3
1993	8.7	8.8	8.8	8.6	8.6	8.7	8.9	8.8	8.7	8.7	8.8	8.9	8.7
1994	7.8	7.7	7.6	7.9	7.8	7.8	7.8	7.7	7.7	7.4	7.4	7.4	7.6
1995	8.0	7.8	7.8	7.8	7.8	7.9	7.8	7.8	7.7	7.6	7.6	7.6	7.7
1996	7.6	7.5	7.5	7.5	7.6	7.7	7.8	7.6	7.5	7.5	7.5	7.5	7.5
1997	7.5	7.5	7.5	7.5	7.5	7.6	7.9	7.8	7.7	7.7	7.8	7.9	7.6
1998	7.6	7.7	7.7	7.7	7.8	7.9	8.0	8.0	7.9	7.6	7.4	7.4	7.7
1999	7.3	7.2	7.3	7.2	7.1	7.2	7.0	7.0	6.9	6.9	6.8	7.0	7.1
2000	7.0	7.1	6.9	6.4	6.3	6.4	6.3	6.3	6.2	5.8	5.8	5.8	6.4
2001	5.3	5.3	5.4	5.2	5.3	5.4	5.4	5.4	5.4	5.3	5.3	5.3	5.3
2002	5.2	5.2	5.2	5.1	5.1	5.1	4.8	4.8	4.6	4.5	4.4	4.4	4.9
2003	4.4	4.4	4.4	4.3	4.3	4.4	4.0	4.0	4.0	4.0	4.0	3.8	4.2
Construction													
1990	12.1	11.7	11.9	11.9	12.0	12.4	12.4	12.6	12.4	12.0	12.0	11.8	12.1
1991	10.7	11.0	11.4	11.4	11.8	12.4	12.2	12.2	11.9	12.0	11.8	11.7	11.7
1992	11.4	11.2	12.0	11.9	12.0	12.3	12.5	12.4	12.1	12.5	12.2	12.1	12.0
1993	12.1	11.7	12.0	12.2	12.6	13.2	13.5	13.4	13.0	13.0	12.9	12.7	12.6
1994	12.7	12.7	13.2	13.6	14.1	14.6	14.4	14.4	14.2	14.5	14.3	14.4	13.9
1995	13.5	13.7	13.7	13.9	14.0	14.5	14.4	14.5	14.2	14.1	14.0	13.8	14.0
1996	13.8	13.8	14.0	14.4	14.8	15.1	14.9	15.0	14.7	14.6	14.6	14.4	14.5
1997	14.0	14.3	14.6	14.8	14.9	15.2	15.5	15.5	15.4	15.9	15.9	15.6	15.1
1998	14.9	15.4	15.8	16.8	17.1	17.5	17.4	17.5	17.4	17.3	17.5	17.4	16.8
1999	17.5	17.5	17.7	18.1	18.6	19.1	19.4	19.3	19.1	19.0	18.6	18.4	18.5
2000	18.4	18.4	19.0	19.2	19.3	19.6	19.7	19.8	19.5	19.5	19.5	19.3	19.3
2001	18.8	19.4	20.0	20.4	20.8	21.3	21.2	21.5	20.8	20.9	20.7	20.7	20.5
2002	20.5	20.4	20.3	20.0	20.3	20.4	20.5	20.8	20.1	19.9	19.6	19.7	20.2
2003	19.1	18.8	19.1	19.7	19.9	20.1	20.2	20.1	19.7	18.3	18.2	17.8	19.3
Manufacturing													
1990	50.8	50.7	51.0	52.0	52.2	52.9	52.7	53.0	53.1	54.0	54.0	54.1	52.5
1991	53.2	52.9	52.9	52.5	52.8	53.0	52.5	52.4	51.7	52.2	51.9	51.6	52.4
1992	51.6	51.3	51.0	51.2	51.0	51.1	50.6	50.8	51.1	51.2	51.0	51.0	51.0
1993	50.8	51.2	51.5	51.2	51.0	51.2	50.8	51.1	51.2	51.7	51.5	51.3	51.2
1994	51.3	51.2	51.2	50.6	50.9	50.8	50.8	51.4	51.8	51.0	51.2	51.6	51.1
1995	51.5	51.6	52.0	51.6	51.7	51.8	51.5	51.5	51.5	51.0	50.9	51.0	51.4
1996	50.8	51.0	51.1	51.2	51.6	52.1	52.0	52.2	52.4	52.5	52.6	52.9	51.8
1997	53.0	53.4	53.5	53.0	53.2	53.8	54.4	54.4	54.5	54.9	55.0	55.4	54.0
1998	55.5	55.9	56.1	56.2	56.4	56.7	56.9	57.0	57.2	57.3	57.2	57.3	56.6
1999	55.5	55.6	55.3	54.2	54.7	55.2	54.6	53.8	53.9	54.0	54.1	54.7	54.6
2000	53.6	53.4	53.7	53.3	53.6	54.1	54.3	54.7	54.7	54.1	54.3	54.8	54.1
2001	53.6	53.6	53.7	54.0	54.2	54.6	54.0	54.1	53.7	52.6	52.8	52.7	53.6
2002	51.9	50.8	50.7	50.7	50.5	50.0	49.0	48.6	48.0	47.4	47.4	47.4	49.4
2003	47.0	46.6	46.4	46.0	45.9	46.1	45.8	45.7	45.5	45.5	45.1	45.2	45.9
Service-providing													
1990	238.2	238.8	240.9	240.8	242.9	246.3	239.6	242.6	248.1	247.3	248.9	250.8	243.7
1991	244.8	246.6	248.5	249.5	250.8	252.2	246.4	248.9	253.6	255.4	254.6	254.9	250.5
1992	250.0	251.0	252.0	254.7	255.8	255.3	250.9	251.9	258.5	259.1	258.5	259.0	254.7
1993	253.6	255.2	257.3	257.4	258.5	260.2	253.2	256.2	261.6	263.1	263.2	266.0	258.7
1994	262.4	263.2	265.4	268.1	268.9	270.5	269.3	271.3	273.8	273.8	274.6	277.2	269.8
1995	269.8	271.0	274.1	273.6	276.9	278.4	274.2	276.3	278.5	280.1	281.8	284.1	276.5
1996	278.3	279.6	282.6	283.7	287.0	287.5	286.1	288.9	290.7	291.1	291.1	293.4	286.6
1997	287.6	289.6	291.8	292.8	296.0	296.9	295.4	297.2	300.1	303.3	304.7	307.3	296.8
1998	302.0	304.3	307.1	309.2	312.9	311.8	310.5	310.4	313.2	314.7	314.8	317.8	310.7
1999	307.2	308.3	309.9	313.7	315.9	315.4	315.7	315.7	317.9	318.1	320.1	320.7	314.9
2000	312.2	313.3	317.3	322.0	325.9	328.0	324.1	326.3	327.5	328.6	330.2	330.7	323.8
2001	320.0	322.7	325.0	328.3	329.5	330.0	326.8	328.0	327.6	327.0	328.7	328.9	326.9
2002	321.4	322.6	323.9	326.2	328.5	324.9	319.9	321.3	321.1	320.8	321.8	321.8	322.9
2003	313.2	313.5	313.9	314.9	315.2	311.6	306.8	307.6	307.8	311.8	315.8	313.4	312.1

Employment by Industry: Oklahoma—*Continued*

(Numbers in thousands. Not seasonally adjusted.)

Industry	January	February	March	April	May	June	July	August	September	October	November	December	Annual Average
TULSA—*Continued*													
Trade, transportation, and utilities													
1990	73.9	73.1	73.8	73.1	73.9	75.0	74.7	75.3	75.1	75.2	76.7	78.0	74.8
1991	73.8	73.0	73.1	72.8	73.6	74.1	74.0	74.1	73.9	73.8	74.6	75.2	73.8
1992	72.9	71.9	72.0	73.3	73.7	73.9	73.8	73.5	73.3	73.4	74.6	75.3	73.4
1993	70.9	70.2	70.5	70.9	71.2	71.8	72.3	73.3	73.4	73.4	74.5	75.8	72.3
1994	72.3	72.4	72.8	73.4	73.5	74.2	74.5	74.8	74.5	74.4	75.6	77.1	74.1
1995	75.0	74.5	74.8	74.7	75.3	75.6	75.7	75.8	75.9	76.3	78.2	79.6	75.9
1996	78.0	77.4	77.7	77.8	78.5	79.0	77.6	78.4	78.2	78.9	80.2	81.7	78.6
1997	78.9	78.5	79.2	79.0	79.8	80.3	80.8	81.3	81.0	81.8	83.7	85.4	80.8
1998	82.9	82.0	82.9	83.0	83.7	83.9	84.9	85.2	84.9	85.7	86.6	87.8	84.4
1999	83.6	83.1	83.6	83.5	84.1	84.3	84.6	84.9	84.6	85.1	86.3	87.3	84.6
2000	84.1	83.6	84.3	85.3	86.0	87.0	86.8	87.4	87.9	87.9	89.9	90.4	86.7
2001	85.8	85.0	85.5	85.3	85.6	85.9	84.5	84.7	83.9	83.7	85.3	85.7	85.0
2002	83.5	82.7	83.2	84.1	84.3	83.9	83.1	83.0	82.9	82.7	84.2	84.8	83.5
2003	82.0	81.1	81.1	81.5	81.5	80.6	79.8	79.9	79.7	80.2	82.0	82.4	81.0
Wholesale trade													
1990	15.8	15.9	16.0	16.1	16.2	16.3	16.5	16.5	16.4	16.1	16.3	16.3	16.2
1991	15.0	15.1	15.1	15.1	15.2	15.2	15.3	15.2	15.2	15.0	14.9	14.9	15.1
1992	14.5	14.3	14.3	14.5	14.6	14.6	14.6	14.5	14.5	14.5	14.6	14.5	14.5
1993	14.1	14.1	14.3	14.6	14.6	14.6	14.6	14.7	14.7	14.6	14.7	14.7	14.5
1994	14.8	14.9	15.0	14.8	14.8	15.0	15.0	15.0	15.1	15.3	15.3	15.4	15.0
1995	15.5	15.6	15.7	15.7	15.8	15.9	15.9	15.9	16.0	16.0	16.1	16.1	15.8
1996	16.0	16.2	16.2	16.3	16.4	16.6	16.6	16.6	16.6	16.7	16.6	16.6	16.4
1997	16.6	16.8	16.8	17.0	17.1	17.2	17.3	17.1	17.1	17.5	17.5	17.5	17.1
1998	17.3	17.2	17.4	17.3	17.4	17.5	17.5	17.5	17.4	17.5	17.3	17.3	17.3
1999	17.1	17.0	17.1	17.0	17.1	17.2	17.3	17.3	17.1	17.2	17.2	17.2	17.2
2000	16.8	16.9	17.1	17.3	17.2	17.5	17.5	17.7	17.7	17.7	17.7	17.7	17.4
2001	17.5	17.5	17.6	17.8	17.9	17.9	17.5	17.4	17.3	17.1	17.3	17.3	17.5
2002	17.4	17.2	17.4	17.5	17.5	17.5	17.5	17.5	17.4	17.2	17.2	17.2	17.4
2003	16.8	16.6	16.7	16.7	16.7	16.7	16.8	16.7	16.7	16.8	16.4	16.3	16.7
Retail trade													
1990	38.1	37.1	37.6	36.8	37.2	37.6	37.2	37.7	37.6	37.6	38.8	39.9	37.7
1991	38.0	37.1	37.2	37.2	37.8	38.0	37.6	37.8	37.7	38.0	39.0	39.6	37.9
1992	37.8	37.2	37.4	38.2	38.5	38.7	38.6	38.4	38.3	38.5	39.6	40.6	38.4
1993	37.4	36.7	36.8	37.2	37.2	37.7	38.0	38.4	38.5	38.8	39.8	40.8	38.1
1994	38.8	38.6	38.9	39.1	39.2	39.7	39.9	40.1	39.9	40.0	41.3	42.6	39.8
1995	40.5	40.0	40.1	40.3	40.7	40.8	41.1	41.4	41.4	41.4	42.8	43.9	41.2
1996	41.3	40.4	40.7	41.0	41.6	41.9	42.0	42.5	42.3	42.6	44.0	45.3	42.1
1997	42.7	42.1	42.2	42.2	42.7	42.8	42.9	43.3	43.0	43.7	45.5	46.9	43.3
1998	44.3	43.6	44.0	44.3	44.8	44.9	45.5	45.9	45.9	46.7	48.0	49.2	45.5
1999	45.2	44.8	45.3	45.5	45.7	45.8	45.7	45.9	45.9	46.5	47.7	48.7	46.1
2000	45.9	45.4	45.8	46.3	47.0	47.4	47.0	47.3	47.8	47.9	49.8	50.2	47.3
2001	46.0	45.1	45.4	45.5	45.6	45.8	44.8	45.0	44.7	44.9	46.3	46.9	45.4
2002	45.0	44.4	44.8	45.1	45.2	44.7	43.9	43.9	43.7	43.7	45.1	45.8	44.6
2003	43.4	42.7	42.7	43.1	43.2	42.9	42.1	42.2	42.2	42.8	44.6	45.2	43.1
Transportation and utilities													
1990	20.0	20.1	20.2	20.2	20.5	21.1	21.0	21.1	21.1	21.5	21.6	21.8	20.8
1991	20.8	20.8	20.8	20.5	20.6	20.9	21.1	21.1	21.0	20.8	20.7	20.7	20.8
1992	20.6	20.4	20.3	20.6	20.6	20.6	20.6	20.6	20.5	20.4	20.4	20.2	20.4
1993	19.4	19.4	19.4	19.1	19.4	19.5	19.7	20.2	20.2	20.0	20.0	20.3	19.7
1994	18.7	18.9	18.9	19.5	19.5	19.5	19.6	19.7	19.5	19.1	19.0	19.1	19.2
1995	19.0	18.9	19.0	18.7	18.8	18.9	18.7	18.5	18.5	18.9	19.3	19.6	18.9
1996	20.7	20.8	20.8	20.5	20.5	20.5	19.0	19.3	19.3	19.6	19.6	19.8	20.0
1997	19.6	19.6	20.2	19.8	20.0	20.3	20.6	20.9	20.9	20.6	20.7	21.0	20.3
1998	21.3	21.2	21.5	21.4	21.5	21.5	21.9	21.8	21.6	21.5	21.3	21.3	21.4
1999	21.3	21.3	21.2	21.0	21.3	21.3	21.6	21.7	21.6	21.4	21.4	21.4	21.4
2000	21.4	21.3	21.4	21.7	21.8	22.1	22.3	22.4	22.4	22.3	22.4	22.5	22.0
2001	22.3	22.4	22.5	22.0	22.1	22.2	22.2	22.3	21.9	21.7	21.7	21.5	22.0
2002	21.1	21.1	21.0	21.5	21.6	21.7	21.7	21.6	21.8	21.8	21.9	21.8	21.6
2003	21.8	21.8	21.7	21.7	21.6	21.0	20.9	21.0	20.8	20.6	21.0	20.9	21.2
Information													
1990	6.9	6.8	6.9	7.0	7.1	7.3	7.2	7.2	7.2	7.3	7.4	7.4	7.1
1991	7.0	7.2	7.2	7.2	7.3	7.4	7.5	7.5	7.5	7.4	7.4	7.5	7.3
1992	7.2	7.2	7.3	7.4	7.5	7.5	7.5	7.5	7.5	7.3	7.3	7.4	7.3
1993	7.3	7.3	7.4	7.4	7.4	7.4	7.4	7.5	7.6	7.2	7.3	7.5	7.3
1994	7.5	7.5	7.5	7.7	7.7	7.9	7.7	7.8	7.8	7.8	7.8	7.9	7.7
1995	7.8	7.8	7.9	7.9	8.0	8.1	8.1	8.2	8.4	8.3	8.3	8.6	8.1
1996	8.5	8.6	8.8	9.0	9.1	9.2	9.3	9.3	9.4	9.6	9.5	9.6	9.1
1997	9.8	9.9	9.9	10.1	10.3	10.4	10.5	10.5	10.6	10.6	10.9	10.9	10.3
1998	11.1	11.1	11.1	11.7	11.9	12.1	12.6	12.5	12.6	12.6	12.8	12.9	12.0
1999	12.1	12.7	12.3	11.7	11.7	11.8	12.7	12.8	12.9	13.7	13.9	13.9	12.7
2000	14.2	14.4	14.4	14.2	14.6	14.8	15.0	15.2	15.5	15.4	15.8	15.8	14.9
2001	14.4	14.5	14.2	14.9	14.7	14.3	14.9	16.0	16.0	16.0	15.7	15.5	15.0
2002	15.6	15.7	15.3	14.5	14.3	14.1	13.9	13.8	13.7	13.6	13.5	13.1	14.3
2003	12.8	12.7	12.4	12.5	12.5	12.4	12.1	11.9	11.8	11.6	11.5	11.3	12.1

Employment by Industry: Oklahoma—*Continued*

(Numbers in thousands. Not seasonally adjusted.)

Industry	January	February	March	April	May	June	July	August	September	October	November	December	Annual Average
TULSA—*Continued*													
Financial activities													
1990	20.0	20.0	20.2	20.3	20.3	20.5	20.4	20.4	20.3	19.8	19.9	19.9	20.1
1991	20.0	20.1	20.2	20.3	20.6	20.9	20.8	20.9	20.8	20.9	20.9	21.0	20.6
1992	20.1	20.2	20.3	20.5	20.7	20.8	20.7	20.8	20.6	20.7	20.7	20.7	20.5
1993	20.2	20.3	20.3	21.0	21.0	21.3	21.3	21.3	21.2	21.7	21.6	21.9	21.0
1994	22.2	22.3	22.5	22.1	22.3	22.5	22.5	22.4	22.4	22.3	22.2	22.4	22.3
1995	22.3	22.4	22.6	22.5	22.9	23.3	23.5	23.6	23.8	23.7	24.2	24.5	23.2
1996	24.2	24.4	24.7	24.5	24.6	24.8	24.7	24.9	24.7	24.7	24.6	24.8	24.6
1997	24.8	24.6	24.5	24.7	24.6	25.2	25.0	25.0	24.8	24.7	24.9	24.9	24.8
1998	24.7	24.8	25.1	25.4	25.5	25.9	25.5	25.5	25.4	24.9	24.9	25.4	25.2
1999	24.3	24.2	24.5	24.5	24.9	25.3	25.2	25.5	25.4	24.3	24.4	24.4	24.7
2000	23.5	23.5	23.5	23.8	24.0	24.5	23.8	23.9	23.9	23.7	23.5	23.7	23.8
2001	24.9	25.1	25.2	25.3	25.4	25.6	25.4	25.5	25.4	25.4	25.4	25.3	25.3
2002	24.9	24.8	24.7	24.7	24.7	24.7	24.7	24.6	24.3	24.1	24.1	24.0	24.5
2003	23.6	23.7	23.7	23.9	24.0	24.1	24.5	24.5	24.4	24.6	24.4	24.1	24.1
Professional and business services													
1990	30.9	30.9	31.4	32.2	32.5	32.6	33.3	33.4	33.7	32.8	32.2	32.0	32.3
1991	32.5	33.2	34.0	34.7	34.9	35.5	35.1	36.0	35.5	36.1	35.5	35.0	34.8
1992	34.6	35.0	34.7	35.1	35.2	35.4	36.3	36.4	36.7	36.8	36.7	35.7	35.7
1993	35.9	36.7	37.3	36.9	37.0	37.6	38.1	38.0	38.0	38.3	37.9	38.0	37.4
1994	38.9	39.0	39.6	40.6	40.9	41.5	42.0	42.9	42.6	43.3	43.3	43.5	41.5
1995	40.5	41.1	42.1	41.7	42.0	42.6	42.4	43.3	43.2	42.8	42.6	42.4	42.2
1996	40.1	40.9	41.7	42.1	43.0	43.4	45.9	46.8	46.9	46.2	45.8	45.6	44.0
1997	43.8	44.7	45.2	46.5	47.7	48.0	50.0	50.5	50.9	50.4	50.2	50.0	48.1
1998	49.1	50.4	51.3	52.1	53.6	53.5	53.4	53.1	53.0	54.1	53.0	53.5	52.5
1999	50.7	49.7	50.1	52.5	53.0	53.0	53.4	52.7	52.9	51.7	51.5	51.5	51.9
2000	50.2	50.5	51.8	54.0	54.5	54.8	55.1	55.6	55.4	56.2	56.0	55.1	54.1
2001	53.0	54.0	54.9	56.3	56.5	57.0	56.8	55.7	54.4	53.4	53.4	53.2	54.8
2002	50.8	51.1	51.3	52.0	52.8	52.2	51.0	51.2	50.6	50.1	49.6	49.5	51.0
2003	48.1	48.3	48.2	48.2	48.1	47.7	46.7	47.5	47.1	47.2	47.6	46.4	47.6
Educational and health services													
1990	34.1	34.7	35.0	34.6	34.0	34.4	34.6	35.0	35.8	36.1	36.3	36.3	35.0
1991	35.7	36.2	36.3	36.2	36.0	35.5	35.5	35.6	36.6	37.2	37.4	37.5	36.3
1992	37.5	37.9	38.3	37.9	37.7	37.4	37.6	37.8	39.2	38.7	38.6	39.0	38.1
1993	39.1	39.5	39.7	38.1	38.0	38.3	38.0	38.1	39.2	38.7	38.7	39.1	38.7
1994	38.8	39.1	39.2	39.0	38.8	39.0	38.4	38.6	39.6	39.8	39.8	40.1	39.1
1995	39.4	39.8	40.3	40.1	40.3	40.3	39.3	39.5	40.8	41.2	41.3	41.4	40.3
1996	40.9	41.3	41.3	41.8	41.8	41.7	41.4	41.5	42.6	42.0	42.2	43.0	41.7
1997	42.5	43.0	43.1	43.3	43.4	43.6	43.5	43.6	44.6	44.8	44.9	45.2	43.7
1998	45.8	46.2	46.4	45.8	45.9	45.7	45.9	46.0	46.1	46.3	47.0	47.1	46.1
1999	46.9	47.2	47.2	46.7	46.5	46.7	47.4	47.4	47.9	47.7	47.7	47.7	47.3
2000	47.1	47.4	47.7	48.2	48.4	48.6	48.5	48.9	49.8	49.0	49.4	49.5	48.5
2001	48.0	48.2	48.7	49.4	49.0	48.8	48.9	49.2	49.9	49.4	50.0	50.1	49.1
2002	50.1	50.5	50.5	50.3	50.0	49.2	49.9	50.9	51.6	51.1	51.9	51.8	50.7
2003	51.4	51.5	51.4	51.5	51.3	50.4	49.9	50.4	50.5	51.9	51.7	51.1	51.1
Leisure and hospitality													
1990	21.5	21.4	21.9	22.8	23.7	24.2	24.0	24.8	24.5	24.1	24.1	24.2	23.4
1991	23.3	23.6	24.3	24.8	25.4	25.9	26.2	26.5	26.2	25.3	24.8	24.8	25.0
1992	24.2	24.4	24.9	26.1	26.4	26.7	26.9	27.2	26.6	26.3	25.7	25.4	25.9
1993	25.3	25.7	26.5	27.7	28.0	28.3	27.5	28.0	28.1	27.8	27.4	27.8	27.3
1994	28.0	27.8	28.3	29.5	29.8	29.9	30.2	30.7	30.4	29.4	29.4	29.3	29.3
1995	29.0	29.1	29.8	30.5	31.6	31.8	31.2	31.2	30.6	30.7	30.1	30.1	30.4
1996	29.6	29.6	30.0	30.4	31.3	31.5	31.2	31.5	31.1	31.0	30.6	30.4	30.6
1997	30.5	30.6	31.3	30.7	31.2	31.6	29.8	30.2	29.7	31.3	30.7	31.0	30.7
1998	30.0	30.2	30.6	31.6	31.9	31.8	31.4	31.3	31.0	30.1	29.5	29.5	30.7
1999	29.8	30.5	30.6	32.6	33.2	33.4	33.7	33.5	33.4	33.7	33.3	33.4	32.6
2000	32.0	32.2	32.8	33.6	33.8	34.4	34.0	34.0	33.3	33.1	32.5	32.4	33.2
2001	31.6	32.2	32.5	33.0	33.4	34.0	34.0	34.3	33.6	33.3	32.9	32.9	33.1
2002	31.7	32.1	32.8	33.6	34.5	34.5	33.3	33.9	33.2	33.0	32.5	32.5	33.1
2003	31.2	31.4	32.0	32.9	33.4	33.3	32.6	33.1	32.3	32.0	32.2	32.3	32.4
Other services													
1990	13.0	13.1	13.1	13.1	13.2	13.6	13.6	13.5	13.5	13.5	13.6	13.6	13.3
1991	13.4	13.5	13.5	13.7	13.7	14.1	13.9	13.8	13.7	13.5	13.3	13.3	13.6
1992	13.2	13.2	13.3	13.4	13.5	13.8	13.8	13.7	13.7	13.7	13.7	13.9	13.5
1993	13.8	13.8	13.8	14.0	14.1	14.3	14.3	14.3	14.2	14.2	14.1	14.1	14.0
1994	14.2	14.3	14.4	14.5	14.6	14.9	15.0	14.9	14.8	14.8	14.7	14.8	14.6
1995	14.7	14.6	14.9	14.9	15.4	15.8	15.4	15.4	15.3	15.3	15.4	15.5	15.2
1996	15.6	15.7	15.8	16.0	16.2	16.4	16.4	16.4	16.3	16.2	16.1	16.1	16.1
1997	15.9	16.0	16.1	16.2	16.3	16.7	16.6	16.6	16.4	16.5	16.5	16.4	16.3
1998	16.3	16.5	16.5	16.7	17.0	17.3	17.4	17.3	17.3	17.2	17.3	17.4	17.0
1999	17.6	17.8	18.1	18.1	18.2	18.5	18.4	18.4	18.2	18.0	18.1	18.0	18.1
2000	17.7	17.6	17.9	18.1	18.2	18.6	18.6	18.4	18.2	18.1	18.1	18.2	18.1
2001	18.6	18.8	19.0	19.1	19.3	19.7	19.7	19.9	19.7	19.7	19.8	19.8	19.4
2002	19.6	19.6	19.7	20.4	20.4	20.7	20.6	20.3	20.1	19.8	19.8	19.7	20.1
2003	19.6	19.7	19.9	19.5	19.6	19.8	19.6	19.4	19.3	19.3	21.5	20.7	19.8

Employment by Industry: Oklahoma—*Continued*

(Numbers in thousands. Not seasonally adjusted.)

Industry	January	February	March	April	May	June	July	August	September	October	November	December	Annual Average
TULSA—*Continued*													
Government													
1990	37.9	38.8	38.6	37.7	38.2	38.7	31.8	33.0	38.0	38.5	38.7	39.4	37.4
1991	39.1	39.8	39.9	39.8	39.3	38.8	33.4	34.5	39.4	41.2	40.7	40.6	38.8
1992	40.3	41.2	41.2	41.0	41.1	39.8	34.3	35.0	40.9	42.2	41.2	41.6	39.9
1993	41.1	41.7	41.8	41.4	41.8	41.2	34.3	35.7	39.9	41.8	41.7	41.8	40.3
1994	40.5	40.8	41.1	41.3	41.3	40.6	39.0	39.2	41.7	42.0	41.8	42.1	40.9
1995	41.1	41.7	41.7	41.3	41.4	40.9	38.6	39.3	40.5	41.8	41.7	42.0	41.0
1996	41.4	41.7	42.6	42.1	42.5	41.5	39.6	40.1	41.5	42.5	42.1	42.2	41.6
1997	41.4	42.3	42.5	42.3	42.7	41.1	39.2	39.5	42.1	43.2	42.9	43.5	41.8
1998	42.1	43.1	43.2	42.9	43.4	41.6	39.4	39.5	42.9	43.8	43.7	44.2	42.4
1999	42.2	43.1	43.5	44.1	44.3	42.4	40.3	40.5	42.6	43.9	44.9	44.5	43.0
2000	43.4	44.1	44.9	44.8	46.4	45.3	42.3	42.9	43.5	45.2	45.0	45.6	44.5
2001	43.7	44.9	45.0	45.0	45.6	44.7	42.6	42.7	44.7	46.1	46.2	46.4	44.8
2002	45.2	46.1	46.4	46.6	47.5	45.6	43.4	43.6	44.7	46.4	46.2	46.4	45.7
2003	44.5	45.1	45.2	44.9	44.8	43.3	41.6	40.9	42.7	45.0	44.9	45.1	44.0
Federal government													
1990	4.8	4.8	4.9	4.7	4.7	4.8	4.9	4.8	4.8	4.8	4.8	4.8	4.8
1991	4.9	4.9	5.0	5.0	5.1	5.1	5.1	5.1	5.1	5.1	5.1	5.1	5.0
1992	5.1	5.1	5.1	5.1	5.1	5.2	5.2	5.1	5.1	5.0	4.9	5.0	5.0
1993	4.9	4.9	4.9	4.9	5.0	5.0	5.0	5.1	5.0	5.0	5.0	5.0	4.9
1994	4.6	4.6	4.6	5.0	5.0	5.0	5.0	5.0	5.0	4.9	4.9	5.0	4.8
1995	4.8	4.9	4.9	4.9	4.9	5.0	4.9	4.9	4.8	4.9	5.1	5.2	4.9
1996	5.1	5.0	5.1	5.1	5.1	5.0	5.0	5.0	5.0	5.0	5.1	5.2	5.0
1997	5.0	5.0	5.0	5.0	5.0	5.1	5.1	5.0	5.0	5.0	5.1	5.3	5.0
1998	5.1	5.1	5.0	5.1	5.1	5.1	5.1	5.1	5.1	5.0	5.1	5.3	5.1
1999	5.1	5.1	5.1	5.2	5.1	5.1	5.1	5.1	5.1	5.1	5.0	5.2	5.1
2000	5.1	5.0	5.3	5.2	6.1	6.2	5.5	5.7	4.8	4.7	4.7	4.9	5.3
2001	4.7	4.7	4.7	4.7	4.8	4.8	4.8	4.7	4.7	4.7	4.7	4.7	4.7
2002	4.7	4.6	4.7	4.6	4.6	4.7	4.6	4.6	4.5	4.7	4.6	4.8	4.6
2003	4.6	4.6	4.6	4.6	4.6	4.6	4.1	4.1	4.1	4.1	4.0	4.1	4.3
State government													
1990	6.1	6.7	6.5	6.5	7.0	6.5	6.1	6.1	6.4	6.4	6.7	6.4	6.4
1991	6.1	6.6	6.4	6.4	6.8	6.3	6.0	6.0	6.3	6.6	6.7	6.6	6.4
1992	6.1	6.8	6.6	6.5	6.6	6.4	6.5	6.2	6.3	6.9	6.5	6.8	6.5
1993	6.1	6.5	6.5	6.4	6.5	6.2	5.9	6.1	6.0	6.3	6.4	6.4	6.2
1994	6.1	6.2	6.2	6.2	6.1	6.0	5.9	5.8	5.9	6.2	6.2	6.3	6.0
1995	6.1	6.3	6.1	6.1	6.2	5.9	5.9	5.7	5.7	6.2	6.2	6.2	6.0
1996	6.1	6.2	6.3	6.3	6.3	6.0	6.1	5.9	6.4	6.4	6.4	6.4	6.2
1997	6.0	6.4	6.5	6.4	6.4	6.2	6.3	6.2	6.2	6.5	6.5	6.2	6.3
1998	6.0	6.5	6.6	6.6	6.6	6.3	6.3	6.1	6.2	6.6	6.9	6.7	6.4
1999	6.1	6.5	6.6	6.6	6.6	6.4	6.3	6.0	6.0	6.5	6.9	6.6	6.4
2000	6.1	6.5	6.9	6.8	6.8	6.6	6.3	6.2	6.5	6.8	6.8	6.8	6.6
2001	5.9	6.7	6.7	6.7	6.7	6.3	6.2	6.0	6.7	6.7	6.8	6.8	6.5
2002	6.0	6.7	6.8	7.0	7.0	6.6	6.5	6.2	6.8	7.1	7.1	7.2	6.8
2003	6.3	6.9	6.9	6.8	6.8	6.4	6.4	6.1	6.7	7.9	8.2	8.3	7.0
Local government													
1990	27.0	27.3	27.2	26.5	26.5	27.4	20.8	22.1	26.8	27.3	27.2	28.2	26.1
1991	28.1	28.3	28.5	28.4	27.4	27.4	22.3	23.4	28.0	29.5	28.9	28.9	27.4
1992	29.1	29.3	29.5	29.4	29.4	28.2	22.6	23.7	29.5	30.3	29.8	29.8	28.3
1993	30.1	30.3	30.4	30.1	30.3	30.0	23.4	24.5	28.9	30.5	30.3	30.4	29.1
1994	29.8	30.0	30.3	30.1	30.2	29.6	28.1	28.4	30.8	30.9	30.7	30.8	29.9
1995	30.2	30.5	30.7	30.3	30.3	30.0	27.8	28.7	30.0	30.7	30.4	30.6	30.0
1996	30.2	30.5	31.2	30.7	31.1	30.5	28.5	29.2	30.1	31.1	30.6	30.6	30.3
1997	30.4	30.9	31.0	30.9	31.3	29.8	27.8	28.3	30.9	31.7	31.3	32.0	30.5
1998	31.0	31.5	31.6	31.2	31.7	30.2	28.0	28.3	31.6	32.2	31.7	32.2	30.9
1999	31.0	31.5	31.8	32.3	32.6	30.9	28.9	29.4	31.5	32.3	33.0	32.7	31.5
2000	32.2	32.6	32.7	32.8	33.5	32.5	30.5	31.0	32.2	33.7	33.5	33.9	32.6
2001	33.1	33.5	33.6	33.6	34.1	33.6	31.6	32.0	33.3	34.7	34.7	34.9	33.6
2002	34.5	34.8	34.9	35.0	35.9	34.3	32.3	32.8	33.4	34.6	34.5	34.4	34.3
2003	33.6	33.6	33.7	33.5	33.4	32.3	31.1	30.7	31.9	33.0	32.7	32.7	32.7

Average Weekly Hours by Industry: Oklahoma

(Not seasonally adjusted.)

Industry	January	February	March	April	May	June	July	August	September	October	November	December	Annual Average
STATEWIDE													
Natural resources and mining													
2001	43.0	44.3	46.3	47.4	47.4	48.4	46.3	44.1	44.7	42.7	41.5	42.0	44.8
2002	40.2	42.1	43.6	39.1	45.6	40.9	43.9	42.0	40.6	40.0	40.2	43.0	41.8
2003	43.9	43.9	44.2	41.0	42.2	44.1	44.8	43.1	42.6	43.5	41.9	42.9	43.2
Manufacturing													
2001	42.4	39.1	39.1	39.6	40.5	38.6	37.7	40.6	38.9	40.0	37.9	38.4	39.4
2002	39.1	39.2	39.3	39.2	39.4	39.3	39.0	39.1	39.4	39.1	39.0	39.1	39.2
2003	38.6	38.1	38.7	38.9	38.1	37.5	39.5	40.3	39.8	39.8	40.9	41.6	39.3
Trade, transportation, and utilities													
2001	34.1	33.7	33.1	33.8	33.8	34.5	35.2	33.6	33.7	33.2	33.4	33.3	33.8
2002	33.0	33.6	33.7	33.3	33.5	34.4	34.3	33.6	33.5	33.5	33.4	34.3	33.7
2003	33.1	33.8	34.1	33.3	34.0	35.1	34.2	34.6	34.1	33.5	33.5	33.7	33.9
Wholesale trade													
2001	39.3	38.9	39.1	39.9	39.3	39.3	38.9	38.9	40.3	39.4	40.4	39.0	39.4
2002	40.2	39.9	39.0	38.8	38.3	40.2	37.6	38.4	38.2	40.4	40.4	40.9	39.3
2003	38.6	38.8	37.7	37.1	37.1	38.9	36.8	37.2	37.3	37.7	38.6	37.1	37.7
OKLAHOMA CITY													
Manufacturing													
2001	41.0	34.7	35.8	37.0	35.8	36.2	33.9	36.8	39.2	42.1	37.3	36.7	37.2
2002	38.0	38.7	39.1	39.3	40.0	39.1	39.5	39.1	39.5	39.5	39.8	40.2	39.3
2003	37.3	38.2	40.5	40.6	39.6	37.8	43.4	43.2	43.2	42.7	43.0	44.5	41.2
TULSA													
Manufacturing													
2001	43.6	42.8	42.9	40.0	41.9	41.2	42.1	41.5	40.3	39.4	39.5	40.3	41.3
2002	38.6	39.6	37.7	37.8	38.8	39.7	38.7	39.7	39.7	39.6	39.7	40.4	39.2
2003	40.8	41.3	41.0	39.4	40.9	40.5	41.0	41.6	41.2	40.8	42.7	42.4	41.1

Average Hourly Earnings by Industry: Oklahoma

(Dollars, not seasonally adjusted.)

Industry	January	February	March	April	May	June	July	August	September	October	November	December	Annual Average
STATEWIDE													
Natural resources and mining													
2001	16.56	16.35	16.97	16.00	15.65	16.48	16.70	15.45	16.73	16.86	16.30	17.05	16.42
2002	16.75	16.81	16.66	16.74	16.73	16.48	16.57	16.01	16.01	15.71	16.22	16.64	16.45
2003	16.16	15.86	16.19	15.79	15.71	15.37	15.55	15.53	15.73	15.53	16.65	15.85	15.82
Manufacturing													
2001	13.01	13.22	13.23	14.04	13.97	13.50	13.55	13.99	13.90	13.72	13.92	13.94	13.66
2002	13.81	14.01	14.12	14.18	14.16	14.13	14.11	14.14	14.17	14.14	14.23	14.17	14.11
2003	14.09	14.21	14.44	14.33	13.88	14.00	14.19	14.21	14.08	13.86	13.84	14.36	14.13
Trade, transportation, and utilities													
2001	10.36	10.68	10.72	10.78	10.78	10.59	10.54	11.05	10.95	11.12	10.91	10.83	10.77
2002	10.76	11.20	11.22	10.95	10.94	10.99	11.14	11.41	11.60	11.31	11.38	11.34	11.19
2003	11.82	11.95	12.06	12.25	12.27	12.03	12.15	12.39	12.77	12.61	12.63	12.48	12.28
Wholesale trade													
2001	10.99	11.48	11.26	11.71	11.68	10.32	10.79	10.87	10.81	10.66	10.76	10.47	10.98
2002	10.54	10.70	10.80	10.40	10.61	10.52	11.27	12.28	12.38	11.11	11.55	11.36	11.12
2003	12.08	12.13	12.39	12.54	12.12	11.54	12.32	12.98	13.82	12.97	13.30	13.00	12.59
OKLAHOMA CITY													
Manufacturing													
2001	12.30	13.46	13.50	13.56	13.79	13.99	14.01	14.00	14.06	14.36	14.60	14.47	13.82
2002	14.17	14.16	14.14	14.66	14.71	15.00	14.73	14.71	14.99	15.02	15.28	15.45	14.75
2003	14.55	15.15	16.17	15.24	14.32	14.25	14.84	14.68	14.61	14.51	13.98	15.08	14.78
TULSA													
Manufacturing													
2001	15.24	15.07	15.10	15.51	15.02	15.40	15.12	15.37	16.29	15.57	15.69	15.75	15.42
2002	15.67	15.49	15.83	15.54	15.04	15.76	15.35	15.63	15.52	15.34	16.05	15.72	15.58
2003	15.51	15.72	15.64	15.65	15.39	15.70	15.53	15.96	16.00	15.96	15.99	16.60	15.80

Average Weekly Earnings by Industry: Oklahoma

(Dollars, not seasonally adjusted.)

Industry	January	February	March	April	May	June	July	August	September	October	November	December	Annual Average
STATEWIDE													
Natural resources and mining													
2001	712.08	724.31	785.71	758.40	741.81	797.63	773.21	681.35	747.83	719.92	676.45	716.10	735.62
2002	673.35	707.70	726.38	654.53	762.89	674.03	727.42	672.42	650.01	628.40	652.04	715.52	687.61
2003	709.42	696.25	715.60	647.39	662.96	677.82	696.64	669.34	670.10	675.56	697.64	679.97	683.42
Manufacturing													
2001	551.62	516.90	517.29	555.98	565.79	521.10	510.84	567.99	540.71	548.80	527.57	535.30	538.20
2002	539.97	549.19	554.92	555.86	557.90	555.31	550.29	552.87	558.30	552.87	554.97	554.05	553.11
2003	543.87	541.40	558.83	557.44	528.83	525.00	560.51	572.66	560.38	551.63	566.06	597.38	555.31
Trade, transportation, and utilities													
2001	353.28	359.92	354.83	364.36	364.36	365.36	371.01	371.28	369.02	369.18	364.39	360.64	364.03
2002	355.08	376.32	378.11	364.64	366.49	378.06	382.10	383.38	388.60	378.89	380.09	388.96	377.10
2003	391.24	403.91	411.25	407.93	417.18	422.25	415.53	428.69	435.46	422.44	423.11	420.58	416.29
Wholesale trade													
2001	431.91	446.57	440.27	467.23	459.02	405.58	419.73	422.84	435.64	420.00	434.70	408.33	432.61
2002	423.71	426.93	421.20	403.52	406.36	422.90	423.75	471.55	472.92	448.84	466.62	464.62	437.02
2003	466.29	470.64	467.10	465.23	449.65	448.91	453.38	482.86	515.49	488.97	513.38	482.30	474.64
OKLAHOMA CITY													
Manufacturing													
2001	504.30	467.06	483.30	501.72	493.68	506.44	474.94	515.20	551.15	604.56	544.58	531.05	514.10
2002	538.46	547.99	552.87	576.14	588.40	586.50	581.84	575.16	592.11	593.29	608.14	621.09	579.68
2003	542.72	578.73	654.89	618.74	567.07	538.65	644.06	634.18	631.15	619.58	601.14	671.06	608.94
TULSA													
Manufacturing													
2001	664.46	645.00	647.79	620.40	629.34	634.48	636.55	637.86	656.49	613.46	619.76	634.73	636.85
2002	604.86	613.40	596.79	587.41	583.55	625.67	594.05	620.51	616.14	607.46	637.19	635.09	610.74
2003	632.81	649.24	641.24	616.61	629.45	635.85	636.73	663.94	659.20	651.17	682.77	703.84	649.38

OREGON AT A GLANCE

(Population and total nonfarm employment numbers in thousands)

Population, Census 2000:	3,421.4
Total nonfarm employment, 2003:	1,562.0
Change in total nonfarm employment	
(Number)	
1990–2003:	315.0
1990–2001:	346.6
2001–2003:	-31.6
(Compound annual rate of change)	
1990–2003:	1.7%
1990–2001:	2.3%
2001–2003:	-1.0%
Unemployment rate	
1990:	5.4%
2001:	6.4%
2003:	8.1%

Average Annual Employment for Total Nonfarm, Goods-Producing, and Service-Providing Industries, 1990–2003

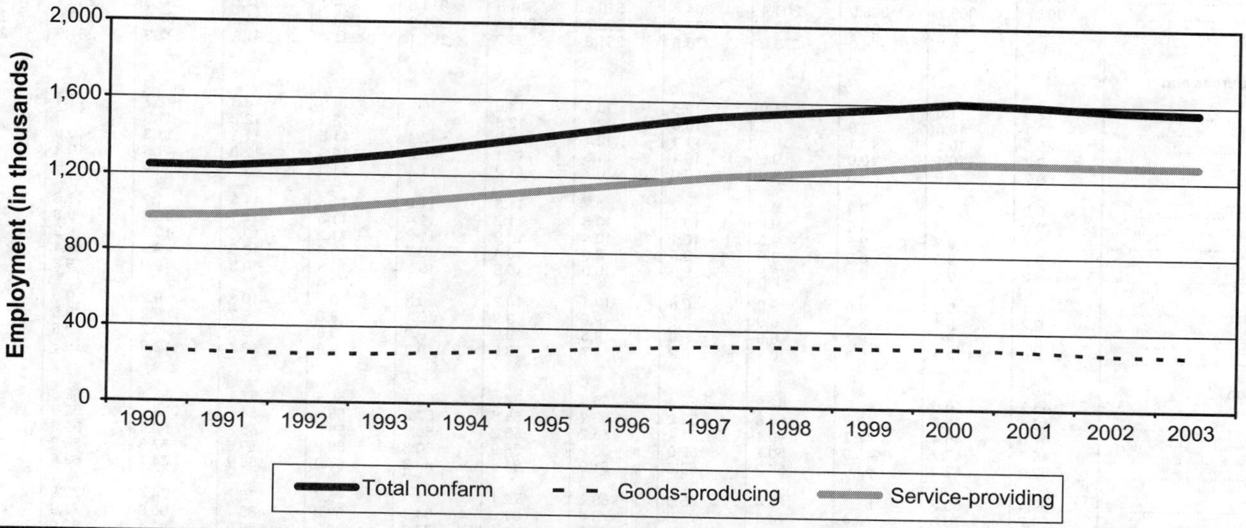

After a sluggish start to the decade, total nonfarm payroll employment rose steadily through the 1990s. But in 2001, employment fell, and continued to decline through 2003. The goods-producing sector was particularly affected by the 2001 contraction, as employment dropped nearly 11 percent from 2000 to 2003. Employment in the service-providing sector also declined during this period, but its decline was much more moderate. While most industries within the service sector decreased from 2000 to 2003, employment in educational and health services increased nearly 9 percent.

Employment by Industry: Oregon

(Numbers in thousands. Not seasonally adjusted.)

Industry	January	February	March	April	May	June	July	August	September	October	November	December	Annual Average
STATEWIDE													
Total nonfarm													
1990	1203.5	1205.8	1220.5	1236.7	1251.6	1266.7	1249.3	1266.4	1268.1	1270.3	1267.8	1257.8	1247.0
1991	1211.2	1217.3	1224.2	1231.3	1242.9	1257.3	1240.4	1250.3	1262.7	1274.1	1265.0	1258.5	1244.6
1992	1222.5	1229.4	1237.2	1254.7	1268.1	1279.5	1272.0	1275.1	1287.7	1298.4	1295.9	1286.9	1267.3
1993	1250.6	1265.0	1276.8	1291.4	1301.8	1318.9	1305.5	1314.9	1333.3	1346.0	1346.2	1346.8	1308.1
1994	1303.6	1315.6	1326.5	1342.6	1356.0	1374.0	1360.3	1373.5	1390.3	1399.3	1405.5	1404.8	1362.7
1995	1359.1	1371.3	1384.8	1394.1	1408.4	1429.5	1411.8	1430.3	1451.6	1457.9	1459.2	1459.9	1418.2
1996	1420.2	1426.4	1440.0	1451.9	1467.6	1484.2	1469.6	1484.7	1502.6	1511.5	1520.6	1515.0	1474.5
1997	1474.2	1485.9	1497.5	1512.0	1529.0	1542.8	1523.8	1531.4	1546.3	1557.0	1556.5	1558.7	1526.3
1998	1508.5	1521.4	1530.2	1543.1	1555.7	1569.1	1545.1	1553.3	1567.8	1574.1	1576.8	1574.2	1551.6
1999	1527.5	1537.1	1550.2	1563.2	1568.8	1583.7	1574.8	1577.1	1591.2	1605.3	1609.6	1610.1	1574.9
2000	1556.6	1570.1	1580.7	1592.2	1610.4	1626.7	1603.3	1609.6	1623.8	1632.7	1638.9	1633.7	1606.6
2001	1581.7	1589.4	1594.4	1595.8	1604.5	1617.5	1585.3	1588.1	1594.0	1598.0	1591.0	1584.0	1593.6
2002	1535.7	1546.2	1554.6	1563.2	1576.7	1589.5	1571.7	1578.6	1586.8	1594.0	1590.6	1582.3	1572.5
2003	1540.0	1545.0	1549.1	1548.9	1560.0	1570.5	1548.7	1559.7	1568.6	1587.0	1584.2	1581.7	1562.0
Total private													
1990	984.0	982.9	995.8	1009.0	1018.5	1033.3	1041.5	1061.2	1052.5	1039.6	1035.3	1028.7	1023.5
1991	986.4	988.4	994.3	1001.4	1010.6	1022.8	1030.3	1042.0	1043.5	1040.9	1030.9	1026.4	1018.2
1992	993.9	996.7	1002.9	1019.8	1030.1	1042.2	1058.2	1063.3	1064.4	1061.2	1052.4	1050.1	1036.3
1993	1017.9	1028.1	1038.1	1052.7	1061.2	1077.3	1091.2	1103.1	1110.8	1108.7	1106.8	1110.1	1075.5
1994	1070.7	1078.9	1089.3	1104.8	1114.4	1133.2	1144.8	1158.5	1162.7	1157.7	1158.6	1161.8	1128.0
1995	1121.2	1129.2	1141.0	1149.7	1160.9	1181.8	1190.7	1209.6	1218.7	1210.0	1209.8	1212.4	1177.9
1996	1176.8	1177.4	1189.2	1200.6	1212.8	1230.0	1242.8	1261.7	1264.1	1259.1	1260.7	1260.5	1228.0
1997	1225.4	1232.0	1242.3	1256.8	1272.3	1285.5	1296.1	1305.3	1303.6	1301.8	1298.1	1301.9	1276.8
1998	1255.9	1264.2	1271.8	1284.9	1293.5	1305.6	1311.9	1320.9	1320.8	1310.6	1307.5	1307.8	1296.3
1999	1267.9	1272.9	1284.4	1296.6	1300.3	1316.0	1332.4	1336.3	1340.3	1337.0	1337.6	1341.8	1313.6
2000	1291.1	1299.5	1308.5	1319.5	1330.4	1348.5	1355.2	1364.1	1367.9	1360.5	1364.7	1361.3	1339.3
2001	1314.7	1315.9	1318.7	1320.8	1325.7	1338.2	1336.8	1340.7	1333.7	1320.2	1311.6	1307.1	1323.7
2002	1262.7	1267.8	1274.3	1284.4	1295.1	1307.1	1318.0	1326.8	1323.6	1317.2	1311.9	1306.6	1299.6
2003	1267.3	1269.3	1273.4	1274.5	1283.7	1295.3	1304.4	1314.7	1312.8	1314.3	1309.3	1309.0	1294.0
Goods-producing													
1990	257.1	255.8	260.6	264.4	268.2	274.8	279.9	287.6	281.3	273.7	268.0	261.4	269.4
1991	250.9	251.2	250.7	251.4	254.9	261.7	267.8	274.2	272.1	267.8	259.0	253.2	259.6
1992	242.2	242.5	243.5	248.1	252.5	260.3	268.1	269.2	264.9	262.4	254.0	249.1	254.7
1993	240.5	243.6	246.7	248.6	251.5	259.9	266.7	272.6	272.5	269.4	262.5	259.2	257.8
1994	251.3	252.9	255.9	260.8	265.6	275.3	282.6	286.6	286.0	282.7	277.2	275.5	271.0
1995	267.0	269.3	271.8	274.2	278.1	288.2	296.7	303.1	305.7	301.5	297.2	295.0	287.3
1996	287.6	287.5	291.4	293.9	296.4	305.3	313.7	320.9	319.2	314.8	310.0	305.6	303.9
1997	299.3	301.0	303.5	308.0	314.2	321.8	328.0	331.7	330.3	327.9	321.4	318.6	317.1
1998	309.3	311.9	313.0	313.2	315.5	322.0	327.5	331.1	327.8	323.3	316.4	312.6	318.6
1999	304.6	304.6	306.8	309.1	310.1	316.6	326.5	327.9	326.4	322.9	317.9	314.7	315.7
2000	304.6	306.0	307.8	309.1	312.2	320.2	324.5	326.5	327.4	321.1	318.3	315.2	316.1
2001	307.7	306.7	305.0	304.4	304.8	310.5	314.8	314.3	309.4	304.0	294.3	290.1	305.5
2002	280.5	280.5	281.6	283.7	287.0	292.7	299.6	301.3	298.3	294.0	287.7	283.5	289.2
2003	276.2	275.7	275.0	273.0	275.6	281.6	286.9	291.1	291.4	291.2	287.3	284.9	282.5
Natural resources and mining													
1990	12.3	11.6	11.5	11.9	12.6	13.4	13.9	14.5	14.3	13.8	12.7	11.4	12.8
1991	10.1	10.5	9.9	9.8	10.8	12.0	12.8	13.3	13.3	12.2	11.9	11.3	11.5
1992	10.6	10.5	10.1	10.5	11.1	12.1	12.8	12.4	11.5	11.8	11.3	10.8	11.3
1993	9.7	10.1	10.0	9.6	10.1	11.3	12.1	12.3	12.3	12.0	11.5	10.8	11.0
1994	9.7	9.9	9.5	9.6	10.0	10.7	11.2	11.1	11.0	10.8	10.4	9.9	10.3
1995	9.2	9.3	9.3	9.3	9.7	10.7	11.3	11.6	11.6	11.6	11.2	10.6	10.5
1996	10.0	9.8	9.8	9.8	10.1	10.5	11.2	11.4	11.3	11.1	10.4	9.8	10.4
1997	9.5	9.8	9.3	9.3	10.1	10.4	10.9	11.3	11.2	10.6	10.2	9.9	10.2
1998	9.2	9.0	8.8	9.0	9.5	9.9	10.4	10.7	10.6	10.3	9.9	9.4	9.7
1999	9.2	9.1	8.9	8.8	9.3	10.0	10.5	10.7	10.5	10.3	10.0	9.8	9.8
2000	9.1	9.2	9.0	9.2	9.6	10.1	10.2	10.3	10.2	10.3	9.9	9.6	9.7
2001	9.2	9.1	8.8	8.6	9.0	9.6	9.9	10.1	9.8	9.7	9.2	8.8	9.3
2002	8.7	8.7	8.7	8.6	9.0	9.5	9.9	9.9	9.8	9.8	9.7	9.5	9.3
2003	8.9	8.9	8.8	8.9	9.2	9.7	9.6	9.8	9.8	9.7	9.6	9.3	9.4
Construction													
1990	46.9	46.6	49.9	52.8	54.4	55.8	57.0	59.1	58.5	57.1	55.1	52.8	53.8
1991	48.4	48.6	49.2	50.6	52.2	53.9	55.5	57.3	56.9	56.5	53.6	52.0	52.9
1992	47.0	46.4	47.7	49.1	51.4	53.2	56.2	56.7	56.0	55.2	52.4	50.0	51.8
1993	45.8	47.7	49.6	50.7	52.9	55.2	58.9	60.3	60.2	59.6	57.8	56.3	54.6
1994	52.9	53.3	54.9	57.2	59.6	61.9	64.6	66.3	67.0	66.2	64.7	63.6	61.0
1995	59.4	60.2	61.7	63.4	65.5	68.6	72.1	75.1	76.7	75.7	74.4	72.9	68.8
1996	69.7	70.3	72.4	74.1	75.5	78.8	81.8	84.1	83.8	83.4	80.9	77.9	77.7
1997	73.9	74.2	75.0	78.2	81.1	84.0	86.1	87.6	87.2	86.5	83.4	82.0	81.6
1998	76.0	76.9	77.6	79.2	80.5	83.9	85.8	87.1	86.6	85.4	82.7	80.9	81.9
1999	76.6	76.3	77.7	79.6	81.0	84.1	87.6	88.8	88.6	87.5	84.6	82.8	82.9
2000	77.3	77.8	78.6	79.7	81.3	84.7	86.0	88.1	88.5	86.1	84.2	82.6	82.9
2001	78.6	78.4	78.9	78.6	79.7	82.2	83.6	85.0	83.2	81.7	78.8	76.8	80.5
2002	72.6	72.9	73.9	75.0	77.2	79.9	82.6	84.9	83.3	81.8	79.1	76.5	78.3
2003	72.1	72.0	72.1	72.7	74.5	77.0	80.3	82.8	82.3	81.7	80.1	78.8	77.2

Employment by Industry: Oregon—*Continued*

(Numbers in thousands. Not seasonally adjusted.)

Industry	January	February	March	April	May	June	July	August	September	October	November	December	Annual Average
STATEWIDE—*Continued*													
Manufacturing													
1990	197.9	197.6	199.2	199.7	201.2	205.6	209.0	214.0	208.5	202.8	200.2	197.2	202.7
1991	192.4	192.1	191.6	191.0	191.9	195.8	199.5	203.6	201.9	199.1	193.5	189.9	195.2
1992	184.6	185.6	185.7	188.5	190.0	195.0	199.1	200.1	197.4	195.4	190.3	188.3	191.7
1993	185.0	185.8	187.1	188.3	188.5	193.4	195.7	200.0	200.0	197.8	193.2	192.1	192.2
1994	188.7	189.7	191.5	194.0	196.0	202.7	206.8	209.2	208.0	205.7	202.1	202.0	199.7
1995	198.4	199.8	200.8	201.5	202.9	208.9	213.3	216.4	217.4	214.2	211.6	211.5	208.1
1996	207.9	207.4	209.2	210.0	210.8	216.0	220.7	225.4	224.1	220.3	218.7	217.9	215.7
1997	215.9	217.0	219.2	220.5	223.0	227.4	231.0	232.8	231.9	230.8	227.8	226.7	225.3
1998	224.1	226.0	226.6	225.0	225.5	228.2	231.3	233.3	230.6	227.6	223.8	222.3	227.0
1999	218.8	219.2	220.2	220.7	219.8	222.5	228.4	228.4	227.3	225.1	223.3	222.1	223.0
2000	218.2	219.0	220.2	220.2	221.3	225.4	228.3	228.1	228.7	224.7	224.2	223.0	223.4
2001	219.9	219.2	217.3	217.2	216.1	218.7	221.3	219.2	216.4	212.6	206.3	204.5	215.7
2002	199.2	198.9	199.0	200.1	200.8	203.3	207.1	206.5	205.2	202.4	198.9	197.5	201.6
2003	195.2	194.8	194.1	191.4	191.9	194.9	197.0	198.5	199.3	199.8	197.6	196.8	195.9
Service-providing													
1990	946.4	950.0	959.9	972.3	983.4	991.9	969.4	978.8	986.8	996.6	999.8	996.4	977.6
1991	960.3	966.1	973.5	979.9	988.0	995.6	972.6	976.1	990.6	1006.3	1006.0	1005.3	985.0
1992	980.3	986.9	993.7	1006.6	1015.6	1019.2	1003.9	1005.9	1022.8	1036.0	1041.9	1037.8	1012.6
1993	1010.1	1021.4	1030.1	1042.8	1050.3	1059.0	1038.8	1042.3	1060.8	1076.6	1083.7	1087.6	1050.3
1994	1052.3	1062.7	1070.6	1081.8	1090.4	1098.7	1077.7	1086.9	1104.3	1116.6	1128.3	1129.3	1091.6
1995	1092.1	1102.0	1113.0	1119.9	1130.3	1141.3	1115.1	1127.2	1145.9	1156.4	1162.0	1164.9	1130.8
1996	1132.6	1138.9	1148.6	1158.0	1171.2	1178.9	1155.9	1163.8	1183.4	1196.7	1210.6	1209.4	1170.7
1997	1174.9	1184.9	1194.0	1204.0	1214.8	1221.0	1195.8	1199.7	1216.0	1229.1	1235.1	1240.1	1209.1
1998	1199.2	1209.5	1217.2	1229.9	1240.2	1247.1	1217.6	1222.2	1240.0	1250.8	1260.4	1261.6	1233.0
1999	1222.9	1232.5	1243.4	1254.1	1258.7	1267.1	1248.3	1249.2	1264.8	1282.4	1291.7	1295.4	1259.2
2000	1252.0	1264.1	1272.9	1283.1	1298.2	1306.5	1278.8	1283.1	1296.4	1311.6	1320.6	1318.5	1290.5
2001	1274.0	1282.7	1289.4	1291.4	1299.7	1307.0	1270.5	1273.8	1284.6	1294.0	1296.7	1293.9	1288.1
2002	1255.2	1265.7	1273.0	1279.5	1289.7	1296.8	1272.1	1277.3	1288.5	1300.0	1302.9	1298.8	1283.3
2003	1263.8	1269.3	1274.1	1275.9	1284.4	1288.9	1261.8	1268.6	1277.2	1295.8	1296.9	1296.8	1279.5
Trade, transportation, and utilities													
1990	257.1	254.0	256.1	258.1	259.8	262.7	264.6	269.0	268.0	266.9	270.8	272.9	263.3
1991	256.7	254.7	255.9	257.4	258.8	260.6	261.2	262.9	264.6	265.9	269.1	271.1	261.6
1992	258.7	257.2	257.7	260.8	262.4	263.7	264.4	266.3	268.0	269.2	272.7	275.4	264.7
1993	262.4	261.8	262.0	264.6	265.9	269.6	271.7	272.2	275.6	278.0	282.6	287.6	271.2
1994	270.8	269.5	270.3	273.3	275.3	278.3	279.8	283.9	285.7	287.1	294.9	299.3	280.7
1995	281.8	280.1	281.5	283.2	285.4	289.2	288.2	292.6	294.6	295.3	301.4	305.5	289.9
1996	290.8	288.1	289.5	292.6	294.9	296.9	299.5	302.2	303.5	306.1	313.4	317.4	299.6
1997	301.7	298.6	299.6	301.6	304.3	307.1	309.8	311.0	311.7	314.4	321.1	326.1	308.9
1998	307.3	307.2	307.4	311.8	313.7	315.5	316.5	317.4	319.1	321.2	327.7	332.0	316.4
1999	313.9	312.0	313.7	315.6	316.5	320.4	320.7	321.1	323.3	325.5	333.0	338.2	321.2
2000	317.8	316.6	317.2	319.4	321.2	323.9	323.6	325.4	326.6	330.0	338.6	339.3	325.0
2001	320.7	316.9	317.6	317.6	318.9	321.4	321.2	321.7	321.0	320.5	325.4	326.7	320.8
2002	309.7	307.4	308.6	310.5	312.5	314.9	316.8	317.2	317.8	318.4	323.2	326.3	315.3
2003	310.4	308.3	308.4	308.6	310.9	312.8	314.8	317.0	317.9	317.3	321.2	321.9	314.1
Wholesale trade													
1990	63.5	63.8	64.7	64.5	64.4	65.1	65.5	66.5	66.3	66.2	66.0	65.8	65.2
1991	63.6	63.9	64.3	64.2	63.8	64.3	64.7	64.7	65.8	66.2	65.1	65.0	64.6
1992	63.7	64.0	64.1	64.4	64.7	65.1	65.5	66.8	67.1	66.3	65.6	65.3	65.2
1993	64.2	64.6	64.6	64.8	64.9	65.8	66.4	66.3	67.5	67.6	66.9	66.9	65.9
1994	65.1	65.4	65.9	66.2	66.4	67.1	67.8	69.0	69.8	69.8	69.7	70.0	67.7
1995	67.8	68.5	69.0	68.8	69.4	70.2	69.9	70.8	71.8	71.4	71.1	71.2	70.0
1996	69.7	70.1	70.7	70.7	70.7	71.0	71.5	72.3	72.7	72.5	72.7	72.6	71.4
1997	71.8	72.2	72.7	72.8	73.2	73.7	75.1	76.3	76.4	75.9	76.0	76.0	74.3
1998	74.7	75.2	75.2	76.3	76.2	76.4	76.4	76.8	77.2	76.5	76.8	76.8	76.2
1999	75.2	75.3	75.5	75.3	75.4	75.6	75.9	75.9	76.4	75.9	76.0	76.3	75.7
2000	75.0	75.3	75.6	75.4	75.4	75.9	76.6	76.6	76.6	77.0	76.9	76.7	76.1
2001	74.7	74.8	75.2	75.0	74.8	75.3	75.7	75.4	75.2	74.1	73.6	73.2	74.8
2002	72.7	72.8	72.8	73.1	73.2	73.7	74.7	74.7	74.6	75.0	74.7	74.7	73.9
2003	73.7	74.0	74.0	74.0	74.2	74.3	75.2	76.2	76.2	74.9	74.3	73.0	74.5
Retail trade													
1990	147.1	143.9	144.6	146.6	147.9	149.8	151.8	154.3	153.5	152.9	157.0	159.2	150.7
1991	147.3	144.9	145.5	147.1	148.5	149.7	149.7	151.3	151.1	151.9	156.4	158.4	150.2
1992	148.8	146.8	147.4	149.7	150.8	151.8	151.9	152.5	153.1	154.8	158.8	161.7	152.3
1993	151.3	149.7	149.9	151.6	152.3	154.4	155.5	156.0	156.8	159.1	163.9	168.1	155.7
1994	155.1	153.3	153.2	155.4	156.7	158.7	159.5	161.9	162.4	163.9	170.6	174.0	160.4
1995	160.8	158.2	158.9	160.3	161.8	164.5	164.0	166.6	166.8	168.2	174.6	178.5	165.3
1996	166.8	164.1	164.9	167.9	170.2	171.7	173.2	174.9	174.7	177.0	184.6	189.2	173.3
1997	176.8	173.3	173.9	175.0	177.4	179.4	180.7	180.3	180.0	183.0	189.4	194.3	180.3
1998	178.3	177.5	177.8	180.5	182.2	183.9	184.5	184.5	184.9	187.1	193.2	197.8	184.4
1999	182.6	180.3	181.6	183.8	184.5	187.9	187.8	188.3	188.9	191.2	197.7	202.4	188.1
2000	185.7	184.1	184.4	186.5	188.2	190.0	189.9	191.0	191.1	194.1	202.4	203.9	190.9
2001	189.5	185.7	186.2	186.6	187.4	189.5	189.2	189.0	188.4	188.5	194.3	196.2	189.2
2002	181.7	179.3	180.5	181.7	183.3	184.9	186.3	186.1	186.6	186.8	192.2	195.4	185.4
2003	181.2	179.0	179.4	179.7	181.7	183.2	184.6	185.5	185.9	186.0	189.9	191.6	184.0

Employment by Industry: Oregon—*Continued*

(Numbers in thousands. Not seasonally adjusted.)

Industry	January	February	March	April	May	June	July	August	September	October	November	December	Annual Average
STATEWIDE—*Continued*													
Transportation and utilities													
1990	46.5	46.3	46.8	47.0	47.5	47.8	47.3	48.2	48.2	47.8	47.8	47.9	47.4
1991	45.8	45.9	46.1	46.1	46.5	46.6	46.8	46.9	47.7	47.8	47.6	47.7	46.8
1992	46.2	46.4	46.2	46.7	46.9	46.8	47.0	47.0	47.8	48.1	48.3	48.4	47.2
1993	46.9	47.5	47.5	48.2	48.7	49.4	49.8	49.9	51.3	51.3	51.8	52.6	49.6
1994	50.6	50.8	51.2	51.7	52.2	52.5	52.5	53.0	53.5	53.4	54.6	55.3	52.6
1995	53.2	53.4	53.6	54.1	54.2	54.5	54.3	55.2	56.0	55.7	55.7	55.8	54.6
1996	54.3	53.9	53.9	54.0	54.0	54.2	54.8	55.0	56.1	56.6	56.1	55.6	54.9
1997	53.1	53.1	53.0	53.8	53.7	54.0	54.0	54.4	55.3	55.5	55.7	55.8	54.3
1998	54.3	54.5	54.4	55.0	55.3	55.2	55.6	56.1	57.0	57.6	57.7	57.4	55.8
1999	56.1	56.4	56.6	56.5	56.6	56.9	57.0	56.9	58.0	58.4	59.3	59.5	57.4
2000	57.1	57.2	57.2	57.5	57.6	58.0	57.1	57.8	58.9	58.9	59.3	58.7	57.9
2001	56.5	56.4	56.2	56.0	56.7	56.6	56.3	57.3	57.4	57.9	57.5	57.3	56.8
2002	55.3	55.3	55.3	55.7	56.0	56.3	55.8	56.4	56.6	56.6	56.3	56.2	56.0
2003	55.5	55.3	55.0	54.9	55.0	55.3	55.0	55.3	55.8	56.4	57.0	57.3	55.7
Information													
1990	26.6	26.7	26.7	26.8	27.0	27.3	26.7	27.0	26.9	26.7	26.8	26.9	26.8
1991	26.6	26.6	26.6	26.8	27.0	27.1	27.3	27.3	27.3	27.3	27.4	27.6	27.1
1992	27.2	27.5	27.6	28.4	28.4	28.3	28.6	28.3	28.7	27.6	26.9	26.9	27.9
1993	26.6	27.0	27.0	27.7	27.4	27.2	27.8	28.3	28.5	28.3	28.7	29.0	27.8
1994	27.8	28.4	28.6	28.9	28.7	28.9	29.5	30.1	29.7	29.6	29.8	29.8	29.2
1995	28.9	29.1	29.0	29.9	29.9	30.3	30.8	31.2	31.6	30.9	30.9	31.4	30.3
1996	30.8	30.9	30.9	31.0	31.3	31.5	31.6	33.0	32.8	32.8	32.6	32.6	31.8
1997	32.2	32.5	33.1	33.7	34.7	33.6	34.2	34.1	33.8	33.9	33.4	33.9	33.6
1998	33.6	33.6	33.8	34.5	34.3	34.4	35.3	35.2	34.9	35.7	35.5	35.3	34.7
1999	35.3	35.5	35.6	35.9	35.8	36.1	36.7	36.6	37.1	37.7	38.0	38.3	36.6
2000	37.9	38.0	38.4	38.4	38.9	39.3	40.0	40.0	40.2	40.9	41.0	41.5	39.5
2001	41.1	40.9	40.8	41.2	41.1	41.8	39.3	39.1	38.5	38.4	38.5	38.5	39.9
2002	38.1	38.2	37.5	36.0	36.0	35.9	35.7	35.7	35.4	35.4	35.3	36.0	36.3
2003	35.0	34.7	34.5	33.7	34.0	33.6	33.4	33.8	33.4	33.3	33.1	33.5	33.8
Financial activities													
1990	69.6	69.9	70.5	71.5	72.2	72.7	72.5	73.3	73.1	73.7	73.3	73.5	72.2
1991	72.8	72.8	73.2	73.5	74.0	74.6	75.4	75.6	75.4	75.7	75.6	75.5	74.5
1992	75.3	75.5	75.9	76.7	77.2	77.6	78.0	78.1	78.0	78.4	78.3	78.8	77.3
1993	77.7	77.8	78.2	79.2	79.9	81.0	81.9	82.3	82.5	82.6	83.1	83.6	80.8
1994	82.4	82.8	83.4	83.7	83.8	84.5	84.5	84.9	84.4	84.2	84.0	84.4	83.9
1995	82.7	83.0	82.9	83.8	83.9	84.9	85.4	85.9	85.6	85.1	85.4	86.0	84.6
1996	84.7	85.0	85.4	85.9	86.5	87.6	88.6	89.3	89.3	89.2	89.2	89.8	87.5
1997	89.0	89.5	89.9	90.5	91.4	91.9	92.6	92.3	91.9	92.1	91.8	92.6	91.3
1998	91.2	91.8	92.3	92.9	93.4	94.5	94.1	94.9	94.5	94.4	94.3	95.1	93.6
1999	93.7	93.6	94.4	94.7	94.7	94.9	95.6	95.8	94.7	94.7	94.1	94.6	94.6
2000	93.6	93.6	93.9	94.8	95.2	95.6	95.6	95.6	95.1	94.3	94.2	94.8	94.7
2001	93.2	93.7	94.2	94.5	95.0	95.8	96.5	96.3	95.8	95.7	95.7	95.8	95.2
2002	93.7	94.1	93.9	93.6	94.1	94.5	96.5	96.9	96.5	96.4	96.3	97.1	95.3
2003	95.9	96.2	96.9	97.7	98.0	99.0	98.4	99.7	99.1	100.2	99.1	98.8	98.3
Professional and business services													
1990	97.2	98.2	100.1	102.1	102.1	103.0	103.5	105.8	105.2	104.4	103.5	102.6	102.3
1991	96.5	97.7	99.6	100.3	100.8	101.5	101.0	103.0	103.4	104.5	102.8	102.6	101.1
1992	100.7	102.0	103.9	107.2	107.9	109.0	112.7	113.8	114.4	115.4	113.7	114.8	109.6
1993	111.3	115.2	117.6	120.2	120.6	120.9	123.3	126.6	128.1	128.1	128.0	129.4	122.4
1994	124.0	126.8	129.1	132.8	133.0	135.7	138.4	140.1	140.7	140.2	140.0	140.2	135.1
1995	135.8	138.5	142.4	142.5	143.5	146.2	145.9	149.9	151.7	151.3	150.6	149.4	145.6
1996	145.7	147.2	149.3	150.1	152.6	155.5	155.8	159.6	161.0	162.0	161.5	161.3	155.1
1997	156.1	159.2	161.2	163.3	165.0	166.5	168.6	171.1	171.3	172.4	170.8	170.0	166.3
1998	162.3	165.2	167.3	169.1	170.1	170.7	172.1	173.2	172.9	170.7	169.8	168.9	169.4
1999	163.2	166.0	169.4	172.1	171.8	173.8	177.5	178.2	179.6	179.9	179.7	180.4	174.3
2000	171.8	174.3	177.1	179.7	180.7	183.4	185.6	187.8	188.7	187.6	186.8	185.1	182.4
2001	180.1	179.4	179.5	178.0	177.9	179.7	178.2	179.4	177.5	173.5	172.2	170.3	177.1
2002	164.6	166.7	168.4	170.4	171.7	174.0	176.1	179.4	177.5	176.4	174.1	171.0	172.5
2003	163.8	165.0	166.0	166.9	168.7	169.9	170.7	173.6	172.0	174.8	173.1	173.5	169.8
Educational and health services													
1990	126.4	127.5	128.3	128.8	129.1	129.0	129.1	129.9	131.5	132.6	132.5	132.1	129.7
1991	130.9	132.3	132.7	133.5	133.8	133.1	132.9	132.8	135.2	137.0	136.7	137.2	134.0
1992	135.3	136.7	136.7	137.3	137.0	135.4	136.1	135.4	137.8	139.3	139.1	138.6	137.1
1993	136.4	137.9	138.4	140.1	139.9	139.1	138.3	137.9	141.0	142.5	142.9	142.4	139.7
1994	140.4	142.3	142.9	142.7	142.8	142.0	140.6	141.1	144.4	145.7	146.2	146.4	143.1
1995	143.5	145.9	146.9	146.5	147.3	146.7	145.9	146.9	150.1	151.6	152.6	153.1	148.1
1996	150.0	152.1	152.8	154.2	154.7	153.4	152.3	153.4	156.6	158.4	159.3	159.4	154.7
1997	157.6	160.0	160.6	161.3	161.3	159.5	157.3	157.5	160.1	162.2	162.4	162.9	160.2
1998	160.4	160.9	161.7	163.2	163.3	161.7	159.1	159.3	163.2	165.0	165.5	165.9	162.4
1999	163.1	165.5	166.0	167.0	167.2	165.4	164.5	164.1	168.5	170.5	170.9	172.0	167.1
2000	167.5	170.7	171.1	171.7	172.5	171.8	169.7	171.0	174.3	175.7	176.6	177.5	172.5
2001	174.4	178.7	179.4	179.7	179.3	176.6	173.2	174.3	179.1	182.4	183.9	184.5	178.8
2002	180.5	184.0	185.1	186.6	186.4	183.4	180.4	180.9	185.2	189.5	190.7	190.1	185.2
2003	186.7	189.4	190.1	189.8	189.5	185.9	185.3	183.7	186.4	188.7	190.3	189.4	187.9

Employment by Industry: Oregon—*Continued*

(Numbers in thousands. Not seasonally adjusted.)

Industry	January	February	March	April	May	June	July	August	September	October	November	December	Annual Average
STATEWIDE—*Continued*													
Leisure and hospitality													
1990	107.0	107.2	109.3	112.0	114.5	117.3	118.3	121.1	119.5	114.5	113.3	112.3	113.9
1991	106.5	107.0	109.3	111.6	114.2	117.2	118.1	119.4	118.4	114.5	112.7	111.9	113.4
1992	107.9	108.2	110.5	114.2	117.1	120.2	122.6	124.3	124.4	120.5	119.8	118.7	117.4
1993	115.8	117.2	120.3	123.9	127.3	130.7	132.9	134.7	133.5	130.4	129.9	129.6	127.2
1994	126.3	128.1	130.7	133.9	136.2	139.3	140.5	142.5	141.9	137.9	136.4	136.2	135.8
1995	132.7	133.8	136.6	139.6	142.4	146.0	147.8	149.6	148.2	143.3	140.9	140.8	141.8
1996	137.0	136.2	138.8	141.6	144.8	148.5	150.3	152.4	150.5	144.8	144.0	143.8	144.4
1997	138.8	140.0	142.9	146.0	148.7	152.6	153.7	155.6	151.8	146.1	144.6	145.1	147.2
1998	140.3	141.5	143.8	147.1	149.8	153.4	154.3	156.7	154.8	146.7	144.8	144.6	148.2
1999	141.4	142.6	145.0	148.5	150.4	155.0	156.9	158.6	156.1	151.7	149.9	149.5	150.5
2000	144.6	146.2	148.3	151.5	154.4	159.0	161.7	162.9	160.0	155.3	153.7	152.7	154.2
2001	141.4	142.6	145.0	148.3	151.4	154.9	156.9	158.9	155.6	149.2	145.6	145.5	149.6
2002	140.8	141.6	143.6	147.4	150.8	155.1	156.6	159.0	156.3	150.5	148.1	146.4	149.7
2003	143.7	144.1	146.2	148.4	150.2	155.8	157.2	158.4	156.1	152.4	149.1	149.8	151.0
Other services													
1990	43.0	43.6	44.2	45.3	45.6	46.5	46.9	47.5	47.0	47.1	47.1	47.0	45.9
1991	45.5	46.1	46.3	46.9	47.1	47.0	46.6	46.8	47.1	48.2	47.6	47.3	46.9
1992	46.6	47.1	47.1	47.1	47.6	47.7	47.7	47.9	48.2	48.4	47.9	47.8	47.6
1993	47.2	47.6	47.9	48.4	48.7	48.9	48.6	48.5	49.1	49.4	49.1	49.3	48.6
1994	47.7	48.1	48.4	48.7	49.0	49.2	48.9	49.3	49.9	50.3	50.1	50.0	49.1
1995	48.8	49.5	49.9	50.0	50.4	50.3	50.0	50.4	51.2	51.0	50.8	51.2	50.3
1996	50.2	50.4	51.1	51.3	51.6	51.3	51.0	50.9	51.2	51.0	50.7	50.6	50.9
1997	50.7	51.2	51.5	52.4	52.7	52.5	51.9	52.0	52.7	52.8	52.6	52.7	52.1
1998	51.5	52.1	52.5	53.1	53.4	53.4	53.0	53.1	53.6	53.6	53.5	53.4	53.0
1999	52.7	53.1	53.5	53.7	53.8	53.8	54.0	54.0	54.6	54.1	54.1	54.1	53.8
2000	53.3	54.1	54.7	54.9	55.3	55.3	54.5	54.9	55.6	55.6	55.5	55.2	54.9
2001	56.1	57.0	57.2	57.1	57.3	57.5	56.7	56.7	56.8	56.5	56.0	55.7	56.7
2002	54.8	55.3	55.6	56.2	56.6	56.6	56.3	56.4	56.6	56.6	56.5	56.2	56.1
2003	55.6	55.9	56.3	56.4	56.8	56.7	57.7	57.4	56.5	56.4	56.1	57.2	56.6
Government													
1990	219.5	222.9	224.7	227.7	233.1	233.4	207.8	205.2	215.6	230.7	232.5	229.1	223.5
1991	224.8	228.9	229.9	229.9	232.3	234.5	210.1	208.3	219.2	233.2	234.1	232.1	226.4
1992	228.6	232.7	234.3	234.9	238.0	237.3	213.8	211.8	223.3	237.2	243.5	236.8	231.0
1993	232.7	236.9	238.7	238.7	240.6	241.6	214.3	211.8	222.5	237.3	239.4	236.7	232.6
1994	232.9	236.7	237.2	237.8	241.6	240.8	215.5	215.0	227.6	241.6	246.9	243.0	234.7
1995	237.9	242.1	243.8	244.4	247.5	247.7	221.1	220.7	232.9	247.9	249.4	247.5	240.2
1996	243.4	249.0	250.8	251.3	254.8	254.2	226.8	223.0	238.5	252.4	259.9	254.5	246.6
1997	248.8	253.9	255.2	255.2	256.7	257.3	227.7	226.1	242.7	255.2	258.4	256.8	249.5
1998	252.6	257.2	258.4	258.2	262.2	263.5	233.2	232.4	247.0	263.5	269.3	266.4	255.3
1999	259.6	264.2	265.8	266.6	268.5	267.7	242.4	240.8	250.9	268.3	272.0	268.3	261.3
2000	265.5	270.6	272.2	272.7	280.0	278.2	248.1	245.5	255.9	272.2	274.2	272.4	267.3
2001	267.0	273.5	275.7	275.0	278.8	279.3	248.5	247.4	260.3	277.8	279.4	276.9	270.0
2002	273.0	278.4	280.3	278.8	281.6	282.4	253.7	251.8	263.2	276.8	278.7	275.7	272.9
2003	272.7	275.7	275.7	274.4	276.3	275.2	244.3	245.0	255.8	272.7	274.9	272.7	268.0
Federal government													
1990	31.7	31.2	31.8	35.1	37.3	37.8	36.6	35.0	34.2	33.4	32.1	32.5	34.1
1991	31.0	30.9	31.0	31.8	32.4	34.3	35.1	34.5	34.3	33.0	32.6	32.4	32.8
1992	31.5	31.5	31.7	32.6	33.2	33.9	35.5	35.3	34.5	33.4	32.6	33.0	33.2
1993	31.7	31.5	31.6	32.0	32.6	33.1	34.0	33.9	33.4	33.1	31.7	31.9	32.5
1994	30.5	30.5	30.6	31.1	31.1	31.3	32.1	32.0	31.7	31.4	30.0	30.4	31.1
1995	29.3	29.3	29.4	29.9	30.5	31.1	32.0	32.0	31.5	30.9	29.7	30.3	30.5
1996	29.3	29.3	29.4	30.0	30.3	30.5	31.3	31.4	31.2	30.2	30.2	30.7	30.3
1997	29.2	29.1	29.1	29.8	30.1	30.4	31.4	31.4	31.2	30.3	30.6	31.0	30.3
1998	29.8	29.2	29.2	29.5	30.3	30.7	31.4	31.4	31.2	30.4	30.5	30.9	30.4
1999	29.8	29.2	29.3	29.8	30.0	30.3	31.5	31.5	31.2	30.7	30.3	30.7	30.4
2000	29.7	29.5	30.2	31.1	35.6	33.4	33.9	33.2	31.2	30.3	30.0	30.9	31.6
2001	29.2	28.8	29.0	28.9	29.5	30.5	31.7	31.4	31.3	30.0	29.4	29.8	30.0
2002	28.5	28.2	28.5	28.7	29.2	30.5	31.6	31.3	31.2	30.1	29.6	30.3	29.8
2003	29.4	29.4	29.9	30.0	30.4	31.1	32.3	32.1	31.8	31.2	30.6	30.8	30.8
State government													
1990	59.5	60.8	61.2	60.8	61.3	62.8	58.2	57.8	57.5	62.6	62.5	61.7	60.6
1991	61.4	62.7	63.1	62.5	62.8	64.0	58.3	58.0	58.6	62.9	63.0	62.3	61.6
1992	61.3	62.6	62.9	62.9	62.8	63.8	58.6	58.2	59.6	62.4	62.3	62.0	61.6
1993	61.1	62.5	62.9	62.6	62.8	64.0	58.5	58.0	59.1	62.3	62.5	62.0	61.5
1994	61.3	62.8	62.9	62.6	62.9	64.2	59.0	59.0	60.0	63.6	64.1	63.5	62.2
1995	62.5	64.2	64.9	64.1	64.8	66.0	60.1	60.0	60.3	64.6	65.6	64.4	63.5
1996	54.6	57.1	57.7	57.1	57.7	58.4	54.1	53.3	53.7	57.3	58.3	57.9	56.4
1997	56.2	58.6	59.0	58.4	58.7	59.9	54.5	54.1	54.1	57.5	58.5	58.3	57.3
1998	57.0	58.8	59.2	58.8	59.2	60.4	55.8	56.0	55.3	60.1	61.2	61.0	58.6
1999	58.5	60.0	60.2	60.0	60.1	60.8	56.0	55.1	54.7	59.6	60.4	59.6	58.8
2000	59.9	60.4	60.7	60.0	60.7	61.4	56.1	57.2	57.0	60.9	61.5	60.6	59.7
2001	58.5	61.6	62.0	61.6	62.1	62.3	58.6	58.0	56.9	62.0	62.4	61.5	60.6
2002	60.6	62.2	62.7	62.2	62.6	63.0	59.7	60.4	59.9	62.0	62.3	62.2	61.7
2003	61.5	62.0	62.4	61.7	62.3	63.0	57.4	57.4	56.8	61.4	62.4	62.2	60.9

Employment by Industry: Oregon—*Continued*

(Numbers in thousands. Not seasonally adjusted.)

Industry	January	February	March	April	May	June	July	August	September	October	November	December	Annual Average
STATEWIDE—*Continued*													
Local government													
1990	128.3	130.9	131.7	131.8	134.5	132.8	113.0	112.4	123.9	134.7	137.9	134.9	128.9
1991	132.4	135.3	135.8	135.6	137.1	136.2	116.7	115.8	126.3	137.3	138.5	137.4	132.0
1992	135.8	138.6	139.7	139.4	142.0	139.6	119.7	118.3	129.2	141.4	148.6	141.8	136.2
1993	139.9	142.9	144.2	144.1	145.2	144.5	121.8	119.9	130.0	141.9	145.2	142.8	138.5
1994	141.1	143.4	143.7	144.1	147.6	145.3	124.4	124.0	135.9	146.6	152.8	149.1	141.5
1995	146.1	148.6	149.5	150.4	152.2	150.6	129.0	128.7	141.1	152.4	154.1	152.8	146.3
1996	159.5	162.6	163.7	164.2	166.8	165.3	141.4	138.3	153.6	164.9	171.4	165.9	159.8
1997	163.4	166.2	167.1	167.0	167.9	167.0	141.8	140.6	157.4	167.4	169.3	167.5	161.9
1998	165.8	169.2	170.0	169.9	172.7	172.4	146.0	145.0	160.5	173.0	177.6	174.5	166.4
1999	171.3	175.0	176.3	176.8	178.4	176.6	154.9	154.2	165.0	178.0	181.3	178.0	172.2
2000	175.9	180.7	181.3	181.6	183.7	183.4	158.1	155.1	167.7	181.0	182.7	180.9	176.0
2001	179.3	183.1	184.7	184.5	187.2	186.5	158.2	158.0	172.1	185.8	187.6	185.6	179.4
2002	183.9	188.0	189.1	187.9	189.8	188.9	162.4	160.1	172.1	184.7	186.8	183.2	181.4
2003	181.8	184.3	183.4	182.7	183.6	181.1	154.6	155.5	167.2	180.1	181.9	179.7	176.3
EUGENE-SPRINGFIELD													
Total nonfarm													
1990	115.4	116.3	116.8	118.5	119.8	120.4	116.7	116.6	118.1	120.1	119.9	118.1	118.1
1991	113.9	113.5	114.1	114.9	116.6	118.3	114.1	114.3	115.4	118.9	118.7	118.4	115.9
1992	114.0	114.6	115.9	116.6	118.1	119.4	116.1	116.3	118.1	120.2	120.1	119.7	117.4
1993	115.3	116.5	117.9	119.8	121.0	122.5	116.9	118.3	121.8	124.5	125.0	125.6	120.4
1994	121.4	123.2	123.5	125.2	126.7	128.8	124.3	125.2	128.3	130.3	130.7	130.5	126.5
1995	125.1	127.0	128.5	129.0	130.0	131.5	127.0	128.0	131.2	133.4	133.7	133.4	129.8
1996	127.7	129.4	131.0	132.1	134.0	135.0	131.4	132.4	134.5	137.1	138.7	137.3	133.4
1997	132.5	134.4	135.5	136.5	138.6	140.0	133.5	134.2	137.3	139.8	141.3	140.9	137.0
1998	136.1	137.5	138.3	139.5	141.7	142.5	136.3	137.1	139.6	142.0	144.3	144.1	139.9
1999	138.1	139.3	140.9	142.5	142.7	143.6	138.9	139.1	142.6	146.1	147.3	147.3	142.4
2000	141.0	142.4	143.3	144.1	145.3	146.4	140.3	141.6	144.3	146.7	146.8	147.0	144.1
2001	140.5	141.2	141.9	141.9	142.6	144.3	138.5	138.3	140.6	141.8	142.2	142.9	141.4
2002	138.1	139.2	140.0	141.0	143.1	144.0	139.5	139.8	142.9	145.0	145.8	145.7	142.0
2003	140.6	141.0	140.6	139.6	141.5	142.4	137.7	138.1	139.4	142.9	143.4	144.3	141.0
Total private													
1990	91.6	91.6	92.1	93.6	94.3	94.5	95.0	96.0	96.0	94.8	94.4	93.0	93.9
1991	89.6	88.5	89.0	90.0	91.5	92.6	92.4	93.6	93.2	93.6	93.2	93.1	91.7
1992	89.3	89.4	90.4	91.1	92.5	93.6	93.8	94.9	95.4	94.9	94.3	94.0	92.8
1993	90.3	91.0	92.5	94.4	95.4	96.3	97.4	99.0	99.8	99.9	100.3	100.8	96.4
1994	97.6	98.5	98.3	100.3	101.5	103.3	103.7	104.9	105.4	105.5	105.5	105.3	102.5
1995	100.8	101.8	103.1	103.8	104.6	105.7	106.3	107.9	108.5	107.9	108.1	107.9	105.5
1996	103.1	103.6	104.9	106.1	107.8	108.8	109.9	111.4	111.0	111.3	112.2	111.0	108.4
1997	107.2	108.3	109.0	110.4	112.1	113.4	113.4	114.2	114.0	114.5	115.3	115.1	112.2
1998	110.8	111.4	111.8	113.4	115.3	116.0	115.5	116.1	115.9	115.6	117.0	117.0	114.7
1999	112.2	112.7	113.9	115.7	115.8	116.6	117.6	118.2	118.8	119.1	120.1	120.4	116.8
2000	114.9	115.4	116.0	117.0	117.6	118.8	118.6	119.7	120.0	119.4	119.2	119.5	118.0
2001	114.6	114.1	114.4	114.6	115.1	116.7	116.1	116.2	115.9	114.8	114.4	115.3	115.2
2002	111.3	111.6	112.2	113.5	115.3	116.2	117.2	118.4	118.2	118.1	118.4	118.4	115.7
2003	113.9	113.7	113.4	112.5	114.0	115.1	115.0	115.5	115.5	115.9	116.2	117.0	114.8
Goods-producing													
1990	23.8	23.6	23.8	23.9	24.3	24.5	25.2	25.8	25.6	24.1	23.3	22.4	24.2
1991	21.3	21.0	21.3	21.5	22.3	22.7	22.9	23.5	23.2	22.8	22.1	21.7	22.2
1992	20.9	20.7	21.1	21.2	21.6	22.2	22.8	23.4	23.2	22.5	21.8	21.3	21.9
1993	20.5	20.8	21.3	21.6	22.0	22.4	23.0	23.7	23.8	23.6	23.0	22.8	22.4
1994	22.0	22.2	22.1	22.7	23.2	24.0	24.5	25.0	25.0	24.9	24.4	23.9	23.7
1995	23.1	23.2	23.5	23.7	23.9	24.5	24.9	25.6	25.7	25.4	25.1	24.6	24.4
1996	23.5	23.7	24.2	24.5	24.6	25.3	26.0	26.8	26.7	26.8	26.5	25.9	25.4
1997	25.1	25.6	25.9	26.6	27.2	27.6	28.2	29.2	29.0	28.9	28.5	28.1	27.5
1998	27.1	27.2	27.3	27.2	27.6	28.0	28.8	29.2	28.9	28.5	28.3	28.1	28.0
1999	27.3	27.7	28.0	28.3	28.4	28.8	29.1	29.7	29.9	29.8	29.5	29.2	28.8
2000	28.6	28.8	28.9	29.3	29.4	29.7	29.8	30.2	30.1	29.8	29.3	29.0	29.4
2001	27.9	27.5	27.5	27.3	27.3	27.6	27.9	27.4	27.3	27.0	26.0	25.7	27.2
2002	25.4	25.4	25.5	25.9	26.4	26.8	27.2	27.3	27.3	27.2	26.8	26.6	26.5
2003	25.9	26.1	25.8	24.8	25.7	26.1	26.3	26.4	26.4	26.2	26.2	26.0	26.0
Natural resources and mining													
1990	1.8	1.7	1.7	1.7	1.7	1.7	1.8	1.9	1.9	1.8	1.6	1.5	1.7
1991	1.3	1.3	1.4	1.3	1.4	1.5	1.5	1.6	1.6	1.5	1.5	1.4	1.4
1992	1.3	1.2	1.3	1.3	1.3	1.4	1.6	1.5	1.3	1.3	1.3	1.4	1.4
1993	1.1	1.2	1.2	1.2	1.2	1.3	1.4	1.4	1.4	1.3	1.2	1.2	1.3
1994	1.1	1.1	1.1	1.1	1.1	1.2	1.2	1.2	1.2	1.2	1.1	1.0	1.1
1995	1.0	1.0	1.0	1.0	1.1	1.1	1.2	1.2	1.2	1.2	1.1	1.1	1.1
1996	1.0	1.1	1.1	1.1	1.1	1.1	1.2	1.2	1.2	1.2	1.1	1.1	1.1
1997	1.0	1.0	1.0	1.0	1.1	1.1	1.1	1.2	1.2	1.2	1.1	1.1	1.1
1998	1.0	1.0	1.0	1.1	1.1	1.1	1.0	1.0	1.1	1.0	1.0	1.0	1.0
1999	0.9	0.9	0.9	0.9	1.0	1.0	1.0	1.0	1.0	1.0	1.0	0.9	1.0
2000	0.9	0.9	0.9	0.9	0.9	1.0	1.0	1.0	1.0	1.1	1.1	1.1	1.0
2001	1.0	1.0	1.0	1.0	1.0	1.0	1.0	1.0	1.0	1.0	0.9	0.9	1.0
2002	0.9	0.9	1.0	1.0	1.0	1.0	1.0	1.0	1.0	1.0	1.0	0.9	1.0
2003	0.9	0.9	0.9	0.9	0.9	1.0	1.0	1.0	1.0	1.0	1.0	0.9	1.0

Employment by Industry: Oregon—*Continued*

(Numbers in thousands. Not seasonally adjusted.)

Industry	January	February	March	April	May	June	July	August	September	October	November	December	Annual Average
EUGENE-SPRINGFIELD *—Continued*													
Construction													
1990	3.9	3.9	4.1	4.3	4.6	4.7	5.0	5.0	5.0	4.8	4.4	4.2	4.5
1991	3.8	3.7	3.8	4.0	4.3	4.5	4.7	4.9	4.9	4.8	4.6	4.5	4.4
1992	4.0	3.9	4.1	4.2	4.5	4.7	4.9	5.0	5.1	4.9	4.5	4.2	4.5
1993	3.9	4.1	4.4	4.5	4.7	5.0	5.3	5.4	5.5	5.4	5.2	5.1	4.9
1994	4.7	4.8	4.8	5.1	5.4	5.7	5.9	6.1	6.1	6.0	5.8	5.5	5.5
1995	5.2	5.2	5.5	5.6	5.7	6.1	6.3	6.5	6.6	6.4	6.3	5.9	5.9
1996	5.5	5.6	6.0	6.1	6.2	6.6	7.0	7.2	7.2	7.2	7.1	6.8	6.5
1997	6.3	6.4	6.5	6.9	7.1	7.4	7.7	7.9	7.8	7.6	7.4	7.5	7.2
1998	6.8	6.7	6.7	6.6	6.9	7.2	7.5	7.5	7.3	7.2	7.0	6.9	7.0
1999	6.5	6.5	6.7	6.8	6.8	7.1	7.3	7.5	7.5	7.3	6.9	6.7	7.0
2000	6.1	6.2	6.2	6.4	6.5	6.8	7.0	7.3	7.1	6.9	6.7	6.4	6.6
2001	6.1	6.1	6.1	6.3	6.4	6.6	6.9	7.0	7.0	6.9	6.6	6.4	6.5
2002	6.0	6.0	6.0	6.3	6.5	6.7	7.1	7.3	7.1	7.0	6.8	6.6	6.6
2003	6.1	6.1	6.1	6.2	6.3	6.5	6.8	6.9	6.9	6.6	6.6	6.5	6.5
Manufacturing													
1990	18.1	18.0	18.0	17.9	18.0	18.1	18.4	18.9	18.7	17.5	17.3	16.7	18.0
1991	16.2	16.0	16.1	16.2	16.6	16.7	16.7	17.0	16.7	16.5	16.0	15.8	16.4
1992	15.6	15.6	15.7	15.7	15.8	16.1	16.3	16.9	16.8	16.3	16.0	15.7	16.0
1993	15.5	15.5	15.7	15.9	16.1	16.1	16.3	16.9	16.9	16.9	16.6	16.5	16.2
1994	16.2	16.3	16.2	16.5	16.7	17.1	17.4	17.7	17.7	17.7	17.5	17.4	17.0
1995	16.9	17.0	17.0	17.1	17.1	17.3	17.4	17.9	17.9	17.8	17.7	17.6	17.4
1996	17.0	17.0	17.1	17.3	17.3	17.6	17.8	18.4	18.3	18.4	18.3	18.0	17.7
1997	17.8	18.2	18.4	18.7	19.0	19.1	19.4	20.1	20.0	20.1	20.0	19.5	19.2
1998	19.3	19.5	19.6	19.5	19.6	19.7	20.3	20.7	20.5	20.3	20.3	20.2	20.0
1999	19.9	20.3	20.4	20.6	20.6	20.7	20.8	21.2	21.4	21.5	21.6	21.6	20.9
2000	21.6	21.7	21.8	22.0	22.0	21.9	21.8	21.9	22.0	21.8	21.5	21.5	21.8
2001	20.8	20.4	20.4	20.0	19.9	20.0	20.0	19.4	19.3	19.1	18.5	18.4	19.7
2002	18.5	18.5	18.5	18.6	18.9	19.1	19.1	19.0	19.2	19.2	19.0	19.1	18.9
2003	18.9	19.1	18.8	17.7	18.5	18.6	18.5	18.5	18.5	18.6	18.6	18.6	18.6
Service-providing													
1990	91.6	92.7	93.0	94.6	95.5	95.9	91.5	90.8	92.5	96.0	96.6	95.7	93.9
1991	92.6	92.5	92.8	93.4	94.3	95.6	91.2	90.8	92.2	96.1	96.6	96.7	93.7
1992	93.1	93.9	94.8	95.4	96.5	97.2	93.3	92.9	94.9	97.7	98.3	98.4	95.5
1993	94.8	95.7	96.6	98.2	99.0	100.1	93.9	94.6	98.0	100.9	102.0	102.8	98.1
1994	99.4	101.0	101.4	102.5	103.5	104.8	99.8	100.2	103.3	105.4	106.3	106.6	102.9
1995	102.0	103.8	105.0	105.3	106.1	107.0	102.1	102.4	105.5	108.0	108.6	108.8	105.4
1996	104.2	105.7	106.8	107.6	109.4	109.7	105.4	105.6	107.8	110.3	112.2	111.4	108.0
1997	107.4	108.8	109.6	109.9	111.4	112.4	105.3	105.0	108.3	110.9	112.8	112.8	109.6
1998	109.0	110.3	111.0	112.3	114.1	114.5	107.5	107.9	110.7	113.5	116.0	116.0	111.9
1999	110.8	111.6	112.9	114.2	114.3	114.8	109.8	109.4	112.7	116.3	117.8	118.1	113.6
2000	112.4	113.6	114.4	114.8	115.9	116.7	110.5	111.4	114.2	116.9	117.5	118.0	114.7
2001	112.6	113.7	114.4	114.6	115.3	116.7	110.6	110.9	113.3	114.8	116.2	117.2	114.2
2002	112.7	113.8	114.5	115.1	116.7	117.2	112.3	112.5	115.6	117.8	119.0	119.1	115.5
2003	114.7	114.9	114.8	114.8	115.8	116.3	111.4	111.7	113.0	116.7	117.2	118.3	115.0
Trade, transportation, and utilities													
1990	22.6	22.3	22.1	22.7	22.7	22.7	22.8	22.9	22.7	22.9	23.7	23.8	22.8
1991	22.3	21.9	21.8	22.0	22.1	22.4	22.3	22.3	22.1	22.5	23.1	23.5	22.4
1992	21.9	21.8	21.8	21.8	22.0	22.3	22.2	22.3	22.3	22.5	22.9	23.2	22.3
1993	22.1	21.9	21.9	22.2	22.5	22.8	22.9	23.1	23.2	23.3	24.2	24.8	22.9
1994	23.0	22.7	22.6	22.9	23.1	23.4	23.5	23.6	23.6	23.6	24.7	25.1	23.5
1995	23.5	23.1	23.3	23.4	23.5	23.7	23.9	24.2	24.2	24.6	25.6	26.2	24.1
1996	24.1	23.9	24.1	24.2	24.4	24.7	24.9	25.0	24.9	25.0	26.1	26.6	24.8
1997	24.8	24.7	24.6	24.9	25.3	25.4	25.6	25.5	25.4	25.5	27.0	27.4	25.5
1998	25.5	25.4	25.3	25.7	26.1	26.3	25.8	25.9	25.9	26.3	27.5	27.9	26.1
1999	25.9	25.7	25.9	26.1	26.2	26.5	26.4	26.5	26.5	26.5	27.7	28.8	26.6
2000	25.9	25.8	25.9	25.9	26.3	26.5	26.4	26.5	26.4	26.5	27.4	28.5	26.5
2001	26.3	26.0	25.9	26.0	26.1	26.4	26.1	26.1	26.0	25.8	26.7	27.7	26.3
2002	25.4	25.1	25.3	25.7	26.0	26.2	26.3	26.6	26.6	26.9	27.9	28.8	26.4
2003	26.0	25.7	25.8	25.9	26.0	26.1	26.1	26.1	26.2	26.5	26.9	27.6	26.2
Wholesale trade													
1990	4.7	4.7	4.7	4.8	4.8	4.8	4.7	4.8	4.7	5.0	4.9	4.9	4.8
1991	4.6	4.6	4.6	4.7	4.7	4.7	4.7	4.7	4.6	4.7	4.7	4.7	4.7
1992	4.4	4.5	4.6	4.5	4.6	4.7	4.6	4.7	4.6	4.6	4.6	4.6	4.6
1993	4.4	4.5	4.5	4.5	4.6	4.7	4.6	4.7	4.7	4.6	4.6	4.7	4.6
1994	4.6	4.6	4.6	4.6	4.6	4.7	4.8	4.9	4.9	4.8	4.8	4.9	4.7
1995	4.7	4.7	4.8	4.9	5.0	5.0	5.1	5.1	5.1	5.2	5.1	5.1	5.0
1996	5.1	5.1	5.2	5.2	5.2	5.3	5.3	5.4	5.3	5.2	5.1	5.2	5.2
1997	5.0	5.1	5.1	5.2	5.3	5.3	5.4	5.4	5.3	5.1	5.1	5.1	5.2
1998	5.1	5.1	5.1	5.1	5.2	5.3	5.3	5.3	5.3	5.3	5.3	5.3	5.2
1999	5.4	5.4	5.5	5.6	5.8	5.9	5.8	5.8	5.7	5.7	5.7	5.8	5.7
2000	5.3	5.4	5.4	5.5	5.6	5.6	5.6	5.6	5.5	5.5	5.4	5.4	5.5
2001	5.3	5.3	5.3	5.3	5.3	5.4	5.3	5.3	5.2	5.1	5.1	5.1	5.3
2002	5.0	4.9	4.9	5.0	5.1	5.1	5.3	5.3	5.2	5.4	5.4	5.4	5.2
2003	5.0	5.0	5.0	5.1	5.1	5.2	5.2	5.2	5.2	5.3	5.2	5.2	5.1

Employment by Industry: Oregon—*Continued*

(Numbers in thousands. Not seasonally adjusted.)

Industry	January	February	March	April	May	June	July	August	September	October	November	December	Annual Average
EUGENE-SPRINGFIELD *—Continued*													
Retail trade													
1990	15.2	14.9	14.7	15.2	15.2	15.2	15.4	15.4	15.2	15.2	16.1	16.2	15.3
1991	15.2	14.7	14.7	14.8	14.9	15.1	15.0	15.0	14.9	15.1	15.8	16.2	15.1
1992	14.9	14.7	14.6	14.7	14.9	15.0	15.0	15.0	15.1	15.3	15.7	16.0	15.1
1993	15.2	15.0	15.0	15.2	15.3	15.4	15.6	15.7	15.7	15.9	16.7	17.1	15.7
1994	15.5	15.2	15.0	15.4	15.6	15.7	15.8	15.8	15.7	15.9	17.0	17.3	15.8
1995	15.9	15.6	15.7	15.6	15.7	15.8	16.0	16.3	16.3	16.6	17.6	18.2	16.3
1996	16.3	16.1	16.2	16.3	16.5	16.7	16.9	16.8	16.8	17.0	18.2	18.5	16.9
1997	17.0	16.8	16.7	16.9	17.2	17.3	17.4	17.3	17.2	17.5	19.0	19.4	17.5
1998	17.6	17.5	17.3	17.7	17.9	18.0	17.5	17.6	17.6	17.9	19.1	19.5	17.9
1999	17.5	17.3	17.4	17.8	17.7	17.9	17.9	18.0	18.0	18.0	19.2	20.2	18.1
2000	17.8	17.6	17.7	17.6	17.8	18.0	18.0	18.0	18.0	18.1	19.1	20.1	18.2
2001	18.0	17.7	17.6	17.8	17.8	18.0	17.9	17.9	17.9	17.9	18.8	19.8	18.1
2002	17.8	17.6	17.8	18.1	18.2	18.3	18.3	18.5	18.6	18.6	19.7	20.5	18.5
2003	18.3	18.0	18.1	18.1	18.2	18.2	18.2	18.2	18.3	18.5	19.0	19.6	18.4
Transportation and utilities													
1990	2.7	2.7	2.7	2.7	2.7	2.7	2.7	2.7	2.8	2.7	2.7	2.7	2.7
1991	2.5	2.6	2.5	2.5	2.5	2.6	2.6	2.6	2.6	2.7	2.6	2.6	2.6
1992	2.6	2.6	2.6	2.6	2.5	2.6	2.6	2.6	2.6	2.6	2.6	2.6	2.6
1993	2.5	2.4	2.4	2.5	2.6	2.7	2.7	2.7	2.8	2.8	2.9	3.0	2.7
1994	2.9	2.9	3.0	2.9	2.9	3.0	2.9	2.9	3.0	2.9	2.9	2.9	2.9
1995	2.9	2.8	2.8	2.9	2.8	2.9	2.8	2.8	2.8	2.8	2.9	2.9	2.8
1996	2.7	2.7	2.7	2.7	2.7	2.7	2.7	2.8	2.8	2.8	2.8	2.9	2.8
1997	2.8	2.8	2.8	2.8	2.8	2.8	2.8	2.8	2.9	2.9	2.9	2.9	2.8
1998	2.8	2.8	2.9	2.9	3.0	3.0	3.0	3.0	3.0	3.1	3.1	3.1	3.0
1999	3.0	3.0	3.0	2.7	2.7	2.7	2.7	2.7	2.8	2.8	2.8	2.8	2.8
2000	2.8	2.8	2.8	2.8	2.9	2.9	2.8	2.9	2.9	2.9	2.9	3.0	2.9
2001	3.0	3.0	3.0	2.9	3.0	3.0	2.9	2.9	2.9	2.8	2.8	2.8	2.9
2002	2.6	2.6	2.6	2.6	2.7	2.8	2.7	2.8	2.8	2.9	2.8	2.9	2.7
2003	2.7	2.7	2.7	2.7	2.7	2.7	2.7	2.7	2.7	2.7	2.7	2.8	2.7
Information													
1990	2.6	2.6	2.5	2.6	2.6	2.6	2.6	2.6	2.6	2.6	2.7	2.7	2.6
1991	2.8	2.8	2.8	2.8	2.8	2.9	2.8	2.8	2.8	2.8	2.9	2.9	2.8
1992	2.8	2.8	2.8	2.9	2.9	2.9	2.8	2.8	2.9	2.9	2.9	2.9	2.9
1993	2.9	2.9	2.9	2.9	2.9	2.9	2.9	2.9	3.0	3.1	3.2	3.2	3.0
1994	3.1	3.2	3.2	3.2	3.2	3.2	3.1	3.1	3.2	3.2	3.3	3.3	3.2
1995	3.2	3.3	3.3	3.6	3.8	3.7	3.7	3.6	3.7	3.7	3.8	3.8	3.6
1996	3.7	3.7	3.6	3.7	3.7	3.8	3.7	3.7	3.7	3.7	3.7	3.7	3.7
1997	3.7	3.7	3.8	3.9	3.8	3.9	3.8	3.8	3.8	4.0	4.0	4.0	3.9
1998	3.8	3.9	3.9	4.3	4.3	4.4	4.3	4.3	4.3	4.3	4.3	4.3	4.2
1999	3.9	3.9	4.0	4.0	3.9	3.9	3.8	3.7	3.8	3.8	3.9	3.9	3.9
2000	3.7	3.6	3.7	3.6	3.6	3.7	3.6	3.7	3.8	3.7	3.8	3.8	3.7
2001	3.8	3.8	3.8	3.9	3.8	3.9	3.8	3.8	3.8	3.8	3.9	3.9	3.8
2002	3.9	3.8	3.8	3.7	3.8	3.7	3.7	3.7	3.7	3.7	3.7	3.7	3.7
2003	3.7	3.7	3.6	3.6	3.6	3.5	3.4	3.4	3.4	3.4	3.4	3.4	3.5
Financial activities													
1990	5.8	5.7	5.8	5.8	5.8	5.8	5.8	5.8	5.9	6.0	5.9	5.9	5.8
1991	5.9	5.8	5.9	5.9	6.0	6.0	6.0	6.0	5.9	5.9	5.9	5.9	5.9
1992	5.9	5.9	6.0	6.1	6.1	6.1	6.1	6.2	6.2	6.2	6.1	6.3	6.1
1993	5.7	5.8	5.9	6.1	6.2	6.3	6.3	6.3	6.4	6.4	6.5	6.5	6.2
1994	6.6	6.6	6.6	6.7	6.8	6.9	6.9	6.9	6.9	6.8	6.8	6.7	6.8
1995	6.6	6.8	6.7	6.8	6.9	7.0	7.1	7.1	7.2	7.2	7.1	7.2	7.0
1996	7.0	7.1	7.2	7.2	7.2	7.3	7.4	7.4	7.4	7.4	7.3	7.3	7.3
1997	7.3	7.3	7.3	7.2	7.3	7.4	7.4	7.3	7.1	7.2	7.1	7.2	7.3
1998	7.2	7.3	7.2	7.4	7.3	7.5	7.3	7.3	7.3	7.2	7.2	7.3	7.3
1999	7.1	7.1	7.2	7.3	7.3	7.4	7.5	7.4	7.3	7.1	7.1	7.2	7.3
2000	6.9	6.9	6.9	7.0	7.0	7.1	7.1	7.1	7.1	6.9	6.9	6.8	7.0
2001	7.0	7.0	7.1	7.1	7.2	7.4	7.4	7.3	7.3	7.3	7.3	7.3	7.2
2002	7.0	7.1	7.0	7.1	7.2	7.2	7.3	7.3	7.3	7.2	7.3	7.3	7.2
2003	7.2	7.2	7.3	7.3	7.4	7.5	7.5	7.6	7.6	7.6	7.6	7.7	7.5
Professional and business services													
1990	9.6	9.7	10.0	10.1	10.2	10.1	10.0	10.2	10.1	10.0	9.8	9.4	9.9
1991	9.0	8.7	8.7	9.0	9.2	9.3	9.3	9.7	9.6	9.6	9.5	9.4	9.3
1992	8.8	9.1	9.4	9.5	9.8	9.9	9.8	10.1	10.3	10.1	10.0	9.8	9.7
1993	9.4	9.7	10.2	10.4	10.5	10.4	10.5	11.5	11.4	11.4	11.4	11.6	10.7
1994	11.8	12.5	12.6	12.8	13.0	13.4	13.3	13.8	13.9	13.8	13.5	13.4	13.2
1995	11.8	12.3	12.8	12.6	12.3	12.6	12.5	13.3	13.2	12.6	12.5	12.2	12.6
1996	12.0	12.0	12.4	12.5	13.4	13.0	13.3	13.7	13.8	13.6	14.1	13.1	13.1
1997	12.7	13.1	13.2	13.4	13.7	13.8	14.1	13.9	13.9	14.2	14.0	13.8	13.7
1998	13.2	13.4	13.7	13.8	14.2	13.9	14.1	14.2	14.2	14.2	14.4	14.4	14.0
1999	13.3	13.5	13.7	14.3	13.9	14.0	14.8	14.9	15.0	15.5	15.7	15.0	14.5
2000	14.3	14.4	14.5	14.9	14.6	14.7	14.9	15.3	15.3	15.1	14.6	14.2	14.7
2001	13.7	13.7	13.7	13.5	13.7	14.0	14.0	14.5	14.6	14.1	14.0	14.3	14.0
2002	14.0	14.3	14.4	14.3	14.5	15.0	15.4	15.8	15.6	15.7	15.4	14.8	14.9
2003	14.4	14.4	14.4	14.3	14.5	14.8	14.5	15.0	14.9	14.9	14.8	15.1	14.7

Employment by Industry: Oregon—*Continued*

(Numbers in thousands. Not seasonally adjusted.)

Industry	January	February	March	April	May	June	July	August	September	October	November	December	Annual Average
EUGENE-SPRINGFIELD *—Continued*													
Educational and health services													
1990	12.4	12.6	12.6	12.7	12.8	12.6	12.6	12.6	12.9	13.2	13.2	13.1	12.8
1991	13.1	13.1	13.2	13.4	13.4	13.3	13.4	13.4	13.9	14.0	13.9	13.9	13.5
1992	13.8	13.9	14.0	14.0	14.0	14.0	13.7	13.5	13.9	14.1	14.0	14.0	13.9
1993	13.9	14.0	14.2	14.5	14.5	14.5	14.4	14.2	14.7	14.8	14.8	14.8	14.4
1994	14.4	14.4	14.2	14.5	14.6	14.4	14.5	14.4	14.7	15.0	14.9	15.0	14.6
1995	14.8	15.1	15.2	15.2	15.3	15.1	15.1	15.0	15.5	15.6	15.5	15.4	15.2
1996	14.8	15.1	15.1	15.4	15.4	15.3	15.5	15.4	15.5	15.8	15.8	15.8	15.4
1997	15.5	15.7	15.9	15.9	15.9	15.8	15.3	15.4	15.8	15.8	15.9	15.9	15.7
1998	16.3	16.3	16.4	16.6	16.7	16.6	16.1	16.2	16.6	16.7	16.9	16.7	16.5
1999	17.0	17.0	17.1	17.3	17.4	17.1	16.9	16.8	17.2	17.7	17.7	17.7	17.2
2000	17.3	17.5	17.5	17.6	17.7	17.6	17.5	17.6	18.1	18.2	18.3	18.3	17.8
2001	17.9	18.1	18.2	18.3	18.2	18.2	17.9	18.0	18.2	18.4	18.4	18.4	18.2
2002	18.2	18.4	18.4	18.6	18.6	18.4	18.2	18.3	18.6	18.6	18.6	18.6	18.5
2003	18.5	18.5	18.4	18.4	18.4	18.3	18.3	18.2	18.5	18.7	18.8	18.7	18.5
Leisure and hospitality													
1990	10.8	11.1	11.2	11.7	11.8	12.1	11.9	12.0	12.0	11.8	11.6	11.5	11.6
1991	11.0	11.0	11.0	11.2	11.4	11.7	11.4	11.6	11.5	11.6	11.4	11.4	11.4
1992	11.0	11.0	11.1	11.4	11.8	11.9	12.1	12.3	12.3	12.2	12.2	12.1	11.8
1993	11.6	11.6	11.8	12.4	12.5	12.6	13.0	12.9	12.8	12.8	12.8	12.7	12.5
1994	12.4	12.6	12.7	13.1	13.2	13.6	13.5	13.7	13.7	13.7	13.4	13.4	13.3
1995	13.3	13.5	13.8	13.8	14.2	14.5	14.5	14.5	14.4	14.2	13.9	13.9	14.0
1996	13.4	13.4	13.6	13.9	14.3	14.6	14.4	14.7	14.2	14.0	13.8	13.7	14.0
1997	13.3	13.4	13.5	13.7	14.0	14.7	14.2	14.2	14.1	13.9	13.8	13.7	13.9
1998	12.8	12.9	13.0	13.4	14.1	14.3	14.2	14.0	13.8	13.5	13.5	13.5	13.6
1999	12.9	12.9	13.1	13.5	13.8	14.0	14.0	14.0	13.9	13.8	13.5	13.6	13.6
2000	13.2	13.4	13.6	13.6	13.9	14.4	14.4	14.3	14.1	14.1	13.9	13.9	13.9
2001	12.9	12.9	13.1	13.4	13.6	14.1	13.9	14.0	13.6	13.3	13.1	13.0	13.4
2002	12.5	12.6	12.8	13.2	13.7	13.8	14.0	14.3	14.0	13.7	13.7	13.5	13.5
2003	13.2	13.1	13.1	13.2	13.4	13.8	13.9	13.8	13.5	13.6	13.5	13.5	13.5
Other services													
1990	4.0	4.0	4.1	4.1	4.1	4.1	4.1	4.1	4.2	4.2	4.2	4.2	4.1
1991	4.2	4.2	4.3	4.2	4.3	4.3	4.3	4.3	4.2	4.4	4.4	4.4	4.3
1992	4.2	4.2	4.2	4.2	4.3	4.3	4.3	4.3	4.3	4.4	4.4	4.4	4.3
1993	4.2	4.3	4.3	4.3	4.3	4.4	4.4	4.4	4.5	4.5	4.4	4.4	4.4
1994	4.3	4.3	4.3	4.4	4.4	4.4	4.4	4.4	4.4	4.5	4.5	4.5	4.4
1995	4.5	4.5	4.5	4.7	4.7	4.6	4.6	4.6	4.6	4.6	4.6	4.6	4.6
1996	4.6	4.7	4.7	4.7	4.8	4.8	4.7	4.7	4.8	5.0	4.9	4.9	4.8
1997	4.8	4.8	4.8	4.8	4.9	4.8	4.8	4.9	4.9	5.0	5.0	5.0	4.9
1998	4.9	5.0	5.0	5.0	5.0	5.0	4.9	5.0	4.9	4.9	4.9	4.8	4.9
1999	4.8	4.9	4.9	4.9	4.9	4.9	5.1	5.2	5.2	4.9	5.0	5.0	5.0
2000	5.0	5.0	5.0	5.1	5.1	5.1	4.9	5.0	5.1	5.1	5.0	5.0	5.0
2001	5.1	5.1	5.1	5.1	5.2	5.1	5.1	5.1	5.1	5.1	5.0	5.0	5.1
2002	4.9	4.9	5.0	5.0	5.1	5.1	5.1	5.1	5.1	5.1	5.0	5.1	5.0
2003	5.0	5.0	5.0	5.0	5.0	5.0	5.0	5.0	5.0	5.0	5.0	5.0	5.0
Government													
1990	23.8	24.7	24.7	24.9	25.5	25.9	21.7	20.6	22.1	25.3	25.5	25.1	24.2
1991	24.3	25.0	25.1	24.9	25.1	25.7	21.7	20.7	22.2	25.3	25.5	25.3	24.2
1992	24.7	25.2	25.5	25.5	25.6	25.8	22.3	21.4	22.7	25.3	25.8	25.7	24.6
1993	25.0	25.5	25.4	25.4	25.6	26.2	19.5	19.3	22.0	24.6	24.7	24.8	24.0
1994	23.8	24.7	25.2	24.9	25.2	25.5	20.6	20.3	22.9	24.8	25.2	25.2	24.0
1995	24.3	25.2	25.4	25.2	25.4	25.8	20.7	20.1	22.7	25.5	25.6	25.5	24.3
1996	24.6	25.8	26.1	26.0	26.2	26.2	21.5	21.0	23.5	25.8	26.5	26.3	25.0
1997	25.3	26.1	26.5	26.1	26.5	26.6	20.1	20.0	23.3	25.3	26.0	25.8	24.8
1998	25.3	26.1	26.5	26.1	26.4	26.5	20.8	21.0	23.7	26.4	27.3	27.1	25.3
1999	25.9	26.6	27.0	26.8	26.9	27.0	21.3	20.9	23.8	27.0	27.2	26.9	25.6
2000	26.1	27.0	27.3	27.1	27.7	27.6	21.7	21.9	24.3	27.3	27.6	27.5	26.1
2001	25.9	27.1	27.5	27.3	27.5	27.6	22.4	22.1	24.7	27.0	27.8	27.6	26.2
2002	26.8	27.6	27.8	27.5	27.8	27.8	22.3	21.4	24.7	26.9	27.4	27.3	26.3
2003	26.7	27.3	27.2	27.1	27.5	27.3	22.7	22.6	23.9	27.0	27.2	27.3	26.2
Federal government													
1990	2.4	2.3	2.4	2.8	2.9	3.1	2.9	2.7	2.6	2.5	2.3	2.4	2.6
1991	2.2	2.2	2.3	2.3	2.3	2.5	2.6	2.5	2.5	2.3	2.3	2.3	2.4
1992	2.2	2.2	2.2	2.3	2.3	2.4	2.5	2.5	2.4	2.3	2.2	2.2	2.3
1993	2.1	2.1	2.0	2.1	2.1	2.1	2.2	2.2	2.2	2.2	2.1	2.1	2.1
1994	2.0	2.0	2.0	2.0	2.0	2.0	2.1	2.1	2.1	2.1	2.0	2.0	2.0
1995	1.9	1.9	1.9	2.0	2.0	2.0	2.1	2.1	2.1	2.1	1.9	1.9	2.0
1996	1.9	1.9	1.9	1.9	2.0	2.0	2.1	2.1	2.0	2.0	2.0	2.0	2.0
1997	1.9	1.9	1.9	1.9	2.0	2.0	2.1	2.2	2.1	2.0	2.0	2.0	2.0
1998	2.0	1.9	1.9	2.0	2.0	2.1	2.2	2.2	2.2	2.1	2.1	2.1	2.1
1999	1.9	1.9	1.9	2.0	2.0	2.0	2.1	2.1	2.1	2.1	2.0	2.0	2.0
2000	2.0	2.0	2.0	2.2	2.6	2.3	2.3	2.3	2.0	2.0	1.9	2.0	2.1
2001	1.9	1.9	1.9	1.9	1.9	2.0	2.1	2.1	2.1	1.9	1.9	1.9	2.0
2002	1.9	1.8	1.8	1.9	1.9	2.0	2.1	2.1	2.0	1.9	1.9	1.9	1.9
2003	1.9	1.9	1.9	1.9	1.9	2.0	2.1	2.1	2.0	2.0	1.9	1.9	2.0

Employment by Industry: Oregon—*Continued*

(Numbers in thousands. Not seasonally adjusted.)

Industry	January	February	March	April	May	June	July	August	September	October	November	December	Annual Average
EUGENE-SPRINGFIELD *—Continued*													
State government													
1990	7.9	8.4	8.4	8.2	8.3	8.5	6.9	6.4	6.7	8.5	8.7	8.4	7.9
1991	8.0	8.5	8.5	8.4	8.4	8.7	7.0	6.7	7.0	8.8	8.9	8.8	8.1
1992	8.3	8.7	8.9	8.8	8.8	8.7	7.2	6.9	7.2	8.5	8.8	8.7	8.3
1993	8.3	8.6	8.6	8.5	8.5	8.8	7.2	6.8	7.1	8.5	8.7	8.7	8.2
1994	8.1	8.7	8.8	8.6	8.7	8.9	7.2	6.9	7.3	8.7	8.9	8.8	8.3
1995	8.3	8.9	9.1	8.8	8.9	9.1	7.3	7.1	7.4	9.0	9.3	9.1	8.5
1996	8.5	9.4	9.5	9.3	9.4	9.4	8.0	7.5	7.8	9.1	9.7	9.6	8.9
1997	8.9	9.5	9.6	9.4	9.5	9.7	7.5	7.2	7.6	8.8	9.2	9.1	8.8
1998	8.6	9.1	9.2	8.9	9.0	9.1	7.2	7.0	7.4	8.6	9.4	9.4	8.6
1999	8.4	8.9	9.0	8.9	9.0	9.1	7.4	6.8	7.1	8.9	9.2	9.0	8.5
2000	8.4	9.1	9.2	8.9	9.0	9.1	7.4	7.2	7.4	9.1	9.4	9.4	8.6
2001	8.5	9.3	9.4	9.3	9.3	9.3	8.1	7.2	7.7	9.2	9.7	9.6	8.9
2002	9.0	9.6	9.7	9.5	9.6	9.6	8.0	7.5	7.8	9.4	9.8	9.7	9.1
2003	9.2	9.7	9.8	9.6	9.7	9.8	7.9	7.7	7.8	9.7	9.9	10.0	9.2
Local government													
1990	13.5	14.0	13.9	13.9	14.3	14.3	11.9	11.5	12.8	14.3	14.5	14.3	13.6
1991	14.1	14.3	14.3	14.2	14.4	14.5	12.1	11.5	12.7	14.2	14.3	14.2	13.7
1992	14.2	14.3	14.4	14.4	14.5	14.7	12.6	12.0	13.1	14.5	14.8	14.8	14.0
1993	14.6	14.8	14.8	14.8	15.0	15.3	10.1	10.3	12.7	13.9	13.9	14.0	13.7
1994	13.7	14.0	14.4	14.3	14.5	14.6	11.3	11.3	13.5	14.0	14.3	14.4	13.7
1995	14.1	14.4	14.4	14.4	14.5	14.7	11.3	10.9	13.2	14.4	14.4	14.5	13.8
1996	14.2	14.5	14.7	14.8	14.8	14.8	11.4	11.4	13.7	14.7	14.8	14.7	14.0
1997	14.5	14.7	15.0	14.8	15.0	14.9	10.5	10.6	13.6	14.5	14.8	14.7	14.0
1998	14.7	15.1	15.4	15.2	15.4	15.3	11.4	11.8	14.1	15.7	15.8	15.6	14.6
1999	15.6	15.8	16.1	15.9	15.9	15.9	11.8	12.0	14.6	16.0	16.0	15.9	15.1
2000	15.7	15.9	16.1	16.0	16.1	16.2	12.0	12.4	14.9	16.2	16.3	16.1	15.3
2001	15.5	15.9	16.2	16.1	16.3	16.3	12.2	12.8	14.9	15.9	16.2	16.1	15.4
2002	15.9	16.2	16.3	16.1	16.3	16.2	12.2	11.8	14.9	15.6	15.7	15.7	15.2
2003	15.6	15.7	15.5	15.6	15.9	15.5	12.7	12.8	14.1	15.3	15.4	15.4	15.0
MEDFORD													
Total nonfarm													
1990	53.1	53.1	53.2	54.2	55.3	55.6	54.3	55.3	56.0	56.9	56.3	55.6	54.9
1991	52.8	52.4	53.0	53.8	54.2	55.2	53.9	54.3	55.7	57.8	57.2	56.8	54.8
1992	53.7	54.6	55.1	56.0	56.7	57.5	56.0	57.1	59.0	59.8	59.5	58.9	57.0
1993	55.8	56.0	56.9	57.3	58.4	58.6	57.5	58.3	60.0	61.8	62.0	61.8	58.7
1994	59.0	59.3	60.1	61.3	61.4	62.2	61.1	61.9	64.1	64.6	65.7	64.9	62.1
1995	61.1	61.4	62.0	62.8	63.3	63.7	62.3	63.8	65.7	65.8	66.3	65.8	63.7
1996	62.5	63.3	63.7	64.2	65.1	65.8	64.6	65.6	67.3	68.3	68.6	69.0	65.7
1997	65.0	65.6	65.9	66.7	67.5	68.1	67.4	68.3	69.5	70.2	71.1	71.5	68.1
1998	67.5	67.6	67.6	68.8	69.7	70.3	68.8	69.4	70.1	71.9	72.1	72.2	69.7
1999	67.6	68.2	68.9	69.9	70.6	71.8	71.1	71.1	72.3	74.6	75.4	74.9	71.4
2000	70.5	70.8	71.7	72.7	74.2	74.5	73.0	72.9	74.6	76.6	78.5	77.0	73.9
2001	72.8	73.3	73.9	73.2	74.0	74.5	72.7	73.3	74.6	75.9	76.5	75.0	74.1
2002	70.6	71.1	71.8	73.3	74.2	74.8	72.0	72.7	75.8	77.1	77.0	77.2	74.0
2003	73.1	73.8	74.3	74.8	76.0	76.4	74.3	74.9	75.9	76.7	76.5	76.8	75.3
Total private													
1990	43.6	43.4	43.4	44.6	45.4	45.5	45.5	46.6	46.8	47.0	46.7	46.0	45.4
1991	43.5	42.7	43.2	43.8	44.2	44.9	45.1	45.6	46.3	47.7	47.2	47.0	45.1
1992	44.0	44.7	45.1	46.0	46.5	47.4	47.1	48.3	49.5	49.6	49.3	48.9	47.2
1993	46.0	46.0	46.6	47.2	48.0	48.1	48.6	49.3	50.5	51.7	51.8	51.8	48.8
1994	49.2	49.2	49.8	51.0	51.1	51.9	52.1	52.8	54.4	54.1	54.7	54.6	52.1
1995	51.1	51.0	51.6	52.3	52.7	53.1	53.2	54.5	55.8	55.1	55.7	55.3	53.5
1996	52.2	52.6	52.9	53.4	54.3	54.9	55.5	56.4	57.5	57.7	58.0	58.5	55.3
1997	55.0	55.0	55.2	56.1	56.7	57.2	57.8	58.9	59.3	59.4	60.1	60.6	57.6
1998	56.8	56.5	56.5	57.7	58.4	59.0	59.2	59.6	59.8	60.5	60.5	60.7	58.8
1999	56.6	56.8	57.4	58.4	58.8	59.9	60.9	61.1	61.7	62.8	63.5	63.2	60.1
2000	58.7	58.9	59.7	60.8	61.7	62.3	62.8	62.8	64.0	64.9	66.7	65.4	62.4
2001	61.1	61.1	61.6	61.4	62.0	62.4	62.5	63.1	63.8	64.1	64.7	63.4	62.6
2002	59.1	59.5	60.1	61.4	62.1	62.6	63.2	63.8	65.0	65.4	65.2	65.4	62.7
2003	61.6	62.1	62.5	63.0	64.0	64.4	64.6	65.2	65.0	65.1	64.8	65.2	64.0
Goods-producing													
1990	9.4	9.4	9.3	9.7	10.0	10.2	10.2	10.3	10.1	9.9	9.6	8.9	9.8
1991	8.6	8.3	8.4	8.5	8.8	9.2	9.5	9.5	9.5	9.9	9.6	9.3	9.1
1992	8.6	8.9	9.2	9.6	9.9	10.2	10.3	10.5	10.4	10.3	10.1	9.7	9.8
1993	9.2	9.1	9.2	9.5	9.8	9.9	10.1	10.3	10.3	10.5	10.3	10.0	9.9
1994	9.7	9.7	9.8	10.1	10.2	10.5	10.9	11.1	11.1	10.9	10.9	10.7	10.5
1995	10.3	10.4	10.5	10.3	10.5	10.9	11.1	11.4	11.4	11.2	11.1	10.8	10.8
1996	10.6	10.6	10.7	11.0	11.0	11.4	11.9	12.1	12.0	12.0	11.7	11.4	11.4
1997	11.0	11.1	11.2	11.5	11.7	12.0	12.4	12.5	12.5	12.5	12.1	11.8	11.9
1998	11.6	11.4	11.4	11.6	11.9	12.3	12.5	12.5	12.3	12.3	12.1	11.7	12.0
1999	11.4	11.3	11.4	11.5	11.8	12.1	12.8	13.0	12.7	12.7	12.8	12.4	12.2
2000	11.8	11.7	12.0	12.3	12.6	13.0	13.3	13.3	13.2	13.1	13.0	12.8	12.7
2001	12.0	12.0	11.8	11.6	11.7	11.8	11.9	11.9	11.8	11.7	11.5	11.2	11.7
2002	10.6	10.7	10.8	11.2	11.3	11.5	11.9	11.9	12.0	11.8	11.8	11.6	11.4
2003	11.2	11.3	11.4	11.4	11.7	11.9	12.0	12.1	12.0	12.0	12.1	12.0	11.8

Employment by Industry: Oregon—*Continued*

(Numbers in thousands. Not seasonally adjusted.)

Industry	January	February	March	April	May	June	July	August	September	October	November	December	Annual Average
MEDFORD—*Continued*													
Natural resources and mining													
1990	0.6	0.6	0.5	0.6	0.7	0.8	0.7	0.7	0.7	0.8	0.7	0.5	0.7
1991	0.4	0.5	0.5	0.6	0.6	0.6	0.6	0.6	0.6	0.6	0.6	0.5	0.6
1992	0.4	0.5	0.5	0.6	0.7	0.7	0.7	0.7	0.6	0.6	0.6	0.5	0.6
1993	0.5	0.5	0.5	0.6	0.6	0.7	0.7	0.8	0.7	0.8	0.7	0.6	0.6
1994	0.6	0.6	0.6	0.7	0.7	0.7	0.8	0.8	0.8	0.7	0.8	0.7	0.7
1995	0.6	0.7	0.7	0.7	0.8	0.9	0.9	1.0	1.0	1.1	1.0	0.9	0.9
1996	0.8	0.8	0.9	0.9	0.8	0.8	0.9	0.9	0.9	0.9	0.8	0.7	0.8
1997	0.7	0.7	0.7	0.8	0.8	0.9	1.0	1.0	1.0	0.9	0.8	0.8	0.8
1998	0.7	0.6	0.5	0.7	0.8	0.8	0.8	0.8	0.8	0.8	0.8	0.7	0.7
1999	0.6	0.6	0.6	0.5	0.7	0.7	0.8	0.8	0.8	0.8	0.8	0.7	0.7
2000	0.7	0.6	0.7	0.7	0.8	0.9	0.9	0.9	0.9	0.9	0.8	0.8	0.8
2001	0.5	0.5	0.5	0.5	0.5	0.5	0.6	0.6	0.6	0.5	0.5	0.4	0.5
2002	0.4	0.4	0.4	0.5	0.5	0.5	0.6	0.6	0.6	0.6	0.6	0.6	0.5
2003	0.5	0.5	0.5	0.5	0.6	0.6	0.6	0.6	0.6	0.6	0.6	0.6	0.6
Construction													
1990	1.9	1.9	1.9	2.1	2.2	2.2	2.4	2.6	2.5	2.4	2.3	2.1	2.2
1991	1.9	1.9	1.9	2.0	2.1	2.2	2.3	2.3	2.3	2.4	2.3	2.2	2.2
1992	1.9	1.9	2.0	2.1	2.1	2.2	2.2	2.3	2.3	2.3	2.2	2.1	2.1
1993	1.9	1.9	2.0	2.1	2.4	2.4	2.5	2.6	2.6	2.7	2.6	2.5	2.4
1994	2.3	2.3	2.4	2.5	2.6	2.7	2.8	2.9	2.9	2.8	2.8	2.7	2.6
1995	2.5	2.6	2.7	2.6	2.6	2.7	2.8	2.9	2.9	2.9	2.8	2.7	2.7
1996	2.5	2.5	2.6	2.7	2.8	3.0	3.2	3.3	3.2	3.2	3.1	3.0	2.9
1997	2.9	2.9	3.0	3.1	3.2	3.3	3.4	3.5	3.5	3.5	3.3	3.1	3.2
1998	3.0	3.0	3.0	2.9	3.0	3.3	3.5	3.5	3.4	3.5	3.4	3.2	3.2
1999	3.1	3.0	3.1	3.2	3.3	3.4	3.6	3.6	3.6	3.6	3.6	3.4	3.4
2000	3.2	3.2	3.3	3.4	3.6	3.8	3.9	3.9	3.9	3.8	3.8	3.7	3.6
2001	3.3	3.4	3.4	3.4	3.5	3.5	3.7	3.8	3.7	3.8	3.7	3.6	3.6
2002	3.2	3.3	3.4	3.5	3.5	3.7	3.9	3.9	3.9	4.0	4.0	3.9	3.7
2003	3.8	3.8	3.9	3.9	4.1	4.3	4.4	4.5	4.4	4.4	4.3	4.2	4.2
Manufacturing													
1990	6.9	6.9	6.9	7.0	7.1	7.2	7.1	7.0	6.9	6.7	6.6	6.3	6.9
1991	6.3	5.9	6.0	5.9	6.1	6.4	6.6	6.6	6.6	6.9	6.7	6.6	6.4
1992	6.3	6.5	6.7	6.9	7.1	7.3	7.4	7.5	7.5	7.4	7.3	7.1	7.1
1993	6.8	6.7	6.7	6.8	6.8	6.8	6.9	6.9	7.0	7.0	7.0	6.9	6.9
1994	6.8	6.8	6.8	6.9	6.9	7.1	7.3	7.4	7.4	7.4	7.3	7.3	7.1
1995	7.2	7.1	7.1	7.0	7.1	7.3	7.4	7.5	7.5	7.2	7.3	7.2	7.2
1996	7.3	7.3	7.2	7.4	7.4	7.6	7.8	7.9	7.9	7.9	7.8	7.7	7.6
1997	7.4	7.5	7.5	7.6	7.7	7.8	8.0	8.0	8.0	8.1	8.0	7.9	7.8
1998	7.9	7.8	7.9	8.0	8.1	8.2	8.2	8.2	8.1	8.0	7.9	7.8	8.0
1999	7.7	7.7	7.7	7.8	7.8	8.0	8.4	8.6	8.3	8.3	8.4	8.3	8.1
2000	7.9	7.9	8.0	8.2	8.2	8.3	8.5	8.5	8.4	8.4	8.4	8.3	8.3
2001	8.2	8.1	7.9	7.7	7.7	7.8	7.6	7.5	7.5	7.4	7.3	7.2	7.7
2002	7.0	7.0	7.0	7.2	7.3	7.3	7.4	7.4	7.5	7.2	7.2	7.1	7.2
2003	6.9	7.0	7.0	7.0	7.0	7.0	7.0	7.0	7.0	7.0	7.2	7.2	7.0
Service-providing													
1990	43.7	43.7	43.9	44.5	45.3	45.4	44.1	45.0	45.9	47.0	46.7	46.7	45.2
1991	44.2	44.1	44.6	45.3	45.4	46.0	44.4	44.8	46.2	47.9	47.6	47.5	45.7
1992	45.1	45.7	45.9	46.4	46.8	47.3	45.7	46.6	48.6	49.5	49.4	49.2	47.2
1993	46.6	46.9	47.7	47.8	48.6	48.7	47.4	48.0	49.7	51.3	51.7	51.8	48.9
1994	49.3	49.6	50.3	51.2	51.2	51.7	50.2	50.8	53.0	53.7	54.8	54.2	51.7
1995	50.8	51.0	51.5	52.5	52.8	52.8	51.2	52.4	54.3	54.6	55.2	55.0	52.8
1996	51.9	52.7	53.0	53.2	54.1	54.4	52.7	53.5	55.3	56.3	56.9	57.6	54.3
1997	54.0	54.5	54.7	55.2	55.8	56.1	55.0	55.8	57.0	57.7	59.0	59.7	56.2
1998	55.9	56.2	56.2	57.2	57.8	58.0	56.3	56.9	57.8	59.6	60.0	60.5	57.7
1999	56.2	56.9	57.5	58.4	58.8	59.7	58.3	58.1	59.6	61.9	62.6	62.5	59.2
2000	58.7	59.1	59.7	60.4	61.6	61.5	59.7	59.6	61.4	63.5	65.5	64.2	61.2
2001	60.8	61.3	62.1	61.6	62.3	62.7	60.8	61.4	62.8	64.2	65.0	63.8	62.4
2002	60.0	60.4	61.0	62.1	62.9	63.3	60.1	60.8	63.8	65.3	65.2	65.6	62.5
2003	61.9	62.5	62.9	63.4	64.3	64.5	62.3	62.8	63.9	64.7	64.4	64.8	63.5
Trade, transportation, and utilities													
1990	13.2	13.0	12.9	13.3	13.3	13.0	12.8	13.7	14.1	14.7	15.1	15.7	13.7
1991	13.7	13.3	13.5	13.5	13.3	13.1	13.1	13.5	14.0	14.7	14.9	15.2	13.8
1992	13.4	13.3	13.3	13.7	13.5	13.4	13.3	13.7	14.5	15.1	15.2	15.5	14.0
1993	13.6	13.5	13.5	13.6	13.6	13.5	13.3	13.9	14.6	15.8	16.3	16.9	14.3
1994	14.7	14.4	14.6	14.8	14.5	14.6	14.5	14.7	16.0	16.1	17.0	17.5	15.3
1995	15.1	14.8	15.0	15.2	15.2	15.1	14.9	15.4	16.3	16.6	17.6	17.8	15.8
1996	15.2	15.0	15.1	14.9	15.1	14.9	14.9	15.3	15.8	16.3	17.6	18.7	15.7
1997	15.8	15.2	15.2	15.3	15.6	15.5	15.7	16.0	16.6	17.3	18.4	19.7	16.4
1998	16.4	16.0	15.8	16.2	16.2	16.2	16.3	16.6	17.0	18.1	18.9	20.1	17.0
1999	16.1	15.9	16.0	16.0	16.3	17.0	16.2	16.3	17.0	18.6	19.1	19.7	17.0
2000	16.5	16.6	16.5	16.3	16.6	16.5	16.6	16.6	17.8	18.9	20.8	20.1	17.5
2001	17.1	16.6	16.8	16.5	17.0	16.8	17.0	17.4	18.1	19.0	20.1	19.2	17.6
2002	16.2	16.2	16.5	16.7	17.0	17.0	17.3	17.7	18.6	19.6	19.8	20.2	17.7
2003	16.4	16.2	16.4	16.5	16.7	16.8	16.7	16.9	17.2	17.6	17.7	18.0	16.9

Employment by Industry: Oregon—*Continued*

(Numbers in thousands. Not seasonally adjusted.)

Industry	January	February	March	April	May	June	July	August	September	October	November	December	Annual Average
MEDFORD—*Continued*													
Wholesale trade													
1990	2.3	2.3	2.3	2.3	2.4	2.4	2.4	2.7	2.7	2.6	2.4	2.3	2.4
1991	2.3	2.3	2.3	2.3	2.2	2.3	2.4	2.4	2.7	2.6	2.3	2.3	2.4
1992	2.3	2.3	2.3	2.3	2.3	2.4	2.4	2.5	2.6	2.4	2.3	2.3	2.4
1993	2.3	2.3	2.3	2.3	2.3	2.3	2.3	2.3	2.4	2.4	2.4	2.3	2.3
1994	2.2	2.2	2.3	2.3	2.3	2.4	2.4	2.4	2.5	2.6	2.5	2.5	2.4
1995	2.4	2.4	2.4	2.5	2.5	2.6	2.5	2.5	2.6	2.7	2.6	2.6	2.5
1996	2.5	2.4	2.4	2.2	2.2	2.2	2.2	2.3	2.3	2.2	2.2	2.1	2.3
1997	2.1	2.1	2.0	2.1	2.1	2.1	2.1	2.3	2.3	2.2	2.2	2.2	2.2
1998	2.2	2.1	2.1	2.1	2.2	2.2	2.2	2.2	2.3	2.3	2.3	2.2	2.2
1999	2.2	2.2	2.2	2.1	2.1	2.1	2.1	2.1	2.2	2.2	2.2	2.2	2.2
2000	2.2	2.2	2.2	2.1	2.1	2.2	2.2	2.2	2.3	2.2	2.2	2.2	2.2
2001	2.1	2.1	2.1	2.1	2.1	2.1	2.2	2.2	2.2	2.1	2.0	2.0	2.1
2002	2.0	2.0	2.1	2.3	2.4	2.4	2.4	2.4	2.4	2.4	2.4	2.4	2.3
2003	2.1	2.1	2.1	2.2	2.2	2.2	2.2	2.2	2.2	2.2	2.2	2.1	2.2
Retail trade													
1990	8.8	8.6	8.5	8.8	8.8	8.5	8.4	8.9	9.3	9.9	10.6	11.3	9.2
1991	9.5	9.0	9.2	9.2	9.1	8.8	8.7	9.1	9.2	10.0	10.6	10.9	9.4
1992	9.2	9.1	9.1	9.4	9.2	9.1	9.0	9.3	9.9	10.8	11.0	11.3	9.7
1993	9.5	9.4	9.4	9.4	9.4	9.2	9.1	9.7	10.2	11.3	11.8	12.5	10.1
1994	10.5	10.1	10.2	10.4	10.1	10.1	10.0	10.2	11.3	11.4	12.4	12.9	10.8
1995	10.6	10.3	10.5	10.6	10.6	10.3	10.3	10.8	11.5	11.7	12.8	13.0	11.1
1996	10.6	10.5	10.6	10.6	10.8	10.5	10.6	10.9	11.3	11.8	13.2	14.4	11.3
1997	11.6	11.0	11.1	11.1	11.3	11.2	11.4	11.5	12.0	12.8	13.9	15.3	12.0
1998	11.9	11.6	11.5	11.8	11.7	11.7	11.8	12.1	12.4	13.5	14.3	15.6	12.5
1999	11.6	11.4	11.5	11.6	11.9	12.5	11.7	11.8	12.4	13.8	14.3	15.0	12.5
2000	11.9	11.9	11.8	11.7	12.0	11.8	11.9	11.9	12.8	14.0	15.9	15.2	12.7
2001	12.6	12.1	12.3	12.1	12.6	12.3	12.5	12.8	13.5	14.5	15.7	14.8	13.2
2002	11.9	11.9	12.1	12.1	12.3	12.2	12.6	12.9	13.8	14.7	14.9	15.3	13.1
2003	11.8	11.6	11.8	11.8	12.0	12.1	12.1	12.3	12.5	12.9	13.0	13.4	12.3
Transportation and utilities													
1990	2.1	2.1	2.1	2.2	2.1	2.1	2.0	2.1	2.1	2.2	2.1	2.1	2.1
1991	1.9	2.0	2.0	2.0	2.0	2.0	2.0	2.0	2.1	2.1	2.0	2.0	2.0
1992	1.9	1.9	1.9	2.0	2.0	1.9	1.9	1.9	2.0	1.9	1.9	1.9	1.9
1993	1.8	1.8	1.8	1.9	1.9	2.0	1.9	1.9	2.0	2.1	2.1	2.1	1.9
1994	2.0	2.1	2.1	2.1	2.1	2.1	2.1	2.1	2.2	2.1	2.1	2.1	2.1
1995	2.1	2.1	2.1	2.1	2.1	2.2	2.1	2.1	2.2	2.2	2.2	2.2	2.1
1996	2.1	2.1	2.1	2.1	2.1	2.2	2.1	2.1	2.2	2.3	2.2	2.2	2.2
1997	2.1	2.1	2.1	2.1	2.2	2.2	2.2	2.2	2.3	2.3	2.3	2.2	2.2
1998	2.3	2.3	2.2	2.3	2.3	2.3	2.3	2.3	2.3	2.3	2.3	2.3	2.3
1999	2.3	2.3	2.3	2.3	2.3	2.4	2.4	2.4	2.4	2.6	2.6	2.5	2.4
2000	2.4	2.5	2.5	2.5	2.5	2.5	2.5	2.5	2.7	2.7	2.7	2.7	2.6
2001	2.4	2.4	2.4	2.3	2.3	2.4	2.3	2.4	2.4	2.4	2.4	2.4	2.4
2002	2.3	2.3	2.3	2.3	2.3	2.4	2.3	2.4	2.4	2.5	2.5	2.5	2.4
2003	2.5	2.5	2.5	2.5	2.5	2.5	2.4	2.4	2.5	2.5	2.5	2.5	2.5
Information													
1990	1.2	1.2	1.1	1.1	1.1	1.1	1.3	1.1	1.0	1.0	1.0	1.0	1.1
1991	1.1	1.1	1.1	1.2	1.2	1.2	1.2	1.2	1.2	1.2	1.2	1.2	1.2
1992	1.2	1.2	1.2	1.2	1.2	1.2	1.2	1.2	1.2	1.2	1.3	1.3	1.2
1993	1.2	1.2	1.2	1.2	1.3	1.2	1.3	1.2	1.2	1.3	1.3	1.2	1.2
1994	1.2	1.2	1.2	1.3	1.2	1.2	1.2	1.3	1.3	1.3	1.3	1.3	1.3
1995	1.3	1.4	1.4	1.4	1.4	1.4	1.3	1.3	1.4	1.4	1.3	1.3	1.4
1996	1.3	1.3	1.3	1.4	1.4	1.4	1.4	1.5	1.5	1.5	1.4	1.4	1.4
1997	1.3	1.3	1.3	1.3	1.3	1.3	1.3	1.4	1.4	1.4	1.4	1.5	1.4
1998	1.5	1.5	1.5	1.5	1.5	1.5	1.5	1.5	1.4	1.5	1.4	1.4	1.5
1999	1.6	1.6	1.6	1.6	1.6	1.6	1.7	1.7	1.7	1.7	1.7	1.7	1.7
2000	1.7	1.7	1.7	1.8	1.8	1.9	1.9	1.9	1.9	2.0	2.0	1.9	1.9
2001	1.9	1.9	1.9	1.8	1.8	1.8	1.8	1.9	1.8	1.8	1.8	1.8	1.8
2002	1.8	1.8	1.7	1.8	1.8	1.8	1.8	1.8	1.8	1.7	1.8	1.8	1.8
2003	1.9	1.9	1.8	1.8	1.9	1.8	1.8	1.8	1.7	1.7	1.7	1.8	1.8
Financial activities													
1990	2.7	2.7	2.7	2.9	2.9	2.8	2.8	2.8	2.8	2.9	2.9	2.8	2.8
1991	2.8	2.8	2.8	2.8	2.9	2.9	2.9	2.9	3.0	3.0	3.0	2.9	2.9
1992	3.0	3.0	3.0	3.0	3.0	3.1	3.1	3.1	3.2	3.2	3.2	3.2	3.1
1993	3.1	3.1	3.1	3.1	3.1	3.1	3.2	3.2	3.2	3.2	3.2	3.2	3.2
1994	3.2	3.2	3.2	3.3	3.3	3.3	3.3	3.4	3.4	3.3	3.3	3.3	3.3
1995	3.2	3.2	3.2	3.2	3.2	3.2	3.2	3.3	3.3	3.2	3.2	3.2	3.2
1996	3.2	3.2	3.2	3.2	3.2	3.3	3.4	3.4	3.4	3.3	3.3	3.4	3.3
1997	3.4	3.4	3.4	3.4	3.4	3.4	3.4	3.5	3.4	3.3	3.4	3.4	3.4
1998	3.4	3.4	3.4	3.2	3.3	3.3	3.3	3.3	3.3	3.3	3.3	3.2	3.3
1999	3.2	3.2	3.3	3.4	3.4	3.4	3.4	3.4	3.4	3.4	3.4	3.4	3.4
2000	3.2	3.2	3.2	3.3	3.3	3.3	3.2	3.2	3.2	3.2	3.2	3.2	3.2
2001	3.4	3.4	3.5	3.6	3.5	3.6	3.5	3.6	3.5	3.6	3.5	3.5	3.5
2002	3.6	3.6	3.6	3.5	3.6	3.7	3.7	3.8	3.8	3.8	3.8	3.8	3.7
2003	3.8	3.8	3.8	3.8	3.9	3.9	3.9	3.9	3.9	4.0	3.9	4.0	3.9

Employment by Industry: Oregon—*Continued*

(Numbers in thousands. Not seasonally adjusted.)

Industry	January	February	March	April	May	June	July	August	September	October	November	December	Annual Average
MEDFORD—*Continued*													
Professional and business services													
1990	3.0	3.1	3.1	3.3	3.4	3.3	3.4	3.4	3.4	3.4	3.4	3.3	3.3
1991	3.1	3.1	3.1	3.2	3.2	3.3	3.3	3.4	3.3	3.4	3.4	3.3	3.3
1992	3.2	3.4	3.3	3.3	3.4	3.5	3.5	3.6	3.7	3.7	3.6	3.6	3.5
1993	3.4	3.6	3.7	3.7	3.7	3.8	4.0	4.0	4.1	4.0	4.1	4.0	3.8
1994	4.3	4.5	4.6	4.7	4.9	5.0	5.0	5.0	5.1	5.2	5.1	4.9	4.9
1995	4.6	4.6	4.7	4.9	5.0	5.0	5.0	5.2	5.2	5.0	5.2	5.0	5.0
1996	4.9	5.1	5.0	5.1	5.4	5.5	5.5	5.5	5.8	5.7	5.4	5.3	5.4
1997	5.5	5.5	5.5	5.6	5.5	5.6	5.4	5.6	5.4	5.3	5.4	5.3	5.5
1998	5.1	5.3	5.4	5.6	5.7	5.8	5.8	5.7	5.9	5.7	5.5	5.5	5.6
1999	5.5	5.6	5.6	6.0	5.9	5.9	6.1	6.1	6.2	6.1	6.1	6.0	5.9
2000	5.8	6.0	6.0	6.3	6.4	6.5	6.4	6.4	6.5	6.6	6.5	6.4	6.3
2001	6.2	6.3	6.3	6.4	6.4	6.4	6.4	6.5	6.5	6.4	6.3	6.2	6.4
2002	5.9	6.1	6.1	6.4	6.5	6.5	6.4	6.4	6.5	6.5	6.3	6.3	6.3
2003	7.0	7.1	7.2	7.3	7.4	7.4	7.5	7.6	7.5	7.5	7.5	7.4	7.4
Educational and health services													
1990	6.6	6.5	6.6	6.6	6.6	6.7	6.6	6.6	6.9	6.9	6.8	6.7	6.7
1991	6.8	6.7	6.8	6.9	6.9	6.9	6.8	6.8	7.0	7.3	7.2	7.3	7.0
1992	7.1	7.3	7.3	7.2	7.2	7.3	7.1	7.2	7.5	7.5	7.5	7.4	7.3
1993	7.4	7.3	7.5	7.5	7.4	7.5	7.4	7.4	7.6	7.7	7.7	7.6	7.5
1994	7.4	7.5	7.5	7.6	7.6	7.5	7.3	7.4	7.6	7.7	7.7	7.7	7.5
1995	7.5	7.6	7.7	7.6	7.7	7.7	7.7	7.8	8.0	8.0	8.0	7.9	7.8
1996	7.9	8.0	8.1	8.2	8.3	8.3	8.2	8.3	8.6	8.7	8.6	8.5	8.3
1997	8.6	8.8	8.8	8.9	8.9	8.9	8.9	9.2	9.3	9.2	9.2	9.1	9.0
1998	9.1	9.1	9.1	9.3	9.3	9.3	9.0	9.1	9.2	9.3	9.2	9.0	9.2
1999	9.1	9.3	9.4	9.5	9.3	9.2	9.4	9.4	9.7	9.6	9.7	9.6	9.4
2000	9.6	9.7	9.8	9.9	9.9	9.9	9.8	9.9	10.0	10.1	10.2	10.1	9.9
2001	10.0	10.2	10.3	10.2	10.2	10.3	10.1	10.1	10.3	10.4	10.5	10.5	10.3
2002	10.3	10.4	10.4	10.4	10.4	10.3	10.3	10.4	10.5	10.6	10.6	10.7	10.4
2003	10.5	10.6	10.6	10.7	10.7	10.7	10.6	10.7	10.8	10.6	10.6	10.6	10.6
Leisure and hospitality													
1990	5.7	5.7	5.9	5.9	6.3	6.6	6.6	6.8	6.7	6.3	6.0	5.8	6.2
1991	5.6	5.5	5.6	5.8	6.0	6.4	6.5	6.4	6.4	6.3	6.0	5.9	6.0
1992	5.6	5.7	5.9	6.1	6.4	6.7	6.7	7.0	7.0	6.6	6.4	6.3	6.4
1993	6.1	6.2	6.4	6.6	7.1	7.1	7.3	7.3	7.4	7.1	6.8	6.8	6.9
1994	6.6	6.6	6.8	7.1	7.3	7.6	7.7	7.7	7.7	7.4	7.2	7.0	7.2
1995	6.9	6.8	6.9	7.5	7.5	7.6	7.8	7.9	7.9	7.5	7.1	7.1	7.4
1996	6.9	7.2	7.3	7.4	7.7	7.9	8.0	8.0	8.1	7.8	7.6	7.5	7.6
1997	7.1	7.3	7.4	7.6	7.8	8.0	8.3	8.3	8.2	7.9	7.7	7.4	7.8
1998	7.3	7.3	7.4	7.8	8.0	8.2	8.3	8.4	8.3	7.9	7.7	7.5	7.8
1999	7.3	7.5	7.7	8.0	8.1	8.3	8.8	8.8	8.6	8.2	8.2	7.9	8.1
2000	7.6	7.5	7.9	8.4	8.5	8.6	9.0	8.9	8.8	8.4	8.4	8.3	8.4
2001	7.9	8.0	8.3	8.6	8.7	9.0	9.1	9.1	9.1	8.6	8.4	8.4	8.6
2002	8.1	8.1	8.4	8.7	8.8	9.1	9.1	9.1	9.0	8.7	8.4	8.3	8.7
2003	8.1	8.4	8.5	8.8	8.9	9.2	9.4	9.5	9.2	9.0	8.6	8.6	8.9
Other services													
1990	1.8	1.8	1.8	1.8	1.8	1.8	1.8	1.9	1.8	1.9	1.9	1.8	1.8
1991	1.8	1.9	1.9	1.9	1.9	1.9	1.8	1.9	1.9	1.9	1.9	1.9	1.9
1992	1.9	1.9	1.9	1.9	1.9	2.0	1.9	2.0	2.0	2.0	2.0	1.9	1.9
1993	2.0	2.0	2.0	2.0	2.0	2.0	2.0	2.0	2.1	2.1	2.1	2.1	2.0
1994	2.1	2.1	2.1	2.1	2.1	2.2	2.2	2.2	2.2	2.2	2.2	2.2	2.2
1995	2.2	2.2	2.2	2.2	2.2	2.2	2.2	2.2	2.3	2.2	2.2	2.2	2.2
1996	2.2	2.2	2.2	2.2	2.2	2.2	2.2	2.3	2.3	2.4	2.4	2.3	2.3
1997	2.3	2.4	2.4	2.5	2.5	2.5	2.4	2.4	2.5	2.5	2.5	2.4	2.4
1998	2.4	2.5	2.5	2.5	2.5	2.4	2.5	2.5	2.4	2.4	2.4	2.3	2.4
1999	2.4	2.4	2.4	2.4	2.4	2.4	2.5	2.4	2.4	2.5	2.5	2.5	2.4
2000	2.5	2.5	2.6	2.5	2.6	2.6	2.6	2.6	2.6	2.6	2.6	2.6	2.6
2001	2.6	2.7	2.7	2.7	2.7	2.7	2.7	2.6	2.7	2.6	2.6	2.6	2.7
2002	2.6	2.6	2.6	2.7	2.7	2.7	2.7	2.7	2.8	2.7	2.7	2.7	2.7
2003	2.7	2.8	2.8	2.7	2.8	2.7	2.7	2.7	2.7	2.7	2.7	2.8	2.7
Government													
1990	9.5	9.7	9.8	9.6	9.9	10.1	8.8	8.7	9.2	9.9	9.6	9.6	9.5
1991	9.3	9.7	9.8	10.0	10.0	10.3	8.8	8.7	9.4	10.1	10.0	9.8	9.7
1992	9.7	9.9	10.0	10.0	10.2	10.1	8.9	8.8	9.5	10.2	10.2	10.0	9.8
1993	9.8	10.0	10.3	10.1	10.4	10.5	8.9	9.0	9.5	10.1	10.2	10.0	9.9
1994	9.8	10.1	10.3	10.3	10.3	10.3	9.0	9.1	9.7	10.5	11.0	10.3	10.1
1995	10.0	10.4	10.4	10.5	10.6	10.6	9.1	9.3	9.9	10.7	10.6	10.5	10.2
1996	10.3	10.7	10.8	10.8	10.8	10.9	9.1	9.2	9.8	10.6	10.6	10.5	10.3
1997	10.0	10.6	10.7	10.6	10.8	10.9	9.6	9.4	10.2	10.8	11.0	10.9	10.5
1998	10.7	11.1	11.1	11.1	11.3	11.3	9.6	9.8	10.3	11.4	11.6	11.5	10.9
1999	11.0	11.4	11.5	11.5	11.8	11.9	10.2	10.0	10.6	11.8	11.9	11.7	11.3
2000	11.8	11.9	12.0	11.9	12.5	12.2	10.2	10.1	10.6	11.7	11.8	11.6	11.5
2001	11.7	12.2	12.3	11.8	12.0	12.1	10.2	10.2	10.8	11.8	11.8	11.6	11.5
2002	11.5	11.6	11.7	11.9	12.1	12.2	8.8	8.9	10.8	11.7	11.8	11.8	11.2
2003	11.5	11.7	11.8	11.8	12.0	12.0	9.7	9.7	10.9	11.6	11.7	11.6	11.3

Employment by Industry: Oregon—*Continued*

(Numbers in thousands. Not seasonally adjusted.)

Industry	January	February	March	April	May	June	July	August	September	October	November	December	Annual Average
MEDFORD—*Continued*													
Federal government													
1990	1.9	1.9	1.9	1.9	2.1	2.1	2.0	1.9	1.9	1.8	1.7	1.8	1.9
1991	1.7	1.7	1.7	1.8	1.8	1.9	1.9	1.8	1.8	1.8	1.7	1.7	1.8
1992	1.6	1.6	1.7	1.8	1.8	1.8	1.9	1.8	1.8	1.8	1.7	1.7	1.8
1993	1.6	1.6	1.7	1.7	1.7	1.7	1.8	1.8	1.8	1.7	1.7	1.7	1.7
1994	1.6	1.6	1.6	1.7	1.6	1.6	1.7	1.7	1.7	1.7	1.6	1.6	1.6
1995	1.5	1.5	1.5	1.6	1.6	1.7	1.7	1.7	1.7	1.7	1.6	1.6	1.6
1996	1.6	1.6	1.6	1.7	1.7	1.7	1.8	1.8	1.7	1.7	1.7	1.7	1.7
1997	1.6	1.6	1.7	1.7	1.7	1.8	1.8	1.8	1.8	1.7	1.7	1.7	1.7
1998	1.7	1.7	1.7	1.7	1.8	1.8	1.8	1.8	1.8	1.7	1.7	1.8	1.8
1999	1.7	1.7	1.7	1.7	1.8	1.8	1.8	1.8	1.8	1.7	1.7	1.7	1.7
2000	1.7	1.6	1.6	1.7	2.0	1.8	1.9	1.8	1.7	1.7	1.7	1.7	1.7
2001	1.7	1.6	1.7	1.7	1.7	1.8	1.8	1.8	1.8	1.7	1.7	1.7	1.7
2002	1.7	1.7	1.7	1.7	1.7	1.7	1.8	1.8	1.8	1.7	1.7	1.8	1.7
2003	1.7	1.7	1.7	1.8	1.8	1.8	1.8	1.8	1.8	1.8	1.7	1.7	1.8
State government													
1990	2.1	2.2	2.2	2.1	2.1	2.2	1.9	1.8	1.8	2.3	2.2	2.1	2.1
1991	2.0	2.1	2.2	2.3	2.3	2.3	1.8	1.8	1.8	2.3	2.2	2.1	2.1
1992	2.1	2.2	2.2	2.1	2.2	2.2	1.9	1.8	1.9	2.3	2.2	2.1	2.1
1993	2.1	2.2	2.3	2.2	2.3	2.4	1.9	1.9	1.9	2.3	2.3	2.1	2.2
1994	2.1	2.3	2.3	2.3	2.3	2.4	2.0	2.0	1.9	2.4	2.4	2.3	2.2
1995	2.2	2.4	2.4	2.4	2.4	2.5	2.0	2.0	2.0	2.4	2.4	2.3	2.3
1996	2.2	2.4	2.4	2.4	2.3	2.4	2.1	2.0	2.0	2.4	2.4	2.3	2.3
1997	1.9	2.4	2.4	2.3	2.3	2.4	2.1	2.0	2.0	2.4	2.5	2.4	2.3
1998	2.3	2.5	2.5	2.5	2.5	2.5	2.0	2.1	1.9	2.5	2.6	2.5	2.4
1999	2.4	2.6	2.6	2.6	2.6	2.7	2.2	2.0	2.0	2.6	2.6	2.5	2.5
2000	2.6	2.6	2.7	2.6	2.7	2.7	2.2	2.2	2.0	2.5	2.6	2.5	2.5
2001	2.3	2.6	2.6	2.6	2.7	2.7	2.3	2.1	2.1	2.6	2.6	2.5	2.5
2002	2.4	2.5	2.5	2.5	2.5	2.6	2.2	2.1	2.1	2.5	2.6	2.5	2.4
2003	2.3	2.4	2.5	2.5	2.5	2.6	2.1	2.1	2.0	2.4	2.5	2.4	2.4
Local government													
1990	5.5	5.6	5.7	5.6	5.7	5.8	4.9	5.0	5.5	5.8	5.7	5.7	5.5
1991	5.6	5.9	5.9	5.9	5.9	6.1	5.1	5.1	5.8	6.0	6.1	6.0	5.8
1992	6.0	6.1	6.1	6.1	6.2	6.1	5.1	5.2	5.8	6.1	6.3	6.2	5.9
1993	6.1	6.2	6.3	6.2	6.4	6.4	5.2	5.3	5.8	6.1	6.2	6.2	6.0
1994	6.1	6.2	6.4	6.3	6.4	6.3	5.3	5.4	6.1	6.4	7.0	6.4	6.2
1995	6.3	6.5	6.5	6.5	6.6	6.4	5.4	5.6	6.2	6.6	6.6	6.6	6.3
1996	6.5	6.7	6.8	6.7	6.8	6.8	5.2	5.4	6.1	6.5	6.5	6.5	6.4
1997	6.5	6.6	6.6	6.6	6.8	6.7	5.7	5.6	6.4	6.7	6.8	6.8	6.5
1998	6.7	6.9	6.9	6.9	7.0	7.0	5.8	5.9	6.6	7.2	7.3	7.2	6.8
1999	6.9	7.1	7.2	7.2	7.4	7.4	6.2	6.2	6.8	7.5	7.6	7.5	7.1
2000	7.5	7.7	7.7	7.6	7.8	7.7	6.1	6.1	6.9	7.5	7.5	7.4	7.3
2001	7.7	8.0	8.0	7.5	7.6	7.6	6.1	6.3	6.9	7.5	7.5	7.4	7.3
2002	7.4	7.4	7.5	7.7	7.9	7.9	4.8	5.0	6.9	7.5	7.5	7.5	7.1
2003	7.5	7.6	7.6	7.5	7.7	7.6	5.8	5.8	7.1	7.4	7.5	7.5	7.2
PORTLAND													
Total nonfarm													
1990	701.7	702.2	712.0	719.4	725.7	732.4	725.7	735.7	735.3	735.1	738.0	736.4	725.0
1991	709.6	713.3	718.8	721.7	727.0	732.3	725.4	726.6	733.4	739.4	738.4	738.5	727.0
1992	719.5	722.3	726.7	734.5	740.0	744.5	741.9	741.4	749.2	757.1	759.5	758.0	741.2
1993	738.1	745.1	750.7	759.5	763.6	771.0	767.9	768.3	776.4	782.9	787.9	791.0	766.9
1994	771.2	778.2	783.4	790.4	795.4	803.3	802.9	805.4	815.3	820.3	829.6	832.5	802.3
1995	807.0	813.9	823.0	826.2	834.8	842.3	835.8	842.9	855.1	859.5	865.7	870.5	839.7
1996	853.0	854.9	863.1	869.3	874.0	881.6	874.8	879.2	889.1	895.2	904.8	908.3	878.9
1997	887.8	894.1	900.6	909.3	917.2	922.5	916.4	915.3	925.0	932.9	938.0	941.7	916.7
1998	914.9	922.5	926.3	932.2	935.6	938.0	931.0	930.2	936.1	940.2	944.5	945.7	933.1
1999	921.7	926.7	933.1	938.1	938.9	944.9	946.5	945.0	949.8	959.3	965.8	966.7	944.7
2000	939.5	948.0	951.6	958.3	966.3	972.6	967.4	968.3	975.3	980.6	988.2	989.0	967.1
2001	964.0	966.7	967.5	966.5	967.9	968.8	950.2	947.4	955.3	954.2	953.0	949.9	959.3
2002	929.0	932.6	935.5	938.8	941.8	944.8	928.1	928.1	938.0	944.4	945.2	941.6	937.3
2003	919.6	921.0	922.5	925.3	928.4	929.1	917.0	917.3	926.3	930.2	931.4	929.8	924.8
Total private													
1990	603.4	602.6	611.6	617.5	621.9	628.6	631.7	643.8	638.4	633.2	634.8	634.4	625.2
1991	608.6	610.7	615.2	618.3	622.8	627.0	628.7	632.7	633.5	634.2	632.2	632.5	624.7
1992	614.6	616.0	619.3	627.0	631.4	635.7	642.2	643.9	647.0	648.7	647.6	649.0	635.2
1993	630.6	636.2	641.1	649.8	653.5	660.5	666.7	669.9	674.9	675.1	678.7	682.9	660.0
1994	663.3	669.0	673.8	680.6	685.0	693.0	701.2	706.1	711.1	710.1	716.2	721.8	694.3
1995	697.8	703.3	711.9	714.3	721.7	730.4	732.3	742.0	748.0	746.9	751.1	756.1	729.7
1996	739.9	740.3	747.4	752.8	757.5	765.3	769.4	777.0	779.3	779.4	785.1	790.6	765.3
1997	772.5	777.8	783.7	792.0	799.9	804.6	808.6	811.1	813.5	816.2	819.5	823.4	801.9
1998	797.9	803.8	806.9	813.0	815.4	817.6	820.9	822.1	822.4	819.6	820.7	823.4	815.3
1999	801.2	804.0	809.6	814.6	815.4	820.5	829.0	829.8	832.0	834.9	838.2	841.0	822.5
2000	815.5	821.5	824.6	830.8	835.8	843.5	847.9	851.9	855.5	853.2	859.7	860.6	841.7
2001	837.2	838.4	838.5	837.8	837.5	839.2	836.4	836.6	831.9	823.5	821.2	818.4	833.1
2002	800.0	801.0	803.1	806.3	808.3	811.3	813.5	816.5	814.5	813.3	812.6	810.2	809.2
2003	790.2	790.5	791.8	794.1	796.2	798.1	798.8	801.1	802.5	800.3	799.6	798.6	796.8

Employment by Industry: Oregon—*Continued*

(Numbers in thousands. Not seasonally adjusted.)

Industry	January	February	March	April	May	June	July	August	September	October	November	December	Annual Average
PORTLAND—*Continued*													
Goods-producing													
1990	157.3	156.4	159.7	161.3	163.1	165.9	167.6	170.6	168.4	164.9	163.6	162.1	163.4
1991	156.1	156.4	157.2	156.9	157.8	160.6	162.5	164.0	162.9	162.1	158.2	156.2	159.2
1992	150.2	150.6	151.9	153.2	155.2	158.2	161.5	161.8	160.9	160.2	157.1	155.6	156.4
1993	151.2	152.1	153.8	155.5	156.4	160.5	163.7	166.1	166.1	164.3	162.1	161.9	159.5
1994	158.5	159.6	161.6	164.3	166.7	172.0	176.3	177.1	178.4	175.4	174.4	174.4	169.9
1995	169.6	171.4	174.0	174.4	177.0	181.4	184.4	187.0	188.7	186.7	185.9	187.3	180.7
1996	184.6	184.6	186.6	187.8	188.3	192.6	195.0	197.1	196.3	194.3	193.4	192.2	191.1
1997	189.2	190.4	192.3	195.2	198.2	201.6	203.5	204.6	205.1	205.1	203.7	202.5	199.3
1998	198.0	199.0	199.9	199.1	199.4	201.4	203.5	203.4	201.5	200.0	197.0	195.4	199.8
1999	190.2	190.2	191.3	193.0	193.2	196.1	200.2	200.2	198.9	197.9	196.1	194.3	195.1
2000	189.6	191.0	192.1	192.6	194.7	198.6	201.2	201.6	203.6	199.9	200.4	199.5	197.1
2001	196.9	196.0	194.2	192.7	192.1	193.3	194.7	194.2	191.3	187.6	183.6	180.8	191.5
2002	175.7	175.4	175.4	175.2	175.6	177.7	180.0	182.1	179.7	177.4	174.8	172.3	176.8
2003	168.3	167.0	166.4	165.7	166.6	168.6	169.4	170.3	170.6	169.7	168.2	166.7	168.1
Natural resources and mining													
1990	1.8	1.7	1.8	1.9	2.0	2.0	2.1	2.1	2.1	2.1	1.9	1.8	1.9
1991	1.6	1.7	1.9	1.8	1.9	2.0	2.1	2.1	2.1	2.0	1.9	1.8	1.9
1992	1.8	1.9	2.0	1.9	1.9	1.9	2.0	1.9	2.0	1.9	1.8	1.7	1.9
1993	1.5	1.6	1.7	1.7	1.8	1.9	2.0	2.0	2.1	2.0	1.9	1.9	1.8
1994	1.7	1.8	1.8	1.7	1.8	1.9	2.0	2.0	2.0	1.9	1.8	1.8	1.9
1995	1.7	1.8	1.8	1.9	1.9	2.0	2.0	2.0	2.0	2.0	1.9	1.9	1.9
1996	1.9	1.8	2.0	2.0	2.0	2.0	2.1	2.2	2.1	2.1	2.0	1.9	2.0
1997	1.9	2.0	2.0	2.0	2.0	2.1	2.2	2.2	2.1	2.0	2.0	2.0	2.0
1998	1.8	1.9	1.9	2.0	2.1	2.1	2.2	2.2	2.2	2.2	2.1	2.0	2.1
1999	1.9	1.9	2.0	2.0	2.0	2.0	2.1	2.1	2.1	2.0	2.0	1.9	2.0
2000	1.8	1.9	1.8	1.8	1.8	1.9	1.8	1.9	1.8	1.8	1.8	1.7	1.8
2001	1.7	1.7	1.7	1.7	1.7	1.7	1.8	1.8	1.8	1.7	1.6	1.6	1.7
2002	1.5	1.5	1.5	1.5	1.6	1.7	1.7	1.7	1.7	1.7	1.7	1.6	1.6
2003	1.6	1.6	1.6	1.6	1.6	1.7	1.7	1.7	1.6	1.5	1.5	1.5	1.6
Construction													
1990	33.1	32.7	35.2	36.8	37.2	37.7	38.4	39.7	39.5	38.0	37.1	35.7	36.8
1991	33.0	33.5	33.8	34.6	35.3	36.2	36.8	37.7	37.3	37.4	35.6	34.7	35.5
1992	31.5	31.2	32.1	32.6	33.7	34.8	36.5	36.6	36.0	36.3	34.7	33.4	34.1
1993	31.1	31.9	32.4	32.9	33.9	35.2	37.6	38.3	38.8	38.5	37.5	36.8	35.4
1994	35.1	35.2	36.1	37.9	38.9	40.6	43.0	44.0	44.5	43.3	42.4	41.8	40.2
1995	39.8	40.1	41.4	42.1	43.0	44.9	46.8	48.8	49.6	49.1	48.7	48.4	45.2
1996	47.2	47.6	48.9	49.6	50.5	52.2	53.3	54.6	54.2	54.5	53.3	51.7	51.5
1997	49.8	50.1	50.6	52.5	54.1	55.6	56.8	57.7	57.8	57.5	56.1	55.2	54.5
1998	51.4	51.6	51.9	52.3	52.4	53.5	55.0	55.8	55.4	54.4	52.7	51.8	53.2
1999	49.0	49.1	49.4	50.8	51.3	52.5	55.2	55.9	55.4	54.7	52.8	51.6	52.3
2000	48.6	49.2	49.8	50.9	51.8	53.4	55.2	56.5	57.0	55.9	54.7	54.0	53.1
2001	53.4	53.4	53.6	52.7	53.3	54.6	55.8	56.7	55.6	54.3	52.6	51.4	54.0
2002	49.2	49.5	49.9	50.0	50.6	51.6	53.5	55.2	54.1	53.4	51.5	49.6	51.5
2003	47.5	47.0	46.8	46.7	47.8	49.0	49.8	50.9	51.1	50.7	49.6	48.2	48.8
Manufacturing													
1990	122.4	122.0	122.7	122.6	123.9	126.2	127.1	128.8	126.8	124.8	124.6	124.6	124.7
1991	121.5	121.2	121.5	120.5	120.6	122.4	123.6	124.2	123.5	122.7	120.7	119.7	121.8
1992	116.9	117.5	117.8	118.7	119.6	121.5	123.0	123.3	122.9	122.0	120.6	120.5	120.4
1993	118.6	118.6	119.7	120.9	120.7	123.4	124.1	125.8	125.2	123.8	122.7	123.2	122.2
1994	121.7	122.6	123.7	124.7	126.0	129.5	131.3	131.1	131.9	130.2	130.2	130.8	127.8
1995	128.1	129.5	130.8	130.4	132.1	134.5	135.6	136.2	137.1	135.6	135.3	137.0	133.5
1996	135.5	135.2	135.7	136.2	135.8	138.4	139.6	140.3	140.0	137.7	138.1	138.6	137.6
1997	137.5	138.3	139.7	140.7	142.1	143.9	144.5	144.7	145.2	145.6	145.6	145.3	142.8
1998	144.8	145.5	146.1	144.8	144.9	145.8	146.3	145.4	143.9	143.4	142.2	141.6	144.6
1999	139.3	139.2	139.9	140.2	139.9	141.6	142.9	142.2	141.4	141.2	141.3	140.8	140.8
2000	139.2	139.9	140.5	139.9	141.1	143.3	144.2	143.2	144.8	142.2	143.9	143.8	142.2
2001	141.8	140.9	138.9	138.3	137.1	137.0	137.1	135.7	133.9	131.6	129.4	127.8	135.8
2002	125.0	124.4	124.0	123.7	123.4	124.4	124.8	125.2	123.9	122.3	121.6	121.1	123.7
2003	119.2	118.4	118.0	117.4	117.2	117.9	117.9	117.7	117.9	117.5	117.1	117.0	117.8
Service-providing													
1990	544.4	545.8	552.3	558.1	562.6	566.5	558.1	565.1	566.9	570.2	574.4	574.3	561.6
1991	553.5	556.9	561.6	564.8	569.2	571.7	562.9	562.6	570.5	577.3	580.2	582.3	567.8
1992	569.3	571.7	574.8	581.3	584.8	586.3	580.4	579.6	588.3	596.9	602.4	602.4	584.9
1993	586.9	593.0	596.9	604.0	607.2	610.5	604.2	602.2	610.3	618.6	625.8	629.1	607.4
1994	612.7	618.6	621.8	626.1	628.7	631.3	626.6	628.3	636.9	644.9	655.2	658.1	632.4
1995	637.4	642.5	649.0	651.8	657.8	660.9	651.4	655.9	666.4	672.8	679.8	683.2	659.1
1996	668.4	670.3	676.5	681.5	685.7	689.0	679.8	682.1	692.8	700.9	711.4	716.1	687.9
1997	698.6	703.7	708.3	714.1	719.0	720.9	712.9	710.7	719.9	727.8	734.3	739.2	717.5
1998	716.9	723.5	726.4	733.1	736.2	736.6	727.5	726.8	734.6	740.2	747.5	750.3	733.3
1999	731.5	736.5	741.8	745.1	745.7	748.8	746.3	744.8	750.9	761.4	769.7	772.4	749.6
2000	749.9	757.0	759.5	765.7	771.6	774.0	766.2	766.7	771.7	780.7	787.8	789.5	770.0
2001	767.1	770.7	773.3	773.8	775.8	775.5	755.5	753.2	764.0	766.6	769.4	769.1	767.8
2002	753.3	757.2	760.1	763.6	766.2	767.1	748.1	746.0	758.3	767.0	770.4	769.3	760.6
2003	751.3	754.0	756.1	759.6	761.8	760.5	747.6	747.0	755.7	760.5	763.2	763.1	756.7

Employment by Industry: Oregon—*Continued*

(Numbers in thousands. Not seasonally adjusted.)

Industry	January	February	March	April	May	June	July	August	September	October	November	December	Annual Average
PORTLAND—*Continued*													
Trade, transportation, and utilities													
1990	153.8	152.3	154.3	155.4	156.4	158.7	158.8	163.3	160.2	159.4	161.9	164.0	158.2
1991	156.0	155.3	156.0	156.5	157.6	159.3	159.2	159.9	159.7	159.5	162.7	164.7	158.9
1992	157.3	156.5	156.3	157.4	158.4	159.3	159.9	159.9	160.4	160.9	163.8	166.8	159.7
1993	158.4	157.8	157.8	159.1	159.6	161.6	162.7	161.8	162.8	163.8	167.5	170.9	162.0
1994	163.1	162.9	162.5	163.5	165.1	167.3	168.9	171.2	171.1	172.0	177.3	180.4	168.8
1995	171.1	170.5	171.3	171.8	173.0	175.8	175.2	177.3	177.1	177.3	182.1	185.4	175.7
1996	179.0	178.0	178.3	179.8	181.0	182.4	183.5	184.7	184.5	185.5	190.1	193.8	183.4
1997	185.3	184.0	184.0	185.6	187.2	188.6	190.4	189.2	190.3	192.1	196.1	199.4	189.4
1998	190.2	189.8	189.5	191.7	192.5	193.5	194.2	194.4	194.0	195.0	199.1	202.8	193.9
1999	192.3	191.0	191.4	193.3	193.6	195.6	197.0	196.8	196.7	198.0	202.1	205.5	196.1
2000	196.0	194.9	194.9	196.5	197.5	199.9	200.1	200.3	199.8	201.3	206.1	208.0	199.6
2001	199.9	198.1	198.0	197.7	197.7	199.5	198.4	198.3	196.5	195.6	197.9	199.3	198.1
2002	191.4	189.7	189.9	190.5	191.6	192.9	193.3	192.5	191.9	191.7	194.6	196.9	192.2
2003	189.2	187.6	187.4	188.4	189.6	190.8	191.2	191.6	191.2	191.0	192.9	193.9	190.4
Wholesale trade													
1990	44.0	44.1	44.7	45.0	45.0	45.7	45.8	46.3	45.8	45.6	45.8	46.0	45.3
1991	44.7	44.8	45.2	45.0	45.0	45.4	45.3	45.4	45.2	45.2	45.1	45.3	45.1
1992	44.7	44.9	45.1	45.1	45.5	45.9	46.6	46.6	46.4	46.2	46.0	46.3	45.8
1993	45.4	45.6	45.7	45.7	45.9	46.7	46.8	46.4	46.5	46.3	46.5	46.6	46.2
1994	46.3	46.7	46.8	47.1	47.1	47.6	47.9	48.6	48.5	48.4	48.8	48.6	47.7
1995	48.1	48.6	48.9	49.5	50.1	50.6	50.3	50.7	50.8	50.4	51.0	51.1	50.0
1996	50.0	50.2	50.4	50.9	51.2	51.5	51.6	51.5	51.5	51.4	52.0	52.1	51.2
1997	52.2	52.2	52.7	52.7	53.2	53.5	54.5	54.8	54.3	54.1	54.6	54.8	53.6
1998	54.2	54.3	54.0	54.8	54.8	54.7	54.7	54.9	54.3	54.0	54.5	54.7	54.5
1999	53.2	53.1	53.0	53.3	53.4	53.5	53.9	54.0	53.8	53.8	53.9	54.0	53.6
2000	54.0	54.2	54.3	54.8	55.1	55.4	56.0	56.2	55.9	56.2	56.4	56.5	55.4
2001	56.6	56.9	57.0	56.8	56.7	57.0	56.7	56.7	56.0	55.3	55.2	54.9	56.3
2002	54.3	54.3	54.2	54.4	54.6	54.7	55.0	55.1	54.8	54.6	54.6	54.7	54.6
2003	54.5	54.6	54.6	54.6	54.7	54.9	55.2	55.1	54.9	54.4	54.4	54.3	54.7
Retail trade													
1990	79.0	77.6	78.4	79.0	79.7	80.9	81.5	85.0	82.5	82.1	84.5	85.9	81.3
1991	80.6	79.6	79.6	80.6	81.6	82.8	82.7	83.3	82.8	82.5	85.7	87.4	82.4
1992	82.3	81.2	81.0	81.8	82.3	82.9	82.7	82.7	82.7	83.3	86.0	88.5	83.1
1993	82.6	81.5	81.3	82.1	82.5	83.5	84.2	83.9	84.1	85.2	88.5	91.5	84.2
1994	85.2	84.6	84.0	85.0	85.7	87.1	88.3	89.6	89.5	90.2	94.1	96.8	88.3
1995	89.6	88.2	88.4	88.2	88.7	90.7	90.1	91.4	90.6	91.1	94.9	97.7	90.8
1996	93.4	92.2	92.1	93.3	94.4	95.2	96.1	97.3	96.7	97.5	101.1	104.4	96.1
1997	97.0	95.8	95.5	96.5	97.6	98.4	99.1	99.1	98.7	100.4	103.5	106.5	99.0
1998	99.2	98.7	98.8	100.1	100.9	101.9	102.3	102.1	102.0	102.8	106.3	110.0	102.1
1999	101.7	100.4	100.8	102.1	102.4	104.1	104.8	104.7	104.4	104.8	108.7	111.8	104.2
2000	104.0	102.9	102.8	103.1	104.0	105.6	105.8	105.6	105.0	106.3	110.4	112.6	105.7
2001	105.6	103.3	103.0	102.7	102.3	103.7	103.1	102.6	101.7	101.5	104.4	106.3	103.4
2002	99.9	98.3	98.5	98.7	99.5	100.5	100.9	100.1	99.8	99.9	103.2	105.4	100.4
2003	98.6	97.4	97.2	97.5	98.4	99.3	99.8	100.0	99.6	99.7	101.6	102.6	99.3
Transportation and utilities													
1990	30.8	30.6	31.2	31.4	31.7	32.1	31.5	32.0	31.9	31.7	31.6	32.1	31.6
1991	30.7	30.9	31.2	30.9	31.0	31.1	31.2	31.2	31.7	31.8	31.9	32.0	31.3
1992	30.3	30.4	30.2	30.5	30.6	30.5	30.6	30.6	31.3	31.4	31.8	32.0	30.9
1993	30.4	30.7	30.8	31.3	31.2	31.4	31.7	31.5	32.2	32.3	32.5	32.8	31.6
1994	31.6	31.6	31.7	31.4	32.3	32.6	32.7	33.0	33.1	33.4	34.4	35.0	32.7
1995	33.4	33.7	34.0	34.1	34.2	34.5	34.8	35.2	35.7	35.8	36.2	36.6	34.9
1996	35.6	35.6	35.8	35.6	35.4	35.7	35.8	35.9	36.3	36.6	37.0	37.3	36.1
1997	36.1	36.0	35.8	36.4	36.4	36.7	36.8	35.3	37.3	37.6	38.0	38.1	36.7
1998	36.8	36.8	36.7	36.8	36.8	36.9	37.2	37.4	37.7	38.2	38.3	38.1	37.3
1999	37.4	37.5	37.6	37.9	37.8	38.0	38.3	38.1	38.5	39.4	39.5	39.7	38.3
2000	38.0	37.8	37.8	38.6	38.4	38.9	38.3	38.5	38.9	38.8	39.3	38.9	38.5
2001	37.7	37.9	38.0	38.2	38.7	38.8	38.6	39.0	38.8	38.8	38.3	38.1	38.4
2002	37.2	37.1	37.2	37.4	37.5	37.7	37.4	37.3	37.3	37.2	36.8	36.8	37.2
2003	36.1	35.6	35.6	36.3	36.5	36.6	36.2	36.5	36.7	36.9	36.9	37.0	36.4
Information													
1990	16.0	16.1	16.0	15.8	16.0	16.3	15.8	16.1	16.1	16.0	16.1	16.0	16.0
1991	15.8	16.0	16.0	16.0	16.1	16.2	16.4	16.4	16.4	16.3	16.3	16.5	16.2
1992	16.7	16.9	16.8	16.9	17.0	17.1	17.3	17.2	17.2	16.9	16.9	17.0	17.0
1993	17.0	17.6	17.6	17.5	17.8	17.7	18.1	18.4	18.4	18.2	18.5	18.4	17.9
1994	17.9	18.3	18.3	18.3	18.5	18.6	18.7	18.8	18.7	18.6	18.9	18.8	18.5
1995	18.5	18.5	18.5	18.9	18.9	19.1	19.0	19.5	19.7	19.5	19.4	19.7	19.1
1996	19.7	19.8	19.9	19.9	20.0	20.2	20.3	20.3	20.4	20.9	20.9	21.3	20.3
1997	21.1	21.2	21.6	22.0	21.9	21.9	22.4	22.3	22.0	22.2	22.1	22.3	21.9
1998	22.5	22.3	22.6	22.9	22.9	23.1	23.5	23.5	23.3	23.8	23.8	24.1	23.2
1999	23.9	24.1	24.1	24.1	23.9	24.4	25.1	25.1	25.4	26.1	26.2	26.6	24.9
2000	25.8	26.1	26.1	26.5	26.8	27.1	27.8	28.0	28.3	28.3	28.4	28.7	27.3
2001	28.8	28.6	28.4	28.1	27.9	27.6	27.3	26.9	26.7	26.4	26.1	26.2	27.4
2002	26.0	25.8	25.3	24.9	24.9	24.9	24.6	24.4	24.3	24.3	24.3	24.5	24.9
2003	24.1	23.8	23.6	23.5	23.4	23.2	23.2	23.3	23.3	23.1	23.2	23.0	23.4

Employment by Industry: Oregon—*Continued*

(Numbers in thousands. Not seasonally adjusted.)

Industry	January	February	March	April	May	June	July	August	September	October	November	December	Annual Average
PORTLAND—*Continued*													
Financial activities													
1990	46.9	47.2	47.7	48.3	48.7	49.0	49.2	49.5	49.5	49.5	49.4	49.4	48.7
1991	48.9	49.0	49.3	49.9	50.2	50.7	51.2	51.2	50.6	50.9	50.8	51.0	50.3
1992	50.2	50.4	50.5	51.6	51.7	51.9	52.1	52.4	52.2	52.4	52.4	52.7	51.7
1993	52.0	52.0	52.3	53.0	53.5	54.0	54.0	54.0	54.1	54.1	54.4	54.9	53.5
1994	54.1	54.2	54.5	55.0	54.9	55.0	55.1	55.2	55.0	54.9	55.1	55.3	54.9
1995	53.9	54.2	54.2	54.5	54.9	55.4	55.5	55.9	55.7	55.6	55.8	56.3	55.2
1996	56.6	56.7	57.1	57.2	57.6	58.2	58.8	59.3	59.5	59.6	59.6	60.1	58.4
1997	59.8	60.2	60.6	61.0	61.7	61.9	62.1	62.3	62.1	62.5	62.6	63.2	61.7
1998	62.0	62.4	62.7	63.2	63.6	63.9	64.2	64.6	64.1	64.6	64.6	64.9	63.7
1999	64.2	64.2	64.5	64.9	65.1	65.1	65.8	65.7	65.0	65.4	65.8	65.6	65.1
2000	64.6	64.6	64.3	64.7	64.8	65.1	65.3	65.1	64.7	64.1	64.3	64.8	64.7
2001	64.3	64.6	65.0	65.0	65.2	65.3	65.5	65.3	65.1	64.9	65.1	65.3	65.1
2002	64.8	65.0	64.8	64.9	65.0	65.2	65.8	66.0	65.7	66.1	66.4	66.8	65.5
2003	66.7	67.0	67.3	67.6	67.7	67.9	67.7	68.0	67.7	67.7	67.2	67.6	67.5
Professional and business services													
1990	72.5	73.4	74.8	75.6	75.7	76.7	77.5	78.8	78.0	78.1	77.9	77.4	76.4
1991	72.3	73.1	74.8	74.8	75.6	76.3	75.9	76.7	77.4	78.3	77.3	77.4	75.8
1992	76.1	76.4	77.9	79.8	80.2	81.2	82.8	83.2	83.2	84.6	83.8	84.0	81.1
1993	80.9	83.3	84.9	86.9	86.8	87.4	89.8	90.5	90.7	91.5	92.2	93.1	88.2
1994	88.0	89.4	90.6	91.9	91.5	93.0	95.3	95.3	95.9	97.7	98.4	99.4	93.9
1995	95.5	97.2	99.5	99.7	101.3	102.9	103.5	106.0	106.9	107.5	107.8	107.0	102.9
1996	103.6	104.2	105.8	106.8	107.0	109.4	109.6	111.5	111.5	112.4	113.1	114.0	109.1
1997	112.5	114.2	116.0	117.0	118.8	120.3	120.6	121.7	121.7	122.0	122.1	122.1	119.1
1998	117.0	119.2	119.4	120.5	120.5	120.9	122.1	121.8	121.0	120.0	119.7	118.5	120.1
1999	115.7	116.9	119.1	119.3	119.3	120.4	121.9	122.6	123.1	123.9	124.2	125.0	121.0
2000	121.0	122.5	123.4	125.0	125.7	127.7	129.4	130.9	130.5	130.7	130.7	129.7	127.3
2001	127.0	127.7	128.4	127.9	127.0	126.9	125.4	125.1	124.0	122.5	121.6	120.0	125.3
2002	119.4	119.7	120.3	121.0	120.3	121.0	122.1	122.6	122.0	121.3	119.7	117.6	120.6
2003	114.6	115.4	115.5	116.3	116.1	116.5	116.9	116.9	117.0	116.8	116.5	116.7	116.3
Educational and health services													
1990	71.6	72.1	72.7	72.7	72.5	71.2	71.7	72.2	73.8	75.3	75.6	75.4	73.1
1991	74.4	75.2	75.1	75.6	75.3	73.0	72.8	72.9	75.2	77.4	77.5	77.3	75.1
1992	76.8	77.6	77.3	78.0	77.7	75.6	75.3	75.2	78.1	79.7	80.0	79.1	77.5
1993	79.3	80.3	80.2	81.7	81.2	79.6	78.8	78.6	82.0	82.9	83.2	82.4	80.9
1994	82.5	84.0	84.4	84.3	83.7	81.9	81.3	81.9	85.4	86.2	86.7	87.4	84.1
1995	85.2	86.3	87.5	87.0	86.8	85.5	84.0	84.6	88.1	89.4	89.9	89.9	87.0
1996	88.8	89.8	90.9	90.9	90.9	88.7	87.6	88.4	91.5	93.8	94.7	94.8	90.9
1997	92.9	95.0	95.0	95.6	95.1	92.5	92.1	92.2	94.9	97.5	97.5	97.4	94.8
1998	95.3	97.2	98.0	98.4	98.0	95.2	94.3	94.4	97.9	100.2	100.5	101.1	97.5
1999	98.6	100.0	100.6	101.0	100.4	97.5	97.1	96.9	101.3	103.1	103.2	103.2	100.2
2000	100.8	103.1	103.3	103.4	102.7	100.2	98.7	99.3	103.2	105.6	106.2	106.2	102.7
2001	104.4	106.5	106.9	107.4	106.8	105.3	103.1	103.7	106.7	108.6	109.7	109.7	106.6
2002	108.1	110.2	111.2	112.0	111.5	109.2	107.4	107.7	110.7	114.1	114.9	114.4	111.0
2003	112.0	114.2	114.8	114.8	114.3	111.5	109.8	109.8	113.2	114.9	115.0	114.6	113.2
Leisure and hospitality													
1990	60.4	60.2	61.1	62.8	63.7	64.5	64.3	66.1	65.6	63.5	63.7	63.5	63.3
1991	59.8	60.1	61.0	62.5	64.0	64.8	64.6	65.4	65.1	63.1	63.0	63.0	63.0
1992	61.3	61.4	62.3	63.7	64.6	65.7	66.6	67.5	68.2	67.1	66.9	67.1	65.2
1993	65.3	66.3	67.5	68.6	70.4	71.9	72.0	73.0	73.1	72.4	72.9	73.2	70.6
1994	72.0	73.0	74.0	75.5	76.6	77.3	77.7	78.4	78.1	76.6	76.7	77.6	76.1
1995	76.1	76.8	78.1	79.5	81.0	81.6	82.1	82.7	82.3	81.2	80.5	80.7	80.2
1996	78.6	78.1	79.3	80.3	82.2	83.3	84.0	84.9	84.8	82.4	82.7	83.5	82.0
1997	81.2	81.9	83.3	84.2	85.3	86.4	86.3	87.4	85.7	83.4	83.8	84.9	84.5
1998	82.1	82.7	83.4	85.6	86.6	87.6	87.5	88.3	88.4	84.0	83.8	84.3	85.4
1999	84.8	85.8	86.6	86.6	87.4	89.0	89.3	90.1	88.8	88.1	88.2	88.3	87.8
2000	85.5	86.7	87.4	88.9	90.0	91.3	92.1	93.2	91.6	89.7	89.8	90.0	89.7
2001	82.5	83.0	83.4	84.7	86.3	86.6	87.8	88.9	87.2	83.7	83.1	83.1	85.0
2002	80.9	81.3	82.1	83.7	85.3	86.5	86.6	87.6	86.5	84.5	83.9	84.0	84.4
2003	81.7	81.8	82.9	84.0	84.4	85.8	86.8	87.2	85.6	83.1	82.7	82.1	84.0
Other services													
1990	24.9	24.9	25.3	25.6	25.8	26.3	26.8	27.2	26.8	26.5	26.6	26.6	26.1
1991	25.3	25.6	25.8	26.1	26.2	26.1	26.1	26.2	26.2	26.6	26.4	26.4	26.1
1992	26.0	26.2	26.3	26.4	26.6	26.7	26.7	26.7	26.8	26.9	26.7	26.7	26.6
1993	26.5	26.8	27.0	27.5	27.8	27.8	27.6	27.5	27.7	27.9	27.9	28.1	27.5
1994	27.2	27.6	27.9	27.8	28.0	27.9	27.9	28.2	28.5	28.7	28.7	28.5	28.1
1995	27.9	28.4	28.8	28.5	28.8	28.7	28.6	29.0	29.5	29.7	29.7	29.8	29.0
1996	29.0	29.1	29.5	30.1	30.5	30.5	30.6	30.8	30.8	30.5	30.6	30.9	30.2
1997	30.5	30.9	30.9	31.4	31.7	31.4	31.2	31.4	31.7	31.4	31.6	31.6	31.3
1998	30.8	31.2	31.4	31.6	31.9	32.0	31.6	31.7	32.2	32.0	32.2	32.3	31.7
1999	31.5	31.8	32.0	32.4	32.5	32.4	32.6	32.4	32.8	32.4	32.4	32.5	32.3
2000	32.2	32.6	33.1	33.2	33.6	33.6	33.3	33.5	33.8	33.6	33.8	33.7	33.3
2001	33.4	33.9	34.2	34.3	34.5	34.7	34.2	34.2	34.4	34.2	34.1	34.0	34.2
2002	33.7	33.9	34.1	34.1	34.1	33.9	33.7	33.6	33.7	33.9	34.0	33.7	33.9
2003	33.6	33.7	33.9	33.8	34.1	33.8	33.8	34.0	33.9	34.0	33.9	34.0	33.9

Employment by Industry: Oregon—*Continued*

(Numbers in thousands. Not seasonally adjusted.)

Industry	January	February	March	April	May	June	July	August	September	October	November	December	Annual Average
PORTLAND—*Continued*													
Government													
1990	98.3	99.6	100.4	101.9	103.8	103.8	94.0	91.9	96.9	101.9	103.2	102.0	99.8
1991	101.0	102.6	103.6	103.4	104.2	105.3	96.7	93.9	99.9	105.2	106.2	106.0	102.3
1992	104.9	106.3	107.4	107.5	108.6	108.8	99.7	97.5	102.2	108.4	111.9	109.0	106.0
1993	107.5	108.9	109.6	109.7	110.1	110.5	101.2	98.4	101.5	107.8	109.2	108.1	106.9
1994	107.9	109.2	109.6	109.8	110.4	110.3	101.7	99.3	104.2	110.2	113.4	110.7	108.1
1995	109.2	110.6	111.1	111.9	113.1	111.9	103.5	100.9	107.1	112.6	114.6	114.4	110.1
1996	113.1	114.6	115.7	116.5	116.5	116.3	105.4	102.2	109.8	115.8	119.7	117.7	113.6
1997	115.3	116.3	116.9	117.3	117.3	117.9	107.8	104.2	111.5	116.7	118.5	118.3	114.8
1998	117.0	118.7	119.4	119.2	120.2	120.4	110.1	108.1	113.7	120.6	123.8	122.3	117.8
1999	120.5	122.7	123.5	123.5	123.5	124.4	117.5	115.2	117.8	124.4	127.6	125.7	122.2
2000	124.0	126.5	127.0	127.5	130.5	129.1	119.5	116.4	119.8	127.4	128.5	128.4	125.4
2001	126.8	128.3	129.0	128.7	130.4	129.6	113.8	110.8	123.4	130.7	131.8	131.5	126.2
2002	129.0	131.6	132.4	132.5	133.5	133.5	114.6	111.6	123.5	131.1	132.6	131.4	128.1
2003	129.4	130.5	130.7	131.2	132.2	131.0	118.2	116.2	123.8	129.9	131.8	131.2	128.0
Federal government													
1990	17.8	17.7	17.9	18.9	20.1	19.7	18.7	18.3	18.1	17.9	17.8	18.0	18.4
1991	17.7	17.6	17.7	17.7	17.9	18.1	18.5	18.4	18.5	18.2	18.2	18.4	18.1
1992	18.2	18.2	18.3	18.4	18.5	18.6	19.1	19.1	19.0	18.8	18.6	19.2	18.7
1993	18.6	18.5	18.4	18.4	18.4	18.5	18.4	18.4	18.3	18.3	18.2	18.6	18.4
1994	18.1	18.0	18.1	18.1	17.8	17.8	17.8	17.7	17.7	17.7	17.5	18.1	17.9
1995	17.5	17.5	17.5	17.5	17.6	17.7	17.9	17.9	17.6	17.5	17.6	18.3	17.7
1996	17.6	17.6	17.6	17.7	17.6	17.5	17.6	17.6	17.7	17.4	17.7	18.3	17.7
1997	17.9	17.6	17.6	17.7	17.6	17.7	17.7	17.8	17.8	17.7	18.2	18.9	17.9
1998	18.0	17.8	17.8	17.6	17.8	17.8	17.9	17.9	17.9	17.9	18.2	18.9	18.0
1999	18.2	17.8	17.8	17.7	17.7	17.6	17.9	18.0	18.0	17.9	18.2	18.8	18.0
2000	18.0	17.9	18.0	18.6	20.7	19.4	19.2	19.2	18.2	18.1	18.1	18.9	18.7
2001	17.9	17.7	17.8	17.7	17.8	17.9	18.2	18.2	18.1	17.9	17.8	18.1	17.9
2002	17.6	17.5	17.5	17.4	17.5	17.8	17.9	18.0	18.0	17.8	17.8	18.3	17.8
2003	18.3	18.3	18.4	18.3	18.3	18.4	18.6	18.5	18.6	18.4	18.4	18.8	18.4
State government													
1990	17.9	18.1	18.3	18.2	18.2	18.8	18.0	17.9	18.1	18.9	18.8	18.6	18.3
1991	18.7	19.1	19.3	19.1	19.2	19.6	18.5	18.4	18.6	19.2	19.3	19.2	19.0
1992	19.0	19.2	19.4	19.5	19.7	19.9	18.8	18.8	19.0	19.7	19.6	19.6	19.4
1993	19.5	19.6	19.8	19.8	19.8	20.0	18.9	18.9	19.0	19.5	19.5	19.6	19.5
1994	19.6	19.8	19.8	19.8	19.9	20.3	19.8	19.9	19.8	20.3	20.4	20.2	20.0
1995	20.2	20.3	20.6	20.4	20.5	20.9	19.4	19.5	20.0	20.7	20.9	20.6	20.3
1996	12.5	12.7	13.0	12.9	13.0	13.2	12.1	12.3	12.5	13.2	13.2	13.0	12.8
1997	13.0	13.2	13.4	13.2	13.3	13.5	12.1	12.2	12.5	13.0	13.1	13.1	13.0
1998	12.9	13.3	13.3	13.1	13.2	13.3	12.0	12.2	12.5	13.4	13.5	13.4	13.0
1999	13.3	13.5	13.7	13.7	13.7	13.7	12.5	12.6	12.7	13.7	13.9	13.8	13.4
2000	13.6	13.9	14.1	14.0	14.1	14.3	12.9	12.9	13.1	14.0	14.2	14.0	13.8
2001	13.9	14.4	14.5	14.5	14.6	14.6	13.4	13.3	13.6	14.6	14.7	14.6	14.2
2002	14.5	14.8	15.0	15.0	15.1	14.9	13.5	13.8	14.2	15.1	15.2	15.1	14.7
2003	15.0	15.2	15.3	15.1	15.4	15.3	13.7	13.6	13.6	14.1	14.5	14.3	14.6
Local government													
1990	62.6	63.8	64.2	64.8	65.5	65.3	57.3	55.7	60.7	65.1	66.6	65.4	63.1
1991	64.6	65.9	66.6	66.6	67.1	67.6	59.7	57.1	62.8	67.8	68.7	68.4	65.2
1992	67.7	68.9	69.7	69.6	70.4	70.3	61.8	59.6	64.2	69.9	73.7	70.2	68.0
1993	69.4	70.8	71.4	71.5	71.9	72.0	63.9	61.1	64.2	70.0	71.5	69.9	69.0
1994	70.2	71.4	71.7	71.9	72.7	72.2	64.1	61.7	66.7	72.2	75.5	72.4	70.2
1995	71.5	72.8	73.0	74.0	75.0	73.3	66.2	63.5	69.5	74.4	76.1	75.5	72.1
1996	83.0	84.3	85.1	85.9	85.9	85.6	75.7	72.3	79.6	85.2	88.8	86.4	83.2
1997	84.4	85.5	85.9	86.4	86.4	86.7	78.0	74.2	81.2	86.0	87.2	86.3	84.0
1998	86.1	87.6	88.3	88.5	89.2	89.3	80.2	78.0	83.3	89.3	92.1	90.0	86.8
1999	89.0	91.4	92.0	92.1	92.1	93.1	87.1	84.6	87.1	92.8	95.5	93.1	90.8
2000	92.4	94.7	94.9	94.9	95.7	95.4	87.4	84.3	88.5	95.3	96.2	95.5	92.9
2001	95.0	96.2	96.7	96.5	98.0	97.1	82.2	79.3	91.7	98.2	99.3	98.8	94.1
2002	96.9	99.3	99.9	100.1	100.9	100.8	83.2	79.8	91.3	98.2	99.6	98.0	95.7
2003	96.1	97.0	97.0	97.8	98.5	97.3	85.9	84.1	91.6	97.4	98.9	98.1	95.0
SALEM													
Total nonfarm													
1990	103.0	103.7	105.5	106.5	108.2	109.0	109.9	113.6	112.8	111.7	110.2	108.4	108.5
1991	104.7	105.8	106.3	106.8	107.1	108.3	107.5	113.0	114.5	114.1	111.1	109.4	109.1
1992	107.2	107.7	108.6	110.7	110.8	112.7	114.1	114.8	117.3	116.8	114.4	112.6	112.3
1993	109.6	111.7	112.2	113.4	114.3	116.5	115.5	118.1	122.1	122.3	119.8	118.2	116.1
1994	115.0	117.0	116.9	118.6	120.5	121.5	120.8	123.9	125.1	124.8	123.6	122.5	120.9
1995	118.4	120.1	120.7	122.1	122.9	125.0	124.9	127.6	129.6	130.1	127.1	126.6	124.6
1996	122.5	123.5	125.1	125.5	127.1	128.3	127.2	131.7	133.8	134.3	132.6	130.1	128.5
1997	126.5	128.2	128.8	129.5	130.9	132.5	131.4	134.2	134.2	134.7	133.3	133.1	131.4
1998	129.6	131.1	132.3	133.3	133.9	135.6	133.7	136.9	139.6	137.2	135.7	135.2	134.5
1999	131.9	133.3	134.3	134.8	135.1	136.3	136.2	138.2	140.5	140.8	139.6	138.4	136.6
2000	134.6	135.7	136.0	136.9	138.2	140.7	138.3	141.0	143.3	142.7	140.9	140.4	139.1
2001	134.6	135.9	136.1	136.1	136.9	139.0	137.7	140.2	141.0	139.8	137.7	137.1	137.7
2002	132.4	133.6	134.6	136.2	137.5	138.3	138.1	139.7	141.8	141.3	139.2	138.0	137.6
2003	133.8	135.0	135.6	135.6	137.8	138.1	136.8	139.0	140.6	142.1	139.3	138.6	137.7

Employment by Industry: Oregon—*Continued*

(Numbers in thousands. Not seasonally adjusted.)

Industry	January	February	March	April	May	June	July	August	September	October	November	December	Annual Average
SALEM—*Continued*													
Total private													
1990	71.6	71.9	73.5	74.2	75.3	76.5	79.5	82.8	82.0	79.3	77.7	76.1	76.7
1991	72.2	72.7	73.4	73.9	74.3	75.6	77.5	82.7	82.7	81.5	78.4	76.8	76.8
1992	74.7	74.7	75.6	77.7	78.0	80.2	84.0	84.6	85.0	83.8	80.5	79.8	79.9
1993	77.0	78.5	78.8	79.7	80.6	83.1	85.1	87.6	89.6	88.8	85.9	85.0	83.3
1994	81.9	83.4	83.5	84.9	86.0	88.0	90.1	92.9	92.3	91.2	89.2	88.8	87.7
1995	84.8	86.1	86.5	87.8	88.4	90.4	93.3	95.8	96.8	95.1	91.9	91.5	90.7
1996	87.6	87.8	89.2	89.7	90.5	92.1	93.3	97.7	99.0	97.7	95.0	93.5	92.8
1997	89.9	91.1	91.7	92.1	93.6	95.0	96.7	99.4	98.6	97.6	96.1	95.7	94.8
1998	92.6	93.6	94.8	95.7	96.0	96.9	98.7	101.6	102.2	98.9	97.1	96.6	97.1
1999	93.4	94.4	95.3	95.9	96.0	97.5	100.2	102.0	102.6	101.3	99.6	98.5	98.1
2000	95.0	96.2	96.5	97.4	98.0	100.2	102.2	104.2	105.1	103.3	101.5	101.2	100.1
2001	95.7	96.2	96.4	96.3	96.8	98.8	100.4	102.4	102.0	100.6	98.4	97.7	98.5
2002	93.1	94.0	94.9	96.5	97.7	98.4	102.0	102.8	103.5	102.2	100.1	99.3	98.7
2003	95.5	96.5	97.0	97.3	99.2	100.0	101.9	103.5	104.4	104.0	101.2	100.7	100.1
Goods-producing													
1990	17.3	17.2	18.0	18.5	19.0	20.1	23.0	25.8	24.3	22.2	20.6	18.7	20.4
1991	17.8	17.7	17.9	18.0	18.1	19.1	21.1	25.0	24.3	22.8	20.0	18.6	20.0
1992	17.6	17.3	17.6	18.0	18.4	20.6	23.8	24.6	23.1	22.1	19.3	18.4	20.1
1993	17.6	18.2	18.2	18.3	18.6	20.3	22.1	24.0	24.8	24.0	21.3	20.0	20.6
1994	19.2	19.7	19.8	20.3	20.9	22.8	25.2	27.0	25.5	24.8	22.3	21.9	22.5
1995	20.9	21.1	21.3	21.5	21.8	23.3	25.9	27.9	27.7	26.5	23.8	23.1	23.7
1996	22.0	21.9	22.6	22.5	23.0	24.2	25.8	29.2	29.0	27.0	25.2	24.0	24.7
1997	23.2	23.3	23.5	23.3	24.0	25.6	27.1	28.8	27.8	26.9	25.0	24.3	25.2
1998	23.1	23.6	24.0	23.8	24.0	25.4	26.6	28.9	28.3	26.6	24.6	23.9	25.2
1999	23.5	23.8	23.7	23.6	23.7	24.3	27.0	28.3	28.1	26.9	25.2	24.4	25.2
2000	23.4	23.6	23.3	23.5	23.5	25.4	26.8	27.9	27.3	26.2	24.4	24.0	24.9
2001	22.7	22.6	22.4	22.0	22.2	23.3	24.6	25.9	25.2	24.0	21.6	21.0	23.1
2002	20.0	19.9	20.3	20.7	21.2	21.7	24.8	25.3	24.9	24.1	22.1	21.5	22.2
2003	20.2	20.4	20.4	20.2	20.8	21.2	22.7	23.9	24.1	23.7	21.7	21.0	21.7
Natural resources and mining													
1990	1.2	1.1	1.2	1.3	1.3	1.4	1.5	1.5	1.5	1.5	1.3	1.3	1.3
1991	1.1	1.2	1.2	1.2	1.2	1.3	1.3	1.4	1.4	1.3	1.2	1.2	1.3
1992	1.2	1.2	1.2	1.2	1.2	1.3	1.3	1.3	1.3	1.3	1.3	1.2	1.3
1993	1.1	1.2	1.2	1.2	1.2	1.3	1.3	1.3	1.3	1.3	1.3	1.2	1.2
1994	1.1	1.2	1.2	1.2	1.3	1.3	1.3	1.3	1.3	1.3	1.3	1.3	1.3
1995	1.2	1.2	1.3	1.3	1.3	1.4	1.4	1.4	1.4	1.5	1.5	1.5	1.4
1996	1.4	1.4	1.4	1.4	1.5	1.5	1.5	1.5	1.6	1.5	1.5	1.4	1.5
1997	1.5	1.4	1.5	1.4	1.4	1.4	1.4	1.5	1.5	1.4	1.4	1.4	1.4
1998	1.3	1.4	1.4	1.4	1.4	1.4	1.4	1.4	1.4	1.4	1.4	1.4	1.4
1999	1.3	1.3	1.3	1.3	1.3	1.3	1.4	1.4	1.4	1.4	1.4	1.4	1.4
2000	1.3	1.3	1.3	1.4	1.4	1.4	1.4	1.4	1.4	1.4	1.4	1.4	1.4
2001	1.3	1.3	1.2	1.2	1.3	1.3	1.3	1.4	1.3	1.3	1.3	1.3	1.3
2002	1.3	1.2	1.2	1.2	1.3	1.3	1.3	1.3	1.3	1.3	1.3	1.3	1.3
2003	1.3	1.3	1.3	1.3	1.3	1.3	1.3	1.4	1.3	1.3	1.3	1.3	1.3
Construction													
1990	4.1	4.0	4.2	4.5	4.7	5.0	5.1	5.4	5.3	5.1	5.0	4.6	4.8
1991	4.3	4.3	4.3	4.4	4.6	4.7	5.1	5.3	5.2	5.1	4.8	4.7	4.7
1992	4.5	4.5	4.7	4.7	4.8	5.1	5.3	5.2	5.3	5.0	4.8	4.6	4.9
1993	4.2	4.4	4.5	4.6	4.8	4.9	5.4	5.5	5.6	5.6	5.5	5.2	5.0
1994	5.0	5.0	5.2	5.3	5.6	5.7	5.8	5.9	6.0	6.0	5.8	5.8	5.6
1995	5.4	5.5	5.5	5.7	5.9	6.1	6.4	6.7	6.8	6.8	6.6	6.5	6.2
1996	6.1	6.1	6.3	6.3	6.5	6.7	7.2	7.5	7.5	7.3	7.1	7.0	6.8
1997	6.8	6.8	6.8	6.9	7.1	7.6	7.6	7.8	7.7	7.7	7.4	7.4	7.3
1998	6.9	6.7	7.0	7.0	7.1	7.9	7.7	7.8	7.9	7.7	7.4	7.3	7.4
1999	6.9	6.8	6.9	7.3	7.3	7.9	8.2	8.1	8.2	8.1	7.8	7.8	7.6
2000	7.2	7.2	7.1	7.1	7.2	7.8	7.6	7.8	7.7	7.4	7.3	7.3	7.4
2001	6.7	6.6	6.6	6.5	6.7	7.2	7.0	7.2	7.0	6.9	6.6	6.3	6.8
2002	6.1	6.1	6.2	6.3	6.6	6.7	7.1	7.2	7.1	7.1	6.8	6.5	6.7
2003	6.0	6.2	6.2	6.0	6.3	6.4	6.8	6.9	6.8	6.8	6.7	6.5	6.5
Manufacturing													
1990	12.0	12.1	12.6	12.7	13.0	13.7	16.4	18.9	17.5	15.6	14.3	12.8	14.3
1991	12.4	12.2	12.4	12.4	12.3	13.1	14.7	18.3	17.7	16.4	14.0	12.7	14.1
1992	11.9	11.6	11.7	12.1	12.4	14.2	17.2	18.1	16.5	15.8	13.2	12.6	13.9
1993	12.3	12.6	12.5	12.5	12.6	14.1	15.4	17.2	17.9	17.1	14.5	13.6	14.4
1994	13.1	13.5	13.4	13.8	14.0	15.8	18.1	19.8	18.2	17.5	15.2	14.8	15.6
1995	14.3	14.4	14.5	14.5	14.6	15.8	18.1	19.8	19.5	18.2	15.7	15.1	16.2
1996	14.5	14.4	14.9	14.8	15.0	16.0	17.1	20.2	19.9	18.2	16.6	15.6	16.4
1997	14.9	15.1	15.2	15.0	15.5	16.6	18.1	19.5	18.6	17.8	16.2	15.5	16.5
1998	14.9	15.5	15.6	15.4	15.5	16.1	17.5	19.7	19.0	17.5	15.8	15.2	16.5
1999	15.3	15.7	15.5	15.0	15.1	15.1	17.4	18.8	18.5	17.4	16.0	15.2	16.3
2000	14.9	15.1	14.9	15.0	14.9	16.2	17.8	18.7	18.2	17.4	15.7	15.3	16.2
2001	14.7	14.7	14.6	14.3	14.2	14.8	16.3	17.3	16.9	15.8	13.7	13.4	15.1
2002	12.6	12.6	12.9	13.2	13.3	13.7	16.4	16.8	16.5	15.7	14.0	13.7	14.3
2003	12.9	12.9	12.9	12.9	13.2	13.5	14.6	15.6	16.0	15.6	13.7	13.2	13.9

Employment by Industry: Oregon—*Continued*

(Numbers in thousands. Not seasonally adjusted.)

Industry	January	February	March	April	May	June	July	August	September	October	November	December	Annual Average
SALEM—*Continued*													
Service-providing													
1990	85.7	86.5	87.5	88.0	89.2	88.9	86.9	87.8	88.5	89.5	89.6	89.7	88.2
1991	86.9	88.1	88.4	88.8	89.0	89.2	86.4	88.0	90.2	91.3	91.1	90.8	89.0
1992	89.6	90.4	91.0	92.7	92.4	92.1	90.3	90.2	94.2	94.7	95.1	94.2	92.2
1993	92.0	93.5	94.0	95.1	95.7	96.2	93.4	94.1	97.3	98.3	98.5	98.2	95.5
1994	95.8	97.3	97.1	98.3	99.6	98.7	95.6	96.9	99.6	100.0	101.3	100.6	98.4
1995	97.5	99.0	99.4	100.6	101.1	101.7	99.0	99.7	101.9	103.6	103.3	103.5	100.9
1996	100.5	101.6	102.5	103.0	104.1	104.1	101.4	102.5	104.8	107.3	107.4	106.1	103.8
1997	103.3	104.9	105.3	106.2	106.9	106.9	104.3	105.4	106.4	107.8	108.3	108.8	106.2
1998	106.5	107.5	108.3	109.5	109.9	110.2	107.1	108.0	111.3	110.6	111.1	111.3	109.3
1999	108.4	109.5	110.6	111.2	111.4	112.0	109.2	109.9	112.4	113.9	114.4	114.0	111.4
2000	111.2	112.1	112.7	113.4	114.7	115.3	111.5	113.1	116.0	116.5	116.5	116.4	114.1
2001	111.9	113.3	113.7	114.1	114.7	115.7	113.1	114.3	115.8	115.8	116.1	116.1	114.6
2002	112.4	113.7	114.3	115.5	116.3	116.6	113.3	114.4	116.9	117.2	117.1	116.5	115.4
2003	113.6	114.6	115.2	115.4	117.0	116.9	114.1	115.1	116.5	118.4	117.6	117.6	116.0
Trade, transportation, and utilities													
1990	17.5	17.3	17.5	17.5	17.7	17.7	18.0	18.0	18.0	17.9	18.1	18.6	17.8
1991	17.2	17.1	17.2	17.3	17.2	17.5	17.5	17.6	17.7	17.8	18.0	18.4	17.5
1992	17.4	17.4	17.7	18.2	18.0	18.2	18.5	18.3	18.7	18.6	18.7	18.9	18.2
1993	18.6	18.5	18.5	18.6	18.6	19.0	19.3	19.3	19.3	19.3	19.6	19.8	19.0
1994	18.6	18.6	18.5	18.7	18.9	19.0	19.2	19.3	19.4	19.5	20.3	20.6	19.2
1995	19.3	19.3	19.3	19.5	19.7	20.0	20.0	20.1	20.3	20.4	20.9	21.0	20.0
1996	19.9	19.8	19.9	20.1	20.2	20.3	20.6	20.7	20.8	21.1	21.3	21.6	20.5
1997	20.1	20.1	20.3	20.5	20.6	20.7	20.8	20.9	20.9	21.1	21.7	21.9	20.8
1998	21.1	21.1	21.2	21.6	21.7	21.6	21.9	21.7	21.9	22.0	22.5	23.1	21.8
1999	21.7	21.6	21.7	22.0	22.2	22.5	22.3	22.4	22.6	23.1	23.6	23.6	22.4
2000	21.9	22.0	22.2	22.3	22.4	22.4	22.5	22.7	23.0	23.3	23.8	24.0	22.7
2001	22.2	21.9	21.9	21.9	21.9	22.2	22.4	22.5	22.3	22.1	22.6	22.8	22.2
2002	21.5	21.3	21.5	21.8	22.1	22.3	22.7	22.8	23.0	23.0	23.5	23.7	22.4
2003	22.6	22.5	22.6	22.6	23.1	23.1	23.0	23.3	23.4	23.6	24.0	24.2	23.2
Wholesale trade													
1990	3.0	3.1	3.1	3.0	3.1	3.1	3.1	3.1	3.1	3.1	3.0	3.2	3.1
1991	3.1	3.1	3.1	3.1	3.0	3.0	3.1	3.1	3.1	3.1	3.0	3.1	3.1
1992	3.0	3.1	2.7	2.9	2.8	2.7	2.8	2.8	2.9	2.9	2.8	2.9	2.9
1993	2.9	2.9	2.9	3.0	2.9	2.9	3.1	3.1	3.1	3.1	3.1	3.0	3.0
1994	3.0	3.0	3.0	3.0	3.0	3.1	3.2	3.2	3.2	3.2	3.1	3.2	3.1
1995	3.1	3.1	3.1	3.0	3.1	3.1	3.1	3.1	3.1	3.2	3.2	3.2	3.1
1996	3.0	3.0	3.1	3.0	3.0	2.9	3.0	3.0	3.1	3.1	3.1	3.1	3.0
1997	2.9	2.9	3.0	3.1	3.1	3.1	3.1	3.1	3.1	3.1	3.1	3.1	3.1
1998	3.0	3.0	3.1	3.2	3.2	3.2	3.4	3.3	3.4	3.3	3.3	3.3	3.2
1999	3.2	3.3	3.3	3.4	3.4	3.4	3.5	3.5	3.5	3.5	3.5	3.5	3.4
2000	3.2	3.3	3.4	3.3	3.3	3.3	3.5	3.5	3.5	3.5	3.4	3.4	3.4
2001	3.2	3.3	3.3	3.3	3.3	3.3	3.6	3.6	3.5	3.4	3.3	3.3	3.4
2002	3.2	3.3	3.3	3.4	3.4	3.4	3.6	3.5	3.5	3.4	3.4	3.4	3.4
2003	3.3	3.4	3.4	3.4	3.6	3.5	3.5	3.5	3.5	3.4	3.4	3.4	3.4
Retail trade													
1990	12.4	12.1	12.3	12.4	12.5	12.6	12.8	12.7	12.7	12.6	12.9	13.3	12.6
1991	12.1	12.0	12.1	12.1	12.1	12.3	12.3	12.4	12.3	12.5	12.8	13.1	12.3
1992	12.3	12.2	12.9	13.1	13.0	13.3	13.4	13.2	13.4	13.3	13.5	13.7	13.1
1993	13.1	13.0	13.0	13.0	13.2	13.5	13.7	13.6	13.5	13.6	13.9	14.1	13.4
1994	13.1	13.0	13.0	13.2	13.4	13.4	13.5	13.5	13.6	13.7	14.5	14.7	13.6
1995	13.6	13.6	13.5	13.9	14.0	14.3	14.3	14.3	14.4	14.5	14.9	15.1	14.2
1996	14.3	14.1	14.1	14.4	14.4	14.6	14.7	14.8	14.7	15.0	15.3	15.5	14.7
1997	14.5	14.5	14.5	14.6	14.7	14.7	14.8	14.8	14.7	14.9	15.5	15.7	14.8
1998	15.1	15.1	15.0	15.3	15.4	15.2	15.4	15.3	15.3	15.5	16.0	16.5	15.4
1999	15.4	15.2	15.3	15.4	15.6	15.8	15.7	15.8	15.8	16.3	16.8	16.8	15.8
2000	15.6	15.6	15.7	15.8	15.9	15.9	15.9	16.0	16.2	16.5	17.0	17.2	16.1
2001	15.8	15.4	15.4	15.4	15.4	15.7	15.7	15.7	15.5	15.4	16.0	16.2	15.6
2002	15.2	14.9	15.1	15.2	15.4	15.7	15.9	16.0	16.1	16.3	16.8	16.9	15.8
2003	16.0	15.8	15.9	15.9	16.2	16.2	16.2	16.4	16.4	16.7	17.1	17.3	16.3
Transportation and utilities													
1990	2.1	2.1	2.1	2.1	2.1	2.0	2.1	2.2	2.2	2.2	2.2	2.1	2.1
1991	2.0	2.0	2.0	2.1	2.1	2.2	2.1	2.1	2.3	2.2	2.2	2.2	2.1
1992	2.1	2.1	2.1	2.2	2.2	2.2	2.3	2.3	2.4	2.4	2.4	2.3	2.3
1993	2.6	2.6	2.6	2.6	2.5	2.6	2.5	2.6	2.7	2.6	2.6	2.7	2.6
1994	2.5	2.6	2.5	2.5	2.5	2.5	2.5	2.6	2.6	2.6	2.7	2.7	2.6
1995	2.6	2.6	2.7	2.6	2.6	2.6	2.6	2.7	2.8	2.7	2.8	2.7	2.7
1996	2.6	2.7	2.7	2.7	2.8	2.8	2.9	2.9	3.0	3.0	2.9	3.0	2.8
1997	2.7	2.7	2.8	2.8	2.8	2.9	2.9	3.0	3.1	3.1	3.1	3.1	2.9
1998	3.0	3.0	3.1	3.1	3.1	3.2	3.1	3.1	3.2	3.2	3.2	3.3	3.1
1999	3.1	3.1	3.1	3.2	3.2	3.3	3.1	3.1	3.3	3.3	3.3	3.3	3.2
2000	3.1	3.1	3.1	3.2	3.2	3.2	3.1	3.2	3.3	3.3	3.4	3.4	3.2
2001	3.2	3.2	3.2	3.2	3.2	3.2	3.1	3.2	3.3	3.3	3.3	3.3	3.2
2002	3.1	3.1	3.1	3.2	3.3	3.2	3.2	3.3	3.4	3.3	3.3	3.4	3.2
2003	3.3	3.3	3.3	3.3	3.3	3.4	3.3	3.4	3.5	3.5	3.5	3.5	3.4

Employment by Industry: Oregon—*Continued*

(Numbers in thousands. Not seasonally adjusted.)

Industry	January	February	March	April	May	June	July	August	September	October	November	December	Annual Average
SALEM—*Continued*													
Information													
1990	1.5	1.5	1.5	1.6	1.6	1.6	1.5	1.5	1.5	1.5	1.5	1.5	1.5
1991	1.6	1.6	1.6	1.6	1.6	1.7	1.7	1.7	1.7	1.7	1.7	1.6	1.7
1992	1.7	1.7	1.7	1.7	1.8	1.8	1.8	1.8	1.8	1.7	1.8	1.7	1.8
1993	1.6	1.7	1.7	1.7	1.7	1.7	1.7	1.7	1.8	1.8	1.7	1.8	1.7
1994	1.7	1.7	1.8	1.7	1.8	1.8	1.8	1.8	1.8	1.8	1.8	1.8	1.8
1995	1.7	1.7	1.7	1.7	1.8	1.7	1.7	1.7	1.7	1.6	1.6	1.6	1.7
1996	1.6	1.6	1.6	1.6	1.6	1.6	1.6	1.6	1.6	1.6	1.6	1.6	1.6
1997	1.6	1.6	1.6	1.5	1.5	1.5	1.5	1.5	1.5	1.6	1.6	1.6	1.6
1998	1.6	1.6	1.6	1.7	1.7	1.8	1.7	1.7	1.7	1.7	1.7	1.7	1.7
1999	1.8	1.8	1.8	1.8	1.8	1.8	1.8	1.8	1.8	1.7	1.8	1.8	1.8
2000	1.7	1.7	1.8	1.9	1.9	1.9	1.9	1.9	1.9	1.9	1.9	2.0	1.9
2001	2.0	2.0	2.0	1.9	1.9	2.0	1.8	1.8	1.8	1.9	1.9	1.9	1.9
2002	1.8	1.8	1.8	1.8	1.7	1.7	1.7	1.7	1.6	1.6	1.7	1.7	1.7
2003	1.6	1.6	1.6	1.6	1.6	1.6	1.6	1.6	1.6	1.6	1.6	1.6	1.6
Financial activities													
1990	5.8	5.9	6.0	6.0	6.1	6.1	6.2	6.3	6.2	6.2	6.2	6.2	6.1
1991	6.0	6.1	6.1	6.0	6.1	6.1	6.2	6.3	6.3	6.2	6.3	6.2	6.2
1992	6.1	6.1	6.1	6.2	6.2	6.1	6.3	6.2	6.2	6.3	6.3	6.4	6.2
1993	6.1	6.2	6.2	6.3	6.4	6.4	6.5	6.7	6.6	6.7	6.8	6.8	6.5
1994	6.6	6.7	6.7	6.9	6.9	6.9	6.9	6.9	6.9	6.9	6.8	6.8	6.8
1995	6.6	6.7	6.6	6.8	6.8	6.9	7.0	6.8	6.8	6.7	6.7	6.8	6.8
1996	6.5	6.6	6.6	6.6	6.6	6.7	6.7	6.8	6.8	6.8	6.9	6.9	6.7
1997	6.7	6.8	6.8	6.7	6.8	6.8	6.8	6.8	6.8	6.7	6.7	6.7	6.8
1998	6.8	6.8	6.8	6.8	6.9	6.9	7.0	7.0	7.1	7.0	7.0	7.0	6.9
1999	6.9	6.9	7.0	6.8	6.8	6.7	6.9	6.9	6.9	6.8	6.8	6.8	6.9
2000	6.8	6.9	6.8	6.7	6.7	6.7	6.8	6.8	6.8	6.8	6.8	6.8	6.8
2001	6.8	6.8	6.8	6.9	6.9	7.1	7.1	7.2	7.2	7.2	7.1	7.2	7.0
2002	6.7	6.8	6.7	6.6	6.6	6.7	6.6	6.7	6.7	6.7	6.7	6.8	6.7
2003	6.7	6.7	6.8	6.7	6.8	6.9	6.9	7.0	6.9	7.0	6.8	6.9	6.8
Professional and business services													
1990	5.4	5.7	5.7	5.6	5.7	5.7	5.9	6.2	6.5	6.0	5.9	5.8	5.8
1991	5.3	5.4	5.5	5.5	5.7	5.6	5.6	6.2	6.2	6.5	6.0	5.8	5.8
1992	6.0	6.1	6.2	6.5	6.6	6.5	6.7	6.6	7.0	7.1	6.6	6.7	6.6
1993	6.3	6.6	6.7	6.8	6.9	7.0	7.0	7.5	7.7	7.8	7.3	7.5	7.1
1994	7.3	7.7	7.8	8.0	8.0	8.1	8.3	8.7	8.4	8.5	8.2	8.1	8.1
1995	8.0	8.2	8.5	8.8	8.8	9.2	9.2	9.3	9.7	9.8	9.2	9.1	9.0
1996	8.4	8.6	8.8	8.5	8.6	8.8	8.6	9.0	9.5	10.0	9.2	8.7	8.9
1997	8.5	8.7	9.0	9.2	9.2	9.2	9.3	9.9	9.8	9.7	9.4	9.6	9.3
1998	8.9	9.0	9.3	9.4	9.4	9.3	9.7	10.2	10.4	9.4	9.2	9.2	9.5
1999	8.6	9.1	9.5	9.8	9.6	9.8	10.2	10.3	10.4	10.4	9.8	9.9	9.8
2000	9.4	9.5	9.9	10.1	10.2	10.3	10.6	11.0	11.2	11.0	10.5	10.5	10.4
2001	9.6	9.5	9.5	9.5	9.6	10.1	10.4	10.6	10.4	10.1	10.0	10.0	9.9
2002	10.0	10.1	10.3	10.8	11.1	11.2	11.7	11.5	11.5	11.6	11.0	11.0	11.0
2003	10.6	10.6	10.9	11.3	11.7	11.9	12.3	12.3	12.2	12.2	11.5	11.8	11.6
Educational and health services													
1990	11.4	11.5	11.7	11.6	11.6	11.6	11.4	11.5	11.6	11.9	12.0	12.0	11.7
1991	11.8	12.1	12.2	12.2	12.2	12.2	11.9	12.1	12.2	12.6	12.7	12.6	12.2
1992	12.6	12.7	12.7	13.0	12.8	12.8	12.8	12.8	13.2	13.2	13.2	13.2	12.9
1993	12.9	13.2	13.2	13.2	13.3	13.4	13.2	13.2	13.5	13.6	13.7	13.7	13.3
1994	13.4	13.6	13.6	13.5	13.6	13.5	13.0	13.1	13.4	13.7	13.8	13.7	13.5
1995	13.6	14.0	14.0	14.0	13.8	13.6	13.5	13.7	14.1	14.3	14.2	14.4	13.9
1996	13.8	14.0	14.2	14.4	14.4	14.2	14.0	14.2	14.6	14.9	14.9	14.8	14.4
1997	14.5	15.0	14.9	14.8	14.9	14.7	14.5	14.4	14.9	15.2	15.4	15.3	14.9
1998	15.3	15.5	15.7	15.9	15.7	15.4	15.3	15.3	15.8	15.9	15.9	15.7	15.6
1999	15.6	15.9	15.9	15.8	15.7	15.7	15.5	15.6	15.8	16.2	16.3	16.3	15.9
2000	16.3	16.8	16.7	16.6	16.7	16.7	16.5	16.6	17.1	17.2	17.3	17.3	16.8
2001	16.6	17.4	17.3	17.3	17.3	16.9	16.7	16.8	17.3	17.8	17.9	17.8	17.3
2002	17.0	17.7	17.7	17.9	17.8	17.3	17.1	17.1	17.7	18.0	18.1	17.9	17.6
2003	17.4	18.1	17.9	17.9	17.9	17.5	17.5	17.5	18.0	18.2	18.3	18.1	17.9
Leisure and hospitality													
1990	8.5	8.5	8.7	8.9	9.1	9.1	8.9	8.9	9.3	8.9	8.7	8.6	8.8
1991	8.1	8.2	8.4	8.6	8.8	8.9	9.0	9.2	9.6	9.1	8.9	8.9	8.8
1992	8.8	8.8	9.0	9.4	9.6	9.5	9.5	9.6	10.1	9.9	9.7	9.7	9.5
1993	9.2	9.3	9.6	10.0	10.1	10.5	10.4	10.4	11.0	10.5	10.5	10.5	10.2
1994	10.3	10.5	10.5	10.8	11.0	11.0	10.8	11.3	11.9	11.1	11.1	11.1	11.0
1995	10.0	10.2	10.2	10.6	10.8	10.9	11.2	11.5	11.6	10.8	10.6	10.6	10.8
1996	10.6	10.5	10.7	11.1	11.2	11.3	11.2	11.4	11.9	11.0	10.8	10.8	11.0
1997	10.4	10.6	10.7	11.0	11.4	11.5	11.7	12.1	11.8	11.2	11.1	11.2	11.2
1998	10.8	10.8	11.0	11.2	11.4	11.5	11.4	11.7	11.8	11.0	10.9	10.8	11.2
1999	10.2	10.2	10.5	10.8	10.9	11.5	11.3	11.5	11.7	10.9	10.8	10.5	10.9
2000	10.4	10.5	10.6	11.1	11.4	11.7	12.0	12.1	12.5	11.6	11.6	11.4	11.4
2001	10.8	10.9	11.3	11.6	11.8	12.0	12.3	12.5	12.6	12.2	12.0	11.8	11.8
2002	11.1	11.2	11.4	11.6	11.9	12.2	12.1	12.4	12.9	11.8	11.7	11.5	11.8
2003	11.3	11.4	11.6	11.8	12.0	12.6	12.7	12.7	13.0	12.4	12.0	11.8	12.1

Employment by Industry: Oregon—*Continued*

(Numbers in thousands. Not seasonally adjusted.)

Industry	January	February	March	April	May	June	July	August	September	October	November	December	Annual Average
SALEM—*Continued*													
Other services													
1990	4.2	4.3	4.4	4.5	4.5	4.6	4.6	4.6	4.6	4.7	4.7	4.7	4.5
1991	4.4	4.5	4.5	4.7	4.6	4.5	4.5	4.6	4.7	4.8	4.8	4.7	4.6
1992	4.5	4.6	4.6	4.7	4.6	4.7	4.6	4.7	4.9	4.9	4.9	4.8	4.7
1993	4.7	4.8	4.7	4.8	5.0	4.8	4.9	4.8	4.9	5.1	5.0	4.9	4.9
1994	4.8	4.9	4.8	5.0	4.9	4.9	4.9	4.8	5.0	4.9	4.9	4.8	4.9
1995	4.7	4.9	4.9	4.9	4.9	4.8	4.8	4.8	4.9	5.0	4.9	4.9	4.9
1996	4.8	4.8	4.8	4.9	4.9	5.0	4.8	4.8	4.8	5.3	5.1	5.1	4.9
1997	4.9	5.0	4.9	5.1	5.2	5.0	5.0	5.0	5.1	5.2	5.2	5.1	5.1
1998	5.0	5.2	5.2	5.3	5.2	5.0	5.1	5.1	5.2	5.3	5.3	5.2	5.2
1999	5.1	5.1	5.2	5.3	5.3	5.2	5.2	5.2	5.3	5.3	5.3	5.2	5.2
2000	5.1	5.2	5.2	5.2	5.2	5.1	5.1	5.2	5.3	5.3	5.2	5.2	5.2
2001	5.0	5.1	5.2	5.2	5.2	5.2	5.1	5.1	5.2	5.3	5.3	5.2	5.2
2002	5.0	5.2	5.2	5.3	5.3	5.3	5.3	5.3	5.2	5.4	5.3	5.2	5.3
2003	5.1	5.2	5.2	5.2	5.3	5.2	5.2	5.2	5.2	5.3	5.3	5.3	5.2
Government													
1990	31.4	31.8	32.0	32.3	32.9	32.5	30.4	30.8	30.8	32.4	32.5	32.3	31.8
1991	32.5	33.1	32.9	32.9	32.8	32.7	30.0	30.3	31.8	32.6	32.7	32.6	32.2
1992	32.5	33.0	33.0	33.0	32.8	32.5	30.1	30.2	32.3	33.0	33.9	32.8	32.4
1993	32.6	33.2	33.4	33.7	33.7	33.4	30.4	30.5	32.5	33.5	33.9	33.2	32.8
1994	33.1	33.6	33.4	33.7	34.5	33.5	30.7	31.0	32.8	33.6	34.4	33.7	33.2
1995	33.6	34.0	34.2	34.3	34.5	34.6	31.6	31.8	32.8	35.0	35.2	35.1	33.9
1996	34.9	35.7	35.9	35.8	36.6	36.2	33.9	34.0	34.8	36.6	37.6	36.6	35.7
1997	36.6	37.1	37.1	37.4	37.3	37.5	34.7	34.8	35.6	37.1	37.2	37.4	36.7
1998	37.0	37.5	37.5	37.6	37.9	38.7	35.0	35.3	37.4	38.3	38.6	38.6	37.5
1999	38.5	38.9	39.0	38.9	39.1	38.8	36.0	36.2	37.9	39.5	40.0	39.9	38.6
2000	39.6	39.5	39.5	39.5	40.2	40.5	36.1	36.8	38.2	39.4	39.4	39.2	39.0
2001	38.9	39.7	39.7	39.8	40.1	40.2	37.3	37.8	39.0	39.2	39.3	39.4	39.2
2002	39.3	39.6	39.7	39.7	39.8	39.9	36.1	36.9	38.3	39.1	39.1	38.7	38.9
2003	38.3	38.5	38.6	38.3	38.6	38.1	34.9	35.5	36.2	38.1	38.1	37.9	37.6
Federal government													
1990	1.7	1.7	1.7	2.0	2.2	2.1	1.9	1.8	1.8	1.7	1.7	1.7	1.8
1991	1.7	1.7	1.7	1.7	1.7	1.8	1.7	1.7	1.8	1.7	1.7	1.7	1.7
1992	1.7	1.7	1.7	1.7	1.7	1.6	1.7	1.7	1.8	1.7	1.7	1.7	1.7
1993	1.6	1.6	1.6	1.7	1.7	1.6	1.6	1.6	1.7	1.7	1.7	1.7	1.7
1994	1.6	1.6	1.6	1.6	1.6	1.6	1.6	1.6	1.7	1.6	1.6	1.7	1.6
1995	1.6	1.6	1.6	1.6	1.7	1.5	1.6	1.6	1.6	1.6	1.6	1.6	1.6
1996	1.6	1.6	1.6	1.6	1.6	1.5	1.5	1.6	1.6	1.6	1.6	1.6	1.6
1997	1.6	1.6	1.6	1.6	1.5	1.5	1.6	1.6	1.7	1.6	1.6	1.7	1.6
1998	1.6	1.6	1.6	1.6	1.6	1.6	1.5	1.5	1.6	1.6	1.6	1.7	1.6
1999	1.6	1.6	1.6	1.6	1.6	1.5	1.5	1.5	1.6	1.6	1.6	1.7	1.6
2000	1.7	1.7	1.7	1.8	2.2	1.8	1.8	1.7	1.6	1.6	1.6	1.6	1.7
2001	1.5	1.5	1.5	1.5	1.5	1.6	1.5	1.5	1.6	1.5	1.5	1.6	1.5
2002	1.5	1.5	1.5	1.5	1.6	1.6	1.6	1.6	1.6	1.6	1.6	1.6	1.6
2003	1.5	1.5	1.5	1.5	1.5	1.6	1.5	1.6	1.6	1.6	1.6	1.6	1.6
State government													
1990	17.3	17.6	17.7	17.7	17.9	18.1	17.8	18.5	17.5	18.0	17.9	17.8	17.8
1991	18.0	18.3	18.3	18.3	18.2	18.3	17.5	17.7	18.4	17.9	17.8	17.8	18.0
1992	17.8	17.9	17.9	18.0	17.8	17.8	17.1	17.3	18.1	17.5	17.4	17.3	17.7
1993	17.4	17.7	17.8	17.9	17.9	17.8	17.1	17.1	17.8	17.5	17.3	17.2	17.5
1994	17.3	17.6	17.5	17.7	17.7	17.6	17.1	17.3	18.0	17.6	17.5	17.5	17.5
1995	17.4	17.7	17.9	17.9	18.0	18.0	17.1	17.4	17.4	17.8	17.7	17.6	17.7
1996	17.6	17.9	18.1	18.2	18.3	18.4	18.1	18.2	18.1	18.4	18.5	18.4	18.2
1997	18.5	18.8	18.9	19.0	19.0	19.1	18.6	19.0	18.4	18.7	18.8	18.5	18.8
1998	18.6	18.9	18.9	19.0	19.1	19.3	18.9	19.7	19.1	19.2	19.3	19.4	19.1
1999	19.5	19.7	19.7	19.8	19.7	19.6	19.1	19.4	19.2	20.0	20.1	19.9	19.6
2000	19.8	19.5	19.5	19.5	19.6	19.6	18.9	19.6	19.0	19.5	19.4	19.2	19.4
2001	19.2	19.6	19.6	19.7	19.8	19.7	19.3	19.8	19.1	19.3	19.3	19.1	19.5
2002	18.9	19.0	19.2	19.3	19.3	19.3	19.0	19.8	19.4	19.4	19.2	19.0	19.2
2003	18.8	18.9	19.0	18.9	19.0	18.8	18.1	18.6	18.2	18.7	18.6	18.5	18.7
Local government													
1990	12.4	12.5	12.6	12.6	12.8	12.3	10.7	10.5	11.5	12.7	12.9	12.8	12.2
1991	12.8	13.1	12.9	12.9	12.9	12.6	10.8	10.9	11.6	13.0	13.2	13.1	12.5
1992	13.0	13.4	13.4	13.3	13.3	13.1	11.3	11.2	12.4	13.8	14.8	13.8	13.1
1993	13.6	13.9	14.0	14.1	14.1	14.0	11.7	11.8	13.0	14.3	14.9	14.3	13.6
1994	14.2	14.4	14.3	14.4	15.2	14.3	12.0	12.1	13.1	14.4	15.3	14.5	14.0
1995	14.6	14.7	14.7	14.8	14.8	15.1	12.9	12.8	13.8	15.6	15.9	15.9	14.6
1996	15.7	16.2	16.2	16.0	16.7	16.3	14.3	14.2	15.1	16.6	17.5	16.6	16.0
1997	16.5	16.7	16.6	16.8	16.8	16.9	14.5	14.2	15.5	16.8	16.8	17.2	16.3
1998	16.8	17.0	17.0	17.0	17.2	17.8	14.6	14.1	16.7	17.5	17.7	17.5	16.7
1999	17.4	17.6	17.7	17.5	17.8	17.7	15.4	15.3	17.1	17.9	18.3	18.3	17.3
2000	18.1	18.3	18.3	18.2	18.4	19.1	15.4	15.5	17.6	18.3	18.4	18.4	17.8
2001	18.2	18.6	18.6	18.6	18.8	18.9	16.5	16.5	18.3	18.4	18.5	18.7	18.2
2002	18.9	19.1	19.0	18.9	18.9	19.0	15.5	15.5	17.3	18.1	18.3	18.1	18.1
2003	18.0	18.1	18.1	17.9	18.1	17.7	15.3	15.3	16.4	17.8	17.9	17.8	17.4

Average Weekly Hours by Industry: Oregon

(Not seasonally adjusted.)

Industry	January	February	March	April	May	June	July	August	September	October	November	December	Annual Average
STATEWIDE													
Manufacturing													
2001	38.4	38.7	39.1	39.9	39.1	39.1	39.0	39.1	39.6	39.0	38.5	39.5	39.1
2002	37.9	38.5	39.0	39.1	38.9	39.9	38.3	40.0	39.9	39.4	38.8	39.3	39.1
2003	38.4	38.9	39.1	38.8	39.1	39.9	38.6	39.6	39.6	39.4	40.3	39.7	39.3
EUGENE-SPRINGFIELD													
Manufacturing													
2001	37.5	38.9	38.9	38.3	39.6	39.4	37.2	41.9	42.0	40.0	40.1	42.0	39.6
2002	39.1	41.5	40.0	40.9	39.9	41.7	39.1	42.0	41.8	41.6	41.7	42.5	41.0
2003	39.4	41.3	40.3	39.0	39.8	43.4	41.5	43.5	41.9	41.0	40.5	41.2	41.1
MEDFORD													
Manufacturing													
2001	37.2	37.9	38.4	39.8	39.8	40.3	39.0	40.1	41.8	40.9	37.0	37.6	39.2
2002	36.6	36.9	36.6	37.0	38.8	40.5	38.4	39.6	40.8	38.1	37.9	38.7	38.3
2003	36.3	40.4	39.3	37.7	39.8	41.3	39.8	40.5	39.2	39.6	40.3	38.3	39.4
PORTLAND													
Manufacturing													
2001	39.1	39.6	39.5	40.5	39.0	38.8	39.1	38.5	39.2	39.2	38.7	39.5	39.2
2002	37.7	38.6	39.3	39.3	38.9	39.5	38.1	39.7	39.3	39.0	39.0	38.9	38.9
2003	37.8	38.2	38.8	38.6	38.8	39.4	38.5	39.1	39.3	39.2	40.2	40.1	39.0
SALEM													
Manufacturing													
2001	36.4	36.9	37.6	37.5	37.7	37.7	35.5	37.5	36.3	37.8	37.3	37.3	37.1
2002	35.5	37.7	39.9	39.0	39.0	39.9	37.8	38.8	39.8	39.1	37.7	39.1	38.7
2003	38.3	37.6	38.3	38.0	37.5	37.1	37.7	39.9	40.9	39.1	37.9	38.8	38.5

Average Hourly Earnings by Industry: Oregon

(Dollars, not seasonally adjusted.)

Industry	January	February	March	April	May	June	July	August	September	October	November	December	Annual Average
STATEWIDE													
Manufacturing													
2001	14.50	14.49	14.51	14.81	14.60	14.76	15.03	14.68	14.80	14.72	14.95	15.02	14.74
2002	15.02	15.04	14.98	14.96	14.99	15.11	15.09	14.93	15.12	15.10	15.10	15.27	15.06
2003	15.30	15.24	15.21	15.22	15.26	15.22	15.24	15.01	15.07	14.96	15.30	15.41	15.20
EUGENE-SPRINGFIELD													
Manufacturing													
2001	13.87	13.83	14.02	13.71	13.88	14.39	14.65	14.46	14.57	14.41	14.32	14.50	14.22
2002	14.55	14.71	14.76	14.60	14.62	14.50	14.70	14.58	15.26	14.94	15.06	14.83	14.77
2003	15.05	14.98	15.33	14.81	14.58	14.90	14.85	14.62	14.89	14.77	15.49	15.14	14.95
MEDFORD													
Manufacturing													
2001	13.96	13.63	13.73	13.95	14.59	14.82	15.49	15.72	15.61	15.71	14.65	14.35	14.69
2002	14.50	14.49	14.39	14.78	15.51	15.69	15.88	15.26	15.84	15.25	14.93	14.51	15.11
2003	15.50	15.04	15.00	15.08	15.03	15.66	15.95	15.26	15.66	15.22	15.17	15.07	15.30
PORTLAND													
Manufacturing													
2001	14.90	14.83	14.81	15.36	15.01	15.27	15.62	15.22	15.24	15.17	15.55	15.48	15.20
2002	15.43	15.37	15.30	15.33	15.33	15.46	15.65	15.43	15.62	15.58	15.73	16.06	15.52
2003	15.94	15.93	15.85	15.84	15.73	15.91	15.81	15.78	15.79	15.62	15.80	15.84	15.82
SALEM													
Manufacturing													
2001	13.20	13.06	13.19	13.16	12.97	13.13	12.86	12.68	13.49	12.64	12.89	13.32	13.04
2002	13.59	13.70	13.53	13.44	13.53	13.31	12.72	12.51	12.64	12.80	12.83	12.72	13.06
2003	13.06	13.65	13.62	14.09	14.10	14.11	13.34	12.73	12.35	12.72	13.76	14.09	13.40

Average Weekly Earnings by Industry: Oregon

(Dollars, not seasonally adjusted.)

Industry	January	February	March	April	May	June	July	August	September	October	November	December	Annual Average
STATEWIDE													
Manufacturing													
2001	556.80	560.76	567.34	590.92	570.86	577.12	586.17	573.99	586.08	574.08	575.58	593.29	576.33
2002	569.26	579.04	584.22	584.94	583.11	602.89	577.95	597.20	603.29	594.94	585.88	600.11	588.85
2003	587.52	592.84	594.71	590.54	596.67	607.28	588.26	594.40	596.77	589.42	616.59	611.78	597.36
EUGENE-SPRINGFIELD													
Manufacturing													
2001	520.13	537.99	545.38	525.09	549.65	566.97	544.98	605.87	611.94	576.40	574.23	609.00	563.11
2002	568.91	610.47	590.40	597.14	583.34	604.65	574.77	612.36	637.87	621.50	628.00	630.28	605.57
2003	592.97	618.67	617.80	577.59	580.28	646.66	616.28	635.97	623.89	605.57	627.35	623.77	614.45
MEDFORD													
Manufacturing													
2001	519.31	516.58	527.23	555.21	580.68	597.25	604.11	630.37	652.50	642.54	542.05	539.56	575.85
2002	530.70	534.68	526.67	546.86	601.79	635.45	609.79	604.30	646.27	581.03	565.85	561.54	578.71
2003	562.65	607.62	589.50	568.52	598.19	646.76	634.81	618.03	613.87	602.71	611.35	577.18	602.82
PORTLAND													
Manufacturing													
2001	582.59	587.27	585.00	622.08	585.39	592.48	610.74	585.97	597.41	594.66	601.79	611.46	595.84
2002	581.71	593.28	601.29	602.47	596.34	610.67	596.27	612.57	613.87	607.62	613.47	624.73	603.73
2003	602.53	608.53	614.98	611.42	610.32	626.85	608.69	617.00	620.55	612.30	635.16	635.18	616.98
SALEM													
Manufacturing													
2001	480.48	481.91	495.94	493.50	488.97	495.00	456.53	475.50	489.69	477.79	480.80	496.84	483.78
2002	482.45	516.49	539.85	524.16	527.67	531.07	480.82	485.39	503.07	500.48	483.69	497.35	505.42
2003	500.20	513.24	521.65	535.42	528.75	523.48	502.92	507.93	505.12	497.35	521.50	546.69	515.90

PENNSYLVANIA AT A GLANCE

(Population and total nonfarm employment numbers in thousands)

Population, Census 2000:	12,281.1
Total nonfarm employment, 2003:	5,602.2
Change in total nonfarm employment	
(Number)	
1990–2003:	432.0
1990–2001:	512.3
2001–2003:	-80.3
(Compound annual rate of change)	
1990–2003:	0.6%
1990–2001:	0.9%
2001–2003:	-0.7%
Unemployment rate	
1990:	5.4%
2001:	4.7%
2003:	5.7%

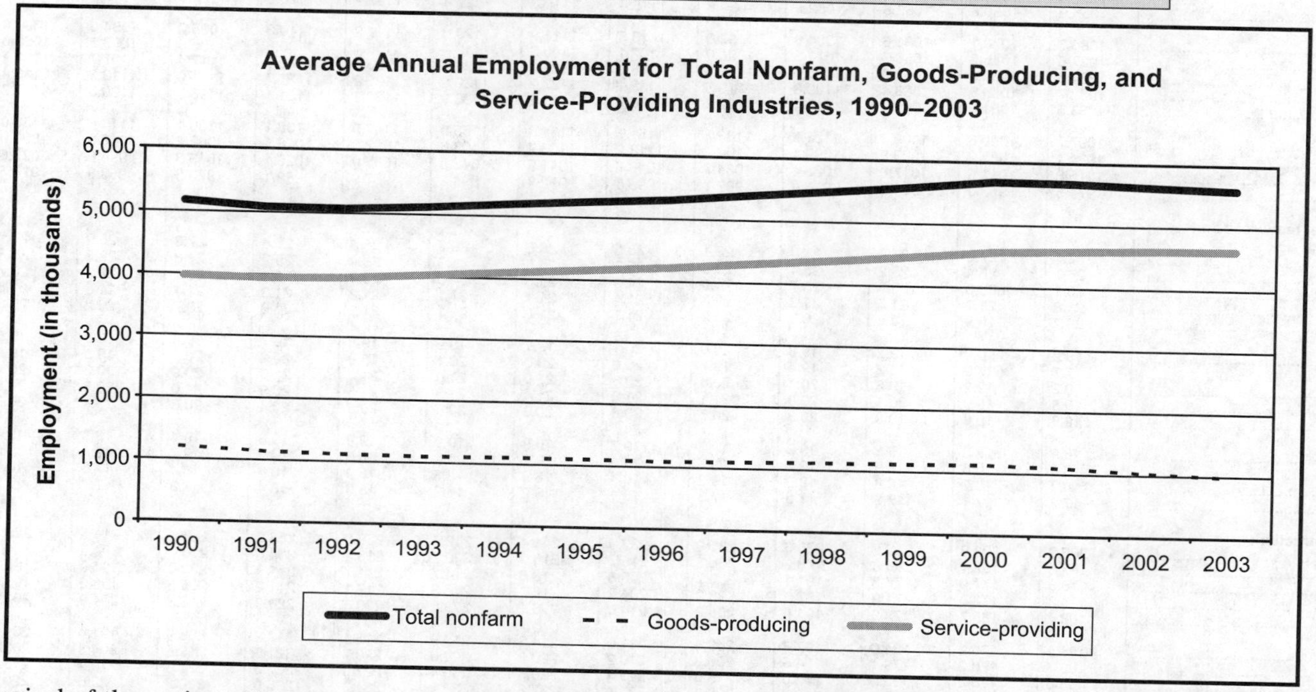

Typical of the nationwide pattern, total nonfarm employment contracted during both recessions and in 2003 remained below its 2000 peak level. Goods-producing industries, which had regained some moderate job growth in the late 1990s, declined significantly in the 2001 recession. Much of this decline was due to a 17 percent drop in manufacturing jobs from 2000 to 2003. The service-providing sector, which had shown strong gains in employment during the 1990s, continued to increase after 2000, but at a much slower rate. Educational and health services, leisure and hospitality, and other services were the only industries to increase by 4 percent or more from 2000 to 2003. Employment in several service-providing industries, including retail trade and professional and business services, decreased.

Employment by Industry: Pennsylvania

(Numbers in thousands. Not seasonally adjusted.)

Industry	January	February	March	April	May	June	July	August	September	October	November	December	Annual Average
STATEWIDE													
Total nonfarm													
1990	5088.1	5106.9	5145.0	5167.2	5202.7	5214.9	5166.2	5164.6	5196.4	5200.1	5201.9	5187.8	5170.2
1991	5027.8	5031.9	5055.8	5082.8	5105.7	5117.9	5054.1	5062.3	5095.2	5117.3	5131.3	5121.1	5083.6
1992	4970.9	4984.0	5012.9	5067.1	5106.0	5117.1	5077.5	5069.3	5095.9	5137.5	5137.6	5130.8	5075.6
1993	5001.7	5035.7	5043.1	5107.5	5144.6	5147.4	5117.4	5116.6	5151.6	5192.4	5205.1	5211.2	5122.9
1994	5029.7	5054.1	5106.0	5170.2	5214.1	5236.9	5191.2	5197.3	5244.8	5273.9	5293.6	5297.3	5192.4
1995	5131.1	5158.7	5202.5	5246.5	5277.2	5293.0	5223.7	5243.4	5286.0	5316.8	5329.4	5329.2	5253.1
1996	5112.6	5192.2	5232.7	5297.1	5336.1	5339.5	5295.4	5306.5	5341.6	5388.3	5413.5	5419.0	5306.2
1997	5263.0	5294.6	5331.6	5383.2	5423.5	5427.0	5392.0	5388.2	5445.8	5493.0	5512.9	5522.3	5406.4
1998	5360.2	5394.8	5428.6	5492.8	5536.5	5520.8	5473.9	5472.1	5516.1	5563.9	5584.9	5593.5	5494.8
1999	5431.6	5480.2	5519.8	5579.1	5609.9	5622.7	5584.6	5579.3	5613.9	5648.6	5672.7	5690.6	5586.1
2000	5547.2	5577.0	5635.7	5690.1	5730.3	5740.2	5688.3	5673.7	5734.4	5744.8	5766.6	5767.1	5691.3
2001	5613.1	5641.0	5676.5	5702.3	5729.1	5738.7	5652.4	5654.8	5690.9	5692.9	5703.4	5694.9	5682.5
2002	5549.6	5575.0	5613.8	5647.0	5680.8	5692.4	5614.3	5614.2	5661.8	5681.0	5689.2	5670.0	5640.8
2003	5522.5	5530.4	5569.3	5611.0	5651.2	5654.4	5580.0	5573.0	5617.0	5637.2	5647.9	5632.0	5602.2
Total private													
1990	4397.1	4398.8	4431.8	4449.4	4484.0	4514.3	4498.0	4509.9	4509.3	4493.1	4489.5	4478.1	4471.1
1991	4335.1	4320.4	4341.4	4369.4	4396.8	4427.0	4400.3	4416.9	4412.9	4412.7	4421.9	4413.7	4389.0
1992	4289.2	4281.4	4306.4	4359.0	4402.3	4423.0	4414.0	4412.8	4419.0	4434.6	4429.2	4424.7	4383.0
1993	4316.6	4327.5	4329.8	4387.1	4428.3	4443.1	4446.9	4454.1	4463.9	4481.3	4484.8	4490.6	4421.2
1994	4339.0	4341.5	4385.9	4446.6	4496.5	4527.1	4520.2	4535.0	4547.5	4554.8	4568.3	4570.6	4486.1
1995	4429.5	4434.5	4475.6	4517.7	4550.1	4580.3	4552.4	4575.6	4585.6	4593.0	4600.2	4599.9	4541.2
1996	4417.4	4465.0	4500.9	4563.2	4605.9	4635.4	4622.3	4636.5	4639.0	4664.7	4684.4	4689.5	4593.7
1997	4555.1	4567.0	4600.3	4649.9	4692.0	4722.7	4718.2	4721.8	4738.5	4765.1	4780.2	4791.4	4691.9
1998	4653.0	4667.9	4698.9	4762.9	4806.8	4828.1	4807.7	4809.8	4808.5	4839.0	4853.4	4863.6	4783.3
1999	4725.4	4754.3	4788.3	4846.4	4881.5	4917.6	4910.6	4909.3	4899.3	4919.4	4936.4	4957.1	4870.5
2000	4828.7	4840.6	4891.3	4943.4	4973.9	5020.4	5010.1	5005.5	5014.5	5009.2	5025.2	5031.7	4966.2
2001	4892.5	4901.0	4933.6	4955.3	4986.1	5020.2	4978.1	4981.6	4962.0	4945.9	4950.1	4944.6	4954.3
2002	4814.1	4819.6	4856.6	4887.4	4926.4	4960.3	4932.1	4938.9	4925.2	4924.7	4925.0	4912.3	4901.9
2003	4783.0	4768.3	4803.1	4844.8	4888.0	4912.5	4891.3	4891.5	4881.2	4881.8	4886.6	4875.6	4859.0
Goods-producing													
1990	1185.7	1179.6	1190.1	1197.1	1209.8	1223.6	1216.6	1222.6	1215.8	1202.6	1189.3	1171.5	1200.4
1991	1131.6	1117.2	1118.6	1131.4	1139.8	1154.9	1148.1	1159.1	1152.8	1147.5	1136.9	1119.7	1138.1
1992	1087.9	1077.8	1084.7	1102.8	1115.3	1129.1	1127.0	1129.5	1125.7	1122.8	1110.3	1094.5	1109.0
1993	1067.5	1064.9	1065.8	1080.7	1094.4	1103.5	1107.9	1112.7	1112.2	1110.5	1104.2	1095.3	1093.3
1994	1055.9	1050.6	1062.5	1082.6	1099.8	1116.4	1119.3	1127.4	1127.9	1126.8	1122.8	1112.8	1100.4
1995	1080.7	1070.1	1081.6	1094.6	1102.0	1115.5	1111.9	1120.3	1117.2	1110.3	1098.7	1084.5	1099.0
1996	1037.0	1045.9	1056.7	1077.5	1091.0	1107.1	1106.3	1112.7	1108.4	1109.6	1105.9	1093.5	1087.6
1997	1064.5	1063.3	1073.0	1090.6	1102.3	1118.1	1121.2	1126.6	1123.8	1123.8	1117.4	1107.7	1102.7
1998	1082.7	1080.5	1088.4	1109.8	1119.3	1132.1	1127.2	1132.0	1126.2	1127.7	1121.9	1113.3	1113.4
1999	1083.5	1084.8	1092.3	1111.4	1122.2	1136.7	1131.2	1133.9	1130.1	1131.1	1128.5	1120.8	1117.2
2000	1097.7	1090.6	1109.8	1123.9	1133.2	1151.7	1151.6	1153.8	1147.9	1138.1	1130.1	1119.8	1129.0
2001	1094.1	1088.2	1093.8	1099.4	1104.2	1113.2	1103.7	1103.6	1092.3	1076.1	1062.2	1049.6	1090.0
2002	1015.8	1011.6	1017.8	1026.4	1034.7	1046.7	1041.9	1043.8	1033.9	1026.1	1013.3	998.0	1025.8
2003	971.5	958.3	964.4	975.6	987.1	995.5	992.3	994.2	987.9	982.1	973.3	958.8	978.4
Natural resources and mining													
1990	27.1	27.0	27.5	27.8	28.1	28.5	28.0	28.2	28.2	27.8	27.3	26.9	27.7
1991	25.7	25.4	25.2	25.4	25.6	25.8	25.5	25.6	25.4	25.2	24.6	23.8	25.3
1992	23.1	23.0	23.3	23.7	24.0	24.3	24.3	24.0	23.9	23.8	23.7	22.7	23.7
1993	21.8	21.7	21.5	21.8	22.3	21.4	21.1	21.1	21.2	21.3	21.1	21.6	21.5
1994	20.2	19.9	19.8	20.5	20.9	21.1	21.0	21.1	21.1	21.0	20.7	20.2	20.6
1995	19.2	18.9	19.2	19.8	20.0	20.1	19.7	19.9	19.8	19.7	19.4	18.8	19.5
1996	17.7	17.9	18.2	19.4	19.7	20.0	20.0	20.1	19.9	20.2	20.1	19.5	19.4
1997	19.2	19.2	19.6	20.1	20.4	20.8	21.0	21.0	21.0	21.0	20.9	20.3	20.4
1998	19.8	19.9	20.1	20.9	21.1	21.3	21.4	21.5	21.5	20.9	21.0	20.5	20.8
1999	19.8	19.8	19.9	20.3	20.7	20.8	20.3	20.5	20.5	20.4	20.3	19.8	20.3
2000	18.9	18.8	19.2	19.2	19.3	19.7	19.9	19.9	19.9	19.6	19.4	19.0	19.4
2001	18.6	18.6	18.9	19.2	19.7	20.0	20.1	20.2	20.0	19.9	19.7	19.3	19.5
2002	18.7	18.7	18.8	18.9	19.2	19.4	18.9	19.3	18.9	18.8	18.4	17.8	18.8
2003	17.2	17.1	17.3	17.5	17.8	18.1	18.2	18.3	18.3	18.4	18.3	17.7	17.9
Construction													
1990	205.9	203.9	212.2	220.6	231.9	239.4	241.4	242.7	238.6	233.2	225.0	211.5	225.5
1991	187.5	182.1	186.3	198.2	208.3	215.7	218.9	220.7	216.2	214.0	206.7	194.5	204.1
1992	176.6	171.9	177.3	191.1	200.7	208.8	213.6	214.7	211.7	211.9	203.0	191.0	197.7
1993	174.3	172.0	171.9	187.2	198.2	204.2	212.0	212.3	212.1	211.2	205.6	196.2	196.4
1994	168.4	165.7	173.3	194.0	206.9	214.0	218.1	220.8	220.6	220.2	215.3	204.9	201.9
1995	184.2	175.2	184.0	197.8	203.5	211.0	214.3	217.8	216.1	212.2	203.9	191.4	201.0
1996	165.7	170.2	179.1	194.9	206.8	216.2	220.8	224.0	220.7	221.7	216.5	204.3	203.4
1997	188.0	186.2	193.5	208.0	215.6	223.4	229.5	230.4	227.0	227.6	221.3	210.9	213.5
1998	193.2	191.3	197.1	215.4	222.8	231.4	237.8	238.2	234.2	235.0	230.2	222.6	220.8
1999	203.2	205.9	211.2	228.8	238.9	247.1	251.9	251.1	248.4	247.4	243.9	235.6	234.5
2000	220.1	215.5	229.9	244.6	254.1	261.3	263.5	264.9	261.9	258.2	252.4	241.2	247.3
2001	225.8	225.0	232.3	244.3	255.3	263.5	265.9	267.4	262.7	259.0	252.8	244.7	249.9
2002	225.0	224.5	231.6	243.5	253.0	260.4	263.6	265.4	260.0	258.2	251.8	240.4	248.1
2003	223.8	218.3	226.1	239.6	251.0	256.7	260.7	262.7	258.6	256.2	250.0	237.4	245.1

Employment by Industry: Pennsylvania—*Continued*

(Numbers in thousands. Not seasonally adjusted.)

Industry	January	February	March	April	May	June	July	August	September	October	November	December	Annual Average
STATEWIDE—*Continued*													
Manufacturing													
1990	952.7	948.7	950.4	948.7	949.8	955.7	947.2	951.7	949.0	941.6	937.0	933.1	947.1
1991	918.4	909.7	907.1	907.8	905.9	913.4	903.7	912.8	911.2	908.3	905.6	901.4	908.8
1992	888.2	882.9	884.1	888.0	890.6	896.0	889.1	890.8	890.1	887.1	883.6	880.8	887.6
1993	871.4	871.2	872.4	871.7	873.9	877.9	874.8	879.3	878.9	878.0	877.5	877.5	875.4
1994	867.3	865.0	869.4	868.1	872.0	881.3	880.2	885.5	886.2	885.6	886.8	887.7	877.9
1995	877.3	876.0	878.4	877.0	878.5	884.4	877.9	882.6	881.3	878.4	875.4	874.3	878.5
1996	853.6	857.8	859.4	863.2	864.5	870.9	865.5	868.6	867.8	867.7	869.3	869.7	864.8
1997	857.3	857.9	859.9	862.5	866.3	873.9	870.7	875.2	875.8	875.2	875.2	876.5	868.9
1998	869.7	869.3	871.2	873.5	875.4	879.4	868.0	872.3	870.5	871.8	870.7	870.2	871.8
1999	860.5	859.1	861.2	862.3	862.6	868.8	859.0	862.3	861.2	863.3	864.3	865.4	862.5
2000	858.7	856.3	860.7	860.1	859.8	870.7	868.2	869.0	866.1	860.3	858.3	859.6	862.3
2001	849.7	844.6	842.6	835.9	829.2	829.7	817.7	816.0	809.6	797.2	789.7	785.6	820.6
2002	772.1	768.4	767.4	764.0	762.5	766.9	759.4	759.1	755.0	749.1	743.1	739.8	758.9
2003	730.5	722.9	721.0	718.5	718.3	720.7	713.4	713.2	711.0	707.5	705.0	703.7	715.5
Service-providing													
1990	3902.4	3927.3	3954.9	3970.1	3992.9	3991.3	3949.6	3942.0	3980.6	3997.5	4012.6	4016.3	3969.8
1991	3896.2	3914.7	3937.2	3951.4	3965.9	3963.0	3906.0	3903.2	3942.4	3969.8	3994.4	4001.4	3945.5
1992	3883.0	3906.2	3928.2	3964.3	3990.7	3988.0	3950.5	3939.8	3970.2	4014.7	4027.3	4036.3	3966.6
1993	3934.2	3970.8	3977.3	4026.8	4050.2	4043.9	4009.5	4003.9	4039.4	4081.9	4100.9	4115.9	4029.6
1994	3973.8	4003.5	4043.5	4087.6	4114.3	4120.5	4071.9	4069.9	4116.9	4147.1	4170.8	4184.5	4092.0
1995	4050.4	4088.6	4120.9	4151.9	4175.2	4177.5	4111.8	4123.1	4168.8	4206.5	4230.7	4244.7	4154.2
1996	4075.6	4146.3	4176.0	4219.6	4245.1	4232.4	4189.1	4193.8	4233.2	4278.7	4307.6	4325.5	4218.6
1997	4198.5	4231.3	4258.6	4292.6	4321.2	4308.9	4270.8	4261.6	4322.0	4369.2	4395.5	4414.6	4303.7
1998	4277.5	4314.3	4340.2	4383.0	4417.2	4388.7	4346.7	4340.1	4389.9	4436.2	4463.0	4480.2	4381.4
1999	4348.1	4395.4	4427.5	4467.7	4487.7	4486.0	4453.4	4445.4	4483.8	4517.5	4544.2	4569.8	4468.9
2000	4449.5	4486.4	4525.9	4566.2	4597.1	4588.5	4536.7	4519.9	4586.5	4606.7	4636.5	4647.3	4562.3
2001	4519.0	4552.8	4582.7	4602.9	4624.9	4625.5	4548.7	4551.2	4598.6	4616.8	4641.2	4645.3	4592.5
2002	4533.8	4563.4	4596.0	4620.6	4646.1	4645.7	4572.4	4570.4	4627.9	4654.9	4675.9	4672.0	4614.9
2003	4551.0	4572.1	4604.9	4635.4	4664.1	4658.9	4587.7	4578.8	4629.1	4655.1	4674.6	4673.2	4623.7
Trade, transportation, and utilities													
1990	1052.3	1041.5	1044.5	1046.9	1053.3	1056.6	1044.5	1047.1	1049.9	1054.5	1068.8	1076.6	1053.0
1991	1026.1	1006.4	1008.0	1008.4	1013.4	1019.1	1006.3	1008.7	1011.2	1017.5	1036.4	1045.2	1017.2
1992	1004.5	988.4	989.6	998.2	1008.9	1010.5	997.1	997.2	1004.0	1017.4	1033.4	1047.1	1008.0
1993	1010.9	1001.2	997.8	1006.8	1013.3	1015.8	1009.4	1011.8	1018.8	1034.2	1048.3	1063.5	1019.3
1994	1020.5	1006.9	1013.8	1015.1	1030.1	1034.2	1023.6	1026.8	1037.2	1053.7	1073.4	1086.4	1035.1
1995	1039.6	1026.8	1032.4	1037.1	1043.5	1046.8	1035.3	1040.5	1047.0	1060.4	1078.9	1093.1	1048.5
1996	1041.3	1035.4	1038.1	1044.3	1053.3	1055.4	1044.8	1048.0	1055.9	1074.7	1096.1	1112.3	1058.3
1997	1068.8	1056.4	1061.1	1059.6	1066.7	1070.0	1058.6	1051.2	1070.7	1087.7	1108.8	1124.7	1073.7
1998	1075.0	1059.5	1062.8	1072.3	1080.5	1081.8	1072.2	1072.8	1082.7	1099.0	1120.0	1134.5	1084.4
1999	1086.8	1078.4	1082.3	1095.1	1103.3	1111.1	1104.3	1104.0	1114.8	1124.3	1145.1	1164.3	1109.5
2000	1118.9	1108.0	1113.1	1125.8	1131.8	1137.9	1125.9	1130.3	1138.3	1149.3	1171.6	1186.2	1136.4
2001	1136.3	1119.0	1122.9	1122.7	1128.5	1132.3	1115.2	1116.9	1122.9	1130.4	1150.4	1161.5	1129.9
2002	1117.9	1101.1	1107.7	1108.3	1118.5	1122.1	1108.9	1111.4	1115.7	1124.5	1142.3	1155.0	1119.5
2003	1107.8	1092.1	1097.1	1104.5	1113.9	1119.9	1108.3	1108.1	1112.5	1122.4	1138.4	1149.3	1114.5
Wholesale trade													
1990	224.8	224.3	225.7	225.4	226.0	227.5	226.1	225.5	223.7	221.6	221.9	221.1	224.5
1991	218.9	216.7	217.2	217.6	218.0	218.6	217.6	217.2	215.6	214.1	214.2	214.5	216.7
1992	210.5	209.2	209.5	211.2	212.4	213.2	212.5	211.5	210.0	211.3	210.1	210.2	211.0
1993	207.4	207.4	207.6	209.2	209.9	210.5	210.3	210.4	209.1	209.4	209.4	210.2	209.2
1994	206.1	205.5	206.9	207.4	208.5	209.7	209.7	210.4	210.1	209.8	210.5	210.6	208.8
1995	207.9	208.0	209.7	211.1	211.6	212.2	211.9	212.4	211.8	211.2	211.7	212.6	211.0
1996	207.8	209.0	209.8	210.0	211.1	212.1	211.4	211.4	210.7	212.2	213.6	214.5	211.1
1997	210.2	210.8	212.2	213.2	214.1	215.3	215.0	215.1	214.7	216.0	216.9	217.8	214.3
1998	213.0	213.1	214.2	217.8	218.3	219.2	218.3	217.8	216.7	218.4	219.0	218.7	217.0
1999	216.9	216.7	217.5	220.6	221.4	223.3	222.0	222.7	223.5	223.7	223.6	224.7	221.4
2000	220.7	221.0	222.7	227.3	227.3	229.1	228.2	228.4	227.4	228.1	228.3	228.6	226.4
2001	226.7	226.4	227.1	227.5	227.8	229.5	229.5	229.2	227.8	226.3	226.3	227.4	227.6
2002	225.1	224.0	224.9	225.0	226.5	228.0	227.6	227.0	225.6	226.2	226.5	227.2	226.1
2003	225.1	224.9	226.4	226.8	228.1	228.9	228.5	227.5	226.4	226.3	226.0	226.4	226.8
Retail trade													
1990	639.4	629.0	629.3	625.8	629.8	632.1	628.4	630.8	629.2	635.3	650.3	659.2	634.9
1991	616.0	599.3	600.4	600.2	603.4	609.8	603.7	605.8	602.8	608.3	627.0	635.4	609.3
1992	603.0	588.6	588.7	593.9	600.9	602.0	598.1	598.8	598.3	606.8	623.3	634.7	603.1
1993	603.7	593.9	589.5	594.3	599.1	601.1	602.2	605.2	605.1	614.2	629.2	644.1	606.8
1994	609.7	597.1	601.4	606.0	612.2	614.6	611.5	615.4	618.7	628.9	649.1	663.0	619.0
1995	626.7	613.9	616.7	619.1	624.4	628.2	623.0	628.0	626.6	633.7	652.6	666.3	629.9
1996	626.0	618.1	619.0	624.9	632.1	634.1	630.0	632.0	632.5	644.1	664.6	681.0	636.5
1997	646.7	633.3	635.1	633.0	638.8	641.7	640.3	643.2	641.5	652.5	673.3	688.4	647.3
1998	648.9	634.7	636.2	639.5	646.1	649.2	645.0	645.8	647.3	658.2	679.1	693.5	652.0
1999	654.3	646.1	648.4	654.2	660.4	666.3	669.6	669.4	669.0	671.7	692.9	710.1	667.7
2000	670.8	660.2	662.2	669.4	674.3	679.8	674.9	679.5	679.0	684.1	706.4	721.5	680.2
2001	678.9	662.5	665.7	663.1	667.3	671.8	663.6	666.6	664.0	668.2	689.1	700.8	671.8
2002	665.4	650.5	655.4	654.4	661.8	666.1	661.0	663.7	659.3	662.5	681.4	694.7	664.7
2003	656.5	642.2	645.8	651.3	658.0	664.6	661.8	663.5	659.2	665.0	682.3	694.0	662.0

Employment by Industry: Pennsylvania—*Continued*

(Numbers in thousands. Not seasonally adjusted.)

Industry	January	February	March	April	May	June	July	August	September	October	November	December	Annual Average
STATEWIDE—*Continued*													
Transportation and utilities													
1990	188.1	188.2	189.5	195.7	197.5	197.0	190.0	190.8	197.0	197.6	196.6	196.3	193.7
1991	191.2	190.4	190.4	190.6	192.0	190.7	185.0	185.7	192.8	195.1	195.2	195.3	191.2
1992	191.0	190.6	191.4	193.1	195.6	195.3	186.5	186.9	195.7	199.3	200.0	202.2	194.0
1993	199.8	199.9	200.7	203.3	204.3	204.2	196.9	196.2	204.6	210.6	209.7	209.2	203.3
1994	204.7	204.3	205.5	201.7	209.4	209.9	202.4	201.0	208.4	215.0	213.8	212.8	207.4
1995	205.0	204.9	206.0	206.9	207.5	206.4	200.4	200.1	208.6	215.5	214.6	214.2	207.5
1996	207.5	208.3	209.3	209.4	210.1	209.2	203.4	204.6	212.7	218.4	217.9	216.8	210.6
1997	211.9	212.3	213.8	213.4	213.8	213.0	203.3	192.9	214.5	219.2	218.6	218.5	212.1
1998	213.1	211.7	212.4	215.0	216.1	213.4	208.9	209.2	218.7	222.4	221.9	222.3	215.4
1999	215.6	215.6	216.4	220.3	221.5	221.5	212.7	211.9	222.3	228.9	228.6	229.5	220.4
2000	227.4	226.8	228.2	229.1	230.2	229.0	222.8	222.4	231.9	237.1	236.9	236.1	229.8
2001	230.7	230.1	230.1	232.1	233.4	231.0	222.1	221.1	231.1	235.9	235.0	233.3	230.5
2002	227.4	226.6	227.4	228.9	230.2	228.0	220.3	220.7	230.8	235.8	234.4	233.1	228.6
2003	226.2	225.0	224.9	226.4	227.8	226.4	218.0	217.1	226.9	231.1	230.1	228.9	225.7
Information													
1990	107.7	107.9	108.2	108.1	108.9	109.6	109.5	109.6	109.2	109.0	109.3	109.9	108.9
1991	108.5	107.9	108.0	107.3	107.4	107.6	107.9	108.1	107.2	106.9	108.0	109.3	107.8
1992	107.3	106.8	107.2	106.5	107.3	107.9	108.2	107.4	106.1	105.8	105.1	105.5	106.8
1993	105.5	105.0	104.6	105.4	105.4	106.0	105.7	105.7	104.8	105.5	105.5	106.2	105.4
1994	106.8	106.5	107.4	107.2	108.2	109.1	109.7	109.9	108.9	109.5	110.2	110.1	108.6
1995	109.6	110.1	110.9	111.9	112.6	113.8	112.7	113.1	112.7	111.8	111.7	112.4	111.9
1996	110.7	111.3	111.7	112.8	113.2	114.2	114.2	114.8	114.1	115.0	115.8	116.7	113.7
1997	114.6	115.2	115.9	117.3	118.6	119.2	119.9	120.3	119.5	120.7	121.3	122.2	118.7
1998	121.2	121.6	122.3	121.3	122.0	122.9	123.6	124.3	123.7	123.7	124.7	125.3	123.1
1999	125.9	126.2	126.6	127.7	128.9	130.0	129.4	130.0	129.9	129.0	130.1	131.1	128.7
2000	132.3	133.0	133.6	133.1	134.5	136.6	138.4	129.2	138.7	138.4	140.0	141.1	135.7
2001	138.0	137.9	137.9	136.2	136.3	136.6	136.3	135.2	133.0	132.4	132.6	132.7	135.4
2002	130.4	130.0	130.7	129.1	129.7	129.4	128.1	127.7	126.1	125.5	125.8	125.7	128.2
2003	124.1	123.5	124.3	123.6	124.0	124.5	123.9	124.1	122.6	122.0	122.2	122.0	123.4
Financial activities													
1990	323.3	323.2	324.0	322.2	324.8	326.6	327.5	327.2	324.5	321.9	321.5	322.7	324.1
1991	320.6	320.5	321.8	320.1	321.4	324.6	325.4	325.6	322.8	321.3	321.4	322.3	322.3
1992	317.7	317.6	318.5	319.0	321.5	323.9	325.9	325.3	323.5	319.2	318.8	320.4	320.9
1993	316.0	316.4	317.1	317.5	319.4	322.3	323.4	325.2	323.5	322.4	322.7	322.0	320.7
1994	320.4	320.1	321.5	322.2	324.2	326.3	325.9	326.1	323.5	320.5	318.9	319.2	322.4
1995	316.6	316.4	317.2	318.5	319.7	322.5	322.5	322.7	321.8	319.5	320.0	320.5	319.8
1996	316.6	317.6	318.7	322.3	322.7	326.3	327.3	328.5	327.5	324.0	324.6	327.0	323.6
1997	322.6	319.0	320.8	320.8	323.1	326.0	321.8	323.4	320.8	323.1	324.0	325.8	322.6
1998	324.1	323.4	324.6	327.7	329.5	332.0	332.7	332.9	329.2	332.1	333.1	336.1	329.8
1999	337.6	332.0	332.4	333.7	334.5	337.0	338.7	338.1	335.9	333.3	333.6	336.0	335.2
2000	335.3	334.8	335.3	336.4	337.4	341.6	341.5	340.8	337.8	337.2	338.2	340.5	338.1
2001	338.8	338.7	340.0	338.3	338.7	341.5	340.7	340.2	336.4	335.2	334.8	336.2	338.3
2002	334.1	333.9	334.9	334.5	335.7	339.1	339.5	340.0	336.8	334.8	335.1	336.5	336.2
2003	335.3	335.2	336.1	336.1	338.2	340.5	341.6	341.7	338.0	336.6	337.3	338.2	337.9
Professional and business services													
1990	442.8	445.7	451.6	454.2	456.9	463.0	461.4	463.0	461.8	457.0	455.2	452.7	455.4
1991	445.5	446.3	451.7	452.3	452.7	456.5	451.9	454.1	452.3	453.6	452.0	450.3	451.6
1992	443.4	443.5	448.0	455.0	455.3	460.3	462.8	463.3	462.4	462.8	459.8	458.0	456.2
1993	452.2	454.7	456.6	466.8	470.3	471.0	474.9	475.1	474.2	474.8	473.6	472.5	468.1
1994	454.6	458.2	466.2	476.3	478.1	483.5	485.6	489.6	488.3	485.2	485.5	485.5	478.1
1995	473.2	477.1	484.3	489.4	491.6	496.9	496.0	501.1	499.7	500.9	501.2	500.0	492.6
1996	481.7	491.2	497.5	506.8	511.9	516.1	517.3	520.5	517.4	520.6	521.9	519.5	510.2
1997	510.6	513.5	520.2	530.3	534.9	543.4	545.8	550.4	548.7	555.1	556.5	558.1	539.0
1998	546.1	548.9	556.6	565.7	572.1	578.6	577.6	581.3	577.7	581.2	583.0	583.9	571.1
1999	572.0	576.4	589.6	589.3	591.6	598.4	602.0	604.5	600.6	599.4	600.4	604.6	594.1
2000	588.0	591.3	602.3	610.0	610.3	618.8	622.3	624.2	620.8	615.8	615.8	615.3	611.2
2001	602.6	605.8	611.1	617.0	618.1	623.9	614.6	619.3	614.9	610.8	607.4	602.4	612.3
2002	587.9	588.8	595.6	603.7	605.9	612.2	610.5	614.4	610.0	609.5	609.3	607.3	604.6
2003	588.6	586.3	591.9	599.7	600.9	602.3	601.5	604.6	602.9	600.6	597.9	593.7	597.6
Educational and health services													
1990	718.5	733.9	737.9	738.4	731.1	720.7	719.4	719.0	741.5	757.8	761.2	761.7	736.8
1991	743.3	762.4	766.4	769.2	761.4	750.9	745.6	745.4	768.9	785.2	790.2	790.4	764.9
1992	771.1	789.2	792.9	797.2	791.0	778.5	775.5	772.1	793.8	814.0	815.9	815.0	792.2
1993	796.8	815.3	817.3	815.4	809.0	796.3	794.5	792.1	814.3	831.8	834.4	835.4	812.7
1994	809.8	829.8	834.8	842.6	834.3	820.8	816.2	814.7	838.1	850.5	853.3	853.3	833.2
1995	824.6	847.9	853.0	853.9	845.4	832.1	819.9	820.5	844.3	862.3	866.3	866.6	844.7
1996	835.4	861.9	865.9	868.3	858.6	844.9	839.8	837.7	861.5	878.1	883.5	883.3	859.9
1997	855.6	879.6	882.5	887.2	877.5	863.2	861.1	859.9	883.6	898.9	903.5	903.7	879.7
1998	876.5	903.7	906.9	911.6	903.1	885.4	876.7	870.7	893.4	910.4	914.5	912.8	897.1
1999	883.6	912.9	913.7	914.4	905.6	889.1	884.5	881.1	894.0	918.4	923.4	921.0	903.5
2000	900.8	924.2	923.2	922.7	914.7	902.1	895.9	894.1	917.8	932.0	938.8	937.2	917.0
2001	915.9	939.6	944.4	943.3	935.6	926.8	922.1	921.0	942.6	954.4	962.2	961.1	939.1
2002	947.3	969.6	973.3	970.0	961.7	951.4	943.8	941.2	963.8	979.1	984.2	975.3	963.4
2003	964.1	984.0	988.2	987.3	978.6	966.6	958.0	953.8	976.3	990.5	997.2	992.6	978.1

Employment by Industry: Pennsylvania—*Continued*

(Numbers in thousands. Not seasonally adjusted.)

Industry	January	February	March	April	May	June	July	August	September	October	November	December	Annual Average
STATEWIDE—*Continued*													
Leisure and hospitality													
1990	360.7	360.3	366.8	373.6	389.0	401.3	406.4	408.6	396.3	380.9	375.0	373.9	382.7
1991	355.7	356.3	362.2	375.1	393.6	404.8	406.0	407.8	392.7	374.7	371.6	370.4	380.9
1992	355.0	355.8	361.7	375.7	396.5	404.8	408.8	410.8	398.2	385.5	379.3	377.2	384.1
1993	363.4	365.6	365.6	387.2	407.3	417.4	419.0	419.8	406.8	391.8	385.1	383.9	392.7
1994	365.1	362.9	370.7	387.9	408.0	421.1	423.0	423.9	409.3	393.8	388.1	387.5	395.1
1995	373.4	373.6	382.0	396.2	417.6	432.4	433.0	435.9	423.8	407.2	401.6	399.6	406.4
1996	377.3	380.7	389.3	406.3	427.8	441.0	440.9	443.0	425.7	412.7	406.0	406.1	413.1
1997	390.3	390.7	395.8	413.7	437.1	448.7	452.6	453.5	438.3	422.0	414.9	414.5	422.7
1998	397.0	399.9	405.6	420.0	444.0	456.9	458.5	457.7	441.3	429.1	420.0	420.4	429.2
1999	402.2	407.3	413.4	434.9	455.3	471.5	473.3	471.3	449.4	440.6	431.3	433.2	440.3
2000	412.5	414.5	426.0	441.7	461.4	477.9	480.2	480.1	463.0	448.2	440.1	440.2	448.8
2001	419.6	423.5	431.0	445.1	468.7	486.6	486.8	487.4	465.1	451.3	444.3	443.7	454.4
2002	426.7	429.2	439.3	457.2	480.4	496.2	496.6	498.5	480.3	466.6	456.6	455.3	465.2
2003	435.7	433.4	443.0	458.6	483.6	498.7	500.9	502.0	482.4	468.3	460.2	460.1	468.9
Other services													
1990	206.1	206.7	208.7	208.9	210.2	212.9	212.7	212.8	210.3	209.4	209.2	209.1	209.8
1991	203.8	203.4	204.7	205.6	207.1	208.6	209.1	208.1	205.0	206.0	205.4	206.1	206.1
1992	202.3	202.3	203.8	204.6	206.5	208.0	208.7	207.2	205.3	207.1	206.6	207.0	205.8
1993	204.3	204.4	205.0	207.3	209.2	210.8	212.1	211.7	209.3	210.3	211.0	211.8	208.9
1994	205.9	206.5	209.0	212.7	213.8	215.7	216.9	216.6	214.3	214.8	216.1	215.8	213.2
1995	211.8	212.5	214.2	216.1	217.7	220.3	221.1	221.5	219.1	220.6	221.8	223.2	218.3
1996	217.4	221.0	223.0	224.9	227.4	230.4	231.7	231.3	228.5	230.0	230.6	231.1	227.3
1997	228.1	229.3	231.0	230.4	231.8	234.1	237.2	236.5	233.1	233.8	233.8	234.7	232.8
1998	230.4	230.4	231.7	234.5	236.3	238.4	239.2	238.1	234.3	235.8	236.2	237.3	235.2
1999	233.8	236.3	238.0	239.9	240.1	243.8	247.2	246.4	244.6	243.3	244.0	246.1	242.0
2000	243.2	244.2	248.0	249.8	250.6	253.8	254.3	253.0	250.2	250.2	250.6	251.4	249.9
2001	247.2	248.3	252.5	253.3	256.0	259.3	258.7	258.0	254.8	255.3	256.2	257.4	254.8
2002	254.0	255.4	257.3	258.2	259.8	263.2	262.8	261.9	258.6	258.6	258.4	259.2	259.0
2003	255.9	255.5	258.1	259.4	261.7	264.5	264.8	263.0	258.6	259.3	260.1	260.9	260.2
Government													
1990	691.0	708.1	713.2	717.8	718.7	700.6	668.2	654.7	687.1	707.0	712.4	709.7	699.0
1991	692.7	711.5	714.4	713.4	708.9	690.9	653.8	645.4	682.3	704.6	709.4	707.4	694.6
1992	681.7	702.6	706.5	708.1	703.7	694.1	663.5	656.5	676.9	702.9	708.4	706.1	692.6
1993	685.1	708.2	713.3	720.4	716.3	704.3	670.5	662.5	687.7	711.1	720.3	720.6	701.7
1994	690.7	712.6	720.1	723.6	717.6	709.8	671.0	662.3	697.3	719.1	725.3	726.7	706.3
1995	701.6	724.2	726.9	728.8	727.1	712.7	671.3	667.8	700.4	723.8	729.2	729.3	711.9
1996	695.2	727.2	731.8	733.9	730.2	704.1	673.1	670.0	702.6	723.6	729.1	729.5	712.5
1997	707.9	727.6	731.3	733.3	731.5	704.3	673.8	666.4	707.3	727.9	732.7	730.9	714.6
1998	707.2	726.9	729.7	729.9	729.7	692.7	666.2	662.3	707.6	724.9	731.5	729.9	711.5
1999	706.2	725.9	731.5	732.7	728.4	705.1	674.0	670.0	714.6	729.2	736.3	733.5	715.6
2000	718.5	736.4	744.4	746.7	756.4	719.8	678.2	668.2	719.9	735.6	741.4	735.4	725.1
2001	720.6	740.0	742.9	747.0	743.0	718.5	674.3	673.2	728.9	747.0	753.3	750.3	728.3
2002	735.5	755.4	757.2	759.6	754.4	732.1	682.2	675.3	736.6	756.3	764.2	757.7	738.9
2003	739.5	762.1	766.2	766.2	763.2	741.9	688.7	681.5	735.8	755.4	761.3	756.4	743.2
Federal government													
1990	132.1	133.0	134.7	138.7	143.1	140.0	138.4	134.6	131.7	130.7	129.6	129.9	134.7
1991	130.1	130.1	130.6	131.4	130.2	131.5	131.0	129.3	128.5	127.3	126.9	127.9	129.6
1992	127.4	127.8	128.1	129.2	129.1	128.6	126.8	126.2	125.6	125.1	124.2	125.9	127.0
1993	123.9	124.1	124.2	127.6	127.2	127.8	126.3	126.4	126.5	124.0	124.3	127.2	125.8
1994	124.4	124.9	125.5	126.8	125.3	125.2	123.1	123.0	123.2	121.8	121.4	123.4	124.0
1995	120.3	120.9	121.4	122.9	121.5	121.4	120.7	120.3	116.6	115.4	114.6	116.1	119.3
1996	115.6	117.1	117.5	119.3	118.0	117.9	116.6	116.0	114.7	113.9	114.5	116.4	116.5
1997	114.3	115.0	115.6	117.5	115.7	115.5	114.4	113.6	112.2	112.2	112.6	115.9	114.5
1998	112.3	113.9	113.5	114.7	115.3	113.4	112.9	113.5	112.8	112.5	112.5	114.6	113.5
1999	110.9	112.6	113.8	114.6	113.0	112.6	111.8	111.7	111.3	110.5	110.4	111.8	112.1
2000	109.3	111.3	116.7	118.4	132.8	119.0	119.6	111.4	109.0	107.2	107.7	109.0	114.3
2001	108.4	108.8	109.5	110.8	110.1	110.2	109.9	108.9	108.2	107.3	108.0	109.1	109.1
2002	108.5	108.7	109.3	109.9	109.3	109.1	108.4	107.3	107.3	107.4	107.7	109.2	108.5
2003	108.2	108.7	109.7	109.9	109.2	107.5	107.2	106.2	105.6	105.1	105.4	106.8	107.5
State government													
1990	151.5	160.0	160.7	160.7	154.5	143.4	145.2	145.4	157.3	160.9	161.2	159.3	155.0
1991	149.8	159.1	158.3	157.8	151.1	140.6	141.3	141.9	152.4	156.2	154.6	153.0	151.3
1992	139.4	149.0	148.2	149.2	142.1	133.7	135.2	136.6	146.2	151.1	152.1	150.9	144.5
1993	142.6	154.7	154.5	159.3	151.3	144.3	145.9	145.9	156.7	162.3	163.2	161.1	153.5
1994	147.7	160.4	161.1	161.8	154.8	147.0	146.8	147.7	158.4	162.8	163.9	163.3	156.3
1995	150.3	163.8	162.9	162.6	157.7	147.1	146.5	149.8	159.2	165.8	166.1	165.5	158.1
1996	146.7	164.4	164.7	166.0	159.2	147.4	148.4	149.2	159.3	163.6	164.7	164.2	158.2
1997	152.5	162.2	161.7	162.5	156.8	145.1	147.1	147.0	161.0	165.1	165.6	162.6	157.4
1998	153.9	162.1	161.3	160.9	156.0	137.4	142.2	144.4	158.5	159.6	161.7	159.6	154.8
1999	150.3	158.3	158.0	159.5	153.6	140.3	141.5	143.1	155.5	157.4	159.1	155.8	152.7
2000	152.6	159.4	158.1	159.0	153.4	141.7	141.4	142.0	156.8	160.2	160.2	154.1	153.2
2001	151.5	161.0	160.4	162.1	157.4	145.2	145.7	146.8	160.3	164.2	164.0	160.3	156.6
2002	154.8	164.2	163.4	165.1	156.6	148.5	145.9	147.7	161.4	165.9	168.4	161.9	158.7
2003	154.4	166.2	166.2	165.8	159.9	149.0	148.1	148.7	159.8	164.3	165.2	161.5	159.1

Employment by Industry: Pennsylvania—*Continued*

(Numbers in thousands. Not seasonally adjusted.)

Industry	January	February	March	April	May	June	July	August	September	October	November	December	Annual Average
STATEWIDE—*Continued*													
Local government													
1990	407.4	415.1	417.8	418.4	421.1	417.2	384.6	374.7	398.1	415.4	421.6	420.5	409.3
1991	412.8	422.3	425.5	424.2	427.6	418.8	381.5	374.2	401.4	421.1	427.9	426.5	413.7
1992	414.9	425.8	430.2	429.7	432.5	431.8	401.5	393.7	405.1	426.7	432.1	429.3	421.1
1993	418.6	429.4	434.6	433.5	437.8	432.2	398.3	390.2	404.5	424.8	432.8	432.3	422.4
1994	418.6	427.3	433.5	435.0	437.5	437.6	401.1	391.6	415.7	434.5	440.0	440.0	426.0
1995	431.0	439.5	442.6	443.3	447.9	444.2	404.1	397.7	424.6	442.6	448.5	447.7	434.5
1996	432.9	445.7	449.6	448.6	453.0	438.8	408.1	404.8	428.6	446.1	449.9	448.9	437.9
1997	441.1	450.4	454.0	453.3	459.0	443.7	412.3	405.8	434.1	450.6	454.5	452.4	442.6
1998	441.0	450.9	454.9	454.3	458.4	441.9	411.1	404.4	436.3	452.8	457.3	455.7	443.3
1999	445.0	455.0	459.7	458.6	461.8	452.2	420.7	415.2	447.8	461.3	466.8	465.9	450.8
2000	456.6	465.7	469.6	469.3	470.2	459.1	417.2	414.8	454.1	468.2	473.5	472.3	457.6
2001	460.7	470.2	473.0	474.1	475.5	463.1	418.7	417.5	460.4	475.5	481.3	480.9	462.6
2002	472.2	482.5	484.5	484.6	488.5	474.5	427.9	420.3	467.9	483.0	488.1	486.6	471.7
2003	476.9	487.2	490.3	490.5	494.1	485.4	433.4	426.6	470.4	486.0	490.7	488.1	476.6
ALLENTOWN-BETHLEHEM													
Total nonfarm													
1990	249.7	250.1	252.7	253.2	255.3	257.3	252.4	254.4	255.7	256.6	256.3	256.3	254.2
1991	248.2	249.4	250.3	251.6	253.6	255.7	251.7	253.6	253.6	252.3	252.9	254.0	252.2
1992	244.6	246.1	247.5	251.2	253.4	252.3	248.8	248.6	251.4	253.4	254.2	253.4	250.4
1993	247.6	250.4	250.6	253.5	255.6	255.2	249.6	250.2	253.1	256.2	256.5	257.1	253.0
1994	247.8	248.9	252.1	255.0	257.1	258.3	254.8	255.9	258.3	258.8	260.2	260.2	255.6
1995	253.1	254.0	256.5	257.3	259.4	260.2	255.8	255.3	258.6	260.1	260.7	260.9	257.7
1996	249.3	253.8	255.4	259.2	261.4	261.8	257.7	257.5	260.3	262.8	264.4	264.6	259.0
1997	260.0	261.5	262.9	264.4	267.8	268.3	265.8	265.9	267.6	271.2	271.5	272.4	266.6
1998	266.8	268.2	270.7	273.4	276.3	275.9	272.3	272.8	274.8	275.6	276.1	277.1	273.3
1999	269.2	272.7	275.1	277.7	280.5	282.2	278.8	280.4	280.8	282.8	283.5	284.7	279.0
2000	278.7	280.2	283.4	285.4	289.0	291.8	287.1	287.0	288.2	290.0	291.3	292.3	287.0
2001	287.1	287.6	290.2	289.3	292.1	294.4	288.4	289.5	289.8	289.4	288.9	288.8	289.6
2002	282.3	282.9	286.3	286.2	289.3	290.9	285.9	286.6	288.9	288.8	288.1	287.7	287.0
2003	282.9	282.4	285.3	287.4	290.3	291.1	285.9	285.5	287.9	289.4	288.5	287.2	287.0
Total private													
1990	223.4	223.0	225.2	225.6	227.4	229.6	226.5	228.7	229.4	229.8	228.9	228.7	227.2
1991	220.9	221.3	222.3	223.9	226.1	228.3	225.2	227.3	227.4	225.1	225.3	226.4	225.0
1992	217.8	218.3	219.5	223.0	225.1	225.3	224.0	223.9	225.4	225.4	226.2	225.2	223.3
1993	220.0	221.9	222.0	224.6	226.6	227.2	224.4	225.0	226.0	227.4	227.6	227.8	225.0
1994	219.8	220.1	223.0	225.8	227.8	229.3	227.3	228.8	230.5	229.4	230.3	230.5	226.9
1995	223.6	224.0	226.3	226.9	228.8	229.9	228.2	228.5	229.9	230.2	230.4	230.6	228.1
1996	220.2	223.6	224.8	228.4	230.3	231.4	229.9	230.2	231.0	232.4	233.4	233.6	229.1
1997	230.0	230.4	231.8	233.3	236.4	237.5	237.6	237.9	238.0	240.4	240.5	241.1	236.2
1998	236.3	236.7	239.0	241.6	244.5	244.9	243.6	244.3	244.7	244.7	244.7	245.8	242.6
1999	238.5	241.1	243.0	246.0	248.6	249.7	249.4	250.6	250.0	250.9	251.3	252.5	247.6
2000	247.0	247.8	250.5	252.6	255.4	258.5	257.0	257.2	257.2	257.2	258.4	259.3	254.8
2001	255.1	254.6	257.0	256.1	258.7	260.6	258.0	258.7	257.3	255.8	255.1	254.9	256.8
2002	249.4	249.2	252.2	252.2	255.1	256.4	255.0	256.1	255.8	254.9	253.9	253.7	253.7
2003	249.5	248.2	250.7	252.8	255.4	256.8	255.5	255.6	255.0	255.6	254.4	253.5	253.6
Goods-producing													
1990	72.2	71.5	72.3	72.1	72.4	73.8	71.7	73.5	73.4	72.3	72.2	71.6	72.4
1991	68.8	68.6	68.6	69.6	69.9	70.9	69.3	71.2	70.8	69.9	69.7	69.3	69.7
1992	66.8	66.2	66.9	67.0	67.4	67.9	67.7	68.2	68.5	67.9	67.8	66.9	67.4
1993	65.7	66.0	66.6	66.7	67.1	67.6	66.5	67.4	67.4	67.4	67.1	66.6	66.8
1994	65.0	64.3	64.9	65.5	66.1	66.9	65.8	67.1	66.8	66.2	66.3	66.0	65.9
1995	64.6	63.9	64.2	64.2	64.2	64.8	64.1	64.7	64.5	64.7	63.9	63.2	64.3
1996	59.9	60.6	60.9	61.9	62.3	63.1	62.4	62.9	62.5	63.4	63.6	63.1	62.2
1997	61.3	61.1	61.4	61.6	62.1	62.8	63.0	63.7	63.1	63.2	63.1	62.7	62.4
1998	61.7	61.3	61.8	62.7	62.3	63.6	62.1	63.1	62.8	62.2	62.1	62.2	62.3
1999	60.8	60.9	61.2	62.3	62.8	63.6	63.1	63.9	63.2	63.3	63.7	63.4	62.7
2000	62.6	62.1	63.0	63.1	63.6	64.7	64.1	65.2	65.0	64.2	64.7	64.7	63.9
2001	64.0	63.6	63.9	63.9	63.9	64.3	63.4	63.8	62.9	61.6	60.4	60.0	63.0
2002	59.1	59.0	59.3	59.1	59.5	59.9	59.2	59.2	58.4	57.5	56.7	56.0	58.6
2003	55.0	54.1	54.2	54.7	55.5	55.9	55.4	55.4	54.8	54.8	54.1	53.4	54.8
Construction and mining													
1990	11.2	10.8	11.3	11.8	12.1	12.7	12.8	12.8	12.7	12.5	12.1	11.5	12.0
1991	10.2	10.0	10.0	10.8	11.3	11.6	11.6	11.9	11.6	11.2	11.0	10.4	11.0
1992	9.3	8.9	9.1	9.2	9.7	10.1	10.3	10.4	10.2	10.1	9.9	9.5	9.7
1993	8.8	8.9	8.8	9.4	9.9	10.2	10.4	10.4	10.3	10.3	10.0	9.8	9.8
1994	8.8	8.6	8.6	9.7	10.4	10.7	10.8	11.1	11.1	10.8	10.7	10.4	10.1
1995	9.5	8.9	9.2	9.8	10.1	10.4	10.7	10.8	10.7	10.5	10.3	9.9	10.1
1996	8.8	9.0	9.4	9.9	10.4	10.7	11.0	11.0	10.6	10.8	10.7	10.3	10.2
1997	9.7	9.5	9.7	10.1	10.5	10.9	11.5	11.4	11.1	11.2	11.0	10.6	10.6
1998	9.8	9.7	9.9	10.9	11.1	11.5	11.8	12.0	12.0	11.8	11.6	11.4	11.1
1999	10.7	10.7	11.0	11.5	11.8	12.3	13.1	13.0	12.8	12.5	12.5	12.3	12.0
2000	11.8	11.3	11.9	12.3	12.6	13.1	13.5	13.6	13.4	13.2	13.2	12.8	12.7
2001	12.2	11.9	12.1	12.6	13.0	13.4	13.7	13.8	13.5	13.2	12.9	12.7	12.9
2002	11.8	11.8	12.3	13.1	13.4	13.9	14.0	13.8	13.4	13.2	13.2	12.8	13.1
2003	12.0	11.6	11.9	12.7	13.4	13.9	14.0	14.0	14.0	13.6	13.2	12.9	13.1

Employment by Industry: Pennsylvania—*Continued*

(Numbers in thousands. Not seasonally adjusted.)

Industry	January	February	March	April	May	June	July	August	September	October	November	December	Annual Average
ALLENTOWN-BETHLEHEM —*Continued*													
Manufacturing													
1990	61.0	60.7	61.0	60.3	60.3	61.1	58.9	60.7	60.7	59.8	60.1	60.1	60.4
1991	58.6	58.6	58.6	58.8	58.6	59.3	57.7	59.3	59.2	58.7	58.7	58.9	58.8
1992	57.5	57.3	57.8	57.8	57.7	57.8	57.4	57.8	58.3	57.8	57.9	57.4	57.7
1993	56.9	57.1	57.8	57.3	57.2	57.4	56.1	57.0	57.1	57.1	57.1	56.8	57.1
1994	56.2	55.7	56.3	55.8	55.7	56.2	55.0	56.0	55.7	55.4	55.6	55.6	55.8
1995	55.1	55.0	55.0	54.4	54.1	54.4	53.4	53.9	53.8	54.2	53.6	53.3	54.2
1996	51.1	51.6	51.5	52.0	51.9	52.4	51.4	51.9	51.9	52.6	52.9	52.8	52.0
1997	51.6	51.6	51.7	51.5	51.6	51.9	51.5	52.3	52.0	52.0	52.1	52.1	51.8
1998	51.9	51.6	51.9	51.8	51.2	52.1	50.3	51.1	50.8	50.4	50.5	50.8	51.2
1999	50.1	50.2	50.2	50.8	51.0	51.3	50.0	50.9	50.4	50.8	51.2	51.1	50.7
2000	50.8	50.8	51.1	50.8	51.0	51.6	50.6	51.6	51.6	51.0	51.5	51.9	51.2
2001	51.8	51.7	51.8	51.3	50.9	50.9	49.7	50.0	49.4	48.4	47.5	47.3	50.1
2002	47.3	47.2	47.0	46.0	46.1	46.0	45.2	45.4	45.0	44.3	43.5	43.2	45.5
2003	43.0	42.5	42.3	42.0	42.1	42.0	41.4	41.4	40.8	41.2	40.9	40.5	41.7
Service-providing													
1990	177.5	178.6	180.4	181.1	182.9	183.5	180.7	180.9	182.3	184.3	184.1	184.7	181.8
1991	179.4	180.8	181.7	182.0	183.7	184.8	182.4	182.4	182.8	182.4	183.2	184.7	182.5
1992	177.8	179.9	180.6	184.2	186.0	184.4	181.1	180.4	182.9	185.5	186.4	186.5	183.0
1993	181.9	184.4	184.0	186.8	188.5	187.6	183.1	182.8	185.7	188.8	189.4	190.5	186.1
1994	182.8	184.6	187.2	189.5	191.0	191.4	189.0	188.8	191.5	192.6	193.9	194.2	189.7
1995	188.5	190.1	192.3	193.1	195.2	195.4	191.7	190.6	194.1	195.4	196.8	197.7	193.4
1996	189.4	193.2	194.5	197.3	199.1	198.7	195.3	194.6	197.8	199.4	200.8	201.5	196.8
1997	198.7	200.4	201.5	202.8	205.7	205.5	202.8	202.2	204.5	208.0	208.4	209.7	204.2
1998	205.1	206.9	208.9	210.7	214.0	212.3	210.2	209.7	212.0	213.4	214.0	214.9	211.0
1999	208.4	211.8	213.9	215.4	217.7	218.6	215.7	216.5	217.6	219.5	219.8	221.3	216.4
2000	216.1	218.1	220.4	222.3	225.4	227.1	223.0	221.8	223.2	225.8	226.6	227.6	223.1
2001	223.1	224.0	226.3	225.4	228.2	230.1	225.0	225.7	226.9	227.8	228.5	228.8	226.7
2002	223.2	223.9	227.0	227.1	229.8	231.0	226.7	227.4	230.5	231.3	231.4	231.7	228.4
2003	227.9	228.3	231.1	232.7	234.8	235.2	230.5	230.1	233.1	234.6	234.4	233.8	232.2
Trade, transportation, and utilities													
1990	49.6	48.8	48.7	48.9	49.1	49.8	49.4	49.7	49.7	49.8	50.7	50.9	49.6
1991	48.2	47.2	47.3	47.5	47.8	48.6	48.1	48.0	48.1	47.7	48.5	49.1	48.0
1992	46.6	46.1	45.8	46.6	46.9	47.0	46.3	46.2	46.8	47.3	48.6	48.8	46.9
1993	47.1	46.5	46.3	46.5	46.8	47.3	46.2	46.0	46.3	47.1	47.9	48.5	46.9
1994	46.6	45.7	45.9	46.1	46.7	46.9	46.4	46.6	47.3	48.4	49.7	50.1	47.2
1995	47.8	47.2	47.1	47.3	47.5	47.7	47.3	47.4	47.9	49.2	50.0	50.5	48.1
1996	48.0	47.6	47.4	48.4	48.5	48.5	48.0	47.9	48.7	49.4	50.4	51.0	48.7
1997	50.7	49.9	50.1	50.1	50.5	50.7	50.6	50.2	51.1	51.8	52.6	53.3	51.0
1998	51.5	50.4	50.7	50.7	50.8	50.9	50.4	50.4	51.4	51.9	52.7	53.1	51.2
1999	51.7	51.3	51.4	52.3	52.8	53.1	52.7	53.4	53.9	54.7	55.5	56.3	53.3
2000	54.4	54.2	54.8	54.9	55.0	55.6	55.0	55.3	55.6	56.6	57.6	58.3	55.6
2001	56.5	55.6	56.0	55.6	56.0	56.9	56.0	56.4	56.2	56.9	58.2	58.8	56.6
2002	56.7	55.8	56.4	56.1	56.9	57.1	56.5	57.1	57.8	58.1	59.2	60.1	57.3
2003	57.7	56.7	57.2	57.5	57.8	58.4	58.0	58.2	58.4	58.9	59.4	60.0	58.2
Wholesale trade													
1990	8.6	8.6	8.6	8.7	8.7	8.9	8.8	8.8	8.7	8.7	8.7	8.7	8.7
1991	8.6	8.6	8.6	8.6	8.6	8.6	8.6	8.5	8.5	8.4	8.4	8.4	8.5
1992	8.3	8.3	8.3	8.6	8.5	8.5	8.7	8.7	8.7	8.8	8.9	8.9	8.6
1993	8.5	8.6	8.7	8.8	8.8	9.0	8.9	8.9	8.9	9.0	8.9	8.8	8.8
1994	8.8	8.7	8.8	8.8	8.9	8.9	8.9	8.9	8.9	8.9	9.0	8.9	8.9
1995	8.8	8.8	8.9	9.1	9.2	9.1	9.2	9.2	9.2	9.2	9.2	9.3	9.1
1996	9.0	9.1	9.1	9.4	9.3	9.4	9.1	9.2	9.2	9.2	9.2	9.2	9.2
1997	9.4	9.4	9.5	9.6	9.7	9.7	9.7	9.8	9.8	9.9	9.9	9.9	9.7
1998	9.8	9.8	9.9	9.9	9.7	9.8	9.8	9.7	9.7	9.6	9.6	9.6	9.7
1999	9.5	9.6	9.6	9.7	9.7	9.8	9.9	10.0	9.9	10.1	10.1	10.2	9.8
2000	10.1	10.2	10.4	10.6	10.5	10.5	10.7	10.7	10.6	10.9	10.9	10.9	10.6
2001	10.9	10.8	10.9	10.7	10.7	10.9	10.8	10.9	10.7	10.6	10.8	10.8	10.8
2002	10.7	10.5	10.6	10.5	10.6	10.7	10.7	10.6	10.5	10.4	10.5	10.6	10.6
2003	10.4	10.3	10.5	10.4	10.4	10.5	10.5	10.5	10.5	10.5	10.5	10.7	10.5
Retail trade													
1990	31.4	30.6	30.5	30.4	30.5	30.8	30.8	31.0	31.0	31.2	32.1	32.5	31.1
1991	29.8	28.8	28.9	29.0	29.2	29.9	29.5	29.5	29.3	29.5	30.2	30.8	29.5
1992	28.7	28.1	27.9	28.3	28.6	28.7	28.2	28.2	28.2	28.5	29.6	29.9	28.6
1993	28.6	28.0	27.7	27.7	28.0	28.2	27.7	27.7	27.6	28.2	29.2	29.9	28.2
1994	27.9	27.2	27.2	27.5	27.8	28.1	27.7	28.0	28.3	29.1	30.2	30.8	28.3
1995	28.8	28.1	28.0	27.8	27.8	28.0	28.1	28.2	28.1	29.1	30.0	30.4	28.5
1996	28.5	27.9	27.7	28.5	28.7	28.8	28.7	28.6	28.8	29.1	30.2	30.8	28.9
1997	30.2	29.3	29.4	29.8	30.0	30.1	30.3	30.2	30.0	30.6	31.4	32.0	30.3
1998	30.2	29.2	29.3	29.0	29.2	29.4	29.2	29.3	29.6	30.2	31.0	31.4	29.8
1999	30.2	29.6	29.7	30.2	30.6	30.8	30.9	31.4	31.5	31.8	32.6	33.3	31.1
2000	31.8	31.5	31.7	31.7	31.8	32.3	32.2	32.4	32.2	32.8	33.8	34.6	32.4
2001	32.7	31.9	32.0	31.7	32.1	32.9	32.5	32.8	32.2	32.9	34.1	34.7	32.7
2002	33.1	32.4	32.6	32.6	33.2	33.5	33.2	33.7	33.5	33.7	34.7	35.5	33.5
2003	33.7	32.9	33.1	33.4	33.7	34.2	34.2	34.3	34.2	34.4	35.1	35.6	34.1

Employment by Industry: Pennsylvania—*Continued*

(Numbers in thousands. Not seasonally adjusted.)

Industry	January	February	March	April	May	June	July	August	September	October	November	December	Annual Average
ALLENTOWN-BETHLEHEM *—Continued*													
Transportation and utilities													
1990	9.6	9.6	9.6	9.8	9.9	10.1	9.8	9.9	10.0	9.9	9.9	9.7	9.8
1991	9.8	9.8	9.8	9.9	10.0	10.1	10.0	10.0	10.3	9.8	9.9	9.9	9.9
1992	9.6	9.7	9.6	9.7	9.8	9.8	9.4	9.3	9.9	10.0	10.1	10.0	9.7
1993	10.0	9.9	9.9	10.0	10.0	10.1	9.6	9.4	9.8	9.9	9.8	9.8	9.9
1994	9.9	9.8	9.9	9.8	10.0	9.9	9.8	9.7	10.1	10.4	10.5	10.4	10.0
1995	10.2	10.3	10.2	10.4	10.5	10.6	10.0	10.0	10.6	10.9	10.8	10.8	10.4
1996	10.5	10.6	10.6	10.5	10.5	10.3	10.2	10.1	10.7	11.1	11.0	11.0	10.6
1997	11.1	11.2	11.2	10.7	10.8	10.9	10.6	10.2	11.3	11.3	11.3	11.4	11.0
1998	11.5	11.4	11.5	11.8	11.9	11.7	11.4	11.4	12.1	12.1	12.1	12.1	11.8
1999	12.0	12.1	12.1	12.4	12.5	12.5	11.9	12.0	12.5	12.8	12.8	12.8	12.4
2000	12.5	12.5	12.7	12.6	12.7	12.8	12.1	12.2	12.8	12.9	12.9	12.8	12.6
2001	12.9	12.9	13.1	13.2	13.2	13.1	12.7	12.7	13.3	13.4	13.3	13.3	13.1
2002	12.9	12.9	13.2	13.0	13.1	12.9	12.6	12.8	13.8	14.0	14.0	14.0	13.3
2003	13.6	13.5	13.6	13.7	13.7	13.7	13.3	13.4	13.7	14.0	13.8	13.7	13.6
Information													
1990	6.0	6.0	6.0	6.1	6.1	6.2	6.1	6.1	6.1	6.0	6.0	6.0	6.1
1991	5.9	5.8	5.8	5.8	5.8	5.8	5.8	5.7	5.7	5.7	5.7	5.7	5.8
1992	5.6	5.6	5.6	5.8	5.8	5.8	5.8	5.8	5.8	5.8	5.7	5.8	5.7
1993	5.9	5.9	5.9	5.9	6.0	6.1	6.0	6.0	6.0	6.0	6.0	6.0	6.0
1994	6.0	6.0	6.0	6.1	6.1	6.2	6.2	6.2	6.1	6.1	6.1	6.2	6.1
1995	6.1	6.1	6.1	6.5	6.6	6.6	6.5	6.5	6.5	6.5	6.5	6.5	6.4
1996	6.4	6.6	6.6	6.6	6.6	6.7	6.7	6.7	6.7	6.7	6.7	6.8	6.7
1997	6.9	7.0	7.0	6.9	7.0	7.1	7.2	7.2	7.1	7.2	7.2	7.3	7.1
1998	7.2	7.2	7.3	7.5	7.5	7.6	7.7	7.7	7.7	7.6	7.6	7.7	7.5
1999	7.6	7.6	7.7	7.7	7.7	7.8	8.0	8.1	8.0	8.0	8.1	8.1	7.9
2000	8.1	8.1	8.2	8.2	8.3	8.6	8.6	8.3	8.2	8.3	8.4	8.6	8.3
2001	8.7	8.6	8.5	8.4	8.4	8.3	8.3	8.1	7.8	7.8	7.6	7.6	8.2
2002	7.5	7.5	7.5	7.5	7.5	7.6	7.5	7.4	7.3	7.3	7.3	7.4	7.4
2003	7.2	7.3	7.4	7.4	7.5	7.6	7.6	7.5	7.4	7.5	7.5	7.4	7.4
Financial activities													
1990	12.8	12.6	12.7	12.5	12.7	12.8	12.8	12.8	12.9	12.9	12.8	12.9	12.8
1991	12.8	12.7	12.7	13.0	13.0	13.3	13.3	13.4	13.4	13.3	13.2	13.3	13.1
1992	13.1	13.1	13.2	13.6	13.6	13.8	13.8	14.0	13.7	13.6	13.6	13.5	13.6
1993	13.4	13.5	13.4	13.4	13.5	13.7	13.7	13.7	13.7	13.6	13.6	13.7	13.6
1994	13.6	13.6	13.7	13.9	14.0	14.1	13.6	13.7	13.6	13.9	13.9	13.9	13.8
1995	13.6	13.6	13.6	13.7	13.7	13.7	13.8	13.8	13.7	13.5	13.5	13.5	13.6
1996	13.3	13.4	13.4	13.8	13.8	13.7	13.7	13.8	13.6	13.8	13.8	13.9	13.7
1997	13.5	13.4	13.4	13.5	13.6	13.8	13.4	13.3	13.3	13.6	13.8	13.8	13.5
1998	14.0	13.9	14.1	14.2	14.3	14.4	14.6	14.8	14.7	14.9	14.9	15.0	14.5
1999	14.9	15.0	14.9	15.3	15.4	15.6	15.2	15.2	15.1	15.0	14.9	15.1	15.1
2000	15.1	15.0	15.2	15.2	15.3	15.5	15.5	15.5	15.4	15.5	15.6	15.8	15.4
2001	16.1	16.0	16.2	15.8	15.7	16.0	16.1	16.2	16.1	16.0	16.0	16.1	16.0
2002	15.9	15.9	15.9	15.9	15.9	16.0	16.1	16.2	16.0	15.8	15.8	16.0	16.0
2003	15.7	15.8	15.8	15.7	15.9	16.0	15.9	15.8	15.7	15.6	15.6	15.7	15.8
Professional and business services													
1990	19.6	19.6	19.9	20.3	20.5	21.0	20.4	20.5	20.4	20.4	20.4	20.1	20.3
1991	20.5	20.7	20.7	20.9	20.8	21.2	20.9	21.1	21.2	20.9	20.9	21.1	20.9
1992	20.5	20.8	21.0	21.4	21.3	21.4	21.2	21.1	21.2	21.1	21.0	20.9	21.1
1993	21.0	21.0	21.1	21.2	21.0	21.0	20.9	21.1	21.0	21.1	21.1	20.7	21.0
1994	19.8	20.3	21.0	22.0	22.2	22.6	22.6	22.5	22.7	22.7	22.4	22.4	21.9
1995	22.0	22.0	22.6	22.7	22.7	23.1	22.9	22.9	23.0	22.6	22.6	22.6	22.6
1996	22.0	22.4	22.5	23.3	23.4	23.7	23.6	23.7	23.6	23.6	23.7	23.5	23.3
1997	23.7	23.6	23.9	24.7	25.0	25.4	25.2	25.4	25.0	25.6	25.6	25.6	24.9
1998	25.5	25.5	26.0	26.7	27.7	27.9	28.1	28.1	27.7	28.3	28.1	27.9	27.3
1999	26.7	27.2	27.3	28.7	28.8	29.0	28.8	28.6	28.4	28.6	28.5	28.3	28.2
2000	27.1	27.1	27.8	28.9	29.0	29.3	29.7	29.2	28.9	29.1	28.8	28.7	28.6
2001	28.4	28.3	28.5	29.1	29.4	29.6	28.9	28.8	28.5	28.6	28.3	28.3	28.7
2002	26.9	26.8	27.3	27.8	27.6	27.8	28.0	28.3	28.0	28.2	27.9	27.7	27.7
2003	27.9	27.9	28.4	29.2	28.8	29.0	28.8	29.4	29.2	29.4	29.1	28.9	28.8
Educational and health services													
1990	34.3	35.6	36.4	35.5	35.5	33.4	33.4	33.5	35.4	36.5	36.6	36.7	35.2
1991	35.0	36.5	37.1	37.1	37.2	35.6	35.2	35.4	37.0	38.0	37.9	37.9	36.7
1992	35.7	37.1	37.6	38.0	38.1	36.2	36.1	36.1	37.7	39.3	39.2	39.0	37.5
1993	37.6	39.0	39.0	39.8	39.8	38.3	38.0	37.8	39.4	40.5	40.4	40.3	39.2
1994	38.4	39.9	40.7	40.7	40.6	39.0	39.0	38.8	40.8	41.2	41.4	41.2	40.1
1995	39.1	40.7	41.7	41.2	41.1	39.5	39.2	39.1	41.4	41.9	42.0	41.8	40.7
1996	39.5	41.5	42.1	41.7	41.6	39.9	40.2	40.0	42.1	42.9	42.9	42.7	41.4
1997	40.9	42.7	43.2	42.9	43.0	41.2	41.2	41.3	43.0	44.3	44.2	44.0	42.7
1998	42.2	44.1	44.9	45.2	45.1	42.6	42.6	42.4	43.8	44.7	45.3	45.3	44.0
1999	42.9	44.7	45.6	44.7	44.5	42.9	42.6	42.9	44.1	45.5	45.8	45.6	44.3
2000	44.1	45.5	45.8	46.2	46.5	45.4	44.8	44.8	46.6	47.1	47.7	47.2	46.0
2001	45.6	46.8	47.6	47.3	47.1	45.9	45.8	46.2	48.1	48.3	48.8	48.5	47.2
2002	46.9	47.7	48.6	48.3	48.2	46.9	46.9	46.9	49.0	49.9	50.3	49.3	48.2
2003	48.5	49.1	50.0	50.1	50.1	49.0	48.8	48.8	50.3	51.4	52.0	51.3	50.0

Employment by Industry: Pennsylvania—*Continued*

(Numbers in thousands. Not seasonally adjusted.)

Industry	January	February	March	April	May	June	July	August	September	October	November	December	Annual Average
ALLENTOWN-BETHLEHEM —*Continued*													
Leisure and hospitality													
1990	17.5	17.5	17.7	18.8	19.6	20.7	20.8	20.8	20.0	20.3	18.5	18.7	19.2
1991	18.1	18.1	18.3	18.8	20.4	21.4	21.1	21.0	20.1	18.4	18.2	18.6	19.4
1992	18.5	18.3	18.3	19.2	20.6	21.6	21.4	20.9	20.3	18.9	18.9	18.8	19.6
1993	18.1	18.7	18.4	19.6	20.8	21.5	21.5	21.6	20.9	20.3	20.1	20.6	20.2
1994	19.3	19.1	19.5	19.9	20.4	21.8	21.7	22.1	21.7	19.3	18.9	19.1	20.2
1995	19.0	19.0	19.4	19.5	21.0	22.2	22.0	21.8	20.9	19.7	19.7	20.1	20.4
1996	19.3	19.3	19.6	20.3	21.6	22.9	22.4	22.3	21.1	20.3	19.9	20.1	20.8
1997	20.6	20.3	20.3	21.0	22.6	23.7	23.9	23.8	22.7	21.8	21.2	21.5	22.0
1998	21.4	21.4	21.3	21.7	23.8	24.8	24.9	24.7	23.8	22.3	21.3	21.7	22.8
1999	21.1	21.4	21.7	21.9	23.5	24.4	25.5	25.1	24.2	22.8	21.6	22.4	23.0
2000	22.4	22.4	22.4	22.9	24.4	25.8	25.8	25.4	24.3	23.2	22.2	22.6	23.7
2001	22.5	22.4	22.7	22.4	24.4	25.6	25.4	25.3	24.1	23.1	22.1	21.9	23.5
2002	22.8	22.9	23.5	23.8	25.7	27.2	26.8	27.2	25.8	24.8	23.5	23.9	24.8
2003	24.4	24.3	24.5	24.9	26.4	27.3	27.1	26.8	25.8	24.5	23.1	23.3	25.2
Other services													
1990	11.4	11.4	11.5	11.4	11.5	11.9	11.9	11.8	11.5	11.6	11.7	11.8	11.6
1991	11.6	11.7	11.8	11.2	11.2	11.5	11.5	11.5	11.1	11.2	11.2	11.4	11.4
1992	11.0	11.1	11.1	11.4	11.4	11.6	11.7	11.6	11.4	11.5	11.4	11.5	11.4
1993	11.2	11.3	11.3	11.5	11.6	11.7	11.6	11.4	11.3	11.4	11.4	11.6	11.4
1994	11.1	11.2	11.3	11.6	11.7	11.8	12.0	11.8	11.5	11.6	11.6	11.6	11.6
1995	11.4	11.5	11.6	11.8	12.0	12.3	12.4	12.3	12.0	12.1	12.2	12.4	12.0
1996	11.8	12.2	12.3	12.4	12.5	12.9	12.9	12.9	12.7	12.3	12.4	12.5	12.5
1997	12.4	12.4	12.5	12.6	12.6	12.8	13.1	13.0	12.7	12.9	12.8	12.9	12.7
1998	12.8	12.9	12.9	12.9	13.0	13.1	13.2	13.1	12.8	12.8	12.7	12.9	12.9
1999	12.8	13.0	13.2	13.1	13.1	13.3	13.5	13.4	13.1	13.0	13.2	13.3	13.2
2000	13.2	13.4	13.3	13.2	13.3	13.6	13.5	13.5	13.2	13.2	13.4	13.4	13.4
2001	13.3	13.3	13.6	13.6	13.8	14.0	14.1	13.9	13.6	13.5	13.7	13.7	13.7
2002	13.6	13.6	13.7	13.7	13.8	13.9	14.0	13.8	13.5	13.3	13.2	13.3	13.6
2003	13.1	13.0	13.2	13.3	13.4	13.6	13.9	13.7	13.4	13.5	13.6	13.5	13.4
Government													
1990	26.3	27.1	27.5	27.6	27.9	27.7	25.9	25.7	26.3	26.8	27.4	27.6	27.0
1991	27.3	28.1	28.0	27.7	27.5	27.4	26.5	26.3	26.2	27.2	27.6	27.6	27.3
1992	26.8	27.8	28.0	28.2	28.3	27.0	24.8	24.7	26.0	28.0	28.0	28.2	27.2
1993	27.6	28.5	28.6	28.9	29.0	28.0	25.2	25.2	27.1	28.8	28.9	29.3	27.9
1994	28.0	28.8	29.1	29.2	29.3	29.0	27.5	27.1	27.8	29.4	29.9	29.7	28.7
1995	29.5	30.0	30.2	30.4	30.6	30.3	27.6	26.8	28.7	29.9	30.3	30.3	29.6
1996	29.1	30.2	30.6	30.8	31.1	30.4	27.8	27.3	29.3	30.4	31.0	31.0	29.9
1997	30.0	31.1	31.1	31.1	31.4	30.8	28.2	28.0	29.6	30.8	31.0	31.3	30.4
1998	30.5	31.5	31.7	31.8	31.8	31.0	28.7	28.5	30.1	30.9	31.4	31.3	30.8
1999	30.7	31.6	32.1	31.7	31.9	32.5	29.4	29.8	30.8	31.9	32.2	32.2	31.4
2000	31.7	32.4	32.9	32.8	33.6	33.3	30.1	29.8	31.0	32.8	32.9	33.0	32.2
2001	32.0	33.0	33.2	33.2	33.4	33.8	30.4	30.8	32.5	33.6	33.8	33.9	32.8
2002	32.9	33.7	34.1	34.0	34.2	34.5	30.9	30.5	33.1	33.9	34.2	34.0	33.3
2003	33.4	34.2	34.6	34.6	34.9	34.3	30.4	29.9	32.9	33.8	34.1	33.7	33.4
Federal government													
1990	2.2	2.4	2.5	2.6	2.8	2.7	2.6	2.4	2.2	2.2	2.2	2.2	2.4
1991	2.4	2.4	2.3	2.3	2.3	2.4	2.4	2.2	2.2	2.2	2.2	2.3	2.3
1992	2.3	2.4	2.4	2.4	2.4	2.4	2.3	2.2	2.2	2.3	2.2	2.4	2.3
1993	2.2	2.3	2.3	2.4	2.3	2.3	2.3	2.3	2.3	2.3	2.2	2.4	2.3
1994	2.2	2.4	2.4	2.4	2.4	2.6	2.7	2.8	2.8	2.8	2.8	3.0	2.6
1995	3.0	3.0	3.1	3.1	3.0	3.1	3.0	3.0	2.9	2.9	2.9	3.0	3.0
1996	3.0	3.0	3.1	3.1	3.1	3.1	2.9	2.9	2.8	2.8	2.9	3.1	3.0
1997	2.9	3.2	3.1	3.0	3.0	3.0	2.8	2.7	2.7	2.7	2.7	2.9	2.9
1998	2.8	3.0	3.0	3.0	3.0	3.0	2.8	2.8	2.7	2.7	2.8	2.9	2.9
1999	2.8	3.0	3.1	3.0	3.0	3.0	2.9	2.9	2.8	2.7	2.8	2.9	2.9
2000	2.8	3.0	3.2	3.2	3.8	3.2	3.3	2.8	2.7	2.7	2.7	2.8	3.0
2001	2.8	2.9	3.0	2.9	2.9	2.9	2.9	2.8	2.7	2.7	2.7	2.8	2.8
2002	2.8	2.9	2.9	2.8	2.8	2.7	2.7	2.4	2.4	2.4	2.3	2.4	2.6
2003	2.5	2.6	2.6	2.6	2.6	2.5	2.4	2.3	2.3	2.3	2.3	2.3	2.4
State government													
1990	2.8	2.7	2.7	2.8	2.7	2.9	3.0	3.0	3.0	3.1	3.2	3.2	2.9
1991	3.1	3.2	3.1	3.0	2.8	2.8	2.8	2.7	2.6	2.6	2.6	2.6	2.8
1992	2.5	2.5	2.4	2.5	2.5	2.5	2.5	2.5	2.5	2.6	2.6	2.6	2.5
1993	2.7	2.8	2.8	2.8	2.7	2.7	2.7	2.7	2.7	2.8	2.8	2.8	2.8
1994	2.7	2.8	2.8	2.8	2.7	2.7	2.7	2.7	2.7	2.8	2.8	2.7	2.7
1995	2.7	2.7	2.6	2.7	2.7	2.7	2.6	2.7	2.6	2.7	2.7	2.7	2.7
1996	2.6	2.7	2.7	2.7	2.7	2.7	2.7	2.7	2.6	2.7	2.7	2.7	2.7
1997	2.7	2.6	2.7	2.7	2.6	2.6	2.7	2.7	2.6	2.6	2.6	2.7	2.7
1998	2.7	2.6	2.7	2.7	2.6	2.6	2.6	2.6	2.6	2.6	2.6	2.6	2.6
1999	2.6	2.5	2.6	2.5	2.5	2.5	2.6	2.6	2.5	2.5	2.5	2.5	2.5
2000	2.5	2.6	2.6	2.6	2.6	2.6	2.6	2.6	2.7	2.7	2.7	2.7	2.6
2001	2.6	2.6	2.6	2.6	2.6	2.6	2.6	2.6	2.7	2.7	2.7	2.7	2.6
2002	2.7	2.6	2.7	2.7	2.6	2.6	2.7	2.7	2.7	2.7	2.8	2.7	2.7
2003	2.8	2.7	2.7	2.7	2.7	2.7	2.7	2.7	2.6	2.7	2.7	2.7	2.7

Employment by Industry: Pennsylvania—*Continued*

(Numbers in thousands. Not seasonally adjusted.)

Industry	January	February	March	April	May	June	July	August	September	October	November	December	Annual Average
ALLENTOWN-BETHLEHEM —*Continued*													
Local government													
1990	21.3	22.0	22.3	22.2	22.4	22.1	20.3	20.3	21.1	21.5	22.0	22.2	21.6
1991	21.8	22.5	22.6	22.4	22.4	22.2	21.3	21.4	21.4	22.4	22.8	22.7	22.2
1992	22.0	22.9	23.2	23.3	23.4	22.1	20.0	20.0	21.3	23.1	23.2	23.2	22.3
1993	22.7	23.4	23.5	23.7	24.0	23.0	20.2	20.2	22.1	23.7	23.9	24.1	22.9
1994	23.1	23.6	23.9	24.0	24.2	23.7	22.1	21.6	22.3	23.8	24.3	24.0	23.4
1995	23.8	24.3	24.5	24.6	24.9	24.5	22.0	21.1	23.2	24.3	24.7	24.6	23.9
1996	23.5	24.5	24.8	25.0	25.3	24.6	22.2	21.7	23.9	24.9	25.4	25.2	24.3
1997	24.4	25.3	25.3	25.4	25.8	25.2	22.7	22.6	24.3	25.5	25.7	25.7	24.8
1998	25.0	25.9	26.0	26.1	26.2	25.4	23.3	23.1	24.8	25.6	26.0	25.8	25.3
1999	25.3	26.1	26.4	26.2	26.4	27.0	23.9	24.3	25.5	26.7	26.9	26.8	26.0
2000	26.4	26.8	27.1	27.0	27.2	27.5	24.2	24.4	25.6	27.4	27.5	27.5	26.6
2001	26.6	27.5	27.6	27.7	27.9	28.3	24.9	25.4	27.1	28.2	28.4	28.4	27.3
2002	27.4	28.2	28.5	28.5	28.8	29.2	25.5	25.4	28.0	28.8	29.1	28.9	28.0
2003	28.1	28.9	29.3	29.3	29.6	29.1	25.3	24.9	28.0	28.8	29.1	28.7	28.3
ERIE													
Total nonfarm													
1990	117.1	117.3	118.3	120.1	121.2	121.9	121.1	120.7	121.6	122.8	123.1	122.3	120.6
1991	119.1	119.3	119.5	120.0	120.3	121.1	120.6	120.2	121.3	121.5	121.5	120.2	120.4
1992	117.7	118.3	118.5	121.3	122.4	123.0	123.1	123.3	123.4	125.0	125.1	124.5	122.1
1993	120.6	121.8	121.9	123.6	123.9	125.5	125.4	124.8	125.8	126.8	126.6	126.5	124.4
1994	120.4	121.1	122.2	123.9	124.9	125.9	126.4	126.3	127.8	126.7	127.0	126.6	124.9
1995	123.6	124.7	125.3	127.2	128.0	128.6	127.7	128.1	128.9	129.0	129.2	129.0	127.4
1996	124.0	125.6	125.6	127.2	127.6	127.8	127.7	127.5	129.3	130.3	129.8	129.2	127.6
1997	126.1	126.9	127.4	127.8	128.7	129.2	129.2	129.1	130.8	131.6	131.3	131.7	129.2
1998	128.3	128.4	129.2	129.9	131.5	131.0	129.7	129.5	132.1	133.5	134.3	133.5	130.9
1999	130.6	131.9	132.3	134.1	134.6	134.3	134.0	133.3	134.6	135.7	135.8	135.0	133.9
2000	132.0	133.0	134.4	137.0	137.8	137.8	136.3	136.8	137.9	137.8	137.7	136.1	136.2
2001	133.2	134.2	134.1	134.8	135.0	133.9	132.0	132.3	133.1	133.7	133.2	132.0	133.5
2002	129.1	129.2	130.0	131.3	132.3	132.2	131.4	132.3	133.4	133.4	133.0	131.6	131.6
2003	127.7	128.1	128.7	130.3	131.3	130.5	127.5	128.4	130.2	131.4	131.7	131.2	129.8
Total private													
1990	103.1	103.2	103.9	105.3	106.5	108.4	108.1	108.5	107.7	108.3	108.5	107.9	106.6
1991	105.1	104.8	104.9	105.6	106.8	108.0	108.1	108.3	107.8	107.0	106.9	105.6	106.6
1992	103.7	103.8	104.2	106.7	108.4	109.4	110.3	110.3	109.7	110.5	110.6	109.9	108.1
1993	106.6	107.2	107.4	109.0	110.0	111.6	112.2	112.2	111.7	111.9	111.5	111.5	110.2
1994	106.6	106.3	107.3	109.1	109.9	111.9	113.1	113.2	113.3	111.5	111.7	111.5	110.5
1995	109.6	109.4	110.0	111.9	112.7	114.1	114.1	114.6	113.7	113.4	113.4	113.4	112.5
1996	109.7	110.1	109.9	111.6	112.2	113.5	114.2	114.0	114.0	114.6	114.1	113.6	112.6
1997	111.1	111.2	111.6	112.2	113.1	114.6	115.4	115.3	115.5	115.7	115.2	115.7	113.9
1998	112.7	112.4	113.1	113.8	115.6	116.2	115.8	115.9	116.2	117.3	118.0	117.7	115.4
1999	115.2	115.8	116.1	117.8	119.0	119.3	119.5	119.4	118.5	119.3	119.4	118.8	118.2
2000	116.0	116.6	118.0	120.2	121.2	122.5	122.0	122.7	121.7	121.1	120.9	119.6	120.2
2001	117.6	117.7	117.6	118.2	118.7	118.8	117.6	117.9	117.0	116.9	116.3	115.3	117.5
2002	113.2	112.4	113.3	114.5	115.5	116.7	116.5	117.3	116.9	116.1	115.6	114.3	115.2
2003	111.1	110.7	111.6	113.2	114.1	115.0	113.1	114.2	113.9	114.3	114.4	114.0	113.3
Goods-producing													
1990	38.0	37.9	38.2	38.8	39.2	40.1	40.0	40.2	39.6	40.3	40.2	39.5	39.3
1991	38.4	38.2	37.9	38.0	38.5	39.0	39.2	39.3	39.3	38.4	37.9	36.8	38.4
1992	36.7	36.9	37.0	37.6	38.4	39.0	39.0	39.2	38.7	39.8	39.6	39.0	38.4
1993	38.0	38.0	38.1	38.9	39.1	39.5	39.8	39.7	39.4	39.5	39.1	39.0	39.0
1994	37.0	36.7	36.9	37.5	37.8	38.5	39.3	39.4	39.5	39.3	38.7	38.4	38.3
1995	38.0	37.6	37.6	38.1	38.5	38.8	39.0	39.1	38.6	38.6	38.7	38.2	38.4
1996	36.9	36.9	36.5	37.2	37.3	38.1	37.8	37.9	37.7	37.9	37.5	37.1	37.4
1997	36.4	36.3	36.3	36.6	36.8	37.3	37.9	37.8	38.1	38.5	38.2	38.2	37.4
1998	37.2	37.2	37.3	37.5	37.8	38.2	38.3	38.3	38.6	38.7	38.7	38.3	38.0
1999	38.0	38.0	38.2	38.7	38.8	38.7	38.9	38.9	38.9	39.0	38.9	38.6	38.6
2000	37.9	37.8	37.7	38.3	38.4	38.9	39.1	39.1	38.9	38.7	38.5	37.5	38.4
2001	36.8	36.6	36.4	36.5	36.4	36.3	35.7	35.7	35.5	35.3	34.7	33.9	35.8
2002	32.9	32.3	32.3	32.8	33.0	33.4	32.6	33.1	33.1	32.7	32.1	31.4	32.6
2003	30.5	30.0	29.9	30.3	30.4	30.7	29.4	30.7	30.5	30.3	30.3	29.8	30.2
Construction and mining													
1990	3.0	2.9	3.1	3.4	3.8	4.3	4.5	4.7	4.4	4.4	4.2	3.8	3.9
1991	3.3	3.1	3.2	3.6	3.9	4.0	4.2	4.4	4.1	4.2	4.0	3.7	3.8
1992	3.6	3.5	3.7	3.9	4.3	4.7	4.7	4.7	4.4	4.6	4.4	4.0	4.2
1993	3.5	3.4	3.4	3.9	4.3	4.5	4.9	4.8	4.6	4.5	4.3	4.0	4.2
1994	3.3	3.2	3.3	3.8	4.1	4.4	4.5	4.6	4.6	4.5	4.3	3.9	4.0
1995	3.6	3.4	3.5	4.1	4.5	4.7	4.8	4.9	4.7	4.4	4.3	4.0	4.2
1996	3.5	3.5	3.5	4.0	4.3	4.8	4.8	4.9	4.6	4.6	4.3	4.0	4.2
1997	3.6	3.6	3.7	4.0	4.3	4.6	4.9	4.8	4.6	4.6	4.4	4.1	4.3
1998	3.8	3.7	3.7	4.2	4.5	4.8	5.1	5.1	4.9	4.8	4.7	4.5	4.5
1999	4.2	4.1	4.2	4.8	5.3	5.4	5.8	5.7	5.6	5.1	4.9	4.7	5.0
2000	4.2	4.1	4.4	4.9	5.2	5.4	5.7	5.8	5.5	5.3	5.1	4.6	5.0
2001	4.2	4.1	4.2	4.8	5.3	5.5	5.6	5.5	5.4	5.2	5.1	4.8	5.0
2002	4.3	4.2	4.3	4.7	5.1	5.3	5.5	5.5	5.5	5.4	5.2	4.9	5.0
2003	4.3	4.1	4.2	4.7	5.0	5.2	5.4	5.4	5.4	5.2	5.1	4.8	4.9

Employment by Industry: Pennsylvania—*Continued*

(Numbers in thousands. Not seasonally adjusted.)

Industry	January	February	March	April	May	June	July	August	September	October	November	December	Annual Average
ERIE—*Continued*													
Manufacturing													
1990	35.0	35.0	35.1	35.4	35.4	35.8	35.5	35.5	35.2	35.9	36.0	35.7	35.5
1991	35.1	35.1	34.7	34.4	34.6	35.0	35.0	34.9	35.2	34.2	33.9	33.1	34.6
1992	33.1	33.4	33.3	33.7	34.1	34.3	34.3	34.5	34.3	35.2	35.2	35.0	34.2
1993	34.5	34.6	34.7	35.0	34.8	35.0	34.9	34.9	34.8	35.0	34.8	35.0	34.8
1994	33.7	33.5	33.6	33.7	33.7	34.1	34.8	34.8	34.9	34.8	34.4	34.5	34.2
1995	34.4	34.2	34.1	34.0	34.0	34.1	34.2	34.2	33.9	34.2	34.4	34.2	34.2
1996	33.4	33.4	33.0	33.2	33.0	33.3	33.0	33.0	33.1	33.3	33.2	33.1	33.2
1997	32.8	32.7	32.6	32.6	32.5	32.7	33.0	33.0	33.5	33.9	33.8	34.1	33.1
1998	33.4	33.5	33.6	33.3	33.3	33.4	33.2	33.2	33.7	33.9	34.0	33.8	33.5
1999	33.8	33.9	34.0	33.9	33.5	33.3	33.1	33.2	33.3	33.9	34.0	33.9	33.7
2000	33.7	33.7	33.3	33.4	33.2	33.5	33.4	33.3	33.4	33.4	33.4	32.9	33.4
2001	32.6	32.5	32.2	31.7	31.1	30.8	30.1	30.2	30.1	30.1	29.6	29.1	30.8
2002	28.6	28.1	28.0	28.1	27.9	28.1	27.1	27.6	27.6	27.3	26.9	26.5	27.7
2003	26.2	25.9	25.7	25.6	25.4	25.5	24.0	25.3	25.1	25.1	25.2	25.0	25.3
Service-providing													
1990	79.1	79.4	80.1	81.3	82.0	81.8	81.1	80.5	82.0	82.5	82.9	82.8	81.3
1991	80.7	81.1	81.6	82.0	81.8	82.1	81.4	80.9	82.0	83.1	83.6	83.4	82.0
1992	81.0	81.4	81.5	83.7	84.0	84.0	84.1	84.1	84.7	85.2	85.5	85.5	83.7
1993	82.6	83.8	83.8	84.7	84.8	86.0	85.6	85.1	86.4	87.3	87.5	87.5	85.4
1994	83.4	84.4	85.3	86.4	87.1	87.4	87.1	86.9	88.3	87.4	88.3	88.2	86.7
1995	85.6	87.1	87.7	89.1	89.5	89.8	88.7	89.0	90.3	90.4	90.5	90.8	89.0
1996	87.1	88.7	89.1	90.0	90.3	89.7	89.9	89.6	91.6	92.4	92.3	92.1	90.2
1997	89.7	90.6	91.1	91.2	91.9	91.9	91.3	91.3	92.7	93.1	93.1	93.5	91.8
1998	91.1	91.2	91.9	92.4	93.7	92.8	91.4	91.2	93.5	94.8	95.6	95.2	92.9
1999	92.6	93.9	94.1	95.4	95.8	95.6	95.1	94.4	95.7	96.7	96.9	96.4	95.2
2000	94.1	95.2	96.7	98.7	99.4	98.9	97.2	97.7	99.0	99.1	99.2	98.6	97.8
2001	96.4	97.6	97.7	98.3	98.6	97.6	96.3	96.6	97.6	98.4	98.5	98.1	97.6
2002	96.2	96.9	97.7	98.5	99.3	98.8	98.8	99.2	100.3	100.7	100.9	100.2	99.0
2003	97.2	98.1	98.8	100.0	100.9	99.8	98.1	97.7	99.7	101.1	101.4	101.4	99.5
Trade, transportation, and utilities													
1990	19.4	19.1	19.1	19.3	19.6	20.0	19.8	19.9	19.6	19.8	20.2	20.3	19.7
1991	19.1	18.6	18.6	18.8	19.0	19.3	19.3	19.4	19.1	19.6	20.1	20.2	19.3
1992	19.1	18.7	18.8	19.1	19.6	19.8	19.8	19.6	19.6	20.0	20.4	20.5	19.6
1993	19.7	19.5	19.4	19.4	19.6	20.2	20.0	20.1	19.9	20.1	20.3	20.6	19.9
1994	19.7	19.5	19.5	19.6	19.7	20.2	20.2	20.2	20.3	20.0	20.5	21.0	20.0
1995	20.0	19.9	19.9	20.5	19.9	20.9	20.6	20.8	20.5	21.0	21.3	21.7	20.6
1996	20.6	20.5	20.5	20.5	20.7	20.9	21.1	21.2	21.5	21.8	22.2	22.3	21.2
1997	21.2	20.9	21.2	21.1	21.3	21.8	21.5	21.4	21.5	22.0	22.3	22.6	21.6
1998	21.4	21.0	21.0	20.9	21.4	21.5	21.5	21.7	21.7	22.5	23.0	23.1	21.7
1999	21.9	21.5	21.5	22.0	22.4	22.3	22.3	22.4	22.1	22.7	23.0	23.2	22.3
2000	22.3	22.2	22.4	23.0	23.1	23.3	22.9	23.3	23.5	23.6	24.1	24.0	23.1
2001	22.8	22.5	22.7	22.8	22.9	22.8	22.5	22.7	22.8	22.9	23.3	23.3	22.8
2002	22.2	21.9	22.4	22.0	22.2	22.4	22.3	22.4	22.4	22.4	22.9	22.9	22.4
2003	21.6	21.5	21.7	21.7	22.0	22.2	21.9	21.9	22.0	22.3	22.8	23.0	22.1
Wholesale trade													
1990	3.9	3.9	3.9	3.9	4.0	4.1	4.0	4.0	4.0	3.9	3.9	3.9	4.0
1991	3.9	3.9	3.9	3.9	3.9	3.9	3.9	3.9	3.9	4.0	3.9	3.9	3.9
1992	3.9	3.9	4.0	4.0	4.0	4.0	4.1	4.0	4.0	4.1	4.0	3.9	4.0
1993	4.0	4.0	4.0	3.9	3.9	4.0	4.0	4.0	3.9	3.9	3.9	4.0	4.0
1994	3.8	3.9	3.9	3.9	3.9	4.0	4.0	4.0	4.0	4.0	4.0	4.0	4.0
1995	4.0	4.0	4.0	4.1	4.0	4.0	4.0	4.0	4.0	3.9	3.9	3.9	4.0
1996	3.9	3.9	3.9	3.9	3.9	3.9	3.9	3.9	3.9	3.9	3.9	3.9	3.9
1997	3.8	3.8	3.9	3.8	3.8	3.9	3.9	3.9	3.9	3.9	3.9	3.9	3.9
1998	3.9	3.9	3.9	3.8	3.9	3.9	3.9	3.9	3.9	3.9	4.0	3.9	3.9
1999	3.9	3.9	3.9	4.0	4.0	4.0	3.9	3.9	3.8	3.9	3.9	3.9	3.9
2000	3.8	3.8	3.8	3.8	3.8	3.9	3.8	3.9	3.8	3.8	3.8	3.8	3.8
2001	3.8	3.7	3.7	3.7	3.8	3.7	3.7	3.6	3.6	3.6	3.6	3.6	3.7
2002	3.6	3.5	3.6	3.6	3.7	3.7	3.7	3.7	3.6	3.6	3.6	3.6	3.6
2003	3.5	3.5	3.6	3.5	3.6	3.6	3.6	3.6	3.5	3.5	3.5	3.5	3.5
Retail trade													
1990	13.2	12.9	12.9	13.0	13.1	13.4	13.4	13.5	13.3	13.7	14.1	14.2	13.4
1991	12.9	12.5	12.5	12.7	12.9	13.1	13.1	13.2	12.9	13.3	13.9	14.0	13.1
1992	13.0	12.7	12.7	12.9	13.3	13.4	13.4	13.3	13.4	13.6	14.1	14.3	13.3
1993	13.5	13.3	13.2	13.3	13.5	13.9	13.9	14.0	13.8	14.0	14.2	14.5	13.8
1994	13.9	13.5	13.6	13.6	13.6	13.9	13.9	13.8	13.9	13.7	14.2	14.5	13.8
1995	13.8	13.6	13.6	13.9	13.4	14.4	14.2	14.5	14.2	14.6	14.9	15.3	14.2
1996	14.2	14.1	14.1	14.0	14.1	14.3	14.5	14.7	14.9	15.1	15.5	15.7	14.6
1997	14.8	14.5	14.6	14.5	14.7	15.0	14.9	14.9	14.8	15.3	15.6	15.9	15.0
1998	14.9	14.5	14.5	14.4	14.8	14.9	14.9	15.1	15.1	15.9	16.3	16.5	15.2
1999	15.4	15.0	15.0	15.2	15.5	15.5	15.6	15.7	15.5	15.9	16.2	16.4	15.6
2000	15.7	15.6	15.8	16.2	16.3	16.4	16.2	16.5	16.7	16.7	17.2	17.3	16.4
2001	16.4	16.2	16.4	16.4	16.4	16.4	16.2	16.6	16.6	16.7	17.1	17.2	16.6
2002	16.2	15.9	16.3	15.9	16.0	16.2	16.2	16.3	16.3	16.3	16.8	16.9	16.3
2003	15.8	15.6	15.8	15.8	16.0	16.2	16.0	16.0	16.1	16.4	16.9	17.1	16.1

Employment by Industry: Pennsylvania—*Continued*

(Numbers in thousands. Not seasonally adjusted.)

Industry	January	February	March	April	May	June	July	August	September	October	November	December	Annual Average
ERIE—*Continued*													
Transportation and utilities													
1990	2.3	2.3	2.3	2.4	2.5	2.5	2.4	2.4	2.3	2.2	2.2	2.2	2.3
1991	2.3	2.2	2.2	2.2	2.2	2.3	2.3	2.3	2.3	2.3	2.3	2.3	2.3
1992	2.2	2.1	2.1	2.2	2.3	2.4	2.3	2.3	2.2	2.3	2.3	2.3	2.3
1993	2.2	2.2	2.2	2.2	2.2	2.3	2.1	2.1	2.2	2.2	2.2	2.1	2.2
1994	2.0	2.1	2.0	2.1	2.2	2.3	2.3	2.4	2.4	2.3	2.3	2.5	2.2
1995	2.2	2.3	2.3	2.5	2.5	2.5	2.4	2.3	2.3	2.5	2.5	2.5	2.4
1996	2.5	2.5	2.5	2.6	2.7	2.7	2.7	2.6	2.7	2.8	2.8	2.7	2.7
1997	2.6	2.6	2.7	2.8	2.8	2.9	2.7	2.6	2.8	2.8	2.8	2.8	2.7
1998	2.6	2.6	2.6	2.7	2.7	2.7	2.7	2.7	2.7	2.7	2.7	2.7	2.7
1999	2.6	2.6	2.6	2.8	2.9	2.8	2.8	2.8	2.8	2.9	2.9	2.9	2.8
2000	2.8	2.8	2.8	3.0	3.0	3.0	2.9	2.9	3.0	3.1	3.1	2.9	2.9
2001	2.6	2.6	2.6	2.7	2.7	2.7	2.6	2.5	2.6	2.6	2.6	2.5	2.6
2002	2.4	2.5	2.5	2.5	2.5	2.5	2.4	2.4	2.5	2.5	2.5	2.4	2.5
2003	2.3	2.4	2.3	2.4	2.4	2.4	2.3	2.3	2.4	2.4	2.4	2.4	2.4
Information													
1990	2.2	2.1	2.1	2.1	2.1	2.2	2.1	2.1	2.2	2.2	2.2	2.2	2.2
1991	2.2	2.2	2.2	2.2	2.2	2.2	2.2	2.2	2.2	2.2	2.2	2.2	2.2
1992	2.1	2.1	2.1	2.2	2.2	2.2	2.2	2.2	2.2	2.2	2.2	2.2	2.2
1993	2.1	2.2	2.2	2.2	2.2	2.2	2.2	2.2	2.2	2.2	2.2	2.2	2.2
1994	2.1	2.1	2.1	2.1	2.2	2.2	2.3	2.3	2.3	2.3	2.3	2.3	2.2
1995	2.3	2.4	2.3	2.3	2.4	2.4	2.4	2.4	2.5	2.5	2.5	2.5	2.4
1996	2.5	2.5	2.6	2.5	2.5	2.6	2.6	2.6	2.7	2.7	2.7	2.7	2.6
1997	2.6	2.7	2.7	2.7	2.7	2.8	2.7	2.7	2.7	2.6	2.7	2.7	2.7
1998	2.6	2.6	2.6	2.6	2.7	2.6	2.6	2.6	2.7	2.6	2.6	2.7	2.6
1999	2.7	2.7	2.7	2.7	2.8	2.8	2.7	2.7	2.7	2.7	2.8	2.8	2.7
2000	2.7	2.7	2.7	2.7	2.7	2.8	2.8	2.8	2.8	2.7	2.7	2.7	2.7
2001	2.7	2.8	2.7	2.8	2.7	2.8	2.7	2.6	2.6	2.6	2.5	2.5	2.7
2002	2.5	2.4	2.4	2.4	2.5	2.5	2.6	2.6	2.6	2.7	2.7	2.7	2.6
2003	2.7	2.7	2.7	2.7	2.7	2.7	2.7	2.8	2.8	2.8	2.8	2.8	2.7
Financial activities													
1990	6.0	5.9	5.9	5.9	5.9	6.1	6.1	6.1	6.0	6.0	6.0	6.0	6.0
1991	6.1	6.0	6.1	6.1	6.2	6.3	6.3	6.2	6.2	6.0	6.1	6.2	6.2
1992	6.0	6.0	5.9	6.0	6.0	6.2	6.1	6.1	6.0	5.8	5.8	5.9	6.0
1993	5.8	5.8	5.8	5.8	5.9	6.0	6.1	6.2	6.2	6.1	6.1	6.1	6.0
1994	6.1	6.1	6.2	6.1	6.1	6.2	6.3	6.3	6.3	6.2	6.2	6.2	6.2
1995	6.1	6.1	6.1	6.2	6.2	6.4	6.3	6.4	6.3	6.1	6.1	6.2	6.2
1996	6.1	6.2	6.1	6.0	6.0	6.2	6.2	6.1	6.1	6.1	6.1	6.1	6.1
1997	6.0	6.0	6.0	6.0	6.0	6.2	6.2	6.2	6.1	6.1	6.1	6.1	6.1
1998	6.1	6.1	6.1	6.1	6.0	6.1	6.0	6.1	5.9	6.0	6.1	6.2	6.1
1999	6.1	6.1	6.1	6.1	6.0	6.1	6.2	6.2	6.1	6.0	6.0	6.1	6.1
2000	6.2	6.1	6.2	6.1	6.1	6.2	6.3	6.3	6.3	6.3	6.3	6.3	6.2
2001	6.6	6.5	6.5	6.4	6.5	6.6	6.4	6.4	6.3	6.4	6.4	6.4	6.5
2002	6.4	6.4	6.4	6.5	6.5	6.7	6.8	6.9	6.8	6.6	6.7	6.7	6.6
2003	6.6	6.6	6.5	6.6	6.7	6.7	6.7	6.8	6.7	6.8	6.9	6.9	6.7
Professional and business services													
1990	6.1	6.4	6.5	6.4	6.5	6.6	7.0	7.1	7.2	7.1	7.1	6.9	6.7
1991	7.0	6.8	7.0	6.8	6.8	6.9	6.8	7.0	7.1	7.1	7.0	6.8	6.9
1992	7.1	7.2	7.2	7.3	7.5	7.5	7.7	7.7	7.8	7.5	7.4	7.3	7.4
1993	6.9	7.3	7.2	7.5	7.7	7.8	7.8	7.8	7.8	7.9	7.9	8.0	7.6
1994	7.6	7.6	8.2	8.1	8.2	8.3	8.4	8.5	8.5	8.1	8.2	8.0	8.1
1995	8.1	8.1	8.4	8.5	8.6	8.6	8.5	8.7	8.7	8.6	8.5	8.3	8.5
1996	7.7	8.0	8.1	8.6	8.7	8.8	8.9	9.0	9.1	9.0	8.9	8.8	8.6
1997	8.5	8.7	8.8	8.7	8.8	9.1	9.2	9.5	9.7	9.4	9.4	9.3	9.1
1998	8.7	8.9	9.2	9.4	9.6	9.9	9.2	9.5	9.6	9.5	9.8	9.6	9.4
1999	9.2	9.7	9.9	9.8	10.1	10.4	10.2	10.3	10.5	10.0	9.9	9.9	10.0
2000	9.2	9.6	10.5	10.7	11.0	11.6	11.2	11.6	11.3	10.9	10.9	11.0	10.8
2001	11.1	11.2	11.0	10.5	10.3	10.5	10.4	10.6	10.5	10.3	10.0	10.0	10.5
2002	10.0	10.3	10.3	10.7	10.9	10.8	11.0	11.1	11.0	10.7	10.5	10.1	10.6
2003	9.5	9.6	9.9	10.1	10.1	10.4	10.3	10.4	10.6	10.6	10.4	10.5	10.2
Educational and health services													
1990	17.5	17.7	17.8	18.0	17.9	17.8	17.7	17.6	18.0	18.5	18.5	18.6	18.0
1991	18.3	18.8	18.7	18.9	18.8	18.7	18.7	18.5	18.7	19.2	19.3	19.2	18.8
1992	18.9	19.1	19.2	19.6	19.5	19.3	19.3	19.2	19.4	19.7	20.0	19.9	19.4
1993	19.4	19.8	19.8	19.6	19.4	19.4	19.3	19.3	19.7	19.9	20.0	19.9	19.6
1994	19.4	19.8	19.6	19.9	19.7	19.8	19.7	19.6	20.1	20.0	20.2	20.2	19.8
1995	20.0	20.2	20.2	20.3	20.4	20.0	19.9	19.8	20.5	20.4	20.5	20.5	20.2
1996	20.4	20.6	20.6	20.6	20.4	20.0	20.2	20.0	20.5	20.6	20.6	20.7	20.4
1997	20.5	20.7	20.6	20.6	20.6	20.3	20.2	20.3	20.9	20.8	20.8	20.8	20.6
1998	21.0	21.0	21.0	20.8	20.9	20.4	20.3	20.1	20.7	21.1	21.2	21.0	20.8
1999	21.0	21.3	21.2	21.0	20.9	20.6	20.3	20.0	20.5	21.3	21.4	20.9	20.9
2000	21.0	21.4	21.5	21.6	21.5	20.9	20.7	20.8	21.2	21.6	21.5	21.3	21.3
2001	21.3	21.7	21.6	21.6	21.7	21.1	21.0	21.1	21.6	21.9	22.0	22.2	21.6
2002	22.1	22.2	22.2	22.3	21.9	21.9	22.0	22.1	22.6	23.0	23.1	23.1	22.4
2003	23.0	23.3	23.5	23.6	23.0	22.7	22.3	22.1	22.7	23.1	23.1	23.1	23.0

Employment by Industry: Pennsylvania—*Continued*

(Numbers in thousands. Not seasonally adjusted.)

Industry	January	February	March	April	May	June	July	August	September	October	November	December	Annual Average
ERIE—*Continued*													
Leisure and hospitality													
1990	9.0	9.2	9.3	9.7	10.2	10.4	10.2	10.3	10.0	9.3	9.2	9.2	9.7
1991	8.9	9.0	9.2	9.8	10.3	10.6	10.4	10.5	10.1	9.4	9.2	9.1	9.7
1992	8.7	8.8	8.9	9.8	10.1	10.2	10.9	11.0	10.7	10.2	9.9	9.8	9.9
1993	9.5	9.4	9.6	10.3	10.7	11.1	11.5	11.4	11.0	10.8	10.5	10.3	10.5
1994	9.5	9.3	9.5	10.3	10.8	11.2	11.3	11.4	10.9	10.2	10.1	10.0	10.4
1995	9.8	9.8	10.1	10.6	11.2	11.5	11.8	11.9	11.2	10.8	10.4	10.5	10.8
1996	10.2	10.0	10.1	10.8	11.3	11.6	12.0	11.8	11.1	11.2	10.7	10.5	10.9
1997	10.5	10.4	10.5	11.0	11.4	11.6	12.0	11.8	11.0	10.8	10.3	10.5	11.0
1998	10.3	10.2	10.4	10.9	11.6	11.9	12.2	12.0	11.5	11.3	11.0	11.1	11.2
1999	10.7	10.8	10.8	11.8	12.3	12.5	13.0	13.0	12.0	11.7	11.4	11.4	11.8
2000	10.8	10.9	11.0	11.7	12.3	12.7	12.8	12.7	11.7	11.3	11.0	10.8	11.6
2001	10.4	10.5	10.7	11.5	12.1	12.5	12.7	12.6	11.6	11.4	11.3	10.8	11.5
2002	10.8	10.6	10.9	11.5	12.2	12.6	12.9	12.9	12.3	11.8	11.4	11.3	11.8
2003	11.1	10.9	11.2	12.0	12.9	13.3	13.4	13.2	12.4	12.1	11.8	11.6	12.2
Other services													
1990	4.9	4.9	5.0	5.1	5.1	5.2	5.2	5.2	5.1	5.1	5.1	5.2	5.1
1991	5.1	5.2	5.2	5.0	5.0	5.0	5.2	5.2	5.1	5.1	5.1	5.1	5.1
1992	5.1	5.0	5.1	5.1	5.1	5.2	5.3	5.3	5.3	5.3	5.3	5.3	5.2
1993	5.2	5.2	5.3	5.3	5.4	5.4	5.5	5.5	5.5	5.4	5.4	5.4	5.4
1994	5.2	5.2	5.3	5.5	5.4	5.5	5.6	5.5	5.4	5.4	5.5	5.4	5.4
1995	5.3	5.3	5.4	5.4	5.5	5.5	5.6	5.5	5.4	5.4	5.4	5.5	5.4
1996	5.3	5.4	5.4	5.4	5.3	5.3	5.4	5.4	5.3	5.3	5.4	5.4	5.4
1997	5.4	5.5	5.5	5.5	5.5	5.5	5.7	5.6	5.5	5.5	5.4	5.5	5.5
1998	5.4	5.4	5.5	5.6	5.6	5.6	5.7	5.6	5.5	5.6	5.6	5.7	5.6
1999	5.6	5.7	5.7	5.7	5.7	5.9	5.9	5.9	5.7	5.9	6.0	5.9	5.8
2000	5.9	5.9	6.0	6.1	6.1	6.1	6.2	6.1	6.0	6.0	5.9	6.0	6.0
2001	5.9	5.9	6.0	6.1	6.1	6.2	6.2	6.2	6.1	6.1	6.1	6.2	6.1
2002	6.3	6.3	6.4	6.3	6.3	6.4	6.3	6.2	6.1	6.2	6.2	6.1	6.3
2003	6.1	6.1	6.2	6.2	6.3	6.3	6.4	6.3	6.2	6.3	6.3	6.3	6.3
Government													
1990	14.0	14.1	14.4	14.8	14.7	13.5	13.0	12.2	13.9	14.5	14.6	14.4	14.0
1991	14.0	14.5	14.6	14.4	13.5	13.1	12.5	11.9	13.5	14.5	14.6	14.6	13.8
1992	14.0	14.5	14.3	14.6	14.0	13.6	12.8	13.0	13.7	14.5	14.5	14.6	14.0
1993	14.0	14.6	14.5	14.6	13.9	13.9	13.2	12.6	14.1	14.9	15.1	15.0	14.2
1994	13.8	14.8	14.9	14.8	15.0	14.0	13.3	13.1	14.5	15.2	15.3	15.1	14.5
1995	14.0	15.3	15.3	15.3	15.3	14.5	13.6	13.5	15.2	15.6	15.8	15.6	14.9
1996	14.3	15.5	15.7	15.6	15.4	14.3	13.5	13.5	15.3	15.7	15.7	15.6	15.0
1997	15.0	15.7	15.8	15.6	15.6	14.6	13.8	13.8	15.3	15.9	16.1	16.0	15.3
1998	15.6	16.0	16.1	16.1	15.9	14.8	13.9	13.6	15.9	16.2	16.3	15.8	15.5
1999	15.4	16.1	16.2	16.3	15.6	15.0	14.5	13.9	16.1	16.4	16.4	16.2	15.7
2000	16.0	16.4	16.4	16.8	16.6	15.3	14.3	14.1	16.2	16.7	16.8	16.5	16.0
2001	15.6	16.5	16.5	16.6	16.3	15.1	14.4	14.4	16.1	16.8	16.9	16.7	16.0
2002	15.9	16.8	16.7	16.8	16.8	15.5	14.9	15.0	16.5	17.3	17.4	17.3	16.4
2003	16.6	17.4	17.1	17.1	17.2	15.5	14.4	14.2	16.3	17.1	17.3	17.2	16.5
Federal government													
1990	1.5	1.5	1.5	1.9	1.9	1.6	1.7	1.6	1.6	1.5	1.5	1.5	1.6
1991	1.5	1.4	1.4	1.4	1.4	1.4	1.4	1.4	1.4	1.5	1.5	1.5	1.4
1992	1.5	1.5	1.5	1.5	1.5	1.5	1.5	1.5	1.4	1.5	1.4	1.4	1.5
1993	1.5	1.5	1.5	1.4	1.4	1.5	1.5	1.5	1.5	1.5	1.5	1.5	1.5
1994	1.5	1.5	1.5	1.5	1.5	1.5	1.5	1.5	1.5	1.5	1.5	1.5	1.5
1995	1.5	1.5	1.5	1.5	1.5	1.5	1.5	1.5	1.5	1.5	1.5	1.5	1.5
1996	1.5	1.5	1.5	1.5	1.5	1.5	1.5	1.5	1.5	1.6	1.6	1.6	1.5
1997	1.6	1.6	1.6	1.6	1.6	1.6	1.6	1.6	1.6	1.6	1.7	1.7	1.6
1998	1.6	1.6	1.6	1.6	1.6	1.6	1.6	1.6	1.6	1.6	1.6	1.7	1.6
1999	1.6	1.6	1.6	1.6	1.6	1.6	1.7	1.7	1.7	1.7	1.7	1.7	1.7
2000	1.6	1.6	1.7	1.8	2.0	1.7	1.7	1.6	1.6	1.5	1.5	1.5	1.7
2001	1.6	1.5	1.5	1.5	1.5	1.5	1.5	1.5	1.5	1.5	1.5	1.5	1.5
2002	1.5	1.5	1.4	1.4	1.4	1.4	1.5	1.5	1.5	1.5	1.5	1.5	1.5
2003	1.5	1.5	1.5	1.5	1.5	1.5	1.5	1.5	1.5	1.5	1.5	1.5	1.5
State government													
1990	3.4	3.2	3.5	3.5	3.4	2.7	2.7	2.7	3.5	3.7	3.6	3.4	3.3
1991	3.2	3.6	3.6	3.5	2.5	2.5	2.5	2.5	3.2	3.5	3.5	3.5	3.1
1992	3.1	3.4	3.2	3.5	2.8	2.7	2.6	2.8	3.4	3.6	3.6	3.6	3.2
1993	3.2	3.6	3.4	3.6	2.7	2.7	2.7	2.8	3.5	3.8	3.9	3.8	3.3
1994	2.9	3.7	3.7	3.6	3.6	2.9	2.9	2.9	3.9	4.0	3.9	3.9	3.5
1995	3.1	4.0	3.9	4.0	3.8	3.1	3.1	3.1	4.0	4.2	4.2	4.1	3.7
1996	3.1	4.1	4.1	4.1	3.8	3.2	3.2	3.2	4.3	4.2	4.2	4.1	3.8
1997	3.8	4.3	4.3	4.1	3.9	3.2	3.2	3.4	4.3	4.3	4.4	4.3	4.0
1998	4.3	4.4	4.4	4.6	4.2	3.3	3.4	3.4	4.6	4.7	4.7	4.2	4.2
1999	4.0	4.5	4.4	4.6	3.8	3.3	3.4	3.4	4.3	4.4	4.4	4.2	4.1
2000	4.3	4.6	4.5	4.6	4.3	3.4	3.5	3.6	4.4	4.7	4.7	4.6	4.3
2001	3.8	4.6	4.6	4.7	4.5	3.6	3.7	3.8	4.4	4.8	4.8	4.7	4.3
2002	3.9	4.8	4.8	4.8	4.7	3.7	3.7	4.0	4.8	5.1	5.1	5.1	4.5
2003	4.7	5.2	5.0	4.9	5.0	3.7	3.7	3.9	4.8	5.0	5.1	5.1	4.7

Employment by Industry: Pennsylvania—*Continued*

(Numbers in thousands. Not seasonally adjusted.)

Industry	January	February	March	April	May	June	July	August	September	October	November	December	Annual Average
ERIE—*Continued*													
Local government													
1990	9.1	9.4	9.4	9.4	9.4	9.2	8.6	7.9	8.8	9.3	9.5	9.5	9.1
1991	9.3	9.5	9.6	9.5	9.6	9.2	8.6	8.0	8.9	9.5	9.6	9.6	9.2
1992	9.4	9.6	9.6	9.6	9.7	9.4	8.7	8.7	8.9	9.4	9.5	9.6	9.3
1993	9.3	9.5	9.6	9.6	9.8	9.7	9.0	8.3	9.1	9.6	9.7	9.7	9.4
1994	9.4	9.6	9.7	9.7	9.9	9.6	8.9	8.7	9.1	9.7	9.9	9.7	9.5
1995	9.4	9.8	9.9	9.8	10.0	9.9	9.0	8.9	9.7	9.9	10.1	10.0	9.7
1996	9.7	9.9	10.1	10.0	10.1	9.6	8.8	8.8	9.5	9.9	9.9	9.9	9.7
1997	9.6	9.8	9.9	9.9	10.1	9.8	9.0	8.8	9.4	10.0	10.0	10.0	9.7
1998	9.7	10.0	10.1	9.9	10.1	9.9	8.9	8.6	9.7	9.9	10.0	9.9	9.7
1999	9.8	10.0	10.2	10.1	10.2	10.1	9.4	8.8	10.1	10.3	10.3	10.3	10.0
2000	10.1	10.2	10.2	10.4	10.3	10.2	9.1	8.9	10.2	10.5	10.6	10.4	10.1
2001	10.2	10.4	10.4	10.4	10.3	10.0	9.2	9.1	10.2	10.5	10.6	10.5	10.2
2002	10.5	10.5	10.5	10.6	10.7	10.4	9.7	9.5	10.2	10.7	10.8	10.7	10.4
2003	10.4	10.7	10.6	10.7	10.7	10.3	9.2	8.8	10.0	10.6	10.7	10.6	10.3
HARRISBURG-LEBANON-CARLISLE													
Total nonfarm													
1990	309.7	310.1	312.3	313.1	316.5	319.2	316.4	316.9	316.9	316.3	317.3	316.5	315.1
1991	311.0	309.3	310.7	312.8	317.0	317.6	316.5	316.7	315.8	316.6	316.7	316.6	314.8
1992	308.4	308.7	311.2	315.3	319.6	320.1	319.4	319.9	320.1	320.5	320.9	321.6	317.1
1993	314.3	315.0	315.1	319.2	323.7	324.1	324.9	324.7	325.5	325.1	325.4	326.4	322.0
1994	318.3	318.7	321.8	324.5	329.9	332.4	330.2	330.8	331.1	334.5	336.2	337.3	328.8
1995	327.8	329.0	331.3	333.7	336.9	338.5	337.0	338.9	338.2	340.3	340.8	341.7	336.2
1996	330.1	335.9	339.3	341.2	346.1	345.3	344.3	345.4	346.1	347.0	347.3	348.5	343.0
1997	343.8	344.9	346.3	349.0	353.2	352.5	351.8	351.1	353.0	353.3	355.0	356.3	350.9
1998	348.6	350.0	351.6	356.0	360.7	361.3	359.4	358.3	360.0	359.4	360.0	360.5	357.2
1999	351.8	353.6	355.3	359.1	360.1	362.8	361.1	359.8	360.1	359.1	360.8	362.7	358.9
2000	354.9	356.0	360.4	362.8	366.7	368.5	365.8	365.4	366.1	365.4	365.9	366.4	363.7
2001	357.3	359.6	361.3	364.6	367.7	369.0	364.5	364.0	364.1	364.7	364.8	365.4	363.9
2002	356.6	359.3	362.2	366.0	367.7	370.5	368.9	369.1	368.8	369.3	370.2	370.0	366.6
2003	360.8	361.3	362.9	366.1	370.7	370.9	368.8	368.1	368.3	368.5	369.6	369.4	367.1
Total private													
1990	245.6	245.4	247.1	247.8	250.9	254.5	253.2	253.9	252.9	251.5	252.1	251.3	250.5
1991	246.7	244.2	245.4	247.8	251.6	253.4	253.7	254.2	252.4	251.9	251.8	251.1	250.4
1992	244.9	243.8	246.0	249.3	253.6	254.3	255.3	255.6	255.1	255.5	255.6	256.2	252.1
1993	249.8	248.5	248.8	252.3	256.8	258.3	261.4	261.8	261.1	259.1	259.1	260.0	256.4
1994	253.3	252.5	255.2	257.8	263.6	265.9	265.4	266.2	266.0	267.8	269.4	269.6	262.7
1995	261.6	261.6	264.0	266.1	269.9	271.6	273.0	274.7	272.8	273.0	273.1	273.8	269.6
1996	265.0	268.2	271.2	273.0	278.0	278.3	280.1	281.3	279.9	279.7	279.2	280.0	276.2
1997	276.4	276.5	277.7	280.0	284.3	285.5	286.6	286.2	285.6	285.3	286.6	288.1	283.2
1998	281.2	281.6	283.2	287.2	292.1	294.3	294.5	293.9	292.3	291.5	291.6	291.9	289.6
1999	284.3	284.9	286.3	290.2	291.6	294.8	295.1	294.3	292.4	291.2	292.0	293.6	290.9
2000	287.0	287.0	291.0	293.6	297.3	299.7	299.5	299.8	298.3	297.1	297.1	298.1	295.5
2001	290.2	290.8	292.2	295.2	298.4	300.4	298.7	298.4	295.6	295.1	295.0	295.9	295.5
2002	288.2	289.3	291.7	295.1	296.3	299.8	301.3	301.9	299.3	298.5	298.7	298.8	296.6
2003	290.9	289.5	291.1	294.1	298.8	300.5	301.1	301.2	298.1	297.6	298.4	298.2	296.6
Goods-producing													
1990	62.3	61.9	62.3	62.8	63.3	64.4	64.4	64.7	64.0	63.0	63.0	62.2	63.2
1991	60.4	58.4	58.6	59.2	59.3	59.8	60.2	60.7	60.3	60.4	59.4	58.6	59.6
1992	57.7	57.0	57.3	58.1	58.6	58.8	59.5	59.7	59.4	59.9	59.3	58.9	58.7
1993	58.0	57.0	56.7	57.0	57.9	58.9	60.3	60.9	60.4	59.7	59.4	59.1	58.8
1994	56.8	56.0	56.2	57.4	58.6	59.7	59.7	60.1	59.8	60.1	60.3	60.1	58.7
1995	57.7	56.9	57.5	57.7	58.1	58.2	58.5	59.0	58.2	57.5	57.1	56.4	57.7
1996	54.4	54.5	55.2	55.6	56.4	56.8	57.7	57.7	56.9	56.5	55.9	55.7	56.1
1997	55.2	54.9	55.2	55.8	56.1	57.0	57.4	57.5	57.3	57.5	57.7	57.7	56.6
1998	56.7	56.5	56.9	58.2	59.7	59.7	59.7	59.6	58.9	58.5	57.7	57.4	58.3
1999	56.5	56.1	56.0	57.0	57.0	58.0	57.1	57.2	56.4	55.3	55.4	55.2	56.4
2000	54.4	53.9	54.9	55.8	56.4	57.2	56.9	56.8	56.9	56.7	56.2	55.7	56.0
2001	54.1	53.7	53.9	53.9	54.0	54.6	54.1	54.1	53.4	52.8	52.4	52.3	53.6
2002	51.2	51.0	51.8	52.1	49.9	51.9	53.0	53.0	52.2	52.1	51.4	50.9	51.7
2003	50.2	49.0	48.8	49.4	50.3	50.9	51.3	51.3	50.4	50.2	49.9	49.5	50.1
Construction and mining													
1990	13.3	13.3	13.6	13.9	14.0	14.4	14.8	14.6	14.2	13.6	13.6	13.1	13.9
1991	12.2	11.8	12.2	12.6	13.1	13.4	13.8	13.9	13.7	13.8	13.1	12.2	13.0
1992	11.6	11.2	11.4	12.3	12.7	12.9	13.2	13.2	13.2	13.6	12.8	12.3	12.5
1993	11.5	11.2	10.9	11.6	12.3	12.8	13.4	13.5	13.3	13.2	12.9	12.5	12.4
1994	11.2	10.8	11.3	11.9	12.8	13.3	13.5	13.5	13.4	13.8	13.5	13.1	12.7
1995	11.8	11.3	11.7	12.3	12.5	12.7	13.1	13.1	12.9	12.4	12.0	11.3	12.3
1996	10.3	10.2	10.9	11.6	12.2	12.7	13.3	13.1	12.7	12.5	12.2	11.8	12.0
1997	11.4	10.9	11.1	11.6	12.0	12.5	13.0	13.0	12.9	12.9	12.9	12.6	12.2
1998	12.2	12.0	12.1	13.2	14.4	13.8	13.9	13.8	13.7	13.6	13.3	13.0	13.3
1999	12.2	12.2	12.3	13.2	13.5	14.1	14.4	14.8	14.9	14.1	14.1	13.9	13.6
2000	13.5	13.1	13.9	14.8	15.1	15.5	15.3	15.5	15.1	14.8	14.4	13.9	14.6
2001	13.5	13.3	13.7	14.3	14.7	15.4	15.3	15.4	14.9	14.9	14.7	14.7	14.6
2002	13.9	13.9	14.4	15.2	15.3	15.8	16.0	16.0	15.5	15.6	15.2	14.6	15.1
2003	14.0	13.5	13.6	13.9	14.6	14.9	15.3	15.4	15.0	14.9	14.6	14.2	14.5

Employment by Industry: Pennsylvania—*Continued*

(Numbers in thousands. Not seasonally adjusted.)

Industry	January	February	March	April	May	June	July	August	September	October	November	December	Annual Average
HARRISBURG-LEBANON-CARLISLE—*Continued*													
Manufacturing													
1990	49.0	48.6	48.7	48.9	49.3	50.0	49.6	50.1	49.8	49.4	49.4	49.1	49.3
1991	48.2	46.6	46.4	46.6	46.2	46.4	46.4	46.8	46.6	46.6	46.3	46.4	46.6
1992	46.1	45.8	45.9	45.8	45.9	45.9	46.3	46.5	46.2	46.3	46.5	46.6	46.2
1993	46.5	45.8	45.8	45.4	45.6	46.1	46.9	47.4	47.1	46.5	46.5	46.6	46.4
1994	45.6	45.2	44.9	45.5	45.8	46.4	46.2	46.6	46.4	46.3	46.8	47.0	46.1
1995	45.9	45.6	45.8	45.4	45.6	45.5	45.4	45.9	45.3	45.1	45.1	45.1	45.5
1996	44.1	44.3	44.3	44.0	44.2	44.1	44.4	44.6	44.2	44.0	43.7	43.9	44.2
1997	43.8	44.0	44.1	44.2	44.1	44.5	44.4	44.5	44.4	44.6	44.8	45.1	44.4
1998	44.5	44.5	44.8	45.0	45.3	45.9	45.8	45.8	45.2	44.9	44.4	44.4	45.0
1999	44.3	43.9	43.7	43.8	43.5	43.9	42.7	42.4	41.5	41.2	41.3	41.3	42.8
2000	40.9	40.8	41.0	41.0	41.3	41.7	41.6	41.3	41.8	41.9	41.8	41.8	41.4
2001	40.6	40.4	40.2	39.6	39.3	39.2	38.8	38.7	38.5	37.9	37.7	37.6	39.0
2002	37.3	37.1	37.4	36.9	34.6	36.1	37.0	37.0	36.7	36.5	36.2	36.3	36.6
2003	36.2	35.5	35.2	35.5	35.7	36.0	36.0	35.9	35.4	35.3	35.3	35.3	35.6
Service-providing													
1990	247.4	248.2	250.0	250.3	253.2	254.8	252.0	252.2	252.9	253.3	254.3	254.3	251.9
1991	250.6	250.9	252.1	253.6	257.7	257.8	256.3	256.0	255.5	256.2	257.3	258.0	255.2
1992	250.7	251.7	253.9	257.2	261.0	261.3	259.9	260.2	260.7	260.6	261.6	262.7	258.5
1993	256.3	258.0	258.4	262.2	265.8	265.2	264.6	263.8	265.1	265.4	266.0	267.3	263.2
1994	261.5	262.7	265.6	267.1	271.3	272.7	270.5	270.7	271.3	274.4	275.9	277.2	270.1
1995	270.1	272.1	273.8	276.0	278.8	280.3	278.5	279.9	280.0	282.8	283.7	285.3	278.4
1996	275.7	281.4	284.1	285.6	289.7	288.5	286.6	287.7	289.2	290.5	291.4	292.8	286.9
1997	288.6	290.0	291.1	293.2	297.1	295.5	294.4	293.6	295.7	295.8	297.3	298.6	294.2
1998	291.9	293.5	294.7	297.8	301.0	301.6	299.7	298.7	301.1	300.9	302.3	303.1	298.9
1999	295.3	297.5	299.3	302.1	303.1	304.8	304.0	302.6	303.7	303.8	305.4	307.5	302.4
2000	300.5	302.1	305.5	307.0	310.3	311.3	308.9	308.6	309.2	308.7	309.7	310.7	307.7
2001	303.2	305.9	307.4	310.7	313.7	314.4	310.4	309.9	310.7	311.9	312.4	313.1	310.3
2002	305.4	308.3	310.4	313.9	317.8	318.6	315.9	316.1	316.6	317.2	318.8	319.1	314.8
2003	310.6	312.3	314.1	316.7	320.4	320.0	317.5	316.8	317.9	318.3	319.7	319.9	317.0
Trade, transportation, and utilities													
1990	65.6	65.1	65.2	65.2	65.5	65.8	64.3	64.2	64.6	65.9	66.5	66.7	65.4
1991	64.6	63.4	63.2	63.8	64.3	64.3	63.6	63.2	63.9	64.1	65.3	65.7	64.1
1992	63.4	62.3	62.6	63.0	63.6	63.4	62.8	62.8	63.0	64.4	65.7	66.6	63.6
1993	64.5	63.5	63.2	64.5	65.0	64.6	65.9	66.2	66.1	66.4	67.4	68.3	65.5
1994	66.1	65.2	65.7	65.4	67.0	66.9	66.7	66.8	67.2	68.6	70.0	70.6	67.2
1995	67.8	67.0	67.4	67.7	68.1	68.0	68.7	68.9	69.0	70.7	71.9	72.7	69.0
1996	70.2	70.0	70.6	70.6	71.5	71.2	71.4	71.3	72.1	73.7	75.0	76.2	72.0
1997	74.2	73.4	73.2	74.1	74.5	74.8	74.7	73.6	75.3	75.8	77.2	78.2	74.9
1998	75.7	74.9	74.9	75.3	75.6	76.2	76.0	75.8	76.4	77.2	78.6	79.5	76.3
1999	76.9	76.3	76.7	76.2	76.3	76.8	77.5	76.9	77.3	78.0	79.3	80.6	77.4
2000	78.6	78.4	79.0	79.1	79.6	79.9	79.6	79.9	79.8	80.1	81.6	82.7	79.9
2001	80.6	80.0	79.9	80.5	80.6	80.4	79.7	79.5	79.5	80.5	81.5	82.4	80.4
2002	79.9	78.8	78.6	79.2	79.8	79.8	79.2	79.4	79.6	80.1	81.2	82.1	79.8
2003	79.4	78.5	78.5	78.4	78.8	79.1	78.9	79.0	78.9	79.9	80.8	81.7	79.3
Wholesale trade													
1990	14.2	14.2	14.4	14.3	14.3	14.4	14.4	14.4	14.4	14.5	14.3	14.3	14.3
1991	14.2	14.0	13.9	14.1	14.1	14.2	14.4	14.4	14.3	14.1	14.1	14.2	14.2
1992	14.0	13.8	13.9	13.8	13.8	13.9	13.8	13.8	13.8	13.9	13.9	13.9	13.9
1993	13.6	13.4	13.5	13.8	13.9	13.9	14.0	14.0	13.9	14.5	14.5	14.5	14.0
1994	14.3	14.2	14.3	14.5	14.6	14.7	14.5	14.7	14.7	14.7	14.7	14.7	14.6
1995	14.6	14.6	14.7	15.1	15.1	15.3	15.3	15.3	15.2	15.3	15.4	15.4	15.1
1996	15.3	15.4	15.6	15.4	15.6	15.6	15.8	15.9	15.8	16.0	16.1	16.3	15.7
1997	16.0	16.0	16.1	16.2	16.3	16.5	16.4	16.5	16.5	16.5	16.5	16.6	16.3
1998	16.3	16.3	16.2	16.3	16.3	16.6	16.6	16.6	16.8	16.8	16.8	16.8	16.5
1999	17.0	17.1	17.1	16.5	16.4	16.5	16.7	16.8	16.7	16.4	16.4	16.6	16.7
2000	16.5	16.4	16.6	16.7	16.8	16.9	16.8	16.8	16.6	16.8	16.8	16.8	16.7
2001	16.6	16.5	16.5	16.6	16.5	16.6	16.5	16.6	16.4	16.5	16.4	16.6	16.5
2002	16.5	16.4	16.3	16.3	16.4	16.4	16.5	16.5	16.5	16.4	16.4	16.5	16.4
2003	16.2	16.2	16.2	16.2	16.3	16.3	16.4	16.4	16.2	16.2	16.2	16.3	16.3
Retail trade													
1990	35.1	34.4	34.3	34.1	34.1	34.4	33.8	33.7	33.6	34.2	35.1	35.5	34.4
1991	33.9	33.0	32.9	33.2	33.6	33.7	33.0	32.7	32.6	33.0	34.0	34.6	33.4
1992	32.9	32.1	32.1	32.5	32.9	32.7	32.9	32.9	32.7	33.5	34.7	35.3	33.1
1993	33.8	33.1	32.6	32.7	33.0	32.7	33.5	33.7	33.3	33.0	34.1	35.0	33.4
1994	33.7	32.8	33.0	33.3	33.5	33.4	33.1	33.3	33.3	33.9	35.3	36.0	33.7
1995	34.4	33.9	34.2	33.9	34.3	34.4	34.5	34.8	34.4	35.2	36.4	37.3	34.8
1996	35.2	35.0	35.3	35.1	35.7	35.6	35.5	35.5	35.8	36.8	38.2	39.4	36.1
1997	38.1	37.3	37.1	36.4	36.8	36.9	37.2	37.5	37.1	37.6	39.0	39.9	37.6
1998	38.3	37.4	37.4	37.2	37.3	37.6	37.5	37.3	37.2	37.8	39.2	40.1	37.9
1999	38.1	37.4	37.7	37.6	37.7	38.1	38.5	38.3	38.0	38.6	39.6	40.7	38.4
2000	38.5	38.0	38.2	38.5	38.8	38.9	38.8	39.0	38.7	38.5	40.0	41.2	38.9
2001	39.7	39.4	39.4	39.5	39.7	39.8	39.6	39.7	39.4	39.7	40.8	41.7	39.9
2002	39.9	38.9	39.0	39.3	39.7	39.7	39.4	39.6	39.3	39.5	40.6	41.6	39.7
2003	39.4	38.6	38.6	38.6	38.8	39.1	39.2	39.3	38.9	39.4	40.6	41.4	39.3

Employment by Industry: Pennsylvania—*Continued*

(Numbers in thousands. Not seasonally adjusted.)

Industry	January	February	March	April	May	June	July	August	September	October	November	December	Annual Average
HARRISBURG-LEBANON-CARLISLE—*Continued*													
Transportation and utilities													
1990	16.3	16.5	16.5	16.8	17.1	17.0	16.1	16.1	16.6	17.2	17.1	16.9	16.7
1991	16.5	16.4	16.4	16.5	16.6	16.4	16.2	16.1	17.0	17.0	17.2	16.9	16.6
1992	16.5	16.4	16.6	16.7	16.9	16.8	16.1	16.1	16.5	17.0	17.1	17.4	16.7
1993	17.1	17.0	17.1	18.0	18.1	18.0	18.4	18.5	18.9	18.9	18.8	18.8	18.1
1994	18.1	18.2	18.4	17.6	18.9	18.8	19.1	18.8	19.2	20.0	20.0	19.9	18.9
1995	18.8	18.5	18.5	18.7	18.7	18.3	18.9	18.8	19.4	20.2	20.1	20.0	19.1
1996	19.7	19.6	19.7	20.1	20.2	20.0	20.1	19.9	20.5	20.9	20.7	20.5	20.2
1997	20.1	20.1	20.0	21.5	21.4	21.4	21.1	19.6	21.7	21.7	21.7	21.7	21.0
1998	21.1	21.2	21.3	21.8	22.0	22.0	21.9	21.9	22.4	22.6	22.6	22.6	22.0
1999	21.8	21.8	21.9	22.1	22.2	22.2	22.3	21.8	22.6	23.0	23.3	23.3	22.4
2000	23.6	24.0	24.2	23.9	24.0	24.1	24.0	24.1	24.5	24.8	24.8	24.7	24.2
2001	24.3	24.1	24.0	24.4	24.4	24.0	23.6	23.2	23.7	24.3	24.3	24.1	24.0
2002	23.5	23.5	23.3	23.6	23.7	23.7	23.3	23.3	23.8	24.2	24.2	24.0	23.7
2003	23.8	23.7	23.7	23.6	23.7	23.7	23.3	23.3	23.8	24.3	24.0	24.0	23.7
Information													
1990	6.6	6.5	6.6	6.7	6.7	6.8	6.7	6.7	6.8	6.6	6.7	6.7	6.7
1991	6.5	6.4	6.5	6.5	6.5	6.5	6.6	6.5	6.3	6.4	6.5	6.5	6.5
1992	6.6	6.5	6.5	6.6	6.7	6.7	6.5	6.5	6.5	6.5	6.5	6.5	6.6
1993	6.5	6.4	6.5	6.4	6.5	6.5	6.6	6.6	6.5	6.5	6.5	6.5	6.5
1994	6.8	6.8	6.9	6.9	7.0	7.0	7.1	7.0	7.0	7.0	7.1	7.2	7.0
1995	7.2	7.2	7.4	7.2	7.2	7.4	7.4	7.4	7.4	7.4	7.4	7.5	7.3
1996	7.5	7.5	7.6	7.7	7.7	7.7	7.7	7.7	7.7	7.8	7.9	7.9	7.7
1997	8.0	8.0	8.0	8.2	8.2	8.2	8.2	8.0	7.9	7.9	7.9	8.0	8.0
1998	7.9	8.0	8.0	7.7	7.7	7.8	7.7	7.7	7.7	7.6	7.6	7.6	7.8
1999	7.7	7.7	7.8	7.8	7.8	7.9	7.6	7.6	7.4	7.5	7.6	7.7	7.7
2000	7.7	7.8	7.8	8.0	8.1	8.2	8.2	7.7	8.3	8.3	8.4	8.5	8.1
2001	8.5	8.6	8.6	8.6	8.6	8.6	8.7	8.7	8.6	8.5	8.5	8.6	8.6
2002	8.5	8.5	8.5	8.5	8.4	8.3	8.3	8.3	8.2	8.0	8.0	7.8	8.3
2003	7.9	7.8	7.8	7.7	7.6	7.7	7.6	7.7	7.6	7.6	7.6	7.6	7.7
Financial activities													
1990	22.1	22.0	22.0	22.1	22.2	22.6	23.0	23.0	22.8	22.5	22.6	22.8	22.5
1991	23.2	23.0	23.1	23.2	23.6	23.7	23.8	23.9	23.6	23.6	23.5	23.6	23.5
1992	22.6	22.5	22.6	22.7	22.9	23.1	22.8	22.8	22.6	22.6	22.6	22.7	22.7
1993	22.7	22.4	22.5	22.6	22.8	23.0	22.9	23.0	22.8	22.9	23.0	23.1	22.8
1994	23.3	23.2	23.3	23.1	23.2	23.4	23.3	23.3	23.1	23.4	23.5	23.6	23.3
1995	23.2	23.2	23.3	23.3	23.4	23.7	23.7	24.0	24.0	24.1	24.4	24.7	23.8
1996	24.8	24.8	25.0	25.5	25.7	26.0	26.4	26.6	26.8	25.7	25.6	25.8	25.7
1997	26.8	26.8	26.7	26.6	26.7	26.8	26.4	25.9	25.8	25.6	25.8	26.0	26.3
1998	25.8	25.7	25.9	26.0	25.8	26.1	26.0	25.9	25.6	25.8	25.8	25.8	25.9
1999	25.4	25.2	25.0	25.3	25.3	25.5	25.5	25.6	25.5	25.3	25.1	25.2	25.3
2000	25.4	25.2	25.2	25.1	25.3	25.4	25.2	25.1	24.9	24.7	24.7	24.8	25.1
2001	25.0	25.1	25.2	25.0	25.1	25.3	25.3	25.3	25.1	25.1	25.3	25.4	25.2
2002	25.4	25.5	25.6	25.6	25.8	26.1	26.4	26.5	26.3	26.2	26.4	26.6	26.0
2003	26.4	26.5	26.5	26.5	26.6	26.8	26.9	27.0	27.1	26.9	27.0	26.9	26.8
Professional and business services													
1990	20.2	20.4	20.6	20.7	20.9	21.1	20.9	21.1	21.2	21.1	20.6	20.3	20.8
1991	21.0	21.1	21.4	21.6	22.0	22.1	22.2	22.6	22.5	22.8	22.7	22.4	22.0
1992	22.4	22.6	23.1	23.9	23.9	24.3	24.9	25.1	25.1	24.5	24.5	24.8	24.1
1993	24.7	24.8	25.1	25.2	25.3	25.3	25.6	25.9	25.9	26.0	25.8	25.9	25.5
1994	25.5	25.9	26.6	26.9	27.1	27.6	27.4	27.9	27.9	28.4	28.5	28.5	27.4
1995	28.3	28.7	28.9	29.3	29.6	30.1	30.2	30.9	30.2	30.7	30.4	30.4	29.8
1996	30.7	31.4	31.6	31.3	31.7	31.7	31.4	32.0	31.4	31.7	31.4	31.3	31.5
1997	31.8	31.3	31.6	31.9	31.8	32.0	33.1	34.0	33.2	33.2	33.0	33.2	32.5
1998	33.3	33.6	33.7	34.1	34.5	35.0	35.5	35.4	35.2	34.9	35.0	34.8	34.6
1999	34.2	34.0	34.3	35.1	34.9	35.6	36.4	35.9	35.5	35.4	35.4	36.0	35.2
2000	35.1	35.0	35.6	35.0	35.1	35.7	36.1	36.4	35.9	35.7	35.3	35.1	35.5
2001	34.6	34.2	34.3	34.9	35.3	35.6	35.1	35.1	34.8	34.8	34.0	33.7	34.7
2002	33.3	33.6	33.6	34.2	34.4	35.0	35.2	35.4	35.3	34.9	35.0	34.6	34.5
2003	33.6	33.3	33.4	33.7	34.2	34.2	34.4	34.5	34.2	34.2	34.1	34.3	34.0
Educational and health services													
1990	34.5	35.3	35.5	35.4	35.4	35.0	34.9	35.2	36.2	36.3	36.6	36.6	35.6
1991	34.9	36.0	36.4	36.5	36.5	35.9	36.1	36.4	37.1	37.5	37.8	37.8	36.6
1992	37.1	37.9	38.2	38.4	38.3	37.7	37.7	37.7	39.0	39.4	39.4	39.2	38.3
1993	37.8	38.8	38.9	39.1	39.2	38.6	38.4	37.7	39.9	39.6	39.5	39.6	38.9
1994	38.7	39.6	39.9	39.8	39.8	38.9	38.7	38.6	40.2	40.6	40.8	40.6	39.7
1995	39.4	40.7	40.9	40.9	41.0	40.1	39.9	40.1	41.5	41.3	41.3	41.5	40.7
1996	39.7	41.6	41.8	41.8	41.8	40.4	40.7	40.9	42.0	42.5	42.7	42.8	41.6
1997	41.6	43.2	43.4	42.9	42.7	41.8	41.8	42.1	43.4	43.7	44.1	44.1	42.9
1998	42.5	43.9	43.9	44.9	44.6	43.8	43.7	43.6	44.8	45.2	45.5	45.2	44.3
1999	43.2	45.0	45.2	45.3	45.3	44.1	44.2	44.4	45.7	45.7	46.1	46.2	45.0
2000	45.4	46.4	46.8	46.7	46.9	45.7	45.8	46.4	47.7	48.2	48.2	48.5	46.9
2001	46.5	48.3	48.2	48.4	48.6	47.5	47.4	47.5	48.7	48.9	49.1	49.3	48.2
2002	47.3	48.8	49.1	49.0	49.4	48.5	48.7	48.7	49.9	50.5	50.6	50.5	49.3
2003	48.7	50.1	50.5	50.6	50.8	49.7	49.7	49.8	50.2	50.4	51.0	50.8	50.2

Employment by Industry: Pennsylvania—*Continued*

(Numbers in thousands. Not seasonally adjusted.)

Industry	January	February	March	April	May	June	July	August	September	October	November	December	Annual Average
HARRISBURG-LEBANON-CARLISLE—*Continued*													
Leisure and hospitality													
1990	21.4	21.3	22.0	21.9	23.9	25.6	26.0	26.1	24.5	22.9	22.9	22.7	23.4
1991	22.1	22.1	22.5	23.5	25.9	27.4	27.4	27.2	25.1	23.2	22.7	22.5	24.3
1992	21.3	21.3	22.0	22.9	25.9	26.5	27.2	27.1	25.6	24.0	23.4	23.1	24.2
1993	21.5	21.5	21.8	23.4	25.8	27.1	27.3	27.1	25.2	23.4	22.8	22.7	24.1
1994	21.4	21.1	21.8	23.4	26.0	27.4	27.5	27.5	25.8	24.3	24.1	24.0	24.5
1995	23.0	22.9	23.6	25.1	27.7	29.3	29.7	29.6	27.7	26.2	25.4	25.3	26.3
1996	22.8	23.3	24.1	25.2	27.6	29.0	29.3	29.6	27.5	26.4	25.4	25.1	26.3
1997	23.7	23.7	24.4	25.2	28.4	29.4	29.7	29.7	27.4	26.3	25.5	25.4	26.6
1998	23.9	23.7	24.5	25.3	28.5	29.8	30.1	30.1	28.1	26.5	25.5	25.7	26.8
1999	24.5	24.6	25.2	27.1	28.9	30.7	30.6	30.5	28.4	27.5	26.6	26.2	27.6
2000	24.0	23.9	25.1	27.3	29.2	30.8	30.8	30.6	27.9	26.7	26.0	26.0	27.4
2001	24.4	24.4	25.5	27.2	29.4	31.3	31.4	31.2	28.6	27.4	27.0	27.0	27.9
2002	25.3	25.7	26.9	28.8	30.8	32.2	32.6	32.5	29.9	28.7	28.0	28.1	29.1
2003	26.6	26.2	27.3	29.2	31.7	33.3	33.4	33.2	31.0	29.5	29.0	28.4	29.9
Other services													
1990	12.9	12.9	12.9	13.0	13.0	13.2	13.0	12.9	12.8	13.2	13.2	13.3	13.0
1991	14.0	13.8	13.7	13.5	13.5	13.7	13.8	13.7	13.6	13.9	13.9	14.0	13.8
1992	13.8	13.7	13.7	13.7	13.7	13.8	13.9	13.9	13.9	14.2	14.2	14.4	13.9
1993	14.1	14.1	14.1	14.1	14.3	14.3	14.4	14.4	14.3	14.6	14.7	14.8	14.4
1994	14.7	14.7	14.8	14.9	14.9	15.0	15.0	15.0	15.0	15.4	15.1	15.0	15.0
1995	15.0	15.0	15.0	14.9	14.8	14.8	14.9	14.8	14.8	15.1	15.2	15.3	15.0
1996	14.9	15.1	15.3	15.3	15.6	15.5	15.5	15.5	15.5	15.4	15.3	15.2	15.3
1997	15.1	15.2	15.2	15.3	15.9	15.5	15.3	15.4	15.3	15.3	15.4	15.5	15.4
1998	15.4	15.3	15.4	15.7	15.7	15.9	15.8	15.8	15.6	15.8	15.9	15.9	15.7
1999	15.9	16.0	16.1	16.4	16.1	16.2	16.2	16.2	16.2	16.5	16.5	16.5	16.2
2000	16.4	16.4	16.6	16.6	16.7	16.8	16.9	16.9	16.9	16.7	16.7	16.8	16.7
2001	16.5	16.5	16.6	16.7	16.8	17.1	17.0	17.0	16.9	17.1	17.2	17.2	16.9
2002	17.3	17.4	17.6	17.7	17.8	18.0	17.9	18.1	17.9	18.0	18.1	18.2	17.8
2003	18.1	18.1	18.3	18.6	18.8	18.8	18.9	18.7	18.7	18.9	19.0	19.0	18.7
Government													
1990	64.1	64.7	65.2	65.3	65.6	64.7	63.2	63.0	64.0	64.8	65.2	65.2	64.6
1991	64.3	65.1	65.3	65.0	65.4	64.2	62.8	62.5	63.4	64.7	64.9	65.5	64.4
1992	63.5	64.9	65.2	66.0	66.0	65.8	64.1	64.3	65.0	65.0	65.3	65.4	65.0
1993	64.5	66.5	66.3	66.9	66.9	65.8	63.5	62.9	64.4	66.0	66.3	66.4	65.5
1994	65.0	66.2	66.6	66.7	66.3	66.5	64.8	64.6	65.1	66.7	66.8	67.7	66.1
1995	66.2	67.4	67.3	67.6	67.0	66.9	64.0	64.2	65.4	67.3	67.7	67.9	66.6
1996	65.1	67.7	68.1	68.2	68.1	67.0	64.2	64.1	66.2	67.3	68.1	68.5	66.9
1997	67.4	68.4	68.6	69.0	68.9	67.0	65.2	64.9	67.4	68.0	68.4	68.2	67.6
1998	67.4	68.4	68.4	68.8	68.6	67.0	64.9	64.4	67.7	67.9	68.4	68.6	67.5
1999	67.5	68.7	69.0	68.9	68.5	68.0	66.0	65.5	67.7	67.9	68.8	69.1	68.0
2000	67.9	69.0	69.4	69.2	69.4	68.8	66.3	65.6	67.8	68.3	68.8	68.3	68.2
2001	67.1	68.8	69.1	69.4	69.3	68.6	65.8	65.6	68.5	69.6	69.8	69.5	68.4
2002	68.4	70.0	70.5	70.9	71.4	70.7	67.6	67.2	69.5	70.8	71.5	71.2	70.0
2003	69.9	71.8	71.8	72.0	71.9	70.4	67.7	66.9	70.2	70.9	71.2	71.2	70.5
Federal government													
1990	13.9	13.9	13.9	14.0	14.4	14.1	13.9	13.7	13.4	13.4	13.4	13.3	13.8
1991	13.3	13.3	13.3	13.2	13.3	13.4	13.3	13.2	13.1	13.0	13.0	13.0	13.2
1992	13.4	13.4	13.4	13.4	13.4	13.4	13.3	13.3	13.2	13.2	13.2	13.3	13.3
1993	13.0	13.0	12.9	13.0	13.0	13.1	13.1	13.1	13.1	12.8	12.8	13.0	13.0
1994	12.7	12.7	12.7	12.7	12.7	12.7	12.6	12.7	12.7	12.5	12.4	12.6	12.6
1995	12.3	12.3	12.3	12.5	12.4	12.4	12.3	12.3	12.3	12.3	12.2	12.4	12.3
1996	12.1	12.2	12.2	12.3	12.3	12.3	12.2	12.3	12.3	12.4	12.7	12.9	12.4
1997	12.8	12.8	12.7	12.7	12.7	12.7	12.7	12.7	12.6	12.6	12.6	12.8	12.7
1998	12.5	12.5	12.4	12.4	12.4	12.4	12.5	12.5	12.4	12.1	12.1	12.3	12.4
1999	12.0	12.0	12.0	11.9	11.9	11.9	11.9	11.9	11.8	11.7	11.8	11.9	11.9
2000	11.6	11.6	11.6	11.8	12.4	11.9	11.9	11.6	11.3	10.9	11.0	11.0	11.6
2001	10.9	10.8	10.8	10.9	10.9	10.9	10.9	10.9	10.8	10.9	11.0	11.0	10.9
2002	11.0	10.8	10.8	10.9	10.9	11.0	10.9	10.8	10.7	10.9	11.0	11.0	10.9
2003	11.0	11.0	10.9	10.8	10.8	10.8	10.8	10.6	10.6	10.6	10.6	10.7	10.8
State government													
1990	29.1	29.2	29.5	29.7	29.6	29.6	29.8	29.9	29.8	30.0	30.1	30.2	29.7
1991	30.0	30.2	30.3	29.8	29.8	29.5	29.8	29.7	29.9	30.0	29.8	30.3	29.9
1992	28.7	29.1	29.1	30.3	30.3	30.2	30.7	30.8	30.7	30.0	29.8	29.8	30.0
1993	29.4	30.5	30.5	30.9	30.7	30.5	30.2	29.8	30.3	31.0	31.0	31.1	30.5
1994	30.8	31.1	31.2	31.2	30.7	31.0	30.9	30.8	30.8	31.3	31.3	31.7	31.1
1995	31.5	31.8	31.7	31.6	31.3	31.1	30.8	31.1	31.0	31.7	31.9	31.9	31.5
1996	30.8	32.0	32.0	32.1	31.8	31.5	31.3	31.2	31.3	31.5	31.7	31.9	31.6
1997	31.6	31.8	31.8	31.9	31.7	31.2	31.6	31.5	31.4	31.6	31.8	31.5	31.6
1998	31.9	32.0	32.1	32.2	31.8	31.2	31.4	31.5	31.8	31.8	32.1	32.1	31.8
1999	32.3	32.4	32.5	32.4	31.9	31.5	31.6	31.8	31.9	31.7	32.0	32.2	32.0
2000	32.1	32.1	32.3	32.1	31.7	31.6	31.6	31.6	32.1	32.4	32.3	31.9	32.0
2001	31.7	32.5	32.6	32.8	32.4	32.5	32.5	32.5	32.8	33.3	33.2	33.0	32.7
2002	32.7	33.6	33.8	34.0	34.2	33.7	33.5	33.4	33.4	33.8	34.0	33.9	33.7
2003	33.8	34.5	34.4	34.4	34.2	33.7	33.6	33.2	33.7	33.7	33.7	33.8	33.9

Employment by Industry: Pennsylvania—*Continued*

(Numbers in thousands. Not seasonally adjusted.)

Industry	January	February	March	April	May	June	July	August	September	October	November	December	Annual Average
HARRISBURG-LEBANON-CARLISLE—*Continued*													
Local government													
1990	21.1	21.6	21.8	21.6	21.6	21.0	19.5	19.4	20.8	21.4	21.7	21.7	21.1
1991	21.0	21.6	21.7	22.0	22.3	21.3	19.7	19.6	20.4	21.7	22.1	22.2	21.3
1992	21.4	22.4	22.7	22.3	22.3	22.2	20.1	20.2	21.1	21.8	22.3	22.3	21.8
1993	22.1	23.0	22.9	23.0	23.2	22.2	20.2	20.0	21.0	22.2	22.5	22.3	22.1
1994	21.5	22.4	22.7	22.8	22.9	22.8	21.3	21.1	21.6	22.9	23.1	23.4	22.4
1995	22.4	23.3	23.3	23.5	23.3	23.4	20.9	20.8	22.1	23.3	23.6	23.6	22.8
1996	22.2	23.5	23.9	23.8	24.0	23.2	20.7	20.6	22.6	23.4	23.7	23.7	22.9
1997	23.0	23.8	24.1	24.4	24.5	23.1	20.9	20.7	23.4	23.8	24.0	23.9	23.3
1998	23.0	23.9	23.9	24.2	24.4	23.4	21.0	20.4	23.5	24.0	24.2	24.2	23.3
1999	23.2	24.3	24.5	24.6	24.7	24.6	22.5	21.8	24.0	24.5	25.0	25.0	24.1
2000	24.2	25.3	25.5	25.3	25.3	25.3	22.8	22.4	24.4	25.0	25.5	25.4	24.7
2001	24.5	25.5	25.7	25.7	26.0	25.2	22.4	22.2	24.9	25.4	25.6	25.5	24.9
2002	24.7	25.6	25.9	26.0	26.3	26.0	23.2	23.0	25.4	26.1	26.5	26.3	25.4
2003	25.1	26.3	26.5	26.8	26.9	25.9	23.3	23.1	25.9	26.6	26.9	26.7	25.8
LANCASTER													
Total nonfarm													
1990	189.3	190.8	193.1	194.7	196.7	196.8	193.8	194.6	195.0	195.0	194.6	193.5	194.0
1991	186.7	188.4	189.7	191.8	192.2	193.5	190.5	190.7	192.5	193.8	193.8	192.8	191.4
1992	187.2	189.7	191.2	193.5	194.5	195.6	193.2	193.0	194.9	196.7	195.8	195.9	193.4
1993	188.9	191.3	191.7	194.9	196.1	196.3	195.7	195.4	196.2	198.6	198.2	198.2	195.1
1994	189.8	191.5	193.6	197.4	199.8	201.7	199.7	199.5	201.6	203.3	203.8	204.0	198.8
1995	196.5	197.8	200.8	203.7	204.9	205.8	203.1	203.4	205.6	205.7	206.7	206.4	203.4
1996	195.3	200.3	202.9	205.7	206.7	207.7	206.0	207.0	210.0	211.0	212.6	212.4	206.5
1997	206.2	207.8	209.7	213.1	214.3	214.8	212.3	213.2	216.0	215.9	216.6	217.3	213.1
1998	209.9	211.5	213.6	216.0	218.1	218.1	218.2	218.2	220.3	220.7	221.0	221.2	217.2
1999	214.3	216.5	218.3	220.8	221.7	222.9	222.5	222.4	223.7	224.9	225.7	226.8	221.7
2000	219.9	221.6	225.0	225.7	227.5	229.0	228.3	228.1	229.4	228.4	228.5	229.1	226.7
2001	221.1	223.2	225.6	226.6	228.1	229.3	227.1	227.3	229.2	228.8	228.8	229.4	227.0
2002	222.3	224.1	226.9	227.1	228.7	230.0	228.2	229.0	230.2	230.3	230.3	230.1	228.1
2003	222.4	222.8	225.5	226.1	228.8	230.4	227.1	227.3	229.1	229.2	229.7	229.1	227.3
Total private													
1990	173.4	173.8	175.5	177.1	178.6	180.0	178.8	179.7	178.6	177.3	176.6	175.8	177.1
1991	170.1	170.4	171.3	174.1	174.8	176.7	175.4	175.8	175.6	176.0	175.8	175.0	174.3
1992	170.6	171.7	172.9	175.1	176.3	178.4	177.9	177.8	178.0	178.4	177.3	177.4	176.0
1993	172.1	172.8	173.2	176.3	177.6	178.7	180.0	179.7	179.8	180.1	179.2	179.6	177.4
1994	172.8	173.0	174.9	178.6	181.0	183.7	183.4	183.8	183.7	184.4	184.7	184.9	180.7
1995	179.2	179.1	181.8	184.6	185.9	188.2	187.2	187.7	187.4	187.0	187.8	187.4	185.3
1996	178.0	181.4	183.6	186.7	187.8	189.7	189.7	190.9	191.7	192.0	193.4	193.1	188.2
1997	188.6	188.9	190.7	194.0	195.2	196.9	196.4	197.3	197.5	196.8	197.4	197.9	194.8
1998	192.0	192.8	194.4	196.9	199.0	200.6	201.3	201.6	201.6	201.7	201.8	202.4	198.8
1999	196.2	197.2	198.7	201.4	202.4	204.9	205.4	205.6	204.8	205.5	206.0	207.5	203.0
2000	201.3	202.1	205.2	205.6	207.1	210.1	210.7	210.9	210.2	208.4	208.3	209.2	207.4
2001	202.1	202.9	205.2	206.2	207.8	210.1	209.4	209.6	209.2	208.3	208.1	208.6	207.3
2002	202.7	203.4	205.9	206.1	208.6	210.1	209.8	210.3	209.5	209.0	208.8	209.3	207.8
2003	202.2	201.5	204.0	204.6	207.7	209.7	208.8	208.9	208.3	207.9	208.2	208.0	206.7
Goods-producing													
1990	70.7	70.5	71.0	71.1	71.7	72.5	71.7	71.9	70.5	69.5	68.9	68.1	70.7
1991	67.3	66.8	66.9	67.1	67.5	68.5	68.3	68.2	67.6	67.3	66.9	66.6	67.4
1992	66.2	66.2	66.0	66.5	67.2	68.6	68.6	68.3	68.2	68.3	68.0	67.6	67.5
1993	66.5	66.4	66.5	66.9	67.5	68.0	68.3	68.1	67.9	67.5	67.0	67.0	67.3
1994	66.0	65.7	65.6	66.7	67.3	68.7	68.9	68.9	68.7	68.6	68.8	68.9	67.7
1995	67.5	67.2	67.7	68.3	68.3	69.3	69.4	69.3	68.8	68.2	68.1	67.8	68.3
1996	66.2	66.7	67.1	67.8	67.5	69.0	68.8	68.8	68.7	69.1	69.5	69.1	68.2
1997	68.2	68.3	68.5	69.7	69.7	70.6	70.2	70.2	70.0	69.6	69.7	69.8	69.5
1998	68.5	68.7	68.9	69.7	70.2	70.7	70.8	70.8	70.2	70.3	70.3	70.2	69.9
1999	69.3	69.1	69.2	70.1	70.2	70.9	70.6	71.0	70.5	70.6	70.6	70.6	70.2
2000	69.8	69.4	70.3	70.5	70.9	72.1	72.0	71.8	71.3	70.3	70.1	70.2	70.7
2001	68.3	67.5	68.0	68.2	68.3	68.9	68.7	68.5	67.8	67.3	66.6	66.5	67.9
2002	65.6	65.6	65.8	66.0	66.0	66.4	66.1	65.8	65.3	64.9	64.6	64.1	65.5
2003	62.9	61.9	62.3	62.2	63.0	63.8	63.1	62.9	62.8	62.3	62.1	61.9	62.6
Construction and mining													
1990	12.0	12.0	12.4	12.6	12.8	13.1	13.3	13.2	12.7	12.5	12.2	11.9	12.6
1991	11.1	10.9	10.9	11.4	11.8	12.1	12.3	12.2	11.8	11.5	11.4	11.0	11.5
1992	10.3	10.2	10.2	10.6	11.0	11.5	11.6	11.6	11.4	11.4	11.3	11.1	11.0
1993	10.6	10.4	10.3	10.9	11.2	11.5	11.7	11.6	11.5	11.6	11.5	11.3	11.2
1994	10.4	10.1	10.3	11.0	11.4	11.7	12.0	12.0	11.9	11.7	11.7	11.7	11.3
1995	10.9	10.5	11.0	11.6	11.7	12.0	11.9	12.0	11.8	11.6	11.6	11.4	11.5
1996	10.5	10.5	10.9	11.6	11.7	12.2	12.4	12.5	12.3	12.1	12.1	11.9	11.7
1997	11.5	11.5	11.7	12.1	12.3	12.6	12.8	12.8	12.6	12.5	12.5	12.5	12.3
1998	11.7	11.6	11.9	12.6	12.9	13.3	13.4	13.5	13.3	13.3	13.3	13.3	12.8
1999	12.9	12.8	13.0	13.7	13.8	14.2	14.6	14.7	14.2	14.2	14.0	14.0	13.8
2000	13.6	13.3	13.9	14.1	14.4	14.9	15.1	15.1	14.9	14.7	14.6	14.5	14.4
2001	14.0	13.9	14.2	14.7	15.1	15.4	15.4	15.5	15.1	15.1	14.9	14.8	14.8
2002	14.4	14.3	14.5	14.9	15.2	15.6	15.9	15.9	15.7	15.7	15.7	15.5	15.3
2003	14.9	14.5	14.9	15.4	15.7	16.1	16.3	16.4	16.1	16.0	16.0	15.8	15.7

Employment by Industry: Pennsylvania—*Continued*

(Numbers in thousands. Not seasonally adjusted.)

Industry	January	February	March	April	May	June	July	August	September	October	November	December	Annual Average
LANCASTER—*Continued*													
Manufacturing													
1990	58.7	58.5	58.6	58.5	58.9	59.4	58.4	58.7	57.8	57.0	56.7	56.2	58.1
1991	56.2	55.9	56.0	55.7	55.7	56.4	56.0	56.0	55.8	55.8	55.5	55.6	55.9
1992	55.9	56.0	55.8	55.9	56.2	57.1	57.0	56.7	56.8	56.9	56.7	56.5	56.5
1993	55.9	56.0	56.2	56.0	56.3	56.5	56.6	56.5	56.4	55.9	55.5	55.7	56.1
1994	55.6	55.6	55.3	55.7	55.9	57.0	56.9	56.9	56.8	56.9	57.1	57.2	56.4
1995	56.6	56.7	56.7	56.7	56.6	57.3	57.5	57.3	57.0	56.6	56.5	56.4	56.8
1996	55.7	56.2	56.2	56.2	55.8	56.8	56.4	56.3	56.4	57.0	57.4	57.2	56.5
1997	56.7	56.8	56.8	57.6	57.4	58.0	57.4	57.4	57.4	57.1	57.2	57.3	57.3
1998	56.8	57.1	57.0	57.1	57.3	57.4	57.4	57.3	56.9	57.0	57.0	56.9	57.1
1999	56.4	56.3	56.2	56.4	56.4	56.7	56.0	56.3	56.3	56.4	56.6	56.6	56.4
2000	56.2	56.1	56.4	56.4	56.5	57.2	56.9	56.7	56.4	55.6	55.5	55.7	56.3
2001	54.3	53.6	53.8	53.5	53.2	53.5	53.3	53.0	52.7	52.2	51.7	51.7	53.0
2002	51.2	51.3	51.3	51.1	50.8	50.8	50.2	49.9	49.6	49.2	48.9	48.6	50.2
2003	48.0	47.4	47.4	46.8	47.3	47.7	46.8	46.5	46.7	46.3	46.1	46.1	46.9
Service-providing													
1990	118.6	120.3	122.1	123.6	125.0	124.3	122.1	122.7	124.5	125.5	125.7	125.4	123.3
1991	119.4	121.6	122.8	124.7	124.7	125.0	122.2	122.5	124.9	126.5	126.9	126.2	124.0
1992	121.0	123.5	125.2	127.0	127.3	127.0	124.6	124.7	126.7	128.4	127.8	128.3	126.0
1993	122.4	124.9	125.2	128.0	128.6	128.3	127.4	127.3	128.3	131.1	131.2	131.2	127.8
1994	123.8	125.8	128.0	130.7	132.5	133.0	130.8	130.6	132.9	134.7	135.0	135.1	131.1
1995	129.0	130.6	133.1	135.4	136.6	136.5	133.7	134.1	136.8	137.5	138.6	138.6	135.0
1996	129.1	133.6	135.8	137.9	139.2	138.7	137.2	138.2	141.3	141.9	143.1	143.3	138.3
1997	138.0	139.5	141.2	143.4	144.6	144.2	142.1	143.0	146.0	146.3	146.9	147.5	143.6
1998	141.4	142.8	144.7	146.3	147.9	147.4	147.4	147.4	150.1	150.4	150.7	151.0	147.3
1999	145.0	147.4	149.1	150.7	151.5	152.0	151.9	151.4	153.2	154.3	155.1	156.2	151.5
2000	150.1	152.2	154.7	155.2	156.6	156.9	156.3	156.3	158.1	158.1	158.4	158.9	156.0
2001	152.8	155.7	157.6	158.4	159.8	160.4	158.4	158.8	161.4	161.5	162.2	162.9	159.2
2002	156.7	158.5	161.1	161.1	162.7	163.6	162.1	163.2	164.9	165.4	165.7	166.0	162.6
2003	159.5	160.9	163.2	163.9	165.8	166.6	164.0	164.4	166.3	166.9	167.6	167.2	164.7
Trade, transportation, and utilities													
1990	40.4	40.2	40.5	40.8	41.1	41.1	40.3	40.6	40.7	40.8	41.2	41.6	40.8
1991	39.7	39.6	39.7	40.5	40.7	40.8	39.7	40.2	40.4	41.2	41.6	41.7	40.5
1992	39.9	39.8	39.8	40.2	40.6	40.7	40.1	39.8	39.9	40.3	40.5	41.2	40.2
1993	39.6	39.3	39.2	39.6	40.0	40.1	40.4	40.1	40.3	41.1	41.4	42.0	40.3
1994	39.7	39.2	39.9	39.7	40.8	41.6	41.3	41.3	41.2	42.0	42.6	43.1	41.0
1995	41.4	41.1	41.7	42.5	42.8	42.9	42.4	42.5	42.6	43.1	43.8	44.1	42.6
1996	41.6	42.0	42.4	43.2	43.1	43.4	43.2	43.6	44.2	44.6	45.6	46.0	43.6
1997	44.2	43.7	44.1	44.2	44.6	44.7	44.5	44.1	44.6	45.1	45.9	46.4	44.7
1998	44.5	44.2	44.5	44.9	45.2	45.0	45.4	45.5	45.8	46.5	46.9	47.4	45.5
1999	45.2	45.1	45.3	45.8	46.1	46.6	46.8	46.9	46.7	47.3	48.3	49.4	46.6
2000	47.4	47.3	47.9	48.2	48.3	48.4	48.2	48.6	48.6	48.3	48.8	49.5	48.3
2001	48.1	47.4	47.7	47.9	48.1	48.4	48.2	48.1	48.3	48.5	49.3	50.4	48.4
2002	48.7	47.5	47.9	48.3	48.8	48.9	48.6	48.7	48.7	49.0	49.8	50.6	48.8
2003	48.9	48.2	48.8	49.3	49.8	49.9	49.7	49.7	49.6	49.9	50.5	51.2	49.6
Wholesale trade													
1990	9.7	9.6	9.6	9.7	9.8	10.0	9.7	9.9	9.9	9.7	9.7	9.7	9.8
1991	9.4	9.3	9.4	9.6	9.5	9.7	9.3	9.6	9.6	9.5	9.4	9.5	9.5
1992	9.5	9.6	9.6	9.6	9.7	9.8	9.7	9.6	9.5	9.6	9.6	9.7	9.6
1993	9.4	9.5	9.6	9.5	9.7	9.7	9.7	9.7	9.6	9.6	9.5	9.6	9.6
1994	9.4	9.3	9.4	9.6	9.6	9.8	9.8	9.8	9.6	9.8	9.9	10.0	9.7
1995	9.7	9.8	9.9	10.2	10.2	10.2	10.2	10.2	10.1	10.1	10.3	10.4	10.1
1996	10.0	10.0	10.1	10.3	10.4	10.5	10.4	10.5	10.5	10.3	10.5	10.5	10.3
1997	10.2	10.2	10.3	10.3	10.5	10.7	10.5	10.7	10.7	10.8	10.9	10.9	10.6
1998	10.7	10.8	10.9	11.1	11.1	11.2	11.2	11.2	11.1	11.0	11.1	11.0	11.0
1999	10.8	10.8	11.0	11.1	11.1	11.3	11.3	11.4	11.2	11.3	11.5	11.6	11.2
2000	11.2	11.3	11.4	11.6	11.7	11.8	11.8	11.8	11.7	11.3	11.1	11.2	11.5
2001	11.0	11.1	11.2	11.1	11.2	11.3	11.4	11.3	11.2	10.8	10.9	11.0	11.1
2002	10.9	10.7	10.7	10.9	11.0	11.2	11.3	11.3	11.3	11.4	11.5	11.7	11.2
2003	11.5	11.7	11.9	12.0	12.2	12.3	12.3	12.2	12.2	12.1	12.2	12.2	12.1
Retail trade													
1990	24.5	24.3	24.5	24.7	25.0	24.8	24.5	24.6	24.5	24.8	25.3	25.7	24.8
1991	24.2	24.2	24.2	24.5	24.8	24.7	24.3	24.5	24.5	25.4	25.8	26.0	24.8
1992	24.1	23.8	23.8	24.1	24.4	24.3	24.0	23.9	24.0	24.3	24.6	25.2	24.2
1993	24.2	23.9	23.7	24.1	24.3	24.3	24.7	24.5	24.5	25.0	25.5	26.0	24.6
1994	24.2	23.8	24.3	24.7	25.0	25.2	25.1	25.2	25.2	25.6	26.2	26.6	25.1
1995	25.3	24.9	25.3	25.7	26.0	26.0	25.7	25.8	25.7	25.9	26.4	26.6	25.8
1996	25.2	25.4	25.6	25.9	26.2	26.3	26.3	26.4	26.8	27.2	27.9	28.4	26.5
1997	27.1	26.6	26.8	27.1	27.4	27.4	27.5	27.4	27.1	27.5	28.2	28.7	27.4
1998	27.1	26.6	26.7	27.0	27.3	27.2	27.6	27.7	27.8	28.5	28.9	29.5	27.7
1999	27.9	27.7	27.7	27.9	28.2	28.5	28.9	28.8	28.6	29.0	29.9	31.0	28.7
2000	29.4	29.2	29.6	29.8	29.9	30.0	29.8	30.1	30.1	30.2	30.9	31.5	30.0
2001	30.3	29.5	29.7	29.8	29.8	30.0	29.7	29.7	29.5	29.9	30.5	31.3	30.0
2002	30.0	29.2	29.5	29.6	29.9	29.8	29.8	29.9	29.6	29.6	30.4	31.0	29.9
2003	29.6	28.8	29.1	29.5	29.8	29.8	29.9	30.0	29.7	29.9	30.4	31.2	29.8

Employment by Industry: Pennsylvania—*Continued*

(Numbers in thousands. Not seasonally adjusted.)

Industry	January	February	March	April	May	June	July	August	September	October	November	December	Annual Average
LANCASTER—*Continued*													
Transportation and utilities													
1990	6.2	6.3	6.4	6.4	6.3	6.3	6.1	6.1	6.3	6.3	6.2	6.2	6.3
1991	6.1	6.1	6.1	6.4	6.4	6.4	6.1	6.1	6.3	6.3	6.4	6.2	6.2
1992	6.3	6.4	6.4	6.5	6.5	6.6	6.4	6.3	6.4	6.4	6.3	6.3	6.4
1993	6.0	5.9	5.9	6.0	6.0	6.1	6.0	5.9	6.2	6.5	6.4	6.4	6.1
1994	6.1	6.1	6.2	5.4	6.2	6.6	6.4	6.3	6.4	6.6	6.5	6.5	6.3
1995	6.4	6.4	6.5	6.6	6.6	6.7	6.5	6.5	6.8	7.1	7.1	7.1	6.7
1996	6.4	6.6	6.7	7.0	6.5	6.6	6.5	6.7	6.9	7.1	7.2	7.1	6.8
1997	6.9	6.9	7.0	6.8	6.7	6.6	6.5	6.0	6.8	6.8	6.8	6.8	6.7
1998	6.7	6.8	6.9	6.8	6.8	6.6	6.6	6.6	6.9	7.0	6.9	6.9	6.8
1999	6.5	6.6	6.6	6.8	6.8	6.8	6.6	6.7	6.9	7.0	6.9	6.8	6.8
2000	6.8	6.8	6.9	6.8	6.7	6.6	6.6	6.7	6.8	6.8	6.8	6.8	6.8
2001	6.8	6.8	6.8	7.0	7.1	7.1	7.1	7.1	7.6	7.8	7.9	8.1	7.3
2002	7.8	7.6	7.7	7.8	7.9	7.9	7.5	7.5	7.8	8.0	7.9	7.9	7.8
2003	7.8	7.7	7.8	7.8	7.8	7.8	7.5	7.5	7.7	7.9	7.9	7.8	7.8
Information													
1990	2.9	3.0	3.0	2.9	3.0	3.0	3.0	3.0	2.9	2.9	2.9	2.9	3.0
1991	2.9	2.8	2.8	2.8	2.8	2.8	2.8	2.7	2.7	2.7	2.7	2.7	2.8
1992	2.8	2.7	2.7	2.7	2.7	2.8	2.7	2.7	2.7	2.6	2.6	2.6	2.7
1993	2.7	2.7	2.7	2.8	2.8	2.8	2.8	2.8	2.8	2.8	2.8	2.8	2.8
1994	2.8	2.8	2.8	2.8	2.9	2.9	3.0	2.9	2.9	3.0	3.0	3.1	2.9
1995	3.1	3.1	3.1	3.1	3.2	3.2	3.3	3.2	3.2	3.2	3.2	3.3	3.2
1996	3.3	3.3	3.3	3.3	3.3	3.3	3.4	3.4	3.4	3.5	3.5	3.5	3.4
1997	3.5	3.5	3.6	3.6	3.6	3.6	3.7	3.7	3.7	3.7	3.7	3.8	3.6
1998	3.8	3.8	3.8	3.8	3.8	3.9	3.9	4.0	4.0	4.0	4.1	4.2	3.9
1999	4.1	4.1	4.1	4.2	4.2	4.2	4.2	4.3	4.3	4.4	4.4	4.3	4.2
2000	4.3	4.3	4.3	4.3	4.3	4.3	4.4	4.2	4.3	4.3	4.3	4.4	4.3
2001	4.1	4.2	4.2	4.2	4.2	4.3	4.3	4.2	4.2	4.1	4.2	4.2	4.2
2002	4.1	4.0	4.1	4.1	4.1	4.1	4.1	4.1	4.0	4.0	4.0	4.0	4.1
2003	4.0	4.0	4.0	4.0	4.0	4.1	4.1	4.1	4.1	4.1	4.1	4.1	4.1
Financial activities													
1990	8.0	8.0	8.0	8.0	8.0	8.3	8.3	8.4	8.3	8.3	8.3	8.3	8.2
1991	8.6	8.6	8.6	8.7	8.8	8.9	8.9	8.9	8.8	8.9	8.9	9.0	8.8
1992	8.9	9.0	9.1	9.3	9.4	9.5	9.6	9.5	9.4	9.4	9.3	9.3	9.3
1993	9.1	9.1	9.3	9.4	9.4	9.6	9.7	9.7	9.7	9.5	9.5	9.6	9.5
1994	9.3	9.4	9.4	9.4	9.3	9.5	9.2	9.3	9.2	9.1	9.1	9.1	9.3
1995	9.1	9.2	9.2	9.2	9.2	9.4	9.3	9.3	9.3	9.3	9.4	9.5	9.3
1996	9.2	9.2	9.3	9.5	9.5	9.7	9.5	9.7	9.7	9.5	9.6	9.7	9.5
1997	9.7	9.7	9.7	9.8	9.8	10.0	9.9	10.1	10.0	10.0	10.1	10.1	9.9
1998	10.0	10.0	10.1	10.2	10.3	10.4	10.4	10.5	10.5	10.5	10.6	10.5	10.3
1999	10.6	10.5	10.6	10.6	10.6	10.8	10.7	10.6	10.5	10.4	10.4	10.5	10.6
2000	10.3	10.3	10.3	10.4	10.5	10.7	10.7	10.7	10.6	10.5	10.5	10.6	10.5
2001	10.7	10.8	10.9	11.0	11.0	11.1	11.3	11.4	11.3	11.2	11.3	11.4	11.1
2002	11.6	11.5	11.5	11.3	11.1	11.0	11.0	10.9	10.6	10.3	10.2	10.1	10.9
2003	10.0	9.9	9.9	10.0	10.1	10.2	10.4	10.3	10.2	10.1	10.1	10.0	10.1
Professional and business services													
1990	9.7	9.8	10.1	10.3	10.4	10.5	10.7	11.0	11.0	10.6	10.6	10.5	10.4
1991	9.5	9.6	9.8	10.2	9.9	10.0	10.1	10.1	10.2	10.3	10.0	9.8	10.0
1992	9.8	10.2	10.2	10.2	10.1	10.5	10.6	10.8	10.5	10.7	10.4	10.5	10.4
1993	10.1	10.4	10.6	11.2	11.2	11.0	11.3	11.5	11.2	11.3	11.1	11.2	11.0
1994	11.1	11.3	11.9	13.0	13.2	13.3	13.3	13.5	13.3	13.3	13.0	12.8	12.8
1995	12.3	12.3	12.7	13.1	13.4	13.6	13.0	13.3	13.0	13.1	13.1	13.2	13.0
1996	12.2	12.9	13.2	13.5	13.8	14.3	14.5	14.6	14.6	14.5	14.4	14.4	13.9
1997	14.5	14.6	14.7	15.5	15.9	16.1	15.8	16.3	16.4	16.2	16.0	16.2	15.7
1998	15.5	15.5	15.9	16.1	16.5	17.0	16.6	16.7	16.8	15.8	15.6	15.8	16.2
1999	16.2	16.3	16.8	16.7	17.0	17.5	17.4	17.4	17.8	17.6	17.5	17.9	17.2
2000	17.4	17.1	17.6	17.0	17.1	17.9	18.4	18.6	18.3	18.0	18.0	18.2	17.8
2001	17.7	18.1	18.6	18.5	18.9	19.3	18.8	19.2	19.4	19.0	18.6	18.4	18.7
2002	17.2	17.6	18.3	18.0	18.5	19.5	19.3	20.2	20.3	20.0	19.8	20.2	19.1
2003	19.1	19.2	19.7	19.5	19.8	19.7	19.5	20.0	20.1	20.0	19.9	19.8	19.7
Educational and health services													
1990	19.3	19.9	20.0	20.4	20.1	19.9	19.7	19.8	20.6	20.9	20.9	20.9	20.2
1991	20.0	20.7	20.7	21.1	20.7	20.6	20.5	20.6	21.4	21.7	21.9	21.7	21.0
1992	20.6	21.2	22.2	22.4	21.2	20.8	20.8	21.0	22.0	22.3	22.2	22.2	21.6
1993	21.3	21.6	21.8	21.8	21.4	21.0	21.1	21.2	22.2	22.9	23.0	22.9	21.9
1994	21.7	22.4	22.4	22.8	22.4	22.0	22.1	22.0	23.1	23.4	23.5	23.4	22.6
1995	22.5	23.1	23.5	23.4	23.1	22.8	22.5	22.6	23.7	23.8	24.1	23.9	23.3
1996	22.5	23.4	23.6	23.6	24.0	22.7	22.7	23.0	24.1	24.5	24.8	24.7	23.6
1997	23.6	24.2	24.5	24.4	24.0	23.5	23.8	23.8	24.8	25.2	25.3	25.2	24.4
1998	24.3	25.0	25.2	25.0	24.8	24.5	24.8	24.7	25.7	26.2	26.3	26.3	25.2
1999	24.7	25.6	25.6	25.7	25.2	25.2	25.0	25.2	26.0	26.0	26.0	26.0	25.5
2000	24.9	26.2	26.5	26.1	25.8	25.7	26.0	25.9	26.8	27.1	27.3	27.2	26.3
2001	26.1	27.5	27.6	27.4	27.1	27.1	27.0	27.1	28.0	28.2	28.6	28.6	27.5
2002	27.7	29.0	29.2	28.9	29.1	28.7	29.0	29.0	29.9	30.4	30.6	30.7	29.4
2003	29.6	30.9	31.1	30.5	30.7	30.7	30.8	30.6	31.0	31.3	31.6	31.6	30.9

Employment by Industry: Pennsylvania—*Continued*

(Numbers in thousands. Not seasonally adjusted.)

Industry	January	February	March	April	May	June	July	August	September	October	November	December	Annual Average
LANCASTER—*Continued*													
Leisure and hospitality													
1990	15.2	15.1	15.6	16.3	16.9	17.4	17.8	17.7	17.4	17.0	16.5	16.2	16.6
1991	14.8	15.0	15.5	16.3	17.0	17.6	17.7	17.7	17.2	16.5	16.3	16.1	16.5
1992	15.0	15.2	15.5	16.3	17.5	17.9	17.9	18.1	17.7	17.3	16.8	16.5	16.8
1993	15.5	15.9	15.8	17.1	17.7	18.5	18.7	18.6	18.0	17.3	16.7	16.3	17.2
1994	14.6	14.6	15.2	16.4	17.2	17.7	17.7	18.0	17.4	17.0	16.7	16.4	16.6
1995	15.3	15.2	15.8	16.8	17.6	18.5	18.9	19.1	18.5	17.9	17.7	17.2	17.4
1996	15.0	15.7	16.4	17.4	18.2	18.8	18.9	19.1	18.4	17.8	17.5	17.3	17.5
1997	16.2	16.1	16.8	17.8	18.6	19.3	19.4	19.9	18.9	17.8	17.4	17.2	18.0
1998	16.3	16.4	16.8	17.8	18.6	19.4	19.7	19.8	19.1	18.8	18.4	18.3	18.3
1999	16.5	16.8	17.3	18.5	19.2	19.7	20.3	19.9	19.0	19.1	18.7	18.6	18.6
2000	17.1	17.4	18.0	18.9	19.9	20.6	20.7	20.7	20.0	19.6	19.0	18.9	19.2
2001	17.0	17.2	17.9	18.7	19.8	20.5	20.7	20.8	20.0	19.7	19.2	18.8	19.2
2002	17.5	17.8	18.6	19.1	20.6	21.0	21.2	21.2	20.4	20.1	19.6	19.3	19.7
2003	17.5	17.3	18.0	18.9	20.1	20.9	20.9	21.0	20.3	19.9	19.6	19.2	19.5
Other services													
1990	7.2	7.3	7.3	7.3	7.4	7.3	7.3	7.3	7.2	7.3	7.3	7.3	7.3
1991	7.3	7.3	7.3	7.4	7.4	7.5	7.4	7.4	7.3	7.4	7.5	7.4	7.4
1992	7.4	7.4	7.4	7.5	7.6	7.6	7.6	7.6	7.6	7.5	7.5	7.5	7.5
1993	7.3	7.4	7.3	7.5	7.6	7.7	7.7	7.7	7.7	7.7	7.7	7.8	7.6
1994	7.6	7.6	7.7	7.8	7.9	8.0	7.9	7.9	7.9	8.0	8.0	8.1	7.9
1995	8.0	7.9	8.1	8.2	8.3	8.5	8.4	8.4	8.3	8.4	8.4	8.4	8.3
1996	8.0	8.2	8.3	8.4	8.4	8.5	8.7	8.7	8.6	8.5	8.5	8.4	8.4
1997	8.7	8.8	8.8	9.0	9.0	9.1	9.1	9.2	9.1	9.2	9.3	9.2	9.0
1998	9.1	9.2	9.2	9.4	9.6	9.7	9.7	9.6	9.5	9.6	9.6	9.7	9.5
1999	9.6	9.7	9.8	9.8	9.9	10.0	10.4	10.3	10.0	10.1	10.1	10.2	10.0
2000	10.1	10.1	10.3	10.2	10.3	10.4	10.3	10.4	10.3	10.3	10.3	10.2	10.3
2001	10.1	10.2	10.3	10.3	10.4	10.5	10.4	10.3	10.2	10.3	10.3	10.3	10.3
2002	10.3	10.4	10.5	10.4	10.4	10.5	10.5	10.4	10.3	10.3	10.2	10.3	10.4
2003	10.2	10.1	10.2	10.2	10.2	10.4	10.3	10.3	10.2	10.3	10.3	10.2	10.2
Government													
1990	15.9	17.0	17.6	17.6	18.1	16.8	15.0	14.9	16.4	17.7	18.0	17.7	16.9
1991	16.6	18.0	18.4	17.7	17.4	16.8	15.1	14.9	16.9	17.8	18.0	17.8	17.1
1992	16.6	18.0	18.3	18.4	18.2	17.2	15.3	15.2	16.9	18.3	18.5	18.5	17.5
1993	16.8	18.5	18.5	18.6	18.5	17.6	15.7	15.7	16.4	18.5	19.0	18.6	17.7
1994	17.0	18.5	18.7	18.8	18.8	18.0	16.3	15.7	17.9	18.9	19.1	19.1	18.1
1995	17.3	18.7	19.0	19.1	19.0	17.6	15.9	15.7	18.2	18.7	18.9	19.0	18.1
1996	17.3	18.9	19.3	19.0	18.9	18.0	16.3	16.1	18.3	19.0	19.2	19.3	18.3
1997	17.6	18.9	19.0	19.1	19.1	17.9	15.9	15.9	18.5	19.1	19.2	19.4	18.3
1998	17.9	18.7	19.2	19.1	19.1	17.5	16.9	16.6	18.7	19.0	19.2	18.8	18.4
1999	18.1	19.3	19.6	19.4	19.3	18.0	17.1	16.8	18.9	19.4	19.7	19.3	18.7
2000	18.6	19.5	19.8	20.1	20.4	18.9	17.6	17.2	19.2	20.0	20.2	19.9	19.3
2001	19.0	20.3	20.4	20.4	20.3	19.2	17.7	17.7	20.0	20.5	20.7	20.8	19.8
2002	19.6	20.7	21.0	21.0	20.1	19.9	18.4	18.7	20.7	21.3	21.5	20.8	20.3
2003	20.2	21.3	21.5	21.5	21.1	20.7	18.3	18.4	20.8	21.3	21.5	21.1	20.6
Federal government													
1990	1.5	1.5	1.6	1.7	1.9	1.7	1.7	1.6	1.5	1.5	1.5	1.5	1.6
1991	1.5	1.5	1.5	1.5	1.5	1.5	1.5	1.5	1.5	1.5	1.5	1.5	1.5
1992	1.5	1.5	1.5	1.5	1.5	1.5	1.5	1.5	1.4	1.4	1.4	1.4	1.5
1993	1.4	1.4	1.4	1.4	1.4	1.4	1.4	1.4	1.5	1.5	1.5	1.5	1.4
1994	1.5	1.5	1.5	1.5	1.5	1.5	1.5	1.5	1.5	1.5	1.5	1.5	1.5
1995	1.5	1.5	1.5	1.5	1.5	1.5	1.5	1.5	1.5	1.5	1.5	1.6	1.5
1996	1.6	1.6	1.6	1.6	1.6	1.6	1.6	1.6	1.6	1.7	1.7	1.8	1.6
1997	1.6	1.6	1.5	1.7	1.6	1.7	1.6	1.6	1.6	1.7	1.7	1.8	1.6
1998	1.6	1.6	1.6	1.6	1.6	1.6	1.6	1.6	1.6	1.6	1.6	1.7	1.6
1999	1.6	1.6	1.7	1.6	1.6	1.6	1.6	1.6	1.6	1.6	1.6	1.7	1.6
2000	1.6	1.6	1.6	1.7	2.0	1.8	1.8	1.6	1.5	1.5	1.6	1.6	1.7
2001	1.6	1.6	1.6	1.6	1.6	1.6	1.6	1.6	1.5	1.5	1.6	1.6	1.6
2002	1.6	1.5	1.5	1.5	1.5	1.6	1.6	1.6	1.6	1.6	1.6	1.6	1.6
2003	1.6	1.6	1.6	1.6	1.6	1.6	1.6	1.6	1.5	1.5	1.5	1.5	1.6
State government													
1990	2.4	3.3	3.6	3.4	3.5	2.4	2.4	2.4	3.0	3.5	3.6	3.4	3.1
1991	2.7	3.5	3.6	3.3	2.7	2.2	2.3	2.2	3.1	3.2	3.2	3.0	2.9
1992	2.2	3.2	3.2	3.3	3.0	2.3	2.2	2.2	3.3	3.5	3.5	3.4	2.9
1993	2.3	3.4	3.3	3.4	3.1	2.4	2.2	2.2	3.3	3.5	3.5	3.4	3.0
1994	2.3	3.4	3.3	3.4	3.2	2.2	2.2	2.2	3.4	3.5	3.5	3.4	3.0
1995	2.3	3.4	3.4	3.4	3.1	2.2	2.2	2.2	3.4	3.4	3.4	3.4	3.0
1996	2.2	3.4	3.5	3.4	3.1	2.2	2.3	2.2	3.2	3.3	3.4	3.4	3.0
1997	2.3	3.4	3.4	3.4	3.3	2.1	2.2	2.4	3.2	3.4	3.4	3.4	3.0
1998	2.5	3.4	3.4	3.4	3.3	2.2	2.3	2.2	3.1	3.3	3.3	2.9	2.9
1999	2.5	3.4	3.5	3.4	3.2	2.2	2.4	2.3	3.2	3.3	3.4	2.9	3.0
2000	2.5	3.3	3.4	3.5	3.4	2.5	2.4	2.4	3.3	3.6	3.5	3.2	3.1
2001	2.6	3.6	3.6	3.6	3.4	2.6	2.6	2.5	3.4	3.6	3.7	3.6	3.2
2002	2.6	3.6	3.7	3.7	2.7	2.8	2.7	2.6	3.5	3.8	3.9	3.3	3.2
2003	2.7	3.7	3.8	3.7	3.2	2.9	2.8	2.6	3.5	3.7	3.7	3.4	3.3

Employment by Industry: Pennsylvania—*Continued*

(Numbers in thousands. Not seasonally adjusted.)

Industry	January	February	March	April	May	June	July	August	September	October	November	December	Annual Average
LANCASTER—*Continued*													
Local government													
1990	12.0	12.2	12.4	12.5	12.7	12.7	10.9	10.9	11.9	12.7	12.9	12.8	12.2
1991	12.4	13.0	13.3	12.9	13.2	13.1	11.3	11.2	12.3	13.1	13.3	13.3	12.7
1992	12.9	13.3	13.6	13.6	13.7	13.4	11.6	11.5	12.2	13.4	13.6	13.7	13.0
1993	13.1	13.7	13.8	13.8	14.0	13.8	12.1	12.1	11.6	13.5	14.0	13.7	13.3
1994	13.2	13.6	13.9	13.9	14.1	14.3	12.6	12.0	13.0	13.9	14.1	14.2	13.6
1995	13.5	13.8	14.1	14.2	14.4	13.9	12.2	12.0	13.3	13.8	14.0	14.0	13.6
1996	13.5	13.9	14.2	14.0	14.2	14.2	12.4	12.3	13.5	14.0	14.1	14.1	13.7
1997	13.7	13.9	14.1	14.0	14.2	14.1	12.1	11.9	13.7	14.0	14.1	14.2	13.7
1998	13.8	13.7	14.2	14.1	14.2	13.7	13.0	12.8	14.0	14.1	14.3	14.2	13.8
1999	14.0	14.3	14.4	14.4	14.5	14.2	13.1	12.9	14.1	14.5	14.7	14.7	14.2
2000	14.5	14.6	14.8	14.9	15.0	14.6	13.4	13.2	14.4	14.9	15.1	15.1	14.5
2001	14.8	15.1	15.2	15.2	15.3	15.0	13.5	13.6	15.1	15.4	15.4	15.6	14.9
2002	15.4	15.6	15.8	15.8	15.9	15.5	14.1	14.5	15.6	15.9	16.0	15.9	15.5
2003	15.9	16.0	16.1	16.2	16.3	16.2	13.9	14.2	15.8	16.1	16.3	16.2	15.8
PHILADELPHIA PMSA													
Total nonfarm													
1990	2210.0	2216.9	2229.6	2225.7	2237.5	2247.2	2220.0	2216.6	2219.2	2226.9	2230.5	2230.6	2225.9
1991	2151.2	2150.7	2158.9	2167.4	2164.9	2165.3	2123.1	2116.7	2133.8	2147.0	2157.6	2161.8	2149.9
1992	2097.0	2101.0	2110.0	2125.9	2132.9	2135.8	2122.7	2110.1	2118.9	2146.2	2153.0	2161.4	2126.2
1993	2105.7	2114.3	2117.8	2136.9	2147.1	2148.2	2133.6	2126.3	2136.1	2162.8	2173.9	2188.5	2140.9
1994	2116.5	2120.2	2143.8	2169.2	2179.3	2187.0	2164.9	2162.1	2181.8	2199.7	2211.1	2224.0	2171.6
1995	2146.1	2154.1	2169.8	2185.7	2190.2	2195.3	2169.0	2175.9	2191.2	2208.9	2223.9	2232.5	2186.9
1996	2142.8	2172.1	2189.7	2213.9	2228.1	2229.4	2214.0	2215.1	2228.3	2248.0	2263.9	2274.8	2218.3
1997	2204.7	2220.4	2238.3	2254.2	2263.8	2268.5	2253.4	2251.0	2276.9	2298.0	2317.0	2331.1	2264.8
1998	2264.5	2278.3	2291.2	2313.8	2325.2	2317.4	2308.7	2314.5	2337.8	2356.9	2373.9	2383.3	2322.1
1999	2309.9	2322.2	2339.7	2367.0	2375.0	2378.7	2353.2	2349.0	2356.8	2377.9	2393.7	2414.0	2361.4
2000	2346.6	2353.0	2375.8	2399.1	2408.9	2418.7	2391.1	2381.4	2406.6	2412.7	2432.1	2444.1	2397.5
2001	2380.2	2389.3	2406.2	2415.8	2423.3	2432.3	2399.0	2393.5	2405.3	2415.3	2432.1	2438.5	2410.9
2002	2377.1	2385.4	2400.7	2409.6	2418.4	2431.7	2394.8	2388.8	2404.4	2421.6	2435.5	2437.8	2408.8
2003	2371.9	2375.4	2392.6	2409.8	2419.1	2424.9	2396.3	2393.3	2403.4	2422.6	2437.4	2442.7	2407.5
Total private													
1990	1908.4	1911.8	1923.3	1918.7	1928.9	1938.8	1922.8	1925.6	1923.1	1924.1	1925.3	1925.6	1923.0
1991	1849.3	1846.1	1854.1	1856.9	1855.8	1859.7	1836.4	1837.7	1842.5	1847.0	1854.5	1859.1	1849.9
1992	1801.0	1799.0	1806.4	1821.5	1830.5	1835.2	1826.3	1821.1	1829.3	1846.8	1851.6	1859.1	1827.3
1993	1810.0	1812.6	1814.8	1832.1	1842.4	1845.9	1842.6	1841.7	1849.8	1866.4	1873.7	1885.0	1843.1
1994	1821.2	1821.3	1841.5	1863.5	1874.6	1883.3	1877.0	1879.8	1889.4	1899.3	1908.5	1918.1	1873.1
1995	1847.2	1852.0	1866.3	1880.6	1886.2	1892.0	1881.6	1892.6	1900.6	1911.6	1924.7	1931.7	1888.9
1996	1847.0	1870.9	1886.1	1910.4	1925.5	1934.4	1925.7	1928.1	1937.8	1951.3	1966.4	1977.1	1921.7
1997	1909.4	1920.8	1936.6	1952.4	1962.4	1974.0	1968.2	1968.9	1987.3	2001.4	2018.4	2031.0	1969.2
1998	1969.7	1978.2	1990.3	2011.8	2022.5	2030.3	2031.9	2038.6	2049.6	2064.2	2079.5	2087.0	2029.5
1999	2016.3	2025.4	2039.4	2063.4	2072.3	2080.2	2070.1	2067.9	2065.9	2078.5	2092.3	2110.5	2065.2
2000	2047.5	2049.0	2068.4	2089.8	2093.5	2110.4	2103.0	2099.1	2108.1	2109.0	2125.5	2136.8	2095.0
2001	2076.3	2080.2	2095.8	2104.0	2113.7	2125.2	2111.3	2109.8	2105.0	2107.2	2120.4	2124.9	2106.2
2002	2066.1	2070.0	2084.7	2092.2	2102.1	2118.3	2103.4	2104.3	2102.0	2110.5	2121.2	2123.2	2099.8
2003	2062.4	2060.6	2075.9	2092.5	2102.6	2112.3	2103.7	2104.3	2104.1	2114.5	2126.4	2131.0	2099.2
Goods-producing													
1990	417.1	416.5	419.9	419.6	422.3	425.3	421.1	422.2	418.5	414.7	409.0	403.5	417.5
1991	382.8	379.7	380.0	383.2	381.9	384.1	378.7	381.2	376.2	378.8	375.8	372.2	379.6
1992	356.8	355.1	357.0	360.1	362.1	365.5	363.0	363.0	362.8	362.6	361.1	358.7	360.7
1993	348.7	348.7	350.3	352.8	355.7	357.3	358.7	360.3	362.4	362.6	361.9	360.6	356.7
1994	345.9	342.9	348.9	355.7	359.2	363.1	363.2	365.7	367.1	367.3	365.7	363.8	359.0
1995	349.8	346.5	350.4	354.7	355.5	358.2	355.8	359.4	360.0	357.8	356.1	352.4	354.7
1996	333.8	338.5	341.8	345.7	348.8	353.0	353.2	355.5	357.1	357.6	357.4	355.9	349.9
1997	345.8	345.7	350.0	354.2	356.4	361.7	360.7	362.9	362.8	361.5	361.2	360.4	356.9
1998	351.9	352.2	354.6	360.4	362.0	365.2	365.8	367.9	368.3	369.0	368.6	366.3	362.7
1999	355.2	355.3	358.4	362.3	364.5	366.9	366.2	367.3	366.0	365.2	365.2	365.1	363.1
2000	355.7	353.3	359.8	366.7	367.0	372.9	370.6	371.8	371.0	368.1	367.6	366.8	365.9
2001	356.2	355.5	358.6	359.5	360.2	361.8	359.9	358.8	356.9	352.8	349.8	347.7	356.5
2002	335.8	333.9	335.3	336.2	339.0	340.6	339.2	340.6	338.3	336.1	333.9	330.8	336.6
2003	321.5	317.6	320.0	324.2	327.3	328.4	328.6	329.1	327.7	325.5	325.9	324.0	325.0
Construction and mining													
1990	93.4	93.1	95.8	96.6	100.0	102.3	102.5	102.2	100.3	98.0	94.5	90.3	97.4
1991	79.6	77.6	78.4	81.1	82.6	84.0	84.1	84.0	83.0	82.9	81.5	78.3	81.4
1992	70.5	69.1	70.7	74.4	75.5	77.7	79.1	79.2	78.3	78.1	77.4	75.7	75.5
1993	70.0	69.7	70.7	73.7	76.0	77.4	79.5	80.2	81.1	81.4	80.8	78.8	76.6
1994	69.0	66.8	70.7	76.8	80.2	82.5	83.8	85.1	85.3	86.1	84.4	82.1	79.4
1995	74.0	70.5	73.2	77.6	78.6	80.7	80.8	82.8	82.9	82.2	80.8	78.3	78.5
1996	67.1	69.8	72.4	77.5	80.7	83.2	85.0	86.4	86.8	87.7	87.4	85.0	80.8
1997	78.4	77.9	81.3	85.5	87.6	90.4	92.9	93.4	92.4	91.8	90.7	88.9	87.6
1998	82.3	82.2	84.1	88.8	90.2	93.1	95.4	96.2	95.4	96.4	95.7	94.2	91.2
1999	86.5	87.4	89.4	94.0	96.4	98.4	99.7	100.4	99.1	99.0	98.3	97.0	95.5
2000	91.0	88.8	94.5	100.0	101.8	104.0	101.9	102.5	102.0	101.1	100.3	98.9	98.9
2001	93.6	93.6	97.0	100.4	102.8	104.7	105.9	106.2	105.7	104.8	103.4	101.7	101.7
2002	94.9	94.7	96.4	98.7	101.3	103.0	104.1	105.5	103.8	103.9	102.8	100.6	100.8
2003	94.7	92.5	94.7	100.8	104.1	105.1	106.6	107.4	106.3	105.6	105.0	103.0	102.2

Employment by Industry: Pennsylvania—*Continued*

(Numbers in thousands. Not seasonally adjusted.)

Industry	January	February	March	April	May	June	July	August	September	October	November	December	Annual Average
PHILADELPHIA PMSA *—Continued*													
Manufacturing													
1990	323.7	323.4	324.1	323.0	322.3	323.0	318.6	320.0	318.2	316.7	314.5	313.2	320.1
1991	303.2	302.1	301.6	302.1	299.3	300.1	294.6	297.2	293.2	295.9	294.3	293.9	298.1
1992	286.3	286.0	286.3	285.7	286.6	287.8	283.9	283.8	284.5	284.5	283.7	283.0	285.2
1993	278.7	279.0	279.6	279.1	279.7	279.9	279.2	280.1	281.3	281.2	281.1	281.8	280.1
1994	276.9	276.1	278.2	278.9	279.0	280.6	279.4	280.6	281.8	281.2	281.3	281.7	279.6
1995	275.8	276.0	277.2	277.1	276.9	277.5	275.0	276.6	277.1	275.6	275.3	274.1	276.2
1996	266.7	268.7	269.4	268.2	268.1	269.8	268.2	269.1	270.3	269.9	270.0	270.9	269.1
1997	267.4	267.8	268.7	268.7	268.8	271.3	267.8	269.5	270.4	269.7	270.5	271.5	269.3
1998	269.6	270.0	270.5	271.6	271.8	272.1	270.4	271.7	272.9	272.6	272.9	272.1	271.5
1999	268.7	267.9	269.0	268.3	268.1	268.5	266.5	266.9	266.9	266.2	266.9	268.1	267.7
2000	264.7	264.5	265.3	266.7	265.2	268.9	268.7	269.3	269.0	267.0	267.3	267.9	267.0
2001	262.6	261.9	261.6	259.1	257.4	257.1	254.0	252.6	251.2	248.0	246.4	246.0	254.8
2002	240.9	239.2	238.9	237.5	237.7	237.6	235.1	235.1	234.5	232.2	231.1	230.2	235.8
2003	226.8	225.1	225.3	223.4	223.2	223.3	222.0	221.7	221.4	219.9	220.9	221.0	222.8
Service-providing													
1990	1792.9	1800.4	1809.7	1806.1	1815.2	1821.9	1798.9	1794.4	1800.7	1812.2	1821.5	1827.1	1808.4
1991	1768.4	1771.0	1778.9	1784.2	1783.0	1781.2	1744.4	1735.5	1757.6	1768.2	1781.8	1789.6	1770.3
1992	1740.2	1745.9	1753.0	1765.8	1770.8	1770.3	1759.7	1747.1	1756.1	1783.6	1791.9	1802.7	1765.6
1993	1757.0	1765.6	1767.5	1784.1	1791.4	1790.9	1774.9	1766.0	1773.7	1800.2	1812.0	1827.9	1784.3
1994	1770.6	1777.3	1794.9	1813.5	1820.1	1823.9	1801.7	1796.4	1814.7	1832.4	1845.4	1860.2	1812.6
1995	1796.3	1807.6	1819.4	1831.0	1834.7	1837.1	1813.2	1816.5	1831.2	1851.1	1867.8	1880.1	1832.2
1996	1809.0	1833.6	1847.9	1868.2	1879.3	1876.4	1860.8	1859.6	1871.2	1890.4	1906.5	1918.9	1868.5
1997	1858.9	1874.7	1888.3	1900.0	1907.4	1906.8	1892.7	1888.1	1914.1	1936.5	1955.8	1970.7	1907.8
1998	1912.6	1926.1	1936.6	1953.4	1963.2	1952.2	1942.9	1946.6	1969.5	1987.9	2005.3	2017.0	1959.4
1999	1954.7	1966.9	1981.3	2004.7	2010.5	2011.8	1987.0	1981.7	1990.8	2012.7	2028.5	2048.9	1998.3
2000	1990.9	1999.7	2016.0	2032.4	2041.9	2045.8	2020.5	2009.6	2035.6	2044.6	2064.5	2077.3	2031.6
2001	2024.0	2033.8	2047.6	2056.3	2063.1	2070.5	2039.1	2034.7	2048.4	2062.5	2082.3	2090.8	2054.4
2002	2041.3	2051.5	2065.4	2073.4	2079.4	2091.1	2055.6	2048.2	2066.1	2085.5	2101.6	2107.0	2072.2
2003	2050.4	2057.8	2072.6	2085.6	2091.8	2096.5	2067.7	2064.2	2075.7	2097.1	2111.5	2118.7	2082.5
Trade, transportation, and utilities													
1990	466.5	461.4	460.2	456.2	457.0	457.9	452.6	454.2	454.3	457.8	465.0	470.7	459.5
1991	441.4	433.5	433.2	431.7	431.3	431.2	424.1	424.3	427.7	429.0	437.1	443.7	432.4
1992	424.1	417.1	416.5	417.8	420.0	419.5	414.1	413.8	418.0	427.2	435.5	444.4	422.3
1993	423.3	418.1	415.9	418.7	420.2	420.5	417.0	416.0	419.3	428.8	435.9	445.6	423.3
1994	428.1	423.1	425.6	428.0	429.7	431.5	428.1	428.4	433.2	441.7	451.3	459.3	434.0
1995	436.6	430.9	430.5	434.1	435.4	435.2	433.7	436.4	438.8	446.0	456.3	463.6	439.8
1996	438.4	436.3	437.2	441.4	444.6	446.2	441.8	441.2	443.8	449.9	459.4	468.3	445.7
1997	445.8	440.2	442.7	440.5	442.5	443.7	440.7	436.9	447.1	454.1	465.5	474.3	447.8
1998	451.4	444.6	445.5	448.3	451.5	453.4	453.3	454.9	460.8	466.0	476.3	484.5	457.5
1999	460.7	456.2	459.0	460.9	462.8	465.4	461.4	462.5	463.5	470.9	481.8	492.4	466.5
2000	468.5	462.3	463.7	468.7	471.5	473.2	468.2	470.6	473.4	478.7	490.0	499.1	474.0
2001	478.0	468.9	470.3	469.7	471.3	473.1	467.1	467.3	468.3	472.5	484.2	491.4	473.5
2002	468.9	461.3	464.4	463.0	465.7	469.0	463.9	465.1	466.5	471.5	480.5	488.7	469.0
2003	467.1	460.3	462.5	465.6	468.7	472.0	467.9	468.4	470.7	477.3	484.9	492.1	471.5
Wholesale trade													
1990	124.4	124.5	124.8	124.0	123.6	123.9	123.0	122.9	122.2	121.5	121.6	121.2	123.1
1991	117.6	117.1	117.3	117.7	117.2	116.9	115.4	114.8	114.7	113.8	113.5	113.8	115.8
1992	110.2	110.1	110.0	110.4	110.3	110.2	109.7	109.1	108.4	109.3	108.7	108.8	109.6
1993	106.6	106.9	106.8	108.0	108.0	107.8	107.6	107.5	107.1	107.6	107.7	108.4	107.5
1994	106.8	106.9	107.2	107.0	107.0	107.2	107.3	107.5	107.4	108.3	108.3	108.7	107.5
1995	107.1	107.7	108.2	109.1	108.6	108.5	108.8	109.0	109.1	108.9	109.1	109.5	108.6
1996	106.6	107.7	107.9	108.3	108.8	109.1	109.6	109.5	109.6	110.4	110.4	111.1	109.1
1997	108.7	109.1	109.9	110.2	110.6	110.9	111.0	111.0	111.0	111.5	111.9	112.6	110.7
1998	110.3	110.5	111.0	112.9	113.0	113.4	113.9	113.9	114.2	114.6	115.0	115.0	113.1
1999	112.3	112.4	113.3	114.0	114.2	114.7	114.8	115.4	114.7	115.7	116.0	116.7	114.5
2000	115.0	115.1	115.7	117.8	118.1	118.7	118.3	118.4	117.9	117.5	117.7	118.3	117.4
2001	117.3	117.2	117.4	118.5	118.5	118.9	119.5	119.0	118.5	118.3	118.8	119.7	118.5
2002	117.1	117.0	117.4	117.1	117.2	117.4	117.2	117.0	116.0	116.4	116.4	116.9	116.9
2003	115.3	115.2	115.7	116.1	116.0	116.3	116.8	116.7	116.5	116.5	116.4	117.0	116.2
Retail trade													
1990	272.7	267.0	265.1	261.8	262.3	262.9	260.6	261.7	261.1	264.5	271.3	277.0	265.7
1991	253.3	245.7	245.1	243.9	243.9	244.1	240.4	241.3	242.5	243.8	251.9	257.7	246.1
1992	243.2	236.3	235.5	236.2	237.8	237.2	235.8	236.2	237.8	245.3	254.0	261.6	241.4
1993	243.1	237.4	235.3	236.6	237.6	238.1	237.3	236.9	237.7	244.0	251.6	260.3	241.3
1994	245.5	240.5	241.9	244.3	246.1	247.2	245.3	246.4	248.9	253.9	264.0	271.9	249.7
1995	254.2	247.5	247.7	249.4	251.3	251.2	250.8	253.9	254.0	258.0	268.1	275.2	255.1
1996	256.4	252.6	253.0	256.0	258.3	259.7	256.0	256.2	255.8	259.1	268.6	277.1	259.1
1997	258.3	252.4	253.0	251.2	253.2	254.2	253.8	255.0	256.4	261.0	271.5	279.8	258.3
1998	262.3	256.2	256.4	256.5	258.8	260.5	260.3	261.7	264.0	267.7	277.8	286.0	264.0
1999	267.8	263.6	265.2	265.0	266.7	268.9	266.2	267.5	267.1	270.1	281.1	290.7	270.0
2000	271.1	265.3	265.9	268.2	270.4	272.3	269.6	272.2	272.2	276.1	287.4	295.2	273.8
2001	276.8	268.3	269.6	266.8	268.3	270.1	266.3	268.2	266.8	269.5	280.9	287.5	271.6
2002	270.2	263.4	265.6	263.4	265.3	268.2	265.6	267.2	266.3	268.3	277.6	285.1	268.9
2003	267.3	261.0	262.9	264.4	267.3	270.8	269.3	270.5	270.3	274.7	282.9	289.6	270.9

Employment by Industry: Pennsylvania—*Continued*

(Numbers in thousands. Not seasonally adjusted.)

Industry	January	February	March	April	May	June	July	August	September	October	November	December	Annual Average
PHILADELPHIA PMSA *—Continued*													
Transportation and utilities													
1990	69.4	69.9	70.3	70.4	71.1	71.1	69.0	69.6	71.0	71.8	72.1	72.5	70.7
1991	70.5	70.7	70.8	70.1	70.2	70.2	68.3	68.2	70.5	71.4	71.7	72.2	70.4
1992	70.7	70.7	71.0	71.2	71.9	72.1	68.6	68.5	71.8	72.6	72.8	74.0	71.3
1993	73.6	73.8	73.8	74.1	74.6	74.6	72.1	71.6	74.5	77.2	76.6	76.9	74.5
1994	75.8	75.7	76.5	76.7	76.6	77.1	75.5	74.5	76.9	79.5	79.0	78.7	76.9
1995	75.3	75.7	74.6	75.6	75.5	75.5	74.1	73.5	75.7	79.1	79.1	78.9	76.1
1996	75.4	76.0	76.3	77.1	77.5	77.4	76.2	75.5	78.4	80.4	80.4	80.1	77.6
1997	78.8	78.7	79.8	79.1	78.7	78.6	75.9	70.9	79.7	81.6	82.1	81.9	78.8
1998	78.8	77.9	78.1	78.9	79.7	79.5	79.1	79.3	82.6	83.7	83.5	83.5	80.4
1999	80.6	80.2	80.5	81.9	81.9	81.8	80.4	79.6	81.7	85.1	84.7	85.0	82.0
2000	82.4	81.9	82.1	82.7	83.0	82.2	80.3	80.0	83.3	85.1	84.9	85.6	82.8
2001	83.9	83.4	83.3	84.4	84.5	84.1	81.3	80.1	83.0	84.7	84.5	84.2	83.5
2002	81.6	80.9	81.4	82.5	83.2	83.4	81.1	80.9	84.2	86.8	86.5	86.7	83.3
2003	84.5	84.1	83.9	85.1	85.4	84.9	81.8	81.2	83.9	86.1	85.6	85.5	84.3
Information													
1990	54.9	55.2	55.2	54.8	55.4	56.0	55.2	55.3	55.0	55.2	55.5	55.6	55.3
1991	55.1	55.2	55.1	55.0	54.6	54.5	54.4	54.2	54.3	54.1	54.1	54.1	54.6
1992	53.7	53.8	54.1	54.9	53.8	54.6	53.2	52.8	53.1	53.6	53.4	53.8	53.7
1993	53.5	53.4	53.0	53.1	53.0	53.1	52.9	53.0	53.0	53.5	53.9	54.1	53.3
1994	53.2	53.3	53.9	53.8	54.0	54.8	55.0	55.0	54.6	55.2	55.6	56.1	54.5
1995	55.1	55.4	55.7	55.8	55.9	56.3	56.1	56.3	56.0	55.7	55.5	55.7	55.8
1996	54.0	54.6	54.6	54.5	54.6	54.8	54.7	55.0	54.9	55.6	56.0	56.3	55.0
1997	54.9	55.3	55.5	56.2	56.4	56.6	57.2	57.4	57.3	57.5	57.8	58.2	56.7
1998	58.2	58.7	58.9	58.5	58.7	59.2	59.4	59.7	59.6	58.8	59.3	59.7	59.1
1999	59.4	59.4	59.9	60.1	60.4	60.5	60.8	60.9	60.4	60.3	60.7	61.3	60.3
2000	62.0	62.1	62.7	62.5	62.8	63.7	65.1	60.3	65.2	64.6	65.2	65.8	63.5
2001	65.1	65.1	64.9	64.1	64.5	64.6	64.7	63.9	63.1	62.9	63.1	63.3	64.1
2002	62.1	61.9	62.4	61.0	61.5	61.2	60.7	60.3	59.7	59.6	59.9	59.7	60.8
2003	58.5	58.2	58.5	58.1	58.3	58.6	59.2	59.3	59.1	59.0	59.5	60.2	58.9
Financial activities													
1990	173.3	174.1	174.6	173.1	174.1	174.5	174.1	173.4	171.5	170.6	170.3	170.9	172.9
1991	169.6	170.6	171.6	169.6	169.4	170.6	170.2	170.0	169.3	168.3	168.2	168.8	169.7
1992	166.9	166.8	166.6	166.2	166.3	166.4	165.5	164.7	164.2	162.9	162.0	162.8	165.1
1993	165.2	165.6	165.8	165.8	166.3	167.4	167.7	169.0	167.2	167.8	168.1	168.6	167.0
1994	166.3	166.7	167.6	168.4	168.9	169.5	169.7	169.6	168.9	168.0	167.0	167.5	168.2
1995	164.2	164.4	164.5	165.2	164.8	165.9	167.1	167.7	166.5	166.4	166.6	167.6	165.9
1996	163.9	164.8	165.6	166.0	166.8	167.0	167.3	168.0	167.8	167.4	168.0	169.4	166.8
1997	166.2	165.9	167.2	168.5	168.8	169.9	170.3	171.0	170.8	170.2	170.7	172.1	169.3
1998	170.3	169.9	170.5	170.7	171.1	172.4	173.8	174.7	174.0	174.9	175.9	177.6	173.0
1999	175.2	174.4	175.2	177.6	178.6	178.7	179.1	178.9	178.2	178.3	178.6	180.0	177.7
2000	178.3	178.5	178.5	178.5	178.8	180.7	180.4	179.8	178.2	178.4	178.8	180.3	179.1
2001	179.2	179.4	180.2	179.3	178.7	179.6	179.2	178.7	176.5	176.4	176.2	177.1	178.4
2002	175.7	175.8	176.1	176.2	176.6	178.7	179.0	179.5	178.4	178.2	178.7	179.6	177.7
2003	178.5	179.3	179.6	179.3	180.0	181.6	181.6	181.2	179.7	179.6	179.6	180.2	180.0
Professional and business services													
1990	248.4	250.7	254.3	256.2	257.5	260.2	258.7	258.8	256.7	255.6	254.6	252.9	255.4
1991	244.3	245.5	248.6	246.3	246.0	246.6	242.5	242.7	242.9	243.2	242.7	242.5	244.5
1992	236.4	237.4	239.7	242.9	243.3	245.2	247.9	247.5	248.2	249.4	248.7	248.7	244.6
1993	241.9	244.8	246.3	250.9	252.9	253.9	254.9	254.5	255.2	256.0	255.8	256.1	251.9
1994	245.3	247.7	251.9	256.4	256.8	258.1	258.9	260.1	261.3	260.1	260.6	261.5	256.6
1995	252.1	255.2	259.1	259.2	260.1	261.3	262.6	265.0	265.5	266.9	268.4	268.8	262.0
1996	258.7	264.7	268.2	273.2	275.6	277.4	278.2	279.7	279.4	282.7	284.2	284.8	275.6
1997	277.4	281.3	285.5	288.4	290.8	295.1	296.6	298.6	299.9	303.1	305.0	306.2	294.0
1998	296.4	298.5	303.8	306.8	309.7	313.1	313.2	314.8	314.8	317.6	319.9	320.0	310.7
1999	308.0	309.7	315.9	319.4	319.9	322.7	321.3	321.5	318.9	320.0	321.0	323.3	318.5
2000	315.4	315.8	321.5	321.1	321.4	325.2	328.0	327.6	327.3	324.1	324.9	325.3	323.1
2001	318.2	319.6	324.0	327.6	329.6	332.1	328.8	332.1	331.0	330.4	330.5	328.2	327.7
2002	321.2	321.5	326.1	330.4	330.4	334.2	330.9	332.3	330.0	331.3	332.4	332.4	329.4
2003	323.4	322.6	327.2	330.3	330.7	331.6	330.6	332.8	331.9	331.9	332.4	332.2	329.8
Educational and health services													
1990	323.7	327.5	329.6	330.1	329.0	327.3	325.8	326.2	334.8	340.5	341.8	342.3	331.6
1991	337.4	342.1	343.4	346.1	343.8	341.1	336.8	336.4	347.3	352.5	355.1	355.0	344.8
1992	350.8	355.2	356.3	358.3	358.0	355.0	353.4	351.9	358.8	366.2	367.7	367.7	358.3
1993	362.1	365.2	366.1	366.7	364.9	361.6	360.6	359.3	366.1	375.2	376.3	377.5	366.8
1994	370.6	375.4	377.4	379.8	378.1	374.4	371.2	370.6	378.1	382.8	383.8	384.1	377.2
1995	373.3	381.0	383.2	382.9	380.1	376.7	368.1	369.3	377.7	386.0	388.9	389.6	379.7
1996	377.1	386.3	388.5	391.4	389.6	385.9	382.0	380.9	390.4	396.4	399.6	399.3	389.0
1997	386.7	398.6	397.4	400.0	396.6	392.2	388.9	388.9	398.2	408.5	411.2	411.6	398.2
1998	402.1	413.8	413.3	416.4	412.6	406.1	405.0	405.4	414.1	421.2	423.4	422.3	413.0
1999	410.3	421.4	418.2	422.0	418.9	411.8	409.8	406.7	413.5	420.8	423.3	423.7	416.7
2000	412.8	421.8	421.0	425.2	420.3	416.7	412.8	412.4	419.6	424.3	428.0	428.0	420.2
2001	419.0	429.4	431.0	432.4	430.5	428.4	425.5	424.5	430.6	437.1	441.3	440.6	430.9
2002	435.1	445.6	446.1	444.3	440.2	438.0	435.0	432.6	439.8	446.4	449.0	445.5	441.5
2003	437.4	447.2	447.2	448.4	444.7	440.7	437.6	436.3	442.7	449.9	453.7	452.2	444.8

Employment by Industry: Pennsylvania—*Continued*

(Numbers in thousands. Not seasonally adjusted.)

Industry	January	February	March	April	May	June	July	August	September	October	November	December	Annual Average
PHILADELPHIA PMSA *—Continued*													
Leisure and hospitality													
1990	139.1	140.0	142.4	141.8	146.2	149.2	147.6	147.8	145.4	142.7	142.4	142.8	144.0
1991	134.5	135.2	137.5	140.7	144.2	146.7	144.7	144.7	141.3	137.2	137.3	138.3	140.2
1992	130.3	131.1	133.2	138.2	143.2	145.1	145.0	144.3	141.2	140.8	139.4	139.2	139.3
1993	132.4	133.7	134.2	140.8	146.0	148.5	146.8	146.4	144.2	140.0	139.3	139.8	141.0
1994	131.4	131.6	134.8	138.7	144.5	147.8	146.0	145.6	141.5	138.9	138.6	139.7	139.9
1995	131.7	133.1	136.2	141.5	147.2	150.5	150.0	150.1	147.9	143.9	143.5	144.2	143.3
1996	133.8	136.6	140.2	147.4	154.1	157.7	156.0	156.0	153.4	150.4	150.3	151.5	149.0
1997	142.7	143.4	147.0	153.9	159.8	163.1	161.0	160.7	159.3	154.9	155.0	155.9	154.7
1998	148.5	149.3	152.0	157.8	163.5	167.2	167.2	166.7	164.3	162.0	161.3	161.8	160.1
1999	154.5	155.4	158.5	166.1	171.5	177.3	174.4	173.0	169.1	166.3	164.6	166.4	166.4
2000	158.1	157.9	162.5	168.2	172.3	177.8	177.3	176.5	174.0	170.5	170.2	170.3	169.6
2001	161.2	162.5	165.3	169.6	176.1	182.0	182.0	180.8	175.8	171.5	171.3	172.1	172.5
2002	163.3	165.2	168.9	174.7	180.2	186.2	184.8	183.8	180.1	179.4	178.7	178.2	177.0
2003	168.9	168.3	172.8	178.0	183.4	188.6	187.1	186.1	182.0	180.5	179.2	178.6	179.5
Other services													
1990	85.4	86.4	87.1	86.9	87.4	88.4	87.7	87.7	86.9	87.0	86.7	86.9	87.0
1991	84.2	84.3	84.7	84.3	84.6	84.9	85.0	84.2	83.5	83.9	84.2	84.5	84.4
1992	82.0	82.5	83.0	83.1	83.8	83.9	84.2	83.1	83.0	84.1	83.8	83.8	83.4
1993	82.9	83.1	83.2	83.3	83.4	83.6	84.0	83.2	82.4	82.5	82.5	82.7	83.1
1994	80.4	80.6	81.4	82.7	83.4	84.1	84.9	84.8	84.7	85.3	85.9	86.1	83.7
1995	84.4	85.5	86.7	87.2	87.2	87.9	88.2	88.4	88.2	88.9	89.4	89.8	87.7
1996	87.3	89.1	90.0	90.8	91.4	92.4	92.5	91.8	91.0	91.3	91.5	91.6	90.9
1997	89.9	90.4	91.3	90.7	91.1	91.7	92.8	92.5	91.9	91.6	92.0	92.3	91.5
1998	90.9	91.2	91.7	92.9	93.4	93.7	94.2	94.5	93.7	94.7	94.8	94.8	93.4
1999	93.0	93.6	94.3	95.0	95.7	96.9	97.1	97.1	96.3	96.7	97.1	98.3	95.9
2000	96.7	97.3	98.7	98.9	99.4	100.2	100.6	100.1	99.4	100.3	100.8	101.2	99.5
2001	99.4	99.8	101.5	101.8	102.8	103.6	104.1	103.7	102.8	103.6	104.0	104.5	102.6
2002	104.0	104.8	105.4	106.4	108.5	110.4	109.9	110.1	109.2	108.0	108.1	108.3	107.8
2003	107.1	107.1	108.1	108.6	109.5	110.8	111.1	111.1	110.3	110.8	111.2	111.5	109.8
Government													
1990	301.6	305.1	306.3	307.0	308.6	308.4	297.2	291.0	296.1	302.8	305.2	305.0	302.9
1991	301.9	304.6	304.8	310.5	309.1	305.6	286.7	279.0	291.3	300.0	303.1	302.7	299.9
1992	296.0	302.0	303.6	304.4	302.4	300.6	296.4	289.0	289.6	299.4	301.4	302.3	298.9
1993	295.7	301.7	303.0	304.8	304.7	302.3	291.0	284.6	286.3	296.4	300.2	303.5	297.9
1994	295.3	298.9	302.3	305.7	304.7	303.7	287.9	282.3	292.4	300.4	302.6	305.9	298.5
1995	298.9	302.1	303.5	305.1	304.0	303.3	287.4	283.3	290.6	297.3	299.2	300.8	298.0
1996	295.8	301.2	303.6	303.5	302.6	295.0	288.3	287.0	290.5	296.7	297.5	297.7	296.6
1997	295.3	299.6	301.7	301.8	301.4	294.5	285.2	282.1	289.6	296.6	298.6	300.1	295.5
1998	294.8	300.1	300.9	302.0	302.7	287.1	276.8	275.9	288.2	292.7	294.4	296.3	292.7
1999	293.6	296.8	300.3	303.6	302.7	298.5	283.1	281.1	290.9	299.4	301.4	303.5	296.2
2000	299.1	304.0	307.4	309.3	315.4	308.3	288.1	282.3	298.5	303.7	306.6	307.3	302.5
2001	303.9	309.1	310.4	311.8	309.6	307.1	287.7	283.7	300.3	308.1	311.7	313.6	304.8
2002	311.0	315.4	316.0	317.4	316.3	313.4	291.4	284.5	302.4	311.1	314.3	314.6	309.0
2003	309.5	314.8	316.7	317.3	316.5	312.6	292.6	289.0	299.3	308.1	311.0	311.7	308.3
Federal government													
1990	73.7	74.5	75.1	76.3	78.0	77.7	77.5	75.6	74.3	73.9	73.0	72.8	75.2
1991	73.1	73.3	73.6	74.7	73.4	73.7	73.2	71.8	71.2	70.4	70.1	70.3	72.4
1992	69.7	70.6	71.0	71.8	71.6	70.8	69.9	69.5	68.7	68.0	67.6	68.8	69.8
1993	67.6	67.8	67.8	70.6	70.4	70.6	69.5	69.3	69.0	67.8	67.8	69.7	69.0
1994	67.3	67.7	68.1	69.8	68.7	68.8	67.5	67.2	66.7	66.0	65.8	67.4	67.6
1995	65.5	65.8	65.9	66.9	65.4	65.1	64.6	64.3	60.9	60.3	59.9	60.5	63.8
1996	60.9	61.6	61.8	63.1	61.3	61.1	59.9	59.5	58.2	57.1	57.3	58.0	60.0
1997	58.0	58.5	58.9	59.4	57.7	57.7	57.0	56.5	55.8	55.5	55.5	57.1	57.3
1998	55.9	57.7	57.3	58.4	58.9	57.1	54.6	54.8	54.8	54.3	53.9	54.8	56.0
1999	56.0	57.7	58.7	59.4	58.4	57.6	56.6	56.2	55.6	55.1	55.3	56.6	56.9
2000	55.8	56.6	58.3	60.4	67.4	62.6	61.4	57.4	56.6	55.4	55.6	56.7	58.7
2001	56.6	56.8	57.7	58.6	57.8	57.7	57.3	56.5	56.3	55.6	55.9	56.9	57.0
2002	57.4	57.3	58.0	58.5	57.9	57.4	56.4	55.7	55.9	55.7	55.9	57.0	56.9
2003	55.6	56.3	57.1	57.5	56.9	55.2	55.0	54.2	53.8	53.9	53.9	54.7	55.3
State government													
1990	36.5	36.7	36.8	36.8	35.8	35.0	34.8	34.5	35.9	36.0	36.2	36.1	35.9
1991	35.6	36.2	36.2	35.8	34.7	33.1	33.0	32.6	33.3	33.9	34.2	33.9	34.4
1992	32.4	34.0	33.8	34.1	32.8	31.6	32.0	31.8	33.5	34.9	34.8	34.4	33.3
1993	33.2	34.8	34.8	35.9	34.9	33.2	32.5	31.7	34.1	34.8	35.0	35.0	34.2
1994	34.4	35.5	35.8	35.9	35.5	34.6	34.1	33.3	35.4	35.9	36.0	36.1	35.2
1995	35.4	36.1	36.1	36.3	36.1	34.8	34.0	33.9	36.0	36.5	36.6	36.5	35.7
1996	36.6	37.1	37.4	37.0	36.8	35.3	34.9	33.9	36.0	36.7	36.8	36.4	36.2
1997	36.0	36.2	36.3	37.0	36.6	35.1	34.0	33.8	36.0	36.2	35.9	35.9	35.8
1998	35.6	35.6	35.5	35.9	35.4	28.8	30.6	30.8	33.8	34.0	33.8	34.0	33.7
1999	34.3	34.1	34.7	34.6	34.1	32.8	32.8	32.0	33.5	34.1	34.1	34.3	33.8
2000	33.8	34.3	34.4	34.6	34.3	33.5	33.4	33.0	35.4	35.4	35.6	35.5	34.4
2001	35.5	36.1	36.2	36.1	35.8	34.7	34.7	34.2	36.2	36.4	36.5	36.4	35.7
2002	36.6	37.1	36.5	37.2	36.6	35.8	34.2	33.8	36.5	36.6	37.2	36.8	36.2
2003	36.6	37.2	37.3	37.2	36.7	36.0	35.7	35.4	36.4	37.1	37.5	37.4	36.7

Employment by Industry: Pennsylvania—*Continued*

(Numbers in thousands. Not seasonally adjusted.)

Industry	January	February	March	April	May	June	July	August	September	October	November	December	Annual Average
PHILADELPHIA PMSA *—Continued*													
Local government													
1990	191.4	193.9	194.4	193.9	194.8	195.7	184.9	180.9	185.9	192.9	196.0	196.1	191.7
1991	193.2	195.1	195.0	200.0	201.0	198.8	180.5	174.6	186.8	195.7	198.8	198.5	193.2
1992	193.9	197.4	198.8	198.5	198.0	198.2	194.5	187.7	187.4	196.5	199.0	199.1	195.8
1993	194.9	199.1	200.4	198.3	199.4	198.5	189.0	183.6	183.2	193.8	197.4	198.8	194.7
1994	193.6	195.7	198.4	200.0	200.5	200.3	186.3	181.8	190.3	198.5	200.8	202.4	195.7
1995	198.0	200.2	201.5	201.9	202.5	203.4	188.8	185.1	193.7	200.5	202.7	203.8	198.5
1996	198.3	202.5	204.4	203.4	204.5	198.6	193.5	193.6	196.3	202.9	203.4	203.3	200.4
1997	201.3	204.9	206.5	205.4	207.1	201.7	194.2	191.8	197.8	204.9	207.2	207.1	202.5
1998	203.3	206.8	208.1	207.7	208.4	201.2	191.6	190.3	199.6	204.4	206.7	207.5	203.0
1999	203.3	205.0	206.9	209.6	210.2	208.1	193.7	192.9	201.8	210.2	212.0	212.6	205.5
2000	209.5	213.1	214.7	214.3	213.7	212.2	193.3	191.9	206.5	212.9	215.4	215.1	209.4
2001	211.8	216.2	216.5	217.1	216.0	214.7	195.7	193.0	207.8	216.1	219.3	220.3	212.0
2002	217.0	221.0	221.5	221.7	221.8	220.2	200.8	195.0	210.0	218.8	221.2	220.8	215.8
2003	217.3	221.3	222.3	222.6	222.9	221.4	201.9	199.4	209.1	217.1	219.6	219.6	216.2
PHILADELPHIA CITY													
Total nonfarm													
1990	747.5	751.9	754.7	749.1	750.9	748.8	742.6	741.2	743.2	743.2	745.9	742.5	746.8
1991	718.9	725.2	725.7	726.7	716.4	713.8	700.9	696.6	705.4	711.0	713.7	712.4	713.9
1992	692.6	696.5	698.4	703.5	699.1	694.9	695.0	687.2	689.7	696.7	697.4	699.1	695.8
1993	684.4	689.9	688.6	694.5	692.1	686.5	684.1	679.8	683.2	691.2	695.1	699.2	689.1
1994	679.2	684.6	689.5	693.0	690.5	686.2	681.9	677.9	685.3	693.1	695.4	695.0	687.6
1995	668.6	677.4	678.7	681.5	678.7	673.7	666.9	667.9	673.9	680.0	682.5	684.1	676.2
1996	657.6	671.6	675.1	681.1	675.8	667.0	667.8	669.6	675.2	679.4	682.1	681.6	673.7
1997	654.4	663.5	664.5	672.0	665.4	661.3	659.3	655.8	668.5	676.9	682.4	686.1	667.5
1998	662.6	672.4	672.1	681.5	679.4	664.7	663.8	666.2	671.2	686.1	690.9	692.9	675.3
1999	667.7	677.0	678.6	686.2	687.1	686.4	679.6	679.2	683.4	693.6	698.9	704.3	685.2
2000	688.2	695.3	696.5	702.8	704.2	699.2	692.7	690.3	694.5	693.1	695.9	698.2	695.9
2001	685.4	692.4	693.2	694.3	690.7	690.5	683.2	681.7	683.6	685.5	689.6	688.7	688.2
2002	674.2	680.6	683.4	686.5	684.1	683.9	682.1	677.2	682.5	687.0	690.1	690.0	683.5
2003	672.9	680.1	681.6	684.4	682.1	678.1	673.8	671.2	675.9	680.2	683.9	683.5	679.0
Total private													
1990	612.9	616.2	618.3	611.5	612.9	610.4	602.3	603.9	607.6	608.1	610.6	607.8	610.2
1991	585.3	591.1	591.1	591.6	583.5	580.9	570.9	570.3	577.7	582.6	584.6	584.4	582.8
1992	565.6	567.7	568.9	573.3	569.8	566.2	560.0	557.8	564.4	570.2	570.9	572.4	567.3
1993	559.7	563.6	561.9	565.2	563.3	558.3	555.2	554.3	561.9	568.9	570.7	573.1	563.0
1994	555.4	559.7	563.9	565.9	565.2	560.6	555.1	554.8	561.9	570.3	572.2	570.9	563.0
1995	546.1	553.3	554.3	556.5	554.9	550.5	544.6	547.6	554.5	560.9	563.5	564.3	554.3
1996	537.7	549.9	552.4	557.5	553.3	549.7	547.1	547.0	555.4	559.5	563.0	562.2	552.9
1997	535.8	543.3	543.3	549.7	544.6	544.5	540.1	538.0	552.3	559.9	565.6	568.4	548.8
1998	545.6	552.9	552.9	561.5	558.9	555.8	549.8	549.0	556.0	570.1	574.6	575.5	558.6
1999	551.9	559.2	559.9	566.6	568.1	568.7	564.4	563.8	567.1	577.4	582.3	586.2	568.0
2000	571.3	576.7	576.4	581.4	579.4	577.1	570.8	569.4	576.3	577.0	579.2	581.1	576.3
2001	568.5	574.6	574.5	574.6	572.5	571.8	563.3	563.2	567.9	569.4	572.5	570.6	570.3
2002	556.2	561.7	564.2	566.4	565.4	566.0	561.6	562.5	568.1	573.6	576.0	575.2	566.4
2003	558.9	564.1	564.7	567.4	565.3	563.9	556.9	557.5	564.1	568.8	571.9	570.7	564.5
Goods-producing													
1990	85.6	85.6	85.6	84.4	85.4	84.8	82.7	84.0	83.7	81.9	80.8	80.2	83.7
1991	76.1	75.8	75.9	76.0	75.0	75.7	73.5	74.3	74.7	74.1	73.2	72.9	74.8
1992	69.3	68.7	69.2	70.3	69.4	69.1	68.2	68.5	69.0	67.0	66.5	67.0	68.5
1993	65.7	65.8	66.0	65.4	65.9	64.8	64.7	65.2	66.2	65.1	65.1	64.9	65.4
1994	63.4	63.0	64.6	64.2	64.4	63.9	63.4	63.6	64.5	63.7	63.2	63.0	63.7
1995	60.2	59.8	59.9	60.8	60.5	59.9	58.7	60.0	61.5	60.1	59.7	59.4	60.0
1996	56.9	58.1	58.5	57.5	57.9	57.6	56.9	57.7	58.6	58.7	58.4	57.5	57.9
1997	55.3	55.8	56.5	56.4	55.6	57.0	57.0	57.7	58.0	57.5	57.4	57.2	56.8
1998	55.5	55.9	55.8	55.6	55.6	55.9	56.4	56.1	56.1	57.1	57.0	56.6	56.1
1999	54.4	54.9	54.9	56.2	56.4	56.8	55.9	56.3	56.5	57.2	57.0	57.3	56.2
2000	55.3	55.0	55.5	56.5	56.6	56.6	55.2	55.5	56.0	56.0	55.2	54.9	55.7
2001	54.2	54.2	54.4	54.7	54.1	53.6	52.5	52.5	53.3	52.7	51.9	51.3	53.3
2002	50.2	49.8	50.3	50.2	50.2	50.6	50.4	50.6	50.5	50.3	49.6	49.1	50.2
2003	47.4	46.7	47.1	46.6	46.8	46.9	46.4	46.3	46.2	45.9	45.4	45.0	46.4
Construction and mining													
1990	15.5	15.4	15.6	15.0	16.1	16.1	16.2	16.3	15.9	15.2	14.4	14.1	15.5
1991	13.6	13.3	13.2	13.0	12.9	12.9	13.3	13.1	13.2	12.5	12.3	12.2	13.0
1992	11.5	11.5	11.7	12.5	11.8	11.5	11.4	11.4	11.3	10.5	10.3	10.6	11.3
1993	10.2	10.1	10.1	10.2	10.4	9.9	10.7	10.7	11.1	10.5	10.9	10.9	10.5
1994	10.2	10.0	10.9	11.2	11.7	11.2	11.2	11.3	11.6	11.0	10.7	10.6	11.0
1995	9.8	9.5	9.6	10.4	10.2	9.8	9.8	10.3	10.8	10.1	9.8	9.5	10.0
1996	9.3	9.9	10.4	10.4	10.8	10.5	10.6	10.9	11.6	11.2	11.0	10.2	10.6
1997	10.0	10.3	11.0	11.7	11.2	12.2	13.1	13.2	13.2	12.0	12.0	11.7	11.8
1998	11.5	11.5	11.7	11.1	11.3	11.8	12.6	12.0	11.6	11.8	11.6	11.2	11.6
1999	10.7	11.0	11.0	12.2	12.5	12.8	12.9	13.0	12.9	12.7	12.5	12.7	12.2
2000	11.7	11.6	12.0	12.8	13.0	13.2	12.2	12.3	12.7	13.2	12.8	12.4	12.5
2001	13.0	13.1	13.4	13.9	13.8	13.4	13.3	13.3	14.2	13.6	13.0	12.4	13.4
2002	11.8	11.8	12.0	12.3	12.6	13.0	13.4	13.6	13.5	13.6	13.3	13.2	12.8
2003	12.2	12.0	12.4	12.5	12.6	12.8	12.7	12.8	12.7	12.5	12.3	12.0	12.5

Employment by Industry: Pennsylvania—*Continued*

(Numbers in thousands. Not seasonally adjusted.)

Industry	January	February	March	April	May	June	July	August	September	October	November	December	Annual Average
PHILADELPHIA CITY *—Continued*													
Manufacturing													
1990	70.1	70.2	70.0	69.4	69.3	68.7	66.5	67.7	67.8	66.7	66.4	66.1	68.2
1991	62.5	62.5	62.7	63.0	62.1	62.8	60.2	61.2	61.5	61.6	60.9	60.7	61.8
1992	57.8	57.2	57.5	57.8	57.6	57.6	56.8	57.1	57.7	56.5	56.2	56.4	57.2
1993	55.5	55.7	55.9	55.2	55.5	54.9	54.0	54.5	55.1	54.6	54.2	54.0	54.9
1994	53.2	53.0	53.7	53.0	52.7	52.7	52.2	52.3	52.9	52.7	52.5	52.4	52.8
1995	50.4	50.3	50.3	50.4	50.3	50.1	48.9	49.7	50.7	50.0	49.9	49.9	50.1
1996	47.6	48.2	48.1	47.1	47.1	47.1	46.3	46.8	47.0	47.5	47.4	47.3	47.3
1997	45.3	45.5	45.5	44.7	44.4	44.8	43.9	44.5	44.8	45.5	45.4	45.5	45.0
1998	44.0	44.4	44.1	44.5	44.3	44.1	43.8	44.1	44.5	45.3	45.4	45.4	44.5
1999	43.7	43.9	43.9	44.0	43.9	44.0	43.0	43.3	43.6	44.5	44.5	44.6	43.9
2000	43.6	43.4	43.5	43.7	43.6	43.4	43.0	43.2	43.3	42.8	42.4	42.5	43.2
2001	41.2	41.1	41.0	40.8	40.3	40.2	39.2	39.2	39.1	39.1	38.9	38.9	39.9
2002	38.4	38.0	38.3	37.9	37.6	37.6	37.0	37.0	37.0	36.7	36.3	35.9	37.3
2003	35.2	34.7	34.7	34.1	34.2	34.1	33.7	33.5	33.5	33.4	33.1	33.0	33.9
Service-providing													
1990	661.9	666.3	669.1	664.7	665.5	664.0	659.9	657.2	659.5	661.3	665.1	662.3	663.1
1991	642.8	649.4	649.8	650.7	641.4	638.1	627.4	622.3	630.7	636.9	640.5	639.5	639.1
1992	623.3	627.8	629.2	633.2	629.7	625.8	626.8	618.7	620.7	629.7	630.9	632.1	627.3
1993	618.7	624.1	622.6	629.1	626.2	621.7	619.4	614.6	617.0	626.1	630.0	634.3	623.7
1994	615.8	621.6	624.9	628.8	626.1	622.3	618.5	614.3	620.8	629.4	632.2	632.0	623.9
1995	608.4	617.6	618.8	620.7	618.2	613.8	608.2	607.9	612.4	619.9	622.8	624.7	616.1
1996	600.7	613.5	616.6	623.6	617.9	609.4	610.9	611.9	616.6	620.7	623.7	624.1	615.8
1997	599.1	607.7	608.0	615.6	609.8	604.3	602.3	598.1	610.5	619.4	625.0	628.9	610.7
1998	607.1	616.5	616.3	625.9	623.8	608.8	607.4	610.1	615.1	629.0	633.9	636.3	619.2
1999	613.3	622.1	623.7	630.0	630.7	629.6	623.7	622.9	626.9	636.4	641.9	647.0	629.0
2000	632.9	640.3	641.0	646.3	647.6	642.6	637.5	634.8	638.5	637.1	640.7	643.3	640.2
2001	631.2	638.2	638.8	639.6	636.6	636.9	630.7	629.2	630.3	632.8	637.7	637.4	635.0
2002	624.0	630.8	633.1	636.3	633.9	633.3	631.7	626.6	632.0	636.7	640.5	640.9	633.3
2003	625.5	633.4	634.5	637.8	635.3	631.2	627.4	624.9	629.7	634.3	638.5	638.5	632.6
Trade, transportation, and utilities													
1990	131.9	129.6	130.2	128.4	128.9	128.3	127.7	128.5	128.3	127.5	127.9	128.3	128.8
1991	120.9	119.8	119.3	119.0	117.4	116.5	114.9	114.7	116.1	116.7	118.2	119.1	117.7
1992	115.1	113.3	113.3	113.2	113.3	112.8	110.5	110.3	112.1	114.6	116.0	117.4	113.5
1993	112.8	111.2	110.0	111.5	111.5	111.4	110.6	109.9	111.8	113.2	114.7	116.6	112.1
1994	110.3	109.0	109.9	110.0	110.9	110.4	108.9	108.5	110.6	112.9	114.7	115.3	111.0
1995	108.7	107.6	107.6	107.2	108.1	107.3	105.3	105.6	107.2	108.4	110.0	111.2	107.9
1996	104.2	104.1	104.7	105.0	104.4	103.9	103.3	102.7	104.5	102.4	103.6	104.5	103.9
1997	99.1	98.5	98.8	99.3	99.4	99.7	98.6	95.7	101.4	103.4	105.5	107.1	100.5
1998	101.6	100.1	99.7	100.5	100.8	100.1	98.4	98.6	101.3	104.4	106.3	107.8	101.6
1999	101.7	101.4	101.4	101.0	101.8	102.6	100.7	100.7	101.8	105.1	107.6	108.8	102.9
2000	103.2	102.5	102.2	103.8	104.2	103.6	100.1	100.6	102.2	102.3	104.6	105.4	102.9
2001	100.3	98.9	99.0	98.6	98.8	98.7	96.0	96.4	98.2	98.5	100.5	101.6	98.8
2002	97.1	95.8	96.3	95.7	96.8	97.5	95.8	96.2	97.8	99.0	100.8	102.6	97.6
2003	97.5	96.2	96.1	96.7	97.0	97.7	96.3	96.2	98.0	99.0	100.9	102.3	97.8
Wholesale trade													
1990	37.0	36.8	37.0	35.4	35.2	35.3	34.6	34.7	34.1	33.8	34.1	33.7	35.1
1991	31.6	31.6	31.6	31.2	31.0	30.6	30.1	30.0	30.0	30.0	29.6	29.5	30.6
1992	29.0	28.9	29.0	28.4	28.1	28.0	27.5	27.4	27.3	27.2	26.9	26.7	27.9
1993	26.3	26.2	26.3	26.3	26.2	26.1	25.6	25.5	25.5	25.4	25.5	25.5	25.9
1994	24.7	24.7	24.8	24.7	24.8	24.6	24.1	24.0	24.1	24.2	24.1	23.9	24.4
1995	23.0	23.1	23.2	23.3	23.2	23.0	22.4	22.3	22.6	22.5	22.5	22.5	22.8
1996	21.8	22.0	22.0	21.7	21.7	21.6	21.6	21.5	21.5	21.6	21.7	21.6	21.7
1997	21.1	21.2	21.2	21.1	21.1	21.1	21.1	21.1	21.2	21.4	21.4	21.4	21.2
1998	21.0	21.1	21.2	21.1	20.8	20.9	20.8	20.6	20.8	21.4	21.4	21.4	21.0
1999	20.7	20.7	20.7	20.6	20.6	20.9	20.9	20.7	20.6	21.4	21.5	21.7	20.9
2000	21.1	21.2	21.3	22.1	22.1	22.2	21.3	21.5	21.3	21.0	21.0	21.0	21.4
2001	20.7	20.5	20.4	20.4	20.3	20.4	20.6	20.5	20.7	20.7	20.8	20.9	20.6
2002	20.8	20.8	20.9	20.9	20.9	21.0	20.8	20.6	20.4	20.3	20.3	20.4	20.7
2003	19.9	19.9	19.9	20.0	20.0	20.0	20.0	19.9	19.9	19.8	19.8	19.9	19.9
Retail trade													
1990	70.5	68.3	68.7	67.9	68.4	68.1	68.3	68.7	69.1	68.8	68.7	69.3	68.7
1991	64.7	63.7	63.4	63.1	62.4	62.1	60.8	60.8	61.2	61.7	63.5	64.5	62.7
1992	61.4	59.7	59.6	59.9	60.2	59.8	59.0	58.9	59.7	61.5	63.4	64.9	60.7
1993	60.5	58.8	58.3	58.8	59.1	59.0	59.6	59.4	60.0	60.7	62.3	64.5	60.1
1994	59.3	57.8	58.3	58.5	59.1	58.9	59.1	59.4	60.3	61.8	64.3	65.4	60.2
1995	61.1	59.7	59.5	59.0	59.8	59.5	58.9	59.3	59.7	60.4	62.2	63.4	60.2
1996	59.1	58.6	58.7	59.2	58.6	58.5	58.1	57.7	58.3	55.9	56.9	58.0	58.1
1997	53.1	52.3	52.4	52.9	53.2	53.3	53.2	53.5	54.3	55.7	57.8	59.4	54.3
1998	55.1	54.5	54.1	55.2	55.5	55.1	54.4	54.4	55.3	57.2	59.0	60.3	55.8
1999	56.1	55.7	55.6	55.3	56.0	56.6	56.0	56.2	56.1	57.8	60.2	61.1	56.9
2000	56.4	55.5	55.1	55.6	55.9	55.6	53.9	54.4	55.0	55.4	57.8	58.8	55.8
2001	54.1	52.9	53.1	52.4	52.6	52.7	51.1	51.7	51.9	51.8	53.8	54.9	52.8
2002	51.1	50.0	50.2	49.4	49.7	50.1	49.6	49.9	50.2	50.7	52.4	53.7	50.6
2003	50.0	48.9	49.1	49.4	49.6	50.5	50.1	50.0	50.3	50.8	52.7	53.9	50.4

Employment by Industry: Pennsylvania—*Continued*

(Numbers in thousands. Not seasonally adjusted.)

Industry	January	February	March	April	May	June	July	August	September	October	November	December	Annual Average
PHILADELPHIA CITY *—Continued*													
Transportation and utilities													
1990	24.4	24.5	24.5	25.1	25.3	24.9	24.8	25.1	25.1	24.9	25.1	25.3	24.9
1991	24.6	24.5	24.3	24.7	24.0	23.8	24.0	23.9	24.9	25.0	25.1	25.1	24.5
1992	24.7	24.7	24.7	24.9	25.0	25.0	24.0	24.0	25.1	25.9	25.7	25.8	25.0
1993	26.0	26.2	25.4	26.4	26.2	26.3	25.4	25.0	26.3	27.1	26.9	26.6	26.2
1994	26.3	26.5	26.8	26.8	27.0	26.9	25.7	25.1	26.2	26.9	26.3	26.0	26.4
1995	24.6	24.8	24.9	24.9	25.1	24.8	24.0	24.0	24.9	25.5	25.3	25.3	24.8
1996	23.3	23.5	24.0	24.1	24.1	23.8	23.6	23.5	24.7	24.9	25.0	24.9	24.1
1997	24.9	25.0	25.2	25.3	25.1	25.3	24.3	21.1	25.9	26.3	26.3	26.3	25.1
1998	25.5	24.5	24.4	24.2	24.5	24.1	23.2	23.6	25.2	25.8	25.9	26.1	24.8
1999	24.9	25.0	25.1	25.1	25.2	25.1	23.8	23.8	25.1	25.9	25.9	26.0	25.1
2000	25.7	25.8	25.8	26.1	26.2	25.8	24.9	24.7	25.9	25.9	25.8	25.6	25.7
2001	25.5	25.5	25.5	25.8	25.9	25.6	24.3	24.2	25.6	26.0	25.9	25.8	25.5
2002	25.2	25.0	25.2	25.4	26.2	26.4	25.4	25.7	27.2	28.0	28.1	28.5	26.4
2003	27.6	27.4	27.1	27.3	27.4	27.2	26.2	26.3	27.8	28.4	28.4	28.5	27.5
Information													
1990	18.8	18.9	19.0	18.7	19.0	19.0	18.7	18.6	18.7	19.1	19.5	19.5	19.0
1991	19.5	19.7	19.5	19.5	19.3	19.3	19.3	19.3	19.2	19.2	19.2	19.2	19.4
1992	18.9	18.9	19.2	18.8	18.9	19.1	19.0	18.6	18.8	18.8	18.6	18.7	18.9
1993	18.3	18.3	18.2	18.3	18.3	18.2	17.8	17.8	17.8	18.0	18.0	18.1	18.1
1994	17.1	17.1	17.4	17.2	17.4	17.7	17.5	17.4	17.6	17.8	17.9	17.9	17.5
1995	16.8	17.0	17.0	17.2	17.2	17.3	17.2	17.2	17.4	17.1	17.0	16.9	17.1
1996	15.2	15.5	15.5	15.7	15.6	15.6	15.6	15.6	15.6	15.7	15.7	15.7	15.6
1997	15.0	15.0	15.1	14.3	14.3	14.4	14.3	14.3	14.5	15.0	15.0	15.0	14.7
1998	15.2	15.3	15.3	15.7	15.6	15.5	15.8	15.7	15.8	15.9	16.0	16.1	15.7
1999	15.7	15.6	15.7	15.9	16.1	15.9	16.3	16.4	16.3	16.3	16.4	16.6	16.1
2000	16.9	16.9	16.7	17.0	17.0	17.2	17.1	15.3	17.1	16.6	16.9	17.2	16.8
2001	17.0	17.1	17.1	16.9	17.0	17.0	17.2	17.0	16.8	16.9	17.1	17.1	17.0
2002	16.9	16.9	17.2	16.9	16.9	16.8	16.8	16.6	16.7	16.7	16.8	16.8	16.8
2003	16.9	16.9	17.1	17.2	17.4	17.5	17.5	17.3	17.6	17.6	17.7	17.8	17.4
Financial activities													
1990	72.1	72.2	72.5	71.0	71.5	71.5	70.9	70.9	70.3	70.0	70.6	70.6	71.2
1991	69.5	69.9	70.2	67.7	66.9	67.5	66.6	66.3	66.1	66.3	66.1	65.9	67.4
1992	63.9	64.1	64.3	64.2	64.2	64.0	61.9	61.4	60.9	61.3	61.2	61.5	62.7
1993	60.5	60.7	60.7	60.3	60.3	60.4	60.8	61.3	61.5	61.6	61.6	61.7	61.0
1994	61.2	61.3	61.5	60.8	60.9	60.7	61.4	61.4	61.6	61.6	61.0	61.0	61.2
1995	58.4	58.4	58.5	58.1	58.1	57.9	57.5	57.7	58.0	56.6	56.9	57.1	57.8
1996	55.7	56.0	56.1	56.9	56.4	56.6	56.2	56.3	56.7	56.5	56.6	56.5	56.4
1997	54.3	54.3	54.2	55.1	54.9	55.0	54.4	54.5	54.7	54.4	54.9	55.2	54.7
1998	53.6	54.1	54.3	54.0	54.0	54.0	53.8	53.7	53.5	53.6	53.9	54.3	53.9
1999	52.3	52.1	51.9	52.4	52.2	52.7	52.5	52.2	51.9	52.7	52.8	53.3	52.4
2000	53.2	53.4	53.0	53.6	53.7	54.0	52.9	52.6	52.3	52.3	52.2	52.6	53.0
2001	52.9	53.1	53.0	52.8	52.3	52.4	52.1	51.8	51.5	51.3	51.4	51.6	52.2
2002	51.1	51.2	51.2	51.4	51.5	52.0	52.4	52.6	52.4	51.8	51.8	52.1	51.8
2003	51.5	51.7	51.7	51.4	51.4	51.6	51.4	51.3	50.9	50.6	50.6	50.8	51.2
Professional and business services													
1990	88.6	89.3	89.9	88.6	88.9	89.2	87.9	87.7	88.3	87.4	87.6	86.3	88.3
1991	82.1	83.5	83.7	82.8	82.0	82.0	80.7	80.7	80.8	80.8	80.7	80.3	81.7
1992	78.2	77.9	78.1	78.6	77.8	78.6	80.3	79.9	80.5	79.4	78.9	78.4	78.9
1993	77.7	78.5	78.7	77.2	76.8	76.8	77.4	77.0	77.5	78.0	77.7	77.6	77.6
1994	75.8	76.4	77.2	77.7	77.4	77.3	77.9	77.9	78.3	78.9	79.3	79.0	77.8
1995	76.4	77.2	77.7	77.5	77.2	77.3	77.5	78.2	79.7	80.4	80.2	80.3	78.3
1996	77.8	79.5	80.1	79.7	79.7	80.0	80.9	80.9	80.9	82.8	83.6	83.2	80.8
1997	80.6	81.7	81.9	82.2	81.7	82.7	82.6	82.9	83.8	84.4	85.2	85.9	83.0
1998	82.2	83.4	84.1	85.7	86.3	87.2	85.5	85.6	85.1	87.0	87.6	87.5	85.6
1999	84.5	85.4	86.1	87.1	86.9	88.0	89.0	89.5	88.4	89.0	89.7	90.7	87.9
2000	88.9	89.6	89.7	89.5	89.2	89.7	89.5	89.5	89.1	87.6	87.5	87.6	89.0
2001	86.3	86.4	86.7	87.0	87.6	88.7	87.7	88.1	87.6	87.8	88.1	87.7	87.5
2002	86.2	86.3	87.2	87.6	87.2	87.9	86.5	86.9	86.9	87.0	87.0	87.1	87.0
2003	85.5	85.5	85.9	85.3	85.1	85.2	84.3	84.4	84.6	84.6	84.7	84.6	85.0
Educational and health services													
1990	141.3	145.2	144.7	145.6	142.8	140.8	140.1	140.0	144.0	147.7	148.9	147.5	144.1
1991	145.9	150.7	149.7	152.1	148.5	145.8	143.9	144.0	149.6	154.8	156.4	155.7	149.8
1992	152.6	156.5	155.4	157.4	154.5	151.6	149.4	149.1	152.5	157.9	158.7	158.6	154.5
1993	155.6	159.4	158.1	159.6	156.5	153.3	152.2	151.9	155.1	161.3	161.8	162.6	157.3
1994	158.8	163.5	162.4	164.3	160.9	157.6	154.6	154.5	158.7	164.1	164.4	163.4	160.6
1995	157.5	163.9	162.8	163.3	159.7	156.7	155.3	155.6	155.8	164.4	165.5	165.3	160.5
1996	157.9	165.2	164.7	165.8	161.8	158.2	157.0	156.6	161.6	166.8	168.1	167.7	162.6
1997	159.5	165.6	163.3	166.2	161.5	159.0	157.5	157.3	162.8	168.4	169.8	170.0	163.4
1998	163.9	169.3	167.9	171.0	166.7	163.4	161.8	161.1	165.4	170.9	171.9	171.5	167.1
1999	164.6	170.5	169.7	171.2	170.2	167.0	165.9	165.1	168.6	172.7	174.7	174.7	169.6
2000	171.2	176.1	174.9	175.6	173.1	170.5	169.9	170.2	173.7	175.7	176.1	176.9	173.7
2001	174.6	180.3	178.9	178.7	175.3	174.1	171.7	171.7	175.6	178.6	180.4	178.7	176.6
2002	174.9	181.0	180.1	181.0	178.2	176.4	175.5	175.7	180.5	184.1	185.2	183.4	179.7
2003	180.7	187.5	186.2	187.9	184.5	181.8	178.5	178.8	183.7	187.5	188.9	187.1	184.4

Employment by Industry: Pennsylvania—*Continued*

(Numbers in thousands. Not seasonally adjusted.)

Industry	January	February	March	April	May	June	July	August	September	October	November	December	Annual Average
PHILADELPHIA CITY *—Continued*													
Leisure and hospitality													
1990	44.6	44.9	45.6	44.7	46.1	46.3	44.3	44.2	44.6	44.7	45.2	45.4	45.1
1991	42.1	42.1	42.9	44.5	44.6	44.4	42.5	41.7	42.3	41.6	41.7	42.2	42.7
1992	39.9	40.3	41.2	42.4	43.2	42.8	42.3	42.0	42.6	42.7	42.7	42.5	42.1
1993	41.3	41.8	42.1	44.6	45.7	45.0	43.3	43.1	43.9	43.5	43.5	43.2	43.4
1994	41.2	41.7	42.6	42.8	44.5	44.4	42.6	42.6	42.1	42.5	42.8	42.7	42.7
1995	39.9	40.7	41.7	43.3	44.9	44.9	43.9	44.0	45.2	44.1	44.3	44.1	43.4
1996	41.3	42.3	43.3	46.9	47.5	47.7	47.2	47.3	47.9	47.2	47.5	47.5	46.1
1997	43.7	43.9	44.7	47.4	48.4	47.9	46.6	46.8	48.5	47.9	48.8	49.0	47.0
1998	45.5	46.3	47.2	50.0	51.0	50.9	49.4	49.5	50.3	52.0	52.5	52.3	49.7
1999	50.7	50.8	51.5	53.9	55.5	56.5	54.8	54.5	54.7	55.2	55.0	55.8	54.1
2000	54.0	54.3	55.3	56.4	56.6	56.5	57.0	56.9	57.4	57.8	57.8	57.5	56.5
2001	54.9	56.1	56.5	56.9	58.1	57.9	56.8	56.5	56.2	54.7	54.0	53.5	56.0
2002	51.0	51.7	52.6	53.9	54.8	54.8	54.4	54.0	53.8	54.7	54.8	54.0	53.7
2003	49.9	50.1	51.0	52.6	53.1	53.0	52.6	53.3	53.4	53.6	53.7	53.0	52.4
Other services													
1990	30.0	30.5	30.8	30.1	30.3	30.5	30.0	30.0	29.7	29.8	30.1	30.0	30.2
1991	29.2	29.6	29.9	30.0	29.8	29.7	29.5	29.3	28.9	29.1	29.1	29.1	29.4
1992	27.7	28.0	28.2	28.4	28.5	28.2	28.4	28.0	28.0	28.5	28.3	28.3	28.2
1993	27.8	27.9	28.1	28.3	28.3	28.4	28.4	28.1	28.1	28.2	28.3	28.4	28.2
1994	27.6	27.7	28.3	28.9	28.8	28.6	28.8	28.9	28.5	28.8	28.9	28.6	28.5
1995	28.2	28.7	29.1	29.1	29.2	29.2	29.2	29.3	29.7	29.8	29.9	30.0	29.3
1996	28.7	29.2	29.5	30.0	30.0	30.1	30.0	29.9	29.6	29.4	29.5	29.6	29.6
1997	28.3	28.5	28.8	28.8	28.8	28.8	29.1	28.8	28.6	28.9	29.0	29.0	28.8
1998	28.1	28.5	28.6	29.0	28.9	28.8	28.7	28.7	28.5	29.2	29.4	29.4	28.8
1999	28.0	28.5	28.7	28.9	29.0	29.2	29.3	29.1	28.9	29.2	29.1	29.0	28.9
2000	28.6	28.9	29.1	29.0	29.0	29.0	29.1	28.8	28.5	28.7	28.9	29.0	28.9
2001	28.3	28.5	28.9	29.0	29.3	29.4	29.3	29.2	28.7	28.9	29.1	29.1	29.0
2002	28.8	29.0	29.3	29.7	29.8	30.0	29.8	29.9	29.5	30.0	30.0	30.1	29.7
2003	29.5	29.5	29.6	29.7	30.0	30.2	29.9	29.9	29.7	30.0	30.0	30.1	29.8
Government													
1990	134.6	135.7	136.4	137.6	138.0	138.4	140.3	137.3	135.6	135.1	135.3	134.7	136.6
1991	133.6	134.1	134.6	135.1	132.9	132.9	130.0	126.3	127.7	128.4	129.1	128.0	131.1
1992	127.0	128.8	129.5	130.2	129.3	128.7	135.0	129.4	125.3	126.5	126.5	126.7	128.6
1993	124.7	126.3	126.7	129.3	128.8	128.2	128.9	125.5	121.3	122.3	124.4	126.1	126.0
1994	123.8	124.9	125.6	127.1	125.3	125.6	126.8	123.1	123.4	122.8	123.2	124.1	124.6
1995	122.5	124.1	124.4	125.0	123.8	123.2	122.3	120.3	119.4	119.1	119.0	119.8	121.9
1996	119.9	121.7	122.7	123.6	122.5	117.3	120.7	122.6	119.8	119.9	119.1	119.4	120.8
1997	118.6	120.2	121.2	122.3	120.8	116.8	119.2	117.8	116.2	117.0	116.8	117.7	118.7
1998	117.0	119.5	119.2	120.0	120.5	108.9	114.0	117.2	115.2	116.0	116.3	117.4	116.8
1999	115.8	117.8	118.7	119.6	119.0	117.7	115.2	115.4	116.3	116.2	116.6	118.1	117.2
2000	116.9	118.6	120.1	121.4	124.8	122.1	121.9	120.9	118.2	116.1	116.7	117.1	119.6
2001	116.9	117.8	118.7	119.7	118.2	118.7	119.9	118.5	115.7	116.1	117.1	118.1	118.0
2002	118.0	118.9	119.2	120.1	118.7	117.9	120.5	114.7	114.4	113.4	114.1	114.8	117.1
2003	114.0	116.0	116.9	117.0	116.8	114.2	116.9	113.7	111.8	111.4	112.0	112.8	114.5
Federal government													
1990	49.4	50.3	50.8	52.0	52.7	52.5	52.0	50.8	50.1	49.8	49.3	49.2	50.7
1991	49.3	49.6	50.0	50.7	49.2	49.3	48.7	47.2	47.0	45.9	45.5	45.2	48.1
1992	45.3	46.1	46.4	47.4	47.1	46.3	45.4	45.1	44.8	44.4	43.8	44.5	45.6
1993	43.7	44.0	44.1	46.8	46.5	46.3	45.1	45.0	44.6	43.9	43.6	44.8	44.9
1994	43.3	43.6	44.3	45.6	44.2	44.2	43.0	42.7	42.3	41.6	41.3	42.0	43.2
1995	41.0	41.8	41.9	42.9	41.4	40.9	40.6	40.3	37.3	36.9	36.4	36.7	39.8
1996	37.6	38.4	38.8	40.0	38.5	38.2	37.3	37.1	36.6	35.6	35.8	36.4	37.5
1997	36.1	37.0	37.5	38.6	37.0	36.8	35.8	35.4	34.9	34.6	34.7	35.3	36.1
1998	35.3	37.1	36.8	38.1	38.4	36.6	35.8	35.7	35.6	35.2	35.1	36.1	36.3
1999	35.4	36.7	37.1	37.8	37.0	36.5	35.5	35.3	35.2	34.8	34.8	35.6	36.0
2000	35.4	36.4	37.5	38.8	42.1	39.6	38.4	36.2	35.8	34.8	35.0	35.5	37.1
2001	36.1	36.3	37.2	38.0	37.3	37.0	36.5	35.9	35.9	35.4	35.4	36.0	36.4
2002	36.6	37.1	37.7	38.2	37.5	36.6	35.7	34.7	34.6	34.0	33.9	34.4	35.9
2003	34.3	35.2	36.1	36.7	36.3	34.4	33.6	32.8	32.6	32.1	32.0	32.5	34.1
State government													
1990	15.5	15.4	15.5	15.5	15.3	15.4	15.2	15.1	15.2	15.1	15.1	15.1	15.3
1991	15.0	14.8	14.7	14.5	14.0	14.0	13.8	13.5	13.3	13.7	13.5	13.2	14.0
1992	13.1	13.1	12.9	13.0	13.1	12.9	13.3	13.3	13.0	13.8	13.8	13.6	13.2
1993	13.3	13.4	13.4	13.5	13.3	13.3	13.6	13.2	13.3	13.5	13.7	13.6	13.4
1994	13.6	13.4	13.6	13.5	13.5	13.7	13.9	13.5	13.7	13.6	13.8	13.9	13.6
1995	13.8	13.9	13.8	13.7	13.8	13.7	13.5	13.5	13.7	13.9	13.9	13.9	13.8
1996	14.0	13.9	14.1	13.9	13.9	13.8	13.7	13.4	13.3	13.9	13.9	13.6	13.8
1997	13.5	13.5	13.5	13.4	13.3	13.1	12.7	12.6	12.7	12.9	12.5	12.4	13.0
1998	12.3	12.2	12.1	11.9	11.9	6.7	9.5	10.9	10.9	11.0	11.0	11.0	11.0
1999	11.0	11.0	11.0	11.1	11.2	11.0	11.0	11.0	11.0	10.9	10.9	11.0	11.0
2000	11.2	10.8	10.9	11.0	11.0	11.0	10.8	10.8	10.9	11.0	11.0	11.1	11.0
2001	11.3	11.3	11.3	11.3	11.3	11.2	11.1	11.1	11.2	11.4	11.4	11.4	11.3
2002	11.4	11.4	11.2	11.4	11.4	11.4	11.2	11.2	11.3	11.1	11.5	11.4	11.3
2003	11.5	11.5	11.5	11.4	11.4	11.3	11.2	11.1	11.0	10.9	11.1	11.2	11.3

Employment by Industry: Pennsylvania—*Continued*

(Numbers in thousands. Not seasonally adjusted.)

Industry	January	February	March	April	May	June	July	August	September	October	November	December	Annual Average
PHILADELPHIA CITY *—Continued*													
Local government													
1990	69.7	70.0	70.1	70.1	70.0	70.5	73.1	71.4	70.3	70.2	70.9	70.4	70.6
1991	69.3	69.7	69.9	69.9	69.7	69.6	67.5	65.6	67.4	68.8	70.1	69.6	68.9
1992	68.6	69.6	70.2	69.8	69.1	69.5	76.3	71.0	67.5	68.3	68.9	68.6	69.8
1993	67.7	68.9	69.2	69.0	69.0	68.6	70.2	67.3	63.4	64.9	67.1	67.7	67.8
1994	66.9	67.9	67.7	68.0	67.6	67.7	69.9	66.9	67.4	67.6	68.1	68.2	67.8
1995	67.7	68.4	68.7	68.4	68.6	68.6	68.2	66.5	68.4	68.3	68.7	69.2	68.3
1996	68.3	69.4	69.8	69.7	70.1	65.3	69.7	72.1	69.9	70.4	69.4	69.4	69.5
1997	69.0	69.7	70.2	70.3	70.5	66.9	70.7	69.8	68.6	69.5	69.6	70.0	69.6
1998	69.4	70.2	70.3	70.0	70.2	65.6	68.7	70.6	68.7	69.8	70.2	70.3	69.5
1999	69.4	70.1	70.6	70.7	70.8	70.2	68.7	69.1	70.1	70.5	70.9	71.5	70.2
2000	70.3	71.4	71.7	71.6	71.7	71.5	72.7	73.9	71.5	70.3	70.7	70.5	71.5
2001	69.5	70.2	70.2	70.4	69.6	70.5	72.3	71.5	68.6	69.3	70.3	70.7	70.3
2002	70.0	70.4	70.3	70.5	69.8	69.9	73.6	68.8	68.5	68.3	68.7	69.0	69.8
2003	68.2	69.3	69.3	68.9	69.1	68.5	72.1	69.8	68.2	68.4	68.9	69.1	69.2
PITTSBURGH													
Total nonfarm													
1990	994.5	999.2	1008.4	1019.3	1027.0	1034.5	1028.2	1024.3	1031.5	1033.2	1034.9	1032.0	1022.3
1991	996.3	995.1	1002.4	1012.9	1017.9	1025.8	1012.3	1012.2	1021.4	1025.6	1030.0	1028.7	1015.1
1992	997.6	996.6	1003.7	1020.6	1030.7	1035.3	1022.2	1020.6	1032.0	1039.3	1037.0	1032.2	1022.3
1993	1007.8	1011.0	1013.7	1027.2	1034.2	1038.2	1029.2	1029.2	1038.2	1048.1	1047.5	1046.4	1030.9
1994	1010.3	1014.8	1024.6	1035.4	1042.9	1051.0	1042.8	1040.4	1052.5	1057.0	1061.3	1060.0	1041.1
1995	1027.1	1029.9	1041.8	1051.1	1057.4	1064.3	1049.0	1046.9	1056.9	1063.1	1065.3	1061.4	1051.2
1996	1028.5	1035.7	1043.9	1057.9	1063.9	1069.6	1061.3	1058.4	1063.6	1074.7	1078.4	1079.0	1059.6
1997	1049.0	1052.2	1061.4	1069.2	1076.9	1082.7	1075.1	1073.0	1081.6	1091.4	1093.9	1094.5	1075.1
1998	1062.4	1065.7	1073.5	1088.7	1098.5	1104.0	1091.3	1088.7	1096.3	1104.5	1107.9	1107.7	1090.8
1999	1070.6	1081.3	1088.9	1105.8	1114.8	1122.7	1114.0	1111.4	1117.9	1119.0	1123.8	1125.1	1107.9
2000	1096.8	1101.4	1113.8	1128.3	1137.2	1140.9	1132.4	1123.2	1135.9	1139.4	1143.6	1141.1	1127.8
2001	1118.8	1123.7	1130.7	1138.5	1144.2	1152.3	1135.6	1131.6	1135.2	1135.1	1138.0	1134.1	1134.8
2002	1105.1	1107.3	1115.6	1123.8	1133.3	1139.5	1123.8	1121.3	1127.6	1130.3	1130.5	1122.6	1123.4
2003	1097.9	1094.0	1103.6	1114.2	1121.5	1125.5	1110.4	1107.5	1113.1	1115.8	1114.5	1110.5	1110.7
Total private													
1990	873.2	874.9	883.0	893.5	902.1	909.4	910.2	910.4	911.2	908.2	909.2	906.9	899.4
1991	875.3	871.0	877.3	888.0	894.5	902.9	901.6	904.1	901.7	902.0	905.3	904.4	894.0
1992	877.0	873.9	879.8	894.6	905.9	911.2	908.2	908.9	910.6	912.5	909.9	906.3	899.9
1993	886.1	886.1	886.9	900.4	907.3	912.5	913.4	915.3	916.9	921.3	919.5	919.1	907.1
1994	888.3	888.5	896.3	907.5	915.6	924.0	926.8	928.2	929.8	929.8	933.6	932.2	916.7
1995	904.3	902.4	913.6	923.1	928.9	937.0	931.8	933.0	934.4	936.2	937.1	933.5	926.3
1996	906.0	908.0	915.5	930.0	938.0	944.9	944.7	944.7	942.4	948.1	950.2	950.8	935.3
1997	922.8	923.7	931.5	939.7	947.7	956.3	957.2	957.9	958.3	964.6	966.3	967.8	949.5
1998	938.6	939.4	946.6	962.6	972.7	979.6	976.4	975.5	973.7	978.2	981.1	981.5	967.2
1999	948.4	956.1	962.6	979.3	988.4	997.7	995.8	996.0	992.9	993.0	996.0	998.9	983.8
2000	972.9	975.3	985.6	1000.3	1007.1	1015.6	1015.9	1010.6	1012.8	1013.0	1015.9	1014.6	1003.3
2001	993.6	996.7	1003.1	1010.5	1016.6	1027.7	1020.4	1018.7	1010.4	1007.2	1008.8	1006.5	1010.0
2002	979.8	978.6	986.9	994.9	1005.5	1012.2	1006.3	1006.7	1002.7	1001.0	999.8	993.3	997.3
2003	971.0	964.3	973.1	984.3	992.4	998.8	992.4	992.3	987.9	986.5	984.3	981.5	984.1
Goods-producing													
1990	173.5	173.1	175.9	178.8	181.9	184.0	185.3	185.9	185.4	182.9	181.3	178.0	180.5
1991	168.9	166.7	167.7	172.5	174.4	177.9	178.6	179.5	177.4	177.4	174.9	172.2	174.0
1992	164.9	163.2	164.7	169.2	172.8	175.2	175.9	176.9	176.7	175.7	171.6	167.5	171.2
1993	162.2	161.0	160.8	165.1	167.4	169.7	171.8	172.0	171.6	172.5	171.0	168.7	167.8
1994	159.7	160.4	162.9	165.3	167.7	170.7	173.4	174.5	174.7	174.3	173.6	170.5	169.0
1995	163.7	162.1	166.0	168.4	170.1	172.4	173.6	174.2	174.0	174.2	171.7	167.0	169.8
1996	159.7	160.4	163.4	168.4	171.6	174.4	176.3	176.9	176.6	177.2	175.2	172.1	171.0
1997	166.2	165.9	168.6	173.6	176.2	178.8	180.4	181.7	180.1	181.7	180.1	177.3	175.9
1998	171.4	171.2	173.3	179.6	181.5	184.2	184.2	185.3	183.6	185.1	183.9	180.0	180.3
1999	171.7	173.9	175.7	181.0	184.3	187.2	187.4	187.7	187.2	186.8	185.7	183.4	182.7
2000	178.7	178.2	182.5	186.4	189.2	191.3	193.4	193.0	192.3	190.7	189.1	185.7	187.5
2001	180.4	181.0	182.0	184.1	186.1	187.9	187.8	187.6	184.7	183.1	179.7	176.4	183.4
2002	168.3	168.8	170.6	174.0	176.7	178.2	176.9	178.2	176.3	175.6	172.4	168.0	173.7
2003	161.3	158.4	161.9	165.5	167.3	169.3	168.7	169.0	167.7	166.2	164.1	161.4	165.1
Construction and mining													
1990	47.0	46.8	49.3	52.1	55.2	56.3	56.6	57.1	56.6	55.6	54.0	51.3	53.2
1991	44.6	43.9	45.4	49.3	52.1	54.4	55.4	56.1	54.8	54.8	52.3	49.9	51.1
1992	45.4	44.7	46.2	50.1	53.0	55.0	56.9	58.0	57.5	56.7	53.3	49.4	52.2
1993	44.2	43.6	43.3	47.4	49.7	51.0	53.7	53.5	53.6	53.3	51.8	49.2	49.5
1994	42.0	42.9	44.8	49.9	52.0	52.9	54.1	54.7	55.2	54.7	53.7	50.4	50.6
1995	44.7	43.3	46.5	49.2	50.4	52.0	53.1	54.0	54.0	54.0	51.5	47.2	50.0
1996	40.5	41.3	43.8	48.5	51.6	53.6	54.9	55.8	55.6	55.9	53.8	50.5	50.5
1997	45.9	46.0	48.6	51.8	53.3	54.7	56.2	56.8	55.3	56.2	54.3	50.9	52.5
1998	46.3	46.0	47.7	53.0	54.4	56.4	58.0	58.9	57.5	58.8	57.4	53.7	54.0
1999	47.3	48.7	50.3	56.2	59.4	61.3	61.9	62.5	62.2	61.8	60.5	57.4	57.5
2000	53.1	52.5	56.4	61.1	63.7	64.6	65.8	65.9	65.5	64.5	62.9	59.0	61.3
2001	55.8	56.8	58.6	61.5	64.8	66.3	67.0	67.4	65.8	65.4	62.9	60.1	62.7
2002	54.5	55.7	57.9	61.5	64.0	65.0	64.7	66.0	64.6	64.0	61.5	57.3	61.4
2003	52.6	51.9	54.7	57.4	59.6	61.1	61.3	62.1	61.6	61.0	59.1	56.6	58.3

Employment by Industry: Pennsylvania—*Continued*

(Numbers in thousands. Not seasonally adjusted.)

Industry	January	February	March	April	May	June	July	August	September	October	November	December	Annual Average
PITTSBURGH—*Continued*													
Manufacturing													
1990	126.5	126.3	126.6	126.7	126.7	127.7	128.7	128.8	128.8	127.3	127.3	126.7	127.3
1991	124.3	122.8	122.3	123.2	122.3	123.5	123.2	123.4	122.6	122.6	122.6	122.3	122.9
1992	119.5	118.5	118.5	119.1	119.8	120.2	119.0	118.9	119.2	119.0	118.3	118.1	119.0
1993	118.0	117.4	117.5	117.7	117.7	118.7	118.1	118.5	118.0	119.2	119.2	119.5	118.3
1994	117.7	117.5	118.1	115.4	115.7	117.8	119.3	119.8	119.5	119.6	119.9	120.1	118.4
1995	119.0	118.8	119.5	119.2	119.7	120.4	120.5	120.2	120.0	120.2	120.2	119.8	119.8
1996	119.2	119.1	119.6	119.9	120.0	120.8	121.4	121.1	121.0	121.3	121.4	121.6	120.5
1997	120.3	119.9	120.0	121.8	122.9	124.1	124.2	124.9	124.8	125.5	125.8	126.4	123.4
1998	125.1	125.2	125.6	126.6	127.1	127.8	126.2	126.4	126.1	126.3	126.5	126.3	126.3
1999	124.4	125.2	125.4	124.8	124.9	125.9	125.5	125.2	125.0	125.0	125.2	126.0	125.2
2000	125.6	125.7	126.1	125.3	125.5	126.7	127.6	127.1	126.8	126.2	126.2	126.7	126.3
2001	124.6	124.2	123.4	122.6	121.3	121.6	120.8	120.2	118.9	117.7	116.8	116.3	120.7
2002	113.8	113.1	112.7	112.5	112.7	113.2	112.2	112.2	111.7	111.6	110.9	110.7	112.3
2003	108.7	106.5	107.2	108.1	107.7	108.2	107.4	106.9	106.1	105.2	105.0	104.8	106.8
Service-providing													
1990	821.0	826.1	832.5	840.5	845.1	850.5	842.9	838.4	846.1	850.3	853.6	854.0	841.8
1991	827.4	828.4	834.7	840.4	843.5	847.9	833.7	832.7	844.0	848.2	855.1	856.5	841.0
1992	832.7	833.4	839.0	851.4	857.9	860.1	846.3	843.7	855.3	863.6	865.4	864.7	851.1
1993	845.6	850.0	852.9	862.1	866.8	868.5	857.4	857.2	866.6	875.6	876.5	877.7	863.1
1994	850.6	854.4	861.7	870.1	875.2	880.3	869.4	865.9	877.8	882.7	887.7	889.5	872.1
1995	863.4	867.8	875.8	882.7	887.3	891.9	875.4	872.7	882.9	888.9	893.6	894.4	881.4
1996	868.8	875.3	880.5	889.5	892.3	895.2	885.0	881.5	887.0	897.5	903.2	906.9	888.6
1997	882.8	886.3	892.8	895.6	900.7	903.9	894.7	891.3	901.5	909.7	913.8	917.2	899.2
1998	891.0	894.5	900.2	909.1	917.0	919.8	907.1	903.4	912.7	919.4	924.0	927.7	910.5
1999	898.9	907.4	913.2	924.8	930.5	935.5	926.6	923.7	930.7	932.2	938.1	941.7	925.3
2000	918.1	923.2	931.3	941.9	948.0	949.6	939.0	930.2	943.6	948.7	954.5	955.4	940.3
2001	938.4	942.7	948.7	954.4	958.1	964.4	947.8	944.0	950.5	952.0	958.3	957.7	951.4
2002	936.8	938.5	945.0	949.8	956.6	961.3	946.9	943.1	951.3	954.7	958.1	954.6	949.7
2003	936.6	935.6	941.7	948.7	954.2	956.2	941.7	938.5	945.4	949.6	950.4	949.1	945.6
Trade, transportation, and utilities													
1990	219.5	218.2	218.9	220.1	222.2	223.0	220.7	220.7	220.7	222.3	225.3	226.9	221.5
1991	216.9	212.8	213.2	215.0	215.4	219.3	217.2	218.5	217.9	219.5	224.0	225.9	218.0
1992	216.3	213.2	213.6	216.1	219.0	219.6	216.9	217.5	218.3	220.4	224.1	225.9	218.4
1993	217.9	216.3	216.1	217.2	218.5	219.6	219.0	220.1	221.1	223.8	225.9	228.5	220.3
1994	219.4	216.1	217.3	217.4	219.9	220.8	219.3	219.7	221.3	225.4	230.5	232.5	221.6
1995	222.7	219.3	221.1	223.2	224.1	225.1	221.8	221.6	222.3	224.9	228.0	230.8	223.7
1996	220.8	217.7	218.4	220.8	223.0	223.5	222.1	222.2	222.7	228.6	233.3	236.9	224.2
1997	226.8	224.2	225.3	225.3	227.1	228.6	226.2	224.5	227.2	231.3	235.6	239.9	228.5
1998	227.4	224.9	225.7	227.8	229.8	230.3	227.3	227.5	229.5	232.1	236.3	239.9	229.9
1999	229.8	228.9	229.2	232.2	233.9	235.4	233.1	233.4	234.1	236.2	240.8	245.2	234.4
2000	234.6	232.1	233.0	237.1	238.2	239.8	237.3	237.0	237.9	240.5	244.5	248.2	238.4
2001	239.2	235.9	236.8	237.2	238.7	239.9	235.5	235.5	235.7	236.5	240.9	241.7	237.8
2002	232.1	229.0	230.0	230.6	232.2	232.9	229.6	229.7	229.9	231.8	235.3	237.0	231.7
2003	226.7	223.5	223.9	225.3	227.1	227.9	224.8	225.2	225.7	226.9	230.0	231.5	226.5
Wholesale trade													
1990	48.1	48.3	48.4	48.6	48.8	49.2	49.0	49.0	48.8	48.9	49.2	48.7	48.8
1991	47.9	47.3	47.4	47.8	47.9	48.1	48.1	48.0	47.6	47.4	47.4	47.4	47.7
1992	47.2	46.8	46.9	47.0	47.4	47.7	47.5	47.4	47.1	47.2	47.0	47.1	47.2
1993	45.9	45.9	46.0	46.3	46.5	46.8	46.9	47.0	46.6	46.7	46.7	46.9	46.5
1994	45.6	45.3	45.8	45.6	46.0	46.4	46.3	46.4	46.5	46.1	46.3	46.4	46.1
1995	45.7	45.5	45.9	46.1	46.2	46.5	46.3	46.2	46.2	46.2	46.1	46.1	46.1
1996	45.3	45.5	45.8	46.1	46.3	46.6	46.3	46.2	46.0	46.4	46.8	47.1	46.2
1997	45.5	45.6	45.7	45.6	45.7	46.1	45.9	45.9	45.6	45.5	45.4	45.8	45.7
1998	44.4	44.5	44.8	45.3	45.5	45.8	45.4	45.4	45.0	45.4	45.4	45.5	45.2
1999	45.3	45.3	45.6	46.3	46.4	47.0	46.6	46.7	46.4	46.1	45.9	46.3	46.2
2000	45.5	45.7	46.0	46.6	46.8	47.1	46.8	46.9	46.6	47.0	47.0	47.0	46.6
2001	46.4	46.5	46.7	46.9	46.9	47.1	47.0	46.9	46.3	45.9	45.8	45.6	46.5
2002	45.0	44.8	44.9	45.3	45.7	46.0	45.6	45.4	45.1	45.3	45.4	45.1	45.3
2003	44.8	44.7	44.8	45.1	45.3	45.2	45.3	45.1	44.9	44.7	44.8	44.6	44.9
Retail trade													
1990	128.1	126.6	126.7	127.1	128.5	129.0	128.4	128.4	127.2	128.4	131.4	133.5	128.6
1991	125.2	121.9	122.5	123.6	123.3	127.4	126.4	127.4	125.9	127.2	132.1	133.6	126.4
1992	125.5	122.6	122.7	124.3	126.1	126.7	125.9	126.4	125.9	127.4	131.1	132.5	126.4
1993	125.4	123.9	123.3	123.7	124.7	125.4	126.4	127.5	127.5	129.0	131.0	133.4	126.8
1994	126.9	124.0	124.5	124.7	126.1	126.6	126.6	127.2	127.3	130.5	135.3	138.1	128.2
1995	129.0	126.0	126.9	128.3	129.0	130.0	128.3	128.3	127.8	129.3	132.6	135.7	129.3
1996	127.4	124.3	124.2	126.0	127.9	128.5	128.5	128.5	128.0	131.6	135.9	139.4	129.2
1997	132.5	129.8	130.3	130.2	131.6	132.8	131.9	132.4	132.0	135.0	139.5	143.1	133.4
1998	133.4	131.1	131.4	132.2	133.8	134.8	133.1	133.5	133.7	135.1	139.3	142.0	134.5
1999	134.4	133.5	133.2	134.8	136.1	136.9	136.9	137.2	136.0	136.8	141.8	145.1	136.9
2000	136.7	134.3	134.4	137.5	138.3	139.5	138.8	138.8	138.2	138.8	142.9	146.2	138.7
2001	139.2	135.9	136.5	136.5	137.5	138.7	136.6	136.7	135.5	135.8	140.5	142.8	137.7
2002	135.4	132.8	133.6	134.0	135.2	136.5	135.8	135.8	134.4	135.4	139.4	142.1	135.9
2003	133.9	131.2	131.7	133.0	134.4	135.9	134.5	135.3	134.3	135.6	138.4	140.6	134.9

Employment by Industry: Pennsylvania—*Continued*

(Numbers in thousands. Not seasonally adjusted.)

Industry	January	February	March	April	May	June	July	August	September	October	November	December	Annual Average
PITTSBURGH—*Continued*													
Transportation and utilities													
1990	43.3	43.3	43.8	44.4	44.9	44.8	43.3	43.3	44.7	45.0	44.7	44.7	44.2
1991	43.8	43.6	43.3	43.6	44.2	43.8	42.7	43.1	44.4	44.9	44.5	44.9	43.9
1992	43.6	43.8	44.0	44.8	45.5	45.2	43.5	43.7	45.3	45.8	46.0	46.3	44.8
1993	46.6	46.5	46.8	47.2	47.3	47.4	45.7	45.6	47.0	48.1	48.2	48.2	47.1
1994	46.9	46.8	47.0	47.1	47.8	47.8	46.4	46.1	47.5	48.8	48.9	48.0	47.4
1995	48.0	47.8	48.3	48.8	48.9	48.6	47.2	47.1	48.3	49.4	49.3	49.0	48.4
1996	48.1	47.9	48.4	48.7	48.8	48.4	47.3	47.5	48.7	50.6	50.6	50.4	48.8
1997	48.8	48.8	49.3	49.5	49.8	49.7	48.4	46.2	49.6	50.8	50.7	51.0	49.4
1998	49.6	49.3	49.5	50.3	50.5	49.7	48.8	48.6	50.8	51.6	51.6	52.4	50.2
1999	50.1	50.1	50.4	51.1	51.4	51.5	49.6	49.5	51.7	53.3	53.1	53.8	51.3
2000	52.4	52.1	52.6	53.0	53.1	53.2	51.7	51.3	53.1	54.7	54.6	55.0	53.1
2001	53.6	53.5	53.6	53.8	54.3	54.1	51.9	51.9	53.9	54.8	54.6	53.3	53.6
2002	51.7	51.4	51.5	51.3	51.3	50.4	48.2	48.5	50.4	51.1	50.5	49.8	50.5
2003	48.0	47.6	47.4	47.2	47.4	46.8	45.0	44.8	46.5	46.6	46.8	46.3	46.7
Information													
1990	20.4	20.5	20.6	20.8	20.8	20.9	21.1	21.0	20.9	20.7	20.6	20.7	20.8
1991	20.2	20.1	20.1	20.3	20.5	20.4	20.3	20.0	19.7	20.1	20.5	20.6	20.2
1992	20.7	20.6	20.7	20.3	20.4	20.4	20.4	20.2	20.0	19.8	19.7	19.8	20.3
1993	20.1	20.6	20.7	20.4	20.5	20.6	20.2	20.2	20.1	20.1	20.2	20.3	20.3
1994	20.4	20.1	20.3	20.3	20.5	20.5	20.8	20.9	20.5	20.6	20.7	20.8	20.5
1995	20.5	20.5	20.8	21.1	21.3	21.5	21.0	21.1	20.9	20.7	20.6	20.8	20.9
1996	20.6	20.6	20.6	21.3	21.4	21.8	21.9	21.9	21.6	21.8	21.9	22.2	21.5
1997	22.1	22.1	22.3	22.0	22.4	22.6	22.7	22.6	22.4	22.6	22.7	22.8	22.4
1998	22.6	22.6	22.9	23.1	23.2	23.3	23.2	23.4	23.5	23.5	23.7	24.0	23.3
1999	23.7	24.2	24.0	24.5	24.7	25.1	25.2	25.3	25.3	25.1	25.1	25.4	24.8
2000	25.6	25.7	25.7	24.9	25.2	25.5	26.1	23.4	26.1	26.5	26.7	26.9	25.7
2001	27.1	27.2	27.2	26.9	27.2	27.4	27.2	27.1	26.8	26.6	26.8	26.8	27.0
2002	26.5	26.2	26.2	26.0	26.1	25.9	25.7	25.7	25.2	25.1	25.4	25.4	25.8
2003	25.4	25.2	25.4	25.1	25.3	25.1	24.9	24.8	24.4	24.4	24.3	24.6	24.9
Financial activities													
1990	57.5	57.7	58.0	58.1	58.4	58.7	59.0	59.2	58.9	58.7	58.6	58.6	58.5
1991	57.6	57.7	57.8	57.8	58.0	58.2	58.7	58.9	58.6	58.1	58.4	58.5	58.2
1992	58.1	57.9	58.1	58.1	58.7	59.2	59.3	59.1	58.7	58.9	58.8	59.1	58.7
1993	58.7	59.0	58.9	59.2	59.5	60.1	60.4	61.1	60.8	60.3	60.2	60.2	59.9
1994	60.1	60.2	60.2	61.4	61.7	62.3	62.9	62.8	62.0	61.2	60.8	60.6	61.4
1995	59.8	59.8	60.2	60.5	61.1	61.6	62.4	62.3	62.0	61.4	61.5	61.8	61.2
1996	61.7	61.8	61.9	62.5	62.7	63.2	64.3	64.5	64.2	63.6	63.7	64.1	63.2
1997	62.8	62.8	63.1	63.1	63.6	64.5	64.4	64.7	64.5	64.7	64.6	64.7	64.0
1998	64.8	64.9	64.9	65.9	66.4	67.0	67.0	66.9	66.4	66.3	66.7	67.0	66.2
1999	66.6	66.1	66.6	66.4	67.1	67.7	68.1	68.3	67.8	66.9	66.9	67.2	67.1
2000	66.4	66.3	66.2	66.8	66.8	67.3	67.2	66.9	66.3	66.2	66.5	66.7	66.6
2001	66.9	67.1	67.3	66.7	67.0	67.7	67.9	67.7	66.9	66.7	67.0	67.2	67.2
2002	67.1	67.4	67.7	67.4	68.0	68.5	68.5	68.5	67.9	67.6	67.7	68.0	67.9
2003	68.4	68.3	68.7	69.0	69.4	69.7	70.2	70.0	69.4	69.1	68.9	69.4	69.2
Professional and business services													
1990	121.5	122.4	123.8	125.2	125.9	128.1	128.4	128.9	128.7	127.0	127.1	126.8	126.2
1991	124.2	124.4	125.4	126.7	126.8	127.4	127.0	127.2	126.3	126.1	126.2	126.0	126.1
1992	124.2	123.9	124.4	127.2	127.3	128.5	127.9	128.4	127.6	127.3	126.6	125.7	126.6
1993	125.6	124.6	124.4	127.9	127.8	127.3	127.5	127.0	126.5	127.1	126.2	125.9	126.5
1994	122.4	122.7	123.6	125.3	125.6	127.2	128.1	128.3	127.7	128.0	127.4	127.1	126.1
1995	124.6	124.9	125.8	127.4	127.9	129.0	128.8	128.8	128.2	128.5	128.5	127.5	127.5
1996	125.3	126.1	127.0	129.9	130.9	131.7	131.1	131.1	129.8	130.3	130.4	129.3	129.4
1997	127.2	127.0	128.2	129.7	130.3	132.0	132.7	133.1	132.3	133.1	132.6	132.6	130.9
1998	129.8	129.7	130.5	132.5	133.8	135.3	135.6	135.5	134.3	134.7	134.6	134.1	133.4
1999	132.3	132.9	133.2	135.9	136.9	137.7	138.6	139.2	138.1	136.6	136.4	136.0	136.2
2000	134.1	134.6	135.6	139.5	139.1	141.3	141.6	141.2	139.7	138.4	138.5	137.8	138.5
2001	137.9	138.3	139.2	141.5	141.0	142.8	141.0	141.6	140.0	139.4	139.4	138.5	140.1
2002	133.9	133.3	133.9	135.6	136.5	137.8	138.7	138.4	136.5	136.0	136.0	136.0	136.1
2003	131.3	130.2	131.1	132.9	133.3	133.0	132.7	133.1	131.2	130.6	130.1	128.9	131.5
Educational and health services													
1990	155.4	156.8	157.6	158.3	156.7	155.3	154.8	153.7	158.4	163.8	164.7	164.5	158.3
1991	159.8	161.9	163.2	163.9	162.2	160.4	160.2	159.7	164.9	167.2	168.2	168.6	163.4
1992	165.6	167.2	168.5	170.1	168.4	167.0	167.0	165.6	170.8	174.3	174.4	174.1	169.4
1993	173.3	175.5	176.1	175.3	172.6	171.5	171.5	171.4	176.2	179.3	179.5	179.4	175.1
1994	175.8	178.7	179.6	179.5	176.8	175.7	175.6	175.9	180.7	180.4	181.2	181.6	178.5
1995	178.1	181.1	182.3	181.3	178.6	177.5	175.8	175.9	180.5	182.2	183.2	183.6	180.0
1996	180.4	183.7	184.3	184.6	180.7	179.1	177.8	177.3	181.3	184.6	185.0	184.6	182.0
1997	181.3	185.1	186.0	185.2	181.6	180.0	180.8	180.9	185.6	188.5	189.3	189.5	184.5
1998	186.5	189.8	190.3	190.8	188.6	187.0	186.8	185.2	189.4	192.8	193.5	193.6	189.5
1999	187.7	191.6	193.9	194.5	191.8	190.4	189.0	188.4	192.3	194.6	195.5	194.6	192.0
2000	192.4	195.8	196.2	196.4	193.6	191.8	192.0	190.9	196.3	199.4	200.3	199.5	195.4
2001	196.4	199.6	200.9	200.1	196.2	197.2	196.7	194.8	199.5	200.5	201.8	202.1	198.8
2002	203.2	205.5	207.0	205.5	203.7	202.7	200.7	199.4	204.5	206.7	207.0	203.0	204.1
2003	207.8	209.7	210.5	209.0	206.7	206.2	204.1	202.1	206.5	209.7	210.3	209.8	207.7

Employment by Industry: Pennsylvania—*Continued*

(Numbers in thousands. Not seasonally adjusted.)

Industry	January	February	March	April	May	June	July	August	September	October	November	December	Annual Average
PITTSBURGH—*Continued*													
Leisure and hospitality													
1990	81.1	81.6	83.2	86.9	90.6	93.3	94.2	94.5	92.1	87.4	86.4	86.2	88.1
1991	81.0	80.8	82.8	85.1	89.8	91.9	91.8	92.6	89.9	86.7	86.2	85.5	87.0
1992	81.5	82.2	83.6	87.1	92.4	93.9	93.5	94.2	91.9	89.1	87.8	87.2	88.7
1993	82.2	82.8	83.1	87.7	93.0	95.4	94.3	94.8	92.7	89.7	87.9	87.5	89.3
1994	83.2	82.8	84.4	89.3	94.0	96.9	96.3	95.9	93.4	90.4	89.6	89.1	90.4
1995	85.8	85.5	87.9	91.2	95.3	99.0	97.2	97.9	96.2	93.4	92.5	90.5	92.7
1996	86.7	86.5	88.4	90.3	94.9	97.9	97.1	97.1	93.5	90.5	89.2	89.9	91.8
1997	85.1	85.6	86.4	89.9	95.3	98.0	97.4	97.9	94.8	90.7	89.4	88.9	91.6
1998	84.3	85.3	87.6	90.2	96.2	98.9	98.3	98.1	94.5	91.1	89.7	89.8	92.0
1999	83.7	85.3	86.6	91.2	96.7	100.6	100.4	99.9	95.1	93.8	92.7	93.6	93.3
2000	86.6	87.7	90.6	94.0	99.9	102.6	102.5	102.5	98.6	95.3	94.1	93.6	95.7
2001	89.6	90.9	92.8	97.1	103.1	106.8	106.4	107.0	100.3	97.8	96.6	97.3	98.8
2002	92.9	92.5	95.0	99.2	105.2	108.3	108.1	109.1	105.7	101.4	99.2	98.9	101.3
2003	94.0	93.0	95.1	100.3	105.9	109.7	108.9	109.9	105.8	102.7	99.7	99.2	102.0
Other services													
1990	44.3	44.6	45.0	45.3	45.6	46.1	46.7	46.5	46.1	45.4	45.2	45.2	45.5
1991	46.7	46.6	47.1	46.7	47.4	47.4	47.8	47.7	47.0	46.9	46.9	47.1	47.1
1992	45.7	45.7	46.2	46.5	46.9	47.4	47.3	47.0	46.6	47.0	46.9	47.0	46.7
1993	46.1	46.3	46.8	47.6	48.0	48.3	48.7	48.7	47.9	48.5	48.6	48.6	47.8
1994	47.3	47.5	48.0	49.0	49.4	49.9	50.4	50.2	49.5	49.5	49.8	50.0	49.2
1995	49.1	49.2	49.5	50.0	50.5	50.9	51.2	51.2	50.3	50.9	51.1	51.5	50.5
1996	50.8	51.2	51.5	52.2	52.8	53.3	54.1	53.7	52.7	51.5	51.5	51.7	52.3
1997	51.3	51.0	51.6	50.9	51.2	51.8	52.6	52.5	51.4	52.0	52.0	52.1	51.7
1998	51.8	51.0	51.4	52.7	53.2	53.6	54.0	53.6	52.5	52.6	52.7	53.1	52.7
1999	52.9	53.2	53.4	53.6	53.0	53.6	54.0	53.8	53.0	53.0	52.9	53.5	53.3
2000	54.5	54.9	55.8	55.2	55.1	56.0	55.8	55.7	55.6	56.0	56.2	56.2	55.6
2001	56.1	56.7	56.9	56.9	57.3	58.0	57.9	57.4	56.5	56.6	56.6	56.5	57.0
2002	55.8	55.9	56.5	56.6	57.1	57.9	58.1	57.7	56.7	56.8	56.8	57.0	56.9
2003	56.1	56.0	56.5	57.2	57.4	57.9	58.1	58.2	57.2	56.9	56.9	56.7	57.1
Government													
1990	121.3	124.3	125.4	125.8	124.9	125.1	118.0	113.9	120.3	125.0	125.7	125.1	122.9
1991	121.0	124.1	125.1	124.9	123.4	122.9	110.7	108.1	119.7	123.6	124.7	124.3	121.0
1992	120.6	122.7	123.9	126.0	124.8	124.1	114.0	111.7	121.4	126.8	127.1	125.9	122.4
1993	121.7	124.9	126.8	126.8	126.9	125.7	115.8	113.9	121.3	126.8	128.0	127.3	123.8
1994	122.0	126.3	128.3	127.9	127.3	127.0	116.0	112.2	122.7	127.2	127.7	127.8	124.4
1995	122.8	127.5	128.2	128.0	128.5	127.3	117.2	113.9	122.5	126.9	128.2	127.9	124.9
1996	122.5	127.7	128.4	127.9	125.9	124.7	116.6	113.7	121.2	126.6	128.2	128.2	124.3
1997	126.2	128.5	129.9	129.5	129.2	126.4	117.9	115.1	123.3	126.8	127.6	126.7	125.6
1998	123.8	126.3	126.9	126.1	125.8	124.4	114.9	113.2	122.6	126.3	126.8	126.2	123.6
1999	122.2	125.2	126.3	126.5	126.4	125.0	118.2	115.4	125.0	126.0	127.8	126.2	124.2
2000	123.9	126.1	128.2	128.0	130.1	125.3	116.5	112.6	123.1	126.4	127.7	126.5	124.5
2001	125.2	127.0	127.6	128.0	127.6	124.6	115.2	112.9	124.8	127.9	129.2	127.6	124.8
2002	125.3	128.7	128.7	128.9	127.8	127.3	117.5	114.6	124.9	129.3	130.7	129.3	126.1
2003	126.9	129.7	130.5	129.9	129.1	126.7	118.0	115.2	125.2	129.3	130.2	129.0	126.6
Federal government													
1990	20.0	20.0	20.3	20.8	21.1	21.0	20.7	20.5	20.3	19.9	19.8	20.3	20.4
1991	20.2	19.9	19.9	19.7	19.8	20.2	20.1	20.1	19.9	20.0	20.0	20.2	20.0
1992	20.3	20.0	20.0	19.9	19.9	20.1	20.3	20.2	20.2	20.3	20.0	20.3	20.1
1993	20.1	20.1	20.0	20.1	20.1	20.3	20.2	20.5	20.7	20.6	20.7	21.3	20.4
1994	21.0	21.0	21.0	20.9	20.9	20.9	20.6	20.6	20.7	20.8	20.7	21.2	20.9
1995	20.5	20.5	20.5	20.3	20.3	20.3	20.2	20.2	20.2	20.1	20.2	20.7	20.3
1996	20.0	20.0	19.9	20.0	19.9	20.0	20.0	20.0	19.9	20.4	20.6	21.3	20.2
1997	20.3	20.2	20.5	20.7	20.5	20.7	20.3	20.3	20.1	20.2	20.3	20.9	20.4
1998	20.2	20.2	20.2	20.2	20.2	20.2	20.2	20.3	20.2	20.1	20.1	20.7	20.2
1999	20.1	20.1	20.1	20.7	20.2	20.2	20.1	20.3	20.2	19.8	20.0	20.3	20.2
2000	19.8	19.9	20.5	20.7	23.4	20.6	21.0	19.8	19.4	19.5	19.7	19.8	20.3
2001	19.8	19.7	19.6	19.7	19.7	19.7	19.8	19.8	19.6	19.6	19.8	19.8	19.7
2002	19.3	19.1	19.0	19.0	19.0	19.1	19.2	19.2	19.3	19.8	19.8	19.8	19.3
2003	19.9	19.7	19.7	19.5	19.4	19.3	19.4	19.4	19.2	19.4	19.3	19.9	19.5
State government													
1990	17.4	18.4	18.4	18.3	16.9	16.6	16.4	16.3	17.6	17.8	17.7	17.5	17.4
1991	16.3	17.4	17.2	17.1	15.5	15.4	15.4	15.4	16.8	16.7	16.6	16.6	16.4
1992	16.7	17.0	16.8	18.1	16.8	16.4	16.4	16.6	18.2	18.7	18.6	18.6	17.4
1993	18.2	18.7	18.5	18.7	17.9	16.7	16.6	16.4	18.3	18.8	18.9	18.5	18.0
1994	16.9	18.6	18.6	18.5	18.0	16.5	16.6	16.5	18.2	18.4	18.5	18.6	17.8
1995	16.7	18.6	18.4	18.3	17.9	16.1	16.2	16.0	17.9	18.2	18.3	18.3	17.6
1996	16.1	18.3	18.1	18.1	16.5	15.8	15.7	15.7	17.6	17.8	17.9	17.9	17.1
1997	17.2	17.6	17.7	17.6	16.3	15.5	15.6	15.6	17.4	17.5	17.6	17.5	16.9
1998	17.1	17.5	17.3	17.2	16.0	15.3	15.4	15.2	17.1	16.9	17.0	17.0	16.6
1999	16.5	17.0	16.8	16.9	16.5	15.0	15.3	15.1	16.7	16.6	16.8	16.2	16.3
2000	16.3	16.7	16.6	16.7	16.2	14.9	14.7	14.6	16.4	16.7	16.7	16.1	16.1
2001	16.3	16.4	16.2	16.4	16.0	14.5	14.5	14.4	16.4	16.5	16.4	15.9	15.8
2002	15.9	16.5	16.4	16.4	14.8	14.6	14.4	14.4	16.2	16.4	16.7	15.9	15.7
2003	15.9	16.5	16.4	16.2	14.9	14.5	14.5	14.4	16.1	16.5	16.5	16.0	15.7

Employment by Industry: Pennsylvania—*Continued*

(Numbers in thousands. Not seasonally adjusted.)

Industry	January	February	March	April	May	June	July	August	September	October	November	December	Annual Average
PITTSBURGH—*Continued*													
Local government													
1990	83.9	85.9	86.7	86.7	86.9	87.5	80.9	77.1	82.4	87.3	88.2	87.3	85.1
1991	84.5	86.8	88.0	88.1	88.1	87.3	75.2	72.6	83.0	86.9	88.1	87.5	84.7
1992	83.6	85.7	87.1	88.0	88.1	87.6	77.3	74.9	83.0	87.8	88.5	87.0	84.9
1993	83.4	86.1	88.3	88.0	88.9	88.7	79.0	77.0	82.3	87.4	88.4	87.5	85.4
1994	84.1	86.7	88.7	88.5	88.4	89.6	78.8	75.1	83.8	88.0	88.5	88.0	85.7
1995	85.6	88.4	89.3	89.4	90.3	90.9	80.8	77.7	84.4	88.6	89.7	88.9	87.0
1996	86.4	89.4	90.4	89.8	89.5	88.9	80.9	78.0	83.7	88.4	89.7	89.0	87.0
1997	88.7	90.7	91.7	91.2	92.4	90.2	82.0	79.2	85.8	89.1	89.7	88.3	88.3
1998	86.5	88.6	89.4	88.7	89.6	88.9	79.3	77.7	85.3	89.3	89.7	88.5	86.8
1999	85.6	88.1	89.4	88.9	89.7	89.8	82.8	80.0	88.1	89.6	91.0	89.7	87.7
2000	87.8	89.5	91.1	90.6	90.5	89.8	80.8	78.2	87.3	90.2	91.3	90.6	88.1
2001	89.1	90.9	91.8	91.9	91.9	90.4	80.9	78.7	88.8	91.8	93.0	91.9	89.3
2002	90.1	93.1	93.3	93.5	94.0	93.6	83.9	81.0	89.4	93.1	94.2	93.6	91.1
2003	91.1	93.5	94.4	94.2	94.8	92.9	84.1	81.4	89.9	93.4	94.4	93.1	91.4
READING													
Total nonfarm													
1990	152.7	152.9	153.9	154.7	156.2	155.5	153.1	152.6	154.8	155.9	156.0	155.8	154.5
1991	149.6	148.0	149.1	149.7	150.5	151.0	148.4	149.8	150.8	152.6	153.5	153.3	150.5
1992	149.6	150.0	150.7	152.1	152.9	153.7	151.2	151.4	152.6	154.3	155.1	154.9	152.4
1993	151.0	151.6	150.7	152.9	153.9	153.8	151.6	152.0	153.3	155.8	157.0	157.4	153.4
1994	150.9	150.1	152.3	155.2	156.6	156.8	153.7	155.9	158.1	159.3	160.2	160.3	155.8
1995	155.1	156.1	156.7	158.5	159.5	159.3	155.6	157.2	160.0	160.9	161.7	161.1	158.5
1996	151.6	156.7	158.2	159.9	161.2	161.6	158.5	160.2	162.8	165.0	165.3	166.1	160.6
1997	161.2	161.8	163.4	164.7	166.1	166.5	162.9	163.9	165.8	167.3	168.0	168.3	165.0
1998	163.8	164.3	164.9	166.4	167.2	166.7	162.9	165.1	166.9	168.3	168.3	169.1	166.2
1999	164.0	164.9	165.3	167.3	168.7	169.0	167.0	167.3	169.9	171.1	172.5	173.5	168.4
2000	168.9	168.5	170.1	170.8	171.6	173.2	170.4	170.5	173.2	173.2	173.7	174.0	171.5
2001	169.5	169.2	170.2	169.9	170.7	171.8	168.1	169.2	170.7	169.4	170.6	170.4	170.0
2002	166.4	166.2	167.1	167.3	168.9	169.3	165.6	166.4	168.2	167.4	167.4	167.1	167.3
2003	161.9	161.1	162.1	163.7	165.1	165.7	161.6	162.9	165.4	166.0	166.7	166.8	164.1
Total private													
1990	135.5	135.0	135.7	136.4	137.2	138.3	137.6	137.1	137.4	137.7	137.7	137.4	136.9
1991	132.3	130.1	130.9	131.6	132.5	133.8	133.1	134.7	134.1	135.1	135.7	135.5	133.3
1992	132.6	132.0	132.7	133.9	134.8	136.4	135.6	136.0	135.5	136.0	136.5	136.3	134.9
1993	133.3	132.8	131.8	134.1	135.4	136.0	135.4	135.9	135.7	137.3	138.2	138.6	135.4
1994	133.5	132.2	134.2	136.6	138.1	139.2	137.9	140.0	140.1	140.2	140.9	141.1	137.8
1995	136.9	136.8	137.2	139.2	140.0	141.0	139.5	140.5	141.7	141.7	142.3	141.5	139.9
1996	133.9	137.7	138.9	140.6	141.7	143.1	142.2	143.9	143.6	145.1	145.9	146.6	141.9
1997	143.2	142.9	144.2	145.6	146.8	148.2	146.5	147.7	147.1	148.0	148.5	148.6	146.4
1998	145.6	145.1	145.5	147.0	147.6	148.4	146.7	148.9	148.3	149.0	148.7	149.3	147.5
1999	145.4	145.4	145.7	147.6	148.7	150.3	150.2	150.7	150.8	151.5	152.5	153.5	149.4
2000	149.9	148.6	150.0	150.7	151.0	154.0	153.5	153.7	153.8	153.4	153.7	154.3	152.2
2001	150.0	148.9	149.8	149.7	150.3	152.4	150.5	151.4	150.8	148.9	149.8	149.4	150.2
2002	146.2	145.2	145.9	146.2	147.6	149.1	148.0	148.5	147.3	146.1	145.8	145.7	146.8
2003	141.0	139.6	140.4	142.1	143.4	144.9	143.6	144.9	144.8	144.5	145.2	145.0	143.3
Goods-producing													
1990	51.6	51.3	51.2	51.6	51.7	52.2	52.3	51.8	52.2	52.2	51.9	51.1	51.8
1991	49.0	47.7	47.7	47.8	48.0	49.0	48.9	49.6	49.4	49.6	49.4	48.9	48.8
1992	48.3	48.0	48.1	48.6	48.3	49.0	49.8	50.0	49.6	49.7	49.7	49.5	49.1
1993	48.3	48.0	47.2	47.6	47.8	48.1	47.7	47.9	47.7	48.9	49.1	49.3	48.1
1994	48.1	47.7	48.1	48.7	49.4	49.9	49.9	50.5	50.3	50.2	50.3	50.4	49.5
1995	48.9	48.7	48.7	49.1	49.3	50.0	50.0	50.4	50.3	49.6	49.5	49.3	49.5
1996	46.3	47.4	47.9	48.4	48.7	49.6	49.5	49.9	49.5	49.6	49.7	49.7	48.9
1997	49.1	49.1	49.3	49.6	49.7	50.2	49.9	50.8	50.4	50.3	50.1	50.0	49.9
1998	49.3	48.8	48.6	49.6	49.3	49.3	47.7	49.5	49.3	48.9	48.4	48.4	48.9
1999	47.8	47.8	47.5	47.9	48.4	49.1	49.3	49.9	49.4	50.0	50.2	50.1	49.0
2000	49.4	48.9	48.9	49.5	49.2	50.3	50.4	50.5	50.4	49.7	48.8	49.2	49.6
2001	48.3	47.8	47.7	47.8	47.7	48.4	47.8	48.1	47.5	46.1	45.8	45.3	47.4
2002	43.8	43.7	43.4	43.6	43.9	44.5	43.9	44.0	43.4	42.9	42.5	42.1	43.5
2003	41.0	40.4	40.3	40.5	41.0	41.3	41.0	41.1	40.8	40.7	40.5	40.0	40.7
Construction and mining													
1990	6.5	6.5	6.8	7.2	7.4	7.8	7.9	7.9	7.7	7.7	7.5	7.1	7.3
1991	6.2	5.8	5.9	6.4	6.7	6.9	7.1	7.1	6.8	6.8	6.7	6.5	6.6
1992	5.9	5.7	5.8	6.2	6.4	6.6	7.0	6.8	6.6	6.5	6.4	6.1	6.3
1993	5.8	5.7	5.6	5.9	6.1	6.4	6.7	6.6	6.4	6.5	6.4	6.3	6.2
1994	5.5	5.3	5.5	6.2	6.6	6.8	7.1	7.4	7.1	7.1	7.0	6.8	6.5
1995	6.1	5.8	6.0	6.6	6.7	7.0	7.3	7.5	7.3	7.1	6.9	6.5	6.7
1996	5.4	5.7	6.1	6.5	6.9	7.2	7.6	7.7	7.4	7.4	7.4	7.1	6.9
1997	6.4	6.4	6.5	6.8	7.2	7.4	7.7	7.7	7.5	7.7	7.5	7.2	7.2
1998	6.7	6.5	6.6	7.0	7.1	7.4	7.7	7.7	7.5	7.3	7.1	7.0	7.1
1999	6.5	6.6	6.7	7.3	7.7	8.0	8.2	8.1	8.0	8.1	8.0	7.8	7.6
2000	7.4	7.0	7.5	8.0	8.1	8.3	8.7	8.8	8.6	8.5	8.4	8.2	8.1
2001	7.8	7.6	7.9	8.3	8.6	9.0	8.9	8.9	8.7	8.5	8.3	8.1	8.4
2002	7.6	7.5	7.7	8.0	8.3	8.7	8.8	8.8	8.6	8.4	8.3	8.1	8.2
2003	7.6	7.3	7.5	8.0	8.5	8.7	8.9	8.9	8.8	8.8	8.6	8.2	8.3

Employment by Industry: Pennsylvania—*Continued*

(Numbers in thousands. Not seasonally adjusted.)

Industry	January	February	March	April	May	June	July	August	September	October	November	December	Annual Average
READING—*Continued*													
Manufacturing													
1990	45.1	44.8	44.4	44.4	44.3	44.4	44.4	43.9	44.5	44.5	44.4	44.0	44.4
1991	42.8	41.9	41.8	41.4	41.3	42.1	41.8	42.5	42.6	42.8	42.7	42.4	42.2
1992	42.4	42.3	42.3	42.4	41.9	42.4	42.8	43.2	43.0	43.2	43.3	43.4	42.7
1993	42.5	42.3	41.6	41.7	41.7	41.7	41.0	41.3	41.3	42.4	42.7	43.0	41.9
1994	42.6	42.4	42.6	42.5	42.8	43.1	42.8	43.1	43.2	43.1	43.3	43.6	42.9
1995	42.8	42.9	42.7	42.5	42.6	43.0	42.7	42.9	43.0	42.5	42.6	42.8	42.8
1996	40.9	41.7	41.8	41.9	41.8	42.4	41.9	42.2	42.1	42.2	42.3	42.6	42.0
1997	42.7	42.7	42.8	42.8	42.5	42.8	42.2	43.1	42.9	42.6	42.6	42.8	42.7
1998	42.6	42.3	42.0	42.6	42.2	41.9	40.0	41.8	41.8	41.6	41.3	41.4	41.8
1999	41.3	41.2	40.8	40.6	40.7	41.1	41.1	41.8	41.4	41.9	42.2	42.3	41.4
2000	42.0	41.9	41.4	41.5	41.1	42.0	41.7	41.7	41.8	41.2	40.4	41.0	41.5
2001	40.5	40.2	39.8	39.5	39.1	39.4	38.9	39.2	38.8	37.6	37.5	37.2	39.0
2002	36.2	36.2	35.7	35.6	35.6	35.8	35.1	35.2	34.8	34.5	34.2	34.0	35.2
2003	33.4	33.1	32.8	32.5	32.5	32.6	32.1	32.2	32.0	31.9	31.9	31.8	32.4
Service-providing													
1990	101.1	101.6	102.7	103.1	104.5	103.3	100.8	100.8	102.6	103.7	104.1	104.7	102.8
1991	100.6	100.3	101.4	101.9	102.5	102.0	99.5	100.2	101.4	103.0	104.1	104.4	101.8
1992	101.3	102.0	102.6	103.5	104.6	104.7	101.4	101.4	103.0	104.6	105.4	105.4	103.3
1993	102.7	103.6	103.5	105.3	106.1	105.7	103.9	104.1	105.6	106.9	107.9	108.1	105.3
1994	102.8	102.4	104.2	106.5	107.2	106.9	103.8	105.4	107.8	109.1	109.9	109.9	106.3
1995	106.2	107.4	108.0	109.4	110.2	109.3	105.6	106.8	109.7	111.3	112.2	111.8	109.0
1996	105.3	109.3	110.3	111.5	112.5	112.0	109.0	110.3	113.3	115.4	115.6	116.4	111.7
1997	112.1	112.7	114.1	115.1	116.4	116.3	113.0	113.1	115.4	117.0	117.9	118.3	115.1
1998	114.5	115.5	116.3	116.8	117.9	117.4	115.2	115.6	117.6	119.4	119.9	120.7	117.2
1999	116.2	117.1	117.8	119.4	120.3	119.9	117.7	117.4	120.5	121.1	122.3	123.4	119.4
2000	119.5	119.6	121.2	121.3	122.4	122.9	120.0	120.0	122.8	123.5	124.9	124.8	121.9
2001	121.2	121.4	122.5	122.1	123.0	123.4	120.3	121.1	123.2	123.3	124.8	125.1	122.6
2002	122.6	122.5	123.7	123.7	125.0	124.8	121.7	122.4	124.8	124.5	124.9	125.0	123.8
2003	120.9	120.7	121.8	123.2	124.1	124.4	120.6	121.8	124.6	125.3	126.2	126.8	123.4
Trade, transportation, and utilities													
1990	30.5	30.4	30.6	30.4	30.4	30.7	30.3	30.4	30.6	30.9	31.3	31.5	30.7
1991	29.5	28.7	28.8	29.0	29.3	29.5	28.7	29.2	29.4	29.5	30.2	30.3	29.3
1992	29.7	29.5	29.7	30.0	30.4	30.6	29.9	30.1	30.3	30.3	31.0	31.4	30.2
1993	30.5	30.1	29.8	30.7	31.1	31.0	31.0	31.1	31.5	31.2	31.9	32.3	31.0
1994	30.2	29.6	29.9	30.2	30.8	30.8	30.4	31.0	31.3	32.1	32.6	32.8	31.0
1995	31.4	31.1	31.1	31.5	31.7	31.8	31.0	31.4	32.2	32.8	33.3	33.5	31.9
1996	31.7	32.1	32.1	32.6	32.8	32.9	32.8	33.4	33.7	34.8	35.7	36.3	33.4
1997	34.6	34.2	34.5	34.4	34.4	34.8	33.9	34.1	34.5	35.2	36.0	36.4	34.8
1998	34.9	34.3	34.1	34.3	34.4	34.4	33.9	34.1	34.6	35.2	35.9	36.4	34.7
1999	34.7	34.4	34.6	34.7	34.8	34.7	34.0	33.9	35.1	35.4	36.0	36.7	34.9
2000	35.5	34.7	34.8	34.6	34.7	34.8	33.6	33.6	34.2	34.8	35.7	36.0	34.8
2001	34.0	33.4	33.3	33.3	33.5	33.9	32.8	32.8	33.3	33.3	34.1	34.4	33.5
2002	33.2	32.3	32.5	32.4	32.9	33.0	32.5	32.8	33.1	32.7	32.8	33.1	32.8
2003	31.3	30.8	31.1	31.5	31.8	31.8	31.5	32.2	32.5	32.2	32.9	33.3	31.9
Wholesale trade													
1990	5.8	5.9	5.9	5.8	5.8	5.9	5.8	5.8	5.7	5.4	5.4	5.4	5.7
1991	5.5	5.4	5.4	5.4	5.5	5.5	5.6	5.5	5.4	5.5	5.5	5.5	5.5
1992	5.5	5.4	5.4	5.5	5.6	5.7	5.6	5.6	5.5	5.6	5.6	5.6	5.6
1993	5.5	5.5	5.5	5.6	5.7	5.7	5.8	5.8	5.7	5.8	5.8	5.8	5.7
1994	5.7	5.7	5.8	5.9	6.0	6.0	6.1	6.2	6.1	6.1	6.1	6.1	6.0
1995	6.0	6.0	6.0	6.1	6.2	6.3	6.2	6.2	6.2	6.2	6.2	6.2	6.2
1996	6.0	6.1	6.2	6.1	6.1	6.1	6.1	6.2	6.1	6.2	6.3	6.3	6.2
1997	6.1	6.1	6.2	6.1	6.2	6.3	6.1	6.2	6.0	6.1	6.2	6.2	6.2
1998	6.0	6.0	6.0	6.0	6.0	6.0	6.1	6.1	6.0	5.9	5.9	5.9	6.0
1999	5.9	5.9	5.9	6.0	6.0	6.1	6.0	6.0	6.0	6.1	6.1	6.2	6.0
2000	6.1	6.1	6.1	6.2	6.3	6.2	6.3	6.4	6.3	6.4	6.4	6.4	6.3
2001	6.3	6.2	6.2	6.2	6.3	6.5	6.3	6.3	6.3	6.3	6.3	6.4	6.3
2002	6.2	6.0	6.1	6.0	6.1	6.3	6.3	6.3	6.3	6.2	6.3	6.3	6.2
2003	6.2	6.2	6.3	6.3	6.4	6.4	6.4	6.4	6.4	6.3	6.4	6.4	6.3
Retail trade													
1990	17.9	17.7	17.8	17.7	17.7	17.8	17.7	17.8	17.8	18.5	18.9	19.0	18.0
1991	17.3	16.7	16.7	17.0	17.1	17.2	16.7	17.2	17.3	17.2	17.8	17.8	17.2
1992	17.4	17.2	17.4	17.7	17.9	18.0	17.8	17.9	17.9	17.8	18.5	18.8	17.9
1993	18.1	17.7	17.5	18.2	18.4	18.3	18.5	18.7	18.9	18.4	19.1	19.4	18.4
1994	17.9	17.5	17.8	17.9	18.1	18.2	18.1	18.5	18.7	19.0	19.6	19.9	18.4
1995	18.7	18.2	18.1	18.2	18.2	18.3	18.0	18.3	18.5	18.7	19.2	19.5	18.5
1996	18.0	18.1	18.0	18.6	18.8	18.9	19.3	19.8	19.8	20.6	21.3	21.8	19.4
1997	20.6	20.2	20.4	20.2	20.2	20.4	20.2	20.5	20.2	20.8	21.5	21.9	20.6
1998	20.5	19.9	19.9	20.1	20.2	20.2	20.0	20.2	20.1	20.6	21.3	21.7	20.4
1999	20.3	20.0	20.1	20.3	20.4	20.6	20.6	20.5	20.7	21.2	21.9	22.4	20.8
2000	21.4	20.8	20.9	20.7	20.8	21.0	20.3	20.4	20.4	20.6	21.3	21.7	20.9
2001	20.3	19.8	19.8	19.9	20.0	20.2	20.0	20.1	20.1	20.1	20.8	21.2	20.2
2002	20.0	19.5	19.7	19.6	19.8	19.9	19.8	20.1	19.9	19.8	20.2	20.6	19.9
2003	19.1	18.6	18.8	19.1	19.3	19.5	19.3	20.0	20.0	19.7	20.2	20.7	19.5

Employment by Industry: Pennsylvania—*Continued*

(Numbers in thousands. Not seasonally adjusted.)

Industry	January	February	March	April	May	June	July	August	September	October	November	December	Annual Average
READING—*Continued*													
Transportation and utilities													
1990	6.8	6.8	6.9	6.9	6.9	7.0	6.8	6.8	7.1	7.0	7.0	7.1	6.9
1991	6.7	6.6	6.7	6.6	6.7	6.8	6.4	6.5	6.7	6.8	6.9	7.0	6.7
1992	6.8	6.9	6.9	6.8	6.9	6.9	6.5	6.6	6.9	6.9	6.9	7.0	6.8
1993	6.9	6.9	6.8	6.9	7.0	7.0	6.7	6.6	6.9	7.0	7.0	7.1	6.9
1994	6.6	6.4	6.3	6.4	6.7	6.6	6.2	6.3	6.5	7.0	6.9	6.8	6.6
1995	6.7	6.9	7.0	7.2	7.3	7.2	6.8	6.9	7.5	7.9	7.9	7.8	7.3
1996	7.7	7.9	7.9	7.9	7.9	7.9	7.4	7.4	7.8	8.0	8.1	8.2	7.8
1997	7.9	7.9	7.9	8.1	8.0	8.1	7.6	7.4	8.3	8.3	8.3	8.3	8.0
1998	8.4	8.4	8.2	8.2	8.2	8.2	7.8	7.8	8.5	8.7	8.7	8.8	8.3
1999	8.5	8.5	8.6	8.4	8.4	8.0	7.4	7.4	8.4	8.1	8.0	8.1	8.2
2000	8.0	7.8	7.8	7.7	7.6	7.6	7.0	6.8	7.5	7.8	8.0	7.9	7.6
2001	7.4	7.4	7.3	7.2	7.2	7.2	6.5	6.4	6.9	6.9	7.0	6.8	7.0
2002	7.0	6.8	6.7	6.8	7.0	6.8	6.4	6.4	6.9	6.7	6.3	6.2	6.7
2003	6.0	6.0	6.0	6.1	6.1	5.9	5.8	5.8	6.1	6.2	6.3	6.2	6.0
Information													
1990	2.0	2.0	2.0	2.0	2.0	2.0	2.0	2.0	1.9	2.0	2.0	2.0	2.0
1991	2.0	1.9	2.0	2.0	2.0	2.0	2.1	2.1	2.0	2.1	2.1	2.1	2.0
1992	2.1	2.0	2.0	2.0	2.0	2.0	2.1	2.1	2.1	2.1	2.0	2.0	2.0
1993	2.0	1.9	1.9	1.9	1.9	2.0	2.0	2.0	1.9	1.9	2.0	2.0	2.0
1994	1.8	1.8	1.8	1.8	1.8	1.9	1.9	1.9	1.9	1.9	1.9	1.9	1.9
1995	1.9	1.9	2.0	2.0	2.0	2.0	2.0	2.0	2.0	2.0	2.0	2.0	2.0
1996	2.0	1.9	1.9	2.0	2.2	2.3	2.1	2.1	2.1	2.2	2.3	2.4	2.1
1997	2.4	2.4	2.4	2.5	2.5	2.5	2.4	2.5	2.4	2.5	2.5	2.5	2.5
1998	2.5	2.5	2.6	2.3	2.3	2.3	2.4	2.4	2.4	2.3	2.3	2.3	2.4
1999	2.3	2.3	2.3	2.3	2.4	2.4	2.4	2.4	2.3	2.0	2.1	2.1	2.3
2000	1.9	1.9	1.9	2.0	2.0	2.0	2.0	1.9	2.0	2.0	2.1	2.1	2.0
2001	2.1	2.0	2.1	2.1	2.1	2.1	2.1	2.1	2.1	2.1	2.1	2.1	2.1
2002	2.0	2.0	2.0	2.0	2.0	2.0	2.0	2.0	2.0	2.0	2.0	2.0	2.0
2003	2.0	1.9	1.9	1.9	1.9	1.9	1.9	1.9	2.0	2.0	2.0	2.0	1.9
Financial activities													
1990	8.8	8.8	8.7	8.5	8.8	8.8	8.7	8.8	8.7	8.6	8.6	8.7	8.7
1991	8.4	8.3	8.4	8.5	8.5	8.5	8.6	8.6	8.5	8.4	8.4	8.4	8.5
1992	8.8	8.8	8.7	8.7	8.7	8.8	8.8	8.8	8.9	8.8	8.8	8.8	8.8
1993	8.7	8.7	8.7	8.6	8.7	8.8	8.8	8.8	8.7	8.8	8.8	8.8	8.7
1994	8.9	8.8	8.9	9.1	9.1	9.3	9.1	9.2	9.2	9.2	9.2	9.2	9.1
1995	9.1	9.0	8.9	8.9	8.9	9.0	8.9	9.0	9.0	8.9	8.9	8.9	9.0
1996	8.8	8.8	8.9	8.8	8.9	8.9	9.0	9.1	9.2	8.8	8.8	8.9	8.9
1997	8.8	8.7	8.8	8.8	8.9	8.9	8.7	8.6	8.4	8.3	8.4	8.4	8.6
1998	8.4	8.4	8.7	8.4	8.4	8.5	8.6	8.6	8.4	8.7	8.7	8.8	8.6
1999	9.0	8.9	8.9	8.7	8.7	8.8	9.1	9.0	8.8	8.6	8.7	8.7	8.8
2000	8.8	8.7	8.8	8.5	8.5	8.7	8.7	8.7	8.5	8.8	8.9	8.9	8.7
2001	8.7	8.7	8.8	8.9	8.9	8.9	8.9	8.8	8.7	8.6	8.6	8.6	8.8
2002	8.6	8.5	8.6	8.5	8.5	8.6	8.5	8.5	8.3	8.2	8.2	8.3	8.4
2003	8.0	8.0	8.1	8.1	8.2	8.3	8.3	8.3	8.3	8.3	8.3	8.3	8.2
Professional and business services													
1990	12.0	12.0	12.2	12.4	12.4	12.4	12.4	12.3	12.1	12.0	12.0	12.0	12.2
1991	12.5	12.3	12.4	12.6	12.5	12.4	12.3	12.6	12.5	12.7	12.6	12.7	12.5
1992	12.1	12.0	12.1	12.1	12.1	12.2	11.8	11.9	11.8	11.8	11.7	11.6	11.9
1993	11.6	11.7	11.8	12.0	12.3	12.1	12.2	12.5	12.4	12.6	12.5	12.5	12.2
1994	12.2	12.1	12.5	13.1	12.9	13.0	12.9	13.3	13.4	13.0	12.9	12.9	12.9
1995	12.4	12.6	12.6	13.2	13.2	13.0	12.8	13.0	13.2	13.3	13.3	13.1	13.0
1996	12.3	13.5	13.6	13.2	13.1	13.1	13.2	13.5	13.4	13.6	13.3	13.2	13.3
1997	13.5	13.2	13.4	13.9	14.1	14.5	14.3	14.5	14.5	14.3	14.2	14.2	14.1
1998	14.2	14.3	14.5	15.2	15.1	15.6	16.1	16.3	16.4	16.2	15.8	16.0	15.5
1999	15.5	15.4	15.5	16.1	16.1	16.3	17.0	17.3	17.2	17.5	17.4	17.5	16.6
2000	17.0	17.0	17.3	17.5	17.3	18.2	18.9	19.3	19.2	19.0	19.2	19.0	18.2
2001	18.8	18.6	18.8	18.5	18.4	18.7	18.6	19.3	19.1	19.0	19.1	18.8	18.8
2002	19.1	18.9	19.1	18.9	18.7	18.9	19.4	19.3	19.3	19.4	19.2	19.2	19.1
2003	18.7	18.5	18.4	18.8	18.5	19.1	19.0	19.5	20.0	19.9	19.7	19.9	19.2
Educational and health services													
1990	14.4	14.4	14.6	14.7	14.6	14.4	14.4	14.2	14.6	14.9	14.9	14.9	14.6
1991	14.8	15.0	15.2	15.1	15.0	14.8	14.8	14.7	15.1	15.5	15.5	15.5	15.1
1992	15.3	15.4	15.5	15.5	15.6	15.9	15.3	15.2	15.5	15.9	16.0	15.8	15.6
1993	15.7	15.9	15.9	16.0	15.9	15.8	15.4	15.3	15.6	16.2	16.3	16.2	15.9
1994	15.7	15.9	16.1	16.1	16.2	16.0	15.6	15.7	16.2	16.5	16.6	16.5	16.1
1995	16.2	16.5	16.6	16.6	16.6	16.3	16.2	16.1	16.7	17.0	17.2	17.0	16.6
1996	16.4	16.9	17.0	17.3	17.2	17.1	16.7	16.7	17.0	17.6	17.7	17.8	17.1
1997	17.3	17.5	17.6	17.8	17.9	17.6	17.5	17.4	17.9	18.4	18.5	18.5	17.8
1998	18.2	18.6	18.7	18.5	18.5	18.2	18.0	17.9	18.2	18.5	18.5	18.4	18.4
1999	17.8	18.0	18.1	18.5	18.4	18.4	18.1	18.1	18.6	18.7	18.9	19.0	18.4
2000	18.6	18.6	18.9	18.9	18.9	19.1	19.1	19.0	19.3	19.3	19.3	19.4	19.0
2001	19.0	19.0	19.5	19.4	19.5	19.6	19.4	19.5	19.7	19.7	20.0	20.2	19.5
2002	20.1	20.1	20.3	20.2	20.3	20.3	20.1	20.1	20.2	20.2	20.5	20.5	20.2
2003	20.2	20.3	20.5	20.5	20.5	20.6	20.4	20.3	20.4	20.8	21.1	21.2	20.6

Employment by Industry: Pennsylvania—*Continued*

(Numbers in thousands. Not seasonally adjusted.)

Industry	January	February	March	April	May	June	July	August	September	October	November	December	Annual Average
READING—*Continued*													
Leisure and hospitality													
1990	9.1	9.2	9.5	9.8	10.2	10.6	10.5	10.6	10.3	10.2	10.2	10.2	10.0
1991	9.2	9.3	9.5	10.0	10.5	10.9	11.1	11.3	10.8	10.7	10.9	10.9	10.4
1992	10.0	9.9	10.2	10.6	11.2	11.4	11.4	11.5	11.0	11.0	10.9	10.8	10.8
1993	10.1	10.1	10.1	10.9	11.2	11.6	11.7	11.7	11.5	11.1	11.0	10.9	11.0
1994	10.1	9.9	10.4	11.0	11.3	11.6	11.6	11.7	11.3	10.9	10.8	10.7	10.9
1995	10.4	10.4	10.7	11.2	11.6	12.1	11.9	11.8	11.7	11.4	11.4	11.0	11.3
1996	10.0	10.4	10.7	11.5	12.0	12.2	12.0	12.2	11.8	11.7	11.6	11.5	11.5
1997	10.8	11.0	11.4	11.8	12.3	12.6	12.7	12.7	12.1	12.0	11.8	11.6	11.9
1998	11.1	11.2	11.3	11.7	12.5	12.9	12.7	12.9	12.0	12.0	11.9	11.8	12.0
1999	11.3	11.5	11.6	12.3	12.7	13.2	13.0	12.9	12.3	12.0	11.9	12.0	12.2
2000	11.3	11.4	11.9	12.2	12.8	13.2	13.0	13.0	12.6	12.1	12.0	12.0	12.3
2001	11.4	11.7	12.0	12.2	12.6	13.1	13.1	13.1	12.8	12.5	12.5	12.3	12.4
2002	11.8	12.0	12.3	12.9	13.5	13.9	13.8	14.0	13.2	12.9	12.9	12.6	13.0
2003	12.1	12.0	12.3	12.9	13.6	13.9	13.6	13.7	13.1	12.8	12.8	12.4	12.9
Other services													
1990	7.1	6.9	6.9	7.0	7.1	7.2	7.0	7.0	7.0	6.9	6.8	7.0	7.0
1991	6.9	6.9	6.9	6.6	6.7	6.7	6.6	6.6	6.4	6.6	6.6	6.7	6.7
1992	6.3	6.4	6.4	6.4	6.5	6.5	6.5	6.4	6.3	6.4	6.4	6.4	6.4
1993	6.4	6.4	6.4	6.4	6.5	6.6	6.6	6.6	6.4	6.6	6.6	6.6	6.5
1994	6.5	6.4	6.5	6.6	6.6	6.7	6.5	6.7	6.5	6.4	6.6	6.7	6.6
1995	6.6	6.6	6.6	6.7	6.7	6.8	6.7	6.8	6.6	6.7	6.7	6.7	6.7
1996	6.4	6.7	6.8	6.8	6.8	7.0	6.9	7.0	6.9	6.8	6.8	6.8	6.8
1997	6.7	6.8	6.8	6.8	7.0	7.1	7.1	7.1	6.9	7.0	7.0	7.0	6.9
1998	7.0	7.0	7.0	7.0	7.1	7.2	7.3	7.2	7.0	7.2	7.2	7.2	7.1
1999	7.0	7.1	7.2	7.1	7.2	7.4	7.3	7.2	7.1	7.3	7.3	7.4	7.2
2000	7.4	7.4	7.5	7.5	7.6	7.7	7.8	7.7	7.6	7.7	7.7	7.7	7.6
2001	7.7	7.7	7.6	7.5	7.6	7.7	7.8	7.7	7.6	7.6	7.6	7.7	7.7
2002	7.6	7.7	7.7	7.7	7.8	7.9	7.8	7.8	7.8	7.8	7.7	7.9	7.8
2003	7.7	7.7	7.8	7.9	7.9	8.0	7.9	7.9	7.7	7.8	7.9	7.9	7.8
Government													
1990	17.2	17.9	18.2	18.3	19.0	17.2	15.5	15.5	17.4	18.2	18.3	18.4	17.6
1991	17.3	17.9	18.2	18.1	18.0	17.2	15.3	15.1	16.7	17.5	17.8	17.8	17.2
1992	17.0	18.0	18.0	18.2	18.1	17.3	15.6	15.4	17.1	18.3	18.6	18.6	17.5
1993	17.7	18.8	18.9	18.8	18.5	17.8	16.2	16.1	17.6	18.5	18.8	18.8	18.0
1994	17.4	17.9	18.1	18.6	18.5	17.6	15.8	15.9	18.0	19.1	19.3	19.2	18.0
1995	18.2	19.3	19.5	19.3	19.5	18.3	16.1	16.7	18.3	19.2	19.4	19.6	18.6
1996	17.7	19.0	19.3	19.3	19.5	18.5	16.3	16.3	19.2	19.9	19.4	19.5	18.7
1997	18.0	18.9	19.2	19.1	19.3	18.3	16.4	16.2	18.7	19.3	19.5	19.7	18.6
1998	18.2	19.2	19.4	19.4	19.6	18.3	16.2	16.2	18.6	19.3	19.6	19.8	18.7
1999	18.6	19.5	19.6	19.7	20.0	18.7	16.8	16.6	19.1	19.6	20.0	20.0	19.0
2000	19.0	19.9	20.1	20.1	20.6	19.2	16.9	16.8	19.4	19.8	20.0	19.7	19.3
2001	19.5	20.3	20.4	20.2	20.4	19.4	17.6	17.8	19.9	20.5	20.8	21.0	19.8
2002	20.2	21.0	21.2	21.1	21.3	20.2	17.6	17.9	20.9	21.3	21.6	21.4	20.5
2003	20.9	21.5	21.7	21.6	21.7	20.8	18.0	18.0	20.6	21.5	21.5	21.8	20.8
Federal government													
1990	1.4	1.4	1.4	1.4	2.2	1.5	1.4	1.4	1.4	1.4	1.3	1.4	1.5
1991	1.3	1.3	1.3	1.4	1.3	1.4	1.4	1.4	1.4	1.4	1.4	1.4	1.4
1992	1.4	1.4	1.3	1.4	1.4	1.4	1.3	1.3	1.3	1.3	1.3	1.3	1.3
1993	1.3	1.3	1.3	1.3	1.3	1.3	1.3	1.3	1.3	1.2	1.2	1.3	1.3
1994	1.2	1.2	1.2	1.3	1.3	1.3	1.3	1.3	1.3	1.3	1.3	1.3	1.3
1995	1.3	1.3	1.3	1.3	1.3	1.3	1.3	1.3	1.3	1.3	1.3	1.3	1.3
1996	1.3	1.3	1.3	1.3	1.3	1.4	1.4	1.4	1.3	1.3	1.3	1.3	1.3
1997	1.2	1.1	1.1	1.2	1.2	1.2	1.2	1.2	1.2	1.2	1.2	1.3	1.2
1998	1.2	1.2	1.2	1.2	1.2	1.2	1.2	1.2	1.2	1.2	1.2	1.3	1.2
1999	1.2	1.2	1.2	1.2	1.2	1.2	1.2	1.2	1.2	1.1	1.2	1.2	1.2
2000	1.2	1.2	1.4	1.3	1.8	1.5	1.4	1.2	1.2	1.1	1.2	1.2	1.3
2001	1.2	1.1	1.2	1.1	1.2	1.2	1.2	1.2	1.1	1.1	1.1	1.2	1.2
2002	1.1	1.1	1.1	1.1	1.1	1.2	1.2	1.2	1.2	1.2	1.2	1.2	1.2
2003	1.2	1.2	1.2	1.2	1.2	1.2	1.2	1.2	1.2	1.2	1.2	1.3	1.2
State government													
1990	3.3	3.8	3.9	3.9	3.8	3.0	3.1	3.0	3.8	4.1	4.1	4.0	3.7
1991	3.4	3.9	3.9	3.9	3.8	3.0	3.1	3.0	3.5	3.7	3.8	3.7	3.6
1992	3.1	3.6	3.6	3.8	3.5	3.1	3.0	3.0	3.6	4.0	4.0	3.9	3.5
1993	3.3	4.1	4.0	4.0	3.6	3.2	3.2	3.1	3.9	4.2	4.2	4.0	3.7
1994	3.4	3.8	3.8	3.9	3.8	3.1	3.1	3.2	4.0	4.1	4.1	4.0	3.7
1995	3.3	4.1	4.2	4.1	4.0	3.1	3.0	3.3	4.0	4.0	4.0	4.0	3.8
1996	3.1	3.8	4.0	4.0	3.9	3.0	3.0	3.1	3.8	3.9	4.1	4.0	3.6
1997	3.2	3.9	4.1	3.9	3.9	2.9	3.1	3.2	4.1	4.1	4.1	4.0	3.7
1998	3.4	4.0	4.0	4.0	3.9	3.0	3.0	3.0	3.7	4.1	4.1	4.0	3.7
1999	3.5	4.1	4.0	4.0	4.0	3.0	3.1	3.1	3.8	4.0	4.1	4.1	3.7
2000	3.6	4.3	4.2	4.2	4.1	3.2	3.1	3.2	4.0	4.1	4.1	3.7	3.8
2001	3.5	4.1	4.0	4.0	3.9	3.1	3.3	3.4	3.8	4.1	4.2	4.2	3.8
2002	3.6	4.2	4.2	4.1	4.1	3.2	3.2	3.4	4.0	4.2	4.2	4.0	3.9
2003	3.7	4.1	4.1	4.1	4.0	3.2	3.1	3.1	3.7	4.0	4.0	4.0	3.8

Employment by Industry: Pennsylvania—*Continued*

(Numbers in thousands. Not seasonally adjusted.)

Industry	January	February	March	April	May	June	July	August	September	October	November	December	Annual Average
READING—*Continued*													
Local government													
1990	12.5	12.7	12.9	13.0	13.0	12.7	11.0	11.1	12.2	12.7	12.9	13.0	12.5
1991	12.6	12.7	13.0	12.8	12.9	12.8	10.8	10.7	11.8	12.4	12.6	12.7	12.3
1992	12.5	13.0	13.1	13.0	13.2	12.8	11.3	11.1	12.2	13.0	13.3	13.4	12.7
1993	13.1	13.4	13.6	13.5	13.6	13.3	11.7	11.7	12.4	13.1	13.4	13.5	13.0
1994	12.8	12.9	13.1	13.4	13.4	13.2	11.4	11.4	12.7	13.7	13.9	13.9	13.0
1995	13.6	13.9	14.0	13.9	14.2	13.9	11.8	12.1	13.0	13.9	14.1	14.3	13.6
1996	13.3	13.9	14.0	14.0	14.3	14.1	11.9	11.8	14.1	14.7	14.0	14.2	13.7
1997	13.6	13.9	14.0	14.0	14.2	14.2	12.1	11.8	13.4	14.0	14.2	14.4	13.7
1998	13.6	14.0	14.2	14.2	14.5	14.1	12.0	12.0	13.7	14.0	14.3	14.5	13.8
1999	13.9	14.2	14.4	14.5	14.8	14.5	12.5	12.3	14.1	14.5	14.7	14.7	14.1
2000	14.2	14.4	14.5	14.6	14.7	14.5	12.4	12.4	14.2	14.6	14.7	14.8	14.2
2001	14.8	15.1	15.2	15.1	15.3	15.1	13.1	13.2	15.0	15.3	15.5	15.6	14.9
2002	15.5	15.7	15.9	15.9	16.1	15.8	13.2	13.3	15.7	15.9	16.2	16.2	15.5
2003	16.0	16.2	16.4	16.3	16.5	16.4	13.7	13.7	15.7	16.3	16.3	16.5	15.8
SCRANTON–WILKES-BARRE													
Total nonfarm													
1990	260.7	262.0	264.2	267.1	268.1	268.3	266.0	266.0	267.7	267.9	267.5	265.4	265.9
1991	257.6	256.4	259.2	261.4	261.4	262.4	259.7	261.8	262.0	263.7	264.2	263.3	261.1
1992	257.4	256.8	258.1	261.1	263.0	263.7	262.2	262.9	263.6	266.1	267.0	265.2	262.3
1993	257.4	259.8	260.2	264.1	266.1	265.3	263.4	264.0	265.1	267.6	268.6	267.9	264.1
1994	257.4	259.4	262.9	267.8	270.2	269.8	266.2	268.7	271.6	273.5	274.5	273.1	267.9
1995	265.3	266.8	269.7	271.3	272.5	273.3	269.6	270.9	272.4	275.0	274.2	273.0	271.2
1996	260.6	265.9	267.5	269.8	273.9	274.1	270.7	272.3	273.2	276.3	278.0	277.3	271.6
1997	268.4	269.8	272.2	273.6	276.3	276.2	272.7	273.2	276.0	278.8	279.5	278.4	274.6
1998	270.1	271.5	274.3	277.1	278.9	279.5	276.6	276.6	277.8	280.7	281.4	280.6	277.1
1999	270.8	273.1	275.4	278.5	280.2	280.1	278.5	278.7	280.1	285.0	286.3	286.6	279.4
2000	278.4	280.3	284.5	287.6	289.8	289.0	285.0	285.3	289.1	288.6	289.5	288.9	286.3
2001	281.5	283.4	285.8	286.4	287.7	286.7	281.8	282.8	284.1	283.3	284.0	283.0	284.2
2002	273.6	275.8	278.7	280.2	280.9	281.5	276.7	278.2	281.3	282.8	283.1	282.2	279.6
2003	274.2	275.2	278.1	280.8	282.6	282.6	278.4	278.6	281.3	283.1	282.8	280.7	279.9
Total private													
1990	228.3	228.1	230.2	232.7	233.7	235.1	233.7	234.4	234.7	234.6	233.6	231.8	232.6
1991	224.5	222.7	225.4	227.6	228.4	230.0	228.1	230.0	229.2	230.1	231.0	229.4	228.0
1992	224.1	222.6	223.9	226.9	229.5	231.1	230.4	230.7	230.7	232.1	232.7	231.3	228.8
1993	224.2	225.1	225.0	229.4	232.0	231.7	230.6	231.3	232.1	233.4	234.3	233.1	230.2
1994	224.7	225.0	228.0	233.2	236.1	236.2	233.8	236.6	237.9	238.9	239.4	238.1	234.0
1995	231.4	232.1	234.7	236.2	237.8	239.2	237.1	238.6	238.4	240.2	239.4	237.6	236.9
1996	226.8	230.1	231.9	234.2	238.3	239.1	237.7	238.8	238.7	241.6	242.7	241.7	236.8
1997	233.5	234.0	236.6	238.3	241.3	241.5	239.0	239.7	241.2	243.7	244.2	243.0	239.7
1998	235.6	236.2	238.7	241.7	244.0	245.0	243.1	243.3	243.2	245.7	246.2	245.3	242.3
1999	235.9	237.4	239.7	243.0	245.0	245.9	245.1	245.3	245.1	249.2	250.1	250.6	244.4
2000	243.2	243.8	247.8	250.8	252.5	253.8	251.3	252.2	253.8	252.9	253.5	253.2	250.7
2001	246.3	246.9	249.4	250.1	251.4	251.5	248.8	249.8	248.8	247.3	247.4	246.2	248.7
2002	237.7	238.7	241.7	243.4	245.0	245.7	242.8	244.1	244.8	245.8	246.0	244.9	243.4
2003	237.6	237.5	240.1	243.3	245.9	246.1	244.2	244.7	244.7	245.6	245.3	243.2	243.2
Goods-producing													
1990	71.4	71.2	72.1	73.0	73.4	74.2	73.7	74.1	73.9	73.0	71.9	70.9	72.7
1991	68.4	67.7	68.7	69.1	69.2	70.6	70.4	71.1	70.6	70.0	69.5	68.1	69.5
1992	66.5	66.0	66.2	66.6	67.5	68.7	68.2	68.7	68.5	67.9	67.6	66.9	67.4
1993	64.4	64.5	64.1	65.3	66.3	66.5	65.8	66.3	66.1	66.2	66.3	64.9	65.6
1994	62.3	62.3	63.6	65.0	66.5	67.2	65.9	67.3	67.4	67.0	67.1	65.9	65.6
1995	63.9	63.4	64.0	64.5	65.6	66.8	65.3	66.4	65.6	65.9	64.8	63.2	65.0
1996	60.0	61.0	61.5	63.2	64.6	65.7	65.0	65.8	65.4	66.4	66.0	64.5	64.1
1997	62.1	62.0	62.5	62.7	64.2	64.5	64.6	65.2	65.1	65.1	64.5	63.3	63.8
1998	61.4	61.5	62.1	62.9	63.8	64.8	64.3	64.3	64.4	64.1	63.6	62.5	63.3
1999	59.9	59.9	60.5	61.7	62.7	63.4	62.9	63.5	63.5	64.1	64.1	63.1	62.4
2000	60.9	60.6	62.1	63.6	64.3	65.4	65.6	66.5	66.3	65.4	65.1	64.3	64.2
2001	62.1	61.9	62.1	62.1	62.6	63.0	61.9	62.5	61.0	59.9	59.4	58.0	61.4
2002	55.5	55.2	55.8	56.3	56.9	58.0	58.1	58.6	58.4	58.0	57.6	56.4	57.1
2003	54.4	53.6	53.8	54.8	55.8	56.4	56.4	56.5	56.1	55.6	55.3	53.9	55.2
Construction and mining													
1990	10.4	10.2	10.6	11.8	12.6	13.2	13.3	13.2	13.1	12.8	12.4	11.5	12.1
1991	9.7	9.4	9.7	10.6	11.2	11.6	11.8	11.7	11.3	11.2	10.9	10.0	10.8
1992	8.8	8.4	8.6	9.4	10.3	10.9	11.2	11.2	10.9	10.7	10.3	9.8	10.0
1993	8.3	8.0	8.0	9.1	9.9	10.3	10.5	10.4	10.4	10.6	10.3	9.6	9.6
1994	7.9	7.6	8.0	9.4	10.6	11.1	11.4	11.5	11.4	11.5	11.4	10.7	10.2
1995	9.4	8.9	9.4	10.4	11.3	12.0	12.1	12.3	11.9	11.7	11.0	9.8	10.9
1996	8.2	8.4	8.8	10.8	11.7	12.5	12.0	12.2	12.0	12.4	12.0	11.1	11.0
1997	9.9	9.4	9.6	10.6	11.6	11.6	12.0	11.9	11.9	11.9	11.5	10.6	11.0
1998	9.2	9.2	9.7	10.6	11.3	11.6	12.1	11.8	11.8	11.7	11.4	10.8	10.9
1999	9.3	9.2	9.5	10.9	11.8	12.1	12.1	12.3	12.3	12.2	12.2	11.4	11.3
2000	9.9	9.5	10.3	11.3	11.9	12.3	12.8	12.9	12.6	12.2	12.0	11.3	11.6
2001	10.2	10.1	10.2	10.9	11.7	12.3	12.5	12.6	12.3	12.2	12.0	11.4	11.5
2002	9.9	9.7	10.2	11.0	11.8	12.2	12.8	12.9	12.6	12.4	12.0	11.1	11.6
2003	9.9	9.5	10.0	10.9	11.7	12.0	12.4	12.5	12.2	12.0	11.7	10.9	11.3

Employment by Industry: Pennsylvania—*Continued*

(Numbers in thousands. Not seasonally adjusted.)

Industry	January	February	March	April	May	June	July	August	September	October	November	December	Annual Average
SCRANTON–WILKES-BARRE—*Continued*													
Manufacturing													
1990	61.0	61.0	61.5	61.2	60.8	61.0	60.4	60.9	60.8	60.2	59.5	59.4	60.6
1991	58.7	58.3	59.0	58.5	58.0	59.0	58.6	59.4	59.3	58.8	58.6	58.1	58.7
1992	57.7	57.6	57.6	57.2	57.2	57.8	57.0	57.5	57.6	57.2	57.3	57.1	57.4
1993	56.1	56.5	56.1	56.2	56.4	56.2	55.3	55.9	55.7	55.6	56.0	55.3	55.9
1994	54.4	54.7	55.6	55.6	55.9	56.1	54.5	55.8	56.0	55.5	55.7	55.2	55.4
1995	54.5	54.5	54.6	54.1	54.3	54.8	53.2	54.1	53.7	54.2	53.8	53.4	54.1
1996	51.8	52.6	52.7	52.4	52.9	53.2	53.0	53.6	53.4	54.0	54.0	53.4	53.1
1997	52.2	52.6	52.9	52.1	52.6	52.9	52.6	53.3	53.2	53.2	53.0	52.7	52.8
1998	52.2	52.3	52.4	52.3	52.5	53.2	52.2	52.5	52.6	52.4	52.2	51.7	52.4
1999	50.6	50.7	51.0	50.8	50.9	51.3	50.8	51.2	51.2	51.9	51.9	51.7	51.2
2000	51.0	51.1	51.8	52.3	52.4	53.1	52.8	53.6	53.7	53.2	53.1	53.0	52.6
2001	51.9	51.8	51.9	51.2	50.9	50.7	49.4	49.9	48.7	47.7	47.4	46.6	49.8
2002	45.6	45.5	45.6	45.3	45.1	45.8	45.3	45.7	45.8	45.6	45.6	45.3	45.5
2003	44.5	44.1	43.8	43.9	44.1	44.4	44.0	44.0	43.9	43.6	43.6	43.0	43.9
Service-providing													
1990	189.3	190.8	192.1	194.1	194.7	194.1	192.3	191.9	193.8	194.9	195.6	194.5	193.2
1991	189.2	188.7	190.5	192.3	192.2	191.8	189.3	190.7	191.4	193.7	194.7	195.2	191.6
1992	190.9	190.8	191.9	194.5	195.5	195.0	194.0	194.2	195.1	198.2	199.4	198.3	194.8
1993	193.0	195.3	196.1	198.8	199.8	198.8	197.6	197.7	199.0	201.4	202.3	203.0	198.6
1994	195.1	197.1	199.3	202.8	203.7	202.6	200.3	201.4	204.2	206.5	207.4	207.2	202.3
1995	201.4	203.4	205.7	206.8	206.9	206.5	204.3	204.5	206.8	209.1	209.4	209.8	206.2
1996	200.6	204.9	206.0	206.6	209.3	208.4	205.7	206.5	207.8	209.9	212.0	212.8	207.5
1997	206.3	207.8	209.7	210.9	212.1	211.7	208.1	208.0	210.9	213.7	215.0	215.1	210.8
1998	208.7	210.0	212.2	214.2	215.1	214.7	212.3	212.3	213.4	216.6	217.8	218.1	213.8
1999	210.9	213.2	214.9	216.8	217.5	216.7	215.6	215.2	216.6	220.9	222.2	223.5	217.0
2000	217.5	219.7	222.4	224.0	225.5	223.6	219.4	218.8	222.8	223.2	224.4	224.6	222.2
2001	219.4	221.5	223.7	224.3	225.1	223.7	219.9	220.3	223.1	223.4	224.6	225.0	222.8
2002	218.1	220.6	222.9	223.9	224.0	223.5	218.6	219.6	222.9	224.8	225.5	225.8	222.5
2003	219.8	221.6	224.3	226.0	226.8	226.2	222.0	222.1	225.2	227.5	227.5	226.8	224.7
Trade, transportation, and utilities													
1990	57.3	56.8	57.0	57.1	57.0	57.5	57.1	57.5	57.8	57.7	58.5	58.7	57.5
1991	56.4	54.9	55.0	56.2	56.4	56.8	55.8	56.1	56.1	56.3	57.5	57.8	56.3
1992	55.8	54.5	54.7	55.5	56.1	56.4	56.0	56.0	56.6	56.6	57.7	58.0	56.2
1993	56.1	55.9	56.0	56.8	57.3	57.2	56.2	56.7	57.4	57.7	58.9	59.4	57.1
1994	57.2	56.2	56.5	56.7	57.1	57.0	56.4	57.3	58.2	58.8	59.3	59.7	57.5
1995	57.0	57.0	57.3	57.4	57.5	57.9	57.1	57.2	57.6	57.8	58.5	58.9	57.6
1996	56.6	56.5	56.2	55.7	56.3	56.6	56.3	56.5	56.9	57.3	58.5	59.2	56.9
1997	57.6	57.2	57.8	57.6	58.4	58.3	57.0	56.7	57.6	58.4	59.5	60.0	58.0
1998	57.8	57.0	57.1	57.7	58.3	58.5	57.8	58.0	58.5	59.2	60.5	61.0	58.5
1999	57.8	57.0	57.4	58.4	59.4	59.6	59.7	60.1	60.6	60.3	61.7	62.3	59.5
2000	59.8	58.9	59.5	60.2	60.7	61.2	60.0	60.3	60.9	61.5	62.5	63.3	60.7
2001	61.2	60.1	60.7	60.8	61.3	61.5	60.7	60.9	61.7	62.4	63.8	64.6	61.6
2002	61.8	61.0	61.6	61.2	61.5	61.5	60.2	60.8	61.1	61.5	62.6	63.4	61.5
2003	61.2	60.5	60.8	61.4	61.8	62.1	61.2	61.5	61.9	62.3	62.9	63.3	61.7
Wholesale trade													
1990	9.7	9.6	9.7	9.8	9.8	9.9	10.0	10.0	9.9	9.8	9.8	9.7	9.8
1991	9.5	9.3	9.4	9.7	9.7	9.7	9.7	9.7	9.6	9.7	9.7	9.7	9.6
1992	9.7	9.5	9.5	9.7	9.9	9.9	9.9	9.8	9.8	9.9	9.8	9.7	9.8
1993	9.4	9.4	9.4	9.5	9.6	9.5	9.5	9.6	9.5	9.2	9.2	9.1	9.4
1994	9.2	9.1	9.2	9.3	9.3	9.4	9.5	9.7	9.7	9.5	9.5	9.5	9.4
1995	9.2	9.2	9.2	9.3	9.3	9.3	9.4	9.4	9.4	9.4	9.4	9.4	9.3
1996	9.3	9.3	9.3	9.2	9.3	9.3	9.4	9.4	9.3	9.3	9.3	9.3	9.3
1997	9.1	9.0	9.1	9.2	9.4	9.4	9.4	9.4	9.4	9.4	9.4	9.4	9.3
1998	9.3	9.3	9.3	9.5	9.6	9.7	9.5	9.5	9.4	9.5	9.5	9.3	9.5
1999	9.3	9.3	9.3	9.5	9.5	9.6	9.7	9.8	9.8	9.7	9.9	9.6	9.6
2000	9.4	9.4	9.5	9.4	9.4	9.5	9.5	9.5	9.6	9.7	9.7	9.8	9.5
2001	10.0	9.9	10.0	10.0	10.1	10.2	10.3	10.4	10.4	10.5	10.5	10.6	10.2
2002	10.6	10.5	10.6	10.6	10.6	10.8	10.6	10.7	10.6	10.6	10.6	10.8	10.6
2003	11.1	11.2	11.4	11.5	11.6	11.7	11.6	11.7	11.6	11.5	11.5	11.4	11.5
Retail trade													
1990	36.1	35.7	35.7	35.5	35.5	35.7	35.5	35.9	35.8	36.0	36.9	37.1	36.0
1991	35.3	34.0	34.0	34.7	34.9	35.2	34.8	35.0	34.7	34.6	35.6	35.9	34.9
1992	34.4	33.5	33.6	34.2	34.4	34.6	34.6	34.6	34.7	34.6	35.6	35.9	34.6
1993	34.1	33.7	33.6	34.0	34.2	34.2	34.0	34.4	34.5	35.0	36.2	36.8	34.6
1994	34.9	34.1	34.3	34.5	34.8	34.6	34.7	35.1	35.2	35.7	36.4	36.9	35.1
1995	34.8	34.8	35.0	35.0	35.2	35.6	35.6	35.5	35.2	35.1	35.8	36.3	35.3
1996	34.0	33.9	34.1	33.7	34.1	34.3	34.4	34.3	34.2	34.4	35.6	36.3	34.4
1997	35.5	35.1	35.4	35.3	35.8	35.9	35.5	35.5	35.3	35.8	36.8	37.3	35.8
1998	35.5	34.8	34.8	35.0	35.4	35.6	35.7	35.8	35.9	36.2	37.4	38.1	35.9
1999	35.5	34.6	35.0	35.6	36.5	36.7	37.1	37.6	37.4	37.5	38.5	39.4	36.8
2000	36.7	36.0	36.3	36.8	37.3	37.6	36.9	37.2	37.1	37.3	38.3	39.0	37.2
2001	37.0	36.0	36.3	36.2	36.5	36.7	36.1	36.2	36.3	36.9	38.2	38.8	36.8
2002	36.7	36.0	36.3	36.1	36.5	36.7	36.0	36.5	36.4	36.8	38.1	38.7	36.7
2003	36.7	36.0	36.1	36.4	36.6	36.8	36.6	36.8	36.8	37.3	38.0	38.6	36.9

Employment by Industry: Pennsylvania—*Continued*

(Numbers in thousands. Not seasonally adjusted.)

Industry	January	February	March	April	May	June	July	August	September	October	November	December	Annual Average
SCRANTON–WILKES-BARRE—*Continued*													
Transportation and utilities													
1990	11.5	11.5	11.6	11.8	11.7	11.9	11.6	11.6	12.1	11.9	11.8	11.9	11.7
1991	11.6	11.6	11.6	11.8	11.8	11.9	11.3	11.4	11.8	12.0	12.2	12.2	11.8
1992	11.7	11.5	11.6	11.6	11.8	11.9	11.5	11.6	12.1	12.1	12.3	12.4	11.8
1993	12.6	12.8	13.0	13.3	13.5	13.5	12.7	12.7	13.4	13.5	13.5	13.5	13.2
1994	13.1	13.0	13.0	12.9	13.0	13.0	12.2	12.5	13.3	13.6	13.4	13.3	13.0
1995	13.0	13.0	13.1	13.1	13.0	13.0	12.1	12.3	13.0	13.3	13.3	13.2	13.0
1996	13.3	13.3	12.8	12.8	12.9	13.0	12.5	12.8	13.4	13.6	13.6	13.6	13.1
1997	13.0	13.1	13.3	13.1	13.2	13.0	12.1	11.8	12.9	13.2	13.3	13.3	12.9
1998	13.0	12.9	13.0	13.2	13.3	13.2	12.6	12.7	13.2	13.5	13.6	13.6	13.2
1999	13.0	13.1	13.1	13.3	13.4	13.3	12.9	12.7	13.4	13.1	13.3	13.3	13.2
2000	13.7	13.5	13.7	14.0	14.0	14.1	13.6	13.6	14.2	14.5	14.5	14.5	14.0
2001	14.2	14.2	14.4	14.6	14.7	14.6	14.3	14.3	15.0	15.0	15.1	15.2	14.6
2002	14.5	14.5	14.7	14.5	14.4	14.0	13.6	13.6	14.1	14.1	13.9	13.9	14.2
2003	13.4	13.3	13.3	13.5	13.6	13.6	13.0	13.0	13.5	13.5	13.4	13.3	13.4
Information													
1990	6.5	6.6	6.5	6.5	6.6	6.6	6.6	6.7	6.5	6.5	6.5	6.5	6.6
1991	6.3	6.2	6.2	6.4	6.3	6.5	6.4	6.4	6.3	6.6	6.6	6.6	6.4
1992	6.6	6.4	6.4	6.4	6.4	6.5	6.6	6.6	6.5	6.7	6.7	6.5	6.5
1993	6.4	6.3	6.3	6.4	6.4	6.5	6.4	6.4	6.3	6.4	6.4	6.4	6.4
1994	6.4	6.3	6.4	6.3	6.4	6.5	6.4	6.5	6.4	6.4	6.4	6.4	6.4
1995	6.4	6.4	6.5	6.3	6.4	6.5	6.4	6.4	6.4	6.3	6.4	6.5	6.4
1996	6.3	6.3	6.3	6.4	6.5	6.6	6.4	6.6	6.5	6.5	6.6	6.6	6.5
1997	6.4	6.4	6.5	6.6	6.6	6.7	6.8	6.9	7.0	7.2	7.2	7.2	6.8
1998	7.2	7.2	7.4	7.2	7.2	7.3	7.4	7.6	7.4	7.3	7.3	7.4	7.3
1999	7.2	7.4	7.3	7.3	7.4	7.5	7.5	7.5	7.6	7.5	7.4	7.4	7.4
2000	7.3	7.5	7.5	7.4	7.5	7.6	7.5	7.0	7.6	7.5	7.6	7.7	7.5
2001	7.4	7.3	7.4	7.5	7.5	7.5	7.4	7.3	7.3	7.3	7.2	7.3	7.4
2002	7.1	7.1	7.1	7.1	7.3	7.2	7.2	7.2	7.0	6.9	6.9	6.8	7.1
2003	6.6	6.6	6.7	6.6	6.7	6.7	6.7	6.7	6.6	6.6	6.6	6.6	6.6
Financial activities													
1990	12.7	12.6	12.7	12.4	12.6	12.8	13.0	13.1	12.9	12.7	12.7	12.6	12.7
1991	12.7	12.6	12.7	12.7	12.9	13.0	12.9	13.0	12.8	12.7	12.8	12.8	12.8
1992	13.0	12.9	12.9	13.0	13.2	13.3	13.3	13.3	13.2	13.1	13.2	13.2	13.1
1993	13.0	13.0	13.0	13.1	13.2	13.4	13.3	13.3	13.3	13.2	13.2	13.2	13.2
1994	13.2	13.3	13.4	13.5	13.3	13.4	13.5	13.5	13.5	13.5	13.4	13.5	13.4
1995	13.7	13.9	14.1	13.9	14.0	14.2	14.3	14.3	14.1	14.2	14.1	14.2	14.1
1996	14.0	14.0	14.2	14.2	14.3	14.5	14.6	14.6	14.5	14.5	14.7	14.7	14.4
1997	14.6	14.5	14.6	14.5	14.7	14.8	14.7	14.8	14.7	14.5	14.4	14.5	14.6
1998	14.5	14.5	14.4	14.6	14.7	14.9	14.9	14.9	14.7	14.7	14.6	14.5	14.7
1999	14.7	14.6	14.6	14.5	14.6	14.9	14.9	14.7	14.4	14.3	14.4	14.6	14.6
2000	14.3	14.2	14.3	14.4	14.5	14.7	14.8	14.8	14.6	14.5	14.6	14.6	14.5
2001	14.8	14.7	14.8	14.7	14.7	15.0	14.9	14.8	14.5	14.4	14.3	14.4	14.7
2002	14.3	14.3	14.3	14.3	14.3	14.5	14.5	14.4	14.3	13.9	13.9	14.0	14.3
2003	14.1	14.1	14.2	14.3	14.5	14.6	14.5	14.5	14.4	14.3	14.3	14.4	14.4
Professional and business services													
1990	14.1	14.1	14.2	14.8	14.9	15.1	14.7	14.7	14.5	14.2	14.1	13.8	14.4
1991	14.2	14.1	14.4	14.2	14.2	14.4	14.5	14.7	14.6	14.7	14.5	14.1	14.4
1992	14.8	14.8	14.9	15.4	15.5	15.8	16.0	16.0	16.0	16.2	15.9	15.8	15.6
1993	15.7	15.8	15.8	16.0	16.3	16.3	16.8	16.8	16.7	16.5	16.4	16.1	16.3
1994	15.9	16.3	16.3	17.1	17.4	17.7	17.6	17.9	17.6	17.5	17.4	17.3	17.2
1995	17.1	17.1	17.4	17.6	17.6	18.2	18.4	18.5	18.2	18.1	17.8	17.6	17.8
1996	16.5	16.8	16.9	17.4	17.9	18.2	18.3	18.4	18.1	18.2	18.2	18.0	17.7
1997	18.0	17.9	18.3	18.6	18.6	19.1	18.7	18.9	18.8	19.2	19.2	19.1	18.7
1998	18.3	18.3	18.4	19.6	19.8	20.2	20.1	20.1	19.9	20.1	20.3	20.3	19.6
1999	20.3	20.8	21.2	20.8	21.0	21.2	21.5	21.4	20.9	22.0	21.8	22.5	21.3
2000	22.8	23.2	23.8	24.6	24.6	24.8	24.1	24.3	24.3	23.9	23.9	23.8	24.0
2001	23.9	23.8	24.1	24.6	24.7	24.5	24.1	24.4	24.0	22.5	21.9	21.3	23.7
2002	20.4	20.6	21.2	21.9	21.9	22.2	21.5	21.6	21.5	22.1	21.9	21.6	21.5
2003	20.6	20.6	21.0	21.5	21.5	21.5	21.3	21.4	21.3	21.5	21.1	20.8	21.2
Educational and health services													
1990	39.4	39.8	40.4	40.4	40.3	39.5	39.4	39.4	40.3	41.5	41.4	41.2	40.3
1991	39.6	40.3	41.0	41.0	40.7	39.7	39.3	39.6	40.3	41.9	42.3	42.3	40.7
1992	40.8	41.6	42.1	42.4	42.4	41.4	41.6	41.1	41.6	43.5	43.7	43.2	42.1
1993	41.8	42.6	43.0	43.3	43.1	42.0	42.2	41.9	42.8	44.3	44.2	44.2	43.0
1994	42.4	43.3	43.9	45.0	44.7	43.4	43.3	43.2	44.0	45.5	45.7	45.5	44.2
1995	44.7	45.7	46.5	46.5	45.9	44.3	44.7	44.5	45.4	47.1	47.4	47.0	45.8
1996	44.9	46.2	47.0	46.5	46.5	45.1	45.1	45.0	45.7	47.7	47.9	48.0	46.3
1997	45.8	47.1	47.6	47.6	47.4	46.2	45.5	45.4	46.3	48.5	48.7	48.5	47.1
1998	47.1	48.3	49.0	48.7	48.5	47.0	46.8	46.6	47.1	49.2	49.2	49.0	48.0
1999	46.5	48.1	48.8	49.0	47.9	46.8	46.6	46.3	47.0	49.2	49.4	49.2	47.9
2000	47.6	49.0	49.5	48.9	48.1	46.9	46.5	46.3	47.6	48.6	48.7	48.6	48.0
2001	46.4	48.2	48.6	48.3	47.5	46.6	46.5	46.7	47.4	48.9	49.2	48.8	47.8
2002	47.3	49.2	49.7	49.8	49.5	48.2	47.8	47.9	49.0	50.5	50.7	50.3	49.2
2003	49.3	50.8	51.7	51.7	51.4	50.1	49.6	49.6	50.6	52.1	52.2	51.9	50.9

Employment by Industry: Pennsylvania—*Continued*

(Numbers in thousands. Not seasonally adjusted.)

Industry	January	February	March	April	May	June	July	August	September	October	November	December	Annual Average
SCRANTON–WILKES-BARRE—*Continued*													
Leisure and hospitality													
1990	17.5	17.6	17.8	18.7	19.1	19.4	19.2	18.9	19.0	19.2	18.8	18.4	18.6
1991	17.3	17.4	17.8	18.5	19.2	19.4	19.2	19.5	19.1	18.4	18.3	18.1	18.5
1992	17.3	17.2	17.5	18.4	19.0	19.6	19.1	19.4	18.9	18.7	18.4	18.2	18.5
1993	17.6	17.8	17.7	19.1	19.9	20.2	20.2	20.2	19.9	19.5	19.3	19.3	19.2
1994	18.0	18.0	18.4	19.7	20.8	21.1	20.7	20.9	20.8	20.2	20.0	19.7	19.9
1995	18.8	18.8	19.0	20.0	20.8	21.2	20.7	21.1	21.0	20.7	20.2	19.9	20.2
1996	18.5	19.1	19.5	20.6	21.8	22.0	21.4	21.3	21.1	20.9	20.7	20.6	20.6
1997	19.2	19.1	19.5	20.8	21.3	21.7	21.4	21.5	21.6	20.8	20.7	20.4	20.7
1998	19.5	19.5	20.3	20.8	21.5	22.0	21.5	21.5	21.2	21.0	20.6	20.5	20.8
1999	19.5	19.6	19.8	20.8	21.5	21.9	21.2	21.3	20.4	21.3	20.9	20.9	20.8
2000	20.1	20.0	20.5	21.1	22.0	22.4	22.0	22.2	21.9	20.9	20.5	20.3	21.2
2001	20.1	20.4	21.1	21.4	22.3	22.6	22.4	22.4	22.3	21.3	21.0	21.2	21.5
2002	20.7	20.7	21.3	22.0	22.8	23.1	22.6	22.8	22.8	22.3	21.8	21.8	22.1
2003	20.9	20.7	21.3	22.4	23.4	23.9	23.6	23.7	23.1	22.5	22.1	21.6	22.4
Other services													
1990	9.4	9.4	9.5	9.8	9.8	10.0	10.0	10.0	9.8	9.8	9.7	9.7	9.7
1991	9.6	9.5	9.6	9.5	9.5	9.6	9.6	9.6	9.4	9.5	9.5	9.6	9.5
1992	9.3	9.2	9.2	9.2	9.4	9.4	9.6	9.6	9.4	9.4	9.5	9.5	9.4
1993	9.2	9.2	9.1	9.4	9.5	9.6	9.7	9.7	9.6	9.6	9.6	9.6	9.5
1994	9.3	9.3	9.5	9.9	9.9	9.9	10.0	10.0	10.0	10.0	10.1	10.1	9.8
1995	9.8	9.8	9.9	10.0	10.0	10.1	10.2	10.2	10.1	10.1	10.2	10.3	10.1
1996	10.0	10.2	10.3	10.2	10.4	10.4	10.6	10.6	10.5	10.1	10.1	10.1	10.3
1997	9.8	9.8	9.8	9.9	10.1	10.2	10.3	10.3	10.1	10.0	10.0	10.0	10.0
1998	9.8	9.9	10.0	10.2	10.2	10.3	10.3	10.3	10.0	10.1	10.1	10.1	10.1
1999	10.0	10.0	10.1	10.5	10.5	10.6	10.8	10.5	10.7	10.5	10.4	10.6	10.4
2000	10.4	10.4	10.6	10.6	10.8	10.8	10.8	10.8	10.6	10.6	10.6	10.6	10.6
2001	10.4	10.5	10.6	10.7	10.8	10.8	10.9	10.8	10.6	10.6	10.6	10.6	10.7
2002	10.6	10.6	10.7	10.8	10.8	11.0	10.9	10.8	10.7	10.6	10.6	10.6	10.7
2003	10.5	10.6	10.6	10.6	10.8	10.8	10.9	10.8	10.7	10.7	10.8	10.7	10.7
Government													
1990	32.4	33.9	34.0	34.4	34.4	33.2	32.3	31.6	33.0	33.3	33.9	33.6	33.3
1991	33.1	33.7	33.8	33.8	33.0	32.4	31.6	31.8	32.8	33.6	33.2	33.9	33.1
1992	33.3	34.2	34.2	34.2	33.5	32.6	31.8	32.2	32.9	34.0	34.3	33.9	33.4
1993	33.2	34.7	35.2	34.7	34.1	33.6	32.8	32.7	33.0	34.2	34.3	34.8	33.9
1994	32.7	34.4	34.9	34.6	34.1	33.6	32.4	32.1	33.7	34.6	35.1	35.0	33.9
1995	33.9	34.7	35.0	35.1	34.7	34.1	32.5	32.3	34.0	34.8	34.8	35.4	34.3
1996	33.8	35.8	35.6	35.6	35.6	35.0	33.0	33.5	34.5	34.7	35.3	35.6	34.8
1997	34.9	35.8	35.6	35.3	35.0	34.7	33.7	33.5	34.8	35.1	35.3	35.4	34.9
1998	34.5	35.3	35.6	35.4	34.9	34.5	33.5	33.3	34.6	35.0	35.2	35.3	34.8
1999	34.9	35.7	35.7	35.5	35.2	34.2	33.4	33.4	35.0	35.8	36.2	36.0	35.1
2000	35.2	36.5	36.7	36.8	37.3	35.2	33.7	33.1	35.3	35.7	36.0	35.7	35.6
2001	35.2	36.5	36.4	36.3	36.3	35.2	33.0	33.0	35.3	36.0	36.6	36.8	35.6
2002	35.9	37.1	37.0	36.8	35.9	35.8	33.9	34.1	36.5	37.0	37.1	37.3	36.2
2003	36.6	37.7	38.0	37.5	36.7	36.5	34.2	33.9	36.6	37.5	37.5	37.5	36.7
Federal government													
1990	4.9	5.1	5.1	5.5	6.0	5.6	5.5	5.0	4.7	4.7	4.8	4.6	5.1
1991	4.6	4.8	4.9	4.9	4.9	5.0	5.1	5.1	5.0	4.8	4.8	5.0	4.9
1992	5.1	5.1	5.0	5.0	5.0	5.0	5.0	5.0	5.0	4.7	4.9	4.8	5.0
1993	4.8	4.8	4.9	4.9	4.8	5.0	5.1	5.1	5.1	4.6	4.6	4.9	4.9
1994	4.7	4.9	4.9	4.9	4.9	4.9	4.9	4.9	5.0	4.9	4.9	4.9	4.9
1995	4.9	4.8	4.8	5.1	5.1	5.1	5.1	5.2	5.2	4.7	4.6	4.9	5.0
1996	4.7	5.2	5.2	5.3	5.3	5.3	5.3	5.3	5.2	4.8	4.8	4.9	5.1
1997	5.0	5.3	5.3	5.2	5.2	5.2	5.2	5.2	5.0	4.9	4.9	5.0	5.1
1998	4.9	4.9	4.9	4.9	4.9	4.9	4.9	4.9	4.8	4.8	4.8	5.0	4.9
1999	4.8	4.8	5.0	4.8	4.8	4.8	5.1	5.2	5.2	5.1	5.1	5.2	5.0
2000	4.6	5.1	5.4	5.5	6.2	5.3	5.5	5.1	4.9	4.5	4.5	4.6	5.1
2001	4.5	5.0	5.0	5.0	5.0	5.0	5.0	4.9	5.0	4.6	4.7	4.7	4.9
2002	4.7	5.0	5.0	5.0	5.0	5.0	5.0	5.0	5.1	4.8	4.8	5.2	5.0
2003	5.2	5.2	5.3	5.2	5.2	5.2	5.2	5.1	5.1	5.1	5.1	5.1	5.2
State government													
1990	7.7	8.6	8.5	8.5	8.0	7.5	7.8	7.6	8.6	8.4	8.6	8.6	8.2
1991	8.4	8.4	8.4	8.4	7.5	7.2	7.3	7.2	8.3	8.1	7.6	8.0	7.9
1992	7.5	7.8	7.6	8.1	7.6	7.2	7.2	7.2	8.0	8.6	8.6	8.1	7.8
1993	7.6	8.4	8.5	8.7	8.0	7.8	7.8	7.7	8.4	8.7	8.7	8.7	8.3
1994	7.8	8.7	8.9	8.8	8.1	7.7	7.8	7.7	8.4	8.9	8.9	8.9	8.4
1995	7.9	8.9	8.9	8.7	8.3	8.0	7.8	7.8	8.6	8.9	8.8	8.8	8.5
1996	7.8	9.0	8.8	8.8	8.3	7.8	7.7	7.7	8.6	8.8	8.9	8.8	8.4
1997	8.5	8.8	8.7	8.8	8.1	7.6	7.7	7.7	8.8	8.9	8.9	8.8	8.4
1998	8.5	8.9	8.8	8.7	8.0	7.4	7.7	7.6	8.4	8.6	8.7	8.6	8.3
1999	8.2	8.7	8.6	8.6	8.3	7.6	7.7	7.8	8.5	8.7	8.9	8.4	8.3
2000	8.5	8.9	8.8	9.0	8.8	7.9	7.8	7.8	8.7	8.9	9.0	8.4	8.5
2001	8.5	8.9	8.8	9.0	8.8	8.1	8.0	8.1	8.9	8.9	9.1	9.2	8.7
2002	8.7	9.1	9.1	9.1	7.9	8.2	8.2	8.4	8.8	9.2	9.3	8.7	8.7
2003	8.6	9.2	9.2	9.1	8.2	8.1	8.1	8.1	8.6	9.0	9.0	8.8	8.7

Employment by Industry: Pennsylvania—*Continued*

(Numbers in thousands. Not seasonally adjusted.)

Industry	January	February	March	April	May	June	July	August	September	October	November	December	Annual Average
SCRANTON–WILKES-BARRE—*Continued*													
Local government													
1990	19.8	20.2	20.4	20.4	20.4	20.1	19.0	19.0	19.7	20.2	20.5	20.4	20.0
1991	20.1	20.5	20.5	20.5	20.6	20.2	19.2	19.5	19.5	20.7	20.8	20.9	20.3
1992	20.7	21.3	21.6	21.1	20.9	20.4	19.6	20.0	19.9	20.7	20.8	21.0	20.7
1993	20.8	21.5	21.8	21.1	21.3	20.8	19.9	19.9	19.5	20.9	21.0	21.2	20.8
1994	20.2	20.8	21.1	20.9	21.1	21.0	19.7	19.5	20.3	20.8	21.3	21.2	20.7
1995	21.1	21.0	21.3	21.3	21.3	21.0	19.6	19.3	20.2	21.2	21.4	21.7	20.9
1996	21.3	21.6	21.6	21.5	22.0	21.9	20.0	20.5	20.7	21.1	21.6	21.9	21.3
1997	21.4	21.7	21.6	21.3	21.7	21.9	20.8	20.6	21.0	21.3	21.5	21.6	21.4
1998	21.1	21.5	21.9	21.8	22.0	22.2	20.9	20.8	21.4	21.6	21.7	21.7	21.6
1999	21.9	22.2	22.1	22.1	22.1	21.8	20.6	20.4	21.3	22.0	22.2	22.4	21.8
2000	22.1	22.5	22.5	22.3	22.3	22.0	20.4	20.2	21.7	22.3	22.5	22.7	22.0
2001	22.2	22.6	22.6	22.3	22.5	22.1	20.0	20.0	21.4	22.5	22.8	22.9	22.0
2002	22.5	23.0	22.9	22.7	23.0	22.6	20.7	20.7	22.6	23.0	23.0	23.4	22.5
2003	22.8	23.3	23.5	23.2	23.3	23.2	20.9	20.7	22.9	23.4	23.4	23.6	22.9
YORK													
Total nonfarm													
1990	153.4	153.3	153.6	152.9	154.6	154.9	153.8	155.3	155.2	154.7	155.6	156.0	154.4
1991	151.5	149.6	150.7	152.9	151.8	152.1	151.0	152.0	152.7	153.2	153.6	153.4	152.0
1992	150.1	149.6	150.2	152.2	152.9	153.1	152.1	152.5	153.1	154.3	155.1	154.7	152.5
1993	151.6	152.1	152.5	154.1	154.0	154.4	153.4	153.6	155.4	155.8	156.6	157.3	154.2
1994	152.7	152.8	154.3	155.4	157.0	157.2	154.1	155.1	157.8	158.3	159.7	160.0	156.2
1995	158.0	158.5	159.1	159.6	160.2	160.5	158.1	158.7	160.6	161.3	161.6	162.3	159.9
1996	155.7	159.7	160.2	160.8	161.8	160.9	159.2	160.2	162.6	163.9	165.0	165.0	161.3
1997	160.8	161.0	161.3	163.0	164.3	163.4	161.4	162.0	163.5	163.6	164.0	164.9	162.8
1998	161.8	162.6	163.4	165.3	166.0	165.1	162.1	162.5	165.2	166.2	166.4	167.5	164.5
1999	164.4	166.3	167.4	167.5	168.3	168.9	167.9	168.2	170.5	170.8	171.9	173.2	168.8
2000	168.5	169.5	171.5	172.4	173.6	174.1	171.9	171.3	174.2	173.7	175.3	175.5	172.6
2001	171.2	171.0	171.7	172.2	172.3	171.4	168.2	168.2	170.9	170.8	171.0	171.7	170.9
2002	167.8	168.0	169.1	169.0	170.0	169.4	167.0	166.9	168.9	168.3	168.4	168.1	168.4
2003	165.2	165.2	166.0	166.8	168.5	168.5	165.8	166.0	168.5	168.7	169.0	168.9	167.3
Total private													
1990	138.4	138.0	138.1	137.1	138.5	139.4	138.9	140.4	140.2	139.2	140.0	140.2	139.0
1991	136.2	134.0	135.2	137.5	136.2	137.3	136.8	137.8	138.3	137.7	137.8	137.6	136.9
1992	135.0	134.1	134.7	136.6	137.6	138.6	138.2	138.6	138.3	138.7	139.3	139.0	137.4
1993	136.3	136.5	136.8	138.3	138.3	139.6	139.3	139.6	140.6	140.4	141.1	141.8	139.1
1994	137.5	137.4	138.7	139.8	141.4	142.0	140.1	141.0	142.8	142.7	143.9	144.3	141.0
1995	142.6	142.8	143.4	143.9	144.5	146.0	144.5	145.1	145.5	145.6	145.7	146.6	144.7
1996	140.5	143.9	144.3	144.8	144.9	145.0	144.4	145.4	146.2	147.1	148.1	148.1	145.2
1997	144.3	144.2	144.5	146.4	147.7	148.2	147.0	147.6	147.5	147.0	147.5	148.3	146.7
1998	145.6	146.3	146.9	148.8	149.4	150.1	148.8	149.0	149.1	149.5	149.7	150.8	148.7
1999	147.8	149.5	150.5	150.9	151.5	152.3	152.6	153.0	154.0	153.9	154.9	156.2	152.3
2000	151.7	152.4	154.5	155.2	155.9	157.3	156.6	156.3	157.7	156.7	158.0	158.3	155.9
2001	154.1	153.7	154.4	154.8	154.8	154.6	152.8	153.0	153.6	153.2	153.1	153.8	153.8
2002	150.3	150.2	151.3	151.5	152.2	152.2	151.1	151.5	151.8	151.0	150.9	150.8	151.2
2003	148.1	147.8	148.6	149.3	150.8	151.4	150.6	150.5	151.1	150.8	151.1	150.8	150.1
Goods-producing													
1990	57.9	57.6	57.6	57.3	57.7	58.3	57.9	58.1	57.8	57.4	57.2	57.1	57.7
1991	55.5	54.6	54.8	55.4	54.6	55.5	55.7	56.0	55.9	55.3	55.0	54.5	55.2
1992	53.0	52.7	52.4	53.1	53.2	54.0	54.1	54.2	53.6	53.7	53.7	53.2	53.4
1993	52.3	52.3	52.3	52.8	53.1	53.9	54.4	54.2	54.2	53.9	53.8	54.1	53.4
1994	52.8	52.6	52.9	53.6	54.2	54.6	53.9	54.1	54.7	54.3	54.8	54.7	53.9
1995	54.7	54.5	54.9	55.1	55.3	56.0	56.3	56.1	55.8	55.7	55.4	55.5	55.4
1996	54.0	55.4	55.2	55.3	55.1	55.5	55.5	55.3	55.4	55.3	55.3	54.9	55.2
1997	54.0	53.9	54.0	54.4	55.1	55.9	55.5	55.6	55.1	55.4	55.1	55.0	54.9
1998	53.9	54.4	54.6	55.3	55.7	55.7	55.5	55.3	54.7	54.8	54.5	54.4	54.9
1999	54.2	54.6	54.7	54.6	54.7	55.3	55.3	55.8	55.7	56.0	56.2	56.4	55.3
2000	55.3	55.2	55.8	55.8	56.0	56.4	56.6	56.3	56.2	56.1	56.1	56.0	56.0
2001	54.9	54.6	54.8	55.0	54.5	54.7	54.3	53.9	53.3	52.8	52.7	52.7	54.0
2002	51.8	51.6	51.8	51.6	51.9	52.5	52.2	52.3	51.7	51.5	50.9	50.6	51.7
2003	50.1	49.8	49.6	49.7	50.1	50.5	50.4	49.9	49.6	49.4	49.0	48.7	49.7
Construction and mining													
1990	8.5	8.4	8.6	8.7	9.0	9.4	9.4	9.4	9.3	9.0	9.0	8.9	9.0
1991	8.1	7.8	7.9	8.0	8.1	8.3	8.3	8.4	8.3	8.1	7.9	7.6	8.1
1992	7.0	6.8	6.8	7.2	7.3	7.8	8.0	8.0	7.8	8.0	7.8	7.4	7.5
1993	6.9	6.9	6.8	7.4	7.6	7.9	8.4	8.4	8.4	8.4	8.1	8.1	7.8
1994	7.1	6.7	6.9	7.7	8.2	8.3	8.5	8.5	8.6	8.4	8.5	8.2	8.0
1995	7.7	7.1	7.6	8.0	8.1	8.4	8.6	8.5	8.4	8.3	8.2	7.8	8.1
1996	7.1	7.8	7.5	8.2	8.5	8.9	8.9	8.8	8.8	8.7	8.6	8.3	8.3
1997	7.9	7.8	7.9	8.4	8.7	9.2	9.0	9.0	8.8	8.9	8.8	8.7	8.6
1998	8.2	8.0	8.2	8.8	9.1	9.5	9.7	9.7	9.4	9.3	9.2	9.0	9.0
1999	8.7	8.8	9.0	9.2	9.6	10.1	10.3	10.4	10.1	10.0	10.0	10.0	9.7
2000	9.7	9.6	10.1	10.4	10.4	10.6	10.7	10.6	10.2	10.1	9.9	9.8	10.2
2001	9.5	9.4	9.7	10.0	10.2	10.6	10.7	10.7	10.4	10.3	10.2	10.1	10.2
2002	9.6	9.7	10.0	10.1	10.4	10.7	10.8	10.9	10.6	10.5	10.3	9.9	10.3
2003	9.7	9.5	9.8	10.2	10.6	10.9	11.0	10.9	10.7	10.7	10.5	10.4	10.4

Employment by Industry: Pennsylvania—*Continued*

(Numbers in thousands. Not seasonally adjusted.)

Industry	January	February	March	April	May	June	July	August	September	October	November	December	Annual Average
YORK—*Continued*													
Manufacturing													
1990	49.4	49.2	49.0	48.6	48.7	48.9	48.5	48.7	48.5	48.4	48.2	48.2	48.7
1991	47.4	46.8	46.9	47.4	46.5	47.2	47.4	47.6	47.6	47.2	47.1	46.9	47.2
1992	46.0	45.9	45.6	45.9	45.9	46.2	46.1	46.2	45.8	45.7	45.9	45.8	45.9
1993	45.4	45.4	45.5	45.4	45.5	46.0	46.0	45.8	45.8	45.5	45.7	46.0	45.7
1994	45.7	45.9	46.0	45.9	46.0	46.3	45.4	45.6	46.1	45.9	46.3	46.5	46.0
1995	47.0	47.4	47.3	47.1	47.2	47.6	47.7	47.6	47.4	47.4	47.2	47.7	47.4
1996	46.9	47.6	47.7	47.1	46.6	46.6	46.6	46.5	46.6	46.6	46.7	46.6	46.8
1997	46.1	46.1	46.1	46.0	46.4	46.7	46.5	46.6	46.3	46.5	46.3	46.3	46.3
1998	45.7	46.4	46.4	46.5	46.6	46.2	45.8	45.6	45.3	45.5	45.3	45.4	45.9
1999	45.5	45.8	45.7	45.4	45.1	45.2	45.0	45.4	45.6	46.0	46.2	46.4	45.6
2000	45.6	45.6	45.7	45.4	45.6	45.8	45.9	45.7	46.0	46.0	46.2	46.2	45.8
2001	45.4	45.2	45.1	45.0	44.3	44.1	43.6	43.2	42.9	42.5	42.5	42.6	43.9
2002	42.2	41.9	41.8	41.5	41.5	41.8	41.4	41.4	41.1	41.0	40.6	40.7	41.4
2003	40.4	40.3	39.8	39.5	39.5	39.6	39.4	39.0	38.9	38.7	38.5	38.3	39.3
Service-providing													
1990	95.5	95.7	96.0	95.6	96.9	96.6	95.9	97.2	97.4	97.3	98.4	98.9	96.8
1991	96.0	95.0	95.9	97.5	97.2	96.6	95.3	96.0	96.8	97.9	98.6	98.9	96.8
1992	97.1	96.9	97.8	99.1	99.7	99.1	98.0	98.3	99.5	100.6	101.4	101.5	99.1
1993	99.3	99.8	100.2	101.3	100.9	100.5	99.0	99.4	101.2	101.9	102.8	103.2	100.8
1994	99.9	100.2	101.4	101.8	102.8	102.6	100.2	101.0	103.1	104.0	104.9	105.3	102.3
1995	103.3	104.0	104.2	104.5	104.9	104.5	101.8	102.6	104.8	105.6	106.2	106.8	104.4
1996	101.7	104.3	105.0	105.5	106.7	105.4	103.7	104.9	107.2	108.6	109.7	110.1	106.1
1997	106.8	107.1	107.3	108.6	109.2	107.5	105.9	106.4	108.4	108.2	108.9	109.9	107.9
1998	107.9	108.2	108.8	110.0	110.3	109.4	106.6	107.2	110.5	111.4	111.9	113.1	109.6
1999	110.2	111.7	112.7	112.9	113.6	113.6	112.6	112.4	114.8	114.8	115.7	116.8	113.5
2000	113.2	114.3	115.7	116.6	117.6	117.7	115.3	115.0	118.0	117.6	119.2	119.5	116.6
2001	116.3	116.4	116.9	117.2	117.8	116.7	113.9	114.3	117.6	118.0	118.3	119.0	116.9
2002	116.0	116.4	117.3	117.4	118.1	116.9	114.8	114.6	117.2	116.8	117.5	117.5	116.7
2003	115.1	115.4	116.4	117.1	118.4	118.0	115.4	116.1	118.9	119.3	120.0	120.2	117.5
Trade, transportation, and utilities													
1990	33.3	33.1	33.1	32.7	33.3	33.3	33.4	33.8	33.6	33.6	34.5	34.8	33.5
1991	33.2	32.2	32.6	33.1	32.8	32.9	32.3	32.7	32.7	32.9	33.3	33.8	32.9
1992	32.8	32.2	32.3	32.4	33.0	33.3	33.0	33.1	33.1	33.3	33.8	33.8	33.0
1993	33.2	33.0	33.1	33.3	33.0	33.5	33.3	33.3	33.4	33.8	34.4	35.0	33.5
1994	33.4	33.2	33.5	32.9	33.8	34.0	32.9	33.2	33.5	34.0	34.7	35.0	33.7
1995	33.7	33.6	33.5	33.2	33.3	33.6	32.6	32.6	32.9	33.3	34.0	34.5	33.4
1996	32.2	32.5	33.0	32.5	32.4	32.5	32.4	32.7	32.9	33.7	34.7	35.2	33.1
1997	33.9	33.4	33.4	33.2	33.3	33.4	33.1	33.2	33.2	33.7	34.5	34.9	33.6
1998	34.1	33.4	33.3	33.7	33.7	33.9	34.0	34.1	34.2	34.9	35.4	36.0	34.2
1999	34.5	34.2	34.5	34.7	35.2	35.3	35.4	35.1	35.4	35.5	36.4	37.2	35.3
2000	35.2	35.2	35.4	35.7	35.9	36.3	36.2	36.2	36.5	36.3	37.4	37.7	36.2
2001	36.5	36.0	35.9	36.0	36.4	36.0	35.6	35.7	36.1	36.7	37.1	37.6	36.3
2002	36.7	36.3	36.5	36.5	37.0	37.0	36.8	36.9	37.0	36.9	37.6	37.9	36.9
2003	36.8	36.3	36.4	36.8	37.2	37.4	36.7	36.8	37.0	37.2	37.9	38.2	37.1
Wholesale trade													
1990	6.4	6.5	6.5	6.4	6.5	6.5	6.5	6.6	6.5	6.5	6.5	6.5	6.5
1991	6.4	6.2	6.3	6.4	6.3	6.5	6.4	6.4	6.3	6.1	6.3	6.3	6.3
1992	6.4	6.3	6.3	6.3	6.4	6.6	6.3	6.3	6.3	6.3	6.3	6.3	6.3
1993	6.4	6.4	6.4	6.3	6.3	6.3	6.3	6.3	6.2	6.3	6.3	6.3	6.3
1994	6.1	6.1	6.1	6.2	6.2	6.3	6.3	6.4	6.3	6.4	6.4	6.4	6.3
1995	6.4	6.4	6.5	6.5	6.5	6.6	6.6	6.6	6.6	6.6	6.5	6.5	6.5
1996	6.4	6.4	6.5	6.5	6.5	6.5	6.5	6.5	6.4	6.5	6.4	6.4	6.5
1997	6.3	6.4	6.4	6.4	6.4	6.4	6.3	6.3	6.2	6.1	6.3	6.3	6.3
1998	6.4	6.3	6.2	6.3	6.4	6.4	6.3	6.3	6.2	6.3	6.2	6.2	6.3
1999	6.3	6.2	6.4	6.4	6.5	6.5	6.5	6.5	6.4	6.5	6.6	6.6	6.5
2000	6.4	6.5	6.5	6.5	6.3	6.3	6.3	6.3	6.3	6.3	6.4	6.4	6.4
2001	6.4	6.4	6.4	6.5	6.5	6.5	6.6	6.5	6.5	6.6	6.5	6.6	6.5
2002	6.6	6.6	6.6	6.7	6.8	6.8	7.0	6.9	7.0	6.8	6.8	6.7	6.8
2003	6.9	6.9	7.0	7.0	7.1	7.1	7.1	7.1	7.1	7.0	7.0	7.0	7.0
Retail trade													
1990	20.2	19.9	19.8	19.7	20.1	20.1	20.4	20.6	20.3	20.3	21.2	21.6	20.4
1991	20.2	19.5	19.7	20.0	19.8	19.9	19.6	19.9	19.8	20.1	20.4	20.8	20.0
1992	19.7	19.3	19.3	19.4	19.7	19.6	19.8	19.8	19.6	19.8	20.2	20.4	19.7
1993	19.4	19.2	19.2	19.4	19.3	19.6	19.6	19.6	19.6	19.6	20.2	20.8	19.6
1994	19.7	19.5	19.7	19.7	20.0	20.0	19.8	19.9	20.0	20.4	21.1	21.5	20.1
1995	20.6	20.4	20.1	20.1	20.2	20.4	20.1	20.1	20.1	20.3	21.2	21.6	20.4
1996	20.0	20.1	20.3	20.2	20.2	20.3	20.1	20.1	20.2	20.8	21.5	22.0	20.5
1997	21.0	20.3	20.3	20.2	20.3	20.3	20.5	20.6	20.4	20.7	21.4	21.9	20.7
1998	20.9	20.3	20.4	20.6	20.7	20.9	20.6	20.6	20.7	21.2	21.8	22.5	20.9
1999	21.1	20.9	21.1	21.2	21.5	21.7	21.9	22.0	21.9	21.7	22.5	23.3	21.7
2000	21.7	21.6	21.7	21.7	22.1	22.4	22.8	22.8	22.6	22.3	23.2	23.6	22.4
2001	22.6	22.0	22.0	22.0	22.4	22.3	22.0	22.1	22.2	22.4	23.0	23.5	22.4
2002	22.5	22.0	22.1	22.0	22.5	22.5	22.5	22.6	22.4	22.4	23.1	23.6	22.5
2003	22.4	21.9	21.9	22.2	22.5	22.7	22.4	22.4	22.2	22.5	23.2	23.5	22.5

Employment by Industry: Pennsylvania—*Continued*

(Numbers in thousands. Not seasonally adjusted.)

Industry	January	February	March	April	May	June	July	August	September	October	November	December	Annual Average
YORK—*Continued*													
Transportation and utilities													
1990	6.7	6.7	6.8	6.6	6.7	6.7	6.5	6.6	6.8	6.8	6.8	6.7	6.7
1991	6.6	6.5	6.6	6.7	6.7	6.5	6.3	6.4	6.6	6.7	6.6	6.7	6.6
1992	6.7	6.6	6.7	6.7	6.9	7.1	6.9	7.0	7.2	7.2	7.3	7.1	7.0
1993	7.4	7.4	7.5	7.6	7.4	7.6	7.4	7.4	7.6	7.9	7.9	7.9	7.6
1994	7.6	7.6	7.7	7.0	7.6	7.7	6.8	6.9	7.2	7.2	7.2	7.1	7.3
1995	6.7	6.8	6.9	6.6	6.6	6.6	5.9	5.9	6.2	6.4	6.3	6.4	6.4
1996	5.8	6.0	6.2	5.8	5.7	5.7	5.8	6.1	6.3	6.4	6.8	6.8	6.1
1997	6.6	6.7	6.7	6.6	6.6	6.7	6.3	6.3	6.6	6.9	6.8	6.7	6.6
1998	6.8	6.8	6.7	6.8	6.6	6.6	7.1	7.2	7.3	7.4	7.4	7.3	7.0
1999	7.1	7.1	7.0	7.1	7.2	7.1	7.0	6.6	7.1	7.3	7.3	7.3	7.1
2000	7.1	7.1	7.2	7.5	7.5	7.6	7.1	7.1	7.6	7.7	7.8	7.7	7.4
2001	7.5	7.6	7.5	7.5	7.5	7.2	7.0	7.1	7.4	7.7	7.6	7.5	7.4
2002	7.6	7.7	7.8	7.8	7.7	7.7	7.3	7.4	7.6	7.7	7.7	7.6	7.6
2003	7.5	7.5	7.5	7.6	7.6	7.6	7.2	7.3	7.7	7.7	7.7	7.7	7.6
Information													
1990	2.0	2.0	2.0	2.0	2.0	2.0	2.1	2.1	2.1	1.9	1.9	1.9	2.0
1991	1.8	1.8	1.8	1.8	1.8	1.8	1.8	1.8	1.8	1.8	1.8	1.8	1.8
1992	1.8	1.8	1.8	1.8	1.8	1.8	1.8	1.8	1.8	1.8	1.8	1.8	1.8
1993	1.8	1.8	1.8	1.9	1.9	1.9	1.8	1.8	1.8	1.8	1.7	1.7	1.8
1994	1.7	1.7	1.7	1.7	1.7	1.8	1.7	1.7	1.7	1.8	1.8	1.8	1.7
1995	1.8	1.8	1.8	1.9	1.9	2.0	2.0	2.0	2.0	2.0	2.0	2.0	1.9
1996	1.9	2.0	2.1	2.0	2.0	2.0	2.0	2.0	2.1	2.2	2.2	2.2	2.1
1997	2.0	2.0	2.0	2.1	2.2	2.2	2.2	2.2	2.1	2.1	2.2	2.2	2.1
1998	2.2	2.2	2.2	2.3	2.4	2.4	2.4	2.5	2.4	2.4	2.4	2.4	2.4
1999	2.5	2.6	2.6	2.6	2.6	2.6	2.6	2.6	2.6	2.6	2.6	2.6	2.6
2000	2.7	2.6	2.6	2.6	2.6	2.6	2.6	2.6	2.6	2.6	2.6	2.6	2.6
2001	2.6	2.6	2.6	2.5	2.4	2.4	2.4	2.3	2.3	2.2	2.2	2.2	2.4
2002	2.0	2.0	2.1	2.0	2.0	2.0	2.1	2.1	2.0	2.0	2.0	2.0	2.0
2003	2.0	1.9	2.0	1.9	1.9	2.0	2.0	2.0	2.0	2.0	2.0	2.0	2.0
Financial activities													
1990	5.1	5.1	5.1	5.1	5.1	5.2	5.1	5.2	5.1	5.1	5.1	5.1	5.1
1991	5.0	5.0	5.0	5.2	5.1	5.2	5.3	5.3	5.2	5.1	5.2	5.2	5.2
1992	5.2	5.2	5.2	5.3	5.4	5.4	5.4	5.3	5.3	5.3	5.3	5.4	5.3
1993	5.4	5.4	5.4	5.4	5.4	5.6	5.3	5.3	5.2	5.2	5.2	5.2	5.3
1994	5.2	5.3	5.3	5.1	5.1	5.2	5.4	5.4	5.4	5.4	5.3	5.3	5.3
1995	5.3	5.3	5.3	5.3	5.3	5.5	5.5	5.5	5.5	5.4	5.3	5.4	5.4
1996	5.4	5.5	5.4	5.5	5.5	5.5	5.5	5.5	5.4	5.4	5.5	5.5	5.5
1997	5.4	5.4	5.4	5.5	5.5	5.5	5.6	5.5	5.4	5.4	5.4	5.4	5.5
1998	5.4	5.3	5.4	5.4	5.5	5.6	5.5	5.5	5.3	5.4	5.4	5.4	5.4
1999	5.6	5.5	5.6	5.5	5.4	5.5	5.6	5.5	5.5	5.5	5.5	5.4	5.5
2000	5.3	5.3	5.2	5.3	5.3	5.4	5.4	5.4	5.4	5.3	5.4	5.4	5.3
2001	5.4	5.4	5.4	5.5	5.6	5.7	5.5	5.5	5.5	5.4	5.4	5.4	5.5
2002	5.4	5.4	5.4	5.4	5.4	5.5	5.4	5.4	5.4	5.3	5.3	5.4	5.4
2003	5.4	5.4	5.5	5.5	5.6	5.7	5.7	5.7	5.6	5.6	5.6	5.7	5.6
Professional and business services													
1990	9.6	9.7	9.8	9.5	9.5	9.6	9.6	10.0	10.0	10.2	10.2	10.1	9.8
1991	10.2	10.2	10.5	10.7	10.7	10.7	10.8	10.9	11.3	11.4	11.4	11.3	10.8
1992	11.6	11.6	12.0	12.2	12.1	11.8	11.8	12.1	12.1	12.2	12.2	12.1	12.0
1993	12.0	12.2	12.5	12.3	12.3	12.2	12.3	12.6	12.8	13.1	13.3	13.1	12.6
1994	12.2	12.3	12.7	12.9	12.7	12.8	12.5	12.9	13.0	13.2	13.3	13.4	12.8
1995	13.3	13.4	13.5	14.0	13.9	14.1	13.6	14.2	13.9	14.2	14.1	13.9	13.8
1996	12.7	13.1	13.0	13.5	13.5	13.6	13.5	13.7	13.7	14.5	14.3	14.0	13.6
1997	13.8	13.8	13.9	14.4	14.6	14.6	14.1	14.3	14.4	13.7	13.6	13.4	14.1
1998	13.9	13.9	14.2	14.9	14.8	15.0	14.4	14.6	14.5	14.5	14.5	14.8	14.5
1999	14.3	14.7	14.8	15.1	15.0	15.2	15.3	15.1	14.9	14.9	15.1	15.0	15.0
2000	15.2	15.7	16.2	16.3	16.3	16.5	16.3	16.2	16.4	16.4	16.4	16.2	16.2
2001	15.6	15.4	15.5	15.4	15.1	15.0	14.5	14.7	14.6	14.3	13.8	13.4	14.8
2002	13.2	13.0	13.0	13.1	13.1	12.9	12.5	12.8	12.6	12.8	12.6	12.3	12.8
2003	12.1	12.1	12.3	12.4	12.5	12.5	12.5	12.8	12.8	13.1	12.9	12.8	12.6
Educational and health services													
1990	12.9	13.1	13.1	13.2	13.2	13.0	12.9	13.0	13.5	13.6	13.7	13.8	13.3
1991	13.4	13.5	13.7	14.0	13.8	13.6	13.5	13.6	13.8	13.9	14.0	13.9	13.7
1992	13.8	14.0	14.2	14.3	14.4	14.2	14.3	14.2	14.4	14.8	15.0	15.1	14.4
1993	14.7	14.9	15.0	15.3	15.1	14.7	14.7	14.7	15.2	15.4	15.5	15.4	15.1
1994	15.2	15.4	15.4	16.1	15.9	15.4	15.5	15.5	16.1	16.4	16.4	16.4	15.8
1995	16.2	16.6	16.6	16.6	16.6	16.2	15.9	16.0	16.5	17.0	17.0	17.0	16.5
1996	16.7	17.2	17.4	17.3	17.2	16.6	16.4	16.8	17.1	17.4	17.6	17.6	17.1
1997	16.8	17.1	17.1	17.7	17.4	16.8	16.7	16.8	17.2	17.7	17.9	18.3	17.3
1998	17.4	18.1	18.2	17.9	17.6	17.4	17.0	16.9	17.6	17.8	18.0	18.2	17.7
1999	17.5	18.4	18.6	18.5	18.1	17.6	17.7	17.8	18.4	18.6	18.7	18.7	18.2
2000	17.8	18.7	18.8	18.8	18.7	18.4	18.2	18.1	18.9	19.0	19.2	19.5	18.7
2001	18.6	19.4	19.4	19.6	19.4	19.1	19.2	19.3	19.8	20.1	20.3	20.7	19.6
2002	20.0	20.7	20.9	20.9	20.6	20.0	19.9	20.0	20.7	20.8	21.0	21.3	20.6
2003	20.6	21.3	21.4	21.5	21.3	20.7	20.8	20.9	21.5	21.7	21.9	21.7	21.3

Employment by Industry: Pennsylvania—*Continued*

(Numbers in thousands. Not seasonally adjusted.)

Industry	January	February	March	April	May	June	July	August	September	October	November	December	Annual Average
YORK—*Continued*													
Leisure and hospitality													
1990	10.8	10.5	10.5	10.4	10.7	10.9	10.8	11.1	11.1	10.4	10.3	10.4	10.7
1991	10.2	9.9	9.9	10.3	10.4	10.6	10.5	10.6	10.8	10.2	10.1	10.1	10.3
1992	9.9	9.8	9.9	10.5	10.7	11.0	10.8	10.9	11.1	10.4	10.3	10.5	10.5
1993	9.9	9.9	9.6	10.2	10.4	10.6	10.4	10.5	10.8	10.0	10.0	10.0	10.2
1994	10.0	9.9	10.1	10.2	10.6	10.9	11.1	11.1	11.2	10.4	10.3	10.4	10.5
1995	10.4	10.3	10.4	10.4	10.7	11.1	11.1	11.1	11.4	10.5	10.4	10.8	10.7
1996	10.3	10.6	10.7	11.1	11.5	11.7	11.6	11.8	12.0	11.3	11.3	11.3	11.3
1997	11.2	11.3	11.4	11.7	12.2	12.4	12.2	12.4	12.6	11.6	11.4	11.6	11.8
1998	11.4	11.6	11.6	11.8	12.3	12.6	12.6	12.6	13.0	12.4	12.2	12.2	12.2
1999	12.1	12.3	12.4	12.6	13.1	13.3	13.3	13.6	13.8	13.2	12.9	13.1	13.0
2000	12.7	12.3	13.0	13.0	13.4	13.9	13.7	13.7	13.9	13.3	13.2	13.4	13.3
2001	13.0	12.9	13.1	13.3	13.8	14.1	13.9	14.0	14.4	14.1	13.9	14.0	13.7
2002	13.7	13.7	13.9	14.4	14.5	14.5	14.5	14.4	14.7	14.0	13.9	13.6	14.2
2003	13.7	13.6	13.8	14.0	14.7	14.9	14.8	14.7	14.9	14.1	14.0	13.9	14.3
Other services													
1990	6.8	6.9	6.9	6.9	7.0	7.1	7.1	7.1	7.0	7.0	7.1	7.0	7.0
1991	6.9	6.8	6.9	7.0	7.0	7.0	6.9	6.9	6.8	7.1	7.0	7.0	6.9
1992	6.9	6.8	6.9	7.0	7.0	7.1	7.0	7.0	6.9	7.2	7.2	7.1	7.0
1993	7.0	7.0	7.1	7.1	7.1	7.2	7.1	7.2	7.2	7.2	7.2	7.3	7.1
1994	7.0	7.0	7.1	7.3	7.4	7.3	7.1	7.1	7.2	7.2	7.3	7.3	7.2
1995	7.2	7.3	7.4	7.4	7.5	7.5	7.5	7.6	7.5	7.5	7.5	7.5	7.5
1996	7.3	7.6	7.5	7.6	7.7	7.6	7.5	7.6	7.6	7.3	7.2	7.4	7.5
1997	7.2	7.3	7.3	7.4	7.4	7.4	7.6	7.6	7.5	7.4	7.4	7.5	7.4
1998	7.3	7.4	7.4	7.5	7.4	7.5	7.4	7.5	7.4	7.3	7.3	7.4	7.4
1999	7.1	7.2	7.3	7.3	7.4	7.5	7.4	7.5	7.7	7.6	7.5	7.8	7.4
2000	7.5	7.4	7.5	7.7	7.7	7.8	7.6	7.8	7.8	7.7	7.7	7.5	7.6
2001	7.5	7.4	7.7	7.5	7.6	7.6	7.4	7.6	7.6	7.6	7.7	7.8	7.6
2002	7.5	7.5	7.7	7.6	7.7	7.8	7.7	7.6	7.7	7.7	7.6	7.7	7.7
2003	7.4	7.4	7.6	7.5	7.5	7.7	7.7	7.7	7.7	7.7	7.8	7.8	7.6
Government													
1990	15.0	15.3	15.5	15.8	16.1	15.5	14.9	14.9	15.0	15.5	15.6	15.8	15.4
1991	15.3	15.6	15.5	15.4	15.6	14.8	14.2	14.2	14.4	15.5	15.8	15.8	15.2
1992	15.1	15.5	15.5	15.6	15.3	14.5	13.9	13.9	14.8	15.6	15.8	15.7	15.1
1993	15.3	15.6	15.7	15.8	15.7	14.8	14.1	14.0	14.8	15.4	15.5	15.5	15.2
1994	15.2	15.4	15.6	15.6	15.6	15.2	14.0	14.1	15.0	15.6	15.8	15.7	15.2
1995	15.4	15.7	15.7	15.7	15.7	14.5	13.6	13.6	15.1	15.7	15.9	15.7	15.2
1996	15.2	15.8	15.9	16.0	16.9	15.9	14.8	14.8	16.4	16.8	16.9	16.9	16.0
1997	16.5	16.8	16.8	16.6	16.6	15.2	14.4	14.4	16.0	16.6	16.5	16.6	16.1
1998	16.2	16.3	16.5	16.5	16.6	15.0	13.3	13.5	16.1	16.7	16.7	16.7	15.8
1999	16.6	16.8	16.9	16.6	16.8	16.6	15.3	15.2	16.5	16.9	17.0	17.0	16.5
2000	16.8	17.1	17.0	17.2	17.7	16.8	15.3	15.0	16.5	17.0	17.3	17.2	16.7
2001	17.1	17.3	17.3	17.4	17.5	16.8	15.4	15.2	17.3	17.6	17.9	17.9	17.1
2002	17.5	17.8	17.8	17.5	17.8	17.2	15.9	15.4	17.1	17.3	17.5	17.3	17.2
2003	17.1	17.4	17.4	17.5	17.7	17.1	15.2	15.5	17.4	17.9	17.9	18.1	17.2
Federal government													
1990	4.5	4.5	4.6	4.7	4.9	4.7	4.6	4.4	4.2	4.1	4.1	4.2	4.5
1991	4.2	4.2	4.2	4.1	4.1	4.1	4.1	4.2	4.2	4.2	4.2	4.3	4.2
1992	4.0	4.1	4.1	4.0	4.0	4.0	4.0	4.0	4.0	4.0	4.0	4.0	4.0
1993	4.0	4.0	4.0	4.0	3.9	3.9	3.9	3.8	3.8	3.6	3.5	3.6	3.8
1994	3.6	3.6	3.6	3.5	3.5	3.5	3.5	3.5	3.5	3.5	3.5	3.5	3.5
1995	3.5	3.4	3.4	3.4	3.4	3.4	3.4	3.4	3.4	3.4	3.4	3.4	3.4
1996	3.4	3.4	3.4	3.5	4.3	4.3	4.2	4.2	4.2	4.2	4.2	4.2	4.0
1997	4.2	4.2	4.2	4.1	4.0	4.0	3.9	3.9	3.8	3.8	3.7	3.8	4.0
1998	3.8	3.8	3.8	3.8	3.8	3.8	3.8	3.8	3.8	3.8	3.8	3.9	3.8
1999	3.8	3.8	3.8	3.7	3.8	3.8	3.8	3.8	3.7	3.7	3.7	3.7	3.8
2000	3.6	3.7	3.7	3.8	4.2	3.7	3.7	3.6	3.5	3.6	3.7	3.7	3.7
2001	3.7	3.6	3.6	3.7	3.7	3.7	3.7	3.7	3.7	3.7	3.8	3.8	3.7
2002	3.8	3.8	3.8	3.7	3.7	3.6	3.6	3.6	3.5	3.2	3.3	3.2	3.6
2003	3.2	3.3	3.3	3.3	3.3	3.4	3.4	3.5	3.5	3.6	3.7	3.7	3.4
State government													
1990	1.0	1.1	1.1	1.1	1.1	1.1	1.1	1.1	1.1	1.1	1.1	1.1	1.1
1991	1.0	1.0	0.9	1.0	0.9	0.8	0.9	0.8	0.9	1.0	1.0	0.9	0.9
1992	0.9	1.0	1.0	1.1	1.0	0.9	0.9	0.9	1.0	1.1	1.1	1.1	1.0
1993	1.0	1.1	1.1	1.1	1.0	0.9	1.0	0.9	1.1	1.1	1.1	1.1	1.0
1994	1.0	1.1	1.1	1.1	1.0	1.0	1.0	1.0	1.0	1.1	1.1	1.1	1.1
1995	1.0	1.1	1.1	1.1	1.0	1.0	1.0	1.0	1.0	1.1	1.1	1.0	1.0
1996	0.9	1.1	1.1	1.1	1.0	1.0	1.0	1.0	1.1	1.1	1.1	1.1	1.1
1997	1.0	1.0	1.0	1.0	0.9	0.9	1.0	1.0	1.1	1.1	1.1	1.1	1.0
1998	1.0	1.0	1.1	1.0	1.0	0.9	1.0	1.0	1.0	1.1	1.1	1.0	1.0
1999	1.0	1.0	1.0	1.0	1.0	1.0	0.9	1.0	0.9	1.0	1.0	1.0	1.0
2000	1.0	1.0	1.0	1.0	1.0	1.0	1.0	1.0	1.1	1.1	1.1	1.0	1.0
2001	1.0	1.0	1.0	1.0	1.0	1.0	1.0	1.0	1.1	1.1	1.1	1.1	1.0
2002	1.0	1.0	1.0	1.0	1.0	1.0	1.0	1.0	1.0	1.1	1.1	1.1	1.0
2003	1.0	1.1	1.1	1.1	1.1	1.0	1.0	1.0	1.1	1.1	1.0	1.1	1.1

Employment by Industry: Pennsylvania—*Continued*

(Numbers in thousands. Not seasonally adjusted.)

Industry	January	February	March	April	May	June	July	August	September	October	November	December	Annual Average
YORK—*Continued*													
Local government													
1990	9.5	9.7	9.8	10.0	10.1	9.7	9.2	9.4	9.7	10.3	10.4	10.5	9.9
1991	10.1	10.4	10.4	10.3	10.6	9.9	9.2	9.2	9.3	10.3	10.6	10.6	10.1
1992	10.2	10.4	10.4	10.5	10.3	9.6	9.0	9.0	9.8	10.5	10.7	10.6	10.1
1993	10.3	10.5	10.6	10.7	10.8	10.0	9.2	9.3	9.9	10.7	10.9	10.8	10.3
1994	10.6	10.7	10.9	11.0	11.1	10.7	9.5	9.6	10.5	11.0	11.2	11.1	10.7
1995	10.9	11.2	11.2	11.2	11.3	10.1	9.2	9.2	10.7	11.2	11.4	11.3	10.7
1996	10.9	11.3	11.4	11.4	11.6	10.6	9.6	9.6	11.1	11.5	11.6	11.6	11.0
1997	11.3	11.6	11.6	11.5	11.7	10.3	9.5	9.5	11.1	11.7	11.7	11.7	11.1
1998	11.4	11.5	11.6	11.7	11.8	10.3	8.5	8.7	11.3	11.8	11.8	11.8	11.0
1999	11.8	12.0	12.1	11.9	12.0	11.8	10.6	10.4	11.9	12.2	12.3	12.3	11.8
2000	12.2	12.4	12.3	12.4	12.5	12.1	10.6	10.4	11.9	12.3	12.5	12.5	12.0
2001	12.4	12.7	12.7	12.7	12.8	12.1	10.7	10.5	12.5	12.8	13.0	13.0	12.3
2002	12.7	13.0	13.0	12.8	13.1	12.6	11.3	10.8	12.6	13.0	13.1	13.0	12.6
2003	12.9	13.0	13.0	13.1	13.3	12.7	10.8	11.0	12.8	13.2	13.2	13.3	12.7

Average Weekly Hours by Industry: Pennsylvania

(Not seasonally adjusted.)

Industry	January	February	March	April	May	June	July	August	September	October	November	December	Annual Average
STATEWIDE													
Manufacturing													
2001	40.6	40.3	40.6	39.7	40.3	40.3	40.2	40.3	40.6	40.2	40.6	40.6	40.4
2002	39.6	39.9	40.5	40.3	40.5	40.6	40.4	40.7	40.7	40.5	40.4	39.8	40.3
2003	39.7	39.3	40.0	39.6	40.0	40.1	39.6	40.0	40.2	40.2	40.7	40.7	40.0
ALLENTOWN-BETHLEHEM													
Manufacturing													
2001	42.0	41.8	41.7	40.8	41.2	41.0	41.0	41.7	41.3	41.5	41.8	41.7	41.4
2002	41.6	42.2	42.3	41.1	41.5	40.1	40.0	40.2	39.8	40.0	39.3	39.3	40.7
2003	39.5	39.3	39.3	38.6	39.1	39.2	39.2	39.7	40.1	39.9	39.4	39.6	39.4
ERIE													
Manufacturing													
2001	42.4	42.6	43.3	41.7	42.2	42.8	43.0	42.2	43.0	43.4	44.1	43.4	42.8
2002	42.6	42.5	42.5	42.5	43.4	42.6	42.1	45.0	45.0	43.9	42.4	43.3	43.2
2003	41.6	42.2	43.2	41.7	42.7	42.8	43.5	42.4	44.2	43.9	44.2	44.8	43.1
HARRISBURG													
Manufacturing													
2001	39.2	38.2	38.1	38.9	39.0	38.9	39.2	39.7	39.5	39.6	39.0	38.5	39.0
2002	37.2	36.8	38.5	37.9	38.3	39.2	40.0	39.7	37.8	37.4	37.1	37.2	38.1
2003	37.6	37.1	38.1	37.9	38.1	38.4	38.7	39.4	38.8	38.8	39.5	39.4	38.5
LANCASTER													
Manufacturing													
2001	38.7	38.0	37.7	37.7	38.3	38.5	37.3	37.8	37.2	37.3	38.0	38.2	37.9
2002	37.1	38.1	38.6	38.0	38.0	38.3	38.4	38.9	37.7	38.2	38.8	38.7	38.2
2003	38.7	38.7	39.4	38.9	39.2	38.9	39.8	40.0	40.1	40.0	40.2	40.9	39.6
PHILADELPHIA PMSA													
Manufacturing													
2001	41.5	40.9	41.9	41.0	41.4	41.6	41.1	40.7	41.5	41.4	41.8	42.0	41.4
2002	40.9	40.6	41.0	41.7	41.8	42.1	41.7	41.6	41.7	41.7	41.0	40.9	41.4
2003	40.4	39.9	41.0	40.4	40.4	40.8	40.7	40.4	40.6	40.5	41.2	41.3	40.6
PITTSBURGH													
Manufacturing													
2001	40.6	40.6	40.8	40.3	39.3	39.4	39.9	39.4	40.1	40.0	40.0	39.5	40.0
2002	39.1	39.8	40.7	40.2	40.2	40.1	40.1	40.8	41.0	40.7	40.4	39.8	40.2
2003	39.1	38.8	39.3	40.1	40.5	40.8	39.7	39.8	40.6	41.2	41.3	42.0	40.3
READING													
Manufacturing													
2001	42.3	40.9	40.6	38.9	40.5	40.7	40.3	41.2	40.9	39.9	40.6	40.4	40.6
2002	38.7	38.3	38.8	39.5	39.6	40.3	39.4	39.6	40.4	39.0	39.9	40.3	39.5
2003	39.7	39.9	40.5	39.9	40.6	40.9	39.9	40.0	39.9	39.9	40.4	40.8	40.2
SCRANTON–WILKES-BARRE													
Manufacturing													
2001	38.8	39.0	39.6	39.3	39.4	40.0	40.0	39.9	40.5	40.0	40.0	39.7	39.7
2002	38.6	39.9	39.5	39.9	40.2	39.8	39.8	39.8	39.9	39.7	39.7	39.5	39.7
2003	39.5	39.7	40.3	40.4	40.8	40.6	38.8	40.4	39.7	39.8	40.3	40.1	40.0
YORK													
Manufacturing													
2001	41.0	41.5	41.9	39.6	41.4	41.7	42.0	41.8	41.9	41.3	42.4	42.6	41.6
2002	42.0	42.0	41.7	41.0	41.7	41.8	41.3	41.3	41.6	41.4	41.6	39.5	41.4
2003	40.5	39.7	41.5	40.2	40.7	41.2	40.8	41.6	41.8	41.2	43.3	42.9	41.3

Average Hourly Earnings by Industry: Pennsylvania

(Dollars, not seasonally adjusted.)

Industry	January	February	March	April	May	June	July	August	September	October	November	December	Annual Average
STATEWIDE													
Manufacturing													
2001	14.26	14.22	14.22	14.23	14.33	14.31	14.41	14.47	14.43	14.43	14.52	14.61	14.37
2002	14.58	14.61	14.62	14.65	14.63	14.66	14.80	14.79	14.91	14.89	14.87	14.99	14.75
2003	14.91	14.97	15.00	14.96	14.93	14.96	14.96	14.97	15.01	14.97	15.04	15.05	14.98
ALLENTOWN-BETHLEHEM													
Manufacturing													
2001	14.58	14.48	14.52	14.34	14.63	14.45	14.73	14.95	14.77	14.85	14.85	15.23	14.69
2002	15.13	15.15	15.16	15.01	15.05	14.97	15.02	15.13	15.10	15.02	15.05	14.95	15.06
2003	14.86	14.97	14.88	14.94	14.65	14.73	14.79	14.99	14.87	14.94	14.97	14.97	14.88
ERIE													
Manufacturing													
2001	15.45	15.62	15.64	15.36	15.60	15.52	15.44	15.61	15.70	15.58	15.72	15.63	15.57
2002	15.43	15.40	15.39	15.24	15.22	15.35	15.29	15.42	15.64	15.55	15.51	15.46	15.41
2003	15.41	15.54	15.68	15.79	15.73	15.60	15.53	15.52	15.66	15.77	15.89	15.87	15.67
HARRISBURG													
Manufacturing													
2001	14.73	14.28	14.40	14.14	14.42	14.40	14.39	14.60	14.26	14.34	14.45	14.42	14.40
2002	14.52	14.60	14.51	14.66	14.41	14.53	14.90	15.02	15.06	15.06	15.13	15.17	14.80
2003	14.89	14.95	15.03	14.81	14.84	15.14	15.09	15.33	15.34	15.22	15.29	15.25	15.11
LANCASTER													
Manufacturing													
2001	14.19	14.14	13.97	14.28	14.17	14.25	14.50	14.51	14.48	14.54	14.84	14.91	14.39
2002	14.49	14.47	14.63	14.64	14.71	14.73	14.74	14.69	14.72	14.78	14.84	14.94	14.70
2003	14.76	14.69	14.82	14.67	14.88	14.88	14.77	14.95	15.11	15.25	15.37	15.43	14.96
PHILADELPHIA PMSA													
Manufacturing													
2001	15.75	15.78	15.89	15.85	15.91	15.87	16.00	15.98	15.90	16.01	16.06	16.20	15.93
2002	16.14	16.15	16.05	15.96	16.09	16.01	16.08	15.90	16.02	15.92	15.88	16.21	16.03
2003	16.12	16.15	16.19	16.02	15.86	15.88	16.02	15.96	16.00	15.94	16.02	16.06	16.02
PITTSBURGH													
Manufacturing													
2001	15.17	15.25	15.30	15.23	15.31	15.34	15.30	15.44	15.56	15.35	15.47	15.51	15.35
2002	15.52	15.69	15.75	15.82	15.77	15.90	15.89	15.95	16.06	16.09	16.06	16.12	15.88
2003	15.95	16.00	16.06	16.24	16.29	16.19	16.24	16.21	16.24	16.26	16.31	16.28	16.19
READING													
Manufacturing													
2001	14.99	14.85	14.72	14.71	14.70	14.72	14.78	14.85	14.77	14.73	14.77	15.06	14.80
2002	15.13	14.84	14.97	14.87	15.13	15.18	14.79	15.13	14.89	14.99	14.92	14.91	14.98
2003	14.97	15.13	15.24	15.20	15.31	15.22	15.30	15.56	15.60	15.60	15.78	16.02	15.41
SCRANTON–WILKES-BARRE													
Manufacturing													
2001	12.56	12.52	12.48	12.62	12.71	12.80	12.76	12.72	12.82	12.96	13.04	13.11	12.75
2002	13.19	13.40	13.39	13.44	13.37	13.45	13.58	13.78	13.62	13.45	13.58	13.67	13.49
2003	13.65	13.64	13.73	13.62	13.66	13.55	13.72	13.64	13.85	13.65	14.03	14.04	13.73
YORK													
Manufacturing													
2001	14.96	14.96	15.03	15.03	15.02	15.06	15.12	15.14	15.14	15.04	15.05	14.93	15.04
2002	15.10	15.14	15.31	15.09	15.06	15.16	15.28	15.21	15.37	15.29	15.23	15.07	15.19
2003	14.98	14.99	14.99	14.78	14.89	14.95	16.12	15.51	15.73	15.58	16.30	16.40	15.44

Average Weekly Earnings by Industry: Pennsylvania

(Dollars, not seasonally adjusted.)

Industry	January	February	March	April	May	June	July	August	September	October	November	December	Annual Average
STATEWIDE													
Manufacturing													
2001	578.96	573.07	577.33	564.93	577.50	576.69	579.28	583.14	585.86	580.09	589.51	593.17	580.55
2002	577.37	582.94	592.11	590.40	592.52	595.20	597.92	601.95	606.84	603.05	600.75	596.60	594.43
2003	591.93	588.32	600.00	592.42	597.20	599.90	592.42	598.80	603.40	601.79	612.13	612.54	599.20
ALLENTOWN-BETHLEHEM													
Manufacturing													
2001	612.36	605.26	605.48	585.07	602.76	592.45	603.93	623.42	610.00	616.28	620.73	635.09	608.17
2002	629.41	639.33	641.27	616.91	624.58	600.30	600.80	608.23	600.98	600.80	591.47	587.54	612.94
2003	586.97	588.32	584.78	576.68	572.82	577.42	579.77	595.10	596.29	596.11	589.82	592.81	586.27
ERIE													
Manufacturing													
2001	655.08	665.41	677.21	640.51	658.32	664.26	663.92	658.74	675.10	676.17	693.25	678.34	666.40
2002	657.32	654.50	654.08	647.70	660.55	653.91	643.71	693.90	703.80	682.65	657.62	669.42	665.71
2003	641.06	655.79	677.38	658.44	671.67	667.68	675.56	658.05	692.17	692.30	702.34	710.98	675.38
HARRISBURG													
Manufacturing													
2001	577.42	545.50	548.64	550.05	562.38	560.16	564.09	579.62	563.27	567.86	563.55	555.17	561.60
2002	540.14	537.28	558.64	555.61	551.90	569.58	596.00	596.29	569.27	563.24	561.32	564.32	563.88
2003	559.86	554.65	572.64	561.30	565.40	581.38	583.98	604.00	595.19	590.54	603.96	600.85	581.74
LANCASTER													
Manufacturing													
2001	549.15	537.32	526.67	538.36	542.71	548.63	540.85	548.48	538.66	542.34	563.92	569.56	545.38
2002	537.58	551.31	564.72	556.32	558.98	564.16	566.02	571.44	554.94	564.60	575.79	578.18	561.54
2003	571.21	568.50	583.91	570.66	583.30	578.83	587.85	598.00	605.91	610.00	617.87	631.09	592.42
PHILADELPHIA PMSA													
Manufacturing													
2001	653.63	645.40	665.79	649.85	658.67	660.19	657.60	650.39	659.85	662.81	671.31	680.40	659.50
2002	660.13	655.69	658.05	665.53	672.56	674.02	670.54	661.44	668.03	663.86	651.08	662.99	663.64
2003	651.25	644.39	663.79	647.21	640.74	647.90	652.01	644.78	649.60	645.57	660.02	663.28	650.41
PITTSBURGH													
Manufacturing													
2001	615.90	619.15	624.24	613.77	601.68	604.40	610.47	608.34	623.96	614.00	618.80	612.65	614.00
2002	606.83	624.46	641.03	635.96	633.95	637.59	637.19	650.76	658.46	654.86	648.82	641.58	638.38
2003	623.65	620.80	631.16	651.22	659.75	660.55	644.73	645.16	659.34	669.91	673.60	683.76	652.46
READING													
Manufacturing													
2001	634.08	607.37	597.63	572.22	595.35	599.10	595.63	611.82	604.09	587.73	599.66	608.42	600.88
2002	585.53	568.37	580.84	587.37	599.15	611.75	582.73	599.15	601.56	584.61	595.31	600.87	591.71
2003	594.31	603.69	617.22	606.48	621.59	622.50	610.47	622.40	622.44	622.44	637.51	653.62	619.48
SCRANTON–WILKES-BARRE													
Manufacturing													
2001	487.33	488.28	494.21	495.97	500.77	512.00	510.40	507.53	519.21	518.40	521.60	520.47	506.18
2002	509.13	534.66	528.91	536.26	537.47	535.31	540.48	548.44	543.44	533.97	539.13	539.97	535.55
2003	539.18	541.51	553.32	550.25	557.33	550.13	532.34	551.06	549.85	543.27	565.41	563.00	549.20
YORK													
Manufacturing													
2001	613.36	620.84	629.76	595.19	621.83	628.00	635.04	632.85	634.37	621.15	638.12	636.02	625.66
2002	634.20	635.88	638.43	618.69	628.00	633.69	631.06	628.17	639.39	633.01	633.57	595.27	628.87
2003	606.69	595.10	622.09	594.16	606.02	615.94	657.70	645.22	657.51	641.90	705.79	703.56	637.67

RHODE ISLAND AT A GLANCE

(Population and total nonfarm employment numbers in thousands)

Population, Census 2000:	1,048.3
Total nonfarm employment, 2003:	483.7
Change in total nonfarm employment	
(Number)	
1990–2003:	32.5
1990–2001:	27.2
2001–2003:	5.3
(Compound annual rate of change)	
1990–2003:	0.5%
1990–2001:	0.5%
2001–2003:	0.6%
Unemployment rate	
1990:	6.1%
2001:	4.6%
2003:	5.4%

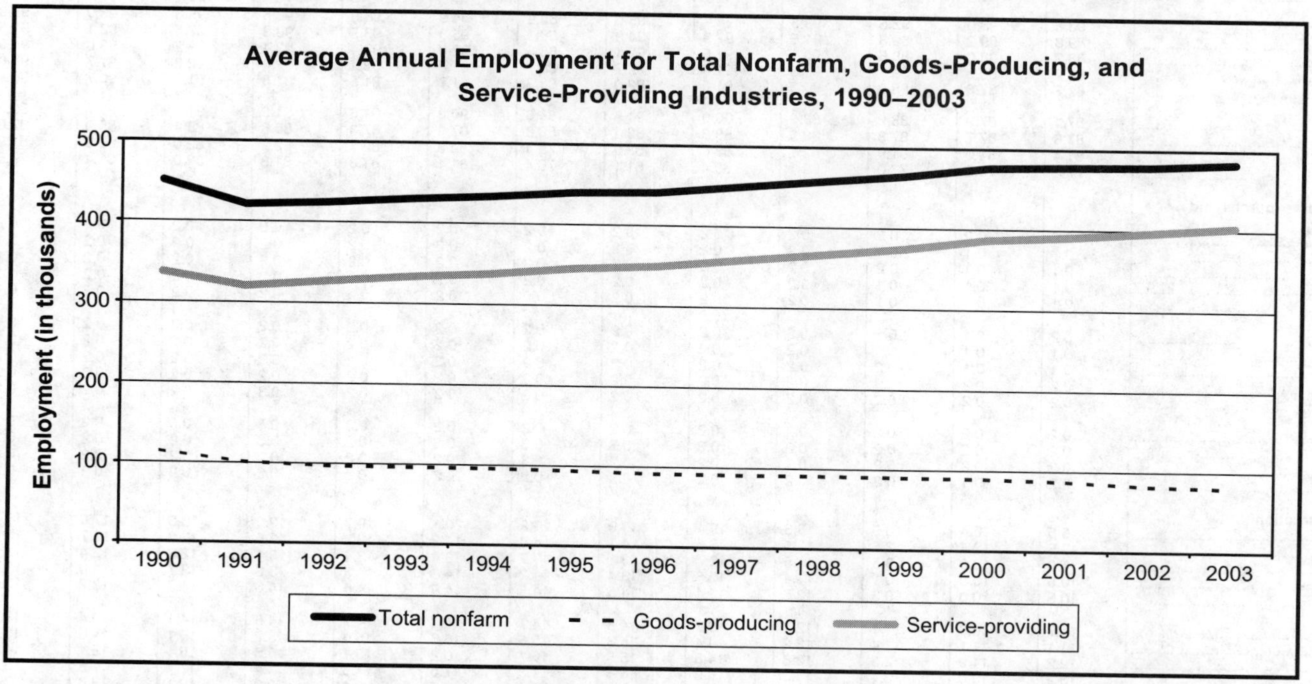

Rhode Island employment was somewhat atypical of national trends during the 1990–2003 period. A steep decline in total nonfarm employment occurred in the 1990–1991 recession, while the 2001 recession had a much more moderate impact. Growth slowed considerably after the 2001 recession, but employment never declined. Jobs in goods-producing industries were particularly hit hard during the 1990–1991 recession, as employment declined over 11 percent. Service-proving sector employment fell off during that first contraction, but continued to expand throughout the 1992–2003 period.

Employment by Industry: Rhode Island

(Numbers in thousands. Not seasonally adjusted.)

Industry	January	February	March	April	May	June	July	August	September	October	November	December	Annual Average
STATEWIDE													
Total nonfarm													
1990	446.7	446.8	449.9	450.5	455.9	458.5	445.2	449.3	455.7	454.0	452.8	449.5	451.2
1991	423.6	420.1	420.3	421.0	426.0	426.9	414.3	418.5	421.9	423.2	422.8	419.8	421.5
1992	410.1	410.7	413.1	422.9	428.3	430.8	422.9	425.0	431.2	434.9	434.5	433.0	424.7
1993	416.4	416.9	418.3	424.2	432.4	435.9	428.6	432.9	437.4	439.0	438.9	439.1	430.0
1994	421.7	421.7	424.8	430.6	435.8	441.1	429.5	437.2	439.5	441.5	444.4	442.1	434.1
1995	428.9	429.2	432.5	437.5	442.5	446.1	434.5	443.3	446.5	447.5	447.4	445.7	440.1
1996	427.1	429.7	432.9	437.4	445.4	448.3	434.5	442.8	448.6	449.3	451.5	451.5	441.5
1997	433.7	435.7	439.6	446.7	452.9	455.6	446.3	451.0	459.7	458.9	459.4	460.4	449.9
1998	442.3	445.3	447.7	454.1	461.9	463.7	456.3	459.1	464.1	466.5	468.2	466.9	458.0
1999	446.7	450.3	453.7	463.2	468.9	469.8	461.9	466.3	471.5	478.0	477.5	478.5	465.5
2000	460.2	462.3	467.3	475.0	482.0	481.8	474.1	476.1	482.2	485.3	486.7	487.6	476.7
2001	468.4	471.0	472.8	479.1	483.2	484.2	474.1	478.5	481.8	482.6	482.1	483.1	478.4
2002	466.0	467.1	471.4	478.6	484.3	485.3	475.4	479.5	484.7	486.0	487.1	487.2	479.4
2003	469.9	469.9	473.5	481.1	488.5	489.9	482.1	484.7	489.6	491.4	491.9	491.9	483.7
Total private													
1990	383.6	383.5	386.7	386.5	390.6	394.0	387.5	392.5	394.2	391.0	389.2	386.0	388.7
1991	360.1	357.1	357.1	359.8	364.6	365.1	357.3	362.3	363.3	361.6	360.9	358.0	360.6
1992	349.5	349.8	351.8	360.6	365.8	367.7	365.6	368.1	371.3	372.0	370.7	369.8	363.5
1993	354.2	354.9	355.7	362.1	369.2	373.6	370.6	375.2	377.5	377.2	376.4	376.3	368.5
1994	359.5	359.1	362.1	368.7	373.5	379.1	371.3	379.6	379.3	379.2	379.7	379.0	372.5
1995	366.7	366.6	370.0	374.6	379.5	385.4	376.6	385.7	387.1	386.0	385.3	382.9	378.8
1996	365.5	367.5	370.3	375.9	382.9	387.4	377.7	386.2	387.5	386.6	388.2	387.6	380.2
1997	370.8	372.2	375.9	382.3	388.3	391.0	386.6	391.6	396.4	395.3	395.3	395.6	386.7
1998	378.5	381.3	383.6	391.0	397.8	400.0	397.1	400.4	402.3	402.8	403.8	402.3	395.0
1999	382.6	386.7	388.8	398.7	403.9	406.0	402.9	407.8	408.9	413.4	412.7	413.3	402.1
2000	395.8	397.9	402.1	409.8	414.5	417.7	412.7	415.9	418.8	420.0	420.9	421.8	412.3
2001	403.0	405.4	407.0	413.2	416.8	418.6	412.4	417.3	417.3	416.4	415.1	415.9	413.2
2002	399.3	400.3	404.3	411.4	416.6	418.6	413.5	417.8	419.4	419.1	419.7	419.6	413.3
2003	402.8	402.8	406.1	414.1	421.0	422.4	419.7	422.3	423.9	423.8	423.9	423.8	417.2
Goods-producing													
1990	113.5	113.2	113.5	113.6	114.3	115.9	110.8	115.5	115.4	115.1	113.6	111.3	113.8
1991	102.8	101.0	100.5	100.3	101.4	101.8	96.4	101.7	102.2	102.1	102.5	100.9	101.1
1992	96.8	96.2	96.2	97.0	97.9	98.8	95.3	97.8	98.3	98.1	98.1	97.0	97.2
1993	93.7	93.3	93.4	95.4	96.8	98.0	94.5	98.1	98.5	98.8	98.5	97.4	96.3
1994	92.9	92.8	92.9	95.2	96.5	98.1	91.9	98.0	98.2	98.6	98.5	96.8	95.8
1995	93.6	93.0	92.5	93.8	94.7	95.6	86.9	94.9	96.0	96.5	95.6	93.9	93.9
1996	89.3	89.2	89.8	91.5	92.9	94.0	86.1	93.3	93.5	93.3	93.5	92.1	91.5
1997	88.2	88.0	88.6	90.1	91.5	92.1	88.5	92.0	93.4	93.4	93.2	93.0	91.0
1998	88.2	89.3	89.6	91.3	91.8	92.7	88.7	91.8	92.4	92.4	92.8	91.7	91.0
1999	87.2	87.8	88.0	90.3	91.0	92.0	88.3	91.7	91.5	91.8	91.8	90.7	90.1
2000	87.1	87.2	88.2	88.6	90.0	91.5	86.6	90.8	91.3	91.6	91.1	90.7	89.5
2001	87.8	87.7	87.8	88.5	88.3	88.4	83.8	87.3	87.3	86.8	85.4	85.0	87.0
2002	81.1	81.0	81.9	82.1	83.0	83.6	79.4	82.8	82.7	82.2	82.0	80.9	81.9
2003	77.5	76.3	77.0	79.1	80.4	81.1	78.4	81.1	81.8	81.8	82.0	81.4	79.8
Natural resources and mining													
1990	0.2	0.2	0.2	0.2	0.2	0.2	0.2	0.2	0.2	0.2	0.2	0.2	0.2
1991	0.1	0.1	0.1	0.2	0.2	0.2	0.2	0.2	0.2	0.2	0.2	0.2	0.1
1992	0.1	0.1	0.2	0.2	0.2	0.2	0.2	0.2	0.2	0.2	0.2	0.2	0.1
1993	0.1	0.1	0.1	0.2	0.2	0.2	0.2	0.2	0.2	0.2	0.2	0.2	0.1
1994	0.1	0.1	0.1	0.2	0.2	0.2	0.2	0.2	0.2	0.2	0.2	0.2	0.1
1995	0.2	0.1	0.1	0.2	0.2	0.2	0.2	0.2	0.2	0.2	0.2	0.2	0.1
1996	0.1	0.1	0.1	0.2	0.2	0.2	0.2	0.2	0.2	0.2	0.2	0.2	0.1
1997	0.1	0.1	0.2	0.2	0.2	0.2	0.2	0.2	0.2	0.2	0.2	0.2	0.1
1998	0.2	0.2	0.2	0.2	0.2	0.2	0.2	0.2	0.2	0.2	0.2	0.2	0.2
1999	0.2	0.2	0.2	0.2	0.2	0.2	0.2	0.2	0.2	0.3	0.2	0.2	0.2
2000	0.2	0.2	0.2	0.2	0.2	0.2	0.2	0.2	0.2	0.3	0.3	0.2	0.2
2001	0.2	0.2	0.2	0.2	0.3	0.3	0.3	0.3	0.2	0.3	0.2	0.2	0.2
2002	0.2	0.2	0.2	0.2	0.2	0.2	0.3	0.2	0.2	0.2	0.2	0.2	0.2
2003	0.2	0.1	0.2	0.2	0.2	0.2	0.2	0.2	0.2	0.2	0.2	0.2	0.2
Construction													
1990	16.6	16.4	16.9	18.3	19.1	19.9	20.2	20.1	19.7	19.0	18.3	17.2	18.4
1991	13.5	12.4	12.5	13.1	13.6	14.1	14.8	14.2	13.8	13.6	13.3	12.7	13.4
1992	11.0	10.6	10.6	11.5	12.4	13.1	13.2	13.4	13.4	13.1	12.8	12.4	12.2
1993	10.5	10.0	10.1	11.4	12.5	13.4	14.2	14.3	14.3	13.8	13.7	13.0	12.6
1994	10.5	10.0	10.3	12.5	13.4	14.5	14.5	14.9	14.5	14.6	14.3	13.7	13.1
1995	11.7	10.8	11.1	12.7	13.7	14.5	14.7	14.8	14.7	14.5	14.1	13.4	13.3
1996	11.1	11.1	11.4	13.2	14.4	15.3	15.6	15.6	15.3	15.2	15.1	14.5	13.9
1997	12.2	11.9	12.5	13.8	14.8	15.5	16.1	16.2	16.1	15.8	15.4	15.1	14.6
1998	13.2	13.0	13.4	15.2	16.0	16.6	17.3	17.5	17.5	17.4	17.4	17.3	15.9
1999	14.7	14.6	15.1	17.3	18.0	18.7	19.4	19.7	19.1	19.2	19.1	18.6	17.7
2000	16.4	15.8	17.0	17.8	18.3	18.9	19.1	19.1	19.1	19.0	18.9	18.4	18.1
2001	16.6	16.5	16.9	18.6	19.2	19.8	20.3	20.5	20.3	20.0	19.8	19.5	19.0
2002	17.4	17.3	18.0	19.1	19.9	20.4	20.4	20.6	20.5	20.1	19.9	19.4	19.4
2003	17.2	16.6	17.3	19.6	21.1	21.8	22.7	22.8	22.8	22.8	22.6	22.1	20.8

Employment by Industry: Rhode Island—*Continued*

(Numbers in thousands. Not seasonally adjusted.)

Industry	January	February	March	April	May	June	July	August	September	October	November	December	Annual Average
STATEWIDE—*Continued*													
Manufacturing													
1990	96.7	96.6	96.4	95.1	95.0	95.8	90.4	95.2	95.5	95.9	95.1	93.9	95.1
1991	89.2	88.5	87.9	87.0	87.6	87.5	81.4	87.3	88.2	88.3	89.0	88.0	87.4
1992	85.7	85.5	85.4	85.3	85.3	85.5	81.9	84.2	84.7	84.8	85.1	84.4	84.8
1993	83.1	83.2	83.2	83.8	84.1	84.4	80.1	83.6	84.0	84.8	84.6	84.2	83.5
1994	82.3	82.7	82.5	82.5	82.9	83.4	77.2	82.9	83.5	83.8	84.0	82.9	82.5
1995	81.7	82.1	81.3	80.9	80.8	80.9	72.0	79.9	81.1	81.8	81.3	80.3	80.3
1996	78.1	78.0	78.3	78.1	78.3	78.5	70.3	77.5	78.0	77.9	78.2	77.4	77.3
1997	75.9	76.0	75.9	76.1	76.5	76.4	72.2	75.6	77.1	77.4	77.6	77.7	76.2
1998	74.8	76.1	76.0	75.9	75.6	75.9	71.2	74.1	74.7	74.8	75.2	74.2	74.8
1999	72.3	73.0	72.7	72.8	72.8	73.1	68.7	71.8	72.2	72.3	72.5	71.9	72.1
2000	70.5	71.2	71.0	70.6	71.5	72.4	67.3	71.5	72.0	72.3	71.9	72.1	71.1
2001	71.0	71.0	70.7	69.7	68.8	68.3	63.2	66.5	66.8	66.5	65.4	65.3	67.8
2002	63.5	63.5	63.7	62.8	62.9	63.0	58.7	62.0	62.0	61.9	61.9	61.3	62.3
2003	60.1	59.6	59.5	59.3	59.1	59.1	55.5	58.1	58.8	58.8	59.2	59.1	58.9
Service-providing													
1990	333.2	333.6	336.4	336.9	341.6	342.6	334.4	333.8	340.3	338.9	339.2	338.2	337.4
1991	320.8	319.1	319.8	320.7	324.6	325.1	317.9	316.8	319.7	321.1	320.3	318.9	320.4
1992	313.3	314.5	316.9	325.9	330.4	332.0	327.6	327.2	332.9	336.8	336.4	336.0	327.4
1993	322.7	323.6	324.9	328.8	335.6	337.9	334.1	334.8	338.9	340.2	340.4	341.7	333.6
1994	328.8	328.9	331.9	335.4	339.3	343.0	337.6	339.2	341.3	342.9	345.9	345.3	338.2
1995	335.3	336.2	340.0	343.7	347.8	350.5	347.6	348.4	350.5	351.0	351.8	351.8	346.2
1996	337.8	340.5	343.1	345.9	352.5	354.3	348.4	349.5	355.1	356.0	358.0	359.4	350.0
1997	345.5	347.7	351.0	356.6	361.4	363.5	357.8	359.0	366.3	365.5	366.2	367.4	358.9
1998	354.1	356.0	358.1	362.8	370.1	371.0	367.6	367.3	371.7	374.1	375.4	375.2	366.9
1999	359.5	362.5	365.7	372.9	377.9	377.8	373.6	374.6	380.0	386.2	385.7	387.8	375.3
2000	373.1	375.1	379.1	386.4	392.0	390.3	387.5	385.3	390.9	393.7	395.6	396.9	387.1
2001	380.6	383.3	385.0	390.6	394.9	395.8	390.3	391.2	394.5	395.8	396.7	398.1	391.4
2002	384.9	386.1	389.5	396.5	401.3	401.7	396.0	396.7	402.0	403.8	405.1	406.3	397.5
2003	392.4	393.6	396.5	402.0	408.1	408.8	403.7	403.6	407.8	409.6	409.9	410.5	403.9
Trade, transportation, and utilities													
1990	79.4	78.0	78.6	76.8	77.3	78.0	75.2	76.3	77.2	77.4	77.5	78.2	77.4
1991	71.4	69.7	69.5	70.9	71.0	71.9	70.6	70.5	71.8	71.4	71.6	72.2	71.0
1992	69.5	68.8	68.9	70.2	71.2	71.8	70.9	71.0	71.9	72.2	72.6	73.7	71.0
1993	69.6	68.6	68.6	69.3	70.3	71.3	70.3	70.7	71.9	73.4	74.5	75.5	71.1
1994	71.6	69.6	70.4	71.1	71.7	72.5	71.6	71.6	72.8	74.3	75.4	76.2	72.4
1995	74.9	74.2	75.2	74.9	75.5	76.2	75.5	76.4	75.5	75.5	76.5	76.9	75.6
1996	72.5	71.7	71.8	72.5	73.8	74.7	73.3	73.5	74.0	74.3	75.1	76.1	73.6
1997	72.2	70.8	70.9	71.2	71.9	72.6	72.6	72.7	74.0	74.0	75.4	76.5	72.9
1998	72.3	71.6	71.9	71.9	74.0	74.8	74.9	75.4	75.9	77.0	78.2	78.3	74.6
1999	72.8	72.5	73.2	72.7	73.8	75.2	75.0	76.5	77.5	78.6	79.3	80.8	75.6
2000	77.5	76.9	77.1	79.0	79.1	79.3	78.3	79.2	80.3	81.3	83.0	84.2	79.6
2001	78.9	77.9	77.7	78.5	78.6	79.7	78.7	78.8	79.2	79.8	81.4	82.4	79.3
2002	79.0	77.7	77.9	79.1	79.9	81.0	80.0	80.1	81.2	82.0	83.3	84.5	80.5
2003	79.6	78.5	78.6	79.3	80.4	81.4	80.2	80.4	81.4	82.1	83.2	84.0	80.8
Wholesale trade													
1990	17.4	17.2	17.3	17.4	16.8	17.1	16.5	17.0	17.1	16.9	16.8	16.7	17.0
1991	15.4	15.7	15.7	15.9	15.8	15.9	15.4	15.4	15.7	15.4	15.6	15.5	15.6
1992	15.1	15.0	15.1	15.2	15.3	15.4	15.1	15.3	15.3	15.3	15.3	15.1	15.2
1993	14.5	14.7	14.7	14.7	14.9	14.9	14.8	14.9	15.0	15.2	15.2	15.2	14.8
1994	14.6	14.3	14.4	14.6	14.6	15.0	14.9	15.0	15.0	15.1	15.2	15.1	14.8
1995	14.5	14.6	14.8	14.9	14.8	14.8	14.8	15.3	15.2	15.2	15.2	15.1	14.9
1996	14.5	14.8	14.8	15.1	15.3	15.4	14.9	15.1	15.1	14.9	15.1	15.2	15.0
1997	14.7	14.7	14.8	14.7	14.7	14.8	14.7	14.9	15.0	14.8	14.9	15.0	14.8
1998	14.6	14.9	15.0	15.0	15.6	15.6	15.7	15.7	15.6	15.7	15.9	15.9	15.4
1999	15.4	15.4	15.6	15.7	15.8	15.9	15.7	15.8	15.7	15.9	15.8	15.8	15.7
2000	15.7	15.9	16.0	16.5	16.5	16.7	16.5	16.7	16.8	17.0	17.1	17.2	16.5
2001	16.0	16.2	16.3	16.5	16.5	16.6	16.6	16.7	16.6	16.7	16.7	16.8	16.5
2002	16.5	16.3	16.4	16.5	16.6	16.7	16.4	16.4	16.3	16.4	16.5	16.4	16.5
2003	16.4	16.2	16.3	16.4	16.6	16.7	16.5	16.4	16.4	16.4	16.4	16.4	16.4
Retail trade													
1990	52.5	51.3	51.8	49.8	50.8	51.0	49.6	50.2	50.2	50.7	51.0	51.6	50.8
1991	46.7	44.9	44.7	45.8	46.0	46.5	46.7	46.6	46.8	46.6	46.8	47.5	46.3
1992	45.2	44.7	44.7	45.1	45.8	46.2	46.2	46.3	46.6	46.9	47.4	48.7	46.1
1993	46.3	45.2	45.1	45.8	46.2	47.1	46.6	47.0	47.3	48.1	49.3	50.3	47.0
1994	47.6	45.8	46.4	46.7	47.3	47.4	47.2	47.2	47.8	48.6	49.8	50.7	47.7
1995	50.6	49.9	50.6	50.3	50.9	51.6	51.3	51.6	50.3	50.1	51.1	51.6	50.8
1996	48.3	47.2	47.2	47.4	48.3	48.9	48.3	48.3	48.4	48.9	49.5	50.4	48.4
1997	47.7	46.2	46.2	46.4	47.0	47.4	47.9	48.0	48.4	48.5	49.8	50.8	47.8
1998	47.6	46.5	46.6	47.1	47.9	48.3	49.0	49.3	49.5	50.6	51.6	51.8	48.8
1999	47.4	47.1	47.3	47.3	47.6	48.6	48.9	50.3	50.7	51.3	52.2	53.8	49.3
2000	51.1	50.4	50.4	51.5	51.5	51.5	51.2	51.7	52.3	53.0	54.7	55.8	52.0
2001	52.0	50.7	50.4	50.7	50.9	51.8	51.3	51.4	51.3	51.7	53.3	54.4	51.7
2002	51.7	50.9	51.0	51.8	52.4	53.1	53.1	53.3	53.7	54.2	55.5	56.8	53.1
2003	52.4	51.5	51.3	51.8	52.4	53.2	52.9	53.3	53.4	53.9	54.9	55.8	53.1

Employment by Industry: Rhode Island—*Continued*

(Numbers in thousands. Not seasonally adjusted.)

Industry	January	February	March	April	May	June	July	August	September	October	November	December	Annual Average
STATEWIDE—*Continued*													
Transportation and utilities													
1990	9.5	9.5	9.5	9.6	9.7	9.9	9.1	9.1	9.9	9.8	9.7	9.9	9.6
1991	9.3	9.1	9.1	9.2	9.2	9.5	8.5	8.5	9.3	9.4	9.2	9.2	9.1
1992	9.2	9.1	9.1	9.9	10.1	10.2	9.6	9.4	10.0	10.0	9.9	9.9	9.7
1993	8.8	8.7	8.8	8.8	9.2	9.3	8.9	8.8	9.6	10.1	10.0	10.0	9.2
1994	9.4	9.5	9.6	9.8	9.8	10.1	9.5	9.4	10.0	10.6	10.4	10.4	9.8
1995	9.8	9.7	9.8	9.7	9.8	9.8	9.4	9.5	10.0	10.2	10.2	10.2	9.8
1996	9.7	9.7	9.8	10.0	10.2	10.4	10.1	10.1	10.5	10.5	10.5	10.5	10.1
1997	9.8	9.9	9.9	10.1	10.2	10.4	10.0	9.8	10.6	10.7	10.7	10.7	10.2
1998	10.1	10.2	10.3	9.8	10.5	10.9	10.2	10.4	10.8	10.7	10.7	10.6	10.4
1999	10.0	10.0	10.3	9.7	10.4	10.7	10.4	10.4	11.1	11.4	11.3	11.2	10.5
2000	10.7	10.6	10.7	11.0	11.1	11.1	10.6	10.8	11.2	11.3	11.2	11.2	10.9
2001	10.9	11.0	11.0	11.3	11.2	11.3	10.8	10.7	11.3	11.4	11.4	11.2	11.1
2002	10.8	10.5	10.5	10.8	10.9	11.2	10.5	10.4	11.2	11.4	11.3	11.3	10.9
2003	10.8	10.8	11.0	11.1	11.4	11.5	10.8	10.7	11.6	11.8	11.9	11.8	11.3
Information													
1990	10.3	10.2	10.1	10.0	10.0	10.1	10.2	10.1	10.1	9.8	9.9	10.0	10.0
1991	9.9	9.9	9.8	9.8	9.8	9.8	9.7	9.7	9.7	9.6	9.7	9.7	9.7
1992	9.7	9.6	9.7	9.6	9.7	9.8	9.8	9.9	9.8	9.8	9.8	9.9	9.7
1993	9.8	9.9	10.0	9.9	9.9	10.0	10.1	10.1	10.2	9.9	10.0	10.1	9.9
1994	10.2	10.2	10.2	10.1	10.2	10.3	10.3	10.3	10.3	10.3	10.3	10.4	10.2
1995	10.6	10.6	10.7	10.5	10.6	10.7	10.6	10.8	10.9	10.5	10.5	10.4	10.6
1996	10.2	10.3	10.3	10.2	10.2	10.2	10.3	10.4	10.4	10.5	10.6	10.6	10.3
1997	10.7	10.5	10.9	10.6	10.7	10.7	10.4	10.5	10.5	10.5	10.6	10.6	10.6
1998	10.5	10.4	10.4	10.4	10.5	10.6	10.7	10.6	10.6	10.6	10.6	10.7	10.5
1999	10.5	10.5	10.5	10.5	10.6	10.6	10.6	10.6	10.6	10.7	10.7	10.6	10.5
2000	10.8	10.9	10.8	10.9	11.0	11.2	11.2	10.0	11.1	11.1	11.1	11.1	10.9
2001	11.1	11.1	11.1	11.2	11.4	11.4	11.4	11.3	11.3	11.2	11.2	11.3	11.3
2002	11.3	11.2	11.3	11.2	11.2	11.3	11.3	11.2	11.2	10.9	11.1	11.2	11.2
2003	11.1	11.1	11.0	11.0	11.0	11.2	11.1	11.1	10.9	10.7	10.7	10.8	11.0
Financial activities													
1990	26.7	26.7	26.9	26.5	26.7	27.1	27.1	26.9	26.8	26.9	26.8	26.5	26.8
1991	25.4	25.4	25.5	25.3	25.6	25.8	25.7	25.6	25.2	24.9	24.9	24.8	25.3
1992	24.6	24.5	24.5	24.2	24.4	24.7	24.8	24.4	24.2	24.2	24.2	23.8	24.3
1993	23.8	23.8	24.0	24.1	24.3	24.6	24.6	24.6	24.5	24.3	24.3	24.5	24.2
1994	24.0	24.2	24.1	24.3	24.4	24.6	24.4	24.3	23.7	22.9	22.9	22.9	23.8
1995	22.4	22.3	22.3	22.7	22.9	23.0	23.3	23.5	23.4	23.0	23.3	23.5	22.9
1996	23.6	23.9	24.0	23.9	24.2	24.3	24.4	24.5	24.5	24.6	24.7	24.9	24.2
1997	24.4	24.7	24.8	25.1	25.3	25.5	25.6	25.8	25.8	25.8	25.9	26.2	25.4
1998	26.7	26.8	27.1	27.2	28.1	28.6	29.0	28.9	28.9	29.1	29.3	29.6	28.2
1999	29.2	29.3	29.4	29.6	29.6	29.9	30.2	30.4	30.0	30.1	30.1	30.5	29.8
2000	30.0	30.0	30.2	30.7	30.5	31.4	32.0	31.7	31.6	31.5	31.7	32.0	31.1
2001	32.0	32.1	32.3	32.0	32.0	32.5	32.5	32.3	32.2	32.2	32.2	32.4	32.2
2002	32.3	32.3	32.2	32.6	32.6	32.9	33.3	33.2	33.1	33.2	33.3	33.6	32.9
2003	33.1	33.2	33.5	33.0	33.3	33.7	34.0	34.0	33.8	33.7	33.8	33.7	33.6
Professional and business services													
1990	39.5	39.9	40.7	41.8	42.3	43.1	44.2	44.3	44.7	43.8	43.8	43.4	42.6
1991	39.4	38.9	39.1	38.5	39.0	38.8	37.9	37.6	37.6	37.2	36.4	35.4	37.9
1992	35.3	35.5	35.9	37.0	37.2	37.7	38.3	38.9	40.2	40.9	40.5	39.9	38.1
1993	37.7	38.1	38.3	39.2	40.3	41.0	41.3	41.8	42.4	41.8	41.7	41.2	40.4
1994	38.7	39.6	40.3	41.2	41.6	42.2	41.7	43.1	43.3	44.0	44.1	44.5	42.0
1995	41.1	41.4	42.3	43.0	43.4	44.4	45.2	44.9	45.6	46.1	45.6	44.6	43.9
1996	40.8	41.3	41.9	42.4	43.2	43.6	43.6	44.7	45.8	45.7	45.6	45.1	43.6
1997	42.5	43.1	43.7	46.5	46.9	47.6	46.6	48.2	49.4	48.7	48.0	47.3	46.5
1998	45.0	45.2	46.2	47.9	47.9	48.9	48.9	49.1	49.4	49.0	48.8	48.6	47.9
1999	44.7	45.7	46.3	49.0	49.6	50.4	50.3	51.1	51.2	51.9	51.9	52.0	49.5
2000	48.2	48.4	49.5	50.9	51.5	52.2	51.0	51.4	51.8	51.9	51.7	51.9	50.8
2001	48.4	48.9	49.0	50.6	50.7	51.1	50.7	51.5	51.6	51.8	50.9	50.6	50.5
2002	47.2	47.0	47.7	49.4	49.4	50.1	48.9	49.3	49.7	49.7	49.4	48.8	48.9
2003	46.4	46.5	47.0	49.2	49.7	50.7	50.6	51.1	51.0	50.6	50.3	49.9	49.4
Educational and health services													
1990	65.8	67.1	67.7	67.7	67.9	65.0	63.0	63.0	65.1	66.7	67.4	67.5	66.1
1991	66.5	67.6	67.9	68.1	68.4	65.0	63.8	64.2	65.6	67.6	68.4	68.2	66.7
1992	68.9	70.0	70.4	73.9	74.0	70.7	70.3	70.2	72.3	74.5	74.6	74.9	72.0
1993	73.2	74.3	74.8	75.1	75.2	72.6	72.0	71.9	74.2	75.7	75.6	76.1	74.2
1994	73.9	74.7	75.1	75.1	74.6	73.8	73.5	73.4	75.1	76.5	76.9	77.2	74.9
1995	75.2	76.2	77.3	77.5	77.4	76.8	75.3	75.1	77.4	78.9	79.4	79.7	77.1
1996	77.6	78.9	79.5	79.8	79.7	78.0	76.7	76.6	78.6	80.4	81.9	82.2	79.1
1997	79.3	80.6	81.7	81.3	81.5	78.7	77.8	77.5	81.1	82.4	83.4	83.4	80.7
1998	80.8	82.4	82.6	83.4	83.6	78.9	78.4	77.9	81.1	83.2	83.8	83.4	81.6
1999	81.6	83.4	83.6	84.6	84.3	78.8	78.9	77.7	81.3	84.5	84.7	84.4	82.3
2000	81.1	83.2	84.0	84.8	84.8	80.2	80.3	80.0	83.2	85.0	86.1	86.1	83.2
2001	83.0	85.4	86.2	86.1	86.3	82.0	81.2	82.1	84.8	86.5	87.5	88.0	84.9
2002	85.6	87.7	88.7	88.9	89.1	84.6	84.0	85.1	88.4	90.3	91.5	92.2	88.0
2003	89.6	91.6	92.6	92.8	92.8	87.7	86.8	86.3	89.5	91.6	92.2	92.6	90.5

Employment by Industry: Rhode Island—*Continued*

(Numbers in thousands. Not seasonally adjusted.)

Industry	January	February	March	April	May	June	July	August	September	October	November	December	Annual Average
STATEWIDE—*Continued*													
Leisure and hospitality													
1990	32.5	32.5	33.2	34.3	36.2	38.8	40.5	40.1	38.7	35.1	34.1	33.1	35.7
1991	29.3	29.3	29.5	31.4	33.8	36.1	37.4	37.2	35.4	32.6	31.2	30.6	32.8
1992	28.5	29.0	29.9	32.1	34.5	37.0	38.6	38.3	37.1	34.6	33.2	32.9	33.8
1993	30.9	31.3	30.9	33.2	36.2	39.6	41.0	41.0	39.0	36.8	35.3	34.9	35.8
1994	32.0	31.6	32.5	35.1	37.9	41.0	41.7	42.7	40.2	37.1	36.4	36.0	37.0
1995	34.4	34.5	35.3	37.6	40.0	43.3	44.1	44.2	42.2	39.6	38.1	37.3	39.2
1996	35.1	35.6	36.0	38.5	41.5	44.8	45.2	45.2	43.0	40.2	39.1	38.8	40.2
1997	36.0	36.9	37.4	39.5	42.2	45.0	46.2	46.1	43.8	42.0	40.4	40.1	41.3
1998	36.7	37.2	37.3	40.2	43.0	46.2	47.0	47.0	45.0	42.0	40.9	40.4	41.9
1999	37.5	38.3	38.4	42.2	45.1	48.8	49.2	49.3	46.9	45.6	44.0	43.9	44.1
2000	41.1	41.2	41.9	44.3	47.0	50.8	52.0	51.4	48.6	46.6	45.4	44.8	46.2
2001	41.1	41.7	42.2	45.4	48.4	51.8	52.4	52.2	49.8	47.0	45.2	44.8	46.8
2002	41.7	42.3	43.4	46.6	49.6	52.7	53.9	53.5	51.0	48.5	46.8	45.8	48.0
2003	43.3	43.4	44.0	47.1	50.5	53.3	55.0	54.9	52.6	50.4	48.7	48.2	49.3
Other services													
1990	15.9	15.9	16.0	15.8	15.9	16.0	16.5	16.3	16.2	16.2	16.1	16.0	16.0
1991	15.4	15.3	15.3	15.5	15.6	15.9	15.8	15.8	15.8	16.2	16.2	16.2	15.7
1992	16.2	16.2	16.3	16.6	16.9	17.2	17.6	17.6	17.5	17.7	17.7	17.7	17.1
1993	15.5	15.6	15.7	15.9	16.2	16.5	16.8	17.0	16.8	16.5	16.5	16.6	16.3
1994	16.2	16.4	16.6	16.6	16.6	16.6	16.2	16.2	15.7	15.5	15.2	15.0	16.0
1995	14.5	14.4	14.4	14.6	15.0	15.4	15.7	15.9	16.1	15.9	16.3	16.6	15.4
1996	16.4	16.6	17.0	17.1	17.4	17.8	18.1	18.0	17.7	17.6	17.7	17.8	17.4
1997	17.5	17.6	17.9	18.0	18.3	18.8	18.9	18.8	18.4	18.5	18.4	18.5	18.3
1998	18.3	18.4	18.5	18.7	18.9	19.3	19.5	19.7	19.0	19.5	19.4	19.6	19.0
1999	19.1	19.2	19.4	19.8	19.9	20.3	20.4	20.5	19.9	20.2	20.2	20.4	19.9
2000	20.0	20.1	20.4	20.6	20.6	21.1	21.3	21.4	20.9	21.0	20.8	21.0	20.7
2001	20.7	20.6	20.7	20.9	21.1	21.7	21.7	21.8	21.1	21.1	21.3	21.4	21.2
2002	21.1	21.1	21.2	21.5	21.8	22.4	22.7	22.6	22.1	22.3	22.3	22.6	22.0
2003	22.2	22.2	22.4	22.6	22.9	23.3	23.6	23.4	22.9	22.9	23.0	23.2	22.9
Government													
1990	63.1	63.3	63.2	64.0	65.3	64.5	57.7	56.8	61.5	63.0	63.6	63.5	62.4
1991	63.5	63.0	63.2	61.2	61.4	61.8	57.0	56.2	58.6	61.6	61.9	61.8	60.9
1992	60.6	60.9	61.3	62.3	62.5	63.1	57.3	56.9	59.9	62.9	63.8	63.2	61.2
1993	62.2	62.0	62.6	62.1	63.2	62.3	58.0	57.7	59.9	61.8	62.5	62.8	61.4
1994	62.2	62.6	62.7	61.9	62.3	62.0	58.2	57.6	60.2	62.3	64.7	63.1	61.6
1995	62.2	62.6	62.5	62.9	63.0	60.7	57.9	57.6	59.4	61.5	62.1	62.8	61.2
1996	61.6	62.2	62.6	61.5	62.5	60.9	56.8	56.6	61.1	62.7	63.3	63.9	61.3
1997	62.9	63.5	63.7	64.4	64.6	64.6	59.7	59.4	63.3	63.6	64.1	64.8	63.2
1998	63.8	64.0	64.1	63.1	64.1	63.7	59.2	58.7	61.8	63.7	64.4	64.6	62.9
1999	64.1	63.6	64.9	64.5	65.0	63.8	59.0	58.5	62.6	64.6	64.8	65.2	63.3
2000	64.4	64.4	65.2	65.2	67.5	64.1	61.4	60.2	63.4	65.3	65.8	65.8	64.3
2001	65.4	65.6	65.8	65.9	66.4	65.6	61.7	61.2	64.5	66.2	67.0	67.2	65.2
2002	66.7	66.8	67.1	67.2	67.7	66.7	61.9	61.7	65.3	66.9	67.4	67.6	66.1
2003	67.1	67.1	67.4	67.0	67.5	67.5	62.4	62.4	65.7	67.6	68.0	68.1	66.5
Federal government													
1990	10.9	10.9	11.0	11.3	12.4	12.0	10.9	10.9	10.8	10.6	10.6	10.6	11.0
1991	10.5	10.5	10.5	10.5	10.5	10.5	10.7	10.7	10.7	10.6	10.6	10.6	10.5
1992	10.7	10.6	10.6	10.6	10.7	10.7	10.8	10.8	10.8	10.4	10.4	10.4	10.6
1993	10.2	10.2	10.2	10.2	10.2	10.3	10.2	10.1	10.1	10.1	10.1	10.5	10.2
1994	10.1	10.1	10.1	10.1	10.1	10.1	10.2	10.2	10.2	10.2	10.3	10.7	10.2
1995	10.4	10.4	10.4	10.4	10.4	10.4	10.4	10.4	10.3	10.3	10.4	10.8	10.4
1996	10.2	10.2	10.2	10.3	10.2	10.3	10.4	10.4	10.5	10.7	10.8	11.4	10.4
1997	10.9	10.9	10.9	11.0	11.0	11.0	11.1	11.1	11.1	10.6	10.7	11.1	10.9
1998	10.6	10.6	10.6	10.6	10.6	10.7	10.6	10.6	10.6	10.5	10.7	11.0	10.6
1999	10.5	10.5	10.7	10.7	10.5	10.5	10.5	10.5	10.4	10.4	10.5	10.8	10.5
2000	10.3	10.4	10.6	11.0	12.6	11.1	11.2	10.7	10.5	10.5	10.6	10.8	10.8
2001	10.4	10.4	10.3	10.4	10.4	10.5	10.7	10.7	10.6	10.5	10.4	10.7	10.5
2002	10.4	10.2	10.3	10.2	10.2	10.2	10.1	10.2	10.2	10.2	10.2	10.5	10.2
2003	10.2	10.1	10.1	10.1	10.1	10.2	10.1	10.1	10.1	10.1	10.0	10.2	10.1
State government													
1990	21.2	21.2	21.1	21.1	21.2	21.2	20.2	19.9	20.3	21.2	21.2	21.1	20.9
1991	21.2	20.8	20.9	20.6	20.5	20.5	20.0	19.3	19.6	20.5	20.3	20.3	20.3
1992	20.2	20.3	20.2	20.3	20.4	20.4	19.7	19.6	20.0	21.0	21.0	20.7	20.3
1993	20.5	20.4	20.5	20.2	20.5	20.5	19.6	19.5	19.1	20.1	20.1	20.0	20.0
1994	19.7	19.7	19.7	19.8	19.9	19.7	18.9	18.5	18.2	19.2	19.1	19.1	19.2
1995	19.0	19.0	19.0	19.1	19.1	19.0	17.9	17.8	17.5	18.5	18.4	18.4	18.5
1996	18.4	18.4	18.4	18.4	18.5	18.4	17.5	17.5	17.2	18.2	18.1	18.0	18.0
1997	18.0	18.0	18.0	18.1	18.2	18.0	17.3	17.3	17.0	18.1	18.0	18.0	17.8
1998	18.0	18.0	18.0	18.1	18.3	18.3	17.5	17.5	17.2	18.3	18.2	18.2	17.9
1999	18.2	18.2	18.4	18.4	18.7	18.6	17.8	17.8	17.6	18.7	18.5	18.5	18.2
2000	18.4	18.5	18.5	18.3	18.6	18.5	17.6	17.6	17.4	18.4	18.3	18.3	18.2
2001	18.2	18.3	18.3	18.3	18.4	18.4	17.7	17.7	17.4	18.5	18.4	18.3	18.2
2002	18.3	18.3	18.3	18.4	18.6	18.4	17.6	17.6	17.2	18.3	18.2	18.1	18.1
2003	18.0	18.0	18.0	18.0	18.0	18.0	17.2	17.1	16.9	17.9	17.9	17.7	17.7

Employment by Industry: Rhode Island—*Continued*

(Numbers in thousands. Not seasonally adjusted.)

Industry	January	February	March	April	May	June	July	August	September	October	November	December	Annual Average
STATEWIDE—*Continued*													
Local government													
1990	31.0	31.2	31.1	31.6	31.7	31.3	26.6	26.0	30.4	31.2	31.8	31.8	30.4
1991	31.8	31.7	31.8	30.1	30.4	30.8	26.3	26.2	28.3	30.5	31.0	30.9	29.9
1992	29.7	30.0	30.5	31.4	31.4	32.0	26.8	26.5	29.1	31.5	32.4	32.1	30.2
1993	31.5	31.4	31.9	31.7	32.5	31.5	28.2	28.1	30.7	31.6	32.3	32.3	31.1
1994	32.4	32.8	32.9	32.0	32.3	32.2	29.1	28.9	31.8	32.9	35.3	33.3	32.1
1995	32.8	33.2	33.1	33.4	33.5	31.3	29.6	29.4	31.6	32.7	33.3	33.6	32.2
1996	33.0	33.6	34.0	32.8	33.8	32.2	28.9	28.7	33.4	33.8	34.4	34.5	32.7
1997	34.0	34.6	34.8	35.3	35.4	35.6	31.3	31.0	35.2	34.9	35.4	35.7	34.4
1998	35.2	35.4	35.5	34.4	35.2	34.7	31.1	30.6	34.0	34.9	35.5	35.4	34.3
1999	35.4	34.9	35.8	35.4	35.8	34.7	30.7	30.2	34.6	35.5	35.8	35.9	34.5
2000	35.7	35.5	36.1	35.9	36.3	34.5	32.6	31.9	35.5	36.4	36.9	36.7	35.3
2001	36.8	36.9	37.2	37.2	37.6	36.7	33.3	32.8	36.5	37.2	38.2	38.2	36.6
2002	38.0	38.3	38.5	38.6	38.9	38.1	34.2	33.9	37.9	38.4	39.0	39.0	37.7
2003	38.9	39.0	39.3	38.9	39.4	39.3	35.1	35.2	38.7	39.6	40.1	40.2	38.6
PROVIDENCE													
Total nonfarm													
1990	499.1	498.6	501.5	500.2	504.7	505.8	487.9	493.8	502.7	501.4	501.0	498.8	499.6
1991	472.0	467.8	468.3	468.5	472.8	472.8	454.7	461.9	467.5	469.4	470.5	467.9	467.8
1992	457.0	457.1	458.8	468.1	472.8	475.5	464.1	467.9	476.6	482.8	483.7	483.7	470.6
1993	465.9	466.5	467.8	473.7	480.9	484.6	472.9	478.2	484.7	489.2	491.8	492.6	479.0
1994	475.1	474.1	477.1	480.1	485.0	489.4	476.8	486.7	493.6	497.6	501.7	501.1	486.5
1995	485.8	486.4	489.2	492.7	496.4	499.1	483.1	494.8	500.6	504.1	505.6	505.1	495.2
1996	484.7	488.0	491.1	494.0	501.2	502.3	484.8	495.4	504.2	507.1	510.9	511.2	497.9
1997	492.5	492.5	495.8	502.1	508.1	510.3	497.7	502.4	514.1	515.8	517.5	519.7	505.7
1998	502.9	504.9	506.4	512.2	519.1	519.3	508.0	511.5	520.6	522.7	525.1	525.0	514.8
1999	505.1	508.9	512.5	521.2	525.0	525.9	513.9	519.6	526.0	534.2	535.8	537.7	522.1
2000	518.7	519.5	524.4	532.1	538.1	537.0	523.2	526.1	537.1	541.6	545.1	547.2	532.5
2001	524.4	525.2	526.9	531.9	534.9	534.9	519.7	526.6	532.2	534.0	535.0	536.3	530.2
2002	518.6	519.4	523.8	531.2	536.0	535.5	521.3	527.5	534.1	536.0	539.1	539.3	530.2
2003	522.9	521.8	524.8	532.3	538.1	538.9	526.1	529.6	537.1	541.2	542.9	543.2	533.2
Total private													
1990	434.8	433.8	436.4	434.6	437.8	440.6	429.7	436.5	439.8	437.0	435.8	433.5	435.8
1991	406.9	403.2	403.5	405.0	409.1	408.6	396.9	404.5	407.6	406.4	407.0	404.5	405.2
1992	394.7	394.4	395.9	404.0	408.5	410.9	406.1	410.4	415.1	418.2	418.3	418.6	407.9
1993	402.0	402.6	403.3	409.7	415.9	420.1	413.4	419.1	423.0	425.3	427.2	427.7	415.7
1994	410.8	409.4	412.3	416.3	420.8	425.1	416.9	427.6	431.4	433.2	435.0	435.8	422.8
1995	421.4	421.4	424.3	427.8	431.3	435.8	423.6	435.4	439.3	440.4	441.1	439.8	431.8
1996	421.7	423.6	426.1	430.2	436.3	439.1	426.7	437.4	441.2	442.4	445.6	445.5	434.6
1997	428.0	427.4	430.6	436.5	442.3	444.3	436.8	442.5	449.7	450.4	451.8	453.2	441.1
1998	437.4	439.1	440.5	447.1	453.0	453.8	447.6	451.5	456.2	456.9	458.6	458.3	450.0
1999	438.9	443.1	445.6	454.5	457.8	459.8	453.0	459.1	461.3	467.3	468.5	470.1	456.5
2000	451.6	452.6	456.7	464.1	467.6	469.4	461.8	466.3	471.0	473.7	476.6	478.5	465.8
2001	456.2	457.1	458.4	463.2	465.9	466.6	455.7	462.9	465.1	465.2	465.4	466.5	462.4
2002	449.4	449.9	454.1	461.2	465.7	466.1	457.5	463.9	466.6	466.9	469.4	469.5	461.7
2003	453.5	452.4	455.3	463.1	468.5	469.4	462.9	466.6	469.4	471.1	472.4	472.8	464.8
Goods-producing													
1990	138.9	138.3	138.2	137.5	138.3	140.3	133.7	139.6	140.4	138.8	137.2	134.5	137.9
1991	123.9	122.2	121.8	122.3	123.2	123.9	116.4	123.7	124.5	123.9	124.0	121.9	122.6
1992	117.6	117.4	117.0	119.3	121.1	122.8	118.3	121.4	122.1	122.2	121.3	120.2	120.0
1993	115.5	115.6	115.3	117.9	119.5	121.2	116.6	120.6	121.4	122.0	122.0	120.9	119.0
1994	116.1	115.3	116.1	118.3	119.4	121.7	115.4	122.2	122.5	122.5	122.4	121.7	119.4
1995	117.3	116.9	117.9	119.1	119.8	120.8	112.1	119.8	120.7	121.6	120.9	119.1	118.8
1996	111.5	111.9	112.5	114.3	116.5	118.3	108.9	117.8	118.2	118.4	118.3	116.5	115.2
1997	111.7	110.5	111.3	113.3	115.1	116.1	111.0	115.1	116.8	116.9	116.9	116.7	114.2
1998	112.9	113.1	112.8	114.6	115.5	116.4	111.7	115.3	116.2	116.0	115.6	114.2	114.5
1999	109.6	110.0	110.5	112.9	113.6	114.3	109.5	113.5	113.2	114.1	113.5	112.3	112.2
2000	107.2	107.4	109.0	110.1	111.2	111.7	106.1	110.7	112.1	112.5	112.0	111.4	110.1
2001	107.8	107.5	107.3	108.0	107.7	107.6	101.0	105.7	106.0	105.6	103.9	103.3	106.0
2002	98.7	98.7	99.7	100.0	101.2	101.5	96.2	100.8	100.8	99.9	99.4	98.3	99.6
2003	94.2	93.1	93.5	96.1	97.3	97.9	93.7	97.1	97.8	97.9	97.9	97.1	96.1
Natural resources and mining													
1990	0.2	0.2	0.2	0.2	0.2	0.2	0.2	0.2	0.2	0.2	0.2	0.2	0.2
1991	0.2	0.1	0.2	0.2	0.2	0.2	0.2	0.2	0.2	0.2	0.2	0.2	0.1
1992	0.2	0.2	0.2	0.2	0.2	0.2	0.2	0.2	0.2	0.2	0.2	0.2	0.2
1993	0.2	0.1	0.2	0.2	0.2	0.2	0.2	0.2	0.2	0.2	0.2	0.2	0.1
1994	0.2	0.2	0.2	0.2	0.2	0.2	0.2	0.2	0.2	0.2	0.2	0.2	0.2
1995	0.2	0.2	0.2	0.2	0.2	0.2	0.2	0.2	0.2	0.2	0.2	0.2	0.2
1996	0.1	0.1	0.2	0.2	0.2	0.2	0.2	0.2	0.2	0.2	0.2	0.2	0.1
1997	0.2	0.2	0.2	0.2	0.3	0.3	0.3	0.3	0.3	0.3	0.3	0.3	0.2
1998	0.2	0.2	0.2	0.3	0.3	0.3	0.3	0.3	0.3	0.3	0.3	0.3	0.2
1999	0.2	0.2	0.3	0.3	0.3	0.3	0.3	0.3	0.3	0.3	0.3	0.3	0.2
2000	0.2	0.2	0.3	0.3	0.3	0.3	0.3	0.3	0.3	0.3	0.3	0.3	0.2
2001	0.2	0.2	0.2	0.3	0.3	0.3	0.3	0.3	0.3	0.3	0.3	0.3	0.3
2002	0.3	0.2	0.3	0.3	0.3	0.3	0.3	0.3	0.3	0.3	0.3	0.3	0.3
2003	0.2	0.2	0.2	0.2	0.2	0.2	0.2	0.2	0.2	0.3	0.3	0.2	0.2

Employment by Industry: Rhode Island—*Continued*

(Numbers in thousands. Not seasonally adjusted.)

Industry	January	February	March	April	May	June	July	August	September	October	November	December	Annual Average
PROVIDENCE—*Continued*													
Construction													
1990	18.5	18.2	18.8	19.9	20.9	21.9	22.1	22.2	21.8	21.0	20.2	18.8	20.3
1991	14.5	13.2	13.3	13.8	14.5	15.2	15.6	15.6	15.2	15.1	14.8	13.9	14.5
1992	11.5	11.6	11.6	12.8	14.0	14.8	14.8	15.0	15.0	14.9	14.5	14.1	13.7
1993	11.7	11.2	11.3	12.9	14.2	15.2	15.8	16.0	16.0	15.9	15.7	15.0	14.2
1994	12.0	11.4	11.7	14.2	15.4	16.6	16.8	17.2	16.8	16.8	16.5	16.0	15.1
1995	13.6	12.3	12.6	14.5	15.5	16.3	16.6	16.9	16.6	16.4	15.9	15.1	15.1
1996	12.3	12.3	12.7	14.7	16.3	17.4	17.7	17.8	17.5	17.3	17.2	16.5	15.8
1997	13.6	13.2	13.8	15.4	16.6	17.5	18.1	18.2	18.1	17.8	17.6	17.2	16.4
1998	15.3	15.1	15.7	17.7	18.6	19.0	19.4	19.5	19.3	19.0	19.0	18.7	18.0
1999	15.9	15.9	16.7	19.1	19.7	20.3	21.0	21.2	20.7	20.7	20.6	20.0	19.3
2000	17.5	17.0	18.4	19.2	19.8	20.6	20.7	20.9	20.9	20.9	20.8	20.1	19.7
2001	18.1	17.9	18.5	20.4	21.1	21.7	22.0	22.2	22.0	21.8	21.6	21.3	20.7
2002	18.9	18.8	19.6	20.8	21.8	22.3	22.3	22.5	22.4	22.0	21.6	21.0	21.2
2003	18.7	17.9	18.6	21.2	22.8	23.6	24.4	24.5	24.5	24.4	24.2	23.8	22.4
Manufacturing													
1990	120.2	119.9	119.2	117.4	117.2	118.2	111.4	117.2	118.4	117.6	116.8	115.5	117.4
1991	109.2	108.9	108.3	108.3	108.5	108.5	100.6	107.9	109.1	108.6	109.0	107.8	107.8
1992	105.9	105.6	105.2	106.3	106.9	107.8	103.3	106.2	106.9	107.1	106.6	105.9	106.1
1993	103.6	104.3	103.8	104.8	105.1	105.8	100.6	104.4	105.2	105.9	106.1	105.7	104.6
1994	103.9	103.7	104.2	103.9	103.8	104.9	98.4	104.8	105.5	105.5	105.7	105.5	104.1
1995	103.5	104.4	105.1	104.4	104.1	104.3	95.3	102.7	103.9	105.0	104.8	103.8	103.4
1996	99.1	99.5	99.6	99.4	100.0	100.7	91.0	99.8	100.5	100.9	100.9	99.8	99.2
1997	97.9	97.1	97.3	97.7	98.2	98.3	92.6	96.6	98.4	98.8	99.0	99.2	97.5
1998	97.4	97.8	96.9	96.6	96.6	97.1	92.0	95.5	96.6	96.7	96.3	95.2	96.2
1999	93.5	93.9	93.5	93.5	93.6	93.7	88.2	92.0	92.2	93.1	92.6	92.0	92.6
2000	89.5	90.2	90.3	90.6	91.1	90.8	85.1	89.5	90.9	91.3	90.9	91.0	90.1
2001	89.5	89.4	88.6	87.3	86.3	85.6	78.7	83.2	83.7	83.5	82.0	81.7	85.0
2002	79.5	79.7	79.8	78.9	79.1	78.9	73.6	78.0	78.1	77.6	77.5	77.0	78.1
2003	75.3	75.0	74.7	74.7	74.3	74.1	69.1	72.4	73.1	73.2	73.4	73.1	73.5
Service-providing													
1990	360.2	360.3	363.3	362.7	366.4	365.5	354.2	354.2	362.3	362.6	363.8	364.3	361.6
1991	348.1	345.6	346.5	346.2	349.6	348.9	338.3	338.2	343.0	345.5	346.5	346.0	345.2
1992	339.4	339.7	341.8	348.8	351.7	352.7	345.8	346.5	354.5	360.6	362.4	363.5	350.6
1993	350.4	350.9	352.5	355.8	361.4	363.4	356.3	357.6	363.3	367.2	369.8	371.7	360.0
1994	359.0	358.8	361.0	361.8	365.6	367.7	361.4	364.5	371.1	375.1	379.3	379.4	367.0
1995	368.5	369.5	371.3	373.6	376.6	378.3	371.0	375.0	379.9	382.5	384.7	386.0	376.4
1996	373.2	376.1	378.6	379.7	384.7	384.0	375.9	377.6	386.0	388.7	392.6	394.7	382.6
1997	380.8	382.0	384.5	388.8	393.0	394.2	386.7	387.3	397.3	398.9	400.6	403.0	391.4
1998	390.0	391.8	393.6	397.6	403.6	402.9	396.3	396.2	404.4	406.7	409.5	410.8	400.2
1999	395.5	398.9	402.0	408.3	411.4	411.6	404.4	406.1	412.8	420.1	422.3	425.4	409.9
2000	411.5	412.1	415.4	422.0	426.9	425.3	417.1	415.4	425.0	429.1	433.1	435.8	422.3
2001	416.6	417.7	419.6	423.9	427.2	427.3	418.7	420.9	426.2	428.4	431.1	433.0	424.2
2002	419.9	420.7	424.1	431.2	434.8	434.0	425.1	426.7	433.3	436.1	439.7	441.0	430.6
2003	428.7	428.7	431.3	436.2	440.8	441.0	432.4	432.5	439.3	443.3	445.0	446.1	437.1
Trade, transportation, and utilities													
1990	91.5	90.5	90.8	89.3	89.8	90.5	86.4	87.3	88.2	88.7	89.9	90.9	89.4
1991	84.4	82.9	82.6	82.2	82.7	83.0	80.6	80.8	82.5	81.7	83.0	84.5	82.5
1992	81.1	80.2	80.4	81.4	82.0	82.8	81.7	82.1	83.3	83.8	85.2	86.8	82.5
1993	82.8	81.8	82.0	82.7	83.5	84.4	82.7	83.8	84.9	86.3	88.7	90.1	84.4
1994	85.2	83.2	83.5	83.5	84.4	85.7	85.2	86.9	88.5	90.3	92.3	93.8	86.8
1995	89.2	88.0	88.1	87.6	88.0	88.7	87.5	89.3	89.5	90.6	92.7	94.1	89.4
1996	88.8	87.5	87.6	88.3	89.1	89.7	88.3	88.5	89.1	88.9	91.6	93.7	89.2
1997	88.5	87.3	87.1	86.5	87.5	87.6	86.9	87.5	88.8	89.1	91.3	93.4	88.4
1998	88.0	87.0	87.1	87.8	89.3	90.2	89.3	89.9	91.2	92.0	94.3	95.8	90.1
1999	89.2	88.6	89.3	89.7	90.7	91.4	89.9	90.7	92.4	94.8	97.6	99.2	91.9
2000	94.9	94.2	94.2	95.7	95.8	95.9	93.7	94.8	95.8	97.3	99.9	101.7	96.1
2001	94.4	92.7	92.4	93.0	93.2	94.4	92.7	93.1	94.2	94.5	97.1	98.7	94.2
2002	94.3	92.8	93.3	94.4	95.0	96.2	94.5	94.7	95.8	96.7	99.2	100.9	95.7
2003	95.0	93.6	93.7	94.3	95.2	96.1	94.6	94.8	95.9	96.9	98.9	100.2	95.8
Wholesale trade													
1990	19.5	19.3	19.4	19.1	19.2	19.3	19.2	19.1	19.0	18.7	18.7	18.5	19.0
1991	17.7	17.5	17.7	17.5	17.6	17.6	17.2	17.4	17.7	17.5	17.5	17.2	17.5
1992	16.8	16.8	16.8	17.2	17.2	17.4	17.1	17.2	17.2	17.3	17.3	17.1	17.1
1993	16.8	16.7	16.8	16.8	16.9	17.0	16.9	17.0	17.0	17.1	17.1	17.1	16.9
1994	16.7	16.6	16.8	16.8	16.9	17.1	17.2	17.6	17.8	17.9	18.0	18.1	17.2
1995	17.6	17.4	17.5	17.5	17.5	17.6	17.6	17.9	17.9	17.7	17.6	17.7	17.6
1996	17.0	17.0	17.0	17.5	17.7	17.9	17.5	17.6	17.6	17.5	17.6	17.7	17.4
1997	17.2	17.2	17.4	17.2	17.4	17.4	17.2	17.4	17.4	17.4	17.6	17.7	17.3
1998	17.5	17.6	17.6	17.8	18.1	18.2	18.4	18.4	18.4	18.8	18.9	18.9	18.2
1999	18.2	18.2	18.3	18.5	18.6	18.7	18.3	18.4	18.4	18.5	18.5	18.6	18.4
2000	18.4	18.5	18.7	19.1	19.1	19.2	19.0	19.3	19.3	19.5	19.5	19.7	19.1
2001	18.9	19.1	19.2	19.5	19.6	19.7	19.7	19.8	19.9	19.7	19.8	20.0	19.6
2002	19.5	19.4	19.5	19.6	19.6	19.7	19.3	19.4	19.3	19.3	19.6	19.5	19.5
2003	19.4	19.2	19.3	19.4	19.6	19.7	19.5	19.4	19.3	19.3	19.2	19.1	19.4

Employment by Industry: Rhode Island—*Continued*

(Numbers in thousands. Not seasonally adjusted.)

Industry	January	February	March	April	May	June	July	August	September	October	November	December	Annual Average
PROVIDENCE—*Continued*													
Retail trade													
1990	61.1	60.3	60.6	59.0	59.3	59.7	56.7	57.8	57.8	58.7	59.9	61.0	59.3
1991	55.9	54.7	54.3	54.0	54.3	54.5	53.5	53.5	53.9	53.3	54.8	56.6	54.4
1992	53.6	52.8	53.0	53.5	53.9	54.4	54.4	54.8	55.3	55.7	57.2	58.9	54.7
1993	55.5	54.8	54.7	55.4	55.9	56.6	55.4	56.5	56.7	57.4	59.8	61.3	56.6
1994	57.4	55.5	55.5	55.5	56.1	57.0	57.2	58.0	59.1	60.4	62.4	63.8	58.1
1995	60.2	59.3	59.2	58.9	59.2	59.8	59.0	60.1	59.9	61.1	63.2	64.5	60.3
1996	60.4	59.1	59.0	59.1	59.5	59.8	59.1	59.2	59.4	59.2	61.8	63.8	59.9
1997	59.9	58.7	58.1	57.6	58.2	58.3	58.3	58.9	59.3	59.5	61.4	63.3	59.2
1998	58.7	57.5	57.5	58.2	58.8	59.3	59.3	59.7	60.4	60.9	63.0	64.5	59.8
1999	59.5	58.8	59.0	59.9	60.3	60.6	60.0	60.8	61.7	63.8	66.7	68.3	61.6
2000	64.6	63.8	63.6	64.4	64.4	64.4	63.1	63.7	64.2	65.4	68.0	69.6	64.9
2001	63.3	61.4	60.9	61.1	61.2	62.2	61.2	61.5	61.8	62.3	64.8	66.4	62.3
2002	62.7	61.5	61.8	62.8	63.3	64.1	63.7	63.8	64.1	64.7	67.0	68.8	64.0
2003	63.4	62.3	62.1	62.5	63.0	63.6	63.1	63.5	63.7	64.4	66.4	67.9	63.8
Transportation and utilities													
1990	10.9	10.9	10.8	11.2	11.3	11.5	10.5	10.4	11.4	11.3	11.3	11.4	11.0
1991	10.8	10.7	10.6	10.7	10.8	10.9	9.9	9.9	10.9	10.9	10.7	10.7	10.6
1992	10.7	10.6	10.6	10.7	10.9	11.0	10.2	10.1	10.8	10.8	10.7	10.8	10.6
1993	10.5	10.3	10.5	10.5	10.7	10.8	10.4	10.3	11.2	11.8	11.8	11.7	10.8
1994	11.1	11.1	11.2	11.2	11.4	11.6	10.8	11.3	11.6	12.0	11.9	11.9	11.4
1995	11.4	11.3	11.4	11.2	11.3	11.3	10.9	11.3	11.7	11.8	11.9	11.9	11.4
1996	11.4	11.4	11.6	11.7	11.9	12.0	11.7	11.7	12.1	12.2	12.2	12.2	11.8
1997	11.4	11.4	11.6	11.7	11.9	11.9	11.4	11.2	12.1	12.2	12.3	12.4	11.7
1998	11.8	11.9	12.0	11.8	12.4	12.7	11.6	11.8	12.4	12.3	12.4	12.4	12.1
1999	11.5	11.6	12.0	11.3	11.8	12.1	11.6	11.5	12.3	12.5	12.4	12.3	11.9
2000	11.9	11.9	11.9	12.2	12.3	12.3	11.6	11.8	12.3	12.4	12.4	12.4	12.1
2001	12.2	12.2	12.3	12.4	12.4	12.5	11.8	11.8	12.5	12.5	12.5	12.3	12.3
2002	12.1	11.9	12.0	12.0	12.1	12.4	11.5	11.5	12.4	12.7	12.6	12.6	12.2
2003	12.2	12.1	12.3	12.4	12.6	12.8	12.0	11.9	12.9	13.2	13.3	13.2	12.6
Information													
1990	10.9	10.6	10.5	10.3	10.3	10.4	10.4	10.4	10.4	10.2	10.2	10.3	10.4
1991	10.1	10.0	10.0	9.9	10.0	10.0	10.0	10.0	9.9	9.9	10.0	9.9	9.9
1992	9.9	9.9	9.9	9.8	9.9	10.0	10.1	10.1	10.0	10.0	10.0	10.1	9.9
1993	10.0	10.2	10.2	9.8	9.8	9.9	10.3	10.4	10.4	10.2	10.3	10.4	10.1
1994	10.5	10.5	10.5	10.4	10.5	10.6	10.6	10.6	10.6	10.7	10.9	10.9	10.6
1995	10.9	11.0	11.0	10.7	10.8	10.9	10.8	11.0	11.1	10.8	10.7	10.7	10.8
1996	10.6	10.7	10.7	10.6	10.6	10.6	10.5	10.6	10.6	10.7	10.7	10.7	10.6
1997	10.8	10.6	10.6	10.4	10.4	10.5	10.3	10.5	10.4	10.5	10.6	10.7	10.5
1998	10.5	10.4	10.6	10.5	10.6	10.6	10.7	10.6	10.6	10.6	10.7	10.7	10.5
1999	10.5	10.5	10.5	10.5	10.6	10.6	10.5	10.5	10.5	10.7	10.7	10.6	10.5
2000	10.8	10.8	10.7	10.9	11.0	11.2	11.2	9.9	11.2	11.1	11.1	11.1	10.9
2001	11.1	11.1	11.2	11.2	11.4	11.5	11.4	11.3	11.3	11.3	11.3	11.3	11.3
2002	11.3	11.3	11.3	11.2	11.3	11.4	11.4	11.3	11.3	11.0	11.3	11.3	11.3
2003	11.2	11.2	11.2	11.1	11.2	11.4	11.2	11.2	11.0	10.8	10.9	10.9	11.1
Financial activities													
1990	29.4	29.4	29.5	29.3	29.4	29.8	29.6	29.4	29.3	29.2	29.0	28.9	29.3
1991	27.8	27.7	27.8	27.6	27.7	27.9	27.7	27.5	27.3	27.0	26.9	26.9	27.4
1992	26.9	26.6	26.5	26.7	26.7	26.8	26.8	26.7	26.2	26.1	26.1	25.8	26.4
1993	25.7	25.6	25.8	25.9	26.0	26.4	26.1	26.1	26.1	25.9	26.0	26.2	25.9
1994	25.8	26.0	25.9	26.0	26.1	26.2	26.0	26.0	25.8	25.8	25.7	25.7	25.9
1995	25.5	25.6	25.8	25.8	25.8	25.6	25.3	25.3	25.2	24.9	25.4	25.5	25.4
1996	25.5	25.5	25.7	25.4	25.6	25.8	25.8	26.0	25.9	26.1	26.2	26.4	25.8
1997	26.0	26.2	26.6	26.8	26.9	27.1	27.1	27.3	27.3	27.3	27.4	27.8	26.9
1998	28.4	28.6	28.9	29.0	29.7	29.8	30.1	30.1	30.1	30.3	30.6	30.8	29.7
1999	30.4	30.6	30.8	30.8	30.8	31.0	31.3	31.5	31.1	31.3	31.3	31.8	31.0
2000	31.2	31.2	31.4	31.8	31.7	32.4	32.6	32.7	32.5	32.5	32.8	33.1	32.1
2001	33.4	33.5	33.7	33.4	33.3	33.8	33.8	33.6	33.4	33.4	33.5	33.8	33.6
2002	33.7	33.7	33.6	34.1	34.2	34.6	34.9	34.9	34.8	35.0	35.2	35.5	34.5
2003	35.0	35.0	35.3	34.9	35.1	35.5	35.7	35.7	35.6	35.5	35.6	35.5	35.4
Professional and business services													
1990	39.9	40.0	40.7	41.6	42.2	42.6	43.0	43.6	43.6	43.2	43.1	43.0	42.2
1991	40.4	39.6	39.8	39.9	40.1	40.1	39.9	40.3	40.2	40.0	39.3	38.4	39.8
1992	37.4	37.5	37.8	38.7	38.4	38.7	39.4	40.2	41.4	42.3	41.9	41.2	39.5
1993	39.2	39.4	39.9	41.4	42.5	43.1	43.3	43.8	44.4	44.2	44.1	43.4	42.3
1994	41.1	41.9	42.1	42.7	43.0	43.5	43.3	44.7	45.1	45.0	45.2	44.8	43.5
1995	43.9	44.1	44.7	45.3	45.6	46.5	45.6	46.8	47.5	47.5	46.9	45.8	45.8
1996	44.7	45.2	45.8	46.3	46.9	46.9	46.8	48.1	49.2	50.5	50.3	49.6	47.5
1997	47.0	47.2	48.2	50.5	50.9	51.8	50.9	52.1	53.4	53.7	52.7	52.0	50.8
1998	50.1	50.4	51.4	52.9	53.2	53.5	53.3	53.4	53.4	53.0	52.7	52.1	52.4
1999	49.3	50.6	51.3	53.6	54.0	54.7	54.5	55.4	55.5	55.9	55.8	56.5	53.9
2000	52.6	52.8	53.9	55.2	55.3	55.6	55.5	55.6	55.9	56.2	56.3	56.3	55.1
2001	52.9	53.0	53.1	54.7	54.8	55.3	54.5	55.8	55.8	55.9	54.8	54.4	54.6
2002	51.2	50.7	51.4	53.0	53.0	53.5	52.0	52.5	52.8	52.9	52.4	51.6	52.3
2003	50.7	50.4	50.6	52.4	53.0	54.1	53.7	54.4	54.3	53.8	53.4	53.0	52.8

Employment by Industry: Rhode Island—*Continued*

(Numbers in thousands. Not seasonally adjusted.)

Industry	January	February	March	April	May	June	July	August	September	October	November	December	Annual Average
PROVIDENCE—*Continued*													
Educational and health services													
1990	71.8	72.7	73.4	73.4	73.4	70.9	69.5	69.4	71.6	73.1	73.5	73.4	72.1
1991	72.1	72.7	73.1	73.5	73.8	71.0	69.4	69.4	71.2	73.1	73.7	73.3	72.1
1992	73.8	74.8	75.1	76.8	77.0	74.6	73.9	74.1	76.6	79.1	79.6	80.2	76.3
1993	78.2	79.1	79.5	79.5	80.0	78.3	77.5	77.3	79.4	81.4	81.3	81.9	79.4
1994	80.3	80.8	81.3	80.3	80.6	78.9	78.5	78.4	81.4	82.2	82.7	83.0	80.7
1995	81.4	82.1	82.7	83.1	83.4	83.6	82.2	82.5	84.9	86.2	86.7	87.1	83.8
1996	84.8	86.4	86.7	86.5	86.4	84.4	83.2	82.8	85.9	87.5	88.5	88.7	85.9
1997	86.4	87.3	87.9	88.3	88.5	86.6	85.8	85.6	89.8	90.4	91.0	90.7	88.1
1998	88.7	90.1	90.1	90.6	90.9	87.7	86.7	86.3	90.0	91.1	91.6	91.6	89.6
1999	90.1	91.9	92.2	92.1	91.7	88.9	89.4	88.8	91.4	93.2	93.1	92.6	91.2
2000	90.5	91.7	92.1	92.9	93.2	90.7	90.7	90.7	93.6	95.0	95.9	96.5	92.7
2001	91.7	93.8	94.8	94.7	94.9	91.0	90.2	91.0	93.6	95.3	96.4	96.7	93.7
2002	94.0	95.9	97.1	97.7	97.8	93.5	92.5	93.7	97.0	98.2	99.4	99.8	96.4
2003	97.5	99.2	100.5	100.8	100.5	96.4	95.4	94.8	97.7	99.9	100.4	100.8	98.7
Leisure and hospitality													
1990	34.3	34.2	35.0	35.2	36.4	38.0	38.6	38.3	38.0	35.4	34.8	34.4	36.0
1991	30.9	31.0	31.2	32.1	33.9	34.8	35.1	35.1	34.3	32.6	31.9	31.5	32.8
1992	29.9	29.9	31.0	32.7	34.5	35.9	36.3	36.2	36.0	34.8	34.1	34.1	33.7
1993	32.5	32.8	32.4	34.4	36.3	38.2	38.5	38.6	37.9	37.2	36.6	36.4	35.9
1994	34.0	33.7	34.7	36.9	38.7	40.3	40.0	40.9	39.9	39.4	38.6	38.8	37.9
1995	36.7	37.2	37.7	39.5	40.9	42.3	42.4	42.7	42.2	40.7	39.7	39.2	40.1
1996	37.8	38.2	38.5	40.2	42.3	44.1	43.6	44.0	43.2	41.5	41.1	40.9	41.2
1997	38.9	39.4	39.8	41.4	43.3	44.4	44.5	44.3	43.6	42.7	42.1	42.0	42.2
1998	39.2	39.8	39.8	41.8	43.7	45.1	45.1	45.1	44.6	43.2	42.4	42.3	42.6
1999	39.6	40.4	40.4	43.7	45.2	47.3	46.2	46.8	46.1	45.7	45.0	45.5	44.3
2000	43.2	43.2	43.9	45.7	47.6	49.6	49.5	49.3	48.0	47.0	46.6	46.2	46.6
2001	43.0	43.6	43.9	46.3	48.5	50.4	49.2	49.4	48.6	47.0	46.0	45.8	46.8
2002	43.8	44.4	45.2	47.9	49.9	51.4	51.5	51.5	50.2	48.8	48.0	47.3	48.3
2003	45.5	45.5	45.9	48.6	51.0	52.5	52.7	52.9	52.0	50.9	49.9	49.8	49.8
Other services													
1990	18.1	18.1	18.3	18.0	18.0	18.1	18.5	18.5	18.3	18.4	18.1	18.1	18.2
1991	17.3	17.1	17.2	17.5	17.7	17.9	17.8	17.7	17.7	18.2	18.2	18.1	17.7
1992	18.1	18.1	18.2	18.6	18.9	19.3	19.6	19.6	19.5	19.9	20.1	20.2	19.1
1993	18.1	18.1	18.2	18.1	18.3	18.6	18.4	18.5	18.5	18.1	18.2	18.4	18.2
1994	17.8	18.0	18.2	18.2	18.1	18.2	17.9	17.9	17.6	17.3	17.2	17.1	17.7
1995	16.5	16.5	16.4	16.7	17.0	17.4	17.7	18.0	18.2	18.1	18.1	18.3	17.4
1996	18.0	18.2	18.6	18.6	18.9	19.3	19.6	19.6	19.1	18.8	18.9	19.0	18.8
1997	18.7	18.9	19.1	19.3	19.7	20.2	20.3	20.1	19.6	19.8	19.8	19.9	19.6
1998	19.6	19.7	19.8	19.9	20.1	20.5	20.7	20.8	20.1	20.7	20.7	20.8	20.2
1999	20.2	20.5	20.6	21.2	21.2	21.6	21.7	21.9	21.1	21.6	21.5	21.6	21.2
2000	21.2	21.3	21.5	21.8	21.8	22.3	22.5	22.6	21.9	22.1	22.0	22.2	21.9
2001	21.9	21.9	22.0	21.9	22.1	22.6	22.9	23.0	22.2	22.2	22.4	22.5	22.3
2002	22.4	22.4	22.5	22.9	23.3	24.0	24.5	24.5	23.9	24.4	24.5	24.8	23.7
2003	24.4	24.4	24.6	24.9	25.2	25.5	25.9	25.7	25.1	25.4	25.4	25.5	25.2
Government													
1990	64.3	64.8	65.1	65.6	66.9	65.2	58.2	57.3	62.9	64.4	65.2	65.3	63.7
1991	65.1	64.6	64.8	63.5	63.7	64.2	57.8	57.4	59.9	63.0	63.5	63.4	62.5
1992	62.3	62.7	62.9	64.1	64.3	64.6	58.0	57.5	61.5	64.6	65.4	65.1	62.7
1993	63.9	63.9	64.5	64.0	65.0	64.5	59.5	59.1	61.7	63.9	64.6	64.9	63.2
1994	64.3	64.7	64.8	63.8	64.2	64.3	59.9	59.1	62.2	64.4	66.7	65.3	63.6
1995	64.4	65.0	64.9	64.9	65.1	63.3	59.5	59.4	61.3	63.7	64.5	65.3	63.4
1996	63.0	64.4	65.0	63.8	64.9	63.2	58.1	58.0	63.0	64.7	65.3	65.7	63.2
1997	64.5	65.1	65.2	65.6	65.8	66.0	60.9	59.9	64.4	65.4	65.7	66.5	64.5
1998	65.5	65.8	65.9	65.1	66.1	65.5	60.4	60.0	64.4	65.8	66.5	66.7	64.8
1999	66.2	65.8	66.9	66.7	67.2	66.1	60.9	60.5	64.7	66.9	67.3	67.6	65.5
2000	67.1	66.9	67.7	68.0	70.5	67.6	61.4	59.8	66.1	67.9	68.5	68.7	66.6
2001	68.2	68.1	68.5	68.7	69.0	68.3	64.0	63.7	67.1	68.8	69.6	69.8	67.8
2002	69.2	69.5	69.7	70.0	70.3	69.4	63.8	63.6	67.5	69.1	69.7	69.8	68.5
2003	69.4	69.4	69.5	69.2	69.6	69.5	63.2	63.0	67.7	70.1	70.5	70.4	68.5
Federal government													
1990	7.3	7.2	7.4	7.7	8.9	8.4	7.4	7.4	7.3	7.1	7.2	7.2	7.5
1991	7.1	7.1	7.1	7.1	7.1	7.1	7.4	7.4	7.4	7.3	7.3	7.3	7.2
1992	7.3	7.3	7.3	7.3	7.3	7.3	7.3	7.3	7.3	7.2	7.1	7.2	7.2
1993	7.0	7.1	7.1	7.0	7.0	7.2	7.1	7.1	7.0	7.0	7.0	7.4	7.0
1994	7.0	7.0	7.0	7.0	7.1	7.1	7.2	7.2	7.2	7.1	7.2	7.6	7.1
1995	7.2	7.3	7.3	7.2	7.2	7.2	7.2	7.2	7.1	7.1	7.3	7.6	7.2
1996	7.1	7.1	7.2	7.2	7.1	7.2	7.2	7.2	7.2	7.2	7.3	7.6	7.2
1997	7.2	7.2	7.1	6.9	6.9	6.9	7.0	7.0	6.9	6.9	6.9	7.3	7.0
1998	6.9	6.9	6.9	6.9	6.9	7.0	7.0	6.9	6.9	6.9	7.1	7.4	6.9
1999	6.9	6.9	7.1	7.1	6.8	6.9	6.9	6.8	6.8	6.8	6.9	7.2	6.9
2000	6.8	6.9	7.1	7.5	9.4	7.8	7.8	7.1	6.9	6.9	7.0	7.2	7.3
2001	7.0	6.8	6.8	7.0	6.9	7.0	7.0	7.1	7.1	6.9	6.8	7.1	7.0
2002	6.7	6.7	6.7	6.7	6.6	6.7	6.5	6.6	6.6	6.7	6.7	7.0	6.7
2003	6.6	6.6	6.6	6.5	6.5	6.5	6.4	6.4	6.4	6.5	6.4	6.6	6.5

Employment by Industry: Rhode Island—*Continued*

(Numbers in thousands. Not seasonally adjusted.)

Industry	January	February	March	April	May	June	July	August	September	October	November	December	Annual Average
PROVIDENCE—*Continued*													
State government													
1990	21.2	21.7	21.8	21.8	21.8	21.8	21.0	20.7	21.0	21.9	21.9	21.8	21.5
1991	21.9	21.5	21.6	21.3	21.3	21.3	20.4	20.1	20.4	21.2	21.0	21.0	21.0
1992	21.0	21.1	21.0	21.1	21.2	21.2	20.5	20.4	20.8	21.8	21.8	21.5	21.1
1993	21.3	21.2	21.3	21.0	21.3	21.3	20.4	20.2	19.9	20.9	20.9	20.8	20.8
1994	20.5	20.5	20.5	20.6	20.6	20.5	19.6	19.3	18.9	20.0	19.9	19.8	20.0
1995	19.8	19.7	19.8	19.8	19.8	19.7	18.6	18.5	18.2	19.2	19.2	19.1	19.2
1996	18.2	19.1	19.2	19.1	19.3	19.1	18.2	18.2	17.9	18.9	18.8	18.7	18.7
1997	18.7	18.7	18.7	18.8	18.9	18.7	18.0	18.0	17.7	18.8	18.7	18.7	18.5
1998	18.7	18.7	18.7	18.8	19.1	19.0	18.2	18.2	17.9	19.0	18.9	18.9	18.6
1999	18.9	19.0	19.1	19.1	19.5	19.3	18.5	18.5	18.3	19.4	19.3	19.2	19.0
2000	19.2	19.2	19.2	19.1	19.4	19.2	18.4	18.3	18.1	19.1	19.0	19.0	18.9
2001	18.9	19.0	19.0	19.1	19.1	19.1	18.3	18.4	18.1	19.2	19.2	19.0	18.9
2002	19.0	19.0	19.1	19.2	19.3	19.1	18.3	18.3	17.9	19.0	18.9	18.8	18.8
2003	18.7	18.7	18.7	18.7	18.7	18.7	17.9	17.8	17.6	18.6	18.6	18.4	18.4
Local government													
1990	35.8	35.9	35.9	36.1	36.2	35.0	29.8	29.2	34.6	35.4	36.1	36.3	34.6
1991	36.1	36.0	36.1	35.1	35.3	35.8	30.0	29.9	32.1	34.5	35.2	35.1	34.2
1992	34.0	34.3	34.6	35.7	35.8	36.1	30.2	29.8	33.4	35.6	36.5	36.4	34.3
1993	35.6	35.6	36.1	36.0	36.7	36.0	32.0	31.8	34.8	36.0	36.7	36.7	35.3
1994	36.8	37.2	37.3	36.2	36.5	36.7	33.1	32.6	36.1	37.3	39.6	37.9	36.4
1995	37.4	38.0	37.8	37.9	38.1	36.4	33.7	33.7	36.0	37.4	38.0	38.6	36.9
1996	37.7	38.2	38.6	37.5	38.5	36.9	32.7	32.6	37.9	38.6	39.2	39.4	37.3
1997	38.6	39.2	39.4	39.9	40.0	40.4	35.9	34.9	39.8	39.7	40.1	40.5	39.0
1998	39.9	40.2	40.3	39.4	40.1	39.5	35.2	34.9	39.6	39.9	40.5	40.4	39.1
1999	40.4	39.9	40.7	40.5	40.9	39.9	35.5	35.2	39.6	40.7	41.1	41.2	39.6
2000	41.1	40.8	41.4	41.4	41.7	40.6	35.2	34.4	41.1	41.9	42.5	42.5	40.3
2001	42.3	42.3	42.7	42.6	43.0	42.2	38.7	38.2	41.9	42.7	43.6	43.7	42.0
2002	43.5	43.8	43.9	44.1	44.4	43.6	39.0	38.7	43.0	43.4	44.1	44.0	43.0
2003	44.1	44.1	44.2	44.0	44.4	44.3	38.9	38.8	43.7	45.0	45.5	45.4	43.5

Average Weekly Hours by Industry: Rhode Island

(Not seasonally adjusted.)

Industry	January	February	March	April	May	June	July	August	September	October	November	December	Annual Average
STATEWIDE													
Manufacturing													
2001	39.2	39.3	39.8	38.2	39.9	40.2	38.5	38.8	40.0	38.7	39.6	40.4	39.4
2002	38.4	38.7	38.4	38.7	38.8	39.3	37.4	37.8	39.4	39.1	38.7	40.0	38.7
2003	38.3	38.4	39.3	38.6	39.6	39.5	38.3	39.1	39.7	39.2	40.1	40.9	39.3
PROVIDENCE													
Manufacturing													
2001	40.2	39.6	40.1	39.4	40.3	40.2	39.0	39.9	40.7	39.9	40.5	40.5	40.0
2002	39.7	40.2	40.8	40.5	40.6	41.1	39.8	40.3	40.6	39.9	39.7	40.1	40.3
2003	39.3	39.5	39.7	39.1	39.2	39.3	38.2	39.5	40.2	39.5	40.5	41.4	39.6

Average Hourly Earnings by Industry: Rhode Island

(Dollars, not seasonally adjusted.)

Industry	January	February	March	April	May	June	July	August	September	October	November	December	Annual Average
STATEWIDE													
Manufacturing													
2001	12.68	12.68	12.68	12.78	12.58	12.66	12.65	12.72	12.77	12.63	12.68	12.70	12.68
2002	12.63	12.76	12.64	12.74	12.72	12.74	12.70	12.79	12.84	12.80	12.81	12.84	12.75
2003	12.78	12.78	12.82	12.84	12.87	12.86	12.87	12.90	12.88	12.93	13.01	12.97	12.88
PROVIDENCE													
Manufacturing													
2001	12.73	12.78	12.82	12.80	12.83	12.93	13.00	13.01	13.06	13.09	13.14	13.08	12.94
2002	13.08	13.09	13.12	13.16	13.16	13.22	13.25	13.26	13.24	13.25	13.28	13.23	13.19
2003	13.21	13.19	13.20	13.22	13.22	13.24	13.26	13.32	13.28	13.32	13.40	13.36	13.27

Average Weekly Earnings by Industry: Rhode Island

(Dollars, not seasonally adjusted.)

Industry	January	February	March	April	May	June	July	August	September	October	November	December	Annual Average
STATEWIDE													
Manufacturing													
2001	497.06	498.32	504.66	488.20	501.94	508.93	487.03	493.54	510.80	488.78	502.13	513.08	499.59
2002	484.99	493.81	485.38	493.04	493.54	500.68	474.98	483.46	505.90	500.48	495.75	513.60	493.43
2003	489.47	490.75	503.83	495.62	509.65	507.97	492.92	504.39	511.34	506.86	521.70	530.47	506.18
PROVIDENCE													
Manufacturing													
2001	511.75	506.09	514.08	504.32	517.05	519.79	507.00	519.10	531.54	522.29	532.17	529.74	517.60
2002	519.28	526.22	535.30	532.98	534.30	543.34	527.35	534.38	537.54	528.68	527.22	530.52	531.56
2003	519.15	521.01	524.04	516.90	518.22	520.33	506.53	526.14	533.86	526.14	542.70	553.10	525.49

SOUTH CAROLINA AT A GLANCE

(Population and total nonfarm employment numbers in thousands)

Population, Census 2000:	4,012
Total nonfarm employment, 2003:	1,812.5
Change in total nonfarm employment	
(Number)	
1990–2003:	267.5
1990–2001:	278.4
2001–2003:	-10.9
(Compound annual rate of change)	
1990–2003:	1.2%
1990–2001:	1.5%
2001–2003:	-0.3%
Unemployment rate	
1990:	4.9%
2001:	5.4%
2003:	6.7%

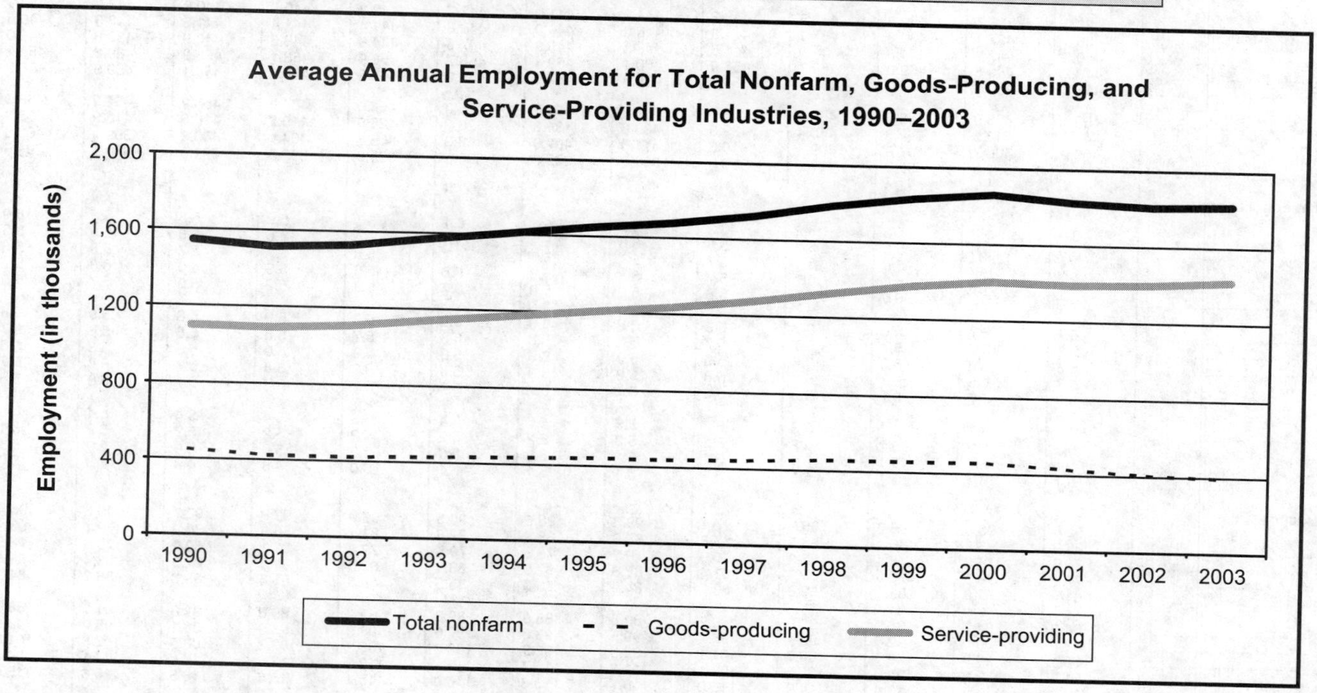

Following national trends, total nonfarm payroll employment dropped in both the 1990–1991 and 2001 recessions and showed some recovery in 2003. Following a recovery from the first recession, jobs in the goods-producing sector rose during the 1990s. Employment began to decline again in 2001 and was nearly 14 percent lower in 2003 than in 1999. Jobs in the service-providing sector, while weakened by the 2001 recession, had recovered by 2003.

Employment by Industry: South Carolina

(Numbers in thousands. Not seasonally adjusted.)

Industry	January	February	March	April	May	June	July	August	September	October	November	December	Annual Average
STATEWIDE													
Total nonfarm													
1990	1502.1	1517.4	1533.3	1546.4	1563.6	1568.9	1539.5	1545.5	1564.0	1555.6	1554.5	1549.4	1545.0
1991	1494.6	1499.9	1513.9	1513.4	1527.3	1528.4	1500.1	1505.7	1514.9	1515.4	1524.5	1524.3	1513.5
1992	1488.4	1496.3	1511.4	1524.4	1537.2	1541.5	1518.8	1526.2	1539.3	1542.8	1556.0	1550.3	1527.7
1993	1518.3	1530.9	1548.0	1571.1	1581.3	1589.7	1567.1	1572.5	1584.8	1587.6	1590.5	1599.3	1570.0
1994	1558.2	1570.5	1590.4	1603.2	1613.6	1626.9	1601.6	1608.8	1622.8	1621.7	1636.7	1633.2	1607.3
1995	1596.4	1606.9	1627.3	1644.5	1658.5	1669.1	1641.4	1651.4	1661.8	1659.6	1664.4	1672.4	1646.1
1996	1625.3	1639.6	1660.6	1670.1	1687.4	1707.9	1653.9	1669.5	1691.4	1689.8	1704.5	1702.2	1675.1
1997	1669.8	1683.9	1704.8	1715.4	1731.1	1739.9	1699.0	1711.0	1739.4	1742.1	1747.7	1758.4	1720.2
1998	1730.0	1740.6	1764.5	1770.2	1788.8	1810.5	1779.3	1784.0	1805.5	1800.8	1807.0	1818.4	1783.3
1999	1781.5	1796.9	1815.5	1830.4	1840.4	1852.1	1812.5	1829.1	1835.6	1848.7	1856.8	1868.5	1830.6
2000	1824.3	1837.0	1862.8	1868.8	1887.5	1900.9	1834.9	1852.3	1851.9	1861.6	1864.8	1866.7	1859.4
2001	1808.9	1817.2	1833.3	1837.6	1843.2	1842.6	1805.3	1827.6	1826.7	1812.5	1814.7	1812.0	1823.4
2002	1762.2	1773.6	1794.8	1813.1	1824.4	1830.1	1785.1	1814.6	1814.6	1814.9	1814.4	1814.4	1804.7
2003	1777.3	1790.2	1806.9	1817.3	1827.2	1827.2	1786.8	1813.3	1824.9	1830.3	1824.4	1823.7	1812.5
Total private													
1990	1225.7	1234.2	1248.0	1260.4	1273.4	1287.3	1279.4	1283.8	1280.1	1264.3	1261.5	1256.1	1262.8
1991	1212.5	1210.1	1221.3	1223.4	1236.1	1245.2	1236.0	1238.3	1231.7	1224.4	1228.1	1227.1	1227.8
1992	1200.3	1202.4	1216.7	1228.8	1241.3	1251.7	1247.1	1252.6	1248.7	1245.2	1245.2	1249.7	1235.8
1993	1224.5	1232.8	1246.4	1269.0	1280.3	1293.2	1289.0	1292.0	1291.8	1287.7	1288.4	1296.8	1274.3
1994	1264.3	1272.0	1290.8	1303.0	1313.0	1330.9	1325.3	1330.9	1330.5	1323.6	1326.2	1333.5	1312.0
1995	1303.3	1309.5	1328.1	1346.4	1359.7	1374.9	1364.3	1370.6	1368.4	1362.7	1365.1	1369.9	1351.9
1996	1330.8	1340.2	1359.5	1370.4	1388.0	1404.7	1394.4	1401.9	1395.5	1389.5	1392.3	1399.4	1380.5
1997	1371.3	1381.2	1400.2	1412.5	1427.2	1440.4	1431.8	1437.2	1436.1	1433.7	1437.4	1446.9	1421.3
1998	1422.5	1428.9	1451.2	1459.5	1477.7	1491.9	1495.5	1494.3	1493.4	1484.1	1488.5	1498.2	1473.8
1999	1466.1	1477.6	1495.5	1510.6	1520.5	1535.9	1528.8	1527.2	1518.7	1527.1	1533.2	1542.6	1515.3
2000	1502.7	1512.4	1534.3	1541.7	1554.5	1570.8	1540.1	1540.4	1531.0	1535.6	1537.0	1538.5	1536.5
2001	1486.2	1490.4	1505.4	1510.7	1516.6	1520.6	1515.6	1514.0	1500.7	1483.7	1484.0	1480.0	1500.6
2002	1436.8	1444.8	1464.8	1483.0	1493.8	1505.7	1494.1	1495.4	1486.1	1484.0	1481.0	1480.8	1479.2
2003	1449.1	1457.2	1473.3	1483.8	1494.5	1501.9	1491.2	1494.7	1493.2	1493.5	1486.0	1483.7	1483.5
Goods-producing													
1990	449.6	451.1	452.4	452.5	453.7	457.2	452.5	452.0	449.5	443.7	440.5	436.8	449.2
1991	426.5	423.6	423.6	419.3	420.7	423.4	420.4	422.1	422.1	421.7	423.5	422.5	422.4
1992	418.2	416.7	417.9	418.8	421.2	423.7	421.8	423.6	424.7	425.0	425.1	425.6	421.8
1993	422.5	422.8	424.5	427.4	428.7	432.1	430.8	431.2	431.4	431.7	432.1	434.3	429.1
1994	429.5	431.0	432.7	431.6	433.2	437.1	435.3	436.7	438.0	438.3	440.1	441.7	435.4
1995	436.2	436.5	439.8	441.5	443.3	444.2	441.0	442.7	442.2	440.3	440.9	443.0	440.9
1996	435.1	437.1	439.8	437.1	441.3	446.6	440.0	442.6	441.4	441.4	441.5	443.3	440.6
1997	440.0	442.2	444.3	444.0	446.5	448.8	445.9	447.3	444.8	448.5	448.9	450.8	446.0
1998	449.2	449.5	452.0	453.7	456.9	460.1	459.4	458.7	458.9	458.1	458.2	460.6	456.2
1999	457.5	456.7	457.0	455.9	456.1	458.8	457.5	455.2	454.6	456.2	458.1	459.6	456.9
2000	453.4	455.9	458.6	458.3	460.0	463.9	454.7	455.0	454.0	454.6	453.9	454.0	456.3
2001	444.1	442.5	442.6	440.4	439.3	436.8	431.3	428.5	425.0	419.2	418.6	415.9	432.0
2002	406.9	406.7	407.8	409.4	410.6	411.6	407.8	408.0	405.6	404.1	400.8	399.4	406.6
2003	397.4	397.9	398.6	397.5	396.3	394.7	392.8	393.2	391.9	392.8	391.9	389.1	394.5
Natural resources and mining													
1990	6.0	6.2	6.3	6.2	6.2	6.2	6.1	6.1	6.1	5.9	5.8	5.8	6.0
1991	5.6	5.6	5.5	5.4	5.5	5.5	5.4	5.4	5.4	5.5	5.6	5.6	5.5
1992	5.7	5.6	5.6	5.6	5.7	5.7	5.7	5.7	5.8	5.7	5.7	5.8	5.6
1993	5.5	5.6	5.6	5.7	5.7	5.8	5.8	5.8	5.8	5.9	6.0	6.0	5.7
1994	6.0	5.9	6.0	5.8	5.8	5.9	5.8	5.7	5.8	5.8	5.8	5.7	5.8
1995	5.7	5.7	5.8	5.7	5.8	5.9	5.8	5.9	5.9	5.9	5.8	5.9	5.8
1996	5.7	5.7	5.7	5.7	5.7	5.8	5.8	5.8	5.7	5.8	5.8	5.8	5.7
1997	5.8	5.8	5.8	5.8	5.9	5.9	5.8	5.8	5.9	5.9	5.8	5.8	5.8
1998	5.7	5.6	5.7	5.7	5.8	5.8	5.9	5.8	5.9	5.8	5.7	5.8	5.7
1999	5.7	5.7	5.7	5.6	5.6	5.7	5.7	5.7	5.7	5.7	5.7	5.8	5.6
2000	5.6	5.7	5.7	5.6	5.7	5.5	5.6	5.4	5.3	5.4	5.4	5.4	5.5
2001	5.2	5.2	5.2	5.2	5.2	5.2	5.2	5.2	5.2	5.2	5.2	5.2	5.1
2002	5.1	5.1	5.1	5.1	5.1	5.1	5.0	5.0	5.0	5.0	5.0	5.0	5.1
2003	5.1	5.1	5.1	5.1	5.1	5.1	5.1	5.1	5.0	4.8	4.8	4.8	5.0
Construction													
1990	92.0	93.9	95.6	95.9	97.1	99.3	98.5	98.5	96.9	93.8	92.7	90.6	95.4
1991	86.0	85.8	86.4	83.9	84.8	84.9	83.1	82.5	81.7	80.9	80.3	79.1	83.2
1992	76.6	76.2	76.4	76.9	78.0	79.2	79.8	79.5	79.6	81.1	80.0	79.8	78.5
1993	77.6	78.5	79.6	80.7	81.4	82.8	83.8	83.4	82.5	82.9	82.5	83.4	81.5
1994	81.3	81.6	83.7	83.6	83.7	84.9	85.0	85.5	85.6	85.0	85.3	86.2	84.2
1995	84.6	84.7	86.9	86.8	88.2	89.8	88.8	89.8	89.9	89.6	89.8	91.1	88.3
1996	87.9	90.0	92.5	93.4	95.7	99.5	98.0	99.6	98.9	98.9	99.1	98.9	96.0
1997	98.1	98.9	100.9	100.5	101.1	102.5	102.9	103.3	103.2	103.3	102.5	102.8	101.6
1998	101.8	102.2	104.0	106.6	109.1	111.2	112.7	112.1	112.3	112.8	112.8	114.1	109.3
1999	112.1	112.4	113.4	114.9	115.0	116.7	116.3	116.0	115.1	115.6	116.5	116.6	115.0
2000	112.7	113.4	116.1	115.4	116.7	118.9	113.3	113.3	112.4	114.4	114.0	114.1	114.5
2001	111.2	111.1	112.9	114.2	115.4	116.0	114.3	114.2	113.0	112.4	112.2	110.9	113.1
2002	107.5	108.8	110.4	112.0	113.4	114.2	113.9	113.8	112.8	112.5	111.8	111.0	111.8
2003	110.7	111.1	112.3	111.7	112.6	113.4	112.9	113.8	112.4	112.6	112.8	112.1	112.4

Employment by Industry: South Carolina—*Continued*

(Numbers in thousands. Not seasonally adjusted.)

Industry	January	February	March	April	May	June	July	August	September	October	November	December	Annual Average
STATEWIDE—*Continued*													
Manufacturing													
1990	351.6	351.0	350.5	350.4	350.4	351.7	347.9	347.4	346.5	344.0	342.0	340.4	347.8
1991	334.9	332.2	331.7	330.0	330.4	333.0	331.9	334.2	335.0	335.3	337.6	337.8	333.6
1992	335.9	334.9	335.9	336.3	337.5	338.8	336.3	338.4	339.3	338.2	339.4	340.0	337.5
1993	339.4	338.7	339.3	341.0	341.6	343.5	341.2	342.0	343.1	342.9	343.6	344.9	341.7
1994	342.2	343.5	343.0	342.2	343.7	346.3	344.5	345.5	346.6	347.5	349.0	349.8	345.3
1995	345.9	346.1	347.1	349.0	349.3	348.5	346.4	347.0	346.4	344.8	345.3	346.0	346.8
1996	341.5	341.4	341.6	338.0	339.9	341.3	336.2	337.2	336.8	336.7	336.6	338.6	338.8
1997	336.1	337.5	337.6	337.7	339.5	340.4	337.2	338.2	335.7	339.3	340.6	342.2	338.5
1998	341.7	341.7	342.3	341.4	342.0	343.1	340.8	340.8	340.7	339.5	339.7	340.7	341.2
1999	339.7	338.6	337.9	335.4	335.5	336.4	335.5	333.5	333.8	334.9	335.9	337.2	336.1
2000	335.1	336.8	336.8	337.3	337.6	339.5	335.8	336.3	336.3	334.8	334.5	334.5	336.2
2001	327.7	326.2	324.5	321.0	318.7	315.6	311.8	309.1	306.8	301.6	301.2	299.8	313.6
2002	294.3	292.8	292.3	292.3	292.1	292.3	288.9	289.2	287.8	286.6	284.0	283.4	289.7
2003	281.6	281.7	281.2	280.7	278.6	276.2	274.8	274.3	274.5	275.4	274.3	272.2	277.1
Service-providing													
1990	1052.5	1066.3	1080.9	1093.9	1109.9	1111.7	1087.0	1093.5	1114.5	1111.9	1114.0	1112.6	1095.7
1991	1068.1	1076.3	1090.3	1094.1	1106.6	1105.0	1079.7	1083.6	1092.8	1093.7	1101.0	1101.8	1091.0
1992	1070.2	1079.6	1093.5	1105.6	1116.0	1117.8	1097.0	1102.6	1114.6	1117.8	1130.9	1124.7	1105.8
1993	1095.8	1108.1	1123.5	1143.7	1152.6	1157.6	1136.3	1141.3	1153.4	1155.9	1158.4	1165.0	1140.9
1994	1128.7	1139.5	1157.7	1171.6	1180.4	1189.8	1166.3	1172.1	1184.8	1183.4	1196.6	1191.5	1171.8
1995	1160.2	1170.4	1187.5	1203.0	1215.2	1224.9	1200.4	1208.7	1219.6	1219.3	1223.5	1229.4	1205.1
1996	1190.2	1202.5	1220.8	1233.0	1246.1	1261.3	1213.9	1226.9	1250.0	1248.4	1263.0	1258.9	1234.5
1997	1229.8	1241.7	1260.5	1271.4	1284.6	1291.1	1253.1	1263.7	1294.6	1293.6	1298.8	1307.6	1274.2
1998	1280.8	1291.1	1312.5	1316.5	1331.9	1350.4	1319.9	1325.3	1346.6	1342.7	1348.8	1357.8	1327.0
1999	1324.0	1340.2	1358.5	1374.5	1384.3	1393.3	1355.0	1373.9	1381.0	1392.5	1398.7	1408.9	1373.7
2000	1370.9	1381.1	1404.2	1410.5	1427.5	1437.0	1380.2	1397.3	1397.9	1407.0	1410.9	1412.7	1403.1
2001	1364.8	1374.7	1390.7	1397.2	1403.9	1405.8	1374.0	1399.1	1401.7	1393.3	1396.1	1396.1	1391.4
2002	1355.3	1366.9	1387.0	1403.7	1413.8	1418.5	1377.3	1406.6	1409.0	1410.8	1413.6	1415.0	1398.1
2003	1379.9	1392.3	1408.3	1419.8	1430.9	1432.5	1394.0	1420.1	1433.0	1437.5	1432.5	1434.6	1418.0
Trade, transportation, and utilities													
1990	299.3	298.6	301.5	304.4	307.3	311.4	311.5	312.9	311.6	308.9	311.7	315.2	307.8
1991	294.3	291.4	293.5	293.4	296.5	298.2	298.2	298.3	295.9	292.1	295.6	299.2	295.5
1992	286.2	284.2	285.9	287.8	290.9	293.9	291.8	294.0	291.8	291.6	293.9	299.3	290.9
1993	287.5	286.9	288.7	293.3	294.9	296.7	297.6	299.6	298.7	301.2	305.8	312.3	296.9
1994	300.3	299.7	302.8	304.5	307.7	311.3	310.9	312.4	312.4	311.8	315.8	321.4	309.2
1995	310.6	309.5	313.2	317.4	321.0	325.1	321.7	322.8	323.0	326.7	331.1	336.2	321.5
1996	322.9	320.3	323.3	325.7	328.4	332.2	331.0	332.9	332.5	334.5	339.5	344.8	330.6
1997	331.8	330.2	334.4	337.8	340.8	343.5	343.6	343.8	345.5	343.7	348.6	356.0	341.6
1998	341.2	339.7	342.6	339.4	344.2	346.3	348.4	348.6	351.2	348.4	354.3	361.0	347.1
1999	345.8	346.2	349.5	351.7	354.4	356.8	358.4	359.0	357.7	360.5	366.7	373.2	356.6
2000	359.4	359.3	364.1	362.7	366.1	368.6	362.6	363.4	362.0	364.3	370.5	373.1	364.6
2001	353.0	350.1	353.4	352.5	354.8	355.7	354.7	354.3	352.0	350.2	354.4	356.3	353.4
2002	340.5	339.6	343.8	346.4	348.2	350.1	347.4	347.2	346.0	346.7	352.1	355.8	347.0
2003	342.3	341.5	344.2	344.9	347.2	350.3	346.7	347.8	347.2	347.9	350.5	352.8	346.9
Wholesale trade													
1990	53.5	53.9	54.3	53.8	54.1	54.4	54.7	54.8	54.9	54.4	54.0	53.9	54.2
1991	51.4	51.2	51.4	51.3	51.7	51.8	52.0	51.9	50.0	50.1	50.0	49.7	51.0
1992	48.9	48.5	48.7	48.3	48.6	49.1	49.2	49.4	49.0	49.0	48.8	49.1	48.8
1993	48.8	48.9	49.3	49.6	49.8	50.0	50.3	50.4	50.5	50.9	50.7	51.3	50.0
1994	50.9	51.1	51.6	51.4	51.5	52.0	52.2	52.3	52.4	52.7	52.8	53.2	52.0
1995	52.6	52.9	53.6	54.1	54.6	55.3	52.7	52.8	52.6	55.1	55.1	55.5	53.9
1996	54.7	54.8	55.0	55.1	55.4	55.8	55.7	55.8	55.8	56.1	56.3	56.6	55.5
1997	56.6	56.9	57.4	57.8	58.2	58.5	58.5	59.0	58.8	56.9	57.1	57.8	57.7
1998	57.2	57.6	57.9	58.5	58.9	59.3	59.9	60.0	59.7	60.0	59.7	60.0	59.0
1999	59.3	59.8	60.2	60.6	60.4	61.1	61.3	61.3	61.4	61.4	61.6	62.2	60.8
2000	62.2	62.4	63.4	63.0	63.4	63.7	63.0	62.9	63.0	63.3	63.4	63.7	63.1
2001	63.0	63.2	63.6	63.6	63.6	64.0	63.8	63.6	63.4	62.8	62.7	62.4	63.3
2002	61.4	62.1	62.7	63.0	63.0	63.7	63.2	62.9	62.6	63.2	63.3	63.2	62.9
2003	62.4	62.8	63.1	63.2	63.2	63.4	62.9	62.9	62.8	62.6	63.1	63.9	63.0
Retail trade													
1990	194.3	192.8	194.9	197.3	199.5	202.6	203.2	203.7	202.5	201.1	204.7	207.9	200.3
1991	191.1	188.2	190.0	190.5	192.9	194.6	193.4	193.4	192.9	189.7	193.2	197.0	192.2
1992	186.0	184.4	186.4	188.5	191.0	192.7	190.8	191.7	190.5	190.2	193.0	197.9	190.2
1993	187.6	186.6	188.1	192.4	193.2	194.4	195.1	196.4	195.0	195.8	200.1	205.8	194.2
1994	196.3	194.8	196.8	199.1	200.9	203.7	203.1	204.3	204.5	203.8	208.3	213.3	202.4
1995	204.3	201.8	204.4	208.0	210.5	213.0	211.8	212.6	213.0	213.6	218.4	223.4	211.2
1996	212.2	209.9	212.0	214.4	216.5	219.3	217.8	219.6	219.6	220.8	225.6	230.6	218.1
1997	218.8	216.8	219.7	221.9	224.2	226.5	227.0	228.6	228.3	228.0	233.2	239.7	226.0
1998	227.2	225.9	228.3	223.9	228.4	229.9	231.3	230.9	233.7	230.2	236.4	242.6	230.7
1999	230.2	229.7	231.9	231.9	233.7	234.7	235.1	235.1	234.3	235.0	240.5	246.2	234.8
2000	234.2	233.1	236.3	235.9	238.4	240.2	234.9	235.5	234.7	235.9	241.8	244.0	237.0
2001	229.2	226.2	228.7	228.3	230.0	230.7	229.4	228.9	227.1	225.9	230.3	232.9	228.9
2002	220.0	217.8	221.4	223.0	224.6	226.3	224.6	224.2	223.3	222.7	227.5	231.6	223.9
2003	219.8	218.3	220.5	221.4	223.3	226.0	223.1	223.6	223.0	224.4	225.2	227.0	223.0

Employment by Industry: South Carolina—*Continued*

(Numbers in thousands. Not seasonally adjusted.)

Industry	January	February	March	April	May	June	July	August	September	October	November	December	Annual Average
STATEWIDE—*Continued*													
Transportation and utilities													
1990	51.5	51.9	52.3	53.3	53.7	54.4	53.6	54.4	54.2	53.4	53.0	53.4	53.2
1991	51.8	52.0	52.1	51.6	51.9	51.8	52.8	53.0	53.0	52.3	52.4	52.5	52.2
1992	51.3	51.3	50.8	51.0	51.3	52.1	51.8	52.9	52.3	52.4	52.1	52.3	51.8
1993	51.1	51.4	51.3	51.3	51.9	52.3	52.2	52.8	53.2	54.5	55.0	55.2	52.6
1994	53.1	53.8	54.4	54.0	55.3	55.6	55.6	55.8	55.5	55.3	54.7	54.9	54.8
1995	53.7	54.8	55.2	55.3	55.9	56.8	57.2	57.4	57.4	58.0	57.6	57.3	56.3
1996	56.0	55.6	56.3	56.2	56.5	57.1	57.5	57.5	57.1	57.6	57.6	57.6	56.8
1997	56.4	56.5	57.3	58.1	58.4	58.5	58.1	56.2	58.4	58.8	58.3	58.5	57.7
1998	56.8	56.2	56.4	57.0	56.9	57.1	57.2	57.7	57.8	58.2	58.2	58.4	57.3
1999	56.3	56.7	57.4	59.2	60.3	61.0	62.0	62.6	62.0	64.1	64.6	64.8	60.9
2000	63.0	63.8	64.4	63.8	64.3	64.7	64.7	65.0	64.3	65.1	65.3	65.4	64.4
2001	60.8	60.7	61.1	60.6	61.2	61.0	61.5	61.8	61.5	61.5	61.4	61.0	61.1
2002	59.1	59.7	59.7	60.4	60.6	60.1	59.6	60.1	60.1	60.8	61.3	61.0	60.2
2003	60.1	60.4	60.6	60.3	60.7	60.9	60.7	61.3	61.4	60.9	62.2	61.9	61.0
Information													
1990	22.2	22.4	22.4	22.6	22.8	23.1	23.9	24.1	24.0	23.9	23.5	23.3	23.1
1991	23.1	23.0	23.3	22.2	22.3	22.4	22.5	22.5	22.4	21.8	22.0	22.1	22.4
1992	22.1	21.9	22.0	21.9	22.1	22.3	22.3	22.4	22.3	22.1	22.3	22.4	22.1
1993	22.0	22.1	22.1	21.9	21.9	22.2	22.0	22.1	22.1	22.2	21.9	22.1	22.0
1994	22.1	22.0	22.2	22.1	22.1	22.7	22.4	22.5	22.3	22.3	22.6	23.0	22.3
1995	22.7	22.7	22.9	23.6	24.1	23.8	23.6	23.5	23.6	23.1	23.4	23.6	23.3
1996	23.3	23.3	23.4	23.3	23.8	23.5	24.1	24.0	23.6	23.5	23.6	23.8	23.6
1997	23.5	23.7	23.7	23.4	23.8	24.5	24.5	24.9	26.1	26.1	27.6	27.7	24.9
1998	26.7	26.8	26.9	27.0	27.6	27.7	27.5	28.0	27.6	28.0	28.0	28.4	27.5
1999	27.7	27.9	28.7	28.2	28.9	29.9	29.1	29.2	29.0	30.0	30.2	30.3	29.0
2000	30.0	30.0	30.4	29.9	30.2	31.0	30.5	30.8	30.7	30.6	30.8	31.2	30.5
2001	29.7	29.8	29.8	29.1	29.1	29.2	28.7	28.7	28.4	27.9	28.1	28.0	28.8
2002	27.7	27.6	27.8	27.5	28.0	28.1	27.8	27.9	27.4	27.9	28.3	28.3	27.9
2003	27.5	27.6	27.5	26.7	26.9	26.9	26.7	26.8	26.4	26.5	26.6	26.8	26.9
Financial activities													
1990	71.2	71.0	70.8	70.8	71.4	72.3	72.3	73.0	71.9	70.7	70.4	69.5	71.2
1991	69.5	69.9	69.5	69.5	70.1	70.8	70.8	70.8	69.8	68.3	68.6	68.2	69.6
1992	68.1	68.1	68.4	69.2	68.9	69.7	70.4	70.3	69.2	68.7	68.6	68.9	69.0
1993	67.8	68.3	68.5	68.9	69.5	70.7	70.5	70.6	70.1	69.5	69.3	69.6	69.4
1994	68.6	69.2	70.1	70.3	71.1	72.4	72.1	71.7	70.9	70.1	70.0	70.5	70.5
1995	69.0	69.0	69.7	69.9	70.5	72.2	72.2	72.5	72.2	71.4	71.7	72.5	71.0
1996	71.9	72.4	73.2	73.3	74.5	75.8	76.3	76.4	75.8	75.4	75.4	76.2	74.7
1997	74.3	74.8	75.7	77.2	78.0	78.9	79.4	79.7	78.4	78.7	78.6	79.9	77.8
1998	79.4	79.6	80.7	81.4	82.4	83.6	84.6	84.4	83.5	84.2	84.6	85.5	82.8
1999	84.7	85.2	86.1	87.3	87.6	88.8	89.5	89.4	87.7	87.2	87.2	88.5	87.4
2000	85.9	86.4	87.0	87.6	88.3	89.7	87.9	88.1	86.7	87.4	87.1	87.3	87.4
2001	85.9	86.5	87.0	87.8	88.1	89.3	90.4	89.9	88.5	87.8	88.2	87.8	88.1
2002	86.4	86.7	87.5	88.9	89.7	90.8	90.4	90.0	89.3	89.2	89.2	89.6	89.0
2003	88.8	88.8	89.5	91.6	92.9	94.1	94.3	94.1	91.4	90.3	90.4	91.1	91.4
Professional and business services													
1990	124.5	126.3	128.3	130.8	133.6	135.1	132.0	133.8	135.3	135.8	136.6	135.4	132.2
1991	130.9	130.9	131.4	131.2	132.6	132.4	130.5	131.6	131.4	132.6	132.7	131.7	131.6
1992	128.0	129.3	130.9	131.7	132.6	134.7	133.4	135.4	135.9	135.7	136.5	137.1	133.4
1993	135.8	137.6	139.1	142.7	145.0	146.8	144.9	145.8	146.3	145.7	145.7	146.5	143.4
1994	141.0	143.1	145.7	149.4	150.7	153.3	152.8	154.7	156.2	154.4	154.4	154.5	150.8
1995	152.7	154.8	156.9	156.9	157.4	160.2	159.4	162.0	162.1	161.3	161.2	159.1	158.6
1996	154.5	157.6	160.5	163.8	166.1	167.9	168.6	170.6	170.5	168.6	169.8	170.6	165.7
1997	168.7	171.1	173.0	172.9	174.2	175.7	172.8	174.5	175.5	172.9	174.1	174.6	173.3
1998	174.9	175.6	178.7	179.4	181.9	183.6	182.5	185.0	185.6	183.0	184.9	184.7	181.6
1999	181.8	184.2	187.3	190.6	190.9	192.2	189.6	190.8	190.4	193.7	195.2	195.5	190.1
2000	186.9	188.2	192.1	195.9	197.8	200.9	197.1	198.1	197.8	197.2	195.9	195.7	195.3
2001	185.3	187.3	188.8	189.6	188.9	188.8	187.7	189.4	187.9	185.0	183.1	182.1	186.9
2002	174.4	176.7	179.4	183.7	184.4	186.6	184.3	187.2	186.5	187.8	185.9	185.4	183.5
2003	180.4	183.0	186.7	187.7	187.7	188.0	188.4	190.1	190.8	191.1	187.1	186.3	187.3
Educational and health services													
1990	95.6	97.3	97.7	98.1	98.4	95.8	94.6	95.4	100.0	101.2	102.0	102.7	98.2
1991	101.5	102.5	103.1	104.7	105.3	104.7	101.6	101.3	103.3	108.6	109.7	110.4	104.7
1992	109.7	111.1	112.1	112.0	112.9	110.8	110.5	110.6	113.7	116.3	117.0	117.2	112.8
1993	114.6	115.8	117.5	118.2	118.4	117.6	116.2	115.6	120.4	121.9	122.4	122.6	118.4
1994	119.7	120.7	121.8	122.4	122.5	121.7	119.7	120.5	123.8	124.3	123.9	124.9	122.1
1995	121.6	122.8	123.0	126.4	126.3	125.8	123.7	124.3	127.0	127.9	128.6	129.0	125.5
1996	125.3	127.3	128.6	128.7	129.0	128.2	125.9	126.7	129.0	128.0	128.4	128.6	127.8
1997	127.0	128.6	129.1	131.0	132.1	131.6	130.4	131.3	134.9	135.5	136.0	137.0	132.0
1998	137.0	138.6	139.5	143.0	143.5	142.8	144.1	143.8	146.5	146.5	147.6	148.4	143.4
1999	146.4	148.3	149.3	150.6	151.0	150.8	149.8	149.9	152.4	154.5	154.9	155.6	151.1
2000	154.6	155.5	156.5	156.4	156.7	156.8	153.2	154.1	156.0	157.7	158.4	159.2	156.2
2001	158.7	160.1	161.3	161.4	162.4	163.3	163.7	165.3	167.9	168.0	169.4	170.4	164.3
2002	168.9	170.2	172.1	171.8	172.4	171.6	171.6	172.5	174.1	174.1	175.2	174.9	172.5
2003	173.2	174.5	175.4	176.2	176.9	176.2	171.8	174.7	181.4	183.5	183.9	183.8	177.6

Employment by Industry: South Carolina—*Continued*

(Numbers in thousands. Not seasonally adjusted.)

Industry	January	February	March	April	May	June	July	August	September	October	November	December	Annual Average
STATEWIDE—*Continued*													
Leisure and hospitality													
1990	117.5	121.3	128.0	134.4	138.8	144.4	143.9	144.4	139.5	132.1	128.9	126.0	133.2
1991	119.5	122.0	129.5	135.8	141.1	144.9	143.5	143.5	138.8	131.9	128.6	125.7	133.7
1992	120.9	124.0	131.4	139.2	144.2	147.6	147.6	147.2	142.4	137.1	133.0	130.2	137.0
1993	125.9	130.4	136.5	146.4	151.3	155.7	155.5	155.8	151.5	144.5	140.8	138.9	144.4
1994	133.6	136.5	145.0	152.1	154.7	160.9	160.5	161.1	155.6	150.9	148.2	146.0	150.4
1995	139.7	143.3	150.8	158.4	164.5	170.1	169.6	170.0	165.6	159.5	156.0	153.9	158.4
1996	146.1	150.0	158.2	165.7	171.7	176.5	175.1	175.3	169.6	165.2	161.4	159.1	164.4
1997	154.1	158.4	167.1	172.9	178.1	183.1	181.7	181.7	176.8	174.1	169.7	167.0	172.0
1998	160.2	164.1	175.1	179.3	184.3	190.3	191.2	188.4	182.7	178.8	173.6	172.2	178.3
1999	166.3	172.6	180.2	188.4	193.5	200.0	196.7	195.6	188.7	186.8	183.1	182.0	186.1
2000	175.1	179.0	186.5	191.2	195.3	199.9	195.8	192.8	185.8	184.6	181.6	179.5	187.2
2001	169.1	173.2	180.4	187.6	191.3	194.8	196.7	195.2	188.4	183.0	179.2	176.5	184.6
2002	169.4	173.9	181.7	191.1	195.6	201.3	200.6	197.9	191.9	190.5	185.7	183.4	188.6
2003	176.1	180.0	186.7	194.4	200.8	205.3	204.5	202.8	199.4	196.1	191.0	189.5	193.9
Other services													
1990	45.8	46.2	46.9	46.8	47.4	48.0	48.7	48.2	48.3	48.0	47.9	47.2	47.4
1991	47.2	46.8	47.4	47.3	47.5	48.4	48.5	48.2	48.0	47.4	47.4	47.3	47.6
1992	47.1	47.1	48.1	48.2	48.5	49.0	49.3	49.1	48.7	48.7	48.8	49.0	48.4
1993	48.4	48.9	49.5	50.2	50.6	51.4	51.5	51.3	51.3	51.0	50.4	50.5	50.4
1994	49.5	49.8	50.5	50.6	51.0	51.5	51.6	51.3	51.3	51.5	51.2	51.5	50.9
1995	50.8	50.9	51.8	52.3	52.6	53.5	53.1	52.8	52.7	52.5	52.2	52.6	52.3
1996	51.7	52.2	52.5	52.8	53.2	54.0	53.4	53.4	53.1	52.9	52.7	53.0	52.9
1997	51.9	52.2	52.9	53.3	53.7	54.3	53.5	54.0	54.1	54.2	53.9	53.9	53.4
1998	53.9	55.0	55.7	56.3	56.9	57.5	57.8	57.4	57.4	57.1	57.3	57.4	56.6
1999	55.9	56.5	57.4	57.9	58.1	58.6	58.2	58.1	58.2	58.2	57.8	57.9	57.7
2000	57.4	58.1	59.1	59.7	60.1	60.0	58.3	58.1	58.0	59.2	58.8	58.5	58.7
2001	60.4	60.9	62.1	62.3	62.7	62.7	62.4	62.7	62.6	62.6	63.0	63.0	62.2
2002	62.6	63.4	64.7	64.2	64.9	65.6	64.2	64.7	65.3	63.7	63.8	64.0	64.3
2003	63.4	63.9	64.7	64.8	65.8	66.4	66.0	65.2	64.7	65.3	64.6	64.3	64.9
Government													
1990	276.4	283.2	285.3	286.0	290.2	281.6	260.1	261.7	283.9	291.3	293.0	293.3	282.1
1991	282.1	289.8	292.6	290.0	291.2	283.2	264.1	267.4	283.2	291.0	296.4	297.2	285.6
1992	288.1	293.9	294.7	295.6	295.9	289.8	271.7	273.6	290.6	297.6	310.8	300.6	291.9
1993	293.8	298.1	301.6	302.1	301.0	296.5	278.1	280.5	293.0	299.9	302.1	302.5	295.7
1994	293.9	298.5	299.6	300.2	300.6	296.0	276.3	277.9	292.3	298.1	310.5	299.7	295.3
1995	293.1	297.4	299.2	298.1	298.8	294.2	277.1	280.8	293.4	296.9	299.3	302.5	294.2
1996	294.5	299.4	301.1	299.7	299.4	303.2	259.5	267.6	295.9	300.3	312.2	302.8	294.6
1997	298.5	302.7	304.6	302.9	303.9	299.5	267.2	273.8	303.3	308.4	310.3	311.5	298.8
1998	307.5	311.7	313.3	310.7	311.1	318.6	283.8	289.7	312.1	316.7	318.5	320.2	309.4
1999	315.4	319.3	320.0	319.8	319.9	316.2	283.7	301.9	316.9	321.6	323.6	325.9	315.3
2000	321.6	324.6	328.5	327.1	333.0	330.1	294.8	311.9	320.9	326.0	327.8	328.2	322.8
2001	322.7	326.8	327.9	326.9	326.6	322.0	289.7	313.6	326.0	328.8	330.7	332.0	322.8
2002	325.4	328.8	330.0	330.1	330.6	324.4	291.0	319.2	328.5	330.9	333.4	333.6	325.5
2003	328.2	333.0	333.6	333.5	332.7	325.3	295.6	318.6	331.7	336.8	338.4	340.0	329.0
Federal government													
1990	39.3	39.3	39.9	40.7	44.8	44.6	41.4	39.7	39.0	39.1	38.8	38.8	40.4
1991	39.3	39.4	39.7	38.4	38.3	38.5	37.9	38.0	37.9	37.3	37.6	37.2	38.2
1992	37.0	36.9	36.4	36.3	36.2	36.3	36.1	35.9	35.8	35.3	35.2	35.4	36.0
1993	34.9	34.8	34.8	34.9	34.7	34.3	34.1	34.0	33.8	33.5	33.4	33.7	34.2
1994	33.1	33.0	32.9	32.8	32.7	32.6	32.3	32.4	32.2	31.7	31.8	32.0	32.4
1995	31.0	30.6	30.5	30.0	30.0	29.9	30.0	29.8	29.8	29.6	29.5	29.7	30.0
1996	28.6	28.7	28.6	28.1	28.1	28.4	28.3	28.2	28.1	28.5	28.6	28.9	28.4
1997	28.4	28.4	28.3	28.4	28.5	28.7	29.2	29.5	29.5	29.6	30.0	30.4	29.0
1998	30.0	29.8	29.8	30.4	30.6	31.9	30.6	30.2	30.1	30.7	31.1	31.9	30.5
1999	30.7	31.0	30.3	30.4	30.1	30.3	30.0	29.7	29.3	29.3	29.5	29.6	30.0
2000	29.0	29.3	30.9	30.6	36.9	36.8	32.7	33.6	28.5	28.8	29.1	29.4	31.3
2001	28.4	28.3	28.3	28.4	28.6	28.7	28.7	28.7	28.5	28.8	28.9	29.0	28.6
2002	28.6	28.3	28.3	28.0	28.1	28.5	28.3	28.2	28.3	28.7	28.6	29.1	28.4
2003	28.0	28.1	27.8	28.2	28.1	28.2	28.3	28.0	28.0	27.7	27.8	28.2	28.0
State government													
1990	89.7	95.3	95.7	96.4	96.4	93.2	92.2	93.0	99.3	101.4	102.4	101.9	96.4
1991	92.7	97.3	99.2	99.3	99.6	97.4	95.4	96.5	100.7	104.0	104.1	103.9	99.1
1992	96.3	101.0	101.6	101.7	101.4	97.7	95.9	96.4	102.2	105.4	116.0	105.3	101.7
1993	99.9	102.8	105.3	105.6	104.1	102.1	100.5	101.2	104.3	106.1	106.0	105.8	103.6
1994	98.5	101.5	102.1	102.6	101.9	99.3	97.7	97.9	102.8	105.2	115.6	105.3	102.5
1995	96.4	99.7	100.3	100.4	100.0	97.3	96.3	96.9	100.5	103.0	103.2	102.8	99.7
1996	97.3	100.1	100.9	100.5	98.8	106.2	96.2	96.6	97.9	99.1	109.3	98.8	100.1
1997	96.0	98.9	99.5	99.8	98.7	96.5	95.8	97.0	99.1	99.8	100.2	100.3	98.4
1998	96.9	100.0	100.6	100.5	99.5	107.2	96.5	97.8	99.7	100.8	100.9	101.3	100.1
1999	98.6	100.8	101.4	101.4	101.1	98.5	96.8	97.0	100.6	101.1	101.5	101.5	100.0
2000	100.2	102.6	103.2	103.1	102.6	100.6	100.3	101.0	102.8	104.0	104.5	104.7	102.4
2001	102.0	103.8	104.3	104.1	102.7	99.8	99.1	99.6	101.4	101.8	101.9	102.2	101.8
2002	99.0	101.0	101.3	101.7	100.8	98.1	97.5	98.5	100.7	101.6	102.0	102.1	100.4
2003	99.3	101.8	102.1	101.6	100.5	97.5	96.4	97.2	102.1	104.4	104.4	105.3	101.1

Employment by Industry: South Carolina—*Continued*

(Numbers in thousands. Not seasonally adjusted.)

Industry	January	February	March	April	May	June	July	August	September	October	November	December	Annual Average
STATEWIDE—*Continued*													
Local government													
1990	147.4	148.6	149.7	148.9	149.0	143.8	126.5	129.0	145.6	150.8	151.8	152.6	145.3
1991	150.1	153.1	153.7	152.3	153.3	147.3	130.8	132.9	144.6	149.7	154.7	156.1	148.2
1992	154.8	156.0	156.7	157.6	158.3	155.8	139.7	141.3	152.6	156.9	159.6	159.9	154.1
1993	159.0	160.5	161.5	161.6	162.2	160.1	143.5	145.3	154.9	160.3	162.7	163.0	157.8
1994	162.3	164.0	164.6	164.8	166.0	164.1	146.3	147.6	157.3	161.2	163.1	162.4	160.3
1995	165.7	167.1	168.4	167.7	168.8	167.0	150.8	154.1	163.1	164.3	166.6	170.0	164.4
1996	168.6	170.6	171.6	171.1	172.5	168.6	135.0	142.8	169.9	172.7	174.3	175.1	166.0
1997	174.1	175.4	176.8	174.7	176.7	174.3	142.2	147.3	174.7	179.0	180.1	180.8	171.3
1998	180.6	181.9	182.9	179.8	181.0	179.5	156.7	161.7	182.3	185.2	186.5	187.0	178.7
1999	186.1	187.5	188.3	188.0	188.7	187.4	156.9	175.2	187.0	191.2	192.6	194.8	185.3
2000	192.4	192.7	194.4	193.4	193.5	192.7	161.8	177.3	189.6	193.2	194.2	194.1	189.1
2001	192.3	194.7	195.3	194.4	195.3	193.5	161.9	185.3	196.1	198.2	199.9	200.8	192.3
2002	197.8	199.5	200.4	200.4	201.7	197.8	165.2	192.5	199.5	200.6	202.8	202.4	196.7
2003	200.9	203.1	203.7	203.7	204.1	199.6	170.9	193.4	201.6	204.7	206.2	206.5	199.9
CHARLESTON													
Total nonfarm													
1990	200.9	202.9	205.4	207.6	210.5	211.2	208.1	207.4	209.7	209.4	210.4	209.8	207.8
1991	203.7	205.5	207.5	206.5	209.2	209.2	206.5	206.8	207.5	207.2	208.0	207.9	207.1
1992	201.8	203.2	204.2	206.2	208.1	208.0	205.3	206.3	208.8	209.4	210.9	211.1	206.9
1993	205.4	206.7	208.5	211.2	212.7	212.1	207.8	208.3	209.0	211.9	213.0	213.9	210.0
1994	209.0	209.5	211.3	211.7	212.5	213.1	207.3	208.8	210.9	210.9	212.9	212.5	210.9
1995	208.7	209.7	211.8	213.6	216.3	216.2	212.9	213.2	215.2	215.2	216.4	217.9	213.9
1996	211.0	212.9	215.6	215.9	219.0	221.7	215.4	218.0	218.6	221.0	223.4	223.4	218.0
1997	219.3	221.7	224.4	226.0	229.9	230.7	228.7	228.8	230.9	232.7	233.2	235.2	228.5
1998	230.7	233.1	235.8	237.4	241.1	244.9	243.7	244.3	246.0	245.3	247.1	248.9	241.5
1999	241.4	244.4	246.9	252.3	254.4	255.6	252.5	252.5	252.5	254.5	255.9	258.0	251.7
2000	255.8	256.5	259.8	259.8	262.8	266.1	256.3	256.6	256.3	259.0	260.3	261.4	259.2
2001	251.8	253.0	255.8	256.6	257.6	258.0	256.4	255.5	256.1	255.3	254.9	255.1	255.5
2002	250.7	254.2	257.1	257.0	259.7	259.5	262.4	263.3	263.6	262.6	262.1	261.9	259.5
2003	257.4	261.3	263.3	260.0	261.5	261.6	257.7	260.1	259.1	260.2	261.0	260.4	260.3
Total private													
1990	147.0	148.5	150.7	153.7	156.1	157.7	157.2	157.7	157.2	155.9	157.0	156.4	154.6
1991	150.4	150.9	152.5	152.0	154.1	154.4	153.7	153.2	152.2	151.8	152.3	152.1	152.5
1992	147.2	147.7	149.0	150.9	152.7	153.5	153.6	154.0	153.8	153.2	153.3	154.5	152.0
1993	150.0	150.7	152.1	154.7	156.5	157.4	156.7	155.8	155.3	156.9	158.0	159.1	155.3
1994	155.4	155.5	157.2	158.1	159.0	161.0	159.2	159.9	159.9	159.1	159.6	160.7	158.7
1995	157.5	158.3	160.5	163.4	165.8	166.9	166.3	166.8	165.8	164.9	166.2	167.4	164.2
1996	162.7	163.5	165.9	167.2	170.3	172.4	170.4	171.7	170.8	172.3	173.0	174.1	169.5
1997	171.2	173.1	175.5	177.2	180.6	182.1	181.6	181.7	181.9	182.5	182.8	184.8	179.6
1998	181.2	183.0	185.5	187.6	190.9	194.0	196.3	196.4	196.8	194.9	196.4	198.0	191.8
1999	191.3	193.8	196.2	201.5	203.6	205.4	204.6	204.6	202.9	204.3	205.3	207.7	201.8
2000	205.5	205.7	208.7	208.9	211.3	214.2	208.7	208.2	207.2	208.9	209.9	210.6	209.0
2001	203.2	203.7	206.1	206.9	208.1	209.6	208.6	208.6	206.9	205.1	204.7	204.9	206.3
2002	201.6	204.2	207.0	206.6	209.3	209.8	213.7	213.9	213.0	211.7	210.9	210.3	209.3
2003	207.5	210.0	212.2	208.3	209.9	211.7	209.2	210.2	208.0	208.9	209.6	208.7	209.5
Goods-producing													
1990	33.9	34.2	34.6	34.7	35.1	35.3	35.4	35.6	35.1	34.8	34.7	34.3	34.8
1991	34.0	33.9	33.8	33.4	33.4	33.1	33.1	33.0	32.6	32.2	32.4	31.9	33.1
1992	31.7	31.7	31.7	31.6	31.7	31.9	31.9	31.7	31.9	31.9	31.9	32.1	31.8
1993	31.8	32.0	31.9	32.1	32.3	32.5	32.1	31.9	31.7	31.8	31.8	31.7	32.0
1994	31.5	31.3	31.1	30.6	30.9	31.1	31.2	31.7	31.8	31.5	31.3	31.6	31.3
1995	31.6	31.8	32.3	32.4	32.8	33.0	32.5	33.0	32.8	32.9	33.1	33.7	32.7
1996	32.9	32.7	33.2	33.7	34.0	34.3	34.1	34.5	34.4	35.5	35.6	35.7	34.2
1997	35.5	35.9	36.2	36.8	37.4	37.7	37.4	37.7	37.8	38.0	38.1	38.4	37.2
1998	38.6	38.9	39.1	39.6	39.7	40.5	41.1	41.1	41.3	40.8	40.8	41.4	40.2
1999	40.5	40.8	41.1	41.8	41.9	42.1	42.2	42.3	42.1	42.5	42.8	43.1	41.9
2000	43.3	43.1	43.6	43.2	43.7	43.6	42.5	42.4	42.2	43.2	43.3	43.4	43.1
2001	42.1	42.1	42.6	42.6	42.9	43.2	42.6	42.6	42.3	42.0	41.9	41.6	42.3
2002	41.3	41.7	42.3	40.9	41.2	41.2	42.6	42.4	42.1	41.7	40.9	40.7	41.6
2003	41.5	41.9	42.3	40.2	40.2	40.6	39.8	40.4	40.6	40.6	40.5	40.9	40.8
Construction and mining													
1990	14.4	14.7	15.1	15.0	15.4	15.5	15.4	15.6	15.2	14.9	14.8	14.5	15.0
1991	14.0	13.9	14.0	13.7	13.7	13.5	13.4	13.2	12.8	12.7	12.8	12.4	13.3
1992	11.7	11.7	11.8	11.7	11.8	12.0	12.1	12.0	12.1	11.9	11.8	11.9	11.9
1993	11.7	11.8	11.9	12.1	12.0	12.2	12.0	11.8	11.7	11.8	11.8	11.8	11.9
1994	11.5	11.4	11.7	11.7	11.7	11.9	11.9	12.3	12.4	12.2	12.0	12.1	11.9
1995	12.0	12.1	12.5	12.8	13.0	13.2	13.1	13.2	13.1	13.3	13.5	13.9	13.0
1996	13.2	13.5	13.8	14.0	14.3	14.4	14.3	14.5	14.6	14.8	14.8	14.7	14.2
1997	14.8	15.0	15.3	15.7	15.9	16.2	16.4	16.5	16.5	16.6	16.6	16.8	16.0
1998	16.8	16.9	17.0	17.8	17.8	18.3	18.6	18.5	18.5	18.5	18.5	18.9	18.0
1999	18.8	19.0	19.2	19.3	19.2	19.3	19.5	19.6	19.4	19.7	19.8	20.0	19.4
2000	19.5	19.4	19.8	20.2	20.6	20.4	19.7	19.6	19.4	20.1	20.2	20.3	19.9
2001	19.7	19.7	20.2	20.2	20.5	20.9	20.7	20.6	20.4	20.7	20.7	20.4	20.4
2002	20.3	20.5	20.9	19.9	20.2	20.2	21.4	21.2	20.9	20.5	19.9	19.8	20.5
2003	19.4	19.7	19.9	19.4	19.5	20.1	19.8	20.0	19.9	20.1	20.1	20.3	19.9

Employment by Industry: South Carolina—*Continued*

(Numbers in thousands. Not seasonally adjusted.)

Industry	January	February	March	April	May	June	July	August	September	October	November	December	Annual Average
CHARLESTON—*Continued*													
Manufacturing													
1990	19.5	19.5	19.5	19.7	19.7	19.8	20.0	20.0	19.9	19.9	19.9	19.8	19.8
1991	20.0	20.0	19.8	19.7	19.7	19.6	19.7	19.8	19.8	19.5	19.6	19.5	19.7
1992	20.0	20.0	19.9	19.9	19.9	19.9	19.8	19.7	19.8	20.0	20.1	20.2	19.9
1993	20.1	20.2	20.0	20.0	20.3	20.3	20.1	20.1	20.0	20.0	20.0	19.9	20.1
1994	20.0	19.9	19.4	18.9	19.2	19.2	19.3	19.4	19.4	19.3	19.3	19.5	19.4
1995	19.6	19.7	19.8	19.6	19.8	19.8	19.4	19.8	19.7	19.6	19.6	19.8	19.7
1996	19.7	19.2	19.4	19.7	19.7	19.9	19.8	20.0	19.8	20.7	20.8	21.0	20.0
1997	20.7	20.9	20.9	21.1	21.5	21.5	21.0	21.2	21.3	21.4	21.5	21.6	21.2
1998	21.8	22.0	22.1	21.8	21.9	22.2	22.5	22.6	22.8	22.3	22.3	22.5	22.2
1999	21.7	21.8	21.9	22.5	22.7	22.8	22.7	22.7	22.7	22.8	23.0	23.1	22.5
2000	23.8	23.7	23.8	23.0	23.1	23.2	22.8	22.8	22.8	23.1	23.1	23.1	23.2
2001	22.4	22.4	22.4	22.4	22.4	22.3	21.9	22.0	21.9	21.3	21.2	21.2	21.9
2002	21.0	21.2	21.4	21.0	21.0	21.0	21.2	21.2	21.2	21.2	21.0	20.9	21.1
2003	22.1	22.2	22.4	20.8	20.7	20.5	20.0	20.4	20.7	20.5	20.4	20.6	20.9
Service-providing													
1990	167.0	168.7	170.8	172.9	175.4	175.9	172.7	171.8	174.6	174.6	175.7	175.5	173.0
1991	169.7	171.6	173.7	173.1	175.8	176.1	173.4	173.8	174.9	175.0	175.6	176.0	174.1
1992	170.1	171.5	172.5	174.6	176.4	176.1	173.4	174.6	176.9	177.5	179.0	179.0	175.1
1993	173.6	174.7	176.6	179.1	180.4	179.6	175.7	176.4	177.3	180.1	181.2	182.2	178.1
1994	177.5	178.2	180.2	181.1	181.6	182.0	176.1	177.1	179.1	179.4	181.6	180.9	179.6
1995	177.1	177.9	179.5	181.2	183.5	183.2	180.4	180.2	182.4	182.3	183.3	184.2	181.3
1996	178.1	180.2	182.4	182.2	185.0	187.4	181.3	183.5	184.2	185.5	187.8	187.7	183.8
1997	183.8	185.8	188.2	189.2	192.5	193.0	191.3	191.1	193.1	194.7	195.1	196.8	191.2
1998	192.1	194.2	196.7	197.8	201.4	204.4	202.6	203.2	204.7	204.5	206.3	207.5	201.3
1999	200.9	203.6	205.8	210.5	212.5	213.5	210.3	210.2	210.4	212.0	213.1	214.9	209.8
2000	212.5	213.4	216.2	216.6	219.1	222.5	213.8	214.2	214.1	215.8	217.0	218.0	216.1
2001	209.7	210.9	213.2	214.0	214.7	214.8	213.8	212.9	213.8	213.3	213.0	213.5	213.1
2002	209.4	212.5	214.8	216.1	218.5	218.3	219.8	220.9	221.5	220.9	221.2	221.2	217.9
2003	215.9	219.4	221.0	219.8	221.3	221.0	217.9	219.7	218.5	219.6	220.5	219.5	219.5
Trade, transportation, and utilities													
1990	40.0	39.8	40.3	41.6	42.2	42.6	42.6	42.8	42.5	43.1	43.8	44.2	42.1
1991	41.2	41.2	41.4	40.7	41.0	41.2	41.1	41.0	40.9	41.3	42.2	42.8	41.3
1992	40.6	40.5	40.5	40.6	41.1	41.5	41.1	41.7	41.4	41.3	41.8	42.9	41.3
1993	41.2	40.8	41.3	42.0	42.2	42.3	42.3	42.1	41.9	43.0	43.9	45.0	42.3
1994	43.0	42.7	43.2	43.0	43.0	43.9	42.9	43.1	43.2	43.4	44.0	45.0	43.4
1995	43.2	43.1	43.6	43.9	44.4	44.6	44.9	44.5	44.6	44.8	45.5	46.3	44.5
1996	44.6	44.2	44.7	45.0	45.3	45.7	45.4	45.5	45.4	46.6	47.5	48.5	45.7
1997	46.5	46.2	46.8	47.1	47.7	47.8	48.4	47.8	47.9	48.8	49.4	50.8	47.9
1998	48.1	48.1	48.6	49.0	49.9	50.8	51.4	51.2	51.6	52.1	52.9	54.1	50.7
1999	51.2	51.2	51.5	52.8	53.3	53.7	55.0	54.9	54.5	54.9	56.0	57.2	53.9
2000	55.3	55.0	55.6	54.7	55.0	56.2	55.4	55.7	55.7	55.9	56.9	57.5	55.7
2001	54.8	54.5	54.8	54.6	54.8	54.9	54.8	55.1	54.8	54.6	55.1	55.6	54.8
2002	53.9	54.1	54.6	54.5	55.2	54.9	55.1	55.3	55.5	55.6	56.2	56.8	55.1
2003	54.2	54.7	55.0	53.9	53.9	54.4	52.9	52.6	52.5	52.7	53.2	53.4	53.6
Wholesale trade													
1990	4.9	4.9	5.0	5.1	5.2	5.2	5.5	5.5	5.5	5.5	5.5	5.5	5.3
1991	5.3	5.4	5.3	5.2	5.4	5.4	5.4	5.3	5.4	5.4	5.4	5.4	5.4
1992	5.2	5.2	5.2	5.1	5.2	5.3	5.3	5.3	5.3	5.3	5.2	5.3	5.2
1993	5.3	5.4	5.5	5.7	5.7	5.6	5.6	5.5	5.5	5.7	5.7	5.7	5.6
1994	5.9	5.8	5.8	5.7	5.5	5.6	5.7	5.7	5.7	5.6	5.6	5.6	5.7
1995	5.6	5.7	5.7	5.8	5.8	5.8	5.9	5.8	5.8	5.9	5.9	6.0	5.8
1996	5.9	5.9	5.9	5.9	6.0	6.1	6.0	6.0	6.0	6.1	6.1	6.2	6.0
1997	6.1	6.1	6.2	6.1	6.2	6.2	6.2	6.1	6.2	6.2	6.3	6.4	6.2
1998	6.2	6.3	6.3	6.4	6.4	6.5	6.7	6.6	6.6	6.7	6.7	6.8	6.5
1999	6.8	6.8	6.8	7.0	7.1	7.1	7.2	7.2	7.1	7.1	7.2	7.3	7.1
2000	7.4	7.4	7.4	7.4	7.4	7.5	7.8	7.8	7.9	7.9	8.0	8.0	7.7
2001	7.9	7.9	8.1	8.0	8.0	8.0	8.1	8.1	8.1	8.0	7.9	8.0	8.0
2002	8.0	8.2	8.4	8.2	8.2	8.2	8.4	8.4	8.5	8.4	8.4	8.5	8.3
2003	8.1	8.2	8.3	8.3	8.1	8.1	7.9	7.9	7.9	7.9	8.0	8.1	8.1
Retail trade													
1990	26.7	26.5	26.8	27.4	27.7	28.2	28.1	28.1	28.1	28.3	29.1	29.5	27.9
1991	27.2	26.9	27.2	26.7	26.9	27.1	27.0	26.8	26.5	26.8	27.6	28.1	27.1
1992	26.4	26.1	26.4	26.5	26.8	26.9	27.0	27.3	27.0	26.9	27.5	28.4	26.9
1993	26.9	26.5	26.7	27.2	27.2	27.3	27.6	27.4	27.2	27.7	28.5	29.5	27.5
1994	27.9	27.6	27.7	27.8	28.0	28.5	27.9	28.1	28.2	28.4	29.1	29.9	28.3
1995	28.4	28.1	28.5	28.8	29.2	29.4	29.5	29.2	29.4	29.3	29.9	30.5	29.2
1996	29.2	28.9	29.0	28.9	29.2	29.4	29.2	29.3	29.2	30.3	30.9	31.9	29.6
1997	30.0	29.7	30.0	30.2	30.7	30.9	30.9	30.8	30.7	31.4	32.0	33.1	30.9
1998	31.0	30.9	31.2	31.6	32.5	33.1	33.6	33.3	33.7	34.0	34.7	35.8	33.0
1999	33.3	33.1	33.3	34.0	34.3	34.5	34.9	34.7	34.4	34.2	34.9	35.9	34.3
2000	34.5	34.2	34.5	34.2	34.5	35.1	34.1	34.3	34.4	34.6	35.4	35.9	34.6
2001	34.2	33.9	34.1	33.9	34.2	34.5	34.1	34.1	34.0	34.0	34.6	35.0	34.2
2002	33.8	33.6	34.0	34.1	34.4	34.7	34.3	34.2	34.3	34.5	35.0	35.8	34.4
2003	34.0	33.9	34.1	33.9	34.2	34.6	33.3	33.2	32.9	33.1	33.3	33.4	33.7

Employment by Industry: South Carolina—*Continued*

(Numbers in thousands. Not seasonally adjusted.)

Industry	January	February	March	April	May	June	July	August	September	October	November	December	Annual Average
CHARLESTON—*Continued*													
Transportation and utilities													
1990	8.4	8.4	8.5	9.1	9.3	9.2	9.0	9.2	8.9	9.3	9.2	9.2	9.0
1991	8.7	8.9	8.9	8.8	8.7	8.7	8.7	8.9	9.0	9.1	9.2	9.3	8.9
1992	9.0	9.2	8.9	9.0	9.1	9.3	8.8	9.1	9.1	9.1	9.1	9.2	9.1
1993	9.0	8.9	9.1	9.1	9.3	9.4	9.1	9.2	9.2	9.6	9.7	9.8	9.3
1994	9.2	9.3	9.7	9.5	9.5	9.8	9.3	9.3	9.3	9.4	9.3	9.5	9.4
1995	9.2	9.3	9.4	9.3	9.4	9.4	9.5	9.5	9.4	9.6	9.7	9.8	9.5
1996	9.5	9.4	9.8	10.2	10.1	10.2	10.2	10.2	10.2	10.2	10.5	10.4	10.1
1997	10.4	10.4	10.6	10.8	10.8	10.7	11.3	10.9	11.0	11.2	11.1	11.3	10.9
1998	10.9	10.9	11.1	11.0	11.0	11.2	11.1	11.3	11.3	11.4	11.5	11.5	11.2
1999	11.1	11.3	11.4	11.8	11.9	12.1	12.9	13.0	13.0	13.6	13.9	14.0	12.5
2000	13.4	13.4	13.7	13.1	13.1	13.6	13.5	13.6	13.4	13.4	13.5	13.6	13.4
2001	12.7	12.7	12.6	12.7	12.6	12.4	12.6	12.9	12.7	12.6	12.6	12.6	12.6
2002	12.1	12.3	12.2	12.2	12.6	12.0	12.4	12.7	12.7	12.7	12.8	12.5	12.4
2003	12.1	12.6	12.6	11.7	11.6	11.7	11.7	11.5	11.7	11.7	11.9	11.9	11.9
Information													
1990	2.8	2.8	2.9	2.9	2.9	3.0	3.1	3.1	3.0	3.0	3.1	3.0	3.0
1991	3.0	3.0	3.0	2.9	2.9	3.0	3.0	3.0	3.0	2.9	2.9	3.0	3.0
1992	2.8	2.8	2.8	2.7	2.8	2.8	2.9	2.9	2.9	2.8	2.9	2.9	2.8
1993	2.9	2.9	2.9	3.0	3.0	3.1	3.0	3.1	3.0	3.1	3.0	3.1	3.0
1994	3.0	3.0	3.0	3.0	3.0	3.0	3.1	3.0	3.0	3.1	3.0	3.0	3.0
1995	3.0	3.0	3.0	3.0	3.0	3.0	3.0	3.0	3.0	2.9	3.0	3.0	3.0
1996	3.0	3.0	3.0	3.0	3.1	3.1	3.2	3.1	3.1	3.2	3.2	3.2	3.1
1997	3.2	3.2	3.2	3.2	3.3	3.3	3.2	3.2	3.3	3.3	3.3	3.4	3.3
1998	3.4	3.4	3.4	3.5	3.7	3.7	3.7	3.7	3.8	3.9	3.8	3.7	3.6
1999	3.8	3.8	3.9	3.8	3.8	4.0	3.9	3.9	3.9	4.0	4.0	4.0	3.9
2000	4.0	4.0	4.1	4.3	4.3	4.4	4.2	4.2	4.2	4.3	4.3	4.3	4.2
2001	4.1	4.1	4.1	4.0	4.0	4.0	4.0	4.0	3.9	3.8	3.9	3.9	3.9
2002	3.9	3.8	3.8	3.6	3.7	3.6	3.9	3.9	3.9	4.3	4.3	4.4	3.9
2003	4.0	4.0	4.0	3.6	3.7	3.7	3.6	3.6	3.7	3.6	3.6	3.5	3.7
Financial activities													
1990	11.2	11.2	11.3	11.1	11.1	11.1	11.1	10.9	11.0	10.7	10.6	10.4	11.0
1991	10.2	10.0	10.0	9.9	10.0	10.1	10.1	10.0	9.9	9.8	9.8	9.9	10.0
1992	9.6	9.5	9.5	9.6	9.6	9.7	9.8	9.8	9.8	9.7	9.6	9.8	9.7
1993	9.4	9.4	9.4	9.4	9.6	9.7	9.8	9.8	9.8	9.7	9.8	9.8	9.6
1994	9.7	9.7	9.9	9.7	9.8	9.9	9.9	9.7	9.7	9.7	9.6	9.6	9.7
1995	9.5	9.5	9.6	9.5	9.5	9.6	9.7	9.7	9.6	9.6	9.7	9.8	9.6
1996	9.6	9.7	9.9	9.8	9.9	10.0	9.9	10.0	9.9	9.9	9.9	10.0	9.9
1997	9.8	9.8	9.9	9.9	10.0	10.1	10.1	10.1	10.0	9.9	9.9	10.0	10.0
1998	9.9	9.9	10.0	10.1	10.2	10.3	10.4	10.3	10.4	10.7	10.6	10.6	10.3
1999	10.2	10.3	10.3	10.7	10.8	11.1	11.1	11.1	10.9	11.0	11.0	11.2	10.8
2000	11.0	11.0	11.0	11.0	11.1	11.3	11.2	11.2	11.0	11.2	11.1	11.2	11.1
2001	10.8	10.9	10.9	11.1	11.1	11.2	11.5	11.4	11.3	11.1	11.0	11.2	11.1
2002	10.7	10.7	10.8	10.4	10.5	10.8	11.0	10.9	10.7	10.5	10.4	10.4	10.7
2003	10.5	10.5	10.5	10.6	10.8	10.9	11.1	11.1	10.9	10.5	10.9	11.0	10.8
Professional and business services													
1990	15.4	15.8	16.0	16.2	16.5	16.8	16.7	17.0	17.1	17.2	17.3	17.3	16.6
1991	16.7	16.9	17.1	17.3	17.6	17.6	17.5	17.5	17.2	17.8	17.1	17.0	17.3
1992	16.0	16.0	16.2	16.3	16.2	16.2	16.8	17.0	17.0	17.4	17.6	17.6	16.7
1993	16.3	16.3	16.5	16.8	17.0	17.1	17.0	16.8	16.6	17.5	17.8	18.2	17.0
1994	18.0	18.2	18.6	19.1	18.9	19.2	19.1	18.9	19.4	19.2	19.4	19.3	18.9
1995	19.2	19.3	19.6	20.4	20.6	20.9	20.5	21.0	20.8	20.9	21.0	21.1	20.4
1996	21.1	21.4	21.7	22.2	22.9	23.5	23.0	23.6	23.5	23.1	23.3	23.4	22.7
1997	24.0	24.6	24.9	25.0	25.7	26.1	26.4	27.4	27.0	26.0	25.9	25.9	25.7
1998	26.2	26.5	26.7	27.4	28.3	28.5	28.6	29.5	29.6	28.4	29.3	29.2	28.2
1999	28.6	28.8	29.2	30.4	30.4	30.5	30.1	30.3	30.0	29.6	30.0	30.6	29.9
2000	30.9	30.9	31.5	32.1	32.7	33.6	32.7	32.9	33.2	32.7	32.7	32.7	32.4
2001	32.3	32.4	32.6	32.8	32.6	32.9	33.1	33.3	33.2	33.1	32.8	32.8	32.8
2002	32.2	33.0	33.2	33.3	33.4	33.8	33.7	34.3	34.5	32.8	32.3	31.8	33.2
2003	32.1	32.9	33.4	33.4	33.5	33.6	33.9	34.8	34.0	34.3	34.4	33.3	33.6
Educational and health services													
1990	15.8	16.1	16.2	16.4	16.3	16.2	16.0	16.1	17.0	16.8	17.0	17.0	16.4
1991	16.8	17.1	17.3	17.5	17.4	17.0	17.0	17.0	17.5	17.8	17.9	17.9	17.4
1992	18.1	18.4	18.6	18.6	18.7	18.3	18.4	18.3	19.0	19.4	19.4	19.3	18.7
1993	19.1	19.1	19.3	19.5	19.5	19.1	19.0	18.9	19.5	20.0	20.1	20.2	19.4
1994	20.0	20.1	20.2	20.5	20.5	20.2	19.9	19.9	20.6	20.5	20.6	20.8	20.3
1995	20.7	20.9	20.9	21.1	21.1	20.8	20.6	20.5	21.2	21.4	21.5	21.3	21.0
1996	20.7	20.9	21.1	20.6	20.6	20.3	20.0	20.2	20.6	20.7	20.7	20.7	20.6
1997	20.7	21.0	21.0	21.0	21.0	20.6	20.5	20.4	21.4	21.8	21.7	21.9	21.1
1998	21.5	21.9	21.6	21.7	21.7	21.4	21.5	21.5	22.1	22.5	22.5	22.7	21.9
1999	22.2	22.7	22.8	23.1	23.3	22.8	22.8	22.9	23.4	23.7	23.5	23.6	23.1
2000	23.9	23.9	24.0	23.9	23.9	23.9	22.9	23.0	23.3	23.9	24.0	24.2	23.7
2001	23.5	23.7	23.9	23.9	23.9	23.9	23.7	24.0	24.2	24.1	24.2	24.4	23.9
2002	24.2	24.5	24.6	25.6	25.9	25.6	26.4	26.3	26.5	27.1	27.3	27.1	25.9
2003	27.1	27.3	27.3	26.7	26.7	26.5	26.8	26.9	26.9	28.6	28.5	28.9	27.4

Employment by Industry: South Carolina—*Continued*

(Numbers in thousands. Not seasonally adjusted.)

Industry	January	February	March	April	May	June	July	August	September	October	November	December	Annual Average
CHARLESTON—*Continued*													
Leisure and hospitality													
1990	20.4	21.0	21.8	23.2	24.2	24.8	24.3	24.3	23.6	22.6	22.8	22.5	23.0
1991	21.0	21.3	22.3	22.8	24.2	24.7	24.2	24.1	23.6	22.8	22.7	22.4	23.0
1992	21.2	21.6	22.4	24.3	25.3	25.7	25.2	25.1	24.5	23.5	22.9	22.7	23.7
1993	22.1	22.9	23.5	24.4	25.3	25.8	25.6	25.4	25.3	24.5	24.3	23.9	24.4
1994	22.9	23.2	23.8	24.9	25.6	26.2	25.6	26.1	25.0	24.7	24.7	24.3	24.8
1995	23.2	23.7	24.4	25.8	27.0	27.4	27.6	27.6	26.5	25.2	25.2	24.9	25.7
1996	23.8	24.5	25.2	25.9	27.6	28.4	27.8	27.8	27.0	26.4	26.0	25.8	26.4
1997	24.7	25.6	26.6	27.3	28.5	29.3	28.5	28.2	27.6	27.7	27.6	27.4	27.4
1998	26.4	27.2	28.7	28.8	29.9	31.2	31.8	31.3	30.3	29.1	29.1	28.9	29.4
1999	27.7	29.0	30.0	31.3	32.5	33.6	31.8	31.6	30.5	31.1	30.5	30.6	30.9
2000	29.7	30.4	31.4	32.2	33.1	33.6	32.5	31.6	30.5	30.5	30.4	30.1	31.3
2001	28.8	29.2	30.2	30.9	31.7	32.3	32.0	31.2	30.3	29.5	29.0	28.5	30.2
2002	28.4	29.2	30.2	31.0	32.0	32.2	33.7	33.4	32.2	32.5	32.2	31.7	31.6
2003	30.9	31.4	32.4	32.4	33.5	34.2	33.3	33.0	31.7	30.9	30.8	30.1	32.1
Other services													
1990	7.5	7.6	7.6	7.6	7.8	7.9	8.0	7.9	7.9	7.7	7.7	7.7	7.7
1991	7.5	7.5	7.6	7.5	7.6	7.7	7.7	7.6	7.5	7.2	7.3	7.2	7.5
1992	7.2	7.2	7.3	7.2	7.3	7.4	7.5	7.5	7.3	7.2	7.2	7.2	7.3
1993	7.2	7.3	7.3	7.5	7.6	7.8	7.9	7.8	7.5	7.3	7.3	7.2	7.5
1994	7.3	7.3	7.4	7.3	7.3	7.5	7.5	7.5	7.2	7.0	7.0	7.1	7.3
1995	7.1	7.0	7.1	7.3	7.4	7.6	7.5	7.5	7.3	7.2	7.2	7.3	7.3
1996	7.0	7.1	7.1	7.0	6.9	7.1	7.0	7.0	6.9	6.9	6.8	6.8	7.0
1997	6.8	6.8	6.9	6.9	7.0	7.2	7.1	6.9	6.9	7.0	6.9	7.0	7.0
1998	7.1	7.1	7.4	7.5	7.5	7.6	7.8	7.8	7.7	7.4	7.4	7.4	7.5
1999	7.1	7.2	7.4	7.6	7.6	7.6	7.7	7.6	7.6	7.5	7.5	7.4	7.5
2000	7.4	7.4	7.5	7.5	7.5	7.6	7.3	7.2	7.1	7.2	7.2	7.2	7.3
2001	6.8	6.8	7.0	7.0	7.1	7.2	6.9	7.0	6.9	6.9	6.8	6.9	6.9
2002	7.0	7.2	7.5	7.3	7.4	7.7	7.3	7.4	7.6	7.2	7.3	7.4	7.4
2003	7.2	7.3	7.3	7.5	7.6	7.8	7.8	7.8	7.7	7.7	7.7	7.6	7.6
Government													
1990	53.9	54.4	54.7	53.9	54.4	53.5	50.9	49.7	52.5	53.5	53.4	53.4	53.2
1991	53.3	54.6	55.0	54.5	55.1	54.8	52.8	53.6	55.3	55.4	55.7	55.8	54.7
1992	54.6	55.5	55.2	55.3	55.4	54.5	51.7	52.3	55.0	56.2	57.6	56.6	55.0
1993	55.4	56.0	56.4	56.5	56.2	54.7	51.1	52.5	53.7	55.0	55.0	54.8	54.8
1994	53.6	54.0	54.1	53.6	53.5	52.1	48.1	48.9	51.0	51.8	53.3	51.8	52.2
1995	51.2	51.4	51.3	50.2	50.5	49.3	46.6	46.4	49.4	50.3	50.2	50.5	49.8
1996	48.3	49.4	49.7	48.7	48.7	49.3	45.0	46.3	47.8	48.7	50.4	49.3	48.5
1997	48.1	48.6	48.9	48.8	49.3	48.6	47.1	47.1	49.0	50.2	50.4	50.4	48.9
1998	49.5	50.1	50.3	49.8	50.2	50.9	47.4	47.9	49.2	50.4	50.7	50.9	49.8
1999	50.1	50.6	50.7	50.8	50.8	50.2	47.9	47.9	49.6	50.2	50.6	50.3	50.0
2000	50.3	50.8	51.1	50.9	51.5	51.9	47.6	48.4	49.1	50.1	50.4	50.8	50.2
2001	48.6	49.3	49.7	49.7	49.5	48.4	47.8	46.9	49.2	50.2	50.2	50.2	49.1
2002	49.1	50.0	50.1	50.4	50.4	49.7	48.7	49.4	50.6	50.9	51.2	51.6	50.2
2003	49.9	51.3	51.1	51.7	51.6	49.9	48.5	49.9	51.1	51.3	51.4	51.7	50.8
Federal government													
1990	19.6	19.6	19.7	19.7	20.0	20.5	19.6	19.3	19.0	18.9	18.7	18.6	19.4
1991	19.1	19.0	19.0	18.5	18.4	18.5	18.3	18.2	18.3	17.5	17.4	17.4	18.3
1992	17.2	17.2	16.5	16.4	16.3	16.4	16.0	16.1	16.1	15.8	15.8	15.9	16.3
1993	15.7	15.7	15.7	15.7	15.5	15.1	14.7	14.7	14.6	14.4	14.4	14.4	15.1
1994	14.1	14.0	13.9	13.8	13.7	13.5	13.2	13.2	13.0	12.5	12.5	12.4	13.3
1995	11.9	11.5	11.3	10.9	10.8	10.6	10.6	10.4	10.5	10.3	10.1	10.2	10.8
1996	9.5	9.5	9.5	8.7	8.7	8.7	8.8	8.7	8.6	9.0	9.0	9.1	9.0
1997	8.8	8.8	8.7	9.0	8.9	8.9	9.2	9.1	9.1	9.3	9.3	9.3	9.0
1998	9.2	9.1	9.1	9.0	9.0	9.0	8.9	8.7	8.7	8.8	8.8	8.9	8.9
1999	8.7	8.7	8.7	9.0	9.0	9.0	9.0	8.8	8.6	8.6	8.7	8.8	8.8
2000	8.6	8.6	8.7	8.8	9.5	10.2	8.8	9.2	8.3	8.3	8.4	8.4	8.8
2001	8.0	8.0	8.0	8.0	8.0	8.0	8.0	8.0	8.0	8.4	8.2	8.1	8.0
2002	8.2	8.1	8.1	8.0	7.9	8.0	8.1	8.0	8.1	8.1	8.1	8.2	8.1
2003	7.9	7.9	7.8	8.0	8.0	8.1	8.1	8.1	8.0	7.9	7.8	8.0	8.0
State government													
1990	15.2	16.0	16.0	16.1	16.0	14.5	14.7	14.6	15.4	16.2	16.2	16.2	15.6
1991	15.9	16.9	17.2	17.0	17.2	16.9	16.6	16.9	17.5	18.1	18.2	18.3	17.2
1992	17.6	18.3	18.6	18.7	18.8	18.7	18.7	19.2	19.8	20.0	21.4	20.1	19.2
1993	19.2	19.7	19.9	20.0	19.8	19.5	19.4	19.2	19.5	19.7	19.6	19.3	19.6
1994	18.7	19.1	19.1	19.0	18.7	18.2	16.8	17.7	18.0	18.2	19.6	18.2	18.4
1995	18.2	18.6	18.6	18.2	18.2	17.8	17.6	17.5	17.9	18.3	18.3	18.4	18.1
1996	17.8	18.3	18.5	18.5	18.3	18.7	17.8	17.7	18.1	18.4	19.9	18.5	18.4
1997	17.9	18.3	18.5	18.6	18.6	18.0	18.1	18.1	18.4	19.0	19.1	19.2	18.5
1998	18.5	19.0	19.1	19.1	19.1	19.5	18.6	18.6	18.8	19.6	19.7	19.8	19.1
1999	19.1	19.4	19.5	19.6	19.4	18.5	18.9	18.7	18.9	19.3	19.4	18.9	19.1
2000	19.4	19.7	19.8	19.5	19.4	18.7	18.6	18.6	18.5	19.2	19.3	19.5	19.2
2001	18.3	18.6	18.9	18.8	18.6	17.8	18.0	18.0	18.5	18.8	18.9	18.9	18.5
2002	18.2	18.7	18.8	18.9	18.8	18.0	18.3	18.4	18.9	19.3	19.4	19.5	18.8
2003	18.8	19.4	19.4	19.5	19.3	18.5	18.6	18.7	19.0	19.1	19.1	19.1	19.0

Employment by Industry: South Carolina—*Continued*

(Numbers in thousands. Not seasonally adjusted.)

Industry	January	February	March	April	May	June	July	August	September	October	November	December	Annual Average
CHARLESTON—*Continued*													
Local government													
1990	19.1	18.8	19.0	18.1	18.4	18.5	16.6	15.8	18.1	18.4	18.5	18.6	18.2
1991	18.3	18.7	18.8	19.0	19.5	19.4	17.9	18.5	19.5	19.8	20.1	20.1	19.1
1992	19.8	20.0	20.1	20.2	20.3	19.4	17.0	17.0	19.1	20.4	20.4	20.6	19.5
1993	20.5	20.6	20.8	20.8	20.9	20.1	17.0	18.6	19.6	20.9	21.0	21.1	20.2
1994	20.8	20.9	21.1	20.8	21.1	20.4	18.1	18.0	20.0	21.1	21.2	21.2	20.4
1995	21.1	21.3	21.4	21.1	21.5	20.9	18.4	18.5	21.0	21.7	21.8	21.9	20.9
1996	21.0	21.6	21.7	21.5	21.7	21.9	18.4	19.9	21.1	21.3	21.5	21.7	21.1
1997	21.4	21.5	21.7	21.2	21.8	21.7	19.8	19.9	21.5	21.9	22.0	21.9	21.4
1998	21.8	22.0	22.1	21.7	22.1	22.4	19.9	20.6	21.7	22.0	22.2	22.2	21.7
1999	22.3	22.5	22.5	22.2	22.4	22.7	20.0	20.4	22.1	22.3	22.5	22.6	22.0
2000	22.3	22.5	22.6	22.6	22.6	23.0	20.2	20.6	22.3	22.6	22.7	22.9	22.2
2001	22.3	22.7	22.8	22.9	22.9	22.6	21.8	20.9	22.7	23.0	23.1	23.2	22.5
2002	22.7	23.2	23.2	23.5	23.7	23.7	22.3	23.0	23.6	23.5	23.7	23.9	23.3
2003	23.2	24.0	23.9	24.2	24.3	23.3	21.8	23.1	24.1	24.3	24.5	24.6	23.8
COLUMBIA													
Total nonfarm													
1990	242.7	244.7	246.3	248.6	250.3	249.7	243.0	244.0	251.9	253.4	253.1	255.5	248.6
1991	243.7	245.9	246.8	248.6	248.9	245.9	239.6	238.6	246.2	247.1	248.1	249.2	245.7
1992	244.0	245.8	247.7	247.9	249.1	250.0	246.6	246.4	247.9	249.7	249.7	250.7	248.0
1993	246.3	248.6	250.6	252.6	253.8	253.6	247.4	249.4	253.9	259.1	259.6	264.1	253.3
1994	255.9	258.4	261.0	263.7	265.4	266.7	263.1	263.4	267.2	268.2	272.8	273.4	264.9
1995	265.8	269.1	271.8	273.0	274.4	273.5	269.3	270.4	274.2	275.6	277.0	279.7	272.8
1996	274.5	275.7	279.3	280.5	283.0	284.3	280.3	281.9	286.6	287.3	289.9	291.2	282.9
1997	286.4	289.7	291.3	291.8	293.7	293.4	289.4	289.0	294.2	294.0	295.8	298.9	292.3
1998	295.0	296.9	299.8	302.6	305.1	306.6	303.6	304.9	307.9	309.6	312.1	314.6	304.9
1999	306.7	310.4	312.8	317.1	318.8	317.9	313.5	314.5	314.7	319.9	321.4	325.0	316.1
2000	317.9	319.4	322.4	313.5	315.6	315.6	307.7	308.3	308.1	312.9	313.8	314.9	314.2
2001	309.0	310.3	312.5	311.8	313.3	312.2	305.5	309.7	309.5	308.9	309.7	310.0	310.2
2002	302.6	304.0	306.8	305.4	306.4	306.1	304.1	309.2	310.8	313.0	313.5	314.8	308.1
2003	307.6	307.9	310.2	303.7	305.3	303.8	302.0	302.9	300.8	300.6	300.4	300.8	303.8
Total private													
1990	176.6	177.0	177.8	179.6	181.3	183.6	181.9	183.5	183.4	184.0	184.0	185.0	181.5
1991	176.2	176.1	176.7	178.5	178.6	179.0	177.4	177.7	178.0	177.8	178.5	179.4	177.8
1992	175.6	176.1	177.4	177.7	178.7	180.4	180.0	180.2	179.4	180.3	180.1	180.9	178.9
1993	177.5	178.9	180.5	182.2	183.5	184.3	183.1	183.7	184.2	188.3	188.5	192.7	184.0
1994	186.2	187.5	189.7	191.4	192.8	195.2	195.5	196.5	197.1	197.7	199.4	201.9	194.2
1995	195.3	196.9	199.1	200.2	201.7	203.0	202.5	203.5	204.5	205.1	205.9	207.1	202.1
1996	203.0	203.3	206.1	207.9	210.3	212.1	213.1	214.5	214.6	214.6	215.4	218.0	211.1
1997	214.9	216.8	217.8	218.3	220.1	221.3	220.1	219.3	220.5	220.0	220.9	223.7	219.5
1998	220.5	221.6	224.2	226.7	229.1	230.8	231.6	232.5	232.3	233.5	235.4	237.8	229.7
1999	231.0	233.1	235.2	239.5	241.2	242.6	241.5	241.4	239.6	243.2	244.2	246.0	239.9
2000	240.8	241.5	243.9	235.4	236.8	239.4	233.6	233.2	234.4	236.9	238.0	239.5	237.8
2001	234.8	235.4	237.2	237.0	238.5	239.3	236.8	237.1	235.7	235.1	235.7	235.7	236.5
2002	229.0	230.1	232.5	230.6	231.4	233.4	235.8	236.6	236.5	238.2	238.3	239.4	234.3
2003	232.6	232.2	234.4	228.5	230.2	230.8	230.9	231.4	228.1	227.4	227.1	227.1	230.1
Goods-producing													
1990	38.2	38.3	38.5	38.5	39.0	39.3	38.7	38.9	38.8	37.9	37.7	37.9	38.5
1991	37.2	37.2	37.2	37.4	37.3	37.5	37.2	37.4	37.4	37.3	37.4	37.3	37.3
1992	37.0	37.0	37.1	37.0	37.3	37.9	37.9	37.8	37.6	37.3	37.3	37.0	37.4
1993	36.7	36.8	37.1	36.9	37.1	37.4	37.6	37.7	37.4	38.1	38.2	38.8	37.5
1994	37.7	37.9	38.4	38.2	38.6	39.2	39.0	39.0	38.9	39.3	39.2	39.7	38.8
1995	38.3	38.2	38.5	38.2	38.5	38.8	38.6	38.6	38.7	38.9	39.0	39.1	38.6
1996	38.6	38.6	39.1	39.6	40.2	40.7	40.6	40.9	40.6	40.7	40.8	41.2	40.1
1997	41.0	41.2	41.3	40.8	41.3	41.6	42.0	41.8	41.8	42.1	42.1	42.5	41.6
1998	42.1	41.8	42.3	42.6	43.2	43.5	43.3	43.8	43.5	43.8	44.2	44.6	43.2
1999	44.3	44.4	44.6	45.1	45.3	45.8	45.8	45.7	45.3	45.1	45.4	45.4	45.2
2000	45.1	45.0	45.2	44.0	44.3	44.9	43.8	44.1	44.0	44.1	43.9	44.1	44.4
2001	43.8	44.0	44.3	44.2	44.5	44.6	44.3	44.0	43.8	43.5	43.3	43.0	43.9
2002	42.2	42.3	42.4	41.4	41.9	42.1	42.7	42.9	42.8	42.5	42.5	42.6	42.4
2003	41.8	41.5	41.9	41.7	42.2	42.3	42.1	41.6	40.2	40.4	39.8	39.4	41.2
Construction and mining													
1990	12.3	12.4	12.6	13.3	13.7	14.0	14.0	13.9	13.8	13.3	13.2	13.0	13.3
1991	12.2	12.3	12.4	12.5	12.5	12.6	12.6	12.7	12.7	12.5	12.5	12.4	12.5
1992	12.0	12.0	12.1	12.2	12.4	12.8	12.9	12.8	12.7	12.4	12.5	12.2	12.4
1993	12.0	11.9	12.1	12.2	12.3	12.5	12.6	12.7	12.6	12.8	12.9	13.1	12.5
1994	12.7	12.7	13.0	12.8	13.1	13.4	13.5	13.4	13.4	13.6	13.6	13.7	13.2
1995	13.3	13.1	13.3	13.3	13.7	14.0	14.0	14.1	14.3	14.4	14.4	14.4	13.9
1996	14.0	14.0	14.4	15.3	15.7	16.0	16.1	16.3	16.0	16.0	15.9	16.0	15.5
1997	15.9	15.9	16.0	15.8	16.1	16.3	16.8	16.6	16.6	16.7	16.6	16.7	16.3
1998	16.4	16.2	16.6	16.8	17.1	17.3	17.4	17.5	17.2	17.2	17.4	17.5	17.1
1999	17.7	17.8	18.0	18.5	18.5	18.9	19.2	19.1	18.7	18.6	18.8	18.8	18.6
2000	18.5	18.4	18.6	18.2	18.4	18.7	18.0	18.1	18.0	18.0	17.9	18.0	18.2
2001	17.8	17.8	18.2	18.2	18.5	18.6	18.4	18.4	18.4	18.1	18.0	17.8	18.1
2002	17.2	17.5	17.6	17.1	17.4	17.6	18.0	18.1	18.1	17.9	18.0	18.1	17.7
2003	17.9	18.0	18.2	17.7	18.1	18.3	18.0	17.7	16.5	16.5	16.1	16.2	17.4

Employment by Industry: South Carolina—*Continued*

(Numbers in thousands. Not seasonally adjusted.)

Industry	January	February	March	April	May	June	July	August	September	October	November	December	Annual Average
COLUMBIA—*Continued*													
Manufacturing													
1990	25.9	25.9	25.9	25.2	25.3	25.3	24.7	25.0	25.0	24.6	24.5	24.9	25.2
1991	25.0	24.9	24.8	24.9	24.8	24.9	24.6	24.7	24.7	24.8	24.9	24.9	24.8
1992	25.0	25.0	25.0	24.8	24.9	25.1	25.0	25.0	24.9	24.9	24.8	24.8	24.9
1993	24.7	24.9	25.0	24.7	24.8	24.9	25.0	25.0	24.8	25.3	25.3	25.7	25.0
1994	25.0	25.2	25.4	25.4	25.5	25.8	25.5	25.6	25.5	25.7	25.6	26.0	25.5
1995	25.0	25.1	25.2	24.9	24.8	24.8	24.6	24.5	24.4	24.5	24.6	24.7	24.8
1996	24.6	24.6	24.7	24.3	24.5	24.7	24.5	24.6	24.6	24.7	24.9	25.2	24.7
1997	25.1	25.3	25.3	25.0	25.2	25.3	25.2	25.2	25.2	25.4	25.5	25.8	25.3
1998	25.7	25.6	25.7	25.8	26.1	26.2	25.9	26.3	26.3	26.6	26.8	27.1	26.2
1999	26.6	26.6	26.6	26.6	26.8	26.9	26.6	26.6	26.6	26.5	26.6	26.6	26.6
2000	26.6	26.6	26.6	25.8	25.9	26.2	25.8	26.0	26.0	26.1	26.0	26.1	26.1
2001	26.0	26.2	26.1	26.0	26.0	26.0	25.9	25.6	25.4	25.4	25.3	25.2	25.7
2002	25.0	24.8	24.8	24.3	24.5	24.5	24.7	24.8	24.7	24.6	24.5	24.5	24.6
2003	23.9	23.5	23.7	24.0	24.1	24.0	24.1	23.9	23.7	23.9	23.7	23.2	23.8
Service-providing													
1990	204.5	206.4	207.8	210.1	211.3	210.4	204.3	205.1	213.1	215.5	215.4	217.6	210.1
1991	206.5	208.7	209.6	211.2	211.6	208.4	202.4	201.2	208.8	209.8	210.7	211.9	208.4
1992	207.0	208.8	210.6	210.9	211.8	212.1	208.7	208.6	210.3	212.4	212.4	213.7	210.6
1993	209.6	211.8	213.5	215.7	216.7	216.2	209.8	211.7	216.5	221.0	221.4	225.3	215.8
1994	218.2	220.5	222.6	225.5	226.8	227.5	224.1	224.4	228.3	228.9	233.6	233.7	226.2
1995	227.5	230.9	233.3	234.8	235.9	234.7	230.7	231.8	235.5	236.7	238.0	240.6	234.2
1996	235.9	237.1	240.2	240.9	242.8	243.6	239.7	241.0	246.0	246.6	249.1	250.0	242.7
1997	245.4	248.5	250.0	251.0	252.4	251.8	247.4	247.2	252.4	251.9	253.7	256.4	250.7
1998	252.9	255.1	257.5	260.0	261.9	263.1	260.3	261.1	264.4	265.8	267.9	270.0	261.7
1999	262.4	266.0	268.2	272.0	273.5	272.1	267.7	268.8	269.4	274.8	276.0	279.6	270.9
2000	272.8	274.4	277.2	269.5	271.3	270.7	263.9	264.2	264.1	268.8	269.9	270.8	269.8
2001	265.2	266.3	268.2	267.6	268.8	267.6	261.2	265.7	265.7	265.4	266.4	267.0	260.1
2002	260.4	261.7	264.4	264.0	264.5	264.0	261.4	266.3	268.0	270.5	271.0	272.2	265.7
2003	265.8	266.4	268.3	262.0	263.1	261.5	259.9	261.3	260.6	260.2	260.6	261.4	262.6
Trade, transportation, and utilities													
1990	46.7	46.2	46.1	46.2	46.7	47.7	47.4	48.0	47.8	48.2	49.0	50.1	47.5
1991	46.4	45.9	46.0	46.7	46.9	47.1	46.8	46.5	46.5	46.7	47.3	48.1	46.7
1992	45.7	45.3	45.5	46.1	46.3	46.9	46.6	46.7	46.6	46.9	47.1	48.1	46.5
1993	46.3	46.3	46.5	47.3	47.5	47.7	47.6	48.3	48.1	49.3	50.2	52.1	48.1
1994	49.8	50.0	50.2	50.3	50.6	51.1	51.1	51.5	51.7	51.5	52.5	53.8	51.2
1995	52.5	52.4	53.3	53.5	53.6	54.1	53.8	54.1	54.4	55.4	56.3	57.3	54.2
1996	54.6	54.0	54.2	54.5	54.9	55.2	55.8	56.4	56.6	57.2	58.2	59.5	55.9
1997	57.0	56.8	57.3	57.5	57.9	58.3	58.7	58.7	59.1	58.8	59.7	61.1	58.4
1998	58.8	58.6	58.4	58.1	57.7	57.7	58.1	58.3	58.7	58.6	59.2	60.4	58.6
1999	57.4	57.5	57.9	58.5	59.3	59.5	59.8	59.8	59.5	60.8	61.8	62.9	59.6
2000	60.3	60.2	60.9	58.8	59.1	59.7	58.3	58.5	58.7	60.0	61.1	62.0	59.8
2001	59.8	59.0	59.3	58.8	59.2	59.4	58.0	57.9	57.6	57.6	58.4	59.2	58.6
2002	56.0	56.1	56.6	56.4	56.7	57.3	56.9	56.9	57.1	57.6	58.9	60.1	57.2
2003	57.6	56.7	57.2	56.1	56.4	56.9	56.0	56.2	54.7	53.6	54.2	54.5	55.8
Wholesale trade													
1990	8.1	8.2	8.2	8.2	8.2	8.5	8.3	8.4	8.4	8.5	8.4	8.5	8.3
1991	8.3	8.4	8.4	8.5	8.5	8.5	8.5	8.4	8.4	8.5	8.5	8.5	8.5
1992	8.4	8.4	8.5	8.5	8.5	8.6	8.8	8.8	8.8	8.8	8.8	8.9	8.7
1993	9.0	9.1	9.2	9.4	9.4	9.5	9.5	9.7	9.7	9.9	9.9	10.2	9.5
1994	10.1	10.1	10.1	10.3	10.3	10.3	10.4	10.5	10.5	10.6	10.7	10.8	10.4
1995	10.8	10.8	10.9	11.0	11.0	11.2	11.0	11.0	11.1	11.2	11.3	11.4	11.1
1996	11.5	11.4	11.3	11.3	11.6	11.6	11.8	11.8	12.0	12.0	12.1	12.0	11.7
1997	11.7	11.8	11.8	12.0	12.1	12.1	12.2	12.2	12.2	12.2	12.2	12.3	12.1
1998	12.1	12.3	12.3	12.4	12.5	12.7	12.9	12.9	12.8	12.8	12.9	12.9	12.6
1999	12.8	12.9	13.0	12.9	13.0	13.1	13.3	13.3	13.2	13.2	13.3	13.3	13.1
2000	13.4	13.4	13.6	13.3	13.4	13.4	13.3	13.4	13.4	13.3	13.4	13.5	13.4
2001	13.9	13.8	13.9	13.6	13.7	13.7	13.5	13.5	13.5	13.4	13.3	13.4	13.6
2002	13.4	13.6	13.7	13.6	13.5	13.6	13.9	13.8	13.7	13.8	13.8	13.7	13.7
2003	13.6	13.6	13.7	13.6	13.7	13.8	13.8	13.8	12.6	11.3	11.4	11.6	13.0
Retail trade													
1990	31.1	30.5	30.4	30.5	30.9	31.5	31.4	31.8	31.6	31.8	32.6	33.7	31.5
1991	30.4	29.9	30.1	30.5	30.7	30.9	30.7	30.4	30.5	30.5	31.1	31.9	30.6
1992	29.7	29.3	29.4	29.8	29.9	30.3	29.8	29.8	29.8	30.1	30.3	31.3	30.0
1993	29.7	29.6	29.7	30.1	30.2	30.3	30.1	30.6	30.5	31.2	32.1	33.4	30.6
1994	31.6	31.6	31.7	31.7	31.9	32.3	32.2	32.5	32.7	32.6	33.5	34.6	32.4
1995	33.6	33.4	34.1	34.0	34.2	34.4	34.0	34.3	34.6	35.1	35.9	36.9	34.5
1996	34.4	34.0	34.3	34.4	34.4	34.8	34.8	35.3	35.4	35.9	36.8	38.0	35.2
1997	36.1	35.8	36.1	36.0	36.3	36.6	37.0	37.3	37.6	37.4	38.5	39.8	37.0
1998	37.8	37.4	37.3	36.5	36.0	35.8	36.0	36.2	36.6	36.3	36.8	37.8	36.7
1999	35.7	35.7	35.9	36.2	36.7	36.7	36.7	36.7	36.8	37.5	38.5	39.4	36.9
2000	37.2	37.1	37.6	36.0	36.2	36.6	35.4	35.5	35.7	36.8	37.9	38.5	36.7
2001	36.4	35.8	36.0	36.0	36.2	36.5	35.3	35.3	35.2	35.2	36.2	37.0	35.9
2002	34.4	34.1	34.5	34.7	35.1	35.6	35.0	35.1	35.4	35.7	37.1	38.2	35.4
2003	35.7	35.1	35.4	34.4	34.6	34.9	34.6	35.0	34.8	34.9	35.4	35.8	35.1

Employment by Industry: South Carolina—*Continued*

(Numbers in thousands. Not seasonally adjusted.)

Industry	January	February	March	April	May	June	July	August	September	October	November	December	Annual Average
COLUMBIA—*Continued*													
Transportation and utilities													
1990	7.5	7.5	7.5	7.5	7.6	7.7	7.7	7.8	7.8	7.9	8.0	7.9	7.7
1991	7.7	7.6	7.5	7.7	7.7	7.7	7.6	7.7	7.6	7.7	7.7	7.7	7.7
1992	7.6	7.6	7.6	7.8	7.9	8.0	8.0	8.1	8.0	8.0	8.0	7.9	7.9
1993	7.6	7.6	7.6	7.8	7.9	7.9	8.0	8.0	7.9	8.2	8.2	8.5	7.9
1994	8.1	8.3	8.4	8.3	8.4	8.5	8.5	8.5	8.5	8.3	8.3	8.4	8.4
1995	8.1	8.2	8.3	8.5	8.4	8.5	8.8	8.8	8.7	9.1	9.1	9.0	8.6
1996	8.7	8.6	8.6	8.8	8.9	8.8	9.2	9.3	9.2	9.3	9.3	9.5	9.0
1997	9.2	9.2	9.4	9.5	9.5	9.6	9.5	9.2	9.3	9.2	9.0	9.0	9.3
1998	8.9	8.9	8.8	9.2	9.2	9.2	9.2	9.2	9.3	9.5	9.5	9.7	9.2
1999	8.9	8.9	9.0	9.4	9.6	9.7	9.8	9.8	9.5	10.1	10.0	10.2	9.6
2000	9.7	9.7	9.7	9.5	9.5	9.7	9.6	9.6	9.6	9.9	9.8	10.0	9.7
2001	9.5	9.4	9.4	9.2	9.3	9.2	9.2	9.1	8.9	9.0	8.9	8.8	9.1
2002	8.2	8.4	8.4	8.1	8.1	8.1	8.0	8.0	8.0	8.1	8.0	8.2	8.1
2003	8.3	8.0	8.1	8.1	8.1	8.2	7.6	7.4	7.3	7.4	7.4	7.1	7.8
Information													
1990	7.8	7.8	7.8	7.9	7.9	8.1	8.1	8.1	8.1	8.3	8.4	8.5	8.1
1991	7.9	7.9	8.1	8.0	7.9	7.9	7.9	7.9	7.9	7.8	7.8	7.9	7.9
1992	8.3	8.2	8.2	8.0	8.1	8.1	8.0	7.9	7.9	7.9	7.9	7.9	8.0
1993	7.7	7.7	7.8	7.6	7.6	7.6	7.6	7.5	7.6	7.7	7.6	7.6	7.6
1994	7.5	7.5	7.6	7.5	7.5	7.7	7.6	7.6	7.6	7.6	7.5	7.4	7.6
1995	7.6	7.6	7.5	7.5	7.6	7.7	7.6	7.6	7.6	7.6	7.6	7.6	7.6
1996	7.5	7.5	7.5	7.7	7.8	7.8	7.7	7.7	7.7	7.6	7.6	7.7	7.7
1997	7.6	7.9	7.9	7.9	7.7	8.0	8.1	8.1	8.2	8.0	8.0	8.1	8.0
1998	7.8	7.8	7.8	7.8	8.0	8.2	8.3	8.2	8.1	8.2	8.3	8.3	8.1
1999	8.4	8.3	8.2	8.4	8.4	8.5	8.5	8.4	8.3	8.2	8.3	8.3	8.4
2000	8.5	8.5	8.3	7.7	7.6	7.8	7.5	7.5	7.5	7.3	7.3	7.3	7.7
2001	7.2	7.1	7.1	6.9	6.9	6.9	6.6	6.6	6.5	6.5	6.5	6.6	6.7
2002	6.4	6.4	6.5	5.8	5.9	6.0	6.4	6.4	6.2	6.1	6.2	6.2	6.2
2003	6.2	6.2	6.2	5.4	5.5	5.5	5.4	5.4	5.3	5.4	5.2	5.6	5.6
Financial activities													
1990	20.9	20.9	20.9	20.4	20.4	20.6	20.6	20.4	20.0	20.0	19.7	19.7	20.4
1991	19.2	19.1	19.1	18.7	18.6	18.8	18.6	18.7	18.7	18.2	18.3	18.5	18.7
1992	19.0	19.1	19.2	18.9	18.9	19.0	19.2	19.1	18.8	19.0	19.0	19.1	19.0
1993	18.6	18.6	18.7	18.3	18.5	18.6	18.9	18.9	19.0	19.1	19.1	19.4	18.8
1994	19.0	19.1	19.2	19.4	19.6	20.0	19.7	19.9	19.7	19.8	20.0	20.2	19.6
1995	19.5	19.7	19.9	19.7	19.6	19.8	20.0	20.2	20.2	20.3	20.6	20.8	20.0
1996	20.4	20.6	20.8	20.6	21.0	21.2	21.2	21.4	21.3	21.4	21.5	21.9	21.1
1997	20.9	21.1	21.3	21.6	21.7	21.9	21.4	21.3	21.4	20.9	21.1	21.5	21.3
1998	22.2	22.4	22.7	23.0	23.4	24.0	24.4	24.3	23.7	24.5	24.9	25.2	23.7
1999	24.4	24.8	24.9	25.3	25.5	25.7	25.6	25.7	25.3	25.3	25.2	25.8	25.3
2000	25.0	25.2	25.3	24.1	24.4	24.7	24.1	24.1	24.2	24.7	24.9	25.0	24.6
2001	24.8	24.7	24.7	25.1	25.2	25.5	25.3	25.3	25.0	25.2	25.7	25.4	25.1
2002	24.8	24.9	25.0	24.6	24.6	24.8	25.2	25.2	25.3	26.1	26.2	26.1	25.2
2003	26.3	26.0	26.1	24.8	25.0	25.2	25.1	25.1	24.5	24.5	24.9	25.3	25.2
Professional and business services													
1990	20.4	20.8	21.1	22.2	22.5	23.1	22.7	23.2	23.3	23.5	23.5	23.2	22.5
1991	21.7	21.6	21.5	22.2	22.3	22.3	22.0	22.2	22.3	22.1	22.3	22.2	22.1
1992	21.4	21.6	21.8	22.3	22.4	23.0	22.9	22.9	22.7	22.6	22.7	22.7	22.4
1993	23.0	23.5	23.7	24.7	24.9	25.3	24.3	24.3	24.2	25.3	25.0	25.6	24.5
1994	25.1	25.3	25.7	26.9	27.2	27.9	28.7	28.9	29.1	28.8	28.9	29.6	27.7
1995	28.6	29.2	29.5	29.5	29.9	30.2	30.3	30.4	30.5	29.1	29.2	29.1	29.6
1996	29.8	30.2	31.1	32.0	32.5	33.1	33.7	33.5	33.6	32.8	33.2	33.5	32.4
1997	34.5	35.0	34.9	34.2	34.5	34.7	33.7	33.4	33.4	33.2	33.3	33.4	34.0
1998	34.4	35.0	35.7	36.4	36.7	36.9	36.4	36.3	36.3	36.0	36.1	36.4	36.1
1999	36.3	36.6	37.4	38.0	38.1	38.5	37.4	37.7	37.1	38.7	38.5	38.4	37.7
2000	37.5	37.6	38.2	38.3	38.6	39.3	38.2	37.8	38.3	38.1	37.7	37.8	38.1
2001	37.2	37.8	38.2	38.5	38.6	38.5	38.2	38.5	38.0	36.6	36.1	36.0	37.6
2002	35.3	35.2	36.0	35.6	35.2	35.8	36.7	37.2	36.9	37.2	36.7	36.6	36.2
2003	34.0	34.4	34.8	33.7	33.6	33.8	33.6	34.2	33.9	33.9	33.1	33.0	33.8
Educational and health services													
1990	16.7	16.8	16.9	17.2	17.1	16.8	16.5	16.6	17.1	17.9	17.9	18.0	17.1
1991	17.4	17.7	17.8	18.1	18.0	17.5	17.3	17.3	17.7	18.2	18.3	18.3	17.8
1992	18.0	18.4	18.6	18.4	18.5	18.0	18.0	18.0	18.4	19.0	19.0	19.1	18.5
1993	18.9	19.1	19.2	19.3	19.2	18.7	18.5	18.4	19.0	19.7	19.7	20.0	19.1
1994	19.5	19.7	19.9	20.2	20.2	19.8	19.8	19.8	20.3	20.9	20.9	20.5	20.1
1995	19.6	20.1	20.2	21.2	21.3	20.9	20.9	20.9	21.3	21.5	21.5	21.6	20.9
1996	21.4	21.6	21.9	21.7	21.7	21.4	21.3	21.4	21.8	21.9	22.0	22.0	21.7
1997	21.9	22.3	22.3	22.8	22.9	22.5	22.9	22.6	23.2	22.9	23.2	23.3	22.7
1998	23.4	23.8	24.1	25.3	26.0	26.1	26.6	27.2	27.5	27.9	28.3	28.3	26.2
1999	27.3	27.9	28.1	28.8	28.6	28.3	28.7	28.6	29.1	29.4	29.4	29.5	28.6
2000	29.1	29.3	29.5	28.3	28.3	28.5	27.9	27.8	28.2	28.5	28.7	28.9	28.6
2001	28.3	28.6	28.8	29.0	29.1	29.2	29.2	29.2	29.7	29.8	30.1	30.1	29.2
2002	29.8	30.1	30.2	31.3	31.3	31.2	32.1	32.1	32.3	32.0	32.2	32.3	31.4
2003	31.8	32.0	32.2	31.9	31.9	31.7	33.3	33.5	33.9	34.1	33.9	33.5	32.8

Employment by Industry: South Carolina—*Continued*

(Numbers in thousands. Not seasonally adjusted.)

Industry	January	February	March	April	May	June	July	August	September	October	November	December	Annual Average
COLUMBIA—*Continued*													
Leisure and hospitality													
1990	17.3	17.5	17.8	18.4	18.9	19.0	19.1	19.5	19.5	19.5	19.2	19.0	18.7
1991	18.1	18.4	18.6	19.1	19.5	19.6	19.2	19.5	19.4	19.3	19.0	19.0	19.1
1992	18.2	18.5	18.9	19.0	19.1	19.3	19.2	19.5	19.2	19.4	19.0	18.9	19.0
1993	18.3	18.8	19.3	19.7	20.3	20.5	20.2	20.2	20.5	20.6	20.3	20.6	19.9
1994	19.5	19.8	20.5	20.7	20.8	21.1	21.3	21.4	21.4	21.3	21.8	22.1	21.0
1995	20.7	21.1	21.5	22.0	22.5	22.7	22.6	23.0	23.2	23.6	23.0	23.0	22.4
1996	22.2	22.3	22.9	23.3	23.6	24.0	24.0	24.4	24.3	24.3	23.4	23.4	23.5
1997	23.4	23.8	24.0	24.6	25.1	25.2	24.2	24.3	24.3	25.2	24.7	24.9	24.5
1998	23.0	23.3	24.2	24.2	24.7	24.8	24.9	24.9	25.1	25.1	25.1	25.3	24.6
1999	23.8	24.4	24.7	25.8	26.3	26.5	25.9	25.8	25.3	26.1	26.1	26.2	25.6
2000	25.8	26.2	26.8	25.1	25.3	25.3	24.8	24.5	24.7	25.1	25.3	25.5	25.4
2001	25.1	25.7	26.1	25.9	26.3	26.3	26.4	26.7	26.3	27.0	26.6	26.4	26.2
2002	25.6	26.1	26.6	26.4	26.6	26.8	26.3	26.2	26.2	27.1	26.1	26.0	26.3
2003	25.4	25.8	26.2	25.8	26.3	26.1	26.3	26.3	26.6	26.4	26.9	26.8	26.2
Other services													
1990	8.6	8.7	8.7	8.8	8.8	9.0	8.8	8.8	8.8	8.7	8.6	8.6	8.7
1991	8.3	8.3	8.4	8.3	8.1	8.3	8.4	8.2	8.1	8.2	8.1	8.1	8.2
1992	8.0	8.0	8.1	8.0	8.1	8.2	8.2	8.3	8.2	8.2	8.1	8.1	8.1
1993	8.0	8.1	8.2	8.4	8.4	8.5	8.4	8.4	8.4	8.5	8.4	8.6	8.4
1994	8.1	8.2	8.2	8.2	8.3	8.4	8.3	8.4	8.4	8.5	8.6	8.6	8.4
1995	8.5	8.6	8.7	8.6	8.7	8.8	8.7	8.7	8.6	8.7	8.7	8.6	8.7
1996	8.5	8.5	8.6	8.5	8.6	8.7	8.8	8.8	8.7	8.7	8.7	8.8	8.7
1997	8.6	8.7	8.8	8.9	9.0	9.1	9.1	9.1	9.1	8.9	8.8	8.9	8.9
1998	8.8	8.9	9.0	9.3	9.4	9.6	9.6	9.5	9.4	9.4	9.3	9.3	9.3
1999	9.1	9.2	9.4	9.6	9.7	9.8	9.8	9.7	9.7	9.6	9.5	9.5	9.6
2000	9.5	9.5	9.7	9.1	9.2	9.2	9.0	8.9	8.8	9.1	9.1	8.9	9.2
2001	8.6	8.5	8.7	8.6	8.7	8.9	8.8	8.9	8.8	8.9	9.0	9.0	8.7
2002	8.9	9.0	9.2	9.1	9.2	9.4	9.5	9.7	9.7	9.6	9.5	9.5	9.4
2003	9.5	9.6	9.8	9.1	9.3	9.3	9.1	9.1	9.0	9.1	9.1	9.0	9.3
Government													
1990	66.1	67.7	68.5	69.0	69.0	66.1	61.1	60.5	68.5	69.4	69.1	70.5	67.1
1991	67.5	69.8	70.1	70.1	70.3	66.9	62.2	60.9	68.2	69.3	69.6	69.8	67.9
1992	68.4	69.7	70.3	70.2	70.4	69.6	66.6	66.2	68.5	69.4	69.6	69.8	69.1
1993	68.8	69.7	70.1	70.4	70.3	69.3	64.3	65.7	69.7	70.8	71.1	71.4	69.3
1994	69.7	70.9	71.3	72.3	72.6	71.5	67.6	66.9	70.1	70.5	73.4	71.5	70.7
1995	70.5	72.2	72.7	72.8	72.7	70.5	66.8	66.9	69.7	70.5	71.1	72.6	70.8
1996	71.5	72.4	73.2	72.6	72.7	72.2	67.2	67.4	72.0	72.7	74.5	73.2	71.8
1997	71.5	72.9	73.5	73.5	73.6	72.1	69.3	69.7	73.7	74.0	74.9	75.2	72.8
1998	74.5	75.3	75.6	75.9	76.0	75.8	72.0	72.4	75.6	76.1	76.7	76.8	75.2
1999	75.7	77.3	77.6	77.6	77.6	75.3	72.0	73.1	75.1	76.7	77.2	79.0	76.2
2000	77.1	77.9	78.5	78.1	78.8	76.2	74.1	75.1	73.7	76.0	75.8	75.4	76.4
2001	74.2	74.9	75.3	74.8	74.8	72.9	68.7	72.6	73.8	73.8	74.0	74.3	67.5
2002	73.6	73.9	74.3	74.8	75.0	72.7	68.3	72.6	74.3	74.8	75.2	75.4	73.7
2003	75.0	75.7	75.8	75.2	75.1	73.0	71.1	71.5	72.7	73.2	73.3	73.7	73.8
Federal government													
1990	7.8	7.8	7.9	8.2	8.5	8.5	8.3	8.0	7.9	7.9	7.8	7.9	8.0
1991	7.8	8.0	8.0	8.0	8.1	8.0	8.2	8.3	8.2	8.2	8.2	8.3	8.1
1992	8.3	8.3	8.3	8.3	8.3	8.4	8.4	8.4	8.3	8.3	8.2	8.2	8.3
1993	8.1	8.1	8.1	8.2	8.1	8.1	8.3	8.1	8.0	7.9	7.9	8.1	8.1
1994	7.9	7.9	7.9	7.9	7.9	8.0	7.9	8.0	8.0	7.8	7.9	8.1	7.9
1995	7.8	7.9	7.9	7.8	7.8	7.9	7.9	7.9	7.9	7.9	7.9	8.2	7.9
1996	7.9	7.9	7.9	8.0	8.0	8.1	8.2	8.2	8.2	8.2	8.3	8.4	8.1
1997	8.4	8.4	8.3	8.4	8.3	8.3	8.0	8.0	8.1	8.0	8.1	8.2	8.2
1998	8.0	8.0	8.0	8.2	8.2	8.2	8.2	8.2	8.3	8.3	8.4	8.5	8.2
1999	8.4	8.4	8.4	8.3	8.2	8.2	8.4	8.3	8.3	8.2	8.4	8.5	8.3
2000	8.1	8.2	8.2	8.5	9.3	9.0	8.5	8.7	8.2	8.2	8.3	8.4	8.5
2001	8.1	8.2	8.3	8.4	8.4	8.4	8.4	8.5	8.4	8.4	8.5	8.6	8.3
2002	8.4	8.3	8.4	8.3	8.4	8.5	8.4	8.5	8.5	8.6	8.6	8.8	8.5
2003	8.4	8.5	8.4	8.4	8.4	8.4	8.4	8.3	8.3	8.3	8.3	8.4	8.4
State government													
1990	37.5	38.8	39.3	39.5	39.5	38.0	35.6	34.2	39.9	40.3	39.9	40.7	38.6
1991	38.5	40.0	40.2	40.1	40.2	39.6	36.3	35.8	39.1	39.0	39.0	38.8	38.9
1992	38.1	39.3	39.7	39.6	39.7	39.1	37.9	37.4	38.7	38.8	38.7	38.8	38.8
1993	38.0	38.8	39.1	39.1	39.0	38.4	37.6	37.7	38.3	38.3	38.3	38.4	38.4
1994	37.3	38.2	38.6	39.6	39.6	38.7	38.3	38.2	38.9	38.6	40.2	39.3	38.8
1995	37.5	38.8	39.3	39.5	39.4	38.6	37.6	37.5	38.5	38.6	38.5	38.6	38.5
1996	38.1	38.8	39.5	38.5	38.4	39.0	37.1	36.9	37.5	37.9	39.3	37.8	38.2
1997	37.1	38.2	38.7	38.6	38.5	38.3	38.0	38.3	39.0	38.8	38.9	39.1	38.5
1998	38.5	39.1	39.3	39.3	39.4	40.2	38.4	38.7	38.9	38.9	38.9	38.9	39.0
1999	38.3	39.6	39.8	39.8	39.8	39.1	37.8	37.9	38.2	38.5	38.6	40.2	39.0
2000	39.0	39.5	39.8	39.8	39.9	39.0	39.1	39.1	39.7	39.9	40.0	40.0	39.6
2001	39.4	39.6	39.8	39.6	39.3	38.4	38.4	37.9	38.0	37.8	37.7	37.7	32.5
2002	37.3	37.5	37.5	38.3	38.1	37.3	37.4	37.3	37.8	37.9	38.1	38.1	37.7
2003	37.9	38.3	38.4	38.1	37.9	37.1	36.7	36.4	36.2	36.1	36.1	36.3	37.1

Employment by Industry: South Carolina—*Continued*

(Numbers in thousands. Not seasonally adjusted.)

Industry	January	February	March	April	May	June	July	August	September	October	November	December	Annual Average
COLUMBIA—*Continued*													
Local government													
1990	20.8	21.1	21.3	21.3	21.0	19.6	17.2	18.3	20.7	21.2	21.4	21.9	20.5
1991	21.2	21.8	21.9	22.0	22.0	19.3	17.7	16.8	20.9	22.1	22.4	22.7	20.9
1992	22.0	22.1	22.3	22.3	22.4	22.1	20.3	20.4	21.5	22.3	22.7	22.8	21.9
1993	22.7	22.8	22.9	23.1	23.2	22.8	18.4	19.9	23.4	24.6	24.9	24.9	22.8
1994	24.5	24.8	24.8	24.8	25.1	24.8	21.4	20.7	23.2	24.1	25.3	24.1	24.0
1995	25.2	25.5	25.5	25.5	25.5	24.0	21.3	21.5	23.3	24.0	24.7	25.8	24.3
1996	25.5	25.7	25.8	26.1	26.3	25.1	21.9	22.3	26.3	26.6	26.9	27.0	25.5
1997	26.0	26.3	26.5	26.5	26.8	25.5	23.3	23.4	26.6	27.2	27.9	27.9	26.2
1998	28.0	28.2	28.3	28.4	28.4	27.4	25.4	25.5	28.4	28.9	29.4	29.4	28.0
1999	29.0	29.3	29.4	29.5	29.6	28.0	25.8	26.9	28.6	30.0	30.2	30.3	28.9
2000	30.0	30.2	30.5	29.8	29.6	28.2	26.5	27.3	25.8	27.9	27.5	27.0	28.4
2001	26.7	27.1	27.2	26.8	27.1	26.1	21.9	26.2	27.4	27.6	27.8	28.0	26.6
2002	27.9	28.1	28.4	28.2	28.5	26.9	22.5	26.8	28.0	28.3	28.5	28.5	27.6
2003	28.7	28.9	29.0	28.7	28.8	27.5	26.0	26.8	28.2	28.8	28.9	29.0	28.3
GREENVILLE-SPARTANBURG													
Total nonfarm													
1990	402.7	405.3	407.5	408.0	412.1	409.2	396.8	402.4	410.8	410.1	410.4	410.5	407.2
1991	398.5	399.7	400.2	399.4	402.1	400.6	388.7	391.3	400.3	399.9	404.6	405.2	399.2
1992	397.5	398.5	401.3	402.6	404.8	406.8	394.1	397.8	407.7	407.7	411.1	411.3	403.4
1993	406.9	409.1	412.4	417.4	419.5	422.3	415.5	414.7	420.7	429.3	432.1	436.1	419.7
1994	423.4	425.3	429.6	433.1	435.3	438.6	431.9	432.3	439.2	438.2	443.3	443.0	434.4
1995	436.9	439.5	443.4	444.4	447.3	450.4	440.1	441.5	451.6	452.5	454.9	455.6	446.5
1996	443.8	447.9	452.1	453.1	456.7	461.1	451.0	452.1	457.4	460.5	464.1	465.7	455.5
1997	457.0	460.2	463.9	465.8	467.8	470.6	461.9	463.9	468.0	468.3	470.8	475.1	466.1
1998	470.0	471.3	475.4	476.2	478.9	484.4	478.6	479.8	487.9	488.0	491.0	494.5	481.3
1999	478.8	480.5	486.4	491.4	493.0	494.1	483.3	485.0	491.1	493.5	496.6	499.1	489.4
2000	488.4	491.1	496.2	500.7	505.0	507.4	494.8	501.9	502.9	504.5	507.2	508.2	500.7
2001	494.5	496.2	499.4	499.1	498.6	497.7	482.6	489.5	487.4	484.2	486.0	484.5	491.6
2002	466.7	468.2	472.3	470.7	472.8	473.7	467.9	477.4	478.6	481.2	483.0	484.3	474.7
2003	472.8	475.4	479.7	474.8	473.2	473.2	463.8	469.4	474.8	476.1	476.0	477.7	473.9
Total private													
1990	352.1	353.7	355.7	355.5	358.8	358.8	353.8	356.6	358.8	357.0	357.0	357.1	356.2
1991	345.0	345.1	345.5	344.8	347.7	347.4	344.0	345.9	346.8	345.5	350.0	350.3	346.5
1992	343.9	344.1	346.6	347.5	350.3	352.3	348.1	350.8	353.4	352.4	354.1	356.0	350.0
1993	352.4	354.0	357.1	362.1	364.9	368.0	367.5	369.7	371.4	374.2	376.7	380.6	366.6
1994	369.4	370.7	374.4	378.3	380.2	383.9	382.2	385.1	387.0	382.6	385.4	387.2	380.5
1995	382.8	384.7	388.3	389.3	392.1	395.3	393.2	395.7	397.2	397.1	399.3	399.9	392.9
1996	389.1	392.4	396.2	397.3	401.3	404.5	403.1	404.1	405.6	404.2	405.8	408.6	401.0
1997	401.0	403.3	406.7	408.7	411.0	413.5	410.4	412.0	412.4	410.1	412.5	416.6	409.9
1998	411.7	412.3	415.9	416.9	419.8	422.8	424.9	426.1	428.3	427.3	429.9	433.3	422.4
1999	418.0	419.3	424.9	430.1	431.6	433.4	428.8	428.9	429.6	431.7	434.5	436.7	429.0
2000	427.0	429.0	433.5	437.5	440.8	444.1	439.6	440.5	440.2	440.9	442.9	444.2	438.4
2001	432.7	433.5	436.5	436.2	435.9	435.6	428.1	428.7	424.8	420.8	422.0	420.4	429.6
2002	403.8	404.4	408.3	406.5	408.8	411.1	412.4	415.5	414.6	416.5	417.3	419.0	411.5
2003	408.5	410.3	414.3	409.2	408.0	409.5	406.9	406.8	409.1	409.7	409.4	411.1	409.4
Goods-producing													
1990	145.7	145.7	145.6	145.1	145.7	145.7	144.1	145.3	145.1	144.0	143.3	142.7	144.8
1991	140.3	139.9	139.3	138.2	138.8	138.9	138.2	138.2	138.3	137.5	139.1	138.9	138.8
1992	138.4	138.0	138.3	138.1	138.6	139.0	138.4	139.4	140.2	138.9	139.3	139.4	138.8
1993	140.1	139.5	140.1	141.0	141.7	142.8	142.9	143.1	143.5	145.0	145.3	146.3	142.6
1994	144.8	144.7	145.3	145.2	145.5	146.8	146.9	147.6	147.5	146.8	147.3	147.4	146.3
1995	147.5	147.8	148.7	148.5	149.0	149.5	148.6	149.3	149.0	148.0	148.1	148.5	148.5
1996	145.5	146.7	147.4	145.7	147.4	147.9	147.5	148.2	147.7	147.1	146.2	146.8	147.0
1997	145.5	146.3	147.1	147.5	148.1	149.0	148.2	148.0	147.1	146.4	146.7	147.5	147.3
1998	146.2	146.4	146.6	148.1	149.0	150.5	150.6	150.7	150.4	150.0	149.6	150.5	149.1
1999	148.1	147.9	148.7	149.7	149.5	150.4	148.3	147.2	147.4	148.2	148.1	148.6	148.5
2000	147.5	148.2	149.0	150.4	151.5	152.8	151.6	152.3	152.1	151.8	151.6	151.7	150.9
2001	148.7	148.3	148.3	148.1	147.5	147.3	143.8	142.9	140.0	138.0	137.0	135.7	143.8
2002	131.8	131.1	131.1	129.9	130.1	131.1	132.5	132.9	131.9	132.1	131.3	131.3	131.4
2003	129.1	129.2	128.9	126.6	125.5	125.3	124.6	122.6	122.5	123.2	123.1	122.6	125.3
Construction and mining													
1990	21.2	21.4	21.6	21.4	21.6	22.1	21.5	21.9	21.5	21.6	21.7	21.5	21.6
1991	20.4	20.5	20.6	20.9	21.3	21.4	21.0	20.9	20.5	20.2	20.4	20.1	20.7
1992	19.6	19.6	19.5	19.5	19.7	19.9	20.3	20.5	20.5	20.5	20.4	20.3	20.0
1993	20.2	20.3	20.6	21.3	21.7	22.2	22.6	22.8	22.6	22.8	23.0	23.3	22.0
1994	23.0	23.4	24.0	24.1	24.4	24.9	25.2	25.2	25.1	24.9	24.9	25.1	24.5
1995	24.7	24.7	25.2	25.1	25.5	26.1	25.8	26.0	26.0	25.6	25.7	25.9	25.5
1996	25.0	25.6	26.2	26.2	26.9	27.6	27.4	27.8	27.7	27.4	27.3	27.3	26.9
1997	27.0	27.4	27.9	28.9	29.6	29.9	30.2	29.9	29.4	29.4	29.3	29.4	29.0
1998	29.0	29.1	29.3	29.7	30.5	31.4	31.9	31.9	32.0	31.9	31.7	31.9	30.9
1999	31.4	31.7	32.2	32.8	33.0	33.7	33.0	32.6	32.7	32.4	32.7	32.5	32.6
2000	31.9	32.0	32.6	32.7	33.1	33.8	32.6	32.9	32.6	33.2	33.2	33.1	32.8
2001	31.8	31.7	32.2	33.1	33.3	33.0	31.9	31.6	30.8	30.9	30.7	30.2	31.7
2002	28.9	29.4	29.6	29.2	29.5	29.9	30.7	30.8	30.6	30.7	30.6	30.4	30.0
2003	30.0	29.7	29.5	28.9	29.3	29.6	29.2	27.9	27.3	27.4	27.5	27.5	28.7

Employment by Industry: South Carolina—*Continued*

(Numbers in thousands. Not seasonally adjusted.)

Industry	January	February	March	April	May	June	July	August	September	October	November	December	Annual Average
GREENVILLE-SPARTANBURG—*Continued*													
Manufacturing													
1990	124.5	124.3	124.0	123.7	124.1	123.6	122.6	123.4	123.6	122.4	121.6	121.2	123.3
1991	119.9	119.4	118.7	117.3	117.5	117.5	117.2	117.3	117.8	117.3	118.7	118.8	118.1
1992	118.8	118.4	118.8	118.6	118.9	119.1	118.1	118.9	119.7	118.4	118.9	119.1	118.8
1993	119.9	119.2	119.5	119.7	120.0	120.6	120.3	120.3	120.9	122.2	122.3	123.0	120.7
1994	121.8	121.3	121.3	121.1	121.1	121.9	121.7	122.4	122.4	121.9	122.4	122.3	121.8
1995	122.8	123.1	123.5	123.4	123.5	123.4	122.8	123.3	123.0	122.4	122.4	122.6	123.0
1996	120.5	121.1	121.2	119.5	120.5	120.3	120.1	120.4	120.0	119.7	118.9	119.5	120.1
1997	118.5	118.9	119.2	118.6	118.5	119.1	118.0	118.1	117.7	117.0	117.4	118.1	118.3
1998	117.2	117.3	117.3	118.4	118.5	119.1	118.7	118.8	118.4	118.1	117.9	118.6	118.2
1999	116.7	116.2	116.5	116.9	116.5	116.7	115.3	114.6	114.7	115.8	115.4	116.1	116.0
2000	115.6	116.2	116.4	117.7	118.4	119.0	119.0	119.4	119.5	118.6	118.4	118.6	118.1
2001	116.9	116.6	116.1	115.0	114.2	114.3	111.9	111.3	109.2	107.1	106.3	105.5	112.0
2002	102.9	101.7	101.5	100.7	100.6	101.2	101.8	102.1	101.3	101.4	100.7	100.9	101.4
2003	99.1	99.5	99.4	97.7	96.2	95.7	95.4	94.7	95.2	95.8	95.6	95.1	96.6
Service-providing													
1990	257.0	259.6	261.9	262.9	266.4	263.5	252.7	257.1	265.7	266.1	267.1	267.8	262.3
1991	258.2	259.8	260.9	261.2	263.3	261.7	250.5	253.1	262.0	262.4	265.5	266.3	260.4
1992	259.1	260.5	263.0	264.5	266.2	267.8	255.7	258.4	267.5	268.8	271.8	271.9	264.6
1993	266.8	269.6	272.3	276.4	277.8	279.5	272.6	271.6	277.2	284.3	286.8	289.8	277.1
1994	278.6	280.6	284.3	287.9	289.8	291.8	285.0	284.7	291.7	291.4	296.0	295.6	288.1
1995	289.4	291.7	294.7	295.9	298.3	300.9	291.5	292.2	302.6	304.5	306.8	307.1	298.0
1996	298.3	301.2	304.7	307.4	309.3	313.2	303.5	303.9	309.7	313.4	317.9	318.9	308.5
1997	311.5	313.9	316.8	318.3	319.7	321.6	313.7	315.9	320.9	321.9	324.1	327.6	318.8
1998	323.8	324.9	328.8	328.1	329.9	333.9	328.0	329.1	337.5	338.0	341.4	344.0	332.3
1999	330.7	332.6	337.7	341.7	343.5	343.7	335.0	337.8	343.7	345.3	348.5	350.5	340.9
2000	340.9	342.9	347.2	350.3	353.5	354.6	343.2	349.6	350.8	352.7	355.6	356.5	349.8
2001	345.8	347.9	351.1	351.0	351.1	350.4	338.8	346.6	347.4	346.2	349.0	348.8	347.8
2002	334.9	337.1	341.2	340.8	342.7	342.6	335.4	344.5	346.7	349.1	351.7	353.0	343.3
2003	343.7	346.2	350.8	348.2	347.7	347.9	339.2	346.8	352.3	352.9	352.9	355.1	348.6
Trade, transportation, and utilities													
1990	81.7	81.8	82.2	82.6	83.4	83.5	83.2	84.1	84.4	84.7	85.5	86.5	83.6
1991	80.2	79.7	79.9	79.7	80.4	80.1	79.8	80.1	80.1	80.2	81.6	82.7	80.4
1992	79.5	78.6	79.1	79.6	80.2	80.4	79.7	80.2	80.2	81.0	81.7	83.1	80.3
1993	80.6	80.6	81.2	82.0	82.4	83.0	83.8	84.5	84.8	86.0	87.5	89.7	83.8
1994	86.2	86.0	86.7	88.4	89.2	89.8	89.6	90.4	90.7	90.6	92.2	93.6	89.5
1995	91.4	91.3	92.1	92.4	93.3	94.1	94.7	95.2	95.4	96.5	98.3	99.8	94.5
1996	96.4	96.3	96.9	96.9	97.9	98.2	98.3	98.4	98.2	99.2	100.8	102.0	98.3
1997	99.4	99.2	99.9	100.7	101.9	102.6	102.2	102.8	102.9	102.8	104.6	106.8	102.2
1998	102.7	102.2	102.8	102.9	103.2	103.8	104.6	105.2	106.8	106.4	108.5	110.3	105.0
1999	103.2	103.2	104.2	104.7	105.2	105.7	106.0	106.1	106.5	107.4	108.8	110.6	106.0
2000	107.2	106.8	108.0	108.5	109.2	109.9	108.9	109.2	109.2	109.8	112.0	112.8	109.3
2001	108.3	106.9	107.8	107.1	107.2	107.3	106.1	106.1	105.2	105.2	107.0	107.0	106.7
2002	101.8	101.1	102.0	101.9	101.9	102.5	101.1	101.6	100.7	100.8	102.6	103.8	101.8
2003	99.5	99.3	99.7	101.0	100.9	102.1	101.3	102.9	103.0	103.3	105.1	107.0	102.1
Wholesale trade													
1990	16.7	16.9	17.0	17.0	17.1	17.2	17.0	17.2	17.4	17.4	17.2	17.3	17.1
1991	16.4	16.5	16.6	16.5	16.7	16.6	16.6	16.6	16.5	16.6	16.6	16.8	16.6
1992	16.4	16.3	16.4	16.4	16.6	16.7	16.6	16.8	16.5	16.6	16.4	16.5	16.5
1993	16.6	16.6	16.8	17.1	17.2	17.5	17.5	17.7	17.7	18.1	18.1	18.5	17.5
1994	18.2	18.2	18.3	18.4	18.5	18.7	18.8	18.9	19.0	19.2	19.4	19.5	18.8
1995	19.2	19.5	19.7	19.6	19.7	19.9	19.9	20.0	20.0	20.1	20.0	20.2	19.8
1996	20.3	20.5	20.5	20.4	20.5	20.6	20.7	20.9	20.8	20.8	20.9	21.0	20.7
1997	21.2	21.4	21.6	21.4	21.8	21.8	21.8	22.2	22.2	22.3	22.5	22.6	21.9
1998	22.7	22.8	22.8	23.1	23.3	23.4	23.7	23.9	24.0	23.8	24.0	24.1	23.5
1999	23.3	23.6	23.7	23.6	23.6	23.7	23.7	23.7	23.8	23.9	23.9	24.3	23.7
2000	24.0	23.9	24.5	24.6	24.8	24.9	24.7	24.6	24.7	24.7	24.7	24.9	24.6
2001	24.7	24.7	24.7	24.7	24.5	24.8	24.4	24.3	23.9	23.7	23.8	23.3	24.2
2002	23.0	23.2	23.2	23.5	23.4	23.8	23.3	23.3	22.9	23.1	23.1	23.2	23.3
2003	22.6	22.8	23.0	22.6	22.7	22.8	22.7	22.6	22.9	23.0	23.3	23.7	22.9
Retail trade													
1990	52.1	51.8	52.0	52.3	52.9	52.9	53.0	53.6	53.7	54.3	55.3	56.2	53.3
1991	51.0	50.5	50.5	50.3	50.8	50.6	50.1	50.3	50.4	50.3	51.6	52.6	50.8
1992	50.1	49.4	49.9	50.3	50.7	50.8	50.0	50.3	50.5	51.0	51.9	53.3	50.7
1993	50.9	50.9	51.2	51.4	51.5	51.6	52.2	52.5	52.7	53.2	54.5	56.0	52.4
1994	53.3	52.8	53.2	54.9	55.3	55.8	55.3	55.8	56.0	55.9	57.2	58.6	55.3
1995	56.8	56.1	56.6	57.1	57.7	58.1	58.6	58.9	59.1	60.0	61.9	63.3	58.7
1996	60.3	59.9	60.3	60.8	61.7	61.9	62.0	62.4	62.4	63.0	64.6	65.8	62.1
1997	62.9	62.4	62.7	63.7	64.2	64.8	64.6	65.1	65.1	64.8	66.4	68.6	64.6
1998	65.2	64.8	65.3	64.4	64.5	64.9	65.1	65.5	67.1	66.7	68.6	70.3	66.0
1999	65.1	64.8	65.4	65.1	65.4	65.6	65.4	65.4	65.9	66.3	67.7	69.0	65.9
2000	65.6	65.1	65.6	65.8	66.1	66.7	66.1	66.5	66.4	66.6	68.8	69.4	66.6
2001	65.3	64.0	64.5	64.0	64.2	64.0	63.1	63.2	62.8	62.9	64.8	65.4	64.0
2002	60.8	59.9	60.7	60.0	60.0	60.2	59.7	60.1	59.6	59.1	60.8	61.9	60.2
2003	58.4	57.9	58.2	59.1	59.0	59.8	59.4	60.7	60.7	60.8	62.2	62.9	59.9

Employment by Industry: South Carolina—*Continued*

(Numbers in thousands. Not seasonally adjusted.)

Industry	January	February	March	April	May	June	July	August	September	October	November	December	Annual Average
GREENVILLE-SPARTANBURG—*Continued*													
Transportation and utilities													
1990	12.9	13.1	13.2	13.3	13.4	13.4	13.2	13.3	13.3	13.0	13.0	13.0	13.2
1991	12.8	12.7	12.8	12.9	12.9	12.9	13.1	13.2	13.2	13.3	13.4	13.3	13.0
1992	13.0	12.9	12.8	12.9	12.9	12.9	13.1	13.1	13.2	13.4	13.4	13.3	13.1
1993	13.1	13.1	13.2	13.5	13.7	13.9	14.1	14.3	14.4	14.7	14.9	15.2	14.0
1994	14.7	15.0	15.2	15.1	15.4	15.3	15.5	15.7	15.7	15.5	15.6	15.5	15.4
1995	15.4	15.7	15.8	15.7	15.9	16.1	16.2	16.3	16.3	16.4	16.4	16.3	16.0
1996	15.8	15.9	16.1	15.7	15.7	15.7	15.6	15.1	15.0	15.4	15.3	15.2	15.5
1997	15.3	15.4	15.6	15.6	15.9	16.0	15.8	15.5	15.6	15.7	15.7	15.6	15.6
1998	14.8	14.6	14.7	15.4	15.4	15.5	15.8	15.8	15.7	15.9	15.9	15.9	15.5
1999	14.8	14.8	15.1	16.0	16.2	16.4	16.9	17.0	16.8	17.2	17.2	17.3	16.3
2000	17.6	17.8	17.9	18.1	18.3	18.3	18.1	18.1	18.1	18.5	18.5	18.5	18.2
2001	18.3	18.2	18.6	18.4	18.5	18.5	18.6	18.6	18.5	18.6	18.4	18.3	18.4
2002	18.0	18.0	18.1	18.4	18.5	18.5	18.1	18.2	18.2	18.6	18.7	18.7	18.3
2003	18.5	18.6	18.5	19.3	19.2	19.5	19.2	19.6	19.4	19.5	19.6	20.4	19.3
Information													
1990	5.5	5.5	5.6	5.7	5.8	5.8	5.9	5.8	5.8	5.6	5.7	5.6	5.7
1991	5.5	5.6	5.7	5.6	5.6	5.7	5.6	5.6	5.5	5.4	5.5	5.5	5.6
1992	5.3	5.3	5.3	5.2	5.2	5.3	5.5	5.5	5.5	5.5	5.5	5.5	5.4
1993	5.4	5.4	5.4	5.4	5.4	5.4	5.4	5.4	5.4	5.5	5.5	5.5	5.4
1994	5.4	5.2	5.3	5.2	5.2	5.4	5.4	5.4	5.5	5.4	5.4	5.5	5.4
1995	5.3	5.3	5.4	5.5	5.7	5.8	5.7	5.8	5.9	5.8	5.9	6.0	5.7
1996	5.9	5.8	5.8	5.8	5.7	6.5	6.5	6.5	6.5	6.6	6.6	6.7	6.2
1997	6.7	6.8	6.7	6.7	6.7	6.8	7.1	7.1	6.9	7.3	7.3	7.4	7.0
1998	7.2	7.3	7.8	8.2	8.3	8.2	7.9	8.2	8.2	8.3	8.4	8.5	8.0
1999	8.1	8.2	8.4	8.7	8.9	9.0	9.0	9.0	8.9	9.2	9.2	9.3	8.8
2000	9.4	9.5	9.6	9.4	9.7	9.9	9.7	9.8	9.8	9.8	9.9	10.1	9.7
2001	9.7	10.0	9.9	9.5	9.4	9.4	9.2	9.4	9.3	9.0	9.1	8.9	9.3
2002	8.7	8.7	8.7	8.2	8.3	8.3	8.5	8.6	8.5	8.7	8.8	8.8	8.6
2003	8.7	8.8	8.8	8.3	8.2	8.2	8.2	8.3	7.9	8.0	8.1	8.3	8.3
Financial activities													
1990	16.5	16.4	16.4	16.4	16.5	16.5	16.5	16.5	16.6	16.7	16.6	16.7	16.5
1991	16.6	16.4	16.2	15.9	16.2	16.1	15.9	16.0	15.9	15.7	15.8	15.9	16.1
1992	15.9	15.9	15.9	15.8	15.9	16.0	16.0	16.1	16.0	15.9	16.0	16.0	16.0
1993	15.8	15.9	15.9	16.2	16.3	16.5	16.6	16.5	16.5	16.6	16.6	16.7	16.3
1994	16.2	16.5	16.5	16.6	16.6	16.7	16.7	16.6	16.6	16.4	16.3	16.4	16.5
1995	16.3	16.1	16.2	16.1	16.2	16.5	16.5	16.7	16.8	16.8	16.8	17.0	16.5
1996	16.7	16.7	16.8	16.8	17.1	17.2	17.3	17.3	17.3	17.4	17.3	17.6	17.1
1997	17.4	17.3	17.6	17.7	17.8	17.9	17.9	17.9	17.8	17.5	17.7	18.1	17.7
1998	18.6	18.6	18.7	18.5	18.7	18.7	19.2	19.4	19.5	19.7	19.8	20.1	19.1
1999	19.3	19.1	19.3	19.5	19.5	19.6	19.7	19.7	19.4	19.4	19.4	19.5	19.5
2000	19.1	19.2	19.3	19.9	20.0	20.0	20.2	19.8	19.6	19.8	19.9	19.9	19.7
2001	19.2	19.5	19.8	19.5	19.3	19.4	19.3	19.1	19.0	18.8	18.9	19.0	19.2
2002	18.9	18.9	19.0	18.9	19.0	19.1	19.5	19.7	19.7	19.5	19.5	19.7	19.3
2003	19.5	19.7	19.8	19.2	19.3	19.5	19.6	19.8	19.3	19.2	18.9	19.1	19.4
Professional and business services													
1990	37.2	38.1	38.6	38.9	39.7	39.7	37.5	37.6	38.5	38.3	38.2	37.9	38.4
1991	36.3	36.7	36.8	36.7	37.0	37.0	36.3	37.1	37.2	37.7	38.2	37.5	37.0
1992	37.7	38.4	39.0	39.0	39.5	40.9	38.8	39.7	40.7	40.4	40.7	41.2	39.7
1993	41.5	42.4	43.6	45.5	46.4	47.4	46.4	47.7	47.8	47.7	48.6	48.7	46.1
1994	45.0	46.0	46.9	48.4	49.0	49.7	49.0	49.7	50.8	48.8	49.5	49.3	48.5
1995	49.5	50.4	51.3	51.2	51.6	52.8	51.9	53.1	53.4	53.3	53.4	51.9	52.0
1996	50.1	51.2	52.1	54.3	54.7	55.9	55.9	56.6	57.6	56.2	56.8	57.3	54.9
1997	56.0	56.7	57.6	56.0	55.8	55.8	54.7	55.1	56.2	54.7	55.0	55.4	55.8
1998	55.7	55.5	56.3	55.1	55.3	56.0	56.7	57.2	56.8	58.0	58.5	58.5	56.6
1999	57.1	57.6	59.1	59.6	60.0	59.9	59.0	59.4	59.3	60.6	62.3	62.0	59.7
2000	57.9	58.3	59.4	60.1	60.6	61.3	60.4	60.6	60.7	60.6	60.6	60.5	60.1
2001	59.2	59.8	60.2	60.3	59.7	59.6	57.5	58.6	58.5	58.4	57.9	57.6	58.9
2002	53.5	54.5	55.6	55.0	55.6	56.0	56.8	57.9	58.3	60.6	60.3	60.5	57.1
2003	57.7	58.3	60.7	59.3	58.2	58.4	58.3	57.2	58.7	58.3	57.2	56.9	58.3
Educational and health services													
1990	24.9	25.2	25.2	25.1	25.1	24.5	24.3	24.6	25.8	25.8	25.7	25.9	25.2
1991	26.0	26.4	26.5	26.7	26.8	26.4	26.0	26.2	27.2	27.8	28.1	28.1	26.9
1992	27.2	27.4	27.6	27.6	27.8	27.1	26.6	26.7	27.9	28.2	28.4	28.4	27.6
1993	27.6	28.0	28.2	28.0	27.8	27.5	27.1	26.8	28.2	28.7	28.9	29.0	28.0
1994	28.3	28.5	28.7	28.7	28.6	28.4	27.6	27.8	28.6	28.5	28.5	28.5	28.4
1995	28.4	29.1	29.1	28.8	28.5	28.1	27.4	27.6	28.7	29.0	29.3	29.1	28.6
1996	28.3	28.9	29.2	29.2	29.0	28.5	27.4	27.3	28.5	28.7	28.8	28.8	28.6
1997	28.3	28.8	28.6	29.5	29.5	29.4	28.6	28.8	29.5	29.9	30.0	30.2	29.3
1998	30.7	31.1	31.1	31.7	31.8	31.1	31.3	31.1	32.1	31.0	31.4	31.5	31.3
1999	30.6	31.0	31.5	32.4	32.4	32.0	31.7	31.7	32.4	32.1	32.2	32.1	31.8
2000	32.6	32.9	33.2	33.7	33.8	33.8	33.3	33.5	33.7	33.8	33.9	34.0	33.5
2001	34.6	35.0	35.2	35.2	35.6	35.9	35.9	36.0	36.5	36.1	36.5	36.4	35.7
2002	36.1	36.6	37.3	37.6	37.9	37.5	37.4	38.3	39.1	39.1	39.3	39.2	38.0
2003	39.0	39.4	39.8	39.0	39.3	39.0	38.5	39.1	39.9	40.5	40.6	40.5	39.6

Employment by Industry: South Carolina—*Continued*

(Numbers in thousands. Not seasonally adjusted.)

Industry	January	February	March	April	May	June	July	August	September	October	November	December	Annual Average
GREENVILLE-SPARTANBURG—*Continued*													
Leisure and hospitality													
1990	28.5	28.8	29.7	29.4	30.1	30.6	29.9	30.3	30.3	29.5	29.8	29.7	29.7
1991	28.6	28.9	29.5	30.3	31.0	31.2	30.5	30.9	30.7	29.7	30.1	30.0	30.1
1992	28.4	29.0	29.8	30.6	31.3	31.6	31.1	31.2	31.0	30.8	30.8	30.5	30.5
1993	29.7	30.3	30.8	32.1	32.9	33.2	33.1	33.5	33.0	32.6	32.2	32.6	32.2
1994	31.7	32.0	32.9	33.9	34.1	34.9	34.7	35.3	35.1	34.0	34.1	34.3	33.9
1995	32.4	32.7	33.3	34.7	35.7	36.3	36.2	35.9	35.9	35.6	35.6	35.5	35.0
1996	34.4	34.9	36.1	36.7	37.4	38.1	38.1	38.0	38.1	37.4	37.7	37.8	37.1
1997	36.2	36.7	37.5	38.7	39.4	40.1	39.8	40.3	40.1	39.6	39.4	39.4	38.9
1998	38.5	39.0	40.4	40.1	41.1	42.0	42.1	41.8	41.9	41.4	41.2	41.5	40.9
1999	40.1	40.7	41.9	43.6	44.1	45.0	43.6	44.2	44.2	43.2	42.9	43.2	43.1
2000	41.8	42.5	43.1	43.5	43.9	44.5	44.0	43.8	43.5	43.4	43.4	43.6	43.4
2001	41.6	42.3	43.3	44.4	45.1	45.1	44.6	45.0	44.6	43.7	43.8	44.0	43.9
2002	41.4	41.6	42.4	42.9	43.8	44.4	44.8	44.7	44.3	44.0	43.8	44.0	43.5
2003	43.3	43.7	44.5	43.7	44.4	44.9	44.3	44.9	45.8	45.1	44.3	44.6	44.5
Other services													
1990	12.1	12.2	12.4	12.3	12.5	12.5	12.4	12.4	12.3	12.4	12.2	12.1	12.3
1991	11.5	11.5	11.6	11.7	11.9	12.0	11.7	11.8	11.9	11.5	11.6	11.7	11.7
1992	11.5	11.5	11.6	11.6	11.8	12.0	12.0	12.0	11.9	11.7	11.7	11.9	11.8
1993	11.7	11.9	11.9	11.9	12.0	12.2	12.2	12.2	12.2	12.1	12.1	12.1	12.0
1994	11.8	11.8	12.1	11.9	12.0	12.2	12.3	12.3	12.2	12.1	12.1	12.2	12.1
1995	12.0	12.0	12.2	12.1	12.1	12.2	12.2	12.1	12.1	12.1	11.9	12.1	12.1
1996	11.8	11.9	11.9	11.9	12.1	12.2	12.1	11.8	11.7	11.6	11.6	11.6	11.9
1997	11.5	11.5	11.7	11.9	11.8	11.9	11.9	12.0	11.9	11.9	11.8	11.8	11.8
1998	12.1	12.2	12.2	12.3	12.4	12.5	12.5	12.5	12.6	12.5	12.5	12.4	12.4
1999	11.5	11.6	11.8	11.9	12.0	11.8	11.5	11.6	11.5	11.6	11.6	11.4	11.7
2000	11.5	11.6	11.9	12.0	12.1	11.9	11.5	11.5	11.6	11.9	11.6	11.6	11.7
2001	11.4	11.7	12.0	12.1	12.1	11.6	11.7	11.6	11.7	11.6	11.8	11.8	11.7
2002	11.6	11.9	12.2	12.1	12.2	12.2	11.8	11.8	12.1	11.7	11.7	11.7	11.9
2003	11.7	11.9	12.1	12.1	12.2	12.1	12.1	12.0	12.0	12.1	12.1	12.1	12.0
Government													
1990	50.6	51.6	51.8	52.5	53.3	50.4	43.0	45.8	52.0	53.1	53.4	53.4	50.9
1991	53.5	54.6	54.7	54.6	54.4	53.2	44.7	45.4	53.5	54.4	54.6	54.9	52.7
1992	53.6	54.4	54.7	55.1	54.5	54.5	46.0	47.0	54.3	55.3	57.0	55.3	53.5
1993	54.5	55.1	55.3	55.3	54.6	54.3	48.0	45.0	49.3	55.1	55.4	55.5	53.1
1994	54.0	54.6	55.2	54.8	55.1	54.7	49.7	47.2	52.2	55.6	57.9	55.8	53.9
1995	54.1	54.8	55.1	55.1	55.2	55.1	46.9	45.8	54.4	55.4	55.6	55.7	53.6
1996	54.7	55.5	55.9	55.8	55.4	56.6	47.9	48.0	51.8	56.3	58.3	57.1	54.4
1997	56.0	56.9	57.2	57.1	56.8	57.1	51.5	51.9	55.6	58.2	58.3	58.5	56.3
1998	58.3	59.0	59.5	59.3	59.1	61.6	53.7	53.7	59.6	60.7	61.1	61.2	58.9
1999	60.8	61.2	61.5	61.3	61.4	60.7	54.5	56.1	61.5	61.8	62.1	62.4	60.4
2000	61.4	62.1	62.7	63.2	64.2	63.3	55.2	61.4	62.7	63.6	64.3	64.0	62.3
2001	61.8	62.7	62.9	62.9	62.7	62.1	54.5	60.8	62.6	63.4	64.0	64.1	62.0
2002	62.9	63.8	64.0	64.2	64.0	62.6	55.5	61.9	64.0	64.7	65.7	65.3	63.2
2003	64.3	65.1	65.4	65.6	65.2	63.7	56.9	62.6	65.7	66.4	66.6	66.6	64.5
Federal government													
1990	2.5	2.5	2.6	2.9	3.9	3.8	3.0	2.7	2.5	2.6	2.5	2.5	2.8
1991	2.5	2.5	2.5	2.5	2.5	2.6	2.6	2.6	2.5	2.5	2.5	2.6	2.5
1992	2.6	2.5	2.5	2.5	2.5	2.5	2.5	2.5	2.5	2.5	2.5	2.5	2.5
1993	2.5	2.5	2.5	2.5	2.5	2.5	2.5	2.5	2.6	2.5	2.5	2.6	2.5
1994	2.6	2.6	2.6	2.5	2.5	2.5	2.6	2.6	2.6	2.6	2.6	2.7	2.6
1995	2.6	2.6	2.6	2.6	2.7	2.7	2.6	2.7	2.7	2.7	2.7	2.8	2.7
1996	2.7	2.7	2.7	2.7	2.7	2.7	2.7	2.7	2.7	2.7	2.7	2.8	2.7
1997	2.7	2.7	2.7	2.8	2.8	2.9	2.9	2.9	2.9	2.9	2.7	2.8	2.8
1998	2.9	2.9	2.9	2.9	2.9	2.9	2.9	2.9	2.9	2.9	3.0	3.1	2.9
1999	3.0	3.0	3.0	3.0	2.9	2.9	2.9	2.9	3.0	3.0	3.1	3.1	3.0
2000	3.1	3.1	3.3	3.4	4.7	4.4	3.8	3.8	2.9	2.9	3.0	3.0	3.5
2001	3.0	3.0	2.9	2.9	2.9	3.0	3.0	3.0	2.9	2.9	3.0	3.0	2.9
2002	3.0	2.9	3.0	2.9	2.9	3.0	2.9	2.9	3.0	3.0	3.0	3.1	3.0
2003	2.9	2.9	2.8	3.0	3.0	3.0	3.0	3.0	2.9	2.9	2.9	3.0	2.9
State government													
1990	13.1	13.8	13.8	13.9	13.9	11.7	11.3	13.7	14.1	14.3	14.3	14.2	13.5
1991	14.3	15.0	15.0	15.0	15.1	14.9	13.3	13.9	14.9	15.1	15.1	15.0	14.7
1992	14.1	14.7	14.9	14.9	14.5	14.7	13.5	13.8	14.9	15.3	16.8	15.1	14.8
1993	14.6	14.9	15.0	15.1	14.4	14.4	13.2	13.3	14.7	14.8	14.9	14.7	14.5
1994	13.5	14.1	14.5	14.4	14.4	14.0	13.2	14.0	14.5	14.8	16.9	14.7	14.4
1995	13.4	13.9	14.0	13.9	13.8	13.5	12.6	13.2	13.5	13.7	13.6	13.5	13.6
1996	13.0	13.5	13.5	13.4	12.6	14.6	12.5	12.9	13.2	13.2	14.9	13.3	13.4
1997	12.6	13.3	13.2	13.3	12.5	12.7	12.2	12.7	13.0	13.2	13.3	13.2	12.9
1998	13.0	13.5	13.7	13.7	13.0	15.6	12.6	13.3	13.7	13.8	13.9	13.9	13.6
1999	13.5	13.8	14.0	14.1	14.0	13.6	13.0	13.4	14.2	13.9	14.0	13.9	13.8
2000	13.7	14.3	14.4	14.4	14.1	13.7	13.5	13.7	14.2	14.3	14.4	14.3	14.1
2001	12.5	12.9	13.0	13.0	12.5	12.3	11.9	12.3	12.6	12.7	12.7	12.8	12.6
2002	12.1	12.6	12.6	13.0	12.5	12.3	11.8	12.3	12.8	12.9	13.0	12.8	12.6
2003	12.3	12.9	12.9	12.9	12.3	11.9	11.1	12.0	13.2	13.4	13.4	13.3	12.6

Employment by Industry: South Carolina—*Continued*

(Numbers in thousands. Not seasonally adjusted.)

Industry	January	February	March	April	May	June	July	August	September	October	November	December	Annual Average
GREENVILLE-SPARTANBURG—*Continued*													
Local government													
1990	35.0	35.3	35.4	35.7	35.5	34.9	28.7	29.4	35.4	36.2	36.6	36.7	34.6
1991	36.7	37.1	37.2	37.1	36.8	35.7	28.8	28.9	36.1	36.8	37.0	37.3	35.5
1992	36.9	37.2	37.3	37.7	37.5	37.3	30.0	30.7	36.9	37.5	37.7	37.7	36.2
1993	37.4	37.7	37.8	37.7	37.7	37.4	32.3	29.2	32.0	37.8	38.0	38.2	36.1
1994	37.9	37.9	38.1	37.9	38.2	38.2	33.9	30.6	35.1	38.2	38.4	38.4	36.9
1995	38.1	38.3	38.5	38.6	38.7	38.9	31.7	29.9	38.2	39.0	39.3	39.4	37.4
1996	39.0	39.3	39.7	39.7	40.1	39.3	32.7	32.4	35.9	40.4	40.7	41.0	38.4
1997	40.7	40.9	41.3	41.0	41.5	41.5	36.4	36.3	39.7	42.1	42.3	42.5	40.5
1998	42.4	42.6	42.9	42.7	43.2	43.1	38.2	37.5	43.0	44.0	44.2	44.2	42.3
1999	44.3	44.4	44.5	44.2	44.5	44.2	38.6	39.8	44.3	44.9	45.0	45.4	43.7
2000	44.6	44.7	45.0	45.4	45.4	45.2	37.9	43.9	45.6	46.4	46.9	46.7	44.8
2001	46.3	46.8	47.0	47.0	47.3	46.8	39.6	45.5	47.1	47.8	48.3	48.3	46.4
2002	47.8	48.3	48.4	48.3	48.6	47.3	40.8	46.7	48.2	48.8	49.7	49.4	47.7
2003	49.1	49.3	49.7	49.7	49.9	48.8	42.8	47.6	49.6	50.1	50.3	50.3	48.9

Average Weekly Hours by Industry: South Carolina

(Not seasonally adjusted.)

Industry	January	February	March	April	May	June	July	August	September	October	November	December	Annual Average
STATEWIDE													
Manufacturing													
2001	41.6	41.5	41.7	41.6	41.8	41.6	40.5	41.0	41.0	40.3	40.7	41.3	41.2
2002	41.0	41.0	41.9	42.2	42.3	42.8	42.3	42.9	42.5	42.1	42.2	42.2	42.1
2003	41.7	42.2	42.1	41.5	41.4	41.1	40.0	40.6	41.3	41.1	41.0	41.1	41.3

Average Hourly Earnings by Industry: South Carolina

(Dollars, not seasonally adjusted.)

Industry	January	February	March	April	May	June	July	August	September	October	November	December	Annual Average
STATEWIDE													
Manufacturing													
2001	13.87	13.78	13.75	13.67	13.87	13.93	13.87	13.92	13.58	13.61	13.79	13.79	13.79
2002	13.95	13.83	13.77	13.82	13.91	14.00	14.20	14.04	14.16	14.10	14.04	14.19	14.00
2003	14.16	14.06	14.05	14.20	13.97	13.97	14.36	14.33	14.23	14.23	14.30	14.49	14.19

Average Weekly Earnings by Industry: South Carolina

(Dollars, not seasonally adjusted.)

Industry	January	February	March	April	May	June	July	August	September	October	November	December	Annual Average
STATEWIDE													
Manufacturing													
2001	576.99	571.87	573.38	568.67	579.77	579.49	561.74	570.72	556.78	548.48	561.25	569.53	568.15
2002	571.95	567.03	576.96	583.20	588.39	599.20	600.66	602.32	601.80	593.61	592.49	598.82	589.40
2003	590.47	593.33	591.51	589.30	578.36	574.17	574.40	581.80	587.70	584.85	586.30	595.54	586.05

SOUTH DAKOTA AT A GLANCE

(Population and total nonfarm employment numbers in thousands)

Population, Census 2000:	754.8
Total nonfarm employment, 2003:	378.2
Change in total nonfarm employment	
(Number)	
1990–2003:	89.5
1990–2001:	89.8
2001–2003:	-0.3
(Compound annual rate of change)	
1990–2003:	2.1%
1990–2001:	2.5%
2001–2003:	0.0%
Unemployment rate	
1990:	3.7%
2001:	3.1%
2003:	3.5%

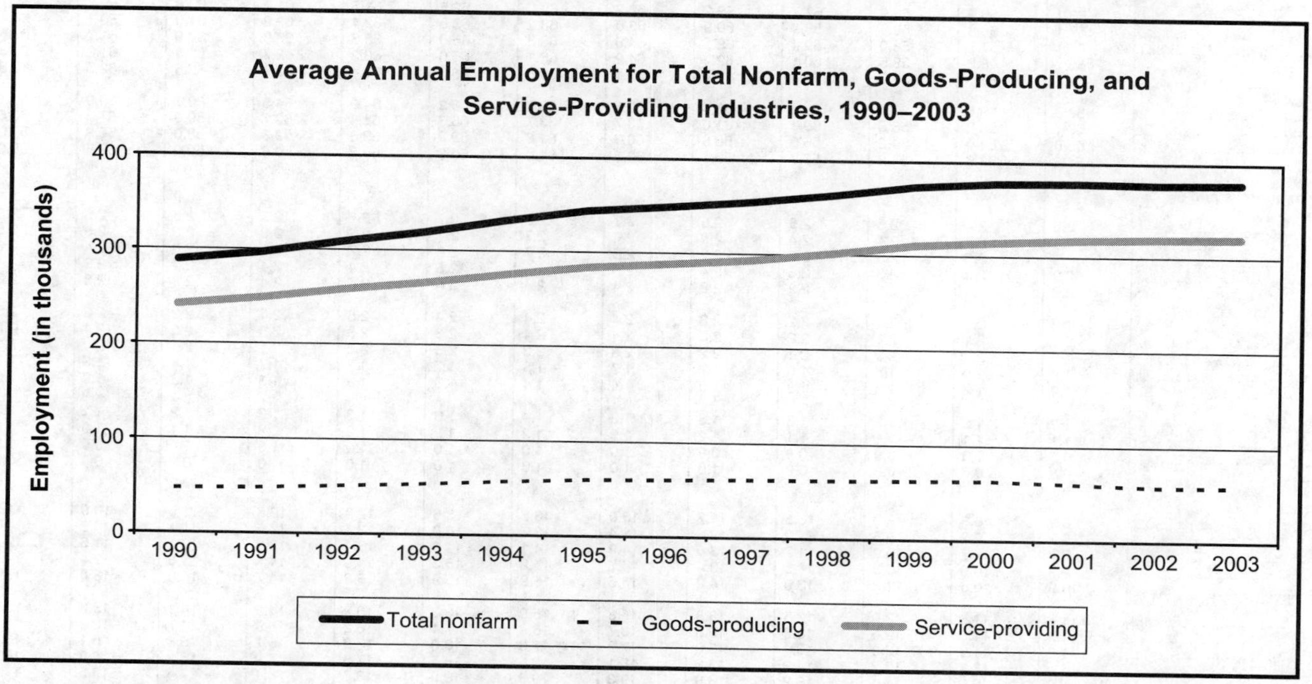

Nonfarm payroll employment rose steadily throughout the 1990s, but leveled off after 2000 due to declines in the goods-producing sector, particularly manufacturing. The number of jobs in the service-providing sector showed strong growth throughout the 1990s before slowing in 2000. Similarly, the goods-producing sector employment had consistent growth through the 1990s, but by 2003 had dropped 8 percent from its peak.

Employment by Industry: South Dakota

(Numbers in thousands. Not seasonally adjusted.)

Industry	January	February	March	April	May	June	July	August	September	October	November	December	Annual Average
STATEWIDE													
Total nonfarm													
1990	275.7	276.4	280.0	284.6	291.9	296.7	293.3	293.7	292.6	293.7	293.0	292.5	288.7
1991	284.5	285.5	288.0	292.9	299.5	304.3	301.3	301.1	299.8	300.4	299.8	300.2	296.4
1992	295.3	297.0	299.0	304.7	311.6	317.1	312.3	314.2	312.7	313.2	312.9	312.0	308.5
1993	303.9	305.3	308.1	313.6	320.7	326.7	322.6	324.4	323.2	325.6	325.6	324.4	318.7
1994	317.5	318.6	322.2	327.6	333.8	341.6	337.3	337.1	336.8	337.0	336.4	337.2	331.9
1995	330.6	331.7	335.5	338.6	345.5	353.6	347.4	349.0	348.4	347.8	347.2	346.4	343.5
1996	338.2	338.4	339.9	345.2	352.6	357.4	352.5	354.0	352.3	353.3	351.6	349.0	348.7
1997	340.4	342.5	345.1	350.2	360.7	364.8	361.2	360.7	359.6	358.6	357.6	357.4	354.9
1998	349.1	350.5	351.6	358.9	367.6	372.5	368.7	369.0	367.7	367.6	367.4	367.3	363.2
1999	359.0	359.4	361.8	369.6	377.5	382.1	377.7	378.8	377.4	378.9	378.3	378.8	373.3
2000	367.2	367.8	371.9	376.8	383.6	388.2	380.9	381.1	379.9	379.9	377.6	377.3	377.7
2001	369.2	369.5	371.4	376.3	385.1	389.4	382.9	383.3	380.1	379.4	378.1	376.8	378.5
2002	365.7	365.7	367.3	373.6	382.9	387.9	382.2	383.4	380.6	380.9	378.7	378.6	377.3
2003	367.9	367.2	368.9	375.0	383.1	387.5	381.7	383.4	380.9	381.7	380.9	380.1	378.2
Total private													
1990	213.3	213.4	216.5	220.1	226.5	231.9	234.5	236.4	231.9	230.4	228.9	228.4	226.0
1991	221.6	222.1	223.9	228.3	234.2	239.5	242.2	242.7	238.0	235.6	234.3	234.5	233.1
1992	230.2	230.6	233.0	238.3	244.2	250.7	251.6	253.1	248.6	246.9	245.3	245.3	243.2
1993	238.0	238.5	241.0	246.2	252.6	258.4	260.5	262.2	257.5	257.7	256.6	256.2	252.1
1994	249.9	250.1	253.7	259.0	264.9	272.1	274.4	275.0	271.0	269.7	268.6	269.3	264.8
1995	259.7	260.2	263.7	265.9	271.9	280.4	280.7	282.8	278.3	276.1	275.4	274.5	272.5
1996	267.2	267.1	268.1	273.2	279.6	285.8	286.5	289.3	283.0	282.4	279.8	278.1	278.3
1997	270.2	271.4	274.0	278.3	287.8	293.2	295.1	295.0	289.7	287.2	285.9	285.6	284.5
1998	278.4	279.0	280.0	287.0	294.9	300.4	301.7	302.9	297.3	295.5	293.6	295.2	292.2
1999	287.7	287.3	289.3	296.9	303.5	309.5	310.1	311.5	305.7	305.5	304.7	304.9	301.4
2000	298.0	297.7	300.6	305.3	310.6	316.3	315.3	315.4	310.0	308.4	306.0	305.2	307.4
2001	296.9	296.5	298.9	302.8	309.7	313.7	313.8	314.0	307.2	305.1	303.5	301.9	305.3
2002	292.4	291.6	293.1	299.3	306.8	311.8	312.0	313.2	307.1	305.9	303.5	303.0	303.3
2003	294.0	292.4	293.8	299.7	306.6	311.5	311.8	312.9	307.1	306.3	305.4	304.2	303.8
Goods-producing													
1990	43.4	43.5	44.4	45.6	47.5	49.6	51.1	50.9	49.7	49.5	48.5	47.2	47.6
1991	44.5	44.7	45.0	46.8	48.7	50.1	50.9	51.4	50.0	50.1	49.0	48.2	48.3
1992	46.7	46.7	47.6	49.7	51.3	53.1	53.4	53.5	52.6	52.5	51.8	51.0	50.8
1993	48.6	49.0	49.4	51.1	53.2	55.4	56.2	56.4	55.3	55.9	55.0	53.7	53.3
1994	52.0	51.6	52.8	54.9	56.7	58.9	60.0	60.1	59.6	59.4	58.8	57.9	56.9
1995	56.1	55.9	56.9	57.7	59.2	62.2	62.5	62.5	61.5	61.3	60.8	59.3	59.7
1996	57.1	56.8	56.9	58.9	60.9	63.0	63.2	63.5	62.1	62.2	61.0	59.1	60.4
1997	57.1	57.3	58.0	59.4	62.5	64.6	65.3	65.0	63.3	63.3	61.9	61.1	61.6
1998	58.7	58.3	58.5	60.1	62.4	64.2	65.1	65.0	63.3	62.7	61.6	61.2	61.8
1999	58.6	58.5	58.9	61.4	63.4	65.1	65.5	65.3	63.8	63.9	63.5	62.3	62.5
2000	59.8	59.5	60.4	62.1	63.4	65.8	66.7	66.2	64.9	64.5	62.7	60.9	63.1
2001	59.1	58.3	58.5	60.1	61.6	63.7	63.7	63.3	61.4	60.7	59.3	57.7	60.6
2002	55.0	54.0	54.2	56.3	58.8	60.6	61.3	60.9	59.6	59.3	58.0	56.9	57.9
2003	54.3	53.6	54.2	56.7	59.1	60.6	61.0	60.8	59.3	59.6	59.0	57.8	58.0
Natural resources and mining													
1990	2.5	2.4	2.5	2.5	2.6	2.7	2.8	2.7	2.7	2.7	2.6	2.5	2.6
1991	2.4	2.4	2.4	2.4	2.6	2.6	2.7	2.7	2.6	2.6	2.6	2.5	2.5
1992	2.5	2.5	2.5	2.6	2.7	2.8	2.7	2.8	2.7	2.7	2.6	2.4	2.6
1993	2.3	2.3	2.3	2.3	2.4	2.5	2.5	2.5	2.4	2.4	2.4	2.3	2.4
1994	2.2	2.1	2.1	2.2	2.3	2.4	2.4	2.4	2.4	2.4	2.4	2.3	2.3
1995	2.2	2.1	2.2	2.2	2.3	2.4	2.4	2.4	2.5	2.4	2.3	2.3	2.3
1996	2.1	2.1	2.1	2.2	2.3	2.4	2.4	2.3	2.3	2.3	2.2	2.1	2.2
1997	2.0	2.0	2.0	2.1	2.2	2.3	2.3	2.3	2.2	2.1	2.1	2.0	2.1
1998	1.9	1.9	1.8	1.6	1.7	1.7	1.8	1.7	1.7	1.7	1.4	1.3	1.7
1999	1.2	1.2	1.3	1.3	1.3	1.4	1.4	1.3	1.3	1.3	1.3	1.2	1.3
2000	1.2	1.2	1.2	1.3	1.3	1.3	1.4	1.3	1.3	1.3	1.2	1.1	1.3
2001	1.1	1.1	1.1	1.1	1.2	1.3	1.2	1.2	1.2	1.2	1.1	1.0	1.1
2002	0.9	0.9	0.9	0.9	0.9	1.0	1.0	1.0	1.0	1.0	1.0	0.9	1.0
2003	0.8	0.8	0.8	0.9	1.0	1.0	1.0	1.0	1.0	1.0	0.9	0.8	0.9
Construction													
1990	8.9	8.8	9.3	10.5	11.7	13.0	13.6	13.6	12.9	12.6	11.9	10.9	11.5
1991	9.2	9.2	9.5	11.0	12.4	13.4	13.7	14.0	13.1	12.5	11.4	10.8	11.7
1992	9.7	9.7	10.2	11.7	13.0	14.0	14.1	14.0	13.4	13.0	12.1	11.5	12.2
1993	9.9	10.0	10.3	11.5	13.4	14.7	15.2	15.3	14.5	14.4	13.6	12.4	12.9
1994	10.9	10.5	11.3	13.0	14.2	15.5	15.9	15.9	15.3	14.7	14.0	13.0	13.7
1995	11.8	11.5	12.0	12.5	13.8	15.8	15.9	16.0	15.2	14.9	14.1	13.3	13.9
1996	11.9	11.6	12.0	13.6	15.3	16.7	16.9	17.1	16.2	15.8	14.7	13.2	14.6
1997	11.8	11.9	12.3	13.4	15.8	17.2	17.6	18.0	17.2	16.7	15.8	15.1	15.2
1998	13.4	13.1	13.2	14.9	16.8	18.1	18.6	18.5	17.5	16.9	16.2	15.8	16.1
1999	13.7	13.6	14.1	16.2	18.0	19.3	19.6	19.5	18.6	18.1	17.4	16.5	17.1
2000	14.9	14.6	15.5	17.3	18.8	20.4	20.9	20.8	19.9	19.2	17.6	16.6	18.0
2001	15.1	14.8	15.3	17.1	19.1	20.9	21.4	21.4	20.4	19.8	18.8	17.6	18.4
2002	15.5	15.2	15.4	17.2	19.6	20.9	21.2	21.1	20.2	19.9	18.9	18.1	18.6
2003	16.0	15.6	16.0	18.2	20.4	21.7	21.9	21.8	20.8	21.0	20.0	18.8	19.4

Employment by Industry: South Dakota—*Continued*

(Numbers in thousands. Not seasonally adjusted.)

Industry	January	February	March	April	May	June	July	August	September	October	November	December	Annual Average
STATEWIDE—*Continued*													
Manufacturing													
1990	32.0	32.3	32.6	32.6	33.2	33.9	34.7	34.6	34.1	34.2	34.0	33.8	33.5
1991	32.9	33.1	33.1	33.4	33.7	34.1	34.5	34.7	34.3	35.0	35.0	34.9	34.1
1992	34.5	34.5	34.9	35.4	35.6	36.3	36.6	36.7	36.5	36.8	37.1	37.1	36.0
1993	36.4	36.7	36.8	37.3	37.4	38.2	38.5	38.6	38.4	39.1	39.0	39.0	38.0
1994	38.9	39.0	39.4	39.7	40.2	41.0	41.7	41.8	41.9	42.3	42.4	42.6	40.9
1995	42.1	42.3	42.7	43.0	43.1	44.0	44.2	44.1	43.8	44.0	44.4	43.7	43.5
1996	43.1	43.1	42.8	43.1	43.3	43.9	43.9	44.1	43.6	44.1	44.1	43.8	43.6
1997	43.3	43.4	43.7	43.9	44.5	45.1	45.4	44.7	43.9	44.5	44.0	44.0	44.2
1998	43.4	43.3	43.5	43.6	43.9	44.4	44.7	44.8	44.1	44.1	44.0	44.1	44.0
1999	43.7	43.7	43.5	43.9	44.1	44.4	44.5	44.5	43.9	44.5	44.8	44.6	44.2
2000	43.7	43.7	43.7	43.5	43.3	44.1	44.4	44.1	43.7	44.0	43.9	43.2	43.8
2001	42.9	42.4	42.1	41.9	41.3	41.5	41.1	40.7	39.8	39.7	39.4	39.1	40.9
2002	38.6	37.9	37.9	38.2	38.3	38.7	39.1	38.8	38.4	38.4	38.1	37.9	38.4
2003	37.5	37.2	37.4	37.6	37.7	37.9	38.1	38.0	37.5	37.6	38.1	38.2	37.7
Service-providing													
1990	232.3	232.9	235.6	239.0	244.4	247.1	242.2	242.8	242.9	244.2	244.5	245.3	241.1
1991	240.0	240.8	243.0	246.1	250.8	254.2	250.4	249.7	249.8	250.3	250.8	252.0	248.2
1992	248.6	250.3	251.4	255.0	260.3	264.0	258.9	260.7	260.1	260.7	261.1	261.0	257.7
1993	255.3	256.3	258.7	262.5	267.5	271.3	266.4	268.0	267.9	269.7	270.6	270.7	265.4
1994	265.5	267.0	269.4	272.7	277.1	282.7	277.3	277.0	277.2	277.6	277.6	279.3	275.0
1995	274.5	275.8	278.6	280.9	286.3	291.4	284.9	286.5	286.9	286.5	286.4	287.1	283.8
1996	281.1	281.6	283.0	286.3	291.7	294.4	289.3	290.5	290.2	291.1	290.6	289.9	288.3
1997	283.3	285.2	287.1	290.8	298.2	300.2	295.9	295.7	296.3	295.3	295.7	296.3	293.3
1998	290.4	292.2	293.1	298.8	305.2	308.3	303.6	304.0	304.4	304.9	305.8	306.1	301.4
1999	300.4	300.9	302.9	308.2	314.1	317.0	312.2	313.5	313.6	315.0	314.8	316.5	310.8
2000	307.4	308.3	311.5	314.7	320.2	322.4	314.2	314.9	315.0	315.4	314.9	316.4	314.6
2001	310.1	311.2	312.9	316.2	323.5	325.7	319.2	320.0	318.7	318.7	318.8	319.1	317.8
2002	310.7	311.7	313.1	317.3	324.1	327.3	320.9	322.5	321.0	321.6	320.7	321.7	319.4
2003	313.6	313.6	314.7	318.3	324.0	326.9	320.7	322.6	321.6	322.1	321.9	322.3	320.2
Trade, transportation, and utilities													
1990	61.8	61.4	61.9	62.8	63.9	64.5	65.3	65.5	64.9	65.6	66.1	66.8	64.2
1991	64.2	63.8	64.0	64.8	66.1	66.3	67.3	66.3	66.0	66.1	67.0	67.8	65.8
1992	65.7	65.3	65.5	66.7	67.7	68.5	68.4	68.7	67.9	67.9	68.3	68.7	67.4
1993	66.6	66.3	66.7	68.1	69.3	69.7	70.2	70.2	69.5	69.8	70.5	71.1	69.0
1994	68.7	68.5	69.1	70.5	71.5	72.2	73.1	72.4	71.9	72.5	73.4	74.2	71.5
1995	71.9	71.7	72.1	72.5	73.4	74.4	74.2	75.0	73.6	74.0	74.8	75.4	73.6
1996	72.5	72.2	72.1	73.0	73.8	73.9	74.2	75.4	73.6	74.2	74.6	74.9	73.7
1997	72.4	71.8	72.2	72.7	75.0	75.2	74.8	74.3	74.1	74.5	75.4	76.0	74.0
1998	73.2	73.2	73.3	74.4	75.8	76.2	75.2	75.5	74.6	75.0	75.4	76.5	74.9
1999	73.7	73.4	73.8	75.2	76.4	76.8	76.7	76.9	75.7	76.4	77.2	77.9	75.8
2000	75.1	74.7	75.0	76.9	77.7	78.0	77.3	77.4	76.5	77.2	78.1	78.4	76.9
2001	75.7	75.7	76.3	76.5	77.9	78.0	77.4	77.4	76.2	77.0	77.9	78.4	77.0
2002	75.0	74.3	74.3	75.9	77.2	77.8	77.0	77.4	76.4	77.1	77.7	78.2	76.5
2003	75.1	74.3	74.5	75.9	77.0	77.4	77.3	77.7	76.7	77.5	77.9	78.4	76.6
Wholesale trade													
1990	14.7	14.6	14.8	14.9	14.9	14.9	15.5	14.9	14.7	14.7	14.5	14.5	14.8
1991	14.4	14.5	14.6	14.8	14.9	14.9	15.9	14.8	14.8	14.7	14.8	14.8	14.8
1992	14.6	14.7	14.8	15.1	15.2	15.2	15.1	15.5	15.1	15.1	15.0	15.0	15.0
1993	14.9	15.0	15.1	15.3	15.5	15.5	15.6	15.6	15.3	15.2	15.3	15.3	15.3
1994	15.1	15.2	15.4	15.7	15.8	15.8	16.7	15.8	15.7	15.6	15.8	15.8	15.7
1995	15.8	15.8	15.9	16.0	16.2	16.1	15.8	16.4	15.7	15.7	15.7	15.8	15.9
1996	15.5	15.6	15.7	16.0	16.0	15.9	15.8	16.6	15.7	15.8	15.8	15.8	15.9
1997	15.5	15.7	15.8	16.0	16.4	16.4	16.2	16.3	16.1	16.1	16.2	16.2	16.1
1998	16.2	16.2	16.3	16.6	16.8	16.7	16.4	16.4	16.1	16.3	16.3	16.3	16.4
1999	16.2	16.2	16.4	16.6	16.8	16.8	16.6	16.6	16.2	16.4	16.4	16.4	16.5
2000	16.3	16.4	16.5	16.7	16.7	16.7	16.5	16.5	16.4	16.5	16.5	16.5	16.5
2001	16.5	16.5	16.6	16.8	17.0	16.9	16.7	16.6	16.4	16.7	16.7	16.7	16.6
2002	16.6	16.6	16.6	16.9	16.9	17.0	16.7	16.6	16.3	16.6	16.6	16.6	16.7
2003	16.4	16.3	16.4	16.7	16.8	16.7	16.8	16.8	16.6	16.9	16.8	16.9	16.7
Retail trade													
1990	37.6	37.2	37.5	38.3	39.0	39.8	40.0	40.7	40.2	40.8	41.5	42.1	39.6
1991	39.9	39.5	39.5	40.1	41.0	41.4	41.3	41.4	40.9	41.0	41.7	42.5	40.9
1992	40.6	40.0	40.1	40.8	41.6	42.4	42.4	42.4	41.8	41.8	42.4	42.8	41.6
1993	40.8	40.5	40.8	41.8	42.5	43.2	43.5	43.5	43.0	43.1	43.8	44.4	42.6
1994	42.5	42.3	42.5	43.4	44.2	44.9	45.0	45.2	44.7	45.1	45.8	46.6	44.4
1995	44.8	44.5	44.7	44.9	45.5	46.5	46.7	46.9	46.1	46.2	47.0	47.5	45.9
1996	45.4	44.9	44.8	45.0	45.8	46.1	46.5	46.9	45.9	46.1	46.6	47.0	45.9
1997	45.2	44.4	44.7	45.0	46.6	47.0	47.0	47.1	46.3	46.3	47.1	47.7	46.2
1998	45.5	45.3	45.3	46.1	47.3	47.8	47.1	47.4	46.5	46.7	47.1	48.2	46.7
1999	45.8	45.4	45.7	46.6	47.6	48.3	48.2	48.5	47.6	47.9	48.7	49.3	47.5
2000	46.9	46.5	46.8	48.3	48.9	49.4	49.0	49.0	47.9	48.4	49.3	49.6	48.3
2001	47.3	47.3	47.7	47.6	48.7	49.0	48.8	49.0	47.7	48.0	49.0	49.5	48.2
2002	46.8	46.1	46.1	47.2	48.3	48.9	48.7	49.1	48.2	48.7	49.4	49.8	48.1
2003	47.2	46.6	46.7	47.8	48.6	49.1	49.1	49.5	48.3	48.8	49.4	49.8	48.4

Employment by Industry: South Dakota—*Continued*

(Numbers in thousands. Not seasonally adjusted.)

Industry	January	February	March	April	May	June	July	August	September	October	November	December	Annual Average
STATEWIDE—*Continued*													
Transportation and utilities													
1990	9.5	9.6	9.6	9.6	10.0	9.8	9.8	9.9	10.0	10.1	10.1	10.2	9.9
1991	9.9	9.8	9.9	9.9	10.2	10.0	10.1	10.1	10.3	10.4	10.5	10.5	10.1
1992	10.5	10.6	10.6	10.8	10.9	10.9	10.9	10.8	11.0	11.0	10.9	10.9	10.8
1993	10.9	10.8	10.8	11.0	11.3	11.0	11.1	11.1	11.2	11.5	11.4	11.4	11.1
1994	11.1	11.0	11.2	11.4	11.5	11.5	11.4	11.4	11.5	11.8	11.8	11.8	11.5
1995	11.3	11.4	11.5	11.6	11.7	11.8	11.7	11.7	11.8	12.1	12.1	12.1	11.7
1996	11.6	11.7	11.6	12.0	12.0	11.9	11.9	11.9	12.0	12.3	12.2	12.1	11.9
1997	11.7	11.7	11.7	11.7	12.0	11.8	11.6	10.9	11.7	12.1	12.1	12.1	11.8
1998	11.5	11.7	11.7	11.7	11.7	11.7	11.7	11.7	12.0	12.0	12.0	12.0	11.8
1999	11.7	11.8	11.7	12.0	12.0	11.7	11.9	11.8	11.9	12.1	12.1	12.2	11.9
2000	11.9	11.8	11.7	11.9	12.1	11.9	11.8	11.9	12.2	12.3	12.3	12.3	12.0
2001	11.9	11.9	12.0	12.1	12.2	12.1	11.9	11.8	12.1	12.3	12.2	12.2	12.0
2002	11.6	11.6	11.6	11.8	12.0	11.9	11.6	11.7	11.9	11.8	11.7	11.8	11.8
2003	11.5	11.4	11.4	11.4	11.6	11.6	11.4	11.4	11.8	11.8	11.7	11.7	11.6
Information													
1990	5.7	5.6	5.5	5.4	5.5	5.5	5.5	5.5	5.5	5.4	5.4	5.4	5.5
1991	5.5	5.5	5.5	5.5	5.5	5.6	5.6	5.6	5.5	5.5	5.6	5.6	5.5
1992	5.5	5.5	5.5	5.6	5.6	5.7	5.6	5.6	5.5	5.6	5.6	5.6	5.6
1993	5.6	5.5	5.5	5.5	5.6	5.6	5.7	5.8	5.7	5.7	5.8	5.8	5.7
1994	5.8	5.9	5.9	5.9	5.9	6.0	5.9	5.9	5.9	5.8	5.8	5.9	5.9
1995	5.9	5.9	5.9	6.0	6.0	6.1	6.1	6.1	6.1	6.2	6.2	6.2	6.1
1996	6.1	6.1	6.1	6.1	6.2	6.3	6.3	6.4	6.3	6.2	6.2	6.2	6.2
1997	6.2	6.2	6.2	6.3	6.4	6.5	6.5	6.5	6.5	6.5	6.6	6.7	6.4
1998	6.5	6.5	6.6	6.6	6.6	6.7	6.8	6.8	6.7	6.7	6.7	6.7	6.7
1999	6.7	6.7	6.8	6.6	6.7	6.8	6.8	6.7	6.6	6.7	6.7	6.8	6.7
2000	6.8	6.7	6.8	6.9	7.0	7.0	7.0	6.9	6.9	6.8	6.9	6.9	6.9
2001	6.8	6.8	6.8	6.7	6.9	6.9	6.9	6.8	6.8	6.8	6.8	6.8	6.8
2002	6.8	6.7	6.8	6.7	6.8	6.9	6.9	6.8	6.7	6.9	6.9	6.9	6.8
2003	6.8	6.7	6.7	6.6	6.7	6.8	6.8	6.6	6.9	6.9	6.9	6.9	6.8
Financial activities													
1990	16.8	16.8	17.0	16.9	17.0	17.2	17.2	17.4	17.2	17.1	17.3	17.5	17.1
1991	17.3	17.3	17.3	17.3	17.3	17.6	17.5	17.6	17.4	17.3	17.4	17.6	17.4
1992	17.7	17.8	17.7	17.8	17.9	18.2	18.4	18.4	18.1	18.0	18.1	18.2	18.0
1993	17.9	18.0	18.3	18.3	18.3	18.6	18.6	18.6	18.5	18.4	18.6	18.8	18.4
1994	18.5	18.4	18.5	18.5	18.7	18.9	18.8	18.9	18.7	18.7	18.8	19.1	18.7
1995	18.6	18.5	18.7	18.5	18.8	19.3	19.2	19.3	19.2	19.2	19.3	19.5	19.0
1996	19.7	19.7	19.8	20.0	20.1	20.4	20.6	20.6	20.3	20.7	20.9	21.2	20.3
1997	20.9	20.9	21.1	21.3	21.4	21.8	21.9	22.0	21.9	22.1	22.3	22.5	21.7
1998	22.4	22.3	22.2	22.6	22.9	23.2	23.5	23.5	23.7	23.8	24.1	24.4	23.2
1999	24.3	24.3	24.5	24.5	24.7	25.3	25.5	25.5	25.4	25.7	25.8	26.0	25.1
2000	25.6	25.6	25.7	25.9	26.0	26.4	26.5	26.4	26.3	26.5	26.7	27.2	26.2
2001	27.5	27.7	27.8	27.8	28.0	28.3	28.4	28.2	28.1	27.9	28.0	28.1	27.9
2002	28.0	28.0	27.9	27.9	27.9	28.1	28.0	28.0	27.7	27.6	27.7	28.0	27.9
2003	27.6	27.6	27.8	27.5	27.4	27.6	27.3	27.6	27.3	27.1	27.6	28.1	27.5
Professional and business services													
1990	10.5	10.6	10.7	10.9	11.0	11.5	11.5	11.7	11.4	11.4	11.3	11.3	11.2
1991	11.2	11.2	11.2	11.3	11.4	11.6	12.2	12.7	12.6	12.0	12.0	12.1	11.8
1992	11.9	12.1	12.1	12.3	12.4	12.7	13.1	13.2	12.8	13.2	13.3	13.2	12.7
1993	12.7	13.0	13.1	13.6	14.2	14.7	14.8	15.1	14.6	15.0	15.2	15.3	14.3
1994	15.1	15.3	15.4	16.1	16.2	16.9	17.1	17.4	17.2	17.4	17.0	17.1	16.5
1995	16.7	16.9	17.3	17.4	17.7	18.4	18.4	18.7	18.8	18.8	18.7	18.7	18.0
1996	18.4	18.7	18.8	19.2	19.5	20.1	20.1	20.4	20.0	20.6	20.3	20.1	19.7
1997	19.8	20.5	20.6	21.3	21.8	22.4	22.4	22.7	22.0	21.8	22.0	21.8	21.6
1998	21.2	21.4	21.6	22.5	23.0	23.5	23.7	23.9	23.2	23.7	23.8	23.8	22.9
1999	23.4	23.4	23.6	25.1	25.1	25.9	25.7	25.9	25.3	25.9	26.2	26.5	25.2
2000	26.6	26.9	27.0	27.2	27.2	27.8	27.7	27.5	27.1	27.1	26.5	26.8	27.1
2001	25.9	25.7	25.7	26.2	26.3	26.4	26.2	26.1	25.4	25.3	24.9	24.7	25.7
2002	24.0	24.4	24.5	24.9	24.9	25.2	24.8	25.1	24.4	24.6	24.7	24.6	24.7
2003	23.9	24.1	23.9	23.9	24.0	24.2	23.7	23.9	23.4	23.7	23.9	23.8	23.9
Educational and health services													
1990	36.4	36.7	37.0	37.0	37.3	36.6	36.0	36.3	37.5	37.7	37.9	37.9	37.0
1991	38.1	38.5	38.8	38.7	38.7	38.8	38.4	38.3	38.9	39.2	39.2	39.4	38.8
1992	39.2	39.5	39.8	40.0	40.4	40.5	40.1	40.3	40.7	41.0	41.1	41.5	40.3
1993	41.3	41.2	41.5	41.4	41.7	41.1	41.0	41.3	42.1	42.5	42.5	42.8	41.7
1994	43.1	43.4	43.7	43.6	43.7	43.5	43.0	43.1	44.2	44.4	44.5	44.8	43.8
1995	44.5	44.7	45.1	45.4	45.5	45.4	44.9	45.0	46.0	46.2	46.4	46.6	45.5
1996	46.2	46.5	46.7	47.1	47.2	47.0	46.7	46.9	47.6	47.5	47.5	47.7	47.1
1997	47.2	47.5	47.6	47.8	48.1	47.8	47.8	48.0	48.5	48.7	49.1	49.3	48.1
1998	49.0	49.4	49.6	49.7	49.8	49.5	49.0	49.1	49.9	50.6	50.7	51.2	49.8
1999	51.1	51.2	51.6	51.3	51.3	50.9	50.6	50.4	51.3	52.0	52.3	52.8	51.4
2000	52.1	52.4	52.7	52.8	52.6	52.0	51.2	51.3	51.9	52.4	52.4	52.6	52.2
2001	51.9	52.5	52.9	53.0	53.1	52.3	52.1	52.2	52.7	53.3	53.9	53.8	52.8
2002	53.3	53.7	54.0	54.4	54.3	54.0	53.5	53.7	54.4	55.0	55.2	55.3	54.2
2003	55.2	55.1	55.2	55.5	55.7	55.2	54.8	55.0	55.5	55.5	55.8	55.7	55.4

Employment by Industry: South Dakota—*Continued*

(Numbers in thousands. Not seasonally adjusted.)

Industry	January	February	March	April	May	June	July	August	September	October	November	December	Annual Average
STATEWIDE—*Continued*													
Leisure and hospitality													
1990	24.8	24.9	25.9	27.7	30.2	32.8	33.7	34.7	31.9	29.4	28.2	27.9	29.3
1991	26.9	27.0	28.1	29.5	31.8	34.6	35.2	35.7	33.0	30.8	29.4	28.9	30.9
1992	28.5	28.7	29.4	30.7	33.3	35.9	36.2	37.0	34.8	32.6	31.1	30.8	32.4
1993	29.5	29.6	30.3	31.9	33.8	36.6	37.6	38.5	35.7	34.1	32.6	32.2	33.5
1994	30.7	30.9	32.1	33.2	35.5	38.7	39.7	40.5	36.9	35.0	33.7	33.7	35.1
1995	30.8	31.1	32.0	32.9	35.6	38.8	39.6	40.2	37.3	35.0	33.9	33.4	35.1
1996	32.2	32.3	32.8	34.0	36.8	39.9	40.5	40.8	38.2	36.0	34.4	33.9	36.0
1997	31.9	32.5	33.3	34.5	37.6	40.0	41.3	41.7	38.8	36.0	34.4	34.0	36.3
1998	33.0	33.1	33.5	35.9	38.6	41.0	41.8	42.4	39.2	36.3	34.6	34.6	37.0
1999	33.1	33.1	33.6	35.8	38.6	41.4	42.2	43.6	40.7	38.0	36.4	36.0	37.7
2000	34.9	35.1	35.8	36.8	39.8	42.5	42.7	43.6	40.6	37.8	36.6	36.3	38.5
2001	34.5	34.3	35.3	36.9	40.1	42.2	43.1	44.0	40.8	38.2	36.9	36.6	38.5
2002	34.7	34.9	35.7	37.4	40.8	43.1	44.3	45.2	41.9	39.4	37.5	37.4	39.4
2003	35.6	35.5	36.0	37.9	40.9	43.8	44.9	45.3	42.0	40.0	38.3	37.5	39.8
Other services													
1990	13.9	13.9	14.1	13.8	14.1	14.2	14.2	14.4	13.8	14.3	14.2	14.4	14.1
1991	13.9	14.1	14.0	14.4	14.7	14.9	15.1	15.1	14.6	14.6	14.7	14.9	14.6
1992	15.0	15.0	15.4	15.5	15.6	16.1	16.4	16.4	16.2	16.1	16.0	16.3	15.8
1993	15.8	15.9	16.2	16.3	16.5	16.7	16.4	16.3	16.1	16.3	16.4	16.5	16.3
1994	16.0	16.1	16.2	16.3	16.7	17.0	16.8	16.7	16.6	16.5	16.6	16.6	16.5
1995	15.2	15.5	15.7	15.5	15.7	15.8	15.8	16.0	15.8	15.4	15.3	15.4	15.6
1996	15.0	14.8	14.9	14.9	15.1	15.2	14.9	15.3	14.9	15.0	14.9	15.0	15.0
1997	14.7	14.7	15.0	15.0	15.0	14.9	15.1	14.8	14.6	14.3	14.2	14.2	14.7
1998	14.4	14.8	14.7	15.2	15.8	16.1	16.6	16.7	16.7	16.7	16.7	16.8	15.9
1999	16.8	16.7	16.5	17.0	17.3	17.3	17.1	17.2	16.9	16.9	16.6	16.6	16.9
2000	17.1	16.8	17.2	16.7	16.9	16.8	16.2	16.1	15.8	16.1	16.1	16.1	16.5
2001	15.5	15.5	15.6	15.6	15.8	15.9	16.0	16.0	15.8	15.9	15.8	15.8	15.7
2002	15.6	15.6	15.7	15.8	16.1	16.1	16.2	16.1	16.0	16.0	15.8	15.7	15.9
2003	15.5	15.5	15.5	15.7	15.8	15.9	16.0	16.0	16.0	16.0	16.0	16.0	15.8
Government													
1990	62.4	63.0	63.5	64.5	65.4	64.8	58.8	57.3	60.7	63.3	64.1	64.1	62.7
1991	62.9	63.4	64.1	64.6	65.3	64.8	59.1	58.4	61.8	64.8	65.5	65.7	63.4
1992	65.1	66.4	66.0	66.4	67.4	66.4	60.7	61.1	64.1	66.3	67.6	66.7	65.4
1993	65.9	66.8	67.1	67.4	68.1	68.3	62.1	62.2	65.7	67.9	69.0	68.2	66.6
1994	67.6	68.5	68.5	68.6	68.9	69.5	62.9	62.1	65.8	67.3	67.8	67.9	67.1
1995	70.9	71.5	71.8	72.7	73.6	73.2	66.7	66.2	70.1	71.7	71.8	71.9	71.0
1996	71.0	71.3	71.8	72.0	73.0	71.6	66.0	64.7	69.3	70.9	71.8	70.9	70.4
1997	70.2	71.1	71.1	71.9	72.9	71.6	66.1	65.7	69.9	71.4	71.7	71.8	70.5
1998	70.7	71.5	71.6	71.9	72.7	72.1	67.0	66.1	70.4	72.1	73.8	72.1	71.0
1999	71.3	72.1	72.5	72.7	74.0	72.6	67.6	67.3	71.7	73.4	73.6	73.9	71.9
2000	69.2	70.1	71.3	71.5	73.0	71.9	65.6	65.7	69.9	71.5	71.6	72.1	70.3
2001	72.3	73.0	72.5	73.5	75.4	75.7	69.1	69.3	72.9	74.3	74.6	74.9	73.1
2002	73.3	74.1	74.2	74.3	76.1	76.1	70.2	70.2	73.5	75.0	75.2	75.6	74.0
2003	73.9	74.8	75.1	75.3	76.5	76.0	69.9	70.5	73.8	75.4	75.5	75.9	74.4
Federal government													
1990	11.2	11.2	11.6	12.4	12.1	11.6	11.7	11.3	11.4	11.1	11.1	11.3	11.5
1991	11.0	11.0	11.0	11.2	11.2	11.3	11.2	11.4	11.4	11.4	11.4	11.4	11.2
1992	11.4	11.3	11.4	11.5	11.5	11.6	11.5	11.7	11.7	11.4	11.3	11.4	11.5
1993	11.3	11.3	11.2	11.3	11.3	11.7	11.4	11.4	11.6	11.6	11.5	11.5	11.4
1994	11.4	11.4	11.4	11.5	11.6	11.9	11.2	11.3	11.6	11.5	11.3	11.3	11.5
1995	11.1	11.1	11.1	11.1	11.2	11.4	11.4	11.3	11.1	11.2	10.9	10.9	11.2
1996	10.8	10.8	10.8	10.9	11.0	11.2	11.2	11.1	11.0	10.9	10.8	10.8	10.9
1997	10.5	10.6	10.6	10.7	10.8	10.9	11.2	11.2	10.9	10.8	10.8	10.7	10.8
1998	10.7	10.6	10.6	10.6	10.7	10.9	11.0	11.1	10.9	10.8	10.8	10.8	10.8
1999	10.7	10.6	10.6	10.7	10.9	10.7	10.8	10.9	11.1	11.1	11.0	11.0	10.8
2000	11.0	11.0	11.9	11.7	12.6	11.3	11.4	11.2	11.2	11.2	11.1	11.3	11.4
2001	10.9	10.7	10.7	10.8	11.0	11.4	11.1	11.4	11.4	11.1	11.1	11.3	11.0
2002	11.1	10.9	11.0	10.9	11.1	11.6	11.3	11.5	11.4	11.2	11.3	11.6	11.2
2003	11.2	11.1	11.2	11.1	11.2	11.7	11.3	11.8	11.6	11.4	11.4	11.7	11.4
State government													
1990	16.9	16.8	17.0	16.8	17.6	17.0	16.2	15.9	15.6	17.1	17.4	17.4	16.8
1991	16.8	17.0	17.2	17.4	17.4	17.1	16.4	16.5	16.0	17.3	17.5	17.5	17.0
1992	17.1	17.4	17.5	17.6	18.0	16.8	16.3	16.9	16.9	17.8	17.8	17.7	17.3
1993	17.3	17.8	17.8	17.8	18.1	17.1	16.9	17.4	17.5	18.1	18.1	18.0	17.7
1994	18.3	18.6	18.6	18.3	18.1	18.0	17.7	17.3	17.7	18.1	18.3	18.2	18.1
1995	17.8	18.0	18.0	18.1	18.1	17.2	16.7	16.6	17.5	18.1	18.2	17.9	17.7
1996	17.4	17.5	17.5	17.5	17.4	15.8	15.4	15.2	16.1	16.9	17.0	16.9	16.7
1997	17.0	17.2	16.7	17.1	16.7	15.0	14.8	15.0	15.7	16.6	16.8	16.7	16.3
1998	16.5	16.7	16.7	16.8	16.6	15.7	15.6	15.3	16.3	16.7	16.7	16.6	16.4
1999	16.5	16.8	16.8	16.9	16.9	15.7	15.6	15.6	16.2	17.0	17.0	17.0	16.5
2000	16.6	16.8	16.9	16.8	16.4	15.9	15.3	15.9	16.6	17.2	17.3	17.2	16.6
2001	17.0	17.3	16.9	17.1	17.7	16.3	15.6	16.2	16.6	17.5	17.6	17.6	17.0
2002	17.2	17.5	17.4	17.3	17.6	16.1	16.1	16.3	16.6	17.5	17.7	17.4	17.1
2003	17.2	17.5	17.4	17.4	17.6	16.4	16.2	16.2	16.6	17.5	17.6	17.5	17.1

Employment by Industry: South Dakota—*Continued*

(Numbers in thousands. Not seasonally adjusted.)

Industry	January	February	March	April	May	June	July	August	September	October	November	December	Annual Average
STATEWIDE—*Continued*													
Local government													
1990	34.3	35.0	34.9	35.3	35.7	36.2	30.9	30.1	33.7	35.1	35.6	35.4	34.4
1991	35.1	35.4	35.9	36.0	36.7	36.4	31.5	30.5	34.4	36.1	36.6	36.8	35.1
1992	36.6	37.7	37.1	37.3	37.9	38.0	32.9	32.5	35.5	37.1	38.5	37.6	36.6
1993	37.3	37.7	38.1	38.3	38.7	39.5	33.8	33.4	36.6	38.2	39.4	38.7	37.5
1994	37.9	38.5	38.5	38.8	39.2	39.6	34.0	33.5	36.5	37.7	38.2	38.4	37.6
1995	42.0	42.4	42.7	43.5	44.3	44.6	38.6	38.3	41.5	42.4	42.7	43.1	42.2
1996	42.8	43.0	43.5	43.6	44.6	44.6	39.4	38.4	42.2	43.1	44.0	43.2	42.7
1997	42.7	43.3	43.8	44.1	45.4	45.7	40.1	39.5	43.3	44.0	44.1	44.4	43.4
1998	43.5	44.2	44.3	44.5	45.4	45.5	40.4	39.7	43.2	44.6	46.3	44.7	43.9
1999	44.1	44.7	45.1	45.1	46.2	46.2	41.2	40.8	44.4	45.3	45.6	45.9	44.6
2000	41.6	42.3	42.5	43.0	44.0	44.7	38.9	38.6	42.1	43.1	43.2	43.6	42.3
2001	44.4	45.0	44.9	45.6	46.7	48.0	42.4	41.7	44.9	45.7	45.9	46.0	45.0
2002	45.0	45.7	45.8	46.1	47.4	48.4	42.8	42.4	45.5	46.3	46.2	46.6	45.7
2003	45.5	46.2	46.5	46.8	47.7	47.9	42.4	42.5	45.6	46.5	46.5	46.7	45.9
RAPID CITY													
Total nonfarm													
1990	36.0	36.0	36.8	37.3	38.9	41.1	41.2	41.1	39.9	39.7	39.1	38.5	38.8
1991	37.3	37.2	37.7	38.3	39.7	41.5	41.8	41.7	41.0	40.4	39.5	39.6	39.6
1992	38.7	38.8	39.3	40.2	41.6	43.2	43.2	43.4	42.1	41.8	40.9	40.7	41.1
1993	39.2	39.6	40.0	41.5	42.6	44.6	44.7	45.2	43.5	43.4	42.9	42.8	42.5
1994	41.0	41.5	41.9	43.3	44.6	46.4	46.2	46.3	44.9	44.7	44.2	44.3	44.1
1995	43.2	43.6	44.1	44.4	45.4	47.0	46.6	46.7	45.9	45.4	44.9	45.3	45.2
1996	43.9	43.6	43.5	44.2	46.0	47.6	47.5	47.9	46.5	46.4	45.7	45.3	45.6
1997	43.9	44.0	44.5	44.8	47.3	48.8	49.1	48.8	47.5	46.6	46.0	46.1	46.4
1998	45.9	45.8	46.0	46.7	48.5	50.2	50.0	50.1	49.3	48.6	48.0	48.4	48.1
1999	46.8	47.0	47.5	48.5	50.1	52.1	51.8	51.6	50.4	49.8	49.7	49.4	49.5
2000	48.2	48.2	48.8	49.9	51.1	53.2	52.9	52.4	51.7	50.6	49.9	50.1	50.5
2001	48.9	48.9	48.9	50.0	51.5	52.8	52.7	52.6	51.4	50.8	50.1	49.9	50.7
2002	48.7	48.6	48.7	49.6	51.4	53.2	53.5	53.5	51.7	51.5	50.9	50.7	51.0
2003	49.2	49.6	49.5	50.6	52.2	53.8	53.6	53.4	51.8	51.1	50.5	50.8	51.3
Total private													
1990	28.8	28.8	29.5	29.9	31.4	33.7	34.5	34.6	32.8	32.4	31.7	31.3	31.6
1991	30.0	29.9	30.3	30.9	32.3	34.1	35.1	35.3	33.9	32.9	32.0	32.1	32.4
1992	31.2	31.2	31.8	32.7	34.1	35.9	36.5	36.9	35.3	34.6	33.8	33.6	33.9
1993	32.0	32.4	32.7	34.0	35.3	37.2	38.1	38.7	36.5	36.0	35.4	35.4	35.3
1994	33.7	34.0	34.4	35.7	37.1	38.9	39.6	39.7	37.9	37.2	36.6	36.8	36.8
1995	35.7	36.0	36.5	36.9	37.8	39.6	40.1	40.1	39.0	38.1	37.5	37.9	37.9
1996	36.6	36.3	36.2	36.9	38.5	40.3	41.1	41.2	39.4	39.1	38.3	38.0	38.4
1997	36.7	36.7	37.1	37.5	39.9	41.4	42.5	42.4	40.6	39.1	38.6	38.7	39.2
1998	38.5	38.3	38.6	39.3	41.0	42.9	43.5	44.0	42.2	41.2	40.5	40.9	40.9
1999	39.5	39.5	40.0	41.0	42.6	44.7	45.2	45.3	43.3	42.3	42.2	41.9	42.2
2000	41.2	41.0	41.6	42.6	43.7	45.9	46.3	45.9	44.6	43.6	42.8	42.9	43.5
2001	41.9	41.7	42.1	43.1	44.5	45.8	46.4	46.4	44.6	43.6	43.1	42.9	43.8
2002	41.7	41.5	41.7	42.6	44.3	46.1	46.7	47.1	44.8	44.3	43.8	43.5	44.0
2003	42.2	42.2	42.3	43.3	44.9	46.6	46.7	46.8	44.7	43.8	43.3	43.5	44.2
Goods-producing													
1990	5.7	5.7	5.9	5.9	6.2	6.6	7.1	7.1	6.9	7.1	6.8	6.6	6.4
1991	6.0	6.1	6.1	6.2	6.4	6.5	6.6	6.8	6.6	6.6	6.3	6.2	6.3
1992	6.2	6.2	6.4	6.7	6.9	7.2	7.1	7.2	7.2	7.0	6.9	6.7	6.8
1993	6.2	6.3	6.3	6.6	7.1	7.2	7.4	7.4	7.1	7.1	7.0	6.8	6.8
1994	6.4	6.2	6.4	6.8	7.2	7.3	7.5	7.5	7.3	7.2	7.2	7.0	7.0
1995	6.8	6.8	6.9	7.0	7.0	7.2	7.2	7.2	7.1	7.3	7.1	7.1	7.0
1996	6.8	6.6	6.4	6.7	6.9	7.2	7.2	7.3	7.1	7.2	7.0	6.7	6.9
1997	6.4	6.5	6.6	6.9	7.4	7.5	7.9	7.9	7.8	7.7	7.6	7.4	7.3
1998	7.0	7.0	6.9	7.2	7.4	7.6	7.8	7.7	7.5	7.5	7.5	7.4	7.3
1999	7.0	7.0	7.1	7.5	7.7	7.9	8.0	7.9	7.6	7.7	7.7	7.6	7.5
2000	7.4	7.4	7.6	8.0	8.0	8.4	8.5	8.4	8.3	8.2	8.1	7.9	8.0
2001	7.5	7.4	7.5	7.8	8.0	8.3	8.3	8.2	8.0	7.8	7.7	7.5	7.8
2002	7.3	6.9	7.0	7.2	7.6	7.8	7.9	7.9	7.6	7.7	7.6	7.5	7.5
2003	7.2	7.1	7.2	7.5	7.9	7.9	7.7	7.6	7.3	7.4	7.3	7.2	7.4
Construction and mining													
1990	2.0	2.0	2.1	2.3	2.4	2.6	2.7	2.7	2.5	2.5	2.5	2.3	2.3
1991	1.9	2.0	2.0	2.1	2.3	2.4	2.5	2.7	2.6	2.5	2.3	2.2	2.2
1992	2.1	2.1	2.2	2.5	2.7	2.9	2.8	2.8	2.8	2.6	2.5	2.4	2.5
1993	2.0	2.1	2.1	2.4	2.8	2.9	3.0	3.0	2.9	2.9	2.8	2.6	2.6
1994	2.3	2.2	2.4	2.7	3.0	3.1	3.1	3.1	3.0	2.9	2.9	2.7	2.7
1995	2.6	2.6	2.6	2.7	2.8	3.1	3.1	3.1	3.0	3.1	2.9	2.8	2.8
1996	2.5	2.4	2.5	2.8	3.0	3.2	3.2	3.3	3.2	3.2	3.0	2.7	2.9
1997	2.5	2.5	2.6	2.7	3.2	3.3	3.4	3.4	3.4	3.3	3.2	3.0	3.0
1998	2.7	2.7	2.6	2.9	3.1	3.2	3.3	3.2	3.1	3.1	3.1	3.0	3.0
1999	2.6	2.6	2.7	3.1	3.3	3.5	3.7	3.6	3.4	3.4	3.4	3.2	3.2
2000	3.1	3.1	3.3	3.6	3.7	4.0	4.0	3.9	3.9	3.7	3.5	3.3	3.5
2001	3.1	3.1	3.1	3.5	3.8	4.0	4.1	4.1	4.0	3.8	3.7	3.5	3.6
2002	3.3	3.2	3.3	3.5	3.9	4.1	4.1	4.1	3.9	3.9	3.8	3.7	3.7
2003	3.4	3.3	3.4	3.7	4.1	4.3	4.2	4.1	3.9	3.9	3.8	3.7	3.8

Employment by Industry: South Dakota—*Continued*

(Numbers in thousands. Not seasonally adjusted.)

Industry	January	February	March	April	May	June	July	August	September	October	November	December	Annual Average
RAPID CITY—*Continued*													
Manufacturing													
1990	3.7	3.7	3.8	3.6	3.8	4.0	4.4	4.4	4.4	4.6	4.3	4.3	4.0
1991	4.1	4.1	4.1	4.1	4.1	4.1	4.1	4.1	4.0	4.1	4.0	4.0	4.0
1992	4.1	4.1	4.2	4.2	4.2	4.3	4.3	4.4	4.4	4.4	4.4	4.3	4.2
1993	4.2	4.2	4.2	4.2	4.3	4.3	4.4	4.4	4.2	4.2	4.2	4.2	4.2
1994	4.1	4.0	4.0	4.1	4.2	4.2	4.4	4.4	4.3	4.3	4.3	4.3	4.2
1995	4.2	4.2	4.3	4.3	4.2	4.1	4.1	4.1	4.1	4.2	4.2	4.3	4.1
1996	4.3	4.2	3.9	3.9	3.9	4.0	4.0	4.0	3.9	4.0	4.0	4.0	4.0
1997	3.9	4.0	4.0	4.2	4.2	4.2	4.5	4.5	4.4	4.4	4.4	4.4	4.2
1998	4.3	4.3	4.3	4.3	4.3	4.4	4.5	4.5	4.4	4.4	4.4	4.4	4.3
1999	4.4	4.4	4.4	4.4	4.4	4.4	4.3	4.3	4.2	4.3	4.3	4.4	4.3
2000	4.3	4.3	4.3	4.4	4.3	4.4	4.5	4.5	4.4	4.5	4.6	4.6	4.4
2001	4.4	4.3	4.4	4.3	4.2	4.3	4.2	4.1	4.0	4.0	4.0	4.0	4.1
2002	4.0	3.7	3.7	3.7	3.7	3.7	3.8	3.8	3.7	3.8	3.8	3.8	3.8
2003	3.8	3.8	3.8	3.8	3.8	3.6	3.5	3.5	3.4	3.5	3.5	3.5	3.6
Service-providing													
1990	30.3	30.3	30.9	31.4	32.7	34.5	34.1	34.0	33.0	32.6	32.3	31.9	32.3
1991	31.3	31.1	31.6	32.1	33.3	35.0	35.2	34.9	34.4	33.8	33.2	33.4	33.2
1992	32.5	32.6	32.9	33.5	34.7	36.0	36.1	36.2	34.9	34.8	34.0	34.0	34.3
1993	33.0	33.3	33.7	34.9	35.5	37.4	37.3	37.8	36.4	36.3	35.9	36.0	35.6
1994	34.6	35.3	35.5	36.5	37.4	39.1	38.7	38.8	37.6	37.5	37.0	37.3	37.1
1995	36.4	36.8	37.2	37.4	38.4	39.8	39.4	39.5	38.8	38.1	37.8	38.2	38.1
1996	37.1	37.0	37.1	37.5	39.1	40.4	40.3	40.6	39.4	39.2	38.7	38.6	38.7
1997	37.5	37.5	37.9	37.9	39.9	41.3	41.2	40.9	39.7	38.9	38.4	38.7	39.1
1998	38.9	38.8	39.1	39.5	41.1	42.6	42.2	42.4	41.8	41.1	40.5	41.0	40.7
1999	39.8	40.0	40.4	41.0	42.4	44.2	43.8	43.7	42.8	42.1	42.0	41.8	42.0
2000	40.8	40.8	41.2	41.9	43.1	44.8	44.4	44.0	43.4	42.4	41.8	42.2	42.5
2001	41.4	41.5	41.4	42.2	43.5	44.5	44.4	44.4	43.4	43.0	42.4	42.4	42.8
2002	41.4	41.7	41.7	42.4	43.8	45.4	45.6	45.6	44.1	43.8	43.3	43.2	43.5
2003	42.0	42.5	42.3	43.1	44.3	45.9	45.9	45.8	44.5	43.7	43.2	43.6	43.9
Trade, transportation, and utilities													
1990	8.5	8.4	8.5	8.8	9.0	9.6	9.4	9.4	9.1	9.0	9.1	9.1	8.9
1991	8.6	8.5	8.7	8.8	9.1	9.5	9.8	9.6	9.4	9.0	9.0	9.1	9.0
1992	8.9	8.8	8.8	9.1	9.3	9.8	10.0	9.9	9.7	9.5	9.4	9.4	9.3
1993	8.9	8.9	9.0	9.4	9.7	9.9	10.2	10.2	9.9	9.8	9.8	9.9	9.6
1994	9.4	9.4	9.4	9.9	10.0	10.5	10.5	10.5	10.2	10.2	10.3	10.4	10.0
1995	9.9	9.9	10.1	10.1	10.3	10.7	10.9	11.0	10.6	10.5	10.5	10.7	10.4
1996	10.1	10.0	10.1	10.1	10.4	10.6	10.9	10.9	10.6	10.5	10.6	10.6	10.4
1997	10.0	9.8	9.9	10.0	10.4	10.8	10.9	10.8	10.4	10.5	10.5	10.7	10.3
1998	10.2	10.1	10.1	10.3	10.8	10.9	10.9	11.1	10.6	10.6	10.7	10.8	10.5
1999	10.3	10.1	10.2	10.4	10.8	11.1	11.2	11.3	10.9	10.7	10.7	10.8	10.7
2000	10.4	10.1	10.3	10.4	10.7	11.0	11.0	10.9	10.7	10.8	10.8	10.9	10.6
2001	10.5	10.4	10.4	10.6	11.0	11.0	11.1	11.3	10.8	11.0	11.1	11.1	10.8
2002	10.5	10.5	10.5	10.7	11.0	11.3	11.2	11.6	11.1	11.1	11.2	11.1	11.0
2003	10.7	10.7	10.6	10.8	11.1	11.5	11.5	11.7	11.2	11.3	11.3	11.4	11.2
Wholesale trade													
1990	1.4	1.4	1.4	1.5	1.5	1.6	1.5	1.5	1.5	1.5	1.5	1.5	1.4
1991	1.4	1.4	1.5	1.5	1.5	1.6	1.6	1.6	1.5	1.5	1.5	1.5	1.5
1992	1.5	1.5	1.6	1.6	1.6	1.6	1.7	1.7	1.6	1.6	1.6	1.6	1.6
1993	1.6	1.6	1.6	1.7	1.7	1.7	1.8	1.8	1.7	1.7	1.7	1.7	1.6
1994	1.7	1.7	1.7	1.8	1.8	1.8	1.8	1.8	1.8	1.8	1.8	1.8	1.7
1995	1.8	1.9	1.9	1.9	1.9	2.0	2.0	2.0	1.9	2.0	1.9	2.0	1.9
1996	1.8	1.8	1.9	1.9	1.9	1.9	2.0	2.0	1.9	1.9	1.9	1.9	1.9
1997	1.8	1.8	1.8	1.9	1.9	1.9	1.9	1.9	1.9	1.9	1.9	1.9	1.8
1998	1.9	1.9	1.9	1.9	2.0	1.9	1.9	1.9	1.9	1.9	1.9	1.9	1.9
1999	1.9	1.8	1.9	1.9	1.9	1.9	1.9	1.9	1.9	1.8	1.8	1.8	1.8
2000	1.8	1.8	1.8	1.8	1.9	1.9	1.9	1.9	1.8	1.8	1.8	1.8	1.8
2001	1.8	1.8	1.8	1.9	1.9	1.9	1.9	1.9	1.8	1.9	1.9	1.8	1.8
2002	1.8	1.9	1.9	1.9	2.0	2.0	1.9	2.0	1.9	1.9	1.9	1.9	1.9
2003	1.9	1.9	1.9	1.9	1.9	2.0	2.0	2.1	2.0	2.1	2.0	2.0	2.0
Retail trade													
1990	5.8	5.7	5.7	5.9	6.1	6.5	6.5	6.5	6.2	6.1	6.2	6.2	6.1
1991	6.0	5.9	6.0	6.1	6.3	6.6	6.8	6.7	6.6	6.3	6.3	6.4	6.3
1992	6.1	6.0	6.0	6.2	6.4	6.8	6.9	6.9	6.7	6.5	6.5	6.5	6.4
1993	6.0	6.0	6.1	6.4	6.6	6.8	7.0	7.0	6.8	6.7	6.7	6.8	6.5
1994	6.4	6.4	6.4	6.7	6.8	7.2	7.3	7.3	7.0	7.0	7.1	7.2	6.9
1995	6.8	6.7	6.8	6.9	7.0	7.3	7.4	7.5	7.2	7.1	7.2	7.3	7.1
1996	7.0	6.9	6.9	6.9	7.1	7.3	7.5	7.5	7.3	7.2	7.3	7.3	7.1
1997	6.9	6.7	6.8	6.8	7.1	7.6	7.7	7.7	7.3	7.2	7.3	7.5	7.2
1998	7.0	6.9	6.9	7.1	7.4	7.6	7.6	7.8	7.3	7.3	7.4	7.5	7.3
1999	7.0	6.9	7.0	7.1	7.5	7.8	7.9	8.0	7.6	7.5	7.5	7.6	7.4
2000	7.2	7.0	7.1	7.2	7.4	7.7	7.7	7.6	7.4	7.5	7.6	7.6	7.4
2001	7.2	7.1	7.1	7.2	7.5	7.6	7.7	7.8	7.5	7.6	7.7	7.8	7.4
2002	7.3	7.2	7.2	7.4	7.5	7.7	7.7	8.0	7.6	7.7	7.8	7.8	7.6
2003	7.4	7.4	7.3	7.5	7.7	8.0	8.0	8.1	7.7	7.7	7.9	8.0	7.7

Employment by Industry: South Dakota—*Continued*

(Numbers in thousands. Not seasonally adjusted.)

Industry	January	February	March	April	May	June	July	August	September	October	November	December	Annual Average
RAPID CITY—*Continued*													
Transportation and utilities													
1990	1.3	1.3	1.4	1.4	1.4	1.5	1.4	1.4	1.4	1.4	1.4	1.4	1.3
1991	1.2	1.2	1.2	1.2	1.3	1.3	1.4	1.3	1.3	1.2	1.2	1.2	1.2
1992	1.3	1.3	1.2	1.3	1.3	1.4	1.4	1.3	1.4	1.4	1.3	1.3	1.3
1993	1.3	1.3	1.3	1.3	1.4	1.4	1.4	1.4	1.4	1.4	1.4	1.4	1.3
1994	1.3	1.3	1.3	1.4	1.4	1.5	1.4	1.4	1.4	1.4	1.4	1.4	1.3
1995	1.3	1.3	1.4	1.3	1.4	1.4	1.5	1.5	1.5	1.4	1.4	1.4	1.4
1996	1.3	1.3	1.3	1.3	1.4	1.4	1.4	1.4	1.4	1.4	1.4	1.4	1.3
1997	1.3	1.3	1.3	1.3	1.4	1.3	1.3	1.2	1.2	1.4	1.3	1.3	1.3
1998	1.3	1.3	1.3	1.3	1.4	1.4	1.4	1.4	1.4	1.4	1.4	1.4	1.3
1999	1.4	1.4	1.3	1.4	1.4	1.4	1.4	1.4	1.4	1.4	1.4	1.4	1.3
2000	1.4	1.3	1.4	1.4	1.4	1.4	1.4	1.4	1.5	1.5	1.4	1.5	1.4
2001	1.5	1.5	1.5	1.5	1.6	1.5	1.5	1.6	1.5	1.5	1.5	1.5	1.5
2002	1.4	1.4	1.4	1.4	1.5	1.6	1.6	1.6	1.6	1.5	1.5	1.4	1.5
2003	1.4	1.4	1.4	1.4	1.5	1.5	1.5	1.5	1.5	1.5	1.4	1.4	1.5
Information													
1990	0.8	0.8	0.8	0.8	0.8	0.8	0.8	0.8	0.7	0.8	0.8	0.8	0.7
1991	0.7	0.7	0.7	0.7	0.7	0.7	0.7	0.7	0.7	0.7	0.7	0.7	0.7
1992	0.7	0.7	0.7	0.7	0.7	0.7	0.7	0.7	0.7	0.7	0.7	0.7	0.7
1993	0.7	0.7	0.7	0.7	0.7	0.7	0.7	0.7	0.7	0.7	0.7	0.7	0.7
1994	0.7	0.8	0.8	0.7	0.7	0.8	0.8	0.8	0.8	0.8	0.8	0.8	0.7
1995	0.8	0.8	0.8	0.8	0.8	0.9	0.8	0.8	0.8	0.8	0.8	0.8	0.8
1996	0.8	0.8	0.8	0.8	0.8	0.8	0.8	0.8	0.8	0.8	0.8	0.8	0.8
1997	0.8	0.8	0.8	0.8	0.8	0.8	0.8	0.8	0.8	0.8	0.8	0.8	0.8
1998	0.8	0.8	0.8	0.8	0.8	0.8	0.8	0.8	0.8	0.8	0.8	0.8	0.8
1999	0.8	0.8	0.8	0.8	0.9	0.9	0.9	0.9	0.9	0.8	0.8	0.9	0.8
2000	0.9	0.9	0.9	1.0	1.0	0.9	0.9	0.9	0.9	0.9	0.9	1.0	0.9
2001	1.0	1.0	1.0	1.0	1.0	1.0	1.0	1.0	1.0	1.0	1.0	1.0	0.9
2002	1.0	1.0	1.0	1.0	1.0	1.0	1.1	1.1	1.0	1.2	1.2	1.2	1.1
2003	1.1	1.1	1.1	1.1	1.1	1.1	1.0	1.0	1.0	1.0	1.1	1.1	1.1
Financial activities													
1990	1.7	1.7	1.8	1.7	1.7	1.8	1.8	1.8	1.8	1.7	1.7	1.7	1.7
1991	1.7	1.7	1.7	1.7	1.8	1.9	1.8	1.8	1.8	1.8	1.8	1.9	1.7
1992	1.8	1.8	1.8	1.8	1.8	1.9	1.9	1.9	1.8	1.8	1.8	1.8	1.8
1993	1.8	1.8	1.8	1.9	1.9	1.9	1.9	2.0	1.9	1.9	1.9	1.9	1.8
1994	1.8	1.9	1.9	1.9	1.9	1.9	2.0	2.0	2.0	1.9	1.9	2.0	1.9
1995	1.8	1.9	1.9	1.9	1.9	2.0	2.0	2.0	2.0	1.9	1.9	2.0	1.9
1996	1.9	1.9	1.9	1.9	1.9	2.0	2.1	2.1	2.0	2.0	2.0	2.0	1.9
1997	2.0	2.0	2.0	2.0	2.1	2.1	2.2	2.2	2.2	2.1	2.1	2.1	2.0
1998	2.9	2.9	3.0	2.9	3.0	3.1	3.1	3.2	3.2	3.1	3.1	3.2	3.0
1999	3.2	3.2	3.2	3.2	3.2	3.4	3.4	3.4	3.3	3.4	3.4	3.4	3.3
2000	3.4	3.4	3.4	3.4	3.5	3.6	3.5	3.5	3.4	3.4	3.4	3.4	3.4
2001	3.4	3.4	3.4	3.4	3.4	3.4	3.4	3.4	3.4	3.3	3.3	3.3	3.3
2002	3.3	3.2	3.2	3.1	3.1	3.2	3.1	3.1	3.1	3.1	3.2	3.1	3.2
2003	3.0	3.0	3.0	3.0	3.0	3.0	2.8	2.8	2.8	2.8	2.8	2.8	2.9
Professional and business services													
1990	2.2	2.2	2.3	2.3	2.4	2.5	2.4	2.5	2.3	2.4	2.4	2.4	2.3
1991	2.2	2.2	2.2	2.3	2.3	2.4	2.5	2.5	2.4	2.5	2.5	2.5	2.3
1992	2.5	2.6	2.7	2.8	2.7	2.8	2.8	3.0	2.9	3.0	3.0	3.0	2.8
1993	2.9	3.1	3.0	2.9	2.9	3.0	3.0	3.2	3.0	3.0	3.1	3.1	3.0
1994	3.0	3.1	3.1	3.2	3.2	3.2	3.3	3.4	3.4	3.4	3.3	3.4	3.2
1995	3.3	3.3	3.3	3.2	3.2	3.3	3.3	3.3	3.2	3.2	3.2	3.3	3.2
1996	3.2	3.2	3.2	3.2	3.3	3.4	3.5	3.6	3.5	3.8	3.6	3.5	3.4
1997	3.4	3.4	3.3	3.3	3.3	3.4	3.3	3.3	3.2	3.1	3.1	3.1	3.2
1998	3.0	3.0	3.1	3.1	3.2	3.3	3.5	3.6	3.4	3.6	3.5	3.5	3.3
1999	3.5	3.4	3.4	3.6	3.7	3.8	3.8	3.8	3.8	3.7	3.8	3.8	3.6
2000	3.7	3.8	3.7	3.8	3.8	3.9	3.8	3.8	3.8	3.7	3.7	3.8	3.7
2001	3.7	3.8	3.8	3.8	3.8	3.8	4.0	4.0	3.8	3.8	3.8	3.7	3.8
2002	3.7	3.8	3.8	3.8	3.8	3.9	3.9	4.0	3.8	3.9	3.8	3.8	3.8
2003	3.8	3.8	3.7	3.7	3.7	3.8	3.8	3.8	3.7	3.7	3.8	3.8	3.8
Educational and health services													
1990	4.0	4.1	4.0	4.0	4.1	4.1	4.2	4.1	4.1	4.3	4.3	4.3	4.1
1991	4.7	4.6	4.6	4.7	4.7	4.7	4.9	4.9	5.0	5.0	5.0	5.0	4.8
1992	4.8	4.8	4.9	4.9	5.1	5.0	5.1	5.2	5.1	5.1	5.2	5.2	5.0
1993	5.1	5.1	5.2	5.3	5.3	5.4	5.4	5.5	5.5	5.6	5.5	5.6	5.3
1994	5.5	5.6	5.6	5.6	5.7	5.6	5.7	5.6	5.7	5.7	5.8	5.8	5.6
1995	5.8	5.9	5.9	6.0	5.9	5.9	5.9	5.9	6.0	6.1	6.1	6.1	5.9
1996	6.1	6.1	6.1	6.2	6.2	6.1	6.1	6.2	6.2	6.3	6.3	6.4	6.1
1997	6.4	6.5	6.5	6.4	6.6	6.5	6.6	6.6	6.6	6.5	6.6	6.7	6.5
1998	6.8	6.7	6.8	6.8	6.7	6.8	6.8	6.9	6.9	6.9	6.9	7.0	6.8
1999	7.0	7.1	7.2	7.1	7.1	7.1	7.1	7.1	7.1	7.1	7.3	7.2	7.1
2000	7.3	7.3	7.4	7.3	7.4	7.4	7.5	7.4	7.6	7.6	7.5	7.6	7.4
2001	7.6	7.5	7.6	7.7	7.7	7.7	7.7	7.7	7.7	7.8	7.8	7.9	7.7
2002	7.8	7.9	7.9	7.9	8.0	7.9	7.9	8.0	8.0	8.1	8.1	8.1	8.0
2003	8.1	8.2	8.2	8.2	8.2	8.2	8.2	8.2	8.2	8.1	8.2	8.3	8.2

Employment by Industry: South Dakota—*Continued*

(Numbers in thousands. Not seasonally adjusted.)

Industry	January	February	March	April	May	June	July	August	September	October	November	December	Annual Average
RAPID CITY—*Continued*													
Leisure and hospitality													
1990	4.1	4.1	4.4	4.6	5.4	6.4	6.8	7.0	6.2	5.2	4.7	4.6	5.2
1991	4.3	4.3	4.5	4.7	5.5	6.5	6.8	7.0	5.9	5.3	4.8	4.8	5.3
1992	4.6	4.6	4.7	4.9	5.8	6.6	6.9	7.1	6.1	5.6	4.9	4.8	5.5
1993	4.6	4.7	4.8	5.2	5.8	7.0	7.5	7.6	6.4	5.9	5.4	5.3	5.8
1994	4.8	4.8	5.1	5.4	6.1	7.3	7.5	7.7	6.3	5.8	5.3	5.3	5.9
1995	5.1	5.2	5.4	5.6	6.4	7.4	7.8	7.7	7.0	6.1	5.8	5.7	6.2
1996	5.5	5.5	5.5	5.8	6.7	8.0	8.4	8.2	7.2	6.3	5.8	5.8	6.5
1997	5.5	5.5	5.8	5.9	6.9	8.0	8.4	8.5	7.2	6.2	5.7	5.6	6.6
1998	5.5	5.5	5.6	5.9	6.8	8.0	8.2	8.3	7.4	6.4	5.7	5.8	6.5
1999	5.3	5.4	5.5	6.0	6.8	8.0	8.3	8.4	7.3	6.4	5.9	5.8	6.5
2000	5.6	5.6	5.8	6.1	6.9	8.1	8.5	8.5	7.4	6.5	6.1	5.9	6.7
2001	5.8	5.8	6.0	6.3	7.1	8.1	8.4	8.3	7.4	6.4	5.9	5.9	6.7
2002	5.6	5.7	5.8	6.4	7.3	8.4	9.0	8.9	7.7	6.8	6.3	6.3	7.0
2003	5.9	5.9	6.1	6.5	7.4	8.5	9.0	9.0	7.8	6.9	6.3	6.3	7.1
Other services													
1990	1.8	1.8	1.8	1.8	1.8	1.9	2.0	1.9	1.7	1.9	1.9	1.8	1.8
1991	1.8	1.8	1.8	1.8	1.8	1.9	2.0	2.0	2.1	2.0	1.9	1.9	1.9
1992	1.7	1.7	1.8	1.8	1.8	1.9	2.0	1.9	1.8	1.9	1.9	2.0	1.8
1993	1.8	1.8	1.9	2.0	1.9	2.1	2.0	2.1	2.0	2.0	2.0	2.1	1.9
1994	2.1	2.2	2.1	2.2	2.3	2.3	2.3	2.2	2.2	2.2	2.0	2.1	2.1
1995	2.2	2.2	2.2	2.3	2.3	2.2	2.2	2.2	2.3	2.2	2.1	2.2	2.2
1996	2.2	2.2	2.2	2.2	2.3	2.2	2.1	2.1	2.0	2.2	2.2	2.2	2.1
1997	2.2	2.2	2.2	2.2	2.4	2.3	2.4	2.3	2.4	2.2	2.2	2.3	2.2
1998	2.3	2.3	2.3	2.3	2.3	2.4	2.4	2.4	2.4	2.3	2.3	2.4	2.3
1999	2.4	2.5	2.6	2.4	2.4	2.5	2.5	2.5	2.4	2.5	2.6	2.4	2.4
2000	2.5	2.5	2.5	2.6	2.4	2.6	2.6	2.5	2.5	2.5	2.3	2.4	2.4
2001	2.4	2.4	2.4	2.5	2.5	2.5	2.5	2.5	2.5	2.5	2.5	2.5	2.4
2002	2.5	2.5	2.5	2.5	2.5	2.6	2.6	2.5	2.5	2.4	2.4	2.4	2.5
2003	2.4	2.4	2.4	2.5	2.5	2.6	2.7	2.7	2.7	2.6	2.5	2.6	2.6
Government													
1990	7.2	7.2	7.3	7.4	7.5	7.4	6.7	6.5	7.1	7.3	7.4	7.2	7.1
1991	7.3	7.3	7.4	7.4	7.4	7.4	6.7	6.4	7.1	7.5	7.5	7.5	7.2
1992	7.5	7.6	7.5	7.5	7.5	7.3	6.7	6.5	6.8	7.2	7.1	7.1	7.1
1993	7.2	7.2	7.3	7.5	7.3	7.4	6.6	6.5	7.0	7.4	7.5	7.4	7.1
1994	7.3	7.5	7.5	7.6	7.5	7.5	6.6	6.6	7.0	7.5	7.6	7.5	7.3
1995	7.5	7.6	7.6	7.5	7.6	7.4	6.5	6.6	6.9	7.3	7.4	7.4	7.2
1996	7.3	7.3	7.3	7.3	7.5	7.3	6.4	6.7	7.1	7.3	7.4	7.3	7.1
1997	7.2	7.3	7.4	7.3	7.4	7.4	6.6	6.4	6.9	7.5	7.4	7.4	7.1
1998	7.4	7.5	7.4	7.4	7.5	7.3	6.5	6.1	7.1	7.4	7.5	7.5	7.2
1999	7.3	7.5	7.5	7.5	7.5	7.4	6.6	6.3	7.1	7.5	7.5	7.5	7.2
2000	7.0	7.2	7.2	7.3	7.4	7.3	6.6	6.5	7.1	7.0	7.1	7.2	7.0
2001	7.0	7.2	6.8	6.9	7.0	7.0	6.3	6.2	6.8	7.2	7.0	7.0	6.8
2002	7.0	7.1	7.0	7.0	7.1	7.1	6.8	6.4	6.9	7.2	7.1	7.2	7.0
2003	7.0	7.4	7.2	7.3	7.3	7.2	6.9	6.6	7.1	7.3	7.2	7.3	7.2
SIOUX FALLS													
Total nonfarm													
1990	76.1	76.3	77.2	78.3	79.3	80.9	80.0	80.2	80.3	80.8	81.1	80.9	79.3
1991	79.5	79.8	80.5	81.6	82.7	83.8	83.1	83.4	83.7	84.1	84.3	84.8	82.6
1992	83.3	83.3	83.8	85.5	86.5	87.9	86.6	87.3	87.0	86.9	87.2	87.1	86.0
1993	85.7	85.8	86.5	87.8	88.7	90.1	89.1	89.5	89.4	90.7	90.8	90.9	88.8
1994	89.2	89.3	90.1	91.1	92.3	94.4	93.3	93.0	93.1	93.8	93.8	94.6	92.3
1995	92.8	92.8	93.8	94.4	95.7	98.4	97.0	97.5	96.9	97.0	97.9	97.8	96.0
1996	96.5	96.3	97.2	98.0	99.1	100.5	99.2	100.3	99.6	100.5	99.8	99.7	98.9
1997	98.4	98.5	99.3	100.8	102.9	104.7	102.9	103.0	103.5	103.4	103.9	104.2	102.1
1998	101.8	102.1	102.7	105.1	106.6	108.3	107.1	107.6	107.6	108.1	108.0	109.5	106.2
1999	107.2	107.1	108.1	110.4	111.7	113.2	113.3	112.5	112.9	113.8	114.2	115.0	111.6
2000	111.6	111.6	113.2	114.4	115.4	117.0	115.0	115.0	114.9	115.1	115.5	115.8	114.5
2001	113.6	113.1	113.4	114.6	116.0	117.3	116.1	115.8	115.6	115.7	116.1	115.6	115.2
2002	113.1	112.9	113.3	115.4	117.1	118.7	117.4	117.1	117.2	117.8	117.1	117.7	116.2
2003	114.8	114.4	114.9	116.6	118.4	119.6	118.0	117.8	117.6	118.7	118.9	117.7	117.3
Total private													
1990	67.6	67.8	68.7	69.5	70.5	71.7	72.1	72.5	71.7	72.2	72.5	72.3	70.8
1991	70.8	71.2	71.8	72.8	73.8	74.5	75.1	75.4	74.9	75.2	75.2	75.8	73.9
1992	74.2	74.3	74.7	76.2	77.2	78.3	78.3	79.0	77.9	77.8	78.0	78.0	77.0
1993	76.5	76.5	77.3	78.4	79.2	80.3	80.7	81.0	80.1	81.2	81.4	81.4	79.5
1994	79.7	79.8	80.6	81.5	82.6	84.2	84.5	84.3	83.5	84.2	84.2	84.8	82.8
1995	83.3	83.3	84.3	84.8	86.1	88.3	88.4	88.8	87.4	87.5	88.4	88.3	86.6
1996	86.9	86.7	87.6	88.3	89.3	90.3	90.5	91.6	89.9	90.8	90.1	90.0	89.3
1997	88.8	88.9	89.6	91.0	93.0	94.4	94.1	94.2	93.9	93.7	94.1	94.4	92.5
1998	92.1	92.3	92.8	95.1	96.5	97.8	98.1	98.6	97.8	98.0	98.0	99.5	96.4
1999	97.2	97.1	98.0	100.2	101.4	102.6	103.6	103.1	102.8	103.7	104.0	104.7	101.5
2000	101.8	101.7	103.1	104.2	105.0	106.3	105.3	105.4	104.9	104.9	105.3	105.6	104.5
2001	103.6	103.1	103.3	104.6	105.9	106.5	106.3	106.3	105.4	105.5	105.9	105.4	105.1
2002	102.9	102.7	103.1	105.1	106.7	107.7	107.7	107.4	106.9	107.4	106.7	107.2	106.0
2003	104.4	103.9	104.3	106.0	107.5	108.3	108.1	107.9	107.1	108.2	108.4	107.2	106.8

Employment by Industry: South Dakota—*Continued*

(Numbers in thousands. Not seasonally adjusted.)

Industry	January	February	March	April	May	June	July	August	September	October	November	December	Annual Average
SIOUX FALLS—*Continued*													
Goods-producing													
1990	12.6	12.6	12.8	13.5	13.9	14.3	14.4	14.3	13.9	13.9	13.6	13.2	13.6
1991	12.8	12.9	13.1	13.6	14.0	14.6	14.9	15.0	14.4	14.5	14.2	14.0	14.0
1992	13.9	13.9	14.1	14.7	15.1	15.4	15.4	15.3	15.0	15.0	14.7	14.6	14.8
1993	14.2	14.3	14.5	14.9	15.3	15.9	15.9	15.9	15.7	16.0	15.8	15.5	15.3
1994	15.3	15.3	15.6	16.0	16.5	17.1	17.3	17.3	17.0	17.1	16.9	16.9	16.5
1995	16.4	16.4	16.5	16.7	17.1	18.1	18.3	18.2	17.7	17.6	17.8	17.4	17.4
1996	16.8	16.7	16.9	17.2	17.7	18.1	18.2	18.2	17.9	17.8	17.5	17.1	17.5
1997	16.6	16.6	17.0	17.3	18.1	18.5	18.7	18.8	18.4	18.4	17.9	17.9	17.9
1998	17.4	17.3	17.6	18.0	18.6	19.2	19.5	19.5	19.0	18.6	18.4	18.6	18.5
1999	18.1	18.0	18.2	18.8	19.3	19.6	20.0	20.0	19.6	19.8	19.5	19.1	19.2
2000	18.4	18.3	18.4	18.9	18.9	19.6	19.9	19.9	19.4	19.4	18.7	18.4	19.0
2001	18.2	17.7	17.7	18.1	18.7	19.2	19.3	19.2	18.7	18.6	18.3	18.0	18.4
2002	17.4	17.3	17.3	18.2	18.9	19.2	19.7	19.4	18.7	18.6	18.2	17.9	18.4
2003	17.3	17.1	17.2	18.0	18.4	19.0	19.2	19.3	18.7	18.7	18.8	17.8	18.3
Construction and mining													
1990	2.9	2.8	3.0	3.4	3.7	4.0	4.1	4.1	3.8	3.8	3.5	3.2	3.5
1991	2.8	2.8	2.9	3.2	3.6	3.9	4.1	4.1	3.8	3.7	3.5	3.4	3.5
1992	3.2	3.3	3.4	3.8	4.1	4.4	4.4	4.3	4.1	4.0	3.8	3.6	3.9
1993	3.2	3.2	3.3	3.6	4.1	4.5	4.6	4.6	4.5	4.5	4.3	3.9	4.0
1994	3.6	3.6	3.8	4.2	4.6	5.0	5.1	5.1	4.8	4.7	4.5	4.3	4.4
1995	3.9	3.9	4.0	4.1	4.4	5.0	5.1	5.1	4.8	4.7	4.5	4.2	4.5
1996	3.8	3.7	3.8	4.2	4.7	5.1	5.2	5.3	5.0	4.9	4.6	4.2	4.5
1997	3.8	3.8	4.0	4.3	5.0	5.4	5.5	5.5	5.3	5.2	4.9	4.7	4.8
1998	4.3	4.3	4.4	4.9	5.5	5.9	6.0	5.9	5.6	5.4	5.1	5.1	5.2
1999	4.7	4.6	4.8	5.3	5.8	6.2	6.3	6.2	6.0	5.9	5.8	5.6	5.6
2000	5.2	5.1	5.5	5.9	6.3	6.8	6.9	6.9	6.7	6.5	6.0	5.8	6.1
2001	5.3	5.2	5.4	5.9	6.5	6.9	7.1	7.1	6.8	6.7	6.4	6.1	6.2
2002	5.5	5.4	5.5	6.0	6.7	7.0	7.2	7.1	6.7	6.5	6.3	6.1	6.3
2003	5.5	5.4	5.5	6.2	6.7	7.1	7.2	7.3	7.0	6.9	6.7	5.8	6.4
Manufacturing													
1990	9.7	9.8	9.8	10.1	10.2	10.3	10.3	10.2	10.1	10.1	10.1	10.0	10.1
1991	10.0	10.1	10.2	10.4	10.4	10.7	10.8	10.9	10.6	10.8	10.7	10.6	10.5
1992	10.7	10.6	10.7	10.9	11.0	11.0	11.0	11.0	10.9	11.0	10.9	11.0	10.9
1993	11.0	11.1	11.2	11.3	11.2	11.4	11.3	11.3	11.2	11.5	11.5	11.6	11.3
1994	11.7	11.7	11.8	11.8	11.9	12.1	12.2	12.2	12.2	12.4	12.4	12.6	12.1
1995	12.5	12.5	12.5	12.6	12.7	13.1	13.2	13.1	12.9	12.9	13.3	13.2	12.9
1996	13.0	13.0	13.1	13.0	13.0	13.0	13.0	12.9	12.9	12.9	12.9	12.9	13.0
1997	12.8	12.8	13.0	13.0	13.1	13.1	13.2	13.3	13.1	13.2	13.0	13.2	13.1
1998	13.1	13.0	13.2	13.1	13.1	13.3	13.5	13.6	13.4	13.2	13.3	13.5	13.3
1999	13.4	13.4	13.4	13.5	13.5	13.4	13.7	13.8	13.6	13.9	13.7	13.5	13.6
2000	13.2	13.2	12.9	13.0	12.6	12.8	13.0	13.0	12.7	12.9	12.7	12.6	12.9
2001	12.9	12.5	12.3	12.2	12.2	12.3	12.2	12.1	11.9	11.9	11.9	11.9	12.1
2002	11.9	11.9	11.8	12.2	12.2	12.2	12.5	12.3	12.0	12.1	11.9	11.8	12.1
2003	11.8	11.7	11.7	11.8	11.7	11.9	12.0	12.0	11.7	11.8	12.1	12.0	11.9
Service-providing													
1990	63.5	63.7	64.4	64.8	65.4	66.6	65.6	65.9	66.4	66.9	67.5	67.7	65.7
1991	66.7	66.9	67.4	68.0	68.7	69.2	68.2	68.4	69.3	69.6	70.1	70.8	68.6
1992	69.4	69.4	69.7	70.8	71.4	72.5	71.2	72.0	72.0	71.9	72.5	72.5	71.3
1993	71.5	71.5	72.0	72.9	73.4	74.2	73.2	73.6	73.7	74.7	75.0	75.4	73.4
1994	73.9	74.0	74.5	75.1	75.8	77.3	76.0	75.7	76.1	76.7	76.9	77.7	75.8
1995	76.4	76.4	77.3	77.7	78.6	80.3	78.7	79.3	79.2	79.4	80.1	80.4	78.7
1996	79.7	79.6	80.3	80.8	81.4	82.4	81.0	82.1	81.7	82.7	82.3	82.6	81.4
1997	81.8	81.9	82.3	83.5	84.8	86.2	84.2	84.2	85.1	85.0	86.0	86.3	84.3
1998	84.4	84.8	85.1	87.1	88.0	89.1	87.6	88.1	88.6	89.5	89.6	90.9	87.7
1999	89.1	89.1	89.9	91.6	92.4	93.6	93.3	92.5	93.3	94.0	94.7	95.9	92.5
2000	93.2	93.3	94.8	95.5	96.5	97.4	95.1	95.1	95.5	95.7	96.8	97.4	95.5
2001	95.4	95.4	95.7	96.5	97.3	98.1	96.8	96.6	96.9	97.1	97.8	97.6	96.7
2002	95.7	95.6	96.0	97.2	98.2	99.5	97.7	97.7	98.5	99.2	98.9	99.8	97.8
2003	97.5	97.3	97.7	98.6	100.0	100.6	98.8	98.5	98.9	100.0	100.1	99.9	99.0
Trade, transportation, and utilities													
1990	18.8	18.6	18.8	19.1	19.1	19.4	19.8	19.9	19.9	20.4	20.8	20.9	19.6
1991	20.2	19.9	19.9	20.2	20.4	20.5	20.4	20.3	20.4	20.7	21.0	21.4	20.4
1992	20.8	20.6	20.6	21.0	21.1	21.4	21.4	21.8	21.3	21.3	21.6	21.8	21.2
1993	21.3	21.2	21.3	21.6	21.8	21.9	22.1	22.2	21.8	22.2	22.7	22.9	21.9
1994	21.9	21.8	22.0	22.3	22.6	22.6	23.1	22.6	22.6	23.0	23.4	23.7	22.6
1995	22.7	22.5	22.7	22.7	23.0	23.1	23.2	23.3	22.8	23.1	23.6	23.9	23.1
1996	22.9	22.7	22.6	22.7	22.8	22.7	23.0	23.6	23.0	23.4	23.6	23.9	23.1
1997	23.1	22.7	22.8	23.0	23.6	23.5	23.3	23.0	23.3	23.4	23.9	24.1	23.3
1998	23.3	23.0	23.1	23.4	23.8	23.9	23.7	23.8	23.8	24.0	24.3	24.8	23.7
1999	23.6	23.6	23.7	24.2	24.3	24.5	24.7	24.6	24.5	25.0	25.4	25.7	24.5
2000	24.7	24.4	24.5	25.3	25.4	25.3	25.2	25.2	25.2	25.5	26.0	26.4	25.3
2001	25.2	25.3	25.3	25.3	25.4	25.5	25.2	25.2	25.0	25.3	26.0	26.0	25.3
2002	25.1	24.6	24.7	25.1	25.3	25.6	25.5	25.3	25.8	26.2	26.5	26.7	25.5
2003	25.5	25.1	25.2	25.8	25.7	25.7	25.5	25.7	25.3	25.8	26.2	26.3	25.7

Employment by Industry: South Dakota—*Continued*

(Numbers in thousands. Not seasonally adjusted.)

Industry	January	February	March	April	May	June	July	August	September	October	November	December	Annual Average
SIOUX FALLS—*Continued*													
Wholesale trade													
1990	4.4	4.4	4.5	4.6	4.5	4.6	4.7	4.7	4.7	4.6	4.6	4.6	4.6
1991	4.7	4.7	4.7	4.7	4.8	4.8	4.9	4.8	4.8	4.8	4.8	4.9	4.8
1992	4.8	4.9	4.9	5.0	5.0	5.2	5.2	5.6	5.2	5.1	5.1	5.1	5.1
1993	5.1	5.1	5.2	5.3	5.3	5.4	5.5	5.6	5.3	5.3	5.3	5.3	5.3
1994	5.2	5.2	5.3	5.4	5.5	5.5	6.0	5.4	5.4	5.3	5.4	5.4	5.4
1995	5.3	5.3	5.4	5.4	5.5	5.4	5.4	5.6	5.2	5.2	5.2	5.3	5.4
1996	5.2	5.2	5.3	5.3	5.3	5.3	5.4	5.9	5.3	5.3	5.3	5.3	5.3
1997	5.3	5.3	5.4	5.5	5.6	5.6	5.5	5.6	5.5	5.4	5.4	5.4	5.5
1998	5.5	5.5	5.5	5.6	5.7	5.7	5.7	5.7	5.7	5.6	5.6	5.6	5.6
1999	5.5	5.6	5.6	5.7	5.8	5.8	5.9	5.8	5.8	5.8	5.8	5.7	5.7
2000	5.7	5.7	5.7	5.8	5.8	5.8	5.8	5.8	5.8	5.8	5.8	5.8	5.8
2001	5.7	5.8	5.8	5.9	5.9	5.9	5.8	5.8	5.7	5.8	5.8	5.7	5.7
2002	5.8	5.8	5.7	5.8	5.8	5.9	5.9	5.8	5.8	5.8	5.8	5.8	5.8
2003	5.7	5.7	5.8	5.9	5.9	5.8	5.8	5.8	5.8	5.8	5.8	5.8	5.8
Retail trade													
1990	11.2	11.0	11.1	11.3	11.4	11.6	11.8	11.9	11.9	12.5	12.8	12.9	11.8
1991	12.1	11.8	11.8	12.1	12.2	12.2	12.0	12.0	12.1	12.3	12.6	12.8	12.2
1992	12.1	11.8	11.8	12.0	12.1	12.2	12.2	12.2	12.1	12.3	12.6	12.8	12.2
1993	12.2	12.1	12.1	12.2	12.4	12.5	12.5	12.5	12.4	12.7	13.2	13.4	12.5
1994	12.6	12.5	12.5	12.7	12.9	13.0	12.9	13.0	13.0	13.4	13.7	14.0	13.0
1995	13.3	13.1	13.1	13.0	13.2	13.4	13.5	13.5	13.3	13.5	14.0	14.2	13.4
1996	13.5	13.3	13.1	13.0	13.1	13.1	13.3	13.4	13.4	13.6	13.8	14.1	13.4
1997	13.4	13.0	13.0	13.0	13.4	13.4	13.4	13.4	13.3	13.5	14.1	14.2	13.4
1998	13.5	13.2	13.2	13.5	13.8	13.9	13.6	13.7	13.6	13.9	14.2	14.7	13.7
1999	13.7	13.6	13.7	14.0	14.1	14.3	14.4	14.4	14.4	14.8	15.2	15.5	14.3
2000	14.6	14.4	14.5	15.1	15.2	15.2	15.1	15.1	15.0	15.3	15.8	16.1	15.1
2001	15.2	15.2	15.2	15.1	15.2	15.3	15.2	15.2	15.0	15.1	15.8	15.9	15.2
2002	15.0	14.6	14.7	15.0	15.2	15.4	15.3	15.3	15.7	16.0	16.4	16.5	15.4
2003	15.5	15.1	15.1	15.6	15.5	15.5	15.4	15.5	15.3	15.8	16.2	16.3	15.6
Transportation and utilities													
1990	3.2	3.2	3.2	3.2	3.2	3.2	3.3	3.3	3.3	3.3	3.4	3.4	3.3
1991	3.4	3.4	3.4	3.4	3.4	3.5	3.5	3.5	3.5	3.6	3.6	3.7	3.5
1992	3.9	3.9	3.9	4.0	4.0	4.0	4.0	4.0	4.0	3.9	3.9	3.9	4.0
1993	4.0	4.0	4.0	4.1	4.1	4.0	4.1	4.1	4.1	4.2	4.2	4.2	4.1
1994	4.1	4.1	4.2	4.2	4.2	4.1	4.2	4.2	4.2	4.3	4.3	4.3	4.2
1995	4.1	4.1	4.2	4.3	4.3	4.3	4.3	4.2	4.3	4.4	4.4	4.4	4.3
1996	4.2	4.2	4.2	4.4	4.4	4.3	4.3	4.3	4.3	4.5	4.5	4.5	4.3
1997	4.4	4.4	4.4	4.5	4.6	4.5	4.4	4.0	4.5	4.5	4.4	4.5	4.4
1998	4.3	4.3	4.4	4.3	4.3	4.3	4.4	4.4	4.5	4.5	4.5	4.5	4.4
1999	4.4	4.4	4.4	4.5	4.4	4.4	4.4	4.4	4.3	4.4	4.4	4.5	4.4
2000	4.4	4.3	4.3	4.4	4.4	4.3	4.3	4.3	4.4	4.4	4.4	4.5	4.4
2001	4.3	4.3	4.3	4.3	4.3	4.3	4.2	4.2	4.3	4.4	4.4	4.4	4.3
2002	4.3	4.2	4.3	4.3	4.3	4.3	4.3	4.2	4.3	4.4	4.3	4.4	4.3
2003	4.3	4.3	4.3	4.3	4.3	4.4	4.3	4.4	4.2	4.2	4.2	4.2	4.3
Information													
1990	2.0	1.9	1.9	1.8	1.8	1.9	1.9	1.9	1.9	1.8	1.8	1.8	1.9
1991	1.9	1.9	1.9	2.0	2.0	2.0	2.0	2.0	2.0	2.0	2.0	2.0	2.0
1992	1.9	1.9	2.0	1.9	2.0	2.0	2.0	2.0	2.0	2.0	2.0	2.0	2.0
1993	2.0	2.0	2.0	1.9	2.0	1.9	2.0	2.0	2.0	2.1	2.1	2.1	2.0
1994	2.1	2.1	2.1	2.1	2.1	2.1	2.1	2.1	2.1	2.1	2.0	2.0	2.1
1995	2.1	2.0	2.1	2.1	2.1	2.1	2.1	2.1	2.1	2.2	2.2	2.2	2.1
1996	2.2	2.1	2.2	2.2	2.2	2.3	2.3	2.3	2.2	2.2	2.2	2.2	2.2
1997	2.2	2.2	2.2	2.2	2.2	2.3	2.3	2.3	2.4	2.4	2.4	2.5	2.3
1998	2.4	2.4	2.4	2.5	2.5	2.5	2.6	2.6	2.6	2.6	2.6	2.6	2.5
1999	2.7	2.7	2.7	2.6	2.6	2.6	2.6	2.5	2.5	2.5	2.6	2.6	2.6
2000	2.6	2.6	2.6	2.7	2.7	2.8	2.8	2.8	2.7	2.7	2.7	2.7	2.7
2001	2.7	2.6	2.6	2.6	2.6	2.6	2.6	2.6	2.6	2.7	2.7	2.6	2.6
2002	2.6	2.6	2.6	2.6	2.6	2.7	2.7	2.6	2.6	2.6	2.6	2.6	2.6
2003	2.6	2.6	2.5	2.5	2.6	2.6	2.5	2.4	2.4	2.4	2.5	2.5	2.5
Financial activities													
1990	8.6	8.6	8.7	8.7	8.7	8.7	8.6	8.7	8.7	8.7	8.8	8.9	8.7
1991	8.8	8.8	8.9	8.9	8.9	8.9	9.0	9.0	8.9	8.9	9.0	9.1	8.9
1992	9.4	9.6	9.4	9.6	9.6	9.7	9.8	9.8	9.7	9.5	9.6	9.6	9.6
1993	9.3	9.4	9.6	9.6	9.5	9.7	9.6	9.6	9.6	9.5	9.6	9.6	9.6
1994	9.6	9.6	9.5	9.5	9.5	9.6	9.6	9.6	9.5	9.6	9.7	9.9	9.6
1995	10.0	10.0	10.1	9.9	10.1	10.3	10.3	10.3	10.3	10.3	10.5	10.5	10.2
1996	10.6	10.6	10.6	10.8	10.9	11.0	11.0	11.0	11.0	11.3	11.5	11.7	11.0
1997	11.6	11.7	11.7	11.9	11.9	12.1	12.1	12.1	12.1	12.4	12.7	12.7	12.1
1998	11.9	11.8	11.7	12.0	12.2	12.4	12.4	12.5	12.7	12.9	13.2	13.3	12.4
1999	13.3	13.4	13.4	13.5	13.6	13.9	14.1	14.1	14.2	14.5	14.5	14.6	13.9
2000	14.4	14.5	14.5	14.5	14.5	14.7	14.7	14.5	14.7	14.7	14.9	15.1	14.6
2001	15.0	15.1	15.1	15.0	15.0	15.1	15.2	15.1	15.0	14.9	14.9	15.0	15.0
2002	15.0	15.1	14.9	14.8	14.8	14.8	14.7	14.6	14.6	14.5	14.4	14.7	14.7
2003	14.5	14.6	14.7	14.4	14.5	14.6	14.5	14.5	14.4	14.5	14.5	14.7	14.5

Employment by Industry: South Dakota—*Continued*

(Numbers in thousands. Not seasonally adjusted.)

Industry	January	February	March	April	May	June	July	August	September	October	November	December	Annual Average
SIOUX FALLS—*Continued*													
Professional and business services													
1990	3.6	3.7	3.7	3.7	3.7	3.8	4.0	3.9	3.9	3.9	3.9	3.8	3.8
1991	4.0	3.9	3.9	4.1	4.1	4.1	4.2	4.2	4.2	4.4	4.4	4.5	4.2
1992	4.2	4.2	4.2	4.3	4.3	4.4	4.5	4.6	4.4	4.6	4.6	4.3	4.4
1993	4.3	4.4	4.4	4.7	4.8	4.9	4.9	5.0	4.9	5.0	4.9	4.9	4.8
1994	5.0	5.0	5.0	5.3	5.3	5.5	5.5	5.6	5.6	5.7	5.5	5.3	5.4
1995	5.1	5.1	5.2	5.4	5.5	5.7	5.6	5.7	5.5	5.6	5.7	5.7	5.5
1996	5.7	6.0	6.0	6.1	6.1	6.3	6.5	6.5	6.4	6.6	6.4	6.1	6.2
1997	6.3	6.4	6.4	6.8	7.0	7.3	7.3	7.5	7.4	7.2	7.4	7.4	7.0
1998	7.0	7.1	7.2	7.6	7.6	7.6	7.7	7.8	7.6	8.0	7.9	8.0	7.6
1999	7.8	7.7	7.7	8.2	8.3	8.5	8.5	8.4	8.4	8.6	8.6	8.9	8.3
2000	8.5	8.5	8.5	8.6	8.5	8.8	8.9	8.8	8.8	8.6	8.7	8.9	8.7
2001	8.6	8.5	8.5	8.9	8.9	9.0	8.7	8.7	8.6	8.7	8.5	8.3	8.6
2002	8.1	8.1	8.2	8.5	8.5	8.7	8.6	8.7	8.4	8.5	8.5	8.4	8.4
2003	8.2	8.3	8.2	8.3	8.5	8.5	8.4	8.7	8.6	8.8	8.8	8.5	8.5
Educational and health services													
1990	11.9	12.2	12.4	12.3	12.4	12.5	12.5	12.6	12.6	12.7	12.8	12.8	12.5
1991	12.5	12.9	13.0	12.8	12.9	12.8	13.1	13.1	13.5	13.5	13.5	13.6	13.1
1992	13.2	13.3	13.4	13.5	13.6	13.7	13.7	13.7	13.9	14.0	14.1	14.1	13.7
1993	14.3	14.2	14.3	14.1	14.1	14.0	14.2	14.2	14.3	14.5	14.5	14.5	14.3
1994	14.3	14.4	14.5	14.3	14.4	14.5	14.3	14.4	14.6	14.7	14.8	14.8	14.5
1995	15.0	15.2	15.2	15.4	15.3	15.4	15.4	15.4	15.7	15.7	15.7	15.7	15.4
1996	15.8	15.8	16.0	16.0	16.0	15.9	15.8	16.0	16.0	16.1	15.9	16.0	15.9
1997	16.2	16.3	16.3	16.2	16.2	16.3	16.2	16.2	16.3	16.3	16.4	16.4	16.3
1998	16.5	16.9	17.0	17.1	17.0	17.0	17.0	17.1	17.4	17.4	17.3	17.6	17.1
1999	17.6	17.6	17.9	18.1	18.1	18.0	18.0	18.1	18.2	18.0	18.3	18.5	18.0
2000	18.4	18.5	18.9	18.7	19.0	18.9	18.3	18.4	18.6	18.7	18.9	18.9	18.7
2001	19.1	19.2	19.2	19.3	19.5	19.0	19.1	19.1	19.5	19.7	20.0	19.8	19.3
2002	19.6	19.8	20.0	20.0	20.1	20.1	19.9	20.1	20.5	20.8	20.8	21.0	20.2
2003	20.8	20.9	21.0	21.1	21.3	21.2	21.0	20.6	21.3	21.5	21.3	21.2	21.1
Leisure and hospitality													
1990	6.7	6.7	6.8	6.9	7.3	7.6	7.4	7.5	7.2	7.0	7.1	7.2	7.1
1991	7.0	7.2	7.4	7.6	7.8	8.1	7.9	8.2	7.7	7.3	7.2	7.2	7.6
1992	7.4	7.4	7.5	7.7	8.0	8.1	8.0	8.3	8.0	7.7	7.6	7.8	7.8
1993	7.4	7.4	7.5	7.8	8.0	8.3	8.2	8.3	8.1	8.1	8.0	8.1	7.9
1994	7.8	7.8	8.1	8.3	8.5	8.9	8.8	8.8	8.4	8.2	8.1	8.4	8.3
1995	8.1	8.2	8.5	8.6	9.0	9.5	9.4	9.6	9.1	8.8	8.7	8.8	8.9
1996	8.7	8.6	8.9	9.0	9.3	9.6	9.4	9.6	9.1	9.0	8.7	8.8	9.1
1997	8.5	8.7	8.8	9.2	9.7	10.0	9.9	10.0	9.8	9.4	9.2	9.3	9.4
1998	9.4	9.3	9.4	9.9	10.3	10.7	10.7	10.8	10.1	9.7	9.6	9.8	10.0
1999	9.4	9.4	9.6	10.0	10.5	10.9	11.0	11.1	10.8	10.6	10.4	10.5	10.4
2000	10.0	10.1	10.6	10.6	11.0	11.3	11.1	11.3	10.8	10.5	10.4	10.4	10.7
2001	10.1	10.0	10.2	10.6	11.0	11.3	11.3	11.5	11.2	10.8	10.7	10.8	10.7
2002	10.3	10.4	10.6	11.0	11.5	11.6	11.6	11.8	11.4	11.2	10.8	11.0	11.1
2003	10.7	10.6	10.7	11.1	11.7	11.9	12.2	11.9	11.6	11.6	11.4	11.3	11.4
Other services													
1990	3.4	3.5	3.6	3.5	3.6	3.5	3.5	3.7	3.6	3.8	3.7	3.7	3.6
1991	3.6	3.7	3.7	3.6	3.7	3.5	3.6	3.6	3.8	3.9	3.9	4.0	3.7
1992	3.4	3.4	3.5	3.5	3.5	3.6	3.5	3.5	3.6	3.7	3.8	3.8	3.6
1993	3.7	3.6	3.7	3.8	3.7	3.7	3.8	3.8	3.7	3.8	3.8	3.8	3.7
1994	3.7	3.8	3.8	3.7	3.7	3.9	3.8	3.9	3.7	3.8	3.8	3.8	3.8
1995	3.9	3.9	4.0	4.0	4.0	4.1	4.1	4.2	4.2	4.2	4.2	4.1	4.1
1996	4.2	4.2	4.4	4.3	4.3	4.4	4.3	4.4	4.3	4.4	4.3	4.2	4.3
1997	4.3	4.3	4.4	4.4	4.3	4.4	4.3	4.3	4.2	4.2	4.2	4.1	4.3
1998	4.2	4.5	4.4	4.6	4.5	4.5	4.5	4.5	4.6	4.8	4.7	4.8	4.6
1999	4.7	4.7	4.8	4.8	4.7	4.6	4.7	4.3	4.6	4.7	4.7	4.8	4.7
2000	4.8	4.8	5.1	4.9	5.0	4.9	4.4	4.5	4.7	4.8	5.0	4.8	4.8
2001	4.7	4.7	4.7	4.8	4.8	4.8	4.9	4.9	4.8	4.8	4.8	4.9	4.8
2002	4.8	4.8	4.8	4.9	5.0	5.0	5.0	4.9	4.9	5.0	4.9	4.9	4.9
2003	4.8	4.7	4.8	4.8	4.8	4.8	4.8	4.8	4.8	4.9	4.9	4.9	4.8
Government													
1990	8.5	8.5	8.5	8.8	8.8	9.2	7.9	7.7	8.6	8.6	8.6	8.6	8.5
1991	8.7	8.6	8.7	8.8	8.9	9.3	8.0	8.0	8.8	8.9	9.1	9.0	8.7
1992	9.1	9.0	9.1	9.3	9.3	9.6	8.3	8.3	9.1	9.1	9.2	9.1	9.0
1993	9.2	9.3	9.2	9.4	9.5	9.8	8.4	8.5	9.3	9.5	9.4	9.5	9.3
1994	9.5	9.5	9.5	9.6	9.7	10.2	8.8	8.7	9.6	9.6	9.6	9.8	9.5
1995	9.5	9.5	9.5	9.6	9.6	10.1	8.6	8.7	9.5	9.5	9.5	9.5	9.4
1996	9.6	9.6	9.6	9.7	9.8	10.2	8.7	8.7	9.7	9.7	9.7	9.7	9.6
1997	9.6	9.6	9.7	9.8	9.9	10.3	8.8	8.8	9.6	9.7	9.8	9.8	9.6
1998	9.7	9.8	9.9	10.0	10.1	10.5	9.0	9.0	9.8	10.1	10.0	10.0	9.8
1999	10.0	10.0	10.1	10.2	10.3	10.6	9.7	9.4	10.1	10.1	10.2	10.3	10.1
2000	9.8	9.9	10.1	10.2	10.4	10.7	9.7	9.6	10.0	10.2	10.2	10.2	10.1
2001	10.0	10.0	10.1	10.0	10.1	10.8	9.8	9.5	10.2	10.2	10.2	10.2	10.0
2002	10.2	10.2	10.2	10.3	10.4	11.0	9.7	9.7	10.3	10.4	10.4	10.5	10.3
2003	10.4	10.5	10.6	10.6	10.9	11.3	9.9	9.9	10.5	10.5	10.5	10.5	10.5

Average Weekly Hours by Industry: South Dakota

(Not seasonally adjusted.)

Industry	January	February	March	April	May	June	July	August	September	October	November	December	Annual Average
STATEWIDE													
Manufacturing													
2001	41.5	40.7	41.8	40.9	41.5	42.0	40.7	42.0	42.9	41.6	42.4	42.0	41.7
2002	40.5	41.0	41.6	42.8	42.4	42.7	41.7	42.5	43.1	43.8	42.3	43.3	42.3
2003	42.6	41.7	42.5	40.9	42.4	42.6	41.8	43.9	41.9	43.2	44.2	42.8	42.6

Average Hourly Earnings by Industry: South Dakota

(Dollars, not seasonally adjusted.)

Industry	January	February	March	April	May	June	July	August	September	October	November	December	Annual Average
STATEWIDE													
Manufacturing													
2001	11.76	11.91	11.90	11.86	12.11	12.13	12.10	12.16	12.33	12.29	12.29	12.46	12.11
2002	12.45	12.48	12.50	12.58	12.57	12.44	12.41	12.43	12.64	12.93	12.77	13.01	12.60
2003	12.79	12.82	12.85	12.90	13.15	13.10	13.17	13.19	13.35	13.33	13.31	13.64	13.13

Average Weekly Earnings by Industry: South Dakota

(Dollars, not seasonally adjusted.)

Industry	January	February	March	April	May	June	July	August	September	October	November	December	Annual Average
STATEWIDE													
Manufacturing													
2001	488.04	484.74	497.42	485.07	502.57	509.46	492.47	510.72	528.96	511.26	521.10	523.32	504.99
2002	504.23	511.68	520.00	538.42	532.97	531.19	517.50	528.28	544.78	566.33	540.17	563.33	532.98
2003	544.85	534.59	546.13	527.61	557.56	558.06	550.51	579.04	559.37	575.86	588.30	583.79	559.34

TENNESSEE AT A GLANCE

(Population and total nonfarm employment numbers in thousands)

Population, Census 2000:	5,689.3
Total nonfarm employment, 2003:	2,667.5
Change in total nonfarm employment	
(Number)	
1990–2003:	474.3
1990–2001:	495.1
2001–2003:	-20.8
(Compound annual rate of change)	
1990–2003:	1.5%
1990–2001:	1.9%
2001–2003:	-0.4%
Unemployment rate	
1990:	5.5%
2001:	4.6%
2003:	5.5%

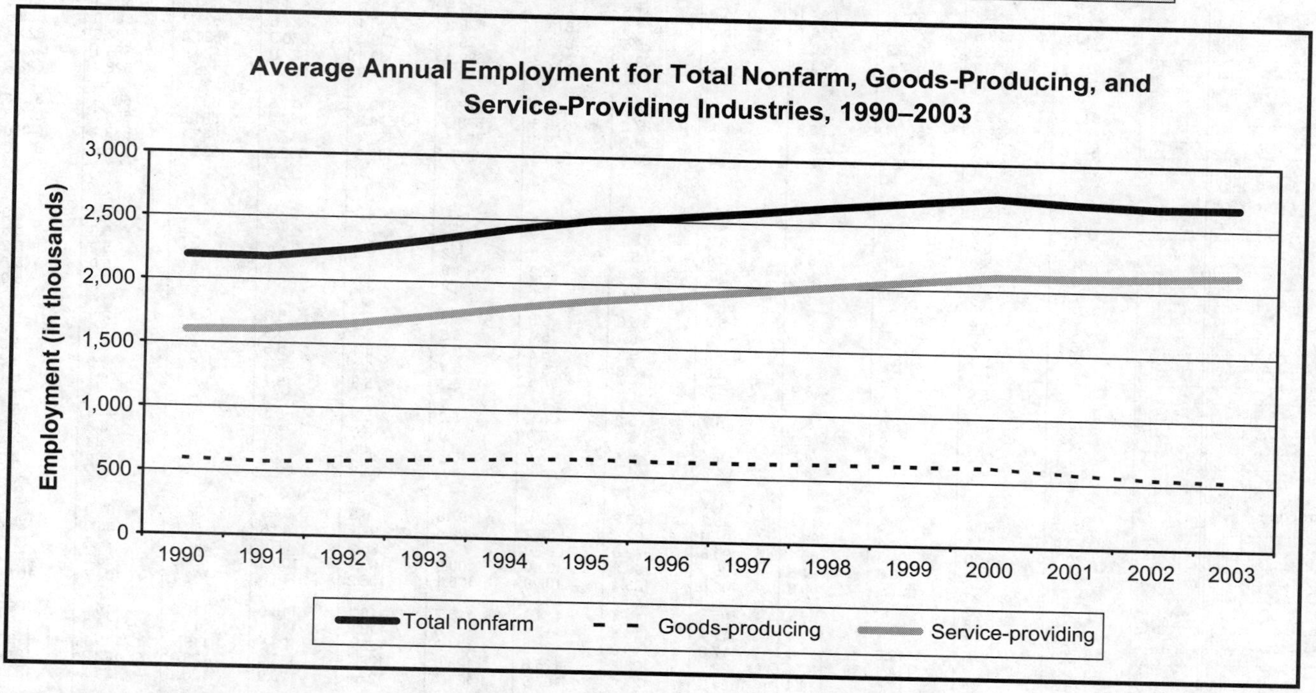

Total nonfarm payroll employment dipped during both the 1990–1991 and 2001 recessions, but showed some moderate signs of recovery in 2003, though still well below its 2000 peak. Employment in the goods-producing sector declined sharply from 2000 to 2001, falling 6.4 percent. Manufacturing employment declined by over 33,000 jobs in that one-year period. The upward trend in employment in the service-providing sector, evident earlier, slowed in 2001.

Employment by Industry: Tennessee

(Numbers in thousands. Not seasonally adjusted.)

Industry	January	February	March	April	May	June	July	August	September	October	November	December	Annual Average
STATEWIDE													
Total nonfarm													
1990	2144.0	2154.3	2175.4	2192.2	2209.7	2215.7	2184.4	2206.4	2219.5	2207.1	2207.1	2202.7	2193.2
1991	2133.0	2138.2	2155.0	2165.7	2185.9	2190.1	2168.8	2194.0	2217.1	2215.8	2220.9	2218.7	2183.6
1992	2166.5	2176.1	2216.0	2223.0	2242.0	2249.5	2235.1	2251.8	2277.0	2294.4	2300.1	2309.0	2245.0
1993	2249.4	2266.4	2281.6	2312.1	2327.2	2335.0	2322.2	2338.1	2365.3	2372.8	2379.8	2392.0	2328.4
1994	2325.0	2346.9	2379.6	2401.0	2426.9	2431.3	2409.4	2431.4	2467.7	2462.5	2500.1	2494.0	2422.9
1995	2425.0	2441.6	2473.3	2479.1	2499.5	2503.5	2476.5	2506.8	2541.7	2534.5	2547.9	2557.4	2498.9
1996	2465.5	2482.2	2536.2	2516.9	2538.7	2535.5	2512.2	2535.7	2562.7	2559.4	2576.0	2579.1	2533.3
1997	2505.3	2526.5	2555.6	2577.0	2588.9	2595.2	2567.0	2588.0	2611.3	2620.5	2631.3	2641.4	2584.0
1998	2563.6	2579.8	2605.8	2623.8	2645.1	2651.2	2628.6	2646.2	2665.7	2672.6	2684.1	2694.1	2638.3
1999	2603.3	2627.0	2654.4	2673.6	2684.6	2691.3	2681.2	2698.0	2715.4	2721.5	2731.9	2741.6	2685.3
2000	2665.1	2683.9	2727.5	2725.7	2740.8	2745.2	2719.4	2737.3	2748.5	2745.9	2753.1	2754.7	2728.9
2001	2673.4	2683.1	2701.2	2705.5	2708.1	2703.2	2666.2	2684.1	2691.2	2676.8	2683.3	2683.0	2688.3
2002	2611.9	2622.8	2643.7	2660.0	2670.2	2672.0	2657.2	2674.7	2684.2	2684.6	2693.5	2698.1	2664.4
2003	2619.4	2627.8	2645.8	2663.9	2672.4	2670.1	2650.4	2673.9	2689.1	2687.5	2700.3	2709.4	2667.5
Total private													
1990	1796.9	1802.1	1820.2	1835.2	1851.6	1869.1	1849.8	1866.8	1863.4	1850.2	1849.5	1846.5	1841.7
1991	1781.0	1781.1	1797.5	1806.5	1829.2	1846.5	1832.9	1852.5	1858.9	1856.1	1861.6	1861.4	1830.4
1992	1812.8	1819.2	1839.8	1863.9	1884.9	1900.9	1899.6	1908.8	1918.4	1930.7	1935.0	1944.1	1888.1
1993	1891.1	1902.7	1916.8	1945.6	1962.1	1979.9	1981.2	1990.9	1997.4	2002.2	2008.8	2019.7	1966.5
1994	1960.1	1976.2	2006.5	2024.6	2050.7	2072.3	2064.5	2078.4	2096.0	2082.8	2099.9	2115.3	2052.2
1995	2055.6	2065.6	2094.6	2099.6	2122.6	2142.3	2127.5	2152.9	2163.2	2149.6	2163.0	2172.6	2125.7
1996	2087.0	2097.4	2128.5	2128.9	2153.1	2163.1	2154.3	2172.4	2179.3	2173.8	2189.4	2193.2	2151.7
1997	2125.7	2141.1	2168.1	2192.1	2206.4	2221.1	2206.8	2222.5	2229.2	2234.0	2243.3	2254.1	2203.7
1998	2184.1	2194.6	2218.1	2233.8	2255.9	2274.2	2262.2	2270.3	2277.7	2278.3	2287.0	2297.9	2252.8
1999	2216.9	2232.4	2257.3	2276.2	2290.2	2310.0	2311.6	2319.2	2328.0	2323.8	2333.3	2343.0	2295.1
2000	2275.0	2285.7	2308.6	2322.4	2332.8	2352.7	2341.2	2349.3	2352.3	2342.3	2347.8	2348.9	2329.9
2001	2275.2	2276.0	2292.1	2295.6	2300.6	2309.2	2285.7	2292.7	2286.5	2266.7	2269.9	2270.9	2285.1
2002	2205.5	2208.0	2226.9	2240.8	2255.1	2266.4	2271.0	2278.9	2275.1	2268.9	2274.5	2278.7	2254.2
2003	2211.0	2212.5	2228.2	2243.7	2254.8	2264.9	2257.9	2271.7	2274.6	2271.9	2282.5	2290.8	2255.4
Goods-producing													
1990	589.7	589.8	593.5	596.2	600.6	604.0	595.2	598.0	597.6	591.6	588.0	584.3	594.0
1991	562.7	562.3	565.6	569.4	574.9	581.6	574.7	581.4	583.5	580.5	579.9	576.5	574.4
1992	568.8	571.2	577.1	583.8	589.3	593.8	591.5	596.1	598.7	598.0	597.1	597.1	588.5
1993	585.9	577.7	593.4	599.1	604.6	612.7	602.1	613.1	615.9	613.4	612.6	612.7	603.6
1994	598.0	601.8	610.5	615.9	621.1	628.6	625.2	628.2	631.0	628.5	629.0	631.0	620.7
1995	622.5	623.6	631.9	633.1	635.5	641.5	633.7	639.5	639.9	634.2	630.6	629.4	632.9
1996	610.9	613.6	620.2	618.7	625.3	625.6	618.7	625.2	626.4	621.8	621.3	620.0	620.6
1997	607.8	609.6	615.2	620.2	621.1	625.5	617.1	626.7	629.4	630.3	626.6	627.6	621.4
1998	617.3	617.8	620.6	625.3	627.5	632.7	625.2	629.4	630.4	627.9	624.5	625.1	625.3
1999	609.5	611.2	616.1	621.1	622.2	627.1	627.7	630.3	631.9	626.3	625.8	626.4	622.9
2000	618.4	619.3	624.0	622.7	625.5	630.0	622.0	622.0	619.8	611.5	607.1	604.4	618.8
2001	593.0	588.5	591.4	588.8	586.8	587.6	579.3	578.8	574.3	565.2	561.8	558.5	579.5
2002	544.6	543.1	544.3	546.3	551.1	554.0	552.0	554.1	552.4	547.8	543.1	543.2	548.0
2003	530.0	528.1	530.2	532.3	534.4	536.9	533.9	537.1	536.5	536.2	535.5	535.9	533.9
Natural resources and mining													
1990	6.2	5.8	6.3	6.4	6.4	6.5	6.5	6.5	6.4	6.3	6.2	6.1	6.3
1991	5.7	5.7	5.8	5.8	5.8	5.7	5.7	5.6	5.6	5.6	5.5	5.3	5.6
1992	4.9	5.0	5.1	5.3	5.4	5.3	5.3	5.3	5.3	5.2	5.2	5.2	5.2
1993	5.0	5.0	5.1	5.2	5.2	5.2	5.2	4.9	4.9	5.1	5.0	5.0	5.0
1994	4.6	4.7	4.9	5.1	5.1	5.2	5.2	5.2	5.2	5.1	5.1	5.1	5.0
1995	5.0	5.0	5.2	5.2	5.2	5.3	5.3	5.3	5.3	5.3	5.4	5.4	5.2
1996	5.1	5.2	5.3	5.4	5.4	5.4	5.4	5.5	5.5	5.5	5.4	5.3	5.3
1997	5.0	5.1	5.2	5.3	5.3	5.3	5.4	5.4	5.4	5.5	5.1	5.4	5.2
1998	5.2	5.1	5.2	5.2	5.3	5.3	5.4	5.4	5.4	5.3	5.2	5.3	5.2
1999	5.0	5.0	5.1	5.2	5.1	5.2	5.2	5.2	5.3	5.1	5.1	5.1	5.1
2000	5.2	5.1	5.2	5.1	5.2	5.2	5.2	5.2	5.2	5.1	5.0	5.0	5.1
2001	4.8	4.9	4.9	5.0	5.0	5.0	5.0	5.0	5.0	5.0	4.9	4.6	4.9
2002	4.4	4.4	4.6	4.6	4.7	4.7	4.7	4.6	4.6	4.4	4.4	4.4	4.5
2003	4.2	4.2	4.2	4.3	4.3	4.3	4.2	4.3	4.3	4.3	4.2	4.2	4.3
Construction													
1990	91.7	90.9	92.5	93.4	95.2	97.2	97.6	97.8	96.3	94.3	93.6	91.3	94.3
1991	80.9	82.4	85.4	88.2	91.0	92.6	92.3	92.6	92.1	89.6	88.5	86.0	88.4
1992	80.1	82.0	84.5	88.1	90.8	92.0	92.8	94.8	96.1	96.6	94.8	93.6	90.5
1993	85.4	86.9	88.8	91.8	96.0	99.2	101.0	100.8	100.7	100.3	99.5	98.2	95.7
1994	90.7	91.4	97.2	100.3	102.9	105.4	105.9	105.1	106.2	106.9	106.1	104.8	101.9
1995	97.9	97.8	102.9	107.1	109.3	113.4	114.3	116.7	118.1	116.0	112.5	110.6	109.7
1996	101.6	103.7	109.1	112.2	117.7	116.8	117.8	118.8	118.6	118.0	116.0	114.8	113.7
1997	107.2	108.6	112.6	117.1	117.9	119.0	122.8	124.3	125.4	123.5	119.7	119.1	118.1
1998	112.1	112.2	114.1	120.1	122.7	125.6	126.8	126.0	125.7	125.0	123.3	123.2	121.4
1999	112.6	114.7	117.0	122.4	124.3	127.4	127.9	127.7	127.4	125.9	125.1	124.7	123.0
2000	120.4	121.5	126.0	125.4	127.9	129.9	127.9	128.4	128.7	125.6	124.1	122.6	125.7
2001	115.2	116.0	119.9	120.8	122.4	124.3	123.7	123.4	121.6	119.5	119.7	117.8	120.4
2002	110.1	109.9	111.3	113.3	115.8	117.8	117.7	118.1	117.7	116.7	115.5	115.7	115.0
2003	109.4	108.3	110.9	114.3	116.7	118.4	118.5	119.2	119.0	117.9	116.8	117.0	115.5

Employment by Industry: Tennessee—*Continued*

(Numbers in thousands. Not seasonally adjusted.)

Industry	January	February	March	April	May	June	July	August	September	October	November	December	Annual Average
STATEWIDE—*Continued*													
Manufacturing													
1990	491.8	493.1	494.7	496.4	499.0	500.3	491.1	493.7	494.9	491.0	488.2	486.9	493.4
1991	476.1	474.2	474.4	475.4	478.1	483.3	476.7	483.2	485.8	485.3	485.9	485.2	480.3
1992	483.8	484.2	487.5	490.4	493.1	496.5	493.4	496.0	497.3	496.2	497.1	498.3	492.8
1993	495.5	485.8	499.5	502.1	503.4	508.3	495.9	507.4	510.3	508.0	508.1	509.5	502.8
1994	502.7	505.7	508.4	510.5	513.1	518.0	514.1	517.9	519.6	516.5	517.8	521.1	513.7
1995	519.6	520.8	523.8	520.8	521.0	522.8	514.1	517.5	516.5	512.9	512.7	513.4	517.9
1996	504.2	504.7	505.8	501.1	502.2	503.4	495.5	500.9	502.3	498.3	499.9	499.9	501.5
1997	495.6	495.9	497.4	497.8	497.9	501.2	488.9	497.0	498.6	501.3	501.8	503.1	498.0
1998	500.0	500.5	501.3	500.0	499.5	501.8	493.0	498.0	499.3	497.6	496.0	496.6	498.6
1999	491.9	491.5	494.0	493.5	492.8	494.5	494.6	497.4	499.2	495.3	495.6	496.6	494.7
2000	492.8	492.7	492.8	492.2	492.4	494.9	488.9	488.4	485.9	480.8	478.0	476.8	488.0
2001	473.0	467.6	466.6	463.0	459.4	458.3	450.6	450.4	447.7	440.7	437.2	436.1	454.2
2002	430.1	428.8	428.4	428.4	430.6	431.5	429.6	431.4	430.1	426.7	423.2	423.1	428.5
2003	416.4	415.6	415.1	413.7	413.4	414.2	411.2	413.6	413.2	414.0	414.5	414.7	414.1
Service-providing													
1990	1554.3	1564.5	1581.9	1596.0	1609.1	1611.7	1589.2	1608.4	1621.9	1615.5	1619.1	1618.4	1599.1
1991	1570.3	1575.9	1589.4	1596.3	1611.0	1608.5	1594.1	1612.6	1633.6	1635.3	1641.0	1642.2	1609.1
1992	1597.7	1604.9	1638.9	1639.2	1652.7	1655.7	1643.6	1655.7	1678.3	1696.4	1703.0	1711.9	1656.5
1993	1663.5	1688.7	1688.2	1713.0	1722.6	1722.3	1720.1	1725.0	1749.4	1759.4	1767.2	1779.3	1724.8
1994	1727.0	1745.1	1769.1	1785.1	1805.8	1802.7	1784.2	1803.2	1836.7	1834.0	1871.1	1863.0	1802.2
1995	1802.5	1818.0	1841.4	1846.0	1864.0	1862.0	1842.8	1867.3	1901.8	1900.3	1917.3	1928.0	1865.9
1996	1854.6	1868.6	1916.0	1898.2	1913.4	1909.9	1893.5	1910.5	1936.3	1937.6	1954.7	1959.1	1912.7
1997	1897.5	1916.9	1940.4	1956.8	1967.8	1969.7	1949.9	1961.3	1981.9	1990.2	2004.7	2013.8	1962.5
1998	1946.3	1962.0	1985.2	1998.5	2017.6	2018.5	2003.4	2016.8	2035.3	2044.7	2059.6	2069.0	2013.0
1999	1993.8	2015.8	2038.3	2052.5	2062.4	2064.2	2053.5	2067.7	2083.5	2095.2	2106.1	2115.2	2062.3
2000	2046.7	2064.6	2103.5	2103.0	2115.3	2115.2	2097.4	2115.3	2128.7	2134.4	2146.0	2150.3	2110.0
2001	2080.4	2094.6	2109.8	2116.7	2121.3	2115.6	2086.9	2105.3	2116.9	2111.6	2121.5	2124.5	2108.8
2002	2067.3	2079.7	2099.4	2113.7	2119.1	2118.0	2105.2	2120.6	2131.8	2136.8	2150.4	2154.9	2116.4
2003	2089.4	2099.7	2115.6	2131.6	2138.0	2133.2	2116.5	2136.8	2152.6	2151.3	2164.8	2173.5	2133.6
Trade, transportation, and utilities													
1990	472.0	468.8	472.2	474.6	478.1	482.4	478.8	483.6	483.9	482.4	488.3	492.1	479.7
1991	470.8	465.1	467.2	466.5	471.1	472.1	470.8	475.3	478.0	481.7	488.1	492.1	474.9
1992	469.2	465.9	468.8	474.1	478.6	481.1	479.7	481.3	484.1	488.2	493.5	498.4	480.2
1993	478.2	478.2	479.8	485.0	488.0	491.9	493.9	495.7	496.3	504.3	512.3	518.9	493.5
1994	497.0	497.3	503.0	503.7	511.8	517.7	513.3	518.4	524.8	520.5	532.7	542.9	515.2
1995	517.1	514.4	518.4	519.2	524.0	530.3	525.7	532.2	536.5	535.6	546.9	553.9	529.5
1996	529.0	526.7	532.6	533.8	534.4	539.3	540.7	542.3	543.5	544.2	559.8	563.8	540.8
1997	538.8	538.5	544.2	546.2	548.2	549.3	549.0	551.1	552.6	557.9	570.2	577.1	551.9
1998	551.1	550.7	554.8	555.3	559.5	563.6	562.7	565.5	568.0	572.0	580.9	586.5	564.2
1999	561.0	561.7	567.2	569.8	572.6	580.0	577.1	580.1	583.2	588.7	596.0	601.4	578.2
2000	574.5	576.0	580.4	583.7	584.2	589.4	587.3	585.4	586.1	589.2	597.4	600.8	586.2
2001	593.1	589.1	591.6	590.6	592.3	592.2	584.8	586.5	586.2	585.5	593.4	596.6	590.2
2002	569.4	566.1	570.1	570.3	572.3	573.6	576.6	576.6	577.5	581.3	590.2	597.1	576.8
2003	571.2	569.1	572.1	573.3	574.4	576.9	576.9	580.0	582.1	586.7	596.1	603.0	580.2
Wholesale trade													
1990	112.7	112.5	113.7	113.6	114.2	115.0	115.2	115.2	114.9	114.1	114.6	114.6	114.1
1991	112.0	111.6	111.9	112.4	113.2	113.7	113.3	113.7	113.6	114.4	114.7	115.1	113.3
1992	111.4	111.4	112.0	113.2	113.7	114.0	113.9	113.5	113.1	113.3	113.2	113.5	113.0
1993	111.6	112.0	112.9	113.1	113.3	114.0	114.8	114.8	115.4	116.4	117.2	118.2	114.4
1994	116.0	116.3	117.3	117.2	117.7	118.7	119.1	119.6	120.1	120.2	121.9	122.7	118.9
1995	120.5	121.0	122.2	121.4	122.5	123.3	121.9	122.9	123.1	123.5	124.2	124.4	122.5
1996	122.2	122.8	123.6	126.1	123.1	123.6	122.9	123.5	123.7	124.4	125.3	125.9	123.9
1997	125.1	125.9	126.7	127.3	127.3	127.4	127.5	127.5	128.2	130.6	131.2	132.0	128.0
1998	130.0	130.5	130.9	130.6	130.9	131.2	130.4	130.4	130.6	130.9	131.0	131.4	130.7
1999	130.0	130.4	131.1	131.2	131.2	132.1	132.2	132.0	132.2	132.4	133.0	133.8	131.8
2000	131.6	132.3	133.2	132.0	131.5	131.7	131.1	130.8	130.7	129.8	129.7	129.8	131.1
2001	128.0	128.1	128.6	128.2	128.1	128.0	126.5	126.9	127.4	126.8	126.9	126.7	127.5
2002	124.7	125.0	125.2	125.4	125.8	126.1	127.0	127.2	127.0	127.8	128.1	128.9	126.5
2003	126.7	127.1	127.2	127.2	127.6	127.9	127.2	127.4	127.8	128.4	129.0	129.8	127.8
Retail trade													
1990	261.6	258.0	259.1	261.8	263.1	265.1	264.1	266.8	266.3	266.4	271.4	274.7	264.8
1991	259.1	253.8	254.3	253.9	257.2	257.4	256.7	259.6	260.9	263.1	268.6	272.2	259.7
1992	256.0	252.5	254.0	257.5	260.0	260.8	260.0	261.3	262.5	264.7	270.2	274.1	261.1
1993	260.2	258.7	258.7	263.7	264.3	266.4	267.7	268.9	269.0	273.4	280.2	285.2	268.0
1994	269.3	267.4	270.4	273.2	276.6	279.9	277.8	280.8	285.2	282.6	291.7	299.2	279.5
1995	282.0	278.8	280.7	283.2	285.7	290.0	288.2	292.2	294.7	293.8	302.3	308.1	289.9
1996	291.0	286.4	290.0	290.1	291.7	295.6	298.3	298.8	298.2	298.5	311.3	314.5	297.0
1997	295.2	292.8	296.7	298.0	299.3	299.9	299.9	301.9	302.5	305.5	315.6	320.9	302.3
1998	299.5	297.4	299.9	300.1	302.4	304.9	305.0	305.9	308.0	311.2	319.1	323.6	306.4
1999	302.8	301.9	305.4	305.1	307.0	309.8	310.3	312.3	313.7	318.0	325.5	330.2	311.8
2000	308.1	307.6	309.9	312.4	313.1	316.9	315.8	316.0	317.1	319.5	327.8	331.6	316.3
2001	322.1	318.4	320.5	319.4	320.0	319.8	314.7	314.8	314.1	314.7	323.7	327.5	319.1
2002	307.8	304.8	307.5	307.7	309.0	310.0	311.2	310.6	312.4	313.9	322.3	328.9	312.2
2003	307.3	304.9	307.0	308.0	308.5	310.0	310.6	312.4	314.0	316.5	325.1	331.6	313.0

Employment by Industry: Tennessee—*Continued*

(Numbers in thousands. Not seasonally adjusted.)

Industry	January	February	March	April	May	June	July	August	September	October	November	December	Annual Average
STATEWIDE—*Continued*													
Transportation and utilities													
1990	97.7	98.3	99.4	99.2	100.8	102.3	99.5	101.6	102.7	101.9	102.3	102.8	100.7
1991	99.7	99.7	101.0	100.2	100.7	101.0	100.8	102.0	103.5	104.2	104.8	104.8	101.8
1992	101.8	102.0	102.8	103.4	104.9	106.3	105.8	106.5	108.5	110.2	110.1	110.8	106.0
1993	106.4	107.5	108.2	108.2	110.4	111.5	111.4	112.0	111.9	114.5	114.9	115.5	111.0
1994	111.7	113.6	115.3	113.3	117.5	119.1	116.4	118.0	119.5	117.7	119.1	121.0	116.8
1995	114.6	114.6	115.5	114.6	115.8	117.0	115.6	117.1	118.7	118.3	120.4	121.4	116.9
1996	115.8	117.5	119.0	117.6	119.6	120.1	119.5	120.0	121.6	121.3	123.2	123.4	119.8
1997	118.5	119.8	120.8	120.9	121.6	122.0	121.6	121.7	121.9	121.8	123.4	124.2	121.5
1998	121.6	122.8	124.0	124.6	126.2	127.5	127.3	129.2	129.4	129.9	130.8	131.5	127.0
1999	128.2	129.4	130.7	133.5	134.4	138.1	134.6	135.8	137.3	138.3	137.5	137.4	134.6
2000	134.8	136.1	137.3	139.3	139.6	140.8	140.4	138.6	138.3	139.9	139.9	139.4	138.7
2001	143.0	142.6	142.5	143.0	144.2	144.4	143.6	144.8	144.7	144.0	142.8	142.4	143.5
2002	136.9	136.3	137.4	137.2	137.5	137.5	138.4	138.8	138.1	139.6	139.8	139.3	138.1
2003	137.2	137.1	137.9	138.1	138.3	139.0	139.1	140.2	140.3	141.8	142.0	141.6	139.4
Information													
1990	44.1	44.3	44.6	44.2	44.2	44.2	44.9	44.8	44.6	44.1	44.3	44.6	44.4
1991	44.6	44.0	44.0	43.9	43.6	43.5	43.2	43.1	42.8	42.4	42.5	42.7	43.3
1992	42.5	42.6	42.7	42.7	42.9	43.4	42.9	43.0	42.5	42.8	43.4	44.2	42.9
1993	43.8	43.7	44.3	44.3	44.7	45.0	44.9	45.0	44.6	44.3	44.6	45.6	44.5
1994	44.0	44.5	45.3	45.7	46.1	46.4	46.2	46.2	46.1	45.7	45.9	46.3	45.7
1995	44.9	44.9	45.3	45.0	45.6	46.1	45.7	46.2	46.1	45.9	46.2	46.7	45.7
1996	49.1	48.4	48.4	47.5	48.0	48.2	48.0	47.9	47.8	48.0	48.3	48.8	48.2
1997	48.0	48.3	48.7	48.3	48.7	49.2	49.3	49.3	49.1	49.8	50.9	51.2	49.2
1998	50.1	50.4	50.4	50.1	51.0	50.9	51.1	50.9	51.4	52.2	52.5	52.9	51.1
1999	51.8	52.2	52.4	52.0	52.5	52.9	52.3	52.6	52.7	53.3	54.3	55.1	52.8
2000	54.6	54.7	55.1	54.1	54.2	54.7	54.1	54.4	54.4	54.6	55.8	56.2	54.7
2001	56.0	56.3	56.5	55.2	55.2	55.7	55.3	55.3	54.5	54.6	55.1	55.4	55.4
2002	54.1	53.9	54.4	53.6	53.8	53.3	52.9	53.0	52.4	52.7	53.1	52.9	53.3
2003	52.1	51.9	51.8	52.0	51.8	51.7	51.7	51.6	51.2	51.5	51.9	52.1	51.8
Financial activities													
1990	110.6	111.0	111.5	112.0	113.0	113.9	113.5	114.0	113.3	112.6	112.3	112.7	112.5
1991	109.8	110.2	110.7	111.0	111.4	111.6	111.7	112.0	111.7	110.9	110.7	111.4	111.0
1992	109.5	110.2	111.0	111.1	111.6	112.7	112.6	112.5	111.7	112.2	112.0	112.7	111.6
1993	112.0	112.5	113.1	113.9	114.5	116.0	116.3	116.7	116.1	116.0	116.5	117.4	115.0
1994	115.9	116.7	117.7	117.5	118.5	120.4	120.5	120.7	120.3	119.8	120.4	121.0	119.1
1995	119.4	119.8	120.8	120.9	122.0	121.9	123.4	123.9	124.1	123.7	125.1	126.6	122.6
1996	124.1	125.4	126.8	125.6	126.7	128.0	128.7	129.2	129.0	128.8	129.6	130.3	127.6
1997	128.0	128.7	129.8	130.2	130.8	132.1	132.5	132.8	132.8	132.5	133.2	134.2	131.4
1998	130.9	131.3	133.0	135.5	135.9	137.3	138.1	138.4	138.4	139.7	139.8	140.5	136.5
1999	140.5	140.7	141.9	139.4	140.0	140.3	142.4	141.4	139.2	139.4	139.4	140.1	140.3
2000	138.9	138.9	139.1	139.0	139.5	140.6	140.0	139.6	139.2	138.4	138.5	139.2	139.2
2001	137.7	138.0	138.6	138.6	138.8	139.9	139.4	139.3	138.3	137.7	137.8	137.6	138.5
2002	137.2	137.6	137.9	137.7	138.2	138.9	138.2	138.5	137.6	138.0	138.8	139.1	138.1
2003	137.8	137.8	138.4	138.6	139.2	140.0	140.1	140.5	139.9	139.5	140.0	140.3	139.3
Professional and business services													
1990	157.8	160.2	163.0	164.1	165.1	167.4	166.2	167.9	168.4	169.1	169.0	168.3	165.5
1991	160.5	163.1	165.6	167.1	168.7	170.9	170.7	172.6	173.8	174.7	174.9	174.6	169.7
1992	172.7	175.1	178.4	180.7	183.1	185.5	183.7	185.6	186.1	190.4	189.7	190.7	183.4
1993	186.4	190.4	191.7	195.1	196.6	200.3	201.2	204.9	204.1	206.4	206.8	207.7	199.3
1994	201.8	206.1	211.8	217.1	219.1	222.8	221.5	224.5	227.0	226.2	227.3	228.9	219.5
1995	219.2	223.3	227.4	229.1	232.3	231.5	231.9	236.2	237.6	239.2	241.7	242.6	232.6
1996	227.8	231.6	237.4	239.2	241.2	244.5	246.3	246.6	248.9	248.3	250.1	248.6	242.5
1997	238.5	243.8	249.5	257.6	259.5	262.1	259.4	263.7	264.9	259.9	260.2	262.0	256.7
1998	250.2	255.4	261.0	263.6	268.4	272.8	269.0	271.8	272.8	276.9	277.7	279.0	268.2
1999	268.2	273.3	278.6	282.0	284.1	287.2	290.3	293.8	295.9	296.4	299.2	301.1	287.5
2000	292.7	295.9	299.9	299.3	299.6	302.0	301.3	305.3	307.3	304.1	302.6	302.4	301.0
2001	299.2	300.5	301.0	299.8	298.3	298.7	296.2	299.4	301.2	297.9	297.4	299.8	299.1
2002	292.3	293.4	297.3	297.4	297.4	297.6	297.8	300.4	298.6	296.2	295.8	293.4	296.5
2003	281.3	282.2	284.0	284.5	286.5	286.9	284.4	289.8	292.0	289.6	290.4	292.3	287.0
Educational and health services													
1990	201.4	204.7	205.7	206.7	207.2	205.5	205.8	209.4	212.0	212.7	213.4	213.6	208.1
1991	211.4	214.2	215.2	216.4	217.3	216.7	216.8	219.3	222.7	223.8	224.6	225.7	218.6
1992	223.4	225.5	226.3	227.4	227.7	224.2	225.4	226.4	233.6	235.9	237.3	238.3	229.2
1993	234.2	237.1	238.4	239.9	239.7	235.7	234.7	235.7	243.5	245.0	245.2	245.7	239.5
1994	241.8	245.0	246.3	247.2	246.8	242.0	242.3	243.3	251.9	252.0	253.6	254.3	247.2
1995	251.3	254.6	256.9	255.4	257.6	253.5	250.8	255.4	261.1	261.6	262.5	263.0	256.9
1996	256.6	259.7	261.3	258.5	259.2	256.5	256.2	257.5	263.1	263.1	264.8	266.3	260.2
1997	259.2	263.0	263.9	265.6	265.6	263.3	266.0	267.7	272.2	272.7	273.3	273.8	267.1
1998	269.2	272.0	273.6	273.4	273.4	270.9	269.5	269.3	273.8	275.0	275.4	276.3	272.6
1999	268.0	270.9	272.3	271.7	272.0	270.2	270.4	270.2	275.6	275.4	276.3	276.8	272.4
2000	271.6	274.3	276.9	278.2	277.2	276.2	276.5	277.5	282.5	284.2	285.4	285.7	278.8
2001	278.0	281.7	283.6	284.7	285.0	284.0	284.4	286.0	289.5	289.9	291.0	291.9	285.8
2002	288.7	291.2	293.8	296.3	297.8	297.6	299.7	301.8	306.3	307.7	309.6	310.5	300.1
2003	307.2	310.5	311.3	312.5	312.2	311.4	310.6	312.2	316.2	316.7	318.1	318.1	313.1

Employment by Industry: Tennessee—*Continued*

(Numbers in thousands. Not seasonally adjusted.)

Industry	January	February	March	April	May	June	July	August	September	October	November	December	Annual Average
STATEWIDE—*Continued*													
Leisure and hospitality													
1990	162.2	164.5	170.4	179.2	185.2	191.5	189.5	190.8	185.5	181.1	177.6	175.4	179.4
1991	164.5	166.1	171.9	179.4	185.4	191.4	189.0	190.0	186.3	180.5	177.7	175.3	179.7
1992	165.9	168.3	174.2	181.8	188.9	194.0	195.3	195.3	192.2	189.6	186.0	183.7	184.6
1993	178.1	180.9	183.2	194.8	200.7	204.7	207.2	207.3	203.7	200.2	197.5	196.8	196.2
1994	187.2	190.5	197.2	206.5	212.5	217.9	217.5	218.1	215.4	207.4	205.9	206.0	206.8
1995	197.2	200.9	208.4	213.4	220.1	226.0	224.2	224.8	222.3	215.2	214.0	213.3	214.9
1996	201.8	203.6	210.8	217.2	223.6	228.6	228.5	228.1	224.3	219.1	218.3	216.9	218.4
1997	202.5	205.5	211.2	222.2	226.8	231.9	229.1	229.5	225.1	220.6	218.4	216.7	219.9
1998	205.2	207.5	217.1	225.6	229.7	233.9	235.5	232.5	226.5	223.7	222.1	221.1	223.3
1999	209.6	212.9	218.4	225.2	229.6	235.7	237.4	234.9	232.2	229.0	227.7	226.2	226.5
2000	216.2	217.3	222.0	231.6	237.9	244.6	244.7	244.9	241.2	234.9	233.4	231.6	233.3
2001	219.0	220.8	228.0	236.5	242.1	247.6	245.4	246.3	240.9	235.4	232.9	231.3	235.5
2002	220.6	223.1	228.9	239.0	243.1	248.7	250.8	252.3	247.4	242.3	241.2	239.7	239.8
2003	229.9	231.6	238.2	247.9	253.1	257.8	256.7	257.6	253.2	248.2	247.2	245.6	247.3
Other services													
1990	59.1	58.8	59.3	58.2	58.2	60.2	55.9	58.3	58.1	56.6	56.6	55.5	57.9
1991	56.7	56.1	57.3	52.8	56.8	58.7	56.0	58.8	60.1	61.6	63.2	63.1	58.4
1992	60.8	60.4	61.3	62.3	62.8	66.2	68.5	68.6	69.5	73.6	76.0	79.0	67.4
1993	72.5	82.2	72.9	73.5	73.3	73.6	80.9	72.5	73.2	72.6	73.3	74.9	74.6
1994	74.4	74.3	74.7	71.0	74.8	76.5	78.0	79.0	79.5	82.7	85.1	84.9	77.9
1995	84.0	84.1	85.5	83.5	85.5	91.5	92.1	94.7	95.6	94.2	96.0	97.1	90.3
1996	87.7	88.4	91.0	88.4	94.7	92.4	87.2	95.6	96.3	100.5	97.2	98.5	93.1
1997	102.9	103.7	105.6	101.8	105.7	107.7	104.4	101.7	103.1	110.3	110.5	111.5	105.7
1998	110.1	109.5	107.6	105.0	110.5	112.1	111.1	112.5	116.4	110.9	114.1	116.5	111.3
1999	108.3	109.5	110.4	115.0	117.2	116.6	114.0	115.9	117.3	115.3	114.6	115.9	114.1
2000	108.1	109.3	111.2	113.8	114.7	115.2	115.3	120.2	121.8	125.4	127.6	128.6	117.6
2001	99.2	101.1	101.4	101.4	102.1	103.5	100.9	101.1	101.6	100.5	100.5	99.8	101.1
2002	98.6	99.6	100.2	100.2	101.4	102.7	103.0	102.2	102.9	102.9	102.7	102.8	101.6
2003	101.5	101.3	102.2	102.6	103.2	103.3	103.6	102.9	103.5	103.5	103.3	103.5	102.9
Government													
1990	347.1	352.2	355.2	357.0	358.1	346.6	334.6	339.6	356.1	356.9	357.6	356.2	351.4
1991	352.0	357.1	357.5	359.2	356.7	343.6	335.9	341.5	358.2	359.7	359.3	357.3	353.1
1992	353.7	356.9	376.2	359.1	357.1	348.6	335.5	343.0	358.6	363.7	365.1	364.9	356.8
1993	358.3	363.7	364.8	366.5	365.1	355.1	341.0	347.2	367.9	370.6	371.0	372.3	361.9
1994	364.9	370.7	373.1	376.4	376.2	359.0	344.9	353.0	371.7	379.7	400.2	378.7	370.7
1995	369.4	376.0	378.7	379.5	376.9	361.2	349.0	353.9	378.5	384.9	384.9	384.8	373.1
1996	378.5	384.8	407.7	388.0	385.6	372.4	357.9	363.3	383.4	385.6	386.6	385.9	381.6
1997	379.6	385.4	387.5	384.9	382.5	374.1	360.2	365.5	382.1	386.5	388.0	387.3	380.3
1998	379.5	385.2	387.7	390.0	389.2	377.0	366.4	375.9	388.0	394.3	397.1	396.2	385.5
1999	386.4	394.6	397.1	397.4	394.4	381.3	369.6	378.8	387.4	397.7	398.6	398.6	390.1
2000	390.1	398.2	418.9	403.3	408.0	392.5	378.2	388.0	396.2	403.6	405.3	405.8	399.0
2001	398.2	407.1	409.1	409.9	407.5	394.0	380.5	391.4	404.7	410.1	413.4	412.1	403.2
2002	406.4	414.8	416.8	419.2	415.1	405.6	386.2	395.8	409.1	415.7	419.0	419.4	410.3
2003	408.4	415.3	417.6	420.2	417.6	405.2	392.5	402.2	414.5	415.6	417.8	418.6	412.1
Federal government													
1990	61.4	62.2	65.0	64.7	67.6	65.1	63.8	63.2	63.2	63.1	62.0	61.9	63.6
1991	61.4	62.9	62.9	62.7	62.2	60.8	60.9	61.3	62.4	62.3	60.8	59.5	61.6
1992	59.3	59.3	59.1	59.1	58.7	58.3	58.2	58.1	58.2	58.0	57.0	57.0	58.3
1993	55.7	55.7	55.9	56.6	56.3	56.1	56.0	55.6	55.5	55.1	54.7	55.0	55.6
1994	55.4	55.9	55.9	56.4	56.1	56.3	55.3	55.2	55.0	54.7	53.3	53.6	55.2
1995	54.3	54.7	55.1	55.4	54.9	55.1	54.7	54.3	54.0	53.7	53.1	53.4	54.3
1996	53.6	54.8	55.1	55.5	54.7	54.7	54.2	53.7	53.7	53.3	53.0	53.3	54.1
1997	52.7	52.8	53.2	52.9	52.3	52.1	51.8	51.5	51.0	50.4	50.5	50.4	51.8
1998	50.1	50.1	50.7	51.4	51.5	50.4	49.9	49.9	50.0	51.5	52.5	52.0	50.8
1999	50.8	51.5	51.6	52.9	51.6	51.4	50.8	50.7	50.5	51.0	50.8	51.1	51.2
2000	50.9	52.2	53.2	53.9	61.2	58.4	55.9	55.4	50.4	50.5	50.7	51.0	53.6
2001	51.0	51.8	51.9	51.9	51.9	51.8	51.7	51.1	51.3	51.1	51.3	51.3	51.5
2002	51.7	52.4	52.6	52.3	52.0	52.2	51.7	50.9	50.9	51.4	51.8	51.9	51.8
2003	51.6	51.9	52.3	52.3	52.0	51.2	51.0	50.4	50.5	50.8	51.1	51.3	51.4
State government													
1990	88.5	91.9	92.0	92.1	88.8	85.8	85.2	86.0	90.5	92.1	92.2	92.2	89.7
1991	89.3	92.7	92.8	93.1	89.8	86.9	87.1	87.1	90.0	91.5	91.7	91.1	90.2
1992	87.7	90.7	90.8	91.0	87.6	84.6	85.4	85.8	89.2	92.4	92.4	92.6	89.1
1993	89.4	92.9	93.5	92.8	90.2	87.9	88.1	88.3	92.6	95.0	94.8	94.7	91.6
1994	90.6	94.5	95.5	95.2	92.5	89.9	89.8	90.2	94.6	96.8	95.5	95.2	93.3
1995	90.8	95.3	96.0	95.3	91.6	87.7	89.2	88.1	94.3	96.4	96.0	95.0	92.9
1996	90.8	95.1	96.1	96.2	93.2	89.8	90.8	90.0	93.8	96.1	95.8	95.0	93.5
1997	91.1	94.7	95.4	94.3	90.9	86.8	87.8	88.5	92.8	96.5	96.3	95.1	92.5
1998	90.0	94.8	95.5	95.5	92.4	88.7	89.7	89.3	94.9	97.1	97.2	96.9	93.5
1999	90.9	96.4	97.5	96.9	92.7	89.2	89.6	89.4	91.3	96.9	97.0	95.8	93.6
2000	90.9	95.5	96.6	96.3	92.6	89.4	88.4	89.3	94.2	96.9	97.0	96.9	93.6
2001	90.8	97.0	97.8	98.5	94.4	90.7	89.7	91.2	96.8	98.3	99.5	98.4	95.3
2002	93.1	98.9	99.5	101.5	97.8	94.2	92.9	94.5	98.9	99.2	100.3	99.6	97.5
2003	93.1	98.3	99.1	100.3	97.4	93.7	92.4	93.2	97.6	97.9	99.0	98.6	96.7

Employment by Industry: Tennessee—*Continued*

(Numbers in thousands. Not seasonally adjusted.)

Industry	January	February	March	April	May	June	July	August	September	October	November	December	Annual Average
STATEWIDE—*Continued*													
Local government													
1990	197.2	198.1	198.2	200.2	201.7	195.7	185.6	190.4	202.4	201.7	203.4	202.1	198.0
1991	201.3	201.5	201.8	203.4	204.7	195.9	187.9	193.1	205.8	205.9	206.8	206.7	201.2
1992	206.7	206.9	226.3	209.0	210.8	205.7	191.9	199.1	211.2	213.3	215.7	215.3	209.3
1993	213.2	215.1	215.4	217.1	218.6	211.1	196.9	203.3	219.8	220.5	221.5	222.6	214.5
1994	218.9	220.3	221.7	224.8	227.6	212.8	199.8	207.6	222.1	228.2	251.4	229.9	222.0
1995	224.3	226.0	227.6	228.8	230.4	218.4	205.1	211.5	230.2	234.8	235.8	236.4	225.7
1996	234.1	234.9	256.5	236.3	237.7	227.9	212.9	219.6	235.9	236.2	237.8	237.6	233.9
1997	235.8	237.9	238.9	237.7	239.3	235.2	220.6	225.5	238.3	239.6	241.2	241.8	235.9
1998	239.4	240.3	241.5	243.1	245.3	237.9	226.8	236.7	243.1	245.7	247.4	247.3	241.2
1999	244.7	246.7	248.0	247.6	250.1	240.7	229.2	238.7	245.6	249.8	250.8	251.7	245.3
2000	248.3	250.5	269.1	253.1	254.2	244.7	233.9	243.3	251.6	256.2	257.6	257.9	251.7
2001	256.4	258.3	259.4	259.5	261.2	251.5	239.1	249.1	256.6	260.7	262.6	262.4	256.4
2002	261.6	263.5	264.7	265.4	265.3	259.2	241.6	250.4	259.3	265.1	266.9	267.9	260.9
2003	263.7	265.1	266.2	267.6	268.2	260.3	249.1	258.6	266.4	266.9	267.7	268.7	264.0
CHATTANOOGA													
Total nonfarm													
1990	197.5	197.8	200.3	200.3	202.5	202.2	199.6	199.3	201.0	200.7	201.1	202.3	200.3
1991	196.4	195.9	196.1	197.5	197.7	198.9	196.5	197.9	201.6	202.8	201.8	202.1	198.7
1992	197.1	196.0	198.6	199.7	201.8	202.0	199.5	200.6	205.0	205.9	207.6	207.5	201.7
1993	202.5	203.2	203.9	206.8	208.7	210.5	209.4	210.1	213.2	213.2	215.7	216.2	209.4
1994	208.9	210.4	212.3	213.5	214.4	215.8	212.9	214.3	217.4	216.1	218.4	217.3	214.3
1995	211.5	212.9	215.4	216.1	217.0	218.3	215.1	217.0	218.8	219.0	221.2	222.6	217.0
1996	213.2	214.0	218.2	218.4	219.6	220.0	217.7	220.0	223.2	223.9	224.0	225.0	219.7
1997	217.6	218.3	220.7	221.4	219.5	218.7	217.6	218.6	220.9	221.0	220.1	220.6	219.5
1998	215.7	216.3	218.1	219.8	220.0	219.7	219.0	220.4	224.0	225.6	226.9	228.3	221.1
1999	221.5	224.3	226.2	231.1	231.0	228.2	229.7	230.3	232.9	234.3	234.0	235.2	229.8
2000	229.9	232.6	235.6	235.4	235.9	235.3	234.1	234.8	238.9	237.7	239.4	238.9	235.7
2001	231.9	232.6	233.4	234.9	235.0	232.3	230.3	230.5	232.9	233.1	234.3	233.9	232.9
2002	229.4	230.9	230.8	232.0	231.1	231.8	230.9	231.8	233.5	235.0	235.9	236.6	232.5
2003	231.9	232.6	234.0	233.0	232.4	231.9	231.3	232.0	234.3	235.1	236.1	236.8	233.5
Total private													
1990	163.7	163.5	164.8	166.1	166.8	167.8	167.8	167.6	166.8	166.3	167.2	166.8	166.2
1991	162.5	161.8	161.9	163.1	163.5	164.7	164.3	165.7	166.4	166.6	166.9	167.7	164.5
1992	162.7	161.8	163.3	165.5	167.6	168.7	167.7	168.8	171.0	171.0	172.8	172.9	167.8
1993	168.0	168.5	169.1	172.4	174.6	176.4	176.7	177.3	178.4	177.7	179.9	180.5	174.9
1994	174.3	175.1	176.9	178.3	179.6	180.7	179.7	180.8	181.8	179.9	181.3	181.5	179.1
1995	176.6	177.2	179.6	180.0	181.3	182.5	180.8	183.0	183.4	182.8	184.9	186.4	181.5
1996	177.5	177.7	180.5	181.8	183.5	185.4	184.1	186.8	188.3	188.8	189.0	190.0	184.4
1997	182.7	183.5	186.0	187.2	186.1	185.7	185.3	186.3	187.7	187.5	186.5	186.7	185.9
1998	182.2	182.6	184.2	186.2	187.0	188.3	188.1	189.5	191.5	192.2	193.1	194.8	188.3
1999	188.7	190.9	192.6	197.8	197.9	199.1	199.0	199.7	200.0	201.0	200.9	202.0	197.4
2000	197.1	199.4	202.0	202.1	202.4	204.1	203.1	203.7	205.4	203.8	205.2	204.4	202.7
2001	198.1	198.3	199.1	200.8	201.3	200.3	198.3	198.2	198.0	198.6	198.8	198.8	199.1
2002	194.8	195.5	195.4	196.9	196.7	197.2	197.0	197.1	197.8	199.4	200.1	200.7	197.4
2003	196.9	197.1	198.5	197.5	197.5	197.9	198.0	197.9	198.7	199.4	200.2	200.6	198.4
Goods-producing													
1990	52.7	52.5	52.6	52.3	52.3	52.5	53.2	53.0	52.7	51.7	51.8	51.3	52.3
1991	49.8	49.1	49.1	48.7	49.0	49.5	49.4	49.6	49.7	49.5	49.4	49.3	49.3
1992	48.4	48.0	48.2	48.4	48.7	49.1	48.9	49.4	49.7	49.9	50.2	49.9	49.0
1993	50.1	50.1	50.4	50.1	50.7	51.3	51.7	52.0	52.2	51.8	52.2	52.6	51.2
1994	51.3	51.2	51.7	52.3	52.3	52.7	52.7	52.9	52.7	52.1	52.2	52.6	52.2
1995	51.6	51.7	52.1	52.5	52.7	53.2	51.3	52.1	51.7	51.5	51.4	51.6	51.9
1996	50.8	50.8	51.3	50.9	50.8	51.2	49.6	51.2	51.3	51.4	51.0	51.1	50.9
1997	50.5	50.3	51.0	52.0	51.5	51.1	51.3	52.2	53.3	52.7	50.9	51.2	51.5
1998	51.6	51.5	51.7	51.6	50.7	51.0	51.6	51.9	52.3	52.4	52.4	52.3	51.7
1999	51.2	51.4	51.6	53.4	53.0	53.4	53.4	53.8	53.8	53.5	53.1	53.3	52.9
2000	53.1	53.4	54.2	53.8	54.2	55.0	54.9	55.0	55.5	54.4	54.4	53.6	54.2
2001	50.9	50.6	50.5	50.6	50.6	50.3	49.6	49.4	49.1	49.2	48.8	48.1	49.8
2002	47.2	47.2	46.6	46.6	46.6	46.8	46.1	46.2	46.1	46.1	45.4	45.3	46.4
2003	44.5	44.8	44.8	44.1	44.0	44.4	44.2	44.3	44.3	44.3	44.0	43.9	44.3
Construction and mining													
1990	7.5	7.2	7.3	7.6	7.6	7.7	8.1	8.2	8.0	7.8	7.8	7.5	7.7
1991	6.8	6.8	6.8	6.9	7.2	7.4	7.5	7.4	7.4	7.5	7.5	7.6	7.2
1992	7.0	6.7	7.0	7.0	7.2	7.2	7.2	7.3	7.3	7.5	7.4	7.1	7.2
1993	7.1	7.0	7.0	7.1	7.4	7.7	7.9	8.0	8.1	8.0	8.2	8.3	7.7
1994	7.5	7.5	7.7	7.8	8.2	8.4	8.6	8.5	8.6	8.2	8.2	8.4	8.1
1995	8.0	7.9	8.2	8.6	8.8	9.1	9.1	9.2	9.1	9.2	9.2	9.3	8.8
1996	8.6	8.7	8.9	9.2	9.6	9.8	9.7	9.7	9.8	10.1	9.8	9.8	9.5
1997	9.5	9.5	10.1	10.4	9.9	9.7	10.2	10.7	11.4	11.1	9.5	9.7	10.1
1998	9.6	9.4	9.6	9.8	9.9	10.0	9.8	9.8	9.9	10.2	9.9	10.0	9.8
1999	8.9	9.1	9.2	10.4	10.0	10.1	10.2	10.5	10.4	10.1	10.0	10.1	9.9
2000	9.6	9.9	10.5	9.7	10.0	10.3	10.4	10.6	11.2	10.6	10.7	10.1	10.3
2001	9.3	9.2	9.4	9.5	9.7	9.8	9.8	9.6	9.4	9.8	9.9	9.3	9.6
2002	8.7	8.6	8.7	8.7	8.8	8.9	8.7	8.8	8.8	8.9	8.8	8.7	8.8
2003	8.7	8.6	8.9	8.6	8.6	9.0	8.9	9.0	9.0	9.1	9.0	8.9	8.9

Employment by Industry: Tennessee—*Continued*

(Numbers in thousands. Not seasonally adjusted.)

Industry	January	February	March	April	May	June	July	August	September	October	November	December	Annual Average
CHATTANOOGA—*Continued*													
Manufacturing													
1990	45.2	45.3	45.3	44.7	44.7	44.8	45.1	44.8	44.7	43.9	44.0	43.8	44.6
1991	43.0	42.3	42.3	41.8	41.8	42.1	41.9	42.2	42.3	42.0	41.9	41.7	42.1
1992	41.4	41.3	41.2	41.4	41.5	41.9	41.7	42.1	42.4	42.4	42.8	42.8	41.9
1993	43.0	43.1	43.4	43.0	43.3	43.6	43.8	44.0	44.1	43.8	44.0	44.3	43.6
1994	43.8	43.7	44.0	44.5	44.1	44.3	44.1	44.4	44.1	43.9	44.0	44.2	44.0
1995	43.6	43.8	43.9	43.9	43.9	44.1	42.2	42.9	42.6	42.3	42.2	42.3	43.1
1996	42.2	42.1	42.4	41.7	41.2	41.4	39.9	41.5	41.5	41.3	41.2	41.3	41.4
1997	41.0	40.8	40.9	41.6	41.6	41.4	41.1	41.5	41.9	41.6	41.4	41.5	41.3
1998	42.0	42.1	42.1	41.8	40.8	41.0	41.8	42.1	42.4	42.2	42.5	42.3	41.9
1999	42.3	42.3	42.4	43.0	43.0	43.3	43.2	43.3	43.4	43.4	43.1	43.2	42.9
2000	43.5	43.5	43.7	44.1	44.2	44.7	44.5	44.4	44.3	43.8	43.7	43.5	43.9
2001	41.6	41.4	41.1	41.1	40.9	40.5	39.8	39.8	39.7	39.4	38.9	38.8	40.2
2002	38.5	38.6	37.9	37.9	37.8	37.9	37.4	37.4	37.3	37.2	36.6	36.6	37.6
2003	35.8	36.2	35.9	35.5	35.4	35.4	35.3	35.3	35.3	35.2	35.0	35.0	35.4
Service-providing													
1990	144.8	145.3	147.7	148.0	150.2	149.7	146.4	146.3	148.3	149.0	149.3	151.0	148.0
1991	146.6	146.8	147.0	148.8	148.7	149.4	147.1	148.3	151.9	153.3	152.4	152.8	149.4
1992	148.7	148.0	150.4	151.3	153.1	152.9	150.6	151.2	155.3	156.0	157.4	157.6	152.7
1993	152.4	153.1	153.5	156.7	158.0	159.2	157.7	158.1	161.0	161.4	163.5	163.6	158.1
1994	157.6	159.2	160.6	161.2	162.1	163.1	160.2	161.4	164.7	164.0	166.2	164.7	162.0
1995	159.9	161.2	163.3	163.6	164.3	165.1	163.8	164.9	167.1	167.5	169.8	171.0	165.1
1996	162.4	163.2	166.9	167.5	168.8	168.8	168.1	168.8	171.9	172.5	173.0	173.9	168.8
1997	167.1	168.0	169.7	169.4	168.0	167.6	166.3	166.4	167.6	168.3	169.2	169.4	168.0
1998	164.1	164.8	166.4	168.2	169.3	168.7	167.4	168.5	171.7	173.2	174.5	176.0	169.4
1999	170.3	172.9	174.6	177.7	178.0	174.8	176.3	176.5	179.1	180.8	180.9	181.9	176.9
2000	176.8	179.2	181.4	181.6	181.7	180.3	179.2	179.8	183.4	183.3	185.0	185.3	181.4
2001	181.0	182.0	182.9	184.3	184.4	182.0	180.7	181.1	183.8	183.9	185.5	185.8	183.1
2002	182.2	183.7	184.2	185.4	184.5	185.0	184.8	185.6	187.4	188.9	190.5	191.3	186.1
2003	187.4	187.8	189.2	188.9	188.4	187.5	187.1	187.7	190.0	190.8	192.1	192.9	189.2
Trade, transportation, and utilities													
1990	40.5	40.3	40.7	41.0	41.3	41.4	41.0	41.1	41.1	40.3	41.2	41.5	40.9
1991	40.5	40.1	40.2	39.8	39.4	39.6	39.6	40.2	40.7	40.2	41.1	41.8	40.2
1992	39.2	38.7	39.1	39.4	40.2	40.1	40.1	40.4	41.1	41.0	41.9	42.2	40.2
1993	40.8	40.6	40.5	40.8	41.3	41.3	41.7	42.0	42.3	42.2	43.7	44.3	41.7
1994	40.9	40.9	41.1	41.6	41.7	42.0	41.7	42.6	42.2	42.4	43.5	44.0	42.0
1995	41.9	41.5	41.9	42.1	42.2	42.7	43.1	44.1	43.8	44.1	45.5	46.5	43.2
1996	43.4	43.0	43.5	43.0	44.1	45.2	45.8	46.9	47.3	48.8	49.6	49.9	45.8
1997	46.6	46.3	46.8	47.0	46.7	46.8	46.3	46.1	46.3	47.0	47.7	48.0	46.8
1998	45.5	45.1	45.6	46.5	47.6	48.7	48.1	49.1	50.0	51.3	52.2	52.8	48.5
1999	50.2	51.0	51.9	53.8	54.1	54.4	53.4	53.9	53.8	55.4	56.0	57.1	53.7
2000	54.5	55.1	55.3	55.6	56.0	55.5	55.4	55.5	55.9	56.4	57.5	57.6	55.8
2001	54.4	53.9	54.4	55.0	55.5	55.3	54.4	54.4	54.2	55.2	55.7	56.1	54.9
2002	54.3	54.2	54.2	54.5	54.3	54.2	54.4	54.5	54.4	55.2	55.9	56.6	54.7
2003	54.5	54.2	54.5	54.6	54.7	54.7	54.8	55.1	55.1	55.6	56.3	57.0	55.1
Wholesale trade													
1990	10.6	10.6	10.6	10.6	10.7	10.8	10.8	10.8	10.8	10.2	10.3	10.4	10.6
1991	10.1	10.1	10.0	10.0	10.1	10.3	10.4	10.7	10.7	10.4	10.4	10.5	10.3
1992	10.1	10.1	10.2	10.2	10.4	10.3	10.3	10.4	10.5	10.2	10.0	10.1	10.2
1993	10.0	10.1	10.1	10.0	10.2	10.1	10.4	10.5	10.5	10.2	10.4	10.4	10.2
1994	9.7	9.9	9.9	9.8	9.7	9.9	9.7	10.0	9.7	9.4	9.3	9.3	9.6
1995	9.3	9.3	9.5	9.2	9.2	9.4	9.2	9.5	9.4	9.2	9.3	9.5	9.3
1996	9.3	9.4	9.4	9.3	9.3	9.3	9.3	9.3	9.4	9.4	9.3	9.3	9.3
1997	9.1	9.1	9.2	9.0	9.0	9.1	9.0	9.2	9.3	9.3	9.4	9.5	9.1
1998	9.2	9.1	9.1	9.1	9.1	9.1	8.9	8.9	9.0	8.8	8.8	8.8	8.9
1999	8.7	8.8	8.8	8.9	8.9	8.9	8.7	8.8	8.8	8.9	8.8	9.0	8.8
2000	8.9	8.9	9.0	8.9	8.9	8.9	8.9	8.9	9.0	9.0	9.2	9.3	8.9
2001	8.4	8.4	8.3	8.3	8.2	8.3	8.2	8.3	8.3	8.4	8.4	8.4	8.3
2002	8.3	8.2	8.1	8.2	8.2	8.2	8.3	8.3	8.4	8.5	8.5	8.7	8.3
2003	8.8	8.8	8.8	8.8	8.9	8.9	8.9	8.9	8.9	8.9	9.0	9.1	8.9
Retail trade													
1990	22.8	22.4	22.7	22.8	23.0	23.0	22.6	22.7	22.5	22.6	23.3	23.5	22.8
1991	23.3	22.9	23.0	22.6	22.6	22.5	22.7	22.9	23.3	23.1	23.9	24.5	23.1
1992	22.7	22.2	22.4	22.7	23.2	23.3	23.6	23.9	24.3	24.6	25.6	25.8	23.6
1993	25.0	24.8	24.6	25.2	25.4	25.4	25.6	25.7	26.0	26.0	27.2	27.8	25.7
1994	25.4	25.1	25.2	25.5	25.6	25.7	25.5	25.9	25.9	26.3	27.4	28.0	25.9
1995	26.1	25.7	25.9	26.4	26.4	26.7	27.1	27.7	27.5	27.9	29.1	30.0	27.2
1996	27.4	26.9	27.2	27.3	27.5	27.5	26.6	26.9	27.1	27.8	28.9	29.6	27.5
1997	27.5	26.8	27.1	27.5	27.1	27.1	26.5	26.0	25.9	26.5	27.2	27.5	26.8
1998	25.7	25.4	25.8	26.3	26.5	26.4	24.9	24.8	25.3	25.6	26.4	27.0	25.8
1999	24.6	25.1	25.6	25.7	25.8	26.0	25.9	26.1	26.1	26.6	27.3	28.3	26.0
2000	25.8	25.8	25.7	25.8	26.0	25.8	25.8	25.6	26.2	26.5	27.4	27.6	26.1
2001	26.3	25.9	26.1	26.2	26.3	26.3	25.9	25.9	26.0	26.5	27.3	27.7	26.4
2002	26.2	26.1	26.3	26.2	26.0	26.0	26.2	26.1	26.0	26.2	26.8	27.2	26.3
2003	25.7	25.6	25.7	25.8	25.8	25.9	26.1	26.2	26.2	26.4	26.9	27.4	26.1

Employment by Industry: Tennessee—*Continued*

(Numbers in thousands. Not seasonally adjusted.)

Industry	January	February	March	April	May	June	July	August	September	October	November	December	Annual Average
CHATTANOOGA—*Continued*													
Transportation and utilities													
1990	7.1	7.3	7.4	7.6	7.6	7.6	7.6	7.6	7.8	7.5	7.6	7.6	7.5
1991	7.1	7.1	7.2	7.2	6.7	6.8	6.5	6.6	6.7	6.7	6.8	6.8	6.8
1992	6.4	6.4	6.5	6.5	6.6	6.5	6.2	6.1	6.3	6.2	6.3	6.3	6.3
1993	5.8	5.7	5.8	5.6	5.7	5.8	5.7	5.8	5.8	6.0	6.1	6.1	5.8
1994	5.8	5.9	6.0	6.3	6.4	6.4	6.5	6.7	6.6	6.7	6.8	6.7	6.4
1995	6.5	6.5	6.5	6.5	6.6	6.6	6.8	6.9	6.9	7.0	7.1	7.0	6.7
1996	6.7	6.7	6.9	6.4	7.3	8.4	9.9	10.7	10.8	11.6	11.4	11.0	8.9
1997	10.0	10.4	10.5	10.5	10.6	10.6	10.8	10.9	11.1	11.2	11.1	11.0	10.7
1998	10.6	10.6	10.7	11.1	12.0	13.2	14.3	15.4	15.7	16.9	17.0	17.0	13.7
1999	16.9	17.1	17.5	19.2	19.4	19.5	18.8	19.0	18.9	19.9	19.9	19.8	18.8
2000	19.8	20.4	20.6	20.9	21.1	20.8	20.7	21.0	20.7	20.9	20.9	20.7	20.7
2001	19.7	19.6	20.0	20.5	21.0	20.7	20.3	20.2	19.9	20.3	20.0	20.0	20.2
2002	19.8	19.9	19.8	20.1	20.1	20.0	19.9	20.1	20.0	20.5	20.6	20.7	20.1
2003	20.0	19.8	20.0	20.0	20.0	19.9	19.8	20.0	20.0	20.3	20.4	20.5	20.1
Information													
1990	2.6	2.6	2.6	2.7	2.6	2.6	2.6	2.6	2.6	2.5	2.6	2.6	2.6
1991	2.7	2.6	2.6	2.6	2.6	2.5	2.6	2.6	2.5	2.6	2.6	2.6	2.5
1992	2.5	2.5	2.5	2.5	2.5	2.5	2.5	2.5	2.5	2.6	2.5	2.5	2.5
1993	2.4	2.4	2.3	2.3	2.3	2.3	2.3	2.3	2.3	2.4	2.4	2.4	2.3
1994	2.4	2.4	2.4	2.5	2.5	2.5	2.4	2.4	2.5	2.5	2.5	2.5	2.4
1995	2.6	2.6	2.6	2.6	2.7	2.7	2.7	2.7	2.7	2.7	2.7	2.8	2.6
1996	2.7	2.6	2.7	2.7	2.7	2.7	2.7	2.7	2.7	2.6	2.6	2.6	2.6
1997	2.6	2.6	2.7	2.6	2.6	2.6	2.6	2.6	2.6	2.6	2.7	2.7	2.6
1998	2.6	2.7	2.7	2.7	2.6	2.6	2.6	2.6	2.7	2.7	2.7	2.8	2.6
1999	2.9	2.9	2.9	2.9	2.9	2.9	2.9	2.9	2.9	2.9	2.8	2.8	2.8
2000	3.0	3.0	3.0	3.0	3.0	3.1	3.0	3.0	3.0	2.9	3.0	3.1	3.0
2001	2.9	2.9	2.8	2.7	2.7	2.7	2.7	2.7	2.7	2.7	2.6	2.6	2.7
2002	2.6	2.6	2.6	2.6	2.6	2.7	2.7	2.7	2.7	2.7	2.8	2.8	2.7
2003	2.7	2.7	2.7	2.7	2.8	2.8	2.8	2.8	2.8	2.8	2.9	2.8	2.8
Financial activities													
1990	12.5	12.5	12.6	12.4	12.5	12.4	12.6	12.6	12.6	12.5	12.6	12.6	12.5
1991	12.8	12.9	12.9	12.8	12.8	12.7	12.8	12.8	12.7	12.7	12.7	12.9	12.7
1992	12.6	12.6	12.7	12.6	12.6	12.7	12.7	12.8	12.7	12.7	12.7	12.7	12.6
1993	12.6	12.4	12.4	12.6	12.7	12.8	12.7	12.7	12.8	12.9	13.1	13.2	12.7
1994	13.1	13.2	13.3	13.2	13.2	13.3	13.4	13.3	13.3	13.2	13.3	13.3	13.2
1995	13.3	13.2	13.3	13.1	13.1	13.3	13.4	13.5	13.5	13.7	13.8	14.0	13.4
1996	13.7	13.8	14.1	14.0	14.1	14.2	14.2	14.3	14.3	14.2	14.3	14.6	14.1
1997	14.7	14.7	14.7	15.0	15.0	15.0	15.0	15.0	15.0	14.8	14.8	14.9	14.8
1998	14.8	14.8	14.9	15.0	15.1	15.1	15.2	15.3	15.4	15.9	15.9	16.1	15.2
1999	15.5	15.6	15.7	16.0	16.1	16.2	15.7	15.7	15.7	15.6	15.6	15.7	15.7
2000	15.6	15.7	15.8	15.7	15.7	15.9	15.4	15.4	15.5	15.5	15.6	15.7	15.6
2001	17.2	17.3	17.5	17.7	17.7	17.8	17.7	17.8	17.7	17.7	17.9	17.9	17.7
2002	17.9	18.0	18.1	18.2	18.2	18.2	18.0	18.0	18.1	18.2	18.4	18.5	18.2
2003	18.1	18.0	18.0	17.7	17.6	17.7	17.7	17.6	17.7	17.8	18.0	18.1	17.8
Professional and business services													
1990	14.7	14.9	15.1	15.3	15.7	15.9	15.3	15.2	15.4	16.5	16.5	16.1	15.5
1991	15.3	15.9	15.7	17.5	17.8	17.9	17.3	18.1	18.2	19.1	19.0	18.9	17.5
1992	17.7	17.8	18.2	18.9	19.4	19.8	19.0	18.8	19.6	20.0	20.3	20.4	19.1
1993	18.0	18.4	18.7	19.7	20.1	20.5	20.2	20.7	21.0	20.7	21.1	20.8	19.9
1994	21.0	21.2	21.6	21.9	22.2	22.1	21.6	21.7	22.4	21.9	22.0	21.8	21.7
1995	21.2	22.0	22.7	22.3	22.5	22.3	21.9	22.3	22.8	22.9	23.1	23.2	22.4
1996	20.8	21.0	21.8	22.6	22.8	23.0	23.4	23.4	23.3	23.5	23.9	23.8	22.7
1997	21.7	22.0	22.4	22.4	22.2	22.9	22.5	23.0	23.2	23.3	23.0	22.6	22.6
1998	21.7	21.9	22.1	22.2	22.3	22.6	22.8	22.9	23.0	22.7	22.8	23.1	22.5
1999	22.6	22.9	22.7	23.0	23.0	23.1	23.7	24.0	23.9	24.2	24.1	24.6	23.4
2000	23.2	23.6	23.8	23.5	23.2	23.4	22.7	23.2	23.4	23.0	22.9	22.3	23.1
2001	24.2	24.3	24.4	24.6	24.4	23.9	23.6	23.4	23.5	23.9	23.7	24.1	24.0
2002	23.5	23.7	23.9	24.1	24.0	24.0	24.6	24.5	24.8	25.3	25.6	25.6	24.5
2003	25.6	25.6	25.9	25.1	25.0	24.9	25.3	25.1	25.4	25.6	25.8	25.8	25.4
Educational and health services													
1990	14.7	14.9	15.1	15.3	15.4	15.3	15.4	15.3	15.2	15.5	15.4	15.4	15.2
1991	15.0	15.3	15.3	15.4	15.5	15.5	15.5	15.7	15.8	16.0	15.9	15.9	15.5
1992	15.6	15.7	16.0	16.5	16.7	16.9	16.7	16.8	17.2	17.1	17.2	17.2	16.6
1993	16.4	16.7	16.8	17.4	17.6	17.9	17.5	17.5	17.7	17.5	17.7	17.5	17.3
1994	17.4	17.5	17.6	17.5	17.5	17.0	17.2	17.3	17.8	17.9	18.0	17.9	17.5
1995	17.4	17.6	17.7	17.9	17.8	17.5	17.5	17.6	18.2	18.5	18.8	18.6	17.9
1996	17.9	17.8	18.0	18.2	18.2	18.3	18.1	18.2	19.0	19.0	19.3	19.5	18.4
1997	18.6	19.0	19.0	19.0	19.0	19.0	19.0	19.0	19.6	19.8	19.7	19.7	19.2
1998	19.8	20.1	20.2	20.0	19.9	19.5	19.0	19.0	19.9	19.8	19.8	20.1	19.7
1999	19.1	19.8	19.9	19.7	19.6	19.3	19.5	19.5	20.0	20.0	20.1	19.8	19.6
2000	19.7	20.2	20.4	20.4	19.9	20.1	20.1	20.2	21.0	21.2	21.4	21.5	20.5
2001	21.1	21.6	21.4	21.3	21.2	21.0	20.7	21.0	21.6	21.7	21.8	21.7	21.3
2002	21.6	21.7	21.6	21.8	21.5	21.5	21.5	21.6	22.3	22.6	22.7	22.7	21.9
2003	22.7	23.0	23.1	23.3	23.1	22.9	22.8	22.8	23.3	23.4	23.3	23.2	23.1

Employment by Industry: Tennessee—*Continued*

(Numbers in thousands. Not seasonally adjusted.)

Industry	January	February	March	April	May	June	July	August	September	October	November	December	Annual Average
CHATTANOOGA—*Continued*													
Leisure and hospitality													
1990	15.9	15.8	16.3	16.7	17.1	17.5	17.4	17.6	17.1	17.3	17.2	17.3	16.9
1991	15.4	15.4	15.9	16.5	16.8	17.3	17.5	17.5	17.3	16.2	16.3	16.3	16.5
1992	15.8	15.7	16.4	16.9	17.3	17.7	18.3	18.5	18.0	17.7	17.7	17.5	17.2
1993	17.1	17.4	17.4	18.6	19.1	19.5	19.8	19.7	19.5	19.2	19.2	19.1	18.8
1994	17.7	17.7	18.3	19.0	19.6	20.1	19.8	20.1	19.8	18.9	18.8	18.8	19.0
1995	17.6	17.7	18.3	18.4	19.2	19.6	19.6	19.6	19.3	18.5	18.7	18.7	18.7
1996	17.5	17.8	18.3	19.8	20.0	20.2	20.1	19.9	19.5	18.9	18.9	18.9	19.1
1997	17.8	17.9	18.5	19.3	19.3	19.8	19.5	19.4	19.0	18.1	18.1	18.1	18.7
1998	17.5	17.4	17.8	18.5	19.1	19.6	19.4	19.4	19.1	18.1	18.1	18.2	18.5
1999	17.7	17.9	18.2	19.1	19.4	20.0	19.7	19.5	19.2	18.6	18.7	18.5	18.8
2000	18.0	18.0	18.5	19.2	19.4	19.9	20.4	20.3	20.0	19.3	19.0	19.1	19.2
2001	17.1	17.4	17.7	18.5	18.8	18.8	18.9	18.9	18.7	17.8	17.9	17.9	18.2
2002	17.4	17.7	18.0	18.6	18.9	19.0	19.0	19.1	18.9	18.7	18.7	18.6	18.6
2003	18.3	18.3	18.9	19.4	19.6	19.7	19.7	19.7	19.5	19.3	19.3	19.2	19.2
Other services													
1990	10.1	10.0	9.8	10.4	9.9	10.2	10.3	10.2	10.1	10.0	9.9	10.0	10.0
1991	11.0	10.5	10.2	9.8	9.6	9.7	9.6	9.2	9.5	10.3	9.9	10.0	9.9
1992	10.9	10.8	10.2	10.3	10.2	9.9	9.5	9.6	10.2	10.0	10.3	10.5	10.2
1993	10.6	10.5	10.6	10.9	10.8	10.8	10.8	10.4	10.6	11.0	10.5	10.6	10.6
1994	10.5	11.0	10.9	10.3	10.6	11.0	10.9	10.5	11.1	11.0	11.0	10.6	10.7
1995	11.0	10.9	11.0	11.1	11.1	11.2	11.3	11.1	11.4	10.9	10.9	11.0	11.0
1996	10.7	10.9	10.8	10.6	10.8	10.6	10.2	10.2	10.9	10.4	9.4	9.6	10.4
1997	10.2	10.7	10.9	9.9	9.8	8.5	9.1	9.0	8.7	9.2	9.6	9.5	9.5
1998	8.7	9.1	9.2	9.7	9.7	9.2	9.4	9.3	9.1	9.3	9.2	9.4	9.2
1999	9.5	9.4	9.7	9.9	9.8	9.8	10.7	10.4	10.7	10.8	10.5	10.2	10.1
2000	10.0	10.4	11.0	10.9	11.0	11.2	11.2	11.1	11.1	11.1	11.4	11.5	10.9
2001	10.3	10.3	10.4	10.4	10.4	10.5	10.7	10.6	10.5	10.4	10.4	10.4	10.4
2002	10.3	10.4	10.4	10.5	10.6	10.8	10.7	10.5	10.5	10.6	10.6	10.6	10.5
2003	10.5	10.5	10.6	10.6	10.7	10.8	10.7	10.5	10.6	10.6	10.6	10.6	10.6
Government													
1990	33.8	34.3	35.5	34.2	35.7	34.4	31.8	31.7	34.2	34.4	33.9	35.5	34.1
1991	33.9	34.1	34.2	34.4	34.2	34.2	32.2	32.2	35.2	36.2	34.9	34.4	34.1
1992	34.4	34.2	35.3	34.2	34.2	33.3	31.8	31.8	34.0	34.9	34.8	34.6	33.9
1993	34.5	34.7	34.8	34.4	34.1	34.1	32.7	32.8	34.8	35.5	35.8	35.7	34.4
1994	34.6	35.3	35.4	35.2	34.8	35.1	33.2	33.5	35.6	36.2	37.1	35.8	35.1
1995	34.9	35.7	35.8	36.1	35.7	35.8	34.3	34.0	35.4	36.2	36.3	36.2	35.5
1996	35.7	36.3	37.7	36.6	36.1	34.6	33.6	33.2	34.9	35.1	35.0	35.0	35.3
1997	34.9	34.8	34.7	34.2	33.4	33.0	32.3	32.3	33.2	33.5	33.6	33.9	33.6
1998	33.5	33.7	33.9	33.6	33.0	31.4	30.9	30.9	32.5	33.4	33.8	33.5	32.8
1999	32.8	33.4	33.6	33.3	33.1	29.1	30.7	30.6	32.9	33.3	33.1	33.2	32.4
2000	32.8	33.2	33.6	33.3	33.5	31.2	31.0	31.1	33.5	33.9	34.2	34.5	32.9
2001	33.8	34.3	34.3	34.1	33.7	32.0	32.0	32.3	34.9	34.5	35.5	35.1	33.9
2002	34.6	35.4	35.4	35.1	34.4	34.6	33.9	34.7	35.7	35.6	35.8	35.9	35.1
2003	35.0	35.5	35.5	35.5	34.9	34.0	33.3	34.1	35.6	35.7	35.9	36.2	35.1
Federal government													
1992	7.7	7.6	7.5	7.5	7.5	7.4	7.4	7.4	7.4	7.5	7.3	7.3	7.4
1993	7.3	7.3	7.3	7.3	7.3	7.3	7.5	7.5	7.5	7.4	7.4	7.4	7.3
1994	7.4	7.4	7.5	7.5	7.5	7.5	8.0	8.1	8.1	8.2	7.8	7.8	7.7
1995	7.7	7.7	7.7	7.7	7.7	7.7	7.7	7.7	7.7	7.7	7.7	7.7	7.7
1996	7.7	7.8	7.8	7.8	7.7	7.7	7.7	7.8	7.7	7.7	7.5	7.6	7.7
1997	7.6	7.5	7.5	7.4	7.4	7.4	7.4	7.3	7.1	7.3	7.3	7.3	7.3
1998	6.9	6.8	6.8	6.7	6.7	6.7	6.7	6.7	6.7	7.0	7.1	7.0	6.8
1999	6.8	6.7	6.7	6.9	6.6	6.5	6.5	6.5	6.5	6.5	6.7	6.7	6.6
2000	6.6	6.5	6.7	6.9	7.7	6.9	7.0	6.8	6.6	6.6	6.7	6.9	6.8
2001	6.7	6.6	6.6	6.7	6.6	6.7	6.7	6.8	6.8	6.8	7.0	7.0	6.8
2002	6.9	6.9	7.0	6.9	6.8	6.8	6.8	6.9	6.9	6.9	7.0	7.0	6.9
2003	6.8	6.8	6.7	6.7	6.7	6.7	6.7	6.7	6.8	6.8	6.9	7.1	6.8
State government													
1992	7.1	7.1	7.1	7.0	6.8	6.7	6.8	6.7	6.9	7.2	7.1	7.0	6.9
1993	7.1	7.3	7.3	6.9	6.5	6.6	6.6	6.6	7.3	7.3	7.3	7.3	7.0
1994	6.7	7.2	7.1	7.1	6.6	6.6	6.6	6.7	7.2	7.4	7.3	7.3	6.9
1995	6.7	7.2	7.3	7.3	6.6	6.4	6.4	6.4	7.2	7.3	7.3	7.3	6.9
1996	6.6	7.1	7.2	7.0	6.5	6.2	6.2	6.1	6.9	7.0	7.0	7.0	6.7
1997	7.0	7.0	6.9	6.8	6.2	5.9	5.9	6.0	6.8	6.9	6.9	6.9	6.6
1998	6.6	6.9	7.0	6.8	6.2	6.1	6.1	6.1	6.8	6.9	6.9	7.0	6.6
1999	6.6	7.0	7.0	7.0	6.2	5.9	5.9	5.8	6.4	6.4	6.3	6.3	6.4
2000	5.8	6.2	6.2	6.2	5.6	5.4	5.5	5.5	6.1	6.2	6.3	6.2	5.9
2001	5.9	6.4	6.4	6.4	5.7	5.6	5.6	5.7	6.3	6.4	6.5	6.5	6.1
2002	6.1	6.5	6.4	6.6	5.9	5.9	5.9	6.0	6.6	6.6	6.6	6.7	6.3
2003	6.1	6.5	6.5	6.5	5.8	5.9	5.8	5.9	6.5	6.6	6.6	6.7	6.3

Employment by Industry: Tennessee—*Continued*

(Numbers in thousands. Not seasonally adjusted.)

Industry	January	February	March	April	May	June	July	August	September	October	November	December	Annual Average
CHATTANOOGA—*Continued*													
Local government													
1992	19.6	19.5	20.7	19.7	19.9	19.2	17.6	17.7	19.7	20.2	20.4	20.3	19.5
1993	20.1	20.1	20.2	20.2	20.3	20.2	18.6	18.7	20.0	20.8	21.1	21.0	20.1
1994	20.5	20.7	20.8	20.6	20.7	21.0	18.6	18.7	20.3	20.6	22.0	20.7	20.4
1995	20.5	20.8	20.8	21.1	21.4	21.7	20.2	19.9	20.5	21.2	21.3	21.2	20.8
1996	21.4	21.4	22.7	21.8	21.9	20.7	19.7	19.3	20.3	20.4	20.5	20.4	20.8
1997	20.3	20.3	20.3	20.0	19.8	19.7	19.0	19.0	19.3	19.3	19.4	19.7	19.6
1998	20.0	20.0	20.1	20.1	20.1	18.6	18.1	18.1	19.0	19.5	19.8	19.5	19.4
1999	19.4	19.7	19.9	19.4	20.3	16.7	18.3	18.3	20.0	20.4	20.1	20.2	19.3
2000	20.4	20.5	20.7	20.2	20.2	18.9	18.5	18.8	20.8	21.1	21.2	21.4	20.2
2001	21.2	21.3	21.3	21.0	21.4	19.7	19.7	19.8	21.8	21.3	22.0	21.6	21.0
2002	21.6	22.0	22.0	21.6	21.7	21.9	21.2	21.8	22.2	22.1	22.2	22.2	21.9
2003	22.1	22.2	22.3	22.3	22.4	21.4	20.8	21.5	22.3	22.3	22.4	22.4	22.0
KNOXVILLE													
Total nonfarm													
1990	258.6	257.6	260.7	264.9	268.8	271.5	265.7	267.9	270.6	269.3	269.5	268.2	266.1
1991	260.2	259.9	263.0	269.6	273.1	276.0	269.0	271.3	276.4	277.2	278.4	278.0	271.0
1992	273.5	273.8	279.6	283.1	286.0	287.7	285.0	287.9	290.2	292.5	291.8	292.1	285.2
1993	284.0	285.3	287.2	296.9	298.1	300.2	299.0	299.8	301.7	302.8	302.9	302.9	296.7
1994	289.1	291.6	295.8	302.2	304.8	306.7	305.3	307.2	309.7	310.7	314.1	312.2	304.1
1995	300.3	301.2	306.5	311.6	314.6	317.4	315.1	318.7	322.3	320.4	318.5	318.7	313.7
1996	303.9	303.5	311.7	313.8	318.9	317.0	315.3	315.8	317.3	317.4	318.1	317.6	314.1
1997	306.1	307.8	311.4	319.7	321.3	323.7	319.6	320.5	322.1	324.1	324.1	325.0	318.7
1998	312.1	314.1	318.7	325.1	329.2	331.6	329.5	329.9	332.3	331.6	332.4	333.5	326.6
1999	320.2	323.5	327.0	331.0	333.0	335.6	334.1	335.0	335.9	336.8	336.9	337.3	332.1
2000	327.4	328.9	335.2	338.1	342.6	344.8	340.9	340.6	343.5	342.1	342.3	342.6	339.0
2001	332.7	333.6	338.2	341.3	343.3	345.8	341.2	340.7	344.0	342.8	343.0	343.1	340.8
2002	333.8	334.4	338.7	346.6	349.5	352.9	350.3	351.1	352.2	355.3	355.3	356.5	348.1
2003	345.8	345.7	349.7	354.4	357.0	358.9	355.9	357.2	360.0	360.5	359.9	360.2	355.4
Total private													
1990	207.6	206.4	209.3	213.1	216.6	220.3	219.1	220.1	219.5	217.8	217.8	216.8	215.3
1991	208.9	208.2	210.9	216.8	220.3	223.7	222.4	223.7	225.2	225.0	225.9	225.4	219.7
1992	220.4	220.3	224.3	229.3	232.3	234.7	235.1	237.0	236.5	237.7	236.9	237.1	231.8
1993	229.4	230.4	232.0	241.1	242.5	244.9	247.8	248.4	246.9	246.8	247.1	247.3	242.0
1994	234.8	236.8	240.8	246.4	248.8	252.0	251.9	253.2	253.5	254.1	255.0	255.5	248.5
1995	245.6	246.0	251.1	255.8	259.0	263.1	262.5	265.8	267.2	264.1	262.1	262.3	258.7
1996	248.1	248.0	253.9	257.8	263.5	262.7	263.2	263.5	262.9	261.5	262.3	262.1	259.1
1997	252.1	252.9	256.5	264.4	266.1	269.5	268.0	268.4	267.8	268.9	268.4	269.4	264.3
1998	258.0	259.5	263.9	270.1	273.9	277.2	277.7	277.4	277.5	275.5	275.8	277.1	271.9
1999	265.5	268.1	271.5	274.9	277.5	281.2	281.8	282.3	281.1	280.6	280.5	281.2	277.1
2000	273.1	273.8	278.3	282.0	285.4	288.8	287.9	288.0	287.6	286.0	286.2	286.4	283.6
2001	276.6	276.6	281.1	285.2	287.1	289.9	288.8	288.1	287.0	284.5	284.7	284.7	284.5
2002	276.7	277.0	281.2	287.5	290.1	293.9	294.2	294.8	293.8	295.4	295.4	296.5	289.7
2003	287.7	287.3	291.0	295.3	297.9	300.2	299.8	300.1	300.4	300.6	299.8	300.2	296.7
Goods-producing													
1990	58.0	57.0	57.3	57.3	57.8	58.0	57.3	57.4	57.7	57.8	57.5	57.3	57.5
1991	55.3	54.6	54.9	55.4	56.0	56.8	55.4	56.5	57.2	57.6	58.3	57.7	56.3
1992	56.6	57.0	58.2	58.8	58.9	59.0	58.7	59.4	59.3	60.0	59.6	59.1	58.7
1993	58.2	58.6	59.2	60.7	61.2	61.1	62.4	61.6	61.3	60.9	61.0	61.1	60.6
1994	58.7	58.8	59.4	60.3	61.0	61.4	62.3	62.9	63.3	63.6	64.1	63.6	61.6
1995	62.4	62.2	63.9	63.9	64.3	65.0	64.6	66.6	67.3	65.9	63.4	62.6	64.3
1996	60.8	60.7	62.3	63.6	66.0	62.4	61.6	61.7	61.8	62.2	61.9	61.5	62.2
1997	61.0	60.8	61.2	62.1	61.8	62.6	62.1	62.5	62.8	64.1	63.6	63.5	62.3
1998	61.7	61.4	62.9	63.8	63.8	63.9	63.9	63.8	64.0	63.2	62.8	62.7	63.1
1999	60.8	61.0	61.6	62.9	63.1	63.4	63.6	63.6	63.9	63.4	63.2	63.5	62.8
2000	62.8	63.0	63.8	63.2	63.3	63.7	63.0	63.1	63.0	62.2	61.9	62.1	62.9
2001	61.3	60.9	61.5	61.0	60.8	61.0	60.1	60.0	59.7	59.1	59.0	58.7	60.3
2002	57.5	57.5	58.2	58.7	59.0	59.8	59.8	59.8	59.5	60.4	60.0	60.2	59.2
2003	58.9	58.5	59.1	59.3	59.6	59.4	59.3	58.9	59.4	59.4	59.3	59.3	59.2
Construction and mining													
1990	13.3	12.5	12.7	13.0	13.1	13.1	13.0	13.0	13.1	13.3	13.2	12.7	13.0
1991	11.5	11.4	11.8	11.9	12.1	12.1	12.1	12.3	12.7	12.5	12.5	12.4	12.1
1992	11.8	12.4	13.3	13.8	13.7	13.6	13.5	13.9	14.4	14.9	14.3	13.5	13.6
1993	12.7	13.1	13.6	14.6	15.2	15.4	15.7	15.3	15.1	15.1	15.1	14.8	14.6
1994	13.4	13.5	14.0	14.6	15.0	15.0	16.1	16.4	16.7	17.4	17.6	17.1	15.6
1995	16.2	16.0	17.4	17.9	18.3	18.6	18.8	20.6	21.4	20.4	17.8	16.9	18.4
1996	16.0	16.0	17.1	18.8	21.1	17.5	16.6	16.5	16.4	16.5	16.1	15.6	17.0
1997	15.1	14.9	15.5	16.2	16.1	16.3	16.7	16.8	16.8	16.9	16.3	16.3	16.2
1998	15.6	15.2	15.8	16.6	16.8	17.0	17.4	17.3	17.2	16.9	16.8	17.2	16.7
1999	15.3	15.8	16.1	16.9	16.9	16.9	16.6	16.6	16.6	16.7	16.7	16.6	16.5
2000	16.2	16.4	17.2	16.8	16.8	17.0	17.0	17.0	17.1	16.6	16.5	16.6	16.8
2001	15.7	15.9	16.4	16.6	16.8	17.2	16.9	16.8	16.8	16.8	16.9	16.7	16.6
2002	15.3	15.4	15.9	16.3	16.6	17.1	17.0	17.0	16.8	17.6	17.2	17.3	16.6
2003	16.5	16.1	16.8	17.1	17.4	17.3	17.4	17.0	17.4	17.4	17.5	17.6	17.1

Employment by Industry: Tennessee—*Continued*

(Numbers in thousands. Not seasonally adjusted.)

Industry	January	February	March	April	May	June	July	August	September	October	November	December	Annual Average
KNOXVILLE—*Continued*													
Manufacturing													
1990	44.7	44.5	44.6	44.3	44.7	44.9	44.3	44.4	44.6	44.5	44.3	44.6	44.5
1991	43.8	43.2	43.1	43.5	43.9	44.7	43.3	44.2	44.5	45.1	45.8	45.3	44.2
1992	44.8	44.6	44.9	45.0	45.2	45.4	45.2	45.5	44.9	45.1	45.3	45.6	45.1
1993	45.5	45.5	45.6	46.1	46.0	45.7	46.7	46.3	46.2	45.8	45.9	46.3	45.9
1994	45.3	45.3	45.4	45.7	46.0	46.4	46.2	46.5	46.6	46.2	46.5	46.5	46.0
1995	46.2	46.2	46.5	46.0	46.0	46.4	45.8	46.0	45.9	45.5	45.6	45.7	45.9
1996	44.8	44.7	45.2	44.8	44.9	44.9	45.0	45.2	45.4	45.7	45.8	45.9	45.1
1997	45.9	45.9	45.7	45.9	45.7	46.3	45.4	45.7	46.0	47.2	47.3	47.2	46.1
1998	46.1	46.2	47.1	47.2	47.0	46.9	46.5	46.5	46.8	46.3	46.0	45.5	46.5
1999	45.5	45.2	45.5	46.0	46.2	46.5	47.0	47.0	47.3	46.7	46.5	46.9	46.3
2000	46.6	46.6	46.6	46.4	46.5	46.7	46.0	46.1	45.9	45.6	45.4	45.5	46.1
2001	45.6	45.0	45.1	44.4	44.0	43.8	43.2	43.2	42.9	42.3	42.1	42.0	43.6
2002	42.2	42.1	42.3	42.4	42.4	42.7	42.8	42.8	42.7	42.8	42.8	42.9	42.6
2003	42.4	42.4	42.3	42.2	42.2	42.1	41.9	41.9	42.0	42.0	41.8	41.7	42.1
Service-providing													
1990	200.6	200.6	203.4	207.6	211.0	213.5	208.4	210.5	212.9	211.5	212.0	210.9	208.5
1991	204.9	205.3	208.1	214.2	217.1	219.2	213.6	214.8	219.2	219.6	220.1	220.3	214.7
1992	216.9	216.8	221.4	224.3	227.1	228.7	226.3	228.5	230.9	232.5	232.2	233.0	226.5
1993	225.8	226.7	228.0	236.2	236.9	239.1	236.6	238.2	240.4	241.9	241.9	241.8	236.1
1994	230.4	232.8	236.4	241.9	243.8	245.3	243.0	244.3	246.4	247.1	250.0	248.6	242.5
1995	237.9	239.0	242.6	247.7	250.3	252.4	250.5	252.1	255.0	254.5	255.1	256.1	249.4
1996	243.1	242.8	249.4	250.2	252.9	254.6	253.7	254.1	255.5	255.2	256.2	256.1	251.9
1997	245.1	247.0	250.2	257.6	259.5	261.1	257.5	258.0	259.3	260.0	260.5	261.5	256.4
1998	250.4	252.7	255.8	261.3	265.4	267.7	265.6	266.1	268.3	268.4	269.6	270.8	263.5
1999	259.4	262.5	265.4	268.1	269.9	272.2	270.5	271.4	272.0	273.4	273.7	273.8	269.3
2000	264.6	265.9	271.4	274.9	279.3	281.1	277.9	277.5	280.5	279.9	280.4	280.5	276.1
2001	271.4	272.7	276.7	280.3	282.5	284.8	281.1	280.7	284.3	283.7	284.0	284.4	280.6
2002	276.3	276.9	280.5	287.9	290.5	293.1	290.5	291.3	292.7	294.9	295.3	296.3	288.9
2003	286.9	287.2	290.6	295.1	297.4	299.5	296.6	298.3	300.6	301.1	300.6	300.9	296.2
Trade, transportation, and utilities													
1990	54.1	53.3	53.7	53.5	53.9	55.0	54.5	54.5	54.4	54.3	55.1	55.6	54.3
1991	53.0	52.0	52.2	52.8	53.4	53.5	53.7	53.9	54.3	54.5	55.2	55.9	53.7
1992	52.9	52.2	52.5	53.8	54.4	54.7	54.5	55.2	55.3	55.7	56.4	57.0	54.5
1993	53.3	53.0	53.0	55.1	54.6	54.9	55.2	55.7	56.3	56.9	58.0	59.0	55.4
1994	55.9	55.9	56.4	57.1	57.5	58.0	57.7	58.1	58.9	59.5	60.7	61.4	58.0
1995	58.6	58.1	58.8	59.7	60.5	61.1	60.8	61.5	62.2	62.4	63.2	64.5	60.9
1996	60.3	59.5	60.8	60.7	61.4	61.8	61.9	62.2	62.5	63.1	64.4	65.3	61.9
1997	60.8	60.9	61.9	62.4	62.7	63.0	62.9	62.8	63.3	65.1	66.2	67.3	63.2
1998	62.9	63.3	63.9	64.8	65.5	66.5	66.2	66.2	66.3	66.6	67.6	68.8	65.7
1999	65.4	65.4	65.9	65.7	66.9	67.0	67.6	67.8	67.8	68.0	68.6	69.4	67.1
2000	66.3	66.2	67.0	68.0	68.6	69.5	69.5	69.4	69.6	70.0	70.9	71.8	68.9
2001	70.4	70.0	70.5	71.3	71.5	71.8	71.9	71.9	72.1	72.6	73.3	74.1	71.8
2002	71.6	71.3	72.3	72.8	72.9	73.1	73.6	73.8	73.8	74.8	75.8	76.9	73.6
2003	73.0	72.6	73.1	73.0	73.6	74.2	75.0	75.1	75.9	76.3	77.2	77.9	74.7
Wholesale trade													
1990	12.8	12.8	12.9	12.6	12.6	12.7	12.6	12.6	12.5	12.5	12.6	12.6	12.6
1991	12.2	12.0	12.1	12.1	12.3	12.3	12.3	12.4	12.4	12.5	12.5	12.5	12.3
1992	12.1	12.0	12.0	12.4	12.4	12.4	12.3	12.3	12.3	12.6	12.5	12.6	12.3
1993	12.0	12.0	12.0	12.1	12.1	12.2	12.2	12.2	12.3	12.3	12.4	12.5	12.1
1994	12.2	12.3	12.3	12.3	12.4	12.5	12.4	12.4	12.4	12.4	12.4	12.5	12.3
1995	12.4	12.4	12.5	12.4	12.5	12.6	12.8	12.8	12.8	12.8	12.8	12.9	12.6
1996	12.6	12.6	12.7	12.6	12.6	12.7	12.5	12.6	12.6	12.7	12.8	12.9	12.6
1997	12.5	12.6	12.7	12.7	12.8	12.8	12.9	12.8	12.9	13.0	13.0	13.1	12.8
1998	12.9	13.0	13.0	13.2	13.4	13.6	13.5	13.5	13.5	13.4	13.4	13.5	13.3
1999	13.2	13.2	13.3	13.0	13.4	13.4	13.6	13.6	13.7	13.7	13.7	13.8	13.4
2000	13.6	13.7	13.8	13.9	13.9	14.2	14.1	13.9	14.1	14.1	14.0	14.2	13.9
2001	14.3	14.4	14.4	14.2	14.3	14.3	14.2	14.1	14.2	14.3	14.2	14.2	14.3
2002	14.1	14.2	14.3	14.3	14.4	14.5	14.9	15.0	15.0	15.3	15.4	15.6	14.8
2003	15.3	15.3	15.4	15.3	15.3	15.5	15.6	15.6	15.8	16.0	16.0	16.1	15.6
Retail trade													
1990	34.3	33.5	33.8	33.9	34.3	35.4	35.0	34.9	34.9	34.9	35.6	36.1	34.7
1991	33.9	33.1	33.2	33.9	34.2	34.4	34.6	34.7	35.1	35.1	35.9	36.5	34.5
1992	34.0	33.4	33.7	34.5	35.1	35.4	35.2	35.9	36.1	36.1	36.8	37.2	35.2
1993	34.3	34.0	34.1	35.8	35.2	35.5	35.8	36.1	36.5	37.0	38.0	38.9	35.9
1994	36.1	35.9	36.2	36.8	37.1	37.5	37.6	37.9	38.5	38.9	40.2	40.8	37.7
1995	38.5	38.0	38.5	39.2	39.6	40.1	39.7	40.3	40.8	41.0	41.8	42.9	40.0
1996	39.5	38.7	39.7	39.7	40.3	40.7	40.9	41.0	41.2	41.6	42.7	43.5	40.7
1997	39.8	39.6	40.4	40.8	40.9	41.3	41.3	41.3	41.5	42.9	44.2	45.2	41.6
1998	41.2	41.4	41.9	42.6	43.1	43.8	43.6	43.4	43.4	43.8	44.9	46.0	43.2
1999	43.0	42.9	43.2	43.3	44.0	44.1	44.6	44.8	44.5	44.8	45.5	46.2	44.2
2000	43.5	43.4	43.9	44.4	45.0	45.7	46.0	46.0	46.0	46.4	47.4	48.2	45.4
2001	46.6	46.0	46.4	47.0	47.1	47.4	47.0	47.0	47.2	47.2	48.2	49.0	47.2
2002	46.9	46.5	47.3	47.7	47.8	47.9	47.9	47.9	48.0	48.4	49.4	50.3	48.0
2003	47.3	46.9	47.3	47.3	47.8	48.2	49.0	49.0	49.1	49.4	50.2	50.9	48.5

Employment by Industry: Tennessee—*Continued*

(Numbers in thousands. Not seasonally adjusted.)

Industry	January	February	March	April	May	June	July	August	September	October	November	December	Annual Average
KNOXVILLE—*Continued*													
Transportation and utilities													
1990	7.0	7.0	7.0	7.0	7.0	6.9	6.9	7.0	7.0	6.9	6.9	6.9	6.9
1991	6.9	6.9	6.9	6.8	6.9	6.8	6.8	6.8	6.8	6.9	6.8	6.9	6.8
1992	6.8	6.8	6.8	6.9	6.9	6.9	7.0	7.0	6.9	7.0	7.1	7.2	6.9
1993	7.0	7.0	6.9	7.2	7.3	7.2	7.2	7.4	7.5	7.6	7.6	7.6	7.2
1994	7.6	7.7	7.9	8.0	8.0	8.0	7.7	7.8	8.0	8.2	8.1	8.1	7.9
1995	7.7	7.7	7.8	8.1	8.4	8.4	8.3	8.4	8.6	8.6	8.6	8.7	8.2
1996	8.2	8.2	8.4	8.4	8.5	8.4	8.5	8.6	8.7	8.8	8.9	8.9	8.5
1997	8.5	8.7	8.8	8.9	9.0	8.9	8.7	8.7	8.9	9.2	9.0	9.0	8.8
1998	8.8	8.9	9.0	9.0	9.0	9.1	9.1	9.3	9.4	9.4	9.3	9.3	9.1
1999	9.2	9.3	9.4	9.4	9.5	9.5	9.4	9.4	9.6	9.5	9.4	9.4	9.4
2000	9.2	9.1	9.3	9.7	9.7	9.6	9.4	9.5	9.5	9.5	9.5	9.4	9.4
2001	9.5	9.6	9.7	10.1	10.1	10.1	10.7	10.8	10.7	11.1	10.9	10.9	10.4
2002	10.6	10.6	10.7	10.8	10.7	10.7	10.8	10.9	10.8	11.1	11.0	11.0	10.8
2003	10.4	10.4	10.4	10.4	10.5	10.5	10.4	10.5	11.0	10.9	11.0	10.9	10.6
Information													
1990	5.7	5.8	5.9	5.9	5.8	5.8	5.9	5.9	5.8	5.7	5.7	5.7	5.8
1991	5.6	5.6	5.7	5.5	5.6	5.6	5.6	5.7	5.6	5.5	5.5	5.5	5.5
1992	5.7	5.7	5.7	5.7	5.7	5.8	5.6	5.8	5.8	5.8	5.8	5.9	5.7
1993	5.9	5.8	5.8	5.9	5.9	5.9	5.9	6.0	5.9	5.9	6.0	6.0	5.9
1994	5.9	5.8	5.9	5.8	5.9	6.0	5.9	6.1	6.0	5.9	5.9	5.9	5.9
1995	5.8	5.8	5.8	5.8	5.8	5.9	5.9	5.9	6.0	5.9	5.9	6.0	5.8
1996	5.9	5.8	5.8	5.8	5.9	5.9	5.8	5.9	5.9	5.8	5.8	5.8	5.8
1997	5.8	5.7	5.7	5.8	5.8	5.9	5.9	6.0	5.9	6.1	6.1	6.2	5.9
1998	5.9	6.0	6.1	6.1	6.1	6.2	6.2	6.2	6.3	6.3	6.3	6.4	6.1
1999	6.0	6.1	6.2	6.5	6.6	6.7	6.8	6.9	6.9	7.0	7.1	7.2	6.6
2000	7.1	7.1	7.2	6.9	6.9	6.9	6.9	6.8	6.8	6.8	6.8	6.8	6.9
2001	6.1	6.1	6.1	6.1	6.0	6.1	6.1	6.0	6.0	6.1	6.1	6.1	6.1
2002	6.1	6.1	6.1	6.2	6.2	6.1	6.2	6.2	6.1	6.3	6.4	6.4	6.2
2003	6.3	6.3	6.2	6.3	6.2	6.2	6.4	6.2	6.3	6.3	6.3	6.3	6.3
Financial activities													
1990	12.0	12.0	12.2	12.1	12.2	12.3	12.2	12.3	12.4	12.2	12.2	12.2	12.1
1991	11.8	11.8	11.9	12.0	11.9	11.8	12.1	12.1	12.1	12.1	12.1	12.0	11.9
1992	12.3	12.3	12.4	12.4	12.4	12.6	12.7	12.7	12.4	12.6	12.4	12.5	12.4
1993	12.7	12.7	12.9	12.9	13.0	13.1	13.4	13.5	13.2	13.2	13.1	13.2	13.0
1994	12.3	12.5	12.7	12.7	12.8	13.3	13.3	13.3	13.0	13.1	13.1	13.1	12.9
1995	12.9	13.0	13.2	13.0	13.1	13.5	13.8	13.7	13.6	13.5	13.6	13.7	13.3
1996	13.4	13.6	13.8	13.7	13.8	13.9	14.1	14.0	13.9	13.9	13.8	13.9	13.8
1997	13.5	13.6	13.7	14.1	14.2	14.5	14.7	14.5	14.5	14.1	14.1	14.2	14.1
1998	13.9	14.1	14.5	14.8	15.0	15.1	15.3	15.3	15.2	15.0	15.0	15.1	14.8
1999	15.0	15.1	15.0	15.0	15.1	15.1	15.2	15.1	15.1	15.1	15.0	15.1	15.0
2000	14.9	14.9	15.0	15.0	15.1	15.3	15.0	15.0	14.9	14.9	15.0	15.0	15.0
2001	15.7	15.8	15.8	15.9	16.0	16.1	16.2	16.1	16.0	16.0	16.1	16.1	16.0
2002	16.0	16.1	16.2	16.3	16.5	16.8	16.8	16.8	16.9	17.2	17.4	17.6	16.7
2003	17.4	17.5	17.7	17.8	18.0	18.2	18.0	18.2	18.3	18.3	18.0	18.2	18.0
Professional and business services													
1990	21.2	21.5	22.0	23.0	23.6	24.3	23.7	24.2	24.3	24.2	24.4	24.3	23.3
1991	23.6	23.7	24.2	25.1	25.4	25.9	26.2	26.2	26.8	26.6	26.5	26.5	25.5
1992	27.0	26.9	27.6	27.8	28.1	28.7	28.4	28.6	28.7	29.0	28.9	28.9	28.2
1993	28.2	28.5	28.5	29.7	29.8	30.7	30.9	31.3	31.0	31.4	31.6	31.5	30.2
1994	29.3	30.3	31.2	31.5	31.8	32.1	31.7	32.1	32.6	32.2	32.2	32.7	31.6
1995	29.4	29.7	30.5	31.1	31.0	31.6	31.2	31.6	32.0	31.6	31.6	31.8	31.0
1996	29.7	29.9	30.7	30.3	30.8	31.0	31.7	31.8	31.9	31.4	31.6	31.3	31.0
1997	30.1	30.2	30.6	32.6	32.6	32.9	31.7	31.6	31.7	31.7	31.6	32.0	31.6
1998	30.7	31.0	31.7	32.1	32.6	32.9	32.0	32.5	32.1	33.2	33.4	33.5	32.3
1999	33.2	33.8	34.9	34.4	34.8	35.2	35.5	36.1	36.0	36.1	36.4	36.6	35.2
2000	36.6	37.2	38.3	38.3	38.6	39.6	38.5	39.0	39.2	38.6	38.7	38.5	38.4
2001	38.4	38.5	39.2	39.8	39.5	39.5	39.6	39.3	39.5	38.5	38.8	39.2	39.2
2002	38.8	38.6	39.4	39.9	40.0	40.3	40.2	40.5	40.5	40.3	39.6	39.5	39.8
2003	39.1	39.2	39.6	41.0	40.9	41.0	40.5	41.0	41.2	40.9	40.1	39.7	40.4
Educational and health services													
1990	23.4	23.5	23.7	23.6	23.7	23.8	23.7	24.0	24.3	24.2	24.4	24.4	23.8
1991	24.2	24.5	24.3	24.7	24.8	25.0	25.3	25.4	25.7	25.7	26.0	26.4	25.1
1992	25.9	26.0	26.3	26.7	26.9	27.1	27.5	27.6	28.0	28.1	28.4	28.6	27.2
1993	28.7	28.9	29.1	29.4	29.3	29.4	29.1	29.2	29.4	29.5	29.5	29.5	29.2
1994	28.8	29.2	29.3	29.3	29.2	29.2	29.0	29.1	29.5	29.7	29.8	29.9	29.3
1995	29.7	30.1	30.3	30.4	30.6	30.9	30.6	30.8	31.3	31.3	31.5	31.5	30.7
1996	30.4	31.0	31.3	31.5	31.3	31.4	31.7	31.9	32.3	32.0	32.3	32.6	31.6
1997	31.7	32.2	32.3	32.7	32.5	32.7	33.0	33.1	33.3	33.1	33.3	33.6	32.7
1998	32.8	33.2	33.6	34.1	34.3	34.4	34.2	34.2	34.8	34.0	34.2	34.2	34.0
1999	33.1	33.3	33.5	33.2	33.4	33.6	33.7	33.8	34.0	33.9	34.1	34.2	33.6
2000	34.0	34.5	34.6	34.6	34.9	35.0	34.7	34.9	35.1	35.3	35.6	35.7	34.9
2001	33.3	33.6	34.0	34.2	34.4	34.6	34.1	34.3	34.3	34.6	34.9	34.9	34.3
2002	34.7	34.9	35.0	35.5	35.7	36.1	35.7	36.0	36.2	36.5	36.8	36.8	35.8
2003	36.8	36.8	37.0	37.4	37.6	37.9	38.0	37.9	37.7	37.9	38.2	38.5	37.6

Employment by Industry: Tennessee—*Continued*

(Numbers in thousands. Not seasonally adjusted.)

Industry	January	February	March	April	May	June	July	August	September	October	November	December	Annual Average
KNOXVILLE—*Continued*													
Leisure and hospitality													
1990	22.5	22.6	23.7	26.5	28.3	29.6	30.2	30.4	29.3	28.2	26.9	25.6	26.9
1991	23.8	24.3	25.4	28.7	30.3	31.6	30.9	30.8	30.4	29.8	28.7	27.8	28.5
1992	25.5	26.0	27.1	30.1	31.9	33.2	33.3	33.4	32.6	31.9	30.2	29.4	30.3
1993	27.4	27.8	28.3	32.1	33.6	34.6	35.8	35.9	34.8	34.0	33.0	32.5	32.4
1994	29.3	29.6	31.0	35.3	36.1	37.2	37.1	37.0	35.6	35.5	34.7	34.0	34.3
1995	30.2	31.0	32.1	35.1	37.1	38.5	39.0	39.2	38.4	37.1	36.3	35.5	35.7
1996	30.8	30.8	32.9	36.0	38.0	39.3	39.5	39.2	38.6	36.9	35.8	35.1	36.0
1997	31.9	32.2	33.7	37.3	38.7	40.0	39.6	39.3	38.4	37.0	35.9	35.2	36.6
1998	32.0	32.7	33.6	37.0	39.0	40.1	41.6	41.0	40.4	39.2	38.1	37.6	37.6
1999	34.4	34.7	36.0	38.3	40.0	41.4	42.0	41.9	40.5	39.9	38.9	38.7	38.8
2000	35.4	35.5	36.9	39.8	41.9	42.0	43.4	43.0	42.7	41.5	40.8	40.0	40.2
2001	37.8	38.0	39.8	43.2	45.1	46.7	46.6	46.4	45.2	43.7	42.6	41.7	43.1
2002	38.0	38.4	39.8	43.7	45.2	46.8	47.1	47.0	45.9	45.1	44.7	44.2	43.8
2003	41.5	41.7	43.5	46.1	47.5	48.5	48.0	48.3	46.7	46.5	45.9	45.0	45.8
Other services													
1990	10.7	10.7	10.8	11.2	11.3	11.5	11.6	11.4	11.3	11.2	11.6	11.7	11.2
1991	11.6	11.7	12.3	12.6	12.9	13.5	13.2	13.1	13.1	13.2	13.6	13.6	12.8
1992	14.5	14.2	14.5	14.0	14.0	13.6	14.4	14.3	14.4	14.6	15.2	15.7	14.4
1993	15.0	15.1	15.2	15.3	15.1	15.2	15.1	15.2	15.0	15.0	14.9	14.5	15.0
1994	14.6	14.7	14.9	14.4	14.5	14.8	14.9	14.6	14.6	14.6	14.5	14.9	14.6
1995	16.6	16.1	16.5	16.8	16.6	16.6	16.6	16.5	16.4	16.4	16.6	16.7	16.5
1996	16.8	16.7	16.3	16.2	16.3	17.0	16.9	16.8	16.0	16.2	16.7	16.6	16.5
1997	17.3	17.3	17.4	17.4	17.8	17.9	18.1	18.6	17.9	17.7	17.6	17.4	17.7
1998	18.1	17.8	17.6	17.4	17.6	18.1	18.3	18.2	18.4	18.0	18.4	18.8	18.0
1999	17.6	18.7	18.4	18.9	17.6	18.8	17.4	17.1	16.9	17.2	17.2	16.5	17.6
2000	16.0	15.4	15.5	16.2	16.1	16.8	16.9	16.8	16.3	16.7	16.5	16.5	16.3
2001	13.6	13.7	14.2	13.7	13.8	14.1	14.2	14.1	14.2	13.9	13.9	13.9	13.9
2002	14.0	14.1	14.2	14.4	14.6	14.9	14.8	14.7	14.9	14.8	14.7	14.9	14.6
2003	14.7	14.7	14.8	14.4	14.5	14.8	14.6	14.5	14.9	15.0	14.8	15.3	14.8
Government													
1990	51.0	51.2	51.4	51.8	52.2	51.2	46.6	47.8	51.1	51.5	51.7	51.4	50.7
1991	51.3	51.7	52.1	52.8	52.8	52.3	46.6	47.6	51.2	52.2	52.5	52.6	51.3
1992	53.1	53.5	55.3	53.8	53.7	53.0	49.9	50.9	53.7	54.8	54.9	55.0	53.4
1993	54.6	54.9	55.2	55.8	55.6	55.3	51.2	51.4	54.8	56.0	55.8	55.6	54.6
1994	54.3	54.8	55.0	55.8	56.0	54.7	53.4	54.0	56.2	56.6	59.1	56.7	55.5
1995	54.7	55.2	55.4	55.8	55.6	54.3	52.6	52.9	55.1	56.3	56.4	56.4	55.0
1996	55.8	55.5	57.8	56.0	55.4	54.3	52.1	52.3	54.4	55.9	55.8	55.5	55.0
1997	54.0	54.9	54.9	55.3	55.2	54.2	51.6	52.1	54.3	55.2	55.7	55.6	54.4
1998	54.1	54.6	54.8	55.0	55.3	54.4	51.8	52.5	54.8	56.1	56.6	56.4	54.7
1999	54.7	55.4	55.5	56.1	55.5	54.4	52.3	52.7	54.8	56.2	56.4	56.1	55.0
2000	54.3	55.1	56.9	56.1	57.2	56.0	53.0	52.6	55.9	56.1	56.1	56.2	55.4
2001	56.1	57.0	57.1	56.1	56.2	55.9	52.4	52.6	57.0	58.3	58.3	58.4	56.3
2002	57.1	57.4	57.5	59.1	59.4	59.0	56.1	56.3	58.4	59.9	59.9	60.0	58.3
2003	58.1	58.4	58.7	59.1	59.1	58.7	56.1	57.1	59.6	59.9	60.1	60.0	58.7
Federal government													
1992	6.5	6.5	6.4	6.6	6.5	6.6	6.5	6.5	6.5	6.6	6.6	6.6	6.5
1993	6.6	6.5	6.6	6.6	6.6	6.6	6.7	6.7	6.6	6.5	6.4	6.4	6.5
1994	6.5	6.5	6.5	6.4	6.4	6.4	6.5	6.5	6.5	6.4	6.0	6.0	6.3
1995	6.0	6.0	6.1	6.1	6.1	6.2	6.3	6.3	6.3	6.2	6.2	6.2	6.1
1996	6.2	6.2	6.2	6.2	6.1	6.2	6.2	6.3	6.3	6.5	6.4	6.4	6.2
1997	6.3	6.3	6.3	6.3	6.3	6.3	6.3	6.3	6.2	5.9	6.1	6.1	6.2
1998	6.0	5.9	5.9	5.9	5.8	5.8	5.8	5.8	5.8	6.0	6.1	6.0	5.9
1999	5.9	5.8	5.8	6.1	5.8	5.8	5.9	5.7	5.7	5.8	5.7	5.7	5.8
2000	5.6	5.6	5.7	5.8	6.9	6.5	6.3	6.2	5.6	5.7	5.7	5.6	5.9
2001	5.6	5.6	5.6	5.6	5.7	5.8	5.8	5.8	5.8	5.8	5.7	5.8	5.7
2002	5.7	5.7	5.7	5.7	5.7	5.8	5.7	5.7	5.8	5.8	5.8	5.8	5.7
2003	5.7	5.7	5.7	5.6	5.6	5.6	5.6	5.6	5.7	5.6	5.6	5.7	5.6
State government													
1992	22.1	22.3	22.2	22.0	21.7	21.1	21.0	21.6	22.4	22.5	22.6	22.5	22.0
1993	22.4	22.7	22.8	22.7	22.3	22.1	21.6	21.8	23.1	23.3	23.2	23.0	22.5
1994	22.1	22.5	22.6	22.1	21.7	20.7	21.2	21.2	22.4	21.8	22.5	22.3	21.9
1995	22.1	22.5	22.4	22.2	21.6	20.4	20.9	21.0	22.0	22.1	22.0	22.1	21.7
1996	21.8	21.5	21.7	21.5	21.0	20.0	20.1	20.1	21.2	21.3	21.3	21.0	21.0
1997	20.4	21.1	21.1	21.3	20.9	19.7	19.5	19.7	20.8	20.7	20.7	20.5	20.5
1998	19.8	20.3	20.4	20.1	19.8	19.0	18.9	19.3	20.2	20.3	20.4	20.2	19.8
1999	19.7	20.3	20.3	20.5	20.0	19.1	19.0	19.4	20.3	20.2	20.3	19.9	19.9
2000	19.3	19.9	20.0	19.9	19.7	19.1	18.7	18.9	20.3	19.8	19.8	19.8	19.6
2001	19.1	19.8	19.9	19.5	19.3	18.8	19.0	19.0	20.5	20.7	20.7	20.7	19.8
2002	19.9	20.2	20.2	20.8	20.8	20.6	19.8	19.8	21.4	21.3	21.3	21.3	20.6
2003	20.7	21.1	21.1	21.4	21.2	20.9	20.1	20.1	21.6	21.6	21.6	21.4	21.1

Employment by Industry: Tennessee—*Continued*

(Numbers in thousands. Not seasonally adjusted.)

Industry	January	February	March	April	May	June	July	August	September	October	November	December	Annual Average
KNOXVILLE—*Continued*													
Local government													
1992	24.5	24.7	26.7	25.2	25.5	25.3	22.4	22.8	24.8	25.7	25.7	25.9	24.9
1993	25.6	25.7	25.8	26.5	26.7	26.6	22.9	22.9	25.1	26.2	26.2	26.2	25.5
1994	25.7	25.8	25.9	27.3	27.9	27.6	25.7	26.3	27.3	28.4	30.6	28.4	27.2
1995	26.6	26.7	26.9	27.5	27.9	27.7	25.4	25.6	26.8	28.0	28.2	28.1	27.1
1996	27.8	27.8	29.9	28.3	28.3	28.1	25.8	25.9	26.9	28.1	28.1	28.1	27.7
1997	27.3	27.5	27.5	27.7	28.0	28.2	25.8	26.1	27.3	28.6	28.9	29.0	27.6
1998	28.3	28.4	28.5	29.0	29.7	29.6	27.1	27.4	28.8	29.8	30.1	30.2	28.9
1999	29.1	29.3	29.4	29.5	29.7	29.5	27.4	27.6	28.8	30.2	30.4	30.5	29.2
2000	29.4	29.6	31.2	30.4	30.6	30.4	28.0	27.5	30.0	30.6	30.6	30.8	29.9
2001	31.4	31.6	31.6	31.0	31.2	31.3	27.6	27.8	30.7	31.8	31.9	31.9	30.8
2002	31.5	31.5	31.6	32.6	32.9	32.6	30.6	30.8	31.2	32.8	32.8	32.9	32.0
2003	31.7	31.6	31.9	32.1	32.3	32.2	30.4	31.4	32.3	32.7	32.9	32.9	32.0
MEMPHIS													
Total nonfarm													
1990	472.0	475.1	478.0	482.4	484.9	487.3	482.5	483.8	489.5	484.4	483.3	483.2	482.2
1991	468.5	470.5	474.0	476.1	478.7	479.8	477.4	481.0	484.3	484.1	485.1	484.3	478.6
1992	473.7	477.2	483.0	481.0	484.0	482.5	480.3	481.4	486.2	488.2	487.4	487.9	482.7
1993	477.2	481.6	485.0	489.6	490.8	492.9	494.3	491.4	498.6	498.8	499.1	501.7	491.7
1994	493.6	495.7	503.5	505.2	509.8	513.1	509.4	513.6	522.5	523.5	531.3	530.6	512.6
1995	519.4	524.4	530.6	525.6	531.3	536.1	531.7	540.1	543.7	541.0	545.1	547.7	534.7
1996	531.2	535.8	545.2	540.0	543.3	546.1	540.8	547.6	551.3	551.6	556.1	557.4	545.5
1997	544.4	549.8	556.7	560.4	563.5	566.4	561.7	569.9	571.1	569.4	572.5	574.6	563.3
1998	556.2	559.9	567.2	571.8	577.0	580.3	578.9	581.8	583.8	583.5	587.3	590.5	576.5
1999	570.2	577.0	581.0	584.2	586.3	589.8	587.1	589.8	593.9	594.5	596.9	599.8	587.5
2000	582.3	586.3	594.5	594.5	596.6	597.8	593.1	600.1	598.9	599.3	599.8	600.3	595.2
2001	585.0	587.2	590.2	596.7	594.3	593.8	589.4	593.2	591.3	589.4	588.9	587.4	590.6
2002	575.6	579.3	581.8	584.8	584.4	583.7	581.7	585.8	585.8	591.2	594.1	594.0	585.2
2003	584.1	585.9	589.4	592.1	591.5	589.0	585.4	589.5	592.3	593.3	594.6	594.8	590.2
Total private													
1990	395.1	396.4	399.7	402.8	406.6	411.3	407.7	410.5	410.7	405.7	404.5	404.4	404.6
1991	390.6	390.8	394.1	395.7	399.2	404.0	402.2	404.3	404.4	403.1	404.4	404.1	399.7
1992	393.7	396.5	398.7	400.0	403.9	407.0	407.0	407.2	407.0	408.3	407.5	408.8	403.8
1993	399.0	402.4	406.1	410.5	412.8	417.9	419.4	419.8	421.5	420.7	421.4	424.4	414.6
1994	416.0	416.7	424.1	425.5	431.3	438.5	438.5	441.7	445.6	443.6	447.7	452.3	435.1
1995	440.3	443.0	448.3	445.2	452.8	458.1	456.7	464.0	465.7	461.5	466.1	469.4	455.9
1996	453.5	455.7	461.2	460.5	465.7	469.8	467.5	473.1	474.6	472.5	477.0	478.9	467.5
1997	466.1	469.7	476.0	479.7	485.4	489.4	487.5	493.9	493.2	490.1	493.7	496.4	485.0
1998	478.9	481.1	487.5	490.4	497.1	502.0	503.7	505.1	505.1	502.1	506.0	509.3	497.3
1999	489.9	494.2	497.8	500.7	504.9	509.9	511.6	513.2	513.7	512.1	514.6	518.2	506.7
2000	502.3	504.0	508.1	511.1	513.8	517.7	516.5	519.6	517.6	515.6	515.9	516.2	513.2
2001	503.0	502.4	505.1	511.1	511.2	514.4	510.9	511.4	507.8	503.2	502.1	502.3	507.1
2002	491.4	492.1	494.3	496.9	498.5	501.7	502.5	502.7	500.2	503.0	504.8	506.1	499.5
2003	497.2	497.0	499.7	503.2	504.9	507.2	506.5	507.2	506.6	505.5	506.6	506.8	504.0
Goods-producing													
1990	82.4	82.9	83.6	84.1	84.7	84.9	84.1	84.3	84.1	82.2	80.6	79.8	83.1
1991	77.1	76.9	77.4	77.9	78.4	78.7	79.0	79.6	80.0	79.3	78.6	77.2	78.3
1992	76.5	76.9	77.7	77.2	78.2	78.4	79.7	80.2	80.2	80.6	79.7	78.9	78.6
1993	77.3	78.2	79.0	79.9	80.5	82.4	83.0	83.3	83.9	82.8	81.7	81.6	81.1
1994	78.9	79.5	81.2	82.6	82.9	84.7	84.6	85.0	85.4	84.1	83.9	83.9	83.0
1995	81.3	81.7	83.7	84.0	84.3	85.0	85.4	86.0	86.1	85.3	84.3	83.9	84.2
1996	81.4	81.9	82.7	82.6	83.7	85.1	85.6	86.7	86.5	84.1	83.4	83.3	83.9
1997	83.2	83.7	85.2	86.5	87.4	88.2	88.5	89.8	90.0	87.7	87.8	86.6	87.0
1998	84.7	85.5	86.1	88.0	88.9	90.2	89.6	89.9	89.1	89.6	89.1	88.8	88.2
1999	84.6	85.4	86.6	86.9	87.4	89.0	88.9	88.9	89.1	87.6	87.1	86.9	87.3
2000	84.4	84.5	85.5	85.1	85.9	86.5	85.7	85.9	85.3	83.7	83.0	82.6	84.8
2001	81.7	81.5	82.1	82.6	82.9	84.0	82.8	82.7	81.6	79.5	78.8	78.2	81.5
2002	75.4	75.2	75.8	76.0	76.7	77.7	78.1	78.1	77.9	77.2	76.4	76.1	76.7
2003	74.3	74.6	74.9	75.8	76.3	76.7	76.9	77.3	77.1	76.1	75.5	75.0	75.9
Construction and mining													
1990	19.6	19.8	20.0	20.2	20.8	21.5	21.4	21.2	20.9	20.3	19.8	19.5	20.4
1991	17.8	17.9	18.2	18.4	18.9	19.4	19.0	19.2	19.2	18.7	18.4	17.7	18.6
1992	16.9	17.0	17.1	17.4	18.1	18.4	18.6	19.0	19.1	19.1	18.7	18.4	18.2
1993	17.0	17.4	17.8	18.0	18.6	19.7	20.2	20.3	20.4	19.6	19.1	18.9	18.9
1994	17.9	18.1	19.1	19.8	20.4	21.3	21.4	21.1	21.2	21.0	20.9	20.8	20.3
1995	19.7	19.8	20.8	21.5	21.8	22.8	23.0	23.4	23.5	23.0	22.6	22.6	22.0
1996	21.2	21.3	22.1	22.4	23.2	24.1	24.9	25.4	25.2	24.5	24.0	23.7	23.5
1997	22.5	22.9	23.8	24.6	25.0	25.3	26.2	26.6	27.0	25.4	25.2	24.6	24.9
1998	23.0	23.4	24.0	25.8	26.3	27.2	26.9	26.8	26.7	26.7	26.3	26.0	25.8
1999	24.3	24.8	25.3	25.9	26.4	27.3	27.1	27.2	27.4	26.5	26.2	25.9	26.2
2000	24.9	25.2	26.3	25.9	26.6	27.1	26.4	26.6	26.7	25.8	25.4	25.1	26.0
2001	24.9	25.1	26.0	26.1	26.4	26.8	26.7	26.6	26.2	24.8	24.9	24.6	25.8
2002	23.7	23.3	23.8	24.1	24.8	25.4	25.6	25.4	25.6	25.0	24.7	24.6	24.7
2003	23.3	23.3	23.6	24.4	24.9	25.1	25.3	25.6	25.8	25.3	24.9	24.8	24.7

Employment by Industry: Tennessee—*Continued*

(Numbers in thousands. Not seasonally adjusted.)

Industry	January	February	March	April	May	June	July	August	September	October	November	December	Annual Average
MEMPHIS—*Continued*													
Manufacturing													
1990	62.8	63.1	63.6	63.9	63.9	63.4	62.7	63.1	63.2	61.9	60.8	60.3	62.7
1991	59.3	59.0	59.2	59.5	59.5	59.3	60.0	60.4	60.8	60.6	60.2	59.5	59.7
1992	59.6	59.9	60.6	59.8	60.1	60.0	61.1	61.2	61.1	61.5	61.0	60.5	60.5
1993	60.3	60.8	61.2	61.9	61.9	62.7	62.8	63.0	63.5	63.2	62.6	62.7	62.2
1994	61.0	61.4	62.1	62.8	62.5	63.4	63.2	63.9	64.2	63.1	63.0	63.1	62.8
1995	61.6	61.9	62.9	62.5	62.5	62.2	62.4	62.6	62.6	62.3	61.7	61.3	62.2
1996	60.2	60.6	60.6	60.2	60.5	61.0	60.7	61.3	61.3	59.6	59.4	59.6	60.4
1997	60.7	60.8	61.4	61.9	62.4	62.9	62.3	63.2	63.0	62.3	62.6	62.0	62.1
1998	61.7	62.1	62.1	62.2	62.6	63.0	62.7	63.1	62.4	62.9	62.8	62.8	62.5
1999	60.3	60.6	61.3	61.0	61.0	61.7	61.8	61.7	61.7	61.1	60.9	61.0	61.1
2000	59.5	59.3	59.2	59.2	59.3	59.4	59.3	59.3	58.6	57.9	57.6	57.5	58.8
2001	56.8	56.4	56.1	56.5	56.5	57.2	56.1	56.1	55.4	54.7	53.9	53.6	55.7
2002	51.7	51.9	52.0	51.9	51.9	52.3	52.5	52.7	52.3	52.2	51.7	51.5	52.1
2003	51.0	51.3	51.3	51.4	51.4	51.6	51.6	51.7	51.3	50.8	50.6	50.2	51.2
Service-providing													
1990	389.6	392.2	394.4	398.3	400.2	402.4	398.4	399.5	405.4	402.2	402.7	403.4	399.0
1991	391.4	393.6	396.6	398.2	400.3	401.1	398.4	401.4	404.3	404.8	406.5	407.1	400.3
1992	397.2	400.3	405.3	403.8	405.8	404.1	400.6	401.2	406.0	407.6	407.7	409.0	404.0
1993	399.9	403.4	406.0	409.7	410.3	410.5	411.3	408.1	414.7	416.0	417.4	420.1	410.6
1994	414.7	416.2	422.3	422.6	426.9	428.4	424.8	428.6	437.1	439.4	447.4	446.7	429.5
1995	438.1	442.7	446.9	441.6	447.0	451.1	446.3	454.1	457.6	455.7	460.8	463.8	450.4
1996	449.8	453.9	462.5	457.4	459.6	461.0	455.2	460.9	464.8	467.5	472.7	474.1	461.6
1997	461.2	466.1	471.5	473.9	476.1	478.2	473.2	480.1	481.1	481.7	484.7	488.0	476.3
1998	471.5	474.4	481.1	483.8	488.1	490.1	489.3	491.9	494.7	493.9	498.2	501.7	488.2
1999	485.6	491.6	494.4	497.3	498.9	500.8	498.2	500.9	504.8	506.9	509.8	512.9	500.1
2000	497.9	501.8	509.0	509.4	510.7	511.3	507.4	514.2	513.6	515.6	516.8	517.7	510.4
2001	503.3	505.7	508.1	514.1	511.4	509.8	506.6	510.5	509.7	509.9	510.1	509.2	509.0
2002	500.2	504.1	506.0	508.8	507.7	506.0	503.6	507.7	507.9	514.0	517.7	517.9	508.5
2003	509.8	511.3	514.5	516.3	515.2	512.3	508.5	512.2	515.2	517.2	519.1	519.8	514.3
Trade, transportation, and utilities													
1990	133.7	133.2	134.1	134.2	135.6	137.5	136.1	137.6	138.3	137.2	138.8	139.8	136.3
1991	133.0	131.5	132.2	131.4	133.2	134.6	132.6	134.0	135.1	136.7	139.2	140.1	134.4
1992	133.9	133.8	134.4	133.6	133.9	134.3	133.7	133.3	134.1	135.0	135.7	137.8	134.4
1993	132.4	132.9	133.6	134.1	134.6	136.4	136.5	136.1	136.9	137.8	139.5	141.9	136.0
1994	136.7	136.4	138.7	138.7	141.2	143.3	142.4	143.7	145.5	145.4	148.7	151.4	142.6
1995	145.2	145.0	145.7	143.9	145.7	149.4	148.7	150.4	152.4	151.3	155.0	157.8	149.2
1996	150.7	150.7	152.1	150.8	153.1	154.3	151.6	153.7	155.8	154.7	158.9	161.4	153.9
1997	154.6	154.8	156.4	156.1	157.5	158.7	157.7	159.9	161.1	161.4	165.4	168.1	159.3
1998	161.4	161.3	162.9	161.4	163.1	165.1	163.9	165.8	168.3	166.1	170.5	173.8	165.3
1999	164.1	166.1	167.5	165.9	167.4	169.3	169.1	170.1	171.1	171.3	173.1	175.6	169.2
2000	167.3	167.1	167.9	170.0	170.2	172.0	168.4	168.9	168.4	170.1	172.2	173.5	169.6
2001	173.5	171.0	170.5	172.1	171.9	172.0	170.7	171.4	170.6	170.1	171.1	171.4	171.4
2002	165.8	163.5	164.2	164.8	165.1	165.4	166.4	166.2	166.2	167.5	170.5	172.1	166.5
2003	167.8	166.5	167.2	167.8	167.7	167.9	167.9	168.3	168.3	168.4	170.5	171.3	168.3
Wholesale trade													
1990	33.4	33.4	33.5	33.2	33.4	33.7	34.1	33.9	33.8	33.6	33.5	33.5	33.5
1991	32.7	32.6	32.7	33.0	33.1	33.2	33.3	33.4	33.4	33.5	33.9	33.8	33.2
1992	32.7	32.8	32.9	32.9	32.7	32.9	32.7	32.3	32.4	32.5	32.6	32.8	32.6
1993	32.1	32.1	32.4	32.3	32.3	32.4	32.4	32.2	32.5	32.5	32.2	32.6	32.3
1994	32.5	32.5	32.9	32.8	32.7	33.0	33.4	33.7	33.9	34.0	34.2	34.5	33.3
1995	34.0	34.2	34.4	34.1	34.5	34.9	34.9	35.1	35.2	34.9	34.9	35.0	34.6
1996	34.7	34.8	34.9	34.9	34.8	34.9	34.9	35.1	35.3	35.4	35.4	35.6	35.0
1997	35.3	35.4	35.5	34.9	34.9	35.1	35.5	35.3	35.3	35.7	35.6	35.8	35.3
1998	35.9	36.1	36.1	35.9	35.9	36.2	36.1	36.0	36.3	36.2	36.0	36.3	36.0
1999	35.8	35.9	35.9	36.3	36.3	36.8	37.1	37.0	36.9	37.0	37.3	37.7	36.6
2000	37.2	37.4	37.2	37.1	37.0	37.2	37.3	37.4	37.4	37.3	37.4	37.5	37.2
2001	36.3	36.2	36.3	37.0	36.8	36.7	36.3	36.6	36.5	36.4	36.4	35.9	36.5
2002	35.9	35.8	35.9	35.9	36.0	36.2	36.1	36.0	36.0	36.7	36.9	37.1	36.2
2003	37.4	37.6	37.5	37.6	37.4	37.6	37.5	37.4	37.5	37.4	37.4	37.6	37.5
Retail trade													
1990	59.8	58.7	59.0	60.0	60.2	60.7	61.0	61.3	61.3	61.6	62.9	63.5	60.8
1991	58.7	57.2	57.2	56.7	58.0	58.8	57.3	57.8	58.3	59.7	61.2	62.2	58.5
1992	58.6	58.0	58.1	57.8	57.7	57.2	56.9	56.6	56.5	57.0	58.2	59.7	57.6
1993	56.5	56.3	56.3	57.4	57.4	58.4	58.8	58.4	58.2	59.0	60.5	61.9	58.2
1994	58.0	57.3	58.4	59.2	59.9	60.8	60.2	60.6	61.7	61.5	63.7	66.1	60.6
1995	61.8	60.6	60.8	60.7	61.7	64.3	63.8	64.5	65.1	64.8	66.9	68.8	63.6
1996	64.6	63.7	63.9	63.3	63.9	64.5	63.5	64.0	64.3	64.4	67.3	68.8	64.6
1997	64.6	63.6	64.2	64.7	64.9	65.2	64.9	65.3	65.2	66.0	68.4	69.9	65.5
1998	64.9	63.5	64.2	63.6	63.9	64.6	64.4	64.8	65.7	65.5	68.8	70.7	65.3
1999	65.0	65.8	66.7	64.9	65.4	66.3	65.9	66.0	66.0	67.3	69.7	71.8	66.7
2000	65.9	65.1	65.7	66.3	66.7	67.1	66.5	66.4	66.1	67.1	69.2	70.5	66.8
2001	70.8	69.4	69.9	69.7	69.7	69.7	69.0	68.2	67.2	67.7	69.5	70.4	69.3
2002	68.1	66.7	67.1	67.4	67.6	67.8	68.1	67.8	68.1	68.2	70.8	72.5	68.4
2003	67.9	66.8	67.4	67.7	67.7	67.6	67.4	67.1	67.3	67.8	69.7	70.7	67.9

Employment by Industry: Tennessee—*Continued*

(Numbers in thousands. Not seasonally adjusted.)

Industry	January	February	March	April	May	June	July	August	September	October	November	December	Annual Average
MEMPHIS—*Continued*													
Transportation and utilities													
1990	40.5	41.1	41.6	41.0	42.0	43.1	41.0	42.4	43.2	42.0	42.4	42.8	41.9
1991	41.6	41.7	42.3	41.7	42.1	42.6	42.0	42.8	43.4	43.5	44.1	44.1	42.6
1992	42.6	43.0	43.4	42.9	43.5	44.2	44.1	44.4	45.2	45.5	44.9	45.3	44.0
1993	43.8	44.5	44.9	44.4	44.9	45.6	45.3	45.5	46.2	46.3	46.8	47.4	45.4
1994	46.2	46.6	47.4	46.7	48.6	49.5	48.8	49.4	49.9	49.9	50.8	50.8	48.7
1995	49.4	50.2	50.5	49.1	49.5	50.2	50.0	50.8	52.1	51.6	53.2	54.0	50.8
1996	51.4	52.2	53.3	52.6	54.4	54.9	53.2	54.6	56.2	54.9	56.2	57.0	54.2
1997	54.7	55.8	56.7	56.5	57.7	58.4	57.3	59.3	60.6	59.7	61.4	62.4	58.3
1998	60.6	61.7	62.6	61.9	63.3	64.3	63.4	65.0	66.3	64.4	65.7	66.8	63.8
1999	63.3	64.4	64.9	64.7	65.7	66.2	66.1	67.1	68.2	67.0	66.1	66.1	65.8
2000	64.2	64.6	65.0	66.6	66.5	67.7	64.6	65.1	64.9	65.7	65.6	65.5	65.5
2001	66.4	65.4	64.3	65.4	65.4	65.6	65.4	66.6	66.9	66.0	65.2	65.1	65.6
2002	61.8	61.0	61.2	61.5	61.5	61.4	62.2	62.4	62.1	62.6	62.8	62.5	61.9
2003	62.5	62.1	62.3	62.5	62.6	62.7	63.0	63.8	63.5	63.2	63.4	63.0	62.9
Information													
1990	8.0	8.1	8.1	8.0	8.0	8.1	8.0	8.0	8.0	7.9	7.9	7.9	8.0
1991	7.9	7.8	7.8	7.8	7.7	7.6	7.6	7.6	7.6	7.5	7.4	7.7	7.6
1992	8.0	8.0	8.0	7.7	7.6	7.8	7.7	7.8	7.7	7.6	7.6	7.8	7.7
1993	7.8	7.8	7.9	7.6	7.8	7.8	7.9	8.0	7.9	7.9	7.8	8.0	7.8
1994	8.0	8.0	8.1	8.2	8.1	8.2	8.3	8.0	8.0	8.3	8.2	8.3	8.1
1995	8.0	8.0	8.1	7.8	8.1	8.0	8.0	8.1	8.0	8.1	8.2	8.3	8.0
1996	8.1	8.0	8.0	8.1	8.2	8.2	8.2	8.1	8.0	8.2	8.2	8.3	8.1
1997	8.3	8.3	8.6	8.4	8.5	8.5	8.6	8.5	8.4	8.6	8.8	8.8	8.5
1998	8.4	8.4	8.4	8.2	8.6	8.4	8.4	8.2	8.3	8.4	8.3	8.5	8.3
1999	8.4	8.6	8.5	8.6	8.5	8.7	8.8	8.9	8.8	9.2	9.5	9.6	8.8
2000	9.5	9.5	9.6	9.5	9.6	9.7	9.4	9.7	9.7	9.7	9.9	10.0	9.6
2001	8.9	8.9	9.0	9.2	9.2	9.5	9.2	9.5	9.4	9.5	9.5	9.5	9.3
2002	9.8	9.7	9.8	9.7	9.7	9.6	9.2	9.6	9.4	9.6	9.7	9.6	9.6
2003	9.5	9.5	9.4	9.7	9.6	9.5	9.2	9.4	9.3	9.3	9.5	9.6	9.5
Financial activities													
1990	26.2	26.2	26.1	26.0	26.0	26.4	26.3	26.3	26.3	26.0	25.8	26.0	26.1
1991	25.9	26.0	26.1	26.4	26.5	26.5	26.9	27.0	26.8	26.6	26.3	26.4	26.4
1992	26.2	26.2	26.4	26.2	26.3	26.6	26.7	26.6	26.3	26.7	26.7	26.7	26.4
1993	26.5	26.6	26.7	26.9	26.8	26.7	26.7	27.0	26.7	26.8	26.8	26.9	26.7
1994	27.2	27.1	27.3	27.0	26.9	27.4	27.4	27.6	27.4	27.2	27.3	27.2	27.2
1995	27.3	27.4	27.5	27.8	28.0	28.2	27.8	27.9	27.8	27.8	27.9	27.9	27.7
1996	28.4	28.5	28.6	27.9	28.2	28.4	28.5	28.5	28.4	28.5	28.7	28.7	28.4
1997	28.0	28.0	28.3	28.5	28.6	28.9	28.9	28.9	28.8	29.6	29.6	30.0	28.8
1998	29.8	29.8	29.9	30.4	30.4	30.5	30.7	30.6	30.5	30.7	30.6	30.7	30.3
1999	30.6	30.5	30.6	31.0	31.0	31.1	31.7	31.4	31.3	31.8	31.6	31.6	31.1
2000	31.5	31.3	31.4	31.7	31.8	32.0	32.5	32.3	32.1	31.4	31.3	31.5	31.7
2001	31.7	31.6	31.6	31.8	31.8	31.9	31.9	32.0	31.9	32.1	32.1	31.8	31.9
2002	31.7	31.8	32.0	32.0	32.1	32.1	31.7	31.8	31.4	31.6	31.8	31.8	31.8
2003	31.9	31.9	32.1	32.1	32.2	32.2	32.2	32.1	32.1	32.3	32.4	32.3	32.2
Professional and business services													
1990	38.2	38.8	39.5	41.2	42.0	42.7	42.8	43.3	43.7	43.0	42.6	42.4	41.6
1991	38.7	39.0	40.2	39.5	39.9	40.9	40.5	41.1	40.9	40.3	40.0	40.1	40.0
1992	38.7	39.6	39.7	39.8	41.0	41.8	41.9	42.3	41.9	41.7	41.7	41.8	40.9
1993	39.6	41.1	41.8	41.9	42.4	43.9	44.3	44.4	43.5	44.5	44.5	45.0	43.0
1994	44.9	44.7	46.8	47.2	47.1	48.8	49.4	50.4	50.7	50.6	51.3	51.9	48.6
1995	51.3	52.1	52.6	52.6	54.7	54.5	55.2	56.7	56.8	56.4	57.3	57.7	54.8
1996	54.8	55.6	57.4	58.1	57.6	58.8	58.3	59.2	59.2	59.6	60.2	59.8	58.2
1997	56.9	58.1	59.5	62.0	62.7	64.0	64.9	66.6	66.1	60.8	60.5	61.1	61.9
1998	60.0	60.6	62.1	63.5	64.8	66.6	67.7	68.0	67.9	67.3	67.5	67.6	65.3
1999	63.2	64.7	65.4	67.6	68.6	69.9	71.3	72.0	72.5	73.2	73.9	74.6	69.7
2000	69.0	69.4	70.6	69.2	70.0	71.0	75.1	76.7	77.5	76.7	75.7	75.6	73.0
2001	74.8	76.0	76.7	78.0	77.1	77.2	77.8	77.3	77.4	75.9	75.4	76.2	76.7
2002	74.9	76.5	75.3	75.0	73.9	74.2	73.9	73.2	72.8	73.6	73.4	73.6	74.2
2003	71.8	71.6	71.7	72.7	73.2	73.3	73.1	72.5	73.0	73.0	73.2	73.4	72.7
Educational and health services													
1990	44.7	45.1	45.1	44.6	44.9	44.9	44.9	45.0	45.4	46.1	46.2	46.2	45.2
1991	46.3	46.8	47.1	47.5	47.4	47.4	47.4	47.6	48.4	48.4	48.6	48.5	47.6
1992	47.8	48.3	48.4	49.1	49.1	49.3	48.9	48.8	50.0	50.5	50.7	50.8	49.3
1993	51.0	51.5	51.9	52.3	52.1	52.0	51.6	51.9	53.3	53.9	54.1	54.1	52.4
1994	53.3	53.5	54.0	52.3	54.1	53.6	53.9	54.1	54.7	54.6	54.9	55.4	54.0
1995	54.5	55.1	55.7	54.9	55.6	55.3	54.9	55.1	56.6	57.2	57.4	57.4	55.8
1996	55.8	56.0	55.7	55.8	55.7	55.6	55.6	55.7	56.7	56.7	57.2	57.3	56.1
1997	56.0	56.8	57.0	57.4	57.6	57.7	57.4	57.7	58.9	58.8	59.0	59.0	57.7
1998	58.1	58.2	58.8	59.4	59.4	59.2	59.1	59.1	59.8	60.1	60.5	60.3	59.3
1999	59.3	59.9	60.1	60.4	60.3	60.0	60.2	60.1	61.1	60.1	60.4	60.5	60.2
2000	59.2	59.6	59.9	60.5	60.5	60.8	60.9	61.0	61.5	62.1	62.5	62.3	60.9
2001	62.5	62.9	63.0	63.4	63.6	63.5	63.7	64.1	64.6	64.1	64.2	64.5	63.7
2002	64.2	64.7	65.3	65.7	65.9	65.5	66.0	66.7	67.5	67.9	68.3	68.3	66.3
2003	68.1	68.5	68.6	68.1	68.3	68.1	67.9	68.4	69.2	69.1	69.2	69.2	68.6

Employment by Industry: Tennessee—*Continued*

(Numbers in thousands. Not seasonally adjusted.)

Industry	January	February	March	April	May	June	July	August	September	October	November	December	Annual Average
MEMPHIS—*Continued*													
Leisure and hospitality													
1990	35.8	36.0	36.7	37.9	38.8	40.7	39.4	39.5	38.5	37.0	36.5	36.2	37.7
1991	36.2	36.5	37.1	38.5	39.3	41.2	40.6	40.3	39.3	37.8	37.8	37.6	38.5
1992	36.1	36.8	37.1	38.8	40.6	41.5	40.9	40.8	39.5	39.6	39.5	39.2	39.2
1993	37.6	38.1	38.4	40.1	41.4	42.0	42.4	41.8	41.3	41.0	40.5	40.7	40.4
1994	40.8	41.7	42.4	43.4	44.9	46.1	45.6	46.0	45.6	44.3	43.8	44.1	44.0
1995	42.4	42.9	43.7	43.7	45.7	47.5	46.5	47.6	46.9	45.1	45.1	44.9	45.1
1996	42.2	42.9	43.7	44.9	46.2	47.3	47.2	46.6	45.5	45.4	44.6	43.9	45.0
1997	42.7	43.7	44.7	45.8	47.5	48.7	49.0	48.5	47.2	45.9	45.5	45.6	46.2
1998	42.9	43.2	44.5	46.0	47.7	49.5	49.3	46.0	45.5	45.0	44.6	44.6	45.7
1999	43.6	44.6	45.1	45.8	46.8	48.1	49.0	47.4	46.0	45.7	45.7	46.6	46.2
2000	45.7	46.2	47.2	48.5	49.3	51.6	51.9	51.6	50.0	48.5	48.0	47.4	48.8
2001	46.2	46.7	48.2	50.1	50.7	52.1	51.0	50.7	48.8	48.7	47.7	47.4	49.0
2002	46.9	48.0	49.1	50.7	52.0	53.7	53.4	53.5	51.5	52.1	51.1	50.8	51.1
2003	50.1	50.6	51.7	52.9	53.5	55.2	54.9	55.0	53.6	53.5	52.3	52.0	52.9
Other services													
1990	26.1	26.1	26.5	26.8	26.6	26.1	26.1	26.5	26.4	26.3	26.1	26.1	26.3
1991	25.5	26.3	26.2	26.7	26.8	27.1	27.6	27.1	26.3	26.5	26.5	26.5	26.5
1992	26.5	26.9	27.0	27.6	27.2	27.3	27.5	27.4	27.3	26.6	25.9	25.8	26.9
1993	26.8	26.2	26.8	27.7	27.2	26.7	27.0	27.3	28.0	26.0	26.5	26.2	26.8
1994	26.2	25.8	25.6	26.1	26.1	26.4	26.9	26.9	28.3	29.1	29.6	30.1	27.2
1995	30.3	30.8	31.3	30.5	30.7	30.2	30.2	32.2	31.1	30.3	30.9	31.5	30.8
1996	32.1	32.1	33.0	32.3	33.0	32.1	32.5	34.6	34.5	35.3	35.8	36.2	33.6
1997	36.4	36.3	36.3	35.0	35.6	34.7	32.5	34.0	32.7	37.3	37.1	37.2	35.4
1998	33.6	34.1	34.8	33.5	34.2	32.5	35.0	37.5	35.7	34.9	34.9	35.0	34.6
1999	36.1	34.4	34.0	34.5	34.9	33.8	32.6	34.4	33.8	33.2	33.3	32.8	33.9
2000	35.7	36.4	36.0	36.6	36.5	34.1	32.6	33.5	33.1	33.4	33.3	33.3	34.5
2001	23.7	23.8	24.0	23.9	24.0	24.2	23.8	23.7	23.5	23.3	23.3	23.3	23.7
2002	22.7	22.7	22.8	23.0	23.1	23.5	23.8	23.6	23.5	23.5	23.6	23.8	23.3
2003	23.7	23.8	24.1	24.1	24.1	24.3	24.4	24.2	24.0	23.8	24.0	24.0	24.0
Government													
1990	76.9	78.7	78.3	79.6	78.3	76.0	74.8	73.3	78.8	78.7	78.8	78.8	77.5
1991	77.9	79.7	79.9	80.4	79.5	75.8	75.2	76.7	79.9	81.0	80.7	80.2	78.9
1992	80.0	80.7	84.3	81.0	80.1	75.5	73.3	74.2	79.2	79.9	79.9	79.1	78.9
1993	78.2	79.2	78.9	79.1	78.0	75.0	74.9	71.6	77.1	78.1	77.7	77.3	77.0
1994	77.6	79.0	79.4	79.7	78.5	74.6	70.9	71.9	76.9	79.9	83.6	78.3	77.5
1995	79.1	81.4	82.3	80.4	78.5	78.0	75.0	76.1	78.0	79.5	79.0	78.3	78.8
1996	77.7	80.1	84.0	79.5	77.6	76.3	73.3	74.5	76.7	79.1	79.1	78.5	78.0
1997	78.3	80.1	80.7	80.7	78.1	77.0	74.2	76.0	77.9	79.3	78.8	78.2	78.2
1998	77.3	78.8	79.7	81.4	79.9	78.3	75.2	76.7	78.7	81.4	81.3	81.2	79.1
1999	80.3	82.8	83.2	83.5	81.4	79.9	75.5	76.6	80.2	82.4	82.3	81.6	80.8
2000	80.0	82.3	86.4	83.4	82.8	80.1	76.6	80.5	81.3	83.7	83.9	84.1	82.0
2001	82.0	84.8	85.1	85.6	83.1	79.4	78.5	81.8	83.5	86.2	86.8	85.1	83.5
2002	84.2	87.2	87.5	87.9	85.9	82.0	79.2	83.1	85.6	88.2	89.3	87.9	85.7
2003	86.9	88.9	89.7	88.9	86.6	81.8	78.9	82.3	85.7	87.8	88.0	88.0	86.1
Federal government													
1992	20.5	20.5	20.6	20.7	20.6	20.0	19.7	19.8	19.9	19.4	18.6	18.6	19.9
1993	18.3	18.6	18.6	18.6	18.0	18.0	17.8	17.5	17.2	17.0	16.6	16.7	17.7
1994	17.4	18.0	18.0	18.3	18.1	18.2	17.1	16.9	16.8	16.9	16.5	16.7	17.4
1995	17.9	18.5	18.8	18.8	18.3	18.3	17.7	17.4	17.1	17.0	16.6	16.7	17.7
1996	16.9	17.4	17.7	17.7	17.1	17.1	16.3	15.7	15.8	15.6	15.4	15.6	16.5
1997	15.9	16.2	16.6	16.5	16.0	15.9	15.6	15.4	15.3	14.0	13.7	13.7	15.4
1998	14.6	14.7	15.2	16.4	16.5	15.6	15.0	15.0	15.1	15.1	15.0	15.1	15.2
1999	15.3	16.3	16.5	16.8	16.4	16.2	15.5	15.3	15.4	15.6	15.4	15.4	15.8
2000	15.5	16.5	16.7	17.0	18.1	19.0	16.6	17.1	15.4	15.5	15.5	15.5	16.5
2001	16.1	16.8	16.9	16.8	16.7	16.5	16.3	16.1	16.3	17.1	17.7	16.7	16.7
2002	16.5	17.8	18.2	18.1	17.9	17.5	16.6	16.7	16.3	17.0	16.9	16.9	17.2
2003	16.6	17.5	18.2	18.3	17.8	17.2	16.4	16.0	16.0	16.6	16.5	16.6	17.0
State government													
1992	13.5	14.2	14.2	14.2	13.3	12.9	12.8	12.5	13.6	14.2	14.3	14.0	13.6
1993	13.9	14.5	14.5	14.5	13.8	13.8	14.0	13.9	13.7	14.3	14.4	14.1	14.1
1994	14.1	14.9	15.0	15.0	13.7	13.7	13.3	13.1	13.5	15.2	15.3	13.9	14.2
1995	13.8	15.2	15.7	14.7	13.1	12.9	13.3	12.8	14.2	15.1	15.2	14.4	14.2
1996	13.8	15.3	15.4	15.0	13.4	13.3	13.5	13.3	14.4	15.8	15.9	15.1	14.5
1997	14.1	15.2	15.3	15.8	13.5	13.3	13.4	13.4	14.2	15.5	15.5	14.9	14.5
1998	13.7	14.9	15.0	15.7	13.9	13.8	13.6	13.6	14.7	16.2	16.4	16.2	14.8
1999	15.1	16.3	16.4	16.5	14.6	14.3	14.3	14.4	15.5	16.2	16.2	15.8	15.4
2000	14.6	15.8	16.1	16.0	14.0	14.0	14.2	14.0	15.2	16.4	16.5	16.8	15.3
2001	14.4	16.0	16.0	15.9	14.0	14.1	14.0	13.9	15.3	16.2	16.3	15.7	15.2
2002	14.6	16.3	16.0	16.1	14.3	14.5	14.4	14.3	15.6	16.3	16.4	16.1	15.4
2003	15.1	16.2	16.2	16.2	14.5	14.6	14.3	14.1	15.6	16.5	16.5	16.3	15.5

Employment by Industry: Tennessee—*Continued*

(Numbers in thousands. Not seasonally adjusted.)

Industry	January	February	March	April	May	June	July	August	September	October	November	December	Annual Average
MEMPHIS—*Continued*													
Local government													
1992	46.0	46.0	49.5	46.1	46.2	42.6	40.8	41.9	45.7	46.3	47.0	46.5	45.3
1993	46.0	46.1	45.8	46.0	46.2	43.2	43.1	40.2	46.2	46.8	46.7	46.5	45.2
1994	46.1	46.1	46.4	46.4	46.7	42.7	40.5	41.9	46.6	47.8	51.8	47.7	45.8
1995	47.4	47.7	47.8	46.9	47.1	46.8	44.0	45.9	46.7	47.4	47.2	47.2	46.8
1996	47.0	47.4	50.9	46.8	47.1	45.9	43.5	45.5	46.5	47.7	47.8	47.8	46.9
1997	48.3	48.7	48.8	48.4	48.6	47.8	45.2	47.2	48.4	49.8	49.6	49.6	48.3
1998	49.0	49.2	49.5	49.3	49.5	48.9	46.6	48.1	48.9	50.1	49.9	49.9	49.0
1999	49.9	50.2	50.3	50.2	50.4	49.4	45.7	46.9	49.3	50.6	50.7	50.4	49.5
2000	49.9	50.0	53.6	50.4	50.7	47.1	45.8	49.4	50.7	51.8	51.9	51.8	50.2
2001	51.5	52.0	52.2	52.9	52.4	48.8	48.2	51.8	51.9	52.9	52.8	52.7	51.7
2002	53.1	53.1	53.3	53.7	53.7	50.0	48.2	52.1	53.7	54.9	56.0	54.9	53.1
2003	55.2	55.2	55.3	54.4	54.3	50.0	48.2	52.2	54.1	54.7	55.0	55.1	53.6
NASHVILLE													
Total nonfarm													
1990	492.2	495.3	501.3	502.4	507.3	506.0	501.7	504.9	506.1	502.4	502.2	501.3	501.9
1991	486.8	487.4	492.4	495.1	501.1	504.9	499.4	504.3	507.9	508.2	508.8	508.5	500.4
1992	497.5	500.2	507.4	510.5	513.0	514.3	509.4	513.4	522.2	527.1	527.7	531.0	514.4
1993	519.4	525.1	529.8	536.9	540.8	545.1	540.4	544.7	549.3	554.0	556.1	560.3	541.8
1994	543.8	549.7	559.2	564.2	570.5	574.0	568.5	575.5	580.9	581.0	590.0	592.0	570.7
1995	577.1	582.4	591.6	589.3	593.5	598.4	590.6	593.0	603.2	604.3	609.2	612.8	595.4
1996	591.4	595.9	605.5	604.3	608.4	608.9	606.1	605.9	616.4	619.8	625.7	625.0	609.4
1997	608.5	615.3	620.6	624.7	629.7	631.6	626.6	631.0	636.8	642.2	646.4	648.9	630.1
1998	635.0	639.7	644.5	647.1	652.1	648.6	649.1	651.8	656.5	663.6	664.0	667.3	651.6
1999	648.2	653.5	660.3	664.6	665.4	665.0	665.3	668.4	675.2	679.4	683.8	687.0	668.0
2000	666.5	670.3	681.0	678.8	682.3	683.2	676.0	680.4	683.7	686.0	688.2	688.8	680.4
2001	670.0	672.2	676.4	679.8	679.5	678.5	674.2	675.4	679.1	675.6	677.9	677.4	676.3
2002	657.3	660.9	665.5	668.0	670.8	668.5	671.5	675.5	679.7	680.6	684.2	685.5	672.3
2003	670.1	671.7	674.8	678.8	680.5	675.8	676.7	683.6	687.3	687.4	691.3	691.8	680.8
Total private													
1990	423.0	425.3	430.6	431.5	434.9	438.1	436.9	438.8	437.2	433.2	432.8	432.5	432.9
1991	417.7	417.3	421.9	424.3	429.6	435.5	434.0	437.3	438.1	437.4	438.0	437.9	430.7
1992	428.4	430.1	434.4	440.1	443.8	449.8	448.3	451.2	451.9	455.7	456.1	458.9	445.7
1993	448.5	452.7	457.1	463.3	467.4	473.2	473.4	475.7	475.7	479.2	480.9	484.2	469.2
1994	469.9	474.3	483.2	487.9	494.6	500.6	499.1	502.2	504.8	504.0	509.1	514.3	495.3
1995	501.3	505.1	513.6	511.6	516.3	523.0	519.9	522.7	525.1	526.3	530.9	534.2	519.1
1996	514.3	516.9	523.0	524.4	528.7	534.0	536.4	535.5	536.9	539.4	544.3	543.8	531.4
1997	528.2	534.0	538.7	543.0	547.5	551.3	552.3	553.3	555.7	560.0	563.3	566.4	549.4
1998	552.6	556.6	560.8	563.9	568.4	570.8	572.2	572.2	573.4	578.4	578.1	581.7	569.0
1999	564.4	567.8	574.3	578.0	580.0	583.7	587.1	587.3	590.5	592.9	596.9	600.0	583.5
2000	581.7	584.1	591.2	591.9	594.1	599.5	595.7	596.5	599.0	599.1	600.7	601.4	594.5
2001	584.1	584.3	588.4	590.7	591.2	594.7	590.4	591.8	591.1	586.7	588.3	588.0	589.1
2002	569.6	571.5	575.3	578.4	581.7	584.5	589.4	591.7	591.6	591.4	594.9	595.8	584.7
2003	580.7	580.9	583.5	587.0	589.6	592.1	594.5	596.3	596.9	596.1	599.8	599.9	591.4
Goods-producing													
1990	105.9	106.1	107.1	106.7	107.5	107.8	107.1	106.5	106.3	105.4	105.1	103.6	106.2
1991	100.3	99.5	100.2	100.0	101.7	103.3	102.3	103.8	103.3	103.2	103.2	102.7	101.9
1992	101.3	101.4	101.7	102.9	103.0	104.0	104.5	105.7	105.4	106.3	106.4	107.2	104.1
1993	105.6	106.0	107.7	107.9	108.2	109.8	109.9	110.4	110.9	111.3	111.6	112.4	109.3
1994	112.0	111.9	115.2	117.6	118.8	120.1	119.5	119.9	120.0	120.9	120.5	121.5	118.1
1995	119.3	120.0	121.5	119.7	120.4	122.4	121.6	121.2	121.4	120.7	121.5	122.1	120.9
1996	117.9	118.2	119.4	119.7	120.5	121.4	120.2	119.2	119.7	119.3	119.1	118.9	119.4
1997	116.9	118.6	119.2	119.6	121.1	121.5	121.3	121.6	121.6	121.3	121.3	122.1	120.5
1998	121.2	122.9	123.1	121.6	120.9	121.9	122.1	121.3	121.3	121.1	120.0	121.3	121.5
1999	119.2	120.2	120.9	122.1	122.8	124.2	124.3	124.0	124.1	124.7	125.2	125.6	123.1
2000	124.3	124.6	125.8	124.9	124.6	125.6	123.6	123.0	122.0	120.9	119.5	119.5	123.1
2001	119.5	118.3	118.8	117.7	117.9	118.8	117.5	117.6	117.1	115.7	114.8	114.7	117.4
2002	110.7	110.1	109.8	111.0	112.1	112.7	112.7	113.0	112.8	112.0	111.6	112.3	111.7
2003	110.5	110.3	110.5	111.0	112.1	112.6	112.1	112.9	112.9	112.4	112.8	112.6	111.9
Construction and mining													
1990	24.1	23.8	24.4	24.2	24.6	24.9	25.2	25.0	24.4	23.9	23.7	23.1	24.3
1991	20.2	20.3	20.9	21.7	22.5	23.3	23.4	23.8	23.2	22.3	22.0	21.2	22.1
1992	19.4	19.4	19.6	20.5	21.0	21.5	22.1	22.5	22.0	22.0	21.9	21.9	21.2
1993	20.6	20.7	21.3	22.2	22.8	23.5	24.0	24.0	24.0	24.2	24.2	24.2	23.0
1994	23.0	23.2	25.0	25.8	26.5	27.0	27.4	27.3	27.0	27.2	26.9	26.7	26.1
1995	25.4	25.3	26.8	27.2	27.7	28.8	29.1	29.2	29.4	29.3	29.4	29.4	28.1
1996	27.5	28.2	29.3	29.6	30.3	31.2	31.5	31.3	31.3	31.2	31.0	30.8	30.3
1997	29.2	29.9	30.5	31.5	31.9	32.6	33.5	33.6	33.3	32.8	32.3	32.2	31.9
1998	31.2	31.4	31.7	32.0	32.8	33.5	34.2	33.9	33.7	33.5	32.9	33.2	32.8
1999	30.3	31.0	31.6	33.3	34.3	35.3	35.8	35.4	35.1	34.8	34.6	34.6	33.8
2000	33.6	33.6	34.7	35.1	36.0	36.4	35.8	35.7	35.1	34.6	34.0	33.8	34.9
2001	31.4	31.6	32.3	32.5	33.0	33.8	33.9	34.0	33.2	32.6	32.5	32.3	32.8
2002	30.2	30.1	30.3	30.6	31.5	32.0	32.6	33.0	33.0	32.6	32.8	32.8	31.8
2003	31.8	31.7	32.3	33.0	33.7	34.4	34.5	34.6	34.4	33.9	34.0	33.9	33.5

Employment by Industry: Tennessee—*Continued*

(Numbers in thousands. Not seasonally adjusted.)

Industry	January	February	March	April	May	June	July	August	September	October	November	December	Annual Average
NASHVILLE—*Continued*													
Manufacturing													
1990	81.8	82.3	82.7	82.5	82.9	82.9	81.9	81.5	81.9	81.5	81.4	80.5	81.9
1991	80.1	79.2	79.3	78.3	79.2	80.0	78.9	80.0	80.1	80.9	81.2	81.5	79.8
1992	81.9	82.0	82.1	82.4	82.0	82.5	82.4	83.2	83.4	84.3	84.5	85.3	83.0
1993	85.0	85.3	86.4	85.7	85.4	86.3	85.9	86.4	86.9	87.1	87.4	88.2	86.3
1994	89.0	88.7	90.2	91.8	92.3	93.1	92.1	92.6	93.0	93.7	93.6	94.8	92.0
1995	93.9	94.7	94.7	92.5	92.7	93.6	92.5	92.0	92.0	91.4	92.1	92.7	92.9
1996	90.4	90.0	90.1	90.1	90.2	90.2	88.7	87.9	88.4	88.1	88.1	88.1	89.1
1997	87.7	88.7	88.7	88.1	89.2	88.9	87.8	88.0	88.3	88.5	89.0	89.9	88.5
1998	90.0	91.5	91.4	89.6	88.1	88.4	87.9	87.4	87.6	87.6	87.1	88.1	88.7
1999	88.9	89.2	89.3	88.8	88.5	88.9	88.5	88.6	89.0	89.9	90.6	91.0	89.2
2000	90.7	91.0	91.1	89.8	88.6	89.2	87.8	87.3	86.9	86.3	85.5	85.7	88.3
2001	88.1	86.7	86.5	85.2	84.9	85.0	83.6	83.6	83.9	83.1	82.3	82.4	84.6
2002	80.5	80.0	79.5	80.4	80.6	80.7	80.1	80.0	79.8	79.4	78.8	79.5	79.9
2003	78.7	78.6	78.2	78.0	78.4	78.2	77.6	78.3	78.5	78.5	78.8	78.7	78.4
Service-providing													
1990	386.3	389.2	394.2	395.7	399.8	398.2	394.6	398.4	399.8	397.0	397.1	397.7	395.6
1991	386.5	387.9	392.2	395.1	399.4	401.6	397.1	400.5	404.6	405.0	405.6	405.8	398.4
1992	396.2	398.8	405.7	407.6	410.0	410.3	404.9	407.7	416.8	420.8	421.3	423.8	410.3
1993	413.8	419.1	422.1	429.0	432.6	435.3	430.5	434.3	438.4	442.7	444.5	447.9	432.5
1994	431.8	437.8	444.0	446.6	451.7	453.9	449.0	455.6	460.9	460.1	469.5	470.5	452.6
1995	457.8	462.4	470.1	469.6	473.1	476.0	469.0	471.8	481.8	483.6	487.7	490.7	474.4
1996	473.5	477.7	486.1	484.6	487.9	487.5	485.9	486.7	496.7	500.5	506.6	506.1	489.9
1997	491.6	496.7	501.4	505.1	508.6	510.1	505.3	509.4	515.2	520.9	525.1	526.8	509.6
1998	513.8	516.8	521.4	525.5	531.2	526.7	527.0	530.5	535.2	542.5	544.0	546.0	530.0
1999	529.0	533.3	539.4	542.5	542.6	540.8	541.0	544.4	551.1	554.7	558.6	561.4	544.9
2000	542.2	545.7	555.2	553.9	557.7	557.6	552.4	557.4	561.7	565.1	568.7	569.3	557.2
2001	550.5	553.9	557.6	562.1	561.6	559.7	556.7	557.8	562.0	559.9	563.1	562.7	559.0
2002	546.6	550.8	555.7	557.0	558.7	555.8	558.8	562.5	566.9	568.6	572.6	573.2	560.6
2003	559.6	561.4	564.3	567.8	568.4	563.2	564.6	570.7	574.4	575.0	578.5	579.2	568.9
Trade, transportation, and utilities													
1990	110.3	109.8	110.7	110.6	111.3	111.6	111.6	112.9	112.5	111.8	113.1	114.1	111.6
1991	107.9	106.9	107.5	108.3	109.3	109.9	109.6	111.7	112.4	112.3	113.5	114.1	110.2
1992	110.2	109.3	109.8	111.5	112.5	113.9	113.3	113.7	115.0	115.2	116.6	117.2	113.1
1993	111.9	112.5	112.7	114.2	115.4	116.3	116.9	117.8	117.4	120.3	122.2	123.4	116.7
1994	116.0	115.9	116.6	115.4	117.6	119.2	118.4	119.4	120.9	121.1	125.3	127.7	119.4
1995	122.2	120.6	121.6	121.0	121.8	122.7	121.6	122.3	123.7	125.4	128.3	129.9	123.4
1996	125.1	123.5	123.8	123.4	124.0	124.7	124.9	125.7	125.7	127.4	130.8	132.4	125.9
1997	127.1	127.1	127.7	127.2	127.3	128.2	128.9	129.2	130.8	133.2	136.8	138.1	130.1
1998	134.6	133.7	133.5	131.4	132.1	132.8	133.6	133.9	134.6	136.6	139.2	140.3	134.6
1999	135.2	134.1	135.0	136.3	135.6	136.8	136.6	136.4	137.4	139.8	142.4	144.6	137.5
2000	136.9	136.5	137.2	137.4	137.2	138.0	139.0	139.6	140.9	143.3	145.4	146.3	139.8
2001	139.4	138.5	138.9	139.5	139.5	139.4	137.9	137.7	137.6	137.5	139.9	140.4	138.9
2002	132.8	131.8	133.1	131.5	132.3	133.0	134.3	134.7	135.4	137.8	140.1	142.4	134.9
2003	136.4	136.1	136.4	136.7	137.0	138.4	139.0	139.7	139.9	140.9	143.0	144.2	139.0
Wholesale trade													
1990	31.8	31.9	32.1	31.7	31.6	31.2	30.9	30.7	30.5	30.1	30.0	29.8	31.0
1991	28.8	28.7	28.7	28.9	29.0	29.1	28.9	29.1	29.0	29.1	29.1	29.2	28.9
1992	28.7	28.7	29.0	29.1	29.2	29.3	29.4	29.2	29.6	29.2	29.2	28.9	29.1
1993	28.5	28.6	28.8	28.8	28.9	29.0	29.9	29.9	30.0	30.7	31.1	31.3	29.6
1994	30.9	31.1	31.1	31.2	31.4	31.7	31.8	32.0	32.2	32.5	33.4	33.5	31.9
1995	33.0	33.2	33.4	32.8	33.0	33.1	32.3	32.5	32.6	32.7	33.2	33.3	32.9
1996	32.8	32.8	32.9	32.8	32.7	32.9	32.7	32.8	33.0	33.2	33.7	34.0	33.0
1997	33.4	33.5	33.4	33.3	33.4	33.7	34.0	34.1	34.7	35.2	35.6	36.1	34.2
1998	35.7	35.7	35.5	34.5	34.4	34.2	34.7	34.7	34.8	34.9	35.0	34.8	34.9
1999	34.7	34.6	34.8	35.1	35.0	35.0	34.8	34.4	34.2	34.2	34.1	34.2	34.5
2000	33.7	33.9	34.0	33.8	33.5	33.5	33.7	33.7	33.8	33.8	33.6	33.7	33.7
2001	33.6	33.7	33.8	34.1	34.1	34.1	33.9	33.7	33.8	33.6	33.5	33.3	33.8
2002	32.5	32.6	32.6	32.9	33.2	33.3	33.7	34.2	34.2	34.8	34.7	34.8	33.6
2003	34.4	34.3	34.3	34.3	34.6	34.7	34.9	35.1	35.1	35.2	35.0	35.1	34.8
Retail trade													
1990	59.8	59.2	59.6	60.0	60.6	60.9	61.1	62.6	62.4	62.2	63.5	64.7	61.3
1991	60.2	59.2	59.6	60.0	60.6	60.9	60.4	62.1	62.4	62.4	63.7	64.2	61.3
1992	61.3	60.7	61.0	61.4	62.0	62.6	62.4	62.9	63.3	63.7	65.0	65.9	62.6
1993	62.2	62.3	62.3	63.8	64.4	65.1	64.7	65.5	65.0	66.5	67.9	69.1	64.9
1994	63.4	62.9	63.7	63.4	64.5	65.8	64.9	65.8	67.3	66.5	69.8	72.3	65.8
1995	67.9	66.5	67.2	66.5	67.2	68.1	68.0	68.5	69.9	70.8	73.4	74.9	69.0
1996	71.5	69.8	70.0	70.0	70.6	71.1	71.3	71.9	71.8	72.6	75.4	76.9	71.9
1997	73.0	72.6	73.1	72.6	72.5	73.0	73.1	73.5	74.3	76.1	79.1	80.0	74.4
1998	76.6	75.6	75.6	74.7	75.3	76.1	75.7	75.8	76.3	77.9	80.6	82.0	76.8
1999	77.5	76.5	77.1	77.1	76.7	78.1	77.8	78.1	79.2	80.8	83.4	85.3	78.9
2000	78.9	78.3	78.7	79.3	79.4	79.9	80.3	80.7	81.8	83.4	85.7	86.6	81.0
2001	80.0	79.1	79.4	79.1	78.9	78.7	77.7	77.7	77.8	78.2	80.9	81.6	79.1
2002	75.3	74.1	75.0	73.5	73.9	74.5	75.4	75.0	75.8	77.1	79.5	81.7	75.9
2003	76.0	75.6	75.7	75.9	75.8	76.8	77.1	77.3	77.7	78.7	81.0	82.1	77.5

Employment by Industry: Tennessee—*Continued*

(Numbers in thousands. Not seasonally adjusted.)

Industry	January	February	March	April	May	June	July	August	September	October	November	December	Annual Average
NASHVILLE—*Continued*													
Transportation and utilities													
1990	18.7	18.7	19.0	18.9	19.1	19.5	19.6	19.6	19.6	19.5	19.6	19.6	19.2
1991	18.9	19.0	19.2	19.4	19.7	19.9	20.3	20.5	21.0	20.8	20.7	20.7	20.0
1992	20.2	19.9	19.8	21.0	21.3	22.0	21.5	21.6	22.1	22.3	22.4	22.4	21.3
1993	21.2	21.6	21.6	21.6	22.1	22.2	22.3	22.4	22.4	23.1	23.2	23.0	22.2
1994	21.7	21.9	21.8	20.8	21.7	21.7	21.7	21.6	21.4	22.1	22.1	21.9	21.7
1995	21.3	20.9	21.0	21.7	21.6	21.5	21.3	21.3	21.2	21.9	21.7	21.7	21.4
1996	20.8	20.9	20.9	20.6	20.7	20.7	20.9	21.0	20.9	21.6	21.7	21.5	21.0
1997	20.7	21.0	21.2	21.3	21.4	21.5	21.8	21.6	21.8	21.9	22.1	22.0	21.5
1998	22.3	22.4	22.4	22.2	22.4	22.5	23.2	23.4	23.5	23.8	23.6	23.5	22.9
1999	23.0	23.0	23.1	24.1	23.9	23.7	24.0	23.9	24.0	24.8	24.9	25.1	23.9
2000	24.3	24.3	24.5	24.3	24.3	24.6	25.0	25.2	25.3	26.1	26.1	26.0	25.0
2001	25.8	25.7	25.7	26.3	26.5	26.6	26.3	26.3	26.0	25.7	25.5	25.5	26.0
2002	25.0	25.1	25.5	25.1	25.2	25.2	25.2	25.5	25.4	25.9	25.9	25.9	25.4
2003	26.0	26.2	26.4	26.5	26.6	26.9	27.0	27.3	27.1	27.0	27.0	27.0	26.8
Information													
1990	15.3	15.3	15.4	15.3	15.3	15.4	15.7	15.7	15.6	15.6	15.5	15.7	15.4
1991	15.6	15.4	15.3	15.5	15.1	15.1	14.8	14.9	15.0	15.2	15.3	15.1	15.1
1992	15.2	15.3	15.3	15.5	15.5	15.7	15.7	15.8	15.5	15.9	16.2	16.8	15.7
1993	16.7	16.7	17.0	17.1	17.2	17.4	17.3	17.3	17.3	17.0	17.0	17.3	17.1
1994	17.0	17.4	17.8	17.5	17.8	17.9	17.7	17.8	17.8	17.9	18.0	18.1	17.7
1995	18.7	18.8	19.0	18.8	18.8	19.0	19.0	19.1	19.2	18.9	19.0	19.2	18.9
1996	19.3	19.3	19.4	18.6	18.9	19.0	18.8	18.9	18.9	19.1	19.1	19.2	19.0
1997	18.9	18.9	18.9	18.7	18.8	19.2	19.3	19.3	19.4	20.0	20.5	20.6	19.3
1998	20.5	20.7	20.4	20.4	20.6	20.5	20.9	20.8	21.3	21.6	21.6	21.4	20.8
1999	21.1	21.0	21.2	20.8	20.9	21.0	20.1	20.1	20.2	20.3	20.6	20.8	20.6
2000	20.7	20.6	20.9	20.8	20.8	20.9	21.2	21.2	21.2	21.3	21.8	22.0	21.1
2001	23.4	23.6	23.6	22.9	22.9	22.9	22.5	22.2	22.0	22.3	22.4	22.5	22.8
2002	21.8	21.8	22.0	21.5	21.3	21.1	21.1	20.9	20.6	20.9	20.7	20.5	21.2
2003	19.7	19.7	19.7	19.6	19.7	19.6	19.6	19.6	19.6	19.5	19.4	19.3	19.6
Financial activities													
1990	35.1	35.3	35.4	35.7	35.8	36.0	36.0	35.9	35.6	35.1	35.0	35.1	35.5
1991	35.9	36.1	36.2	36.0	36.1	36.3	35.8	36.2	36.2	36.0	36.1	36.4	36.1
1992	35.7	35.9	36.0	35.8	36.0	36.3	36.1	36.3	36.3	36.1	36.0	36.3	36.0
1993	36.1	36.6	36.7	36.5	36.7	37.0	37.0	37.1	37.1	37.0	37.3	37.6	36.8
1994	37.1	37.5	37.7	37.7	38.0	38.6	38.4	38.6	38.5	38.3	38.6	39.1	38.1
1995	38.4	38.6	39.0	39.7	40.1	40.7	40.9	41.3	41.6	41.4	41.0	41.5	40.3
1996	41.3	41.8	42.2	42.3	42.5	43.0	43.0	43.4	43.6	43.3	43.7	43.9	42.8
1997	43.4	43.7	43.9	43.0	43.5	44.1	44.2	44.4	44.5	45.1	45.5	45.8	44.2
1998	45.7	46.2	46.4	46.8	47.1	47.5	47.5	47.6	47.3	48.2	48.1	48.4	47.2
1999	48.4	48.5	48.9	47.9	47.9	47.9	49.2	48.7	48.3	47.2	47.3	47.5	48.1
2000	46.6	46.7	46.7	46.4	46.4	46.7	46.6	46.2	45.9	45.5	45.7	45.7	46.2
2001	43.3	43.6	43.8	44.0	44.0	44.2	44.2	44.0	43.5	43.1	42.9	42.6	43.6
2002	42.1	42.2	42.1	42.5	42.7	43.3	43.2	43.4	43.2	43.5	43.7	43.8	43.0
2003	43.8	43.9	44.1	44.2	44.3	44.6	44.3	44.4	44.2	44.4	44.7	44.7	44.3
Professional and business services													
1990	40.4	41.0	41.4	41.6	41.9	42.3	42.2	42.9	43.0	42.9	43.0	42.8	42.1
1991	37.7	38.0	38.8	38.9	39.4	39.9	39.7	40.1	40.7	41.1	41.5	41.3	39.7
1992	40.4	41.1	42.0	43.4	43.8	44.2	43.5	44.3	44.1	45.2	44.5	44.5	43.4
1993	44.7	45.7	46.6	47.3	48.0	49.2	49.3	50.0	50.1	51.2	50.9	51.3	48.6
1994	49.0	50.2	51.6	53.6	54.0	54.8	55.2	56.0	56.6	56.0	56.1	56.6	54.1
1995	54.6	55.9	57.3	58.1	58.7	58.8	58.0	59.4	59.7	60.9	61.6	61.5	58.7
1996	57.7	59.4	60.8	61.6	62.3	63.2	63.3	64.4	65.3	65.1	65.9	65.3	62.8
1997	62.5	64.9	66.0	66.2	67.1	68.0	67.4	68.2	68.7	69.3	69.5	70.2	67.3
1998	67.4	69.8	71.7	72.0	73.9	74.2	74.6	75.9	75.9	77.5	76.9	77.4	73.9
1999	75.7	77.3	79.0	81.3	82.3	82.5	83.2	84.7	85.5	86.2	86.7	86.1	82.5
2000	84.7	86.1	87.8	87.7	88.4	88.7	87.7	88.6	89.8	90.0	89.9	89.9	88.2
2001	84.5	84.4	85.1	86.0	85.4	85.6	86.4	87.6	88.0	86.8	87.0	87.3	86.2
2002	84.0	85.4	86.5	86.9	87.2	86.9	87.6	88.3	87.6	86.3	87.1	85.9	86.6
2003	81.6	81.4	81.8	81.7	82.4	82.6	83.0	83.2	83.0	82.6	83.0	82.5	82.4
Educational and health services													
1990	56.5	57.0	57.2	57.7	57.6	57.7	57.8	58.0	59.3	59.2	59.3	59.3	58.0
1991	59.1	59.7	60.0	59.8	60.1	60.4	59.7	60.4	61.5	62.2	62.2	62.7	60.6
1992	62.5	62.9	62.9	63.0	63.2	63.4	63.1	63.6	64.8	66.3	66.5	67.3	64.1
1993	65.7	66.1	66.6	67.2	67.2	67.1	67.1	67.6	68.9	68.7	68.9	69.1	67.5
1994	68.3	69.1	69.3	69.5	69.8	69.3	69.4	70.0	71.6	72.1	72.7	73.1	70.3
1995	72.9	74.1	74.7	73.6	74.0	74.1	74.2	75.2	76.5	76.9	77.4	77.7	75.1
1996	75.3	76.0	76.3	75.8	75.7	75.6	75.5	75.9	77.1	77.5	77.9	78.2	76.4
1997	76.6	77.4	77.5	77.3	77.6	77.0	78.0	78.5	80.0	79.5	79.9	80.1	78.2
1998	81.4	82.2	82.4	80.7	80.9	80.0	79.9	79.7	80.6	80.9	80.3	80.9	80.8
1999	78.5	79.2	79.2	79.4	79.1	78.6	78.9	78.6	80.2	80.7	80.5	80.9	79.4
2000	78.8	79.5	80.3	81.3	80.7	80.7	80.8	80.8	81.7	82.1	82.6	82.5	80.9
2001	81.6	82.6	83.0	84.4	84.3	84.8	85.0	85.0	85.3	85.0	85.3	85.9	84.4
2002	85.4	86.2	86.6	87.7	88.2	88.1	90.1	90.1	90.4	90.6	90.8	90.7	88.7
2003	91.1	91.7	91.8	92.9	92.9	92.9	94.1	93.5	93.7	94.0	94.1	94.4	93.1

Employment by Industry: Tennessee—*Continued*

(Numbers in thousands. Not seasonally adjusted.)

Industry	January	February	March	April	May	June	July	August	September	October	November	December	Annual Average
NASHVILLE—*Continued*													
Leisure and hospitality													
1990	41.2	42.3	44.8	45.2	46.8	48.3	47.7	48.1	46.1	44.8	43.5	43.5	45.1
1991	43.1	43.5	45.7	47.5	49.3	51.5	53.4	51.4	50.1	48.4	47.1	46.4	48.1
1992	44.2	45.1	47.6	48.5	50.2	52.2	52.0	51.8	50.6	50.0	49.2	48.7	49.1
1993	47.1	48.1	48.7	51.6	53.1	54.5	54.1	53.9	52.5	52.1	51.3	51.4	51.5
1994	48.9	50.3	52.8	54.3	56.2	58.0	57.7	57.7	56.7	54.9	54.9	55.2	54.8
1995	52.6	54.1	57.1	56.6	58.3	60.7	60.7	60.6	59.3	58.0	58.0	58.1	57.8
1996	53.9	54.7	56.8	58.9	60.5	62.4	65.6	63.1	61.7	63.0	63.0	60.9	60.3
1997	57.7	58.7	60.8	64.3	66.0	67.2	66.0	66.0	65.0	64.7	63.6	63.4	63.6
1998	55.7	54.7	56.2	64.8	66.1	66.6	67.0	66.3	65.4	65.2	64.8	64.6	63.1
1999	60.5	61.6	63.6	64.6	65.5	66.3	67.7	67.8	67.6	66.3	66.4	66.4	65.3
2000	63.8	63.9	65.7	66.7	69.0	71.2	70.0	70.1	70.1	68.8	68.6	68.9	68.0
2001	65.6	66.0	67.5	68.0	68.8	70.1	68.6	69.3	68.5	67.1	67.0	66.5	67.8
2002	64.7	65.4	66.7	68.3	68.4	69.6	70.3	71.4	70.9	69.0	70.0	69.7	68.7
2003	67.1	67.9	69.2	70.7	70.8	71.9	72.6	73.4	73.2	71.3	72.2	72.0	71.0
Other services													
1990	18.3	18.5	18.6	18.7	18.7	19.0	18.8	18.8	18.8	18.4	18.3	18.4	18.6
1991	18.1	18.2	18.2	18.3	18.6	19.1	18.7	18.8	18.9	19.0	19.1	19.2	18.6
1992	18.9	19.1	19.1	19.5	19.6	20.1	20.1	20.0	20.2	20.7	20.7	20.9	19.9
1993	20.7	21.0	21.1	21.5	21.6	21.9	21.8	21.6	21.5	21.6	21.7	21.7	21.4
1994	21.6	22.0	22.2	22.3	22.4	22.7	22.8	22.8	22.7	22.8	23.0	23.0	22.5
1995	22.6	23.0	23.4	24.1	24.2	24.6	23.9	23.6	23.7	24.1	24.1	24.2	23.7
1996	23.8	24.0	24.3	24.1	24.3	24.7	25.1	24.9	24.9	24.7	24.8	25.0	24.5
1997	25.1	24.7	24.7	26.7	26.1	26.1	27.2	26.1	25.7	26.9	26.2	26.1	25.9
1998	26.1	26.4	27.1	26.2	26.8	27.3	26.6	26.7	27.0	27.3	27.2	27.4	26.8
1999	25.8	25.9	26.5	25.6	25.9	26.4	27.1	27.0	27.2	27.7	27.8	28.1	26.7
2000	25.9	26.2	26.8	26.7	27.0	27.7	26.8	27.0	27.4	27.2	27.2	26.6	26.8
2001	26.8	27.3	27.7	28.2	28.4	28.9	28.3	28.4	29.1	29.2	29.0	28.1	28.3
2002	28.1	28.6	28.5	29.0	29.5	29.8	30.1	29.9	30.7	31.3	30.9	30.5	29.7
2003	30.5	29.9	30.0	30.2	30.4	29.5	29.8	29.6	30.4	31.0	30.6	30.2	30.2
Government													
1990	69.2	70.0	70.7	70.9	72.4	67.9	64.8	66.1	68.9	69.2	69.4	68.8	69.0
1991	69.1	70.1	70.5	70.8	71.5	69.4	65.4	67.0	69.8	70.8	70.8	70.6	69.6
1992	69.1	70.1	73.0	70.4	69.2	64.5	61.1	62.2	70.3	71.4	71.6	72.1	68.7
1993	70.9	72.4	72.7	73.6	73.4	71.9	67.0	69.0	73.6	74.8	75.2	76.1	72.5
1994	73.9	75.4	76.0	76.3	75.9	73.4	69.4	73.3	76.1	77.0	80.9	77.7	75.4
1995	75.8	77.3	78.0	77.7	77.2	75.4	70.7	70.3	78.1	78.0	78.3	78.6	76.2
1996	77.1	79.0	82.5	79.9	79.7	74.9	69.7	70.4	79.5	80.4	81.4	81.2	77.9
1997	80.3	81.3	81.9	81.7	82.2	80.3	74.3	77.7	81.1	82.2	83.1	82.5	80.7
1998	82.4	83.1	83.7	83.2	83.7	77.8	76.9	79.6	83.1	85.2	85.9	85.6	82.5
1999	83.8	85.7	86.0	86.6	85.4	81.3	78.2	81.1	84.7	86.5	86.9	87.0	84.4
2000	84.8	86.2	89.8	86.9	88.2	83.7	80.3	83.9	84.7	86.9	87.5	87.4	85.8
2001	85.9	87.9	88.0	89.1	88.3	83.8	83.8	83.6	88.0	88.9	89.6	89.4	87.2
2002	87.7	89.4	90.2	89.6	89.1	84.0	82.1	83.8	88.1	89.2	89.3	89.7	87.7
2003	89.4	90.8	91.3	91.8	90.9	83.7	82.2	87.3	90.4	91.3	91.5	91.9	89.4
Federal government													
1990	10.2	10.1	10.5	10.8	13.1	11.6	11.1	10.5	10.2	10.5	10.2	10.2	10.7
1991	10.1	10.1	10.4	10.4	10.5	10.7	10.6	10.6	10.7	10.6	10.3	10.1	10.4
1992	9.9	9.8	9.8	9.7	9.7	9.7	9.6	9.6	9.6	9.7	9.7	9.8	9.7
1993	9.9	9.9	9.9	10.1	10.1	10.2	10.1	10.1	10.2	10.1	10.1	10.3	10.0
1994	10.1	10.1	10.0	10.1	10.0	10.0	10.5	10.5	10.5	10.4	10.4	10.5	10.2
1995	10.5	10.4	10.4	10.4	10.4	10.5	10.4	10.4	10.4	10.4	10.3	10.5	10.4
1996	10.6	11.2	11.2	11.3	11.2	11.3	11.3	11.3	11.3	11.2	11.4	11.5	11.2
1997	11.5	11.5	11.5	11.4	11.4	11.3	11.3	11.3	11.3	11.2	11.3	11.4	11.3
1998	11.4	11.4	11.6	11.3	11.4	11.3	11.3	11.3	11.3	11.4	11.6	11.9	11.4
1999	11.5	11.4	11.4	11.8	11.4	11.4	11.4	11.4	11.4	11.4	11.4	11.6	11.4
2000	11.6	11.6	11.6	11.8	13.4	13.0	12.2	12.3	11.2	11.2	11.3	11.3	11.8
2001	11.2	11.2	11.2	11.1	11.2	11.2	11.2	11.2	11.2	11.1	11.2	11.3	11.2
2002	11.2	11.1	11.1	11.0	10.9	11.0	11.0	10.9	11.1	11.2	11.3	11.3	11.1
2003	11.2	11.2	11.0	11.1	11.0	11.1	11.1	11.1	11.3	11.3	11.4	11.4	11.2
State government													
1990	24.1	24.7	24.8	24.8	23.9	22.8	22.9	22.7	23.9	24.4	24.6	24.3	23.9
1991	23.3	24.0	23.9	24.0	24.2	23.9	22.7	22.2	23.0	23.5	23.5	23.2	23.4
1992	22.5	23.3	23.4	23.4	21.8	21.5	21.9	21.8	23.1	23.7	23.5	23.7	22.8
1993	23.0	23.9	24.1	24.5	23.9	22.5	22.5	22.4	23.8	24.5	24.7	24.6	23.7
1994	23.5	24.6	25.1	24.8	24.1	22.9	23.4	23.5	24.3	24.8	25.1	24.8	24.2
1995	23.9	25.0	25.2	24.9	24.2	23.7	23.7	22.9	24.6	25.0	25.1	24.9	24.4
1996	23.6	24.8	25.0	25.0	24.6	23.7	23.7	23.0	24.3	25.7	25.9	25.8	24.5
1997	25.0	25.6	25.7	25.5	25.3	23.5	23.3	23.5	24.7	25.6	25.9	25.2	24.9
1998	25.0	25.6	25.7	25.3	25.1	24.0	23.8	24.0	25.8	26.6	26.7	26.3	25.3
1999	25.3	26.9	26.8	26.9	25.8	24.5	24.2	24.6	25.7	26.5	26.6	26.3	25.8
2000	25.4	26.5	26.7	26.5	25.9	24.7	25.0	25.0	25.5	26.7	26.9	26.9	25.9
2001	25.8	27.2	27.2	27.3	26.6	25.6	25.6	25.7	26.8	27.7	27.9	27.5	26.7
2002	25.8	27.5	27.8	27.8	27.2	25.7	23.9	26.0	26.3	26.7	26.4	26.8	26.5
2003	27.0	28.4	28.5	28.3	27.5	26.1	24.6	26.5	26.8	27.1	26.9	27.3	27.1

Employment by Industry: Tennessee—*Continued*

(Numbers in thousands. Not seasonally adjusted.)

Industry	January	February	March	April	May	June	July	August	September	October	November	December	Annual Average
NASHVILLE—*Continued*													
Local government													
1990	34.9	35.2	35.4	35.3	35.4	33.5	30.8	32.9	34.8	34.3	34.6	34.3	34.2
1991	35.7	36.0	36.2	36.4	36.8	34.8	32.1	34.2	36.1	36.7	37.0	37.3	35.7
1992	36.7	37.0	39.8	37.3	37.7	33.3	29.6	30.8	37.6	38.0	38.4	38.6	36.2
1993	38.0	38.6	38.7	39.0	39.4	39.2	34.4	36.5	39.6	40.2	40.4	41.2	38.7
1994	40.3	40.7	40.9	41.4	41.8	40.5	35.5	39.3	41.3	41.8	45.4	42.4	40.9
1995	41.4	41.9	42.4	42.4	42.6	41.2	36.6	37.0	43.1	42.6	42.9	43.2	41.4
1996	42.9	43.0	46.3	43.6	43.9	39.9	34.7	36.1	43.9	43.5	44.1	43.9	42.1
1997	43.8	44.2	44.7	44.8	45.5	45.5	39.7	42.9	45.1	45.4	45.9	45.9	44.4
1998	46.0	46.1	46.4	46.6	47.2	42.5	41.8	44.3	46.0	47.2	47.6	47.4	45.7
1999	47.0	47.4	47.8	47.9	48.2	45.4	42.6	45.1	47.6	48.6	48.9	49.1	47.1
2000	47.8	48.1	51.5	48.6	48.9	46.0	43.1	46.6	48.0	49.0	49.3	49.2	48.0
2001	48.9	49.5	49.6	50.7	50.5	47.0	47.0	46.7	50.0	50.1	50.5	50.6	49.3
2002	50.7	50.8	51.3	50.8	51.0	47.3	47.2	46.9	50.7	51.3	51.6	51.6	50.1
2003	51.2	51.2	51.8	52.4	52.4	46.5	46.5	49.7	52.3	52.9	53.2	53.2	51.1

Average Weekly Hours by Industry: Tennessee

(Not seasonally adjusted.)

Industry	January	February	March	April	May	June	July	August	September	October	November	December	Annual Average
STATEWIDE													
Manufacturing													
2001	38.5	38.1	37.9	37.1	38.7	38.9	38.9	39.7	39.8	39.3	39.8	40.2	38.9
2002	39.8	39.7	40.1	39.6	39.5	40.1	39.9	40.5	40.7	40.3	40.1	40.7	40.1
2003	39.4	39.4	39.2	39.3	39.4	39.9	39.0	40.4	40.3	39.9	40.3	40.8	39.8
CHATTANOOGA													
Manufacturing													
2001	39.7	38.9	39.6	38.6	40.5	39.7	40.3	41.2	41.1	39.7	40.2	42.0	40.1
2002	41.5	42.7	43.4	42.0	42.3	42.7	42.8	42.1	41.8	39.4	39.7	40.5	41.8
2003	42.2	41.2	40.2	39.6	39.4	40.5	40.3	41.8	42.3	41.9	41.1	41.3	41.0
KNOXVILLE													
Manufacturing													
2001	41.3	40.2	41.1	41.1	41.6	41.2	41.1	41.9	41.9	41.3	42.7	42.4	41.5
2002	41.6	41.2	41.4	41.5	41.1	41.8	41.1	42.4	42.3	40.7	40.8	41.0	41.4
2003	40.1	40.2	39.3	39.9	40.6	40.3	40.0	40.4	40.9	40.6	40.3	43.5	40.5
MEMPHIS													
Manufacturing													
2001	40.3	39.4	40.0	39.9	39.6	39.9	40.6	42.0	42.4	42.4	42.4	41.1	40.8
2002	40.8	39.2	40.8	40.3	40.0	40.0	40.6	41.5	41.3	41.6	42.0	40.9	40.8
2003	40.3	39.6	41.0	41.4	41.1	41.8	42.3	41.4	40.4	41.9	41.9	40.7	41.2
NASHVILLE													
Manufacturing													
2001	37.3	37.0	36.9	36.3	37.1	37.6	37.0	38.8	38.6	38.5	39.3	39.8	37.8
2002	40.0	39.2	40.1	39.3	39.3	40.1	38.6	39.8	39.2	39.7	40.6	40.6	39.7
2003	38.2	38.9	37.7	38.4	38.5	39.6	38.4	39.7	39.3	39.5	39.8	39.7	39.0

Average Hourly Earnings by Industry: Tennessee

(Dollars, not seasonally adjusted.)

Industry	January	February	March	April	May	June	July	August	September	October	November	December	Annual Average
STATEWIDE													
Manufacturing													
2001	12.95	12.97	12.99	12.92	12.75	12.88	12.83	12.72	12.79	12.81	12.89	13.05	12.88
2002	13.09	13.01	13.13	13.00	13.07	13.18	13.11	13.13	13.16	13.19	13.28	13.47	13.15
2003	13.47	13.59	13.45	13.56	13.57	13.50	13.63	13.55	13.58	13.52	13.60	13.71	13.56
CHATTANOOGA													
Manufacturing													
2001	12.94	12.89	12.76	13.04	12.94	13.18	12.92	12.88	12.86	12.77	12.63	12.76	12.88
2002	12.66	12.69	12.56	12.40	12.46	12.66	12.71	12.62	12.67	12.62	12.81	12.72	12.63
2003	12.81	12.95	13.10	13.43	13.95	13.55	13.72	13.39	13.31	12.96	13.31	13.04	13.24
KNOXVILLE													
Manufacturing													
2001	13.88	14.08	14.10	14.15	14.14	14.21	14.16	13.94	13.81	13.82	13.68	13.94	14.00
2002	13.55	13.64	13.83	13.79	13.81	13.74	13.83	13.76	13.62	13.80	13.73	13.94	13.75
2003	14.06	14.23	13.70	14.07	14.09	13.78	13.89	14.26	14.40	14.08	14.66	13.99	14.10
MEMPHIS													
Manufacturing													
2001	13.83	14.06	14.16	14.16	13.97	14.09	13.85	13.96	13.91	14.15	14.25	14.10	14.04
2002	14.62	14.16	14.90	14.63	14.55	14.90	14.66	14.50	14.92	14.81	14.88	15.67	14.77
2003	15.16	14.99	15.23	15.19	15.28	15.30	14.99	14.87	15.08	14.02	14.17	15.26	14.96
NASHVILLE													
Manufacturing													
2001	13.49	13.51	13.42	13.48	13.46	13.74	13.41	13.68	13.74	13.52	13.65	13.80	13.58
2002	13.90	13.88	13.92	13.85	14.20	13.99	13.68	14.21	14.10	14.15	14.59	14.37	14.07
2003	14.78	14.54	14.38	14.50	14.42	14.37	14.39	14.26	14.24	14.43	14.44	14.50	14.44

Average Weekly Earnings by Industry: Tennessee

(Dollars, not seasonally adjusted.)

Industry	January	February	March	April	May	June	July	August	September	October	November	December	Annual Average
STATEWIDE													
Manufacturing													
2001	498.58	494.16	492.32	479.33	493.43	501.03	499.09	504.98	509.04	503.43	513.02	524.61	501.03
2002	520.98	516.50	526.51	514.80	516.27	528.52	523.09	531.77	535.61	531.56	532.53	548.23	527.32
2003	530.72	535.45	527.24	532.91	534.66	538.65	531.57	547.42	547.27	539.45	548.08	559.37	539.69
CHATTANOOGA													
Manufacturing													
2001	513.72	501.42	505.30	503.34	524.07	523.25	520.68	530.66	528.55	506.97	507.73	535.92	516.49
2002	525.39	541.86	545.10	520.80	527.06	540.58	543.99	531.30	529.61	497.23	508.56	515.16	527.93
2003	540.58	533.54	526.62	531.83	549.63	548.78	552.92	559.70	563.01	543.02	547.04	538.55	542.84
KNOXVILLE													
Manufacturing													
2001	573.24	566.02	579.51	581.57	588.22	585.45	581.98	584.09	578.64	570.77	584.14	591.06	581.00
2002	563.68	561.97	572.56	572.29	567.59	574.33	568.41	583.42	576.13	561.66	560.18	571.54	569.25
2003	563.81	572.05	538.41	561.39	572.05	555.33	555.60	576.10	588.96	571.65	590.80	608.57	571.05
MEMPHIS													
Manufacturing													
2001	557.35	553.96	566.40	564.98	553.21	562.19	562.31	586.32	589.78	599.96	604.20	579.51	572.83
2002	596.50	555.07	607.92	589.59	582.00	596.00	595.20	601.75	616.20	616.10	624.96	640.90	602.62
2003	610.95	593.60	624.43	628.87	628.01	639.54	634.08	615.62	609.23	587.44	593.72	621.08	616.35
NASHVILLE													
Manufacturing													
2001	503.18	499.87	495.20	489.32	499.37	516.62	496.17	530.78	530.36	520.52	536.45	549.24	513.32
2002	556.00	544.10	558.19	544.31	558.06	561.00	528.05	565.56	552.72	561.76	592.35	583.42	558.58
2003	564.60	565.61	542.13	556.80	555.17	569.05	552.58	566.12	559.63	569.99	574.71	575.65	563.16

TEXAS AT A GLANCE

(Population and total nonfarm employment numbers in thousands)

Population, Census 2000:	20,851.8
Total nonfarm employment, 2003:	9,373.1
Change in total nonfarm employment	
(Number)	
1990–2003:	2,277.8
1990–2001:	2,423.1
2001–2003:	-145.3
(Compound annual rate of change)	
1990–2003:	2.2%
1990–2001:	2.7%
2001–2003:	-0.8%
Unemployment rate	
1990:	6.4%
2001:	5.0%
2003:	6.7%

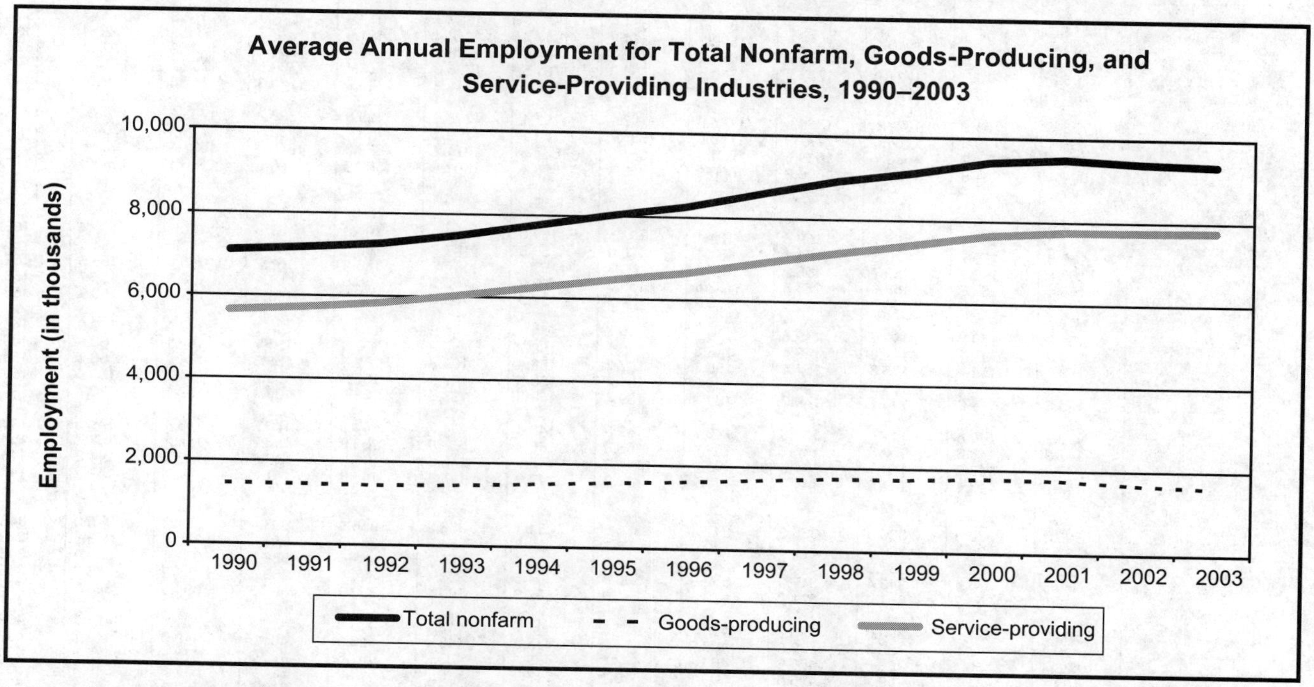

Total nonfarm employment rose substantially through the 1990s, peaking in 2001 and declining thereafter. The goods-producing industries were largely responsible for this trend, declining by more than 9 percent from 2001 to 2003. During this time, employment declined by over 125,000 in manufacturing, as well as 29,000 in construction. Employment in the service-providing sector showed an upward trend in the 1990s but it moderated during the 2001 recession. Government employment showed the largest increase among the service-providing industries, adding over 60,000 jobs from 2001 to 2003.

Employment by Industry: Texas

(Numbers in thousands. Not seasonally adjusted.)

Industry	January	February	March	April	May	June	July	August	September	October	November	December	Annual Average
STATEWIDE													
Total nonfarm													
1990	6890.9	6939.0	6989.6	7043.6	7113.5	7147.6	7101.6	7126.3	7172.3	7192.7	7212.5	7214.1	7095.3
1991	7040.2	7088.8	7131.9	7146.5	7192.7	7215.3	7147.4	7162.9	7221.1	7232.2	7252.4	7264.4	7174.7
1992	7097.1	7145.4	7186.3	7235.5	7272.9	7286.8	7269.0	7276.3	7298.9	7369.5	7384.1	7406.7	7269.0
1993	7272.0	7334.8	7378.1	7428.0	7462.7	7494.1	7496.2	7519.4	7556.3	7584.1	7604.2	7647.8	7481.5
1994	7498.8	7541.7	7603.6	7692.4	7721.0	7757.9	7765.7	7799.2	7835.9	7884.2	7932.9	7977.4	7750.9
1995	7811.8	7878.4	7929.1	7966.5	8010.4	8043.1	8001.9	8042.4	8093.6	8120.7	8164.0	8209.5	8022.6
1996	8024.8	8080.4	8134.0	8194.5	8249.7	8261.8	8238.8	8279.4	8310.5	8388.2	8443.7	8467.6	8256.1
1997	8317.4	8403.1	8475.5	8529.1	8594.5	8628.4	8592.7	8647.2	8713.0	8752.2	8800.9	8842.5	8608.0
1998	8691.3	8768.1	8827.3	8880.2	8933.7	8953.9	8909.0	8962.0	9030.7	9064.1	9103.2	9158.3	8940.2
1999	8957.6	9032.4	9097.4	9106.8	9137.6	9170.8	9108.8	9157.5	9229.5	9256.5	9297.4	9359.1	9159.3
2000	9196.2	9276.0	9358.2	9371.1	9446.2	9474.0	9389.8	9457.5	9523.6	9524.5	9566.9	9616.8	9433.4
2001	9426.9	9496.8	9553.9	9551.5	9578.9	9587.8	9465.5	9516.1	9537.2	9494.0	9504.0	9508.4	9518.4
2002	9312.0	9366.3	9423.6	9429.6	9475.9	9459.0	9354.9	9408.2	9458.1	9436.4	9469.3	9481.1	9422.9
2003	9289.0	9335.4	9369.7	9385.6	9414.0	9398.3	9289.4	9341.1	9382.9	9398.8	9431.4	9441.8	9373.1
Total private													
1990	5641.8	5669.8	5713.1	5761.2	5809.8	5896.8	5898.2	5931.6	5913.7	5908.5	5918.2	5920.4	5831.9
1991	5767.5	5795.2	5839.9	5849.9	5891.5	5943.4	5926.7	5941.8	5924.3	5910.7	5920.5	5934.5	5887.2
1992	5782.3	5806.6	5845.2	5893.9	5929.2	5978.2	5980.7	5985.1	5961.4	6006.3	6010.4	6037.0	5934.7
1993	5916.8	5952.5	5995.4	6037.5	6070.6	6139.5	6168.4	6184.1	6178.6	6183.3	6197.7	6241.5	6105.5
1994	6107.4	6127.7	6187.3	6267.2	6293.4	6362.7	6398.1	6425.1	6422.8	6442.2	6481.9	6531.0	6337.2
1995	6385.6	6424.1	6473.3	6504.1	6548.6	6617.7	6605.9	6641.4	6648.7	6652.5	6685.9	6735.0	6576.9
1996	6581.2	6613.0	6666.3	6719.5	6776.4	6832.0	6836.1	6870.1	6853.9	6903.1	6950.1	6979.4	6798.4
1997	6851.6	6911.2	6979.7	7027.0	7095.3	7172.6	7170.2	7209.8	7225.3	7241.1	7281.2	7332.1	7124.8
1998	7199.4	7250.5	7307.8	7360.3	7410.8	7478.1	7490.9	7519.1	7518.0	7528.2	7555.9	7612.5	7436.0
1999	7432.7	7479.3	7540.4	7552.6	7584.6	7662.7	7659.2	7683.5	7687.2	7693.5	7728.2	7790.2	7624.5
2000	7649.1	7699.8	7774.3	7786.8	7838.7	7937.0	7914.6	7957.8	7959.2	7940.8	7974.5	8025.0	7871.5
2001	7861.2	7902.1	7953.9	7950.3	7976.9	8028.1	7971.3	7993.3	7934.1	7869.9	7867.7	7877.6	7932.2
2002	7706.6	7728.3	7778.5	7784.9	7828.5	7859.4	7824.6	7857.4	7825.6	7768.3	7791.4	7809.5	7796.9
2003	7646.2	7657.6	7693.6	7708.0	7737.0	7763.3	7726.7	7765.3	7744.9	7732.7	7754.9	7772.4	7725.2
Goods-producing													
1990	1416.0	1423.1	1432.8	1438.9	1450.2	1471.4	1473.9	1482.1	1478.0	1479.7	1474.2	1462.9	1456.9
1991	1442.5	1451.9	1463.0	1452.8	1457.8	1470.9	1462.7	1460.9	1454.4	1446.5	1441.4	1431.6	1453.0
1992	1402.3	1404.9	1412.5	1422.9	1434.2	1446.6	1448.7	1447.5	1440.5	1449.6	1442.1	1437.7	1432.5
1993	1412.0	1420.9	1433.3	1432.9	1444.0	1463.6	1466.8	1469.1	1469.5	1476.0	1471.3	1475.2	1452.9
1994	1450.8	1453.2	1467.2	1479.4	1487.2	1506.7	1512.4	1519.4	1524.5	1528.0	1529.0	1533.4	1499.3
1995	1514.9	1525.5	1535.3	1537.7	1547.9	1564.9	1560.2	1567.4	1572.6	1575.1	1572.8	1579.7	1554.5
1996	1556.4	1567.6	1580.4	1585.5	1599.3	1614.2	1617.4	1624.4	1621.5	1627.6	1628.8	1626.4	1604.1
1997	1611.0	1631.4	1645.5	1645.8	1664.0	1681.0	1684.1	1696.3	1699.4	1704.2	1702.9	1707.4	1672.8
1998	1695.2	1710.7	1721.9	1727.3	1740.5	1756.6	1761.5	1765.6	1763.4	1760.6	1752.4	1754.7	1742.5
1999	1718.8	1730.0	1738.9	1729.5	1731.2	1747.2	1746.6	1748.3	1749.8	1749.3	1747.8	1753.6	1740.9
2000	1738.4	1754.4	1772.6	1764.6	1775.3	1798.1	1791.1	1795.2	1795.8	1786.2	1783.2	1786.4	1778.4
2001	1766.9	1779.8	1788.6	1777.2	1778.4	1785.7	1768.2	1769.7	1753.1	1732.3	1719.4	1706.8	1760.5
2002	1673.5	1674.2	1680.7	1669.9	1674.5	1681.5	1668.5	1671.2	1659.0	1640.4	1631.1	1622.6	1662.3
2003	1601.6	1601.8	1601.3	1600.8	1606.3	1610.4	1598.4	1601.5	1598.8	1590.8	1586.1	1583.5	1598.4
Natural resources and mining													
1990	158.2	158.1	158.7	159.8	161.1	163.4	164.0	164.4	164.6	167.8	168.3	169.4	163.2
1991	170.3	170.7	170.8	171.1	171.1	170.0	169.6	167.8	165.9	164.5	163.8	164.2	168.3
1992	162.4	160.2	159.7	158.2	157.8	158.7	157.5	156.7	156.4	155.7	155.0	155.5	157.8
1993	155.4	153.5	153.6	153.5	153.5	155.5	155.9	155.5	155.6	157.4	156.8	156.7	155.2
1994	156.1	154.4	154.2	153.9	153.0	154.3	152.9	153.0	152.8	153.1	152.8	153.2	153.6
1995	151.6	150.2	149.6	149.6	149.3	149.4	149.7	149.5	149.3	148.7	147.9	149.0	149.5
1996	147.3	147.1	147.8	148.4	148.3	149.7	150.7	150.9	150.6	151.7	152.1	153.6	149.9
1997	153.7	154.4	155.3	154.4	155.7	157.7	162.0	162.8	162.4	163.6	164.2	166.1	159.4
1998	166.0	165.2	162.5	161.1	161.0	161.7	160.5	159.0	157.5	155.6	154.2	153.4	159.8
1999	145.8	144.2	143.4	140.3	139.0	139.4	138.3	138.5	138.5	139.0	139.1	140.7	140.5
2000	140.7	140.6	141.6	139.6	140.7	142.3	143.4	144.2	144.7	146.2	146.4	149.5	143.3
2001	147.0	148.8	150.5	151.3	152.4	155.3	156.0	156.9	155.8	155.2	154.2	153.7	153.0
2002	147.8	146.9	146.1	144.6	145.4	146.3	145.0	145.6	145.6	143.8	143.9	144.2	145.4
2003	142.7	143.4	144.5	144.7	145.9	147.2	147.9	148.8	148.3	147.7	147.1	147.3	146.3
Construction													
1990	325.3	330.3	336.5	338.3	347.4	356.3	354.1	358.2	356.6	353.4	351.2	345.6	346.1
1991	331.6	339.4	349.7	346.3	349.3	355.7	353.6	354.0	352.8	354.2	350.6	343.8	348.4
1992	323.7	328.5	337.2	343.9	349.6	352.8	355.5	355.7	351.5	356.3	351.1	345.0	345.9
1993	330.5	335.4	343.4	347.3	352.9	360.8	364.5	366.1	364.4	368.4	364.8	366.7	355.4
1994	352.6	355.2	364.4	371.2	373.3	381.9	387.5	390.1	392.3	395.3	394.5	395.2	379.5
1995	384.3	391.6	398.6	398.7	406.7	414.5	415.7	418.4	420.9	423.8	421.2	421.7	409.7
1996	410.2	417.4	425.6	429.8	438.2	444.9	445.9	448.4	445.0	450.8	449.0	443.7	437.4
1997	436.4	450.4	456.6	456.6	466.3	473.1	478.4	483.2	481.6	482.3	478.5	475.8	468.3
1998	469.1	481.3	489.1	495.5	503.1	510.1	517.9	520.7	518.9	521.7	517.8	519.5	505.4
1999	508.6	520.2	528.1	531.4	533.4	543.4	545.4	546.2	547.3	548.5	546.1	546.5	537.1
2000	539.7	550.7	563.2	561.4	567.6	579.9	577.4	580.2	578.5	571.5	567.9	567.6	567.1
2001	564.5	575.8	584.7	581.7	586.8	591.8	586.5	590.7	584.0	576.8	574.4	568.8	580.5
2002	556.6	563.2	572.8	569.7	575.5	579.9	574.3	577.8	571.4	564.0	559.0	553.1	568.1
2003	545.8	547.4	550.0	551.0	557.9	559.6	553.6	556.3	554.0	548.6	546.2	544.9	551.3

Employment by Industry: Texas—*Continued*

(Numbers in thousands. Not seasonally adjusted.)

Industry	January	February	March	April	May	June	July	August	September	October	November	December	Annual Average
STATEWIDE—*Continued*													
Manufacturing													
1990	932.5	934.7	937.6	940.8	941.7	951.7	955.8	959.5	956.8	958.5	954.7	947.9	947.7
1991	940.6	941.8	942.5	935.4	937.4	945.2	939.5	939.1	935.7	927.8	927.0	923.6	936.3
1992	916.2	916.2	915.6	920.8	926.8	935.1	935.7	935.1	932.6	937.6	936.0	937.2	928.7
1993	926.1	932.0	936.3	932.1	937.6	947.3	946.4	947.5	949.5	950.2	949.7	951.8	942.2
1994	942.1	943.6	948.6	954.3	960.9	970.5	972.0	976.3	979.4	979.6	981.7	985.0	966.2
1995	979.0	983.7	987.1	989.4	991.9	1001.0	994.8	999.5	1002.4	1002.6	1003.7	1009.0	995.3
1996	998.9	1003.1	1007.0	1007.3	1012.8	1019.6	1020.8	1025.1	1025.9	1025.1	1027.7	1029.1	1016.9
1997	1020.9	1026.6	1033.6	1034.8	1042.0	1050.2	1043.7	1050.3	1055.4	1058.3	1060.2	1065.5	1045.1
1998	1060.1	1064.2	1070.3	1070.7	1076.4	1084.8	1083.1	1085.9	1087.0	1083.3	1080.4	1081.8	1077.3
1999	1064.4	1065.6	1067.4	1057.8	1058.8	1064.4	1062.9	1063.6	1064.0	1061.8	1062.6	1066.4	1063.3
2000	1058.0	1063.1	1067.8	1063.6	1067.0	1075.9	1070.3	1070.8	1072.6	1068.5	1068.9	1069.3	1068.0
2001	1055.4	1055.2	1053.4	1044.2	1039.2	1038.6	1025.7	1022.1	1013.3	1000.3	990.8	984.3	1026.8
2002	969.1	964.1	961.8	955.6	953.6	955.3	949.2	947.8	942.0	932.6	928.2	925.3	948.7
2003	913.1	911.0	906.8	905.1	902.5	903.6	896.9	896.4	896.5	894.5	892.8	891.3	900.9
Service-providing													
1990	5474.9	5515.9	5556.8	5604.7	5663.3	5676.2	5627.7	5644.2	5694.3	5713.0	5738.3	5751.2	5638.4
1991	5597.7	5636.9	5668.9	5693.7	5734.9	5744.4	5684.7	5702.0	5766.7	5785.7	5811.0	5832.8	5721.6
1992	5694.8	5740.5	5773.8	5812.6	5838.7	5840.2	5820.3	5828.8	5858.4	5919.9	5942.0	5969.0	5836.6
1993	5860.0	5913.9	5944.8	5995.1	6018.7	6030.5	6029.4	6050.3	6086.8	6108.1	6132.9	6172.6	6028.6
1994	6048.0	6088.5	6136.4	6213.0	6233.8	6251.2	6253.3	6279.8	6311.4	6356.2	6403.9	6444.0	6251.6
1995	6296.9	6352.9	6393.8	6428.8	6462.5	6478.2	6441.7	6475.0	6521.0	6545.6	6591.2	6629.8	6468.1
1996	6468.4	6512.8	6553.6	6609.0	6650.4	6647.6	6621.4	6655.0	6689.0	6760.6	6814.9	6841.2	6652.0
1997	6706.4	6771.7	6830.0	6883.3	6930.5	6947.4	6908.6	6950.9	7013.6	7048.0	7098.0	7135.1	6935.3
1998	6996.1	7057.4	7105.4	7152.9	7193.2	7197.3	7147.5	7196.4	7267.3	7303.5	7350.8	7403.6	7197.6
1999	7238.8	7302.4	7358.5	7377.3	7406.4	7423.6	7362.2	7409.2	7479.7	7507.2	7549.6	7605.5	7418.4
2000	7457.8	7521.6	7585.6	7606.5	7670.9	7675.9	7598.7	7662.3	7727.8	7738.3	7783.7	7830.4	7655.0
2001	7660.0	7717.0	7765.3	7774.3	7800.5	7802.1	7697.3	7746.4	7784.1	7761.7	7784.6	7801.6	7757.9
2002	7638.5	7692.1	7742.9	7759.7	7801.4	7777.5	7686.4	7737.0	7799.1	7796.0	7838.2	7858.5	7760.6
2003	7687.4	7733.6	7768.4	7784.8	7807.7	7787.9	7691.0	7739.6	7784.1	7808.0	7845.3	7858.3	7774.7
Trade, transportation, and utilities													
1990	1559.7	1547.4	1554.2	1554.6	1563.0	1579.4	1577.2	1583.7	1583.7	1586.9	1606.4	1623.5	1576.6
1991	1570.4	1555.1	1560.9	1555.7	1567.7	1581.2	1576.0	1584.0	1585.7	1586.7	1604.2	1625.3	1579.4
1992	1562.4	1553.5	1557.7	1569.0	1575.4	1587.8	1581.4	1583.9	1585.3	1603.0	1622.8	1650.4	1586.1
1993	1592.4	1583.8	1584.7	1598.4	1604.3	1616.3	1633.1	1637.6	1638.5	1647.3	1673.4	1704.2	1626.2
1994	1642.2	1633.3	1640.1	1648.5	1658.7	1673.0	1671.3	1682.6	1688.7	1701.2	1731.4	1764.0	1677.9
1995	1701.7	1691.2	1695.4	1696.9	1702.8	1717.9	1717.6	1729.0	1734.6	1741.7	1772.9	1802.7	1725.4
1996	1737.4	1724.7	1731.2	1741.0	1752.5	1763.8	1755.1	1764.4	1760.7	1776.9	1809.3	1835.4	1762.7
1997	1772.7	1764.5	1774.5	1777.2	1787.1	1801.6	1802.7	1807.2	1817.0	1833.5	1864.3	1893.4	1808.0
1998	1836.3	1828.5	1838.2	1846.2	1856.8	1866.3	1868.1	1878.0	1880.5	1892.4	1926.1	1961.4	1873.2
1999	1888.9	1884.7	1895.5	1894.2	1902.4	1920.2	1921.6	1933.3	1934.5	1950.8	1983.5	2020.4	1927.5
2000	1951.3	1947.7	1954.5	1952.5	1963.9	1984.7	1977.9	1996.8	1991.4	2002.8	2040.3	2075.3	1986.6
2001	1997.4	1985.7	1992.9	1989.4	1994.7	2003.4	1994.8	2002.8	1991.9	1988.8	2006.4	2027.5	1997.9
2002	1958.5	1946.3	1953.6	1952.1	1960.1	1964.9	1960.2	1965.1	1957.7	1953.0	1980.5	2005.5	1963.1
2003	1926.7	1912.2	1915.2	1912.9	1912.8	1917.6	1912.8	1926.8	1924.4	1932.6	1960.3	1977.6	1927.7
Wholesale trade													
1990	364.3	365.4	367.6	368.3	369.6	374.4	375.9	376.7	375.5	375.4	376.0	375.3	372.0
1991	369.9	370.8	371.9	370.5	370.8	374.1	372.9	373.2	371.2	370.2	369.9	369.6	371.3
1992	362.3	362.6	364.2	366.5	367.4	370.7	367.9	367.7	366.7	371.3	371.2	372.4	367.6
1993	368.0	369.5	371.7	373.5	375.2	377.9	377.6	376.8	377.1	376.8	376.7	378.4	374.9
1994	374.1	374.4	376.2	379.1	379.1	382.1	383.6	383.5	383.6	383.8	385.2	387.6	381.0
1995	382.8	385.2	387.9	388.3	390.1	393.5	394.9	395.4	396.3	397.0	397.4	399.3	392.3
1996	394.2	396.7	399.0	401.4	403.4	406.5	407.7	409.2	408.3	409.9	411.4	413.2	405.1
1997	409.1	413.4	417.3	417.8	420.9	425.3	426.7	428.3	428.7	428.9	430.0	432.7	423.3
1998	433.6	436.5	439.1	442.5	444.3	446.6	447.6	448.7	448.6	449.5	450.6	452.9	445.0
1999	449.2	451.4	454.3	451.0	452.9	456.3	457.2	458.4	459.6	459.9	460.7	463.8	456.2
2000	459.7	461.8	463.2	463.9	465.8	470.5	470.9	471.6	472.5	471.6	472.9	475.4	468.3
2001	472.9	474.5	476.7	475.8	475.8	477.1	476.0	475.6	472.9	470.0	467.5	468.1	473.5
2002	460.9	460.7	463.3	461.7	463.3	465.4	465.3	465.9	465.0	462.9	463.8	464.7	463.6
2003	457.2	456.8	458.0	457.0	457.9	460.1	458.7	459.2	458.9	458.5	459.3	459.2	458.4
Retail trade													
1990	899.0	884.6	887.8	889.4	894.7	902.4	897.8	902.7	901.9	906.3	925.2	940.1	902.7
1991	895.0	877.6	880.1	876.7	885.0	892.0	888.7	895.2	898.6	899.0	917.6	936.7	895.2
1992	890.3	880.7	881.8	891.4	895.9	902.0	900.9	902.8	904.6	918.2	937.9	961.7	905.7
1993	913.3	903.4	900.6	910.8	912.7	918.9	925.0	929.8	928.8	936.2	959.8	985.0	927.0
1994	938.0	927.3	930.9	939.0	944.7	952.5	947.9	958.0	964.6	974.9	1000.8	1026.4	958.8
1995	974.6	961.7	960.9	962.1	965.6	976.1	973.2	983.6	987.4	995.1	1024.0	1047.1	984.3
1996	995.7	979.5	982.9	988.4	996.6	1003.6	996.0	1002.1	1001.4	1011.9	1040.6	1064.2	1005.2
1997	1008.5	996.0	1001.7	1002.1	1008.0	1015.8	1013.0	1022.9	1021.3	1031.8	1062.0	1087.6	1022.6
1998	1032.4	1020.4	1026.4	1028.0	1033.8	1040.0	1038.4	1044.9	1047.5	1054.0	1085.6	1113.8	1047.1
1999	1055.9	1048.0	1056.1	1056.0	1062.0	1073.7	1073.4	1080.7	1080.6	1091.5	1122.1	1151.9	1079.3
2000	1094.5	1086.9	1092.2	1089.6	1097.3	1109.5	1103.0	1117.8	1110.6	1121.3	1155.5	1182.4	1113.4
2001	1118.3	1106.1	1111.4	1110.3	1113.6	1119.6	1112.7	1119.3	1112.3	1112.4	1138.4	1160.0	1119.5
2002	1106.9	1096.1	1101.2	1101.7	1106.0	1107.7	1101.7	1103.9	1099.6	1095.1	1122.5	1146.0	1107.4
2003	1081.3	1068.7	1070.9	1070.4	1072.0	1074.9	1073.5	1084.6	1083.5	1089.7	1114.2	1130.1	1084.5

Employment by Industry: Texas—*Continued*

(Numbers in thousands. Not seasonally adjusted.)

Industry	January	February	March	April	May	June	July	August	September	October	November	December	Annual Average
STATEWIDE—*Continued*													
Transportation and utilities													
1990	296.4	297.4	298.8	296.9	298.7	302.6	303.5	304.3	306.3	305.2	305.2	308.1	302.0
1991	305.5	306.7	308.9	308.5	311.9	315.1	314.4	315.6	315.9	317.5	316.7	319.0	313.0
1992	309.8	310.2	311.7	311.1	312.1	315.1	312.6	313.4	314.0	313.5	313.7	316.3	312.8
1993	311.1	310.9	312.4	314.1	316.4	319.5	330.5	331.0	332.6	334.3	336.9	340.8	324.2
1994	330.1	331.6	333.0	330.4	334.9	338.4	339.8	341.1	340.5	342.5	345.4	350.0	338.1
1995	344.3	344.3	346.6	346.5	347.1	348.3	349.5	350.0	350.9	349.6	351.5	356.3	348.7
1996	347.5	348.5	349.3	351.2	352.5	353.7	351.4	353.1	351.0	355.1	357.3	358.0	352.4
1997	355.1	355.1	355.5	357.3	358.2	360.5	363.0	356.0	367.0	372.8	372.3	373.1	362.2
1998	370.3	371.6	372.7	375.7	378.7	379.7	382.1	384.4	384.4	388.9	389.9	394.7	381.1
1999	383.8	385.3	385.1	387.2	387.5	390.2	391.0	394.2	394.3	399.4	400.7	404.7	392.0
2000	397.1	399.0	399.1	399.0	400.8	404.7	404.0	407.4	408.3	409.9	411.9	417.5	404.9
2001	406.2	405.1	404.8	403.3	405.3	406.7	406.1	407.9	406.7	406.4	400.5	399.4	404.8
2002	390.7	389.5	389.1	388.7	390.8	391.8	393.2	395.3	393.1	395.0	394.2	394.8	392.2
2003	388.2	386.7	386.3	385.5	382.9	382.6	380.6	383.0	382.0	384.4	386.8	388.3	384.8
Information													
1990	173.6	173.8	174.6	175.1	175.8	177.8	180.7	180.0	178.5	177.4	178.3	178.4	177.0
1991	177.2	176.0	176.8	177.9	177.9	177.7	178.5	177.5	176.0	177.4	178.8	180.5	177.7
1992	174.2	174.4	175.2	175.9	176.7	177.5	176.7	175.3	173.8	175.0	175.2	176.8	175.6
1993	175.3	175.4	176.5	177.1	178.0	180.1	179.8	178.7	177.4	178.2	178.8	180.2	178.0
1994	177.5	177.8	178.7	179.6	180.3	182.5	186.5	185.9	185.2	186.3	188.8	191.9	183.4
1995	190.4	192.7	194.5	192.4	192.2	195.4	195.4	196.1	195.3	196.4	198.7	201.9	195.1
1996	196.8	198.3	199.5	202.2	203.9	205.9	206.8	207.7	207.2	211.2	214.9	216.6	205.9
1997	216.7	218.8	219.1	222.7	225.1	228.9	230.0	231.1	230.2	231.2	235.6	236.1	227.1
1998	229.8	231.9	234.8	235.0	237.3	239.8	242.0	242.7	243.0	244.9	247.3	249.4	239.8
1999	245.4	246.5	248.0	248.9	251.3	253.2	251.1	252.2	253.0	253.6	256.5	259.4	251.6
2000	258.2	259.7	262.3	266.5	269.8	275.5	276.7	278.7	279.9	278.3	280.6	280.7	272.2
2001	273.4	274.6	274.9	273.7	273.3	273.6	269.7	268.7	266.5	264.8	264.1	261.9	269.9
2002	258.3	256.3	255.2	251.9	251.8	251.5	247.9	246.7	244.4	243.8	243.2	242.6	249.5
2003	238.6	237.9	237.5	235.8	235.9	236.3	235.9	235.0	232.6	232.3	231.5	231.0	235.0
Financial activities													
1990	450.5	453.4	454.9	459.1	461.4	466.3	463.5	464.1	462.3	457.5	455.9	458.4	458.9
1991	446.0	447.5	449.0	450.0	450.6	453.6	453.2	453.7	450.8	450.8	449.6	451.7	450.5
1992	444.3	445.3	447.1	446.9	448.1	451.3	449.5	449.2	444.9	449.4	448.3	449.5	447.8
1993	447.9	449.2	451.3	452.0	454.0	459.6	463.0	463.1	460.4	461.0	460.8	463.6	457.2
1994	459.2	460.2	463.5	469.4	470.5	473.8	474.9	474.1	471.6	472.5	472.5	474.9	469.8
1995	464.7	465.0	466.9	469.7	471.5	475.9	476.2	476.3	476.1	473.9	475.1	477.9	472.4
1996	473.9	475.0	477.3	478.4	480.8	485.5	486.9	488.3	485.9	489.8	492.8	494.4	484.1
1997	490.3	492.4	496.0	498.8	503.1	507.9	508.7	509.0	509.3	516.6	517.9	522.8	506.1
1998	512.9	515.9	519.8	530.2	533.0	537.0	542.6	544.4	544.7	548.6	547.8	552.0	535.7
1999	545.5	547.3	551.4	552.8	555.2	560.2	564.5	565.4	562.9	562.7	563.2	566.9	558.2
2000	558.8	560.5	563.4	564.3	565.6	570.4	571.6	571.7	570.6	570.7	571.6	575.6	567.9
2001	569.5	572.5	574.9	576.1	577.9	582.7	582.6	582.6	579.5	578.3	577.4	580.3	577.8
2002	575.2	575.9	577.2	576.6	580.0	582.8	583.1	583.7	580.8	580.3	581.9	583.1	580.1
2003	577.8	579.8	581.2	582.8	585.5	588.4	589.5	591.4	588.5	587.4	585.9	587.0	585.4
Professional and business services													
1990	581.9	590.2	601.1	614.7	622.5	641.9	640.6	647.1	648.7	651.2	652.5	652.5	628.7
1991	621.6	630.3	638.6	639.3	644.3	649.6	648.6	651.8	647.9	648.5	648.2	645.8	642.9
1992	628.4	634.6	641.8	647.5	650.1	656.0	660.3	660.9	658.8	665.6	661.5	665.1	652.6
1993	648.6	656.9	664.7	676.8	681.7	690.7	699.1	702.4	705.4	706.7	705.0	706.5	687.0
1994	693.9	700.4	712.9	732.4	727.7	739.7	754.5	759.8	759.6	757.4	761.4	765.2	738.7
1995	742.8	755.5	766.2	772.8	776.3	786.8	784.1	793.0	794.9	801.6	805.1	808.7	782.3
1996	782.9	795.6	805.6	814.1	818.3	826.3	839.7	846.5	846.3	859.6	863.1	865.8	830.3
1997	847.7	862.8	877.1	895.2	902.1	919.7	919.5	930.8	934.4	936.7	941.6	950.7	909.9
1998	937.1	951.8	962.2	968.8	973.0	990.9	993.8	997.5	997.2	1009.2	1008.8	1017.5	984.0
1999	994.6	1010.1	1022.8	1025.7	1026.1	1041.3	1045.7	1047.8	1049.0	1049.5	1050.5	1062.8	1035.5
2000	1046.8	1057.6	1073.4	1079.4	1085.4	1107.9	1109.0	1117.5	1122.1	1118.3	1117.1	1122.3	1096.4
2001	1095.9	1101.7	1107.7	1104.1	1101.9	1109.2	1098.6	1101.3	1089.8	1073.4	1069.6	1068.1	1093.4
2002	1037.1	1042.0	1049.6	1055.3	1057.1	1061.4	1059.3	1069.3	1063.8	1055.8	1055.3	1053.1	1054.9
2003	1027.9	1032.2	1038.5	1043.5	1043.7	1044.2	1040.7	1048.6	1049.3	1052.1	1051.8	1052.3	1043.7
Educational and health services													
1990	651.8	660.9	664.8	668.6	671.4	672.9	674.5	683.4	689.5	692.5	694.9	693.4	676.6
1991	685.4	695.9	701.1	706.6	709.9	709.3	710.7	716.4	723.2	725.7	729.5	729.8	712.0
1992	721.5	730.1	733.6	738.0	739.4	741.2	745.2	749.4	755.4	760.5	762.1	763.9	745.0
1993	760.7	768.2	773.0	774.4	777.3	779.8	779.6	784.5	791.2	789.5	791.2	792.9	780.2
1994	784.0	790.8	795.4	805.3	807.9	809.2	813.0	819.0	826.7	827.8	831.8	836.4	812.3
1995	824.3	832.8	839.0	845.3	849.3	849.6	849.0	856.7	867.2	868.7	872.6	874.9	852.5
1996	863.1	869.9	875.3	879.3	884.7	883.4	882.0	891.9	900.6	906.4	912.7	913.8	888.6
1997	903.6	913.8	920.6	927.6	933.2	932.4	932.3	942.0	952.2	951.6	953.8	956.7	935.0
1998	944.1	952.0	956.2	957.9	959.3	958.2	955.2	962.9	972.1	970.5	976.0	977.8	961.9
1999	962.1	967.0	970.6	973.1	974.4	975.8	970.5	977.5	989.2	988.2	991.8	993.2	977.8
2000	981.0	989.1	994.6	996.1	1000.1	999.7	996.8	1006.1	1018.8	1016.4	1019.9	1022.2	1003.4
2001	1013.8	1024.5	1030.3	1032.0	1037.0	1041.5	1039.1	1048.1	1054.4	1056.4	1060.7	1063.3	1041.7
2002	1054.8	1066.2	1071.0	1074.5	1080.4	1077.1	1077.6	1090.1	1101.2	1097.0	1103.0	1105.7	1083.2
2003	1098.8	1107.8	1112.4	1114.3	1118.4	1113.9	1112.1	1122.0	1129.8	1131.3	1135.7	1136.8	1119.4

Employment by Industry: Texas—*Continued*

(Numbers in thousands. Not seasonally adjusted.)

Industry	January	February	March	April	May	June	July	August	September	October	November	December	Annual Average
STATEWIDE—*Continued*													
Leisure and hospitality													
1990	554.5	565.6	573.6	590.6	603.2	619.1	618.7	621.8	606.6	597.5	591.2	587.7	594.2
1991	563.8	576.2	586.0	600.7	614.1	626.8	622.4	623.9	614.6	604.2	598.8	597.8	602.4
1992	578.4	591.0	603.1	616.1	627.8	635.9	637.7	639.8	625.8	624.1	621.0	615.8	618.0
1993	601.4	617.6	629.6	641.9	645.8	659.9	655.9	659.0	648.0	637.0	630.8	631.2	638.2
1994	614.7	625.8	640.3	660.1	668.1	680.2	686.4	686.7	670.9	670.1	668.2	666.3	661.5
1995	650.4	664.1	675.7	687.4	703.7	718.1	714.8	714.5	700.6	689.5	683.9	683.6	690.5
1996	667.0	676.7	689.8	707.8	724.0	735.8	731.4	730.6	717.1	715.2	711.6	709.9	709.7
1997	695.2	709.9	726.6	737.3	755.1	770.8	764.4	765.3	756.7	742.4	740.4	739.5	742.0
1998	721.4	734.9	748.2	764.4	778.4	794.2	791.2	792.4	783.3	768.3	764.5	765.2	767.2
1999	746.7	760.5	777.8	792.4	805.4	821.7	815.2	814.9	806.2	798.4	794.2	792.1	793.8
2000	776.0	789.6	808.8	817.8	831.1	848.0	840.0	840.9	829.9	819.2	813.7	813.8	819.1
2001	793.7	810.3	827.8	840.8	854.7	868.3	861.3	863.2	845.4	826.3	820.2	820.0	836.0
2002	801.5	816.3	835.3	848.3	865.1	877.0	869.3	872.2	860.5	843.3	840.2	840.8	847.5
2003	821.9	831.9	848.8	859.0	873.8	886.8	875.6	879.4	864.2	852.1	849.3	849.6	857.7
Other services													
1990	253.8	255.4	257.1	259.6	262.3	268.0	269.1	269.4	266.4	265.8	264.8	263.6	262.9
1991	260.6	262.3	264.5	266.9	269.2	274.3	274.6	273.6	271.7	270.9	270.0	272.0	269.2
1992	270.8	272.8	274.2	277.6	277.5	281.9	281.2	279.1	276.9	279.1	277.4	277.8	277.2
1993	278.5	280.5	282.3	284.0	285.5	289.5	291.1	289.7	288.2	287.6	286.4	287.7	285.9
1994	285.1	286.2	289.2	292.5	293.0	297.6	299.1	297.6	295.6	298.9	298.8	298.9	294.4
1995	296.4	297.3	300.3	301.9	304.9	309.1	308.6	308.4	307.4	305.6	304.8	305.6	304.2
1996	303.7	305.2	307.2	311.2	312.9	317.1	316.8	316.3	314.6	316.4	316.9	317.1	313.0
1997	314.4	317.6	320.3	322.4	325.6	330.3	328.5	328.1	326.1	324.9	324.7	325.5	324.0
1998	322.6	324.8	326.5	330.5	332.5	335.1	336.5	335.6	333.8	333.7	333.0	334.5	331.6
1999	330.7	333.2	335.4	336.0	338.6	343.1	344.0	344.1	342.6	341.0	340.7	341.8	339.3
2000	338.6	341.2	344.7	345.6	347.5	352.7	351.5	350.9	350.7	348.9	348.1	348.7	347.4
2001	350.6	353.0	356.8	357.0	359.0	363.7	357.0	356.9	353.5	349.6	349.9	349.7	354.7
2002	347.7	351.1	355.9	356.3	359.5	363.2	358.7	359.1	358.2	354.7	356.2	356.1	356.4
2003	352.9	354.0	358.7	358.9	360.6	365.7	361.7	360.6	357.3	354.1	354.3	354.6	357.8
Government													
1990	1249.1	1269.2	1276.5	1282.4	1303.7	1250.8	1203.4	1194.7	1258.6	1284.2	1294.3	1293.7	1263.4
1991	1272.7	1293.6	1292.0	1296.6	1301.2	1271.9	1220.7	1221.1	1296.8	1321.5	1331.9	1329.9	1287.5
1992	1314.8	1338.8	1341.1	1341.6	1343.7	1308.6	1288.3	1291.2	1337.5	1363.2	1373.7	1369.7	1334.4
1993	1355.2	1382.3	1382.7	1390.5	1392.1	1354.6	1327.8	1335.3	1377.7	1400.8	1406.5	1406.3	1376.0
1994	1391.4	1414.0	1416.3	1425.2	1427.6	1395.2	1367.6	1374.1	1413.1	1442.0	1451.0	1446.4	1413.7
1995	1426.2	1454.3	1455.8	1462.4	1461.8	1425.4	1396.0	1401.0	1444.9	1468.2	1478.1	1474.5	1445.7
1996	1443.6	1467.4	1467.7	1475.0	1473.3	1429.8	1402.7	1409.3	1456.6	1485.1	1493.6	1488.2	1457.7
1997	1465.8	1491.9	1495.8	1502.1	1499.2	1455.8	1422.5	1437.4	1487.7	1511.1	1519.7	1510.4	1483.3
1998	1491.9	1517.6	1519.5	1519.9	1522.9	1475.8	1418.1	1442.9	1512.7	1535.9	1547.3	1545.8	1504.2
1999	1524.9	1553.1	1557.0	1554.2	1553.0	1508.1	1449.6	1474.0	1542.3	1563.0	1569.2	1568.9	1534.8
2000	1547.1	1576.2	1583.9	1584.3	1607.5	1537.0	1475.2	1499.7	1564.4	1583.7	1592.4	1591.8	1561.9
2001	1565.7	1594.7	1600.0	1601.2	1602.0	1559.7	1494.2	1522.8	1603.1	1624.1	1636.3	1630.8	1586.2
2002	1605.4	1638.0	1645.1	1644.7	1647.4	1599.6	1530.3	1550.8	1632.5	1668.1	1677.9	1671.6	1626.0
2003	1642.8	1677.8	1676.1	1677.6	1677.0	1635.0	1562.7	1575.8	1638.0	1666.1	1676.5	1669.4	1647.9
Federal government													
1990	199.5	200.0	203.2	206.9	226.3	211.7	213.3	203.7	200.7	198.5	199.3	200.0	205.3
1991	198.3	197.7	196.8	198.0	199.3	200.4	198.5	197.5	195.6	196.6	197.0	199.1	197.9
1992	198.4	198.0	198.2	198.1	197.1	197.2	197.4	196.7	196.0	194.9	194.3	195.4	196.8
1993	195.0	195.0	194.8	194.2	193.4	193.6	192.9	192.5	192.6	192.7	191.6	193.6	193.5
1994	192.2	192.5	191.1	193.5	192.8	192.8	189.8	188.8	188.5	187.5	187.7	190.6	190.7
1995	188.1	188.6	188.8	189.4	188.9	189.7	187.4	187.7	187.2	187.0	187.9	189.2	188.3
1996	186.3	186.9	187.0	189.1	187.5	188.2	187.1	187.2	186.6	186.0	186.6	188.6	187.3
1997	185.8	186.4	187.2	188.4	186.7	187.2	186.7	186.7	186.4	185.4	186.1	188.5	186.8
1998	185.2	185.3	185.2	185.1	186.0	185.3	185.7	186.2	186.6	186.0	187.0	189.6	186.1
1999	186.5	187.3	189.0	187.3	185.5	185.4	183.5	183.2	181.3	181.6	181.0	184.4	184.7
2000	182.0	183.2	187.5	190.3	214.0	191.5	192.7	181.0	177.8	177.2	176.7	179.9	186.2
2001	178.0	177.3	177.7	177.4	177.7	179.0	180.3	179.6	179.1	178.6	178.3	177.7	178.4
2002	176.8	176.9	177.7	177.9	177.7	179.1	178.9	177.6	178.4	181.9	182.3	183.0	179.0
2003	181.3	181.9	181.4	181.6	181.6	180.4	180.5	179.5	178.0	179.0	177.9	178.2	180.1
State government													
1990	267.1	273.4	274.2	275.7	274.9	264.7	266.3	266.0	272.5	280.1	281.8	280.7	273.1
1991	270.8	276.1	275.7	276.6	275.3	266.1	269.1	267.9	280.7	290.7	292.6	287.9	277.5
1992	283.7	290.8	290.4	289.4	288.5	277.6	280.8	281.7	290.4	297.1	299.0	298.4	289.0
1993	295.3	302.6	303.0	307.0	306.6	296.1	295.8	296.0	302.5	308.4	307.7	306.7	302.3
1994	301.0	307.2	306.8	312.9	312.6	303.5	305.3	305.7	312.5	321.7	323.1	320.0	311.0
1995	314.1	322.9	323.0	324.3	322.2	309.8	310.0	309.1	319.6	325.9	327.6	325.4	319.5
1996	314.0	319.7	319.6	322.8	320.3	303.0	308.0	307.3	320.2	327.4	328.7	324.8	318.0
1997	320.8	328.6	328.4	329.8	327.8	309.2	312.2	311.3	327.2	331.8	332.1	324.8	323.7
1998	320.7	328.6	327.7	325.3	325.0	310.8	308.0	306.3	320.0	328.5	330.3	328.0	321.6
1999	322.2	332.4	332.2	333.3	331.2	316.8	313.1	309.9	323.2	332.2	333.2	330.3	325.8
2000	323.8	333.6	333.9	333.5	331.8	316.5	314.3	314.9	325.3	334.3	335.1	333.0	327.5
2001	325.6	335.9	337.2	338.7	337.0	321.5	322.0	322.0	336.0	343.9	346.3	343.9	334.1
2002	337.0	344.6	347.4	346.9	346.7	329.8	330.1	327.2	344.7	351.8	351.4	349.8	342.3
2003	343.5	353.9	353.3	352.0	348.8	332.8	328.9	325.6	337.1	344.5	345.9	343.0	342.4

Employment by Industry: Texas—*Continued*

(Numbers in thousands. Not seasonally adjusted.)

Industry	January	February	March	April	May	June	July	August	September	October	November	December	Annual Average
STATEWIDE—*Continued*													
Local government													
1990	782.5	795.8	799.1	799.8	802.5	774.4	723.8	725.0	785.4	805.6	813.2	813.0	785.0
1991	803.6	819.8	819.5	822.0	826.6	805.4	753.1	755.7	820.5	834.2	842.3	842.9	812.1
1992	832.7	850.0	852.5	854.1	858.1	833.8	810.1	812.8	851.1	871.2	880.4	875.9	848.6
1993	864.9	884.7	884.9	889.3	892.1	864.9	839.1	846.8	882.6	899.7	907.2	906.0	880.2
1994	898.2	914.3	918.4	918.8	922.2	898.9	872.5	879.6	912.1	932.8	940.2	935.8	912.0
1995	924.0	942.8	944.0	948.7	950.7	925.9	898.6	904.2	938.1	955.3	962.6	959.9	937.9
1996	943.3	960.8	961.1	963.1	965.5	938.6	907.6	914.8	949.8	971.7	978.3	974.8	952.5
1997	959.2	976.9	980.2	983.9	984.7	959.4	923.6	939.4	974.1	993.9	1001.5	997.1	972.8
1998	986.0	1003.7	1006.6	1009.5	1011.9	979.7	924.4	950.4	1006.1	1021.4	1030.0	1028.2	996.5
1999	1016.2	1033.4	1035.8	1033.6	1036.3	1005.9	953.0	980.9	1037.8	1049.2	1055.0	1054.2	1024.3
2000	1041.3	1059.4	1062.5	1060.5	1061.7	1029.0	968.2	1003.8	1061.3	1072.2	1080.6	1078.9	1048.3
2001	1062.1	1081.5	1085.1	1085.1	1087.3	1059.2	991.9	1021.2	1088.0	1101.6	1111.7	1109.2	1073.6
2002	1091.6	1116.5	1120.0	1119.9	1123.0	1090.7	1021.3	1046.0	1109.4	1134.4	1144.2	1138.8	1104.7
2003	1118.0	1142.0	1141.4	1144.0	1146.6	1121.8	1053.3	1070.7	1122.9	1142.6	1152.7	1148.2	1125.4
ABILENE													
Total nonfarm													
1990	48.7	48.5	48.4	48.6	49.1	47.5	47.2	46.7	48.7	48.9	48.9	49.3	48.3
1991	48.5	48.8	48.8	48.7	49.0	48.1	47.5	47.3	48.6	49.0	49.4	49.8	48.6
1992	49.3	49.2	49.2	49.8	49.7	48.6	49.0	49.0	50.3	50.8	50.8	51.3	49.7
1993	50.5	50.1	50.3	50.0	49.8	49.0	49.4	48.9	50.0	50.1	50.3	50.5	49.9
1994	49.9	49.9	49.9	50.6	50.3	49.4	49.6	49.8	51.0	52.1	52.3	52.5	50.6
1995	52.3	52.5	52.1	52.6	52.3	51.8	51.8	51.9	53.2	53.5	53.4	53.8	52.6
1996	52.5	52.6	53.1	53.8	54.0	53.1	52.9	53.1	54.3	54.8	55.1	55.1	53.7
1997	54.4	54.5	54.9	55.0	55.2	55.0	54.8	54.9	56.0	56.6	57.1	57.0	55.4
1998	56.2	56.7	56.8	56.8	56.8	56.1	56.1	56.0	56.8	56.5	56.8	56.6	56.5
1999	55.5	55.4	55.6	56.6	56.1	55.7	55.4	55.5	56.0	56.3	56.3	56.2	55.8
2000	55.1	55.4	55.9	56.2	56.1	55.6	54.6	55.0	55.6	55.2	55.0	55.7	55.4
2001	54.8	55.3	55.3	55.2	55.1	55.1	54.7	54.5	54.6	54.8	55.5	55.4	55.0
2002	54.2	54.9	55.7	55.3	55.7	56.0	55.2	55.6	56.3	55.4	56.1	56.9	55.6
2003	55.2	55.4	56.0	56.0	56.8	57.1	55.7	56.1	56.8	57.0	57.2	57.2	56.4
Total private													
1990	39.6	39.3	39.2	39.3	39.8	38.4	38.5	38.1	39.5	39.6	39.5	39.9	39.2
1991	39.2	39.5	39.6	39.5	39.7	39.0	38.8	38.6	39.6	39.8	40.1	40.4	39.4
1992	40.0	39.8	39.9	40.4	40.2	39.4	40.1	40.0	40.8	41.2	41.2	41.7	40.3
1993	40.9	40.5	40.7	40.4	40.2	39.5	40.2	39.7	40.3	40.3	40.5	40.7	40.3
1994	40.2	40.2	40.3	40.9	40.5	40.1	40.5	40.7	41.4	42.3	42.5	42.7	41.0
1995	42.5	42.7	42.4	43.0	42.6	42.4	42.5	42.5	43.3	43.3	43.3	43.7	42.8
1996	42.6	42.7	43.1	43.9	44.1	43.5	43.6	43.8	44.5	44.9	45.1	45.1	43.9
1997	44.4	44.6	44.9	45.2	45.2	45.2	45.2	45.3	45.9	46.4	46.7	46.6	45.4
1998	46.1	46.5	46.6	46.7	46.6	46.1	46.4	46.4	46.7	46.4	46.6	46.4	46.4
1999	45.4	45.4	45.6	46.4	46.0	45.9	45.9	45.9	46.0	46.1	46.1	46.1	45.9
2000	45.1	45.2	45.6	46.1	45.7	45.5	45.0	45.5	45.7	45.3	45.2	45.9	45.4
2001	45.2	45.6	45.6	45.5	45.4	45.6	45.5	45.4	45.1	45.3	45.8	45.9	45.4
2002	44.7	45.3	46.1	45.8	46.2	46.4	46.1	46.5	46.9	45.8	46.4	47.1	46.1
2003	45.7	45.9	46.5	46.5	47.2	47.6	46.6	47.2	47.5	47.6	47.7	47.7	47.0
Goods-producing													
1990	7.9	7.8	7.7	7.6	7.8	7.1	7.0	7.0	7.2	7.2	7.3	7.2	7.4
1991	7.2	7.1	7.0	7.0	7.0	6.9	6.7	6.6	6.9	6.8	6.8	6.8	6.9
1992	6.9	6.8	6.9	6.9	6.9	6.7	7.1	7.0	7.0	7.2	7.0	7.0	6.9
1993	6.9	6.8	6.9	6.8	6.8	6.7	6.7	6.6	6.5	6.5	6.5	6.5	6.6
1994	6.5	6.5	6.5	6.7	6.6	6.6	6.6	6.7	6.6	6.9	6.9	6.9	6.6
1995	6.9	6.9	6.8	6.8	6.9	6.8	6.9	6.8	6.9	7.0	6.9	6.8	6.8
1996	6.7	6.6	6.7	6.8	7.1	6.9	7.1	7.1	7.2	7.4	7.4	7.4	7.0
1997	7.3	7.2	7.3	7.3	7.3	7.4	7.4	7.4	7.4	7.5	7.5	7.4	7.3
1998	7.3	7.3	7.2	7.1	7.1	7.0	7.1	7.0	7.0	6.7	6.8	6.6	7.0
1999	6.4	6.5	6.6	6.5	6.6	6.5	6.6	6.5	6.5	6.4	6.3	6.3	6.4
2000	6.3	6.3	6.3	6.3	6.3	6.5	6.5	6.5	6.5	6.5	6.4	6.5	6.4
2001	6.3	6.4	6.4	6.3	6.3	6.4	6.4	6.4	6.2	6.3	6.3	6.4	6.3
2002	6.1	6.2	6.3	6.3	6.4	6.5	6.4	6.6	6.5	6.1	6.2	6.3	6.3
2003	6.0	6.1	6.2	6.2	6.3	6.3	6.1	6.3	6.3	6.2	6.2	6.2	6.2
Natural resources and mining													
1990	1.4	1.4	1.4	1.3	1.4	1.3	1.3	1.3	1.4	1.4	1.5	1.5	1.3
1991	1.6	1.5	1.5	1.4	1.4	1.4	1.3	1.2	1.3	1.3	1.3	1.3	1.3
1992	1.3	1.3	1.3	1.3	1.3	1.2	1.3	1.3	1.3	1.4	1.4	1.4	1.3
1993	1.4	1.3	1.3	1.3	1.3	1.3	1.3	1.3	1.3	1.3	1.3	1.3	1.3
1994	1.2	1.2	1.2	1.3	1.2	1.2	1.2	1.3	1.3	1.3	1.3	1.3	1.2
1995	1.3	1.3	1.3	1.3	1.3	1.3	1.3	1.3	1.4	1.3	1.3	1.3	1.3
1996	1.4	1.3	1.3	1.4	1.5	1.4	1.4	1.4	1.4	1.6	1.6	1.6	1.4
1997	1.7	1.6	1.6	1.6	1.6	1.6	1.6	1.6	1.6	1.7	1.7	1.7	1.6
1998	1.6	1.6	1.6	1.4	1.4	1.4	1.4	1.3	1.3	1.1	1.1	1.0	1.3
1999	0.8	0.7	0.7	0.6	0.6	0.5	0.6	0.6	0.6	0.6	0.6	0.6	0.6
2000	0.7	0.7	0.7	0.7	0.7	0.8	0.8	0.8	0.8	0.9	0.9	0.9	0.7
2001	0.9	0.9	0.9	0.9	0.9	0.9	0.9	0.9	0.9	0.9	0.9	0.9	0.9
2002	0.8	0.8	0.8	0.8	0.8	0.8	0.8	0.9	0.9	0.8	0.8	0.8	0.8
2003	0.8	0.8	0.8	0.9	0.9	0.9	0.9	0.9	0.9	0.9	0.9	0.9	0.9

Employment by Industry: Texas—*Continued*

(Numbers in thousands. Not seasonally adjusted.)

Industry	January	February	March	April	May	June	July	August	September	October	November	December	Annual Average
ABILENE—*Continued*													
Construction													
1990	1.5	1.5	1.4	1.4	1.4	1.4	1.4	1.5	1.5	1.4	1.4	1.3	1.4
1991	1.4	1.4	1.4	1.5	1.5	1.5	1.5	1.5	1.6	1.5	1.5	1.5	1.4
1992	1.5	1.5	1.6	1.7	1.7	1.6	1.8	1.7	1.7	1.7	1.6	1.6	1.6
1993	1.5	1.5	1.6	1.7	1.7	1.8	1.9	1.8	1.7	1.7	1.8	1.8	1.7
1994	1.9	1.9	1.9	1.9	1.9	2.0	2.0	2.0	1.9	2.1	2.1	2.1	1.9
1995	2.2	2.2	2.2	2.1	2.2	2.2	2.2	2.1	2.1	2.2	2.1	2.0	2.1
1996	1.9	1.9	2.0	2.0	2.1	2.1	2.2	2.2	2.2	2.2	2.2	2.2	2.1
1997	2.1	2.1	2.1	2.2	2.2	2.2	2.2	2.2	2.2	2.2	2.2	2.1	2.1
1998	2.2	2.2	2.2	2.3	2.3	2.3	2.4	2.4	2.3	2.3	2.3	2.3	2.2
1999	2.3	2.4	2.4	2.4	2.5	2.5	2.5	2.4	2.4	2.3	2.3	2.3	2.3
2000	2.3	2.3	2.3	2.2	2.2	2.3	2.3	2.3	2.3	2.3	2.2	2.3	2.2
2001	2.2	2.3	2.4	2.3	2.3	2.4	2.4	2.4	2.3	2.4	2.4	2.4	2.3
2002	2.3	2.4	2.5	2.5	2.6	2.8	2.8	2.9	2.8	2.6	2.7	2.8	2.6
2003	2.6	2.6	2.7	2.6	2.7	2.7	2.5	2.6	2.6	2.6	2.6	2.6	2.6
Manufacturing													
1990	5.0	4.9	4.9	4.9	5.0	4.4	4.3	4.2	4.3	4.4	4.4	4.4	4.5
1991	4.2	4.2	4.1	4.1	4.1	4.0	3.9	3.9	4.0	4.0	4.0	4.0	4.0
1992	4.1	4.0	4.0	3.9	3.9	3.9	4.0	4.0	4.0	4.1	4.0	4.0	3.9
1993	4.0	4.0	4.0	3.8	3.8	3.6	3.5	3.5	3.5	3.5	3.4	3.4	3.6
1994	3.4	3.4	3.4	3.5	3.5	3.4	3.4	3.4	3.4	3.5	3.5	3.5	3.4
1995	3.4	3.4	3.3	3.4	3.4	3.3	3.4	3.4	3.4	3.5	3.5	3.5	3.4
1996	3.4	3.4	3.4	3.4	3.5	3.4	3.5	3.5	3.6	3.6	3.6	3.6	3.4
1997	3.5	3.5	3.6	3.5	3.5	3.6	3.6	3.6	3.6	3.6	3.6	3.6	3.5
1998	3.5	3.5	3.4	3.4	3.4	3.3	3.3	3.3	3.4	3.3	3.4	3.3	3.3
1999	3.3	3.4	3.5	3.5	3.5	3.5	3.5	3.5	3.5	3.5	3.4	3.4	3.4
2000	3.3	3.3	3.3	3.4	3.4	3.4	3.4	3.4	3.4	3.3	3.3	3.3	3.3
2001	3.2	3.2	3.1	3.1	3.1	3.1	3.1	3.1	3.0	3.0	3.0	3.1	3.0
2002	3.0	3.0	3.0	3.0	3.0	2.9	2.8	2.8	2.8	2.7	2.7	2.7	2.9
2003	2.6	2.7	2.7	2.7	2.7	2.7	2.7	2.8	2.8	2.7	2.7	2.7	2.7
Service-providing													
1990	40.8	40.7	40.7	41.0	41.3	40.4	40.2	39.7	41.5	41.7	41.6	42.1	40.9
1991	41.3	41.7	41.8	41.7	42.0	41.2	40.8	40.7	41.7	42.2	42.6	43.0	41.7
1992	42.4	42.4	42.3	42.9	42.8	41.9	41.9	42.0	43.3	43.6	43.8	44.3	42.8
1993	43.6	43.3	43.4	43.2	43.0	42.3	42.7	42.3	43.5	43.6	43.8	44.0	43.2
1994	43.4	43.4	43.4	43.9	43.7	42.8	43.0	43.1	44.4	45.2	45.4	45.6	43.9
1995	45.4	45.6	45.3	45.8	45.4	45.0	44.9	45.1	46.3	46.5	46.5	47.0	45.7
1996	45.8	46.0	46.4	47.0	46.9	46.2	45.8	46.0	47.1	47.4	47.7	47.7	46.6
1997	47.1	47.3	47.6	47.7	47.9	47.6	47.4	47.5	48.6	49.1	49.6	49.6	48.0
1998	48.9	49.4	49.6	49.7	49.7	49.1	49.0	49.0	49.8	49.8	50.0	50.0	49.5
1999	49.1	48.9	49.0	50.1	49.5	49.2	48.8	49.0	49.5	49.9	50.0	49.9	49.4
2000	48.8	49.1	49.6	49.9	49.8	49.1	48.1	48.5	49.1	48.7	48.6	49.2	49.0
2001	48.5	48.9	48.9	48.9	48.8	48.7	48.3	48.1	48.4	48.5	49.2	49.0	48.6
2002	48.1	48.7	49.4	49.0	49.3	49.5	48.8	49.0	49.8	49.3	49.9	50.6	49.3
2003	49.2	49.3	49.8	49.8	50.5	50.8	49.6	49.8	50.5	50.8	51.0	51.0	50.2
Trade, transportation, and utilities													
1990	11.1	10.8	10.8	10.8	11.0	10.7	10.7	10.4	10.8	10.8	10.8	11.1	10.8
1991	11.0	11.0	11.0	10.6	10.7	10.4	10.5	10.4	10.7	10.8	11.2	11.4	10.8
1992	11.0	10.9	10.8	10.9	10.8	10.6	10.7	10.8	11.0	11.2	11.3	11.6	10.9
1993	11.0	10.8	10.7	10.7	10.6	10.4	10.7	10.6	10.8	10.8	11.0	11.3	10.7
1994	11.1	10.9	10.9	11.0	10.9	10.8	11.1	11.1	11.2	11.4	11.5	11.7	11.1
1995	11.3	11.1	11.1	11.1	11.1	11.2	11.2	11.3	11.5	11.4	11.6	11.9	11.3
1996	11.3	11.3	11.4	11.4	11.3	11.1	11.1	11.3	11.4	11.5	11.7	11.8	11.3
1997	11.2	11.2	11.0	11.0	10.9	10.9	10.9	11.0	11.1	11.4	11.7	11.7	11.1
1998	11.4	11.3	11.4	11.5	11.5	11.5	11.5	11.4	11.4	11.5	11.7	11.9	11.5
1999	11.3	11.2	11.2	11.5	11.4	11.3	11.3	11.3	11.3	11.5	11.7	11.7	11.3
2000	11.3	11.1	11.1	11.5	11.5	11.3	11.2	11.4	11.3	11.3	11.5	11.8	11.3
2001	11.4	11.4	11.2	11.3	11.3	11.4	11.3	11.3	11.2	11.3	11.6	11.6	11.3
2002	11.2	11.1	11.2	11.0	11.1	11.2	11.1	11.2	11.4	11.0	11.2	11.3	11.2
2003	10.9	10.8	10.8	10.8	10.9	11.0	10.6	10.8	10.9	11.1	11.2	11.3	10.9
Wholesale trade													
1990	2.0	1.9	1.9	1.9	1.9	1.9	1.9	1.8	1.9	1.9	1.9	1.9	1.9
1991	2.0	2.0	2.0	2.0	2.0	2.0	2.0	1.9	1.9	1.9	1.8	1.9	1.9
1992	2.0	2.0	2.0	2.0	2.0	1.9	1.9	1.9	2.0	2.0	2.0	2.0	1.9
1993	2.0	2.0	2.0	2.0	2.0	1.9	2.0	1.9	2.0	2.0	2.0	2.0	1.9
1994	2.1	2.0	2.0	2.1	2.0	2.0	2.1	2.1	2.1	2.1	2.1	2.1	2.0
1995	2.1	2.1	2.1	2.1	2.1	2.1	2.1	2.1	2.1	2.1	2.1	2.1	2.1
1996	2.0	2.0	2.0	2.0	2.0	2.0	2.0	2.1	2.1	2.1	2.1	2.1	2.0
1997	2.0	2.1	2.1	2.1	2.0	2.1	2.1	2.1	2.1	2.2	2.2	2.2	2.1
1998	2.2	2.2	2.3	2.3	2.3	2.3	2.3	2.3	2.2	2.2	2.2	2.2	2.2
1999	2.1	2.1	2.1	2.2	2.2	2.2	2.2	2.2	2.2	2.3	2.3	2.3	2.2
2000	2.3	2.2	2.2	2.3	2.3	2.3	2.3	2.3	2.3	2.3	2.3	2.3	2.2
2001	2.3	2.3	2.3	2.4	2.4	2.4	2.4	2.4	2.4	2.4	2.4	2.4	2.3
2002	2.4	2.4	2.4	2.3	2.4	2.4	2.4	2.4	2.4	2.3	2.3	2.3	2.4
2003	2.3	2.3	2.3	2.3	2.4	2.4	2.3	2.3	2.4	2.4	2.4	2.4	2.4

Employment by Industry: Texas—*Continued*

(Numbers in thousands. Not seasonally adjusted.)

Industry	January	February	March	April	May	June	July	August	September	October	November	December	Annual Average
ABILENE—*Continued*													
Retail trade													
1990	7.0	6.8	6.8	6.9	7.0	6.8	6.8	6.7	6.9	6.9	7.0	7.3	6.9
1991	7.1	7.1	7.1	6.7	6.8	6.6	6.6	6.6	6.8	7.0	7.4	7.5	6.9
1992	7.1	7.0	6.9	6.9	6.9	6.8	6.8	6.9	7.0	7.1	7.2	7.5	7.0
1993	7.0	6.9	6.8	6.8	6.7	6.6	6.7	6.7	6.8	6.8	7.0	7.2	6.8
1994	6.9	6.8	6.8	6.8	6.8	6.7	6.9	7.0	7.1	7.2	7.4	7.6	7.0
1995	7.3	7.1	7.1	7.1	7.1	7.2	7.2	7.3	7.5	7.4	7.6	7.9	7.3
1996	7.5	7.5	7.6	7.5	7.5	7.3	7.3	7.4	7.5	7.5	7.7	7.8	7.5
1997	7.4	7.3	7.3	7.3	7.3	7.2	7.2	7.3	7.4	7.5	7.8	7.8	7.4
1998	7.6	7.5	7.5	7.5	7.5	7.6	7.5	7.4	7.5	7.6	7.7	7.9	7.5
1999	7.5	7.4	7.4	7.6	7.5	7.4	7.4	7.4	7.4	7.4	7.6	7.7	7.4
2000	7.3	7.2	7.2	7.4	7.4	7.3	7.1	7.3	7.3	7.3	7.5	7.7	7.3
2001	7.4	7.4	7.3	7.3	7.3	7.3	7.2	7.3	7.2	7.2	7.5	7.5	7.3
2002	7.2	7.1	7.2	7.1	7.1	7.1	7.1	7.2	7.3	7.1	7.3	7.4	7.2
2003	7.1	7.0	7.0	7.0	7.0	7.1	6.9	7.0	7.1	7.2	7.3	7.4	7.1
Transportation and utilities													
1990	2.1	2.1	2.1	2.0	2.1	2.0	2.0	1.9	2.0	2.0	1.9	1.9	2.0
1991	1.9	1.9	1.9	1.9	1.9	1.8	1.9	1.9	2.0	1.9	2.0	2.0	1.9
1992	1.9	1.9	1.9	2.0	1.9	1.9	2.0	2.0	2.0	2.1	2.1	2.1	1.9
1993	2.0	1.9	1.9	1.9	1.9	1.9	2.0	2.0	2.0	2.0	2.0	2.1	1.9
1994	2.1	2.1	2.1	2.1	2.1	2.1	2.1	2.0	2.0	2.1	2.0	2.0	2.0
1995	1.9	1.9	1.9	1.9	1.9	1.9	1.9	1.9	1.9	1.9	1.9	1.9	1.9
1996	1.8	1.8	1.8	1.9	1.8	1.8	1.8	1.8	1.8	1.9	1.9	1.9	1.8
1997	1.8	1.8	1.6	1.6	1.6	1.6	1.6	1.6	1.6	1.7	1.7	1.7	1.6
1998	1.6	1.6	1.6	1.7	1.7	1.6	1.7	1.7	1.7	1.7	1.8	1.8	1.6
1999	1.7	1.7	1.7	1.7	1.7	1.7	1.7	1.7	1.7	1.8	1.8	1.7	1.7
2000	1.7	1.7	1.7	1.8	1.8	1.7	1.8	1.8	1.7	1.7	1.7	1.8	1.7
2001	1.7	1.7	1.6	1.6	1.6	1.7	1.7	1.6	1.6	1.7	1.7	1.7	1.6
2002	1.6	1.6	1.6	1.6	1.6	1.7	1.6	1.6	1.7	1.6	1.6	1.6	1.6
2003	1.5	1.5	1.5	1.5	1.5	1.5	1.4	1.5	1.4	1.5	1.5	1.5	1.5
Information													
1990	1.1	1.1	1.1	1.1	1.1	1.1	1.1	1.1	1.1	1.1	1.1	1.1	1.1
1991	1.1	1.1	1.1	1.1	1.1	1.1	1.1	1.1	1.1	1.1	1.1	1.1	1.1
1992	1.0	1.0	1.1	1.0	1.0	1.0	1.0	1.0	1.0	1.0	1.0	1.0	1.0
1993	1.0	1.0	1.0	1.0	1.0	1.0	1.0	1.0	1.0	1.0	0.9	0.9	0.9
1994	0.9	0.9	0.9	0.9	0.9	0.9	0.9	0.9	1.0	1.0	1.0	1.0	0.9
1995	1.0	1.0	1.0	1.0	1.0	1.0	0.9	1.0	1.0	1.0	1.0	1.0	0.9
1996	1.0	1.0	1.0	1.0	1.1	1.1	1.0	1.0	1.0	1.1	1.0	1.0	1.0
1997	1.0	1.0	1.0	1.1	1.0	1.1	1.1	1.1	1.1	1.1	1.1	1.2	1.0
1998	1.1	1.2	1.2	1.2	1.2	1.2	1.2	1.2	1.2	1.2	1.2	1.2	1.1
1999	1.2	1.2	1.2	1.2	1.2	1.2	1.2	1.2	1.2	1.2	1.2	1.2	1.2
2000	1.2	1.2	1.2	1.2	1.2	1.2	1.2	1.2	1.2	1.1	1.1	1.2	1.1
2001	1.1	1.1	1.1	1.1	1.1	1.1	1.1	1.1	1.1	1.1	1.1	1.1	1.1
2002	1.1	1.1	1.1	1.1	1.1	1.1	1.1	1.1	1.2	1.1	1.2	1.1	1.1
2003	1.1	1.1	1.1	1.1	1.1	1.2	1.2	1.1	1.1	1.1	1.1	1.1	1.1
Financial activities													
1990	2.3	2.3	2.3	2.3	2.4	2.3	2.4	2.3	2.4	2.4	2.3	2.3	2.3
1991	2.3	2.3	2.3	2.3	2.3	2.3	2.2	2.2	2.2	2.2	2.3	2.2	2.2
1992	2.2	2.2	2.2	2.2	2.2	2.2	2.2	2.2	2.2	2.3	2.3	2.3	2.2
1993	2.3	2.2	2.3	2.2	2.3	2.2	2.3	2.3	2.3	2.3	2.3	2.3	2.2
1994	2.2	2.2	2.2	2.2	2.2	2.2	2.2	2.2	2.2	2.2	2.2	2.2	2.2
1995	2.3	2.3	2.2	2.2	2.2	2.2	2.2	2.2	2.2	2.3	2.2	2.3	2.2
1996	2.3	2.3	2.3	2.3	2.3	2.3	2.3	2.3	2.4	2.4	2.4	2.4	2.3
1997	2.4	2.6	2.6	2.5	2.6	2.6	2.6	2.6	2.6	2.6	2.6	2.6	2.5
1998	2.7	2.7	2.7	2.7	2.7	2.7	2.7	2.7	2.7	2.7	2.7	2.7	2.7
1999	2.7	2.7	2.7	2.7	2.7	2.7	2.7	2.7	2.7	2.7	2.7	2.7	2.7
2000	2.7	2.7	2.7	2.8	2.7	2.7	2.7	2.7	2.7	2.8	2.8	2.8	2.7
2001	2.8	2.8	2.8	2.7	2.7	2.7	2.8	2.7	2.7	2.7	2.7	2.7	2.7
2002	2.7	2.7	2.7	2.7	2.7	2.8	2.8	2.7	2.7	2.7	2.7	2.8	2.7
2003	2.7	2.7	2.8	2.8	2.8	2.8	2.8	2.8	2.8	2.8	2.8	2.8	2.8
Professional and business services													
1990	2.5	2.5	2.5	2.5	2.4	2.3	2.5	2.4	2.6	2.7	2.7	2.8	2.5
1991	2.7	2.8	2.8	2.9	2.9	2.9	2.9	2.9	2.8	3.0	2.9	3.0	2.8
1992	3.0	2.9	2.9	3.0	2.9	2.9	3.0	2.9	3.0	3.0	3.0	3.1	2.9
1993	3.0	3.0	3.0	2.9	2.9	2.8	2.8	2.7	2.8	2.8	2.8	2.8	2.8
1994	2.7	2.7	2.6	2.6	2.5	2.5	2.6	2.6	2.6	2.7	2.7	2.7	2.6
1995	2.7	2.8	2.8	3.0	2.8	2.8	2.9	2.9	2.9	3.0	2.9	2.9	2.8
1996	2.8	2.9	3.0	3.0	3.0	3.0	3.0	2.9	2.9	2.9	3.0	3.0	2.9
1997	3.1	3.1	3.1	3.4	3.3	3.3	3.5	3.4	3.4	3.5	3.6	3.5	3.3
1998	3.5	3.7	3.6	3.7	3.6	3.5	3.7	3.7	3.7	3.7	3.7	3.6	3.6
1999	3.6	3.6	3.6	3.9	3.8	3.8	3.8	3.8	3.9	3.9	3.9	3.9	3.7
2000	3.9	4.0	4.1	4.1	4.0	4.0	4.0	4.0	4.1	3.8	3.8	3.9	3.9
2001	3.9	4.0	4.1	4.1	4.0	4.1	4.0	3.9	3.9	3.9	3.9	3.9	3.9
2002	3.9	4.0	4.1	4.0	4.0	3.9	3.8	3.8	3.9	3.9	4.0	4.1	4.0
2003	4.0	4.1	4.1	4.1	4.2	4.2	4.1	4.1	4.3	4.3	4.3	4.2	4.2

Employment by Industry: Texas—*Continued*

(Numbers in thousands. Not seasonally adjusted.)

Industry	January	February	March	April	May	June	July	August	September	October	November	December	Annual Average
ABILENE—*Continued*													
Educational and health services													
1990	8.3	8.3	8.3	8.4	8.5	8.3	8.3	8.4	8.8	8.8	8.8	8.9	8.5
1991	8.6	8.8	8.8	8.9	8.9	8.7	8.6	8.7	9.0	9.0	9.0	9.1	8.8
1992	9.1	9.2	9.2	9.3	9.3	9.1	9.1	9.1	9.5	9.3	9.5	9.5	9.2
1993	9.5	9.6	9.6	9.6	9.5	9.3	9.5	9.5	9.9	9.9	9.9	9.8	9.6
1994	9.8	9.9	10.0	10.2	10.1	10.0	9.9	10.0	10.4	10.6	10.7	10.7	10.1
1995	10.8	11.0	10.9	11.0	10.8	10.6	10.6	10.7	11.0	10.9	11.0	11.0	10.8
1996	10.8	11.0	11.0	11.3	11.2	11.0	11.0	11.1	11.5	11.5	11.6	11.5	11.2
1997	11.4	11.4	11.5	11.6	11.5	11.3	11.2	11.2	11.6	11.7	11.7	11.7	11.4
1998	11.7	11.7	11.8	11.7	11.6	11.4	11.4	11.5	11.7	11.8	11.8	11.6	11.6
1999	11.5	11.5	11.5	11.7	11.4	11.3	11.4	11.4	11.6	11.8	11.8	11.8	11.5
2000	11.5	11.6	11.7	11.7	11.5	11.3	11.1	11.4	11.5	11.6	11.5	11.5	11.4
2001	11.6	11.6	11.6	11.5	11.4	11.3	11.3	11.4	11.4	11.7	11.8	11.8	11.5
2002	11.6	11.8	11.9	12.0	12.1	12.1	12.1	12.3	12.4	12.4	12.6	12.6	12.2
2003	12.4	12.5	12.6	12.8	12.9	13.0	13.0	13.1	13.2	13.4	13.4	13.4	13.0
Leisure and hospitality													
1990	4.2	4.2	4.2	4.3	4.3	4.2	4.2	4.3	4.3	4.3	4.2	4.2	4.2
1991	4.0	4.1	4.2	4.3	4.4	4.3	4.4	4.4	4.5	4.5	4.4	4.4	4.3
1992	4.4	4.4	4.4	4.6	4.6	4.5	4.5	4.6	4.6	4.7	4.6	4.7	4.5
1993	4.7	4.6	4.7	4.7	4.7	4.7	4.7	4.6	4.6	4.5	4.6	4.6	4.6
1994	4.5	4.5	4.6	4.7	4.7	4.6	4.7	4.7	4.8	4.9	4.9	4.9	4.7
1995	4.9	5.0	5.0	5.2	5.2	5.2	5.2	5.1	5.2	5.1	5.1	5.2	5.1
1996	5.1	5.0	5.1	5.4	5.5	5.5	5.5	5.5	5.4	5.4	5.3	5.3	5.3
1997	5.3	5.4	5.6	5.6	5.8	5.9	5.8	5.8	5.9	5.7	5.7	5.7	5.6
1998	5.6	5.8	5.9	6.0	6.1	6.0	6.1	6.1	6.3	6.0	6.0	6.0	5.9
1999	5.9	5.9	6.0	6.0	6.1	6.2	6.1	6.2	6.1	5.9	5.8	5.8	6.0
2000	5.6	5.6	5.8	5.8	5.9	5.8	5.7	5.7	5.8	5.6	5.5	5.6	5.7
2001	5.5	5.6	5.7	5.8	5.9	5.9	5.9	5.9	5.9	5.6	5.7	5.7	5.7
2002	5.5	5.7	6.0	6.0	6.0	6.0	6.0	6.0	6.0	5.8	5.8	6.1	5.9
2003	5.8	5.8	6.0	5.9	6.1	6.2	5.9	6.1	6.0	5.9	5.9	5.9	6.0
Other services													
1990	2.2	2.3	2.3	2.3	2.3	2.4	2.3	2.2	2.3	2.3	2.3	2.3	2.2
1991	2.3	2.3	2.4	2.4	2.4	2.4	2.4	2.3	2.4	2.4	2.4	2.4	2.3
1992	2.4	2.4	2.4	2.5	2.5	2.4	2.5	2.4	2.5	2.5	2.5	2.5	2.4
1993	2.5	2.5	2.5	2.5	2.4	2.4	2.5	2.4	2.4	2.5	2.5	2.5	2.4
1994	2.5	2.6	2.6	2.6	2.6	2.5	2.5	2.5	2.6	2.6	2.6	2.6	2.5
1995	2.6	2.6	2.6	2.7	2.6	2.6	2.6	2.5	2.6	2.6	2.6	2.6	2.6
1996	2.6	2.6	2.6	2.7	2.6	2.6	2.6	2.6	2.7	2.7	2.7	2.7	2.6
1997	2.7	2.7	2.8	2.7	2.8	2.7	2.7	2.8	2.8	2.9	2.8	2.8	2.7
1998	2.8	2.8	2.8	2.8	2.8	2.8	2.7	2.8	2.7	2.8	2.7	2.8	2.7
1999	2.8	2.8	2.8	2.9	2.8	2.9	2.8	2.8	2.7	2.7	2.7	2.7	2.7
2000	2.6	2.7	2.7	2.7	2.6	2.7	2.6	2.6	2.6	2.6	2.6	2.6	2.6
2001	2.6	2.7	2.7	2.7	2.7	2.7	2.7	2.7	2.7	2.7	2.7	2.7	2.6
2002	2.6	2.7	2.8	2.7	2.8	2.8	2.8	2.8	2.8	2.8	2.7	2.8	2.8
2003	2.8	2.8	2.9	2.8	2.9	2.9	2.9	2.9	2.9	2.8	2.8	2.8	2.9
Government													
1990	9.1	9.2	9.2	9.3	9.3	9.1	8.7	8.6	9.2	9.3	9.4	9.4	9.1
1991	9.3	9.3	9.2	9.2	9.3	9.1	8.7	8.7	9.0	9.2	9.3	9.4	9.1
1992	9.3	9.4	9.3	9.4	9.5	9.2	8.9	9.0	9.5	9.6	9.6	9.6	9.3
1993	9.6	9.6	9.6	9.6	9.6	9.5	9.2	9.2	9.7	9.8	9.8	9.8	9.5
1994	9.7	9.7	9.6	9.7	9.8	9.3	9.1	9.1	9.6	9.8	9.8	9.8	9.5
1995	9.8	9.8	9.7	9.6	9.7	9.4	9.3	9.4	9.9	10.2	10.1	10.1	9.7
1996	9.9	9.9	10.0	9.9	9.9	9.6	9.3	9.3	9.8	9.9	10.0	10.0	9.7
1997	10.0	9.9	10.0	9.8	10.0	9.8	9.6	9.6	10.1	10.2	10.4	10.4	9.9
1998	10.1	10.2	10.2	10.1	10.2	10.0	9.7	9.6	10.1	10.1	10.2	10.2	10.0
1999	10.1	10.0	10.0	10.2	10.1	9.8	9.5	9.6	10.0	10.2	10.2	10.1	9.9
2000	10.0	10.2	10.3	10.1	10.4	10.1	9.6	9.5	9.9	9.9	9.8	9.8	9.9
2001	9.6	9.7	9.7	9.7	9.7	9.5	9.2	9.1	9.5	9.5	9.7	9.5	9.5
2002	9.5	9.6	9.6	9.5	9.5	9.6	9.1	9.1	9.4	9.6	9.7	9.8	9.5
2003	9.5	9.5	9.5	9.5	9.6	9.5	9.1	8.9	9.3	9.4	9.5	9.5	9.4
Federal government													
1990	1.4	1.4	1.5	1.6	1.6	1.5	1.5	1.4	1.4	1.4	1.5	1.5	1.4
1991	1.4	1.4	1.3	1.4	1.4	1.4	1.4	1.3	1.3	1.3	1.4	1.4	1.3
1992	1.3	1.3	1.3	1.3	1.3	1.3	1.3	1.3	1.3	1.3	1.3	1.3	1.3
1993	1.4	1.3	1.3	1.3	1.3	1.3	1.3	1.3	1.3	1.4	1.3	1.3	1.3
1994	1.3	1.3	1.3	1.3	1.3	1.3	1.3	1.3	1.3	1.3	1.3	1.3	1.3
1995	1.3	1.3	1.3	1.2	1.2	1.3	1.3	1.6	1.5	1.6	1.6	1.6	1.4
1996	1.5	1.5	1.5	1.5	1.5	1.5	1.5	1.5	1.5	1.5	1.6	1.6	1.5
1997	1.6	1.5	1.5	1.5	1.5	1.6	1.6	1.6	1.6	1.6	1.8	1.8	1.6
1998	1.5	1.5	1.5	1.5	1.5	1.6	1.5	1.5	1.5	1.5	1.6	1.6	1.5
1999	1.5	1.4	1.4	1.6	1.4	1.5	1.5	1.5	1.5	1.5	1.5	1.5	1.4
2000	1.4	1.5	1.5	1.5	1.7	1.6	1.5	1.4	1.4	1.4	1.3	1.4	1.4
2001	1.3	1.2	1.2	1.2	1.2	1.2	1.3	1.3	1.2	1.2	1.3	1.2	1.2
2002	1.2	1.2	1.2	1.2	1.2	1.3	1.3	1.3	1.2	1.2	1.3	1.3	1.2
2003	1.2	1.2	1.2	1.2	1.2	1.2	1.3	1.2	1.2	1.2	1.2	1.2	1.2

Employment by Industry: Texas—*Continued*

(Numbers in thousands. Not seasonally adjusted.)

Industry	January	February	March	April	May	June	July	August	September	October	November	December	Annual Average
ABILENE—*Continued*													
State government													
1990	2.5	2.5	2.5	2.5	2.5	2.5	2.5	2.5	2.5	2.5	2.5	2.5	2.5
1991	2.5	2.5	2.5	2.4	2.5	2.5	2.5	2.5	2.4	2.4	2.4	2.4	2.4
1992	2.4	2.4	2.4	2.4	2.4	2.4	2.4	2.4	2.4	2.4	2.4	2.4	2.4
1993	2.4	2.4	2.4	2.4	2.4	2.4	2.4	2.4	2.4	2.3	2.3	2.3	2.3
1994	2.3	2.3	2.2	2.3	2.3	2.3	2.3	2.3	2.3	2.4	2.4	2.4	2.3
1995	2.4	2.4	2.4	2.3	2.3	2.3	2.4	2.3	2.3	2.3	2.2	2.2	2.3
1996	2.2	2.2	2.2	2.2	2.2	2.2	2.2	2.2	2.2	2.2	2.2	2.2	2.2
1997	2.2	2.2	2.2	2.2	2.2	2.2	2.2	2.2	2.2	2.2	2.2	2.2	2.2
1998	2.2	2.2	2.2	2.2	2.2	2.2	2.2	2.2	2.2	2.2	2.2	2.2	2.2
1999	2.2	2.2	2.2	2.2	2.2	2.2	2.2	2.2	2.2	2.2	2.2	2.2	2.2
2000	2.2	2.2	2.2	2.1	2.1	2.1	2.1	2.1	2.1	2.1	2.0	2.0	2.1
2001	2.0	2.0	2.0	2.0	2.0	2.0	2.0	2.0	2.1	2.0	2.0	2.0	2.0
2002	2.0	2.0	2.0	2.0	2.0	2.0	2.0	2.0	2.0	2.0	2.0	2.0	2.0
2003	2.0	2.0	2.0	2.0	2.0	2.0	2.0	2.0	2.0	2.0	2.0	2.0	2.0
Local government													
1990	5.2	5.3	5.2	5.2	5.2	5.1	4.7	4.7	5.3	5.4	5.4	5.4	5.1
1991	5.4	5.4	5.4	5.4	5.4	5.2	4.8	4.9	5.3	5.5	5.5	5.6	5.3
1992	5.6	5.7	5.6	5.7	5.8	5.5	5.2	5.3	5.8	5.9	5.9	5.9	5.6
1993	5.8	5.9	5.9	5.9	5.9	5.8	5.5	5.5	6.0	6.1	6.2	6.2	5.8
1994	6.1	6.1	6.1	6.1	6.2	5.7	5.5	5.5	6.0	6.1	6.1	6.1	5.9
1995	6.1	6.1	6.0	6.1	6.2	5.8	5.6	5.5	6.1	6.3	6.3	6.3	6.0
1996	6.2	6.2	6.3	6.2	6.2	5.9	5.6	5.6	6.1	6.2	6.2	6.2	6.0
1997	6.2	6.2	6.3	6.1	6.3	6.0	5.8	5.8	6.3	6.4	6.4	6.4	6.1
1998	6.4	6.5	6.5	6.4	6.5	6.2	6.0	5.9	6.4	6.4	6.4	6.4	6.3
1999	6.4	6.4	6.4	6.4	6.5	6.1	5.8	5.9	6.3	6.5	6.5	6.4	6.3
2000	6.4	6.5	6.6	6.5	6.6	6.4	6.0	6.0	6.4	6.4	6.5	6.4	6.3
2001	6.3	6.5	6.5	6.5	6.5	6.3	5.9	5.8	6.2	6.3	6.4	6.3	6.2
2002	6.3	6.4	6.4	6.3	6.3	6.3	5.8	5.8	6.2	6.4	6.4	6.5	6.3
2003	6.3	6.3	6.3	6.3	6.4	6.3	5.8	5.7	6.1	6.2	6.3	6.3	6.2
AUSTIN													
Total nonfarm													
1990	380.1	382.8	385.6	389.1	390.1	388.5	383.6	385.6	395.7	399.5	403.4	402.9	390.6
1991	395.3	398.6	400.6	402.5	403.4	399.3	393.7	395.4	406.5	410.1	414.3	414.0	402.8
1992	410.3	414.1	416.1	421.7	422.4	420.7	416.4	417.1	431.3	438.7	440.0	441.2	424.2
1993	436.1	442.2	445.3	452.1	452.9	449.3	446.9	450.4	463.3	467.2	468.6	468.9	453.6
1994	463.7	468.6	472.6	481.2	481.7	481.5	477.8	481.2	494.6	500.5	504.2	505.4	484.4
1995	497.4	504.6	508.2	512.6	516.0	515.3	507.7	513.2	525.9	529.6	533.3	534.0	516.5
1996	524.0	531.3	535.5	540.8	541.6	538.4	533.0	539.7	545.5	551.0	555.0	554.6	540.9
1997	544.1	553.8	557.9	562.1	562.5	561.4	562.3	567.5	575.6	579.6	585.1	583.8	566.3
1998	577.3	586.0	590.8	596.3	598.4	600.5	594.5	602.0	608.1	615.0	619.2	619.7	600.7
1999	610.0	618.9	624.1	627.9	630.2	635.3	631.9	640.2	645.1	649.5	654.7	657.0	635.4
2000	646.2	655.5	662.7	663.8	670.4	674.8	670.2	679.9	682.3	685.9	690.3	690.1	672.7
2001	675.2	679.8	682.8	679.2	678.3	677.7	666.7	672.6	671.5	669.6	669.2	666.2	674.0
2002	652.4	656.5	659.8	661.0	662.5	656.9	652.2	658.1	659.1	658.9	662.7	660.4	658.4
2003	646.4	648.7	649.4	653.4	655.1	652.7	645.0	652.7	654.0	655.4	658.1	656.1	652.3
Total private													
1990	270.4	271.0	273.0	275.0	276.5	279.7	281.2	283.7	283.0	284.5	287.4	288.0	279.5
1991	280.0	281.0	283.2	284.8	286.7	287.9	289.8	291.3	291.7	293.6	296.7	297.9	288.7
1992	293.7	295.5	297.4	301.9	304.0	307.5	309.7	310.4	312.0	317.1	317.8	320.7	307.3
1993	315.2	318.2	321.5	327.0	329.2	331.7	335.9	337.7	339.6	342.0	344.1	346.1	332.4
1994	340.2	342.5	346.3	353.3	354.7	359.5	363.6	365.4	367.6	371.0	374.3	376.9	359.6
1995	368.5	372.4	375.9	379.9	383.9	388.9	390.5	394.5	398.0	401.1	404.9	407.5	388.8
1996	398.6	403.0	407.5	410.5	413.6	417.2	417.0	420.0	419.7	423.0	426.1	427.8	415.3
1997	418.1	423.8	427.9	431.4	434.7	440.0	444.1	446.8	449.4	450.7	455.2	457.3	440.0
1998	450.6	455.4	460.2	464.2	467.3	471.9	473.8	476.1	477.9	480.6	483.9	487.5	470.8
1999	478.4	484.3	489.5	491.6	495.5	503.3	505.4	508.1	510.3	512.8	517.4	522.8	501.6
2000	511.2	517.0	523.6	525.1	531.0	540.4	540.5	544.9	545.2	547.2	550.5	553.4	535.8
2001	538.6	540.0	541.9	538.4	537.9	540.5	533.8	533.8	528.2	525.1	522.8	523.1	533.6
2002	509.7	510.9	513.0	513.9	516.4	517.8	514.4	516.7	514.1	510.7	512.9	512.8	513.6
2003	499.8	499.6	500.8	503.8	506.7	508.3	507.6	510.7	510.1	508.9	510.5	510.6	506.5
Goods-producing													
1990	58.3	58.3	58.9	58.8	59.3	60.5	61.3	62.2	61.8	62.5	62.8	62.6	60.6
1991	62.8	63.5	63.8	64.2	64.7	65.6	66.6	66.6	66.1	66.6	67.0	67.0	65.4
1992	66.7	66.9	67.2	68.3	69.0	70.3	71.3	71.3	71.1	72.5	72.4	72.9	70.0
1993	72.5	73.2	73.9	74.3	74.6	76.1	77.7	77.7	77.7	78.0	79.0	79.8	76.2
1994	79.4	79.5	80.2	81.6	82.1	83.8	85.5	86.0	86.3	86.5	86.8	87.1	83.7
1995	86.7	87.4	88.5	89.6	90.6	91.9	91.9	92.6	93.2	94.6	95.3	96.0	91.5
1996	95.8	97.0	98.3	99.2	100.0	100.7	101.0	101.0	100.4	100.4	100.5	100.5	99.6
1997	99.3	100.5	101.8	101.6	102.8	104.9	105.9	106.4	107.1	108.0	108.8	109.2	104.7
1998	108.7	110.1	111.1	111.9	112.1	113.6	114.2	114.5	114.9	115.2	115.1	115.3	113.1
1999	112.7	112.2	113.3	113.2	114.1	116.0	117.7	117.8	118.0	118.4	119.0	120.0	116.0
2000	117.6	119.2	121.8	121.9	122.9	125.9	126.1	126.8	126.7	126.6	126.8	126.8	124.1
2001	125.0	124.8	124.5	120.9	120.0	120.4	117.6	116.6	113.7	111.9	109.8	108.8	117.8
2002	105.4	104.7	104.7	103.0	103.0	103.7	102.1	101.4	99.5	98.6	97.5	96.8	101.7
2003	95.9	95.2	95.2	95.1	95.4	95.9	95.2	94.9	94.4	94.3	94.3	93.7	95.0

Employment by Industry: Texas—*Continued*

(Numbers in thousands. Not seasonally adjusted.)

Industry	January	February	March	April	May	June	July	August	September	October	November	December	Annual Average
AUSTIN—*Continued*													
Natural resources and mining													
1990	1.1	1.1	1.1	1.1	1.1	1.1	1.1	1.1	1.1	1.1	1.2	1.2	1.1
1991	1.2	1.2	1.2	1.2	1.2	1.2	1.2	1.2	1.2	1.1	1.1	1.2	1.2
1992	1.2	1.2	1.1	1.1	1.2	1.2	1.2	1.2	1.1	1.1	1.1	1.1	1.2
1993	1.1	1.0	1.1	1.0	1.0	1.0	1.0	1.0	1.0	1.0	1.0	1.0	1.0
1994	1.0	1.0	1.0	1.0	1.0	1.0	1.1	1.0	1.0	1.0	1.1	1.0	1.0
1995	1.0	1.0	1.1	1.1	1.1	1.1	1.1	1.1	1.1	1.1	1.2	1.2	1.1
1996	1.1	1.1	1.1	1.2	1.2	1.2	1.2	1.2	1.2	1.3	1.3	1.2	1.2
1997	1.2	1.3	1.3	1.4	1.3	1.4	1.4	1.4	1.4	1.4	1.4	1.4	1.4
1998	1.4	1.4	1.4	1.5	1.5	1.5	1.5	1.5	1.5	1.5	1.5	1.5	1.5
1999	1.3	1.3	1.3	1.3	1.4	1.4	1.4	1.4	1.4	1.4	1.4	1.5	1.4
2000	1.4	1.5	1.5	1.5	1.5	1.5	1.5	1.6	1.6	1.6	1.6	1.6	1.5
2001	1.5	1.6	1.6	1.7	1.7	1.8	1.8	1.8	1.8	1.8	1.8	1.8	1.7
2002	1.7	1.8	1.8	1.8	1.7	1.8	1.7	1.8	1.7	1.7	1.7	1.6	1.7
2003	1.5	1.5	1.5	1.5	1.5	1.5	1.5	1.5	1.5	1.5	1.5	1.5	1.5
Construction													
1990	11.2	11.2	11.4	11.4	11.8	12.4	12.6	12.9	12.5	12.4	12.3	12.2	12.0
1991	11.9	12.2	12.4	12.7	13.0	13.4	13.7	13.7	13.5	13.9	13.8	13.8	13.2
1992	13.8	13.7	14.1	14.7	14.9	15.3	15.7	15.8	15.6	16.0	16.0	16.2	15.2
1993	15.9	16.5	16.9	17.3	17.3	18.2	19.0	18.9	19.0	19.4	19.7	19.8	18.2
1994	19.6	19.4	20.1	21.0	21.4	22.4	23.1	23.6	23.5	23.4	23.5	23.7	22.1
1995	23.2	23.5	24.1	24.7	25.1	25.6	25.7	25.7	25.8	26.2	26.1	26.3	25.2
1996	26.1	27.0	27.7	28.3	28.7	29.0	29.4	29.3	28.9	28.9	28.9	28.9	28.4
1997	27.8	28.4	28.7	28.9	29.5	30.3	31.1	31.4	31.4	31.3	31.4	31.5	30.1
1998	31.3	31.9	32.4	33.2	33.4	33.9	33.9	34.1	33.9	34.2	34.2	34.4	33.4
1999	33.6	34.5	35.4	36.0	36.4	37.6	38.0	37.9	38.1	38.3	38.1	38.2	36.8
2000	36.9	37.7	39.0	39.4	39.9	41.1	40.8	41.0	41.1	40.5	40.1	39.9	39.8
2001	38.9	39.8	40.4	40.3	40.9	41.5	40.9	40.8	40.0	39.0	37.9	37.4	39.8
2002	35.9	36.2	36.9	36.7	37.1	37.6	37.5	37.2	36.2	35.9	35.4	34.9	36.5
2003	35.0	35.0	35.1	35.7	36.3	36.7	36.3	36.4	36.0	35.7	35.5	35.1	35.7
Manufacturing													
1990	46.0	46.0	46.4	46.3	46.4	47.0	47.6	48.2	48.2	49.0	49.3	49.2	47.5
1991	49.7	50.1	50.2	50.3	50.5	51.0	51.7	51.7	51.4	51.6	52.1	52.0	51.0
1992	51.7	52.0	52.0	52.5	52.9	53.8	54.4	54.3	54.4	55.4	55.3	55.6	53.7
1993	55.5	55.7	55.9	56.0	56.3	56.9	57.7	57.8	57.7	57.6	58.3	59.0	57.0
1994	58.8	59.1	59.1	59.6	59.7	60.4	61.3	61.4	61.8	62.1	62.2	62.4	60.7
1995	62.5	62.9	63.3	63.8	64.4	65.2	65.1	65.8	66.3	67.3	68.0	68.5	65.3
1996	68.6	68.9	69.5	69.7	70.1	70.5	70.4	70.5	70.3	70.2	70.3	70.4	70.0
1997	70.3	70.8	71.8	71.3	72.0	73.2	73.4	73.6	74.3	75.3	76.0	76.3	73.2
1998	76.0	76.8	77.3	77.2	77.2	78.2	78.8	78.9	79.5	79.5	79.4	79.4	78.2
1999	77.8	76.4	76.6	75.9	76.3	77.0	78.3	78.5	78.5	78.7	79.5	80.3	77.8
2000	79.3	80.0	81.3	81.0	81.5	83.3	83.8	84.2	84.0	84.5	85.1	85.3	82.8
2001	84.6	83.4	82.5	78.9	77.4	77.1	74.9	74.0	71.9	71.1	70.1	69.6	76.2
2002	67.8	66.7	66.0	64.5	64.2	64.3	62.9	62.4	61.6	61.0	60.4	60.3	63.5
2003	59.4	58.7	58.6	57.9	57.6	57.7	57.4	57.0	56.9	57.1	57.3	57.1	57.7
Service-providing													
1990	321.8	324.5	326.7	330.3	330.8	328.0	322.3	323.4	333.9	337.0	340.6	340.3	330.0
1991	332.5	335.1	336.8	338.3	338.7	333.7	327.1	328.8	340.4	343.5	347.3	347.0	337.4
1992	343.6	347.2	348.9	353.4	353.4	350.4	345.1	345.8	360.2	366.2	367.6	368.3	354.2
1993	363.6	369.0	371.4	377.8	378.3	373.2	369.2	372.7	385.6	389.2	389.6	389.1	377.4
1994	384.3	389.1	392.4	399.6	399.6	397.7	392.3	395.2	408.3	414.0	417.4	418.3	400.7
1995	410.7	417.2	419.7	423.0	425.4	423.4	415.8	420.6	432.7	435.0	438.0	438.0	425.0
1996	428.2	434.3	437.2	441.6	441.6	437.7	432.0	438.7	445.1	450.6	454.5	454.1	441.3
1997	444.8	453.3	456.1	460.5	459.7	456.5	456.4	461.1	468.5	471.6	476.3	474.6	461.6
1998	468.6	475.9	479.7	484.4	486.3	486.9	480.3	487.5	493.2	499.8	504.1	504.4	487.6
1999	497.3	506.7	510.8	514.7	516.1	519.3	514.2	522.4	527.1	531.1	535.7	537.0	519.4
2000	528.6	536.3	540.9	541.9	547.5	548.9	544.1	553.1	555.6	559.3	563.5	563.3	548.6
2001	550.2	555.0	558.3	558.3	558.3	557.3	549.1	556.0	557.8	557.7	559.4	557.4	556.2
2002	547.0	551.8	555.1	558.0	559.5	553.2	550.1	556.7	559.6	560.3	565.2	563.6	556.7
2003	550.5	553.5	554.2	558.3	559.7	556.8	549.8	557.8	559.6	561.1	563.8	562.4	557.3
Trade, transportation, and utilities													
1990	61.9	60.8	60.7	59.4	59.5	59.6	60.0	59.9	60.4	60.7	62.2	63.2	60.7
1991	59.9	58.1	58.4	57.7	57.8	58.3	58.6	59.1	59.1	59.8	61.4	62.9	59.3
1992	60.8	60.2	60.4	61.1	61.2	61.5	61.7	62.2	63.1	64.2	65.4	67.0	62.4
1993	64.9	64.5	65.0	65.7	66.1	65.9	66.9	67.8	68.4	69.6	71.0	72.4	67.4
1994	69.7	69.8	70.2	71.5	71.6	71.9	72.0	73.0	73.9	75.4	77.5	79.3	73.0
1995	76.4	76.3	76.4	77.0	77.5	79.3	80.8	82.4	84.2	85.2	87.3	88.8	81.0
1996	85.4	85.1	85.2	85.4	86.3	87.2	86.6	87.8	87.9	89.0	91.0	92.7	87.5
1997	88.9	88.6	88.9	89.0	89.5	90.3	91.2	92.2	93.3	94.5	96.8	98.4	91.8
1998	95.4	95.1	96.0	96.2	96.9	97.2	97.6	98.4	98.9	100.4	102.5	104.7	98.3
1999	103.1	103.8	104.7	104.9	105.6	106.8	107.8	108.8	108.9	110.9	113.5	115.7	107.9
2000	111.4	111.6	111.9	111.9	112.8	114.0	114.6	116.2	116.0	117.6	120.5	122.5	115.1
2001	118.6	116.8	116.4	116.6	116.7	116.2	115.5	115.7	115.3	115.9	116.9	118.6	116.6
2002	113.8	112.7	112.7	112.9	113.0	113.1	112.6	113.0	112.2	112.4	114.7	116.6	113.3
2003	110.9	109.7	109.6	109.7	110.0	110.6	111.7	113.0	113.1	113.5	115.3	116.7	112.0

Employment by Industry: Texas—*Continued*

(Numbers in thousands. Not seasonally adjusted.)

Industry	January	February	March	April	May	June	July	August	September	October	November	December	Annual Average
AUSTIN—*Continued*													
Wholesale trade													
1990	12.5	12.4	12.4	12.3	12.1	12.3	12.3	12.2	12.4	12.3	12.4	12.4	12.3
1991	12.5	11.6	11.6	11.6	11.6	11.7	11.6	11.6	11.5	11.6	11.8	11.9	11.7
1992	11.3	10.8	10.9	11.0	11.1	11.3	11.7	11.9	12.0	12.3	12.5	12.7	11.6
1993	12.7	12.7	13.0	13.3	13.5	13.5	13.9	14.0	13.9	13.9	13.9	13.9	13.5
1994	14.0	14.2	14.3	14.7	14.7	14.9	15.1	15.2	15.3	15.7	15.8	15.9	15.0
1995	15.8	16.2	16.4	16.4	16.6	17.7	18.8	19.0	19.3	19.2	19.5	19.6	17.9
1996	19.7	20.0	20.1	20.3	20.5	20.8	20.8	21.1	21.1	21.2	21.3	21.6	20.7
1997	21.1	21.3	21.5	21.8	22.2	22.6	23.0	23.1	23.6	24.1	24.4	24.7	22.8
1998	25.4	25.5	25.8	25.7	25.9	26.3	26.8	26.9	27.2	27.1	27.2	27.4	26.4
1999	29.7	30.1	30.4	30.5	30.8	31.2	31.6	32.1	32.3	33.0	33.4	33.6	31.6
2000	33.0	33.5	33.5	33.8	34.1	35.0	35.1	35.4	35.7	36.2	36.6	36.9	34.9
2001	37.0	36.5	36.1	36.5	36.3	35.4	35.5	35.1	34.6	34.5	34.3	34.5	35.5
2002	33.9	33.9	34.0	33.9	33.9	34.2	34.2	34.1	34.0	33.8	33.7	33.7	33.9
2003	33.4	33.4	33.3	33.3	33.5	33.7	33.9	34.0	33.8	33.9	34.1	34.3	33.7
Retail trade													
1990	43.5	42.5	42.4	41.5	41.7	41.6	41.8	41.9	42.0	42.4	43.7	44.7	42.5
1991	41.7	40.8	41.1	40.4	40.5	40.8	41.1	41.4	41.4	42.0	43.4	44.7	41.6
1992	43.2	43.0	43.1	43.5	43.6	43.5	43.4	43.6	44.2	45.1	46.0	47.4	44.1
1993	45.0	44.6	44.7	45.1	45.3	45.1	45.6	46.2	46.9	47.9	49.2	50.6	46.4
1994	48.1	47.8	48.2	49.1	49.1	49.2	49.2	50.0	50.6	51.6	53.4	54.9	50.1
1995	52.4	51.8	51.7	51.9	52.1	53.1	53.3	54.3	55.6	56.5	58.2	59.4	54.2
1996	56.4	55.8	55.7	55.5	56.1	56.6	56.1	56.9	57.0	57.9	59.8	61.0	57.1
1997	58.0	57.5	57.5	57.9	57.9	58.3	58.6	59.3	59.4	60.0	62.0	63.3	59.1
1998	59.8	59.3	59.8	60.1	60.5	60.5	60.4	60.9	61.1	62.5	64.4	66.4	61.3
1999	63.0	63.1	63.6	63.5	63.9	64.9	65.7	65.8	65.6	66.8	68.9	70.9	65.5
2000	67.6	67.3	67.6	67.7	68.2	68.7	69.0	70.0	69.4	70.5	72.9	74.4	69.4
2001	70.3	69.1	69.1	68.9	69.1	69.6	68.8	69.3	69.3	69.9	71.2	72.7	69.7
2002	68.7	67.7	67.6	67.9	68.0	67.9	67.3	67.7	67.2	67.5	69.9	71.8	68.3
2003	67.0	65.9	65.9	66.0	66.1	66.5	67.3	68.4	68.7	69.0	70.5	71.7	67.8
Transportation and utilities													
1990	5.9	5.9	5.9	5.6	5.7	5.7	5.9	5.8	6.0	6.0	6.1	6.1	5.9
1991	5.7	5.7	5.7	5.7	5.7	5.8	5.9	6.1	6.2	6.2	6.2	6.3	5.9
1992	6.3	6.4	6.4	6.6	6.5	6.7	6.6	6.7	6.9	6.8	6.9	6.9	6.6
1993	7.2	7.2	7.3	7.3	7.3	7.3	7.4	7.6	7.6	7.8	7.9	7.9	7.5
1994	7.6	7.8	7.7	7.7	7.8	7.8	7.7	7.8	8.0	8.1	8.3	8.5	7.9
1995	8.2	8.3	8.3	8.7	8.8	8.5	8.7	9.1	9.3	9.5	9.6	9.8	8.9
1996	9.3	9.3	9.4	9.6	9.7	9.8	9.7	9.8	9.8	9.9	9.9	10.1	9.7
1997	9.8	9.8	9.9	9.3	9.4	9.4	9.6	9.8	10.3	10.4	10.4	10.4	9.9
1998	10.2	10.3	10.4	10.4	10.5	10.4	10.4	10.6	10.6	10.8	10.9	10.9	10.5
1999	10.4	10.6	10.7	10.9	10.9	10.7	10.5	10.9	11.0	11.1	11.2	11.2	10.8
2000	10.8	10.8	10.8	10.4	10.5	10.3	10.5	10.8	10.9	10.9	11.0	11.2	10.7
2001	11.3	11.2	11.2	11.2	11.3	11.2	11.2	11.3	11.4	11.5	11.4	11.4	11.3
2002	11.2	11.1	11.1	11.1	11.1	11.0	11.1	11.2	11.0	11.1	11.1	11.1	11.1
2003	10.5	10.4	10.4	10.4	10.4	10.4	10.5	10.6	10.6	10.6	10.7	10.7	10.5
Information													
1990	10.1	10.2	10.2	10.4	10.4	10.5	10.5	10.5	10.5	10.6	10.6	10.6	10.4
1991	11.3	11.3	11.3	11.0	11.1	11.2	11.4	11.5	11.4	11.4	11.4	11.5	11.3
1992	11.3	11.2	11.3	11.4	11.5	11.5	11.7	11.7	11.5	11.8	11.9	11.9	11.6
1993	11.8	11.9	12.0	12.2	12.3	12.3	12.4	12.5	12.4	12.4	12.4	12.5	12.3
1994	12.2	11.8	12.0	12.1	12.2	12.3	12.4	12.4	12.5	12.6	12.7	13.0	12.4
1995	13.1	13.3	13.4	13.3	13.5	13.7	13.8	13.9	14.0	14.3	14.5	14.6	13.8
1996	14.3	14.5	14.6	14.7	14.9	15.2	15.2	15.4	15.5	15.4	15.6	15.7	15.1
1997	15.9	16.3	16.5	16.5	16.6	16.9	17.2	17.2	17.2	17.3	17.5	17.8	16.9
1998	17.7	17.9	18.0	18.0	18.1	18.5	18.4	18.6	18.7	19.1	19.4	19.7	18.5
1999	19.4	19.4	19.4	19.5	20.1	20.6	20.7	20.9	21.2	21.2	21.4	22.0	20.5
2000	21.9	22.3	22.7	23.5	24.1	25.0	25.5	25.7	25.5	25.0	25.1	25.3	24.3
2001	24.1	23.8	23.2	23.0	23.0	23.0	23.3	23.3	23.2	23.0	23.1	23.0	23.2
2002	23.0	22.9	23.0	22.9	22.8	23.0	22.7	22.5	22.3	22.1	22.0	21.8	22.6
2003	21.5	21.4	21.3	20.9	20.9	21.0	21.0	20.9	20.7	20.5	20.3	20.2	20.9
Financial activities													
1990	23.6	23.8	23.7	24.7	24.8	24.8	24.8	24.9	24.7	24.5	24.6	24.8	24.5
1991	23.0	23.0	23.3	23.4	23.5	23.7	23.9	23.8	23.9	24.0	24.0	24.1	23.6
1992	24.4	24.4	24.4	24.3	24.5	24.9	25.1	25.2	25.2	25.6	25.6	25.7	24.9
1993	25.5	25.6	25.7	25.9	26.1	26.5	26.7	26.9	26.9	26.5	26.5	26.8	26.3
1994	26.3	26.4	26.8	27.2	27.8	28.2	28.4	28.5	28.5	28.9	28.8	28.9	27.9
1995	28.5	28.6	28.8	29.2	29.5	29.6	29.5	29.7	29.6	29.7	29.7	29.9	29.4
1996	30.0	30.4	30.6	30.3	30.5	30.8	30.9	30.8	30.5	31.0	31.1	31.4	30.7
1997	31.1	31.2	31.5	31.3	31.6	31.9	31.5	31.9	31.8	31.5	31.6	32.0	31.6
1998	32.0	31.9	32.2	32.4	32.5	32.7	33.0	33.5	33.6	33.7	33.6	34.0	32.9
1999	33.4	33.7	34.0	34.4	34.6	35.0	34.7	35.0	35.0	34.7	34.9	35.3	34.6
2000	34.6	34.9	34.9	35.0	35.0	35.4	35.4	35.6	35.4	35.6	35.5	35.8	35.3
2001	35.5	35.9	36.1	36.3	36.5	36.9	37.0	36.8	36.4	36.6	36.4	36.9	36.4
2002	36.7	36.9	37.0	37.4	37.7	38.1	38.2	38.4	38.5	38.7	38.9	39.1	38.0
2003	38.5	38.6	38.7	39.1	39.3	39.5	39.6	39.8	39.6	39.8	40.0	40.3	39.4

Employment by Industry: Texas—*Continued*

(Numbers in thousands. Not seasonally adjusted.)

Industry	January	February	March	April	May	June	July	August	September	October	November	December	Annual Average
AUSTIN—*Continued*													
Professsional and business services													
1990	34.0	34.1	34.6	35.9	36.4	36.8	37.0	37.5	37.6	38.0	38.2	38.6	36.6
1991	37.4	37.9	38.5	39.3	39.6	38.9	38.5	39.4	39.1	39.5	40.4	40.0	39.0
1992	39.6	40.2	40.6	41.1	41.7	42.3	43.0	43.3	43.6	44.3	44.2	45.0	42.4
1993	43.6	44.6	45.3	46.2	46.3	47.3	48.0	48.4	49.0	50.0	50.3	50.0	47.4
1994	49.5	50.3	51.0	52.3	52.1	53.1	54.6	54.9	55.2	56.4	57.1	57.4	53.7
1995	56.4	57.4	58.0	58.0	59.0	60.1	61.1	61.6	61.9	62.2	62.2	62.3	60.0
1996	59.7	60.7	61.7	62.8	63.0	63.7	64.3	64.7	64.7	65.5	65.6	66.0	63.5
1997	64.0	65.6	66.1	68.7	68.9	70.1	71.7	72.5	72.8	72.7	73.1	73.1	69.9
1998	71.4	72.9	73.4	75.0	75.8	77.3	78.3	78.3	78.2	77.8	78.4	78.6	76.3
1999	78.0	79.9	80.7	81.9	82.6	84.0	85.0	85.7	85.5	86.1	86.0	86.9	83.5
2000	86.5	87.0	88.6	88.9	90.3	92.7	93.5	94.2	94.4	95.0	95.4	95.8	91.9
2001	92.7	93.0	93.7	92.6	91.8	91.5	91.4	91.6	90.3	89.6	89.1	88.8	91.3
2002	86.3	86.4	86.7	87.0	87.4	88.0	87.6	88.8	87.7	86.9	87.1	86.6	87.2
2003	84.6	84.6	84.8	85.4	86.1	86.2	85.9	86.1	86.3	85.8	85.6	85.0	85.5
Educational and health services													
1990	34.8	35.1	35.6	35.7	35.6	36.0	35.9	36.6	36.5	36.9	37.5	37.5	36.1
1991	37.1	37.7	37.9	38.0	37.9	38.0	38.5	38.6	39.6	39.9	40.4	40.3	38.7
1992	39.8	40.3	40.4	41.5	41.4	41.3	41.5	41.4	42.0	42.8	42.5	42.5	41.5
1993	42.3	42.7	43.0	44.4	44.4	44.1	44.4	44.4	44.8	45.0	45.2	45.2	44.2
1994	45.0	45.5	45.8	46.4	46.2	46.4	46.1	46.1	46.7	46.9	47.2	47.5	46.3
1995	45.9	46.5	46.7	47.5	47.6	47.3	47.0	47.7	48.7	49.0	49.6	49.8	47.8
1996	48.9	49.4	50.0	50.4	50.2	50.3	49.4	50.3	51.1	51.5	52.2	52.0	50.5
1997	51.1	52.0	52.3	52.6	52.4	52.5	53.2	53.4	53.9	53.8	54.2	54.4	53.0
1998	54.1	54.8	55.5	55.7	55.7	55.6	56.3	56.6	57.6	58.3	58.7	58.8	56.5
1999	57.4	59.0	59.4	59.3	59.1	59.8	59.2	59.4	60.7	60.8	61.5	61.6	59.8
2000	60.3	61.2	61.5	61.8	62.6	62.6	61.4	62.3	63.5	63.6	63.5	63.5	62.3
2001	61.5	62.7	63.3	63.5	63.3	64.5	62.5	62.8	63.7	63.8	63.8	63.7	63.2
2002	62.7	63.9	64.0	64.7	64.9	64.1	64.0	64.7	65.7	65.7	66.1	65.8	64.7
2003	64.6	65.4	65.1	66.0	66.2	65.1	64.8	65.7	66.3	66.3	66.6	66.5	65.7
Leisure and hospitality													
1990	32.7	33.5	34.0	35.0	35.3	35.9	35.9	36.2	36.0	35.8	36.0	35.4	35.1
1991	33.4	34.3	34.6	35.6	36.4	36.3	36.1	36.3	36.6	36.5	36.3	36.2	35.7
1992	35.2	36.3	36.9	37.9	38.4	39.0	38.8	38.8	39.0	39.1	39.2	39.0	38.1
1993	38.1	39.2	40.0	41.2	42.3	42.2	42.5	42.8	43.0	43.2	42.5	42.3	41.6
1994	41.1	42.2	43.0	44.4	45.0	45.7	46.3	46.5	46.4	46.1	46.0	45.5	44.9
1995	43.6	44.7	45.7	46.8	47.5	48.2	47.8	48.1	47.9	47.6	47.7	47.4	46.9
1996	45.9	47.1	48.1	48.6	49.6	50.0	50.3	50.6	50.1	50.6	50.4	50.0	49.3
1997	48.4	50.0	51.0	51.5	52.4	52.8	52.8	52.6	52.8	52.5	52.6	51.8	51.8
1998	50.8	52.0	53.1	54.1	55.2	55.9	55.0	55.2	55.2	55.3	55.4	55.5	54.4
1999	53.6	55.2	56.7	57.2	58.1	59.5	58.7	58.9	59.2	58.8	59.3	59.3	57.9
2000	57.1	58.9	60.1	59.9	60.9	62.1	61.5	61.7	61.3	61.4	61.3	61.1	60.6
2001	58.6	60.2	61.7	62.1	63.0	64.0	63.0	63.5	62.5	61.3	60.7	60.4	61.7
2002	58.8	60.1	61.4	62.4	63.5	63.6	63.1	63.6	63.6	62.3	62.4	62.3	62.3
2003	60.3	61.0	62.2	63.6	64.6	65.3	64.7	65.2	64.7	63.7	63.5	63.5	63.5
Other services													
1990	15.0	15.2	15.3	15.1	15.2	15.6	15.8	15.9	15.5	15.5	15.5	15.3	15.4
1991	15.1	15.2	15.4	15.6	15.7	15.9	16.2	16.0	15.9	15.9	15.8	15.9	15.7
1992	15.9	16.0	16.2	16.3	16.3	16.7	16.6	16.5	16.5	16.8	16.6	16.7	16.4
1993	16.5	16.5	16.6	17.1	17.1	17.3	17.3	17.2	17.4	17.3	17.2	17.1	17.1
1994	17.0	17.0	17.3	17.8	17.7	18.1	18.3	18.0	18.1	18.2	18.2	18.2	17.8
1995	17.9	18.2	18.4	18.5	18.7	18.8	18.6	18.5	18.5	18.5	18.6	18.7	18.5
1996	18.6	18.8	19.0	19.1	19.1	19.3	19.3	19.4	19.5	19.6	19.7	19.5	19.2
1997	19.4	19.6	19.8	20.2	20.5	20.6	20.6	20.6	20.5	20.4	20.6	20.6	20.3
1998	20.5	20.7	20.9	20.9	21.0	21.1	21.0	21.0	20.8	20.8	20.8	20.9	20.9
1999	20.8	21.1	21.3	21.2	21.3	21.6	21.6	21.6	21.8	21.9	21.8	22.0	21.5
2000	21.8	21.9	22.1	22.2	22.4	22.7	22.5	22.4	22.4	22.4	22.4	22.6	22.3
2001	22.6	22.8	23.0	23.4	23.6	24.0	23.5	23.5	23.1	23.0	23.0	22.9	23.2
2002	23.0	23.3	23.5	23.6	24.1	24.2	24.1	24.3	24.6	24.0	24.2	23.8	23.9
2003	23.5	23.7	23.9	24.0	24.2	24.7	24.7	25.1	25.0	25.0	24.9	24.7	24.5
Government													
1990	109.7	111.8	112.6	114.1	113.6	108.8	102.4	101.9	112.7	115.0	116.0	114.9	111.1
1991	115.3	117.6	117.4	117.7	116.7	111.4	103.9	104.1	114.8	116.5	117.6	116.1	114.1
1992	116.6	118.6	118.7	119.8	118.4	113.2	106.7	106.7	119.3	121.6	122.2	120.5	116.9
1993	120.9	124.0	123.8	125.1	123.7	117.6	111.0	112.7	123.7	125.2	124.5	122.8	121.3
1994	123.5	126.1	126.3	127.9	127.0	122.0	114.2	115.8	127.0	129.5	129.9	128.5	124.8
1995	128.9	132.2	132.3	132.7	132.1	126.4	117.2	118.7	127.9	128.5	128.4	126.5	127.7
1996	125.4	128.3	128.0	130.3	128.0	121.2	116.0	119.7	125.8	128.0	128.9	126.8	125.5
1997	126.0	130.0	130.0	130.7	127.8	121.4	118.2	120.7	126.2	128.9	129.9	126.5	126.4
1998	126.7	130.6	130.6	132.1	131.1	128.6	120.7	125.9	130.2	134.4	135.3	132.2	129.9
1999	131.6	134.6	134.6	136.3	134.7	132.0	126.5	132.1	134.8	136.7	137.3	134.2	133.8
2000	135.0	138.5	139.1	138.7	139.4	134.4	129.7	135.0	137.1	138.7	139.8	136.7	136.8
2001	136.6	139.8	140.9	140.8	140.4	137.2	132.9	138.8	143.3	144.5	146.4	143.1	140.3
2002	142.7	145.6	146.8	147.1	146.1	139.1	137.8	141.4	145.0	148.2	149.8	147.6	144.8
2003	146.6	149.1	148.6	149.6	148.4	144.4	137.4	142.0	143.9	146.5	147.6	145.5	145.8

Employment by Industry: Texas—*Continued*

(Numbers in thousands. Not seasonally adjusted.)

Industry	January	February	March	April	May	June	July	August	September	October	November	December	Annual Average
AUSTIN—*Continued*													
Federal government													
1990	11.6	12.6	13.1	14.3	14.0	13.6	13.0	12.8	12.9	12.8	12.9	12.9	13.0
1991	12.7	13.0	12.9	13.1	12.9	12.0	11.6	11.6	11.1	11.4	11.3	11.2	12.1
1992	11.8	12.0	12.1	12.5	11.8	11.4	11.2	11.2	11.3	10.9	10.7	10.7	11.5
1993	11.3	12.1	12.0	12.4	11.8	11.4	10.9	10.6	10.2	10.3	10.0	9.9	11.1
1994	10.7	11.2	11.5	12.2	11.7	11.7	10.5	10.5	10.4	10.3	10.1	10.1	10.9
1995	10.8	11.7	11.8	12.3	11.4	11.3	11.0	11.0	10.7	10.7	10.1	9.8	11.1
1996	10.7	11.4	11.4	11.9	10.9	10.6	10.2	10.1	9.7	9.3	9.2	9.2	10.4
1997	9.6	10.9	11.6	11.7	10.4	10.0	9.6	9.5	9.2	9.2	9.0	9.0	10.0
1998	9.5	10.5	10.9	11.0	10.3	10.1	9.8	9.8	9.7	9.3	9.1	9.2	9.9
1999	9.6	10.7	11.1	11.9	10.8	10.4	9.9	9.8	9.6	9.4	9.2	9.2	10.1
2000	10.2	11.3	11.8	12.1	13.1	10.9	10.6	9.7	9.4	9.2	9.1	9.0	10.5
2001	9.1	10.2	10.6	10.6	10.4	10.1	10.0	9.9	9.8	9.8	9.7	9.6	9.9
2002	9.5	10.5	10.8	11.2	10.7	10.4	10.0	10.3	10.2	9.9	10.6	9.7	10.3
2003	10.3	11.1	11.1	11.2	10.5	10.3	10.0	10.0	9.6	9.5	9.3	9.2	10.2
State government													
1990	57.9	58.6	58.6	58.8	58.1	54.5	54.8	54.4	58.7	59.9	60.2	59.4	57.8
1991	60.4	61.5	61.2	61.3	60.3	57.2	57.0	57.9	61.4	61.6	62.2	61.1	60.3
1992	61.0	62.1	61.8	62.4	61.6	57.8	58.4	59.0	63.2	63.9	64.6	63.3	61.6
1993	63.2	64.8	64.6	65.0	64.3	59.3	60.5	60.9	65.0	65.4	64.9	63.3	63.4
1994	63.2	64.8	64.6	64.9	64.3	59.8	60.9	61.1	65.4	66.8	66.7	65.5	64.0
1995	65.6	67.1	67.1	66.5	66.5	61.9	61.3	60.9	65.1	65.7	66.0	64.6	64.9
1996	63.2	64.5	63.9	64.7	63.5	58.4	59.7	59.2	63.5	64.7	65.3	63.5	62.8
1997	63.5	65.2	64.4	65.0	63.6	58.9	60.2	59.3	63.5	65.0	65.2	62.0	63.0
1998	61.9	64.0	63.6	63.9	63.5	62.5	60.5	60.6	62.6	66.1	66.2	64.4	63.3
1999	64.5	66.1	65.6	65.9	64.9	63.8	63.6	63.7	64.4	65.9	66.1	64.1	64.9
2000	64.1	65.8	65.4	65.3	64.6	63.3	63.6	64.3	65.0	66.5	66.2	65.1	64.9
2001	65.3	66.7	66.9	66.6	66.1	64.5	64.5	65.1	67.3	67.7	68.2	66.9	66.3
2002	67.3	68.3	68.3	68.1	67.0	62.6	66.0	66.1	68.4	69.6	69.3	68.1	67.4
2003	69.2	70.2	69.4	69.1	67.8	66.0	65.4	65.7	66.5	67.6	67.7	66.4	67.6
Local government													
1990	40.2	40.6	40.9	41.0	41.5	40.7	34.6	34.7	41.1	42.3	42.9	42.6	40.3
1991	42.2	43.1	43.3	43.3	43.5	42.2	35.3	34.6	42.3	43.5	44.1	43.8	41.8
1992	43.8	44.5	44.8	44.9	45.0	44.0	37.1	36.5	44.8	46.8	46.9	46.5	43.8
1993	46.4	47.1	47.2	47.7	47.6	46.9	39.6	41.2	48.5	49.5	49.6	49.6	46.7
1994	49.6	50.1	50.2	50.8	51.0	50.5	42.8	44.2	51.2	52.4	53.1	52.9	49.9
1995	52.5	53.4	53.4	53.9	54.2	53.2	44.9	46.8	52.1	52.1	52.3	52.1	51.7
1996	51.5	52.4	52.7	53.7	53.6	52.2	46.1	50.4	52.6	54.0	54.4	54.1	52.3
1997	52.9	53.9	54.0	54.0	53.8	52.5	48.4	51.9	53.5	54.7	55.7	55.5	53.4
1998	55.3	56.1	56.1	57.2	57.3	56.0	50.4	55.5	57.9	59.0	60.0	58.6	56.6
1999	57.5	57.8	57.9	58.5	59.0	57.8	53.0	58.6	60.8	61.4	62.0	60.9	58.8
2000	60.7	61.4	61.9	61.3	61.7	60.2	55.5	61.0	62.7	63.0	64.5	62.6	61.4
2001	62.2	62.9	63.4	63.6	63.9	62.6	58.4	63.8	66.2	67.0	68.5	66.6	64.0
2002	65.9	66.8	67.7	67.8	68.4	66.1	61.8	65.0	66.4	68.7	69.9	69.8	67.0
2003	67.1	67.8	68.1	69.3	70.1	68.1	62.0	66.3	67.8	69.4	70.6	69.9	68.0
BEAUMONT-PORT ARTHUR													
Total nonfarm													
1990	138.8	138.2	139.5	140.7	141.0	142.4	142.0	142.1	143.8	144.9	145.2	146.8	142.1
1991	147.4	148.1	150.0	148.5	149.7	150.4	150.1	151.0	151.8	152.0	152.6	152.6	150.3
1992	148.9	149.3	149.6	150.5	150.9	151.6	150.4	150.4	151.9	152.1	150.5	150.2	150.5
1993	147.7	148.3	148.7	148.9	149.0	148.8	149.0	148.7	150.0	149.8	149.9	151.0	149.1
1994	148.3	148.4	148.0	147.9	148.6	148.1	146.0	147.0	150.0	150.0	150.6	151.8	148.7
1995	149.4	149.8	149.7	150.5	151.7	151.4	149.4	150.2	152.4	151.4	151.7	152.0	150.8
1996	150.0	149.5	150.0	150.6	150.9	150.9	148.8	150.5	151.5	152.7	153.7	154.2	151.1
1997	151.9	154.7	154.6	155.0	156.8	156.5	157.1	158.0	159.0	160.7	160.9	161.1	157.1
1998	157.4	159.5	160.6	159.5	160.0	160.9	159.8	160.5	160.5	160.6	161.7	162.1	160.2
1999	159.4	160.7	160.0	159.7	159.1	158.3	157.2	159.2	159.9	159.7	160.8	162.1	159.6
2000	158.9	160.4	161.9	161.2	161.8	161.6	159.2	160.9	161.2	161.2	161.8	162.6	161.0
2001	160.6	161.6	162.3	158.6	158.0	158.0	155.3	156.5	157.0	156.4	157.0	158.0	158.2
2002	156.8	157.5	158.3	157.0	157.4	158.0	153.0	155.4	156.5	155.5	156.7	156.9	156.6
2003	155.0	155.3	155.5	156.8	158.1	156.2	154.7	155.4	157.4	156.5	156.8	156.6	156.2
Total private													
1990	117.4	116.5	117.9	118.9	118.8	121.4	121.8	122.3	122.6	123.3	123.5	124.9	120.7
1991	125.5	126.1	127.9	126.4	127.4	128.7	129.7	130.7	130.1	129.9	130.3	130.2	128.5
1992	126.6	126.9	127.1	127.9	128.2	129.9	129.8	129.7	129.5	129.1	127.3	126.9	128.2
1993	124.5	125.0	125.2	125.6	125.5	126.2	127.2	127.1	126.4	125.7	125.6	126.7	125.8
1994	124.3	124.2	123.8	123.7	124.3	124.7	123.6	124.5	125.5	125.2	125.6	126.8	124.6
1995	124.4	124.7	124.6	125.5	126.6	127.0	126.3	126.7	127.1	125.7	125.8	126.2	125.8
1996	124.3	123.7	124.2	124.7	125.1	125.7	124.7	126.2	125.7	126.5	127.3	127.8	125.4
1997	125.8	128.5	128.2	128.6	130.2	130.8	132.5	133.2	132.9	134.0	133.9	134.6	131.1
1998	130.9	133.0	134.1	133.1	133.6	135.1	135.2	135.8	134.6	134.1	134.9	135.3	134.1
1999	132.7	133.9	133.1	132.4	132.0	132.7	132.7	133.3	132.9	132.5	133.4	134.6	133.0
2000	131.5	132.8	134.2	133.6	133.7	135.1	133.9	134.9	134.2	133.7	134.2	135.0	133.9
2001	133.1	134.1	134.7	131.2	130.5	130.4	129.7	130.2	129.8	128.6	129.0	130.1	130.9
2002	129.0	129.6	130.3	129.2	129.6	130.5	128.5	129.3	129.2	127.8	128.6	128.7	129.2
2003	127.1	127.3	127.7	128.8	130.1	129.3	129.3	130.0	129.7	129.1	129.0	128.9	128.9

Employment by Industry: Texas—*Continued*

(Numbers in thousands. Not seasonally adjusted.)

Industry	January	February	March	April	May	June	July	August	September	October	November	December	Annual Average
BEAUMONT-PORT ARTHUR *—Continued*													
Goods-producing													
1990	35.8	35.4	36.0	36.9	36.5	37.7	37.5	37.8	38.0	38.9	39.4	40.1	37.5
1991	40.9	41.6	43.2	41.3	41.6	42.1	42.7	43.1	43.0	43.1	43.1	42.2	42.3
1992	40.7	40.6	41.1	41.4	41.1	41.8	42.2	42.5	42.4	41.2	39.8	38.8	41.1
1993	38.6	38.5	38.8	38.9	38.6	38.6	39.1	39.2	38.9	38.8	38.4	38.3	38.7
1994	38.2	38.2	37.6	37.3	37.3	37.4	36.2	36.9	37.6	37.7	37.1	37.5	37.4
1995	37.0	37.4	36.6	36.3	36.7	36.3	36.0	36.4	37.3	37.2	36.7	36.4	36.6
1996	36.2	36.0	36.6	35.9	35.7	35.8	36.0	36.8	36.8	37.4	37.9	37.9	36.5
1997	37.2	39.4	38.3	38.6	39.5	39.9	41.5	42.1	41.5	42.2	41.9	41.7	40.3
1998	39.9	42.1	42.5	41.1	41.0	42.0	42.6	42.9	42.3	42.4	42.8	42.4	42.0
1999	41.2	43.0	42.0	41.3	40.8	40.9	41.1	41.2	41.1	40.9	41.2	41.5	41.3
2000	40.2	41.3	41.8	42.2	42.2	42.5	42.5	42.6	42.5	41.8	41.5	41.3	41.8
2001	41.4	42.7	42.9	39.6	38.2	37.8	37.5	37.6	37.4	36.9	36.8	36.6	38.7
2002	36.9	37.3	37.7	36.5	36.3	35.9	35.1	35.3	35.4	35.2	35.0	34.8	36.0
2003	34.5	34.7	34.6	35.2	36.1	35.3	35.8	36.3	36.2	36.0	35.2	34.7	35.4
Natural resources and mining													
1990	1.3	1.4	1.3	1.4	1.5	1.6	1.5	1.5	1.4	1.5	1.5	1.6	1.4
1991	1.4	1.3	1.3	1.4	1.3	1.3	1.3	1.3	1.3	1.3	1.3	1.3	1.3
1992	1.2	1.1	1.1	1.1	1.1	1.1	1.0	1.0	1.0	1.0	1.0	1.0	1.0
1993	0.9	0.9	0.9	0.9	0.9	0.9	0.9	0.9	1.0	0.9	0.9	0.9	0.9
1994	0.9	0.9	0.9	0.9	0.9	0.9	0.8	0.8	0.8	0.8	0.8	0.8	0.8
1995	0.8	0.8	0.8	0.8	0.8	0.8	0.7	0.7	0.7	0.7	0.7	0.7	0.7
1996	0.7	0.7	0.7	0.7	0.7	0.7	0.7	0.7	0.7	0.7	0.7	0.7	0.7
1997	0.7	0.7	0.7	0.7	0.7	0.8	0.8	0.8	0.8	0.8	0.8	0.9	0.7
1998	0.9	0.9	0.8	0.8	0.8	0.8	0.8	0.7	0.7	0.7	0.7	0.7	0.7
1999	0.6	0.6	0.7	0.7	0.7	0.7	0.7	0.7	0.7	0.7	0.7	0.7	0.6
2000	0.7	0.6	0.6	0.7	0.7	0.8	0.6	0.7	0.7	0.6	0.6	0.6	0.6
2001	0.7	0.7	0.7	0.7	0.7	0.7	0.7	0.7	0.7	0.7	0.7	0.7	0.6
2002	0.6	0.6	0.7	0.7	0.7	0.7	0.7	0.8	0.8	0.8	0.7	0.6	0.7
2003	0.7	0.7	0.7	0.7	0.8	0.8	0.8	0.8	0.7	0.7	0.7	0.7	0.7
Construction													
1990	11.0	10.8	11.2	12.0	11.3	12.0	12.1	12.4	12.7	13.3	13.8	14.3	12.2
1991	15.0	15.7	17.6	15.5	15.8	16.0	16.1	16.4	16.3	16.5	16.3	15.5	16.0
1992	14.0	13.9	14.3	14.8	14.5	15.0	15.1	15.4	15.3	14.8	13.8	12.7	14.4
1993	12.4	12.4	12.8	12.9	12.7	12.7	13.3	13.6	13.3	13.4	13.1	12.9	12.9
1994	13.2	13.2	12.4	12.1	12.1	12.1	11.3	12.1	12.8	12.8	12.4	12.9	12.4
1995	12.7	13.4	12.8	12.7	13.0	12.7	12.5	13.0	13.8	13.8	13.3	13.1	13.0
1996	12.3	12.1	12.6	12.1	11.8	11.7	11.5	12.0	12.1	12.6	13.2	13.2	12.2
1997	13.0	14.9	13.8	13.8	14.7	14.6	16.1	16.4	16.0	16.5	16.1	15.9	15.1
1998	14.2	16.3	16.6	15.1	14.9	15.5	15.7	15.8	15.2	15.7	16.0	16.0	15.5
1999	16.1	17.8	16.8	16.2	15.9	15.7	15.8	15.7	15.7	15.6	15.8	16.2	16.1
2000	16.0	17.1	18.0	19.0	19.0	19.3	19.0	18.7	18.5	18.4	18.2	18.1	18.2
2001	18.1	19.5	19.6	16.3	15.6	15.5	15.4	15.6	15.4	15.1	15.0	15.1	16.3
2002	15.2	15.5	15.8	15.2	14.8	14.4	14.1	14.5	14.7	14.6	14.6	14.6	14.8
2003	14.3	14.4	14.4	14.8	15.5	14.8	14.9	15.4	15.3	15.2	14.6	14.3	14.8
Manufacturing													
1990	23.5	23.2	23.5	23.5	23.7	24.1	23.9	23.9	23.9	24.1	24.1	24.2	23.8
1991	24.5	24.6	24.3	24.4	24.5	24.8	25.3	25.4	25.4	25.3	25.5	25.4	24.9
1992	25.5	25.6	25.7	25.5	25.5	25.7	26.1	26.1	26.1	25.4	25.0	25.1	25.6
1993	25.3	25.2	25.1	25.1	25.0	25.0	24.9	24.7	24.6	24.5	24.4	24.5	24.8
1994	24.1	24.1	24.3	24.3	24.3	24.4	24.1	24.0	24.0	24.1	23.9	23.8	24.1
1995	23.5	23.2	23.0	22.8	22.9	22.8	22.8	22.7	22.8	22.7	22.7	22.6	22.8
1996	23.2	23.2	23.3	23.1	23.2	23.4	23.8	24.1	24.0	24.1	24.0	24.0	23.6
1997	23.5	23.8	23.8	24.1	24.1	24.5	24.6	24.9	24.7	24.9	25.0	24.9	24.4
1998	24.8	24.9	25.1	25.2	25.3	25.7	26.1	26.4	26.4	26.0	26.1	25.7	25.6
1999	24.5	24.6	24.5	24.4	24.2	24.5	24.6	24.8	24.7	24.6	24.7	24.6	24.5
2000	23.5	23.6	23.2	22.5	22.5	22.4	22.9	23.2	23.3	22.8	22.7	22.6	22.9
2001	22.6	22.5	22.6	22.6	21.9	21.6	21.4	21.3	21.3	21.1	21.1	20.8	21.7
2002	21.1	21.2	21.2	20.6	20.8	20.8	20.3	20.0	19.9	19.8	19.7	19.6	20.4
2003	19.5	19.6	19.5	19.7	19.8	19.7	20.1	20.1	20.2	20.1	19.9	19.7	19.8
Service-providing													
1990	103.0	102.8	103.5	103.8	104.5	104.7	104.5	104.3	105.8	106.0	105.8	106.7	104.6
1991	106.5	106.5	106.8	107.2	108.1	108.3	107.4	107.9	108.8	108.9	109.5	110.4	108.0
1992	108.2	108.7	108.5	109.1	109.8	109.8	108.2	107.9	109.5	110.9	110.7	111.4	109.3
1993	109.1	109.8	109.9	110.0	110.4	110.2	109.9	109.5	111.1	111.0	111.5	112.7	110.4
1994	110.1	110.2	110.4	110.6	111.3	110.7	109.8	110.1	112.4	112.3	113.5	114.3	111.3
1995	112.4	112.4	113.1	114.2	115.0	115.1	113.4	113.8	115.1	114.2	115.0	115.6	114.1
1996	113.8	113.5	113.4	114.7	115.2	115.1	112.8	113.7	114.7	115.3	115.8	116.3	114.5
1997	114.7	115.3	116.3	116.4	117.3	116.6	115.6	115.9	117.5	118.5	119.0	119.4	116.8
1998	117.5	117.4	118.1	118.4	119.0	118.9	117.2	117.6	118.2	118.2	118.9	119.7	118.2
1999	118.2	117.7	118.0	118.4	118.3	117.4	116.1	118.0	118.8	118.8	119.6	120.6	118.3
2000	118.7	119.1	120.1	119.0	119.6	119.1	116.7	118.3	118.7	119.4	120.3	121.3	119.1
2001	119.2	118.9	119.4	119.0	119.8	120.2	117.8	118.9	119.6	119.5	120.2	121.4	119.4
2002	119.9	120.2	120.6	120.5	121.1	122.1	117.9	120.1	121.1	120.3	121.7	122.1	120.6
2003	120.5	120.6	120.9	121.6	122.0	120.9	118.9	119.1	121.2	120.5	121.6	121.9	120.8

Employment by Industry: Texas—*Continued*

(Numbers in thousands. Not seasonally adjusted.)

Industry	January	February	March	April	May	June	July	August	September	October	November	December	Annual Average
BEAUMONT-PORT ARTHUR *—Continued*													
Trade, transportation, and utilities													
1990	31.4	31.1	31.0	30.9	30.5	30.9	31.4	31.2	31.7	32.0	32.1	32.5	31.3
1991	32.3	31.6	31.5	31.4	31.7	32.2	32.4	32.8	33.0	33.5	34.0	34.2	32.5
1992	32.9	32.7	32.4	32.6	32.6	33.1	32.4	32.2	32.2	32.6	32.7	33.2	32.6
1993	31.7	31.8	31.7	31.6	31.6	31.7	31.7	31.5	31.7	31.3	31.7	32.5	31.7
1994	31.1	30.5	30.4	30.2	30.6	30.8	31.0	30.8	31.1	30.9	31.6	32.1	30.9
1995	30.7	30.6	30.7	31.0	31.2	31.5	31.5	31.4	31.3	31.0	31.5	32.0	31.2
1996	31.1	30.5	30.3	30.5	30.6	30.9	30.4	30.6	30.4	30.6	31.1	31.4	30.7
1997	30.4	30.3	30.4	30.6	30.8	30.9	30.7	30.8	30.8	31.2	31.6	32.0	30.8
1998	30.6	30.4	30.6	30.5	30.6	30.8	30.7	30.9	30.7	30.4	31.1	31.6	30.7
1999	30.0	30.0	30.1	29.8	30.0	30.2	30.3	30.5	30.4	30.4	31.2	31.7	30.3
2000	30.6	30.2	30.3	29.9	30.0	30.4	29.9	30.2	30.2	30.0	30.6	31.3	30.3
2001	30.0	29.9	29.9	29.9	29.8	29.9	29.8	29.8	29.7	29.4	29.9	30.7	29.8
2002	30.1	30.0	29.9	29.8	30.0	30.0	29.9	30.1	30.0	29.7	30.4	30.8	30.1
2003	30.0	29.8	30.0	29.8	29.8	29.9	29.5	29.5	29.4	29.2	29.8	30.3	29.8
Wholesale trade													
1990	4.4	4.3	4.4	4.4	4.4	4.5	4.8	4.7	4.8	4.8	4.9	4.7	4.5
1991	5.0	5.0	5.0	5.0	5.0	5.2	5.1	5.1	5.0	5.2	5.2	5.2	5.0
1992	5.2	5.1	5.2	5.2	5.2	5.3	5.0	5.0	5.0	5.1	5.0	5.0	5.1
1993	4.9	5.0	5.0	4.9	4.8	4.9	4.8	4.8	4.8	4.7	4.8	4.8	4.8
1994	4.7	4.6	4.6	4.6	4.7	4.7	4.7	4.5	4.5	4.4	4.4	4.5	4.5
1995	4.4	4.4	4.5	4.4	4.4	4.6	4.4	4.4	4.4	4.4	4.3	4.4	4.4
1996	4.2	4.2	4.2	4.3	4.3	4.3	4.3	4.3	4.3	4.3	4.3	4.3	4.2
1997	4.3	4.4	4.4	4.4	4.4	4.5	4.5	4.5	4.5	4.4	4.4	4.4	4.4
1998	4.4	4.5	4.5	4.4	4.4	4.5	4.5	4.5	4.5	4.4	4.4	4.4	4.4
1999	4.2	4.1	4.1	4.0	4.0	4.1	4.3	4.3	4.3	4.2	4.2	4.3	4.1
2000	4.2	4.2	4.3	4.2	4.2	4.2	4.2	4.2	4.2	4.1	4.1	4.2	4.1
2001	4.1	4.2	4.2	4.2	4.2	4.2	4.2	4.1	4.1	4.1	4.1	4.2	4.1
2002	4.1	4.1	4.1	4.1	4.2	4.2	4.2	4.2	4.3	4.2	4.3	4.3	4.2
2003	4.3	4.3	4.3	4.3	4.3	4.3	4.1	4.1	4.1	4.0	4.0	4.0	4.2
Retail trade													
1990	18.8	18.4	18.5	18.5	18.4	18.6	18.8	18.8	18.7	19.1	19.4	19.7	18.8
1991	19.0	18.5	18.5	18.5	18.7	18.8	19.2	19.6	20.0	20.1	20.2	20.6	19.3
1992	19.6	19.4	19.2	19.4	19.4	19.7	19.4	19.2	19.3	19.7	19.9	20.3	19.5
1993	19.3	19.2	19.1	19.1	19.1	19.1	19.2	19.3	19.2	19.1	19.4	20.1	19.2
1994	19.2	19.0	19.0	18.9	19.2	19.3	19.0	19.2	19.2	19.2	19.8	20.3	19.2
1995	19.5	19.4	19.3	19.7	20.0	20.2	20.2	20.3	20.2	20.2	20.8	21.2	20.0
1996	20.6	20.1	20.0	20.2	20.3	20.4	20.1	20.3	20.2	20.3	20.8	21.2	20.3
1997	20.3	20.0	20.1	20.2	20.3	20.3	20.1	20.3	20.2	20.6	21.2	21.5	20.4
1998	20.3	20.1	20.2	20.3	20.4	20.4	20.5	20.7	20.6	20.4	21.1	21.6	20.5
1999	20.4	20.5	20.6	20.4	20.6	20.7	20.6	20.7	20.6	20.7	21.4	21.8	20.7
2000	20.8	20.5	20.6	20.4	20.6	20.9	20.4	20.6	20.5	20.5	21.0	21.5	20.6
2001	20.3	20.1	20.1	20.0	20.1	20.2	20.1	20.2	20.0	19.8	20.3	20.9	20.1
2002	20.2	20.1	20.1	20.1	20.2	20.3	20.1	20.3	20.1	20.0	20.5	21.0	20.3
2003	20.0	19.8	19.8	19.8	20.0	20.1	20.1	20.1	20.0	20.0	20.6	21.0	20.1
Transportation and utilities													
1990	8.2	8.4	8.1	8.0	7.7	7.8	7.8	7.7	8.2	8.1	7.8	8.1	7.9
1991	8.3	8.1	8.0	7.9	8.0	8.2	8.1	8.1	8.0	8.2	8.6	8.4	8.1
1992	8.1	8.2	8.0	8.0	8.0	8.1	8.0	8.0	7.9	7.8	7.8	7.9	7.9
1993	7.5	7.6	7.6	7.6	7.7	7.7	7.7	7.4	7.7	7.5	7.5	7.6	7.5
1994	7.2	6.9	6.8	6.7	6.7	6.8	7.3	7.1	7.4	7.3	7.4	7.3	7.0
1995	6.8	6.8	6.9	6.9	6.8	6.7	6.9	6.7	6.7	6.4	6.4	6.4	6.7
1996	6.3	6.2	6.1	6.0	6.0	6.2	6.0	6.0	5.9	6.0	6.0	5.9	6.0
1997	5.8	5.9	5.9	6.0	6.1	6.1	6.1	6.0	6.1	6.2	6.0	6.1	6.0
1998	5.9	5.8	5.9	5.8	5.8	5.9	5.7	5.7	5.6	5.6	5.6	5.6	5.7
1999	5.4	5.4	5.4	5.4	5.4	5.4	5.4	5.5	5.5	5.5	5.6	5.6	5.4
2000	5.6	5.5	5.4	5.3	5.2	5.3	5.3	5.4	5.5	5.4	5.5	5.6	5.4
2001	5.6	5.6	5.6	5.7	5.5	5.5	5.5	5.5	5.6	5.5	5.5	5.6	5.5
2002	5.8	5.8	5.7	5.6	5.6	5.5	5.6	5.6	5.6	5.5	5.6	5.5	5.6
2003	5.7	5.7	5.9	5.7	5.5	5.5	5.3	5.3	5.3	5.2	5.2	5.3	5.5
Information													
1990	2.4	2.3	2.3	2.3	2.3	2.3	2.4	2.4	2.3	2.3	2.3	2.3	2.3
1991	2.3	2.3	2.3	2.3	2.3	2.3	2.4	2.3	2.3	2.4	2.4	2.4	2.3
1992	2.2	2.2	2.2	2.2	2.3	2.3	2.3	2.2	2.3	2.3	2.3	2.3	2.2
1993	2.1	2.1	2.1	2.0	2.0	2.1	2.1	2.1	2.0	2.0	2.0	2.0	2.0
1994	2.0	2.0	2.0	2.0	2.0	2.1	2.1	2.1	2.1	2.0	2.1	2.1	2.0
1995	2.0	2.0	2.0	2.1	2.1	2.1	2.2	2.2	2.2	2.1	2.2	2.2	2.1
1996	2.2	2.2	2.2	2.3	2.3	2.3	2.2	2.3	2.3	2.3	2.3	2.3	2.2
1997	2.3	2.3	2.3	2.3	2.4	2.3	2.4	2.4	2.5	2.6	2.5	2.5	2.4
1998	2.4	2.4	2.5	2.5	2.5	2.5	2.6	2.6	2.6	2.6	2.6	2.6	2.5
1999	2.6	2.5	2.5	2.5	2.5	2.5	2.5	2.6	2.5	2.5	2.5	2.6	2.5
2000	2.6	2.6	2.6	2.7	2.8	2.8	2.8	2.7	2.7	2.8	2.8	2.8	2.7
2001	2.8	2.8	2.8	2.8	2.8	2.8	2.9	2.9	2.9	2.9	2.9	2.9	2.8
2002	2.8	2.8	2.8	2.7	2.8	2.8	2.8	2.8	2.8	2.8	2.9	2.9	2.8
2003	2.9	2.8	2.8	2.8	2.8	2.8	2.8	2.8	2.8	2.7	2.7	2.7	2.8

Employment by Industry: Texas—*Continued*

(Numbers in thousands. Not seasonally adjusted.)

Industry	January	February	March	April	May	June	July	August	September	October	November	December	Annual Average
BEAUMONT-PORT ARTHUR —*Continued*													
Financial activities													
1990	6.0	5.9	6.0	5.8	5.8	5.9	5.8	5.7	5.7	5.5	5.5	5.7	5.7
1991	5.4	5.4	5.4	5.4	5.5	5.4	5.5	5.5	5.5	5.4	5.4	5.4	5.4
1992	5.3	5.2	5.3	5.3	5.4	5.4	5.4	5.4	5.4	5.4	5.3	5.3	5.3
1993	5.3	5.3	5.2	5.3	5.2	5.3	5.3	5.4	5.4	5.4	5.3	5.4	5.3
1994	5.3	5.3	5.3	5.3	5.3	5.3	5.4	5.4	5.3	5.4	5.4	5.4	5.3
1995	5.4	5.3	5.4	5.5	5.4	5.5	5.5	5.5	5.5	5.5	5.5	5.5	5.4
1996	5.4	5.5	5.4	5.5	5.5	5.5	5.5	5.5	5.5	5.5	5.5	5.6	5.4
1997	5.5	5.5	5.5	5.6	5.7	5.7	5.7	5.8	5.8	5.9	5.9	6.0	5.7
1998	5.9	5.9	5.9	6.0	6.0	6.1	6.1	6.1	6.1	6.0	6.1	6.1	6.0
1999	6.0	6.0	6.0	6.1	6.1	6.2	6.2	6.2	6.2	6.2	6.3	6.4	6.1
2000	6.1	6.1	6.2	6.0	6.0	6.1	6.1	6.1	6.1	6.1	6.2	6.3	6.1
2001	6.0	6.0	6.1	6.0	6.0	6.0	5.9	6.0	5.9	5.9	5.9	6.0	5.9
2002	5.7	5.7	5.8	5.9	6.0	6.1	6.1	6.1	6.1	6.1	6.2	6.2	6.0
2003	6.2	6.2	6.2	6.2	6.2	6.2	6.2	6.2	6.2	6.3	6.3	6.3	6.2
Professional and business services													
1990	9.0	9.0	9.2	9.6	10.0	10.2	10.3	10.8	10.6	10.5	10.4	10.4	10.0
1991	10.7	10.9	10.9	11.3	11.0	10.9	10.8	10.9	10.7	10.4	10.1	9.9	10.7
1992	9.9	10.2	10.1	10.0	10.2	10.4	10.6	10.6	10.4	10.8	10.6	10.6	10.3
1993	10.2	10.3	10.2	10.2	10.0	10.2	10.5	10.4	10.2	10.2	10.3	10.4	10.2
1994	10.3	10.4	10.4	10.6	10.5	10.5	10.9	11.1	11.2	11.1	11.0	11.1	10.7
1995	11.1	11.1	11.2	11.3	11.3	11.4	11.3	11.3	11.3	11.2	11.0	11.0	11.2
1996	10.7	10.7	10.8	10.6	10.3	10.3	10.4	10.4	10.3	10.5	10.5	10.5	10.5
1997	10.6	10.7	10.9	10.8	10.8	10.8	10.9	11.0	11.2	11.2	11.0	11.2	10.9
1998	11.3	11.4	11.5	11.3	11.6	11.6	11.5	11.5	11.3	11.6	11.5	11.6	11.4
1999	11.3	11.4	11.4	11.7	11.8	11.9	11.8	11.9	11.9	11.8	11.9	12.0	11.7
2000	11.8	12.1	12.3	12.0	11.8	11.9	11.7	11.9	11.9	12.0	11.9	12.1	11.9
2001	12.2	12.2	12.2	12.2	12.4	12.6	12.5	12.6	12.8	12.9	12.9	13.1	12.5
2002	13.0	12.9	13.0	13.1	13.0	13.6	12.8	13.0	12.9	12.6	12.5	12.4	12.9
2003	12.2	12.2	12.2	12.5	12.5	12.2	12.3	12.5	12.5	12.6	12.4	12.6	12.4
Educational and health services													
1990	17.5	17.6	17.9	17.6	17.7	17.9	17.9	17.9	18.1	18.2	18.0	18.1	17.8
1991	17.6	17.9	18.0	18.4	18.6	18.8	18.9	18.9	18.6	18.4	18.5	19.2	18.4
1992	19.4	19.6	19.5	19.6	19.8	19.9	19.8	19.9	20.0	20.0	19.9	20.0	19.7
1993	20.0	20.1	20.2	20.4	20.7	20.8	20.7	20.8	20.8	20.8	20.8	20.9	20.5
1994	20.8	20.9	20.9	21.0	21.0	20.8	20.4	20.5	20.7	20.8	20.8	20.8	20.7
1995	20.8	20.9	21.1	21.5	21.6	21.6	21.5	21.4	21.2	21.0	21.0	21.1	21.2
1996	21.0	21.1	21.1	21.4	21.9	21.9	21.5	21.6	21.6	21.7	21.8	21.8	21.5
1997	21.9	22.0	22.3	22.2	22.3	22.4	22.3	22.3	22.4	22.5	22.6	22.6	22.3
1998	22.4	22.4	22.6	22.4	22.4	22.3	22.0	22.1	22.0	21.9	21.8	21.9	22.1
1999	22.5	21.5	21.4	21.3	21.2	21.3	21.1	21.1	21.2	21.2	21.0	21.0	21.3
2000	21.1	21.1	21.2	21.3	21.4	21.6	21.4	21.7	21.4	21.9	21.9	21.9	21.4
2001	21.6	21.6	21.7	21.8	21.9	21.9	21.8	21.9	22.0	22.0	22.1	22.2	21.8
2002	22.1	22.3	22.3	22.2	22.3	22.3	22.3	22.5	22.6	22.3	22.3	22.3	22.3
2003	22.1	22.3	22.4	22.9	23.0	22.9	22.9	22.7	22.7	22.5	22.7	22.4	22.6
Leisure and hospitality													
1990	10.3	10.3	10.5	10.9	11.1	11.3	11.4	11.4	11.2	10.9	10.8	10.8	10.9
1991	11.2	11.3	11.4	11.1	11.4	11.5	11.5	11.7	11.6	11.4	11.5	11.6	11.4
1992	11.1	11.2	11.3	11.6	11.6	11.6	11.7	11.6	11.5	11.5	11.4	11.4	11.4
1993	11.4	11.6	11.7	11.8	11.9	12.0	12.2	12.2	12.0	11.8	11.8	11.8	11.8
1994	11.4	11.6	11.9	11.9	12.1	12.3	12.1	12.3	12.1	12.0	12.2	12.3	12.0
1995	12.0	12.0	12.2	12.3	12.7	12.8	12.6	12.7	12.6	12.2	12.3	12.4	12.4
1996	12.1	12.1	12.2	12.8	13.0	13.1	12.8	13.1	12.9	12.7	12.5	12.5	12.6
1997	12.3	12.5	12.7	12.6	12.7	12.8	12.9	12.8	12.7	12.5	12.5	12.7	12.6
1998	12.5	12.4	12.5	13.2	13.3	13.5	13.4	13.5	13.4	13.1	13.0	13.0	13.0
1999	12.9	13.2	13.4	13.6	13.5	13.6	13.4	13.6	13.4	13.4	13.2	13.2	13.3
2000	13.1	13.3	13.7	13.4	13.4	13.6	13.2	13.4	13.3	13.0	13.1	13.1	13.3
2001	13.0	12.9	13.1	12.9	13.3	13.3	13.3	13.4	13.2	12.7	12.6	12.7	13.0
2002	12.4	12.6	12.8	12.9	13.0	13.4	13.3	13.3	13.2	13.0	13.2	13.2	13.0
2003	13.1	13.2	13.4	13.4	13.5	13.7	13.5	13.7	13.7	13.6	13.8	13.8	13.5
Other services													
1990	5.0	4.9	5.0	4.9	4.9	5.2	5.1	5.1	5.0	5.0	5.0	5.0	5.0
1991	5.1	5.1	5.2	5.2	5.3	5.5	5.5	5.5	5.4	5.3	5.3	5.3	5.3
1992	5.1	5.2	5.2	5.2	5.2	5.4	5.4	5.3	5.3	5.3	5.3	5.3	5.2
1993	5.2	5.3	5.3	5.4	5.5	5.5	5.6	5.5	5.4	5.4	5.3	5.4	5.4
1994	5.2	5.3	5.3	5.4	5.5	5.5	5.5	5.4	5.4	5.3	5.4	5.5	5.3
1995	5.4	5.4	5.4	5.5	5.6	5.8	5.7	5.8	5.7	5.5	5.6	5.6	5.5
1996	5.6	5.6	5.6	5.7	5.8	5.9	5.9	5.9	5.9	5.8	5.7	5.8	5.7
1997	5.6	5.8	5.8	5.9	6.0	6.0	6.1	6.0	6.0	5.9	5.9	5.9	5.9
1998	5.9	6.0	6.0	6.1	6.2	6.3	6.3	6.2	6.2	6.1	6.0	6.1	6.1
1999	6.2	6.3	6.3	6.1	6.1	6.1	6.3	6.2	6.2	6.1	6.1	6.2	6.1
2000	6.0	6.1	6.1	6.1	6.1	6.2	6.3	6.3	6.1	6.1	6.2	6.2	6.1
2001	6.1	6.0	6.0	6.0	6.1	6.1	6.0	6.0	5.9	5.9	5.9	5.9	5.9
2002	6.0	6.0	6.0	6.1	6.2	6.4	6.2	6.2	6.2	6.1	6.1	6.1	6.1
2003	6.1	6.1	6.1	6.0	6.2	6.3	6.3	6.3	6.2	6.2	6.1	6.1	6.2

Employment by Industry: Texas—*Continued*

(Numbers in thousands. Not seasonally adjusted.)

Industry	January	February	March	April	May	June	July	August	September	October	November	December	Annual Average
BEAUMONT-PORT ARTHUR *—Continued*													
Government													
1990	21.4	21.7	21.6	21.8	22.2	21.0	20.2	19.8	21.2	21.6	21.7	21.9	21.3
1991	21.9	22.0	22.1	22.1	22.3	21.7	20.4	20.3	21.7	22.1	22.3	22.4	21.7
1992	22.3	22.4	22.5	22.6	22.7	21.7	20.6	20.7	22.4	23.0	23.2	23.3	22.2
1993	23.2	23.3	23.5	23.3	23.5	22.6	21.8	21.6	23.6	24.1	24.3	24.3	23.2
1994	24.0	24.2	24.2	24.2	24.3	23.4	22.4	22.5	24.5	24.8	25.0	25.0	24.0
1995	25.0	25.1	25.1	25.0	25.1	24.4	23.1	23.5	25.3	25.7	25.9	25.8	24.9
1996	25.7	25.8	25.8	25.9	25.8	25.2	24.1	24.3	25.8	26.2	26.4	26.4	25.6
1997	26.1	26.2	26.4	26.4	26.6	25.7	24.6	24.8	26.1	26.7	27.0	26.5	26.0
1998	26.5	26.5	26.5	26.4	26.4	25.8	24.6	24.7	25.9	26.5	26.8	26.8	26.1
1999	26.7	26.8	26.9	27.3	27.1	25.6	24.5	25.9	27.0	27.2	27.4	27.5	26.6
2000	27.4	27.6	27.7	27.6	28.1	26.5	25.3	26.0	27.0	27.5	27.6	27.6	27.1
2001	27.5	27.5	27.6	27.4	27.5	27.6	25.6	26.3	27.2	27.8	28.0	27.9	27.3
2002	27.8	27.9	28.0	27.8	27.8	27.5	24.5	26.1	27.3	27.7	28.1	28.2	27.4
2003	27.9	28.0	27.8	28.0	28.0	26.9	25.4	25.4	27.7	27.4	27.8	27.7	27.3
Federal government													
1990	1.4	1.4	1.5	1.7	2.0	1.8	1.7	1.4	1.4	1.4	1.4	1.5	1.5
1991	1.4	1.4	1.4	1.4	1.4	1.4	1.4	1.4	1.4	1.4	1.4	1.4	1.4
1992	1.3	1.4	1.4	1.4	1.4	1.4	1.3	1.4	1.4	1.4	1.4	1.4	1.3
1993	1.4	1.4	1.4	1.3	1.3	1.4	1.4	1.4	1.4	1.4	1.4	1.4	1.3
1994	1.3	1.3	1.3	1.4	1.4	1.4	1.6	1.7	1.8	1.7	1.7	1.7	1.5
1995	1.7	1.7	1.7	1.7	1.7	1.8	1.7	1.8	2.0	2.0	2.2	2.2	1.8
1996	2.1	2.1	2.1	2.1	2.0	2.0	2.0	2.1	2.1	2.2	2.4	2.5	2.1
1997	2.5	2.5	2.5	2.6	2.6	2.6	2.7	2.7	2.8	2.8	2.8	2.8	2.6
1998	2.7	2.7	2.7	2.6	2.6	2.7	2.7	2.6	2.7	2.8	2.9	3.1	2.7
1999	2.9	3.0	2.9	3.1	2.9	2.9	2.9	2.9	2.8	2.8	2.9	3.0	2.9
2000	2.9	2.9	2.9	3.0	3.6	2.9	2.9	2.8	2.7	2.7	2.7	2.8	2.9
2001	2.7	2.7	2.7	2.7	2.7	2.9	3.0	3.0	3.1	3.0	3.1	3.1	2.9
2002	3.1	3.1	3.1	3.0	3.0	3.2	3.2	3.3	3.3	3.3	3.6	3.6	3.2
2003	3.5	3.5	3.4	3.4	3.4	3.3	3.3	3.2	3.3	3.4	3.5	3.5	3.4
State government													
1990	4.4	4.6	4.4	4.4	4.5	3.9	3.8	3.8	4.2	4.4	4.4	4.4	4.2
1991	4.4	4.4	4.5	4.5	4.5	4.1	3.9	3.9	4.1	4.4	4.4	4.4	4.2
1992	4.4	4.4	4.4	4.4	4.4	3.8	3.7	3.8	4.2	4.4	4.4	4.5	4.2
1993	4.5	4.5	4.6	4.6	4.7	4.0	4.6	4.5	5.2	5.3	5.3	5.2	4.7
1994	5.1	5.2	5.2	5.2	5.2	4.7	4.6	4.7	5.4	5.6	5.7	5.7	5.1
1995	5.7	5.7	5.7	5.7	5.7	5.2	5.1	5.2	5.9	6.1	6.1	6.0	5.6
1996	6.1	6.0	6.0	6.1	6.0	5.5	5.5	5.5	6.1	6.2	6.2	6.1	5.9
1997	6.1	6.0	6.1	6.0	6.1	5.8	5.7	5.7	5.9	6.1	6.2	6.1	5.9
1998	6.1	6.0	6.0	6.0	6.0	5.7	5.6	5.6	5.8	6.0	6.0	6.0	5.9
1999	6.0	6.0	6.1	6.1	6.1	5.7	5.8	5.6	5.9	6.1	6.1	6.1	5.9
2000	6.1	6.1	6.1	6.1	6.1	5.7	5.8	5.7	5.6	5.9	5.9	5.9	5.9
2001	5.9	5.9	5.9	5.9	6.0	6.0	5.7	5.7	5.7	6.0	6.1	6.0	5.8
2002	6.1	6.0	6.0	6.1	6.1	5.8	5.8	5.7	5.8	6.1	6.1	6.1	6.0
2003	6.1	6.1	6.1	6.2	6.2	5.7	5.8	5.7	5.7	6.0	6.1	6.0	6.0
Local government													
1990	15.6	15.7	15.7	15.7	15.7	15.3	14.7	14.6	15.6	15.8	15.9	16.0	15.5
1991	16.1	16.2	16.2	16.2	16.4	16.2	15.1	15.0	16.2	16.3	16.5	16.6	16.0
1992	16.6	16.6	16.7	16.8	16.9	16.5	15.6	15.5	16.8	17.2	17.4	17.4	16.6
1993	17.3	17.4	17.5	17.4	17.5	17.2	15.8	15.7	17.0	17.4	17.6	17.7	17.1
1994	17.6	17.7	17.7	17.6	17.7	17.3	16.2	16.1	17.3	17.5	17.6	17.6	17.3
1995	17.6	17.7	17.7	17.6	17.7	17.4	16.3	16.5	17.4	17.6	17.6	17.6	17.3
1996	17.5	17.7	17.7	17.7	17.8	17.7	16.6	16.7	17.6	17.8	17.8	17.8	17.5
1997	17.5	17.7	17.8	17.8	17.9	17.3	16.2	16.4	17.4	17.8	18.0	17.6	17.4
1998	17.7	17.8	17.8	17.8	17.8	17.4	16.3	16.5	17.4	17.7	17.9	17.7	17.4
1999	17.8	17.8	17.9	18.1	18.1	17.0	15.8	17.4	18.3	18.3	18.4	18.4	17.7
2000	18.4	18.6	18.7	18.5	18.4	17.9	16.6	17.5	18.7	18.9	19.0	18.9	18.3
2001	18.9	18.9	19.0	18.8	18.8	18.7	16.9	17.6	18.4	18.8	18.8	18.8	18.5
2002	18.6	18.8	18.9	18.7	18.7	18.5	15.5	17.1	18.2	18.3	18.4	18.5	18.2
2003	18.3	18.4	18.3	18.4	18.4	17.9	16.3	16.5	18.7	18.0	18.2	18.2	18.0
BROWNSVILLE-HARLINGEN													
Total nonfarm													
1990	74.2	74.6	75.3	75.6	76.1	76.3	76.3	77.0	76.5	76.8	77.5	78.5	76.2
1991	76.8	76.9	78.0	76.6	76.8	78.0	77.2	78.6	79.1	78.3	78.8	80.1	77.9
1992	78.5	79.5	80.5	80.8	81.7	81.5	80.3	81.7	82.0	82.4	83.5	84.0	81.3
1993	84.0	84.8	85.9	86.0	86.4	86.1	85.1	86.0	86.9	86.7	87.1	87.7	86.0
1994	87.5	88.4	89.6	89.9	90.3	91.1	90.3	91.1	90.8	91.5	92.6	92.9	90.5
1995	91.7	92.1	92.8	92.2	91.9	92.1	90.5	91.1	92.1	92.4	92.5	93.2	92.0
1996	92.2	92.5	92.6	93.5	93.8	93.7	93.0	94.7	94.6	95.4	95.6	95.9	93.9
1997	95.5	96.4	97.1	97.1	97.0	97.6	97.3	97.7	97.6	97.9	98.2	98.8	97.3
1998	98.0	98.2	99.6	99.5	99.6	100.3	99.4	99.2	99.7	100.3	100.8	101.1	99.6
1999	100.8	100.8	101.7	103.0	103.3	105.4	104.3	104.1	104.5	104.9	105.7	107.0	103.7
2000	106.1	106.4	108.0	108.0	109.1	110.7	109.5	110.6	110.5	110.2	111.4	112.5	109.4
2001	110.7	111.4	112.4	112.0	112.3	111.5	109.6	111.0	111.3	110.0	111.2	112.6	111.3
2002	111.8	112.6	113.7	114.6	115.1	115.2	114.1	114.5	115.3	115.0	115.4	115.8	114.4
2003	114.8	114.4	115.1	114.8	115.1	114.7	114.1	113.9	114.3	114.1	114.9	115.2	114.6

Employment by Industry: Texas—*Continued*

(Numbers in thousands. Not seasonally adjusted.)

Industry	January	February	March	April	May	June	July	August	September	October	November	December	Annual Average
BROWNSVILLE-HARLINGEN—*Continued*													
Total private													
1990	56.7	57.0	57.7	58.0	58.4	59.5	60.0	60.4	59.2	59.3	60.0	60.9	58.9
1991	59.1	59.2	60.4	59.0	59.2	60.7	60.6	61.4	61.1	60.1	60.3	61.7	60.2
1992	60.2	60.9	62.0	62.1	63.0	62.9	63.1	64.0	63.2	63.3	63.8	64.5	62.7
1993	64.2	64.9	65.9	65.8	66.3	66.4	67.3	67.4	67.0	66.3	66.5	67.1	66.2
1994	66.8	67.4	68.7	69.0	69.4	70.8	71.0	71.1	69.9	70.1	70.6	71.2	69.6
1995	70.2	70.3	71.0	70.3	70.1	70.9	70.5	70.4	70.5	70.4	70.4	71.2	70.5
1996	70.5	70.3	70.5	71.4	71.7	72.4	72.7	73.7	72.4	72.8	72.8	73.2	72.0
1997	73.3	73.6	74.3	74.2	74.2	75.5	76.1	75.8	74.8	74.6	74.7	75.3	74.7
1998	74.4	74.7	76.0	76.0	75.8	77.3	77.4	77.0	76.4	76.6	77.0	77.3	76.3
1999	76.9	76.8	77.7	79.0	79.3	81.8	81.9	81.1	80.4	80.5	81.0	82.3	79.8
2000	81.2	81.5	82.8	82.8	83.6	85.8	86.2	86.6	85.6	84.2	85.3	86.3	84.3
2001	84.6	85.1	85.8	85.8	86.4	86.6	86.2	86.7	85.8	84.0	84.9	86.3	85.6
2002	85.6	86.3	87.2	88.1	88.9	89.5	89.8	89.9	89.5	88.6	89.0	89.2	88.5
2003	88.6	88.1	88.6	88.1	88.8	88.7	89.4	89.0	88.4	87.5	88.3	88.9	88.5
Goods-producing													
1990	12.9	12.8	12.7	12.9	13.2	13.5	13.8	14.1	14.0	14.0	14.1	14.0	13.5
1991	12.9	12.8	12.8	12.4	12.4	12.8	12.6	13.1	13.1	12.9	12.9	13.1	12.8
1992	12.6	12.8	12.9	13.2	13.6	13.6	13.6	13.6	13.6	13.8	13.9	14.0	13.4
1993	14.1	14.2	14.6	14.7	15.1	15.2	15.3	15.5	15.4	15.3	15.2	15.1	14.9
1994	15.2	15.3	15.4	15.7	15.7	15.9	15.9	16.0	15.9	15.9	16.1	16.3	15.7
1995	16.2	16.5	16.4	16.4	16.4	16.5	16.2	16.4	16.4	16.1	16.1	16.1	16.3
1996	15.8	15.7	15.5	16.0	16.0	16.3	16.0	16.2	16.2	16.5	16.5	16.6	16.1
1997	16.4	16.4	16.4	16.0	16.0	16.2	16.2	16.3	16.3	16.1	15.9	16.0	16.1
1998	15.9	15.9	16.2	16.2	16.1	16.2	16.3	16.4	16.4	16.5	16.5	16.3	16.2
1999	15.9	15.5	15.7	15.9	16.2	16.4	16.5	16.6	16.1	15.8	15.5	15.7	15.9
2000	15.4	15.5	15.6	16.0	16.1	16.4	16.7	16.8	16.8	16.4	16.6	16.6	16.2
2001	16.2	16.4	16.3	16.3	16.2	15.9	15.8	15.8	15.7	15.1	14.9	15.0	15.8
2002	14.4	14.3	13.8	14.6	14.6	14.6	14.9	15.0	14.8	14.4	14.2	13.9	14.5
2003	13.7	13.6	13.4	13.3	13.4	13.3	13.3	13.2	13.1	12.9	12.8	12.8	13.2
Construction and mining													
1990	2.3	2.3	2.3	2.3	2.4	2.5	2.6	2.6	2.5	2.4	2.5	2.4	2.4
1991	2.3	2.3	2.3	2.3	2.3	2.3	2.2	2.3	2.3	2.4	2.4	2.4	2.3
1992	2.3	2.3	2.3	2.3	2.5	2.4	2.3	2.3	2.2	2.3	2.3	2.2	2.3
1993	2.3	2.3	2.3	2.5	2.6	2.6	2.7	2.8	2.7	2.7	2.6	2.6	2.5
1994	2.7	2.6	2.7	2.7	2.6	2.7	2.8	2.7	2.6	2.6	2.7	2.7	2.6
1995	2.8	3.0	3.0	3.0	3.1	3.1	3.1	3.1	3.1	3.0	3.0	3.0	3.0
1996	2.8	2.8	2.7	2.9	2.9	3.0	2.9	2.9	3.0	3.1	3.1	3.1	2.9
1997	3.1	3.1	3.1	3.2	3.3	3.4	3.3	3.3	3.3	3.2	3.2	3.2	3.2
1998	3.3	3.3	3.4	3.4	3.4	3.4	3.6	3.5	3.5	3.5	3.5	3.5	3.4
1999	3.5	3.5	3.5	3.5	3.5	3.6	3.8	3.8	3.8	3.7	3.7	3.8	3.6
2000	3.6	3.6	3.7	3.8	3.9	4.0	4.2	4.2	4.2	4.2	4.2	4.2	3.9
2001	4.4	4.5	4.5	4.6	4.6	4.7	4.6	4.6	4.5	4.3	4.2	4.2	4.4
2002	4.1	4.0	4.1	4.2	4.3	4.3	4.4	4.4	4.4	4.3	4.2	4.1	4.2
2003	4.2	4.2	4.1	3.9	4.0	3.9	3.9	4.0	3.9	3.8	3.8	3.8	4.0
Manufacturing													
1990	10.6	10.5	10.4	10.6	10.8	11.0	11.2	11.5	11.5	11.6	11.6	11.6	11.0
1991	10.6	10.5	10.5	10.1	10.1	10.5	10.4	10.8	10.8	10.5	10.5	10.7	10.5
1992	10.3	10.5	10.6	10.9	11.1	11.2	11.3	11.3	11.4	11.5	11.6	11.8	11.1
1993	11.8	11.9	12.3	12.2	12.5	12.6	12.6	12.7	12.7	12.6	12.6	12.5	12.4
1994	12.5	12.7	12.7	13.0	13.1	13.2	13.1	13.3	13.3	13.3	13.4	13.6	13.1
1995	13.4	13.5	13.4	13.4	13.3	13.4	13.1	13.3	13.3	13.1	13.1	13.1	13.2
1996	13.0	12.9	12.8	13.1	13.1	13.3	13.1	13.3	13.2	13.4	13.4	13.5	13.1
1997	13.3	13.3	13.3	12.8	12.7	12.8	12.9	13.0	13.0	12.9	12.7	12.8	12.9
1998	12.6	12.6	12.8	12.8	12.7	12.8	12.7	12.9	12.9	13.0	13.0	12.8	12.8
1999	12.4	12.0	12.2	12.4	12.7	12.8	12.7	12.8	12.3	12.1	11.8	11.9	12.3
2000	11.8	11.9	11.9	12.2	12.2	12.4	12.5	12.6	12.6	12.2	12.4	12.4	12.2
2001	11.8	11.9	11.8	11.7	11.6	11.2	11.2	11.2	11.2	10.8	10.7	10.8	11.3
2002	10.3	10.3	9.7	10.4	10.3	10.3	10.5	10.6	10.4	10.1	10.0	9.8	10.2
2003	9.5	9.4	9.3	9.4	9.4	9.4	9.4	9.2	9.2	9.1	9.0	9.0	9.3
Service-providing													
1990	61.3	61.8	62.6	62.7	62.9	62.8	62.5	62.9	62.5	62.8	63.4	64.5	62.7
1991	63.9	64.1	65.2	64.2	64.4	65.2	64.6	65.5	66.0	65.4	65.9	67.0	65.1
1992	65.9	66.7	67.6	67.6	68.1	67.9	66.7	68.1	68.4	68.6	69.6	70.0	67.9
1993	69.9	70.6	71.3	71.3	71.3	70.9	69.8	70.5	71.5	71.4	71.9	72.6	71.0
1994	72.3	73.1	74.2	74.2	74.6	75.2	74.4	75.1	74.9	75.6	76.5	76.6	74.7
1995	75.5	75.6	76.4	75.8	75.5	75.6	74.3	74.7	75.7	76.3	76.4	77.1	75.7
1996	76.4	76.8	77.1	77.5	77.8	77.4	77.0	78.5	78.4	78.9	79.1	79.3	77.8
1997	79.1	80.0	80.7	81.1	81.0	81.4	81.1	81.4	81.3	81.8	82.3	82.8	81.1
1998	82.1	82.3	83.4	83.3	83.5	84.1	83.1	82.8	83.3	83.8	84.3	84.8	83.4
1999	84.9	85.3	86.0	87.1	87.1	89.0	87.8	87.5	88.4	89.1	90.2	91.3	87.8
2000	90.7	90.9	92.4	92.0	93.0	94.3	92.8	93.8	93.7	93.8	94.8	95.9	93.1
2001	94.5	95.0	96.1	95.7	96.1	95.6	93.8	95.2	95.6	94.9	96.3	97.6	95.5
2002	97.4	98.3	99.9	100.0	100.5	100.6	99.2	99.5	100.5	100.6	101.2	101.9	100.0
2003	101.1	100.8	101.7	101.5	101.7	101.4	100.8	100.7	101.2	101.2	102.1	102.4	101.4

Employment by Industry: Texas—*Continued*

(Numbers in thousands. Not seasonally adjusted.)

Industry	January	February	March	April	May	June	July	August	September	October	November	December	Annual Average
BROWNSVILLE-HARLINGEN—*Continued*													
Trade, transportation, and utilities													
1990	16.8	16.6	16.7	16.8	16.8	17.0	17.1	17.4	17.1	17.0	17.4	17.8	17.0
1991	17.8	17.6	18.1	17.9	18.0	18.2	18.2	18.4	18.5	18.5	18.6	19.0	18.2
1992	18.1	18.1	18.3	18.5	18.8	18.8	19.0	19.0	18.8	19.2	19.6	19.9	18.8
1993	19.0	19.1	18.8	18.9	18.8	18.7	18.8	18.9	19.1	18.7	19.1	19.6	18.9
1994	18.8	18.8	19.0	19.1	19.2	19.4	19.2	19.4	19.3	19.7	19.9	20.3	19.3
1995	19.4	19.0	19.0	18.9	18.6	18.8	18.6	18.6	18.9	19.2	19.3	19.8	19.0
1996	19.0	18.7	18.5	19.0	19.1	19.2	19.3	19.6	19.2	19.4	19.5	19.7	19.1
1997	19.2	19.1	19.1	19.2	19.2	19.6	19.6	19.4	19.4	19.8	20.2	20.4	19.5
1998	19.5	19.5	19.8	19.8	19.8	19.9	20.0	19.9	19.9	20.3	20.6	20.9	19.9
1999	20.5	20.2	20.3	20.5	20.5	21.2	21.3	21.1	21.0	21.5	22.1	22.6	21.0
2000	21.3	20.9	21.1	21.6	21.7	21.6	21.7	21.8	21.7	22.0	22.7	23.2	21.7
2001	22.7	22.4	22.4	22.6	22.8	22.8	22.8	22.6	22.4	22.0	22.6	23.1	22.6
2002	22.4	22.0	22.2	22.4	22.7	22.8	23.0	22.9	23.0	22.7	23.1	23.7	22.7
2003	22.8	22.3	22.3	22.3	22.2	22.2	22.7	22.4	22.4	22.5	23.1	23.4	22.6
Wholesale trade													
1990	2.9	2.9	3.0	3.0	3.1	3.1	3.1	3.1	3.0	3.0	3.0	3.1	3.0
1991	3.3	3.3	3.4	3.4	3.4	3.5	3.5	3.5	3.5	3.6	3.5	3.5	3.4
1992	3.4	3.4	3.5	3.4	3.5	3.5	3.5	3.5	3.5	3.6	3.6	3.5	3.4
1993	3.3	3.4	3.1	3.3	3.3	3.3	3.3	3.3	3.4	3.3	3.3	3.3	3.3
1994	3.1	3.1	3.1	3.1	3.2	3.2	3.1	3.1	3.1	3.1	3.1	3.1	3.1
1995	3.1	3.1	3.2	3.1	3.1	3.1	3.1	3.1	3.1	3.2	3.1	3.2	3.1
1996	3.2	3.2	3.2	3.3	3.3	3.3	3.4	3.5	3.4	3.3	3.2	3.2	3.2
1997	3.2	3.2	3.2	3.3	3.3	3.3	3.3	3.2	3.2	3.2	3.2	3.2	3.2
1998	3.1	3.1	3.2	3.2	3.2	3.2	3.2	3.1	3.1	3.1	3.1	3.1	3.1
1999	3.2	3.2	3.2	3.5	3.5	3.5	3.5	3.5	3.5	3.5	3.5	3.6	3.4
2000	3.5	3.4	3.5	3.5	3.6	3.5	3.5	3.6	3.6	3.6	3.6	3.7	3.5
2001	3.6	3.7	3.7	3.8	3.8	3.8	3.7	3.8	3.8	3.7	3.7	3.7	3.7
2002	3.7	3.7	3.7	3.7	3.8	3.8	3.8	3.8	3.8	3.8	3.7	3.8	3.8
2003	3.7	3.7	3.7	3.6	3.6	3.6	3.6	3.6	3.6	3.6	3.6	3.6	3.6
Retail trade													
1990	11.7	11.5	11.5	11.6	11.5	11.7	11.7	11.9	11.8	11.7	12.1	12.4	11.7
1991	12.2	11.9	12.1	11.9	11.9	12.1	12.1	12.2	12.2	12.1	12.3	12.7	12.1
1992	12.0	11.9	12.0	12.4	12.5	12.5	12.8	12.8	12.7	12.9	13.3	13.7	12.6
1993	13.1	13.1	13.1	12.9	12.8	12.7	12.7	12.8	12.8	12.7	13.1	13.5	12.9
1994	12.9	12.9	13.1	13.2	13.2	13.3	13.3	13.4	13.4	13.8	14.0	14.4	13.4
1995	13.5	13.2	13.1	12.9	12.7	12.8	12.6	12.6	12.8	13.0	13.2	13.6	13.0
1996	12.8	12.5	12.4	12.7	12.8	12.9	12.8	12.9	12.7	13.0	13.2	13.4	12.8
1997	12.9	12.7	12.7	12.6	12.6	12.9	12.9	12.9	12.8	13.1	13.4	13.7	12.9
1998	12.8	12.7	12.8	12.8	12.9	13.0	13.0	13.1	13.0	13.5	13.8	14.1	13.1
1999	13.5	13.2	13.3	13.1	13.1	13.7	13.8	13.6	13.5	14.0	14.5	14.9	13.6
2000	13.8	13.5	13.5	13.9	13.9	13.8	13.9	13.8	13.7	14.1	14.8	15.2	13.9
2001	14.6	14.2	14.2	14.5	14.7	14.7	14.8	14.5	14.3	14.1	14.7	15.2	14.5
2002	14.6	14.2	14.4	14.6	14.7	14.8	15.0	14.8	14.9	14.8	15.3	15.8	14.8
2003	15.1	14.6	14.7	14.8	14.7	14.7	15.1	14.8	14.7	14.9	15.5	15.8	15.0
Transportation and utilities													
1990	2.2	2.2	2.2	2.2	2.2	2.2	2.3	2.4	2.3	2.3	2.3	2.3	2.2
1991	2.3	2.4	2.6	2.6	2.7	2.6	2.6	2.7	2.8	2.8	2.8	2.8	2.6
1992	2.7	2.8	2.8	2.7	2.8	2.8	2.7	2.7	2.6	2.7	2.7	2.7	2.7
1993	2.6	2.6	2.6	2.7	2.7	2.7	2.8	2.8	2.9	2.7	2.7	2.8	2.7
1994	2.8	2.8	2.8	2.8	2.8	2.9	2.8	2.9	2.8	2.8	2.8	2.8	2.8
1995	2.8	2.7	2.7	2.9	2.8	2.9	2.9	2.9	3.0	3.0	3.0	3.0	2.8
1996	3.0	3.0	2.9	3.0	3.0	3.0	3.1	3.2	3.1	3.1	3.1	3.1	3.0
1997	3.1	3.2	3.2	3.3	3.3	3.4	3.4	3.3	3.4	3.5	3.6	3.5	3.3
1998	3.6	3.7	3.8	3.8	3.7	3.7	3.8	3.7	3.8	3.7	3.7	3.7	3.7
1999	3.8	3.8	3.8	3.9	3.9	4.0	4.0	4.0	4.0	4.0	4.1	4.1	3.9
2000	4.0	4.0	4.1	4.2	4.2	4.3	4.3	4.4	4.4	4.3	4.3	4.3	4.2
2001	4.5	4.5	4.5	4.3	4.3	4.3	4.3	4.3	4.3	4.2	4.2	4.2	4.3
2002	4.1	4.1	4.1	4.1	4.2	4.2	4.2	4.3	4.3	4.1	4.1	4.1	4.2
2003	4.0	4.0	3.9	3.9	3.9	3.9	4.0	4.0	4.1	4.0	4.0	4.0	4.0
Information													
1990	1.2	1.2	1.2	1.3	1.3	1.3	1.4	1.3	1.3	1.3	1.3	1.4	1.2
1991	1.3	1.3	1.3	1.3	1.3	1.3	1.3	1.3	1.2	1.2	1.2	1.2	1.2
1992	1.2	1.2	1.2	1.2	1.2	1.2	1.2	1.2	1.2	1.3	1.3	1.3	1.2
1993	1.4	1.4	1.4	1.5	1.5	1.5	1.5	1.5	1.5	1.5	1.5	1.6	1.4
1994	1.5	1.5	1.6	1.4	1.4	1.5	1.5	1.5	1.4	1.4	1.5	1.5	1.4
1995	1.5	1.5	1.5	1.5	1.5	1.5	1.6	1.5	1.6	1.6	1.6	1.6	1.5
1996	1.6	1.6	1.6	1.7	1.7	1.7	1.7	1.7	1.6	1.6	1.5	1.5	1.6
1997	1.5	1.5	1.4	1.4	1.4	1.4	1.4	1.4	1.4	1.4	1.4	1.4	1.4
1998	1.3	1.4	1.4	1.4	1.4	1.4	1.4	1.4	1.4	1.4	1.3	1.3	1.3
1999	1.3	1.3	1.3	1.4	1.4	1.4	1.4	1.4	1.4	1.4	1.4	1.4	1.3
2000	1.4	1.4	1.5	1.4	1.4	1.5	1.5	1.5	1.5	1.5	1.5	1.5	1.4
2001	1.5	1.5	1.5	1.5	1.5	1.6	1.4	1.5	1.5	1.5	1.5	1.5	1.5
2002	1.5	1.5	1.5	1.5	1.5	1.5	1.5	1.5	1.5	1.5	1.5	1.5	1.5
2003	1.5	1.5	1.5	1.4	1.4	1.4	1.4	1.4	1.4	1.4	1.4	1.4	1.4

Employment by Industry: Texas—*Continued*

(Numbers in thousands. Not seasonally adjusted.)

Industry	January	February	March	April	May	June	July	August	September	October	November	December	Annual Average
BROWNSVILLE-HARLINGEN—*Continued*													
Financial activities													
1990	3.9	3.9	4.0	3.9	3.9	4.0	4.0	4.0	3.9	3.9	3.9	3.9	3.9
1991	3.8	3.8	3.9	3.8	3.8	3.9	3.8	3.8	3.8	3.7	3.7	3.8	3.8
1992	3.6	3.6	3.7	3.6	3.6	3.6	3.7	3.6	3.6	3.6	3.6	3.6	3.6
1993	3.5	3.5	3.6	3.7	3.7	3.8	3.8	3.8	3.8	3.8	3.8	3.7	3.7
1994	3.7	3.7	3.8	3.8	3.8	3.9	3.9	3.9	3.8	3.8	3.7	3.7	3.7
1995	3.8	3.7	3.8	3.8	3.8	3.9	4.0	4.0	3.9	3.8	3.8	3.9	3.8
1996	3.8	3.8	3.9	4.0	4.0	4.1	4.1	4.1	4.0	4.0	4.0	4.0	3.9
1997	4.1	4.1	4.2	4.1	4.1	4.3	4.3	4.2	4.1	4.1	4.0	4.0	4.1
1998	4.0	4.0	4.1	4.1	4.1	4.2	4.2	4.2	4.1	4.1	4.1	4.1	4.1
1999	4.1	4.1	4.1	4.3	4.3	4.4	4.3	4.3	4.2	4.2	4.2	4.2	4.2
2000	4.2	4.2	4.2	4.2	4.2	4.3	4.3	4.4	4.3	4.2	4.2	4.3	4.2
2001	4.2	4.2	4.3	4.2	4.3	4.3	4.3	4.3	4.3	4.1	4.1	4.1	4.2
2002	4.1	4.2	4.3	4.3	4.4	4.4	4.5	4.5	4.4	4.3	4.3	4.3	4.3
2003	4.4	4.4	4.5	4.5	4.6	4.6	4.6	4.5	4.5	4.4	4.4	4.4	4.5
Professional and business services													
1990	4.2	4.3	4.3	4.3	4.3	4.4	4.4	4.5	4.5	4.7	4.7	4.7	4.4
1991	4.1	4.2	4.3	4.1	4.2	4.3	4.3	4.3	4.4	4.7	4.7	4.8	4.3
1992	4.8	4.9	4.9	4.8	4.8	4.7	4.6	4.7	4.7	4.6	4.6	4.6	4.7
1993	4.5	4.5	4.5	4.5	4.5	4.4	4.4	4.4	4.4	4.3	4.3	4.3	4.4
1994	4.3	4.3	4.3	4.2	4.2	4.2	4.2	4.1	4.1	4.1	4.1	4.0	4.1
1995	4.0	4.0	4.0	4.0	3.9	3.9	3.9	3.8	3.8	3.8	3.8	3.8	3.8
1996	3.8	3.7	3.7	3.7	3.7	3.7	3.6	3.7	3.6	3.6	3.6	3.7	3.6
1997	3.8	3.9	3.9	4.0	4.0	4.1	4.1	4.1	4.0	4.0	4.0	4.1	4.0
1998	4.7	4.8	4.7	4.6	4.5	4.6	4.4	4.5	4.6	4.6	4.7	4.7	4.6
1999	4.9	5.0	5.0	5.1	5.1	5.3	5.1	5.2	5.4	5.7	5.8	6.0	5.3
2000	6.1	6.2	6.2	6.0	5.9	6.1	6.3	6.5	6.8	6.7	6.6	6.7	6.3
2001	6.7	6.7	6.4	6.3	6.3	6.3	6.2	6.4	6.4	6.6	6.6	6.8	6.4
2002	7.1	7.2	7.2	7.2	7.2	7.4	7.3	7.3	7.4	7.7	8.0	7.8	7.4
2003	7.7	7.5	7.3	7.2	7.3	7.1	7.0	7.2	7.2	7.2	7.3	7.3	7.3
Educational and health services													
1990	8.2	8.4	8.5	8.5	8.6	8.9	9.0	8.8	8.3	8.4	8.4	8.5	8.5
1991	8.4	8.5	8.6	8.8	8.9	9.5	9.6	9.6	9.1	8.6	8.8	9.0	8.9
1992	9.3	9.4	9.4	9.5	9.7	10.0	10.0	10.7	10.3	10.0	10.1	10.3	9.8
1993	11.0	11.2	11.4	11.2	11.3	11.4	12.0	11.9	11.5	11.7	11.7	11.8	11.5
1994	12.1	12.1	12.3	12.8	13.0	13.6	13.9	13.8	13.5	13.5	13.6	13.8	13.1
1995	13.5	13.6	13.6	13.6	13.7	14.0	13.9	14.0	14.1	14.3	14.4	14.5	13.9
1996	14.8	14.9	14.9	14.7	15.2	15.2	15.7	16.1	16.0	16.1	16.2	16.1	15.4
1997	16.5	16.6	16.7	16.9	17.0	17.3	17.7	17.8	17.3	17.2	17.3	17.5	17.1
1998	17.0	16.8	16.8	16.6	16.7	17.6	17.7	17.2	17.0	17.1	17.2	17.4	17.0
1999	17.4	17.5	17.5	17.9	17.8	18.7	19.4	18.6	18.5	18.5	18.7	18.9	18.2
2000	18.9	19.1	19.2	18.6	18.6	19.6	19.5	19.8	19.1	19.0	19.3	19.5	19.1
2001	19.6	19.7	19.8	20.0	20.2	20.3	20.5	20.9	21.0	21.3	21.7	21.9	20.5
2002	22.3	22.5	22.7	22.9	23.1	23.1	23.1	23.3	23.4	23.6	23.6	23.6	23.1
2003	23.9	24.1	24.2	24.5	24.7	24.6	25.0	25.1	25.1	25.1	25.2	25.4	24.7
Leisure and hospitality													
1990	6.5	6.9	7.3	7.3	7.2	7.4	7.4	7.4	7.2	6.9	7.1	7.5	7.1
1991	7.7	7.8	8.2	7.5	7.5	7.7	7.7	7.8	7.7	7.2	7.1	7.5	7.6
1992	7.4	7.7	8.3	8.0	8.0	7.9	7.9	7.9	7.7	7.5	7.4	7.5	7.7
1993	7.5	7.8	8.3	8.1	8.1	8.2	8.2	8.2	7.9	7.6	7.5	7.6	7.9
1994	7.9	8.3	8.8	8.7	8.7	8.9	8.9	8.9	8.5	8.2	8.2	8.2	8.5
1995	8.4	8.6	9.2	8.7	8.7	8.8	8.8	8.6	8.3	8.0	7.8	7.9	8.4
1996	8.1	8.3	8.8	8.6	8.3	8.5	8.5	8.5	8.1	7.9	7.8	7.9	8.2
1997	8.0	8.2	8.8	8.7	8.5	8.6	8.7	8.6	8.3	8.2	8.1	8.1	8.4
1998	8.2	8.5	9.1	9.3	9.2	9.4	9.4	9.4	9.0	8.6	8.6	8.6	8.9
1999	8.9	9.3	9.9	9.9	10.0	10.3	9.9	9.9	9.8	9.4	9.3	9.5	9.6
2000	9.9	10.2	11.0	10.9	11.6	12.2	12.1	11.7	11.4	10.3	10.3	10.4	11.0
2001	10.3	10.8	11.7	11.4	11.6	11.8	11.6	11.6	11.0	10.1	10.1	10.6	11.0
2002	10.5	11.2	12.0	11.7	11.9	12.1	12.0	11.9	11.5	11.0	10.9	11.0	11.5
2003	11.2	11.3	11.9	11.5	11.7	12.0	11.8	11.7	11.2	10.5	10.6	10.7	11.3
Other services													
1990	3.0	2.9	3.0	3.0	3.1	3.0	2.9	2.9	2.9	3.1	3.1	3.1	3.0
1991	3.1	3.2	3.2	3.2	3.1	3.0	3.1	3.1	3.3	3.3	3.3	3.3	3.1
1992	3.2	3.2	3.3	3.3	3.3	3.1	3.1	3.3	3.3	3.3	3.3	3.3	3.2
1993	3.2	3.2	3.3	3.2	3.3	3.2	3.3	3.2	3.4	3.4	3.4	3.4	3.2
1994	3.3	3.4	3.5	3.3	3.4	3.4	3.5	3.5	3.4	3.5	3.5	3.4	3.4
1995	3.4	3.4	3.5	3.4	3.5	3.5	3.5	3.5	3.5	3.6	3.6	3.6	3.5
1996	3.6	3.6	3.6	3.7	3.7	3.7	3.8	3.8	3.7	3.7	3.7	3.7	3.6
1997	3.8	3.8	3.8	3.9	4.0	4.0	4.1	4.0	4.0	3.8	3.8	3.8	3.9
1998	3.8	3.8	3.9	4.0	4.0	4.0	4.0	4.0	4.0	4.0	4.0	4.0	3.9
1999	3.9	3.9	3.9	4.0	4.0	4.1	4.0	4.0	4.0	4.0	4.0	4.0	3.9
2000	4.0	4.0	4.0	4.1	4.1	4.1	4.1	4.1	4.0	4.1	4.1	4.1	4.0
2001	3.4	3.4	3.4	3.5	3.5	3.6	3.6	3.6	3.5	3.3	3.4	3.3	3.4
2002	3.3	3.4	3.5	3.5	3.5	3.6	3.5	3.5	3.5	3.4	3.4	3.4	3.5
2003	3.4	3.4	3.5	3.4	3.5	3.5	3.6	3.5	3.5	3.5	3.5	3.5	3.5

Employment by Industry: Texas—*Continued*

(Numbers in thousands. Not seasonally adjusted.)

Industry	January	February	March	April	May	June	July	August	September	October	November	December	Annual Average
BROWNSVILLE-HARLINGEN—*Continued*													
Government													
1990	17.5	17.6	17.6	17.6	17.7	16.8	16.3	16.6	17.3	17.5	17.5	17.6	17.3
1991	17.7	17.7	17.6	17.6	17.6	17.3	16.6	17.2	18.0	18.2	18.5	18.4	17.7
1992	18.3	18.6	18.5	18.7	18.7	18.6	17.2	17.7	18.8	19.1	19.7	19.5	18.6
1993	19.8	19.9	20.0	20.2	20.1	19.7	17.8	18.6	19.9	20.4	20.6	20.6	19.8
1994	20.7	21.0	20.9	20.9	20.9	20.3	19.3	20.0	20.9	21.4	22.0	21.7	20.8
1995	21.5	21.8	21.8	21.9	21.8	21.2	20.0	20.7	21.6	22.0	22.1	22.0	21.5
1996	21.7	22.2	22.1	22.1	22.1	21.3	20.3	21.0	22.2	22.6	22.8	22.7	21.9
1997	22.2	22.8	22.8	22.9	22.8	22.1	21.2	21.9	22.8	23.3	23.5	23.5	22.6
1998	23.6	23.5	23.6	23.5	23.8	23.0	22.0	22.2	23.3	23.7	23.8	23.8	23.3
1999	23.9	24.0	24.0	24.0	24.0	23.6	22.4	23.0	24.1	24.4	24.7	24.7	23.9
2000	24.9	24.9	25.2	25.2	25.5	24.9	23.3	24.0	24.9	26.0	26.1	26.2	25.0
2001	26.1	26.3	26.6	26.2	25.9	24.9	23.4	24.3	25.5	26.0	26.3	26.3	25.6
2002	26.2	26.3	26.5	26.5	26.2	25.7	24.3	24.6	25.8	26.4	26.4	26.6	26.0
2003	26.2	26.3	26.5	26.7	26.3	26.0	24.7	24.9	25.9	26.6	26.6	26.3	26.1
Federal government													
1990	1.2	1.2	1.2	1.2	1.2	1.2	1.2	1.2	1.2	1.2	1.2	1.2	1.2
1991	1.2	1.2	1.2	1.2	1.2	1.2	1.3	1.3	1.2	1.2	1.2	1.2	1.2
1992	1.2	1.2	1.2	1.2	1.2	1.3	1.3	1.4	1.3	1.3	1.3	1.3	1.2
1993	1.3	1.3	1.3	1.3	1.3	1.3	1.3	1.4	1.4	1.4	1.3	1.3	1.3
1994	1.3	1.3	1.3	1.4	1.4	1.4	1.4	1.4	1.4	1.4	1.4	1.4	1.3
1995	1.4	1.4	1.4	1.4	1.4	1.4	1.4	1.4	1.4	1.4	1.4	1.4	1.4
1996	1.4	1.4	1.4	1.4	1.4	1.4	1.5	1.5	1.5	1.5	1.5	1.5	1.4
1997	1.5	1.6	1.6	1.6	1.6	1.6	1.6	1.6	1.7	1.7	1.7	1.7	1.6
1998	1.8	1.7	1.8	1.8	1.9	1.9	1.9	2.0	2.0	2.1	2.1	2.1	1.9
1999	2.1	2.1	2.1	2.1	2.1	2.2	2.2	2.2	2.2	2.2	2.2	2.2	2.1
2000	2.2	2.2	2.4	2.4	2.7	2.3	2.4	2.3	2.3	2.3	2.3	2.3	2.3
2001	2.3	2.3	2.3	2.3	2.3	2.3	2.3	2.3	2.3	2.3	2.3	2.3	2.3
2002	2.3	2.2	2.3	2.2	2.3	2.3	2.3	2.2	2.2	2.3	2.3	2.4	2.3
2003	2.3	2.3	2.3	2.4	2.4	2.4	2.4	2.4	2.4	2.5	2.4	2.4	2.4
State government													
1990	2.2	2.2	2.2	2.1	2.2	2.0	2.1	2.1	2.0	2.1	2.1	2.1	2.1
1991	2.1	2.1	2.1	2.1	2.2	2.1	2.2	2.2	2.1	2.2	2.3	2.3	2.1
1992	2.3	2.3	2.3	2.3	2.3	2.3	2.3	2.3	2.3	2.3	2.4	2.4	2.3
1993	3.4	3.4	3.3	3.3	3.3	3.3	3.1	3.1	3.4	3.4	3.5	3.4	3.3
1994	3.3	3.5	3.4	3.5	3.5	3.3	3.3	3.3	3.6	3.7	3.8	3.7	3.4
1995	3.6	3.8	3.7	3.8	3.8	3.6	3.6	3.5	3.5	3.6	3.6	3.5	3.6
1996	3.3	3.6	3.6	3.6	3.6	3.4	3.4	3.4	3.6	3.7	3.8	3.7	3.5
1997	3.4	3.7	3.7	3.8	3.7	3.5	3.5	3.5	3.7	3.9	3.9	3.9	3.6
1998	3.9	3.8	3.8	3.8	3.9	3.8	3.6	3.8	3.7	3.7	3.7	3.7	3.7
1999	3.8	3.8	3.8	3.8	3.8	3.8	3.5	3.6	3.7	3.8	3.8	3.8	3.7
2000	3.9	3.9	3.8	3.8	3.8	3.8	3.8	3.8	3.8	4.0	4.0	4.0	3.8
2001	3.9	3.9	3.9	3.9	3.9	3.7	3.7	3.8	3.9	4.2	4.2	4.2	3.9
2002	4.2	4.2	4.2	4.2	3.8	3.8	3.9	3.7	4.0	4.2	4.2	4.2	4.1
2003	3.9	3.9	4.1	4.1	3.7	3.7	3.7	3.6	3.8	4.1	4.1	3.8	3.9
Local government													
1990	14.1	14.2	14.2	14.3	14.3	13.6	13.0	13.3	14.1	14.2	14.2	14.3	13.9
1991	14.4	14.4	14.3	14.3	14.2	14.0	13.1	13.7	14.7	14.8	15.0	14.9	14.3
1992	14.8	15.1	15.0	15.2	15.2	15.0	13.6	14.0	15.2	15.5	16.0	15.8	15.0
1993	15.1	15.2	15.4	15.6	15.5	15.1	13.4	14.1	15.1	15.6	15.8	15.9	15.1
1994	16.1	16.2	16.2	16.0	16.0	15.6	14.6	15.3	15.9	16.3	16.8	16.6	15.9
1995	16.5	16.6	16.7	16.7	16.6	16.2	15.0	15.8	16.7	17.0	17.1	17.1	16.5
1996	17.0	17.2	17.1	17.1	17.1	16.5	15.4	16.1	17.1	17.4	17.5	17.5	16.9
1997	17.3	17.5	17.5	17.5	17.5	17.0	16.1	16.8	17.4	17.7	17.9	17.9	17.3
1998	17.9	18.0	18.0	17.9	18.0	17.3	16.5	16.4	17.6	17.9	18.0	18.0	17.6
1999	18.0	18.1	18.1	18.1	18.1	17.6	16.7	17.2	18.2	18.4	18.7	18.7	17.9
2000	18.8	18.8	19.0	19.0	19.0	18.8	17.1	17.9	18.8	19.7	19.8	19.9	18.8
2001	19.9	20.1	20.4	20.0	19.7	18.9	17.4	18.2	19.3	19.5	19.8	19.8	19.4
2002	19.7	19.9	20.0	20.1	20.1	19.6	18.1	18.7	19.6	19.9	19.9	20.0	19.6
2003	20.0	20.1	20.1	20.2	20.2	19.9	18.6	18.9	19.7	20.0	20.1	20.1	19.8
CORPUS CHRISTI													
Total nonfarm													
1990	130.7	131.3	134.5	133.9	136.0	137.3	135.0	134.9	136.3	135.3	135.2	135.0	134.6
1991	131.0	133.7	135.4	134.7	136.2	136.8	134.2	134.8	135.1	135.2	135.9	136.0	134.9
1992	132.7	134.3	136.4	136.6	138.5	138.7	135.3	136.5	137.3	138.9	139.3	140.3	137.0
1993	136.9	138.3	140.7	139.8	139.6	140.3	138.9	139.7	140.5	140.8	140.8	142.7	139.9
1994	139.2	139.8	141.6	142.8	142.9	144.1	142.5	143.4	145.2	145.0	145.3	145.6	143.1
1995	142.2	143.8	145.3	146.2	146.7	147.5	144.8	145.2	146.3	146.0	147.1	147.3	145.7
1996	144.5	145.5	147.4	149.1	151.9	151.8	150.8	151.4	153.2	153.5	153.3	153.6	150.5
1997	151.6	152.8	154.0	154.7	154.3	154.7	152.3	152.4	154.4	154.6	155.6	155.2	153.8
1998	153.8	154.8	155.5	156.1	155.9	156.9	156.4	156.7	157.9	157.5	158.0	159.4	156.5
1999	156.8	157.0	158.0	157.7	158.1	159.6	157.6	156.8	158.8	158.5	158.4	159.6	158.0
2000	158.2	158.1	159.1	159.5	160.5	160.5	159.3	159.8	160.2	159.4	160.2	161.0	159.6
2001	160.6	161.7	162.4	160.8	160.6	161.5	159.1	160.1	160.8	160.0	160.2	160.4	160.6
2002	158.4	159.7	160.2	160.6	160.7	160.5	158.0	158.9	161.2	161.3	162.0	162.1	160.3
2003	158.7	160.7	161.1	161.3	161.5	161.5	159.4	160.1	161.2	161.3	161.0	161.4	160.8

Employment by Industry: Texas—*Continued*

(Numbers in thousands. Not seasonally adjusted.)

Industry	January	February	March	April	May	June	July	August	September	October	November	December	Annual Average
CORPUS CHRISTI *—Continued*													
Total private													
1990	101.0	101.4	104.4	103.9	105.5	107.7	106.9	106.8	106.9	105.6	105.3	105.0	105.0
1991	101.5	103.4	105.2	104.3	105.5	107.0	106.3	106.8	106.0	105.4	105.9	105.9	105.2
1992	102.9	104.2	106.2	106.5	108.4	108.8	107.4	108.1	107.7	108.4	108.8	109.8	107.2
1993	106.6	107.6	109.9	109.0	109.2	110.2	110.2	110.6	110.0	110.0	109.9	111.7	109.5
1994	108.5	109.1	110.9	112.1	112.2	113.5	114.1	114.7	114.8	114.0	114.2	114.5	112.7
1995	111.5	112.4	114.0	114.5	115.3	116.5	115.9	116.3	115.6	114.6	115.6	115.9	114.8
1996	113.8	114.2	115.7	117.6	120.2	120.6	121.0	121.2	121.1	122.6	122.5	122.9	119.4
1997	121.3	122.0	123.2	123.3	123.5	124.5	123.9	124.0	124.0	124.0	124.8	124.5	123.5
1998	123.5	124.0	124.7	125.4	125.1	126.7	127.7	128.0	127.2	126.5	127.0	128.5	126.1
1999	126.4	126.2	127.2	126.8	127.3	129.1	129.2	128.4	128.2	127.6	127.5	128.7	127.7
2000	127.6	127.2	127.9	128.5	128.8	129.9	130.3	130.7	129.7	128.6	129.3	130.3	129.0
2001	130.4	131.1	131.8	130.0	129.8	131.0	130.3	130.9	129.9	128.9	128.9	129.2	130.1
2002	127.4	128.6	129.2	129.3	129.2	129.8	129.2	130.1	130.2	129.8	130.1	130.4	129.4
2003	127.7	129.1	129.3	129.6	129.9	130.5	130.4	130.8	130.4	129.9	129.4	129.8	129.7
Goods-producing													
1990	23.3	23.6	25.3	23.8	24.9	25.1	24.4	24.4	24.6	24.8	24.7	24.4	24.4
1991	24.4	25.5	26.2	25.3	25.7	26.3	25.8	26.0	25.9	26.2	26.6	26.5	25.8
1992	24.4	24.4	25.6	24.7	25.3	25.1	24.4	24.7	24.9	26.3	26.3	26.5	25.2
1993	25.5	26.2	27.3	26.4	26.3	26.3	25.8	25.8	25.8	25.6	25.5	25.7	26.0
1994	24.3	24.3	24.9	24.6	24.6	25.0	25.6	25.7	26.6	26.4	26.1	26.0	25.3
1995	25.4	25.7	25.9	25.6	26.0	26.3	25.9	25.7	25.6	25.4	25.5	24.9	25.6
1996	24.7	24.8	25.2	26.4	27.5	27.0	27.3	27.4	27.8	27.7	27.1	27.3	26.6
1997	27.4	27.8	27.5	27.3	26.6	26.3	26.3	26.0	26.3	26.8	27.2	26.5	26.8
1998	27.3	27.4	27.4	26.8	26.2	26.4	26.6	26.4	26.1	26.5	26.2	26.5	26.6
1999	27.1	26.8	27.0	27.1	26.9	27.4	27.3	27.2	27.5	27.9	27.5	27.7	27.2
2000	28.8	28.1	28.2	28.2	28.5	28.2	28.3	28.6	27.9	27.9	27.8	28.4	28.2
2001	29.2	29.9	29.8	28.2	27.4	27.5	27.8	28.2	28.2	28.3	28.4	28.1	28.4
2002	27.8	28.8	28.8	28.4	28.6	28.5	28.2	28.6	29.1	29.3	29.4	29.1	28.7
2003	28.8	28.7	29.0	29.3	29.1	28.9	28.6	28.8	28.5	28.9	28.2	28.2	28.8
Natural resources and mining													
1990	3.2	3.1	3.2	3.1	3.2	3.2	3.2	3.2	3.2	3.3	3.2	3.2	3.1
1991	3.1	3.2	3.1	3.1	3.0	2.9	2.8	2.8	2.7	2.8	2.7	2.7	2.9
1992	2.5	2.4	2.4	2.5	2.5	2.5	2.5	2.5	2.4	2.3	2.4	2.5	2.4
1993	2.3	2.3	2.3	2.3	2.3	2.3	2.3	2.3	2.2	2.3	2.3	2.3	2.2
1994	2.3	2.2	2.3	2.4	2.3	2.4	2.3	2.4	2.3	2.3	2.3	2.2	2.3
1995	2.1	2.1	2.1	2.1	2.2	2.2	2.2	2.2	2.2	2.2	2.2	2.2	2.1
1996	2.1	2.1	2.0	2.1	2.2	2.2	2.2	2.2	2.2	2.1	2.2	2.2	2.1
1997	2.3	2.3	2.3	2.2	2.2	2.2	2.3	2.3	2.3	2.4	2.4	2.5	2.3
1998	2.4	2.4	2.4	2.2	2.3	2.2	2.2	2.2	2.1	2.1	2.1	2.2	2.2
1999	2.1	2.1	2.1	1.8	1.8	1.8	1.8	1.8	1.8	1.8	1.8	1.9	1.8
2000	1.9	1.9	1.9	1.8	1.8	1.8	1.8	1.9	1.9	1.9	1.9	2.0	1.8
2001	1.9	1.9	2.0	2.1	2.1	2.2	2.3	2.3	2.2	2.2	2.2	2.2	2.1
2002	2.3	2.4	2.4	2.3	2.4	2.4	2.4	2.5	2.7	2.6	2.6	2.6	2.5
2003	2.7	2.6	2.7	2.8	2.8	2.8	2.8	2.8	2.8	2.8	2.8	2.8	2.8
Construction													
1990	9.4	9.7	11.2	9.6	10.4	10.6	9.9	9.9	10.2	10.2	10.2	10.0	10.1
1991	9.7	10.5	11.1	10.5	10.9	11.5	11.1	11.3	11.1	11.5	12.0	11.8	11.0
1992	10.2	10.2	11.3	10.5	10.9	10.7	10.0	10.3	10.6	12.0	11.9	11.9	10.8
1993	11.0	11.8	12.7	11.9	11.8	11.8	11.3	11.1	11.2	10.9	10.8	10.9	11.4
1994	9.7	9.8	10.1	9.7	9.8	10.0	10.6	10.5	11.5	11.5	11.2	11.1	10.4
1995	10.7	11.1	11.3	11.0	11.3	11.4	11.4	11.4	11.4	11.4	11.5	10.8	11.2
1996	10.7	10.9	11.4	12.4	13.3	12.7	12.9	13.0	13.4	13.6	13.0	13.1	12.5
1997	13.1	13.5	13.0	13.2	12.4	12.1	12.1	11.7	11.9	12.3	12.6	11.8	12.4
1998	12.7	12.8	12.7	12.3	11.6	11.7	12.1	11.9	11.7	11.9	11.7	11.9	12.0
1999	12.7	12.3	12.4	12.7	12.2	12.5	12.3	12.1	12.3	13.0	12.6	12.6	12.4
2000	13.7	13.1	13.2	13.5	13.8	13.5	13.5	13.8	13.0	13.2	13.1	13.6	13.4
2001	14.7	15.3	15.1	13.5	12.7	12.6	12.9	13.4	13.5	13.8	14.0	13.7	13.7
2002	13.5	14.6	14.6	14.4	14.5	14.4	14.1	14.4	14.8	15.2	15.2	15.0	14.6
2003	14.5	14.4	14.6	14.7	14.5	14.3	13.9	14.1	14.0	14.4	13.8	13.9	14.3
Manufacturing													
1990	10.7	10.8	10.9	11.1	11.3	11.3	11.3	11.3	11.2	11.3	11.3	11.2	11.1
1991	11.6	11.8	12.0	11.7	11.8	11.9	11.9	11.9	12.1	11.9	11.9	12.0	11.8
1992	11.7	11.8	11.9	11.7	11.9	11.9	11.9	11.9	11.9	12.0	12.0	12.1	11.8
1993	12.2	12.1	12.3	12.2	12.2	12.2	12.2	12.4	12.4	12.4	12.4	12.5	12.2
1994	12.3	12.3	12.5	12.5	12.5	12.6	12.7	12.8	12.8	12.6	12.6	12.7	12.5
1995	12.6	12.5	12.5	12.5	12.5	12.7	12.3	12.1	12.0	11.8	11.8	11.9	12.2
1996	11.9	11.8	11.8	11.9	12.0	12.1	12.2	12.2	12.2	12.0	11.9	12.0	12.0
1997	12.0	12.0	12.2	11.9	12.0	12.0	11.9	12.0	12.1	12.1	12.2	12.2	12.0
1998	12.2	12.2	12.3	12.3	12.3	12.5	12.3	12.3	12.3	12.5	12.4	12.4	12.3
1999	12.3	12.4	12.5	12.6	12.9	13.1	13.2	13.3	13.4	13.1	13.1	13.2	12.9
2000	13.2	13.1	13.1	12.9	12.9	12.9	13.0	12.9	13.0	12.8	12.8	12.8	12.9
2001	12.6	12.7	12.7	12.6	12.6	12.7	12.6	12.5	12.5	12.3	12.2	12.2	12.5
2002	12.0	11.8	11.8	11.7	11.7	11.7	11.7	11.7	11.6	11.5	11.6	11.5	11.7
2003	11.6	11.7	11.7	11.8	11.8	11.8	11.9	11.9	11.7	11.7	11.6	11.5	11.7

Employment by Industry: Texas—*Continued*

(Numbers in thousands. Not seasonally adjusted.)

Industry	January	February	March	April	May	June	July	August	September	October	November	December	Annual Average
CORPUS CHRISTI *—Continued*													
Service-providing													
1990	107.4	107.7	109.2	110.1	111.1	112.2	110.6	110.5	111.7	110.5	110.5	110.6	110.1
1991	106.6	108.2	109.2	109.4	110.5	110.5	108.4	108.8	109.2	109.0	109.3	109.5	109.0
1992	108.3	109.9	110.8	111.9	113.2	113.6	110.9	111.8	112.4	112.6	113.0	113.8	111.8
1993	111.4	112.1	113.4	113.4	113.3	114.0	113.1	113.9	114.7	115.2	115.3	117.0	113.9
1994	114.9	115.5	116.7	118.2	118.3	119.1	116.9	117.7	118.6	118.6	119.2	119.6	117.7
1995	116.8	118.1	119.4	120.6	120.7	121.2	118.9	119.5	120.7	120.6	121.6	122.4	120.0
1996	119.8	120.7	122.2	122.7	124.4	124.8	123.5	124.0	125.4	125.8	126.2	126.3	123.8
1997	124.2	125.0	126.5	127.4	127.7	128.4	126.0	126.4	128.1	127.8	128.4	128.7	127.0
1998	126.5	127.4	128.1	129.3	129.7	130.5	129.8	130.3	131.8	131.0	131.8	132.9	129.9
1999	129.7	130.2	131.0	130.6	131.2	132.2	130.3	129.6	131.3	130.6	130.9	131.9	130.7
2000	129.4	130.0	130.9	131.3	132.0	132.3	131.0	131.2	132.3	131.5	132.4	132.6	131.4
2001	131.4	131.8	132.6	132.6	133.2	134.0	131.3	131.9	132.6	131.7	131.8	132.3	132.2
2002	130.6	130.9	131.4	132.2	132.1	132.0	129.8	130.3	132.1	132.0	132.6	133.0	131.6
2003	129.9	132.0	132.1	132.0	132.4	132.6	130.8	131.3	132.7	132.4	132.8	133.2	132.0
Trade, transportation, and utilities													
1990	26.6	26.3	26.4	26.5	27.2	27.1	27.0	26.6	26.7	26.6	26.8	26.9	26.7
1991	25.6	25.7	26.1	25.7	25.8	26.1	26.3	26.3	26.3	25.9	26.1	26.4	26.0
1992	25.5	25.9	26.0	26.0	26.3	26.6	26.6	26.7	26.8	26.9	27.4	28.4	26.5
1993	26.8	26.7	26.8	26.7	26.6	26.7	26.8	27.0	26.8	26.9	27.3	28.5	26.9
1994	27.5	27.5	27.8	28.0	27.9	27.9	27.8	27.9	27.8	27.9	28.3	28.7	27.9
1995	27.6	27.6	27.5	27.4	27.5	27.6	27.6	27.7	27.7	27.5	28.1	28.8	27.7
1996	27.3	27.2	27.4	27.3	27.6	27.8	27.8	27.7	27.7	27.6	28.1	28.7	27.6
1997	27.3	27.0	27.3	27.0	27.1	27.5	27.7	27.7	27.8	27.7	28.3	28.7	27.5
1998	27.8	27.4	27.5	27.8	27.9	28.4	28.3	28.3	28.1	28.1	28.5	29.3	28.1
1999	27.7	27.6	27.9	27.9	27.9	28.3	28.3	28.0	28.0	28.0	28.6	29.2	28.1
2000	28.1	28.1	28.1	28.4	28.6	28.9	28.6	28.8	28.7	28.7	29.4	29.8	28.6
2001	28.5	28.2	28.5	28.5	28.7	29.0	28.6	28.6	28.2	28.2	28.5	28.9	28.5
2002	28.0	27.8	27.9	28.0	28.1	28.6	28.3	28.3	28.3	28.1	28.5	28.9	28.2
2003	27.4	28.2	27.7	27.8	27.7	27.9	27.9	27.9	28.0	27.9	28.4	28.9	28.0
Wholesale trade													
1990	4.9	4.9	5.0	5.0	5.2	5.2	5.3	5.2	5.2	5.2	5.2	5.2	5.1
1991	5.1	5.2	5.2	5.2	5.3	5.4	5.4	5.3	5.3	5.2	5.2	5.2	5.2
1992	5.1	5.1	5.1	5.1	5.1	5.2	5.4	5.3	5.3	5.2	5.3	5.3	5.2
1993	5.3	5.3	5.3	5.3	5.3	5.3	5.5	5.4	5.3	5.2	5.2	5.2	5.3
1994	5.1	5.1	5.1	5.2	5.2	5.4	5.4	5.3	5.2	5.1	5.1	5.2	5.2
1995	5.0	5.1	5.1	5.0	5.1	5.1	5.1	5.0	5.1	5.0	4.9	4.9	5.0
1996	4.8	4.9	4.9	4.9	4.9	5.0	5.1	5.1	5.1	5.1	5.0	5.1	4.9
1997	4.9	4.9	5.0	5.0	5.0	5.1	5.2	5.1	5.1	5.1	5.1	5.2	5.0
1998	5.1	5.1	5.1	5.2	5.1	5.3	5.4	5.3	5.3	5.2	5.2	5.3	5.2
1999	5.0	5.0	5.0	5.0	5.0	5.1	5.1	5.0	5.0	5.0	5.0	5.0	5.0
2000	5.0	5.0	5.0	5.0	5.0	5.1	5.1	5.1	5.1	5.0	5.1	5.1	5.0
2001	5.0	5.0	5.1	5.1	5.1	5.2	5.2	5.2	5.1	5.1	5.1	5.1	5.0
2002	5.0	5.0	5.1	5.0	5.0	5.1	5.1	5.0	5.0	4.9	4.9	4.9	5.0
2003	4.8	4.8	4.8	4.8	4.8	4.8	4.9	4.8	4.8	4.7	4.7	4.7	4.8
Retail trade													
1990	17.3	16.9	16.8	17.1	17.5	17.3	17.1	17.0	16.9	17.0	17.2	17.3	17.1
1991	16.2	16.1	16.2	16.2	16.2	16.4	16.4	16.6	16.5	16.1	16.4	16.8	16.3
1992	16.0	16.2	16.3	16.4	16.6	16.8	16.6	16.8	16.9	17.1	17.4	18.3	16.7
1993	17.0	16.9	17.0	16.9	16.8	16.9	16.8	17.0	16.9	17.1	17.5	18.5	17.1
1994	17.6	17.6	17.9	18.0	18.0	17.8	17.7	18.0	18.0	18.2	18.6	19.0	18.0
1995	18.2	18.0	18.0	17.8	17.7	17.9	17.8	18.0	17.9	17.8	18.5	19.1	18.0
1996	18.0	17.7	17.9	17.8	18.0	18.1	18.0	18.1	18.1	18.1	18.6	19.1	18.1
1997	18.0	17.7	17.9	17.6	17.7	17.9	17.9	18.1	18.0	17.9	18.5	18.8	18.0
1998	17.8	17.5	17.6	17.8	17.9	18.1	18.1	18.2	18.1	18.1	18.5	19.1	18.0
1999	18.0	17.9	18.2	18.2	18.1	18.3	18.3	18.2	18.1	18.0	18.6	19.2	18.2
2000	18.1	18.1	18.1	18.2	18.3	18.4	18.3	18.5	18.3	18.5	19.0	19.4	18.4
2001	18.1	17.8	18.0	18.0	18.2	18.3	18.0	18.0	17.7	17.7	18.0	18.4	18.0
2002	17.7	17.5	17.6	17.6	17.8	18.1	17.9	17.9	17.9	17.9	18.3	18.7	17.9
2003	17.5	17.5	17.7	17.7	17.8	17.9	17.8	17.8	17.9	18.0	18.4	18.9	17.9
Transportation and utilities													
1990	4.4	4.5	4.6	4.4	4.5	4.6	4.6	4.4	4.6	4.4	4.4	4.4	4.4
1991	4.3	4.4	4.7	4.3	4.3	4.3	4.5	4.4	4.5	4.6	4.5	4.4	4.4
1992	4.4	4.6	4.6	4.5	4.6	4.6	4.6	4.6	4.6	4.6	4.7	4.8	4.6
1993	4.5	4.5	4.5	4.5	4.5	4.5	4.5	4.6	4.6	4.6	4.6	4.8	4.5
1994	4.8	4.8	4.8	4.8	4.7	4.7	4.7	4.6	4.6	4.6	4.6	4.5	4.6
1995	4.4	4.5	4.4	4.6	4.7	4.6	4.7	4.7	4.7	4.7	4.7	4.8	4.6
1996	4.5	4.6	4.6	4.6	4.7	4.7	4.7	4.5	4.5	4.4	4.5	4.5	4.5
1997	4.4	4.4	4.4	4.4	4.4	4.5	4.6	4.5	4.7	4.7	4.7	4.7	4.5
1998	4.9	4.8	4.8	4.8	4.9	5.0	4.8	4.8	4.7	4.8	4.8	4.9	4.8
1999	4.7	4.7	4.7	4.7	4.8	4.9	4.9	4.8	4.9	5.0	5.0	5.0	4.8
2000	5.0	5.0	5.0	5.2	5.3	5.4	5.2	5.2	5.3	5.2	5.3	5.3	5.2
2001	5.4	5.4	5.4	5.4	5.4	5.5	5.4	5.4	5.4	5.4	5.4	5.4	5.4
2002	5.3	5.3	5.2	5.4	5.3	5.4	5.3	5.4	5.4	5.3	5.3	5.3	5.3
2003	5.1	5.9	5.2	5.3	5.1	5.2	5.2	5.3	5.3	5.2	5.3	5.3	5.3

Employment by Industry: Texas—*Continued*

(Numbers in thousands. Not seasonally adjusted.)

Industry	January	February	March	April	May	June	July	August	September	October	November	December	Annual Average
CORPUS CHRISTI *—Continued*													
Information													
1990	2.7	2.7	2.7	2.7	2.8	2.8	2.8	2.8	2.7	2.7	2.7	2.7	2.7
1991	2.7	2.8	2.8	2.7	2.8	2.8	2.7	2.7	2.7	2.7	2.7	2.7	2.7
1992	2.7	2.7	2.7	2.7	2.8	2.8	2.8	2.8	2.8	2.8	2.8	2.8	2.7
1993	2.7	2.7	2.8	2.7	2.8	2.8	2.8	2.8	2.8	2.8	2.8	2.8	2.7
1994	2.6	2.6	2.6	2.5	2.5	2.5	2.5	2.5	2.5	2.4	2.4	2.5	2.5
1995	2.4	2.5	2.5	2.6	2.6	2.6	2.6	2.6	2.6	2.6	2.6	2.6	2.5
1996	2.6	2.6	2.6	2.7	2.7	2.7	2.7	2.7	2.7	2.7	2.7	2.7	2.6
1997	2.7	2.7	2.7	2.7	2.7	2.8	2.8	2.8	2.7	2.8	2.7	2.8	2.7
1998	2.7	2.7	2.7	2.8	2.8	2.8	2.9	2.9	2.9	2.9	3.0	3.0	2.8
1999	3.0	3.0	3.0	3.0	3.1	3.1	3.1	3.1	3.1	3.0	3.1	3.1	3.0
2000	3.1	3.1	3.0	3.1	3.1	3.1	3.1	3.1	3.1	3.1	3.1	3.1	3.0
2001	3.0	3.0	3.0	2.9	3.0	3.0	2.9	2.9	2.9	2.9	2.8	2.9	2.9
2002	2.9	2.9	2.9	3.0	3.0	2.9	2.9	2.9	2.8	2.8	2.8	2.8	2.9
2003	2.7	2.7	2.7	2.7	2.7	2.7	2.7	2.6	2.6	2.6	2.7	2.7	2.7
Financial activities													
1990	6.9	6.9	7.0	7.1	7.4	7.3	7.2	7.3	7.6	7.5	7.2	7.0	7.2
1991	6.6	6.7	6.8	6.9	6.8	6.8	6.6	6.7	6.5	6.5	6.5	6.5	6.6
1992	6.4	6.5	6.6	6.7	6.8	6.8	6.9	6.9	6.8	6.7	6.7	6.8	6.7
1993	6.7	6.7	6.8	6.8	6.7	6.9	7.0	7.1	7.0	7.0	6.9	7.0	6.8
1994	6.8	6.8	6.9	7.1	7.1	7.2	7.3	7.4	7.2	7.1	7.1	7.1	7.0
1995	7.0	7.0	7.1	7.1	7.1	7.3	7.3	7.3	7.2	7.2	7.3	7.3	7.1
1996	7.3	7.4	7.4	7.3	7.4	7.5	7.5	7.5	7.5	7.4	7.5	7.5	7.4
1997	7.3	7.3	7.4	7.4	7.5	7.5	7.3	7.3	7.2	7.2	7.2	7.2	7.3
1998	7.2	7.2	7.3	7.4	7.4	7.5	7.5	7.5	7.4	7.4	7.4	7.5	7.3
1999	7.2	7.2	7.2	7.4	7.5	7.6	7.6	7.6	7.5	7.5	7.5	7.5	7.4
2000	7.4	7.4	7.5	7.4	7.5	7.6	7.6	7.6	7.6	7.5	7.5	7.6	7.5
2001	7.2	7.3	7.3	7.2	7.3	7.4	7.3	7.3	7.2	7.1	7.1	7.1	7.2
2002	7.1	7.1	7.1	7.2	7.3	7.4	7.5	7.4	7.4	7.4	7.5	7.5	7.3
2003	7.4	7.4	7.5	7.5	7.5	7.6	7.6	7.6	7.6	7.6	7.6	7.6	7.5
Professional and business services													
1990	9.7	9.8	10.2	10.4	10.7	10.8	10.8	10.8	10.9	10.9	10.8	10.7	10.5
1991	10.6	10.6	10.6	10.6	10.7	10.6	10.6	10.6	10.6	10.6	10.6	10.5	10.6
1992	10.4	10.4	10.3	10.3	10.3	10.3	9.9	9.8	9.8	9.8	9.6	9.7	10.0
1993	9.7	9.8	10.0	10.0	10.1	10.2	10.4	10.3	10.4	10.6	10.4	10.6	10.2
1994	10.6	10.7	10.8	11.2	10.9	11.1	10.9	10.9	10.9	10.9	10.9	11.0	10.9
1995	10.8	10.8	11.0	10.9	11.0	11.2	11.1	11.3	11.2	11.5	11.6	11.8	11.1
1996	11.8	11.8	11.8	12.1	12.3	12.4	12.2	12.2	12.2	12.5	12.4	12.3	12.1
1997	12.3	12.2	12.3	13.0	12.9	13.1	13.2	13.4	13.4	13.9	14.1	14.3	13.1
1998	13.6	13.8	13.9	14.1	13.9	14.1	14.7	14.8	14.8	15.4	15.3	15.3	14.4
1999	14.8	15.0	15.1	15.3	15.3	15.6	16.1	16.1	15.9	15.8	15.6	15.8	15.5
2000	15.2	15.4	15.4	15.6	15.2	15.5	15.9	15.8	15.9	15.9	16.2	16.1	15.6
2001	16.0	16.0	16.0	15.9	15.7	15.9	15.9	15.6	15.5	15.5	15.4	15.5	15.7
2002	15.3	15.5	15.4	15.6	14.9	14.9	14.8	14.9	14.9	15.1	14.9	15.2	15.1
2003	15.2	15.4	15.1	14.8	14.8	14.8	15.2	15.3	15.2	15.1	14.9	14.8	15.1
Educational and health services													
1990	13.0	13.0	13.2	13.4	11.8	13.6	13.5	13.8	13.8	13.3	13.0	13.4	13.2
1991	13.4	13.5	13.6	13.7	13.8	13.9	13.7	13.8	13.8	13.6	13.6	13.5	13.6
1992	14.6	14.9	15.0	15.3	15.6	15.6	15.5	15.6	15.7	15.6	15.7	15.6	15.3
1993	15.6	15.7	15.7	15.8	15.9	16.0	15.9	16.1	16.3	16.4	16.5	16.6	16.0
1994	16.5	16.7	16.8	17.1	17.2	17.3	17.5	17.8	18.0	17.9	18.1	18.1	17.4
1995	17.9	18.0	18.3	18.5	18.5	18.5	18.4	18.5	18.7	18.5	18.8	18.8	18.4
1996	18.8	19.0	19.2	19.1	19.3	19.4	19.2	19.3	19.5	21.5	21.6	21.5	19.7
1997	22.0	22.2	22.3	22.0	22.3	22.4	22.0	22.2	22.4	22.2	22.3	22.3	22.2
1998	22.3	22.5	22.5	22.6	22.6	22.7	22.7	22.9	22.9	22.6	22.7	22.8	22.6
1999	22.3	22.5	22.6	22.1	22.2	22.2	21.9	21.9	22.2	22.3	22.2	22.4	22.2
2000	22.3	22.3	22.4	22.1	22.1	22.1	22.4	22.7	22.9	22.7	22.8	22.9	22.4
2001	24.0	24.0	24.0	23.7	23.8	23.8	23.7	24.0	24.1	23.9	24.1	24.2	23.9
2002	23.7	23.6	23.6	23.5	23.6	23.4	23.3	23.8	23.9	23.8	23.9	23.9	23.7
2003	23.6	23.7	23.7	23.8	24.0	24.0	24.0	24.2	24.3	24.2	24.3	24.3	24.0
Leisure and hospitality													
1990	11.6	11.9	12.3	12.7	13.2	13.5	13.8	13.7	13.2	12.6	13.0	12.9	12.8
1991	11.6	11.8	12.3	12.5	12.9	13.5	13.5	13.6	13.2	12.9	12.9	12.9	12.8
1992	12.5	12.8	13.4	14.0	14.4	14.6	14.4	14.6	14.0	13.4	13.5	13.2	13.7
1993	12.7	13.0	13.6	13.6	13.8	14.2	14.3	14.3	13.8	13.6	13.4	13.4	13.6
1994	13.1	13.4	14.0	14.4	14.8	15.2	15.1	15.1	14.5	14.1	14.0	13.8	14.2
1995	13.3	13.6	14.2	14.9	15.0	15.3	15.4	15.3	14.6	14.1	13.9	13.9	14.4
1996	13.5	13.6	14.2	14.8	15.3	15.6	16.1	16.2	15.6	15.2	15.1	14.8	15.0
1997	14.4	14.9	15.6	15.9	16.3	16.7	16.6	16.4	16.1	15.4	15.3	15.0	15.7
1998	14.9	15.3	15.7	16.1	16.4	16.8	16.9	17.0	16.6	15.7	15.8	15.9	16.0
1999	16.1	16.3	16.9	16.8	17.2	17.6	17.7	17.4	16.9	16.3	16.2	16.1	16.7
2000	16.0	16.1	16.6	17.0	17.0	17.5	17.5	17.3	16.8	16.0	15.9	15.8	16.6
2001	15.9	16.1	16.5	16.9	17.1	17.5	17.3	17.5	17.1	16.4	16.0	16.0	16.6
2002	16.0	16.3	16.9	16.9	17.0	17.3	17.5	17.6	17.3	16.8	16.6	16.6	16.9
2003	16.3	16.6	17.1	17.2	17.5	17.9	17.8	17.9	17.8	17.2	16.9	16.9	17.3

Employment by Industry: Texas—*Continued*

(Numbers in thousands. Not seasonally adjusted.)

Industry	January	February	March	April	May	June	July	August	September	October	November	December	Annual Average
CORPUS CHRISTI *—Continued*													
Other services													
1990	7.2	7.2	7.3	7.3	7.5	7.5	7.4	7.4	7.4	7.2	7.1	7.0	7.2
1991	6.6	6.8	6.8	6.9	7.0	7.0	7.1	7.1	7.0	7.0	6.9	6.9	6.9
1992	6.4	6.6	6.6	6.8	6.9	7.0	6.9	7.0	6.9	6.9	6.8	6.8	6.8
1993	6.9	6.8	6.9	7.0	7.0	7.1	7.2	7.2	7.1	7.1	7.1	7.1	7.0
1994	7.1	7.1	7.1	7.2	7.2	7.3	7.4	7.4	7.3	7.3	7.3	7.3	7.2
1995	7.1	7.2	7.5	7.5	7.6	7.7	7.6	7.9	8.0	7.8	7.8	7.8	7.6
1996	7.8	7.8	7.9	7.9	8.1	8.2	8.2	8.2	8.1	8.0	8.0	8.1	8.0
1997	7.9	7.9	8.1	8.0	8.1	8.2	8.0	8.2	8.1	8.0	7.7	7.7	7.9
1998	7.7	7.7	7.7	7.8	7.9	8.0	8.1	8.2	8.4	7.9	8.1	8.2	7.9
1999	8.2	7.8	7.5	7.2	7.2	7.3	7.2	7.1	7.1	6.8	6.8	6.9	7.2
2000	6.7	6.7	6.7	6.7	6.8	7.0	6.9	6.8	6.8	6.8	6.6	6.6	6.7
2001	6.6	6.6	6.7	6.7	6.8	6.9	6.8	6.8	6.7	6.6	6.6	6.5	6.7
2002	6.6	6.6	6.6	6.7	6.7	6.8	6.7	6.6	6.5	6.5	6.5	6.4	6.6
2003	6.3	6.4	6.5	6.5	6.6	6.7	6.6	6.5	6.4	6.4	6.4	6.4	6.5
Government													
1990	29.7	29.9	30.1	30.0	30.5	29.6	28.1	28.1	29.4	29.7	29.9	30.0	29.5
1991	29.5	30.3	30.2	30.4	30.7	29.8	27.9	28.0	29.1	29.8	30.0	30.1	29.6
1992	29.8	30.1	30.2	30.1	30.1	29.9	27.9	28.4	29.6	30.5	30.5	30.5	29.8
1993	30.3	30.7	30.8	30.8	30.4	30.1	28.7	29.1	30.5	30.8	30.9	31.0	30.3
1994	30.7	30.7	30.7	30.7	30.7	30.6	28.4	28.7	30.4	31.0	31.1	31.1	30.4
1995	30.7	31.4	31.3	31.7	31.4	31.0	28.9	28.9	30.7	31.4	31.5	31.4	30.8
1996	30.7	31.3	31.7	31.5	31.7	31.2	29.8	30.2	32.1	30.9	30.8	30.7	31.0
1997	30.3	30.8	30.8	31.4	30.8	30.2	28.4	28.4	30.4	30.6	30.8	30.7	30.3
1998	30.3	30.8	30.8	30.7	30.8	30.2	28.7	28.7	30.7	31.0	31.0	30.9	30.3
1999	30.4	30.8	30.8	30.9	30.8	30.5	28.4	28.4	30.6	30.9	30.9	30.9	30.3
2000	30.6	30.9	31.2	31.0	31.7	30.6	29.0	29.1	30.5	30.8	30.9	30.7	30.5
2001	30.2	30.6	30.6	30.8	30.8	30.5	28.8	29.2	30.9	31.1	31.3	31.2	30.5
2002	31.0	31.1	31.0	31.3	31.5	30.7	28.8	28.8	31.0	31.5	31.9	31.7	30.9
2003	31.0	31.6	31.8	31.7	31.6	31.0	29.0	29.3	30.8	31.4	31.6	31.6	31.0
Federal government													
1990	7.5	7.5	7.6	7.5	7.8	7.6	7.7	7.3	7.3	7.1	7.0	7.0	7.4
1991	7.0	7.2	7.3	7.3	7.3	7.3	7.3	7.0	6.8	6.7	6.7	6.7	7.0
1992	6.6	6.6	6.6	6.6	6.6	6.6	6.5	6.4	6.4	6.4	6.3	6.3	6.4
1993	6.3	6.3	6.3	6.1	6.0	6.0	6.0	6.0	6.0	6.0	6.0	6.0	6.0
1994	5.9	5.8	5.8	5.8	5.8	5.8	5.8	5.9	5.9	5.9	5.9	5.9	5.8
1995	5.9	5.9	5.9	5.9	5.9	5.9	5.9	5.9	5.9	5.9	5.8	5.8	5.8
1996	5.8	5.7	5.8	5.7	5.8	5.8	6.0	6.1	6.1	6.1	6.1	6.2	5.9
1997	6.2	6.2	6.2	6.2	6.2	6.3	6.2	6.0	6.0	5.9	5.9	5.9	6.1
1998	5.9	5.9	5.9	5.8	5.8	5.9	5.8	5.8	5.8	5.8	5.8	5.8	5.8
1999	5.7	5.7	5.7	5.8	5.7	5.8	5.7	5.8	5.8	5.8	5.7	5.7	5.7
2000	5.7	5.7	5.8	5.8	6.4	5.7	6.0	5.8	5.7	5.7	5.7	5.7	5.8
2001	5.7	5.6	5.7	5.7	5.7	5.8	5.9	6.0	6.1	6.0	6.0	6.0	5.8
2002	5.9	5.8	5.8	5.8	5.8	5.9	5.9	5.9	6.0	6.0	6.0	6.0	5.9
2003	5.9	5.9	5.9	5.9	5.9	5.9	6.1	6.2	6.2	6.2	6.1	6.2	6.0
State government													
1990	3.1	3.1	3.1	3.4	3.4	3.4	3.4	3.4	3.4	3.4	3.4	3.4	3.3
1991	3.3	3.4	3.4	3.4	3.3	3.3	3.3	3.3	3.3	3.4	3.4	3.4	3.3
1992	3.5	3.5	3.5	3.5	3.5	3.5	3.5	3.5	3.5	3.6	3.6	3.6	3.5
1993	3.7	3.7	3.7	3.7	3.7	3.6	3.7	3.6	3.7	3.6	3.6	3.7	3.6
1994	3.6	3.7	3.6	3.6	3.6	3.6	3.6	3.6	3.8	3.9	3.9	3.9	3.7
1995	3.8	3.9	3.9	4.0	3.9	3.8	3.8	3.7	4.0	4.1	4.1	4.1	3.9
1996	3.9	4.0	4.0	4.1	4.1	3.9	4.0	4.0	4.1	4.2	4.2	4.2	4.0
1997	4.1	4.2	4.2	4.2	4.2	3.9	4.0	4.0	4.3	4.3	4.3	4.2	4.1
1998	4.2	4.3	4.3	4.3	4.3	4.0	4.1	4.0	4.3	4.4	4.4	4.4	4.2
1999	4.4	4.4	4.4	4.4	4.4	4.1	4.2	3.7	4.4	4.4	4.4	4.4	4.3
2000	4.4	4.4	4.4	4.4	4.4	4.1	4.1	4.0	4.3	4.4	4.4	4.4	4.3
2001	4.3	4.4	4.4	4.4	4.4	4.2	4.2	4.2	4.5	4.4	4.5	4.4	4.3
2002	4.4	4.5	4.5	4.5	4.5	4.1	4.2	4.0	4.5	4.5	4.6	4.5	4.4
2003	4.3	4.6	4.6	4.5	4.5	4.0	4.1	4.1	4.4	4.5	4.5	4.5	4.4
Local government													
1990	19.1	19.3	19.4	19.1	19.3	18.6	17.0	17.4	18.7	19.2	19.5	19.6	18.8
1991	19.2	19.7	19.5	19.7	20.1	19.2	17.3	17.7	19.0	19.7	19.9	20.0	19.2
1992	19.7	20.0	20.1	20.0	20.0	19.8	17.9	18.5	19.7	20.5	20.6	20.6	19.7
1993	20.3	20.7	20.8	21.0	20.7	20.5	19.0	19.5	20.8	21.2	21.3	21.3	20.5
1994	21.2	21.2	21.3	21.3	21.3	21.2	19.0	19.2	20.7	21.2	21.3	21.3	20.8
1995	21.0	21.6	21.5	21.8	21.6	21.3	19.2	19.3	20.8	21.4	21.6	21.5	21.0
1996	21.0	21.6	21.9	21.7	21.8	21.5	19.8	20.1	21.9	20.6	20.5	20.3	21.0
1997	20.0	20.4	20.4	21.0	20.4	20.0	18.2	18.4	20.1	20.4	20.6	20.6	20.0
1998	20.2	20.6	20.6	20.6	20.7	20.3	18.8	18.9	20.6	20.8	20.8	20.7	20.3
1999	20.3	20.7	20.7	20.7	20.7	20.6	18.5	18.9	20.4	20.7	20.8	20.8	20.3
2000	20.5	20.8	21.0	20.8	20.9	20.8	18.9	19.3	20.5	20.7	20.8	20.6	20.4
2001	20.2	20.6	20.5	20.7	20.7	20.5	18.7	19.0	20.3	20.7	20.8	20.8	20.2
2002	20.7	20.8	20.7	21.0	21.2	20.7	18.7	18.9	20.5	21.0	21.3	21.2	20.6
2003	20.8	21.1	21.3	21.3	21.2	21.1	18.8	19.0	20.2	20.7	21.0	20.9	20.6

Employment by Industry: Texas—*Continued*

(Numbers in thousands. Not seasonally adjusted.)

Industry	January	February	March	April	May	June	July	August	September	October	November	December	Annual Average
DALLAS													
Total nonfarm													
1990	1384.6	1391.4	1399.1	1405.0	1415.9	1426.3	1422.6	1431.5	1436.1	1439.3	1444.6	1450.8	1420.6
1991	1400.0	1404.4	1409.8	1414.6	1423.3	1426.7	1421.4	1423.6	1426.7	1431.8	1432.9	1437.5	1421.1
1992	1398.0	1405.6	1411.7	1422.3	1429.5	1431.6	1428.4	1428.6	1435.0	1449.1	1448.0	1454.1	1428.5
1993	1426.8	1437.9	1446.6	1457.4	1465.8	1476.2	1476.7	1484.3	1490.4	1497.3	1501.6	1512.8	1472.8
1994	1478.9	1485.9	1496.9	1509.8	1521.3	1533.9	1537.7	1546.4	1554.9	1563.7	1573.6	1586.1	1532.4
1995	1551.6	1564.2	1574.7	1580.9	1590.2	1600.9	1593.3	1605.8	1614.1	1617.8	1629.5	1640.0	1596.9
1996	1604.7	1616.5	1629.8	1641.6	1655.3	1666.5	1662.6	1675.1	1680.6	1696.8	1710.5	1719.6	1663.3
1997	1690.6	1704.5	1720.5	1734.9	1751.4	1765.3	1755.3	1770.8	1783.5	1791.7	1801.1	1811.1	1756.7
1998	1778.2	1791.0	1802.8	1819.3	1830.8	1843.5	1842.4	1856.2	1863.0	1875.3	1885.2	1900.3	1840.7
1999	1856.6	1870.5	1885.6	1892.9	1898.6	1912.0	1904.7	1915.9	1925.6	1937.9	1945.2	1961.2	1908.9
2000	1924.6	1936.9	1953.6	1965.3	1977.5	1998.8	1985.9	1995.5	2006.2	2010.5	2015.7	2026.1	1983.1
2001	1987.8	1996.1	2007.5	2007.4	2006.2	2010.9	1982.3	1987.9	1987.6	1971.3	1966.6	1964.0	1989.6
2002	1923.4	1926.7	1936.0	1934.9	1940.2	1934.1	1919.1	1926.4	1930.6	1926.8	1930.5	1930.3	1929.9
2003	1886.5	1891.6	1894.5	1901.3	1904.7	1905.1	1891.5	1899.4	1903.1	1910.7	1912.5	1917.7	1901.6
Total private													
1990	1219.6	1224.9	1231.5	1235.9	1244.4	1261.1	1261.2	1271.3	1266.7	1267.9	1271.3	1277.4	1252.8
1991	1230.1	1231.3	1236.0	1239.5	1247.6	1255.4	1255.8	1257.9	1252.0	1255.3	1254.9	1258.9	1247.9
1992	1223.2	1227.0	1232.7	1242.9	1249.0	1255.7	1259.4	1258.5	1255.4	1268.9	1266.7	1272.3	1251.0
1993	1248.4	1255.4	1263.7	1274.5	1282.2	1295.8	1301.3	1304.5	1306.0	1311.9	1315.5	1325.9	1290.4
1994	1294.3	1298.9	1309.1	1321.2	1332.3	1348.5	1357.8	1363.8	1365.2	1373.3	1382.0	1393.4	1345.0
1995	1361.1	1371.2	1380.9	1387.3	1396.5	1411.2	1410.0	1420.9	1422.7	1426.4	1436.5	1446.5	1405.9
1996	1414.5	1424.5	1437.3	1449.6	1463.5	1477.7	1480.7	1488.5	1487.8	1501.8	1513.9	1522.6	1471.9
1997	1495.4	1507.2	1522.7	1538.2	1554.5	1573.9	1568.7	1579.2	1584.8	1592.0	1599.1	1608.7	1560.4
1998	1579.1	1589.4	1601.1	1617.6	1628.5	1644.9	1651.7	1658.2	1660.0	1667.5	1675.6	1688.4	1638.5
1999	1647.5	1660.1	1674.9	1683.5	1688.8	1704.8	1708.2	1714.7	1714.1	1724.0	1730.0	1742.2	1699.4
2000	1708.9	1719.7	1735.7	1747.5	1756.0	1781.1	1780.0	1787.2	1788.3	1792.3	1796.0	1803.5	1766.4
2001	1768.3	1773.9	1785.0	1785.2	1783.5	1790.4	1774.9	1775.9	1762.4	1744.1	1737.2	1733.6	1767.9
2002	1697.0	1694.5	1702.7	1703.8	1707.9	1711.0	1704.2	1705.9	1698.3	1689.3	1691.2	1692.1	1699.8
2003	1654.7	1652.2	1655.7	1662.1	1664.9	1669.2	1665.5	1673.3	1666.2	1670.6	1671.1	1676.7	1665.2
Goods-producing													
1990	285.7	286.1	286.1	285.7	287.2	290.8	291.9	292.4	291.8	290.9	289.1	287.1	288.7
1991	279.8	280.9	280.3	276.6	277.2	279.1	280.5	279.5	278.6	275.7	274.9	273.3	278.0
1992	269.4	269.7	271.1	273.7	275.7	277.1	279.4	278.4	277.6	277.7	276.1	275.8	275.1
1993	274.1	275.7	277.8	278.0	280.1	283.8	286.4	286.1	286.1	287.8	287.1	286.9	282.5
1994	282.3	283.0	284.8	286.6	288.7	293.0	293.2	295.3	296.1	294.1	294.3	294.5	290.5
1995	293.1	295.1	296.8	298.7	300.0	304.0	302.4	304.7	306.3	307.0	307.1	307.5	301.9
1996	301.9	305.0	307.4	308.6	311.9	315.2	315.5	316.4	316.0	317.7	318.4	318.6	312.7
1997	315.3	317.9	322.3	323.7	327.8	330.6	334.1	336.2	336.4	336.0	334.8	335.0	329.2
1998	330.8	333.6	336.3	340.3	343.2	346.7	349.2	350.7	350.7	349.8	348.5	348.6	344.0
1999	342.2	345.5	348.6	348.6	349.0	352.4	352.9	353.4	353.4	352.8	352.7	352.4	350.3
2000	350.3	353.3	357.0	357.9	359.5	364.8	364.1	364.4	364.4	363.0	361.4	360.0	360.0
2001	359.4	360.3	361.6	358.7	358.2	359.6	353.9	353.1	348.6	341.6	337.7	333.7	352.2
2002	327.1	325.7	326.5	325.0	325.3	327.2	325.0	323.5	320.2	315.1	313.4	310.3	322.0
2003	304.7	304.8	304.6	304.8	306.3	307.9	306.9	307.0	305.4	303.7	302.1	300.6	304.9
Natural resources and mining													
1990	14.9	14.8	14.8	14.9	15.0	15.1	15.1	15.1	15.2	15.1	15.1	15.3	15.0
1991	15.5	15.5	15.4	15.5	15.4	15.5	15.7	15.5	15.3	15.2	15.0	14.9	15.4
1992	15.4	15.3	15.3	14.8	14.6	14.6	14.7	14.7	14.6	14.4	14.5	14.8	14.8
1993	14.9	14.6	14.5	14.4	14.2	14.3	13.9	13.7	13.6	14.1	14.6	14.6	14.3
1994	14.6	14.0	13.7	12.6	12.4	12.5	11.9	12.0	12.3	12.4	12.3	12.3	12.8
1995	11.9	11.7	11.7	11.4	11.3	11.3	11.1	11.1	11.1	10.9	10.7	10.7	11.2
1996	10.8	10.6	10.6	10.8	10.7	10.8	10.8	10.6	10.5	10.8	10.8	10.9	10.7
1997	10.6	10.5	10.5	10.5	10.5	10.4	10.5	10.3	10.3	10.3	10.3	10.3	10.4
1998	10.1	9.8	9.9	9.9	9.8	9.7	9.6	9.6	9.5	9.4	9.2	9.3	9.7
1999	8.6	8.5	8.4	7.8	7.9	8.2	7.9	7.9	7.8	7.5	7.4	7.5	8.0
2000	7.7	7.3	7.1	6.6	6.8	7.0	6.9	6.9	6.9	6.5	6.5	6.7	6.9
2001	6.7	6.9	6.9	6.9	7.0	7.2	7.0	7.1	7.1	7.0	7.0	7.1	7.0
2002	7.1	7.1	7.1	7.4	7.3	7.4	7.3	7.3	7.2	7.0	7.0	7.0	7.2
2003	6.8	6.7	6.7	6.5	6.6	6.6	6.7	6.7	6.7	6.6	6.5	6.5	6.6
Construction													
1990	48.0	48.1	48.2	48.3	49.2	50.6	50.7	51.7	51.8	51.1	50.7	50.0	49.9
1991	46.1	47.6	48.4	48.3	49.3	50.3	51.5	51.0	50.5	49.7	48.9	48.0	49.1
1992	45.9	46.7	48.3	50.6	51.2	51.6	53.5	53.1	52.3	52.6	51.2	50.7	50.6
1993	49.3	50.2	51.8	53.1	54.6	56.4	57.7	57.9	57.8	58.3	57.3	57.0	55.1
1994	54.4	54.9	56.7	59.9	60.7	62.9	63.6	64.7	64.6	64.4	64.2	64.1	61.3
1995	61.4	62.6	64.4	65.7	67.0	69.1	69.9	71.0	71.7	71.5	71.5	71.1	68.1
1996	69.4	71.1	72.7	73.4	75.1	76.7	76.7	76.9	76.2	77.4	77.6	77.4	75.1
1997	76.0	77.7	80.0	81.6	83.5	84.7	85.1	85.9	85.4	85.4	84.4	83.8	82.8
1998	81.5	83.9	86.0	88.4	90.1	91.4	92.9	94.0	94.1	94.3	93.6	93.3	90.3
1999	90.9	93.7	96.1	98.9	98.9	101.2	102.1	102.9	103.1	103.5	103.3	102.8	99.8
2000	100.7	103.4	106.6	107.4	108.4	111.6	112.8	113.6	113.8	113.0	112.0	111.6	109.6
2001	111.4	112.4	114.1	113.9	114.7	115.9	113.9	113.9	111.7	108.5	107.0	105.5	111.9
2002	102.4	102.4	103.7	103.4	104.4	105.9	104.8	105.1	103.1	100.9	100.6	99.0	103.0
2003	96.1	96.4	96.8	97.5	99.1	100.2	100.9	101.0	100.1	98.4	97.1	95.7	98.3

Employment by Industry: Texas—*Continued*

(Numbers in thousands. Not seasonally adjusted.)

Industry	January	February	March	April	May	June	July	August	September	October	November	December	Annual Average
DALLAS—*Continued*													
Manufacturing													
1990	222.8	223.2	223.1	222.5	223.0	225.1	226.1	225.6	224.8	224.7	223.3	221.8	223.8
1991	218.2	217.8	216.5	212.8	212.5	213.3	213.3	213.0	212.8	210.8	211.0	210.4	213.5
1992	208.1	207.7	207.5	208.3	209.9	210.9	211.2	210.6	210.7	210.7	210.4	210.3	209.7
1993	209.9	210.9	211.5	210.5	211.3	213.1	214.8	214.5	214.7	215.4	215.2	215.3	213.1
1994	213.3	214.1	214.4	214.1	215.6	217.6	217.7	218.6	219.2	217.3	217.8	218.1	216.5
1995	219.8	220.8	220.7	221.6	221.7	223.6	221.4	222.6	223.5	224.6	224.9	225.7	222.6
1996	221.7	223.3	224.1	224.4	226.1	227.7	228.0	228.9	229.3	229.5	230.0	230.3	226.9
1997	228.7	229.7	231.8	231.6	233.8	235.5	238.5	240.0	240.7	240.3	240.1	240.9	236.0
1998	239.2	239.9	240.4	242.0	243.3	245.6	246.7	247.1	247.1	246.1	245.7	246.0	244.1
1999	242.7	243.3	244.1	241.9	242.2	243.0	242.9	242.6	242.5	241.8	242.0	242.1	242.6
2000	241.9	242.6	243.3	243.9	244.3	246.2	244.4	243.9	243.7	243.5	242.9	241.7	243.5
2001	241.3	241.0	240.6	237.9	236.5	236.5	233.0	232.1	229.8	226.1	223.7	221.1	233.3
2002	217.6	216.2	215.7	214.2	213.6	213.9	212.9	211.1	209.9	207.2	205.8	204.3	211.9
2003	201.8	201.7	201.1	200.8	200.6	201.1	199.3	199.3	198.6	198.7	198.5	198.4	200.0
Service-providing													
1990	1098.9	1105.3	1113.0	1119.3	1128.7	1135.5	1130.7	1139.1	1144.3	1148.4	1155.5	1163.7	1131.9
1991	1120.2	1123.5	1129.5	1138.0	1146.1	1147.6	1140.9	1144.1	1148.1	1156.1	1158.0	1164.2	1143.0
1992	1128.6	1135.9	1140.6	1148.6	1153.8	1154.5	1149.0	1150.2	1157.4	1171.4	1171.9	1178.3	1153.4
1993	1152.7	1162.2	1168.8	1179.4	1185.7	1192.4	1190.3	1198.2	1204.3	1209.5	1214.5	1225.9	1190.3
1994	1196.6	1202.9	1212.1	1223.2	1232.6	1240.9	1244.5	1251.1	1258.8	1269.6	1279.3	1291.6	1241.9
1995	1258.5	1269.1	1277.9	1282.2	1290.2	1296.9	1290.9	1301.1	1307.8	1310.8	1322.4	1332.5	1295.0
1996	1302.8	1311.5	1322.4	1333.0	1343.4	1351.3	1347.1	1358.7	1364.6	1379.1	1392.1	1401.0	1350.6
1997	1375.3	1386.6	1398.2	1411.2	1423.6	1434.7	1421.2	1434.6	1447.1	1455.7	1466.3	1476.1	1427.6
1998	1447.4	1457.4	1466.5	1479.0	1487.6	1496.8	1493.2	1505.5	1512.3	1525.5	1536.7	1551.7	1496.6
1999	1514.4	1525.0	1537.0	1544.3	1549.6	1559.6	1551.8	1562.5	1572.2	1585.1	1592.5	1608.8	1558.6
2000	1574.3	1583.6	1596.6	1607.4	1618.0	1634.0	1621.8	1631.1	1641.8	1647.5	1654.3	1666.1	1623.0
2001	1628.4	1635.8	1645.9	1648.7	1648.0	1651.3	1628.4	1634.8	1639.0	1629.7	1628.9	1630.3	1637.4
2002	1596.3	1601.0	1609.5	1609.9	1614.9	1606.9	1594.1	1602.9	1610.4	1611.7	1617.1	1620.0	1607.9
2003	1581.8	1586.8	1589.9	1596.5	1598.4	1597.2	1584.6	1592.4	1597.7	1607.0	1610.4	1617.1	1596.7
Trade, transportation and utilities													
1990	319.3	317.5	319.3	317.8	319.2	323.3	322.0	323.5	323.0	323.8	328.9	333.9	322.6
1991	320.9	316.8	318.0	317.0	319.0	321.8	321.3	322.5	321.4	323.3	327.3	331.7	321.8
1992	317.5	315.5	315.3	317.8	318.8	320.8	320.5	320.8	321.2	325.1	328.4	333.4	321.3
1993	320.5	318.4	319.6	324.3	324.9	326.6	328.2	330.1	330.5	332.4	337.6	344.7	328.2
1994	329.4	327.9	329.7	330.8	335.1	339.2	337.7	340.5	341.9	345.7	352.6	360.2	339.2
1995	344.6	343.7	345.4	345.0	347.1	350.1	350.5	353.1	353.1	354.2	362.1	367.7	351.4
1996	355.5	353.4	355.5	357.1	359.1	362.7	362.0	363.8	363.9	365.5	372.5	378.0	362.4
1997	364.3	363.4	365.4	370.1	373.0	376.5	375.6	377.1	378.5	382.4	388.2	394.1	375.7
1998	383.9	382.8	385.2	387.9	389.6	392.1	392.7	395.6	396.4	400.0	408.7	415.5	394.2
1999	400.2	400.0	402.3	403.3	405.2	409.0	408.7	411.2	411.8	417.0	424.6	433.0	410.5
2000	418.4	417.4	418.9	420.0	422.4	428.4	427.3	431.7	431.2	435.3	444.0	451.5	428.9
2001	436.5	433.8	435.9	433.5	432.7	434.7	433.3	435.6	435.0	433.4	435.1	438.1	434.8
2002	423.9	420.8	421.4	419.5	419.9	420.8	421.0	422.0	420.2	419.2	423.7	429.5	421.8
2003	412.1	407.8	407.4	408.0	407.4	407.7	404.7	409.2	408.3	413.1	417.8	421.9	410.5
Wholesale trade													
1990	99.7	100.1	100.2	100.7	100.9	101.7	101.7	102.4	102.2	102.3	102.6	102.8	101.4
1991	100.7	100.9	101.2	99.8	100.1	100.9	100.5	100.8	99.9	99.8	99.5	99.7	100.3
1992	97.7	97.9	98.1	98.7	98.9	99.5	99.4	99.2	99.2	99.9	99.7	99.8	99.0
1993	98.1	98.3	99.0	102.8	103.1	103.6	102.9	103.0	103.6	103.6	103.6	103.9	102.1
1994	100.2	100.6	101.0	102.2	102.4	103.1	102.9	103.3	103.2	104.6	105.2	106.0	102.9
1995	102.7	103.1	103.6	105.3	105.7	106.7	106.6	107.1	107.3	107.0	107.2	107.6	105.8
1996	106.5	106.9	107.4	107.9	108.5	109.5	110.0	110.8	110.9	110.2	110.4	111.0	109.2
1997	110.9	111.9	112.9	114.9	115.8	117.0	117.6	118.0	118.1	118.6	118.5	119.4	116.1
1998	121.0	121.9	122.5	124.2	125.0	125.7	126.2	126.9	126.4	127.5	128.1	128.4	125.3
1999	126.4	127.2	127.9	127.2	128.1	128.8	129.1	129.3	129.3	128.9	129.5	130.7	128.5
2000	129.5	129.8	131.2	133.0	133.3	134.8	133.3	133.5	133.4	133.7	134.2	134.6	132.9
2001	134.7	135.5	136.2	135.4	134.7	135.1	134.2	134.2	133.2	132.6	131.4	131.3	134.0
2002	129.3	129.1	130.0	129.1	128.9	129.1	129.3	129.3	129.0	128.0	128.3	128.6	129.0
2003	126.1	125.9	126.2	125.6	125.2	125.3	124.5	124.7	124.4	124.4	124.1	123.4	125.0
Retail trade													
1990	171.4	168.5	169.7	169.0	169.6	172.2	171.5	171.8	171.4	172.4	177.2	181.4	172.2
1991	170.3	166.3	167.3	166.8	167.6	169.3	169.5	170.4	169.8	171.0	175.3	179.0	170.2
1992	168.7	166.2	166.0	167.3	168.1	168.9	169.3	169.5	169.6	171.3	175.4	179.6	170.0
1993	169.8	167.8	168.0	168.8	169.1	170.3	172.7	174.3	173.7	174.9	179.6	184.5	172.8
1994	174.5	172.3	172.6	175.0	177.1	179.2	178.4	180.6	182.2	183.7	188.7	194.0	179.9
1995	183.6	182.2	182.8	181.5	182.8	185.3	184.7	186.4	186.2	187.6	194.7	199.1	186.4
1996	189.1	186.4	187.7	188.4	189.7	191.9	190.5	191.2	190.9	192.7	198.8	203.8	191.8
1997	192.2	189.7	190.6	191.2	192.7	194.4	192.7	194.5	194.4	196.7	201.9	206.8	194.8
1998	196.1	193.9	195.3	195.3	196.1	197.6	197.5	198.9	200.0	202.3	209.5	215.2	199.8
1999	204.3	203.0	204.4	205.0	206.0	208.6	208.1	209.7	210.1	213.9	220.7	227.3	210.1
2000	215.8	214.6	214.6	213.2	214.8	218.5	219.0	222.1	221.4	224.3	231.8	237.8	220.7
2001	226.9	223.9	225.1	223.9	223.3	224.5	223.8	225.6	225.8	224.6	228.7	232.0	225.7
2002	221.4	219.2	218.6	217.5	217.7	217.9	217.5	218.1	217.0	216.1	220.7	226.4	219.0
2003	213.1	209.4	208.7	209.3	209.4	209.8	208.4	211.7	211.3	214.1	218.8	222.8	212.2

Employment by Industry: Texas—*Continued*

(Numbers in thousands. Not seasonally adjusted.)

Industry	January	February	March	April	May	June	July	August	September	October	November	December	Annual Average
DALLAS—*Continued*													
Transportation and utilities													
1990	48.2	48.9	49.4	48.1	48.7	49.4	48.8	49.3	49.4	49.1	49.1	49.7	49.0
1991	49.9	49.6	49.5	50.4	51.3	51.6	51.3	51.3	51.7	52.5	52.5	53.0	51.2
1992	51.1	51.4	51.2	51.8	51.8	52.4	51.8	52.1	52.4	53.9	53.3	54.0	52.3
1993	52.6	52.3	52.6	52.7	52.7	52.7	52.6	52.8	53.2	53.9	54.4	56.3	53.2
1994	54.7	55.0	56.1	53.6	55.6	56.9	56.4	56.6	56.5	57.4	58.7	60.2	56.5
1995	58.3	58.4	59.0	58.2	58.6	58.1	59.2	59.6	59.6	59.6	60.2	61.0	59.2
1996	59.9	60.1	60.4	60.8	60.9	61.3	61.5	61.8	62.1	62.6	63.3	63.2	61.5
1997	61.2	61.8	61.9	64.0	64.5	65.1	65.3	64.6	66.0	67.1	67.8	67.9	64.8
1998	66.8	67.0	67.4	68.4	68.5	68.8	69.0	69.8	70.0	70.2	71.1	71.9	69.1
1999	69.5	69.8	70.0	71.1	71.1	71.6	71.5	72.2	72.4	74.2	74.4	75.0	71.9
2000	73.1	73.0	73.1	73.8	74.3	75.1	75.0	76.1	76.4	77.3	78.0	79.1	75.4
2001	74.9	74.4	74.6	74.2	74.7	75.1	75.3	75.8	76.0	76.2	75.0	74.8	75.1
2002	73.2	72.5	72.8	72.9	73.3	73.8	74.2	74.6	74.2	75.1	74.7	74.5	73.8
2003	72.9	72.5	72.5	73.1	72.8	72.6	71.8	72.8	72.6	74.6	74.9	75.7	73.2
Information													
1990	61.9	62.0	62.7	62.5	62.6	63.3	64.7	64.6	64.0	64.5	65.0	65.4	63.6
1991	63.1	62.3	62.4	64.3	64.6	63.4	64.0	63.5	62.8	63.8	64.2	64.8	63.6
1992	61.4	61.6	61.5	61.5	61.7	61.7	61.7	61.2	60.5	61.3	61.7	62.5	61.5
1993	62.0	62.3	62.6	62.9	63.2	64.0	63.8	63.3	62.8	63.3	63.4	63.9	63.1
1994	64.2	64.4	64.9	65.1	65.7	66.5	67.9	67.8	67.9	68.7	70.0	71.7	67.1
1995	72.2	73.5	73.8	74.0	74.5	74.9	74.9	75.6	75.0	75.3	76.3	77.8	74.8
1996	75.3	76.2	77.2	78.1	79.4	80.1	80.5	81.0	80.8	82.9	84.7	85.8	80.2
1997	87.4	88.2	87.3	87.9	88.9	90.4	90.3	90.7	90.3	91.1	92.1	92.5	89.8
1998	92.1	92.2	92.3	92.7	93.8	94.5	95.1	95.5	95.5	95.5	96.3	97.4	94.4
1999	94.7	95.5	95.9	97.3	98.4	98.1	96.5	97.2	97.2	97.6	98.7	99.4	97.2
2000	98.0	99.7	100.7	101.1	101.7	103.7	104.3	105.2	105.4	105.6	106.6	106.5	103.2
2001	103.0	103.1	104.0	103.2	102.7	102.2	100.5	99.9	98.6	98.0	97.0	95.6	100.7
2002	94.8	93.8	93.7	91.3	90.6	89.7	87.5	86.6	85.7	85.2	85.2	84.7	89.1
2003	83.2	82.9	82.5	81.6	81.2	80.8	80.6	80.4	79.4	79.3	77.7	77.8	80.6
Financial activities													
1990	132.1	133.6	133.8	135.1	135.6	136.8	136.7	137.3	136.0	135.7	135.5	136.1	135.4
1991	134.0	134.0	133.9	134.0	133.9	134.0	135.2	135.8	134.3	135.0	134.5	134.9	134.5
1992	132.6	132.2	132.6	131.2	131.2	131.5	132.8	132.0	130.6	132.0	131.8	131.6	131.8
1993	133.3	133.6	134.0	133.5	133.4	134.5	136.1	136.5	135.9	136.7	136.9	137.8	135.2
1994	137.9	138.8	139.8	139.8	140.3	140.7	139.7	139.2	138.6	139.8	139.8	140.3	139.6
1995	137.8	138.1	138.7	138.8	139.0	140.5	140.7	140.9	141.4	140.3	140.7	141.8	139.9
1996	140.9	141.4	142.2	141.2	141.9	143.4	142.8	143.9	143.8	145.0	146.0	146.2	143.2
1997	147.1	147.8	148.8	150.6	152.2	154.1	153.3	154.3	154.7	156.5	158.4	159.2	153.1
1998	158.9	160.1	161.7	163.1	164.3	165.3	167.4	167.9	167.7	168.8	168.8	169.8	165.3
1999	167.7	167.8	168.8	169.1	169.3	170.0	171.1	171.1	169.8	169.8	169.3	169.8	169.5
2000	167.9	168.0	169.0	170.3	170.1	170.6	170.7	169.9	169.0	169.1	168.5	169.4	169.4
2001	164.6	165.5	166.1	166.3	166.6	168.2	167.8	168.1	167.3	167.4	167.7	168.4	167.0
2002	167.5	167.3	167.8	167.1	167.5	167.9	168.0	168.2	167.4	166.7	167.2	167.2	167.5
2003	165.6	166.2	166.1	166.7	167.4	168.1	168.9	169.5	168.9	169.4	169.8	170.0	168.1
Professional and business services													
1990	148.1	149.4	151.8	152.6	154.1	157.7	159.0	161.4	162.7	162.3	163.2	164.5	157.2
1991	152.5	153.3	155.0	154.7	156.2	157.6	157.1	157.6	157.0	158.3	157.2	156.6	156.1
1992	153.2	154.0	156.3	159.7	160.3	161.6	162.3	161.5	162.0	164.5	163.3	162.9	160.1
1993	158.2	160.5	162.2	167.3	168.6	171.5	174.2	174.4	176.5	177.7	177.1	177.9	170.5
1994	173.5	174.7	177.1	182.1	181.8	184.9	193.5	194.3	195.2	194.2	195.3	195.8	186.9
1995	189.2	192.7	195.6	197.4	198.2	200.1	200.2	203.0	203.4	204.6	207.0	207.2	199.9
1996	202.3	206.6	209.4	216.5	218.7	221.2	226.5	228.4	228.8	232.2	234.5	235.0	221.7
1997	227.2	230.9	235.0	239.6	240.9	245.8	242.9	246.6	249.3	251.2	252.1	254.1	243.0
1998	249.1	252.0	254.8	258.4	259.2	264.2	265.5	266.0	266.5	271.0	270.6	273.6	262.6
1999	268.4	273.5	277.5	278.4	277.2	282.2	285.2	286.3	286.8	288.8	288.9	291.4	282.1
2000	286.1	289.2	292.9	297.0	298.6	307.0	306.0	308.3	310.0	309.2	308.9	309.6	301.9
2001	299.0	299.7	301.0	301.3	299.8	299.7	296.0	294.8	291.4	284.8	282.9	281.2	294.3
2002	272.9	272.1	273.5	274.9	275.9	276.4	277.1	278.7	277.6	276.0	275.2	273.7	275.3
2003	266.4	265.7	266.2	268.7	268.4	269.4	269.4	270.8	270.4	270.7	270.2	271.7	269.0
Educational and health services													
1990	111.2	113.7	114.1	114.4	115.3	115.5	115.4	119.3	119.4	119.9	120.7	121.0	116.7
1991	116.9	119.1	120.1	121.1	121.4	121.1	123.6	124.7	125.2	126.3	126.7	127.2	122.8
1992	125.5	127.7	127.9	127.9	128.1	127.9	129.3	131.2	132.0	133.5	133.2	133.7	129.8
1993	130.8	132.3	133.1	131.8	132.2	132.3	130.4	131.1	132.4	132.7	133.0	133.6	132.1
1994	130.4	131.8	132.3	133.9	134.2	134.7	135.9	136.6	137.6	138.5	139.3	139.8	135.4
1995	136.8	138.6	139.6	141.4	142.1	142.5	143.0	144.5	145.9	147.2	148.1	148.7	143.2
1996	145.8	147.2	148.6	147.8	148.9	148.7	148.1	149.5	150.8	152.5	153.6	154.1	149.6
1997	152.9	155.1	156.4	156.1	158.0	158.1	159.1	160.8	162.6	161.0	161.3	161.5	158.6
1998	158.1	159.8	160.2	161.2	161.5	161.5	161.8	162.5	163.5	162.0	163.1	163.4	161.6
1999	160.2	161.4	161.9	161.6	161.7	161.5	163.0	164.3	165.6	165.9	166.2	166.6	163.3
2000	163.2	164.3	165.6	165.5	166.4	166.2	167.3	168.1	170.2	169.5	169.6	169.9	167.2
2001	169.4	171.5	172.3	173.2	174.4	175.9	176.3	177.0	177.9	177.7	178.1	178.4	175.2
2002	177.3	179.2	179.7	181.0	182.0	181.0	180.9	182.3	183.6	183.6	184.5	184.9	181.7
2003	185.0	186.3	186.9	187.1	187.7	187.3	188.5	189.2	190.1	190.6	191.0	191.6	188.4

Employment by Industry: Texas—*Continued*

(Numbers in thousands. Not seasonally adjusted.)

Industry	January	February	March	April	May	June	July	August	September	October	November	December	Annual Average
DALLAS—*Continued*													
Leisure and hospitality													
1990	109.8	110.8	111.6	114.5	116.7	119.2	117.2	118.4	116.0	117.5	115.9	116.4	115.3
1991	110.1	111.9	113.0	118.2	121.2	123.1	119.1	119.6	118.3	118.6	115.8	115.9	117.1
1992	109.6	111.9	113.3	115.4	118.0	118.8	117.1	118.1	116.7	120.1	117.7	117.6	116.2
1993	114.4	117.2	118.6	121.1	123.8	126.0	125.1	126.1	125.5	124.7	124.0	124.3	122.6
1994	120.3	121.8	123.6	125.6	128.9	130.7	131.1	131.5	129.5	133.2	131.2	131.4	128.2
1995	128.5	130.5	131.7	132.4	135.4	137.5	136.8	137.5	136.5	137.2	134.6	135.0	134.5
1996	132.7	134.0	136.0	138.4	141.2	142.9	142.1	142.5	141.2	143.1	141.1	141.3	139.7
1997	138.4	140.7	144.1	146.5	149.2	152.9	148.8	148.9	149.0	149.8	147.8	147.6	147.0
1998	142.9	145.0	146.6	148.9	151.5	154.3	153.3	153.5	153.5	154.3	153.3	153.1	150.9
1999	148.2	150.0	153.0	157.9	160.2	162.5	161.7	162.2	161.5	163.7	161.2	160.9	158.6
2000	156.4	158.7	161.2	164.6	166.1	168.6	168.5	168.2	167.1	169.4	166.0	165.7	165.0
2001	164.4	167.3	170.1	175.0	175.5	175.3	174.2	174.8	171.9	170.6	167.8	167.2	171.2
2002	163.5	164.8	167.7	171.7	173.4	173.9	172.0	172.0	171.3	171.3	169.4	169.0	170.0
2003	165.6	166.0	167.5	170.7	172.5	173.2	172.1	173.4	171.0	171.2	170.1	170.7	170.3
Other services													
1990	51.5	51.8	52.1	53.3	53.7	54.5	54.3	54.4	53.8	53.3	53.0	53.0	53.2
1991	52.8	53.0	53.3	53.6	54.1	55.3	55.0	54.7	54.4	54.3	54.3	54.5	54.1
1992	54.0	54.4	54.7	55.7	55.2	56.3	56.3	55.3	54.8	54.7	54.5	54.8	55.1
1993	55.1	55.4	55.8	55.6	56.0	57.1	57.1	56.9	56.3	56.6	56.4	56.8	56.3
1994	56.3	56.5	56.9	57.3	57.6	58.8	58.8	58.6	58.4	59.1	59.5	59.7	58.1
1995	58.9	59.0	59.3	59.6	60.2	61.6	61.5	61.6	61.1	60.6	60.6	60.8	60.4
1996	60.1	60.7	61.0	61.9	62.4	63.5	63.2	63.0	62.5	62.9	63.1	63.6	62.3
1997	62.8	63.2	63.4	63.7	64.5	65.5	64.6	64.6	64.0	64.0	64.4	64.7	64.1
1998	63.3	63.9	64.0	65.1	65.4	66.3	66.7	66.5	66.2	66.1	66.3	67.0	65.6
1999	65.9	66.4	66.9	67.3	67.8	69.1	69.1	69.0	68.0	68.4	68.4	68.7	67.9
2000	68.6	69.1	70.4	71.1	71.2	71.8	71.8	71.4	71.0	71.2	71.0	70.9	70.8
2001	72.0	72.7	74.0	74.0	73.6	74.8	72.9	72.6	71.7	70.6	70.9	71.0	72.6
2002	70.0	70.8	72.4	73.3	73.3	74.1	72.7	72.6	72.3	72.2	72.6	72.8	72.4
2003	72.1	72.5	74.5	74.5	74.0	74.8	74.4	73.8	72.7	72.6	72.4	72.4	73.4
Government													
1990	165.0	166.5	167.6	169.1	171.5	165.2	161.4	160.2	169.4	171.4	173.3	173.4	167.8
1991	169.9	173.1	173.8	175.1	175.7	171.3	165.6	165.7	174.7	176.5	178.0	178.6	173.2
1992	174.8	178.6	179.0	179.4	180.5	175.9	169.0	170.1	179.6	180.2	181.3	181.8	177.5
1993	178.4	182.5	182.9	182.9	183.6	180.4	175.4	179.8	184.4	185.4	186.1	186.9	182.4
1994	184.6	187.0	187.8	188.6	189.0	185.4	179.9	182.6	189.7	190.4	191.6	192.7	187.4
1995	190.5	193.0	193.8	193.6	193.7	189.7	183.3	184.9	191.4	191.4	193.0	193.5	191.0
1996	190.2	192.0	192.5	192.0	191.8	188.8	181.9	186.6	192.8	195.0	196.6	197.0	191.4
1997	195.2	197.3	197.8	196.7	196.9	191.4	186.6	191.6	198.7	199.7	202.0	202.4	196.4
1998	199.1	201.6	201.7	201.7	202.3	198.6	190.7	198.0	203.0	207.8	209.6	211.9	202.2
1999	209.1	210.4	210.7	209.4	209.8	207.2	196.5	201.2	211.5	213.9	215.2	219.0	209.5
2000	215.7	217.2	217.9	217.8	221.5	217.7	205.9	208.3	217.9	218.2	219.7	222.6	216.7
2001	219.5	222.2	222.5	222.2	222.7	220.5	207.4	212.0	225.2	227.2	229.4	230.4	221.8
2002	226.4	232.2	233.3	231.1	232.3	223.1	214.9	220.5	232.3	237.5	239.3	238.2	230.1
2003	231.8	239.4	238.8	239.2	239.8	235.9	226.0	226.1	236.9	240.1	241.4	241.0	236.4
Federal government													
1990	29.8	29.8	30.1	30.4	32.4	32.3	32.9	31.7	31.4	31.3	31.7	31.9	31.3
1991	31.8	31.8	32.1	32.2	32.3	32.2	32.2	32.2	32.2	32.1	31.9	32.5	32.1
1992	32.1	31.8	31.9	31.8	31.6	31.6	31.6	31.5	32.1	32.0	31.5	31.8	31.8
1993	31.7	31.7	31.6	31.3	31.3	31.8	32.0	31.8	31.8	31.9	31.4	32.1	31.7
1994	31.9	31.9	31.7	32.2	32.1	31.9	31.5	31.4	31.5	31.3	31.5	32.6	31.8
1995	31.8	31.5	31.5	31.2	31.0	30.7	30.3	30.2	30.1	29.9	30.0	31.0	30.8
1996	28.4	28.5	28.5	28.9	28.6	28.7	28.6	28.7	29.1	28.9	29.4	30.3	28.9
1997	29.9	29.7	29.9	29.8	29.7	29.8	30.0	30.3	30.3	29.9	30.8	31.6	30.1
1998	30.0	30.0	29.9	30.5	30.6	30.4	30.6	31.1	31.3	31.8	32.3	33.5	31.0
1999	32.3	31.2	31.1	31.4	31.2	31.1	31.0	31.2	31.1	31.3	31.3	33.1	31.4
2000	32.1	31.3	31.5	32.3	36.0	33.1	32.8	31.2	31.0	31.1	31.2	32.2	32.2
2001	31.8	30.9	30.9	30.8	30.7	30.9	31.1	31.0	31.0	31.1	31.0	30.8	30.9
2002	30.5	30.5	30.7	30.3	30.4	30.6	30.7	30.7	30.9	31.6	31.5	31.6	30.8
2003	31.1	31.0	30.8	30.7	30.7	30.5	30.4	30.3	30.0	30.4	29.9	29.9	30.5
State government													
1990	22.0	22.4	22.5	22.6	22.6	21.4	20.9	21.2	22.5	23.5	23.7	23.6	22.4
1991	22.9	23.4	23.4	23.5	23.4	22.0	21.6	22.1	23.0	24.1	24.5	24.4	23.2
1992	24.0	24.8	24.4	25.0	24.9	24.3	23.5	23.9	25.0	24.9	25.1	25.5	24.6
1993	25.2	25.7	25.6	25.7	25.5	24.3	24.7	24.5	25.8	26.2	26.1	25.7	25.4
1994	25.5	26.1	26.2	26.3	26.0	25.1	25.4	24.9	26.3	27.1	27.1	26.7	26.1
1995	26.5	27.3	27.3	27.4	27.2	25.9	25.7	25.4	27.2	27.3	27.4	26.9	26.8
1996	27.3	27.3	27.1	27.2	26.6	25.6	25.4	25.2	26.7	27.9	27.7	27.3	26.8
1997	27.4	27.7	27.6	26.8	26.4	24.3	24.8	24.2	27.1	27.1	27.1	26.7	26.4
1998	26.8	27.1	26.9	26.7	26.6	26.0	24.5	24.4	25.4	26.4	26.6	27.3	26.2
1999	27.1	27.4	27.2	27.3	27.0	26.5	25.1	24.6	25.7	26.3	26.5	27.8	26.5
2000	27.2	27.7	27.6	27.7	27.3	27.0	25.3	25.2	25.6	26.5	26.8	28.1	26.8
2001	27.6	28.7	28.7	28.7	28.3	28.1	26.9	26.6	27.0	29.0	29.6	29.8	28.2
2002	29.5	30.4	30.6	30.3	30.1	29.0	28.2	27.2	29.2	30.1	30.2	30.4	29.6
2003	29.6	30.6	30.3	30.1	30.0	28.5	27.9	26.8	29.1	30.1	30.3	30.3	29.5

Employment by Industry: Texas—*Continued*

(Numbers in thousands. Not seasonally adjusted.)

Industry	January	February	March	April	May	June	July	August	September	October	November	December	Annual Average
DALLAS—*Continued*													
Local government													
1990	113.2	114.3	115.0	116.1	116.5	111.5	107.6	107.3	115.5	116.6	117.9	117.9	114.1
1991	115.2	117.9	118.3	119.4	120.0	117.1	111.8	111.4	119.5	120.3	121.6	121.7	117.9
1992	118.7	122.0	122.7	122.6	124.0	120.0	113.9	114.7	122.5	123.3	124.7	124.5	121.1
1993	121.5	125.1	125.7	125.9	126.8	124.3	118.7	123.5	126.8	127.3	128.6	129.1	125.3
1994	127.2	129.0	129.9	130.1	130.9	128.4	123.0	126.3	131.9	132.0	133.0	133.4	129.6
1995	132.2	134.2	135.0	135.0	135.5	133.1	127.3	129.3	134.1	134.2	135.6	135.6	133.4
1996	134.5	136.2	136.9	135.9	136.6	134.5	127.9	132.7	137.0	138.2	139.5	139.4	135.8
1997	137.9	139.9	140.3	140.1	140.8	137.3	131.8	137.1	141.3	142.7	144.1	144.1	139.8
1998	142.3	144.5	144.9	144.5	145.1	142.2	135.6	142.5	146.3	149.6	150.7	151.1	144.9
1999	149.7	151.8	152.4	150.7	151.6	149.6	140.4	145.4	154.7	156.3	157.4	158.1	151.5
2000	156.4	158.2	158.8	157.8	158.2	157.6	147.8	151.9	161.3	160.6	161.7	162.3	157.7
2001	160.1	162.6	162.9	162.7	163.7	161.5	149.4	154.4	167.2	167.1	168.8	169.8	162.5
2002	166.4	171.3	172.0	170.5	171.8	163.5	156.0	162.6	172.2	175.8	177.6	176.2	169.7
2003	171.1	177.8	177.7	178.4	179.1	176.9	167.7	169.0	177.8	179.6	181.2	180.8	176.4
EL PASO													
Total nonfarm													
1990	204.8	206.1	206.3	207.2	209.2	209.8	209.3	210.0	210.4	210.7	211.0	210.9	208.8
1991	207.1	206.9	207.9	209.1	210.5	210.5	210.5	212.3	214.1	213.8	213.8	215.8	211.0
1992	211.1	212.1	214.3	215.6	216.6	217.5	217.7	218.1	220.0	223.8	223.2	223.6	217.8
1993	218.7	221.4	221.0	223.5	224.1	224.3	225.3	226.8	228.8	228.3	227.9	228.5	224.9
1994	223.2	224.4	226.1	227.7	228.7	229.8	230.9	233.3	234.8	236.4	237.6	237.5	230.9
1995	231.8	233.3	234.0	233.9	235.1	235.1	234.1	236.8	237.9	235.4	234.9	237.5	235.0
1996	231.4	232.5	233.7	234.6	236.2	235.3	235.3	238.1	238.5	240.7	241.4	242.4	236.7
1997	236.2	237.8	239.4	240.8	242.9	243.3	243.0	244.7	247.1	246.3	247.2	248.9	243.1
1998	243.3	243.9	245.9	247.0	249.0	248.4	246.3	248.6	249.6	250.6	251.0	251.7	247.9
1999	246.3	248.2	248.7	250.0	250.9	250.5	249.9	251.4	253.6	254.0	254.9	256.9	251.3
2000	252.0	253.6	255.4	255.0	256.3	255.9	254.3	256.7	259.1	257.9	259.5	260.7	256.4
2001	254.9	255.6	257.6	255.1	256.3	255.5	251.4	254.7	257.0	253.9	254.8	254.7	255.1
2002	251.6	251.9	254.7	255.3	255.7	254.7	251.7	256.1	261.0	258.6	260.2	261.1	256.1
2003	254.3	255.1	255.4	255.9	255.2	251.2	249.3	253.5	257.0	256.5	257.6	258.1	254.9
Total private													
1990	161.0	161.8	162.0	162.7	164.4	165.9	166.3	168.0	166.6	165.3	165.4	165.7	164.6
1991	162.6	161.6	162.7	163.3	164.6	165.9	166.4	168.0	168.3	166.7	166.6	168.1	165.4
1992	165.2	165.1	167.0	168.0	168.9	171.7	171.5	172.4	172.7	174.2	173.3	173.9	170.3
1993	171.1	172.1	172.6	174.8	175.2	176.8	177.6	179.5	180.0	178.9	178.2	179.0	176.3
1994	174.3	174.5	175.8	177.8	179.4	181.2	183.3	185.7	186.4	186.2	187.5	188.9	181.8
1995	183.7	184.3	185.2	184.5	185.5	186.5	185.6	187.7	187.9	184.6	184.1	187.0	185.6
1996	182.3	182.8	183.6	183.9	185.4	186.0	186.0	188.3	188.1	187.7	188.4	189.2	186.0
1997	184.3	184.9	186.4	187.6	189.8	191.4	191.6	192.9	194.0	192.8	193.4	195.2	190.4
1998	190.2	189.7	191.7	192.9	194.8	195.7	193.9	195.8	195.4	196.0	196.2	196.9	194.1
1999	191.9	192.7	193.5	194.6	195.5	196.7	196.3	197.4	198.2	197.8	198.5	200.3	196.1
2000	196.0	196.5	198.2	197.5	198.7	200.6	198.9	201.1	202.8	200.8	202.3	203.3	199.7
2001	197.4	197.2	199.1	196.5	197.6	198.4	197.0	198.8	198.3	195.3	195.7	196.5	197.3
2002	193.2	192.5	195.5	196.6	197.9	199.0	198.3	201.1	201.6	198.4	199.8	201.7	198.0
2003	195.0	194.4	194.8	195.4	195.6	194.5	193.7	196.3	196.3	195.5	196.5	196.7	195.4
Goods-producing													
1990	48.8	49.1	49.1	49.1	49.3	50.3	50.4	51.8	50.8	49.9	49.5	48.9	49.8
1991	48.2	48.1	48.1	48.1	48.8	49.2	49.8	50.6	51.7	50.6	50.4	50.4	49.5
1992	49.4	49.2	50.4	51.0	51.9	52.9	52.7	53.8	54.1	54.5	53.9	54.0	52.3
1993	52.4	52.9	52.9	53.4	53.6	54.5	54.8	56.2	56.8	56.0	55.2	55.2	54.5
1994	53.1	53.0	53.2	53.8	54.1	54.7	55.4	57.5	58.3	57.0	57.2	57.3	55.4
1995	55.4	56.0	56.4	55.9	56.1	56.8	56.1	57.4	58.1	55.3	54.5	56.0	56.2
1996	54.5	54.6	54.3	54.1	54.7	55.4	55.0	56.4	56.7	55.7	55.5	55.7	55.2
1997	54.1	54.3	54.6	54.4	55.2	55.5	55.0	55.9	56.3	55.8	55.2	55.9	55.2
1998	54.8	53.8	54.7	54.5	55.2	55.3	53.9	54.9	55.5	55.3	54.1	54.5	54.7
1999	52.7	52.3	52.6	52.3	52.5	52.5	52.5	52.8	53.4	52.8	52.3	52.3	52.6
2000	51.5	51.5	51.4	50.2	50.5	50.7	49.4	50.7	51.0	49.6	49.5	49.2	50.4
2001	47.7	47.7	47.7	46.0	46.1	46.2	45.7	46.3	46.3	44.9	44.2	44.1	46.0
2002	42.9	41.6	42.4	42.1	41.7	42.0	41.6	43.1	43.2	41.5	40.9	40.8	42.0
2003	39.7	39.6	39.4	39.0	38.5	38.1	37.6	38.2	38.4	37.5	37.5	37.4	38.4
Construction and mining													
1990	8.3	8.2	8.2	8.5	8.6	9.1	9.0	9.1	9.0	9.0	8.8	8.5	8.7
1991	8.2	8.1	8.1	8.0	8.4	8.2	8.2	8.2	8.1	7.9	7.7	7.7	8.1
1992	7.6	7.6	7.9	8.1	8.3	8.7	8.6	8.7	8.5	8.5	8.4	8.3	8.3
1993	8.1	8.3	8.2	8.3	8.3	8.5	8.4	8.6	8.6	8.8	8.8	8.9	8.5
1994	8.8	8.7	8.9	8.8	8.8	9.1	9.5	9.6	9.8	9.9	10.0	10.2	9.3
1995	10.3	10.6	10.9	10.5	10.4	10.7	10.4	10.4	10.3	10.4	10.3	10.3	10.5
1996	10.3	10.3	10.3	10.5	10.9	11.0	11.2	11.3	11.2	11.4	11.4	11.7	11.0
1997	11.3	11.5	11.6	11.6	11.9	12.0	11.5	11.5	11.6	11.6	11.5	11.7	11.6
1998	11.5	11.7	11.9	12.1	12.6	12.4	11.4	11.6	11.9	12.5	12.4	12.6	12.1
1999	12.2	12.3	12.5	13.0	13.0	13.1	13.2	12.9	13.0	13.1	13.1	13.1	12.9
2000	12.9	12.8	12.9	12.6	12.8	12.9	12.5	12.6	12.7	12.5	12.5	12.6	12.7
2001	12.5	12.5	12.7	11.6	11.8	11.8	11.9	12.0	12.3	11.9	11.8	11.8	12.0
2002	11.7	11.7	12.0	11.6	11.5	11.8	11.7	12.0	12.0	11.7	11.7	11.6	11.8
2003	11.9	11.9	11.9	11.8	11.9	11.9	11.8	12.0	12.0	11.9	12.0	11.9	11.9

Employment by Industry: Texas—*Continued*

(Numbers in thousands. Not seasonally adjusted.)

Industry	January	February	March	April	May	June	July	August	September	October	November	December	Annual Average
EL PASO—*Continued*													
Manufacturing													
1990	40.5	40.9	40.9	40.6	40.7	41.2	41.4	42.7	41.8	40.9	40.7	40.4	41.1
1991	40.0	40.0	40.0	40.1	40.4	41.0	41.6	42.4	43.6	42.7	42.7	42.7	41.4
1992	41.8	41.6	42.5	42.9	43.6	44.2	44.1	45.1	45.6	46.0	45.5	45.7	44.1
1993	44.3	44.6	44.7	45.1	45.3	46.0	46.4	47.6	48.2	47.2	46.4	46.3	46.0
1994	44.3	44.3	44.3	45.0	45.3	45.6	45.9	47.9	48.5	47.1	47.2	47.1	46.0
1995	45.1	45.4	45.5	45.4	45.7	46.1	45.7	47.0	47.8	44.9	44.2	45.7	45.7
1996	44.2	44.3	44.0	43.6	43.8	44.4	43.8	45.1	45.5	44.3	44.1	44.0	44.3
1997	42.8	42.8	43.0	42.8	43.3	43.5	43.5	44.4	44.7	44.2	43.7	44.2	43.6
1998	43.3	42.1	42.8	42.4	42.6	42.9	42.5	43.3	43.6	42.8	41.7	41.9	42.7
1999	40.5	40.0	40.1	39.3	39.5	39.4	39.3	39.9	40.4	39.7	39.2	39.2	39.7
2000	38.6	38.7	38.5	37.6	37.7	37.8	36.9	38.1	38.3	37.1	37.0	36.6	37.7
2001	35.2	35.2	35.0	34.4	34.3	34.4	33.8	34.3	34.0	33.0	32.4	32.3	34.0
2002	31.2	29.9	30.4	30.5	30.2	30.2	29.9	31.1	31.2	29.8	29.2	29.2	30.2
2003	27.8	27.7	27.5	27.2	26.6	26.2	25.8	26.2	26.4	25.6	25.5	25.5	26.5
Service-providing													
1990	156.0	157.0	157.2	158.1	159.9	159.5	158.9	158.2	159.6	160.8	161.5	162.0	159.1
1991	158.9	158.8	159.8	161.0	161.7	161.3	160.7	161.7	162.4	163.2	163.4	165.4	161.5
1992	161.7	162.9	163.9	164.6	164.7	164.6	165.0	164.3	165.9	169.3	169.3	169.6	165.5
1993	166.3	168.5	168.1	170.1	170.5	169.8	170.5	170.6	172.0	172.3	172.7	173.3	170.4
1994	170.1	171.4	172.9	173.9	174.6	175.1	175.5	175.8	176.5	179.4	180.4	180.2	175.5
1995	176.4	177.3	177.6	178.0	179.0	178.3	178.0	179.4	179.8	180.1	180.4	181.5	178.8
1996	176.9	177.9	179.4	180.5	181.5	179.9	180.3	181.7	181.8	185.0	185.9	186.7	181.5
1997	182.1	183.5	184.8	186.4	187.7	187.8	188.0	188.8	190.8	190.5	192.0	193.0	188.0
1998	188.5	190.1	191.2	192.5	193.8	193.1	192.4	193.7	194.1	195.3	196.9	197.2	193.2
1999	193.6	195.9	196.1	197.7	198.4	198.0	197.4	198.6	200.2	201.2	202.6	204.6	198.7
2000	200.5	202.1	204.0	204.8	205.8	205.2	204.9	206.0	208.1	208.3	210.0	211.5	205.9
2001	207.2	207.9	209.9	209.1	210.2	209.3	205.7	208.4	210.7	209.0	210.6	210.6	209.0
2002	208.7	210.3	212.3	213.2	214.0	212.7	210.1	213.0	217.8	217.1	219.3	220.3	214.1
2003	214.6	215.5	216.0	216.9	216.7	213.1	211.7	215.3	218.6	219.0	220.1	220.7	216.5
Trade, transportation, and utilities													
1990	46.2	46.0	45.7	45.6	46.2	46.5	46.6	46.9	47.0	47.2	47.9	48.4	46.7
1991	46.4	45.5	45.9	45.9	46.1	46.4	46.2	46.6	46.4	46.5	46.9	47.8	46.4
1992	46.3	46.0	46.2	46.6	46.6	47.2	47.1	47.0	47.3	48.3	48.5	49.1	47.2
1993	48.2	47.8	47.6	48.0	47.8	47.7	48.2	48.3	48.5	48.8	49.3	50.1	48.4
1994	48.7	48.2	48.5	49.3	49.6	50.0	49.6	49.6	49.7	50.4	51.5	52.9	49.8
1995	50.9	50.3	49.9	49.1	49.2	49.3	49.5	49.9	50.0	49.9	50.4	51.4	50.0
1996	49.6	49.1	49.1	48.9	49.0	49.0	49.2	49.1	49.1	49.7	50.6	51.4	49.5
1997	49.1	48.6	48.9	49.0	49.3	49.7	49.9	49.7	50.1	50.1	51.2	51.9	49.8
1998	49.8	49.7	49.8	50.6	50.9	50.9	51.2	51.4	51.2	51.6	52.8	53.6	51.1
1999	51.3	51.1	51.2	51.8	51.9	52.2	52.2	52.6	52.6	54.0	54.8	55.8	52.6
2000	53.4	52.7	53.2	53.2	53.8	54.2	53.9	54.3	54.7	55.0	56.3	57.0	54.3
2001	54.6	53.6	54.2	53.7	53.8	53.7	53.7	53.8	53.1	52.9	54.1	54.8	53.8
2002	53.0	52.2	53.0	53.2	53.8	54.1	53.7	54.1	54.4	54.6	55.6	56.7	54.0
2003	54.3	53.4	53.9	54.4	54.6	54.6	54.6	55.6	55.4	55.8	56.4	56.8	55.0
Wholesale trade													
1990	10.3	10.3	10.2	10.2	10.3	10.4	10.4	10.5	10.5	10.4	10.4	10.4	10.4
1991	9.8	9.8	9.9	9.9	9.9	9.9	9.9	9.9	9.8	9.8	9.7	9.7	9.8
1992	9.6	9.7	9.7	9.7	9.6	9.7	9.6	9.6	9.5	9.7	9.6	9.6	9.6
1993	9.9	9.9	10.0	9.8	9.7	9.7	9.7	9.7	9.6	9.6	9.6	9.6	9.7
1994	9.4	9.4	9.4	9.5	9.5	9.6	9.6	9.6	9.6	9.8	9.8	9.9	9.6
1995	9.7	9.8	9.7	9.6	9.7	9.8	9.9	10.0	10.1	9.9	9.9	10.0	9.8
1996	10.0	10.0	10.1	10.0	10.0	10.0	10.1	10.2	10.2	10.2	10.2	10.2	10.1
1997	10.1	10.2	10.3	10.1	10.2	10.3	10.2	10.2	10.3	10.3	10.3	10.4	10.2
1998	10.3	10.3	10.4	10.6	10.6	10.5	10.5	10.6	10.5	10.7	10.7	10.8	10.5
1999	10.4	10.4	10.5	10.3	10.3	10.3	10.3	10.3	10.4	10.4	10.4	10.5	10.4
2000	10.4	10.3	10.4	10.4	10.5	10.5	10.3	10.3	10.3	10.2	10.2	10.3	10.3
2001	10.1	10.1	10.2	10.1	10.1	10.1	10.1	10.1	10.1	9.9	9.9	9.9	10.0
2002	9.7	9.7	9.8	9.8	9.9	9.9	9.8	9.9	9.8	9.7	9.6	9.7	9.8
2003	9.6	9.5	9.6	9.6	9.7	9.7	9.7	9.8	9.7	9.7	9.7	9.7	9.7
Retail trade													
1990	27.8	27.5	27.4	27.5	27.9	28.0	28.2	28.4	28.4	28.6	29.4	29.7	28.2
1991	28.6	27.8	27.9	27.7	27.8	28.0	27.7	28.0	27.9	28.2	28.7	29.4	28.1
1992	28.1	27.7	27.7	28.3	28.3	28.7	28.6	28.5	28.8	29.6	29.9	30.5	28.7
1993	29.0	28.5	28.3	28.7	28.6	28.5	29.0	29.1	29.4	29.7	30.2	30.8	29.2
1994	29.7	29.2	29.4	30.1	30.3	30.4	29.9	29.9	29.9	30.4	31.5	32.6	30.3
1995	30.9	30.2	29.8	29.3	29.3	29.3	29.4	29.5	29.5	29.5	29.9	30.6	29.8
1996	29.4	28.8	28.6	28.6	28.8	28.8	28.8	29.0	29.0	29.5	30.3	31.1	29.2
1997	29.5	28.9	29.0	29.0	29.0	29.1	29.5	29.5	29.4	29.3	30.3	30.9	29.5
1998	29.0	28.8	28.8	29.3	29.5	29.6	30.0	30.0	29.9	29.8	30.9	31.6	29.8
1999	29.8	29.4	29.5	29.9	30.0	30.2	30.0	30.3	30.1	31.3	31.9	32.7	30.4
2000	30.8	30.1	30.5	30.6	30.9	31.1	31.1	31.4	31.7	32.3	33.5	34.0	31.5
2001	32.3	31.5	32.0	31.6	31.6	31.5	31.7	32.0	31.2	31.3	32.5	33.1	31.8
2002	31.7	30.9	31.5	31.6	32.0	32.3	31.8	32.1	32.5	32.6	33.6	34.5	32.3
2003	32.6	31.9	32.2	32.6	32.7	32.7	32.7	33.5	33.4	33.7	34.6	34.7	33.1

Employment by Industry: Texas—*Continued*

(Numbers in thousands. Not seasonally adjusted.)

Industry	January	February	March	April	May	June	July	August	September	October	November	December	Annual Average
EL PASO—*Continued*													
Transportation and utilities													
1990	8.1	8.2	8.1	7.9	8.0	8.1	8.0	8.0	8.1	8.2	8.1	8.3	8.1
1991	8.0	7.9	8.1	8.3	8.4	8.5	8.6	8.7	8.7	8.5	8.5	8.7	8.4
1992	8.6	8.6	8.8	8.6	8.7	8.8	8.9	8.9	9.0	9.0	9.0	9.0	8.8
1993	9.3	9.4	9.3	9.5	9.5	9.5	9.5	9.5	9.5	9.5	9.5	9.7	9.5
1994	9.6	9.6	9.7	9.7	9.8	10.0	10.1	10.1	10.2	10.2	10.2	10.4	10.0
1995	10.3	10.3	10.4	10.2	10.2	10.2	10.2	10.4	10.4	10.5	10.6	10.8	10.4
1996	10.2	10.3	10.4	10.3	10.2	10.2	10.3	9.9	9.9	10.0	10.1	10.1	10.2
1997	9.5	9.5	9.6	9.9	10.1	10.3	10.2	10.0	10.4	10.5	10.6	10.6	10.1
1998	10.5	10.6	10.6	10.7	10.8	10.8	10.7	10.8	10.8	11.1	11.2	11.2	10.8
1999	11.1	11.3	11.2	11.6	11.6	11.7	11.9	12.0	12.1	12.3	12.5	12.6	11.8
2000	12.2	12.3	12.3	12.2	12.4	12.6	12.5	12.6	12.7	12.5	12.6	12.7	12.5
2001	12.2	12.0	12.0	12.0	12.1	12.1	11.9	11.7	11.8	11.7	11.7	11.8	11.9
2002	11.6	11.6	11.7	11.8	11.9	11.9	12.1	12.1	12.1	12.3	12.4	12.5	12.0
2003	12.1	12.0	12.1	12.2	12.2	12.2	12.2	12.3	12.3	12.4	12.1	12.4	12.2
Information													
1990	3.4	3.5	3.5	3.5	3.6	3.6	3.6	3.5	3.5	3.5	3.5	3.6	3.5
1991	3.6	3.6	3.7	3.6	3.5	3.6	3.7	3.6	3.5	3.4	3.5	3.6	3.6
1992	3.6	3.7	3.7	3.6	3.6	3.6	3.6	3.5	3.5	3.6	3.7	3.7	3.6
1993	3.6	3.6	3.6	3.7	3.7	3.8	3.7	3.6	3.5	3.5	3.6	3.6	3.6
1994	3.5	3.6	3.5	3.7	3.7	3.8	3.9	3.8	3.7	3.7	3.7	3.9	3.7
1995	4.0	3.9	4.0	4.0	4.0	4.0	3.9	3.8	3.8	3.8	3.9	4.0	3.9
1996	4.0	4.0	4.1	4.1	4.2	4.2	4.2	4.2	4.2	4.3	4.5	4.6	4.2
1997	4.4	4.3	4.5	4.5	4.5	4.5	4.5	4.6	4.6	4.4	4.4	4.4	4.5
1998	4.3	4.4	4.4	4.2	4.2	4.3	4.3	4.3	4.3	4.4	4.5	4.6	4.4
1999	4.5	4.5	4.6	4.9	5.0	4.9	5.0	5.0	5.0	5.0	5.1	5.1	4.9
2000	4.9	4.8	4.9	4.9	4.9	4.9	4.9	4.9	4.9	4.8	4.9	5.0	4.9
2001	4.8	4.8	4.8	4.9	5.0	5.1	4.9	4.9	5.0	4.9	5.0	4.9	4.9
2002	5.0	4.9	4.9	5.0	5.0	5.0	5.1	5.2	5.2	5.2	5.3	5.5	5.1
2003	5.5	5.5	5.4	5.5	5.5	5.4	5.4	5.4	5.2	5.4	5.4	5.4	5.4
Financial activities													
1990	9.4	9.3	9.3	9.3	9.4	9.5	9.3	9.3	9.2	9.0	8.9	9.0	9.2
1991	9.0	8.9	8.9	8.9	8.9	8.9	8.8	8.7	8.7	8.7	8.8	8.8	8.8
1992	8.7	8.7	8.8	8.8	8.8	8.9	8.9	8.9	8.8	9.0	8.9	9.1	8.9
1993	9.1	9.1	9.2	9.2	9.2	9.2	9.2	9.3	9.2	9.1	9.1	9.1	9.2
1994	9.0	9.1	9.1	9.3	9.3	9.4	9.3	9.4	9.3	9.4	9.4	9.4	9.3
1995	9.5	9.5	9.5	9.3	9.4	9.4	9.4	9.4	9.4	9.3	9.3	9.4	9.4
1996	9.2	9.2	9.4	9.4	9.5	9.6	9.5	9.5	9.5	9.6	9.6	9.6	9.5
1997	9.4	9.5	9.6	9.7	9.8	9.8	9.7	9.7	9.5	9.5	9.6	9.6	9.6
1998	9.9	9.9	10.0	9.9	9.9	9.9	10.1	10.1	10.1	10.2	10.2	10.2	10.0
1999	10.2	10.2	10.1	10.3	10.3	10.3	10.3	10.4	10.3	10.3	10.4	10.4	10.3
2000	10.2	10.1	10.1	10.1	10.1	10.3	10.3	10.3	10.3	10.3	10.3	10.4	10.2
2001	10.9	10.9	11.2	11.0	11.1	11.3	11.6	11.7	11.7	11.7	11.7	11.8	11.3
2002	11.8	11.9	12.0	11.8	11.8	11.8	11.8	11.7	11.7	11.8	12.0	12.0	11.8
2003	12.0	12.0	12.1	12.0	12.0	11.9	12.0	12.0	11.9	11.8	12.0	12.0	12.0
Professional and business services													
1990	13.4	13.7	13.9	13.9	14.0	14.1	14.3	14.0	13.9	13.9	14.0	14.1	13.9
1991	13.6	13.7	13.8	14.3	14.3	14.4	14.4	14.5	14.4	14.1	13.7	14.1	14.1
1992	14.2	14.4	14.6	14.7	14.5	14.8	15.0	15.2	15.3	14.9	14.7	14.8	14.8
1993	14.3	14.7	14.8	15.4	15.4	15.5	15.5	15.2	15.8	15.6	15.8	15.4	15.3
1994	15.1	15.8	15.9	15.5	15.7	16.0	17.1	17.2	17.2	17.5	17.6	17.2	16.5
1995	16.8	17.3	17.3	17.3	17.2	17.3	17.2	17.7	17.6	17.6	17.6	17.5	17.4
1996	17.0	17.4	17.9	18.0	18.2	18.1	18.1	18.9	18.8	19.2	19.1	18.7	18.3
1997	18.4	18.9	18.8	18.9	19.3	19.8	20.6	21.4	21.6	22.4	22.5	22.7	20.4
1998	21.8	21.9	22.2	22.6	22.7	23.3	22.3	22.6	22.4	23.2	23.1	23.0	22.6
1999	22.7	23.2	23.1	22.5	22.2	23.2	22.9	23.0	23.4	23.0	23.2	23.7	23.0
2000	23.8	24.6	25.4	25.2	25.2	25.6	25.0	25.3	25.8	26.0	26.3	26.5	25.4
2001	25.3	25.5	25.7	25.3	25.1	25.2	24.4	24.9	24.9	25.1	24.6	24.7	25.0
2002	24.9	25.5	25.8	26.1	26.1	26.3	26.5	26.8	27.1	27.4	27.3	27.9	26.5
2003	25.6	25.5	24.8	25.1	25.0	24.3	24.1	24.6	25.2	25.3	25.4	25.3	25.0
Educational and health services													
1990	15.6	15.9	16.0	16.0	16.1	15.9	16.2	16.4	16.4	16.6	16.7	16.6	16.2
1991	17.0	17.1	17.2	17.1	17.2	17.2	17.2	17.6	17.6	17.6	17.8	17.9	17.4
1992	17.6	17.8	17.7	17.1	17.0	17.4	17.3	17.5	17.6	18.0	17.8	17.8	17.6
1993	18.1	18.2	18.3	17.9	18.0	18.2	18.4	18.8	18.9	19.0	18.9	19.2	18.5
1994	19.1	19.2	19.6	19.6	20.0	20.0	20.6	20.6	21.0	21.2	21.3	21.3	20.3
1995	20.7	20.7	20.9	21.0	21.2	21.2	21.2	21.3	21.5	21.6	21.5	21.6	21.2
1996	21.4	21.7	21.8	21.7	21.8	21.6	21.3	21.5	21.5	21.6	21.7	21.8	21.6
1997	22.1	22.2	22.4	22.5	22.6	22.7	22.7	22.6	23.0	22.7	22.8	22.9	22.6
1998	22.6	22.8	22.8	22.7	22.9	22.8	23.1	23.3	23.3	23.0	23.3	23.2	23.0
1999	23.1	23.2	23.3	23.8	23.9	23.6	23.5	23.7	23.8	23.7	23.8	24.0	23.6
2000	23.6	24.0	24.0	23.8	24.0	24.1	24.4	24.7	25.1	25.1	25.3	25.5	24.5
2001	25.1	25.3	25.6	25.6	25.8	26.2	26.1	26.3	26.5	26.0	26.2	26.4	25.9
2002	26.3	26.6	26.8	27.2	27.6	27.7	28.1	28.5	28.5	27.6	27.8	28.0	27.6
2003	27.7	28.0	28.3	28.5	28.6	28.6	28.6	28.8	28.9	28.9	28.9	28.9	28.6

Employment by Industry: Texas—*Continued*

(Numbers in thousands. Not seasonally adjusted.)

Industry	January	February	March	April	May	June	July	August	September	October	November	December	Annual Average
EL PASO—*Continued*													
Leisure and hospitality													
1990	16.9	16.9	17.1	17.9	18.4	18.6	18.4	18.6	18.3	17.7	17.4	17.6	17.8
1991	17.2	17.1	17.5	17.8	18.1	18.5	18.5	18.6	18.3	17.8	17.6	17.7	17.9
1992	17.5	17.5	17.8	18.3	18.6	18.9	18.7	18.5	18.3	17.9	17.8	17.6	18.1
1993	17.2	17.5	18.0	18.8	19.1	19.5	19.4	19.6	19.1	18.8	18.4	18.6	18.7
1994	18.2	18.2	18.6	19.0	19.3	19.6	19.7	19.9	19.6	19.3	19.1	19.3	19.2
1995	18.8	19.0	19.4	20.3	20.5	20.8	20.4	20.3	19.8	19.5	19.4	19.6	19.8
1996	19.3	19.4	19.6	20.3	20.4	20.5	20.9	20.9	20.7	20.2	20.0	20.1	20.2
1997	19.5	19.8	20.1	21.2	21.7	22.0	21.8	21.7	21.6	20.6	20.5	20.6	20.9
1998	20.0	20.1	20.6	21.3	21.8	21.9	21.7	21.9	21.3	21.1	21.0	20.7	21.1
1999	20.4	21.1	21.5	21.9	22.5	22.7	22.6	22.6	22.4	21.7	21.5	21.6	21.9
2000	21.3	21.4	21.7	22.6	22.8	23.2	23.3	23.2	23.3	22.3	22.1	22.2	22.5
2001	21.5	21.8	22.2	22.3	22.9	22.9	22.9	23.0	23.0	22.0	22.1	22.0	22.3
2002	21.6	22.0	22.6	23.2	23.8	24.0	23.6	23.8	23.7	22.6	23.1	23.1	23.1
2003	22.7	22.8	23.3	23.3	23.9	24.0	23.9	24.1	23.8	23.4	23.5	23.6	23.5
Other services													
1990	7.3	7.4	7.4	7.4	7.4	7.4	7.5	7.5	7.5	7.5	7.5	7.5	7.4
1991	7.6	7.6	7.6	7.6	7.7	7.7	7.8	7.8	7.7	8.0	7.9	7.8	7.7
1992	7.9	7.8	7.8	7.9	7.9	8.0	8.2	8.0	7.8	8.0	8.0	7.8	7.9
1993	8.2	8.3	8.2	8.4	8.4	8.4	8.4	8.5	8.2	8.1	7.9	7.8	8.2
1994	7.6	7.4	7.4	7.6	7.7	7.7	7.7	7.7	7.6	7.7	7.7	7.6	7.6
1995	7.6	7.6	7.8	7.6	7.9	7.7	7.9	7.9	7.7	7.6	7.5	7.5	7.7
1996	7.3	7.4	7.4	7.4	7.6	7.6	7.8	7.8	7.6	7.4	7.4	7.3	7.5
1997	7.3	7.3	7.5	7.4	7.4	7.4	7.4	7.3	7.3	7.3	7.2	7.2	7.3
1998	7.0	7.1	7.2	7.1	7.2	7.3	7.3	7.3	7.3	7.2	7.2	7.1	7.2
1999	7.0	7.1	7.1	7.1	7.2	7.3	7.3	7.3	7.3	7.3	7.4	7.4	7.2
2000	7.3	7.4	7.5	7.5	7.4	7.6	7.7	7.7	7.7	7.7	7.6	7.5	7.6
2001	7.5	7.6	7.7	7.7	7.8	7.8	7.7	7.9	7.8	7.8	7.8	7.8	7.7
2002	7.7	7.8	8.0	8.0	8.1	8.1	7.9	7.9	7.8	7.7	7.8	7.7	7.9
2003	7.5	7.6	7.6	7.6	7.5	7.6	7.5	7.6	7.5	7.4	7.4	7.3	7.5
Government													
1990	43.8	44.3	44.3	44.5	44.8	43.9	43.0	42.0	43.8	45.4	45.6	45.2	44.2
1991	44.5	45.3	45.2	45.8	45.9	44.6	44.1	44.3	45.8	47.1	47.2	47.7	45.6
1992	45.9	47.0	47.3	47.6	47.7	45.8	46.2	45.7	47.3	49.6	49.9	49.7	47.5
1993	47.6	49.3	48.4	48.7	48.9	47.5	47.7	47.3	48.8	49.4	49.7	49.5	48.6
1994	48.9	49.9	50.3	49.9	49.3	48.6	47.6	47.6	48.4	50.2	50.1	48.6	49.1
1995	48.1	49.0	48.8	49.4	49.6	48.6	48.5	49.1	50.0	50.8	50.8	50.5	49.4
1996	49.1	49.7	50.1	50.7	50.8	49.3	49.3	49.8	50.4	53.0	53.0	53.2	50.7
1997	51.9	52.9	53.0	53.2	53.1	51.9	51.4	51.8	53.1	53.5	53.8	53.7	52.8
1998	53.1	54.2	54.2	54.1	54.2	52.7	52.4	52.8	54.2	54.6	54.8	54.8	53.8
1999	54.4	55.5	55.2	55.4	55.4	53.8	53.6	54.0	55.4	56.2	56.4	56.6	55.2
2000	56.0	57.1	57.2	57.5	57.6	55.3	55.4	55.6	56.3	57.1	57.2	57.4	56.6
2001	57.5	58.4	58.5	58.6	58.7	57.1	54.4	55.9	58.7	58.6	59.1	58.2	57.8
2002	58.4	59.4	59.2	58.7	57.8	55.7	53.4	55.0	59.4	60.2	60.4	59.4	58.1
2003	59.3	60.7	60.6	60.5	59.6	56.7	55.6	57.2	60.7	61.0	61.1	61.4	59.5
Federal government													
1990	9.2	9.3	9.3	9.5	9.7	9.4	9.6	9.3	9.1	9.1	9.1	9.1	9.3
1991	9.1	9.1	9.1	9.3	9.2	9.3	9.2	9.2	9.2	9.1	9.1	9.2	9.2
1992	9.2	9.2	9.3	9.4	9.4	9.4	9.4	9.3	9.2	9.2	9.2	9.2	9.3
1993	9.2	9.2	9.1	8.9	8.9	9.0	9.0	9.0	9.0	9.1	9.1	9.1	9.1
1994	9.0	9.0	9.0	8.9	8.8	8.7	8.6	8.5	8.4	8.4	8.3	8.3	8.7
1995	8.2	8.2	8.2	8.3	8.4	8.4	8.4	8.5	8.4	8.4	8.3	8.3	8.3
1996	8.1	8.1	8.1	8.2	8.3	8.4	8.5	8.6	8.6	8.7	8.7	8.8	8.4
1997	8.8	8.8	8.8	8.9	8.7	8.7	8.8	8.8	8.8	8.8	8.8	8.8	8.8
1998	8.7	8.7	8.7	8.7	8.7	8.7	8.7	8.8	8.8	8.6	8.6	8.6	8.7
1999	8.6	8.5	8.5	8.6	8.6	8.7	8.6	8.6	8.7	8.6	8.6	8.6	8.6
2000	8.7	8.7	8.8	9.1	9.5	8.8	8.9	8.7	8.7	8.7	8.7	8.8	8.8
2001	8.6	8.6	8.6	8.6	8.7	8.7	8.8	8.7	8.7	8.7	8.7	8.7	8.6
2002	8.7	8.6	8.7	8.7	8.7	8.7	8.7	8.5	8.7	8.8	8.8	8.8	8.7
2003	8.7	8.7	8.7	8.7	8.8	8.8	8.8	8.8	8.9	8.9	8.9	8.8	8.8
State government													
1990	5.1	5.0	5.0	4.9	4.9	5.0	4.9	4.3	5.0	5.2	5.3	5.1	5.0
1991	5.4	5.3	5.3	5.3	5.2	5.2	5.1	4.6	5.2	5.7	5.8	5.8	5.3
1992	6.1	6.0	6.0	6.1	6.1	5.7	5.8	5.4	6.0	6.1	6.2	6.1	6.0
1993	6.3	6.3	6.3	6.4	6.5	6.2	6.2	5.2	5.9	6.0	6.0	6.0	6.1
1994	6.1	6.1	6.2	6.2	6.3	5.9	6.1	5.6	6.4	6.5	6.5	6.5	6.2
1995	6.7	6.6	6.6	6.6	6.7	6.4	6.4	6.3	6.8	7.1	7.1	7.0	6.7
1996	7.0	7.3	7.4	7.5	7.5	7.0	7.0	7.1	7.6	7.9	7.8	7.9	7.4
1997	7.9	8.0	8.1	8.1	8.2	7.8	7.5	7.5	8.3	8.3	8.3	8.3	8.0
1998	8.4	8.4	8.4	8.3	8.3	7.8	7.6	7.4	8.3	8.4	8.4	8.4	8.2
1999	8.4	8.5	8.6	8.6	8.6	7.9	7.9	7.6	8.5	8.5	8.6	8.6	8.4
2000	8.7	8.7	8.7	8.7	8.7	8.0	8.1	7.8	8.5	8.6	8.7	8.7	8.5
2001	8.8	8.7	8.8	8.8	8.9	8.3	8.3	8.1	8.9	8.9	8.9	9.0	8.6
2002	9.2	9.0	9.0	9.0	9.1	8.2	8.3	8.0	9.1	9.3	9.3	9.3	8.9
2003	9.5	9.3	9.2	9.2	9.3	8.2	8.0	7.9	9.0	9.1	9.1	9.1	8.9

Employment by Industry: Texas—*Continued*

(Numbers in thousands. Not seasonally adjusted.)

Industry	January	February	March	April	May	June	July	August	September	October	November	December	Annual Average
EL PASO—*Continued*													
Local government													
1990	29.5	30.0	30.0	30.1	30.2	29.5	28.5	28.4	29.7	31.1	31.2	31.0	29.9
1991	30.0	30.9	30.8	31.2	31.5	30.1	29.8	30.5	31.4	32.3	32.3	32.7	31.1
1992	30.6	31.8	32.0	32.1	32.2	30.7	31.0	31.0	32.1	34.3	34.5	34.4	32.2
1993	32.1	33.8	33.0	33.4	33.5	32.3	32.5	33.1	33.9	34.3	34.6	34.4	33.4
1994	33.8	34.8	35.1	34.8	34.2	34.0	32.9	33.5	33.6	35.3	35.3	33.8	34.3
1995	33.2	34.2	34.0	34.5	34.5	33.8	33.7	34.3	34.8	35.3	35.4	35.2	34.4
1996	34.0	34.3	34.6	35.0	35.0	33.9	33.8	34.1	34.2	36.4	36.5	36.5	34.9
1997	35.2	36.1	36.1	36.2	36.2	35.4	35.1	35.5	36.0	36.4	36.7	36.6	36.0
1998	36.0	37.1	37.1	37.1	37.2	36.2	36.1	36.6	37.1	37.6	37.8	37.8	37.0
1999	37.4	38.5	38.1	38.2	38.2	37.2	37.1	37.8	38.2	39.1	39.2	39.4	38.2
2000	38.6	39.7	39.7	39.7	39.4	38.5	38.4	39.1	39.1	39.8	39.8	39.9	39.3
2001	40.1	41.1	41.1	41.2	41.1	40.1	37.3	39.1	41.1	41.0	41.5	40.5	40.4
2002	40.5	41.8	41.5	41.0	40.0	38.8	36.4	38.5	41.6	42.1	42.3	41.3	40.5
2003	41.1	42.7	42.7	42.6	41.5	39.7	38.8	40.5	42.8	43.0	43.1	43.5	41.8
FT. WORTH-ARLINGTON													
Total nonfarm													
1990	579.5	585.5	587.3	591.6	594.0	599.9	596.6	600.7	601.5	600.4	602.7	602.4	595.2
1991	589.1	588.3	590.6	593.3	597.2	600.9	591.3	594.0	596.8	595.9	597.3	596.2	594.2
1992	581.1	584.0	584.1	593.4	598.7	602.3	597.2	596.9	600.2	601.5	603.8	605.7	595.7
1993	594.3	600.0	602.9	608.1	610.8	616.9	613.1	614.2	620.3	619.7	621.7	622.9	612.1
1994	612.0	614.2	620.6	630.1	633.5	637.5	633.2	636.7	640.4	640.9	645.5	647.1	632.6
1995	631.8	639.2	644.7	650.4	656.4	660.2	654.8	657.9	662.6	662.7	665.7	670.5	654.7
1996	659.3	663.9	669.1	674.5	680.5	684.1	679.4	684.1	686.6	687.8	692.3	695.2	679.7
1997	679.6	685.1	694.1	700.4	707.4	712.4	710.2	713.5	719.9	720.4	724.4	729.2	708.1
1998	716.4	722.1	727.5	734.6	740.4	744.4	738.8	743.3	748.9	749.6	753.8	760.1	740.0
1999	743.4	750.5	755.9	762.0	764.7	770.5	766.1	770.6	774.8	776.7	780.4	786.6	766.9
2000	772.4	777.5	785.0	787.7	796.9	800.6	794.4	798.7	801.2	797.8	802.3	806.4	793.4
2001	785.2	790.3	794.5	797.4	800.5	804.1	797.6	802.0	798.4	791.0	790.0	790.9	795.1
2002	776.5	780.0	785.8	787.7	791.8	792.3	784.1	787.4	787.0	782.6	785.9	787.1	785.7
2003	769.2	771.9	774.7	777.2	780.8	781.1	772.5	777.1	778.3	778.3	779.7	781.6	776.9
Total private													
1990	504.3	509.2	511.0	514.8	517.2	524.6	525.8	529.9	527.3	525.1	525.8	525.5	520.0
1991	513.0	511.2	513.7	515.9	519.3	523.3	518.6	520.2	518.3	515.8	516.6	515.5	516.8
1992	500.5	502.3	502.1	511.2	516.4	521.0	520.0	519.6	517.8	517.9	519.3	521.5	514.1
1993	510.2	514.8	517.6	523.1	525.4	532.7	533.9	534.3	535.4	534.0	535.7	536.6	527.8
1994	527.0	527.5	534.0	543.6	546.8	552.2	552.9	555.7	554.2	553.8	557.4	558.8	547.0
1995	544.8	550.6	556.4	561.8	567.8	573.5	573.0	575.6	575.2	574.4	576.5	580.9	567.5
1996	571.2	574.6	579.5	584.4	590.8	596.1	596.1	599.2	597.0	597.6	601.4	604.2	591.0
1997	590.0	594.2	602.6	608.7	615.2	622.1	624.1	626.2	628.1	627.1	631.0	635.5	617.1
1998	624.3	627.9	633.1	640.2	645.6	651.7	650.3	653.4	654.4	653.8	657.3	663.4	646.3
1999	648.1	653.5	658.7	664.8	667.1	674.7	674.6	676.9	676.6	677.3	680.1	686.4	669.9
2000	674.0	677.4	684.7	686.4	693.6	699.7	697.6	700.5	699.9	695.4	698.7	702.7	692.6
2001	684.0	686.5	690.6	694.5	697.9	703.2	700.2	703.9	696.4	686.9	685.2	686.3	692.9
2002	673.5	674.4	680.3	682.4	686.1	688.9	685.1	687.4	682.5	675.4	676.7	677.8	680.9
2003	662.5	663.2	666.4	668.7	671.5	672.9	669.8	673.6	671.0	668.5	669.2	671.2	669.0
Goods-producing													
1990	144.3	145.3	145.7	146.4	145.0	146.6	146.2	148.0	147.1	147.0	146.0	143.8	146.0
1991	140.0	138.8	139.5	138.5	138.1	138.5	133.8	133.4	132.8	131.7	130.9	128.5	135.4
1992	125.0	124.7	122.3	124.0	126.0	126.5	128.4	128.0	127.2	127.5	127.3	127.0	126.2
1993	123.2	126.1	127.2	125.6	127.1	129.1	127.9	128.2	129.4	131.0	130.3	129.4	127.9
1994	127.3	126.3	128.0	130.2	130.7	132.5	133.1	134.0	134.4	135.0	134.7	134.2	131.7
1995	130.8	132.6	133.6	135.7	136.4	137.6	137.0	136.7	136.8	136.2	135.4	135.7	135.4
1996	135.4	136.8	138.1	138.9	140.5	142.0	143.0	143.5	143.0	142.4	142.6	143.0	140.8
1997	140.8	141.7	143.7	144.1	145.9	147.6	148.6	148.9	149.3	147.7	147.7	147.9	146.2
1998	147.6	148.6	150.1	150.8	152.4	153.9	154.6	154.8	155.6	154.9	155.1	155.3	152.8
1999	151.8	153.1	154.0	154.2	154.6	156.6	157.5	157.2	157.6	157.3	157.3	157.8	155.8
2000	157.3	158.3	159.8	158.8	160.4	161.8	161.2	160.3	159.3	157.7	157.0	156.7	159.1
2001	153.4	154.0	154.6	154.9	155.6	157.1	156.1	156.8	154.7	152.0	150.4	149.4	154.0
2002	146.8	147.1	148.1	148.9	149.9	151.5	150.8	151.2	149.9	147.3	146.8	146.5	148.7
2003	143.9	144.0	144.1	144.3	145.2	145.8	145.2	145.5	145.2	143.3	142.2	142.3	144.3
Natural resources and mining													
1990	4.1	4.2	4.2	4.3	4.3	4.4	4.4	4.3	4.3	4.3	4.4	4.4	4.3
1991	4.3	4.3	4.3	4.5	4.5	4.5	4.5	4.5	4.5	4.4	4.4	4.4	4.4
1992	4.4	4.3	4.3	4.4	4.4	4.4	4.4	4.4	4.4	4.4	4.4	4.4	4.4
1993	4.3	4.3	4.3	4.3	4.4	4.4	4.4	4.4	4.4	4.5	4.5	4.5	4.4
1994	4.4	4.4	4.5	4.5	4.5	4.5	4.5	4.5	4.5	4.4	4.4	4.4	4.5
1995	4.3	4.3	4.3	4.5	4.5	4.5	4.5	4.6	4.6	4.5	4.4	4.3	4.4
1996	4.2	4.3	4.4	4.3	4.4	4.5	4.6	4.6	4.6	4.4	4.4	4.4	4.4
1997	4.4	4.4	4.4	4.2	4.3	4.4	4.6	4.6	4.6	4.6	4.6	4.6	4.5
1998	4.6	4.6	4.7	4.7	4.7	4.7	4.8	4.7	4.8	4.7	4.7	4.7	4.7
1999	4.5	4.5	4.5	4.5	4.3	4.2	4.2	4.3	4.3	4.2	4.2	4.2	4.3
2000	4.2	4.2	4.2	4.1	4.1	4.2	4.1	4.1	4.0	4.0	4.0	4.0	4.1
2001	3.9	4.0	4.0	4.1	4.1	4.2	4.2	4.3	4.3	4.3	4.3	4.2	4.1
2002	4.2	4.3	4.3	4.3	4.2	4.3	4.2	4.2	4.1	4.1	4.1	4.1	4.2
2003	3.8	3.8	3.8	3.9	3.9	4.0	4.0	4.0	3.9	3.9	3.9	3.8	3.9

Employment by Industry: Texas—*Continued*

(Numbers in thousands. Not seasonally adjusted.)

Industry	January	February	March	April	May	June	July	August	September	October	November	December	Annual Average
FT. WORTH-ARLINGTON *—Continued*													
Construction													
1990	22.2	22.4	22.2	23.0	23.4	24.5	23.7	23.8	23.7	23.2	23.1	22.8	23.2
1991	21.3	21.6	22.0	22.7	22.7	23.0	22.8	22.4	22.2	21.5	21.2	20.8	22.0
1992	19.3	19.8	20.4	21.5	21.9	22.2	23.1	23.3	23.0	22.7	22.3	22.0	21.8
1993	21.5	22.0	22.6	22.8	23.4	24.4	24.9	25.1	24.9	25.5	25.2	25.0	23.9
1994	23.0	23.3	24.3	25.7	25.8	26.7	26.9	27.2	27.3	27.0	26.8	26.9	25.9
1995	25.8	26.7	27.2	28.2	28.6	29.4	29.7	29.5	29.6	29.9	29.8	30.1	28.7
1996	29.7	30.3	30.9	32.4	33.3	34.0	34.1	34.2	33.6	33.6	33.5	33.5	32.8
1997	32.4	33.4	34.3	34.4	35.3	35.9	37.0	37.4	37.3	36.4	36.2	36.2	35.5
1998	35.4	36.2	37.0	37.8	38.9	39.6	40.8	40.8	40.8	40.5	40.3	40.4	39.0
1999	38.9	39.9	40.6	41.5	42.0	42.9	43.2	42.9	43.0	42.9	42.6	42.6	41.9
2000	42.2	43.3	44.9	44.8	46.2	47.7	47.8	47.3	46.5	45.4	44.9	44.8	45.5
2001	42.8	43.1	44.0	44.8	46.0	47.5	47.5	48.1	46.9	46.1	45.3	45.0	45.5
2002	43.6	44.0	45.0	45.6	46.4	47.3	47.2	47.2	46.2	44.7	44.4	44.0	45.5
2003	43.1	43.1	43.4	43.8	44.3	44.7	44.8	44.8	44.5	43.2	42.4	42.2	43.7
Manufacturing													
1990	118.0	118.7	119.3	119.1	117.3	117.7	118.1	119.9	119.1	119.5	118.5	116.6	118.5
1991	114.4	112.9	113.2	111.3	110.9	111.0	106.5	106.5	106.1	105.8	105.3	103.3	108.9
1992	101.3	100.6	97.6	98.1	99.7	99.9	100.9	100.3	99.8	100.4	100.6	100.6	100.0
1993	97.4	99.8	100.3	98.5	99.3	100.3	98.6	98.7	100.1	101.0	100.6	99.9	99.5
1994	99.9	98.6	99.2	100.0	100.4	101.3	101.7	102.3	102.6	103.6	103.5	102.9	101.3
1995	100.7	101.6	102.1	103.0	103.3	103.7	102.8	102.6	102.6	101.8	101.2	101.3	102.2
1996	101.5	102.2	102.8	102.2	102.8	103.5	104.3	104.7	104.8	104.4	104.7	105.1	103.6
1997	104.0	103.9	105.0	105.5	106.3	107.3	107.0	106.9	107.4	106.7	106.9	107.1	106.2
1998	107.6	107.8	108.4	108.3	108.8	109.6	109.0	109.3	110.0	109.7	110.1	110.2	109.1
1999	108.4	108.7	108.9	108.2	108.3	109.5	110.1	110.0	110.3	110.2	110.5	111.0	109.5
2000	110.9	110.8	110.7	109.9	110.1	109.9	109.3	108.9	108.8	108.3	108.1	107.9	109.5
2001	106.7	106.9	106.6	106.0	105.5	105.4	104.4	104.4	103.5	101.6	100.8	100.2	104.3
2002	99.0	98.8	98.8	99.0	99.3	99.9	99.4	99.8	99.6	98.5	98.3	98.4	99.1
2003	97.0	97.1	96.9	96.6	97.0	97.1	96.4	96.7	96.8	96.2	95.9	96.3	96.7
Service-providing													
1990	435.2	440.2	441.6	445.2	449.0	453.3	450.4	452.7	454.4	453.4	456.7	458.6	449.2
1991	449.1	449.5	451.1	454.8	459.1	462.4	457.5	460.6	464.0	464.2	466.4	467.7	458.9
1992	456.1	459.3	461.8	469.4	472.7	475.8	468.8	468.9	473.0	474.0	476.5	478.7	469.6
1993	471.1	473.9	475.7	482.5	483.7	487.8	485.2	486.0	490.9	488.7	491.4	493.5	484.2
1994	484.7	487.9	492.6	499.9	502.8	505.0	500.1	502.7	506.0	505.9	510.8	512.9	500.9
1995	501.0	506.6	511.1	514.7	520.0	522.6	517.8	521.2	525.8	526.5	530.3	534.8	519.4
1996	523.9	527.1	531.0	535.6	540.0	542.1	536.4	540.6	543.6	545.4	549.7	552.2	539.0
1997	538.8	543.4	550.4	556.3	561.5	564.8	561.6	564.6	570.6	572.7	576.7	581.3	561.9
1998	568.8	573.5	577.4	583.8	588.0	590.5	584.2	588.5	593.3	594.7	598.7	604.8	587.2
1999	591.6	597.4	601.9	607.8	610.1	613.9	608.6	613.4	617.2	619.4	623.1	628.8	611.1
2000	615.1	619.2	625.2	628.9	636.5	638.8	633.2	638.4	641.9	640.1	645.3	649.7	634.4
2001	631.8	636.3	639.9	642.5	644.9	647.0	641.5	645.2	643.7	639.0	639.6	641.5	641.0
2002	629.7	632.9	637.7	638.8	641.9	640.8	633.3	636.2	637.1	635.3	639.1	640.6	637.0
2003	625.3	627.9	630.6	632.9	635.6	635.3	627.3	631.6	633.1	635.0	637.5	639.3	632.6
Trade, transportation, and utilities													
1990	149.6	149.5	150.2	150.5	151.6	153.1	155.4	156.7	157.4	157.1	159.0	160.5	154.2
1991	153.4	150.6	151.2	151.6	152.6	153.8	154.3	155.4	155.7	157.0	158.4	159.9	154.5
1992	152.5	151.2	151.4	154.9	155.5	156.9	156.3	156.1	156.3	156.7	158.4	160.5	155.6
1993	156.0	155.0	154.7	156.2	154.4	155.8	158.2	157.9	157.5	157.9	161.0	162.4	157.3
1994	158.5	157.6	157.5	160.0	160.9	162.2	162.3	163.1	163.5	164.2	167.5	170.2	162.3
1995	164.0	163.9	164.6	165.7	167.0	167.8	168.2	171.6	172.2	173.8	177.5	180.5	169.7
1996	173.9	173.5	173.5	173.6	174.5	174.8	173.4	173.5	173.3	174.9	178.0	181.0	174.8
1997	175.2	174.3	174.7	173.4	174.9	175.8	175.9	176.7	176.9	179.7	182.5	185.6	177.1
1998	179.9	179.5	180.7	182.1	183.3	184.1	183.7	184.9	184.9	186.3	189.8	193.4	184.4
1999	187.0	187.0	188.1	190.4	190.8	192.6	193.0	194.3	194.9	196.6	199.6	203.5	193.2
2000	196.4	196.6	197.8	197.8	199.5	201.2	201.1	202.5	202.5	204.1	207.9	211.1	201.5
2001	203.8	202.6	203.2	203.2	203.6	204.4	203.4	203.8	202.1	200.0	200.3	201.8	202.6
2002	196.2	194.9	196.1	196.2	196.3	196.3	196.6	195.8	194.2	193.2	195.2	196.6	195.6
2003	188.8	187.3	187.2	186.8	186.8	186.7	185.5	187.1	186.7	186.7	188.3	189.9	187.3
Wholesale trade													
1990	27.3	27.6	27.7	28.1	28.2	28.4	28.9	29.0	28.8	28.6	28.6	28.6	28.3
1991	28.6	28.4	28.4	28.7	28.8	29.0	28.9	28.8	28.6	28.8	28.5	28.2	28.6
1992	27.6	27.3	27.2	27.9	28.0	28.3	27.8	27.7	27.5	27.6	27.7	28.0	27.7
1993	27.7	27.7	27.8	28.4	28.3	28.6	28.7	28.4	28.5	28.0	28.3	28.4	28.2
1994	28.6	28.5	28.8	29.0	29.1	29.3	29.6	29.7	29.6	29.3	29.4	29.7	29.2
1995	29.1	29.4	29.7	30.5	30.6	30.9	30.9	30.8	30.7	30.9	30.9	31.1	30.5
1996	30.6	30.9	31.1	31.4	31.9	32.1	32.0	32.1	31.9	32.2	32.3	32.6	31.8
1997	32.1	32.4	32.8	32.0	32.3	32.5	32.5	32.6	32.6	32.9	32.7	32.7	32.5
1998	32.6	33.0	33.1	33.6	34.1	34.2	33.7	34.0	34.2	34.3	34.6	34.8	33.9
1999	34.5	34.9	35.1	35.8	36.0	36.1	36.7	36.9	36.9	37.1	37.0	37.4	36.2
2000	37.2	37.3	37.7	37.8	38.0	38.0	38.1	38.2	38.3	38.4	38.4	38.5	38.0
2001	38.5	38.6	38.7	38.4	38.4	38.7	38.5	38.3	37.9	37.5	37.4	37.2	38.1
2002	36.9	37.0	37.1	36.9	37.1	37.3	37.2	37.1	37.1	37.1	36.9	37.0	37.1
2003	36.5	36.3	36.4	36.5	36.6	36.8	36.9	36.7	36.6	36.6	36.4	36.4	36.6

Employment by Industry: Texas—*Continued*

(Numbers in thousands. Not seasonally adjusted.)

Industry	January	February	March	April	May	June	July	August	September	October	November	December	Annual Average
FT. WORTH-ARLINGTON —*Continued*													
Retail trade													
1990	78.2	77.6	78.2	78.1	78.6	79.3	79.5	79.7	79.4	79.9	81.8	83.3	79.5
1991	76.9	74.9	75.3	75.4	76.0	76.5	76.4	76.9	77.3	77.6	79.0	80.6	76.9
1992	75.2	74.1	73.9	75.6	76.0	76.6	76.8	76.7	77.1	77.7	79.4	81.0	76.7
1993	77.2	76.2	76.0	77.2	75.6	76.0	78.0	78.1	77.8	79.1	81.7	83.3	78.0
1994	79.5	78.6	78.3	79.4	79.8	80.6	80.2	80.8	81.1	82.3	84.9	86.9	81.0
1995	82.6	82.0	82.5	82.6	83.4	83.8	83.9	84.2	84.7	86.1	89.3	91.5	84.7
1996	86.5	85.5	85.5	85.6	86.2	87.0	86.5	87.3	87.2	88.2	91.2	93.7	87.5
1997	88.8	87.2	87.9	88.0	89.0	89.4	89.2	89.6	89.4	91.5	94.8	97.8	90.2
1998	92.0	90.8	91.5	91.5	91.7	92.4	92.7	93.1	92.9	93.6	96.5	99.4	93.2
1999	94.1	93.3	93.6	94.4	94.4	95.6	95.3	95.8	96.0	97.2	100.2	103.1	96.1
2000	96.9	96.5	97.1	97.1	98.2	99.3	98.9	99.9	99.4	100.7	104.0	106.6	99.6
2001	99.4	98.1	98.7	98.8	99.1	99.3	98.6	98.5	98.1	98.6	100.9	102.8	99.2
2002	97.6	96.2	97.0	97.1	96.7	96.5	97.1	96.3	94.9	94.1	96.8	98.4	96.6
2003	91.8	90.8	90.8	91.0	91.1	91.4	91.2	92.8	92.6	92.4	94.3	95.4	92.1
Transportation and utilities													
1990	44.1	44.3	44.3	44.3	44.8	45.4	47.0	48.0	49.2	48.6	48.6	48.6	46.4
1991	47.9	47.3	47.5	47.5	47.8	48.3	49.0	49.7	49.8	50.6	50.9	51.1	49.0
1992	49.7	49.8	50.3	51.4	51.5	52.0	51.7	51.7	51.7	51.4	51.3	51.5	51.2
1993	51.1	51.1	50.9	50.6	50.5	51.2	51.5	51.4	51.2	50.8	51.0	50.7	51.0
1994	50.4	50.5	50.4	51.6	52.0	52.3	52.5	52.6	52.8	52.6	53.2	53.6	52.0
1995	52.3	52.5	52.4	52.6	53.0	53.1	53.4	56.6	56.8	56.8	57.3	57.9	54.6
1996	56.8	57.1	56.9	56.6	56.4	55.7	54.9	54.1	54.2	54.5	54.5	54.7	55.5
1997	54.3	54.7	54.0	53.4	53.6	53.9	54.2	54.5	54.9	55.3	55.0	55.1	54.4
1998	55.3	55.7	56.1	57.0	57.5	57.5	57.3	57.8	57.8	58.4	58.7	59.2	57.4
1999	58.4	58.8	59.4	60.2	60.4	60.9	61.0	61.6	62.0	62.3	62.4	63.0	60.9
2000	62.3	62.8	63.0	62.9	63.3	63.9	64.1	64.4	64.8	65.0	65.5	66.0	64.0
2001	65.9	65.9	65.8	66.0	66.1	66.4	66.3	67.0	66.1	63.9	62.0	61.8	65.2
2002	61.7	61.7	62.0	62.2	62.5	62.5	62.3	62.4	62.2	62.0	61.5	61.2	62.0
2003	60.5	60.2	60.0	59.3	59.1	58.5	57.4	57.6	57.5	57.7	57.6	58.1	58.6
Information													
1990	10.0	9.7	9.5	9.6	9.8	9.9	10.3	10.1	9.9	10.2	10.1	10.1	9.9
1991	10.5	10.2	10.2	9.9	9.9	10.1	10.4	10.2	10.1	10.2	11.1	11.1	10.3
1992	10.9	11.0	11.0	11.0	11.1	11.1	10.7	10.8	10.7	10.8	10.7	10.8	10.9
1993	10.9	10.9	10.9	11.0	10.9	11.1	11.2	11.1	11.0	10.9	10.9	11.0	11.0
1994	10.8	10.8	10.8	11.2	11.2	11.4	11.4	11.3	11.2	11.3	11.4	11.6	11.2
1995	11.9	12.0	12.1	11.8	11.8	12.0	11.9	11.9	11.8	11.7	11.9	12.1	11.9
1996	11.7	11.8	11.9	12.4	12.6	12.8	13.1	13.3	13.1	13.8	14.2	14.1	12.9
1997	13.8	14.0	14.7	15.0	15.3	15.7	15.9	16.1	16.2	16.4	16.6	16.8	15.5
1998	17.2	17.3	17.6	17.4	17.6	17.8	17.6	17.7	17.8	18.5	18.8	18.8	17.8
1999	18.8	18.8	18.7	17.8	18.0	18.1	18.1	18.1	18.0	17.8	18.0	18.4	18.2
2000	18.2	18.1	18.2	18.9	19.1	19.4	19.3	19.1	19.4	19.6	19.7	19.8	19.1
2001	19.9	19.9	20.1	20.0	20.0	20.1	20.1	20.1	19.9	19.7	19.9	20.1	19.9
2002	19.6	19.4	19.1	18.9	18.8	19.0	18.9	18.9	18.6	18.4	18.0	17.9	18.8
2003	17.7	17.6	17.8	17.7	17.8	18.0	18.0	17.9	17.7	17.7	17.9	18.0	17.8
Financial activities													
1990	29.3	29.3	29.4	29.3	29.1	29.3	29.3	29.3	29.0	28.9	28.8	29.1	29.2
1991	27.8	27.6	27.7	28.1	28.2	28.2	28.4	28.5	28.5	28.2	28.2	28.3	28.1
1992	28.6	28.5	28.8	29.0	29.0	29.2	28.4	28.4	28.3	28.1	28.1	28.5	28.6
1993	27.8	27.9	27.9	28.2	28.2	28.8	28.9	29.0	29.0	28.7	28.8	28.8	28.5
1994	29.0	29.1	29.3	29.9	30.0	30.1	30.1	30.1	29.9	29.9	30.0	30.0	29.8
1995	29.7	29.7	29.9	30.4	30.6	30.8	31.0	30.9	30.8	31.0	31.1	31.4	30.6
1996	31.1	31.3	31.4	31.6	32.2	32.5	32.9	33.1	32.9	32.9	33.2	33.1	32.4
1997	32.7	32.7	33.0	32.4	32.6	32.9	33.6	33.5	33.6	34.6	34.6	35.1	33.4
1998	34.5	34.6	35.0	35.8	36.0	36.5	36.8	36.9	37.1	37.4	37.4	37.8	36.3
1999	37.4	37.6	37.9	38.3	38.7	39.1	39.7	40.1	40.1	40.4	40.4	40.7	39.2
2000	40.4	40.5	40.8	41.4	41.8	42.2	42.5	42.9	43.1	43.4	43.8	44.3	42.3
2001	43.5	43.7	43.8	44.3	44.6	45.1	45.4	45.6	45.5	45.9	46.1	46.4	44.9
2002	45.8	46.1	46.0	46.1	46.3	46.4	46.2	46.2	46.0	46.0	46.1	45.9	46.1
2003	45.7	45.9	45.6	45.5	45.7	46.0	45.9	46.0	45.7	45.7	45.6	45.7	45.8
Professional and business services													
1990	42.0	42.5	42.9	43.8	43.9	45.6	45.5	45.8	45.7	45.2	45.7	46.0	44.6
1991	45.9	46.9	47.3	47.7	48.2	49.1	48.5	48.9	48.6	48.4	48.2	48.4	48.0
1992	47.0	47.5	48.2	49.1	49.9	50.6	50.4	50.6	50.8	51.5	51.3	51.9	49.9
1993	50.4	50.6	51.1	53.2	54.4	55.0	55.4	55.8	56.9	57.1	57.0	57.7	54.6
1994	56.3	56.3	57.3	60.3	60.0	60.4	60.4	60.9	61.0	59.8	59.7	59.2	59.3
1995	56.6	57.6	59.2	60.3	60.8	61.5	61.4	61.7	62.0	61.9	62.0	62.7	60.6
1996	62.2	62.4	64.1	64.0	64.1	64.6	66.3	67.6	67.7	67.5	67.6	66.9	65.4
1997	65.8	66.4	68.9	73.6	73.6	74.7	75.7	76.7	77.0	76.4	76.5	76.8	73.5
1998	75.8	75.7	76.6	77.4	77.7	78.9	79.1	79.2	79.2	79.7	79.2	80.2	78.2
1999	78.4	79.6	81.0	81.8	81.4	83.2	83.0	83.4	83.5	82.5	82.3	83.2	81.9
2000	82.1	82.7	84.5	84.8	85.1	86.3	85.6	86.5	87.9	85.3	84.8	84.8	85.0
2001	82.2	82.5	82.5	83.8	84.1	84.9	84.3	86.0	85.1	82.6	82.0	82.0	83.5
2002	80.2	80.4	81.4	81.4	81.6	81.7	79.9	81.7	81.0	80.2	80.7	80.9	80.9
2003	78.6	78.9	80.2	80.9	80.8	80.9	81.3	82.4	83.0	83.4	83.7	83.7	81.5

Employment by Industry: Texas—*Continued*

(Numbers in thousands. Not seasonally adjusted.)

Industry	January	February	March	April	May	June	July	August	September	October	November	December	Annual Average
FT. WORTH-ARLINGTON —*Continued*													
Educational and health services													
1990	53.4	54.8	55.3	55.6	56.3	56.3	56.1	56.8	57.6	58.4	58.6	58.7	56.5
1991	58.8	59.1	59.5	60.1	60.7	60.3	59.8	60.3	60.8	60.4	60.4	60.3	60.0
1992	59.0	59.5	59.7	60.8	60.9	61.2	60.4	60.4	60.9	60.9	61.4	61.9	60.6
1993	61.3	61.6	61.9	62.5	62.5	62.9	62.5	63.1	64.0	62.5	62.8	62.9	62.5
1994	63.3	63.7	64.0	64.8	64.8	64.9	63.6	64.8	65.4	65.8	65.9	66.1	64.8
1995	65.5	66.3	66.8	66.6	67.1	67.1	67.9	68.1	69.1	68.6	68.5	68.7	67.5
1996	67.6	68.4	68.6	69.0	69.3	69.7	69.6	70.5	71.0	71.0	71.3	71.5	69.8
1997	71.2	71.6	72.2	72.4	72.9	73.3	73.4	74.0	75.0	74.9	74.9	75.0	73.4
1998	74.3	74.3	74.1	74.8	75.3	75.2	74.4	75.3	76.0	76.4	77.0	77.2	75.4
1999	76.0	76.9	77.1	77.7	77.4	77.4	76.8	77.5	77.5	77.9	78.0	78.1	77.4
2000	77.7	77.8	78.3	78.7	79.0	78.5	77.8	78.3	78.6	79.1	79.4	79.7	78.6
2001	78.3	78.9	79.6	79.8	80.0	80.2	80.3	81.0	81.3	81.5	81.7	81.8	80.3
2002	80.6	81.2	81.6	81.8	82.3	81.9	82.1	83.5	84.0	83.7	84.1	84.0	82.6
2003	83.3	83.9	84.0	84.4	84.8	84.2	84.2	85.1	85.0	84.9	85.0	84.8	84.5
Leisure and hospitality													
1990	52.9	55.2	55.0	56.4	58.0	59.8	59.1	59.3	57.0	54.8	54.1	53.8	56.3
1991	52.7	54.3	54.3	55.5	57.0	58.4	58.1	58.2	56.9	55.1	54.6	54.2	55.8
1992	52.9	55.0	55.5	56.9	58.4	59.4	59.5	59.7	58.2	56.7	56.4	55.3	57.0
1993	54.8	56.8	57.8	59.8	61.4	63.2	62.6	62.4	61.2	59.4	58.3	57.8	59.6
1994	55.9	57.8	60.0	60.7	62.8	63.9	65.1	64.8	62.3	61.2	61.4	60.6	61.4
1995	59.3	61.4	62.7	63.6	66.3	68.3	67.2	66.5	64.4	63.3	62.2	61.7	63.9
1996	61.6	62.5	63.8	66.6	68.9	70.6	68.9	68.9	67.3	66.4	65.7	65.7	66.4
1997	61.9	64.6	66.2	68.5	70.5	72.3	71.6	71.0	70.6	68.0	68.9	68.8	68.6
1998	66.2	68.8	69.6	72.1	73.3	75.4	74.0	74.6	73.7	70.4	69.9	70.4	71.5
1999	68.8	70.3	71.5	73.7	75.1	76.4	74.9	74.7	73.4	73.0	72.7	72.8	73.1
2000	70.5	71.6	73.4	74.1	76.6	77.6	77.9	78.5	77.0	74.4	74.4	74.5	75.0
2001	71.4	73.2	74.9	76.8	78.0	78.9	78.7	78.6	76.2	74.0	73.5	73.5	75.6
2002	73.0	73.9	76.1	77.1	78.6	79.7	78.4	78.0	76.7	75.0	74.2	74.6	76.3
2003	73.4	74.3	76.0	77.4	78.4	79.3	77.8	77.9	76.0	75.2	74.9	75.0	76.3
Other services													
1990	22.8	22.9	23.0	23.2	23.5	24.0	23.9	23.9	23.6	23.5	23.5	23.5	23.4
1991	23.9	23.7	24.0	24.5	24.6	24.9	25.3	25.3	24.9	24.8	24.8	24.8	24.6
1992	24.6	24.9	25.2	25.5	25.6	26.1	25.9	25.6	25.4	25.7	25.7	25.6	25.5
1993	25.8	25.9	26.1	26.6	26.5	26.8	27.2	26.8	26.4	26.5	26.6	26.6	26.5
1994	25.9	25.9	27.1	26.5	26.4	26.8	26.9	26.7	26.5	26.6	26.8	26.9	26.6
1995	27.0	27.1	27.5	27.7	27.8	28.4	28.4	28.2	28.1	27.9	27.9	28.1	27.8
1996	27.7	27.9	28.1	28.3	28.7	29.1	28.9	28.8	28.7	28.7	28.8	28.9	28.6
1997	28.6	28.9	29.2	29.3	29.5	29.8	29.4	29.3	29.5	29.4	29.3	29.5	29.3
1998	28.8	29.1	29.4	29.8	30.0	29.9	30.1	30.0	30.1	30.2	30.1	30.3	29.8
1999	29.9	30.2	30.4	30.9	31.1	31.3	31.6	31.6	31.6	31.8	31.8	31.9	31.2
2000	31.4	31.8	31.9	31.9	32.1	32.7	32.2	32.4	32.1	31.8	31.7	31.8	32.0
2001	31.5	31.7	31.9	31.7	32.0	32.5	31.9	32.0	31.6	31.2	31.3	31.3	31.7
2002	31.3	31.4	31.9	32.0	32.3	32.4	32.2	32.1	32.1	31.6	31.6	31.4	31.9
2003	31.1	31.3	31.5	31.7	32.0	32.0	31.9	31.7	31.7	31.6	31.6	31.8	31.7
Government													
1990	75.2	76.3	76.3	76.8	76.8	75.3	70.8	70.8	74.2	75.3	76.9	76.9	75.1
1991	76.1	77.1	76.9	77.4	77.9	77.6	72.7	73.8	78.5	80.1	80.7	80.7	77.5
1992	80.6	81.7	82.0	82.2	82.3	81.3	77.2	77.3	82.4	83.6	84.5	84.2	81.6
1993	84.1	85.2	85.3	85.0	85.4	84.2	79.2	79.9	84.9	85.7	86.0	86.3	84.3
1994	85.0	86.7	86.6	86.5	86.7	85.3	80.3	81.0	86.2	87.1	88.1	88.3	85.7
1995	87.0	88.6	88.3	88.6	88.6	86.7	81.8	82.3	87.4	88.3	89.2	89.6	87.2
1996	88.1	89.3	89.6	90.1	89.7	88.0	83.3	84.9	89.6	90.2	90.9	91.0	88.7
1997	89.6	90.9	91.5	91.7	92.2	90.3	86.1	87.3	91.8	93.3	93.4	93.7	91.0
1998	92.1	94.2	94.4	94.4	94.8	92.7	88.5	89.9	94.5	95.8	96.5	96.7	93.7
1999	95.3	97.0	97.2	97.2	97.6	95.8	91.5	93.7	98.2	99.4	100.3	100.2	97.0
2000	98.4	100.1	100.3	101.3	103.3	100.9	96.8	98.2	101.3	102.4	103.6	103.7	100.9
2001	101.2	103.8	103.9	102.9	102.6	100.9	97.4	98.1	102.0	104.1	104.8	104.6	102.1
2002	103.0	105.6	105.5	105.3	105.7	103.4	99.0	100.0	104.5	107.2	109.2	109.3	104.8
2003	106.7	108.7	108.3	108.5	109.3	108.2	102.7	103.5	107.3	109.8	110.5	110.4	107.8
Federal government													
1990	13.2	13.1	13.1	13.2	13.2	13.4	13.5	13.5	13.6	13.3	13.3	13.5	13.3
1991	13.3	13.3	13.2	13.6	13.7	13.9	13.9	13.9	13.9	13.9	13.9	13.9	13.7
1992	13.9	13.8	13.8	13.8	13.7	13.8	13.8	13.7	13.8	13.7	13.6	13.6	13.8
1993	13.7	13.6	13.6	13.6	13.5	13.6	13.5	13.6	13.6	13.9	13.8	14.0	13.7
1994	13.6	13.7	13.7	13.8	13.7	13.6	13.5	13.5	13.5	13.3	13.4	13.7	13.6
1995	13.4	13.4	13.3	13.3	13.2	13.3	13.3	13.3	13.3	13.2	13.3	13.5	13.3
1996	13.3	13.3	13.2	13.3	13.3	13.4	13.5	13.6	13.7	13.7	13.9	14.2	13.5
1997	14.0	13.8	13.9	14.1	14.1	14.2	14.1	14.1	14.2	14.1	14.2	14.4	14.1
1998	14.0	14.0	14.0	14.0	14.1	14.1	14.0	14.0	14.0	14.2	14.4	14.8	14.1
1999	14.2	14.2	14.1	14.1	14.0	14.1	13.9	13.9	13.9	14.0	14.0	14.3	14.1
2000	14.0	14.0	14.3	14.5	16.1	14.7	14.5	13.9	13.8	13.9	13.9	14.2	14.3
2001	13.9	13.9	13.9	13.9	13.9	14.0	14.2	14.2	14.1	14.1	14.0	14.1	14.0
2002	14.1	14.0	14.2	14.0	14.0	14.1	14.1	14.1	14.5	15.4	15.7	15.7	14.5
2003	15.6	15.4	15.4	15.4	15.4	15.2	15.2	15.1	15.0	15.0	14.8	14.7	15.2

Employment by Industry: Texas—*Continued*

(Numbers in thousands. Not seasonally adjusted.)

Industry	January	February	March	April	May	June	July	August	September	October	November	December	Annual Average
FT. WORTH-ARLINGTON *—Continued*													
State government													
1990	8.5	8.9	8.8	9.2	9.1	9.2	8.9	8.9	8.6	9.0	9.1	9.1	8.9
1991	9.1	9.3	9.0	9.1	9.3	9.3	8.9	9.0	8.9	9.1	9.4	9.3	9.1
1992	9.4	9.7	9.6	9.8	10.0	9.8	9.6	9.5	9.6	10.0	10.1	10.1	9.8
1993	10.3	10.3	10.3	10.1	10.3	10.2	9.8	9.8	10.4	10.2	10.1	10.1	10.2
1994	9.6	9.9	9.6	9.7	9.9	9.8	9.5	9.5	9.6	9.6	9.7	9.7	9.7
1995	9.4	9.8	9.6	9.5	9.5	9.1	9.0	8.9	9.2	9.1	9.1	9.2	9.3
1996	8.8	9.2	9.1	9.3	9.2	8.9	8.6	8.7	9.0	8.9	9.0	8.9	9.0
1997	8.6	9.0	9.1	9.1	9.1	8.9	8.5	8.5	8.7	9.1	9.1	9.0	8.9
1998	8.6	9.1	9.1	9.1	9.1	8.9	8.5	8.5	8.8	9.2	9.2	9.1	8.9
1999	8.9	9.2	9.2	9.3	9.2	9.1	8.6	8.6	8.9	9.3	9.4	9.2	9.1
2000	9.0	9.3	9.3	9.4	9.4	9.2	9.0	9.1	9.1	9.6	9.7	9.6	9.3
2001	9.3	9.7	9.7	9.7	9.7	9.6	9.3	9.3	9.4	9.8	9.9	9.9	9.5
2002	9.5	10.0	10.0	9.9	10.0	9.8	9.3	9.2	9.4	10.0	10.1	10.1	9.8
2003	9.7	10.1	10.1	10.1	10.1	9.9	9.2	9.1	9.3	9.8	9.9	9.9	9.8
Local government													
1990	53.5	54.3	54.4	54.4	54.5	52.7	48.4	48.4	52.0	53.0	54.5	54.3	52.9
1991	53.7	54.5	54.7	54.7	54.9	54.4	49.9	50.9	55.7	57.1	57.4	57.5	54.6
1992	57.3	58.2	58.6	58.6	58.6	57.7	53.8	54.1	59.0	59.9	60.8	60.5	58.1
1993	60.1	61.3	61.4	61.3	61.6	60.4	55.9	56.5	60.9	61.6	62.1	62.2	60.4
1994	61.8	63.1	63.3	63.0	63.1	61.9	57.3	58.0	63.1	64.2	65.0	64.9	62.4
1995	64.2	65.4	65.4	65.8	65.9	64.3	59.5	60.1	64.9	66.0	66.8	66.9	64.6
1996	66.0	66.8	67.3	67.5	67.2	65.7	61.2	62.6	66.9	67.6	68.0	67.9	66.2
1997	67.0	68.1	68.5	68.5	69.0	67.2	63.5	64.7	68.9	70.1	70.1	70.3	68.0
1998	69.5	71.1	71.3	71.3	71.6	69.7	66.0	67.4	71.7	72.4	72.9	72.8	70.6
1999	72.2	73.6	73.9	73.8	74.4	72.6	69.0	71.2	75.4	76.1	76.9	76.7	73.8
2000	75.4	76.8	76.7	77.4	77.8	77.0	73.3	75.2	78.4	78.9	80.0	79.9	77.2
2001	78.0	80.2	80.3	79.3	79.0	77.3	73.9	74.6	78.5	80.2	80.9	80.6	78.5
2002	79.4	81.6	81.3	81.4	81.7	79.5	75.6	76.7	80.6	81.8	83.4	83.5	80.5
2003	81.4	83.2	82.8	83.0	83.8	83.1	78.3	79.3	83.0	85.0	85.8	85.8	82.9
GALVESTON-TEXAS CITY													
Total nonfarm													
1990	73.6	74.5	75.1	76.4	77.1	78.1	78.4	78.3	78.1	77.6	77.4	77.1	76.8
1991	75.7	76.4	77.3	77.7	78.3	79.3	79.1	79.4	79.1	80.6	79.7	79.6	78.5
1992	78.8	78.8	79.2	79.9	80.7	81.3	80.7	80.6	80.7	81.2	82.1	81.9	80.5
1993	81.3	82.7	83.4	83.8	84.1	84.7	83.9	83.8	84.5	84.1	83.8	83.8	83.7
1994	82.2	83.1	83.4	84.2	84.3	84.7	83.9	83.8	84.0	84.9	85.4	85.3	84.1
1995	83.8	84.8	85.9	86.1	86.7	87.9	87.8	87.8	88.6	88.7	89.0	88.6	87.1
1996	86.5	87.4	88.1	87.5	87.1	87.7	87.6	87.1	86.2	86.4	86.7	86.6	87.1
1997	85.2	85.8	86.5	86.8	87.9	88.6	87.3	87.7	87.4	87.8	88.2	88.9	87.3
1998	87.1	88.4	88.7	88.9	90.2	90.7	89.7	89.6	89.3	89.2	89.4	90.1	89.3
1999	87.8	88.8	89.3	88.7	88.7	89.3	88.2	87.6	88.0	87.8	87.6	87.9	88.3
2000	86.6	87.3	87.6	87.4	88.5	88.7	87.8	88.0	87.7	88.0	88.3	88.2	87.8
2001	86.3	86.9	87.8	87.6	88.2	88.8	87.6	87.3	86.6	86.1	86.6	86.1	87.1
2002	86.0	87.0	87.9	87.9	88.6	89.4	87.8	88.0	87.6	87.5	88.0	88.5	87.9
2003	87.1	87.4	88.6	89.0	88.9	89.7	87.8	87.7	88.3	88.3	88.4	88.7	88.3
Total private													
1990	51.8	52.3	52.9	54.3	54.7	55.6	56.3	56.6	55.9	55.1	54.9	54.6	54.6
1991	53.4	53.7	54.8	55.3	55.8	56.9	57.0	57.3	56.8	57.5	56.5	56.3	55.9
1992	56.0	55.6	55.9	56.3	56.7	57.2	57.7	57.8	57.0	57.2	58.0	57.8	56.9
1993	57.0	58.0	58.5	58.9	59.1	59.8	59.9	60.0	59.9	59.1	58.6	58.7	59.0
1994	57.2	57.9	58.1	59.0	59.1	59.7	59.5	59.4	58.8	59.3	59.6	59.6	58.9
1995	58.2	58.7	59.6	60.0	60.4	61.5	62.0	62.1	61.8	61.7	62.0	61.7	60.8
1996	59.6	59.3	59.6	59.5	59.7	60.4	60.8	60.7	59.5	59.5	59.8	60.1	59.9
1997	58.9	59.2	59.8	60.3	61.0	61.9	61.6	61.5	60.9	60.9	61.0	61.8	60.7
1998	60.1	61.3	61.5	61.8	62.8	63.5	63.4	63.2	62.5	62.8	63.0	63.7	62.5
1999	62.0	62.8	63.5	63.0	63.1	64.0	63.7	63.5	62.7	62.1	62.0	62.2	62.9
2000	61.1	61.6	61.7	61.7	62.3	63.1	63.0	62.8	62.0	62.9	62.9	63.1	62.4
2001	61.3	61.6	62.3	62.2	62.7	63.3	62.7	62.3	61.2	60.5	60.9	60.7	61.8
2002	60.3	61.1	62.0	62.0	62.4	63.3	62.8	62.9	61.7	61.4	61.6	61.9	62.0
2003	61.1	61.3	62.3	62.8	62.9	63.6	63.3	63.1	63.1	62.8	62.7	63.4	62.7
Goods-producing													
1990	13.4	13.8	13.5	13.5	13.5	13.5	14.1	14.2	14.1	14.0	14.0	13.6	13.8
1991	13.2	13.1	14.0	14.0	13.5	13.7	13.7	14.1	14.2	14.6	14.3	13.9	13.9
1992	14.8	14.4	14.2	14.2	14.2	14.5	14.6	14.9	15.0	15.3	15.0	14.7	14.7
1993	14.7	14.8	15.0	14.7	14.5	14.4	14.0	13.8	14.2	14.2	14.0	13.9	14.4
1994	13.5	13.8	13.9	13.4	13.6	13.4	13.5	13.4	13.5	14.0	14.1	14.2	13.7
1995	14.1	14.2	14.5	13.7	13.8	14.1	14.4	14.7	14.7	15.3	15.4	14.9	14.5
1996	14.2	14.3	14.2	13.7	13.3	13.3	13.8	13.8	13.4	13.6	13.6	13.3	13.7
1997	13.2	13.4	13.3	12.9	13.0	13.0	13.0	12.9	12.9	13.1	13.3	13.4	13.1
1998	13.6	14.0	13.9	13.9	13.7	13.6	13.7	13.7	13.7	14.1	13.8	14.2	13.8
1999	14.6	14.8	14.6	13.7	13.6	13.6	13.3	13.2	13.2	12.8	12.7	12.9	13.6
2000	13.1	13.3	13.3	12.9	12.8	12.8	12.7	12.8	12.9	13.3	13.2	13.1	13.0
2001	13.0	13.1	13.3	12.8	12.7	12.7	12.3	12.1	12.0	12.2	12.2	12.3	12.5
2002	12.0	12.1	12.3	12.3	12.0	12.1	12.0	12.0	12.0	12.2	12.2	12.1	12.1
2003	12.1	12.1	12.1	12.1	11.3	11.5	11.5	11.3	12.2	12.4	12.4	12.3	11.9

Employment by Industry: Texas—*Continued*

(Numbers in thousands. Not seasonally adjusted.)

Industry	January	February	March	April	May	June	July	August	September	October	November	December	Annual Average
GALVESTON-TEXAS CITY *—Continued*													
Construction and mining													
1990	5.2	5.6	5.3	5.3	5.4	5.3	5.4	5.5	5.4	5.5	5.6	5.3	5.4
1991	4.9	4.9	5.8	5.7	5.0	5.1	4.9	5.2	5.6	5.9	5.6	5.2	5.3
1992	6.1	5.7	5.5	5.5	5.5	5.7	5.6	6.0	6.2	6.6	6.3	6.0	5.9
1993	6.1	6.2	6.3	6.1	5.9	5.8	5.4	5.3	5.7	5.8	5.6	5.4	5.8
1994	5.1	5.4	5.5	5.3	5.5	5.3	5.2	5.2	5.3	5.9	5.9	5.8	5.5
1995	6.1	6.1	6.3	5.7	5.7	6.0	6.3	6.5	6.6	7.2	7.1	6.7	6.4
1996	6.3	6.4	6.2	5.8	5.4	5.4	5.8	5.8	5.5	5.9	5.5	5.2	5.8
1997	4.9	5.2	5.1	4.8	4.9	4.9	5.0	4.9	4.9	4.9	5.0	5.0	5.0
1998	5.3	5.7	5.4	5.6	5.7	5.5	5.5	5.5	5.5	6.2	5.7	6.0	5.6
1999	6.3	6.7	6.3	5.6	5.7	5.7	5.3	5.2	5.2	5.0	5.0	4.9	5.6
2000	5.1	5.1	5.1	4.5	4.5	4.6	4.7	4.7	4.8	4.9	4.8	4.7	4.8
2001	4.8	4.9	5.2	4.9	4.8	4.9	4.8	4.8	4.6	4.7	4.8	5.0	4.8
2002	4.7	4.8	5.0	5.0	4.8	4.9	4.9	5.0	4.9	4.7	4.7	4.7	4.8
2003	4.8	4.9	4.8	4.8	4.9	5.1	5.0	5.0	5.1	5.0	5.0	5.0	5.0
Manufacturing													
1990	8.2	8.2	8.2	8.2	8.1	8.2	8.7	8.7	8.7	8.5	8.4	8.3	8.4
1991	8.3	8.2	8.2	8.3	8.5	8.6	8.8	8.9	8.6	8.7	8.7	8.7	8.5
1992	8.7	8.7	8.7	8.7	8.7	8.8	9.0	8.9	8.8	8.7	8.7	8.7	8.8
1993	8.6	8.6	8.7	8.6	8.6	8.6	8.6	8.5	8.5	8.4	8.4	8.5	8.6
1994	8.4	8.4	8.4	8.1	8.1	8.1	8.3	8.2	8.2	8.1	8.2	8.4	8.2
1995	8.0	8.1	8.2	8.0	8.1	8.1	8.1	8.2	8.1	8.1	8.3	8.2	8.1
1996	7.9	7.9	8.0	7.9	7.9	7.9	8.0	8.0	7.9	7.7	8.1	8.1	7.9
1997	8.3	8.2	8.2	8.1	8.1	8.1	8.0	8.0	8.0	8.2	8.3	8.4	8.2
1998	8.3	8.3	8.5	8.3	8.0	8.1	8.2	8.2	8.2	7.9	8.1	8.2	8.2
1999	8.3	8.1	8.3	8.1	7.9	7.9	8.0	8.0	8.0	7.8	7.7	8.0	8.0
2000	8.0	8.2	8.2	8.4	8.3	8.2	8.0	8.1	8.1	8.4	8.4	8.4	8.2
2001	8.2	8.2	8.1	7.9	7.9	7.8	7.5	7.3	7.4	7.5	7.4	7.3	7.7
2002	7.3	7.3	7.3	7.3	7.2	7.2	7.1	7.0	7.1	7.5	7.5	7.4	7.3
2003	7.3	7.2	7.3	7.3	6.4	6.4	6.5	6.3	7.1	7.4	7.4	7.3	7.0
Service-providing													
1990	60.2	60.7	61.6	62.9	63.6	64.6	64.3	64.1	64.0	63.6	63.4	63.5	63.0
1991	62.5	63.3	63.3	63.7	64.8	65.6	65.4	65.3	64.9	66.0	65.4	65.7	64.7
1992	64.0	64.4	65.0	65.7	66.5	66.8	66.1	65.7	65.7	65.9	67.1	67.2	65.8
1993	66.6	67.9	68.4	69.1	69.6	70.3	69.9	70.0	70.3	69.9	69.8	69.9	69.3
1994	68.7	69.3	69.5	70.8	70.7	71.3	70.4	70.4	70.5	70.9	71.3	71.1	70.4
1995	69.7	70.6	71.4	72.4	72.9	73.8	73.4	73.1	73.9	73.4	73.6	73.7	72.7
1996	72.3	73.1	73.9	73.8	73.8	74.4	73.8	73.3	72.8	72.8	73.1	73.3	73.4
1997	72.0	72.4	73.2	73.9	74.9	75.6	74.3	74.8	74.5	74.7	74.9	75.5	74.2
1998	73.5	74.4	74.8	75.0	76.5	77.1	76.0	75.9	75.6	75.1	75.6	75.9	75.5
1999	73.2	74.0	74.7	75.0	75.1	75.7	74.9	74.4	74.8	75.0	74.9	75.0	74.7
2000	73.5	74.0	74.3	74.5	75.7	75.9	75.1	75.2	74.8	74.7	75.1	75.1	74.8
2001	73.3	73.8	74.5	74.8	75.5	76.1	75.3	75.2	74.6	73.9	74.4	73.8	74.6
2002	74.0	74.9	75.6	75.6	76.6	77.3	75.8	76.0	75.6	75.3	75.8	76.4	75.7
2003	75.0	75.3	76.5	76.9	77.6	78.2	76.3	76.4	76.1	75.9	76.0	76.4	76.4
Trade, transportation, and utilities													
1990	13.4	13.2	13.5	13.8	13.5	13.8	13.7	13.7	13.5	13.3	13.1	13.1	13.5
1991	12.7	12.6	12.4	13.0	13.3	13.6	13.6	13.6	13.5	13.9	13.7	13.6	13.3
1992	13.0	13.0	12.9	12.9	13.1	12.9	13.1	13.0	12.7	13.1	13.2	13.1	13.0
1993	13.0	13.2	13.1	13.5	13.4	13.4	13.8	13.9	13.8	13.7	13.7	14.0	13.5
1994	13.4	13.6	13.3	13.8	14.0	14.0	13.7	13.8	13.7	13.8	14.0	14.2	13.8
1995	13.7	13.5	13.8	14.2	14.2	14.3	14.4	14.5	14.6	14.3	14.6	14.8	14.2
1996	14.3	14.1	14.2	13.9	14.1	14.2	14.0	14.1	14.0	14.1	14.3	14.6	14.2
1997	13.9	13.7	13.9	13.8	13.8	14.0	13.9	14.2	14.0	13.7	14.0	14.3	13.9
1998	13.6	13.7	13.7	13.9	14.2	14.3	14.3	14.4	14.4	14.5	15.0	15.1	14.3
1999	14.2	14.3	14.6	14.5	14.4	14.6	14.8	14.8	14.7	14.8	15.0	15.2	14.7
2000	14.5	14.3	14.4	14.3	14.5	14.7	14.8	14.9	14.5	14.9	15.0	15.2	14.7
2001	14.0	13.9	13.9	13.7	13.7	13.9	13.8	13.9	13.7	13.6	13.7	13.8	13.8
2002	13.6	14.1	14.2	14.2	14.2	14.6	14.3	14.3	14.1	14.1	14.5	14.7	14.2
2003	14.2	14.3	14.5	14.5	14.5	14.6	14.5	14.5	14.4	14.4	14.5	15.1	14.5
Wholesale trade													
1990	1.4	1.4	1.4	1.6	1.6	1.7	1.6	1.7	1.7	1.7	1.6	1.6	1.6
1991	1.5	1.5	1.5	1.5	1.5	1.5	1.5	1.5	1.5	1.5	1.5	1.5	1.5
1992	1.5	1.5	1.5	1.5	1.6	1.5	1.6	1.6	1.5	1.5	1.5	1.5	1.5
1993	1.4	1.4	1.5	1.5	1.5	1.5	1.5	1.5	1.5	1.5	1.5	1.5	1.5
1994	1.4	1.5	1.4	1.5	1.5	1.5	1.5	1.5	1.5	1.5	1.5	1.6	1.5
1995	1.5	1.5	1.5	1.5	1.5	1.6	1.6	1.6	1.6	1.5	1.6	1.6	1.6
1996	1.5	1.5	1.5	1.6	1.6	1.6	1.6	1.6	1.6	1.6	1.6	1.7	1.6
1997	1.6	1.6	1.7	1.6	1.6	1.7	1.7	1.7	1.7	1.7	1.6	1.6	1.7
1998	1.6	1.7	1.7	1.6	1.6	1.6	1.6	1.6	1.6	1.6	1.6	1.6	1.6
1999	1.6	1.6	1.7	1.6	1.6	1.6	1.6	1.6	1.6	1.7	1.6	1.6	1.6
2000	1.6	1.6	1.6	1.6	1.6	1.7	1.7	1.7	1.6	1.7	1.6	1.6	1.6
2001	1.6	1.6	1.6	1.6	1.6	1.6	1.6	1.6	1.6	1.6	1.6	1.6	1.5
2002	1.5	1.5	1.5	1.6	1.6	1.6	1.6	1.7	1.7	1.6	1.6	1.6	1.6
2003	1.6	1.6	1.6	1.6	1.6	1.6	1.6	1.6	1.6	1.6	1.6	1.7	1.6

Employment by Industry: Texas—*Continued*

(Numbers in thousands. Not seasonally adjusted.)

Industry	January	February	March	April	May	June	July	August	September	October	November	December	Annual Average
GALVESTON-TEXAS CITY *—Continued*													
Retail trade													
1990	8.0	8.0	8.0	8.0	8.0	8.1	8.1	8.1	8.1	8.0	8.1	8.0	8.0
1991	7.8	7.7	7.6	8.1	8.3	8.4	8.4	8.5	8.6	8.6	8.7	8.6	8.3
1992	8.3	8.2	8.2	8.2	8.3	8.4	8.4	8.4	8.2	8.5	8.6	8.6	8.4
1993	8.5	8.6	8.5	8.8	8.8	8.8	9.1	9.2	9.0	9.0	9.1	9.2	8.9
1994	8.9	8.8	8.8	8.9	9.0	9.1	8.8	8.8	8.8	9.0	9.2	9.4	9.0
1995	9.1	8.9	9.1	9.5	9.5	9.7	9.6	9.7	9.7	9.6	9.8	10.0	9.5
1996	9.6	9.2	9.3	9.4	9.5	9.7	9.5	9.5	9.4	9.6	9.7	9.9	9.5
1997	9.4	9.2	9.3	9.4	9.4	9.5	9.6	9.8	9.6	9.3	9.7	9.9	9.5
1998	9.5	9.4	9.4	9.7	9.9	10.0	10.0	10.1	10.0	10.0	10.5	10.8	9.9
1999	10.0	10.1	10.2	10.1	10.0	10.3	10.5	10.4	10.3	10.3	10.5	10.8	10.3
2000	10.2	9.9	10.1	10.0	10.2	10.3	10.4	10.4	10.2	10.4	10.6	10.8	10.3
2001	9.9	9.7	9.7	9.6	9.6	9.7	9.7	9.7	9.5	9.4	9.6	9.8	9.6
2002	9.7	10.2	10.3	10.1	10.1	10.5	10.3	10.1	9.9	10.0	10.4	10.6	10.2
2003	10.1	10.3	10.4	10.4	10.3	10.5	10.5	10.4	10.2	10.2	10.3	10.8	10.4
Transportation and utilities													
1990	4.0	3.8	4.1	4.2	3.9	4.0	4.0	3.9	3.7	3.6	3.4	3.5	3.8
1991	3.4	3.4	3.3	3.4	3.5	3.7	3.7	3.6	3.4	3.8	3.5	3.5	3.5
1992	3.2	3.3	3.2	3.2	3.2	3.0	3.1	3.0	3.0	3.1	3.1	3.0	3.1
1993	3.1	3.2	3.1	3.2	3.1	3.1	3.2	3.2	3.3	3.2	3.1	3.3	3.2
1994	3.1	3.3	3.1	3.4	3.5	3.4	3.4	3.5	3.4	3.3	3.3	3.2	3.3
1995	3.1	3.1	3.2	3.2	3.2	3.0	3.2	3.2	3.3	3.2	3.2	3.2	3.2
1996	3.2	3.4	3.4	2.9	3.0	2.9	2.9	3.0	3.0	2.9	3.0	3.0	3.1
1997	2.9	2.9	2.9	2.8	2.8	2.8	2.6	2.7	2.7	2.7	2.7	2.8	2.8
1998	2.5	2.6	2.6	2.6	2.7	2.7	2.7	2.7	2.8	2.9	2.9	2.7	2.7
1999	2.6	2.6	2.7	2.8	2.8	2.7	2.7	2.8	2.8	2.8	2.9	2.8	2.8
2000	2.7	2.8	2.7	2.7	2.7	2.7	2.7	2.8	2.7	2.8	2.8	2.8	2.7
2001	2.5	2.6	2.6	2.5	2.5	2.6	2.5	2.6	2.6	2.6	2.5	2.4	2.5
2002	2.4	2.4	2.4	2.5	2.5	2.5	2.4	2.5	2.5	2.5	2.5	2.5	2.5
2003	2.5	2.4	2.5	2.5	2.6	2.5	2.4	2.5	2.6	2.6	2.6	2.6	2.5
Information													
1990	1.0	1.0	1.0	1.1	1.2	1.2	1.2	1.2	1.2	1.2	1.2	1.2	1.1
1991	1.3	1.3	1.3	1.3	1.3	1.3	1.4	1.4	1.4	1.4	1.3	1.3	1.3
1992	1.4	1.4	1.4	1.3	1.3	1.3	1.3	1.3	1.3	1.2	1.2	1.2	1.3
1993	1.2	1.2	1.2	1.1	1.1	1.1	1.1	1.1	1.1	1.1	1.1	1.1	1.1
1994	1.1	1.1	1.1	1.0	1.0	1.0	1.1	1.0	1.0	1.1	1.1	1.1	1.1
1995	1.1	1.1	1.1	1.1	1.1	1.1	1.1	1.1	1.1	1.1	1.1	1.1	1.1
1996	1.1	1.1	1.1	1.0	1.0	1.0	1.0	1.0	1.0	1.0	1.0	1.1	1.0
1997	1.0	1.0	1.0	1.0	1.0	1.0	1.0	1.0	1.0	1.0	1.0	1.1	1.0
1998	0.9	0.9	0.9	1.0	1.0	1.0	1.0	1.0	1.0	1.0	1.0	1.0	1.0
1999	1.0	1.0	1.0	1.0	1.0	1.0	0.9	0.9	0.9	0.9	0.9	1.0	1.0
2000	0.9	0.9	0.9	0.9	0.9	1.0	1.0	0.9	0.9	0.9	0.9	0.9	0.9
2001	0.8	0.8	0.9	0.8	0.8	0.8	0.8	0.8	0.8	0.9	0.9	0.8	0.8
2002	0.8	0.8	0.8	0.8	0.8	0.8	0.8	0.8	0.8	0.8	0.8	0.8	0.8
2003	0.8	0.8	0.8	0.8	0.8	0.8	0.8	0.8	0.8	0.8	0.8	0.8	0.8
Financial activities													
1990	4.9	5.0	5.0	5.0	5.0	5.2	5.2	5.2	5.3	5.3	5.3	5.2	5.1
1991	5.3	5.4	5.4	5.4	5.4	5.5	5.5	5.6	5.4	5.6	5.5	5.4	5.5
1992	5.6	5.5	5.6	5.6	5.6	5.7	5.8	5.9	5.8	5.7	5.7	5.6	5.7
1993	5.6	5.6	5.7	5.7	5.7	5.7	5.8	5.7	5.7	5.6	5.5	5.5	5.7
1994	5.5	5.5	5.5	5.6	5.5	5.6	5.5	5.5	5.5	5.5	5.5	5.5	5.5
1995	5.3	5.3	5.4	5.5	5.5	5.6	5.5	5.5	5.5	5.5	5.5	5.5	5.5
1996	5.4	5.5	5.5	5.5	5.5	5.6	5.6	5.6	5.6	5.6	5.6	5.6	5.6
1997	5.6	5.6	5.6	5.6	5.6	5.6	5.8	5.7	5.7	5.8	5.8	5.8	5.7
1998	5.9	5.9	5.9	6.1	6.1	6.1	6.1	6.0	6.1	6.1	6.1	6.1	6.0
1999	6.0	5.9	6.0	5.8	5.8	5.8	5.8	5.8	5.8	5.7	5.7	5.7	5.8
2000	5.7	5.8	5.7	5.7	5.6	5.7	5.8	5.8	5.8	5.7	5.7	5.7	5.7
2001	5.7	5.7	5.7	5.7	5.7	5.8	5.8	5.9	5.8	5.8	5.9	5.8	5.7
2002	5.9	5.8	5.9	5.9	6.0	6.0	6.0	6.0	6.0	6.0	5.9	6.0	6.0
2003	5.9	5.9	5.9	5.9	6.0	6.0	6.1	6.1	6.0	6.0	6.0	6.1	6.0
Professional and business services													
1990	2.9	2.8	3.0	3.4	3.6	3.6	3.6	3.6	3.7	3.5	3.6	3.9	3.4
1991	3.2	3.6	3.8	3.9	3.9	4.0	3.9	3.7	3.9	3.6	3.7	4.0	3.8
1992	3.9	3.8	3.9	3.9	3.8	3.8	3.7	3.3	3.4	3.4	3.4	3.7	3.7
1993	3.4	3.6	3.6	3.7	3.8	3.9	3.9	3.9	4.0	3.7	3.7	3.7	3.7
1994	3.8	3.8	4.0	4.0	3.9	4.0	3.8	3.7	3.8	3.8	3.8	3.8	3.9
1995	3.6	3.7	3.7	3.8	3.8	3.9	3.8	3.8	3.9	3.9	3.9	3.9	3.8
1996	3.7	3.7	3.8	3.8	3.8	3.8	3.9	3.9	3.8	3.9	3.9	3.9	3.8
1997	3.9	4.0	4.1	4.1	4.2	4.2	4.2	4.3	4.2	4.2	4.2	4.2	4.2
1998	3.9	4.0	4.0	3.7	3.8	3.8	3.7	3.8	3.7	3.7	3.7	3.8	3.8
1999	3.6	3.7	3.7	3.6	3.6	3.6	3.5	3.6	3.5	3.6	3.5	3.5	3.6
2000	3.5	3.6	3.6	3.7	3.7	3.7	3.7	3.8	3.9	3.9	3.9	3.9	3.7
2001	3.9	3.9	4.0	4.3	4.4	4.1	4.2	4.2	4.1	4.1	4.2	4.1	4.1
2002	4.1	4.2	4.3	4.3	4.4	4.4	4.4	4.5	4.5	4.5	4.6	4.6	4.4
2003	4.7	4.8	4.9	4.9	5.0	4.9	4.9	5.0	5.0	5.0	4.9	4.9	4.9

Employment by Industry: Texas—*Continued*

(Numbers in thousands. Not seasonally adjusted.)

Industry	January	February	March	April	May	June	July	August	September	October	November	December	Annual Average
GALVESTON-TEXAS CITY *—Continued*													
Educational and health services													
1990	5.7	5.7	5.7	5.7	5.7	5.7	5.9	6.1	6.1	6.0	6.1	6.0	5.9
1991	6.0	5.9	5.9	5.8	5.9	5.9	5.9	6.0	6.0	6.2	6.1	6.1	6.0
1992	5.8	5.8	5.8	5.9	5.9	6.0	5.9	6.1	6.2	6.1	6.1	6.1	6.0
1993	6.0	6.0	6.1	6.1	6.2	6.4	6.7	6.8	6.9	6.9	6.9	6.9	6.5
1994	6.5	6.6	6.7	7.0	6.9	6.9	6.8	6.9	7.0	7.1	7.1	7.1	6.9
1995	6.8	6.9	6.9	7.0	7.0	7.0	7.1	7.2	7.3	7.3	7.3	7.4	7.1
1996	7.2	6.9	6.8	7.0	7.0	7.1	6.9	7.0	7.0	7.1	7.2	7.3	7.0
1997	7.3	7.3	7.4	7.3	7.3	7.3	7.4	7.4	7.6	7.7	7.7	7.8	7.5
1998	7.6	7.7	7.8	7.7	7.8	7.8	7.8	7.7	7.7	7.8	7.8	7.8	7.8
1999	7.9	7.9	7.9	8.1	8.1	8.2	8.1	8.2	8.3	8.2	8.3	8.2	8.1
2000	8.1	8.1	7.9	7.8	7.9	7.8	8.0	8.1	8.2	8.3	8.3	8.4	8.1
2001	8.4	8.5	8.5	8.5	8.6	8.6	8.6	8.6	8.7	8.5	8.6	8.6	8.5
2002	8.5	8.5	8.5	8.6	8.6	8.5	8.4	8.5	8.5	8.3	8.3	8.3	8.5
2003	8.2	8.2	8.3	8.4	8.4	8.3	8.2	8.4	8.4	8.4	8.4	8.4	8.3
Leisure and hospitality													
1990	7.4	7.6	8.1	8.5	8.9	9.3	9.3	9.3	8.7	8.5	8.3	8.4	8.5
1991	8.4	8.5	8.7	8.7	9.2	9.6	9.7	9.5	9.0	8.9	8.6	8.7	9.0
1992	8.3	8.4	8.8	9.1	9.4	9.6	9.9	9.9	9.3	9.1	10.1	10.1	9.3
1993	9.9	10.3	10.5	10.9	11.2	11.6	11.4	11.5	10.9	10.7	10.5	10.4	10.8
1994	10.1	10.2	10.3	10.7	10.9	11.4	11.8	11.8	11.0	10.7	10.6	10.4	10.8
1995	10.3	10.6	10.8	11.3	11.6	12.0	12.2	11.9	11.3	10.9	10.8	10.7	11.2
1996	10.4	10.4	10.6	11.2	11.6	11.9	12.1	11.8	11.2	10.7	10.7	10.8	11.1
1997	10.5	10.7	10.9	11.9	12.4	13.0	12.5	12.3	11.8	11.7	11.4	11.5	11.7
1998	10.9	11.3	11.7	11.8	12.5	13.1	13.0	12.8	12.2	11.8	11.8	11.9	12.1
1999	11.1	11.5	12.0	12.6	12.9	13.5	13.5	13.2	12.6	12.5	12.3	12.1	12.5
2000	11.7	12.0	12.3	12.7	13.3	13.7	13.3	12.9	12.2	12.4	12.4	12.3	12.6
2001	11.9	12.1	12.4	12.8	13.2	13.7	13.5	13.2	12.5	11.8	11.8	11.7	12.5
2002	11.8	12.0	12.4	12.3	12.8	13.3	13.3	13.2	12.2	11.9	11.7	11.8	12.4
2003	11.5	11.6	12.2	12.5	13.2	13.8	13.7	13.4	12.6	12.2	12.1	12.2	12.6
Other services													
1990	3.1	3.2	3.1	3.3	3.3	3.3	3.3	3.3	3.3	3.3	3.3	3.2	3.3
1991	3.3	3.3	3.3	3.2	3.3	3.3	3.3	3.4	3.4	3.3	3.3	3.3	3.3
1992	3.2	3.3	3.3	3.4	3.4	3.4	3.4	3.4	3.3	3.3	3.3	3.3	3.3
1993	3.2	3.3	3.3	3.2	3.2	3.3	3.2	3.3	3.3	3.2	3.2	3.2	3.2
1994	3.3	3.3	3.3	3.5	3.3	3.4	3.3	3.3	3.3	3.3	3.4	3.3	3.3
1995	3.3	3.4	3.4	3.4	3.4	3.5	3.5	3.4	3.4	3.4	3.4	3.4	3.4
1996	3.3	3.3	3.4	3.4	3.4	3.5	3.5	3.5	3.5	3.5	3.5	3.5	3.4
1997	3.5	3.5	3.6	3.7	3.7	3.8	3.8	3.7	3.7	3.7	3.6	3.7	3.7
1998	3.7	3.8	3.6	3.7	3.7	3.8	3.8	3.8	3.7	3.8	3.8	3.8	3.8
1999	3.6	3.7	3.7	3.7	3.7	3.7	3.8	3.8	3.7	3.6	3.6	3.6	3.7
2000	3.6	3.6	3.6	3.7	3.6	3.7	3.7	3.6	3.6	3.5	3.5	3.6	3.6
2001	3.6	3.6	3.6	3.6	3.6	3.7	3.7	3.6	3.6	3.6	3.6	3.6	3.6
2002	3.6	3.6	3.6	3.6	3.6	3.6	3.6	3.6	3.6	3.6	3.6	3.6	3.6
2003	3.7	3.6	3.6	3.7	3.7	3.7	3.6	3.6	3.7	3.6	3.6	3.6	3.6
Government													
1990	21.8	22.2	22.2	22.1	22.4	22.5	22.1	21.7	22.2	22.5	22.5	22.5	22.2
1991	22.3	22.7	22.5	22.4	22.5	22.4	22.1	22.1	22.3	23.1	23.2	23.3	22.6
1992	22.8	23.2	23.3	23.6	24.0	24.1	23.0	22.8	23.7	24.0	24.1	24.1	23.6
1993	24.3	24.7	24.9	24.9	25.0	24.9	24.0	23.8	24.6	25.0	25.2	25.1	24.7
1994	25.0	25.2	25.3	25.2	25.2	25.0	24.4	24.4	25.2	25.6	25.8	25.7	25.2
1995	25.6	26.1	26.3	26.1	26.3	26.4	25.8	25.7	26.8	27.0	27.0	26.9	26.3
1996	26.9	28.1	28.5	28.0	27.4	27.3	26.8	26.4	26.7	26.9	26.9	26.5	27.2
1997	26.3	26.6	26.7	26.5	26.9	26.7	25.7	26.2	26.5	26.9	27.2	27.1	26.6
1998	27.0	27.1	27.2	27.1	27.4	27.2	26.3	26.4	26.8	26.4	26.4	26.4	26.8
1999	25.8	26.0	25.8	25.7	25.6	25.3	24.5	24.1	25.3	25.7	25.6	25.7	25.4
2000	25.5	25.7	25.9	25.7	26.2	25.6	24.8	25.2	25.7	25.1	25.4	25.1	25.5
2001	25.0	25.3	25.5	25.4	25.5	25.5	24.9	25.0	25.4	25.6	25.7	25.4	25.3
2002	25.7	25.9	25.9	25.9	26.2	26.1	25.0	25.1	25.9	26.1	26.4	26.6	25.9
2003	26.0	26.1	26.3	26.2	26.0	26.1	24.5	24.6	25.2	25.5	25.7	25.3	25.6
Federal government													
1990	1.0	1.0	1.0	1.0	1.2	1.1	1.1	1.0	0.9	0.9	0.9	0.9	1.0
1991	0.9	0.9	0.9	0.9	0.9	0.9	1.0	1.0	0.9	1.0	1.0	1.0	0.9
1992	1.0	1.0	1.0	1.0	1.0	1.0	1.0	1.0	1.0	1.0	1.0	1.0	1.0
1993	1.0	1.0	1.0	1.0	1.0	1.0	1.0	1.0	1.0	1.0	1.0	1.0	1.0
1994	1.0	1.0	1.0	1.0	1.0	1.0	1.0	1.0	1.0	1.0	1.0	1.0	1.0
1995	1.0	1.0	1.0	1.0	1.0	1.0	1.0	1.0	1.0	1.0	1.0	1.0	1.0
1996	1.0	1.0	1.0	1.0	1.0	1.0	1.0	1.0	1.0	0.9	0.9	1.0	1.0
1997	1.0	1.0	1.0	0.9	0.9	0.9	0.9	0.9	0.9	0.9	0.9	0.9	0.9
1998	0.9	0.9	0.9	0.9	0.9	0.9	0.9	0.9	0.9	0.9	0.9	0.9	0.9
1999	0.9	0.9	0.9	0.9	0.9	0.9	0.9	0.9	0.9	1.0	0.9	0.9	0.9
2000	0.9	1.0	1.0	1.0	1.5	1.1	1.0	1.0	0.9	0.9	0.9	0.9	1.0
2001	0.9	0.9	0.9	0.9	0.9	0.9	0.9	0.9	0.9	0.9	0.9	0.9	0.9
2002	0.9	0.9	0.9	0.9	0.9	0.9	0.9	0.9	0.9	0.9	0.9	0.9	0.9
2003	0.9	0.9	0.9	0.9	0.9	0.9	0.9	0.9	0.9	0.9	0.9	0.9	0.9

Employment by Industry: Texas—*Continued*

(Numbers in thousands. Not seasonally adjusted.)

Industry	January	February	March	April	May	June	July	August	September	October	November	December	Annual Average
GALVESTON-TEXAS CITY *—Continued*													
State government													
1990	9.6	9.7	9.6	9.6	9.7	9.9	9.9	9.9	9.6	9.9	9.9	9.9	9.8
1991	9.8	9.9	9.8	9.9	9.9	10.1	10.2	10.3	10.2	10.4	10.4	10.4	10.1
1992	10.3	10.5	10.6	10.8	11.1	11.5	11.2	11.2	11.1	11.2	11.2	11.2	11.0
1993	11.6	11.7	11.7	11.8	11.8	12.2	12.0	12.0	11.9	12.3	12.3	12.2	12.0
1994	12.2	12.3	12.3	12.2	12.2	12.5	12.6	12.7	12.5	12.6	12.7	12.7	12.5
1995	12.8	13.0	13.1	13.0	13.2	13.6	13.7	13.8	13.7	13.8	13.8	13.8	13.4
1996	13.8	15.0	15.2	14.6	14.0	14.1	14.2	13.8	13.8	13.6	13.6	13.2	14.1
1997	12.8	13.0	13.0	13.0	13.2	13.3	13.5	13.4	13.2	13.4	13.6	13.5	13.2
1998	13.5	13.4	13.5	13.3	13.6	13.6	13.5	13.5	13.2	12.9	12.7	12.7	13.3
1999	12.5	12.4	12.1	12.0	11.8	11.8	11.8	11.4	11.5	11.9	11.8	11.9	11.9
2000	11.9	11.8	11.9	11.9	11.9	12.0	11.9	12.0	12.1	11.4	11.6	11.6	11.8
2001	11.5	11.6	11.7	11.6	11.6	11.7	11.7	11.7	11.6	11.8	11.8	11.8	11.6
2002	11.8	11.8	11.8	11.8	11.8	11.8	11.8	11.9	11.9	11.9	12.1	12.2	11.9
2003	12.3	12.2	12.3	12.1	11.9	11.8	11.4	11.5	11.3	11.3	11.3	11.2	11.7
Local government													
1990	11.2	11.5	11.6	11.5	11.5	11.5	11.1	10.8	11.7	11.7	11.7	11.7	11.5
1991	11.6	11.9	11.8	11.6	11.7	11.4	10.9	10.8	11.2	11.7	11.8	11.9	11.5
1992	11.5	11.7	11.7	11.8	11.9	11.6	10.8	10.6	11.6	11.8	11.9	11.9	11.6
1993	11.7	12.0	12.2	12.1	12.2	11.7	11.0	10.8	11.7	11.7	11.9	11.9	11.7
1994	11.8	11.9	12.0	12.0	12.0	11.5	10.8	10.7	11.7	12.0	12.1	12.0	11.7
1995	11.8	12.1	12.2	12.1	12.1	11.8	11.1	10.9	12.1	12.2	12.2	12.1	11.9
1996	12.1	12.1	12.3	12.4	12.4	12.2	11.6	11.6	11.9	12.4	12.4	12.3	12.1
1997	12.5	12.6	12.7	12.6	12.8	12.5	11.3	11.9	12.4	12.6	12.7	12.7	12.4
1998	12.6	12.8	12.8	12.9	12.9	12.7	11.9	12.0	12.7	12.6	12.8	12.8	12.6
1999	12.4	12.7	12.8	12.8	12.9	12.6	11.8	11.8	12.9	12.8	12.9	12.9	12.6
2000	12.7	12.9	13.0	12.8	12.8	12.5	11.9	12.2	12.7	12.8	12.9	12.6	12.7
2001	12.6	12.8	12.9	12.9	13.0	12.9	12.3	12.4	12.9	12.9	13.0	12.7	12.7
2002	13.0	13.2	13.2	13.2	13.5	13.4	12.3	12.3	13.1	13.3	13.4	13.5	13.1
2003	12.8	13.0	13.1	13.2	13.2	13.4	12.2	12.2	13.0	13.3	13.5	13.2	13.0
HOUSTON													
Total nonfarm													
1990	1545.8	1560.7	1575.2	1588.1	1610.1	1626.7	1621.4	1627.5	1632.8	1637.7	1646.1	1661.5	1611.1
1991	1605.8	1617.4	1630.1	1633.7	1643.8	1655.4	1632.9	1632.5	1639.7	1640.8	1647.1	1651.0	1635.9
1992	1611.7	1619.9	1626.3	1634.1	1642.0	1643.6	1633.1	1632.0	1633.4	1650.3	1656.6	1664.9	1637.3
1993	1626.5	1634.2	1643.2	1653.7	1660.5	1669.1	1666.0	1670.2	1675.7	1682.8	1690.0	1704.5	1664.7
1994	1662.5	1672.2	1682.8	1699.6	1705.5	1713.1	1706.9	1715.4	1720.3	1735.7	1749.7	1759.4	1710.3
1995	1722.1	1736.4	1747.7	1750.6	1761.3	1773.8	1763.5	1772.0	1778.9	1785.9	1795.1	1808.5	1766.3
1996	1765.2	1779.7	1787.2	1796.7	1809.2	1814.0	1808.0	1816.2	1821.7	1845.9	1858.6	1861.4	1813.7
1997	1829.6	1848.5	1861.8	1866.9	1884.6	1894.8	1884.9	1901.9	1918.2	1931.4	1946.8	1962.2	1894.3
1998	1928.0	1946.4	1961.8	1970.1	1983.9	1995.7	1992.7	2006.7	2018.3	2023.1	2032.5	2049.3	1992.4
1999	1995.7	2010.1	2023.1	2012.5	2018.7	2028.5	2019.1	2028.6	2041.3	2046.0	2055.1	2068.9	2029.0
2000	2026.2	2044.9	2060.6	2063.8	2078.8	2087.4	2073.4	2084.2	2102.6	2103.5	2112.0	2127.4	2080.4
2001	2084.1	2103.8	2114.9	2118.0	2126.5	2128.1	2111.3	2124.3	2129.4	2124.2	2129.6	2130.3	2118.7
2002	2089.1	2102.6	2111.5	2109.3	2120.2	2120.0	2101.8	2111.4	2117.6	2115.1	2119.7	2125.4	2112.0
2003	2087.2	2094.0	2100.6	2094.5	2101.0	2101.4	2076.7	2086.5	2095.6	2097.0	2106.1	2109.0	2095.8
Total private													
1990	1341.8	1351.6	1365.6	1377.3	1395.6	1418.3	1418.7	1427.2	1426.1	1425.3	1431.8	1446.3	1402.1
1991	1391.5	1400.8	1412.3	1414.8	1425.1	1439.6	1427.9	1428.0	1421.9	1419.0	1423.5	1427.1	1419.3
1992	1392.0	1395.8	1402.5	1408.0	1416.5	1422.1	1419.5	1417.7	1409.5	1419.3	1424.8	1435.8	1413.6
1993	1399.5	1401.9	1411.7	1419.7	1427.3	1441.4	1446.2	1451.0	1447.0	1449.2	1455.1	1470.1	1435.0
1994	1429.9	1433.8	1443.5	1459.3	1464.8	1478.8	1480.2	1487.2	1486.6	1492.3	1504.6	1517.1	1473.2
1995	1481.7	1491.1	1503.9	1504.5	1515.0	1534.0	1529.6	1537.3	1537.4	1536.7	1543.7	1559.9	1522.9
1996	1521.7	1531.3	1540.7	1546.8	1559.8	1574.2	1575.0	1581.6	1578.3	1592.1	1604.1	1610.4	1568.0
1997	1581.5	1594.8	1607.0	1612.3	1630.4	1649.0	1649.6	1662.0	1664.3	1672.5	1686.5	1705.2	1642.9
1998	1674.3	1686.9	1702.0	1711.1	1725.1	1744.4	1752.1	1761.8	1760.1	1760.6	1768.0	1785.4	1736.0
1999	1735.0	1745.3	1757.3	1746.7	1753.6	1769.6	1772.7	1778.2	1776.8	1777.6	1786.3	1800.8	1766.7
2000	1762.7	1775.7	1791.1	1792.9	1802.7	1825.0	1821.8	1832.7	1831.9	1831.9	1841.0	1856.3	1813.8
2001	1818.7	1833.3	1843.3	1844.4	1853.0	1864.5	1855.0	1862.3	1850.8	1844.2	1847.8	1848.9	1847.1
2002	1811.7	1818.8	1826.7	1824.2	1834.6	1842.5	1833.4	1840.6	1831.4	1821.7	1826.6	1832.9	1828.8
2003	1799.0	1800.2	1806.5	1800.6	1807.0	1814.5	1801.1	1807.3	1802.1	1797.2	1804.7	1808.6	1804.1
Goods-producing													
1990	333.1	339.4	344.4	346.2	353.3	358.3	357.5	360.2	360.1	360.1	361.1	362.2	353.0
1991	349.3	354.0	358.1	356.0	356.2	360.3	356.7	354.9	353.5	354.3	352.8	351.1	354.8
1992	340.1	342.7	344.3	347.2	348.4	349.7	347.2	344.3	342.1	346.1	344.2	343.0	344.9
1993	333.3	333.1	335.0	338.3	339.2	343.8	344.0	344.0	343.1	346.4	344.9	350.0	341.3
1994	341.7	343.5	347.1	350.2	350.8	353.9	354.9	356.9	358.9	360.2	362.0	363.4	353.6
1995	357.1	360.1	364.3	361.6	365.1	369.1	369.9	371.0	372.4	372.9	372.7	376.4	367.7
1996	372.1	376.1	380.0	378.5	382.1	387.0	387.5	388.8	389.2	392.1	391.8	389.6	384.6
1997	385.3	392.2	395.0	393.2	396.8	400.5	400.4	404.0	405.1	408.6	410.3	412.4	400.3
1998	409.4	413.6	416.2	418.6	421.7	426.0	427.5	428.7	428.6	429.4	426.8	429.6	423.0
1999	418.1	420.7	419.8	415.4	413.9	415.3	412.9	413.3	413.2	414.9	414.9	415.7	415.7
2000	411.3	416.9	421.1	420.0	422.7	427.3	425.9	428.4	429.4	428.2	428.8	431.0	424.3
2001	428.0	434.9	437.4	439.3	440.2	440.2	437.2	439.4	437.6	435.7	434.7	430.6	436.2
2002	424.1	426.8	427.9	425.6	426.6	427.3	424.9	425.9	423.8	422.5	419.4	417.5	424.4
2003	413.5	413.8	413.1	410.8	412.5	413.8	408.5	409.0	408.8	408.2	407.2	407.4	410.6

Employment by Industry: Texas—*Continued*

(Numbers in thousands. Not seasonally adjusted.)

Industry	January	February	March	April	May	June	July	August	September	October	November	December	Annual Average
HOUSTON—*Continued*													
Natural resources and mining													
1990	56.6	57.0	57.4	58.5	59.0	60.4	60.4	60.6	60.3	61.2	61.8	62.9	59.7
1991	59.9	60.0	60.3	60.4	60.5	61.5	62.4	62.0	61.3	61.0	60.6	60.6	60.9
1992	61.4	60.5	60.1	60.2	59.9	60.1	59.3	58.5	58.1	57.8	57.5	58.3	59.3
1993	58.1	57.1	57.3	57.5	57.6	58.4	58.8	58.5	58.4	58.9	58.4	59.5	58.2
1994	59.7	59.3	59.4	60.7	60.3	60.9	60.1	60.1	60.3	60.0	60.3	60.4	60.1
1995	58.3	57.9	58.0	57.8	58.0	58.5	58.6	58.4	58.3	57.8	57.5	58.1	58.1
1996	57.6	57.7	58.2	57.6	57.8	58.4	58.9	58.9	58.7	59.1	59.5	60.0	58.5
1997	59.3	59.7	59.7	60.4	61.0	61.7	62.2	62.9	62.6	63.1	63.6	64.6	61.7
1998	64.0	64.2	64.3	64.2	64.5	65.3	65.4	65.2	64.9	64.2	63.7	64.7	64.6
1999	61.3	61.0	60.6	61.1	60.0	60.0	59.2	59.0	58.7	58.8	58.7	59.5	59.8
2000	58.2	58.2	58.7	59.3	59.6	60.1	61.0	61.3	61.4	62.1	62.1	64.1	60.5
2001	61.5	62.5	63.0	62.9	63.2	64.0	64.5	65.0	64.4	64.7	64.8	64.5	63.7
2002	61.6	61.3	60.9	60.4	60.7	61.3	61.6	61.7	61.5	61.7	62.0	62.2	61.4
2003	62.2	62.2	62.4	62.6	62.9	63.4	64.3	64.4	63.9	63.9	63.9	64.2	63.4
Construction													
1990	108.9	112.5	115.5	115.8	121.1	121.9	119.3	120.9	121.1	120.4	119.9	118.6	118.0
1991	110.7	114.2	117.0	115.0	114.3	115.7	113.0	112.5	113.4	115.3	114.6	113.2	114.1
1992	104.0	108.1	110.0	110.9	112.3	112.3	111.7	110.5	109.4	113.1	112.1	109.9	110.4
1993	102.5	103.0	104.4	106.4	107.1	109.2	108.5	109.1	108.4	110.5	109.4	112.5	107.6
1994	106.2	108.1	110.5	110.4	110.4	110.3	111.7	113.2	115.0	116.9	117.4	117.2	112.3
1995	113.7	116.1	118.6	115.5	118.1	119.3	120.1	120.7	122.4	123.9	123.1	124.5	119.7
1996	120.3	122.9	125.2	124.3	126.7	129.0	129.0	129.2	129.9	131.5	130.1	126.5	127.1
1997	124.5	128.9	130.8	127.2	128.6	129.9	129.1	131.0	131.6	132.8	132.6	131.9	129.9
1998	130.2	133.2	135.1	137.9	139.7	141.2	142.9	144.2	144.5	147.3	145.4	146.2	140.7
1999	142.9	146.3	148.2	147.6	148.2	148.6	148.4	149.0	149.6	151.7	151.3	150.8	148.6
2000	149.4	153.4	156.1	153.9	155.6	158.2	156.0	157.3	158.2	156.5	156.0	155.4	155.5
2001	156.3	160.6	162.2	164.4	164.7	163.1	161.2	163.2	163.0	162.9	163.4	160.8	162.1
2002	159.8	162.9	165.0	164.5	165.7	165.3	163.9	164.9	164.4	164.7	162.4	160.3	163.7
2003	159.2	160.5	160.4	158.8	160.3	159.8	156.0	156.8	157.5	157.5	156.7	156.0	158.3
Manufacturing													
1990	167.6	169.9	171.5	171.9	173.2	176.0	177.8	178.7	178.7	178.5	179.4	180.7	175.3
1991	178.7	179.8	180.8	180.6	181.4	183.1	181.3	180.4	178.8	178.0	177.6	177.3	179.8
1992	174.7	174.1	174.2	176.1	176.2	177.3	176.2	175.3	174.6	175.2	174.6	174.8	175.3
1993	172.7	173.0	173.3	174.4	174.5	176.2	176.7	176.4	176.3	177.0	177.1	178.0	175.5
1994	175.8	176.1	177.2	179.1	180.1	182.7	183.1	183.6	183.6	183.3	184.3	185.8	181.2
1995	185.1	186.1	187.7	188.3	189.0	191.3	191.2	191.9	191.7	191.2	192.1	193.8	190.0
1996	194.2	195.5	196.6	196.6	197.6	199.6	199.6	200.7	200.6	201.5	202.2	203.1	199.0
1997	201.5	203.6	204.5	205.6	207.2	208.9	209.1	210.1	210.9	212.7	214.1	215.9	208.7
1998	215.2	216.2	216.8	216.5	217.5	219.5	219.2	219.3	219.2	217.9	217.7	218.7	217.8
1999	213.9	213.4	211.0	206.7	205.7	206.7	205.3	205.3	204.9	204.4	204.9	205.4	207.3
2000	203.7	205.3	206.3	206.8	207.5	209.0	208.9	209.8	209.8	209.6	210.7	211.5	208.2
2001	210.2	211.8	212.2	212.0	212.3	213.1	211.5	211.2	210.2	208.1	206.5	205.3	210.3
2002	202.7	202.6	202.0	200.7	200.2	200.7	199.4	199.3	197.9	196.1	195.0	195.0	199.3
2003	192.1	191.1	190.3	189.4	189.3	190.6	188.2	187.8	187.4	186.8	186.6	187.2	188.9
Service-providing													
1990	1212.7	1221.3	1230.8	1241.9	1256.8	1268.4	1263.9	1267.3	1272.7	1277.6	1285.0	1299.3	1258.1
1991	1256.5	1263.4	1272.0	1277.7	1287.6	1295.1	1276.2	1277.6	1286.2	1286.5	1294.3	1299.9	1281.1
1992	1271.6	1277.2	1282.0	1286.9	1293.6	1293.9	1285.9	1287.7	1291.3	1304.2	1312.4	1321.9	1292.4
1993	1293.2	1301.1	1308.2	1315.4	1321.3	1325.3	1322.0	1326.2	1332.6	1336.4	1345.1	1354.5	1323.4
1994	1320.8	1328.7	1335.7	1349.4	1354.7	1359.2	1352.0	1358.5	1361.4	1375.5	1387.7	1396.0	1356.6
1995	1365.0	1376.3	1383.4	1389.0	1396.2	1404.7	1393.6	1401.0	1406.5	1413.0	1422.4	1432.1	1398.6
1996	1393.1	1403.6	1407.2	1418.2	1427.1	1427.0	1420.5	1427.4	1432.5	1453.8	1466.8	1471.8	1429.1
1997	1444.3	1456.3	1466.8	1473.7	1487.8	1494.3	1484.5	1497.9	1513.1	1522.8	1536.5	1549.8	1494.0
1998	1518.6	1532.8	1545.6	1551.5	1562.2	1569.7	1565.2	1578.0	1589.7	1593.7	1605.7	1619.7	1569.4
1999	1577.6	1589.4	1603.3	1597.1	1604.8	1613.2	1606.2	1615.3	1628.1	1631.1	1640.2	1653.2	1613.3
2000	1614.9	1628.0	1639.5	1643.8	1656.1	1660.1	1647.5	1655.8	1673.2	1675.3	1683.2	1696.4	1656.2
2001	1656.1	1668.9	1677.5	1678.7	1686.3	1687.9	1674.1	1684.9	1691.8	1688.5	1694.9	1699.7	1682.4
2002	1665.0	1675.8	1683.6	1683.7	1693.6	1692.7	1676.9	1685.5	1693.8	1692.6	1700.3	1707.9	1687.6
2003	1673.7	1680.2	1687.5	1683.7	1688.5	1687.6	1668.2	1677.5	1686.8	1688.8	1698.9	1701.6	1685.3
Trade, transportation, and utilities													
1990	367.9	367.3	369.7	369.5	372.0	375.9	376.2	377.8	379.7	379.8	384.7	392.2	376.1
1991	374.0	369.9	371.8	370.7	374.2	377.9	375.5	376.5	374.4	372.7	376.2	382.3	374.7
1992	370.2	366.0	367.4	367.3	368.7	370.8	367.9	368.8	367.9	370.7	377.6	385.4	370.7
1993	372.7	369.2	370.4	368.0	372.1	375.8	377.2	378.1	376.1	380.1	387.7	396.4	377.0
1994	379.2	376.6	376.9	380.1	380.3	384.0	381.5	383.9	386.3	391.5	398.8	407.7	385.6
1995	394.5	391.9	394.1	393.2	394.3	399.9	397.4	399.6	400.5	400.5	406.6	415.3	399.0
1996	399.1	396.9	397.9	400.3	402.6	404.9	404.6	406.4	404.4	409.0	416.6	422.3	405.4
1997	407.5	405.7	406.2	407.5	410.2	414.7	415.5	418.3	419.9	423.5	432.1	440.1	416.8
1998	425.6	423.2	425.0	427.7	431.4	434.5	437.1	440.4	440.0	442.3	450.6	461.6	436.6
1999	442.0	441.3	441.1	439.4	441.2	446.0	447.6	450.1	449.0	451.7	457.8	467.9	447.9
2000	450.0	448.7	450.4	449.5	451.0	455.0	454.0	457.8	455.1	458.5	466.1	475.8	456.0
2001	457.9	456.3	456.8	455.7	458.0	460.9	460.9	462.9	459.8	461.8	466.0	470.0	460.5
2002	454.7	452.4	453.3	451.2	452.6	453.6	451.9	453.1	450.7	450.0	456.2	463.4	453.6
2003	445.0	439.7	439.6	436.6	435.5	438.6	438.5	440.8	439.2	440.2	446.6	450.2	440.9

Employment by Industry: Texas—*Continued*

(Numbers in thousands. Not seasonally adjusted.)

Industry	January	February	March	April	May	June	July	August	September	October	November	December	Annual Average
HOUSTON—*Continued*													
Wholesale trade													
1990	95.9	97.0	98.1	98.0	98.4	98.3	98.2	98.5	98.6	98.8	98.7	98.9	98.1
1991	95.9	96.1	96.8	96.9	97.5	98.5	98.5	98.6	97.9	97.8	97.7	97.7	97.5
1992	96.8	96.6	96.9	96.6	96.9	97.7	96.1	96.3	95.8	96.6	96.8	97.5	96.7
1993	95.6	95.9	96.5	96.6	96.5	97.0	96.4	96.1	96.3	96.7	96.7	97.2	96.5
1994	95.2	95.2	96.4	97.2	96.8	97.6	97.8	97.8	98.0	98.4	98.9	99.5	97.4
1995	98.1	98.9	99.7	99.1	99.6	100.5	100.6	100.8	100.9	101.4	101.6	102.3	100.3
1996	100.6	101.3	101.8	102.4	102.9	104.0	104.0	104.2	103.9	104.4	105.0	105.4	103.3
1997	103.9	105.2	105.9	105.8	106.6	107.9	108.7	109.5	109.7	109.7	110.1	110.8	107.8
1998	110.4	111.2	111.8	112.4	113.1	113.8	113.7	114.1	114.4	114.3	114.8	115.8	113.3
1999	113.6	114.2	113.7	112.5	112.7	113.1	113.7	113.8	113.8	113.6	113.4	114.0	113.5
2000	112.3	112.6	113.3	113.6	113.7	114.4	114.4	114.4	114.5	113.4	113.6	114.2	113.7
2001	113.6	114.4	115.2	114.4	114.7	115.4	115.8	116.1	115.7	115.3	115.0	115.0	115.0
2002	113.5	113.8	114.3	113.6	113.9	114.1	113.9	114.1	114.1	113.9	114.3	114.2	114.0
2003	112.9	112.8	113.0	112.3	112.7	113.4	113.2	113.5	113.5	113.3	113.0	113.1	113.1
Retail trade													
1990	184.7	182.3	183.0	183.1	184.2	187.1	187.3	188.8	189.4	190.5	195.1	200.6	188.0
1991	186.3	181.1	181.5	181.0	182.7	184.2	183.2	184.2	183.3	182.6	187.1	192.1	184.1
1992	183.5	179.8	180.1	181.9	182.3	183.3	184.1	184.3	183.8	186.9	192.1	198.2	185.0
1993	188.5	184.9	184.9	182.3	185.7	187.9	190.0	191.3	189.3	191.9	197.8	205.7	190.0
1994	192.9	189.5	188.3	189.9	190.6	192.8	189.6	191.7	194.2	198.0	204.3	211.0	194.4
1995	199.5	196.3	196.7	197.1	198.0	201.0	199.5	201.8	202.5	203.3	208.9	214.9	201.6
1996	203.3	200.0	200.5	200.8	202.1	203.2	201.1	202.1	201.9	203.7	210.4	215.9	203.8
1997	203.1	199.8	200.1	200.1	201.5	203.6	203.3	206.2	205.5	208.1	216.1	223.1	205.9
1998	210.8	207.2	208.9	208.0	209.5	211.6	211.8	214.2	213.8	213.8	222.4	229.6	213.5
1999	216.3	214.2	215.5	216.0	217.9	221.0	221.5	223.6	223.4	225.9	231.6	238.9	222.2
2000	226.3	223.1	224.4	222.6	223.7	225.7	224.6	227.4	224.8	228.3	235.3	241.9	227.3
2001	227.5	225.2	225.6	225.3	226.2	227.9	227.3	228.7	226.3	227.6	233.9	239.6	228.4
2002	227.3	225.1	226.8	225.7	226.6	226.7	224.4	225.1	223.8	223.3	229.4	235.4	226.6
2003	221.1	217.8	218.2	216.3	216.6	218.4	217.9	219.8	219.3	220.5	226.6	230.6	220.3
Transportation and utilities													
1990	87.3	88.0	88.6	88.4	89.4	90.5	90.7	90.5	91.7	90.5	90.9	92.7	89.9
1991	91.8	92.7	93.5	92.8	94.0	95.2	93.8	93.7	93.2	92.3	91.4	92.5	93.1
1992	89.9	89.6	90.4	88.8	89.5	89.8	87.7	88.2	88.3	87.2	88.7	89.7	89.0
1993	88.6	88.4	89.0	89.1	89.9	90.9	90.8	90.7	90.5	91.5	93.2	93.5	90.5
1994	91.1	91.9	92.2	93.0	92.9	93.6	94.1	94.4	94.1	95.1	95.6	97.2	93.8
1995	96.9	96.7	97.7	97.0	96.7	98.4	97.3	97.0	97.1	95.8	96.1	98.1	97.1
1996	95.2	95.6	95.6	97.1	97.6	97.7	99.5	100.1	98.6	100.9	101.2	101.0	98.3
1997	100.5	100.7	100.2	101.6	102.1	103.2	103.5	102.6	104.7	105.7	105.9	106.2	103.1
1998	104.4	104.8	104.3	107.3	108.8	109.1	111.6	112.1	111.8	114.2	113.4	116.2	109.8
1999	112.1	112.9	111.9	110.9	110.6	111.9	112.4	112.7	111.8	112.2	112.8	115.0	112.3
2000	111.4	113.0	112.7	113.3	113.6	114.9	115.0	116.0	115.8	116.8	117.2	119.7	115.0
2001	116.8	116.7	116.0	116.0	117.1	117.6	117.8	118.1	117.8	118.9	117.1	115.4	117.1
2002	113.9	113.5	112.2	111.9	112.1	112.8	113.6	113.9	112.8	112.8	112.5	113.8	113.0
2003	111.0	109.1	108.4	108.0	106.2	106.8	107.4	107.5	106.4	106.4	107.0	106.5	107.6
Information													
1990	33.3	33.8	33.8	33.6	33.9	34.4	34.4	34.4	34.0	33.7	33.9	34.3	34.0
1991	32.5	32.4	32.6	32.3	32.1	32.3	32.7	32.6	32.1	32.5	32.5	33.0	32.5
1992	32.1	32.0	32.0	32.5	32.8	32.8	32.4	32.1	31.8	31.9	31.9	32.2	32.2
1993	31.3	31.2	31.3	31.4	31.2	31.6	31.6	31.5	31.6	31.4	31.3	31.4	31.4
1994	31.4	31.6	31.3	31.3	31.2	31.5	32.9	33.0	32.9	33.3	33.5	33.7	32.3
1995	32.7	33.1	33.2	32.6	31.8	32.1	32.5	32.8	32.9	33.6	34.0	34.7	33.0
1996	33.7	33.9	33.4	33.9	34.0	34.2	34.5	34.7	34.4	34.6	35.3	36.3	34.4
1997	35.8	36.1	36.2	37.2	37.9	38.6	38.7	38.8	38.8	38.7	39.4	40.0	38.0
1998	38.8	39.1	39.7	39.2	39.9	40.5	40.6	40.8	40.9	41.0	41.7	42.0	40.4
1999	41.1	41.4	41.8	41.7	42.1	42.5	42.7	42.9	42.8	43.4	43.7	44.1	42.5
2000	44.0	44.3	44.5	45.0	45.4	45.8	46.0	46.3	46.4	46.5	46.8	47.0	45.7
2001	46.3	46.6	46.6	46.5	46.0	45.9	44.3	44.1	43.2	42.8	42.7	42.3	44.7
2002	41.2	40.8	40.6	39.7	39.7	39.9	39.4	39.1	38.7	38.5	38.2	38.1	39.5
2003	37.8	37.7	37.7	37.5	37.5	37.5	37.6	37.3	36.9	36.9	36.9	36.7	37.3
Financial activities													
1990	103.4	104.6	105.0	106.4	106.9	108.7	107.1	107.1	107.1	106.1	106.3	108.1	106.4
1991	104.4	105.0	105.0	104.7	104.9	105.8	104.7	104.8	103.9	104.0	103.5	104.3	104.6
1992	103.1	103.7	104.0	104.2	105.1	104.9	104.6	105.0	104.1	104.4	104.3	104.9	104.4
1993	103.5	103.9	104.2	104.3	104.1	105.6	106.0	105.6	105.3	106.0	105.5	105.9	105.0
1994	104.3	104.4	104.8	106.1	105.8	106.5	107.1	106.9	106.2	106.2	106.4	107.0	106.0
1995	102.5	101.7	101.8	102.9	103.2	104.0	103.9	103.8	103.5	102.8	103.1	103.6	103.1
1996	102.7	103.0	103.4	102.8	103.1	104.0	104.5	104.9	104.5	104.9	105.5	105.4	104.1
1997	105.0	105.4	105.7	106.8	107.5	108.5	109.1	109.7	109.5	111.4	111.5	113.2	108.6
1998	111.0	111.8	112.5	113.6	114.3	115.5	117.0	117.6	117.7	119.1	118.5	119.8	115.7
1999	118.5	119.4	120.5	120.3	120.9	121.1	122.2	122.2	121.9	122.3	122.4	122.7	121.2
2000	121.8	122.0	122.2	122.7	122.9	124.0	125.3	125.4	125.4	125.4	125.8	126.3	124.1
2001	125.0	125.5	125.9	125.8	126.0	126.4	126.1	125.9	125.2	124.2	123.7	123.9	125.3
2002	123.1	123.3	123.3	123.1	123.5	124.1	123.9	123.8	123.0	123.4	123.4	123.5	123.5
2003	122.4	122.7	123.4	123.8	124.5	125.0	124.9	125.6	124.8	125.3	125.5	125.6	124.5

Employment by Industry: Texas—*Continued*

(Numbers in thousands. Not seasonally adjusted.)

Industry	January	February	March	April	May	June	July	August	September	October	November	December	Annual Average
HOUSTON—*Continued*													
Professsional and business services													
1990	184.6	189.1	192.0	197.2	200.5	205.4	205.0	206.6	206.2	207.8	208.5	210.9	201.2
1991	207.5	208.8	211.5	214.6	217.0	219.3	216.6	217.7	216.0	213.5	215.1	213.4	214.3
1992	209.4	210.3	211.5	209.8	210.7	211.6	214.1	213.8	211.4	213.0	212.4	214.7	211.9
1993	209.6	210.3	213.7	216.8	217.2	218.8	222.3	223.7	222.9	221.6	221.5	221.3	218.3
1994	218.1	218.8	220.4	222.3	222.2	226.1	226.7	227.5	225.1	225.9	226.6	227.5	223.9
1995	224.7	229.1	232.6	234.1	235.4	238.9	237.6	240.5	240.9	242.0	242.4	243.8	236.8
1996	234.5	238.0	240.4	241.1	242.7	244.8	246.6	248.7	248.9	252.8	254.2	255.8	245.7
1997	251.1	254.9	257.9	260.3	263.9	269.0	268.5	271.1	272.2	272.9	275.2	278.9	266.3
1998	275.1	280.3	284.6	284.4	285.5	291.3	294.0	296.5	295.9	297.9	299.8	299.5	290.4
1999	291.1	292.6	295.5	291.0	291.0	295.5	297.3	297.7	298.0	295.5	296.9	300.2	295.2
2000	292.0	295.3	298.8	299.8	301.3	308.5	309.4	312.7	313.9	313.2	312.9	314.6	306.0
2001	306.8	309.6	311.1	310.8	310.5	313.7	311.7	311.5	308.8	306.2	306.5	305.9	309.4
2002	298.6	299.5	301.7	301.8	302.8	303.7	302.1	304.4	301.9	299.3	299.0	298.5	301.1
2003	293.9	295.2	296.2	296.1	294.6	294.5	291.7	292.7	292.2	289.9	289.8	289.1	293.0
Educational and health services													
1990	153.3	145.9	147.5	147.6	148.0	148.8	149.0	150.2	152.9	152.2	153.2	153.5	150.2
1991	149.5	151.9	152.5	153.3	154.2	153.9	153.4	154.7	156.1	157.2	158.3	158.1	154.4
1992	155.9	157.1	157.5	158.9	159.7	159.5	160.0	161.1	162.6	163.1	164.3	165.5	160.4
1993	163.5	164.7	166.1	166.8	166.1	165.9	166.6	168.0	169.5	167.9	168.3	168.8	166.9
1994	165.6	166.9	167.5	169.3	170.0	169.5	170.8	172.7	174.2	171.7	172.3	173.3	170.3
1995	170.7	172.2	173.3	174.3	174.9	175.1	173.8	175.8	176.7	175.8	176.6	177.3	174.7
1996	174.5	175.8	176.2	176.1	177.9	178.1	177.8	179.9	181.3	183.8	185.1	185.6	179.3
1997	183.0	182.1	186.3	187.5	188.7	188.5	188.1	190.5	192.5	193.2	193.4	194.8	189.1
1998	191.5	193.7	195.3	195.3	196.3	195.8	195.3	197.7	199.6	196.9	196.8	198.0	196.0
1999	194.2	195.1	199.6	200.4	201.3	201.7	201.9	203.3	205.6	206.3	207.1	206.9	202.0
2000	204.8	206.3	208.1	208.7	209.1	208.5	208.3	209.0	210.8	210.2	210.9	211.8	208.9
2001	209.5	211.6	213.0	213.3	215.3	215.2	215.2	218.4	220.6	221.5	222.7	223.6	216.6
2002	222.3	224.5	225.5	225.9	226.7	227.0	226.7	229.1	230.1	228.7	230.1	230.3	227.2
2003	229.2	230.8	232.2	232.0	233.4	232.6	231.6	233.2	235.5	236.3	238.0	238.3	233.6
Leisure and hospitality													
1990	112.3	116.7	117.9	121.1	124.5	128.3	130.3	131.2	127.4	126.6	125.2	125.8	123.9
1991	116.6	120.5	122.1	124.5	127.2	129.5	127.9	126.7	126.5	125.4	125.9	125.9	124.9
1992	120.1	122.2	124.1	125.8	128.8	129.8	130.2	129.6	127.0	127.0	127.5	127.2	126.6
1993	122.9	126.1	127.3	129.5	132.7	134.5	132.6	134.4	132.9	130.6	130.8	131.0	130.4
1994	124.6	126.5	129.8	132.8	137.1	139.1	137.5	137.6	135.2	134.7	135.9	135.6	133.9
1995	131.6	134.8	135.6	136.9	141.1	144.7	143.9	143.3	140.2	139.0	138.5	138.7	139.0
1996	134.9	136.9	138.5	142.6	145.6	147.9	146.8	145.4	142.9	141.5	142.1	141.9	142.3
1997	140.4	143.7	145.2	144.8	149.5	152.4	152.2	152.7	149.9	147.5	147.8	148.6	147.9
1998	146.3	148.0	150.9	153.9	156.7	161.2	160.7	160.4	158.2	154.3	154.1	154.5	154.9
1999	150.7	154.5	158.5	157.9	162.0	165.6	165.3	165.4	163.9	160.9	160.9	160.6	160.5
2000	157.2	159.9	163.3	164.6	167.4	171.7	168.5	169.0	166.7	165.5	165.0	164.8	165.3
2001	161.1	164.2	167.2	167.9	171.4	175.9	174.4	175.0	171.0	167.6	167.1	168.0	169.2
2002	163.8	166.9	169.2	172.1	176.9	180.1	178.1	178.9	177.2	173.7	174.4	175.4	173.9
2003	171.0	173.9	177.1	177.6	182.2	184.8	181.1	182.1	178.6	175.0	175.6	176.6	178.0
Other services													
1990	53.9	54.8	55.3	55.7	56.5	58.5	59.2	59.7	58.7	59.0	58.9	59.3	57.5
1991	57.7	58.3	58.7	58.7	59.3	60.6	60.4	60.1	59.4	59.4	59.2	59.0	59.2
1992	61.1	61.8	61.7	62.3	62.3	63.0	63.1	63.0	62.6	63.1	62.6	62.9	62.5
1993	62.7	63.4	63.7	64.6	64.7	65.4	65.9	65.7	65.6	65.2	65.1	65.3	64.8
1994	65.0	65.5	65.7	67.2	67.4	68.2	68.8	68.7	67.8	68.8	69.1	68.9	67.6
1995	67.9	68.2	69.0	68.9	69.2	70.2	70.6	70.5	70.3	70.1	69.8	70.1	69.6
1996	70.2	70.7	70.9	71.5	71.8	73.3	72.7	72.8	72.7	73.4	73.5	73.5	72.3
1997	73.4	74.7	74.5	75.0	75.9	76.8	77.1	76.9	76.4	76.7	76.8	77.2	76.0
1998	76.6	77.2	77.8	78.4	79.3	79.6	79.9	79.7	79.2	79.7	79.7	80.4	79.0
1999	79.3	80.3	80.5	80.6	81.2	81.9	82.8	83.3	82.4	82.6	82.6	82.7	81.7
2000	81.6	82.3	82.7	82.6	82.9	84.2	84.4	84.1	84.2	84.4	84.7	85.0	83.6
2001	84.1	84.6	85.3	85.1	85.6	86.3	85.2	85.1	84.6	84.4	84.4	84.6	84.9
2002	83.9	84.6	85.2	84.8	85.8	86.8	86.4	86.3	86.0	85.6	85.9	86.2	85.6
2003	86.2	86.4	87.2	86.2	86.8	87.7	87.2	86.6	86.1	85.4	85.1	84.7	86.3
Government													
1990	204.0	209.1	209.6	210.8	214.5	208.4	202.7	200.3	206.7	212.4	214.3	215.2	209.0
1991	214.3	216.6	217.8	218.9	218.7	215.8	205.0	204.5	217.8	221.8	223.6	223.9	216.6
1992	219.7	224.1	223.8	226.1	225.5	221.5	213.6	214.3	223.9	231.0	231.8	229.1	223.7
1993	227.0	232.3	231.5	234.0	233.2	227.7	219.8	219.2	228.7	233.6	234.9	234.4	229.7
1994	232.6	238.4	239.3	240.3	240.7	234.3	226.7	228.2	233.7	243.4	245.1	242.3	237.1
1995	240.4	245.3	243.8	246.1	246.3	239.8	233.9	234.7	241.5	249.2	251.4	248.6	243.4
1996	243.5	248.4	246.5	249.9	249.4	239.8	233.0	234.6	243.4	253.8	254.5	251.0	245.7
1997	248.1	253.7	254.8	254.6	254.2	245.8	235.3	239.9	253.9	258.9	260.3	257.0	251.4
1998	253.7	259.5	259.8	259.0	258.8	251.3	240.6	244.9	258.2	262.5	264.5	263.9	256.4
1999	260.7	264.8	265.8	265.8	265.1	258.9	246.4	250.4	264.5	268.4	268.8	268.1	262.3
2000	263.5	269.2	269.5	270.9	276.1	262.4	251.6	251.5	270.7	271.6	271.0	271.1	266.6
2001	265.4	270.5	271.6	273.6	273.5	263.6	256.3	262.0	278.6	280.0	281.8	281.4	271.5
2002	277.4	283.8	284.8	285.1	285.6	277.5	268.4	270.8	286.2	293.4	293.1	292.5	283.2
2003	288.2	293.8	294.1	293.9	294.0	286.9	275.6	279.2	293.5	299.8	301.4	300.4	291.7

Employment by Industry: Texas—*Continued*

(Numbers in thousands. Not seasonally adjusted.)

Industry	January	February	March	April	May	June	July	August	September	October	November	December	Annual Average
HOUSTON—*Continued*													
Federal government													
1990	25.5	25.5	25.7	26.1	28.7	27.8	27.7	26.1	25.8	25.9	26.0	26.5	26.4
1991	26.2	26.2	26.4	26.6	26.8	27.0	26.8	26.5	26.4	26.5	26.5	27.0	26.6
1992	26.6	26.5	26.4	26.4	26.3	26.5	26.5	26.3	26.6	26.2	26.0	26.3	26.4
1993	25.9	25.8	25.8	25.7	25.7	25.9	25.9	25.7	25.7	25.6	25.6	26.2	25.8
1994	25.6	25.6	25.6	25.6	25.6	25.5	25.0	24.8	24.6	24.5	24.6	25.5	25.2
1995	24.8	24.7	24.8	24.7	24.8	24.9	24.9	24.8	24.7	24.5	24.5	25.0	24.8
1996	24.5	24.4	24.8	24.9	24.9	25.1	25.0	25.1	25.2	25.2	25.3	25.9	25.0
1997	25.4	25.5	25.8	25.4	25.4	25.4	25.5	25.5	25.5	25.6	25.5	26.3	25.6
1998	25.8	25.7	25.7	25.4	25.4	25.5	25.6	25.7	26.1	26.2	26.3	26.9	25.9
1999	26.2	26.2	26.1	26.2	26.0	26.0	26.0	26.1	26.1	26.1	26.1	26.8	26.2
2000	26.0	26.1	26.5	27.4	32.7	29.2	28.6	26.3	26.1	25.9	25.8	26.4	27.3
2001	25.9	25.9	25.9	25.8	25.9	25.8	26.4	26.3	26.1	25.9	25.7	25.7	25.9
2002	25.5	25.3	25.5	25.4	25.4	25.7	25.5	25.5	25.5	26.6	26.6	26.6	25.8
2003	26.4	26.3	26.4	26.5	26.4	26.3	26.2	26.1	26.0	26.2	26.0	25.9	26.2
State government													
1990	37.7	38.7	39.0	39.4	39.2	38.2	38.8	38.2	39.0	39.8	40.2	39.9	39.0
1991	39.6	40.5	40.9	41.9	41.0	39.0	39.5	38.7	41.4	42.4	43.0	42.3	40.9
1992	40.3	41.6	41.8	42.7	42.1	40.5	41.3	41.5	41.6	44.2	43.6	43.6	42.1
1993	41.4	42.9	43.0	43.1	42.2	42.0	41.6	41.1	42.1	41.7	41.7	42.3	42.1
1994	43.1	44.0	43.6	44.4	44.0	42.9	43.0	42.6	41.9	44.4	45.2	43.9	43.6
1995	44.3	44.7	44.3	44.5	43.9	43.5	43.4	42.9	43.0	44.1	45.2	45.2	44.1
1996	43.5	43.7	43.5	44.2	43.6	41.3	41.3	41.4	43.0	45.1	44.7	43.5	43.2
1997	42.9	44.0	43.9	44.0	43.9	41.9	41.5	41.0	44.2	44.5	44.7	43.8	43.4
1998	43.6	45.2	45.4	45.2	44.9	43.4	42.3	42.5	44.0	44.1	44.8	44.1	44.1
1999	44.8	45.8	46.0	46.3	46.1	44.8	44.1	43.6	45.3	46.7	46.7	45.5	45.5
2000	45.8	47.0	47.2	47.3	47.3	44.7	44.4	44.2	48.2	48.5	48.3	47.9	46.7
2001	47.0	48.7	48.7	49.2	48.6	45.3	46.1	45.8	49.5	49.2	49.7	49.0	48.0
2002	49.5	50.7	50.8	51.4	51.5	49.0	48.2	48.4	52.1	52.5	52.2	51.8	50.7
2003	51.2	52.9	53.0	53.2	53.1	51.4	50.9	51.1	53.3	53.6	54.1	53.5	52.6
Local government													
1990	140.8	144.9	144.9	145.3	146.6	142.4	136.2	136.0	141.9	146.7	148.1	148.8	143.6
1991	148.5	149.9	150.5	150.4	150.9	149.8	138.7	139.3	150.0	152.9	154.1	154.6	149.1
1992	152.8	156.0	155.6	157.0	157.1	154.5	145.8	146.5	155.7	160.6	162.2	159.2	155.3
1993	159.7	163.6	162.7	165.2	165.3	159.8	152.3	152.4	160.9	166.3	167.6	165.9	161.8
1994	163.9	168.8	170.1	170.3	171.1	165.9	158.7	160.8	167.2	174.5	175.3	172.9	168.3
1995	171.3	175.9	174.7	176.9	177.6	171.4	165.6	167.0	173.8	180.6	181.7	178.4	174.6
1996	175.5	180.3	178.2	180.8	180.9	173.4	166.7	168.1	175.2	183.5	184.5	181.6	177.4
1997	179.8	184.2	185.1	185.2	184.9	178.5	168.3	173.4	184.2	188.8	190.1	186.9	182.5
1998	184.3	188.6	188.7	188.4	188.5	182.4	172.7	176.7	188.1	192.2	193.4	192.9	186.4
1999	189.7	192.8	193.7	193.3	193.0	188.1	176.3	180.7	193.1	195.6	196.0	195.8	190.7
2000	191.7	196.1	195.8	196.2	196.1	188.5	178.6	181.0	196.4	197.2	196.9	196.8	192.6
2001	192.5	195.9	197.0	198.6	199.0	192.5	183.8	189.9	203.0	204.9	206.4	206.7	197.5
2002	202.4	207.8	208.5	208.3	208.7	202.8	194.7	196.9	208.6	214.3	214.3	214.1	206.8
2003	210.6	214.6	214.7	214.2	214.5	209.2	198.5	202.0	214.2	220.0	221.3	221.0	212.9
SAN ANGELO													
Total nonfarm													
1990	36.5	36.1	36.3	36.6	36.2	36.3	36.1	35.8	36.0	36.4	36.9	36.9	36.3
1991	36.2	36.9	37.3	37.6	37.4	37.3	37.3	37.2	37.9	38.4	38.2	38.5	37.5
1992	38.0	38.2	38.6	38.3	38.6	38.5	38.2	38.3	38.7	39.3	38.8	39.2	38.6
1993	38.8	39.0	39.1	39.3	39.1	38.9	38.8	38.7	39.3	39.7	39.5	39.6	39.2
1994	38.5	38.8	39.5	39.7	39.4	39.8	39.8	40.0	40.8	40.7	40.7	40.9	39.9
1995	40.3	40.5	41.0	40.9	40.6	41.0	40.9	41.0	41.3	41.7	41.7	41.6	41.0
1996	41.5	41.8	41.7	41.5	41.8	41.2	41.8	41.8	42.8	42.6	42.8	43.0	42.0
1997	42.8	43.3	43.1	43.4	43.7	43.7	43.0	43.5	43.7	43.8	44.1	44.3	43.5
1998	43.6	43.9	44.1	44.3	44.5	44.0	43.6	43.7	43.6	43.3	43.7	43.7	43.8
1999	42.7	42.9	43.2	43.4	43.2	43.5	42.9	43.6	44.0	43.9	44.2	44.4	43.5
2000	43.7	43.9	43.9	44.1	44.3	43.8	43.8	43.9	43.8	43.8	44.0	44.2	43.9
2001	43.7	44.1	44.3	44.4	44.6	44.7	44.0	44.3	44.9	44.3	44.4	44.4	44.3
2002	43.9	44.1	44.5	44.5	44.7	44.6	43.7	44.0	43.9	43.6	43.8	43.9	44.1
2003	42.9	43.6	43.7	43.6	43.7	44.0	43.3	43.6	43.8	43.8	44.2	44.1	43.7
Total private													
1990	29.1	28.7	28.8	29.0	28.6	28.8	28.9	28.7	28.4	28.7	29.2	29.2	28.8
1991	28.6	29.1	29.7	29.8	29.7	30.1	30.1	30.0	30.3	30.7	30.5	30.8	30.0
1992	30.2	30.3	30.8	30.5	30.8	31.1	30.9	31.1	31.0	31.4	30.9	31.4	30.9
1993	30.9	31.2	31.2	31.4	31.3	31.6	31.4	31.3	31.3	31.7	31.5	31.6	31.4
1994	30.4	30.8	31.4	31.6	31.4	32.2	32.1	32.1	32.4	32.3	32.3	32.6	31.8
1995	31.8	32.0	32.5	32.4	32.2	33.1	32.7	32.9	32.8	33.2	33.2	33.1	32.7
1996	32.9	33.2	33.2	33.0	33.2	33.2	33.7	33.6	34.1	33.8	34.0	34.3	33.5
1997	34.1	34.4	34.3	34.7	34.9	35.0	34.7	35.0	34.8	34.9	35.1	35.4	34.8
1998	34.8	34.8	35.1	35.4	35.5	35.3	35.1	35.1	34.6	34.3	34.7	34.8	35.0
1999	33.9	33.8	34.0	34.4	34.2	35.0	34.5	34.9	34.9	34.8	35.0	35.2	34.6
2000	34.6	34.6	34.6	35.0	35.1	35.3	35.2	35.1	34.6	34.6	34.9	35.1	34.9
2001	34.6	34.9	35.1	35.3	35.4	35.8	35.5	35.8	35.8	35.3	35.4	35.5	35.3
2002	35.0	35.1	35.4	35.4	35.8	35.8	35.3	35.3	35.0	34.6	34.8	35.0	35.2
2003	34.0	34.6	34.7	34.6	34.8	35.3	35.0	35.3	35.0	35.0	35.3	35.3	34.9

Employment by Industry: Texas—*Continued*

(Numbers in thousands. Not seasonally adjusted.)

Industry	January	February	March	April	May	June	July	August	September	October	November	December	Annual Average
SAN ANGELO—*Continued*													
Goods-producing													
1990	6.0	5.9	5.8	6.0	5.8	6.0	5.9	5.8	5.8	6.0	6.1	6.0	5.9
1991	6.0	6.1	6.3	6.2	6.1	6.3	6.4	6.3	6.2	6.2	6.2	6.2	6.2
1992	6.1	6.1	6.1	6.1	6.3	6.4	6.3	6.4	6.5	6.6	6.5	6.5	6.3
1993	6.4	6.3	6.3	6.3	6.4	6.3	6.5	6.5	6.5	6.6	6.6	6.5	6.4
1994	6.4	6.4	6.5	6.5	6.5	6.8	6.7	6.7	6.7	6.8	6.8	6.9	6.6
1995	6.8	6.8	6.9	6.7	6.6	6.9	6.9	6.9	6.8	6.8	6.8	6.8	6.8
1996	6.8	6.8	6.8	6.7	6.8	6.8	7.0	7.1	7.2	7.0	7.1	7.1	6.9
1997	7.3	7.3	7.2	7.3	7.3	7.4	7.4	7.6	7.5	7.4	7.4	7.4	7.4
1998	7.2	7.2	7.3	7.2	7.3	7.2	7.1	7.2	6.9	6.8	6.9	6.9	7.1
1999	6.8	6.8	6.8	6.9	6.8	7.2	7.2	7.2	7.2	7.3	7.1	7.2	7.0
2000	7.3	7.3	7.3	7.2	7.3	7.4	7.3	7.2	7.0	7.2	7.2	7.2	7.2
2001	7.3	7.3	7.4	7.4	7.6	7.5	7.4	7.4	7.3	7.3	7.2	7.2	7.3
2002	7.1	6.9	6.8	6.7	6.8	6.8	6.8	6.8	6.7	6.5	6.4	6.5	6.7
2003	6.4	6.6	6.6	6.5	6.4	6.7	6.6	6.6	6.6	6.5	6.5	6.5	6.5
Natural resources and mining													
1990	0.4	0.4	0.4	0.4	0.3	0.4	0.4	0.4	0.4	0.4	0.4	0.4	0.4
1991	0.5	0.6	0.6	0.6	0.6	0.6	0.6	0.5	0.5	0.5	0.5	0.5	0.6
1992	0.5	0.5	0.5	0.5	0.5	0.5	0.5	0.5	0.6	0.6	0.6	0.6	0.5
1993	0.6	0.5	0.5	0.5	0.5	0.5	0.5	0.5	0.6	0.5	0.6	0.6	0.5
1994	0.5	0.5	0.6	0.5	0.5	0.5	0.5	0.5	0.5	0.5	0.5	0.5	0.5
1995	0.5	0.5	0.5	0.5	0.5	0.5	0.5	0.4	0.4	0.5	0.5	0.5	0.5
1996	0.5	0.5	0.5	0.5	0.5	0.5	0.6	0.6	0.6	0.5	0.5	0.5	0.5
1997	0.6	0.6	0.6	0.6	0.6	0.6	0.6	0.7	0.7	0.7	0.7	0.7	0.6
1998	0.6	0.6	0.7	0.6	0.6	0.7	0.7	0.7	0.6	0.6	0.6	0.6	0.6
1999	0.5	0.5	0.5	0.5	0.5	0.6	0.6	0.6	0.6	0.7	0.7	0.7	0.6
2000	0.7	0.7	0.7	0.7	0.7	0.8	0.8	0.8	0.8	0.8	0.8	0.8	0.8
2001	0.8	0.9	0.9	0.9	1.0	1.0	1.0	1.0	1.0	1.0	1.0	1.0	0.9
2002	1.0	0.8	0.7	0.6	0.6	0.6	0.6	0.6	0.7	0.7	0.6	0.6	0.7
2003	0.6	0.7	0.7	0.7	0.6	0.7	0.7	0.7	0.7	0.7	0.7	0.7	0.7
Construction													
1990	1.0	1.0	1.0	1.0	1.0	1.1	1.0	1.0	1.0	1.0	1.1	1.0	1.0
1991	1.0	1.0	1.0	1.0	1.0	1.1	1.1	1.1	1.1	1.1	1.1	1.1	1.1
1992	1.0	1.0	1.0	1.1	1.2	1.2	1.2	1.2	1.2	1.2	1.2	1.2	1.1
1993	1.2	1.2	1.2	1.2	1.3	1.3	1.4	1.5	1.4	1.5	1.5	1.4	1.3
1994	1.4	1.4	1.4	1.5	1.5	1.6	1.6	1.5	1.5	1.6	1.6	1.6	1.5
1995	1.6	1.6	1.6	1.6	1.6	1.7	1.7	1.8	1.7	1.7	1.7	1.7	1.7
1996	1.7	1.7	1.7	1.7	1.7	1.7	1.7	1.7	1.7	1.7	1.8	1.8	1.7
1997	1.8	1.8	1.8	1.8	1.8	1.8	1.9	1.9	1.9	1.8	1.8	1.8	1.8
1998	1.8	1.8	1.8	1.9	2.0	1.9	2.0	2.0	1.9	1.9	1.9	2.0	1.9
1999	2.0	2.0	2.0	2.1	2.1	2.2	2.3	2.2	2.2	2.2	2.1	2.2	2.1
2000	2.2	2.2	2.2	2.2	2.3	2.3	2.2	2.2	2.1	2.2	2.2	2.2	2.2
2001	2.2	2.1	2.2	2.2	2.3	2.2	2.2	2.2	2.2	2.2	2.1	2.1	2.1
2002	2.1	2.1	2.1	2.1	2.1	2.1	2.1	2.1	2.0	1.9	1.9	1.9	2.0
2003	1.8	1.9	1.9	1.9	1.9	2.0	2.0	2.0	2.1	2.0	2.0	2.0	2.0
Manufacturing													
1990	4.6	4.5	4.4	4.6	4.5	4.5	4.5	4.4	4.4	4.6	4.6	4.6	4.5
1991	4.5	4.5	4.7	4.6	4.5	4.6	4.7	4.7	4.6	4.6	4.6	4.6	4.6
1992	4.6	4.6	4.6	4.5	4.6	4.7	4.6	4.7	4.7	4.8	4.7	4.7	4.7
1993	4.6	4.6	4.6	4.6	4.6	4.5	4.6	4.5	4.5	4.6	4.5	4.5	4.6
1994	4.5	4.5	4.5	4.5	4.5	4.7	4.6	4.7	4.7	4.7	4.7	4.8	4.6
1995	4.7	4.7	4.8	4.6	4.5	4.7	4.7	4.7	4.7	4.6	4.6	4.6	4.7
1996	4.6	4.6	4.6	4.5	4.6	4.6	4.7	4.8	4.9	4.8	4.8	4.8	4.7
1997	4.9	4.9	4.8	4.9	4.9	5.0	4.9	5.0	4.9	4.9	4.9	4.9	4.9
1998	4.8	4.8	4.8	4.7	4.7	4.6	4.4	4.5	4.4	4.3	4.4	4.3	4.6
1999	4.3	4.3	4.3	4.3	4.2	4.4	4.3	4.4	4.4	4.4	4.3	4.3	4.3
2000	4.4	4.4	4.4	4.3	4.3	4.3	4.3	4.2	4.1	4.2	4.2	4.2	4.3
2001	4.3	4.3	4.3	4.3	4.3	4.3	4.2	4.2	4.1	4.1	4.1	4.1	4.2
2002	4.0	4.0	4.0	4.0	4.1	4.1	4.1	4.1	4.0	3.9	3.9	4.0	4.0
2003	4.0	4.0	4.0	3.9	3.9	4.0	3.9	3.9	3.8	3.8	3.8	3.8	3.9
Service-providing													
1990	30.5	30.2	30.5	30.6	30.4	30.3	30.2	30.0	30.2	30.4	30.8	30.9	30.4
1991	30.2	30.8	31.0	31.4	31.3	31.0	30.9	30.9	31.7	32.2	32.0	32.3	31.3
1992	31.9	32.1	32.5	32.2	32.3	32.1	31.9	31.9	32.2	32.7	32.3	32.7	32.2
1993	32.4	32.7	32.8	33.0	32.7	32.6	32.3	32.2	32.8	33.1	32.9	33.1	32.7
1994	32.1	32.4	33.0	33.2	32.9	33.0	33.1	33.3	34.1	33.9	33.9	34.0	33.2
1995	33.5	33.7	34.1	34.2	34.0	34.1	34.0	34.1	34.5	34.9	34.9	34.8	34.2
1996	34.7	35.0	34.9	34.8	35.0	34.4	34.8	34.7	35.6	35.6	35.7	35.9	35.1
1997	35.5	36.0	35.9	36.1	36.4	36.3	35.6	35.9	36.2	36.4	36.7	36.9	36.2
1998	36.4	36.7	36.8	37.1	37.2	36.8	36.5	36.5	36.7	36.5	36.8	36.8	36.7
1999	35.9	36.1	36.4	36.5	36.4	36.3	35.7	36.4	36.8	36.6	37.1	37.2	36.5
2000	36.4	36.6	36.6	36.9	37.0	36.4	36.5	36.7	36.8	36.6	36.8	37.0	36.7
2001	36.4	36.8	36.9	37.0	37.0	37.2	36.6	36.9	37.6	37.0	37.2	37.2	36.9
2002	36.8	37.2	37.7	37.8	37.9	37.8	36.9	37.2	37.2	37.1	37.4	37.4	37.4
2003	36.5	37.0	37.1	37.1	37.3	37.3	36.7	37.0	37.2	37.3	37.7	37.6	37.2

Employment by Industry: Texas—*Continued*

(Numbers in thousands. Not seasonally adjusted.)

Industry	January	February	March	April	May	June	July	August	September	October	November	December	Annual Average
SAN ANGELO—*Continued*													
Trade, transportation, and utilities													
1990	6.8	6.6	6.6	6.7	6.7	6.7	6.6	6.5	6.5	6.5	6.7	6.8	6.6
1991	6.5	6.6	6.6	6.5	6.5	6.7	6.6	6.6	7.2	7.3	7.2	7.3	6.8
1992	6.8	6.6	6.8	6.7	6.8	7.0	6.8	6.9	7.0	7.1	6.9	7.1	6.9
1993	6.9	6.9	6.9	7.0	6.9	7.0	7.0	6.9	6.9	7.0	7.1	7.3	7.0
1994	6.7	6.7	6.9	6.9	6.9	7.0	7.1	7.2	7.3	7.4	7.4	7.5	7.1
1995	7.2	7.1	7.1	7.1	7.1	7.3	7.1	7.2	7.1	7.4	7.5	7.5	7.2
1996	7.4	7.4	7.5	7.4	7.4	7.4	7.4	7.4	7.4	7.3	7.5	7.7	7.4
1997	7.4	7.4	7.3	7.5	7.5	7.5	7.6	7.6	7.6	7.6	7.7	7.9	7.6
1998	7.6	7.5	7.5	7.6	7.6	7.7	7.6	7.6	7.6	7.6	7.8	7.8	7.6
1999	7.4	7.3	7.3	7.3	7.2	7.3	7.3	7.4	7.4	7.3	7.6	7.7	7.4
2000	7.4	7.3	7.3	7.4	7.4	7.4	7.4	7.4	7.3	7.3	7.5	7.6	7.4
2001	7.4	7.4	7.5	7.5	7.5	7.5	7.6	7.6	7.6	7.4	7.6	7.7	7.5
2002	7.5	7.5	7.5	7.5	7.6	7.6	7.4	7.5	7.5	7.5	7.6	7.7	7.5
2003	7.3	7.3	7.4	7.4	7.4	7.4	7.4	7.5	7.3	7.5	7.7	7.8	7.5
Wholesale trade													
1990	1.2	1.2	1.2	1.3	1.3	1.3	1.2	1.2	1.2	1.2	1.2	1.2	1.2
1991	1.2	1.2	1.2	1.3	1.3	1.3	1.3	1.3	1.3	1.4	1.4	1.4	1.3
1992	1.3	1.2	1.3	1.3	1.3	1.3	1.3	1.3	1.3	1.4	1.3	1.3	1.3
1993	1.4	1.3	1.4	1.4	1.4	1.4	1.4	1.4	1.3	1.4	1.4	1.4	1.4
1994	1.3	1.3	1.4	1.4	1.4	1.4	1.4	1.4	1.4	1.5	1.5	1.5	1.4
1995	1.4	1.4	1.4	1.4	1.4	1.5	1.4	1.4	1.3	1.4	1.4	1.3	1.4
1996	1.3	1.4	1.4	1.4	1.4	1.4	1.4	1.4	1.4	1.4	1.4	1.4	1.4
1997	1.4	1.4	1.4	1.5	1.5	1.5	1.5	1.5	1.5	1.5	1.5	1.5	1.5
1998	1.5	1.5	1.5	1.5	1.5	1.6	1.6	1.6	1.6	1.5	1.6	1.5	1.5
1999	1.5	1.5	1.5	1.5	1.5	1.5	1.5	1.5	1.5	1.5	1.6	1.6	1.5
2000	1.5	1.5	1.5	1.5	1.5	1.5	1.6	1.5	1.5	1.5	1.5	1.5	1.5
2001	1.5	1.5	1.5	1.5	1.5	1.5	1.6	1.6	1.6	1.5	1.5	1.5	1.5
2002	1.5	1.5	1.5	1.5	1.5	1.6	1.5	1.5	1.5	1.5	1.5	1.5	1.5
2003	1.5	1.5	1.5	1.5	1.5	1.5	1.5	1.5	1.5	1.5	1.5	1.5	1.5
Retail trade													
1990	4.9	4.7	4.7	4.7	4.7	4.7	4.7	4.6	4.6	4.6	4.8	4.9	4.7
1991	4.6	4.6	4.6	4.5	4.5	4.6	4.5	4.5	5.1	5.1	5.0	5.1	4.7
1992	4.8	4.7	4.7	4.7	4.8	4.9	4.8	4.8	4.9	4.9	4.8	5.0	4.8
1993	4.7	4.8	4.7	4.8	4.7	4.8	4.8	4.7	4.8	4.8	4.9	5.0	4.8
1994	4.6	4.6	4.7	4.7	4.7	4.8	4.9	5.0	5.1	5.1	5.1	5.2	4.9
1995	5.0	4.9	4.9	4.9	4.9	5.0	4.9	5.0	5.0	5.2	5.3	5.4	5.0
1996	5.3	5.2	5.3	5.2	5.2	5.2	5.2	5.2	5.2	5.1	5.3	5.5	5.2
1997	5.2	5.2	5.1	5.2	5.2	5.2	5.3	5.3	5.3	5.3	5.4	5.6	5.3
1998	5.3	5.2	5.2	5.3	5.3	5.3	5.2	5.2	5.2	5.3	5.4	5.5	5.3
1999	5.1	5.0	5.0	5.0	4.9	5.0	5.0	5.1	5.1	5.0	5.2	5.3	5.1
2000	5.1	5.0	5.0	5.1	5.1	5.1	5.0	5.1	5.0	5.0	5.2	5.3	5.1
2001	5.1	5.1	5.2	5.2	5.2	5.2	5.2	5.2	5.2	5.1	5.3	5.4	5.2
2002	5.2	5.2	5.2	5.2	5.3	5.2	5.1	5.2	5.2	5.2	5.3	5.4	5.2
2003	5.0	5.0	5.1	5.1	5.1	5.1	5.1	5.2	5.1	5.2	5.4	5.5	5.2
Transportation and utilities													
1990	0.7	0.7	0.7	0.7	0.7	0.7	0.7	0.7	0.7	0.7	0.7	0.7	0.7
1991	0.7	0.8	0.8	0.7	0.7	0.8	0.8	0.8	0.8	0.8	0.8	0.8	0.8
1992	0.7	0.7	0.8	0.7	0.7	0.8	0.7	0.8	0.8	0.8	0.8	0.8	0.8
1993	0.8	0.8	0.8	0.8	0.8	0.8	0.8	0.8	0.8	0.8	0.8	0.9	0.8
1994	0.8	0.8	0.8	0.8	0.8	0.8	0.8	0.8	0.8	0.8	0.8	0.8	0.8
1995	0.8	0.8	0.8	0.8	0.8	0.8	0.8	0.8	0.8	0.8	0.8	0.8	0.8
1996	0.8	0.8	0.8	0.8	0.8	0.8	0.8	0.8	0.8	0.8	0.8	0.8	0.8
1997	0.8	0.8	0.8	0.8	0.8	0.8	0.8	0.8	0.8	0.8	0.8	0.8	0.8
1998	0.8	0.8	0.8	0.8	0.8	0.8	0.8	0.8	0.8	0.8	0.8	0.8	0.8
1999	0.8	0.8	0.8	0.8	0.8	0.8	0.8	0.8	0.8	0.8	0.8	0.8	0.8
2000	0.8	0.8	0.8	0.8	0.8	0.8	0.8	0.8	0.8	0.8	0.8	0.8	0.8
2001	0.8	0.8	0.8	0.8	0.8	0.8	0.8	0.8	0.8	0.8	0.8	0.8	0.7
2002	0.8	0.8	0.8	0.8	0.8	0.8	0.8	0.8	0.8	0.8	0.8	0.8	0.8
2003	0.8	0.8	0.8	0.8	0.8	0.8	0.8	0.8	0.7	0.8	0.8	0.8	0.8
Information													
1990	2.4	2.4	2.4	2.4	2.4	2.4	2.3	2.3	2.2	2.2	2.3	2.3	2.3
1991	2.3	2.3	2.4	2.4	2.4	2.3	2.3	2.3	2.3	2.4	2.4	2.4	2.4
1992	2.4	2.4	2.4	2.4	2.4	2.3	2.4	2.4	2.3	2.3	2.3	2.3	2.4
1993	2.3	2.4	2.4	2.4	2.4	2.4	2.2	2.2	2.1	2.2	2.1	2.1	2.3
1994	2.0	2.1	2.1	2.1	2.1	2.1	2.1	2.0	1.9	1.9	1.9	2.0	2.0
1995	1.8	1.9	2.0	1.9	1.9	2.0	2.0	2.0	2.1	2.1	2.0	2.0	2.0
1996	2.0	2.0	2.1	1.9	1.8	1.8	1.8	1.8	2.0	2.0	2.0	2.1	1.9
1997	2.1	2.1	2.2	2.0	2.1	2.1	2.1	2.1	2.1	2.1	2.2	2.3	2.1
1998	2.5	2.4	2.5	2.5	2.6	2.6	2.6	2.5	2.6	2.5	2.6	2.7	2.6
1999	2.6	2.6	2.5	2.6	2.7	2.7	2.6	2.6	2.6	2.6	2.7	2.7	2.6
2000	2.6	2.6	2.6	2.6	2.6	2.6	2.5	2.5	2.5	2.4	2.4	2.5	2.5
2001	2.4	2.4	2.5	2.4	2.4	2.4	2.4	2.3	2.3	2.3	2.3	2.3	2.3
2002	2.4	2.4	2.4	2.3	2.3	2.3	2.2	2.2	2.2	2.1	2.1	2.1	2.3
2003	2.1	2.1	2.1	2.0	2.0	2.0	2.0	2.0	2.0	2.0	2.0	2.0	2.0

Employment by Industry: Texas—*Continued*

(Numbers in thousands. Not seasonally adjusted.)

Industry	January	February	March	April	May	June	July	August	September	October	November	December	Annual Average
SAN ANGELO—*Continued*													
Financial activities													
1990	1.6	1.5	1.5	1.4	1.4	1.4	1.6	1.6	1.5	1.5	1.5	1.5	1.5
1991	1.4	1.4	1.4	1.5	1.5	1.5	1.5	1.5	1.5	1.5	1.5	1.5	1.5
1992	1.5	1.5	1.6	1.5	1.6	1.6	1.6	1.6	1.6	1.6	1.6	1.6	1.6
1993	1.6	1.6	1.6	1.6	1.6	1.7	1.6	1.6	1.6	1.6	1.6	1.6	1.6
1994	1.5	1.6	1.6	1.6	1.6	1.7	1.7	1.7	1.7	1.6	1.6	1.6	1.6
1995	1.5	1.5	1.5	1.6	1.6	1.6	1.6	1.6	1.6	1.6	1.6	1.6	1.6
1996	1.6	1.6	1.6	1.6	1.6	1.7	1.7	1.7	1.7	1.7	1.7	1.7	1.7
1997	1.7	1.7	1.7	1.7	1.8	1.8	1.8	1.8	1.8	1.8	1.7	1.8	1.8
1998	1.8	1.8	1.8	1.9	1.9	1.9	1.9	1.9	1.9	1.9	1.9	1.9	1.9
1999	1.8	1.8	1.9	1.9	1.9	1.9	1.9	1.9	1.9	1.9	1.9	1.9	1.9
2000	1.8	1.8	1.8	1.9	1.9	1.9	2.0	1.9	1.9	1.9	1.9	1.9	1.9
2001	1.9	1.9	1.9	1.9	1.9	1.9	1.9	1.9	1.9	1.9	1.9	1.9	1.9
2002	1.8	1.9	1.9	1.8	1.9	1.9	1.9	1.9	1.9	1.9	1.9	1.9	1.9
2003	1.9	1.9	1.9	2.0	2.0	2.0	2.0	2.0	2.0	2.0	2.0	2.0	2.0
Professional and business services													
1990	3.0	3.0	3.1	2.9	2.9	2.9	2.9	2.9	2.8	2.9	2.9	2.9	2.9
1991	3.1	3.1	3.1	3.2	3.2	3.2	3.2	3.2	3.1	3.2	3.1	3.1	3.2
1992	3.3	3.4	3.4	3.5	3.4	3.4	3.4	3.4	3.3	3.2	3.1	3.2	3.3
1993	3.2	3.4	3.3	3.3	3.3	3.2	3.2	3.3	3.4	3.4	3.2	3.2	3.3
1994	3.2	3.2	3.2	3.2	3.2	3.2	3.2	3.3	3.4	3.4	3.3	3.3	3.3
1995	3.3	3.3	3.3	3.3	3.2	3.2	3.2	3.2	3.1	3.3	3.3	3.3	3.3
1996	3.3	3.3	3.3	3.2	3.3	3.2	3.2	3.2	3.3	3.3	3.3	3.3	3.3
1997	3.3	3.3	3.3	3.4	3.3	3.3	3.3	3.3	3.3	3.4	3.5	3.4	3.3
1998	3.4	3.4	3.5	3.5	3.4	3.2	3.2	3.2	3.1	3.0	2.9	2.9	3.2
1999	2.9	2.9	3.0	3.0	2.9	3.0	2.9	2.9	2.9	3.1	3.1	3.1	3.0
2000	2.9	2.9	2.9	2.9	2.8	2.8	2.7	2.8	2.7	2.9	3.0	3.1	2.9
2001	3.2	3.3	3.2	3.2	3.1	3.3	3.2	3.4	3.4	3.4	3.5	3.5	3.3
2002	3.3	3.4	3.6	3.7	3.6	3.6	3.4	3.3	3.1	3.2	3.3	3.3	3.4
2003	3.1	3.3	3.3	3.3	3.4	3.5	3.4	3.5	3.4	3.4	3.5	3.4	3.4
Educational and health services													
1990	4.8	4.7	4.7	4.9	4.8	4.7	4.8	4.8	4.8	4.9	4.9	4.9	4.8
1991	5.0	5.1	5.2	5.3	5.2	5.3	5.4	5.4	5.4	5.4	5.5	5.5	5.3
1992	5.6	5.6	5.7	5.6	5.6	5.6	5.6	5.6	5.6	5.7	5.6	5.7	5.6
1993	5.7	5.8	5.8	5.8	5.8	5.9	5.9	5.8	5.8	5.8	5.9	5.9	5.8
1994	5.7	5.8	5.9	6.1	6.0	6.1	6.0	6.0	6.1	6.1	6.1	6.1	6.0
1995	6.1	6.2	6.4	6.5	6.5	6.6	6.5	6.6	6.6	6.5	6.6	6.5	6.5
1996	6.6	6.8	6.7	6.9	7.0	6.9	7.0	7.0	7.1	7.1	7.1	7.1	6.9
1997	7.1	7.2	7.2	7.3	7.3	7.3	7.0	7.0	7.0	7.0	7.0	7.0	7.1
1998	7.0	7.0	7.0	7.0	7.0	7.0	6.9	7.0	6.9	6.9	7.0	7.0	7.0
1999	6.9	6.8	6.9	7.0	7.0	7.1	6.9	7.0	7.1	6.9	6.9	6.9	7.0
2000	7.0	7.0	7.0	7.0	7.0	7.0	7.0	7.1	7.1	7.0	7.0	6.9	7.0
2001	6.8	6.9	6.9	6.9	6.9	7.0	7.0	7.1	7.1	7.1	7.1	7.1	6.9
2002	7.1	7.1	7.2	7.1	7.2	7.2	7.2	7.3	7.3	7.2	7.3	7.3	7.2
2003	7.1	7.2	7.2	7.2	7.3	7.3	7.3	7.4	7.4	7.4	7.4	7.4	7.3
Leisure and hospitality													
1990	3.0	3.1	3.1	3.2	3.1	3.1	3.3	3.3	3.3	3.2	3.3	3.3	3.2
1991	2.8	3.0	3.1	3.1	3.2	3.1	3.1	3.1	3.0	3.1	3.0	3.1	3.1
1992	2.9	3.1	3.1	3.1	3.1	3.1	3.2	3.2	3.1	3.3	3.3	3.3	3.2
1993	3.2	3.2	3.2	3.3	3.2	3.4	3.4	3.4	3.3	3.4	3.3	3.3	3.3
1994	3.2	3.3	3.5	3.5	3.4	3.5	3.6	3.5	3.5	3.4	3.5	3.5	3.5
1995	3.4	3.5	3.6	3.7	3.6	3.7	3.7	3.8	3.8	3.8	3.7	3.7	3.7
1996	3.5	3.6	3.5	3.6	3.6	3.7	3.9	3.7	3.7	3.7	3.6	3.6	3.6
1997	3.5	3.7	3.7	3.8	3.8	3.8	3.8	3.9	3.8	3.9	3.9	3.9	3.8
1998	3.6	3.8	3.8	3.9	3.9	3.9	4.0	3.9	3.9	3.9	3.9	3.9	3.9
1999	3.8	3.9	3.9	4.0	4.0	4.0	4.0	4.1	4.1	4.0	4.0	4.0	4.0
2000	3.9	4.0	4.0	4.3	4.4	4.4	4.5	4.5	4.4	4.2	4.2	4.2	4.3
2001	3.9	4.0	4.0	4.3	4.3	4.4	4.3	4.4	4.5	4.2	4.1	4.1	4.2
2002	4.1	4.2	4.3	4.5	4.6	4.6	4.6	4.5	4.5	4.4	4.4	4.4	4.4
2003	4.3	4.4	4.4	4.4	4.5	4.6	4.5	4.5	4.5	4.4	4.4	4.4	4.4
Other services													
1990	1.5	1.5	1.6	1.5	1.5	1.6	1.5	1.5	1.5	1.5	1.5	1.5	1.5
1991	1.5	1.5	1.6	1.6	1.6	1.7	1.6	1.6	1.6	1.6	1.6	1.7	1.6
1992	1.6	1.6	1.7	1.6	1.6	1.7	1.6	1.6	1.6	1.6	1.6	1.7	1.6
1993	1.6	1.6	1.7	1.7	1.7	1.7	1.6	1.6	1.7	1.7	1.7	1.7	1.7
1994	1.7	1.7	1.7	1.7	1.7	1.8	1.7	1.7	1.8	1.7	1.7	1.7	1.7
1995	1.7	1.7	1.7	1.6	1.7	1.8	1.7	1.6	1.7	1.7	1.7	1.7	1.7
1996	1.7	1.7	1.7	1.7	1.7	1.7	1.7	1.7	1.7	1.7	1.7	1.7	1.7
1997	1.7	1.7	1.7	1.7	1.8	1.8	1.7	1.7	1.7	1.7	1.7	1.7	1.7
1998	1.7	1.7	1.7	1.8	1.8	1.8	1.8	1.8	1.7	1.7	1.7	1.7	1.7
1999	1.7	1.7	1.7	1.7	1.7	1.8	1.7	1.8	1.7	1.7	1.7	1.7	1.7
2000	1.7	1.7	1.7	1.7	1.7	1.8	1.8	1.7	1.7	1.7	1.7	1.7	1.7
2001	1.7	1.7	1.7	1.7	1.7	1.8	1.7	1.7	1.7	1.7	1.7	1.7	1.7
2002	1.7	1.7	1.7	1.8	1.8	1.8	1.8	1.8	1.8	1.8	1.8	1.8	1.8
2003	1.8	1.8	1.8	1.8	1.8	1.8	1.8	1.8	1.8	1.8	1.8	1.8	1.8

Employment by Industry: Texas—*Continued*

(Numbers in thousands. Not seasonally adjusted.)

Industry	January	February	March	April	May	June	July	August	September	October	November	December	Annual Average
SAN ANGELO—*Continued*													
Government													
1990	7.4	7.4	7.5	7.6	7.6	7.5	7.2	7.1	7.6	7.7	7.7	7.7	7.5
1991	7.6	7.8	7.6	7.8	7.7	7.2	7.2	7.2	7.6	7.7	7.7	7.7	7.6
1992	7.8	7.9	7.8	7.8	7.8	7.4	7.3	7.2	7.7	7.9	7.9	7.8	7.7
1993	7.9	7.8	7.9	7.9	7.8	7.3	7.4	7.4	8.0	8.0	8.0	8.0	7.8
1994	8.1	8.0	8.1	8.1	8.0	7.6	7.7	7.9	8.4	8.4	8.4	8.3	8.1
1995	8.5	8.5	8.5	8.5	8.4	7.9	8.2	8.1	8.5	8.5	8.5	8.5	8.4
1996	8.6	8.6	8.5	8.5	8.6	8.0	8.1	8.2	8.7	8.8	8.8	8.7	8.5
1997	8.7	8.9	8.8	8.7	8.8	8.7	8.3	8.5	8.9	8.9	9.0	8.9	8.8
1998	8.8	9.1	9.0	8.9	9.0	8.7	8.5	8.6	9.0	9.0	9.0	8.9	8.9
1999	8.8	9.1	9.2	9.0	9.0	8.5	8.4	8.7	9.1	9.1	9.2	9.2	8.9
2000	9.1	9.3	9.3	9.1	9.2	8.5	8.6	8.8	9.2	9.2	9.1	9.1	9.0
2001	9.1	9.2	9.2	9.1	9.2	8.9	8.5	8.5	9.1	9.0	9.0	8.9	8.9
2002	8.9	9.0	9.1	9.1	8.9	8.8	8.4	8.7	8.9	9.0	9.0	8.9	8.9
2003	8.9	9.0	9.0	9.0	8.9	8.7	8.3	8.3	8.8	8.8	8.9	8.8	8.8
Federal government													
1990	1.2	1.2	1.3	1.4	1.5	1.4	1.4	1.3	1.3	1.3	1.3	1.3	1.3
1991	1.2	1.3	1.2	1.3	1.3	1.3	1.3	1.3	1.2	1.2	1.2	1.2	1.3
1992	1.2	1.2	1.2	1.2	1.2	1.2	1.2	1.2	1.2	1.2	1.2	1.2	1.2
1993	1.2	1.2	1.2	1.2	1.2	1.2	1.2	1.2	1.2	1.2	1.2	1.2	1.2
1994	1.2	1.2	1.2	1.2	1.2	1.2	1.2	1.3	1.3	1.3	1.3	1.3	1.2
1995	1.3	1.3	1.3	1.3	1.3	1.3	1.4	1.3	1.3	1.3	1.3	1.3	1.3
1996	1.3	1.3	1.2	1.3	1.3	1.3	1.3	1.3	1.3	1.3	1.3	1.3	1.3
1997	1.3	1.3	1.3	1.3	1.3	1.4	1.4	1.4	1.3	1.3	1.3	1.3	1.3
1998	1.3	1.3	1.3	1.3	1.3	1.4	1.4	1.4	1.3	1.3	1.3	1.3	1.3
1999	1.3	1.3	1.4	1.3	1.3	1.4	1.4	1.4	1.4	1.4	1.4	1.4	1.4
2000	1.3	1.4	1.4	1.4	1.4	1.4	1.4	1.4	1.3	1.3	1.3	1.3	1.4
2001	1.3	1.3	1.3	1.3	1.3	1.3	1.3	1.3	1.3	1.3	1.3	1.3	1.3
2002	1.3	1.3	1.3	1.4	1.4	1.4	1.4	1.4	1.4	1.4	1.4	1.4	1.4
2003	1.4	1.4	1.4	1.4	1.4	1.4	1.4	1.3	1.3	1.3	1.3	1.3	1.4
State government													
1990	2.3	2.3	2.3	2.3	2.2	2.2	2.3	2.4	2.4	2.4	2.4	2.4	2.3
1991	2.4	2.4	2.3	2.4	2.3	2.2	2.3	2.3	2.4	2.3	2.3	2.3	2.3
1992	2.4	2.4	2.3	2.3	2.3	2.2	2.3	2.3	2.3	2.4	2.4	2.3	2.3
1993	2.4	2.3	2.4	2.3	2.3	2.2	2.3	2.2	2.3	2.3	2.3	2.3	2.3
1994	2.3	2.3	2.3	2.3	2.3	2.3	2.4	2.4	2.4	2.4	2.4	2.3	2.3
1995	2.5	2.4	2.4	2.4	2.4	2.3	2.5	2.4	2.5	2.4	2.4	2.4	2.4
1996	2.5	2.4	2.4	2.4	2.4	2.2	2.3	2.2	2.3	2.4	2.4	2.3	2.4
1997	2.4	2.4	2.3	2.3	2.3	2.1	2.2	2.2	2.4	2.3	2.4	2.3	2.3
1998	2.3	2.4	2.3	2.3	2.3	2.2	2.3	2.2	2.3	2.4	2.4	2.3	2.3
1999	2.3	2.4	2.4	2.4	2.3	2.2	2.3	2.2	2.4	2.5	2.5	2.4	2.4
2000	2.5	2.5	2.4	2.4	2.4	2.2	2.3	2.2	2.5	2.5	2.5	2.4	2.4
2001	2.5	2.5	2.5	2.5	2.5	2.3	2.4	2.3	2.6	2.6	2.6	2.5	2.4
2002	2.5	2.6	2.6	2.6	2.5	2.3	2.4	2.4	2.6	2.6	2.6	2.5	2.5
2003	2.5	2.6	2.6	2.6	2.5	2.3	2.3	2.3	2.6	2.6	2.7	2.6	2.5
Local government													
1990	3.9	3.9	3.9	3.9	3.9	3.9	3.5	3.4	3.9	4.0	4.0	4.0	3.9
1991	4.0	4.1	4.1	4.1	4.1	3.7	3.6	3.6	4.0	4.2	4.2	4.2	4.0
1992	4.2	4.3	4.3	4.3	4.3	4.0	3.8	3.7	4.2	4.3	4.3	4.3	4.2
1993	4.3	4.3	4.3	4.4	4.3	3.9	3.9	4.0	4.5	4.5	4.5	4.5	4.3
1994	4.6	4.5	4.6	4.6	4.5	4.1	4.1	4.2	4.7	4.7	4.7	4.7	4.5
1995	4.7	4.8	4.8	4.8	4.7	4.3	4.3	4.4	4.7	4.8	4.8	4.8	4.7
1996	4.8	4.9	4.9	4.8	4.9	4.5	4.5	4.7	5.1	5.1	5.1	5.1	4.9
1997	5.0	5.2	5.2	5.1	5.2	5.2	4.7	4.9	5.2	5.3	5.3	5.3	5.1
1998	5.2	5.4	5.4	5.3	5.4	5.1	4.8	5.0	5.4	5.3	5.3	5.3	5.2
1999	5.2	5.4	5.4	5.3	5.4	4.9	4.7	5.1	5.3	5.2	5.3	5.4	5.2
2000	5.3	5.4	5.5	5.3	5.4	4.9	4.9	5.2	5.4	5.4	5.3	5.4	5.3
2001	5.3	5.4	5.4	5.3	5.4	5.3	4.8	4.9	5.2	5.1	5.1	5.1	5.1
2002	5.1	5.1	5.2	5.1	5.0	5.1	4.6	4.9	4.9	5.0	5.0	5.0	5.0
2003	5.0	5.0	5.0	5.0	5.0	5.0	4.6	4.7	4.9	4.9	4.9	4.9	4.9
SAN ANTONIO													
Total nonfarm													
1990	516.1	519.2	522.6	524.8	528.7	530.7	521.7	523.5	529.5	531.6	533.3	533.9	526.3
1991	519.6	523.1	527.7	528.7	531.7	532.7	527.2	530.4	541.3	539.2	542.2	544.0	532.3
1992	528.4	534.6	539.1	546.7	551.4	552.0	550.7	550.5	555.8	559.8	561.9	563.9	549.6
1993	552.8	560.9	565.1	570.5	573.1	572.9	569.6	571.0	575.0	576.6	579.7	583.0	570.9
1994	572.5	580.1	585.2	593.5	595.0	595.8	594.9	593.5	600.8	605.4	609.9	615.2	595.2
1995	600.4	607.8	612.6	616.0	622.1	623.1	619.1	620.3	625.5	626.1	629.9	633.5	619.7
1996	618.7	624.1	628.0	632.4	637.7	638.4	631.8	635.5	639.7	645.3	650.0	652.1	636.1
1997	639.7	647.8	655.3	658.5	663.3	665.1	658.9	662.0	667.5	670.4	671.8	675.4	661.3
1998	665.7	670.8	675.8	677.2	680.1	680.2	679.1	682.8	688.5	690.9	693.4	697.0	681.8
1999	685.1	690.8	695.4	700.8	705.0	707.3	701.5	704.9	711.1	708.3	709.4	713.5	702.8
2000	702.0	709.2	712.6	718.1	725.3	725.4	718.9	721.2	726.0	722.2	724.4	728.4	719.5
2001	712.1	721.0	727.0	728.1	734.0	737.9	727.5	732.7	730.9	724.3	724.3	725.8	727.1
2002	711.3	719.2	725.1	728.6	734.0	732.4	724.4	729.8	733.0	729.7	731.0	731.1	727.5
2003	713.3	719.6	724.9	726.4	729.6	730.0	722.6	726.0	727.5	725.3	727.4	727.9	725.0

Employment by Industry: Texas—*Continued*

(Numbers in thousands. Not seasonally adjusted.)

Industry	January	February	March	April	May	June	July	August	September	October	November	December	Annual Average
SAN ANTONIO—*Continued*													
Total private													
1990	395.4	396.9	400.1	402.9	405.5	410.5	409.0	410.4	409.9	409.7	411.0	412.0	406.1
1991	398.6	401.1	405.8	406.5	409.5	413.2	413.4	415.0	416.3	415.9	417.7	419.2	411.0
1992	405.3	410.3	414.2	420.3	424.5	428.1	432.7	432.2	430.3	433.3	434.5	436.5	425.2
1993	426.3	432.8	437.0	442.6	444.8	449.1	451.6	451.6	449.1	448.5	450.8	453.0	444.8
1994	444.1	450.2	455.5	464.5	465.2	469.6	473.8	472.4	471.2	476.2	479.8	484.8	467.3
1995	472.1	477.4	481.8	485.2	490.4	494.2	495.0	495.4	494.9	494.9	497.9	501.3	490.0
1996	487.9	491.5	495.2	499.6	504.3	508.3	508.6	509.2	507.2	511.6	515.2	517.4	504.7
1997	506.8	512.7	519.9	523.3	527.9	533.1	533.0	532.6	533.0	534.2	535.6	539.1	527.6
1998	530.8	535.3	539.4	541.5	544.2	549.5	552.1	551.9	553.2	555.7	557.7	561.4	547.7
1999	550.3	554.5	559.3	564.9	568.9	575.7	576.1	576.5	578.2	575.6	576.5	580.9	569.8
2000	570.2	575.1	578.1	583.3	588.2	595.0	593.5	594.9	594.9	589.7	591.4	595.6	587.5
2001	580.4	587.8	593.5	594.4	600.2	606.9	602.7	604.8	598.8	591.2	589.8	591.4	595.1
2002	578.6	583.5	589.0	592.8	597.4	600.6	598.4	601.8	598.9	593.0	593.7	594.1	593.5
2003	578.6	582.4	587.8	588.7	591.8	596.4	593.9	595.9	593.8	589.2	590.5	591.4	590.0
Goods-producing													
1990	69.1	69.2	69.1	69.1	68.6	69.8	68.5	69.1	68.7	69.2	68.8	68.8	69.0
1991	68.7	68.5	68.8	68.3	69.1	69.9	69.7	70.3	70.5	70.5	70.8	70.6	69.6
1992	68.4	68.7	69.1	69.9	70.5	71.3	72.2	72.0	72.1	72.7	72.7	72.2	71.0
1993	71.4	72.7	73.3	73.5	73.9	74.2	75.0	75.2	74.9	74.9	75.0	75.4	74.1
1994	73.7	74.5	75.5	76.8	77.0	78.4	79.2	78.8	79.1	79.9	79.9	80.5	77.8
1995	78.9	80.0	80.8	80.5	81.5	81.8	82.2	82.1	82.6	82.5	82.0	82.1	81.4
1996	80.6	81.1	81.6	81.8	82.5	83.0	83.4	83.6	83.3	84.4	84.7	84.8	82.9
1997	83.4	84.3	85.5	85.4	86.6	87.3	87.3	86.9	87.2	88.3	87.9	88.0	86.5
1998	87.9	88.3	88.7	88.0	89.0	89.9	90.6	90.5	90.7	91.3	91.5	91.9	89.9
1999	91.0	92.0	93.3	92.7	92.9	93.9	94.8	95.0	95.0	94.8	94.3	94.9	93.7
2000	93.2	94.0	94.2	94.3	95.6	97.3	96.6	96.4	96.7	95.8	95.3	96.2	95.5
2001	93.8	94.6	95.6	95.4	96.1	97.1	97.1	97.2	96.9	94.9	93.5	93.6	95.4
2002	91.4	91.3	92.1	91.9	92.2	93.0	92.4	92.0	90.6	89.3	88.8	88.8	91.2
2003	87.5	87.8	87.7	88.0	88.2	88.7	88.0	88.0	87.6	86.7	86.4	86.4	87.6
Natural resources and mining													
1990	2.2	2.2	2.3	2.3	2.3	2.2	2.3	2.3	2.3	2.3	2.3	2.3	2.3
1991	2.3	2.3	2.3	2.2	2.2	2.2	2.1	2.1	2.1	2.2	2.2	2.2	2.2
1992	2.1	2.1	2.0	2.0	2.0	2.0	1.9	1.9	1.9	2.0	2.0	2.0	2.0
1993	2.1	2.1	2.1	2.1	2.2	2.1	2.1	2.1	2.0	2.0	2.0	2.1	2.1
1994	2.0	2.0	2.0	2.1	2.0	2.0	2.0	2.0	2.1	2.0	2.0	2.0	2.0
1995	2.1	2.1	2.1	2.1	2.2	2.2	2.2	2.1	2.1	2.0	2.0	2.0	2.1
1996	2.0	2.0	2.0	2.0	2.0	2.0	2.0	2.1	2.1	2.1	2.1	2.1	2.0
1997	2.0	2.0	2.1	2.1	2.1	2.1	2.1	2.1	2.1	2.1	2.1	2.1	2.1
1998	2.1	2.0	2.0	2.0	2.0	2.0	2.0	2.0	2.0	2.0	2.0	2.0	2.0
1999	2.0	2.0	2.0	2.0	2.0	2.0	2.0	2.0	2.0	2.0	2.0	2.0	2.0
2000	2.0	2.0	2.0	2.0	2.0	2.0	2.0	2.0	2.0	2.1	2.1	2.1	2.0
2001	2.1	2.1	2.1	2.2	2.2	2.2	2.3	2.3	2.3	2.4	2.4	2.4	2.2
2002	2.4	2.4	2.4	2.4	2.4	2.4	2.4	2.4	2.4	2.3	2.3	2.3	2.4
2003	2.3	2.3	2.3	2.3	2.3	2.3	2.3	2.3	2.3	2.2	2.2	2.2	2.3
Construction													
1990	22.4	22.3	22.4	22.3	22.5	23.4	23.1	23.1	22.8	22.9	22.4	22.1	22.6
1991	22.6	23.0	23.4	23.3	23.8	24.0	24.2	24.3	24.2	24.4	24.4	23.8	23.8
1992	22.6	22.7	23.0	23.8	24.1	24.5	25.3	25.2	25.1	25.4	24.9	24.4	24.3
1993	23.9	24.3	24.8	25.3	25.6	26.0	26.7	26.9	26.7	26.8	26.8	26.8	25.9
1994	26.6	26.9	27.5	28.3	28.1	28.7	29.6	29.5	29.5	30.1	30.1	30.5	28.8
1995	29.5	30.2	30.8	30.7	31.2	31.3	31.8	31.9	32.1	31.9	31.5	31.4	31.2
1996	30.9	31.2	31.6	31.6	31.9	32.2	32.7	33.0	32.6	33.0	33.2	33.3	32.3
1997	32.9	33.5	34.2	34.1	35.1	35.4	35.5	35.3	35.3	35.6	35.2	35.0	34.8
1998	35.5	35.7	36.1	35.1	35.7	36.3	37.1	37.3	37.2	36.9	37.0	37.5	36.5
1999	36.8	37.4	38.4	38.0	37.9	38.9	39.4	39.3	39.2	38.9	38.6	38.7	38.5
2000	38.1	38.5	38.8	38.5	39.1	40.1	40.1	40.5	40.5	39.7	39.7	39.9	39.5
2001	39.2	39.9	40.8	40.8	41.6	42.9	43.3	43.9	43.5	42.0	41.9	41.7	41.7
2002	40.5	40.8	41.3	41.4	41.9	42.4	42.1	42.3	41.3	40.5	40.1	39.8	41.2
2003	39.4	39.2	39.4	39.7	40.2	40.7	40.5	40.7	40.2	39.7	39.6	39.8	39.9
Manufacturing													
1990	44.5	44.7	44.4	44.5	43.8	44.2	43.1	43.7	43.6	44.0	44.1	44.4	44.1
1991	43.8	43.2	43.1	42.8	43.1	43.7	43.4	43.9	44.2	43.9	44.2	44.6	43.7
1992	43.7	43.9	44.1	44.1	44.4	44.8	45.0	44.9	45.1	45.3	45.8	45.8	44.7
1993	45.4	46.3	46.4	46.1	46.1	46.1	46.2	46.2	46.2	46.1	46.2	46.5	46.2
1994	45.1	45.6	46.0	46.4	46.9	47.7	47.6	47.3	47.5	47.8	47.8	48.0	47.0
1995	47.3	47.7	47.9	47.7	48.1	48.3	48.2	48.1	48.4	48.6	48.5	48.7	48.1
1996	47.7	47.9	48.0	48.2	48.6	48.8	48.7	48.5	48.6	49.3	49.4	49.4	48.6
1997	48.5	48.8	49.2	49.2	49.4	49.8	49.7	49.5	49.8	50.6	50.6	50.9	49.7
1998	50.3	50.6	50.6	50.9	51.3	51.6	51.5	51.2	51.5	52.4	52.5	52.4	51.4
1999	52.2	52.6	52.9	52.7	53.0	53.0	53.4	53.7	53.8	53.9	53.7	54.2	53.3
2000	53.1	53.5	53.4	53.8	54.5	55.2	54.5	53.9	54.2	54.0	53.5	54.2	54.0
2001	52.5	52.6	52.7	52.4	52.3	52.0	51.5	51.0	51.1	50.5	49.2	49.5	51.4
2002	48.5	48.1	48.4	48.1	47.9	48.2	47.9	47.3	46.9	46.5	46.4	46.7	47.6
2003	45.8	46.3	46.0	46.0	45.7	45.7	45.2	45.0	45.1	44.8	44.6	44.4	45.4

Employment by Industry: Texas—*Continued*

(Numbers in thousands. Not seasonally adjusted.)

Industry	January	February	March	April	May	June	July	August	September	October	November	December	Annual Average
SAN ANTONIO—*Continued*													
Service-providing													
1990	447.0	450.0	453.5	455.7	460.1	460.9	453.2	454.4	460.8	462.4	464.5	465.1	457.3
1991	450.9	454.6	458.9	460.4	462.6	462.8	457.5	460.1	470.8	468.7	471.4	473.4	462.7
1992	460.0	465.9	470.0	476.8	480.9	480.7	478.5	478.5	483.7	487.1	489.2	491.7	478.6
1993	481.4	488.2	491.8	497.0	499.2	498.7	494.6	495.8	500.1	501.7	504.7	507.6	496.7
1994	498.8	505.6	509.7	516.7	518.0	517.4	515.7	514.7	521.7	525.5	530.0	534.7	517.4
1995	521.5	527.8	531.8	535.5	540.6	541.3	536.9	538.2	542.9	543.6	547.9	551.4	538.3
1996	538.1	543.0	546.4	550.6	555.2	555.4	548.4	551.9	556.4	560.9	565.3	567.3	553.2
1997	556.3	563.5	569.8	573.1	576.7	577.8	571.6	575.1	580.3	582.1	583.9	587.4	574.8
1998	577.8	582.5	587.1	589.2	591.1	590.3	588.5	592.3	597.8	599.6	601.9	605.1	591.9
1999	594.1	598.8	602.1	608.1	612.1	613.4	606.7	609.9	616.1	613.5	615.1	618.6	609.0
2000	608.8	615.2	618.4	623.8	629.7	628.1	622.3	624.8	629.3	626.4	629.1	632.2	624.0
2001	618.3	626.4	631.4	632.7	637.9	640.8	630.4	635.5	634.0	629.4	630.8	632.2	631.6
2002	619.9	627.9	633.0	636.7	641.8	639.4	632.0	637.8	642.4	640.4	642.2	642.3	636.3
2003	625.8	631.8	637.2	638.4	641.4	641.3	634.6	638.0	639.9	638.6	641.0	641.5	637.5
Trade, transportation, and utilities													
1990	101.0	100.2	100.5	100.0	100.0	100.9	100.6	101.0	100.9	102.0	103.8	105.5	101.4
1991	101.0	99.5	99.9	100.5	100.8	102.5	102.4	102.9	103.3	103.6	105.4	107.2	102.4
1992	101.5	100.9	101.1	102.5	103.7	104.7	105.0	105.1	105.3	108.1	109.9	113.3	105.1
1993	107.8	107.1	107.3	107.7	108.0	108.8	110.3	110.5	110.5	111.5	114.1	115.5	109.9
1994	111.2	111.1	111.3	113.0	112.4	113.3	113.5	113.8	113.3	114.9	117.4	119.6	113.7
1995	115.0	114.1	114.0	113.9	114.3	115.8	116.0	116.8	116.8	117.6	120.6	123.3	116.5
1996	117.7	116.4	116.8	117.4	118.9	119.3	119.1	119.7	119.2	120.7	122.8	124.7	119.4
1997	119.1	118.2	119.0	119.7	120.2	121.1	120.9	121.3	120.9	123.8	125.7	128.6	121.5
1998	123.4	123.0	123.5	123.8	124.4	125.1	125.4	125.7	126.5	127.8	130.0	132.2	125.9
1999	126.5	125.9	126.6	126.5	127.4	128.4	128.3	129.3	130.0	130.4	132.6	135.3	128.9
2000	129.2	128.7	128.6	129.4	130.0	131.6	131.8	133.2	132.9	134.2	137.1	139.3	132.2
2001	133.3	133.2	134.1	133.7	134.1	134.2	133.2	133.7	132.9	132.7	134.8	136.0	133.8
2002	130.8	129.6	130.3	131.1	131.7	131.6	131.3	131.8	132.0	131.4	133.8	134.9	131.7
2003	129.0	128.2	129.1	128.8	128.8	129.0	129.0	129.5	129.9	130.2	132.6	133.5	129.8
Wholesale trade													
1990	20.5	20.4	20.5	20.0	20.0	20.1	20.2	20.2	20.1	20.0	20.1	20.1	20.2
1991	19.6	19.3	19.3	19.4	19.4	19.5	19.6	19.7	19.7	19.9	19.9	19.9	19.6
1992	19.7	19.8	19.9	20.1	20.3	20.6	20.6	20.2	20.4	20.7	20.6	20.8	20.3
1993	20.8	21.4	21.5	21.4	21.5	21.7	22.1	21.9	21.9	21.9	21.8	21.9	21.7
1994	21.5	21.5	21.5	21.5	21.6	21.7	22.0	22.0	22.0	22.2	22.1	22.3	21.8
1995	22.1	22.2	22.3	22.7	22.9	23.0	23.1	23.0	23.0	23.0	22.8	22.9	22.8
1996	22.8	22.9	22.9	22.8	23.0	23.2	23.4	23.6	23.5	23.3	23.4	23.4	23.2
1997	23.2	23.3	23.5	23.6	23.7	23.9	23.8	23.8	23.7	23.8	23.9	24.1	23.7
1998	23.8	23.9	24.1	24.4	24.5	24.8	24.8	24.9	24.9	25.0	25.0	25.1	24.6
1999	24.8	25.0	25.2	25.3	25.4	25.7	25.8	25.9	26.0	26.0	26.0	26.2	25.6
2000	25.5	25.7	25.9	25.8	25.9	26.2	26.4	26.4	26.6	26.6	26.4	26.6	26.2
2001	26.3	26.4	26.5	26.7	26.9	27.0	26.9	27.0	26.9	26.7	26.7	26.9	26.7
2002	26.1	26.1	26.2	26.2	26.3	26.5	26.5	26.5	26.4	26.3	26.4	26.4	26.3
2003	25.8	25.9	26.0	26.0	26.2	26.4	26.5	26.5	26.6	26.7	26.7	26.8	26.3
Retail trade													
1990	68.3	67.5	67.6	67.7	67.7	68.5	68.3	68.6	68.6	69.9	71.5	73.2	69.0
1991	68.1	66.8	67.1	67.9	68.0	69.2	69.0	69.4	69.7	69.7	71.4	73.1	69.1
1992	68.1	67.3	67.5	68.3	69.1	69.5	69.6	70.0	70.0	72.3	74.2	77.1	70.3
1993	71.6	70.2	70.2	71.0	71.0	71.3	72.3	72.6	72.5	73.5	76.1	77.2	72.5
1994	73.1	72.9	73.2	74.5	73.6	74.2	74.3	74.7	74.4	75.9	78.5	80.4	75.0
1995	76.6	75.7	75.4	74.7	74.8	76.0	75.9	76.8	76.8	77.5	80.7	82.8	77.0
1996	78.0	76.6	76.7	77.4	78.6	78.7	78.4	78.7	78.4	79.9	82.0	83.8	78.9
1997	79.0	77.9	78.4	78.7	78.9	79.6	79.4	79.7	79.5	81.9	83.6	86.3	80.2
1998	81.3	80.7	80.9	80.6	81.0	81.4	81.5	81.7	82.6	83.5	85.5	87.4	82.3
1999	82.7	81.9	82.7	82.2	83.0	83.5	83.5	84.3	84.9	85.0	87.3	89.7	84.2
2000	84.6	84.1	84.0	84.7	85.1	86.2	86.3	87.4	86.9	87.8	90.6	92.4	86.7
2001	87.1	87.1	87.9	87.3	87.4	87.6	87.0	87.4	86.8	87.4	89.7	90.9	87.8
2002	86.7	85.4	85.8	86.5	86.6	86.1	85.9	86.2	86.7	86.1	88.2	89.3	86.6
2003	84.0	83.2	83.9	83.8	83.7	83.8	83.9	84.5	84.7	85.0	87.3	88.1	84.7
Transportation and utilities													
1990	12.2	12.3	12.4	12.3	12.3	12.3	12.1	12.2	12.2	12.1	12.2	12.2	12.2
1991	13.3	13.4	13.5	13.2	13.4	13.8	13.8	13.8	13.9	14.0	14.1	14.2	13.7
1992	13.7	13.8	13.7	14.1	14.3	14.6	14.8	14.9	14.9	15.1	15.1	15.4	14.5
1993	15.4	15.5	15.6	15.3	15.5	15.8	15.9	16.0	16.1	16.1	16.2	16.4	15.8
1994	16.6	16.7	16.6	17.0	17.2	17.4	17.2	17.1	16.9	16.8	16.8	16.9	16.9
1995	16.3	16.2	16.3	16.5	16.6	16.8	17.0	17.0	17.0	17.1	17.1	17.6	16.8
1996	16.9	16.9	17.2	17.2	17.3	17.4	17.3	17.4	17.3	17.5	17.4	17.5	17.3
1997	16.9	17.0	17.1	17.4	17.6	17.6	17.7	17.8	17.7	18.1	18.2	18.2	17.6
1998	18.3	18.4	18.5	18.8	18.9	18.9	19.1	19.1	19.0	19.3	19.5	19.7	19.0
1999	19.0	19.0	18.7	19.0	19.0	19.2	19.0	19.1	19.1	19.4	19.3	19.4	19.1
2000	19.1	18.9	18.7	18.9	19.0	19.2	19.1	19.4	19.4	19.8	20.1	20.3	19.3
2001	19.9	19.7	19.7	19.7	19.8	19.6	19.3	19.3	19.2	18.6	18.4	18.2	19.2
2002	18.0	18.1	18.3	18.4	18.8	19.0	18.9	19.1	18.9	19.0	19.2	19.2	18.7
2003	19.2	19.1	19.2	19.0	18.9	18.8	18.6	18.5	18.6	18.5	18.6	18.6	18.8

Employment by Industry: Texas—*Continued*

(Numbers in thousands. Not seasonally adjusted.)

Industry	January	February	March	April	May	June	July	August	September	October	November	December	Annual Average
SAN ANTONIO—*Continued*													
Information													
1990	13.6	13.7	13.7	14.2	14.1	14.3	15.0	14.8	14.8	14.4	14.6	14.6	14.3
1991	13.8	13.8	14.0	14.7	14.7	14.7	13.9	13.9	14.0	14.8	14.9	15.2	14.4
1992	14.6	14.4	14.8	14.8	14.9	15.0	14.7	14.3	14.1	14.3	14.1	14.3	14.5
1993	14.4	14.0	14.4	14.9	15.0	15.1	15.2	15.1	15.0	15.5	15.6	15.7	15.0
1994	15.1	15.3	15.5	15.6	15.4	15.5	16.0	15.8	15.8	16.4	16.7	17.0	15.8
1995	16.2	16.3	16.5	16.7	16.7	17.1	17.1	16.9	16.6	16.7	16.8	17.0	16.7
1996	16.8	17.0	17.1	17.4	17.4	17.6	17.6	17.5	17.4	18.2	18.4	18.3	17.6
1997	18.0	18.0	18.4	19.0	18.9	19.2	19.3	19.2	19.2	19.3	19.5	19.4	19.0
1998	19.6	19.8	20.2	20.2	20.3	20.2	20.5	20.7	20.8	21.0	21.1	21.0	20.5
1999	21.4	21.5	21.7	21.6	21.7	22.0	22.3	22.3	23.0	22.7	22.9	23.2	22.2
2000	23.3	23.4	23.3	24.4	24.9	25.3	25.7	25.9	26.2	25.9	26.1	25.8	25.0
2001	24.9	25.0	25.0	25.3	25.2	25.6	25.6	25.7	25.4	25.6	25.5	25.6	25.3
2002	25.3	25.3	25.0	24.8	24.8	24.7	23.9	23.9	23.5	23.7	23.8	23.5	24.4
2003	23.2	23.1	23.2	23.3	23.4	23.6	23.8	23.7	23.6	23.7	23.8	24.0	23.5
Financial activities													
1990	42.8	42.9	43.1	43.1	43.1	43.4	42.6	42.7	42.6	41.7	41.5	42.2	42.6
1991	40.8	41.2	41.5	41.2	41.4	41.4	41.5	41.5	41.5	41.1	41.0	41.6	41.3
1992	40.7	41.0	41.0	41.3	41.5	41.9	42.1	42.0	41.7	41.5	41.5	41.6	41.5
1993	41.0	41.4	41.8	42.2	42.7	43.0	43.2	43.2	42.9	42.8	43.0	43.3	42.5
1994	42.9	43.3	43.6	44.3	44.5	45.0	45.3	45.2	45.2	45.1	45.2	45.4	44.6
1995	44.5	44.6	44.7	44.7	44.9	45.2	45.6	45.6	45.6	45.5	45.6	45.5	45.2
1996	45.0	45.1	45.1	46.3	46.4	46.9	46.8	46.9	46.7	47.4	47.9	47.8	46.5
1997	47.1	47.4	47.9	47.7	47.9	48.3	48.2	48.0	48.1	48.5	48.4	48.9	48.0
1998	48.4	48.7	48.7	48.8	49.0	49.4	50.2	50.2	50.5	50.9	51.1	51.5	49.8
1999	51.1	51.5	52.0	52.4	52.8	53.6	54.0	54.2	54.3	54.5	54.5	54.8	53.3
2000	54.4	54.8	54.9	55.5	55.5	56.0	55.7	55.4	55.4	55.6	55.7	56.2	55.4
2001	55.7	56.3	56.7	56.8	57.4	58.0	58.0	58.3	58.1	57.2	57.4	57.7	57.3
2002	57.1	57.2	57.5	57.8	58.3	58.5	58.4	58.7	58.6	58.8	59.0	59.4	58.3
2003	58.4	58.8	59.0	58.7	58.9	59.2	59.4	59.5	59.2	59.5	59.5	59.8	59.2
Professional and business services													
1990	41.6	42.1	43.0	43.6	44.5	45.2	46.2	47.1	47.5	47.9	48.4	48.1	45.4
1991	46.5	47.8	48.4	46.9	46.8	46.8	47.7	48.1	47.6	47.9	47.6	47.4	47.5
1992	46.0	47.2	47.8	48.8	49.2	49.6	49.9	50.0	49.8	50.7	50.5	50.6	49.2
1993	50.2	51.8	52.1	54.1	53.7	53.7	53.3	53.8	54.0	53.8	54.0	54.0	53.2
1994	53.8	54.9	56.1	57.3	57.1	57.8	58.4	58.4	58.3	59.7	60.1	61.1	57.8
1995	60.5	61.5	62.1	62.9	63.0	64.0	63.9	63.7	63.5	64.6	64.7	65.8	63.4
1996	64.4	65.2	65.3	65.6	65.4	66.7	67.8	66.6	66.6	67.4	67.7	68.6	66.4
1997	69.8	72.1	71.8	71.9	72.4	74.1	74.6	74.1	73.4	72.8	72.6	73.5	72.8
1998	72.6	73.8	74.4	75.1	74.5	76.5	77.3	76.8	76.5	77.9	78.3	79.4	76.1
1999	78.9	80.1	80.4	81.7	82.4	85.2	84.8	83.7	83.6	85.0	84.2	85.5	83.0
2000	84.0	84.6	85.0	87.2	88.6	90.6	91.1	91.1	90.1	89.2	88.4	89.0	88.2
2001	86.9	87.7	88.0	88.4	88.8	90.8	89.3	89.3	87.1	84.5	83.3	84.2	87.3
2002	82.1	83.3	83.9	85.4	85.8	86.6	87.4	88.8	88.8	87.7	86.7	86.4	86.1
2003	83.0	83.9	85.2	85.1	86.2	86.8	86.5	87.3	87.0	86.4	86.3	86.0	85.8
Educational and health services													
1990	55.1	56.0	56.2	57.0	56.8	56.7	56.6	56.5	58.1	58.9	59.3	59.2	57.2
1991	57.2	58.5	59.3	60.2	60.2	59.3	58.7	59.3	61.0	61.5	61.8	61.7	59.9
1992	60.3	61.8	62.2	62.8	62.3	61.6	63.3	63.9	64.3	65.4	65.8	65.6	63.3
1993	64.3	65.6	65.8	65.8	65.5	65.4	65.9	65.9	67.0	67.6	68.3	68.1	66.3
1994	67.0	68.2	68.7	69.9	69.7	68.5	69.6	70.1	71.5	73.2	73.8	73.7	70.3
1995	72.4	73.6	74.0	74.6	75.2	74.0	74.5	75.2	76.9	78.5	78.8	78.7	75.5
1996	76.7	77.5	78.3	79.1	79.4	77.9	77.8	79.1	80.5	81.8	81.9	81.8	79.3
1997	80.8	81.3	82.3	83.1	82.9	81.3	81.9	82.6	85.1	85.7	86.0	85.9	83.2
1998	85.1	86.7	87.1	86.9	86.3	85.7	84.6	85.6	87.6	88.2	88.5	88.0	86.7
1999	85.4	86.6	86.7	87.1	87.3	86.1	85.6	86.8	89.0	88.1	88.0	88.0	87.1
2000	87.0	88.6	88.3	87.7	87.8	86.4	85.9	86.7	89.3	88.0	88.3	88.1	87.7
2001	87.2	89.4	90.0	89.5	90.2	89.7	89.1	90.7	91.8	92.5	93.0	92.9	90.5
2002	91.7	93.3	93.6	93.9	94.2	93.0	92.2	93.8	95.7	96.0	96.5	96.5	94.2
2003	94.9	96.0	96.2	96.5	96.4	96.4	94.9	96.3	98.2	97.4	97.6	97.7	96.5
Leisure and hospitality													
1990	51.2	51.8	53.5	54.9	56.8	58.2	57.7	57.3	55.5	53.9	52.8	52.0	54.6
1991	49.9	51.2	52.9	53.7	55.2	56.9	57.4	57.0	56.5	54.7	54.5	53.8	54.5
1992	52.5	54.9	56.6	58.5	60.4	61.8	63.3	62.9	61.1	58.6	58.1	56.9	58.8
1993	54.8	57.6	59.7	61.7	63.3	65.8	65.3	64.7	61.7	59.7	58.1	58.2	60.9
1994	57.9	60.2	61.9	64.2	65.7	67.3	67.8	66.6	64.5	63.2	63.0	63.6	63.8
1995	61.2	63.7	66.1	68.0	70.4	72.0	71.4	70.8	68.7	65.5	65.2	64.9	67.3
1996	62.9	65.3	67.0	67.6	69.7	71.8	70.9	70.6	68.4	66.6	66.4	66.3	67.8
1997	64.0	66.4	69.5	70.9	73.3	75.5	74.6	74.4	73.2	70.2	69.8	69.3	70.9
1998	68.5	69.6	71.2	72.9	74.5	76.2	76.8	75.7	74.0	72.0	70.8	70.9	72.8
1999	69.8	70.5	72.1	76.3	77.5	79.2	78.7	77.7	75.9	73.2	73.1	72.4	74.7
2000	72.7	74.4	77.0	77.7	78.5	79.9	78.9	78.5	76.7	74.2	73.6	73.9	76.3
2001	71.9	74.7	76.8	78.2	81.0	83.5	82.6	82.1	79.2	76.9	75.1	74.5	78.0
2002	73.5	76.4	79.3	80.4	82.6	84.9	85.0	84.9	81.8	78.6	77.1	76.9	80.1
2003	75.5	77.5	79.9	81.0	82.5	84.9	84.9	84.3	81.3	78.6	77.4	77.1	80.4

Employment by Industry: Texas—*Continued*

(Numbers in thousands. Not seasonally adjusted.)

Industry	January	February	March	April	May	June	July	August	September	October	November	December	Annual Average
SAN ANTONIO—*Continued*													
Other services													
1990	21.0	21.0	21.0	21.0	21.6	22.0	21.8	21.9	21.8	21.7	21.8	21.6	21.5
1991	20.7	20.6	21.0	21.0	21.3	21.7	22.1	22.0	21.9	21.8	21.7	21.7	21.5
1992	21.3	21.4	21.6	21.7	22.0	22.2	22.2	22.0	21.9	22.0	21.9	22.0	21.9
1993	22.4	22.6	22.6	22.7	22.7	23.1	23.4	23.2	23.1	22.7	22.7	22.8	22.8
1994	22.5	22.7	22.9	23.4	23.4	23.8	24.0	23.7	23.5	23.8	23.7	23.9	23.4
1995	23.4	23.6	23.6	23.9	24.4	24.3	24.3	24.3	24.2	24.0	24.2	24.0	24.0
1996	23.8	23.9	24.0	24.4	24.6	25.1	25.2	25.2	25.1	25.1	25.4	25.1	24.7
1997	24.6	25.0	25.5	25.6	25.7	26.3	26.2	26.1	25.9	25.6	25.7	25.5	25.6
1998	25.3	25.4	25.6	25.8	26.2	26.5	26.7	26.7	26.6	26.6	26.4	26.5	26.2
1999	26.2	26.4	26.5	26.6	26.9	27.3	27.6	27.5	27.4	26.9	26.9	26.8	26.9
2000	26.4	26.6	26.8	27.1	27.3	27.9	27.8	27.7	27.6	26.8	26.9	27.1	27.2
2001	26.7	26.9	27.3	27.1	27.4	28.0	27.8	27.8	27.4	26.9	27.2	26.9	27.2
2002	26.7	27.1	27.3	27.5	27.8	28.3	27.8	27.9	27.9	27.5	28.0	27.7	27.6
2003	27.1	27.1	27.5	27.3	27.4	27.8	27.4	27.3	27.0	26.7	26.9	26.9	27.2
Government													
1990	120.7	122.3	122.5	121.9	123.2	120.2	112.7	113.1	119.6	121.9	122.3	121.9	120.2
1991	121.0	122.0	121.9	122.2	122.2	119.5	113.8	115.4	125.0	123.3	124.5	124.8	121.3
1992	123.1	124.3	124.9	126.4	126.9	123.9	118.0	118.3	125.5	126.5	127.4	127.4	124.4
1993	126.5	128.1	128.1	127.9	128.3	123.8	118.0	119.4	125.9	128.1	128.9	130.0	126.1
1994	128.4	129.9	129.7	129.0	129.8	126.2	121.1	121.1	129.6	129.2	130.1	130.4	127.9
1995	128.3	130.4	130.8	130.8	131.7	128.9	124.1	124.9	130.6	131.2	132.0	132.2	129.7
1996	130.8	132.6	132.8	132.8	133.4	130.1	123.2	126.3	132.5	133.7	134.8	134.7	131.5
1997	132.9	135.1	135.4	135.2	135.4	132.0	125.9	129.4	134.5	136.2	136.2	136.3	133.7
1998	134.9	135.5	136.4	135.7	135.9	130.7	127.0	130.9	135.3	135.2	135.7	135.6	134.1
1999	134.8	136.3	136.1	135.9	136.1	131.6	125.4	128.4	132.9	132.7	132.9	132.6	133.0
2000	131.8	134.1	134.5	134.8	137.1	130.4	125.4	126.3	131.1	132.5	133.0	132.8	132.0
2001	131.7	133.2	133.5	133.7	133.8	131.0	124.8	127.9	132.1	133.1	134.5	134.4	131.9
2002	132.7	135.7	136.1	135.8	136.6	131.8	126.0	128.0	134.1	136.7	137.3	137.0	134.0
2003	134.7	137.2	137.1	137.7	137.8	133.6	128.7	130.1	133.7	136.1	136.9	136.5	135.0
Federal government													
1990	44.3	44.6	44.8	44.6	45.7	45.6	45.6	44.9	43.2	43.7	43.5	43.3	44.5
1991	42.9	42.8	42.6	42.7	42.8	43.2	43.7	43.5	43.5	43.2	43.3	43.5	43.1
1992	43.6	43.5	43.8	43.5	43.5	43.3	43.3	43.0	43.0	42.8	42.7	43.0	43.3
1993	42.7	42.6	42.2	41.8	41.8	41.8	41.8	41.5	40.5	40.4	40.5	40.7	41.5
1994	40.4	40.5	39.7	39.8	40.0	40.0	39.9	39.1	38.9	38.5	38.7	38.9	39.5
1995	38.1	38.2	38.2	38.2	38.7	39.1	39.0	38.6	38.3	37.8	37.8	38.0	38.3
1996	37.8	38.1	38.2	38.4	38.4	38.6	38.7	38.6	38.5	38.2	38.5	38.7	38.4
1997	38.5	38.6	38.7	38.8	38.9	39.0	39.0	38.7	38.7	38.4	38.3	38.6	38.7
1998	38.2	38.0	37.8	37.2	37.3	37.2	37.3	37.0	36.7	36.1	36.0	36.0	37.1
1999	35.9	35.7	35.6	35.3	35.3	35.1	34.3	33.7	32.2	32.0	31.9	32.0	34.1
2000	31.8	32.1	32.2	32.3	34.5	31.7	32.4	30.9	29.8	29.4	29.2	29.4	31.3
2001	29.1	29.1	29.1	28.6	28.6	29.0	29.1	28.8	28.6	28.4	28.3	28.0	28.7
2002	27.8	28.1	28.1	28.1	28.2	28.5	28.6	28.3	28.5	28.7	28.6	28.7	28.4
2003	28.5	28.9	28.7	28.6	28.5	28.5	28.4	28.2	27.8	27.8	27.7	27.7	28.3
State government													
1990	11.9	11.9	12.0	12.2	12.1	12.3	12.3	12.2	12.4	12.5	12.6	12.5	12.2
1991	12.8	12.8	12.8	12.7	12.8	12.9	12.9	12.9	12.8	12.8	12.9	12.9	12.8
1992	13.1	13.0	13.1	13.5	13.5	13.4	13.5	13.4	13.5	13.6	13.8	13.6	13.4
1993	13.8	13.8	13.8	13.8	13.8	13.6	13.9	13.8	13.6	13.6	13.7	13.9	13.8
1994	14.0	14.0	14.2	14.1	14.1	13.8	14.0	13.8	14.3	14.3	14.5	14.4	14.1
1995	14.7	14.8	14.7	14.7	14.6	14.4	14.7	14.4	15.0	14.9	14.8	14.8	14.7
1996	15.0	14.8	14.7	14.8	14.8	14.3	14.3	14.2	14.9	14.8	14.9	14.8	14.7
1997	14.9	15.0	15.1	14.9	14.8	14.4	14.5	14.3	14.8	14.9	14.9	14.8	14.8
1998	14.9	14.9	14.9	14.9	14.7	14.3	14.5	14.2	15.0	15.1	15.1	14.9	14.8
1999	15.1	15.1	15.1	15.2	15.2	14.6	14.3	14.2	15.0	15.1	15.1	15.0	14.9
2000	15.0	15.0	15.0	14.9	14.9	14.3	14.3	14.2	14.7	14.9	15.1	15.0	14.8
2001	14.9	15.2	15.2	15.2	15.3	14.5	14.6	14.5	15.2	15.3	15.3	15.3	15.0
2002	15.3	15.5	15.4	15.4	15.5	14.1	14.7	14.6	15.3	15.4	15.4	15.5	15.2
2003	15.4	15.6	15.6	15.5	15.5	14.6	14.7	14.5	15.2	15.3	15.4	15.3	15.2
Local government													
1990	64.5	65.8	65.7	65.1	65.4	62.3	54.8	56.0	64.0	65.7	66.2	66.1	63.5
1991	65.3	66.4	66.5	66.8	66.6	63.4	57.2	59.0	68.7	67.3	68.3	68.4	65.3
1992	66.4	67.8	68.0	69.4	69.9	67.2	61.2	61.9	69.0	70.1	70.9	70.8	67.7
1993	70.0	71.7	72.1	72.3	72.7	68.4	62.3	64.1	71.8	74.1	74.7	75.4	70.8
1994	74.0	75.4	75.8	75.1	75.7	72.4	67.2	68.2	76.4	76.4	76.9	77.1	74.2
1995	75.5	77.4	77.9	77.9	78.4	75.4	70.4	71.9	77.3	78.5	79.4	79.4	76.6
1996	78.0	79.7	79.9	79.6	80.2	77.2	70.2	73.5	79.1	80.7	81.4	81.2	78.4
1997	79.5	81.5	81.6	81.5	81.7	78.6	72.4	76.4	81.0	82.9	83.0	82.9	80.3
1998	81.8	82.6	83.7	83.6	83.9	79.2	75.2	79.7	83.6	84.0	84.6	84.7	82.2
1999	83.8	85.5	85.4	85.4	85.6	81.9	76.8	80.5	85.7	85.6	85.9	85.6	84.0
2000	85.0	87.0	87.3	87.6	87.7	84.4	78.7	81.2	86.6	88.2	88.7	88.4	85.9
2001	87.7	88.9	89.2	89.9	89.9	87.5	81.1	84.6	88.3	89.4	90.9	91.1	88.2
2002	89.6	92.1	92.6	92.3	92.9	89.2	82.7	85.1	90.3	92.6	93.3	92.8	90.5
2003	90.8	92.7	92.8	93.6	93.8	90.5	85.6	87.4	90.7	93.0	93.8	93.5	91.5

Average Weekly Hours by Industry: Texas

(Not seasonally adjusted.)

Industry	January	February	March	April	May	June	July	August	September	October	November	December	Annual Average
STATEWIDE													
Natural resources and mining													
2001	46.0	47.7	47.2	49.1	48.0	48.7	48.6	48.3	49.8	49.4	48.8	47.7	48.3
2002	46.0	45.9	46.1	45.4	46.5	47.5	46.1	47.5	45.3	45.7	43.8	45.1	45.9
2003	44.0	44.7	43.2	41.6	43.3	43.4	44.8	45.0	46.8	45.3	46.1	45.1	44.5
Manufacturing													
2001	42.4	41.7	41.8	40.4	41.6	41.5	41.6	41.7	41.7	41.3	41.7	41.9	41.6
2002	41.2	40.4	40.9	40.6	41.0	42.1	41.1	41.7	41.4	40.8	40.9	41.6	41.1
2003	41.6	41.3	41.7	41.1	41.3	41.5	41.0	41.7	41.5	41.2	41.4	41.5	41.4
Trade, transportation, and utilities													
2001	35.1	35.2	35.5	35.5	35.2	35.4	36.1	35.7	35.6	35.5	35.5	36.0	35.5
2002	35.1	35.3	35.1	35.3	35.1	35.5	35.1	34.9	34.5	34.3	34.1	34.5	34.9
2003	34.1	34.6	34.7	34.2	34.6	35.5	34.9	34.7	34.3	34.7	34.4	34.4	34.6
Wholesale trade													
2001	39.4	39.5	39.6	39.6	38.7	39.6	40.6	40.7	41.1	40.3	41.1	41.3	40.1
2002	39.5	39.5	38.5	39.1	38.4	39.2	38.3	38.0	37.1	36.8	36.8	37.6	38.2
2003	37.4	37.9	37.6	37.2	38.2	38.2	37.4	36.9	36.6	37.3	37.3	37.8	37.5
Retail trade													
2001	31.8	31.5	31.9	32.1	31.7	32.1	32.7	32.4	32.2	32.1	31.9	32.6	32.1
2002	32.1	32.3	32.3	32.0	32.3	32.8	32.5	32.0	31.7	31.7	31.3	31.7	32.1
2003	31.4	31.5	31.5	31.1	31.4	32.2	31.8	31.9	31.4	31.5	31.2	31.5	31.5
DALLAS													
Manufacturing													
2001	41.2	40.4	40.2	38.9	39.0	39.3	39.2	39.1	39.1	38.8	39.4	38.9	39.5
2002	39.2	39.3	39.6	39.3	39.4	39.6	39.1	39.7	39.4	38.9	39.3	39.1	39.3
2003	39.1	39.6	40.2	39.9	40.0	39.5	38.5	39.3	38.8	39.3	39.5	39.3	39.4
FT. WORTH-ARLINGTON													
Manufacturing													
2001	41.7	41.3	40.5	40.2	40.2	41.4	40.6	40.5	39.7	40.6	39.6	39.9	40.5
2002	40.0	38.9	40.1	40.1	39.6	40.1	40.0	41.4	41.1	40.6	40.1	40.2	40.2
2003	40.3	40.2	39.7	41.4	41.1	41.5	41.5	42.0	42.5	41.8	42.0	42.3	41.4
HOUSTON													
Manufacturing													
2001	45.2	44.1	45.2	43.3	45.2	44.4	44.5	43.3	43.9	43.8	44.2	44.6	44.3
2002	43.6	42.7	43.2	42.2	42.7	43.4	43.8	43.2	43.4	42.8	42.8	44.5	43.2
2003	43.7	43.3	43.7	42.9	42.5	43.5	42.9	42.0	42.7	42.1	42.8	42.3	42.9
SAN ANTONIO													
Manufacturing													
2001	41.8	40.1	40.4	40.4	40.7	40.4	40.2	39.8	38.9	39.0	38.6	37.8	39.9
2002	37.6	37.7	37.7	37.0	36.9	37.4	36.8	37.2	37.6	37.5	37.7	38.3	37.4
2003	38.4	37.9	37.9	38.0	39.3	39.4	39.1	39.3	39.4	39.1	39.0	39.5	38.9

Average Hourly Earnings by Industry: Texas

(Dollars, not seasonally adjusted.)

Industry	January	February	March	April	May	June	July	August	September	October	November	December	Annual Average
STATEWIDE													
Natural resources and mining													
2001	15.50	15.21	15.61	15.31	15.50	15.41	15.46	15.37	15.21	15.43	15.50	15.38	15.41
2002	15.42	15.39	15.46	15.42	15.45	15.56	15.66	15.53	15.37	15.46	15.41	15.56	15.47
2003	15.51	15.50	15.36	15.59	15.10	15.15	15.08	15.05	15.19	15.20	15.11	15.26	15.25
Manufacturing													
2001	14.07	14.02	14.14	14.02	13.98	14.03	14.07	14.03	14.04	13.97	14.00	14.05	14.04
2002	13.97	13.95	13.95	13.91	13.83	13.92	13.97	13.92	14.00	13.90	13.90	13.95	13.93
2003	13.95	13.87	13.91	13.97	13.95	13.91	13.97	13.94	13.93	13.92	14.01	13.98	13.94
Trade, transportation, and utilities													
2001	12.56	12.74	12.87	12.77	12.70	12.71	12.79	12.77	12.75	12.71	12.72	12.74	12.74
2002	12.80	12.74	12.75	12.82	12.72	12.83	12.78	12.76	12.89	12.93	12.88	12.88	12.81
2003	12.97	13.07	13.08	13.05	12.98	13.04	12.96	12.99	13.00	13.01	13.04	12.95	13.01
Wholesale trade													
2001	15.20	15.41	15.43	15.36	15.30	15.18	15.24	15.15	15.23	15.18	15.08	15.20	15.25
2002	15.31	15.33	15.25	15.35	15.25	15.31	15.40	15.44	15.49	15.50	15.58	15.61	15.40
2003	15.51	15.55	15.49	15.43	15.50	15.54	15.60	15.62	15.66	15.62	15.69	15.68	15.57
Retail trade													
2001	10.93	11.04	11.11	11.11	11.08	11.06	11.09	11.07	11.14	11.10	11.07	11.00	11.07
2002	11.04	11.04	11.03	11.03	11.00	11.00	10.99	10.97	10.99	11.00	10.94	10.91	10.99
2003	10.97	10.95	10.98	10.98	10.97	10.94	10.92	10.96	10.99	11.02	10.98	10.97	10.97
DALLAS													
Manufacturing													
2001	14.09	14.14	13.93	13.89	13.78	13.87	13.62	13.79	13.64	13.48	13.48	13.85	13.81
2002	13.95	14.09	14.05	13.80	13.65	13.73	13.86	13.85	13.70	13.60	13.61	13.63	13.80
2003	13.63	13.58	13.53	13.49	13.44	13.44	13.44	13.50	13.53	13.47	13.47	13.47	13.50
FT. WORTH-ARLINGTON													
Manufacturing													
2001	17.32	17.26	17.11	17.38	17.23	17.27	17.35	17.30	17.30	17.40	17.29	17.58	17.31
2002	17.73	17.63	17.73	17.87	17.78	17.61	17.55	17.48	17.52	17.51	17.33	17.38	17.59
2003	17.32	17.35	17.27	17.24	17.32	17.20	17.06	17.19	17.19	17.10	16.92	17.05	17.18
HOUSTON													
Manufacturing													
2001	16.94	17.09	17.16	17.11	17.10	17.09	17.20	17.18	17.30	17.08	17.11	16.99	17.11
2002	17.00	17.05	17.02	17.05	17.05	16.99	16.94	17.02	17.03	16.91	16.90	16.98	17.00
2003	17.00	17.01	17.05	17.17	17.09	17.04	17.15	17.20	17.23	17.33	17.37	17.38	17.16
SAN ANTONIO													
Manufacturing													
2001	10.57	10.68	10.75	10.77	10.76	10.78	10.81	10.75	10.68	10.66	10.70	10.66	10.71
2002	10.69	10.74	10.68	10.71	10.71	10.67	10.61	10.69	10.69	10.72	10.74	10.83	10.71
2003	10.80	10.80	10.81	10.82	10.86	10.83	10.85	10.86	10.88	10.94	10.93	10.89	10.85

Average Weekly Earnings by Industry: Texas

(Dollars, not seasonally adjusted.)

Industry	January	February	March	April	May	June	July	August	September	October	November	December	Annual Average
STATEWIDE													
Natural resources and mining													
2001	713.00	725.52	736.79	751.72	744.00	750.47	751.36	742.37	757.46	762.24	756.40	733.63	744.30
2002	709.32	706.40	712.71	700.07	718.43	739.10	721.93	737.68	696.26	706.52	674.96	701.76	710.07
2003	682.44	692.85	663.55	648.54	653.83	657.51	675.58	677.25	710.89	688.56	696.57	688.23	678.63
Manufacturing													
2001	596.57	584.63	591.05	566.41	581.57	582.25	585.31	585.05	585.47	576.96	583.80	588.70	584.06
2002	575.56	563.58	570.56	564.75	567.03	586.03	574.17	580.46	579.60	567.12	568.51	580.32	572.52
2003	580.32	572.83	580.05	574.17	576.14	577.27	572.77	581.30	578.10	573.50	580.01	580.17	577.12
Trade, transportation, and utilities													
2001	440.86	448.45	456.89	453.34	447.04	449.93	461.72	455.89	453.90	451.21	451.56	458.64	452.27
2002	449.28	449.72	447.53	452.55	446.47	455.47	448.58	445.32	444.71	443.50	439.21	444.36	447.07
2003	442.28	452.22	453.88	446.31	449.11	462.92	452.30	450.75	445.90	451.45	448.58	445.48	450.15
Wholesale trade													
2001	598.88	608.70	611.03	608.26	592.11	601.13	618.74	616.61	625.95	611.75	619.79	627.76	611.53
2002	604.75	605.54	587.13	600.19	585.60	600.15	589.82	586.72	574.68	570.40	573.34	586.94	588.28
2003	580.07	589.35	582.42	574.00	592.10	593.63	583.44	576.38	573.16	582.63	585.24	592.70	583.88
Retail trade													
2001	347.57	347.76	354.41	356.63	351.24	355.03	362.64	358.67	358.71	356.31	353.13	358.60	355.35
2002	354.38	356.59	356.27	352.96	355.30	360.80	357.18	351.04	348.38	348.70	342.42	345.85	352.78
2003	344.46	344.93	345.87	341.48	344.46	352.27	347.26	349.62	345.09	347.13	342.58	345.56	345.56
DALLAS													
Manufacturing													
2001	580.51	571.26	559.99	540.32	537.42	545.09	533.90	539.19	533.32	523.02	531.11	538.77	545.50
2002	546.84	553.74	556.38	542.34	537.81	543.71	541.93	549.85	539.78	529.04	534.87	532.93	542.34
2003	532.93	537.77	543.91	538.25	537.60	530.88	517.44	530.55	524.96	529.37	532.07	529.37	531.90
FT. WORTH-ARLINGTON													
Manufacturing													
2001	722.24	712.84	692.96	698.68	692.65	714.98	704.41	700.65	686.81	706.44	684.68	701.44	701.06
2002	709.20	685.81	710.97	716.59	704.09	706.16	702.00	723.67	720.07	710.91	694.93	698.68	707.12
2003	698.00	697.47	685.62	713.74	711.85	713.80	707.99	721.98	730.58	714.78	710.64	721.22	711.25
HOUSTON													
Manufacturing													
2001	765.69	753.67	775.63	740.86	772.92	758.80	765.40	743.89	759.47	748.10	756.26	757.75	757.97
2002	741.20	728.04	735.26	719.51	728.04	737.37	741.97	735.26	739.10	723.75	723.32	755.61	734.40
2003	742.90	736.53	745.09	736.59	726.33	741.24	735.74	722.40	735.72	729.59	743.44	735.17	736.16
SAN ANTONIO													
Manufacturing													
2001	441.83	428.27	434.30	435.11	437.93	435.51	434.56	427.85	415.45	415.74	413.02	402.95	427.33
2002	401.94	404.90	402.64	396.27	395.20	399.06	390.45	397.67	401.94	402.00	404.90	414.79	400.55
2003	414.72	409.32	409.70	411.16	426.80	426.70	424.24	426.80	428.67	427.75	426.27	430.16	422.07

UTAH AT A GLANCE

(Population and total nonfarm employment numbers in thousands)

Population, Census 2000:	2,233.2
Total nonfarm employment, 2003:	1,073.8
Change in total nonfarm employment	
(Number)	
1990–2003:	350.2
1990–2001:	357.7
2001–2003:	-7.5
(Compound annual rate of change)	
1990–2003:	3.1%
1990–2001:	3.7%
2001–2003:	-0.3%
Unemployment rate	
1990:	4.4%
2001:	4.4%
2003:	5.7%

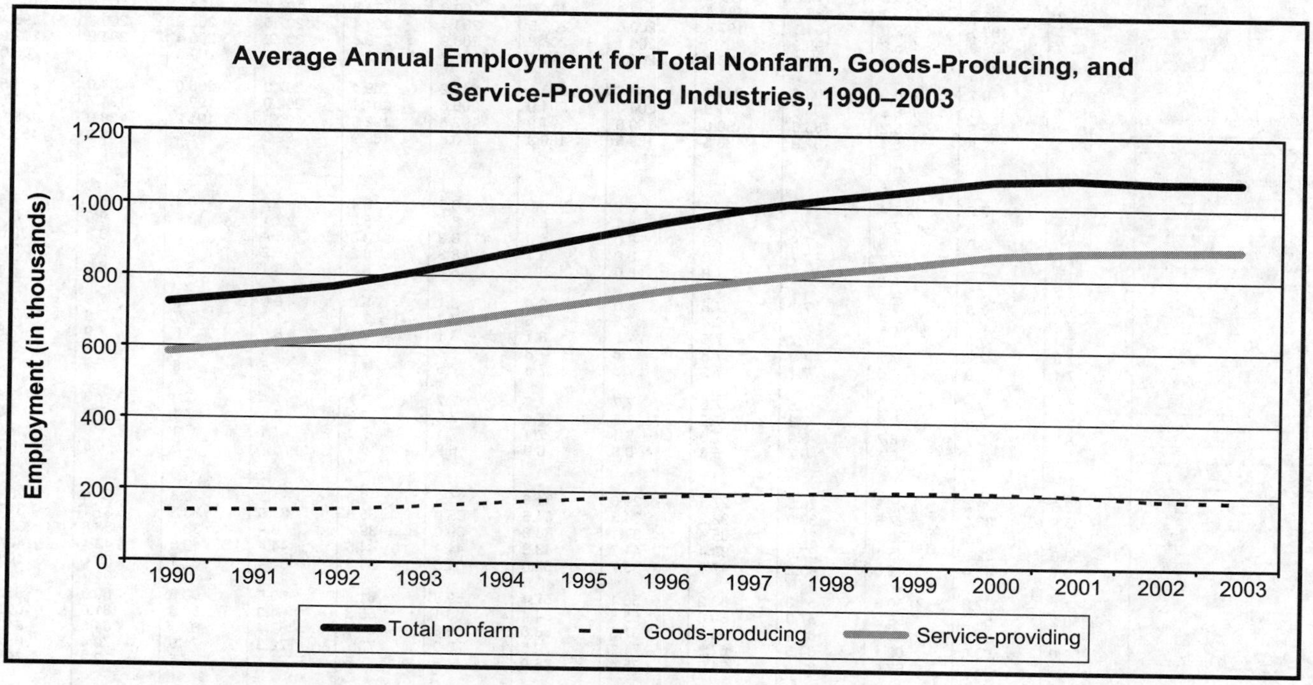

Following the pattern of many of the western states, total nonfarm payroll employment rose steadily in the 1990s and edged off slightly following the 2001 recession. Goods-producing employment, which peaked in 1999, continued to decline each year thereafter, losing about 20,000 jobs by 2003. The service-providing sector experienced job growth throughout the period, albeit at a slower rate from 2001 to 2003.

Employment by Industry: Utah

(Numbers in thousands. Not seasonally adjusted.)

Industry	January	February	March	April	May	June	July	August	September	October	November	December	Annual Average
STATEWIDE													
Total nonfarm													
1990	697.9	700.7	707.6	716.1	720.6	729.6	717.7	724.3	737.0	739.4	745.4	747.3	723.6
1991	724.9	729.6	735.4	737.1	743.5	750.5	739.8	745.5	755.7	756.5	762.7	762.4	745.3
1992	742.6	748.3	754.7	759.8	766.5	771.9	762.9	769.2	779.9	783.5	790.6	793.9	768.6
1993	774.5	780.5	789.8	798.2	803.2	814.6	806.3	813.3	825.5	831.1	837.4	843.2	809.8
1994	823.3	829.4	838.8	846.9	853.9	864.8	856.1	864.4	878.7	878.6	888.1	893.7	859.7
1995	870.8	880.2	890.0	895.6	899.4	911.0	901.1	910.5	928.3	925.8	935.7	942.5	907.5
1996	921.0	927.9	935.5	942.4	949.4	959.9	948.8	958.2	970.6	969.5	982.9	987.1	954.4
1997	960.5	970.2	980.7	985.0	992.0	998.8	988.6	993.2	1007.7	1007.1	1016.9	1021.7	993.5
1998	992.4	1002.3	1009.7	1014.7	1019.9	1029.5	1018.8	1025.0	1038.4	1035.8	1043.9	1047.8	1023.2
1999	1016.6	1025.6	1035.1	1043.8	1044.2	1055.4	1042.2	1048.6	1062.8	1062.1	1069.9	1075.5	1048.5
2000	1044.9	1053.3	1063.1	1071.1	1074.0	1083.5	1067.3	1073.8	1088.4	1089.0	1094.5	1101.7	1075.4
2001	1069.2	1072.9	1080.2	1083.5	1084.3	1091.3	1073.4	1078.4	1088.4	1083.5	1085.3	1085.7	1081.3
2002	1062.8	1069.6	1065.7	1073.4	1072.0	1077.1	1063.3	1066.5	1079.1	1080.3	1084.4	1087.1	1073.4
2003	1058.2	1059.0	1062.3	1069.7	1070.6	1076.5	1064.3	1071.6	1083.0	1085.5	1090.0	1094.6	1073.8
Total private													
1990	547.9	549.3	555.6	562.2	564.9	576.3	575.9	583.5	588.0	586.2	591.9	595.5	573.1
1991	571.9	574.3	580.1	580.7	585.4	595.3	594.5	600.4	602.4	599.7	605.0	606.9	591.3
1992	586.4	589.8	596.2	599.9	605.0	613.4	615.9	622.1	624.1	623.8	630.0	634.7	611.7
1993	614.7	618.5	627.4	636.0	639.8	652.5	656.8	663.8	667.5	669.7	675.2	682.0	650.3
1994	661.7	665.8	675.3	682.2	688.2	701.3	705.5	714.2	718.1	714.1	723.3	729.8	698.2
1995	707.7	714.4	723.4	727.6	731.0	744.9	748.6	758.8	766.1	760.3	768.7	776.7	744.0
1996	755.6	759.0	765.8	771.2	777.6	790.9	794.4	803.6	805.1	800.6	810.9	816.4	787.5
1997	790.2	796.0	805.5	809.0	814.7	824.4	827.7	833.3	836.5	832.4	839.9	845.4	821.3
1998	818.4	823.7	830.2	835.2	838.9	851.0	853.2	860.1	859.9	856.5	862.9	867.6	846.5
1999	840.1	844.1	851.9	860.2	860.0	874.3	876.6	882.3	882.0	879.1	885.7	891.9	869.0
2000	863.7	866.4	874.6	880.7	882.2	895.7	894.7	901.7	902.7	900.5	905.2	912.1	890.0
2001	882.6	881.0	887.5	889.5	890.1	898.0	896.4	901.3	897.1	890.1	890.4	890.7	891.2
2002	868.5	874.6	867.7	874.5	874.4	879.3	878.9	883.6	883.3	882.5	885.9	888.7	878.5
2003	860.1	859.3	862.4	868.6	870.8	878.5	879.3	886.6	885.8	886.2	889.3	893.6	876.7
Goods-producing													
1990	131.2	131.2	132.6	136.4	138.2	142.0	143.1	145.3	146.1	145.0	144.5	143.6	139.9
1991	136.2	136.8	138.6	138.8	141.2	144.0	144.3	145.9	147.7	145.9	145.5	143.0	142.3
1992	138.2	137.9	139.7	141.3	144.4	147.6	149.0	150.8	151.0	151.1	150.6	149.2	145.9
1993	143.6	143.6	146.8	149.8	152.3	156.4	158.1	160.4	161.2	161.8	161.6	160.5	154.6
1994	155.9	155.9	158.8	161.8	165.2	169.7	172.2	175.0	176.5	175.9	176.0	174.7	168.1
1995	169.4	170.4	173.8	174.8	177.0	181.1	181.1	184.2	187.4	186.9	188.3	188.7	180.2
1996	182.2	181.3	183.2	185.5	188.5	193.0	194.0	196.8	196.6	194.4	194.4	193.2	190.2
1997	187.5	189.1	192.0	194.1	197.4	200.6	202.5	204.4	203.4	202.6	203.0	200.8	198.1
1998	193.9	195.0	196.8	198.9	201.8	206.1	206.8	208.9	208.6	206.2	206.4	204.9	202.9
1999	196.4	197.4	199.8	203.2	205.0	209.7	210.5	211.7	212.0	209.9	209.6	206.9	206.0
2000	200.2	199.7	200.9	203.6	205.4	209.6	208.8	210.2	209.4	207.3	206.0	204.5	205.5
2001	198.4	197.1	198.5	198.5	201.3	204.2	204.9	206.5	204.1	202.0	199.6	194.7	200.8
2002	185.4	182.0	183.2	185.6	188.6	190.8	191.9	192.8	192.5	192.3	191.2	188.9	188.8
2003	181.3	179.8	180.4	182.9	186.5	188.6	189.3	190.8	189.9	189.2	188.4	185.9	186.1
Natural resources and mining													
1990	7.5	7.5	7.4	7.7	7.9	7.9	8.0	8.2	8.4	8.2	8.1	8.1	7.9
1991	7.7	7.8	7.8	7.7	7.9	8.1	8.3	8.3	8.3	8.1	8.2	8.0	8.0
1992	8.0	8.0	7.8	7.8	7.9	8.0	8.0	8.3	8.3	8.4	8.3	8.2	8.0
1993	7.8	7.7	7.7	7.7	7.8	8.0	8.1	8.3	8.2	8.2	8.3	8.3	8.0
1994	7.8	7.7	7.7	7.7	7.8	8.0	8.1	8.2	8.2	8.1	8.1	8.1	7.9
1995	7.6	7.6	7.6	7.7	7.8	8.0	8.0	8.1	8.2	8.0	8.0	7.9	7.8
1996	7.2	7.2	7.2	7.3	7.4	7.5	7.6	7.7	7.7	7.7	7.7	7.6	7.4
1997	7.4	7.5	7.6	7.7	7.5	7.7	8.1	8.1	8.1	8.0	8.0	7.9	7.8
1998	7.8	7.7	7.7	7.6	7.6	7.8	7.8	7.8	7.7	7.5	7.5	7.4	7.7
1999	7.1	7.0	7.0	7.1	7.2	7.3	7.4	7.5	7.5	7.5	7.5	7.3	7.3
2000	7.2	7.2	7.3	7.5	7.6	7.7	7.7	7.7	7.7	7.4	7.3	7.3	7.5
2001	7.2	7.2	7.3	7.3	7.5	7.5	7.4	7.5	7.3	7.1	7.1	7.0	7.3
2002	6.7	6.7	6.7	6.9	7.0	7.1	7.1	7.1	7.2	7.1	7.1	7.0	7.0
2003	6.6	6.5	6.6	6.7	6.8	6.8	6.9	6.8	6.8	6.7	6.6	6.5	6.7
Construction													
1990	23.6	23.4	24.3	26.5	27.8	29.6	31.0	31.9	32.0	31.5	30.8	29.5	28.4
1991	25.9	26.3	27.5	30.0	32.2	34.3	34.5	35.9	35.8	34.5	33.3	31.1	31.7
1992	28.9	29.1	30.8	33.4	35.4	37.1	38.3	39.0	39.2	38.9	38.1	36.8	35.4
1993	33.0	32.9	35.1	37.5	39.4	41.7	43.3	44.4	44.5	44.4	43.8	42.4	40.2
1994	40.1	40.4	42.8	45.2	47.8	50.7	52.0	53.6	54.3	53.4	52.1	50.4	48.5
1995	47.1	47.9	50.3	51.3	53.2	56.1	57.4	59.8	61.5	60.8	60.6	60.3	55.5
1996	56.2	54.9	56.2	57.9	60.6	63.6	64.4	66.1	65.3	64.0	63.5	61.8	61.2
1997	56.9	57.6	60.0	62.1	65.4	67.6	68.8	69.8	68.8	67.4	67.1	64.8	64.7
1998	59.6	60.6	62.1	64.5	67.8	71.1	72.5	73.9	73.7	72.3	71.9	70.4	68.4
1999	65.8	65.7	67.6	69.9	71.7	75.4	76.9	77.8	77.5	76.1	75.5	73.3	72.8
2000	68.0	67.9	68.9	71.0	72.8	75.8	75.5	76.5	75.4	74.1	72.7	71.3	72.5
2001	65.9	65.4	66.8	68.3	71.2	74.1	75.2	77.0	75.7	75.0	73.7	70.5	71.6
2002	63.9	61.5	62.9	65.1	67.6	69.5	70.8	71.6	71.4	71.3	70.4	68.3	67.9
2003	62.6	62.0	62.5	64.5	67.4	69.2	70.3	71.7	71.0	70.4	69.4	67.1	67.3

Employment by Industry: Utah—*Continued*

(Numbers in thousands. Not seasonally adjusted.)

Industry	January	February	March	April	May	June	July	August	September	October	November	December	Annual Average
STATEWIDE—*Continued*													
Manufacturing													
1990	100.1	100.3	100.9	102.2	102.5	104.5	104.1	105.2	105.7	105.3	105.6	106.0	103.5
1991	102.6	102.7	103.3	101.1	101.1	101.6	101.5	101.7	103.6	103.3	104.0	103.9	102.5
1992	101.3	100.8	101.1	100.1	101.1	102.5	102.7	103.5	103.5	103.8	104.2	104.2	102.4
1993	102.8	103.0	104.0	104.6	105.1	106.7	106.7	107.7	108.5	109.2	109.5	109.8	106.4
1994	108.0	107.8	108.3	108.9	109.6	111.0	112.1	113.2	114.0	114.4	115.8	116.2	111.6
1995	114.7	114.9	115.9	115.8	116.0	117.0	115.7	116.3	117.7	118.1	119.7	120.5	116.8
1996	118.8	119.2	119.8	120.3	120.5	121.9	122.0	123.0	123.6	122.7	123.2	123.8	121.5
1997	123.2	124.0	124.4	124.3	124.5	125.3	125.6	126.5	126.5	127.2	127.9	128.1	125.6
1998	126.5	126.7	127.0	126.8	126.4	127.2	126.5	127.2	127.2	126.4	127.0	127.1	126.8
1999	123.5	124.7	125.2	126.2	126.1	127.0	126.2	126.4	127.0	126.3	126.6	126.3	126.0
2000	125.0	124.6	124.7	125.1	125.0	126.1	125.6	126.0	126.3	125.8	126.0	125.9	125.5
2001	125.3	124.5	124.4	122.9	122.6	122.6	122.3	122.0	121.1	119.9	118.8	117.2	122.0
2002	114.8	113.8	113.6	113.6	114.0	114.2	114.0	114.1	113.9	113.9	113.7	113.6	113.9
2003	112.1	111.3	111.3	111.7	112.3	112.6	112.1	112.3	112.1	112.1	112.4	112.3	112.1
Service-providing													
1990	566.7	569.5	575.0	579.7	582.4	587.6	574.6	579.0	590.9	594.4	600.9	603.7	583.7
1991	588.7	592.8	596.8	598.3	602.3	606.5	595.5	599.6	608.0	610.6	617.2	619.4	602.9
1992	604.4	610.4	615.0	618.5	622.1	624.3	613.9	618.4	628.9	632.4	640.0	644.7	622.7
1993	630.9	636.9	643.0	648.4	650.9	658.2	648.2	652.9	664.3	669.3	675.8	682.7	655.1
1994	667.4	673.5	680.0	685.1	688.7	695.1	683.9	689.4	702.2	702.7	712.1	719.0	691.5
1995	701.4	709.8	716.2	720.8	722.4	729.9	720.0	726.3	740.9	738.9	747.4	753.8	727.3
1996	738.8	746.6	752.3	756.9	760.9	766.9	754.8	761.4	774.0	775.1	788.5	793.9	764.1
1997	773.0	781.1	788.7	790.9	794.6	798.2	786.1	788.8	804.3	804.5	813.9	820.9	795.4
1998	798.5	807.3	812.9	815.8	818.1	823.4	812.0	816.1	829.8	829.6	837.5	842.9	820.3
1999	820.2	828.2	835.3	840.6	839.2	845.7	831.7	836.9	850.8	852.2	860.3	868.6	842.5
2000	844.7	853.6	862.2	867.5	868.6	873.9	858.5	863.6	879.0	881.7	888.5	897.2	869.9
2001	870.8	875.8	881.7	885.0	883.0	887.1	868.5	871.9	884.3	881.5	885.7	891.0	880.5
2002	877.4	887.6	882.5	887.8	883.4	886.3	871.4	873.7	886.6	888.0	893.2	898.2	884.7
2003	876.9	879.2	881.9	886.8	884.1	887.9	875.0	880.8	893.1	896.3	901.6	908.7	887.7
Trade, transportation, and utilities													
1990	150.5	148.9	149.8	148.9	150.1	152.9	152.7	154.5	156.1	156.6	160.8	163.0	153.7
1991	155.0	152.6	153.1	153.1	154.4	157.1	156.2	157.5	157.9	158.1	163.1	165.6	156.9
1992	157.7	156.7	157.6	157.9	159.6	161.6	161.6	162.5	162.9	163.7	168.4	171.6	161.8
1993	162.8	162.0	163.0	164.8	165.7	168.5	169.8	171.4	172.0	173.5	178.4	182.2	169.5
1994	173.0	171.9	173.1	173.5	176.0	179.6	180.6	182.5	183.2	183.3	189.4	192.3	179.8
1995	183.6	182.9	184.2	185.2	185.9	188.3	189.1	190.9	192.1	191.7	197.3	200.7	189.3
1996	191.7	190.4	190.9	191.1	192.8	195.5	196.3	197.9	197.1	198.3	204.9	208.8	196.3
1997	198.6	198.1	199.4	199.6	200.3	202.2	204.1	203.4	205.8	207.2	212.8	217.6	204.1
1998	207.8	206.5	207.3	206.9	207.6	209.5	210.3	211.9	212.2	213.0	218.7	222.3	211.2
1999	212.0	209.7	211.0	212.5	212.5	214.1	214.9	216.0	215.7	216.8	222.2	226.9	215.4
2000	216.9	214.7	215.7	216.4	216.5	219.1	219.3	220.9	221.6	223.4	228.1	231.4	220.3
2001	219.8	218.1	218.6	219.0	218.7	218.9	218.4	218.8	217.6	217.1	220.7	222.4	219.0
2002	214.2	212.5	211.7	213.5	215.2	215.5	215.3	216.1	215.1	216.2	220.0	221.8	215.6
2003	211.1	209.6	210.0	210.5	212.1	212.7	212.7	214.2	213.8	215.1	219.0	221.8	213.6
Wholesale trade													
1990	28.0	28.0	28.2	28.7	28.7	29.0	29.3	29.6	29.7	29.7	30.0	29.9	29.0
1991	29.0	28.9	29.1	29.2	29.3	29.6	29.6	29.7	29.6	29.5	29.5	29.5	29.3
1992	29.1	29.1	29.4	29.4	29.5	29.7	29.7	29.7	29.7	29.8	29.8	29.8	29.5
1993	29.3	29.4	29.7	30.0	30.1	30.6	30.8	31.0	30.9	31.1	31.2	31.3	30.4
1994	30.5	30.6	30.8	31.2	31.5	32.2	32.4	32.5	32.9	33.0	33.2	33.2	32.0
1995	32.3	32.6	33.0	33.0	33.1	33.8	33.8	34.1	34.2	34.1	34.3	34.7	33.5
1996	34.0	34.1	34.3	34.2	34.4	35.0	35.3	35.4	35.4	35.7	36.0	36.3	35.0
1997	35.3	35.6	36.0	36.2	36.3	36.6	36.6	36.8	37.0	36.8	36.8	37.1	36.4
1998	36.6	36.9	37.3	37.7	37.9	38.1	38.0	38.2	38.2	37.8	38.1	38.1	37.7
1999	38.1	38.1	38.5	38.7	38.9	39.2	39.2	39.4	39.4	39.4	39.6	39.9	39.0
2000	39.5	39.7	39.9	39.9	40.1	40.5	40.7	40.8	40.9	41.1	41.0	41.3	40.5
2001	40.9	41.1	41.3	41.2	41.4	41.5	41.5	41.4	41.1	40.9	40.9	40.9	41.2
2002	39.9	40.0	40.0	40.1	40.6	40.5	40.5	40.6	40.4	40.5	40.4	40.5	40.3
2003	39.8	39.8	39.9	40.1	40.4	40.5	40.2	40.4	40.2	40.3	40.5	40.5	40.2
Retail trade													
1990	86.5	84.7	85.2	85.8	87.0	89.1	88.6	89.7	91.1	91.2	95.2	97.0	89.2
1991	91.0	89.1	89.5	89.4	90.4	92.3	91.1	92.2	92.8	93.3	98.0	100.2	92.4
1992	93.3	92.0	92.4	92.7	94.1	95.4	95.1	95.9	96.3	96.8	101.2	103.7	95.7
1993	96.2	95.1	95.5	96.9	97.6	99.1	99.8	100.6	100.6	101.8	106.1	109.4	99.8
1994	101.4	99.9	100.5	101.8	103.2	105.3	106.5	108.0	108.3	108.6	114.4	116.9	106.2
1995	109.7	108.8	109.8	110.5	111.4	112.9	113.8	114.9	115.8	115.5	120.6	123.0	113.8
1996	115.6	114.0	114.1	115.1	116.6	118.5	119.6	120.8	119.7	120.3	126.2	129.0	119.1
1997	120.8	119.9	120.6	120.2	121.2	122.6	123.0	123.7	123.5	124.5	129.5	132.8	123.5
1998	124.5	122.7	122.7	122.3	123.0	124.4	124.8	126.0	126.0	127.0	132.1	135.2	125.9
1999	126.8	124.6	125.2	126.6	127.1	128.4	128.5	129.5	129.0	129.7	134.7	138.2	129.0
2000	129.3	127.0	127.5	128.2	128.6	130.1	129.7	130.9	131.3	132.7	137.1	139.5	131.0
2001	131.6	129.8	130.0	130.6	130.8	131.0	130.4	130.8	129.9	129.7	133.9	135.5	131.2
2002	129.6	127.5	127.5	129.0	130.1	130.6	130.3	131.0	130.5	130.9	135.0	137.1	130.8
2003	127.7	126.3	126.7	127.1	128.2	128.8	128.9	130.1	129.9	130.7	134.9	137.3	129.7

Employment by Industry: Utah—*Continued*

(Numbers in thousands. Not seasonally adjusted.)

Industry	January	February	March	April	May	June	July	August	September	October	November	December	Annual Average
STATEWIDE—*Continued*													
Transportation and utilities													
1990	36.0	36.2	36.4	34.4	34.4	34.8	34.8	35.2	35.3	35.7	35.6	36.1	35.4
1991	35.0	34.6	34.5	34.5	34.7	35.2	35.5	35.6	35.5	35.3	35.6	35.9	35.1
1992	35.3	35.6	35.8	35.8	36.0	36.5	36.8	36.9	36.9	37.1	37.4	38.1	36.5
1993	37.3	37.5	37.8	37.9	38.0	38.8	39.2	39.8	40.5	40.6	41.1	41.5	39.1
1994	41.1	41.4	41.8	40.5	41.3	42.1	41.7	42.0	42.0	41.7	41.8	42.2	41.6
1995	41.6	41.5	41.4	41.7	41.4	41.6	41.5	41.9	42.1	42.1	42.4	43.0	41.8
1996	42.1	42.3	42.5	41.8	41.8	42.0	41.4	41.7	42.0	42.3	42.7	43.5	42.1
1997	42.5	42.6	42.8	43.2	42.8	43.0	44.5	42.9	45.3	45.9	46.5	47.7	44.1
1998	46.7	46.9	47.3	46.9	46.7	47.0	47.5	47.7	48.0	48.2	48.5	49.0	47.5
1999	47.1	47.0	47.3	47.2	46.5	46.5	47.2	47.1	47.3	47.7	47.9	48.8	47.3
2000	48.1	48.0	48.3	48.3	47.8	48.5	48.9	49.2	49.4	49.6	50.0	50.6	48.9
2001	47.3	47.2	47.3	47.2	46.5	46.4	46.5	46.6	46.6	46.5	45.9	46.0	46.7
2002	44.7	45.0	44.2	44.4	44.5	44.4	44.5	44.5	44.2	44.8	44.6	44.2	44.5
2003	43.6	43.5	43.4	43.3	43.5	43.4	43.6	43.7	43.7	44.1	43.6	44.0	43.6
Information													
1990	12.3	12.8	12.8	13.1	13.0	13.5	13.7	13.8	13.8	13.8	14.0	14.1	13.3
1991	12.8	12.7	12.7	12.7	12.8	13.0	13.4	13.5	13.2	13.5	13.5	13.4	13.1
1992	13.5	14.4	14.5	14.7	14.7	15.2	15.5	15.7	15.7	16.0	16.7	17.0	15.3
1993	16.4	16.7	16.9	17.0	17.3	17.8	17.5	17.7	17.7	17.9	18.2	18.5	17.4
1994	18.5	18.9	19.2	19.8	20.3	20.8	20.8	21.5	21.3	21.2	21.6	22.6	20.5
1995	20.9	21.3	21.5	21.2	21.4	22.1	23.1	23.4	23.6	22.9	22.8	23.0	22.2
1996	23.6	24.0	25.7	25.6	26.0	26.6	26.7	27.4	27.8	27.3	27.5	27.6	26.3
1997	26.1	26.7	27.3	27.0	27.4	27.8	27.9	28.2	28.3	28.0	28.1	28.4	27.6
1998	27.7	28.5	28.7	29.0	29.0	29.5	30.8	31.0	31.0	31.0	31.5	31.5	29.9
1999	31.0	31.6	31.4	31.8	31.9	32.9	33.0	33.5	33.6	34.2	35.1	34.7	32.9
2000	34.2	34.3	34.6	34.5	35.3	35.8	35.7	36.2	36.3	35.9	36.2	36.1	35.4
2001	34.5	33.9	33.8	33.8	34.1	34.2	33.7	33.4	33.0	32.5	32.9	32.5	33.5
2002	31.8	31.7	31.1	30.9	31.3	31.1	31.0	30.7	30.5	30.5	30.8	30.7	31.0
2003	30.1	30.0	29.9	29.4	30.1	30.3	30.1	30.2	30.0	30.1	30.5	30.6	30.1
Financial activities													
1990	34.1	34.3	34.5	34.6	34.3	34.8	34.8	35.2	35.3	34.9	35.1	35.4	34.7
1991	34.9	35.5	35.8	35.7	36.0	36.4	36.6	36.9	36.8	36.5	36.9	37.5	36.2
1992	37.3	37.5	37.7	37.8	37.9	38.0	38.2	38.4	38.7	38.8	39.0	39.7	38.2
1993	39.6	39.8	40.5	40.9	41.0	41.7	42.2	42.7	43.4	44.4	45.1	45.9	42.2
1994	45.7	46.1	46.8	46.5	46.2	46.4	46.3	46.6	46.8	46.3	46.7	47.2	46.4
1995	46.1	46.8	47.1	46.8	47.0	47.5	47.7	48.3	49.0	48.9	49.3	50.1	47.8
1996	49.7	50.0	50.6	50.8	50.8	51.1	51.0	51.3	51.6	51.6	52.4	53.2	51.1
1997	52.4	52.7	53.4	53.3	53.2	53.5	53.1	53.6	54.1	54.1	54.5	54.9	53.6
1998	54.2	54.4	54.8	55.2	55.2	55.9	56.6	56.9	57.2	57.5	57.6	58.0	56.1
1999	57.4	57.4	57.8	57.6	57.4	57.8	57.6	58.1	57.8	57.9	58.5	59.3	57.9
2000	58.6	58.4	58.7	58.5	58.3	58.6	58.9	59.2	59.2	59.3	59.8	60.6	59.0
2001	61.2	61.5	61.8	61.6	61.7	62.2	62.6	63.1	63.0	62.7	63.3	63.9	62.4
2002	63.4	63.4	62.9	63.0	63.3	63.4	63.0	63.3	62.9	63.7	63.8	64.6	63.4
2003	64.1	64.8	64.4	64.7	65.0	64.7	64.9	65.1	64.4	64.6	64.8	65.6	64.8
Professional and business services													
1990	70.6	70.5	71.8	72.7	73.4	75.4	75.0	76.6	77.0	77.9	78.9	78.8	74.8
1991	76.4	77.5	78.8	78.8	80.3	81.5	81.8	82.6	82.0	81.5	81.8	80.9	80.3
1992	75.9	76.8	77.7	78.6	79.2	80.1	80.4	82.0	81.9	82.2	83.1	82.7	80.0
1993	81.1	81.8	82.7	84.1	84.7	86.7	87.1	88.1	88.8	89.4	89.4	90.0	86.1
1994	87.4	88.5	90.5	91.8	92.1	93.6	94.7	96.2	97.0	96.6	97.9	99.0	93.7
1995	97.3	99.2	100.5	102.0	102.6	105.5	107.1	109.5	111.1	109.8	110.1	111.0	105.4
1996	108.4	110.0	109.3	110.8	112.9	115.4	116.5	118.4	119.3	118.9	120.0	120.5	115.0
1997	116.5	116.4	117.3	119.2	120.6	123.0	122.5	123.9	124.7	123.2	123.4	124.3	121.3
1998	119.4	120.5	121.8	123.7	124.2	127.1	126.6	127.6	127.6	128.2	128.5	128.7	125.3
1999	124.9	126.6	127.8	129.6	129.6	132.3	133.0	134.4	134.1	135.0	135.6	137.3	131.7
2000	131.1	132.4	134.8	136.8	137.0	140.0	139.1	140.7	141.6	142.0	141.6	142.7	138.3
2001	136.8	135.9	137.0	137.3	137.9	138.1	137.4	138.3	136.3	134.7	132.9	131.8	136.2
2002	129.5	132.7	129.6	131.2	132.4	132.6	132.1	133.4	133.3	132.9	133.1	132.0	132.1
2003	126.5	126.4	127.0	129.5	131.1	132.2	132.9	134.9	134.3	134.6	134.2	133.8	131.5
Educational and health services													
1990	65.5	67.0	67.5	68.0	67.2	66.6	65.5	65.8	68.2	69.6	70.1	70.2	67.6
1991	68.7	70.5	70.9	71.2	70.6	70.0	68.6	69.4	71.7	72.9	73.4	73.3	70.9
1992	72.1	73.9	74.4	74.4	73.9	73.1	72.4	72.9	75.3	76.9	77.4	77.5	74.5
1993	75.7	77.6	78.2	78.7	77.9	77.0	77.0	77.0	79.5	80.7	81.2	81.0	78.4
1994	79.2	80.9	81.3	81.3	80.7	79.8	79.3	80.0	82.4	83.4	84.1	84.2	81.3
1995	82.0	83.8	84.2	84.4	83.8	83.1	82.9	83.4	85.7	87.1	87.6	88.0	84.6
1996	86.1	88.2	89.2	89.2	88.5	87.8	87.2	87.5	90.3	91.5	92.6	92.5	89.2
1997	91.3	93.5	94.2	93.6	93.1	91.8	91.2	92.0	94.6	96.1	96.8	97.0	93.8
1998	94.8	97.0	97.6	97.3	96.7	95.4	94.7	94.9	97.1	98.8	99.4	99.3	96.9
1999	97.0	98.9	99.5	100.0	99.1	99.0	98.4	98.4	101.4	101.5	102.4	102.4	99.8
2000	99.9	102.6	103.1	103.8	103.4	102.5	101.7	102.4	105.1	106.2	107.4	108.2	103.9
2001	107.6	109.0	109.6	109.9	106.8	107.5	105.6	106.4	111.0	112.1	113.1	113.9	109.4
2002	111.7	112.9	113.4	114.5	110.8	110.7	110.0	111.6	116.3	117.6	118.1	119.2	113.9
2003	117.4	118.4	119.1	119.2	115.2	115.7	114.3	115.3	120.0	121.9	122.0	122.0	118.4

Employment by Industry: Utah—*Continued*

(Numbers in thousands. Not seasonally adjusted.)

Industry	January	February	March	April	May	June	July	August	September	October	November	December	Annual Average
STATEWIDE—*Continued*													
Leisure and hospitality													
1990	59.3	60.0	61.8	63.2	63.4	65.3	64.8	65.9	65.5	62.7	62.8	64.5	63.2
1991	62.2	62.9	64.4	64.6	64.1	66.8	66.7	67.7	66.8	65.3	64.7	67.1	65.2
1992	65.8	66.5	68.3	68.6	68.5	70.6	71.2	72.1	71.6	68.4	68.0	70.2	69.1
1993	68.8	70.0	72.0	73.2	73.2	75.9	76.2	77.4	76.2	73.6	72.6	75.1	73.6
1994	73.4	74.8	76.5	78.2	78.3	81.1	80.9	81.7	80.6	77.4	77.5	79.6	78.3
1995	78.6	79.9	81.7	83.0	82.9	86.2	86.2	87.4	85.9	82.1	82.3	84.0	83.3
1996	83.2	84.2	86.1	87.0	86.8	89.6	90.2	91.6	90.1	86.5	86.8	88.2	87.5
1997	86.2	87.7	89.9	90.2	90.5	93.0	93.4	94.7	93.1	89.1	89.2	90.1	90.6
1998	88.8	89.8	91.1	91.8	91.9	94.7	94.0	95.4	93.7	89.8	88.9	90.9	91.7
1999	89.6	90.6	92.6	93.7	92.8	96.4	96.6	97.8	95.8	92.6	91.4	93.7	93.6
2000	92.5	94.2	96.7	96.8	95.9	99.2	100.0	100.9	98.8	96.4	95.9	98.4	97.1
2001	94.9	96.0	98.5	99.2	98.9	101.4	101.5	102.1	100.2	97.1	95.7	99.1	98.7
2002	100.5	106.3	103.3	103.1	100.0	102.1	102.1	102.2	99.9	96.8	96.1	99.0	101.0
2003	97.7	98.4	99.5	100.2	98.4	101.5	101.9	102.7	100.8	98.1	97.6	101.1	99.8
Other services													
1990	24.4	24.6	24.8	25.3	25.3	25.8	26.3	26.4	26.0	25.7	25.7	25.9	25.5
1991	25.7	25.8	25.8	25.8	26.0	26.5	26.9	26.9	26.3	26.0	26.1	26.1	26.1
1992	25.9	26.1	26.3	26.6	26.8	27.2	27.6	27.7	27.0	26.7	26.8	26.8	26.7
1993	26.7	27.0	27.3	27.5	27.7	28.5	28.9	29.1	28.7	28.4	28.7	28.8	28.1
1994	28.6	28.8	29.1	29.3	29.4	30.3	30.7	30.7	30.3	30.0	30.1	30.2	29.7
1995	29.8	30.1	30.4	30.2	30.4	31.1	31.4	31.7	31.3	30.9	31.0	31.2	30.7
1996	30.7	30.9	30.8	31.2	31.3	31.9	32.5	32.7	32.3	32.1	32.3	32.4	31.7
1997	31.6	31.8	32.0	32.0	32.2	32.5	33.0	33.1	32.5	32.1	32.1	32.3	32.3
1998	31.8	32.0	32.1	32.4	32.5	32.8	33.4	33.5	32.5	32.0	31.9	32.0	32.4
1999	31.8	31.9	32.0	31.8	31.7	32.1	32.6	32.4	31.6	31.2	30.9	30.7	31.7
2000	30.3	30.1	30.1	30.3	30.4	30.9	31.2	31.2	30.7	30.0	30.2	30.2	30.5
2001	29.4	29.5	29.7	30.2	30.7	31.5	32.3	32.7	31.9	31.9	32.2	32.4	31.2
2002	32.0	33.1	32.5	32.7	32.8	33.1	33.5	33.5	32.8	32.5	32.8	32.5	32.8
2003	31.9	31.9	32.1	32.2	32.4	32.8	33.2	33.4	32.6	32.6	32.8	32.8	32.6
Government													
1990	150.0	151.4	152.0	153.9	155.7	153.3	141.8	140.8	149.0	153.2	153.5	151.8	150.5
1991	153.0	155.3	155.3	156.4	158.1	155.2	145.3	145.1	153.3	156.8	157.7	155.5	153.9
1992	156.2	158.5	158.5	159.9	161.5	158.5	147.0	147.1	155.8	159.7	160.6	159.2	156.8
1993	159.8	162.0	162.4	162.2	163.4	162.1	149.5	149.5	158.0	161.4	162.2	161.2	159.4
1994	161.6	163.6	163.5	164.7	165.7	163.5	150.6	150.2	160.6	164.5	164.8	163.9	161.4
1995	163.1	165.8	166.6	168.0	168.4	166.1	152.5	151.7	162.2	165.5	167.0	165.8	163.5
1996	165.4	168.9	169.7	171.2	171.8	169.0	154.4	154.6	165.5	168.9	172.0	170.7	166.8
1997	170.3	174.2	175.2	176.0	177.3	174.4	160.9	159.9	171.2	174.7	177.0	176.3	172.3
1998	174.0	178.6	179.5	179.5	181.0	178.5	165.6	164.9	178.5	179.3	181.0	180.2	176.7
1999	176.5	181.5	183.2	183.6	184.2	181.1	165.6	166.3	180.8	183.0	184.2	183.6	179.5
2000	181.2	186.9	188.5	190.4	191.8	187.8	172.6	172.1	185.7	188.5	189.3	189.6	185.4
2001	186.6	191.9	192.7	194.0	194.2	193.3	177.0	177.1	191.3	193.4	194.9	195.0	190.1
2002	194.3	195.0	198.0	198.9	197.6	197.8	184.4	182.9	195.8	197.8	198.5	198.4	195.0
2003	198.1	199.7	199.9	201.1	199.8	198.0	185.0	185.0	197.2	199.3	200.7	201.0	197.1
Federal government													
1990	39.8	40.0	40.4	41.1	41.3	41.7	41.4	40.4	39.8	39.0	38.2	38.6	40.1
1991	38.6	39.0	39.2	39.4	39.5	39.7	39.3	38.8	38.8	38.0	37.3	37.3	38.7
1992	38.2	38.7	38.7	38.6	38.6	38.6	38.0	37.6	37.3	36.5	35.8	36.0	37.7
1993	36.2	36.7	36.8	35.3	35.2	35.4	34.8	34.6	33.9	33.5	32.4	32.6	34.7
1994	32.6	33.1	33.2	33.4	32.9	33.4	33.1	33.1	32.7	32.2	31.5	31.6	32.7
1995	31.7	32.1	32.5	33.0	32.4	32.6	32.5	32.3	31.7	31.3	30.5	30.7	31.9
1996	30.6	31.8	32.1	32.4	31.9	32.0	31.7	31.4	31.1	30.2	30.1	30.5	31.3
1997	30.7	31.8	32.1	32.5	31.9	32.0	32.0	31.4	31.1	30.1	30.1	30.4	31.3
1998	30.1	31.3	31.6	31.9	32.3	31.6	31.1	30.8	30.8	29.7	29.7	29.6	30.9
1999	29.8	31.5	31.7	32.3	31.7	31.9	31.1	31.1	31.1	30.9	30.4	30.6	31.2
2000	30.5	32.4	33.7	34.1	35.9	33.4	33.6	32.7	32.2	31.6	31.2	31.8	32.8
2001	31.8	33.3	33.5	34.0	34.1	34.8	35.1	34.6	34.5	33.6	33.7	33.8	33.9
2002	33.7	34.5	35.0	35.3	35.9	36.7	36.9	36.4	36.1	35.4	34.9	35.3	35.5
2003	35.9	36.1	36.0	35.8	36.2	36.0	36.2	36.0	35.6	35.2	35.1	35.7	35.8
State government													
1990	41.9	42.6	42.0	42.3	42.7	41.2	39.8	39.7	39.9	43.3	44.0	42.2	41.8
1991	43.6	44.7	43.9	44.5	44.9	43.3	42.1	42.1	42.3	45.4	46.5	44.6	43.9
1992	45.6	46.8	46.0	46.5	46.8	45.3	43.6	43.7	43.8	46.7	48.0	46.8	45.8
1993	47.7	48.8	48.2	49.0	48.8	47.7	46.6	45.9	46.3	49.4	50.5	48.8	48.1
1994	49.4	50.4	49.4	50.1	50.5	48.6	47.7	47.7	47.8	51.0	51.4	50.3	49.5
1995	50.3	51.5	50.7	51.7	51.6	50.7	49.4	48.7	48.8	51.1	52.3	51.0	50.6
1996	51.7	52.9	52.4	53.2	53.0	52.0	50.1	49.6	49.4	52.0	53.8	52.7	51.9
1997	53.1	54.4	54.2	53.5	53.7	52.8	51.6	51.0	50.8	53.7	55.3	54.4	53.2
1998	53.8	56.0	55.9	55.6	55.0	55.0	54.0	54.2	56.8	56.7	57.3	56.5	55.6
1999	54.5	56.7	57.0	56.6	55.8	54.6	52.9	53.8	56.9	57.2	57.8	56.8	55.9
2000	55.6	58.3	58.2	58.6	57.4	56.1	54.5	55.8	58.4	59.0	59.4	58.8	57.5
2001	57.1	59.7	59.7	60.1	59.0	57.7	55.4	56.7	60.0	60.4	60.6	60.3	58.9
2002	60.1	58.9	61.1	61.2	57.1	57.3	55.8	56.9	60.3	60.8	61.0	60.6	59.3
2003	60.1	60.5	60.5	61.1	57.3	57.7	56.3	57.6	60.5	60.9	61.2	60.9	59.6

Employment by Industry: Utah—*Continued*

(Numbers in thousands. Not seasonally adjusted.)

Industry	January	February	March	April	May	June	July	August	September	October	November	December	Annual Average
STATEWIDE—*Continued*													
Local government													
1990	68.3	68.8	69.6	70.5	71.7	70.4	60.6	60.7	69.3	70.9	71.3	71.0	68.5
1991	70.8	71.6	72.2	72.5	73.7	72.2	63.9	64.2	72.2	73.4	73.9	73.6	71.1
1992	72.4	73.0	73.8	74.8	76.1	74.6	65.4	65.8	74.7	76.5	76.8	76.4	73.3
1993	75.9	76.5	77.4	77.9	79.4	79.0	68.1	69.0	77.8	78.5	79.3	79.8	76.5
1994	79.6	80.1	80.9	81.2	82.3	81.5	69.8	69.4	80.1	81.3	81.9	82.0	79.1
1995	81.1	82.2	83.4	83.3	84.4	82.8	70.6	70.7	81.7	83.1	84.2	84.1	80.9
1996	83.1	84.2	85.2	85.6	86.9	85.0	72.6	73.6	85.0	86.7	88.1	87.5	83.6
1997	86.5	88.0	88.9	90.0	91.7	89.6	77.3	77.5	89.3	90.9	91.6	91.5	87.7
1998	90.1	91.3	92.0	92.0	93.7	91.9	80.5	79.9	90.9	92.9	94.0	94.1	90.3
1999	92.2	93.3	94.5	94.7	96.7	94.6	81.6	81.4	92.8	94.9	96.0	96.2	92.4
2000	95.1	96.2	96.6	97.7	98.5	98.3	84.5	83.6	95.1	97.9	98.7	99.0	95.1
2001	97.7	98.9	99.5	99.9	101.1	100.8	86.5	85.8	96.8	99.4	100.6	100.9	97.3
2002	100.5	101.6	101.9	102.4	104.6	103.8	91.7	89.6	99.4	101.6	102.6	102.5	100.2
2003	102.1	103.1	103.4	104.2	106.3	104.3	92.5	91.4	101.1	103.2	104.4	104.4	101.7
PROVO-OREM													
Total nonfarm													
1990	88.9	90.3	91.7	93.0	91.1	92.6	90.7	92.5	97.6	99.5	100.8	101.0	94.1
1991	96.6	98.0	98.5	98.6	96.4	98.0	97.0	98.5	101.7	102.5	103.9	103.6	99.4
1992	97.9	99.6	100.7	100.8	98.9	100.0	99.3	100.8	105.1	106.2	107.3	108.0	102.1
1993	103.4	104.4	105.6	107.3	104.9	106.9	105.7	106.6	111.4	112.1	113.4	113.9	108.0
1994	111.0	112.6	114.5	115.1	112.8	114.7	114.1	115.5	120.7	120.1	121.0	121.0	116.1
1995	117.4	119.1	120.6	121.1	118.3	119.7	119.6	122.3	128.3	128.9	130.8	132.1	123.2
1996	126.7	127.9	128.4	128.3	126.3	126.7	126.4	128.2	133.1	133.6	136.3	136.5	129.9
1997	131.1	133.1	134.6	135.8	132.6	133.2	131.3	134.4	139.1	138.2	140.0	140.0	135.3
1998	136.3	138.4	139.5	140.4	138.8	140.7	138.5	140.8	145.8	146.2	147.8	148.3	141.8
1999	142.5	143.9	145.4	145.9	144.0	145.4	142.5	144.7	149.7	151.1	152.7	154.0	146.8
2000	148.5	149.9	151.3	151.8	150.2	152.5	148.9	151.3	157.0	157.0	157.9	158.5	152.9
2001	154.1	154.0	155.2	155.8	152.6	153.5	150.0	151.4	155.7	155.7	156.3	154.8	154.1
2002	149.9	149.8	150.7	153.0	150.0	150.8	147.6	148.6	154.5	155.5	156.4	156.9	152.0
2003	150.9	151.1	152.0	153.2	150.4	151.2	147.6	149.0	155.5	156.2	157.1	157.8	152.7
Total private													
1990	74.4	75.7	76.9	78.1	75.9	77.5	77.5	78.7	83.0	84.5	85.6	85.9	79.5
1991	81.5	82.8	83.1	83.2	81.0	83.0	83.1	84.0	86.2	86.8	88.1	87.9	84.2
1992	82.6	84.0	84.9	85.1	83.2	84.6	85.4	86.5	89.6	90.1	91.1	91.9	86.6
1993	87.6	88.4	89.2	90.9	88.6	90.3	90.6	91.4	94.9	95.4	96.7	97.3	91.8
1994	94.4	95.8	97.5	98.0	95.9	98.4	99.2	100.1	103.5	102.9	103.9	103.8	99.5
1995	100.3	101.7	102.9	103.4	101.0	103.4	104.9	107.0	110.8	111.3	113.0	114.5	106.2
1996	109.2	110.2	110.6	110.4	108.8	110.8	112.0	112.5	115.3	115.1	117.6	117.9	112.5
1997	112.7	114.4	115.7	116.4	113.3	115.6	116.2	117.6	119.9	118.9	120.6	120.6	116.8
1998	117.1	119.1	120.0	120.5	119.0	121.5	121.7	123.4	126.2	126.3	127.7	128.4	122.6
1999	122.9	124.2	125.3	125.7	123.9	126.6	125.9	127.1	129.8	130.6	132.1	133.4	127.3
2000	127.9	129.0	130.2	130.5	129.0	131.8	131.4	132.9	136.2	135.6	136.5	137.1	132.3
2001	132.7	132.5	133.6	133.9	131.0	131.9	131.5	132.0	134.1	133.4	133.8	132.6	132.8
2002	127.7	127.3	128.0	129.9	127.3	128.3	128.3	128.7	132.0	132.8	133.5	134.2	129.8
2003	128.2	128.2	128.9	129.8	127.0	128.9	128.4	129.2	132.7	133.1	133.9	134.8	130.3
Goods-producing													
1990	15.8	16.0	16.2	16.9	16.7	17.0	17.1	17.0	17.5	18.2	18.3	18.3	17.1
1991	17.4	17.6	17.8	18.1	18.1	18.6	18.6	18.7	19.0	18.7	18.8	18.5	18.3
1992	18.1	17.3	17.7	17.9	18.1	18.4	19.0	19.1	19.5	19.2	18.8	19.0	18.5
1993	18.1	18.1	18.6	19.1	19.1	19.6	19.6	19.8	20.2	20.3	20.4	20.2	19.4
1994	19.9	20.1	20.9	21.4	21.5	22.1	22.4	22.7	23.2	23.2	23.7	23.4	22.0
1995	22.9	23.3	23.9	24.0	23.9	24.7	25.2	26.3	27.4	27.6	28.5	28.7	25.5
1996	27.4	27.1	27.2	27.1	27.1	27.5	28.0	27.9	27.9	27.6	28.3	27.7	27.6
1997	26.2	26.9	27.0	27.7	27.7	28.4	29.2	29.5	29.4	29.3	29.5	28.9	28.3
1998	27.8	28.4	28.9	29.0	29.3	29.8	29.8	30.3	30.7	30.2	30.2	29.7	29.5
1999	28.2	28.3	28.8	29.2	29.3	30.2	30.0	30.1	30.4	30.5	30.5	29.9	29.6
2000	29.0	29.2	29.5	29.9	30.3	31.0	31.2	31.4	31.6	31.1	31.3	31.3	30.6
2001	30.2	30.1	30.4	30.3	30.7	30.9	31.3	31.2	30.9	30.2	29.8	28.3	30.4
2002	26.6	26.1	26.4	27.0	27.5	27.9	28.2	28.4	28.5	28.6	28.6	28.0	27.7
2003	26.7	26.0	25.9	26.1	26.5	27.1	27.2	27.3	27.3	27.2	27.3	27.0	26.8
Construction and mining													
1990	2.7	2.7	2.8	3.2	3.3	3.4	3.5	3.6	3.7	4.2	4.3	4.1	3.5
1991	3.6	3.7	3.9	4.4	4.7	5.1	5.2	5.3	5.3	4.6	4.4	4.2	4.5
1992	4.5	4.5	4.8	5.0	5.3	5.5	5.9	5.8	6.0	5.7	5.5	5.5	5.3
1993	4.9	4.9	5.1	5.6	5.8	6.1	6.3	6.3	6.3	6.3	6.2	6.0	5.8
1994	5.7	5.7	6.2	6.6	6.9	7.2	7.3	7.4	7.4	7.2	7.3	7.0	6.8
1995	6.6	6.8	7.3	7.5	7.8	8.4	9.1	10.1	10.9	11.0	11.6	11.6	9.1
1996	10.5	9.9	9.5	9.1	9.4	9.7	9.9	10.0	9.8	9.6	9.8	9.2	9.7
1997	8.1	8.4	8.5	9.0	9.3	9.8	10.2	10.4	10.1	9.9	10.0	9.5	9.4
1998	8.8	9.1	9.5	9.8	10.3	10.8	10.9	11.1	11.3	11.0	10.9	10.6	10.3
1999	9.8	9.8	10.2	10.5	10.6	11.2	11.2	11.3	11.3	11.3	11.2	10.7	10.8
2000	10.1	10.3	10.5	10.7	11.0	11.4	11.6	11.5	11.5	11.3	11.2	11.0	11.0
2001	9.9	9.9	10.2	10.4	10.8	11.1	11.6	11.6	11.5	11.2	11.2	10.8	10.9
2002	9.6	9.3	9.6	10.0	10.5	10.8	11.0	11.3	11.5	11.7	11.7	11.1	10.7
2003	10.1	9.8	9.8	9.9	10.3	10.7	10.8	11.0	10.9	10.9	10.9	10.6	10.5

Employment by Industry: Utah—*Continued*

(Numbers in thousands. Not seasonally adjusted.)

Industry	January	February	March	April	May	June	July	August	September	October	November	December	Annual Average
PROVO-OREM—*Continued*													
Manufacturing													
1990	13.1	13.3	13.4	13.7	13.4	13.6	13.6	13.4	13.8	14.0	14.0	14.2	13.6
1991	13.8	13.9	13.9	13.7	13.4	13.5	13.4	13.4	13.7	14.1	14.4	14.3	13.8
1992	13.6	12.8	12.9	12.9	12.8	12.9	13.1	13.3	13.5	13.5	13.3	13.5	13.2
1993	13.2	13.2	13.5	13.5	13.3	13.5	13.3	13.5	13.9	14.0	14.2	14.2	13.6
1994	14.2	14.4	14.7	14.8	14.6	14.9	15.1	15.3	15.8	16.0	16.4	16.4	15.2
1995	16.3	16.5	16.6	16.5	16.1	16.3	16.1	16.2	16.5	16.6	16.9	17.1	16.5
1996	16.9	17.2	17.7	18.0	17.7	17.8	18.1	17.9	18.1	18.0	18.5	18.5	17.9
1997	18.1	18.5	18.5	18.7	18.4	18.6	19.0	19.1	19.3	19.4	19.5	19.4	18.9
1998	19.0	19.3	19.4	19.2	19.0	19.0	18.9	19.2	19.4	19.2	19.3	19.1	19.2
1999	18.4	18.5	18.6	18.7	18.7	19.0	18.8	18.8	19.1	19.2	19.3	19.2	18.9
2000	18.9	18.9	19.0	19.2	19.3	19.6	19.6	19.9	20.1	19.8	20.1	20.3	19.6
2001	20.3	20.2	20.2	19.9	19.9	19.8	19.7	19.6	19.4	19.0	18.6	17.5	19.5
2002	17.0	16.8	16.8	17.0	17.0	17.1	17.2	17.1	17.0	16.9	16.9	16.9	17.0
2003	16.6	16.2	16.1	16.2	16.2	16.4	16.4	16.3	16.4	16.3	16.4	16.4	16.3
Service-providing													
1990	73.1	74.3	75.5	76.1	74.4	75.6	73.6	75.5	80.1	81.3	82.5	82.7	77.1
1991	79.2	80.4	80.7	80.5	78.3	79.4	78.4	79.8	82.7	83.8	85.1	85.1	81.1
1992	79.8	82.3	83.0	82.9	80.8	81.6	80.3	81.7	85.6	87.0	88.5	89.0	83.5
1993	85.3	86.3	87.0	88.2	85.8	87.3	86.1	86.8	91.2	91.8	93.0	93.7	88.5
1994	91.1	92.5	93.6	93.7	91.3	92.6	91.7	92.8	97.5	96.9	97.3	97.6	94.1
1995	94.5	95.8	96.7	97.1	94.4	95.0	94.4	96.0	100.9	101.3	102.3	103.4	97.7
1996	99.3	100.8	101.2	101.2	99.2	99.2	98.4	100.3	105.2	106.0	108.0	108.8	102.3
1997	104.9	106.2	107.6	108.1	104.9	104.8	102.1	104.9	109.7	108.9	110.5	111.1	107.0
1998	108.5	110.0	110.6	111.4	109.5	110.9	108.7	110.5	115.1	116.0	117.6	118.6	112.3
1999	114.3	115.6	116.6	116.7	114.7	115.2	112.5	114.6	119.3	120.6	122.2	124.1	117.2
2000	119.5	120.7	121.8	121.9	119.9	121.5	117.7	119.9	125.4	125.9	126.6	127.2	122.3
2001	123.9	123.9	124.8	125.5	121.9	122.6	118.7	120.2	124.8	125.5	126.5	126.5	123.7
2002	123.3	123.7	124.3	126.0	122.5	122.9	119.4	120.2	126.0	126.9	127.8	128.9	124.3
2003	124.2	125.1	126.1	127.1	123.9	124.1	120.4	121.7	128.2	129.0	129.8	130.8	125.9
Trade, transportation, and utilities													
1990	17.2	17.3	17.5	17.4	17.3	17.6	17.6	17.8	18.7	19.0	19.7	19.9	18.1
1991	18.9	18.7	18.6	18.6	18.0	18.3	18.1	18.4	18.9	19.1	19.8	20.0	18.8
1992	18.8	19.0	18.9	18.7	18.3	18.4	18.7	18.8	19.0	19.1	19.7	20.0	19.0
1993	18.7	18.7	18.6	19.1	18.7	18.8	18.9	19.2	19.7	19.9	20.6	21.1	19.3
1994	19.8	19.8	19.8	20.2	19.9	20.4	20.6	20.7	21.1	21.1	21.6	21.7	20.6
1995	20.7	20.6	21.0	21.2	21.1	21.2	21.8	22.0	22.6	22.7	23.3	23.7	21.8
1996	22.2	22.4	22.7	22.8	22.8	23.0	23.5	23.6	23.8	23.9	24.8	25.3	23.4
1997	23.9	24.2	24.4	24.4	24.2	24.1	24.3	24.6	24.6	24.6	25.4	25.9	24.6
1998	24.3	24.3	23.7	23.5	23.3	23.6	23.8	24.4	24.5	24.9	25.9	26.8	24.4
1999	25.5	25.2	25.4	25.4	25.4	25.6	25.6	25.9	25.9	26.1	27.2	27.9	25.9
2000	26.2	25.9	25.7	25.6	25.6	25.7	25.6	26.1	26.5	26.8	27.4	27.5	26.2
2001	25.6	25.1	25.3	25.4	25.4	25.4	25.2	25.3	24.9	25.0	25.8	25.8	25.4
2002	24.7	24.2	24.5	24.8	24.8	24.9	24.8	24.8	24.9	24.9	25.7	26.0	24.9
2003	24.4	24.2	24.2	24.4	24.6	24.6	24.6	25.0	25.1	25.1	25.8	26.2	24.9
Wholesale trade													
1990	3.2	3.3	3.3	3.3	3.2	3.3	3.3	3.3	3.4	3.4	3.5	3.5	3.3
1991	3.5	3.5	3.4	3.4	3.3	3.3	3.4	3.4	3.4	3.4	3.5	3.4	3.4
1992	3.4	3.4	3.4	3.4	3.4	3.4	3.5	3.5	3.5	3.5	3.5	3.5	3.5
1993	3.4	3.4	3.4	3.5	3.4	3.5	3.6	3.5	3.6	3.7	3.7	3.7	3.5
1994	3.5	3.5	3.5	3.6	3.5	3.7	3.8	3.6	3.7	3.7	3.7	3.7	3.6
1995	3.7	3.7	3.8	3.8	3.8	3.8	3.9	4.0	4.0	4.0	4.0	4.1	3.9
1996	3.9	4.0	4.1	4.0	4.1	4.1	4.2	4.2	4.2	4.2	4.3	4.2	4.1
1997	4.0	4.1	4.2	4.1	4.1	4.1	4.1	4.2	4.2	4.2	4.2	4.2	4.1
1998	4.1	4.2	4.2	4.3	4.3	4.2	4.2	4.3	4.3	4.3	4.4	4.4	4.3
1999	4.3	4.3	4.4	4.3	4.3	4.2	4.4	4.3	4.3	4.3	4.3	4.4	4.3
2000	4.2	4.3	4.3	4.3	4.4	4.4	4.5	4.5	4.6	4.6	4.5	4.4	4.4
2001	4.3	4.2	4.2	4.2	4.2	4.2	4.2	4.1	4.0	4.0	4.0	4.0	4.1
2002	3.9	3.9	3.9	3.9	3.9	3.9	3.9	3.8	3.8	3.8	3.8	3.8	3.9
2003	3.8	3.8	3.8	3.8	3.8	3.8	3.7	3.7	3.7	3.7	3.7	3.7	3.8
Retail trade													
1990	11.6	11.6	11.8	11.5	11.5	11.7	11.8	12.0	12.8	13.0	13.7	13.9	12.2
1991	12.9	12.7	12.8	12.8	12.4	12.7	12.4	12.7	13.1	13.3	13.9	14.1	13.0
1992	13.0	13.2	13.1	13.1	12.8	12.9	13.0	13.1	13.4	13.5	14.1	14.4	13.3
1993	13.3	13.3	13.2	13.5	13.2	13.1	13.0	13.4	13.9	14.0	14.6	15.1	13.6
1994	14.0	13.9	13.9	14.2	14.0	14.4	14.4	14.7	15.0	15.1	15.7	15.8	14.6
1995	14.9	14.8	15.1	15.3	15.2	15.3	15.6	15.8	16.3	16.4	17.1	17.4	15.8
1996	16.2	16.2	16.4	16.5	16.5	16.7	17.0	17.1	17.3	17.3	18.1	18.7	17.0
1997	17.4	17.6	17.7	17.7	17.6	17.5	17.5	17.9	18.0	18.1	18.9	19.4	17.9
1998	18.0	17.8	17.3	17.0	16.9	17.3	17.5	18.0	18.2	18.6	19.5	20.2	18.0
1999	18.8	18.5	18.5	18.7	18.6	18.9	18.7	18.9	19.0	19.1	20.1	20.6	19.0
2000	19.1	18.8	18.8	18.6	18.5	18.6	18.4	18.8	19.0	19.3	20.0	20.2	19.0
2001	19.2	18.9	19.1	19.2	19.2	19.2	18.9	19.1	18.9	19.0	19.8	19.9	19.2
2002	18.9	18.5	18.7	19.0	19.0	19.1	19.0	19.2	19.2	19.2	20.0	20.4	19.2
2003	18.8	18.6	18.6	18.8	18.9	19.0	19.1	19.5	19.6	19.6	20.3	20.6	19.3

Employment by Industry: Utah—*Continued*

(Numbers in thousands. Not seasonally adjusted.)

Industry	January	February	March	April	May	June	July	August	September	October	November	December	Annual Average
PROVO-OREM—*Continued*													
Transportation and utilities													
1990	2.4	2.4	2.4	2.6	2.6	2.6	2.5	2.5	2.5	2.6	2.5	2.5	2.5
1991	2.5	2.5	2.4	2.4	2.3	2.3	2.3	2.3	2.4	2.4	2.4	2.5	2.4
1992	2.4	2.4	2.4	2.2	2.1	2.1	2.2	2.2	2.1	2.1	2.1	2.1	2.2
1993	2.0	2.0	2.0	2.1	2.1	2.2	2.3	2.3	2.2	2.2	2.3	2.3	2.2
1994	2.3	2.4	2.4	2.4	2.4	2.3	2.4	2.4	2.4	2.3	2.2	2.2	2.3
1995	2.1	2.1	2.1	2.1	2.1	2.1	2.3	2.2	2.3	2.3	2.2	2.2	2.2
1996	2.1	2.2	2.2	2.3	2.2	2.2	2.3	2.3	2.3	2.4	2.4	2.4	2.3
1997	2.5	2.5	2.5	2.6	2.5	2.5	2.7	2.5	2.4	2.3	2.3	2.3	2.5
1998	2.2	2.3	2.2	2.2	2.1	2.1	2.1	2.1	2.0	2.0	2.0	2.2	2.1
1999	2.4	2.4	2.5	2.4	2.5	2.5	2.5	2.7	2.6	2.7	2.8	2.9	2.6
2000	2.9	2.8	2.6	2.7	2.7	2.7	2.7	2.8	2.9	2.9	2.9	2.9	2.8
2001	2.1	2.0	2.0	2.0	2.0	2.0	2.1	2.1	2.0	2.0	2.0	1.9	2.0
2002	1.9	1.8	1.9	1.9	1.9	1.9	1.9	1.8	1.9	1.9	1.9	1.8	1.9
2003	1.8	1.8	1.8	1.8	1.9	1.8	1.8	1.8	1.8	1.8	1.8	1.9	1.8
Information													
1990	2.1	2.2	2.3	2.4	2.5	2.7	2.8	2.8	2.9	3.0	3.1	3.1	2.7
1991	3.0	3.1	3.2	3.1	3.1	3.2	3.2	3.2	3.2	3.3	3.3	3.3	3.2
1992	3.5	4.3	4.3	4.3	4.4	4.5	4.6	4.6	4.8	5.0	5.3	5.5	4.6
1993	5.3	5.5	5.5	5.5	5.4	5.5	5.5	5.5	5.7	5.7	5.8	5.9	5.6
1994	5.9	5.8	5.9	6.0	6.1	6.2	6.3	6.3	6.4	6.4	6.3	6.4	6.2
1995	6.3	6.4	6.3	6.4	6.3	6.3	6.4	6.4	6.5	6.5	6.4	6.5	6.4
1996	6.4	6.4	6.4	5.9	5.9	5.9	6.0	5.9	6.0	5.8	5.8	5.9	6.0
1997	5.8	5.8	5.9	5.8	5.6	5.7	5.6	5.6	5.7	5.6	5.7	5.7	5.7
1998	5.9	6.0	6.0	6.5	6.5	6.6	6.6	6.8	6.9	6.9	6.9	7.0	6.6
1999	7.0	7.2	7.3	7.4	7.5	7.8	7.8	8.0	8.2	8.4	8.6	8.8	7.8
2000	8.8	9.0	9.1	9.0	9.1	9.1	9.1	9.0	9.0	8.7	8.6	8.6	8.9
2001	7.9	7.9	7.8	7.6	7.5	7.4	7.3	7.2	7.1	7.0	7.0	6.9	7.4
2002	6.6	6.5	6.5	6.5	6.6	6.7	6.6	6.7	6.7	6.6	6.6	6.7	6.6
2003	6.7	6.7	6.7	6.7	6.7	6.8	6.6	6.6	6.6	6.7	6.6	6.7	6.7
Financial activities													
1990	2.8	2.9	2.9	2.9	2.8	2.9	2.9	2.9	3.0	2.9	2.9	2.9	2.9
1991	2.8	2.9	2.8	2.8	2.7	2.7	2.7	2.8	2.8	2.8	2.7	2.8	2.8
1992	2.7	2.8	2.8	2.8	2.8	2.9	2.8	2.9	3.0	3.0	3.0	3.0	2.9
1993	3.0	3.1	3.2	3.1	3.1	3.1	3.2	3.2	3.3	3.5	3.6	3.6	3.3
1994	3.7	3.8	3.9	3.8	3.7	3.7	3.8	3.8	3.9	3.7	3.7	3.7	3.8
1995	3.6	3.7	3.8	3.7	3.6	3.6	3.6	3.6	3.7	3.7	3.8	3.9	3.7
1996	3.8	3.8	3.9	4.0	4.0	4.1	4.1	4.1	4.1	4.0	4.0	4.1	4.0
1997	4.0	4.0	4.1	4.1	4.1	4.1	3.9	4.1	4.1	4.0	4.2	4.1	4.1
1998	4.1	4.1	4.2	4.3	4.3	4.4	4.3	4.4	4.5	4.7	4.7	4.8	4.4
1999	4.7	4.8	4.8	4.7	4.6	4.7	4.7	4.6	4.6	4.6	4.5	4.6	4.7
2000	4.4	4.4	4.5	4.4	4.5	4.5	4.5	4.5	4.6	4.6	4.6	4.7	4.5
2001	4.8	4.8	4.9	4.9	4.9	5.0	5.0	5.1	5.2	5.2	5.3	5.4	5.1
2002	5.2	5.2	5.2	5.3	5.3	5.3	5.3	5.4	5.4	5.5	5.6	5.8	5.4
2003	5.5	5.6	5.7	5.6	5.7	5.8	5.8	5.9	5.8	5.9	6.0	6.2	5.8
Professional and business services													
1990	13.6	13.8	14.2	14.4	14.2	14.5	14.7	15.3	15.8	16.2	16.2	16.1	14.9
1991	14.5	14.8	14.9	14.8	15.0	15.6	16.1	16.1	16.1	16.2	16.9	16.8	15.7
1992	13.7	14.2	14.5	14.5	14.5	14.6	14.7	15.1	15.2	15.9	16.3	16.2	15.0
1993	15.1	15.1	15.2	15.2	15.1	15.8	15.9	15.9	16.2	16.3	16.3	16.4	15.7
1994	15.6	16.2	16.6	15.9	15.9	16.3	16.6	16.9	17.1	16.8	16.6	16.5	16.4
1995	15.4	15.5	15.6	15.6	15.3	16.1	16.6	16.9	16.9	16.9	16.7	16.9	16.2
1996	16.0	16.3	15.2	15.1	15.3	15.9	16.2	16.3	16.6	16.8	17.4	17.6	16.2
1997	16.7	16.6	16.7	16.7	16.3	17.2	17.2	17.1	17.2	16.7	16.9	17.2	16.9
1998	16.8	17.2	17.4	17.5	17.8	18.7	18.8	18.8	18.9	18.9	18.9	18.7	18.2
1999	17.3	17.8	17.7	17.8	17.7	18.0	18.0	18.3	18.5	19.1	19.2	20.1	18.3
2000	17.8	18.0	18.5	18.5	18.6	19.5	19.2	19.7	19.8	19.9	19.8	19.9	19.1
2001	18.7	18.3	18.6	18.9	18.9	18.7	18.6	18.7	18.4	17.9	17.9	17.5	18.4
2002	17.4	17.4	17.3	17.8	18.2	18.2	18.0	17.8	17.7	17.9	18.0	18.0	17.8
2003	16.8	17.1	17.2	17.4	18.0	18.4	18.3	18.4	18.3	18.3	18.3	18.2	17.9
Educational and health services													
1990	13.8	14.2	14.5	14.5	13.0	13.2	12.8	13.1	14.9	15.1	15.4	15.5	14.2
1991	15.5	16.1	16.2	16.0	14.5	14.7	14.4	14.6	15.8	16.2	16.2	16.2	15.5
1992	16.0	16.4	16.5	16.6	15.0	15.2	14.9	15.2	17.2	17.3	17.5	17.7	16.3
1993	17.4	17.8	17.8	18.2	16.7	16.8	16.7	16.9	18.6	18.8	18.9	19.1	17.8
1994	18.7	19.0	19.2	19.2	17.5	17.9	17.7	17.8	19.6	19.8	20.1	20.2	18.9
1995	19.6	20.1	20.1	20.2	18.6	18.9	18.7	19.0	20.9	21.3	21.6	21.9	20.1
1996	21.3	21.8	22.3	22.4	20.6	21.0	20.7	20.8	23.0	23.3	23.6	23.7	22.0
1997	23.3	23.8	24.1	24.1	22.1	22.5	22.3	22.5	24.6	24.9	25.3	25.3	23.7
1998	25.1	25.8	26.2	26.1	24.2	24.5	24.3	24.5	26.6	27.0	27.2	27.4	25.7
1999	26.9	27.4	27.6	27.4	25.5	25.9	25.5	25.9	28.1	28.2	28.4	28.3	27.1
2000	28.4	28.9	29.1	29.2	27.2	27.7	27.3	27.6	30.1	30.0	30.3	30.8	28.9
2001	30.8	31.4	31.6	31.4	27.7	28.2	27.4	27.8	31.4	32.4	32.4	32.8	30.4
2002	32.0	32.5	32.7	32.9	29.0	29.0	28.8	29.0	32.6	33.6	33.5	33.9	31.6
2003	33.1	33.4	33.8	33.9	29.6	29.9	29.4	29.4	33.2	34.0	34.1	34.5	32.4

Employment by Industry: Utah—*Continued*

(Numbers in thousands. Not seasonally adjusted.)

Industry	January	February	March	April	May	June	July	August	September	October	November	December	Annual Average
PROVO-OREM—*Continued*													
Leisure and hospitality													
1990	6.2	6.3	6.3	6.5	6.5	6.6	6.5	6.8	7.1	7.0	6.9	7.0	6.6
1991	6.4	6.6	6.6	6.8	6.7	6.9	6.9	7.1	7.3	7.4	7.3	7.3	6.9
1992	6.7	6.9	7.1	7.1	6.9	7.2	7.3	7.4	7.7	7.3	7.2	7.2	7.2
1993	6.8	6.9	7.0	7.3	7.2	7.3	7.3	7.5	7.7	7.4	7.6	7.5	7.3
1994	7.3	7.5	7.6	7.9	7.8	8.0	8.0	8.1	8.4	8.2	8.2	8.2	7.9
1995	8.1	8.3	8.4	8.6	8.7	8.9	8.8	8.9	9.0	8.8	8.9	9.1	8.7
1996	8.6	8.8	9.1	9.5	9.6	9.7	9.7	10.1	10.1	10.0	10.0	9.9	9.6
1997	9.2	9.4	9.8	9.9	9.7	10.0	9.9	10.4	10.5	10.1	10.0	9.8	9.9
1998	9.6	9.7	10.0	9.9	10.1	10.2	10.3	10.5	10.5	10.2	10.4	10.6	10.2
1999	9.9	10.0	10.2	10.3	10.5	10.7	10.6	10.7	10.7	10.3	10.4	10.5	10.4
2000	10.1	10.4	10.5	10.6	10.5	10.9	11.1	11.2	11.3	11.3	11.3	11.1	10.9
2001	11.3	11.5	11.6	11.9	12.2	12.5	12.6	12.6	12.4	11.9	11.8	12.0	12.0
2002	11.4	11.6	11.5	11.7	12.0	12.2	12.5	12.5	12.3	11.8	11.6	11.8	11.9
2003	11.2	11.3	11.5	11.8	11.9	12.2	12.4	12.5	12.5	12.0	11.9	12.0	11.9
Other services													
1990	2.9	3.0	3.0	3.1	2.9	3.0	3.1	3.0	3.1	3.1	3.1	3.1	3.0
1991	3.0	3.0	3.0	3.0	2.9	3.0	3.1	3.1	3.1	3.1	3.1	3.0	3.0
1992	3.1	3.1	3.1	3.2	3.2	3.4	3.4	3.4	3.2	3.3	3.3	3.3	3.3
1993	3.2	3.2	3.3	3.4	3.3	3.4	3.5	3.4	3.5	3.5	3.5	3.5	3.4
1994	3.5	3.6	3.6	3.6	3.5	3.8	3.8	3.8	3.8	3.7	3.7	3.7	3.7
1995	3.7	3.8	3.8	3.7	3.5	3.7	3.8	3.9	3.8	3.8	3.8	3.8	3.8
1996	3.5	3.6	3.8	3.6	3.5	3.7	3.8	3.8	3.8	3.7	3.7	3.7	3.7
1997	3.6	3.7	3.7	3.7	3.6	3.6	3.8	3.8	3.8	3.7	3.6	3.7	3.7
1998	3.5	3.6	3.6	3.7	3.5	3.7	3.8	3.7	3.6	3.5	3.5	3.4	3.6
1999	3.4	3.5	3.5	3.5	3.4	3.7	3.7	3.6	3.4	3.4	3.3	3.3	3.5
2000	3.2	3.2	3.3	3.3	3.2	3.4	3.4	3.4	3.3	3.2	3.2	3.2	3.3
2001	3.4	3.4	3.4	3.5	3.6	3.8	4.0	4.0	3.8	3.8	3.8	3.9	3.7
2002	3.8	3.8	3.9	3.9	3.9	4.1	4.1	4.1	3.9	3.9	3.9	4.0	3.9
2003	3.8	3.9	3.9	3.9	4.0	4.1	4.1	4.1	3.9	3.9	3.9	4.0	4.0
Government													
1990	14.5	14.6	14.8	14.9	15.2	15.1	13.2	13.8	14.6	15.0	15.2	15.1	14.7
1991	15.1	15.2	15.4	15.4	15.4	15.0	13.9	14.5	15.5	15.7	15.8	15.7	15.2
1992	15.3	15.6	15.8	15.7	15.7	15.4	13.9	14.3	15.5	16.1	16.2	16.1	15.5
1993	15.8	16.0	16.4	16.4	16.3	16.6	15.1	15.2	16.5	16.7	16.7	16.6	16.2
1994	16.6	16.8	17.0	17.1	16.9	16.3	14.9	15.4	17.2	17.2	17.1	17.2	16.6
1995	17.1	17.4	17.7	17.7	17.3	16.3	14.7	15.3	17.5	17.6	17.8	17.6	17.0
1996	17.5	17.7	17.8	17.9	17.5	15.9	14.4	15.7	17.8	18.5	18.7	18.6	17.3
1997	18.4	18.7	18.9	19.4	19.3	17.6	15.1	16.8	19.2	19.3	19.4	19.4	18.5
1998	19.2	19.3	19.5	19.9	19.8	19.2	16.8	17.4	19.6	19.9	20.1	19.9	19.2
1999	19.6	19.7	20.1	20.2	20.1	18.8	16.6	17.6	19.9	20.5	20.6	20.6	19.5
2000	20.6	20.9	21.1	21.3	21.2	20.7	17.5	18.4	20.8	21.4	21.4	21.4	20.6
2001	21.4	21.5	21.6	21.9	21.6	21.6	18.5	19.4	21.6	22.3	22.5	22.2	21.3
2002	22.2	22.5	22.7	23.1	22.7	22.5	19.3	19.9	22.5	22.7	22.9	22.7	22.1
2003	22.7	22.9	23.1	23.4	23.4	22.3	19.2	19.8	22.8	23.1	23.2	23.0	22.4
Federal government													
2001	1.1	1.0	1.0	1.1	1.1	1.2	1.2	1.2	1.2	1.1	1.1	1.1	1.1
2002	1.1	1.0	1.0	1.1	1.1	1.2	1.2	1.2	1.2	1.1	1.1	1.1	1.1
2003	1.0	1.0	1.0	1.0	1.1	1.1	1.1	1.1	1.1	1.1	1.1	1.1	1.1
State government													
2001	5.7	5.7	5.7	5.7	5.1	5.1	5.1	5.3	5.8	5.9	5.9	5.7	5.6
2002	5.8	5.9	6.0	6.0	5.4	5.3	5.2	5.4	5.8	5.8	5.8	5.7	5.7
2003	5.8	5.8	5.9	5.9	5.3	5.3	5.2	5.4	5.9	5.9	5.9	5.8	5.7
Local government													
2001	14.6	14.8	14.9	15.1	15.4	15.3	12.2	12.9	14.6	15.3	15.5	15.4	14.7
2002	15.3	15.6	15.7	16.0	16.2	16.0	12.9	13.3	15.5	15.8	16.0	15.9	15.4
2003	15.9	16.1	16.2	16.5	17.0	15.9	12.9	13.3	15.8	16.1	16.2	16.1	15.7
SALT LAKE CITY-OGDEN													
Total nonfarm													
1990	477.9	478.6	483.0	488.7	493.8	499.3	493.8	497.9	502.1	502.9	506.7	508.4	494.4
1991	492.4	495.2	499.1	501.0	507.5	511.0	505.5	508.4	512.0	512.5	516.8	517.0	506.5
1992	504.3	507.4	511.7	515.4	521.5	524.3	519.2	523.0	526.5	527.6	534.3	536.7	520.9
1993	524.8	528.1	535.0	540.2	544.7	551.5	548.7	552.0	556.4	560.0	566.6	569.8	548.1
1994	556.4	559.6	565.1	570.3	577.0	583.4	578.8	583.7	590.4	590.0	598.0	602.1	579.5
1995	588.7	594.6	600.0	604.0	608.2	615.0	608.8	615.8	623.0	621.5	629.3	632.8	611.8
1996	620.4	625.0	629.8	634.1	640.4	647.0	641.4	647.6	651.9	651.9	661.6	664.3	642.9
1997	647.4	653.9	659.6	661.6	668.9	673.0	668.0	669.0	676.1	677.0	683.3	686.8	668.7
1998	666.8	672.8	676.4	679.8	686.5	692.5	687.1	690.0	695.8	693.6	699.5	702.8	687.0
1999	682.3	688.4	693.5	698.1	701.2	706.6	700.4	703.6	708.4	707.5	713.9	717.7	701.8
2000	698.5	704.4	710.3	714.7	719.1	723.0	715.4	718.5	724.5	726.0	729.6	734.1	718.2
2001	713.4	716.1	719.4	720.6	723.1	726.1	716.9	718.8	720.7	717.7	719.5	720.3	719.4
2002	707.4	712.7	705.4	708.0	708.7	711.0	706.4	706.4	708.7	709.4	712.3	712.9	709.1
2003	697.4	697.1	697.7	702.1	705.1	708.0	704.8	707.2	707.8	710.4	713.9	716.6	705.7

Employment by Industry: Utah—*Continued*

(Numbers in thousands. Not seasonally adjusted.)

Industry	January	February	March	April	May	June	July	August	September	October	November	December	Annual Average
SALT LAKE CITY-OGDEN *—Continued*													
Total private													
1990	379.8	379.5	383.9	388.1	392.6	399.1	398.8	404.4	404.8	402.8	406.7	409.8	395.8
1991	392.7	394.0	398.0	399.2	404.8	409.7	409.0	413.0	412.7	411.5	415.3	416.8	406.3
1992	402.7	404.4	408.8	411.4	416.7	421.2	421.7	425.6	424.7	423.9	429.6	432.8	418.6
1993	420.1	422.3	429.0	434.3	438.5	446.0	449.7	453.8	454.1	456.0	461.9	465.9	444.3
1994	451.3	452.8	458.8	463.0	469.4	476.7	479.0	484.7	486.5	483.8	491.4	496.1	474.4
1995	482.5	486.6	492.0	494.8	499.2	506.7	508.3	515.8	518.2	514.3	521.6	526.3	505.5
1996	513.7	515.7	520.5	523.6	529.7	537.1	539.8	546.7	546.1	543.5	551.6	555.5	535.2
1997	537.7	541.5	546.6	548.2	555.2	560.0	562.2	565.4	567.2	565.3	570.5	575.0	557.9
1998	555.0	558.1	561.3	564.2	569.7	577.3	579.0	583.1	582.1	580.5	584.8	589.0	573.7
1999	569.9	571.7	576.1	580.1	583.5	590.3	592.2	595.9	593.2	591.8	597.0	601.5	586.9
2000	583.2	584.7	590.2	593.1	596.5	603.5	602.8	607.2	606.4	606.5	609.6	613.8	599.8
2001	594.6	593.4	596.5	596.6	599.2	603.0	601.0	603.8	599.2	595.1	595.7	596.0	597.8
2002	582.6	588.4	579.0	581.0	582.5	584.6	583.8	587.1	584.4	583.8	586.3	587.1	584.2
2003	570.1	569.2	570.1	574.3	578.3	581.7	582.4	586.9	583.9	584.5	587.5	590.1	579.9
Goods-producing													
1990	83.3	83.6	84.5	86.8	88.7	90.7	91.8	93.6	93.6	92.2	91.8	91.3	89.3
1991	86.7	87.1	88.3	88.7	90.3	91.4	91.6	92.9	94.0	93.0	92.7	91.1	90.6
1992	87.5	87.8	89.3	90.4	92.6	94.5	95.1	96.1	95.9	95.7	96.0	95.2	93.0
1993	91.7	91.8	93.9	95.4	96.7	99.1	100.7	102.1	102.2	102.1	102.3	101.3	98.2
1994	98.3	98.1	99.8	101.6	103.9	106.6	108.5	110.5	111.0	110.4	109.9	108.9	105.6
1995	106.3	106.7	109.0	109.9	111.7	113.8	113.5	115.1	116.2	115.9	116.4	117.0	112.6
1996	113.6	113.2	114.8	116.2	118.2	121.0	121.7	123.7	123.4	121.4	121.3	120.7	119.1
1997	117.3	118.2	119.9	120.3	123.1	125.1	125.9	127.0	126.8	125.6	125.3	123.8	123.2
1998	121.0	121.7	122.5	123.7	126.0	128.8	129.7	130.6	130.4	129.0	128.7	128.1	126.7
1999	125.0	124.9	126.3	127.9	129.4	132.0	133.0	133.9	133.4	131.8	131.4	130.0	129.9
2000	125.9	125.7	126.5	127.8	129.3	131.4	130.9	132.0	131.3	130.1	129.2	128.2	129.0
2001	124.8	124.1	124.8	123.9	125.4	127.2	127.6	128.4	127.4	126.1	124.5	121.8	125.5
2002	116.1	113.6	114.0	114.8	116.6	118.0	118.3	119.0	118.4	117.9	116.9	115.8	116.6
2003	112.3	111.8	112.0	113.6	115.5	116.3	116.5	117.4	117.0	116.6	115.8	114.9	115.0
Construction and mining													
1990	18.4	18.5	19.1	20.5	21.7	22.7	23.9	24.8	24.7	23.7	23.2	22.3	21.9
1991	19.7	20.0	20.7	22.8	24.1	25.0	25.3	26.4	26.3	25.9	25.3	23.7	23.7
1992	21.7	21.7	22.8	24.6	26.0	27.0	27.6	28.1	28.2	27.8	27.7	26.8	25.8
1993	24.4	24.4	26.0	27.4	28.5	30.1	31.6	32.5	32.4	32.3	32.2	31.1	29.4
1994	29.3	29.5	30.9	32.4	34.0	36.0	37.1	38.5	39.1	38.4	37.2	35.9	34.8
1995	33.7	34.2	35.7	36.2	37.4	39.0	39.7	40.9	41.4	40.7	40.0	40.2	38.2
1996	37.3	36.8	38.2	39.8	41.6	43.4	44.2	45.5	44.9	43.8	43.7	42.8	41.8
1997	40.1	40.8	42.5	43.5	45.9	47.3	47.8	48.5	47.9	47.1	46.5	45.1	45.3
1998	41.9	42.6	43.4	44.6	46.7	49.0	50.1	50.8	50.7	49.8	49.2	48.3	47.3
1999	45.3	45.3	46.4	47.8	49.2	51.5	52.7	53.4	53.0	52.1	51.7	50.3	49.9
2000	46.8	46.7	47.4	48.5	49.9	51.7	51.4	52.2	51.5	50.5	49.5	48.5	49.6
2001	45.8	45.5	46.4	46.3	48.0	49.8	50.2	51.1	50.4	49.9	48.9	46.8	48.3
2002	42.6	40.8	41.5	42.7	44.1	45.4	46.0	46.3	45.6	45.3	44.7	43.7	44.1
2003	40.9	40.6	40.9	42.3	43.9	44.8	45.4	46.2	45.8	45.5	44.6	43.9	43.7
Manufacturing													
1990	64.9	65.1	65.4	66.3	67.0	68.0	67.9	68.8	68.9	68.5	68.6	69.0	67.3
1991	67.0	67.1	67.6	65.9	66.2	66.4	66.3	66.5	67.7	67.1	67.4	67.4	66.8
1992	65.8	66.1	66.5	65.8	66.6	67.5	67.5	68.0	67.7	67.9	68.3	68.4	67.1
1993	67.3	67.4	67.9	68.0	68.2	69.0	69.1	69.6	69.8	69.8	70.1	70.2	68.8
1994	69.0	68.6	68.9	69.2	69.9	70.6	71.4	72.0	71.9	72.0	72.7	73.0	70.7
1995	72.6	72.5	73.3	73.7	74.3	74.8	73.8	74.2	74.8	75.2	76.4	76.8	74.3
1996	76.3	76.4	76.6	76.4	76.6	77.6	77.5	78.2	78.5	77.6	77.6	77.9	77.2
1997	77.2	77.4	77.4	76.8	77.2	77.8	78.1	78.5	78.9	78.5	78.8	78.7	77.9
1998	79.1	79.1	79.1	79.1	79.3	79.8	79.6	79.8	79.7	79.2	79.5	79.8	79.4
1999	79.7	79.6	79.9	80.1	80.2	80.5	80.3	80.5	80.4	79.7	79.7	79.7	80.0
2000	79.1	79.0	79.1	79.3	79.4	79.7	79.5	79.8	79.8	79.6	79.7	79.7	79.5
2001	79.0	78.6	78.4	77.6	77.4	77.4	77.4	77.3	77.0	76.2	75.6	75.0	77.2
2002	73.5	72.8	72.5	72.1	72.5	72.6	72.3	72.7	72.8	72.6	72.2	72.1	72.6
2003	71.4	71.2	71.1	71.3	71.6	71.5	71.1	71.2	71.2	71.1	71.2	71.0	71.2
Service-providing													
1990	394.6	395.0	398.5	401.9	405.1	408.6	402.0	404.3	408.5	410.7	414.9	417.1	405.1
1991	405.7	408.1	410.8	412.3	417.2	419.6	413.9	415.5	418.0	419.5	424.1	425.9	415.8
1992	416.8	419.6	422.4	425.0	428.9	429.8	424.1	426.9	430.6	431.9	438.3	441.5	427.9
1993	433.1	436.3	441.1	444.8	448.0	452.4	448.0	449.9	454.2	457.9	464.3	468.5	449.8
1994	458.1	461.5	465.3	468.7	473.1	476.8	470.3	473.2	479.4	479.6	488.1	493.2	473.9
1995	482.4	487.9	491.0	494.1	496.5	501.2	495.3	500.7	506.8	505.6	512.9	515.8	499.1
1996	506.8	511.8	515.0	517.9	522.2	526.0	519.7	523.9	528.5	530.5	540.3	543.6	523.8
1997	530.1	535.7	539.7	541.3	545.8	547.9	542.1	542.0	549.3	551.4	558.0	563.0	545.5
1998	545.8	551.1	553.9	556.1	560.5	563.7	557.4	559.4	565.4	564.6	570.8	574.7	560.3
1999	557.3	563.5	567.2	570.2	571.8	574.6	567.4	569.7	575.0	575.7	582.5	587.7	571.9
2000	572.6	578.7	583.8	586.9	589.8	591.6	584.5	586.5	593.2	595.9	600.4	605.9	589.2
2001	588.6	592.0	594.6	596.7	597.7	598.9	589.3	590.4	593.3	591.6	595.0	598.5	593.9
2002	591.3	599.1	591.4	593.2	592.1	593.0	588.1	587.4	590.3	591.5	595.4	597.1	592.5
2003	585.1	585.3	585.7	588.5	589.6	591.7	588.3	589.8	590.8	593.8	598.1	601.7	590.7

Employment by Industry: Utah—*Continued*

(Numbers in thousands. Not seasonally adjusted.)

Industry	January	February	March	April	May	June	July	August	September	October	November	December	Annual Average
SALT LAKE CITY-OGDEN —*Continued*													
Trade, transportation and utilities													
1990	109.4	108.3	108.7	107.7	109.2	111.0	110.7	112.1	112.4	113.0	116.3	117.9	111.3
1991	111.1	109.3	109.7	109.9	111.6	113.2	112.6	113.6	113.3	113.8	117.7	119.7	112.9
1992	113.4	112.4	113.0	113.5	114.9	116.2	115.8	116.4	116.0	116.4	120.0	122.8	115.9
1993	116.5	115.7	116.7	117.7	118.8	120.8	122.3	122.8	122.4	123.7	127.7	130.5	121.3
1994	123.7	122.7	123.6	123.3	125.8	127.9	129.0	130.3	130.2	130.1	135.1	138.2	128.3
1995	131.4	130.6	131.2	131.7	132.6	134.2	134.3	135.6	135.6	135.2	139.9	142.4	134.5
1996	135.9	134.9	135.0	135.0	136.6	138.4	139.0	140.1	138.8	139.9	144.8	147.8	138.8
1997	139.9	139.3	139.9	140.0	140.8	142.0	143.9	143.8	144.1	146.0	149.8	153.7	143.6
1998	145.8	144.3	144.2	144.2	145.4	146.8	148.0	148.7	148.4	148.9	153.0	155.9	147.8
1999	147.0	145.5	146.1	147.1	147.8	148.4	149.6	149.8	149.1	149.5	153.6	157.0	149.2
2000	149.8	148.3	149.3	149.4	150.2	151.8	152.0	152.6	152.6	154.0	157.2	159.8	152.3
2001	155.2	153.9	153.9	153.6	153.3	153.1	152.5	152.5	151.7	151.8	154.1	155.4	153.4
2002	150.1	148.9	147.4	148.0	148.9	149.3	149.1	149.4	148.8	149.5	152.2	153.4	149.6
2003	146.4	144.9	145.0	144.8	146.0	146.4	146.5	147.6	147.1	148.2	151.6	153.7	147.4
Wholesale trade													
1990	23.6	23.6	23.8	24.2	24.4	24.5	24.8	25.1	25.0	25.1	25.3	25.2	24.5
1991	24.3	24.2	24.5	24.5	24.8	25.0	24.9	25.1	24.9	24.8	24.7	24.9	24.7
1992	24.5	24.4	24.6	24.7	24.8	24.9	24.8	24.8	24.7	24.8	24.7	24.8	24.7
1993	24.5	24.6	24.8	25.1	25.2	25.6	25.8	25.8	25.7	25.7	25.8	25.9	25.3
1994	25.4	25.3	25.6	25.9	26.3	26.7	26.9	27.1	27.3	27.3	27.6	28.0	26.6
1995	26.7	26.9	27.1	27.2	27.4	28.0	27.9	28.2	28.2	28.0	28.2	28.5	27.6
1996	27.9	28.0	28.2	28.2	28.5	28.9	29.1	29.3	29.2	29.4	29.6	30.0	28.8
1997	29.2	29.5	29.7	29.9	30.1	30.3	30.4	30.5	30.5	30.5	30.5	30.6	30.1
1998	29.7	29.5	29.6	29.7	30.0	30.3	30.3	30.4	30.4	30.0	30.1	30.2	30.0
1999	30.1	30.2	30.4	30.6	30.9	31.2	31.3	31.5	31.5	31.4	31.5	31.8	31.0
2000	31.6	31.7	31.9	32.0	32.2	32.4	32.7	32.8	32.8	32.8	32.8	33.1	32.4
2001	33.1	33.3	33.4	33.3	33.5	33.6	33.5	33.5	33.2	33.2	33.1	33.1	33.3
2002	32.4	32.5	32.4	32.4	32.7	32.7	32.8	32.8	32.7	32.7	32.7	32.7	32.6
2003	32.2	32.1	32.2	32.4	32.6	32.7	32.5	32.7	32.6	32.8	32.9	32.9	32.6
Retail trade													
1990	58.8	57.5	57.5	58.1	59.1	60.4	59.8	60.4	60.8	61.1	64.0	65.3	60.2
1991	60.6	59.3	59.5	59.4	60.6	61.7	61.0	61.7	61.8	62.5	66.2	67.7	61.8
1992	62.3	61.1	61.3	61.7	62.8	63.5	63.1	63.5	63.3	63.4	66.9	68.8	63.4
1993	63.4	62.4	62.9	63.6	64.5	65.5	66.4	66.5	65.9	67.0	70.5	72.9	65.9
1994	66.9	65.8	66.1	66.8	68.0	69.3	70.5	71.3	71.1	71.3	75.9	78.0	70.0
1995	72.9	72.1	72.5	72.7	73.6	74.5	74.9	75.6	75.7	75.5	79.6	81.3	75.0
1996	75.8	74.4	74.3	74.8	76.1	77.3	78.3	79.1	77.7	78.4	82.9	84.7	77.8
1997	79.0	78.0	78.2	77.8	78.6	79.6	80.2	79.9	79.9	81.0	84.7	87.4	80.4
1998	81.5	80.1	79.8	79.8	80.5	81.4	81.9	82.3	81.9	82.7	86.6	88.9	82.3
1999	82.2	80.6	80.8	81.5	82.2	82.8	83.2	83.7	83.0	83.3	87.1	89.6	83.3
2000	83.0	81.5	81.9	82.1	82.8	83.7	83.2	83.6	83.7	84.9	87.9	89.8	84.0
2001	85.3	84.0	83.8	83.8	83.9	83.8	83.3	83.4	82.9	82.9	85.9	87.2	84.2
2002	83.4	81.9	81.4	81.8	82.5	83.0	82.6	83.1	82.8	83.1	86.0	87.5	83.3
2003	81.3	80.2	80.2	80.1	81.0	81.3	81.5	82.2	82.0	82.6	86.1	87.8	82.2
Transportation and utilities													
1990	27.0	27.2	27.4	25.4	25.7	26.1	26.1	26.6	26.6	26.8	27.0	27.4	26.6
1991	26.2	25.8	25.7	26.0	26.2	26.5	26.7	26.8	26.6	26.5	26.8	27.1	26.4
1992	26.6	26.9	27.1	27.1	27.3	27.8	27.9	28.1	28.0	28.2	28.4	29.2	27.7
1993	28.6	28.7	29.0	29.0	29.1	29.7	30.1	30.5	30.8	31.0	31.4	31.7	29.9
1994	31.4	31.6	31.9	30.6	31.5	31.9	31.6	31.9	31.8	31.5	31.6	32.2	31.6
1995	31.8	31.6	31.6	31.8	31.6	31.7	31.5	31.8	31.7	31.7	32.1	32.6	31.7
1996	32.2	32.5	32.5	32.0	32.0	32.2	31.6	31.7	31.9	32.1	32.3	33.1	32.1
1997	31.7	31.8	32.0	32.3	32.1	32.1	33.3	33.4	33.7	34.5	34.6	35.7	33.1
1998	34.6	34.7	34.8	34.7	34.9	35.1	35.8	36.0	36.1	36.2	36.3	36.8	35.5
1999	34.7	34.7	34.9	35.0	34.7	34.4	35.1	34.6	34.6	34.8	35.0	35.6	34.8
2000	35.2	35.1	35.5	35.3	35.2	35.7	36.1	36.2	36.1	36.3	36.5	36.9	35.8
2001	36.8	36.6	36.7	36.5	35.9	35.7	35.7	35.6	35.6	35.7	35.1	35.1	35.9
2002	34.3	34.5	33.6	33.8	33.7	33.6	33.7	33.5	33.3	33.7	33.5	33.2	33.7
2003	32.9	32.6	32.6	32.3	32.4	32.4	32.5	32.7	32.5	32.8	32.6	33.0	32.6
Information													
1990	10.7	10.6	10.6	10.8	10.6	10.8	10.9	11.0	11.0	10.9	11.0	11.2	10.8
1991	9.8	9.7	9.6	9.7	9.7	9.8	10.2	10.3	10.0	10.3	10.2	10.2	9.9
1992	10.0	10.2	10.2	10.4	10.4	10.7	10.9	11.0	10.9	11.0	11.4	11.5	10.7
1993	11.1	11.3	11.4	11.6	11.8	12.3	12.0	12.1	12.0	12.1	12.4	12.5	11.8
1994	12.5	12.8	13.2	13.6	13.9	14.3	14.2	14.5	14.5	14.4	14.8	14.9	13.9
1995	14.2	14.5	14.7	14.4	14.5	15.1	16.0	16.4	16.4	15.8	15.7	15.9	15.3
1996	16.5	16.8	16.9	17.4	17.6	18.1	18.4	19.0	19.4	19.1	19.0	19.1	18.1
1997	17.7	18.3	18.9	18.6	19.0	19.4	19.6	19.9	19.8	19.7	19.7	19.8	19.2
1998	19.2	19.8	19.9	19.8	19.9	20.3	21.5	21.6	21.4	21.3	21.8	21.9	20.7
1999	21.3	21.7	21.4	21.6	21.6	22.3	22.3	22.6	22.5	23.0	23.5	23.2	22.3
2000	22.5	22.4	22.7	22.7	23.4	24.0	24.0	24.5	24.6	24.6	24.9	24.7	23.8
2001	23.7	23.1	23.1	23.2	23.6	23.8	23.4	23.3	22.9	22.5	23.0	22.7	23.2
2002	22.3	22.3	21.6	21.4	21.6	21.4	21.4	20.9	20.8	20.9	21.0	20.8	21.4
2003	20.3	20.1	20.0	19.6	20.1	20.3	20.2	20.3	20.2	20.2	20.4	20.4	20.2

Employment by Industry: Utah—*Continued*

(Numbers in thousands. Not seasonally adjusted.)

Industry	January	February	March	April	May	June	July	August	September	October	November	December	Annual Average
SALT LAKE CITY-OGDEN *—Continued*													
Financial activities													
1990	27.1	27.3	27.5	27.8	27.9	28.3	28.2	28.6	28.6	28.5	28.6	28.8	28.1
1991	28.1	28.6	28.9	29.2	29.7	30.1	30.3	30.4	30.2	29.9	30.3	30.8	29.7
1992	30.5	30.6	30.8	30.8	31.1	31.2	31.3	31.6	31.5	31.6	31.7	32.0	31.2
1993	32.0	32.1	32.8	33.3	33.6	34.1	34.5	35.1	35.4	36.2	36.9	37.4	34.4
1994	37.1	37.3	37.9	37.8	37.8	37.8	37.9	38.1	38.0	37.7	37.9	38.3	37.8
1995	37.4	38.0	38.2	38.1	38.6	38.9	39.1	39.7	40.2	40.0	40.4	40.8	39.1
1996	40.3	40.6	41.1	41.3	41.6	41.7	41.6	41.9	42.0	42.2	42.8	43.4	41.7
1997	42.6	42.8	43.3	43.5	43.8	43.9	43.7	43.9	44.3	44.3	44.4	44.9	43.8
1998	44.3	44.3	44.7	45.0	45.4	45.9	46.6	46.9	47.0	47.3	47.1	47.4	46.0
1999	46.6	46.6	46.9	46.8	47.0	47.4	47.5	47.7	47.3	47.7	48.1	48.7	47.4
2000	48.1	47.9	48.1	48.2	48.2	48.4	48.6	48.9	48.8	48.9	49.2	49.7	48.6
2001	50.1	50.4	50.5	50.4	50.6	51.0	51.3	51.5	51.4	51.1	51.5	51.8	51.0
2002	51.2	51.1	50.6	50.7	51.1	51.2	50.9	51.1	50.9	51.3	51.2	51.6	51.1
2003	51.5	52.0	51.5	51.9	52.3	51.8	52.1	52.1	51.5	51.9	52.0	52.2	51.9
Professional and business services													
1990	50.7	50.4	51.6	52.1	53.1	54.4	54.1	55.1	54.7	54.7	55.3	55.5	53.4
1991	54.8	55.9	57.1	57.2	58.2	58.8	58.5	59.0	58.3	57.5	57.0	56.2	57.3
1992	54.1	54.5	55.5	56.3	57.0	57.5	57.6	58.5	58.1	57.7	58.1	57.7	56.8
1993	57.3	57.9	58.8	60.0	60.8	61.8	62.0	62.6	63.0	63.4	63.5	63.8	61.2
1994	61.8	62.1	63.5	65.0	65.5	66.3	67.2	68.3	68.3	67.7	69.0	70.1	66.2
1995	69.7	71.3	72.3	73.6	74.4	76.2	77.3	79.5	80.3	79.0	79.4	79.7	76.0
1996	78.1	79.6	80.5	82.0	83.7	85.3	85.9	87.3	87.6	86.8	87.5	87.8	84.3
1997	86.0	86.3	87.0	88.8	90.4	92.1	91.5	92.6	93.9	92.7	92.6	93.7	90.6
1998	89.2	90.1	91.1	92.4	93.4	95.4	94.6	95.8	95.6	95.8	95.8	96.5	93.8
1999	94.0	95.1	96.1	97.4	98.2	99.9	100.6	101.8	100.9	101.4	101.7	103.1	99.2
2000	99.2	100.4	102.5	103.4	104.1	105.6	105.7	106.5	106.8	107.0	106.2	107.2	104.6
2001	101.0	100.7	101.3	101.3	101.7	101.9	100.8	101.6	99.8	98.6	96.9	96.4	100.2
2002	94.8	97.9	94.9	95.6	96.0	96.1	96.3	97.7	97.3	96.8	97.0	96.0	96.4
2003	92.5	92.3	93.0	94.7	95.6	96.4	96.9	98.4	97.6	97.3	97.3	96.6	95.7
Educational and health services													
1990	43.3	43.5	43.7	43.9	43.8	43.3	42.6	42.7	44.1	45.0	45.3	45.4	43.8
1991	43.9	44.9	45.2	45.5	45.4	44.9	44.3	44.7	46.1	47.0	47.3	47.4	45.5
1992	46.5	47.6	47.9	47.9	47.8	47.1	46.7	47.1	48.5	49.5	49.9	49.8	48.0
1993	48.8	49.9	50.4	50.7	50.3	49.6	49.6	49.7	51.1	51.9	52.3	52.2	50.5
1994	51.1	52.1	52.4	52.5	52.4	51.7	50.2	50.5	53.1	53.8	54.3	54.3	52.3
1995	52.9	54.1	54.4	54.3	54.2	53.5	53.1	53.5	55.0	55.8	56.2	56.2	54.4
1996	55.6	56.4	56.9	57.0	56.6	55.6	55.3	55.7	57.5	58.4	59.0	58.8	56.9
1997	58.2	59.5	59.7	59.1	59.0	57.7	57.2	57.3	58.9	59.9	60.2	60.2	58.9
1998	58.7	59.8	59.8	59.7	59.3	58.4	57.1	57.4	58.9	59.9	60.2	60.1	59.1
1999	58.1	59.3	59.7	59.9	59.5	58.8	58.1	58.2	60.1	60.2	60.6	60.5	59.4
2000	59.6	61.1	61.2	61.4	61.2	61.1	59.3	59.7	61.3	61.8	62.2	62.8	61.1
2001	61.3	61.9	62.1	62.5	62.8	62.9	62.0	62.4	63.2	63.4	64.1	64.3	62.7
2002	63.2	63.8	63.8	64.3	64.4	64.4	63.9	65.0	65.9	66.2	66.7	67.2	64.9
2003	66.2	66.7	67.0	66.8	67.0	67.3	66.7	67.2	67.9	68.2	68.4	68.7	67.3
Leisure and hospitality													
1990	37.8	38.1	39.4	40.7	40.8	41.8	41.3	41.9	41.5	39.8	39.8	40.9	40.3
1991	39.5	39.7	40.4	40.2	40.8	42.1	41.8	42.4	41.7	41.1	41.2	42.5	41.1
1992	42.0	42.5	43.2	42.9	43.5	44.4	44.4	44.9	44.4	42.8	43.3	44.6	43.5
1993	43.6	44.3	45.4	45.9	46.5	47.8	47.7	48.4	47.4	46.2	46.2	47.5	46.4
1994	46.3	47.1	47.6	48.3	49.0	50.4	49.9	50.4	49.7	48.2	48.9	49.8	48.8
1995	49.4	50.0	50.6	51.3	51.4	52.7	52.6	53.3	52.2	50.7	51.6	52.1	51.4
1996	51.9	52.3	53.1	52.7	53.1	54.3	54.8	55.6	54.5	52.9	54.3	54.9	53.7
1997	53.5	54.5	55.2	55.1	56.1	56.7	56.8	57.3	56.3	54.3	55.6	56.0	55.6
1998	54.9	55.5	56.0	56.2	56.8	58.0	57.2	57.9	56.9	55.0	55.0	55.9	56.3
1999	54.9	55.6	56.5	56.3	56.9	58.3	57.5	58.3	57.0	55.6	55.6	56.6	56.6
2000	56.0	57.0	57.9	58.0	57.8	58.7	59.4	60.0	58.5	58.0	58.6	59.4	58.3
2001	57.4	58.0	59.4	60.0	59.8	60.7	60.4	60.8	60.1	58.9	58.7	60.6	59.6
2002	62.1	67.0	63.5	63.0	60.6	60.9	60.3	60.3	59.1	58.2	58.1	59.4	61.0
2003	58.4	58.9	59.1	60.2	59.0	60.3	60.2	60.5	59.6	59.1	58.7	60.4	59.5
Other services													
1990	17.5	17.7	17.9	18.3	18.5	18.8	19.2	19.4	18.9	18.7	18.6	18.8	18.5
1991	18.8	18.8	18.8	18.8	19.1	19.4	19.7	19.7	19.1	18.9	18.9	18.9	19.0
1992	18.7	18.8	18.9	19.2	19.4	19.6	19.9	20.0	19.4	19.2	19.2	19.2	19.2
1993	19.1	19.3	19.6	19.7	20.0	20.5	20.9	21.0	20.6	20.4	20.6	20.7	20.2
1994	20.5	20.6	20.8	20.9	21.1	21.7	22.1	22.1	21.7	21.5	21.5	21.6	21.3
1995	21.2	21.4	21.6	21.5	21.8	22.3	22.4	22.7	22.3	21.9	22.0	22.2	21.9
1996	21.8	21.9	22.2	22.0	22.3	22.7	23.1	23.4	22.9	22.8	22.9	23.0	22.5
1997	22.5	22.6	22.7	22.8	23.0	23.1	23.6	23.6	23.1	22.8	22.9	22.9	23.0
1998	21.9	22.6	23.1	23.2	23.5	23.7	24.3	24.2	23.5	23.3	23.2	23.2	23.3
1999	23.0	23.0	23.1	23.1	23.1	23.2	23.6	23.6	22.9	22.6	22.5	22.4	23.0
2000	22.1	21.9	22.0	22.2	22.3	22.5	22.9	23.0	22.5	22.1	22.1	22.0	22.3
2001	21.1	21.3	21.4	21.7	22.0	22.4	23.0	23.3	22.7	22.7	22.9	23.0	22.3
2002	22.8	23.8	23.2	23.2	23.3	23.3	23.6	23.7	23.2	23.0	23.2	22.9	23.3
2003	22.5	22.5	22.5	22.7	22.8	22.9	23.3	23.4	23.0	23.0	23.3	23.2	22.9

Employment by Industry: Utah—*Continued*

(Numbers in thousands. Not seasonally adjusted.)

Industry	January	February	March	April	May	June	July	August	September	October	November	December	Annual Average
SALT LAKE CITY-OGDEN *—Continued*													
Government													
1990	98.1	99.1	99.1	100.6	101.2	100.2	95.0	93.5	97.3	100.1	100.0	98.6	98.5
1991	99.7	101.2	101.1	101.8	102.7	101.3	96.5	95.4	99.3	101.0	101.5	100.2	100.1
1992	101.6	103.0	102.9	104.0	104.8	103.1	97.5	97.4	101.8	103.7	104.7	103.9	102.3
1993	104.7	105.8	106.0	105.9	106.2	105.5	99.0	98.2	102.3	104.0	104.7	103.9	103.8
1994	105.1	106.8	106.3	107.3	107.6	106.7	99.8	99.0	103.9	106.2	106.6	106.0	105.1
1995	106.2	108.0	108.0	109.2	109.0	108.3	100.5	100.0	104.8	107.2	107.7	106.5	106.2
1996	106.7	109.3	109.3	110.5	110.7	109.9	101.6	100.9	105.8	108.4	110.0	108.8	107.6
1997	109.7	112.4	113.0	113.4	113.7	113.0	105.8	103.6	108.9	111.7	112.8	111.8	110.8
1998	111.8	114.7	115.1	115.6	116.8	115.2	108.1	106.9	113.7	113.1	114.7	113.8	113.3
1999	112.4	116.7	117.4	118.0	117.7	116.3	108.2	107.7	115.2	115.7	116.9	116.2	114.9
2000	115.3	119.7	120.1	121.6	122.6	119.5	112.6	111.3	118.1	119.5	120.0	120.3	118.4
2001	118.8	122.7	122.9	124.0	123.9	123.1	115.9	115.0	121.5	122.6	123.8	124.3	121.5
2002	124.8	124.3	126.4	127.0	126.2	126.4	122.6	119.3	124.3	125.6	126.0	125.8	124.9
2003	127.3	127.9	127.6	127.8	126.8	126.3	122.4	120.3	123.9	125.9	126.4	126.5	125.8
Federal government													
2001	26.0	27.5	27.5	28.0	27.6	27.7	27.8	27.5	27.3	26.9	27.2	27.4	27.4
2002	27.8	28.7	28.9	29.2	29.3	29.3	29.4	29.1	28.8	28.7	28.4	28.6	28.9
2003	29.9	30.0	29.7	29.5	29.4	28.6	28.7	28.6	28.2	28.3	28.3	28.4	29.0
State government													
2001	38.7	40.6	40.5	41.0	40.7	39.0	38.5	39.7	41.2	41.2	41.4	41.4	40.3
2002	41.7	39.6	41.6	41.8	39.6	39.3	39.4	39.5	41.3	41.4	41.5	41.3	40.7
2003	41.3	41.4	41.2	41.7	39.6	39.8	39.5	39.7	40.8	41.3	41.5	41.5	40.8
Local government													
2001	54.1	54.6	54.9	55.0	55.6	56.4	49.6	47.8	53.0	54.5	55.2	55.5	53.9
2002	55.3	56.0	55.9	56.0	57.3	57.8	53.8	50.7	54.2	55.5	56.1	55.9	55.4
2003	56.1	56.5	56.7	56.6	57.8	57.9	54.2	52.0	54.9	56.3	56.6	56.6	56.0

Average Weekly Hours by Industry: Utah

(Not seasonally adjusted.)

Industry	January	February	March	April	May	June	July	August	September	October	November	December	Annual Average
STATEWIDE													
Natural resources and mining													
2001	42.2	41.4	41.2	41.8	41.2	41.6	43.3	41.8	43.7	42.5	42.9	44.1	42.3
2002	43.7	43.1	45.6	44.4	42.5	44.0	45.5	43.9	44.3	46.0	45.5	43.9	44.4
2003	44.1	42.7	43.9	43.9	44.7	42.8	42.7	42.6	44.3	45.9	46.6	44.7	44.1
Manufacturing													
2001	38.6	39.2	38.8	38.1	38.2	38.4	38.1	38.7	38.5	37.7	38.3	38.3	38.4
2002	37.4	36.1	37.4	36.6	37.2	37.9	37.4	38.8	38.1	38.0	39.5	39.5	37.8
2003	38.5	40.1	39.8	40.4	40.1	39.8	38.6	40.5	39.8	40.0	38.8	39.9	39.7
Wholesale trade													
2001	36.5	36.4	36.4	38.2	37.2	37.4	38.9	37.5	37.2	36.5	36.8	37.0	37.2
2002	35.9	36.6	36.6	36.0	37.3	38.2	38.3	38.6	39.0	38.5	38.5	38.3	37.7
2003	39.3	39.4	39.4	38.5	38.1	38.0	37.1	38.1	38.2	38.2	37.8	37.6	38.3
Retail trade													
2001	27.9	28.0	28.2	28.9	28.7	29.2	29.7	29.1	29.0	28.7	28.1	28.9	28.7
2002	28.2	28.3	28.6	29.0	29.1	29.8	29.9	29.4	29.5	29.0	28.5	29.8	29.1
2003	27.9	28.5	29.1	29.0	29.2	30.1	29.8	29.6	29.6	29.2	28.4	29.3	29.1
Information													
2001	40.6	39.5	40.0	40.0	40.3	41.1	41.2	40.0	39.3	38.4	37.5	39.1	39.8
2002	37.0	38.5	37.3	35.2	35.2	37.2	36.3	35.9	35.9	36.3	35.5	37.5	36.5
2003	36.4	37.3	38.0	36.0	35.1	37.2	34.8	34.6	34.3	35.1	36.2	34.8	35.8
SALT LAKE CITY-OGDEN													
Construction and mining													
2001	37.5	38.0	38.4	37.8	39.5	37.9	39.8	40.9	40.4	40.1	39.6	38.2	39.0
2002	37.9	37.5	38.4	37.4	38.4	38.4	37.9	37.9	38.3	39.4	37.9	37.5	38.1
2003	37.5	37.2	38.2	37.6	37.9	38.3	38.4	39.7	38.6	39.1	39.0	37.8	38.3
Manufacturing													
2001	38.6	38.8	38.7	38.4	38.2	38.3	38.6	38.3	39.1	37.8	38.3	37.7	38.4
2002	35.7	35.5	36.9	35.6	35.8	37.0	36.9	38.1	38.4	37.2	38.0	38.4	37.0
2003	36.9	38.3	38.0	38.6	38.5	38.7	37.4	39.4	38.6	38.9	37.6	38.7	38.3
Trade, transportation, and utilities													
2001	32.1	32.6	32.5	33.2	33.8	33.9	33.9	33.3	34.1	33.4	32.8	33.5	33.3
2002	32.4	33.2	33.4	32.7	33.4	32.9	33.1	32.4	34.0	34.1	32.8	33.7	33.2
2003	33.2	34.3	34.5	34.1	33.8	33.2	33.1	33.5	33.6	33.8	33.4	33.1	33.6
Wholesale trade													
2001	37.2	37.5	37.5	39.2	37.7	37.3	39.1	37.7	38.1	37.1	37.8	38.1	37.9
2002	36.5	38.0	38.5	36.6	37.4	38.6	39.3	39.0	39.6	39.1	39.2	39.0	38.4
2003	39.1	39.9	40.2	38.4	38.7	38.6	38.1	38.8	38.8	38.4	38.0	37.0	38.7
Retail trade													
2001	28.3	28.4	28.6	29.5	29.1	29.6	29.9	29.5	29.7	29.3	28.4	29.2	29.1
2002	28.3	28.5	28.8	29.2	29.4	29.9	29.7	29.6	30.0	29.3	28.6	30.0	29.3
2003	28.1	29.2	29.9	29.9	29.7	30.5	30.1	30.2	30.2	29.8	28.8	30.0	29.7
Information													
2001	40.8	39.5	40.0	39.8	40.2	40.9	40.9	39.6	38.4	39.3	38.9	39.7	39.8
2002	37.5	39.3	37.3	34.6	34.7	36.9	36.6	35.9	35.4	35.0	34.8	34.9	36.1
2003	33.8	35.3	36.3	35.1	34.5	35.5	34.1	33.4	32.7	33.4	33.8	32.3	34.1

Average Hourly Earnings by Industry: Utah

(Dollars, not seasonally adjusted.)

Industry	January	February	March	April	May	June	July	August	September	October	November	December	Annual Average
STATEWIDE													
Natural resources and mining													
2001	15.09	15.03	15.15	15.23	15.15	15.39	15.35	15.34	15.55	15.70	15.89	15.76	15.38
2002	15.74	15.76	15.51	15.69	15.38	14.98	15.13	16.23	16.40	16.10	16.27	16.57	15.82
2003	16.11	16.38	15.89	16.12	16.00	18.08	18.69	19.56	19.51	19.25	19.03	19.67	17.88
Manufacturing													
2001	13.59	13.57	13.66	13.77	13.62	13.76	13.91	13.89	13.85	13.81	13.80	13.90	13.76
2002	13.75	14.08	14.09	14.19	13.80	14.27	14.28	14.17	14.39	14.17	13.80	14.45	14.12
2003	14.68	14.71	14.71	14.82	14.63	14.67	14.79	15.02	15.01	15.05	15.26	15.42	14.90
Wholesale trade													
2001	14.54	14.35	14.29	14.45	14.18	14.70	14.61	14.17	14.73	14.42	14.37	14.94	14.48
2002	15.35	15.01	14.67	15.07	14.65	15.51	15.74	15.62	15.82	15.76	15.58	16.13	15.42
2003	16.01	16.26	16.08	16.60	16.30	16.66	17.06	16.87	17.55	17.01	16.80	16.34	16.63
Retail trade													
2001	10.70	10.62	10.69	10.63	10.63	10.62	10.73	10.52	10.75	10.62	10.65	10.73	10.66
2002	11.01	10.81	11.09	10.79	10.96	11.24	11.17	11.06	11.58	11.18	10.87	11.13	11.08
2003	11.47	11.37	11.35	11.92	11.64	11.53	11.69	11.48	11.49	11.50	11.04	10.57	11.41
Information													
2001	17.08	17.08	17.03	17.46	17.41	17.46	16.96	16.83	17.50	17.62	17.71	17.52	17.30
2002	17.95	17.71	18.10	17.69	16.90	16.88	17.20	16.92	18.00	17.47	18.08	18.17	17.59
2003	17.92	19.36	19.34	19.47	20.12	21.22	22.55	22.13	22.91	23.04	23.13	23.77	21.27
SALT LAKE CITY-OGDEN													
Construction and mining													
2001	17.69	17.11	17.26	17.10	16.86	17.20	17.57	17.72	17.93	17.87	18.39	18.76	17.63
2002	18.92	19.26	19.03	19.12	18.63	17.74	17.74	18.50	18.62	19.10	18.96	19.77	18.77
2003	18.97	18.52	18.06	18.03	17.89	17.80	17.85	17.69	18.00	18.17	17.63	17.58	18.00
Manufacturing													
2001	13.40	13.36	13.48	13.53	13.51	13.68	13.79	13.86	13.85	13.89	13.90	14.21	13.70
2002	14.40	14.31	14.48	14.60	14.33	14.40	14.29	14.16	14.29	14.26	14.32	14.29	14.34
2003	14.25	14.43	14.30	14.13	14.22	14.30	14.45	14.50	14.51	14.95	14.67	14.81	14.46
Trade, transportation, and utilities													
2001	13.77	13.52	13.46	13.53	13.40	13.66	14.04	13.19	13.43	13.36	13.47	13.60	13.54
2002	13.72	13.44	12.65	12.87	13.23	13.92	14.06	14.02	14.26	14.03	13.81	14.12	13.68
2003	14.37	16.03	14.58	14.93	14.68	14.94	14.98	14.73	15.03	15.12	14.93	14.29	14.88
Wholesale trade													
2001	15.46	15.01	15.03	15.35	14.90	15.73	15.72	14.95	15.18	15.15	14.95	15.25	15.22
2002	15.79	14.99	14.55	15.28	14.95	15.94	16.54	16.17	16.38	16.20	15.83	16.51	15.77
2003	16.40	16.77	16.39	16.97	16.24	16.80	16.80	16.62	17.55	17.07	16.93	16.75	16.77
Retail trade													
2001	11.39	11.22	11.34	11.21	11.33	11.17	11.43	11.07	11.32	11.16	11.13	11.38	11.26
2002	11.64	11.37	11.78	11.44	11.77	12.03	12.09	11.93	12.89	12.38	11.93	12.18	11.96
2003	12.60	12.41	12.46	13.05	12.69	12.55	12.75	12.42	12.49	12.43	11.95	11.34	12.42
Information													
2001	16.89	16.94	17.24	17.70	17.67	18.62	17.97	17.84	18.69	18.05	17.79	17.65	17.75
2002	18.11	18.12	18.31	18.03	17.08	17.20	17.38	17.01	18.35	17.80	17.59	16.13	17.62
2003	16.64	17.38	16.96	17.66	18.29	18.55	19.78	19.19	19.51	20.03	18.86	19.36	18.51

Average Weekly Earnings by Industry: Utah

(Dollars, not seasonally adjusted.)

Industry	January	February	March	April	May	June	July	August	September	October	November	December	Annual Average
STATEWIDE													
Natural resources and mining													
2001	636.80	622.24	624.18	636.61	624.18	640.22	6[illegible]4.66	641.21	679.54	667.25	681.68	695.02	650.57
2002	687.84	679.26	707.26	696.64	653.65	659.12	6[illegible]8.42	712.50	726.52	740.60	740.29	727.42	702.41
2003	710.45	699.43	697.57	707.67	715.20	773.82	7[illegible]8.06	833.26	864.29	883.58	886.80	879.25	788.51
Manufacturing													
2001	524.57	531.94	530.01	524.64	520.28	528.38	5[illegible]9.97	537.54	533.23	520.64	528.54	532.37	528.38
2002	514.25	508.29	526.97	519.35	513.36	540.83	5[illegible]4.07	549.80	548.26	538.46	545.10	570.78	533.74
2003	565.18	589.87	585.46	598.73	586.66	583.87	5[illegible]0.89	608.31	597.40	602.00	592.09	615.26	591.53
Wholesale trade													
2001	530.71	522.34	520.16	551.99	527.50	549.78	[illegible]8.33	531.38	547.96	526.33	528.82	552.78	538.66
2002	551.07	549.37	536.92	542.52	546.45	592.48	[illegible]2.84	602.93	616.98	606.76	599.83	617.78	581.33
2003	629.19	640.64	633.55	639.10	621.03	633.08	[illegible]2.93	642.75	670.41	649.78	635.04	614.38	636.93
Retail trade													
2001	298.53	297.36	301.46	307.21	305.08	310.10	[illegible]18.68	306.13	311.75	304.79	299.27	310.10	305.94
2002	310.48	305.92	317.17	312.91	318.94	334.95	[illegible]33.98	325.16	341.61	324.22	309.80	331.67	322.43
2003	320.01	324.05	330.29	345.68	339.89	347.05	[illegible]48.36	339.81	340.10	335.80	313.54	309.70	332.03
Information													
2001	693.45	674.66	681.20	698.40	701.62	717.61	[illegible]98.75	673.20	687.75	676.61	664.13	685.03	688.54
2002	664.15	681.84	675.13	622.69	594.88	627.94	[illegible]24.36	607.43	646.20	634.16	641.84	681.38	642.04
2003	652.29	722.13	734.92	700.92	706.21	789.38	[illegible]84.74	765.70	785.81	808.70	837.31	827.20	761.47
SALT LAKE CITY-OGDEN													
Construction and mining													
2001	663.38	650.18	662.78	646.38	665.97	651.88	[illegible]99.29	724.75	724.37	716.59	728.24	716.63	687.57
2002	717.07	722.25	730.75	715.09	715.39	681.22	[illegible]72.35	701.15	713.15	752.54	718.58	741.38	715.14
2003	711.38	688.94	689.89	677.93	678.03	681.74	[illegible]85.44	702.29	694.80	710.45	687.57	664.52	689.40
Manufacturing													
2001	517.24	518.37	521.68	519.55	516.08	523.94	532.29	530.84	541.54	525.04	532.37	535.72	526.08
2002	514.08	508.01	534.31	519.76	513.01	532.80	527.30	539.50	548.74	530.47	544.16	548.74	530.58
2003	525.83	552.67	543.40	545.42	547.47	553.41	540.43	571.30	560.09	581.56	551.59	573.15	553.82
Trade, transportation, and utilities													
2001	442.02	440.75	437.45	449.20	452.92	463.07	475.96	439.23	457.96	446.22	441.82	455.60	450.88
2002	444.53	446.21	422.51	420.85	441.88	457.97	465.39	454.25	484.84	478.42	452.97	475.84	454.18
2003	477.08	549.83	503.01	509.11	496.18	496.01	495.84	493.46	505.01	511.06	498.66	473.00	499.97
Wholesale trade													
2001	575.11	562.88	563.63	601.72	561.73	586.73	614.65	563.62	578.36	562.07	565.11	581.03	576.84
2002	576.34	569.62	560.18	559.25	559.13	615.28	650.02	630.63	648.65	633.42	620.54	643.89	605.57
2003	641.24	669.12	658.88	651.65	628.49	648.48	640.08	644.86	680.94	655.49	643.34	619.75	649.00
Retail trade													
2001	322.34	318.65	324.32	330.70	329.70	330.63	341.76	326.57	336.20	326.99	316.09	332.30	327.67
2002	329.41	324.05	339.26	334.05	346.04	359.70	359.07	353.13	386.70	362.73	341.20	365.40	350.43
2003	354.06	362.37	372.55	390.20	376.89	382.78	383.78	375.08	377.20	370.41	344.16	340.20	368.87
Information													
2001	689.11	669.13	689.60	704.46	710.33	761.56	734.97	706.46	717.70	709.37	692.03	700.71	706.45
2002	679.13	712.12	682.96	623.84	592.68	634.68	636.11	610.66	649.59	623.00	612.13	562.94	636.08
2003	562.43	613.51	615.65	619.87	631.01	658.53	674.50	640.95	637.98	669.00	637.47	625.33	631.19

VERMONT AT A GLANCE

(Population and total nonfarm employment numbers in thousands)

Population, Census 2000:	608.8
Total nonfarm employment, 2003:	298.6
Change in total nonfarm employment	
(Number)	
1990–2003:	40.9
1990–2001:	44.4
2001–2003:	-3.5
(Compound annual rate of change)	
1990–2003:	1.1%
1990–2001:	1.5%
2001–2003:	-0.6%
Unemployment rate	
1990:	4.9%
2001:	3.3%
2003:	4.5%

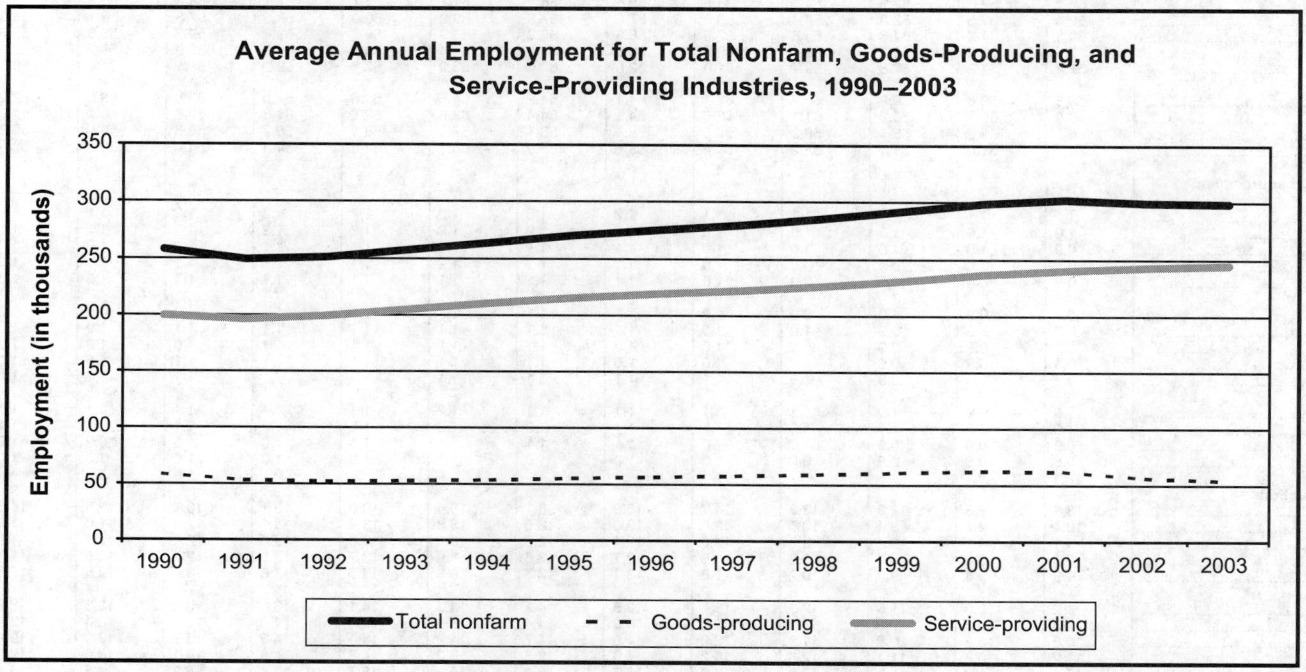

Total nonfarm employment declined more significantly in the early 1990s than in the 2001 recession, however it showed steady growth between these two contractions. The number of jobs in the goods-producing sector fell substantially in both recessions. Employment in the service-providing sector grew steadily following the earlier recession, and continued to grow throughout the 1990s, slowing marginally after 2000. From 2000 to 2003, educational and health services, wholesale trade, and government employment grew the fastest.

Employment by Industry: Vermont

(Numbers in thousands. Not seasonally adjusted.)

Industry	January	February	March	April	May	June	July	August	September	October	November	December	Annual Average
STATEWIDE													
Total nonfarm													
1990	258.7	258.2	257.8	255.6	257.1	259.9	256.3	257.1	259.3	259.5	255.5	257.2	257.7
1991	248.4	247.3	246.6	244.5	245.4	247.9	247.1	248.8	253.1	254.6	252.1	253.7	249.1
1992	244.6	249.0	248.3	246.6	246.8	249.8	248.8	250.2	256.7	259.3	256.6	257.6	251.2
1993	251.2	254.6	253.5	252.6	253.4	257.8	254.6	256.3	262.7	264.8	262.9	264.2	257.4
1994	256.8	260.5	262.1	259.0	260.9	264.2	260.6	261.8	268.5	270.6	269.4	272.9	263.9
1995	265.2	268.3	269.6	266.6	266.8	269.0	266.2	267.5	274.6	276.6	274.5	277.5	270.2
1996	270.6	273.6	273.8	272.2	273.6	275.3	269.6	271.9	278.7	280.7	278.5	282.5	275.1
1997	272.7	277.3	276.7	275.3	276.9	279.1	275.6	276.3	283.2	286.8	284.0	288.8	279.4
1998	278.8	283.9	284.1	283.1	284.1	285.5	281.0	281.3	288.5	289.7	287.8	292.3	285.0
1999	284.7	289.0	289.3	288.5	289.6	291.0	287.6	287.3	294.2	298.2	297.9	301.3	291.6
2000	293.7	296.9	299.0	293.6	297.2	300.0	293.6	293.8	301.3	304.2	302.4	308.7	298.7
2001	301.7	302.6	302.0	299.6	301.2	304.6	297.8	297.5	303.7	305.3	303.1	306.0	302.1
2002	299.4	299.4	299.1	297.1	299.4	302.1	294.0	293.9	300.8	302.6	300.2	304.1	299.3
2003	297.2	297.8	296.9	293.6	298.0	301.2	293.7	294.7	301.4	303.1	301.0	304.9	298.6
Total private													
1990	216.5	214.4	213.2	208.8	210.8	215.9	218.7	219.7	216.3	214.3	210.2	211.5	214.2
1991	204.6	201.9	200.8	198.9	200.3	204.7	209.4	211.1	209.2	208.9	205.8	208.0	205.3
1992	200.9	203.6	202.5	200.9	201.8	206.7	211.3	213.2	213.1	213.5	210.0	211.9	207.5
1993	207.1	209.1	208.0	206.5	207.6	213.5	217.9	219.9	218.6	218.5	216.2	218.2	213.4
1994	212.7	214.5	215.6	212.5	214.2	219.2	223.3	224.8	223.6	223.5	221.2	225.5	219.2
1995	220.1	221.5	222.2	219.4	220.2	224.1	228.4	230.0	229.8	229.3	226.7	229.9	225.1
1996	225.6	226.5	226.4	224.5	226.1	230.5	231.9	234.4	232.7	233.4	230.1	234.2	229.7
1997	228.3	229.7	229.4	227.4	229.3	234.0	237.5	238.2	236.9	238.2	235.3	239.9	233.7
1998	233.7	235.6	236.0	235.1	236.4	240.2	242.9	243.2	241.6	240.6	238.2	242.5	238.8
1999	238.0	239.8	239.8	239.2	240.0	244.1	248.1	248.3	245.9	247.5	246.5	250.0	243.9
2000	244.8	246.1	246.7	242.1	244.8	251.1	252.4	252.8	251.4	252.5	250.2	256.4	249.3
2001	251.6	251.0	250.3	247.9	249.4	254.7	256.1	255.8	252.6	251.9	249.6	252.4	251.9
2002	248.1	246.8	246.4	244.2	246.7	251.1	252.2	251.8	249.6	248.6	245.8	250.7	248.5
2003	245.1	243.9	243.1	239.7	244.1	249.3	250.5	251.9	248.7	248.4	246.3	250.0	246.8
Goods-producing													
1990	57.9	56.6	56.3	57.1	58.4	60.1	60.4	60.9	59.6	58.8	57.0	55.6	58.2
1991	51.6	50.3	50.1	51.2	52.5	54.0	55.2	55.5	54.7	54.7	54.0	52.5	53.0
1992	48.6	49.0	49.1	50.0	51.3	53.0	53.8	54.5	54.2	54.1	53.3	52.1	51.9
1993	49.1	49.3	49.3	50.4	51.9	53.9	55.1	55.4	54.8	54.5	54.3	53.0	52.6
1994	49.9	49.8	50.3	51.2	52.7	54.2	55.1	55.7	55.5	55.7	55.8	54.7	53.4
1995	52.1	52.0	52.6	54.1	54.8	55.5	56.2	57.1	57.1	57.1	56.6	55.3	55.0
1996	52.4	52.5	52.8	54.4	56.3	57.8	57.9	59.2	59.0	58.5	57.8	56.7	56.3
1997	54.5	54.2	54.6	55.6	57.6	58.8	59.2	59.9	59.3	59.6	59.3	58.8	57.6
1998	55.9	55.8	56.3	58.1	59.7	60.8	61.2	61.4	60.6	60.2	59.9	59.7	59.1
1999	57.3	57.2	57.6	59.7	61.0	62.0	63.0	63.0	62.4	62.2	62.1	61.6	60.8
2000	58.8	58.6	59.2	60.7	62.1	64.1	64.2	64.5	63.8	64.0	63.6	63.0	62.2
2001	60.9	60.1	60.2	61.1	62.6	64.1	64.4	63.8	62.6	61.8	60.6	60.1	61.9
2002	56.5	55.3	55.1	56.2	57.6	58.4	58.1	57.0	56.4	56.2	55.3	54.0	56.3
2003	51.7	51.0	51.1	52.2	54.4	55.6	55.9	56.1	54.6	54.8	54.4	53.9	53.8
Natural resources and mining													
1990	1.1	1.1	1.1	1.1	1.1	1.2	1.3	1.2	1.2	1.2	1.2	1.1	1.2
1991	1.0	1.0	1.0	1.0	1.0	1.2	1.2	1.2	1.2	1.2	1.1	1.1	1.1
1992	0.9	1.0	1.0	1.0	1.0	1.1	1.1	1.1	1.1	1.1	1.0	1.0	1.0
1993	0.9	1.0	0.9	0.9	1.0	1.1	1.1	1.2	1.1	1.1	1.1	1.1	1.0
1994	0.9	0.8	0.9	0.9	1.0	1.1	1.1	1.1	1.1	1.1	1.1	1.0	1.0
1995	0.9	0.9	1.0	0.9	1.0	1.1	1.1	1.1	1.1	1.1	1.0	0.9	1.0
1996	0.8	0.8	0.9	1.0	1.0	1.1	1.1	1.1	1.1	1.1	1.1	1.0	1.0
1997	0.8	0.9	0.9	0.9	1.0	1.0	1.1	1.1	1.1	1.1	1.0	1.0	1.0
1998	0.9	0.9	0.9	1.0	1.0	1.0	1.1	1.1	1.1	1.1	1.1	1.0	1.0
1999	0.9	0.9	0.9	1.0	1.1	1.1	1.1	1.1	1.2	1.1	1.1	1.1	1.1
2000	1.0	0.9	1.0	1.1	1.1	1.1	1.1	1.2	1.1	1.1	1.1	1.1	1.1
2001	1.0	1.0	1.1	1.0	1.1	1.1	1.2	1.2	1.2	1.2	1.1	1.1	1.1
2002	0.9	0.9	0.9	1.0	1.0	1.1	1.1	1.1	1.1	1.0	1.0	0.9	1.0
2003	0.8	0.8	0.9	0.9	1.0	1.0	1.0	1.0	1.0	1.0	1.0	1.0	1.0
Construction													
1990	13.5	12.5	12.3	13.3	14.7	15.8	16.1	16.4	16.0	15.1	13.7	12.5	14.3
1991	10.4	9.7	9.4	10.5	12.0	13.0	13.6	13.8	13.4	13.1	12.3	11.0	11.9
1992	9.1	8.7	8.7	9.5	11.0	12.1	12.8	13.1	13.0	13.0	12.4	11.4	11.2
1993	9.5	8.8	8.7	9.8	11.6	12.7	13.6	14.0	13.7	13.5	12.7	11.5	11.7
1994	9.8	9.4	9.3	10.2	11.8	13.1	13.5	13.8	13.7	13.6	13.4	12.5	12.0
1995	11.2	10.8	11.0	12.3	13.0	13.5	14.1	14.3	14.1	13.8	13.2	12.3	12.8
1996	10.3	9.8	9.9	11.0	12.8	13.9	14.4	15.1	15.0	14.3	13.4	12.4	12.7
1997	10.8	10.2	10.2	11.2	12.9	14.0	14.7	14.9	14.4	14.3	13.7	12.9	12.9
1998	11.2	10.8	11.1	12.6	14.2	14.9	15.3	15.3	14.8	14.6	14.1	13.6	13.5
1999	12.1	11.9	11.8	13.9	14.9	15.7	16.3	16.2	15.7	15.4	15.0	14.3	14.4
2000	12.7	12.3	12.5	13.9	15.2	16.3	16.7	16.6	16.1	16.0	15.3	14.6	14.9
2001	13.2	12.7	12.8	13.8	15.5	16.6	17.2	17.2	16.5	16.1	15.6	15.1	15.2
2002	13.4	12.9	12.8	13.9	15.3	15.8	16.3	16.3	15.8	15.8	15.3	14.3	14.8
2003	13.0	12.4	12.5	13.7	15.6	16.6	17.2	17.4	16.9	16.6	16.2	15.6	15.3

Employment by Industry: Vermont—*Continued*

(Numbers in thousands. Not seasonally adjusted.)

Industry	January	February	March	April	May	June	July	August	September	October	November	December	Annual Average
STATEWIDE—*Continued*													
Manufacturing													
1990	43.3	43.0	42.9	42.7	42.6	43.1	43.0	43.3	42.4	42.5	42.1	42.0	42.7
1991	40.2	39.6	39.7	39.7	39.5	39.8	40.4	40.5	40.1	40.4	40.6	40.4	40.1
1992	38.6	39.3	39.4	39.5	39.3	39.8	39.9	40.3	40.1	40.0	39.9	39.7	39.7
1993	38.7	39.5	39.7	39.7	39.3	40.1	40.4	40.2	40.0	39.9	40.5	40.4	39.9
1994	39.2	39.6	40.1	40.1	39.9	40.0	40.5	40.8	40.7	41.0	41.3	41.2	40.4
1995	40.0	40.3	40.6	40.9	40.8	40.9	41.0	41.7	41.9	42.2	42.4	42.1	41.2
1996	41.3	41.9	42.0	42.4	42.5	42.8	42.4	43.0	42.9	43.1	43.3	43.3	42.6
1997	42.9	43.1	43.5	43.5	43.7	43.8	43.4	43.9	43.8	44.2	44.6	44.9	43.8
1998	43.8	44.1	44.3	44.5	44.5	44.9	44.8	45.0	44.7	44.5	44.7	45.1	44.6
1999	44.3	44.4	44.9	44.8	45.0	45.2	45.6	45.7	45.5	45.7	46.0	46.2	45.3
2000	45.1	45.4	45.7	45.7	45.8	46.7	46.4	46.7	46.6	46.9	47.2	47.3	46.3
2001	46.7	46.4	46.3	46.3	46.0	46.4	46.0	45.4	44.9	44.5	43.9	43.9	45.6
2002	42.2	41.5	41.4	41.3	41.3	41.5	40.7	39.6	39.5	39.4	39.0	38.8	40.5
2003	37.9	37.8	37.7	37.6	37.8	38.0	37.7	37.7	36.7	37.2	37.2	37.3	37.6
Service-providing													
1990	200.8	201.6	201.5	198.5	198.7	199.8	195.9	196.2	199.7	200.7	198.5	201.6	199.5
1991	196.8	197.0	196.5	193.3	192.9	193.9	191.9	193.3	198.4	199.9	198.1	201.2	196.1
1992	196.0	200.0	199.2	196.6	195.5	196.8	195.0	195.7	202.5	205.2	203.3	205.5	199.3
1993	202.1	205.3	204.2	202.2	201.5	203.9	199.5	200.9	207.9	210.3	208.6	211.2	204.8
1994	206.9	210.7	211.8	207.8	208.2	210.0	205.5	206.1	213.0	214.9	213.6	218.2	210.6
1995	213.1	216.3	217.0	212.5	212.0	213.5	210.0	210.4	217.5	219.5	217.9	222.2	215.2
1996	218.2	221.1	221.0	217.8	217.3	217.5	211.7	212.7	219.7	222.2	220.7	225.8	218.8
1997	218.2	223.1	222.1	219.7	219.3	220.3	216.4	216.4	223.9	227.2	224.7	230.0	221.8
1998	222.9	228.1	227.8	225.0	224.4	224.7	219.8	219.9	227.9	229.5	227.9	232.6	225.9
1999	227.4	231.8	231.7	228.8	228.6	229.0	224.6	224.3	231.8	236.0	235.8	239.7	230.8
2000	234.9	238.3	239.8	232.9	235.1	235.9	229.4	229.3	237.5	240.2	238.8	245.7	236.5
2001	240.8	242.5	241.8	238.5	238.6	240.5	233.4	233.7	241.1	243.5	242.5	245.9	240.2
2002	242.9	244.1	244.0	240.9	241.8	243.7	235.9	236.9	244.4	246.4	244.9	250.1	243.0
2003	245.5	246.8	245.8	241.4	243.6	245.6	237.8	238.6	246.8	248.3	246.6	251.0	244.8
Trade, transportation, and utilities													
1990	51.4	50.7	50.6	50.3	50.6	51.4	51.6	51.9	51.1	50.9	51.1	51.7	51.1
1991	49.7	48.4	48.2	48.5	48.1	49.0	49.1	49.4	49.0	49.2	49.3	50.0	49.0
1992	47.7	47.6	47.4	48.2	48.5	49.3	49.8	50.1	50.0	50.8	51.3	51.7	49.4
1993	49.8	49.8	49.7	50.2	50.4	51.4	51.8	52.2	51.9	52.6	53.0	53.4	51.4
1994	51.0	51.2	51.2	50.9	51.9	52.7	53.2	53.2	52.9	53.4	53.8	54.8	52.5
1995	52.4	52.4	52.5	53.0	53.4	53.9	54.0	53.9	53.8	54.5	54.7	55.5	53.7
1996	53.6	53.2	53.2	53.4	53.8	54.2	54.0	54.5	54.0	54.8	55.5	56.6	54.2
1997	54.1	54.0	54.3	54.4	54.4	55.1	55.7	55.6	55.3	56.1	56.5	57.2	55.2
1998	54.5	54.4	54.4	55.2	55.4	55.9	56.0	56.0	56.0	56.4	57.0	58.2	55.8
1999	55.4	55.4	55.3	55.7	55.8	56.1	56.8	56.7	56.6	57.5	58.6	59.6	56.6
2000	57.2	57.0	56.9	56.9	57.2	57.9	58.0	58.1	58.0	58.7	59.5	60.5	58.0
2001	58.1	57.6	57.5	57.7	58.4	58.9	58.4	58.5	58.3	59.2	60.1	61.1	58.7
2002	58.3	57.7	57.9	57.9	58.7	59.2	59.1	59.2	58.7	59.1	59.7	60.5	58.8
2003	57.9	57.4	56.8	57.0	57.6	58.4	57.8	58.1	57.8	58.5	58.8	59.6	58.0
Wholesale trade													
1990	9.4	9.3	9.3	9.5	9.4	9.4	9.6	9.5	9.4	9.3	9.3	9.3	9.4
1991	9.3	9.2	9.2	9.3	9.2	9.3	9.3	9.2	9.1	9.1	9.2	9.2	9.2
1992	8.9	8.9	9.0	9.1	9.2	9.3	9.5	9.5	9.5	9.6	9.6	9.6	9.3
1993	9.4	9.6	9.6	9.7	9.7	9.9	10.0	10.0	9.8	9.9	9.8	9.8	9.8
1994	9.5	9.6	9.7	9.6	9.8	9.9	10.0	9.8	9.8	9.7	9.8	9.8	9.8
1995	9.6	9.7	9.7	9.8	9.9	9.9	10.1	10.0	10.0	10.1	10.1	10.3	9.9
1996	9.8	9.7	9.8	9.9	9.9	9.8	9.6	9.7	9.6	9.6	9.6	9.7	9.7
1997	9.5	9.6	9.6	9.6	9.6	9.6	9.7	9.6	9.6	9.7	9.7	9.7	9.6
1998	9.4	9.5	9.4	9.5	9.5	9.6	9.7	9.6	9.6	9.5	9.6	9.5	9.5
1999	9.3	9.4	9.4	9.4	9.4	9.3	9.4	9.4	9.4	9.5	9.6	9.7	9.4
2000	9.7	9.7	9.8	9.9	9.8	9.8	9.9	9.9	9.8	9.8	9.9	9.9	9.8
2001	9.9	10.0	10.0	10.1	10.0	10.1	10.1	10.1	10.1	10.1	10.1	10.3	10.1
2002	9.9	9.9	10.0	10.0	10.1	10.1	10.2	10.2	10.3	10.2	10.3	10.4	10.1
2003	10.1	10.1	10.1	10.1	10.2	10.3	10.2	10.3	10.3	10.4	10.4	10.5	10.3
Retail trade													
1990	34.4	33.8	33.6	33.2	33.6	34.1	34.2	34.5	33.8	33.7	34.0	34.5	34.0
1991	32.6	31.6	31.5	31.7	31.5	32.2	32.5	32.8	32.4	32.6	32.6	33.3	32.3
1992	31.3	31.1	30.9	31.4	31.6	32.1	32.5	32.7	32.5	33.1	33.5	33.9	32.2
1993	32.2	32.0	31.9	32.2	32.4	33.1	33.7	34.1	33.9	34.2	34.8	35.2	33.3
1994	33.5	33.5	33.3	33.2	33.8	34.4	34.9	35.1	34.7	35.0	35.3	36.3	34.4
1995	34.6	34.4	34.5	34.7	35.0	35.5	35.9	35.8	35.4	35.7	36.0	36.6	35.3
1996	35.5	35.1	35.1	35.1	35.4	35.9	36.3	36.6	36.0	36.5	37.2	38.2	36.1
1997	36.3	36.0	36.3	36.4	36.4	37.0	37.4	37.6	37.1	37.6	38.1	38.7	37.1
1998	36.6	36.4	36.5	37.0	37.2	37.6	37.9	37.9	37.6	38.0	38.6	39.9	37.6
1999	37.5	37.3	37.3	37.7	37.8	38.1	39.0	38.9	38.3	39.0	40.2	41.1	38.5
2000	38.9	38.7	38.5	38.5	38.9	39.5	39.6	39.8	39.4	40.0	40.7	41.8	39.5
2001	39.6	39.0	39.0	39.0	39.8	40.0	39.9	40.0	39.4	40.2	41.1	41.9	39.9
2002	39.7	39.2	39.3	39.2	39.8	40.3	40.5	40.5	39.7	40.0	40.5	41.2	40.0
2003	39.2	38.8	38.3	38.4	38.9	39.4	39.6	39.7	39.0	39.4	39.6	40.2	39.2

Employment by Industry: Vermont—*Continued*

(Numbers in thousands. Not seasonally adjusted.)

Industry	January	February	March	April	May	June	July	August	September	October	November	December	Annual Average
STATEWIDE—*Continued*													
Transportation and utilities													
1990	7.6	7.6	7.7	7.6	7.6	7.9	7.8	7.9	7.9	7.9	7.8	7.9	7.8
1991	7.8	7.6	7.5	7.5	7.4	7.5	7.3	7.4	7.5	7.5	7.5	7.5	7.5
1992	7.5	7.6	7.5	7.7	7.7	7.9	7.8	7.9	8.0	8.1	8.2	8.2	7.8
1993	8.2	8.2	8.2	8.3	8.3	8.4	8.1	8.1	8.2	8.5	8.4	8.4	8.3
1994	8.0	8.1	8.2	8.1	8.3	8.4	8.3	8.3	8.4	8.7	8.7	8.7	8.4
1995	8.2	8.3	8.3	8.5	8.5	8.5	8.0	8.1	8.4	8.7	8.6	8.6	8.4
1996	8.3	8.4	8.3	8.4	8.5	8.5	8.1	8.2	8.4	8.7	8.7	8.7	8.4
1997	8.3	8.4	8.4	8.4	8.4	8.5	8.6	8.4	8.6	8.8	8.7	8.8	8.5
1998	8.5	8.5	8.5	8.7	8.7	8.7	8.4	8.5	8.8	8.9	8.8	8.8	8.7
1999	8.6	8.7	8.6	8.6	8.6	8.7	8.4	8.4	8.9	9.0	8.8	8.8	8.7
2000	8.6	8.6	8.6	8.5	8.5	8.6	8.5	8.4	8.8	8.9	8.9	8.8	8.6
2001	8.6	8.6	8.5	8.6	8.6	8.8	8.4	8.4	8.8	8.9	8.9	8.9	8.7
2002	8.7	8.6	8.6	8.7	8.8	8.8	8.4	8.5	8.7	8.9	8.9	8.9	8.7
2003	8.6	8.5	8.4	8.5	8.5	8.7	8.0	8.1	8.5	8.7	8.8	8.9	8.5
Information													
1990	5.5	5.5	5.5	5.5	5.5	5.5	5.5	5.5	5.5	5.4	5.4	5.5	5.5
1991	5.5	5.4	5.4	5.4	5.4	5.4	5.7	5.7	5.6	5.6	5.6	5.7	5.5
1992	5.5	5.6	5.6	5.6	5.5	5.6	5.5	5.5	5.6	5.6	5.6	5.6	5.6
1993	5.5	5.6	5.6	5.7	5.6	5.7	5.8	5.8	5.8	5.8	5.9	5.8	5.7
1994	5.8	5.8	5.9	5.9	5.9	5.9	6.0	6.0	6.0	5.9	5.9	6.0	5.9
1995	5.9	5.9	6.0	5.9	5.9	5.9	6.0	6.1	6.2	6.2	6.3	6.3	6.1
1996	6.3	6.3	6.3	6.4	6.3	6.4	6.3	6.3	6.3	6.3	6.2	6.3	6.3
1997	6.1	6.2	6.2	6.2	6.2	6.3	6.3	6.3	6.3	6.4	6.3	6.4	6.3
1998	6.4	6.5	6.6	6.6	6.7	6.7	6.6	6.6	6.5	6.4	6.5	6.5	6.6
1999	6.4	6.4	6.4	6.5	6.5	7.1	7.0	7.0	6.8	6.8	6.9	6.9	6.7
2000	6.7	6.8	6.8	6.8	6.8	6.9	6.9	6.3	6.9	6.9	7.0	7.0	6.8
2001	6.9	7.0	6.8	6.8	6.8	6.9	6.7	6.7	6.6	6.7	6.8	6.8	6.8
2002	6.7	6.7	6.7	6.8	6.7	6.7	6.7	6.7	6.6	6.5	6.6	6.6	6.7
2003	6.5	6.4	6.5	6.4	6.5	6.6	6.5	6.5	6.5	6.4	6.5	6.5	6.5
Financial activities													
1990	13.9	13.7	13.6	13.4	13.5	13.6	13.6	13.5	13.3	13.3	13.2	13.4	13.5
1991	13.1	12.9	13.0	12.9	12.9	12.9	13.0	12.9	12.6	12.6	12.6	12.7	12.8
1992	12.7	12.7	12.6	12.3	12.5	12.7	12.8	12.8	12.7	12.6	12.5	12.7	12.6
1993	12.3	12.3	12.3	12.3	12.3	12.6	12.7	12.7	12.5	12.5	12.4	12.6	12.5
1994	12.8	12.8	12.8	12.5	12.6	12.7	12.9	12.9	12.8	12.6	12.6	12.9	12.7
1995	12.7	12.7	12.7	12.6	12.6	12.9	12.9	12.9	12.7	12.6	12.6	12.8	12.7
1996	12.5	12.6	12.6	12.5	12.7	12.7	12.9	12.9	12.7	12.6	12.7	12.8	12.7
1997	12.6	12.6	12.6	12.6	12.7	13.0	13.0	13.0	12.8	12.7	12.7	12.7	12.8
1998	12.7	12.7	12.7	12.7	12.7	12.9	12.9	13.0	12.9	12.7	12.7	12.9	12.8
1999	13.1	13.1	13.1	13.1	13.2	13.4	13.4	13.4	13.0	13.1	13.0	13.0	13.2
2000	13.0	12.9	13.0	12.8	13.0	13.1	12.9	13.0	12.7	13.0	12.9	13.2	13.0
2001	12.9	13.0	13.1	12.9	13.1	13.4	13.4	13.4	13.3	13.2	13.2	13.3	13.2
2002	13.0	13.0	13.0	12.9	13.1	13.3	13.5	13.5	13.2	13.2	13.0	13.2	13.2
2003	13.0	13.0	13.0	13.0	13.2	13.4	13.5	13.5	13.3	13.2	13.1	13.2	13.2
Professional and business services													
1990	14.0	14.1	14.0	14.2	14.3	14.5	14.4	14.4	14.2	14.1	14.0	13.9	14.2
1991	13.5	13.4	13.4	13.5	13.8	13.9	14.2	14.5	14.2	14.3	14.2	14.2	13.9
1992	13.7	14.1	14.1	14.4	14.2	14.4	14.7	14.9	14.8	15.2	14.7	14.6	14.5
1993	14.2	14.5	14.2	14.4	14.9	15.5	15.4	15.8	16.0	16.1	16.0	16.0	15.3
1994	15.3	15.6	15.7	16.0	16.3	16.7	16.7	16.8	16.8	16.7	16.5	16.8	16.3
1995	15.7	16.1	16.1	16.7	16.6	16.8	17.1	17.2	17.2	17.1	17.1	16.9	16.7
1996	16.5	16.7	16.8	17.2	17.4	17.8	18.0	18.2	18.2	18.4	17.8	17.9	17.6
1997	17.0	17.3	17.3	17.6	18.0	18.4	19.1	19.2	19.2	19.2	18.9	18.8	18.3
1998	18.5	18.9	19.1	19.5	19.7	20.2	20.7	20.5	20.3	19.9	19.8	19.8	19.7
1999	19.6	19.8	20.0	20.5	20.6	20.9	20.9	21.0	20.5	21.0	21.0	21.0	20.6
2000	19.5	19.8	20.3	20.7	21.0	21.5	21.4	21.3	20.9	21.0	20.7	20.9	20.8
2001	20.1	20.3	20.4	20.7	21.3	21.4	21.4	21.3	20.8	20.5	20.2	20.0	20.7
2002	19.2	19.2	19.3	20.0	20.5	20.6	20.7	20.9	21.0	20.9	20.4	20.3	20.3
2003	19.3	19.4	19.3	20.0	20.6	21.0	21.0	21.1	20.7	20.5	20.4	20.2	20.3
Educational and health services													
1990	35.2	35.4	35.6	34.8	34.7	34.3	34.0	34.0	34.5	35.0	35.1	35.1	34.8
1991	34.3	35.0	35.0	35.5	35.0	34.6	34.8	34.7	36.1	36.8	37.0	37.4	35.5
1992	36.0	37.2	37.4	37.8	36.9	36.4	36.3	36.1	37.6	38.2	38.4	38.2	37.2
1993	37.5	38.5	38.9	38.8	38.0	37.5	37.7	37.5	38.8	39.4	39.8	39.7	38.5
1994	38.9	40.1	40.6	40.1	39.4	38.7	39.0	38.7	40.0	40.8	41.2	41.2	39.9
1995	40.4	41.5	41.9	41.6	40.9	40.1	40.5	40.3	41.8	42.3	42.6	42.6	41.4
1996	41.7	42.7	43.0	43.0	42.3	41.2	40.7	40.5	41.4	42.6	42.8	42.9	42.1
1997	41.8	42.8	43.0	42.9	42.5	41.5	41.3	41.2	42.4	43.2	43.5	43.7	42.5
1998	42.6	43.8	43.9	43.8	43.4	42.6	42.6	42.2	43.2	44.0	44.1	44.0	43.4
1999	43.1	44.2	44.4	44.6	44.3	43.3	43.4	43.1	44.4	45.3	45.7	45.8	44.3
2000	45.1	46.2	46.2	46.0	45.5	44.7	44.9	44.8	46.3	47.1	47.3	47.4	46.0
2001	46.8	47.5	47.7	47.7	47.7	47.2	47.1	46.8	48.6	49.0	49.2	49.7	47.9
2002	49.0	49.7	50.0	50.1	50.3	49.5	49.5	49.2	50.7	50.9	51.3	51.5	50.1
2003	50.9	51.4	51.8	52.0	52.2	51.7	51.7	51.7	53.0	53.5	53.7	53.9	52.3

Employment by Industry: Vermont—*Continued*

(Numbers in thousands. Not seasonally adjusted.)

Industry	January	February	March	April	May	June	July	August	September	October	November	December	Annual Average
STATEWIDE—*Continued*													
Leisure and hospitality													
1990	31.0	30.8	29.9	25.7	25.8	28.5	31.1	31.4	30.0	28.7	26.5	28.4	29.0
1991	29.3	28.9	28.1	24.1	24.7	26.9	29.4	30.4	29.0	27.8	25.3	27.6	27.6
1992	29.3	29.9	28.7	24.8	25.1	27.3	30.2	31.1	30.0	28.8	26.0	28.9	28.3
1993	30.7	31.0	29.9	26.5	26.3	28.4	30.7	31.8	30.3	29.1	26.4	29.3	29.2
1994	30.7	30.8	30.7	27.5	27.0	29.7	31.6	32.6	30.9	29.8	26.8	30.5	29.9
1995	32.6	32.5	32.0	27.1	27.5	30.2	32.7	33.4	32.1	30.6	28.0	31.6	30.9
1996	33.8	33.7	32.8	28.6	28.3	31.1	32.6	33.5	31.8	30.9	28.1	31.8	31.4
1997	33.5	33.7	32.5	29.2	28.8	31.5	33.5	33.6	32.3	31.6	28.8	33.0	31.8
1998	34.0	34.3	33.7	29.8	29.4	31.5	33.1	33.8	32.6	31.5	29.1	32.3	32.1
1999	34.2	34.7	33.9	29.9	29.4	31.9	34.0	34.6	32.8	32.1	29.8	32.6	32.5
2000	35.1	35.3	34.7	28.6	29.5	33.0	34.2	34.9	33.1	32.1	29.6	34.7	32.9
2001	36.1	35.8	34.9	31.2	29.6	32.6	34.3	35.1	32.5	31.5	29.5	31.4	32.9
2002	35.6	35.5	34.6	30.4	29.8	33.0	34.1	34.9	32.7	31.7	29.5	34.4	33.0
2003	35.9	35.4	34.6	29.1	29.5	32.2	33.8	34.6	32.6	31.5	29.4	32.6	32.6
Other services													
1990	7.6	7.6	7.7	7.8	8.0	8.0	8.1	8.1	8.1	8.1	7.9	7.9	7.9
1991	7.6	7.6	7.6	7.8	7.9	8.0	8.0	8.0	8.0	7.9	7.8	7.9	7.8
1992	7.4	7.5	7.6	7.8	7.8	8.0	8.2	8.2	8.2	8.2	8.2	8.1	7.9
1993	8.0	8.1	8.1	8.2	8.2	8.5	8.7	8.7	8.5	8.5	8.4	8.4	8.4
1994	8.3	8.4	8.4	8.4	8.4	8.6	8.8	8.9	8.7	8.6	8.6	8.6	8.6
1995	8.3	8.4	8.4	8.4	8.5	8.8	9.0	9.1	8.9	8.9	8.8	8.9	8.7
1996	8.8	8.8	8.9	9.0	9.0	9.3	9.5	9.3	9.3	9.3	9.2	9.2	9.1
1997	8.7	8.9	8.9	8.9	9.1	9.4	9.4	9.4	9.3	9.4	9.3	9.3	9.2
1998	9.1	9.2	9.3	9.4	9.4	9.6	9.8	9.7	9.5	9.5	9.1	9.1	9.4
1999	8.9	9.0	9.1	9.2	9.2	9.4	9.6	9.5	9.4	9.5	9.4	9.5	9.3
2000	9.4	9.5	9.6	9.6	9.7	9.9	9.9	9.9	9.7	9.7	9.6	9.7	9.7
2001	9.8	9.7	9.7	9.8	9.9	10.2	10.4	10.2	9.9	10.0	10.0	10.0	10.0
2002	9.8	9.7	9.8	9.9	10.0	10.4	10.5	10.4	10.3	10.1	10.0	10.2	10.1
2003	9.9	9.9	10.0	10.0	10.1	10.4	10.3	10.3	10.2	10.0	10.0	10.1	10.1
Government													
1990	42.2	43.8	44.6	46.8	46.3	44.0	37.6	37.4	43.0	45.2	45.3	45.7	43.5
1991	43.8	45.4	45.8	45.6	45.1	43.2	37.7	37.7	43.9	45.7	46.3	45.7	43.8
1992	43.7	45.4	45.8	45.7	45.0	43.1	37.5	37.0	43.6	45.8	46.6	45.7	43.7
1993	44.1	45.5	45.5	46.1	45.8	44.3	36.7	36.4	44.1	46.3	46.7	46.0	44.0
1994	44.1	46.0	46.5	46.5	46.7	45.0	37.3	37.0	44.9	47.1	48.2	47.4	44.7
1995	45.1	46.8	47.4	47.2	46.6	44.9	37.8	37.5	44.8	47.3	47.8	47.6	45.1
1996	45.0	47.1	47.4	47.7	47.5	44.8	37.7	37.5	46.0	47.3	48.4	48.3	45.4
1997	44.4	47.6	47.3	47.9	47.6	45.1	38.1	38.1	46.3	48.6	48.7	48.9	45.7
1998	45.1	48.3	48.1	48.0	47.7	45.3	38.1	38.1	46.9	49.1	49.6	49.8	46.2
1999	46.7	49.2	49.5	49.3	49.6	46.9	39.5	39.0	48.3	50.7	51.4	51.3	47.6
2000	48.9	50.8	52.3	51.5	52.4	48.9	41.2	41.0	49.9	51.7	52.2	52.3	49.4
2001	50.1	51.6	51.7	51.7	51.8	49.9	41.7	41.7	51.1	53.4	53.5	53.6	50.2
2002	51.3	52.6	52.7	52.9	52.7	51.0	41.8	42.1	51.2	54.0	54.4	53.4	50.8
2003	52.1	53.9	53.8	53.9	53.9	51.9	43.2	42.8	52.7	54.7	54.7	54.9	51.9
Federal government													
1990	5.3	5.3	5.5	7.4	7.2	6.1	5.8	5.4	5.4	5.3	5.3	5.4	5.8
1991	5.3	5.3	5.3	5.3	5.3	5.4	5.5	5.4	5.5	5.4	5.4	5.5	5.4
1992	5.4	5.4	5.4	5.4	5.4	5.4	5.5	5.6	5.6	5.6	5.5	5.6	5.5
1993	5.5	5.5	5.4	5.6	5.6	5.6	5.6	5.6	5.5	5.5	5.5	5.6	5.5
1994	5.5	5.5	5.5	5.6	5.6	5.6	5.5	5.5	5.5	5.5	5.5	5.5	5.5
1995	5.4	5.4	5.5	5.4	5.5	5.5	5.6	5.6	5.5	5.5	5.4	5.6	5.5
1996	5.4	5.4	5.4	5.5	5.5	5.5	5.5	5.5	5.5	5.4	5.5	5.5	5.5
1997	5.4	5.4	5.4	5.4	5.4	5.4	5.4	5.4	5.4	5.4	5.4	5.5	5.4
1998	5.5	5.5	5.5	5.5	5.6	5.6	5.5	5.6	5.5	5.4	5.5	5.6	5.5
1999	5.5	5.5	5.5	5.6	5.6	5.6	5.6	5.6	5.7	5.6	5.7	5.8	5.6
2000	5.7	5.7	6.8	6.4	6.9	6.2	6.3	5.9	5.7	5.7	5.7	5.8	6.1
2001	5.7	5.7	5.6	5.7	5.7	5.8	5.9	5.9	5.8	5.9	5.7	5.8	5.8
2002	5.7	5.7	5.7	5.7	5.8	5.9	5.9	6.1	6.1	6.1	6.2	6.3	5.9
2003	6.2	6.2	6.2	6.2	6.2	6.2	6.2	6.2	6.2	6.2	6.2	6.2	6.2
State government													
1990	13.8	15.2	15.4	15.7	15.1	14.1	14.3	14.1	14.8	15.7	15.2	15.5	14.9
1991	14.4	15.4	15.7	15.8	14.8	13.6	14.0	13.7	15.4	15.8	16.0	15.3	15.0
1992	14.1	15.3	15.5	15.7	14.6	13.5	13.8	13.6	14.7	15.5	15.7	14.7	14.7
1993	14.1	15.1	14.6	15.4	14.8	13.7	13.6	13.4	14.9	15.6	15.7	14.7	14.6
1994	13.9	15.4	15.7	15.5	15.1	13.9	14.2	13.8	14.8	15.9	15.9	15.6	15.0
1995	14.5	15.8	15.9	15.8	15.2	13.8	13.7	13.6	14.7	15.9	16.1	15.3	15.0
1996	13.9	15.6	15.7	15.9	15.2	13.6	13.7	13.5	15.2	15.7	16.1	15.8	15.0
1997	13.6	15.9	15.6	16.0	15.1	13.7	13.7	13.7	15.3	16.2	16.3	16.1	15.1
1998	13.6	15.9	15.7	15.9	14.7	13.5	13.6	13.8	15.5	16.6	16.6	16.4	15.2
1999	14.4	16.1	16.2	16.3	15.9	13.8	13.9	14.0	15.6	16.9	17.0	16.8	15.6
2000	15.1	16.6	16.8	16.8	16.4	14.9	14.7	14.8	16.2	17.1	17.2	17.0	16.1
2001	15.3	16.8	16.9	16.9	16.5	15.4	14.9	15.0	16.6	17.5	17.6	17.4	16.4
2002	15.9	17.0	17.1	17.1	16.5	15.2	14.9	14.9	16.5	17.6	17.6	16.4	16.4
2003	15.8	17.2	17.3	17.3	16.7	15.3	15.5	15.4	17.3	18.3	18.2	18.3	16.9

Employment by Industry: Vermont—*Continued*

(Numbers in thousands. Not seasonally adjusted.)

Industry	January	February	March	April	May	June	July	August	September	October	November	December	Annual Average
STATEWIDE—*Continued*													
Local government													
1990	23.1	23.3	23.7	23.7	24.0	23.8	17.5	17.9	22.8	24.2	24.8	24.8	22.8
1991	24.1	24.7	24.8	24.5	25.0	24.2	18.2	18.6	23.0	24.5	24.9	24.9	23.5
1992	24.2	24.7	24.9	24.6	25.0	24.2	18.2	17.8	23.3	24.7	25.4	25.4	23.5
1993	24.5	24.9	25.5	25.1	25.4	25.0	17.5	17.4	23.7	25.2	25.5	25.7	23.8
1994	24.7	25.1	25.3	25.4	26.0	25.5	17.6	17.7	24.6	25.7	26.8	26.3	24.2
1995	25.2	25.6	26.0	26.0	25.9	25.6	18.5	18.3	24.6	25.9	26.3	26.7	24.6
1996	25.7	26.1	26.3	26.3	26.8	25.7	18.5	18.5	25.3	26.2	26.8	27.0	24.9
1997	25.4	26.3	26.3	26.5	27.1	26.0	19.0	19.0	25.6	27.0	27.0	27.3	25.2
1998	26.0	26.9	26.9	26.6	27.4	26.2	19.0	18.7	25.9	27.1	27.5	27.8	25.5
1999	26.8	27.6	27.8	27.4	28.1	27.5	20.0	19.4	27.0	28.2	28.7	28.7	26.4
2000	28.1	28.5	28.7	28.3	29.1	27.8	20.2	20.3	28.0	28.9	29.3	29.5	27.2
2001	29.1	29.1	29.2	29.1	29.6	28.7	20.9	20.8	28.7	30.0	30.2	30.4	28.0
2002	29.7	29.9	29.9	30.1	30.4	29.9	21.0	21.1	28.6	30.3	30.6	30.7	28.5
2003	30.1	30.5	30.3	30.4	31.0	30.4	21.5	21.2	29.2	30.2	30.3	30.4	28.8
BARRE-MONTPELIER													
Total nonfarm													
1990	29.1	28.5	28.6	28.0	28.5	28.7	28.1	28.4	28.9	28.6	28.4	28.3	28.5
1991	27.5	27.5	27.5	27.0	27.5	28.4	26.4	27.9	28.1	28.0	27.7	27.8	27.6
1992	27.1	27.5	27.1	26.5	27.6	28.1	27.1	27.5	28.2	28.3	28.1	28.4	27.6
1993	27.5	28.1	28.5	27.9	28.5	29.4	28.1	28.3	29.5	29.2	29.3	29.4	28.6
1994	28.6	28.5	29.0	28.8	29.6	30.2	28.7	29.0	30.4	30.2	30.3	30.5	29.5
1995	29.7	29.8	30.2	29.7	30.3	31.0	29.5	29.4	30.9	30.5	30.3	30.9	30.2
1996	30.2	30.3	30.1	29.9	30.6	31.0	29.6	30.0	31.3	31.1	30.8	31.1	30.5
1997	30.1	30.3	30.4	30.0	29.9	30.5	30.0	30.1	30.5	30.8	30.4	30.9	30.3
1998	30.3	30.3	30.5	30.3	30.9	31.7	30.7	31.3	31.9	31.8	31.6	32.3	31.1
1999	31.4	31.8	31.8	32.0	32.6	33.3	32.4	32.5	33.1	33.4	33.1	33.6	32.6
2000	33.0	33.2	33.6	33.4	33.8	34.4	33.3	33.4	34.1	33.9	33.8	34.4	33.7
2001	33.9	34.0	34.2	33.6	34.3	35.1	34.3	34.5	34.9	34.9	34.7	35.0	34.5
2002	34.0	33.9	34.1	33.9	34.2	35.0	33.9	33.9	34.4	34.2	33.6	34.2	34.1
2003	33.4	33.5	33.5	33.4	33.9	34.5	33.6	34.0	34.6	34.4	34.8	34.6	34.0
Total private													
1990	22.1	21.5	21.6	21.1	21.3	21.4	21.7	21.9	21.6	21.5	21.2	21.2	21.5
1991	20.2	20.2	20.2	19.9	20.4	21.0	19.9	21.2	21.0	20.8	20.4	20.6	20.5
1992	20.1	20.3	20.0	19.4	20.3	20.8	21.0	21.3	21.0	21.2	20.9	21.3	20.6
1993	20.6	21.1	21.4	20.8	21.2	22.0	22.1	22.3	22.4	22.1	22.1	22.2	21.7
1994	22.0	21.8	22.3	22.0	22.5	23.1	22.8	23.1	23.1	23.1	23.0	23.2	22.7
1995	22.4	22.4	22.6	22.2	22.6	23.2	23.2	23.1	23.3	23.0	22.7	23.3	22.8
1996	22.8	22.9	22.6	22.5	23.0	23.4	23.5	23.6	23.7	23.7	23.4	23.6	23.2
1997	23.2	23.2	23.3	22.9	22.7	23.4	23.7	23.9	23.7	23.8	23.5	23.9	23.4
1998	23.1	23.1	23.3	23.1	23.5	24.2	24.3	24.3	24.5	24.2	24.0	24.7	23.9
1999	23.8	24.0	24.0	24.2	24.7	25.3	25.4	25.5	25.1	25.3	25.1	25.6	24.8
2000	25.1	25.3	25.4	25.3	25.6	26.0	26.0	26.2	25.8	25.9	25.6	26.2	25.7
2001	25.6	25.7	25.8	25.4	25.9	26.5	26.5	26.6	26.3	26.3	26.1	26.3	26.1
2002	25.6	25.5	25.7	25.5	25.6	26.2	26.0	26.0	25.7	25.5	25.2	25.8	25.7
2003	25.0	25.0	25.0	24.9	25.1	25.6	25.7	26.0	25.7	25.6	25.9	25.7	25.4
Goods-producing													
1990	4.5	4.3	4.3	4.3	4.6	4.6	4.5	4.7	4.7	4.5	4.4	4.1	4.5
1991	3.5	3.4	3.5	3.8	4.2	4.3	4.1	4.3	4.2	4.1	3.9	3.8	3.9
1992	3.2	3.3	3.2	3.4	3.8	4.0	4.0	4.2	4.2	4.3	4.2	4.0	3.8
1993	3.4	3.5	3.7	3.8	4.1	4.3	4.4	4.4	4.3	4.4	4.3	4.1	4.1
1994	3.6	3.7	3.8	3.9	4.3	4.6	4.4	4.6	4.6	4.6	4.5	4.4	4.3
1995	3.9	3.8	4.1	4.3	4.5	4.7	5.0	4.8	4.8	4.9	4.7	4.5	4.5
1996	4.0	4.0	4.1	4.4	4.7	4.9	4.9	4.9	4.9	5.0	5.0	4.8	4.6
1997	4.3	4.3	4.3	4.4	4.5	4.7	4.7	4.7	4.8	4.7	4.7	4.6	4.6
1998	4.1	4.1	4.2	4.5	4.7	4.9	5.0	5.0	4.9	4.9	5.0	4.8	4.7
1999	4.3	4.3	4.4	4.8	5.1	5.3	5.4	5.4	5.4	5.5	5.4	5.3	5.1
2000	4.9	5.1	5.2	5.4	5.7	5.9	5.6	5.9	5.7	5.7	5.6	5.5	5.5
2001	4.9	5.0	5.0	5.1	5.4	5.6	5.6	5.6	5.6	5.4	5.3	5.1	5.3
2002	4.5	4.4	4.5	4.7	4.9	5.0	5.0	5.0	4.9	4.8	4.6	4.5	4.7
2003	3.9	3.9	4.1	4.4	4.6	4.8	4.9	4.9	4.9	4.9	4.8	4.7	4.6
Construction and mining													
1990	1.5	1.3	1.3	1.4	1.6	1.7	1.8	1.9	1.8	1.7	1.6	1.4	1.6
1991	1.1	1.0	1.0	1.3	1.6	1.7	1.7	1.7	1.6	1.5	1.4	1.2	1.4
1992	0.9	0.9	0.8	1.0	1.2	1.4	1.5	1.5	1.5	1.5	1.4	1.2	1.2
1993	0.9	0.9	0.9	1.0	1.2	1.4	1.5	1.5	1.4	1.5	1.3	1.2	1.2
1994	0.9	0.9	0.9	1.0	1.2	1.5	1.5	1.5	1.5	1.5	1.4	1.3	1.3
1995	1.0	0.9	1.1	1.3	1.5	1.6	1.7	1.6	1.6	1.6	1.4	1.3	1.4
1996	1.0	0.9	1.0	1.2	1.5	1.6	1.6	1.6	1.6	1.6	1.6	1.4	1.4
1997	1.1	1.1	1.1	1.2	1.4	1.5	1.6	1.6	1.6	1.6	1.6	1.4	1.4
1998	1.2	1.1	1.2	1.4	1.6	1.7	1.8	1.8	1.7	1.6	1.7	1.5	1.5
1999	1.2	1.1	1.1	1.4	1.6	1.7	1.7	1.7	1.6	1.7	1.5	1.5	1.5
2000	1.3	1.3	1.3	1.5	1.7	1.8	1.8	1.8	1.7	1.7	1.6	1.5	1.6
2001	1.3	1.2	1.2	1.4	1.6	1.8	1.8	1.8	1.8	1.7	1.7	1.5	1.6
2002	1.3	1.2	1.3	1.4	1.6	1.7	1.8	1.8	1.7	1.7	1.6	1.5	1.6
2003	1.2	1.1	1.2	1.4	1.6	1.7	1.8	1.8	1.8	1.8	1.7	1.6	1.6

Employment by Industry: Vermont—*Continued*

(Numbers in thousands. Not seasonally adjusted.)

Industry	January	February	March	April	May	June	July	August	September	October	November	December	Annual Average
BARRE-MONTPELIER *—Continued*													
Manufacturing													
1990	3.0	3.0	3.0	2.9	3.0	2.9	2.7	2.8	2.9	2.8	2.8	2.7	2.9
1991	2.4	2.4	2.5	2.5	2.6	2.6	2.4	2.6	2.6	2.6	2.5	2.6	2.5
1992	2.3	2.4	2.4	2.4	2.6	2.6	2.5	2.7	2.7	2.8	2.8	2.8	2.6
1993	2.5	2.6	2.8	2.8	2.9	2.9	2.9	2.9	2.9	2.9	3.0	2.9	2.8
1994	2.7	2.8	2.9	2.9	3.1	3.1	2.9	3.1	3.1	3.1	3.1	3.1	3.0
1995	2.9	2.9	3.0	3.0	3.0	3.1	3.3	3.2	3.2	3.3	3.3	3.2	3.1
1996	3.0	3.1	3.1	3.2	3.2	3.3	3.3	3.3	3.3	3.4	3.4	3.4	3.3
1997	3.2	3.2	3.2	3.2	3.1	3.2	3.1	3.1	3.2	3.1	3.1	3.2	3.2
1998	2.9	3.0	3.0	3.1	3.1	3.2	3.2	3.2	3.2	3.3	3.3	3.3	3.2
1999	3.1	3.2	3.3	3.4	3.5	3.6	3.7	3.7	3.8	3.8	3.9	3.8	3.6
2000	3.6	3.8	3.9	3.9	4.0	4.1	3.8	4.1	4.0	4.0	4.0	4.0	3.9
2001	3.6	3.8	3.8	3.7	3.8	3.8	3.8	3.8	3.8	3.7	3.6	3.6	3.7
2002	3.2	3.2	3.2	3.3	3.3	3.3	3.2	3.2	3.2	3.1	3.0	3.0	3.2
2003	2.7	2.8	2.9	3.0	3.0	3.1	3.1	3.1	3.1	3.1	3.1	3.1	3.0
Service-providing													
1990	24.6	24.2	24.3	23.7	23.9	24.1	23.6	23.7	24.2	24.1	24.0	24.2	24.1
1991	24.0	24.1	24.0	23.2	23.3	24.1	22.3	23.6	23.9	23.9	23.8	24.0	23.7
1992	23.9	24.2	23.9	23.1	23.8	24.1	23.1	23.3	24.0	24.0	23.9	24.4	23.8
1993	24.1	24.6	24.8	24.1	24.4	25.1	23.7	23.9	25.2	24.8	25.0	25.3	24.6
1994	25.0	24.8	25.2	24.9	25.3	25.6	24.3	24.4	25.8	25.6	25.8	26.1	25.2
1995	25.8	26.0	26.1	25.4	25.8	26.3	24.5	24.6	26.1	25.6	25.6	26.4	25.7
1996	26.2	26.3	26.0	25.5	25.9	26.1	24.7	25.1	26.4	26.1	25.8	26.3	25.9
1997	25.8	26.0	26.1	25.6	25.4	25.8	25.3	25.4	25.7	26.1	25.7	26.3	25.8
1998	26.2	26.2	26.3	25.8	26.2	26.8	25.7	26.3	27.0	26.9	26.6	27.5	26.5
1999	27.1	27.5	27.4	27.2	27.5	28.0	27.0	27.1	27.7	27.9	27.7	28.3	27.5
2000	28.1	28.1	28.4	28.0	28.1	28.5	27.7	27.5	28.4	28.2	28.2	28.9	28.2
2001	29.0	29.0	29.2	28.5	28.9	29.5	28.7	28.9	29.3	29.5	29.4	29.9	29.2
2002	29.5	29.5	29.6	29.2	29.3	30.0	28.9	28.9	29.5	29.4	29.0	29.7	29.4
2003	29.5	29.6	29.4	29.0	29.3	29.7	28.7	29.1	29.7	29.5	30.0	29.9	29.5
Trade, transportation, and utilities													
1990	5.3	5.0	5.0	5.1	5.2	5.3	5.4	5.4	5.3	5.4	5.3	5.4	5.3
1991	5.0	5.0	5.0	5.1	5.2	5.2	4.9	5.3	5.2	5.1	5.1	5.2	5.1
1992	5.1	5.1	5.0	4.9	5.2	5.3	5.3	5.3	5.2	5.3	5.3	5.4	5.2
1993	5.2	5.3	5.3	5.3	5.4	5.6	5.5	5.5	5.6	5.6	5.8	5.7	5.5
1994	5.5	5.4	5.5	5.6	5.8	5.9	5.7	5.7	5.8	5.8	5.8	5.9	5.7
1995	5.5	5.6	5.5	5.6	5.7	5.8	5.5	5.5	5.6	5.6	5.6	5.7	5.6
1996	5.6	5.6	5.4	5.4	5.5	5.7	5.7	5.7	5.6	5.7	5.7	5.7	5.6
1997	5.7	5.6	5.6	5.6	5.7	5.8	5.8	5.8	5.7	5.7	5.8	5.8	5.7
1998	5.6	5.5	5.6	5.5	5.5	5.7	5.6	5.6	5.7	5.7	5.7	6.0	5.6
1999	5.6	5.6	5.6	5.8	5.8	5.9	5.9	5.8	5.8	5.8	5.9	6.0	5.8
2000	5.9	5.8	5.8	5.9	5.9	5.8	5.8	5.8	5.8	5.9	6.0	6.1	5.9
2001	5.8	5.8	5.9	5.9	6.0	6.0	6.0	6.0	6.0	6.1	6.2	6.3	6.0
2002	6.0	5.8	5.9	5.9	6.0	6.0	5.9	5.9	5.9	5.9	5.9	6.1	5.9
2003	5.8	5.7	5.7	5.7	5.7	5.9	5.7	5.8	5.8	5.8	6.1	5.9	5.8
Wholesale trade													
1990	0.9	0.8	0.8	0.9	0.8	0.9	0.9	0.9	0.9	0.9	0.9	0.9	0.9
1991	0.8	0.8	0.8	0.9	0.9	0.9	0.8	0.9	0.9	0.9	0.8	0.9	0.9
1992	0.9	0.9	0.8	0.8	0.9	0.9	0.9	0.9	0.9	0.9	0.9	0.9	0.9
1993	0.8	0.9	0.9	0.9	0.9	0.9	0.9	0.9	0.9	1.0	1.0	0.9	0.9
1994	0.9	0.9	0.9	0.9	0.9	0.9	0.9	0.9	0.9	0.9	0.9	0.9	0.9
1995	0.8	0.8	0.8	0.8	0.8	0.9	0.9	0.9	0.9	0.9	0.9	0.9	0.9
1996	0.9	0.9	0.9	0.9	0.9	0.9	0.9	0.9	0.9	0.9	0.9	0.9	0.9
1997	1.0	1.0	1.0	1.0	1.0	1.0	1.0	1.0	1.0	1.0	1.0	1.0	1.0
1998	1.0	1.0	1.0	0.9	0.9	1.0	1.0	1.0	1.0	1.0	1.0	1.0	1.0
1999	0.9	0.9	0.9	1.0	0.9	1.0	1.0	1.0	1.0	1.0	1.0	1.0	1.0
2000	1.0	1.0	1.0	1.0	1.0	1.0	1.0	1.0	1.0	1.0	1.0	1.0	1.0
2001	0.9	0.9	1.0	1.0	1.0	1.0	1.0	1.0	1.0	1.0	1.0	1.0	1.0
2002	1.0	0.9	1.0	1.0	1.0	1.0	1.0	1.0	1.0	1.0	1.0	1.1	1.0
2003	1.0	1.0	1.0	0.9	0.9	1.0	0.9	0.9	0.9	0.9	1.0	0.9	0.9
Retail trade													
1990	3.7	3.5	3.5	3.5	3.6	3.7	3.7	3.7	3.6	3.7	3.6	3.7	3.6
1991	3.5	3.4	3.4	3.4	3.5	3.5	3.3	3.5	3.5	3.4	3.5	3.5	3.5
1992	3.4	3.4	3.4	3.4	3.5	3.5	3.5	3.5	3.4	3.5	3.5	3.6	3.5
1993	3.5	3.4	3.4	3.4	3.5	3.7	3.6	3.6	3.7	3.6	3.8	3.8	3.6
1994	3.6	3.6	3.7	3.7	3.8	3.9	3.8	3.8	3.8	3.8	3.8	3.9	3.8
1995	3.6	3.7	3.6	3.7	3.8	3.8	3.7	3.7	3.7	3.7	3.7	3.8	3.7
1996	3.7	3.7	3.7	3.7	3.8	4.0	4.1	4.1	3.9	4.0	4.0	4.0	3.9
1997	3.9	3.8	3.8	3.8	3.9	4.0	4.1	4.1	3.9	3.9	4.0	4.0	3.9
1998	3.8	3.7	3.8	3.8	3.8	3.9	3.9	3.9	3.9	3.9	3.9	4.2	3.9
1999	4.0	4.0	3.9	4.0	4.1	4.1	4.1	4.1	4.0	4.0	4.1	4.2	4.1
2000	4.1	4.1	4.1	4.1	4.1	4.1	4.1	4.1	4.0	4.1	4.2	4.3	4.1
2001	4.1	4.1	4.1	4.1	4.2	4.2	4.2	4.3	4.2	4.2	4.3	4.4	4.2
2002	4.2	4.1	4.1	4.1	4.2	4.2	4.2	4.2	4.1	4.1	4.2	4.2	4.2
2003	4.1	4.0	4.0	4.1	4.1	4.2	4.2	4.2	4.2	4.2	4.3	4.3	4.2

Employment by Industry: Vermont—*Continued*

(Numbers in thousands. Not seasonally adjusted.)

Industry	January	February	March	April	May	June	July	August	September	October	November	December	Annual Average
BARRE-MONTPELIER *—Continued*													
Transportation and utilities													
1990	0.7	0.7	0.7	0.7	0.8	0.7	0.8	0.8	0.8	0.8	0.8	0.8	0.8
1991	0.7	0.8	0.8	0.8	0.8	0.8	0.8	0.9	0.8	0.8	0.8	0.8	0.8
1992	0.8	0.8	0.8	0.7	0.8	0.9	0.9	0.9	0.9	0.9	0.9	0.9	0.9
1993	0.9	1.0	1.0	1.0	1.0	1.0	1.0	1.0	1.0	1.0	1.0	1.0	1.0
1994	1.0	0.9	0.9	1.0	1.1	1.1	1.0	1.0	1.1	1.1	1.1	1.1	1.0
1995	1.1	1.1	1.1	1.1	1.1	1.1	0.9	0.9	1.0	1.0	1.0	1.0	1.0
1996	1.0	1.0	0.8	0.8	0.8	0.8	0.7	0.7	0.8	0.8	0.8	0.8	0.8
1997	0.8	0.8	0.8	0.8	0.8	0.8	0.7	0.7	0.8	0.8	0.8	0.8	0.8
1998	0.8	0.8	0.8	0.8	0.8	0.8	0.7	0.7	0.8	0.8	0.8	0.8	0.8
1999	0.7	0.7	0.8	0.8	0.8	0.8	0.8	0.7	0.8	0.8	0.8	0.8	0.8
2000	0.8	0.7	0.7	0.8	0.8	0.7	0.7	0.7	0.8	0.8	0.8	0.8	0.8
2001	0.8	0.8	0.8	0.8	0.8	0.8	0.8	0.7	0.8	0.9	0.9	0.9	0.8
2002	0.8	0.8	0.8	0.8	0.8	0.8	0.7	0.7	0.8	0.8	0.7	0.8	0.8
2003	0.7	0.7	0.7	0.7	0.7	0.7	0.6	0.7	0.7	0.7	0.8	0.7	0.7
Information													
1990	0.6	0.6	0.6	0.6	0.6	0.6	0.6	0.6	0.6	0.6	0.6	0.6	0.6
1991	0.5	0.5	0.5	0.5	0.5	0.5	0.5	0.5	0.5	0.5	0.5	0.5	0.5
1992	0.5	0.5	0.5	0.5	0.5	0.5	0.5	0.5	0.5	0.5	0.5	0.5	0.5
1993	0.5	0.5	0.5	0.5	0.5	0.6	0.6	0.6	0.6	0.6	0.6	0.6	0.6
1994	0.6	0.6	0.6	0.6	0.6	0.6	0.7	0.7	0.6	0.6	0.6	0.6	0.6
1995	0.6	0.6	0.6	0.6	0.6	0.6	0.6	0.6	0.6	0.6	0.6	0.6	0.6
1996	0.6	0.6	0.6	0.6	0.6	0.6	0.6	0.6	0.6	0.6	0.6	0.6	0.6
1997	0.6	0.6	0.6	0.6	0.6	0.7	0.7	0.7	0.7	0.7	0.6	0.7	0.7
1998	0.6	0.6	0.6	0.6	0.6	0.6	0.7	0.6	0.7	0.6	0.6	0.7	0.6
1999	0.7	0.7	0.7	0.7	0.7	0.7	0.7	0.7	0.7	0.7	0.7	0.7	0.7
2000	0.7	0.7	0.7	0.7	0.7	0.7	0.7	0.7	0.7	0.7	0.7	0.7	0.7
2001	0.7	0.7	0.7	0.7	0.7	0.7	0.7	0.7	0.7	0.7	0.7	0.7	0.7
2002	0.7	0.7	0.7	0.7	0.7	0.7	0.7	0.7	0.7	0.7	0.7	0.7	0.7
2003	0.7	0.7	0.7	0.7	0.7	0.7	0.7	0.7	0.7	0.7	0.7	0.7	0.7
Financial activities													
1990	2.8	2.8	2.8	2.7	2.6	2.6	2.6	2.6	2.6	2.5	2.5	2.5	2.6
1991	2.5	2.5	2.5	2.4	2.4	2.5	2.5	2.5	2.4	2.4	2.4	2.4	2.5
1992	2.4	2.4	2.4	2.4	2.4	2.4	2.4	2.5	2.4	2.4	2.4	2.4	2.4
1993	2.5	2.5	2.5	2.4	2.5	2.6	2.6	2.6	2.6	2.5	2.5	2.6	2.5
1994	2.6	2.6	2.6	2.5	2.5	2.6	2.5	2.5	2.5	2.5	2.5	2.5	2.5
1995	2.5	2.5	2.5	2.5	2.5	2.5	2.4	2.5	2.5	2.4	2.4	2.5	2.5
1996	2.4	2.4	2.4	2.4	2.5	2.5	2.4	2.5	2.5	2.4	2.5	2.4	2.4
1997	2.5	2.5	2.5	2.5	2.5	2.5	2.5	2.5	2.4	2.4	2.3	2.3	2.5
1998	2.3	2.3	2.3	2.3	2.4	2.4	2.4	2.4	2.4	2.4	2.4	2.5	2.4
1999	2.4	2.4	2.4	2.4	2.5	2.5	2.5	2.6	2.5	2.5	2.5	2.6	2.5
2000	2.5	2.5	2.5	2.5	2.6	2.6	2.6	2.6	2.6	2.6	2.5	2.6	2.6
2001	2.7	2.7	2.7	2.7	2.7	2.8	2.8	2.8	2.8	2.7	2.7	2.8	2.7
2002	2.7	2.7	2.7	2.7	2.7	2.8	2.8	2.8	2.8	2.7	2.7	2.8	2.7
2003	2.7	2.7	2.7	2.7	2.7	2.7	2.7	2.7	2.7	2.7	2.7	2.7	2.7
Professional and business services													
1990	1.2	1.2	1.2	1.3	1.2	1.3	1.3	1.3	1.2	1.3	1.3	1.2	1.3
1991	1.2	1.2	1.2	1.2	1.2	1.3	1.2	1.3	1.4	1.4	1.3	1.2	1.3
1992	1.2	1.3	1.3	1.3	1.3	1.3	1.4	1.4	1.4	1.4	1.3	1.4	1.3
1993	1.3	1.4	1.4	1.4	1.5	1.5	1.5	1.5	1.6	1.6	1.5	1.5	1.5
1994	1.4	1.4	1.4	1.5	1.5	1.5	1.6	1.6	1.5	1.5	1.5	1.5	1.5
1995	1.5	1.4	1.4	1.5	1.5	1.6	1.6	1.5	1.5	1.4	1.4	1.4	1.5
1996	1.4	1.4	1.4	1.4	1.6	1.5	1.5	1.5	1.6	1.6	1.5	1.5	1.5
1997	1.4	1.4	1.5	1.5	1.4	1.5	1.5	1.6	1.6	1.7	1.6	1.6	1.5
1998	1.5	1.5	1.6	1.6	1.7	1.8	1.8	1.8	1.8	1.7	1.7	1.7	1.7
1999	1.7	1.8	1.8	1.8	1.9	1.9	2.0	2.0	1.8	1.8	1.8	1.8	1.8
2000	1.7	1.7	1.7	1.8	1.9	2.0	2.0	2.0	1.9	1.8	1.8	1.8	1.8
2001	1.8	1.8	1.8	1.8	1.9	2.0	1.9	2.0	1.9	1.9	1.9	1.9	1.9
2002	1.8	1.9	1.9	1.9	1.9	2.0	2.0	1.9	1.9	1.9	1.9	1.9	1.9
2003	1.8	1.8	1.8	1.9	1.9	2.0	2.0	2.0	2.0	2.0	2.0	1.9	1.9
Educational and health services													
1990	3.7	3.6	3.7	3.6	3.8	3.7	3.7	3.7	3.7	3.7	3.7	3.7	3.7
1991	3.7	3.8	3.8	3.8	3.8	3.8	3.4	3.6	3.8	3.8	3.9	3.9	3.8
1992	3.7	3.8	3.8	3.7	3.8	3.8	3.8	3.8	3.8	3.9	3.9	3.9	3.8
1993	3.9	3.9	4.0	4.0	3.9	3.9	3.8	3.9	4.0	4.0	4.1	4.1	4.0
1994	4.1	4.1	4.2	4.2	4.1	4.1	3.9	3.9	4.1	4.2	4.2	4.2	4.1
1995	4.1	4.2	4.3	4.3	4.3	4.2	4.1	4.2	4.3	4.3	4.3	4.3	4.2
1996	4.2	4.3	4.3	4.4	4.5	4.3	4.3	4.2	4.4	4.3	4.4	4.4	4.3
1997	4.3	4.4	4.4	4.4	4.3	4.3	4.3	4.4	4.4	4.6	4.6	4.6	4.4
1998	4.6	4.6	4.6	4.7	4.7	4.7	4.6	4.6	4.7	4.8	4.7	4.7	4.7
1999	4.5	4.7	4.7	4.8	4.8	4.8	4.7	4.7	4.7	4.8	4.8	4.8	4.7
2000	4.7	4.8	4.9	4.9	4.9	4.8	4.9	4.8	4.9	5.0	4.9	5.0	4.9
2001	5.0	5.0	5.0	5.0	5.1	5.1	5.0	5.1	5.1	5.3	5.3	5.3	5.1
2002	5.1	5.2	5.3	5.3	5.3	5.3	5.2	5.3	5.3	5.2	5.3	5.3	5.3
2003	5.3	5.3	5.3	5.3	5.4	5.3	5.3	5.4	5.3	5.3	5.4	5.4	5.3

Employment by Industry: Vermont—*Continued*

(Numbers in thousands. Not seasonally adjusted.)

Industry	January	February	March	April	May	June	July	August	September	October	November	December	Annual Average
BARRE-MONTPELIER —*Continued*													
Leisure and hospitality													
1990	2.9	2.9	2.9	2.4	2.2	2.2	2.5	2.5	2.5	2.4	2.4	2.7	2.5
1991	2.8	2.8	2.7	2.1	2.1	2.3	2.3	2.6	2.4	2.4	2.3	2.6	2.5
1992	3.0	2.9	2.8	2.2	2.3	2.4	2.5	2.5	2.4	2.4	2.2	2.6	2.5
1993	2.8	3.0	2.9	2.3	2.2	2.3	2.5	2.6	2.5	2.3	2.2	2.6	2.5
1994	3.1	3.0	3.1	2.6	2.5	2.6	2.8	2.9	2.7	2.7	2.7	2.9	2.8
1995	3.2	3.2	3.1	2.3	2.4	2.6	2.8	2.8	2.8	2.7	2.6	3.1	2.8
1996	3.4	3.4	3.2	2.7	2.4	2.7	2.8	2.9	2.8	2.8	2.5	3.0	2.9
1997	3.3	3.3	3.2	2.7	2.5	2.7	2.8	2.9	2.8	2.7	2.6	3.0	2.9
1998	3.1	3.2	3.1	2.6	2.6	2.8	2.8	2.9	2.9	2.7	2.6	3.0	2.9
1999	3.3	3.2	3.1	2.6	2.6	2.8	2.8	2.9	2.8	2.9	2.7	3.1	2.9
2000	3.4	3.4	3.3	2.8	2.6	2.8	2.9	2.9	2.8	2.8	2.7	3.1	3.0
2001	3.4	3.4	3.3	2.9	2.7	2.9	3.0	3.0	2.8	2.8	2.6	2.8	3.0
2002	3.4	3.4	3.3	2.9	2.7	3.0	2.9	2.9	2.7	2.8	2.7	3.1	3.0
2003	3.4	3.5	3.3	2.8	2.7	2.8	3.0	3.0	2.9	2.8	2.8	3.0	3.0
Other services													
1990	1.1	1.1	1.1	1.1	1.1	1.1	1.1	1.1	1.0	1.1	1.0	1.0	1.1
1991	1.0	1.0	1.0	1.0	1.0	1.1	1.0	1.1	1.1	1.1	1.0	1.0	1.0
1992	1.0	1.0	1.0	1.0	1.0	1.1	1.1	1.1	1.1	1.0	1.1	1.1	1.1
1993	1.0	1.0	1.1	1.1	1.1	1.2	1.2	1.2	1.2	1.1	1.1	1.0	1.1
1994	1.1	1.0	1.1	1.1	1.2	1.2	1.2	1.2	1.3	1.2	1.2	1.2	1.2
1995	1.1	1.1	1.1	1.1	1.1	1.2	1.2	1.2	1.2	1.1	1.1	1.2	1.1
1996	1.2	1.2	1.2	1.2	1.2	1.2	1.3	1.3	1.3	1.3	1.2	1.2	1.2
1997	1.1	1.1	1.2	1.2	1.2	1.2	1.4	1.3	1.3	1.3	1.3	1.3	1.2
1998	1.3	1.3	1.3	1.3	1.3	1.3	1.4	1.4	1.4	1.4	1.3	1.3	1.3
1999	1.3	1.3	1.3	1.3	1.3	1.4	1.4	1.4	1.4	1.3	1.3	1.3	1.3
2000	1.3	1.3	1.3	1.3	1.3	1.4	1.5	1.5	1.4	1.4	1.4	1.4	1.4
2001	1.3	1.3	1.4	1.3	1.4	1.4	1.5	1.4	1.4	1.4	1.4	1.4	1.4
2002	1.4	1.4	1.4	1.4	1.4	1.4	1.5	1.5	1.5	1.5	1.4	1.4	1.4
2003	1.4	1.4	1.4	1.4	1.4	1.4	1.4	1.5	1.4	1.4	1.4	1.4	1.4
Government													
1990	7.0	7.0	7.0	6.9	7.2	7.3	6.4	6.5	7.3	7.1	7.2	7.1	7.0
1991	7.3	7.3	7.3	7.1	7.1	7.4	6.5	6.7	7.1	7.2	7.3	7.2	7.1
1992	7.0	7.2	7.1	7.1	7.3	7.3	6.1	6.2	7.2	7.1	7.2	7.1	7.0
1993	6.9	7.0	7.1	7.1	7.3	7.4	6.0	6.0	7.1	7.1	7.2	7.2	7.0
1994	6.6	6.7	6.7	6.8	7.1	7.1	5.9	5.9	7.3	7.1	7.3	7.3	6.8
1995	7.3	7.4	7.6	7.5	7.7	7.8	6.3	6.3	7.6	7.5	7.6	7.6	7.4
1996	7.4	7.4	7.5	7.4	7.6	7.6	6.1	6.4	7.6	7.4	7.4	7.5	7.3
1997	6.9	7.1	7.1	7.1	7.2	7.1	6.3	6.2	6.8	7.0	6.9	7.0	6.9
1998	7.2	7.2	7.2	7.2	7.4	7.5	6.4	7.0	7.4	7.6	7.6	7.6	7.3
1999	7.6	7.8	7.8	7.8	7.9	8.0	7.0	7.0	8.0	8.1	8.0	8.0	7.8
2000	7.9	7.9	8.2	8.1	8.2	8.4	7.3	7.2	8.3	8.0	8.2	8.2	8.0
2001	8.3	8.3	8.4	8.2	8.4	8.6	7.8	7.9	8.6	8.6	8.6	8.7	8.4
2002	8.4	8.4	8.4	8.4	8.6	8.8	7.9	7.9	8.7	8.7	8.4	8.4	8.4
2003	8.4	8.5	8.5	8.5	8.8	8.9	7.9	8.0	8.9	8.8	8.9	8.9	8.6
Federal government													
1990	0.4	0.4	0.4	0.4	0.4	0.4	0.4	0.4	0.4	0.4	0.4	0.4	0.4
1991	0.4	0.4	0.4	0.4	0.3	0.4	0.4	0.4	0.4	0.4	0.4	0.4	0.4
1992	0.4	0.4	0.4	0.4	0.4	0.4	0.4	0.3	0.4	0.3	0.3	0.3	0.4
1993	0.3	0.3	0.3	0.3	0.3	0.3	0.3	0.3	0.3	0.3	0.3	0.3	0.3
1994	0.3	0.3	0.3	0.3	0.4	0.4	0.3	0.3	0.3	0.3	0.3	0.3	0.3
1995	0.3	0.3	0.3	0.3	0.3	0.3	0.3	0.3	0.3	0.3	0.3	0.3	0.3
1996	0.3	0.3	0.3	0.3	0.3	0.3	0.3	0.4	0.4	0.3	0.3	0.3	0.3
1997	0.3	0.3	0.3	0.3	0.3	0.3	0.3	0.3	0.3	0.3	0.3	0.4	0.3
1998	0.3	0.3	0.3	0.3	0.3	0.3	0.3	0.3	0.3	0.3	0.3	0.3	0.3
1999	0.3	0.3	0.3	0.3	0.3	0.3	0.3	0.3	0.4	0.4	0.4	0.4	0.3
2000	0.4	0.3	0.6	0.5	0.5	0.4	0.4	0.4	0.4	0.3	0.4	0.4	0.4
2001	0.4	0.4	0.4	0.3	0.3	0.4	0.4	0.4	0.4	0.4	0.3	0.4	0.4
2002	0.4	0.3	0.3	0.3	0.3	0.4	0.3	0.4	0.3	0.4	0.3	0.3	0.3
2003	0.3	0.3	0.3	0.3	0.3	0.3	0.3	0.3	0.3	0.3	0.3	0.3	0.3
State government													
1990	3.8	3.8	3.8	3.8	3.9	4.0	4.1	4.2	4.1	3.9	3.9	3.8	3.9
1991	4.0	3.9	3.9	3.9	3.9	4.0	4.1	4.1	4.0	3.9	3.9	3.8	4.0
1992	3.8	3.9	3.8	3.8	3.9	4.0	4.1	4.1	4.0	3.9	3.9	3.8	3.9
1993	3.8	3.8	3.9	3.9	4.0	4.1	4.2	4.1	4.0	3.9	3.9	3.9	4.0
1994	3.5	3.5	3.5	3.6	3.7	3.7	4.1	4.1	4.2	3.9	4.0	4.0	3.8
1995	4.2	4.2	4.3	4.3	4.4	4.5	4.5	4.5	4.5	4.3	4.3	4.2	4.4
1996	4.2	4.2	4.2	4.2	4.3	4.3	4.3	4.3	4.3	4.1	4.1	4.1	4.2
1997	3.8	3.8	3.8	3.8	3.9	3.9	3.9	3.8	3.7	3.6	3.6	3.5	3.8
1998	3.9	3.9	3.9	3.9	4.0	4.1	3.7	4.2	4.2	4.2	4.2	4.2	4.0
1999	4.2	4.3	4.3	4.3	4.4	4.5	4.5	4.5	4.5	4.5	4.4	4.4	4.4
2000	4.4	4.4	4.4	4.5	4.5	4.7	4.6	4.6	4.6	4.5	4.6	4.5	4.5
2001	4.7	4.7	4.8	4.7	4.8	4.9	4.9	5.0	4.9	4.8	4.9	4.8	4.8
2002	4.8	4.8	4.8	4.8	4.9	5.0	5.0	5.0	5.0	4.9	4.7	4.7	4.9
2003	4.7	4.8	4.8	4.8	5.0	5.1	5.1	5.1	5.1	5.1	5.1	5.1	5.0

Employment by Industry: Vermont—*Continued*

(Numbers in thousands. Not seasonally adjusted.)

Industry	January	February	March	April	May	June	July	August	September	October	November	December	Annual Average
BARRE-MONTPELIER —*Continued*													
Local government													
1990	2.8	2.8	2.8	2.7	2.9	2.9	1.9	1.9	2.8	2.8	2.9	2.9	2.7
1991	2.9	3.0	3.0	2.8	2.9	3.0	2.0	2.2	2.7	2.9	3.0	3.0	2.8
1992	2.8	2.9	2.9	2.9	3.0	2.9	1.6	1.8	2.8	2.9	3.0	3.0	2.7
1993	2.8	2.9	2.9	2.9	3.0	3.0	1.5	1.6	2.8	2.9	3.0	3.0	2.7
1994	2.8	2.9	2.9	2.9	3.0	3.0	1.5	1.5	2.8	2.9	3.0	3.0	2.7
1995	2.8	2.9	3.0	2.9	3.0	3.0	1.5	1.5	2.8	2.9	3.0	3.1	2.7
1996	2.9	2.9	3.0	2.9	3.0	3.0	1.5	1.7	2.9	3.0	3.0	3.1	2.7
1997	2.8	3.0	3.0	3.0	3.0	2.9	2.1	2.1	2.8	3.1	3.0	3.1	2.8
1998	3.0	3.0	3.0	3.0	3.1	3.1	2.4	2.5	2.9	3.1	3.1	3.1	2.9
1999	3.1	3.2	3.2	3.2	3.2	3.2	2.2	2.2	3.1	3.2	3.2	3.2	3.0
2000	3.1	3.2	3.2	3.1	3.2	3.3	2.3	2.2	3.3	3.2	3.2	3.3	3.1
2001	3.2	3.2	3.2	3.2	3.3	3.3	2.5	2.5	3.3	3.4	3.4	3.5	3.2
2002	3.2	3.3	3.3	3.3	3.4	3.4	2.6	2.5	3.4	3.4	3.4	3.4	3.2
2003	3.4	3.4	3.4	3.4	3.5	3.5	2.5	2.6	3.5	3.4	3.5	3.5	3.3
BURLINGTON													
Total nonfarm													
1990	85.0	86.0	85.9	86.4	86.6	87.5	84.5	84.7	86.8	88.4	86.8	87.1	86.3
1991	83.2	83.6	83.2	85.1	85.6	85.1	81.4	83.6	85.5	86.4	86.1	86.3	84.5
1992	83.2	84.2	84.5	85.1	85.7	85.6	83.8	84.3	87.8	88.6	88.9	87.9	85.8
1993	85.1	85.7	85.5	87.1	88.8	88.9	88.5	88.0	90.9	91.0	91.4	90.8	88.4
1994	86.7	88.3	88.6	89.9	91.3	91.8	89.7	89.9	92.4	94.1	94.2	95.0	90.9
1995	91.3	91.4	92.7	92.6	94.0	95.0	92.4	92.7	96.1	94.7	95.4	94.9	93.6
1996	93.4	94.6	94.8	96.9	97.5	98.2	95.3	95.9	98.6	98.5	99.1	99.0	96.8
1997	94.5	96.4	96.4	97.2	98.4	98.3	97.2	96.4	100.1	101.6	101.7	102.0	98.3
1998	97.6	99.4	99.5	101.1	101.7	101.8	100.4	100.0	103.2	104.1	104.7	105.2	101.5
1999	100.4	102.1	102.0	103.7	104.6	104.4	104.0	103.4	105.6	107.3	107.7	108.3	104.4
2000	105.1	105.6	106.4	107.6	108.6	108.2	106.6	106.2	108.6	110.5	110.8	111.7	107.9
2001	108.7	109.3	109.4	110.1	110.7	111.1	109.3	108.4	109.9	110.9	110.6	111.1	110.0
2002	106.7	107.1	107.2	108.4	109.3	108.8	107.1	105.8	108.6	108.9	109.4	108.8	108.0
2003	105.4	106.2	106.0	107.2	108.7	108.4	107.1	106.9	108.4	109.6	110.2	110.1	107.9
Total private													
1990	71.7	71.4	71.4	71.8	72.8	74.2	74.0	74.2	74.0	73.6	72.5	72.2	72.8
1991	68.9	68.6	68.5	69.9	71.0	71.6	71.7	72.4	72.0	71.4	70.8	70.6	70.6
1992	69.3	69.5	69.7	70.2	71.5	72.1	72.3	73.2	73.8	73.6	73.5	73.4	71.8
1993	71.0	70.8	70.9	71.9	74.0	74.9	76.1	76.4	76.6	75.7	76.0	76.2	74.2
1994	72.9	73.3	73.5	74.7	76.4	77.7	77.9	78.4	78.6	78.4	78.2	78.9	76.5
1995	76.5	76.0	77.3	77.5	79.4	80.8	81.1	81.4	81.8	80.7	81.3	80.8	79.5
1996	79.0	79.0	79.1	80.9	82.4	83.7	83.6	84.1	83.6	82.6	82.6	82.5	81.9
1997	80.1	80.1	80.7	81.0	82.8	84.0	84.6	84.1	84.5	85.3	85.1	85.5	83.1
1998	83.0	83.1	83.6	84.9	86.1	87.3	87.7	87.4	87.7	87.4	87.8	88.3	86.1
1999	85.2	85.3	85.5	86.9	88.2	89.3	90.7	90.4	89.6	90.1	90.2	90.9	88.5
2000	88.6	88.3	88.9	90.1	91.1	92.6	92.4	92.5	92.1	93.1	93.1	93.9	91.3
2001	91.8	91.6	91.9	92.5	93.4	94.9	94.7	94.3	92.9	93.1	92.6	92.7	93.0
2002	89.6	89.2	89.3	90.3	91.6	92.6	92.4	91.5	91.1	90.3	90.4	90.7	90.8
2003	87.5	87.5	87.3	88.5	90.0	91.5	91.3	91.4	90.3	90.5	90.5	90.5	89.7
Goods-producing													
1990	20.3	20.1	20.0	19.9	20.2	20.8	20.8	21.0	20.4	20.2	19.6	19.3	20.2
1991	18.2	18.1	18.1	18.3	18.6	18.9	19.1	19.2	18.7	18.8	18.7	18.3	18.5
1992	17.8	17.7	17.8	17.9	18.5	18.9	19.2	19.5	19.4	19.0	18.9	18.6	18.6
1993	18.0	18.0	18.0	18.5	19.2	19.8	20.3	20.0	19.6	19.1	19.4	19.3	19.1
1994	18.3	18.4	18.4	18.8	19.4	19.9	20.2	20.2	20.1	20.2	20.3	20.1	19.5
1995	19.5	19.1	19.6	19.6	20.2	20.8	21.2	21.6	21.5	21.4	21.6	21.1	20.6
1996	20.4	20.4	20.2	20.9	21.7	22.3	22.3	22.6	22.4	21.9	21.7	21.5	21.5
1997	20.9	20.8	20.9	21.0	21.7	22.2	22.3	22.3	22.0	22.2	22.3	22.3	21.7
1998	21.7	21.5	21.6	22.0	22.5	22.9	23.1	23.1	22.9	22.7	22.8	23.0	22.4
1999	22.3	22.1	22.4	22.9	23.3	23.7	24.2	24.2	23.8	23.9	23.7	23.8	23.3
2000	23.2	23.0	23.4	23.6	24.0	24.7	25.1	25.3	25.1	25.3	25.4	25.2	24.4
2001	24.9	24.7	24.8	24.8	25.0	25.5	25.4	25.1	24.5	24.2	23.8	23.7	24.7
2002	22.8	22.1	22.0	22.3	22.5	22.6	22.3	21.3	21.2	21.1	20.9	20.7	21.8
2003	20.2	20.1	20.0	20.4	20.7	21.1	21.3	21.2	20.2	20.3	20.3	20.2	20.5
Construction and mining													
1990	4.3	4.1	4.1	4.3	4.6	4.9	4.9	5.0	4.9	4.5	4.1	3.8	4.4
1991	3.4	3.3	3.3	3.5	3.8	4.1	4.2	4.3	4.1	4.0	3.8	3.5	3.7
1992	3.1	2.9	2.9	3.1	3.6	3.9	4.2	4.3	4.3	4.3	4.1	3.9	3.7
1993	3.3	3.1	3.1	3.5	4.0	4.4	4.7	4.7	4.5	4.5	4.4	4.2	4.0
1994	3.6	3.5	3.4	3.6	4.2	4.6	4.7	4.7	4.6	4.6	4.6	4.4	4.2
1995	3.9	3.7	3.9	4.1	4.5	4.8	5.0	5.2	5.0	4.9	4.8	4.5	4.5
1996	3.9	3.8	3.7	4.0	4.6	5.0	5.1	5.2	5.1	5.0	4.8	4.6	4.5
1997	4.2	4.0	4.0	4.1	4.6	5.0	5.2	5.2	5.0	5.0	4.9	4.8	4.6
1998	4.4	4.2	4.3	4.7	5.1	5.3	5.4	5.4	5.3	5.3	5.2	5.2	4.9
1999	4.8	4.8	4.8	5.4	5.6	5.8	6.0	6.0	5.8	5.7	5.6	5.4	5.4
2000	5.0	4.9	5.0	5.3	5.6	5.9	6.0	6.0	5.8	5.8	5.6	5.4	5.5
2001	5.1	5.0	5.0	5.2	5.5	5.9	6.0	5.9	5.7	5.6	5.5	5.4	5.5
2002	4.9	4.8	4.7	4.8	5.1	5.2	5.2	5.2	5.1	5.1	5.1	4.9	5.0
2003	4.6	4.5	4.5	4.8	5.2	5.5	5.7	5.7	5.6	5.5	5.5	5.4	5.2

Employment by Industry: Vermont—*Continued*

(Numbers in thousands. Not seasonally adjusted.)

Industry	January	February	March	April	May	June	July	August	September	October	November	December	Annual Average
BURLINGTON—*Continued*													
Manufacturing													
1990	16.0	16.0	15.9	15.6	15.6	15.9	15.9	16.0	15.5	15.7	15.5	15.5	15.7
1991	14.8	14.8	14.8	14.8	14.8	14.8	14.9	14.9	14.6	14.8	14.9	14.8	14.8
1992	14.7	14.8	14.9	14.8	14.9	15.0	15.0	15.2	15.1	14.7	14.8	14.7	14.8
1993	14.7	14.9	14.9	15.0	15.2	15.4	15.6	15.3	15.1	14.6	15.0	15.1	15.0
1994	14.7	14.9	15.0	15.2	15.2	15.3	15.5	15.5	15.5	15.6	15.7	15.7	15.3
1995	15.6	15.4	15.7	15.5	15.7	16.0	16.2	16.4	16.5	16.5	16.8	16.6	16.0
1996	16.5	16.6	16.5	16.9	17.1	17.3	17.2	17.4	17.3	16.9	16.9	16.9	16.9
1997	16.7	16.8	16.9	16.9	17.1	17.2	17.1	17.1	17.0	17.2	17.4	17.5	17.0
1998	17.3	17.3	17.3	17.3	17.4	17.6	17.7	17.7	17.6	17.4	17.6	17.8	17.5
1999	17.5	17.3	17.6	17.5	17.7	17.9	18.2	18.2	18.0	18.2	18.1	18.4	17.8
2000	18.2	18.1	18.4	18.3	18.4	18.8	19.1	19.3	19.3	19.5	19.8	19.8	18.9
2001	19.8	19.7	19.8	19.6	19.5	19.6	19.4	19.2	18.8	18.6	18.3	18.3	19.2
2002	17.9	17.3	17.3	17.5	17.4	17.4	17.1	16.1	16.1	16.0	15.8	15.8	16.8
2003	15.6	15.6	15.5	15.6	15.5	15.6	15.6	15.5	14.6	14.8	14.8	14.8	15.3
Service-providing													
1990	64.7	65.9	65.9	66.5	66.4	66.7	63.7	63.7	66.4	68.2	67.2	67.8	66.0
1991	65.0	65.5	65.1	66.8	67.0	66.2	62.3	64.4	66.8	67.6	67.4	68.0	66.0
1992	65.4	66.5	66.7	67.2	67.2	66.7	64.6	64.8	68.4	69.6	70.0	69.3	67.2
1993	67.1	67.7	67.5	68.6	69.6	69.1	68.2	68.0	71.3	71.9	72.0	71.5	69.3
1994	68.4	69.9	70.2	71.1	71.9	71.9	69.5	69.7	72.3	73.9	73.9	74.9	71.4
1995	71.8	72.3	73.1	73.0	73.8	74.2	71.2	71.1	74.6	73.3	73.8	73.8	73.0
1996	73.0	74.2	74.6	76.0	75.8	75.9	73.0	73.3	76.2	76.6	77.4	77.5	75.2
1997	73.6	75.6	75.5	76.2	76.7	76.1	74.9	74.1	78.1	79.4	79.4	79.7	76.6
1998	75.9	77.9	77.9	79.1	79.2	78.9	77.3	76.9	80.3	81.4	81.9	82.2	79.0
1999	78.1	80.0	79.6	80.8	81.3	80.7	79.8	79.2	81.8	83.4	84.0	84.5	81.1
2000	81.9	82.6	83.0	84.0	84.6	83.5	81.5	80.9	83.5	85.2	85.4	86.5	83.5
2001	83.8	84.6	84.6	85.3	85.7	85.6	83.9	83.3	85.4	86.7	86.8	87.4	85.3
2002	83.9	85.0	85.2	86.1	86.8	86.2	84.8	84.5	87.4	87.8	88.5	88.1	86.2
2003	85.2	86.1	86.0	86.8	88.0	87.3	85.8	85.7	88.2	89.3	89.9	89.9	87.4
Trade, transportation, and utilities													
1990	17.3	16.9	16.9	17.1	17.3	17.4	17.4	17.4	17.4	17.4	17.5	17.7	17.3
1991	16.7	16.2	16.2	16.4	16.5	16.8	16.6	16.7	16.5	16.4	16.4	16.6	16.5
1992	16.2	16.0	16.0	16.2	16.4	16.6	16.5	16.6	16.6	16.8	17.1	17.3	16.5
1993	16.5	16.2	16.3	16.4	16.8	17.0	17.2	17.4	17.4	17.5	17.7	18.1	17.0
1994	17.1	16.9	17.0	17.1	17.5	17.7	17.8	17.9	17.7	17.8	18.0	18.2	17.5
1995	17.7	17.4	17.7	17.7	18.0	18.3	18.3	18.3	18.1	18.0	18.4	18.6	18.0
1996	18.0	17.6	17.7	17.9	18.3	18.5	18.5	18.7	18.5	18.5	19.0	19.2	18.3
1997	18.5	18.3	18.6	18.6	18.9	19.1	19.2	18.9	18.9	19.3	19.4	19.9	18.9
1998	19.0	18.9	19.0	19.4	19.5	19.8	19.8	19.8	19.8	20.0	20.5	20.8	19.6
1999	19.6	19.4	19.3	19.5	19.6	19.9	20.1	19.9	19.7	20.2	20.8	21.4	19.9
2000	20.0	19.8	19.6	20.1	20.3	20.5	20.4	20.4	20.1	20.5	20.9	21.4	20.3
2001	20.3	20.1	20.2	20.4	20.9	20.9	20.8	20.9	20.7	21.2	21.7	22.0	20.8
2002	20.8	20.9	20.7	20.8	21.2	21.3	21.5	21.4	21.1	21.3	21.8	22.2	21.3
2003	21.0	20.9	20.4	20.7	21.0	21.3	21.1	21.0	20.9	21.2	21.4	21.5	21.0
Wholesale trade													
1990	3.7	3.6	3.6	3.7	3.7	3.7	3.8	3.8	3.8	3.8	3.7	3.8	3.7
1991	3.8	3.8	3.8	3.8	3.8	3.9	3.7	3.7	3.6	3.6	3.6	3.6	3.7
1992	3.6	3.6	3.6	3.5	3.5	3.5	3.6	3.6	3.5	3.5	3.5	3.5	3.5
1993	3.4	3.5	3.5	3.4	3.5	3.5	3.6	3.6	3.6	3.6	3.6	3.6	3.5
1994	3.4	3.4	3.4	3.4	3.4	3.4	3.5	3.5	3.5	3.5	3.5	3.5	3.4
1995	3.6	3.6	3.6	3.7	3.7	3.7	3.8	3.7	3.7	3.7	3.7	3.7	3.6
1996	3.6	3.6	3.6	3.6	3.6	3.7	3.6	3.7	3.7	3.6	3.6	3.6	3.6
1997	3.6	3.6	3.7	3.6	3.7	3.7	3.7	3.6	3.6	3.6	3.6	3.6	3.6
1998	3.6	3.6	3.5	3.6	3.6	3.7	3.7	3.7	3.7	3.7	3.8	3.7	3.6
1999	3.7	3.7	3.7	3.6	3.6	3.6	3.6	3.5	3.5	3.6	3.6	3.7	3.6
2000	3.5	3.5	3.5	3.6	3.6	3.6	3.7	3.7	3.6	3.6	3.6	3.7	3.6
2001	3.7	3.7	3.7	3.7	3.7	3.7	3.7	3.7	3.6	3.6	3.6	3.6	3.7
2002	3.6	3.6	3.6	3.6	3.7	3.7	3.8	3.7	3.7	3.7	3.8	3.9	3.7
2003	3.9	3.8	3.8	3.8	3.8	3.8	3.8	3.8	3.8	3.8	3.9	3.8	3.8
Retail trade													
1990	11.1	10.8	10.9	10.9	11.1	11.1	11.0	11.1	11.1	11.0	11.2	11.4	11.0
1991	10.5	10.1	10.1	10.3	10.4	10.5	10.5	10.6	10.5	10.4	10.5	10.7	10.4
1992	10.2	10.0	10.0	10.2	10.4	10.5	10.4	10.5	10.5	10.7	11.0	11.2	10.4
1993	10.6	10.3	10.3	10.5	10.8	10.9	10.9	11.1	11.1	11.2	11.4	11.8	10.9
1994	11.1	10.9	10.9	11.0	11.3	11.4	11.4	11.5	11.4	11.4	11.6	11.9	11.3
1995	11.4	11.1	11.3	11.2	11.5	11.7	11.6	11.7	11.5	11.4	11.8	12.0	11.5
1996	11.6	11.2	11.2	11.4	11.7	11.7	11.8	11.9	11.7	11.8	12.3	12.5	11.7
1997	12.0	11.8	12.0	12.1	12.2	12.3	12.4	12.4	12.3	12.6	12.8	13.2	12.3
1998	12.4	12.3	12.5	12.7	12.8	12.9	12.9	12.9	12.9	13.1	13.6	14.0	12.9
1999	12.9	12.7	12.6	12.9	12.9	13.1	13.3	13.2	13.0	13.4	14.1	14.6	13.2
2000	13.5	13.3	13.2	13.5	13.6	13.7	13.6	13.6	13.4	13.8	14.3	14.7	13.6
2001	13.7	13.5	13.6	13.7	14.2	14.2	14.0	14.1	14.0	14.5	15.1	15.4	14.2
2002	14.2	14.3	14.2	14.2	14.4	14.5	14.5	14.5	14.3	14.4	14.8	15.1	14.5
2003	14.1	14.1	13.7	13.9	14.1	14.3	14.3	14.2	14.0	14.3	14.4	14.6	14.2

Employment by Industry: Vermont—*Continued*

(Numbers in thousands. Not seasonally adjusted.)

Industry	January	February	March	April	May	June	July	August	September	October	November	December	Annual Average
BURLINGTON—*Continued*													
Transportation and utilities													
1990	2.5	2.5	2.4	2.5	2.5	2.6	2.6	2.5	2.5	2.6	2.6	2.5	2.5
1991	2.4	2.3	2.3	2.3	2.3	2.4	2.4	2.4	2.4	2.4	2.3	2.3	2.3
1992	2.4	2.4	2.4	2.5	2.5	2.6	2.5	2.5	2.6	2.6	2.6	2.6	2.5
1993	2.5	2.4	2.5	2.5	2.5	2.6	2.7	2.7	2.7	2.7	2.7	2.7	2.6
1994	2.6	2.6	2.7	2.7	2.8	2.9	2.9	2.9	2.8	2.9	2.9	2.8	2.7
1995	2.7	2.7	2.8	2.8	2.8	2.9	2.9	2.9	2.9	2.9	2.9	2.9	2.8
1996	2.8	2.8	2.9	2.9	3.0	3.1	3.1	3.1	3.1	3.1	3.1	3.1	3.0
1997	2.9	2.9	2.9	2.9	3.0	3.1	3.1	2.9	3.0	3.1	3.0	3.1	2.9
1998	3.0	3.0	3.0	3.1	3.1	3.2	3.2	3.2	3.2	3.2	3.1	3.1	3.1
1999	3.0	3.0	3.0	3.0	3.1	3.2	3.2	3.2	3.2	3.2	3.1	3.1	3.1
2000	3.0	3.0	2.9	3.0	3.1	3.2	3.1	3.1	3.1	3.1	3.0	3.0	3.0
2001	2.9	2.9	2.9	3.0	3.0	3.0	3.1	3.1	3.1	3.1	3.0	3.0	3.0
2002	3.0	3.0	2.9	3.0	3.1	3.1	3.2	3.2	3.1	3.2	3.2	3.2	3.1
2003	3.0	3.0	2.9	3.0	3.1	3.2	3.0	3.0	3.1	3.1	3.1	3.1	3.1
Information													
1990	2.0	2.0	2.1	2.1	2.1	2.1	2.1	2.1	2.1	2.0	2.0	2.1	2.0
1991	2.1	2.1	2.1	2.2	2.2	2.2	2.3	2.4	2.3	2.3	2.3	2.3	2.2
1992	2.3	2.3	2.4	2.4	2.4	2.4	2.3	2.3	2.3	2.3	2.3	2.3	2.3
1993	2.3	2.3	2.3	2.4	2.4	2.4	2.5	2.4	2.5	2.5	2.5	2.4	2.4
1994	2.4	2.4	2.4	2.5	2.5	2.5	2.5	2.5	2.4	2.5	2.5	2.5	2.4
1995	2.5	2.5	2.5	2.4	2.5	2.5	2.5	2.5	2.7	2.7	2.7	2.8	2.5
1996	2.8	2.8	2.8	2.8	2.8	2.8	2.8	2.8	2.8	2.7	2.8	2.8	2.7
1997	2.7	2.7	2.7	2.6	2.7	2.7	2.7	2.7	2.7	2.8	2.8	2.8	2.7
1998	2.9	2.9	3.0	3.1	3.2	3.2	3.1	3.1	3.1	3.0	3.1	3.1	3.0
1999	3.0	3.0	3.0	3.0	3.1	3.1	3.2	3.2	3.2	3.2	3.2	3.2	3.1
2000	3.2	3.2	3.1	3.2	3.2	3.2	3.2	2.9	3.2	3.3	3.3	3.3	3.1
2001	3.3	3.3	3.3	3.2	3.2	3.2	3.0	3.0	3.0	3.0	3.1	3.1	3.1
2002	3.0	3.1	3.2	3.1	3.2	3.2	3.2	3.2	3.1	3.0	3.1	3.1	3.1
2003	3.0	3.0	3.1	3.0	3.1	3.1	3.1	3.1	3.1	3.2	3.2	3.2	3.1
Financial activities													
1990	4.7	4.7	4.7	4.9	4.9	5.0	5.0	5.0	4.9	4.9	4.9	4.9	4.8
1991	4.8	4.8	4.8	4.8	4.8	4.9	4.9	4.9	4.8	4.7	4.6	4.6	4.7
1992	4.6	4.6	4.6	4.6	4.6	4.7	4.7	4.7	4.7	4.7	4.7	4.8	4.6
1993	4.5	4.5	4.5	4.5	4.5	4.6	4.7	4.7	4.7	4.6	4.6	4.6	4.5
1994	4.7	4.7	4.7	4.6	4.7	4.8	4.9	4.9	4.8	4.8	4.8	4.9	4.7
1995	4.9	4.9	4.9	4.9	4.9	5.0	5.0	5.0	4.9	4.8	4.7	4.8	4.8
1996	4.7	4.8	4.8	4.8	4.9	4.9	5.0	5.1	4.9	4.9	4.9	4.9	4.8
1997	4.9	4.9	4.9	4.9	4.9	5.1	5.1	5.1	5.0	5.0	5.0	4.9	4.9
1998	5.1	5.0	5.0	5.0	5.1	5.2	5.2	5.3	5.3	5.2	5.2	5.3	5.1
1999	5.3	5.4	5.4	5.4	5.6	5.6	5.6	5.5	5.3	5.4	5.3	5.3	5.4
2000	5.3	5.3	5.2	5.3	5.3	5.4	5.1	5.1	5.0	5.2	5.2	5.3	5.2
2001	5.2	5.2	5.3	5.3	5.3	5.5	5.5	5.5	5.4	5.4	5.4	5.4	5.4
2002	5.2	5.3	5.3	5.2	5.3	5.3	5.4	5.4	5.3	5.4	5.3	5.3	5.3
2003	5.1	5.2	5.2	5.2	5.3	5.5	5.5	5.5	5.3	5.4	5.3	5.3	5.3
Professional and business services													
1990	5.8	5.8	5.8	5.9	5.9	6.0	5.8	5.8	5.8	5.8	5.8	5.8	5.8
1991	5.7	5.8	5.7	6.0	6.2	6.1	6.1	6.2	6.1	6.1	6.1	6.1	6.0
1992	6.0	6.1	6.0	6.0	6.2	6.1	6.1	6.3	6.3	6.6	6.4	6.5	6.2
1993	6.4	6.5	6.3	6.2	6.6	6.8	6.6	6.9	7.1	7.0	7.1	7.2	6.7
1994	6.9	7.1	7.0	7.3	7.5	7.7	7.4	7.5	7.7	7.6	7.6	7.8	7.4
1995	7.1	7.2	7.2	7.5	7.7	7.7	7.6	7.5	7.5	7.4	7.6	7.4	7.4
1996	7.6	7.6	7.7	7.9	8.0	8.2	8.2	8.2	8.0	8.1	7.9	7.9	7.9
1997	7.9	7.9	8.0	8.1	8.3	8.4	8.7	8.7	8.8	8.8	8.7	8.8	8.4
1998	8.4	8.4	8.5	8.8	8.8	8.9	9.0	8.9	8.9	8.9	9.0	9.0	8.7
1999	9.0	9.1	9.0	9.3	9.3	9.4	9.5	9.6	9.4	9.4	9.6	9.7	9.3
2000	9.4	9.5	9.8	10.0	10.2	10.3	10.0	10.0	9.8	9.9	9.9	10.0	9.9
2001	9.7	9.7	9.8	9.8	9.9	10.0	10.0	9.9	9.7	9.6	9.5	9.4	9.8
2002	9.0	8.9	9.1	9.4	9.6	9.6	9.6	9.8	10.0	9.4	9.6	9.6	9.5
2003	9.1	9.2	9.1	9.6	9.7	9.9	9.9	10.0	9.8	9.6	9.7	9.7	9.6
Educational and health services													
1990	11.6	11.7	11.7	11.6	11.6	11.6	11.4	11.4	11.7	12.0	11.9	11.9	11.6
1991	11.5	11.8	11.7	11.9	11.8	11.6	11.7	11.6	12.1	12.3	12.3	12.4	11.8
1992	12.4	12.7	12.8	12.8	12.5	12.3	12.2	12.2	12.8	13.0	13.2	13.1	12.6
1993	13.0	13.1	13.2	13.2	13.1	12.8	12.9	12.8	13.3	13.4	13.6	13.6	13.1
1994	13.2	13.4	13.5	13.6	13.5	13.3	13.2	13.3	13.8	13.9	13.9	14.1	13.5
1995	13.9	14.1	14.4	14.3	14.3	14.2	14.0	14.0	14.5	14.6	14.8	14.8	14.3
1996	14.4	14.6	14.6	14.8	14.6	14.4	14.1	14.0	14.3	14.6	14.8	14.7	14.4
1997	14.3	14.6	14.6	14.5	14.4	14.3	14.0	14.0	14.6	14.9	15.1	15.1	14.5
1998	14.7	15.1	15.2	15.1	15.1	15.0	14.9	14.8	15.3	15.4	15.7	15.6	15.1
1999	15.2	15.4	15.4	15.3	15.4	15.3	15.2	15.2	15.6	15.7	15.9	15.7	15.4
2000	15.9	15.9	16.1	16.0	15.9	15.8	15.8	15.8	16.1	16.2	16.3	16.3	16.0
2001	16.6	16.6	16.6	16.7	16.6	16.6	16.5	16.4	16.6	16.9	16.9	17.0	16.7
2002	16.9	16.9	16.9	17.0	17.0	16.9	16.8	16.7	17.0	17.3	17.4	17.5	17.0
2003	17.3	17.3	17.6	17.5	17.5	17.3	17.0	17.0	17.7	18.1	18.0	18.0	17.5

Employment by Industry: Vermont—*Continued*

(Numbers in thousands. Not seasonally adjusted.)

Industry	January	February	March	April	May	June	July	August	September	October	November	December	Annual Average
BURLINGTON—*Continued*													
Leisure and hospitality													
1990	7.2	7.4	7.4	7.4	7.9	8.4	8.6	8.5	8.7	8.3	7.8	7.5	7.9
1991	7.0	6.9	7.0	7.3	7.9	8.1	8.1	8.4	8.5	7.8	7.4	7.3	7.6
1992	7.1	7.2	7.2	7.4	7.9	8.1	8.3	8.6	8.7	8.2	7.8	7.7	7.8
1993	7.3	7.2	7.3	7.6	8.3	8.4	8.7	9.0	8.8	8.4	7.9	7.8	8.0
1994	7.2	7.3	7.4	7.6	8.1	8.5	8.6	8.8	8.8	8.3	7.8	8.0	8.0
1995	7.7	7.6	7.7	7.9	8.5	8.8	9.1	9.1	9.2	8.4	8.1	7.9	8.3
1996	7.7	7.8	7.9	8.3	8.6	9.0	9.1	9.2	9.1	8.4	8.0	8.0	8.4
1997	7.6	7.6	7.7	7.9	8.5	8.7	9.1	8.9	9.0	8.8	8.2	8.1	8.3
1998	7.7	7.8	7.8	8.0	8.4	8.7	8.9	8.8	8.8	8.5	8.1	8.1	8.3
1999	7.5	7.6	7.7	8.1	8.5	8.9	9.5	9.4	9.2	8.8	8.3	8.3	8.4
2000	8.1	8.1	8.2	8.4	8.7	9.2	9.2	9.4	9.3	9.1	8.5	8.8	8.7
2001	8.3	8.5	8.4	8.8	9.0	9.6	9.7	9.8	9.4	9.1	8.5	8.4	9.0
2002	8.3	8.5	8.6	8.9	9.2	9.8	9.9	10.0	9.8	9.2	8.7	8.7	9.1
2003	8.2	8.2	8.3	8.5	9.1	9.6	9.8	10.0	9.7	9.1	9.0	9.0	9.0
Other services													
1990	2.8	2.8	2.8	2.9	2.9	2.9	2.9	3.0	3.0	3.0	3.0	3.0	2.9
1991	2.9	2.9	2.9	3.0	3.0	3.0	2.9	3.0	3.0	3.0	3.0	3.0	2.9
1992	2.9	2.9	2.9	2.9	3.0	3.0	3.0	3.0	3.0	3.0	3.1	3.1	2.9
1993	3.0	3.0	3.0	3.1	3.1	3.1	3.2	3.2	3.2	3.2	3.2	3.2	3.1
1994	3.1	3.1	3.1	3.2	3.2	3.3	3.3	3.3	3.3	3.3	3.3	3.3	3.2
1995	3.2	3.2	3.3	3.2	3.3	3.5	3.4	3.4	3.4	3.4	3.4	3.4	3.3
1996	3.4	3.4	3.4	3.5	3.5	3.6	3.6	3.5	3.6	3.5	3.5	3.5	3.5
1997	3.3	3.3	3.3	3.4	3.4	3.5	3.5	3.5	3.5	3.5	3.6	3.6	3.4
1998	3.5	3.5	3.5	3.5	3.5	3.6	3.7	3.6	3.6	3.7	3.4	3.4	3.5
1999	3.3	3.3	3.3	3.4	3.4	3.4	3.4	3.4	3.4	3.5	3.4	3.5	3.3
2000	3.5	3.5	3.5	3.5	3.5	3.5	3.6	3.6	3.5	3.6	3.6	3.6	3.5
2001	3.5	3.5	3.5	3.5	3.5	3.6	3.8	3.7	3.6	3.7	3.7	3.7	3.6
2002	3.6	3.5	3.5	3.6	3.6	3.9	3.7	3.7	3.6	3.6	3.6	3.6	3.6
2003	3.6	3.6	3.6	3.6	3.6	3.7	3.6	3.6	3.6	3.6	3.6	3.6	3.6
Government													
1990	13.3	14.6	14.5	14.6	13.8	13.3	10.5	10.5	12.8	14.8	14.3	14.9	13.4
1991	14.3	15.0	14.7	15.2	14.6	13.5	9.7	11.2	13.5	15.0	15.3	15.7	13.9
1992	13.9	14.7	14.8	14.9	14.2	13.5	11.5	11.1	14.0	15.0	15.4	14.5	13.9
1993	14.1	14.9	14.6	15.2	14.8	14.0	12.4	11.6	14.3	15.3	15.4	14.6	14.2
1994	13.8	15.0	15.1	15.2	14.9	14.1	11.8	11.5	13.8	15.7	16.0	16.1	14.4
1995	14.8	15.4	15.4	15.1	14.6	14.2	11.3	11.3	14.3	14.0	14.1	14.1	14.0
1996	14.4	15.6	15.7	16.0	15.1	14.5	11.7	11.8	15.0	15.9	16.5	16.5	14.8
1997	14.4	16.3	15.7	16.2	15.6	14.3	12.6	12.3	15.6	16.3	16.6	16.5	15.2
1998	14.6	16.3	15.9	16.2	15.6	14.5	12.7	12.6	15.5	16.7	16.9	16.9	15.3
1999	15.2	16.8	16.5	16.8	16.4	15.1	13.3	13.0	16.0	17.2	17.5	17.4	15.9
2000	16.5	17.3	17.5	17.5	17.5	15.6	14.2	13.7	16.5	17.4	17.7	17.8	16.6
2001	16.9	17.7	17.5	17.6	17.3	16.2	14.6	14.1	17.0	17.8	18.0	18.4	16.9
2002	17.1	17.9	17.9	18.1	17.7	16.2	14.7	14.3	17.5	18.6	19.0	18.1	17.3
2003	17.9	18.7	18.7	18.7	18.7	16.9	15.8	15.5	18.1	19.1	19.7	19.6	18.1
Federal government													
1990	2.0	2.0	2.1	2.0	2.0	2.1	2.1	2.1	2.1	2.1	2.1	2.1	2.0
1991	2.1	2.1	2.1	2.1	2.1	2.1	2.1	2.1	2.1	2.1	2.1	2.2	2.1
1992	2.1	2.1	2.1	2.1	2.1	2.1	2.3	2.3	2.3	2.3	2.3	2.3	2.2
1993	2.3	2.3	2.3	2.3	2.3	2.3	2.3	2.3	2.3	2.3	2.2	2.3	2.2
1994	2.2	2.2	2.2	2.3	2.3	2.3	2.2	2.2	2.2	2.2	2.2	2.2	2.2
1995	2.2	2.2	2.2	2.2	2.3	2.3	2.3	2.3	2.2	2.2	2.2	2.2	2.2
1996	2.2	2.2	2.2	2.2	2.2	2.2	2.3	2.2	2.2	2.2	2.2	2.2	2.2
1997	2.2	2.2	2.2	2.2	2.2	2.2	2.2	2.2	2.2	2.2	2.2	2.2	2.2
1998	2.2	2.2	2.2	2.2	2.2	2.3	2.2	2.2	2.3	2.2	2.3	2.3	2.2
1999	2.3	2.3	2.3	2.3	2.3	2.3	2.3	2.3	2.3	2.4	2.4	2.4	2.3
2000	2.4	2.5	2.6	2.6	2.7	2.6	2.6	2.5	2.4	2.4	2.4	2.5	2.5
2001	2.5	2.4	2.4	2.4	2.4	2.5	2.6	2.5	2.5	2.6	2.4	2.4	2.5
2002	2.4	2.4	2.5	2.5	2.5	2.5	2.5	2.7	2.8	2.9	2.9	3.0	2.6
2003	2.9	2.9	2.9	2.9	2.9	2.9	2.9	2.9	2.9	2.9	2.9	2.9	2.9
State government													
1990	5.2	6.4	6.2	6.3	5.6	5.1	4.6	4.6	4.8	6.2	5.6	6.2	5.5
1991	5.8	6.3	6.2	6.6	6.0	5.3	3.7	4.9	5.4	6.5	6.7	7.0	5.8
1992	5.4	6.0	6.2	6.3	5.5	5.1	5.1	5.0	5.6	6.2	6.5	5.6	5.7
1993	5.3	5.9	5.5	6.3	5.9	5.0	5.1	4.9	5.7	6.4	6.5	5.6	5.6
1994	5.2	6.3	6.4	6.4	5.9	5.0	4.7	4.4	5.1	6.7	7.0	7.0	5.8
1995	5.9	6.4	6.4	5.9	5.4	5.0	5.0	5.0	5.4	5.0	5.0	4.9	5.4
1996	5.3	6.4	6.5	6.7	5.7	5.2	5.3	5.2	6.0	6.8	7.3	7.2	6.1
1997	5.6	7.1	6.7	7.1	6.3	5.4	5.4	5.1	6.4	7.0	7.2	7.1	6.3
1998	5.6	7.0	6.7	7.0	6.3	5.4	5.3	5.3	6.4	7.3	7.4	7.3	6.4
1999	5.8	7.2	6.9	7.2	6.8	5.6	5.6	5.5	6.6	7.4	7.6	7.5	6.6
2000	6.6	7.2	7.3	7.4	7.1	5.8	5.7	5.6	6.7	7.4	7.6	7.5	6.8
2001	6.7	7.4	7.4	7.4	7.1	6.0	5.9	5.9	7.0	7.6	7.8	8.2	7.0
2002	6.9	7.5	7.5	7.6	7.2	5.9	5.9	5.8	6.9	7.5	7.7	6.7	6.9
2003	6.7	7.5	7.6	7.6	7.4	6.1	6.1	6.1	7.2	7.9	8.3	8.2	7.2

Employment by Industry: Vermont—*Continued*

(Numbers in thousands. Not seasonally adjusted.)

Industry	January	February	March	April	May	June	July	August	September	October	November	December	Annual Average
BURLINGTON—*Continued*													
Local government													
1990	6.1	6.2	6.2	6.3	6.2	6.1	3.8	3.8	5.9	6.5	6.6	6.6	5.8
1991	6.4	6.6	6.4	6.5	6.5	6.1	3.9	4.2	6.0	6.4	6.5	6.5	6.0
1992	6.4	6.6	6.5	6.5	6.6	6.3	4.1	3.8	6.1	6.5	6.6	6.6	6.0
1993	6.5	6.7	6.8	6.6	6.6	6.7	5.0	4.4	6.3	6.6	6.7	6.7	6.3
1994	6.4	6.5	6.5	6.5	6.7	6.8	4.9	4.9	6.5	6.8	6.8	6.9	6.3
1995	6.7	6.8	6.8	7.0	6.9	6.9	4.0	4.0	6.7	6.8	6.9	7.0	6.3
1996	6.9	7.0	7.0	7.1	7.2	7.1	4.1	4.4	6.8	6.9	7.0	7.1	6.5
1997	6.6	7.0	6.8	6.9	7.1	6.7	5.0	5.0	7.0	7.1	7.2	7.2	6.6
1998	6.8	7.1	7.0	7.0	7.1	6.8	5.2	5.1	6.8	7.2	7.2	7.3	6.7
1999	7.1	7.3	7.3	7.3	7.3	7.2	5.4	5.2	7.1	7.4	7.5	7.5	6.9
2000	7.5	7.6	7.6	7.5	7.7	7.2	5.9	5.6	7.4	7.6	7.7	7.8	7.2
2001	7.7	7.9	7.7	7.8	7.8	7.7	6.1	5.7	7.5	7.6	7.8	7.8	7.4
2002	7.8	8.0	7.9	8.0	8.0	7.8	6.3	5.8	7.8	8.2	8.4	8.4	7.7
2003	8.3	8.3	8.2	8.2	8.4	7.9	6.8	6.5	8.0	8.3	8.5	8.5	8.0

Average Weekly Hours by Industry: Vermont

(Not seasonally adjusted.)

Industry	January	February	March	April	May	June	July	August	September	October	November	December	Annual Average
STATEWIDE													
Goods-producing													
2001	39.6	39.3	39.6	39.7	39.8	39.8	40.0	40.3	40.0	40.1	39.2	39.8	39.7
2002	39.5	39.8	40.1	40.1	39.9	40.2	40.2	40.4	40.3	39.6	39.6	39.1	39.9
2003	39.5	39.6	39.6	39.7	39.7	40.3	40.1	40.3	40.3	40.4	40.3	40.2	40.0
Natural resources and mining													
2001	32.9	32.0	31.3	33.3	32.7	32.9	33.1	33.1	32.5	32.3	31.1	32.1	32.6
2002	31.9	31.2	31.1	33.4	33.3	32.4	33.4	33.5	33.6	33.1	32.0	31.9	32.6
2003	31.7	31.4	31.5	33.5	33.5	33.7	33.8	33.9	33.9	33.9	33.8	33.7	33.3
Construction													
2001	39.0	39.5	39.9	40.4	41.8	41.7	41.6	41.9	41.7	40.5	39.2	39.2	40.6
2002	38.5	39.5	39.2	39.8	40.4	41.6	41.5	41.7	41.8	40.3	39.1	38.7	40.3
2003	38.8	38.9	39.0	39.1	39.2	41.0	41.1	41.3	41.3	41.3	41.0	41.0	40.4
Manufacturing													
2001	39.9	39.3	39.7	39.8	39.3	39.4	39.6	39.8	39.5	40.1	39.5	40.2	39.6
2002	40.0	40.1	40.6	40.3	39.9	39.9	39.9	40.1	40.0	39.5	40.0	39.4	40.0
2003	39.8	39.9	40.0	40.1	40.1	40.2	39.9	40.0	40.1	40.1	40.2	40.0	40.0
Wholesale trade													
2001	33.8	34.0	34.9	34.8	35.1	34.9	35.9	38.8	37.6	37.2	36.8	36.6	35.9
2002	34.1	35.0	34.9	35.5	35.7	36.0	36.4	36.5	36.6	36.4	36.3	35.9	35.8
2003	34.6	34.7	34.8	34.9	35.0	35.1	35.5	35.6	35.6	35.6	35.7	35.7	35.2
Retail trade													
2001	30.4	28.8	29.2	29.6	29.0	29.7	30.9	30.0	29.9	29.8	29.6	30.2	29.8
2002	29.9	29.4	29.3	29.1	29.4	30.3	30.5	30.5	30.3	30.1	29.9	30.6	29.9
2003	30.3	30.4	30.4	30.6	30.5	30.7	30.8	30.9	30.9	30.9	30.9	30.8	30.7
BURLINGTON													
Manufacturing													
2001	38.3	36.9	37.0	36.1	36.7	37.3	37.2	36.9	37.9	37.4	36.8	37.4	37.1
2002	37.4	38.0	38.9	38.8	38.6	38.0	38.1	38.2	38.3	38.2	37.4	37.6	38.1
2003	37.5	37.7	37.6	37.7	37.7	37.8	37.5	37.6	37.6	37.7	37.7	37.2	37.6

Average Hourly Earnings by Industry: Vermont

(Dollars, not seasonally adjusted.)

Industry	January	February	March	April	May	June	July	August	September	October	November	December	Annual Average
STATEWIDE													
Goods-producing													
2001	14.33	14.35	14.34	14.36	14.47	14.49	14.51	14.56	14.55	14.51	14.51	14.50	14.46
2002	14.50	14.52	14.52	14.57	14.59	14.61	14.63	14.63	14.63	14.69	14.67	14.66	14.60
2003	14.69	14.68	14.69	14.72	14.75	14.80	14.81	14.84	14.84	14.83	14.83	14.83	14.78
Natural resources and mining													
2001	13.38	13.39	13.39	13.37	13.37	13.35	13.43	13.38	13.44	13.43	13.40	13.42	13.40
2002	13.36	13.38	13.45	13.51	13.60	13.65	13.68	13.69	13.70	13.62	13.65	13.66	13.59
2003	13.60	13.62	13.65	13.68	13.69	13.72	13.73	13.75	13.76	13.76	13.76	13.77	13.71
Construction													
2001	15.23	15.21	15.25	15.27	15.36	15.41	15.45	15.49	15.50	15.42	15.38	15.30	15.37
2002	15.26	15.32	15.34	15.33	15.40	15.44	15.45	15.46	15.47	15.46	15.49	15.35	15.41
2003	15.33	15.35	15.37	15.39	15.41	15.46	15.47	15.49	15.49	15.49	15.49	15.50	15.44
Manufacturing													
2001	14.12	14.14	14.12	14.12	14.19	14.17	14.16	14.21	14.21	14.20	14.22	14.27	14.18
2002	14.29	14.30	14.31	14.35	14.32	14.31	14.31	14.30	14.31	14.40	14.38	14.44	14.33
2003	14.51	14.49	14.50	14.51	14.52	14.54	14.55	14.57	14.56	14.56	14.57	14.57	14.54
Wholesale trade													
2001	17.70	17.75	17.80	17.74	17.84	17.81	17.77	17.75	17.77	17.71	17.79	17.72	17.76
2002	17.77	17.82	17.84	17.80	17.85	17.80	17.81	17.83	17.84	17.77	17.73	17.83	17.81
2003	17.89	17.90	17.89	17.90	17.91	17.93	17.94	17.97	17.97	17.97	17.97	17.98	17.94
Retail trade													
2001	11.60	11.63	11.68	11.71	11.70	11.69	11.77	11.74	11.79	11.73	11.76	11.70	11.71
2002	11.62	11.67	11.71	11.76	11.81	11.75	11.82	11.85	11.87	11.88	11.94	11.88	11.80
2003	11.84	11.83	11.85	11.86	11.88	11.90	11.91	11.93	11.93	11.93	11.93	11.92	11.89
BURLINGTON													
Manufacturing													
2001	14.85	14.84	14.77	14.80	14.83	14.78	14.73	14.72	14.69	14.75	14.79	14.84	14.78
2002	14.88	14.95	15.01	15.06	15.02	15.03	15.02	15.02	15.03	15.07	15.03	15.08	15.02
2003	15.14	15.15	15.14	15.16	15.17	15.18	15.19	15.21	15.22	15.21	15.22	15.30	15.19

Average Weekly Earnings by Industry: Vermont

(Dollars, not seasonally adjusted.)

Industry	January	February	March	April	May	June	July	August	September	October	November	December	Annual Average
STATEWIDE													
Goods-producing													
2001	567.47	563.96	567.86	570.09	575.91	576.70	580.40	586.77	582.00	581.85	568.79	577.10	574.06
2002	572.75	577.90	582.25	584.26	582.14	587.32	588.13	591.05	589.59	581.72	580.93	573.21	582.54
2003	580.26	581.33	581.72	584.38	585.58	596.44	593.88	598.05	598.05	599.13	597.65	596.17	591.20
Natural resources and mining													
2001	440.20	428.48	419.11	445.22	437.20	439.22	444.53	442.88	436.80	433.79	416.74	430.78	436.84
2002	426.18	417.46	418.30	451.23	452.88	442.26	456.91	458.62	460.32	450.82	436.80	435.75	443.03
2003	431.12	427.67	429.98	458.28	458.62	462.36	464.07	466.13	466.46	466.46	465.09	464.05	456.54
Construction													
2001	593.97	600.80	608.48	616.91	642.05	642.60	642.72	649.03	646.35	624.51	602.90	599.76	624.02
2002	587.51	605.14	601.33	610.13	622.16	642.30	641.18	644.68	646.65	623.04	605.66	594.05	621.02
2003	594.80	597.12	599.43	601.75	604.07	633.86	635.82	639.74	639.74	639.74	635.09	635.50	623.78
Manufacturing													
2001	563.39	555.70	560.56	561.98	557.67	558.30	560.74	565.56	561.30	569.42	561.69	573.65	561.53
2002	571.60	573.43	580.99	578.31	571.37	570.97	570.97	573.43	572.40	568.80	575.20	568.94	573.20
2003	577.50	578.15	580.00	581.85	582.25	584.51	580.55	582.80	583.86	583.86	585.71	582.80	581.60
Wholesale trade													
2001	598.26	603.50	621.22	617.35	626.18	621.57	637.94	688.70	668.15	658.81	654.67	648.55	637.58
2002	605.96	623.70	622.62	631.90	637.25	640.80	648.28	650.80	652.94	646.83	643.60	640.10	637.60
2003	618.99	621.13	622.57	624.71	626.85	629.34	636.87	639.73	639.73	639.73	641.53	641.89	631.49
Retail trade													
2001	352.64	334.94	341.06	346.62	339.30	347.19	363.69	352.20	352.52	349.55	348.10	353.34	348.96
2002	347.44	343.10	343.10	342.22	347.21	356.03	360.51	361.43	359.66	357.59	357.01	363.53	352.82
2003	358.75	359.63	360.24	362.92	362.34	365.33	366.83	368.64	368.64	368.64	368.64	367.14	365.02
BURLINGTON													
Manufacturing													
2001	568.76	547.60	546.49	534.28	544.26	551.29	547.96	543.17	556.75	551.65	544.27	555.02	548.34
2002	556.51	568.10	583.89	584.33	579.77	571.14	572.26	573.76	575.65	575.67	562.12	567.01	572.26
2003	567.75	571.16	569.26	571.53	571.91	573.80	569.63	571.90	572.27	573.42	573.79	569.16	571.14

VIRGINIA AT A GLANCE

(Population and total nonfarm employment numbers in thousands)

Population, Census 2000:	7,078.5
Total nonfarm employment, 2003:	3,500.3
Change in total nonfarm employment	
(Number)	
1990–2003:	604.1
1990–2001:	620.3
2001–2003:	-16.2
(Compound annual rate of change)	
1990–2003:	1.5%
1990–2001:	1.8%
2001–2003:	-0.2%
Unemployment rate	
1990:	4.4%
2001:	3.2%
2003:	4.1%

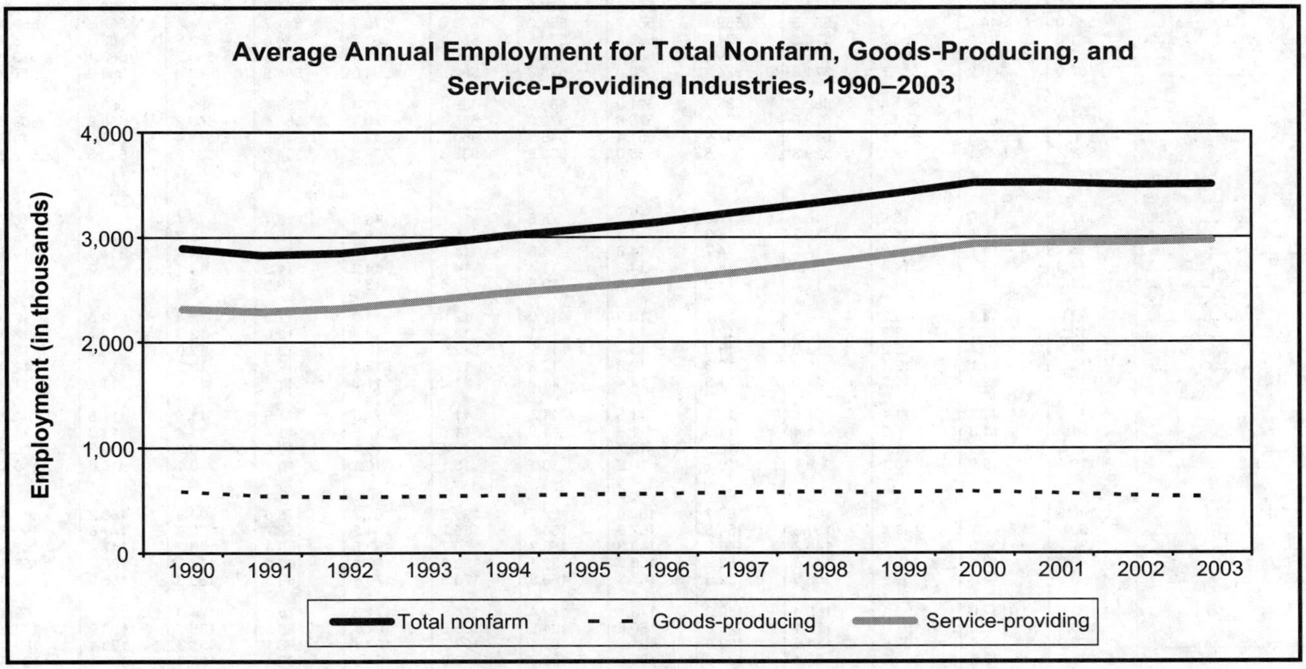

Total nonfarm payroll employment fell off in the 1990–1991 recession, but showed robust growth throughout the rest of the 1990s. During the 2001 recession, employment edged down, but appeared to have regained momentum in 2003. Employment in the goods-producing industries declined steeply in both recessions, and in 2003 was well below its 1990 level. From 1990 to 2003, goods-producing employment declined 9 percent. In the service-providing sector, employment leveled off between 2001 and 2002, but appeared to be recovering in 2003.

Employment by Industry: Virginia

(Numbers in thousands. Not seasonally adjusted.)

Industry	January	February	March	April	May	June	July	August	September	October	November	December	Annual Average
STATEWIDE													
Total nonfarm													
1990	2846.7	2858.1	2881.9	2890.0	2917.9	2940.5	2898.1	2901.0	2915.9	2898.6	2903.6	2903.1	2896.2
1991	2803.9	2791.9	2807.9	2815.9	2838.6	2861.2	2815.2	2819.3	2841.5	2841.5	2851.9	2858.0	2828.9
1992	2783.2	2786.7	2805.6	2829.3	2853.9	2873.2	2846.9	2845.7	2870.1	2884.2	2898.1	2904.3	2848.4
1993	2836.6	2849.9	2861.5	2895.0	2923.1	2947.2	2921.1	2919.4	2948.0	2963.5	2975.6	2986.0	2918.9
1994	2906.4	2912.1	2949.4	2982.7	3005.4	3037.5	3008.7	3013.2	3040.3	3047.0	3065.7	3075.3	3003.6
1995	3002.4	3009.4	3039.7	3054.6	3076.3	3107.3	3063.1	3063.4	3088.5	3094.0	3112.2	3125.2	3069.6
1996	3019.9	3053.3	3089.1	3107.8	3131.0	3162.5	3138.5	3144.8	3167.6	3185.9	3209.8	3220.5	3135.8
1997	3148.1	3159.6	3192.3	3207.4	3230.9	3259.4	3226.7	3228.3	3255.9	3272.1	3292.3	3309.1	3231.8
1998	3215.0	3230.5	3258.8	3288.3	3319.7	3352.8	3319.7	3329.6	3364.2	3364.9	3388.0	3408.2	3319.9
1999	3316.6	3338.2	3367.4	3392.0	3406.8	3440.9	3401.2	3411.4	3436.3	3459.1	3481.4	3497.1	3412.3
2000	3408.5	3423.7	3469.9	3492.2	3520.4	3557.4	3517.3	3521.3	3545.7	3560.5	3584.5	3596.9	3516.5
2001	3472.6	3484.7	3513.0	3519.6	3537.9	3568.1	3516.5	3515.6	3520.7	3507.4	3519.9	3522.4	3516.5
2002	3433.6	3444.5	3472.7	3490.6	3510.2	3538.4	3484.7	3487.0	3504.9	3509.3	3524.1	3529.5	3494.1
2003	3437.3	3435.8	3464.0	3481.5	3507.8	3536.5	3493.4	3499.2	3517.1	3532.3	3550.6	3547.5	3500.3
Total private													
1990	2272.3	2274.5	2296.1	2305.1	2327.7	2357.8	2341.1	2349.6	2341.0	2315.4	2317.4	2317.0	2317.9
1991	2223.7	2205.8	2221.4	2228.3	2251.7	2278.3	2259.0	2269.3	2267.0	2253.4	2257.5	2265.1	2248.3
1992	2196.8	2194.6	2211.4	2232.9	2258.2	2283.0	2280.8	2285.7	2285.5	2286.2	2291.8	2302.0	2259.0
1993	2241.5	2248.1	2257.8	2289.6	2320.2	2348.3	2344.3	2351.7	2352.9	2357.1	2364.4	2377.0	2321.0
1994	2306.6	2306.5	2338.7	2369.5	2395.4	2429.0	2427.2	2439.3	2443.3	2437.1	2449.6	2463.3	2400.4
1995	2400.8	2400.0	2429.5	2444.6	2469.4	2505.5	2495.1	2499.0	2500.1	2493.4	2505.8	2521.9	2472.0
1996	2428.0	2453.0	2485.7	2501.8	2528.1	2563.0	2564.2	2577.6	2577.6	2582.8	2600.4	2613.9	2539.6
1997	2550.2	2556.0	2587.3	2600.2	2628.4	2659.8	2655.8	2661.7	2666.6	2669.5	2683.8	2703.5	2635.2
1998	2617.6	2625.0	2650.3	2679.7	2713.6	2748.7	2741.3	2757.2	2766.2	2755.4	2769.9	2790.8	2717.9
1999	2712.5	2725.2	2748.8	2772.7	2793.7	2829.7	2814.1	2829.9	2828.9	2836.7	2851.7	2869.5	2801.1
2000	2794.5	2802.8	2841.7	2857.5	2883.8	2925.4	2912.5	2919.7	2927.7	2929.3	2946.6	2960.4	2891.8
2001	2847.3	2849.4	2876.6	2882.5	2904.7	2933.8	2907.0	2911.7	2898.9	2874.6	2878.3	2883.1	2887.3
2002	2803.3	2807.2	2832.3	2849.1	2870.5	2898.5	2870.3	2877.0	2875.5	2865.1	2876.7	2885.2	2859.2
2003	2803.4	2795.7	2822.3	2838.1	2866.3	2892.5	2878.0	2887.7	2881.4	2882.7	2894.5	2896.8	2861.6
Goods-producing													
1990	585.9	587.0	590.6	588.9	591.7	597.1	591.2	590.9	586.9	579.1	574.1	567.0	585.8
1991	545.6	538.1	537.3	539.1	543.2	548.8	543.7	547.4	547.2	546.3	544.2	540.5	543.4
1992	525.3	523.8	526.8	530.2	533.8	538.3	535.9	537.8	539.0	537.6	535.1	534.2	533.1
1993	521.4	523.4	524.6	531.3	536.6	542.5	542.6	544.9	545.4	547.7	544.8	543.1	537.3
1994	525.5	525.1	531.6	539.9	545.4	551.8	552.6	554.9	558.1	558.6	557.9	557.0	546.5
1995	544.2	541.7	547.9	551.9	555.3	561.8	559.8	560.4	561.4	561.5	560.7	559.7	555.5
1996	534.0	544.7	551.3	553.5	559.1	564.7	566.3	569.0	570.1	571.2	571.4	569.6	560.4
1997	561.3	561.6	568.3	570.5	574.7	580.1	579.5	580.1	581.7	584.8	583.8	583.5	575.8
1998	563.5	562.9	566.7	575.4	579.8	585.1	584.1	586.1	589.4	587.6	584.7	585.1	579.2
1999	567.6	568.2	569.7	571.8	574.2	580.8	576.6	582.5	584.0	584.5	583.2	583.8	577.2
2000	574.0	573.8	581.4	582.2	585.7	591.0	585.6	589.4	591.8	588.7	589.1	588.9	585.1
2001	571.2	569.7	573.6	572.5	573.1	576.6	572.3	575.4	570.4	562.4	560.2	556.8	569.5
2002	539.1	538.5	542.5	544.4	547.9	551.4	546.9	550.1	547.5	545.6	543.4	541.2	544.9
2003	528.3	525.1	529.1	529.3	534.6	536.0	536.8	538.6	536.3	534.2	534.6	530.3	532.8
Natural resources and mining													
1990	17.4	17.6	16.9	16.8	17.0	17.1	16.8	16.7	16.5	16.1	16.1	16.1	16.7
1991	16.2	15.6	15.7	15.3	15.3	15.4	15.1	15.0	15.1	15.3	15.3	15.1	15.3
1992	14.7	14.7	14.8	14.7	14.7	14.8	14.5	14.5	14.6	14.5	14.4	14.4	14.6
1993	14.3	14.2	14.4	14.3	14.3	14.3	14.4	14.2	14.2	14.3	14.1	14.2	14.2
1994	14.0	13.9	14.0	14.0	13.9	14.0	13.5	13.5	13.5	13.2	13.2	13.3	13.6
1995	13.4	13.4	13.7	13.1	13.1	13.2	12.9	12.9	13.0	12.3	12.4	12.5	12.9
1996	12.0	12.2	12.3	12.4	12.3	12.4	12.1	12.2	12.3	12.6	12.6	12.7	12.3
1997	12.9	13.1	13.2	13.0	13.2	13.4	12.9	12.9	13.0	13.0	13.0	13.0	13.0
1998	12.3	12.1	12.4	12.3	12.3	12.3	12.2	12.3	12.4	12.3	12.2	12.2	12.2
1999	12.1	12.0	11.9	11.5	11.3	11.4	11.2	11.2	11.3	11.4	11.4	11.4	11.5
2000	11.4	11.3	11.4	11.4	11.4	11.5	11.5	11.5	11.5	11.5	11.5	11.6	11.4
2001	11.2	11.3	11.3	11.4	11.5	11.6	11.5	11.6	11.5	11.4	11.4	11.3	11.4
2002	11.0	10.9	11.0	10.7	10.8	10.7	10.5	10.4	10.4	10.2	10.2	10.2	10.6
2003	10.0	9.9	10.1	9.9	10.1	10.2	10.1	10.1	10.1	10.1	10.1	10.0	10.1
Construction													
1990	180.5	182.0	185.9	184.7	187.1	190.0	186.5	185.5	181.7	176.8	173.9	168.2	181.9
1991	150.8	147.7	149.4	151.8	154.6	157.3	154.8	155.7	154.5	152.7	150.8	147.6	152.3
1992	137.7	137.0	139.6	143.2	146.3	149.3	150.7	150.7	150.5	149.4	148.2	147.4	145.8
1993	140.0	142.1	143.5	147.8	152.2	156.3	159.1	159.3	159.1	160.0	157.8	156.7	152.8
1994	145.5	145.3	150.9	158.5	162.5	167.3	169.8	170.3	170.1	169.3	168.3	166.9	162.0
1995	159.0	157.0	163.1	166.4	169.3	173.4	173.4	174.3	174.2	175.2	174.3	173.3	169.4
1996	155.7	162.3	167.9	172.1	176.8	180.6	184.8	185.5	184.7	186.3	185.7	183.9	177.1
1997	178.9	179.0	183.5	184.4	188.5	191.5	193.1	193.7	192.1	193.1	191.3	190.4	188.2
1998	177.6	177.6	180.3	187.4	191.0	195.2	198.6	199.8	199.9	197.1	195.8	196.1	191.3
1999	187.4	189.2	191.0	198.7	200.1	203.8	202.8	203.5	202.3	202.4	202.4	202.7	198.8
2000	196.0	196.9	204.4	207.4	210.3	214.6	214.7	216.4	216.1	215.2	215.1	214.4	210.1
2001	205.9	207.7	213.1	215.9	219.8	223.4	223.3	224.3	221.5	217.7	216.1	214.5	216.9
2002	205.0	206.0	210.0	213.0	216.4	218.9	219.7	220.5	217.7	216.5	214.5	212.9	214.3
2003	204.4	202.6	208.1	211.6	218.4	220.3	224.1	225.7	223.7	224.9	225.9	223.8	217.8

Employment by Industry: Virginia—*Continued*

(Numbers in thousands. Not seasonally adjusted.)

Industry	January	February	March	April	May	June	July	August	September	October	November	December	Annual Average
STATEWIDE—*Continued*													
Manufacturing													
1990	388.0	387.4	387.8	387.4	387.6	390.0	387.9	388.7	388.7	386.2	384.1	382.7	387.2
1991	378.6	374.8	372.2	372.0	373.3	376.1	373.8	376.7	377.6	378.3	378.1	377.8	375.7
1992	372.9	372.1	372.4	372.3	372.8	374.2	370.7	372.6	373.9	373.7	372.5	372.4	372.7
1993	367.1	367.1	366.7	369.2	370.1	371.9	369.1	371.4	372.1	373.4	372.9	372.2	370.2
1994	366.0	365.9	366.7	367.4	369.0	370.5	369.3	371.1	374.5	376.1	376.4	376.8	370.8
1995	371.8	371.3	371.1	372.4	372.9	375.2	373.5	373.2	374.2	374.0	374.0	373.9	373.1
1996	366.3	370.2	371.1	369.0	370.0	371.7	369.4	371.3	373.1	372.3	373.1	373.0	370.8
1997	369.5	369.5	371.6	373.1	373.0	375.2	373.5	373.5	376.6	378.7	379.5	380.1	374.4
1998	373.6	373.2	374.0	375.7	376.5	377.6	373.3	374.0	377.1	378.2	376.7	376.8	375.5
1999	368.1	367.0	366.8	361.6	362.8	365.6	362.6	367.8	370.4	370.7	369.4	369.7	366.8
2000	366.6	365.6	365.6	363.4	364.0	364.9	359.4	361.5	364.2	362.0	362.5	362.9	363.5
2001	354.1	350.7	349.2	345.2	341.8	341.6	337.5	339.5	337.4	333.3	332.7	331.0	341.2
2002	323.1	321.6	321.5	320.7	320.7	321.8	316.7	319.2	319.4	318.9	318.7	318.1	320.0
2003	313.9	312.6	310.9	307.8	306.1	305.5	302.6	302.8	302.5	299.2	298.6	296.5	304.9
Service-providing													
1990	2260.8	2271.1	2291.3	2301.1	2326.2	2343.4	2306.9	2310.1	2329.0	2319.5	2329.5	2336.1	2310.4
1991	2258.3	2253.8	2270.6	2276.8	2295.4	2312.4	2271.5	2271.9	2294.3	2295.2	2307.7	2317.5	2285.4
1992	2257.9	2262.9	2278.8	2299.1	2320.1	2334.9	2311.0	2307.9	2331.1	2346.6	2363.0	2370.1	2315.2
1993	2315.2	2326.5	2336.9	2363.7	2386.5	2404.7	2378.5	2374.5	2402.6	2415.8	2430.8	2442.9	2381.5
1994	2380.9	2387.0	2417.8	2442.8	2460.0	2485.7	2456.1	2458.3	2482.2	2488.4	2507.8	2518.3	2457.1
1995	2458.2	2467.7	2491.8	2502.7	2521.0	2545.5	2503.3	2503.0	2527.1	2532.5	2551.5	2565.5	2514.1
1996	2485.9	2508.6	2537.8	2554.3	2571.9	2597.8	2572.2	2575.8	2597.5	2614.7	2638.4	2650.9	2575.4
1997	2586.8	2598.0	2624.0	2636.9	2656.2	2679.3	2647.2	2648.2	2674.2	2687.3	2708.5	2725.6	2656.0
1998	2651.5	2667.6	2692.1	2712.9	2739.9	2767.7	2735.6	2743.5	2774.8	2777.3	2803.3	2823.1	2740.7
1999	2749.0	2770.0	2797.7	2820.2	2832.6	2860.1	2824.6	2828.9	2852.3	2874.6	2898.2	2913.3	2835.1
2000	2834.5	2849.9	2888.5	2910.0	2934.7	2966.4	2931.7	2931.9	2953.9	2971.8	2995.4	3008.0	2931.3
2001	2901.4	2915.0	2939.4	2947.1	2964.8	2991.5	2944.2	2940.2	2950.3	2945.0	2959.7	2965.6	2947.0
2002	2894.5	2906.0	2930.2	2946.2	2962.3	2987.0	2937.8	2936.9	2957.4	2963.7	2980.7	2988.3	2949.3
2003	2909.0	2910.7	2934.9	2952.2	2973.2	3000.5	2956.6	2960.6	2980.8	2998.1	3016.0	3017.2	2967.5
Trade, transportation, and utilities													
1990	574.6	563.9	567.5	565.9	571.1	576.4	572.1	576.2	574.0	576.0	585.1	591.5	574.5
1991	557.4	546.2	547.0	544.0	547.8	551.8	547.3	549.3	549.9	551.1	561.6	570.5	551.9
1992	540.2	532.3	531.7	534.2	540.5	545.4	544.2	545.2	545.5	550.5	559.2	570.1	544.9
1993	545.5	539.6	539.2	543.4	551.3	555.7	554.9	557.8	558.7	569.3	582.9	594.0	557.6
1994	566.3	559.8	565.0	567.9	573.5	579.2	576.3	579.3	582.0	587.3	600.1	610.5	578.9
1995	581.3	572.2	575.0	574.3	579.1	585.2	581.7	583.7	586.3	592.1	606.6	615.9	586.1
1996	585.8	581.4	585.3	585.0	588.7	596.2	595.3	600.2	602.1	609.6	625.6	634.7	599.1
1997	600.6	592.9	598.2	595.2	600.4	605.4	603.9	607.0	611.8	619.6	634.2	643.6	609.4
1998	605.5	599.1	602.2	602.9	610.1	615.4	612.8	619.6	625.1	631.1	645.9	655.6	618.7
1999	622.4	616.9	622.7	625.0	629.6	636.2	632.7	636.3	639.2	647.1	662.7	673.3	637.0
2000	637.7	633.8	638.1	637.3	642.8	648.1	645.3	649.2	651.3	661.3	676.8	686.8	650.7
2001	644.0	634.8	638.3	635.0	640.7	645.2	642.9	643.8	641.6	646.0	658.7	664.9	644.7
2002	632.9	623.7	625.5	626.3	630.8	636.2	634.6	636.3	634.8	639.2	652.9	663.7	636.4
2003	625.3	618.4	621.0	623.1	628.9	633.3	632.9	636.3	634.3	642.3	654.8	662.8	634.5
Wholesale trade													
1990	107.5	107.8	108.5	107.7	108.1	109.0	109.4	109.6	109.3	109.7	109.5	109.2	108.7
1991	106.3	105.8	106.3	105.8	105.7	106.1	105.4	105.3	105.5	105.3	105.0	105.2	105.6
1992	103.7	103.3	103.5	103.7	104.3	104.9	105.6	105.4	105.1	105.5	104.9	105.8	104.6
1993	103.3	103.5	104.0	104.5	104.8	105.2	105.6	105.4	105.5	105.6	105.2	105.7	104.8
1994	105.8	105.7	106.2	107.3	107.9	108.8	108.6	108.9	109.8	109.5	109.7	110.4	108.2
1995	107.3	107.3	108.1	108.2	108.6	109.7	108.9	109.1	109.2	109.7	109.6	110.1	108.8
1996	107.9	108.9	109.7	109.1	108.9	109.9	109.8	109.9	110.1	109.9	110.1	110.5	109.5
1997	109.1	109.5	110.5	109.2	109.7	110.5	109.9	110.1	110.4	110.2	110.7	111.1	110.0
1998	107.5	108.3	109.0	108.9	109.5	110.3	109.6	110.0	110.8	110.5	110.8	111.4	109.7
1999	109.8	110.4	110.7	111.5	111.6	112.4	111.8	111.6	111.6	111.9	112.1	112.4	111.4
2000	111.2	111.8	112.7	113.5	114.0	114.9	113.9	114.4	114.5	116.3	116.7	117.4	114.2
2001	113.9	114.1	115.1	115.2	115.1	115.9	115.2	115.0	114.4	114.1	114.3	114.4	114.7
2002	112.4	112.2	112.6	112.8	113.0	113.4	112.8	113.0	112.6	112.7	113.1	113.5	112.8
2003	112.3	112.3	112.6	112.5	113.3	113.5	113.5	113.6	113.0	113.7	114.5	114.8	113.3
Retail trade													
1990	365.8	358.0	359.7	359.0	363.8	366.7	362.8	366.1	364.1	365.6	374.7	380.9	365.6
1991	353.3	342.8	343.5	341.0	344.6	346.8	343.3	345.2	345.3	346.5	357.0	364.6	347.8
1992	338.4	331.6	330.9	333.2	337.9	340.7	339.1	339.5	339.4	344.1	353.2	361.8	340.8
1993	340.9	335.1	334.3	336.9	342.8	344.7	341.8	344.0	343.7	351.4	364.7	374.8	346.2
1994	349.6	342.6	345.6	348.1	352.4	356.2	353.7	356.6	358.9	363.7	377.1	387.6	357.6
1995	364.7	356.0	357.4	357.3	361.4	365.1	361.7	363.4	366.1	369.0	383.6	392.6	366.5
1996	368.0	361.8	364.4	365.0	368.6	373.3	371.5	375.7	377.6	381.5	396.4	405.0	375.7
1997	376.2	368.0	371.9	370.8	374.4	377.7	376.4	379.1	382.8	388.6	402.9	411.1	381.6
1998	380.4	373.3	375.3	376.0	381.0	384.6	381.9	387.4	392.1	396.7	411.6	420.3	388.3
1999	392.5	386.4	390.6	391.4	394.9	399.5	395.9	399.4	402.0	407.3	422.7	433.3	401.3
2000	401.9	397.4	400.5	398.9	403.6	407.3	404.6	407.9	410.2	415.8	431.2	440.8	410.0
2001	405.2	395.9	398.2	395.6	400.6	404.0	402.3	404.0	402.9	407.9	421.9	429.1	405.6
2002	402.8	394.7	396.1	396.4	400.1	403.6	401.6	402.8	402.2	405.3	418.1	428.6	404.4
2003	395.8	389.6	391.3	393.0	397.5	401.0	399.4	402.9	402.4	408.9	422.2	429.0	402.8

Employment by Industry: Virginia—*Continued*

(Numbers in thousands. Not seasonally adjusted.)

Industry	January	February	March	April	May	June	July	August	September	October	November	December	Annual Average
STATEWIDE—*Continued*													
Transportation and utilities													
1990	101.3	98.1	99.3	99.2	99.2	100.7	99.9	100.5	100.6	100.7	100.9	101.4	100.1
1991	97.8	97.6	97.2	97.2	97.5	98.9	98.6	98.8	99.1	99.3	99.6	100.7	98.5
1992	98.1	97.4	97.3	97.3	98.3	99.8	99.5	100.3	101.0	100.9	101.1	102.5	99.4
1993	101.3	101.0	100.9	102.0	103.7	105.8	107.5	108.4	109.5	112.3	113.0	113.5	106.5
1994	110.9	111.5	113.2	112.5	113.2	114.2	114.0	113.8	113.3	114.1	113.3	112.5	113.0
1995	109.3	108.9	109.5	108.8	109.1	110.4	111.1	111.2	111.0	113.4	113.4	113.2	110.7
1996	109.9	110.7	111.2	110.9	111.2	113.0	114.0	114.6	114.4	118.2	119.1	119.2	113.8
1997	115.3	115.4	115.8	115.2	116.3	117.2	117.6	117.8	118.6	120.8	120.6	121.4	117.6
1998	117.6	117.5	117.9	118.0	119.6	120.5	121.3	122.2	122.2	123.9	123.5	123.9	120.6
1999	120.1	120.1	121.4	122.1	123.1	124.3	125.0	125.3	125.6	127.9	127.9	127.6	124.2
2000	124.6	124.6	124.9	124.9	125.2	125.9	126.8	126.9	126.6	129.2	128.9	128.6	126.4
2001	124.9	124.8	125.0	124.2	125.0	125.3	125.4	124.8	124.3	124.0	122.5	121.4	124.3
2002	117.7	116.8	116.8	117.1	117.7	119.2	120.2	120.5	120.0	121.2	121.7	121.6	119.2
2003	117.2	116.5	117.1	117.6	118.1	118.8	120.0	119.8	118.9	119.7	118.1	119.0	118.4
Information													
1990	72.2	72.5	72.9	73.9	74.1	75.2	75.7	75.5	75.4	74.4	74.4	74.4	74.2
1991	75.4	75.0	75.3	74.0	74.9	75.6	75.4	75.4	75.1	74.9	75.0	74.9	75.0
1992	74.1	74.2	74.2	74.3	74.7	74.8	75.5	75.3	74.9	76.4	76.8	77.3	75.2
1993	73.6	73.7	74.2	73.1	73.7	74.2	73.5	74.2	74.1	74.2	74.6	74.7	73.9
1994	74.2	74.1	74.5	75.0	75.5	76.4	76.5	77.5	77.3	76.6	77.1	76.9	75.9
1995	79.4	79.7	80.4	80.3	80.5	81.3	80.9	81.5	81.9	80.6	81.0	81.5	80.7
1996	82.5	82.7	83.3	83.9	84.5	85.6	86.0	86.7	86.8	86.6	87.5	88.0	85.3
1997	87.2	88.2	88.9	94.6	95.1	96.4	97.1	97.2	96.8	97.1	98.0	99.7	94.6
1998	97.7	98.2	98.4	98.6	100.0	101.2	100.5	101.2	101.1	101.0	101.7	103.0	100.2
1999	98.1	99.1	99.4	103.9	105.0	106.2	106.3	107.0	108.0	108.3	109.3	110.6	105.1
2000	112.6	113.5	114.7	115.5	117.7	120.0	121.2	116.4	123.3	123.4	124.3	125.3	118.9
2001	123.9	124.2	124.0	121.3	121.2	119.7	119.2	118.0	116.6	114.4	113.4	112.8	119.1
2002	109.9	109.4	108.8	107.4	107.5	107.3	104.9	104.4	102.6	102.2	102.9	102.6	105.8
2003	101.3	101.6	101.5	100.5	100.9	101.8	101.6	101.1	100.0	100.6	101.1	101.3	101.1
Financial activities													
1990	140.7	141.5	142.6	143.2	144.5	146.9	145.8	145.9	144.8	142.8	142.7	143.1	143.7
1991	140.2	139.7	140.4	139.3	140.3	142.5	141.0	141.3	140.8	138.1	138.0	139.0	140.0
1992	135.6	136.0	136.7	136.0	137.3	139.2	140.3	140.7	139.8	139.0	139.0	140.6	138.3
1993	138.0	138.6	139.1	139.9	141.4	143.8	145.1	145.7	145.6	146.0	145.8	147.7	143.0
1994	146.3	146.9	148.5	148.2	149.6	151.8	151.4	152.2	151.6	149.3	149.4	150.4	149.6
1995	146.4	146.5	147.4	147.1	148.1	150.4	150.2	150.3	149.9	148.0	148.9	150.1	148.6
1996	149.3	150.2	151.3	150.7	151.6	154.0	153.3	154.1	152.9	155.3	155.9	157.2	152.9
1997	156.0	156.5	157.8	156.9	158.2	160.4	160.1	160.0	159.1	158.9	159.0	160.4	158.6
1998	160.1	159.0	160.1	161.9	164.1	167.5	166.5	167.7	167.8	168.6	168.7	170.4	165.2
1999	168.7	170.1	171.0	172.1	173.4	175.8	174.9	175.7	174.8	173.9	174.4	175.7	173.3
2000	173.8	174.3	175.3	176.4	178.0	180.7	180.1	181.0	180.4	181.3	181.8	183.4	178.8
2001	176.9	177.8	178.9	179.0	180.2	182.6	182.5	183.0	181.1	178.2	178.9	179.9	179.9
2002	179.0	179.7	180.4	180.3	181.6	184.0	183.9	183.9	182.6	182.4	183.4	184.4	182.1
2003	182.6	183.3	184.2	184.9	186.6	189.0	190.2	190.6	188.5	188.6	189.1	189.7	187.3
Professional and business services													
1990	338.4	342.9	347.3	348.4	350.0	354.4	350.3	352.8	352.5	346.7	345.3	344.5	347.7
1991	333.8	333.9	338.2	339.2	340.9	345.0	342.5	345.0	346.0	343.0	341.6	342.7	340.9
1992	340.6	342.5	347.8	351.1	352.0	357.5	359.3	360.2	362.8	364.0	365.5	366.5	355.8
1993	362.0	366.2	369.6	376.6	378.9	384.1	381.4	382.4	384.7	385.6	386.5	387.2	378.7
1994	375.5	379.2	385.5	390.0	391.8	398.3	400.0	404.3	407.8	406.8	407.2	410.5	396.4
1995	404.7	409.5	417.7	419.6	423.8	431.0	428.8	431.8	432.1	431.9	433.3	438.2	425.2
1996	422.9	431.2	438.8	441.2	444.8	451.0	449.7	454.9	456.6	460.1	460.7	462.7	447.8
1997	455.0	459.2	462.6	464.4	466.5	473.5	472.6	476.1	478.8	477.5	479.5	485.3	470.9
1998	483.8	489.8	497.0	500.3	504.0	512.1	512.2	517.2	519.0	516.2	518.7	523.4	507.8
1999	517.6	524.7	530.9	532.2	534.1	543.4	540.0	544.7	543.3	548.9	549.9	553.3	538.5
2000	542.0	548.4	558.0	563.1	564.1	575.2	572.9	575.6	576.1	578.1	579.3	583.4	568.0
2001	554.8	557.8	563.1	561.2	561.2	567.0	563.5	565.2	559.6	554.4	552.2	554.3	559.5
2002	537.1	541.5	547.3	548.4	548.5	552.0	550.3	551.7	548.1	545.7	546.1	546.9	547.0
2003	535.9	535.9	541.4	544.1	545.3	549.5	551.4	555.7	552.7	555.5	559.6	558.3	548.8
Educational and health services													
1990	231.2	233.6	235.6	236.5	237.9	238.7	236.2	237.6	243.0	245.0	247.0	247.6	239.1
1991	245.1	246.5	248.7	248.8	250.2	250.2	248.2	248.8	254.0	256.6	257.8	259.2	251.1
1992	256.0	258.2	259.8	260.3	261.6	261.3	258.1	257.7	262.3	265.3	265.8	266.2	261.0
1993	263.8	265.8	266.8	267.4	268.2	267.7	265.4	265.0	269.6	270.7	270.8	271.4	267.7
1994	269.6	271.2	273.5	274.7	276.1	275.7	271.7	271.6	277.3	281.2	282.7	284.0	275.7
1995	279.1	282.1	283.8	283.4	284.6	284.6	280.7	280.6	287.3	288.3	288.5	290.1	284.4
1996	284.3	288.4	290.0	292.8	293.1	292.6	290.6	291.3	296.9	298.7	300.9	303.1	293.5
1997	301.0	303.9	307.1	305.0	307.4	306.7	304.0	304.5	310.3	312.4	314.1	315.9	307.6
1998	309.2	312.6	313.8	314.5	316.5	315.0	312.5	312.7	319.7	318.0	319.8	321.4	315.4
1999	320.8	322.9	324.2	326.0	326.2	324.6	320.6	320.5	325.9	329.9	331.5	332.4	325.4
2000	326.2	329.1	331.9	329.1	330.7	330.7	330.3	330.6	335.0	336.7	338.1	339.2	332.3
2001	339.5	342.8	344.6	345.2	346.5	346.7	331.6	332.0	350.1	353.7	355.1	356.5	345.4
2002	355.9	360.2	362.1	363.8	363.5	363.0	343.9	345.4	367.4	370.8	373.0	372.9	361.8
2003	368.2	369.7	371.8	373.4	372.4	371.4	352.2	353.7	372.5	374.0	374.4	375.4	369.1

Employment by Industry: Virginia—*Continued*

(Numbers in thousands. Not seasonally adjusted.)

Industry	January	February	March	April	May	June	July	August	September	October	November	December	Annual Average
STATEWIDE—*Continued*													
Leisure and hospitality													
1990	213.3	216.4	221.9	230.6	239.6	248.8	249.8	250.5	245.2	232.9	230.0	228.4	233.9
1991	212.0	212.6	219.4	228.3	237.9	246.6	244.5	245.5	238.3	228.4	224.2	223.0	230.0
1992	211.9	214.1	220.4	232.2	243.1	249.9	250.8	252.6	245.2	237.2	234.3	230.5	235.1
1993	222.0	225.1	227.7	240.5	251.5	260.4	260.7	261.1	254.7	243.6	238.8	237.9	243.6
1994	228.8	229.3	237.3	251.5	260.8	271.5	274.2	275.1	265.2	254.5	252.2	250.5	254.2
1995	243.2	244.9	252.8	263.8	272.9	284.6	286.5	284.1	275.0	264.5	260.8	259.8	266.0
1996	245.0	248.8	258.5	266.7	277.1	288.0	292.0	289.8	280.7	269.2	265.3	264.8	270.4
1997	255.5	259.0	267.4	276.6	287.4	296.5	297.3	295.2	286.5	277.3	272.6	271.5	278.5
1998	255.6	259.8	266.6	279.6	290.7	301.2	301.6	300.5	291.8	280.3	277.3	277.6	281.8
1999	264.1	268.6	274.7	284.8	293.8	303.5	304.5	305.0	296.2	285.9	282.7	281.8	287.1
2000	272.2	273.1	283.9	294.2	304.6	317.7	314.8	315.2	307.7	297.3	294.5	290.4	297.1
2001	275.1	279.5	289.9	299.8	311.9	324.4	324.0	323.2	309.9	296.9	291.1	289.1	301.2
2002	275.8	279.2	289.3	301.5	312.3	324.5	326.4	326.2	314.4	302.7	298.5	296.2	303.9
2003	283.5	282.7	292.0	303.4	317.1	328.7	330.2	329.3	316.0	306.8	299.6	297.5	307.2
Other services													
1990	116.0	116.7	117.7	117.7	118.8	120.3	120.0	120.2	119.2	118.5	118.8	120.5	118.7
1991	114.2	113.8	115.1	115.6	116.5	117.8	116.4	116.6	115.7	115.0	115.1	115.3	115.5
1992	113.1	113.5	114.0	114.6	115.2	116.6	116.7	116.2	116.0	116.2	116.1	116.6	115.4
1993	115.2	115.7	116.6	117.4	118.6	119.9	120.7	120.6	120.1	120.0	120.2	121.0	118.8
1994	120.4	120.9	122.8	122.3	122.7	124.3	124.5	124.4	124.0	122.8	123.0	123.5	122.9
1995	122.5	123.4	124.5	124.2	125.1	126.6	126.5	126.6	126.2	126.5	126.0	126.6	125.3
1996	124.2	125.6	127.2	128.0	129.2	130.9	131.0	131.6	131.5	132.1	133.1	133.8	129.8
1997	133.6	134.7	137.0	137.0	138.7	140.8	141.3	141.6	141.6	141.9	142.6	143.6	139.5
1998	142.2	143.6	145.5	146.5	148.4	151.2	151.1	152.2	152.3	152.6	153.1	154.3	149.4
1999	153.2	154.7	156.2	156.9	157.4	159.2	158.5	158.2	157.5	158.2	158.0	158.6	157.2
2000	156.0	156.8	158.4	159.7	160.2	162.0	162.3	162.3	162.1	162.5	162.7	163.0	160.6
2001	161.9	162.8	164.2	168.5	169.9	171.6	171.0	171.1	169.6	168.6	168.7	168.8	168.1
2002	173.6	175.0	176.4	177.0	178.4	180.1	179.4	179.0	178.1	176.5	176.5	177.3	177.3
2003	178.3	179.0	181.3	179.4	180.5	182.8	182.7	182.4	181.1	180.7	181.3	181.5	180.9
Government													
1990	574.4	583.6	585.8	584.9	590.2	582.7	557.0	551.4	574.9	583.2	586.2	586.1	578.3
1991	580.2	586.1	586.5	587.6	586.9	582.9	556.2	550.0	574.5	588.1	594.4	592.9	580.5
1992	586.4	592.1	594.2	596.4	595.7	590.2	566.1	560.0	584.6	598.0	606.3	602.3	589.3
1993	595.1	601.8	603.7	605.4	602.9	598.9	576.8	567.7	595.1	606.4	611.2	609.0	597.8
1994	599.8	605.6	610.7	613.2	610.0	608.5	581.5	573.9	597.0	609.9	616.1	612.0	603.1
1995	601.6	609.4	610.2	610.0	606.9	601.8	568.0	564.4	588.4	600.6	606.4	603.3	597.5
1996	591.9	600.3	603.4	606.0	602.9	599.5	574.3	567.2	590.0	603.1	609.4	606.6	596.2
1997	597.9	603.6	605.0	607.2	602.5	599.6	570.9	566.6	589.3	602.6	608.5	605.6	596.6
1998	597.4	605.5	608.5	608.6	606.1	604.1	578.4	572.4	598.0	609.5	618.1	617.4	602.0
1999	604.1	613.0	618.6	619.3	613.1	611.2	587.1	581.5	607.4	622.4	629.7	627.6	611.2
2000	614.0	620.9	628.2	634.7	636.6	632.0	604.8	601.6	618.0	631.2	637.9	636.5	624.7
2001	625.3	635.3	636.4	637.1	633.2	634.3	609.5	603.9	621.8	632.8	641.6	639.3	629.2
2002	630.3	637.3	640.4	641.5	639.7	639.9	614.4	610.0	629.4	644.2	647.4	644.3	634.9
2003	633.9	640.1	641.7	643.4	641.5	644.0	615.4	611.5	635.7	649.6	656.1	650.7	638.6
Federal government													
1990	177.8	177.5	178.8	177.1	182.7	180.3	179.5	177.2	174.4	174.5	174.4	174.8	177.4
1991	175.8	175.0	175.0	175.7	177.2	178.6	180.0	178.5	177.5	177.4	177.6	178.7	177.2
1992	178.5	178.4	178.8	178.6	179.1	180.4	181.7	180.5	178.6	177.9	177.4	178.2	179.0
1993	177.9	176.9	176.6	176.2	176.0	177.1	179.1	177.9	175.0	174.0	172.9	174.0	176.1
1994	173.2	172.5	172.0	171.4	171.2	172.1	172.6	171.9	169.9	169.3	169.2	169.9	171.2
1995	169.4	168.4	168.0	167.5	167.9	167.7	168.0	167.7	166.5	165.7	164.8	165.9	167.2
1996	164.0	163.7	163.2	163.8	163.8	164.4	165.1	164.7	163.0	161.3	161.6	162.4	163.4
1997	160.1	158.3	157.6	157.5	157.0	157.5	157.1	156.6	154.1	153.3	153.8	154.7	156.4
1998	152.4	151.8	151.8	151.2	151.7	152.1	152.9	152.8	151.6	151.0	152.1	153.4	152.0
1999	150.8	149.6	149.6	150.5	149.1	149.8	150.7	150.6	149.5	149.7	150.2	151.5	150.1
2000	150.0	149.5	152.2	154.0	160.8	158.7	155.8	155.9	149.5	149.2	149.6	151.2	153.0
2001	149.5	147.9	148.1	147.2	147.3	148.8	149.5	146.7	146.0	145.1	145.1	146.1	147.3
2002	144.9	144.3	145.1	145.2	145.6	147.6	147.9	147.3	147.0	147.7	147.3	148.8	146.6
2003	146.9	146.5	146.7	146.7	147.1	147.8	148.9	148.9	148.7	149.3	149.0	150.5	148.1
State government													
1990	137.4	143.5	142.5	142.7	140.5	133.1	128.6	128.2	140.1	141.5	141.9	140.8	138.4
1991	135.4	140.9	139.5	141.3	137.7	131.7	126.2	124.6	137.5	141.6	142.5	141.2	136.6
1992	137.3	142.6	142.1	143.4	139.7	131.0	127.4	126.2	140.4	145.0	145.7	144.8	138.8
1993	139.6	145.8	145.6	147.4	143.1	136.1	132.8	133.2	147.0	149.9	151.0	148.5	143.3
1994	143.6	149.8	151.0	153.1	147.5	140.6	136.4	134.9	147.3	150.8	151.3	147.7	146.1
1995	141.4	148.2	147.5	149.2	143.9	136.0	127.3	125.5	138.0	141.4	143.6	139.5	140.1
1996	134.2	142.0	142.5	143.1	137.2	132.1	130.2	126.7	136.9	142.5	143.6	141.7	137.7
1997	136.2	142.1	141.6	144.1	136.7	131.9	128.7	126.8	139.7	141.4	142.3	139.9	137.6
1998	135.3	142.5	143.4	144.3	138.8	135.4	132.7	132.1	142.7	145.0	146.4	145.1	140.3
1999	136.4	144.3	147.9	147.9	141.8	136.1	133.3	133.0	145.6	149.0	150.3	148.1	142.8
2000	138.4	146.2	147.2	150.4	144.8	139.4	137.3	137.0	146.7	149.8	151.1	149.3	144.8
2001	142.6	151.4	151.3	152.2	146.2	141.6	140.1	138.8	145.4	147.9	150.7	148.3	146.4
2002	142.8	148.2	149.2	149.8	144.6	141.2	137.5	136.8	145.2	148.8	148.3	145.2	144.8
2003	139.7	145.0	144.7	145.5	141.3	139.5	137.1	137.4	146.3	150.5	151.3	146.1	143.7

Employment by Industry: Virginia—*Continued*

(Numbers in thousands. Not seasonally adjusted.)

Industry	January	February	March	April	May	June	July	August	September	October	November	December	Annual Average
STATEWIDE—*Continued*													
Local government													
1990	259.2	262.6	264.5	265.1	267.0	269.3	248.9	246.0	260.4	267.2	269.9	270.5	262.5
1991	269.0	270.2	272.0	270.6	272.0	272.6	250.0	246.9	259.5	269.1	274.3	273.0	266.6
1992	270.6	271.1	273.3	274.4	276.9	278.8	257.0	253.3	265.6	275.1	283.2	279.3	271.5
1993	277.6	279.1	281.5	281.8	283.8	285.7	264.9	256.6	273.1	282.5	287.3	286.5	278.3
1994	283.0	283.3	287.7	288.7	291.3	295.8	272.5	267.1	279.8	289.8	295.6	294.4	285.7
1995	290.8	292.8	294.7	293.3	295.1	298.1	272.7	271.2	283.9	293.5	298.0	297.9	290.1
1996	293.7	294.6	297.7	299.1	301.9	303.0	279.0	275.8	290.1	299.3	304.2	302.5	295.0
1997	301.6	303.2	305.8	305.6	308.8	310.2	285.1	283.2	295.5	307.9	312.4	311.0	302.5
1998	309.7	311.2	313.3	313.1	315.6	316.6	292.8	287.5	303.7	313.5	319.6	318.9	309.6
1999	316.9	319.1	321.1	320.9	322.2	325.3	303.1	297.9	312.3	323.7	329.2	328.0	318.3
2000	325.6	325.2	328.8	330.3	331.0	333.9	311.7	308.7	321.8	332.2	337.2	336.0	326.8
2001	333.2	336.0	337.0	337.7	339.7	343.9	319.9	318.4	330.4	339.8	345.8	344.9	335.6
2002	342.6	344.8	346.1	346.5	349.5	351.1	329.0	325.9	337.2	347.7	351.8	350.3	343.5
2003	347.3	348.6	350.3	351.2	353.1	356.7	329.4	325.2	340.7	349.8	355.8	354.1	346.9
CHARLOTTESVILLE													
Total nonfarm													
1990	70.8	72.0	72.7	73.3	72.3	71.4	69.9	69.4	71.7	71.3	71.8	71.7	71.5
1991	67.8	69.1	68.0	69.9	67.9	68.4	67.5	66.7	69.5	70.2	70.4	70.6	68.8
1992	68.3	68.4	68.8	70.3	69.1	68.4	68.0	67.6	70.2	71.5	71.9	71.9	69.5
1993	69.0	70.6	70.7	72.8	72.3	71.2	70.8	69.3	72.8	73.9	74.1	73.9	71.7
1994	71.0	71.8	72.9	74.5	72.6	74.0	74.3	72.6	75.6	76.3	76.6	75.8	74.0
1995	73.6	75.1	74.7	75.9	74.0	76.1	75.4	74.5	75.7	77.8	78.1	78.0	75.7
1996	74.5	77.1	77.6	78.6	76.6	78.6	77.0	76.5	79.0	80.2	80.6	80.8	78.0
1997	77.7	79.6	79.9	81.2	79.7	81.0	80.0	79.5	80.3	82.3	83.0	83.5	80.6
1998	78.7	81.9	82.4	84.1	84.5	86.3	84.1	83.0	83.8	85.1	85.0	85.2	83.6
1999	81.9	84.1	84.2	86.2	86.4	86.2	83.6	83.4	85.4	87.1	87.3	87.6	85.2
2000	84.6	86.5	88.7	88.6	88.1	88.3	87.2	86.7	88.9	88.8	89.5	90.0	87.9
2001	86.4	88.3	88.7	90.1	89.9	90.6	86.2	86.2	87.3	86.3	87.0	87.7	87.9
2002	84.6	85.3	86.0	85.8	86.9	88.7	85.1	85.7	88.1	87.5	88.2	88.4	86.7
2003	86.0	86.7	87.2	85.9	86.4	87.4	84.3	83.7	86.9	87.2	87.8	87.8	86.4
Total private													
1990	48.1	48.3	48.7	49.0	49.3	49.7	49.3	49.4	49.0	48.6	49.0	49.1	48.9
1991	46.4	46.4	46.2	46.9	46.9	47.8	47.7	47.4	47.5	47.4	47.4	47.7	47.1
1992	45.8	45.5	45.9	47.2	47.1	47.5	47.6	47.6	47.6	48.1	48.3	48.2	47.2
1993	46.6	47.0	47.2	48.7	49.1	49.7	49.7	49.3	49.5	49.7	49.7	50.1	48.8
1994	48.0	47.9	48.8	50.0	50.5	51.2	51.3	50.8	51.5	51.3	51.6	51.2	50.3
1995	50.1	50.2	50.7	50.8	51.2	52.3	52.4	52.8	52.7	52.7	52.8	53.1	51.8
1996	50.4	51.6	52.1	52.9	53.6	54.4	53.9	54.2	54.2	54.5	54.6	54.8	53.4
1997	53.2	53.6	53.7	55.0	55.4	56.1	55.6	55.7	55.5	55.7	56.3	56.7	55.2
1998	54.7	55.1	55.4	57.1	57.6	58.2	57.6	57.2	57.8	57.8	57.7	58.2	57.0
1999	56.5	57.2	57.2	58.7	58.9	60.0	59.3	59.4	59.7	59.8	60.0	60.5	58.9
2000	59.1	59.3	60.3	60.3	60.9	61.8	61.6	61.0	61.2	60.5	61.0	61.5	60.7
2001	59.5	59.1	59.5	61.0	61.7	62.2	61.9	61.4	61.7	61.5	61.7	61.9	61.1
2002	59.6	60.0	60.3	61.0	61.7	62.5	61.4	61.6	62.2	61.5	62.1	62.3	61.4
2003	59.9	60.6	60.8	60.2	60.5	61.3	60.3	60.0	60.2	60.3	60.8	60.9	60.5
Goods-producing													
1990	12.3	12.3	12.5	12.4	12.4	12.6	12.4	12.5	12.1	11.7	11.7	11.6	12.2
1991	11.2	11.2	10.9	11.3	11.3	11.5	11.0	11.0	11.0	10.9	10.8	10.8	11.0
1992	10.3	10.3	10.4	10.8	10.7	10.9	11.3	11.2	11.1	10.8	10.7	10.6	10.7
1993	10.4	10.5	10.5	10.7	11.0	11.2	11.3	11.3	11.4	11.1	11.0	11.0	10.9
1994	10.8	10.8	10.9	11.0	11.3	11.3	11.5	11.3	11.5	11.1	11.0	10.9	11.1
1995	10.9	10.9	10.7	10.9	10.9	11.3	11.1	11.2	11.1	11.1	11.0	11.0	11.0
1996	10.6	11.0	11.0	11.0	11.3	11.6	11.7	12.0	11.7	11.7	11.5	11.4	11.3
1997	11.1	11.1	11.2	11.4	11.5	11.7	11.8	11.6	11.5	11.5	11.6	11.6	11.4
1998	11.2	11.2	11.3	11.6	11.9	12.0	11.9	11.9	12.0	11.8	11.6	11.6	11.6
1999	11.4	11.5	11.5	12.0	12.2	12.4	12.1	12.1	12.2	12.0	11.9	11.9	11.9
2000	11.9	11.9	12.3	12.2	12.4	12.6	12.6	12.5	12.8	11.6	12.2	12.5	12.2
2001	12.1	11.6	11.7	11.7	11.8	11.9	11.8	11.7	11.8	11.5	11.4	11.5	11.7
2002	10.9	11.0	11.1	11.3	11.4	11.6	11.5	11.7	11.7	11.3	11.4	11.4	11.4
2003	10.9	10.9	10.8	10.5	10.2	10.3	10.2	10.2	10.0	9.9	10.0	9.9	10.3
Construction and mining													
1990	4.4	4.4	4.5	4.5	4.5	4.6	4.6	4.6	4.4	4.1	4.1	4.0	4.3
1991	3.6	3.6	3.6	3.6	3.7	3.9	3.9	3.9	3.8	3.7	3.6	3.6	3.7
1992	3.4	3.4	3.5	3.7	3.7	3.9	3.9	3.9	3.8	3.6	3.5	3.5	3.6
1993	3.3	3.4	3.4	3.7	3.9	4.1	4.2	4.3	4.3	4.1	4.0	4.0	3.8
1994	3.8	3.8	3.9	4.2	4.4	4.4	4.5	4.4	4.4	4.4	4.3	4.2	4.2
1995	4.0	4.0	4.0	4.1	4.2	4.4	4.3	4.4	4.2	4.1	4.1	4.1	4.1
1996	3.8	4.0	4.1	4.3	4.5	4.7	4.7	4.7	4.5	4.6	4.5	4.5	4.4
1997	4.2	4.3	4.4	4.6	4.7	4.8	4.9	4.8	4.6	4.6	4.6	4.6	4.5
1998	4.3	4.3	4.3	4.6	4.8	4.9	4.9	4.9	4.9	4.7	4.6	4.6	4.6
1999	4.5	4.6	4.6	5.0	5.2	5.3	5.2	5.2	5.2	5.0	5.0	5.0	4.9
2000	5.1	5.1	5.4	5.4	5.5	5.7	5.7	5.6	5.6	5.5	5.4	5.5	5.4
2001	5.3	5.3	5.5	5.7	5.8	6.0	6.0	6.0	5.9	5.7	5.6	5.6	5.7
2002	5.4	5.4	5.4	5.6	5.7	5.9	6.0	6.0	5.8	5.7	5.6	5.6	5.7
2003	5.4	5.4	5.4	5.6	5.7	5.9	6.0	6.0	5.8	5.8	5.8	5.7	5.7

Employment by Industry: Virginia—*Continued*

(Numbers in thousands. Not seasonally adjusted.)

Industry	January	February	March	April	May	June	July	August	September	October	November	December	Annual Average
CHARLOTTESVILLE *—Continued*													
Manufacturing													
1990	7.9	7.9	8.0	7.9	7.9	8.0	7.8	7.9	7.7	7.6	7.6	7.6	7.8
1991	7.6	7.6	7.3	7.7	7.6	7.6	7.1	7.1	7.2	7.2	7.2	7.2	7.3
1992	6.9	6.9	6.9	7.1	7.0	7.0	7.4	7.3	7.3	7.2	7.2	7.1	7.1
1993	7.1	7.1	7.1	7.0	7.1	7.1	7.1	7.0	7.1	7.0	7.0	7.0	7.0
1994	7.0	7.0	7.0	6.8	6.9	6.9	7.0	6.9	7.1	6.7	6.7	6.7	6.8
1995	6.9	6.9	6.7	6.8	6.7	6.9	6.8	6.8	6.9	7.0	6.9	6.9	6.8
1996	6.8	7.0	6.9	6.7	6.8	6.9	7.0	7.3	7.2	7.1	7.0	6.9	6.9
1997	6.9	6.8	6.8	6.8	6.8	6.9	6.9	6.8	6.9	6.9	7.0	7.0	6.8
1998	6.9	6.9	7.0	7.0	7.1	7.1	7.0	7.0	7.1	7.1	7.0	7.0	7.0
1999	6.9	6.9	6.9	7.0	7.0	7.1	6.9	6.9	7.0	7.0	6.9	6.9	6.9
2000	6.8	6.8	6.9	6.8	6.9	6.9	6.9	6.9	7.2	6.1	6.8	7.0	6.8
2001	6.8	6.3	6.2	6.0	6.0	5.9	5.8	5.7	5.9	5.8	5.8	5.9	6.0
2002	5.5	5.6	5.7	5.7	5.7	5.7	5.5	5.7	5.9	5.6	5.8	5.8	5.7
2003	5.5	5.5	5.4	4.9	4.5	4.4	4.2	4.2	4.2	4.1	4.2	4.2	4.6
Service-providing													
1990	58.5	59.7	60.2	60.9	59.9	58.8	57.5	56.9	59.6	59.6	60.1	60.1	59.3
1991	56.6	57.9	57.1	58.6	56.6	56.9	56.5	55.7	58.5	59.3	59.6	59.8	57.7
1992	58.0	58.1	58.4	59.5	58.4	57.5	56.7	56.4	59.1	60.7	61.2	61.3	58.7
1993	58.6	60.1	60.2	62.1	61.3	60.0	59.5	58.0	61.4	62.8	63.1	62.9	60.8
1994	60.2	61.0	62.0	63.5	61.3	62.7	62.8	61.3	64.1	65.2	65.6	64.9	62.8
1995	62.7	64.2	64.0	65.0	63.1	64.8	64.3	63.3	64.6	66.7	67.1	67.0	64.7
1996	63.9	66.1	66.6	67.6	65.3	67.0	65.3	64.5	67.3	68.5	69.1	69.4	66.7
1997	66.6	68.5	68.7	69.8	68.2	69.3	68.2	67.9	68.8	70.8	71.4	71.9	69.1
1998	67.5	70.7	71.1	72.5	72.6	74.3	72.2	71.1	71.8	73.3	73.4	73.6	72.0
1999	70.5	72.6	72.7	74.2	74.2	73.8	71.5	71.3	73.2	75.1	75.4	75.7	73.3
2000	72.7	74.6	76.4	76.4	75.7	75.7	74.6	74.2	76.1	77.2	77.3	77.5	75.7
2001	74.3	76.7	77.0	78.4	78.1	78.7	74.4	74.5	75.5	74.8	75.6	76.2	76.2
2002	73.7	74.3	74.9	74.5	75.5	77.1	73.6	74.0	76.4	76.2	76.8	77.0	75.3
2003	75.1	75.8	76.4	75.4	76.2	77.1	74.1	73.5	76.9	77.3	77.8	77.9	76.1
Trade, transportation, and utilities													
1990	11.3	11.2	11.1	11.1	11.3	11.3	11.3	11.3	11.3	11.3	11.7	11.9	11.3
1991	10.9	10.7	10.6	10.6	10.7	10.7	10.8	10.8	10.9	10.8	11.1	11.5	10.8
1992	10.6	10.4	10.3	10.5	10.4	10.4	10.3	10.3	10.5	10.9	11.3	11.6	10.6
1993	10.7	10.5	10.4	10.6	10.7	10.9	10.8	10.7	10.7	11.1	11.4	11.7	10.8
1994	10.9	10.6	11.0	11.1	11.2	11.4	11.4	11.2	11.5	11.6	11.9	12.1	11.3
1995	11.5	11.3	11.3	11.2	11.3	11.3	11.3	11.3	11.3	11.7	11.9	12.1	11.4
1996	11.1	11.1	11.2	11.4	11.4	11.5	11.5	11.6	11.6	11.6	11.8	12.2	11.5
1997	11.3	11.3	11.2	11.5	11.5	11.6	11.4	11.5	11.4	11.6	12.1	12.5	11.5
1998	11.5	11.4	11.5	11.6	11.7	11.7	11.7	11.8	11.8	11.8	12.0	12.6	11.7
1999	11.7	12.0	12.0	12.1	12.1	12.4	12.3	12.4	12.5	12.8	13.3	13.7	12.4
2000	12.6	12.5	12.6	12.4	12.5	12.4	12.4	12.4	12.5	13.0	13.0	13.1	12.6
2001	12.4	12.2	12.4	12.4	12.6	12.7	12.7	12.8	12.6	12.9	13.2	13.5	12.7
2002	12.7	12.6	12.7	12.7	12.8	12.8	12.7	12.8	12.8	12.7	13.0	13.3	12.8
2003	12.3	12.3	12.3	12.3	12.4	12.6	12.6	12.6	12.5	12.6	13.0	13.3	12.6
Wholesale trade													
1990	1.5	1.5	1.5	1.4	1.4	1.4	1.5	1.5	1.4	1.4	1.4	1.5	1.4
1991	1.4	1.4	1.4	1.4	1.4	1.4	1.4	1.4	1.4	1.4	1.3	1.4	1.3
1992	1.3	1.3	1.3	1.4	1.3	1.3	1.3	1.3	1.3	1.3	1.3	1.3	1.3
1993	1.2	1.2	1.2	1.3	1.3	1.3	1.3	1.3	1.3	1.3	1.3	1.3	1.2
1994	1.3	1.2	1.3	1.3	1.3	1.4	1.4	1.3	1.4	1.4	1.4	1.4	1.3
1995	1.4	1.4	1.4	1.4	1.4	1.4	1.4	1.4	1.4	1.4	1.3	1.4	1.3
1996	1.3	1.3	1.3	1.4	1.4	1.4	1.4	1.4	1.4	1.4	1.4	1.4	1.3
1997	1.4	1.4	1.4	1.4	1.4	1.4	1.4	1.4	1.4	1.4	1.4	1.4	1.4
1998	1.3	1.3	1.3	1.3	1.3	1.3	1.3	1.3	1.3	1.4	1.3	1.4	1.3
1999	1.2	1.3	1.3	1.3	1.3	1.4	1.4	1.4	1.4	1.4	1.4	1.5	1.3
2000	1.4	1.4	1.4	1.4	1.4	1.4	1.3	1.3	1.3	1.4	1.3	1.3	1.3
2001	1.4	1.4	1.5	1.4	1.5	1.5	1.4	1.4	1.4	1.4	1.4	1.4	1.4
2002	1.4	1.4	1.5	1.5	1.5	1.5	1.4	1.5	1.5	1.4	1.5	1.5	1.5
2003	1.4	1.4	1.4	1.4	1.4	1.4	1.4	1.4	1.4	1.5	1.5	1.5	1.4
Retail trade													
1990	8.4	8.3	8.2	8.3	8.5	8.5	8.4	8.4	8.5	8.5	8.9	9.0	8.4
1991	8.2	8.0	7.9	7.9	8.0	8.0	8.0	8.0	8.1	8.0	8.4	8.7	8.1
1992	8.0	7.8	7.7	7.7	7.7	7.7	7.6	7.6	7.8	8.2	8.6	8.8	7.9
1993	8.1	7.9	7.8	7.9	7.9	8.1	7.9	7.9	7.9	8.2	8.5	8.8	8.0
1994	8.0	7.9	8.1	8.2	8.3	8.4	8.4	8.4	8.6	8.7	9.0	9.2	8.4
1995	8.7	8.5	8.5	8.4	8.5	8.5	8.4	8.5	8.6	8.9	9.2	9.4	8.6
1996	8.6	8.6	8.7	8.7	8.7	8.8	8.8	8.9	8.9	8.9	9.1	9.5	8.8
1997	8.7	8.7	8.6	8.8	8.8	8.9	8.7	8.8	8.8	8.9	9.4	9.8	8.9
1998	9.0	8.9	9.0	9.0	9.1	9.1	9.1	9.2	9.2	9.1	9.4	9.9	9.1
1999	9.3	9.4	9.4	9.5	9.5	9.6	9.5	9.6	9.7	9.9	10.5	10.8	9.7
2000	9.9	9.8	9.9	9.7	9.8	9.7	9.8	9.8	9.9	10.2	10.3	10.5	9.9
2001	9.7	9.5	9.6	9.7	9.8	9.9	9.9	10.0	9.9	10.1	10.4	10.7	9.9
2002	10.0	9.9	9.9	9.9	9.9	10.0	9.9	9.9	9.9	9.8	10.1	10.3	10.0
2003	9.6	9.6	9.6	9.6	9.7	9.8	9.8	9.8	9.8	9.8	10.2	10.5	9.8

Employment by Industry: Virginia—*Continued*

(Numbers in thousands. Not seasonally adjusted.)

Industry	January	February	March	April	May	June	July	August	September	October	November	December	Annual Average
CHARLOTTESVILLE *—Continued*													
Transportation and utilities													
1990	1.4	1.4	1.4	1.4	1.4	1.4	1.4	1.4	1.4	1.4	1.4	1.4	1.4
1991	1.3	1.3	1.3	1.3	1.3	1.3	1.4	1.4	1.4	1.4	1.4	1.4	1.3
1992	1.3	1.3	1.3	1.4	1.4	1.4	1.4	1.4	1.4	1.4	1.4	1.5	1.3
1993	1.4	1.4	1.4	1.4	1.5	1.5	1.6	1.5	1.5	1.6	1.6	1.6	1.5
1994	1.6	1.5	1.6	1.6	1.6	1.6	1.6	1.5	1.5	1.5	1.5	1.5	1.5
1995	1.4	1.4	1.4	1.4	1.4	1.4	1.5	1.4	1.3	1.4	1.4	1.3	1.3
1996	1.2	1.2	1.2	1.3	1.3	1.3	1.3	1.3	1.3	1.3	1.3	1.3	1.2
1997	1.2	1.2	1.2	1.3	1.3	1.3	1.3	1.3	1.2	1.3	1.3	1.3	1.2
1998	1.2	1.2	1.2	1.3	1.3	1.3	1.3	1.3	1.3	1.3	1.3	1.3	1.2
1999	1.2	1.3	1.3	1.3	1.3	1.4	1.4	1.4	1.4	1.5	1.4	1.4	1.3
2000	1.3	1.3	1.3	1.3	1.3	1.3	1.3	1.3	1.3	1.4	1.4	1.3	1.3
2001	1.3	1.3	1.3	1.3	1.3	1.3	1.4	1.4	1.3	1.4	1.4	1.4	1.3
2002	1.3	1.3	1.3	1.3	1.4	1.3	1.4	1.4	1.4	1.5	1.4	1.5	1.4
2003	1.3	1.3	1.3	1.3	1.3	1.4	1.4	1.4	1.3	1.3	1.3	1.3	1.3
Information													
1990	2.1	2.1	2.1	2.2	2.2	2.2	2.3	2.3	2.3	2.2	2.2	2.2	2.2
1991	2.2	2.2	2.2	2.1	2.1	2.1	2.1	2.1	2.1	2.1	2.1	2.1	2.1
1992	2.0	2.0	2.1	2.1	2.1	2.1	2.0	2.1	2.0	2.0	2.0	2.0	2.0
1993	2.1	2.1	2.1	2.1	2.1	2.1	2.1	2.1	2.1	2.1	2.1	2.1	2.1
1994	2.0	2.0	2.1	2.1	2.1	2.2	2.1	2.1	2.1	2.1	2.1	2.1	2.0
1995	2.1	2.0	2.1	2.0	2.0	2.1	2.1	2.1	2.1	2.1	2.1	2.2	2.0
1996	2.2	2.2	2.3	2.3	2.3	2.3	2.3	2.3	2.3	2.4	2.4	2.4	2.3
1997	2.3	2.4	2.4	2.3	2.3	2.4	2.4	2.4	2.4	2.4	2.4	2.4	2.3
1998	2.4	2.4	2.4	2.5	2.5	2.5	2.5	2.5	2.5	2.5	2.5	2.5	2.4
1999	2.4	2.4	2.4	2.5	2.5	2.6	2.5	2.6	2.6	2.6	2.6	2.7	2.5
2000	2.7	2.8	2.8	2.7	2.7	2.8	2.8	2.7	2.7	2.6	2.6	2.7	2.7
2001	2.6	2.6	2.6	2.7	2.8	2.7	2.8	2.7	2.7	2.7	2.7	2.7	2.7
2002	2.5	2.6	2.5	2.6	2.6	2.6	2.6	2.6	2.5	2.5	2.5	2.5	2.6
2003	2.4	2.4	2.5	2.4	2.4	2.4	2.4	2.3	2.3	2.3	2.3	2.4	2.4
Financial activities													
1990	2.7	2.7	2.7	2.8	2.8	2.8	2.9	2.8	2.8	2.8	2.8	2.9	2.7
1991	2.7	2.7	2.7	2.7	2.7	2.8	2.8	2.8	2.8	2.7	2.7	2.8	2.7
1992	2.7	2.7	2.7	2.8	2.8	2.9	2.9	2.9	2.8	2.8	2.8	2.8	2.8
1993	2.8	2.8	2.8	2.9	2.9	2.9	2.9	2.9	2.9	2.9	2.9	3.0	2.8
1994	2.9	2.9	2.9	2.9	3.0	3.1	3.0	3.0	3.0	3.0	3.0	3.0	2.9
1995	2.9	3.0	3.0	2.9	3.0	3.0	3.0	3.1	3.0	3.0	3.0	3.0	2.9
1996	3.0	3.0	3.1	3.1	3.2	3.2	3.1	3.1	3.1	3.1	3.1	3.2	3.1
1997	3.1	3.1	3.1	3.1	3.2	3.2	3.3	3.3	3.3	3.3	3.3	3.3	3.2
1998	3.4	3.4	3.3	3.4	3.4	3.4	3.1	3.1	3.2	3.4	3.3	3.4	3.3
1999	3.3	3.2	3.2	3.4	3.3	3.4	3.4	3.4	3.4	3.3	3.3	3.3	3.3
2000	3.3	3.3	3.3	3.4	3.4	3.5	3.5	3.5	3.4	3.4	3.3	3.3	3.3
2001	3.4	3.4	3.5	3.6	3.6	3.7	3.7	3.7	3.7	3.6	3.6	3.6	3.6
2002	3.5	3.4	3.4	3.5	3.5	3.7	3.7	3.7	3.6	3.6	3.7	3.7	3.6
2003	3.5	3.5	3.6	3.5	3.6	3.7	3.7	3.7	3.7	3.7	3.7	3.7	3.6
Professional and business services													
1990	5.5	5.7	5.8	5.7	5.8	5.9	5.8	5.9	5.7	5.6	5.7	5.7	5.7
1991	5.8	5.9	5.9	5.9	5.9	6.3	6.2	6.1	6.0	6.1	6.1	6.0	6.0
1992	6.0	6.1	6.1	6.1	6.1	6.2	6.0	6.1	6.1	6.3	6.2	6.1	6.1
1993	5.9	6.2	6.2	6.5	6.5	6.6	6.4	6.4	6.4	6.5	6.4	6.3	6.3
1994	6.2	6.3	6.3	6.5	6.5	6.7	6.7	6.6	6.6	6.7	6.8	6.6	6.5
1995	6.5	6.5	6.7	7.0	7.1	7.3	7.5	7.7	7.7	7.4	7.4	7.4	7.1
1996	6.9	7.3	7.3	7.6	7.5	7.6	7.5	7.6	7.7	7.8	7.8	7.7	7.5
1997	7.8	7.9	7.8	8.1	8.0	8.2	7.9	8.0	7.9	7.8	7.9	8.1	7.9
1998	8.0	8.1	8.0	8.4	8.4	8.5	8.4	8.4	8.4	8.5	8.4	8.3	8.3
1999	8.4	8.4	8.4	8.4	8.3	8.4	8.3	8.3	8.3	8.6	8.4	8.5	8.3
2000	8.6	8.7	8.7	8.9	8.8	9.0	9.1	9.1	8.8	8.9	8.9	9.0	8.8
2001	8.7	8.7	8.6	9.0	8.9	9.0	9.1	9.0	8.9	8.9	8.9	8.9	8.9
2002	8.7	8.7	8.7	8.4	8.5	8.5	8.5	8.5	8.5	8.8	8.8	8.9	8.6
2003	8.9	8.9	8.9	9.0	9.0	9.0	9.0	9.0	9.0	9.1	9.0	9.0	9.0
Educational and health services													
1990	5.1	5.1	5.2	5.2	5.1	5.1	4.9	4.9	5.1	5.5	5.3	5.4	5.1
1991	4.9	5.0	5.1	5.2	5.1	5.0	5.3	5.2	5.2	5.3	5.2	5.2	5.1
1992	5.3	5.2	5.3	5.5	5.4	5.4	5.4	5.3	5.4	5.6	5.6	5.6	5.4
1993	5.6	5.7	5.7	5.8	5.8	5.8	5.8	5.7	5.8	5.9	5.9	6.0	5.7
1994	5.9	5.9	6.0	6.2	6.2	6.1	6.1	6.1	6.3	6.3	6.3	6.4	6.1
1995	6.5	6.6	6.6	6.6	6.7	6.8	6.8	6.7	6.9	6.8	6.8	6.9	6.7
1996	6.8	6.9	7.0	7.1	7.2	7.3	7.1	7.0	7.2	7.4	7.4	7.5	7.1
1997	7.4	7.4	7.5	7.6	7.6	7.6	7.7	7.6	7.7	7.8	7.8	7.8	7.6
1998	7.8	7.8	7.9	8.1	8.2	8.1	8.1	7.9	8.2	8.2	8.3	8.3	8.0
1999	8.2	8.3	8.2	8.5	8.5	8.5	8.3	8.3	8.5	8.4	8.5	8.5	8.3
2000	8.3	8.3	8.5	8.4	8.5	8.5	8.5	8.3	8.6	8.6	8.7	8.7	8.4
2001	8.9	8.9	8.9	9.1	9.2	9.1	8.6	8.4	9.3	9.3	9.4	9.4	9.0
2002	9.5	9.6	9.7	9.7	9.6	9.8	9.0	8.8	9.8	9.7	9.9	9.9	9.6
2003	9.6	10.3	10.3	9.7	9.7	9.9	9.1	8.9	9.6	9.6	9.7	9.7	9.7

Employment by Industry: Virginia—*Continued*

(Numbers in thousands. Not seasonally adjusted.)

Industry	January	February	March	April	May	June	July	August	September	October	November	December	Annual Average
CHARLOTTESVILLE *—Continued*													
Leisure and hospitality													
1990	6.3	6.4	6.5	6.8	6.9	7.0	6.8	6.8	6.9	6.7	6.8	6.6	6.7
1991	5.9	6.0	6.1	6.3	6.3	6.5	6.6	6.5	6.6	6.7	6.6	6.5	6.3
1992	6.1	6.1	6.2	6.6	6.7	6.7	6.8	6.8	6.8	6.8	6.7	6.5	6.5
1993	6.2	6.3	6.6	7.1	7.1	7.2	7.4	7.2	7.2	7.1	7.0	6.9	6.9
1994	6.3	6.4	6.6	7.1	7.1	7.3	7.4	7.5	7.4	7.4	7.4	7.0	7.0
1995	6.6	6.8	7.1	7.1	7.1	7.4	7.5	7.6	7.5	7.5	7.5	7.3	7.2
1996	6.7	7.0	7.1	7.1	7.3	7.5	7.4	7.3	7.2	7.2	7.2	7.0	7.1
1997	6.9	7.0	7.1	7.6	7.8	7.9	7.7	7.8	7.8	7.8	7.7	7.5	7.5
1998	6.9	7.2	7.4	7.9	7.9	8.3	8.1	7.8	7.9	7.8	7.8	7.7	7.7
1999	7.3	7.5	7.6	7.9	8.0	8.2	8.4	8.3	8.2	8.1	8.0	7.8	7.9
2000	7.6	7.7	8.0	8.2	8.5	8.8	8.6	8.4	8.3	8.2	8.2	8.1	8.2
2001	7.6	7.9	8.0	8.6	8.8	9.1	9.2	9.1	8.8	8.7	8.6	8.4	8.6
2002	7.8	8.0	8.2	8.7	9.2	9.3	9.3	9.2	9.1	8.8	8.8	8.6	8.8
2003	8.2	8.2	8.4	8.7	9.1	9.2	9.2	9.2	9.0	9.0	9.0	8.8	8.8
Other services													
1990	2.8	2.8	2.8	2.8	2.8	2.8	2.9	2.9	2.8	2.8	2.8	2.8	2.8
1991	2.8	2.7	2.7	2.8	2.8	2.9	2.9	2.9	2.9	2.8	2.8	2.8	2.8
1992	2.8	2.7	2.8	2.8	2.9	2.9	2.9	2.9	2.9	2.9	3.0	3.0	2.8
1993	2.9	2.9	2.9	3.0	3.0	3.0	3.0	3.0	3.0	3.0	3.0	3.1	2.9
1994	3.0	3.0	3.0	3.1	3.1	3.1	3.1	3.0	3.1	3.1	3.1	3.1	3.0
1995	3.1	3.1	3.2	3.1	3.1	3.1	3.1	3.1	3.1	3.1	3.1	3.2	3.1
1996	3.1	3.1	3.1	3.3	3.4	3.4	3.3	3.3	3.4	3.3	3.4	3.4	3.2
1997	3.3	3.4	3.4	3.4	3.5	3.5	3.4	3.5	3.5	3.5	3.5	3.5	3.4
1998	3.5	3.6	3.6	3.6	3.6	3.7	3.8	3.8	3.8	3.8	3.8	3.8	3.7
1999	3.8	3.9	3.9	3.9	4.0	4.1	4.0	4.0	4.0	4.0	4.0	4.1	3.9
2000	4.1	4.1	4.1	4.1	4.1	4.2	4.1	4.1	4.1	4.2	4.1	4.1	4.1
2001	3.8	3.8	3.8	3.9	4.0	4.0	4.0	4.0	3.9	3.9	3.9	3.9	3.9
2002	4.0	4.1	4.0	4.1	4.1	4.2	4.1	4.3	4.2	4.1	4.0	4.0	4.1
2003	4.1	4.1	4.0	4.1	4.1	4.2	4.1	4.1	4.1	4.1	4.1	4.1	4.1
Government													
1990	22.7	23.7	24.0	24.3	23.0	21.7	20.6	20.0	22.7	22.7	22.8	22.6	22.5
1991	21.4	22.7	21.8	23.0	21.0	20.6	19.8	19.3	22.0	22.8	23.0	22.9	21.6
1992	22.5	22.9	22.9	23.1	22.0	20.9	20.4	20.0	22.6	23.4	23.6	23.7	22.3
1993	22.4	23.6	23.5	24.1	23.2	21.5	21.1	20.0	23.3	24.2	24.4	23.8	22.9
1994	23.0	23.9	24.1	24.5	22.1	22.8	23.0	21.8	24.1	25.0	25.0	24.6	23.6
1995	23.5	24.9	24.0	25.1	22.8	23.8	23.0	21.7	23.0	25.1	25.3	24.9	23.9
1996	24.1	25.5	25.5	25.7	23.0	24.2	23.1	22.3	24.8	25.7	26.0	26.0	24.6
1997	24.5	26.0	26.2	26.2	24.3	24.9	24.4	23.8	24.8	26.6	26.7	26.8	25.4
1998	24.0	26.8	27.0	27.0	26.9	28.1	26.5	25.8	26.0	27.3	27.3	27.0	26.6
1999	25.4	26.9	27.0	27.5	27.5	26.2	24.3	24.0	25.7	27.3	27.3	27.1	26.3
2000	25.5	27.2	28.4	28.3	27.2	26.5	25.6	25.7	27.7	28.3	28.5	28.5	27.2
2001	26.9	29.2	29.2	29.1	28.2	28.4	24.3	24.8	25.6	24.8	25.3	25.8	26.8
2002	25.0	25.3	25.7	24.8	25.2	26.2	23.7	24.1	25.9	26.0	26.1	26.1	25.3
2003	26.1	26.1	26.4	25.7	25.9	26.1	24.0	23.7	26.7	26.9	27.0	26.9	26.0
Federal government													
1990	1.3	1.3	1.4	1.5	1.5	1.6	1.5	1.4	1.3	1.3	1.3	1.3	1.3
1991	1.3	1.3	1.3	1.3	1.3	1.3	1.3	1.3	1.3	1.3	1.3	1.3	1.3
1992	1.3	1.3	1.3	1.3	1.3	1.3	1.3	1.3	1.3	1.3	1.3	1.3	1.3
1993	1.3	1.3	1.3	1.3	1.3	1.3	1.3	1.3	1.3	1.3	1.3	1.3	1.3
1994	1.3	1.3	1.3	1.3	1.3	1.3	1.3	1.3	1.3	1.3	1.3	1.3	1.3
1995	1.3	1.3	1.3	1.3	1.3	1.3	1.3	1.3	1.3	1.3	1.3	1.3	1.3
1996	1.3	1.3	1.3	1.3	1.3	1.3	1.3	1.3	1.3	1.3	1.3	1.3	1.3
1997	1.3	1.3	1.3	1.3	1.3	1.3	1.3	1.3	1.3	1.3	1.3	1.4	1.3
1998	1.3	1.3	1.3	1.3	1.3	1.3	1.3	1.3	1.3	1.3	1.4	1.4	1.3
1999	1.3	1.3	1.3	1.4	1.4	1.4	1.3	1.3	1.3	1.4	1.4	1.4	1.3
2000	1.4	1.4	1.9	1.7	2.0	2.0	1.7	1.8	1.4	1.4	1.4	1.4	1.6
2001	1.3	1.3	1.3	1.4	1.4	1.4	1.4	1.4	1.4	1.4	1.4	1.4	1.4
2002	1.4	1.4	1.4	1.4	1.4	1.4	1.4	1.5	1.4	1.5	1.5	1.5	1.4
2003	1.4	1.4	1.5	1.4	1.5	1.4	1.4	1.4	1.4	1.4	1.4	1.5	1.4
State government													
1990	16.0	16.9	17.1	17.2	15.9	14.4	14.4	13.9	15.8	15.9	15.8	15.7	15.7
1991	14.5	15.7	14.8	15.9	14.0	13.5	13.5	13.0	15.2	15.9	16.0	15.8	14.8
1992	15.6	16.0	15.9	16.0	14.9	13.7	14.0	13.7	15.7	16.2	16.3	16.3	15.3
1993	15.1	16.3	16.1	16.7	15.8	14.0	14.2	13.8	16.1	16.7	16.9	16.3	15.6
1994	15.5	16.4	16.6	16.9	14.4	15.0	15.8	15.3	16.5	17.3	17.2	16.9	16.1
1995	15.9	17.2	16.2	17.3	15.0	15.9	15.6	15.0	15.4	17.3	17.3	17.0	16.2
1996	16.3	17.7	17.6	17.7	15.0	16.0	15.2	14.7	16.9	17.6	17.8	17.9	16.7
1997	16.5	17.9	18.0	18.0	16.1	16.6	17.1	16.6	16.7	18.3	18.4	18.4	17.3
1998	15.9	18.6	18.7	18.7	18.6	19.7	19.2	18.6	17.8	18.9	18.7	18.5	18.4
1999	17.1	18.5	18.6	18.9	18.8	17.5	17.1	16.8	17.3	18.6	18.5	18.4	18.0
2000	16.8	18.5	19.1	19.1	17.8	16.9	17.1	17.4	19.0	19.3	19.5	19.6	18.3
2001	18.1	20.3	20.3	20.0	19.1	19.1	17.0	17.2	16.7	15.7	16.1	16.5	18.0
2002	15.8	16.1	16.4	15.6	15.9	16.9	15.8	16.3	16.8	16.5	16.6	16.6	16.3
2003	16.8	16.9	17.1	16.4	16.5	16.7	16.5	16.1	17.5	17.5	17.5	17.3	16.9

Employment by Industry: Virginia—*Continued*

(Numbers in thousands. Not seasonally adjusted.)

Industry	January	February	March	April	May	June	July	August	September	October	November	December	Annual Average
CHARLOTTESVILLE *—Continued*													
Local government													
1990	5.4	5.5	5.5	5.6	5.6	5.7	4.7	4.7	5.6	5.5	5.7	5.6	5.4
1991	5.6	5.7	5.7	5.8	5.7	5.8	5.0	5.0	5.5	5.6	5.7	5.8	5.5
1992	5.6	5.6	5.7	5.8	5.8	5.9	5.1	5.0	5.6	5.9	6.0	6.1	5.6
1993	6.0	6.0	6.1	6.1	6.1	6.2	5.6	4.9	5.9	6.2	6.2	6.2	5.9
1994	6.2	6.2	6.2	6.3	6.4	6.5	5.9	5.2	6.3	6.4	6.5	6.4	6.2
1995	6.3	6.4	6.5	6.5	6.5	6.6	6.1	5.4	6.3	6.5	6.7	6.6	6.3
1996	6.5	6.5	6.6	6.7	6.7	6.9	6.6	6.3	6.6	6.8	6.9	6.8	6.6
1997	6.7	6.8	6.9	6.9	6.9	7.0	6.0	5.9	6.8	7.0	7.0	7.0	6.7
1998	6.8	6.9	7.0	7.0	7.0	7.1	6.0	5.9	6.9	7.1	7.2	7.1	6.8
1999	7.0	7.1	7.1	7.2	7.3	7.3	5.9	5.9	7.1	7.3	7.4	7.3	6.9
2000	7.3	7.3	7.4	7.5	7.4	7.6	6.8	6.5	7.3	7.6	7.6	7.5	7.3
2001	7.5	7.6	7.6	7.7	7.7	7.9	5.9	6.2	7.5	7.7	7.8	7.9	7.4
2002	7.8	7.8	7.9	7.8	7.9	7.9	6.5	6.3	7.7	8.0	8.0	8.0	7.6
2003	7.9	7.8	7.8	7.9	7.9	8.0	6.1	6.2	7.8	8.0	8.1	8.1	7.6
LYNCHBURG													
Total nonfarm													
1990	89.3	89.1	89.5	90.4	91.0	90.8	89.3	90.0	90.9	90.2	90.1	89.9	90.0
1991	88.7	88.6	88.6	89.0	89.3	89.4	88.5	88.3	89.8	89.8	91.0	90.8	89.3
1992	88.8	88.5	88.6	89.7	89.6	89.7	88.3	88.9	90.3	90.0	90.6	91.3	89.5
1993	90.2	90.3	90.5	92.3	93.0	92.7	90.6	91.5	93.3	93.7	94.6	95.2	92.3
1994	92.9	92.7	94.1	94.1	94.9	94.9	93.4	93.2	94.3	95.9	96.8	97.0	94.5
1995	94.1	94.1	94.7	96.4	95.7	96.8	95.1	95.2	96.4	96.7	97.7	98.1	95.9
1996	92.9	94.9	95.2	96.4	96.6	96.1	95.4	95.8	96.5	97.8	98.9	98.7	96.2
1997	94.7	95.9	96.6	96.6	96.5	96.5	95.8	96.0	97.4	98.9	99.1	99.1	96.9
1998	96.1	97.2	98.2	97.8	97.9	98.8	97.5	97.5	99.4	101.2	101.8	102.7	98.8
1999	99.8	100.6	101.1	102.1	101.7	102.3	100.9	100.8	102.3	103.4	104.5	104.9	102.0
2000	102.3	102.5	103.9	104.3	104.7	104.4	103.0	102.9	104.3	105.2	105.4	105.1	104.0
2001	101.8	102.1	102.6	104.3	103.9	104.3	102.6	102.4	101.6	102.4	102.3	102.3	102.7
2002	99.5	100.0	100.6	100.8	100.6	100.1	100.4	100.8	100.9	101.0	101.6	100.4	100.6
2003	97.9	98.0	98.5	99.2	98.7	98.4	97.6	98.7	98.6	99.5	100.1	99.7	98.7
Total private													
1990	77.6	77.3	77.6	78.4	78.7	78.6	77.6	78.2	78.8	78.2	78.0	77.8	78.0
1991	76.6	76.5	76.4	76.9	77.1	77.3	76.7	76.7	78.2	78.1	79.2	79.0	77.3
1992	77.1	76.8	76.9	77.9	77.9	77.9	76.8	77.5	78.7	78.3	78.9	79.5	77.8
1993	78.4	78.5	78.6	80.1	80.7	80.4	79.0	79.8	81.4	81.6	82.4	82.9	80.3
1994	80.6	80.4	81.7	81.7	82.5	82.5	81.2	81.3	82.2	83.6	84.4	84.6	82.2
1995	81.8	81.8	82.4	83.9	83.4	84.4	83.9	83.9	84.2	84.3	85.2	85.5	83.7
1996	80.3	82.3	82.6	83.7	84.0	83.3	83.1	83.7	84.2	85.0	85.9	85.7	83.6
1997	81.9	83.1	83.7	83.8	83.6	83.5	83.1	83.4	85.0	86.3	86.3	86.3	84.1
1998	83.3	84.4	85.3	85.0	85.0	85.8	84.9	85.1	86.9	88.3	88.7	89.4	86.0
1999	86.8	87.4	87.8	88.7	88.6	89.1	88.1	88.0	89.6	89.9	90.9	91.1	88.8
2000	89.0	89.2	90.3	90.8	90.9	90.6	90.2	90.4	91.4	91.8	92.2	91.6	90.7
2001	88.7	88.9	89.4	91.0	90.7	90.9	89.8	89.6	89.0	88.9	88.5	88.8	89.5
2002	85.9	86.4	86.8	87.1	87.0	86.8	87.3	87.7	88.0	87.6	87.9	86.8	87.1
2003	84.5	84.5	85.1	85.7	85.0	85.0	84.8	85.8	85.6	86.3	86.8	86.5	85.5
Goods-producing													
1990	27.7	27.5	27.7	27.9	27.8	28.0	27.7	27.9	28.0	27.7	27.3	27.0	27.6
1991	27.2	27.2	27.1	27.2	27.2	27.4	27.2	27.3	27.6	27.3	27.5	27.2	27.2
1992	27.2	27.1	27.0	27.3	27.2	27.2	27.2	27.3	27.7	27.6	27.6	27.7	27.3
1993	27.4	27.5	27.6	27.9	28.1	28.2	27.9	28.1	28.6	28.9	28.8	29.0	28.1
1994	28.1	28.1	28.2	28.1	28.5	28.4	28.1	28.1	28.7	28.8	28.9	28.9	28.4
1995	28.6	28.7	28.8	29.3	29.2	29.5	30.0	30.2	30.2	30.6	30.5	30.7	29.6
1996	29.0	29.6	29.8	30.1	30.4	30.2	30.4	30.5	30.5	30.6	30.6	30.5	30.1
1997	29.8	30.1	30.4	30.1	30.2	30.2	30.0	29.9	30.2	30.6	30.5	30.4	30.2
1998	30.6	31.0	31.2	30.9	31.3	31.7	31.3	31.2	31.7	31.8	31.7	31.9	31.3
1999	31.0	31.2	31.3	31.7	31.6	31.6	31.4	31.3	31.7	31.4	31.4	31.4	31.4
2000	31.5	31.2	31.5	31.1	30.9	31.0	31.0	31.2	31.5	31.5	31.5	31.3	31.2
2001	29.3	29.0	29.0	29.0	28.8	29.1	28.9	28.7	27.6	27.5	27.1	26.9	28.4
2002	26.0	26.0	26.1	25.8	25.9	26.1	26.1	26.1	26.5	26.0	25.8	25.7	26.0
2003	25.3	25.2	25.4	25.3	25.4	25.3	25.2	25.3	24.9	24.8	25.0	24.9	25.2
Construction and mining													
1990	5.0	5.0	5.1	5.3	5.4	5.5	5.4	5.4	5.4	5.3	5.3	5.1	5.2
1991	5.0	5.0	5.1	5.3	5.5	5.6	5.4	5.5	5.5	5.3	5.2	5.1	5.2
1992	4.8	4.8	4.8	5.0	5.0	5.0	5.1	5.1	5.2	5.0	5.0	5.0	4.9
1993	4.7	4.8	4.8	5.1	5.3	5.4	5.5	5.6	5.7	5.7	5.7	5.8	5.3
1994	5.2	5.2	5.1	5.3	5.5	5.6	5.5	5.5	5.6	5.6	5.6	5.6	5.4
1995	5.4	5.5	5.8	5.8	5.9	6.1	6.3	6.4	6.3	6.4	6.4	6.6	6.0
1996	5.4	5.6	5.7	5.7	5.8	5.9	6.0	6.0	5.9	5.9	5.9	5.8	5.8
1997	5.7	5.7	5.9	6.0	6.1	6.1	6.2	6.2	6.1	6.2	6.0	6.1	6.0
1998	5.6	5.7	5.8	5.9	6.0	6.2	6.4	6.3	6.3	6.3	6.2	6.3	6.0
1999	5.8	5.9	6.0	6.3	6.3	6.4	6.4	6.3	6.2	6.2	6.2	6.2	6.1
2000	6.1	6.1	6.3	6.3	6.4	6.5	6.5	6.7	6.6	6.8	6.8	6.8	6.4
2001	6.2	6.0	6.0	6.5	6.5	6.8	7.0	7.2	6.9	6.9	6.7	6.7	6.6
2002	6.2	6.2	6.3	6.4	6.6	6.7	6.9	6.9	7.2	6.9	6.7	6.7	6.6
2003	6.4	6.3	6.5	6.6	6.9	6.8	6.9	6.9	6.8	6.9	6.8	6.8	6.7

Employment by Industry: Virginia—*Continued*

(Numbers in thousands. Not seasonally adjusted.)

Industry	January	February	March	April	May	June	July	August	September	October	November	December	Annual Average
LYNCHBURG—*Continued*													
Manufacturing													
1990	22.7	22.5	22.6	22.6	22.4	22.5	22.3	22.5	22.6	22.4	22.0	21.9	22.4
1991	22.2	22.2	22.0	21.9	21.7	21.8	21.8	21.8	22.1	22.0	22.3	22.1	21.9
1992	22.4	22.3	22.2	22.3	22.2	22.2	22.1	22.2	22.5	22.6	22.6	22.7	22.3
1993	22.7	22.7	22.8	22.8	22.8	22.8	22.4	22.5	22.9	23.2	23.1	23.2	22.8
1994	22.9	22.9	23.1	22.8	23.0	22.8	22.6	22.6	23.1	23.2	23.3	23.3	22.9
1995	23.2	23.2	23.0	23.5	23.3	23.4	23.7	23.8	23.9	24.2	24.1	24.1	23.6
1996	23.6	24.0	24.1	24.4	24.6	24.3	24.4	24.5	24.6	24.7	24.7	24.7	24.3
1997	24.1	24.4	24.5	24.1	24.1	24.1	23.8	23.7	24.1	24.4	24.5	24.3	24.1
1998	25.0	25.3	25.4	25.0	25.3	25.5	24.9	24.9	25.4	25.5	25.5	25.6	25.2
1999	25.2	25.3	25.3	25.4	25.3	25.2	25.0	25.0	25.5	25.2	25.2	25.2	25.2
2000	25.4	25.1	25.2	24.8	24.5	24.5	24.5	24.5	24.9	24.7	24.7	24.5	24.7
2001	23.1	23.0	23.0	22.5	22.3	22.3	21.9	21.5	20.7	20.6	20.4	20.2	21.8
2002	19.8	19.8	19.8	19.4	19.3	19.4	19.2	19.2	19.3	19.1	19.1	19.0	19.4
2003	18.9	18.9	18.9	18.7	18.5	18.5	18.3	18.4	18.1	17.9	18.2	18.1	18.5
Service-providing													
1990	61.6	61.6	61.8	62.5	63.2	62.8	61.6	62.1	62.9	62.5	62.8	62.9	62.3
1991	61.5	61.4	61.5	61.8	62.1	62.0	61.3	61.0	62.2	62.5	63.5	63.6	62.0
1992	61.6	61.4	61.6	62.4	62.4	62.5	61.1	61.6	62.6	62.4	63.0	63.6	62.1
1993	62.8	62.8	62.9	64.4	64.9	64.5	62.7	63.4	64.7	64.8	65.8	66.2	64.1
1994	64.8	64.6	65.9	66.0	66.4	66.5	65.3	65.1	65.6	67.1	67.9	68.1	66.1
1995	65.5	65.4	65.9	67.1	66.5	67.3	65.1	65.0	66.2	66.1	67.2	67.4	66.2
1996	63.9	65.3	65.4	66.3	66.2	65.9	65.0	65.3	66.0	67.2	68.3	68.2	66.0
1997	64.9	65.8	66.2	66.5	66.3	66.3	65.8	66.1	67.2	68.3	68.6	68.7	66.7
1998	65.5	66.2	67.0	66.9	66.6	67.1	66.2	66.3	67.7	69.4	70.1	70.8	67.4
1999	68.8	69.4	69.8	70.4	70.1	70.7	69.5	69.5	70.6	72.0	73.1	73.5	70.6
2000	70.8	71.3	72.4	73.2	73.8	73.4	72.0	71.7	72.8	73.7	73.9	73.8	72.7
2001	72.5	73.1	73.6	75.3	75.1	75.2	73.7	73.7	74.0	74.9	75.2	75.4	74.3
2002	73.5	74.0	74.5	75.0	74.7	74.0	74.3	74.7	74.4	75.0	75.8	74.7	74.6
2003	72.6	72.8	73.1	73.9	73.3	73.1	72.4	73.4	73.7	74.7	75.1	74.8	73.6
Trade, transportation, and utilities													
1990	21.4	21.1	21.1	20.7	20.8	20.8	20.5	20.8	21.0	20.7	21.1	21.2	20.9
1991	20.7	20.4	20.3	20.2	20.3	20.3	20.0	20.0	20.5	20.9	21.7	21.7	20.5
1992	20.5	20.1	20.0	20.0	20.1	20.2	19.9	19.9	19.9	19.9	20.5	20.9	20.1
1993	20.6	20.3	20.1	20.4	20.4	20.4	19.7	20.0	20.4	20.9	21.7	22.3	20.6
1994	21.2	20.6	21.1	20.9	20.9	21.0	20.5	20.6	20.8	21.5	22.5	22.7	21.1
1995	21.0	20.7	20.7	20.8	20.5	20.9	20.4	20.3	20.4	20.4	21.4	21.8	20.7
1996	19.9	20.0	20.0	20.2	20.0	19.9	19.8	19.9	19.9	20.4	21.6	21.6	20.2
1997	19.6	19.5	19.5	19.2	19.1	19.1	18.9	19.1	19.5	20.5	21.2	21.1	19.6
1998	18.3	18.3	18.5	18.1	17.9	18.0	18.0	18.0	18.5	19.0	19.6	19.7	18.4
1999	18.4	18.5	18.6	18.6	18.4	18.6	18.4	18.4	18.9	19.3	19.8	19.9	18.8
2000	18.6	18.8	18.8	18.9	19.0	19.2	19.1	19.0	19.2	19.7	20.4	20.3	19.2
2001	19.4	19.2	19.2	19.6	19.7	19.8	19.7	19.4	19.4	19.6	20.1	20.4	19.6
2002	19.2	18.9	19.0	18.9	18.9	18.9	18.9	18.9	18.9	18.8	19.2	19.4	19.0
2003	18.2	18.1	18.3	18.4	18.6	18.7	18.5	18.8	18.7	18.8	19.0	19.3	18.6
Wholesale trade													
1990	6.2	6.2	6.2	6.1	6.1	6.0	5.9	6.0	6.1	6.0	6.0	6.0	6.0
1991	6.1	6.1	6.1	6.0	6.1	6.0	6.0	6.1	6.2	6.1	6.2	6.1	6.0
1992	6.0	5.8	5.7	5.6	5.6	5.5	5.5	5.5	5.5	5.5	5.5	5.5	5.6
1993	5.6	5.6	5.6	5.6	5.6	5.5	5.4	5.4	5.5	5.6	5.5	5.5	5.5
1994	5.6	5.4	5.5	5.4	5.4	5.4	5.2	5.3	5.4	5.5	5.5	5.5	5.4
1995	5.5	5.5	5.5	5.3	5.1	5.1	5.1	5.1	5.1	5.0	5.1	4.9	5.1
1996	4.8	4.8	4.9	5.0	4.9	4.9	4.8	4.8	4.8	4.9	4.9	4.9	4.8
1997	4.7	4.7	4.7	4.6	4.6	4.6	4.5	4.5	4.6	4.7	4.7	4.7	4.6
1998	3.0	3.1	3.1	2.9	2.9	2.9	2.9	2.8	2.9	2.9	2.9	2.9	2.9
1999	2.8	2.9	2.9	2.7	2.7	2.7	2.8	2.7	2.8	2.9	2.8	2.8	2.7
2000	2.8	2.8	2.8	2.9	2.8	2.9	2.8	2.8	2.8	2.9	2.8	2.8	2.8
2001	3.3	3.3	3.3	3.2	3.3	3.3	3.3	3.3	3.3	3.3	3.3	3.4	3.3
2002	3.3	3.3	3.3	3.4	3.4	3.4	3.5	3.6	3.7	3.5	3.6	3.7	3.5
2003	3.6	3.6	3.7	3.7	3.7	3.7	3.7	3.7	3.8	3.8	3.8	3.8	3.7
Retail trade													
1990	12.2	11.8	11.8	11.6	11.7	11.8	11.7	11.8	11.9	11.8	12.1	12.2	11.8
1991	11.9	11.6	11.5	11.5	11.5	11.6	11.4	11.3	11.6	12.1	12.8	12.9	11.8
1992	11.9	11.7	11.7	11.7	11.8	12.0	11.7	11.7	11.6	11.7	12.3	12.6	11.8
1993	12.3	12.0	11.8	12.0	12.0	12.1	11.5	11.8	12.0	12.3	13.2	13.7	12.2
1994	12.6	12.1	12.4	12.4	12.4	12.5	12.3	12.3	12.4	13.0	14.1	14.3	12.7
1995	12.8	12.5	12.5	12.7	12.7	13.1	12.6	12.5	12.6	12.7	13.7	14.3	12.8
1996	12.7	12.8	12.7	12.8	12.7	12.6	12.6	12.7	12.7	13.1	14.3	14.3	13.0
1997	12.6	12.4	12.4	12.3	12.2	12.2	12.1	12.3	12.6	13.4	14.1	14.0	12.7
1998	13.0	12.8	13.0	12.7	12.5	12.6	12.6	12.8	13.1	13.5	14.1	14.2	13.0
1999	13.1	13.0	13.1	13.3	13.1	13.3	13.0	13.1	13.5	13.8	14.4	14.4	13.4
2000	13.3	13.5	13.5	13.5	13.6	13.7	13.7	13.7	13.9	14.3	15.1	15.0	13.9
2001	13.2	13.0	13.0	13.3	13.3	13.4	13.3	13.0	13.0	13.3	13.8	13.9	13.3
2002	13.0	12.8	12.8	12.6	12.6	12.6	12.5	12.4	12.3	12.4	12.7	12.7	12.6
2003	11.8	11.7	11.7	11.8	11.9	12.0	11.9	12.1	11.9	12.0	12.3	12.4	12.0

Employment by Industry: Virginia—*Continued*

(Numbers in thousands. Not seasonally adjusted.)

Industry	January	February	March	April	May	June	July	August	September	October	November	December	Annual Average
LYNCHBURG—*Continued*													
Transportation and utilities													
1990	3.0	3.1	3.1	3.0	3.0	3.0	2.9	3.0	3.0	2.9	3.0	3.0	3.0
1991	2.7	2.7	2.7	2.7	2.7	2.7	2.6	2.6	2.7	2.7	2.7	2.7	2.6
1992	2.6	2.6	2.6	2.7	2.7	2.7	2.7	2.7	2.8	2.7	2.7	2.8	2.6
1993	2.7	2.7	2.7	2.8	2.8	2.8	2.8	2.8	2.9	3.0	3.0	3.1	2.8
1994	3.0	3.1	3.2	3.1	3.1	3.1	3.0	3.0	3.0	3.0	2.9	2.9	3.0
1995	2.7	2.7	2.7	2.8	2.7	2.7	2.7	2.7	2.7	2.7	2.6	2.6	2.6
1996	2.4	2.4	2.4	2.4	2.4	2.4	2.4	2.4	2.4	2.4	2.4	2.4	2.4
1997	2.3	2.4	2.4	2.3	2.3	2.3	2.3	2.3	2.3	2.4	2.4	2.4	2.3
1998	2.3	2.4	2.4	2.5	2.5	2.5	2.5	2.4	2.5	2.6	2.6	2.6	2.4
1999	2.5	2.6	2.6	2.6	2.6	2.6	2.6	2.6	2.6	2.6	2.6	2.7	2.6
2000	2.5	2.5	2.5	2.5	2.6	2.6	2.6	2.5	2.5	2.5	2.5	2.5	2.5
2001	2.9	2.9	2.9	3.1	3.1	3.1	3.1	3.1	3.1	3.0	3.0	3.1	3.0
2002	2.9	2.8	2.9	2.9	2.9	2.9	2.9	2.9	2.9	2.9	2.9	3.0	2.9
2003	2.8	2.8	2.9	2.9	3.0	3.0	2.9	3.0	3.0	3.0	2.9	3.1	2.9
Information													
1990	1.3	1.3	1.3	1.3	1.3	1.3	1.3	1.3	1.4	1.3	1.3	1.4	1.3
1991	1.3	1.3	1.3	1.3	1.3	1.4	1.3	1.3	1.3	1.3	1.3	1.3	1.3
1992	1.3	1.3	1.3	1.3	1.3	1.3	1.3	1.3	1.3	1.3	1.3	1.3	1.3
1993	1.3	1.3	1.3	1.3	1.3	1.3	1.3	1.3	1.3	1.3	1.3	1.3	1.3
1994	1.4	1.4	1.4	1.4	1.3	1.4	1.3	1.4	1.3	1.3	1.3	1.4	1.3
1995	1.4	1.3	1.3	1.3	1.3	1.4	1.3	1.3	1.3	1.3	1.3	1.3	1.3
1996	1.2	1.3	1.2	1.3	1.3	1.3	1.3	1.3	1.3	1.3	1.2	1.2	1.2
1997	1.2	1.2	1.3	1.3	1.3	1.3	1.3	1.3	1.3	1.3	1.3	1.3	1.2
1998	1.3	1.3	1.4	1.3	1.3	1.3	1.3	1.3	1.3	1.4	1.4	1.5	1.3
1999	1.3	1.3	1.4	1.4	1.4	1.4	1.3	1.3	1.3	1.3	1.3	1.3	1.3
2000	1.3	1.3	1.4	1.3	1.2	1.2	1.2	1.1	1.2	1.2	1.3	1.2	1.2
2001	1.2	1.2	1.2	1.2	1.2	1.2	1.2	1.2	1.2	1.1	1.1	1.1	1.2
2002	1.0	1.0	1.0	1.0	1.0	1.0	0.9	0.9	0.9	0.9	0.9	0.9	1.0
2003	0.9	1.0	1.0	1.0	1.0	1.0	1.0	1.0	0.9	1.0	1.0	1.0	1.0
Financial activities													
1990	3.7	3.7	3.7	3.7	3.7	3.7	3.6	3.6	3.6	3.6	3.6	3.6	3.6
1991	3.8	3.8	3.8	3.8	3.8	3.8	3.8	3.8	3.8	3.8	3.8	3.8	3.8
1992	3.7	3.8	3.8	3.7	3.7	3.6	3.6	3.6	3.6	3.7	3.7	3.7	3.6
1993	3.7	3.7	3.7	3.7	3.8	3.8	3.7	3.7	3.8	3.8	3.8	3.9	3.7
1994	3.8	3.8	3.9	3.9	4.0	4.0	3.9	3.8	3.8	3.9	3.9	3.9	3.8
1995	3.8	3.8	3.8	3.9	3.9	4.0	4.0	4.0	4.0	4.0	4.0	4.0	3.9
1996	3.9	4.0	4.0	4.0	4.0	4.1	4.1	4.1	4.0	4.1	4.1	4.1	4.0
1997	4.0	4.1	4.1	4.1	4.1	4.2	4.3	4.2	4.3	4.2	4.2	4.3	4.1
1998	4.4	4.4	4.4	4.4	4.3	4.3	4.2	4.3	4.3	4.3	4.3	4.4	4.3
1999	4.4	4.4	4.3	4.3	4.3	4.4	4.3	4.3	4.3	4.5	4.5	4.6	4.3
2000	4.4	4.4	4.4	4.5	4.4	4.4	4.5	4.5	4.5	4.5	4.4	4.4	4.4
2001	4.3	4.4	4.4	4.4	4.4	4.5	4.4	4.4	4.3	4.3	4.3	4.3	4.4
2002	4.1	4.2	4.2	4.2	4.3	4.3	4.3	4.3	4.2	4.0	4.1	4.0	4.2
2003	4.1	4.1	4.1	4.1	4.2	4.3	4.3	4.3	4.2	4.2	4.2	4.2	4.2
Professional and business services													
1990	5.6	5.7	5.8	5.4	5.4	5.5	5.4	5.5	5.4	5.4	5.4	5.3	5.4
1991	5.4	5.5	5.5	5.7	5.6	5.6	5.7	5.6	5.7	5.7	5.8	5.8	5.6
1992	5.9	5.9	5.9	6.1	6.0	6.0	6.0	6.1	6.4	6.6	6.6	6.6	6.1
1993	6.8	6.8	7.0	7.2	7.3	7.2	7.1	7.2	7.4	7.4	7.6	7.3	7.1
1994	7.1	7.2	7.5	7.5	7.5	7.6	7.5	7.5	7.6	7.9	7.8	7.6	7.5
1995	7.5	7.6	7.7	7.9	7.9	7.8	7.5	7.5	7.4	7.5	7.5	7.6	7.6
1996	7.3	7.7	7.8	7.8	7.8	7.7	7.6	7.8	8.1	8.2	8.1	8.2	7.8
1997	7.7	8.2	8.2	8.7	8.4	8.4	8.4	8.5	8.8	8.7	8.3	8.3	8.3
1998	7.9	8.0	8.2	8.5	8.4	8.5	8.3	8.4	8.5	9.0	8.8	8.9	8.4
1999	9.7	9.7	9.7	9.7	9.7	10.0	9.7	9.7	9.8	10.2	10.4	10.6	9.9
2000	10.4	10.5	10.7	11.1	11.2	10.8	10.5	10.4	10.3	10.4	10.2	10.3	10.5
2001	8.5	8.5	8.7	9.3	9.4	9.4	9.5	9.5	9.1	8.9	8.4	8.7	9.0
2002	8.3	8.4	8.6	8.7	8.8	8.9	8.8	8.9	8.9	9.0	8.9	9.0	8.8
2003	8.6	8.5	8.4	8.6	8.5	8.6	8.6	8.6	8.6	8.5	8.4	8.3	8.5
Educational and health services													
1990	9.0	9.1	9.0	10.2	10.3	9.9	10.0	9.9	10.2	10.4	10.4	10.4	9.9
1991	9.6	9.7	9.7	9.6	9.6	9.5	9.4	9.5	9.9	9.9	9.9	9.9	9.6
1992	9.6	9.8	9.8	9.9	9.8	9.8	9.3	9.6	10.1	9.7	9.8	9.8	9.7
1993	9.8	10.0	10.0	10.1	10.1	9.9	9.7	9.8	10.2	9.8	9.8	9.8	9.9
1994	10.0	10.1	10.2	10.0	10.0	9.8	9.7	9.7	9.9	10.1	10.1	10.1	9.9
1995	9.9	10.0	10.1	10.3	10.2	10.1	9.9	9.9	10.2	10.1	10.1	10.0	10.0
1996	9.5	9.9	9.8	10.0	10.0	9.7	9.6	9.7	9.9	10.0	10.0	9.9	9.8
1997	9.8	10.1	10.1	10.1	10.1	9.9	9.9	10.0	10.4	10.6	10.6	10.6	10.1
1998	10.7	11.0	11.1	11.1	10.9	10.9	10.8	10.9	11.3	11.4	11.5	11.5	11.0
1999	11.4	11.5	11.5	11.7	11.7	11.6	11.6	11.7	12.1	12.1	12.2	12.1	11.7
2000	12.1	12.3	12.5	12.3	12.3	12.2	12.2	12.3	12.5	12.6	12.6	12.6	12.3
2001	15.0	15.4	15.5	15.7	15.2	14.7	14.2	14.3	15.4	16.1	16.0	16.0	15.3
2002	16.0	16.3	16.3	16.5	15.8	15.2	16.1	16.2	16.2	16.7	16.8	15.7	16.2
2003	15.7	15.9	16.0	15.9	15.0	14.7	14.8	15.3	16.0	16.7	16.9	16.8	15.8

Employment by Industry: Virginia—*Continued*

(Numbers in thousands. Not seasonally adjusted.)

Industry	January	February	March	April	May	June	July	August	September	October	November	December	Annual Average
LYNCHBURG—*Continued*													
Leisure and hospitality													
1990	5.8	5.8	5.9	6.1	6.3	6.3	6.1	6.1	6.1	6.0	5.9	5.9	6.0
1991	5.7	5.7	5.8	6.2	6.4	6.4	6.4	6.4	6.5	6.4	6.3	6.4	6.2
1992	6.0	5.9	6.1	6.6	6.8	6.8	6.5	6.7	6.7	6.5	6.4	6.5	6.4
1993	5.8	5.9	5.9	6.4	6.6	6.5	6.5	6.6	6.6	6.3	6.3	6.2	6.3
1994	5.9	6.1	6.2	6.7	7.1	7.1	7.0	7.0	6.9	6.9	6.7	6.8	6.7
1995	6.4	6.5	6.7	7.1	7.2	7.4	7.5	7.4	7.4	7.1	7.0	6.8	7.0
1996	6.3	6.5	6.7	6.9	7.1	7.0	6.8	6.9	7.0	6.9	6.8	6.7	6.8
1997	6.3	6.4	6.5	6.7	6.7	6.7	6.6	6.7	6.7	6.6	6.4	6.4	6.5
1998	6.3	6.6	6.6	6.8	6.9	7.0	6.9	6.8	7.0	7.0	6.9	7.0	6.8
1999	6.4	6.6	6.7	7.0	7.1	7.1	7.0	6.9	7.0	6.6	6.7	6.6	6.8
2000	6.4	6.4	6.6	7.1	7.4	7.3	7.2	7.4	7.5	7.1	7.0	6.7	7.0
2001	6.4	6.6	6.7	7.1	7.3	7.4	7.2	7.4	7.4	6.8	6.9	6.8	7.0
2002	6.5	6.7	6.7	7.0	7.3	7.4	7.3	7.5	7.5	7.3	7.3	7.2	7.1
2003	6.8	6.8	6.9	7.4	7.4	7.5	7.5	7.6	7.5	7.5	7.4	7.1	7.3
Other services													
1990	3.1	3.1	3.1	3.1	3.1	3.1	3.0	3.1	3.1	3.1	3.0	3.0	3.0
1991	2.9	2.9	2.9	2.9	2.9	2.9	2.9	2.8	2.9	2.8	2.9	2.9	2.8
1992	2.9	2.9	3.0	3.0	3.0	3.0	3.0	3.0	3.0	3.0	3.0	3.0	2.9
1993	3.0	3.0	3.0	3.1	3.1	3.1	3.1	3.1	3.1	3.2	3.1	3.1	3.0
1994	3.1	3.1	3.2	3.2	3.2	3.2	3.2	3.2	3.2	3.2	3.2	3.2	3.1
1995	3.2	3.2	3.3	3.3	3.2	3.3	3.3	3.3	3.3	3.3	3.4	3.3	3.2
1996	3.2	3.3	3.3	3.4	3.4	3.4	3.5	3.5	3.5	3.5	3.5	3.5	3.4
1997	3.5	3.5	3.6	3.6	3.7	3.7	3.7	3.7	3.8	3.8	3.8	3.9	3.6
1998	3.8	3.8	3.9	3.9	4.0	4.1	4.1	4.2	4.3	4.4	4.5	4.5	4.1
1999	4.2	4.2	4.3	4.3	4.4	4.4	4.4	4.4	4.5	4.5	4.6	4.6	4.4
2000	4.3	4.3	4.4	4.5	4.5	4.5	4.5	4.5	4.7	4.8	4.8	4.8	4.5
2001	4.6	4.6	4.7	4.7	4.7	4.8	4.7	4.7	4.6	4.6	4.6	4.6	4.7
2002	4.8	4.9	4.9	5.0	5.0	5.0	4.9	4.9	4.9	4.9	4.9	4.9	4.9
2003	4.9	4.9	5.0	5.0	4.9	4.9	4.9	4.9	4.8	4.8	4.9	4.9	4.9
Government													
1990	11.7	11.8	11.9	12.0	12.3	12.2	11.7	11.8	12.1	12.0	12.1	12.1	11.9
1991	12.1	12.1	12.2	12.1	12.2	12.1	11.8	11.6	11.6	11.7	11.8	11.8	11.9
1992	11.7	11.7	11.7	11.8	11.7	11.8	11.5	11.4	11.6	11.7	11.7	11.8	11.6
1993	11.8	11.8	11.9	12.2	12.3	12.3	11.6	11.7	11.9	12.1	12.2	12.3	12.0
1994	12.3	12.3	12.4	12.4	12.4	12.4	12.2	11.9	12.1	12.3	12.4	12.4	12.2
1995	12.3	12.3	12.3	12.5	12.3	12.4	11.2	11.3	12.2	12.4	12.5	12.6	12.1
1996	12.6	12.6	12.6	12.7	12.6	12.8	12.3	12.1	12.3	12.8	13.0	13.0	12.6
1997	12.8	12.8	12.9	12.8	12.9	13.0	12.7	12.6	12.4	12.6	12.8	12.8	12.7
1998	12.8	12.8	12.9	12.8	12.9	13.0	12.6	12.4	12.5	12.9	13.1	13.3	12.8
1999	13.0	13.2	13.3	13.4	13.1	13.2	12.8	12.8	12.7	13.5	13.6	13.8	13.2
2000	13.3	13.3	13.6	13.5	13.8	13.8	12.8	12.5	12.9	13.4	13.2	13.5	13.3
2001	13.1	13.2	13.2	13.3	13.2	13.4	12.8	12.8	12.6	13.5	13.8	13.5	13.2
2002	13.6	13.6	13.8	13.7	13.6	13.3	13.1	13.1	12.9	13.4	13.7	13.6	13.5
2003	13.4	13.5	13.4	13.5	13.7	13.4	12.8	12.9	13.0	13.2	13.3	13.2	13.3
Federal government													
1990	0.7	0.7	0.8	0.8	0.9	0.8	0.8	0.8	0.7	0.7	0.7	0.7	0.7
1991	0.7	0.7	0.7	0.7	0.7	0.7	0.7	0.7	0.7	0.7	0.7	0.7	0.7
1992	0.7	0.7	0.7	0.7	0.7	0.7	0.7	0.7	0.7	0.7	0.6	0.6	0.6
1993	0.6	0.6	0.6	0.7	0.7	0.7	0.7	0.7	0.7	0.7	0.7	0.7	0.6
1994	0.7	0.7	0.7	0.7	0.7	0.7	0.7	0.7	0.7	0.7	0.7	0.7	0.7
1995	0.7	0.7	0.7	1.1	1.1	1.1	1.1	1.2	1.2	1.2	1.2	1.2	1.0
1996	1.2	1.2	1.2	1.2	1.2	1.2	1.2	1.2	1.2	1.2	1.3	1.3	1.2
1997	1.2	1.2	1.2	1.2	1.2	1.2	1.2	1.2	1.2	1.2	1.2	1.2	1.2
1998	1.2	1.2	1.2	1.2	1.2	1.2	1.2	1.2	1.2	1.2	1.3	1.4	1.2
1999	1.2	1.2	1.1	1.4	1.1	1.1	1.1	1.1	1.1	1.1	1.1	1.2	1.1
2000	1.1	1.1	1.2	1.1	1.3	1.2	1.1	1.1	0.9	0.8	0.8	0.9	1.0
2001	0.8	0.8	0.8	0.8	0.8	0.8	0.8	0.8	0.8	0.8	0.8	0.8	0.8
2002	0.8	0.8	0.8	0.8	0.8	0.8	0.8	0.8	0.8	0.8	0.8	0.8	0.8
2003	0.8	0.8	0.8	0.8	0.8	0.8	0.8	0.8	0.8	0.8	0.8	0.8	0.8
State government													
1990	4.0	4.0	4.0	4.0	4.1	4.1	4.1	4.2	4.2	3.9	3.9	3.9	4.0
1991	3.9	3.9	3.9	3.9	4.0	4.0	4.0	4.0	3.8	3.8	3.8	3.8	3.9
1992	3.8	3.8	3.8	3.8	3.8	3.8	3.7	3.7	3.7	3.7	3.7	3.7	3.7
1993	3.9	3.9	3.9	4.0	4.0	4.0	3.8	3.8	3.8	3.9	3.9	3.9	3.9
1994	3.9	3.9	3.9	3.9	3.9	3.9	3.8	3.8	3.7	3.8	3.8	3.7	3.8
1995	3.7	3.7	3.6	3.6	3.4	3.4	3.3	3.3	3.3	3.3	3.3	3.3	3.4
1996	3.3	3.3	3.3	3.3	3.3	3.3	3.2	3.2	3.2	3.3	3.3	3.3	3.2
1997	3.3	3.3	3.3	3.3	3.3	3.3	3.2	3.2	3.2	3.2	3.2	3.2	3.2
1998	3.2	3.2	3.2	3.2	3.2	3.2	3.2	3.2	3.2	3.2	3.2	3.2	3.2
1999	3.2	3.2	3.2	3.2	3.2	3.2	3.1	3.1	3.1	3.2	3.2	3.2	3.1
2000	3.1	3.1	3.1	3.1	3.1	3.2	3.1	3.1	3.1	3.1	3.1	3.1	3.1
2001	3.1	3.1	3.1	3.1	3.2	3.2	3.1	3.1	3.1	3.2	3.3	3.3	3.2
2002	3.3	3.3	3.3	3.3	3.3	3.3	3.2	3.2	3.2	3.3	3.3	3.3	3.3
2003	3.2	3.2	3.2	3.2	3.3	3.3	3.1	3.2	3.2	3.2	3.2	3.2	3.2

Employment by Industry: Virginia—*Continued*

(Numbers in thousands. Not seasonally adjusted.)

Industry	January	February	March	April	May	June	July	August	September	October	November	December	Annual Average
LYNCHBURG—*Continued*													
Local government													
1990	7.0	7.1	7.1	7.2	7.3	7.3	6.8	6.8	7.2	7.4	7.5	7.5	7.1
1991	7.5	7.5	7.6	7.5	7.5	7.4	7.1	6.9	7.1	7.2	7.3	7.3	7.3
1992	7.2	7.2	7.2	7.3	7.2	7.3	7.1	7.0	7.2	7.3	7.4	7.5	7.2
1993	7.3	7.3	7.4	7.5	7.6	7.6	7.1	7.2	7.4	7.5	7.6	7.7	7.4
1994	7.7	7.7	7.8	7.8	7.8	7.8	7.7	7.4	7.7	7.8	7.9	8.0	7.7
1995	7.9	7.9	8.0	7.8	7.8	7.9	6.8	6.8	7.7	7.9	8.0	8.1	7.7
1996	8.1	8.1	8.1	8.2	8.1	8.3	7.9	7.7	7.9	8.3	8.4	8.4	8.1
1997	8.3	8.3	8.4	8.3	8.4	8.5	8.3	8.2	8.0	8.2	8.4	8.4	8.3
1998	8.4	8.4	8.5	8.4	8.5	8.6	8.2	8.0	8.1	8.5	8.6	8.7	8.4
1999	8.6	8.8	9.0	8.8	8.8	8.9	8.6	8.6	8.5	9.2	9.3	9.4	8.8
2000	9.1	9.1	9.3	9.3	9.4	9.4	8.6	8.3	8.9	9.5	9.3	9.5	9.1
2001	9.2	9.3	9.3	9.4	9.2	9.4	8.9	8.9	8.7	9.5	9.7	9.4	9.2
2002	9.5	9.5	9.7	9.6	9.5	9.2	9.1	9.1	8.9	9.3	9.6	9.5	9.4
2003	9.4	9.5	9.4	9.5	9.6	9.3	8.9	8.9	9.0	9.2	9.3	9.2	9.3
NORFOLK-VIRGINIA BEACH-NEWPORT NEWS													
Total nonfarm													
1990	585.5	586.8	592.6	596.4	605.4	614.3	608.2	609.3	608.5	605.7	606.3	607.5	602.2
1991	581.8	578.3	584.3	587.7	595.4	605.2	599.2	600.7	602.3	599.5	598.1	600.7	594.4
1992	581.5	584.4	588.9	593.7	601.6	607.3	602.9	604.6	607.4	604.7	607.0	606.4	599.2
1993	589.6	592.9	596.5	602.8	608.8	615.6	608.5	608.8	608.3	606.9	608.0	609.9	604.7
1994	592.5	594.1	602.2	612.1	619.0	626.3	625.1	628.0	631.1	623.0	624.3	626.5	617.0
1995	610.4	613.1	619.4	624.4	633.9	642.3	633.3	634.4	637.5	638.2	640.1	640.6	630.6
1996	621.4	623.0	631.1	633.8	640.1	648.6	647.6	651.6	655.3	654.2	657.5	657.7	643.4
1997	648.3	650.0	657.1	660.0	668.0	676.4	667.3	669.3	673.3	675.7	679.4	681.1	667.1
1998	658.7	660.5	667.7	671.7	682.6	689.4	691.9	694.5	694.7	689.6	693.3	695.5	682.5
1999	670.4	675.8	683.0	686.3	692.2	700.1	688.8	697.3	698.1	698.3	701.3	702.9	691.2
2000	683.0	686.8	695.7	696.8	704.1	714.4	704.8	707.0	707.5	706.8	711.4	711.2	702.4
2001	691.3	694.3	702.6	714.9	722.1	731.7	723.4	725.9	724.8	721.9	726.8	726.3	717.2
2002	702.5	707.1	713.3	718.2	725.2	734.0	720.3	724.3	723.5	727.1	730.1	733.5	721.6
2003	712.4	713.4	720.3	723.5	732.9	740.0	732.5	735.4	733.8	737.0	743.0	744.9	730.8
Total private													
1990	447.2	448.0	453.5	456.6	464.0	473.2	473.0	474.6	469.3	465.1	465.3	466.7	463.0
1991	442.1	438.0	443.9	448.6	455.7	465.0	463.8	465.8	463.2	458.2	456.1	458.9	454.9
1992	441.4	442.8	446.8	451.0	458.0	465.4	466.1	468.1	465.7	461.1	462.7	462.1	457.6
1993	446.7	448.9	451.6	458.4	464.6	471.9	470.5	471.7	468.1	467.5	467.4	469.3	463.0
1994	454.6	454.5	461.6	471.2	478.0	484.9	490.6	493.7	492.4	483.9	484.0	486.3	477.9
1995	472.2	474.0	479.7	485.9	495.1	504.3	501.4	502.3	501.8	500.4	500.8	501.3	493.2
1996	485.3	486.0	493.3	497.2	503.3	512.4	518.0	522.6	520.6	518.0	519.9	520.1	508.0
1997	506.8	507.3	513.8	516.4	524.3	532.5	531.2	533.8	532.3	531.9	533.9	536.2	525.0
1998	516.0	516.6	522.7	527.4	537.8	545.5	551.1	553.9	550.5	545.3	547.3	550.0	538.6
1999	527.9	531.5	538.1	541.3	547.4	555.7	547.8	557.0	555.6	553.4	555.4	557.6	547.3
2000	538.3	541.4	549.2	550.3	555.9	566.7	562.2	564.6	563.1	560.6	563.9	564.9	556.7
2001	546.3	547.6	555.6	568.0	575.2	583.6	579.5	582.4	578.6	574.0	577.6	577.9	570.5
2002	555.7	558.8	563.9	569.0	575.1	583.4	575.9	579.7	575.4	576.9	579.6	583.3	573.1
2003	563.7	563.7	569.8	573.7	582.7	588.9	585.6	589.1	584.8	585.9	591.0	593.0	581.0
Goods-producing													
1990	101.2	101.0	102.0	101.5	102.8	105.0	105.6	105.5	104.3	102.8	102.1	101.0	102.9
1991	96.8	96.0	96.4	98.1	98.5	100.7	100.6	101.2	100.7	100.1	99.5	98.8	98.9
1992	95.3	95.2	95.5	95.3	95.9	97.0	96.7	97.4	97.9	97.7	97.0	96.6	96.4
1993	94.4	95.2	95.6	96.1	96.5	97.4	97.1	96.9	95.7	96.5	95.8	95.3	96.0
1994	92.4	92.3	94.2	94.6	95.6	96.0	97.4	97.8	98.1	97.7	97.7	97.7	95.9
1995	96.8	96.7	98.0	98.2	99.9	102.0	101.4	101.4	101.4	103.2	103.2	103.0	100.4
1996	100.5	101.4	102.7	101.8	102.5	103.4	104.9	105.4	105.3	105.0	105.3	104.6	103.5
1997	104.1	104.4	105.0	104.0	105.3	106.3	105.9	106.3	106.0	106.8	106.9	107.6	105.7
1998	103.8	103.1	104.2	104.3	104.9	106.0	106.8	107.0	106.6	106.0	105.0	105.3	105.2
1999	103.2	103.5	104.0	98.8	99.9	101.3	100.3	105.3	105.1	106.0	105.8	106.1	103.2
2000	104.1	104.6	105.7	106.0	106.7	108.0	107.5	107.3	107.2	107.7	107.6	107.7	106.6
2001	104.2	104.5	105.9	108.2	108.8	109.5	108.5	110.3	109.2	108.2	108.1	108.1	107.8
2002	103.7	103.8	104.1	103.9	104.5	105.2	103.4	105.0	104.2	104.9	104.9	105.2	104.4
2003	103.1	102.5	103.6	103.2	105.0	105.4	103.8	105.7	104.9	105.0	105.2	105.7	104.4
Construction and mining													
1990	35.7	35.6	36.2	35.7	36.1	36.9	36.3	36.1	35.2	34.4	34.2	33.3	35.4
1991	30.1	29.5	30.0	30.9	31.6	32.3	32.3	32.6	32.3	31.7	31.6	31.2	31.3
1992	29.3	29.2	29.4	30.2	30.6	31.1	31.6	31.6	32.0	31.6	31.6	31.4	30.8
1993	29.9	30.6	30.9	31.1	31.7	32.4	32.7	32.4	32.1	32.2	31.6	31.7	31.6
1994	30.5	30.5	31.7	32.4	33.0	33.6	34.4	34.3	34.2	33.8	33.7	33.8	32.9
1995	33.4	33.4	34.6	34.6	35.4	36.5	36.5	36.6	36.8	37.9	37.7	37.9	35.9
1996	35.6	36.7	37.6	38.0	38.8	39.4	40.5	40.6	40.1	40.1	40.2	39.9	38.9
1997	39.3	39.5	39.8	39.3	40.3	41.1	41.3	41.5	40.8	40.7	40.4	40.6	40.3
1998	38.4	38.1	38.9	39.7	40.4	41.0	41.6	41.8	41.4	40.4	40.2	40.6	40.2
1999	39.2	39.7	39.8	40.6	40.7	41.4	41.0	41.1	40.3	40.4	40.1	40.6	40.4
2000	39.4	39.8	40.7	41.3	41.7	42.7	42.5	42.6	42.4	42.3	42.5	42.6	41.7
2001	41.8	42.2	43.2	45.7	46.4	47.1	47.4	47.6	46.8	45.9	45.6	45.5	45.4
2002	43.3	43.7	44.3	44.2	44.7	45.3	45.3	45.0	44.1	44.7	44.4	44.6	44.5
2003	43.1	42.7	43.4	43.3	45.3	45.5	45.8	46.0	45.2	44.9	45.1	45.8	44.7

Employment by Industry: Virginia—*Continued*

(Numbers in thousands. Not seasonally adjusted.)

Industry	January	February	March	April	May	June	July	August	September	October	November	December	Annual Average
NORFOLK-VIRGINIA BEACH-NEWPORT NEWS —*Continued*													
Manufacturing													
1990	65.5	65.4	65.8	65.8	66.7	68.1	69.3	69.4	69.1	68.4	67.9	67.7	67.4
1991	66.7	66.5	66.4	67.2	66.9	68.4	68.3	68.6	68.4	68.4	67.9	67.6	67.6
1992	66.0	66.0	66.1	65.1	65.3	65.9	65.1	65.8	65.9	66.1	65.4	65.2	65.6
1993	64.5	64.6	64.7	65.0	64.8	65.0	64.4	64.5	63.6	64.3	64.2	63.6	64.4
1994	61.9	61.8	62.5	62.2	62.6	62.4	63.0	63.5	63.9	63.9	64.0	63.9	62.9
1995	63.4	63.3	63.4	63.6	64.5	65.5	64.9	64.8	64.6	65.3	65.5	65.1	64.4
1996	64.9	64.7	65.1	63.8	63.7	64.0	64.4	64.8	65.2	64.9	65.1	64.7	64.6
1997	64.8	64.9	65.2	64.7	65.0	65.2	64.6	64.8	65.2	66.1	66.5	67.0	65.3
1998	65.4	65.0	65.3	64.6	64.5	65.0	65.2	65.2	65.2	65.6	64.8	64.7	65.0
1999	64.0	63.8	64.2	58.2	59.2	59.9	59.3	64.2	64.8	65.6	65.7	65.5	62.8
2000	64.7	64.8	65.0	64.7	65.0	65.3	65.0	64.7	64.8	65.4	65.1	65.1	64.9
2001	62.4	62.3	62.7	62.5	62.4	62.4	61.1	62.7	62.4	62.3	62.5	62.6	62.4
2002	60.4	60.1	59.8	59.7	59.8	59.9	58.1	60.0	60.1	60.2	60.5	60.6	59.9
2003	60.0	59.8	60.2	59.9	59.7	59.9	58.0	59.7	59.7	60.1	60.1	59.9	59.8
Service-providing													
1990	484.3	485.8	490.6	494.9	502.6	509.3	502.6	503.8	504.2	502.9	504.2	506.5	499.3
1991	485.0	482.3	487.9	489.6	496.9	504.5	498.6	499.5	501.6	499.4	498.6	501.9	495.4
1992	486.2	489.2	493.4	498.4	505.7	510.3	506.2	507.2	509.5	507.0	510.0	509.8	502.7
1993	495.2	497.7	500.9	506.7	512.3	518.2	511.4	511.9	512.6	510.4	512.2	514.6	508.6
1994	500.1	501.8	508.0	517.5	523.4	530.3	527.7	530.2	533.0	525.3	526.6	528.8	521.0
1995	513.6	516.4	521.4	526.2	534.0	540.3	531.9	533.0	536.1	535.0	536.9	537.6	530.2
1996	520.9	521.6	528.4	532.0	537.6	545.2	542.7	546.2	550.0	549.2	552.2	553.1	539.9
1997	544.2	545.6	552.1	556.0	562.7	570.1	561.4	563.0	567.3	568.9	572.5	573.5	561.4
1998	554.9	557.4	563.5	567.4	577.7	583.4	585.1	587.5	588.1	583.6	588.3	590.2	577.2
1999	567.2	572.3	579.0	587.5	592.3	598.8	588.5	592.0	593.0	592.3	595.5	596.8	587.9
2000	578.9	582.2	590.0	590.8	597.4	606.4	597.3	599.7	600.3	599.1	603.8	603.5	595.7
2001	587.1	589.8	596.7	606.7	613.3	622.2	614.9	615.6	615.6	613.7	618.7	618.2	609.4
2002	598.8	603.3	609.2	614.3	620.7	628.8	616.9	619.3	619.3	622.2	625.2	628.3	617.2
2003	609.3	610.9	616.7	620.3	627.9	634.6	628.7	629.7	628.9	632.0	637.8	639.2	626.3
Trade, transportation, and utilities													
1990	119.0	117.4	118.2	117.6	118.4	120.2	118.8	120.1	118.5	121.4	123.0	124.4	119.7
1991	114.4	112.0	112.1	111.1	112.2	114.1	114.4	115.3	115.4	115.5	117.2	119.5	114.4
1992	111.4	110.5	110.4	110.6	112.2	113.6	113.1	113.9	113.8	114.2	115.9	116.8	113.0
1993	110.3	108.9	108.6	109.1	110.6	111.9	112.3	113.2	112.9	115.8	119.1	120.8	112.7
1994	114.0	112.8	113.4	114.0	115.4	116.5	117.6	118.7	120.1	120.0	121.7	123.0	117.2
1995	115.6	114.3	114.5	115.0	116.5	117.9	117.1	117.8	118.2	121.3	124.3	124.5	118.0
1996	119.1	117.0	117.3	117.2	118.1	120.5	120.8	123.5	124.2	125.4	129.1	129.5	121.8
1997	121.8	119.3	120.2	120.0	121.4	122.9	122.8	124.0	125.5	127.9	130.7	131.0	123.9
1998	122.8	121.0	122.0	121.4	123.7	124.8	125.8	127.6	128.7	130.8	134.3	134.6	126.4
1999	125.7	124.7	126.4	127.5	128.8	130.1	128.5	130.2	130.5	131.9	135.8	137.0	129.7
2000	128.2	128.0	128.3	128.2	129.5	130.8	130.0	131.5	132.0	134.8	138.4	139.9	131.6
2001	134.2	131.9	132.4	132.8	134.4	135.3	134.4	135.3	136.0	137.3	140.6	141.9	135.5
2002	133.7	132.0	131.0	132.1	133.7	135.5	134.1	134.6	134.3	136.8	140.5	142.7	135.1
2003	132.2	130.4	130.8	131.1	132.3	133.4	133.7	135.2	134.9	136.8	143.3	145.1	134.9
Wholesale trade													
1990	19.0	19.0	19.1	18.7	18.9	19.0	18.9	19.0	18.8	19.1	19.0	19.1	18.9
1991	18.0	17.8	18.0	17.9	17.9	18.2	18.1	18.0	18.0	18.3	18.2	18.2	18.0
1992	18.1	18.1	18.2	18.1	18.4	18.5	18.5	18.5	18.4	18.4	18.5	18.4	18.3
1993	17.3	17.3	17.5	17.6	17.5	17.6	17.6	17.5	17.5	17.7	17.6	17.9	17.5
1994	17.5	17.5	17.5	18.2	18.3	18.4	18.7	18.9	19.1	18.9	18.7	18.9	18.3
1995	17.8	17.8	17.9	17.6	17.7	17.9	17.9	18.0	18.0	18.1	18.0	18.1	17.9
1996	17.9	17.9	18.1	17.9	17.8	18.0	18.1	18.1	18.0	18.1	18.1	18.1	18.0
1997	18.0	18.3	18.4	18.2	18.5	18.7	18.5	18.6	18.5	18.7	18.6	18.8	18.4
1998	18.9	19.0	19.1	19.2	19.4	19.5	19.6	19.6	19.5	19.5	19.6	19.7	19.3
1999	19.8	19.8	20.0	20.3	20.4	20.6	20.3	20.3	20.0	19.9	19.9	20.1	20.1
2000	20.1	20.3	20.4	20.5	20.6	20.7	20.7	20.8	20.7	20.9	21.0	21.1	20.6
2001	23.1	23.3	23.5	23.3	23.4	23.6	23.6	23.5	23.5	23.4	23.5	23.6	23.4
2002	22.8	22.8	22.8	23.0	23.1	23.1	22.8	22.8	22.7	22.9	23.0	23.0	22.9
2003	22.5	22.5	22.5	22.7	22.9	23.0	23.0	23.0	22.8	22.5	22.9	22.8	22.8
Retail trade													
1990	78.4	77.0	77.4	77.3	78.6	79.8	78.6	79.6	78.1	80.2	82.1	82.8	79.1
1991	75.6	73.1	73.5	72.7	73.9	75.1	75.7	76.6	76.5	76.2	78.1	80.1	75.5
1992	72.8	72.1	71.9	71.7	73.5	74.5	73.9	74.6	74.8	74.9	76.7	77.2	74.0
1993	72.7	71.4	71.0	71.2	72.7	73.3	73.2	74.4	74.2	76.3	79.7	80.9	74.2
1994	74.7	73.3	73.5	73.8	75.0	75.7	76.6	77.6	78.8	78.7	81.0	82.1	76.7
1995	76.4	75.1	75.0	75.9	77.1	78.2	77.5	77.9	78.6	80.5	83.5	83.6	78.2
1996	78.6	76.5	76.5	76.9	78.0	79.6	79.6	82.0	82.8	83.4	86.9	87.3	80.6
1997	80.2	77.6	78.4	78.5	79.4	80.6	80.8	82.2	83.5	85.1	88.1	87.9	81.8
1998	81.0	79.2	79.9	79.5	81.2	82.0	82.8	84.4	85.9	87.3	91.0	91.1	83.7
1999	83.4	82.3	83.5	84.0	84.8	85.9	84.6	86.3	86.9	87.9	91.9	93.0	86.2
2000	84.6	84.1	84.2	83.8	84.9	86.0	85.0	86.2	87.1	88.8	92.6	94.0	86.7
2001	86.4	84.0	84.0	84.8	86.0	86.5	85.9	87.1	87.6	88.7	92.2	93.4	87.2
2002	86.9	85.0	84.0	84.9	86.1	87.3	86.3	87.0	86.9	88.7	92.2	94.2	87.5
2003	85.4	83.9	84.0	84.6	85.7	86.6	86.1	87.5	87.4	89.2	95.0	96.4	87.7

Employment by Industry: Virginia—*Continued*

(Numbers in thousands. Not seasonally adjusted.)

Industry	January	February	March	April	May	June	July	August	September	October	November	December	Annual Average
NORFOLK-VIRGINIA BEACH-NEWPORT NEWS *—Continued*													
Transportation and utilities													
1990	21.6	21.4	21.7	21.6	20.9	21.4	21.3	21.5	21.6	22.1	21.9	22.5	21.6
1991	20.8	21.1	20.6	20.5	20.4	20.8	20.6	20.7	20.9	21.0	20.9	21.2	20.7
1992	20.5	20.3	20.3	20.8	20.3	20.6	20.7	20.8	20.6	20.9	20.7	21.2	20.6
1993	20.3	20.2	20.1	20.3	20.4	21.0	21.5	21.3	21.2	21.8	21.8	22.0	20.9
1994	21.8	22.0	22.4	22.0	22.1	22.4	22.3	22.2	22.2	22.4	22.0	22.0	22.1
1995	21.4	21.4	21.6	21.5	21.7	21.8	21.7	21.9	21.6	22.7	22.8	22.8	21.9
1996	22.6	22.6	22.7	22.4	22.3	22.9	23.1	23.4	23.4	23.9	24.1	24.1	23.1
1997	23.6	23.4	23.4	23.3	23.5	23.6	23.5	23.2	23.5	24.1	24.0	24.3	23.6
1998	22.9	22.8	23.0	22.7	23.1	23.3	23.4	23.6	23.3	24.0	23.7	23.8	23.3
1999	22.5	22.6	22.9	23.2	23.6	23.6	23.6	23.6	23.6	24.1	24.0	23.9	23.4
2000	23.5	23.6	23.7	23.9	24.0	24.1	24.3	24.5	24.2	25.1	24.8	24.8	24.2
2001	24.7	24.6	24.9	24.7	25.0	25.2	24.9	24.7	24.9	25.2	24.9	24.9	24.9
2002	24.0	24.2	24.2	24.2	24.5	25.1	25.0	24.8	24.7	25.2	25.3	25.5	24.7
2003	24.3	24.0	24.3	23.8	23.7	23.8	24.6	24.7	24.7	25.1	25.4	25.9	24.5
Information													
1990	9.5	9.6	9.6	10.4	10.6	10.7	10.8	10.8	10.8	11.0	10.7	10.8	10.4
1991	10.7	10.7	10.7	10.5	11.3	11.0	11.1	11.2	11.1	11.4	11.3	11.4	11.0
1992	10.6	10.6	10.5	10.8	11.2	11.0	11.1	10.7	10.7	11.4	11.9	12.2	11.0
1993	11.4	11.5	11.6	11.1	11.1	11.2	10.9	11.4	11.4	11.4	11.5	11.5	11.3
1994	11.9	11.7	11.8	11.7	11.9	12.0	11.7	12.1	12.2	12.1	12.2	12.4	11.9
1995	12.7	12.7	12.6	12.4	12.8	12.4	12.6	13.2	13.3	13.2	13.0	12.6	12.7
1996	13.1	13.0	13.2	12.8	13.0	13.3	13.2	13.4	13.2	13.3	13.3	13.3	13.1
1997	13.3	13.1	13.0	12.8	12.9	12.8	13.1	13.3	13.3	13.2	13.3	13.4	13.1
1998	13.3	13.3	13.3	12.7	13.2	13.1	13.4	13.2	12.9	13.3	12.7	12.7	13.0
1999	13.0	12.9	12.8	13.0	13.2	13.3	13.1	13.1	13.1	12.9	13.0	13.2	13.0
2000	13.4	13.3	13.3	13.3	13.6	13.7	13.8	12.6	13.8	13.6	13.5	13.6	13.4
2001	15.1	15.0	15.1	15.2	15.4	15.7	16.0	16.0	16.1	16.2	16.5	16.6	15.7
2002	16.1	16.1	16.1	16.1	16.3	16.3	16.2	16.2	16.1	16.1	16.4	16.5	16.2
2003	16.2	16.3	16.3	16.0	16.1	16.3	16.2	15.8	15.9	16.0	16.0	16.1	16.1
Financial activities													
1990	27.5	27.8	28.1	28.1	28.6	29.6	29.4	29.5	29.0	27.9	28.0	28.0	28.4
1991	27.1	26.9	27.1	26.3	26.8	27.9	27.8	27.8	27.5	26.7	26.4	26.7	27.0
1992	25.8	25.8	25.9	26.0	26.6	27.1	27.4	27.5	26.8	26.6	26.4	26.9	26.5
1993	26.1	26.4	26.3	27.3	27.6	28.5	28.2	28.4	28.0	28.2	28.0	28.2	27.6
1994	28.1	28.1	28.4	30.0	30.4	31.3	31.9	31.9	31.6	30.3	30.1	30.3	30.2
1995	29.3	29.5	29.4	30.3	30.6	31.5	31.3	31.3	31.1	30.3	30.2	30.6	30.4
1996	30.4	30.4	30.5	29.3	29.4	30.2	31.6	31.8	31.3	30.7	30.9	31.1	30.6
1997	31.3	31.4	31.7	31.4	31.7	32.5	32.4	32.5	31.9	31.5	31.4	31.8	31.7
1998	31.6	31.9	32.4	33.2	33.6	34.6	35.0	34.9	34.4	34.0	33.9	34.1	33.6
1999	34.2	34.5	34.7	35.7	35.8	36.7	35.9	36.0	35.6	35.2	35.1	35.4	35.4
2000	34.2	34.5	34.6	35.4	35.6	36.9	36.5	36.8	36.5	36.0	35.9	36.2	35.7
2001	35.0	35.2	35.4	35.9	36.2	37.1	37.2	37.2	36.6	35.8	35.8	35.7	36.1
2002	34.9	35.2	35.4	35.7	36.2	37.3	36.5	36.8	36.1	36.6	36.7	36.9	36.2
2003	36.6	36.9	37.1	37.7	38.3	39.2	39.0	39.1	38.6	37.8	37.6	37.5	38.0
Professional and business services													
1990	56.8	57.9	58.7	58.5	58.9	60.3	59.7	59.9	59.9	59.6	59.4	59.5	59.0
1991	58.4	58.2	59.5	61.1	61.3	62.3	61.6	62.2	62.1	61.6	61.1	61.1	60.8
1992	62.2	62.7	63.6	64.5	63.8	65.2	66.0	66.4	66.7	64.3	65.4	65.3	64.6
1993	65.2	66.1	66.7	67.3	67.6	68.6	67.5	67.4	67.1	67.2	66.8	67.5	67.0
1994	64.7	65.5	66.5	67.5	67.8	69.1	70.6	72.2	72.0	70.1	69.7	70.5	68.8
1995	69.4	70.8	72.3	72.7	74.5	76.2	74.6	75.4	75.9	74.0	73.5	73.9	73.6
1996	72.5	73.8	75.2	76.2	76.6	77.9	79.2	81.0	81.5	81.9	81.5	81.3	78.2
1997	80.2	81.0	82.8	82.7	83.1	84.5	83.8	85.4	85.5	85.1	86.1	87.0	83.9
1998	84.6	86.0	87.1	85.8	87.0	88.8	89.5	91.3	91.4	89.8	91.1	92.6	88.7
1999	88.9	90.6	92.0	92.8	93.4	95.5	95.0	96.7	96.4	96.3	96.2	96.6	94.2
2000	91.6	93.8	95.5	94.5	93.2	96.1	94.6	95.6	94.3	93.6	94.3	94.4	94.2
2001	93.3	94.4	95.7	98.3	98.4	99.7	98.8	100.4	100.7	100.4	101.2	101.4	98.6
2002	97.6	99.7	101.4	101.1	100.4	101.3	99.9	101.5	100.4	100.0	100.2	100.0	100.3
2003	96.5	97.5	98.5	98.6	97.9	97.8	98.4	99.2	98.4	100.2	101.1	101.3	98.8
Educational and health services													
1990	54.1	54.7	55.2	54.7	55.3	55.5	54.6	55.0	56.2	57.0	57.7	58.0	55.6
1991	58.4	58.4	59.1	58.4	58.8	59.3	58.2	57.9	59.6	60.1	60.1	60.7	59.0
1992	59.6	60.3	60.6	60.0	60.5	60.3	59.5	59.5	60.7	61.3	61.6	61.6	60.4
1993	60.8	61.1	61.5	61.7	61.9	61.5	60.9	60.6	61.6	61.9	61.7	62.0	61.4
1994	62.0	62.4	63.1	62.9	63.3	63.1	60.9	60.8	62.6	64.6	64.8	65.2	62.9
1995	64.1	64.9	65.3	64.9	65.4	65.7	64.5	64.7	66.2	65.9	65.7	66.4	65.3
1996	64.9	65.5	65.6	66.2	66.1	65.9	65.2	65.4	67.0	66.9	67.0	67.6	66.1
1997	66.6	67.2	67.8	67.4	68.4	68.4	66.7	67.2	68.8	68.9	69.2	69.5	68.0
1998	69.0	69.6	70.1	69.9	70.8	70.4	70.9	70.8	72.4	71.8	72.1	72.4	70.8
1999	68.8	69.6	70.0	70.4	70.7	70.2	67.5	67.5	69.2	69.4	69.4	69.8	69.3
2000	70.6	71.3	71.6	69.5	70.6	70.4	70.2	70.2	71.0	71.1	71.4	71.6	70.7
2001	70.4	70.9	71.2	72.7	73.3	73.6	72.6	72.6	74.3	74.4	75.1	75.4	73.0
2002	74.2	75.1	75.8	75.2	75.9	76.1	73.2	73.7	76.7	77.6	78.1	78.4	75.8
2003	76.6	77.1	77.5	78.2	78.8	78.9	76.4	76.4	79.1	79.5	79.0	79.3	78.1

Employment by Industry: Virginia—*Continued*

(Numbers in thousands. Not seasonally adjusted.)

Industry	January	February	March	April	May	June	July	August	September	October	November	December	Annual Average
NORFOLK-VIRGINIA BEACH-NEWPORT NEWS —*Continued*													
Leisure and hospitality													
1990	54.9	55.4	57.4	61.4	64.6	66.7	69.0	68.6	65.6	60.6	59.6	58.9	61.8
1991	53.0	52.8	55.6	59.6	62.9	65.4	66.2	66.2	63.0	59.1	56.8	57.0	59.8
1992	53.3	54.4	56.8	60.4	64.2	67.1	68.1	68.8	65.3	61.6	60.5	58.9	61.6
1993	55.3	56.5	57.8	62.0	65.4	68.7	69.2	69.4	67.0	62.2	60.3	59.6	62.7
1994	57.0	57.3	59.2	64.3	67.4	70.4	73.5	73.4	68.9	63.8	62.8	62.2	65.0
1995	59.7	60.2	62.4	67.5	70.3	73.0	74.3	72.9	70.1	66.8	65.5	64.8	67.2
1996	60.0	60.1	63.8	68.5	72.2	75.4	77.3	76.2	72.3	68.8	66.8	66.6	69.0
1997	63.5	64.8	66.8	71.4	74.3	77.5	78.7	77.1	73.3	70.9	68.6	68.3	71.2
1998	63.6	64.1	65.5	71.9	75.9	78.7	80.4	79.6	74.5	70.2	69.0	69.0	71.8
1999	65.0	66.3	68.3	72.9	75.5	78.1	77.7	78.1	75.8	71.5	70.2	69.6	72.4
2000	66.6	66.0	70.0	73.1	76.2	80.1	78.9	79.8	77.5	73.1	72.1	71.0	73.7
2001	66.9	68.3	72.0	76.1	79.6	83.3	84.0	82.6	77.9	74.1	72.9	71.6	75.8
2002	67.5	68.6	71.4	76.3	79.4	82.7	83.6	83.0	78.7	75.9	74.0	73.2	76.2
2003	69.7	70.3	72.6	75.6	80.8	84.2	84.5	83.9	79.2	77.0	75.1	74.1	77.3
Other services													
1990	24.2	24.2	24.3	24.4	24.8	25.2	25.1	25.2	25.0	24.8	24.8	26.1	24.8
1991	23.3	23.0	23.4	23.5	23.9	24.3	23.9	24.0	23.8	23.7	23.7	23.7	23.6
1992	23.2	23.3	23.5	23.4	23.6	24.1	24.2	23.9	23.8	24.0	24.0	23.8	23.7
1993	23.2	23.2	23.5	23.8	23.9	24.1	24.4	24.4	24.4	24.3	24.2	24.4	23.9
1994	24.5	24.4	25.0	26.2	26.2	26.5	27.0	26.8	26.9	25.3	25.0	25.0	25.7
1995	24.6	24.9	25.2	24.9	25.1	25.6	25.6	25.6	25.6	25.7	25.4	25.5	25.3
1996	24.8	24.8	25.0	25.2	25.4	25.8	25.8	25.9	25.8	26.0	26.0	26.1	25.5
1997	26.0	26.1	26.5	26.7	27.2	27.6	27.8	28.0	28.0	27.6	27.7	27.6	27.2
1998	27.3	27.6	28.1	28.2	28.7	29.1	29.3	29.5	29.6	29.4	29.2	29.3	28.7
1999	29.1	29.4	29.9	30.2	30.1	30.5	29.8	30.1	29.9	30.2	29.9	29.9	29.9
2000	29.6	29.9	30.2	30.3	30.5	30.7	30.7	30.8	30.8	30.7	30.7	30.5	30.4
2001	27.2	27.4	27.9	28.8	29.1	29.4	28.0	28.0	27.8	27.6	27.4	27.2	28.0
2002	28.0	28.3	28.7	28.6	28.7	29.0	29.0	28.9	28.9	29.0	28.8	30.4	28.9
2003	32.8	32.7	33.4	33.3	33.5	33.7	33.6	33.8	33.8	33.6	33.7	33.9	33.5
Government													
1990	138.3	138.8	139.1	139.8	141.4	141.1	135.2	134.7	139.2	140.6	141.0	140.8	139.1
1991	139.7	140.3	140.4	139.1	139.7	140.2	135.4	134.9	139.1	141.3	142.0	141.8	139.4
1992	140.1	141.6	142.1	142.7	143.6	141.9	136.8	136.5	141.7	143.6	144.3	144.3	141.6
1993	142.9	144.0	144.9	144.4	144.2	143.7	138.0	137.1	140.2	139.4	140.6	140.6	141.6
1994	137.9	139.6	140.6	140.9	141.0	141.4	134.5	134.3	138.7	139.1	140.3	140.2	139.0
1995	138.2	139.1	139.7	138.5	138.8	138.0	131.9	132.1	135.7	137.8	139.3	139.3	137.3
1996	136.1	137.0	137.8	136.6	136.8	136.2	129.6	129.0	134.7	136.2	137.6	137.6	135.4
1997	141.5	142.7	143.3	143.6	143.7	143.9	136.1	135.5	141.0	143.8	145.5	144.9	142.1
1998	142.7	143.9	145.0	144.3	144.8	143.9	140.8	140.6	144.2	144.3	146.0	145.5	143.8
1999	142.5	144.3	144.9	145.0	144.8	144.4	141.0	140.3	142.5	144.9	145.9	145.3	143.8
2000	144.7	145.4	146.5	146.5	148.2	147.7	142.6	142.4	144.4	146.2	147.5	146.3	145.7
2001	145.0	146.7	147.0	146.9	146.9	148.1	143.9	143.5	146.2	147.9	149.2	148.4	146.6
2002	146.8	148.3	149.4	149.2	150.1	150.6	144.4	144.6	148.1	150.2	150.5	150.2	148.5
2003	148.7	149.7	150.5	149.8	150.2	151.1	146.9	146.3	149.0	151.1	152.0	151.9	149.8
Federal government													
1990	56.3	56.2	56.3	56.3	57.7	56.8	56.4	56.2	55.6	55.5	55.3	55.3	56.1
1991	55.2	55.0	54.9	54.9	55.1	55.4	55.6	55.3	55.3	55.4	55.5	55.5	55.2
1992	55.4	55.4	55.3	55.1	55.2	55.5	55.6	55.6	55.2	55.0	55.1	55.1	55.2
1993	55.0	54.5	54.4	54.1	53.5	53.6	53.8	53.6	51.2	49.4	49.5	49.4	52.6
1994	49.1	48.8	48.7	48.7	48.5	48.4	48.2	48.2	47.6	47.4	47.3	47.1	48.1
1995	46.6	46.3	46.1	45.7	45.8	45.5	45.8	45.8	45.3	44.9	45.0	45.0	45.6
1996	44.5	44.1	43.8	43.8	43.8	43.8	44.0	44.0	43.2	42.7	43.0	43.2	43.6
1997	49.1	48.8	48.8	48.7	48.7	48.8	48.6	48.6	48.3	48.3	48.4	48.4	48.6
1998	47.7	47.7	47.6	47.5	47.4	47.7	48.0	47.9	47.7	47.0	47.1	47.1	47.5
1999	46.7	46.5	46.6	46.3	46.3	46.4	47.1	46.8	46.5	46.4	46.4	46.6	46.5
2000	46.3	46.2	46.3	47.0	48.2	48.1	47.5	47.7	46.2	45.9	45.9	46.1	46.7
2001	45.3	45.1	45.1	45.1	45.1	45.3	45.4	45.5	45.3	45.0	44.8	45.2	45.2
2002	45.0	44.9	45.2	45.3	45.4	45.8	45.9	46.1	46.1	46.3	46.1	46.5	45.7
2003	45.9	46.0	45.9	46.0	46.0	46.1	46.2	46.4	46.1	45.8	45.9	46.0	46.0
State government													
1990	19.9	19.9	19.8	20.1	20.1	19.9	17.5	17.4	20.1	20.6	20.7	20.6	19.7
1991	20.0	20.6	20.3	20.2	20.0	19.7	17.2	17.0	20.1	21.1	21.1	20.8	19.8
1992	20.1	20.9	21.2	21.4	21.1	19.6	17.0	16.8	21.3	21.7	21.6	21.6	20.3
1993	20.5	21.5	21.6	21.1	21.3	20.7	18.8	18.5	21.5	22.0	22.0	22.2	20.9
1994	21.0	21.9	22.1	22.1	21.2	21.3	19.0	18.9	22.1	22.3	22.1	22.2	21.3
1995	21.3	21.8	22.0	21.9	21.7	21.0	18.1	17.6	21.5	21.6	21.8	21.7	21.0
1996	20.1	21.2	21.4	21.2	20.3	19.7	17.3	16.8	20.4	20.2	19.9	20.1	19.8
1997	19.1	19.7	19.9	20.0	19.5	19.4	17.5	17.1	19.7	19.6	20.0	19.8	19.2
1998	18.2	19.0	19.9	19.6	19.6	18.7	19.0	19.0	20.2	19.6	20.0	19.9	19.3
1999	17.8	19.2	19.4	19.4	19.1	18.6	18.5	18.4	20.1	19.1	19.3	19.4	19.0
2000	18.2	18.9	19.2	19.0	19.2	19.3	18.8	18.5	20.0	19.6	19.7	19.2	19.1
2001	18.6	19.5	20.0	19.6	19.3	19.7	19.4	19.4	20.6	20.0	20.2	19.3	19.6
2002	18.7	19.5	20.0	19.9	20.0	20.4	18.6	18.7	20.9	19.9	20.0	19.6	19.7
2003	18.9	19.5	19.6	19.7	19.8	20.2	19.4	18.9	20.8	20.9	21.1	21.0	20.0

Employment by Industry: Virginia—*Continued*

(Numbers in thousands. Not seasonally adjusted.)

Industry	January	February	March	April	May	June	July	August	September	October	November	December	Annual Average
NORFOLK-VIRGINIA BEACH-NEWPORT NEWS *—Continued*													
Local government													
1990	62.1	62.7	63.0	63.4	63.6	64.4	61.3	61.1	63.5	64.5	65.0	64.9	63.2
1991	64.5	64.7	65.2	64.0	64.6	65.1	62.6	62.6	63.7	64.8	65.4	65.5	64.3
1992	64.6	65.3	65.6	66.2	67.3	66.8	64.2	64.1	65.2	66.9	67.6	67.6	65.9
1993	67.4	68.0	68.9	69.2	69.4	69.4	65.4	65.0	67.5	68.0	69.1	69.0	68.0
1994	67.8	68.9	69.8	70.1	71.3	71.7	67.3	67.2	69.0	69.4	70.9	70.9	69.5
1995	70.3	71.0	71.6	70.9	71.3	71.5	68.0	68.7	68.9	71.3	72.5	72.6	70.7
1996	71.5	71.7	72.6	71.6	72.7	72.7	68.3	68.2	71.1	73.3	74.7	74.3	71.8
1997	73.3	74.2	74.6	74.9	75.5	75.7	70.0	69.8	73.0	75.9	77.1	76.7	74.2
1998	76.8	77.2	77.5	77.2	77.8	77.5	73.8	73.7	76.3	77.7	78.9	78.5	76.9
1999	78.0	78.6	78.9	79.3	79.4	79.4	75.4	75.1	75.9	79.4	80.2	79.3	78.2
2000	80.2	80.3	81.0	80.5	80.8	80.3	76.3	76.2	78.2	80.7	81.9	81.0	79.7
2001	81.1	82.1	81.9	82.2	82.5	83.1	79.1	78.6	80.3	82.9	84.2	83.9	81.8
2002	83.1	83.9	84.2	84.0	84.7	84.4	79.9	79.8	81.1	84.0	84.4	84.1	83.1
2003	83.9	84.2	85.0	84.1	84.4	84.8	81.3	81.0	82.1	84.4	85.0	84.9	83.8
NORTHERN VIRGINIA													
Total nonfarm													
1990	839.1	838.9	845.1	845.9	856.4	864.8	856.1	853.7	852.4	847.4	849.4	851.7	850.0
1991	823.0	819.3	822.8	823.5	832.0	840.8	829.5	826.1	827.4	825.0	829.7	834.3	827.7
1992	813.6	811.9	819.2	823.9	835.4	843.0	840.2	836.1	839.1	844.0	849.8	855.2	834.2
1993	835.3	839.1	841.8	849.8	861.9	871.8	869.4	865.5	869.2	874.3	883.5	891.1	862.7
1994	866.7	865.0	876.6	887.2	896.8	911.2	905.5	905.7	909.7	914.0	922.7	931.3	899.3
1995	909.9	909.3	919.3	919.2	927.8	938.7	928.7	927.1	930.9	934.1	942.8	950.8	928.2
1996	916.5	926.7	937.7	941.9	952.7	967.4	961.3	961.9	964.5	969.2	979.0	986.3	955.4
1997	972.7	973.8	984.1	986.7	997.7	1008.6	1005.1	1005.5	1005.5	1009.0	1017.8	1027.8	999.5
1998	999.8	1005.4	1015.0	1024.1	1035.5	1050.1	1045.3	1044.9	1050.3	1049.5	1061.4	1071.6	1037.7
1999	1046.1	1050.7	1059.9	1071.0	1078.0	1094.3	1090.5	1092.9	1099.2	1109.7	1119.6	1129.1	1086.7
2000	1105.8	1109.3	1125.6	1133.3	1144.8	1162.2	1154.9	1155.3	1161.9	1171.3	1181.9	1191.0	1149.7
2001	1161.1	1163.5	1174.4	1193.4	1203.0	1216.1	1200.2	1193.4	1189.8	1185.8	1188.7	1192.0	1188.5
2002	1161.8	1161.5	1171.0	1173.5	1182.4	1194.5	1183.4	1179.9	1183.3	1182.4	1191.7	1195.2	1180.1
2003	1165.5	1164.3	1173.6	1178.9	1192.0	1206.7	1198.3	1198.7	1202.2	1210.3	1219.6	1226.6	1194.7
Total private													
1990	676.2	674.6	680.3	680.6	687.8	696.7	692.5	693.2	688.0	679.3	680.0	681.5	684.2
1991	654.9	649.9	653.0	653.2	660.3	668.6	661.9	662.2	659.0	653.6	657.2	660.8	657.8
1992	641.3	639.1	645.0	650.1	659.1	666.0	668.6	668.4	666.9	669.1	672.5	678.7	660.4
1993	661.3	664.0	666.5	674.6	685.2	694.4	695.9	697.6	696.1	698.4	705.4	713.6	687.7
1994	691.4	689.1	699.6	710.1	718.5	731.3	731.1	733.8	733.1	735.2	742.2	751.3	722.2
1995	732.5	730.1	739.9	741.5	748.9	760.3	756.5	757.8	755.7	756.4	764.5	772.6	751.3
1996	741.9	749.8	760.1	764.4	773.9	788.0	789.4	791.4	788.7	793.1	801.5	809.9	779.3
1997	792.5	792.9	802.6	805.1	815.8	827.1	829.8	832.2	828.7	829.9	837.8	849.5	820.3
1998	823.3	827.2	835.8	845.1	856.0	869.8	869.7	872.4	870.8	869.5	878.5	888.4	858.8
1999	866.1	868.9	877.0	887.4	895.1	909.7	912.9	916.6	914.8	924.3	932.3	941.4	903.8
2000	919.9	922.7	937.7	944.6	954.2	971.5	972.9	975.2	974.2	981.7	990.6	998.9	962.0
2001	971.5	974.1	983.1	1001.2	1010.4	1021.4	1012.3	1009.6	1000.1	992.9	994.0	996.9	997.3
2002	970.0	969.8	976.7	979.3	986.9	997.1	993.0	992.7	988.6	984.6	992.8	996.2	985.6
2003	970.5	967.9	976.3	981.4	993.0	1006.1	1005.0	1007.0	1002.6	1007.3	1014.7	1021.6	996.1
Goods-producing													
1990	102.3	102.2	103.0	101.9	102.3	102.7	100.4	99.6	98.1	95.7	93.8	91.4	99.4
1991	83.7	82.0	81.9	81.5	82.8	83.9	82.3	82.3	80.7	80.9	79.9	78.7	81.7
1992	74.8	74.2	75.1	75.8	77.0	78.3	78.9	79.0	78.7	78.9	78.3	77.9	77.2
1993	73.7	74.3	74.7	77.6	78.9	80.5	82.0	82.4	82.1	83.1	83.1	83.0	79.6
1994	78.3	78.0	80.0	83.4	85.0	86.7	87.9	88.3	88.1	88.4	88.2	88.3	85.0
1995	84.4	83.3	85.4	86.6	87.7	88.9	89.1	89.7	89.8	89.7	89.5	89.0	87.7
1996	81.9	84.9	87.3	88.0	89.4	91.6	92.5	92.9	92.9	93.6	93.8	93.2	90.1
1997	91.3	91.2	93.6	94.2	95.6	97.2	98.4	99.3	98.8	100.0	99.5	99.1	96.5
1998	94.3	95.0	95.2	98.0	99.4	101.3	102.1	102.7	102.8	101.9	102.0	101.6	99.6
1999	93.1	93.9	94.7	97.3	98.4	100.0	100.7	101.3	101.6	102.1	102.0	102.1	98.9
2000	99.9	100.7	103.8	104.5	105.6	107.8	108.5	109.1	109.2	109.0	109.5	109.1	106.3
2001	106.2	107.1	108.8	112.9	114.5	116.0	115.5	115.7	115.0	113.0	112.8	112.0	112.5
2002	108.0	108.4	109.6	109.6	111.1	112.1	111.2	111.5	110.2	109.4	108.6	108.0	109.8
2003	105.2	105.0	105.9	106.6	109.0	110.5	111.9	112.4	112.1	111.9	111.8	111.9	109.5
Construction and mining													
1990	65.4	65.8	66.5	64.4	64.8	65.1	63.1	62.4	60.9	58.8	57.2	55.0	62.4
1991	47.9	46.3	46.3	46.2	47.3	48.3	47.0	47.2	46.6	45.8	44.9	43.7	46.4
1992	40.7	40.1	41.0	42.0	43.2	44.5	45.3	45.5	45.5	45.6	45.1	44.7	43.6
1993	42.0	42.5	42.7	44.1	45.5	47.0	48.8	49.2	49.0	49.8	49.8	49.7	46.6
1994	45.5	45.2	47.1	50.4	51.9	53.7	55.0	55.3	55.2	55.3	54.9	54.8	52.0
1995	51.0	49.9	51.7	52.9	53.9	55.0	55.0	55.5	55.5	55.3	55.2	54.6	53.7
1996	48.1	50.7	52.7	53.8	55.1	56.7	57.9	58.2	58.1	58.7	58.7	58.0	55.5
1997	56.0	55.9	57.6	58.0	59.3	60.2	61.0	61.2	60.8	61.5	61.0	60.5	59.4
1998	57.0	57.5	57.7	60.2	61.4	63.1	64.3	64.8	64.8	63.8	64.0	63.6	61.8
1999	60.9	61.8	62.3	64.7	65.8	67.3	67.8	68.3	68.6	69.0	69.0	68.9	66.2
2000	67.1	67.8	70.6	71.2	72.4	74.0	74.9	75.5	75.7	75.4	75.7	75.4	72.9
2001	72.4	73.3	75.1	79.7	81.4	82.8	82.5	82.8	82.3	80.9	80.6	79.9	79.5
2002	76.5	76.8	78.0	79.1	80.6	81.5	81.2	81.7	80.4	80.2	79.6	78.7	79.5
2003	75.1	74.7	76.3	78.0	80.5	81.8	83.2	83.8	83.4	84.0	84.0	83.7	80.7

Employment by Industry: Virginia—*Continued*

(Numbers in thousands. Not seasonally adjusted.)

Industry	January	February	March	April	May	June	July	August	September	October	November	December	Annual Average
NORTHERN VIRGINIA *—Continued*													
Manufacturing													
1990	36.9	36.4	36.5	37.5	37.5	37.6	37.3	37.2	37.2	36.9	36.6	36.4	37.0
1991	35.8	35.7	35.6	35.3	35.5	35.6	35.3	35.1	34.1	35.1	35.0	35.0	35.2
1992	34.1	34.1	34.1	33.8	33.8	33.8	33.6	33.5	33.2	33.3	33.2	33.2	33.6
1993	31.7	31.8	32.0	33.5	33.4	33.5	33.2	33.2	33.1	33.3	33.3	33.3	32.9
1994	32.8	32.8	32.9	33.0	33.1	33.0	32.9	33.0	32.9	33.1	33.3	33.5	33.0
1995	33.4	33.4	33.7	33.7	33.8	33.9	34.1	34.2	34.3	34.4	34.3	34.4	33.9
1996	33.8	34.2	34.6	34.2	34.3	34.9	34.6	34.7	34.8	34.9	35.1	35.2	34.6
1997	35.3	35.3	36.0	36.2	36.3	37.0	37.4	38.1	38.0	38.5	38.5	38.6	37.1
1998	37.3	37.5	37.5	37.8	38.0	38.2	37.8	37.9	38.0	38.1	38.0	38.0	37.8
1999	32.2	32.1	32.4	32.6	32.6	32.7	32.9	33.0	33.0	33.1	33.0	33.2	32.7
2000	32.8	32.9	33.2	33.3	33.2	33.8	33.6	33.6	33.5	33.6	33.8	33.7	33.4
2001	33.8	33.8	33.7	33.2	33.1	33.2	33.0	32.9	32.7	32.1	32.2	32.1	33.0
2002	31.5	31.6	31.6	30.5	30.5	30.6	30.0	29.8	29.8	29.2	29.0	29.3	30.3
2003	30.1	30.3	29.6	28.6	28.5	28.7	28.7	28.6	28.7	27.9	27.8	28.2	28.8
Service-providing													
1990	736.8	736.7	742.1	744.0	754.1	762.1	755.7	754.1	754.3	751.7	755.6	760.3	750.6
1991	739.3	737.3	740.9	742.0	749.2	756.9	747.2	743.8	746.7	744.1	749.8	755.6	746.0
1992	738.8	737.7	744.1	748.1	758.4	764.7	761.3	757.1	760.4	765.1	771.5	777.3	757.0
1993	761.6	764.8	767.1	772.2	783.0	791.3	787.4	783.1	787.1	791.2	800.4	808.1	783.1
1994	788.4	787.0	796.6	803.8	811.8	824.5	817.6	817.4	821.6	825.6	834.5	843.0	814.3
1995	825.5	826.0	833.9	832.6	840.1	849.8	839.6	837.4	841.1	844.4	853.3	861.8	840.4
1996	834.6	841.8	850.4	853.9	863.3	875.8	868.8	869.0	871.6	875.6	885.2	893.1	865.2
1997	881.4	882.6	890.5	892.5	902.1	911.4	906.7	906.2	906.7	909.0	918.3	928.7	903.0
1998	905.5	910.4	919.8	926.1	936.1	948.8	943.2	942.2	947.5	947.6	959.4	970.0	938.0
1999	953.0	956.8	965.2	973.7	979.6	994.3	989.8	991.6	997.6	1007.6	1017.6	1027.0	987.8
2000	1005.9	1008.6	1021.8	1028.8	1039.2	1054.4	1046.4	1046.2	1052.7	1062.3	1072.4	1081.9	1043.3
2001	1054.9	1056.4	1065.6	1080.5	1088.5	1100.1	1084.7	1077.7	1074.8	1072.8	1075.9	1080.0	1076.0
2002	1053.8	1053.1	1061.4	1063.9	1071.3	1082.4	1072.2	1068.4	1073.1	1073.0	1083.1	1087.2	1070.2
2003	1060.3	1059.3	1067.7	1072.3	1083.0	1096.2	1086.4	1086.3	1090.1	1098.4	1107.8	1114.7	1085.2
Trade, transportation, and utilities													
1990	174.1	168.6	169.5	169.0	171.4	173.2	171.5	172.3	171.2	171.1	173.4	176.3	171.8
1991	167.3	163.3	163.0	161.3	162.8	164.0	163.3	163.3	162.5	161.6	165.1	168.4	163.8
1992	160.2	156.9	156.9	158.9	160.6	162.0	162.0	161.9	161.1	162.4	165.9	171.6	161.7
1993	164.9	162.8	162.6	162.9	166.1	168.1	167.6	168.0	167.5	170.5	175.6	181.3	168.1
1994	173.4	169.6	171.4	172.4	174.6	177.1	176.7	176.5	176.4	178.5	183.9	189.7	176.6
1995	179.6	175.3	175.9	174.7	175.4	177.0	175.4	175.2	175.3	177.4	183.0	187.6	177.6
1996	176.3	174.5	175.0	173.1	174.6	177.0	176.3	176.9	176.2	180.0	185.2	190.3	177.9
1997	179.1	175.5	177.6	176.3	178.4	180.2	179.8	180.8	181.0	183.3	188.6	193.9	181.2
1998	180.9	178.4	179.0	180.2	182.3	185.0	183.6	184.6	184.8	187.0	192.3	196.7	184.5
1999	188.0	185.2	187.1	187.8	189.5	192.3	192.7	193.1	193.4	196.1	201.3	206.5	192.7
2000	195.1	192.4	194.1	193.4	195.7	197.9	197.2	198.2	197.7	202.2	208.3	213.6	198.8
2001	200.2	197.1	198.3	199.9	202.4	204.7	204.2	203.8	201.2	201.9	205.9	208.5	202.3
2002	198.5	195.2	196.1	196.1	198.0	200.0	199.5	199.4	199.1	200.5	204.7	209.5	199.7
2003	197.6	195.6	196.5	196.7	198.9	201.4	201.2	201.9	201.5	203.1	207.8	212.1	201.2
Wholesale trade													
1990	28.9	29.1	29.1	29.1	29.2	29.4	29.6	29.6	29.4	29.5	29.4	29.3	29.3
1991	28.3	28.3	28.3	28.3	28.2	28.3	28.6	28.3	28.3	27.9	27.9	28.0	28.2
1992	27.5	27.5	27.5	27.7	27.8	27.9	28.0	28.0	27.8	27.6	27.4	28.5	27.7
1993	27.8	28.0	28.1	28.0	28.1	28.2	28.3	28.3	28.3	28.0	28.1	28.4	28.1
1994	29.3	29.3	29.4	30.1	30.3	30.5	30.3	30.1	30.3	30.1	30.2	30.6	30.0
1995	30.0	29.9	30.1	30.4	29.8	30.2	29.8	29.7	29.8	30.3	30.5	30.8	30.1
1996	30.4	30.8	30.9	29.9	29.8	30.1	30.1	30.2	30.1	30.1	30.3	30.5	30.2
1997	30.1	30.1	30.4	30.0	30.1	30.4	29.9	30.1	30.1	29.9	30.1	30.2	30.1
1998	28.6	28.9	29.1	29.6	29.6	30.0	29.8	29.8	29.7	29.7	29.7	29.9	29.5
1999	30.2	30.3	30.3	30.6	30.5	30.8	30.6	30.5	30.6	30.9	31.1	31.1	30.6
2000	30.7	30.9	31.0	31.3	31.7	32.0	31.6	31.8	31.8	33.0	33.2	33.5	31.8
2001	35.5	35.5	35.7	36.4	36.4	36.6	36.2	36.1	35.8	35.6	35.7	35.7	35.9
2002	35.2	35.1	35.2	35.1	35.2	35.3	35.2	35.1	34.9	35.2	35.3	35.5	35.2
2003	35.1	35.2	35.3	35.2	35.3	35.4	35.3	35.3	35.0	35.5	35.7	36.1	35.4
Retail trade													
1990	112.7	110.1	110.6	110.1	111.9	112.9	111.0	111.6	110.8	110.8	113.1	116.2	111.8
1991	107.8	103.9	103.8	102.2	103.3	104.0	102.7	103.3	102.6	102.5	105.8	108.8	104.2
1992	102.0	99.1	99.2	100.8	102.1	103.0	102.6	102.2	101.9	103.5	106.9	111.2	102.8
1993	105.3	103.0	102.9	103.0	105.2	106.2	104.8	105.1	104.3	106.9	111.6	116.6	106.2
1994	108.9	105.4	106.6	107.1	108.7	110.6	109.9	110.0	110.1	112.3	117.7	123.3	110.8
1995	114.7	110.7	111.2	110.2	111.5	112.3	111.4	111.9	112.1	113.7	119.4	123.9	113.5
1996	114.7	112.3	113.0	112.4	113.7	115.3	114.2	114.6	114.4	116.2	121.0	125.7	115.6
1997	116.1	112.5	113.8	113.1	114.5	115.7	115.5	116.1	116.4	118.1	123.1	128.2	116.9
1998	117.4	114.7	114.9	115.1	116.5	118.2	116.6	117.6	118.1	120.1	125.2	129.4	118.6
1999	121.0	118.0	119.3	119.5	120.6	122.4	122.6	123.1	123.2	125.0	130.0	135.0	123.3
2000	124.4	121.6	122.9	122.0	123.6	125.0	124.7	125.5	125.3	127.3	133.1	138.2	126.1
2001	123.8	120.8	121.7	121.9	123.9	125.9	125.4	125.4	123.9	125.8	130.7	134.0	125.3
2002	125.5	122.5	123.3	123.3	124.8	126.2	125.2	125.3	125.7	126.5	130.3	135.1	126.1
2003	124.5	122.6	123.3	123.6	125.3	127.5	126.9	127.8	128.2	129.4	133.5	137.3	127.5

Employment by Industry: Virginia—*Continued*

(Numbers in thousands. Not seasonally adjusted.)

Industry	January	February	March	April	May	June	July	August	September	October	November	December	Annual Average
NORTHERN VIRGINIA *—Continued*													
Transportation and utilities													
1990	32.5	29.4	29.8	29.8	30.3	30.9	30.9	31.1	31.0	30.8	30.9	30.8	30.6
1991	31.2	31.1	30.9	30.8	31.3	31.7	32.0	31.7	31.6	31.2	31.4	31.6	31.3
1992	30.7	30.3	30.2	30.4	30.7	31.1	31.4	31.7	31.4	31.3	31.6	31.9	31.0
1993	31.8	31.8	31.6	31.9	32.8	33.7	34.5	34.6	34.9	35.6	35.9	36.3	33.7
1994	35.2	34.9	35.4	35.2	35.6	36.0	36.5	36.4	36.0	36.1	36.0	35.8	35.7
1995	34.9	34.7	34.6	34.1	34.1	34.5	34.2	33.6	33.4	33.4	33.1	32.9	33.9
1996	31.2	31.4	31.1	30.8	31.1	31.6	32.0	32.1	31.7	33.7	33.9	34.1	32.0
1997	32.9	32.9	33.4	33.2	33.8	34.1	34.4	34.6	34.5	35.3	35.4	35.5	34.1
1998	34.9	34.8	35.0	35.5	36.2	36.8	37.2	37.2	37.0	37.2	37.4	37.4	36.3
1999	36.8	36.9	37.5	37.7	38.4	39.1	39.5	39.5	39.6	40.2	40.2	40.4	38.8
2000	40.0	39.9	40.2	40.1	40.4	40.9	40.9	40.9	40.6	41.9	42.0	41.9	40.8
2001	40.9	40.8	40.9	41.6	42.1	42.2	42.6	42.3	41.5	40.5	39.5	38.8	41.1
2002	37.8	37.6	37.6	37.7	38.0	38.5	39.1	39.0	38.5	38.8	39.1	38.9	38.4
2003	38.0	37.8	37.9	37.9	38.3	38.5	39.0	38.8	38.3	38.2	38.6	38.7	38.3
Information													
1990	37.2	37.5	37.8	37.8	37.9	38.5	38.8	38.6	38.2	37.6	37.8	37.9	37.9
1991	39.1	39.0	39.1	38.3	38.3	39.0	38.9	38.7	38.7	38.5	38.5	38.4	38.7
1992	39.5	39.7	39.6	39.1	39.2	39.6	40.5	40.5	40.3	40.8	40.6	40.8	40.0
1993	39.1	39.1	39.2	39.2	39.4	39.7	39.5	39.7	39.7	39.8	39.9	40.3	39.5
1994	39.5	39.6	39.8	39.4	39.6	40.4	41.2	41.5	41.4	40.8	41.2	40.4	40.4
1995	42.4	42.7	43.3	43.8	44.5	45.2	44.6	45.0	45.4	44.7	45.1	45.8	44.3
1996	46.5	46.5	46.9	47.4	48.0	48.7	48.7	49.2	49.3	48.8	49.6	49.9	48.2
1997	49.2	50.2	50.8	51.7	52.0	52.8	52.9	53.1	52.9	53.0	53.6	54.8	52.2
1998	54.3	54.6	54.7	56.1	56.6	57.6	57.1	57.6	57.6	57.6	58.5	59.4	56.8
1999	58.9	59.5	59.8	60.3	60.5	61.6	62.4	63.2	63.8	65.1	65.8	66.7	62.3
2000	66.9	67.8	68.9	69.6	70.9	72.6	73.7	73.2	75.4	76.5	77.0	77.5	72.5
2001	79.7	79.9	79.7	78.6	78.3	76.5	75.5	74.4	73.2	70.9	69.5	68.8	75.4
2002	66.7	66.3	65.6	64.3	64.2	63.8	62.2	61.7	60.3	60.2	60.3	59.8	63.0
2003	59.4	59.4	59.2	58.6	58.9	59.3	59.4	59.4	58.6	59.2	59.7	59.9	59.3
Financial activities													
1990	48.5	49.0	49.1	48.8	49.2	49.7	49.4	49.4	49.0	48.7	48.6	48.9	49.0
1991	49.3	48.9	49.3	49.4	49.7	50.2	49.4	49.4	49.5	48.7	48.8	49.3	49.3
1992	47.6	47.7	48.1	48.0	48.4	48.8	49.3	49.5	49.2	48.6	48.8	49.1	48.5
1993	49.7	49.8	50.0	50.1	50.6	51.3	52.9	52.9	52.7	53.5	54.1	54.3	51.8
1994	53.6	53.8	54.4	54.3	54.4	54.8	53.9	54.3	54.1	54.1	54.1	54.6	54.2
1995	52.8	52.7	53.1	52.2	52.4	52.9	52.7	52.6	52.7	52.2	52.6	52.9	52.6
1996	52.7	53.1	53.7	53.5	53.9	54.8	54.2	54.5	54.1	54.5	54.7	55.2	54.0
1997	55.1	55.3	55.9	55.3	56.0	56.5	56.7	56.6	56.3	56.5	57.0	57.8	56.2
1998	58.5	56.9	57.4	58.0	58.9	60.0	59.9	60.2	60.1	60.1	60.1	60.7	59.2
1999	59.4	59.9	60.1	60.1	60.5	61.2	61.4	61.6	61.2	60.9	61.2	61.5	60.7
2000	61.6	61.9	62.5	62.0	62.3	62.8	63.0	63.0	62.6	63.0	63.1	63.5	62.6
2001	61.2	61.5	62.0	62.7	63.1	63.9	63.9	63.9	63.3	63.1	63.4	63.7	63.0
2002	63.6	63.9	64.1	63.8	63.8	64.4	64.1	64.3	63.9	64.0	64.6	65.0	64.1
2003	66.1	66.0	66.3	66.5	67.1	67.9	68.4	68.4	67.6	68.5	68.8	69.0	67.6
Professional and business services													
1990	144.4	145.6	147.9	149.6	149.8	151.1	151.1	151.7	151.2	147.4	146.9	147.1	148.6
1991	141.4	141.6	143.6	143.6	143.9	145.2	144.5	144.8	145.1	143.3	143.1	143.8	143.6
1992	142.6	143.3	145.7	146.2	147.2	149.2	150.4	150.4	151.6	152.6	153.2	153.5	148.8
1993	150.3	152.3	153.4	155.7	156.7	158.2	157.8	158.2	159.4	159.5	160.6	161.3	156.9
1994	154.9	156.0	158.6	161.3	161.7	164.7	164.8	166.4	167.5	168.4	169.2	171.2	163.7
1995	168.5	169.8	173.6	174.0	175.7	178.6	178.5	179.3	178.5	180.6	182.5	184.3	176.9
1996	177.6	179.9	183.4	187.5	189.2	192.9	194.1	194.8	194.5	197.5	198.1	199.6	190.7
1997	197.5	198.6	197.5	199.2	200.2	203.0	204.8	205.4	205.2	205.1	205.9	209.5	202.6
1998	209.6	212.8	217.4	217.7	219.4	222.6	224.4	225.2	225.1	223.6	224.7	227.3	220.8
1999	229.6	231.6	234.1	236.7	238.0	242.3	243.3	245.0	244.8	249.2	250.1	252.5	241.4
2000	251.4	252.9	256.6	258.9	259.8	265.4	265.2	266.8	266.9	269.6	270.8	272.7	263.0
2001	282.1	283.7	285.7	294.9	294.6	297.1	295.6	294.8	291.3	289.4	288.4	289.3	290.6
2002	281.0	281.6	283.8	284.0	284.3	286.0	285.4	284.9	282.8	283.8	284.0	284.9	283.9
2003	281.5	281.3	283.5	286.1	287.5	290.5	292.8	294.4	293.1	294.1	294.4	296.1	289.6
Educational and health services													
1990	62.5	63.4	63.7	63.4	64.0	64.6	64.6	64.7	65.6	66.0	66.6	66.9	64.6
1991	65.7	66.3	66.4	67.4	68.1	68.1	66.9	67.2	68.1	68.7	69.3	69.7	67.6
1992	68.7	69.2	69.8	69.9	70.5	70.2	69.3	69.0	69.7	71.2	71.1	71.4	70.0
1993	71.1	71.9	72.3	72.5	72.8	72.8	72.2	72.2	73.2	73.8	74.1	74.5	72.7
1994	74.5	74.9	75.8	75.9	76.4	76.6	75.9	75.9	76.9	78.3	78.8	79.2	76.5
1995	78.6	79.6	80.2	79.8	80.0	80.1	79.0	78.8	80.1	80.8	81.2	81.7	79.9
1996	79.7	81.4	82.3	82.5	83.1	83.1	82.8	83.0	83.8	84.9	85.8	86.6	83.2
1997	86.1	86.9	88.4	88.2	89.1	89.1	89.0	89.1	89.7	91.0	91.9	92.4	89.2
1998	88.7	90.3	90.6	90.6	91.3	90.9	90.2	89.8	91.1	93.0	93.8	94.3	91.2
1999	92.7	93.1	93.4	94.5	94.5	94.2	94.3	94.2	95.4	97.9	98.3	98.2	95.0
2000	94.4	95.8	96.9	97.8	98.0	98.3	98.6	98.6	99.2	100.0	100.4	100.6	98.2
2001	96.4	97.8	98.6	100.0	100.6	100.9	96.1	95.8	100.4	101.8	102.3	102.5	99.4
2002	103.0	104.1	104.8	105.5	105.9	106.0	101.2	101.7	105.6	107.0	107.8	107.5	105.0
2003	106.0	106.3	107.2	108.2	108.1	108.0	101.9	101.6	105.6	106.8	107.1	107.2	106.2

Employment by Industry: Virginia—*Continued*

(Numbers in thousands. Not seasonally adjusted.)

Industry	January	February	March	April	May	June	July	August	September	October	November	December	Annual Average
NORTHERN VIRGINIA *—Continued*													
Leisure and hospitality													
1990	66.4	67.2	67.9	68.6	71.3	74.5	74.2	74.4	72.7	70.6	70.6	70.6	70.7
1991	67.5	68.0	68.5	70.3	72.9	75.9	74.8	74.7	73.0	71.0	71.5	71.3	71.6
1992	67.7	67.8	69.4	71.5	75.1	76.5	76.9	76.9	75.0	73.1	73.3	72.8	73.0
1993	71.2	72.1	72.3	74.6	78.2	80.7	80.9	81.1	78.6	75.5	75.2	75.4	76.3
1994	73.8	73.5	75.5	78.8	82.0	85.3	85.3	85.4	83.4	81.0	80.9	81.5	80.5
1995	80.2	80.3	81.7	83.5	86.1	90.0	89.5	89.3	86.3	83.0	82.7	83.1	84.6
1996	79.3	81.0	82.5	83.4	86.2	89.9	91.1	90.1	87.9	83.6	83.7	84.0	85.2
1997	83.1	83.8	86.4	87.8	91.6	94.7	94.4	94.1	91.0	87.0	87.1	87.3	89.0
1998	82.7	84.5	86.3	88.6	91.8	95.2	95.2	94.8	91.8	88.7	89.1	90.0	89.8
1999	86.0	86.9	88.6	91.1	93.7	97.6	97.5	97.6	94.1	92.3	92.6	92.7	92.5
2000	90.6	91.0	94.3	96.9	100.2	104.5	103.8	103.5	100.5	97.8	97.7	97.9	98.2
2001	92.2	93.2	95.8	97.6	101.5	106.4	105.5	105.1	100.3	97.4	96.2	96.5	99.0
2002	93.5	94.4	96.5	99.8	103.1	108.0	108.2	108.2	104.1	100.8	101.0	100.5	101.5
2003	97.0	95.8	98.0	100.9	105.3	109.8	110.5	110.2	106.0	106.0	106.4	106.1	104.3
Other services													
1990	40.8	41.1	41.4	41.5	41.9	42.4	42.5	42.5	42.0	42.2	42.3	42.4	41.9
1991	40.9	40.8	41.2	41.4	41.8	42.3	41.8	41.8	41.4	40.9	41.0	41.2	41.3
1992	40.2	40.3	40.4	40.7	41.1	41.4	41.3	41.2	41.3	41.5	41.3	41.6	41.0
1993	41.3	41.7	42.0	42.0	42.5	43.1	43.0	43.1	42.9	42.7	42.8	43.5	42.5
1994	43.4	43.7	44.1	44.6	44.8	45.7	45.4	45.5	45.3	45.7	45.9	46.4	45.0
1995	46.0	46.4	46.7	46.9	47.1	47.6	47.7	47.9	47.6	48.0	47.9	48.2	47.3
1996	47.9	48.5	49.0	49.0	49.5	50.0	49.7	50.0	50.0	50.2	50.6	51.1	49.6
1997	51.1	51.4	52.4	52.4	52.9	53.6	53.8	53.8	53.8	54.0	54.2	54.7	53.1
1998	54.3	54.7	55.2	55.9	56.3	57.2	57.2	57.5	57.5	57.6	58.0	58.4	56.6
1999	58.4	58.8	59.2	59.6	60.0	60.5	60.6	60.6	60.5	60.7	61.0	61.2	60.0
2000	60.0	60.2	60.6	61.5	61.7	62.2	62.9	62.8	62.7	63.6	63.8	64.0	62.1
2001	53.5	53.8	54.2	54.6	55.4	55.9	56.0	56.1	55.4	55.4	55.5	55.6	55.1
2002	55.7	55.9	56.2	56.2	56.5	56.8	61.2	61.0	62.6	58.9	61.8	61.0	58.7
2003	57.7	58.5	59.7	57.8	58.2	58.7	58.9	58.7	58.1	57.7	58.7	59.3	58.5
Government													
1990	162.9	164.3	164.8	165.3	168.6	168.1	163.6	160.5	164.4	168.1	169.4	170.2	165.8
1991	168.1	169.4	169.8	170.3	171.7	172.2	167.6	163.9	168.4	171.4	172.5	173.5	169.9
1992	172.3	172.8	174.2	173.8	176.3	177.0	171.6	167.7	172.2	174.9	177.3	176.5	173.8
1993	174.0	175.1	175.3	175.2	176.7	177.4	173.5	167.9	173.1	175.9	178.1	177.5	174.9
1994	175.3	175.9	177.0	177.1	178.3	179.9	174.4	171.9	176.6	178.8	180.5	180.0	177.1
1995	177.4	179.2	179.4	177.7	178.9	178.4	172.2	169.3	175.2	177.7	178.3	178.2	176.8
1996	174.6	176.9	177.6	177.5	178.8	179.4	171.9	170.5	175.8	176.1	177.5	176.4	176.0
1997	180.2	180.9	181.5	181.6	181.9	181.5	175.3	173.3	176.8	179.1	180.0	178.3	179.2
1998	176.5	178.2	179.2	179.0	179.5	180.3	175.6	172.5	179.5	180.0	182.9	183.2	178.8
1999	180.0	181.8	182.9	183.6	182.9	184.6	177.6	176.3	184.4	185.4	187.3	187.7	182.8
2000	185.9	186.6	187.9	188.7	190.6	190.7	182.0	180.1	187.7	189.6	191.3	192.1	187.7
2001	189.6	189.4	191.3	192.2	192.6	194.7	187.9	183.8	189.7	192.9	194.7	195.1	191.2
2002	191.8	191.7	194.3	194.2	195.5	197.4	190.4	187.2	194.7	197.8	198.9	199.0	194.4
2003	195.0	196.4	197.3	197.5	199.0	200.6	193.3	191.7	199.6	203.0	204.9	205.0	198.6
Federal government													
1990	75.9	75.8	75.6	75.5	77.0	77.2	77.3	76.2	75.2	75.5	75.6	76.5	76.1
1991	76.7	76.5	76.5	77.5	78.5	79.4	80.2	79.3	78.6	78.9	78.8	79.5	78.3
1992	79.3	79.4	79.9	80.0	81.0	81.8	82.1	81.3	80.3	79.9	79.5	80.1	80.3
1993	79.7	79.3	79.4	79.4	79.9	80.6	81.6	80.8	79.9	79.5	79.6	80.8	80.0
1994	79.8	79.5	79.3	79.1	79.3	80.2	80.9	80.2	79.1	78.9	78.7	79.3	79.5
1995	79.1	78.7	78.6	78.3	78.8	78.7	79.2	78.6	78.2	78.0	77.2	77.9	78.4
1996	76.6	76.6	76.4	76.5	76.7	77.3	77.6	77.2	76.4	75.3	75.4	75.6	76.4
1997	79.9	78.7	78.5	78.4	78.0	78.1	77.9	77.4	75.4	75.0	74.8	75.0	77.2
1998	74.2	73.8	73.8	73.7	74.1	74.5	75.2	75.3	74.6	74.2	74.4	74.7	74.3
1999	74.2	73.7	73.7	73.9	73.6	74.1	74.5	74.7	74.0	74.1	74.1	74.5	74.0
2000	73.9	73.5	73.8	74.5	76.5	75.9	75.1	75.3	73.1	73.2	73.2	73.8	74.3
2001	73.7	72.6	72.8	73.9	74.0	75.1	75.4	72.6	72.2	71.7	71.7	71.9	73.1
2002	71.3	70.9	71.4	71.4	71.9	73.0	73.3	72.7	72.3	72.8	72.7	73.2	72.2
2003	72.4	72.2	72.3	72.6	72.9	73.7	74.4	74.4	74.9	75.4	75.3	75.8	73.9
State government													
1990	12.7	13.2	13.4	13.3	13.8	12.9	12.0	12.1	13.6	13.7	13.8	13.6	13.1
1991	12.9	13.7	13.7	13.7	13.9	13.2	12.3	12.1	13.5	14.1	14.2	14.3	13.4
1992	14.0	14.6	14.8	14.8	14.7	14.1	13.6	13.3	14.3	15.2	15.3	15.5	14.5
1993	14.5	15.4	15.4	15.6	15.6	15.0	13.8	13.5	15.5	15.7	15.9	14.7	15.0
1994	14.8	15.7	15.9	16.1	16.4	15.2	14.6	14.3	15.9	16.3	16.5	15.2	15.5
1995	15.2	16.1	16.2	16.2	16.1	15.0	13.5	13.1	15.2	15.1	15.3	14.1	15.0
1996	13.8	15.0	15.3	15.3	15.0	14.3	13.5	13.0	15.3	15.1	15.3	14.0	14.5
1997	13.8	15.1	15.3	15.5	15.2	14.5	14.2	13.6	15.8	15.5	15.6	13.6	14.8
1998	14.1	15.5	15.6	15.6	14.3	14.3	14.6	14.3	15.9	15.7	15.9	15.4	15.1
1999	14.2	15.7	16.0	16.2	15.2	14.8	14.1	14.1	16.7	16.3	16.7	16.0	15.5
2000	15.2	16.7	17.0	17.0	16.3	15.6	15.1	15.0	17.3	17.2	17.4	17.0	16.4
2001	15.8	16.5	17.3	17.2	16.1	15.8	15.1	15.0	15.4	17.7	17.8	17.3	16.4
2002	16.4	16.1	17.9	17.8	17.0	16.2	15.0	15.1	17.1	18.0	17.8	17.3	16.8
2003	15.5	17.0	17.2	16.7	16.6	16.0	15.1	14.8	16.0	16.9	17.1	17.1	16.3

Employment by Industry: Virginia—*Continued*

(Numbers in thousands. Not seasonally adjusted.)

Industry	January	February	March	April	May	June	July	August	September	October	November	December	Annual Average
NORTHERN VIRGINIA *—Continued*													
Local government													
1990	74.3	75.3	75.8	76.5	77.8	78.0	74.3	72.2	75.6	78.9	80.0	80.1	76.5
1991	78.5	79.2	79.6	79.1	79.3	79.6	75.1	72.5	76.3	78.4	79.5	79.7	78.0
1992	79.0	78.8	79.5	79.0	80.6	81.1	75.9	73.1	77.6	79.8	82.5	80.9	78.9
1993	79.8	80.4	80.5	80.2	81.2	81.8	78.1	73.6	77.7	80.7	82.6	82.0	79.8
1994	80.7	80.7	81.8	81.9	82.6	84.5	78.9	77.4	81.6	83.6	85.3	85.5	82.0
1995	83.1	84.4	84.6	83.2	84.0	84.7	79.5	77.6	81.8	84.6	85.8	86.2	83.2
1996	84.2	85.3	85.9	85.7	87.1	87.8	80.8	80.3	84.1	85.7	86.8	86.8	85.0
1997	86.5	87.1	87.7	87.7	88.7	88.9	83.2	82.3	85.6	88.6	89.6	89.7	87.1
1998	88.2	88.9	89.8	89.7	91.1	91.5	85.8	82.9	89.0	90.1	92.6	93.1	89.3
1999	91.6	92.4	93.2	93.5	94.1	95.7	89.0	87.5	93.7	95.0	96.5	97.2	93.2
2000	96.8	96.4	97.1	97.2	97.8	99.2	91.8	89.8	97.3	99.2	100.7	101.3	97.0
2001	100.1	100.3	101.2	101.1	102.5	103.8	97.4	96.2	102.1	103.5	105.2	105.9	101.6
2002	104.1	104.7	105.0	105.0	106.6	108.2	102.1	99.4	105.3	107.0	108.4	108.5	105.4
2003	107.1	107.2	107.8	108.2	109.5	110.9	103.8	102.5	108.7	110.7	112.5	112.1	108.4
RICHMOND-PETERSBURG													
Total nonfarm													
1990	467.8	470.3	473.5	474.0	476.0	480.4	474.4	475.4	477.7	474.7	476.0	476.1	474.6
1991	462.6	460.6	464.6	464.6	466.5	470.3	461.7	462.4	464.4	462.9	465.5	465.8	464.3
1992	456.1	456.5	457.6	463.0	465.2	468.5	463.4	461.1	465.0	468.2	471.4	472.9	464.0
1993	463.1	465.6	467.4	470.9	474.4	478.8	473.8	473.2	476.5	480.6	482.8	485.3	474.3
1994	474.6	476.8	484.5	489.0	491.4	496.3	493.6	492.9	495.6	497.7	500.5	501.8	491.2
1995	492.8	494.9	499.4	501.2	502.6	507.1	501.6	501.0	503.9	502.7	507.4	510.1	502.0
1996	493.5	498.0	504.1	506.3	507.9	512.3	507.1	507.2	510.5	513.4	518.2	520.1	508.2
1997	512.4	514.8	518.1	522.6	524.4	529.6	523.7	522.9	526.3	531.2	534.4	536.6	524.7
1998	525.0	526.3	530.9	532.5	535.7	539.8	532.6	533.1	538.4	539.4	544.0	547.4	535.4
1999	535.5	539.2	542.5	546.3	547.4	551.0	545.1	544.2	547.9	549.9	556.7	557.3	546.9
2000	547.1	549.3	554.7	557.2	560.2	563.7	555.7	553.5	560.0	561.8	566.0	569.2	558.2
2001	558.6	561.9	565.3	576.4	578.2	581.2	576.4	575.6	575.2	571.9	574.7	576.1	572.6
2002	561.8	566.5	569.8	570.1	572.6	575.2	568.1	567.4	566.4	567.4	570.7	571.4	569.0
2003	558.8	558.6	563.2	565.3	567.9	570.5	562.4	562.4	561.1	565.2	567.1	566.8	564.1
Total private													
1990	371.1	371.3	374.6	375.9	378.2	383.1	380.2	381.6	381.5	377.2	378.3	378.7	377.6
1991	366.2	363.3	367.3	366.7	370.6	374.6	370.2	371.9	370.0	367.3	368.1	369.5	368.8
1992	359.8	359.1	360.6	365.0	368.8	372.3	370.2	370.1	370.6	370.7	371.9	374.5	367.8
1993	365.1	366.2	367.7	371.1	375.6	379.3	377.3	378.5	378.6	379.6	380.2	383.8	375.2
1994	374.5	375.2	382.2	386.5	389.9	394.6	394.2	395.5	397.0	396.9	397.4	400.6	390.3
1995	392.6	393.2	398.1	400.1	403.0	408.1	406.5	407.8	408.3	406.0	408.6	412.3	403.7
1996	397.6	400.8	406.9	407.8	410.8	415.1	412.7	414.4	415.0	416.1	418.4	421.7	411.4
1997	413.9	415.2	419.3	421.7	424.4	428.6	426.9	426.8	427.8	429.7	430.9	433.9	424.9
1998	423.1	423.2	426.9	429.5	433.7	438.6	434.6	436.8	439.2	437.3	439.4	443.5	433.8
1999	432.8	435.2	438.9	442.2	444.3	448.2	445.4	446.8	447.0	446.7	450.6	452.6	444.2
2000	443.7	444.6	449.3	451.8	454.6	458.9	454.8	453.6	457.2	457.1	460.1	463.1	454.0
2001	454.3	455.0	459.1	470.2	472.5	476.0	473.4	473.1	471.8	465.8	466.8	468.3	467.2
2002	455.7	458.5	462.3	461.7	465.0	467.9	463.9	463.7	462.9	460.6	463.0	463.9	462.4
2003	452.7	451.3	456.7	457.5	461.2	464.2	460.1	461.7	459.0	461.0	461.3	461.0	459.0
Goods-producing													
1990	86.5	86.8	87.1	86.4	86.7	87.4	86.8	87.1	86.8	85.7	85.0	84.2	86.3
1991	82.2	81.2	81.6	81.3	81.9	82.7	81.5	81.7	81.6	81.7	81.5	81.2	81.6
1992	80.1	79.8	80.5	80.5	80.6	81.3	80.6	80.5	81.0	80.8	80.9	81.1	80.6
1993	79.7	80.0	80.0	80.1	80.6	80.6	79.9	80.2	80.3	80.3	79.7	79.6	80.0
1994	77.6	77.7	78.7	80.1	80.6	81.2	81.0	81.4	81.6	82.4	82.1	82.5	80.5
1995	80.1	80.3	81.0	82.2	82.3	83.2	82.6	83.2	83.3	83.5	83.9	83.7	82.4
1996	80.1	81.7	82.5	82.6	83.5	84.1	84.8	84.8	85.5	85.1	85.3	85.4	83.7
1997	83.3	83.3	84.1	87.1	87.4	88.3	88.0	87.9	88.2	88.5	88.7	88.5	86.9
1998	86.5	85.8	86.4	86.7	87.2	87.6	87.4	87.8	88.0	88.0	88.0	88.4	87.3
1999	85.9	86.0	86.8	88.0	87.9	88.5	87.7	88.1	88.7	88.6	89.3	89.6	87.9
2000	87.9	88.0	89.0	89.3	89.4	89.8	89.0	89.3	89.9	89.6	89.9	90.6	89.3
2001	88.7	89.0	89.5	90.1	89.9	90.1	89.2	89.0	88.4	87.2	87.2	86.9	88.8
2002	84.2	84.5	85.2	85.5	86.2	86.7	85.8	86.4	86.0	85.9	85.8	85.6	85.7
2003	83.6	83.1	84.2	84.2	84.5	84.2	84.1	84.4	83.8	84.1	83.7	82.2	83.8
Construction and mining													
1990	29.8	30.0	30.5	30.5	30.8	31.1	31.1	31.2	30.7	30.2	29.7	29.0	30.3
1991	26.6	26.0	26.4	27.0	27.2	27.7	27.0	27.0	27.0	27.1	27.0	26.7	26.8
1992	25.2	25.3	25.8	26.0	26.4	27.0	26.4	26.3	26.4	26.5	26.6	26.7	26.2
1993	26.0	26.3	26.5	26.8	27.2	27.5	27.1	27.3	27.3	27.3	26.8	26.7	26.9
1994	25.6	25.6	26.4	27.1	27.5	28.1	28.1	28.3	28.3	28.4	28.4	28.5	27.5
1995	27.6	27.6	28.4	28.8	29.1	29.8	30.0	30.2	30.4	30.5	30.7	30.7	29.4
1996	27.8	29.0	29.8	30.1	30.8	31.3	32.1	31.9	32.3	32.1	32.1	32.3	30.9
1997	31.5	31.6	32.1	32.9	33.4	34.0	34.3	34.3	34.0	34.0	34.0	33.5	33.3
1998	31.6	31.4	31.6	32.7	33.0	33.4	34.0	34.1	34.0	33.8	33.6	33.7	33.0
1999	32.7	32.9	33.6	34.7	34.4	34.5	34.4	34.6	34.6	34.6	35.0	35.2	34.2
2000	33.8	33.9	35.0	36.1	36.3	36.8	36.4	36.7	36.7	36.7	36.8	36.7	35.9
2001	35.4	35.6	36.7	38.3	38.7	38.9	38.9	38.8	38.4	37.6	37.7	37.4	37.7
2002	35.9	36.1	37.1	37.7	38.4	38.5	38.4	38.9	38.6	38.5	38.4	38.1	37.9
2003	36.9	36.7	38.1	38.2	38.8	38.8	39.4	39.7	39.2	39.5	39.4	37.8	38.5

Employment by Industry: Virginia—*Continued*

(Numbers in thousands. Not seasonally adjusted.)

Industry	January	February	March	April	May	June	July	August	September	October	November	December	Annual Average
RICHMOND-PETERSBURG —*Continued*													
Manufacturing													
1990	56.7	56.8	56.6	55.9	55.9	56.3	55.7	55.9	56.1	55.5	55.3	55.2	55.9
1991	55.6	55.2	55.2	54.3	54.7	55.0	54.5	54.7	54.6	54.6	54.5	54.5	54.7
1992	54.9	54.5	54.7	54.5	54.2	54.3	54.2	54.2	54.6	54.3	54.3	54.4	54.4
1993	53.7	53.7	53.5	53.3	53.4	53.1	52.8	52.9	53.0	53.0	52.9	52.9	53.1
1994	52.0	52.1	52.3	53.0	53.1	53.1	52.9	53.1	53.3	54.0	53.7	54.0	53.0
1995	52.5	52.7	52.6	53.4	53.2	53.4	52.6	53.0	52.9	53.0	53.2	53.0	52.9
1996	52.3	52.7	52.7	52.5	52.7	52.8	52.7	52.9	53.2	53.0	53.2	53.1	52.8
1997	51.8	51.7	52.0	54.2	54.0	54.3	53.7	53.6	54.2	54.5	54.7	55.0	53.6
1998	54.9	54.4	54.8	54.0	54.2	54.2	53.4	53.7	54.0	54.2	54.4	54.7	54.2
1999	53.2	53.1	53.2	53.3	53.5	54.0	53.3	53.5	54.1	54.0	54.3	54.4	53.6
2000	54.1	54.1	54.0	53.2	53.1	53.0	52.6	52.6	53.2	52.9	53.1	53.9	53.3
2001	53.3	53.4	52.8	51.8	51.2	51.2	50.3	50.2	50.0	49.6	49.5	49.5	51.1
2002	48.3	48.4	48.1	47.8	47.8	48.2	47.4	47.5	47.4	47.4	47.4	47.5	47.8
2003	46.7	46.4	46.1	46.0	45.7	45.4	44.7	44.7	44.6	44.6	44.3	44.4	45.3
Service-providing													
1990	381.3	383.5	386.4	387.6	389.3	393.0	387.6	388.3	390.9	389.0	391.0	391.9	388.3
1991	380.4	379.4	383.0	383.3	384.6	387.6	380.2	380.7	382.8	381.2	384.0	384.6	382.6
1992	376.0	376.7	377.1	382.5	384.6	387.2	382.8	380.6	384.0	387.4	390.5	391.8	383.4
1993	383.4	385.6	387.4	390.8	393.8	398.2	393.9	393.0	396.2	400.3	403.1	405.7	394.2
1994	397.0	399.1	405.8	408.9	410.8	415.1	412.6	411.5	414.0	415.3	418.4	419.3	410.6
1995	412.7	414.6	418.4	419.0	420.3	423.9	419.0	417.8	420.6	419.2	423.5	426.4	419.6
1996	413.4	416.3	421.6	423.7	424.4	428.2	422.3	422.4	425.0	428.3	432.9	434.7	424.4
1997	429.1	431.5	434.0	435.5	437.0	441.3	435.7	435.0	438.1	442.7	445.7	448.1	437.8
1998	438.5	440.5	444.5	445.8	448.5	452.2	445.2	445.3	450.4	451.4	456.0	459.0	448.1
1999	449.6	453.2	455.7	458.3	459.5	462.5	457.4	456.1	459.2	461.3	467.4	467.7	458.9
2000	459.2	461.3	465.7	467.9	470.8	473.9	466.7	464.2	470.1	472.2	476.1	478.6	468.8
2001	469.9	472.9	475.8	486.3	488.3	491.1	487.2	486.6	486.8	484.7	487.5	489.2	483.9
2002	477.6	482.0	484.6	484.6	486.4	488.5	482.3	481.0	480.4	481.5	484.9	485.8	483.3
2003	475.2	475.5	479.0	481.1	483.4	486.3	478.3	478.0	477.3	481.1	483.4	484.6	480.3
Trade, transportation, and utilities													
1990	92.0	90.0	90.3	89.2	89.7	90.2	89.9	90.8	90.0	90.6	92.7	94.1	90.7
1991	89.5	87.7	87.9	87.9	88.4	88.8	87.6	87.9	87.7	88.2	90.5	91.9	88.6
1992	87.9	86.4	85.2	86.5	87.3	87.6	87.4	87.1	87.4	88.5	90.0	91.6	87.7
1993	88.0	87.4	87.7	87.3	88.4	88.8	89.3	89.8	90.4	92.1	94.4	96.7	90.0
1994	92.4	92.2	93.0	93.8	94.5	95.5	94.6	95.2	95.7	97.4	98.7	100.5	95.2
1995	96.7	95.3	95.6	95.1	95.3	95.7	95.9	95.7	96.4	96.7	99.0	101.1	96.5
1996	96.5	95.0	95.8	95.6	96.3	97.0	97.1	98.0	98.8	99.1	101.6	103.6	97.8
1997	98.8	98.5	99.1	98.1	98.4	99.0	98.7	98.8	99.2	100.2	102.3	104.3	99.6
1998	98.9	98.3	98.2	97.5	98.5	99.1	98.6	99.3	101.0	101.7	104.2	106.2	100.1
1999	100.8	100.0	100.7	101.3	101.8	102.5	101.7	102.3	102.8	105.1	107.8	109.5	103.0
2000	104.3	103.8	104.5	103.6	104.2	104.4	104.1	104.8	105.0	106.1	108.4	110.2	105.2
2001	109.4	108.2	108.5	109.4	109.9	110.0	109.6	109.6	109.3	110.2	112.1	113.1	109.9
2002	108.4	107.1	107.6	107.6	108.0	108.3	107.5	107.8	107.3	108.4	110.2	111.9	108.3
2003	106.5	105.6	105.7	105.8	106.9	107.3	106.9	107.4	107.1	108.5	109.9	110.8	107.4
Wholesale trade													
1990	21.1	21.1	21.2	21.0	21.0	21.1	21.5	21.4	21.3	21.3	21.3	21.3	21.2
1991	20.7	20.7	20.8	20.7	20.7	20.7	20.3	20.2	20.1	20.1	20.0	20.1	20.4
1992	20.0	20.0	19.9	20.2	20.4	20.5	20.6	20.5	20.4	20.7	20.7	20.7	20.3
1993	20.4	20.6	20.6	20.6	20.8	20.8	21.2	21.1	21.0	21.0	20.9	20.9	20.8
1994	21.1	21.1	21.1	21.8	21.9	22.2	22.1	22.2	22.4	22.5	22.5	22.7	21.9
1995	21.8	21.9	21.9	21.7	21.9	22.0	22.4	22.4	22.4	22.3	22.4	22.5	22.1
1996	22.1	22.2	22.3	22.7	22.7	22.8	22.7	22.9	23.0	22.5	22.5	22.6	22.5
1997	22.2	22.3	22.4	22.6	22.5	22.6	22.7	22.6	22.6	22.7	22.7	22.8	22.5
1998	22.7	23.0	23.0	22.4	22.6	22.7	22.6	22.8	23.2	22.9	23.0	23.2	22.8
1999	22.6	22.7	22.6	23.3	23.2	23.3	23.2	23.2	23.2	23.3	23.3	23.4	23.1
2000	22.9	22.9	23.1	23.1	23.1	23.2	23.3	23.4	23.5	23.7	23.8	23.9	23.3
2001	25.9	25.9	26.0	26.5	26.3	26.3	26.1	25.9	25.8	25.9	25.8	25.8	26.0
2002	25.5	25.5	25.7	25.7	25.6	25.6	25.6	25.6	25.5	25.7	25.6	25.7	25.6
2003	25.4	25.5	25.6	25.4	25.7	25.7	25.7	25.8	25.5	25.7	25.7	25.5	25.6
Retail trade													
1990	56.8	54.8	54.8	54.2	54.6	54.7	54.3	55.1	54.4	54.9	57.0	58.2	55.3
1991	55.0	53.3	53.2	53.0	53.4	53.5	52.9	53.0	53.0	53.4	55.4	56.5	53.8
1992	53.1	51.5	50.5	51.0	51.5	51.5	51.3	51.0	51.1	51.9	53.4	54.8	51.8
1993	51.5	50.6	50.7	50.2	51.0	51.1	51.0	51.3	51.8	52.8	55.0	57.2	52.0
1994	53.5	52.9	53.4	53.4	53.8	54.2	53.5	54.0	54.3	55.6	57.3	59.1	54.5
1995	56.8	55.2	55.4	55.1	55.4	55.7	55.1	55.1	55.9	55.9	58.1	60.2	56.1
1996	56.8	55.3	55.9	55.1	55.8	56.4	56.2	56.8	57.6	58.1	60.4	62.4	57.2
1997	58.8	58.3	58.8	58.0	58.3	58.7	58.3	58.5	58.9	59.3	61.6	63.3	59.2
1998	58.7	57.9	57.9	57.6	58.3	58.7	58.2	58.7	59.8	60.7	63.1	64.8	59.5
1999	60.5	59.7	60.3	60.0	60.6	61.2	60.3	60.8	61.3	62.9	65.5	67.3	61.7
2000	63.0	62.5	62.9	62.1	62.8	62.9	62.2	62.8	63.0	63.7	65.8	67.5	63.4
2001	63.6	62.4	62.7	62.7	63.3	63.5	63.5	63.5	63.3	64.3	66.6	67.8	63.9
2002	63.9	62.8	63.2	62.9	63.4	63.6	62.9	63.1	62.8	63.5	65.3	66.9	63.7
2003	62.9	61.9	61.9	62.1	62.9	63.2	62.7	63.2	63.3	64.3	66.0	67.0	63.5

Employment by Industry: Virginia—*Continued*

(Numbers in thousands. Not seasonally adjusted.)

Industry	January	February	March	April	May	June	July	August	September	October	November	December	Annual Average
RICHMOND-PETERSBURG *—Continued*													
Transportation and utilities													
1990	14.1	14.1	14.3	14.0	14.1	14.4	14.1	14.3	14.3	14.4	14.4	14.6	14.2
1991	13.8	13.7	13.9	14.2	14.3	14.6	14.4	14.7	14.6	14.7	15.1	15.3	14.4
1992	14.8	14.9	14.8	15.3	15.4	15.6	15.5	15.6	15.9	15.9	15.9	16.1	15.4
1993	16.1	16.2	16.4	16.5	16.6	16.9	17.1	17.4	17.6	18.3	18.5	18.6	17.1
1994	17.8	18.2	18.5	18.6	18.8	19.1	19.0	19.0	19.0	19.3	18.9	18.7	18.7
1995	18.1	18.2	18.3	18.3	18.0	18.0	18.4	18.2	18.1	18.5	18.5	18.4	18.2
1996	17.6	17.5	17.6	17.8	17.8	17.8	18.2	18.3	18.2	18.5	18.7	18.6	18.0
1997	17.8	17.9	17.9	17.5	17.6	17.7	17.7	17.7	17.7	18.2	18.0	18.2	17.8
1998	17.5	17.4	17.3	17.5	17.6	17.7	17.8	17.8	18.0	18.1	18.1	18.2	17.7
1999	17.7	17.6	17.8	18.0	18.0	18.0	18.2	18.3	18.3	18.9	19.0	18.8	18.2
2000	18.4	18.4	18.5	18.4	18.3	18.3	18.6	18.6	18.5	18.7	18.8	18.8	18.5
2001	19.9	19.9	19.8	20.2	20.3	20.2	20.0	20.2	20.2	20.0	19.7	19.5	20.0
2002	19.0	18.8	18.7	19.0	19.0	19.1	19.0	19.1	19.0	19.2	19.3	19.3	19.0
2003	18.2	18.2	18.2	18.3	18.3	18.4	18.5	18.4	18.3	18.5	18.2	18.3	18.3
Information													
1990	11.4	11.4	11.5	11.3	11.2	11.4	11.7	11.7	11.9	11.7	11.6	11.5	11.5
1991	11.2	11.1	11.1	11.1	11.3	11.4	11.3	11.5	11.3	11.1	11.2	11.1	11.2
1992	10.3	10.1	10.2	10.0	10.1	10.0	9.8	9.8	9.9	9.9	10.0	10.0	10.0
1993	9.3	9.3	9.4	9.3	9.4	9.4	9.3	9.2	9.2	9.3	9.2	9.2	9.2
1994	9.2	9.1	9.2	9.3	9.4	9.5	9.4	9.5	9.5	9.4	9.5	9.6	9.3
1995	9.8	9.9	10.0	9.8	9.8	9.9	9.9	9.9	9.9	9.5	9.6	9.7	9.8
1996	9.7	9.8	9.8	9.6	9.6	9.6	9.7	9.7	9.7	9.7	9.8	9.9	9.7
1997	9.8	9.8	9.9	9.9	9.8	9.9	9.8	9.8	9.8	10.3	10.4	10.5	9.9
1998	9.9	10.0	9.9	10.4	10.5	10.6	10.4	10.4	10.5	10.2	10.3	10.4	10.2
1999	10.7	10.7	10.8	10.8	11.0	11.1	11.0	11.1	11.2	11.1	11.2	11.3	11.0
2000	11.1	11.0	11.2	11.2	11.4	11.6	11.5	9.6	11.8	11.7	11.8	12.0	11.3
2001	12.4	12.3	12.4	12.3	12.3	12.2	12.3	12.3	12.2	12.1	12.1	12.1	12.3
2002	12.3	12.3	12.3	12.2	12.3	12.2	12.0	12.0	11.9	11.5	11.9	11.9	12.1
2003	11.7	11.9	12.0	11.7	11.7	11.8	11.7	11.7	11.5	11.1	11.2	11.1	11.6
Financial activities													
1990	33.3	33.3	33.5	34.6	34.7	35.1	34.9	34.7	34.5	34.5	34.5	34.5	34.3
1991	32.6	32.5	32.6	33.0	33.0	33.4	33.3	33.3	33.1	32.5	32.5	32.6	32.8
1992	32.3	32.4	32.5	32.1	32.4	32.7	32.7	32.8	33.0	32.6	32.5	32.8	32.5
1993	31.2	31.2	31.3	30.6	31.0	31.3	31.4	31.5	31.7	31.7	31.8	32.1	31.4
1994	32.0	32.2	32.7	32.3	32.7	33.2	33.6	33.7	33.8	33.3	33.3	33.3	33.0
1995	32.7	32.8	33.0	33.3	33.6	34.1	34.4	34.6	34.6	34.4	34.8	35.1	33.9
1996	34.9	35.1	35.1	35.4	35.5	35.9	35.1	35.2	35.2	37.0	37.2	37.5	35.7
1997	37.5	37.6	37.6	37.3	37.4	37.6	37.2	37.0	36.8	37.0	36.6	36.6	37.1
1998	35.7	35.7	35.8	35.9	36.3	37.1	36.5	37.0	37.2	37.9	38.1	38.5	36.8
1999	38.4	38.7	39.1	39.4	39.7	40.1	40.1	40.5	40.7	40.5	40.7	40.9	39.9
2000	40.5	40.5	40.6	41.5	41.7	42.1	42.1	42.1	42.4	43.5	43.9	44.6	42.1
2001	43.9	44.2	44.3	45.1	45.2	45.7	45.7	46.0	45.8	44.4	44.6	44.9	45.0
2002	45.8	45.9	46.0	46.0	46.3	46.5	46.4	45.9	45.8	45.8	46.0	46.0	46.0
2003	45.0	45.3	45.4	45.6	45.8	46.1	46.2	46.4	46.1	46.2	46.4	46.5	45.9
Professional and business services													
1990	60.0	60.7	61.3	62.1	62.6	63.1	61.5	61.8	61.7	60.8	60.9	60.6	61.4
1991	59.9	59.5	60.2	59.4	60.3	61.2	61.3	61.9	61.7	60.5	60.1	60.0	60.5
1992	58.5	58.5	59.0	59.6	60.8	61.5	61.5	61.6	61.4	62.1	62.3	62.8	60.8
1993	62.1	62.8	63.0	65.4	65.9	67.2	66.2	66.5	66.8	67.9	67.7	68.1	65.8
1994	67.4	67.7	69.4	69.5	69.8	70.4	70.7	71.0	72.4	72.1	72.1	72.5	70.4
1995	72.3	72.8	73.8	74.2	74.8	76.0	74.7	76.0	76.0	74.8	75.2	76.5	74.7
1996	74.0	75.4	76.9	76.5	76.9	77.6	75.4	76.2	76.3	77.3	77.1	77.2	76.4
1997	77.1	77.6	78.1	77.8	77.9	78.5	78.7	79.1	79.9	80.3	80.5	81.0	78.8
1998	82.7	83.0	84.4	85.4	85.9	86.8	86.2	86.8	87.2	87.1	86.7	87.3	85.7
1999	86.0	87.3	87.8	86.7	86.3	87.2	85.9	86.1	86.1	85.2	85.7	85.0	86.2
2000	85.3	86.1	86.8	88.8	89.3	90.0	88.5	88.2	89.4	88.6	88.7	89.0	88.2
2001	86.3	86.6	87.1	91.0	91.3	92.0	91.0	90.6	89.3	87.6	87.7	88.0	89.0
2002	85.5	86.6	87.2	87.3	87.6	87.6	86.9	86.5	86.5	84.5	85.1	84.8	86.3
2003	83.2	82.5	83.8	82.6	83.1	83.6	82.9	82.9	82.2	81.9	82.2	82.0	82.7
Educational and health services													
1990	39.0	39.3	39.6	39.6	39.7	40.0	39.7	40.0	41.3	41.4	41.8	41.7	40.2
1991	41.1	41.3	41.9	41.4	41.7	41.5	40.8	40.9	41.4	42.1	42.3	42.7	41.5
1992	41.8	42.3	42.5	43.0	43.2	43.3	42.9	42.8	43.5	43.8	44.0	44.1	43.1
1993	43.3	43.6	43.7	43.7	44.0	43.9	43.5	43.6	44.2	43.9	44.1	43.9	43.7
1994	43.1	43.3	43.7	43.8	44.0	43.8	43.8	43.7	44.9	44.6	44.9	45.3	44.0
1995	44.8	45.3	45.4	45.2	45.5	45.4	44.7	44.6	46.6	47.0	47.2	47.3	45.7
1996	46.3	46.7	47.1	47.4	47.3	47.3	46.8	47.0	48.0	47.7	48.1	48.4	47.3
1997	48.7	48.9	49.2	48.8	49.0	48.9	48.4	48.4	49.5	49.4	49.7	50.1	49.0
1998	48.9	49.0	48.9	48.8	49.0	48.5	47.5	47.6	48.8	47.5	47.7	48.1	48.3
1999	48.8	49.2	49.2	49.9	49.9	49.6	48.9	49.1	49.7	50.3	50.7	50.8	49.6
2000	50.4	50.5	50.9	49.4	49.4	49.3	48.8	49.0	49.7	50.2	50.7	50.9	49.9
2001	51.0	51.4	51.5	52.4	52.5	52.4	50.6	50.7	53.9	54.4	54.5	54.5	52.5
2002	54.6	55.1	55.4	55.9	55.4	55.6	54.4	54.6	56.9	57.4	57.8	57.5	55.9
2003	58.0	58.0	58.1	58.4	58.1	57.9	55.5	57.1	58.8	60.2	60.5	61.0	58.5

Employment by Industry: Virginia—*Continued*

(Numbers in thousands. Not seasonally adjusted.)

Industry	January	February	March	April	May	June	July	August	September	October	November	December	Annual Average
RICHMOND-PETERSBURG *—Continued*													
Leisure and hospitality													
1990	30.3	31.1	32.3	33.9	34.8	36.8	36.7	36.5	36.4	33.8	33.0	33.2	34.0
1991	31.5	31.7	33.5	34.2	35.5	37.0	35.9	36.2	34.9	32.8	31.7	31.7	33.8
1992	30.9	31.6	32.7	35.1	36.2	37.6	37.0	37.2	36.1	34.7	33.9	33.7	34.7
1993	33.1	33.4	34.1	36.1	37.6	39.2	38.6	38.5	36.9	35.4	34.2	35.0	36.0
1994	33.8	34.0	36.1	38.0	39.2	41.2	41.0	40.9	39.1	37.6	36.8	36.6	37.8
1995	36.1	36.6	38.9	39.9	41.1	43.0	43.5	42.9	40.7	39.4	38.2	38.2	39.8
1996	36.3	37.0	39.3	40.2	41.1	42.7	42.6	42.3	40.4	39.0	38.0	38.4	39.7
1997	37.4	38.0	39.4	41.0	42.6	44.1	43.9	43.7	42.3	41.4	40.0	40.1	41.1
1998	37.9	38.5	40.1	41.8	42.9	45.0	44.2	43.9	42.8	40.7	40.1	39.9	41.4
1999	37.9	38.7	39.7	41.2	42.7	43.9	44.7	44.5	42.8	40.7	40.0	40.2	41.4
2000	39.2	39.6	40.8	42.5	43.8	46.0	45.2	45.0	43.4	41.7	41.1	40.1	42.3
2001	39.9	40.3	42.6	44.3	45.4	47.4	47.5	47.1	45.2	42.6	41.1	41.1	43.7
2002	39.7	40.6	42.7	43.0	44.7	46.4	46.5	46.1	44.3	42.9	41.9	41.9	43.4
2003	40.7	40.7	43.0	44.7	46.5	48.4	48.1	47.4	45.2	44.6	42.7	42.5	44.5
Other services													
1990	18.6	18.7	19.0	18.8	18.8	19.1	19.0	19.0	18.9	18.7	18.8	18.9	18.8
1991	18.2	18.3	18.5	18.4	18.5	18.6	18.5	18.5	18.3	18.4	18.3	18.3	18.4
1992	18.0	18.0	18.0	18.2	18.2	18.3	18.3	18.3	18.3	18.3	18.3	18.4	18.2
1993	18.4	18.5	18.5	18.6	18.7	18.9	19.1	19.2	19.1	19.0	19.1	19.2	18.8
1994	19.0	19.0	19.4	19.7	19.7	19.8	20.1	20.1	20.0	20.1	20.0	20.3	19.7
1995	20.1	20.2	20.4	20.4	20.6	20.8	20.8	20.9	20.8	20.7	20.7	20.7	20.5
1996	19.8	20.1	20.4	20.5	20.6	20.9	21.2	21.2	21.1	21.2	21.3	21.3	20.8
1997	21.3	21.5	21.9	21.7	21.9	22.3	22.2	22.1	22.1	22.6	22.7	22.8	22.0
1998	22.6	22.9	23.2	23.0	23.4	23.9	23.8	24.0	23.7	24.2	24.3	24.7	23.6
1999	24.3	24.6	24.8	24.9	25.0	25.3	25.4	25.1	25.0	25.2	25.2	25.3	25.0
2000	25.0	25.1	25.5	25.5	25.4	25.7	25.6	25.6	25.6	25.7	25.6	25.7	25.5
2001	22.7	23.0	23.2	25.6	26.0	26.2	27.5	27.8	27.7	27.3	27.5	27.7	26.0
2002	25.2	26.4	25.9	24.2	24.5	24.6	24.4	24.4	24.2	24.2	24.3	24.3	24.7
2003	24.0	24.2	24.5	24.5	24.6	24.9	24.7	24.4	24.3	24.4	24.7	24.9	24.5
Government													
1990	96.7	99.0	98.9	98.1	97.8	97.3	94.2	93.8	96.2	97.5	97.7	97.4	97.0
1991	96.4	97.3	97.3	97.9	95.9	95.7	91.5	90.5	94.4	95.6	97.4	96.3	95.5
1992	96.3	97.4	97.0	98.0	96.4	96.2	93.2	91.0	94.4	97.5	99.5	98.4	96.2
1993	98.0	99.4	99.7	99.8	98.8	99.5	96.5	94.7	97.9	101.0	102.6	101.5	99.1
1994	100.1	101.6	102.3	102.5	101.5	101.7	99.4	97.4	98.6	100.8	103.1	101.2	100.8
1995	100.2	101.7	101.3	101.1	99.6	99.0	95.1	93.2	95.6	96.7	98.8	97.8	98.3
1996	95.9	97.2	97.2	98.5	97.1	97.2	94.4	92.8	95.5	97.3	99.8	98.4	96.7
1997	98.5	99.6	98.8	100.9	100.0	101.0	96.8	96.1	98.5	101.5	103.5	102.7	99.8
1998	101.9	103.1	104.0	103.0	102.0	101.2	98.0	96.3	99.2	102.1	104.6	103.9	101.6
1999	102.7	104.0	103.6	104.1	103.1	102.8	99.7	97.4	100.9	103.2	106.1	104.7	102.6
2000	103.4	104.7	105.4	105.4	105.6	104.8	100.9	99.9	102.8	104.7	105.9	106.1	104.1
2001	104.3	106.9	106.2	106.2	105.7	105.2	103.0	102.5	103.4	106.1	107.9	107.8	105.4
2002	106.1	108.0	107.5	108.4	107.6	107.3	104.2	103.7	103.5	106.8	107.7	107.5	106.5
2003	106.1	107.3	106.5	107.8	106.7	106.3	102.3	100.7	102.1	104.2	105.8	105.8	105.1
Federal government													
1990	17.1	17.2	17.3	16.9	17.5	17.1	16.8	16.7	16.4	16.6	16.5	16.5	16.8
1991	17.0	16.6	16.6	16.3	16.1	16.1	16.2	16.1	16.0	15.7	15.9	16.3	16.2
1992	16.4	16.3	16.2	15.8	15.7	15.7	15.8	15.7	15.5	15.5	15.6	15.8	15.8
1993	16.1	16.0	15.7	15.5	15.3	15.6	15.6	15.4	15.9	15.9	15.9	16.2	15.7
1994	16.4	16.3	16.1	15.9	15.6	15.8	15.6	15.6	15.5	15.4	15.8	16.0	15.8
1995	16.1	16.0	15.7	15.6	15.4	15.5	15.5	15.4	15.4	15.3	15.4	15.6	15.5
1996	15.7	15.7	15.5	15.6	15.4	15.4	15.4	15.4	15.4	15.3	15.5	15.8	15.5
1997	16.5	16.4	16.2	16.4	16.1	16.3	16.3	16.3	16.3	16.1	16.5	17.0	16.3
1998	16.7	16.8	16.8	16.0	16.1	15.8	15.8	15.7	15.6	15.5	15.6	15.8	16.0
1999	15.8	15.6	15.5	15.4	15.3	15.3	15.2	15.2	15.2	15.3	15.5	16.0	15.4
2000	15.9	15.7	15.6	15.6	16.9	16.0	15.8	15.6	15.0	15.2	15.5	15.9	15.7
2001	15.8	15.6	15.6	15.1	15.1	15.1	15.2	15.2	15.1	14.9	15.1	15.3	15.3
2002	15.2	15.1	15.1	15.0	15.0	15.1	15.0	14.8	14.8	14.9	15.0	15.4	15.0
2003	15.3	15.1	15.1	15.0	15.0	14.8	14.9	14.9	14.6	14.9	14.9	15.5	15.0
State government													
1990	41.3	43.0	42.0	42.3	41.6	41.4	41.5	41.4	41.9	42.5	42.6	41.9	41.9
1991	40.5	41.8	41.3	42.7	40.8	40.8	40.3	40.0	41.0	41.6	41.5	40.9	41.1
1992	40.6	41.5	41.1	42.2	40.7	40.4	40.7	40.0	40.5	42.0	42.3	41.9	41.1
1993	41.2	42.6	42.8	43.2	42.5	42.8	42.1	41.9	42.5	43.9	44.2	43.4	42.7
1994	42.5	44.0	44.3	44.7	43.9	43.2	42.8	42.4	42.9	43.5	43.5	43.0	43.3
1995	41.7	42.9	42.5	42.5	41.3	40.3	39.1	38.8	39.7	40.0	40.3	39.8	40.7
1996	38.2	39.7	39.3	39.9	38.8	38.6	37.8	37.2	38.6	38.9	39.4	38.9	38.7
1997	38.6	39.7	38.8	39.6	38.9	38.7	38.4	38.3	39.1	40.2	40.1	40.0	39.2
1998	39.5	40.4	40.9	40.9	39.7	39.3	38.9	38.5	39.8	40.7	41.1	41.5	40.1
1999	40.5	41.7	41.2	41.9	40.9	40.6	40.3	39.6	40.5	41.5	42.0	41.3	41.0
2000	40.3	41.5	41.9	42.1	41.0	40.9	41.0	40.4	41.8	42.0	42.0	42.0	41.4
2001	40.3	42.5	41.6	42.1	41.6	41.0	42.4	42.1	41.8	42.6	42.8	42.8	42.0
2002	41.3	42.6	41.9	42.8	41.9	41.3	42.5	42.0	40.9	41.6	41.5	41.1	41.8
2003	39.7	40.8	40.2	41.3	40.3	40.1	39.6	39.3	40.4	41.1	41.6	41.1	40.5

Employment by Industry: Virginia—*Continued*

(Numbers in thousands. Not seasonally adjusted.)

Industry	January	February	March	April	May	June	July	August	September	October	November	December	Annual Average
RICHMOND-PETERSBURG *—Continued*													
Local government													
1990	38.3	38.8	39.6	38.9	38.7	38.8	35.9	35.7	37.9	38.4	38.6	39.0	38.2
1991	38.9	38.9	39.4	38.9	39.0	38.8	35.0	34.4	37.4	38.3	40.0	39.1	38.1
1992	39.3	39.6	39.7	40.0	40.0	40.1	36.7	35.3	38.4	40.0	41.6	40.7	39.2
1993	40.7	40.8	41.2	41.1	41.0	41.1	38.8	37.4	39.5	41.2	42.5	41.9	40.6
1994	41.2	41.3	41.9	41.9	42.0	42.7	41.0	39.4	40.2	41.9	43.8	42.2	41.6
1995	42.4	42.8	43.1	43.0	42.9	43.2	40.5	39.0	40.5	41.4	43.1	42.4	42.0
1996	42.0	41.8	42.4	43.0	42.9	43.2	41.2	40.2	41.5	43.1	44.9	43.7	42.4
1997	43.4	43.5	43.8	44.9	45.0	46.0	42.1	41.5	43.1	45.2	46.9	45.7	44.2
1998	45.7	45.9	46.3	46.1	46.2	46.1	43.3	42.1	43.8	45.9	47.9	46.6	45.4
1999	46.4	46.7	46.9	46.8	46.9	46.9	44.2	42.6	45.2	46.4	48.6	47.4	46.2
2000	47.2	47.5	47.9	47.7	47.7	47.9	44.1	43.9	46.0	47.5	48.4	48.2	47.0
2001	48.2	48.8	49.0	49.0	49.0	49.1	45.4	45.2	46.5	48.6	50.0	49.7	48.2
2002	49.6	50.3	50.5	50.6	50.7	50.9	46.7	46.9	47.8	50.3	51.2	51.0	49.7
2003	51.1	51.4	51.2	51.5	51.4	51.4	47.8	46.5	47.1	48.2	49.3	49.2	49.7

Average Weekly Hours by Industry: Virginia

(Not seasonally adjusted.)

Industry	January	February	March	April	May	June	July	August	September	October	November	December	Annual Average
STATEWIDE													
Manufacturing													
2001	40.1	39.7	40.0	38.9	40.0	40.7	40.1	39.9	40.7	40.1	40.3	40.8	40.1
2002	40.5	40.4	40.7	40.7	40.8	41.1	40.4	41.1	40.7	40.1	41.2	41.3	40.8
2003	40.3	40.2	41.0	40.0	40.9	41.2	40.0	40.9	40.6	41.1	41.7	41.6	40.8
LYNCHBURG													
Manufacturing													
2001	41.2	41.7	42.2	40.9	39.8	41.7	41.3	39.9	42.6	39.2	43.1	44.4	41.5
2002	41.0	42.4	44.6	42.0	42.0	42.5	40.0	41.9	43.7	41.4	44.0	42.9	42.4
2003	41.8	42.5	44.6	42.4	43.1	43.8	39.9	43.0	42.8	42.4	42.5	42.5	42.6
NORFOLK-VIRGINIA BEACH-NEWPORT NEWS													
Manufacturing													
2001	42.9	43.4	44.2	43.2	43.8	43.7	43.2	43.5	44.2	43.9	44.3	44.4	43.7
2002	44.2	44.4	44.9	43.7	43.6	43.5	43.0	44.0	42.9	43.3	47.1	47.2	44.3
2003	46.6	46.7	46.7	45.2	47.3	48.5	46.9	47.1	47.0	48.2	49.9	46.3	47.2
NORTHERN VIRGINIA													
Manufacturing													
2001	38.6	38.4	39.0	38.7	39.2	39.5	39.1	40.5	38.3	39.6	39.9	38.3	39.1
2002	38.6	39.5	38.3	39.2	38.7	38.6	40.8	41.7	40.1	37.8	40.1	39.0	39.4
2003	39.0	39.0	40.6	39.5	37.3	40.7	38.2	38.3	39.3	39.4	39.5	38.6	39.1
RICHMOND-PETERSBURG													
Manufacturing													
2001	40.7	40.4	40.5	40.2	40.0	40.3	39.7	40.2	41.1	40.4	40.7	40.5	40.4
2002	38.8	38.8	39.4	38.5	39.3	39.3	39.1	36.6	33.8	35.0	35.1	36.0	37.5
2003	35.5	35.6	35.9	35.7	35.4	35.3	34.6	35.4	34.9	35.2	35.1	34.4	35.2

Average Hourly Earnings by Industry: Virginia

(Dollars, not seasonally adjusted.)

Industry	January	February	March	April	May	June	July	August	September	October	November	December	Annual Average
STATEWIDE													
Manufacturing													
2001	14.24	14.36	14.39	14.40	14.37	14.46	14.39	14.47	14.60	14.48	14.81	14.93	14.49
2002	14.99	14.88	14.93	14.97	15.21	15.09	15.17	15.37	15.47	15.49	15.57	15.81	15.25
2003	15.62	15.47	15.77	15.78	15.77	16.05	15.79	15.76	16.00	15.94	16.26	16.29	15.88
LYNCHBURG													
Manufacturing													
2001	14.84	14.67	14.71	15.39	14.81	14.52	14.72	14.67	14.63	14.74	14.63	14.40	14.73
2002	14.52	14.45	14.35	14.62	14.32	14.20	14.49	14.14	14.51	14.60	14.57	14.60	14.45
2003	14.56	14.44	14.12	14.34	14.19	14.36	14.32	14.39	14.29	14.52	14.52	14.43	14.37
NORFOLK-VIRGINIA BEACH-NEWPORT NEWS													
Manufacturing													
2001	17.52	17.62	17.71	17.37	17.59	17.58	17.52	17.66	17.74	17.68	17.73	17.82	17.63
2002	17.90	17.98	18.01	17.87	17.91	17.89	17.60	18.10	17.97	18.13	18.08	18.24	17.98
2003	18.35	18.13	18.50	18.19	18.30	18.16	17.73	17.87	18.16	18.26	18.86	18.71	18.27
NORTHERN VIRGINIA													
Manufacturing													
2001	15.21	15.00	15.17	15.12	15.44	15.29	15.02	15.66	15.49	15.41	15.58	15.66	15.33
2002	15.40	15.70	15.61	15.15	15.19	15.50	14.93	14.93	15.17	14.94	15.64	16.15	15.36
2003	16.27	16.27	16.36	16.30	15.75	15.13	15.34	15.34	15.34	15.78	15.83	15.51	15.78
RICHMOND-PETERSBURG													
Manufacturing													
2001	15.34	15.51	15.54	15.86	15.69	15.60	15.52	15.65	15.62	15.68	15.78	15.89	15.64
2002	15.78	15.61	15.38	15.43	15.63	15.48	15.64	15.45	15.72	15.40	16.49	16.50	15.69
2003	16.40	16.63	16.60	16.40	16.70	16.46	16.58	16.57	16.56	16.64	16.34	16.76	16.55

Average Weekly Earnings by Industry: Virginia

(Dollars, not seasonally adjusted.)

Industry	January	February	March	April	May	June	July	August	September	October	November	December	Annual Average
STATEWIDE													
Manufacturing													
2001	571.02	570.09	575.60	560.16	574.80	588.52	577.04	577.35	594.22	580.65	596.84	609.14	581.05
2002	607.10	601.15	607.65	609.28	620.57	620.20	612.87	631.71	629.63	621.15	641.48	652.95	622.20
2003	629.49	621.89	646.57	631.20	644.99	661.26	631.60	644.58	649.60	655.13	678.04	677.66	647.90
LYNCHBURG													
Manufacturing													
2001	611.41	611.74	620.76	629.45	589.44	605.48	607.94	585.33	623.24	577.81	630.55	639.36	611.30
2002	595.32	612.68	640.01	614.04	601.44	603.50	579.60	592.47	634.09	604.44	641.08	626.34	612.68
2003	608.61	613.70	629.75	608.02	611.59	628.97	571.37	618.77	611.61	615.65	617.10	613.28	612.16
NORFOLK-VIRGINIA BEACH-NEWPORT NEWS													
Manufacturing													
2001	751.61	764.71	782.78	750.38	770.44	768.25	756.86	768.21	784.11	776.15	785.44	791.21	770.43
2002	791.18	798.31	808.65	780.92	780.88	778.22	756.80	796.40	770.91	785.03	851.57	860.93	796.51
2003	855.11	846.67	863.95	822.19	865.59	880.76	831.54	841.68	853.52	880.13	941.11	866.27	862.34
NORTHERN VIRGINIA													
Manufacturing													
2001	587.11	576.00	591.63	585.14	605.25	603.96	587.28	634.23	593.27	610.24	621.64	599.78	599.40
2002	594.44	620.15	597.86	593.88	587.85	598.30	609.14	622.58	608.32	564.73	627.16	629.85	605.18
2003	634.53	634.53	664.22	643.85	587.48	615.79	585.99	587.52	602.86	621.73	625.29	598.69	617.00
RICHMOND-PETERSBURG													
Manufacturing													
2001	624.34	626.60	629.37	637.57	627.60	628.68	616.14	629.13	641.98	633.47	642.25	643.55	631.86
2002	612.26	605.67	605.97	594.06	614.26	608.36	611.52	565.47	531.34	539.00	578.80	594.00	588.38
2003	582.20	592.03	595.94	585.48	591.18	581.04	573.67	586.58	577.94	585.73	573.53	576.54	582.56

WASHINGTON AT A GLANCE

(Population and total nonfarm employment numbers in thousands)

Population, Census 2000:	5,894.1
Total nonfarm employment, 2003:	2,659.4
Change in total nonfarm employment	
(Number)	
1990–2003:	516.4
1990–2001:	554.0
2001–2003:	-37.6
(Compound annual rate of change)	
1990–2003:	1.7%
1990–2001:	2.1%
2001–2003:	-0.7%
Unemployment rate	
1990:	5.1%
2001:	6.2%
2003:	7.4%

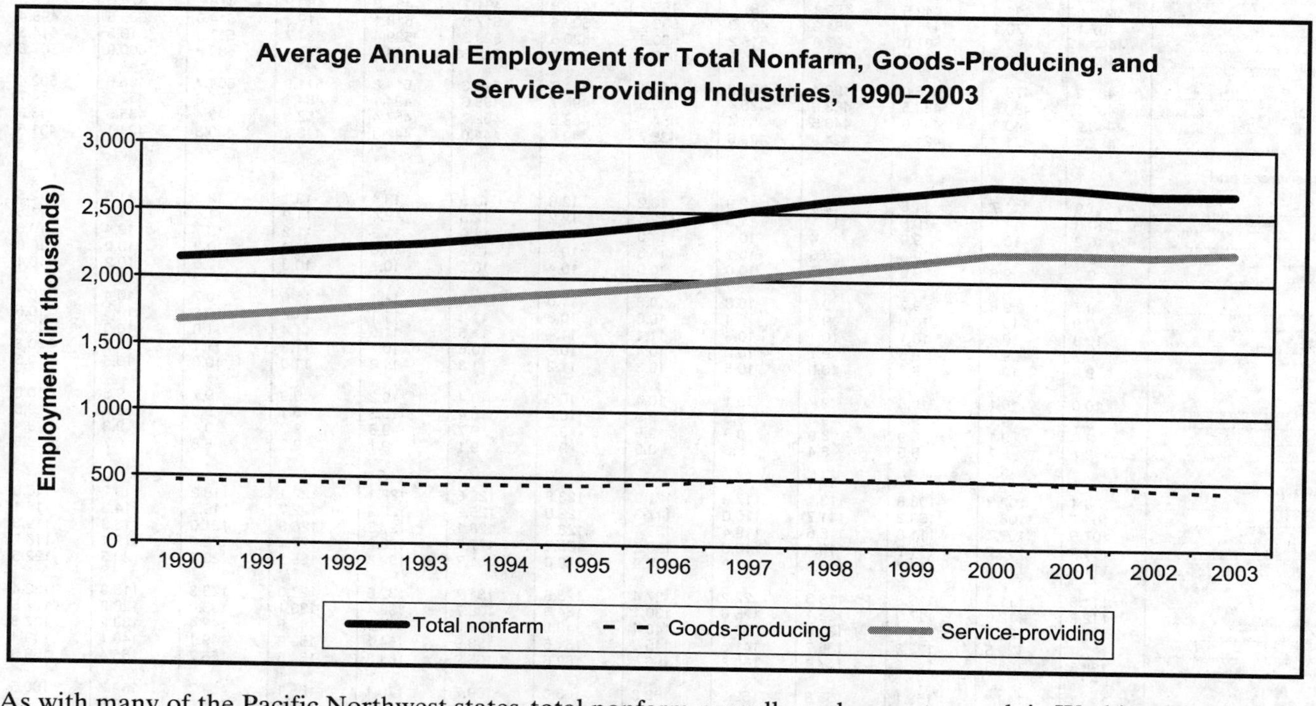

As with many of the Pacific Northwest states, total nonfarm payroll employment growth in Washington was steady throughout the 1990s and began to decline in 2001. Goods-producing industries accounted for most of the job losses. Employment in this sector peaked in 1998, but by 2003 had dropped over 16 percent. In the service-providing sector, employment rose steadily until 2000, when employment leveled off. However, it showed some signs of recovery in 2003, when over 22,000 jobs were added.

Employment by Industry: Washington

(Numbers in thousands. Not seasonally adjusted.)

Industry	January	February	March	April	May	June	July	August	September	October	November	December	Annual Average
STATEWIDE													
Total nonfarm													
1990	2065.6	2076.5	2100.6	2122.7	2149.8	2177.4	2152.2	2167.3	2190.2	2169.9	2177.8	2166.3	2143.0
1991	2108.7	2117.5	2139.3	2155.0	2184.8	2198.4	2182.9	2187.9	2219.4	2212.9	2215.9	2205.6	2177.3
1992	2155.1	2167.6	2188.3	2205.6	2229.4	2246.8	2224.0	2228.0	2260.5	2256.2	2256.9	2250.4	2222.4
1993	2178.6	2194.5	2214.8	2236.7	2260.1	2282.9	2255.4	2251.4	2289.9	2288.0	2294.3	2289.1	2252.9
1994	2227.9	2242.3	2256.6	2280.8	2303.1	2328.6	2301.3	2313.0	2352.5	2341.7	2356.0	2347.7	2304.2
1995	2282.7	2296.9	2320.7	2332.3	2354.2	2385.4	2340.4	2352.3	2389.8	2358.9	2369.0	2380.7	2346.9
1996	2324.6	2337.8	2365.9	2383.4	2412.5	2435.0	2418.5	2429.3	2457.8	2466.6	2479.1	2476.6	2415.5
1997	2414.2	2433.6	2459.2	2481.4	2514.7	2545.5	2524.5	2526.3	2554.0	2562.9	2575.0	2579.1	2514.2
1998	2507.5	2528.6	2548.1	2570.2	2600.1	2623.7	2605.8	2603.1	2629.9	2635.0	2644.0	2642.9	2594.9
1999	2572.8	2585.5	2611.8	2621.6	2641.3	2665.5	2658.7	2658.1	2679.6	2690.9	2698.3	2700.1	2648.6
2000	2638.8	2645.3	2688.2	2687.0	2721.2	2744.6	2709.3	2721.1	2739.6	2741.7	2749.6	2749.0	2711.2
2001	2670.9	2677.0	2694.5	2699.1	2718.3	2736.6	2700.7	2697.1	2705.5	2697.8	2691.5	2674.9	2697.0
2002	2606.2	2611.2	2623.0	2637.6	2663.7	2679.4	2661.3	2660.3	2674.8	2678.5	2683.4	2669.4	2654.1
2003	2609.0	2618.0	2624.3	2638.3	2663.5	2679.7	2663.1	2664.4	2680.6	2692.8	2692.9	2686.4	2659.4
Total private													
1990	1676.5	1676.4	1702.9	1722.2	1745.1	1772.2	1771.6	1792.4	1797.2	1765.8	1764.2	1758.8	1745.4
1991	1705.2	1708.0	1726.4	1739.7	1764.2	1779.1	1787.4	1802.7	1810.2	1792.7	1788.3	1785.5	1765.7
1992	1736.9	1740.8	1757.9	1778.4	1796.2	1817.1	1824.1	1833.2	1840.8	1825.3	1817.6	1817.3	1798.8
1993	1750.7	1762.7	1778.2	1801.4	1822.8	1844.9	1847.0	1852.4	1864.6	1852.3	1846.8	1851.9	1822.9
1994	1795.2	1800.6	1816.7	1840.0	1858.6	1882.4	1888.1	1906.4	1920.0	1895.1	1900.2	1901.5	1867.0
1995	1840.8	1847.5	1867.2	1881.3	1899.2	1929.4	1918.4	1939.9	1954.7	1911.0	1911.2	1929.7	1902.5
1996	1878.4	1883.5	1907.2	1927.3	1952.1	1976.3	1986.8	2010.6	2015.3	2011.4	2013.8	2017.4	1965.0
1997	1960.3	1975.0	1997.0	2018.0	2048.7	2075.1	2082.7	2098.3	2104.9	2100.5	2103.0	2111.2	2056.2
1998	2044.2	2058.1	2077.4	2098.8	2126.7	2147.9	2157.1	2169.1	2173.5	2164.3	2163.3	2167.6	2129.0
1999	2101.7	2109.7	2130.4	2142.3	2160.3	2182.0	2202.0	2212.0	2214.4	2210.6	2209.9	2217.4	2174.3
2000	2159.5	2158.1	2198.6	2198.9	2221.6	2249.7	2245.5	2266.0	2268.7	2255.1	2255.9	2258.0	2227.9
2001	2170.6	2170.9	2183.8	2188.3	2204.4	2221.0	2212.9	2222.2	2211.9	2185.0	2169.9	2158.0	2191.6
2002	2093.9	2092.1	2102.0	2115.9	2139.2	2154.7	2163.1	2175.3	2170.7	2154.9	2150.5	2142.8	2137.9
2003	2088.3	2091.7	2097.0	2111.0	2130.7	2149.3	2162.2	2175.2	2174.0	2164.5	2156.6	2156.1	2138.1
Goods-producing													
1990	446.7	444.9	453.7	459.9	466.7	473.8	476.8	484.6	484.4	472.1	465.6	456.1	465.4
1991	439.0	440.9	444.3	448.3	455.6	459.6	465.3	472.1	473.2	467.6	459.5	451.3	456.3
1992	437.9	437.3	442.5	450.6	456.8	462.0	467.7	469.3	468.3	464.6	455.8	448.3	455.0
1993	428.5	431.2	434.0	438.7	444.0	449.4	441.3	444.9	446.6	455.8	447.1	440.1	441.8
1994	426.9	425.8	429.8	437.9	442.9	449.5	451.8	459.2	463.0	455.0	448.6	441.8	444.3
1995	432.4	433.4	438.8	444.0	447.8	456.3	454.5	459.0	463.2	432.7	427.6	441.7	444.2
1996	432.9	433.9	442.5	450.1	457.1	465.2	471.8	481.7	484.5	483.2	478.6	474.6	463.0
1997	467.1	470.1	476.1	484.3	493.3	503.2	509.6	517.2	518.1	519.3	514.0	509.5	498.4
1998	492.4	496.2	501.0	507.8	515.2	520.8	526.8	529.3	529.4	524.7	517.8	510.5	514.3
1999	493.9	493.4	496.8	503.4	506.6	513.6	518.1	522.3	519.7	517.1	508.3	500.9	507.8
2000	489.2	476.7	496.0	498.4	503.2	510.1	511.7	516.3	514.8	511.9	504.7	496.6	502.4
2001	483.6	480.5	483.5	483.9	488.4	493.6	494.7	498.3	494.1	484.1	471.6	459.7	484.7
2002	443.7	440.2	440.6	443.5	450.4	454.1	458.8	462.7	457.4	452.3	443.4	435.5	448.6
2003	422.4	421.7	421.3	424.9	429.8	435.7	440.6	444.0	442.3	440.3	430.8	424.1	431.5
Natural resources and mining													
1990	11.9	11.7	11.6	12.3	12.9	13.2	12.6	13.5	13.4	13.1	12.6	11.8	12.5
1991	10.8	11.0	10.8	11.1	11.8	12.1	12.2	12.3	12.4	11.9	11.6	11.2	11.6
1992	10.2	10.2	9.9	10.4	10.8	11.0	11.2	11.0	11.3	11.2	10.7	10.4	10.6
1993	9.0	9.4	9.5	9.6	10.1	10.5	10.8	10.5	10.8	10.6	10.3	10.0	10.0
1994	9.3	9.6	9.6	9.8	10.0	10.3	10.4	10.2	10.7	10.6	10.5	10.2	10.1
1995	9.7	9.8	9.7	9.9	10.3	10.8	11.0	10.8	11.1	11.0	10.7	10.4	10.4
1996	9.9	10.0	10.0	9.9	10.4	10.6	10.8	11.2	11.1	11.2	10.8	10.6	10.5
1997	10.3	10.4	10.1	10.1	10.6	11.1	11.4	11.5	11.6	11.4	11.0	10.5	10.8
1998	9.7	9.6	9.5	9.7	10.2	10.4	10.5	10.6	10.7	11.3	11.1	10.7	10.3
1999	9.9	10.0	9.9	10.0	10.5	10.8	11.2	11.3	11.3	11.0	10.6	10.5	10.5
2000	10.0	10.1	9.8	9.7	10.1	10.4	10.3	10.4	10.2	9.9	9.7	9.5	10.0
2001	9.9	9.7	9.2	9.0	9.5	9.9	10.4	10.4	10.3	10.1	9.8	9.4	9.8
2002	9.0	9.1	8.9	8.9	9.3	9.5	9.7	9.7	9.8	9.7	9.4	9.3	9.4
2003	8.7	8.7	8.5	8.4	8.6	8.9	9.1	9.1	9.1	9.2	8.8	8.7	8.8
Construction													
1990	103.4	102.3	108.8	113.4	117.8	121.9	123.8	128.8	128.1	122.1	118.2	113.2	116.8
1991	104.7	106.5	109.2	111.7	116.0	117.3	122.0	125.2	125.2	122.7	118.5	114.2	116.1
1992	107.5	107.7	111.8	115.6	119.4	123.4	126.8	128.1	127.3	126.3	121.0	116.9	119.3
1993	104.9	108.7	111.2	113.4	116.0	120.2	125.2	127.9	128.2	127.3	122.5	119.1	118.7
1994	111.6	111.0	114.7	118.9	122.2	126.0	129.0	131.7	132.8	128.9	123.8	120.3	122.5
1995	111.5	111.9	116.6	118.3	122.2	127.4	128.5	131.7	132.6	127.0	123.3	118.9	122.4
1996	112.8	112.6	117.9	122.1	125.6	130.1	134.6	138.7	138.4	136.1	133.0	128.2	127.5
1997	123.8	124.7	126.9	131.8	136.2	140.4	143.3	147.0	146.1	145.9	142.4	139.2	137.3
1998	127.4	129.5	132.8	136.7	141.8	145.3	151.5	153.9	154.1	153.2	149.1	146.1	143.4
1999	138.5	138.8	142.6	147.5	150.8	156.8	162.6	165.2	164.5	164.6	158.7	155.4	153.8
2000	146.7	149.2	153.1	155.8	159.3	163.8	166.6	169.7	170.1	168.1	164.7	159.7	160.5
2001	152.0	150.9	155.4	155.5	159.4	163.3	165.4	168.6	166.5	162.5	155.6	149.8	158.7
2002	143.2	143.5	144.6	148.4	153.6	156.6	161.3	166.0	163.9	161.2	156.5	151.6	154.2
2003	144.9	145.2	145.8	149.3	154.2	158.2	163.2	166.9	165.4	165.2	160.2	155.2	156.1

Employment by Industry: Washington—*Continued*

(Numbers in thousands. Not seasonally adjusted.)

Industry	January	February	March	April	May	June	July	August	September	October	November	December	Annual Average
STATEWIDE—*Continued*													
Manufacturing													
1990	331.4	330.9	333.3	334.2	336.0	338.7	340.4	342.3	342.9	336.9	334.8	331.1	336.0
1991	323.5	323.4	324.3	325.5	327.8	330.2	331.1	334.6	335.6	333.0	329.4	325.9	328.6
1992	320.2	319.4	320.8	324.6	326.6	327.6	329.7	330.2	329.7	327.1	324.1	321.0	325.0
1993	314.6	313.1	313.3	315.7	317.9	318.7	305.3	306.5	307.6	317.9	314.3	311.0	312.9
1994	306.0	305.2	305.5	309.2	310.7	313.2	312.4	317.3	319.5	315.5	314.3	311.3	311.6
1995	311.2	311.7	312.5	315.8	315.3	318.1	315.0	316.5	319.5	294.7	293.6	312.4	311.3
1996	310.2	311.3	314.6	318.1	321.1	324.5	326.4	331.8	335.0	335.9	334.8	335.8	324.9
1997	333.0	335.0	339.1	342.4	346.5	351.7	354.9	358.7	360.4	362.0	360.6	359.8	350.3
1998	355.3	357.1	358.7	361.4	363.2	365.1	364.8	364.8	364.6	360.2	357.6	353.7	360.5
1999	345.5	344.6	344.3	345.9	345.3	346.0	344.3	345.8	343.9	341.5	339.0	335.0	343.4
2000	332.5	317.4	333.1	332.9	333.8	335.9	334.8	336.2	334.5	333.9	330.3	327.4	331.8
2001	321.7	319.9	318.9	319.4	319.5	320.4	318.9	319.3	317.3	311.5	306.2	300.5	316.1
2002	291.5	287.6	287.1	286.2	287.5	288.0	287.8	287.0	283.7	281.4	277.5	274.6	285.0
2003	268.8	267.8	267.0	267.2	267.0	268.6	268.3	268.0	267.8	265.9	261.8	260.2	266.5
Service-providing													
1990	1618.9	1631.6	1646.9	1662.8	1683.1	1703.6	1675.4	1682.7	1705.8	1697.8	1712.2	1710.2	1677.5
1991	1669.7	1676.6	1695.0	1706.7	1729.2	1738.8	1717.6	1715.8	1746.2	1745.3	1756.4	1754.3	1720.9
1992	1717.2	1730.3	1745.8	1755.0	1772.6	1784.8	1756.3	1758.7	1792.2	1791.6	1801.1	1802.1	1767.3
1993	1750.1	1763.3	1780.8	1798.0	1816.1	1833.5	1814.1	1806.5	1843.3	1832.2	1847.2	1849.0	1811.1
1994	1801.0	1816.5	1826.8	1842.9	1860.2	1879.1	1849.5	1853.8	1889.5	1886.7	1907.4	1905.9	1859.9
1995	1850.3	1863.5	1881.9	1888.3	1906.4	1929.1	1885.9	1893.3	1926.6	1926.2	1941.4	1939.0	1902.6
1996	1891.7	1903.9	1923.4	1933.3	1955.4	1969.8	1946.7	1947.6	1973.3	1983.4	2000.5	2002.0	1952.5
1997	1947.1	1963.5	1983.1	1997.1	2021.4	2042.3	2014.9	2009.1	2035.9	2043.6	2061.0	2069.6	2015.7
1998	2015.1	2032.4	2047.1	2062.4	2084.9	2102.9	2079.0	2073.8	2100.5	2110.3	2126.2	2132.4	2080.5
1999	2078.9	2092.1	2115.0	2118.2	2134.7	2151.9	2140.6	2135.8	2159.9	2173.8	2190.0	2199.2	2140.8
2000	2149.6	2168.6	2192.2	2188.6	2218.0	2234.5	2197.6	2204.8	2224.8	2229.8	2244.9	2252.4	2208.8
2001	2187.3	2196.5	2211.0	2215.2	2229.9	2243.0	2206.0	2198.8	2211.4	2213.7	2219.9	2215.2	2212.3
2002	2162.5	2171.0	2182.4	2194.1	2213.3	2225.3	2202.5	2197.6	2217.4	2226.2	2240.0	2233.9	2205.5
2003	2186.6	2196.3	2203.0	2213.4	2233.7	2244.0	2222.5	2220.4	2238.3	2252.5	2262.1	2262.3	2227.9
Trade, transportation, and utilities													
1990	419.2	415.1	421.0	424.4	430.8	438.9	436.4	440.0	441.8	436.9	444.7	448.9	433.1
1991	428.4	422.1	425.4	427.6	433.8	438.3	438.4	440.6	443.0	439.4	446.5	450.2	436.1
1992	428.7	426.9	429.6	433.5	438.0	444.3	442.6	445.7	448.0	445.7	451.0	455.9	440.8
1993	432.0	431.4	432.5	436.7	442.1	448.4	453.9	452.8	457.2	449.8	455.5	463.2	446.2
1994	438.1	436.6	439.1	442.3	447.4	456.0	455.1	459.8	463.8	462.4	472.6	479.0	454.3
1995	455.8	451.7	453.8	457.0	460.7	470.8	469.3	474.1	477.2	477.9	485.0	488.5	468.4
1996	467.3	463.0	465.6	467.5	471.9	478.1	482.8	486.4	487.2	490.8	498.5	503.6	480.2
1997	468.7	469.5	474.2	481.7	488.4	496.0	495.7	494.5	498.4	500.6	508.3	514.2	490.8
1998	488.7	486.8	489.1	495.4	500.1	505.9	508.7	509.7	512.3	517.1	525.5	532.5	505.9
1999	505.1	502.8	504.9	506.9	511.0	515.8	522.4	522.5	525.6	529.8	537.6	544.8	519.1
2000	520.6	518.8	523.6	522.5	527.1	533.5	530.2	533.0	533.3	539.2	548.2	552.5	531.8
2001	523.5	518.3	520.9	520.4	522.0	527.2	526.3	526.0	523.5	522.2	526.1	527.8	523.7
2002	505.1	498.9	500.1	501.3	505.7	509.9	512.5	512.0	512.8	512.6	518.3	522.2	509.3
2003	502.2	498.0	498.3	500.1	504.6	509.8	513.9	514.8	515.2	516.2	523.3	528.9	510.4
Wholesale trade													
1990	97.2	97.6	99.1	99.8	100.8	104.2	103.5	103.2	103.7	103.1	102.5	101.7	101.3
1991	99.7	99.9	100.8	101.7	102.3	103.3	103.1	103.4	103.9	103.0	102.8	102.0	102.1
1992	98.8	99.4	101.3	101.5	102.6	105.2	104.2	104.6	104.2	104.7	103.7	102.9	102.7
1993	100.7	101.3	101.9	103.1	104.2	105.2	107.0	106.5	107.6	106.6	106.2	105.7	104.6
1994	101.3	102.4	103.7	104.4	104.8	107.9	106.2	106.9	107.7	107.2	107.2	107.8	105.6
1995	105.6	106.3	106.7	107.9	108.8	112.4	110.6	110.7	111.8	111.0	109.8	109.3	109.2
1996	107.4	108.0	109.1	110.8	111.4	113.1	114.0	113.9	114.6	115.1	114.2	113.8	112.1
1997	110.8	111.9	112.9	113.1	114.7	117.5	117.5	117.6	117.8	118.5	118.0	117.0	115.6
1998	112.8	113.4	114.5	115.9	116.8	118.0	118.1	118.7	118.0	119.7	119.2	118.1	116.9
1999	117.4	117.4	117.9	118.5	119.2	119.6	120.8	120.9	121.2	120.5	119.6	119.0	119.3
2000	118.0	118.8	120.2	120.0	120.6	123.3	121.7	122.4	122.0	123.2	122.6	122.1	121.2
2001	119.3	119.4	120.1	120.1	120.6	122.0	121.5	120.7	119.6	119.0	118.1	116.4	119.7
2002	114.8	115.0	115.3	115.0	115.8	116.3	116.4	116.5	116.4	116.2	115.6	114.5	115.7
2003	113.6	113.8	114.3	115.0	115.3	116.2	117.0	117.1	117.1	116.9	116.3	115.7	115.7
Retail trade													
1990	240.5	236.6	239.7	242.4	245.8	249.2	248.0	250.4	250.9	248.9	258.4	262.6	247.7
1991	245.0	239.9	241.5	243.2	247.4	249.9	248.7	251.1	251.0	249.8	257.4	261.8	248.8
1992	247.3	244.8	245.4	248.6	251.4	254.0	252.5	255.6	256.8	255.4	262.8	267.5	253.5
1993	248.7	246.7	247.2	250.0	253.6	257.7	260.7	260.7	262.4	259.5	267.6	273.4	257.3
1994	254.6	252.1	252.5	254.6	258.3	262.0	263.1	266.6	268.0	266.6	276.9	283.0	263.1
1995	265.2	260.5	261.8	263.5	266.2	271.3	270.3	274.8	275.3	276.1	285.1	289.3	271.6
1996	273.1	267.9	269.3	271.3	274.5	277.4	278.2	281.5	281.3	281.6	291.4	296.8	278.6
1997	269.1	268.4	271.9	278.4	282.9	286.3	287.3	288.2	287.6	292.1	301.3	308.0	285.1
1998	286.2	283.5	284.6	287.3	290.4	294.4	296.4	295.8	297.7	301.3	310.6	318.4	295.5
1999	296.7	293.8	294.9	295.8	299.1	302.8	306.5	306.9	307.9	311.1	320.9	329.0	305.4
2000	310.0	307.1	309.5	308.9	312.9	315.4	312.6	314.4	314.8	316.7	327.3	332.9	315.2
2001	312.3	307.4	308.9	307.9	308.7	311.1	311.6	312.4	310.9	309.6	317.1	321.2	311.6
2002	303.2	297.2	298.3	299.3	302.1	304.8	306.6	306.3	306.4	306.1	314.1	319.5	305.3
2003	301.7	297.8	298.0	299.1	302.7	305.9	308.6	309.3	308.4	309.5	317.7	323.1	306.8

Employment by Industry: Washington—*Continued*

(Numbers in thousands. Not seasonally adjusted.)

Industry	January	February	March	April	May	June	July	August	September	October	November	December	Annual Average
STATEWIDE—*Continued*													
Transportation and utilities													
1990	81.5	80.9	82.2	82.2	84.2	85.5	84.9	86.4	87.2	84.9	83.8	84.6	84.0
1991	83.7	82.3	83.1	82.7	84.1	85.1	86.6	86.1	88.1	86.6	86.3	86.4	85.0
1992	82.6	82.7	82.9	83.4	84.0	85.1	85.9	85.5	87.0	85.6	84.5	85.5	84.5
1993	82.6	83.4	83.4	83.6	84.3	85.5	86.2	85.6	87.2	83.7	81.7	84.1	84.2
1994	82.2	82.1	82.9	83.3	84.3	86.1	85.8	86.3	88.1	88.6	88.5	88.2	85.5
1995	85.0	84.9	85.3	85.6	85.7	87.1	88.4	88.6	90.1	90.8	90.1	89.9	87.6
1996	86.8	87.1	87.2	85.4	86.0	87.6	90.6	91.0	91.3	94.1	92.9	93.0	89.4
1997	88.8	89.2	89.4	90.2	90.8	92.2	90.9	88.7	93.0	90.0	89.0	89.2	90.1
1998	89.7	89.9	90.0	92.2	92.9	93.5	94.2	95.2	96.6	96.1	95.7	96.0	93.5
1999	91.0	91.6	92.1	92.6	92.7	93.4	95.1	94.7	96.5	98.2	97.1	96.8	94.3
2000	92.6	92.9	93.9	93.6	93.6	94.8	95.9	96.2	96.5	99.3	98.3	97.5	95.4
2001	91.9	91.5	91.9	92.4	92.7	94.1	93.2	92.9	93.0	93.6	90.9	90.2	92.4
2002	87.1	86.7	86.5	87.0	87.8	88.8	89.5	89.2	90.0	90.3	88.6	88.2	88.3
2003	86.9	86.4	86.0	86.0	86.6	87.7	88.3	88.4	89.7	89.8	89.3	90.1	87.9
Information													
1990	48.7	49.0	48.7	48.8	49.2	50.0	50.1	50.9	50.6	49.5	49.5	49.7	49.5
1991	48.8	49.3	49.7	49.7	50.3	50.7	51.5	51.9	51.7	51.3	51.9	52.4	50.7
1992	51.6	51.8	52.1	52.4	52.4	53.0	54.0	53.9	53.6	53.6	53.7	53.8	52.9
1993	53.9	54.1	54.6	54.9	55.6	56.3	57.3	57.7	57.3	56.4	56.5	57.1	55.9
1994	56.7	57.1	57.4	57.7	58.2	58.6	58.8	59.2	59.3	60.6	61.1	61.6	58.8
1995	60.7	61.4	62.0	62.7	63.3	64.5	64.8	65.0	65.5	65.9	66.8	67.2	64.1
1996	66.5	66.8	67.4	67.7	68.6	69.2	68.9	69.1	68.8	68.8	68.8	69.5	68.3
1997	70.5	71.1	71.9	70.5	71.4	72.6	73.4	73.6	73.2	73.0	73.5	74.4	72.4
1998	74.2	74.9	75.2	74.2	76.6	77.4	78.0	78.8	78.5	78.6	79.2	80.3	77.1
1999	81.5	82.3	82.7	81.9	83.8	84.6	86.8	87.7	88.1	86.2	87.7	89.0	85.1
2000	90.5	92.0	93.5	94.1	95.9	98.7	99.9	101.0	102.0	100.9	101.6	101.9	97.6
2001	101.6	101.8	101.0	99.4	99.6	100.3	99.3	99.1	97.0	96.3	96.1	96.7	99.0
2002	94.2	93.9	93.5	93.2	93.3	93.8	93.9	94.0	93.1	93.3	93.4	93.3	93.6
2003	92.2	92.0	91.5	91.1	91.7	92.0	92.4	93.2	92.4	92.5	92.4	93.2	92.2
Financial activities													
1990	109.8	110.4	111.5	112.5	113.6	114.8	114.8	115.1	114.8	113.6	113.3	113.3	113.1
1991	112.5	113.0	114.0	115.0	116.0	116.6	116.8	117.6	117.0	115.4	115.3	115.5	115.3
1992	113.5	113.9	114.5	115.4	116.2	117.3	117.7	117.9	119.0	119.3	119.0	120.0	116.9
1993	117.0	117.6	118.7	119.8	120.7	121.9	124.1	124.5	124.6	122.9	123.5	124.4	121.6
1994	123.4	124.1	124.5	124.1	124.3	124.7	124.5	124.8	123.7	121.9	121.4	121.5	123.5
1995	119.2	119.7	119.8	119.8	120.7	121.9	122.3	123.5	123.4	123.1	123.1	123.5	121.6
1996	121.9	122.8	123.3	123.5	124.5	126.1	126.3	127.0	126.3	125.4	125.3	126.1	124.8
1997	124.4	125.0	125.6	126.0	127.0	127.9	128.8	129.8	129.3	132.0	132.4	133.5	128.4
1998	129.2	130.5	131.1	134.4	135.4	136.7	138.2	138.8	138.5	140.7	140.7	141.5	136.3
1999	138.9	139.5	140.5	141.3	141.8	142.7	144.0	143.9	142.2	145.9	146.4	146.7	142.8
2000	141.9	142.6	142.5	141.7	142.2	142.6	142.6	143.0	142.9	141.3	141.6	142.7	142.3
2001	142.4	143.3	143.1	143.4	144.3	145.2	147.2	147.7	147.9	145.9	145.7	146.1	145.2
2002	143.0	143.6	144.0	144.7	145.6	146.2	147.1	148.1	147.8	147.1	148.1	148.7	146.2
2003	148.2	148.9	149.7	150.9	152.2	153.2	155.1	156.0	155.3	154.3	154.3	154.9	152.8
Professional and business services													
1990	187.3	187.9	191.8	194.4	196.0	199.6	201.7	204.8	205.1	201.1	200.8	200.2	197.5
1991	194.4	195.8	198.6	199.9	201.6	202.7	205.7	208.7	208.6	206.5	204.5	204.2	202.6
1992	202.2	203.3	205.9	207.2	208.0	210.4	210.8	210.9	212.1	209.5	208.9	209.0	208.1
1993	205.2	207.4	210.9	213.7	215.7	218.2	222.0	222.7	224.1	222.7	221.0	222.1	217.1
1994	216.6	218.5	222.4	227.8	228.4	231.5	235.3	236.8	238.8	237.8	238.8	238.3	230.9
1995	227.1	229.8	233.9	230.0	231.9	234.4	232.0	236.6	239.2	238.2	236.5	235.4	233.7
1996	228.3	230.6	234.5	238.0	239.9	242.1	244.4	248.6	249.6	250.0	250.4	250.6	242.2
1997	245.3	249.8	254.5	257.3	260.5	262.7	263.5	266.7	268.0	267.3	268.3	269.9	261.1
1998	263.5	266.3	270.3	269.9	272.1	274.9	276.2	278.5	277.9	277.8	277.8	277.2	273.5
1999	269.6	272.6	278.0	280.5	282.6	285.8	290.1	293.7	294.5	295.0	296.1	298.1	286.3
2000	290.3	293.1	298.3	298.6	300.7	305.2	305.9	311.6	312.8	309.8	309.0	310.6	303.8
2001	296.8	296.9	299.6	300.7	300.6	301.3	297.8	299.0	296.5	293.9	290.3	287.5	296.7
2002	279.8	282.3	284.6	287.1	288.6	291.5	293.2	297.2	297.1	295.3	294.9	291.3	290.2
2003	282.3	284.6	285.6	287.7	288.5	290.1	293.0	297.4	297.3	297.7	297.2	296.3	291.5
Educational and health services													
1990	199.1	202.0	203.8	204.5	205.8	205.9	203.3	205.1	209.4	211.0	212.5	213.4	206.3
1991	213.2	215.9	217.7	217.6	219.1	218.9	217.2	218.7	222.7	225.6	227.2	227.9	220.1
1992	226.3	229.1	229.7	229.8	230.1	230.0	229.9	230.5	235.3	235.6	237.6	238.9	231.9
1993	234.7	238.1	239.9	242.3	243.1	242.9	237.2	237.1	241.0	243.5	244.0	244.2	240.6
1994	242.7	245.6	246.0	246.1	245.9	245.1	244.9	246.0	250.7	246.8	248.6	250.0	246.5
1995	244.2	247.4	249.2	252.6	253.5	253.6	250.6	251.5	255.7	253.4	254.8	254.9	251.7
1996	253.0	257.0	258.2	258.0	259.5	259.3	255.1	256.8	259.6	263.8	265.1	265.9	259.2
1997	265.8	266.1	267.2	267.4	268.6	267.8	264.6	265.8	270.1	269.9	270.9	271.9	268.0
1998	272.7	276.8	278.2	277.4	279.7	278.4	274.3	275.0	278.8	282.2	282.6	283.4	278.2
1999	277.1	279.5	281.1	280.6	282.0	280.8	279.0	278.9	282.7	284.6	285.6	286.6	281.5
2000	285.4	289.8	292.8	290.1	291.2	291.0	289.5	291.3	293.3	294.9	296.3	297.1	291.8
2001	292.4	296.8	298.0	298.6	299.7	298.1	291.6	292.9	299.2	302.5	305.1	305.0	298.3
2002	301.7	305.6	307.3	307.7	309.4	306.2	300.8	301.5	306.7	311.1	312.8	312.0	306.9
2003	307.8	311.4	312.6	313.9	314.5	311.7	307.9	307.3	311.7	315.0	316.3	316.3	312.2

Employment by Industry: Washington—*Continued*

(Numbers in thousands. Not seasonally adjusted.)

Industry	January	February	March	April	May	June	July	August	September	October	November	December	Annual Average
STATEWIDE—*Continued*													
Leisure and hospitality													
1990	178.3	179.5	183.7	188.7	193.4	198.4	197.3	200.4	199.9	192.1	188.5	187.8	190.6
1991	180.6	182.6	187.6	192.0	197.6	201.4	201.0	203.1	202.2	196.0	192.6	192.9	194.1
1992	186.8	188.8	193.1	198.2	203.2	207.7	208.6	212.8	212.8	206.2	201.4	201.0	201.7
1993	190.9	194.0	198.4	205.1	210.5	215.4	216.9	218.8	220.2	209.3	207.6	208.2	207.9
1994	199.6	201.1	204.6	210.8	217.3	221.9	221.3	224.0	224.3	215.8	214.6	214.0	214.1
1995	207.0	209.3	213.8	218.8	224.2	229.6	226.2	231.2	232.0	223.0	221.2	220.7	221.4
1996	212.0	212.3	217.8	224.0	231.3	235.7	236.9	240.2	239.3	229.9	227.5	227.2	227.8
1997	219.2	223.2	226.9	229.8	237.4	242.0	243.5	246.8	244.8	236.0	233.4	235.1	234.8
1998	223.5	226.7	231.0	237.4	244.6	249.5	250.2	254.2	254.0	239.3	235.8	238.0	240.3
1999	232.6	236.1	242.2	243.4	247.8	253.1	256.0	257.7	256.6	247.8	244.2	246.6	247.0
2000	237.8	240.6	246.4	249.2	254.7	261.2	258.5	261.7	261.9	250.4	248.1	250.1	251.7
2001	235.0	237.7	241.2	245.4	252.4	256.7	257.6	260.6	256.6	243.7	238.9	239.1	247.1
2002	231.4	232.2	236.0	241.2	248.1	253.7	256.7	259.7	257.0	245.4	241.8	242.1	245.4
2003	235.7	237.2	239.6	243.6	249.8	256.0	258.7	261.7	259.6	249.2	243.1	242.8	248.1
Other services													
1990	87.4	87.6	88.7	89.0	89.6	90.8	91.2	91.5	91.2	89.5	89.3	89.4	89.6
1991	88.3	88.4	89.1	89.6	90.2	90.9	91.5	90.0	91.8	90.9	90.8	91.1	90.2
1992	89.9	89.7	90.5	91.3	91.5	92.4	92.8	92.2	91.7	90.8	90.2	90.4	91.1
1993	88.5	88.9	89.2	90.2	91.1	92.4	94.3	93.9	93.6	91.9	91.6	92.6	91.5
1994	91.2	91.8	92.9	93.3	94.2	95.1	96.4	96.6	96.4	94.8	94.5	95.3	94.3
1995	94.4	94.8	95.9	96.4	97.1	98.3	98.7	99.0	98.5	96.8	96.2	97.8	96.9
1996	96.5	97.1	97.9	98.5	99.3	100.6	100.6	100.8	100.0	99.5	99.6	99.9	99.1
1997	99.3	100.2	100.6	101.0	102.1	102.9	103.6	103.9	103.0	102.4	102.2	102.7	101.9
1998	100.0	99.9	101.5	102.3	103.0	104.3	104.7	104.8	104.1	103.9	103.9	104.2	103.0
1999	103.0	103.5	104.2	104.3	104.7	105.6	105.6	105.3	105.0	104.2	104.0	104.7	104.5
2000	103.8	104.5	105.5	104.3	106.6	107.4	107.2	108.1	107.7	106.7	106.4	106.5	106.2
2001	95.3	95.6	96.5	96.5	97.4	98.6	98.4	98.6	97.1	96.4	96.1	96.1	96.9
2002	95.0	95.4	95.9	97.2	98.1	99.3	100.1	100.1	98.8	97.8	97.8	97.7	97.8
2003	97.5	97.9	98.4	98.8	99.6	100.8	100.6	100.8	100.2	99.3	99.2	99.6	99.4
Government													
1990	389.1	400.1	397.7	400.5	404.7	405.2	380.6	374.9	393.0	404.1	413.6	407.5	397.5
1991	403.5	409.5	412.9	415.3	420.6	419.3	395.5	385.2	409.2	420.2	427.6	420.1	411.5
1992	418.2	426.8	430.4	427.2	433.2	429.7	399.9	394.8	419.7	430.9	439.3	433.1	423.6
1993	427.9	431.8	436.6	435.3	437.3	438.0	408.4	399.0	425.3	435.7	447.5	437.2	430.0
1994	432.7	441.7	439.9	440.8	444.5	446.2	413.2	406.6	432.5	446.6	455.8	446.2	437.2
1995	441.9	449.4	453.5	451.0	455.0	456.0	422.0	412.4	435.1	447.9	457.8	451.0	444.4
1996	446.2	454.3	458.7	456.1	460.4	458.7	431.7	418.7	442.5	455.2	465.3	459.2	450.5
1997	453.9	458.6	462.2	463.4	466.0	470.4	441.8	428.0	449.1	462.4	472.0	467.9	457.9
1998	463.3	470.5	470.7	471.4	473.4	475.8	448.7	434.0	456.4	470.7	480.7	475.3	465.9
1999	471.1	475.8	481.4	479.3	481.0	483.5	456.7	446.1	465.2	480.3	488.4	482.7	474.2
2000	479.3	487.2	489.6	488.1	499.6	494.9	463.8	455.1	470.9	486.6	493.7	491.0	483.3
2001	500.3	506.1	510.7	510.8	513.9	515.6	487.8	474.9	493.6	512.8	521.6	516.9	505.4
2002	512.3	519.1	521.0	521.7	524.5	524.7	498.2	485.0	504.1	523.6	532.9	526.6	516.1
2003	520.7	526.3	527.3	527.3	532.8	530.4	500.9	489.2	506.6	528.3	536.3	530.3	521.4
Federal government													
1990	72.8	72.8	73.8	75.2	77.1	75.9	75.3	73.1	72.5	71.9	71.8	72.3	73.7
1991	71.0	70.9	71.0	72.0	72.6	73.9	75.2	75.0	74.7	73.0	72.8	73.0	72.9
1992	72.3	72.2	72.3	72.8	73.0	74.0	74.8	74.7	74.5	73.6	72.8	73.3	73.3
1993	72.9	72.7	72.6	71.7	72.4	72.9	72.9	72.9	72.5	71.5	71.0	71.9	72.3
1994	70.8	70.6	70.7	71.2	71.6	71.9	72.5	72.4	72.3	71.7	71.0	71.6	71.5
1995	70.1	70.1	70.1	69.9	70.7	70.9	70.5	70.5	70.0	70.0	68.9	69.9	70.1
1996	68.5	68.3	68.5	68.9	69.0	69.2	69.0	69.2	69.0	67.8	67.7	68.7	68.6
1997	67.5	66.9	66.9	67.3	67.7	68.1	68.8	68.8	68.5	67.4	67.7	68.9	67.8
1998	67.6	66.3	66.3	66.1	66.7	67.2	68.0	68.1	67.8	67.1	67.4	68.3	67.2
1999	67.5	66.6	67.9	66.6	67.1	67.5	68.1	68.2	67.9	67.7	67.6	68.6	67.6
2000	66.8	66.9	67.1	69.5	79.2	73.9	70.6	72.0	68.2	67.7	68.1	68.8	69.9
2001	66.8	66.2	66.6	66.6	67.2	68.3	69.2	69.4	69.1	68.2	68.1	69.1	67.9
2002	67.7	66.9	67.3	67.5	68.2	69.3	70.4	70.4	70.3	70.4	70.8	71.6	69.2
2003	69.5	69.0	69.3	69.4	70.0	70.5	71.2	71.1	70.9	70.4	69.9	71.2	70.2
State government													
1990	113.4	116.1	116.8	116.2	116.4	115.1	103.3	102.8	109.7	119.2	119.4	118.2	113.8
1991	119.1	121.6	122.4	122.7	122.6	120.7	105.4	106.7	115.0	126.4	126.9	124.8	119.5
1992	124.5	126.7	127.3	125.3	125.4	122.1	107.4	107.8	115.7	126.1	127.4	125.7	121.7
1993	126.3	127.0	129.3	128.2	127.4	125.7	107.9	109.0	116.0	126.7	128.0	125.5	123.0
1994	126.0	127.0	127.6	127.6	127.7	126.9	110.1	112.6	117.7	130.5	131.2	128.2	124.4
1995	129.6	131.4	131.2	131.6	131.9	129.9	111.8	113.3	120.0	130.8	132.1	129.8	126.9
1996	129.7	131.7	133.3	132.3	132.8	130.6	113.7	115.5	122.2	133.2	134.7	133.0	128.5
1997	133.0	134.9	136.4	135.8	135.7	134.3	116.2	118.0	124.8	135.8	136.7	136.1	131.4
1998	135.7	137.6	139.3	138.4	138.7	137.8	118.9	118.8	127.5	139.1	140.9	138.5	134.2
1999	139.0	141.4	142.9	142.4	142.1	140.9	122.6	124.0	130.5	142.1	143.4	140.9	137.6
2000	142.1	144.4	146.3	144.2	144.3	141.7	124.7	126.0	132.7	144.8	147.4	144.8	140.2
2001	144.9	146.7	148.4	148.1	148.6	145.9	127.9	130.1	135.9	150.4	150.8	148.9	143.9
2002	148.8	150.6	151.6	150.6	150.9	147.7	129.6	131.0	137.8	151.3	152.6	150.7	146.1
2003	149.4	151.0	151.7	151.1	151.3	149.3	130.8	132.3	138.9	150.3	151.4	148.6	146.3

Employment by Industry: Washington—*Continued*

(Numbers in thousands. Not seasonally adjusted.)

Industry	January	February	March	April	May	June	July	August	September	October	November	December	Annual Average
STATEWIDE—*Continued*													
Local government													
1990	202.9	211.2	207.1	209.1	211.2	214.2	202.0	199.0	210.8	213.0	222.4	217.0	209.9
1991	213.4	217.0	219.5	220.6	225.4	224.7	214.9	203.5	219.5	220.8	227.9	222.3	219.1
1992	221.4	227.9	230.8	229.1	234.8	233.6	217.7	212.3	229.5	231.2	239.1	234.1	228.4
1993	228.7	232.1	234.7	235.4	237.5	239.4	227.6	217.1	236.8	237.5	248.5	239.8	234.5
1994	235.9	244.1	241.6	242.0	245.2	247.4	230.6	221.6	242.5	244.4	253.6	246.4	241.2
1995	242.2	247.9	252.2	249.5	252.4	255.2	239.7	228.6	245.1	247.1	256.8	251.3	247.3
1996	248.0	254.3	256.9	254.9	258.6	258.9	249.0	234.0	251.3	254.2	262.9	257.5	253.3
1997	253.4	256.8	258.9	260.3	262.6	268.0	256.8	241.2	255.8	259.2	267.6	262.9	258.6
1998	260.0	266.6	265.1	266.9	268.0	270.8	261.8	247.1	261.1	264.5	272.4	268.5	264.4
1999	264.6	267.8	270.6	270.3	271.8	275.1	266.0	253.9	266.8	270.5	277.4	273.2	269.0
2000	270.4	275.9	276.2	274.4	276.1	279.3	268.5	257.1	270.0	274.1	278.2	277.4	273.1
2001	288.6	293.2	295.7	296.1	298.1	301.4	290.7	275.4	288.6	294.2	302.7	298.9	293.6
2002	295.8	301.6	302.1	303.6	305.4	307.7	298.2	283.6	296.0	301.9	309.5	304.3	300.8
2003	301.8	306.3	306.3	306.8	311.5	310.6	298.9	285.8	296.8	307.6	315.0	310.5	304.8
SEATTLE													
Total nonfarm													
1990	1085.7	1090.9	1100.2	1103.9	1116.5	1130.8	1123.9	1132.1	1138.5	1126.5	1137.5	1132.2	1118.2
1991	1100.0	1101.5	1111.1	1111.2	1125.5	1131.5	1127.3	1127.9	1140.6	1134.5	1142.8	1140.4	1124.5
1992	1116.7	1122.1	1128.8	1130.3	1140.5	1146.5	1137.7	1136.5	1149.4	1147.1	1153.9	1154.2	1138.6
1993	1121.2	1126.3	1134.2	1138.2	1143.4	1153.0	1142.4	1141.7	1154.6	1150.1	1158.8	1161.5	1143.7
1994	1130.1	1138.0	1137.3	1146.2	1153.5	1163.6	1153.7	1157.6	1176.6	1170.5	1186.4	1186.7	1158.3
1995	1155.3	1161.7	1171.6	1170.5	1180.9	1194.2	1176.8	1185.8	1201.1	1172.1	1186.4	1207.1	1180.2
1996	1180.2	1189.4	1201.4	1203.6	1216.6	1228.9	1225.5	1228.7	1244.4	1247.7	1267.6	1270.8	1225.4
1997	1239.6	1250.2	1262.8	1272.6	1288.3	1306.0	1298.7	1300.4	1313.0	1318.5	1334.7	1342.5	1293.9
1998	1307.9	1320.9	1328.3	1336.4	1351.7	1363.0	1358.6	1359.1	1371.0	1373.0	1386.8	1390.1	1353.9
1999	1354.7	1359.9	1370.0	1371.7	1380.0	1390.0	1388.4	1390.5	1399.0	1400.8	1414.1	1420.3	1386.6
2000	1386.7	1382.5	1408.6	1400.7	1415.0	1428.8	1414.0	1420.4	1430.8	1430.2	1438.6	1445.3	1416.8
2001	1402.9	1404.5	1408.9	1404.2	1410.3	1416.0	1399.3	1396.7	1397.1	1386.1	1386.9	1380.9	1399.5
2002	1346.2	1345.6	1346.3	1346.3	1356.5	1363.3	1353.0	1352.9	1354.0	1352.4	1361.3	1354.5	1352.7
2003	1324.0	1327.8	1326.7	1329.2	1340.4	1345.4	1341.1	1341.4	1345.2	1346.3	1350.9	1353.2	1339.3
Total private													
1990	938.3	938.1	950.0	953.2	963.8	977.1	979.3	988.8	987.3	974.1	978.4	977.9	967.1
1991	946.8	946.0	954.4	953.8	964.3	971.6	975.1	982.4	982.9	974.9	977.8	980.8	967.5
1992	957.7	958.0	963.2	967.6	973.4	982.0	984.9	986.6	986.4	981.5	983.0	987.2	975.9
1993	956.9	960.7	966.7	971.6	975.6	983.9	984.3	988.1	987.8	982.4	984.2	992.6	977.9
1994	963.9	965.6	968.6	976.1	982.6	991.4	995.6	1003.4	1007.1	999.5	1008.2	1014.0	989.6
1995	985.2	988.1	995.1	997.6	1006.5	1017.5	1013.3	1027.5	1030.0	999.3	1006.7	1032.3	1008.2
1996	1006.8	1011.1	1021.8	1027.3	1038.0	1051.0	1056.8	1068.5	1070.3	1072.5	1085.5	1094.2	1050.3
1997	1064.2	1073.1	1084.1	1093.8	1108.1	1121.0	1126.3	1135.1	1135.6	1139.1	1149.3	1160.6	1115.8
1998	1127.2	1136.1	1145.0	1152.6	1166.8	1176.2	1181.9	1189.2	1188.2	1189.1	1196.1	1202.5	1170.9
1999	1169.1	1173.1	1181.3	1183.9	1190.8	1199.4	1207.6	1214.3	1212.8	1212.4	1219.9	1229.7	1199.5
2000	1198.1	1189.1	1216.1	1209.2	1219.6	1233.8	1232.1	1241.3	1242.6	1239.1	1244.8	1251.5	1226.4
2001	1208.5	1208.2	1211.3	1206.8	1211.9	1216.4	1208.9	1212.4	1202.6	1188.1	1182.6	1179.7	1203.1
2002	1146.9	1143.2	1144.2	1144.2	1153.6	1160.3	1159.4	1164.6	1156.2	1150.9	1153.3	1151.2	1152.3
2003	1121.8	1122.4	1122.2	1124.9	1132.4	1140.0	1145.8	1150.9	1146.6	1142.3	1141.5	1147.4	1136.5
Goods-producing													
1990	273.6	272.4	276.2	276.0	278.1	280.7	284.0	285.9	284.7	278.7	276.8	274.0	278.4
1991	267.6	267.1	268.5	267.7	270.0	271.6	275.3	278.2	277.8	275.1	272.7	271.3	271.9
1992	266.7	266.0	267.9	268.6	270.8	271.8	274.6	273.4	271.5	268.9	266.8	265.1	269.3
1993	254.9	256.1	256.8	256.1	254.8	255.6	245.4	246.3	244.6	254.2	250.4	249.6	252.0
1994	242.2	240.9	240.6	241.8	242.4	243.9	245.8	248.0	248.9	246.2	244.9	244.3	244.1
1995	243.6	243.7	244.5	244.5	244.2	245.7	243.2	245.7	245.4	219.3	218.8	239.2	239.8
1996	236.3	237.6	241.1	243.2	245.6	248.9	251.9	256.2	258.0	259.6	261.9	263.7	250.3
1997	262.8	264.2	267.5	270.7	274.3	278.9	282.9	286.7	286.5	291.3	292.4	293.2	279.2
1998	285.6	288.0	290.0	292.4	295.6	297.9	299.9	301.0	300.8	299.5	298.2	296.1	295.4
1999	287.8	286.5	286.2	287.7	287.3	288.1	288.0	289.3	286.5	286.5	283.8	281.3	286.5
2000	276.4	262.2	279.3	277.3	278.3	280.6	280.3	281.4	280.9	279.8	278.2	277.0	277.6
2001	271.5	269.8	270.9	269.8	270.8	271.8	272.4	273.2	270.9	265.6	259.9	255.4	268.5
2002	248.4	246.0	245.1	243.4	245.3	245.5	245.0	246.3	242.8	240.2	236.9	234.0	243.2
2003	227.2	226.4	225.5	225.6	226.7	227.6	228.9	229.6	228.1	227.4	224.5	223.8	226.8
Natural resources and mining													
1990	1.8	1.8	1.8	2.0	2.0	2.1	2.1	2.1	2.1	2.1	2.0	1.9	1.9
1991	1.7	1.8	1.8	1.8	1.9	1.9	1.8	1.9	1.9	1.8	1.8	1.7	1.8
1992	1.5	1.6	1.6	1.5	1.6	1.6	1.6	1.6	1.6	1.6	1.6	1.5	1.5
1993	1.5	1.5	1.6	1.6	1.7	1.7	1.7	1.7	1.7	1.6	1.6	1.6	1.6
1994	1.5	1.5	1.5	1.6	1.6	1.6	1.6	1.6	1.6	1.6	1.6	1.5	1.5
1995	1.5	1.6	1.6	1.6	1.6	1.7	1.7	1.7	1.7	1.6	1.6	1.5	1.6
1996	1.6	1.6	1.6	1.6	1.6	1.6	1.6	1.7	1.8	1.7	1.6	1.7	1.6
1997	1.8	1.8	1.7	1.7	1.8	1.9	1.9	2.0	2.0	2.0	2.0	1.8	1.8
1998	1.7	1.7	1.7	1.7	1.8	1.8	2.0	2.0	2.0	2.3	2.3	2.2	1.9
1999	2.1	2.0	2.0	2.1	2.1	2.1	2.3	2.2	2.2	2.2	2.1	2.0	2.1
2000	2.0	2.0	2.1	2.1	2.1	2.2	2.2	2.2	2.2	2.2	2.1	2.0	2.1
2001	2.2	2.1	2.1	2.1	2.0	2.1	2.1	2.0	2.0	1.9	1.8	1.7	2.0
2002	1.7	1.6	1.7	1.6	1.6	1.6	1.6	1.6	1.7	1.6	1.6	1.6	1.6
2003	1.5	1.5	1.5	1.4	1.3	1.3	1.3	1.3	1.3	1.3	1.2	1.2	1.3

Employment by Industry: Washington—*Continued*

(Numbers in thousands. Not seasonally adjusted.)

Industry	January	February	March	April	May	June	July	August	September	October	November	December	Annual Average
SEATTLE—*Continued*													
Construction													
1990	58.4	58.0	60.7	61.8	63.8	65.6	66.9	69.0	68.2	64.4	62.5	60.1	63.2
1991	56.7	57.1	58.2	58.0	59.5	60.4	63.0	65.2	65.0	63.9	62.2	60.9	60.8
1992	57.9	58.0	59.6	60.7	62.6	64.3	66.3	66.3	66.0	64.8	62.6	61.5	62.5
1993	55.8	57.5	58.2	57.6	57.5	58.9	61.6	63.2	62.5	61.7	59.5	58.7	59.3
1994	55.1	55.0	55.4	56.4	57.5	58.8	60.7	62.1	62.4	61.4	59.8	58.8	58.6
1995	55.3	55.6	56.7	56.7	58.1	60.5	61.9	63.3	63.1	61.0	59.4	57.7	59.1
1996	55.4	55.7	57.3	58.3	59.6	61.1	63.1	65.3	65.8	65.0	64.3	63.7	61.2
1997	61.8	62.0	62.6	63.8	65.6	67.5	69.6	71.4	70.6	71.3	70.6	70.1	67.2
1998	65.4	66.5	67.6	68.9	71.5	73.3	76.2	77.2	77.4	77.4	76.0	75.3	72.7
1999	72.3	72.0	73.6	75.7	77.1	79.4	82.5	84.1	83.5	84.2	81.9	80.5	78.9
2000	77.8	79.1	81.2	81.7	83.3	85.4	86.7	88.0	88.4	87.5	86.5	85.4	84.2
2001	82.0	81.2	82.5	81.3	82.6	83.8	85.0	85.9	84.9	82.2	78.9	76.5	82.2
2002	74.3	74.8	74.9	74.6	76.6	77.4	79.0	81.4	80.2	78.5	76.5	74.6	76.9
2003	71.2	71.4	71.5	72.7	74.8	76.1	77.9	79.6	79.0	78.7	77.1	76.1	75.5
Manufacturing													
1990	213.4	212.6	213.7	212.2	212.3	213.0	215.0	214.8	214.4	212.2	212.3	212.0	213.1
1991	209.2	208.2	208.5	207.9	208.6	209.3	210.5	211.1	210.9	209.4	208.7	208.7	209.2
1992	207.3	206.4	206.7	206.4	206.6	205.9	206.7	205.5	203.9	202.5	202.6	202.1	205.2
1993	197.6	197.1	197.0	196.9	195.6	195.0	182.1	181.4	180.4	190.9	189.3	189.3	191.0
1994	185.6	184.4	183.7	183.8	183.3	183.5	183.5	184.3	184.9	183.2	183.5	184.0	183.9
1995	186.8	186.5	186.2	186.2	184.5	183.5	179.6	180.7	180.6	156.7	157.8	180.0	179.0
1996	179.3	180.3	182.2	183.3	184.4	186.2	187.2	189.2	190.4	192.9	196.0	198.3	187.4
1997	199.2	200.4	203.2	205.2	206.9	209.5	211.4	213.3	213.9	218.0	219.8	221.3	210.1
1998	218.5	219.8	220.7	221.8	222.3	222.8	221.7	221.8	221.4	219.8	219.9	218.6	220.7
1999	213.4	212.5	210.6	209.9	208.1	206.6	203.2	203.0	200.8	200.1	199.8	198.8	205.5
2000	196.6	181.1	196.0	193.5	192.9	193.0	191.4	191.2	190.3	190.1	189.6	189.6	191.2
2001	187.3	186.5	186.3	186.4	186.2	185.9	185.3	185.3	184.0	181.5	179.2	177.2	184.3
2002	172.4	169.6	168.5	167.2	167.1	166.5	164.4	163.3	160.9	160.1	158.8	157.8	164.7
2003	154.5	153.5	152.5	151.5	150.6	150.2	149.7	148.7	147.8	147.4	146.2	146.5	149.9
Service-providing													
1990	812.1	818.5	824.0	827.9	838.4	850.1	839.9	846.2	853.8	847.8	860.7	858.2	839.8
1991	832.4	834.4	842.6	843.5	855.5	859.9	852.0	849.7	862.8	859.4	870.1	869.1	852.6
1992	850.0	856.1	860.9	861.7	869.7	874.7	863.1	863.1	877.9	878.2	887.1	889.1	869.3
1993	866.3	870.2	877.4	882.1	888.6	897.4	897.0	895.4	910.0	895.9	908.4	911.9	891.7
1994	887.9	897.1	896.7	904.4	911.1	919.7	907.9	909.6	927.7	924.3	941.5	942.4	914.1
1995	911.7	918.0	927.1	926.0	936.7	948.5	933.6	940.1	955.7	952.8	967.6	967.9	940.4
1996	943.9	951.8	960.3	960.4	971.0	980.0	973.6	972.5	986.4	988.1	1005.7	1007.1	975.0
1997	976.8	986.0	995.3	1001.9	1014.0	1027.1	1015.8	1013.7	1026.5	1027.2	1042.3	1049.3	1014.6
1998	1022.3	1032.9	1038.3	1044.0	1056.1	1065.1	1058.7	1058.1	1070.2	1073.5	1088.6	1094.0	1058.4
1999	1066.9	1073.4	1083.8	1084.0	1092.7	1101.9	1100.4	1101.2	1112.5	1114.3	1130.3	1139.0	1100.0
2000	1110.3	1120.3	1129.3	1123.4	1136.7	1148.2	1133.7	1139.0	1149.9	1150.4	1160.4	1168.3	1139.1
2001	1131.4	1134.7	1138.0	1134.4	1139.5	1144.2	1126.9	1123.5	1126.2	1120.5	1127.0	1125.5	1131.0
2002	1097.8	1099.6	1101.2	1102.9	1111.2	1117.8	1108.0	1106.6	1111.2	1112.2	1124.4	1120.5	1109.5
2003	1096.8	1101.4	1101.2	1103.6	1113.7	1117.8	1112.2	1111.8	1117.1	1118.9	1126.4	1129.4	1112.5
Trade, transportation, and utilities													
1990	225.6	222.9	224.7	225.3	228.7	232.0	231.5	233.8	233.3	233.2	238.6	241.2	230.9
1991	228.1	224.3	225.4	225.3	227.5	230.2	230.3	231.9	231.9	229.8	235.0	237.5	229.7
1992	226.4	225.0	224.8	226.0	227.3	229.5	228.9	229.8	229.4	230.4	233.5	237.2	229.0
1993	226.3	225.5	224.5	225.0	226.4	229.2	234.7	234.3	234.7	228.8	232.4	237.9	229.9
1994	226.1	224.8	224.6	225.7	227.7	230.7	231.4	233.7	234.4	233.1	239.1	243.3	231.2
1995	232.5	230.1	230.9	231.3	233.5	237.1	237.6	241.7	241.2	241.5	247.3	250.8	237.9
1996	242.4	239.9	240.8	239.9	241.9	244.6	247.8	249.8	249.5	251.7	257.4	261.4	247.2
1997	245.8	245.5	247.1	250.6	253.4	256.4	257.3	256.5	258.0	258.4	263.5	267.8	255.0
1998	257.3	256.9	257.9	260.2	261.6	264.6	266.8	267.3	267.9	270.7	276.5	281.5	265.7
1999	268.1	267.1	269.7	268.6	270.2	272.1	275.3	276.2	276.9	279.5	285.1	290.9	274.9
2000	276.3	274.9	276.3	276.1	278.2	280.5	279.9	281.5	281.0	283.9	288.7	292.0	280.7
2001	279.0	276.1	276.5	274.9	274.8	276.1	275.7	275.8	274.0	271.6	274.2	276.3	275.4
2002	265.1	261.4	260.6	260.5	262.3	264.2	264.7	264.8	263.5	263.2	266.9	269.5	263.9
2003	260.0	257.4	256.9	256.9	258.3	260.3	262.3	262.6	261.9	262.0	266.0	270.5	261.3
Wholesale trade													
1990	58.8	58.9	59.4	59.2	59.9	60.9	61.6	61.2	61.1	61.1	60.9	60.8	60.3
1991	59.9	59.7	60.0	59.9	60.1	60.4	60.4	60.7	60.7	59.8	60.6	60.0	60.1
1992	59.3	59.3	59.5	59.5	59.8	60.4	60.5	60.5	60.1	61.1	60.7	60.7	60.1
1993	60.3	60.5	60.4	60.6	60.9	61.1	62.7	62.6	62.3	61.4	61.5	61.8	61.3
1994	60.0	60.4	60.2	60.5	60.6	61.2	61.5	62.2	62.1	61.8	62.0	62.7	61.2
1995	62.5	62.9	63.1	63.2	63.7	64.2	64.0	64.4	64.4	63.8	64.2	64.6	63.7
1996	64.2	64.5	64.9	66.0	66.2	66.6	67.3	67.5	67.3	67.1	67.3	67.5	66.3
1997	66.0	66.6	67.1	67.1	67.5	68.1	68.8	69.3	69.0	69.4	69.7	69.8	68.2
1998	67.6	68.1	68.6	68.9	69.2	69.5	69.9	70.1	69.5	70.5	70.8	70.7	69.4
1999	70.2	70.3	70.3	70.7	70.9	71.1	71.8	72.0	71.6	71.5	71.4	71.9	71.1
2000	71.1	71.6	72.2	72.1	72.3	73.1	73.1	73.5	73.2	73.7	73.4	73.8	72.7
2001	72.0	72.3	72.3	72.3	72.2	72.5	72.2	72.5	72.0	71.0	70.6	70.5	71.9
2002	70.0	70.0	69.9	69.5	69.7	69.7	69.2	69.5	68.9	68.1	68.0	68.0	69.2
2003	67.9	68.0	68.1	68.1	68.2	68.2	68.6	68.8	68.4	68.5	68.2	68.8	68.3

Employment by Industry: Washington—*Continued*

(Numbers in thousands. Not seasonally adjusted.)

Industry	January	February	March	April	May	June	July	August	September	October	November	December	Annual Average
SEATTLE—*Continued*													
Retail trade													
1990	119.0	116.6	117.2	117.5	118.9	120.8	119.8	121.1	120.8	121.9	127.5	129.9	120.9
1991	117.8	114.9	115.2	115.7	117.0	118.8	117.9	119.3	118.9	118.5	122.8	125.6	118.5
1992	118.1	116.7	116.3	117.2	117.8	119.1	118.2	119.3	119.4	119.4	123.2	126.1	119.2
1993	117.3	116.0	115.6	116.2	117.4	119.3	121.9	121.7	122.0	119.9	124.1	127.6	119.9
1994	117.7	116.3	116.1	116.9	118.2	119.9	120.5	121.8	122.1	121.2	126.7	130.0	120.6
1995	121.5	119.0	119.6	119.8	121.0	123.5	123.3	126.4	126.0	126.7	131.9	134.9	124.4
1996	127.8	125.1	125.2	125.5	126.7	128.5	128.4	129.9	129.6	130.3	135.9	139.5	129.3
1997	127.4	126.5	127.5	130.5	132.5	134.1	134.9	135.3	134.6	137.6	142.5	146.4	134.1
1998	135.8	134.8	135.2	136.4	137.1	139.5	141.0	140.8	141.5	143.8	148.9	153.5	140.6
1999	143.5	142.2	141.8	142.6	143.8	145.4	147.7	148.3	148.8	150.6	156.1	161.3	147.6
2000	150.5	148.6	149.2	148.9	150.8	152.0	151.2	152.0	152.1	153.2	158.1	161.1	152.3
2001	151.4	148.4	149.0	147.7	147.7	148.6	149.2	149.5	148.5	147.7	151.7	154.1	149.5
2002	144.8	141.1	141.1	141.4	142.3	143.7	144.0	143.7	143.2	143.7	147.9	150.9	144.0
2003	142.1	140.0	139.7	139.7	140.7	142.2	143.7	143.6	143.2	143.6	147.8	151.3	143.1
Transportation and utilities													
1990	47.8	47.4	48.1	48.6	49.9	50.3	50.1	51.5	51.4	50.2	50.2	50.5	49.6
1991	50.4	49.7	50.2	49.7	50.4	51.0	52.0	51.9	52.3	51.5	51.6	51.9	51.0
1992	49.0	49.0	49.0	49.3	49.7	50.0	50.2	50.0	49.9	49.9	49.6	50.4	49.6
1993	48.7	49.0	48.5	48.2	48.1	48.8	50.1	50.0	50.4	47.5	46.8	48.5	48.7
1994	48.4	48.1	48.3	48.3	48.9	49.6	49.4	49.7	50.2	50.1	50.4	50.6	49.3
1995	48.5	48.2	48.2	48.3	48.8	49.4	50.3	50.9	50.8	51.0	51.2	51.3	49.7
1996	50.4	50.3	50.7	48.4	49.0	49.5	52.1	52.4	52.6	54.3	54.2	54.4	51.5
1997	52.4	52.4	52.5	53.0	53.4	54.2	53.6	51.9	54.4	51.4	51.3	51.6	52.6
1998	53.9	54.0	54.1	54.9	55.3	55.6	55.9	56.4	56.9	56.4	56.8	57.3	55.6
1999	54.4	54.6	57.6	55.3	55.5	55.6	55.8	55.9	56.5	57.4	57.6	57.7	56.1
2000	54.7	54.7	54.9	55.1	55.1	55.4	55.6	56.0	55.7	57.0	57.2	57.1	55.7
2001	55.6	55.4	55.2	54.9	54.9	55.0	54.3	53.8	53.5	52.9	51.9	51.7	54.1
2002	50.3	50.3	49.6	49.6	50.3	50.8	51.5	51.6	51.4	51.4	51.0	50.6	50.7
2003	50.0	49.4	49.1	49.1	49.4	49.9	50.0	50.2	50.3	49.9	50.0	50.4	49.8
Information													
1990	31.6	31.8	31.3	31.2	31.5	32.0	32.4	33.1	32.6	31.8	31.7	31.8	31.9
1991	32.0	32.5	32.7	32.8	33.3	33.7	34.3	34.5	34.5	34.2	34.6	35.1	33.6
1992	34.6	34.7	35.0	35.0	35.0	35.3	36.4	36.2	35.9	36.3	36.4	36.5	35.6
1993	36.5	36.6	37.0	37.3	37.6	38.0	39.4	39.8	39.5	38.5	38.6	38.9	38.1
1994	38.8	39.2	39.3	39.7	40.0	40.3	40.6	40.9	41.0	42.6	43.1	43.3	40.7
1995	42.8	43.4	43.9	44.4	45.0	46.2	46.6	47.2	47.7	48.1	49.0	48.3	46.0
1996	48.5	49.0	49.4	49.9	50.5	51.0	50.6	50.7	50.4	50.5	50.9	51.4	50.2
1997	51.4	51.7	52.3	52.4	53.1	53.9	55.4	55.5	55.0	54.9	55.1	55.8	53.8
1998	55.5	56.0	56.2	54.9	57.1	57.5	58.2	58.9	58.5	58.5	59.1	60.0	57.5
1999	61.1	61.8	62.0	61.6	63.0	63.4	66.2	67.0	67.5	66.0	67.3	68.2	64.5
2000	70.0	71.3	72.4	72.5	73.9	76.3	77.6	78.5	79.4	78.9	79.5	79.8	75.8
2001	78.8	79.2	78.5	77.2	77.4	77.9	77.1	77.0	75.4	75.4	75.3	75.8	77.1
2002	73.7	73.4	73.2	72.8	72.9	73.2	73.5	73.6	72.8	72.9	73.1	72.9	73.2
2003	71.8	71.8	71.4	71.2	71.6	71.8	72.3	73.1	72.6	72.6	72.5	73.5	72.2
Financial activities													
1990	68.2	68.6	69.2	69.4	70.1	70.8	70.6	70.8	70.7	69.9	69.9	69.9	69.8
1991	68.4	68.7	69.2	69.8	70.3	70.5	70.3	70.5	70.3	69.7	69.9	70.0	69.8
1992	69.4	69.6	69.7	70.0	70.5	71.3	71.6	71.8	72.3	72.7	72.7	73.3	71.2
1993	71.6	71.9	72.5	72.9	73.0	73.5	75.5	75.9	76.0	74.4	75.0	75.6	73.9
1994	75.8	76.3	76.5	75.7	75.4	75.4	75.2	75.5	74.7	73.4	73.2	73.3	75.0
1995	71.6	71.9	71.7	71.4	72.0	72.8	73.4	74.2	73.7	73.9	74.1	74.6	72.9
1996	73.3	73.9	74.1	74.1	74.7	75.8	75.7	76.1	75.7	75.2	75.7	76.2	75.0
1997	74.3	74.7	75.0	75.8	76.4	77.1	77.4	78.2	77.9	79.1	79.6	80.5	77.1
1998	77.3	78.3	78.6	81.7	82.2	82.8	84.1	84.4	84.1	86.5	87.0	87.3	82.8
1999	85.7	86.4	86.8	87.1	87.2	87.9	88.9	88.9	87.8	87.5	88.3	88.8	87.6
2000	87.2	87.8	87.5	87.3	87.3	87.8	87.2	87.6	87.3	87.1	87.5	88.6	87.5
2001	87.8	88.5	88.4	88.2	88.6	88.9	90.4	90.6	91.0	89.8	89.9	90.4	89.4
2002	87.3	87.9	88.2	88.1	88.5	88.6	88.8	89.1	89.1	88.9	89.7	89.8	88.7
2003	89.5	90.0	90.2	90.3	91.1	91.5	92.8	93.2	92.7	91.5	91.5	91.9	91.4
Professional and business services													
1990	117.8	119.4	121.5	123.1	123.7	126.2	127.5	129.3	130.1	127.8	128.1	127.6	125.1
1991	121.5	122.0	123.7	123.1	124.3	124.7	126.2	127.3	127.5	127.5	126.8	126.9	125.1
1992	125.5	125.5	127.0	126.3	126.7	127.4	126.7	126.7	127.6	126.7	126.9	127.0	126.6
1993	126.0	126.8	128.9	130.3	131.0	132.4	135.7	137.1	137.7	135.4	135.5	136.4	132.7
1994	132.4	133.4	135.3	138.8	138.9	140.6	143.3	144.6	145.9	146.2	147.8	148.6	141.3
1995	140.8	142.5	145.4	142.8	144.6	146.3	145.5	149.3	150.7	150.7	151.1	151.2	146.7
1996	146.2	147.9	150.3	152.0	153.7	155.3	157.1	160.1	160.8	161.3	163.6	163.9	156.0
1997	159.1	162.3	165.5	167.5	169.6	171.1	171.4	173.5	174.5	174.4	176.1	178.0	170.2
1998	173.1	175.4	177.6	176.2	178.2	180.0	181.7	183.9	182.7	182.9	184.2	184.2	180.0
1999	179.1	180.9	183.3	186.3	187.9	190.0	193.1	195.2	196.0	196.5	198.5	200.8	190.6
2000	194.6	195.9	199.4	198.7	200.1	203.7	205.3	208.7	209.8	207.4	207.8	209.2	203.3
2001	196.3	195.8	196.8	195.1	195.3	194.1	189.9	190.2	188.0	186.0	183.7	181.6	191.1
2002	176.4	177.3	177.7	178.2	179.2	180.1	181.2	183.1	182.3	181.5	182.1	179.7	179.9
2003	174.1	175.3	175.5	176.2	176.6	177.2	179.3	181.5	181.5	182.3	182.5	182.7	178.7

Employment by Industry: Washington—*Continued*

(Numbers in thousands. Not seasonally adjusted.)

Industry	January	February	March	April	May	June	July	August	September	October	November	December	Annual Average
SEATTLE—*Continued*													
Educational and health services													
1990	94.9	96.3	97.6	97.0	97.4	97.9	96.1	96.9	98.8	99.6	100.3	100.6	97.7
1991	100.3	101.7	103.0	102.5	103.3	103.4	102.1	102.6	104.8	105.5	106.0	106.4	103.4
1992	105.9	107.3	107.4	107.6	107.5	108.0	107.6	107.8	109.6	110.3	111.4	112.3	108.5
1993	110.4	111.7	112.6	113.6	113.7	113.5	109.3	109.3	111.2	113.4	113.8	114.0	112.2
1994	112.9	114.0	114.3	113.7	113.8	113.6	112.5	113.1	115.2	114.4	115.8	116.3	114.1
1995	111.8	113.3	114.0	116.4	117.1	116.9	115.5	115.7	117.8	116.9	117.5	117.5	115.8
1996	116.2	117.8	118.5	117.5	118.2	118.5	115.6	116.3	118.0	120.4	121.7	122.2	118.4
1997	121.1	122.6	123.3	123.6	123.5	123.1	120.1	121.1	123.1	122.3	123.5	124.1	122.6
1998	125.4	127.4	127.8	127.7	129.1	128.1	125.2	125.5	127.6	129.8	130.4	130.4	127.8
1999	127.3	128.3	128.6	127.0	127.9	127.3	125.3	125.4	127.5	129.2	129.6	130.0	127.7
2000	129.3	131.3	132.6	129.8	130.1	129.9	129.2	129.5	130.5	131.8	133.0	132.9	130.8
2001	129.7	131.6	131.7	132.4	132.5	132.8	128.8	129.7	131.5	133.5	134.9	135.0	132.0
2002	134.1	135.6	135.9	135.6	136.1	135.7	132.4	132.6	134.1	136.4	137.6	137.2	135.3
2003	135.4	136.9	137.2	137.8	137.6	137.2	135.0	134.5	135.8	137.3	138.2	138.1	136.8
Leisure and hospitality													
1990	87.2	87.0	89.2	91.0	93.6	96.2	95.8	97.2	95.6	92.4	92.4	92.1	92.4
1991	89.5	90.2	92.1	92.7	95.4	97.0	95.6	96.2	95.0	92.5	92.2	92.9	93.4
1992	89.3	90.2	91.5	93.8	95.2	97.7	97.9	99.7	99.4	96.1	95.3	95.6	95.1
1993	92.1	92.9	94.9	96.7	99.0	101.0	102.3	103.4	102.3	97.1	97.8	98.9	98.2
1994	94.9	95.8	96.5	99.0	102.2	104.2	103.4	104.0	103.5	101.3	101.9	102.1	100.7
1995	99.4	100.3	101.4	103.4	106.0	107.7	106.1	108.1	108.3	105.3	105.5	106.1	104.8
1996	100.3	101.2	103.5	106.4	108.7	111.4	112.5	113.4	112.5	109.1	109.4	110.2	108.2
1997	104.9	107.0	107.8	107.9	111.9	113.9	114.9	116.5	114.1	112.6	112.9	114.5	111.5
1998	108.6	110.1	111.6	113.9	117.2	118.7	119.1	121.2	119.8	114.7	114.1	116.0	115.4
1999	114.3	116.2	118.6	119.5	121.1	123.6	124.1	125.5	123.8	121.1	120.9	122.8	120.9
2000	118.0	119.2	121.6	121.1	123.6	126.5	123.7	124.9	124.7	121.8	121.7	123.5	122.5
2001	118.0	119.6	120.6	121.3	124.3	125.8	125.8	126.8	123.6	118.8	117.1	117.5	121.6
2002	114.3	113.9	115.6	117.2	120.4	123.4	124.0	125.1	122.3	119.1	118.1	119.1	119.4
2003	115.6	116.2	116.9	118.2	121.4	124.7	125.7	126.7	124.9	120.8	117.7	118.1	120.6
Other services													
1990	39.4	39.7	40.3	40.2	40.7	41.3	41.4	41.8	41.5	40.7	40.6	40.7	40.6
1991	39.4	39.5	39.8	39.9	40.2	40.5	41.0	41.2	41.1	40.6	40.6	40.7	40.3
1992	39.9	39.7	39.9	40.3	40.4	41.0	41.2	41.2	40.7	40.1	40.0	40.2	40.3
1993	39.1	39.2	39.5	39.7	40.1	40.7	42.0	42.0	41.8	40.6	40.7	41.3	40.5
1994	40.8	41.2	41.5	41.7	42.2	42.7	43.4	43.6	43.5	42.3	42.4	42.8	42.3
1995	42.7	42.9	43.3	43.4	44.1	44.8	45.4	45.6	45.2	43.6	43.4	44.6	44.0
1996	43.6	43.8	44.1	44.3	44.7	45.5	45.6	45.9	45.4	44.7	44.9	45.2	44.8
1997	44.8	45.1	45.6	45.3	45.9	46.6	46.9	47.1	46.5	46.1	46.2	46.7	46.0
1998	44.4	44.0	45.3	45.6	45.8	46.6	46.9	47.0	46.8	46.5	46.6	47.0	46.0
1999	45.7	45.9	46.1	46.1	46.2	47.0	46.7	46.8	46.8	46.1	46.4	46.9	46.3
2000	46.3	46.5	47.0	46.4	48.1	48.5	48.9	49.2	49.0	48.4	48.4	48.5	47.9
2001	47.4	47.6	47.9	47.9	48.2	49.0	48.8	49.1	48.2	47.4	47.6	47.7	48.1
2002	47.6	47.7	47.9	48.4	48.9	49.6	49.8	50.0	49.3	48.7	48.9	49.0	48.8
2003	48.2	48.4	48.6	48.7	49.1	49.7	49.5	49.7	49.1	48.4	48.6	48.8	48.9
Government													
1990	147.4	152.8	150.2	150.7	152.7	153.7	144.6	143.3	151.2	152.4	159.1	154.3	151.0
1991	153.2	155.5	156.7	157.4	161.2	159.9	152.2	145.5	157.7	159.6	165.0	159.6	156.9
1992	159.0	164.1	165.6	162.7	167.1	164.5	152.8	149.9	163.0	165.6	170.9	167.0	162.6
1993	164.3	165.6	167.5	166.6	167.8	169.1	158.1	153.6	166.8	167.7	174.6	168.9	165.8
1994	166.2	172.4	168.7	170.1	170.9	172.2	158.1	154.2	169.5	171.0	178.2	172.7	168.6
1995	170.1	173.6	176.5	172.9	174.4	176.7	163.5	158.3	171.1	172.8	179.7	174.8	172.0
1996	173.4	178.3	179.6	176.3	178.6	177.9	168.7	160.2	174.1	175.2	182.1	176.6	175.0
1997	175.4	177.1	178.7	178.8	180.2	185.0	172.4	165.3	177.4	179.4	185.4	181.9	178.0
1998	180.7	184.8	183.3	183.8	184.9	186.8	176.7	169.9	182.8	183.9	190.7	187.6	182.9
1999	185.6	186.8	188.7	187.8	189.2	190.6	180.8	176.2	186.2	188.4	194.2	190.6	187.0
2000	188.6	193.4	192.5	191.5	195.4	195.0	181.9	179.1	188.2	191.1	193.8	193.8	190.3
2001	194.4	196.3	197.6	197.4	198.4	199.6	190.4	184.3	194.5	198.0	204.3	201.2	196.4
2002	199.3	202.4	202.1	202.1	202.9	203.0	193.6	188.3	197.8	201.5	208.0	203.3	200.4
2003	202.2	205.4	204.5	204.3	208.0	205.4	195.3	190.5	198.6	204.0	209.4	205.8	202.8
Federal government													
1990	22.9	22.8	23.1	23.3	24.0	23.5	23.7	22.9	22.7	22.5	22.5	22.9	23.0
1991	22.7	22.6	22.6	22.7	22.8	23.1	23.3	23.3	23.3	23.1	22.9	23.5	22.9
1992	23.1	23.0	23.0	23.1	23.1	23.3	23.4	23.3	23.3	23.3	23.2	23.7	23.2
1993	23.5	23.5	23.5	23.5	23.7	23.9	24.0	24.1	24.0	23.8	23.7	24.3	23.7
1994	23.7	23.7	23.7	23.8	23.8	23.8	23.8	23.8	23.8	23.7	23.6	24.3	23.7
1995	23.3	23.3	23.3	23.3	23.3	23.5	23.4	23.4	23.3	23.3	23.1	23.7	23.3
1996	23.2	23.2	23.2	23.2	23.1	23.1	23.0	23.0	23.0	22.8	23.0	23.7	23.1
1997	23.2	22.9	22.9	23.0	23.1	23.2	23.3	23.4	23.4	23.1	23.3	23.9	23.2
1998	24.3	23.4	23.4	23.6	23.7	23.8	23.9	24.0	24.1	24.1	24.4	25.3	24.0
1999	25.1	24.3	24.7	24.2	24.3	24.4	24.2	24.3	24.3	24.4	24.6	25.4	24.5
2000	24.5	24.6	24.6	25.4	28.6	26.9	25.1	25.9	24.4	24.4	24.9	25.3	25.3
2001	25.2	24.9	25.0	24.9	24.9	24.9	25.1	25.1	25.1	25.1	25.5	25.9	25.1
2002	25.4	25.0	25.0	25.0	25.0	25.2	25.4	25.3	25.2	26.3	26.7	27.2	25.6
2003	26.7	26.3	26.3	26.3	26.3	26.2	26.3	26.2	26.1	26.2	26.3	26.8	26.3

Employment by Industry: Washington—*Continued*

(Numbers in thousands. Not seasonally adjusted.)

Industry	January	February	March	April	May	June	July	August	September	October	November	December	Annual Average
SEATTLE—*Continued*													
State government													
1990	43.5	44.0	44.5	44.6	44.8	45.1	39.3	39.2	41.6	45.9	46.1	45.6	43.6
1991	45.8	46.5	46.9	47.0	47.0	47.7	40.9	40.8	43.4	48.8	49.1	48.6	46.0
1992	48.4	49.0	49.3	48.5	48.8	48.8	42.5	42.1	44.7	49.6	50.1	49.7	47.6
1993	49.4	49.8	50.5	49.9	50.0	50.5	42.6	42.5	45.2	49.9	50.2	49.6	48.3
1994	49.5	50.0	49.7	50.2	50.5	50.9	43.7	43.8	45.9	51.0	51.4	50.7	48.9
1995	51.0	51.5	52.0	51.5	51.7	52.3	44.3	44.2	47.1	51.5	52.1	51.0	50.0
1996	51.1	52.0	52.4	52.0	52.3	52.6	45.4	45.3	47.8	52.2	52.7	51.1	50.5
1997	52.1	52.7	53.4	53.2	53.5	54.3	46.4	46.5	49.0	53.5	53.5	53.8	51.8
1998	53.3	54.0	54.9	54.6	54.9	55.8	47.5	47.5	50.5	54.3	55.1	54.3	53.0
1999	54.6	55.5	56.3	56.0	56.2	57.0	49.1	49.1	52.0	56.3	56.8	56.0	54.5
2000	55.6	56.7	57.3	56.8	57.0	57.3	50.0	50.2	53.1	57.3	58.0	57.4	55.5
2001	57.5	58.3	58.8	58.6	58.9	59.0	51.9	52.0	54.4	59.4	60.0	59.6	57.4
2002	59.7	60.2	60.5	60.1	60.2	60.1	53.3	52.9	55.3	59.9	60.9	59.3	58.5
2003	60.1	60.8	61.3	60.9	61.3	61.6	54.1	53.9	56.9	60.6	61.1	60.6	59.4
Local government													
1990	81.0	86.0	82.6	82.8	83.9	85.1	81.6	81.2	86.9	84.0	90.5	85.8	84.2
1991	84.7	86.4	87.2	87.7	91.4	89.1	88.0	81.4	91.0	87.7	93.0	87.5	87.9
1992	87.5	92.1	93.3	91.1	95.2	92.4	86.9	84.5	95.0	92.7	97.6	93.6	91.8
1993	91.4	92.3	93.5	93.2	94.1	94.7	91.5	87.0	97.6	94.0	100.7	95.0	93.7
1994	93.0	98.7	95.3	96.1	96.6	97.5	90.6	86.6	99.8	96.3	103.2	97.7	95.9
1995	95.8	98.8	101.2	98.1	99.4	100.9	95.8	90.7	100.7	98.0	104.5	100.1	98.6
1996	99.1	103.1	104.0	101.1	103.2	102.2	100.3	91.9	103.3	100.2	106.4	101.8	101.3
1997	100.1	101.5	102.4	102.6	103.6	107.5	102.7	95.4	105.0	102.8	108.6	104.2	103.0
1998	103.1	107.4	105.0	105.6	106.3	107.2	105.3	98.4	108.2	105.5	111.2	108.0	105.9
1999	105.8	107.0	107.6	107.6	108.6	109.2	107.5	102.9	109.9	107.8	112.8	109.2	107.9
2000	108.5	112.1	110.6	109.3	109.8	110.8	106.8	103.0	110.7	109.4	110.9	111.1	109.4
2001	111.7	113.1	113.8	113.9	114.6	115.7	113.4	107.2	115.0	113.5	118.8	115.7	113.9
2002	114.2	117.2	116.6	117.0	117.7	117.7	114.9	110.1	117.3	115.3	120.4	116.8	116.3
2003	115.4	118.3	116.9	117.1	120.4	117.6	114.9	110.4	115.6	117.2	122.0	118.4	117.0
SPOKANE													
Total nonfarm													
1990	145.7	146.0	148.1	149.8	152.0	154.2	150.9	151.7	154.9	154.5	155.0	154.4	151.4
1991	149.4	149.8	151.8	154.6	156.9	159.2	156.5	157.3	160.0	159.4	159.9	159.8	156.2
1992	154.9	155.7	158.4	160.3	162.4	164.2	161.2	162.2	164.3	166.1	165.9	166.3	161.8
1993	159.3	160.8	163.2	167.4	169.0	170.2	167.2	165.9	171.1	172.6	173.1	172.7	167.7
1994	167.4	168.9	171.8	173.9	176.1	176.5	173.5	175.0	178.4	179.5	179.7	177.7	174.8
1995	172.0	173.3	175.9	178.1	179.4	181.5	176.4	177.4	180.7	182.4	182.6	181.5	178.4
1996	174.3	174.8	177.1	180.5	182.8	184.1	180.9	181.9	184.3	185.4	186.0	185.1	181.4
1997	178.1	179.4	181.2	183.1	186.0	187.0	184.7	184.4	187.3	188.0	188.5	188.5	184.6
1998	182.8	183.9	186.3	188.2	190.3	191.1	186.6	186.9	190.4	190.2	189.9	190.2	188.0
1999	185.3	185.8	188.8	188.9	191.0	192.3	189.9	190.9	192.9	196.0	196.3	196.3	191.2
2000	188.0	190.0	192.2	194.4	197.2	197.9	193.6	195.1	198.1	201.1	201.3	200.1	195.7
2001	196.1	196.8	198.2	200.1	200.7	201.6	196.3	197.3	199.0	200.7	200.8	198.3	198.8
2002	190.8	191.7	192.7	194.9	197.1	197.7	194.2	194.0	197.6	198.5	199.3	198.5	195.6
2003	193.4	194.3	195.6	197.2	199.3	200.1	196.2	196.3	199.2	201.1	201.3	200.1	197.8
Total private													
1990	122.2	121.9	123.8	125.5	127.4	129.4	129.1	130.2	131.1	129.7	129.9	129.4	127.4
1991	124.7	124.5	126.4	128.5	130.5	132.5	132.7	133.8	134.5	132.7	133.3	133.2	130.6
1992	128.7	129.0	131.5	133.2	135.1	136.8	137.1	138.1	138.3	138.8	138.5	139.0	135.3
1993	130.7	131.7	133.7	137.7	139.0	140.0	141.1	141.1	143.1	142.9	143.1	143.0	138.9
1994	138.1	139.1	141.8	143.7	145.9	146.2	147.1	148.9	150.0	149.1	149.1	147.5	145.5
1995	142.1	142.8	145.3	147.4	148.4	150.4	149.8	151.2	152.3	152.2	151.9	151.0	148.7
1996	144.2	144.2	146.3	149.7	151.7	153.0	154.0	155.3	155.5	154.7	155.0	154.1	151.4
1997	147.4	148.4	150.0	151.8	154.3	155.3	157.0	156.9	157.9	156.9	157.1	157.0	154.1
1998	151.7	152.4	154.5	156.3	158.0	158.9	158.7	159.2	160.5	158.2	157.6	157.9	156.9
1999	153.6	153.4	156.2	156.1	158.2	159.4	161.3	162.4	162.2	163.2	163.3	163.7	159.4
2000	156.3	157.5	159.5	161.5	163.4	164.6	164.2	166.4	167.0	168.3	167.8	167.0	163.6
2001	162.7	162.6	163.8	165.7	166.0	166.8	166.2	167.5	167.1	166.5	166.4	164.0	165.4
2002	156.8	157.3	158.3	160.4	162.3	163.1	163.8	164.0	165.2	164.0	164.3	163.7	161.9
2003	158.9	159.6	160.9	162.4	164.0	164.8	165.3	165.8	166.4	166.6	166.8	165.6	163.9
Goods-producing													
1990	24.0	23.8	24.5	25.5	26.1	26.8	27.1	27.4	27.7	27.1	26.8	26.1	26.0
1991	24.4	24.5	25.2	26.1	26.9	27.7	27.9	28.2	29.0	27.7	27.4	26.4	26.7
1992	25.1	25.1	25.8	26.7	27.4	28.0	28.0	28.4	28.3	28.5	27.9	26.9	27.1
1993	24.7	25.3	26.0	27.6	28.2	28.7	29.3	29.4	30.1	30.2	29.7	29.0	28.1
1994	27.8	28.1	29.0	30.0	30.6	30.9	31.2	31.8	32.0	31.7	31.1	30.2	30.3
1995	28.9	29.1	30.1	31.3	31.8	32.7	33.1	33.6	33.8	33.2	32.6	32.1	31.8
1996	30.2	29.9	30.7	32.5	33.2	33.8	34.3	34.7	35.7	34.3	33.6	32.2	32.9
1997	30.5	30.7	31.3	32.4	33.2	33.8	34.5	34.6	34.9	34.4	33.6	32.4	33.0
1998	30.3	30.7	31.3	31.9	32.5	32.9	33.3	33.5	33.6	32.3	31.7	31.2	32.1
1999	29.7	29.7	30.9	31.8	32.2	32.9	33.5	34.0	33.6	33.8	33.5	32.8	32.3
2000	30.8	30.9	31.6	32.3	33.0	33.7	34.1	34.5	34.3	35.2	33.8	32.5	33.0
2001	31.0	30.4	30.7	31.3	31.8	32.1	31.8	32.3	31.5	30.9	30.0	28.4	31.0
2002	26.9	26.6	26.8	27.5	28.1	28.8	29.2	29.3	29.2	28.8	28.3	27.6	28.1
2003	26.7	26.9	27.0	27.6	27.9	28.6	29.0	29.4	29.4	29.5	29.0	27.7	28.2

Employment by Industry: Washington—*Continued*

(Numbers in thousands. Not seasonally adjusted.)

Industry	January	February	March	April	May	June	July	August	September	October	November	December	Annual Average
SPOKANE—*Continued*													
Construction and mining													
1990	5.9	5.8	6.3	7.0	7.3	7.8	8.0	8.4	8.5	8.2	7.8	7.3	7.3
1991	6.4	6.5	6.9	7.6	8.1	8.5	8.9	9.2	9.1	9.0	8.8	8.1	8.0
1992	7.2	7.3	7.8	8.4	8.9	9.3	9.8	10.2	10.0	9.9	9.4	8.5	8.8
1993	7.2	7.4	7.8	9.0	9.5	10.1	10.5	10.8	11.1	11.3	10.8	10.1	9.6
1994	9.0	8.9	9.4	10.1	10.6	11.0	11.0	11.3	11.3	11.1	10.5	9.7	10.3
1995	8.5	8.4	9.1	9.8	10.2	10.8	11.2	11.7	11.7	11.4	11.1	10.4	10.3
1996	9.0	8.6	9.4	10.6	11.2	11.7	12.1	12.4	12.3	11.9	11.5	10.3	10.9
1997	9.4	9.3	9.6	10.4	10.9	11.3	11.7	11.8	11.9	11.4	10.9	9.9	10.7
1998	8.5	8.6	9.0	9.7	10.2	10.7	11.1	11.3	11.3	11.1	10.5	10.2	10.1
1999	9.1	9.1	9.7	10.5	10.9	11.4	11.9	12.2	11.9	12.1	11.8	11.2	10.9
2000	9.5	9.7	10.2	10.7	11.3	11.7	12.0	12.4	12.3	11.9	11.5	10.5	11.1
2001	9.5	9.6	10.2	10.7	11.1	11.5	11.7	12.1	11.9	11.8	11.3	10.2	11.0
2002	9.1	9.0	9.2	9.8	10.5	11.0	11.3	11.4	11.5	11.3	11.0	10.3	10.5
2003	9.7	9.7	9.9	10.4	10.9	11.4	11.7	12.1	12.1	12.2	11.8	10.7	11.1
Manufacturing													
1990	18.1	18.0	18.2	18.5	18.8	19.0	19.1	19.0	19.2	18.9	19.0	18.8	18.7
1991	18.0	18.0	18.3	18.5	18.8	19.2	19.0	19.0	19.9	18.7	18.6	18.3	18.6
1992	17.9	17.8	18.0	18.3	18.5	18.7	18.2	18.2	18.3	18.6	18.5	18.4	18.2
1993	17.5	17.9	18.2	18.6	18.7	18.6	18.8	18.6	19.0	18.9	18.9	18.9	18.5
1994	18.8	19.2	19.6	19.9	20.0	19.9	20.2	20.5	20.7	20.6	20.6	20.5	20.0
1995	20.4	20.7	21.0	21.5	21.6	21.9	21.9	21.9	22.1	21.8	21.5	21.7	21.5
1996	21.2	21.3	21.3	21.9	22.0	22.1	22.2	22.3	23.4	22.4	22.1	21.9	22.0
1997	21.1	21.4	21.7	22.0	22.3	22.5	22.8	22.8	23.0	23.0	22.7	22.5	22.3
1998	21.8	22.1	22.3	22.2	22.3	22.2	22.2	22.2	22.3	21.2	21.2	21.0	21.9
1999	20.6	20.6	21.2	21.3	21.3	21.5	21.6	21.8	21.7	21.7	21.7	21.6	21.3
2000	21.3	21.2	21.4	21.6	21.7	22.0	22.1	22.1	22.0	23.3	22.3	22.0	21.9
2001	21.5	20.8	20.5	20.6	20.7	20.6	20.1	20.2	19.6	19.1	18.7	18.2	20.1
2002	17.8	17.6	17.6	17.7	17.6	17.8	17.9	17.9	17.7	17.5	17.3	17.3	17.6
2003	17.0	17.2	17.1	17.2	17.0	17.2	17.3	17.3	17.3	17.3	17.2	17.0	17.2
Service-providing													
1990	121.7	122.2	123.6	124.3	125.9	127.4	123.8	124.3	127.2	127.4	128.2	128.3	125.4
1991	125.0	125.3	126.6	128.5	130.0	131.5	128.6	129.1	131.0	131.7	132.5	133.4	129.4
1992	129.8	130.6	132.6	133.6	135.0	136.2	133.2	133.8	136.0	137.6	138.0	139.4	134.7
1993	134.6	135.5	137.2	139.8	140.8	141.5	137.9	136.5	141.0	142.4	143.4	143.7	139.5
1994	139.6	140.8	142.8	143.9	145.5	145.6	142.3	143.2	146.4	147.8	148.6	147.5	144.5
1995	143.1	144.2	145.8	146.8	147.6	148.8	143.3	143.8	146.9	149.2	150.0	149.4	146.5
1996	144.1	144.9	146.4	148.0	149.6	150.3	146.6	147.2	148.6	151.1	152.4	152.9	148.5
1997	147.6	148.7	149.9	150.7	152.8	153.2	150.2	149.8	152.4	153.6	154.9	156.1	151.6
1998	152.5	153.2	155.0	156.3	157.8	158.2	153.3	153.4	156.8	157.9	158.2	159.0	155.9
1999	155.6	156.1	157.9	157.1	158.8	159.4	156.4	156.9	159.3	162.2	162.8	163.5	158.8
2000	157.2	159.1	160.6	162.1	164.2	164.2	159.5	160.6	163.8	165.9	167.5	167.6	162.6
2001	165.1	166.4	167.5	168.8	168.9	169.5	164.5	165.0	167.5	169.8	170.8	169.9	167.8
2002	163.9	165.1	165.9	167.4	169.0	168.9	165.0	164.7	168.4	169.7	171.0	170.9	167.5
2003	166.7	167.4	168.6	169.6	171.4	171.5	167.2	166.9	169.8	171.6	172.3	172.4	169.6
Trade, transportation, and utilities													
1990	33.1	32.8	33.1	33.5	33.9	34.5	34.3	34.5	34.5	34.3	34.7	35.1	34.0
1991	33.4	32.8	32.8	32.9	33.3	33.6	33.4	33.5	33.6	33.8	34.5	34.9	33.5
1992	32.6	32.6	33.1	33.1	33.3	33.6	33.6	33.9	33.9	34.0	34.6	36.0	33.6
1993	33.5	33.3	33.6	34.4	34.6	34.9	35.3	35.2	35.5	35.4	36.3	36.9	34.9
1994	34.9	34.7	35.3	35.3	35.8	36.1	36.0	36.4	36.6	36.9	37.5	37.6	36.0
1995	35.8	35.3	35.6	36.0	36.1	36.7	36.8	37.1	37.5	38.3	38.9	39.1	36.9
1996	36.6	36.2	36.5	37.2	37.4	37.6	37.9	38.0	37.7	38.2	39.2	39.3	37.6
1997	36.1	35.9	36.1	36.7	37.5	37.8	38.4	37.9	38.3	38.7	39.7	40.3	37.7
1998	38.5	38.2	38.2	38.6	39.1	39.4	39.3	39.1	39.5	39.9	40.6	41.3	39.3
1999	39.7	39.5	39.6	39.4	39.8	40.0	40.5	40.6	41.0	41.2	42.0	42.4	40.4
2000	40.7	40.9	41.2	40.9	41.4	41.5	41.2	41.7	41.8	42.8	43.8	44.0	41.8
2001	41.3	40.7	40.8	41.0	40.9	41.3	41.2	41.4	41.1	41.7	42.2	42.3	41.3
2002	40.2	40.1	40.1	40.4	40.7	40.8	40.7	40.5	40.7	40.6	41.3	41.6	40.6
2003	39.9	39.5	39.7	39.9	40.4	40.6	40.7	40.8	40.6	40.8	41.7	42.1	40.6
Wholesale trade													
1990	8.8	8.9	9.0	9.0	9.1	9.3	9.4	9.4	9.4	9.4	9.4	9.3	9.2
1991	8.9	8.9	8.9	9.1	9.1	9.2	9.3	9.3	9.3	9.3	9.2	9.2	9.1
1992	8.4	8.4	8.8	8.8	8.9	9.0	9.0	9.2	9.1	8.8	8.8	9.7	8.9
1993	8.6	8.7	8.8	8.8	8.8	9.0	9.2	9.2	9.1	9.1	9.0	9.0	8.9
1994	8.4	8.6	9.0	8.9	8.9	9.1	8.9	9.0	9.0	9.0	8.6	8.7	8.8
1995	8.6	8.6	8.7	8.8	8.8	8.9	8.8	8.8	8.9	8.8	8.8	8.8	8.7
1996	8.8	8.8	8.8	9.0	9.0	9.2	9.3	9.3	9.1	9.1	9.1	9.0	9.0
1997	9.0	9.1	9.2	9.2	9.3	9.3	9.6	9.5	9.5	9.4	9.6	9.6	9.3
1998	9.6	9.6	9.7	9.8	9.9	10.1	10.3	10.2	10.3	10.3	10.3	10.3	10.0
1999	10.6	10.6	10.6	10.3	10.4	10.5	10.6	10.6	10.9	10.5	10.5	10.5	10.5
2000	10.5	10.7	10.7	10.2	10.4	10.5	10.5	10.6	10.5	10.6	10.6	10.6	10.5
2001	10.4	10.3	10.3	10.3	10.2	10.2	10.0	10.0	9.8	9.9	9.8	9.7	10.1
2002	9.5	9.6	9.5	9.5	9.6	9.6	9.7	9.6	9.6	9.5	9.5	9.5	9.6
2003	9.6	9.5	9.6	9.7	9.8	9.8	9.8	9.8	9.8	9.8	9.9	9.9	9.8

Employment by Industry: Washington—*Continued*

(Numbers in thousands. Not seasonally adjusted.)

Industry	January	February	March	April	May	June	July	August	September	October	November	December	Annual Average
SPOKANE—*Continued*													
Retail trade													
1990	19.8	19.5	19.6	20.1	20.3	20.6	20.4	20.5	20.5	20.5	20.9	21.2	20.3
1991	20.1	19.6	19.6	19.5	19.9	20.0	19.9	20.0	20.0	20.1	20.9	21.2	20.0
1992	19.6	19.6	19.7	19.6	19.7	19.9	19.9	20.1	20.2	20.5	21.1	21.5	20.1
1993	20.4	20.1	20.2	20.5	20.7	20.8	21.0	21.0	21.2	21.1	22.2	22.6	20.9
1994	21.4	21.0	21.1	21.1	21.5	21.6	21.8	22.0	22.1	22.1	23.1	23.2	21.8
1995	21.8	21.4	21.5	21.6	21.7	22.2	22.1	22.4	22.5	23.1	23.8	24.0	22.3
1996	22.4	22.0	22.2	22.6	22.9	22.8	22.8	22.9	22.8	23.2	24.2	24.5	22.9
1997	21.9	21.6	21.6	22.1	22.7	23.0	23.2	23.2	23.2	23.7	24.5	25.0	22.9
1998	23.4	23.1	23.0	23.2	23.5	23.6	23.3	23.1	23.3	23.9	24.6	25.2	23.6
1999	23.5	23.3	23.4	23.4	23.7	23.8	24.1	24.1	24.2	24.7	25.5	26.0	24.1
2000	24.5	24.5	24.7	24.8	25.2	25.2	24.8	25.1	25.3	26.0	27.1	27.4	25.3
2001	25.2	24.8	24.9	24.8	24.9	25.2	25.1	25.3	25.3	25.6	26.2	26.4	25.3
2002	24.9	24.7	24.8	24.9	25.1	25.1	25.1	25.0	25.1	25.0	25.7	26.1	25.1
2003	24.5	24.1	24.2	24.3	24.7	24.8	25.0	25.1	24.8	25.0	25.8	26.1	24.9
Transportation and utilities													
1990	4.5	4.4	4.5	4.4	4.5	4.6	4.5	4.6	4.6	4.4	4.4	4.6	4.5
1991	4.4	4.3	4.3	4.3	4.3	4.4	4.2	4.2	4.3	4.4	4.4	4.5	4.3
1992	4.6	4.6	4.6	4.7	4.7	4.7	4.7	4.6	4.6	4.7	4.7	4.8	4.6
1993	4.5	4.5	4.6	5.1	5.1	5.1	5.1	5.0	5.2	5.2	5.1	5.3	4.9
1994	5.1	5.1	5.2	5.3	5.4	5.4	5.3	5.4	5.5	5.8	5.8	5.7	5.4
1995	5.4	5.3	5.4	5.6	5.6	5.6	5.9	5.9	6.1	6.4	6.3	6.3	5.8
1996	5.4	5.4	5.5	5.6	5.5	5.6	5.8	5.8	5.8	5.9	5.9	5.8	5.6
1997	5.2	5.2	5.3	5.4	5.5	5.5	5.6	5.2	5.6	5.6	5.6	5.7	5.4
1998	5.5	5.5	5.5	5.6	5.7	5.7	5.7	5.8	5.9	5.7	5.7	5.8	5.6
1999	5.6	5.6	5.6	5.7	5.7	5.7	5.8	5.9	5.9	6.0	6.0	5.9	5.7
2000	5.7	5.7	5.8	5.9	5.8	5.8	5.9	6.0	6.0	6.2	6.1	6.0	5.9
2001	5.7	5.6	5.6	5.9	5.8	5.9	6.1	6.1	6.0	6.2	6.2	6.2	5.9
2002	5.8	5.8	5.8	6.0	6.0	6.1	5.9	5.9	6.0	6.1	6.1	6.0	6.0
2003	5.8	5.9	5.9	5.9	5.9	6.0	5.9	5.9	6.0	6.0	6.0	6.1	5.9
Information													
1990	3.4	3.4	3.4	3.6	3.6	3.7	3.5	3.6	3.7	3.6	3.6	3.6	3.5
1991	3.5	3.5	3.7	3.6	3.7	3.6	3.6	3.7	3.6	3.5	3.6	3.5	3.5
1992	3.4	3.3	3.4	3.4	3.4	3.5	3.5	3.5	3.4	3.5	3.5	3.5	3.4
1993	3.4	3.4	3.4	3.3	3.4	3.4	3.4	3.4	3.4	3.4	3.4	3.5	3.4
1994	3.4	3.5	3.5	3.4	3.4	3.5	3.4	3.5	3.5	3.4	3.4	3.4	3.4
1995	3.4	3.4	3.5	3.4	3.3	3.4	3.4	3.4	3.4	3.4	3.4	3.4	3.4
1996	3.5	3.4	3.4	3.3	3.3	3.4	3.3	3.3	3.4	3.4	3.4	3.4	3.3
1997	3.3	3.3	3.3	3.4	3.4	3.4	3.3	3.3	3.4	3.3	3.3	3.4	3.3
1998	3.5	3.5	3.6	3.4	3.5	3.5	3.4	3.5	3.5	3.4	3.4	3.4	3.4
1999	3.3	3.4	3.5	3.3	3.4	3.4	3.3	3.4	3.4	3.4	3.4	3.4	3.3
2000	3.3	3.3	3.4	3.7	3.7	3.8	3.6	3.7	3.7	3.6	3.7	3.7	3.6
2001	3.5	3.5	3.5	3.4	3.4	3.4	3.4	3.4	3.3	3.2	3.2	3.2	3.4
2002	3.0	3.0	3.0	2.9	2.9	2.9	2.8	2.8	2.8	2.8	2.8	2.9	2.9
2003	2.9	2.9	2.9	2.9	2.9	2.9	2.9	2.9	2.9	2.9	2.9	2.9	2.9
Financial activities													
1990	9.0	9.1	9.1	9.1	9.2	9.3	9.2	9.2	9.2	9.1	9.1	9.0	9.1
1991	9.0	9.0	9.1	9.1	9.2	9.4	9.4	9.5	9.5	9.3	9.3	9.4	9.2
1992	9.1	9.2	9.2	9.2	9.3	9.5	9.5	9.6	9.6	9.7	9.6	9.7	9.4
1993	9.8	9.8	9.9	9.9	10.0	10.0	10.1	10.1	10.2	10.2	10.2	10.3	10.0
1994	10.1	10.2	10.2	10.5	10.6	10.5	10.5	10.6	10.6	10.7	10.6	10.5	10.4
1995	10.6	10.6	10.7	10.5	10.6	10.6	10.5	10.6	10.7	10.8	10.8	10.7	10.6
1996	10.3	10.5	10.6	10.6	10.7	10.7	10.8	10.9	10.8	10.7	10.7	10.9	10.6
1997	10.7	10.7	10.8	10.8	10.8	10.7	10.9	10.9	10.9	10.9	10.9	11.0	10.8
1998	11.1	11.1	11.2	11.2	11.2	11.3	11.2	11.3	11.3	11.0	10.9	11.0	11.1
1999	11.1	11.0	11.0	11.1	11.1	11.1	11.2	11.1	11.1	11.2	11.1	11.1	11.1
2000	11.4	11.4	11.4	11.3	11.4	11.4	11.6	11.6	11.7	11.4	11.4	11.4	11.4
2001	11.5	11.5	11.5	11.5	11.6	11.6	11.6	11.7	11.7	11.6	11.7	11.7	11.6
2002	11.6	11.7	11.6	11.9	12.1	12.2	12.5	12.6	12.7	12.5	12.7	12.9	12.3
2003	13.0	13.1	13.3	13.5	13.6	13.8	13.8	13.9	13.8	13.7	13.7	13.6	13.6
Professional and business services													
1990	10.7	10.7	11.1	10.6	10.7	10.9	11.6	11.7	11.8	11.7	11.5	11.4	11.2
1991	10.8	10.9	11.2	11.6	11.8	11.9	11.9	12.2	11.9	11.9	11.8	11.7	11.6
1992	12.3	12.3	12.7	13.3	13.6	13.8	13.6	13.5	13.7	13.8	13.7	13.7	13.3
1993	12.8	13.1	13.1	13.9	14.1	14.2	14.3	14.1	14.6	14.5	14.2	14.2	13.9
1994	14.0	14.2	14.6	15.1	15.5	15.5	15.4	15.6	15.9	15.9	16.2	15.6	15.2
1995	14.6	15.1	15.6	15.7	15.8	15.9	15.2	15.3	15.5	15.5	15.2	14.9	15.3
1996	13.5	13.8	14.0	14.4	14.6	14.8	14.9	15.1	15.2	15.1	14.9	14.9	14.6
1997	14.9	15.5	15.6	15.8	15.9	16.1	15.9	15.9	15.9	16.0	16.1	16.1	15.8
1998	16.1	16.2	16.6	16.9	17.1	17.0	17.0	16.7	17.0	16.9	16.8	16.1	16.7
1999	15.7	15.9	16.7	16.6	17.0	17.1	17.5	18.1	18.2	18.6	18.2	18.2	17.3
2000	17.0	17.5	17.6	18.1	18.3	18.5	17.9	18.4	18.5	18.8	18.6	18.2	18.1
2001	18.4	18.6	18.8	19.6	19.0	19.2	19.3	19.5	19.5	19.3	19.1	18.5	19.1
2002	17.9	18.0	18.3	19.0	19.3	19.5	19.4	19.9	20.0	19.7	19.5	19.2	19.1
2003	18.5	18.5	18.7	19.2	19.4	19.6	19.8	19.7	19.5	19.5	19.2	19.1	19.2

Employment by Industry: Washington—*Continued*

(Numbers in thousands. Not seasonally adjusted.)

Industry	January	February	March	April	May	June	July	August	September	October	November	December	Annual Average
SPOKANE—*Continued*													
Educational and health services													
1990	21.4	21.6	21.6	21.9	22.1	22.2	22.0	22.2	22.5	22.3	22.5	22.7	22.0
1991	22.8	23.0	23.2	23.4	23.4	23.7	23.8	23.9	23.8	24.0	24.3	24.5	23.6
1992	24.6	24.9	25.0	24.7	24.8	24.9	25.1	25.2	25.3	25.2	25.3	25.5	25.0
1993	24.3	24.5	24.7	25.0	24.8	24.9	24.6	24.8	24.8	24.9	25.0	25.2	24.7
1994	24.8	24.9	25.1	25.0	24.8	24.9	25.3	25.4	25.4	25.1	25.0	25.2	25.0
1995	25.2	25.5	25.6	25.6	25.6	25.7	26.0	26.1	25.8	25.9	26.0	25.9	25.7
1996	26.5	26.7	26.8	26.9	27.0	26.9	27.5	27.6	26.9	27.5	27.7	27.9	27.1
1997	27.4	27.8	27.9	27.8	27.8	27.7	28.4	28.5	28.5	27.9	28.0	28.1	27.9
1998	28.0	28.3	28.6	28.6	28.6	28.5	28.5	28.9	29.1	29.1	29.1	29.3	28.7
1999	29.0	29.1	29.2	29.1	29.3	29.2	29.5	29.4	29.2	29.6	29.6	29.8	29.3
2000	29.2	29.5	29.7	30.1	30.1	30.2	30.5	30.7	30.8	30.8	30.8	31.1	30.2
2001	31.0	31.8	32.0	32.0	31.8	31.4	31.2	31.3	31.9	32.0	32.1	32.0	31.7
2002	30.9	31.4	31.7	31.8	31.9	31.0	31.3	31.1	31.9	32.0	32.1	32.2	31.6
2003	31.4	32.2	32.4	32.4	32.4	31.6	31.7	31.5	32.4	32.8	32.9	32.9	32.2
Leisure and hospitality													
1990	13.4	13.4	13.8	14.0	14.4	14.5	14.0	14.1	14.3	14.3	14.4	14.3	14.0
1991	13.6	13.7	14.0	14.6	14.9	15.2	15.3	15.5	15.8	15.3	15.2	15.5	14.8
1992	14.6	14.6	15.2	15.6	16.1	16.2	16.4	16.6	16.7	16.7	16.5	16.3	15.9
1993	14.8	14.9	15.5	16.0	16.3	16.1	16.5	16.5	16.9	16.6	16.7	16.3	16.0
1994	15.8	16.2	16.6	16.8	17.5	17.2	17.5	17.8	18.1	17.5	17.5	17.2	17.1
1995	16.1	16.2	16.6	17.1	17.5	17.7	17.1	17.4	17.9	17.3	17.3	17.2	17.1
1996	16.2	16.2	16.7	17.2	17.8	18.0	17.5	17.9	18.0	17.8	17.7	17.7	17.3
1997	17.0	16.9	17.3	17.1	17.8	18.0	17.8	18.0	18.2	17.8	17.8	18.0	17.6
1998	16.7	16.9	17.4	18.0	18.3	18.6	18.3	18.5	18.8	18.0	17.5	18.0	17.9
1999	17.6	17.4	17.7	17.2	17.8	18.0	18.2	18.1	18.1	17.8	17.9	18.3	17.8
2000	16.5	16.6	17.2	17.5	17.8	17.9	17.9	18.1	18.4	17.8	17.7	18.2	17.6
2001	17.5	17.5	17.8	18.1	18.4	18.7	18.7	18.7	18.8	18.4	18.7	18.6	18.3
2002	17.8	17.9	18.0	18.2	18.6	19.0	19.1	19.0	19.1	18.7	18.7	18.5	18.6
2003	17.8	17.7	17.9	17.8	18.2	18.5	18.4	18.6	18.7	18.3	18.2	18.2	18.2
Other services													
1990	7.2	7.1	7.2	7.3	7.4	7.5	7.4	7.5	7.4	7.3	7.3	7.2	7.3
1991	7.2	7.1	7.2	7.2	7.3	7.4	7.4	7.3	7.3	7.2	7.2	7.3	7.2
1992	7.0	7.0	7.1	7.2	7.2	7.3	7.4	7.4	7.4	7.4	7.4	7.4	7.2
1993	7.4	7.4	7.5	7.6	7.6	7.8	7.6	7.6	7.6	7.7	7.6	7.6	7.5
1994	7.3	7.3	7.5	7.6	7.7	7.6	7.8	7.8	7.9	7.9	7.8	7.8	7.6
1995	7.5	7.6	7.6	7.8	7.7	7.7	7.7	7.7	7.7	7.8	7.7	7.7	7.6
1996	7.4	7.5	7.6	7.6	7.7	7.8	7.8	7.8	7.8	7.7	7.8	7.8	7.6
1997	7.5	7.6	7.7	7.8	7.9	7.8	7.8	7.8	7.8	7.9	7.7	7.7	7.7
1998	7.5	7.5	7.6	7.7	7.7	7.7	7.7	7.7	7.7	7.6	7.6	7.6	7.6
1999	7.5	7.4	7.6	7.6	7.6	7.7	7.6	7.7	7.6	7.6	7.6	7.7	7.6
2000	7.4	7.4	7.4	7.6	7.7	7.6	7.4	7.7	7.8	7.9	8.0	7.9	7.6
2001	8.5	8.6	8.7	8.8	9.1	9.1	9.0	9.2	9.3	9.4	9.4	9.3	9.0
2002	8.5	8.6	8.8	8.7	8.7	8.9	8.8	8.8	8.8	8.9	8.9	8.8	8.8
2003	8.7	8.8	9.0	9.1	9.2	9.2	9.0	9.0	9.1	9.1	9.2	9.1	9.0
Government													
1990	23.5	24.1	24.3	24.3	24.6	24.8	21.8	21.5	23.8	24.8	25.1	25.0	24.0
1991	24.7	25.3	25.4	26.1	26.4	26.7	23.8	23.5	25.5	26.7	26.6	26.6	25.6
1992	26.2	26.7	26.9	27.1	27.3	27.4	24.1	24.1	26.0	27.3	27.4	27.3	26.5
1993	28.6	29.1	29.5	29.7	30.0	30.2	26.1	24.8	28.0	29.7	30.0	29.7	28.7
1994	29.3	29.8	30.0	30.2	30.2	30.3	26.4	26.1	28.4	30.4	30.6	30.2	29.3
1995	29.9	30.5	30.6	30.7	31.0	31.1	26.6	26.2	28.4	30.2	30.7	30.5	29.7
1996	30.1	30.6	30.8	30.8	31.1	31.1	26.9	26.6	28.8	30.7	31.0	31.0	29.9
1997	30.7	31.0	31.2	31.3	31.7	31.7	27.7	27.5	29.4	31.1	31.4	31.5	30.5
1998	31.1	31.5	31.8	31.9	32.3	32.2	27.9	27.7	29.9	32.0	32.3	32.3	31.0
1999	31.7	32.4	32.6	32.8	32.8	32.9	28.6	28.5	30.7	32.8	33.0	32.6	31.7
2000	31.7	32.5	32.7	32.9	33.8	33.3	29.4	28.7	31.1	32.8	33.5	33.1	32.1
2001	33.4	34.2	34.4	34.4	34.7	34.8	30.1	29.8	31.9	34.2	34.4	34.3	33.4
2002	34.0	34.4	34.4	34.5	34.8	34.6	30.4	30.0	32.4	34.5	35.0	34.8	33.7
2003	34.5	34.7	34.7	34.8	35.3	35.3	30.9	30.5	32.8	34.5	34.5	34.5	33.9
Federal government													
1990	3.6	3.6	3.6	3.6	3.6	3.7	3.6	3.6	3.6	3.5	3.5	3.6	3.6
1991	3.4	3.5	3.4	3.9	4.0	4.0	4.2	4.2	4.2	4.1	4.1	4.1	3.9
1992	4.2	4.2	4.2	4.2	4.2	4.2	4.3	4.3	4.3	4.3	4.3	4.3	4.3
1993	4.4	4.3	4.3	4.3	4.4	4.4	4.4	4.4	4.4	4.5	4.5	4.6	4.4
1994	4.5	4.5	4.5	4.4	4.4	4.4	4.5	4.5	4.5	4.5	4.5	4.5	4.4
1995	4.4	4.4	4.4	4.3	4.3	4.4	4.4	4.4	4.4	4.4	4.3	4.5	4.3
1996	4.4	4.3	4.4	4.3	4.3	4.3	4.3	4.3	4.3	4.3	4.3	4.5	4.3
1997	4.4	4.3	4.3	4.3	4.3	4.3	4.4	4.4	4.4	4.3	4.3	4.5	4.3
1998	4.3	4.3	4.3	4.3	4.3	4.3	4.3	4.3	4.3	4.4	4.4	4.7	4.3
1999	4.4	4.4	4.4	4.4	4.3	4.3	4.4	4.4	4.4	4.4	4.4	4.5	4.3
2000	4.4	4.4	4.4	4.6	5.1	4.6	4.6	4.6	4.4	4.5	4.4	4.6	4.5
2001	4.5	4.4	4.4	4.4	4.4	4.5	4.5	4.6	4.6	4.5	4.5	4.6	4.5
2002	4.5	4.4	4.4	4.4	4.5	4.5	4.5	4.6	4.6	4.7	4.7	4.8	4.6
2003	4.7	4.6	4.6	4.6	4.7	4.7	4.7	4.7	4.7	4.7	4.7	4.8	4.7

Employment by Industry: Washington—*Continued*

(Numbers in thousands. Not seasonally adjusted.)

Industry	January	February	March	April	May	June	July	August	September	October	November	December	Annual Average
SPOKANE—*Continued*													
State government													
1990	6.8	7.0	7.1	7.1	7.1	7.0	6.2	6.3	6.8	7.2	7.3	7.2	6.9
1991	7.3	7.5	7.5	7.6	7.6	7.6	6.5	6.6	7.1	7.6	7.6	7.6	7.3
1992	7.4	7.6	7.7	7.5	7.5	7.5	6.4	6.5	7.0	7.5	7.5	7.5	7.3
1993	9.4	9.6	9.8	9.8	9.8	9.7	7.0	7.2	8.4	9.7	9.8	9.5	9.1
1994	9.4	9.6	9.6	9.6	9.6	9.5	7.0	7.4	8.3	9.6	9.7	9.3	9.0
1995	9.4	9.7	9.6	9.7	9.9	9.8	7.1	7.4	8.4	9.6	9.9	9.5	9.1
1996	9.5	9.8	9.7	9.6	9.8	9.7	7.1	7.6	8.4	9.7	9.8	9.6	9.1
1997	9.7	9.9	10.0	9.9	10.0	10.0	7.3	7.8	8.7	9.9	10.0	9.9	9.4
1998	9.8	10.0	10.2	10.2	10.4	10.2	7.7	8.1	9.0	10.2	10.4	10.2	9.7
1999	10.2	10.5	10.6	10.6	10.6	10.5	7.9	8.3	9.2	10.4	10.6	10.3	9.9
2000	10.1	10.5	10.6	10.5	10.6	10.5	8.0	8.3	9.3	10.3	10.8	10.3	9.9
2001	10.4	10.8	10.9	10.8	10.9	10.7	8.2	8.6	9.3	10.8	11.0	10.8	10.3
2002	10.8	11.1	11.0	10.9	10.9	10.7	8.3	8.7	9.5	10.8	11.2	10.9	10.4
2003	10.8	11.0	11.0	10.9	11.0	10.8	8.5	8.6	9.5	10.9	11.0	10.9	10.4
Local government													
1990	13.1	13.5	13.6	13.6	13.9	14.1	12.0	11.6	13.4	14.1	14.3	14.2	13.5
1991	14.0	14.3	14.5	14.6	14.8	15.1	13.1	12.7	14.2	15.0	14.9	14.9	14.3
1992	14.6	14.9	15.0	15.4	15.6	15.7	13.4	13.3	14.7	15.5	15.6	15.5	14.9
1993	14.8	15.2	15.4	15.6	15.8	16.1	14.7	13.2	15.2	15.5	15.7	15.6	15.2
1994	15.4	15.7	15.9	16.2	16.2	16.4	14.9	14.2	15.6	16.3	16.4	16.4	15.8
1995	16.1	16.4	16.6	16.7	16.8	16.9	15.1	14.4	15.6	16.2	16.5	16.5	16.1
1996	16.2	16.5	16.7	16.9	17.0	17.1	15.5	14.7	16.1	16.7	16.9	16.9	16.4
1997	16.6	16.8	16.9	17.1	17.4	17.4	16.0	15.3	16.3	16.9	17.1	17.1	16.7
1998	17.0	17.2	17.3	17.4	17.6	17.7	15.9	15.3	16.6	17.4	17.5	17.4	17.0
1999	17.1	17.5	17.6	17.8	17.9	18.1	16.3	15.8	17.1	18.0	18.0	17.8	17.4
2000	17.2	17.6	17.7	17.8	18.1	18.2	16.8	15.8	17.4	18.0	18.3	18.2	17.5
2001	18.5	19.0	19.1	19.2	19.4	19.6	17.4	16.6	18.0	18.9	18.9	18.9	18.6
2002	18.7	18.9	19.0	19.2	19.4	19.4	17.6	16.7	18.3	19.0	19.1	19.1	18.7
2003	19.0	19.1	19.1	19.3	19.6	19.8	17.7	17.2	18.6	18.9	18.8	18.8	18.8
TACOMA													
Total nonfarm													
1990	187.2	188.6	190.0	193.3	195.8	196.5	196.0	196.8	198.0	198.7	197.6	198.1	194.7
1991	190.9	191.2	193.2	194.8	196.0	196.7	197.3	196.6	198.5	200.5	199.3	198.9	196.1
1992	194.6	195.8	197.9	199.5	201.8	201.4	199.8	199.8	202.9	204.5	202.9	203.6	200.3
1993	200.9	202.0	204.5	205.9	206.3	207.4	205.6	205.3	210.3	210.0	210.0	211.3	206.6
1994	205.6	206.5	208.2	210.9	212.3	213.6	211.1	213.4	217.9	215.6	216.3	216.5	212.3
1995	211.7	212.7	215.5	216.5	218.1	219.0	215.9	217.3	221.8	219.5	218.9	219.3	217.1
1996	215.0	216.1	217.6	218.6	220.5	221.6	220.7	222.2	225.2	227.2	226.7	227.4	221.5
1997	222.4	224.1	226.4	228.6	230.0	230.9	229.3	229.3	233.4	232.5	232.3	233.6	229.4
1998	228.0	229.6	231.3	233.3	235.7	237.9	235.5	235.9	239.4	239.3	238.9	240.8	235.4
1999	232.3	233.7	236.9	238.4	239.3	241.4	241.3	239.4	241.8	242.3	242.3	243.9	239.4
2000	237.4	239.2	242.8	244.4	246.0	246.9	243.9	245.0	246.7	246.0	247.0	247.7	244.4
2001	240.8	241.3	242.7	243.2	244.7	245.7	245.4	243.7	247.0	244.6	243.9	244.3	243.9
2002	237.5	238.6	239.7	241.8	243.5	245.6	245.9	245.0	248.8	247.7	248.5	248.9	244.3
2003	243.1	243.7	245.4	246.9	248.3	249.5	247.8	248.6	252.8	252.8	253.5	253.8	248.9
Total private													
1990	146.0	145.8	148.3	150.9	152.6	153.5	153.6	155.5	156.8	155.6	153.5	153.8	152.1
1991	148.0	147.9	149.6	150.7	152.0	152.3	153.4	154.2	156.1	156.8	155.0	154.8	152.5
1992	150.7	151.7	153.6	155.0	157.2	156.7	157.0	157.6	159.9	160.0	158.0	158.7	156.3
1993	156.3	156.9	159.0	160.7	160.8	161.9	162.1	162.3	166.2	164.3	163.7	164.8	161.5
1994	160.6	161.2	162.5	165.0	165.7	166.7	166.6	169.1	172.5	169.2	169.4	169.7	166.5
1995	165.4	166.0	168.4	169.3	170.2	171.2	170.4	172.5	176.3	173.4	172.2	172.5	170.6
1996	168.7	169.5	170.6	171.5	173.0	173.5	175.1	176.9	179.5	180.6	179.6	180.0	174.8
1997	175.2	176.7	178.7	181.0	182.0	182.8	182.2	184.1	187.6	185.2	184.3	185.5	182.1
1998	180.1	181.7	183.0	184.7	186.7	188.6	188.1	190.0	192.9	190.7	189.8	191.5	187.3
1999	183.9	185.0	187.7	189.2	189.9	191.3	192.4	192.3	194.4	193.2	192.5	193.8	190.4
2000	188.2	189.6	192.9	194.3	194.5	195.0	194.2	196.2	198.2	195.9	195.9	196.6	194.2
2001	189.8	189.7	190.7	191.3	192.5	193.1	194.3	194.5	196.6	192.8	191.5	191.6	192.4
2002	185.3	186.0	187.0	189.0	190.6	192.1	193.9	195.4	197.7	195.1	195.4	195.9	192.0
2003	190.3	190.6	192.0	193.6	194.6	195.5	196.8	198.6	201.2	199.3	199.6	199.8	196.0
Goods-producing													
1990	31.0	30.6	31.5	31.7	31.8	32.3	32.4	33.0	32.4	31.8	30.9	30.0	31.6
1991	28.4	28.3	28.7	28.9	29.2	29.7	30.2	30.5	30.3	30.2	29.5	28.8	29.3
1992	27.4	27.3	27.8	29.0	29.5	29.9	30.1	30.1	30.1	29.8	29.4	28.8	29.1
1993	28.5	28.8	29.3	29.6	29.6	29.8	31.4	31.8	32.0	32.1	31.5	31.2	30.4
1994	30.0	30.1	30.3	30.7	30.9	31.4	31.6	32.4	32.6	32.1	32.0	31.4	31.2
1995	30.8	30.7	31.4	31.9	32.6	33.1	33.5	34.1	34.6	33.9	33.2	33.1	32.7
1996	33.0	33.4	33.7	34.4	34.9	35.4	36.9	37.8	38.0	38.2	37.3	36.9	35.8
1997	36.2	36.2	36.6	37.3	37.7	38.2	38.5	39.4	39.3	39.1	38.7	38.5	37.9
1998	37.3	37.8	38.0	38.4	39.1	39.6	40.2	40.8	40.4	40.1	39.3	39.1	39.1
1999	37.8	37.7	38.3	38.2	38.6	39.2	39.9	40.2	40.0	39.7	38.9	38.6	38.9
2000	37.3	37.6	38.3	39.4	39.2	39.2	39.2	39.7	39.7	39.2	38.7	38.1	38.8
2001	37.7	37.5	37.7	37.6	38.2	38.9	39.4	40.1	39.8	38.6	37.9	37.0	38.4
2002	35.6	35.7	35.4	36.2	36.7	37.6	37.8	38.2	37.8	37.4	36.9	36.1	36.8
2003	35.4	35.2	35.5	35.9	36.5	37.2	37.9	38.7	38.7	38.6	38.3	37.9	37.2

Employment by Industry: Washington—*Continued*

(Numbers in thousands. Not seasonally adjusted.)

Industry	January	February	March	April	May	June	July	August	September	October	November	December	Annual Average
TACOMA—*Continued*													
Natural resources and mining													
1990	0.4	0.3	0.3	0.4	0.4	0.4	0.4	0.4	0.4	0.4	0.4	0.4	0.3
1991	0.3	0.4	0.4	0.4	0.4	0.4	0.4	0.4	0.4	0.4	0.4	0.4	0.3
1992	0.4	0.4	0.4	0.4	0.4	0.4	0.4	0.4	0.4	0.4	0.4	0.4	0.4
1993	0.3	0.4	0.4	0.4	0.4	0.4	0.4	0.4	0.4	0.4	0.4	0.4	0.3
1994	0.4	0.4	0.4	0.4	0.4	0.4	0.4	0.4	0.4	0.4	0.4	0.4	0.4
1995	0.4	0.4	0.4	0.5	0.5	0.5	0.5	0.5	0.5	0.5	0.4	0.4	0.4
1996	0.4	0.4	0.4	0.4	0.4	0.4	0.5	0.5	0.5	0.4	0.4	0.4	0.4
1997	0.4	0.4	0.4	0.4	0.4	0.4	0.4	0.4	0.4	0.4	0.4	0.4	0.4
1998	0.4	0.4	0.4	0.5	0.5	0.5	0.5	0.5	0.5	0.5	0.5	0.5	0.4
1999	0.4	0.5	0.5	0.5	0.5	0.5	0.5	0.5	0.5	0.5	0.5	0.5	0.4
2000	0.4	0.5	0.5	0.5	0.5	0.5	0.4	0.5	0.5	0.5	0.4	0.4	0.4
2001	0.5	0.5	0.5	0.4	0.5	0.5	0.6	0.6	0.6	0.6	0.6	0.6	0.5
2002	0.5	0.6	0.6	0.6	0.6	0.6	0.6	0.6	0.6	0.6	0.6	0.6	0.6
2003	0.5	0.5	0.6	0.6	0.6	0.6	0.6	0.6	0.6	0.6	0.6	0.6	0.6
Construction													
1990	10.8	10.7	11.6	11.9	12.0	12.3	12.1	12.5	12.2	12.2	11.8	11.4	11.7
1991	10.5	10.3	10.5	10.7	10.8	10.9	11.3	11.6	11.4	11.7	11.0	10.8	10.9
1992	10.6	10.6	11.0	11.2	11.4	11.5	11.6	11.7	11.5	11.6	11.2	10.9	11.2
1993	10.8	11.2	11.4	11.3	11.4	11.6	11.9	12.0	12.2	12.5	12.1	12.0	11.7
1994	11.2	11.2	11.4	12.0	12.2	12.5	12.5	13.0	12.8	12.4	12.0	11.7	12.0
1995	11.1	11.1	11.5	11.6	12.0	12.5	12.4	12.7	12.9	12.2	11.9	11.7	11.9
1996	11.5	11.6	11.8	12.1	12.3	12.8	13.2	13.7	13.7	13.2	12.6	12.2	12.5
1997	11.8	12.1	12.1	12.7	13.0	13.3	13.5	14.0	13.9	13.7	13.3	13.1	13.0
1998	12.2	12.6	12.9	13.3	13.7	14.0	14.5	15.0	15.0	15.0	14.8	14.5	13.9
1999	14.2	13.9	14.3	14.5	14.7	15.2	15.7	16.0	15.9	16.0	15.5	15.4	15.1
2000	14.7	15.1	15.5	15.9	15.9	16.0	16.2	16.6	16.5	16.3	16.1	15.9	15.8
2001	15.5	15.5	15.6	15.7	16.2	16.6	17.0	17.5	17.3	16.6	16.2	15.6	16.3
2002	15.1	15.2	15.0	15.6	16.0	16.7	16.9	17.4	17.3	17.0	16.7	16.2	16.3
2003	16.0	16.0	16.1	16.5	17.1	17.8	18.4	19.0	19.0	19.0	18.8	18.5	17.7
Manufacturing													
1990	19.8	19.6	19.6	19.4	19.4	19.6	19.9	20.1	19.8	19.2	18.7	18.2	19.4
1991	17.6	17.6	17.8	17.8	18.0	18.4	18.5	18.5	18.5	18.1	18.1	17.6	18.0
1992	16.4	16.3	16.4	17.4	17.7	18.0	18.1	18.0	18.2	17.8	17.8	17.5	17.4
1993	17.4	17.2	17.5	17.9	17.8	17.8	19.1	19.4	19.4	19.2	19.0	18.8	18.3
1994	18.4	18.5	18.5	18.3	18.3	18.5	18.7	19.0	19.4	19.3	19.6	19.3	18.8
1995	19.3	19.2	19.5	19.8	20.1	20.1	20.6	20.9	21.2	21.2	20.9	21.0	20.3
1996	21.1	21.4	21.5	21.9	22.2	22.2	23.2	23.6	23.8	24.6	24.3	24.3	22.8
1997	24.0	23.7	24.1	24.2	24.3	24.5	24.6	25.0	25.0	25.0	25.0	25.0	24.5
1998	24.7	24.8	24.7	24.6	24.9	25.1	25.2	25.3	24.9	24.6	24.0	24.1	24.7
1999	23.2	23.3	23.5	23.2	23.4	23.5	23.7	23.7	23.6	23.2	22.9	22.7	23.3
2000	22.2	22.0	22.3	23.0	22.8	22.7	22.6	22.6	22.7	22.4	22.2	21.8	22.4
2001	21.7	21.5	21.6	21.5	21.5	21.8	21.8	22.0	21.9	21.4	21.1	20.8	21.6
2002	20.0	19.9	19.8	20.0	20.1	20.3	20.3	20.2	19.9	19.8	19.6	19.3	19.9
2003	18.9	18.7	18.8	18.8	18.8	18.8	18.9	19.1	19.1	19.0	18.9	18.8	18.9
Service-providing													
1990	156.2	158.0	158.5	161.6	164.0	164.2	163.6	163.8	165.6	166.9	166.7	168.1	163.1
1991	162.5	162.9	164.5	165.9	166.8	167.0	167.1	166.1	168.2	170.3	169.8	170.1	166.7
1992	167.2	168.5	170.1	170.5	172.3	171.5	169.7	169.7	172.8	174.7	173.5	174.8	171.2
1993	172.4	173.2	175.2	176.3	176.7	177.6	174.2	173.5	178.3	177.9	178.5	180.1	176.1
1994	175.6	176.4	177.9	180.2	181.4	182.2	179.5	181.0	185.3	183.5	184.3	185.1	181.0
1995	180.9	182.0	184.1	184.6	185.5	185.9	182.4	183.2	187.2	185.6	185.7	186.2	184.4
1996	182.0	182.7	183.9	184.2	185.6	186.2	183.8	184.4	187.2	189.0	189.4	190.5	185.7
1997	186.2	187.9	189.8	191.3	192.3	192.7	190.8	189.9	194.1	193.4	193.6	195.1	191.4
1998	190.7	191.8	193.3	194.9	196.6	198.3	195.3	195.1	199.0	199.2	199.6	201.7	196.2
1999	194.5	196.0	198.6	200.2	200.7	202.2	201.4	199.2	201.8	202.6	203.4	205.3	200.4
2000	200.1	201.6	204.5	205.0	206.8	207.7	204.7	205.3	207.0	206.8	208.3	209.6	205.6
2001	203.1	203.8	205.0	205.6	206.5	206.8	206.0	203.6	207.2	206.0	206.0	207.3	205.6
2002	201.9	202.9	204.3	205.6	206.8	208.0	208.1	206.8	211.0	210.3	211.6	212.8	207.5
2003	207.7	208.5	209.9	211.0	211.8	212.3	209.9	209.9	214.1	214.2	215.2	215.9	211.7
Trade, transportation, and utilities													
1990	39.1	38.5	39.1	39.5	40.2	40.2	40.2	40.4	40.7	40.0	41.1	41.9	40.0
1991	40.1	39.4	39.9	40.1	40.8	40.6	40.5	40.7	41.2	40.7	41.5	42.1	40.6
1992	39.9	39.9	40.9	41.0	41.7	41.5	41.4	41.8	42.2	41.8	42.7	43.3	41.5
1993	42.1	41.6	42.0	42.5	43.0	43.2	43.1	43.1	43.5	43.1	43.9	44.8	42.9
1994	41.6	41.7	42.6	42.7	43.4	43.4	43.5	44.5	45.4	45.1	46.0	46.8	43.8
1995	44.7	44.7	45.0	45.3	45.4	45.5	44.9	45.6	46.3	46.6	47.2	47.5	45.7
1996	44.2	43.9	43.7	43.9	44.3	44.4	44.7	44.7	44.8	45.1	45.7	46.7	44.6
1997	42.8	42.9	43.8	45.0	45.3	45.5	44.9	44.7	45.2	45.5	46.3	47.3	44.9
1998	44.3	44.0	44.2	44.7	45.2	45.7	45.9	45.9	46.1	46.9	47.8	49.0	45.8
1999	45.1	44.9	45.4	45.1	45.4	46.0	46.2	46.0	46.1	46.8	48.1	49.1	46.1
2000	46.2	46.0	46.6	47.1	47.3	47.6	47.0	47.2	47.4	48.3	49.7	50.4	47.5
2001	47.8	47.0	47.0	47.1	47.0	47.3	47.4	47.0	47.0	47.4	47.8	48.5	47.4
2002	46.3	45.6	45.9	45.8	46.3	47.0	47.5	47.5	47.8	48.1	48.9	50.0	47.2
2003	46.9	46.4	46.6	46.6	47.1	47.4	48.1	48.0	48.0	48.5	49.3	49.7	47.7

Employment by Industry: Washington—*Continued*

(Numbers in thousands. Not seasonally adjusted.)

Industry	January	February	March	April	May	June	July	August	September	October	November	December	Annual Average
TACOMA—*Continued*													
Wholesale trade													
1990	8.1	8.2	8.3	8.3	8.5	8.5	8.6	8.7	8.7	8.5	8.5	8.5	8.4
1991	8.0	8.1	8.2	8.2	8.3	8.2	8.2	8.2	8.2	8.0	8.1	8.1	8.1
1992	7.4	7.5	8.4	8.4	8.6	8.6	8.7	8.6	8.6	8.5	8.6	8.6	8.3
1993	8.8	8.8	8.9	9.0	9.1	9.1	9.2	9.2	9.1	9.0	9.0	9.0	9.0
1994	7.9	8.0	8.9	8.8	8.9	9.0	9.1	9.1	9.3	9.1	9.1	9.2	8.8
1995	9.0	9.1	9.2	9.2	9.2	9.3	9.3	9.3	9.4	9.4	9.2	9.1	9.2
1996	9.3	9.4	9.4	9.6	9.8	9.8	9.8	9.8	9.8	9.7	9.7	9.8	9.6
1997	9.3	9.5	9.5	9.6	9.7	9.9	9.8	9.7	9.7	9.6	9.4	9.4	9.5
1998	9.2	9.3	9.3	9.5	9.5	9.6	9.4	9.3	9.1	9.4	9.3	9.4	9.3
1999	9.1	9.2	9.3	9.2	9.3	9.4	9.3	9.3	9.3	9.2	9.2	9.3	9.2
2000	9.5	9.5	9.6	9.7	9.8	9.9	9.8	9.7	9.6	9.6	9.5	9.5	9.6
2001	9.5	9.5	9.6	9.6	9.5	9.7	9.7	9.5	9.5	9.3	9.2	9.2	9.5
2002	8.9	8.9	9.1	9.0	9.1	9.3	9.3	9.2	9.2	9.1	9.1	9.1	9.1
2003	9.0	9.0	9.1	9.1	9.2	9.2	9.3	9.2	9.2	9.2	9.1	9.0	9.1
Retail trade													
1990	24.2	23.6	23.9	24.4	24.7	24.7	24.6	24.7	24.8	24.5	25.6	26.1	24.6
1991	24.7	24.2	24.2	24.4	24.9	24.7	24.6	24.8	25.0	25.0	25.7	26.3	24.8
1992	25.0	24.7	24.8	24.8	25.2	25.1	24.9	25.4	25.6	25.4	26.4	26.9	25.3
1993	25.5	25.1	25.3	25.5	25.9	26.1	25.9	26.0	26.3	26.4	27.3	28.0	26.1
1994	26.2	26.2	26.1	26.4	26.7	26.7	26.7	27.8	28.2	28.0	28.8	29.5	27.2
1995	27.8	27.6	27.7	27.9	28.0	28.0	27.6	28.3	28.6	28.8	29.5	30.0	28.3
1996	27.2	26.8	26.6	26.6	26.7	26.7	26.9	27.0	27.1	27.5	28.2	28.9	27.1
1997	26.1	25.9	26.9	27.7	27.7	27.9	27.7	27.7	28.0	28.6	29.7	30.7	27.8
1998	28.2	27.8	27.9	28.1	28.4	28.9	29.2	29.2	29.5	30.2	31.1	32.1	29.2
1999	28.7	28.2	28.5	28.5	28.8	29.1	29.3	29.2	29.3	29.8	30.9	31.9	29.3
2000	28.8	28.6	28.9	29.0	29.3	29.3	28.9	29.1	29.4	29.8	31.2	32.1	29.5
2001	29.6	28.9	28.9	28.9	28.9	28.9	28.9	28.6	28.8	29.1	29.6	30.3	29.1
2002	28.8	28.1	28.2	28.1	28.5	28.8	29.1	29.2	29.5	29.5	30.4	31.2	29.1
2003	28.8	28.3	28.3	28.3	28.7	28.9	29.2	29.2	29.1	29.4	30.5	31.0	29.1
Transportation and utilities													
1990	6.8	6.7	6.9	6.8	7.0	7.0	7.0	7.0	7.2	7.0	7.0	7.3	6.9
1991	7.4	7.1	7.5	7.5	7.6	7.7	7.7	7.7	8.0	7.7	7.7	7.7	7.6
1992	7.5	7.7	7.7	7.8	7.9	7.8	7.8	7.8	8.0	7.9	7.7	7.8	7.7
1993	7.8	7.7	7.8	8.0	8.0	8.0	8.0	7.9	8.1	7.7	7.6	7.8	7.8
1994	7.5	7.5	7.6	7.5	7.8	7.7	7.7	7.6	7.9	8.0	8.1	8.1	7.7
1995	7.9	8.0	8.1	8.2	8.2	8.2	8.0	8.0	8.3	8.4	8.5	8.4	8.1
1996	7.7	7.7	7.7	7.7	7.8	7.9	8.0	7.9	7.9	7.9	7.8	8.0	7.8
1997	7.4	7.5	7.4	7.7	7.9	7.7	7.4	7.3	7.5	7.3	7.2	7.2	7.4
1998	6.9	6.9	7.0	7.1	7.3	7.2	7.3	7.4	7.5	7.3	7.4	7.5	7.2
1999	7.3	7.5	7.6	7.4	7.3	7.5	7.6	7.5	7.5	7.8	8.0	7.9	7.5
2000	7.9	7.9	8.1	8.4	8.2	8.4	8.3	8.4	8.4	8.9	9.0	8.8	8.3
2001	8.7	8.6	8.5	8.6	8.6	8.7	8.8	8.9	8.7	9.0	9.0	9.0	8.8
2002	8.6	8.6	8.6	8.7	8.7	8.9	9.1	9.1	9.1	9.5	9.4	9.7	9.0
2003	9.1	9.1	9.2	9.2	9.2	9.3	9.6	9.6	9.7	9.9	9.7	9.7	9.4
Information													
1990	3.0	3.0	3.0	3.0	3.1	3.1	3.1	3.1	3.1	3.1	3.1	3.2	3.0
1991	3.1	3.1	3.2	3.1	3.1	3.2	3.3	3.3	3.2	3.2	3.2	3.3	3.1
1992	3.2	3.2	3.2	3.2	3.2	3.2	3.2	3.1	3.1	3.1	3.1	3.1	3.1
1993	3.0	3.1	3.1	3.2	3.3	3.3	3.2	3.2	3.2	3.2	3.1	3.1	3.1
1994	3.1	3.1	3.1	3.1	3.1	3.1	3.1	3.1	3.1	3.1	3.0	3.0	3.0
1995	3.0	3.0	3.1	3.2	3.2	3.2	3.1	3.1	3.1	3.0	3.0	3.0	3.0
1996	3.0	3.0	3.1	3.1	3.1	3.2	3.2	3.2	3.1	3.2	3.2	3.1	3.1
1997	3.2	3.2	3.2	3.1	3.2	3.1	2.9	2.9	2.9	2.9	3.0	3.0	3.0
1998	2.8	2.9	2.9	2.9	3.0	3.0	3.0	3.1	3.1	3.2	3.1	3.2	3.0
1999	3.3	3.4	3.4	3.5	3.6	3.6	3.6	3.6	3.6	3.3	3.4	3.4	3.4
2000	3.4	3.4	3.6	3.6	3.7	3.7	4.0	4.1	4.1	4.0	4.0	4.0	3.8
2001	3.8	3.7	3.8	3.7	3.7	3.7	3.6	3.5	3.4	3.2	3.3	3.3	3.6
2002	3.2	3.2	3.1	3.0	3.0	3.0	3.0	2.9	2.9	2.9	2.9	3.0	3.0
2003	3.0	3.0	2.9	3.0	2.9	3.0	2.9	2.9	2.9	2.9	3.0	3.0	3.0
Financial activities													
1990	9.9	10.0	10.1	10.3	10.4	10.4	10.5	10.6	10.5	10.5	10.5	10.5	10.3
1991	11.0	11.1	11.2	11.2	11.4	11.3	11.4	11.4	11.4	11.1	11.2	11.3	11.2
1992	10.0	10.0	10.1	10.1	10.2	10.1	10.1	10.1	10.3	10.4	10.4	10.5	10.1
1993	10.2	10.2	10.3	10.4	10.4	10.5	10.4	10.3	10.3	10.6	10.7	10.7	10.4
1994	10.3	10.3	10.3	10.4	10.4	10.4	10.5	10.4	10.5	10.2	10.1	10.1	10.3
1995	10.0	10.1	10.3	10.3	10.3	10.3	10.2	10.4	10.6	10.5	10.5	10.6	10.3
1996	10.6	10.6	10.7	10.6	10.6	10.6	10.7	10.8	10.8	10.8	10.8	10.9	10.7
1997	11.1	11.2	11.2	11.3	11.2	11.2	11.1	11.2	11.2	11.4	11.5	11.5	11.2
1998	11.2	11.4	11.5	11.8	11.9	12.0	12.1	12.3	12.4	12.3	12.3	12.5	11.9
1999	12.0	12.1	12.3	13.1	13.2	13.2	13.2	13.1	13.0	13.7	13.9	13.8	13.0
2000	13.2	13.3	13.4	13.3	13.3	13.2	13.1	13.2	13.3	13.0	13.1	13.1	13.2
2001	13.0	13.0	13.0	13.1	13.0	13.1	13.1	13.0	12.9	12.7	12.6	12.6	12.9
2002	12.7	12.7	12.7	12.8	12.9	12.9	13.0	13.2	13.1	13.1	13.2	13.3	13.0
2003	13.1	13.1	13.2	13.4	13.5	13.6	13.5	13.7	13.6	13.6	13.6	13.7	13.5

Employment by Industry: Washington—*Continued*

(Numbers in thousands. Not seasonally adjusted.)

Industry	January	February	March	April	May	June	July	August	September	October	November	December	Annual Average
TACOMA—Continued													
Professional and business services													
1990	13.6	13.6	13.9	14.3	14.7	15.0	15.1	15.5	15.5	14.8	14.7	14.6	14.6
1991	13.4	13.3	13.5	13.9	14.0	14.0	14.3	14.4	14.4	13.8	13.4	13.5	13.8
1992	14.3	14.8	15.0	15.2	15.3	15.5	15.8	15.9	16.0	15.6	15.3	15.5	15.3
1993	15.3	15.3	16.0	15.2	15.3	15.6	15.2	15.4	15.6	15.8	15.4	15.3	15.4
1994	15.7	15.7	15.8	16.4	16.3	16.7	16.9	17.2	17.3	16.7	16.6	16.4	16.4
1995	16.1	16.2	16.7	16.1	16.1	16.3	16.4	16.8	17.1	16.7	16.1	16.3	16.4
1996	15.8	16.0	16.4	16.4	16.5	16.5	16.8	17.1	17.1	17.9	17.5	17.2	16.7
1997	17.8	17.8	18.2	17.7	17.8	17.8	17.8	18.3	18.4	18.1	17.7	18.0	17.9
1998	18.4	18.3	18.6	18.3	18.5	18.8	17.8	18.3	18.3	18.6	18.4	18.5	18.4
1999	18.0	18.0	18.2	18.2	18.0	18.2	18.0	18.0	18.1	17.9	17.9	17.8	18.0
2000	18.1	18.3	18.5	17.7	17.8	18.1	18.0	18.3	18.5	18.4	18.0	18.4	18.1
2001	18.3	18.2	18.5	18.7	18.6	19.3	19.6	19.5	19.5	19.2	19.1	19.0	19.0
2002	18.2	18.5	18.8	19.5	19.5	19.8	20.0	20.7	20.8	20.6	20.9	20.5	19.8
2003	19.9	20.1	20.1	20.3	20.3	20.6	20.8	21.3	21.2	21.1	21.1	20.7	20.6
Educational and health services													
1990	25.0	25.4	25.6	26.3	26.6	26.5	25.9	26.2	26.7	27.6	27.6	27.6	26.4
1991	27.2	27.5	27.6	27.8	27.9	27.5	27.9	28.1	28.5	29.7	30.0	29.6	28.2
1992	29.5	29.8	29.6	29.3	29.5	29.0	29.0	29.0	29.7	29.6	29.9	29.8	29.4
1993	29.7	29.9	30.2	30.5	30.5	30.4	29.8	29.9	30.4	30.5	30.5	30.5	30.2
1994	31.6	32.0	31.8	32.2	32.2	31.9	31.5	31.6	32.4	32.1	32.2	32.2	31.9
1995	31.6	31.8	32.0	32.4	32.4	32.3	32.1	32.3	32.9	32.8	33.0	32.8	32.3
1996	33.0	33.6	33.6	33.6	33.6	33.4	33.1	33.1	33.7	34.7	35.0	35.1	33.7
1997	33.8	34.3	34.2	34.5	34.5	34.3	34.0	34.2	35.0	35.1	35.1	35.1	34.5
1998	34.7	35.2	35.2	35.2	35.4	35.4	34.7	34.8	35.2	35.6	35.6	35.5	35.2
1999	34.9	35.1	35.4	36.0	36.0	35.8	35.7	35.8	36.0	36.3	36.3	36.3	35.8
2000	36.3	36.7	37.3	37.4	37.5	37.0	36.9	37.1	37.6	37.7	37.6	37.4	37.2
2001	35.1	35.9	36.0	36.2	36.3	34.6	34.7	34.8	36.1	36.5	36.7	36.6	35.8
2002	36.1	36.8	37.2	37.3	37.5	36.5	36.4	36.4	37.1	38.1	38.2	38.1	37.1
2003	37.3	37.7	38.0	38.3	38.5	37.5	36.9	37.0	37.7	38.0	38.1	38.0	37.8
Leisure and hospitality													
1990	16.8	17.1	17.5	18.1	18.0	18.2	18.5	18.8	19.9	19.8	17.7	18.1	18.2
1991	17.1	17.5	17.7	17.9	17.9	18.2	18.0	18.0	19.1	20.1	18.2	18.2	18.1
1992	18.3	18.5	18.8	19.0	19.5	19.2	19.1	19.6	20.5	21.5	19.1	19.5	19.3
1993	19.1	19.6	19.7	20.7	20.3	20.6	20.4	20.2	22.8	20.7	20.4	20.9	20.4
1994	20.0	20.0	20.2	21.0	20.9	21.0	20.7	21.1	22.3	21.3	21.0	21.1	20.8
1995	20.6	20.8	21.1	21.2	21.4	21.7	21.3	21.4	22.8	21.2	20.7	20.5	21.2
1996	20.3	20.2	20.5	20.5	21.0	20.9	20.6	21.0	22.9	21.6	21.1	21.1	20.9
1997	21.2	21.9	22.3	22.8	22.9	23.2	23.5	23.7	26.1	23.6	22.5	22.6	23.0
1998	21.9	22.5	22.9	23.5	23.6	24.1	24.3	24.7	27.4	23.8	23.1	23.5	23.7
1999	22.6	23.6	24.4	24.7	24.6	24.8	25.2	25.1	27.2	25.2	23.8	24.5	24.6
2000	23.6	24.0	24.7	25.4	25.2	25.6	25.6	26.2	27.2	25.0	24.6	24.9	25.1
2001	23.4	23.7	23.9	24.1	24.7	24.9	25.0	25.1	26.5	23.9	22.9	23.3	24.3
2002	22.5	22.7	23.0	23.3	23.5	23.9	24.5	24.7	26.6	23.6	23.1	23.4	23.7
2003	23.3	23.6	24.1	24.6	24.1	24.4	24.7	25.1	27.2	24.9	24.6	25.1	24.6
Other services													
1990	7.6	7.6	7.6	7.7	7.8	7.8	7.9	7.9	8.0	8.0	7.9	7.9	7.8
1991	7.7	7.7	7.8	7.8	7.7	7.8	7.8	7.8	8.0	8.0	8.0	8.0	7.8
1992	8.1	8.2	8.2	8.2	8.3	8.3	8.3	8.0	8.0	8.2	8.1	8.2	8.1
1993	8.4	8.4	8.4	8.6	8.4	8.5	8.6	8.4	8.4	8.3	8.2	8.3	8.4
1994	8.3	8.3	8.4	8.5	8.5	8.8	8.8	8.8	8.9	8.6	8.5	8.7	8.5
1995	8.6	8.7	8.8	8.9	8.8	8.8	8.9	8.8	8.9	8.7	8.5	8.7	8.7
1996	8.8	8.8	8.9	9.0	9.0	9.1	9.1	9.2	9.1	9.1	9.0	9.0	9.0
1997	9.1	9.2	9.2	9.3	9.4	9.5	9.5	9.7	9.5	9.5	9.5	9.5	9.4
1998	9.5	9.6	9.7	9.9	10.0	10.0	10.1	10.1	10.0	10.2	10.2	10.2	9.9
1999	10.2	10.2	10.3	10.4	10.5	10.5	10.6	10.5	10.4	10.3	10.2	10.3	10.3
2000	10.1	10.3	10.5	10.4	10.5	10.6	10.4	10.4	10.4	10.3	10.2	10.3	10.3
2001	10.7	10.7	10.8	10.8	11.0	11.3	11.5	11.5	11.4	11.3	11.2	11.3	11.1
2002	10.7	10.8	10.9	11.1	11.2	11.4	11.7	11.8	11.6	11.3	11.3	11.5	11.3
2003	11.4	11.5	11.6	11.5	11.7	11.8	12.0	11.9	11.9	11.7	11.6	11.7	11.7
Government													
1990	41.2	42.8	41.7	42.4	43.2	43.0	42.4	41.3	41.2	43.1	44.1	44.3	42.5
1991	42.9	43.3	43.6	44.1	44.0	44.4	43.9	42.4	42.4	43.7	44.3	44.1	43.5
1992	43.9	44.1	44.3	44.5	44.6	44.7	42.8	42.2	43.0	44.5	44.9	44.9	44.0
1993	44.6	45.1	45.5	45.2	45.5	45.5	43.5	43.0	44.1	45.7	46.3	46.5	45.0
1994	45.0	45.3	45.7	45.9	46.6	46.9	44.5	44.3	45.4	46.4	46.9	46.8	45.8
1995	46.3	46.7	47.1	47.2	47.9	47.8	45.5	44.8	45.5	46.1	46.7	46.8	46.5
1996	46.3	46.6	47.0	47.1	47.5	48.1	45.6	45.3	45.7	46.6	47.1	47.4	46.6
1997	47.2	47.4	47.7	47.6	48.0	48.1	47.1	45.2	45.8	47.3	48.0	48.1	47.2
1998	47.9	47.9	48.3	48.6	49.0	49.3	47.4	45.9	46.5	48.6	49.1	49.3	48.1
1999	48.4	48.7	49.2	49.2	49.4	50.1	48.9	47.1	47.4	49.1	49.8	50.1	48.9
2000	49.2	49.6	49.9	50.1	51.5	51.9	49.7	48.8	48.5	50.1	51.1	51.1	50.1
2001	51.0	51.6	52.0	51.9	52.2	52.6	51.1	49.2	50.4	51.8	52.4	52.7	51.6
2002	52.2	52.6	52.7	52.8	52.9	53.5	52.0	49.6	51.1	52.6	53.1	53.0	52.3
2003	52.8	53.1	53.4	53.3	53.7	54.0	51.0	50.0	51.6	53.5	53.9	54.0	52.9

Employment by Industry: Washington—*Continued*

(Numbers in thousands. Not seasonally adjusted.)

Industry	January	February	March	April	May	June	July	August	September	October	November	December	Annual Average
TACOMA—*Continued*													
Federal government													
1990	11.3	11.4	11.3	11.5	12.1	11.8	11.9	11.4	11.3	11.0	11.1	11.2	11.4
1991	11.2	11.1	11.1	11.4	11.5	11.5	11.7	11.8	11.6	11.1	11.2	11.2	11.3
1992	11.1	11.0	11.0	11.0	10.9	11.0	11.1	11.1	11.0	11.2	11.1	11.2	11.0
1993	11.3	11.2	11.1	11.2	11.2	11.1	11.2	11.2	11.1	10.9	11.0	11.1	11.1
1994	10.9	10.8	10.7	10.8	11.0	11.1	11.3	11.3	11.3	11.0	11.1	11.1	11.0
1995	11.0	10.9	10.9	10.9	11.3	11.0	11.1	11.1	11.0	10.8	10.8	11.0	10.9
1996	10.8	10.7	10.7	10.7	10.8	10.8	10.7	10.8	10.7	10.6	10.7	10.9	10.7
1997	10.8	10.6	10.6	10.7	10.8	10.9	10.9	10.8	10.7	10.5	10.5	10.7	10.7
1998	10.8	10.5	10.5	10.6	10.6	10.7	10.8	10.7	10.6	10.8	10.8	10.9	10.6
1999	10.4	10.3	10.5	10.3	10.4	10.5	10.5	10.5	10.4	10.3	10.4	10.6	10.4
2000	10.2	10.2	10.2	10.5	11.7	11.6	10.7	11.1	10.4	10.3	10.6	10.7	10.6
2001	9.6	9.4	9.5	9.5	9.6	9.8	9.8	9.8	9.8	9.6	9.6	9.8	9.7
2002	9.6	9.5	9.6	9.5	9.6	9.8	9.9	10.0	10.0	9.8	9.8	9.9	9.8
2003	9.6	9.6	9.6	9.6	9.7	9.9	9.9	9.9	9.9	9.9	9.7	10.1	9.8
State government													
1990	7.6	7.8	7.8	7.8	7.9	7.9	7.6	7.5	7.5	7.9	8.2	8.2	7.8
1991	8.1	8.3	8.3	8.4	8.4	8.5	7.9	8.0	8.6	9.5	9.6	9.4	8.5
1992	9.4	9.5	9.5	9.4	9.4	9.4	8.3	8.6	8.7	9.3	9.4	9.3	9.1
1993	9.3	9.4	9.8	9.4	9.5	9.6	8.4	8.7	8.9	9.5	9.5	9.5	9.2
1994	9.5	9.6	9.7	9.7	10.0	9.8	8.7	9.0	9.3	9.9	10.0	9.9	9.5
1995	9.8	9.9	9.8	10.0	10.0	10.1	8.9	9.1	9.3	9.8	9.9	9.8	9.7
1996	9.8	10.0	9.9	10.0	10.0	10.0	8.9	9.2	9.6	10.1	10.1	10.1	9.8
1997	10.1	10.2	10.3	10.2	10.3	10.3	9.1	9.4	9.9	10.3	10.4	10.2	10.0
1998	10.2	10.3	10.5	10.5	10.6	10.5	9.3	9.8	10.2	10.7	10.8	10.8	10.3
1999	10.7	10.9	11.0	11.0	10.9	11.0	9.9	10.1	10.5	11.1	11.1	11.0	10.7
2000	10.8	11.0	11.0	10.9	11.0	11.1	10.0	10.2	10.7	11.1	11.2	11.1	10.8
2001	10.9	11.2	11.3	11.2	11.2	11.3	10.2	10.6	11.1	11.4	11.5	11.4	11.1
2002	11.3	11.4	11.4	11.4	11.4	11.4	10.2	10.3	11.2	11.3	11.3	11.2	11.2
2003	11.3	11.3	11.4	11.3	11.3	11.3	10.1	10.2	10.6	11.3	11.5	11.4	11.1
Local government													
1990	22.3	23.6	22.6	23.1	23.2	23.3	22.9	22.4	22.4	24.2	24.8	24.9	23.3
1991	23.6	23.9	24.2	24.3	24.1	24.4	24.3	22.6	22.2	23.1	23.5	23.5	23.6
1992	23.4	23.6	23.8	24.1	24.3	24.3	23.4	22.5	23.3	24.0	24.4	24.4	23.7
1993	24.0	24.5	24.6	24.6	24.8	24.8	23.9	23.1	24.1	25.3	25.8	25.9	24.6
1994	24.6	24.9	25.3	25.4	25.6	26.0	24.5	24.0	24.8	25.5	25.8	25.8	25.1
1995	25.5	25.9	26.4	26.3	26.6	26.7	25.5	24.6	25.2	25.5	26.0	26.0	25.8
1996	25.7	25.9	26.4	26.4	26.7	27.3	26.0	25.3	25.4	25.9	26.3	26.4	26.1
1997	26.3	26.6	26.8	26.7	26.9	26.9	27.1	25.0	25.2	26.5	27.1	27.2	26.5
1998	26.9	27.1	27.3	27.5	27.8	28.1	27.3	25.4	25.7	27.1	27.5	27.6	27.1
1999	27.3	27.5	27.7	27.9	28.1	28.6	28.5	26.5	26.5	27.7	28.3	28.5	27.7
2000	28.2	28.4	28.7	28.7	28.8	29.2	29.0	27.5	27.4	28.7	29.3	29.3	28.6
2001	30.5	31.0	31.2	31.2	31.4	31.5	31.1	28.8	29.5	30.8	31.3	31.5	30.8
2002	31.3	31.7	31.7	31.9	31.9	32.3	31.9	29.3	29.9	31.5	32.0	31.9	31.4
2003	31.9	32.2	32.4	32.4	32.7	32.8	31.0	29.9	31.1	32.3	32.7	32.5	32.0

Average Weekly Hours by Industry: Washington

(Not seasonally adjusted.)

Industry	January	February	March	April	May	June	July	August	September	October	November	December	Annual Average
STATEWIDE													
Construction													
2001	36.3	35.0	35.9	36.0	36.8	36.1	37.0	37.3	37.4	36.3	35.1	35.3	36.2
2002	35.3	36.0	34.9	35.6	35.8	36.8	36.2	37.0	37.5	37.2	35.7	35.0	36.1
2003	35.4	36.1	35.7	36.1	36.9	37.3	36.5	37.4	37.4	36.2	37.0	35.8	36.5
Manufacturing													
2001	39.6	39.7	40.2	39.7	39.8	40.0	40.0	40.2	40.7	40.6	39.8	40.2	40.0
2002	39.8	40.2	40.3	39.9	40.0	40.7	39.5	40.1	40.6	40.7	40.0	39.7	40.1
2003	38.9	39.8	39.8	38.7	39.1	40.5	38.0	39.7	40.1	40.0	39.8	39.3	39.5
Trade, transportation, and utilities													
2001	32.8	33.4	33.5	34.0	33.4	33.8	34.2	33.8	33.8	33.2	32.9	34.1	33.6
2002	32.3	33.4	33.1	33.6	33.8	34.7	34.1	34.4	35.0	34.2	33.6	34.8	33.9
2003	32.8	34.4	34.2	34.1	34.2	35.1	34.4	34.8	34.5	34.2	34.4	33.8	34.2
Wholesale trade													
2001	37.0	37.4	37.7	38.5	37.7	37.8	38.6	37.4	38.1	37.0	37.2	38.4	37.7
2002	36.3	36.5	36.6	37.2	37.0	38.2	37.2	37.4	38.3	37.5	37.4	38.7	37.4
2003	36.7	38.6	38.4	37.8	37.8	39.0	37.1	37.5	37.7	38.0	38.7	36.8	37.8
Retail trade													
2001	30.6	31.1	31.2	31.9	31.2	31.5	32.1	31.6	31.6	31.0	30.6	31.8	31.4
2002	30.1	31.4	30.9	31.3	31.5	32.4	32.1	32.1	32.5	31.7	31.2	32.5	31.7
2003	30.7	32.3	32.0	32.0	32.0	32.8	32.6	33.0	32.4	31.9	32.0	32.0	32.1

Average Hourly Earnings by Industry: Washington

(Dollars, not seasonally adjusted.)

Industry	January	February	March	April	May	June	July	August	September	October	November	December	Annual Average
STATEWIDE													
Construction													
2001	21.85	21.61	21.71	21.60	21.50	21.54	21.76	21.95	22.16	22.05	22.09	22.27	21.84
2002	22.53	22.44	22.23	22.28	22.21	22.23	22.54	22.93	22.76	22.70	22.66	23.08	22.56
2003	23.02	23.05	22.89	22.77	22.76	22.66	23.02	23.27	22.87	23.42	22.58	22.71	22.92
Manufacturing													
2001	17.75	17.65	17.94	17.72	17.65	17.74	17.93	17.82	18.17	18.10	18.52	18.59	17.96
2002	18.79	18.65	18.54	18.41	18.24	18.41	18.43	17.89	17.74	17.51	17.78	17.41	18.15
2003	18.12	18.00	18.01	18.06	17.88	17.66	17.98	17.86	18.01	18.07	18.29	18.40	18.03
Trade, transportation, and utilities													
2001	14.39	14.32	14.27	14.48	14.53	14.53	14.56	14.49	14.81	14.63	14.61	14.68	14.53
2002	14.89	14.98	14.93	15.01	14.93	15.15	14.96	15.02	15.25	15.13	14.91	14.89	15.01
2003	15.02	15.38	15.40	15.12	15.20	15.28	15.33	15.31	15.36	15.36	15.40	15.32	15.29
Wholesale trade													
2001	16.20	16.24	15.95	16.23	16.48	16.48	16.48	16.36	16.65	16.39	16.40	16.68	16.38
2002	16.40	17.04	16.60	16.51	16.60	16.73	16.68	16.82	17.30	17.03	17.15	17.18	16.84
2003	17.17	17.48	17.52	17.34	17.56	17.66	17.98	17.67	17.83	17.99	18.52	18.83	17.80
Retail trade													
2001	12.72	12.67	12.65	12.78	12.76	12.80	12.84	12.71	13.09	13.05	13.08	13.00	12.85
2002	13.35	13.19	13.35	13.40	13.36	13.64	13.38	13.39	13.56	13.31	13.05	13.03	13.33
2003	13.15	13.35	13.43	13.19	13.18	13.26	13.20	13.23	13.35	13.31	13.26	13.08	13.25

Average Weekly Earnings by Industry: Washington

(Dollars, not seasonally adjusted.)

Industry	January	February	March	April	May	June	July	August	September	October	November	December	Annual Average
STATEWIDE													
Construction													
2001	793.16	756.35	779.39	777.60	791.20	777.59	805.12	818.74	828.78	800.42	775.36	786.13	790.61
2002	795.31	807.84	775.83	793.17	795.12	818.06	815.95	848.41	853.50	844.44	808.96	807.80	814.42
2003	814.91	832.11	817.17	822.00	839.84	845.22	840.23	870.30	855.34	847.80	835.46	813.02	836.58
Manufacturing													
2001	702.90	700.71	721.19	703.48	702.47	709.60	717.20	716.36	739.52	734.86	737.10	747.32	718.40
2002	747.84	749.73	747.16	734.56	729.60	749.29	727.99	717.39	720.24	712.66	711.20	691.18	727.82
2003	704.87	716.40	716.80	698.92	699.11	715.23	683.24	709.04	722.20	722.80	727.94	723.12	712.19
Trade, transportation, and utilities													
2001	471.99	478.29	478.05	492.32	485.30	491.11	497.95	489.76	500.58	485.72	480.67	500.59	488.21
2002	480.95	500.33	494.18	504.34	504.63	525.71	510.14	516.69	533.75	517.45	500.98	518.17	508.84
2003	492.66	529.07	526.68	515.59	519.84	536.33	527.35	532.79	529.92	525.31	529.76	517.82	522.92
Wholesale trade													
2001	599.40	607.38	601.32	624.86	621.30	622.94	636.13	611.86	634.37	606.43	610.08	640.51	617.53
2002	595.32	621.96	607.56	614.17	614.20	639.09	620.50	629.07	662.59	638.63	641.41	664.87	629.82
2003	630.14	674.73	672.77	655.45	663.77	688.74	667.06	662.63	672.19	683.62	716.72	692.94	672.84
Retail trade													
2001	389.23	394.04	394.68	407.68	398.11	403.20	412.16	401.64	413.64	404.55	400.25	413.40	403.49
2002	401.84	414.17	412.52	419.42	420.84	441.94	429.50	429.82	440.70	421.93	407.16	423.48	422.56
2003	403.71	431.21	429.76	422.08	421.76	434.93	430.32	436.59	432.54	424.59	424.32	418.56	425.33

WEST VIRGINIA AT A GLANCE

(Population and total nonfarm employment numbers in thousands)

Population, Census 2000:	1,808.3
Total nonfarm employment, 2003:	726.3
Change in total nonfarm employment	
(Number)	
1990–2003:	96.3
1990–2001:	105.2
2001–2003:	-8.9
(Compound annual rate of change)	
1990–2003:	1.1%
1990–2001:	1.4%
2001–2003:	-0.6%
Unemployment rate	
1990:	8.6%
2001:	5.2%
2003:	6.0%

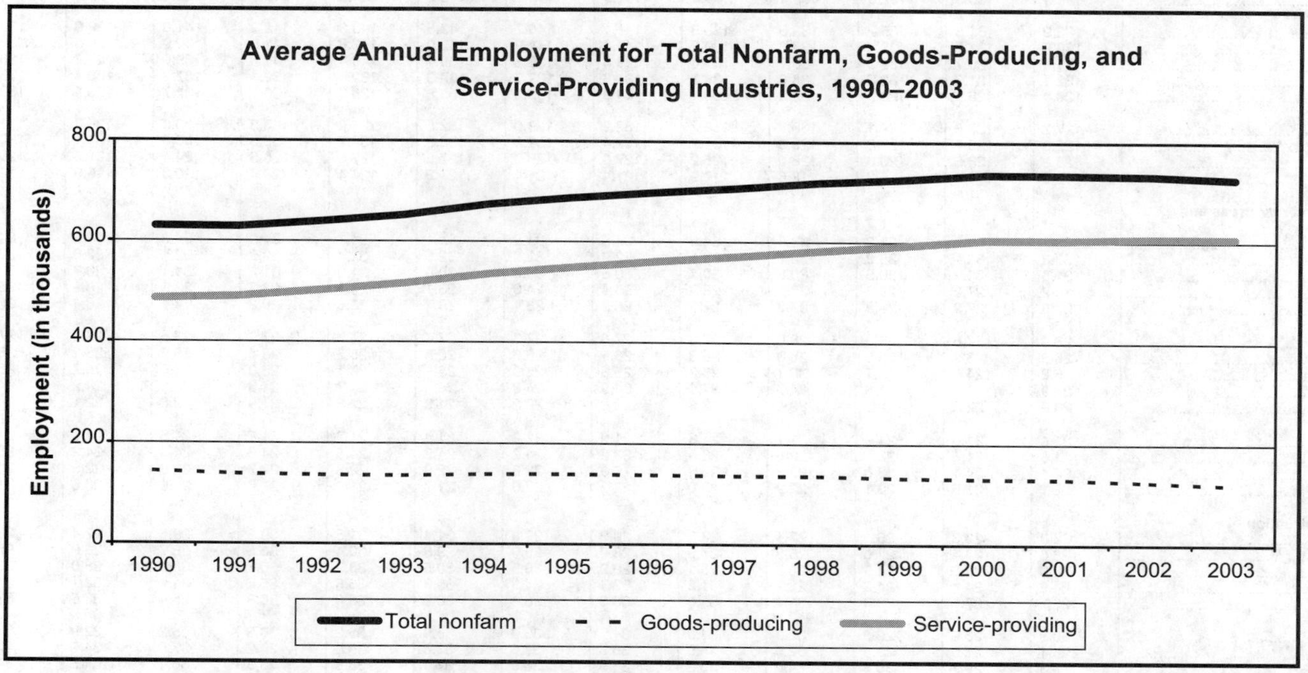

Following the 1990–1991 recession, total nonfarm payroll employment in West Virginia rose until the onset of the 2001 recession. Goods-producing industries experienced a decline in employment since 1995, and dropped substantially following the 2001 recession. In 2003, employment in this sector was well below its 1990 level. Employment in the service-providing sector supplied a better source of growth, rising steadily during the 1990s and only leveling off during the 2001 contraction. Over 120,000 service-providing jobs were added from 1990 to 2003. Employment in educational and health services grew the fastest from 2000 to 2003, rising by 8.3 percent.

Employment by Industry: West Virginia

(Numbers in thousands. Not seasonally adjusted.)

Industry	January	February	March	April	May	June	July	August	September	October	November	December	Annual Average
STATEWIDE													
Total nonfarm													
1990	610.5	611.6	620.9	626.4	645.4	637.6	638.2	630.7	633.9	636.3	634.4	634.2	630.0
1991	615.7	615.3	619.8	624.0	632.4	633.5	635.7	628.7	633.1	636.4	636.0	635.3	628.8
1992	621.0	619.8	625.1	633.0	653.4	640.2	649.9	640.7	643.4	649.6	649.8	651.2	639.8
1993	632.5	631.6	636.0	647.6	656.3	654.1	660.3	653.3	659.0	664.5	663.7	670.0	652.4
1994	641.2	645.8	655.3	667.2	689.2	678.1	680.6	679.5	684.0	685.4	698.1	688.6	674.4
1995	666.4	665.4	675.6	683.8	691.6	692.8	693.4	692.6	696.0	699.0	698.4	699.0	687.8
1996	671.5	675.2	684.6	690.6	714.9	704.9	705.4	702.7	706.7	708.5	710.0	708.2	698.6
1997	688.3	687.4	696.0	702.6	710.3	713.0	712.6	709.1	713.7	719.2	720.5	720.7	707.8
1998	696.0	697.9	704.4	711.4	731.3	724.3	726.2	721.9	725.8	729.8	730.4	731.6	719.3
1999	705.0	707.3	714.2	724.2	730.3	732.0	731.3	727.5	729.5	736.5	736.0	738.2	726.0
2000	714.1	714.1	728.6	733.1	751.5	741.1	742.1	733.8	739.8	741.7	744.9	744.8	735.8
2001	719.0	721.9	730.5	735.2	739.6	742.1	734.8	737.8	737.8	740.3	742.2	741.9	735.2
2002	717.2	719.9	727.5	731.5	747.3	737.1	733.8	735.4	735.6	735.9	738.2	737.2	733.1
2003	714.4	711.1	719.6	727.4	732.0	734.5	728.5	729.8	730.5	729.6	729.3	728.5	726.3
Total private													
1990	485.7	485.5	493.6	499.3	505.3	509.9	507.9	511.4	511.4	508.5	506.2	506.2	502.6
1991	491.0	489.3	492.5	495.7	502.4	506.7	505.5	507.1	507.9	505.9	505.0	504.8	501.2
1992	493.0	491.6	494.6	501.8	507.6	510.3	513.1	514.4	515.4	516.2	515.7	516.2	507.5
1993	502.0	499.9	502.8	514.0	521.4	522.4	524.9	527.1	528.1	530.1	528.2	534.1	519.6
1994	510.3	513.7	520.4	532.4	540.0	543.9	545.1	548.6	552.1	549.3	548.9	550.3	537.9
1995	532.7	530.6	538.6	546.9	553.3	556.4	555.7	559.8	562.5	560.5	559.7	560.2	551.4
1996	536.8	539.0	545.6	552.4	562.3	566.6	567.5	569.6	571.9	569.0	569.7	568.2	559.9
1997	551.3	549.4	555.6	562.6	569.2	574.3	573.2	574.6	577.2	579.0	578.6	579.3	568.7
1998	559.6	559.3	564.1	571.7	579.1	586.1	585.0	586.1	587.4	587.5	586.9	589.0	578.5
1999	566.7	567.8	571.9	581.3	587.3	591.2	589.4	591.4	591.1	594.4	593.8	594.8	585.1
2000	574.9	574.0	583.7	589.6	594.1	599.1	597.1	595.6	600.7	599.9	601.7	601.7	592.7
2001	581.0	581.3	587.7	592.6	597.3	601.2	596.6	599.4	598.8	597.9	598.5	598.2	594.2
2002	578.1	578.9	583.8	588.1	592.8	594.9	596.0	597.0	595.0	592.6	593.1	592.3	590.2
2003	573.6	568.8	575.6	582.4	586.8	590.7	589.6	590.7	590.7	587.4	585.9	585.4	584.0
Goods-producing													
1990	138.2	138.3	142.0	143.2	145.5	147.3	146.9	148.2	148.0	146.8	144.0	142.4	144.2
1991	137.1	136.0	136.5	137.2	139.5	141.6	140.7	141.2	141.7	141.3	139.1	137.2	139.1
1992	133.3	132.3	133.0	134.9	136.7	137.9	139.6	140.0	139.9	140.4	139.9	137.2	137.1
1993	133.3	130.7	132.5	136.3	138.6	137.3	137.3	137.2	137.8	137.6	135.5	137.9	136.0
1994	128.9	130.5	132.9	138.1	140.6	142.3	142.5	143.2	144.8	143.0	142.1	140.2	139.1
1995	133.9	131.8	135.2	139.0	139.8	141.1	140.7	142.5	143.3	142.9	141.6	139.0	139.2
1996	130.5	131.5	133.4	135.6	139.2	141.4	141.9	142.0	143.8	141.6	140.0	136.5	138.1
1997	131.8	130.7	132.3	135.7	137.4	139.3	138.3	139.4	140.4	141.5	139.0	137.2	136.9
1998	132.1	131.3	132.2	135.6	138.2	139.8	139.7	139.3	139.7	139.1	137.2	136.4	136.7
1999	128.4	128.1	128.3	132.2	134.1	134.5	135.2	135.5	136.0	136.1	134.7	133.1	133.0
2000	127.2	125.6	129.1	130.9	132.2	132.9	133.0	132.5	134.0	133.8	133.3	130.4	131.2
2001	125.0	125.1	127.6	129.9	131.2	132.4	132.0	132.9	133.2	133.8	133.0	131.1	130.6
2002	123.8	123.5	123.9	126.0	126.2	127.0	126.7	127.2	127.0	125.6	124.4	121.3	125.2
2003	116.0	113.6	116.3	118.6	119.9	121.4	121.4	121.2	121.4	120.4	120.3	116.9	119.0
Natural resources and mining													
1990	33.7	33.6	33.8	33.7	34.0	34.5	34.2	34.1	34.1	34.0	34.3	34.2	34.0
1991	33.6	33.1	33.0	32.7	32.6	32.9	32.5	32.5	32.4	32.2	32.1	32.0	32.6
1992	31.6	30.9	30.5	30.8	30.7	30.5	30.4	30.8	31.0	31.2	31.1	30.7	30.9
1993	30.2	27.2	29.2	28.7	28.2	25.4	24.0	23.1	23.4	23.2	23.1	28.2	26.2
1994	27.9	27.9	28.2	27.8	27.9	28.3	28.4	28.7	28.6	28.3	28.4	28.4	28.2
1995	28.4	27.6	28.0	28.0	27.8	27.6	27.3	27.7	27.7	27.6	27.6	27.3	27.7
1996	26.8	26.3	25.9	26.0	26.3	26.6	26.5	26.5	26.7	26.4	25.5	25.2	26.2
1997	25.2	24.9	25.1	25.1	25.2	25.3	25.0	25.1	25.1	25.3	25.0	25.2	25.1
1998	24.9	24.6	24.6	24.7	24.9	24.9	24.8	24.6	24.7	24.3	24.3	24.2	24.6
1999	23.0	22.8	22.3	22.4	22.3	22.6	22.2	21.9	22.3	21.9	22.0	22.1	22.3
2000	21.4	21.0	21.0	21.1	21.3	21.0	21.2	21.4	21.7	21.8	21.8	21.8	21.4
2001	21.8	21.8	22.1	22.6	23.0	23.8	24.2	24.2	24.3	24.6	24.8	24.9	23.5
2002	24.4	24.1	23.6	23.3	22.9	22.9	22.6	22.8	22.8	22.7	22.9	22.5	23.1
2003	22.1	21.6	22.1	22.2	22.0	22.2	22.0	21.7	21.7	21.0	21.0	20.6	21.7
Construction													
1990	23.3	23.3	26.1	27.1	28.8	29.2	29.9	31.4	31.5	30.8	29.5	27.4	28.2
1991	23.6	23.4	24.0	26.3	27.9	28.9	29.0	29.8	30.4	30.5	28.7	26.9	27.5
1992	23.9	23.8	24.5	26.2	28.1	28.9	30.5	30.5	30.2	30.7	30.0	28.0	27.9
1993	24.6	24.4	24.3	28.7	31.2	32.4	34.3	35.3	35.6	35.6	34.1	32.1	31.1
1994	25.7	27.1	29.0	33.7	35.6	36.3	36.4	36.9	38.0	36.8	35.4	33.5	33.7
1995	28.3	26.6	29.0	32.9	34.0	34.7	35.2	35.9	36.2	36.3	35.2	32.9	33.1
1996	26.1	27.6	29.5	32.0	34.9	36.5	37.6	37.8	39.4	38.2	37.6	34.7	34.3
1997	30.3	29.7	30.8	34.0	35.2	36.5	36.9	37.4	38.6	38.8	36.4	34.5	34.9
1998	30.1	29.4	29.9	33.3	34.9	36.4	37.0	36.8	37.1	37.2	35.5	34.7	34.4
1999	29.3	29.3	29.4	33.0	35.0	35.3	35.9	36.2	36.0	36.9	35.7	33.9	33.8
2000	28.9	28.1	31.6	33.9	35.2	35.5	35.7	35.5	36.8	36.8	36.4	33.7	34.0
2001	29.3	29.7	32.1	34.1	35.1	35.6	35.6	37.0	37.8	38.7	37.9	35.8	34.8
2002	29.7	30.0	31.0	33.4	34.0	34.9	35.4	35.8	35.7	35.2	34.3	31.8	33.4
2003	28.4	27.1	29.3	31.4	33.0	34.2	34.5	34.9	35.2	34.8	34.7	32.9	32.5

Employment by Industry: West Virginia—*Continued*

(Numbers in thousands. Not seasonally adjusted.)

Industry	January	February	March	April	May	June	July	August	September	October	November	December	Annual Average
STATEWIDE—*Continued*													
Manufacturing													
1990	81.2	81.4	82.1	82.4	82.7	83.6	82.8	82.7	82.4	82.0	80.2	80.8	82.0
1991	79.9	79.5	79.5	78.2	79.0	79.8	79.2	78.9	78.9	78.6	78.3	78.3	79.0
1992	77.8	77.6	78.0	77.9	77.9	78.5	78.7	78.7	78.7	78.5	78.8	78.5	78.3
1993	78.5	79.1	79.0	78.9	79.2	79.5	79.0	78.8	78.8	78.8	78.3	77.6	78.8
1994	75.3	75.5	75.7	76.6	77.1	77.7	77.7	77.6	78.2	77.9	78.3	78.3	77.2
1995	77.2	77.6	78.2	78.1	78.0	78.8	78.2	78.9	79.4	79.0	78.8	78.8	78.4
1996	77.6	77.6	78.0	77.6	78.0	78.3	77.8	77.7	77.7	77.0	76.9	76.6	77.6
1997	76.3	76.1	76.4	76.6	77.0	77.5	76.4	76.9	76.7	77.4	77.6	77.5	76.9
1998	77.1	77.3	77.7	77.6	78.4	78.5	77.9	77.9	77.9	77.6	77.4	77.5	77.7
1999	76.1	76.0	76.6	76.8	76.8	76.6	77.1	77.4	77.7	77.3	77.0	77.1	76.9
2000	76.9	76.5	76.5	75.9	75.7	76.4	76.1	75.6	75.5	75.2	75.1	74.9	75.9
2001	73.9	73.6	73.4	73.2	73.1	73.0	72.2	71.7	71.1	70.5	70.3	70.4	72.2
2002	69.7	69.4	69.3	69.3	69.3	69.2	68.7	68.6	68.5	67.7	67.2	67.0	68.7
2003	65.5	64.9	64.9	65.0	64.9	65.0	64.9	64.6	64.5	64.6	64.6	63.4	64.7
Service-providing													
1990	472.3	473.3	478.9	483.2	499.9	490.3	491.3	482.5	485.9	489.5	490.4	491.8	485.8
1991	478.6	479.3	483.3	486.8	492.9	491.9	495.0	487.5	491.4	495.1	496.9	498.1	489.7
1992	487.7	487.5	492.1	498.1	516.7	502.3	510.3	500.7	503.5	509.2	509.9	514.0	502.7
1993	499.2	500.9	503.5	511.3	517.7	516.8	523.0	516.1	521.2	526.9	528.2	532.1	516.4
1994	512.3	515.3	522.4	529.1	548.6	535.8	538.1	536.3	539.2	542.4	556.0	548.4	535.3
1995	532.5	533.6	540.4	544.8	551.8	551.7	552.7	550.1	552.7	556.1	556.8	560.0	548.6
1996	541.0	543.7	551.2	555.0	575.7	563.5	563.5	560.7	562.9	566.9	570.0	571.7	560.5
1997	556.5	556.7	563.7	566.9	572.9	573.7	574.3	569.7	573.3	577.7	581.5	583.5	570.9
1998	563.9	566.6	572.2	575.8	593.1	584.5	586.5	582.6	586.1	590.7	593.2	595.2	582.5
1999	576.6	579.2	585.9	592.0	596.2	597.5	596.1	592.0	593.5	600.4	601.3	605.1	593.0
2000	586.9	588.5	599.5	602.2	619.3	608.2	609.1	601.3	605.8	607.9	611.6	614.4	604.6
2001	594.0	596.8	602.9	605.3	608.4	609.7	602.8	604.9	604.6	606.5	609.2	610.8	604.6
2002	593.4	596.4	603.6	605.5	621.1	610.1	607.1	608.2	608.6	610.3	613.8	615.9	607.8
2003	598.4	597.5	603.3	608.8	612.1	613.1	607.1	608.6	609.1	609.2	609.0	611.6	607.3
Trade, transportation, and utilities													
1990	133.4	132.0	133.0	134.0	135.3	136.3	135.9	136.8	136.8	136.3	138.0	139.1	135.6
1991	132.7	131.5	132.1	132.2	133.4	134.2	134.5	134.4	134.0	134.0	135.9	137.0	133.8
1992	132.6	131.0	131.6	132.9	134.1	134.5	134.8	134.8	134.7	135.0	136.4	138.4	134.2
1993	132.7	132.1	132.3	134.6	136.1	137.4	138.6	139.7	139.6	140.9	142.3	145.4	137.6
1994	138.4	137.9	139.1	140.9	142.2	143.1	142.9	144.0	144.4	144.1	145.9	147.5	142.5
1995	141.5	140.4	141.3	142.1	143.7	144.3	143.8	144.8	145.5	145.1	146.9	148.4	144.0
1996	140.8	140.4	141.5	142.4	143.8	144.6	144.1	144.8	145.1	144.1	146.9	148.0	143.9
1997	141.2	139.8	140.9	141.6	143.1	143.9	143.6	143.1	143.8	144.3	147.0	147.9	143.4
1998	141.0	140.1	140.9	141.6	143.2	144.5	144.1	145.1	144.9	145.0	147.1	148.3	143.8
1999	141.8	141.0	141.8	143.7	145.2	146.2	144.9	145.4	145.4	147.4	149.1	150.4	145.2
2000	142.6	141.3	142.6	142.9	144.3	145.5	144.9	145.4	145.1	145.0	147.9	148.8	144.7
2001	140.1	138.4	139.0	139.5	140.5	141.3	139.6	140.0	139.5	139.1	141.3	142.1	140.0
2002	136.1	134.9	135.9	136.2	137.4	137.7	137.1	136.9	136.2	136.6	138.6	139.7	136.9
2003	133.5	131.7	132.9	134.4	135.6	136.2	135.8	136.4	136.2	136.7	136.1	139.0	135.4
Wholesale trade													
1990	23.6	23.6	23.8	23.9	23.9	24.1	24.2	24.2	24.1	24.2	24.1	24.0	24.0
1991	23.7	23.7	23.9	23.6	23.8	23.8	23.6	23.4	23.3	23.1	23.0	22.9	23.5
1992	22.4	22.3	22.4	22.6	22.8	22.8	23.0	22.9	22.9	22.9	22.7	22.7	22.7
1993	21.8	21.8	21.9	22.3	22.4	22.5	22.7	22.6	22.5	22.5	22.4	22.5	22.3
1994	21.8	21.9	22.0	22.4	22.5	22.7	22.7	22.8	22.9	22.7	22.8	22.8	22.5
1995	22.4	22.5	22.7	22.8	22.9	22.9	22.8	22.8	23.0	22.8	22.8	22.8	22.8
1996	22.2	22.2	22.4	22.7	22.9	22.9	22.9	23.0	23.0	23.1	23.0	23.1	22.8
1997	22.7	22.7	23.3	24.0	24.3	24.5	24.6	24.5	24.5	24.3	24.3	24.4	24.0
1998	24.1	24.2	24.3	24.3	24.4	24.5	24.6	24.4	24.3	24.2	24.1	24.2	24.3
1999	23.9	23.9	24.0	24.3	24.3	24.5	24.3	24.3	24.2	24.6	24.4	24.4	24.3
2000	23.7	23.8	24.0	24.0	24.1	24.1	24.1	24.2	24.3	24.0	24.2	24.1	24.1
2001	23.7	23.8	24.0	24.2	24.2	24.5	24.1	23.9	23.9	23.7	23.6	23.7	23.9
2002	23.0	23.2	23.4	23.5	23.5	23.4	23.3	23.2	23.1	23.0	23.0	23.0	23.2
2003	22.4	22.3	22.6	22.7	22.9	23.0	22.9	23.0	22.9	22.9	22.7	22.6	22.7
Retail trade													
1990	81.5	80.1	80.5	81.1	82.0	82.5	82.0	82.8	83.0	82.2	84.1	85.4	82.3
1991	80.6	79.4	79.7	80.0	80.8	81.2	81.5	81.6	81.4	81.7	83.8	85.2	81.4
1992	81.1	79.8	80.0	80.8	81.4	81.6	81.9	82.2	81.9	82.3	84.1	85.9	81.9
1993	81.6	80.8	81.1	82.3	83.2	83.8	84.4	85.2	85.0	85.8	87.4	90.1	84.2
1994	84.1	83.0	83.5	85.0	86.1	86.8	86.6	87.8	88.4	88.4	90.4	92.4	86.9
1995	87.5	86.4	87.2	87.9	89.3	89.9	89.5	90.4	91.1	90.6	92.7	94.5	89.8
1996	88.6	88.0	88.7	89.3	90.4	91.2	90.5	91.1	91.5	90.8	93.7	95.0	90.7
1997	89.5	88.0	88.2	88.9	89.8	90.2	89.7	89.9	90.0	91.0	93.8	94.6	90.3
1998	88.7	87.6	88.2	88.8	90.1	91.1	90.9	92.1	92.1	92.5	94.8	95.9	91.1
1999	90.1	89.3	89.9	91.2	92.6	93.1	92.3	92.6	92.7	94.3	96.3	97.6	92.7
2000	91.7	90.4	91.2	91.7	92.8	93.7	93.2	93.7	93.2	93.6	96.5	97.7	93.3
2001	90.3	88.4	88.8	88.9	89.7	90.0	89.0	89.6	89.2	89.0	91.4	92.1	89.7
2002	87.2	86.0	86.9	87.1	88.1	88.3	88.2	88.1	87.8	88.2	90.4	91.5	88.2
2003	86.0	84.5	85.3	86.7	87.5	88.0	87.8	88.2	88.2	88.8	88.4	91.5	87.6

Employment by Industry: West Virginia—*Continued*

(Numbers in thousands. Not seasonally adjusted.)

Industry	January	February	March	April	May	June	July	August	September	October	November	December	Annual Average
STATEWIDE—*Continued*													
Transportation and utilities													
1990	28.3	28.3	28.7	29.0	29.4	29.7	29.7	29.8	29.7	29.9	29.8	29.7	29.3
1991	28.4	28.4	28.5	28.6	28.8	29.2	29.4	29.4	29.3	29.2	29.1	28.9	28.9
1992	29.1	28.9	29.2	29.5	29.9	30.1	29.9	29.7	29.9	29.8	29.6	29.8	29.6
1993	29.3	29.5	29.3	30.0	30.5	31.1	31.5	31.9	32.1	32.6	32.5	32.8	31.1
1994	32.5	33.0	33.6	33.5	33.6	33.6	33.6	33.4	33.1	33.0	32.7	32.3	33.2
1995	31.6	31.5	31.4	31.4	31.5	31.5	31.5	31.6	31.4	31.7	31.4	31.1	31.5
1996	30.0	30.2	30.4	30.4	30.5	30.5	30.7	30.7	30.6	30.2	30.2	29.9	30.4
1997	29.0	29.1	29.4	28.7	29.0	29.2	29.3	28.7	29.3	29.0	28.9	28.9	29.0
1998	28.2	28.3	28.4	28.5	28.7	28.9	28.6	28.6	28.5	28.3	28.2	28.2	28.5
1999	27.8	27.8	27.9	28.2	28.3	28.6	28.3	28.5	28.5	28.5	28.4	28.4	28.3
2000	27.2	27.1	27.4	27.2	27.4	27.7	27.6	27.5	27.6	27.4	27.2	27.0	27.4
2001	26.1	26.2	26.2	26.4	26.6	26.8	26.5	26.5	26.4	26.4	26.3	26.3	26.3
2002	25.9	25.7	25.6	25.6	25.8	26.0	25.6	25.6	25.3	25.4	25.2	25.2	25.6
2003	25.1	24.9	25.0	25.0	25.2	25.2	25.1	25.2	25.1	25.0	25.0	24.9	25.1
Information													
1990	11.7	11.8	11.8	12.1	12.0	12.1	12.1	12.0	12.0	12.0	12.0	12.2	12.0
1991	12.0	12.0	11.9	11.9	12.0	12.0	12.1	12.1	12.1	12.1	12.1	12.1	12.0
1992	11.9	12.0	12.0	12.0	12.0	12.1	12.1	12.1	12.0	12.1	12.1	12.1	12.0
1993	11.8	11.8	11.8	11.8	11.9	12.0	12.1	12.1	12.0	12.2	12.2	12.3	12.0
1994	12.0	12.0	12.0	12.1	12.2	12.3	12.5	12.5	12.5	12.4	12.4	12.7	12.3
1995	11.7	11.7	11.9	12.5	12.5	12.7	12.5	12.4	12.5	12.5	12.6	12.7	12.4
1996	12.4	12.4	12.6	12.7	12.8	12.9	12.8	12.9	12.9	12.8	12.9	13.0	12.8
1997	12.8	12.8	13.0	13.2	13.1	13.2	12.9	12.9	12.8	12.8	12.9	12.9	12.9
1998	13.3	13.3	13.2	13.4	13.4	13.6	13.5	13.5	13.6	13.5	13.5	13.5	13.4
1999	13.2	13.4	13.7	13.8	13.9	14.2	14.4	14.5	14.5	14.1	14.2	14.2	14.0
2000	14.0	14.1	14.1	14.2	14.2	14.3	14.4	11.7	14.3	14.3	14.5	14.7	14.1
2001	14.2	14.3	14.3	14.2	14.2	14.3	14.1	14.1	13.9	13.8	13.8	13.8	14.0
2002	13.4	13.4	13.4	13.2	13.3	13.3	13.3	13.3	13.2	13.2	13.4	13.4	13.3
2003	12.9	12.8	12.8	12.8	12.8	12.8	12.9	12.8	12.7	12.5	12.7	12.6	12.8
Financial activities													
1990	26.0	25.9	26.0	26.0	26.2	26.4	26.2	26.3	26.4	26.2	26.1	26.2	26.2
1991	26.1	26.1	26.2	26.0	26.2	26.3	26.2	26.1	26.0	26.0	26.0	26.2	26.1
1992	25.7	25.6	25.6	25.6	26.0	26.2	26.3	26.3	26.2	26.3	26.3	26.4	26.0
1993	26.1	26.1	26.1	26.4	26.6	26.7	26.8	26.9	26.9	26.8	26.9	26.9	26.6
1994	26.5	26.5	26.7	27.1	27.3	27.6	27.6	27.7	27.8	27.6	27.6	27.9	27.3
1995	27.6	27.4	27.5	27.7	27.9	28.1	28.2	28.3	28.2	28.1	28.0	28.1	27.9
1996	27.6	27.6	27.9	28.2	28.4	28.6	28.4	28.4	28.4	28.5	28.5	28.8	28.3
1997	28.6	28.6	28.9	29.1	29.4	29.5	29.6	29.7	29.7	29.8	29.7	29.9	29.4
1998	29.3	29.3	29.5	29.6	29.6	30.0	30.0	29.8	29.9	29.7	29.8	30.5	29.8
1999	30.1	30.1	30.3	30.3	30.7	31.0	31.0	31.1	30.7	30.7	30.7	30.9	30.6
2000	30.7	30.8	31.2	31.1	31.3	31.6	31.3	31.4	31.1	31.1	31.2	31.6	31.2
2001	30.6	30.5	30.6	30.7	30.8	30.9	30.8	30.6	30.5	30.6	30.5	30.7	30.6
2002	30.2	30.4	30.7	30.8	31.0	31.3	31.5	31.7	31.5	31.6	31.6	31.8	31.2
2003	30.8	30.8	30.8	31.0	30.7	31.0	31.0	31.0	31.2	31.1	31.0	31.1	31.0
Professional and business services													
1990	31.0	31.3	32.2	32.9	33.2	33.7	32.9	33.1	33.1	33.0	33.0	33.0	32.7
1991	32.2	32.3	32.8	33.2	33.0	33.3	33.7	33.7	33.8	33.8	33.8	33.7	33.3
1992	33.4	33.7	33.8	34.7	34.8	35.3	35.6	35.5	35.7	36.2	35.7	35.9	35.0
1993	35.3	36.0	36.0	37.0	37.2	37.2	37.6	38.0	38.6	38.8	38.7	38.5	37.4
1994	36.7	37.7	38.2	39.0	39.2	40.2	40.5	40.7	41.0	41.2	41.1	41.4	39.7
1995	40.5	40.7	41.5	42.6	43.1	43.5	43.7	43.8	44.1	44.1	44.3	44.7	43.1
1996	43.0	43.7	43.9	44.8	45.4	45.7	46.3	46.2	46.1	46.7	47.2	47.3	45.5
1997	45.7	45.9	46.9	47.5	47.5	48.1	48.4	48.3	48.6	48.2	49.1	49.5	47.8
1998	47.3	47.8	48.5	49.2	49.9	51.4	51.1	51.7	51.9	54.1	54.5	54.4	51.0
1999	51.6	52.6	53.0	53.3	53.3	54.4	53.8	54.6	53.6	54.7	54.8	54.9	53.7
2000	52.9	53.6	54.8	56.5	56.1	57.2	56.6	56.5	56.8	56.3	56.6	57.0	55.9
2001	56.1	56.7	57.4	57.4	57.6	58.3	57.7	57.9	57.2	57.3	57.2	57.4	57.3
2002	54.5	54.8	55.6	56.5	56.6	57.4	57.8	58.4	57.7	56.8	57.0	57.5	56.7
2003	55.5	55.4	55.8	56.3	56.1	56.9	56.5	56.7	56.7	56.5	56.8	57.4	56.4
Educational and health services													
1990	67.4	68.3	69.3	69.5	69.8	69.4	69.5	69.7	70.6	71.7	72.1	72.5	70.0
1991	72.5	73.0	73.8	74.1	74.8	75.1	74.4	75.2	76.3	76.6	76.9	77.5	75.0
1992	76.8	77.3	78.0	78.5	78.5	78.3	78.5	78.9	80.2	81.5	81.9	82.4	79.2
1993	81.4	81.8	82.4	83.1	83.1	82.8	83.0	83.3	84.0	85.5	85.5	85.9	83.5
1994	84.2	84.7	85.4	86.2	86.7	85.7	85.9	86.0	87.4	88.8	89.2	89.6	86.7
1995	88.5	89.2	89.8	89.3	89.6	88.7	88.4	88.5	89.9	91.1	91.1	91.3	89.6
1996	90.0	90.4	91.0	91.0	91.5	90.1	90.0	90.1	90.7	92.3	92.5	92.7	91.0
1997	91.7	91.7	92.1	92.6	92.8	92.1	92.9	93.1	94.2	96.2	96.5	96.8	93.6
1998	95.3	95.8	96.7	96.8	96.7	96.2	95.9	96.2	97.0	98.1	98.4	98.7	96.8
1999	97.1	97.4	98.4	98.7	98.3	97.2	96.6	96.7	97.6	99.2	99.2	99.7	98.0
2000	97.5	98.6	99.6	100.1	99.9	99.1	98.1	98.6	100.1	101.7	102.0	102.6	99.8
2001	100.8	101.8	102.7	102.8	102.9	102.4	101.5	102.3	103.9	105.1	105.9	106.7	103.2
2002	105.4	106.7	107.4	106.9	107.3	106.0	106.3	105.9	107.0	108.5	109.3	109.7	107.2
2003	108.4	108.2	108.7	108.7	108.9	107.7	106.7	107.1	108.2	108.4	108.3	107.7	108.1

Employment by Industry: West Virginia—*Continued*

(Numbers in thousands. Not seasonally adjusted.)

Industry	January	February	March	April	May	June	July	August	September	October	November	December	Annual Average
STATEWIDE—*Continued*													
Leisure and hospitality													
1990	44.2	44.3	45.5	47.8	49.2	50.5	50.2	51.0	50.0	48.1	46.6	46.3	47.8
1991	44.4	44.6	45.3	47.1	49.1	49.9	49.7	50.4	49.7	48.1	47.3	46.9	47.7
1992	45.3	45.7	46.6	48.9	51.1	51.7	51.6	52.3	51.9	50.2	49.1	49.1	49.5
1993	47.2	47.4	47.5	50.1	52.8	53.8	54.2	54.7	53.7	52.9	51.5	51.3	51.4
1994	48.2	48.8	50.3	52.5	55.1	56.1	56.6	57.8	57.3	55.4	53.6	53.9	53.8
1995	52.2	52.5	54.4	56.4	58.8	60.1	60.3	61.2	60.4	57.9	56.1	56.5	57.2
1996	53.4	53.5	55.4	57.1	59.7	61.4	61.6	62.3	61.5	59.2	57.4	57.1	58.3
1997	54.8	54.8	55.8	57.2	60.0	62.4	62.0	62.6	62.1	60.6	58.9	59.4	59.2
1998	56.1	56.6	57.8	59.7	61.8	63.9	63.7	63.7	63.1	60.4	58.4	58.7	60.3
1999	56.5	56.8	57.7	60.0	62.1	63.6	63.4	63.4	62.7	61.3	59.9	60.0	60.6
2000	58.3	57.8	59.4	61.0	62.8	64.7	64.8	65.4	64.8	62.9	61.2	61.2	62.0
2001	59.2	59.4	60.8	62.6	64.4	65.8	65.6	66.4	65.3	63.1	61.8	61.2	62.9
2002	59.8	60.2	61.7	63.0	65.3	66.6	67.9	68.2	67.1	65.2	63.8	63.7	64.4
2003	61.8	61.7	63.3	65.3	67.6	69.2	69.8	70.2	68.6	66.4	65.4	65.3	66.2
Other services													
1990	33.8	33.6	33.8	33.8	34.1	34.2	34.2	34.3	34.5	34.4	34.4	34.5	34.1
1991	34.0	33.8	33.9	34.0	34.4	34.3	34.2	34.0	34.3	34.0	33.9	34.2	34.1
1992	34.0	34.0	34.0	34.3	34.4	34.3	34.6	34.5	34.8	34.5	34.3	34.7	34.4
1993	34.2	34.0	34.2	34.7	35.1	35.2	35.3	35.2	35.5	35.4	35.6	35.9	35.0
1994	35.4	35.6	35.8	36.5	36.7	36.6	36.6	36.7	36.9	36.8	37.0	37.1	36.5
1995	36.8	36.9	37.0	37.3	37.9	37.9	38.1	38.3	38.6	38.8	39.1	39.5	38.0
1996	39.1	39.5	39.9	40.6	41.5	41.9	42.4	42.9	43.4	43.8	44.3	44.8	42.0
1997	44.7	45.1	45.7	45.7	45.9	45.8	45.5	45.5	45.6	45.6	45.5	45.7	45.5
1998	45.2	45.1	45.3	45.8	46.3	46.7	47.0	46.8	47.3	47.6	48.0	48.5	46.6
1999	48.0	48.4	48.7	49.3	49.7	50.1	50.1	50.2	50.6	50.9	51.2	51.6	49.9
2000	51.7	52.2	52.9	52.9	53.3	53.8	54.0	54.1	54.5	54.8	55.0	55.4	53.7
2001	55.0	55.1	55.3	55.5	55.7	55.8	55.3	55.2	55.3	55.1	55.0	55.2	55.2
2002	54.9	55.0	55.2	55.5	55.7	55.6	55.4	55.4	55.3	55.1	55.0	55.2	55.3
2003	54.7	54.6	55.0	55.3	55.2	55.5	55.5	55.3	55.7	55.4	55.3	55.4	55.2
Government													
1990	124.8	126.1	127.3	127.1	140.1	127.7	130.3	119.3	122.5	127.8	128.2	128.0	127.4
1991	124.7	126.0	127.3	128.3	130.0	126.8	130.2	121.6	125.2	130.5	131.0	130.5	127.7
1992	128.0	128.2	130.5	131.2	145.8	129.9	136.8	126.3	128.0	133.4	134.1	135.0	132.3
1993	130.5	131.7	133.2	133.6	134.9	131.7	135.4	126.2	130.9	134.4	135.5	135.9	132.8
1994	130.9	132.1	134.9	134.8	149.2	134.2	135.5	130.9	131.9	136.1	149.2	138.3	136.5
1995	133.7	134.8	137.0	136.9	138.3	136.4	137.7	132.8	133.5	138.5	138.7	138.8	136.4
1996	134.7	136.2	139.0	138.2	152.6	138.3	137.9	133.1	134.8	139.5	140.3	140.0	138.7
1997	137.0	138.0	140.4	140.0	141.1	138.7	139.4	134.5	136.5	140.2	141.9	141.4	139.1
1998	136.4	138.6	140.3	139.7	152.2	138.2	141.2	135.8	138.4	142.3	143.5	142.6	140.8
1999	138.3	139.5	142.3	142.9	143.0	140.8	141.9	136.1	138.4	142.1	142.2	143.4	140.9
2000	139.2	140.1	144.9	143.5	157.4	142.0	145.0	138.2	139.1	141.8	143.2	143.1	143.1
2001	138.0	140.6	142.8	142.6	142.3	140.9	138.2	138.4	139.0	142.4	143.7	143.7	141.0
2002	139.1	141.0	143.7	143.4	154.5	142.2	137.8	138.4	140.6	143.3	145.1	144.9	142.8
2003	140.8	142.3	144.0	145.0	145.2	143.8	138.9	139.1	139.8	142.2	143.4	143.1	142.3
Federal government													
1990	16.2	16.2	17.2	17.5	19.5	19.4	18.2	16.8	16.5	16.5	16.4	16.5	17.2
1991	16.2	16.2	16.3	16.8	16.9	17.2	17.1	17.2	17.1	17.2	17.3	17.3	16.9
1992	17.1	17.0	17.1	17.5	17.5	17.7	17.7	17.6	17.6	17.9	17.6	17.8	17.5
1993	17.3	17.3	17.3	17.6	17.8	17.9	17.9	17.8	18.0	17.8	17.8	18.0	17.7
1994	17.8	17.8	17.8	18.0	18.1	18.5	18.5	18.5	18.6	18.6	18.5	18.7	18.3
1995	18.6	18.6	18.7	18.9	19.1	19.5	19.7	19.7	19.6	19.7	19.6	19.7	19.3
1996	19.5	19.6	19.6	19.6	19.7	19.9	20.0	20.3	20.0	20.0	20.3	20.4	19.9
1997	20.3	20.3	20.5	20.7	20.9	21.3	21.5	21.6	21.5	21.5	21.7	21.8	21.1
1998	21.3	21.1	21.1	21.1	21.3	21.3	21.6	22.0	22.0	22.9	23.3	22.2	21.8
1999	21.5	21.5	21.5	22.2	21.5	21.6	21.7	21.7	21.8	21.9	21.8	22.1	21.7
2000	21.9	21.9	23.6	22.6	25.2	22.7	23.3	22.2	21.7	21.5	21.8	21.9	22.5
2001	21.7	21.5	21.5	21.5	21.7	22.0	22.1	22.0	22.0	21.8	21.8	22.0	21.7
2002	21.7	21.6	21.7	21.7	21.8	22.1	22.3	21.9	21.9	21.9	22.1	22.3	21.9
2003	22.0	21.9	21.9	21.9	21.9	22.1	22.1	22.0	21.9	21.8	21.8	22.1	22.0
State government													
1990	38.4	39.3	39.4	38.8	38.0	35.3	44.3	34.7	37.0	40.5	40.6	40.3	38.9
1991	38.0	39.0	40.1	40.1	40.8	36.5	44.6	36.2	37.5	42.3	42.2	41.8	39.9
1992	40.5	40.7	42.6	42.5	43.0	38.8	50.2	40.2	40.2	43.6	43.9	44.1	42.5
1993	41.4	42.1	43.7	43.4	43.8	39.5	47.5	38.4	41.3	44.1	44.4	44.5	42.8
1994	41.0	42.0	44.1	43.3	44.2	40.4	46.0	41.4	41.1	43.8	44.3	45.4	43.1
1995	41.7	42.6	44.3	44.0	44.7	41.2	46.8	41.9	41.3	45.1	45.1	44.9	43.6
1996	41.9	42.3	45.2	44.5	45.2	42.6	46.2	41.2	42.0	45.4	45.4	45.0	43.9
1997	42.8	43.4	44.8	44.4	44.7	40.8	46.1	41.0	42.6	45.2	44.8	45.4	43.8
1998	41.7	43.7	45.2	44.5	44.0	41.2	47.0	40.8	43.7	45.5	45.7	45.8	44.1
1999	43.1	43.5	46.2	45.8	45.9	42.6	47.4	41.6	43.4	45.9	45.8	46.7	44.8
2000	43.1	44.1	46.3	46.0	45.5	42.7	48.7	42.7	43.9	46.2	46.9	46.6	45.2
2001	42.6	44.9	46.7	46.5	45.4	42.7	43.6	43.6	44.1	46.7	47.5	47.2	45.1
2002	43.9	45.4	47.4	47.0	46.1	43.9	43.1	43.7	45.3	47.4	48.2	47.8	45.8
2003	44.6	46.2	47.5	47.5	47.0	44.8	44.0	43.7	44.4	46.3	46.9	46.4	45.8

Employment by Industry: West Virginia—*Continued*

(Numbers in thousands. Not seasonally adjusted.)

Industry	January	February	March	April	May	June	July	August	September	October	November	December	Annual Average
STATEWIDE—*Continued*													
Local government													
1990	70.2	70.6	70.7	70.8	82.6	73.0	67.8	67.8	69.0	70.8	71.2	71.2	71.3
1991	70.5	70.8	70.9	71.4	72.3	73.1	68.5	68.2	70.6	71.0	71.5	71.4	70.9
1992	70.4	70.5	70.8	71.2	85.3	73.4	68.9	68.5	70.2	71.9	72.6	73.1	72.2
1993	71.8	72.3	72.2	72.6	73.3	74.3	70.0	70.0	71.6	72.5	73.3	73.4	72.3
1994	72.1	72.3	73.0	73.5	86.9	75.3	71.0	71.0	72.2	73.7	86.4	74.2	75.1
1995	73.4	73.6	74.0	74.0	74.5	75.7	71.2	71.2	72.6	73.7	74.0	74.2	73.5
1996	73.3	74.3	74.2	74.1	87.7	75.8	71.7	71.6	72.8	74.1	74.6	74.6	74.9
1997	73.9	74.3	75.1	74.9	75.5	76.6	71.8	71.9	72.4	73.5	75.4	74.2	74.1
1998	73.4	73.8	74.0	74.1	86.9	75.7	72.6	73.0	72.7	73.9	74.5	74.6	74.9
1999	73.7	74.5	74.6	74.9	75.6	76.6	72.8	72.8	73.2	74.3	74.6	74.6	74.4
2000	74.2	74.1	75.0	74.9	86.7	76.6	73.0	73.3	73.5	74.1	74.5	74.6	75.4
2001	73.7	74.2	74.6	74.6	75.2	76.2	72.5	72.8	72.9	73.9	74.4	74.5	74.1
2002	73.5	74.0	74.6	74.7	86.6	76.2	72.4	72.8	73.4	74.0	74.8	74.8	75.2
2003	74.2	74.2	74.6	75.6	76.3	76.9	72.8	73.4	73.5	74.1	74.7	74.6	74.6
CHARLESTON													
Total nonfarm													
1990	108.2	108.7	110.4	110.4	112.9	112.3	112.2	111.3	111.6	110.9	111.3	111.3	111.0
1991	108.6	109.2	110.2	110.3	112.0	112.9	113.5	113.3	112.8	112.5	112.7	112.8	111.7
1992	111.1	110.7	111.7	112.4	114.3	114.4	115.5	115.8	115.1	115.5	116.2	117.4	114.2
1993	113.7	115.0	115.1	116.8	118.4	120.1	121.3	122.0	120.4	120.8	121.5	121.8	118.9
1994	117.3	118.0	119.8	121.7	123.9	124.1	125.3	125.0	125.0	124.6	126.0	126.0	123.1
1995	121.7	121.5	123.1	124.0	125.5	127.0	127.3	126.9	126.9	127.2	126.5	126.9	125.4
1996	122.5	123.5	124.3	125.7	128.7	129.3	130.1	129.5	129.5	129.7	130.4	130.9	127.8
1997	127.4	127.5	128.7	129.4	130.4	131.4	132.1	131.3	130.9	131.0	132.9	132.4	130.5
1998	128.8	129.0	130.0	131.2	132.8	134.0	135.4	135.4	134.5	134.4	134.4	134.8	132.9
1999	131.5	132.2	132.9	134.9	135.7	137.5	137.7	137.3	136.6	137.1	137.5	137.3	135.7
2000	133.4	133.7	135.9	136.6	138.7	138.6	139.0	136.2	138.0	137.6	138.2	138.8	137.1
2001	134.6	134.8	135.7	136.0	136.8	138.1	137.7	137.5	136.0	135.4	135.6	135.7	136.1
2002	132.3	132.4	133.8	134.4	136.0	135.2	136.0	135.8	134.6	134.9	135.4	135.5	134.7
2003	131.2	130.4	132.0	133.1	133.6	134.4	133.8	134.0	132.8	133.7	133.8	134.0	133.1
Total private													
1990	88.4	88.7	90.2	90.3	91.2	92.0	91.9	92.0	92.1	91.4	91.7	91.6	91.0
1991	89.3	89.6	90.5	90.8	92.0	92.7	93.0	93.6	93.1	92.8	92.9	92.9	91.9
1992	91.0	90.8	91.4	92.2	92.5	93.3	93.7	93.9	94.2	94.3	95.0	96.0	93.2
1993	92.7	93.5	93.3	95.4	96.6	98.0	98.6	99.7	99.0	99.3	99.6	100.1	97.2
1994	95.8	96.4	97.8	99.8	100.4	101.7	102.0	102.5	103.2	102.3	102.5	103.3	100.6
1995	99.5	99.1	100.5	101.5	102.6	103.7	103.5	103.4	104.6	104.3	103.8	104.0	102.5
1996	100.0	100.5	101.3	102.9	104.3	105.8	106.6	106.8	106.8	106.6	107.1	107.4	104.7
1997	104.3	104.0	105.0	105.8	106.5	107.4	108.3	108.1	108.0	107.8	108.4	108.4	106.8
1998	105.5	105.5	106.4	107.6	107.9	110.0	111.0	111.9	111.1	111.1	110.6	110.9	109.1
1999	107.8	108.2	108.6	110.5	111.4	112.9	112.8	113.4	112.9	113.4	113.7	113.2	111.6
2000	109.4	109.8	111.7	112.5	112.8	113.9	113.9	112.2	114.1	113.7	114.0	114.4	112.7
2001	110.9	110.9	111.5	111.9	112.8	113.5	112.9	112.8	112.2	111.4	111.4	111.4	111.9
2002	108.3	108.2	109.3	110.0	110.2	110.3	111.3	111.1	110.3	110.2	110.5	110.5	110.0
2003	106.5	105.4	106.8	108.1	108.5	109.2	109.2	109.4	108.8	109.2	108.9	109.2	108.3
Goods-producing													
1990	15.7	15.8	16.4	16.5	16.7	16.9	17.1	17.2	17.2	17.2	17.1	16.8	16.7
1991	16.4	16.6	16.7	17.1	17.4	17.6	17.5	17.7	17.7	17.8	17.5	17.4	17.3
1992	16.6	16.4	16.4	16.6	16.9	17.1	17.4	17.5	17.6	17.8	17.8	17.5	17.1
1993	17.0	16.7	16.9	17.4	17.8	18.2	18.3	18.3	18.2	18.3	18.1	17.7	17.7
1994	16.3	16.5	16.8	17.9	18.2	18.3	18.4	18.6	18.9	18.5	18.2	18.0	17.9
1995	17.1	16.8	17.5	17.8	17.8	18.2	18.4	18.1	18.5	18.6	18.2	17.8	17.9
1996	16.3	16.6	17.0	17.5	18.0	18.5	18.9	18.8	18.8	18.6	18.4	18.2	18.0
1997	17.2	17.1	17.2	17.6	17.8	18.2	18.7	18.9	19.0	19.1	18.8	18.4	18.2
1998	17.8	17.9	18.2	18.4	18.5	18.9	19.6	19.6	19.4	19.3	18.8	18.8	18.8
1999	17.7	17.7	17.8	18.7	19.1	19.2	19.3	19.5	19.5	19.1	18.7	18.4	18.7
2000	17.5	17.3	18.0	18.5	18.6	18.8	19.0	18.8	19.3	19.2	19.1	18.8	18.6
2001	18.1	18.2	18.4	18.8	19.1	19.3	19.0	18.8	18.8	18.7	18.4	18.1	18.6
2002	17.3	17.4	17.4	17.5	17.4	17.6	17.9	17.8	17.8	17.6	17.4	17.1	17.5
2003	16.1	15.4	15.9	16.4	16.7	16.7	16.7	16.8	17.0	16.8	16.9	16.4	16.5
Construction and mining													
1990	5.6	5.7	6.2	6.3	6.4	6.6	6.7	6.9	6.9	7.1	7.0	6.7	6.5
1991	5.9	6.1	6.2	6.8	7.0	7.1	7.1	7.3	7.3	7.5	7.3	7.1	6.9
1992	6.1	6.0	6.1	6.4	6.7	6.8	7.1	7.3	7.4	7.7	7.8	7.4	6.9
1993	6.9	6.6	6.6	7.3	7.8	8.2	8.5	8.5	8.5	8.6	8.4	8.0	7.8
1994	6.7	6.9	7.3	8.3	8.7	8.7	8.7	9.1	9.2	8.9	8.7	8.4	8.3
1995	7.5	7.1	7.7	8.3	8.4	8.6	8.8	8.7	9.0	9.0	8.7	8.2	8.3
1996	6.8	7.0	7.4	8.0	8.5	9.0	9.3	9.3	9.3	9.0	8.9	8.6	8.4
1997	7.7	7.6	7.7	8.2	8.3	8.7	9.0	9.2	9.3	9.4	9.1	8.7	8.6
1998	7.9	8.0	8.2	8.5	8.6	8.9	9.5	9.5	9.4	9.4	9.0	9.0	8.8
1999	7.9	7.9	7.9	8.8	9.2	9.2	9.3	9.4	9.4	9.2	8.9	8.6	8.8
2000	7.6	7.4	7.9	8.6	8.9	9.1	9.3	9.2	9.6	9.5	9.5	9.1	8.8
2001	8.4	8.5	8.7	9.2	9.4	9.6	9.7	9.9	10.0	10.0	9.8	9.4	9.4
2002	8.6	8.7	8.7	8.9	8.9	9.1	9.4	9.4	9.4	9.4	9.3	8.9	9.1
2003	8.1	7.7	8.1	8.7	9.0	9.0	9.1	9.3	9.4	9.3	9.4	9.0	8.8

Employment by Industry: West Virginia—*Continued*

(Numbers in thousands. Not seasonally adjusted.)

Industry	January	February	March	April	May	June	July	August	September	October	November	December	Annual Average
CHARLESTON—*Continued*													
Manufacturing													
1990	10.1	10.1	10.2	10.2	10.3	10.3	10.4	10.3	10.3	10.1	10.1	10.1	10.2
1991	10.5	10.5	10.5	10.3	10.4	10.5	10.4	10.4	10.4	10.3	10.2	10.3	10.4
1992	10.5	10.4	10.3	10.2	10.2	10.3	10.3	10.2	10.2	10.1	10.0	10.1	10.2
1993	10.1	10.1	10.3	10.1	10.0	10.0	9.8	9.8	9.7	9.7	9.7	9.7	9.9
1994	9.6	9.6	9.5	9.6	9.5	9.6	9.7	9.5	9.7	9.6	9.5	9.6	9.6
1995	9.6	9.7	9.8	9.5	9.4	9.6	9.6	9.4	9.5	9.6	9.5	9.6	9.6
1996	9.5	9.6	9.6	9.5	9.5	9.5	9.6	9.5	9.5	9.6	9.5	9.6	9.5
1997	9.5	9.5	9.5	9.4	9.5	9.5	9.7	9.7	9.7	9.7	9.7	9.7	9.6
1998	9.9	9.9	10.0	9.9	9.9	10.0	10.1	10.1	10.0	9.9	9.8	9.8	9.9
1999	9.8	9.8	9.9	9.9	9.9	10.0	10.0	10.1	10.1	9.9	9.8	9.8	9.9
2000	9.9	9.9	10.1	9.9	9.7	9.7	9.7	9.6	9.7	9.7	9.6	9.7	9.8
2001	9.7	9.7	9.7	9.6	9.7	9.7	9.3	8.9	8.8	8.7	8.6	8.7	9.2
2002	8.7	8.7	8.7	8.6	8.5	8.5	8.5	8.4	8.4	8.2	8.1	8.2	8.5
2003	8.0	7.7	7.8	7.7	7.7	7.7	7.6	7.5	7.6	7.5	7.5	7.4	7.6
Service-providing													
1990	92.5	92.9	94.0	93.9	96.2	95.4	95.1	94.1	94.4	93.7	94.2	94.5	94.2
1991	92.2	92.6	93.5	93.2	94.6	95.3	96.0	95.6	95.1	94.7	95.2	95.4	94.5
1992	94.5	94.3	95.3	95.8	97.4	97.3	98.1	98.3	97.5	97.7	98.4	99.9	97.0
1993	96.7	98.3	98.2	99.4	100.6	101.9	103.0	103.7	102.2	102.5	103.4	104.1	101.2
1994	101.0	101.5	103.0	103.8	105.7	105.8	106.9	106.4	106.1	106.1	107.8	108.0	105.2
1995	104.6	104.7	105.6	106.2	107.7	108.8	108.9	108.8	108.4	108.6	108.3	109.1	107.5
1996	106.2	106.9	107.3	108.2	110.7	110.8	111.2	110.7	110.7	111.1	112.0	112.7	109.9
1997	110.2	110.4	111.5	111.8	112.6	113.2	113.4	112.4	111.9	111.9	114.1	114.0	112.3
1998	111.0	111.1	111.8	112.8	114.3	115.1	115.8	115.8	115.1	115.1	115.6	116.0	114.1
1999	113.8	114.5	115.1	116.2	116.6	118.3	118.4	117.8	117.1	118.0	118.8	118.9	117.0
2000	115.9	116.4	117.9	118.1	120.1	119.8	120.0	117.4	118.7	118.4	119.1	120.0	118.5
2001	116.5	116.6	117.3	117.2	117.7	118.8	118.7	118.7	117.2	116.7	117.2	117.6	117.5
2002	115.0	115.0	116.4	116.9	118.6	117.6	118.1	118.0	116.8	117.3	118.0	118.4	117.2
2003	115.1	115.0	116.1	116.7	116.9	117.7	117.1	117.2	115.8	116.9	116.9	117.6	116.6
Trade, transportation, and utilities													
1990	26.8	26.6	26.8	26.8	27.1	27.3	27.2	27.2	27.4	27.7	28.3	28.6	27.3
1991	26.7	26.3	26.5	26.4	26.8	26.7	27.0	27.2	26.9	26.8	27.3	27.4	26.8
1992	26.5	26.3	26.4	26.5	26.6	26.9	26.6	26.7	26.8	26.8	27.2	27.9	26.8
1993	26.4	26.7	26.6	27.0	27.2	27.6	27.9	28.5	28.3	28.8	29.2	29.8	27.8
1994	28.2	28.1	28.4	28.4	28.6	29.1	28.9	29.0	29.4	29.2	29.6	30.1	28.9
1995	28.6	28.4	28.6	28.4	28.7	28.8	28.5	28.6	28.9	28.9	29.2	29.4	28.8
1996	27.5	27.1	27.1	27.7	28.1	28.5	28.4	28.7	28.9	28.5	29.1	29.5	28.3
1997	28.4	28.2	28.1	28.5	28.8	28.8	28.6	28.5	28.4	28.2	28.8	29.2	28.5
1998	27.9	27.6	27.7	28.0	27.9	28.2	28.3	29.0	28.7	28.6	28.8	29.0	28.3
1999	28.2	27.9	27.9	28.3	28.5	28.7	28.4	28.7	28.5	29.1	29.7	29.9	28.7
2000	27.9	27.8	27.9	27.5	27.7	27.7	27.5	27.6	27.6	27.8	28.5	28.7	27.9
2001	27.5	27.1	27.1	27.0	27.2	27.3	27.2	27.4	27.3	27.1	27.6	27.9	27.3
2002	26.9	26.6	26.6	26.5	26.6	26.6	26.5	26.6	26.5	26.8	27.2	27.4	26.7
2003	26.1	25.8	26.1	26.1	26.2	26.4	26.4	26.7	26.6	26.9	26.6	27.5	26.5
Wholesale trade													
1990	5.6	5.6	5.6	5.5	5.6	5.6	5.7	5.6	5.6	5.6	5.5	5.6	5.6
1991	5.7	5.7	5.7	5.6	5.7	5.6	5.7	5.7	5.7	5.6	5.6	5.5	5.7
1992	5.5	5.5	5.5	5.5	5.6	5.5	5.7	5.6	5.6	5.6	5.6	5.6	5.6
1993	5.5	5.6	5.6	5.6	5.6	5.6	5.6	5.7	5.7	5.7	5.7	5.8	5.6
1994	5.6	5.6	5.7	5.7	5.8	5.9	5.8	5.8	5.8	5.8	5.9	5.9	5.8
1995	5.7	5.7	5.8	5.8	5.8	5.8	5.8	5.8	5.9	5.9	5.8	5.8	5.8
1996	5.7	5.6	5.6	5.7	5.8	5.8	5.8	5.9	5.9	5.9	5.9	5.9	5.8
1997	5.9	5.9	5.9	5.9	6.0	5.9	5.9	5.9	5.8	5.8	5.8	5.9	5.9
1998	5.9	5.9	5.9	5.8	5.7	5.8	5.8	5.8	5.8	5.8	5.7	5.8	5.8
1999	5.7	5.7	5.7	5.8	5.8	5.8	5.8	5.8	5.8	5.8	5.8	5.8	5.8
2000	5.7	5.7	5.8	5.8	5.8	5.8	5.8	5.9	5.9	5.9	6.1	6.0	5.9
2001	5.9	5.9	5.9	5.9	5.9	6.0	6.0	6.0	6.0	5.9	5.9	6.0	5.9
2002	5.9	5.9	5.9	5.9	5.8	5.8	5.8	5.8	5.8	5.8	5.7	5.7	5.8
2003	5.6	5.6	5.7	5.7	5.7	5.8	5.9	5.9	5.9	6.0	6.0	6.0	5.8
Retail trade													
1990	14.6	14.3	14.5	14.4	14.6	14.7	14.6	14.7	14.9	15.0	15.7	16.1	14.8
1991	14.4	14.0	14.1	14.2	14.4	14.4	14.5	14.7	14.4	14.4	14.9	15.2	14.5
1992	14.2	14.0	14.1	14.1	14.1	14.5	14.2	14.3	14.3	14.4	14.8	15.4	14.4
1993	14.3	14.5	14.4	14.7	14.8	15.1	15.3	15.7	15.4	15.7	16.1	16.5	15.2
1994	15.3	15.1	15.2	15.2	15.3	15.6	15.6	15.8	16.2	16.0	16.3	16.9	15.7
1995	15.8	15.6	15.7	15.6	15.9	16.1	15.9	16.1	16.3	16.3	16.8	17.1	16.1
1996	16.0	15.8	15.8	15.7	16.0	16.3	16.1	16.2	16.3	15.8	16.4	16.8	16.1
1997	15.7	15.4	15.3	15.5	15.6	15.7	15.3	15.4	15.3	15.4	16.0	16.2	15.6
1998	15.1	14.8	14.8	15.1	15.2	15.4	15.6	16.3	16.1	16.1	16.5	16.7	15.6
1999	16.0	15.8	15.8	16.0	16.3	16.4	16.1	16.3	16.1	16.7	17.2	17.4	16.3
2000	15.9	15.9	15.9	15.8	15.9	15.9	15.7	15.7	15.7	15.9	16.4	16.7	16.0
2001	15.5	15.2	15.2	15.1	15.2	15.2	15.1	15.3	15.2	15.1	15.6	15.8	15.2
2002	15.0	14.8	14.9	14.8	14.9	14.9	14.9	15.0	15.0	15.1	15.6	15.9	15.1
2003	14.7	14.5	14.7	14.7	14.8	14.9	14.8	15.1	15.0	15.1	14.9	15.7	14.9

Employment by Industry: West Virginia—*Continued*

(Numbers in thousands. Not seasonally adjusted.)

Industry	January	February	March	April	May	June	July	August	September	October	November	December	Annual Average
CHARLESTON—*Continued*													
Transportation and utilities													
1990	6.6	6.7	6.7	6.9	6.9	7.0	6.9	6.9	6.9	7.1	7.1	6.9	6.9
1991	6.6	6.6	6.7	6.6	6.7	6.7	6.8	6.8	6.8	6.8	6.8	6.7	6.7
1992	6.8	6.8	6.8	6.9	6.9	6.9	6.7	6.8	6.9	6.8	6.8	6.9	6.8
1993	6.6	6.6	6.6	6.7	6.8	6.9	7.0	7.1	7.2	7.4	7.4	7.5	7.0
1994	7.3	7.4	7.5	7.5	7.5	7.6	7.5	7.4	7.4	7.4	7.4	7.3	7.4
1995	7.1	7.1	7.1	7.0	7.0	6.9	6.8	6.7	6.7	6.7	6.6	6.5	6.9
1996	5.8	5.7	5.7	6.3	6.3	6.4	6.5	6.6	6.7	6.8	6.8	6.8	6.4
1997	6.8	6.9	6.9	7.1	7.2	7.2	7.4	7.2	7.3	7.0	7.0	7.1	7.1
1998	6.9	6.9	7.0	7.1	7.0	7.0	6.9	6.9	6.8	6.7	6.6	6.5	6.9
1999	6.5	6.4	6.4	6.5	6.4	6.5	6.5	6.6	6.6	6.6	6.7	6.7	6.5
2000	6.3	6.2	6.2	5.9	6.0	6.0	6.0	6.0	6.0	6.0	6.0	6.0	6.1
2001	6.1	6.0	6.0	6.0	6.1	6.1	6.1	6.1	6.1	6.1	6.1	6.1	6.0
2002	6.0	5.9	5.8	5.8	5.9	5.9	5.8	5.8	5.7	5.9	5.9	5.8	5.9
2003	5.8	5.7	5.7	5.7	5.7	5.7	5.7	5.7	5.7	5.8	5.7	5.8	5.7
Information													
1990	3.6	3.6	3.6	3.8	3.7	3.8	3.7	3.7	3.7	3.6	3.6	3.6	3.7
1991	3.6	3.6	3.6	3.4	3.5	3.5	3.5	3.6	3.6	3.5	3.5	3.6	3.5
1992	3.4	3.5	3.5	3.6	3.6	3.6	3.7	3.7	3.6	3.6	3.7	3.7	3.6
1993	3.6	3.6	3.6	3.5	3.5	3.6	3.6	3.6	3.6	3.7	3.7	3.7	3.6
1994	3.6	3.6	3.6	3.6	3.6	3.6	3.7	3.7	3.6	3.6	3.6	3.7	3.6
1995	3.1	3.0	3.0	3.4	3.4	3.4	3.2	3.2	3.2	3.2	3.2	3.2	3.2
1996	3.1	3.1	3.1	3.2	3.2	3.3	3.3	3.3	3.3	3.4	3.4	3.4	3.3
1997	3.3	3.3	3.4	3.4	3.4	3.4	3.3	3.3	3.3	3.2	3.3	3.3	3.3
1998	3.7	3.7	3.7	3.6	3.6	3.6	3.6	3.6	3.6	3.6	3.6	3.6	3.6
1999	3.6	3.6	3.8	3.5	3.6	3.7	3.8	3.8	3.9	3.9	3.9	3.9	3.8
2000	4.0	4.0	4.0	4.0	4.0	4.1	4.0	2.5	3.9	3.9	3.9	4.0	3.9
2001	3.9	3.9	3.9	3.8	3.8	3.8	3.8	3.7	3.7	3.7	3.7	3.7	3.7
2002	3.6	3.6	3.6	3.5	3.5	3.5	3.5	3.5	3.5	3.5	3.5	3.5	3.5
2003	3.5	3.5	3.5	3.5	3.4	3.5	3.4	3.4	3.4	3.3	3.3	3.3	3.4
Financial activities													
1990	6.8	6.8	6.9	6.8	6.8	6.9	6.7	6.7	6.8	6.6	6.6	6.6	6.8
1991	6.3	6.3	6.4	6.5	6.6	6.7	6.6	6.5	6.5	6.4	6.5	6.5	6.5
1992	6.4	6.3	6.4	6.3	6.4	6.5	6.6	6.5	6.5	6.5	6.5	6.7	6.5
1993	6.5	6.5	6.5	6.6	6.8	6.8	6.8	6.8	6.8	6.7	6.8	6.9	6.7
1994	6.8	6.8	6.8	7.0	7.1	7.2	7.1	7.1	7.2	7.1	7.2	7.3	7.1
1995	7.3	7.3	7.3	7.2	7.3	7.3	7.3	7.3	7.4	7.4	7.3	7.4	7.3
1996	7.3	7.4	7.4	7.5	7.4	7.5	7.4	7.3	7.3	7.6	7.5	7.6	7.4
1997	7.6	7.6	7.8	7.9	7.9	7.9	8.0	8.0	8.1	8.2	8.1	8.2	7.9
1998	8.0	8.1	8.2	8.3	8.3	8.5	8.6	8.7	8.6	8.5	8.5	8.7	8.4
1999	8.5	8.5	8.5	8.4	8.5	8.7	8.6	8.7	8.6	8.6	8.6	8.6	8.6
2000	8.4	8.4	8.5	8.4	8.5	8.6	8.6	8.6	8.6	8.5	8.3	8.5	8.5
2001	8.2	8.2	8.2	8.0	8.1	8.1	8.1	8.1	8.0	8.1	8.1	8.1	8.0
2002	7.9	7.9	7.9	7.9	7.9	7.9	8.0	8.0	7.9	8.1	8.1	8.1	8.0
2003	7.9	7.9	7.8	8.0	8.0	8.0	8.1	8.0	8.0	8.2	8.1	8.2	8.0
Professional and business services													
1990	8.3	8.4	8.6	8.5	8.7	8.7	8.7	8.7	8.6	8.4	8.5	8.5	8.6
1991	8.7	8.8	9.1	9.2	9.2	9.4	9.5	9.5	9.5	9.5	9.3	9.4	9.3
1992	9.2	9.4	9.5	9.4	9.3	9.4	9.5	9.4	9.6	9.8	9.9	10.0	9.5
1993	9.8	10.1	9.9	10.3	10.5	10.5	10.6	10.6	10.7	10.6	10.7	10.7	10.4
1994	10.5	10.6	10.8	11.0	11.0	11.3	11.4	11.4	11.3	11.4	11.3	11.4	11.1
1995	11.1	11.1	11.3	11.9	12.1	12.2	12.2	12.1	12.3	12.3	12.2	12.2	11.9
1996	12.3	12.5	12.5	12.6	12.7	12.7	12.9	13.0	12.7	13.1	13.0	13.1	12.8
1997	12.9	12.9	13.1	13.1	13.1	13.2	13.5	13.3	13.3	13.2	13.3	13.3	13.2
1998	12.5	12.5	12.6	12.9	12.9	13.4	13.4	13.7	13.6	14.1	14.0	13.9	13.3
1999	13.5	13.8	13.8	14.1	14.0	14.4	14.5	14.8	14.6	14.9	14.6	14.6	14.3
2000	14.5	14.8	15.2	15.4	15.1	15.3	15.2	15.1	15.1	15.0	15.1	15.2	15.1
2001	14.8	14.7	14.9	14.7	14.7	14.7	14.7	14.7	14.5	14.7	14.5	14.4	14.6
2002	13.8	13.8	14.3	14.6	14.6	14.4	14.5	14.5	14.2	13.8	13.9	13.8	14.2
2003	13.4	13.3	13.4	13.4	13.3	13.3	13.6	13.5	13.5	13.5	13.7	13.6	13.5
Educational and health services													
1990	13.3	13.5	13.6	13.4	13.5	13.5	13.6	13.6	13.7	13.7	13.8	13.7	13.6
1991	13.8	14.0	14.0	14.1	13.9	14.0	14.2	14.3	14.3	14.4	14.5	14.4	14.2
1992	14.8	14.7	14.8	15.0	14.6	14.6	14.8	14.9	15.1	15.3	15.2	15.4	14.9
1993	14.9	15.2	15.1	15.3	15.2	15.3	15.4	15.6	15.5	15.7	15.7	15.7	15.4
1994	15.5	15.7	15.7	15.8	15.7	15.6	15.8	15.8	16.1	16.1	16.1	16.3	15.9
1995	16.2	16.4	16.4	16.3	16.4	16.4	16.6	16.7	16.9	16.9	16.7	16.8	16.6
1996	16.8	16.8	16.8	16.8	16.8	16.8	17.0	17.0	17.1	17.2	17.3	17.2	17.0
1997	16.9	17.0	17.1	17.1	17.1	17.2	17.3	17.2	17.3	17.6	17.7	17.6	17.3
1998	17.4	17.5	17.6	17.5	17.6	17.6	17.7	17.7	17.7	17.9	17.9	17.8	17.7
1999	17.5	17.7	17.6	17.7	17.5	17.5	17.5	17.5	17.5	17.7	17.8	17.7	17.6
2000	17.2	17.4	17.6	17.7	17.7	17.9	18.1	18.2	18.2	18.2	18.1	18.2	17.9
2001	17.3	17.6	17.6	17.8	17.8	18.1	18.2	18.3	18.4	18.2	18.2	18.2	17.9
2002	18.2	18.2	18.3	18.4	18.5	18.4	18.7	18.6	18.5	18.7	18.8	18.8	18.5
2003	18.4	18.4	18.4	18.6	18.7	18.8	18.4	18.4	18.3	18.5	18.5	18.3	18.5

Employment by Industry: West Virginia—*Continued*

(Numbers in thousands. Not seasonally adjusted.)

Industry	January	February	March	April	May	June	July	August	September	October	November	December	Annual Average
CHARLESTON—*Continued*													
Leisure and hospitality													
1990	7.9	8.0	8.2	8.4	8.6	8.8	8.7	8.7	8.5	8.0	7.8	7.7	8.3
1991	7.7	7.9	8.1	8.0	8.4	8.6	8.4	8.6	8.4	8.2	8.1	8.0	8.2
1992	7.9	8.0	8.1	8.6	8.8	9.0	8.8	8.9	8.7	8.3	8.4	8.5	8.5
1993	8.3	8.5	8.4	8.9	9.1	9.5	9.5	9.8	9.4	9.0	8.9	8.9	9.0
1994	8.5	8.7	9.1	9.5	9.6	9.9	10.0	10.2	10.0	9.7	9.7	9.6	9.5
1995	9.3	9.3	9.5	9.7	10.0	10.4	10.3	10.4	10.3	9.8	9.7	9.8	9.9
1996	9.4	9.6	9.9	10.0	10.3	10.7	10.7	10.7	10.6	9.9	10.0	9.9	10.1
1997	9.6	9.5	9.7	9.9	10.1	10.5	10.5	10.5	10.2	9.9	10.0	10.0	10.0
1998	9.8	9.8	9.9	10.4	10.5	11.2	11.0	10.9	10.7	10.3	10.1	10.1	10.4
1999	9.9	10.0	10.1	10.5	10.9	11.2	11.2	11.0	10.7	10.5	10.7	10.4	10.6
2000	10.2	10.2	10.5	11.0	11.2	11.5	11.4	11.4	11.3	11.1	11.1	11.1	11.0
2001	10.6	10.6	10.8	11.2	11.5	11.6	11.5	11.5	11.2	10.7	10.7	10.8	11.0
2002	10.4	10.4	10.8	11.2	11.3	11.4	11.7	11.6	11.4	11.2	11.1	11.2	11.1
2003	10.9	10.9	11.4	11.7	11.8	12.1	12.1	12.2	11.7	11.5	11.4	11.5	11.6
Other services													
1990	6.0	6.0	6.1	6.1	6.1	6.1	6.2	6.2	6.2	6.2	6.0	6.1	6.1
1991	6.1	6.1	6.1	6.1	6.2	6.2	6.3	6.2	6.2	6.2	6.2	6.2	6.2
1992	6.2	6.2	6.3	6.2	6.3	6.2	6.3	6.3	6.3	6.2	6.3	6.3	6.3
1993	6.2	6.2	6.3	6.4	6.5	6.5	6.5	6.5	6.5	6.5	6.5	6.7	6.4
1994	6.4	6.4	6.6	6.6	6.6	6.7	6.7	6.7	6.7	6.7	6.8	6.9	6.7
1995	6.8	6.8	6.9	6.8	6.9	7.0	7.0	7.0	7.1	7.2	7.3	7.4	7.0
1996	7.3	7.4	7.5	7.6	7.8	7.8	8.0	8.0	8.1	8.3	8.4	8.5	7.9
1997	8.4	8.4	8.6	8.3	8.3	8.2	8.4	8.4	8.4	8.4	8.4	8.4	8.4
1998	8.4	8.4	8.5	8.5	8.6	8.6	8.8	8.7	8.8	8.8	8.9	9.0	8.7
1999	8.9	9.0	9.1	9.3	9.3	9.5	9.5	9.4	9.6	9.6	9.7	9.7	9.4
2000	9.7	9.9	10.0	10.0	10.0	10.0	10.1	10.0	10.1	10.0	9.9	9.9	10.0
2001	10.5	10.6	10.6	10.6	10.6	10.6	10.4	10.3	10.3	10.2	10.2	10.2	10.4
2002	10.2	10.3	10.4	10.4	10.4	10.5	10.5	10.5	10.5	10.5	10.5	10.6	10.4
2003	10.2	10.2	10.3	10.4	10.4	10.4	10.5	10.4	10.3	10.5	10.4	10.4	10.4
Government													
1990	19.8	20.0	20.2	20.1	21.7	20.3	20.3	19.3	19.5	19.5	19.6	19.7	20.0
1991	19.3	19.6	19.7	19.5	20.0	20.2	20.5	19.7	19.7	19.7	19.8	19.9	19.8
1992	20.1	19.9	20.3	20.2	21.8	21.1	21.8	21.9	20.9	21.2	21.2	21.4	21.0
1993	21.0	21.5	21.8	21.4	21.8	22.1	22.7	22.3	21.4	21.5	21.9	21.7	21.8
1994	21.5	21.6	22.0	21.9	23.5	22.4	23.3	22.5	21.8	22.3	23.5	22.7	22.4
1995	22.2	22.4	22.6	22.5	22.9	23.3	23.8	23.5	22.3	22.9	22.7	22.9	22.8
1996	22.5	23.0	23.0	22.8	24.4	23.5	23.5	22.7	22.7	23.1	23.3	23.5	23.2
1997	23.1	23.5	23.7	23.6	23.9	24.0	23.8	23.2	22.9	23.2	24.5	24.0	23.6
1998	23.3	23.5	23.6	23.6	24.9	24.0	24.4	23.5	23.4	23.3	23.8	23.9	23.8
1999	23.7	24.0	24.3	24.4	24.3	24.6	24.9	23.9	23.7	23.7	23.8	24.1	24.1
2000	24.0	23.9	24.2	24.1	25.9	24.7	25.1	24.0	23.9	23.9	24.2	24.4	24.4
2001	23.7	23.9	24.2	24.1	24.0	24.6	24.8	24.7	23.8	24.0	24.2	24.3	24.1
2002	24.0	24.2	24.5	24.4	25.8	24.9	24.7	24.7	24.3	24.7	24.9	25.0	24.7
2003	24.7	25.0	25.2	25.0	25.1	25.2	24.6	24.6	24.0	24.5	24.9	24.8	24.8
Federal government													
1990	1.8	1.8	1.9	2.0	2.2	2.1	2.0	1.9	1.9	1.9	1.9	1.9	1.9
1991	1.9	1.9	1.9	2.0	2.0	2.1	2.1	2.1	2.1	2.0	2.0	2.0	2.0
1992	2.0	2.0	2.0	2.0	2.0	2.0	2.0	2.0	2.0	2.0	1.9	2.0	2.0
1993	1.9	1.9	1.9	1.9	2.0	2.0	2.0	2.0	2.0	2.0	2.0	2.1	2.0
1994	2.0	2.0	2.0	2.1	2.1	2.2	2.2	2.3	2.3	2.4	2.5	2.5	2.2
1995	2.4	2.4	2.4	2.4	2.4	2.4	2.4	2.4	2.4	2.3	2.3	2.4	2.4
1996	2.3	2.3	2.3	2.3	2.3	2.3	2.4	2.6	2.5	2.6	2.7	2.7	2.4
1997	2.7	2.7	2.7	2.7	2.7	2.7	2.7	2.7	2.7	2.7	2.8	2.7	2.7
1998	2.6	2.6	2.6	2.6	2.6	2.6	2.6	2.6	2.6	2.6	2.8	2.7	2.6
1999	2.6	2.6	2.6	2.7	2.5	2.5	2.5	2.5	2.5	2.5	2.6	2.7	2.6
2000	2.7	2.5	2.7	2.6	3.0	2.7	2.7	2.5	2.5	2.5	2.6	2.7	2.6
2001	2.6	2.5	2.5	2.4	2.4	2.6	2.6	2.6	2.6	2.6	2.6	2.6	2.5
2002	2.6	2.5	2.6	2.6	2.6	2.6	2.7	2.7	2.7	2.7	2.8	2.9	2.7
2003	2.8	2.8	2.7	2.7	2.7	2.6	2.6	2.6	2.5	2.5	2.7	2.7	2.7
State government													
1990	9.5	9.7	9.7	9.5	9.3	9.2	9.9	9.1	9.0	9.0	9.1	9.2	9.4
1991	8.8	9.1	9.2	8.9	9.3	9.2	9.9	9.2	9.0	9.2	9.3	9.4	9.2
1992	9.6	9.5	9.8	9.7	10.0	10.1	11.1	11.2	9.8	10.1	10.0	10.0	10.1
1993	9.8	10.1	10.4	10.2	10.4	10.4	11.5	11.0	10.2	10.0	10.1	10.1	10.4
1994	10.1	10.2	10.5	10.2	10.5	10.5	11.9	11.2	10.2	10.3	10.3	10.5	10.5
1995	10.3	10.5	10.6	10.4	10.8	10.9	12.1	12.1	10.5	10.8	10.6	10.7	10.9
1996	10.5	10.7	10.9	10.6	10.9	11.1	11.6	10.9	10.6	10.7	10.6	10.8	10.8
1997	10.5	10.8	10.9	10.8	11.0	10.9	11.4	10.8	10.6	10.5	10.6	11.1	10.8
1998	10.6	10.8	10.8	10.7	10.8	11.0	12.0	11.1	10.8	10.7	10.9	11.0	10.9
1999	10.9	11.1	11.3	11.2	11.3	11.3	12.3	11.3	11.0	11.0	11.0	11.2	11.2
2000	11.1	11.2	11.3	11.2	11.3	11.5	12.5	11.4	11.1	11.3	11.4	11.5	11.4
2001	11.0	11.3	11.6	11.5	11.4	11.6	12.4	12.3	11.4	11.4	11.5	11.6	11.5
2002	11.4	11.7	11.8	11.6	11.6	11.9	12.0	12.0	11.7	11.8	11.9	11.9	11.8
2003	11.8	12.0	12.2	11.9	11.9	11.9	12.0	11.9	11.6	11.7	11.8	11.8	11.9

Employment by Industry: West Virginia—*Continued*

(Numbers in thousands. Not seasonally adjusted.)

Industry	January	February	March	April	May	June	July	August	September	October	November	December	Annual Average
CHARLESTON—*Continued*													
Local government													
1990	8.5	8.5	8.6	8.6	10.2	9.0	8.4	8.3	8.6	8.6	8.6	8.6	8.7
1991	8.6	8.6	8.6	8.6	8.7	8.9	8.5	8.4	8.6	8.5	8.5	8.5	8.6
1992	8.5	8.4	8.5	8.5	9.8	9.0	8.7	8.7	9.1	9.1	9.3	9.4	8.9
1993	9.3	9.5	9.5	9.3	9.4	9.7	9.2	9.3	9.2	9.5	9.8	9.5	9.4
1994	9.4	9.4	9.5	9.6	10.9	9.7	9.2	9.0	9.3	9.6	10.7	9.7	9.7
1995	9.5	9.5	9.6	9.7	9.7	10.0	9.3	9.0	9.4	9.8	9.8	9.8	9.6
1996	9.7	10.0	9.8	9.9	11.2	10.1	9.5	9.2	9.6	9.8	10.0	10.0	9.9
1997	9.9	10.0	10.1	10.1	10.2	10.4	9.7	9.7	9.6	10.0	11.1	10.2	10.1
1998	10.1	10.1	10.2	10.3	11.5	10.4	9.8	9.8	10.0	10.0	10.1	10.2	10.2
1999	10.2	10.3	10.4	10.5	10.5	10.8	10.1	10.1	10.2	10.2	10.2	10.2	10.3
2000	10.2	10.2	10.2	10.3	11.6	10.5	9.9	10.1	10.3	10.1	10.2	10.2	10.3
2001	10.1	10.1	10.1	10.2	10.2	10.4	9.8	9.8	9.8	10.0	10.1	10.1	10.0
2002	10.0	10.0	10.1	10.2	11.6	10.4	10.0	10.0	9.9	10.2	10.2	10.2	10.2
2003	10.1	10.2	10.3	10.4	10.5	10.7	10.0	10.1	9.9	10.3	10.4	10.3	10.3
HUNTINGTON-ASHLAND													
Total nonfarm													
1990	108.3	107.6	109.9	111.0	113.4	112.2	111.7	112.2	112.6	112.2	113.3	112.4	111.4
1991	109.5	108.9	109.8	110.5	111.6	111.3	109.6	110.3	110.6	111.4	112.1	112.1	110.6
1992	109.1	110.0	110.8	112.0	114.1	113.3	111.7	112.0	113.7	115.4	115.4	114.7	112.6
1993	110.7	110.1	110.6	112.1	113.5	113.6	112.6	112.6	113.2	115.8	116.6	116.3	113.1
1994	110.0	112.7	114.2	116.1	117.7	116.9	112.9	114.3	116.5	117.5	119.2	118.7	115.5
1995	114.8	115.2	116.7	118.6	118.7	118.7	117.0	118.0	118.8	118.9	120.4	120.8	118.0
1996	115.6	116.4	118.3	118.0	119.9	120.7	118.2	118.9	120.3	121.4	122.5	122.4	119.3
1997	117.3	117.6	119.0	120.5	120.8	121.4	120.1	122.0	121.7	122.8	124.0	124.4	120.9
1998	119.5	120.2	121.2	122.6	123.1	122.1	121.5	121.1	122.4	124.8	125.5	126.3	122.5
1999	119.7	120.4	122.9	123.3	123.8	123.2	122.6	122.5	122.8	125.0	125.0	125.3	123.0
2000	120.5	121.2	123.1	123.1	124.1	123.3	122.4	122.4	123.5	123.4	124.5	125.4	123.1
2001	120.6	120.9	121.6	122.3	122.0	122.4	119.2	120.2	121.7	121.7	122.4	121.9	121.4
2002	118.5	119.4	120.8	121.0	121.3	121.5	118.6	119.2	120.1	120.9	122.2	122.4	120.5
2003	119.3	119.4	121.3	122.7	122.5	122.3	119.3	119.7	121.2	122.0	123.4	123.6	121.4
Total private													
1990	89.1	88.2	89.9	91.3	92.2	93.2	94.0	94.6	94.2	92.4	93.5	92.6	92.1
1991	90.2	89.1	89.8	90.5	91.5	92.1	91.6	92.2	91.5	91.4	91.8	91.7	91.1
1992	89.3	89.8	90.5	91.7	93.2	94.0	93.5	93.8	94.3	95.0	95.0	94.3	92.8
1993	91.0	90.0	90.3	91.7	93.1	94.1	94.1	94.1	93.9	94.9	95.5	95.1	93.1
1994	90.1	91.9	93.2	94.9	96.5	96.9	95.5	96.0	96.8	96.3	97.2	97.3	95.2
1995	94.0	94.2	95.1	97.3	97.8	98.5	98.9	99.4	99.2	97.8	99.0	99.5	97.5
1996	95.3	95.7	97.0	96.8	98.5	100.3	99.7	99.8	100.0	99.8	100.7	100.6	98.6
1997	96.6	96.4	97.3	98.7	99.5	100.6	101.1	102.7	101.0	101.1	102.0	102.5	99.9
1998	98.7	98.6	99.2	100.6	101.1	102.0	102.1	101.9	102.0	102.9	103.5	104.3	101.4
1999	98.7	98.8	100.9	101.3	102.6	102.5	103.1	103.0	102.2	102.9	103.0	103.1	101.8
2000	99.7	99.8	100.7	100.6	101.3	101.9	101.4	101.6	102.1	101.4	102.2	103.1	101.3
2001	99.4	99.4	99.8	100.6	100.8	101.4	100.3	100.9	101.1	100.2	100.4	99.8	100.3
2002	97.7	97.8	99.0	99.1	99.7	100.6	100.0	100.0	99.7	99.4	100.2	100.3	99.5
2003	98.6	98.3	99.8	101.1	101.5	101.5	101.1	100.8	101.0	100.7	101.7	101.7	100.7
Goods-producing													
1990	24.3	23.8	24.2	24.6	25.1	25.5	25.6	26.0	26.0	25.1	25.9	24.7	25.0
1991	23.9	23.2	23.4	23.6	24.1	24.3	24.3	24.4	24.2	24.1	24.0	23.4	23.9
1992	22.9	23.6	24.1	24.2	25.0	25.2	24.9	25.1	26.0	26.1	26.3	25.0	24.8
1993	23.5	23.0	22.8	23.2	23.6	24.3	24.3	24.1	24.0	24.4	24.5	23.5	23.7
1994	21.9	23.3	24.0	24.1	24.4	24.7	23.4	23.6	23.8	24.0	24.1	23.5	23.7
1995	22.3	22.5	22.5	23.5	23.3	23.8	23.9	24.2	23.9	23.3	23.5	23.2	23.3
1996	22.1	22.2	22.7	21.7	22.8	23.8	23.3	23.5	23.7	23.4	23.4	23.0	22.9
1997	22.0	21.9	22.3	23.0	22.9	23.1	23.5	25.3	23.5	23.2	23.3	23.3	23.1
1998	22.1	22.3	22.1	22.9	22.8	22.9	23.1	23.1	22.7	22.7	22.5	22.2	22.6
1999	20.4	20.3	21.0	21.6	21.8	21.9	22.4	22.3	21.9	22.1	22.0	21.5	21.6
2000	20.5	20.6	20.6	19.9	20.3	20.5	20.8	20.8	20.7	20.2	20.3	20.2	20.5
2001	18.7	18.5	18.6	18.8	18.7	19.0	18.8	19.2	19.6	18.9	18.4	17.8	18.7
2002	17.2	17.3	17.4	17.2	17.3	17.6	17.6	17.6	17.7	17.3	17.3	17.4	17.4
2003	16.7	16.6	17.2	17.8	17.8	17.7	17.6	17.7	17.4	17.6	17.4	17.3	17.4
Construction and mining													
1990	6.2	6.0	6.2	6.5	6.8	6.9	7.0	7.3	7.3	6.9	7.5	6.4	6.7
1991	5.8	5.4	5.6	6.1	6.4	6.3	6.4	6.4	6.4	6.4	6.3	5.8	6.1
1992	5.3	6.1	6.5	6.5	7.2	7.2	7.1	7.2	8.1	8.2	8.3	7.2	7.0
1993	5.9	5.8	5.8	6.4	6.8	7.4	7.7	7.6	7.6	7.8	7.8	6.9	6.9
1994	6.4	7.9	8.4	8.2	8.3	8.4	7.3	7.5	7.6	7.8	7.8	7.1	7.7
1995	5.8	5.7	5.9	6.9	6.7	7.0	7.4	7.4	7.3	7.1	7.1	6.8	6.7
1996	6.1	6.1	6.6	7.0	7.4	8.2	7.7	7.8	7.9	7.6	7.5	7.1	7.2
1997	6.5	6.4	6.8	7.5	7.4	7.6	8.0	9.4	7.8	7.5	7.5	7.3	7.4
1998	6.5	6.6	6.5	7.4	7.3	7.5	7.6	7.6	7.1	7.1	7.0	7.0	7.1
1999	5.8	5.8	6.0	6.6	6.7	6.9	7.5	7.4	7.1	7.2	7.2	6.8	6.7
2000	6.0	6.1	6.2	6.3	6.8	6.9	7.1	7.1	7.0	6.9	7.0	6.8	6.7
2001	6.1	6.0	6.2	6.5	6.5	6.8	6.7	7.1	7.7	7.0	6.6	6.1	6.6
2002	5.5	5.6	5.7	5.8	5.9	6.1	6.1	6.1	6.1	6.1	6.1	6.1	5.9
2003	5.8	5.7	6.2	7.1	7.4	7.3	7.3	7.3	6.9	7.1	6.9	6.9	6.8

Employment by Industry: West Virginia—*Continued*

(Numbers in thousands. Not seasonally adjusted.)

Industry	January	February	March	April	May	June	July	August	September	October	November	December	Annual Average
HUNTINGTON-ASHLAND *—Continued*													
Manufacturing													
1990	18.1	17.8	18.0	18.1	18.3	18.6	18.6	18.7	18.7	18.2	18.4	18.3	18.3
1991	18.1	17.8	17.8	17.5	17.7	18.0	17.9	18.0	17.8	17.7	17.7	17.6	17.8
1992	17.6	17.5	17.6	17.7	17.8	18.0	17.8	17.9	17.9	17.9	18.0	17.8	17.7
1993	17.6	17.2	17.0	16.8	16.8	16.9	16.6	16.5	16.4	16.6	16.7	16.6	16.8
1994	15.5	15.4	15.6	15.9	16.1	16.3	16.1	16.1	16.2	16.2	16.3	16.4	16.0
1995	16.5	16.8	16.6	16.6	16.6	16.8	16.5	16.8	16.6	16.2	16.4	16.4	16.5
1996	16.0	16.1	16.1	14.7	15.4	15.6	15.6	15.7	15.8	15.8	15.9	15.9	15.7
1997	15.5	15.5	15.5	15.5	15.5	15.5	15.5	15.9	15.7	15.7	15.8	16.0	15.6
1998	15.6	15.7	15.6	15.5	15.5	15.4	15.5	15.5	15.6	15.6	15.5	15.2	15.5
1999	14.6	14.5	15.0	15.0	15.1	15.0	14.9	14.9	14.8	14.9	14.8	14.7	14.8
2000	14.5	14.5	14.4	13.6	13.5	13.6	13.7	13.7	13.7	13.3	13.3	13.4	13.8
2001	12.6	12.5	12.4	12.3	12.2	12.2	12.1	12.1	11.9	11.9	11.8	11.7	12.1
2002	11.7	11.7	11.7	11.4	11.4	11.5	11.5	11.5	11.6	11.2	11.2	11.3	11.5
2003	10.9	10.9	11.0	10.7	10.4	10.4	10.3	10.4	10.5	10.5	10.5	10.4	10.6
Service-providing													
1990	84.0	83.8	85.7	86.4	88.3	86.7	86.1	86.2	86.6	87.1	87.4	87.7	86.3
1991	85.6	85.7	86.4	86.9	87.5	87.0	85.3	85.9	86.4	87.3	88.1	88.7	86.7
1992	86.2	86.4	86.7	87.8	89.1	88.1	86.8	86.9	87.7	89.3	89.1	89.7	87.8
1993	87.2	87.1	87.8	88.9	89.9	89.3	88.3	88.5	89.2	91.4	92.1	92.8	89.3
1994	88.1	89.4	90.2	92.0	93.3	92.2	89.5	90.7	92.7	93.5	95.1	95.2	91.8
1995	92.5	92.7	94.2	95.1	95.4	94.9	93.1	93.8	94.9	95.6	96.9	97.6	94.7
1996	93.5	94.2	95.6	96.3	97.1	96.9	94.9	95.4	96.6	98.0	99.1	99.4	96.4
1997	95.3	95.7	96.7	97.5	97.9	98.3	96.6	96.7	98.2	99.6	100.7	101.1	97.8
1998	97.4	97.9	99.1	99.7	100.3	99.2	98.4	98.0	99.7	102.1	103.0	104.1	99.9
1999	99.3	100.1	101.9	101.7	102.0	101.3	100.2	100.2	100.9	102.9	103.0	103.8	101.4
2000	100.0	100.6	102.5	103.2	103.8	102.8	101.6	101.6	102.8	103.2	104.2	105.2	102.6
2001	101.9	102.4	103.0	103.5	103.3	103.4	100.4	101.0	102.1	102.8	104.0	104.1	102.6
2002	101.3	102.1	103.4	103.8	104.0	103.9	101.0	101.6	102.4	103.6	104.9	105.0	103.1
2003	102.6	102.8	104.1	104.9	104.7	104.6	101.7	102.0	103.8	104.4	106.0	106.3	104.0
Trade, transportation, and utilities													
1990	25.8	25.3	25.8	25.7	26.0	26.0	26.1	26.1	25.9	25.8	26.2	26.4	25.9
1991	25.3	24.8	25.0	25.0	25.2	25.3	25.1	25.5	25.3	25.2	25.8	26.1	25.3
1992	25.2	25.0	25.0	25.1	25.4	25.6	25.4	25.4	25.4	25.7	26.0	26.4	25.4
1993	24.9	24.5	24.7	24.8	25.2	25.4	25.3	25.3	25.2	25.7	26.3	26.7	25.3
1994	25.2	25.1	25.5	25.7	26.3	26.3	26.2	26.3	26.3	26.2	26.8	27.2	26.0
1995	26.1	25.7	26.0	26.3	26.6	26.8	26.8	26.9	26.9	26.8	27.5	27.9	26.6
1996	26.4	26.2	26.5	26.6	26.9	27.1	26.9	27.0	27.1	27.2	28.1	28.3	27.0
1997	26.3	25.9	26.1	26.2	26.3	26.5	26.6	26.6	26.5	26.7	27.4	27.7	26.5
1998	25.9	25.4	25.6	25.8	26.0	26.1	26.3	26.3	26.8	27.3	27.7	28.1	26.4
1999	25.9	25.7	26.1	26.3	26.7	26.6	26.7	26.9	26.9	27.4	27.6	27.7	26.7
2000	26.4	26.1	26.4	26.4	26.7	26.6	26.3	26.5	26.6	26.9	27.6	28.1	26.7
2001	26.9	26.5	26.5	26.6	26.7	26.6	26.5	26.5	26.4	26.8	27.4	27.5	26.7
2002	26.4	26.1	26.3	26.2	26.4	26.4	25.9	26.0	25.9	25.9	26.5	26.6	26.2
2003	25.7	25.3	25.5	25.8	25.9	25.9	26.0	26.0	26.2	26.2	27.2	27.4	26.1
Wholesale trade													
1990	4.5	4.4	4.5	4.5	4.6	4.6	4.6	4.6	4.5	4.7	4.7	4.7	4.5
1991	4.7	4.6	4.7	4.7	4.7	4.7	4.7	4.7	4.6	4.5	4.6	4.6	4.6
1992	4.5	4.5	4.5	4.5	4.4	4.5	4.5	4.5	4.5	4.5	4.4	4.4	4.4
1993	4.1	4.0	4.0	4.0	4.1	4.1	4.1	4.0	4.0	4.1	4.1	4.1	4.0
1994	3.9	3.9	3.9	3.9	4.0	4.0	4.0	4.0	4.0	3.9	4.0	4.0	3.9
1995	4.0	3.9	4.0	4.2	4.2	4.2	4.2	4.2	4.2	4.1	4.2	4.2	4.1
1996	4.1	4.1	4.1	4.2	4.2	4.2	4.2	4.2	4.2	4.2	4.2	4.3	4.1
1997	4.2	4.1	4.2	4.2	4.2	4.2	4.3	4.3	4.3	4.2	4.2	4.2	4.2
1998	4.0	4.0	4.0	4.2	4.2	4.2	4.2	4.2	4.2	4.2	4.2	4.2	4.1
1999	4.1	4.1	4.2	4.1	4.1	4.1	4.1	4.2	4.1	4.5	4.4	4.4	4.2
2000	4.1	4.1	4.1	4.0	4.1	4.1	4.0	4.1	4.1	3.9	3.9	3.9	4.0
2001	3.8	3.8	3.8	3.8	3.8	3.8	3.8	3.7	3.7	3.7	3.7	3.7	3.7
2002	3.7	3.7	3.7	3.7	3.7	3.7	3.8	3.8	3.8	3.7	3.6	3.6	3.7
2003	3.5	3.5	3.6	3.6	3.6	3.6	3.6	3.6	3.6	3.6	3.6	3.6	3.6
Retail trade													
1990	16.9	16.5	16.8	16.7	16.8	16.8	16.8	16.8	16.7	16.5	16.9	17.0	16.7
1991	16.2	15.8	15.9	15.9	16.1	16.1	16.0	16.4	16.3	16.3	16.8	17.1	16.2
1992	16.3	16.1	16.1	16.2	16.5	16.6	16.4	16.5	16.5	16.7	17.2	17.5	16.5
1993	16.4	16.1	16.3	16.5	16.7	16.8	16.7	16.8	16.7	17.1	17.6	18.0	16.8
1994	16.7	16.6	16.9	17.0	17.4	17.4	17.4	17.5	17.6	17.7	18.3	18.7	17.4
1995	17.6	17.3	17.5	17.7	18.0	18.2	18.2	18.3	18.4	18.4	19.0	19.5	18.1
1996	18.2	17.9	18.1	18.2	18.4	18.6	18.4	18.5	18.6	18.6	19.5	19.7	18.5
1997	18.0	17.7	17.7	17.9	18.0	18.1	18.1	18.2	18.1	18.3	18.9	19.3	18.1
1998	17.8	17.4	17.5	17.6	17.8	17.8	18.0	18.1	18.6	19.1	19.6	19.9	18.2
1999	18.0	17.8	18.0	18.3	18.6	18.5	18.6	18.7	18.9	19.0	19.3	19.3	18.5
2000	18.4	18.1	18.3	18.5	18.7	18.5	18.4	18.5	18.6	18.7	19.2	19.5	18.6
2001	17.8	17.4	17.5	17.5	17.6	17.5	17.3	17.4	17.3	17.7	18.3	18.4	17.6
2002	17.2	16.9	17.1	17.1	17.2	17.2	16.9	17.0	17.0	17.0	17.7	17.9	17.2
2003	16.9	16.5	16.6	16.9	17.0	17.0	17.1	17.1	17.2	17.4	18.2	18.5	17.2

Employment by Industry: West Virginia—*Continued*

(Numbers in thousands. Not seasonally adjusted.)

Industry	January	February	March	April	May	June	July	August	September	October	November	December	Annual Average
HUNTINGTON-ASHLAND *—Continued*													
Transportation and utilities													
2001	1.8	1.7	1.7	1.8	1.8	1.8	1.7	1.7	1.7	1.7	1.7	1.7	1.7
2002	5.5	5.5	5.5	5.4	5.5	5.5	5.2	5.2	5.1	5.2	5.2	5.1	5.3
2003	5.3	5.3	5.3	5.3	5.3	5.3	5.3	5.3	5.4	5.2	5.4	5.3	5.3
Information													
1990	1.8	1.8	1.9	2.0	2.0	2.1	2.0	2.0	2.0	2.0	2.0	2.0	1.9
1991	2.0	2.0	2.0	2.0	2.0	2.0	2.0	2.0	1.9	2.0	2.0	2.1	2.0
1992	2.0	2.0	2.0	1.9	1.9	1.9	2.0	2.0	1.9	1.9	1.9	1.9	1.9
1993	1.9	1.9	1.9	1.8	1.8	1.9	1.8	1.9	1.8	2.0	1.9	2.0	1.8
1994	2.0	1.9	1.8	1.8	2.0	1.9	1.9	1.9	1.9	1.9	1.9	1.9	1.9
1995	1.9	1.9	2.0	2.0	2.0	2.0	2.0	1.9	2.0	1.9	1.9	2.1	1.9
1996	1.9	1.9	1.9	1.9	2.0	2.0	2.0	2.0	1.9	1.8	1.8	1.8	1.9
1997	1.7	1.8	1.8	1.8	1.8	1.8	1.9	1.8	1.8	1.7	1.7	1.7	1.7
1998	1.7	1.7	1.7	1.7	1.7	1.8	1.7	1.7	1.7	1.7	1.7	1.7	1.7
1999	1.8	1.8	1.8	1.8	1.8	1.8	1.8	1.8	1.7	1.7	1.7	1.7	1.7
2000	1.7	1.7	1.7	1.7	1.6	1.7	1.7	1.6	1.7	1.7	1.7	1.7	1.7
2001	1.6	1.6	1.6	1.6	1.7	1.6	1.6	1.6	1.6	1.6	1.6	1.6	1.6
2002	1.6	1.6	1.6	1.6	1.6	1.6	1.6	1.6	1.5	1.5	1.5	1.5	1.6
2003	1.6	1.6	1.6	1.6	1.6	1.6	1.6	1.6	1.6	1.6	1.6	1.6	1.6
Financial activities													
1990	4.5	4.5	4.5	4.6	4.6	4.7	4.7	4.7	4.7	4.6	4.7	4.6	4.6
1991	4.7	4.6	4.7	4.7	4.7	4.8	4.7	4.7	4.6	4.6	4.6	4.6	4.6
1992	4.5	4.5	4.4	4.5	4.6	4.7	4.7	4.7	4.6	4.6	4.6	4.5	4.5
1993	4.5	4.5	4.5	4.5	4.5	4.6	4.6	4.6	4.5	4.5	4.5	4.5	4.5
1994	4.4	4.4	4.4	4.6	4.6	4.7	4.7	4.7	4.7	4.5	4.6	4.6	4.5
1995	4.6	4.6	4.5	4.5	4.6	4.6	4.6	4.6	4.5	4.5	4.4	4.4	4.5
1996	4.4	4.4	4.5	4.5	4.5	4.5	4.6	4.6	4.6	4.6	4.6	4.5	4.5
1997	4.5	4.5	4.6	4.6	4.7	4.7	4.7	4.7	4.6	4.6	4.6	4.7	4.6
1998	4.7	4.7	4.7	4.7	4.7	4.8	4.7	4.6	4.6	4.6	4.9	5.2	4.7
1999	5.2	5.2	5.4	5.4	5.5	5.5	5.6	5.6	5.5	5.7	5.6	5.8	5.5
2000	5.8	5.8	5.8	5.9	5.9	5.9	5.8	5.8	5.8	5.9	5.9	5.8	5.8
2001	5.6	5.6	5.6	5.8	5.7	5.9	5.8	5.8	5.8	5.8	5.8	5.8	5.7
2002	5.7	5.7	5.7	5.7	5.7	5.9	5.8	5.7	5.7	5.8	5.8	5.8	5.8
2003	5.7	5.7	5.7	5.6	5.5	5.3	5.0	4.9	4.9	5.1	5.1	5.3	5.3
Professional and business services													
1990	6.7	6.8	7.1	7.5	7.5	7.6	7.7	7.7	7.4	7.3	7.2	7.3	7.3
1991	7.1	7.0	7.0	7.1	7.1	7.2	7.3	7.3	7.3	7.4	7.2	7.3	7.1
1992	7.2	7.1	7.2	7.3	7.2	7.4	7.5	7.5	7.3	7.5	7.3	7.4	7.3
1993	7.3	7.3	7.2	7.6	7.7	7.5	7.6	7.6	7.6	7.6	7.6	7.7	7.5
1994	7.3	7.5	7.6	7.8	7.8	7.9	7.8	7.9	8.0	8.1	8.1	8.3	7.8
1995	7.6	7.9	8.0	8.4	8.5	8.4	8.6	8.7	8.6	8.6	8.8	9.0	8.4
1996	8.2	8.4	8.4	8.6	8.5	8.7	8.7	8.6	8.4	8.5	8.5	8.4	8.4
1997	8.4	8.6	8.6	9.0	9.0	9.3	9.1	9.2	9.5	9.7	9.8	9.8	9.1
1998	9.8	9.9	9.9	10.0	10.0	10.2	9.9	9.9	9.8	10.4	10.5	10.7	10.0
1999	10.2	10.3	10.6	10.2	10.1	10.0	10.0	9.9	9.8	9.8	9.8	9.9	10.0
2000	9.6	9.8	9.9	10.2	10.1	10.4	10.1	10.1	10.6	10.3	10.4	10.6	10.2
2001	10.1	10.5	10.6	10.7	10.7	10.7	10.5	10.5	10.5	10.1	10.2	10.2	10.4
2002	9.8	10.0	10.3	10.3	10.1	10.4	10.4	10.3	10.2	10.3	10.3	10.2	10.2
2003	10.7	10.8	11.0	11.1	11.0	11.0	11.0	10.8	11.1	11.1	11.1	10.9	11.0
Educational and health services													
1990	12.5	12.6	12.7	12.7	12.7	12.8	12.9	13.0	13.1	13.0	13.1	13.1	12.8
1991	13.0	13.2	13.3	13.4	13.4	13.5	13.6	13.6	13.6	13.9	14.1	14.1	13.5
1992	13.8	13.9	14.0	14.3	14.3	14.5	14.3	14.3	14.4	14.7	14.7	14.7	14.3
1993	14.6	14.6	14.8	15.0	15.0	15.0	15.0	15.0	15.1	15.2	15.2	15.3	14.9
1994	14.9	15.0	15.0	15.4	15.4	15.4	15.5	15.6	15.7	15.7	15.7	15.9	15.4
1995	16.0	16.1	16.1	16.2	16.1	16.2	16.2	16.3	16.3	16.2	16.3	16.4	16.2
1996	16.2	16.4	16.4	16.5	16.5	16.5	16.5	16.5	16.7	16.8	16.9	17.0	16.5
1997	16.9	16.9	16.9	17.0	17.1	17.2	17.1	17.0	17.1	17.3	17.3	17.4	17.1
1998	17.4	17.4	17.6	17.7	17.6	17.8	18.0	18.0	18.0	18.1	18.1	18.3	17.8
1999	18.0	18.1	18.4	18.2	18.3	18.2	18.3	18.2	18.2	18.3	18.3	18.4	18.2
2000	18.1	18.2	18.4	18.4	18.4	18.4	18.5	18.5	18.5	18.3	18.3	18.7	18.4
2001	18.3	18.4	18.5	18.5	18.5	18.7	18.5	18.6	18.6	18.6	18.7	18.8	18.5
2002	19.1	19.1	19.3	19.4	19.4	19.6	19.7	19.7	19.7	19.7	19.8	19.9	19.5
2003	19.9	20.0	20.2	20.1	20.2	20.4	20.5	20.6	20.7	20.3	20.3	20.4	20.3

Employment by Industry: West Virginia—*Continued*

(Numbers in thousands. Not seasonally adjusted.)

Industry	January	February	March	April	May	June	July	August	September	October	November	December	Annual Average
HUNTINGTON-ASHLAND *—Continued*													
Leisure and hospitality													
1990	7.8	7.7	8.0	8.4	8.5	8.9	9.3	9.4	9.3	8.8	8.6	8.7	8.6
1991	8.4	8.4	8.5	9.0	9.2	9.3	9.1	9.2	9.0	8.6	8.5	8.5	8.8
1992	8.1	8.1	8.3	8.8	9.2	9.2	9.2	9.4	9.2	9.0	8.7	8.8	8.8
1993	8.6	8.6	8.7	9.0	9.5	9.7	9.7	9.8	9.8	9.6	9.4	9.4	9.3
1994	8.5	8.7	9.0	9.4	9.8	9.9	10.0	10.0	10.3	9.7	9.7	9.6	9.5
1995	9.3	9.3	9.8	10.2	10.4	10.6	10.8	10.8	10.9	10.3	10.3	10.2	10.2
1996	9.8	9.8	10.2	10.7	10.9	11.3	11.3	11.2	11.1	10.8	10.7	10.8	10.7
1997	10.3	10.3	10.6	10.8	11.4	11.7	11.6	11.5	11.4	11.2	11.2	11.1	11.0
1998	10.3	10.4	10.8	11.0	11.4	11.5	11.4	11.3	11.3	11.0	10.9	10.9	11.0
1999	10.2	10.3	10.6	10.9	11.4	11.5	11.4	11.4	11.2	11.0	11.0	11.0	10.9
2000	10.5	10.4	10.7	10.9	11.1	11.2	11.0	11.1	11.1	10.9	10.8	10.8	10.9
2001	10.2	10.2	10.3	10.6	10.8	10.9	10.7	10.9	10.7	10.4	10.3	10.2	10.5
2002	10.0	10.1	10.5	10.7	11.1	11.1	11.1	11.2	11.1	10.8	10.9	10.8	10.8
2003	10.2	10.2	10.5	10.9	11.3	11.5	11.3	11.2	11.0	10.7	10.8	10.7	10.9
Other services													
1990	5.7	5.7	5.7	5.8	5.8	5.6	5.7	5.7	5.8	5.8	5.8	5.8	5.7
1991	5.8	5.9	5.9	5.7	5.8	5.7	5.5	5.5	5.6	5.6	5.6	5.6	5.6
1992	5.6	5.6	5.5	5.6	5.6	5.5	5.5	5.4	5.5	5.5	5.5	5.6	5.5
1993	5.7	5.6	5.7	5.8	5.8	5.7	5.8	5.8	5.9	5.9	6.1	6.0	5.8
1994	5.9	6.0	5.9	6.1	6.2	6.1	6.0	6.0	6.1	6.2	6.3	6.3	6.0
1995	6.2	6.2	6.2	6.2	6.3	6.1	6.0	6.0	6.1	6.2	6.3	6.3	6.1
1996	6.3	6.4	6.4	6.3	6.4	6.4	6.4	6.4	6.5	6.7	6.7	6.8	6.4
1997	6.5	6.5	6.4	6.3	6.3	6.3	6.6	6.6	6.6	6.7	6.7	6.8	6.5
1998	6.8	6.8	6.8	6.8	6.9	6.9	7.0	7.0	7.1	7.1	7.2	7.2	6.9
1999	7.0	7.1	7.0	6.9	7.0	7.0	6.9	6.9	7.0	6.9	7.0	7.1	6.9
2000	7.1	7.2	7.2	7.2	7.2	7.2	7.2	7.2	7.1	7.2	7.2	7.2	7.2
2001	8.0	8.1	8.1	8.0	8.0	8.0	7.9	7.8	7.9	8.0	8.0	7.9	7.9
2002	7.9	7.9	7.9	8.0	8.1	8.0	7.9	7.9	7.9	8.1	8.1	8.1	8.0
2003	8.1	8.1	8.1	8.2	8.2	8.1	8.1	8.0	8.1	8.1	8.2	8.1	8.1
Government													
1990	19.2	19.4	20.0	19.7	21.2	19.0	17.7	17.6	18.4	19.8	19.8	19.8	19.3
1991	19.3	19.8	20.0	20.0	20.1	19.2	18.0	18.1	19.1	20.0	20.3	20.4	19.5
1992	19.8	20.2	20.3	20.3	20.9	19.3	18.2	18.2	19.4	20.4	20.4	20.4	19.8
1993	19.7	20.1	20.3	20.4	20.4	19.5	18.5	18.5	19.3	20.9	21.1	21.2	19.9
1994	19.9	20.8	21.0	21.2	21.2	20.0	17.4	18.3	19.7	21.2	22.0	21.4	20.3
1995	20.8	21.0	21.6	21.3	20.9	20.2	18.1	18.6	19.6	21.1	21.4	21.3	20.4
1996	20.3	20.7	21.3	21.2	21.4	20.4	18.5	19.1	20.3	21.6	21.8	21.8	20.7
1997	20.7	21.2	21.7	21.8	21.3	20.8	19.0	19.3	20.7	21.7	22.0	21.9	21.0
1998	20.8	21.6	22.0	22.0	22.0	20.1	19.4	19.2	20.4	21.9	22.0	22.0	21.1
1999	21.0	21.6	22.0	22.0	21.2	20.7	19.5	19.5	20.6	22.1	22.0	22.2	21.2
2000	20.8	21.4	22.4	22.5	22.8	21.4	21.0	20.8	21.4	22.0	22.3	22.3	21.8
2001	21.2	21.5	21.8	21.7	21.2	21.0	18.9	19.3	20.6	21.5	22.0	22.1	21.0
2002	20.8	21.6	21.8	21.9	21.6	20.9	18.6	19.2	20.4	21.5	22.0	22.1	21.0
2003	20.7	21.1	21.5	21.6	21.0	20.8	18.2	18.9	20.2	21.3	21.7	21.9	20.7
Federal government													
1990	2.8	2.8	3.1	3.1	3.7	3.2	3.1	3.0	2.9	2.8	2.8	2.8	3.0
1991	2.8	2.9	2.9	2.9	2.9	3.0	3.0	3.0	3.0	3.0	3.0	3.0	2.9
1992	3.0	3.0	3.0	3.1	3.1	3.1	3.2	3.2	3.2	3.2	3.2	3.2	3.1
1993	3.2	3.2	3.2	3.2	3.2	3.2	3.2	3.1	3.2	3.1	3.2	3.2	3.1
1994	3.1	3.1	3.1	3.2	3.1	3.2	3.2	3.1	3.1	3.1	3.1	3.1	3.1
1995	3.1	3.1	3.1	3.1	3.1	3.2	3.2	3.2	3.2	3.1	3.1	3.1	3.1
1996	3.1	3.1	3.1	3.1	3.1	3.1	3.1	3.1	3.1	3.0	3.0	3.1	3.0
1997	3.0	3.0	3.0	3.0	3.0	3.0	3.0	3.0	3.0	2.9	3.0	2.9	2.9
1998	2.9	2.9	2.9	2.9	2.9	2.9	2.9	2.9	2.9	2.9	2.9	2.9	2.9
1999	2.9	2.9	2.9	2.9	2.9	2.9	2.9	2.9	2.9	2.9	2.9	2.9	2.9
2000	2.9	3.0	3.2	3.1	3.6	3.2	3.2	3.1	2.9	2.9	2.9	2.9	3.1
2001	2.9	2.9	2.9	2.9	2.9	3.0	3.0	3.0	3.0	2.9	3.0	3.0	2.9
2002	3.0	2.9	2.9	2.9	2.9	3.0	3.0	2.9	2.9	2.9	3.0	3.0	2.9
2003	2.9	2.9	2.9	2.9	2.9	3.0	3.0	3.0	3.0	3.0	3.0	3.1	3.0
State government													
1990	4.7	4.9	5.0	4.9	5.0	4.2	4.5	3.9	4.5	5.1	5.1	5.1	4.7
1991	4.7	5.0	5.2	5.2	5.1	4.4	4.7	4.5	4.9	5.1	5.3	5.4	4.9
1992	4.9	5.2	5.3	5.2	5.1	4.4	4.4	4.3	5.1	5.3	5.3	5.3	4.9
1993	4.8	5.0	5.2	5.2	5.1	4.4	4.9	4.5	5.0	5.6	5.6	5.6	5.0
1994	4.7	5.5	5.6	5.6	5.2	4.6	4.9	4.6	5.1	5.7	5.8	5.8	5.2
1995	5.2	5.4	5.8	5.7	5.2	4.7	5.0	4.6	4.8	5.6	5.8	5.7	5.2
1996	4.8	5.0	5.6	5.6	5.1	4.9	4.8	4.6	5.3	5.8	5.9	5.9	5.2
1997	4.8	5.3	5.7	5.6	5.0	4.7	4.7	4.4	5.1	5.5	5.7	5.7	5.1
1998	4.7	5.4	5.7	5.7	4.9	4.5	4.9	4.3	5.0	5.7	5.8	5.7	5.1
1999	4.8	5.4	5.7	5.8	4.9	4.5	4.8	4.4	5.0	5.7	5.6	5.9	5.2
2000	4.7	5.1	5.8	5.8	5.0	4.7	4.7	4.7	5.2	5.8	5.9	5.8	5.3
2001	5.3	5.5	5.8	5.7	5.0	4.9	4.7	4.7	5.3	5.9	6.1	6.1	5.4
2002	4.9	5.7	5.8	5.9	5.0	4.9	4.7	4.7	5.4	5.8	6.0	6.1	5.4
2003	4.9	5.3	5.6	5.8	5.2	4.9	4.5	4.4	5.3	5.7	5.9	5.9	5.3

Employment by Industry: West Virginia—*Continued*

(Numbers in thousands. Not seasonally adjusted.)

Industry	January	February	March	April	May	June	July	August	September	October	November	December	Annual Average
HUNTINGTON-ASHLAND *—Continued*													
Local government													
1990	11.7	11.7	11.9	11.7	12.5	11.6	10.1	10.7	11.0	11.9	11.9	11.9	11.5
1991	11.8	11.9	11.9	11.9	12.1	11.8	10.3	10.6	11.2	11.9	12.0	12.0	11.6
1992	11.9	12.0	12.0	12.0	12.7	11.8	10.6	10.7	11.1	11.9	11.9	11.9	11.7
1993	11.7	11.9	11.9	12.0	12.1	11.9	10.4	10.9	11.1	12.2	12.3	12.4	11.7
1994	12.1	12.2	12.3	12.4	12.9	12.2	9.3	10.6	11.5	12.4	13.1	12.5	11.9
1995	12.5	12.5	12.7	12.5	12.6	12.3	9.9	10.8	11.6	12.4	12.5	12.5	12.0
1996	12.4	12.6	12.6	12.5	13.2	12.4	10.6	11.4	11.9	12.8	12.9	12.8	12.3
1997	12.9	12.9	13.0	13.2	13.3	13.1	11.3	11.9	12.6	13.3	13.3	13.3	12.8
1998	13.2	13.3	13.4	13.4	14.2	12.7	11.6	12.0	12.5	13.3	13.3	13.4	13.0
1999	13.3	13.3	13.4	13.3	13.4	13.3	11.8	12.2	12.7	13.5	13.5	13.4	13.0
2000	13.2	13.3	13.4	13.6	14.2	13.5	13.1	13.0	13.3	13.3	13.5	13.6	13.4
2001	13.0	13.1	13.1	13.1	13.3	13.1	11.2	11.6	12.3	12.7	12.9	13.0	12.7
2002	12.9	13.0	13.1	13.1	13.7	13.0	10.9	11.6	12.1	12.8	13.0	13.0	12.7
2003	12.9	12.9	13.0	12.9	12.9	12.9	10.7	11.5	11.9	12.6	12.8	12.9	12.5
PARKERSBURG-MARIETTA													
Total nonfarm													
1990	60.4	60.3	61.0	61.7	62.4	62.8	62.2	61.6	62.0	62.2	62.5	62.4	61.7
1991	60.7	60.2	60.2	61.1	62.0	62.2	62.0	62.3	62.7	62.0	62.7	62.2	61.6
1992	61.3	61.3	61.4	62.4	63.4	63.5	63.9	63.5	63.4	63.7	63.8	64.1	62.9
1993	62.4	62.5	62.1	63.6	64.2	64.4	64.8	64.9	65.0	65.6	65.7	65.2	64.2
1994	62.6	63.3	64.1	65.2	66.2	66.3	65.7	66.3	67.0	67.1	67.7	66.9	65.7
1995	64.9	65.3	65.4	66.4	66.8	67.5	67.1	67.6	68.0	68.7	68.3	68.3	67.0
1996	65.5	66.2	66.7	67.5	68.9	69.0	69.0	68.9	69.6	69.1	69.4	69.6	68.2
1997	67.0	66.9	68.1	68.9	69.2	70.6	69.8	69.4	69.7	69.5	69.6	70.1	69.0
1998	67.7	67.4	67.6	68.6	69.9	70.3	69.0	69.3	70.3	70.5	70.6	70.5	69.3
1999	67.3	68.2	68.3	69.6	70.1	70.5	69.7	69.7	70.1	70.9	71.3	71.8	69.7
2000	69.1	69.0	69.5	70.3	71.2	71.6	71.0	70.6	70.9	71.0	72.1	72.3	70.7
2001	69.6	69.4	70.0	70.1	70.7	70.5	69.7	70.0	70.0	70.6	70.4	70.3	70.1
2002	68.4	68.7	69.5	70.2	71.3	71.1	71.7	72.3	72.3	70.5	71.1	71.2	70.7
2003	68.9	68.1	68.5	69.2	70.1	70.4	69.7	69.9	70.2	70.2	70.8	70.5	69.7
Total private													
1990	50.9	50.7	51.2	51.9	52.1	52.9	52.8	52.3	52.5	52.2	52.5	52.3	52.0
1991	50.9	50.3	50.2	51.0	51.7	52.1	52.6	52.8	52.9	52.0	52.6	52.2	51.7
1992	51.2	51.1	51.2	52.1	52.5	53.3	53.6	53.5	53.3	53.2	53.3	53.5	52.6
1993	52.2	52.0	51.6	53.0	53.5	54.0	54.6	54.9	54.6	54.9	54.9	54.6	53.7
1994	52.3	52.8	53.4	54.5	55.0	55.7	55.7	56.2	56.7	56.4	56.5	56.3	55.1
1995	54.4	54.7	54.7	55.8	56.1	57.0	56.9	57.6	57.7	58.0	57.6	57.7	56.5
1996	55.1	55.6	56.0	56.8	57.7	58.3	58.8	58.7	59.1	58.5	58.7	59.0	57.6
1997	56.5	56.4	57.5	58.2	58.3	59.7	60.6	60.3	60.6	60.0	60.1	60.7	59.0
1998	58.4	58.0	58.2	59.1	59.9	60.8	59.8	60.3	61.1	61.0	61.0	61.0	59.8
1999	58.1	58.8	58.9	60.1	60.6	61.0	60.4	60.6	60.9	61.3	61.7	62.2	60.3
2000	59.6	59.4	59.8	60.6	60.9	61.7	61.4	61.3	61.5	61.4	62.4	62.7	61.0
2001	60.0	59.7	60.3	60.5	60.9	60.7	60.4	60.7	60.5	60.9	60.6	60.6	60.4
2002	58.9	59.0	59.8	60.5	61.0	61.3	62.3	62.9	62.8	60.8	61.3	61.6	61.0
2003	59.3	58.4	58.8	59.4	60.3	60.5	60.3	60.6	60.7	60.3	60.9	60.9	60.0
Goods-producing													
1990	17.0	17.0	17.3	17.4	17.6	17.9	17.8	17.6	17.5	17.7	17.6	17.5	17.4
1991	16.7	16.4	16.5	16.8	17.2	17.3	17.5	17.6	17.5	17.2	17.2	16.8	17.0
1992	16.5	16.3	16.4	16.6	16.6	16.9	16.9	16.9	16.8	17.0	16.8	16.7	16.7
1993	16.0	16.0	15.9	16.3	16.4	16.6	17.1	17.1	16.9	17.1	16.6	16.3	16.5
1994	15.3	15.5	15.8	16.4	16.6	16.9	16.9	17.1	17.3	17.3	17.4	17.1	16.6
1995	16.2	16.1	16.1	16.6	16.5	16.9	17.2	17.5	17.7	17.7	17.5	17.4	16.9
1996	16.6	16.5	16.7	17.1	17.4	17.7	18.1	18.0	17.9	17.8	17.6	17.6	17.4
1997	16.7	16.6	16.9	17.3	17.4	17.8	18.2	18.2	18.0	17.9	17.7	17.8	17.5
1998	17.0	17.0	16.8	16.9	17.3	17.5	17.2	17.5	17.7	17.8	17.5	17.0	17.2
1999	16.3	16.7	16.5	17.1	17.2	17.3	16.8	17.2	17.6	17.8	17.5	17.5	17.1
2000	16.5	16.3	16.7	16.5	16.7	17.0	16.8	16.9	17.0	17.1	17.2	16.9	16.8
2001	15.9	15.9	16.0	16.0	16.0	16.0	16.1	16.0	15.8	15.8	15.4	15.3	15.8
2002	15.3	15.3	15.7	15.9	16.3	16.3	16.8	17.2	17.1	15.6	15.5	15.4	16.0
2003	14.6	14.2	14.3	14.4	14.6	14.6	14.6	14.7	15.0	14.7	15.0	14.8	14.6
Construction and mining													
1990	3.2	3.3	3.6	3.5	3.7	3.9	3.8	3.8	3.9	4.0	3.9	3.8	3.7
1991	3.2	3.2	3.3	3.8	4.0	4.0	4.1	4.2	4.1	4.0	3.8	3.5	3.7
1992	3.3	3.2	3.3	3.7	3.9	3.9	3.9	3.9	3.9	4.1	3.9	3.8	3.7
1993	3.3	3.3	3.4	3.6	3.8	3.9	4.3	4.4	4.2	4.2	4.0	3.9	3.8
1994	3.3	3.5	3.7	4.0	4.2	4.4	4.5	4.6	4.6	4.9	4.8	4.6	4.2
1995	3.8	3.6	3.8	4.1	4.2	4.5	4.7	4.8	5.1	5.3	5.0	4.8	4.4
1996	3.9	3.8	4.1	4.4	4.7	4.8	5.2	5.2	5.1	5.2	5.2	4.9	4.7
1997	4.3	4.3	4.5	4.7	5.0	5.1	5.4	5.6	5.4	5.3	5.1	5.1	4.9
1998	4.5	4.4	4.3	4.4	4.6	5.0	4.9	5.1	5.3	5.8	5.4	4.8	4.8
1999	3.9	4.1	4.0	4.4	4.5	4.6	4.6	4.8	4.8	5.0	4.8	4.7	4.5
2000	4.0	3.8	4.0	4.1	4.3	4.4	4.4	4.5	4.7	4.7	4.7	4.5	4.3
2001	3.8	3.8	3.9	4.2	4.3	4.4	4.5	4.5	4.3	4.3	4.0	3.9	4.1
2002	4.2	4.4	4.8	5.3	5.8	6.0	6.6	7.1	6.8	5.4	5.3	5.1	5.6
2003	4.6	4.3	4.4	4.5	4.7	4.8	4.8	4.9	5.1	4.9	5.1	5.1	4.8

Employment by Industry: West Virginia—*Continued*

(Numbers in thousands. Not seasonally adjusted.)

Industry	January	February	March	April	May	June	July	August	September	October	November	December	Annual Average
PARKERSBURG-MARIETTA *—Continued*													
Manufacturing													
1990	13.8	13.7	13.7	13.9	13.9	14.0	14.0	13.8	13.6	13.7	13.7	13.7	13.7
1991	13.5	13.2	13.2	13.0	13.2	13.3	13.4	13.4	13.4	13.2	13.4	13.3	13.2
1992	13.2	13.1	13.1	12.9	12.7	13.0	13.0	13.0	12.9	12.9	12.9	12.9	12.9
1993	12.7	12.7	12.5	12.7	12.6	12.7	12.8	12.7	12.7	12.9	12.6	12.4	12.6
1994	12.0	12.0	12.1	12.4	12.4	12.5	12.4	12.5	12.7	12.4	12.6	12.5	12.3
1995	12.4	12.5	12.3	12.5	12.3	12.4	12.5	12.7	12.6	12.4	12.5	12.6	12.4
1996	12.7	12.7	12.6	12.7	12.7	12.9	12.9	12.8	12.8	12.6	12.4	12.7	12.7
1997	12.4	12.3	12.4	12.6	12.4	12.7	12.8	12.6	12.6	12.6	12.6	12.7	12.5
1998	12.5	12.6	12.5	12.5	12.7	12.5	12.3	12.4	12.4	12.0	12.1	12.2	12.3
1999	12.4	12.6	12.5	12.7	12.7	12.7	12.2	12.4	12.8	12.8	12.7	12.8	12.6
2000	12.5	12.5	12.7	12.4	12.4	12.6	12.4	12.4	12.3	12.4	12.5	12.4	12.4
2001	12.1	12.1	12.1	11.8	11.7	11.6	11.6	11.5	11.5	11.5	11.4	11.4	11.6
2002	11.1	10.9	10.9	10.6	10.5	10.3	10.2	10.1	10.3	10.2	10.2	10.3	10.5
2003	10.0	9.9	9.9	9.9	9.9	9.8	9.8	9.8	9.9	9.8	9.9	9.7	9.9
Service-providing													
1990	43.4	43.3	43.7	44.3	44.8	44.9	44.4	44.0	44.5	44.5	44.9	44.9	44.3
1991	44.0	43.8	43.7	44.3	44.8	44.9	44.5	44.7	45.2	44.8	45.5	45.4	44.6
1992	44.8	45.0	45.0	45.8	46.8	46.6	47.0	46.6	46.6	46.7	47.0	47.4	46.2
1993	46.4	46.5	46.2	47.3	47.8	47.8	47.7	47.8	48.1	48.5	49.1	48.9	47.6
1994	47.3	47.8	48.3	48.8	49.6	49.4	48.8	49.2	49.7	49.8	50.3	49.8	49.0
1995	48.7	49.2	49.3	49.8	50.3	50.6	49.9	50.1	50.3	51.0	50.8	50.9	50.0
1996	48.9	49.7	50.0	50.4	51.5	51.3	50.9	50.9	51.7	51.3	51.8	52.0	50.8
1997	50.3	50.3	51.2	51.6	51.8	52.8	51.6	51.2	51.7	51.6	51.9	52.3	51.5
1998	50.7	50.4	50.8	51.7	52.6	52.8	51.8	51.8	52.6	52.7	53.1	53.5	52.0
1999	51.0	51.5	51.8	52.5	52.9	53.2	52.9	52.5	52.5	53.1	53.8	54.3	52.6
2000	52.6	52.7	52.8	53.8	54.5	54.6	54.2	53.7	53.9	53.9	54.9	55.4	53.9
2001	53.7	53.5	54.0	54.1	54.7	54.5	53.6	54.0	54.2	54.8	55.0	55.0	54.2
2002	53.1	53.4	53.8	54.3	55.0	54.8	54.9	55.1	55.2	54.9	55.6	55.8	54.7
2003	54.3	53.9	54.2	54.8	55.5	55.8	55.1	55.2	55.2	55.5	55.8	55.7	55.1
Trade, transportation, and utilities													
1990	13.0	12.8	12.8	12.9	12.9	12.9	13.1	13.0	13.0	13.0	13.4	13.4	13.0
1991	12.8	12.6	12.5	12.6	12.7	12.8	12.7	12.8	12.8	12.7	13.1	13.2	12.7
1992	12.5	12.5	12.5	12.7	12.8	12.8	13.0	13.1	13.1	13.1	13.4	13.7	12.9
1993	13.1	13.0	12.9	13.3	13.3	13.5	13.6	13.7	13.7	13.7	14.0	14.2	13.5
1994	13.6	13.8	13.9	13.8	13.8	13.9	14.0	14.1	14.2	14.1	14.4	14.5	14.0
1995	13.8	13.8	13.8	13.7	13.9	14.1	14.0	14.1	14.1	14.4	14.4	14.5	14.0
1996	13.5	13.7	13.8	13.9	14.2	14.2	14.1	14.2	14.3	14.3	14.6	14.9	14.1
1997	13.2	13.2	13.3	13.4	13.5	13.7	13.9	13.8	14.0	14.0	14.3	14.5	13.7
1998	13.8	13.6	13.7	14.0	14.0	14.2	14.0	14.1	14.4	14.2	14.6	14.7	14.1
1999	13.7	13.7	13.9	14.1	14.2	14.4	14.5	14.4	14.4	14.5	14.9	15.5	14.3
2000	14.8	14.5	14.4	14.4	14.5	14.7	14.8	14.9	14.9	15.0	15.6	16.0	14.8
2001	14.5	14.0	14.1	14.1	14.3	14.3	13.9	14.1	14.0	13.9	14.2	14.3	14.1
2002	13.6	13.4	13.5	13.4	13.5	13.7	13.6	13.8	13.9	14.1	14.5	14.7	13.8
2003	13.9	13.5	13.5	13.5	13.8	13.8	13.9	13.8	13.9	14.3	14.6	14.9	14.0
Wholesale trade													
1990	2.0	2.0	2.0	2.0	2.0	2.0	2.0	2.0	2.0	2.0	2.1	2.1	2.0
1991	2.0	2.0	2.0	1.9	2.0	2.0	2.0	2.0	2.0	2.0	2.0	2.0	1.9
1992	1.8	1.9	1.9	1.9	1.9	1.9	2.0	2.0	2.0	2.0	2.0	2.0	1.9
1993	2.0	2.0	2.0	2.1	2.1	2.1	2.2	2.2	2.2	2.1	2.1	2.0	2.0
1994	2.1	2.1	2.1	2.0	2.0	2.0	2.1	2.1	2.1	2.0	2.0	2.0	2.0
1995	2.0	2.0	2.0	2.0	2.0	2.1	2.1	2.1	2.2	2.2	2.1	2.1	2.0
1996	2.2	2.3	2.3	2.2	2.3	2.3	2.3	2.3	2.3	2.3	2.3	2.3	2.2
1997	2.2	2.3	2.3	2.3	2.3	2.3	2.4	2.4	2.4	2.4	2.4	2.4	2.3
1998	2.3	2.3	2.3	2.3	2.3	2.3	2.3	2.3	2.4	2.3	2.3	2.4	2.3
1999	2.3	2.3	2.3	2.3	2.3	2.3	2.3	2.3	2.3	2.3	2.3	2.3	2.3
2000	2.3	2.2	2.2	2.2	2.2	2.2	2.3	2.3	2.3	2.2	2.2	2.2	2.2
2001	2.2	2.2	2.2	2.2	2.2	2.2	2.1	2.1	2.1	2.0	1.9	1.9	2.1
2002	1.9	1.8	1.8	1.8	1.8	1.8	1.8	1.8	1.8	1.8	1.8	1.8	1.8
2003	1.8	1.7	1.7	1.7	1.8	1.8	1.8	1.7	1.7	1.7	1.7	1.7	1.7
Retail trade													
1990	8.7	8.5	8.5	8.6	8.6	8.6	8.7	8.6	8.6	8.6	8.9	9.0	8.6
1991	8.5	8.3	8.3	8.4	8.4	8.5	8.4	8.5	8.5	8.4	8.7	8.9	8.4
1992	8.5	8.4	8.4	8.6	8.6	8.6	8.7	8.8	8.8	8.8	9.1	9.4	8.7
1993	8.9	8.8	8.7	8.9	8.9	9.0	9.0	9.1	9.0	9.1	9.3	9.6	9.0
1994	8.8	8.9	9.0	9.0	9.0	9.1	9.1	9.2	9.3	9.3	9.6	9.8	9.1
1995	9.1	9.1	9.1	9.2	9.4	9.4	9.4	9.5	9.4	9.6	9.8	9.9	9.4
1996	9.1	9.1	9.2	9.4	9.5	9.5	9.4	9.5	9.5	9.5	9.8	10.1	9.4
1997	9.0	8.9	9.0	9.0	9.1	9.2	9.3	9.3	9.4	9.4	9.7	9.9	9.2
1998	9.3	9.1	9.2	9.4	9.4	9.6	9.5	9.6	9.8	9.9	10.3	10.3	9.6
1999	9.3	9.3	9.5	9.7	9.8	10.0	10.1	10.0	10.0	10.3	10.7	11.2	9.9
2000	10.7	10.5	10.4	10.4	10.5	10.7	10.7	10.8	10.8	10.9	11.6	12.0	10.8
2001	10.5	10.1	10.2	10.1	10.3	10.3	10.1	10.3	10.2	10.2	10.6	10.7	10.2
2002	10.0	9.8	9.9	9.8	9.9	10.0	9.9	10.0	10.1	10.3	10.7	10.9	10.1
2003	10.1	9.8	9.8	10.0	10.1	10.1	10.2	10.2	10.3	10.7	11.0	11.3	10.3

Employment by Industry: West Virginia—*Continued*

(Numbers in thousands. Not seasonally adjusted.)

Industry	January	February	March	April	May	June	July	August	September	October	November	December	Annual Average
PARKERSBURG-MARIETTA —*Continued*													
Transportation and utilities													
1990	2.3	2.3	2.3	2.3	2.3	2.3	2.4	2.4	2.4	2.4	2.4	2.3	2.3
1991	2.3	2.3	2.2	2.3	2.3	2.3	2.3	2.3	2.3	2.3	2.4	2.3	2.3
1992	2.2	2.2	2.2	2.2	2.3	2.3	2.3	2.3	2.3	2.3	2.3	2.3	2.2
1993	2.2	2.2	2.2	2.3	2.3	2.4	2.4	2.4	2.5	2.5	2.6	2.6	2.3
1994	2.7	2.8	2.8	2.8	2.8	2.8	2.8	2.8	2.8	2.8	2.8	2.7	2.7
1995	2.7	2.7	2.7	2.5	2.5	2.6	2.5	2.5	2.5	2.6	2.5	2.5	2.5
1996	2.2	2.3	2.3	2.3	2.4	2.4	2.4	2.4	2.5	2.5	2.5	2.5	2.3
1997	2.0	2.0	2.0	2.1	2.1	2.2	2.2	2.1	2.2	2.2	2.2	2.2	2.1
1998	2.2	2.2	2.2	2.3	2.3	2.3	2.2	2.2	2.2	2.0	2.0	2.0	2.1
1999	2.1	2.1	2.1	2.1	2.1	2.1	2.1	2.1	2.1	1.9	1.9	2.0	2.0
2000	1.8	1.8	1.8	1.8	1.8	1.8	1.8	1.8	1.8	1.9	1.8	1.8	1.8
2001	1.8	1.7	1.7	1.8	1.8	1.8	1.7	1.7	1.7	1.7	1.7	1.7	1.7
2002	1.7	1.8	1.8	1.8	1.8	1.9	1.9	2.0	2.0	2.0	2.0	2.0	1.9
2003	2.0	2.0	2.0	1.8	1.9	1.9	1.9	1.9	1.9	1.9	1.9	1.9	1.9
Information													
1990	0.9	0.9	0.9	0.8	0.8	0.8	0.9	0.9	0.9	0.8	0.9	0.9	0.8
1991	0.9	0.9	0.9	0.9	0.9	0.9	0.9	0.9	0.9	0.9	0.9	0.9	0.9
1992	0.9	0.9	0.9	0.8	0.8	0.9	0.9	0.9	0.8	0.8	0.8	0.9	0.8
1993	1.0	1.0	0.9	0.9	1.0	1.0	1.0	1.0	1.0	1.0	1.0	1.0	0.9
1994	1.0	1.0	1.1	1.0	1.0	1.0	1.0	1.0	1.0	1.0	1.0	1.0	1.0
1995	1.0	1.0	1.0	1.1	1.1	1.1	1.1	1.1	1.1	1.1	1.1	1.2	1.0
1996	1.2	1.2	1.2	1.3	1.3	1.3	1.4	1.4	1.4	1.3	1.4	1.4	1.3
1997	1.2	1.2	1.2	1.1	1.1	1.2	1.2	1.2	1.2	1.2	1.1	1.2	1.1
1998	1.1	1.1	1.1	1.1	1.1	1.1	1.1	1.1	1.1	1.1	1.1	1.1	1.1
1999	1.0	1.0	1.0	1.1	1.1	1.1	1.1	1.1	1.1	1.0	1.0	1.0	1.0
2000	1.0	1.0	1.0	1.0	1.0	1.0	1.1	0.9	1.1	1.0	1.1	1.1	1.0
2001	1.1	1.1	1.1	1.1	1.1	1.0	1.0	1.0	1.0	1.0	1.0	1.0	1.0
2002	1.0	1.0	1.0	1.0	1.0	1.0	1.0	1.0	1.0	0.9	1.0	1.0	1.0
2003	1.0	1.0	1.0	1.0	1.0	1.0	1.0	1.0	1.0	1.0	1.0	1.0	1.0
Financial activities													
1990	2.4	2.4	2.4	2.4	2.4	2.5	2.5	2.5	2.5	2.5	2.5	2.5	2.4
1991	2.6	2.6	2.5	2.5	2.5	2.5	2.5	2.5	2.6	2.5	2.5	2.5	2.5
1992	2.5	2.5	2.5	2.5	2.5	2.6	2.6	2.6	2.6	2.6	2.6	2.6	2.5
1993	2.5	2.5	2.5	2.6	2.6	2.6	2.6	2.5	2.6	2.6	2.6	2.6	2.5
1994	2.6	2.5	2.5	2.6	2.6	2.6	2.6	2.6	2.6	2.6	2.6	2.6	2.5
1995	2.6	2.6	2.6	2.6	2.6	2.6	2.6	2.7	2.6	2.6	2.6	2.6	2.6
1996	2.5	2.6	2.6	2.8	2.8	2.8	2.8	2.8	2.8	2.8	2.8	2.8	2.7
1997	2.7	2.7	2.8	2.8	2.8	2.9	2.9	2.9	3.0	2.9	3.0	3.0	2.8
1998	2.9	2.9	2.9	2.9	2.9	2.9	2.9	2.9	2.9	2.9	2.9	2.9	2.9
1999	2.9	2.9	2.9	3.0	3.0	3.0	3.0	3.0	3.0	3.0	3.0	3.0	2.9
2000	3.0	3.0	3.0	2.9	3.0	3.0	3.0	3.0	3.0	3.0	3.1	3.1	3.0
2001	2.8	2.8	2.8	2.8	2.9	2.9	3.0	3.0	3.0	3.0	3.0	3.0	2.9
2002	3.0	3.0	3.1	3.3	3.3	3.3	3.3	3.3	3.3	3.3	3.3	3.3	3.2
2003	3.1	3.0	3.0	3.0	3.0	3.1	3.1	3.1	3.1	3.0	3.0	3.0	3.0
Professional and business services													
1990	3.5	3.5	3.6	3.7	3.7	3.8	3.6	3.5	3.6	3.5	3.5	3.4	3.5
1991	3.4	3.4	3.4	3.5	3.4	3.5	3.6	3.5	3.6	3.5	3.5	3.4	3.4
1992	3.4	3.5	3.4	3.7	3.7	3.8	3.8	3.7	3.8	3.7	3.7	3.7	3.6
1993	3.7	3.8	3.8	3.9	3.9	3.9	3.9	4.0	3.8	3.9	4.0	3.8	3.8
1994	3.7	3.8	3.8	3.9	4.0	4.1	4.2	4.4	4.5	4.4	4.1	4.1	4.0
1995	3.9	4.0	4.1	4.1	4.1	4.2	4.1	4.2	4.2	4.2	4.2	4.2	4.1
1996	4.3	4.4	4.4	4.0	4.1	4.2	4.3	4.3	4.5	4.5	4.6	4.5	4.3
1997	4.2	4.3	4.5	4.6	4.6	4.8	4.8	4.8	4.8	4.6	4.6	4.8	4.6
1998	4.5	4.5	4.6	4.6	4.9	5.1	5.0	5.0	5.2	5.5	5.5	5.7	5.0
1999	5.1	5.0	5.1	4.7	4.8	4.8	4.7	4.8	4.7	5.0	5.2	5.0	4.9
2000	4.7	4.7	4.7	5.2	5.2	5.3	4.9	4.8	4.7	4.7	4.8	4.9	4.8
2001	4.8	4.7	4.8	5.0	5.0	5.0	4.7	4.8	4.7	4.8	4.7	4.7	4.7
2002	4.5	4.4	4.5	4.7	4.8	4.8	5.1	5.1	5.0	4.9	4.9	5.0	4.8
2003	4.9	4.9	4.9	5.1	5.0	5.0	5.0	5.1	5.1	4.9	4.9	4.9	5.0
Educational and health services													
1990	5.8	5.9	5.9	6.1	6.0	6.0	5.9	5.9	6.1	6.1	6.1	6.1	5.9
1991	6.1	6.2	6.1	6.2	6.2	6.1	6.4	6.4	6.6	6.5	6.6	6.6	6.3
1992	6.7	6.7	6.7	6.7	6.6	6.6	6.6	6.6	6.7	6.6	6.6	6.6	6.6
1993	6.7	6.7	6.7	6.6	6.6	6.6	6.6	6.7	6.8	6.8	6.9	6.9	6.7
1994	6.8	6.8	6.8	6.9	6.9	6.8	6.8	6.8	7.0	7.0	7.1	7.1	6.9
1995	7.1	7.2	7.2	7.3	7.3	7.3	7.2	7.2	7.4	7.5	7.4	7.4	7.2
1996	7.2	7.2	7.2	7.2	7.2	7.1	7.0	7.0	7.2	7.1	7.1	7.2	7.1
1997	8.2	8.3	8.4	8.4	8.3	8.2	8.5	8.5	8.7	8.7	8.7	8.7	8.4
1998	8.7	8.7	8.8	8.9	8.9	8.8	8.7	8.8	9.0	9.0	9.0	9.1	8.8
1999	9.1	9.3	9.3	9.4	9.4	9.3	9.2	9.2	9.3	9.4	9.4	9.5	9.3
2000	9.2	9.5	9.5	10.0	9.7	9.7	9.8	9.9	10.0	10.0	10.1	10.2	9.8
2001	10.4	10.7	10.8	10.5	10.2	10.1	10.1	10.2	10.6	11.0	11.0	11.0	10.5
2002	10.7	11.0	11.0	10.9	10.6	10.6	10.8	10.8	11.0	10.9	10.9	11.0	10.9
2003	10.9	11.1	11.1	11.1	11.3	11.3	11.1	11.2	11.3	11.2	11.2	11.2	11.2

Employment by Industry: West Virginia—*Continued*

(Numbers in thousands. Not seasonally adjusted.)

Industry	January	February	March	April	May	June	July	August	September	October	November	December	Annual Average
PARKERSBURG-MARIETTA *—Continued*													
Leisure and hospitality													
1990	4.3	4.3	4.4	4.6	4.7	4.8	4.8	4.8	4.7	4.5	4.4	4.4	4.5
1991	4.3	4.3	4.4	4.5	4.7	4.8	4.8	4.9	4.8	4.7	4.7	4.7	4.6
1992	4.6	4.6	4.7	5.0	5.3	5.4	5.4	5.5	5.3	5.3	5.2	5.1	5.1
1993	4.9	4.9	4.9	5.3	5.5	5.5	5.6	5.6	5.6	5.6	5.6	5.5	5.3
1994	5.1	5.2	5.4	5.7	5.9	6.1	5.9	5.9	5.8	5.8	5.7	5.7	5.6
1995	5.6	5.8	5.9	6.1	6.3	6.5	6.4	6.5	6.3	6.3	6.2	6.1	6.1
1996	5.7	5.8	5.9	6.1	6.3	6.5	6.5	6.4	6.4	6.1	6.0	5.9	6.1
1997	5.7	5.6	5.8	6.1	6.2	6.6	6.5	6.4	6.4	6.2	6.2	6.2	6.1
1998	5.9	5.9	6.0	6.3	6.4	6.7	6.5	6.6	6.5	6.2	6.1	6.2	6.2
1999	5.8	5.9	5.9	6.3	6.5	6.6	6.6	6.5	6.4	6.1	6.2	6.2	6.2
2000	6.0	5.9	6.0	6.1	6.3	6.4	6.4	6.4	6.3	6.1	6.0	5.9	6.1
2001	5.6	5.6	5.8	6.1	6.4	6.4	6.5	6.6	6.4	6.4	6.3	6.2	6.1
2002	5.9	5.9	6.0	6.4	6.5	6.6	6.7	6.7	6.6	6.4	6.5	6.4	6.4
2003	6.1	6.0	6.2	6.5	6.7	6.8	6.8	6.9	6.6	6.5	6.5	6.4	6.5
Other services													
1990	4.0	3.9	3.9	4.0	4.0	4.2	4.2	4.1	4.2	4.1	4.1	4.1	4.0
1991	4.1	3.9	3.9	4.0	4.1	4.2	4.2	4.2	4.1	4.0	4.1	4.1	4.0
1992	4.1	4.1	4.1	4.1	4.2	4.3	4.4	4.2	4.2	4.1	4.2	4.2	4.1
1993	4.3	4.1	4.0	4.1	4.2	4.3	4.2	4.3	4.2	4.2	4.2	4.3	4.2
1994	4.2	4.2	4.1	4.2	4.2	4.3	4.3	4.3	4.3	4.2	4.2	4.2	4.2
1995	4.2	4.2	4.0	4.3	4.3	4.3	4.3	4.3	4.3	4.2	4.2	4.3	4.2
1996	4.1	4.2	4.2	4.4	4.4	4.5	4.6	4.6	4.6	4.6	4.6	4.7	4.4
1997	4.6	4.5	4.6	4.5	4.4	4.5	4.6	4.5	4.5	4.5	4.5	4.5	4.5
1998	4.5	4.3	4.3	4.4	4.4	4.5	4.4	4.3	4.3	4.3	4.3	4.3	4.3
1999	4.2	4.3	4.3	4.4	4.4	4.5	4.5	4.4	4.4	4.5	4.5	4.5	4.4
2000	4.4	4.5	4.5	4.5	4.5	4.6	4.6	4.5	4.5	4.5	4.5	4.6	4.5
2001	4.9	4.9	4.9	4.9	5.0	5.0	5.1	5.0	5.0	5.0	5.0	5.1	4.9
2002	4.9	5.0	5.0	4.9	5.0	5.0	5.0	5.0	4.9	4.7	4.7	4.8	4.9
2003	4.8	4.7	4.8	4.8	4.9	4.9	4.8	4.8	4.7	4.7	4.7	4.7	4.8
Government													
1990	9.5	9.6	9.8	9.8	10.3	9.9	9.4	9.3	9.5	10.0	10.0	10.1	9.7
1991	9.8	9.9	10.0	10.1	10.3	10.1	9.4	9.5	9.8	10.0	10.1	10.0	9.9
1992	10.1	10.2	10.2	10.3	10.9	10.2	10.3	10.0	10.1	10.5	10.5	10.6	10.3
1993	10.2	10.5	10.5	10.6	10.7	10.4	10.2	10.0	10.4	10.7	10.8	10.6	10.4
1994	10.3	10.5	10.7	10.7	11.2	10.6	10.0	10.1	10.3	10.7	11.2	10.6	10.5
1995	10.5	10.6	10.7	10.6	10.7	10.5	10.2	10.0	10.3	10.7	10.7	10.6	10.5
1996	10.4	10.6	10.7	10.7	11.2	10.7	10.2	10.2	10.5	10.6	10.7	10.6	10.5
1997	10.5	10.5	10.6	10.7	10.9	10.9	9.2	9.1	9.1	9.5	9.5	9.4	9.9
1998	9.3	9.4	9.4	9.5	10.0	9.5	9.2	9.0	9.2	9.5	9.6	9.5	9.4
1999	9.2	9.4	9.4	9.5	9.5	9.5	9.3	9.1	9.2	9.6	9.6	9.6	9.4
2000	9.5	9.6	9.7	9.7	10.3	9.9	9.6	9.3	9.4	9.6	9.7	9.6	9.6
2001	9.6	9.7	9.7	9.6	9.8	9.8	9.3	9.3	9.5	9.7	9.8	9.7	9.6
2002	9.5	9.7	9.7	9.7	10.3	9.8	9.4	9.4	9.5	9.7	9.8	9.6	9.7
2003	9.6	9.7	9.7	9.8	9.8	9.9	9.4	9.3	9.5	9.9	9.9	9.6	9.7
Federal government													
1990	1.7	1.7	1.8	1.8	1.9	1.9	2.0	1.9	1.9	1.9	1.8	1.9	1.8
1991	1.8	1.8	1.8	1.9	1.9	1.9	1.9	1.9	1.9	1.8	1.9	1.8	1.8
1992	1.9	1.9	1.9	1.9	1.9	1.9	2.0	2.0	2.0	2.0	2.0	2.0	1.9
1993	2.0	2.0	2.0	2.0	2.0	2.0	2.1	2.1	2.1	2.1	2.1	2.0	2.0
1994	2.0	2.1	2.1	2.1	2.1	2.1	2.1	2.1	2.1	2.1	2.1	2.1	2.0
1995	2.1	2.1	2.1	2.1	2.1	2.1	2.1	2.1	2.1	2.1	2.1	2.1	2.1
1996	2.1	2.1	2.1	2.1	2.1	2.1	2.1	2.1	2.1	2.0	2.0	2.0	2.0
1997	2.0	2.0	2.1	2.1	2.1	2.1	2.2	2.2	2.1	2.1	2.1	2.1	2.1
1998	2.1	2.1	2.1	2.1	2.1	2.1	2.2	2.2	2.2	2.2	2.2	2.2	2.1
1999	2.1	2.1	2.1	2.1	2.1	2.1	2.2	2.2	2.2	2.2	2.2	2.2	2.1
2000	2.2	2.2	2.3	2.3	2.4	2.3	2.3	2.2	2.2	2.2	2.2	2.2	2.2
2001	2.2	2.2	2.2	2.2	2.2	2.2	2.2	2.2	2.2	2.2	2.2	2.2	2.2
2002	2.2	2.2	2.2	2.2	2.2	2.2	2.3	2.3	2.3	2.2	2.2	2.2	2.2
2003	2.2	2.2	2.2	2.2	2.2	2.2	2.2	2.2	2.2	2.3	2.2	2.2	2.2
State government													
1990	1.1	1.1	1.2	1.2	1.2	1.0	1.1	1.0	1.0	1.2	1.2	1.2	1.1
1991	1.1	1.1	1.2	1.2	1.2	1.0	1.0	1.1	1.1	1.2	1.2	1.2	1.1
1992	1.2	1.3	1.3	1.3	1.3	1.1	1.4	1.1	1.2	1.3	1.3	1.3	1.2
1993	1.1	1.3	1.3	1.3	1.3	1.1	1.3	1.1	1.2	1.2	1.3	1.3	1.2
1994	1.2	1.2	1.3	1.3	1.2	1.1	1.1	1.2	1.2	1.3	1.3	1.3	1.2
1995	1.2	1.3	1.3	1.3	1.3	1.1	1.3	1.2	1.2	1.3	1.3	1.3	1.2
1996	1.1	1.2	1.3	1.3	1.3	1.2	1.2	1.2	1.3	1.3	1.3	1.3	1.2
1997	1.2	1.2	1.2	1.2	1.3	1.3	1.3	1.1	1.1	1.2	1.2	1.2	1.2
1998	1.1	1.2	1.2	1.2	1.2	1.1	1.3	1.1	1.1	1.2	1.2	1.2	1.1
1999	1.1	1.2	1.2	1.2	1.2	1.1	1.3	1.1	1.1	1.2	1.2	1.2	1.1
2000	1.2	1.2	1.2	1.2	1.2	1.2	1.4	1.2	1.2	1.2	1.2	1.2	1.2
2001	1.2	1.2	1.2	1.2	1.2	1.2	1.2	1.2	1.2	1.2	1.2	1.2	1.2
2002	1.2	1.2	1.2	1.2	1.2	1.2	1.2	1.2	1.2	1.2	1.2	1.2	1.1
2003	1.2	1.2	1.2	1.2	1.2	1.2	1.2	1.2	1.2	1.2	1.2	1.2	1.2

Employment by Industry: West Virginia—*Continued*

(Numbers in thousands. Not seasonally adjusted.)

Industry	January	February	March	April	May	June	July	August	September	October	November	December	Annual Average
PARKERSBURG-MARIETTA *—Continued*													
Local government													
1990	6.7	6.8	6.8	6.8	7.2	7.0	6.3	6.4	6.6	6.9	7.0	7.0	6.7
1991	6.9	7.0	7.0	7.0	7.2	7.2	6.5	6.5	6.8	7.0	7.0	7.0	6.9
1992	7.0	7.0	7.0	7.1	7.7	7.2	6.9	6.9	6.9	7.2	7.2	7.3	7.1
1993	7.1	7.2	7.2	7.3	7.4	7.3	6.8	6.8	7.1	7.4	7.4	7.3	7.1
1994	7.1	7.2	7.3	7.3	7.9	7.4	6.8	6.8	7.0	7.3	7.8	7.2	7.2
1995	7.2	7.2	7.3	7.2	7.3	7.3	6.8	6.7	7.0	7.3	7.3	7.2	7.1
1996	7.2	7.3	7.3	7.3	7.8	7.4	6.9	6.9	7.1	7.3	7.4	7.3	7.2
1997	7.3	7.3	7.3	7.4	7.5	7.5	5.7	5.8	5.9	6.2	6.2	6.1	6.6
1998	6.1	6.1	6.1	6.2	6.7	6.3	5.7	5.7	5.9	6.1	6.2	6.1	6.1
1999	6.0	6.1	6.1	6.2	6.2	6.3	5.8	5.8	5.9	6.2	6.2	6.2	6.0
2000	6.1	6.2	6.2	6.2	6.7	6.4	5.9	5.9	6.0	6.2	6.3	6.2	6.1
2001	6.2	6.3	6.3	6.2	6.4	6.4	5.9	5.9	6.1	6.3	6.4	6.3	6.2
2002	6.1	6.3	6.3	6.3	6.9	6.4	5.9	5.9	6.0	6.3	6.4	6.2	6.3
2003	6.2	6.3	6.3	6.4	6.4	6.5	6.0	5.9	6.1	6.4	6.5	6.2	6.3
WHEELING													
Total nonfarm													
1990	58.9	58.9	59.7	60.1	61.2	61.0	61.0	60.7	60.9	61.2	61.5	61.2	60.5
1991	58.9	59.1	58.8	59.5	60.8	60.6	60.6	60.1	60.0	60.2	60.3	60.5	59.9
1992	58.6	58.2	58.7	58.8	60.0	60.0	60.0	59.5	59.2	59.8	60.1	59.9	59.4
1993	58.6	59.0	59.1	59.9	60.5	60.3	60.2	59.7	59.8	60.7	61.1	61.7	60.0
1994	58.9	58.9	59.8	61.5	62.3	62.2	63.0	62.9	63.2	63.0	63.6	63.6	61.9
1995	61.7	61.4	62.0	62.2	63.2	63.6	63.1	63.0	63.4	63.9	64.2	64.5	63.0
1996	61.6	61.5	62.3	63.3	65.2	64.4	64.5	64.9	65.5	64.5	64.8	65.1	63.9
1997	62.6	62.9	63.4	64.3	65.4	66.0	65.4	65.6	65.7	66.1	66.7	66.7	65.0
1998	64.4	64.5	65.2	65.6	66.9	67.1	66.5	66.4	66.5	67.3	68.1	68.0	66.3
1999	65.1	65.4	66.1	66.2	67.0	67.1	68.6	66.7	67.0	67.3	67.8	67.8	66.8
2000	65.4	64.9	66.0	67.5	68.5	67.6	67.7	67.7	67.8	67.7	67.8	67.7	67.1
2001	65.6	66.0	66.6	66.9	67.2	67.5	67.4	67.2	66.8	67.7	67.6	68.0	67.0
2002	65.4	65.6	66.2	66.9	67.8	67.5	67.0	66.9	66.8	67.7	67.5	67.5	66.9
2003	64.9	64.6	65.1	66.5	66.9	67.0	66.8	66.6	66.9	66.9	67.0	66.6	66.3
Total private													
1990	49.8	49.8	50.1	50.9	50.9	51.5	52.0	51.8	52.0	51.7	51.8	51.8	51.1
1991	49.7	49.7	49.5	49.9	51.1	51.0	51.4	51.1	50.8	50.7	50.7	50.9	50.5
1992	49.4	48.9	49.4	49.4	49.7	50.5	50.7	50.5	50.1	50.3	50.5	50.4	49.9
1993	49.2	49.6	49.6	50.2	50.8	50.5	50.7	50.5	50.6	50.9	51.1	51.8	50.4
1994	49.5	49.5	50.2	51.6	51.8	52.1	53.4	53.3	53.6	53.0	53.1	53.5	52.0
1995	51.9	51.5	52.2	52.2	52.9	53.1	52.9	53.0	53.2	53.6	53.8	54.1	52.8
1996	51.5	51.3	52.0	53.1	54.2	53.9	54.3	55.1	55.4	54.2	54.5	54.8	53.6
1997	52.6	52.8	53.2	54.2	55.2	55.8	55.3	55.6	55.9	55.9	56.4	56.4	54.9
1998	54.6	54.3	55.0	55.5	56.1	56.7	56.2	56.4	56.3	56.9	57.6	57.6	56.1
1999	55.0	55.2	55.7	55.7	56.3	56.3	58.2	56.5	56.8	56.9	57.1	57.2	56.4
2000	55.2	54.6	55.4	57.0	57.1	56.7	57.2	57.1	57.5	57.1	57.0	57.1	56.5
2001	55.3	55.6	56.1	56.4	56.6	56.8	56.9	56.8	56.3	57.0	56.8	57.2	56.4
2002	55.1	55.3	55.8	56.4	56.8	56.9	57.0	57.1	57.0	57.1	57.0	56.9	56.5
2003	54.7	54.3	54.6	55.9	56.2	56.5	56.5	56.4	56.8	56.4	56.7	56.2	55.9
Goods-producing													
1990	10.5	10.6	10.6	10.9	11.1	11.3	11.5	11.6	11.6	11.5	11.2	11.1	11.1
1991	10.6	10.4	10.5	10.5	10.9	11.1	11.3	11.2	10.8	11.1	10.7	10.6	10.8
1992	10.0	9.6	9.7	9.8	9.9	10.2	10.3	10.5	10.4	10.5	10.4	9.9	10.1
1993	9.4	9.5	9.5	9.9	10.2	10.0	9.6	9.5	9.6	9.6	9.5	9.8	9.6
1994	9.1	9.3	9.6	9.9	9.8	10.0	10.4	10.7	10.7	10.2	10.0	9.9	9.9
1995	9.4	9.2	9.4	9.7	9.8	9.9	9.9	10.1	10.1	10.1	9.9	9.6	9.7
1996	9.0	9.1	9.2	9.4	9.7	9.7	10.1	10.4	10.4	9.7	9.4	9.3	9.6
1997	8.7	8.8	8.9	9.2	9.5	9.7	9.9	10.0	10.2	10.4	10.2	10.2	9.6
1998	9.4	9.3	9.4	9.8	10.0	10.1	10.3	10.4	10.2	10.2	10.2	10.1	9.9
1999	9.3	9.4	9.5	9.8	9.9	10.0	10.4	10.1	10.1	10.2	10.1	9.9	9.8
2000	9.5	9.2	9.5	9.9	10.0	9.8	10.1	10.2	10.1	9.9	9.8	9.6	9.8
2001	8.7	8.7	9.0	9.1	9.3	9.4	9.5	9.5	9.4	9.8	9.5	9.4	9.2
2002	8.9	9.0	9.0	9.3	9.5	9.6	9.7	9.7	9.7	9.8	9.7	9.7	9.5
2003	9.3	9.1	9.2	9.5	9.7	9.7	9.8	9.8	10.0	9.3	9.3	9.2	9.5
Construction and mining													
1990	3.9	3.9	3.9	4.1	4.3	4.4	4.5	4.5	4.5	4.5	4.3	4.1	4.2
1991	3.8	3.7	3.8	3.9	4.2	4.3	4.5	4.5	4.4	4.5	4.3	4.1	4.1
1992	3.8	3.5	3.5	3.8	3.9	4.1	4.2	4.3	4.3	4.4	4.3	3.8	3.9
1993	3.4	3.4	3.4	3.8	4.0	3.8	3.5	3.3	3.4	3.5	3.4	4.0	3.5
1994	3.3	3.5	3.8	3.9	3.8	3.9	4.4	4.7	4.7	4.3	4.1	3.9	4.0
1995	3.5	3.2	3.4	3.6	3.7	3.8	3.9	4.1	4.0	4.1	4.0	3.7	3.7
1996	3.3	3.4	3.5	3.7	4.0	4.1	4.4	4.5	4.6	4.4	4.1	4.0	4.0
1997	3.6	3.6	3.7	3.9	4.1	4.3	4.5	4.5	4.6	4.6	4.4	4.3	4.1
1998	3.9	3.8	3.8	4.2	4.4	4.5	4.7	4.7	4.6	4.6	4.6	4.5	4.3
1999	3.8	3.9	4.0	4.3	4.4	4.5	4.7	4.6	4.6	4.6	4.6	4.5	4.3
2000	4.1	3.8	4.1	4.2	4.3	4.3	4.5	4.6	4.5	4.3	4.3	4.1	4.2
2001	3.6	3.6	3.8	3.9	4.1	4.2	4.3	4.3	4.3	4.6	4.4	4.3	4.1
2002	3.8	3.9	3.9	4.1	4.2	4.3	4.4	4.4	4.4	4.5	4.5	4.4	4.2
2003	4.2	4.1	4.3	4.5	4.6	4.6	4.7	4.8	5.0	4.4	4.4	4.3	4.5

Employment by Industry: West Virginia—*Continued*

(Numbers in thousands. Not seasonally adjusted.)

Industry	January	February	March	April	May	June	July	August	September	October	November	December	Annual Average
WHEELING—*Continued*													
Manufacturing													
1990	6.6	6.7	6.7	6.8	6.8	6.9	7.0	7.1	7.1	7.0	6.9	7.0	6.8
1991	6.8	6.7	6.7	6.6	6.7	6.8	6.8	6.7	6.4	6.6	6.4	6.5	6.6
1992	6.2	6.1	6.2	6.0	6.0	6.1	6.1	6.2	6.1	6.1	6.1	6.1	6.1
1993	6.0	6.1	6.1	6.1	6.2	6.2	6.1	6.2	6.2	6.1	6.1	5.8	6.1
1994	5.8	5.8	5.8	6.0	6.0	6.1	6.0	6.0	6.0	5.9	5.9	6.0	5.9
1995	5.9	6.0	6.0	6.1	6.1	6.1	6.0	6.0	6.1	6.0	5.9	5.9	6.0
1996	5.7	5.7	5.7	5.7	5.7	5.6	5.7	5.9	5.8	5.3	5.3	5.3	5.6
1997	5.1	5.2	5.2	5.3	5.4	5.4	5.4	5.5	5.6	5.8	5.8	5.9	5.4
1998	5.5	5.5	5.6	5.6	5.6	5.6	5.6	5.7	5.6	5.6	5.6	5.6	5.5
1999	5.5	5.5	5.5	5.5	5.5	5.5	5.7	5.5	5.5	5.6	5.5	5.4	5.5
2000	5.4	5.4	5.4	5.7	5.7	5.5	5.6	5.6	5.6	5.6	5.5	5.5	5.5
2001	5.1	5.1	5.2	5.2	5.2	5.2	5.2	5.2	5.1	5.2	5.1	5.1	5.1
2002	5.1	5.1	5.1	5.2	5.3	5.3	5.3	5.3	5.3	5.3	5.2	5.3	5.2
2003	5.1	5.0	4.9	5.0	5.1	5.1	5.1	5.0	5.0	4.9	4.9	4.9	5.0
Service-providing													
1990	48.4	48.3	49.1	49.2	50.1	49.7	49.5	49.1	49.3	49.7	50.3	50.1	49.4
1991	48.3	48.7	48.3	49.0	49.9	49.5	49.3	48.9	49.2	49.1	49.6	49.9	49.1
1992	48.6	48.6	49.0	49.0	50.1	49.8	49.7	49.0	48.8	49.3	49.7	50.0	49.3
1993	49.2	49.5	49.6	50.0	50.3	50.3	50.6	50.2	50.2	51.1	51.6	51.9	50.3
1994	49.8	49.6	50.2	51.6	52.5	52.2	52.6	52.2	52.5	52.8	53.6	53.7	51.9
1995	52.3	52.2	52.6	52.5	53.4	53.7	53.2	52.9	53.3	53.8	54.3	54.9	53.2
1996	52.6	52.4	53.1	53.9	55.5	54.7	54.4	54.5	55.1	54.8	55.4	55.8	54.3
1997	53.9	54.1	54.5	55.1	55.9	56.3	55.5	55.6	55.5	55.7	56.5	56.5	55.4
1998	55.0	55.2	55.8	55.8	56.9	57.0	56.2	56.0	56.3	57.1	57.9	57.9	56.4
1999	55.8	56.0	56.6	56.4	57.1	57.1	58.2	56.6	56.9	57.1	57.7	57.9	56.9
2000	55.9	55.7	56.5	57.6	58.5	57.8	57.6	57.5	57.7	57.8	58.0	58.1	57.3
2001	56.9	57.3	57.6	57.8	57.9	58.1	57.9	57.7	57.4	57.9	58.1	58.6	57.7
2002	56.5	56.6	57.2	57.6	58.3	57.9	57.3	57.2	57.1	57.9	57.8	57.8	57.4
2003	55.6	55.5	55.9	57.0	57.2	57.3	57.0	56.8	56.9	57.6	57.7	57.4	56.8
Trade, transportation, and utilities													
1990	14.0	13.8	13.9	14.0	13.9	14.1	14.2	14.2	14.1	14.0	14.3	14.4	14.0
1991	13.5	13.5	13.3	13.5	13.9	13.7	13.7	13.8	13.7	13.6	13.9	14.1	13.6
1992	13.6	13.4	13.4	13.5	13.5	13.6	13.7	13.7	13.4	13.5	13.7	14.0	13.5
1993	13.4	13.5	13.5	13.4	13.6	13.5	13.8	13.7	13.6	14.0	14.2	14.4	13.7
1994	13.4	13.4	13.4	13.7	13.8	13.8	14.2	14.0	14.1	14.1	14.3	14.7	13.9
1995	14.1	13.9	14.1	13.8	13.9	14.0	13.8	13.8	13.9	14.0	14.2	14.5	14.0
1996	13.7	13.6	13.7	13.9	14.1	14.0	14.0	14.2	14.4	14.2	14.7	15.1	14.1
1997	14.0	13.8	13.7	14.1	14.2	14.6	14.5	14.6	14.5	14.4	14.9	14.9	14.3
1998	14.6	14.4	14.3	14.0	14.1	14.3	14.2	14.2	14.0	14.1	14.6	14.7	14.2
1999	14.0	13.9	14.1	14.0	14.2	14.2	14.8	14.4	14.5	14.5	14.8	14.9	14.3
2000	14.1	13.9	14.0	14.4	14.3	14.3	14.4	14.3	14.1	14.3	14.5	14.6	14.2
2001	13.4	13.2	13.2	13.4	13.3	13.4	13.3	13.3	13.1	12.9	12.9	13.1	13.2
2002	12.6	12.3	12.3	12.5	12.4	12.5	12.5	12.5	12.4	12.2	12.3	12.4	12.4
2003	11.8	11.8	11.8	12.0	12.1	12.2	12.2	12.0	12.1	12.2	12.7	12.7	12.1
Wholesale trade													
1990	2.2	2.2	2.2	2.2	2.2	2.2	2.3	2.3	2.3	2.3	2.3	2.2	2.2
1991	2.2	2.2	2.2	2.2	2.3	2.3	2.3	2.3	2.3	2.3	2.2	2.2	2.2
1992	2.2	2.2	2.2	2.1	2.1	2.2	2.1	2.1	2.1	2.1	2.1	2.1	2.1
1993	2.1	2.1	2.1	2.1	2.1	2.1	2.2	2.1	2.0	2.1	2.1	2.1	2.1
1994	2.0	2.0	2.0	2.0	2.0	2.0	2.1	2.0	2.1	2.1	2.1	2.1	2.0
1995	2.1	2.1	2.1	2.2	2.2	2.2	2.2	2.1	2.2	2.2	2.2	2.2	2.1
1996	2.2	2.2	2.2	2.2	2.2	2.2	2.2	2.2	2.2	2.2	2.2	2.2	2.2
1997	2.2	2.2	2.2	2.2	2.2	2.4	2.5	2.5	2.4	2.4	2.5	2.4	2.3
1998	2.4	2.4	2.4	2.4	2.4	2.5	2.5	2.5	2.4	2.4	2.5	2.5	2.4
1999	2.5	2.5	2.5	2.5	2.5	2.5	2.7	2.6	2.6	2.6	2.6	2.6	2.5
2000	2.5	2.5	2.6	2.6	2.5	2.5	2.5	2.5	2.5	2.5	2.5	2.5	2.5
2001	2.4	2.4	2.4	2.5	2.4	2.4	2.3	2.3	2.2	2.2	2.1	2.1	2.3
2002	2.1	2.0	2.0	2.0	2.0	2.0	2.0	2.1	2.1	2.1	2.0	2.1	2.0
2003	2.0	2.1	2.1	2.1	2.1	2.1	2.1	2.0	2.1	2.0	2.0	2.0	2.1
Retail trade													
1990	9.5	9.3	9.3	9.4	9.3	9.4	9.5	9.5	9.4	9.4	9.7	9.9	9.4
1991	9.0	9.0	8.9	9.1	9.3	9.1	9.1	9.2	9.1	9.1	9.5	9.7	9.1
1992	9.2	9.0	9.0	9.2	9.2	9.2	9.3	9.3	9.1	9.2	9.4	9.7	9.2
1993	9.1	9.1	9.1	9.1	9.2	9.2	9.3	9.3	9.3	9.6	9.8	10.0	9.3
1994	9.2	9.1	9.1	9.4	9.4	9.4	9.6	9.6	9.6	9.6	9.9	10.2	9.5
1995	9.6	9.4	9.5	9.2	9.3	9.4	9.2	9.4	9.4	9.5	9.7	10.1	9.4
1996	9.3	9.2	9.3	9.6	9.7	9.7	9.6	9.8	10.0	9.9	10.4	10.7	9.7
1997	9.7	9.5	9.5	9.7	9.8	10.0	9.8	9.9	9.9	9.8	10.2	10.3	9.8
1998	10.1	9.9	9.8	9.6	9.6	9.7	9.7	9.7	9.6	9.7	10.1	10.2	9.8
1999	9.7	9.6	9.8	9.8	9.9	9.9	10.3	10.0	10.1	10.1	10.4	10.5	10.0
2000	9.9	9.7	9.7	10.1	10.1	10.1	10.2	10.1	9.9	10.1	10.3	10.5	10.0
2001	9.4	9.2	9.2	9.2	9.2	9.2	9.3	9.3	9.2	9.0	9.2	9.4	9.2
2002	8.9	8.7	8.7	8.9	8.8	8.9	8.9	8.8	8.7	8.5	8.7	8.8	8.8
2003	8.3	8.2	8.2	8.4	8.5	8.6	8.6	8.5	8.5	8.7	9.2	9.2	8.6

Employment by Industry: West Virginia—*Continued*

(Numbers in thousands. Not seasonally adjusted.)

Industry	January	February	March	April	May	June	July	August	September	October	November	December	Annual Average
WHEELING—*Continued*													
Transportation and utilities													
1990	2.3	2.3	2.4	2.4	2.4	2.5	2.4	2.4	2.4	2.3	2.3	2.3	2.3
1991	2.3	2.3	2.2	2.2	2.3	2.3	2.3	2.3	2.3	2.2	2.2	2.2	2.2
1992	2.2	2.2	2.2	2.2	2.2	2.2	2.3	2.3	2.2	2.2	2.2	2.2	2.2
1993	2.2	2.3	2.3	2.2	2.3	2.2	2.3	2.3	2.3	2.3	2.3	2.3	2.2
1994	2.2	2.3	2.3	2.3	2.4	2.4	2.5	2.4	2.4	2.4	2.3	2.4	2.3
1995	2.4	2.4	2.5	2.4	2.4	2.4	2.4	2.3	2.3	2.3	2.3	2.2	2.3
1996	2.2	2.2	2.2	2.1	2.2	2.1	2.2	2.2	2.2	2.1	2.1	2.2	2.1
1997	2.1	2.1	2.0	2.2	2.2	2.2	2.2	2.2	2.2	2.2	2.2	2.2	2.1
1998	2.1	2.1	2.1	2.0	2.1	2.1	2.0	2.0	2.0	2.0	2.0	2.0	2.0
1999	1.8	1.8	1.8	1.7	1.8	1.8	1.8	1.8	1.8	1.8	1.8	1.8	1.7
2000	1.7	1.7	1.7	1.7	1.7	1.7	1.7	1.7	1.7	1.7	1.7	1.6	1.6
2001	1.6	1.6	1.6	1.7	1.7	1.8	1.7	1.7	1.7	1.7	1.6	1.6	1.6
2002	1.6	1.6	1.6	1.6	1.6	1.6	1.6	1.6	1.6	1.6	1.6	1.5	1.6
2003	1.5	1.5	1.5	1.5	1.5	1.5	1.5	1.5	1.5	1.5	1.5	1.5	1.5
Information													
1990	1.2	1.2	1.2	1.2	1.2	1.2	1.2	1.2	1.2	1.2	1.2	1.2	1.2
1991	1.2	1.2	1.1	1.2	1.2	1.2	1.2	1.2	1.2	1.2	1.2	1.3	1.2
1992	1.2	1.2	1.3	1.3	1.3	1.3	1.2	1.2	1.2	1.2	1.2	1.2	1.2
1993	1.2	1.2	1.2	1.2	1.2	1.2	1.2	1.2	1.2	1.2	1.2	1.2	1.2
1994	1.2	1.2	1.2	1.2	1.3	1.4	1.4	1.3	1.3	1.2	1.2	1.2	1.2
1995	1.1	1.1	1.1	1.1	1.1	1.1	1.1	1.1	1.1	1.1	1.2	1.2	1.1
1996	1.2	1.2	1.2	1.2	1.3	1.3	1.1	1.1	1.1	1.1	1.1	1.1	1.1
1997	1.2	1.3	1.3	1.3	1.4	1.4	1.3	1.3	1.3	1.4	1.5	1.5	1.3
1998	1.4	1.4	1.4	1.4	1.4	1.4	1.3	1.3	1.3	1.5	1.5	1.5	1.4
1999	1.4	1.5	1.5	1.5	1.6	1.6	1.6	1.5	1.4	1.4	1.4	1.4	1.4
2000	1.3	1.4	1.4	1.4	1.4	1.4	1.4	1.2	1.3	1.3	1.3	1.3	1.3
2001	1.1	1.2	1.2	1.2	1.2	1.2	1.3	1.3	1.2	1.3	1.3	1.3	1.2
2002	1.2	1.2	1.2	1.2	1.2	1.2	1.1	1.1	1.1	1.2	1.2	1.2	1.2
2003	1.2	1.2	1.2	1.2	1.2	1.2	1.2	1.2	1.2	1.2	1.2	1.2	1.2
Financial activities													
1990	3.1	3.2	3.2	3.2	3.2	3.3	3.3	3.3	3.3	3.3	3.3	3.3	3.2
1991	3.2	3.2	3.2	3.3	3.3	3.3	3.2	3.2	3.2	3.2	3.2	3.2	3.2
1992	3.1	3.1	3.2	3.1	3.1	3.2	3.2	3.1	3.1	3.1	3.1	3.1	3.1
1993	3.2	3.2	3.2	3.2	3.2	3.3	3.3	3.2	3.2	3.2	3.2	3.3	3.2
1994	3.2	3.1	3.2	3.2	3.2	3.2	3.3	3.3	3.3	3.2	3.2	3.3	3.2
1995	3.2	3.1	3.1	3.1	3.1	3.1	3.1	3.0	3.0	3.1	3.1	3.1	3.0
1996	3.0	3.0	3.0	3.0	3.1	3.1	3.1	3.1	3.0	3.1	3.1	3.1	3.0
1997	3.1	3.1	3.1	3.1	3.1	3.1	3.1	3.1	3.1	3.1	3.1	3.1	3.1
1998	3.1	3.1	3.1	3.1	3.1	3.1	3.1	3.1	3.1	3.1	3.1	3.2	3.1
1999	3.2	3.1	3.1	3.2	3.2	3.2	3.2	3.1	3.1	3.1	3.1	3.2	3.1
2000	3.1	3.0	3.0	3.0	3.1	3.0	3.1	3.1	3.1	3.1	3.1	3.1	3.0
2001	2.9	2.9	2.9	2.9	2.9	3.0	2.9	2.9	2.9	2.9	2.9	2.9	2.8
2002	2.9	2.9	2.9	2.8	2.9	2.9	2.9	2.9	2.9	2.9	2.9	2.9	2.9
2003	2.9	2.9	2.9	2.9	2.9	2.9	2.9	2.9	2.9	2.9	2.9	2.9	2.9
Professional and business services													
1990	2.8	2.8	2.9	3.0	2.9	2.9	2.8	2.8	2.8	2.9	2.9	2.8	2.8
1991	3.0	3.1	3.0	3.0	3.0	2.9	3.0	3.0	3.0	2.9	3.0	2.9	2.9
1992	3.0	3.0	3.0	3.2	3.1	3.2	3.2	3.2	3.2	3.1	3.0	3.1	3.1
1993	3.2	3.2	3.2	3.3	3.3	3.3	3.3	3.4	3.4	3.4	3.5	3.4	3.3
1994	3.6	3.6	3.6	3.6	3.5	3.5	3.6	3.7	3.8	3.8	3.7	3.7	3.6
1995	3.8	3.8	3.9	3.8	4.0	3.9	3.9	3.9	4.0	4.0	4.1	4.2	3.9
1996	3.9	3.9	3.9	4.5	4.5	4.5	4.6	4.6	4.7	4.6	4.7	4.5	4.4
1997	4.3	4.4	4.5	4.6	4.6	4.6	4.4	4.4	4.5	4.4	4.5	4.5	4.4
1998	4.3	4.3	4.5	4.7	4.7	4.9	4.6	4.8	4.8	5.2	5.2	5.0	4.7
1999	4.8	5.0	4.9	4.6	4.5	4.6	4.9	4.8	4.8	4.8	4.9	4.9	4.7
2000	4.6	4.6	4.6	4.9	4.7	4.7	4.8	4.8	5.0	4.8	4.8	5.0	4.7
2001	4.7	4.7	4.8	4.7	4.5	4.6	4.5	4.5	4.3	4.5	4.5	4.8	4.5
2002	4.6	4.5	4.7	4.7	4.6	4.7	4.8	4.9	4.9	4.6	4.7	4.6	4.7
2003	4.6	4.5	4.5	4.6	4.6	4.7	4.7	4.8	4.7	4.7	4.6	4.6	4.6
Educational and health services													
1990	9.9	9.9	9.9	10.0	9.9	10.0	10.1	10.0	10.2	10.2	10.2	10.2	10.0
1991	10.1	10.3	10.3	10.2	10.4	10.5	10.4	10.5	10.7	10.7	10.7	10.8	10.4
1992	10.8	10.8	10.9	10.6	10.6	10.7	10.9	10.7	10.8	10.9	10.9	11.0	10.8
1993	11.0	11.1	11.1	11.0	11.0	10.9	11.2	11.2	11.3	11.3	11.3	11.4	11.1
1994	11.3	11.3	11.4	11.7	11.7	11.7	11.9	11.7	11.8	12.1	12.3	12.3	11.7
1995	12.3	12.4	12.4	12.3	12.3	12.3	12.2	12.2	12.2	12.5	12.5	12.6	12.3
1996	12.2	12.3	12.3	12.2	12.4	12.2	12.2	12.3	12.4	12.3	12.3	12.4	12.2
1997	12.3	12.4	12.4	12.4	12.5	12.5	12.4	12.5	12.7	12.8	12.8	12.9	12.5
1998	12.7	12.8	12.9	13.0	12.9	13.0	12.9	12.9	13.0	13.2	13.3	13.4	13.0
1999	12.9	12.9	12.9	12.8	12.9	12.7	13.0	12.7	12.9	12.9	12.9	13.0	12.8
2000	12.7	12.7	12.8	13.1	13.1	13.0	13.1	13.1	13.3	13.3	13.3	13.3	13.0
2001	13.5	13.8	13.7	13.5	13.5	13.2	13.4	13.3	13.5	13.8	13.8	13.8	13.5
2002	13.3	13.8	13.8	13.8	13.9	13.6	13.4	13.5	13.5	13.9	13.8	13.9	13.7
2003	13.1	13.2	13.2	13.5	13.4	13.2	13.0	13.1	13.3	13.4	13.4	13.2	13.3

Employment by Industry: West Virginia—*Continued*

(Numbers in thousands. Not seasonally adjusted.)

Industry	January	February	March	April	May	June	July	August	September	October	November	December	Annual Average
WHEELING—*Continued*													
Leisure and hospitality													
1990	5.3	5.3	5.4	5.6	5.7	5.7	5.9	5.7	5.8	5.6	5.6	5.7	5.6
1991	5.1	5.0	5.1	5.2	5.4	5.3	5.6	5.2	5.2	5.0	5.0	5.0	5.1
1992	4.7	4.8	4.9	4.9	5.1	5.2	5.1	5.1	5.0	5.0	5.2	5.1	5.0
1993	4.8	4.8	4.8	5.1	5.2	5.2	5.2	5.2	5.2	5.1	5.1	5.1	5.0
1994	4.6	4.6	4.7	5.1	5.3	5.3	5.4	5.4	5.4	5.2	5.2	5.2	5.1
1995	4.9	4.9	5.0	5.2	5.4	5.5	5.6	5.6	5.6	5.5	5.5	5.5	5.3
1996	5.2	4.9	5.4	5.5	5.7	5.7	5.8	5.9	5.9	5.7	5.7	5.7	5.5
1997	5.5	5.5	5.7	5.9	6.3	6.3	6.1	6.1	6.0	5.8	5.8	5.7	5.8
1998	5.5	5.5	5.8	5.9	6.2	6.2	6.1	6.0	6.2	5.9	5.9	5.9	5.9
1999	5.6	5.6	5.8	5.9	6.1	6.0	6.2	6.0	6.0	6.0	5.9	5.9	5.9
2000	5.8	5.7	6.0	6.1	6.3	6.3	6.2	6.3	6.4	6.2	6.1	6.1	6.1
2001	5.6	5.6	5.8	6.1	6.4	6.5	6.5	6.5	6.4	6.3	6.4	6.4	6.2
2002	6.1	6.2	6.4	6.6	6.8	6.9	7.1	7.0	7.0	7.0	6.9	6.7	6.7
2003	6.3	6.2	6.3	6.7	6.8	7.1	7.2	7.1	7.1	7.2	7.1	6.9	6.8
Other services													
1990	3.0	3.0	3.0	3.0	3.0	3.0	3.0	3.0	3.0	3.0	3.1	3.1	3.0
1991	3.0	3.0	3.0	3.0	3.0	3.0	3.0	3.0	3.0	3.0	3.0	3.0	3.0
1992	3.0	3.0	3.0	3.0	3.1	3.1	3.1	3.0	3.0	3.0	3.0	3.0	3.0
1993	3.0	3.1	3.1	3.1	3.1	3.1	3.1	3.1	3.1	3.1	3.1	3.2	3.1
1994	3.1	3.0	3.1	3.2	3.2	3.2	3.2	3.2	3.2	3.2	3.2	3.2	3.1
1995	3.1	3.1	3.2	3.2	3.3	3.3	3.3	3.3	3.3	3.3	3.3	3.4	3.2
1996	3.3	3.3	3.3	3.4	3.4	3.4	3.4	3.5	3.5	3.5	3.5	3.6	3.4
1997	3.5	3.5	3.6	3.6	3.6	3.6	3.6	3.6	3.6	3.6	3.6	3.6	3.5
1998	3.6	3.5	3.6	3.6	3.7	3.7	3.7	3.7	3.7	3.7	3.8	3.8	3.6
1999	3.8	3.8	3.9	3.9	3.9	4.0	4.1	3.9	4.0	4.0	4.0	4.0	3.9
2000	4.1	4.1	4.1	4.2	4.2	4.2	4.1	4.1	4.2	4.2	4.1	4.1	4.1
2001	...	5.5	5.5	5.5	5.5	5.5	5.5	5.5	5.5	5.5	5.5	5.5	...
2002	5.5	5.4	5.5	5.5	5.5	5.5	5.5	5.5	5.5	5.5	5.5	5.5	5.5
2003	5.5	5.4	5.5	5.5	5.5	5.5	5.5	5.5	5.5	5.5	5.5	5.5	5.5
Government													
1990	9.1	9.1	9.6	9.2	10.3	9.5	9.0	8.9	8.9	9.5	9.7	9.4	9.3
1991	9.2	9.4	9.3	9.6	9.7	9.6	9.2	9.0	9.2	9.5	9.6	9.6	9.4
1992	9.2	9.3	9.3	9.4	10.3	9.5	9.3	9.0	9.1	9.5	9.6	9.5	9.4
1993	9.4	9.4	9.5	9.7	9.7	9.8	9.5	9.2	9.2	9.8	10.0	9.9	9.5
1994	9.4	9.4	9.6	9.9	10.5	10.1	9.6	9.6	9.6	10.0	10.5	10.1	9.8
1995	9.8	9.9	9.8	10.0	10.3	10.5	10.2	10.0	10.2	10.3	10.4	10.4	10.1
1996	10.1	10.2	10.3	10.2	11.0	10.5	10.2	9.8	10.1	10.3	10.3	10.3	10.2
1997	10.0	10.1	10.2	10.1	10.2	10.2	10.1	10.0	9.8	10.2	10.3	10.3	10.1
1998	9.8	10.2	10.2	10.1	10.8	10.4	10.3	10.0	10.2	10.4	10.5	10.4	10.2
1999	10.1	10.2	10.4	10.5	10.7	10.8	10.4	10.2	10.2	10.4	10.7	10.6	10.4
2000	10.2	10.3	10.6	10.5	11.4	10.9	10.5	10.6	10.3	10.6	10.8	10.6	10.6
2001	10.3	10.4	10.5	10.5	10.6	10.7	10.5	10.4	10.5	10.7	10.8	10.8	10.5
2002	10.3	10.3	10.4	10.5	11.0	10.6	10.0	9.8	9.8	10.6	10.5	10.6	10.4
2003	10.2	10.3	10.5	10.6	10.7	10.5	10.3	10.2	10.1	10.5	10.3	10.4	10.4
Federal government													
1990	0.7	0.7	0.7	0.7	0.9	0.8	0.7	0.7	0.7	0.7	0.7	0.7	0.7
1991	0.7	0.7	0.7	0.7	0.7	0.7	0.7	0.7	0.7	0.7	0.7	0.7	0.7
1992	0.7	0.7	0.7	0.7	0.7	0.7	0.7	0.7	0.7	0.7	0.7	0.7	0.7
1993	0.7	0.7	0.7	0.7	0.7	0.7	0.7	0.7	0.7	0.7	0.7	0.7	0.7
1994	0.6	0.6	0.6	0.7	0.7	0.7	0.7	0.7	0.7	0.7	0.7	0.7	0.6
1995	0.7	0.7	0.7	0.7	0.7	0.7	0.7	0.7	0.7	0.7	0.7	0.7	0.7
1996	0.7	0.7	0.7	0.7	0.7	0.7	0.7	0.6	0.6	0.7	0.6	0.7	0.6
1997	0.7	0.7	0.7	0.7	0.7	0.7	0.7	0.7	0.7	0.7	0.7	0.7	0.7
1998	0.7	0.7	0.7	0.7	0.7	0.7	0.7	0.7	0.7	0.7	0.7	0.7	0.7
1999	0.7	0.7	0.7	0.7	0.7	0.7	0.7	0.7	0.7	0.7	0.7	0.7	0.7
2000	0.7	0.7	0.8	0.8	0.9	0.8	0.8	0.8	0.7	0.7	0.7	0.7	0.7
2001	0.8	0.7	0.7	0.8	0.7	0.8	0.8	0.8	0.8	0.8	0.8	0.8	0.7
2002	0.8	0.7	0.7	0.7	0.7	0.7	0.8	0.8	0.7	0.8	0.7	0.8	0.7
2003	0.8	0.8	0.8	0.8	0.8	0.8	0.8	0.8	0.7	0.7	0.7	0.7	0.8
State government													
1990	1.7	1.7	2.1	1.8	1.9	1.6	1.5	1.5	1.6	1.9	2.0	1.9	1.7
1991	1.8	1.9	1.9	2.0	1.9	1.7	1.5	1.5	1.7	1.9	2.0	2.0	1.8
1992	1.8	1.9	1.9	2.0	2.0	1.6	1.8	1.6	1.7	2.0	2.0	1.9	1.8
1993	1.9	1.9	2.0	2.0	1.9	1.8	1.8	1.6	1.6	1.9	2.0	1.9	1.8
1994	1.8	1.8	1.9	2.0	2.0	1.9	1.7	1.7	1.7	1.9	2.0	2.0	1.8
1995	1.9	1.9	1.9	2.0	2.1	2.0	2.1	1.9	2.0	2.1	2.2	2.2	2.0
1996	2.1	2.1	2.2	2.2	2.3	2.1	2.1	1.9	2.1	2.1	2.2	2.1	2.1
1997	2.1	2.1	2.2	2.2	2.2	2.0	2.1	2.0	2.0	2.3	2.3	2.3	2.1
1998	2.0	2.3	2.3	2.2	2.2	2.1	2.2	2.0	2.2	2.3	2.4	2.3	2.2
1999	2.3	2.3	2.4	2.4	2.5	2.3	2.2	2.1	2.2	2.4	2.5	2.5	2.3
2000	2.3	2.4	2.5	2.4	2.5	2.3	2.2	2.2	2.3	2.5	2.6	2.5	2.3
2001	2.3	2.4	2.5	2.4	2.5	2.2	2.2	2.2	2.3	2.4	2.4	2.4	2.3
2002	2.2	2.3	2.4	2.4	2.4	2.2	1.7	1.6	1.7	2.4	2.4	2.4	2.2
2003	2.2	2.3	2.4	2.3	2.3	2.0	2.1	2.1	2.2	2.5	2.4	2.4	2.3

Employment by Industry: West Virginia—*Continued*

(Numbers in thousands. Not seasonally adjusted.)

Industry	January	February	March	April	May	June	July	August	September	October	November	December	Annual Average
WHEELING—*Continued*													
Local government													
1990	6.7	6.7	6.8	6.7	7.5	7.1	6.8	6.7	6.6	6.9	7.0	6.8	6.8
1991	6.7	6.8	6.7	6.9	7.1	7.2	7.0	6.8	6.8	6.9	6.9	6.9	6.8
1992	6.7	6.7	6.7	6.7	7.6	7.2	6.8	6.7	6.7	6.8	6.9	6.9	6.8
1993	6.8	6.8	6.8	7.0	7.1	7.3	7.0	6.9	6.9	7.2	7.3	7.3	7.0
1994	7.0	7.0	7.1	7.2	7.8	7.5	7.2	7.2	7.2	7.4	7.8	7.4	7.3
1995	7.2	7.3	7.2	7.3	7.5	7.8	7.4	7.4	7.5	7.5	7.5	7.5	7.4
1996	7.3	7.4	7.4	7.3	8.0	7.7	7.4	7.3	7.4	7.5	7.5	7.5	7.4
1997	7.2	7.3	7.3	7.2	7.3	7.5	7.3	7.3	7.1	7.2	7.3	7.3	7.2
1998	7.1	7.2	7.2	7.2	7.9	7.6	7.4	7.3	7.3	7.4	7.4	7.4	7.3
1999	7.1	7.2	7.3	7.4	7.5	7.8	7.5	7.4	7.3	7.3	7.5	7.4	7.3
2000	7.2	7.2	7.3	7.3	8.0	7.8	7.5	7.6	7.3	7.4	7.5	7.4	7.4
2001	7.2	7.3	7.3	7.3	7.4	7.7	7.5	7.4	7.4	7.5	7.6	7.6	7.4
2002	7.3	7.3	7.3	7.4	7.9	7.7	7.5	7.4	7.4	7.4	7.4	7.4	7.5
2003	7.2	7.2	7.3	7.5	7.6	7.7	7.4	7.3	7.2	7.3	7.2	7.3	7.4

Average Weekly Hours by Industry: West Virginia

(Not seasonally adjusted.)

Industry	January	February	March	April	May	June	July	August	September	October	November	December	Annual Average
STATEWIDE													
Total private													
2001	33.7	34.0	34.0	34.3	34.5	34.5	34.3	34.4	34.6	34.5	34.5	34.7	34.3
2002	33.9	34.0	34.1	34.2	34.2	34.8	34.4	34.7	34.8	34.7	34.6	34.7	34.4
2003	33.8	34.0	34.2	34.1	34.3	34.4	34.1	34.3	34.3	34.3	34.5	34.1	34.2
Natural resources and mining													
2001	43.8	44.0	44.2	45.4	46.3	46.1	44.7	45.8	45.1	45.2	44.4	45.3	45.0
2002	45.4	45.8	45.0	44.8	44.6	46.0	44.6	46.3	46.4	46.0	46.0	47.0	45.7
2003	46.6	46.9	46.5	46.2	46.3	46.1	44.4	46.9	46.9	46.9	46.3	46.6	46.4
Construction													
2001	37.8	35.5	37.2	37.3	38.5	38.2	38.6	38.7	39.1	38.7	38.9	38.6	38.2
2002	37.1	37.4	37.6	38.3	37.7	38.1	38.7	39.4	39.5	38.9	38.7	38.5	38.4
2003	37.9	37.0	38.3	37.5	39.3	39.3	39.5	40.3	40.5	38.9	38.5	38.8	38.9
Manufacturing													
2001	40.9	41.1	41.3	41.3	41.4	41.1	40.3	40.6	41.5	41.4	41.4	41.3	41.1
2002	40.8	40.9	41.0	41.6	41.6	41.7	40.9	41.3	42.0	41.7	42.2	41.6	41.4
2003	40.9	40.7	41.5	41.2	41.0	41.2	40.7	40.9	41.7	41.5	42.5	41.8	41.3
Trade, transportation, and utilities													
2001	34.5	34.7	34.7	35.2	35.3	35.7	35.7	35.6	35.7	35.4	35.4	35.8	35.3
2002	34.3	34.7	34.8	34.8	35.4	36.0	36.0	36.1	35.9	35.7	35.5	35.9	35.4
2003	34.2	34.7	35.0	35.4	35.7	35.7	36.0	35.6	35.3	35.5	35.7	35.5	35.4
Wholesale trade													
2001	39.7	39.8	39.7	39.8	39.7	40.8	39.9	40.6	40.4	40.2	40.4	40.0	40.1
2002	39.5	39.0	39.4	39.3	40.1	41.1	40.6	41.3	41.2	40.7	41.7	40.5	40.4
2003	39.8	39.3	40.0	39.7	40.2	40.8	40.0	40.2	40.8	40.1	41.8	40.1	40.3
Retail trade													
2001	31.5	31.3	31.6	32.2	32.6	32.6	33.2	32.7	32.7	32.5	32.7	33.4	32.4
2002	31.1	31.8	31.9	31.9	32.5	33.1	33.3	33.1	32.7	32.5	32.4	33.1	32.5
2003	30.9	31.5	32.0	32.4	32.8	32.8	33.1	32.6	32.0	32.4	32.4	32.9	32.3
Financial activities													
2001	35.2	34.7	34.4	35.0	34.5	35.0	35.0	34.3	34.2	33.9	33.5	34.3	34.5
2002	33.8	34.1	34.3	34.3	33.7	34.4	33.8	34.1	34.4	33.4	33.1	33.9	33.9
2003	33.3	33.9	33.6	32.5	33.3	33.9	32.7	33.1	32.8	33.3	33.8	32.7	33.3
Professional and business services													
2001	34.6	37.0	37.3	37.0	37.1	37.0	36.2	36.2	36.9	37.5	38.2	38.7	37.0
2002	36.5	36.9	37.8	38.1	37.4	38.7	38.4	39.0	39.0	39.2	38.1	37.7	38.1
2003	36.5	36.9	37.3	36.5	36.4	36.6	35.5	36.1	35.9	36.1	36.4	34.3	36.2
Leisure and hospitality													
2001	26.7	26.9	26.9	27.1	27.6	27.8	28.0	28.4	28.1	28.2	27.8	27.8	27.6
2002	27.8	27.5	27.4	27.3	27.8	28.5	28.3	28.3	28.0	28.1	27.2	26.9	27.8
2003	26.9	26.9	26.9	27.4	27.6	27.7	27.8	28.0	28.1	28.2	27.9	27.6	27.6
CHARLESTON													
Total private													
2001	33.8	34.5	34.7	34.9	35.0	34.9	34.9	34.6	34.8	34.7	34.4	34.8	34.7
2002	34.2	34.6	34.8	34.7	34.6	34.6	34.1	34.4	34.8	34.4	34.7	34.9	34.6
2003	34.4	34.5	34.8	35.0	34.8	34.9	34.2	34.6	34.4	34.3	34.4	34.4	34.5
Trade, transportation, and utilities													
2001	35.6	36.0	36.2	36.0	36.7	36.9	37.5	36.5	36.7	36.0	36.0	36.7	36.4
2002	35.4	35.8	36.3	36.4	36.9	36.3	36.5	36.2	36.4	35.8	35.7	36.5	36.2
2003	35.6	35.9	36.0	36.6	37.0	37.6	37.3	37.2	36.8	36.6	36.3	36.4	36.6
Retail trade													
2001	31.6	31.9	32.1	32.5	33.7	33.4	34.0	33.2	32.9	32.4	32.7	33.9	32.8
2002	32.1	32.6	32.8	33.4	34.0	33.1	32.8	32.7	32.4	32.4	32.4	33.2	32.8
2003	32.1	32.2	32.3	33.6	33.7	34.2	33.9	34.0	33.6	32.5	32.7	32.9	33.2
Financial activities													
2001	35.9	34.1	34.1	36.0	33.7	33.2	32.6	33.1	32.9	33.2	32.3	33.0	33.7
2002	32.0	33.0	32.8	33.2	32.1	32.7	31.5	32.8	33.9	33.5	34.7	35.1	33.2
2003	34.2	34.5	34.7	34.6	35.0	35.0	33.1	34.9	34.7	35.2	34.9	35.0	34.7
Professional and business services													
2001	34.1	39.3	39.6	39.5	39.7	39.3	38.9	37.9	39.9	39.5	39.3	39.7	38.9
2002	38.1	38.8	39.4	39.7	39.9	39.7	38.8	40.4	40.1	39.8	39.4	39.1	39.4
2003	38.7	38.9	39.3	39.5	38.8	38.1	37.3	37.3	36.6	36.2	36.1	34.8	37.6

Average Weekly Hours by Industry: West Virginia—*Continued*

(Not seasonally adjusted.)

Industry	January	February	March	April	May	June	July	August	September	October	November	December	Annual Average
HUNTINGTON-ASHLAND													
Total private													
2001	34.0	34.2	34.4	34.7	34.5	34.8	35.1	34.9	34.7	34.6	34.7	35.1	34.7
2002	34.9	35.0	34.9	35.0	35.2	35.1	35.0	35.3	35.2	35.5	35.1	35.0	35.1
2003	34.4	34.5	34.8	35.0	34.9	34.9	34.6	34.9	34.2	34.8	35.0	35.1	34.7
Manufacturing													
2001	41.8	41.3	42.4	42.5	42.5	43.5	43.8	43.8	43.4	43.2	43.7	43.3	43.0
2002	41.2	41.8	42.0	42.2	42.9	42.8	43.1	43.2	42.9	43.4	43.7	43.0	42.7
2003	41.0	41.3	41.6	41.4	42.1	42.2	42.1	42.7	41.0	42.8	43.9	42.9	42.1
Trade, transportation, and utilities													
2001	34.9	34.9	34.4	34.9	35.2	36.0	36.0	35.8	36.0	35.4	35.1	35.8	35.4
2002	34.6	34.9	34.5	35.0	34.8	34.6	35.3	35.1	35.0	35.2	34.6	35.1	34.9
2003	34.7	35.3	35.4	35.3	35.5	35.2	35.0	34.7	33.5	35.0	34.9	35.5	35.0
Retail trade													
2001	32.8	32.6	32.3	33.3	33.6	34.4	35.0	34.6	35.1	34.2	33.8	34.9	33.9
2002	33.3	34.1	33.5	34.1	34.1	33.8	34.7	34.5	34.2	34.0	33.9	34.5	34.1
2003	33.4	34.2	34.3	34.0	34.4	34.4	34.2	33.9	32.6	33.9	34.1	34.9	34.0
PARKERSBURG-MARIETTA													
Total private													
2001	33.7	33.5	33.8	33.7	34.1	34.1	34.4	34.3	34.7	34.5	34.5	34.2	34.2
2002	33.0	32.9	33.2	33.4	33.3	33.6	34.0	34.1	33.9	33.9	33.9	34.0	33.6
2003	33.1	33.2	33.4	33.5	33.6	33.7	34.2	34.2	34.3	34.3	34.1	35.2	33.9
Professional and business services													
2001	30.5	30.6	30.0	29.2	30.0	30.7	30.3	30.4	30.7	31.5	30.5	29.6	30.2
2002	28.2	29.0	29.8	29.5	29.1	28.2	28.9	29.4	28.2	30.0	28.3	29.3	29.0
2003	29.9	30.8	31.7	30.2	31.2	33.9	34.1	33.7	33.2	32.0	30.1	33.5	32.0
WHEELING													
Total private													
2001	32.7	32.7	33.0	32.8	33.1	32.7	33.0	32.8	32.9	32.9	33.1	33.0	32.9
2002	31.1	31.8	32.3	31.9	31.9	32.5	31.7	31.9	32.3	31.5	31.8	32.0	31.9
2003	30.9	31.2	31.6	31.2	31.6	32.3	32.1	32.2	31.8	31.7	31.1	32.0	31.7
Retail trade													
2001	25.6	24.7	25.2	26.2	27.7	26.7	27.0	27.0	27.2	26.4	26.6	27.7	26.5
2002	25.0	25.9	27.3	27.4	27.4	28.0	27.4	27.3	26.7	26.0	26.5	28.3	26.9
2003	25.6	25.5	26.6	26.4	27.3	28.2	28.4	28.3	27.0	27.0	26.6	28.7	27.2
Professional and business services													
2001	36.0	36.4	35.9	35.2	33.8	32.4	32.5	31.6	33.4	32.8	33.0	33.5	33.9
2002	31.9	31.3	32.0	31.9	30.7	32.9	32.4	31.6	32.4	32.6	32.5	32.6	32.0
2003	32.0	32.4	33.5	32.3	30.7	31.6	30.2	31.5	31.8	30.5	31.9	30.9	31.5

Average Hourly Earnings by Industry: West Virginia

(Dollars, not seasonally adjusted.)

Industry	January	February	March	April	May	June	July	August	September	October	November	December	Annual Average
STATEWIDE													
Total private													
2001	11.80	11.80	11.86	11.92	11.87	11.90	11.96	11.96	12.05	12.07	12.09	12.10	11.95
2002	12.20	12.19	12.19	12.17	12.10	12.14	12.12	12.15	12.25	12.27	12.34	12.37	12.21
2003	12.45	12.45	12.46	12.49	12.46	12.52	12.54	12.59	12.74	12.68	12.78	12.75	12.58
Natural resources and mining													
2001	17.82	18.08	18.06	17.93	18.15	18.09	18.12	18.06	18.26	18.20	18.23	18.37	18.12
2002	18.30	18.43	18.28	18.05	18.09	18.06	18.09	18.17	18.19	18.21	18.30	18.47	18.22
2003	18.16	18.02	18.28	18.18	18.17	18.09	18.10	18.15	18.03	17.76	17.69	18.28	18.08
Construction													
2001	15.61	15.44	15.63	15.88	15.83	15.72	15.75	15.88	15.76	15.85	15.70	15.69	15.74
2002	15.66	15.78	15.77	15.83	15.67	15.71	15.85	15.77	15.81	15.68	15.86	15.82	15.77
2003	15.83	15.79	15.71	15.82	16.01	16.08	16.30	16.39	16.59	16.50	16.63	16.78	16.23
Manufacturing													
2001	14.66	14.58	14.51	14.84	14.57	14.84	14.80	14.86	14.90	14.91	15.03	15.10	14.80
2002	15.17	15.04	15.05	15.23	15.35	15.40	15.47	15.35	15.49	15.55	15.83	15.93	15.40
2003	16.07	15.93	16.02	16.19	15.96	16.12	16.06	16.09	16.02	15.99	16.13	16.03	16.05
Trade, transportation, and utilities													
2001	10.56	10.69	10.66	10.66	10.55	10.49	10.57	10.58	10.70	10.65	10.68	10.64	10.62
2002	10.84	10.87	10.98	10.81	10.79	10.83	10.82	10.85	10.89	10.86	10.71	10.76	10.83
2003	10.85	11.03	11.07	11.08	11.09	11.22	11.24	11.33	11.45	11.46	11.41	11.24	11.21
Wholesale trade													
2001	13.61	13.79	13.87	13.56	13.39	13.27	13.48	13.33	13.64	13.50	13.61	13.68	13.56
2002	13.68	13.90	13.94	13.85	13.83	13.90	13.84	13.86	13.73	13.98	13.80	13.79	13.84
2003	13.89	14.04	14.09	14.12	14.27	14.39	14.50	14.70	14.92	14.80	14.78	14.92	14.46
Retail trade													
2001	8.37	8.46	8.45	8.49	8.42	8.37	8.51	8.52	8.58	8.54	8.62	8.66	8.50
2002	8.69	8.68	8.80	8.60	8.61	8.70	8.73	8.82	8.93	8.81	8.71	8.83	8.74
2003	8.82	8.98	9.01	8.93	8.92	9.06	9.01	8.99	8.98	9.07	9.02	8.93	8.98
Financial activities													
2001	9.78	9.91	9.93	9.91	9.95	9.87	9.92	9.83	9.98	10.04	10.19	10.19	9.96
2002	10.21	10.23	10.13	10.15	10.07	10.02	10.06	10.08	10.25	10.41	10.62	10.50	10.23
2003	10.59	10.62	10.42	10.63	10.63	10.49	10.68	10.76	10.85	11.01	11.17	11.04	10.74
Professional and business services													
2001	11.29	11.35	11.51	11.59	11.55	11.76	12.03	11.81	12.04	11.89	11.99	12.00	11.74
2002	12.26	12.36	12.39	12.32	12.11	12.40	12.19	12.08	12.39	12.49	12.62	12.55	12.35
2003	12.88	12.89	12.67	12.98	12.94	12.89	12.84	12.61	12.85	12.68	12.75	12.97	12.83
Leisure and hospitality													
2001	6.98	6.89	6.89	6.85	6.87	6.90	6.92	6.85	6.80	6.83	6.82	6.82	6.87
2002	7.02	6.96	6.99	7.04	7.06	7.01	7.07	7.18	7.12	7.21	7.07	7.14	7.07
2003	6.87	6.85	6.91	6.84	6.89	6.95	6.92	6.97	6.98	6.98	6.89	6.95	6.92
CHARLESTON													
Total private													
2001	13.31	13.25	13.29	13.42	13.43	13.53	13.63	13.75	13.80	13.71	13.66	13.65	13.54
2002	13.70	13.71	13.65	13.71	13.63	13.73	13.74	13.77	13.90	13.76	13.85	13.76	13.74
2003	13.75	13.76	13.70	13.78	13.81	13.93	14.03	14.11	14.11	14.06	14.29	14.19	13.96
Trade, transportation, and utilities													
2001	12.83	12.83	12.92	12.92	12.94	12.91	12.90	13.00	13.19	13.06	12.98	12.83	12.94
2002	13.04	13.01	13.19	13.04	13.01	13.08	13.01	13.18	13.35	13.25	13.01	12.95	13.09
2003	12.96	13.06	13.01	12.80	12.89	12.81	12.80	12.95	12.67	12.93	12.89	12.84	12.88
Retail trade													
2001	10.15	10.13	10.10	10.04	9.94	10.07	10.06	10.17	10.29	10.23	10.19	10.01	10.11
2002	10.02	9.94	10.11	10.12	10.04	10.15	10.13	10.31	10.54	10.36	10.23	10.40	10.20
2003	10.24	10.42	10.33	10.11	10.33	10.13	10.26	10.19	10.01	10.18	10.09	10.21	10.21
Financial activities													
2001	10.53	10.66	10.65	10.78	11.22	11.29	11.38	11.33	11.37	11.46	11.49	11.59	11.13
2002	11.44	11.59	11.47	11.52	11.23	11.50	11.67	11.59	11.63	11.88	12.02	11.54	11.59
2003	11.72	11.78	11.43	11.38	11.28	11.37	11.71	11.82	11.90	11.77	12.12	12.38	11.73
Professional and business services													
2001	10.62	10.85	10.92	11.12	10.89	11.01	11.39	11.31	11.27	11.10	11.12	11.25	11.08
2002	11.37	11.38	11.16	11.39	11.16	11.26	11.01	10.71	10.96	10.71	11.07	10.86	11.09
2003	11.05	11.37	11.42	11.68	11.84	12.35	12.69	12.69	12.92	12.73	13.13	13.38	12.24

Average Hourly Earnings by Industry: West Virginia—*Continued*

(Dollars, not seasonally adjusted.)

Industry	January	February	March	April	May	June	July	August	September	October	November	December	Annual Average
HUNTINGTON-ASHLAND													
Total private													
2001	12.47	12.32	12.37	12.46	12.36	12.45	12.39	12.42	12.49	12.56	12.61	12.61	12.46
2002	12.67	12.63	12.65	12.63	12.55	12.66	12.57	12.53	12.58	12.58	12.62	12.48	12.60
2003	12.59	12.70	12.74	12.70	12.75	12.74	12.70	12.59	12.68	12.64	12.59	12.42	12.65
Manufacturing													
2001	15.07	14.83	14.73	14.85	14.80	14.95	14.88	15.02	15.12	15.21	15.10	15.18	14.98
2002	15.29	15.31	15.63	15.61	15.75	15.80	15.51	15.67	15.62	15.57	15.65	15.79	15.60
2003	15.66	15.50	15.75	15.69	15.71	15.43	15.35	15.50	15.11	15.26	15.33	15.42	15.48
Trade, transportation, and utilities													
2001	10.18	10.38	10.22	10.24	10.25	10.17	10.11	10.21	10.12	10.33	10.39	10.45	10.26
2002	10.18	10.16	10.21	10.07	10.19	10.21	10.20	10.21	10.08	10.04	9.90	9.83	10.11
2003	10.08	10.30	10.44	10.46	10.40	10.61	10.49	10.36	10.64	10.45	10.25	9.98	10.37
Retail trade													
2001	8.76	8.91	8.76	8.81	8.78	8.65	8.66	8.64	8.55	8.71	8.87	8.95	8.75
2002	9.04	8.96	9.06	9.00	9.06	9.10	9.16	9.20	9.10	9.06	8.96	8.88	9.05
2003	8.87	9.16	9.42	9.43	9.16	9.50	9.34	9.20	9.41	9.31	9.09	8.93	9.23
PARKERSBURG-MARIETTA													
Total private													
2001	12.29	12.38	12.30	12.27	12.21	12.29	12.35	12.31	12.32	12.39	12.42	12.38	12.33
2002	13.04	13.11	13.08	13.17	13.21	13.33	13.22	13.35	13.29	13.04	13.14	13.20	13.18
2003	13.29	13.44	13.17	13.14	13.16	13.32	13.22	13.33	13.33	13.14	13.30	13.14	13.25
Professional and business services													
2001	7.53	7.50	7.39	7.67	7.73	7.55	7.49	7.83	7.66	7.85	7.97	8.17	7.69
2002	7.83	7.71	7.97	8.01	7.93	8.04	7.79	7.76	7.90	7.97	8.09	8.49	7.96
2003	8.67	8.69	8.73	8.93	8.90	9.75	9.89	9.54	9.99	10.10	10.76	10.23	9.56
WHEELING													
Total private													
2001	11.41	11.63	11.60	11.60	11.64	11.65	11.70	11.77	11.61	11.68	11.65	11.61	11.63
2002	11.34	11.39	11.18	11.22	11.34	11.41	11.26	11.33	11.43	11.23	11.30	11.54	11.33
2003	11.73	11.84	11.89	11.97	11.98	12.14	12.18	12.21	12.42	12.21	12.33	12.27	12.10
Retail trade													
2001	8.31	8.29	8.39	8.22	8.32	8.30	8.23	8.42	8.25	8.38	8.28	8.28	8.31
2002	8.37	8.51	8.41	8.18	8.29	8.23	8.23	8.25	8.51	8.39	8.25	8.25	8.32
2003	8.38	8.78	8.69	8.90	8.97	9.11	9.06	9.04	9.12	8.93	8.85	8.61	8.87
Professional and business services													
2001	10.85	11.44	11.04	10.96	10.98	11.22	11.31	11.43	11.42	11.26	11.00	10.98	11.15
2002	11.37	11.26	10.93	11.17	11.03	11.28	10.91	11.25	11.29	10.99	10.73	11.03	11.10
2003	11.20	11.24	10.95	10.81	10.69	10.57	10.57	10.06	9.74	9.68	9.31	9.08	10.33

Average Weekly Earnings by Industry: West Virginia

(Dollars, not seasonally adjusted.)

Industry	January	February	March	April	May	June	July	August	September	October	November	December	Annual Average
STATEWIDE													
Total private													
2001	397.66	401.20	403.24	408.86	409.52	410.55	410.23	411.42	416.93	416.42	417.11	419.87	409.89
2002	413.58	414.46	415.68	416.21	413.82	422.47	416.93	421.61	426.30	425.77	426.96	429.24	420.02
2003	420.81	423.30	426.13	425.91	427.38	430.69	427.61	431.84	436.98	434.92	440.91	434.78	430.24
Natural resources and mining													
2001	780.52	795.52	798.25	814.02	840.35	833.95	809.96	827.15	823.53	822.64	809.41	832.16	815.40
2002	830.82	844.09	822.60	808.64	806.81	830.76	806.81	841.27	844.02	837.66	841.80	868.09	832.65
2003	846.26	845.14	850.02	839.92	841.27	833.95	803.64	851.24	845.61	832.94	819.05	851.85	838.91
Construction													
2001	590.06	548.12	581.44	592.32	609.46	600.50	607.95	614.56	616.22	613.40	610.73	605.63	601.27
2002	580.99	590.17	592.95	606.29	590.76	598.55	613.40	621.34	624.50	609.95	613.78	609.07	605.57
2003	599.96	584.23	601.69	593.25	629.19	631.94	643.85	660.52	671.90	641.85	640.26	651.06	631.35
Manufacturing													
2001	599.59	599.24	599.26	612.89	603.20	609.92	596.44	603.32	618.35	617.27	622.24	623.63	608.28
2002	618.94	615.14	617.05	633.57	638.56	642.18	632.72	633.96	650.58	648.44	668.03	662.69	637.56
2003	657.26	648.35	664.83	667.03	654.36	664.14	653.64	658.08	668.03	663.59	685.53	670.05	662.87
Trade, transportation, and utilities													
2001	364.32	370.94	369.90	375.23	372.42	374.49	377.35	376.65	381.99	377.01	378.07	380.91	374.89
2002	371.81	377.19	382.10	376.19	381.97	389.88	389.52	391.69	390.95	387.70	380.21	386.28	383.38
2003	371.07	382.74	387.45	392.23	395.91	400.55	404.64	403.35	404.19	406.83	407.34	399.02	396.83
Wholesale trade													
2001	540.32	548.84	550.64	539.69	531.58	541.42	537.85	541.20	551.06	542.70	549.84	547.20	543.76
2002	540.36	542.10	549.24	544.31	554.58	571.29	561.90	572.42	565.68	568.99	575.46	558.50	559.14
2003	552.82	551.77	563.60	560.56	573.65	587.11	580.00	590.94	608.74	593.48	617.80	598.29	582.74
Retail trade													
2001	263.66	264.80	267.02	273.38	274.49	272.86	282.53	278.60	280.57	277.55	281.87	289.24	275.40
2002	270.26	276.02	280.72	274.34	279.83	287.97	290.71	291.94	292.01	286.33	282.20	292.27	284.05
2003	272.54	282.87	288.32	289.33	292.58	297.17	298.23	293.07	287.36	293.87	292.25	293.80	290.05
Financial activities													
2001	344.26	343.88	341.59	346.85	343.28	345.45	347.20	337.17	341.32	340.36	341.37	349.52	343.62
2002	345.10	348.84	347.46	348.15	339.36	344.69	340.03	343.73	352.60	347.69	351.52	355.95	346.80
2003	352.65	360.02	350.11	345.48	353.98	355.61	349.24	356.16	355.88	366.63	377.55	361.01	357.64
Professional and business services													
2001	390.63	419.95	429.32	428.83	428.51	435.12	435.49	427.52	444.28	445.88	458.02	464.40	434.38
2002	447.49	456.08	468.34	469.39	452.91	479.88	468.10	471.12	483.21	489.61	480.82	473.14	470.54
2003	470.12	475.64	472.59	473.77	471.02	471.77	455.82	455.22	461.32	457.75	464.10	444.87	464.45
Lesiure and hospitality													
2001	186.37	185.34	185.34	185.64	189.61	191.82	193.76	194.54	191.08	192.61	189.60	189.60	189.61
2002	195.16	191.40	191.53	192.19	196.27	199.79	200.08	203.19	199.36	202.60	192.30	192.07	196.55
2003	184.80	184.27	185.88	187.42	190.16	192.52	192.38	195.16	196.14	196.84	192.23	191.82	190.99
CHARLESTON													
Total private													
2001	449.88	457.13	461.16	468.36	470.05	472.20	475.69	475.75	480.24	475.74	469.90	475.02	469.84
2002	468.54	474.37	475.02	475.74	471.60	475.06	468.53	473.69	483.72	473.34	480.60	480.22	475.40
2003	473.00	474.72	476.76	482.30	480.59	486.16	479.83	488.21	485.38	482.26	491.58	488.14	481.62
Trade, transportation, and utilities													
2001	456.75	461.88	467.70	465.12	474.90	476.38	483.75	474.50	484.07	470.16	467.28	470.86	471.02
2002	461.62	465.76	478.80	474.66	480.07	474.80	474.87	477.12	485.94	474.35	464.46	472.68	473.86
2003	461.38	468.85	468.36	468.48	476.93	481.66	477.44	481.74	466.26	473.24	467.91	467.38	471.41
Retail trade													
2001	320.74	323.15	324.21	326.30	334.98	336.34	342.04	337.64	338.54	331.45	333.21	339.34	331.61
2002	321.64	324.04	331.61	338.01	341.36	335.97	332.26	337.14	341.50	335.66	331.45	345.28	334.56
2003	328.70	335.52	333.66	339.70	348.12	346.45	347.81	346.46	336.34	330.85	329.94	335.91	338.97
Financial activities													
2001	378.03	363.51	363.17	388.08	378.11	374.83	370.99	375.02	374.07	380.47	371.13	382.47	375.08
2002	366.08	382.47	376.22	382.46	360.48	376.05	367.61	380.15	394.26	397.98	417.09	405.05	384.79
2003	400.82	406.41	396.62	393.75	394.80	397.95	387.60	412.52	412.93	414.30	422.99	433.30	407.03
Professional and business services													
2001	362.14	426.41	432.43	439.24	432.33	432.69	443.07	428.65	449.67	438.45	437.02	446.63	431.01
2002	433.20	441.54	439.70	452.18	445.28	447.02	427.19	432.68	439.50	426.26	436.16	424.63	436.95
2003	427.64	442.29	448.81	461.36	459.39	470.54	473.34	473.34	472.87	460.83	473.99	465.62	460.22

Average Weekly Earnings by Industry: West Virginia—*Continued*

(Dollars, not seasonally adjusted.)

Industry	January	February	March	April	May	June	July	August	September	October	November	December	Annual Average
HUNTINGTON-ASHLAND													
Total private													
2001	423.98	421.34	425.53	432.36	426.42	433.26	434.89	433.46	433.40	434.58	437.57	442.61	432.36
2002	442.18	442.05	441.49	442.05	441.76	444.37	439.95	442.31	442.82	446.59	442.96	436.80	442.26
2003	433.10	438.15	443.35	444.50	444.98	444.63	439.42	439.39	433.66	439.87	440.65	435.94	438.96
Manufacturing													
2001	629.93	612.48	624.55	631.13	629.00	650.33	651.74	657.88	656.21	657.07	659.87	657.29	644.14
2002	629.95	639.96	656.46	658.74	675.68	676.24	668.48	676.94	670.10	675.74	683.91	678.97	666.12
2003	642.06	640.15	655.20	649.57	661.39	651.15	646.24	661.85	619.51	653.13	672.99	661.52	651.71
Trade, transportation, and utilities													
2001	355.28	362.26	351.57	357.38	360.80	366.12	363.96	365.52	364.32	365.68	364.69	374.11	363.20
2002	352.23	354.58	352.25	352.45	354.61	353.27	360.06	358.37	352.80	353.41	342.54	345.03	352.84
2003	349.78	363.59	369.58	369.24	369.20	373.47	367.15	359.49	356.44	365.75	357.73	354.29	362.95
Retail trade													
2001	287.33	290.47	282.95	293.37	295.01	297.56	303.10	298.94	300.11	297.88	299.81	312.36	296.63
2002	301.03	305.54	303.51	306.90	308.95	307.58	317.85	317.40	311.22	308.04	303.74	306.36	308.61
2003	296.26	313.27	323.11	320.62	315.10	326.80	319.43	311.88	306.77	315.61	309.97	311.66	313.82
PARKERSBURG-MARIETTA													
Total private													
2001	414.17	414.73	415.74	413.50	416.36	419.09	424.84	422.23	427.50	427.46	428.49	423.40	421.69
2002	430.32	431.32	434.26	439.88	439.89	447.89	449.48	455.24	450.53	442.06	445.45	448.80	442.85
2003	439.90	446.21	439.88	440.19	442.18	448.88	452.12	455.89	457.22	450.70	453.53	462.53	449.18
Professional and business services													
2001	229.67	229.50	221.70	223.96	231.90	231.79	226.95	238.03	235.16	247.28	243.09	241.83	232.24
2002	220.81	223.59	237.51	236.30	230.76	226.73	225.13	228.14	222.78	239.10	228.95	248.76	230.84
2003	259.23	267.65	276.74	269.69	277.68	330.53	337.25	321.50	331.67	323.20	323.88	342.71	305.92
WHEELING													
Total private													
2001	373.11	380.30	382.80	380.48	385.28	380.96	386.10	386.06	381.97	384.27	385.62	383.13	382.63
2002	352.67	362.20	361.11	357.92	361.75	370.83	356.94	361.43	369.19	353.75	359.34	369.28	361.43
2003	362.46	369.41	375.72	373.46	378.57	392.12	390.98	393.16	394.96	387.06	383.46	392.64	383.57
Retail trade													
2001	212.74	204.76	211.43	215.36	230.46	221.61	222.21	227.34	224.40	221.23	220.25	229.36	220.22
2002	209.25	220.41	229.59	224.13	227.15	230.44	225.50	225.23	227.22	218.14	218.63	233.48	223.81
2003	214.53	223.89	231.15	234.96	244.88	256.90	257.30	255.83	246.24	241.11	235.41	247.11	241.26
Professional and business services													
2001	390.60	416.42	396.34	385.79	371.12	363.53	367.58	361.19	381.43	369.33	363.00	367.83	377.99
2002	362.70	352.44	349.76	356.32	338.62	371.11	353.48	355.50	365.80	358.27	348.73	359.58	355.20
2003	358.40	364.18	366.83	349.16	328.18	334.01	319.21	316.89	309.73	295.24	296.99	280.57	325.40

WISCONSIN AT A GLANCE

(Population and total nonfarm employment numbers in thousands)

Population, Census 2000:	5,363.7
Total nonfarm employment, 2003:	2,778.9
Change in total nonfarm employment	
(Number)	
1990–2003:	487.4
1990–2001:	522.4
2001–2003:	-35.0
(Compound annual rate of change)	
1990–2003:	1.5%
1990–2001:	1.9%
2001–2003:	-0.6%
Unemployment rate	
1990:	4.3%
2001:	4.4%
2003:	5.6%

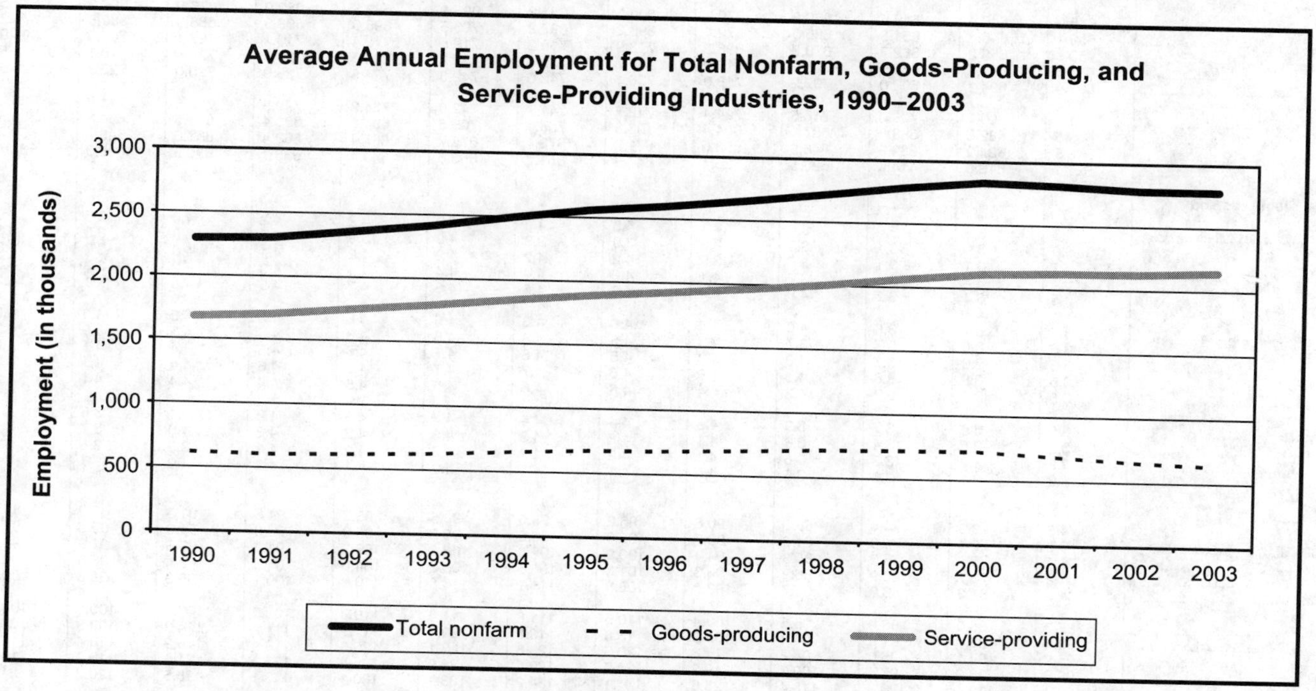

Following the nationwide pattern, total nonfarm payroll employment recovered smoothly in the mid and late 1990s from the earlier recession, but declined again starting in 2001. This was largely attributable to a decline in the goods-producing sector, where the number of jobs fell substantially. Over 87,000 jobs were eliminated in manufacturing from 2000 to 2003. Employment in the service-providing sector continued to increase through the 2001 recession, although at a much slower rate.

Employment by Industry: Wisconsin

(Numbers in thousands. Not seasonally adjusted.)

Industry	January	February	March	April	May	June	July	August	September	October	November	December	Annual Average
STATEWIDE													
Total nonfarm													
1990	2206.7	2220.8	2236.0	2268.6	2298.0	2333.7	2309.7	2315.8	2331.7	2329.5	2329.5	2317.9	2291.5
1991	2232.9	2237.6	2251.3	2275.5	2303.8	2335.5	2313.5	2323.2	2333.3	2341.8	2341.1	2335.1	2302.1
1992	2269.0	2277.3	2287.9	2335.2	2366.4	2392.8	2374.9	2380.1	2398.3	2404.8	2406.3	2401.6	2357.9
1993	2324.9	2341.8	2355.4	2377.4	2416.6	2443.4	2424.8	2431.5	2450.4	2461.3	2461.4	2463.2	2412.7
1994	2383.8	2397.7	2421.7	2456.1	2487.2	2523.2	2512.9	2512.5	2543.7	2541.1	2556.0	2553.0	2490.7
1995	2476.9	2488.3	2512.9	2533.6	2559.6	2601.1	2571.5	2579.6	2596.5	2594.6	2594.1	2594.3	2558.6
1996	2523.8	2520.0	2545.7	2564.0	2604.7	2638.6	2611.4	2627.4	2635.7	2642.5	2648.5	2644.4	2600.6
1997	2559.9	2569.5	2584.6	2617.7	2659.6	2696.1	2671.4	2679.6	2695.6	2708.4	2711.7	2715.3	2655.8
1998	2625.2	2639.2	2651.8	2691.8	2726.7	2760.1	2731.5	2738.5	2746.5	2760.8	2768.4	2775.8	2718.0
1999	2686.4	2699.9	2718.3	2761.0	2788.1	2827.2	2808.5	2811.1	2815.5	2827.1	2829.2	2835.6	2784.0
2000	2748.9	2759.7	2785.1	2820.3	2846.9	2885.5	2852.5	2858.5	2859.3	2864.1	2869.9	2854.7	2833.8
2001	2770.7	2776.5	2788.9	2813.6	2840.1	2861.6	2829.3	2829.1	2825.0	2820.8	2812.6	2798.4	2813.9
2002	2719.4	2717.6	2735.9	2766.1	2799.4	2823.1	2795.4	2800.5	2798.5	2814.2	2816.5	2801.8	2782.4
2003	2710.5	2718.4	2726.6	2761.6	2796.0	2823.8	2797.6	2804.8	2798.3	2809.9	2805.0	2793.9	2778.9
Total private													
1990	1877.1	1876.0	1888.5	1913.4	1945.5	1988.9	1989.4	2001.1	1987.8	1978.2	1972.6	1964.8	1948.6
1991	1897.1	1885.6	1897.6	1917.3	1949.9	1988.8	1990.9	2004.0	1989.3	1987.1	1983.7	1976.1	1955.6
1992	1921.9	1916.7	1926.5	1967.3	2003.1	2037.2	2042.6	2050.6	2039.4	2040.3	2033.7	2033.1	2001.0
1993	1971.8	1973.0	1987.3	2007.5	2046.1	2082.0	2087.9	2097.3	2090.5	2091.4	2089.2	2089.8	2051.2
1994	2026.2	2026.5	2047.1	2077.2	2111.9	2156.2	2168.3	2176.0	2177.1	2167.8	2173.6	2175.7	2123.6
1995	2102.4	2103.8	2126.0	2142.1	2172.9	2219.6	2215.9	2231.2	2221.5	2209.5	2206.8	2207.4	2179.9
1996	2144.1	2135.5	2156.0	2175.7	2215.7	2252.5	2251.4	2270.2	2252.1	2251.4	2250.0	2250.6	2217.1
1997	2178.2	2177.3	2191.0	2222.0	2264.8	2307.2	2311.1	2324.2	2312.8	2312.3	2311.1	2317.5	2269.1
1998	2239.1	2240.8	2253.2	2287.9	2324.5	2365.6	2363.5	2375.0	2356.0	2360.4	2361.2	2370.6	2324.8
1999	2291.4	2296.4	2314.3	2352.2	2379.2	2426.7	2434.0	2439.8	2421.7	2420.7	2418.1	2427.2	2385.1
2000	2349.3	2350.9	2373.0	2401.6	2429.5	2472.2	2471.4	2480.1	2461.6	2454.1	2452.2	2442.6	2428.2
2001	2368.4	2358.8	2367.9	2388.5	2415.6	2445.5	2441.9	2445.1	2413.4	2396.8	2386.0	2374.1	2400.2
2002	2310.8	2296.1	2309.7	2337.9	2373.3	2409.8	2411.7	2420.4	2394.5	2387.5	2383.7	2375.6	2367.6
2003	2306.2	2293.5	2300.4	2333.0	2371.6	2404.5	2415.6	2426.1	2401.2	2391.6	2385.1	2376.0	2367.1
Goods-producing													
1990	591.5	590.8	594.6	603.4	614.8	630.5	633.0	638.0	631.0	625.8	617.3	606.7	614.8
1991	582.8	576.0	578.8	589.1	600.9	618.2	622.6	627.3	622.1	617.0	609.7	600.4	603.7
1992	584.8	580.8	583.6	597.2	610.3	625.9	633.6	635.9	630.7	628.7	622.8	615.9	612.5
1993	598.1	597.9	602.4	609.1	623.0	637.5	642.1	645.0	641.5	641.5	636.9	631.3	625.5
1994	610.9	608.4	617.3	633.0	645.9	666.0	672.6	675.4	674.9	671.0	670.0	664.0	650.8
1995	648.0	646.4	649.5	660.8	670.5	690.3	691.2	695.8	689.5	682.0	676.9	669.3	672.5
1996	650.1	645.8	651.5	665.5	679.4	696.2	697.2	705.5	696.9	693.3	688.6	680.5	679.2
1997	659.3	658.2	662.7	678.9	696.5	713.9	716.2	719.5	713.4	710.1	707.1	703.0	694.9
1998	683.6	682.7	685.9	703.2	715.8	731.7	731.3	737.2	727.9	723.9	720.4	718.1	713.5
1999	693.4	694.1	699.0	709.2	718.0	736.1	742.0	742.6	734.6	728.9	725.0	723.3	720.5
2000	701.3	700.7	708.0	716.5	724.4	742.7	741.7	742.5	734.2	729.5	722.6	711.8	723.0
2001	689.5	682.5	683.2	687.1	694.4	706.8	706.1	705.6	694.6	685.4	674.5	664.8	689.5
2002	643.5	634.9	638.6	646.8	658.0	671.8	673.1	675.7	667.4	662.4	657.0	645.7	656.2
2003	621.1	613.0	614.0	623.5	636.4	647.2	651.7	653.6	643.4	638.1	635.5	626.9	633.7
Natural resources and mining													
1990	3.5	3.5	3.6	3.8	4.1	4.3	4.2	4.2	4.2	4.2	4.0	3.5	3.9
1991	3.0	3.0	3.1	3.3	3.8	3.9	3.9	4.0	3.9	3.9	3.6	3.3	3.6
1992	3.1	3.1	3.1	3.5	3.9	4.2	4.2	4.2	4.2	4.1	4.0	3.7	3.8
1993	3.4	3.4	3.5	3.7	4.1	4.3	4.4	4.4	4.4	4.3	4.2	3.9	4.0
1994	3.5	3.4	3.7	4.0	4.4	4.6	4.6	4.6	4.7	4.6	4.5	4.1	4.2
1995	3.8	3.7	3.8	4.0	4.4	4.6	4.6	4.6	4.6	4.5	4.3	4.0	4.2
1996	3.6	3.6	3.7	3.7	4.3	4.5	4.6	4.6	4.6	4.6	4.3	3.9	4.2
1997	3.5	3.6	3.7	3.8	4.3	4.5	4.6	4.7	4.6	4.5	4.4	4.1	4.2
1998	3.6	3.8	3.6	4.1	4.5	4.6	4.7	4.7	4.7	4.6	4.4	4.1	4.3
1999	3.5	3.7	3.7	4.2	4.4	4.6	4.6	4.5	4.5	4.4	4.4	4.1	4.2
2000	3.5	3.6	3.7	3.9	4.3	4.4	4.4	4.4	4.3	4.2	4.1	3.6	4.0
2001	3.2	3.3	3.4	3.6	4.1	4.3	4.3	4.3	4.2	4.2	4.0	3.7	3.9
2002	3.2	3.2	3.3	3.6	4.1	4.2	4.2	4.2	4.2	4.1	3.9	3.6	3.8
2003	3.2	3.1	3.2	3.5	4.0	4.1	4.1	4.2	4.1	4.2	4.0	3.7	3.8
Construction													
1990	74.3	72.9	74.4	83.0	90.6	96.2	98.0	98.5	95.7	94.5	91.5	85.0	87.9
1991	73.9	72.1	74.0	81.6	89.7	95.0	96.8	98.2	95.9	96.0	91.9	85.6	87.6
1992	77.7	75.7	76.3	85.3	94.4	100.2	102.0	102.3	99.7	101.0	97.3	91.6	92.0
1993	81.2	79.7	80.9	86.2	96.3	101.3	105.5	105.2	104.0	105.3	102.4	96.5	95.4
1994	84.3	81.3	86.0	94.7	103.0	108.8	111.1	110.8	110.3	109.1	106.3	99.6	100.4
1995	87.7	85.0	88.8	95.5	103.4	110.5	111.8	111.4	110.3	109.2	106.1	100.1	101.7
1996	90.6	88.0	91.5	98.4	108.8	115.6	118.8	120.1	117.9	117.2	114.3	107.8	107.4
1997	95.9	94.1	96.0	104.2	114.3	120.5	123.6	123.1	120.6	119.4	116.2	110.4	111.5
1998	96.8	96.0	97.4	109.7	119.2	124.7	129.6	128.9	125.8	124.3	121.6	118.2	116.0
1999	103.4	103.4	106.9	116.4	123.6	131.1	134.2	133.1	130.1	129.1	126.5	120.7	121.5
2000	107.6	106.1	111.2	121.3	128.7	135.3	137.3	137.5	133.6	131.7	127.7	119.9	124.8
2001	109.3	108.0	110.1	118.1	128.0	134.6	138.1	138.8	134.8	133.3	129.0	122.3	125.4
2002	108.7	105.7	108.0	117.9	127.2	133.4	136.7	136.7	133.1	132.0	129.2	120.9	124.1
2003	108.6	105.0	106.6	116.1	127.8	133.5	135.9	135.7	132.1	130.5	128.6	121.8	123.5

Employment by Industry: Wisconsin—*Continued*

(Numbers in thousands. Not seasonally adjusted.)

Industry	January	February	March	April	May	June	July	August	September	October	November	December	Annual Average
STATEWIDE—*Continued*													
Manufacturing													
1990	513.7	514.4	516.6	516.6	520.1	530.0	530.8	535.3	531.1	527.1	521.8	518.2	523.0
1991	505.9	500.9	501.7	504.2	507.4	519.3	521.9	525.1	522.3	517.1	514.2	511.5	512.6
1992	504.0	502.0	504.2	508.4	512.0	521.5	527.4	529.4	526.8	523.6	521.5	520.6	516.8
1993	513.5	514.8	518.0	519.2	522.6	531.9	532.2	535.4	533.1	531.9	530.3	530.9	526.2
1994	523.1	523.7	527.6	534.3	538.5	552.6	556.9	560.0	559.9	557.3	559.2	560.3	546.1
1995	556.5	557.7	556.9	561.3	562.7	575.2	574.8	579.8	574.6	568.3	566.5	565.2	566.6
1996	555.9	554.2	556.3	563.4	566.3	576.1	573.8	580.8	574.4	571.5	570.0	568.8	567.6
1997	559.9	560.5	563.0	570.9	577.9	588.9	588.0	591.7	588.2	586.2	586.5	588.5	579.2
1998	583.2	582.9	584.9	589.4	592.1	602.4	597.0	603.6	597.4	595.0	594.4	595.8	593.2
1999	586.5	587.0	588.4	588.6	590.0	600.4	603.2	605.0	600.0	595.4	594.1	598.5	594.8
2000	590.2	591.0	593.1	591.3	591.4	603.0	600.0	600.6	596.3	593.6	590.8	588.3	594.1
2001	577.0	571.2	569.7	565.4	562.3	567.9	563.7	562.5	555.6	547.9	541.5	538.8	560.3
2002	531.6	526.0	527.3	525.3	526.7	534.2	532.2	534.8	530.1	526.3	523.9	521.2	528.3
2003	509.3	504.9	504.2	503.9	504.6	509.6	511.7	513.7	507.2	503.4	502.9	501.4	506.4
Service-providing													
1990	1615.2	1630.0	1641.4	1665.2	1683.2	1703.2	1676.7	1677.8	1700.7	1703.7	1712.2	1711.2	1676.7
1991	1650.1	1661.6	1672.5	1686.4	1702.9	1717.3	1690.9	1695.9	1711.2	1724.8	1731.4	1734.7	1698.3
1992	1684.2	1696.5	1704.3	1738.0	1756.1	1766.9	1741.3	1744.2	1767.6	1776.1	1783.5	1785.7	1745.4
1993	1726.8	1743.9	1753.0	1768.3	1793.6	1805.9	1782.7	1786.5	1808.9	1819.8	1824.5	1831.9	1787.2
1994	1772.9	1789.3	1804.4	1823.1	1841.3	1857.2	1840.3	1837.1	1868.8	1870.1	1886.0	1889.0	1840.0
1995	1828.9	1841.9	1863.4	1872.8	1889.1	1910.8	1880.3	1883.8	1907.0	1912.6	1917.2	1925.0	1886.1
1996	1873.7	1874.2	1894.2	1898.5	1925.3	1942.4	1914.2	1921.9	1938.8	1949.2	1959.9	1963.9	1921.4
1997	1900.6	1911.3	1921.9	1938.8	1963.1	1982.2	1955.2	1960.1	1982.2	1998.3	2004.6	2012.3	1960.9
1998	1941.6	1956.5	1965.9	1988.6	2010.9	2028.4	2000.2	2001.3	2018.6	2036.9	2048.0	2057.7	2004.6
1999	1993.0	2005.8	2019.3	2051.8	2070.1	2091.1	2066.5	2068.5	2080.9	2098.2	2104.2	2112.3	2063.5
2000	2047.6	2059.0	2077.1	2103.8	2122.5	2142.8	2110.8	2116.0	2125.1	2134.6	2147.3	2142.9	2110.8
2001	2081.2	2094.0	2105.7	2126.5	2145.7	2154.8	2123.2	2123.5	2130.4	2135.4	2138.1	2133.6	2124.3
2002	2075.9	2082.7	2097.3	2119.3	2141.4	2151.3	2122.3	2124.8	2131.1	2151.8	2159.5	2156.1	2126.1
2003	2089.4	2105.4	2112.6	2138.1	2159.6	2176.6	2145.9	2151.2	2154.9	2171.8	2169.5	2167.0	2145.2
Trade, transportation, and utilities													
1990	448.0	441.2	443.5	447.6	454.3	462.6	459.0	463.7	464.8	467.4	474.5	477.8	458.7
1991	454.4	446.6	448.2	449.7	456.6	461.0	458.9	463.4	462.7	467.4	475.3	477.8	460.2
1992	456.2	449.7	450.4	455.1	462.3	468.0	463.0	466.4	467.8	473.7	480.0	484.3	464.7
1993	459.8	454.9	456.9	461.5	468.4	474.7	471.8	474.2	477.8	483.1	491.8	496.3	472.6
1994	473.4	469.2	472.9	476.8	483.5	489.3	487.7	491.1	496.8	502.8	513.0	517.7	489.5
1995	489.7	485.4	489.3	492.9	498.9	504.3	499.2	503.4	507.0	512.9	520.6	524.9	502.4
1996	500.2	491.3	494.1	494.5	502.6	506.3	502.4	506.2	507.3	515.2	525.0	529.3	506.2
1997	504.2	497.9	500.0	501.5	509.2	514.6	512.6	517.4	520.3	525.7	535.0	541.9	515.0
1998	512.5	507.3	509.5	511.6	519.4	525.1	521.7	524.9	527.6	538.8	548.0	556.0	525.2
1999	526.7	522.4	526.2	529.2	534.8	541.4	539.2	541.3	543.0	553.0	562.6	569.6	540.8
2000	541.4	535.8	539.4	543.9	548.4	550.6	549.2	552.0	555.7	564.7	574.9	578.7	552.9
2001	549.2	540.0	541.7	544.1	549.2	549.8	543.5	546.2	544.2	548.0	557.2	558.8	547.7
2002	533.0	524.7	527.4	528.9	535.8	538.2	533.5	534.9	535.4	540.8	552.4	555.9	536.7
2003	528.3	521.9	521.8	528.5	536.1	540.5	541.0	545.2	541.3	546.7	552.4	554.8	538.2
Wholesale trade													
1990	91.0	90.7	91.5	92.6	93.5	96.1	96.5	97.0	96.2	96.2	94.5	95.1	94.2
1991	93.4	93.1	93.4	94.6	95.5	97.8	98.0	97.9	96.7	95.5	95.2	95.2	95.5
1992	93.4	93.1	93.6	95.1	96.6	98.4	98.5	98.9	98.0	97.4	96.5	96.8	96.4
1993	94.5	94.3	95.2	96.1	97.0	98.3	99.8	99.6	98.7	98.1	98.1	98.4	97.3
1994	96.6	96.5	97.4	98.6	99.4	101.0	100.8	100.7	100.4	100.4	100.8	101.0	99.5
1995	99.4	99.6	100.7	102.3	103.0	104.3	104.4	104.4	103.7	103.3	103.2	103.8	102.7
1996	100.8	100.5	101.2	102.0	103.0	104.0	104.3	104.5	103.6	103.7	104.0	104.5	103.0
1997	103.3	103.5	104.0	105.2	106.3	107.9	108.8	109.0	108.9	108.4	108.3	109.2	106.9
1998	107.8	107.6	108.2	109.0	109.9	111.3	111.7	111.5	110.5	111.1	111.1	111.7	110.1
1999	111.2	111.3	112.1	112.8	113.4	114.9	115.4	114.9	113.7	114.4	114.4	115.0	113.6
2000	114.1	114.2	114.9	115.2	115.7	117.1	117.5	117.4	116.3	116.4	116.6	117.0	116.0
2001	115.4	115.2	115.5	115.4	116.4	117.5	117.2	116.8	115.4	115.3	114.8	114.9	115.8
2002	113.2	112.7	113.2	113.9	114.8	115.5	116.1	115.6	114.4	113.6	113.7	113.6	114.2
2003	111.3	111.1	111.3	112.3	112.9	113.9	114.3	114.4	114.2	114.0	113.2	113.1	113.0
Retail trade													
1990	273.7	266.6	267.3	269.6	273.6	279.4	278.0	281.4	280.1	283.0	292.2	294.5	278.3
1991	275.0	267.7	268.2	268.4	272.5	274.5	274.9	279.0	277.2	281.6	289.7	292.9	276.8
1992	275.0	268.7	268.5	270.7	274.8	278.0	276.5	279.7	278.4	284.6	292.8	297.0	278.7
1993	277.2	272.3	272.7	274.6	278.6	282.3	281.3	282.9	283.5	287.5	296.0	300.1	282.4
1994	282.9	277.6	279.1	281.6	285.8	290.0	290.9	293.6	296.4	301.0	311.5	316.6	292.3
1995	294.8	290.0	291.7	292.4	296.3	300.4	298.3	301.7	302.7	307.5	316.0	319.9	301.0
1996	303.9	295.2	296.5	295.7	301.3	304.4	303.1	305.6	305.2	311.1	321.7	326.3	305.8
1997	306.2	299.5	300.7	300.2	305.4	309.3	309.6	313.0	312.5	317.0	326.9	333.2	311.1
1998	308.6	303.4	304.8	304.8	309.9	314.1	312.7	314.5	314.7	323.8	334.1	341.4	315.6
1999	316.3	311.7	313.8	314.5	318.1	323.1	322.9	324.5	324.3	332.0	342.3	348.5	324.3
2000	325.0	319.2	321.3	323.5	326.2	328.5	328.3	330.5	331.6	338.2	349.1	353.2	331.2
2001	326.4	317.7	318.8	319.6	322.4	323.6	320.4	323.0	319.6	323.1	333.6	336.3	323.7
2002	317.1	309.9	311.3	310.5	314.5	317.6	315.8	317.4	315.0	319.8	331.5	336.4	318.1
2003	314.2	308.0	307.2	310.9	316.0	318.9	321.1	324.6	319.2	324.5	330.4	333.5	319.0

Employment by Industry: Wisconsin—*Continued*

(Numbers in thousands. Not seasonally adjusted.)

Industry	January	February	March	April	May	June	July	August	September	October	November	December	Annual Average
STATEWIDE—*Continued*													
Transportation and utilities													
1990	83.3	83.9	84.7	85.4	87.2	87.1	84.5	85.3	88.5	88.2	87.8	88.2	86.2
1991	86.0	85.8	86.6	86.7	88.6	88.7	86.0	86.5	88.8	90.3	90.4	89.7	87.8
1992	87.8	87.9	88.3	89.3	90.9	91.6	88.0	87.8	91.4	91.7	90.7	90.5	89.7
1993	88.1	88.3	89.0	90.8	92.8	94.1	90.7	91.7	95.6	97.5	97.7	97.8	92.8
1994	93.9	95.1	96.4	96.6	98.3	98.3	96.0	96.8	100.0	101.4	100.7	100.1	97.8
1995	95.5	95.8	96.9	98.2	99.6	99.6	96.5	97.3	100.6	102.1	101.4	101.2	98.7
1996	95.5	95.6	96.4	96.8	98.3	97.9	95.0	96.1	98.5	100.4	99.3	98.5	97.4
1997	94.7	94.9	95.3	96.1	97.5	97.4	94.2	95.4	98.9	100.3	99.8	99.5	97.0
1998	96.1	96.3	96.5	97.8	99.6	99.7	97.3	98.9	102.4	103.9	102.8	102.9	99.5
1999	99.2	99.4	100.3	101.9	103.3	103.4	100.9	101.9	105.0	106.6	105.9	106.1	102.8
2000	102.3	102.4	103.2	105.2	106.5	105.0	103.4	104.1	107.8	110.1	109.2	108.5	105.6
2001	107.4	107.1	107.4	109.1	110.4	108.7	105.9	106.4	109.2	109.6	108.8	107.6	108.1
2002	102.7	102.1	102.9	104.5	106.5	105.1	101.6	101.9	106.0	107.4	107.2	105.9	104.5
2003	102.8	102.8	103.3	105.3	107.2	107.7	105.6	106.2	107.9	108.2	108.8	108.2	106.2
Information													
1990	43.4	43.5	43.6	43.9	44.2	44.6	44.6	44.7	44.7	44.7	45.3	45.5	44.4
1991	43.7	43.5	43.6	43.2	43.5	43.7	43.3	43.3	43.1	43.8	44.5	44.8	43.7
1992	43.0	43.0	42.8	43.1	43.3	43.3	43.2	43.3	43.2	43.5	44.1	44.2	43.3
1993	43.5	43.4	43.4	42.9	43.1	43.4	43.5	43.5	43.4	43.6	44.3	44.4	43.5
1994	43.9	43.8	44.0	43.5	43.6	44.0	44.1	44.2	44.5	44.3	45.0	45.4	44.2
1995	44.9	44.7	45.1	44.1	44.2	44.9	45.0	45.3	45.5	45.2	46.5	46.6	45.2
1996	45.2	44.7	45.3	44.4	44.8	45.2	45.6	45.8	45.6	46.3	47.1	47.3	45.6
1997	46.0	46.0	45.9	45.8	46.0	46.6	46.5	46.8	46.9	46.6	47.4	48.0	46.5
1998	48.4	48.3	48.7	48.6	48.8	49.6	49.7	49.9	49.1	49.9	50.5	50.7	49.4
1999	50.4	50.6	50.9	51.1	51.7	52.2	50.9	52.0	52.1	52.6	53.2	53.2	51.7
2000	52.5	52.4	52.5	52.6	52.9	53.4	53.8	53.9	53.8	54.6	55.6	55.6	53.6
2001	53.8	53.6	53.8	54.0	53.4	53.7	53.3	53.1	52.6	52.5	52.8	52.5	53.3
2002	51.8	51.3	51.2	51.1	51.0	51.1	51.1	51.2	50.6	50.8	51.2	51.4	51.2
2003	50.7	50.1	50.1	49.7	49.6	49.8	50.2	49.5	48.9	49.2	48.8	49.5	49.7
Financial activities													
1990	120.6	121.0	121.6	122.5	123.9	125.6	125.7	125.4	124.4	125.0	124.9	126.0	123.9
1991	124.9	124.6	124.8	124.7	125.5	127.2	127.3	127.5	125.9	125.8	125.9	126.9	125.9
1992	126.1	126.3	126.4	127.3	128.2	130.1	130.8	130.8	129.8	129.5	129.4	130.8	128.8
1993	130.0	130.3	131.0	130.8	131.6	132.8	133.5	133.4	132.4	131.7	131.7	132.5	131.8
1994	131.5	131.6	131.8	132.6	133.1	134.8	135.1	134.9	133.9	132.8	132.8	133.8	133.2
1995	132.7	132.6	133.6	133.5	133.9	135.9	135.4	135.8	134.8	134.1	134.3	135.1	134.3
1996	134.2	133.9	134.9	135.1	135.5	137.1	137.6	137.7	136.4	135.7	135.0	135.8	135.7
1997	135.8	135.9	136.6	136.6	137.0	139.0	139.7	140.0	139.0	138.7	138.7	140.1	138.1
1998	140.2	139.2	139.4	139.4	140.0	141.1	141.7	142.1	140.8	141.0	141.6	143.0	140.8
1999	141.4	141.7	142.0	145.1	145.5	147.6	147.6	147.9	146.0	146.6	146.5	148.4	145.5
2000	146.7	146.6	146.8	148.1	148.6	150.6	151.0	150.8	149.8	149.7	150.0	150.9	149.1
2001	150.0	150.0	151.0	150.6	151.5	153.4	153.8	153.6	152.2	151.4	151.7	151.8	151.8
2002	151.4	151.7	151.7	152.4	153.1	154.8	155.6	156.0	154.5	154.2	154.8	155.5	153.8
2003	154.3	154.9	155.0	155.9	157.0	158.7	159.0	159.0	159.0	158.9	160.1	160.1	157.7
Professional and business services													
1990	145.0	146.8	148.7	152.9	152.7	156.8	156.3	157.6	157.0	157.7	156.1	155.2	153.6
1991	149.8	150.6	152.4	154.8	155.4	157.8	158.3	159.9	159.5	162.9	162.0	160.8	157.0
1992	158.3	159.3	160.1	168.6	169.4	172.0	173.8	175.5	175.0	176.1	174.8	174.5	169.8
1993	170.1	171.8	173.7	177.4	180.3	182.4	185.9	187.3	188.5	189.5	188.0	186.5	181.8
1994	185.2	187.8	190.3	194.3	195.0	198.6	202.4	204.6	205.2	205.4	205.2	204.3	198.2
1995	198.0	199.8	204.8	203.8	205.4	207.9	210.2	212.2	213.6	210.2	208.5	208.4	206.9
1996	203.8	204.2	207.0	208.9	210.9	212.4	213.6	217.9	217.7	219.4	218.6	218.3	212.7
1997	211.2	213.6	216.0	219.3	221.1	226.6	225.9	228.7	228.9	232.0	230.5	230.8	223.7
1998	219.4	221.9	224.7	229.2	230.0	234.6	237.0	237.0	234.5	237.3	236.7	236.6	231.6
1999	225.6	225.9	229.2	237.8	238.1	244.0	245.7	248.2	247.4	249.1	247.0	247.6	240.5
2000	236.5	238.7	242.0	245.5	248.8	252.4	250.0	253.0	252.1	250.4	249.4	245.0	247.0
2001	235.3	235.4	235.1	239.0	240.5	242.4	242.3	244.1	240.2	238.5	235.7	233.1	238.5
2002	228.8	229.5	233.1	239.8	241.5	244.2	245.1	247.1	244.6	244.5	240.8	238.7	239.8
2003	234.9	236.4	238.3	243.1	243.7	246.1	249.4	253.0	252.4	248.8	248.2	244.3	244.9
Educational and health services													
1990	232.3	234.4	235.8	234.5	235.6	236.6	235.9	236.6	239.1	241.1	243.2	243.3	237.4
1991	240.6	243.0	244.7	245.2	246.1	248.0	245.9	246.3	249.7	252.9	254.9	255.6	247.7
1992	253.4	255.8	256.7	259.1	259.5	259.3	258.7	258.2	260.9	263.7	264.5	265.0	259.6
1993	262.4	265.3	265.6	267.2	267.4	267.0	266.8	266.9	269.3	271.3	272.3	272.4	267.8
1994	267.9	270.4	271.3	272.4	273.0	273.2	272.2	272.1	274.6	274.9	277.6	277.9	273.1
1995	273.0	276.0	278.0	277.2	278.4	279.3	278.3	279.4	282.8	285.5	288.0	289.1	280.4
1996	287.8	290.9	293.2	292.9	293.7	294.0	292.9	292.4	295.0	298.2	299.8	300.3	294.3
1997	296.0	298.8	299.2	299.5	300.5	301.1	301.5	301.3	304.3	307.1	308.9	309.7	302.3
1998	304.8	308.1	309.9	311.9	311.8	312.9	309.1	310.1	313.8	317.6	320.3	321.8	312.7
1999	319.5	323.5	325.1	328.2	327.7	328.5	328.9	327.7	330.1	332.5	334.3	335.0	328.4
2000	331.2	334.3	336.6	338.8	338.0	340.2	339.7	340.7	341.3	342.6	345.2	346.3	339.6
2001	341.9	347.6	349.0	349.5	349.3	349.0	347.9	347.9	350.0	352.6	355.2	355.3	349.6
2002	350.3	352.3	353.0	355.6	356.1	358.7	356.5	357.9	358.1	360.9	363.5	363.0	357.2
2003	359.8	361.6	361.9	364.3	364.1	364.8	364.9	365.2	369.9	374.3	374.6	373.9	366.6

Employment by Industry: Wisconsin—*Continued*

(Numbers in thousands. Not seasonally adjusted.)

Industry	January	February	March	April	May	June	July	August	September	October	November	December	Annual Average
STATEWIDE—*Continued*													
Leisure and hospitality													
1990	181.0	182.4	184.7	192.4	203.2	214.8	217.7	218.3	210.2	200.0	194.0	192.8	199.3
1991	184.8	185.0	188.7	194.6	205.3	215.7	217.9	219.6	209.6	200.2	194.3	192.3	200.7
1992	185.7	187.1	189.5	200.0	212.0	220.4	221.2	222.6	214.1	206.7	199.6	199.4	204.9
1993	191.6	192.7	195.7	200.4	213.5	223.7	224.7	228.1	218.4	210.9	204.6	204.9	209.1
1994	195.6	196.8	199.4	204.9	218.3	228.9	233.3	233.3	226.2	215.0	208.8	209.5	214.2
1995	198.2	200.6	205.1	210.1	221.8	235.1	236.5	239.2	227.7	218.5	211.3	211.0	217.9
1996	202.7	203.9	207.3	212.9	227.1	237.9	239.9	243.1	231.7	221.4	214.3	215.3	221.5
1997	204.8	206.1	208.5	216.9	231.6	241.9	245.3	247.0	236.1	228.1	220.1	220.5	225.6
1998	207.5	210.0	210.5	219.6	233.8	244.6	247.7	249.0	237.7	227.1	218.7	219.2	227.1
1999	210.2	212.8	216.4	226.1	238.5	251.3	254.4	254.5	243.4	232.1	224.6	224.6	232.4
2000	215.5	216.9	221.6	230.1	242.4	254.8	259.6	261.3	248.3	235.9	228.0	226.4	236.7
2001	219.4	220.1	223.0	233.9	246.7	257.7	263.0	262.4	247.8	236.8	227.6	224.7	238.6
2002	221.0	220.7	222.5	231.4	245.8	256.9	264.2	265.0	251.9	241.7	232.0	232.1	240.4
2003	225.6	224.0	226.6	235.7	252.1	262.7	267.9	269.2	255.9	245.0	238.2	237.0	245.0
Other services													
1990	115.3	115.9	116.0	116.2	116.8	117.4	117.2	116.8	116.6	116.5	117.3	117.5	116.6
1991	116.1	116.3	116.4	116.0	116.6	117.2	116.7	116.7	116.7	117.1	117.1	117.5	116.7
1992	114.4	114.7	117.0	116.9	118.1	118.2	118.3	117.9	117.9	118.4	118.5	119.0	117.4
1993	116.3	116.7	118.6	118.2	118.8	120.5	119.6	118.9	119.2	119.8	119.6	121.5	119.0
1994	117.8	118.5	120.1	119.7	119.5	121.4	120.9	120.4	121.0	121.6	121.2	123.1	120.4
1995	117.9	118.3	120.6	119.7	119.8	121.9	120.1	120.1	120.6	121.1	120.7	123.0	120.3
1996	120.1	120.8	122.7	121.5	121.7	123.4	122.2	121.6	121.5	121.9	121.6	123.8	121.9
1997	120.9	120.8	122.1	123.5	122.9	123.5	123.4	123.5	123.9	124.0	123.4	123.5	123.0
1998	122.7	123.3	124.6	124.4	124.9	126.0	125.3	124.8	124.6	124.8	125.0	125.2	124.6
1999	124.2	125.4	125.5	125.5	124.9	125.6	125.3	125.6	125.1	125.9	124.9	125.5	125.3
2000	124.2	125.5	126.1	126.1	126.0	127.5	126.4	125.9	126.4	126.7	126.5	127.9	126.3
2001	129.3	129.6	131.1	130.3	130.6	132.7	132.0	132.2	131.8	131.6	131.3	133.1	131.3
2002	131.0	131.0	132.2	131.9	132.0	134.1	132.6	132.6	132.0	132.2	132.0	133.3	132.2
2003	131.5	131.6	132.7	132.3	132.6	134.7	131.5	131.4	130.4	130.6	127.3	129.5	131.3
Government													
1990	329.6	344.8	347.5	355.2	352.5	344.8	320.3	314.7	343.9	351.3	356.9	353.1	342.9
1991	335.8	352.0	353.7	358.2	353.9	346.7	322.6	319.2	344.0	354.7	357.4	359.0	346.4
1992	347.1	360.6	361.4	367.9	363.3	355.6	332.3	329.5	358.9	364.5	372.6	368.5	356.9
1993	353.1	368.8	368.1	369.9	370.5	361.4	336.9	334.2	359.9	369.9	372.2	373.4	361.5
1994	357.6	371.2	374.6	378.9	375.3	367.0	344.6	336.5	366.6	373.3	382.4	377.3	367.1
1995	374.5	384.5	386.9	391.5	386.7	381.5	355.6	348.4	375.0	385.1	387.3	386.9	378.7
1996	379.7	384.5	389.7	388.3	389.0	386.1	360.0	357.2	383.6	391.1	398.5	393.8	383.5
1997	381.7	392.2	393.6	395.7	394.8	388.9	360.3	355.4	382.8	396.1	400.6	397.8	386.7
1998	386.1	398.4	398.6	403.9	402.2	394.5	368.0	363.5	390.5	400.4	407.2	405.2	393.2
1999	395.0	403.5	404.0	408.8	408.9	400.5	374.5	371.3	393.8	406.4	411.1	408.4	398.9
2000	399.6	408.8	412.1	418.7	417.4	413.3	381.1	378.4	397.7	410.0	417.7	412.1	405.6
2001	402.3	417.7	421.0	425.1	424.5	416.1	387.4	384.0	411.6	424.0	426.6	424.3	413.7
2002	408.6	421.5	426.2	428.2	426.1	413.3	383.7	380.1	404.0	426.7	432.8	426.2	414.8
2003	404.3	424.9	426.2	428.6	424.4	419.3	382.0	378.7	397.1	418.3	419.9	417.9	411.8
Federal government													
1990	29.4	29.4	29.9	32.2	34.1	31.7	31.3	30.2	29.6	29.2	29.2	29.7	30.5
1991	29.2	29.1	29.1	29.3	29.4	29.9	29.5	29.2	29.1	28.9	29.1	29.8	29.3
1992	29.6	29.3	29.4	29.2	29.3	29.5	30.1	29.9	29.8	29.7	29.5	30.1	29.6
1993	29.7	29.6	29.6	29.6	29.7	30.1	30.3	30.4	30.2	30.3	30.4	31.2	30.1
1994	30.4	30.4	30.4	30.4	30.4	30.7	30.6	30.6	30.4	30.3	30.2	30.7	30.5
1995	30.1	30.0	30.1	30.1	30.1	30.3	30.4	30.4	30.1	30.0	29.8	30.1	30.1
1996	29.9	30.0	30.0	30.2	30.1	30.3	30.4	30.4	30.2	29.8	30.0	30.7	30.2
1997	29.4	29.3	29.3	29.5	29.6	29.8	29.8	29.8	29.6	29.4	29.7	30.2	29.6
1998	29.1	29.1	29.1	29.3	29.4	29.7	29.8	29.8	29.7	29.8	30.5	31.2	29.7
1999	30.2	29.7	29.8	30.9	30.0	30.0	29.9	30.1	30.1	29.9	30.4	31.1	30.2
2000	30.5	30.5	32.0	33.5	37.6	38.3	33.5	35.1	29.8	29.7	30.4	30.6	32.6
2001	29.9	29.7	29.8	29.9	30.0	30.3	30.4	30.4	30.2	30.0	30.1	30.2	30.1
2002	29.7	29.6	29.6	29.5	29.6	30.2	30.1	30.0	29.8	30.1	30.1	30.4	29.9
2003	29.8	29.8	29.7	29.7	29.7	30.0	30.1	29.9	29.8	29.8	29.5	30.2	29.8
State government													
1990	81.1	89.3	89.7	90.8	90.0	84.5	81.4	81.3	89.1	92.2	92.9	90.4	87.7
1991	82.3	91.0	91.6	92.4	91.3	84.4	82.8	83.9	90.1	92.5	93.7	92.0	89.0
1992	86.8	94.2	93.6	94.2	94.1	86.5	86.3	87.5	92.2	95.9	96.6	94.7	91.9
1993	92.3	94.9	93.9	95.6	96.1	87.6	87.5	88.9	93.6	97.1	97.9	94.9	93.4
1994	88.1	96.2	97.4	98.4	98.0	89.3	88.8	88.7	92.0	96.2	97.3	95.0	93.8
1995	90.6	93.7	94.5	96.0	94.2	87.4	87.0	86.5	90.8	95.1	96.0	93.4	92.1
1996	93.9	93.1	94.2	96.4	94.8	89.4	87.6	87.7	92.9	97.7	99.7	96.6	93.7
1997	92.7	96.6	98.3	99.1	96.9	90.0	90.1	90.0	94.3	99.6	101.3	97.8	95.6
1998	94.0	98.4	99.7	101.4	100.3	92.5	92.9	93.4	97.3	101.0	102.7	101.4	97.9
1999	96.6	100.1	100.7	103.5	101.9	95.6	94.7	94.9	97.9	103.0	104.0	100.7	99.5
2000	97.2	100.5	101.9	104.1	100.7	96.2	91.7	91.8	93.5	98.4	100.8	98.2	97.9
2001	91.9	102.1	103.4	104.7	104.3	96.7	96.2	95.7	101.3	104.2	105.3	102.4	100.7
2002	92.6	100.1	102.6	105.0	101.8	93.3	91.4	94.6	99.0	104.6	107.7	103.4	99.7
2003	92.6	102.2	103.8	105.6	103.1	96.7	91.0	93.7	99.2	102.1	103.0	100.7	99.5

Employment by Industry: Wisconsin—*Continued*

(Numbers in thousands. Not seasonally adjusted.)

Industry	January	February	March	April	May	June	July	August	September	October	November	December	Annual Average
STATEWIDE—*Continued*													
Local government													
1990	219.1	226.1	228.0	232.2	228.4	228.6	207.7	203.2	225.2	229.9	234.9	233.0	224.7
1991	224.3	231.9	233.0	236.6	233.2	232.5	210.3	206.0	224.7	233.3	234.6	237.2	228.1
1992	230.8	237.2	238.3	244.5	239.8	239.5	215.9	212.1	236.9	238.8	246.5	243.6	235.3
1993	231.1	244.2	244.6	244.7	244.6	243.8	219.1	214.9	236.1	242.5	243.9	247.3	238.1
1994	239.2	244.5	246.7	250.1	246.9	247.0	225.2	217.3	244.2	246.8	254.9	251.5	242.9
1995	253.8	260.8	262.4	265.4	262.4	263.8	238.3	231.5	254.1	260.1	261.5	263.4	256.5
1996	255.9	261.4	265.5	261.8	264.0	266.3	242.0	239.2	260.5	263.7	268.8	266.4	259.6
1997	259.6	266.3	265.9	267.1	268.3	269.1	240.4	235.5	258.8	267.0	269.6	269.9	261.5
1998	263.0	270.9	269.7	273.2	272.6	272.3	245.4	240.3	263.5	269.6	274.1	272.7	265.6
1999	268.2	273.7	273.5	274.4	277.0	274.8	249.8	246.3	265.8	273.5	276.7	276.5	269.2
2000	271.9	277.8	278.2	281.1	279.1	278.8	255.9	251.5	274.4	281.9	286.4	283.3	275.0
2001	280.5	285.9	287.8	290.5	290.2	289.1	260.8	257.9	280.1	289.8	291.2	291.7	283.0
2002	286.3	291.8	294.0	293.7	294.7	289.8	262.2	255.5	275.2	292.0	295.0	292.4	285.2
2003	281.9	292.9	292.7	293.3	291.6	292.6	260.9	255.1	268.1	286.4	287.4	287.0	282.5
APPLETON-OSHKOSH-NEENAH													
Total nonfarm													
1990	155.6	155.5	157.0	159.0	160.1	163.4	162.8	163.2	164.0	163.3	163.8	162.8	160.8
1991	158.4	159.1	159.3	160.9	163.4	166.0	165.4	167.6	167.2	168.1	167.7	167.7	164.2
1992	162.7	163.3	164.4	167.6	168.7	172.0	170.6	171.4	172.8	173.6	173.4	173.4	169.4
1993	168.3	169.2	170.1	172.1	173.8	177.0	175.0	175.3	175.9	178.3	178.6	178.6	174.3
1994	172.4	172.5	174.5	177.0	178.4	181.8	181.7	180.8	182.9	184.4	184.8	185.1	179.6
1995	180.2	180.1	182.1	184.2	184.1	187.9	186.9	187.1	187.7	187.4	187.5	187.8	185.2
1996	183.3	183.2	185.5	187.2	188.8	191.9	190.5	191.3	190.2	192.6	192.7	191.8	189.0
1997	187.0	186.7	187.5	190.3	192.6	195.7	194.6	195.3	195.4	195.7	195.3	195.5	192.6
1998	190.8	190.9	192.4	194.7	196.7	200.1	199.8	200.4	199.6	200.3	200.5	201.3	197.2
1999	195.4	195.8	197.5	199.6	200.9	204.4	202.6	203.0	201.7	203.1	204.2	205.6	201.1
2000	200.8	201.3	203.1	205.1	206.6	209.8	208.8	209.5	208.7	208.6	209.4	208.6	206.6
2001	204.4	203.6	204.7	205.4	206.5	209.5	208.5	208.3	206.8	207.7	207.4	207.0	206.7
2002	201.8	200.7	201.9	203.6	205.7	208.0	205.9	206.7	205.6	207.1	208.1	207.3	205.2
2003	201.4	200.6	201.3	202.7	205.6	207.9	204.6	204.1	202.2	204.3	204.1	203.2	203.5
Total private													
1990	138.3	137.7	138.7	140.3	142.2	145.8	146.3	147.0	146.8	145.2	144.8	144.2	143.1
1991	140.9	140.3	140.8	142.3	145.0	148.1	149.0	150.9	149.9	149.6	148.8	148.8	146.2
1992	144.8	144.4	145.5	148.2	149.8	153.4	153.6	154.6	154.4	154.6	153.8	154.0	150.9
1993	149.7	149.8	150.9	152.2	154.4	157.2	157.5	158.1	157.6	158.8	159.0	158.9	155.3
1994	153.3	152.8	154.7	156.7	158.5	161.9	163.0	163.2	164.0	164.2	164.0	164.7	160.0
1995	159.7	158.9	160.5	162.4	162.9	166.8	166.8	167.6	167.1	165.6	165.3	165.9	164.1
1996	162.0	161.2	163.2	165.3	167.0	170.1	170.0	171.0	168.9	170.3	170.2	169.5	167.3
1997	165.2	164.8	165.1	167.7	169.8	173.6	174.2	175.0	174.1	173.1	172.8	173.5	170.7
1998	169.2	169.0	169.9	172.0	173.9	177.3	177.6	179.0	177.0	177.2	177.4	178.1	174.8
1999	172.9	172.6	174.2	176.3	177.5	181.4	180.7	181.7	179.8	179.8	180.5	182.1	178.2
2000	178.0	177.8	179.6	181.2	182.8	186.5	186.4	187.6	186.1	185.0	185.4	184.9	183.4
2001	181.2	180.1	180.9	181.4	182.8	186.1	186.6	186.7	184.1	183.3	182.8	182.5	183.2
2002	178.2	176.5	177.5	179.3	181.3	184.7	184.1	185.3	183.3	182.9	183.4	183.4	181.7
2003	178.1	176.5	177.0	178.5	181.2	184.1	182.7	182.3	180.3	180.4	180.2	179.4	180.1
Goods-producing													
1990	57.1	57.0	57.4	57.7	58.8	60.9	61.7	61.7	60.9	59.7	58.9	58.1	59.1
1991	57.0	56.4	56.4	57.4	59.0	61.4	62.5	63.0	62.5	61.4	60.5	60.0	59.7
1992	58.3	57.8	58.2	59.0	59.9	62.6	63.4	63.6	62.8	62.4	61.3	61.2	60.8
1993	59.3	59.4	59.9	60.4	61.6	63.3	63.3	63.4	62.9	63.1	62.3	62.1	61.7
1994	59.9	59.5	60.3	60.9	62.0	64.3	65.2	65.4	65.1	64.5	64.3	63.9	62.9
1995	62.6	62.0	62.3	63.0	63.1	65.5	66.3	66.2	65.8	64.4	63.9	63.5	64.0
1996	62.4	62.1	63.0	64.2	65.2	67.5	68.1	67.9	67.1	66.7	66.4	65.4	65.5
1997	64.4	63.8	63.7	64.7	65.7	68.1	68.7	68.6	67.6	66.3	65.9	65.7	66.1
1998	65.0	64.7	65.1	66.1	67.4	69.2	69.6	69.5	69.2	67.9	67.8	67.7	67.4
1999	66.7	66.6	67.1	68.3	69.1	71.6	71.9	72.1	71.1	70.1	70.2	70.5	69.6
2000	69.8	69.3	70.0	70.7	71.8	73.9	73.8	73.6	72.4	71.7	71.4	71.0	71.6
2001	69.6	69.0	69.0	68.9	69.4	71.0	71.4	70.4	69.2	68.2	67.3	66.7	69.2
2002	64.4	63.3	63.1	64.1	64.7	66.7	67.2	67.0	66.1	65.7	65.4	64.4	65.2
2003	59.0	58.1	58.2	58.4	59.5	60.8	60.3	59.9	59.1	59.2	59.3	58.5	59.2
Construction and mining													
1990	7.2	7.1	7.1	7.7	8.2	8.8	9.0	9.1	9.0	8.8	8.6	8.1	8.2
1991	7.2	7.0	7.1	7.6	8.6	9.3	9.4	9.6	9.6	9.6	9.6	9.3	8.6
1992	8.4	8.0	8.0	8.3	8.8	9.6	9.4	9.3	9.1	9.6	9.3	9.0	8.9
1993	8.3	8.2	8.3	8.6	9.7	9.9	10.3	10.3	10.3	10.2	9.9	9.4	9.4
1994	8.6	8.2	8.9	9.4	9.9	10.4	11.0	10.9	11.0	10.8	10.5	9.9	9.9
1995	8.9	8.5	8.7	9.5	10.0	10.7	10.9	10.6	10.7	10.6	10.6	10.1	9.9
1996	9.4	9.1	9.5	9.8	10.7	11.6	11.9	12.0	11.9	11.9	11.7	10.9	10.8
1997	9.9	9.5	9.7	10.3	11.0	11.7	12.1	12.0	11.7	11.4	11.2	10.7	10.9
1998	9.9	9.7	9.7	10.7	11.5	11.9	12.4	12.2	12.2	12.0	11.9	11.9	11.3
1999	10.8	10.7	11.0	11.8	12.5	13.2	13.4	13.5	13.1	12.8	12.8	12.6	12.3
2000	11.7	11.7	12.1	13.2	14.0	14.5	14.4	14.5	14.1	14.0	13.9	13.4	13.4
2001	11.8	11.8	11.9	12.3	13.1	13.7	13.9	13.8	13.5	13.4	13.1	12.6	12.9
2002	11.4	11.2	11.3	12.0	12.7	13.4	13.8	13.8	13.6	13.6	13.6	13.0	12.8
2003	11.9	11.4	11.7	12.3	13.1	13.7	13.6	13.2	12.9	13.0	13.0	12.5	12.7

Employment by Industry: Wisconsin—*Continued*

(Numbers in thousands. Not seasonally adjusted.)

Industry	January	February	March	April	May	June	July	August	September	October	November	December	Annual Average
APPLETON-OSHKOSH-NEENAH—*Continued*													
Manufacturing													
1990	49.9	49.9	50.3	50.0	50.6	52.1	52.7	52.6	51.9	50.9	50.3	50.0	50.9
1991	49.8	49.4	49.3	49.8	50.4	52.1	53.1	53.4	52.9	51.8	50.9	50.7	51.1
1992	49.9	49.8	50.2	50.7	51.1	53.0	54.0	54.3	53.7	52.8	52.0	52.2	51.9
1993	51.0	51.2	51.6	51.8	51.9	53.4	53.0	53.1	52.6	52.9	52.4	52.7	52.3
1994	51.3	51.3	51.4	51.5	52.1	53.9	54.2	54.5	54.1	53.7	53.8	54.0	52.9
1995	53.7	53.5	53.6	53.5	53.1	54.8	55.4	55.6	55.1	53.8	53.3	53.4	54.0
1996	53.0	53.0	53.5	54.4	54.5	55.9	56.2	55.9	55.2	54.8	54.7	54.5	54.6
1997	54.5	54.3	54.0	54.4	54.7	56.4	56.6	56.6	55.9	54.9	54.7	55.0	55.1
1998	55.1	55.0	55.4	55.4	55.9	57.3	57.2	57.3	57.0	55.9	55.9	55.8	56.1
1999	55.9	55.9	56.1	56.5	56.6	58.4	58.5	58.6	58.0	57.3	57.4	57.9	57.2
2000	58.1	57.6	57.9	57.5	57.8	59.4	59.4	59.1	58.3	57.7	57.5	57.6	58.1
2001	57.8	57.2	57.1	56.6	56.3	57.3	57.5	56.6	55.7	54.8	54.2	54.1	56.3
2002	53.0	52.1	51.8	52.1	52.0	53.3	53.4	53.2	52.5	52.1	51.8	51.4	52.4
2003	47.1	46.7	46.5	46.1	46.4	47.1	46.7	46.7	46.2	46.2	46.3	46.0	46.5
Service-providing													
1990	98.5	98.5	99.6	101.3	101.3	102.5	101.1	101.5	103.1	103.6	104.9	104.7	101.7
1991	101.4	102.7	102.9	103.5	104.4	104.6	102.9	104.6	104.7	106.7	107.2	107.7	104.4
1992	104.4	105.5	106.2	108.6	108.8	109.4	107.2	107.8	110.0	111.2	112.1	112.2	108.6
1993	109.0	109.8	110.2	111.7	112.2	113.7	111.7	111.9	113.0	115.2	116.3	116.5	112.6
1994	112.5	113.0	114.2	116.1	116.4	117.5	116.5	115.4	117.8	119.9	120.5	121.2	116.7
1995	117.6	118.1	119.8	121.2	121.0	122.4	120.6	120.9	121.9	123.0	123.6	124.3	121.2
1996	120.9	121.1	122.5	123.0	123.6	124.4	122.4	123.4	123.1	125.9	126.3	126.4	123.5
1997	122.6	122.9	123.8	125.6	126.9	127.6	125.9	126.7	127.8	129.4	129.4	129.8	126.5
1998	125.8	126.2	127.3	128.6	129.3	130.9	130.2	130.9	130.4	132.4	132.7	133.6	129.8
1999	128.7	129.2	130.4	131.3	131.8	132.8	130.7	130.9	130.6	133.0	134.0	135.1	131.5
2000	131.0	132.0	133.1	134.4	134.8	135.9	135.0	135.9	136.3	136.9	138.0	137.6	135.0
2001	134.8	134.6	135.7	136.5	137.1	138.5	137.1	137.9	137.6	139.5	140.1	140.3	137.5
2002	137.4	137.4	138.8	139.5	141.0	141.3	138.7	139.7	139.5	141.4	142.7	142.9	140.0
2003	142.4	142.5	143.1	144.3	146.1	147.1	144.3	144.2	143.1	145.1	144.8	144.7	144.3
Trade, transportation, and utilities													
1990	27.9	27.4	27.4	27.4	27.7	28.3	28.1	28.7	29.5	29.4	29.9	30.0	28.4
1991	28.3	28.0	27.9	28.2	28.5	28.6	28.7	29.1	29.5	29.6	29.9	30.2	28.8
1992	28.5	28.1	28.3	29.0	29.4	29.7	29.4	29.9	30.5	31.0	31.4	31.7	29.7
1993	29.9	29.4	29.4	30.0	30.3	30.9	30.9	31.0	31.3	32.1	33.0	33.0	30.9
1994	30.8	30.4	30.5	30.9	31.3	31.7	31.7	31.9	32.7	33.7	34.1	34.5	32.0
1995	32.3	31.9	32.0	32.4	32.5	33.1	32.8	32.9	33.5	33.8	34.3	34.7	33.0
1996	33.1	32.5	32.7	32.9	33.1	33.4	33.0	33.3	33.7	34.9	35.5	35.6	33.6
1997	33.0	32.6	32.5	33.0	33.5	33.7	33.5	33.9	34.7	35.0	35.7	36.1	33.9
1998	33.9	33.8	34.1	34.4	34.7	35.0	34.9	35.2	35.1	36.3	37.0	37.6	35.1
1999	35.7	35.3	35.7	35.9	36.0	36.6	36.5	36.5	36.5	37.8	38.6	39.3	36.7
2000	37.3	37.5	37.7	37.8	38.0	38.1	38.2	38.5	38.8	39.5	40.1	40.4	38.4
2001	38.6	37.9	38.0	38.1	38.3	38.7	38.0	38.2	38.1	38.5	39.3	39.3	38.4
2002	37.3	36.4	36.5	36.7	37.1	37.3	36.9	37.3	37.1	37.3	38.3	38.5	37.2
2003	36.4	36.1	35.9	36.2	36.8	37.3	37.0	37.3	37.6	37.5	38.1	38.4	37.1
Wholesale trade													
1990	5.0	4.9	4.9	4.9	4.9	5.1	5.1	5.2	5.2	5.1	5.1	5.1	5.0
1991	5.2	5.2	5.2	5.2	5.3	5.3	5.3	5.3	5.2	5.2	5.1	5.2	5.2
1992	5.2	5.1	5.2	5.2	5.3	5.3	5.3	5.3	5.2	5.2	5.2	5.3	5.2
1993	5.4	5.3	5.3	5.3	5.4	5.5	5.6	5.6	5.4	5.4	5.5	5.5	5.4
1994	5.4	5.4	5.6	5.5	5.5	5.6	5.6	5.7	5.6	5.6	5.6	5.7	5.5
1995	5.6	5.7	5.7	5.7	5.7	5.8	5.9	5.8	5.8	5.8	5.8	5.8	5.7
1996	5.9	5.8	5.9	6.0	6.0	6.0	6.1	6.1	6.0	6.1	6.1	6.1	6.0
1997	6.0	6.0	6.0	6.2	6.3	6.4	6.4	6.4	6.4	6.4	6.5	6.5	6.2
1998	6.5	6.5	6.6	6.5	6.5	6.6	6.6	6.6	6.5	6.5	6.5	6.6	6.5
1999	6.5	6.5	6.5	6.7	6.7	6.8	6.7	6.6	6.6	6.7	6.7	6.8	6.6
2000	6.6	6.6	6.6	6.7	6.8	6.8	6.9	6.9	6.8	6.8	6.8	6.8	6.7
2001	6.9	6.9	6.9	6.8	6.9	6.9	6.9	6.9	6.9	6.8	6.7	6.7	6.9
2002	6.7	6.7	6.8	6.8	6.8	6.9	7.0	7.0	6.9	6.8	6.8	6.8	6.8
2003	6.8	6.7	6.7	6.8	6.8	6.9	6.8	6.9	6.9	6.7	6.7	6.7	6.8
Retail trade													
1990	18.1	17.7	17.7	17.6	17.8	18.2	18.2	18.6	19.2	19.1	19.6	19.6	18.4
1991	18.2	17.9	17.8	18.0	18.2	18.3	18.4	18.8	19.2	19.2	19.6	19.7	18.6
1992	18.1	17.7	17.7	18.2	18.5	18.8	18.7	19.1	19.7	20.1	20.5	20.7	18.9
1993	19.0	18.7	18.7	19.0	19.2	19.6	19.6	19.6	19.9	20.6	21.4	21.4	19.7
1994	19.7	19.3	19.1	19.3	19.6	19.9	20.0	20.1	20.9	21.5	22.0	22.3	20.3
1995	20.5	20.0	20.0	20.2	20.3	20.9	20.7	21.0	21.4	21.6	22.1	22.4	20.9
1996	20.9	20.4	20.4	20.4	20.6	21.0	20.9	21.1	21.5	22.5	23.1	23.3	21.3
1997	21.0	20.6	20.5	20.7	21.0	21.1	21.2	21.3	21.9	22.1	22.7	23.1	21.4
1998	21.0	20.9	21.0	21.2	21.4	21.7	21.7	21.9	21.8	22.8	23.5	23.9	21.9
1999	22.1	21.8	22.0	22.0	22.1	22.5	22.5	22.6	22.5	23.6	24.3	24.8	22.7
2000	23.1	23.3	23.4	23.3	23.4	23.5	23.5	23.8	24.1	24.6	25.3	25.5	23.9
2001	23.6	23.0	23.1	23.6	23.9	24.3	23.9	24.2	24.1	24.7	25.7	25.8	24.2
2002	23.9	23.0	23.0	22.9	23.2	23.4	23.0	23.3	23.0	23.3	24.2	24.4	23.4
2003	22.6	22.4	22.3	22.4	22.9	23.3	23.2	23.3	23.5	23.6	24.2	24.5	23.2

Employment by Industry: Wisconsin—*Continued*

(Numbers in thousands. Not seasonally adjusted.)

Industry	January	February	March	April	May	June	July	August	September	October	November	December	Annual Average
APPLETON-OSHKOSH-NEENAH—*Continued*													
Transportation and utilities													
1990	4.8	4.8	4.8	4.9	5.0	5.0	4.8	4.9	5.1	5.2	5.2	5.3	4.9
1991	4.9	4.9	4.9	5.0	5.0	5.0	5.0	5.0	5.1	5.2	5.2	5.3	5.0
1992	5.2	5.3	5.4	5.6	5.6	5.6	5.4	5.5	5.6	5.7	5.7	5.7	5.5
1993	5.5	5.4	5.4	5.7	5.7	5.8	5.7	5.8	6.0	6.1	6.1	6.1	5.7
1994	5.7	5.7	5.8	6.1	6.2	6.2	6.1	6.1	6.2	6.6	6.5	6.5	6.1
1995	6.2	6.2	6.3	6.5	6.5	6.4	6.2	6.1	6.3	6.4	6.4	6.5	6.3
1996	6.3	6.3	6.4	6.5	6.5	6.4	6.0	6.1	6.2	6.3	6.3	6.2	6.2
1997	6.0	6.0	6.0	6.1	6.2	6.2	5.9	6.2	6.4	6.5	6.5	6.5	6.2
1998	6.4	6.4	6.5	6.7	6.8	6.7	6.6	6.7	6.8	7.0	7.0	7.1	6.7
1999	7.1	7.0	7.2	7.2	7.2	7.3	7.3	7.3	7.4	7.5	7.6	7.7	7.3
2000	7.6	7.6	7.7	7.8	7.8	7.8	7.8	7.8	7.9	8.1	8.0	8.1	7.8
2001	8.1	8.0	8.0	7.7	7.5	7.5	7.2	7.1	7.1	7.0	6.9	6.8	7.4
2002	6.7	6.7	6.7	7.0	7.1	7.0	6.9	7.0	7.2	7.2	7.3	7.3	7.0
2003	7.0	7.0	6.9	7.0	7.1	7.1	7.0	7.1	7.2	7.2	7.2	7.2	7.1
Information													
1990	2.3	2.3	2.3	2.3	2.3	2.3	2.3	2.4	2.3	2.3	2.3	2.3	2.3
1991	2.4	2.4	2.4	2.4	2.4	2.4	2.4	2.4	2.4	2.4	2.4	2.4	2.4
1992	2.3	2.3	2.3	2.3	2.3	2.3	2.3	2.3	2.3	2.2	2.3	2.3	2.2
1993	2.3	2.2	2.3	2.2	2.2	2.3	2.4	2.4	2.3	2.3	2.3	2.3	2.2
1994	2.3	2.3	2.4	2.3	2.3	2.4	2.5	2.5	2.5	2.4	2.4	2.5	2.4
1995	2.5	2.5	2.6	2.5	2.5	2.5	2.5	2.5	2.5	2.5	2.5	2.5	2.5
1996	2.4	2.4	2.4	2.4	2.4	2.5	2.5	2.5	2.4	2.5	2.5	2.5	2.4
1997	2.5	2.5	2.5	2.4	2.4	2.5	2.4	2.5	2.4	2.4	2.4	2.5	2.4
1998	2.4	2.4	2.4	2.5	2.5	2.6	2.7	2.7	2.6	2.5	2.6	2.6	2.5
1999	2.6	2.6	2.6	2.7	2.7	2.7	2.6	2.6	2.6	2.6	2.6	2.7	2.6
2000	2.6	2.6	2.6	2.7	2.7	2.8	2.7	2.7	2.7	2.7	2.8	2.8	2.7
2001	3.0	3.0	3.0	3.1	3.2	3.3	3.4	3.4	3.5	3.6	3.7	3.7	3.3
2002	3.7	3.7	3.8	3.7	3.7	3.8	3.7	3.7	3.6	3.6	3.7	3.7	3.7
2003	3.7	3.7	3.7	3.6	3.6	3.7	3.7	3.6	3.5	3.6	3.6	3.6	3.6
Financial activities													
1990	7.3	7.3	7.3	7.3	7.3	7.4	7.5	7.5	7.4	7.4	7.4	7.5	7.3
1991	7.4	7.4	7.4	7.4	7.5	7.6	7.6	7.6	7.6	7.5	7.5	7.6	7.5
1992	7.7	7.8	7.8	7.9	8.0	8.1	8.2	8.2	8.1	8.1	8.2	8.2	8.0
1993	8.1	8.1	8.2	8.3	8.4	8.6	8.6	8.6	8.5	8.6	8.6	8.7	8.4
1994	8.3	8.3	8.3	8.3	8.4	8.5	8.8	8.7	8.7	8.5	8.5	8.6	8.4
1995	8.4	8.4	8.4	8.7	8.6	8.7	8.8	8.7	8.6	8.5	8.5	8.6	8.5
1996	8.5	8.5	8.5	8.6	8.5	8.6	8.8	8.7	8.6	8.6	8.5	8.5	8.5
1997	8.6	8.6	8.6	8.9	8.9	9.1	9.1	9.1	9.1	9.2	9.2	9.3	8.9
1998	9.4	9.1	9.0	8.9	8.8	9.0	9.2	9.3	9.2	9.2	9.1	9.1	9.1
1999	9.2	9.3	9.2	9.2	9.2	9.3	9.2	9.2	9.2	9.2	9.2	9.3	9.2
2000	9.2	9.1	9.2	9.2	9.2	9.4	9.6	9.5	9.6	9.7	9.7	9.8	9.4
2001	9.6	9.6	9.8	9.7	9.8	10.0	10.2	10.2	10.2	10.4	10.5	10.6	10.1
2002	10.6	10.7	10.7	10.7	10.8	10.9	10.8	10.9	10.7	10.8	10.8	10.8	10.8
2003	10.8	10.9	10.9	10.8	10.9	11.0	10.8	10.8	10.7	10.9	10.8	10.8	10.8
Professional and business services													
1990	8.6	8.8	8.8	9.4	9.5	9.7	9.3	9.4	9.3	9.1	9.2	9.1	9.1
1991	9.3	9.4	9.5	9.7	10.0	10.1	10.3	10.5	10.3	10.6	10.7	10.7	10.0
1992	10.5	10.5	10.6	11.2	11.1	11.3	11.2	11.3	11.4	11.4	11.3	11.2	11.0
1993	11.1	11.2	11.4	11.3	11.4	11.5	11.7	11.8	12.1	12.1	12.1	11.8	11.6
1994	12.6	12.4	12.9	13.3	13.5	13.6	13.5	13.7	13.5	13.8	13.6	13.8	13.3
1995	13.8	13.6	14.1	14.1	14.3	14.6	14.5	14.5	14.7	14.6	14.6	14.7	14.3
1996	14.5	14.3	14.8	15.0	15.3	15.4	15.2	15.5	15.1	14.9	14.9	15.0	14.9
1997	15.2	15.5	15.7	15.8	16.1	16.6	16.5	16.8	16.5	16.7	16.4	16.5	16.1
1998	15.5	15.6	15.7	16.1	16.3	16.7	17.3	17.4	17.1	17.7	17.6	17.7	16.7
1999	16.1	15.9	16.0	16.5	16.4	16.7	16.5	16.6	16.4	16.4	16.4	16.5	16.3
2000	16.4	16.5	16.5	16.6	16.7	16.8	16.9	17.3	17.0	16.8	16.6	16.1	16.6
2001	16.0	16.1	16.1	16.2	16.3	16.5	16.9	17.1	16.8	16.9	16.6	16.6	16.5
2002	16.9	17.1	17.4	17.8	18.2	18.5	18.1	18.5	18.3	18.5	18.3	18.3	18.0
2003	21.2	21.0	21.1	21.5	21.8	22.3	22.2	22.0	21.4	21.6	21.4	21.1	21.6
Educational and health services													
1990	14.5	14.3	14.4	14.8	14.9	15.3	15.3	15.2	15.3	15.5	15.5	15.6	15.0
1991	15.4	15.6	15.7	15.6	15.6	15.9	15.8	15.9	16.0	16.3	16.2	16.2	15.8
1992	16.4	16.6	16.7	16.8	16.6	16.8	16.7	16.7	16.8	16.8	16.8	16.8	16.7
1993	16.7	16.9	16.9	16.7	16.8	16.9	17.1	17.1	17.0	17.1	17.2	17.3	16.9
1994	16.8	16.9	17.0	17.1	17.0	17.3	17.3	17.1	17.5	17.5	17.6	17.7	17.2
1995	17.8	18.0	18.1	18.2	18.2	18.6	18.4	18.4	18.4	18.4	18.4	18.7	18.3
1996	18.3	18.4	18.6	18.6	18.6	18.5	18.4	18.4	18.3	18.8	18.8	18.8	18.5
1997	18.5	18.6	18.7	18.8	18.8	19.1	19.5	19.4	19.4	19.5	19.5	19.5	19.1
1998	19.7	19.6	19.7	19.5	19.4	19.6	19.1	19.3	19.2	19.2	19.3	19.3	19.4
1999	18.9	18.9	19.1	19.0	19.0	19.0	19.0	19.0	19.1	19.2	19.2	19.2	19.0
2000	19.0	19.0	19.2	19.3	19.2	19.5	19.5	19.8	19.9	19.9	20.3	20.0	19.5
2001	20.3	20.3	20.5	20.4	20.4	20.8	20.8	20.7	20.7	20.6	20.7	20.6	20.6
2002	20.8	20.9	21.0	21.0	21.0	21.3	21.2	21.2	21.3	21.2	21.2	21.3	21.1
2003	21.2	21.2	21.3	21.5	21.5	21.7	21.6	21.4	21.6	21.6	21.4	21.4	21.5

Employment by Industry: Wisconsin—*Continued*

(Numbers in thousands. Not seasonally adjusted.)

Industry	January	February	March	April	May	June	July	August	September	October	November	December	Annual Average
APPLETON-OSHKOSH-NEENAH—*Continued*													
Leisure and hospitality													
1990	11.4	11.4	11.7	12.2	12.6	12.6	12.8	12.9	12.9	12.5	12.3	12.3	12.3
1991	11.7	11.7	12.0	12.3	12.7	12.7	12.2	13.0	12.2	12.4	12.2	12.2	12.2
1992	11.7	11.9	12.1	12.5	12.9	12.9	12.7	12.8	12.8	13.0	12.8	12.8	12.5
1993	12.5	12.7	12.8	13.3	13.7	13.7	13.5	13.7	13.4	13.4	13.4	13.5	13.3
1994	12.5	12.8	13.1	13.7	13.9	13.9	13.8	13.7	13.8	13.6	13.3	13.5	13.4
1995	13.0	13.2	13.6	14.0	14.3	14.3	14.0	14.9	14.2	13.9	13.7	13.9	13.9
1996	13.4	13.6	13.8	14.2	14.6	14.7	14.6	15.4	14.3	14.4	14.2	14.2	14.2
1997	13.6	13.8	13.9	14.5	14.9	15.0	14.9	15.2	14.9	14.5	14.2	14.4	14.4
1998	13.7	14.1	14.3	14.9	15.2	15.5	15.2	15.9	14.9	14.7	14.4	14.5	14.7
1999	14.0	14.3	14.7	14.9	15.3	15.6	15.2	15.9	15.0	14.7	14.4	14.7	14.8
2000	13.9	13.9	14.4	15.0	15.4	15.9	15.7	16.3	15.5	14.8	14.5	14.6	14.9
2001	14.5	14.6	14.8	15.4	15.8	16.0	16.1	16.8	15.7	15.4	15.0	15.0	15.4
2002	14.7	14.6	14.9	15.4	16.0	16.2	16.3	16.6	16.3	16.0	15.9	16.4	15.8
2003	15.9	15.6	15.9	16.5	17.2	17.2	17.1	17.1	16.3	16.0	15.7	15.5	16.3
Other services													
1990	9.2	9.2	9.4	9.2	9.1	9.3	9.3	9.2	9.2	9.3	9.3	9.3	9.2
1991	9.4	9.4	9.5	9.3	9.3	9.4	9.5	9.4	9.4	9.4	9.4	9.5	9.4
1992	9.4	9.4	9.5	9.5	9.6	9.7	9.7	9.8	9.7	9.7	9.7	9.8	9.6
1993	9.8	9.9	10.0	10.0	10.0	10.0	10.0	10.1	10.1	10.1	10.1	10.2	10.0
1994	10.1	10.2	10.2	10.2	10.1	10.2	10.2	10.2	10.2	10.2	10.2	10.2	10.1
1995	9.3	9.3	9.4	9.5	9.4	9.5	9.5	9.5	9.4	9.5	9.4	9.3	9.4
1996	9.4	9.4	9.4	9.4	9.3	9.5	9.4	9.3	9.4	9.5	9.4	9.5	9.4
1997	9.4	9.4	9.5	9.6	9.5	9.5	9.6	9.5	9.5	9.5	9.5	9.5	9.5
1998	9.6	9.7	9.6	9.6	9.6	9.7	9.6	9.7	9.7	9.7	9.6	9.6	9.6
1999	9.7	9.7	9.8	9.8	9.8	9.9	9.8	9.8	9.9	9.8	9.9	9.9	9.8
2000	9.8	9.9	10.0	9.9	9.8	10.1	10.0	9.9	10.2	9.9	10.0	10.2	9.9
2001	9.6	9.6	9.7	9.6	9.6	9.8	9.8	9.9	9.9	9.7	9.7	10.0	9.7
2002	9.8	9.8	10.1	9.9	9.8	10.0	9.9	10.1	9.9	9.8	9.8	10.0	9.9
2003	9.9	9.9	10.0	10.0	9.9	10.1	10.0	10.2	10.1	10.0	9.9	10.1	10.0
Government													
1990	17.3	17.8	18.3	18.7	17.9	17.6	16.5	16.2	17.2	18.1	19.0	18.6	17.7
1991	17.5	18.8	18.5	18.6	18.4	17.9	16.4	16.7	17.3	18.5	18.9	18.9	18.0
1992	17.9	18.9	18.9	19.4	18.9	18.6	17.0	16.8	18.4	19.0	19.6	19.4	18.5
1993	18.6	19.4	19.2	19.9	19.4	19.8	17.5	17.2	18.3	19.5	19.6	19.7	19.0
1994	19.1	19.7	19.8	20.3	19.9	19.9	18.7	17.6	18.9	20.2	20.8	20.4	19.6
1995	20.5	21.2	21.6	21.8	21.2	21.1	20.1	19.5	20.6	21.8	22.2	21.9	21.1
1996	21.3	22.0	22.3	21.9	21.8	21.8	20.5	20.3	21.3	22.3	22.5	22.3	21.6
1997	21.8	21.9	22.4	22.6	22.8	22.1	20.4	20.3	21.3	22.6	22.5	22.0	21.8
1998	21.6	21.9	22.5	22.7	22.8	22.8	22.2	21.4	22.6	23.1	23.1	23.2	22.4
1999	22.5	23.2	23.3	23.3	23.4	23.0	21.9	21.3	21.9	23.3	23.7	23.5	22.8
2000	22.8	23.5	23.5	23.9	23.8	23.3	22.4	21.9	22.6	23.6	24.0	23.7	23.2
2001	23.2	23.5	23.8	24.0	23.7	23.4	21.9	21.6	22.7	24.4	24.6	24.5	23.4
2002	23.6	24.2	24.4	24.3	24.4	23.3	21.8	21.4	22.3	24.2	24.7	23.9	23.5
2003	23.3	24.1	24.3	24.2	24.4	23.8	21.9	21.8	21.9	23.9	23.9	23.8	23.4
Federal government													
2001	1.1	1.1	1.1	1.1	1.1	1.1	1.1	1.1	1.1	1.1	1.1	1.1	1.0
2002	1.1	1.1	1.1	1.0	1.0	1.0	1.0	1.0	1.0	1.0	1.1	1.1	1.0
2003	1.1	1.1	1.1	1.1	1.1	1.1	1.1	1.1	1.1	1.1	1.1	1.1	1.1
State government													
2001	5.0	5.0	5.3	5.3	5.2	4.6	4.7	4.6	4.5	5.5	5.6	5.5	5.0
2002	4.8	5.1	5.4	5.5	5.4	4.6	4.5	4.6	4.3	5.6	5.7	5.1	5.1
2003	4.7	5.1	5.5	5.3	5.4	4.7	4.4	4.5	4.5	5.3	5.4	5.3	5.0
Local government													
2001	17.1	17.4	17.4	17.6	17.4	17.7	16.1	15.9	17.1	17.8	17.9	17.9	17.2
2002	17.7	18.0	17.9	17.8	18.0	17.7	16.3	15.8	17.0	17.6	17.9	17.7	17.5
2003	17.5	17.9	17.7	17.8	17.9	18.0	16.4	16.2	16.3	17.5	17.4	17.4	17.3
GREEN BAY													
Total nonfarm													
1990	101.9	102.1	102.8	104.2	105.5	107.6	106.5	107.2	107.7	107.2	107.8	106.6	105.5
1991	104.6	105.4	105.9	106.6	107.3	109.3	108.2	109.3	109.9	110.7	110.3	110.5	108.1
1992	108.2	108.7	109.2	111.8	113.1	114.6	112.8	112.9	113.8	115.2	115.6	115.3	112.6
1993	111.9	112.4	113.2	114.6	115.9	117.5	116.7	117.5	118.0	119.0	119.8	119.5	116.3
1994	116.2	116.6	118.2	119.8	121.6	123.1	122.6	122.4	123.9	124.6	125.3	125.3	121.6
1995	123.6	123.9	125.2	126.0	127.4	129.3	127.5	127.9	128.7	129.2	129.4	129.7	127.3
1996	126.9	127.4	128.1	128.8	130.2	132.6	131.2	132.6	133.0	132.9	133.3	134.4	130.9
1997	130.5	131.2	131.4	133.0	134.3	135.6	133.7	134.6	134.0	135.7	135.8	136.0	133.8
1998	133.5	133.7	134.6	135.9	136.9	138.2	137.7	137.9	138.8	140.7	141.1	142.4	137.6
1999	139.5	140.0	141.2	141.7	142.1	143.9	143.7	144.6	144.6	146.3	147.5	147.9	143.5
2000	142.1	142.8	143.7	145.1	146.2	148.0	147.2	148.2	148.8	148.2	148.4	147.6	146.3
2001	144.6	144.9	145.0	145.8	146.3	147.5	146.2	146.1	145.5	146.1	145.3	144.4	145.6
2002	142.4	142.0	142.9	144.7	146.6	147.7	146.2	147.1	147.3	147.7	148.2	147.1	145.8
2003	144.1	143.3	143.7	146.1	147.2	148.4	147.6	148.8	150.1	151.6	151.3	150.9	147.8

Employment by Industry: Wisconsin—*Continued*

(Numbers in thousands. Not seasonally adjusted.)

Industry	January	February	March	April	May	June	July	August	September	October	November	December	Annual Average
GREEN BAY—*Continued*													
Total private													
1990	90.5	90.3	91.0	92.3	93.6	95.7	95.6	96.5	96.1	95.4	95.6	94.6	93.9
1991	92.6	93.1	93.5	94.3	94.9	96.6	97.1	98.2	97.9	98.1	97.7	98.0	96.0
1992	95.9	95.9	96.5	98.8	100.5	101.6	101.5	101.8	101.4	102.7	102.6	102.6	100.1
1993	99.4	99.6	100.4	101.6	103.1	104.6	105.4	106.1	105.7	106.3	107.0	106.6	103.8
1994	103.5	103.8	105.2	106.5	108.6	110.0	110.2	110.4	111.0	111.6	111.8	112.0	108.7
1995	108.4	108.5	109.7	110.4	112.1	113.7	113.2	114.0	113.8	114.0	114.0	114.3	112.1
1996	111.4	111.6	112.4	113.2	114.5	116.6	116.6	118.0	117.2	117.1	117.2	118.6	115.3
1997	114.8	115.3	115.4	116.8	118.2	119.5	119.2	119.9	118.4	119.7	119.4	119.8	118.0
1998	117.4	117.6	118.4	119.6	120.6	121.8	122.6	122.8	123.2	124.3	124.7	126.0	121.5
1999	123.2	123.7	124.8	125.0	125.4	127.1	128.1	129.1	128.7	129.6	130.7	131.0	127.2
2000	125.5	125.9	126.8	128.0	128.8	130.9	131.6	132.2	132.3	131.0	130.7	130.3	129.5
2001	127.6	127.3	127.5	128.3	128.7	129.9	129.8	129.8	128.4	128.3	127.3	126.5	128.3
2002	125.0	124.2	124.8	126.6	128.3	129.7	129.7	130.8	130.0	129.8	130.0	129.2	128.2
2003	126.8	125.3	125.7	128.2	129.4	130.6	131.3	132.4	133.5	133.9	133.5	133.3	130.3
Goods-producing													
1990	26.9	26.8	26.8	26.6	27.6	28.9	29.4	29.8	29.0	28.5	27.9	26.9	27.9
1991	26.2	26.2	26.2	26.6	27.1	28.3	29.0	29.4	28.7	28.3	27.6	27.5	27.5
1992	27.0	27.0	27.0	28.5	29.3	30.0	30.6	30.7	30.1	29.9	29.6	29.0	29.0
1993	28.2	28.0	28.3	28.9	29.6	30.3	31.2	31.7	31.2	31.1	30.9	30.2	29.9
1994	29.5	29.3	29.8	30.5	31.6	32.6	32.9	32.9	32.4	32.2	32.2	31.6	31.4
1995	31.6	31.5	31.8	32.3	32.9	34.2	34.6	34.7	34.0	33.9	33.6	33.0	33.1
1996	31.6	31.4	31.4	32.1	32.8	34.0	34.6	35.1	34.4	33.9	33.6	33.7	33.2
1997	32.6	32.5	32.4	33.1	34.0	35.1	35.6	35.6	34.6	34.6	34.4	33.8	34.0
1998	33.5	33.3	33.7	33.9	34.4	35.7	36.4	36.4	36.2	35.8	35.6	35.4	35.0
1999	34.7	34.9	35.2	35.3	35.8	36.8	37.5	37.6	37.2	36.9	37.0	36.6	36.2
2000	35.3	35.4	35.6	35.9	36.7	38.0	38.2	38.1	37.7	36.8	36.7	36.2	36.7
2001	35.6	35.1	35.2	35.3	35.6	36.5	36.7	36.6	36.0	35.8	35.1	34.6	35.7
2002	34.2	34.0	34.2	34.7	35.4	36.0	36.2	36.3	35.6	34.9	34.6	34.1	35.0
2003	33.5	33.1	33.4	33.9	34.7	35.3	35.7	35.4	35.4	35.6	35.4	34.9	34.7
Construction and mining													
1990	4.2	4.2	4.2	4.6	4.9	5.3	5.3	5.3	5.1	5.1	4.9	4.5	4.8
1991	4.0	4.0	4.0	4.5	4.9	5.2	5.4	5.4	5.3	5.5	5.4	5.3	4.9
1992	5.0	5.1	5.0	5.6	6.0	6.2	6.4	6.1	6.2	6.2	5.9	5.6	5.7
1993	5.0	4.9	5.1	5.3	5.7	5.9	6.1	6.1	6.1	6.2	6.0	5.6	5.6
1994	5.0	4.8	5.3	5.7	6.2	6.6	6.4	6.3	6.3	6.2	6.1	5.8	5.8
1995	5.4	5.3	5.6	6.1	6.6	7.0	6.8	6.6	6.7	6.6	6.5	6.1	6.2
1996	5.5	5.4	5.6	5.9	6.7	7.1	7.3	7.5	7.5	7.3	7.2	6.9	6.6
1997	6.0	5.9	5.8	6.2	6.9	7.2	7.4	7.2	7.1	7.0	6.8	6.3	6.6
1998	5.5	5.5	5.7	6.2	6.8	7.2	7.5	7.5	7.5	7.3	7.2	7.0	6.7
1999	6.4	6.6	6.7	7.1	7.5	7.9	8.1	7.9	7.9	7.9	7.9	7.5	7.4
2000	6.8	6.8	7.0	7.5	8.2	8.5	8.6	8.5	8.4	8.1	8.0	7.6	7.8
2001	7.3	7.1	7.2	7.4	7.9	8.3	8.6	8.7	8.5	8.5	8.2	7.9	8.0
2002	7.3	7.3	7.5	8.0	8.4	8.6	8.8	8.8	8.5	8.3	8.1	7.7	8.1
2003	7.1	7.1	7.1	7.5	8.1	8.3	8.5	8.4	8.2	8.1	8.0	7.6	7.8
Manufacturing													
1990	22.7	22.6	22.6	22.0	22.7	23.6	24.1	24.5	23.9	23.4	23.0	22.4	23.1
1991	22.2	22.2	22.2	22.1	22.2	23.1	23.6	24.0	23.4	22.8	22.2	22.2	22.6
1992	22.0	21.9	22.0	22.9	23.3	23.8	24.2	24.6	23.9	23.7	23.7	23.4	23.2
1993	23.2	23.1	23.2	23.6	23.9	24.4	25.1	25.6	25.1	24.9	24.9	24.6	24.3
1994	24.5	24.5	24.5	24.8	25.4	26.0	26.5	26.6	26.1	26.0	26.1	25.8	25.5
1995	26.2	26.2	26.2	26.2	26.3	27.2	27.8	28.1	27.3	27.3	27.1	26.9	26.9
1996	26.1	26.0	25.8	26.2	26.1	26.9	27.3	27.6	26.9	26.6	26.4	26.8	26.5
1997	26.6	26.6	26.6	26.9	27.1	27.9	28.2	28.4	27.5	27.6	27.6	27.5	27.3
1998	28.0	27.8	28.0	27.7	27.6	28.5	28.9	28.9	28.7	28.5	28.4	28.4	28.2
1999	28.3	28.3	28.5	28.2	28.3	28.9	29.4	29.7	29.3	29.0	29.1	29.1	28.8
2000	28.5	28.6	28.6	28.4	28.5	29.5	29.6	29.6	29.3	28.7	28.7	28.6	28.8
2001	28.3	28.0	28.0	27.9	27.7	28.2	28.1	27.9	27.5	27.3	26.9	26.7	27.7
2002	26.9	26.7	26.7	26.7	27.0	27.4	27.4	27.5	27.1	26.6	26.5	26.4	26.9
2003	26.4	26.0	26.3	26.4	26.6	27.0	27.2	27.0	27.2	27.5	27.4	27.3	26.9
Service-providing													
1990	75.0	75.3	76.0	77.6	77.9	78.7	77.1	77.4	78.7	78.7	79.9	79.7	77.6
1991	78.4	79.2	79.7	80.0	80.2	81.0	79.2	79.9	81.2	82.4	82.7	83.0	80.5
1992	81.2	81.7	82.2	83.3	83.8	84.6	82.2	82.2	83.7	85.3	86.0	86.3	83.5
1993	83.7	84.4	84.9	85.7	86.3	87.2	85.5	85.8	86.8	87.9	88.9	89.3	86.3
1994	86.7	87.3	88.4	89.3	90.0	90.5	89.7	89.5	91.5	92.4	93.1	93.7	90.1
1995	92.0	92.4	93.4	93.7	94.5	95.1	92.9	93.2	94.7	95.3	95.8	96.7	94.1
1996	95.3	96.0	96.7	96.7	97.4	98.6	96.6	97.5	98.6	99.0	99.7	100.7	97.7
1997	97.9	98.7	99.0	99.9	100.3	100.5	98.1	99.0	99.4	101.1	101.4	102.2	99.7
1998	100.0	100.4	100.9	102.0	102.5	102.5	101.3	101.5	102.6	104.9	105.5	107.0	102.5
1999	104.8	105.1	106.0	106.4	106.3	107.1	106.2	107.0	107.4	109.4	110.5	111.3	107.2
2000	106.8	107.4	108.1	109.2	109.5	110.0	109.0	110.1	111.1	111.4	111.7	111.4	109.6
2001	109.0	109.8	109.8	110.5	110.7	111.0	109.5	109.5	109.5	110.3	110.2	109.8	110.0
2002	108.2	108.0	108.7	110.0	111.2	111.7	110.0	110.8	111.7	112.8	113.6	113.0	110.8
2003	110.6	110.2	110.3	112.2	112.5	113.1	111.9	113.4	114.7	116.0	115.9	116.0	113.1

Employment by Industry: Wisconsin—*Continued*

(Numbers in thousands. Not seasonally adjusted.)

Industry	January	February	March	April	May	June	July	August	September	October	November	December	Annual Average
GREEN BAY—*Continued*													
Trade, transportation, and utilities													
1990	24.4	24.3	24.5	24.9	25.0	25.7	25.6	25.5	25.5	25.5	25.9	26.0	25.2
1991	24.8	24.8	24.9	24.9	25.0	25.1	25.1	25.2	25.2	25.2	25.5	25.6	25.1
1992	24.8	24.6	24.7	25.1	25.2	25.2	24.8	25.0	24.9	25.5	25.7	25.8	25.1
1993	25.1	25.0	25.1	25.0	25.5	25.8	25.9	26.0	25.9	26.3	26.7	26.8	25.7
1994	25.8	25.8	26.1	26.3	26.7	26.9	26.6	26.7	27.0	27.4	27.6	27.8	26.7
1995	27.6	27.5	27.6	27.5	28.0	28.1	27.9	27.9	28.0	28.1	28.4	28.7	27.9
1996	28.3	28.5	28.5	28.6	29.1	29.3	29.0	29.2	29.2	29.4	29.8	30.2	29.0
1997	28.9	28.8	29.1	29.1	29.6	29.7	29.5	29.5	29.4	29.8	29.8	30.0	29.4
1998	29.0	29.1	29.3	29.5	29.7	29.7	29.6	29.8	30.1	30.6	30.9	31.3	29.8
1999	30.2	30.3	30.5	30.5	30.7	30.8	30.8	31.0	31.0	31.7	32.1	32.6	31.0
2000	30.8	30.9	31.0	31.2	31.3	31.5	31.5	31.6	31.9	32.0	32.1	32.3	31.5
2001	31.6	31.3	31.2	31.5	31.6	31.9	32.2	32.2	31.8	31.7	31.9	31.8	31.7
2002	31.4	31.1	31.4	31.3	31.5	31.9	32.1	32.2	32.4	32.6	33.1	33.4	32.0
2003	31.7	31.4	31.4	31.7	32.3	32.5	32.3	32.6	32.3	32.5	32.7	32.9	32.2
Wholesale trade													
1990	5.1	5.0	5.0	5.2	5.2	5.4	5.4	5.3	5.2	5.1	5.1	5.1	5.1
1991	4.7	4.7	4.7	4.7	4.7	4.8	4.9	4.9	4.9	4.8	4.8	4.8	4.7
1992	4.6	4.6	4.6	4.7	4.7	4.8	4.8	4.8	4.7	4.7	4.7	4.7	4.7
1993	4.7	4.8	4.8	4.8	4.9	5.0	5.1	5.1	5.0	5.1	5.1	5.1	4.9
1994	5.0	5.0	5.0	5.1	5.1	5.2	5.2	5.2	5.2	5.2	5.1	5.2	5.1
1995	5.2	5.2	5.2	5.2	5.3	5.4	5.4	5.4	5.4	5.4	5.4	5.4	5.3
1996	5.3	5.3	5.3	5.2	5.3	5.4	5.4	5.5	5.5	5.4	5.5	5.5	5.3
1997	5.4	5.4	5.5	5.5	5.6	5.6	5.6	5.6	5.6	5.7	5.6	5.7	5.5
1998	5.5	5.6	5.6	5.6	5.7	5.7	5.8	5.8	5.8	5.8	5.8	5.9	5.7
1999	5.8	5.8	5.8	5.8	5.8	5.8	5.8	5.8	5.8	5.9	5.9	6.0	5.8
2000	5.8	5.8	5.8	5.9	6.0	6.1	6.2	6.2	6.2	6.1	6.1	6.1	6.0
2001	6.2	6.1	6.1	6.1	6.2	6.2	6.1	6.1	6.0	5.9	5.9	5.9	6.1
2002	5.9	5.8	5.8	5.9	5.9	6.0	6.0	6.0	6.0	6.0	5.9	5.9	5.9
2003	5.8	5.8	5.9	5.9	5.9	6.0	6.1	6.1	6.0	6.0	5.9	5.9	5.9
Retail trade													
1990	12.2	12.1	12.3	12.5	12.5	13.0	12.9	12.8	12.7	12.8	13.1	13.2	12.6
1991	12.7	12.6	12.6	12.7	12.7	12.7	12.6	12.7	12.6	12.7	13.0	13.2	12.7
1992	12.6	12.4	12.4	12.8	12.8	12.7	12.4	12.6	12.5	13.1	13.4	13.5	12.7
1993	12.7	12.5	12.5	12.5	12.7	12.8	12.7	12.7	12.7	12.9	13.3	13.4	12.7
1994	12.8	12.7	12.9	13.0	13.2	13.2	13.0	13.1	13.3	13.6	14.0	14.1	13.2
1995	13.8	13.7	13.8	13.6	13.8	13.8	13.7	13.8	13.8	13.8	14.1	14.4	13.8
1996	14.1	14.3	14.3	14.3	14.6	14.6	14.5	14.6	14.6	14.8	15.1	15.5	14.6
1997	14.3	14.1	14.3	14.3	14.6	14.6	14.4	14.5	14.3	14.5	14.6	14.8	14.4
1998	14.0	14.0	14.1	14.1	14.2	14.2	14.1	14.2	14.3	14.6	15.0	15.2	14.3
1999	14.5	14.5	14.7	14.6	14.8	14.7	14.7	14.8	14.8	15.3	15.7	16.0	14.9
2000	14.8	14.7	14.8	14.9	14.8	14.9	14.8	14.9	15.2	15.4	15.6	15.7	15.0
2001	14.5	14.3	14.3	14.8	14.9	15.3	15.9	16.1	15.9	16.1	16.5	16.7	15.4
2002	16.3	16.1	16.3	16.1	16.1	16.3	16.3	16.4	16.4	16.7	17.3	17.6	16.5
2003	16.5	16.2	16.1	16.3	16.6	16.6	16.2	16.5	16.2	16.3	16.5	16.6	16.4
Transportation and utilities													
1990	7.1	7.2	7.2	7.2	7.3	7.3	7.3	7.4	7.6	7.6	7.7	7.7	7.3
1991	7.4	7.5	7.6	7.5	7.6	7.6	7.6	7.6	7.7	7.7	7.7	7.6	7.5
1992	7.6	7.6	7.7	7.6	7.7	7.7	7.6	7.6	7.7	7.7	7.6	7.6	7.6
1993	7.7	7.7	7.8	7.7	7.9	8.0	8.1	8.2	8.2	8.3	8.3	8.3	8.0
1994	8.0	8.1	8.2	8.2	8.4	8.5	8.4	8.4	8.5	8.6	8.5	8.5	8.3
1995	8.6	8.6	8.6	8.7	8.9	8.9	8.8	8.7	8.8	8.9	8.9	8.9	8.7
1996	8.9	8.9	8.9	9.1	9.2	9.3	9.1	9.1	9.1	9.2	9.2	9.2	9.1
1997	9.2	9.3	9.3	9.3	9.4	9.5	9.5	9.4	9.5	9.6	9.6	9.5	9.4
1998	9.5	9.5	9.6	9.8	9.8	9.8	9.7	9.8	10.0	10.2	10.1	10.2	9.8
1999	9.9	10.0	10.0	10.1	10.1	10.3	10.3	10.4	10.4	10.5	10.5	10.6	10.2
2000	10.2	10.4	10.4	10.4	10.5	10.5	10.5	10.5	10.5	10.5	10.4	10.5	10.4
2001	10.9	10.9	10.8	10.6	10.5	10.4	10.2	10.0	9.9	9.7	9.5	9.2	10.2
2002	9.2	9.2	9.3	9.3	9.5	9.6	9.8	9.8	10.0	9.9	9.9	9.9	9.6
2003	9.4	9.4	9.4	9.5	9.8	9.9	10.0	10.0	10.1	10.2	10.3	10.4	9.9
Information													
1990	1.7	1.7	1.7	1.7	1.8	1.8	1.8	1.9	1.9	1.9	1.9	1.9	1.8
1991	2.0	2.1	2.0	2.1	2.1	2.1	2.1	2.1	2.1	2.1	2.1	2.1	2.0
1992	2.0	2.0	2.0	2.0	2.0	2.1	2.1	2.0	2.0	2.0	2.0	2.0	2.0
1993	2.0	2.1	2.1	2.1	2.1	2.2	2.2	2.2	2.1	2.2	2.2	2.2	2.1
1994	2.0	2.0	2.0	2.0	2.0	2.0	2.0	2.0	2.0	2.0	2.0	2.0	2.0
1995	2.0	2.0	2.0	1.9	1.9	1.9	2.0	2.0	2.0	2.0	2.0	2.0	1.9
1996	2.0	2.1	2.0	2.0	2.0	2.0	2.1	2.1	2.1	2.2	2.3	2.3	2.1
1997	2.2	2.2	2.1	2.1	2.1	2.0	2.1	2.1	2.1	2.2	2.2	2.2	2.1
1998	2.2	2.3	2.2	2.2	2.2	2.2	2.3	2.3	2.3	2.4	2.4	2.5	2.2
1999	2.4	2.4	2.4	2.3	2.3	2.2	2.3	2.3	2.4	2.3	2.4	2.4	2.3
2000	2.4	2.4	2.3	2.4	2.4	2.5	2.6	2.6	2.6	2.6	2.6	2.6	2.5
2001	2.6	2.6	2.6	2.5	2.5	2.5	2.5	2.4	2.4	2.4	2.4	2.5	2.5
2002	2.5	2.5	2.4	2.3	2.3	2.3	2.4	2.4	2.5	2.5	2.5	2.6	2.4
2003	2.5	2.4	2.4	2.4	2.4	2.4	2.5	2.5	2.5	2.5	2.5	2.6	2.5

Employment by Industry: Wisconsin—*Continued*

(Numbers in thousands. Not seasonally adjusted.)

Industry	January	February	March	April	May	June	July	August	September	October	November	December	Annual Average
GREEN BAY—*Continued*													
Financial activities													
1990	5.4	5.5	5.5	5.7	5.7	5.8	5.8	5.8	5.8	5.8	5.9	6.0	5.7
1991	6.1	6.1	6.2	6.3	6.3	6.4	6.4	6.5	6.4	6.4	6.5	6.6	6.3
1992	6.6	6.6	6.6	6.7	6.7	6.9	6.8	6.9	6.9	6.9	6.9	6.9	6.7
1993	6.9	7.0	7.0	7.2	7.3	7.5	7.5	7.6	7.5	7.6	7.7	7.8	7.3
1994	7.7	7.8	7.8	8.1	8.1	8.2	8.3	8.4	8.4	8.4	8.6	8.8	8.2
1995	8.9	9.0	9.1	9.0	9.1	9.3	9.2	9.2	9.3	9.3	9.4	9.6	9.2
1996	9.9	9.9	10.0	9.8	9.8	9.8	9.8	9.8	9.7	9.6	9.3	9.4	9.7
1997	9.7	9.7	9.5	9.5	9.4	9.4	9.3	9.3	9.2	9.3	9.2	9.3	9.4
1998	9.6	9.7	9.7	9.9	9.8	9.9	9.9	10.0	10.0	10.2	10.3	10.5	9.9
1999	11.0	11.2	11.1	10.8	10.8	11.0	10.9	10.9	10.9	10.8	10.9	11.0	10.9
2000	11.0	11.0	11.1	11.1	11.0	11.0	11.0	10.9	10.8	10.7	10.7	10.7	10.9
2001	10.9	10.8	10.7	10.7	10.7	10.7	10.4	10.3	10.2	10.2	10.2	10.2	10.5
2002	10.2	10.2	10.2	10.3	10.4	10.5	10.4	10.5	10.5	10.4	10.5	10.5	10.4
2003	10.4	10.4	10.5	10.7	10.7	10.7	10.7	10.8	10.9	10.8	10.9	10.9	10.7
Professional and business services													
1990	8.0	8.0	8.0	8.2	8.2	8.2	8.3	8.4	8.6	8.5	8.6	8.5	8.2
1991	8.5	8.6	8.6	8.5	8.5	8.5	8.6	8.7	8.7	9.1	9.0	9.0	8.6
1992	8.8	8.8	8.9	9.4	9.4	9.5	9.7	9.7	9.6	10.0	9.8	9.8	9.4
1993	9.3	9.3	9.4	9.8	9.8	9.9	9.9	9.8	9.9	9.9	10.0	9.9	9.7
1994	9.7	9.8	10.1	10.1	10.3	10.4	10.5	10.5	10.7	10.9	10.6	10.6	10.3
1995	10.1	10.1	10.4	10.5	10.7	10.9	10.5	10.6	10.8	10.9	10.8	10.6	10.5
1996	10.2	10.1	10.3	10.5	10.5	10.6	10.7	10.8	10.8	11.0	11.2	11.3	10.6
1997	11.0	11.5	11.6	11.8	11.8	11.9	11.8	12.0	11.9	12.3	12.3	12.5	11.8
1998	11.8	11.9	11.9	12.3	12.4	12.5	12.6	12.4	12.4	13.0	13.0	13.1	12.4
1999	12.6	12.4	12.6	12.4	12.2	12.3	12.7	12.9	12.9	13.1	13.5	13.5	12.7
2000	12.4	12.5	12.6	12.7	12.6	12.7	13.3	13.6	13.7	13.3	13.2	13.0	12.9
2001	12.9	12.9	12.9	12.9	13.0	13.1	13.2	13.4	12.9	13.0	12.9	12.6	13.0
2002	12.6	12.5	12.6	12.7	12.7	13.0	13.0	13.3	13.2	13.3	13.2	12.9	12.9
2003	12.7	12.7	12.6	13.3	13.1	13.4	13.5	13.6	13.7	13.6	13.2	13.2	13.2
Educational and health services													
1990	10.9	10.9	11.0	11.3	11.3	11.4	11.2	11.3	11.4	11.6	11.7	11.8	11.3
1991	11.4	11.5	11.6	11.7	11.7	11.8	11.8	11.9	12.1	12.2	12.2	12.3	11.8
1992	12.3	12.3	12.4	12.5	12.4	12.4	12.1	12.1	12.2	12.4	12.5	12.6	12.3
1993	12.3	12.5	12.5	12.5	12.6	12.6	12.6	12.6	12.7	12.7	12.9	12.8	12.6
1994	12.6	12.7	12.7	12.8	12.8	12.8	13.0	12.9	13.1	13.3	13.4	13.3	12.9
1995	13.3	13.4	13.5	13.6	13.9	13.7	13.7	13.8	14.0	14.0	14.1	14.1	13.7
1996	14.1	14.2	14.3	14.4	14.2	14.5	14.5	14.4	14.5	14.7	14.7	14.8	14.4
1997	14.4	14.7	14.7	14.7	14.7	14.8	14.7	14.7	14.7	14.8	14.9	14.9	14.7
1998	14.7	14.9	15.0	14.9	15.0	14.7	14.8	14.6	14.9	15.1	15.1	15.2	14.9
1999	15.0	15.2	15.3	15.7	15.6	15.7	15.9	15.9	15.9	16.2	16.1	16.2	15.7
2000	15.8	16.0	16.1	16.4	16.3	16.6	16.8	16.7	16.7	16.8	16.8	16.9	16.4
2001	16.2	16.8	16.9	17.0	16.8	16.6	16.7	16.4	16.7	16.8	16.6	16.6	16.7
2002	16.3	16.5	16.4	17.3	17.6	17.8	17.6	17.6	17.5	17.7	17.7	17.1	17.3
2003	17.6	17.6	17.6	17.7	17.7	17.7	18.2	18.4	18.6	18.7	18.4	18.4	18.1
Leisure and hospitality													
1990	8.3	8.2	8.4	8.7	8.8	8.7	8.5	8.8	9.0	8.7	8.7	8.5	8.6
1991	8.8	8.9	9.0	9.2	9.3	9.3	9.3	9.6	9.8	9.9	9.9	9.9	9.4
1992	9.6	9.7	9.9	9.6	10.4	10.5	10.6	10.6	10.9	11.1	11.2	11.5	10.4
1993	10.7	10.7	10.9	11.2	11.2	11.3	11.3	11.4	11.5	11.6	11.7	11.9	11.2
1994	11.4	11.4	11.6	11.7	12.1	12.2	12.0	12.1	12.4	12.5	12.5	12.9	12.0
1995	9.9	9.9	10.0	10.3	10.4	10.4	10.3	10.7	10.5	10.5	10.7	11.1	10.3
1996	10.4	10.3	10.6	10.7	11.0	11.3	11.1	11.8	11.5	11.2	11.2	11.6	11.0
1997	10.9	10.8	10.7	11.2	11.3	11.3	11.0	11.5	11.3	11.3	11.1	11.5	11.1
1998	11.1	10.7	10.7	11.2	11.4	11.4	11.4	11.7	11.7	11.7	11.7	12.3	11.4
1999	11.5	11.4	11.6	11.8	11.9	12.1	11.9	12.4	12.3	12.2	12.3	12.2	11.9
2000	11.5	11.3	11.5	11.7	12.0	12.1	11.9	12.4	12.5	12.3	12.2	12.1	11.9
2001	11.6	11.5	11.6	12.0	12.2	12.3	12.0	12.3	12.1	12.1	12.0	12.0	12.0
2002	11.6	11.1	11.2	11.6	12.0	11.9	11.9	12.3	12.0	12.1	12.1	12.2	11.8
2003	12.1	11.4	11.5	12.1	12.2	12.4	12.3	12.9	13.9	14.0	14.2	14.2	12.8
Other services													
1990	4.9	4.9	5.1	5.2	5.2	5.2	5.0	5.0	4.9	4.9	5.0	5.0	5.0
1991	4.8	4.9	5.0	5.0	4.9	5.1	4.8	4.8	4.9	4.9	4.9	5.0	4.9
1992	4.8	4.9	5.0	5.0	5.1	5.0	4.8	4.8	4.8	4.9	4.9	5.0	4.9
1993	4.9	5.0	5.1	4.9	5.0	5.0	4.8	4.8	4.9	4.9	4.9	5.0	4.9
1994	4.8	5.0	5.1	5.0	5.0	4.9	4.9	4.9	5.0	4.9	4.9	5.0	4.9
1995	5.0	5.1	5.3	5.3	5.2	5.2	5.0	5.1	5.2	5.3	5.0	5.2	5.1
1996	4.9	5.1	5.3	5.1	5.1	5.1	4.8	4.8	5.0	5.1	5.1	5.3	5.0
1997	5.1	5.1	5.3	5.3	5.3	5.3	5.2	5.2	5.2	5.4	5.5	5.6	5.2
1998	5.5	5.7	5.9	5.7	5.7	5.7	5.6	5.6	5.6	5.5	5.7	5.7	5.6
1999	5.8	5.9	6.1	6.2	6.1	6.2	6.1	6.1	6.1	6.4	6.4	6.5	6.1
2000	6.3	6.4	6.6	6.6	6.5	6.5	6.3	6.3	6.4	6.5	6.4	6.5	6.4
2001	6.2	6.3	6.4	6.4	6.3	6.3	6.1	6.2	6.3	6.3	6.2	6.2	6.3
2002	6.2	6.3	6.4	6.4	6.4	6.3	6.1	6.2	6.3	6.3	6.3	6.4	6.3
2003	6.3	6.3	6.3	6.4	6.3	6.2	6.1	6.2	6.2	6.2	6.2	6.2	6.2

Employment by Industry: Wisconsin—*Continued*

(Numbers in thousands. Not seasonally adjusted.)

Industry	January	February	March	April	May	June	July	August	September	October	November	December	Annual Average
GREEN BAY—*Continued*													
Government													
1990	11.4	11.8	11.8	11.9	11.9	11.9	10.9	10.7	11.6	11.8	12.2	12.0	11.6
1991	12.0	12.3	12.4	12.3	12.4	12.7	11.1	11.1	12.0	12.6	12.6	12.5	12.1
1992	12.3	12.8	12.7	13.0	12.6	13.0	11.3	11.1	12.4	12.5	13.0	12.7	12.4
1993	12.5	12.8	12.8	13.0	12.8	12.9	11.3	11.4	12.3	12.7	12.8	12.9	12.5
1994	12.7	12.8	13.0	13.3	13.0	13.1	12.4	12.0	12.9	13.0	13.5	13.3	12.9
1995	15.2	15.4	15.5	15.6	15.3	15.6	14.3	13.9	14.9	15.2	15.4	15.4	15.1
1996	15.5	15.8	15.7	15.6	15.7	16.0	14.6	14.6	15.8	15.8	16.1	15.8	15.5
1997	15.7	15.9	16.0	16.2	16.1	16.1	14.5	14.7	15.6	16.0	16.4	16.2	15.7
1998	16.1	16.1	16.2	16.3	16.3	16.4	15.1	15.1	15.6	16.4	16.4	16.4	16.0
1999	16.3	16.3	16.4	16.7	16.7	16.8	15.6	15.5	15.9	16.7	16.8	16.9	16.3
2000	16.6	16.9	16.9	17.1	17.4	17.1	15.6	16.0	16.5	17.2	17.7	17.3	16.8
2001	17.0	17.6	17.5	17.5	17.6	17.6	16.4	16.3	17.1	17.8	18.0	17.9	17.4
2002	17.4	17.8	18.1	18.1	18.3	18.0	16.5	16.3	17.3	17.9	18.2	17.9	17.7
2003	17.3	18.0	18.0	17.9	17.8	17.8	16.3	16.4	16.6	17.7	17.8	17.6	17.4
Federal governmnet													
2001	1.0	1.0	1.0	1.0	1.0	1.0	1.0	1.0	1.0	1.0	1.0	1.0	1.0
2002	1.0	1.0	1.0	1.0	1.0	1.0	1.0	1.0	1.0	1.1	1.1	1.1	1.0
2003	1.1	1.1	1.1	1.0	1.0	1.0	1.0	1.0	1.0	1.0	1.0	1.0	1.0
State government													
2001	2.9	3.0	2.9	2.9	2.9	2.6	2.5	2.5	2.9	2.9	2.9	3.0	2.8
2002	2.6	2.9	2.9	2.9	3.0	2.6	2.5	2.5	2.7	2.8	2.8	2.9	2.8
2003	2.5	2.6	2.7	2.7	2.6	2.4	2.3	2.3	2.5	2.6	2.7	2.6	2.5
Local government													
2001	13.1	13.6	13.6	13.6	13.7	14.0	12.9	12.8	13.2	13.9	14.1	13.9	13.5
2002	13.8	13.9	14.2	14.2	14.3	14.4	13.0	12.8	13.6	14.0	14.3	13.9	13.9
2003	13.7	14.3	14.2	14.2	14.2	14.4	13.0	13.1	13.1	14.1	14.1	14.0	13.9
MADISON													
Total nonfarm													
1990	209.5	214.7	216.2	219.6	221.4	222.7	223.5	223.2	226.5	226.9	228.3	226.1	221.6
1991	216.9	220.3	221.5	223.7	225.1	225.1	225.2	227.1	228.0	229.4	230.4	228.9	225.1
1992	221.9	226.0	226.8	231.0	233.1	234.6	232.5	234.6	236.8	239.4	240.4	239.8	233.1
1993	232.3	235.4	236.4	238.5	241.9	242.1	242.2	243.1	246.2	249.9	251.2	250.7	242.5
1994	238.0	241.6	244.0	246.8	248.1	249.0	248.9	248.7	253.3	253.9	256.7	255.2	248.7
1995	247.6	250.4	252.7	253.8	255.0	256.3	254.1	255.6	258.0	258.9	261.0	259.5	255.2
1996	252.7	254.2	256.7	258.8	261.2	263.5	259.8	261.1	264.0	266.6	269.9	268.1	261.4
1997	258.7	261.4	262.9	265.8	267.9	268.6	267.1	268.8	270.6	271.5	273.9	272.3	267.5
1998	268.2	269.4	270.7	274.6	275.3	277.1	274.9	275.4	276.5	278.9	282.0	282.7	275.5
1999	275.2	275.1	276.8	281.7	281.6	285.0	283.6	284.6	285.4	286.5	288.5	288.1	282.7
2000	281.0	281.6	283.7	288.4	287.9	291.6	288.1	288.3	289.9	292.5	295.7	293.9	288.6
2001	288.0	289.4	291.5	296.0	296.2	298.6	294.5	294.7	297.0	297.6	298.9	296.6	294.9
2002	288.6	290.8	292.6	295.7	295.6	294.9	293.3	295.5	295.2	299.2	302.8	300.4	295.4
2003	288.5	291.5	292.0	296.7	297.0	301.1	297.0	299.2	298.0	300.6	302.9	302.8	297.3
Total private													
1990	153.7	155.0	155.7	157.8	159.7	162.5	163.8	164.3	164.5	164.9	165.5	164.4	161.0
1991	158.3	158.1	158.8	161.0	162.6	163.8	164.9	166.0	164.8	165.7	166.2	165.2	163.0
1992	160.8	161.5	162.1	165.1	167.4	170.3	169.2	170.4	170.5	172.5	173.0	173.5	168.0
1993	167.0	168.3	169.4	171.1	174.0	176.8	177.5	178.1	178.9	181.5	182.5	182.9	175.7
1994	172.7	173.2	175.0	177.6	179.8	182.7	183.7	184.2	185.0	184.5	186.5	186.0	180.9
1995	180.1	181.0	182.8	183.4	185.3	188.4	188.9	190.5	190.0	189.9	191.2	190.3	186.8
1996	184.9	184.6	186.6	187.6	190.4	194.2	193.8	195.4	194.9	195.6	196.8	196.9	191.8
1997	190.0	190.5	191.9	193.9	196.5	199.4	200.2	202.0	201.8	200.8	201.7	201.7	197.5
1998	197.8	197.4	198.3	201.0	202.9	206.2	205.7	206.2	204.7	206.1	207.7	209.4	203.6
1999	202.3	201.5	203.0	206.2	207.9	212.3	212.5	213.8	213.1	213.1	214.3	215.0	209.6
2000	208.5	208.1	209.5	212.2	214.2	217.4	217.8	218.7	217.6	218.7	219.6	219.3	215.1
2001	214.0	212.8	213.5	216.2	218.0	221.3	221.1	222.1	219.6	220.0	220.2	220.1	218.2
2002	214.9	215.1	216.1	217.3	219.5	222.6	222.5	223.8	221.9	222.7	224.1	224.2	220.4
2003	216.8	216.5	216.5	219.4	221.6	224.9	225.9	227.1	224.7	225.9	227.4	228.1	222.9
Goods-producing													
1990	31.4	31.2	31.5	32.2	33.1	34.4	35.4	35.6	35.1	34.4	34.2	33.3	33.5
1991	31.9	31.1	31.4	32.3	33.3	34.3	34.6	35.0	33.9	33.7	33.0	32.3	33.1
1992	31.3	31.2	31.4	32.4	33.5	34.9	35.3	35.6	35.1	34.5	34.6	33.9	33.6
1993	33.2	32.9	33.2	33.8	35.2	36.1	37.0	36.9	36.6	36.5	36.5	36.1	35.3
1994	34.1	33.8	34.6	35.8	36.7	38.1	38.4	38.8	38.5	37.8	37.6	37.0	36.8
1995	35.4	35.1	35.8	36.0	36.9	38.3	39.1	39.5	38.9	38.2	38.0	37.1	37.4
1996	36.5	36.1	36.8	38.0	39.0	40.0	40.5	41.0	40.3	39.9	39.6	39.0	38.9
1997	38.1	38.0	38.5	39.5	40.7	41.8	42.4	42.8	42.2	41.4	40.9	40.4	40.6
1998	39.4	39.4	39.6	41.4	42.3	43.7	44.0	44.1	42.9	42.3	42.2	42.1	42.0
1999	40.9	41.0	41.3	42.2	43.0	44.5	44.9	45.1	44.4	44.6	44.6	44.1	43.4
2000	43.1	42.8	43.4	44.4	45.2	46.7	46.8	46.6	45.7	45.8	45.1	44.5	45.0
2001	42.3	41.6	41.6	42.4	43.3	44.9	45.1	45.3	44.1	43.2	42.1	41.5	43.1
2002	39.9	39.9	40.1	40.8	41.6	43.0	43.0	43.5	42.4	42.3	42.2	41.5	41.7
2003	40.1	39.6	39.8	41.0	41.6	43.1	43.5	43.8	42.8	42.2	42.2	42.1	41.8

Employment by Industry: Wisconsin—*Continued*

(Numbers in thousands. Not seasonally adjusted.)

Industry	January	February	March	April	May	June	July	August	September	October	November	December	Annual Average
MADISON—*Continued*													
Construction and mining													
1990	7.3	7.3	7.5	8.3	8.9	9.4	9.7	9.9	9.5	9.3	9.1	8.6	8.7
1991	7.4	7.1	7.2	8.0	8.8	9.3	9.5	9.7	9.2	9.3	8.8	8.3	8.6
1992	7.7	7.6	7.7	8.8	9.6	10.3	10.4	10.5	10.1	10.0	9.8	9.2	9.3
1993	8.5	8.3	8.4	8.9	9.8	10.2	10.6	10.6	10.4	10.6	10.5	10.0	9.7
1994	8.6	8.3	8.8	9.9	10.6	11.2	11.4	11.4	11.2	10.8	10.5	9.9	10.2
1995	9.3	9.0	9.4	9.9	10.5	11.2	11.2	11.2	11.0	10.9	10.7	10.1	10.4
1996	9.7	9.5	10.0	10.8	11.6	12.3	12.7	12.7	12.3	12.2	12.0	11.6	11.5
1997	10.6	10.5	10.8	11.5	12.4	13.0	13.4	13.4	13.0	12.7	12.5	12.0	12.2
1998	10.9	10.9	11.0	12.1	12.8	13.7	14.0	14.0	13.4	13.5	13.3	13.1	12.7
1999	11.8	12.0	12.3	13.3	13.9	14.8	15.0	15.0	14.6	14.5	14.3	13.7	13.8
2000	12.7	12.5	13.0	13.7	14.2	15.0	15.2	15.1	14.7	14.7	14.4	13.9	14.1
2001	12.9	12.9	12.9	14.0	14.6	15.5	15.9	16.0	15.3	15.1	14.8	14.4	14.5
2002	13.0	13.0	13.1	13.9	14.6	15.4	15.7	15.6	14.9	14.8	14.7	14.1	14.4
2003	13.2	12.9	13.0	13.9	14.8	15.8	15.8	16.0	15.1	15.2	15.0	14.7	14.6
Manufacturing													
1990	24.1	23.9	24.0	23.9	24.2	25.0	25.7	25.7	25.6	25.1	25.1	24.7	24.8
1991	24.5	24.0	24.2	24.3	24.5	25.0	25.1	25.3	24.7	24.4	24.2	24.0	24.5
1992	23.6	23.6	23.7	23.6	23.9	24.6	24.9	25.1	25.0	24.5	24.8	24.7	24.3
1993	24.7	24.6	24.8	24.9	25.4	25.9	26.4	26.3	26.2	25.9	26.0	26.1	25.6
1994	25.5	25.5	25.8	25.9	26.1	26.9	27.0	27.4	27.3	27.0	27.1	27.1	26.6
1995	26.1	26.1	26.4	26.1	26.4	27.1	27.9	28.3	27.9	27.3	27.3	27.0	27.0
1996	26.8	26.6	26.8	27.2	27.4	27.7	27.8	28.3	28.0	27.7	27.6	27.4	27.4
1997	27.5	27.5	27.7	28.0	28.3	28.8	29.0	29.4	29.2	28.7	28.4	28.4	28.4
1998	28.5	28.5	28.6	29.3	29.5	30.0	30.0	30.1	29.5	28.8	28.9	29.0	29.2
1999	29.1	29.0	29.0	28.9	29.1	29.7	29.9	30.1	29.8	30.1	30.3	30.4	29.6
2000	30.4	30.3	30.4	30.7	31.0	31.7	31.6	31.5	31.0	31.1	30.7	30.6	30.9
2001	29.4	28.7	28.7	28.4	28.7	29.4	29.2	29.3	28.8	28.1	27.3	27.1	28.6
2002	26.9	26.9	27.0	26.9	27.0	27.6	27.3	27.9	27.5	27.5	27.5	27.4	27.3
2003	26.9	26.7	26.8	27.1	26.8	27.3	27.7	27.8	27.7	27.0	27.2	27.4	27.2
Service-providing													
1990	178.1	183.5	184.7	187.4	188.3	188.3	188.1	187.6	191.4	192.5	194.1	192.8	188.1
1991	185.0	189.2	190.1	191.4	191.8	190.8	190.6	192.1	194.1	195.7	197.4	196.6	192.1
1992	190.6	194.8	195.4	198.6	199.6	199.7	197.2	199.0	201.7	204.9	205.8	205.9	199.4
1993	199.1	202.5	203.2	204.7	206.7	206.0	205.2	206.2	209.6	213.4	214.7	214.6	207.2
1994	203.9	207.8	209.4	211.0	211.4	210.9	210.5	209.9	214.8	216.1	219.1	218.2	211.9
1995	212.2	215.3	216.9	217.8	218.1	218.0	215.0	216.1	219.1	220.7	223.0	222.4	217.9
1996	216.2	218.1	219.9	220.8	222.2	223.5	219.3	220.1	223.7	226.7	230.3	229.1	222.5
1997	220.6	223.4	224.4	226.3	227.2	226.8	224.7	226.0	228.4	230.1	233.0	231.9	226.9
1998	228.8	230.0	231.1	233.2	233.0	233.4	230.9	231.3	233.6	236.6	239.8	240.6	233.5
1999	234.3	234.1	235.5	239.5	238.6	240.5	238.7	239.5	241.0	241.9	243.9	244.0	239.3
2000	237.9	238.8	240.3	244.0	242.7	244.9	241.3	241.7	244.2	246.7	250.6	249.4	243.5
2001	245.7	247.8	249.9	253.6	252.9	253.7	249.4	249.4	252.9	254.4	256.8	255.1	251.8
2002	248.7	250.9	252.5	254.9	254.0	251.9	250.3	252.0	252.8	256.9	260.6	258.9	253.7
2003	248.4	251.9	252.2	255.7	255.4	258.0	253.5	255.4	255.2	258.4	260.7	260.7	255.5
Trade, transportation, and utilities													
1990	39.0	38.3	38.3	39.0	39.4	40.0	40.0	40.2	40.7	41.4	42.3	42.5	40.1
1991	38.6	38.1	37.9	38.5	38.8	38.5	39.1	39.7	40.0	41.0	41.9	42.2	39.5
1992	39.3	38.9	38.8	39.2	39.6	39.8	38.6	38.8	39.5	40.7	41.4	42.0	39.7
1993	38.9	38.8	39.1	39.4	39.7	40.3	40.2	40.6	41.2	42.4	43.2	44.0	40.7
1994	40.3	39.9	40.1	40.6	41.1	41.8	42.3	42.5	43.3	43.9	45.7	45.9	42.3
1995	42.8	42.5	42.4	42.3	42.6	43.1	43.3	43.7	44.1	44.9	46.3	46.4	43.7
1996	43.2	41.9	41.9	42.0	42.5	43.5	43.6	44.1	44.5	45.6	47.1	47.7	44.0
1997	44.1	43.2	43.3	43.5	43.8	44.3	44.8	45.6	46.1	46.3	47.3	47.8	45.0
1998	46.4	44.6	44.5	44.2	44.7	45.1	45.3	45.6	46.1	47.6	49.2	50.7	46.2
1999	47.7	45.8	45.8	45.8	46.2	47.0	47.3	47.9	48.6	49.1	50.8	51.7	47.8
2000	48.5	46.8	46.8	47.5	47.8	48.1	48.1	48.7	49.2	50.5	52.1	52.9	48.9
2001	51.7	49.1	49.2	49.4	49.5	49.5	49.2	50.0	49.8	50.7	52.0	52.7	50.2
2002	49.2	48.2	48.2	48.2	48.5	48.7	48.7	49.1	49.4	50.3	52.0	53.0	49.5
2003	49.0	48.2	47.8	48.3	49.0	49.4	50.1	50.9	50.2	51.9	52.4	53.2	50.0
Wholesale trade													
1990	6.9	6.9	7.0	7.3	7.3	7.5	7.5	7.6	7.7	7.8	7.8	7.8	7.4
1991	7.1	7.2	7.2	7.7	7.7	7.8	8.0	8.0	8.0	8.1	8.1	8.1	7.8
1992	7.6	7.6	7.7	7.9	8.0	8.1	8.2	8.1	8.1	7.9	7.8	7.9	7.9
1993	7.7	7.8	7.9	8.0	8.1	8.3	8.3	8.4	8.6	8.7	8.7	8.8	8.3
1994	8.4	8.3	8.4	8.7	8.8	8.9	8.9	8.9	9.0	8.9	8.9	8.9	8.8
1995	8.8	8.9	8.9	8.9	8.8	9.0	8.9	8.9	8.9	8.7	8.7	8.7	8.8
1996	8.7	8.7	8.8	8.8	8.9	9.0	8.8	8.9	8.8	8.8	8.9	8.9	8.8
1997	8.9	8.9	9.0	9.1	9.2	9.4	9.5	9.4	9.4	9.2	9.3	9.4	9.2
1998	9.4	9.3	9.3	9.4	9.4	9.6	9.7	9.7	9.6	9.7	9.7	9.7	9.5
1999	9.8	9.8	9.8	9.8	9.9	10.0	10.2	10.2	10.1	10.1	10.1	10.2	10.0
2000	10.2	10.3	10.4	10.4	10.5	10.7	10.7	10.8	10.5	10.5	10.6	10.7	10.5
2001	10.5	10.6	10.6	10.6	10.6	10.7	10.7	10.7	10.5	10.4	10.3	10.2	10.5
2002	10.1	10.2	10.2	10.3	10.4	10.4	10.5	10.4	10.4	10.2	10.2	10.3	10.3
2003	10.2	10.3	10.2	10.4	10.4	10.5	10.6	10.7	10.4	10.6	10.7	10.9	10.5

Employment by Industry: Wisconsin—*Continued*

(Numbers in thousands. Not seasonally adjusted.)

Industry	January	February	March	April	May	June	July	August	September	October	November	December	Annual Average
MADISON—*Continued*													
Retail trade													
1990	26.1	25.4	25.3	25.7	26.0	26.5	26.6	26.8	27.0	27.6	28.6	28.7	26.7
1991	25.8	25.1	24.9	25.0	25.2	24.9	25.4	26.0	26.1	26.9	27.7	28.0	25.9
1992	25.7	25.3	25.1	25.2	25.3	25.4	24.2	24.5	25.0	26.4	27.3	27.8	25.6
1993	25.1	24.9	25.0	25.2	25.4	25.7	25.6	25.9	26.3	27.3	28.2	28.9	26.1
1994	25.8	25.4	25.5	25.7	26.1	26.7	27.1	27.3	28.0	28.5	30.3	30.5	27.2
1995	27.7	27.4	27.3	27.2	27.5	27.8	28.2	28.6	28.9	29.8	31.2	31.4	28.6
1996	28.6	27.3	27.1	27.1	27.4	28.3	28.7	29.0	29.4	30.3	31.7	32.4	28.9
1997	29.0	28.0	28.0	28.1	28.2	28.7	29.2	30.0	30.3	30.5	31.4	31.9	29.4
1998	30.7	29.0	28.8	28.3	28.7	29.0	28.9	29.2	29.5	30.7	32.4	33.9	29.9
1999	31.0	29.1	29.0	28.9	29.2	29.9	30.0	30.6	31.2	31.6	33.4	34.2	30.7
2000	31.4	29.5	29.4	29.8	30.0	30.2	30.3	30.8	31.4	32.5	34.0	34.7	31.2
2001	33.9	31.2	31.2	31.4	31.5	31.4	31.2	31.9	31.8	32.8	34.3	35.0	32.3
2002	31.9	30.8	30.8	30.6	30.8	30.9	31.0	31.5	31.6	32.5	34.3	35.2	31.8
2003	31.5	30.6	30.4	30.7	31.4	31.5	32.0	32.7	32.3	33.9	34.3	35.0	32.2
Transportation and utilities													
1990	6.0	6.0	6.0	6.0	6.1	6.0	5.9	5.8	6.0	6.0	5.9	6.0	6.0
1991	5.7	5.8	5.8	5.8	5.9	5.8	5.7	5.7	5.9	6.0	6.1	6.1	5.9
1992	6.0	6.0	6.0	6.1	6.3	6.3	6.2	6.2	6.4	6.4	6.3	6.3	6.2
1993	6.1	6.1	6.2	6.2	6.2	6.3	6.3	6.3	6.3	6.4	6.3	6.3	6.3
1994	6.1	6.2	6.2	6.2	6.2	6.2	6.3	6.3	6.3	6.5	6.5	6.5	6.3
1995	6.3	6.2	6.2	6.2	6.3	6.3	6.2	6.2	6.3	6.4	6.4	6.3	6.3
1996	5.9	5.9	6.0	6.1	6.2	6.2	6.1	6.2	6.3	6.5	6.5	6.4	6.2
1997	6.2	6.3	6.3	6.3	6.4	6.2	6.1	6.2	6.4	6.6	6.6	6.5	6.3
1998	6.3	6.3	6.4	6.5	6.6	6.5	6.7	6.7	7.0	7.2	7.1	7.1	6.7
1999	6.9	6.9	7.0	7.1	7.1	7.1	7.1	7.1	7.3	7.4	7.3	7.3	7.1
2000	6.9	7.0	7.0	7.3	7.3	7.2	7.1	7.1	7.3	7.5	7.5	7.5	7.2
2001	7.3	7.3	7.4	7.4	7.4	7.4	7.3	7.4	7.5	7.5	7.4	7.5	7.4
2002	7.2	7.2	7.2	7.3	7.3	7.4	7.2	7.2	7.4	7.6	7.5	7.5	7.3
2003	7.3	7.3	7.2	7.2	7.2	7.4	7.5	7.5	7.5	7.4	7.4	7.3	7.4
Information													
1990	4.6	4.8	4.8	4.6	4.6	4.6	4.6	4.6	4.7	4.7	4.7	4.7	4.7
1991	4.6	4.7	4.8	4.9	4.9	4.8	4.8	4.8	4.9	4.9	5.0	4.9	4.8
1992	4.7	4.8	4.8	4.8	4.8	4.8	4.8	4.8	5.0	4.9	5.0	5.0	4.9
1993	5.0	5.0	5.0	4.9	4.8	4.7	4.8	4.8	4.8	4.9	5.1	5.1	4.9
1994	4.9	4.9	5.0	4.9	4.9	4.9	4.9	5.0	4.9	5.0	5.2	5.1	5.0
1995	5.1	5.2	5.2	5.3	5.2	5.3	5.3	5.3	5.4	5.6	5.7	5.6	5.4
1996	5.5	5.5	5.5	5.5	5.5	5.6	5.7	5.7	5.7	5.9	6.0	6.0	5.7
1997	5.8	5.9	5.8	5.8	5.8	5.8	5.9	6.0	6.1	6.3	6.4	6.5	6.0
1998	6.7	6.8	6.9	7.0	6.9	7.1	7.0	6.9	6.9	7.0	7.1	7.1	7.0
1999	6.9	6.9	7.0	7.2	7.2	7.3	7.2	7.1	7.2	7.2	7.2	7.1	7.1
2000	6.8	6.8	6.7	6.7	6.9	6.9	7.0	7.1	7.0	7.1	7.2	7.2	7.0
2001	7.1	7.1	7.1	7.1	7.0	6.8	6.8	6.7	6.6	6.5	6.5	6.4	6.8
2002	6.4	6.5	6.4	6.4	6.4	6.4	6.5	6.5	6.4	6.5	6.5	6.5	6.5
2003	6.7	6.7	6.7	6.7	6.6	6.6	6.7	6.7	6.6	6.7	6.8	6.9	6.7
Financial activities													
1990	18.9	19.1	19.2	19.5	19.7	20.0	20.3	20.3	20.1	20.1	20.2	20.4	19.8
1991	19.8	19.8	19.8	19.4	19.5	19.7	19.7	19.7	19.3	19.2	19.2	19.3	19.5
1992	19.2	19.3	19.4	19.6	19.7	19.9	20.1	20.1	19.9	19.9	20.0	20.4	19.8
1993	20.2	20.3	20.5	20.6	20.7	21.0	21.1	21.0	20.7	20.9	20.8	20.9	20.7
1994	20.2	20.2	20.0	20.5	20.6	20.8	20.7	20.7	20.5	20.3	20.3	20.3	20.4
1995	20.8	20.6	20.7	20.8	20.7	21.1	21.0	21.0	20.7	20.4	20.5	20.5	20.7
1996	20.4	20.2	20.5	20.3	20.3	20.7	20.7	20.8	20.5	20.3	20.3	20.2	20.4
1997	20.4	20.5	20.6	20.7	20.6	20.9	21.2	21.2	21.0	21.0	21.0	21.0	20.8
1998	21.2	21.1	21.2	21.4	21.4	21.8	21.7	21.8	21.5	21.5	21.5	21.7	21.5
1999	21.4	21.4	21.6	21.9	21.9	22.5	22.2	22.3	21.8	22.1	22.1	22.2	22.0
2000	22.0	22.0	22.1	22.5	22.4	22.7	22.7	22.7	22.6	22.6	22.5	22.6	22.5
2001	22.3	22.5	22.7	22.9	23.0	23.2	23.7	23.8	23.6	23.6	23.6	23.7	23.2
2002	24.1	24.3	24.3	24.3	24.5	24.8	24.9	25.0	24.7	24.7	24.7	24.8	24.6
2003	24.9	25.1	25.0	25.2	25.4	25.7	26.0	25.8	26.0	25.8	25.8	26.0	25.6
Professional and business services													
1990	15.2	15.4	15.5	16.3	16.3	16.6	16.9	17.1	17.1	17.1	16.9	16.7	16.4
1991	18.3	18.6	18.6	19.3	19.3	19.6	19.7	19.7	19.8	20.1	19.9	19.6	19.4
1992	19.7	19.8	20.0	20.8	21.2	21.6	22.0	22.6	22.6	22.5	22.1	22.2	21.4
1993	21.1	21.7	21.8	21.9	22.5	23.1	23.0	23.3	23.4	23.1	23.1	22.8	22.6
1994	22.4	22.8	23.0	23.2	23.4	23.6	23.7	23.8	23.9	24.1	24.1	24.2	23.5
1995	23.8	24.4	24.7	24.9	24.9	25.3	25.5	26.0	25.7	25.5	25.2	25.4	25.1
1996	24.7	25.4	25.8	25.5	26.1	26.4	26.2	26.3	26.3	26.4	26.5	26.4	26.0
1997	25.8	26.4	26.9	27.4	28.0	28.5	28.1	28.4	28.0	27.3	27.2	27.3	27.4
1998	26.6	26.9	27.2	27.3	27.3	27.7	27.7	27.8	27.1	27.6	27.8	27.8	27.4
1999	26.6	26.7	27.2	28.4	28.5	29.4	29.3	29.6	29.4	29.0	28.7	29.1	28.5
2000	28.1	28.4	28.5	28.3	28.9	29.3	29.4	29.7	29.3	29.4	29.2	29.1	29.0
2001	28.7	29.5	29.5	30.2	30.4	31.3	30.4	30.4	30.1	31.3	31.3	31.2	30.4
2002	30.9	31.0	31.6	31.8	31.7	32.2	32.4	32.3	32.1	32.1	31.9	31.5	31.8
2003	30.2	30.4	30.4	31.0	30.8	31.0	30.4	31.0	30.5	30.6	31.0	31.1	30.7

Employment by Industry: Wisconsin—*Continued*

(Numbers in thousands. Not seasonally adjusted.)

Industry	January	February	March	April	May	June	July	August	September	October	November	December	Annual Average
MADISON—*Continued*													
Educational and health services													
1990	17.0	17.1	17.2	17.1	17.1	17.1	16.9	16.8	17.1	17.2	17.3	17.2	17.1
1991	17.1	17.3	17.5	17.4	17.4	17.4	17.2	17.3	17.5	17.8	18.0	18.0	17.5
1992	18.0	18.3	18.4	18.6	18.5	18.6	18.6	18.5	18.8	19.9	20.0	20.1	18.9
1993	19.8	20.0	20.1	20.4	20.3	20.4	20.3	20.5	20.8	21.4	21.5	21.5	20.6
1994	21.0	21.1	21.3	21.4	21.4	21.5	21.4	21.4	21.7	21.8	21.9	21.9	21.5
1995	21.9	22.0	22.2	22.3	22.5	22.5	22.4	22.5	22.8	23.0	23.3	23.3	22.6
1996	23.8	24.1	24.5	24.6	24.5	24.6	24.4	24.5	24.7	25.2	25.1	25.2	24.6
1997	24.9	25.1	25.2	25.2	25.1	25.2	25.0	24.9	25.1	25.2	25.4	25.2	25.1
1998	25.2	25.5	25.5	25.7	25.7	25.8	25.4	25.5	25.7	26.1	26.2	26.4	25.7
1999	26.5	26.6	26.6	26.4	26.3	26.3	26.1	26.0	26.1	26.2	26.1	26.0	26.3
2000	26.1	26.4	26.5	26.8	26.8	27.0	26.7	26.7	26.7	26.9	26.9	26.7	26.7
2001	26.4	26.7	26.9	27.0	27.2	27.3	27.3	27.3	27.1	27.2	27.3	27.4	27.1
2002	27.5	27.6	27.8	27.8	28.1	28.3	28.0	28.2	28.2	28.2	28.5	28.6	28.1
2003	28.5	28.8	28.9	28.9	29.1	29.3	29.6	29.4	29.2	29.8	29.9	30.1	29.3
Leisure and hospitality													
1990	17.6	18.9	19.0	18.7	19.0	19.1	19.1	19.1	19.2	19.2	19.3	19.2	19.0
1991	18.0	18.4	18.7	19.1	19.3	19.4	19.6	19.7	19.4	19.0	19.1	18.8	19.0
1992	18.9	19.4	19.5	19.8	20.1	20.4	19.6	19.9	19.6	19.8	19.7	19.7	19.7
1993	18.8	19.3	19.4	19.6	20.2	20.5	20.4	20.4	20.7	21.4	21.5	21.7	20.3
1994	19.6	20.0	20.4	20.6	21.1	21.3	21.6	21.4	21.6	20.8	21.0	21.0	20.9
1995	19.8	20.5	21.0	20.9	21.6	21.8	21.5	21.7	21.6	21.4	21.4	21.1	21.2
1996	20.2	20.6	20.7	20.8	21.5	22.2	21.7	22.1	22.1	21.4	21.3	21.2	21.3
1997	20.1	20.5	20.7	20.8	21.4	21.5	21.4	21.7	21.9	21.8	21.9	21.6	21.3
1998	20.6	21.1	21.2	21.6	22.3	22.5	22.1	22.1	22.1	21.6	21.4	21.2	21.7
1999	20.1	20.7	20.9	21.6	22.2	22.5	22.6	22.7	22.5	21.8	21.8	21.7	21.8
2000	20.8	21.6	21.9	22.3	22.7	23.1	23.3	23.4	23.3	22.7	22.8	22.5	22.5
2001	21.7	22.3	22.5	23.1	23.6	24.1	24.3	24.4	24.2	23.4	23.2	22.9	23.3
2002	22.5	23.1	23.1	23.4	24.2	24.4	24.3	24.6	24.2	24.0	23.7	23.7	23.8
2003	22.9	23.0	23.2	23.7	24.5	24.9	24.8	24.7	24.6	24.1	24.5	23.9	24.1
Other services													
1990	10.0	10.2	10.2	10.4	10.5	10.7	10.6	10.6	10.5	10.8	10.6	10.4	10.5
1991	10.0	10.1	10.1	10.1	10.1	10.1	10.2	10.1	10.0	10.0	10.1	10.1	10.1
1992	9.7	9.8	9.8	9.9	10.0	10.3	10.2	10.1	10.0	10.3	10.2	10.2	10.0
1993	10.0	10.3	10.3	10.5	10.6	10.7	10.7	10.6	10.7	10.9	10.8	10.8	10.6
1994	10.2	10.5	10.6	10.6	10.6	10.7	10.7	10.6	10.6	10.8	10.7	10.6	10.6
1995	10.5	10.7	10.8	10.9	10.9	11.0	10.8	10.8	10.8	10.9	10.8	10.9	10.8
1996	10.6	10.8	10.9	10.9	11.0	11.2	11.0	10.9	10.8	10.9	10.9	11.2	10.9
1997	10.8	10.9	10.9	11.0	11.1	11.4	11.4	11.4	11.4	11.5	11.6	11.9	11.3
1998	11.7	12.0	12.2	12.4	12.3	12.5	12.5	12.4	12.4	12.4	12.3	12.4	12.3
1999	12.2	12.4	12.6	12.7	12.6	12.8	12.9	13.1	13.1	13.1	13.0	13.1	12.8
2000	13.1	13.3	13.6	13.7	13.5	13.6	13.8	13.8	13.8	13.7	13.8	13.8	13.6
2001	13.8	14.0	14.0	14.1	14.0	14.2	14.3	14.2	14.1	14.1	14.2	14.3	14.1
2002	14.4	14.5	14.6	14.6	14.5	14.8	14.7	14.6	14.5	14.6	14.6	14.6	14.6
2003	14.5	14.7	14.7	14.6	14.6	14.9	14.8	14.8	14.8	14.8	14.8	14.8	14.7
Government													
1990	55.8	59.7	60.5	61.8	61.7	60.2	59.7	58.9	62.0	62.0	62.8	61.7	60.6
1991	58.6	62.2	62.7	62.7	62.5	61.3	60.3	61.1	63.2	63.7	64.2	63.7	62.2
1992	61.1	64.5	64.7	65.9	65.7	64.3	63.3	64.2	66.3	66.9	67.4	66.3	65.1
1993	65.3	67.1	67.0	67.4	67.9	65.3	64.7	65.0	67.3	68.4	68.7	67.8	66.8
1994	65.3	68.4	69.0	69.2	68.3	66.3	65.2	64.5	68.3	69.4	70.2	69.2	67.8
1995	67.5	69.4	69.9	70.4	69.7	67.9	65.2	65.1	68.0	69.0	69.8	69.2	68.4
1996	67.8	69.6	70.1	71.2	70.8	69.3	66.0	65.7	69.1	71.0	73.1	71.2	69.6
1997	68.7	70.9	71.0	71.9	71.4	69.2	66.9	66.8	68.8	70.7	72.2	70.6	69.9
1998	70.4	72.0	72.4	73.6	72.4	70.9	69.2	69.2	71.8	72.8	74.3	73.3	71.9
1999	72.9	73.6	73.8	75.5	73.7	72.7	71.1	70.8	72.3	73.4	74.2	73.1	73.1
2000	72.5	73.5	74.2	76.2	73.7	74.2	70.3	69.6	72.3	73.8	76.1	74.6	73.4
2001	74.0	76.6	78.0	79.8	78.2	77.3	73.4	72.6	77.4	77.6	78.7	76.5	76.7
2002	73.7	75.7	76.5	78.4	76.1	72.3	70.8	71.7	73.3	76.5	78.7	76.2	75.0
2003	71.7	75.0	75.5	77.3	75.4	76.2	71.1	72.1	73.3	74.7	75.5	74.7	74.4
Federal government													
1990	3.5	3.5	3.5	3.7	3.9	3.6	3.7	3.6	3.5	3.5	3.5	3.5	3.6
1991	3.5	3.5	3.5	3.5	3.5	3.6	3.5	3.6	3.5	3.5	3.6	3.6	3.5
1992	3.6	3.6	3.6	3.6	3.6	3.6	3.7	3.7	3.7	3.7	3.7	3.7	3.7
1993	3.8	3.7	3.7	3.7	3.8	3.8	3.8	3.8	3.8	3.8	3.8	3.8	3.8
1994	3.8	3.8	3.8	3.8	3.8	3.8	3.7	3.7	3.7	3.7	3.6	3.7	3.7
1995	3.8	3.7	3.8	3.7	3.7	3.8	3.8	3.8	3.7	3.7	3.7	3.8	3.8
1996	3.9	3.9	3.9	3.9	3.9	3.9	3.9	4.0	3.9	4.2	4.3	4.3	4.0
1997	4.2	4.2	4.2	4.2	4.3	4.3	4.3	4.3	4.2	4.2	4.3	4.3	4.3
1998	4.2	4.2	4.2	4.2	4.2	4.3	4.3	4.3	4.3	4.3	4.3	4.4	4.3
1999	4.3	4.3	4.3	4.3	4.2	4.2	4.3	4.2	4.3	4.2	4.2	4.4	4.3
2000	4.4	4.3	4.3	4.6	4.7	4.9	4.6	4.7	4.4	4.4	4.4	4.6	4.5
2001	4.4	4.4	4.4	4.5	4.5	4.4	4.6	4.5	4.5	4.5	4.5	4.5	4.5
2002	4.5	4.4	4.4	4.4	4.3	4.4	4.5	4.5	4.5	4.6	4.6	4.7	4.5
2003	4.6	4.6	4.6	4.6	4.6	4.6	4.6	4.6	4.6	4.6	4.6	4.7	4.6

Employment by Industry: Wisconsin—*Continued*

(Numbers in thousands. Not seasonally adjusted.)

Industry	January	February	March	April	May	June	July	August	September	October	November	December	Annual Average
MADISON—*Continued*													
State government													
1990	38.3	40.7	41.3	42.4	42.2	41.4	41.4	41.0	43.2	42.7	42.9	41.9	41.6
1991	39.6	42.3	42.7	43.4	43.2	42.5	42.2	43.1	43.6	43.7	44.1	42.9	42.8
1992	41.0	43.9	43.8	44.9	45.1	44.0	44.1	45.1	45.8	45.9	46.1	45.1	44.6
1993	45.3	46.1	45.7	46.6	47.0	45.4	45.8	45.9	46.7	47.2	47.3	46.3	46.3
1994	44.4	46.9	47.2	47.6	46.9	45.3	45.2	45.2	47.4	47.7	48.2	47.2	46.6
1995	46.6	47.6	47.7	48.3	47.4	45.6	45.3	45.0	46.8	46.8	47.4	46.7	46.8
1996	46.1	47.0	47.3	48.6	48.1	46.7	45.3	45.3	46.7	47.3	49.1	47.4	47.1
1997	46.2	47.6	47.5	48.4	47.8	46.3	46.1	46.0	46.2	47.0	48.4	46.9	47.0
1998	46.9	47.9	48.3	49.3	48.2	47.4	47.2	47.5	47.7	48.1	49.3	48.4	48.0
1999	48.4	48.8	49.0	50.5	49.0	48.3	48.0	47.8	47.8	48.5	49.0	47.9	48.6
2000	47.5	48.1	48.7	50.5	47.9	47.8	47.1	46.3	46.1	47.0	48.9	47.3	47.8
2001	47.1	49.9	50.0	51.6	49.9	49.2	48.8	48.1	50.0	49.4	50.2	48.1	49.4
2002	45.3	47.8	48.2	50.1	47.7	45.4	44.7	46.6	47.6	48.0	50.5	47.9	47.5
2003	45.1	48.1	48.5	50.3	48.0	48.8	44.9	46.4	47.2	47.8	48.7	47.6	47.6
Local government													
1990	14.1	15.5	15.7	15.7	15.6	15.1	14.6	14.3	15.3	15.8	16.3	16.3	15.4
1991	15.5	16.4	16.5	15.8	15.7	15.3	14.6	14.4	16.0	16.4	16.5	17.1	15.9
1992	16.4	17.0	17.3	17.4	17.1	16.7	15.5	15.3	16.9	17.3	17.6	17.6	16.8
1993	16.2	17.3	17.5	17.1	17.1	16.1	15.1	15.3	16.8	17.4	17.6	17.7	16.8
1994	17.1	17.7	17.9	17.7	17.6	17.2	16.2	15.6	17.2	18.0	18.4	18.3	17.4
1995	17.2	18.0	18.5	18.4	18.6	18.6	16.1	16.3	17.5	18.4	18.6	18.7	17.9
1996	17.8	18.7	19.0	18.7	18.8	18.7	16.8	16.4	18.5	19.5	19.7	19.5	18.5
1997	18.2	19.1	19.2	19.3	19.4	18.7	16.5	16.5	18.3	19.4	19.5	19.4	18.6
1998	19.3	19.9	19.9	20.0	20.0	19.2	17.6	17.4	19.7	20.4	20.7	20.5	19.6
1999	20.2	20.5	20.6	20.7	20.4	20.1	18.8	18.8	20.3	20.7	20.9	20.9	20.2
2000	20.6	21.1	21.1	21.1	21.1	21.5	18.6	18.6	21.8	22.4	22.7	22.7	21.1
2001	22.5	22.3	23.6	23.7	23.8	23.7	20.0	20.0	22.9	23.7	24.0	23.9	22.8
2002	23.9	23.5	23.9	23.9	24.1	22.5	21.6	20.6	21.2	23.9	23.6	23.6	23.0
2003	22.0	22.3	22.4	22.4	22.8	22.8	21.6	21.1	21.5	22.3	22.2	22.4	22.2
MILWAUKEE													
Total nonfarm													
1990	743.2	745.0	749.3	753.2	759.0	766.0	756.9	759.2	762.9	763.4	765.4	767.0	757.5
1991	744.1	742.3	744.6	745.7	749.9	756.3	745.7	748.1	749.5	755.9	759.1	757.8	749.9
1992	741.4	743.6	744.1	756.4	762.6	769.1	762.1	762.4	765.2	769.1	770.9	773.7	760.1
1993	751.4	756.6	759.8	762.4	771.1	778.6	771.8	774.8	781.3	785.1	787.3	792.6	772.7
1994	766.7	770.9	776.7	780.6	786.2	794.3	789.8	790.5	799.5	799.7	804.3	806.3	788.8
1995	787.3	789.9	796.2	798.0	802.5	811.2	802.4	804.3	811.6	812.4	814.7	817.7	804.0
1996	800.1	798.1	804.0	804.3	811.2	819.2	812.8	817.4	817.9	819.2	823.2	827.2	812.9
1997	806.8	808.3	811.4	817.3	824.3	837.0	826.4	828.7	836.1	841.3	845.6	850.6	827.8
1998	825.1	830.4	834.0	840.1	845.8	857.3	846.7	847.1	849.7	853.5	859.2	863.4	846.0
1999	839.3	844.4	848.1	858.2	863.4	872.2	864.5	866.0	867.7	871.8	872.9	877.2	862.1
2000	850.2	852.9	857.9	865.9	869.5	879.4	869.1	871.7	871.6	874.2	878.0	874.9	867.9
2001	856.5	856.5	858.7	863.1	864.3	866.0	856.1	855.0	853.6	853.6	849.9	849.1	856.9
2002	829.0	828.2	832.4	839.3	843.8	848.7	840.3	840.5	839.0	844.7	845.0	843.6	839.5
2003	820.0	822.8	824.9	831.2	834.3	840.2	831.8	833.2	826.4	838.1	835.2	834.1	831.0
Total private													
1990	659.8	659.2	662.7	665.6	671.1	678.1	676.0	678.9	676.6	675.5	677.6	679.2	671.7
1991	658.9	654.7	656.3	656.9	662.0	667.8	664.9	668.2	664.1	667.7	670.9	669.2	663.5
1992	655.1	654.1	654.9	666.1	672.5	678.8	679.6	679.6	676.4	679.5	680.4	683.3	671.7
1993	667.5	666.2	669.2	672.3	680.5	687.6	689.1	691.7	692.2	695.2	697.3	701.6	684.2
1994	677.9	680.2	685.5	690.0	695.1	703.0	705.5	707.1	709.4	708.9	712.3	714.9	699.2
1995	696.9	698.5	704.8	704.9	709.6	718.8	717.7	721.7	722.4	722.6	725.0	728.9	714.3
1996	711.2	709.0	714.1	715.8	722.2	728.3	727.3	731.2	729.2	730.3	732.8	735.7	723.9
1997	717.6	718.1	721.7	728.2	734.5	744.7	743.7	747.1	748.6	751.5	754.4	758.6	739.1
1998	736.1	739.2	743.2	747.9	754.3	764.0	762.8	764.1	761.4	762.9	765.8	770.3	756.0
1999	748.2	751.7	756.4	766.2	769.9	779.1	779.9	781.7	779.1	781.2	780.7	785.3	771.6
2000	759.5	760.9	765.4	771.2	775.7	782.5	781.8	784.0	781.0	780.4	783.3	782.2	775.7
2001	763.6	761.1	763.4	766.7	768.9	771.7	770.0	768.5	760.7	757.7	754.3	752.7	763.3
2002	734.8	731.1	734.9	742.6	747.8	752.4	753.0	753.2	747.6	746.6	746.5	745.3	744.7
2003	726.6	725.5	728.1	734.1	739.6	745.1	747.5	748.5	739.5	743.8	742.1	740.4	738.4
Goods-producing													
1990	188.6	188.7	188.9	189.5	191.0	192.1	191.6	192.0	191.5	190.5	189.8	188.4	190.2
1991	182.2	180.4	180.1	181.5	182.6	184.2	182.4	183.5	183.1	184.2	183.1	180.6	182.3
1992	179.6	178.6	178.6	179.1	181.6	184.5	184.5	184.1	183.2	184.2	183.8	183.1	182.1
1993	179.4	179.1	179.8	180.4	183.2	185.0	185.7	185.8	185.9	186.6	186.9	187.2	183.8
1994	179.9	179.8	181.9	184.3	186.5	190.1	190.9	191.0	191.4	191.0	191.8	191.9	187.5
1995	187.7	188.2	189.2	190.0	191.5	195.3	194.3	195.0	194.4	194.1	193.8	193.4	192.2
1996	189.0	187.9	188.8	189.4	191.8	194.3	194.2	194.9	193.6	192.8	192.8	192.0	191.8
1997	188.5	188.9	189.9	193.9	197.0	200.8	200.8	201.7	201.5	201.6	202.3	202.1	197.4
1998	196.7	197.0	197.8	199.6	201.9	204.7	203.5	203.9	203.1	202.1	201.9	202.2	201.2
1999	195.5	196.6	197.4	200.1	201.1	204.1	203.8	203.5	201.9	202.3	201.4	201.4	200.8
2000	195.0	195.1	196.1	198.5	199.7	202.3	201.6	201.9	200.2	199.0	198.5	196.6	198.7
2001	191.9	190.3	190.3	189.3	189.4	191.2	190.3	190.4	188.4	186.6	184.1	182.7	188.7
2002	176.5	174.9	175.4	176.8	178.1	179.8	178.4	179.4	178.0	177.5	176.7	174.6	177.2
2003	169.1	167.9	167.9	169.5	170.8	172.3	172.0	172.5	169.6	169.4	169.1	165.2	169.6

Employment by Industry: Wisconsin—*Continued*

(Numbers in thousands. Not seasonally adjusted.)

Industry	January	February	March	April	May	June	July	August	September	October	November	December	Annual Average
MILWAUKEE—*Continued*													
Natural resources and mining													
1990	0.3	0.3	0.3	0.3	0.3	0.3	0.3	0.3	0.3	0.3	0.3	0.3	0.3
1991	0.3	0.3	0.3	0.3	0.3	0.3	0.3	0.3	0.3	0.3	0.3	0.3	0.3
1992	0.3	0.3	0.3	0.3	0.3	0.3	0.3	0.3	0.3	0.3	0.3	0.3	0.3
1993	0.3	0.3	0.3	0.3	0.3	0.3	0.3	0.3	0.3	0.3	0.3	0.3	0.3
1994	0.3	0.3	0.3	0.3	0.3	0.3	0.3	0.4	0.3	0.3	0.3	0.3	0.3
1995	0.3	0.3	0.3	0.3	0.3	0.4	0.4	0.4	0.3	0.3	0.3	0.3	0.3
1996	0.3	0.3	0.3	0.3	0.3	0.3	0.3	0.3	0.3	0.3	0.3	0.3	0.3
1997	0.3	0.3	0.3	0.3	0.4	0.4	0.4	0.4	0.4	0.4	0.4	0.4	0.4
1998	0.4	0.4	0.4	0.4	0.4	0.4	0.4	0.4	0.4	0.4	0.4	0.4	0.4
1999	0.4	0.4	0.4	0.5	0.5	0.5	0.5	0.5	0.5	0.5	0.5	0.5	0.5
2000	0.4	0.4	0.4	0.4	0.5	0.5	0.5	0.5	0.5	0.5	0.5	0.4	0.5
2001	0.4	0.4	0.4	0.4	0.5	0.5	0.5	0.5	0.5	0.5	0.4	0.4	0.5
2002	0.4	0.4	0.4	0.4	0.4	0.5	0.5	0.5	0.5	0.4	0.4	0.4	0.4
2003	0.4	0.4	0.4	0.4	0.4	0.5	0.5	0.5	0.4	0.4	0.5	0.4	0.4
Construction													
1990	25.9	25.6	25.9	27.3	29.0	29.9	30.5	30.6	29.9	29.6	29.2	28.0	28.5
1991	24.7	24.4	24.8	26.1	27.8	28.9	29.2	29.4	28.8	29.2	28.2	26.8	27.4
1992	24.7	24.3	24.2	26.2	28.2	29.9	30.1	30.2	29.3	30.0	29.5	28.4	27.9
1993	25.3	25.1	25.2	26.1	28.2	29.4	30.6	30.5	30.2	30.4	29.9	28.9	28.3
1994	25.3	24.6	25.5	27.1	29.0	30.4	30.9	30.9	30.9	30.5	30.0	28.6	28.6
1995	25.4	24.9	25.4	26.8	28.4	29.8	30.4	30.5	30.2	30.3	29.6	28.5	28.4
1996	25.8	25.1	25.8	27.2	29.2	30.5	31.5	31.8	31.5	31.1	30.7	29.6	29.2
1997	26.7	26.6	27.0	28.5	30.6	32.0	32.8	32.8	32.4	32.4	32.0	31.1	30.4
1998	27.2	27.1	27.4	29.6	31.5	32.9	33.7	33.6	33.1	32.8	32.3	31.7	31.1
1999	28.0	28.6	29.4	32.3	33.9	35.5	36.4	35.9	35.3	35.2	34.6	33.6	33.2
2000	30.2	29.9	30.9	33.1	34.6	36.0	36.2	36.4	35.6	35.0	34.3	32.6	33.7
2001	30.8	30.8	31.3	32.7	34.5	35.8	36.7	36.8	35.9	35.4	34.6	33.5	34.1
2002	29.7	28.9	29.5	32.2	34.0	35.1	35.9	36.1	35.6	35.7	34.9	33.0	33.4
2003	29.9	29.2	29.4	31.5	33.6	34.7	36.1	36.2	35.4	35.0	33.5	30.8	32.9
Manufacturing													
1990	162.4	162.8	162.7	161.9	161.7	161.9	160.8	161.1	161.3	160.6	160.3	160.1	161.5
1991	157.2	155.7	155.0	155.1	154.5	155.0	152.9	153.8	154.0	154.7	154.6	153.5	154.7
1992	154.6	154.0	154.1	152.6	153.1	154.3	154.1	153.6	153.6	153.9	154.0	154.4	153.9
1993	153.8	153.7	154.3	154.0	154.7	155.3	154.8	155.0	155.4	155.9	156.7	158.0	155.1
1994	154.3	154.9	156.1	156.9	157.2	159.4	159.7	159.7	160.2	160.2	161.5	163.0	158.6
1995	162.0	163.0	163.5	162.9	162.8	165.1	163.5	164.1	163.9	163.5	163.9	164.6	163.6
1996	162.9	162.5	162.7	161.9	162.3	163.5	162.4	162.8	161.8	161.4	161.8	162.1	162.3
1997	161.5	162.0	162.6	165.1	166.0	168.4	167.6	168.5	168.7	168.8	169.9	170.6	166.6
1998	169.1	169.5	170.0	169.6	170.0	171.4	169.4	169.9	169.6	168.9	169.2	170.1	169.7
1999	167.1	167.6	167.6	167.3	166.7	168.1	166.9	167.1	166.1	166.6	166.3	167.3	167.1
2000	164.4	164.8	164.8	165.0	164.6	165.8	164.9	165.0	164.1	163.5	163.7	163.6	164.5
2001	160.7	159.1	158.6	156.2	154.4	154.9	153.1	153.1	152.0	150.7	149.1	148.8	154.2
2002	146.4	145.6	145.5	144.2	143.7	144.2	142.0	142.8	141.9	141.4	141.4	141.2	143.4
2003	138.8	138.3	138.1	137.6	136.8	137.1	135.4	135.8	133.8	134.0	135.1	134.0	136.2
Service-providing													
1990	554.6	556.3	560.4	563.7	568.0	573.9	565.3	567.2	571.4	572.9	575.6	578.6	567.3
1991	561.9	561.9	564.5	564.2	567.3	572.1	563.3	564.6	566.4	571.7	576.0	577.2	567.6
1992	561.8	565.0	565.5	577.3	581.0	584.6	577.6	578.3	582.0	584.9	587.1	590.6	578.0
1993	572.0	577.5	580.0	582.0	587.9	593.6	586.1	589.0	595.4	598.5	600.4	605.4	589.0
1994	586.8	591.1	594.8	596.3	599.7	604.2	598.9	599.5	608.1	608.7	612.5	614.4	601.3
1995	599.6	601.7	607.0	608.0	611.0	615.9	608.1	609.3	617.2	618.3	620.9	624.3	611.8
1996	611.1	610.2	615.2	614.9	619.4	624.9	618.6	622.5	624.3	626.4	630.4	635.2	621.1
1997	618.3	619.4	621.5	623.4	627.3	636.2	625.6	627.0	634.6	639.7	643.3	648.5	630.4
1998	628.4	633.4	636.2	640.5	643.9	652.6	643.2	643.2	646.6	651.4	657.3	661.2	644.8
1999	643.8	647.8	650.7	658.1	662.3	668.1	660.7	662.5	665.8	669.5	671.5	675.8	661.4
2000	655.2	657.8	661.8	667.4	669.8	677.1	667.5	669.8	671.4	675.2	679.5	678.3	669.2
2001	664.6	666.2	668.4	673.8	674.9	674.8	665.8	664.6	665.2	667.0	665.8	666.4	668.1
2002	652.5	653.3	657.0	662.5	665.7	668.9	661.9	661.1	661.0	667.2	668.3	669.0	662.4
2003	650.9	654.9	657.0	661.7	663.5	667.9	659.8	660.7	656.8	668.7	666.1	668.9	661.4
Trade, transportation, and utilities													
1990	143.2	141.2	141.5	140.7	142.1	143.5	141.6	143.3	143.4	144.0	147.7	149.5	143.5
1991	143.7	141.1	141.1	139.7	141.0	141.5	140.4	141.4	140.4	142.0	145.8	146.9	142.1
1992	141.1	138.9	138.8	141.2	142.2	143.1	141.6	142.3	142.7	144.3	147.0	148.8	142.7
1993	142.2	139.9	140.2	140.9	142.0	143.4	141.9	142.7	144.0	146.7	149.7	151.7	143.8
1994	144.9	144.0	144.9	144.9	145.9	146.8	146.0	147.1	148.2	150.3	153.5	155.1	147.6
1995	149.8	148.1	149.1	149.6	151.0	152.5	150.8	152.2	152.9	154.7	157.9	159.9	152.4
1996	153.9	150.5	151.0	150.6	152.1	152.4	151.1	152.3	152.6	154.1	158.0	159.7	153.2
1997	153.3	151.4	152.1	150.9	151.6	153.1	151.1	152.7	153.6	156.6	159.7	162.3	154.0
1998	153.2	152.3	153.3	152.2	154.3	155.2	153.7	155.0	155.9	159.2	162.1	164.5	155.9
1999	157.4	156.6	157.7	157.8	158.2	159.6	159.4	160.2	160.4	162.9	164.6	166.8	160.1
2000	159.5	157.6	157.9	158.5	159.1	158.9	159.6	160.4	161.2	162.4	164.8	166.7	160.6
2001	163.1	160.5	160.8	160.6	160.9	159.9	157.6	157.9	156.9	157.5	159.5	160.0	159.6
2002	155.6	152.9	153.7	153.5	154.8	154.6	153.0	152.7	153.4	153.9	157.2	159.1	154.5
2003	152.3	150.4	150.6	151.3	152.5	153.3	150.9	150.9	148.8	151.6	154.0	155.8	151.9

Employment by Industry: Wisconsin—*Continued*

(Numbers in thousands. Not seasonally adjusted.)

Industry	January	February	March	April	May	June	July	August	September	October	November	December	Annual Average
MILWAUKEE—*Continued*													
Wholesale trade													
1990	35.7	35.7	35.8	35.5	35.8	36.2	36.3	36.4	36.0	35.8	35.8	36.0	35.9
1991	36.1	36.1	36.0	35.9	36.0	36.4	36.4	36.2	35.6	35.5	35.7	35.6	36.0
1992	35.4	35.5	35.4	35.9	36.2	36.5	36.5	36.5	36.2	36.3	36.5	36.6	36.1
1993	35.6	35.6	35.8	36.1	36.1	36.5	36.9	36.6	36.4	36.6	36.6	36.8	36.3
1994	36.3	36.3	36.5	36.7	36.7	37.3	37.3	37.4	37.1	37.4	37.5	37.6	37.0
1995	37.4	37.6	37.8	38.5	39.2	39.8	39.8	39.9	39.9	39.7	39.7	40.2	39.1
1996	39.4	39.3	39.4	40.0	40.1	40.2	40.6	40.7	40.6	40.5	40.8	40.9	40.2
1997	40.7	40.9	41.0	40.9	41.0	41.6	41.7	41.7	41.6	41.8	41.8	42.2	41.4
1998	41.4	41.6	41.9	42.0	42.1	42.3	42.4	42.5	42.2	42.3	42.5	42.6	42.2
1999	42.3	42.5	42.6	42.9	42.8	43.0	43.3	43.4	42.8	43.0	42.9	42.9	42.9
2000	42.6	42.8	42.8	42.9	43.1	43.4	43.2	43.2	42.8	42.8	42.9	43.1	43.0
2001	42.8	42.9	43.0	42.6	42.6	42.8	42.4	42.4	41.8	41.6	41.4	41.5	42.3
2002	41.1	41.0	41.0	40.8	40.9	41.0	41.1	40.9	40.5	40.2	40.2	40.2	40.7
2003	40.0	40.0	40.0	40.0	40.0	40.4	40.1	39.3	39.3	39.5	39.8	40.0	39.9
Retail trade													
1990	80.8	78.6	78.7	78.0	78.8	79.8	78.9	80.0	79.2	80.6	84.3	85.6	80.3
1991	79.5	77.2	77.1	75.8	76.7	76.9	76.8	77.8	76.7	77.9	81.2	82.6	78.0
1992	77.4	75.2	75.2	76.0	76.6	76.8	76.4	77.2	76.6	77.9	80.7	82.5	77.4
1993	77.6	75.5	75.5	75.3	76.1	76.7	76.7	77.3	77.7	79.2	82.0	83.6	77.8
1994	77.9	76.7	76.8	76.9	77.3	77.7	77.4	78.0	78.5	80.2	83.1	84.8	78.8
1995	79.9	78.0	78.6	77.9	78.5	79.4	78.3	79.2	79.8	81.4	84.5	86.0	80.1
1996	81.7	79.3	79.9	78.9	80.2	80.4	79.6	80.5	80.2	81.2	84.9	86.5	81.1
1997	81.9	79.7	80.2	79.0	79.6	80.2	79.6	80.9	80.5	82.7	86.0	88.1	81.5
1998	80.7	79.6	80.4	79.3	80.7	81.4	80.7	81.2	81.1	84.2	86.9	89.2	82.1
1999	83.0	82.2	83.0	82.4	82.9	84.0	84.4	84.9	84.4	85.9	88.0	90.2	84.6
2000	83.9	82.0	82.3	82.2	82.7	83.2	84.0	84.7	84.7	84.9	87.6	89.3	84.3
2001	86.6	84.3	84.7	84.5	84.9	84.8	83.7	83.8	82.5	83.1	85.7	86.6	84.6
2002	84.3	81.9	82.5	82.5	83.5	84.2	83.0	83.0	82.5	82.9	86.3	88.2	83.7
2003	82.3	80.3	80.5	80.7	81.8	82.3	80.7	81.5	79.0	81.2	82.9	84.6	81.5
Transportation and utilities													
1990	26.7	26.9	27.0	27.2	27.5	27.5	26.4	26.9	28.2	27.6	27.6	27.9	27.3
1991	28.1	27.8	28.0	28.0	28.3	28.2	27.2	27.4	28.1	28.6	28.9	28.7	28.1
1992	28.3	28.2	28.2	29.3	29.4	29.8	28.7	28.6	29.9	30.1	29.8	29.7	29.2
1993	29.0	28.8	28.9	29.5	29.8	30.2	28.3	28.8	29.9	30.9	31.1	31.3	29.7
1994	30.7	31.0	31.6	31.3	31.9	31.8	31.3	31.7	32.6	32.7	32.9	32.7	31.9
1995	32.5	32.5	32.7	33.2	33.3	33.3	32.7	33.1	33.2	33.6	33.7	33.7	33.1
1996	32.8	31.9	31.7	31.7	31.8	31.8	30.9	31.1	31.8	32.4	32.3	32.3	31.9
1997	30.7	30.8	30.9	31.0	31.0	31.3	29.8	30.1	31.5	32.1	31.9	32.0	31.1
1998	31.1	31.1	31.0	30.9	31.5	31.5	30.6	31.3	32.6	32.7	32.7	32.7	31.6
1999	32.1	31.9	32.1	32.5	32.5	32.6	31.7	31.9	33.2	34.0	33.7	33.7	32.7
2000	33.0	32.8	32.8	33.4	33.3	32.3	32.4	32.5	33.7	34.7	34.3	34.3	33.3
2001	33.7	33.3	33.1	33.5	33.4	32.3	31.5	31.7	32.6	32.8	32.4	31.9	32.7
2002	30.2	30.0	30.2	30.2	30.4	29.4	28.9	28.8	30.4	30.8	30.7	30.7	30.1
2003	30.0	30.1	30.1	30.6	30.7	30.6	30.1	30.1	30.5	30.9	31.3	31.2	30.5
Information													
1990	18.9	19.0	19.2	18.8	18.8	19.0	18.9	18.9	18.8	19.0	19.0	18.9	18.9
1991	18.6	18.5	18.4	18.2	18.2	18.2	18.2	18.2	18.1	18.3	18.4	18.5	18.3
1992	18.2	18.4	18.2	18.6	18.7	18.5	18.2	18.3	18.1	18.4	18.4	18.5	18.4
1993	18.6	18.6	18.6	18.2	18.3	18.4	18.5	18.4	18.4	18.5	18.5	18.5	18.5
1994	18.7	18.7	18.8	18.6	18.6	18.6	18.6	18.6	18.6	18.4	18.5	18.6	18.6
1995	18.4	18.5	18.6	18.2	18.0	18.2	18.2	18.2	18.2	18.2	18.3	18.4	18.3
1996	18.4	18.3	18.4	18.3	18.5	18.6	18.8	19.0	18.8	18.8	18.9	19.0	18.7
1997	18.5	18.6	18.7	19.1	19.2	19.5	19.3	19.1	19.3	18.9	18.9	19.1	19.0
1998	19.6	19.6	19.9	19.9	19.9	20.1	20.0	20.1	19.9	20.0	20.1	20.0	19.9
1999	19.2	19.4	19.5	20.0	20.3	20.5	20.5	20.5	20.3	20.5	20.7	20.7	20.2
2000	19.9	20.1	20.2	20.2	20.3	20.4	20.4	20.5	20.6	20.7	20.8	20.9	20.4
2001	19.7	19.7	19.9	20.1	19.9	20.0	20.0	19.9	19.8	19.9	19.9	19.9	19.9
2002	19.7	19.5	19.6	19.5	19.3	19.3	19.2	19.2	18.9	18.8	18.8	18.8	19.2
2003	18.8	18.6	18.6	18.5	18.4	18.4	18.6	18.6	18.8	19.4	19.2	19.2	18.8
Financial activities													
1990	51.8	51.9	52.1	52.2	52.7	53.1	52.9	52.7	52.4	52.6	52.5	52.9	52.5
1991	52.9	52.8	52.8	52.9	53.1	53.5	53.5	53.6	52.9	52.9	53.0	53.2	53.1
1992	52.0	52.1	52.3	52.2	52.5	52.9	53.4	53.2	52.8	52.6	52.4	52.8	52.6
1993	52.6	53.1	53.3	51.8	52.1	52.8	53.1	53.1	53.1	52.8	52.9	53.2	52.8
1994	52.9	53.0	53.3	53.2	53.1	53.7	53.7	53.4	53.0	52.6	52.5	52.7	53.1
1995	52.1	52.4	52.5	52.7	52.7	53.3	53.0	53.2	53.0	53.0	53.2	53.6	52.9
1996	52.6	52.7	53.0	53.6	53.6	54.2	54.4	54.6	54.2	54.0	54.1	54.2	53.8
1997	54.0	53.9	54.1	54.0	54.0	54.6	54.7	54.7	54.5	54.3	54.3	54.7	54.3
1998	54.8	55.3	55.3	55.4	55.5	56.2	56.8	56.8	56.4	56.2	56.7	57.2	56.1
1999	57.0	57.1	57.3	57.0	57.1	57.7	57.8	58.0	57.1	57.4	57.4	58.0	57.4
2000	56.5	56.6	56.5	56.9	57.1	57.9	58.1	58.0	57.7	58.2	58.7	59.1	57.6
2001	58.4	58.1	58.2	58.3	58.4	59.0	58.7	58.4	57.8	57.3	57.4	57.1	58.1
2002	57.1	57.1	57.0	57.3	57.4	57.9	58.6	58.6	57.9	57.8	58.1	58.1	57.7
2003	57.8	58.0	58.0	58.2	58.5	59.0	59.8	59.8	58.9	59.5	60.9	61.8	59.2

Employment by Industry: Wisconsin—*Continued*

(Numbers in thousands. Not seasonally adjusted.)

Industry	January	February	March	April	May	June	July	August	September	October	November	December	Annual Average
MILWAUKEE—*Continued*													
Professional and business services													
1990	73.6	74.2	75.4	76.8	76.9	78.8	78.4	79.0	78.3	78.8	77.7	77.6	77.1
1991	73.2	73.0	73.4	73.9	74.0	75.1	75.3	76.0	75.6	77.5	77.6	76.8	75.1
1992	74.3	74.9	74.8	79.2	79.6	80.7	82.1	82.6	82.1	82.7	82.3	82.1	79.8
1993	79.4	79.7	80.3	82.3	83.6	84.7	87.0	87.9	88.6	89.0	88.0	87.9	84.9
1994	84.9	86.5	87.6	88.3	89.1	90.5	93.5	94.9	95.8	95.7	96.0	95.3	91.5
1995	91.3	92.2	94.4	93.3	93.8	94.4	95.7	97.2	97.8	95.9	95.2	95.6	94.7
1996	92.7	92.9	94.2	95.1	95.3	95.4	95.5	97.9	98.5	99.6	98.9	98.9	96.2
1997	95.8	96.7	96.9	98.9	99.2	100.9	100.7	102.0	103.3	104.4	104.3	104.5	100.6
1998	100.8	101.9	103.3	104.3	103.7	106.0	107.2	106.8	106.6	107.1	106.8	107.4	105.2
1999	103.8	104.5	105.9	109.7	109.4	111.5	111.8	113.9	114.1	114.4	113.3	113.6	110.5
2000	108.2	109.4	110.3	110.5	111.7	112.9	111.4	111.9	112.7	111.5	112.0	109.5	111.0
2001	105.9	104.9	104.9	106.7	106.6	106.6	106.8	107.3	105.6	103.7	102.3	101.7	105.3
2002	100.1	100.1	101.6	105.3	105.6	105.7	106.3	106.9	106.0	105.6	103.5	102.8	104.1
2003	100.9	101.3	102.5	103.8	103.2	103.6	105.9	105.2	105.2	104.6	102.3	100.2	103.2
Educational and health services													
1990	90.0	90.2	90.8	90.9	90.9	90.6	90.9	91.3	92.5	93.0	93.5	93.6	91.5
1991	92.8	93.8	94.2	94.2	94.5	94.5	93.9	94.3	95.4	96.4	96.9	97.1	94.8
1992	97.0	98.1	98.5	99.5	99.7	99.0	99.4	99.2	100.0	100.6	100.6	101.0	99.4
1993	101.0	102.0	102.0	102.5	102.4	101.9	102.1	102.1	103.5	104.0	103.9	104.3	102.6
1994	102.4	103.9	104.1	103.6	103.6	103.2	102.5	102.2	103.9	104.2	104.4	104.6	103.6
1995	103.1	104.1	104.6	104.0	104.1	104.6	103.9	104.3	106.2	107.8	108.8	109.6	105.4
1996	108.9	110.5	111.3	110.7	110.9	110.8	110.3	110.3	111.3	113.0	113.1	113.4	111.2
1997	112.0	113.0	113.2	113.5	113.4	113.5	113.2	113.3	114.9	115.0	115.2	116.0	113.9
1998	114.3	115.8	116.7	116.9	117.3	117.4	116.7	117.1	117.8	118.6	119.1	118.8	117.2
1999	118.0	119.2	120.0	120.5	120.5	120.4	121.1	120.6	122.2	122.2	122.5	123.0	120.9
2000	121.3	122.5	123.6	124.1	124.0	123.7	123.3	124.1	124.3	126.1	126.8	127.5	124.3
2001	122.9	125.8	126.6	126.2	126.3	125.4	125.5	125.6	126.4	128.0	128.2	128.2	126.3
2002	124.4	125.3	125.7	125.9	126.2	125.9	126.0	126.4	126.5	127.9	128.6	128.0	126.4
2003	125.8	128.0	128.1	128.4	128.2	127.8	128.4	128.5	131.2	134.3	134.7	134.6	129.8
Leisure and hospitality													
1990	55.1	55.1	55.9	58.1	59.6	61.4	62.6	62.7	60.7	58.8	58.5	58.8	58.9
1991	56.4	56.1	56.8	57.5	59.4	60.9	61.3	61.7	59.1	56.9	56.6	56.2	58.2
1992	53.9	54.2	54.4	57.3	59.1	60.3	60.8	60.8	58.2	57.3	56.6	56.8	57.5
1993	55.2	54.6	55.2	56.3	58.8	60.7	60.4	61.2	58.2	57.1	56.8	57.5	57.7
1994	54.5	54.4	54.8	57.0	58.4	59.8	60.4	60.1	58.4	56.4	55.4	56.0	57.1
1995	54.7	55.1	55.9	56.8	58.3	60.6	62.3	62.3	60.2	58.8	57.9	58.8	58.5
1996	56.3	56.5	57.1	58.1	60.1	62.3	63.0	62.4	60.5	58.2	57.4	58.3	59.2
1997	56.0	56.4	57.1	58.0	60.2	62.4	64.0	63.6	61.3	60.1	59.0	59.2	59.8
1998	56.8	57.3	57.0	59.8	61.9	64.7	65.2	64.6	61.9	59.8	58.8	60.0	60.7
1999	57.5	58.2	59.1	61.6	63.6	65.8	66.2	65.7	63.4	61.7	61.0	61.7	62.1
2000	60.0	60.1	60.9	62.4	63.6	65.9	67.2	67.2	64.2	62.2	61.3	61.2	63.0
2001	60.5	60.7	61.3	64.9	66.7	68.3	69.8	67.9	64.7	63.7	61.9	61.6	64.3
2002	60.4	60.3	60.7	63.0	65.2	67.3	70.0	68.6	65.8	63.8	62.5	62.4	64.2
2003	60.9	60.5	61.3	63.2	67.0	68.9	70.6	71.4	66.5	64.8	62.0	63.2	65.0
Other services													
1990	38.6	38.9	38.9	38.6	39.1	39.6	39.1	39.0	39.0	38.8	38.9	39.5	39.0
1991	39.1	39.0	39.5	39.0	39.2	39.9	39.9	39.5	39.5	39.5	39.5	39.9	39.5
1992	39.0	38.9	39.3	39.0	39.1	39.8	39.6	39.1	39.3	39.4	39.3	40.2	39.3
1993	39.1	39.2	39.8	39.9	40.1	40.7	40.4	40.5	40.5	40.5	40.6	41.3	40.2
1994	39.7	39.9	40.1	40.1	39.9	40.3	39.9	39.8	40.1	40.3	40.2	40.7	40.1
1995	39.8	39.9	40.5	40.3	40.2	39.9	39.5	39.3	39.7	40.1	39.9	39.6	39.9
1996	39.4	39.7	40.3	40.0	39.9	40.3	40.0	39.8	39.7	39.8	39.6	40.2	39.9
1997	39.5	39.2	39.7	39.9	39.9	39.9	39.9	40.0	40.2	40.6	40.7	40.7	40.0
1998	39.9	40.0	39.9	39.8	39.8	39.7	39.7	39.8	39.8	39.9	40.3	40.2	39.9
1999	39.8	40.1	39.5	39.5	39.7	39.5	39.3	39.3	39.7	39.8	39.8	40.1	39.7
2000	39.1	39.5	39.9	40.1	40.2	40.5	40.2	40.0	40.1	40.3	40.4	40.7	40.1
2001	41.2	41.1	41.4	40.6	40.7	41.3	41.3	41.1	41.1	41.0	41.0	41.5	41.1
2002	41.0	41.0	41.2	41.3	41.2	41.9	41.5	41.4	41.1	41.3	41.1	41.5	41.3
2003	41.0	40.8	41.1	41.2	41.0	41.8	41.3	41.6	40.5	40.2	39.9	40.4	40.9
Government													
1990	83.4	85.8	86.6	87.6	87.9	87.9	80.9	80.3	86.3	87.9	87.8	87.8	85.9
1991	85.2	87.6	88.3	88.8	87.9	88.5	80.8	79.9	85.4	88.2	88.2	88.6	86.5
1992	86.3	89.5	89.2	90.3	90.1	90.3	82.5	82.8	88.8	89.6	90.5	90.4	88.4
1993	83.9	90.4	90.6	90.1	90.6	91.0	82.7	83.1	89.1	89.9	90.0	91.0	88.5
1994	88.8	90.7	91.2	90.6	91.1	91.3	84.3	83.4	90.1	90.8	92.0	91.4	89.6
1995	90.4	91.4	91.4	93.1	92.9	92.4	84.7	82.6	89.2	89.8	89.7	88.8	89.7
1996	88.9	89.1	89.9	88.5	89.0	90.9	85.5	86.2	88.7	88.9	90.4	91.5	89.0
1997	89.2	90.2	89.7	89.1	89.8	92.3	82.7	81.6	87.5	89.8	91.2	92.0	88.8
1998	89.0	91.2	90.8	92.2	91.5	93.3	83.9	83.0	88.3	90.6	93.4	93.1	90.0
1999	91.1	92.7	91.7	92.0	93.5	93.1	84.6	84.3	88.6	90.6	92.2	91.9	90.5
2000	90.7	92.0	92.5	94.7	93.8	96.9	87.3	87.7	90.6	93.8	94.7	92.7	92.3
2001	92.9	95.4	95.3	96.4	95.4	94.3	86.1	86.5	92.9	95.9	95.6	96.4	93.6
2002	94.2	97.1	97.5	96.7	96.0	96.3	87.3	87.3	91.4	98.1	98.5	98.3	94.9
2003	93.4	97.3	96.8	97.1	94.7	95.1	84.3	84.7	86.9	94.3	93.1	93.7	92.6

Employment by Industry: Wisconsin—*Continued*

(Numbers in thousands. Not seasonally adjusted.)

Industry	January	February	March	April	May	June	July	August	September	October	November	December	Annual Average
MILWAUKEE—*Continued*													
Federal government													
2001	11.3	11.2	11.3	11.3	11.3	11.3	11.3	11.3	11.3	11.3	11.5	11.6	11.3
2002	11.2	11.2	11.2	11.2	11.2	11.1	11.2	11.2	11.1	11.3	11.4	11.7	11.3
2003	11.4	11.4	11.4	11.3	11.2	11.2	11.2	11.1	11.1	11.2	11.0	11.5	11.3
State government													
2001	10.1	11.3	11.5	11.3	11.5	11.0	10.8	11.8	11.7	11.9	11.8	11.7	11.3
2002	11.2	11.7	11.9	11.8	11.8	11.4	11.1	12.3	11.8	11.9	12.0	11.8	11.7
2003	11.3	11.7	11.8	11.7	11.7	11.3	11.1	12.4	11.7	11.9	11.8	11.7	11.7
Local government													
1990	63.2	65.4	66.1	66.9	66.6	67.7	60.9	59.7	65.5	67.2	67.2	67.0	65.3
1991	64.5	66.9	67.4	68.2	67.1	68.4	60.8	58.9	64.8	67.4	67.3	67.5	65.8
1992	65.7	68.3	68.1	69.2	68.9	69.9	62.0	61.3	67.7	68.3	69.4	68.9	67.3
1993	62.7	69.4	69.6	69.2	69.5	70.4	62.2	61.6	68.0	68.7	68.7	69.2	67.4
1994	67.9	69.5	69.9	69.4	69.7	70.3	63.3	61.4	68.7	69.2	70.5	69.7	68.3
1995	69.0	70.1	70.2	71.8	71.6	71.6	63.7	60.7	68.0	68.8	68.7	67.7	68.5
1996	67.9	68.0	68.8	67.4	67.7	70.0	64.7	64.2	67.4	67.4	68.6	69.3	67.6
1997	67.6	68.3	67.8	67.3	67.8	70.4	60.8	58.7	65.7	67.7	68.8	69.2	66.7
1998	67.2	69.2	68.8	70.2	69.4	71.2	61.9	60.0	66.3	68.2	70.3	69.3	67.7
1999	68.1	70.1	69.1	69.2	71.0	70.7	62.2	60.7	66.1	67.9	69.3	68.5	67.7
2000	67.9	69.3	69.4	71.1	69.0	71.1	66.0	64.4	70.7	73.5	73.8	71.9	69.8
2001	71.5	72.9	72.5	73.8	72.6	72.0	64.0	63.4	69.9	72.7	72.3	73.1	70.9
2002	71.8	74.2	74.4	73.7	73.0	73.8	65.0	63.8	68.5	74.9	75.1	74.8	71.9
2003	70.7	74.2	73.6	74.1	71.8	72.6	62.0	61.2	64.1	71.2	70.3	70.5	69.7

Average Weekly Hours by Industry: Wisconsin

(Not seasonally adjusted.)

Industry	January	February	March	April	May	June	July	August	September	October	November	December	Annual Average
STATEWIDE													
Manufacturing													
2001	40.5	39.7	40.5	39.1	40.3	39.9	40.2	40.4	40.9	39.8	39.6	41.1	40.2
2002	40.2	40.1	40.6	40.2	40.2	40.8	39.9	40.6	40.8	40.7	40.6	40.8	40.5
2003	40.2	40.3	40.3	40.3	40.0	40.7	39.2	40.0	40.5	40.1	40.9	40.9	40.3
APPLETON-OSHKOSH-NEENAH													
Manufacturing													
2001	41.9	41.0	41.3	39.0	41.1	40.8	41.5	41.5	42.2	40.6	39.7	42.7	41.1
2002	41.0	39.3	40.3	40.1	40.3	42.8	41.3	42.6	42.2	41.4	42.1	42.4	41.3
2003	39.9	40.5	40.8	41.0	41.6	42.4	41.2	40.9	42.3	41.8	42.3	42.6	41.4
GREEN BAY													
Manufacturing													
2001	43.4	40.6	41.0	40.3	40.6	41.4	40.2	38.8	42.5	39.8	39.9	41.9	40.9
2002	41.8	40.2	39.9	39.0	38.5	41.0	37.9	38.9	40.7	41.2	40.0	41.9	40.1
2003	41.7	40.6	40.2	38.7	39.8	42.7	38.3	42.3	40.6	38.8	40.5	39.1	40.3
MADISON													
Manufacturing													
2001	40.6	43.7	44.3	43.0	43.8	44.3	40.9	42.2	40.7	40.0	42.2	43.2	42.4
2002	41.8	43.9	44.1	42.5	43.0	43.1	41.1	41.9	42.2	42.2	42.6	41.4	42.5
2003	41.6	41.7	42.0	40.7	38.5	38.9	36.5	38.9	38.9	39.5	39.7	39.2	39.7
MILWAUKEE													
Manufacturing													
2001	39.1	38.0	38.8	36.9	38.5	38.0	38.4	38.9	39.6	39.7	39.4	40.2	38.8
2002	38.7	39.1	39.9	40.1	40.2	40.1	39.7	40.3	40.8	40.5	41.1	41.5	40.2
2003	41.1	40.3	40.2	40.8	39.6	40.5	39.0	39.7	40.3	40.4	40.8	41.6	40.4

Average Hourly Earnings by Industry: Wisconsin

(Dollars, not seasonally adjusted.)

Industry	January	February	March	April	May	June	July	August	September	October	November	December	Annual Average
STATEWIDE													
Manufacturing													
2001	15.14	15.09	15.34	15.27	15.40	15.44	15.46	15.48	15.65	15.60	15.68	15.80	15.44
2002	15.82	15.85	15.96	15.82	15.87	15.80	15.71	15.69	15.85	15.90	15.94	16.13	15.86
2003	16.03	16.07	16.02	16.06	16.09	16.11	16.01	16.05	16.19	16.18	16.19	16.39	16.12
APPLETON-OSHKOSH-NEENAH													
Manufacturing													
2001	16.38	16.31	16.21	16.32	16.53	16.51	16.69	16.63	16.93	16.94	17.23	16.72	16.61
2002	16.86	16.78	16.93	16.96	17.20	17.02	17.20	17.37	17.79	17.49	17.44	17.51	17.22
2003	17.31	17.50	17.47	17.51	17.38	17.25	17.53	17.63	17.76	17.88	18.21	18.12	17.63
GREEN BAY													
Manufacturing													
2001	14.07	14.06	14.20	14.35	14.19	14.35	14.26	14.37	14.84	14.12	14.65	14.76	14.35
2002	14.43	14.10	14.50	14.04	14.07	14.40	14.16	14.19	14.19	14.40	14.04	14.16	14.23
2003	14.12	14.02	13.77	13.91	14.03	14.25	14.29	14.46	14.52	13.92	14.29	14.56	14.18
MADISON													
Manufacturing													
2001	14.76	14.78	14.80	15.51	15.21	15.22	15.26	14.98	14.90	15.21	14.81	15.10	15.05
2002	15.23	14.99	15.02	15.02	15.48	15.14	15.35	15.06	15.26	15.59	15.39	15.61	15.26
2003	15.31	15.30	15.11	15.04	15.42	15.43	15.25	15.52	15.44	15.15	15.07	15.21	15.27
MILWAUKEE													
Manufacturing													
2001	16.54	16.57	16.60	16.50	16.67	16.70	16.70	16.74	16.76	16.71	16.93	17.17	16.71
2002	16.90	17.23	17.15	16.98	16.96	16.78	16.69	16.72	16.80	16.73	16.70	17.04	16.89
2003	16.73	16.88	16.88	16.84	16.89	16.94	16.58	16.92	17.07	16.90	17.10	17.48	16.94

Average Weekly Earnings by Industry: Wisconsin

(Dollars, not seasonally adjusted.)

Industry	January	February	March	April	May	June	July	August	September	October	November	December	Annual Average
STATEWIDE													
Manufacturing													
2001	613.17	599.07	621.27	597.06	620.62	616.06	621.49	625.39	640.09	620.88	620.93	649.38	620.69
2002	635.96	635.59	647.98	635.96	637.97	644.64	626.83	637.01	646.68	647.13	647.16	658.10	642.33
2003	644.41	647.62	645.61	647.22	643.60	655.68	627.59	642.00	655.70	648.82	662.17	670.35	649.64
APPLETON-OSHKOSH-NEENAH													
Manufacturing													
2001	686.32	668.71	669.47	636.48	679.38	673.61	692.64	690.15	714.45	687.76	684.03	713.94	682.67
2002	691.26	659.45	682.28	680.10	693.16	728.46	710.36	739.96	750.74	724.09	734.22	742.42	711.19
2003	690.67	708.75	712.78	717.91	723.01	731.40	722.24	721.07	751.25	747.38	770.28	771.91	729.88
GREEN BAY													
Manufacturing													
2001	610.64	570.84	582.20	578.31	576.11	594.09	573.25	557.56	630.70	561.98	584.54	618.44	586.92
2002	603.17	566.82	578.55	547.56	541.70	590.40	536.66	551.99	577.53	593.28	561.60	593.30	570.62
2003	588.80	569.21	553.55	538.32	558.39	608.48	547.31	611.66	589.51	540.10	578.75	569.30	571.45
MADISON													
Manufacturing													
2001	599.26	645.89	655.64	666.93	666.20	674.25	624.13	632.16	606.43	608.40	624.98	652.32	638.12
2002	636.61	658.06	662.38	638.35	665.64	652.53	630.89	631.01	643.97	657.90	655.61	646.25	648.55
2003	636.90	638.01	634.62	612.13	593.67	600.23	556.63	603.73	600.62	598.43	598.28	596.23	606.22
MILWAUKEE													
Manufacturing													
2001	646.71	629.66	644.08	608.85	641.80	634.60	641.28	651.19	663.70	663.39	667.04	690.23	648.35
2002	654.03	673.69	684.29	680.90	681.79	672.88	662.59	673.82	685.44	677.57	686.37	707.16	678.98
2003	687.60	680.26	678.58	687.07	668.84	686.07	646.62	671.72	687.92	682.76	697.68	727.17	684.38

WYOMING AT A GLANCE

(Population and total nonfarm employment numbers in thousands)

Population, Census 2000:	493.8
Total nonfarm employment, 2003:	250.0
Change in total nonfarm employment	
(Number)	
1990–2003:	51.5
1990–2001:	46.9
2001–2003:	4.6
(Compound annual rate of change)	
1990–2003:	1.8%
1990–2001:	1.9%
2001–2003:	0.9%
Unemployment rate	
1990:	5.3%
2001:	3.9%
2003:	4.4%

Average Annual Employment for Total Nonfarm, Goods-Producing, and Service-Providing Industries, 1990–2003

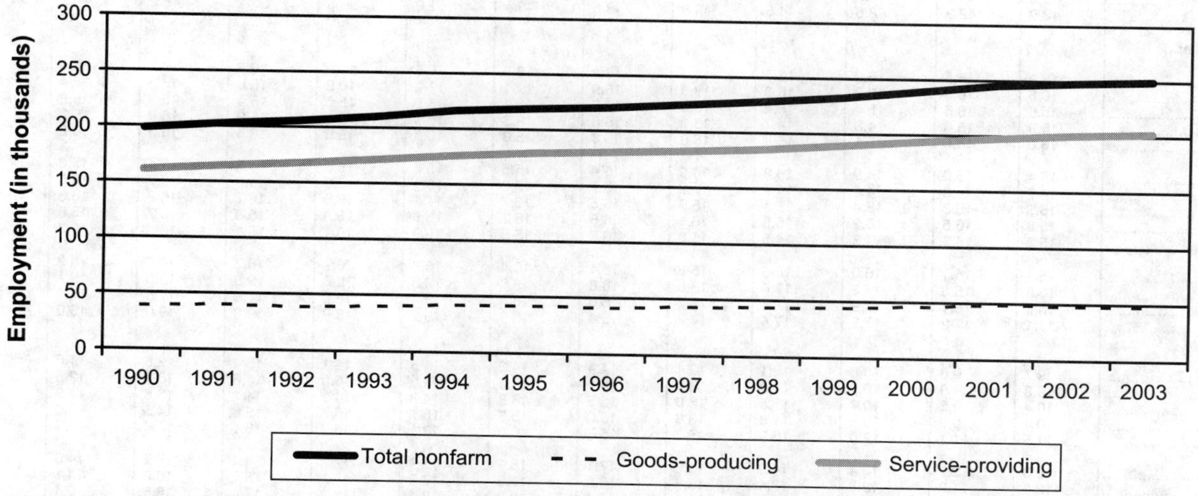

Total nonfarm payroll employment grew steadily from 1990 to 2003. Employment in the service-providing sector followed a similar pattern, increasing each year. However, employment in professional and business services and educational health services grew rapidly. From 1990 to 2003, employment in professional and business services increased by over 75 percent, and in educational and health services employment grew nearly 64 percent, from 12,700 to 20,800. Employment in the goods-producing sector remained steady, and declined only slightly after the 2001 recession.

Employment by Industry: Wyoming

(Numbers in thousands. Not seasonally adjusted.)

Industry	January	February	March	April	May	June	July	August	September	October	November	December	Annual Average
STATEWIDE													
Total nonfarm													
1990	186.8	187.2	190.2	194.4	200.3	208.7	203.0	203.9	206.3	202.0	200.1	199.2	198.5
1991	192.4	192.6	195.3	197.6	205.8	213.7	207.9	208.6	211.3	207.4	202.3	202.1	203.0
1992	195.9	195.8	197.5	199.8	208.2	214.7	209.0	210.9	213.4	209.7	207.2	205.2	205.6
1993	199.3	198.5	200.2	203.5	211.4	220.7	215.7	216.5	220.1	215.5	211.2	211.8	210.3
1994	205.3	204.8	206.8	210.3	218.3	227.0	221.9	224.8	225.7	221.0	218.6	217.4	216.8
1995	210.3	209.6	211.9	213.5	220.2	231.1	223.5	224.1	228.3	223.7	217.9	218.0	219.3
1996	211.0	210.7	212.1	214.7	223.5	231.7	225.4	228.1	229.8	225.8	221.6	219.1	221.1
1997	212.7	212.2	214.7	217.4	227.1	234.0	232.0	232.8	233.4	229.4	224.3	224.7	224.5
1998	217.9	217.9	219.3	222.3	232.3	238.0	234.6	234.8	235.2	231.8	227.6	227.9	228.3
1999	221.0	220.7	224.4	227.1	234.8	242.9	240.5	240.2	241.0	237.7	233.0	233.9	233.1
2000	227.8	228.5	232.2	234.1	241.7	248.8	246.4	247.1	245.0	242.9	238.2	239.3	239.3
2001	233.1	233.5	236.8	239.4	247.2	256.6	252.8	254.5	251.4	248.8	245.5	245.3	245.4
2002	237.9	237.7	240.2	242.4	250.2	258.2	255.7	255.4	254.2	250.5	246.5	246.1	247.9
2003	238.9	238.4	240.0	243.1	250.8	259.7	257.3	258.7	257.4	254.5	250.7	251.0	250.0
Total private													
1990	131.8	131.4	133.9	137.4	142.2	152.1	154.5	155.1	150.5	145.4	142.6	142.0	143.2
1991	136.9	136.5	138.4	140.7	147.9	156.7	159.0	159.4	154.5	149.4	144.4	144.1	147.3
1992	139.0	138.2	139.5	141.4	148.7	156.7	159.5	160.0	156.3	151.9	147.2	146.9	148.7
1993	141.8	140.4	141.5	144.7	151.5	162.0	165.4	165.9	162.5	156.7	152.5	153.1	153.1
1994	147.2	146.2	147.8	150.9	157.9	168.1	170.6	171.6	167.4	161.4	157.3	157.6	158.6
1995	151.5	150.5	152.2	153.7	159.9	171.6	173.3	173.7	170.5	164.3	158.8	158.8	161.5
1996	152.2	151.6	152.3	154.8	162.4	171.9	175.0	176.3	171.3	166.2	161.7	160.1	162.9
1997	154.5	153.7	155.6	158.2	166.4	175.3	179.7	179.9	174.8	169.8	164.9	165.3	166.5
1998	159.3	158.9	159.8	162.3	171.1	178.9	182.4	182.3	176.1	171.5	167.5	167.9	169.8
1999	161.8	161.0	163.9	166.3	172.9	182.4	185.7	185.5	181.5	177.1	172.6	173.3	173.6
2000	167.7	167.9	169.9	172.1	178.1	187.5	190.1	190.6	184.8	180.8	176.2	177.3	178.5
2001	172.3	172.1	174.6	177.4	184.1	193.3	195.4	196.6	190.2	186.1	182.8	181.9	183.9
2002	176.0	175.4	176.8	179.4	186.1	194.1	197.2	197.0	191.5	186.3	182.2	181.0	185.3
2003	175.6	174.7	175.5	179.1	185.8	194.8	198.1	199.5	194.5	189.4	185.8	185.7	186.5
Goods-producing													
1990	34.3	33.6	34.6	36.2	37.6	39.7	40.2	40.5	40.2	39.9	39.0	37.6	37.7
1991	35.4	35.1	35.6	37.1	39.3	41.2	41.7	41.8	41.0	40.8	39.0	38.0	38.8
1992	35.2	34.8	34.9	35.6	37.6	38.5	39.3	40.1	39.9	40.6	39.3	37.7	37.7
1993	35.8	34.2	34.5	35.7	38.1	40.4	41.6	41.9	41.9	41.8	40.4	39.6	38.8
1994	37.2	36.3	37.1	38.8	40.8	43.0	43.2	43.8	43.7	43.1	42.1	40.9	40.8
1995	38.3	37.4	38.0	38.6	39.9	42.6	42.5	42.8	43.2	42.4	40.9	39.9	40.5
1996	37.1	36.2	36.3	37.8	40.5	42.0	42.3	43.5	43.1	42.9	42.1	39.8	40.3
1997	37.3	37.2	38.0	39.3	42.1	44.0	45.1	45.8	45.6	45.0	43.8	42.6	42.1
1998	40.4	39.8	39.9	40.8	43.9	44.8	45.6	45.6	44.7	44.0	43.4	42.4	42.9
1999	39.8	39.2	39.9	41.2	43.6	45.1	46.1	46.1	45.9	46.1	45.0	44.3	43.5
2000	42.1	42.0	42.7	43.7	45.2	46.6	47.3	48.0	47.4	47.4	45.6	45.2	45.2
2001	43.0	43.0	43.9	45.6	47.7	49.9	50.6	51.3	50.4	51.2	50.3	48.1	47.9
2002	45.5	44.2	44.7	45.9	48.2	49.0	49.4	50.2	49.4	48.7	47.0	45.1	47.3
2003	42.9	42.3	42.6	44.6	46.8	48.5	49.4	51.0	50.5	50.1	48.9	47.9	47.1
Natural resources and mining													
1990	15.8	15.5	15.3	15.4	15.7	16.1	16.6	16.8	16.6	16.7	16.8	16.6	16.1
1991	16.5	16.3	16.3	16.3	16.5	16.9	17.1	17.2	16.9	16.6	16.3	16.4	16.6
1992	15.8	15.5	15.4	15.2	15.5	15.7	16.1	16.2	16.0	16.4	16.3	16.2	15.8
1993	15.9	15.0	14.8	14.7	15.0	15.8	16.3	16.3	16.3	15.9	15.9	16.2	15.6
1994	16.0	15.6	15.5	15.4	15.8	16.3	16.3	16.5	16.5	16.4	16.3	16.2	16.0
1995	15.4	15.0	14.9	14.8	14.9	15.4	15.5	15.5	15.6	15.3	15.1	15.0	15.2
1996	14.7	14.6	14.4	14.7	15.2	15.7	15.8	16.1	15.8	15.6	15.7	15.5	15.3
1997	15.3	15.3	15.4	15.4	15.8	16.5	16.7	17.1	16.8	16.7	16.8	16.8	16.2
1998	16.8	16.5	16.2	15.8	16.1	16.5	16.7	16.6	16.2	15.8	15.7	15.8	16.2
1999	15.2	14.7	14.6	14.5	15.0	15.5	15.8	15.9	16.1	16.1	16.1	16.3	15.4
2000	16.1	16.1	16.0	15.5	15.8	16.1	16.4	16.8	16.7	16.7	16.7	16.9	16.3
2001	16.6	16.8	17.3	17.4	18.0	18.8	19.0	19.3	19.3	19.5	19.3	19.1	18.4
2002	18.4	18.1	17.9	17.4	17.7	18.0	18.3	18.4	18.0	17.8	17.5	17.3	17.9
2003	17.1	17.2	17.2	17.4	17.8	18.4	18.9	19.2	18.9	19.0	19.0	19.0	18.3
Construction													
1990	9.7	9.6	10.6	12.1	13.1	14.4	14.3	14.5	14.1	13.4	12.6	11.6	12.5
1991	9.8	9.9	10.5	11.9	13.9	15.1	15.5	15.5	15.0	14.6	13.4	12.3	13.1
1992	10.4	10.3	10.7	11.5	13.0	13.5	13.8	14.3	14.1	14.1	13.3	11.9	12.5
1993	10.4	10.0	10.5	11.8	13.8	15.0	15.5	15.7	15.7	15.6	14.5	13.6	13.5
1994	11.5	11.1	12.0	13.9	15.3	16.7	16.8	17.1	16.7	16.1	15.4	14.4	14.7
1995	12.8	12.7	13.4	14.2	15.2	17.1	16.9	17.1	17.2	16.4	15.2	14.5	15.2
1996	12.6	11.9	12.3	13.4	15.4	16.2	16.3	17.2	17.1	16.7	16.0	14.1	14.9
1997	12.3	12.4	13.1	14.2	16.4	17.4	18.2	18.4	18.3	17.4	16.5	15.4	15.8
1998	13.7	13.4	13.9	15.1	17.8	18.0	18.5	18.6	18.1	17.5	17.1	16.1	16.4
1999	14.5	14.6	15.4	16.6	18.5	19.3	19.9	19.9	19.5	19.3	18.4	17.5	17.7
2000	15.9	15.8	16.7	18.0	19.1	20.0	20.3	20.7	20.3	19.8	18.1	17.5	18.5
2001	16.1	16.0	16.5	18.2	19.9	21.2	21.6	22.0	21.2	21.4	20.9	19.3	19.5
2002	17.6	17.0	17.5	19.2	21.1	21.5	21.6	22.2	21.9	21.2	19.8	18.2	19.9
2003	16.6	16.2	16.6	18.2	19.9	20.8	21.1	22.3	22.2	21.3	20.1	19.1	19.5

Employment by Industry: Wyoming—*Continued*

(Numbers in thousands. Not seasonally adjusted.)

Industry	January	February	March	April	May	June	July	August	September	October	November	December	Annual Average
STATEWIDE—*Continued*													
Manufacturing													
1990	8.8	8.5	8.7	8.7	8.8	9.2	9.3	9.2	9.5	9.8	9.6	9.4	9.1
1991	9.1	8.9	8.8	8.9	8.9	9.2	9.1	9.1	9.1	9.6	9.3	9.3	9.1
1992	9.0	9.0	8.8	8.9	9.1	9.3	9.4	9.6	9.8	10.1	9.7	9.6	9.3
1993	9.5	9.2	9.2	9.2	9.3	9.6	9.8	9.9	9.9	10.3	10.0	9.8	9.6
1994	9.7	9.6	9.6	9.5	9.7	10.0	10.1	10.2	10.5	10.6	10.4	10.3	10.0
1995	10.1	9.7	9.7	9.6	9.8	10.1	10.1	10.2	10.4	10.7	10.6	10.4	10.1
1996	9.8	9.7	9.6	9.7	9.9	10.1	10.2	10.2	10.2	10.6	10.4	10.2	10.0
1997	9.7	9.5	9.5	9.7	9.9	10.1	10.2	10.3	10.5	10.9	10.5	10.4	10.1
1998	9.9	9.9	9.8	9.9	10.0	10.3	10.4	10.4	10.4	10.7	10.6	10.5	10.2
1999	10.1	9.9	9.9	10.1	10.1	10.3	10.4	10.3	10.3	10.7	10.5	10.5	10.2
2000	10.1	10.1	10.0	10.2	10.3	10.5	10.6	10.5	10.4	10.9	10.8	10.8	10.4
2001	10.3	10.2	10.1	10.0	9.8	9.9	10.0	10.0	9.9	10.3	10.1	9.7	10.0
2002	9.5	9.1	9.3	9.3	9.4	9.5	9.5	9.6	9.5	9.7	9.7	9.6	9.5
2003	9.2	8.9	8.8	9.0	9.1	9.3	9.4	9.5	9.4	9.8	9.8	9.8	9.3
Service-providing													
1990	152.5	153.6	155.6	158.2	162.7	169.0	162.8	163.4	166.1	162.1	161.1	161.6	160.7
1991	157.0	157.5	159.7	160.5	166.5	172.5	166.2	166.8	170.3	166.6	163.3	164.1	164.2
1992	160.7	161.0	162.6	164.2	170.6	176.2	169.7	170.8	173.5	169.1	167.9	167.5	167.8
1993	163.5	164.3	165.7	167.8	173.3	180.3	174.1	174.6	178.2	173.7	170.8	172.2	171.5
1994	168.1	168.5	169.7	171.5	177.5	184.0	178.7	181.0	182.0	177.9	176.5	176.5	175.9
1995	172.0	172.2	173.9	174.9	180.3	188.5	181.0	181.3	185.1	181.3	177.0	178.1	178.8
1996	173.9	174.5	175.8	176.9	183.0	189.7	183.1	184.6	186.7	182.9	179.5	179.3	180.8
1997	175.4	175.0	176.7	178.1	185.0	190.0	186.9	187.0	187.8	184.4	180.5	182.1	182.4
1998	177.5	178.1	179.4	181.5	188.4	193.2	189.0	189.2	190.5	187.8	184.2	185.5	185.3
1999	181.2	181.5	184.5	185.9	191.2	197.8	194.4	194.1	195.1	191.6	188.0	189.6	189.5
2000	185.7	186.5	189.5	190.4	196.5	202.2	199.1	199.1	197.6	195.5	192.6	194.1	194.0
2001	190.1	190.5	192.9	193.8	199.5	206.7	202.2	203.2	201.0	197.6	195.2	197.2	197.5
2002	192.4	193.5	195.5	196.5	202.0	209.2	206.3	205.2	204.8	201.8	199.5	201.0	200.6
2003	196.0	196.1	197.4	198.5	204.0	211.2	207.9	207.7	206.9	204.4	201.8	203.1	202.9
Trade, transportation, and utilities													
1990	39.7	39.6	40.0	40.5	41.7	43.0	43.4	43.6	43.0	42.2	42.5	42.9	41.8
1991	41.2	40.8	40.8	41.0	42.2	43.4	43.5	43.9	43.0	41.8	42.4	42.7	42.2
1992	41.3	40.8	41.0	41.5	42.5	43.8	44.4	44.6	44.3	43.3	43.0	43.6	42.8
1993	41.8	41.4	41.4	42.1	43.0	44.5	45.0	45.3	45.1	44.0	44.0	44.3	43.4
1994	42.1	41.7	41.8	42.0	43.7	45.2	45.8	46.3	45.7	44.2	44.3	45.0	43.9
1995	42.9	42.4	42.6	42.4	43.5	45.5	45.5	45.9	45.4	44.2	44.3	44.6	44.1
1996	43.3	43.0	42.7	43.2	44.3	45.8	46.6	46.8	45.9	45.1	45.3	45.5	44.7
1997	44.1	43.4	43.8	44.1	45.3	46.7	47.2	47.2	46.3	45.5	45.5	46.2	45.4
1998	44.2	44.0	44.1	44.5	46.3	47.2	47.5	47.5	46.2	46.0	46.1	46.5	45.8
1999	44.7	44.1	44.9	45.6	46.3	47.7	48.3	48.5	47.6	47.1	47.2	47.8	46.6
2000	46.3	46.0	45.9	46.6	47.7	48.9	49.7	50.0	49.1	48.7	49.1	49.4	48.1
2001	47.5	46.9	47.3	47.8	49.0	50.2	50.2	50.1	49.1	48.1	48.1	48.6	48.6
2002	47.0	46.4	46.7	47.2	48.5	49.7	50.0	50.0	49.1	48.7	49.0	49.2	48.5
2003	47.1	46.5	46.5	47.2	48.2	49.6	50.2	50.3	49.4	48.4	48.9	48.9	48.4
Wholesale trade													
1990	5.0	5.1	5.1	5.1	5.2	5.3	5.4	5.3	5.3	5.3	5.3	5.3	5.2
1991	5.1	5.0	5.1	5.2	5.2	5.2	5.2	5.3	5.2	5.2	5.2	5.1	5.1
1992	5.1	5.1	5.1	5.2	5.2	5.2	5.3	5.2	5.3	5.3	5.3	5.3	5.2
1993	5.2	5.2	5.3	5.3	5.4	5.4	5.4	5.5	5.4	5.5	5.5	5.5	5.3
1994	5.4	5.4	5.4	5.5	5.6	5.6	5.7	5.8	5.8	5.7	5.8	5.8	5.6
1995	5.6	5.5	5.6	5.7	5.7	5.7	5.8	5.8	5.8	5.7	5.7	5.7	5.6
1996	5.6	5.6	5.6	5.7	5.8	5.8	5.9	5.9	5.8	5.8	5.8	5.8	5.7
1997	5.8	5.8	5.9	6.0	6.1	6.1	6.2	6.2	6.2	6.2	6.1	6.2	6.0
1998	6.1	6.1	6.2	6.2	6.3	6.3	6.3	6.2	6.2	6.2	6.1	6.2	6.2
1999	6.0	6.0	6.1	6.2	6.1	6.2	6.2	6.3	6.3	6.2	6.2	6.2	6.1
2000	6.1	6.2	6.2	6.3	6.3	6.5	6.5	6.5	6.5	6.4	6.4	6.5	6.3
2001	6.5	6.5	6.6	6.8	6.9	7.0	7.0	7.1	7.0	7.0	7.0	7.1	6.9
2002	7.0	7.0	7.0	7.0	7.0	7.1	7.1	7.1	7.0	7.0	7.0	7.0	7.0
2003	6.9	6.8	6.8	6.9	6.9	7.0	7.1	7.1	7.0	6.9	7.0	7.0	7.0
Retail trade													
1990	23.6	23.3	23.6	24.0	25.0	26.0	26.2	26.5	25.9	25.2	25.5	26.0	25.0
1991	24.6	24.3	24.3	24.3	25.4	26.6	26.6	26.9	26.2	25.1	25.7	26.2	25.5
1992	24.9	24.4	24.7	25.0	25.8	27.0	27.4	27.7	27.3	26.4	26.2	26.7	26.1
1993	25.2	24.8	24.8	25.4	26.1	27.5	27.8	28.1	27.8	26.8	26.9	27.2	26.5
1994	25.9	25.5	25.6	25.9	27.2	28.3	28.7	29.0	28.5	27.3	27.4	27.8	27.2
1995	26.5	26.1	26.2	26.1	27.1	28.7	28.6	29.0	28.6	27.7	27.9	28.2	27.5
1996	26.9	26.5	26.4	26.6	27.5	28.8	29.4	29.6	28.9	28.1	28.2	28.5	27.9
1997	27.4	26.7	27.0	27.2	28.2	29.4	29.7	29.8	28.8	28.2	28.4	28.8	28.3
1998	27.4	27.0	27.1	27.5	29.0	29.8	30.0	30.0	28.9	28.7	28.9	29.1	28.6
1999	27.8	27.3	27.7	28.1	28.9	29.8	30.4	30.6	29.8	29.5	29.5	30.0	29.1
2000	28.7	28.4	28.3	28.8	29.9	30.7	31.5	31.7	31.0	30.5	30.8	31.0	30.1
2001	29.5	29.2	29.5	29.7	30.8	31.7	31.6	31.4	30.6	29.7	29.8	30.2	30.3
2002	28.9	28.4	28.7	29.1	30.3	31.2	31.5	31.4	30.7	30.1	30.4	30.6	30.1
2003	28.8	28.3	28.3	28.9	29.7	30.8	31.2	31.2	30.7	29.8	30.1	30.2	29.8

Employment by Industry: Wyoming—*Continued*

(Numbers in thousands. Not seasonally adjusted.)

Industry	January	February	March	April	May	June	July	August	September	October	November	December	Annual Average
STATEWIDE—*Continued*													
Transportation and utilities													
1990	11.1	11.2	11.3	11.4	11.5	11.7	11.8	11.8	11.8	11.7	11.7	11.6	11.5
1991	11.5	11.5	11.4	11.5	11.6	11.6	11.7	11.7	11.6	11.5	11.5	11.4	11.5
1992	11.3	11.3	11.2	11.3	11.5	11.6	11.7	11.7	11.7	11.6	11.5	11.6	11.5
1993	11.4	11.4	11.3	11.4	11.5	11.6	11.8	11.7	11.9	11.7	11.6	11.6	11.5
1994	10.8	10.8	10.8	10.6	10.9	11.3	11.4	11.5	11.4	11.2	11.1	11.4	11.1
1995	10.8	10.8	10.8	10.6	10.7	11.1	11.1	11.1	11.0	10.8	10.7	10.7	10.8
1996	10.8	10.9	10.7	10.9	11.0	11.2	11.3	11.3	11.2	11.2	11.3	11.2	11.0
1997	10.9	10.9	10.9	10.9	11.0	11.2	11.3	11.2	11.3	11.1	11.0	11.2	11.0
1998	10.7	10.9	10.8	10.8	11.0	11.1	11.2	11.3	11.1	11.1	11.1	11.2	11.0
1999	10.9	10.8	11.1	11.3	11.3	11.7	11.7	11.6	11.5	11.4	11.5	11.6	11.3
2000	11.5	11.4	11.4	11.5	11.5	11.7	11.7	11.8	11.6	11.8	11.9	11.9	11.6
2001	11.5	11.2	11.2	11.3	11.3	11.5	11.6	11.6	11.5	11.4	11.3	11.3	11.4
2002	11.1	11.0	11.0	11.1	11.2	11.4	11.4	11.5	11.4	11.6	11.6	11.6	11.3
2003	11.4	11.4	11.4	11.4	11.6	11.8	11.9	12.0	11.7	11.7	11.8	11.7	11.7
Information													
1990	3.6	3.6	3.6	3.6	3.6	3.7	3.8	3.8	3.7	3.6	3.7	3.7	3.6
1991	3.6	3.6	3.6	3.6	3.7	3.8	3.8	3.8	3.7	3.7	3.6	3.7	3.6
1992	3.6	3.6	3.7	3.6	3.6	3.7	3.8	3.8	3.7	3.6	3.6	3.7	3.6
1993	3.6	3.6	3.6	3.5	3.6	3.7	3.7	3.7	3.6	3.6	3.6	3.6	3.6
1994	3.6	3.6	3.6	3.6	3.7	3.7	3.6	3.6	3.5	3.4	3.4	3.5	3.5
1995	3.4	3.4	3.4	3.4	3.5	3.6	3.6	3.6	3.5	3.5	3.5	3.5	3.4
1996	3.4	3.4	3.4	3.5	3.6	3.7	3.7	3.7	3.6	3.6	3.6	3.6	3.5
1997	3.6	3.6	3.6	3.6	3.6	3.7	3.7	3.7	3.6	3.5	3.5	3.6	3.6
1998	3.5	3.5	3.6	3.6	3.6	3.8	3.8	3.8	3.8	3.8	3.8	3.9	3.7
1999	3.9	3.8	3.8	3.9	3.9	4.0	4.1	4.0	4.0	4.0	4.0	4.0	3.9
2000	4.0	3.9	3.9	4.0	4.0	4.1	4.1	4.0	4.0	3.9	4.0	4.0	3.9
2001	4.0	3.9	3.9	3.9	4.0	4.1	4.1	4.2	4.2	4.1	4.2	4.2	4.1
2002	4.2	4.2	4.2	4.2	4.1	4.2	4.2	4.1	4.1	4.0	4.1	4.1	4.1
2003	4.1	4.1	4.2	4.1	4.2	4.2	4.2	4.2	4.1	4.2	4.2	4.2	4.2
Financial activities													
1990	7.7	7.7	7.9	7.9	7.9	8.1	8.1	8.2	7.9	7.9	7.9	7.9	7.9
1991	7.8	7.7	7.9	7.8	7.9	8.0	8.1	8.0	7.9	7.8	7.7	7.8	7.8
1992	7.8	7.7	7.9	8.0	8.0	8.2	8.2	8.2	8.1	8.0	8.0	8.1	8.0
1993	8.0	8.0	8.0	8.0	8.2	8.3	8.4	8.4	8.3	8.2	8.1	8.3	8.1
1994	8.1	8.1	8.1	8.3	8.2	8.5	8.5	8.5	8.3	8.2	8.0	8.2	8.2
1995	8.0	8.0	8.1	8.2	8.3	8.5	8.4	8.5	8.4	8.2	8.2	8.2	8.2
1996	8.2	8.2	8.3	8.2	8.4	8.6	8.6	8.6	8.5	8.5	8.5	8.6	8.4
1997	8.5	8.5	8.5	8.7	8.7	8.9	9.1	9.0	9.0	8.9	8.9	8.9	8.8
1998	8.9	8.9	9.0	9.0	9.2	9.4	9.4	9.3	9.2	9.1	9.1	9.3	9.1
1999	9.0	9.0	9.0	9.1	9.2	9.4	9.3	9.3	9.2	9.2	9.1	9.2	9.1
2000	9.0	8.9	9.1	9.1	9.2	9.4	9.3	9.4	9.2	9.2	9.1	9.3	9.1
2001	9.0	9.0	9.1	9.3	9.4	9.7	9.7	9.9	9.7	9.6	9.6	9.6	9.5
2002	9.6	9.7	9.7	9.8	10.0	10.3	10.4	10.4	10.3	10.0	9.9	9.9	10.0
2003	9.8	9.8	10.0	10.0	10.1	10.4	10.5	10.5	10.4	10.3	10.5	10.5	10.2
Professional and business services													
1990	7.9	8.0	8.3	8.8	9.0	9.4	9.6	9.6	9.3	9.1	8.8	8.7	8.8
1991	8.6	8.6	9.0	9.4	9.7	10.2	10.4	10.1	9.8	9.7	9.4	9.3	9.5
1992	9.5	9.2	9.3	9.5	10.0	10.2	10.5	10.2	10.0	10.0	9.7	9.5	9.8
1993	9.2	9.4	9.5	10.0	10.2	10.9	10.9	10.9	10.8	10.7	10.4	10.3	10.2
1994	9.9	10.0	10.3	10.7	11.2	11.7	11.7	11.7	11.3	11.3	11.2	10.9	10.9
1995	10.6	10.9	11.1	11.5	11.8	12.6	12.7	12.5	12.1	11.9	11.6	11.4	11.7
1996	11.0	11.3	11.3	11.6	12.0	12.5	12.9	13.0	12.6	12.4	12.0	11.9	12.0
1997	11.4	11.4	11.7	12.0	12.6	13.1	13.8	13.6	13.2	13.1	12.7	12.4	12.5
1998	12.2	12.1	12.5	13.1	13.8	14.2	14.4	14.4	13.9	13.9	13.5	13.5	13.4
1999	13.1	13.5	13.9	14.2	14.5	15.1	15.2	15.1	14.9	14.8	14.7	14.4	14.4
2000	13.6	13.8	14.2	14.6	15.0	15.5	15.5	15.4	15.0	14.8	14.6	14.4	14.7
2001	14.9	15.0	15.3	15.8	16.0	16.3	16.4	16.5	15.9	15.6	15.4	15.1	15.7
2002	14.5	14.8	15.0	15.5	15.7	16.2	16.6	16.4	15.7	15.8	15.5	15.2	15.6
2003	14.3	14.5	14.5	15.2	15.7	16.4	16.6	16.7	16.2	15.8	15.3	15.3	15.5
Educational and health services													
1990	12.5	12.4	12.4	12.7	12.9	12.6	12.4	12.6	12.9	13.0	12.9	13.1	12.7
1991	13.3	13.3	13.6	13.6	13.7	13.6	13.6	14.0	13.9	14.1	14.1	14.2	13.7
1992	14.0	14.1	14.3	14.4	14.5	14.4	14.2	14.4	14.6	14.4	14.3	14.2	14.3
1993	14.1	14.4	14.5	14.6	14.8	14.6	14.6	14.8	15.1	15.2	15.2	15.3	14.7
1994	15.2	15.5	15.7	15.5	15.6	15.4	15.3	15.6	16.0	16.1	16.1	16.3	15.6
1995	16.0	16.2	16.3	16.3	16.3	16.2	16.4	16.5	16.7	16.7	16.7	16.9	16.4
1996	16.4	16.6	16.6	16.6	16.6	16.5	16.3	16.5	16.7	16.8	16.9	17.0	16.6
1997	16.6	16.7	16.7	17.0	17.0	16.7	16.7	16.7	16.9	17.2	17.2	17.2	16.8
1998	16.9	17.1	17.2	17.1	17.1	17.0	17.2	17.3	17.4	17.5	17.6	17.7	17.2
1999	17.4	17.4	17.7	17.6	17.6	17.6	17.5	17.5	17.9	17.5	17.6	17.8	17.5
2000	17.6	17.9	18.1	18.0	18.2	18.3	18.2	18.4	18.3	18.7	18.5	18.7	18.2
2001	18.8	18.9	19.2	19.1	19.2	19.2	19.3	19.6	19.3	19.5	19.8	19.6	19.3
2002	19.3	19.7	19.8	19.7	19.9	20.0	20.0	20.1	20.0	19.9	20.1	20.2	19.9
2003	20.4	20.5	20.4	20.7	21.0	20.8	20.8	20.8	20.8	21.1	21.3	21.4	20.8

Employment by Industry: Wyoming—*Continued*

(Numbers in thousands. Not seasonally adjusted.)

Industry	January	February	March	April	May	June	July	August	September	October	November	December	Annual Average
STATEWIDE—*Continued*													
Leisure and hospitality													
1990	19.8	20.2	20.7	21.2	22.8	28.8	30.1	29.9	26.7	22.8	20.9	21.2	23.7
1991	20.3	20.7	21.1	21.4	24.5	29.4	30.8	30.7	28.2	24.6	21.3	21.4	24.5
1992	20.8	21.2	21.5	21.6	25.1	30.4	31.4	31.1	28.2	24.4	21.8	22.6	25.0
1993	22.0	22.0	22.5	23.2	25.8	31.6	33.2	32.8	29.8	25.4	23.1	23.9	26.2
1994	23.4	23.4	23.5	24.2	26.8	32.4	34.2	33.8	30.8	27.0	24.1	24.7	27.3
1995	24.3	24.2	24.6	25.2	28.3	34.1	35.7	35.3	32.8	29.1	25.4	26.0	28.7
1996	24.8	24.9	25.6	25.8	28.9	34.5	36.3	36.0	33.0	29.0	25.5	25.9	29.1
1997	25.2	25.2	25.5	25.7	29.1	33.9	35.8	35.5	31.9	28.4	25.0	26.0	28.9
1998	25.0	25.2	25.1	25.8	28.7	33.7	35.7	35.5	32.2	28.6	25.4	26.0	28.9
1999	25.5	25.6	26.2	26.2	29.1	34.6	36.2	35.9	33.1	29.6	26.2	26.9	29.5
2000	26.2	26.4	26.9	27.0	29.6	35.4	36.7	36.1	32.7	29.0	26.2	27.2	29.9
2001	26.3	26.5	26.9	26.8	29.5	34.5	35.7	35.5	32.2	28.6	26.0	27.2	29.6
2002	26.6	27.0	27.2	27.5	29.9	34.9	36.7	35.9	33.2	29.6	27.1	27.7	30.3
2003	27.5	27.5	27.7	27.8	30.2	35.2	36.6	36.2	33.5	29.8	27.2	28.0	30.6
Other services													
1990	6.3	6.3	6.4	6.5	6.7	6.8	6.9	6.9	6.8	6.9	6.9	6.9	6.6
1991	6.7	6.7	6.8	6.8	6.9	7.1	7.1	7.1	7.0	6.9	6.9	7.0	6.9
1992	6.8	6.8	6.9	7.2	7.4	7.5	7.7	7.6	7.5	7.6	7.5	7.5	7.3
1993	7.3	7.4	7.5	7.6	7.8	8.0	8.0	8.1	7.9	7.8	7.7	7.8	7.7
1994	7.7	7.6	7.7	7.8	7.9	8.2	8.3	8.3	8.1	8.1	8.1	8.1	7.9
1995	8.0	8.0	8.1	8.1	8.3	8.5	8.5	8.6	8.4	8.3	8.2	8.3	8.2
1996	8.0	8.0	8.1	8.1	8.1	8.3	8.3	8.2	7.9	7.9	7.8	7.8	8.0
1997	7.8	7.7	7.8	7.8	8.0	8.3	8.3	8.4	8.3	8.2	8.3	8.4	8.1
1998	8.2	8.3	8.4	8.4	8.5	8.8	8.8	8.9	8.7	8.6	8.6	8.6	8.5
1999	8.4	8.4	8.5	8.5	8.7	8.9	9.0	9.1	8.9	8.8	8.8	8.9	8.7
2000	8.9	9.0	9.1	9.1	9.2	9.3	9.3	9.3	9.1	9.1	9.1	9.1	9.1
2001	8.8	8.9	9.0	9.1	9.3	9.4	9.4	9.5	9.4	9.4	9.4	9.5	9.3
2002	9.3	9.4	9.5	9.6	9.8	9.8	9.9	9.9	9.7	9.6	9.5	9.6	9.6
2003	9.5	9.5	9.6	9.5	9.6	9.7	9.8	9.8	9.6	9.7	9.5	9.5	9.6
Government													
1990	55.0	55.8	56.3	57.0	58.1	56.6	48.5	48.8	55.8	56.6	57.5	57.2	55.2
1991	55.5	56.1	56.9	56.9	57.9	57.0	48.9	49.2	56.8	58.0	57.9	58.0	55.7
1992	56.9	57.6	58.0	58.4	59.5	58.0	49.5	50.9	57.1	57.8	60.0	58.3	56.8
1993	57.5	58.1	58.7	58.8	59.9	58.7	50.3	50.6	57.6	58.8	58.7	58.7	57.2
1994	58.1	58.6	59.0	59.4	60.4	58.9	51.3	53.2	58.3	59.6	61.3	59.8	58.1
1995	58.8	59.1	59.7	59.8	60.3	59.5	50.2	50.4	57.8	59.4	59.1	59.2	57.7
1996	58.8	59.1	59.8	59.9	61.1	59.8	50.4	51.8	58.5	59.6	59.9	59.0	58.1
1997	58.2	58.5	59.1	59.2	60.7	58.7	52.3	52.9	58.6	59.6	59.4	59.4	58.0
1998	58.6	59.0	59.5	60.0	61.2	59.1	52.2	52.5	59.1	60.3	60.1	60.0	58.4
1999	59.2	59.7	60.5	60.8	61.9	60.5	54.8	54.7	59.5	60.6	60.4	60.6	59.4
2000	60.1	60.6	62.3	62.0	63.6	61.3	56.3	56.5	60.2	62.1	62.0	62.0	60.7
2001	60.8	61.4	62.2	62.0	63.1	63.3	57.4	57.9	61.2	62.7	62.7	63.4	61.5
2002	61.9	62.3	63.4	63.0	64.1	64.1	58.5	58.4	62.7	64.2	64.3	65.1	62.7
2003	63.3	63.7	64.5	64.0	65.0	64.9	59.2	59.2	62.9	65.1	64.9	65.3	63.5
Federal government													
1990	7.1	7.0	7.1	7.7	7.9	8.4	8.6	8.2	7.9	7.3	7.0	7.3	7.6
1991	6.8	6.8	6.8	6.9	7.2	8.0	8.3	8.2	7.9	7.5	7.2	7.1	7.3
1992	7.0	7.0	7.0	7.0	7.3	8.1	8.3	8.2	8.0	7.5	7.2	7.1	7.4
1993	7.1	7.0	7.0	7.1	7.4	8.0	8.2	8.2	7.9	7.5	7.2	7.1	7.4
1994	7.0	7.0	6.9	7.1	7.3	7.8	8.0	8.0	7.9	7.7	7.4	7.4	7.4
1995	7.2	7.2	7.1	7.2	7.4	7.9	8.0	8.0	7.7	7.5	7.2	7.2	7.4
1996	7.1	7.1	7.0	7.1	7.3	7.7	7.8	7.8	7.5	7.2	6.8	6.8	7.2
1997	6.7	6.6	6.6	6.7	7.2	7.6	7.7	7.7	7.5	7.0	6.8	6.7	7.0
1998	6.6	6.6	6.6	6.7	7.2	7.6	7.8	7.9	7.7	7.1	6.9	6.8	7.1
1999	6.7	6.6	6.6	6.8	7.2	7.6	7.9	7.9	7.7	7.3	6.9	6.8	7.1
2000	6.7	6.7	7.6	7.5	8.2	8.1	8.1	8.0	7.6	7.2	6.9	7.0	7.4
2001	6.7	6.6	6.7	6.7	7.2	8.1	8.2	8.1	8.1	7.3	7.0	7.6	7.4
2002	6.8	6.7	6.8	6.8	7.2	8.2	8.4	8.2	8.3	7.6	7.3	8.0	7.5
2003	7.1	7.1	7.2	7.1	7.5	8.4	8.6	8.5	8.4	7.8	7.5	7.4	7.7
State government													
1990	13.4	13.6	13.7	13.6	14.0	13.6	13.3	13.0	13.0	13.9	13.9	13.9	13.5
1991	13.8	13.9	14.0	14.1	14.2	13.7	13.6	13.4	13.4	14.1	14.0	14.0	13.8
1992	13.8	13.9	13.9	14.0	14.1	13.5	13.5	13.2	13.3	14.0	14.1	14.0	13.7
1993	14.0	14.1	14.1	14.2	14.2	13.7	13.6	13.3	13.3	14.1	14.1	14.1	13.9
1994	14.0	14.1	14.1	14.1	14.2	13.7	13.4	13.1	13.3	14.0	14.0	14.0	13.8
1995	13.9	13.8	14.0	14.0	14.0	13.6	13.0	12.8	13.1	13.7	13.7	13.6	13.6
1996	13.5	13.4	13.6	13.7	13.8	13.3	13.0	13.0	13.2	13.7	13.7	13.6	13.4
1997	13.5	13.4	13.5	13.7	13.8	13.4	13.1	13.1	13.2	13.8	13.7	13.7	13.4
1998	13.5	13.5	13.6	13.7	13.9	13.4	13.1	12.9	13.0	13.7	13.7	13.7	13.4
1999	13.5	13.6	13.7	13.8	13.8	13.3	13.2	12.7	13.1	13.8	13.8	13.8	13.5
2000	13.6	13.7	13.9	13.8	13.9	13.5	13.2	13.0	13.2	14.1	14.2	14.1	13.6
2001	14.0	14.0	14.1	14.2	14.3	14.0	13.6	13.3	13.5	14.4	14.5	14.5	14.0
2002	14.3	14.3	14.6	14.6	14.8	14.5	14.0	13.7	14.1	14.9	15.0	15.0	14.5
2003	14.9	14.8	15.0	14.9	15.0	14.7	14.2	13.8	14.3	15.2	15.3	15.5	14.8

Employment by Industry: Wyoming—*Continued*

(Numbers in thousands. Not seasonally adjusted.)

Industry	January	February	March	April	May	June	July	August	September	October	November	December	Annual Average
STATEWIDE—*Continued*													
Local government													
1990	34.5	35.2	35.5	35.7	36.2	34.6	26.6	27.6	34.9	35.4	36.6	36.0	34.0
1991	34.9	35.4	36.1	35.9	36.5	35.3	27.0	27.6	35.5	36.4	36.7	36.9	34.5
1992	36.1	36.7	37.1	37.4	38.1	36.4	27.7	29.5	35.8	36.3	38.7	37.2	35.5
1993	36.4	37.0	37.6	37.5	38.3	37.0	28.5	29.1	36.4	37.2	37.4	37.5	35.8
1994	37.1	37.5	38.0	38.2	38.9	37.4	29.9	32.1	37.1	37.9	39.9	38.4	36.8
1995	37.7	38.1	38.6	38.6	38.9	38.0	29.2	29.6	37.0	38.2	38.2	38.4	36.7
1996	38.2	38.6	39.2	39.1	40.0	38.8	29.6	31.0	37.8	38.7	39.4	38.6	37.4
1997	38.0	38.5	39.0	38.8	39.7	37.7	31.5	32.1	37.9	38.8	38.9	39.0	37.4
1998	38.5	38.9	39.3	39.6	40.1	38.1	31.3	31.7	38.4	39.5	39.5	39.5	37.8
1999	39.0	39.5	40.2	40.2	40.9	39.6	33.7	34.1	38.7	39.5	39.7	40.0	38.7
2000	39.8	40.2	40.8	40.7	41.5	39.7	35.0	35.5	39.4	40.8	40.9	40.9	39.6
2001	40.1	40.8	41.4	41.1	41.6	41.2	35.6	36.5	39.6	41.0	41.2	41.3	40.1
2002	40.8	41.3	42.0	41.6	42.1	41.4	36.1	36.5	40.3	41.7	42.0	42.1	40.7
2003	41.3	41.8	42.3	42.0	42.5	41.8	36.4	36.9	40.2	42.1	42.1	42.4	41.0
CASPER													
Total nonfarm													
1990	26.7	27.0	27.7	28.4	28.6	29.1	28.9	29.1	29.0	29.1	29.1	29.3	28.5
1991	28.1	27.8	28.2	28.3	28.8	29.7	28.8	29.0	29.1	29.1	29.5	29.5	28.8
1992	27.3	27.5	27.7	27.5	28.2	28.8	28.1	28.1	28.4	28.6	28.6	28.2	28.0
1993	27.3	27.2	27.3	27.8	28.4	29.2	28.6	29.1	29.8	29.4	28.9	29.0	28.5
1994	27.8	27.9	28.4	28.5	28.9	29.4	28.8	29.5	29.8	29.9	29.8	29.5	29.0
1995	28.6	28.8	29.0	29.0	29.6	30.3	29.6	29.7	30.1	30.1	29.4	29.9	29.5
1996	28.6	28.4	28.9	28.9	29.7	30.0	29.3	29.6	30.1	29.7	29.6	29.7	29.3
1997	29.3	29.3	29.6	29.7	30.2	30.8	30.4	30.3	30.6	30.5	30.4	30.6	30.1
1998	29.7	29.6	30.0	30.3	31.3	31.6	30.7	30.7	30.8	31.0	30.8	31.2	30.6
1999	30.3	30.4	31.0	31.0	31.5	31.8	31.4	31.5	32.2	31.9	32.0	32.0	31.4
2000	30.9	31.2	31.6	32.1	32.5	32.5	31.9	31.8	32.0	32.8	32.6	32.5	32.0
2001	31.5	31.6	32.1	32.6	33.1	33.5	32.9	32.9	33.1	33.0	33.0	33.2	32.7
2002	32.4	32.5	32.9	33.1	33.8	34.4	33.8	34.1	33.8	34.1	33.8	33.9	33.6
2003	32.9	33.1	33.5	33.9	34.5	34.8	34.6	34.5	34.5	34.8	34.5	34.7	34.2
Total private													
1990	21.8	21.9	22.5	23.2	23.3	23.7	24.1	24.3	23.9	24.1	24.0	24.1	23.4
1991	22.9	22.7	22.9	23.2	23.5	24.2	24.0	24.1	23.9	24.0	24.2	24.2	23.6
1992	21.9	22.2	22.3	22.2	22.8	23.1	23.4	23.0	23.2	23.4	23.2	22.9	22.8
1993	22.0	21.9	21.9	22.5	23.0	23.6	24.0	24.3	24.4	24.0	23.5	23.5	23.2
1994	22.4	22.4	22.8	23.1	23.3	23.8	24.2	24.5	24.4	24.4	24.0	23.9	23.6
1995	23.2	23.3	23.4	23.6	23.9	24.7	24.7	24.8	24.6	24.5	23.8	24.2	24.0
1996	23.2	22.9	23.3	23.4	24.1	24.4	24.7	24.9	24.9	24.4	24.3	24.3	24.0
1997	24.0	24.0	24.1	24.4	24.7	25.4	25.6	25.6	25.3	25.2	25.1	25.2	24.8
1998	24.3	24.3	24.5	24.9	25.8	26.2	26.0	25.9	25.5	25.4	25.3	25.6	25.3
1999	24.8	24.9	25.4	25.3	25.7	26.1	26.5	26.5	26.7	26.3	26.4	26.4	25.9
2000	25.3	25.5	25.7	26.3	26.6	26.9	27.0	27.0	26.6	27.2	27.1	26.8	26.5
2001	26.0	26.0	26.3	27.0	27.4	27.9	28.1	27.9	27.7	27.3	27.4	27.4	27.2
2002	26.9	26.9	27.2	27.5	28.1	28.7	28.9	29.1	28.5	28.4	28.1	28.1	28.0
2003	27.3	27.4	27.7	28.1	28.6	29.1	29.6	29.7	29.5	29.2	28.9	28.9	28.7
Goods-producing													
1990	4.8	4.8	5.1	5.3	5.3	5.5	5.8	5.8	5.9	5.9	5.7	5.8	5.4
1991	5.3	5.1	5.2	5.6	5.8	6.1	6.0	6.0	5.8	5.9	5.9	5.8	5.7
1992	4.7	4.6	4.8	4.7	5.0	5.2	5.3	5.2	5.2	5.3	5.2	5.0	5.0
1993	4.7	4.7	4.5	4.5	4.7	5.0	5.4	5.4	5.5	5.4	5.1	5.0	4.9
1994	4.6	4.6	4.7	4.9	5.0	5.2	5.3	5.3	5.4	5.4	5.2	5.1	5.0
1995	4.9	4.7	4.8	4.9	5.1	5.4	5.3	5.3	5.3	5.2	5.0	5.0	5.0
1996	4.8	4.6	4.7	4.7	5.0	5.1	5.1	5.3	5.3	5.1	5.0	4.9	4.9
1997	4.7	4.9	4.9	5.0	5.1	5.4	5.5	5.6	5.5	5.5	5.6	5.5	5.2
1998	5.3	5.2	5.3	5.3	5.5	5.8	5.7	5.6	5.6	5.4	5.3	5.5	5.4
1999	5.0	5.0	5.0	5.0	5.1	5.4	5.6	5.5	5.5	5.4	5.4	5.4	5.2
2000	5.0	5.1	5.1	5.1	5.1	5.4	5.5	5.6	5.5	5.7	5.6	5.5	5.3
2001	5.3	5.4	5.4	5.6	5.7	5.9	6.0	6.0	6.0	5.9	5.9	5.7	5.7
2002	5.5	5.4	5.4	5.4	5.8	5.9	5.9	6.2	5.9	6.0	5.9	5.8	5.8
2003	5.5	5.6	5.7	5.8	6.2	6.3	6.7	6.8	6.7	6.7	6.6	6.6	6.3
Natural resources and mining													
1990	2.3	2.3	2.2	2.3	2.3	2.4	2.5	2.5	2.6	2.5	2.4	2.5	2.4
1991	2.4	2.3	2.3	2.5	2.5	2.6	2.6	2.6	2.6	2.6	2.5	2.6	2.5
1992	2.3	2.1	2.2	2.1	2.1	2.2	2.3	2.2	2.2	2.4	2.3	2.3	2.2
1993	2.1	2.0	1.9	1.8	1.9	2.0	2.2	2.3	2.4	2.3	2.2	2.2	2.1
1994	2.0	2.0	2.0	2.0	2.0	2.0	2.0	2.0	2.1	2.1	2.1	2.0	2.0
1995	1.9	1.8	1.8	1.8	1.9	1.9	1.9	1.8	2.0	1.9	1.8	1.8	1.8
1996	1.8	1.7	1.7	1.6	1.7	1.7	1.8	1.9	1.9	1.8	1.8	1.8	1.7
1997	1.7	1.8	1.8	1.9	1.9	2.0	2.1	2.1	2.1	2.1	2.1	2.2	1.9
1998	2.1	2.1	2.1	2.0	2.0	2.1	2.2	2.1	2.1	2.0	1.9	2.0	2.0
1999	1.6	1.6	1.6	1.5	1.6	1.7	1.8	1.8	1.9	1.9	1.9	2.0	1.7
2000	1.8	1.9	1.9	1.8	1.8	1.9	2.0	2.0	2.0	2.1	2.1	2.1	1.9
2001	2.0	2.1	2.1	2.1	2.2	2.3	2.3	2.3	2.3	2.3	2.3	2.2	2.2
2002	2.1	2.0	1.9	1.8	2.0	2.0	2.1	2.2	2.1	2.2	2.2	2.1	2.1
2003	2.0	2.1	2.1	2.1	2.3	2.3	2.5	2.6	2.6	2.6	2.6	2.7	2.4

Employment by Industry: Wyoming—*Continued*

(Numbers in thousands. Not seasonally adjusted.)

Industry	January	February	March	April	May	June	July	August	September	October	November	December	Annual Average
CASPER—*Continued*													
Construction													
1990	1.3	1.3	1.7	1.8	1.7	1.8	2.0	2.0	2.0	2.0	1.9	1.9	1.7
1991	1.5	1.5	1.6	1.8	2.0	2.2	2.1	2.1	2.0	2.0	2.1	1.9	1.9
1992	1.2	1.2	1.3	1.3	1.5	1.6	1.6	1.6	1.6	1.5	1.6	1.3	1.4
1993	1.2	1.2	1.2	1.3	1.4	1.5	1.7	1.7	1.6	1.6	1.5	1.4	1.4
1994	1.2	1.2	1.3	1.5	1.6	1.7	1.8	1.8	1.7	1.7	1.5	1.5	1.5
1995	1.4	1.4	1.5	1.6	1.7	1.9	1.9	1.9	1.7	1.7	1.6	1.6	1.6
1996	1.4	1.3	1.4	1.5	1.7	1.8	1.7	1.8	1.8	1.7	1.6	1.5	1.6
1997	1.4	1.5	1.5	1.5	1.6	1.8	1.8	1.9	1.8	1.8	1.9	1.7	1.6
1998	1.6	1.5	1.6	1.7	1.9	2.0	1.9	1.9	1.9	1.8	1.8	1.8	1.7
1999	1.7	1.7	1.8	1.9	1.9	2.0	2.1	2.1	2.0	1.9	1.9	1.8	1.9
2000	1.7	1.7	1.7	1.8	1.9	2.0	2.0	2.1	2.0	2.1	1.9	1.8	1.8
2001	1.7	1.7	1.7	1.9	1.9	2.0	2.1	2.1	2.1	2.0	2.0	1.9	1.9
2002	1.8	1.9	2.0	2.1	2.3	2.4	2.3	2.4	2.2	2.2	2.1	2.1	2.2
2003	2.0	2.0	2.1	2.2	2.4	2.5	2.6	2.6	2.5	2.5	2.4	2.3	2.3
Manufacturing													
1990	1.2	1.2	1.2	1.2	1.3	1.3	1.3	1.3	1.3	1.4	1.4	1.4	1.2
1991	1.4	1.3	1.3	1.3	1.3	1.3	1.3	1.3	1.2	1.3	1.3	1.3	1.3
1992	1.2	1.3	1.3	1.3	1.4	1.4	1.4	1.4	1.4	1.4	1.3	1.4	1.3
1993	1.4	1.5	1.4	1.4	1.4	1.5	1.5	1.4	1.5	1.5	1.4	1.4	1.4
1994	1.4	1.4	1.4	1.4	1.4	1.5	1.5	1.5	1.6	1.6	1.6	1.6	1.4
1995	1.6	1.5	1.5	1.5	1.5	1.6	1.5	1.6	1.6	1.6	1.6	1.6	1.5
1996	1.6	1.6	1.6	1.6	1.6	1.6	1.6	1.6	1.6	1.6	1.6	1.6	1.6
1997	1.6	1.6	1.6	1.6	1.6	1.6	1.6	1.6	1.6	1.6	1.6	1.6	1.6
1998	1.6	1.6	1.6	1.6	1.6	1.7	1.6	1.6	1.6	1.6	1.6	1.7	1.6
1999	1.7	1.7	1.6	1.6	1.6	1.7	1.7	1.6	1.6	1.6	1.6	1.6	1.6
2000	1.5	1.5	1.5	1.5	1.4	1.5	1.5	1.5	1.5	1.5	1.6	1.6	1.5
2001	1.6	1.6	1.6	1.6	1.6	1.6	1.6	1.6	1.6	1.6	1.6	1.6	1.6
2002	1.6	1.5	1.5	1.5	1.5	1.5	1.5	1.6	1.6	1.6	1.6	1.6	1.6
2003	1.5	1.5	1.5	1.5	1.5	1.5	1.6	1.6	1.6	1.6	1.6	1.6	1.6
Service-providing													
1990	21.9	22.2	22.6	23.1	23.3	23.6	23.1	23.3	23.1	23.2	23.4	23.5	23.0
1991	22.8	22.7	23.0	22.7	23.0	23.6	22.8	23.0	23.3	23.2	23.6	23.7	23.1
1992	22.6	22.9	22.9	22.8	23.2	23.6	22.8	22.9	23.2	23.3	23.4	23.2	23.0
1993	22.6	22.5	22.8	23.3	23.7	24.2	23.2	23.7	24.3	24.0	23.8	24.0	23.5
1994	23.2	23.3	23.7	23.6	23.9	24.2	23.5	24.2	24.4	24.5	24.6	24.4	23.9
1995	23.7	24.1	24.2	24.1	24.5	24.9	24.3	24.4	24.8	24.9	24.4	24.9	24.4
1996	23.8	23.8	24.2	24.2	24.7	24.9	24.2	24.3	24.8	24.6	24.6	24.8	24.4
1997	24.6	24.4	24.7	24.7	25.1	25.4	24.9	24.7	25.1	25.0	24.8	25.1	24.8
1998	24.4	24.4	24.7	25.0	25.8	25.8	25.0	25.1	25.2	25.6	25.5	25.7	25.1
1999	25.3	25.4	26.0	26.0	26.4	26.4	25.8	26.0	26.7	26.5	26.6	26.6	26.1
2000	25.9	26.1	26.5	27.0	27.4	27.1	26.4	26.2	26.5	27.1	27.0	27.0	26.6
2001	26.2	26.2	26.7	27.0	27.4	27.6	26.9	26.9	27.1	27.1	27.1	27.5	27.0
2002	26.9	27.1	27.5	27.7	28.0	28.5	27.9	27.9	27.9	28.1	27.9	28.1	27.8
2003	27.4	27.5	27.8	28.1	28.3	28.5	27.9	27.7	27.8	28.1	27.9	28.1	27.9
Trade, transportation, and utilities													
1990	6.5	6.5	6.5	6.6	6.7	6.7	6.7	6.7	6.7	6.6	6.8	7.0	6.6
1991	6.6	6.5	6.5	6.5	6.6	6.7	6.6	6.7	6.7	6.8	7.2	7.2	6.7
1992	6.8	6.8	6.7	6.7	6.7	6.8	6.8	6.7	6.7	6.8	6.9	6.9	6.7
1993	6.7	6.6	6.5	6.7	6.8	6.8	6.8	6.9	7.1	7.0	7.0	7.1	6.8
1994	6.9	6.7	6.7	6.6	6.7	6.7	6.8	7.0	6.9	6.9	7.0	7.0	6.8
1995	6.8	6.8	6.7	6.6	6.7	6.9	6.8	6.9	6.8	6.8	6.8	7.1	6.8
1996	6.9	6.8	6.8	6.8	6.9	7.0	7.0	7.0	6.9	6.9	7.0	7.2	6.9
1997	7.2	7.0	7.0	7.0	7.0	7.2	7.1	7.1	7.1	7.0	7.0	7.2	7.0
1998	7.0	7.0	7.0	7.0	7.3	7.3	7.2	7.2	7.1	7.0	7.1	7.2	7.1
1999	7.2	7.0	7.2	7.1	7.3	7.3	7.4	7.5	7.6	7.6	7.8	7.9	7.4
2000	7.6	7.6	7.6	7.8	7.8	7.8	7.9	7.9	7.9	8.1	8.1	8.2	7.8
2001	7.7	7.5	7.6	7.8	7.8	7.8	7.9	7.8	7.9	7.7	7.9	8.0	7.8
2002	7.9	7.7	7.8	7.9	7.9	8.0	8.0	7.9	7.9	8.0	8.1	8.2	7.9
2003	7.7	7.7	7.8	7.8	7.8	7.8	7.9	7.9	7.8	7.8	7.8	7.9	7.8
Wholesale trade													
1990	1.8	1.8	1.8	1.9	1.9	1.9	1.9	1.9	1.9	1.9	1.9	1.9	1.8
1991	1.8	1.8	1.8	1.8	1.8	1.9	1.9	1.9	1.8	1.8	1.8	1.8	1.8
1992	1.8	1.8	1.7	1.8	1.8	1.8	1.8	1.8	1.8	1.8	1.8	1.8	1.7
1993	1.8	1.8	1.8	1.8	1.8	1.8	1.8	1.8	1.8	1.8	1.8	1.8	1.8
1994	1.8	1.8	1.8	1.8	1.8	1.8	1.8	1.9	1.9	1.9	1.9	1.9	1.8
1995	1.8	1.9	1.9	1.9	1.9	1.9	1.9	1.9	1.9	1.8	1.8	1.9	1.8
1996	1.9	1.9	1.9	1.9	1.9	2.0	2.0	2.0	1.9	1.9	1.9	1.9	1.9
1997	2.0	2.0	2.0	2.0	2.0	2.0	2.0	2.0	2.0	2.0	2.0	2.0	2.0
1998	2.0	2.0	2.1	2.0	2.1	2.1	2.0	2.0	2.0	2.0	2.0	2.0	2.0
1999	2.0	1.9	2.0	2.0	2.0	2.0	2.0	2.0	2.0	2.0	2.0	2.0	1.9
2000	2.0	2.0	2.1	2.1	2.1	2.1	2.1	2.1	2.1	2.2	2.1	2.2	2.1
2001	2.1	2.1	2.2	2.2	2.2	2.2	2.2	2.2	2.2	2.2	2.2	2.2	2.2
2002	2.3	2.2	2.3	2.2	2.3	2.2	2.2	2.2	2.2	2.2	2.2	2.2	2.2
2003	2.1	2.1	2.1	2.1	2.1	2.1	2.2	2.2	2.1	2.1	2.1	2.1	2.1

Employment by Industry: Wyoming—*Continued*

(Numbers in thousands. Not seasonally adjusted.)

Industry	January	February	March	April	May	June	July	August	September	October	November	December	Annual Average
CASPER—*Continued*													
Retail trade													
1990	3.7	3.7	3.7	3.7	3.8	3.8	3.8	3.8	3.8	3.7	3.9	4.0	3.7
1991	3.7	3.6	3.6	3.7	3.8	3.8	3.7	3.8	3.8	3.9	4.3	4.3	3.8
1992	4.0	3.9	3.9	4.0	4.0	4.0	4.0	4.0	4.0	4.0	4.1	4.1	4.0
1993	3.9	3.8	3.8	3.9	4.0	4.0	4.0	4.1	4.2	4.1	4.2	4.3	4.0
1994	4.1	3.9	3.9	4.0	4.1	4.1	4.1	4.2	4.1	4.1	4.2	4.2	4.0
1995	4.1	4.0	3.9	3.9	4.0	4.1	4.0	4.1	4.0	4.1	4.1	4.3	4.0
1996	4.1	4.0	4.0	4.0	4.1	4.1	4.1	4.1	4.1	4.1	4.2	4.3	4.1
1997	4.2	4.0	4.0	4.0	4.0	4.1	4.0	4.0	4.0	4.0	4.0	4.1	4.0
1998	3.9	3.9	3.8	4.0	4.1	4.1	4.1	4.1	4.0	3.9	4.0	4.1	4.0
1999	4.1	4.0	4.1	4.0	4.2	4.2	4.2	4.3	4.4	4.4	4.6	4.7	4.2
2000	4.4	4.4	4.3	4.5	4.5	4.5	4.6	4.6	4.6	4.7	4.8	4.8	4.5
2001	4.4	4.3	4.3	4.4	4.4	4.4	4.4	4.3	4.4	4.3	4.5	4.6	4.4
2002	4.5	4.4	4.4	4.6	4.6	4.7	4.7	4.6	4.6	4.7	4.8	4.9	4.6
2003	4.5	4.5	4.6	4.6	4.6	4.6	4.6	4.6	4.6	4.6	4.6	4.7	4.6
Transportation and utilities													
1990	1.0	1.0	1.0	1.0	1.0	1.0	1.0	1.0	1.0	1.0	1.0	1.1	1.0
1991	1.1	1.1	1.1	1.0	1.0	1.0	1.0	1.0	1.1	1.1	1.1	1.1	1.0
1992	1.0	1.1	1.1	0.9	0.9	1.0	1.0	0.9	0.9	1.0	1.0	1.0	0.9
1993	1.0	1.0	0.9	1.0	1.0	1.0	1.0	1.0	1.1	1.1	1.0	1.0	1.0
1994	1.0	1.0	1.0	0.8	0.8	0.8	0.9	0.9	0.9	0.9	0.9	0.9	0.9
1995	0.9	0.9	0.9	0.8	0.8	0.9	0.9	0.9	0.9	0.9	0.9	0.9	0.8
1996	0.9	0.9	0.9	0.9	0.9	0.9	0.9	0.9	0.9	0.9	0.9	1.0	0.9
1997	1.0	1.0	1.0	1.0	1.0	1.1	1.1	1.1	1.1	1.0	1.0	1.1	1.0
1998	1.1	1.1	1.1	1.0	1.1	1.1	1.1	1.1	1.1	1.1	1.1	1.1	1.0
1999	1.1	1.1	1.1	1.1	1.1	1.1	1.2	1.2	1.2	1.2	1.2	1.2	1.1
2000	1.2	1.2	1.2	1.2	1.2	1.2	1.2	1.2	1.2	1.2	1.2	1.2	1.2
2001	1.2	1.1	1.1	1.2	1.2	1.2	1.3	1.3	1.3	1.2	1.2	1.2	1.2
2002	1.1	1.1	1.1	1.1	1.0	1.1	1.1	1.1	1.1	1.1	1.1	1.1	1.1
2003	1.1	1.1	1.1	1.1	1.1	1.1	1.1	1.1	1.1	1.1	1.1	1.1	1.1
Information													
1990	0.6	0.6	0.6	0.6	0.6	0.6	0.6	0.6	0.6	0.7	0.7	0.7	0.6
1991	0.7	0.7	0.7	0.7	0.7	0.7	0.6	0.6	0.6	0.6	0.6	0.6	0.6
1992	0.6	0.6	0.6	0.6	0.6	0.6	0.6	0.6	0.6	0.6	0.6	0.6	0.6
1993	0.6	0.5	0.5	0.6	0.6	0.6	0.6	0.6	0.6	0.5	0.5	0.5	0.5
1994	0.6	0.6	0.6	0.6	0.6	0.6	0.6	0.6	0.6	0.6	0.6	0.6	0.6
1995	0.6	0.6	0.6	0.6	0.6	0.6	0.6	0.6	0.6	0.6	0.6	0.6	0.6
1996	0.6	0.6	0.6	0.6	0.6	0.6	0.6	0.6	0.6	0.6	0.6	0.6	0.6
1997	0.6	0.6	0.6	0.6	0.6	0.6	0.6	0.6	0.6	0.6	0.6	0.6	0.6
1998	0.6	0.6	0.6	0.6	0.6	0.6	0.6	0.6	0.6	0.6	0.6	0.6	0.6
1999	0.6	0.6	0.6	0.6	0.6	0.6	0.6	0.6	0.6	0.6	0.6	0.6	0.6
2000	0.6	0.6	0.6	0.6	0.7	0.6	0.6	0.6	0.6	0.6	0.6	0.6	0.6
2001	0.6	0.6	0.6	0.6	0.6	0.6	0.6	0.6	0.6	0.6	0.6	0.6	0.6
2002	0.6	0.6	0.6	0.5	0.5	0.6	0.6	0.6	0.6	0.6	0.5	0.6	0.6
2003	0.5	0.5	0.5	0.5	0.5	0.5	0.5	0.5	0.5	0.5	0.5	0.5	0.5
Financial activities													
1990	1.6	1.6	1.7	1.6	1.6	1.6	1.6	1.7	1.5	1.6	1.6	1.5	1.6
1991	1.5	1.5	1.5	1.4	1.4	1.4	1.4	1.5	1.4	1.4	1.4	1.5	1.4
1992	1.4	1.4	1.4	1.4	1.4	1.4	1.4	1.4	1.4	1.4	1.4	1.4	1.4
1993	1.4	1.4	1.4	1.4	1.4	1.4	1.4	1.4	1.4	1.4	1.4	1.4	1.4
1994	1.4	1.3	1.4	1.4	1.4	1.4	1.4	1.4	1.4	1.4	1.3	1.4	1.3
1995	1.4	1.4	1.4	1.4	1.4	1.4	1.4	1.4	1.4	1.4	1.4	1.4	1.4
1996	1.3	1.3	1.4	1.4	1.4	1.4	1.4	1.4	1.4	1.4	1.4	1.4	1.3
1997	1.4	1.4	1.4	1.4	1.4	1.5	1.5	1.5	1.5	1.5	1.5	1.5	1.4
1998	1.4	1.5	1.5	1.5	1.6	1.6	1.6	1.6	1.6	1.6	1.6	1.6	1.5
1999	1.6	1.6	1.6	1.6	1.6	1.6	1.6	1.6	1.6	1.6	1.6	1.6	1.6
2000	1.5	1.5	1.5	1.5	1.5	1.5	1.5	1.5	1.5	1.5	1.5	1.5	1.5
2001	1.4	1.4	1.4	1.5	1.5	1.5	1.5	1.5	1.5	1.6	1.6	1.6	1.5
2002	1.7	1.7	1.7	1.8	1.9	2.0	2.0	2.0	1.9	1.8	1.7	1.7	1.8
2003	1.8	1.8	1.8	1.8	1.8	1.9	1.8	1.8	1.8	1.8	1.8	1.8	1.8
Professional and business services													
1990	2.1	2.1	2.2	2.4	2.4	2.5	2.5	2.6	2.5	2.4	2.3	2.3	2.3
1991	2.2	2.2	2.2	2.2	2.2	2.3	2.5	2.4	2.4	2.4	2.3	2.3	2.3
1992	2.1	2.2	2.1	2.1	2.2	2.1	2.4	2.2	2.3	2.2	2.1	2.1	2.1
1993	1.9	2.0	2.0	2.2	2.3	2.5	2.5	2.5	2.5	2.4	2.4	2.4	2.3
1994	1.9	1.9	2.0	2.1	2.1	2.2	2.3	2.3	2.2	2.2	2.1	2.0	2.1
1995	2.0	2.1	2.1	2.3	2.3	2.4	2.5	2.4	2.4	2.4	2.2	2.2	2.2
1996	2.1	2.1	2.2	2.2	2.3	2.4	2.4	2.4	2.4	2.3	2.2	2.2	2.2
1997	2.2	2.3	2.3	2.4	2.5	2.6	2.6	2.7	2.6	2.4	2.4	2.4	2.4
1998	2.3	2.3	2.4	2.5	2.7	2.8	2.8	2.8	2.7	2.9	2.8	2.8	2.6
1999	2.7	2.9	3.0	3.0	3.0	3.0	3.1	3.0	3.0	3.0	2.9	2.9	2.9
2000	2.8	2.8	2.8	2.9	2.9	3.0	2.8	2.8	2.7	2.7	2.7	2.6	2.7
2001	2.7	2.7	2.8	2.9	3.0	3.1	3.0	3.0	2.9	2.9	2.9	2.9	2.9
2002	2.7	2.8	2.9	3.0	3.0	3.1	3.1	3.1	3.0	2.9	2.9	2.8	2.9
2003	2.8	2.8	2.8	2.9	3.0	3.1	3.3	3.3	3.2	3.1	2.9	2.9	3.0

Employment by Industry: Wyoming—*Continued*

(Numbers in thousands. Not seasonally adjusted.)

Industry	January	February	March	April	May	June	July	August	September	October	November	December	Annual Average
CASPER—*Continued*													
Educational and health services													
1990	2.5	2.5	2.5	2.6	2.6	2.6	2.5	2.5	2.6	2.6	2.6	2.6	2.5
1991	2.7	2.7	2.7	2.7	2.7	2.7	2.7	2.7	2.7	2.7	2.7	2.7	2.7
1992	2.6	2.7	2.7	2.7	2.7	2.7	2.6	2.7	2.7	2.8	2.9	2.9	2.7
1993	2.9	3.0	3.0	3.0	3.0	3.0	3.0	3.1	3.1	3.1	3.1	3.2	3.0
1994	3.2	3.3	3.3	3.3	3.3	3.3	3.3	3.3	3.4	3.4	3.4	3.5	3.3
1995	3.4	3.5	3.5	3.5	3.4	3.4	3.5	3.5	3.5	3.5	3.5	3.5	3.4
1996	3.5	3.5	3.5	3.5	3.5	3.4	3.4	3.4	3.6	3.6	3.7	3.7	3.5
1997	3.7	3.7	3.6	3.7	3.7	3.7	3.7	3.6	3.6	3.8	3.7	3.7	3.6
1998	3.6	3.6	3.6	3.6	3.6	3.6	3.6	3.6	3.6	3.7	3.7	3.7	3.6
1999	3.7	3.8	3.8	3.8	3.8	3.8	3.8	3.9	3.9	3.8	3.9	3.9	3.8
2000	3.8	3.9	4.0	4.1	4.1	4.1	4.0	4.0	4.0	4.1	4.2	4.2	4.0
2001	4.0	4.0	4.0	4.0	4.0	4.1	4.0	4.1	4.0	4.0	4.0	4.0	4.0
2002	4.1	4.2	4.2	4.2	4.2	4.2	4.2	4.2	4.2	4.2	4.2	4.2	4.2
2003	4.3	4.3	4.3	4.3	4.3	4.3	4.3	4.3	4.4	4.4	4.4	4.4	4.3
Leisure and hospitality													
1990	2.5	2.6	2.7	2.9	2.9	3.0	3.1	3.1	2.9	3.0	3.0	2.9	2.8
1991	2.6	2.7	2.8	2.8	2.8	2.9	2.9	2.9	3.0	2.9	2.8	2.8	2.8
1992	2.5	2.7	2.7	2.8	2.9	3.0	3.0	2.9	3.0	3.0	2.9	2.8	2.8
1993	2.6	2.5	2.8	2.9	3.0	3.0	3.0	3.1	2.9	2.9	2.8	2.7	2.8
1994	2.6	2.8	2.9	2.9	2.9	3.0	3.1	3.2	3.1	3.1	3.0	2.9	2.9
1995	2.8	2.8	2.9	2.9	3.0	3.2	3.2	3.2	3.2	3.2	3.0	3.0	3.0
1996	2.7	2.7	2.8	2.8	3.0	3.1	3.4	3.4	3.4	3.2	3.1	3.0	3.0
1997	2.9	2.8	3.0	3.0	3.1	3.1	3.3	3.2	3.1	3.1	3.0	3.0	3.0
1998	2.8	2.8	2.8	3.0	3.1	3.1	3.1	3.1	3.0	2.9	2.8	2.8	2.9
1999	2.7	2.7	2.8	2.8	2.9	3.0	3.0	3.0	3.1	2.9	2.8	2.7	2.8
2000	2.6	2.6	2.7	2.8	3.0	3.0	3.2	3.1	3.0	3.0	2.9	2.8	2.8
2001	2.7	2.8	2.9	3.0	3.1	3.2	3.3	3.2	3.1	2.9	2.8	2.9	3.0
2002	2.8	2.8	2.9	3.0	3.1	3.2	3.3	3.3	3.3	3.2	3.1	3.1	3.1
2003	3.0	3.0	3.1	3.3	3.3	3.5	3.4	3.4	3.4	3.2	3.2	3.1	3.2
Other services													
1990	1.2	1.2	1.2	1.2	1.2	1.2	1.3	1.3	1.2	1.3	1.3	1.3	1.2
1991	1.3	1.3	1.3	1.3	1.3	1.4	1.3	1.3	1.3	1.3	1.3	1.3	1.3
1992	1.2	1.2	1.3	1.2	1.3	1.3	1.3	1.3	1.3	1.3	1.2	1.2	1.2
1993	1.2	1.2	1.2	1.2	1.2	1.3	1.3	1.3	1.3	1.3	1.2	1.2	1.2
1994	1.2	1.2	1.2	1.3	1.3	1.4	1.4	1.4	1.4	1.4	1.4	1.4	1.3
1995	1.3	1.4	1.4	1.4	1.4	1.4	1.4	1.5	1.4	1.4	1.3	1.4	1.3
1996	1.3	1.3	1.3	1.4	1.4	1.4	1.4	1.4	1.3	1.3	1.3	1.3	1.3
1997	1.3	1.3	1.3	1.3	1.3	1.3	1.3	1.3	1.3	1.3	1.3	1.3	1.3
1998	1.3	1.3	1.3	1.4	1.4	1.4	1.4	1.4	1.3	1.3	1.4	1.4	1.3
1999	1.3	1.3	1.4	1.4	1.4	1.4	1.4	1.4	1.4	1.4	1.4	1.4	1.3
2000	1.4	1.4	1.4	1.5	1.5	1.5	1.5	1.5	1.4	1.5	1.5	1.4	1.4
2001	1.6	1.6	1.6	1.6	1.7	1.7	1.8	1.7	1.7	1.7	1.7	1.7	1.7
2002	1.6	1.7	1.7	1.7	1.7	1.7	1.8	1.8	1.7	1.7	1.7	1.7	1.7
2003	1.7	1.7	1.7	1.7	1.7	1.7	1.7	1.7	1.7	1.7	1.7	1.7	1.7
Government													
1990	4.9	5.1	5.2	5.2	5.3	5.4	4.8	4.8	5.1	5.0	5.1	5.2	5.0
1991	5.2	5.1	5.3	5.1	5.3	5.5	4.8	4.9	5.2	5.1	5.3	5.3	5.1
1992	5.4	5.3	5.4	5.3	5.4	5.7	4.7	5.1	5.2	5.2	5.4	5.3	5.2
1993	5.3	5.3	5.4	5.3	5.4	5.6	4.6	4.8	5.4	5.4	5.4	5.5	5.2
1994	5.4	5.5	5.6	5.4	5.6	5.6	4.6	5.0	5.4	5.5	5.8	5.6	5.4
1995	5.4	5.5	5.6	5.4	5.7	5.6	4.9	4.9	5.5	5.6	5.6	5.7	5.4
1996	5.4	5.5	5.6	5.5	5.6	5.6	4.6	4.7	5.2	5.3	5.3	5.4	5.3
1997	5.3	5.3	5.5	5.3	5.5	5.4	4.8	4.7	5.3	5.3	5.3	5.4	5.2
1998	5.4	5.3	5.5	5.4	5.5	5.4	4.7	4.8	5.3	5.6	5.5	5.6	5.3
1999	5.5	5.5	5.6	5.7	5.8	5.7	4.9	5.0	5.5	5.6	5.6	5.6	5.5
2000	5.6	5.7	5.9	5.8	5.9	5.6	4.9	4.8	5.4	5.6	5.5	5.7	5.5
2001	5.5	5.6	5.8	5.6	5.7	5.6	4.8	5.0	5.4	5.7	5.6	5.8	5.5
2002	5.5	5.6	5.7	5.6	5.7	5.7	4.9	5.0	5.3	5.7	5.7	5.8	5.5
2003	5.6	5.7	5.8	5.8	5.9	5.7	5.0	4.8	5.0	5.6	5.6	5.8	5.5
Federal government													
2001	0.6	0.6	0.6	0.6	0.6	0.7	0.7	0.7	0.7	0.7	0.7	0.7	0.7
2002	0.6	0.6	0.6	0.6	0.6	0.7	0.7	0.7	0.7	0.7	0.7	0.7	0.7
2003	0.7	0.7	0.7	0.7	0.7	0.7	0.7	0.7	0.7	0.7	0.7	0.7	0.7
State government													
2001	0.7	0.7	0.7	0.7	0.7	0.7	0.7	0.7	0.7	0.7	0.7	0.7	0.7
2002	0.7	0.7	0.7	0.7	0.7	0.7	0.8	0.7	0.8	0.7	0.7	0.7	0.7
2003	0.7	0.7	0.7	0.7	0.7	0.7	0.7	0.7	0.7	0.7	0.7	0.7	0.7

Employment by Industry: Wyoming—*Continued*

(Numbers in thousands. Not seasonally adjusted.)

Industry	January	February	March	April	May	June	July	August	September	October	November	December	Annual Average
CASPER—*Continued*													
Local government													
1990	3.5	3.7	3.7	3.7	3.8	3.9	3.2	3.3	3.7	3.6	3.7	3.8	3.6
1991	3.8	3.7	3.9	3.7	3.9	4.0	3.4	3.4	3.7	3.7	3.8	3.9	3.7
1992	3.9	3.9	4.0	3.8	3.9	4.2	3.2	3.7	3.8	3.8	4.0	3.9	3.8
1993	3.9	3.9	4.0	3.8	4.0	4.2	3.1	3.4	3.9	3.9	3.9	4.1	3.8
1994	4.0	4.1	4.2	4.0	4.2	4.1	3.2	3.6	4.0	4.0	4.4	4.2	4.0
1995	4.0	4.1	4.2	4.0	4.3	4.2	3.4	3.5	4.0	4.1	4.2	4.3	4.0
1996	4.1	4.1	4.2	4.1	4.3	4.3	3.3	3.4	3.9	3.9	4.0	4.1	3.9
1997	4.0	4.0	4.2	4.0	4.2	4.0	3.5	3.3	4.0	4.0	4.0	4.1	3.9
1998	4.1	4.0	4.2	4.1	4.2	4.0	3.3	3.4	3.9	4.2	4.1	4.2	3.9
1999	4.1	4.2	4.3	4.2	4.3	4.2	3.4	3.5	4.1	4.2	4.2	4.2	4.0
2000	4.2	4.3	4.4	4.3	4.4	4.2	3.4	3.4	4.0	4.2	4.2	4.3	4.1
2001	4.2	4.3	4.5	4.3	4.4	4.2	3.4	3.6	4.0	4.3	4.2	4.4	4.2
2002	4.2	4.3	4.4	4.3	4.4	4.3	3.4	3.6	3.8	4.3	4.3	4.4	4.1
2003	4.2	4.3	4.4	4.4	4.5	4.3	3.6	3.4	3.6	4.2	4.2	4.4	4.1

Average Weekly Hours by Industry: Wyoming

(Not seasonally adjusted.)

Industry	January	February	March	April	May	June	July	August	September	October	November	December	Annual Average
STATEWIDE													
Manufacturing													
2001	39.3	37.1	38.1	38.6	37.6	37.9	38.5	39.0	39.9	38.5	38.7	39.5	38.6
2002	37.6	37.6	37.2	38.6	38.7	41.1	40.6	39.3	41.1	39.4	39.1	40.5	39.3
2003	39.6	40.5	39.6	40.7	41.1	43.8	39.2	40.3	38.4	39.4	39.9	40.6	40.2

Average Hourly Earnings by Industry: Wyoming

(Dollars, not seasonally adjusted.)

Industry	January	February	March	April	May	June	July	August	September	October	November	December	Annual Average
STATEWIDE													
Manufacturing													
2001	16.73	16.96	16.76	17.37	17.28	17.43	17.73	17.54	17.87	17.08	17.01	17.43	17.26
2002	17.67	17.90	17.62	17.56	17.51	17.68	18.04	17.68	18.23	17.91	17.33	17.52	17.72
2003	18.02	18.40	17.60	17.53	16.95	16.59	16.35	15.98	16.37	15.87	15.79	15.86	16.74

Average Weekly Earnings by Industry: Wyoming

(Dollars, not seasonally adjusted.)

Industry	January	February	March	April	May	June	July	August	September	October	November	December	Annual Average
STATEWIDE													
Manufacturing													
2001	657.49	629.22	638.56	670.48	649.73	660.60	682.61	684.06	713.01	657.58	658.29	688.49	666.24
2002	664.39	673.04	655.46	677.82	677.64	726.65	732.42	694.82	749.25	705.65	677.60	709.56	696.40
2003	713.59	745.20	696.96	713.47	696.65	726.64	640.92	643.99	628.61	625.28	630.02	643.92	672.95

Appendix. Geographical Boundary Components

State and area	Type of area	Components
Alabama		
Birmingham	MSA	Blount, Jefferson, St. Clair, and Shelby Counties
Huntsville	MSA	Limestone and Madison Counties
Mobile	MSA	Baldwin and Mobile Counties
Montgomery	MSA	Autauga, Elmore, and Montgomery Counties
Tuscaloosa	MSA	Tuscaloosa County
Alaska		
Anchorage	MSA	Anchorage Borough
Arizona		
Phoenix	MSA	Maricopa and Pinal Counties
Tucson	MSA	Pima County
Arkansas		
Fayetteville-Springdale	MSA	Benton and Washington Counties
Fort Smith	MSA	Crawford and Sebastian Counties, AR; Sequoyah County, OK
Little Rock-North Little Rock	MSA	Faulkner, Lonoke, Pulaski, and Saline Counties
California		
Bakersfield	MSA	Kern County
Fresno	MSA	Fresno and Madera Counties
Los Angeles-Long Beach	PMSA	Los Angeles County
Oakland	PMSA	Alameda and Contra Costa Counties
Sacramento	PMSA	El Dorado, Placer, and Sacramento Counties
San Diego	MSA	San Diego County
San Francisco	PMSA	Marin, San Francisco, and San Mateo Counties
San Jose	PMSA	Santa Clara County
Stockton	MSA	San Joaquin County
Vallejo-Fairfield-Napa	PMSA	Napa and Solano Counties
Ventura	PMSA	Ventura County
Colorado		
Boulder-Longmont	PMSA	Boulder County
Colorado Springs	MSA	El Paso County
Denver	PMSA	Adams, Arapahoe, Broomfield, Denver, Douglas, and Jefferson Counties
Connecticut		
Bridgeport-Milford	PMSA	Bridgeport and Shelton cities, and Easton, Fairfield, Monroe, Stratford, and Trumbull towns in Fairfield County; Ansonia, Derby, and Milford cities, and Beacon Falls, Oxford, and Seymour towns in New Haven County
Hartford	MSA	Bristol, Hartford, and New Britain cities, and Avon, Berlin, Bloomfield, Burlington, Canton, East Granby, East Hartford, East Windsor, Enfield, Farmington, Glastonbury, Granby, Manchester, Marlborough, Newington, Plainville, Rocky Hill, Simsbury, Southington, South Windsor, Suffield, West Hartford, Wethersfield, Windsor, and Windsor Locks towns in Hartford County; Barkhamsted, Harwinton, New Hartford, Plymouth, and Winchester towns in Litchfield County; Middletown city, and Cromwell, Durham, East Haddam, East Hampton, Haddam, Middlefield, and Portland towns in Middlesex County; Colchester and Lebanon towns in New London County; Andover, Bolton, Columbia, Coventry, Ellington, Hebron, Mansfield, Somers, Stafford, Tolland, Vernon, and Willington towns in Tolland County; Ashford, Chaplin, and Windham towns in Windham County
New Haven-Meriden	PMSA	Clinton and Killingworth towns in Middlesex County; Meriden, New Haven, and West Haven cities, and Bethany, Branford, Cheshire, East Haven, Guilford, Hamden, Madison, North Branford, North Haven, Orange, Wallingford, and Woodbridge towns in New Haven County

Appendix. Geographical Boundary Components—*Continued*

State and area	Type of area	Components
Connecticut—*Continued*		
New London-Norwich	MSA	Old Saybrook town in Middlesex County; New London and Norwich cities, and Bozrah, East Lyme, Franklin, Griswold, Groton, Ledyard, Lisbon, Montville, North Stonington, Old Lyme, Preston, Salem, Sprague, Stonington, and Waterford towns in New London County; Canterbury and Plainfield towns in Windham County; Hopkinton and Westerly towns in Washington County, RI
Stamford	PMSA	Norwalk and Stamford cities, and Darien, Greenwich, New Canaan, Weston, Westport, and Wilton towns in Fairfield County
Delaware		
Dover	MSA	Kent County
Wilmington	PMSA	New Castle County, DE; Cecil County MD
District of Columbia		
Washington	MSA	District of Columbia; Calvert, Charles, Frederick, Montgomery, and Prince George's Counties, MD; Alexandria, Fairfax, Falls Church, Fredericksburg, Manassas, and Manassas Park cities, and Arlington, Clarke, Culpeper, Fairfax, Fauquier, King George, Loudoun, Prince William, Spotsylvania, Stafford, and Warren Counties, VA; Berkeley and Jefferson Counties, WV
Florida		
Fort Lauderdale-Hollywood-Pompano Beach	PMSA	Broward County
Jacksonville	MSA	Clay, Duval, Nassau, and St. Johns Counties
Miami-Hialeh	PMSA	Miami-Dade County
Orlando	MSA	Lake, Orange, Osceola, and Seminole Counties
Sarasota	MSA	Manatee and Sarasota Counties
Tallahassee	MSA	Gadsen and Leon Counties
Tampa-St. Petersburg-Clearwater	MSA	Hernando, Hillsborough, Pasco, and Pinellas Counties
West Palm Beach-Boca Raton-Delray Beach	MSA	Palm Beach County
Georgia		
Atlanta	MSA	Barrow, Bartow, Carroll, Cherokee, Clayton, Cobb, Coweta, DeKalb, Douglas, Fayette, Forsyth, Fulton, Gwinnett, Henry, Newton, Paulding, Pickens, Rockdale, Spalding, and Walton Counties
Macon-Warner Robins	MSA	Bibb, Houston, Jones, Peach, and Twiggs Counties
Savannah	MSA	Bryan, Chatham, and Effingham Counties
Hawaii		
Honolulu	MSA	Honolulu County
Idaho		
Boise City	MSA	Ada and Canyon Counties
Illinois		
Champaign-Urbana-Rantoul	MSA	Champaign County
Chicago	PMSA	Cook, DeKalb, DuPage, Grundy, Kane, Kendall, Lake, McHenry, and Will Counties
Springfield	MSA	Menard and Sangamon Counties
Indiana		
Fort Wayne	MSA	Adams, Allen, DeKalb, Huntington, Wells, and Whitley Counties
Gary-Hammond	PMSA	Lake and Porter Counties
Indianapolis	MSA	Boone, Hamilton, Hancock, Hendricks, Johnson, Madison, Marion, Morgan, and Shelby Counties
Muncie	MSA	Delaware County
South Bend-Mishawaka	MSA	St. Joseph County
Iowa		
Cedar Rapids	MSA	Linn County
Des Moines	MSA	Dallas, Polk, and Warren Counties
Iowa City	MSA	Johnson City
Sioux City	MSA	Woodbury County, IA; Dakota County, NE
Waterloo-Cedar Falls	MSA	Black Hawk County

Appendix. Geographical Boundary Components—*Continued*

State and area	Type of area	Components
Kansas		
Lawrence	MSA	Douglas County
Topeka	MSA	Shawnee County
Wichita	MSA	Butler, Harvey, and Sedgwick Counties
Kentucky		
Lexington-Fayette	MSA	Bourbon, Clark, Fayette, Jessamine, Madison, Scott, and Woodford Counties
Louisville	MSA	Bullitt, Jefferson, and Oldham Counties, KY; Clark, Floyd, Harrison, and Scott Counties, IN
Louisiana		
Baton Rouge	MSA	Ascension, East Baton Rouge, Livingston, and West Baton Rouge Parishes
Lafayette	MSA	Acadia, Lafayette, St. Landry, and St. Martin Parishes
New Orleans	MSA	Jefferson, Orleans, Plaquemines, St. Bernard, St. Charles, St. James, St. John the Baptist, and St. Tammany Parishes
Shreveport	MSA	Bossier, Caddo, and Webster Parishes
Maine		
Lewiston-Auburn	MSA	Auburn and Lewiston cities, and Greene, Lisbon, Mechanic Falls, Poland, Sabattus, Turner, and Wales towns in Androscoggin County
Portland	MSA	Portland, South Portland, and Westbrook cities, and Cape Elizabeth, Casco, Cumberland, Falmouth, Freeport, Gorham, Gray, Long Island, North Yarmouth, Raymond, Scarborough, Standish, Windham, and Yarmouth towns in Cumberland County; Buxton, Hollis, Limington, and Old Orchard Beach towns in York County
Maryland		
Baltimore	MSA	Baltimore city, Anne Arundel, Baltimore, Carroll, Harford, Howard, and Queen Anne's Counties
Baltimore City		Baltimore city
Suburban Maryland-D.C		Calvert, Charles, Frederick, Montgomery, and Prince George's Counties
Massachusetts		
Barnstable-Yarmouth	MSA	Barnstable city, and Brewster, Chatham, Dennis, Eastham, Harwich, Mashpee, Orleans, Sandwich, and Yarmouth towns in Barnstable County
Boston	PMSA	Taunton city, and Berkley, Dighton, Mansfield, and Norton towns in Bristol County; Beverly, Gloucester, Lynn, Newburyport, Peabody, and Salem cities, and Amesbury, Danvers, Essex, Hamilton, Ipswich, Lynnfield, Manchester-by-the-Sea, Marblehead, Middleton, Nahant, Newbury, Rockport, Rowley, Salisbury, Saugus, Swampscott, Topsfield, and Wenham towns in Essex County; Cambridge, Everett, Malden, Marlborough, Medford, Melrose, Newton, Somerville, Waltham, Watertown, and Woburn cities, and Acton, Arlington, Ashland, Ayer, Bedford, Belmont, Boxborough, Burlington, Carlisle, Concord, Framingham, Holliston, Hopkinton, Hudson, Lexington, Lincoln, Littleton, Maynard, Natick, North Reading, Reading, Sherborn, Shirley, Stoneham, Stow, Sudbury, Townsend, Wakefield, Wayland, Weston, Wilmington, and Winchester towns in Middlesex County; Franklin and Quincy cities, and Bellingham, Braintree, Brookline, Canton, Cohasset, Dedham, Dover, Foxborough, Holbrook, Medfield, Medway, Millis, Milton, Needham, Norfolk, Norwood, Plainville, Randolph, Sharon, Stoughton, Walpole, Wellesley, Westwood, Weymouth, and Wrentham towns in Norfolk County; Carver, Duxbury, Hanover, Hingham, Hull, Kingston, Marshfield, Norwell, Pembroke, Plymouth, Rockland, Scituate, and Wareham towns in Plymouth County; Boston, Chelsea, and Revere cities, and Winthrop town in Suffolk County; Berlin, Blackstone, Bolton, Harvard, Hopedale, Lancaster, Mendon, Milford, Millville, Southborough, and Upton towns in Worcester County, MA; Seabrook and South Hampton towns in Rockingham County, NH
Lawrence-Haverhill	PMSA	Haverhill, Lawrence, and Methuen cities, and Andover, Boxford, Georgetown, Groveland, Merrimac, North Andover, and West Newbury towns in Essex County, MA; Atkinson, Chester, Danville, Derry, Fremont, Hampstead, Kingston, Newton, Plaistow, Raymond, Salem, Sandown, and Windham towns in Rockingham County, NH
Lowell	PMSA	Lowell city, and Billerica, Chelmsford, Dracut, Dunstable, Groton, Pepperell, Tewksbury, Tyngsborough, and Westford towns in Middlesex County, MA; Pelham town in Hillsborough County, NH

Appendix. Geographical Boundary Components—*Continued*

State and area	Type of area	Components
Massachusetts—*Continued*		
New Bedford	PMSA	New Bedford city, and Acushnet, Dartmouth, Fairhaven, and Freetown towns in Bristol County; Marion, Mattapoisett, and Rochester towns in Plymouth County
Springfield	MSA	Sunderland town in Franklin County; Agawam, Chicopee, Holyoke, Springfield, and Westfield cities, and East Longmeadow, Hampden, Longmeadow, Ludlow, Monson, Montgomery, Palmer, Russell, Southwick, West Springfield, and Wilbraham towns in Hampden County; Northampton city, and Amherst, Belchertown, Easthampton, Granby, Hadley, Hatfield, Huntington, Southampton, South Hadley, Ware, and Williamsburg towns in Hampshire County
Worcester	PMSA	Holland town in Hampden County; Worcester city, and Auburn, Barre, Boylston, Brookfield, Charlton, Clinton, Douglas, Dudley, East Brookfield, Grafton, Holden, Leicester, Millbury, Northborough, Northbridge, North Brookfield, Oakham, Oxford, Paxton, Princeton, Rutland, Shrewsbury, Southbridge, Spencer, Sterling, Sturbridge, Sutton, Uxbridge, Webster, Westborough, West Boylston, and West Brookfield towns in Worcester County, MA; Thompson town in Windham County, CT
Michigan		
Ann Arbor	PMSA	Lenawee, Livingston, and Washtenaw Counties
Detroit	PMSA	Lapeer, Macomb, Monroe, Oakland, St. Clair, and Wayne Counties
Flint	PMSA	Genesee County
Grand Rapids	MSA	Allegan, Kent, Muskegon, and Ottawa Counties
Kalamazoo	MSA	Calhoun, Kalamazoo, and Van Buren Counties
Lansing-East Lansing	MSA	Clinton, Eaton, and Ingham Counties
Minnesota		
Duluth	MSA	St. Louis County, MN; Douglas County, WI
Minneapolis-St. Paul	MSA	Anoka, Carver, Chisago, Dakota, Hennepin, Isanti, Ramsey, Scott, Sherburne, Washington, and Wright Counties, MN; Pierce and St. Croix Counties, WI
Rochester	MSA	Olmsted County
St. Cloud	MSA	Benton and Stearns Counties
Mississippi		
Jackson	MSA	Hinds, Madison, and Rankin Counties
Missouri		
Kansas City	MSA	Cass, Clay, Clinton, Jackson, Lafayette, Platte, and Ray Counties, MO; Johnson, Leavenworth, Miami, and Wyandotte Counties, KS
St. Louis	MSA	St. Louis city, and Franklin, Jefferson, Lincoln, St. Charles, St. Louis, and Warren Counties, MO; Clinton, Jersey, Madison, Monroe, and St. Clair Counties, IL
Springfield	MSA	Christian, Greene, and Webster Counties
Montana		
Billings	MSA	Yellowstone County
Nebraska		
Lincoln	MSA	Lancaster County
Omaha	MSA	Cass, Douglas, Sarpy, and Washington Counties, NE; Pottawattamie County, IA
Nevada		
Las Vegas	MSA	Clark and Nye Counties, NV; Mohave County, AZ
Reno	MSA	Washoe County
New Hampshire		
Manchester	PMSA	Manchester city, and Bedford, Goffstown, and Weare towns in Hillsborough County; Allenstown and Hooksett towns in Merrimack County; Auburn, Candia, and Londonderry towns in Rockingham County
Portsmouth-Dover-Rochester	PMSA	Portsmouth city and Brentwood, East Kingston, Epping, Exeter, Greenland, Hampton, Hampton Falls, Kensington, New Castle, Newfields, Newington, Newmarket, North Hampton, Rye, and Stratham towns in Rockingham County; Dover, Rochester, and Somersworth cities, and Barrington, Durham, Farmington, Lee, Madbury, Milton, and Rollinsford towns in Strafford County, NH; and Berwick, Eliot, Kittery, South Berwick, and York towns in York County, ME

Appendix. Geographical Boundary Components—*Continued*

State and area	Type of area	Components
New Jersey		
Atlantic City	PMSA	Atlantic and Cape May Counties
Bergen-Passaic	PMSA	Bergen and Passaic Counties
Camden	PMSA	Burlington, Camden, and Gloucester Counties
Jersey City	PMSA	Hudson County
Middlesex-Somerset-Hunterdon	PMSA	Hunterdon, Middlesex, and Somerset Counties
Monmouth-Ocean	PMSA	Monmouth and Ocean Counties
Newark	PMSA	Essex, Morris, Sussex, Union, and Warren Counties
Trenton	PMSA	Mercer County
Vineland-Millville-Bridgeton	PMSA	Cumberland County
New Mexico		
Albuquerque	MSA	Bernalillo, Sandoval, and Valencia Counties
Las Cruces	MSA	Dona Ana County
Santa Fe	MSA	Los Alamos and Santa Fe Counties
New York		
Albany-Schenectady-Troy	MSA	Albany, Montgomery, Rensselaer, Saratoga, Schenectady, and Schoharie Counties
Buffalo	MSA	Erie and Niagara Counties
Nassau-Suffolk	PMSA	Nassau and Suffolk Counties
New York	PMSA	Bronx, Kings, New York, Putnam, Queens, Richmond, Rockland, and Westchester Counties
New York City		Bronx, Kings, New York, Queens, and Richmond Counties
Rochester	MSA	Genesee, Livingston, Monroe, Ontario, Orleans, and Wayne Counties
Syracuse	MSA	Cayuga, Madison, Onondaga, and Oswego Counties
Westchester County	MSA	Westchester County
North Carolina		
Charlotte-Gastonia-Rock Hill	MSA	Cabarrus, Gaston, Lincoln, Mecklenburg, Rowan, and Union Counties, NC; York County, SC
Greensboro–Winston-Salem–High Point	MSA	Alamance, Davidson, Davie, Forsyth, Guilford, Randolph, Stokes, and Yadkin Counties
Raleigh-Durham	MSA	Chatham, Durham, Franklin, Johnston, Orange, and Wake Counties
North Dakota		
Bismarck	MSA	Burleigh and Morton Counties
Fargo-Moorhead	MSA	Cass County, ND; Clay County, MN
Grand Forks	MSA	Grand Forks County, ND; Polk County, MN
Ohio		
Akron	PMSA	Portage and Summit Counties
Canton	MSA	Carroll and Stark Counties
Cincinnati	PMSA	Brown, Clermont, Hamilton, and Warren Counties, OH; Boone, Campbell, Gallatin, Grant, Kenton, and Pendleton Counties, KY; Dearborn and Ohio Counties, IN
Cleveland	PMSA	Ashtabula, Cuyahoga, Geauga, Lake, Lorain, and Medina Counties
Columbus	MSA	Delaware, Fairfield, Franklin, Licking, Madison, and Pickaway Counties
Hamilton-Middletown	PMSA	Butler County
Steubenville-Weirton	MSA	Jefferson County, OH; Brooke and Hancock Counties, WV
Youngstown-Warren	MSA	Columbiana, Mahoning, and Trumbull Counties
Oklahoma		
Lawton	MSA	Comanche County
Oklahoma City	MSA	Canadian, Cleveland, Logan, McClain, Oklahoma, and Pottawatomie Counties
Tulsa	MSA	Creek, Osage, Rogers, Tulsa, and Wagoner Counties
Oregon		
Eugene-Springfield	MSA	Lane County
Medford	MSA	Jackson County
Portland	PMSA	Clackamas, Columbia, Multnomah, Washington, and Yamhill Counties, OR; Clark County, WA
Salem	PMSA	Marion and Polk Counties

Appendix. Geographical Boundary Components—*Continued*

State and area	Type of area	Components
Pennsylvania		
Allentown-Bethlehem	MSA	Carbon, Lehigh, and Northampton Counties
Erie	MSA	Erie County
Harrisburg-Lebanon-Carlisle	MSA	Cumberland, Dauphin, Lebanon, and Perry Counties
Lancaster	MSA	Lancaster County
Philadelphia	PMSA	Bucks, Chester, Delaware, Montgomery, and Philadelphia Counties, PA; Burlington, Camden, Gloucester, and Salem Counties, NJ
Philadelphia City		Philadelphia County
Pittsburgh	MSA	Allegheny, Beaver, Butler, Fayette, Washington, and Westmoreland Counties
Reading	MSA	Berks County
Scranton–Wilkes-Barre	MSA	Columbia, Lackawanna, Luzerne, and Wyoming Counties
York	MSA	York County
Rhode Island		
Providence	MSA	Barrington, Bristol, and Warren towns in Bristol County; Warwick city, and Coventry, East Greenwich, West Greenwich, and West Warwick towns in Kent County; Jamestown, Little Compton, and Tiverton towns in Newport County; Central Falls, Cranston, East Providence, Pawtucket, Providence, and Woonsocket cities, and Burrillville, Cumberland, Foster, Glocester, Johnston, Lincoln, North Providence, North Smithfield, Scituate, and Smithfield towns in Providence County; Charlestown, Exeter, Narragansett, North Kingstown, Richmond, and South Kingstown towns in Washington County, RI; Attleboro and Fall River cities, and North Attleborough, Rehoboth, Seekonk, Somerset, Swansea, and Westport towns in Bristol County, MA
South Carolina		
Charleston	MSA	Berkeley, Charleston, and Dorchester Counties
Columbia	MSA	Lexington and Richland Counties
Greenville-Spartanburg	MSA	Anderson, Cherokee, Greenville, Pickens, and Spartanburg Counties
South Dakota		
Rapid City	MSA	Pennington County
Sioux Falls	MSA	Lincoln and Minnehaha Counties
Tennessee		
Chattanooga	MSA	Hamilton and Marion Counties, TN; Catoosa, Dade, and Walker Counties, GA
Knoxville	MSA	Anderson, Blount, Knox, Loudon, Sevier, and Union Counties
Memphis	MSA	Fayette, Shelby, and Tipton Counties, TN; Crittenden County, AR; DeSoto County, MS
Nashville	MSA	Cheatham, Davidson, Dickson, Robertson, Rutherford, Sumner, Williamson, and Wilson Counties
Texas		
Abilene	MSA	Taylor Counties
Austin	MSA	Bastrop, Caldwell, Hays, Travis, and Williamson Counties
Beaumont-Port Arthur	MSA	Hardin, Jefferson, and Orange Counties
Brownsville-Harlingen	MSA	Cameron County
Corpus Christi	MSA	Nueces and San Patricio Counties
Dallas	PMSA	Collin, Dallas, Denton, Ellis, Henderson, Hunt, Kaufman, and Rockwall Counties
El Paso	MSA	El Paso County
Fort Worth-Arlington	PMSA	Hood, Johnson, Parker, and Tarrant Counties
Galveston-Texas City	PMSA	Galveston
Houston	PMSA	Chambers, Fort Bend, Harris, Libert, Montgomery, and Waller Counties
San Angelo	MSA	Tom Green County
San Antonio	MSA	Bexar, Comal, Guadalupe, and Wilson Counties

Appendix. Geographical Boundary Components—*Continued*

State and area	Type of area	Components
Utah		
Provo-Orem	MSA	Utah County
Salt Lake City-Ogden	MSA	Davis, Salt Lake, and Weber Counties
Vermont		
Barre-Montpelier		East Granville town in Addison County; Groton and Ryegate towns in Caledonia County; Bolton and Huntington towns in Chittenden County; Bradford, Braintree, Brookfield, Chelsea, Corinth, Fairlee, Newbury, Orange, Randolph, Topsham, Vershire, Washington, West Fairlee, and Williamstown towns in Orange County; and Barre city and Barre, Berlin, Cabot, Calais, Duxbury, East Montpelier, Fayston, Marshfield, Middlesex, Montpelier, Moretown, Northfield, Plainfield, Roxbury, Waitsfield, Warren, and Waterbury towns in Washington County
Burlington	MSA	Burlington, South Burlington, and Winooski cities, and Charlotte, Colchester, Essex, Hinesburg, Jericho, Milton, Richmond, St. George, Shelburne, and Williston towns in Chittenden County; St. Albans city, and Fairfax, Georgia, St. Albans, and Swanton towns in Franklin County; Grand Isle and South Hero towns in Grand Isle County
Virginia		
Charlottesville	MSA	Charlottesville city, and Albemarle, Fluvanna, and Greene Counties
Lynchburg	MSA	Bedford and Lynchburg cities, and Amherst, Bedford, and Campbell Counties
Norfolk-Virginia Beach-Newport News	MSA	Chesapeake, Hampton, Newport News, Norfolk, Poquoson, Portsmouth, Suffolk, Virginia Beach, and Williamsburg cities, and Gloucester, Isle of Wight, James City, Mathews, and York Counties, VA; Currituck County, NC
Northern Virginia		Alexandria, Fairfax, Falls Church, Fredericksburg, Manassas, and Manassas Park cities, and Arlington, Clarke, Culpeper, Fairfax, Fauquier, King George, Loudoun, Prince William, Spotsylvania, Stafford, and Warren Counties
Richmond-Petersburg	MSA	Colonial Heights, Hopewell, Petersburg, and Richmond cities, and Charles City, Chesterfield, Dinwiddie, Goochland, Hanover, Henrico, New Kent, Powhatan, and Prince George Counties
Washington		
Seattle	PMSA	Island, King, and Snohomish Counties
Spokane	MSA	Spokane County
Tacoma	PMSA	Pierce County
West Virginia		
Charleston	MSA	Kanawah and Putnam Counties
Huntington-Ashland	MSA	Cabell and Wayne Counties, WV; Boyd, Carter, and Greenup Counties, KY; Lawrence County, OH
Parkersburg-Marietta	MSA	Wood County, WV; Washington County, OH
Wheeling	MSA	Marshall and Ohio Counties, WV; Belmont County, OH
Wisconsin		
Appleton-Oshkosh-Neenah	MSA	Calumet, Outagamie, and Winnebago Counties
Green Bay	MSA	Brown County
Madison	MSA	Dane County
Milwaukee	PMSA	Milwaukee, Ozaukee, Washington, and Waukesha Counties
Wyoming		
Casper	MSA	Natrona County